AGE, WEIGHT & DISTANCE TABLE

Timeform's scale of weight-for-age for the flat

Dist	Age	Jan		Feb		Mar		Apr		May		June	
		1-16	17-31	1-16	17-28	1-16	17-31	1-16	17-30	1-16	17-31	1-16	17-30
5f	4	10–0	10–0	10–0	10–0	10–0	10–0	10–0	10–0	10–0	10–0	10–0	10–0
	3	9–5	9–5	9–6	9–7	9–7	9–8	9–8	9–9	9–9	9–10	9–10	9–11
	2						8–0	8–1	8–3	8–4	8–5	8–6	8–7
6f	4	10–0	10–0	10–0	10–0	10–0	10–0	10–0	10–0	10–0	10–0	10–0	10–0
	3	9–2	9–3	9–4	9–5	9–5	9–6	9–7	9–7	9–8	9–8	9–9	9–9
	2									8–0	8–2	8–3	8–4
7f	4	9–13	9–13	10–0	10–0	10–0	10–0	10–0	10–0	10–0	10–0	10–0	10–0
	3	9–0	9–1	9–2	9–3	9–4	9–4	9–5	9–6	9–6	9–7	9–8	9–8
	2											7–13	8–1
1m	4	9–13	9–13	9–13	9–13	10–0	10–0	10–0	10–0	10–0	10–0	10–0	10–0
	3	8–12	8–13	9–0	9–1	9–2	9–2	9–3	9–4	9–5	9–5	9–6	9–7
	2												
9f	4	9–12	9–12	9–12	9–13	9–13	9–13	9–13	10–0	10–0	10–0	10–0	10–0
	3	8–10	8–11	8–12	8–13	9–0	9–1	9–2	9–2	9–3	9–4	9–5	9–5
	2												
1¼m	4	9–11	9–12	9–12	9–12	9–13	9–13	9–13	9–13	9–13	10–0	10–0	10–0
	3	8–8	8–9	8–10	8–11	8–12	8–13	9–0	9–1	9–2	9–2	9–3	9–4
	2												
11f	4	9–10	9–11	9–11	9–12	9–12	9–12	9–13	9–13	9–13	9–13	9–13	10–0
	3	8–6	8–7	8–8	8–9	8–10	8–11	8–12	8–13	9–0	9–1	9–2	9–2
1½m	4	9–10	9–10	9–10	9–11	9–11	9–12	9–12	9–12	9–13	9–13	9–13	9–13
	3	8–4	8–5	8–6	8–7	8–8	8–9	8–10	8–11	8–12	8–13	9–0	9–1
13f	4	9–9	9–9	9–10	9–10	9–11	9–11	9–11	9–12	9–12	9–12	9–13	9–13
	3	8–2	8–3	8–4	8–5	8–7	8–8	8–9	8–10	8–11	8–12	8–13	9–0
1¾m	4	9–8	9–8	9–9	9–9	9–10	9–10	9–11	9–11	9–12	9–12	9–12	9–13
	3	8–0	8–2	8–3	8–4	8–5	8–6	8–7	8–8	8–9	8–10	8–11	8–12
15f	4	9–7	9–8	9–8	9–9	9–9	9–10	9–10	9–11	9–11	9–11	9–12	9–12
	3	7–13	8–0	8–1	8–2	8–4	8–5	8–6	8–7	8–8	8–9	8–10	8–11
2m	4	9–6	9–7	9–7	9–8	9–9	9–9	9–10	9–10	9–11	9–11	9–11	9–12
	3	7–11	7–12	7–13	8–1	8–2	8–3	8–4	8–5	8–6	8–7	8–8	8–9
2¼m	4	9–5	9–5	9–6	9–7	9–7	9–8	9–9	9–9	9–10	9–10	9–10	9–11
	3	7–8	7–9	7–11	7–12	7–13	8–0	8–2	8–3	8–4	8–5	8–6	8–7
2½m	4	9–3	9–4	9–5	9–6	9–6	9–7	9–7	9–8	9–9	9–9	9–10	9–10
	3	7–5	7–7	7–8	7–9	7–11	7–12	7–13	8–1	8–2	8–3	8–4	8–5

For 5-y-o's and older, use 10-0 in all cases
Race distances in the above tables are shown only at 1 furlong intervals.
For races over odd distances, the nearest distance shown in the table should be used:
thus for races of 1m to 1m 109 yards, use the table weights for 1m;
for 1m 110 yards to 1m 219 yards use the 9f table

The age, weight and distance table covering July to December appears on the end paper at the back of the book

RACEHORSES OF 2009

Price £75.00

A TIMEFORM PUBLICATION

CONTENTS

The age, weight and distance tables, for use in applying the ratings in races involving horses of different ages, appear on the end papers at the front and back of the book

Compiled and produced by

G. Greetham (Publishing Editor), C. S. Williams (Managing Editor & Handicapper), J. Ingles (Essays, 'Top Horses Abroad' & Editor for pedigrees), E. K. Wilkinson (Essays & Editor), A. J. Mealor (Handicapper & Editor), D. W. Johnson, S. Molyneux (Handicappers), J. Early, D. P. Cleary, P. E. Turner (Essays), S. Khoshsokhan, K. T. Melrose, J. A. Todd (Short Commentaries), S. Wright (pedigrees, database updates), G. Crowther, G. Johnstone (proof checking), D. Holdsworth, W. Muncaster, R. Todd, C. Wright (Production)

ISBN 978 1 901570 76 2

Racehorses of 2009

Introduction

'When the One Great Scorer
comes to mark against your name,
He writes, not that you won or lost,
but how you played the game.'

The words of Grantland Rice, the best known American sports writer of the early-'twentieth century, seem strangely irrelevant to modern professional sport in which gamesmanship and cheating are in danger of becoming almost part and parcel of the game. Too many governing bodies convey the impression of just wanting such problems to go away, rather than confronting them head-on and taking a firm stand. When the Arsenal striker Eduardo was banned for two Champions League matches by UEFA for deceiving a referee to win a penalty in a match against Celtic in August, it seemed to be the start of a fight back against cheating (surely the clampdown would have to apply to *all* players at *all* clubs through the season). UEFA's apparent hard line rebounded, however, when Arsenal successfully exposed UEFA's impotence by questioning, among other things, the fact that a dive spotted by a referee is punished with a yellow card, while one spotted by UEFA's disciplinary committee leads to a two-match ban. UEFA's own appeal court overturned the ban after also taking into account the match referee's testimony that he stood by his original decision. The case was a fiasco, one camera angle making the incident look like a dive while another suggested contact, leading two teams of UEFA officials to arrive at different decisions after viewing and hearing basically the same evidence! There was a furore over another yellow card offence when Thierry Henry got away with a handball in a move leading up to the goal which knocked the Republic of Ireland out of the World Cup in a play-off in Paris. 'We've been robbed,' was the cry, with the Football Association of Ireland asking for a replay and Henry himself labelled a cheat by sections of the media—as if he was the only player who had ever perpetrated a sly handball. The silence of the football authorities was deafening.

Athletics and cycling are two sports in much more serious trouble than football but at least they have been trying to address their particular problems. They have recognised that if they do not do so they will alienate their audiences. Formula One imposed life bans on the Renault team principal Flavio Briatore (who later won an appeal in the French courts) and his number-two (though Renault itself escaped lightly) after an investigation into the 2008 Singapore Grand Prix heard evidence that driver Nelson Piquet Jnr—granted immunity from prosecution in return for his co-operation—staged a crash to bring out the safety car and close the pit lane, which benefited his teammate Fernando Alonso, who had refuelled early and was able to move through the field on the restart and win. If this was the most despicable act of cheating in sport uncovered during 2009—if for no other reason than it could have cost lives—then there were others that were nearly as disgraceful. The Renault saga was dubbed 'Crashgate' by the popular media which also reported widely on 'Bloodgate' which tarnished the reputation of rugby union, once renowned for its old school values ('If you have to cheat to win, what is the quality of the victory?'). England rugby legend Dean Richards was exposed over an illegal substitution to allow a recognised kicker—who missed a last-gasp drop kick that would have won the match—to come on with five minutes to go in a

Heineken Cup match between Harlequins (for whom Richards was director of rugby) and Leinster. The player who came off, Tom Williams, faked a blood injury and later claimed his mouth was cut after the game to cover up the use of a concealed blood capsule. Although misconduct charges against Richards and others were initially dismissed—Williams was banned for twelve months and Harlequins given a heavy fine (half of it suspended)—Richards resigned (crucially, without coming clean about his role) and the club ordered an internal review. Williams' testimony at a subsequent European Rugby Cup appeal hearing led to a worldwide three-year ban for Richards and an increased fine for Harlequins (though the club escaped a ban from the Heineken Cup competition and did not suffer a points deduction, its lawyers successfully pleading that 'a substantial number of innocent persons would thereby have suffered possible redundancy and financial consequences'). Richards was quoted, in a subsequent interview with the *Daily Telegraph*, as saying: 'I did cheat, I knew it was wrong but I thought it was an accepted practice in rugby.'

Figuring high up among the other stories of sporting heroes dislodged from their pedestals was the sorry tale surrounding the runaway women's 800 metre gold medallist at the athletics world championships in August, eighteen-year-old Caster Semenya of South Africa. The president of Athletics South Africa Leonard Chuene—who originally accused the IAAF of racism when it was announced at the championships that Semenya had failed a gender test—admitted in the end that he and others had known all along that Semenya's gender was an issue (unconfirmed reports suggested that Semenya, who looks set to keep her medal, possesses internal male testes which would account for her high levels of testosterone). Former tennis idol Andre Agassi revealed in an autobiography published during the year that he tested positive for recreational drugs twelve years earlier and then duped the Association of Tennis Professionals with the excuse that he accidentally took a gulp of a spiked drink, after which the case was covered up. Agassi might well have lost sponsors and the image of his sport been damaged had he been exposed at the time, something which applies to two others who are facing the consequences of 'cheating' of another kind. The downfall of champion golfer Tiger Woods, who, at the time of writing, is taking an 'indefinite' break after revelations about his infidelity, was followed early in 2010 by the decision of Mr Justice Tugendhat to lift a High Court injunction granted to the England football captain John Terry, to prevent details of an affair being published. Terry's use of the privacy laws, based on the Human Rights Act that guarantees 'respect for private and family life' in the European Union countries, was suspected by the judge of having been motivated more by the desire to protect his earnings from sponsorship than by the desire to protect the woman with whom he had been conducting the liaison. Stressing that Terry's conduct was not unlawful, Mr Justice Tugendhat said: 'Freedom to live as one chooses [within the law] is one of the most valuable freedoms, but so is the freedom to criticise the conduct of others as being socially harmful, or wrong.' If the ruling arguably struck a blow for freedom—the media had a field day—it was damaging for Terry who, among other things, lost the England captaincy.

In probably the most infamous of all 'match fixing' scandals, back in 1919, several Chicago White Sox baseball players conspired to 'throw' the World Series (Cincinnati Reds beat them 5-3). The following year, seven of the players were acquitted of criminal charges, two of the accused having recanted confessions made earlier to a Chicago grand jury. Baseball issued its own verdict, the day after the acquittal, by banning the players for life. 'Regardless of the verdict of juries, no player who throws a ball game, no player who undertakes or promises to throw a ball game, no player who sits in confidence

Mixed fortunes for three of the figures involved in the BHA's wide-ranging 'race-fixing' investigations: six-times champion jockey Kieren Fallon (centre) began his comeback with 'fresh focus' in early-September; trainer Karl Burke (left) started a twelve-month ban in July for passing inside information for reward to warned-off owner Miles Rodgers; jockey Darren Williams served a three-month ban but was then refused a licence when he tried to resume his career in October

with a bunch of crooked ball players and gamblers, where the ways and means of throwing a game are discussed and does not promptly tell his club about it, will ever play professional baseball.' The players had undermined, in the words of F. Scott Fitzgerald, 'the faith of fifty million people' and baseball felt that, whatever the legal niceties, it had to make an example of the conspirators. It is often tempting to feel sorry for someone deprived of their livelihood but, as a general rule, sporting bodies should err on the side of being too harsh, rather than too lenient, in disciplinary matters. British racing's governing bodies have been accused on occasions of being too harsh but the British Horseracing Authority deserves credit for navigating a path through some high profile cases in recent times. The review of evidence from the collapsed Old Bailey 'race-fixing' trial in 2007, the BHA focussing on lay betting on Betfair on twelve races in 2004, was finally concluded in 2009. Six-times champion Kieren Fallon was allowed to return to riding in September, once an eighteen-month worldwide ban imposed for a drug offence had expired; he co-operated with the BHA investigation and admitted that he had been 'reckless' with inside information rules and convinced the BHA that he had 'fresh focus'. Fergal Lynch was, for a time, allowed by the racing authorities in Pennsylvania to continue his career in America after being fined £50,000 by the BHA in a plea bargain involving an undertaking not to apply for a licence in Britain for twelve months (a review of the BHA evidence did result later in Lynch being banned for a year from riding at Philadelphia Park, where he had become the top jockey). Trainer Karl Burke, who had not faced criminal charges at the Old Bailey, at first denied nearly all the allegations made against him but, after finally making a clean breast of things, he was disqualified for twelve months by the BHA in July for supplying inside information to former owner Miles Rodgers. Rodgers had been a disqualified person since 2004 and he himself became the subject of an indefinite ban from racing after admitting betting on the basis of information supplied by Burke, Lynch and Williams.

The ban on Burke seemed to draw a line under the investigations relating to the Old Bailey evidence, but there was a sting in the tail when Darren

Williams was turned down after applying to renew his licence. Williams, who had, like Lynch, been suspended with loss of earnings compensation for eighteen months in the lead-up to the Old Bailey trial, had been banned in July for three months for breaching inside information rules in his association with Rodgers. Williams had, however, among other things, refused to comply with a BHA order to disclose details of his Old Bailey defence case. The BHA announced: 'We consider it fundamental to the integrity of the sport that those who seek to corrupt racing no longer assume that they can simply return as a licensed individual once they have served a period of disqualification . . . they must establish that they no longer pose an ongoing threat to the integrity of the sport and they are a "fit and proper person" to hold a licence . . . anybody returning from a suspension or disqualification for serious offences can in future expect a similar level of scrutiny.' The punishments meted out by the BHA should prove a deterrent to others and are a warning that times have changed. There are still difficulties, however, with finding a universally understood definition of 'inside information' (where exactly is the boundary between opinion and inside information?). Furthermore, Williams maintained he had been unfairly treated and 'it is one law for one and one for another'; Kieren Fallon had 'not had to appear before a committee to show that he was a fit and proper person' after failing drugs tests and being involved in the same trial as him; while Lynch [unlike him] had 'stopped a horse for material reward [Bond City at Ripon in August 2004] and was only fined.' The accusation that Fallon had had special treatment was untrue. Like other jockeys who have reapplied for a licence after being suspended or disqualified, he was interviewed by the BHA's Licensing Committee. The Licensing Committee also pointed out that 'Mr Williams could have chosen to make an unqualified apology in relation to his past conduct, with a promise that he would do everything he could to see that nothing like it happened again. He chose not to do so . . . the committee remained concerned as to Mr Williams' apparent lack of remorse.'

The British Horseracing Authority is also set to tighten up its drug testing of horses in 2010, enhancing the deterrent effect by 'making increased use of information and intelligence' and doing more testing in training. Most of the positive tests recorded in British racing result from errors in administering medication. There are very few cases of deliberate doping to win or lose. The most high profile disqualification in Britain in the latest season was that of **Delegator** who was stripped of the Celebration Mile at an inquiry in December after failing a dope test. Runner-up in the Two Thousand Guineas and the St James's Palace Stakes, Delegator was purchased privately in the summer by Godolphin and his disqualification came as a result of a medication infringement and spoiled a particularly good second half of the year for Godolphin. Godolphin's ambitions are global—it won a record 202 races around the world in 2009—and nine of its thirteen Group/Grade 1 winners during the year came in the States, where the permitted use of some drugs gives rise to cynicism and suspicion in some quarters. The essay on **Rip Van Winkle** outlines the progress being made by American racing (the use of steroids is now banned in most of the thirty-eight separate jurisdictions) but raceday use of lasix is still a burning issue. Rip Van Winkle and others in the Ballydoyle contingent at the Breeders' Cup did not run on lasix and, if others followed the example, it would make Europe's strict drugs policy more tenable and would put pressure on the Breeders' Cup organisers to come into line. The essay on **Jealous Again**, one of the American-trained two-year-olds who won at Royal Ascot, provides further insight into the routine use of drugs in American racing.

Rip Van Winkle is a top-class racehorse—he put up the best performance seen in the Sussex Stakes for thirty years—but he was beaten three times by

Sea The Stars who dominated the European season and remained unbeaten in six genuine championship events at a mile to a mile and a half, winning six Group 1s in a row (Two Thousand Guineas, Derby, Eclipse, International, Irish Champion and Arc). The wide-ranging essay on Sea The Stars criticises the World Thoroughbred Rankings which awarded Sea The Stars only the eighth highest figure since its forerunner the International Classifications was established in 1977. 'The Derby is the Derby' was the reply of Sea The Stars's trainer John Oxx when asked at the end of the year to nominate his personal highlight of Sea The Stars's magnificent campaign. The Derby is Britain's most valuable race but, because of the weakness of the pound, it fell from thirteenth to forty-second in the list of the world's most valuable races compiled by the International Racing Bureau. The economic recession spells further trouble ahead for British racing, with the number of horses in training (down 3% in 2009) and the number of owners (down over 5%) set to fall again in 2010. Worrying glances were also cast in the direction of Dubai when Dubai World, the driving force behind the country's rapid expansion, called in accountants to advise on a financial restructuring after it asked creditors for a moratorium on the repayment of multi-billion-dollar loans. The Maktoum family's support of British racing was shown again at Tattersalls' October Yearling Sales, for example, when the Maktoum family and its associates accounted for nearly thirty per cent of the aggregate (the family was, however, absent from the December Sales where other overseas buyers—notably from Japan and Australia—bolstered trade for the 980 horses catalogued, the smallest number since 1993). The reductions in the numbers of broodmares and foals was modest in the circumstances in Britain (down marginally to 10,624 and 5,595 respectively), but in Ireland—whose problems are outlined in the essay on **Termagant** and in 'Top Horses Abroad'—the falls were marked. The number of registered broodmares in Ireland fell from 20,038 in 2008 to 18,851 in 2009 and the number of foals from 12,419 to 10,167 (the numbers were down more than ten per cent in North America where the foal crop is now around 30,000 and the number of registered mares around 50,000). 2009 marked the twenty-fifth season of the European Breeders' Fund which has put over £22m into racing, raised from a voluntary levy on stallion fees through which the stallion's offspring qualify for EBF-supported races (at least seventy per cent of two-year-old maidens in the participating countries must be confined to EBF eligible horses). A new yearling bonus scheme, funded by contributions from yearling vendors and purchasers and by the Thoroughbred Breeders' Associations in Britain and Ireland, will also provide a stimulus in 2010 by offering a bonus to eligible winners of selected two-year-old maiden races, including EBF events.

John Magnier observed that had it not been for Sea The Stars, Ballydoyle would have cleaned up in 2009. As well as winning the Eclipse with Rip Van Winkle, it would have won the International with **Mastercraftsman** and the Derby and Irish Champion with **Fame And Glory**, instead of those horses all coming second. Ballydoyle could, however, be thankful that Sea The Stars missed the Irish Derby, leaving the Coolmore partners to win their eleventh successive Irish classic, ten of them won by horses trained by Aidan O'Brien who now needs only five more to match the twenty-seven won by Vincent O'Brien (and two more to match his illustrious predecessor's sixteen British classics). Vincent O'Brien died during Derby week and a tribute to him appears in the essay on Fame And Glory who won the Irish Derby after coming second at Epsom with stable companions in third, fourth and fifth. Mastercraftsman was third in the pecking order at Ballydoyle for much of the season, though he won both the Irish Two Thousand Guineas and the St James's Palace Stakes

Johnny Murtagh and some of the team who worked with Yeats at Ballydoyle are ecstatic after the stayer's record-breaking fourth victory in the Gold Cup at Royal Ascot, witnessed by a crowd of 68,983 (down 5% on the previous year) and a TV audience of 1.8m (200,000 up on 2008)

(and also had the distinction of recording the best performance in Europe on an artificial surface when winning the Diamond Stakes at Dundalk). Ballydoyle also sent out **Yeats** to win a fourth successive Gold Cup at Royal Ascot. The now-retired Yeats has the distinction of having had more Timeform essays—seven in all—than any other horse in the history of the *Racehorses* annual. Twelve-year-old **Caracciola**, who also became the oldest horse to win a listed race when successful at York in May, became the oldest Royal Ascot winner, fittingly in the Queen Alexandra Stakes, the race Brown Jack won six times.

Another of the memorable Royal Ascot performances came from **Ghanaati** who followed up her One Thousand Guineas win (achieved on her first outing on turf) in a very strong Coronation Stakes. Her owner Hamdan Al Maktoum won the owners' title in Britain for the sixth time, finishing in the top three for the twenty-second consecutive year. Ghanaati's essay looks at the successs that her grandam Height of Fashion has brought to Sheikh Hamdan's Shadwell Stud and points out that the mating which produced Ghanaati, who is by the American-based Coolmore stallion Giant's Causeway, was one of the last arranged before the final parting of the ways between the Maktoums and Coolmore, the Maktoums having not used Coolmore stallions, or purchased yearlings by Coolmore stallions, since relations turned sour in the middle of the decade. Sheikh Hamdan's Shadwell stallion roster in 2010 will include **Aqlaam**, winner of the Prix du Moulin, and he can look forward to the three-year-old careers of the unbeaten pair **Arcano**, who won the Prix Morny after Sheikh Hamdan purchased him (he doesn't buy horses in training with anything like the regularity of his brother Sheikh Mohammed) and **Awzaan**, who won the Shadwell-sponsored Middle Park.

The trainers' championship and the jockeys' championship went, respectively, to Sir Michael Stoute and his stable-jockey Ryan Moore who were both decisive winners. It was the tenth domestic trainers' title for Stoute who had a one, two, three, with **Conduit**, **Tartan Bearer** and **Ask**, in Britain's most important all-aged championship the King George VI and Queen Elizabeth Stakes which carried total prize money of £1m in its first year sponsored by Betfair. The first two both carried the colours of Ballymacoll Stud whose history, from the days of Dorothy Paget and through the Sobell/Weinstock era, is one of the subjects dealt with in Conduit's essay, which also looks at the change that the King George field has undergone since the 'nineties (no Derby winner has won since Galileo in 2001) and at ideas that could be considered to restore the race to its former glories. Ascot has a fine record, for example, of attracting overseas challengers—**Scenic Blast** provided the latest success for a top Australian sprinter at the Royal meeting—and the King George could have its profile raised by being linked, perhaps through a massive bonus, with other global championship events.

Stoute's latest title put him level with Henry Cecil for the number of championships (they are two behind the twentieth century record holder Alec Taylor). Cecil himself had another good season as Warren Place continued its resurgence (Cecil's last title was in 1993). The traditional standard that flies after a Group 1 winner was raised following the successes of **Midday** (Nassau Stakes and Breeders' Cup Filly & Mare Turf) and **Twice Over** (Champion Stakes). The essay on Twice Over looks at an idea gathering momentum to stage a new domestic championship meeting in September as a finale to the Flat, incorporating races from Champions Day and the Queen Elizabeth II Stakes meeting at Ascot. Racing for Change, the latest initiative launched to 'rebrand' the sport and broaden its appeal, is taking time to develop its clear

Rip Van Winkle won the Queen Elizabeth II Stakes at Ascot (left) and Twice Over took the Champion Stakes at Newmarket; the two autumn championship events are being mooted as the basis for an end-of-season Festival to rotate around some of the top courses

plan for racing's future ('2009 was all about building the case . . . 2010 is all about delivery'). Meanwhile, racing's share of betting shop turnover continues to decline—now said to be at thirty-seven per cent —and the 2008/9 statutory levy on bookmakers' profits on horseracing is forecast to produce around £91m, one of its lowest for several years. The Levy Board has announced cuts to its contribution to prize money in 2010 of 8.8% (down to £57m), with a further drop expected in 2011 (total prize money was a record £110.7m in 2009). The move by Hills and Ladbrokes to transfer internet operations to Gibraltar is expected to result in a £4m loss in revenue for the levy (Betfair is the only major betting operator that makes a voluntary payment from its offshore business). The chief executive of Hills, Ralph Topping, made a telling comment in an interview in the latest season. 'The world has moved on. You can't stop competition [from other betting products] but racing hasn't risen to the challenge. There's an Oliver Twist mentality. "Please sir, can we have some more" . . . bookmakers have worked hard at attracting new customers, finding out what they wanted and providing it. But we are making less money from horseracing. My solution would be to work with racing to make more money for both of us.' Unfortunately, the racing hierarchy and the bookmakers are cast as adversaries, and there are those who think that the sport has already gone too far in making the fixture list 'bookmaker [therefore levy] friendly'. A full programme of 'twilight' fixtures staged at the floodlit tracks, running from the end of afternoon racing to the middle of the evening, was introduced over the latest winter. In a further development in the saga of the Tote, the Government has announced that it plans to dispose of it on the open market. Racing had hoped, only a few years ago, that it might be able to acquire the Tote for nothing but a warning from the European Commission about state-aid laws undermined a proposed sale to a racing trust. How much will racing get from the proceeds of any sale? Treasury minister Lord Myners seemed to offer a clear indication that it won't be much, if anything at all—'public assets are disposed of for the public good, rather than for individual sectoral interest.' The Government's assumption of ownership of the Tote—from which historically the profits have been ploughed back into racing—is scandalous since its effective nationalisation in 2003 was understood to be a mechanism by which it could be sold to the proposed racing trust, a figure of £50m discussed before the European Commission intervened.

Despite the worsening economy, a number of trainers enjoyed their best seasons, the greatest achievement among those being Mark Johnston's 216 domestic winners, though that was pushed close by the remarkable season enjoyed by another northern trainer Richard Fahey (dealt with in the entry on the ill-fated **Utmost Respect**). Johnston became the first trainer on the Flat in Britain to top the two-hundred-winner mark in a calendar year (Martin Pipe achieved a double century over jumps on eight occasions). Johnston's 1,2,3 earnings of £2,607,701, which put him in third place in the trainers' table behind Sir Michael Stoute and Aidan O'Brien, were also a new personal best, while five wins on foreign soil included a very lucrative sales-race victory by Shakespearean in the Goffs Million Mile and **Jukebox Jury**'s Group 1 win in the Preis von Europa. Johnston also trained **Mastery** in the early part of the year before the horse was transferred to Godolphin, for whom he won the Derby Italiano (a race which lost its Group 1 status) and the St Leger, his success at Doncaster being Godolphin's first win in a British classic for five years. **Gladiatorus**, **Schiaparelli** and the two-year-old **Passion For Gold** were the other Group 1 winners for Godolphin in Europe, while **Cavalryman**, transferred from Sheikh Mohammed to Godolphin SNC before his Arc trial, carried the Godolphin SNC beige colours into third in the Arc. Godolphin's

It was a record-breaking year for the Godolphin team which won 202 races worldwide and won more races in Britain than any other owner; Saeed bin Suroor was also the leading British-based trainer by earnings on foreign soil

sixty-two individual two-year-old winners in Britain (also including **Vale of York** who went on to win the Breeders' Cup Juvenile) was bettered only by the yard of Richard Hannon which had set a new overall numerical record of 189 victories in 2008 (*Racehorses*, which recorded 190 winners, went to press before the disqualification in February 2009 of Rebecca de Winter who failed a dope test after winning at Lingfield in November). Hannon's 2009 achievements are summarised in the essay on the stable's best two-year-old **Canford Cliffs** whose season, like that of the stable's best older horse **Paco Boy**, was unfortunately cut short before the autumn big-race programme got under way. Hannon's leading contender for the 2010 fillies' classics **Pollenator** beat the subsequent Fillies' Mile winner **Hibaayeb** in the May Hill Stakes. Ballydoyle's best two-year-old filly **You'll Be Mine** was a very promising third in the Fillies' Mile, though no two-year-old filly made a bigger impression than the Cheveley Park winner **Special Duty**, trained by Criquette Head-Maarek who has already saddled three winners of the One Thousand Guineas and may well have another. Ballydoyle was, as usual, very well represented by its two-year-old colts, the Racing Post Trophy winner **St Nicholas Abbey** looking an outstanding classic candidate and backed up by Criterium International winner **Jan Vermeer**, Royal Lodge winner **Joshua Tree**, Phoenix Stakes winner **Alfred Nobel** and the first, second and fourth in a blanket finish to the Dewhurst, **Beethoven**, **Fencing Master** and the highly regarded **Steinbeck**, among others. Alfred Nobel ran eight times and Beethoven eleven, illustrating once again that Aidan O'Brien has a more traditional approach to the two-year-old programme than most of the other leading trainers.

Among the sprinters, **Fleeting Spirit** finally managed a Group 1 win in the July Cup, which was as strong a championship sprint as any run in Europe. The Golden Jubilee Stakes, in which **Art Connoisseur** held off American challenger Cannonball, is now the most valuable race at Royal Ascot and the highlight of the Saturday card which attracted a crowd of 78,790 (a record for a single day at the meeting) and a peak TV audience of 2.1m (up 800,000 on the previous year). **Borderlescott** won the Nunthorpe for the second year in a row, **Total Gallery** beat Fleeting Spirit in the Prix de l'Abbaye to maintain Britain's dominance of France's most prestigious sprint and **Regal Parade** beat Fleeting Spirit in the Sprint Cup to become the latest in a long line of horses improved by David Nicholls after being with another stable. Regal Parade was a bargain buy at the end of his three-year-old days when Nicholls picked him up from Mark Johnston's stable for 16,000 guineas at the Newmarket Autumn Sales. The season featured a number of other horses whose achievements provide food for the optimist. **Well Armed** won the world's most valuable race, the Dubai World Cup, after a career in which he has overcome a succession of injuries. **Vision d'Etat**, bought more as a prospective jumper, took his career earnings on the Flat to over £2.2m, adding three more Group 1s in the latest season to the Prix du Jockey Club he won the previous year. Italian Marco Botti, who trains at Newmarket, pulled off a Grade 1 win in the States with **Gitano Hernando** (the first big winner for Kieren Fallon on his return) who went from winning a minor event on the all-weather at Wolverhampton in September to success in the Goodwood Stakes at Santa Anita the following month. Veteran Irish trainer Kevin Prendergast won Group 1s with bargain buys **Kingsfort** (whose essay recounts one of the wettest summers on record) and Termagant to continue a revival in the fortunes of his stable which topped £1m in prize money for the third time in four seasons. **Sariska** continued the recent run of success by small-scale owner-breeders in the Oaks and then went on to complete the Oaks double with a facile success at the Curragh (ending the winning run of Coolmore in the Irish classics). The Stoute stable produced two unusual stories, the sprinter **Kingsgate Native** successfully returning to action after proving infertile (his essay looks at others who have had short-lived stud careers) and **Spanish Moon** winning the Grand Prix de Saint-Cloud while serving a ban from racing in Britain because of bad behaviour at the start (his entry traces the history of starting stalls and points out the importance placed on starting by American trainers).

The most notable achievement by an owner-breeder was the Aga Khan's seven winners—five of them at Group 1—at Longchamp on Arc weekend. **Alandi**, **Shalanaya** and **Varenar** were three of the Aga Khan's Group 1 winners but the most significant may turn out to be the two-year-olds **Siyouni** and **Rosanara** who were in the first crop bred from the Lagardere broodmare band to matings planned by the Aga Khan, Siyouni's victory in the race named after the late Jean-Luc Lagardere being a particularly appropriate one. The Lagardere bloodstock, much of it with North American origins, was added to the Aga Khan's Studs in 2005. British-owned **Dar Re Me**, descended from one of the Aga Khan's long-standing Boussac families, was the subject of a controversial disqualification after beating the Prix de Diane winner **Stacelita** in the Prix Vermeille. As the essay on Dar Re Mi points out, the rules on interference differ between some of the major racing countries, sometimes causing confusion, and they need standardising for the good of the sport's global image. Stacelita, who won three Group 1s, and the Poule d'Essai des Pouliches winner **Elusive Wave** gave their owner Martin Schwartz and trainer Jean-Claude Rouget a double in the fillies' classics in France. Rouget, who also saddled the Prix du Jockey Club winner **Le Havre**, was champion trainer in France for the first time, his year covered in most detail in the essay on another of his Group 1 winners **Never On Sunday**. Rouget didn't train the best horse in France, though, which was the superb filly **Goldikova** who took her total of Group 1 wins to seven when successful for the second time in the Breeders' Cup Mile. Her wide-margin victory in the Prix Jacques le Marois was one of the best by a filly at a mile in Timeform's long experience (her essay names the handful of others who have recorded performances that bear comparison).

The significant fall in the value of sterling after the global banking crisis made races on foreign soil even more attractive to British trainers, who won £24,574,470 abroad in 2009, according to the IRB figures, smashing the previous record set in 2006. Saeed bin Suroor (£3,361,108) was the most successful, followed by Sir Michael Stoute (£3,295,452), Luca Cumani (£2,626,018) and Mick Channon (£2,279,794). Stoute's top earner abroad was the same horse who won most for the stable at home, **Conduit**, winner of the Breeders' Cup Turf for the second time, while Cumani's top earner was the globe-trotting **Presvis**. Mick Channon's most successful year yet, in terms of overall prize money, owed plenty to the overseas exploits of such as **Lahaleeb**, **Eva's Request** and, in particular, **Youmzain** whose second in the Arc—a position he has now filled three years in a row—earned connections £838,899 (at prevailing exchange rates), more than the first prize for any race run in Britain in 2009. Youmzain has been beaten by three-year-olds in the last two Arcs and his essay discusses the weight-for-age concession that three-year-olds receive from older horses (a concession that some advocate abolishing in championship races).

The opening of a new racecourse, Ffos Las in Wales, went smoothly but the same could not be said for Great Leighs in Essex which lost its racing dates from January onwards, after barely nine months of operation, and was unable to bid for fixtures in 2010. The administrators were called in because of mounting debts, among them money owed to the British Horseracing Authority and to the Levy Board, whose chairman Rob Hughes retired at the end of September after eleven years holding racing's purse strings. The most

Mark Johnston became the first Flat trainer in Britain to win two hundred races in a calendar year; thirteen times champion jockey in Ireland Michael Kinane was the season's most significant retirement, Sea The Stars giving him his third victory in both the Derby and the Prix de l'Arc de Triomphe

significant retirement among the jockeys and trainers was thirteen-times champion jockey in Ireland, Michael Kinane, who hung up his saddle after partnering Sea The Stars to his six Group 1 successes and also winning the Irish St Leger and Prix du Cadran on Alandi. Sea The Stars was Kinane's fourth winner of the Two Thousand Guineas and his third in the Derby and the Arc. He won big races all round the world, highlights including the Belmont Stakes on Go And Go in 1990 and the Melbourne Cup on Vintage Crop in 1993, both for Dermot Weld in a fifteen-year association during which he was the dominant jockey in Ireland. Kinane was first jockey at Ballydoyle in a very successful five-year period when his winners included High Chaparral in the Irish Derby, the Irish Champion and two editions of the Breeders' Cup Turf, and Galileo in the Derby, Irish Derby and King George (a race he won five times), as well as Rock of Gibraltar and Giant's Causeway, among others. In Galileo's year, Kinane rode seventeen of Ballydoyle's worldwide total of twenty-three Group/Grade 1 victories. Very much a man for the big occasion, but also a man of few words, Kinane announced his retirement quietly, after riding in an international jockeys' competition in Japan in early-December. Breeding horses, rather than training them, looks like being Kinane's future; he is already a successful breeder, his mare Funsie producing 2007 Derby winner Authorized, making him the only Derby-winning jockey to also breed a winner of the race.

The deaths of apprentice jockeys Jamie Kyne (18) and Jan Wilson (19) in a suspected arson attack on a house in Malton in September cast a shadow over the season. The trophy awarded to the season's leading apprentice—who, in 2009, was also based at Malton—has been named in honour of the pair. Frederik Tylicki won the title, contested over the turf season, by one winner from David Probert, though Probert rode more winners in the calendar year. Among the other deaths in the year were those of racehorse owner, punter and columnist Sir Clement Freud who was commemorated with a race at Epsom on Derby Day. Racing for Change would do well to note the following Freudian wisdom on the racecourse experience: 'The average racegoer's modest ambition is to find a place from which the opportunities to eat, drink, watch the race and urinate are no more than a minute away.' Freud was frequently in contact with *Timeform* about the performances of his horses—he must have been a nightmare to deal with as an owner judged by some of the views he expressed—and *Timeform* lost another friend in Ivan Allan, who died at only sixty-eight in November. Allan, who trained successfully in Singapore and Hong Kong, owned horses in Britain for a long time, the most successful of them Commanche Run. All of Allan's British-owned horses were given names beginning with the letter C, dating back to a time when the relevant dozen or so pages of the weekly *Timeform Black Book* could be torn out and posted to him, something which was maintained until the advent of the fax machine.

As usual, the horses whose names appear in bold in this Introduction are among those who have been given extended entries in the A to Z. The Irish Supplement makes its third appearance so that *Racehorses* provides a comprehensive record of the achievements of all the thoroughbreds who ran on the Flat in Britain and Ireland in 2009. The Supplement contains ratings and commentaries for all horses that ran on the Flat in Ireland but are not included in *Racehorses*. Some Irish-trained horses that ran in Britain, but did not win here, appear in the Supplement. Ireland still merits a section in 'Top Horses Abroad' which, given the increasingly international nature of racing, is a very important reference, providing Timeform ratings for the leading horses in all the major countries.

February 2010

TIMEFORM CHAMPIONS IN EUROPE 2009

HORSE OF THE YEAR
BEST THREE-YEAR-OLD COLT
BEST MIDDLE-DISTANCE HORSE RATED AT 140

SEA THE STARS

BEST TWO-YEAR-OLD FILLY RATED AT 119

JEALOUS AGAIN

BEST TWO-YEAR-OLD COLT RATED AT 126p

ST NICHOLAS ABBEY

JOINT-BEST THREE-YEAR-OLD FILLIES RATED AT 123

SARISKA and **STACELITA**

BEST OLDER FEMALE RATED AT 133

GOLDIKOVA

JOINT-BEST OLDER HORSES RATED AT 130

CONDUIT and **YOUMZAIN**

BEST SPRINTER RATED AT 128

SCENIC BLAST

BEST MILER RATED AT 134

RIP VAN WINKLE

BEST STAYER RATED AT 126

YEATS

BEST PERFORMANCE IN A HANDICAP IN BRITAIN

MAIN AIM

ran to 123
when winning Berry Bros & Rudd Handicap at Newbury

BEST PERFORMANCE ON ALL-WEATHER IN BRITAIN

KIRKLEES

ran to 123
when winning totesport.com September Stakes at Kempton

THE TIMEFORM 'TOP HUNDRED'

Here are listed the 'Top 100' two-year-olds, three-year-olds and older horses in the annual. Fillies and mares are denoted by (f).

2 YEAR OLDS

126p St Nicholas Abbey
122p Arcano
122 Canford Cliffs
119p Awzaan
119p Jan Vermeer
119p Passion For Gold
119 Jealous Again (f)
118 Hearts of Fire
118 Special Duty (f)
117 Beethoven
117 Showcasing
117 Siyouni
117 Vale of York
116p Elusive Pimpernel
116p Fencing Master
116+ Arctic
116 Xtension
115p Joshua Tree
115p Kingsfort
115p Steinbeck
115 Emerald Commander
115 Lady of The Desert (f)
115 Orpen Grey
115 Radiohead
114p Chabal
114p Waseet
114 Poet's Voice
113p Our Jonathan
112p Pounced
112 Zanzibari
111p Al Zir
111p Music Show (f)
111p Pollenator (f)
111p Termagant (f)
111 Dick Turpin
111 Free Judgement
111 Layla's Hero
111 Lucky General
111 Orpen Shadow
111 Silver Grecian
111 Tabassum (f)
111 Viscount Nelson
110p Cape Blanco
110+ Mister Manannan
110 Alfred Nobel
110 Atasari (f)
110 Hibaayeb (f)
110 Layali Al Andalus
110 Long Lashes (f)
110 Love Lockdown
110 Monsieur Chevalier
110 Rosanara (f)
110 Taajub
109 Azizi
109 Buzzword
109 Dolled Up (f)
109 Iver Bridge Lad
109 Lady Darshaan (f)
109 Lucky Like
109 Misheer (f)
109 Party Doctor
108p Behkabad
108 Air Chief Marshal
108 Awesome Act
108 Colonial
108 Frozen Power
108 Habaayib (f)
108 Lope de Vega
108 Mikhail Glinka
107p Black Quartz
107p Midas Touch
107p Prompter
107p Song of My Heart (f)
107 Morana
107 Queen's Grace (f)
107 Sand Vixen (f)
106P Workforce
106 Citrus Star
106 Lillie Langtry (f)
106 Puff (f)
106 Shakespearean
106 Shamandar (f)
105P You'll Be Mine (f)
105p Beyond Desire (f)
105p Dancing David
105p Kalypso King
105p Zeitoper
105 Above Limits (f)
105 Azmeel
105 Blue Maiden (f)
105 Cabaret (f)
105 Mon Cadeaux
105 Red Jazz
105 Singeur
105 Society Rock
105 Walk On Bye (f)
104p Eightfold Path
104p Prizefighting
104p Seta (f)
104p Timepiece (f)
104p Wedding March (f)
104+ High Twelve
104+ Nurture (f)
104 Ask Frank
104 Bould Mover
104 Carnaby Street
104 Circumvent
104 Corporal Maddox
104 Emirates Dream
104 Famous (f)
104 In The Slips (f)
104 Mr David
104 Mudaaraah (f)
104 Pleasant Day
104 Sir Parky

3 YEAR OLDS

140 Sea The Stars
134 Rip Van Winkle
133 Fame And Glory
130 Cavalryman
130 Rachel Alexandra (f)
129 Mastercraftsman
126 Zacinto
125 Delegator
124 Gitano Hernando
124 Le Havre
124 Wiener Walzer
123 Jukebox Jury
123 Man of Iron
123 Sariska (f)
123 Stacelita (f)
123 Total Gallery
122 Alwaary
122 Amour Propre
122 Finjaan
122 Gan Amhras
122 Ghanaati (f)
122 Golden Sword
122 Mastery
122 Midday (f)
122 Monitor Closely
122 Ouqba
122 Regal Ransom
122 Sayif
122 Silver Frost
122 Varenar
122d Masterofthehorse
121 Art Connoisseur
121 Kite Wood
121 Lahaleeb (f)
121 Libano
121 Lord Shanakill
121 Mourayan
120p Daryakana (f)
120 Elusive Wave (f)
120 Fuisse
120 Prince Siegfried
120 Rainbow View (f)
120 Shalanaya (f)
120 Turati
120 Wajir
120 Zafisio
119 Border Patrol
119 Cirrus des Aigles
119 Manighar
119 Secrecy

119 Sweet Hearth (f)
118p Age of Aquarius
118p Laaheb
118 Ashalanda (f)
118 Cashelgar
118 Changingoftheguard
118 Deposer
118 Donativum
118 Eliot
118 Harbinger
118 High Heeled (f)
118 Oiseau de Feu
118 Rayeni
117p Anmar
117p Strawberrydaiquiri (f)
117p Whispering Gallery
117 Holberg
117 Roses For The Lady (f)
117 Tamazirte (f)
117 Westphalia
117§ Father Time
116+ Antara (f)
116 Able Master
116 Alaivan
116 Board Meeting (f)
116 Evasive
116 Fantasia (f)
116 Glass Harmonium
116 Grand Ducal
116 Moneycantbuymelove (f)
116 Naaqoos
116 Reggane (f)
116 Triple Aspect
116 Yankee Doodle
115 Again (f)
115 Desert Party
115 Firebet
115 Night Magic (f)
115 Proportional (f)
115 Sri Putra
114p Darley Sun
114p Prince of Dance
114 Ashram
114 Black Bear Island
114 Chock A Block
114 Debussy
114 Fergus McIver
114 Freemantle
114 Intense Focus
114 Moonlife (f)
114 Nashmiah (f)
114 Palavicini
114 Roman Empress (f)
114 Secret Society
114 Soul City
114 Spin Cycle
114 Vocalised

OLDER HORSES
133 Goldikova (f)
131 Zenyatta (f)
130 Conduit
130 Gio Ponti
130 Sacred Kingdom
130 Youmzain
129 Paco Boy
129 Well Armed
128 Gladiatorus
128 Scenic Blast
128 Takeover Target
127 Getaway
127 Twice Over
127 Vision d'Etat
126 Archipenko
126 Ask
126 Good Ba Ba
126 Mawatheeq
126 Presvis
126 Tartan Bearer
126 Yeats
125 Aqlaam
125 Never On Sunday
125 Vodka (f)
124 Dar Re Mi (f)
124 Fleeting Spirit (f)
124 Kingsgate Native
124 Patkai
123 Borderlescott
123 Bronze Cannon
123 Casual Conquest
123 Doctor Fremantle
123 Eastern Anthem
123 Famous Name
123 Gloria de Campeao
123 Kirklees
123 Main Aim
123 Purple Moon
123 Regal Parade
123 Spanish Moon
123 Utmost Respect
123d Cesare
122 Alexandros
122 Benbaun
122 Cannonball
122 Duff
122 Kasbah Bliss
122 Russian Sage
122 Virtual
122§ Geordieland
121 Alandi
121 Arabian Gleam
121 Balthazaar's Gift
121 Cat Junior
121 J J The Jet Plane
121 King's Apostle
121 Pipedreamer
121 Poet
121 Vertigineux
121§ Asset
120 Balius
120 Crossharbour
120 Duncan
120 Gris de Gris
120 Mac Love
120 Pressing
120 Quijano
120 Schiaparelli
120 War Artist
119 Alpine Rose (f)
119 Beacon Lodge
119 Buccellati
119 Campanologist
119 Coastal Path
119 Confront
119 Crystal Capella (f)
119 Imbongi
119 Lady Marian (f)
119 Look Here (f)
119 Mourilyan
119 Racinger
119 Summit Surge
119 Tranquil Tiger
119 Veracity
118 Askar Tau
118 Bankable
118 Chief Editor
118 Chinchon
118 City Leader
118 Crime Scene
118 Curtain Call
118 Flamingo Fantasy
118 Ialysos
118 Loup Breton
118 Magadan
118 Mariol
118 Ordnance Row
118 Premio Loco
118 Profound Beauty (f)
118 Proviso (f)
118 Rio de La Plata
118 Sahpresa (f)
118 Stotsfold
118 Strike The Deal
118 Trincot
118 Voila Ici

2009 STATISTICS

The following tables cover Jan 1–Dec 31. The prize money statistics, compiled by *Timeform*, relate to first-three prize money and win money. Win money was traditionally used to decide the trainers' championship until, in 1994, the BHB and the National Trainers' Federation established a championship decided by total prize money as determined by *Racing Post*. Since 2007, the trainers' and owners' championships have been decided over the turf season (March 28th-November 7th in 2009). The jockeys' championship has traditionally been decided by the number of winners ridden during the year, though since 1997 the Jockeys' Association has recognised a championship that runs for the turf season.

	OWNERS (1,2,3 earnings)	*Horses*	*Indiv'l Wnrs*	*Races Won*	*Runs*	*%*	*Stakes £*
1	Mr Hamdan Al Maktoum	219	98	134	678	19.7	2,959,686
2	Godolphin	182	116	148	530	27.9	2,559,242
3	Mr K. Abdulla	110	51	74	312	23.7	1,973,568
4	Mr Christopher Tsui	1	1	4	4	100.0	1,575,935
5	Sheikh Hamdan bin Mohammed Al Maktoum	126	71	103	504	20.4	1,245,851
6	Ballymacoll Stud	16	9	10	47	21.2	1,187,651
7	Mr D. Smith, Mrs John Magnier, Mr M. Tabor	12	3	3	21	14.2	937,254
8	Mr M. Tabor, D. Smith & Mrs John Magnier	10	3	3	19	15.7	836,850
9	Cheveley Park Stud	65	38	48	251	19.1	830,803
10	Mr Saeed Manana	63	21	35	307	11.4	606,772
11	H. R. H. Princess Haya of Jordan	50	24	32	182	17.5	599,150
12	Mrs M. E. Slade	5	4	5	21	23.8	596,974

Note: Mr Hamdan Al Maktoum was also leading owner in the turf season

	OWNERS (win money, £1m+)	*Horses*	*Indiv'l Wnrs*	*Races Won*	*Runs*	*%*	*Stakes £*
1	Mr Hamdan Al Maktoum	219	98	134	678	19.7	2,218,068
2	Godolphin	182	116	148	530	27.9	1,743,074
3	Mr Christopher Tsui	1	1	4	4	100.0	1,575,935
4	Mr K. Abdulla	110	51	74	312	23.7	1,463,437

	TRAINERS (1,2,3 earnings)	*Horses*	*Indiv'l Wnrs*	*Races Won*	*Runs*	*%*	*Stakes £*
1	Sir Michael Stoute	133	71	99	429	23.0	3,296,912
2	A. P. O'Brien, Ireland	42	11	12	78	15.3	2,677,212
3	M. Johnston	250	141	216	1227	17.6	2,607,701
4	Saeed bin Suroor	182	116	148	530	27.9	2,559,242
5	R. Hannon	255	121	188	1371	13.7	2,504,367
6	J. H. M. Gosden	159	72	88	516	17.0	2,067,124
7	B. W. Hills	140	64	88	566	15.5	1,795,016
8	J. Oxx, Ireland	8	2	5	12	41.6	1,614,717
9	R. A. Fahey	186	94	165	1106	14.9	1,553,016
10	H. R. A. Cecil	94	45	63	324	19.4	1,311,631
11	W. J. Haggas	96	45	69	346	19.9	1,258,304
12	M. L. W. Bell	92	38	48	369	12.7	1,140,732

Note: Sir Michael Stoute was also leading trainer in the turf season

TRAINERS (win money, £1m+)	Horses	Indiv'l Wnrs	Races Won	Runs	%	Stakes £
1 Sir Michael Stoute	133	71	99	429	23.0	2,076,616
2 R. Hannon	255	121	188	1371	13.7	1,751,648
3 M. Johnston	250	141	216	1227	17.6	1,746,758
4 Saeed bin Suroor	182	116	148	530	27.9	1,743,074
5 J. Oxx, Ireland	8	2	5	12	41.6	1,599,639
6 A. P. O'Brien, Ireland	42	11	12	78	15.3	1,593,836
7 J. H. M. Gosden	159	72	88	516	17.0	1,447,852
8 B. W. Hills	140	64	88	566	15.5	1,359,890
9 R. A. Fahey	186	94	165	1106	14.9	1,123,058

TRAINERS (with 100+ winners)	Horses	Indiv'l Wnrs	Races Won	2nd	3rd	Runs	%
1 M. Johnston	250	141	216	164	140	1227	17.6
2 R. Hannon	255	121	188	164	156	1371	13.7
3 R. A. Fahey	186	94	165	138	145	1106	14.9
4 Saeed bin Suroor	182	116	148	82	72	530	27.9
5 P. D. Evans	125	56	114	104	98	955	11.9
6 M. R. Channon	157	69	108	134	145	1119	9.6

JOCKEYS (by winners)	1st	2nd	3rd	Unpl	Mts	%
1 Ryan Moore	178	140	112	444	874	20.4
2 Richard Hughes	144	98	92	434	768	18.7
3 Jamie Spencer	130	110	82	373	695	18.7
4 Chris Catlin	126	137	110	916	1289	9.7
5 N. Callan	120	125	85	558	888	13.5
6 Jim Crowley	120	112	124	710	1066	11.2
7 Robert Winston	120	110	116	592	938	12.7
8 Paul Hanagan	119	115	128	637	999	11.9
9 Joe Fanning	113	93	74	432	712	15.8
10 Philip Makin	111	75	80	495	761	14.5
11 T. P. Queally	109	93	100	524	826	13.1
12 Seb Sanders	106	77	91	516	790	13.4

Note: Ryan Moore was leading jockey in the turf season with 174 winners

JOCKEYS (1,2,3 earnings)	Races Won	Rides	%	Stakes £
1 Ryan Moore	178	874	20.4	4,617,458
2 R. Hills	98	424	23.1	2,635,730
3 Jimmy Fortune	74	587	12.6	2,170,812
4 L. Dettori	103	429	24.0	2,113,668
5 J. Murtagh	15	83	18.0	2,100,175
6 Richard Hughes	144	768	18.7	2,086,522
7 T. P. Queally	109	826	13.1	1,997,109
8 M. J. Kinane	5	31	16.1	1,896,249
9 Jamie Spencer	130	695	18.7	1,618,649
10 N. Callan	120	888	13.5	1,453,510
11 Seb Sanders	106	790	13.4	1,284,357
12 Ted Durcan	94	616	15.2	1,210,046

JOCKEYS (win money, £1m+)	Won	Rides	%	£
1 Ryan Moore	178	874	20.4	3,092,033
2 R. Hills	98	424	23.1	1,986,104
3 M. J. Kinane	5	31	16.1	1,599,639
4 J. Murtagh	15	83	18.0	1,502,820

5	T. P. Queally	109	826	13.1	1,495,492
6	L. Dettori	103	429	24.0	1,401,361
7	Richard Hughes	144	768	18.7	1,375,512
8	Jimmy Fortune	74	587	12.6	1,339,455
9	Jamie Spencer	130	695	18.7	1,070,058
10	Seb Sanders	106	790	13.4	1,063,531
11	N. Callan	120	888	13.5	1,010,913

	APPRENTICES (by winners)	*1st*	*2nd*	*3rd*	*Unpl*	*Mts*	*%*
1	David Probert	81	62	72	474	689	11.7
2	Frederik Tylicki	71	84	53	287	495	14.3
3	Andrea Atzeni	47	48	63	307	465	10.1

Note: Tylicki was leading apprentice in the turf season with 68 winners (one more than Probert)

	SIRES OF WINNERS (1,2,3 earnings)	*Races Won*	*Runs*	*%*	*Stakes £*
1	Cape Cross (by Green Desert)	135	852	15.8	2,897,835
2	Oasis Dream (by Green Desert)	100	615	16.2	2,564,661
3	Pivotal (by Polar Falcon)	110	658	16.7	1,826,198
4	Danehill Dancer (by Danehill)	77	719	10.7	1,451,866
5	Galileo (by Sadler's Wells)	39	293	13.3	1,401,061
6	Sadler's Wells (by Northern Dancer)	35	251	13.9	1,238,106
7	Montjeu (by Sadler's Wells)	49	412	11.8	1,209,584
8	Dansili (by Danehill)	83	661	12.5	1,159,078
9	Invincible Spirit (by Green Desert)	80	650	12.3	1,059,372
10	Exceed And Excel (by Danehill)	75	542	13.8	1,036,356
11	Bahamian Bounty (by Cadeaux Genereux)	93	779	11.9	865,179
12	Giant's Causeway (by Storm Cat)	40	308	12.9	852,291

	SIRES OF WINNERS (win money)	*Horses*	*Indiv'l Wnrs*	*Races Won*	*Stakes £*
1	Cape Cross (by Green Desert)	150	81	135	2,549,893
2	Oasis Dream (by Green Desert)	125	66	100	1,639,076
3	Pivotal (by Polar Falcon)	134	69	110	1,252,521
4	Danehill Dancer (by Danehill)	155	56	77	1,051,976
5	Sadler's Wells (by Northern Dancer)	78	23	35	776,754
6	Galileo (by Sadler's Wells)	87	29	39	768,379
7	Dalakhani (by Darshaan)	38	11	12	696,802
8	Dansili (by Danehill)	117	50	83	690,981
9	Invincible Spirit (by Green Desert)	115	59	80	668,782
10	Montjeu (by Sadler's Wells)	109	38	49	666,200

	LEADING HORSES (1,2,3 earnings)	*Races Won*	*Runs*	*Stakes £*
1	Sea The Stars 3 b.c Cape Cross – Urban Sea	4	4	1,575,935
2	Conduit 4 ch.c Dalakhani – Well Head	1	3	635,538
3	Oasis Dancer 2 br.c Oasis Dream – Good Enough	1	3	542,760
4	Ghanaati 3 b.f Giant's Causeway – Sarayir	2	4	457,128
5	Lillie Langtry 2 b.f Danehill Dancer – Hoity Toity	1	2	448,424
6	Rip Van Winkle 3 b.c Galileo – Looking Back	2	5	419,835
7	Fleeting Spirit 4 b.f Invincible Spirit – Millennium Tale	1	3	353,736
8	Tartan Bearer 4 ch.c Spectrum – Highland Gift	1	3	348,941
9	Mastery 3 b.c Sulamani – Moyesii	1	4	345,499
10	Sariska 3 b.f Pivotal – Maycocks Bay	2	5	342,857
11	Ask 6 b.h Sadler's Wells – Request	2	3	324,287
12	Paco Boy 4 b.c. Desert Style – Tappen Zee	2	5	288,802

EXPLANATORY NOTES

'Racehorses of 2009' deals individually, in alphabetical sequence, with every British-trained horse that ran on the Flat in 2009, plus a good number of overseas-trained horses. For each of these horses is given (1) its age, colour and sex followed by the name of its sire, its dam and the sire of the dam, with highest Timeform Annual rating where the information is available, (2) its breeding, and for most horses, where this information has not been given in a previous Racehorses Annual, a family outline, (3) a form summary giving its Timeform rating at the end of the previous year, followed by an abbreviated summary of all its performances during the past year and the date of its last run, (4) a Timeform rating, or ratings, of its merit in 2009 (which appears in the margin), (5) a Timeform commentary on its racing or general characteristics as a racehorse, with some suggestions, perhaps, regarding its prospects for 2010, and (6) the name of its trainer when it last ran. For each two-year-old the foaling date is also given.

TIMEFORM RATINGS

The Timeform Rating is a measure of the *best* form a horse displayed, expressed in pounds. Without going into complexities, the scale used for Timeform ratings represents around 3 lb a length at five furlongs, 2 lb a length at a mile and a quarter and 1 lb at two miles. When a horse has raced on turf and on an artificial surface and its form on one is significantly different from the other, the two ratings are given, the one for artificial surfaces set out below the turf preceded by 'a'. Some of the ratings may be different from those in the final issue of the 2009 Timeform Black Book series. The 'Racehorses Annual' figure is the definitive Timeform Rating.

The following may be attached to, or appear instead of, a rating:-

- p likely to improve.
- P capable of *much* better form.
- \+ the horse may be better than we have rated it.
- d the horse appears to have deteriorated, and might no longer be capable of running to the rating given.
- § unreliable (for temperamental or other reasons).
- §§ so temperamentally unsatisfactory as not to be worth a rating.
- ? the horse's rating is suspect. If used without a rating the symbol implies that the horse can't be assessed with confidence, or, if used in the in-season Timeform publications, that the horse is out of form.

RATINGS AND WEIGHT-FOR-AGE

The ratings in this book embrace all the horses in training it is possible to weigh up, ranging from tip-top performers, with ratings from 130 to 145, through categories such as high-class, very smart, smart, useful, fairly useful, fair and modest, down to the poorest, rated around the 20 mark. All the ratings are at weight-for-age, so that equal ratings mean horses of equal merit: the Timeform handicap is really not a single handicap, but four handicaps side by side: one for two-year-olds, one for three-year-olds, one for four-year-olds and one for older horses. Thus, a three-year-old rated, for argument's sake, at 117 is deemed to be identical in point of 'merit' with a four-year-old also rated at 117: but for them to have equal chances in, say, a mile race in May, the three-year-old would need to be receiving 9 lb from the four-year-old, the weight difference specified by the Age, Weight and Distance Tables on the end papers at the front and back of the book.

USING THE RATINGS

A. Horses of the Same Age

If the horses all carry the same weight there are no adjustments to be made, and the horses with the highest ratings have the best chances. If the horses carry different weights, jot down their ratings, and to the rating of each horse add one point for every pound the horse is set to carry less than 10 st, or subtract one point for every pound it has to carry more than 10 st.

B. Horses of Different Ages

Treat each horse separately, and compare the weight it has to carry with the weight for age prescribed for it in the tables, according to the age of the horse, the distance of the race and the time of the year. Then, add one point to the rating for each pound the horse has to carry less than the weight given in the tables: or, subtract one point from the rating for every pound it has to carry more than the weight prescribed by the tables.

For the purposes of rating calculations it should, in general, be assumed that any allowance a rider is able to claim is nullified by his or her inexperience.

WEIGHING UP A RACE

The ratings tell you which horses in a race are most favoured by the weights; but the commentaries should also be studied carefully to see if there is any reason—suitability of going and distance among the most important points to consider—why the horse might be expected not to run up to its rating or indeed, with a lightly raced or inexperienced horse, might improve on it. The quality of jockeyship is also an important factor when deciding between horses with similar chances.

In setting out the various characteristics, requirements and peculiarities of each horse in its commentary, we have expressed ourselves in as critical a manner as possible, endeavouring to say just as much, and no more, than the facts seem to warrant. Where there are clear indications, and conclusions can be drawn with fair certainty, we have drawn them; if it is a matter of probability or possibility we have put it that way; and where real conclusions are not to be drawn, we have been content to state the facts.

THE FORM SUMMARIES

The distance of each race is given in furlongs, fractional distances being expressed in the decimal notation to the nearest tenth of a furlong. The prefix 'a' signifies a race on an artificial surface (except for 'f' for fibresand at Southwell, and 'p' for polytrack at Great Leighs, Kempton, Lingfield, Wolverhampton, Dundalk and some US tracks).

The going is symbolised as follows: f=firm (turf) or fast (artificial surface); m=good to firm, or standard to fast (artificial surface); g=good (turf) or standard (artificial surface); d=good to soft/dead, or standard to slow (artificial surface); s=soft (turf) or slow, sloppy, muddy or wet (artificial surface); v=heavy.

Placings are indicated, up to sixth place, by the use of superior figures, an asterisk being used to denote a win.

Where sale prices are considered relevant F denotes the price as a foal, Y the price as a yearling, 2-y-o as a two-year-old, and so on. These are given in guineas unless prefixed by $ (American dollars) or € (euros). Other currencies are converted approximately into guineas or pounds sterling at the prevailing exchange rate.

RACEHORSES OF 2009

Horse *Commentary* *Rating*

AAHAYGIRL (IRE) 3 b.f. Choisir (AUS) 126 – Siem Reap (USA) (El Gran Senor (USA) 136) [2009 84: p6g f6d^{3} 6d^{3} 6s^{5} 6m^{2} 6d^{3} 7m^{6} Jun 25] sturdy filly: just fair performer in 2009: stays 6f: acts on good to firm and good to soft ground, probably on soft: blinkered/visored last 3 starts: races prominently. *K. R. Burke* **65**

AAHAYGRAN (USA) 3 b.f. Gulch (USA) – Boundless Beauty (USA) (Copelan (USA)) [2009 61: 7d^{6} Mar 31] big, good-bodied filly: modest form in maidens at 2 yrs: well held only outing in 2009: should prove best up to 7f. *K. R. Burke* **–**

AAIM TO PROSPER (IRE) 5 br.g. Val Royal (FR) 127 – Bint Al Balad (IRE) 63 (Ahonoora 122) [2009 12s 12m^{4} 14g^{4} p16g^{6} 16d* 21g 16g* 16.4m^{3} 18m 16g* Oct 30] leggy gelding: useful handicapper: missed 2007/8: won at Newbury in July, Ascot in August and, having left M. Channon after eighth start, Newmarket in October: stays 2m: acts on polytrack, good to firm and good to soft ground: effective with/without visor/blinkers. *B. J. Meehan* **96**

AAJEL (USA) 5 gr.g. Aljabr (USA) 125 – Awtaan (USA) 77 (Arazi (USA) 135) [2009 16g* Aug 30] big gelding: useful handicapper: missed 2008: gelded, won 4-runner event at Yarmouth readily by 5 lengths from Amerigo, dictating: stays 2m: acts on polytrack, raced only on good ground or firmer on turf. *M. P. Tregoning* **106**

AAKEF (IRE) 3 b.g. Exceed And Excel (AUS) 126 – Bush Baby § (Zamindar (USA) 116) [2009 82: 5.2d* 6.1m 6m Sep 25] stocky gelding: fairly useful handicapper: won at Yarmouth in April by neck from Bouvardia: below form after: may prove best at 5f/6f: acts on good to soft going (hung on firm): sold only 1,500 gns. *M. A. Jarvis* **93**

AALSMEER 2 b.f. (Feb 15) Invincible Spirit (IRE) 121 – Flower Market 68 (Cadeaux Genereux 131) [2009 5m^{3} 5s^{2} 5d^{2} 6d^{2} 5m^{3} 5g Oct 10] £32,000Y: compact filly: first foal: dam, 2-y-o 6f winner, half-sister to smart 7f to 8.5f winner Green Line: fairly useful maiden: best efforts when placed in listed events at York and Ayr (third to Mister Manannan) second/fifth starts: seemed amiss in Cornwallis Stakes at Ascot final outing: raced mainly at 5f: acts on soft and good to firm going: sold 30,000 gns. *E. S. McMahon* **91**

AALYA (IRE) 2 b.f. (Mar 8) Peintre Celebre (USA) 137 – Weqaar (USA) 83 (Red Ransom (USA)) [2009 8.3m^{6} Sep 1] leggy filly: third foal: dam, 1¼m winner, half-sister to top-class 1¼m/1½m performer Sakhee: 11/2, encouraging sixth to Quiet in maiden at Leicester, slowly away and not knocked about: bred to be suited by 1¼m+: open to improvement. *J. L. Dunlop* **58 p**

AAMAN (IRE) 3 gr.c. Dubai Destination (USA) 127 – Amellnaa (IRE) 86 (Sadler's Wells (USA) 132) [2009 57: 8.3g 12.1v 11.9f^{2} 16g* p16f^{3} 15.4m Sep 22] tall, unfurnished colt: modest handicapper: won maiden event at Goodwood in August: stays 2m: acts on polytrack and firm ground: often makes running. *E. F. Vaughan* **64**

AASIFA (USA) 3 b.f. Diesis 133 – Lady's Truth (USA) (Riverman (USA) 131) [2009 9.9g May 20] $45,000F, 42,000Y: half-sister to several winners, including fairly useful 1999 2-y-o 6f winner Miraki (by Miswaki): dam, 9f winner in France, sister to US Grade 2 9f winner Minneapple: 12/1, in rear in maiden at Goodwood: sold 800 gns. *C. E. Brittain* **–**

AATTASH (IRE) 2 b.c. (Apr 12) Clodovil (IRE) 116 – Mothers Footprints (IRE) (Maelstrom Lake 118) [2009 6m 6m^{3} 7.2g^{4} p8m^{5} 8.3m^{3} 8m^{5} 8g Oct 19] €50,000F, 100,000Y: rather leggy colt: seventh foal: half-brother to fairly useful 2004 2-y-o 6f/7f winner Lamh Eile (by Lend A Hand) and winner in Italy by Goldmark: dam unraced: fair maiden: stays 8.3f: acts on polytrack and good to firm going: visored (weakened tamely) final start. *M. R. Channon* **74**

ABANDAGOLD (IRE) 2 b.f. (Apr 16) Orpen (USA) 116 – Rainbow Java (IRE) (Fairy King (USA)) [2009 5m^{6} 6g^{4} 6m^{2} 7g* 7.1g^{2} Jul 3] €5,000F, €6,000Y: sixth foal: half-sister to winner in Italy by Glen Jordan: dam, Italian 5f winner, half-sister to Gold Cup winner Mr Dinos: fair performer: left A. Haynes, won 5-runner maiden at Chester in June: good second in minor event at Warwick final start: stays 7f: races up with pace. *P. D. Evans* **72**

ABAYAAN 3 gr.c. Sadler's Wells (USA) 132 – Showdown 65 (Darshaan 133) [2009 f11f* Dec 17] 46,000Y, 50,000 2-y-o: third foal: brother to fairly useful 1½m and 14.6f winner Phreeze: dam once-raced sister to useful performers up to 1½m Approach and Intrigued and half-sister to Poule d'Essai des Poulains winner Aussie Rules, out of very smart 1¼m performer Last Second: 3/1, won maiden at Southwell by neck from Outrageous Request, leading over 1f out: should be suited by 1½m+: looks sure to improve. *Jane Chapple-Hyam* **89 p**

ABBASHINKO 3 b.f. Shinko Forest (IRE) – Abbaleva 60 (Shaddad (USA) 75) [2009 p7.1g⁴ 6g p6m³ Oct 28] 22,000Y: first foal: dam, 7f winner, half-sister to useful sprinters Abbajabba and Blue Iris: modest form in maidens: likely to prove best at 5f/6f. *Tom Dascombe* **58 +**

ABBEY EXPRESS 4 b.g. Bahamian Bounty 116 – Glimpse 77 (Night Shift (USA)) [2009 –: 8.3s Aug 12] little form: tried blinkered/tongue tied. *M. A. Barnes* **–**

ABBEYGATE 8 b.g. Unfuwain (USA) 131 – Ayunli 81 (Chief Singer 131) [2009 –, a55: p8g p9.5g p10g p8g⁵ 10.2d Aug 11] strong gelding: poor performer nowadays: stays easy 1½m: acts on all-weather, little form on turf: sometimes blinkered/in cheekpieces: tried tongue tied. *T. Keddy* **– a41**

ABBEY STEPS (IRE) 3 b.g. Choisir (AUS) 126 – Hello Mary (IRE) (Dolphin Street (FR) 125) [2009 54: 5m⁴ 6s⁴ 6m 5.9m 7g Jul 8] close-coupled gelding: modest maiden handicapper: looked increasingly moody first 3 starts: stays 6f: acts on soft and good to firm ground: usually blinkered. *T. D. Easterby* **58**

ABBI JICARO 2 b.f. (May 2) Passing Glance 119 – Makeover (Priolo (USA) 127) [2009 6g⁴ 7g⁴ 7.2g⁶ 6d⁴ 6m 8g Oct 16] tall, leggy, narrow filly: third foal: dam unraced: poor maiden: should stay 7f. *Mrs L. Williamson* **44**

ABBONDANZA (IRE) 6 b.g. Cape Cross (IRE) 129 – Ninth Wonder (USA) (Forty Niner (USA)) [2009 99: p7g⁴ p8.6g² p8g* p7g* p7g* 8.3m⁴ 7m 7g⁶ 6m 7m Oct 3] lengthy, good-topped gelding: smart performer on all-weather, useful on turf: won handicaps at Lingfield in March (2) and May (beat Capricorn Run by head): best effort on turf when 4¼ lengths fourth to Ordnance Row in listed race at Windsor: has won over 1¼m, best at 7f/1m: acts on polytrack and good to firm ground: usually wears cheekpieces, visored eighth start: front runner. *I. Semple* **106 a111**

ABHAINN (IRE) 3 ch.g. Hawk Wing (USA) 136 – Grannys Reluctance (IRE) 63 (Anita's Prince 126) [2009 61: p8.6g p7g⁴ p7.1g 7f⁶ 6m³ 6.1g³ 6m 6.1d* 6m* Sep 29] close-coupled-gelding: fair handicapper: made all at Chepstow and Warwick in September: best efforts at 6f: acts on polytrack, good to firm and good to soft ground: tried visored/in cheekpieces at 2 yrs. *B. Palling* **67**

ABIIAR (USA) 2 b.c. (Mar 20) Essence of Dubai (USA) 118 – Jocey's Dance (USA) (Seattle Dancer (USA) 119) [2009 p7g p6m⁶ Nov 28] little impact in maidens (bit reportedly slipped through mouth on debut). *J. R. Best* **50**

ABIGAILS ANGEL 2 b.f. (Mar 12) Olden Times 121 – Make Ready 76 (Beveled (USA)) [2009 p8g 8d p8g³ Nov 21] fifth foal: half-sister to 2003 2-y-o 1m seller winner Xpressions (by Turtle Island): dam 5f (at 2 yrs)/6f winner: form only when third in seller at Lingfield: will stay 1¼m. *B. R. Johnson* **52**

A BIG SKY BREWING (USA) 5 b.g. Arch (USA) 127 – Runalpharun (USA) (Thunder Rumble (USA) 116) [2009 68, a76: p7.1g² p7.1g⁶ 7.5m 7.5m p7.1g f6g f6g p6g p7.1g³ f6f p7.1g Dec 12] big, strong gelding: fair handicapper, better on all-weather: best at 7f: acts on polytrack and good to soft going: often blinkered. *T. D. Barron* **– a72**

ABLE DARA 6 b.g. Lahib (USA) 129 – Nishara (Nishapour (FR) 125) [2009 50: 8.5m 14.1m 16g 9.9g 12.1m 12g Aug 14] tall gelding: poor maiden: barely stays 1¾m: acts on fibresand and good to firm ground: tried in blinkers/cheekpieces. *N. Bycroft* **47**

ABLE MASTER (IRE) 3 b.g. Elusive City (USA) 117 – Foresta Verde (USA) 46 (Green Forest (USA) 134) [2009 91: 5g⁴ 6s² 6m 6g³ 6m³ 6d* 7m² 7d⁵ 6s⁵ Nov 7] smallish, strong gelding: type to carry condition: smart performer: much improved when winning handicap at York in September by 2½ lengths from Kaldoun Kingdom: good neck second to Musaalem in listed race at Redcar, best effort after: effective at 6f/7f: acts on soft and good to firm going. *B. Smart* **116**

ABOUKIR 3 b.g. Almutawakel 126 – Conquestadora 98 (Hernando (FR) 127) [2009 70p: 11m 8m⁶ 9.9f f8g³ 8.3d 10d Aug 7] modest performer: should stay 1¼m+: acts on fibresand and good to firm ground: tried tongue tied: looks reluctant. *P. F. I. Cole* **62 §**

Mr J. Hanson's "Above Average"

ABOVE AVERAGE (IRE) 3 b.c. High Chaparral (IRE) 132 – Crystal Valkyrie (IRE) **110**
81 (Danehill (USA) 126) [2009 73p: 10.3g^2 10m* 12.3m 12m 13m^3 12m^5 14.6m 16m^3 Oct 17] tall colt: smart performer: much improved, and won bet365 Classic Trial at Sandown (beat Big Bound by head) in April: best effort when length third to Akmal in Jockey Club Cup at Newmarket final start: stays 2m: raced only on good/good to firm ground: sold privately, and to join L. Freedman in Australia. *B. W. Hills*

ABOVE LIMITS (IRE) 2 b.f. (Apr 3) Exceed And Excel (AUS) 126 – Cin Isa Luv **105**
(USA) (Private Account (USA)) [2009 p5.1g^3 5g* 6f^6 5.2d 5.2m^3 5m^3 5g^6 Oct 10] €16,000Y: lengthy filly: half-sister to several winners, including fairly useful 2002 2-y-o 1m winner Bugatti Royale (by Dynaformer): dam, US 1m winner, half-sister to US Grade 1 2-y-o 8.5f winner Script Ohio: useful performer: won maiden at Sandown in May: much improved when length third to Strike The Deal in listed event at Doncaster penultimate start: just respectable sixth in Cornwallis Stakes at Ascot next time, unable to lead: will prove best at 5f/6f: front runner: sold 65,000 gns. *Tom Dascombe*

ABRAHAM LINCOLN (IRE) 5 b.h. Danehill (USA) 126 – Moon Drop 103 **102**
(Dominion 123) [2009 114: p6g^5 5.8s^6 6g^2 6s^3 6m 6g 6m^3 Jul 2] strong, good-bodied horse: just useful performer in 2009: creditable efforts when placed at Haydock (minor event, 5¼ lengths third to Royal Rock) and York (handicap) in May: below form after: best at 6f: acts on polytrack, soft and good to firm going: sold 65,000 gns later in July, resold 30,000 gns in October. *D. Nicholls*

ABRIACHAN 2 b.c. (Mar 31) Celtic Swing 138 – Cape Finisterre (IRE) (Cape Cross **83**
(IRE) 129) [2009 p7.1g^3 7m* 7d Sep 6] £16,000Y: first foal: dam unraced out of close

relation to smart performer up to 14.6f Startino: fairly useful form: won maiden at Folkestone in August easily by 1½ lengths from Yarra River: well held in nursery at York next time: should be suited by 1m+. *M. G. Quinlan*

ABSA LUTTE (IRE) 6 b.m. Darnay 117 – Zenana (IRE) 74 (Lucky Guest 109) [2009 **81**
82: 10s 6s^2 7s p6g^6 a6g^3 7m p6g^3 p5g* p6m* 5v^2 p6f* Dec 13] tall, lengthy mare: fairly useful performer: left J. Nash in Ireland, won 2 claimers at Kempton within 3 days in October and, having been trained on tenth start only by Gay Kelleway, handicap at Kempton in December: effective at 5f to easy 7f: acts on sand/polytrack and any turf going: usually tongue tied: sometimes slowly away. *Pat Morris*

ABSHER (IRE) 2 b.c. (Jan 22) Noverre (USA) 125 – Turn To Vodka (FR) (Polish **–**
Precedent (USA) 131) [2009 p5.1g^5 5.1m Apr 18] soon outpaced in maidens: sent to Saudi Arabia. *Pat Morris*

ABSINTHE (IRE) 3 b.g. King's Best (USA) 132 – Triple Try (IRE) 89 (Sadler's Wells **85**
(USA) 132) [2009 81p: 8.3f^3 p10g^2 10d^2 Sep 16] tall gelding: fairly useful maiden: good second in handicaps at Kempton and Sandown (veered right, gelded after): stays 1¼m: acts on polytrack and good to soft ground. *W. R. Swinburn*

ABSOLUTE MUSIC (USA) 2 b. or br.f. (Jan 26) Consolidator (USA) 121 – Allegro **98**
Lady (USA) (Souvenir Copy (USA) 113) [2009 5m^2 5m* 6f 5m^4 5s^2 5.2m 5d* 6s^3 7s^2 Nov 3] $95,000Y: close-coupled filly: second foal: dam, US maiden, out of half-sister to smart performer up to 1¼m Worldly Manner: useful performer: won maiden at Leicester in May and minor event at Ripon in September: best efforts in France, placed in listed race at Vichy fifth start and in Prix Eclipse at Chantilly and Prix Miesque at Maisons-Laffitte (2 lengths second to Lixirova): stays 7f: best form on soft ground. *R. M. H. Cowell*

ABSOLUT POWER (GER) 8 ch.g. Acatenango (GER) 127 – All Our Dreams **79**
(Caerleon (USA) 132) [2009 88: 16m 16d^4 21g^6 16m^4 16g^5 Oct 8] lengthy gelding: fair handicapper nowadays: stays 21f: acts on polytrack, good to firm and good to soft going: tried visored: races prominently: fair but temperamental hurdler/chaser. *J. A. Geake*

ABSTRACT FOLLY (IRE) 7 b.g. Rossini (USA) 118 – Cochiti 35 (Kris 135) [2009 **68**
75: 16d^4 15.9m^5 14m^4 14.1g^2 15.8s p16.5g^5 Nov 30] leggy gelding: good mover: fair handicapper: stays 2m: acts on polytrack, firm and good to soft going: has worn blinkers: held up. *J. D. Bethell*

ABU DERBY (IRE) 3 b.g. Fath (USA) 116 – Solas Abu (IRE) 82 (Red Sunset 120) **65**
[2009 74: f6s^3 p5g^6 6m^6 f6g^4 f5m 6m^4 f6g^4 p6f f7g^5 a6.8g* Dec 13] modest performer: sold from J. Given 3,000 gns before winning minor event at Taby in December: stays 6.8f: acts on dirt/fibresand and good to firm going: tongue tied last 4 starts in Britain, tried blinkered: often finishes weakly. *Catharina Vang, Sweden*

ABU DUBAI (IRE) 3 b.f. Kheleyf (USA) 116 – Boudica (IRE) (Alhaarth (IRE) 126) **68**
[2009 p6g p7g^5 p7g^6 p8.6g^2 p9.5g^2 p8.6g^5 8m p9.5g^5 Jun 5] fair maiden: stays 9.5f: raced only on polytrack and good to firm ground. *C. A. Dwyer*

ABULHARITH 3 b.g. Medicean 128 – Limuru (Salse (USA) 128) [2009 69: 10m^6 **66**
11.6m 11m^5 10.2g 11.7g^2 p11g^3 10m 10m^3 p9.5g Oct 15] good-bodied gelding: fair maiden: left P. Chapple-Hyam 5,500 gns/gelded after fourth start: stays 11f: acts on polytrack and good to firm ground: none too consistent (has reportedly bled). *R. A. Harris*

ACADEMY OF WAR (USA) 3 b. or br.g. Royal Academy (USA) 130 – Lover Come **–**
Back (USA) (Dynaformer (USA)) [2009 59: 6m 6g 7d p8g^5 12m Aug 23] little form at 3 yrs. *J. M. Bradley*

ACCEDE 3 b.f. Acclamation 118 – Here To Me 78 (Muhtarram (USA) 125) [2009 81: **88**
8m 7d 9.9m 10m^2 10s^2 10.2g^5 10g p8g p10g^6 Nov 13] lengthy, good-topped filly: fairly useful performer: second in 2 handicaps at Newbury: stays 1¼m: acts on polytrack, soft and good to firm ground: held up. *J. G. Portman*

ACCLABEN (IRE) 3 b.g. Acclamation 118 – Jour de Grace (SWE) (Steve's Friend **56**
(USA)) [2009 57p: 8m^5 8g^5 Jul 6] good-topped gelding: modest maiden: stays 1m: raced only on good/good to firm going. *G. A. Swinbank*

ACCLAIMED (IRE) 4 b.g. Hawk Wing (USA) 136 – Park Charger 105 (Tirol 127) **98**
[2009 105: p8.6g^5 p10m^6 Sep 26] good-bodied, attractive gelding: useful performer, lightly raced: respectable efforts in minor events at Wolverhampton (7 lengths fifth to Gitano Hernando) and Kempton (none too keen) in 2009: stays 9f: raced on polytrack and good/good to soft going: bandaged final start: sold 13,500 gns, joined John Joseph Hanlon, Ireland and gelded. *J. Noseda*

ACCLAIM TO FAME (IRE) 3 b.g. Acclamation 118 – Khafaya 68 (Unfuwain **52**
(USA) 131) [2009 –: 12m 10g^4 11.5g^6 10.1m^6 Aug 13] tall gelding: modest maiden: left S. Parr after reappearance, then trained by K. R. Burke next 2 starts: stays 1¼m: acts on good to firm going: tongue tied once: sold £2,300, and gelded. *A. P. Jarvis*

ACCORDING TO PETE 8 b.g. Accordion – Magic Bloom (Full of Hope 125) [2009 **62**
76: 17.5m 18g Oct 10] good-topped gelding: fairly useful maiden handicapper at best, just modest in 2009 (useful hurdler/chaser): should stay 2m: acts on soft going. *J. M. Jefferson*

ACCOUNTABLE 2 b.c. (Apr 24) Avonbridge 123 – Fair Compton 69 (Compton Place **42**
125) [2009 6m^5 p6g Sep 2] rather leggy colt: poor form in maidens. *B. G. Powell*

ACCUMULATION (UAE) 3 ch.f. Halling (USA) 133 – Roseate (USA) (Mt Liver- **–**
more (USA)) [2009 –: 8m^5 14.1m Aug 29] no sign of ability: blinkered final start. *M. W. Easterby*

ACE CLUB 8 ch.g. Indian Rocket 115 – Presently 48 (Cadeaux Genereux 131) [2009 **– §**
–§, a48§: p5.1g^5 f5g^6 p6g p5.1g Apr 20] angular gelding: poor performer: effective at 5f **a43 §**
to 7f: acts on all-weather, had form on turf earlier in career: wears headgear: unreliable. *Garry Moss*

ACE OF HEARTS 10 b.g. Magic Ring (IRE) 115 – Lonely Heart 101 (Midyan (USA) **106**
124) [2009 104: p8g^5 p10g^2 p8.6g^2 8m 8m* 8.1m p8f^2 Dec 19] short-backed gelding: useful handicapper: won at Newmarket in May by ½ length from Final Verse: best at 1m/1¼m: acts on polytrack, firm and soft going: genuine and consistent. *C. F. Wall*

ACE OF SPIES (IRE) 4 b.g. Machiavellian (USA) 123 – Nadia 116 (Nashwan (USA) **66**
135) [2009 71d: 7m^6 8.5m^3 7.5m^2 6g* 7m^2 8.5m 5.9g^6 7.5m 6m^6 7.1m^5 7m 6m^5 Sep 23] angular gelding: fair handicapper: won at Newcastle in April: best at 6f/7f: acts on polytrack and good to firm ground: often in cheekpieces/visor: reportedly had breathing problem eighth start. *G. A. Harker*

A CHAILIN MO CHROI (IRE) 4 ch.f. Daggers Drawn (USA) 114 – Clangigi (IRE) **–**
63§ (Paris House 123) [2009 51: 14d 12.5m p9.5g p13.9g Dec 14] little form in 2009: left T. McCourt after second start: tried in headgear. *Aidan Anthony Howard, Ireland*

ACHAK (IRE) 3 b.g. Invincible Spirit (IRE) 121 – She's So Lovely 106 (Distant **93**
Relative 128) [2009 93: p7g^4 7m p5g* 6.5f^2 6.5f* Nov 4] tall gelding: fairly useful performer: won minor event at Dundalk in August (left Ger Lyons in Ireland after) and claimer at Santa Anita in November: stays 7f: acts on polytrack and firm going: blinkered (well held in handicap at Ascot) second start. *P. Gallagher, USA*

ACHIEVED 6 b.g. Lahib (USA) 129 – Equity's Darling (IRE) 65 (Law Society (USA) **–**
130) [2009 10g Jun 15] little form in bumper/novice hurdles: 200/1, tailed off in maiden at Windsor. *D. C. O'Brien*

ACHROMATIC 3 gr.g. Green Desert (USA) 127 – Pericardia 60 (Petong 126) [2009 **62**
54p: 8.3f^4 8.1g p8g^4 p9.5g p8.6g^2 Dec 14] modest maiden handicapper: gelded after second start: stays 8.6f: acts on polytrack and firm going: twice visored: quirky. *W. R. Swinburn*

ACOL 2 ch.g. (Mar 25) Domedriver (IRE) 128 – Bridge Pal 70 (First Trump 118) [2009 **–**
7.2m 8d 7.2v Oct 31] well held in maidens. *A. G. Foster*

ACQUAINTED 2 b.f. (Feb 26) Shamardal (USA) 129 – Love Everlasting 112 (Pursuit **– p**
of Love 124) [2009 7g Oct 31] third foal: dam, 7.5f (at 2 yrs) to 1½m winner, half-sister to smart winner around 1¼m Baron Ferdinand, out of half-sister to Shirley Heights: 50/1, signs of ability in maiden at Newmarket: should improve. *M. L. W. Bell*

ACQUAVELLA 3 b.f. Danehill Dancer (IRE) 117 – Oh So Well (IRE) (Sadler's Wells **71**
(USA) 132) [2009 8.3m^3 11.1g^3 10.3s 10.3m^5 11.1g^3 12m Oct 5] useful-looking filly: has scope: closely related to 2007 2-y-o 7f winner Annaliesse (by Rock of Gibraltar) and half-sister to several winners, notably very smart 7f (at 2 yrs) to 12.5f winner Dark Moondancer (by Anshan): dam unraced out of high-class sprinter Soba: fair maiden: stays 11f: best efforts on good ground. *R. A. Fahey*

ACQUAVIVA 2 ch.f. (Apr 28) Medicean 128 – Amazing Bay 100 (Mazilier (USA) 107) **–**
[2009 6m 5.1g Jul 4] 11,500F, €10,000Y: angular filly: half-sister to several winners, including 7-y-o Scartozz: dam 2-y-o 5f/6f winner: well beaten in maidens. *Eve Johnson Houghton*

ACQUIESCED (IRE) 3 b.f. Refuse To Bend (IRE) 128 – North East Bay (USA) **85**
(Prospect Bay (CAN) 117) [2009 85: p7g 7m^2 7d^5 May 16] good-topped, attractive filly: fairly useful handicapper: should stay 1m: acts on good to firm going. *R. Hannon*

ACQUISITION 3 b.f. Dansili 127 – Quota 102 (Rainbow Quest (USA) 134) [2009 10m^4 11.8m* 12m* 12m* 14v* 12m^3 p13g Oct 29] angular filly: seventh living foal: half-sister to several winners, including 2001 2-y-o 7f winner Protectress (by Hector Protector) who stayed 1¼m, and 1½m to 14.8f winner Market Forces (by Lomitas), both useful: dam, 1¼m winner, sister to Racing Post Trophy winner/St Leger second Armiger: fairly useful form: won maiden at Leicester in June, and handicaps at Ripon in July, Salisbury in August and Haydock in September: looked laboured in listed race at Lingfield final start: stayed 1¾m: unraced on firm going, acted on any other: genuine: visits Zamindar. *H. R. A. Cecil* **94**

ACROPOLIS (IRE) 8 b.g. Sadler's Wells (USA) 132 – Dedicated Lady (IRE) 101 (Pennine Walk 120) [2009 102§: p16g^3 14m^6 12d 12d^4 12f p13.9m^6 p12.2g^2 f11m^5 p12g^6 Dec 31] strong, sturdy gelding: just fair performer at best nowadays: trained on reappearance only by A. Carroll: regressive after, left Mrs J. Le Brocq in Jersey after sixth outing: barely stays 2m: acts on any going: tried in headgear/tongue tie: irresolute. *B. G. Powell* **73 d**

ACROSS THE SANDS 3 b.c. Oasis Dream 129 – Well Beyond (IRE) 101 (Don't Forget Me 127) [2009 p5.1g p5g^3 p6g p5.1g^5 p5.1g^4 f5g Dec 22] modest maiden: best efforts at 5f: raced only on all-weather. *C. N. Kellett* **60**

ACROSS THE SEA (USA) 2 gr. or ro.g. (May 23) Giant's Causeway (USA) 132 – Trust Your Heart (USA) (Relaunch (USA)) [2009 8g Sep 30] $200,000Y: sixth foal: half-brother to several winners in USA: dam US 2-y-o 1m winner: 8/1, very green when seventh of 8 in maiden at Newcastle: gelded after: will do better. *T. P. Tate* **51 p**

ACROSSTHEUNIVERSE (USA) 3 b. or br.f. Forestry (USA) 121 – Belong To Lassie (USA) (Belong To Me (USA)) [2009 60p: p5g^3 p5.1g^5 Oct 9] modest maiden: will stay 6f: raced only on polytrack. *J. R. Gask* **63**

ACROSTIC 4 ch.g. Tobougg (IRE) 125 – Royal Dream 81 (Ardkinglass 114) [2009 99: 8m^4 8.9g^4 8.1m* 8g^6 8m^3 Aug 20] sturdy gelding: smart handicapper: generally progressive, and won valuable event at Sandown (beat Crackdown by head) in July: good 2 lengths third to Roaring Forte at York final start: stays 1m (stamina stretched over 9f): acts on polytrack, soft and good to firm ground. *L. M. Cumani* **109**

ACTABOU 4 b.g. Tobougg (IRE) 125 – Carreamia 62 (Weldnaas (USA) 112) [2009 72: 9.3m 8.3m^4 6m^6 6g 6g 7.5g 5.9d^6 Aug 19] strong, workmanlike gelding: fair handicapper in 2008: well below form in 2009 (including over hurdles): should stay 7f: acts on good to firm going: tried tongue tied: blinkered last 3 starts. *F. P. Murtagh* **50 d**

ACT GREEN 3 ch.f. Haafhd 129 – Roaring Twenties 81 (Halling (USA) 133) [2009 84: 10.2g^3 8.3m^6 8m^2 8d^5 6g 8m^3 Aug 6] good-bodied filly: fairly useful handicapper: placed 3 times: best efforts at 1m: acts on polytrack, good to firm and good to soft going: tried visored: attitude under suspicion: sold 11,000 gns. *M. L. W. Bell* **80**

ACTING ELEGANT 2 b.f. (Apr 25) Needwood Blade 117 – Diamond Vanessa (IRE) (Distinctly North (USA) 115) [2009 5.5f^6 6g^3 6g^5 6d^4 p5.1m 7g 6.1s Oct 7] narrow filly: half-sister to 5f (at 2 yrs) to 1m winner Wizby (by Wizard King) and winner in Italy by Puissance: dam of little account: poor maiden: should stay 7f: acts on firm and good to soft going. *P. D. Evans* **46**

ACTION GIRL 4 gr.f. Act One 124 – Mohican Girl 112 (Dancing Brave (USA) 140) [2009 10m^6 8.3g^4 9g 9.7m p10m p8m p12.2g^6 Dec 12] sturdy filly: half-sister to several winners, including 7.6f to 9f winner The Prince (by Machiavellian) and 11f/1½m winner Susie May (by Hernando), both useful: dam, 1¼m/11.4f winner, half-sister to Yorkshire Oaks winners Untold and Sally Brown: little impact in bumpers: modest maiden: should be suited by 1¼m+: raced on polytrack and good/good to firm ground: in cheekpieces last 3 starts. *R. M. H. Cowell* **63**

Coral Challenge (Heritage Handicap), Sandown—
Acrostic (near side) shows a smart turn of foot to peg back Crackdown; Mirrored leads the chasing group

ACTION IMPACT (ARG) 5 b.g. Bernstein (USA) 115 – Valeur (ARG) (Lode (USA)) [2009 84: p10g⁶ p12g² p12g⁶ p11g* Jul 8] tall gelding: fairly useful handicapper: improved when winning at Kempton in July: stays easy 1½m: acts on polytrack, soft and good to firm ground. *G. L. Moore* **89**

ACTIVATE 2 b.g. (Apr 16) Motivator 131 – Princess Manila (CAN) (Manila (USA)) [2009 7d 8.1d⁶ 8d² Oct 22] 70,000F, 100,000Y: small, sturdy gelding: half-brother to several winners abroad, notably very smart Italian 1m to 1¼m performer Prince Kirk (by Selkirk): dam, ran once in US, half-sister to Derby Italiano winner Hailsham: still green, easily best effort in maidens when head second to Tertiary at Brighton, staying on strongly (gelded after): bred to be suited 1¼m+: open to further improvement. *M. L. W. Bell* **82 p**

ACTIVE ASSET (IRE) 7 ch.g. Sinndar (IRE) 134 – Sacristy 54 (Godswalk (USA) 130) [2009 78: 8g 10m⁶ 10m 10g p12.2g⁵ p12.2g³ p12.2g Dec 26] good-topped gelding: fair handicapper: stays 1½m: acts on polytrack, firm and good to soft ground: tried tongue tied: often races freely held up. *J. A. Glover* **66**

ACTODOS (IRE) 5 gr.g. Act One 124 – Really Gifted (IRE) (Cadeaux Genereux 131) [2009 p16g p12g p13.9g³ Sep 25] big, angular gelding: fairly useful performer in 2007: missed 2008: fair at best at 5 yrs: stays 1¾m: acts on all-weather, good to firm and good to soft going: often front runs. *B. R. Millman* **74**

ACT OF KALANISI (IRE) 3 b.g. Kalanisi (IRE) 132 – Act of The Pace (IRE) 86 (King's Theatre (IRE) 128) [2009 11.1g⁵ 12g* 12.3m² 15.9m* 12m⁶ Sep 13] first foal: dam, 1½m winner who stayed 15f, closely related to very smart middle-distance stayer Yavana's Pace: fairly useful form: won 4-runner maiden at Catterick in June and 5-runner handicap at Chester (by a head from Zuwaar) in July: inadequate test final start: will be suited by 2m+. *M. Johnston* **93**

ACTRESS ANNIE 4 gr.f. Act One 124 – Kembla 59 (Known Fact (USA) 135) [2009 –: p8g Jan 6] little form. *Mike Murphy* **–**

ACT THREE 5 b.m. Beat Hollow 126 – Rada's Daughter 107 (Robellino (USA) 127) [2009 76: 13.1d³ 13.3m 13.3g³ 14.1m⁶ p12m Oct 7] tall mare: modest maiden handicapper nowadays: stays 1¾m: acts on soft ground: temperamental. *Mouse Hamilton-Fairley* **64 §**

ACTUALITY 7 b.g. So Factual (USA) 120 – Cottage Maid (Inchinor 119) [2009 55: f7g f8g Feb 5] lengthy gelding: modest handicapper in 2008: well held at 7 yrs: stays 1m: acts on polytrack, sand and good to firm going: tried tongue tied/in cheekpieces. *J. Balding* **–**

ACUZIO 8 b.g. Mon Tresor 113 – Veni Vici (IRE) (Namaqualand (USA)) [2009 p16.5g Dec 5] sturdy, compact gelding: fair handicapper at 6 yrs: missed 2008: well below form sole start in 2009: barely stays 2m: acts on polytrack, firm and good to soft going: tried blinkered/in cheekpieces/tongue tied. *S. Wynne* **–**

ADAB (IRE) 4 b.g. Invincible Spirit (IRE) 121 – Acate (IRE) (Classic Music (USA)) [2009 66: 7m 5m 6d 5m Sep 14] strong, sturdy gelding: maiden: no form in 2009: tried visored/in cheekpieces. *Miss Tracy Waggott* **–**

ADAGE 6 b.m. Vettori (IRE) 119 – Aymara 85 (Darshaan 133) [2009 66: p16.5g⁵ p13g⁴ 16g⁶ 16g p16g³ p13.9g p16.5g p16g p16m⁴ p13.9g Dec 14] lengthy, quite good-topped mare: modest handicapper: stays 2m: acts on polytrack, soft and good to firm going: tried in cheekpieces/blinkers: tongue tied: has looked irresolute. *David Pinder* **53**

ADAM DE BEAULIEU (USA) 2 b.g. (Mar 28) Broken Vow (USA) 117 – Gambling Champ (USA) (Fabulous Champ (USA)) [2009 f5m Dec 5] 16/1, tongue tied and very green, last in maiden at Southwell. *P. C. Haslam* **–**

ADARE (GER) 6 b.g. Saddlers' Hall (IRE) 126 – Aughamore Beauty (IRE) (Dara Monarch 128) [2009 f12g Mar 27] fairly useful form in bumpers in 2007: only second start on Flat when tailed off in maiden at Southwell. *R. Brotherton* **–**

ADA RIVER 4 b.f. Dansili 127 – Miss Meltemi (IRE) 100 (Miswaki Tern (USA) 120) [2009 99: 8.1g² 8.1d² 8m p8m Nov 29] strong filly: useful performer: improved efforts when runner-up in listed events at Sandown first 2 starts, beaten 4½ lengths by Strawberrydaiquiri and then length by Bankable: below form after: stays 1¼m: acts on polytrack and good to soft ground. *A. M. Balding* **102**

ADDAHAB (USA) 2 b.f. (Feb 9) Rock Hard Ten (USA) 126 – Compassionate (USA) (Housebuster (USA)) [2009 8d⁵ p8.6g* Oct 29] seventh foal: half-sister to winners in USA by Storm Cat and Coronado's Quest: dam, US Grade 3 2-y-o 9f winner, out of US **78**

Grade 1 8.5f winner Adored: in cheekpieces, easily better effort in maidens when winning at Wolverhampton by length from Reallymissgreeley: should stay 9f+. *Saeed bin Suroor*

ADDICTIVE DREAM (IRE) 2 ch.g. (Mar 15) Kheleyf (USA) 116 – Nottambula (IRE) (Thatching 131) [2009 p6g Sep 9] 50/1 and very green, down the field in maiden at Kempton: gelded after. *W. R. Swinburn* **54**

ADDIENA 5 b.m. Golan (IRE) 129 – Nurse Goodbody (USA) (Personal Hope (USA) 118) [2009 72: 12.1g^{6} p12.2g 8.1m^{5} 8.3v p12.2g Nov 21] close-coupled mare: just modest handicapper in 2009: likely to prove best up to 1m: acts on heavy and good to firm going: often races freely. *B. Palling* **57**

ADDIKT (IRE) 4 b.c. Diktat 126 – Frond 85 (Alzao (USA) 117) [2009 84: 8.9d^{4} 8.5m^{4} 9.9m 8s 8m 10m Oct 13] lengthy, angular colt: fairly useful handicapper: well below form after second start: stays 10.3f: acts on polytrack, soft and good to firm ground. *G. A. Harker* **82 d**

ADDISON DE WITT 3 ch.g. Where Or When (IRE) 124 – Star Entry 67 (In The Wings 128) [2009 40: 8m 12m^{2} 12.1m^{4} 14.1m 12.1m^{4} 12.1m^{4} 12g^{2} 10.1m* 12d^{2} 14.1m^{3} Sep 14] workmanlike gelding: fair handicapper: won at Newcastle in August: stayed 1¾m: acted on good to firm and good to soft ground: in cheekpieces/visor last 5 starts: fair juvenile hurdler: dead. *Micky Hammond* **69**

ADDWAITYA 4 b.g. Xaar 132 – Three White Sox 73 (Most Welcome 131) [2009 73: 10f^{3} 9m* 8d^{6} 8.5m^{2} 9.7m^{5} 10g^{2} p10m^{5} p10m Dec 9] leggy gelding: fairly useful handicapper: won amateur event at Goodwood in June: left C. Wall 18,000 gns after sixth outing: stays 1¼m: acts on polytrack, firm and good to soft going: in cheekpieces last 2 starts. *Mrs L. J. Mongan* **85**

ADELE BLANC SEC (FR) 2 b.f. (Mar 31) Marchand de Sable (USA) 117 – Plead (FR) (Bering 136) [2009 6f^{2} p6g* Aug 27] €22,000Y: useful-looking filly: fourth foal: half-sister to 3 winners in France, including 1¼m winner Pleando and 1½m winner Quart de Cidre (both by Hernando): dam, French 11f winner, half-sister to smart French performer up to 12.5f Playact: very promising both starts, winning 12-runner maiden at Lingfield comfortably by 3½ lengths from Rakaan: bred to be suited by 1m+: useful prospect. *Tom Dascombe* **93 p**

ADLERFLUG (GER) 5 ch.h. In The Wings 128 – Aiyana (GER) (Last Tycoon 131) [2009 123: 10.5g^{3} Apr 26] very smart performer at best: successful in Deutsches Derby at Hamburg in 2007 and Deutschland Preis at Dusseldorf in 2008 and runner-up in Grosser Preis von Baden at Baden-Baden both years: shaped well only outing in 2009, despite inadequate test/not best of runs in straight, when staying-on ¾-length third to Vision d'Etat in Prix Ganay at Longchamp: underwent operation after fracturing cannon bone in training month later: stayed 1½m: went well on soft/heavy ground, unraced on firmer than good: to stand at Gestut Harzburg, Germany, fee €5,500, live foal. *J. Hirschberger, Germany* **117**

ADMIN (IRE) 2 ch.g. (Feb 28) Namid 128 – Night Rhapsody (IRE) 81 (Mujtahid (USA) 118) [2009 5g^{3} 6g^{5} 5g^{2} p5g^{2} p5m^{3} p5g* Oct 11] €22,000Y: useful-looking gelding: fourth foal: half-brother to fairly useful 2007 2-y-o 6f/7f winner Golan Knight (by Golan), later successful up to 1½m in Switzerland, and Irish 3-y-o Monivea: dam Irish 1m winner: fairly useful form: 13/8-on, made hard work of winning maiden at Lingfield: gelded after: best effort when second in nursery there fourth start: raced mainly at 5f: acts on polytrack: has found little. *R. M. Beckett* **81**

ADMIRABLE DUCHESS 2 gr.f. (May 6) Compton Place 125 – Smart Hostess 101 (Most Welcome 131) [2009 6.1m^{5} 6m^{3} 5g^{4} 5.7m^{5} 6m Oct 1] 20,000Y: lengthy, workmanlike filly: second foal: half-sister to 3-y-o Lenny Bee: dam, 5f/6f winner, half-sister to smart sprinter Smart Predator: fair maiden: stays 6f. *D. J. S. ffrench Davis* **66**

ADMIRABLE DUQUE (IRE) 3 b.g. Selkirk (USA) 129 – Stunning (USA) 103 (Nureyev (USA) 131) [2009 69: 11.6m^{3} 12.6g* 12m 14g 11.6g^{5} 14.1m 14g 13.3m 12d p12g p12.2g* p12m Nov 21] lengthy gelding: fairly useful handicapper: won at Warwick in May and Wolverhampton in October: stays 12.6f: acts on polytrack and good to firm ground: tried blinkered, in cheekpieces last 2 outings: unreliable. *D. J. S. ffrench Davis* **80 §**

ADMIRAL ARRY 4 ch.g. Compton Admiral 121 – Loreto Rose 76 (Lahib (USA) 129) [2009 –: 7d 5.7m 10m^{6} Jun 1] no form: tried in visor/cheekpieces. *J. M. Bradley* **–**

ADMIRAL BOND (IRE) 4 ch.g. Titus Livius (FR) 115 – Where's Charlotte 53 (Sure Blade (USA) 130) [2009 72: p5.1g^{2} p5g^{5} p5.1g^{5} p5.1m^{2} f5g^{5} 6m p5.1g p5.1g^{5} p6g 5g^{5} f5f^{6} f5g^{6} Dec 22] strong gelding: modest handicapper nowadays: best at 5f: acts on all-weather and good to soft going: wears headgear: held up. *G. R. Oldroyd* **62**

ADMIRAL BREESE 2 b.g. (May 10) Halling (USA) 133 – Covet (Polish Precedent (USA) 131) [2009 8.3v f7g³ f7f³ Dec 17] good-topped gelding: seemingly best effort in maidens when 10 lengths third to Solicitor at Southwell second start. *R. Hollinshead* **60 ?**

ADMIRAL COCHRANE (IRE) 2 b.c. (Mar 5) Noverre (USA) 125 – Michelle Hicks 92 (Ballad Rock 122) [2009 6s⁶ 5g⁴ 6g p6f³ f6m³ p7g² p6g* p7f³ Dec 20] 12,500F, 12,000Y: useful-looking colt: half-brother to several winners, notably useful 2003 2-y-o 6f winner Malvern Light (by Zieten): dam 2-y-o 7.5f winner: fair performer: won nursery at Wolverhampton in December: effective at 6f/7f: acts on all-weather. *W. Jarvis* **76**

ADMIRAL DUNDAS (IRE) 4 b.g. Noverre (USA) 125 – Brandish (Warning 136) [2009 91: 8.5m 8.9d² 8g 10g 9g⁶ 10.1m⁴ 9.2g* p9.5g⁵ 9.9s⁶ 10.3g Oct 24] angular gelding: fairly useful performer: won claimer at Hamilton in September: stays easy 9.4f: acts on polytrack, soft and good to firm going: below par in cheekpieces/blinkers: sold 16,000 gns. *W. Jarvis* **88**

ADMIRAL (IRE) 8 b.g. Alhaarth (IRE) 126 – Coast Is Clear (IRE) 60 (Rainbow Quest (USA) 134) [2009 12.1m⁴ 14.6g 12.3m 16.2g 15m 12.1g Jun 17] rangy, good sort: fluent mover: useful handicapper in 2006: lightly raced and no form since: tried in blinkers/cheekpieces/tongue tie. *S. Parr* **–**

ADMIRAL OF THE DEE (IRE) 3 b.g. Catcher In The Rye (IRE) 115 – Grandmette (IRE) 54 (Grand Lodge (USA) 125) [2009 7.5m⁶ Jun 23] 28/1, well-held last in maiden at Beverley. *Pat Morris* **–**

ADMIRAL SANDHOE (USA) 3 ch.g. Diesis 133 – Dancing Sea (USA) 80 (Storm Cat (USA)) [2009 79: 8.3g 7.1m² p8g 7m p7g⁴ 7m⁶ 7g Aug 29] strong gelding: fair maiden handicapper: stays 1m: acts on soft and good to firm going: gelded after final start: unreliable. *Mrs A. J. Perrett* **72 §**

ADMIRALS WAY 4 ch.g. Observatory (USA) 131 – Dockage (CAN) (Riverman (USA) 131) [2009 65§: f8g p7g⁴ p7g p7g* p5g⁴ p8g Apr 2] medium-sized gelding: modest handicapper: won apprentice event at Kempton in March: stays 9f, effective at shorter: acts on polytrack, soft and good to firm going: carries head awkwardly. *C. N. Kellett* **59**

ADMIRE THE VIEW (IRE) 2 ch.f. (Apr 21) Dubawi (IRE) 129 – Miss Honorine (IRE) 109 (Highest Honor (FR) 124) [2009 6.1m 7d* 7g Aug 8] 55,000Y: small, stocky filly: third foal: half-sister to useful 2007 2-y-o 6f winner Master Chef (by Oasis Dream), later successful up to 7f in Scandinavia: dam, Irish 1m/1¼m winner, out of sister to US Grade 1 8.5f winner Louis Cyphre: fairly useful form: won maiden at Thirsk in July by 7 lengths from Mad Millie: seemed amiss in Sweet Solera Stakes at Newmarket final start: should stay 1m. *D. R. Lanigan* **87**

ADNAMS 3 b.g. Nayef (USA) 129 – Bedford Joy (GER) (Big Shuffle (USA) 122) [2009 8m⁵ 10.1g⁵ 10m 11.5s⁶ p11g Sep 9] big gelding: has scope: first foal: dam, ran 3 times in Germany, half-sister to useful German performers Bedford Set (miler) and Bedford Forrest (up to 2m): fair maiden: looked ungainly final start: should prove best at 1½m: sold 3,500 gns. *C. F. Wall* **65**

ADORING (IRE) 3 b.f. One Cool Cat (USA) 123 – Refined (IRE) 95 (Statoblest 120) [2009 7m* 7g⁵ 8m⁶ Aug 15] 70,000Y: sixth foal: closely related to 7f winner Savannah Poppy (by Statue of Liberty) and half-sister to several winners, notably 7-y-o Galeota and useful 11f/13f winner Loulwa (by Montjeu): dam 2-y-o 5f winner: fairly useful form: won maiden at Newmarket in May: failed to build on that in handicaps there subsequently, though failed to see out longer trip final start: stays 7f: sold 42,000 gns. *W. J. Haggas* **86**

ADORN 3 b.f. Kyllachy 129 – Red Tiara (USA) 60 (Mr Prospector (USA)) [2009 105p: 6v⁵ 5m 6s 6m Aug 16] useful-looking filly: useful form in 2008: well below form in 2009: likely to prove best at 5f/6f: acts on polytrack and good to firm going. *J. Noseda* **79**

ADOZEN DREAMS 3 b.f. Monsieur Bond (IRE) 120 – Chicago Bond (USA) 64 (Real Quiet (USA) 131) [2009 60: 5m 5d 5g 6m 5m 8.5m 10m Oct 3] good-topped filly: modest winner at 2 yrs: no form in 2009: virtually refused to race fourth outing: tried in cheekpieces. *N. Bycroft* **–**

A DREAM COME TRUE 4 b.f. Where Or When (IRE) 124 – Katy Ivory (IRE) 68 (Night Shift (USA)) [2009 65, a69: 8d 10s p10m Aug 20] good-topped filly: fair handicapper at best: little impact in 2009: stays 1¼m: acts on polytrack: has carried head awkwardly. *D. K. Ivory* **–**

totesport.com Challenge Cup (Heritage Handicap), Ascot—
Advanced (noseband) holds off Axiom (spots on sleeves) to give apprentice Amy Ryan her biggest win; Something (cheekpieces and partially obscured by winner) and Proclaim (rail) dead-heat for third

ADVANCED 6 b.g. Night Shift (USA) – Wonderful World (GER) (Dashing Blade 117) **113**
[2009 105: 6m^{2} 6m* 5g^{3} 6m^{6} 6d 7g^{4} 6m^{3} 6m 7m* 7.5m^{4} 7d^{4} 6s Nov 3] good-topped gelding: smart performer: won handicaps at Pontefract in April and Ascot (28-runner totesport.com Challenge Cup, by neck from Axiom, well drawn and showed good attitude) in September: creditable 1½ lengths fourth to Duff in Concorde Stakes at Tipperary tenth start: below form last 2 outings: needs good test at 5f, stays 7f: acts on polytrack, firm and soft going: twice tongue tied at 2 yrs: tried in cheekpieces, blinkered final start: races prominently. *K. A. Ryan*

ADVENTURE STORY 2 ch.f. (Mar 19) Bold Edge 123 – Birthday Venture 65 (Soviet **73 +**
Star (USA) 128) [2009 6.5g^{6} 5g^{2} 6m^{2} 6s* Nov 7] good-topped filly: fifth foal: sister to 6f winner Born To Be Bold: dam 7f to 1¼m winner: fair performer: best effort when winning maiden at Doncaster by ¾ length from Jarrow, settling better: should stay 7f. *R. Hannon*

ADVERSANE 5 ch.g. Alhaarth (IRE) 126 – Cragreen (Green Desert (USA) 127) [2009 **–**
f12g f12d p12g Mar 18] rangy gelding: has a quick action: maiden handicapper: little form since mid-2007 (no form over hurdles for Mary Meek in 2008): tried visored/in cheekpieces. *A. J. Lidderdale*

ADVERTISE 3 b.g. Passing Glance 119 – Averami 68 (Averti (IRE) 117) [2009 77: **72**
7.1f^{6} 7m^{5} 7.1m^{2} 7m^{4} 7m 7d^{4} Oct 15] leggy gelding: fair handicapper: raced mainly at 7f: acts on good to firm and good to soft ground: has finished tamely. *A. M. Balding*

ADVERTISEMENT (USA) 2 b. or br.c. (Feb 8) Mr Greeley (USA) 122 – Banner **79**
(USA) (A P Indy (USA) 131) [2009 6m^{4} p8m^{3} Aug 8] $400,000F: well-made colt: second foal: dam unraced out of half-sister to Breeders' Cup Distaff winner Sacahuista, herself dam of high-class 1¼m/1½m performer Ekraar: fair form in maidens at Ascot and Lingfield (odds on, still green): should prove suited by 1m+. *J. Noseda*

ADVISOR (FR) 3 gr.g. Anabaa (USA) 130 – Armilina (FR) 100 (Linamix (FR) 127) **86**
[2009 78p: 8d^{5} 8.3g* 9g^{6} 9.9m^{4} 10.1g^{4} 12s^{2} 11.9g^{6} Aug 6] tall gelding: fairly useful handicapper: won at Windsor in April: best effort when second at Doncaster: stays 1½m: acts on soft and good to firm going: joined P. Nicholls and gelded, won juvenile event on hurdling debut. *M. L. W. Bell*

AEGEAN DANCER 7 b.g. Piccolo 121 – Aegean Flame 86 (Anshan 119) [2009 101: **92**
5m^{2} 5g 5.4m Aug 18] close-coupled gelding: fairly useful handicapper: returned lame after struck into at York final outing: was best at 5f: acted on all-weather and firm going: was sometimes slowly away: dead. *B. Smart*

AEGEAN DESTINY 2 b.f. (Mar 18) Beat Hollow 126 – Starlist (Observatory (USA) **67**
131) [2009 5m^{6} 6f 5.1g^{3} 7m* 8m^{2} p7m f8m p8g^{5} p7.1m^{4} p8.6g Dec 17] leggy filly: first **a54**
foal: dam unraced half-sister to useful 1½m/1¾m winner Big Moment, out of sister to Park Hill Stakes winner Eva Luna, herself dam of St Leger winner Brian Boru: fair performer, better on turf than all-weather: won seller at Leicester in September: left R. Hannon after sixth start: stays 1m: acts on good to firm going. *R. A. Harris*

AEGEAN KING 3 b.g. Falbrav (IRE) 133 – Aegean Dream (IRE) 97 (Royal Academy **62**
(USA) 130) [2009 p5g^{6} 5m^{6} 5m^{5} 5m^{3} Jul 4] modest maiden: gelded after final outing: likely to stay 6f: sold £800 in December. *M. Wigham*

AEGEAN PRIDE 4 b.f. Sakhee (USA) 136 – Aegean Dream (IRE) 97 (Royal Academy (USA) 130) [2009 68: f7g^{6} p8.6g p7.1g 7.1m 7s 6m Jun 10] lengthy filly: maiden: fair at 3 yrs: little form in 2009. *A. Berry* **–**

AEGEAN PRINCE 5 b.g. Dr Fong (USA) 128 – Dizzydaisy 57 (Sharpo 132) [2009 89: 14.1g^{2} p12.2g^{6} 12g p11g 14.8g p13.9g Oct 9] compact gelding: fairly useful handicapper: left R. Hannon £17,000 after 4 yrs: well below form after second outing: stays easy 1¾m: acts on polytrack, good to soft and good to firm ground: tried in cheekpieces/blinkers: held up: sold 3,500 gns. *P. Howling* **87 d**

AEGEAN ROSE 4 br.f. Superior Premium 122 – Lady Sabina 61 (Bairn (USA) 126) [2009 p8.6g p8g^{4} p8g 10.9m p12g p10g May 12] no solid form. *M. Blanshard* **–**

AEGEAN SHADOW 3 ch.f. Sakhee (USA) 136 – Noble View (USA) 68 (Distant View (USA) 126) [2009 6d* p8f Sep 10] third foal: half-sister to 5-y-o Silver Hotspur: dam, maiden (stayed 9f), half-sister to Poule d'Essai des Pouliches winner Houseproud: 33/1, won maiden at Leicester in July by length from Mata Hari Blue: never a threat in apprentice handicap at Kempton next time: sold 17,000 gns. *M. Wigham* **71**

AEGEAN (USA) 2 b.f. (Feb 27) Northern Afleet (USA) 117 – Apt To Star (USA) (Aptitude (USA) 128) [2009 p4.5f* a5g* 6f a5.5f^{4} a6f Dec 19] $70,000Y: compact filly: first foal: dam ran once in USA: won maiden at Keeneland and Grade 3 Kentucky Juvenile Stakes at Churchill Downs (beat stable-companion Jealous Again 1¼ lengths), both in April: 11/4, only mid-field in 22-runner Albany Stakes at Royal Ascot next time: odds on, not discredited when fourth in non-graded stakes at Monmouth: off over 4 months, well below form final outing: should stay 6f: acts on polytrack and dirt: blinkered first 3 outings, also tongue tied at Royal Ascot. *Wesley A. Ward, USA* **102**

AERODYNAMIC (IRE) 2 b.c. (Apr 6) Oratorio (IRE) 128 – Willowbridge (IRE) (Entrepreneur 123) [2009 6.1g* 7m^{6} Jun 20] 95,000F, 200,000Y: attractive colt: fourth foal: closely related to 5-y-o Willow Dancer and half-brother to winner in Greece by Fasliyev: dam unraced close relation to Breeders' Cup Turf winner Northern Spur: won maiden at Nottingham easily by length from Ballodair: still green and stiff task when only sixth to Big Audio in listed race at Royal Ascot 9 days later: should stay 7f. *Pat Eddery* **82**

AEROPLANE 6 b.h. Danehill Dancer (IRE) 117 – Anita At Dawn (IRE) 77 (Anita's Prince 126) [2009 103+: p7g* p6g^{4} p7.1g^{3} p7.1g^{3} p7g^{6} 7m p7.1g* p7g* p7f^{6} p8f^{2} Dec 20] medium-sized horse: smart performer: won handicap at Kempton in January and claimers at Wolverhampton in September (left S. Callaghan) and Lingfield in November (left Ian Williams £15,000): back to near best when ¾-length second to Falcativ in handicap at Kempton final start: best at 7f: acts on polytrack, soft and good to firm going: sometimes in cheekpieces: hard ride. *P. D. Evans* **110**

AESTIVAL 3 b.g. Falbrav (IRE) 133 – Summer Night 94 (Nashwan (USA) 135) [2009 –p: 10g Oct 19] little form: withdrawn at stall intended reappearance. *Sir Mark Prescott* **–**

AETOS 2 b.c. (Apr 22) Royal Applause 124 – Hagwah (USA) 109 (Dancing Brave (USA) 140) [2009 6g^{4} Jul 28] €50,000F, 72,000Y: big, well-made colt: half-brother to several winners, including useful 1¼m/1½m winner Trust Rule (by Selkirk) and 3-y-o Nizhoni Dancer: dam, 1m to 1½m winner, half-sister to very smart US performer up to 11f Sarafan: second favourite, green and not knocked about when 9¼ lengths fourth to Lowdown in maiden at Goodwood: should stay at least 1m: should improve. *M. P. Tregoning* **69 p**

AFFIRMABLE 2 b.f. (Apr 1) Doyen (IRE) 132 – Bella Bellisimo (IRE) 84 (Alzao (USA) 117) [2009 7g^{6} Aug 14] sixth foal: half-sister to 7f winner Scroll (by Mark of Esteem), later successful in Belgium, and German 1¼m winner Nico's Friend (by Nayef): dam, 2-y-o 6f winner (stayed 1¼m), out of half-sister to Oaks second Wind In Her Hair, herself dam of top-class Japanese colt Deep Impact: 100/1, shaped well when 7 lengths sixth of 16 to Destination Aim in maiden at Newmarket, smooth headway before green under pressure: bred to stay 1m+: should progress. *J. W. Hills* **64 p**

AFFIRMATIVELY 4 b.f. Diktat 126 – Circlet 74 (Lion Cavern (USA) 117) [2009 71d: p6g p7g p5.1g^{4} p5g^{3} p5g^{2} p5.1g 5f 5m^{3} 6m 5.5g^{5} 6m p5g Jul 22] leggy, useful-looking filly: modest handicapper: stays easy 7f: acts on polytrack and good to firm going: usually blinkered/tongue tied nowadays: signs of temperament. *A. W. Carroll* **51**

AFFLUENT 3 b.f. Oasis Dream 129 – Valencia 79 (Kenmare (FR) 125) [2009 78P: p5g^{2} 5g^{3} 5g* 5m^{5} 5g^{5} 5.7f^{4} Aug 22] attractive filly: fairly useful handicapper: won at Windsor in May: below form after: should have stayed 6f: acted on polytrack and soft ground: stud. *R. Charlton* **89**

AFLAAM (IRE) 4 b.g. Dubai Destination (USA) 127 – Arjuzah (IRE) 110 (Ahonoora 122) [2009 82: p8g 7m 8m4 p7.1g 7g5 8.3m3 8m p7m p10m p10m Dec 10] tall, good-topped gelding: fairly useful handicapper: left P. Howling prior to final start: stays 8.3f: acts on good to firm and good to soft ground: tried tongue tied: held up. *R. A. Harris* **86**

AFRICAN ART (USA) 3 ch.c. Johannesburg (USA) 127 – Perovskia (USA) (Stravinsky (USA) 133) [2009 70p: 8.1m* 8m4 8m 8m5 8m3 p7g Oct 24] good-topped colt: fairly useful performer: won maiden at Haydock in April: best effort when third in handicap at Pontefract: stays 1m: acts on good to firm ground: sold 22,000 gns, sent to Switzerland. *B. J. Meehan* **94**

AFRICAN CHEETAH 3 ch.c. Pivotal 124 – Miss Queen (USA) (Miswaki (USA) 124) [2009 7m3 7.1m6 8.5g3 10.1s* 10d4 9.7m4 12.4g3 12g5 10g6 p8.6g* Dec 7] 200,000Y: rangy colt: sixth foal: half-brother to several winners, including useful 6.5f to 1m winner Mandobi (by Mark of Esteem) and smart 6f (at 2 yrs) to 1m winner Prince of Light (by Fantastic Light): dam, US 6f winner, half-sister to useful 6f/7f winner Tajannub: fairly useful form: won maiden at Newcastle in May and, having left M. Johnston £19,000, handicap at Wolverhampton in December: effective at 8.6f, barely stays 12.4f: acts on polytrack, soft and good to firm going. *R. Hollinshead* **84**

AFRICAN ROSE 4 ch.f. Observatory (USA) 131 – New Orchid (USA) 106 (Quest For Fame 127) [2009 119: 5m4 6m6 6.5g Aug 9] good-topped filly: smart performer: won Sprint Cup at Doncaster in 2008: respectable efforts first 2 starts at 4 yrs, fourth to Tax Free in Prix du Gros-Chene at Chantilly and sixth to Fleeting Spirit in July Cup at Newmarket: reportedly bled when well held in Prix Maurice de Gheest at Deauville final start: had form at 1m, very best efforts around 6f on good to soft ground: visits Oasis Dream. *Mme C. Head-Maarek, France* **113**

AFRICA'S STAR (IRE) 3 br.f. Johannesburg (USA) 127 – Grable (IRE) 76 (Sadler's Wells (USA) 132) [2009 63: 6m 5m3 5m 5m4 5g 7v Sep 4] rangy filly: modest maiden: stays 7f: acts on fibresand and good to firm going: tried blinkered/in cheekpieces. *M. Dods* **63**

AFTER THE SHOW 8 b.g. Royal Applause 124 – Tango Teaser (Shareef Dancer (USA) 135) [2009 82: p5g2 p5g3 f5m 5v p5g 5.1d f6m p6g4 p6m p5f4 Dec 19] useful-looking gelding: fair handicapper nowadays: effective at 5f/6f: acts on all-weather, soft and good to firm going: tried in cheekpieces/blinkers: held up. *Rae Guest* **68**

AFTON VIEW (IRE) 4 gr.g. Clodovil (IRE) 116 – Moonlight Partner (IRE) 81 (Red Sunset 120) [2009 64: f8g5 f6g6 p6g p6g2 f6g2 f8g f8d Mar 10] angular gelding: modest maiden handicapper: effective at 6f to 8.6f: acts on all-weather, firm and good to soft ground: tried in blinkers/cheekpieces: tried tongue tied. *S. Parr* **58**

AGAIN (IRE) 3 b.f. Danehill Dancer (IRE) 117 – Cumbres (FR) (Kahyasi 130) [2009 108: 8v* 8f 8d3 10g Oct 4] **115**

While Ballydoyle had plenty to choose from for its multiple entries in the colts' classics, it was a different story with the fillies. Its sole representative Heart Shaped made the frame in the One Thousand Guineas, but Ballydoyle's Oaks contender, the Cheshire Oaks winner Perfect Truth, finished last. The situation was even worse in the Irish One Thousand Guineas and Oaks in which the Ballydoyle fillies were well beaten. The Coolmore partners still won the boylesports.com Irish One Thousand Guineas, however, with the David Wachman-trained Again, whose victory gave them a tenth successive Irish classic (Fame And Glory extended the sequence to eleven—ten of the wins for Aidan O'Brien-trained horses—in the Irish Derby until British-trained Sariska broke the sequence in the Irish Oaks).

Again's success improved the subsequent collective record of winners of the Moyglare Stud Stakes, whose achievements have fallen short of those of the winners of other Group 1s such as the Cheveley Park Stakes and the Fillies' Mile. Doubt was cast in *Racehorses* on whether Again would prove a genuine classic contender, especially as she had been well beaten afterwards in the Prix Marcel Boussac. In the event, Again progressed enough over the winter to make a winning start to her three-year-old season in the Irish One Thousand Guineas, providing David Wachman, who plays a significant role within the Coolmore set-up, with his first classic success. In terms of form, the latest edition of the Irish One Thousand Guineas, a strongly-run race on heavy going, was nothing out of the ordinary and, furthermore, the form completely failed to work out. Until British-trained runner-up Lahaleeb won the Grade 1 E. P. Taylor Stakes at Woodbine in October,

boylesports.com Irish 1000 Guineas, the Curragh—Again (right) wanders markedly under pressure as she wears down Lahaleeb; Oh Goodness Me (centre) takes third; 25/1-shot Totally Devoted finishes in the rear in Aidan O'Brien's attempt at a tenth successive Irish classic

the sixteen fillies who ran at the Curragh in May had managed to win only three of their fifty-four subsequent races—two maidens and a minor event. With neither the Newmarket One Thousand Guineas winner nor any of the leading French-trained fillies taking part, Again was sent off the 5/2 favourite for the Irish One Thousand Guineas. Cuis Ghaire and Super Sleuth had followed Ghanaati home at Newmarket three weeks earlier, but both seemed all at sea under far more testing conditions at the Curragh. Again was off the bridle from halfway and hung badly right and then left away from the whip under a very strong ride before knuckling down to lead near the line and win by a neck from Lahaleeb, who had finished tenth at Newmarket on firm ground. Third-placed Oh Goodness Me finished three and a half lengths behind Lahaleeb, with nearly a dozen lengths separating Again from the best of her three other stablemates in the line-up, Chintz in fifth (Ballydoyle-trained Totally Devoted came fourteenth of sixteen).

It may well be that Again's extremely hard race at the Curragh took the edge off her for the remainder of the season, but there is no doubt she wasn't the same filly afterwards. Her yard was admittedly under something of a cloud when Again flopped in the Coronation Stakes at Royal Ascot, though on that occasion the under-foot conditions were vastly different to those at the Curragh. Whilst not discredited in finishing third to Rainbow View in the Matron Stakes at Leopardstown after a three-month break, Again was disappointing, stepped up in trip, in the Prix de l'Opera at Longchamp on her final outing, the fitting of cheekpieces making little difference, though it was noticeable that she had gone in her coat and she also moved short to post.

Again (IRE) (b.f. 2006)	Danehill Dancer (IRE) (b 1993)	Danehill (b 1986)	Danzig
			Razyana
		Mira Adonde (b or br 1986)	Sharpen Up
			Lettre d'Amour
	Cumbres (FR) (b 1993)	Kahyasi (b 1985)	Ile de Bourbon
			Kadissya
		Floripedes (b 1985)	Top Ville
			Toute Cy

A Group 1 winner at two and three, Again could not significantly enhance her racing record by being kept in training and she has been retired to the paddocks, with a visit to Galileo the plan in 2010. The Coolmore partners have reason to be doubly grateful to Again as her classic victory helped her sire Danehill Dancer to pip the Darley stallion Cape Cross in a closely-run race to top the sire's table. Danehill Dancer sired the winners of seventeen pattern races in Europe (more than any other sire) in the latest season, and his Anglo-Irish sires' title was the twentieth in a row for Coolmore. Again's pedigree on the distaff side was covered at length in *Racehorses of 2008*, and all that needs adding is that a yearling filly out of Cumbres and by the Australian sire Danroad—making her a close relation of Again—was sold at Tattersalls in October for 75,000 guineas. The strong, angular Again is certainly no oil-painting but she was a smart filly at her best and a good example of 'handsome is that handsome does.' Again looked sure to be suited by further than a mile at three—she was given an Oaks entry—and should have stayed a mile and a quarter. All her best form came on soft or heavy going and she was probably unsuited by firm, her victory on good to firm coming in a maiden at two. *David Wachman, Ireland*

AGAINST THE RULES 3 b.g. Diktat 126 – Bella Bellisimo (IRE) 84 (Alzao (USA) **–**
117) [2009 56: p8g Sep 2] close-coupled gelding: modest maiden at 2 yrs: well held only outing in 2009: tried in cheekpieces. *J. A. R. Toller*

AGAPANTHUS (GER) 4 b.g. Tiger Hill (IRE) 127 – Astilbe (GER) (Monsun (GER) **74**
124) [2009 95d: 10.1d* 10d^{6} 10s 10m 10.3g 10.2v^{6} Nov 4] sturdy gelding: fair handicapper nowadays: won at Yarmouth in April: stays 11f: acts on good to soft going: tried in cheekpieces. *B. J. Curley*

AGEEBAH 3 b.f. Acclamation 118 – Flag (Selkirk (USA) 129) [2009 59: p8g^{2} p8g* **71**
p7.1g^{5} Mar 7] angular filly: fair handicapper: won at Kempton in February: stays 1m: acts on polytrack: sold 3,200 gns in July. *C. E. Brittain*

AGENT ARCHIE (USA) 2 b.c. (Mar 22) Smart Strike (CAN) 121 – Dans La Ville **71 +**
(CHI) (Winning (USA)) [2009 7d^{6} 9m* Sep 23] $180,000Y: sixth foal: half-brother to German 1¼m winner Martin's Friend (by Grand Slam): dam unraced: much better effort in maidens when winning 9-runner event at Goodwood by 1½ lengths from Regal Guest, dictating: will stay 1¼m. *J. R. Best*

AGENT BOO 2 b.c. (Feb 10) Monsieur Bond (IRE) 120 – Silca Boo 99 (Efisio 120) **61**
[2009 5m 5g^{5} f5g^{6} p6g^{3} f7g 6d* p6m^{6} Sep 28] close-coupled colt: modest performer: won nursery at Ayr in August: stays 6f well: acts on good to soft ground and on all-weather: blinkered last 2 starts: sold £2,600, sent to Norway. *E. S. McMahon*

AGENTE PARMIGIANO (IRE) 3 ch.c. Captain Rio 122 – Kama's Wheel 51 **93**
(Magic Ring (IRE) 115) [2009 92: p9g p8g^{4} 6s^{3} 7g^{6} 7m^{4} 7m^{5} p7g^{4} 7m^{3} 7m Oct 16] **a103**
workmanlike colt: useful handicapper on all-weather, fairly useful on turf: best effort when length fourth to Khor Dubai at Kempton seventh start: likely to prove best short of 1m: acts on polytrack and good to firm going: tried in cheekpieces, tongue tied last 3 starts: sent to Bahrain. *G. A. Butler*

AGENTE ROMANO (USA) 4 b. or br.c. Street Cry (IRE) 130 – Dixie Bay (USA) **76**
(Dixieland Band (USA)) [2009 78: 10.1m^{6} 14.1m^{5} 13.3m 13m^{2} 12m^{5} 11.8m^{2} Jul 16] sturdy colt: fair maiden: stays 1¾m: acts on polytrack and good to firm ground: blinkered last 3 outings: tried tongue tied: suspect attitude: joined Evan Williams £5,000, fair hurdler (successful in September). *G. A. Butler*

AGENT STONE (IRE) 3 ch.g. Night Shift (USA) – Just One Smile (IRE) 71 (Desert **76**
Prince (IRE) 130) [2009 67: 6m 6g* 6g^{6} May 15] sturdy gelding: fair performer: best effort when winning maiden at Doncaster in May: stays 6f: visored last 2 starts, tongue tied previous 3 outings: sold £5,200 later in May. *D. Nicholls*

AGE OF AQUARIUS (IRE) 3 b.c. Galileo (IRE) 134 – Clara Bow (FR) (Top Ville **118 p**
129) [2009 106p: 11.5m* 12g 12g^{2} Jul 14] useful-looking colt: has scope: smart performer: won totesport.com Lingfield Derby Trial in May by neck from Montaff: creditable 8½ lengths seventh to Sea The Stars in Derby at Epsom next time: best effort when 1½ lengths second to Cavalryman in Grand Prix de Paris at Longchamp, leading before home turn: favourite, withdrawn at 48-hour stage from St Leger at Doncaster in September (reportedly met with slight setback): will stay 1¾m: unraced on firm going, acts on any other and polytrack: races prominently: should do better still, particularly when stamina is tested more. *A. P. O'Brien, Ireland*

AGE OF COUTURE 3 ch.f. Hold That Tiger (USA) 117 – Three Wishes 87 (Sadler's **51**
Wells (USA) 132) [2009 48: 7m Jun 5] modest form in 7f maidens: sold 2,000 gns in July. *W. Jarvis*

AGE OF REASON (UAE) 4 b.g. Halling (USA) 133 – Time Changes (USA) (Danzig **116**
(USA)) [2009 108: 12d^3 12m* 12g* 12m^2 12g^5 13.3m^3 11.6m^4 p12m^2 Nov 4] rangy gelding: smart performer: improved in 2009, winning handicap at Nad Al Sheba (beat Young Mick by 4¾ lengths) in January and very valuable event at Doha (Qatar) in February: best effort after when length second to Quijano in Gran Premio di Milano at Milan fourth start: should stay 1¾m: acts on polytrack and firm ground. *Saeed bin Suroor*

AGGBAG 5 b.g. Fath (USA) 116 – Emaura 61 (Dominion 123) [2009 63: p8g^5 p7.1g^4 **63**
p7.1g^3 f7g^2 p7.1g^2 7m^4 f7g 8.3m^4 8f 8.1g* 8.1g^2 7g^3 f8g^3 p8.6m p8.6g Sep 25] strong gelding: modest handicapper: left B. Baugh, won apprentice race at Warwick in June: left J. Mackie after eleventh outing: stays easy 8.6f: acts on all-weather and good to firm going: tried in cheekpieces. *Miss M. E. Rowland*

AGGLESTONE ROCK 4 b.g. Josr Algarhoud (IRE) 118 – Royalty (IRE) (Fairy King **73**
(USA)) [2009 62: p16.5g^3 p13g* 10.1s 16.5s 15.8s^2 Oct 27] big, workmanlike gelding: fair handicapper: won at Lingfield in February: stays 15.8f: acts on polytrack and soft ground: progressive hurdler/chaser. *P. A. Kirby*

AGGRAVATION 7 b.g. Sure Blade (USA) 130 – Confection (Formidable (USA) 125) **71**
[2009 79: 8g^3 p8g^3 8d 8.3g^5 8m 8.5m^3 8d^6 8.3g Oct 5] compact, deep-girthed gelding: fair handicapper: stays 9f: acts on polytrack, firm and good to soft ground: effective visored/tongue tied: held up: sold 7,500 gns, joined C. Grant. *D. R. C. Elsworth*

AGILETE 7 b.g. Piccolo 121 – Ingerence (FR) (Akarad (FR) 130) [2009 p9.5g* p9.5g^2 **89**
p9.5g* p9.5g* 10.1d^4 p8g 10.4g^2 10g* 10.4g* 11.9g^3 10g 10.1m* 10.2s p8.6g p9.5m^4 Nov 28] workmanlike gelding: fairly useful handicapper: better than ever in 2009, winning at Wolverhampton in January (minor event), February and March, Sandown (apprentices) in July, Haydock in August and Yarmouth in September: effective at 9f to 12.6f: acts on all-weather, firm and good to soft going: tried in cheekpieces/blinkers: tongue tied once: usually travels strongly held up. *J. Pearce*

AGNES LOVE 3 gr.f. Piccolo 121 – Erracht 76 (Emarati (USA) 74) [2009 –, a62: 5f **–**
5.3f^6 p5g^2 p5g^5 p5g* p6g^3 p6g p6g Nov 25] sturdy filly: fair handicapper on all-weather: **a66**
won at Kempton in August: stays 6f: acts on polytrack, no form on turf. *J. Akehurst*

AGONY AND ECSTASY 2 ch.f. (Mar 14) Captain Rio 122 – Agony Aunt 81 (Formidable (USA) 125) [2009 6g^6 7.1m^5 7.6d* p8m^5 8.3d* f8m^3 Nov 6] smallish filly: seventh foal: half-sister to several winners, including useful UAE sprinter Doctor Hilary (2-y-o 6f winner in Britain, by Mujahid) and fairly useful 6f winner Cool Tune (by Piccolo): dam 1¼m winner: fairly useful performer: won maiden at Lingfield in August and nursery at Windsor (very awkward on bend) in October: respectable effort in cheekpieces final start: stays 8.3f: acts on good to soft ground, probably on all-weather: races up with pace. *R. M. Beckett* **84**

AGRICULTURAL 3 b.c. Daylami (IRE) 138 – Rustic (IRE) 99 (Grand Lodge (USA) **–**
125) [2009 9g^6 11.1g Jul 16] well beaten in maidens. *Mrs L. B. Normile*

totesport.com Derby Trial Stakes, Lingfield—
Age of Aquarius (rail) rallies to regain the lead from Montaff (centre), Father Time close up in third

AHLA WASAHL 3 br.f. Dubai Destination (USA) 127 – In Full Cry (USA) (Seattle Slew (USA)) [2009 84: 8m^2 8s^5 7.1g 8.1g^4 8m* p8g^2 Oct 29] strong filly: smart performer, much improved: won listed handicap at Ascot in September by ½ length from Alsace Lorraine: good 2¼ lengths second to Moonlife in listed race at Lingfield final start: stays 1m: acts on polytrack and good to firm going. *D. M. Simcock* **111**

AHLAWY (IRE) 6 gr.g. Green Desert (USA) 127 – On Call 103 (Alleged (USA) 138) [2009 78: p9.5g* p9.5g* p12.2g^3 p9.5g* p9.5g* p10g 10.3m^6 10.1g^2 10.1m^2 Aug 20] close-coupled gelding: useful performer on all-weather, fairly useful on turf: won seller and handicap in January, claimer in March and handicap in April, all at Wolverhampton: stays 10.5f: acts on polytrack, firm and soft going: blinkered nowadays, also tongue tied in 2009. *F. Sheridan* **82 a96**

AHMEDY (IRE) 6 b.g. Polish Precedent (USA) 131 – Nawaji (USA) 45 (Trempolino (USA) 135) [2009 p12.2g* 10.3d Oct 24] sparely-made gelding: fairly useful handicapper: missed 2007/8: won at Wolverhampton in October: stays 1½m: acts on polytrack, firm and good to soft going: sometimes slowly away. *J. J. Quinn* **81**

AHWAHNEE 2 ch.f. (Apr 10) Compton Place 125 – Tahara (IRE) (Caerleon (USA) 132) [2009 p5g Oct 22] sister to 6-y-o Godfrey Street and half-sister to several winners, including 3-y-o Gilt Edge Girl: dam ran twice: 13/2, clear signs of ability when last of 7 in maiden at Kempton: should improve. *R. M. Beckett* **– p**

AILSA CARMEL (IRE) 2 b.f. (Feb 15) Antonius Pius (USA) 123§ – Dancing Duchess (IRE) 93 (Danehill Dancer (IRE) 117) [2009 5.2g^3 5g^6 6g* 5.9m* 6m^2 5m^4 Jun 28] 9,000Y, 16,000 2-y-o: sturdy filly: first foal: dam Irish 2-y-o 5f winner: fair performer: won maidens in June at Brighton (awarded race after winner failed dope test) and Carlisle: better at 6f than 5f: sold 2,500 gns in October, sent to Sweden. *M. R. Channon* **77**

AILSA CRAIG (IRE) 3 b.f. Chevalier (IRE) 115 – Sharplaw Destiny (IRE) 55 (Petardia 113) [2009 63p: 7.1g^6 6d^3 6.1m^2 7m^2 7.1v^5 8m* 8d^3 8m f8g^6 Nov 17] good-topped filly: fair handicapper: won at Bath in August: left R. Hannon 5,500 gns prior to final start: stays 1m: acts on fibresand, good to firm and good to soft going: tried in cheekpieces. *E. W. Tuer* **74**

AIMEESKEEPINGFAITH 2 b.f. (Mar 11) Beckett (IRE) 116 – Keeping The Faith (IRE) 88 (Ajraas (USA) 88) [2009 7s 6m p6g Sep 18] poor form in maidens: dead. *M. R. Channon* **44**

AIM TO ACHIEVE (IRE) 3 b.f. Galileo (IRE) 134 – Sabander Bay (USA) 51 (Lear Fan (USA) 130) [2009 –: 8g^4 p8g* 8g^3 Jul 18] sturdy filly: fairly useful form: won maiden at Kempton in June: further improvement when ½-length third of 4 to Bravo Echo in handicap at Newmarket: will be suited by 1¼m+: raced only on polytrack and good ground: sold 20,000 gns in November. *B. W. Hills* **81**

AINE (IRE) 4 ch.f. Danehill Dancer (IRE) 117 – Antinnaz (IRE) 111 (Thatching 131) [2009 102: 5d^4 6v 6m 6s* 6v^6 5s^3 5v^5 7.5v Sep 10] lengthy filly: useful performer: won listed race at Fairyhouse in July by neck from Snaefell: good third to Perfect Polly in similar event at Tipperary, best effort after: should stay easy 7f: acts on heavy and good to firm going: blinkered (ran poorly) second start. *T. Stack, Ireland* **105**

AINE'S DELIGHT (IRE) 3 b.f. King's Best (USA) 132 – Gentle Thoughts 73 (Darshaan 133) [2009 –: 8.3f 8f 8g* 7.6g^4 8.1m 8g^4 10g* Oct 19] useful-looking filly: fair handicapper: won at Salisbury (apprentices) in June and Windsor in October: stays 1¼m: acts on firm going: none too consistent. *Andrew Turnell* **72**

AINIA 4 b.f. Alhaarth (IRE) 126 – Vayavaig 78 (Damister (USA) 123) [2009 83: 8.1g^2 9m* 8d^6 12d^6 9.9g 8d Oct 18] leggy filly: fairly useful performer: won handicap at Musselburgh in June: stiff tasks in listed events last 3 starts: stays 1¼m: acts on good to firm and heavy going. *D. M. Simcock* **83**

AINTGOTTANAME 2 b.f. (Mar 11) Trade Fair 124 – Emouna (Cadeaux Genereux 131) [2009 p7g p8g p8m Dec 4] 2,200Y: first foal: dam French 1¼m winner: well held in maidens. *M. J. McGrath* **–**

AINTHEGORGEOUS 2 b.c. (Mar 27) Dr Fong (USA) 128 – Free Spirit (IRE) (Caerleon (USA) 132) [2009 7.5m 7.5g 6g Aug 31] sturdy colt: well held in maidens/seller. *P. T. Midgley* **–**

AIN'T TALKIN' 3 ch.c. Zaha (CAN) 106 – Royal Ivy 71 (Mujtahid (USA) 118) [2009 49: p7g* Jan 23] strong colt: modest performer: well backed, won handicap at Lingfield in January: stays 7f: acts on polytrack. *M. J. Attwater* **51**

AINTWOGRAND (IRE) 2 b.f. (Jan 24) Acclamation 118 – Rebel Clan (IRE) (Tagula (IRE) 116) [2009 5.1m^{6} 6g^{5} 5g^{6} 6d^{5} p6g^{5} Aug 7] third foal: half-sister to 7f winner Rebel Pearl (by Barathea): dam unraced half-sister to Cheveley Park Stakes winner Capricciosa: modest maiden: below form in sellers last 2 starts. *M. R. Channon* **53**

AIR CHIEF MARSHAL (IRE) 2 b.c. (Mar 25) Danehill Dancer (IRE) 117 – Hawala (IRE) 97 (Warning 136) [2009 6d^{2} 7v* 5v^{3} 6m 6.3s^{6} 6v^{2} 6v^{2} 7s^{4} 6g^{5} 7d^{4} Oct 26] €320,000Y: useful-looking colt: sixth foal: brother to smart 6f (at 2 yrs)/7f winner Misu Bond and half-brother to 3 winners, including useful Irish 5f to 8.7f (including 6f at 2 yrs) winner Slip Dance (by Celtic Swing) and 3-y-o Winged Harriet: dam 1m winner: useful performer: won maiden at Gowran in May by 8 lengths: best effort when ½-length second to Alfred Nobel in Phoenix Stakes at the Curragh sixth start: will stay 1m: seems best on ground softer than good (hung when well held on good to firm in Coventry Stakes at Royal Ascot fourth outing): sometimes slowly into stride. *A. P. O'Brien, Ireland* **108**

AIR LION (USA) 3 b.g. Lion Heart (USA) 124 – Swigert (USA) (Fusaichi Pegasus (USA) 130) [2009 f5g^{2} f5g^{3} f5m^{6} Jul 21] modest form in maidens at Southwell, then gelded: has looked awkward. *R. M. H. Cowell* **62**

AIR MAZE 3 b.f. Dansili 127 – Begueule (FR) (Bering 136) [2009 p7.1g^{2} f8g^{2} p9.5m* 10.2g* 10d^{3} 12d^{2} p13.9g^{3} 12g Oct 6] €600,000Y: close-coupled filly: third foal: half-sister to useful 1¼m/11f winner Pivotal Answer (by Pivotal): dam useful French 7f/1m winner: fairly useful performer: won maiden at Wolverhampton in February and, after 5-month absence, handicap at Bath in July: good placed efforts next 3 starts but shaped as if amiss final outing: barely stays 1¾m: acts on polytrack and good to soft going. *Sir Mark Prescott* **80**

AJAAN 5 br.h. Machiavellian (USA) 123 – Alakananda 92 (Hernando (FR) 127) [2009 112: 18.7m^{2} 16.1d 14.1s^{4} 18m^{5} Oct 17] smallish horse: useful handicapper: held form well through light campaign, neck second to Daraahem in Chester Cup and 9 lengths fifth to Darley Sun in Cesarewitch at Newmarket: stays 18.7f: acts on firm and soft going: blinkered: often held up: quirky. *H. R. A. Cecil* **106**

AJARA BOY 2 ch.c. (Jan 20) Avonbridge 123 – Cultural Role 95 (Night Shift (USA)) [2009 6g 6m^{6} p5g^{6} p8.6g Oct 17] sturdy, compact colt: showed little in maidens (trained by N. Vaughan on debut): should be suited by 7f+: visored final start (seemed amiss). *Tom Dascombe* **–**

AJARA (IRE) 3 b.f. Elusive City (USA) 117 – My-Lorraine (IRE) 77 (Mac's Imp (USA) 116) [2009 74+: p7.1g Jan 23] fair winner at 2 yrs: ran poorly in handicap only start in 2009: raced only at Wolverhampton: joined Tom Dascombe. *N. J. Vaughan* **–**

AJHAR (USA) 5 b.g. Diesis 133 – Min Alhawa (USA) 108 (Riverman (USA) 131) [2009 110: p10g 10g* Aug 14] strong, compact gelding: type to carry condition: useful performer: won minor event at Newmarket in August by 3¼ lengths from Classic Punch, easily better effort in 2009: stays 1½m: acts on polytrack, soft and good to firm ground: sold 65,000 gns, to join L. Freedman in Australia. *M. P. Tregoning* **108**

AJIGOLO 6 ch.g. Piccolo 121 – Ajig Dancer 86 (Niniski (USA) 125) [2009 100, a104: 6m 5m 5m 6s 6g 6d 6m 6g p6g p6m Nov 21] tall, good-topped gelding: useful handicapper at best: left M. Channon, deteriorated in 2009: was best at 5f/6f: acted on polytrack and good to firm going: tried visored/blinkered: held up: dead. *N. Wilson* **–**

AJJAADD (USA) 3 b.g. Elusive Quality (USA) – Millstream (USA) 107 (Dayjur (USA) 137) [2009 80: p5g^{2} p6m^{2} Dec 9] tall, useful-looking gelding: just fair maiden in 2009: effective at 5f to 7f: raced only on polytrack and good to firm going. *T. E. Powell* **69**

AJOOL (USA) 2 ch.f. (Apr 18) Aljabr (USA) 125 – Tamgeed (USA) 66 (Woodman (USA) 126) [2009 7g^{5} Oct 31] sturdy filly: seventh foal: half-sister to 3 winners, including fairly useful 1¼m to 13f winner Mutamaasek (by Swain): dam, maiden (should have proved best at 1¼m/1½m), out of close relative to Irish 1000 Guineas winner Mehthaaf and July Cup winner Elnadim: 12/1 and better for run, travelled smoothly long way and not knocked about when 4 lengths fifth of 20 to Revered in maiden at Newmarket: will do better. *B. W. Hills* **73 p**

AKABAR 3 b.g. Piccolo 121 – Fredora 93 (Inchinor 119) [2009 6d 6m^{4} 6m^{6} 7g Aug 12] modest maiden: stays 6f: blinkered final outing. *R. M. Beckett* **59**

AKAMON 2 ch.f. (Mar 22) Monsun (GER) 124 – Akanta (GER) (Wolfhound (USA) 126) [2009 p6g^{6} p7.1g^{2} Nov 6] leggy, rather unfurnished filly: fourth foal: sister to German 11f winner Allegrette: dam German 7f winner: better effort in maidens when ¾-length second to Sea of Heartbreak at Wolverhampton, finishing well: will stay 1m: open to further improvement. *E. A. L. Dunlop* **66 p**

Jockey Club Cup, Newmarket—Akmal makes all in a slowly-run race; Nehaam and Above Average (right) fill the minor placings, and the visored Oasis Knight finishes fifth

AKASH (IRE) 9 b.g. Dr Devious (IRE) 127 – Akilara (IRE) 87 (Kahyasi 130) [2009 p12.2g f14g Jan 27] well-made gelding: one-time useful performer: little form since 2004: tried blinkered/tongue tied. *K. M. Prendergast* –

AKBABEND 3 b.g. Refuse To Bend (IRE) 128 – Akdariya (IRE) 103 (Shirley Heights 130) [2009 76p: 9m² 9d 10d⁵ 12g² p12.2g* p12g³ Oct 26] rangy gelding: fairly useful performer: first past post in maiden at Catterick (subsequently demoted) in August and handicap at Wolverhampton in October: stays 1½m: acts on polytrack, best turf effort on good going: races prominently: hangs left. *M. Johnston* 89

AKHENATEN 3 b.c. High Chaparral (IRE) 132 – Lady Adnil (IRE) (Stravinsky (USA) 133) [2009 98: p8.6g* p9g 10s 8m⁶ 6m² 6f² 7g⁴ 6g 6g 7d³ 7m³ 7m* 7m 10g⁶ Dec 24] tall, close-coupled colt: useful performer: won minor event at Wolverhampton in March and handicap at Doncaster (by ¾ length from Vitoria) in September: placed 4 times in between: sold from M. Channon 100,000 gns before final outing: effective at 6f to 8.6f: acts on polytrack, firm and good to soft going. *M. Mubarak, Qatar* 101

AKMAL 3 ch.g. Selkirk (USA) 129 – Ayun (USA) 99 (Swain (IRE) 134) [2009 76: 10m² 12m³ 11.5g* 12f* 12f² 14m* 12g⁵ 14m* 14.1m* 14m* 16m* Oct 17] sturdy gelding: smart performer: won maiden at Lingfield in May, handicaps at Thirsk in June, York in July and August (Sky Bet Melrose Stakes, beat Alanbrooke ¾ length), Yarmouth in September, then listed race (by ¾ length from Nehaam) and Jockey Club Cup (beat same rival ½ length), typically doing no more than necessary for last 2 wins, both at Newmarket in October: stays 2m: acts on firm going (well held on heavy): blinkered once: tactically versatile: thoroughly game and genuine, a credit to connections. *J. L. Dunlop* 112

AKRAM (IRE) 7 b.g. Night Shift (USA) – Akdariya (IRE) 103 (Shirley Heights 130) [2009 8m 10.9m⁵ Sep 29] neat gelding: formerly useful: fair at best nowadays: stays 11f: acts on good to firm ground: tried tongue tied/in cheekpieces: fairly useful hurdler, won in November. *Jonjo O'Neill* 65

AKTIA (IRE) 2 b.f. (Apr 28) Danehill Dancer (IRE) 117 – La Gandilie (FR) 106 (Highest Honor (FR) 124) [2009 8.1m⁶ 8g p7g³ Nov 18] 42,000Y: good-topped filly: fifth foal: closely related to useful 2007 2-y-o 6f winner Fashion Rocks (by Rock of Gibraltar) and half-sister to Irish 3-y-o Art Broker: dam French 2-y-o 1m winner: similar form in maidens: considerately handled first 2 starts, inadequate trip next time (third to Hypnotized at Kempton): should be suited by 1m+: capable of better. *L. M. Cumani* 69 p

AKUBRA (IRE) 2 b.f. (Mar 9) One Cool Cat (USA) 123 – Dreaming Waters 62 (Groom Dancer (USA) 128) [2009 p6f p6f Dec 13] €15,000F, €6,000Y, resold £800Y: first foal: dam, maiden, half-sister to Oaks runner-up Something Exciting: well held in maidens at Kempton. *Norma Twomey* –

AKULA (IRE) 2 ch.c. (Feb 12) Soviet Star (USA) 128 – Danielli (IRE) 79 (Danehill (USA) 126) [2009 7s³ 7d 8m Sep 18] €30,000Y: first foal: dam, Irish maiden (stayed 13f), half-sister to 4-y-o Eva's Request: form in maidens only when 7½ lengths third of 10 to Nideeb at Yarmouth (66/1). *M. H. Tompkins* 76

ALACITY (IRE) 3 b.f. Elusive City (USA) 117 – Minamala (IRE) 81 (Desert King (IRE) 129) [2009 –: 6f^3 7m^6 8d^4 6d 7v^6 5g^3 6g^6 5s^5 5.1s^2 Nov 4] modest maiden: best efforts at 5f: acts on soft ground: usually races prominently. *N. Bycroft* **63**

AL ADHAM 2 b.c. (May 12) Dansili 127 – Miss Meggy 97 (Pivotal 124) [2009 6m^6 6g a6f Dec 11] form in maidens only on debut: left Saeed bin Suroor after next start. *M. bin Shafya, UAE* **54**

ALAINMAAR (FR) 3 b.g. Johar (USA) 130 – Lady Elgar (IRE) (Sadler's Wells (USA) 132) [2009 8m^2 10m* 10m* Oct 2] €240,000Y: good-topped gelding: sixth foal: half-brother to 3 winners, notably very smart US 11f/1½m performer Grand Couturier (by Grand Lodge): dam, well beaten in France only start, sister to smart Irish performer up to 1½m Desert Fox: useful form: progressive, winning maiden at Pontefract in September and handicap at Newmarket (beat Rumble of Thunder 2½ lengths in 3-runner event) in October: will be suited by 1½m: type to hold his own in listed/pattern events. *M. A. Jarvis* **108 p**

ALAIVAN (IRE) 3 b.g. Kalanisi (IRE) 132 – Alaya (IRE) 89 (Ela-Mana-Mou 132) [2009 10g^5 12v* 10v^2 12s* Jul 6] fifth foal: half-brother to very smart Irish 7f (at 2 yrs) to 1¼m winner Alayan (by Sri Pekan) and 5-y-o Alarazi: dam, Irish 1½m winner, half-sister to top-class 1½m performer Alamshar: smart performer: progressed to win minor event at Gowran (by 5 lengths from Fergus McIver) in May and listed race at Roscommon (by 3½ lengths from Von Jawlensky) in July: creditable head second to Grand Ducal in Gallinule Stakes at the Curragh in between: should be suited by 1¾m/2m: acts on heavy ground: joined E. O'Grady, and won over hurdles in December. *John M. Oxx, Ireland* **116**

ALANBROOKE 3 gr.c. Hernando (FR) 127 – Alouette 105 (Darshaan 133) [2009 82p: 11d^2 12.5g^6 12d 14m* 16g* 16g^2 12g^6 14m^2 14v^3 18m^2 18m 16d^3 Oct 28] well-made colt: useful handicapper: won at Sandown and Ascot in July: placed several other times, including when second at York (beaten ¾ length by Akmal in Melrose Stakes) and Newmarket (went down by 4½ lengths to Bernie The Bolt, pair well clear): stays 2¼m: unraced on firm going, acts on any other: blinkered nowadays: races prominently: reliable. *M. Johnston* **108**

ALAN DEVONSHIRE 4 b.g. Mtoto 134 – Missed Again 84 (High Top 131) [2009 99: 7m 8m 10m 9s p7.1g 6.1s 8g 7m Oct 26] rather leggy, close-coupled gelding: useful performer at best: deteriorated badly in 2009. *M. H. Tompkins* **–**

ALANDI (IRE) 4 b.c. Galileo (IRE) 134 – Aliya (IRE) 105 (Darshaan 133) [2009 83p: 13s* 14g^2 14d^2 14d^5 14s* 14s* 20g* Oct 4] **121**

Zarkava's retirement to stud at the end of 2008 removed the brightest star from the Aga Khan's racing firmament but there appeared still to be a great deal for that filly's owner-breeder to look forward to. Impressive Grand Prix de Paris winner Montmartre and Blandford Stakes winner and Prix de l'Opera third Katiyra looked set for more success as four-year-olds, while among the classic hopes were Arazan, successful in the Futurity Stakes, the Killavullan Stakes winner Rayeni and Beresford Stakes runner-up Mourayan. In the event, as reported in *Racehorses of 2008*, Montmartre had to be retired to stud in February because of a recurrence of the leg injury he had sustained when gaining his big win. Sent to the French National Stud, he showed little interest at first in his mares but reportedly got four non-thoroughbreds in foal late in the year. Arazan did not race either, firstly because early in the year the ground was deemed too firm, and then because he succumbed to a bad chest infection. Reportedly he stays in training. Katiyra ran twice without making much impact, Rayeni finished second in the Irish Two Thousand Guineas, but had to wait until October before gaining his only success from four runs, in a listed race at the Curragh, and Mourayan, for all that he ran third in the Irish Derby, was something of a disappointment and did not win before being sold to Australia. Such is the strength of the Aga Khan's breeding operation, though, that he still had his colours carried to victory by seven Group 1 winners, with another horse that he had bred but sold, Alpine Rose, making the score eight, his highest ever. Leaving Alpine Rose and two-year-olds Rosanara and Siyouni out of the equation, forecasting top-level success for any of the remainder was virtually impossible. Shalanaya, who won the Prix de l'Opera, and Daryakana, who ended the latest campaign with victory in the Hong Kong Vase, were unraced at two (as were Group 2 scorers Ashalanda, and Manighar), while Varenar (Prix de la Foret) had notched just a small race at Compiegne from three starts in 2008. The real eye-opener, however, was arguably four-year-old Alandi, who did not reach the racecourse until October 20th, 2008 but still went on to prove himself a fine stayer, compiling a record of four wins from seven starts in the latest season, his wins including the Irish St Leger and Prix du Cadran, before he too was sold to Australia with a view to being aimed at the 2010 Melbourne Cup.

It's a safe bet that the Aga Khan received considerably more for selling Alandi than he would have done if the colt had, as initially intended, gone through the ring at the Goffs horses in training sale a few days after his only start as a three-year-old. He started a warm favourite in a field of thirteen that day at the Curragh, winning decisively, after which John Oxx revealed that Alandi had had various niggling problems earlier in the year. Alandi's reappearance came in the listed Vintage Crop Stakes at Navan at the end of April, a race in which Yeats was also having his first run of the season. Yeats ran poorly, unlike Alandi, who looked set for a good year after challenging long-time leader Hindu Kush and The Betchworth Kid over a furlong out and galloping away to win by three and half lengths. After the win Oxx said: 'We had plenty of offers to buy him as a hurdler at the end of last season, but we decided to hold on to him as he's very well bred.' A wise move as things turned out, but it was four months before Alandi won again. He suffered three reverses, running creditably in the listed Saval Beg Stakes at Leopardstown (a length behind Hindu Kush) and the Curragh Cup (beaten a neck by Profound Beauty after being squeezed out over a furlong from home) but beating only one home in the listed Challenge Stakes also won by Profound Beauty at Leopardstown again. Despite this last defeat, Alandi started at a shade of odds on for the listed Ballycullen Stakes at Fairyhouse towards the end of August and justified the confidence in style, leading two furlongs out and drawing clear to beat his stable-companion (and half-sister) Aliyfa eased down by five lengths, value ten. An impressive and improved performance which augured very well for the autumn.

Significantly, the going for the Ballycullen Stakes was soft, as it had been for the Vintage Crop Stakes—the ground had been good for one and good to soft for Alandi's two other defeats. Alandi did not need to make a great deal of improvement to take a hand in the finish of his next race, the Irish Field St Leger at the Curragh three weeks later. There was confidence behind him in a renewal better than some recent editions, with six of the eight runners having been successful in pattern or listed company. Alandi was sent off second favourite behind Goodwood Cup and Prix Kergorlay winner Schiaparelli, ahead of Profound Beauty, Yeats, who was having his first run since winning the Gold Cup, and All The Aces, a smart performer over middle distances but unproven at a mile and three quarters. There

Irish Field St Leger, the Curragh—Alandi (centre) gets the better of Clowance (right) to complete a memorable eight days for John Oxx and Michael Kinane; the weakening Schiaparelli takes third

Qatar Prix du Cadran, Longchamp—a seventh pattern-race win of the Arc weekend for owner-breeder the Aga Khan as Alandi stays on strongly ahead of Kasbah Bliss (right) and Yeats

was one other British-trained challenger, 2008 Oaks fourth Clowance making her seasonal reappearance, and just one three-year-old, Yeats's stable-companion Moon Indigo. Conditions were testing, which played to Alandi's strengths. Ridden close to a strong pace set by Schiaparelli—Alandi's rider Michael Kinane later said 'I couldn't believe the pace they went. My horse was never on the bridle'—Alandi looked bound for second place for most of the straight as he was rousted along with the leader still galloping strongly. The picture changed a furlong out, however, as Schiaparelli's stride started to shorten dramatically and Alandi, under a tremendously strong ride by Kinane, hit the front two hundred yards out. Schiaparelli was beaten but Kinane still had to keep Alandi going at full tilt because Clowance came with a good run on his outside and almost drew level. Superior fitness, and the combined never-say-die attitude of horse and jockey, told in the end, however, and Alandi passed the post half a length to the good with Schiaparelli five lengths further behind Clowance in third. Yeats finished last.

This was the second time the Aga Khan had won the Irish St Leger, following Kastoria in 2006, and the fourth win for Oxx who had saddled Kastoria and, before her, Eurobird and Petite Ile in 1987 and 1989. Such a hard race might have been expected to leave its mark on the principals but the first three all ran well subsequently. Schiaparelli took the Gran Premio del Jockey Club and finished second in the Prix Royal-Oak, a race in which Clowance came fourth, while Alandi crowned his European career with victory in the Qatar Prix du Cadran at Longchamp just over three weeks after his Curragh triumph. The Aga Khan had bred three winners of this race before, Shafaraz in 1980, Karkour in 1983 and Tajoun in 1999—the first two had raced for other owners—but Oxx was attempting to become the first Irish trainer to triumph since Seamus McGrath with Levmoss forty years earlier. In fact Alandi's participation was in some doubt in the run-up to the race owing to a quarter crack, and Oxx said: 'It hasn't been an ideal preparation and the ground looks like being faster than ideal, but we wanted to run him on it over an extreme distance to see how he fares on both counts with next year in mind.' The going was good, on the firm side if anything, which seemingly wasn't entirely in Alandi's favour, though an extra six furlongs certainly was. In what was the strongest renewal of the Cadran since the mid-'nineties, Alandi and Kinane had to show their battling qualities again to win the day. Alandi started third favourite of twelve behind Yeats, who was making his farewell appearance, and French-trained Kasbah Bliss, a good staying hurdler capable of mixing it with the best stayers on the Flat as well, as he showed when landing the Prix Gladiateur three weeks earlier. The other runners included Doncaster Cup winner Askar Tau, Prix de Pomone winner Armure and Pouvoir Absolu, who had bustled up Jukebox Jury in the Grand Prix de Deauville. After Windsor Palace had made the running for Yeats, the latter took over half a mile out with Alandi in pursuit. Yeats was in better form than on

H.H. Aga Khan's "Alandi"

the previous occasions the two had met, though not in the form he had shown at Royal Ascot and Alandi was able to pass him with a furlong and a half to go. Any thoughts that the race was effectively in the bag soon evaporated as Kasbah Bliss came with a rattle to launch a challenge after being waited with. The post came just in time for the game Alandi, who prevailed by a short head, with Yeats a length and a half away third. With Kasbah Bliss running well in the Hong Kong Vase subsequently, the form was as good as the Irish St Leger, and Alandi looked a worthy contender for the Gold Cup as a five-year-old until news came through of his sale.

With Galileo, Darshaan and Relko in the first three generations Alandi's pedigree contains more influences for stamina than those of the vast majority of modern thoroughbreds. His dam Aliya won the Oyster Stakes, a listed event over a mile and a half, a race also won by Alandi's three-year-old half-sister Aliyfa, a daughter of miler Spinning World already mentioned as runner-up to Alandi in the Ballycullen Stakes over two furlongs further. Aliya's five previous foals included minor winners by Entrepreneur and Daylami; her two-year old filly Aliwiyya (by Anabaa) showed modest form when beaten a total of fifty-three lengths in four starts and there is a yearling colt by Barathea. Another daughter, unraced Alizaya (by Highest Honor), was sold in foal to Oratorio for €140,000 at Deauville in December and visits Sea The Stars. This is an excellent family. Aliya's sister Aliysa won the Oaks, only to be disqualified controversially for failing a drugs test, and her foals included the dam of outstanding middle-distance colt Alamshar, successful in the Irish Derby and King George VI and Queen Elizabeth Stakes in 2003. The next dam, Alannya, showed smart form at a mile to a mile and a quarter and was out of Nucciolina who figures in the bottom line of the pedigrees of Yesterday, Alborada and Albanova.

Alandi (IRE) (b.c. 2005)	Galileo (IRE) (b 1998)	Sadler's Wells (b 1981)	Northern Dancer
			Fairy Bridge
		Urban Sea (ch 1989)	Miswaki
			Allegretta
	Aliya (IRE) (b 1994)	Darshaan (br 1981)	Shirley Heights
			Delsy
		Alannya (b 1972)	Relko
			Nucciolina

Alandi, a tall colt who is suited by a test of stamina, acts well on soft and heavy going—he has yet to encounter firm. He should be an interesting candidate for the Melbourne Cup if he can handle the very firm conditions that usually prevail. He may be chasing shadows earlier in the Australian season though, since there are not many good races over a mile and three quarters or more in the calendar there and Alandi is far from certain to have the speed to be effective in some of the races over shorter distances often used as lead-up events to the Melbourne Cup. *John M. Oxx, Ireland*

ALANNAH (IRE) 4 b.f. Alhaarth (IRE) 126 – Aljeeza (Halling (USA) 133) [2009 –: 10.2g 11.7g^4 11.8m Oct 13] poor maiden: stays 11.7f: best effort on good ground. *Mrs P. N. Dutfield* **47**

ALARAZI (IRE) 5 b.g. Spectrum (IRE) 126 – Alaya (IRE) 89 (Ela-Mana-Mou 132) [2009 113: p10g^5 8s p10g^3 10f 10g^3 Aug 8] big gelding: useful performer nowadays: best effort in 2009 when 2¾ lengths third to Whispering Gallery in handicap at Newmarket final outing: stays 1¼m, seemingly not 1¾m: acts on heavy going, probably on polytrack: usually blinkered (not entirely straightforward): joined Mrs L. Wadham. *T. G. Mills* **104**

ALAZEYAB (USA) 3 b.c. El Prado (IRE) 119 – Itnab 116 (Green Desert (USA) 127) [2009 97p: 10m^5 10d 10g* 10.4m 9.9g 8m^2 8m^4 9m Oct 3] sturdy colt: useful handicapper: won at Newmarket in June by a length from Wintercast: ran well in frame after at York (second to Roaring Forte) and Doncaster (fourth to Manassas): stays 1¼m: raced mainly on good/good to firm going (laboured on good to soft): tongue tied twice at 2 yrs: front runner: sent to UAE. *M. A. Jarvis* **108**

AL AZY (IRE) 4 b.c. Nayef (USA) 129 – Nasheed (USA) 113 (Riverman (USA) 131) [2009 69: p12g^5 p10g p9.5g p16.5g^3 15.8g 14.1m* 12m 11.5g* 12m^6 14v 14g Sep 19] sturdy colt: fair handicapper: won at Yarmouth in May and July (apprentice event), then left D. Simcock 11,500 gns: free-going sort, but stays easy 16.5f: acts on polytrack, soft and good to firm going: tried blinkered: usually races up with pace: none too consistent. *G. Keane, Ireland* **69**

ALBAASHA (IRE) 3 ch.c. Lemon Drop Kid (USA) 131 – Cozy Maria (USA) 105 (Cozzene (USA)) [2009 51: 10m^5 9d^5 12m^2 p16g^5 11.9m^6 Jul 6] fair maiden handicapper: best effort at 1½m: acts on good to firm ground, probably on polytrack: visored last 3 starts: one to treat with caution: sold 27,000 gns, sent to Qatar. *Sir Michael Stoute* **71 §**

ALBACOCCA 2 gr.f. (Jan 26) With Approval (CAN) – Ballymac Girl 63 (Niniski (USA) 125) [2009 p8.6g p8m 8.1m Sep 26] leggy filly: half-sister to 2007 2-y-o 5f winner Alizadora (by Zilzal) and useful 1¼m and 13f winner Coat of Honour (by Mark of Esteem): dam, 1½m to 15f winner, closely related to smart stayer Alleluia, and half-sister to Last Second and to dams of Alborada/Albanova and Quarter Moon/Yesterday: no form in 3 maidens within 16 days in September, looking in need of experience: bred to be well suited by 1¼m+: capable of better. *Sir Mark Prescott* **– p**

ALBAHER 3 b.c. Oasis Dream 129 – Dance Sequence (USA) 105 (Mr Prospector (USA)) [2009 82p: 8.1m^4 8.1m 8m 10.4g Oct 10] big, good-bodied colt: won maiden at Ascot only start at 2 yrs: well below form in 2009: sold 5,000 gns. *J. L. Dunlop* **–**

ALBAQAA 4 ch.g. Medicean 128 – Basbousate Nadia 92 (Wolfhound (USA) 126) [2009 99: p11g^5 10m^3 10.4m^4 8.9g^2 10.4m^3 Jul 11] compact gelding: useful handicapper: career-best efforts when placed at York last 2 outings, neck second to Kavachi, then 5¼ lengths third to Sirvino in John Smith's Cup: stays 11f: acts on polytrack, soft and good to firm ground: tried visored: edgy sort, sometimes takes good hold and has run well when sweating: consistent. *R. A. Fahey* **101**

AL BARQ (IRE) 2 ch.f. (Mar 2) Traditionally (USA) 117 – Prayer (IRE) 83 (Rainbow Quest (USA) 134) [2009 6g 7g 6g Aug 31] leggy filly: second foal: half-sister to 4-y-o **–**

Without A Prayer: dam ran twice in Ireland: no form, including in seller: sold £800. *Miss D. Mountain*

ALBASEET (IRE) 3 b.g. Desert Style (IRE) 121 – Double Eight (IRE) 77 (Common **66**
Grounds 118) [2009 77: 6m^{3} Aug 17] angular gelding: fair maiden: speedy, raced only at 5f/6f: acts on polytrack and soft going: sold 6,000 gns in October, sent to Bahrain. *M. P. Tregoning*

ALBEED 2 b.f. (Mar 7) Tiger Hill (IRE) 127 – Ayun (USA) 99 (Swain (IRE) 134) [2009 **60 p**
7g 7.1m 8g Oct 23] third foal: half-sister to 3-y-o Akmal and winner in Greece by Sakhee: dam, 1m/1¼m winner, closely related to smart 7f to 9f performer Haami, out of smart half-sister to Derby winner Erhaab: best effort in maidens when tenth of 21 at Doncaster (hung briefly, again not knocked about) final start: should continue to progress in handicaps at 1¼m+. *J. L. Dunlop*

ALBERO DI GIUDA (IRE) 4 b.f. Clodovil (IRE) 116 – All Away (IRE) (Glow **56**
(USA)) [2009 p5.1g^{4} p7.1g^{6} p7.1g f5m^{3} p5.1g^{5} p5.1g^{3} 7f f5f^{5} p7m Dec 30] half-sister to 3 winners in Italy: dam unraced: winner of 7 of 23 starts in Italy, including at Rome (4) and Tagliacozzo in 2008: left G. Attilio, modest and patchy form in Britain in 2009: effective at 5f to 7.5f: acts on all-weather/sand and heavy ground: tried in cheekpieces: tongue tied in Britain. *F. Sheridan*

ALBERTINE ROSE 3 gr.f. Namid 128 – Barathiki 81 (Barathea (IRE) 127) [2009 89: **–**
5m 5v 5g Aug 3] workmanlike filly: fairly useful at 2 yrs: well held in 2009. *W. R. Muir*

ALBERTS STORY (USA) 5 b.g. Tale of The Cat (USA) 113 – Hazino (USA) **54**
(Hazaam (USA) 113) [2009 64: p10g^{4} f12g^{3} f12g Feb 10] lengthy, rather leggy gelding: modest handicapper: stays 1½m: acts on all-weather, soft and good to firm going: tried blinkered/in cheekpieces. *R. A. Fahey*

ALBIERA (IRE) 4 b.f. Xaar 132 – Madam Waajib (IRE) (Waajib 121) [2009 8.3d **–**
p9.5g p9.5g p12m Dec 6] 12,000Y: fourth foal: half-sister to 2006 2-y-o 5f winner Deadshot Keen (by Invincible Spirit), later 1m winner in USA, and 8-y-o Play Master: dam lightly raced at 2 yrs: well held in maidens/handicap. *H. Morrison*

ALCALDE 3 b.g. Hernando (FR) 127 – Alexandrine (IRE) 78 (Nashwan (USA) 135) **97**
[2009 95p: 12s 12m^{2} 14m 10.3m 10.9m* 10.2d^{6} 12d^{3} Oct 24] rangy gelding: useful handicapper: won at Warwick (by ¾ length from Crackentorp) in October: good third to Hunterview at Doncaster final outing: gelded after: should stay 1¾m: acts on soft and good to firm going: tried blinkered: suspect temperament. *M. Johnston*

ALDAADO (IRE) 3 b.g. Alhaarth (IRE) 126 – Zobaida (IRE) 77 (Green Desert (USA) **82**
127) [2009 8m 10.1s^{4} 7.5m^{3} 8.5g* 8.3m* 8.5m^{5} 8.1g^{3} 10.4g Oct 10] €30,000F, 32,000Y: lengthy gelding: sixth foal: half-brother to Irish 7-y-o Dand Nee and Irish 1½m winner Agamard (by Red Ransom): dam, 7f winner who stayed 8.5f, out of half-sister to Zilzal: fairly useful handicapper: won at Beverley (dead-heat) in May and Hamilton in June: may prove best at 1¼m: acts on good to firm ground. *M. Dods*

AL DAFA (USA) 2 ch.c. (Feb 12) Kingmambo (USA) 125 – Crimson Conquest (USA) **63**
85 (Diesis 133) [2009 6m^{4} 7d Sep 15] closely related to 3 winners, notably very smart 6f (at 2 yrs) to 1¼m winner Crimplene (by Lion Cavern), and half-sister to several winners, including smart 1¼m/1½m winner Dutch Gold (by Lahib): dam 2-y-o 6f winner (stayed 1¼m): better effort in maidens at Lingfield when fourth to Dubai Set: should be suited by 1m+: has left Godolphin. *Saeed bin Suroor*

ALDERBED 3 b.g. Bahri (USA) 125 – Tanasie (Cadeaux Genereux 131) [2009 48: **49**
11.6d^{6} 10m^{6} Jun 18] quite attractive gelding: poor maiden: stays 11.6f: acts on polytrack, unraced on extremes of going on turf: tried visored/blinkered. *George Baker*

ALDERMOOR (USA) 3 b.g. Tale of The Cat (USA) 113 – Notting Hill (BRZ) (Jules **96**
(USA) 110) [2009 105p: 6m^{4} 5g 6m 6g 6m 6d 7m* 6g 7s Nov 7] strong gelding: useful handicapper: won at Newmarket (beat One Way Or Another by head) in October: stays 7f: acts on firm going: tongue tied once: none too consistent: gelded after final start. *S. C. Williams*

ALDIRUOS (IRE) 9 ch.g. Bigstone (IRE) 126 – Ball Cat (FR) (Cricket Ball (USA) **–**
124) [2009 p16g^{5} p13g Feb 10] won 1½m claimer at Longchamp for J-C. Rouget in 2003: well held in handicaps in Britain: tried blinkered: fair but ungenuine hurdler. *A. W. Carroll*

ALDORABLE 2 ch.f. (Feb 28) Starcraft (NZ) 128 – Aldora 109 (Magic Ring (IRE) **54**
115) [2009 p7g 6m^{4} 6m^{4} p6f Oct 14] compact filly: first foal: dam, 5f (at 2 yrs) to 9f winner, half-sister to smart performer up to 1½m Polar Red: modest maiden: bred to stay 1m+: form only on turf. *R. A. Teal*

ALEATRICIS 4 br. or gr.g. Kingmambo (USA) 125 – Alba Stella 92 (Nashwan (USA) **90**
135) [2009 79: 12.1m^2 12m^2 12d* 13.1m^4 15.9m^3 18m Sep 19] lengthy gelding: fairly useful handicapper: won at Pontefract in May: best effort after when close third at Chester: stays easy 2m: acts on good to firm and good to soft ground: blinkered final start in 2008. *J. J. Quinn*

ALEQA 2 b.f. (Feb 10) Oasis Dream 129 – Vanishing Point (USA) (Caller I D (USA)) **–**
[2009 6.5g Oct 8] 50,000Y: compact filly: fifth foal: half-sister to 5-y-o Royal Rock and 6-y-o Gold Express: dam US 6f (including at 2 yrs)/6.5f winner: 16/1, tailed off in maiden at Newbury. *C. F. Wall*

ALERON (IRE) 11 b.g. Sadler's Wells (USA) 132 – High Hawk 124 (Shirley Heights **66**
130) [2009 71: 15.8m 15.8g^2 16.2g^5 16d^3 Sep 1] tall gelding: fair handicapper: barely stays 2m: acts on dirt/fibresand, soft and good to firm going: tried in tongue tie/visor, usually wears cheekpieces: has hung/found little: useful chaser. *J. J. Quinn*

ALESSANO 7 ch.g. Hernando (FR) 127 – Alessandra 101 (Generous (IRE) 139) [2009 **85**
14m^5 16.1g p12g^5 14.1s Oct 12] workmanlike gelding: useful handicapper at 4 yrs: off 2½ years, fairly useful form on reappearance: well held after, pulled up lame final outing: stays 1¾m: acts on polytrack, firm and good to soft going, probably on soft: tried in cheekpieces, usually blinkered. *G. L. Moore*

ALEXANDER FAMILY (IRE) 3 b.f. Danetime (IRE) 121 – Villa Nova (IRE) 55 **65**
(Petardia 113) [2009 63: p7.1g* p7g^5 Feb 14] fair handicapper, ex-Irish: won at Wolverhampton in January: raced too freely next time: not sure to stay much beyond 7f: acts on polytrack. *E. F. Vaughan*

ALEXANDER GULCH (USA) 3 b.g. Thunder Gulch (USA) 129 – Lovely Later **86**
(USA) (Green Dancer (USA) 132) [2009 86: p8g^2 p10g^2 10.3m^5 Mar 29] strong, close-coupled gelding: fairly useful handicapper: in cheekpieces, twice good second at Lingfield: ran poorly next time (gelded after): stays 1¼m: acts on polytrack: edgy sort: joined Mrs L. Wadham. *K. A. Ryan*

ALEXANDER GURU 5 ch.g. Ishiguru (USA) 114 – Superspring (Superlative 118) **62**
[2009 66, a72: p9.5g p8g p9.5g^5 Feb 17] workmanlike gelding: modest performer: stays 1½m: acts on polytrack and good to firm going: often races freely. *M. Blanshard*

ALEXANDER LOYALTY (IRE) 3 b.f. Invincible Spirit (IRE) 121 – Nassma (IRE) **64**
95 (Sadler's Wells (USA) 132) [2009 68p: p5g 6.1g p7g 8.3m^5 Jun 28] stocky filly: modest maiden: stays 8.3f: acts on soft and good to firm ground: visored final outing. *E. F. Vaughan*

ALEXANDROS 4 ch.c. Kingmambo (USA) 125 – Arlette (IRE) (King of Kings (IRE) **122**
125) [2009 113: 8g* 9g* 8.9g^3 8d 8d^2 8m 8.3v* 8g Dec 13] neat, attractive colt: very smart performer: improved in 2009, winning handicaps at Nad Al Sheba in January and February (beat Biarritz by 3½ lengths), and minor event at Nottingham in November (straightforward task): also ran well when nose second to Virtual in Lockinge Stakes at Newbury (rider lost whip 1f out): reportedly lame when well held in Queen Anne Stakes at Royal Ascot next time (off over 4 months afterwards): respectable seventh to Good Ba Ba in Hong Kong Mile at Sha Tin final start: stays 9f: acts on heavy ground. *Saeed bin Suroor*

ALFALASTEENI 2 ch.g. (Apr 19) Kyllachy 129 – Mrs Nash 66 (Night Shift (USA)) **–**
[2009 6v 5g 6s^6 5s Aug 1] close-coupled gelding: no form: tried blinkered: possibly ungenuine. *Ian Williams*

ALFALEVVA 2 b.g. (Mar 15) Piccolo 121 – Evanesce 72 (Lujain (USA) 119) [2009 6s **61**
6m 7f^6 7m p8m^4 p9.5g^2 p10m Nov 21] good-topped gelding: modest maiden: stays 9.5f: acts on polytrack. *M. R. Channon*

ALFATHAA 4 b.g. Nayef (USA) 129 – Arctic Char 102 (Polar Falcon (USA) 126) **107**
[2009 107: 8m^5 8.1m^5 9.9g^5 8m^6 10.3m^6 8m^2 9m Oct 3] big, rangy, good-topped gelding: useful handicapper: mostly creditable efforts in competitive events in 2009, ½-length second to Elna Bright at Ascot: effective at 1m/1¼m: acts on firm and good to soft going: tried blinkered, in cheekpieces of late: held up: sold 78,000 gns. *W. J. Haggas*

ALFIE FLITS 7 b.g. Machiavellian (USA) 123 – Elhilmeya (IRE) 94 (Unfuwain **99**
(USA) 131) [2009 109: 10.4m Aug 8] tall, good-topped gelding: useful performer nowadays: respectable eighth to Libel Law in valuable handicap at Haydock sole Flat outing in 2009: effective at 1¼m (granted test) to easy 1¾m: acts on heavy and good to firm going, below form sole start on polytrack: useful hurdler. *G. A. Swinbank*

ALFIE LEE (IRE) 12 ch.g. Case Law 113 – Nordic Living (IRE) 53 (Nordico (USA)) [2009 46: 5m^5 5m Jun 29] compact, well-made gelding: poor performer: well held in 2009: sometimes wears headgear: tongue tied. *D. A. Nolan* **–**

ALFIES EXPRESS 5 br.g. My Best Valentine 122 – Ali Rose 47 (Cigar 68) [2009 p9.5g p12g p12m Nov 27] no show in bumpers/novice hurdles for F. Sutherland: little sign of ability in maidens/seller. *S. Curran* **–**

ALFIE TUPPER (IRE) 6 ch.g. Soviet Star (USA) 128 – Walnut Lady 91 (Forzando 122) [2009 82: 10m p10g 10g p10g p8g Dec 7] leggy, attractive gelding: handicapper, just modest in 2009: stays easy 1½m: acts on polytrack and good to firm ground: free-going sort. *J. R. Boyle* **59**

ALFONSO THE WISE (IRE) 2 b.c. (May 22) Galileo (IRE) 134 – Dalawara (IRE) (Top Ville 129) [2009 8g Oct 8] rangy colt: closely related to 2 middle-distance winners in France by Sadler's Wells and half-brother to smart 1m (at 2 yrs) to 1¾m winner Heron Island (by Shirley Heights) who stayed 2½m: dam, French maiden, sister to Prix Vermeille winner Darara (dam of 4-y-o Dar Re Mi) and half-sister to Prix du Jockey Club winner Darshaan: 16/1, green and in need of race, tenth of 16 in well-contested maiden won by Dancing David at Newbury: will do better. *J. Noseda* **– p**

ALFRED NOBEL (IRE) 2 b.c. (Jan 23) Danehill Dancer (IRE) 117 – Glinting Desert (IRE) 73 (Desert Prince (IRE) 130) [2009 5d^2 6v^3 7g* 6g* 6v* 7s^6 7m^5 a8.5f Nov 7] **110**

Alfred Nobel's name does not normally crop up in a sporting context, but it did so on a couple of occasions in 2009. Somewhat bizarrely, he was mentioned in a post-match interview with the England football manager Fabio Capello, who was commenting on the fact that David Beckham had received the man of the match award after coming on as substitute and spending only around half an hour on the pitch in the game against Belarus. Capello, displaying a wry sense of humour, likened it to Barack Obama being awarded the Nobel Peace Prize after just nine months as United States President. Far less surprising, given their predilection for naming horses after famous people, was that the Coolmore partners had a two-year-old colt called Alfred Nobel racing for them. He was no Horatio Nelson, nor a George Washington, two of the best Coolmore-owned juveniles of recent years, but Alfred Nobel did show himself to be smart when winning the Camas Park & Ashtown House Studs Phoenix Stakes at the Curragh in July.

The Group 1 Phoenix Stakes had been won by Alfred Nobel's trainer Aidan O'Brien on nine occasions previously, including with George Washington, and Alfred Nobel was one of four of his stable's representatives as he attempted to equal

NetJets Railway Stakes, the Curragh—a tenth win in the last eleven runnings of this race for Aidan O'Brien as Alfred Nobel, despite carrying his head awkwardly, proves too strong for In Some Respect (left), King Ledley (noseband) and Kitty Kiernan

Camas Park & Ashton House Studs Phoenix Stakes, the Curragh—Alfred Nobel completes his hat-trick and gives Aidan O'Brien a tenth win in the race in the last twelve years; stablemate Air Chief Marshal gives him most to do in a 1,2,3 for sire Danehill Dancer

Paddy Prendergast's record for the number of wins in the race by a trainer. Alfred Nobel was on a hat-trick, having got off the mark, at the third attempt, in a maiden at Leopardstown in May and then followed up in the NetJets Railway Stakes at the Curragh in June. He won the latter by a length and a quarter from In Some Respect despite looking none too straightforward under pressure, carrying his head very awkwardly and edging right. The runner-up was one of three to reoppose him in the Phoenix, in which Alfred Nobel just shaded favouritism ahead of Walk On Bye, the latter the unbeaten winner of a maiden and the Anglesey Stakes, both at the Curragh. It was, however, one of Alfred Nobel's unconsidered stablemates who provided him with the sternest opposition. Air Chief Marshal, a 33/1-shot, led for much of the way and Alfred Nobel, who was produced latest of all out wide, collared him only in the last fifty yards, carrying his head very high but winning going away by half a length, with Walk On Bye a further two and a half lengths back in third. It was a substandard Phoenix Stakes and the form didn't work out. Alfred Nobel himself did nothing for it in three subsequent starts, finishing last of six in the National Stakes at the Curragh, fifth of twenty-two in the Tattersalls Timeform Million at Newmarket and tenth of thirteen in the Breeders' Cup Juvenile at Santa Anita. However, he reportedly returned with a swollen hock on the first occasion and did run far better than his position suggests at Newmarket, well on top in the stand-side group in a race dominated by those who raced on the far side: his final race was not only his first away from turf but also his first over further than seven furlongs, and he weakened after making some headway turning for home, appearing not to get the extended mile.

Alfred Nobel (IRE) (b.c. Jan 23, 2007)	Danehill Dancer (IRE) (b 1993)	Danehill (b 1986)	Danzig
			Razyana
		Mira Adonde (b or br 1986)	Sharpen Up
			Lettre d'Amour
	Glinting Desert (IRE) (b 2002)	Desert Prince (b 1995)	Green Desert
			Flying Fairy
		Dazzling Park (br 1996)	Warning
			Park Express

Alfred Nobel's sire Danehill Dancer, who won the Phoenix Stakes himself and is the sire of the 2008 winner Mastercraftsman, had the distinction of being responsible for the first three home in the latest edition. Danehill Dancer didn't stay when tried twice at a mile as a three-year-old, and, although some of his better progeny have been suited by middle distances the majority are not. Alfred Nobel, a 220,000-guinea yearling, is the first foal of Glinting Desert, who raced solely at two at up to seven furlongs, winning a maiden at that trip on her final start. Glinting Desert, by the top-class miler Desert Prince, is a daughter of the smart Irish filly Dazzling Park. Dazzling Park won three races including the Matron Stakes at a mile and a listed event over nine furlongs, and then showed she stayed a mile and a quarter when runner-up in the Irish Champion Stakes, a race won by her dam Park Express. A top racemare, Park Express also made a name for herself at stud, her other winners including the Japanese Group 1 six-furlong winner Shinko Forest and, of course, New Approach. The useful-looking Alfred Nobel showed in the Phoenix Stakes that he acts well on heavy ground, while good to firm seemed no problem for him at Newmarket. *A. P. O'Brien, Ireland*

ALFREDTHEORDINARY 4 b.g. Hunting Lion (IRE) 115 – Solmorin (Fraam 114) **64**
[2009 65: p10g p8g* p8g^2 p8.6g^6 p8g p8.6g Dec 5] close-coupled gelding: modest handicapper: won apprentice event at Lingfield in March: stays 1¼m: acts on polytrack, firm and good to soft ground. *M. R. Channon*

ALFRESCO 5 b.g. Mtoto 134 – Maureena (IRE) (Grand Lodge (USA) 125) [2009 88, **84**
a102: p8g^6 p7g^3 p8g^5 6m* 6m^2 5m 5d 6g p6f 8m p7g^4 p7g p8m Dec 1] useful-looking **a89**
gelding: fairly useful handicapper, better on all-weather: won at Goodwood in May: patchy form after: effective at 6f to 1m: acts on polytrack, firm and soft going: wears headgear: quirky. *J. R. Best*

ALF TUPPER 6 b.g. Atraf 116 – Silvery 67 (Petong 126) [2009 61: p9.5g^4 p8.6g* p8g^3 **69**
p8g p8f 12s 8g Sep 19] tall, rangy gelding: fair handicapper: won at Wolverhampton in **a76**
January: third at Dundalk, only good effort after: left A. McGuinness after fifth outing: effective at 1m/9f: acts on polytrack, good to firm and good to soft going (seemingly not on softer): tried blinkered (ran as if amiss): usually held up. *John J. Walsh, Ireland*

AL GHAZAL (USA) 2 b.c. (Mar 9) Motivator 131 – Mansfield Park 107 (Green **94**
Desert (USA) 127) [2009 6g^3 7.1g* 10m* 8d Oct 24] strong, good sort: second foal: half-brother to fairly useful French 1¼m (including at 2 yrs) winner Rushworth (by Halling): dam, 7f (at 2 yrs)/1m winner, sister to high-class miler Cape Cross: fairly useful form: won maiden at Sandown in August and 3-runner minor event at Leicester (made all, by 5 lengths) in October: only eighth of 11 to St Nicholas Abbey in Racing Post Trophy at Doncaster: stays 1¼m. *Saeed bin Suroor*

AL GILLANI (IRE) 4 b.g. Monashee Mountain (USA) 115 – Whisper Dawn (IRE) **–**
(Fasliyev (USA) 120) [2009 90: p6g* p6g 6g^6 p6g^2 Aug 11] fairly useful handicapper **a90**
on all-weather: won at Kempton in March: creditable effort after only when second at Lingfield: best at 6f: acts on polytrack (well held all starts on turf): usually races prominently. *J. R. Boyle*

ALHAQUE (USA) 3 ch.g. Galileo (IRE) 134 – Safeen (USA) (Storm Cat (USA)) **79**
[2009 84: 11.8m^3 10m 10.9g^6 p12m^2 14m^2 Oct 1] close-coupled gelding: has fluent action: fair maiden: left P. Chapple-Hyam after second start: probably stays 1¾m: raced only on polytrack and good/good to firm going: sold 27,000 gns, joined G. L. Moore, then gelded. *W. J. Haggas*

ALHENA (IRE) 2 b.f. (Mar 11) Alhaarth (IRE) 126 – Mail Boat (Formidable (USA) **53**
125) [2009 6m 8.1m Sep 26] €60,000Y: strong filly: eighth foal: half-sister to 3 winners, including smart 2002 2-y-o 6f/7f winner Mail The Desert (by Desert Prince) and useful Irish 7f (at 2 yrs)/9f winner Amarula Ridge (by Indian Ridge): dam unraced half-sister to smart 1¼m/1½m performer Dry Dock: green, encouraging seventh in maiden at Redcar: seemed amiss next time: should be suited by 7f/1m. *K. A. Ryan*

ALICANTE 3 gr.f. Pivotal 124 – Alba Stella 92 (Nashwan (USA) 135) [2009 60p: 8m^5 **80**
11.1d* 11.5d* 12d 12m^6 Sep 13] angular filly: has quick, unimpressive action: fairly useful handicapper: much improved when winning at Hamilton and Yarmouth within 5 days in July: below form after: should stay 1½m: acts on good to soft going. *Sir Mark Prescott*

ALICE ALLEYNE (IRE) 2 b.f. (Feb 2) Oasis Dream 129 – Vas Y Carla (USA) 80 **80**
(Gone West (USA)) [2009 p6g^2 6m^2 p7.1g* Oct 1] second foal: dam, maiden (raced only at 7f/1m), out of Oaks winner Lady Carla: fairly useful form: made all in maiden at Wolverhampton (beat Pictures 1¼ lengths): stays 7f. *Sir Michael Stoute*

ALICE CULLEN 2 b.f. (Mar 11) Bertolini (USA) 125 – Albavilla 82 (Spectrum (IRE) 126) [2009 7g Oct 31] unfurnished filly: second foal: half-sister to 3-y-o Antinori: dam, 1¾m winner, half-sister to very smart performer up to 1¾m Barolo: 100/1 and green, eleventh of 20 to Revered in maiden at Newmarket, taking time to wind up: will be suited by 1¼m+: sure to do better. *W. R. Swinburn* **54 p**

ALIMARR (IRE) 3 ch.f. Noverre (USA) 125 – Tiger Desert (GER) (Desert King (IRE) 129) [2009 67: p5g⁵ f8g f5g⁵ f7d⁶ Feb 26] sturdy filly: modest maiden at 2 yrs: well held in 2009: tried in cheekpieces/blinkers/tongue tie. *S. Parr* **–**

ALINGHI (IRE) 2 b.f. (Mar 14) Oratorio (IRE) 128 – The Stick 61 (Singspiel (IRE) 133) [2009 p6g⁵ Oct 21] good-quartered filly: second foal: dam, maiden (should have stayed 1¼m), out of Musidora Stakes winner Fatah Flare: 7/1, 3¼ lengths fifth to Hulcote Rose in maiden at Kempton, slowly away and green early: should stay at least 1m: sold 4,000 gns and sent to Greece. *R. Hannon* **56**

ALIS AQUILAE (IRE) 3 b.g. Captain Rio 122 – Garnock Academy (USA) (Royal Academy (USA) 130) [2009 6.1f⁵ 5m Jun 16] tall, lengthy gelding: third foal: half-brother to 8.5f/11.5f winner in Italy by Daggers Drawn: dam unraced half-sister to useful performer up to 2m Hearthstead Wings: better effort in maidens when 4½ lengths fifth of 17 to Devil You Know at Nottingham. *T. J. Etherington* **72**

ALITTLEMOREFLAIR 3 ch.f. Grape Tree Road 122 – Native Flair 87 (Be My Native (USA) 122) [2009 p8g p9.5g⁴ p12.2g⁵ p12g p12g³ 12.1m 14.1s p12g 12g³ 16m 16m⁵ Sep 17] rather leggy filly: half-sister to several winners, including 1m/1¼m winner Holy Smoke (by Statoblest) and 1½m/2m winner Chater Flair (by Efisio): dam 1¼m/1½m winner: modest maiden handicapper: best effort at 1½m on polytrack: visored last 3 starts: ungenuine. *J. Pearce* **63 §**

ALIYBEE (IRE) 3 b.f. Barathea (IRE) 127 – Aliyshan (IRE) 80 (Darshaan 133) [2009 50: p9.5g Jan 12] modest maiden: should stay beyond 1m: raced only on all-weather. *E. J. O'Neill* **–**

ALIYFA (IRE) 3 b.f. Spinning World (USA) 130 – Aliya (IRE) 105 (Darshaan 133) [2009 91: p10.7g² 11.3d* 11.3m³ 12g⁵ 14d³ 12s⁴ 14s² 12v* 12s Oct 11] smart performer: won handicap at Limerick in April and listed race at Galway (by ½ length from The Bull Hayes) in August: good efforts when third in listed race at Leopardstown (1½ lengths behind Profound Beauty) and fourth in handicap at Galway (behind Drunken Sailor) fifth/sixth outings: stays 1¾m: acts on polytrack, heavy and good to firm going: often blanketed for stall entry: usually races up with pace: game. *John M. Oxx, Ireland* **112**

AL JAADL 2 b.f. (Mar 15) Shamardal (USA) 129 – Three Wishes 87 (Sadler's Wells (USA) 132) [2009 7m⁵ Oct 6] 40,000Y: compact filly: fifth foal: half-sister to useful French 2004 2-y-o 9f winner Todman Avenue (by Lear Fan) and Italian 7.5f winner Snowstream (by Diesis): dam, Irish maiden (stayed 1¼m), sister to useful Irish winner up to 1¼m Sister Bella: 33/1 and green, encouraging 13¼ lengths fifth of 15 to Marie de Medici in maiden at Leicester, stuck wide and late headway under considerate ride: bred to stay 1m+: should improve. *W. Jarvis* **55 p**

AL JATHAAB (USA) 4 gr.g. Aljabr (USA) 125 – Al Ihsas (IRE) 99 (Danehill (USA) 126) [2009 p8g p8.6g⁵ p8g³ Mar 11] modest maiden: raced around 1m on polytrack. *M. Wigham* **60**

AL JOZA 2 b.f. (Mar 26) Dubawi (IRE) 129 – Avila 76 (Ajdal (USA) 130) [2009 p6g⁴ 8m 7m Oct 3] unfurnished filly: half-sister to several winners, notably Racing Post Trophy/Dante Stakes winner Dilshaan (by Darshaan): dam, third at 7f, half-sister to Chester Vase winner Nomrood: modest form in maidens first 2 starts: shaped as if amiss in valuable sales race at Newmarket: bred to be suited by 1m+. *C. E. Brittain* **63**

ALKHAFIF 3 b.g. Royal Applause 124 – My First Romance 61 (Danehill (USA) 126) [2009 99p: p8g 7m Sep 9] strong, lengthy gelding: won maiden at Newmarket sole start in 2008: suffered setback after and tailed off in 2009: dead. *E. A. L. Dunlop* **–**

AL KHALEEJ (IRE) 5 b.g. Sakhee (USA) 136 – Mood Swings (IRE) 77 (Shirley Heights 130) [2009 114: 6g 7g Aug 8] lengthy, good-bodied gelding: type to carry condition: smart handicapper at 4 yrs: reportedly suffered injury and off 14 months, shaped well both starts in 2009, at York and Newmarket (not knocked about): effective at 7f/1m: acts on polytrack and good to firm going: usually travels strongly. *E. A. L. Dunlop* **102 +**

ALKHATAAF (USA) 2 b.c. (May 14) Green Desert (USA) 127 – Elrafa Ah (USA) 105 (Storm Cat (USA)) [2009 6m Sep 18] rather leggy colt: brother to useful 6f/7f winner **–**

Shmookh, closely related to 2 winners, notably high-class 1998 2-y-o 6f/7f (Dewhurst Stakes) winner Mujahid (by Danzig), and half-brother to 7f winner Raajiya (by Gulch): dam 5f (at 2 yrs) and 6f winner who stayed 1m: 4/1, always towards rear in maiden at Newbury: bred to do better. *J. L. Dunlop*

AL KHAWAREZMI 2 b.c. (Mar 30) Shamardal (USA) 129 – Mrs Ting (USA) 54 (Lyphard (USA) 132) [2009 6s 7m Oct 13] strong, useful-looking colt: well beaten in maidens: sold £2,200. *M. Johnston* **–**

AL KHIMIYA (IRE) 2 b.f. (Jan 27) Van Nistelrooy (USA) 108 – Golden Flyer (FR) (Machiavellian (USA) 123) [2009 p6g 7m^{2} 7m^{3} 7.1m^{6} p7.1g^{4} p7m* p8.6g^{3} p8m* p8m^{4} p7f* Dec 20] leggy filly: second foal: dam unraced daughter of US Grade 2 8.5f winner Shir Dar: fair performer: won claimers in September and October (left S. Callaghan £6,000) and nursery in December, all at Kempton: effective at 7f/1m: acts on polytrack and good to firm going. *S. Woodman* **77**

ALL ABOUT YOU (IRE) 3 b.g. Mind Games 121 – Expectation (IRE) 59 (Night Shift (USA)) [2009 91p: 6.1m^{3} 7g 7.1m^{4} 8g^{5} 8s 7m^{4} 8m^{3} p7g^{6} p6m Nov 26] good-bodied gelding: fairly useful handicapper: didn't train on as expected in 2009, leaving W. Haggas 16,000 gns prior to final start (gelded after): stays 1m: acts on good to firm going: tried blinkered: has looked awkward. *P. Howling* **89 d**

ALLANIT (GER) 5 b.g. Tiger Hill (IRE) 127 – Astilbe (GER) (Monsun (GER) 124) [2009 106d: p12g p10g p10g p12.2m Aug 21] ex-German: useful performer at best: disappointing in handicaps in Britain, racing too freely in 2009. *B. J. Curley* **–**

ALLANNAH ABU 2 b.f. (Apr 23) Dubawi (IRE) 129 – Alexandrine (IRE) 78 (Nashwan (USA) 135) [2009 p7g p7g p7g Oct 29] 180,000Y: good-topped filly: fifth foal: half-sister to several winners, including 1½m to 1¾m winner Alambic (by Cozzene) and 3-y-o Alcalde, both useful: dam, 1¼m to 13f winner, half-sister to very smart 1¼m performer Last Second and to dams of Alborada/Albanova and Yesterday/Quarter Moon: slowly away and outpaced in maidens: bred to be well suited by 1¼m+: type to do better in handicaps. *Sir Mark Prescott* **– p**

ALLEXES (IRE) 3 b. or br.f. Exceed And Excel (AUS) 126 – Lizanne (USA) (Theatrical 128) [2009 –: 8m 7g 6.1g p7g p7g p10m Sep 26] rather unfurnished filly: modest maiden handicapper: in cheekpieces final start. *J. R. Boyle* **55**

ALLEZ FRANK (GER) 8 b.g. Macanal (USA) 114 – Agua Clara (GER) (Roi Dagobert 128) [2009 60: 12.1v^{3} Jul 24] modest hurdler/fair chaser: modest form on Flat in Britain: stays 14.5f: acts on polytrack and heavy ground. *A. E. Jones* **64**

ALLFORMARY 3 b.f. Tobougg (IRE) 125 – Bollin Rita 82 (Rambo Dancer (CAN) 107) [2009 72: 8.1m^{3} 8d 7g f8m^{5} 10g^{5} 8s* 8m^{2} f8g 7g Oct 17] useful-looking filly: fairly useful handicapper: won at Thirsk in September: stays 1m: acts on heavy and good to firm going: has found little: sold £18,000. *B. Smart* **82**

ALL FOR YOU (IRE) 3 b.f. High Chaparral (IRE) 132 – Quatre Saisons (FR) (Homme de Loi (IRE) 120) [2009 62p: 8g 8.3g^{2} 7m* 7.1m^{3} 7g^{5} p7.1g p7.1g^{3} Oct 2] tall, good-bodied filly: has scope: fair handicapper: won at Lingfield in June: stays 1m: raced only on polytrack and good/good to firm ground: in cheekpieces last 2 outings: sold 26,000 gns. *M. Botti* **76**

ALL GUNS FIRING (IRE) 3 b.g. High Chaparral (IRE) 132 – Lili Cup (FR) (Fabulous Dancer (USA) 124) [2009 85p: 10m 14m^{3} 12d^{6} f11f^{4} Dec 17] strong gelding: fair maiden: left M. Jarvis 11,000 gns prior to final outing: acts on heavy and good to firm going: stays 1¾m: tried tongue tied (said to have had breathing problem). *D. Carroll* **79**

ALLIED POWERS (IRE) 4 b.c. Invincible Spirit (IRE) 121 – Always Friendly 111 (High Line 125) [2009 113: 10.1g 12.1d* 10m 10.4g^{2} 12v^{3} 10d^{2} 12m Oct 17] tall, good-topped colt: smart performer: won listed handicap at Hamilton in May by 4½ lengths from Lady Jane Digby: good efforts when second in York Stakes (beaten 1¼ lengths by Kirklees) and Kilternan Stakes at Leopardstown (4½ lengths behind Poet): effective at 1¼m/1½m (at least when conditions aren't testing): best on good ground or softer (acts on heavy). *M. L. W. Bell* **115**

ALL IN THE RED (IRE) 4 ch.g. Redback 116 – Light-Flight (IRE) (Brief Truce (USA) 126) [2009 76: f8g* p8g* p8.6g^{3} 10.3m 10.2m* f8g f11g^{5} 12m 10.4v^{2} 10.1d 11.9m^{3} 11.5m 10m 10g 10m^{3} Jul 29] lengthy gelding: fair performer: won seller at Southwell and claimer at Kempton (left B. Pollock £6,000 after next start) in February **78**

and handicap at Nottingham in April: stays 1½m: acts on all-weather, heavy and good to firm ground: wears headgear (usually cheekpieces): often starts slowly/races lazily: held up. *A. Crook*

ALL MOVING PARTS (USA) 2 b. or br.g. (Feb 8) Forest Camp (USA) 114 – Smooth Player (USA) 115 (Bertrando (USA) 127) [2009 6m 6g 8.3s^6 8g^6 Oct 20] $15,000Y, £22,000 2-y-o: lengthy, deep-girthed gelding: modest maiden: sixth in nursery at Yarmouth: stays 8.3f: acts on soft going. *J. S. Wainwright* **61**

ALLORO 5 ch.g. Auction House (USA) 120 – Minette 55 (Bishop of Cashel 122) [2009 –: p8g f8g Jan 15] compact gelding: maiden: little form since 2007: tried in cheekpieces: won over hurdles in February. *A. Kirtley* **–**

ALL RIGHT NOW 2 b.c. (Apr 13) Night Shift (USA) – Cookie Cutter (IRE) 71 (Fasliyev (USA) 120) [2009 p7.1g Dec 28] 16,000Y: first foal: dam 6f winner: 25/1, very green when well held in maiden at Wolverhampton. *S. Kirk* **–**

ALL SPIN (IRE) 3 ch.g. Spinning World (USA) 130 – Mad Annie (USA) (Anabaa (USA) 130) [2009 70: 6g^6 7g^4 p6g^3 5m^4 5g 5m Aug 31] rather leggy gelding: fair maiden handicapper: hampered and fell heavily at Newcastle final start: was effective at 5f/6f: acted on polytrack and good to firm going: once visored (ran to form): dead. *A. P. Jarvis* **70**

ALL THE ACES (IRE) 4 b.g. Spartacus (IRE) 107 – Lili Cup (FR) (Fabulous Dancer (USA) 124) [2009 113: 13.3d^2 12g* 12m^5 p12m^2 14s^5 12v^6 Oct 24] strong, good sort: smart performer: suffered hairline fracture of hock and off 11 months before reappearance: won listed event at Newmarket in June by 6 lengths from Wasan: good effort after only when ¾-length second to Kirklees in September Stakes at Kempton: should stay 1¾m: acts on polytrack, firm and good to soft going: races prominently: gelded after final start. *M. A. Jarvis* **117**

ALL THE NINES (IRE) 3 b.f. Elusive City (USA) 117 – Sagaing (Machiavellian (USA) 123) [2009 –: p7.1g^6 f6g* 6g* 6m* 6m^5 6m^6 f6g 6d Jul 31] quite good-topped filly: fairly useful handicapper: won at Southwell (maiden) in April and Hamilton (2) in May: below form after: should stay 7f: acts on all-weather and good to firm going: races prominently. *Mrs D. J. Sanderson* **88**

ALL YOU NEED (IRE) 5 b.g. Iron Mask (USA) 117 – Choice Pickings (IRE) (Among Men (USA) 124) [2009 67: p7.1g p8.6g^5 p6g* p6m 7.5m f6g^6 6m* 6m^5 8m 6d^6 p6g^4 p8g p6g^6 Nov 20] rather leggy gelding: modest performer nowadays: won minor event at Wolverhampton in February and seller at Leicester in June: stays 7f: acts on polytrack and firm going: wears headgear. *R. Hollinshead* **60**

ALMADAA 2 b.c. (Feb 1) Exceed And Excel (AUS) 126 – Masaader (USA) 96 (Wild Again (USA)) [2009 6g p6g^3 p6g^4 6g Oct 9] neat colt: fair maiden: looked awkward when well held in nursery at York: stays 6f: acts on polytrack: sold 8,000 gns. *E. A. L. Dunlop* **65**

ALMAHAZA (IRE) 5 b.g. Alzao (USA) 117 – Morna's Moment (USA) 59 (Timeless Moment (USA)) [2009 p8.6g f8g* p10g f8g* p10g^4 p13.9g f8g^2 f12g^4 p10m f8f^4 f8f^2 Dec 17] rangy gelding: fair handicapper: missed 2008 and gelded prior to reappearance: won at Southwell in February and March: effective at 1m to 1½m: acts on all-weather, unraced on extremes of going on turf: sometimes wears blinkers/cheekpieces: held up: quirky. *A. J. Chamberlain* **70**

ALMAMIA 4 b.f. Hernando (FR) 127 – Alborada 122 (Alzao (USA) 117) [2009 f12g^6 Jan 15] leggy filly: fair maiden in 2007: off 14 months, never dangerous sole start at 4 yrs: should be suited by 1½m. *Sir Mark Prescott* **–**

ALMATLAIE (USA) 3 b.f. Elusive Quality (USA) – Hachiyah (IRE) 91 (Generous (IRE) 139) [2009 43p: p5.1g^6 p6g Sep 12] ex-Irish: poor form in maidens: bred to stay 7f+. *J. W. Unett* **36**

ALMATY EXPRESS 7 b.g. Almaty (IRE) 113§ – Express Girl 75 (Sylvan Express 117) [2009 –, a92: p5g^5 p5.1g p5.1g* p5.1g* p5g 5g p5g 5m p5.1g p5.1g p5.1g p5.1g^6 p5.1g p6g^6 Dec 19] smallish gelding: fairly useful handicapper on all-weather, no form on turf: won at Wolverhampton in March and April (eleventh course win): below form after: best at 5f: raced mostly on polytrack nowadays: blinkered. *J. R. Weymes* **–** **a87 d**

ALMAZAR 3 b.g. Green Desert (USA) 127 – Zaqrah (USA) 80 (Silver Hawk (USA) 123) [2009 58: 8.1g^5 7g^5 May 28] lengthy gelding: modest maiden: will prove best short of 1m: has looked awkward: sold 5,000 gns in July, sent to Greece. *J. L. Dunlop* **52**

John Smith's Stakes (Heritage Handicap), Newbury—Almiqdaad shows much improved form; Drunken Sailor (blinkers) and Sweet Lightning are next to finish

ALMIQDAAD 3 b.c. Haafhd 129 – Etizaaz (USA) 117 (Diesis 133) [2009 96p: 10d[5] 10m 10m* 9m Oct 3] strong, well-made colt: powerful galloper with long stride: useful handicapper: improved to win John Smith's Stakes at Newbury (beat Drunken Sailor 1¼ lengths) in September: joint-favourite, only eleventh in Cambridgeshire at Newmarket next time: stays 1¼m: acts on good to firm going. *M. A. Jarvis* **109**

ALMORA GURU 5 b.m. Ishiguru (USA) 114 – Princess Almora 88 (Pivotal 124) [2009 –: p8g p8g p8.6g[5] p8.6m[5] p7.1g[4] p8.6g[4] Mar 30] close-coupled mare: modest performer: stays easy 8.6f: acts on polytrack and firm going, probably on soft: tried in cheekpieces. *W. M. Brisbourne* **53**

ALMOST MARRIED (IRE) 5 b.g. Indian Ridge 123 – Shining Hour (USA) 104 (Red Ransom (USA)) [2009 68: 5m 6f 6m Oct 1] lengthy gelding: fair handicapper at 4 yrs: below form in 2009. *J. S. Goldie* **–**

ALMOWJ 6 b.g. Fasliyev (USA) 120 – Tiriana (Common Grounds 118) [2009 50: 10.2g 8.1g 10.2g Jul 23] sturdy gelding: modest maiden at best: well held in 2009: tried blinkered/in cheekpieces. *G. H. Jones* **–**

AL MUGTAREB (IRE) 3 b.c. Acclamation 118 – Billie Bailey (USA) (Mister Baileys 123) [2009 70p: 6m* 7g 6g[2] 6g[5] 7m 7.6m[5] 8g 7d Aug 26] sturdy colt: fair performer: won maiden at Catterick in April: inconsistent in handicaps after: stays 7.6f: acts on polytrack and good to firm going: blinkered final start (pulled hard): sold 2,000 gns, sent to Bahrain. *M. Johnston* **72**

AL MUHEER (IRE) 4 b.c. Diktat 126 – Dominion Rose (USA) 65 (Spinning World (USA) 130) [2009 104: p8.6g[4] p10g[6] p8g* p7.1g* p7g[3] p7g p7g[5] 7f[5] 7f[2] 7m 7m* 7m 7m Sep 26] close-coupled colt: smart performer: won minor event at Lingfield in February and handicaps at Wolverhampton in March and Ascot (much improved, beat Secret **113**

Abu Dhabi International Stakes (Heritage Handicap), Ascot—
40/1-shot Al Muheer shows improved form with the blinkers refitted;
Secret Society (right), Redford (partially obscured by winner) and Genki (left) also make the frame

Society ½ length in Abu Dhabi International Stakes) in July: also ran well when 1¾ lengths second to Giganticus in Buckingham Palace Stakes (handicap) at Royal Ascot: stays 1m, effective at shorter: acts on polytrack and firm going: tried in cheekpieces/tongue tie, best in blinkers: tactically versatile. *C. E. Brittain*

AL MUKAALA (IRE) 3 ch.g. Cadeaux Genereux 131 – Crescent Moon (Mr Prospector (USA)) [2009 71: f8g Mar 11] lengthy gelding: fair maiden at 2 yrs: well held in seller only outing in 2009: tried tongue tied. *B. N. Pollock* **–**

ALMUKTAHEM 3 b.c. Green Desert (USA) 127 – Nasanice (IRE) 97 (Nashwan (USA) 135) [2009 7d^5 7m^4 8.5m^2 9m* 10d^3 10.3m p10f^3 Sep 4] useful-looking colt: seventh foal: brother to fairly useful 1m winner Safwa and half-brother to 3 winners, including high-class 1m (at 2 yrs) to 1½m winner Maraahel (by Alzao) and smart 7f/1m winner Mostashaar (by Intikhab): dam Irish 9f winner: useful form: won maiden at Lingfield in July: improved when third to Bab Al Salam in handicap there final outing: stays 1¼m: acts on polytrack, unraced on extremes of going on turf: visored last 4 starts: often front runner: joined E. Charpy in UAE. *Sir Michael Stoute* **95**

ALMUNTASER (IRE) 2 b.g. (Mar 9) Celtic Swing 138 – Fire Reply (IRE) (Royal Academy (USA) 130) [2009 5g^4 6g 6s^5 6m 6.1s^5 6g Oct 19] rather leggy gelding: modest maiden: stays 6f: acts on soft ground: blinkered last 2 starts: sold £2,800. *Ian Williams* **53**

ALMUTAHAM (USA) 2 b. or br.c. (May 1) Dynaformer (USA) – Forest Lady (USA) (Woodman (USA) 126) [2009 7g 8.1d Aug 31] $260,000Y: third foal: half-brother to 3-y-o Natural Flair and a winner in USA by War Chant: dam unraced sister to very smart performer up to 1½m Ciro: green and spared hard race in maidens at Ascot and Chepstow: sure to do better. *J. L. Dunlop* **– p**

ALMUTAWAAZIN 3 b.g. Nayef (USA) 129 – Crown Water (USA) (Chief's Crown (USA)) [2009 –p: 8s 12m May 7] big, strong gelding: no form in maidens: sold 7,000 gns in July. *M. P. Tregoning* **–**

ALNADANA (IRE) 4 gr.f. Danehill Dancer (IRE) 117 – Alnamara (FR) 105 (Linamix (FR) 127) [2009 107: 8d^2 8d^5 8.5g^2 8g* 9.5g^2 8m Oct 3] lengthy, good-topped filly: first foal: dam, French 1¼m/1½m winner, out of half-sister to Prix de l'Arc de Triomphe winner Sakhee: smart performer: won newcomers race at Deauville at 2 yrs (when trained by A. Fabre) and listed race at Maisons-Laffitte in 2008: improved in 2009, winning Prix Messidor at Maisons-Laffitte (made all, beat Mr Brock 3 lengths) in July and good 1¼ lengths second to Dynaforce in Beverly D Stakes at Arlington next start: would also have won Princess Elizabeth Stakes at Epsom third outing but for hanging badly left down camber (beaten length by Eva's Request): stayed 9.5f: acted on good to soft going, well below form on good to firm in Sun Chariot Stakes at Newmarket final start: slowly away second outing: visits Sinndar. *A. de Royer Dupre, France* **115**

AL NAOUWEE (USA) 2 b. or br.c. (Feb 17) Forest Camp (USA) 114 – Dancehall Deelites (CAN) (Afternoon Deelites (USA) 122) [2009 7m^3 7m^2 p7.1g^4 6d Oct 24] $30,000F, $15,000Y, £40,000 2-y-o: tall colt: first foal: dam Canadian winner around 1m, including at 2 yrs: easily best effort when ¾-length second of 5 to Court Gown in minor event at Redcar: stays 7f: joined A. Al Raihe in UAE. *B. Smart* **78**

ALNWICK 5 b.g. Kylian (USA) – Cebwob 85 (Rock City 120) [2009 81: p16g³ p16g p16g² p16g⁴ 16m⁴ 15g p16g⁴ 16d² 21g⁵ p16g* 15g³ 16m p16.5g⁴ 16g³ Oct 30] tall, close-coupled gelding: fairly useful handicapper: won at Kempton in August: good third at Newmarket final outing: best form at 2m: acts on polytrack, firm and good to soft going: below form only try in cheekpieces: races prominently: reliable. *P. D. Cundell* **87**

ALONG THE NILE 7 b.g. Desert Prince (IRE) 130 – Golden Fortune 102 (Forzando 122) [2009 –: 10m 10g 10.2v Nov 4] strong, lengthy gelding: one-time fairly useful handicapper: little form since 2007: often tongue tied, tried in cheekpieces: fairly useful hurdler. *K. G. Reveley* **–**

ALOTAGO (IRE) 2 ch.f. (Feb 11) Tagula (IRE) 116 – Batool (USA) 73 (Bahri (USA) 125) [2009 7.5g 7.5f⁶ 8g p8.6g Oct 9] tall, close-coupled filly: first foal: dam maiden (stayed 1¼m): little form, including in nursery. *D. Nicholls* **–**

A LOT OF RED (IRE) 3 b.c. Barathea (IRE) 127 – A Lot of Kir (IRE) (Selkirk (USA) 129) [2009 8m 6m⁶ 6d 7f 6m 8.1m⁵ 8.3m Sep 30] lengthy, good-topped colt: modest maiden: tongue tied, also blinkered last 2 starts. *P. J. O'Gorman* **51**

ALPEN GLEN 3 ch.f. Halling (USA) 133 – Anne d'Autriche (IRE) 75 (Rainbow Quest (USA) 134) [2009 12.1m* 10.3g* 10m⁶ 9.9g 9.9f p10g⁵ p12.2g Dec 11] 65,000Y: lengthy, unfurnished filly: fifth foal: half-sister to useful 2005 2-y-o 1m winner Austrian and 5-y-o Aureate (both by Jade Robbery): dam, 11.5f winner, sister to smart 1½m/15f winner Pozarica and half-sister to very smart 1¼m/1½m winner Annaba: useful form: won maiden at Chepstow (by 6 lengths) and handicap at Chester (beat Eastern Aria 2¾ lengths), both in June: below form after: likely to prove best at 1½m+. *M. Johnston* **96**

ALPES MARITIMES 5 b.g. Danehill Dancer (IRE) 117 – Miss Riviera 103 (Kris 135) [2009 93: p10g p10g⁵ p10g⁵ 10g⁶ p10g³ p10g Jun 17] big, strong gelding: fairly useful performer: stays 1¼m: acts on polytrack, good to firm and good to soft going: tried in cheekpieces: sold 8,000 gns. *G. L. Moore* **80**

ALPHACINO 2 b.g. (Apr 2) Hunting Lion (IRE) 115 – Fading Away (Fraam 114) [2009 5d⁴ p5.1g³ 6.1g² 6f⁵ 7s⁵ 7.5m⁴ 7d² 7d* 7.5m⁵ 7g p8.6g Nov 30] fair performer: claimed from M. Channon £6,000 prior to winning claimer at Thirsk in July: stays 7f: acts on good to soft ground: in cheekpieces last 4 starts (seemed amiss final one). *P. C. Haslam* **64**

ALPHA TAURI (USA) 3 b.c. Aldebaran (USA) 126 – Seven Moons (JPN) (Sunday Silence (USA)) [2009 65: 7.1m² 6m 6d 6m Aug 8] smallish, sturdy colt: fair maiden: well held after reappearance (said to have finished lame second outing): stays 7f: acts on good to firm going: blinkered final outing: sold 2,500 gns in October, sent to Italy. *H. R. A. Cecil* **81 d**

ALPHA VEGA (IRE) 3 b.f. Marju (IRE) 127 – Szabo (IRE) 88 (Anabaa (USA) 130) [2009 8.3g p11g⁴ p12m³ Nov 29] 72,000F, 150,000Y: second foal: half sister to Italian 1¼m winner Fuente Apache (by Hawk Wing): dam, Irish/French maiden (stayed 1½m), half-sister to useful performers Nightbird (sprinter) and Night Air (miler): modest form in maidens: visored last 2 starts: sold 3,000 gns. *J. R. Fanshawe* **63**

ALPINE ROSE (FR) 4 gr.f. Linamix (FR) 127 – Fragrant Hill 104 (Shirley Heights 130) [2009 104: 10g³ 10.5g* 12m² 10m* 10g⁴ 10m Oct 17] tall, lengthy filly: sister to several at least useful winners in France, notably very smart 10.5f to 1½m winner Fragrant Mix and smart 1¼m/1½m winner Fracassant, and half-sister to 2 winners, including smart 1m (at 2 yrs)/1½m winner Fraloga (by Grand Lodge): dam 7f (at 2 yrs) **119**

Darley Prix Jean Romanet, Deauville—
Alpine Rose (near side) and Lady Marian fight out the finish of a race run as a Group 1 contest for the first time, the pair clear of La Boum (pale colours) and Danse Grecque

and 11f winner: smart performer: won maiden at Chantilly and minor event at Clairefontaine in 2008: sold from J-C. Rouget €550,000 after final 3-y-o start: improved in 2009, winning Prix Corrida at Saint-Cloud in May and Prix Jean Romanet at Deauville (by short head from Lady Marian after good duel) in August: good 1½ lengths second to Spanish Moon in Grand Prix de Saint-Cloud in between: not at best last 2 starts, in Prix de l'Opera at Longchamp and Champion Stakes at Newmarket: stayed 12.5f: acted on firm and soft ground: raced prominently: stud. *A. de Royer Dupre, France*

ALQAAHIR (USA) 7 b.h. Swain (IRE) 134 – Crafty Example (USA) (Crafty **75**
Prospector (USA)) [2009 77: 8g 7d 7s p8.6g* p8.6g* p8.6g p8.6g^6 Dec 7] rangy horse: fair handicapper: won twice at Wolverhampton in October: stays 1¼m: acts on polytrack, firm and soft ground: has joined P. Burgoyne. *L. Smyth, Ireland*

ALQAFFAY (IRE) 4 b.c. King's Best (USA) 132 – Spirit of Tara (IRE) 106 (Sadler's **82**
Wells (USA) 132) [2009 76: 9.9g^2 12d^3 10m^3 9.9m^2 10.1m^2 Sep 9] fairly useful maiden: stays 1½m: acts on polytrack, good to firm and good to soft going: sold 24,000 gns. *J. H. M. Gosden*

AL QASI (IRE) 6 b.h. Elnadim (USA) 128 – Delisha (Salse (USA) 128) [2009 118: 7g^6 **105**
7s^4 6d 7m Oct 17] rather leggy, attractive horse: smart performer at best: not as good at 6 yrs, best effort when 4½ lengths fourth to Three Rocks in Minstrel Stakes at the Curragh: stays 7f: seems best on good going or softer (won on polytrack and firm at 3 yrs): sometimes bandaged fore joints. *P. W. Chapple-Hyam*

AL QEDDAAF (IRE) 3 b.g. Alhaarth (IRE) 126 – Just Special 109 (Cadeaux **87**
Genereux 131) [2009 71p: 6d^5 8s* 8m p10m p10g^3 Oct 22] tall gelding: fairly useful handicapper: won at Yarmouth in June: creditable third at Kempton final outing: stays 1¼m: acts on polytrack and soft going: sold 80,000 gns, joined D. McCain Jnr. *W. J. Haggas*

ALRAFID (IRE) 10 ch.g. Halling (USA) 133 – Ginger Tree (USA) 86 (Dayjur (USA) **66**
137) [2009 p16g^2 f12g^4 p13g^5 Feb 4] fair performer on Flat nowadays (successful over hurdles in April): seems to stay 2m: acts on polytrack, soft and good to firm going: blinkered in 2009: usually held up/takes good hold. *G. L. Moore*

ALRASM (IRE) 2 b.g. (Mar 29) Acclamation 118 – New Deal 76 (Rainbow Quest **99**
(USA) 134) [2009 6d^2 6f* 6m 6m 8g^2 Oct 23] £150,000Y: tall, attractive gelding: second foal: dam French 1m winner: useful performer: won maiden at Doncaster in May: excellent length second of 19 to Antoniola in nursery at same course final outing, strong at finish (gelded after): stays 1m: acts on firm and good to soft going. *M. A. Jarvis*

AL RAYANAH 6 b.m. Almushtarak (IRE) 122 – Desert Bloom (FR) (Last Tycoon 131) **60**
[2009 60: 8.1g^2 8.1g^6 8d f8g^5 8g^4 8m 8g^4 p8.6g^6 Oct 30] modest performer: best short of 1¼m: acts on all-weather, firm and soft going: wears cheekpieces/blinkers nowadays: held up: has hung. *G. Prodromou*

AL SABAHEYA 3 b.f. Kheleyf (USA) 116 – Baalbek 76 (Barathea (IRE) 127) [2009 **89**
92: p8g 10f^5 8.1g^2 8.5g 7g^5 8m^5 7g 7d^4 p7f^6 9.7m 7d^3 p8g^3 Oct 14] workmanlike filly: fairly useful handicapper: placed 3 times in 2009: stays 1m: acts on polytrack, good to firm and good to soft going: tried blinkered (including last 3 starts): sold 7,000 gns. *C. E. Brittain*

ALSACE LORRAINE (IRE) 4 b.f. Giant's Causeway (USA) 132 – Mer de Corail **102**
(IRE) 111 (Sadler's Wells (USA) 132) [2009 73: 8d* 8m* 8m^2 9g* 9.9g^4 8m^2 Sep 26] well-made filly: useful handicapper: much improved at 4 yrs, winning at Yarmouth in April, Doncaster in June and Goodwood (beat Full of Love by neck) in July: unlucky ½-length second of 17 to Ahla Wasahl in listed event at Ascot final outing, suffering interference over 1f out: should stay 1¼m: acts on good to firm and good to soft ground: held up. *J. R. Fanshawe*

ALSADAA (USA) 6 b.g. Kingmambo (USA) 125 – Aljawza (USA) 86 (Riverman **80**
(USA) 131) [2009 84: p11g^6 12m Sep 10] close-coupled, quite attractive gelding: fairly useful handicapper: stays 1½m: acts on all-weather and good to firm ground: tongue tied at 3 yrs: useful hurdler. *Mrs L. J. Mongan*

ALSAHIL (USA) 3 ch.c. Diesis 133 – Tayibah (IRE) 81 (Sadler's Wells (USA) 132) **84**
[2009 75p: 8g* p8f^6 Dec 16] fairly useful form: won maiden at Brighton in April: left M. Tregoning 12,500 gns and off 8 months prior to final start: likely to stay 1¼m: raced only on polytrack and good ground. *Micky Hammond*

ALSERAAJ (USA) 4 ch.f. El Prado (IRE) 119 – Barzah (IRE) 98 (Darshaan 133) **56**
[2009 73d: p8.6g f12g p10g^3 Apr 4] lengthy, good-bodied filly: modest maiden handi-

capper nowadays: stays 1¼m: acts on polytrack and good to firm going: tried tongue tied (has had breathing problem). *Ian Williams*

AL SHABABIYA (IRE) 2 b.f. (May 3) Dubawi (IRE) 129 – Multaka (USA) 66 (Gone West (USA)) [2009 p8m p8.6g[2] Dec 19] 38,000F: third foal: half-sister to 4-y-o Watson's Bay and 3-y-o Palacefield: dam, ran 4 times, closely related to very smart performer up to 1¼m Bahhare and half-sister to high-class miler Bahri: modest form in polytrack maidens: stays 8.6f. *D. M. Simcock* **64**

ALSUFOOH (USA) 2 ch.f. (Feb 9) Haafhd 129 – Dufoof (USA) (Kingmambo (USA) 125) [2009 7g[5] 7.2v[5] Oct 31] second foal: dam unraced half-sister to smart performer up to 9f Iqte Saab: fifth in maidens at Catterick (better effort, beaten 8¼ lengths by Madam Macie) and Ayr (not knocked about). *M. Johnston* **57 +**

ALTERNATIVE CHOICE (USA) 3 b.g. Grand Slam (USA) 120 – Northern Fleet (USA) (Afleet (CAN)) [2009 62: p7g[5] p8g[2] Mar 30] modest maiden: gelded after final outing: stays 1m: raced only on polytrack. *N. P. Littmoden* **62**

ALTHABEA 2 b.c. (Feb 23) Avonbridge 123 – Mandolin (IRE) 69 (Sabrehill (USA) 120) [2009 p7.1g 5m[6] 7.1g 6.1s 6g Oct 19] close-coupled colt: poor maiden: seemed amiss in nursery final start (blinkered): sold £800. *Ian Williams* **42**

ALTILHAR (USA) 6 b.g. Dynaformer (USA) – Al Desima 93 (Emperor Jones (USA) 119) [2009 86: p16g[4] Feb 12] robust gelding: fairly useful handicapper: off 13 months, shaped as if retaining ability when fourth at Kempton: stays 2m: acts on polytrack and good to firm going: sometimes blinkered: fairly useful hurdler. *G. L. Moore* **78**

ALTIMATUM (USA) 3 ch.c. Rahy (USA) 115 – Aldiza (USA) (Storm Cat (USA)) [2009 65: 8f[2] 8.1m p8g 8.3g[4] p12m[4] p8.6g[6] Dec 7] good-topped colt: fair maiden: first past post at Brighton in July, but later demoted: often looked temperamental after: stays 1m: acts on polytrack and firm going: tried blinkered/tongue tied: one to treat with caution. *P. F. I. Cole* **70 §**

ALTO SINGER (IRE) 4 b.f. Alhaarth (IRE) 126 – Sonatina 103 (Distant Relative 128) [2009 66: p8g p8g Feb 12] compact filly: form only when fourth at Windsor on 3-y-o reappearance: tried in cheekpieces. *L. A. Dace* **–**

ALTOS REALES 5 b.m. Mark of Esteem (IRE) 137 – Karsiyaka (IRE) (Kahyasi 130) [2009 66: p9.5g p11g p11g 12.4s[5] f11m[2] 10.1m f11g f14m[2] p12.2g* f12g Dec 22] modest handicapper nowadays, better on all-weather: left J. Given £1,500 after seventh start: won at Wolverhampton in December: barely stays 1¾m: acts on all-weather and soft ground. *M. J. Scudamore* **51 a57**

ALUBARI 2 b.c. (May 10) Tiger Hill (IRE) 127 – Why So Silent (Mill Reef (USA) 141) [2009 p7m[6] Oct 26] closely related to several at least useful winners, notably 7f to 1¼m winner Leporello and 7f (at 2 yrs) to 1½m winner Poppy Carew, both smart, and half-brother to 3 winners: dam unraced close relation of dual Chester Cup winner Top Cees: 50/1 and green, encouraging sixth to Prizefighting in maiden at Kempton: should stay 1m+: sure to do better. *W. R. Swinburn* **50 p**

ALUCICA 6 b.m. Celtic Swing 138 – Acicula (IRE) 96 (Night Shift (USA)) [2009 48, a64: f8s p8g[3] p7g[5] p10g Feb 11] modest handicapper: stays easy 1m: acts on polytrack: visored: has raced freely: none too consistent. *D. Shaw* **57**

ALVEE (IRE) 4 br.f. Key of Luck (USA) 126 – Alleluia 117 (Caerleon (USA) 132) [2009 75p: 16d 15g p13.9g Sep 17] compact filly: modest maiden: probably stays 2m: raced on polytrack and good ground or softer: visored final outing. *J. R. Fanshawe* **63**

ALWAARY (USA) 3 b.c. Dynaformer (USA) – Tabrir (IRE) (Unfuwain (USA) 131) [2009 99p: 11.5m[4] 11g* 12m[2] 12m[4] 12m[6] Aug 18] good sort: very smart performer: won listed race at Goodwood in May: much better form against elders next 2 starts, in Princess of Wales's Stakes at Newmarket (badly hampered when ¾-length third (promoted) to Doctor Fremantle) and King George VI and Queen Elizabeth Stakes at Ascot (stayed on from well off pace when 4¼ lengths fourth to Conduit): sweated up, below form in Great Voltigeur Stakes at York final outing, refusing to settle: will stay beyond 1½m: raced only on polytrack and good/good to firm going: held up. *J. H. M. Gosden* **122**

ALWARQAA 2 b.f. (Apr 1) Oasis Dream 129 – Al Sifaat 88 (Unfuwain (USA) 131) [2009 7g Oct 31] second foal: dam, 2-y-o 6f winner, out of half-sister to 2000 Guineas/Champion Stakes winner Haafhd: 25/1, very green and no show in maiden at Newmarket: sold 3,000 gns. *B. W. Hills* **–**

AL WASEF (USA) 4 b.g. Danzig (USA) – Widady (USA) (Gone West (USA)) [2009 71: 7s 6d 7.2m^5 7.2g^3 8m 8.3m^6 Jul 11] useful-looking gelding: fair maiden: stays 1m: acts on soft going: signs of temperament. *J. S. Goldie* **71**

ALWAYS BEST 5 b.g. Best of The Bests (IRE) 122 – Come To The Point (Pursuit of Love 124) [2009 59: 13m^3 15m^4 12d 13g 12.1v^6 12.4d Sep 7] tall gelding: poor handicapper nowadays: stays 1¾m: acts on polytrack, firm and soft going: tried in headgear/tongue tie: none too consistent. *R. Allan* **45**

ALWAYS BOLD (IRE) 4 ch.g. King's Best (USA) 132 – Tarakana (USA) 101 (Shahrastani (USA) 135) [2009 96: 20m 15.8g^2 21g 16g^3 Aug 8] tall, good-topped gelding: fairly useful handicapper: placed at Catterick and Ascot: best form up to 2m: acts on polytrack, heavy and good to firm ground: progressive hurdler. *D. McCain Jnr* **94**

ALWAYS CERTAIN (USA) 4 ch.g. Giant's Causeway (USA) 132 – Mining Missharriet (USA) (Mining (USA)) [2009 73: p12g^6 p16g^5 f14g Mar 3] good-topped gelding: modest handicapper nowadays: best form around 1¼m: acts on polytrack and firm going: temperament under suspicion. *P. G. Murphy* **60**

ALWAYS DAZZLING 2 ch.f. (Apr 17) Cadeaux Genereux 131 – Woodlass (USA) (Woodman (USA) 126) [2009 6m^2 Jul 13] second foal: half-sister to useful 7f (in France at 2 yrs)/8.5f (in USA) winner Duke of Homberg (by Dynaformer): dam useful French 6.5f (at 2 yrs)/1m winner: 12/1, encouraging ¾-length second to Lord Aeryn in maiden at Ayr, green and leading over 1f out: injured after: should do better. *M. Johnston* **59 p**

ALWAYS DE ONE 2 b.f. (May 6) Fruits of Love (USA) 127 – Yes Virginia (USA) (Roanoke (USA)) [2009 7.5m 7m^4 8g p8.6g Nov 30] small filly: half-sister to several winners, including 4-y-o Yankee Storm: dam US 1m/8.5f winner: modest maiden: well held in nursery: should stay 1m. *M. Johnston* **61**

Hamdan Al Maktoum's "Alwaary"

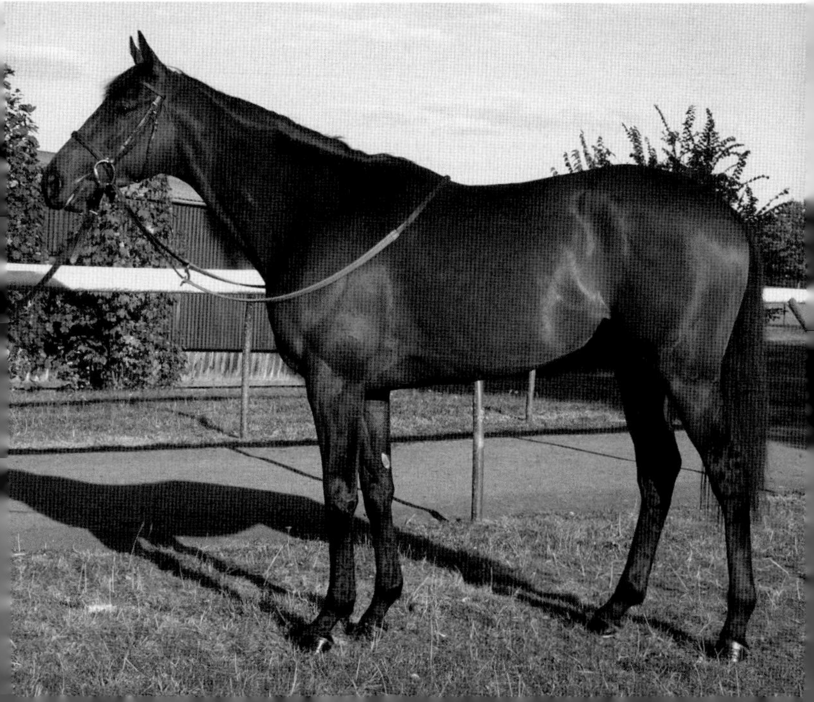

ALWAYS DIXIE (IRE) 2 b.f. (Feb 25) Lucky Story (USA) 128 – Jerre Jo Glanville (USA) (Skywalker (USA)) [2009 5m³ f7f⁵ p7.1g p7g Dec 31] half-sister to several winners, including 8-y-o Parkview Love: dam US 2-y-o 6f winner: modest maiden: well held in nursery final start: stays 7f. *M. Johnston* **56**

ALWAYS ENGAGED 4 b.f. Compton Place 125 – Good Standing (USA) 93 (Distant View (USA) 126) [2009 –: f6s f5g⁶ Feb 3] little form: dead. *J. R. Norton* **–**

ALWAYS ROSES 2 ch.f. (Mar 14) Generous (IRE) 139 – Arcady 69 (Slip Anchor 136) [2009 10m f8m⁵ p8m Nov 19] half sister to 7f seller winner Heaven's Gates (by Most Welcome): dam, 13f to 2m winner, half-sister to useful 6f to 1m winner Atavus: well held in maidens. *C. C. Bealby* **–**

ALWAYS THE SUN 3 b.f. Intikhab (USA) 135 – Dane Dancing (IRE) 68 (Danehill (USA) 126) [2009 –: f8g p7g 10m⁵ 6d⁴ 6m 6g p8.6g⁵ p7g⁶ p7g⁵ p8m⁶ Dec 6] modest maiden: stays 7f: acts on polytrack and good to soft going: sometimes in cheekpieces. *P. Leech* **57**

ALYARF (USA) 3 b.c. Dixie Union (USA) 121 – Tabheej (IRE) 100 (Mujtahid (USA) 118) [2009 101p: 8m⁴ 7m* May 23] sturdy, compact colt: smart form: confirmed reappearance promise (non-staying fourth to Delegator in Craven Stakes at Newmarket) when winning listed race on same course in May impressively by 1¾ lengths from Nasri, soon in control after leading 2f out: will prove best at 6f/7f: raced only on good/good to firm going. *B. W. Hills* **110**

ALYSEVE 4 b.f. Averti (IRE) 117 – Leen 68 (Distant Relative 128) [2009 –: 6g 7m 6g⁶ 6m 10m⁶ Jun 23] neat filly: little form: tried in cheekpieces. *Mrs C. A. Dunnett* **–**

AL ZAEEM 2 b.c. (Mar 29) Mujahid (USA) 125 – Tycho's Star (Mystiko (USA) 124) [2009 7d 8.3m⁵ p8.6g Oct 1] workmanlike colt: well beaten in sellers/claimer: tried visored: sold £1,500. *Miss D. Mountain* **–**

AL ZIR (USA) 2 b.c. (Feb 11) Medaglia d'Oro (USA) 129 – Bayou Plans (USA) (Bayou Hebert (USA)) [2009 7d* 7m* 8d³ Oct 24] $1,600,000 2-y-o: strong, lengthy, good-topped colt: has scope: seventh foal: half-brother to several winners in USA, notably very smart Grade 1 7f winner Midas Eyes (by Touch Gold) and Grade 3 7.5f to 8.5f winner Bayou's Lassie (by Outflanker): dam US 5f to 8.5f winner, including at 2 yrs: created big impression when winning maiden at Newmarket (easily by 4 lengths from from Awesome Act) in August and 3-runner minor event at Doncaster (by 5 lengths) in September: still learning, creditable 6¼ lengths third to St Nicholas Abbey in Racing Post Trophy at Doncaster: stays 1m: already smart, and looks type to progress further at 3 yrs. *Saeed bin Suroor* **111 p**

AMANDA CARTER 5 b.m. Tobougg (IRE) 125 – Al Guswa 98 (Shernazar 131) [2009 92: 10g³ 12.1d 10m⁵ 10.3g⁴ 9.8g 12m⁶ 16.4d⁶ 13.1m* 13.1m⁵ 12d⁵ Oct 24] leggy mare: useful handicapper: won at Ayr in September by 8 lengths: generally respectable efforts otherwise: stays 13f: acts on firm and good to soft going: has raced freely. *R. A. Fahey* **92**

AMANJENA 4 b.f. Beat Hollow 126 – Placement (Kris 135) [2009 99: 10.3g⁶ 10.3g⁵ 10.1m 10m Sep 25] lengthy filly: useful performer at 3 yrs: below form in 2009: stays 1¼m: acts on polytrack and good to firm going. *A. M. Balding* **86**

AMARILLO SLIM (IRE) 5 b.g. Danehill Dancer (IRE) 117 – Jungle Story (IRE) 74 (Alzao (USA) 117) [2009 –: 11.5m Jun 4] maiden: little form since 2 yrs, including over jumps: tried blinkered. *S. Curran* **–**

AMARY (IRE) 2 b.f. (Feb 2) Acclamation 118 – Amistad (GER) (Winged Love (IRE) 121) [2009 6m* 6m² 6m 7m⁶ Oct 2] €97,000F, 65,000Y: lengthy filly: has scope: third foal: dam, German 2-y-o 7f winner, sister to smart German 1½m performer Acamani: fairly useful performer: won maiden at Newcastle in May: good 5 lengths second to Awzaan in minor event at Newmarket: well below that level in Firth of Clyde Stakes at Ayr and Oh So Sharp Stakes at Newmarket: should stay at least 7f. *C. E. Brittain* **84**

AMATARA (IRE) 3 b.f. Indian Haven 119 – Mother's Hope (IRE) (Idris (IRE) 118) [2009 –: p8g f8g p10g Apr 8] tall, leggy filly: little sign of ability: tried in cheekpieces. *B. G. Powell* **–**

AMAZING BLUE SKY 3 b.g. Barathea (IRE) 127 – Azure Lake (USA) (Lac Ouimet (USA)) [2009 64: p9.5m f8g³ f11g³ f8g² 12m⁶ f11g² 8s 8.5g f12g⁵ 10g² 8.3g 12m 10.2g² 8g³ 10.3d* 10.3g* 9.9m³ 10d* Aug 6] workmanlike gelding: fair handicapper: improved to win at Doncaster (2) in July and Sandown in August: stays 11f: acts on all-weather, good to firm and good to soft going: tried blinkered: front runner. *Mrs R. A. Carr* **76**

AMAZING KING (IRE) 5 b.g. King Charlemagne (USA) 120 – Kraemer (USA) (Lyphard (USA) 132) [2009 77: 9.9g 12m^6 11.5g* 11.1s^2 12.5m^2 12.4d Oct 13] rather leggy gelding: fair handicapper: won at Yarmouth in July: stays 12.5f: acts on polytrack, soft and good to firm going: fairly useful hurdler. *P. A. Kirby* **76**

AMAZING MEMORIES (IRE) 3 b.c. Barathea (IRE) 127 – Early Memory (USA) 83 (Devil's Bag (USA)) [2009 –: 7m Oct 6] no form in minor event (for T. O'Mara in Ireland) and maiden nearly 12 months apart. *John A. Harris*

AMAZING TIGER (GER) 3 b.c. Tiger Hill (IRE) 127 – Allure (GER) (Konigsstuhl (GER)) [2009 10.3g^5 8m* p12g 8.5m^6 p8g^2 7g Oct 17] 30,000Y: useful-looking colt: has scope: fourth foal: half-brother to 3 winners in Germany, including useful 1m/9f winner Alianthus (by Hernando): dam, German 9.5f winner, half-sister to smart German 1½m performer Acamani: fairly useful form: won maiden at Musselburgh in June: best effort when second in handicap at Lingfield: stays 1m: acts on polytrack and good to firm going: races freely: sold £16,000. *M. Johnston* **87**

AMAZING VALOUR (IRE) 7 b.g. Sinndar (IRE) 134 – Flabbergasted (IRE) (Sadler's Wells (USA) 132) [2009 16g Jul 21] good-bodied gelding: one-time fair maiden: well held on belated Flat return: tried blinkered: modest and lazy staying jumper. *P. Bowen* **–**

AMBER GLOW 5 ch.m. Tumbleweed Ridge 117 – Sweet Victoria (IRE) (Mukaddamah (USA) 125) [2009 10.3m 12v Nov 3] second foal: dam unraced: ran out halfway in bumper at Market Rasen: looked very reluctant when pulled up in maidens: one to avoid. *A. Berry* **§§**

AMBER GREY (IRE) 2 ch.c. (Apr 2) Galileo (IRE) 134 – Grecian Glory (IRE) 88 (Zafonic (USA) 130) [2009 8g^3 7d^4 Oct 26] €175,000F: fourth foal: dam, 1m winner, half-sister to smart 1¼m/13f winner Dark Shell, out of very smart French performer up to 1¼m Grecian Urn: in frame in maidens at Navan and Leopardstown (3¾ lengths fourth to Don Carlos): should be suited by 1¼m/1½m: should improve further. *A. P. O'Brien, Ireland* **86 p**

AMBER MOON 4 ch.f. Singspiel (IRE) 133 – Merewood (USA) 74 (Woodman (USA) 126) [2009 52: p7.1g^2 f7g^2 p8.6g^4 f8g^3 p8g^3 p8.6m* f8d* p9.5g^5 f8g^6 10.9m f8g^5 7.1g 8g p8.6g Jul 7] modest performer: won handicap at Wolverhampton and claimer at Southwell (left J. Osborne £5,000) within a week in March: stays 8.6f: acts on all-weather: blinkered: not straightforward. *Miss A. Stokell* **66**

AMBER RIDGE 4 b.g. Tumbleweed Ridge 117 – Amber Brown 67 (Thowra (FR)) [2009 –: f8g p9.5g p9.5g^6 10.1g 8.1g^3 8d 8f^2 8m^2 8.1m 8d 8.1g 8.1m Aug 20] tall gelding: modest maiden handicapper: stays 1m (too free at 1¼m): acts on firm and soft ground: tried tongue tied/in cheekpieces/visor: inconsistent. *B. P. J. Baugh* **58**

AMBER SUNSET 3 b.f. Monsieur Bond (IRE) 120 – Quantum Lady 79 (Mujadil (USA) 119) [2009 83: 7.6m 7g 7.1g p7.1g p7.1g p7g^4 f8g p7.1g^5 Dec 28] good-topped filly: just fair handicapper at 3 yrs: stays 7f: acts on polytrack and soft going: races prominently. *J. Jay* **72**

AMBROGINA 2 b.f. (Feb 28) Osorio (GER) 114 – Oh Bej Oh Bej (IRE) 113 (Distinctly North (USA) 115) [2009 6v^5 p7m f8g^2 Dec 18] 22,000Y: fourth foal: half-sister to Italian 7f/1m winner Dr Bej (by Dr Fong): dam Italian 5f (including at 2 yrs)/6f winner: best effort in maidens (modest form) when head second to Lily Lily at Southwell final outing: stays 1m: open to further improvement. *M. Botti* **60 p**

AMBROSE PRINCESS (IRE) 4 b.f. Chevalier (IRE) 115 – Mark One 85 (Mark of Esteem (IRE) 137) [2009 63: 16g^2 16g* Jul 25] close-coupled, angular filly: fair performer: improved to win handicap at Lingfield: stays 2m: acts on polytrack, good to firm and good to soft going: ran once in cheekpieces (below form). *M. J. Scudamore* **68**

AMEEQ (USA) 7 b. or br.g. Silver Hawk (USA) 123 – Haniya (IRE) 92 (Caerleon (USA) 132) [2009 –: p12g p16g^5 p12.2g 14g^2 17.1m^3 Aug 16] quite good-topped gelding: fair handicapper: left G. L. Moore after second outing: stays easy 2m: acts on polytrack, good to firm and good to soft going: tried tongue tied/blinkered: fairly useful hurdler. *Dr R. D. P. Newland* **79**

AMEER (IRE) 2 b.c. (Apr 5) Monsun (GER) 124 – Ailette (Second Set (IRE) 127) [2009 7g* 8m* 8d^3 Oct 9] 205,000F, 240,000Y: well-made colt: fourth foal: half-brother to German 2006 2-y-o 7.5f winner Asinara (by Big Shuffle): dam, German 2-y-o 6f winner, half-sister to German 2000 Guineas winner Aviso: won maiden at Newmarket (by head from Awesome Act) in August and minor event at Newbury (beat Private Story readily by ¾ length) in September: similar form when 1½ lengths third of 4 to Circumvent **98 p**

in Prix Thomas Bryon at Saint-Cloud, again dictating: stays 1m: already useful and probably capable of better still. *Saeed bin Suroor*

AMENABLE (IRE) 2 b.g. (Mar 4) Bertolini (USA) 125 – Graceful Air (IRE) 69 (Danzero (AUS)) [2009 5g 6g f6g* Sep 29] second foal: dam, 9.3f/1¼m winner, half-sister to useful sprinter Mystical Land: 100/1, form in maidens only when winning at Southwell, making most: stays 6f: acts on fibresand. *D. Nicholls* **75**

AMERICAN AGENT (USA) 2 b.c. (May 16) Eavesdropper (USA) – Storm Season (USA) (Storm Cat (USA)) [2009 p7f^5 p5.1g^4 Dec 26] modest form in maidens at Lingfield and Wolverhampton (unsuited by drop in trip). *P. F. I. Cole* **56 +**

AMERICAN CHAMP (IRE) 3 b.g. Pyrus (USA) 106 – Sandy Fitzgerald (IRE) (Last Tycoon 131) [2009 p8.6g Dec 14] never dangerous in maiden at Wolverhampton. *Pat Morris* **–**

AMERICAN LIGHT 3 b.g. Statue of Liberty (USA) 115 – Break of Dawn (USA) (Mt Livermore (USA)) [2009 76: 6d 5g^3 p5g p5.1g^2 Dec 11] lengthy gelding: fair maiden: left J. Burns in Ireland €5,700 prior to final start: best at 5f: acts on polytrack, form on turf only on good going. *D. M. Simcock* **75**

AMERICAN SPIN 5 ch.g. Groom Dancer (USA) 128 – Sea Vixen 87 (Machiavellian (USA) 123) [2009 p11g* p12.2g^2 p12g^4 16g 21.7m^5 p16g Jul 8] useful-looking gelding: fairly useful performer: missed 2007/8: won maiden at Kempton in January: in frame in handicaps at Wolverhampton and Lingfield: probably flattered in Queen Alexandra Stakes at Royal Ascot: seems to stay 21f, but probably best at 1½m to 2m: acts on polytrack, good to firm and good to soft ground. *L. A. Dace* **82**

AMERIGO (IRE) 4 gr.g. Daylami (IRE) 138 – Geminiani (IRE) 106 (King of Kings (IRE) 125) [2009 109: 18.7m^5 16.2g 21.7m^3 16.4m^6 16g^2 Aug 30] well-made gelding: useful performer: good 2½ lengths fifth to Daraahem in Chester Cup: creditable placed efforts at Royal Ascot and Yarmouth (handicap) after: thorough stayer: raced only on good going or firmer. *M. A. Jarvis* **105**

AMES SOUER (IRE) 6 b.m. Fayruz 116 – Taispeain (IRE) 86 (Petorius 117) [2009 p6g^6 Jan 6] leggy mare: poor performer: won minor event (first win) at Ostend in 2008: left J. Dekeyser in Belgium before return: stays 7f: acts on all-weather, firm and good to soft ground. *P. D. Evans* **49**

AMETHYST DAWN (IRE) 3 ro.f. Act One 124 – A L'Aube (IRE) (Selkirk (USA) 129) [2009 85: 9.9m 8g^5 8.3m 9.8m^5 12m^2 12d^3 14.1g^5 12.4d 8.5g^2 8g^2 7g 8.3v* Nov 4] big filly: fair handicapper nowadays: won at Nottingham in November: has form at 1½m, probably best at shorter (effective at 1m): acts on heavy and good to firm going: races prominently. *T. D. Easterby* **76**

AM I BLUE 3 b.f. Dubai Destination (USA) 127 – Seal Indigo (IRE) 93 (Glenstal (USA) 118) [2009 61p: 10.2g^4 p9.5g 14m 11.5s p12.2g 15.4m^2 15m^5 Oct 5] fair maiden: stays 15.4f: acts on good to firm ground: tried blinkered: joined T. Vaughan. *H. J. L. Dunlop* **65**

AMICAL RISKS (FR) 5 bl.g. Take Risks (FR) 116 – Miss High (FR) (Concorde Jr (USA)) [2009 65: 11.6g^4 12.1g 12s^3 Oct 27] workmanlike gelding: modest handicapper nowadays: stays easy 1½m: acts on polytrack and good to soft ground: sold 6,000 gns. *W. J. Musson* **57**

AMIR PASHA (UAE) 4 br.g. Halling (USA) 133 – Clarinda (IRE) 91 (Lomond (USA) 128) [2009 64: 16m^3 16m 17.2g Jul 4] well-made gelding: modest maiden: stays easy 2m: acts on polytrack, yet to race on extremes of going on turf: tried visored/in cheekpieces. *Micky Hammond* **63**

AMITOLA (IRE) 2 ch.f. (Mar 20) Choisir (AUS) 126 – Emly Express (IRE) (High Estate 127) [2009 6m* 6g^5 Oct 30] €15,000Y, £36,000 2-y-o: strong filly: fifth foal: half-sister to 3 winners, including 6-y-o Damika and Irish 7-y-o Quai du Roi: dam French 11.5f winner: fairly useful form both starts: won maiden at Ayr (by 6 lengths) in October: again well backed, 4½ lengths fifth to Queen's Grace in listed race at Newmarket, still needing experience: should stay 7f. *T. D. Barron* **92 +**

AMJAD 12 ch.g. Cadeaux Genereux 131 – Babita 107 (Habitat 134) [2009 –: 13.8m Jun 5] lengthy, useful-looking gelding: fair handicapper in 2002: well held both starts on Flat since: sometimes blinkered/visored: poor hurdler. *S. G. West* **–**

AMNO DANCER (IRE) 2 b.g. (Mar 2) Namid 128 – Special Dancer (Shareef Dancer (USA) 135) [2009 p6g^6 6g^5 6g^3 5g 7d^5 f6m Nov 11] €15,000F, €12,000Y: fourth foal: half-brother to 3-y-o Ja One and French/Belgian 1¼m to 15f winner Special Reggae (by **72**

Xaar): dam, useful winner in Italy up to 1½m, half-sister to smart Irish 1¼m/1½m winner Cajarian and to dam of very smart 7f/1m performer Caradak: fair maiden: stays 6f: seemed amiss fourth start, gelded after final one. *M. H. Tompkins*

AMOSITE 3 b.f. Central Park (IRE) 123 – Waterline Dancer (IRE) 69 (Danehill Dancer (IRE) 117) [2009 73§: p6g⁴ 6g 5.1m* 5m³ 5m 5m³ 5g³ 5g Aug 13] lightly-made filly: fair handicapper: won at Nottingham in April: effective at 5f/6f: acts on polytrack and good to firm going: usually visored/blinkered: usually front runner: temperamental and unreliable. *J. R. Jenkins* **79 §**

AMOURETTA 4 b.f. Daylami (IRE) 138 – Allumette (Rainbow Quest (USA) 134) [2009 –: 15.4m Sep 22] quite good-topped filly: no form: tried visored/in cheekpieces. *T. T. Clement* **–**

AMOUREUSE 2 b.f. (Mar 28) Needwood Blade 117 – Good Health 78 (Magic Ring (IRE) 115) [2009 5.1m 5g 5d f5g Jun 2] £13,000Y: compact, workmanlike filly: second foal: closely related to 3-y-o The Magic of Rio: dam 2-y-o 5f winner: no form in maidens: tried in cheekpieces. *I. W. McInnes* **–**

AMOUR PROPRE 3 ch.c. Paris House 123 – Miss Prim (Case Law 113) [2009 111: 5m* 5m 5m⁵ Aug 21] good-topped colt: very smart performer: further improvement at 3 yrs, winning stanjames.com Palace House Stakes at Newmarket in May by 2½ lengths from Hoh Hoh Hoh: much better effort after (found to have ripped off front shoe in King's Stand Stakes at Royal Ascot next time) when respectable 1¾ lengths fifth to Borderlescott in Nunthorpe Stakes at York (reportedly returned with bruised feet): speedy, will prove best kept to 5f: acts on firm ground. *H. Candy* **122**

AMRON HILL 6 b.g. Polar Prince (IRE) 117 – Maradata (IRE) 68 (Shardari 134) [2009 58: f16g³ f14g³ Jan 27] workmanlike gelding: modest handicapper: stayed 2m: acted on all-weather: dead. *R. Hollinshead* **52**

AMROTH 3 b.f. Rock of Gibraltar (IRE) 133 – Gwen John (USA) 70 (Peintre Celebre (USA) 137) [2009 10d 11.8g⁴ 10.3m⁵ 11.6d p16.5g Oct 30] 30,000Y: angular filly: first foal: dam, maiden (stayed 9f), half-sister to Queen Mary Stakes/US Grade 2 1m winner Dance Parade and US Grade 3 9f winner Ocean Queen: modest maiden: no easy ride last 3 starts: stays 1½m: tried visored. *P. D. Evans* **64**

AMTAAR 2 b.f. (Feb 17) Nayef (USA) 129 – Emerald Fire 86 (Pivotal 124) [2009 7m p7g³ p6g² 7.5g⁴ Sep 22] 65,000Y: compact filly: second foal: dam 6f (including at 2 yrs) winner: modest maiden: should stay 7f. *C. E. Brittain* **63**

AMWELL BRAVE 8 b.g. Pyramus (USA) 78 – Passage Creeping (IRE) 75 (Persian Bold 123) [2009 65d: p11g³ p13.3g* p13.9g³ p12g p12g⁵ 11.5m⁴ f14g⁵ 13.1f 12m Sep 23] rather leggy gelding: modest performer nowadays: won minor event at Great Leighs in January: effective at 11f to easy 2m: acts on all-weather, firm and soft ground: tried visored/tongue tied: held up: no battler. *J. R. Jenkins* **55**

AMWELL HOUSE 4 gr.g. Auction House (USA) 120 – Amwell Star (USA) 46 (Silver Buck (USA)) [2009 57: p8g p8g⁴ p8g³ p8g p8g Mar 11] close-coupled gelding: modest maiden: stays 1½m: acts on all-weather, yet to race on extremes of going on turf. *J. R. Jenkins* **54**

stanjames.com Palace House Stakes, Newmarket—the three-year-old Amour Propre shows impressive speed ahead of Hoh Hoh Hoh (left), Borderlescott and Strike The Deal (visor)

AMYLYN 2 b.f. (May 15) Starcraft (NZ) 128 – Skirt Around 69 (Deploy 131) [2009 8.3v Nov 4] 2,200Y: sturdy filly: third foal: half-sister to 4-y-o This Ones For Eddy: dam, French 11f winner, out of sister to 1000 Guineas winner Fairy Footsteps: 150/1, always behind in maiden at Nottingham. *J. R. Holt* **–**

ANACOT STEEL (IRE) 4 ch.g. Danehill Dancer (IRE) 117 – Paper Moon (IRE) 92 (Lake Coniston (IRE) 131) [2009 8.1v 9.3d Jul 26] non-stayer in bumper: well beaten in maidens. *Pat Morris* **–**

ANACREON (IRE) 3 b.g. Dansili 127 – Anbella (FR) (Common Grounds 118) [2009 64p: p7g² p6g* 10m 6m Jul 20] compact gelding: has round action: fair performer: landed odds in maiden at Lingfield in April: well below form next 2 starts 3 months apart (unsuitable trip first occasion): probably better at 6f than 7f: best efforts on polytrack: gelded after final start. *J. H. M. Gosden* **76**

ANAGRAM 3 b.f. Efisio 120 – Saint Ann (USA) 66 (Geiger Counter (USA)) [2009 5.7g p6g³ p7.1g² 6s⁶ f7m Nov 12] half-sister to 3 winners, including useful performer up to 1½m Sienna Storm, 1m winner at 2 yrs, and 1¼m winner White Moss (both by Peintre Celebre): dam, ran 4 times at 2 yrs (looked rather temperamental), out of half-sister to very smart sprinter Primo Dominie: modest maiden: stays 7f: acts on polytrack: blinkered after debut. *W. R. Muir* **64**

ANA MOUTABAHI 2 b.c. (May 8) Anabaa (USA) 130 – Runaway Venus (USA) (Runaway Groom (CAN)) [2009 p7m p7g² p7.1g⁴ Dec 18] fair form when in frame in maidens at Kempton and Wolverhampton: raced only at 7f on polytrack. *C. G. Cox* **66**

ANANDA KANDA (USA) 2 b.f. (Mar 11) Hero's Tribute (USA) – Roja (USA) (L'Enjoleur (CAN)) [2009 5m 6v* p7g 6d⁴ f8g⁵ 8g⁶ Sep 17] €15,000Y: small filly: half-sister to smart but untrustworthy Irish 1¼m/1¾m winner Red Moloney (by Sahm) and several winners in USA: dam sprint maiden in USA: fair performer: won maiden at Haydock in May: good fourth in nursery at Newcastle: should be suited by 1m+: best efforts on ground softer than good (acts on heavy): sweated up badly third start. *B. Ellison* **76**

ANASY (USA) 3 b.f. Gone West (USA) – Blue Moon (FR) 114 (Lomitas 129) [2009 –: p7m 7.1m p9.5g Oct 16] little form: left D. Simcock 3,200 gns before reappearance. *T. Keddy* **–**

ANAYA 2 b.f. (Mar 14) Tobougg (IRE) 125 – Nacho Venture (FR) 88 (Rainbow Quest (USA) 134) [2009 8.1d 8m 8.1m³ 8d² p8m² p8.6g² p8m⁴ p8f⁵ Dec 20] 10,000Y: sturdy filly: third foal: sister to Irish 4-y-o Mexican Venture: dam maiden (should have stayed 1½m): fair maiden: will stay 1¼m: acts on polytrack, good to firm and good to soft going: races prominently. *M. R. Channon* **72**

ANCHORAGE BOY (USA) 2 b.g. (Jan 27) Southern Image (USA) 129 – Alaskan Winter (USA) (Gulch (USA)) [2009 7g 7d 7g⁵ Aug 5] first sign of ability in maidens when fifth at Yarmouth: gelded. *Miss Amy Weaver* **49 ?**

ANCIEN REGIME (IRE) 4 b.g. King's Best (USA) 132 – Sadalsud (IRE) (Shaadi (USA) 126) [2009 117: 6d² 6m 6s³ p6m* 6m 6g Oct 10] tall gelding: smart performer: not quite so good in 2009, but still won minor event at Lingfield in August by 1½ lengths from Judd Street: ran as if amiss next 2 outings and gelded after: best at 5f/6f: yet to race on heavy ground, acts on any other and polytrack. *Saeed bin Suroor* **111**

ANCIENT CROSS 5 b.g. Machiavellian (USA) 123 – Magna Graecia (IRE) 112 (Warning 136) [2009 76: 7m⁶ f7g³ 7s⁴ f7g² 7s⁴ 7m³ 6.9g⁵ 7.5g² 9.9f⁴ 8d³ 7.1m* 7m² 7g* Oct 17] good-bodied gelding: fairly useful handicapper: won at Musselburgh in September and Catterick (better than ever) in October: stays 1m: acts on all-weather, soft and good to firm going: tried blinkered: tongue tied last 7 starts: held up. *M. W. Easterby* **90**

ANCIENT KINGDOM (USA) 2 ch.c. (Apr 12) Giant's Causeway (USA) 132 – Measure (USA) (Seeking The Gold (USA)) [2009 7d³ Oct 26] sixth foal: dam, ran once in France, closely related to very smart French performer up to 1m Jade Robbery from family of Sadler's Wells and Nureyev: 20/1, 3½ lengths third to Don Carlos in maiden at Leopardstown, green/edging left before keeping on well under hands and heels: sure to do fair bit better. *A. P. O'Brien, Ireland* **87 p**

ANCIENT LIGHTS 4 b.c. High Chaparral (IRE) 132 – Fascinating Hill (FR) (Danehill (USA) 126) [2009 90: p10g³ May 1] good-topped colt: type to carry condition: useful form, lightly raced: off 9½ months, improved when 1½ lengths third to Lady Jane Digby on handicap debut at Lingfield: will stay 1½m: sent to Germany. *H. R. A. Cecil* **100**

ANCIENT OAK 2 ch.c. (Mar 3) Compton Place 125 – Dolce Piccata 88 (Piccolo 121) [2009 5m 6m⁶ Sep 25] workmanlike colt: tailed off in maidens: dead. *H. A. McWilliams* **–**

ANDAMAN SUNSET 4 b.c. Red Ransom (USA) – Miss Amanpuri 92 (Alzao (USA) 117) [2009 83: p10g p12.2g p10g p9.5g p10g p11f Dec 16] sturdy colt: handicapper: little impact in 2009: tried in cheekpieces/blinkers/tongue strap. *J. L. Spearing* –

AND A PARTRIDGE 3 ch.g. Compton Place 125 – Dunloe (IRE) 54 (Shaadi (USA) 126) [2009 p8.6g^{3} 10m p12g^{3} May 30] modest maiden: stays 8.6f. *J. A. Osborne* **55**

ANDEAN MARGIN (IRE) 3 b.g. Giant's Causeway (USA) 132 – Spiritual Air 93 (Royal Applause 124) [2009 73: p8g^{2} p7g^{2} p7g^{2} 8m^{3} f7g 7.5f 7.5g p9.5g Oct 15] rangy gelding: fair handicapper: placed first 4 starts (left S. Callaghan 25,000 gns after third outing): below form after: stays 1m: acts on all-weather and good to firm going: often blinkered: possibly not straightforward: sold 4,000 gns. *M. W. Easterby* **75**

ANDHAAR 3 b. or br.g. Bahri (USA) 125 – Deraasaat 92 (Nashwan (USA) 135) [2009 78: 9.7g^{3} 10.1m^{2} p10g* 10.1g 9.8m^{3} 12m^{3} 11m^{3} p9.5g^{3} Dec 3] good-topped gelding: fairly useful performer: won maiden at Lingfield in June: good third in handicaps last 3 starts, leaving E. Dunlop 60,000 gns prior to final one: stays 1½m: acts on polytrack and good to firm going. *S. Gollings* **90**

ANDINA (IRE) 2 ch.f. (Apr 15) Singspiel (IRE) 133 – Fragrant Oasis (USA) 113 (Rahy (USA) 115) [2009 6m^{3} 8f* Oct 10] 11,000Y: seventh foal: sister to 6-y-o Forbidden and half-sister to 3 winners, including 5-y-o Desert Vision: dam 7f winner, including at 2 yrs: promising third in maiden at Newbury: left J. Hills/off 4½ months, won similar event at Santa Anita by ½ length from Warren's Jitterbug: stays 1m: should improve further. *B. D. A. Cecil, USA* **79 p**

ANDORN (GER) 5 b.h. Monsun (GER) 124 – Anthyllis (GER) (Lycius (USA) 124) [2009 90d: 7m p8.6g^{3} 9.8m^{2} 12d 12m^{3} 12.3m^{5} 12g^{6} 12.5m* 13.8g^{6} Oct 17] ex-German horse: fair performer nowadays: claimed from B. Curley £6,000 after second start: won seller at Musselburgh in September: stays 12.5f: acts on polytrack, soft and good to firm ground: races prominently. *P. A. Kirby* **70**

ANDRASTA 4 b.f. Bertolini (USA) 125 – Real Popcorn (IRE) 52 (Jareer (USA) 115) [2009 63§: p6g^{5} 6m 6g 5d* 5v 5m 5m 6g^{6} 6g^{4} 6g^{4} 5g^{5} 5f* 5m^{5} 5s^{5} 5m^{6} 5g 5g 5s^{6} p5g Nov 18] good-topped filly: modest handicapper: won at Hamilton in May and Ayr in August: left A. Berry after fourteenth start: stays 6f: acts on fibresand, firm and soft ground: tried in cheekpieces: not to be trusted. *S. A. Harris* **61 §**

ANDURIL 8 ch.g. Kris 135 – Attribute 69 (Warning 136) [2009 59§: f8s p8.6g^{5} p8.6g 8g p8.6g Dec 18] workmanlike gelding: modest handicapper: left I. McInnes prior to final start: stays easy 1¼m: acts on all-weather, firm and soft ground: usually wears headgear: unreliable. *D. Carroll* **52 §**

ANESSIA 3 b.f. Fantastic Light (USA) 134 – Lamarque (IRE) (Nureyev (USA) 131) [2009 p10g^{4} 10.2v^{5} 10.3s p12m Sep 16] €47,000Y: sixth foal: half-sister to fairly useful winner around 1¼m (including at 2 yrs) La Mouline (by Nashwan) and 2007 2-y-o 7f winner Mafioso (by Red Ransom): dam unraced close relation to Arc winner Carnegie out of Arc winner Detroit: modest maiden: should be suited by 1½m. *Tom Dascombe* **59**

ANFIELD ROAD 4 ch.g. Dr Fong (USA) 128 – Mackenzie's Friend (Selkirk (USA) 129) [2009 80: p16g p12.2g 12v p12.2g^{5} Dec 5] lengthy, rather leggy gelding: fair performer: modest form for D. Gandolfo over hurdles between second and third starts: stays 13.3f: acts on polytrack and heavy going: tried visored/in cheekpieces. *L. Corcoran* **73**

ANFIELD STAR (IRE) 3 b.g. Celtic Swing 138 – Shenkara (IRE) 79 (Night Shift (USA)) [2009 53: p5f^{6} p7m p6g Oct 23] poor form: tried blinkered. *Pat Morris* **46**

ANGARIC (IRE) 6 ch.g. Pivotal 124 – Grannys Reluctance (IRE) 63 (Anita's Prince 126) [2009 82: f6g 6m^{3} 7.1m* 7.1m 7.1m 6g 6d^{4} 6m f6g Dec 8] neat gelding: fair handicapper: won at Musselburgh in May: effective at 6f to 8.3f: acts on polytrack, firm and good to soft ground: tried tongue tied. *B. Smart* **72**

ANGELA JONES 2 ch.f. (May 15) Cape Town (IRE) 119 – Full English (Perugino (USA) 84) [2009 6d 5.2g Aug 12] third foal: dam well beaten both starts: well beaten in sellers at Yarmouth. *D. K. Ivory* –

ANGELENA BALLERINA (IRE) 2 ch.f. (Apr 24) Indian Haven 119 – Nom Francais 39§ (First Trump 118) [2009 5.1m^{4} 6m^{2} 5g^{4} 6g^{2} 6g 6g^{6} p7.1g^{5} 6d^{6} p8.6g^{2} Oct 17] 9,500F, €5,000Y: unfurnished filly: fifth foal: half-sister to 3 winners, including 6-y-o The London Gang: dam, maiden who seemed to stay 2m (probably ungenuine), closely related to smart sprinter Perryston View: fair maiden: best form at 6f: acts on polytrack and good to firm ground: in cheekpieces last 5 starts, looking unwilling last 2: sold 8,500 gns. *A. Bailey* **78**

ANGELICA'S ART (IRE) 3 b.f. Marju (IRE) 127 – Flatter (IRE) (Barathea (IRE) 127) [2009 7m 8.3f 9.9m 12m p11g Aug 5] 47,000Y: good-topped filly: second foal: dam unraced half-sister to high-class Hong Kong performer up to 1½m Viva Pataca (by Marju), smart as 2-y-o in Britain when named Comic Strip: modest maiden: well held at 11f+: blinkered, looked very awkward final outing. *B. J. Meehan* **58**

ANGEL OF FASHION (IRE) 2 b.f. (Feb 4) Invincible Spirit (IRE) 121 – Vanitycase (IRE) 61 (Editor's Note (USA) 125) [2009 5.2s 5g^2 5.5f^4 5g^5 p6g^6 6m* 6g 7d 6m* 6m^6 Oct 5] £16,000Y: compact filly: first foal: dam, Irish maiden, out of unraced half-sister to St Leger winner Scorpion: fair performer: best efforts when winning nurseries at Leicester in July and September: stays 6f: acts on firm going: sold £7,500. *B. W. Hills* **79**

ANGELOFTHENORTH 7 b.m. Tomba 119 – Dark Kristal (IRE) 66 (Gorytus (USA) 132) [2009 55: 6g 5m^6 5m 5g^4 5m^3 5d^5 5g^2 5m^3 5.1g Aug 14] leggy mare: modest performer: best at 5f: acts on heavy and good to firm going: tried blinkered: usually held up. *C. J. Teague* **52**

ANGELO POLIZIANO 3 ch.g. Medicean 128 – Helen Sharp (Pivotal 124) [2009 65: 7.1m 6m^4 7.1m 6m 5m^6 p5.1g* p6g^4 5m^5 5g^4 5d^4 5m* 5s 5m p6g f5m Nov 12] big, strong gelding: fair handicapper: won at Wolverhampton in June and Newcastle in August: stays 6f: acts on polytrack and good to firm going: in headgear since former win. *Mrs A. Duffield* **76**

ANGEL ROCK (IRE) 4 b.c. Rock of Gibraltar (IRE) 133 – Nomothetis (IRE) (Law Society (USA) 130) [2009 100: 10s 8.1v* 8.9g^5 8.1m^5 10.1m 8v Nov 8] rangy, quite attractive colt: fairly useful handicapper: won at Haydock in May: below form after: stays 1¼m: acts on polytrack, heavy and good to firm going: tried in cheekpieces (below form). *M. Botti* **92**

ANGELS AND DEMONS (IRE) 3 b.f. Golan (IRE) 129 – I Want You Now (IRE) (Nicolotte 118) [2009 f6g 8.3d 8g 12.5m^5 12.5m Sep 27] first foal: dam lightly-raced maiden: well held in varied company, leaving G. Moss after third start. *R. C. Guest* **–**

ANGELSBEMINE 3 b.f. Almaty (IRE) 113§ – Undercover Girl (IRE) 51 (Barathea (IRE) 127) [2009 –: f6s Jan 4] leggy filly: no sign of ability: tried visored. *J. R. Norton* **–**

ANGEL SONG 3 b.f. Dansili 127 – Something Blue (Petong 126) [2009 f6g* f6g^3 7d^4 p5g^6 f6m Nov 11] 75,000Y: seventh foal: half-sister to several winners, including 5-y-o Mood Music and 6-y-o Memphis Man: dam, ran 3 times, half-sister to dam of smart sprinters Astonished and Bishops Court: fair performer: won maiden at Southwell in January: may prove best at 5f/6f: acts on all-weather and good to soft ground. *Sir Mark Prescott* **68**

ANGEL'S PURSUIT (IRE) 2 ch.c. (Mar 15) Pastoral Pursuits 127 – Midnight Angel (Machiavellian (USA) 123) [2009 5m* 5m 5m^3 6m^6 5.1g^2 5g^2 p6g 6m* 6m^2 6m Oct 3] £45,000Y, £190,000 2-y-o: sturdy colt: has a fluent action: sixth foal: half-brother to several winners, notably smart 2007 2-y-o 5f/6f (Middle Park Stakes) winner Dark Angel (by Acclamation): dam unraced out of useful sprinter Night At Sea: useful performer: won maiden at Newmarket in May and minor event at Doncaster (by ¾ length from Roodle) in September: seemed to excel himself when 1¼ lengths second to Awzaan in Mill Reef Stakes at Newbury penultimate start: poorly drawn final outing: stays 6f: raced mainly on good/good to firm ground. *R. Hannon* **99**

ANGEL VOICES (IRE) 6 b.m. Tagula (IRE) 116 – Lithe Spirit (IRE) 74 (Dancing Dissident (USA) 119) [2009 75: p6g^2 p6g^6 p8g^6 p6g p6g Apr 25] good-bodied mare: has a moderate, quick action: modest performer nowadays: effective at 6f to 1m: acts on polytrack, soft and good to firm ground: usually wears cheekpieces/visor. *K. R. Burke* **58**

ANGIE'S NAP (USA) 2 ch.f. (Apr 27) Lion Heart (USA) 124 – Magick Top (USA) (Topsider (USA)) [2009 5m 5g 5.2g^2 f5g p5g 6d^6 f5g^2 p5g f5g* f6g* f5m* f6m^4 f5m^6 f5g^5 f7d^3 Dec 29] $52,000F, £25,000Y: small filly: half-sister to several winners in USA: dam, US 6f (at 2 yrs) to 8.5f winner, out of half-sister to Roberto: modest performer: left E. Dunlop after third start: won nurseries in September and October and claimer in November, all at Southwell: stays 6f: best efforts on fibresand: tried visored, usually in cheekpieces: temperament firmly under suspicion. *P. S. McEntee* **57 a62**

ANGLE OF ATTACK (IRE) 4 b.g. Acclamation 118 – Travel Spot Girl (Primo Dominie 121) [2009 85: 5f 5g 5m 5v f6g^6 5m 6m 5.1g f7f f6d* Dec 29] lengthy gelding: modest handicapper nowadays: dropped in weights and visored, won at Southwell in December: best at 5f/6f: acts on all-weather, soft and good to firm ground: tried in headgear: often makes running. *A. D. Brown* **63**

ANGLEZARKE (IRE) 3 br.f. Acclamation 118 – Welsh Mist 102 (Damister (USA) **109**
123) [2009 101: 5g* 5g^{2} 5m^{3} 5m^{6} Jul 4] good-topped filly: useful performer: won minor event at York in May by a length from Rievaulx World: good efforts after, including when 3½ lengths third to Scenic Blast in King's Stand Stakes at Royal Ascot, well drawn: raced mainly at 5f, should stay 6f: acts on firm and soft going: genuine. *T. D. Easterby*

ANGUS NEWZ 6 ch.m. Compton Place 125 – Hickleton Lady (IRE) 64 (Kala Shikari **100**
125) [2009 102: 5.2s 5.1g^{4} 5.1m^{3} 6d^{5} 6v 5g^{4} 5m 5.1m^{5} 5d^{4} 6.1g 5.1d^{3} 5m^{3} 6m^{3} 6m^{5} 6m^{6} 5g Oct 17] lengthy, plain mare: useful performer: in-and-out form in 2009: stays 6f: acts on heavy and good to firm going: effective with or without visor: looks ungainly (tends to hang/carry head high): usually makes running/races prominently. *M. Quinn*

ANHAR (USA) 2 b. or br.c. (Mar 1) Kingmambo (USA) 125 – Because (IRE) 87 **96 p**
(Sadler's Wells (USA) 132) [2009 8.3s* 10g^{2} Oct 31] $950,000F: rangy, attractive colt: second foal: dam, Irish maiden (stayed 1½m), sister to Quarter Moon (won Moyglare Stud Stakes), Yesterday (Irish 1000 Guineas winner) and All My Loving, all placed in Oaks: won maiden at Nottingham by ½ length from Desert Sage: better form when short-head second to Take It To The Max in 6-runner minor event at Newmarket later in month, still learning and idling (wandered): will stay 1½m: already useful and sure to progress further. *Saeed bin Suroor*

ANICE STELLATO (IRE) 3 br.f. Dalakhani (IRE) 133 – Summer Spice (IRE) 88 **98**
(Key of Luck (USA) 126) [2009 90p: 11.5m^{5} 12m 10m^{2} 12m* 12m^{5} Oct 1] neat filly: useful form: won handicap at Newmarket in September by neck from Storyland: stays 1½m: raced only on good to firm going: raced freely when blinkered in Ribblesdale Stakes on second start. *R. M. Beckett*

ANIMATOR 4 b.g. Act One 124 – Robsart (IRE) 91 (Robellino (USA) 127) [2009 82: **68**
10.2f 10.4v May 21] sturdy gelding: fair handicapper nowadays: free-going sort, not sure to stay beyond 1¼m: acts on polytrack and firm going: has looked none too keen: sold £1,800 in August. *C. Grant*

ANITA'S LUCK (IRE) 2 b.g. (Apr 8) Key of Luck (USA) 126 – Anita's Contessa **70**
(IRE) 68 (Anita's Prince 126) [2009 5m^{4} Apr 2] unfurnished gelding: sixth foal: half-brother to several winners, including 10-y-o A One and Irish 5-y-o Napoleon Dynamite: dam 6f/7f winner: 11/1, 5¾ lengths fourth to Archers Road in maiden at Leicester: will stay at least 7f. *B. Palling*

ANITRA'S DANCE 2 b.f. (May 7) Tobougg (IRE) 125 – Dancemma 76 (Emarati –
(USA) 74) [2009 p6g 6d p6g Jul 13] sturdy, close-coupled filly: fourth foal: half-sister to winner in Czech Republic by Bahamian Bounty: dam sprint maiden: well held in maidens. *P. Howling*

ANJOMARBA (IRE) 2 b.f. (Feb 16) Tillerman 123 – Golden Charm (IRE) 63 **83**
(Common Grounds 118) [2009 5d 5g^{3} 5m^{2} p5.1g^{4} 6g^{5} 6g* 6f* 6d* 6m 5g^{4} 6m^{5} 6g 6s **a67**
p7m^{4} p6g^{3} p6f^{3} Dec 19] angular filly: sixth foal: half-sister to 3 winners, including 1m winner English Rocket (by Indian Rocket) and 2007 2-y-o 5f seller winner Golden Dane (by Danetime): dam 2-y-o 6f winner: fairly useful performer, better on turf than all-weather: won sellers at Yarmouth in May, and Thirsk and York in June: below form after: best at 5f/6f: acts on firm and good to soft going: tried in cheekpieces: usually front runner. *W. G. M. Turner*

ANMAR (USA) 3 ch.c. Rahy (USA) 115 – Ranin 112 (Unfuwain (USA) 131) [2009 **117 p**
101: p10g* Nov 11] good-topped colt: smart form: off 13 months and visored, improved when winning minor event at Kempton in November by 5 lengths from Pachattack, quickening away: will stay 1½m: acts on polytrack and soft ground: will make mark in pattern company. *Saeed bin Suroor*

ANNABELLE'S CHARM (IRE) 4 ch.f. Indian Ridge 123 – Kylemore (IRE) **107**
(Sadler's Wells (USA) 132) [2009 76: p10g* p10g^{5} 10.1d^{3} 9.7m* 10g^{2} 8.1f^{4} 8m* 8m 8d^{2} 10.5s Nov 11] well-made filly: useful performer: progressive in 2009, won maiden at Lingfield (simple task) in January, handicap at Folkestone in April and listed race at Bath (by length from Please Sing) in August: ran well (plenty to do) when neck second to Ravenel in Premio Sergio Cumani at Milan penultimate start: better at 1m than 1¼m: acts on polytrack, good to firm and good to soft ground: can race freely. *L. M. Cumani*

ANNACABOE (IRE) 2 b.f. (Apr 16) Footstepsinthesand 120 – Alexandria (IRE) –
(Irish River (FR) 131) [2009 5g Aug 12] €2,000Y: fourth foal: half-sister to 1½m winner George Henson (by Desert Style): dam unraced: 100/1, always in rear in maiden at Sandown: bred to be suited by 1m+. *Mrs L. C. Jewell*

ANNAMBO 9 ch.g. In The Wings 128 – Anna Matrushka (Mill Reef (USA) 141) [2009 11.6m 14.1m^3 11.6m^6 12g p12.2g^4 13.1f^3 p12.2g^2 p13.9g p12m* Sep 24] smallish, lengthy gelding: unimpressive mover: missed 2008: fair handicapper nowadays: visor refitted, won at Kempton: stays 16.5f: acts on polytrack, firm and good to soft going: tried in cheekpieces: signs of temperament. *Andrew Reid* **71**

ANNAN ROCK (IRE) 3 b.g. Statue of Liberty (USA) 115 – My Enigma (Rainbow Quest (USA) 134) [2009 p8.6g p8g^6 8.3g Jul 27] good-topped gelding: well beaten in maidens/claimer: sold 2,200 gns in October. *W. J. Musson* **–**

ANNA'S BOY 2 ch.g. (Mar 20) Reel Buddy (USA) 118 – Simianna 101 (Bluegrass Prince (IRE) 110) [2009 6s 6s^6 6g^3 Sep 30] maiden: almost certainly flattered when third of 5 to The Only Boss at Newcastle. *A. Berry* **47 ?**

ANN BIRKETT 3 ch.f. Beat Hollow 126 – Blue Gentian (USA) 96 (Known Fact (USA) 135) [2009 10.1g Jul 2] 3,000F, 4,000Y: fifth foal: half-sister to 7-y-o Bavarica and winner in Belgium by Distant Music: dam 2-y-o 7f winner: 150/1, always behind in maiden at Yarmouth: sold £1,000 in August. *Miss J. Feilden* **–**

ANNELKO 2 b.c. (Mar 24) Sulamani (IRE) 130 – Creeking 65 (Persian Bold 123) [2009 8g Oct 21] 66/1 and green, always behind in maiden at Bath. *A. B. Haynes* **–**

ANNE OF KIEV (IRE) 4 b.f. Oasis Dream 129 – Top Flight Queen 82 (Mark of Esteem (IRE) 137) [2009 91: p5.1g p5.1g* Dec 4] well-made filly: fairly useful performer, lightly raced: tongue tied, won handicap at Wolverhampton in December: will prove best at 5f/6f: raced on polytrack and good ground or softer: has carried head awkwardly. *J. R. Gask* **87**

ANNES ROCKET (IRE) 4 b.c. Fasliyev (USA) 120 – Aguilas Perla (IRE) (Indian Ridge 123) [2009 64: p8g p8g p7g^6 p7g^6 7m^2 8.1g* 7m* 7d 8f 8m 8f 7g^2 p7.1g p7m 8g^4 p7m* p7m Oct 26] lengthy colt: fair handicapper: won at Warwick (apprentices) and Brighton in May and Kempton in October: stays 1m: acts on polytrack and good to firm going: often slowly away/held up. *J. C. Fox* **64**

ANNES SOUND (IRE) 3 gr.f. Mull of Kintyre (USA) 114 – Striking Sound (USA) 56 (Rubiano (USA)) [2009 46: 10.3m 11.1m 10.2g 10.1m 10m Sep 12] sturdy filly: maiden: well held at 3 yrs. *Pat Morris* **–**

ANNIA GALERIA (IRE) 2 b.f. (Jan 26) Antonius Pius (USA) 123§ – Jay Gee (IRE) 93 (Second Set (IRE) 127) [2009 5m* 6d^3 p5g p5g^5 p5g 5m Sep 14] €5,000Y: smallish filly: sixth foal: half-sister to 4-y-o Bookiebasher Babe and 6-y-o Collateral Damage: dam 2-y-o 6f winner: modest performer: won seller at Leicester in July: claimed from A. Haynes £5,000 after second start: no improvement in nurseries: raced mainly at 5f: acts on polytrack and good to firm going. *C. A. Dwyer* **53**

ANNIA (IRE) 2 b.f. (Apr 23) Antonius Pius (USA) 123§ – Floosie (IRE) 32 (Night Shift (USA)) [2009 p5g^6 p5f 6s 5.2m p5.1g 5.7m p6m f8m p5.1g f5f Dec 17] smallish filly: first foal: dam poor maiden: fair maiden: left David Marnane in Ireland after fourth start, regressive after: likely to prove best at 5f: acts on polytrack and good to firm going: tried tongue tied: often makes running: none too consistent and signs of temperament. *N. P. Littmoden* **66 d**

ANNIBALE CARO 7 b.g. Mtoto 134 – Isabella Gonzaga 75 (Rock Hopper 124) [2009 80: 11.5m 10.3m 12.1m 10s Aug 26] good-topped gelding: fair performer at best nowadays: stays 1½m: acts on good to firm and good to soft going: patiently ridden. *J. S. Goldie* **70**

ANOTHER BOTTLE (IRE) 8 b.g. Cape Cross (IRE) 129 – Aster Aweke (IRE) 87 (Alzao (USA) 117) [2009 79: p8g p8g 9.7m^5 12d^4 10m May 30] round-barrelled gelding: one-time useful performer: just fair in 2009: stayed 1¼m: acted on firm and good to soft ground: won over hurdles in June: dead. *Mrs S. Leech* **76**

ANOTHER CHARACTER (USA) 2 b. or br.c. (Feb 9) Giant's Causeway (USA) 132 – Mambo Halo (USA) (Southern Halo (USA)) [2009 p8f p9.5g Nov 14] well held in maidens. *M. Blanshard* **–**

ANOTHER DECREE 4 b.g. Diktat 126 – Akhira 90 (Emperor Jones (USA) 119) [2009 72: 8m^6 6d 7.2g^5 7m^3 7g 7m^3 p8.6m 12g Oct 17] tall gelding: modest performer nowadays: stays 7f: acts on firm and good to soft going: tried tongue tied/in cheekpieces of late: held up: sold £1,400. *M. Dods* **63**

ANOTHER ECHO 3 b.f. Bahamian Bounty 116 – Blue Nile (IRE) 70 (Bluebird (USA) 125) [2009 –: 8m Aug 31] no form. *W. Storey* **–**

ANOTHER GENEPI (USA) 6 br.m. Stravinsky (USA) 133 – Dawn Aurora (USA) (Night Shift (USA)) [2009 –, a78: f7g4 f7g Mar 19] angular mare: fair performer: below form in 2009: best up to 7f: acts on all-weather and firm going: tried in cheekpieces, usually blinkered: sent to Syrian Arab Republic. *E. J. Creighton* **– a62**

ANOTHER GRAND (IRE) 2 b.g. (Apr 28) Statue of Liberty (USA) 115 – Fallacy (Selkirk (USA) 129) [2009 6s 6f f5g6 6m Jun 16] poor form, including in seller. *Mrs R. A. Carr* **41**

ANOTHER LUKE (IRE) 3 b.c. Captain Rio 122 – Belalzao (IRE) 71 (Alzao (USA) 117) [2009 66: 8f 7.1m 5m 6g 6g Oct 16] workmanlike colt: modest maiden at 2 yrs: little form in 2009. *T. J. Etherington* **–**

ANOTHER MAGIC MAN (USA) 2 b. or br.c. (Mar 31) Chief Seattle (USA) 116 – Georgia Anna (USA) (Stutz Blackhawk (USA)) [2009 7m p7m5 7d3 9d6 p7.1g3 Oct 30] $4,500F: sixth foal: half-brother to several winners in USA: dam US 1m/8.5f winner: fair maiden: has raced freely, but should stay beyond 7f: acts on polytrack and good to soft going. *J. R. Best* **70**

ANOTHER SOCKET 4 b.f. Overbury (IRE) 116 – Elsocko 76 (Swing Easy (USA) 126) [2009 75: p5g p5.1g2 Mar 30] sturdy filly: just modest performer in 2009: raced at 5f, will stay 6f: acts on polytrack, good to firm and good to soft ground. *E. S. McMahon* **59**

ANOTHER SOLD 2 ch.f. (Feb 16) Auction House (USA) 120 – Countrywide Girl (IRE) 67 (Catrail (USA) 123) [2009 5g 5m 5.1m6 Jun 27] £800Y: first foal: dam 5f (at 2 yrs) to 7f winner: no sign of ability. *A. Berry* **–**

ANOTHER TRY (IRE) 4 b.g. Spinning World (USA) 130 – Mad Annie (USA) (Anabaa (USA) 130) [2009 66: p7g p8g f6g* 6f* 7g6 p7g3 7m4 6s5 6g* p6f p7.1g2 Dec 19] strong gelding: fair handicapper: won at Southwell in May, Lingfield in June and Yarmouth in October: seems best at 6f/7f: acts on all-weather and firm ground. *A. P. Jarvis* **75**

ANSELLS PRIDE (IRE) 6 b.g. King Charlemagne (USA) 120 – Accounting (Sillery (USA) 122) [2009 93: 10.2d 8m 8.5m 8.1m 8g p8.6g p8.6g3 p8.6g2 f8g5 Dec 27] fairly useful handicapper on turf, fair on all-weather: stays 1m: acts on all-weather, firm and soft ground: usually races close up. *B. Smart* **82 a76**

AN TADH (IRE) 6 b.g. Halling (USA) 133 – Tithcar 67 (Cadeaux Genereux 131) [2009 106§: p5g* 5.1m 5g p6g Aug 15] good-topped gelding: useful performer: won minor event at Dundalk (for second successive year) in April: respectable efforts at best in handicaps after, including at Chester second outing: best at 5f to 7f: acts on polytrack, good to firm and good to soft ground: tried in blinkers/cheekpieces: often races close up: unreliable. *G. M. Lyons, Ireland* **100 §**

ANTARA (GER) 3 b.f. Platini (GER) 126 – Auenpracht (GER) (General Assembly (USA)) [2009 8g3 8g3 8g3 8g* 8g* 10g* Oct 3] second foal: half-sister to German 6f/7f winner Anastra (by Seattle Dancer): dam, German 5f winner (including at 2 yrs), half-sister to useful German performer up to 1½m Auenteufel: smart performer: won maiden at Hoppegarten and auction event at Munich at 2 yrs, another auction event at Munich in August, listed race at Hanover in September and Westminster Preis der Deutschen Einheit at Hoppegarten (best effort, by 8 lengths from Liang Kay) in October: stays 1¼m: acts on soft ground. *R. Dzubasz, Germany* **116 +**

ANTARCTIC DESERT (IRE) 2 b.g. (Feb 18) Green Desert (USA) 127 – Arctic Silk 80 (Selkirk (USA) 129) [2009 7s4 6g 6m2 Sep 24] €16,000Y: tall, good-topped gelding: second foal: dam, maiden (stayed 1m), out of 1000 Guineas winner Cape Verdi: easily best effort in maidens when 5 lengths second to Racy at Pontefract (gelded after): will prove best at 7f+: acts on good to firm ground: type to do better at 3 yrs. *K. A. Ryan* **74 p**

ANTHEMION (IRE) 12 ch.g. Night Shift (USA) – New Sensitive (Wattlefield 117) [2009 59: 9.2m 7.1g Jul 6] good-topped gelding: fair handicapper at best: well held in 2009. *Mrs J. C. McGregor* **–**

ANTHOLOGY 3 b.c. Haafhd 129 – Annapurna (IRE) 101 (Brief Truce (USA) 126) [2009 98: 8m5 8m 9.8m3 Jun 2] strong colt: fairly useful handicapper: third at Ripon final outing: barely stays 9.8f: raced only on good to firm/good to soft going. *B. Smart* **86**

ANTIGUA SUNRISE (IRE) 3 b.f. Noverre (USA) 125 – Staff Approved 94 (Teenoso (USA) 135) [2009 72p: 7.1m3 9.9m3 12s* 12.1g* 12d* 14m5 10.4g3 9.8m4 13g Sep 20] close-coupled filly: fairly useful handicapper: won at York and Beverley in May, and Ripon in June: good third at York after: stays 13f: acts on soft going. *R. A. Fahey* **85**

ANTILLIA 4 b.f. Red Ransom (USA) – Milly of The Vally 93 (Caerleon (USA) 132) [2009 82p: p13.9g p13g³ Feb 21] sturdy filly: fair handicapper: stays easy 13f: acts on polytrack: reportedly finished lame first 4-y-o start. *C. F. Wall* **72**

ANTINORI (IRE) 3 b.g. Fasliyev (USA) 120 – Albavilla 82 (Spectrum (IRE) 126) [2009 85p: p8g² 10m³ 10g* 10.4g³ 10m² 10m Sep 19] lengthy gelding: has scope: useful handicapper: won at Sandown in May: better still when placed at York (wandered) and Sandown (neck second to Fanjura): stays 10.4f: acts on polytrack, soft and good to firm ground: in cheekpieces last 2 starts: travels well, but not straightforward: has joined Godolphin. *W. R. Swinburn* **103**

ANTIPODEAN (UAE) 3 ch.g. Halling (USA) 133 – Anka Britannia (USA) (Irish River (FR) 131) [2009 f8g³ f8g⁶ f11g⁶ 10m³ 9.9m 10g 12m⁶ 10m 7.5m 9.9g Sep 22] poor maiden: well below form after fourth start: stays 1¼m: acts on fibresand and good to firm ground: blinkered last 2 outings. *P. T. Midgley* **49 d**

ANTIQUE DIAMOND (IRE) 2 b.f. (Apr 14) Chineur (FR) 123 – Flash And Dazzle (IRE) 64 (Bertolini (USA) 125) [2009 6g 5.1m 6m 8.3m 6g p7.1g Oct 30] £4,000Y: sturdy filly: first foal: dam, maiden (ran only at 2 yrs, barely stayed 7f), half-sister to useful 1997 2-y-o sprinter Crazee Mental: no form in maidens. *Lucinda Featherstone* **–**

ANT MUSIC (IRE) 2 b.g. (Mar 6) Antonius Pius (USA) 123§ – Day Is Dawning (IRE) (Green Forest (USA) 134) [2009 5m⁶ 6g⁴ 7m⁴ 7m p8.6g⁴ Dec 18] smallish, angular gelding: fair maiden: gelded prior to final start: stays 7f: acts on good to firm ground. *J. S. Moore* **65**

ANTOELLA (IRE) 2 gr.f. (Apr 28) Antonius Pius (USA) 123§ – Bella Estella (GER) (Sternkoenig (IRE) 122) [2009 6.1g 7.1m⁶ p7g Oct 20] plain filly: second foal: dam German 1m winner: signs of a little ability in maidens. *Ian Williams* **–**

ANTONIOLA (IRE) 2 b.g. (Feb 18) Antonius Pius (USA) 123§ – Balliamo (IRE) (Royal Academy (USA) 130) [2009 6m² 6g³ 7m³ 8g* Oct 23] 7,500Y: big, lengthy gelding: second foal: closely related to French 1m winner Gayala (by Iron Mask): dam, Italian winner around 11f, half-sister to smart performers Desert Magic (6f/7f) and Farasan (up to 1½m): fairly useful and progressive form: won 19-runner nursery at Doncaster by length from Alrasm, well on top despite hanging left: stays 1m. *T. D. Easterby* **91 +**

ANTONIUS MORIS (IRE) 2 b.c. (Apr 25) Antonius Pius (USA) 123§ – Suaad (IRE) 88 (Fools Holme (USA)) [2009 5.5m* 5m⁴ 5m 6.1m³ 6.1v² 6d 7m⁴ 7g⁴ Sep 30] strong colt: fairly useful performer: won maiden at Warwick in May: stayed 7f: acted on heavy and good to firm going: dead. *Tom Dascombe* **82**

ANY DAY (IRE) 2 b.f. (Feb 15) Kheleyf (USA) 116 – Daylight Ahead (IRE) (Tenby 125) [2009 p5g⁶ p5g² p6g³ 5.2g⁶ p5g* 5.1m³ 6m³ 5.7m³ p5.1g Oct 16] €26,000F, £15,500 2-y-o: rather leggy filly: second foal: closely related to winner in Hong Kong by Desert Story: dam unraced half-sister to smart miler Hurricane Alan: fair performer: won nursery at Lingfield in July: effective at 5f/6f: acts on polytrack and good to firm going: sold 3,800 gns, sent to UAE. *R. M. Beckett* **70**

ANY GIVEN MOMENT (IRE) 3 b.g. Alhaarth (IRE) 126 – Shastri (USA) 73 (Alleged (USA) 138) [2009 p8g 8g 8m⁶ 11.5m⁵ 13.1d³ p16m Sep 16] tall, good-topped gelding: modest maiden: should stay 2m: unraced on extremes of ground. *D. M. Simcock* **58**

ANY SECRETS 3 b.g. Compton Place 125 – Anyhow (IRE) 75 (Distant Relative 128) [2009 8.1g p8.6g 7g p8.6g p7g Oct 8] little form: in cheekpieces/visor last 2 starts. *Karen George* **–**

A ONE (IRE) 10 b.g. Alzao (USA) 117 – Anita's Contessa (IRE) 68 (Anita's Prince 126) [2009 55: 8m 10g 7m f12m Nov 11] rather leggy gelding: modest at 9 yrs: no form in 2009. *Mrs H. J. Manners* **–**

APACHE DAWN 5 ch.g. Pursuit of Love 124 – Taza (Persian Bold 123) [2009 81d: p10m⁵ p10g⁴ p13.9g 8f⁵ 10.2g³ 9.9m f11m Jul 21] big, good-topped gelding: modest performer nowadays: claimed from G. L. Moore £5,000 after second start: stays easy 1¼m: acts on polytrack and heavy going: tried blinkered/tongue tied: temperamental. *A. Sadik* **57 §**

APACHE FORT 6 b.g. Desert Prince (IRE) 130 – Apogee 113 (Shirley Heights 130) [2009 83: p13g p12.2g³ p12g³ p13g⁶ p12g⁴ p12g p13g p12.2g² 12m⁶ 11.6f⁴ p12.2g p16.5g⁵ p13.9g Oct 2] good-topped gelding: fair handicapper: below form after eighth start: effective at 1½m to 2m: acts on polytrack, soft and good to firm going: wears blinkers: tried tongue tied: travels strongly, but tends to find little: untrustworthy. *T. Keddy* **76 d**

APACHE KID (IRE) 2 b.c. (Mar 29) Antonius Pius (USA) 123§ – She's The Tops 83 **47**
(Shernazar 131) [2009 7.1m 9m^5 Sep 23] poor form in maidens at Chepstow and Goodwood: should stay at least 1m. *B. R. Millman*

APACHE MOON 3 ch.g. Monsieur Bond (IRE) 120 – Mighty Squaw 58 (Indian Ridge **–**
123) [2009 f7g Mar 26] 14/1, well held in maiden at Southwell. *R. Curtis*

APACHE NATION (IRE) 6 b.g. Fruits of Love (USA) 127 – Rachel Green (IRE) 46 **64**
(Case Law 113) [2009 66: 8g 7.9g^4 8d^2 9.1g^6 8s 8m 9.1v Oct 31] good-bodied gelding: modest handicapper nowadays: stays 9f: acts on good to firm going, 4 of 5 wins on soft/heavy: has been blinkered. *M. Dods*

APACHE RIDGE (IRE) 3 ch.g. Indian Ridge 123 – Seraphina (IRE) 99 (Pips Pride **74**
117) [2009 66p: 5.1d^6 6s* 6m^2 May 25] fair form: won maiden at Hamilton in May: good second in handicap at Leicester (gelded after): stays 6f: acts on good to firm and soft going. *K. A. Ryan*

APEX 8 ch.g. Efisio 120 – Royal Loft 105 (Homing 130) [2009 p8g 7.1m p8g^5 p8g 8.1m **74**
Sep 29] leggy, angular gelding: has a short, round action: missed 2008: fair handicapper nowadays: has form up to 11f, though best efforts at 1m: acts on all-weather, soft and good to firm going: tried blinkered/in cheekpieces: has been slowly away: has found little. *M. Hill*

APHRODISIA 5 b.m. Sakhee (USA) 136 – Aegean Dream (IRE) 97 (Royal Academy **84**
(USA) 130) [2009 82, a77: p8g* p8.6g^3 p10g p12g^5 10.3m* 12.3m^4 10g^5 Jul 4] good- **a72**
topped mare: fairly useful handicapper on turf, fair on all-weather: won at Kempton in January and Doncaster in April: has form at 1½m but better at shorter (effective at 1m): acts on polytrack and good to firm ground: held up. *Ian Williams*

APHRODITE'S ROCK 3 ch.f. Falbrav (IRE) 133 – Comtesse Noire (CAN) 67 **70**
(Woodman (USA) 126) [2009 –p: 7m^6 7g 7f^5 9.7m^2 10.1m Aug 13] lightly-made filly: fair maiden: stays 9.6f: acts on good to firm ground. *Miss Gay Kelleway*

A P LING 2 b.f. (Feb 26) Antonius Pius (USA) 123§ – Spain 62 (Polar Falcon (USA) **46**
126) [2009 8.3d 8.3v p7.1g^5 Dec 4] workmanlike filly: fifth foal: half-sister to winner in Spain by Dr Fong: dam twice-raced half-sister to smart 1991 2-y-o sprinter Magic Ring: poor maiden: should be suited by 1m: acts on polytrack. *C. N. Kellett*

A POCKETFUL OF RYE (IRE) 2 b.f. (Feb 20) Acclamation 118 – Rye (IRE) 75 **71**
(Charnwood Forest (IRE) 125) [2009 p6g^5 7m^2 p8g^6 p8.6g Oct 23] €90,000F: second foal: sister to 3-y-o River Rye: dam 1m winner: fair maiden: seemed amiss in nursery final start: stays 1m: sold 10,000 gns. *J. A. Osborne*

APOLLO SHARK (IRE) 4 ch.g. Spartacus (IRE) 107 – Shot of Redemption (Shirley **81**
Heights 130) [2009 76: 7s 5.9m^6 7m^6 7d* 7d Aug 28] rather leggy, lengthy gelding: fairly useful handicapper: won at Thirsk in July: best form at 6f/easy 7f: acts on good to soft ground. *J. Howard Johnson*

APOSTLE OF ROME (IRE) 2 b.g. (May 13) Oratorio (IRE) 128 – Novelette **60**
(Darshaan 133) [2009 7.1g^4 7s 6m^6 p8.6g^6 Oct 9] useful-looking gelding: modest form last 2 starts, including in nursery: will be suited by 1¼m+. *Tom Dascombe*

APOTHEOSIS 4 ch.g. Dr Fong (USA) 128 – Carradale 73 (Pursuit of Love 124) [2009 **72**
67p: p8g^5 p8.6g p10g* 10.2m^4 10d^2 p10g 10g^3 10m^6 p10m^3 Sep 26] good-bodied gelding: fair handicapper: won at Kempton in March: stays 1¼m: acts on polytrack and good to soft ground: sold 8,000 gns, then gelded. *W. R. Swinburn*

APPALACHIAN TRAIL (IRE) 8 b.g. Indian Ridge 123 – Karinski (USA) (Palace **102**
Music (USA) 129) [2009 114: 7.1g 7.1s^3 8g^5 7.1g^5 8m^3 7g 7d 7s p8.6g* p8m^3 f7g Dec 22] sturdy gelding: useful performer: best efforts in 2009 when fifth in listed race at Pontefract (to Khateeb) and third in handicap at Ayr (beaten 2 lengths by Extraterrestrial) third/fifth outings: below form later in year, though won claimer at Wolverhampton in November (left I. Semple after next start): effective at 7f to 8.6f: acts on polytrack, heavy and good to firm ground: tried visored, usually blinkered nowadays: has hung: waited with. *N. Wilson*

APPEAL TO REASON (USA) 2 b.c. (Mar 16) Successful Appeal (USA) 118 – **?**
Grand Mirage (USA) (Southern Halo (USA)) [2009 7d^6 7m 7.5s^5 Dec 20] good-bodied colt: sold from J. R. Best 2,500 gns after second start: first form in maidens when fifth at Dos Hermanas final outing. *B. Rama, Spain*

APPELOUSE 4 b.f. Zaha (CAN) 106 – Appelone (Emperor Jones (USA) 119) [2009 **65**
f8g^4 f7g^5 p7.1g^5 p8.6g^5 f8g* 8s p9.5g Sep 18] third foal: half-sister to 5-y-o Glenridding:

dam unraced: fair handicapper: left M. Dods £800 after second start: won apprentice race at Southwell in July: best efforts on fibresand: will stay 1¼m: sold £400. *D. W. Thompson*

APPLAUDE 4 b.g. Royal Applause 124 – Flossy 107 (Efisio 120) [2009 86: 8d 10g 11.1m³ 10d⁵ 12g 10.4g* f11g² 12d 10g* 10.4m⁵ 9.1g³ 10.2v f12m⁵ p8.6g p9.5g f11g Dec 27] lengthy, deep-girthed gelding: fair performer: won claimer at Haydock (left G. A. Swinbank £8,000) in August and seller at Ayr in September: left J. A. Harris after tenth start: stays 11f: acts on fibresand, good to firm and good to soft going: blinkered/in cheekpieces of late: increasingly temperamental, and one to treat with plenty of caution. *R. C. Guest* **77 d**

APPLAUSE (IRE) 3 b.f. Danehill Dancer (IRE) 117 – Sniffle (IRE) 60 (Shernazar 131) [2009 80p: 8.3g* 8m* 8m⁶ 9m⁴ Oct 3] leggy, close-coupled filly: useful form: won maiden at Windsor and handicap at Redcar (beat Wannabe King 2¾ lengths) in July: good fourth to Supaseus in Cambridgeshire at Newmarket final start, racing away from main action: stays 9f: acts on polytrack and good to firm going: sent to USA: should do better still. *J. Noseda* **102 p**

APPLE CHARLOTTE 3 b.f. Royal Applause 124 – Maid of Camelot 102 (Caerleon (USA) 132) [2009 82p: 8m* 10d* 10m² 10f p8g³ Oct 29] leggy filly: useful performer: won minor event at Ascot in April and listed race at Newbury (by 2¼ lengths from The Miniver Rose) in May: creditable placed efforts in listed events after at Newbury (short-head second to Splashdown) and Lingfield (third to Moonlife): not entirely discredited in American Oaks at Hollywood in between: stays 1¼m: acts on polytrack, good to firm and good to soft going: sold 260,000 gns. *H. R. A. Cecil* **108**

APPLESNAP (IRE) 4 b.f. Clodovil (IRE) 116 – Apple Brandy (USA) (Cox's Ridge (USA)) [2009 77: 6m 7m 7m⁵ 7d p8g⁴ 8m 9m Aug 6] good-topped filly: modest handicapper nowadays: trained on reappearance by J. Ryan: stays 7f: acts on polytrack and good to firm ground: often in headgear: ungenuine. *Miss Amy Weaver* **66 §**

APRES SKI (IRE) 6 b.g. Orpen (USA) 116 – Miss Kinabalu 50 (Shirley Heights 130) [2009 54: 7g Jun 20] modest in 2008: well held sole outing in 2009: effective at 6f to 1m: acts on all-weather, soft and good to firm going: often races freely. *J. F. Coupland* **–**

APRIL FOOL 5 ch.g. Pivotal 124 – Palace Affair 113 (Pursuit of Love 124) [2009 78: p8g⁶ 8d⁵ 8f* 8.3g 8f* 8g⁶ 8m 8m p8g Sep 9] close-coupled, compact gelding: fair handicapper: won at Bath in May and June: free-going sort, best up to 1m: acts on polytrack, firm and good to soft ground: visored: usually front runner. *J. A. Geake* **79**

APRIL LADY (IRE) 3 b.f. Tagula (IRE) 116 – Dusty Diamond (IRE) 76 (Royal Abjar (USA) 121) [2009 f6s p5.1g f6g 6m 5g May 28] €5,000Y: first foal: dam Irish maiden (stayed 17f): poor maiden. *A. Berry* **42**

APRIL'S DAUGHTER 4 b.f. Kyllachy 129 – April Stock 97 (Beveled (USA)) [2009 63: 10d 10g³ 11.6m 10.2g⁴ 11.9m Aug 5] deep-girthed filly: modest maiden: stays 1¼m: acts on good to soft going. *B. R. Millman* **55**

APRIL THE SECOND 5 b.g. Tomba 119 – Little Kenny 50 (Warning 136) [2009 58: f11g f12g Dec 22] workmanlike gelding: maiden, lightly raced: well held in 2009: stays 11f: acts on good to soft ground. *R. J. Price* **–**

APURNA 4 ch.f. Rock of Gibraltar (IRE) 133 – Dance Lesson 47 (In The Wings 128) [2009 10.2s Oct 7] lengthy, useful-looking filly: fair maiden at 2 yrs for J. Bolger in Ireland (sold 800 gns July 2008): shaped as if amiss on belated return: bred to stay 1m: in cheekpieces (best effort) final 2-y-o start. *John A. Harris* **–**

AQLAAM 4 b.c. Oasis Dream 129 – Bourbonella (Rainbow Quest (USA) 134) [2009 124: 8d 8m³ 8m* 8m² 8g* 8m⁴ Sep 26] **125**

In what turned out to be his final season Aqlaam tackled six races, twice as many as in his first two put together. More opportunities, coupled with a step up in trip, helped Aqlaam to push his form to a higher level and in winning the Prix du Moulin de Longchamp in September he showed himself a high-class miler. He now joins his owner's stallions Haafhd, Nayef and Sakhee at the Nunnery Stud, his fee set at £7,000 for 2010. Aqlaam, a lengthy, quite attractive individual, should make up into a good-looking stallion and, as the first son of Oasis Dream to go to stud, he is likely to prove popular, especially with smaller commercial breeders.

It says much for Aqlaam that he eventually achieved so much as he did, given that he suffered a knee injury at two and a pelvic injury at three. The pelvic injury came after he had won his first two starts that season, a maiden at Newbury

Prix du Moulin de Longchamp, Longchamp—
Aqlaam puts up a high-class performance to gain his first Group 1 win;
Famous Name, Virtual (partially obscured by winner), Oiseau de Feu (right) and Gladiatorus come next

and the Jersey Stakes at Royal Ascot, after which he was sidelined for eleven months. Aqlaam made an inauspicious return in the Lockinge Stakes at Newbury, beating only one home, possibly unsuited by the softish ground even though he had shaped encouragingly on a similar surface on his debut. Back on a sound surface, Aqlaam showed he had lost none of his ability, following a third behind Paco Boy and Cesare in the Queen Anne Stakes at the Royal meeting with victory back at Ascot in the totesport.com Summer Mile. Racing on a round course for the first time, Aqlaam started favourite for the Group 2 Summer Mile and, with Cesare nowhere near his best, didn't need to improve to justify his market position. The race wasn't truly run and Aqlaam failed to settle, but he still found enough to peg back Confront who had kicked on turning for home, winning by half a length.

Aqlaam's three subsequent races were all Group 1s, the first two in France. Although no match for the outstanding filly Goldikova in the Prix Jacques le Marois at Deauville, he did finish well clear of the remainder headed by Lockinge winner Virtual. There was no Goldikova to worry about in the Prix du Moulin, and the race was weakened still further when the favourite, the Poule d'Essai des Pouliches winner Elusive Wave, refused to race after banging her nose on the gate as the stall opened. Aqlaam was keen to get on with things and the strong pace set by Gladiatorus helped his rider settle him, Aqlaam racing in second until taking over approaching the final furlong and never looking in much danger thereafter. Irish challenger Famous Name, attempting a four-timer, was beaten a length and a half into second, with a further two and a half lengths back to Virtual, again third. At least Aqlaam had remained sound for long enough to fulfil his potential, but less than three weeks later he was found to be sore after trailing home last of four in the Queen Elizabeth II Stakes at Ascot. According to Richard Hills, who rode Aqlaam in all of his races, he was never moving well, although he set a very strong gallop for much of the way. Aqlaam won the Jersey on firm and the Summer Mile on good to firm, but his best run came on the good ground he encountered at Longchamp.

Aqlaam is from Oasis Dream's first crop and was the most expensive of his yearlings sold at auction in 2006, fetching 260,000 guineas. A bargain buy as it turned out, with Aqlaam's total earnings on the racecourse alone amounting to nearly £500,000. Aqlaam is the second foal of Bourbonella, an unraced half-sister to several at least useful stayers, most notably Persian Punch, whose twenty victories included three Jockey Club Cups and two Goodwood Cups. Their dam

Mr Hamdan Al Maktoum's "Aqlaam"

Aqlaam (b.c. 2005)	Oasis Dream (b 2000)	Green Desert (b 1983)	Danzig
			Foreign Courier
		Hope (b 1991)	Dancing Brave
			Bahamian
	Bourbonella (b 2000)	Rainbow Quest (b 1981)	Blushing Groom
			I Will Follow
		Rum Cay (ch 1985)	Our Native
			Oraston

Rum Cay won at an extended fourteen furlongs, and she was also successful in a bumper at Towcester. Aqlaam's great grandam Oraston was a smart mile and a quarter performer who won the Premio Lydia Tesio. Bourbonella's only other foal to reach the racecourse is Curacao (by Sakhee), who won a couple of races at up to a mile and three quarters in the latest season. The dam also has a two-year-old full brother to Aqlaam named Madlool and a yearling filly by Cape Cross who fetched 300,000 guineas at Newmarket in October. Bourbonella is reportedly in foal to Oasis Dream again. *W. J. Haggas*

AQUAPARK 3 b.g. Shinko Forest (IRE) – Waterpark 75 (Namaqualand (USA)) [2009 6g 6g f12f^{4} Dec 12] well held in maidens. *R. Craggs* –

AQUARIAN DANCER 4 b.f. Mujahid (USA) 125 – Admonish 57 (Warning 136) [2009 51: f7g^{5} 8m 9.2d 10m Sep 23] close-coupled, workmanlike filly: poor maiden handicapper: stays 1m: acts on fibresand and soft ground. *Jedd O'Keeffe* 49

AQUARIAN SPIRIT 2 b.g. (Feb 9) Fantastic Light (USA) 134 – Notable Lady (IRE) 95 (Victory Note (USA) 120) [2009 7m^3 7d^3 7d* 7.5m^2 8m^3 8m^2 Sep 19] 15,000F, 20,000 2-y-o: second foal: half-brother to 3-y-o Equinity: dam 2-y-o 5f winner: fairly useful performer: won maiden at Newcastle in July: good efforts when placed in nurseries after: stays 1m: acts on good to firm and good to soft ground: gelded. *R. A. Fahey* **85**

AQUARIUS STAR (IRE) 2 ch.f. (Feb 16) Danehill Dancer (IRE) 117 – Easter Heroine (IRE) 72 (Exactly Sharp (USA) 121) [2009 7.5m^2 7m^5 Aug 9] 100,000F, 230,000Y: unfurnished filly: seventh foal: half-sister to useful 2001 2-y-o 5f/6f winner Doc Holiday (by Dr Devious) and fairly useful 1¼m winner Greek Easter (by Namid): dam, Irish maiden who stayed 1¼m, half-sister to useful sprinter Ocker: much better effort in maidens when 2 lengths second to Spying at Beverley. *Pat Eddery* **76**

AQUA VITAE (IRE) 2 ch.f. (Mar 30) Camacho 118 – Baileys Cream 79 (Mister Baileys 123) [2009 6m^5 Sep 10] €32,000F, £65,000Y, 130,000 2-y-o: fifth foal: half-sister to 3-y-o Baileys Cacao and Italian 1m/9f winner Rich of Promises (by Imperial Ballet): dam 2-y-o 7f winner: 11/4 and very green, very slowly away and uncomfortable on track when fifth of 8 in maiden at Epsom: has left Godolphin. *Saeed bin Suroor* **–**

AQWAAL (IRE) 3 b.c. Red Ransom (USA) – Mubkera (IRE) 100 (Nashwan (USA) 135) [2009 83p: 10m* 10d* 12f^5 10m^6 Jul 9] well-made colt: useful performer: won handicaps at Sandown in April and Newbury (by a head from Decision) in May: good efforts last 2 starts, in King Edward VII Stakes at Royal Ascot (7¼ lengths fifth to Father Time) and quite valuable handicap at Newmarket (sixth behind Firebet): stayed 1½m: acted on firm and soft ground: dead. *E. A. L. Dunlop* **105**

AQWAAS (USA) 3 ch.f. Diesis 133 – Jinaan (USA) 72 (Mr Prospector (USA)) [2009 68p: 8g^2 7.5m* 7g^2 9.3g 8g 10g Dec 24] quite attractive filly: fairly useful form: landed odds in maiden at Beverley in June: left Sir Michael Stoute after, then sold 32,000 gns: stays 1m: acts on good to firm going. *I. Al Malki, Qatar* **80**

ARABIAN FLAME (IRE) 3 b.g. King's Best (USA) 132 – Frappe (IRE) 93 (Inchinor 119) [2009 82: 8s^4 Apr 18] quite attractive gelding: fairly useful maiden: ran respectably only outing on Flat in 2009: should stay 1¼m: sold 4,500 gns, joined Seamus Fahey, Ireland. *M. R. Channon* **77**

ARABIAN GLEAM 5 b.h. Kyllachy 129 – Gleam of Light (IRE) 81 (Danehill (USA) 126) [2009 122: 7.1g^3 8m 7m^3 7m* Oct 17] small, good-bodied horse: very smart performer: won Victor Chandler Challenge Stakes at Newmarket by neck from Ouqba, getting first run and finding plenty for pressure: creditable efforts when third earlier, behind Main Aim in John of Gaunt Stakes at Haydock and Duff in Park Stakes at Doncaster (off 3 months prior to being beaten ½ length): effective at 7f/easy 1m: acts on polytrack, good to firm and good to soft going: in cheekpieces nowadays: seemingly amiss in Queen Anne Stakes at Royal Ascot second outing. *J. Noseda* **121**

Victor Chandler Challenge Stakes, Newmarket—Arabian Gleam finds plenty to hold off the unlucky-in-running Ouqba (right), Donativum (grey) and Main Aim

ARABIAN JEWEL 2 b.f. (Feb 17) Kheleyf (USA) 116 – Lady Liesel 63 (Bin Ajwaad (IRE) 119) [2009 6m May 30] 36,000Y: first foal: dam, maiden (stayed 1m), out of half-sister to dam of Golan and Tartan Bearer: 8/1 and very green, last in maiden at Lingfield, slowly away and considerately handled. *D. M. Simcock* **–**

ARABIAN MIRAGE 3 b.f. Oasis Dream 129 – Bathilde (IRE) 102 (Generous (IRE) 139) [2009 88p: 7m^4 8m 7g Jul 8] leggy filly: fairly useful form: creditable 10 lengths fourth to Fantasia in Nell Gwyn Stakes at Newmarket on reappearance: below form in handicaps after: should stay 1m: acts on polytrack and good to firm ground: forces pace. *B. J. Meehan* **87**

ARABIAN MOONLIGHT 3 b.f. Barathea (IRE) 127 – Ludynosa (USA) 98 (Cadeaux Genereux 131) [2009 –p: 8.3m 10m^5 p16g Jun 25] compact filly: little form over varied trips: sold 4,000 gns in July, sent to Greece. *E. F. Vaughan* **–**

ARABIAN PEARL (IRE) 3 b.f. Refuse To Bend (IRE) 128 – Intercede (Pursuit of Love 124) [2009 –: 10s 8.3f^2 7.5g* 6.9m^2 7m^4 p7m p7f Oct 14] tall, unfurnished ex-Irish filly: fairly useful performer: won maiden at Beverley in May: good second in handicap at Carlisle next time: will be suited by return to 1m: acts on firm going: races up with pace. *P. W. Chapple-Hyam* **82**

ARABIAN PRIDE 2 b.g. (Feb 16) Cadeaux Genereux 131 – Noble Peregrine (Lomond (USA) 128) [2009 6s^3 6m^2 6m^4 6g^2 6m* 6g^5 7m^5 Sep 18] 110,000Y: workmanlike gelding: half-brother to several winners, including 1m/9f winner Wannabe Around (by Primo Dominie), 6f (including at 2 yrs)/7f winner Grantley Adams (by Dansili) and 5-y-o Dubai's Touch, all smart: dam Italian 1¼m winner: fairly useful performer: won maiden at Newmarket (made all) in August: well below form in listed event/nursery after (then gelded): should stay 7f: acts on soft and good to firm going. *D. M. Simcock* **80**

ARABIAN SILK (IRE) 3 b.f. Barathea (IRE) 127 – Anthyllis (IRE) (Night Shift (USA)) [2009 –: p8g p8g 10.3d 10m^2 p12g 11.9d^6 Oct 22] strong filly: modest maiden handicapper: stays 1¼m: acts on good to firm going, seemingly on polytrack: sold 6,000 gns, joined D. McCain Jnr. *D. M. Simcock* **54**

ARABIAN SPIRIT 4 b.g. Oasis Dream 129 – Royal Flame (IRE) 72 (Royal Academy (USA) 130) [2009 99: p8g^4 8s^2 7m 8.1m p8m^5 7d 7.2m p7m^6 p8.6g Oct 16] close-coupled gelding: has a quick, fluent action: fairly useful handicapper: creditable second to Extraterrestrial in Spring Cup at Newbury: lost way after: stays 1m: acts on polytrack, soft and good to firm going: sold 33,000 gns, joined R. Fahey. *E. A. L. Dunlop* **97**

ARABIAN SUN 5 b.g. Singspiel (IRE) 133 – Bright Halo (IRE) (Bigstone (IRE) 126) [2009 65: 17.2d p16g Jun 24] compact gelding: fair handicapper in first half of 2008: has completely lost way (including over jumps): wears headgear, tongue tied final start. *C. P. Morlock* **–**

ARAB LEAGUE (IRE) 4 b.g. Dubai Destination (USA) 127 – Johnny And Clyde (USA) (Sky Classic (CAN)) [2009 8.1g^6 10.9d^2 11m^2 12.1v^2 14.1m^2 13.1g* 11.9d^3 16g* 16g^3 Oct 28] rather leggy gelding: fair handicapper: won at Bath (amateurs) in September and Newbury (apprentices) in October: stays 2m: unraced on firm ground, acts on any other. *R. J. Price* **70**

ARACHNOPHOBIA (IRE) 3 b.g. Redback 116 – La Mata (IRE) (Danehill Dancer (IRE) 117) [2009 70: p6g^3 p7.1g* p7g^3 f7g^2 p6g p7g* 6d^6 p7g^5 p7m* p7g^4 p7m^2 Oct 31] strong, compact gelding: fairly useful handicapper: won at Wolverhampton in April, and Kempton in July and September: good second at latter course final outing: stays 7f: acts on all-weather and good to soft going: usually races prominently. *Pat Eddery* **90**

ARANEL (IRE) 3 ch.c. Hawk Wing (USA) 136 – Antinnaz (IRE) 111 (Thatching 131) [2009 8g* 8g^5 8g* 7m 7g^3 8g* 6g* 6s^5 Nov 3] €37,000Y: lengthy colt: fifth foal: half-brother to 2 winners, including 4-y-o Aine: dam 5f/6f winner, including at 2 yrs: useful performer: won minor events at Madrid in April and May, €28,000 contest at San Sebastian in August and minor event at Madrid in October: better than bare result when eighth of 16 to Ouqba in Jersey Stakes at Royal Ascot fourth start, meeting trouble: good 2½ lengths fifth to Dunkerque in Prix de Seine-et-Oise at Maisons-Laffitte final outing: effective at 6f to 1m: acts on soft ground. *M. Delcher-Sanchez, Spain* **106**

ARASHI 3 b.g. Fantastic Light (USA) 134 – Arriving 105 (Most Welcome 131) [2009 10.1m^6 8.1g^6 10m^2 10s^4 10m p9.5g^3 p8.6m^2 p9.5g^3 p8.6g p12.2g^5 p12.2g^4 p9.5g^4 p12.2g^6 Dec 17] good-topped gelding: fair maiden handicapper: effective at 8.6f to 1½m: acts on polytrack and good to firm ground: in cheekpieces after second outing: refused to enter stall intended third outing. *Lucinda Featherstone* **73**

ARCANO (IRE) 2 b.c. (Feb 14) Oasis Dream 129 – Tariysha (IRE) (Daylami (IRE) 138) [2009 6m* 6m* 6m* Aug 23] **122 p**

Hamdan Al Maktoum doesn't buy horses in training with anything like the regularity of his brother Sheikh Mohammed but proportionately his success rate is higher. Three purchases which provided spectacular returns were Height of Fashion, who became one of the best broodmares of the modern era (there is more about her in the essay on Ghanaati); Jeune, who won the Melbourne Cup; and Invasor. The last-named, bought for a sum reported to be in the region of 1,400,000 dollars after being named Uruguayan Horse of the Year in 2005, won six of his seven starts for his new owner including the Breeders' Cup Classic and Dubai World Cup. He was named Horse of the Year in America in 2006. Inevitably there have been some failures, among them four-year-olds Bruges and Kalahari Gold, neither of whom won after being purchased on Hamdan Al Maktoum's behalf in 2007 and 2008 respectively. Albertus Maximus, bought after winning the 2008 Breeders' Cup Dirt Mile, did gain a notable victory in the Donn Handicap in January but wasn't seen out again after finishing sixth behind Well Armed in the Dubai World Cup. Two purchases of juveniles during the latest season look as if they might well end up on the right side of the balance sheet. Joanna, snapped up in the wake of her success in the Prix du Calvados, finished a creditable third in the Prix Marcel Boussac, and Arcano, already winner of the July Stakes, confirmed he was one of the best colts of his generation when landing the Darley Prix Morny.

The Prix Morny consistently maintains its standing among the best French races for two-year-olds, bolstered by being the only one in which fillies have regularly taken on the colts. Although there were only five runners at Deauville—none trained by Aidan O'Brien, who scratched his three entries led by Phoenix Stakes winner Alfred Nobel—the race looked strong. Wide-margin Coventry Stakes winner Canford Cliffs was odds on, ahead of the filly Special Duty, successful in the Prix Robert Papin, Arcano, the Andre Fabre-trained Prix de Cabourg winner Zanzibari and the outsider Dolled Up, who had finished third in the Robert Papin. Arcano arrived at Deauville unbeaten in two starts, his debut in a thirteen-runner maiden at Newbury early in June having resulted in a head victory from another colt set to go on to better things, Showcasing (the subsequent Goffs Million Sprint winner Lucky General was fifth). Arcano then started favourite against ten opponents in the TNT July Stakes at Newmarket including Reignier

TNT July Stakes, Newmarket—Arcano and Orpen Grey pull clear of the remainder

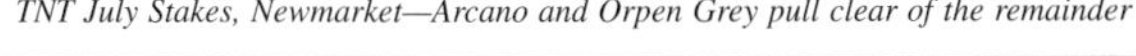

Darley Prix Morny, Deauville—not much between the five runners but the course record is broken as Arcano, in new colours, maintains his unbeaten record, accounting for Special Duty (No.4), Canford Cliffs (rail), Dolled Up and Zanzibari

and Tawaabb who had both been placed in the Norfolk Stakes. The second favourite, however, was Orpen Grey, a winner at Warwick and Salisbury, and he was the only one to make a race of it with Arcano, doing the donkey work until the patiently-ridden favourite produced a good turn of speed to hit the front inside the final furlong. Arcano finished three quarters of a length ahead of Orpen Grey with third-placed Red Jazz three lengths away. The Timeform computer timefigure for the winner, equating to a timerating of 118, was one of the best of the year by a two-year-old, albeit not so good as the figure recorded by Canford Cliffs in the Coventry.

The Prix Morny seemed a good choice for Arcano, especially as the going was good to firm, as for both his earlier races, conditions which favour horses of his type whose most telling weapon is a good turn of foot. Special Duty set a strong pace at Deauville, pursued by Canford Cliffs, with Arcano held up in last, though never far behind. Zanzibari was already in trouble soon after halfway and, with just over a furlong left, Arcano and Canford Cliffs were both under the whip as well. It looked as if Special Duty would hold on, but Arcano produced a decisive burst of speed after being switched to the outside, getting up to beat Special Duty by a short neck with Canford Cliffs a neck away third, Dolled Up a neck further back in fourth and Zanzibari keeping on again and beaten only a further head. The fact that Arcano's time of 1m 07.90sec broke a course record which had stood since Gallanta set it in 1984 seemed slightly odd in view of the fact that all the runners had finished together but there is no reason to question the time, and, despite the blanket finish, there is no reason to question the value of the winner's performance. Dolled Up was beaten in the Prix d'Arenberg next time and Canford Cliffs, who, in the view of connections at least, was never showing the same form after Royal Ascot, was not seen again, nor was Zanzibari. Special Duty, though, upheld the form when a decisive winner of the Cheveley Park Stakes. The Prix Morny resulted in Arcano's replacing Canford Cliffs as favourite for the Two Thousand Guineas, at around 8/1 at the time, though by the end of the year he was 10/1 in a market headed by the impressive Racing Post Trophy winner St Nicholas Abbey. The Dewhurst Stakes was pencilled in as Arcano's next target but he did not meet his engagement in that race, the trainer using his website—an increasingly useful way of imparting information—to explain. 'Arcano worked very well last week but since then we have not been happy with him. After consultation with the colt's owner, we have decided to put him away for the season.'

The Aga Khan bred eight horses successful in Group 1 races during the year and Arcano also comes from one of his families. The dam, Tariysha, was culled from the Aga Khan's Studs, making €140,000 as an unraced three-year-old. Arcano is her first foal, followed by a Medicean colt which fetched 450,000 guineas on Hamdan Al Maktoum's behalf at Tattersalls in October, the same sale at which Arcano had made 90,000 guineas a year earlier. The latest offspring of Tariysha is a full sister to Arcano. Generally this is a family noted for producing precocious individuals. The grandam Tarwiya won the C. L. Weld Park Stakes and ran second in the Moyglare Stud Stakes at two before finishing third in the Irish One Thousand Guineas. Several of her daughters have now produced two-year-old stakes winners, among them the Flying Childers winner Godfrey Street and Big Audio, winner of the latest Chesham Stakes. Tarwiya is a half-sister to the speedy Blue Dakota, winner of the Norfolk Stakes, and the family traces to the brilliant Prix de l'Abbaye winner Texana.

Arcano (IRE) (b.c. Feb 14, 2007)	Oasis Dream (b 2000)	Green Desert (b 1983)	Danzig
			Foreign Courier
		Hope (b 1991)	Dancing Brave
			Bahamian
	Tariysha (IRE) (b 2002)	Daylami (gr 1994)	Doyoun
			Daltawa
		Tarwiya (b 1989)	Dominion
			Touraya

With his distaff family and a Middle Park Stakes winner who developed into a champion sprinter as his sire, Arcano is no certainty on breeding to be suited by a mile at three, though he himself shows no propensity to being headstrong, racing in a pretty relaxed manner. There are also some staying elements in his pedigree. His dam is by an influence for stamina in Daylami out of a mare who stayed a mile and, while the majority of Oasis Dream's offspring are best at up to seven furlongs, he is getting good winners over further, including, in the latest season, the middle-distance performers Midday and Monitor Closely and the miler Aqlaam. Oasis Dream had an excellent year, with such as Main Aim, Misheer and Showcasing also flying the flag, and it has resulted in his fee at Banstead Manor Stud going up from £30,000 to £65,000 for 2010. Oasis Dream's popularity at the yearling sales was predictable, given the year he had, and eleven of his yearlings fetched at least 150,000 guineas, one of them knocked down to Demi O'Byrne for 700,000 guineas at Tattersalls, the highest price the agent paid for any yearling during the year and a major compliment to Oasis Dream especially as Coolmore buys few progeny nowadays of stallions based at other studs. John Magnier paid 480,000 guineas for an Oasis Dream yearling subsequently named Jacamar in 2007, though the colt ran only twice and made 12,000 guineas when sold out of Aidan O'Brien's stable at the end of his two-year-old days. To return to Arcano, he is a compact colt who probably has improvement in him and, all being well, will return refreshed as a three-year-old. While St Nicholas Abbey has more obvious claims in the Guineas, Arcano remains one to keep on the right side. *B. J. Meehan*

ARCH 6 ch.g. Arkadian Hero (USA) 123 – Loriner's Lass 80 (Saddlers' Hall (IRE) 126) [2009 –: 12m Jun 14] no form on Flat: poor maiden hurdler. *A. M. Crow* –

ARCHERS ROAD (IRE) 2 b.g. (Mar 15) Titus Livius (FR) 115 – Somoushe (IRE) (Black Minnaloushe (USA) 123) [2009 5m^2 5m* 5m* 5m^2 5.1m^2 5g^2 5g* 5g^5 5.1m^3 5.2d^3 5g^3 5m^6 5m^5 5m^4 6g 6d^4 Oct 24] smallish, sturdy gelding: first foal: dam unraced half-sister to smart German 1¼m/1½m performer Ransom O'War: useful performer: won maiden at Leicester and minor event at Newcastle within 3 days in April, and minor event at Beverley in May: largely held form after, particularly good effort when 2¼ lengths third to Monsieur Chevalier in Molecomb Stakes at Goodwood eleventh start: raced at 5f/6f: acts on good to firm and good to soft ground: tough and reliable: sold 52,000 gns, then gelded. *M. R. Channon* 100

ARCH EVENT 4 ch.f. Umistim 119 – Arch Angel (IRE) 55 (Archway (IRE) 115) [2009 –: p9.5g^{6} p7g p8.6g Dec 28] lengthy, plain filly: no form: tried in cheekpieces. *A. W. Carroll* **–**

ARCHIE RICE (USA) 3 b.g. Arch (USA) 127 – Gold Bowl (USA) (Seeking The Gold (USA)) [2009 101p: 6m 7g 8m 7m^{5} 8.1m p7g Oct 11] rangy gelding: fairly useful handicapper: stays 7f: raced only on polytrack and good/good to firm ground: raced freely penultimate start: none too consistent: sold 18,000 gns. *W. Jarvis* **93**

ARCHIMBOLDO (USA) 6 ch.g. Woodman (USA) 126 – Awesome Strike (USA) 84 (Theatrical 128) [2009 61§: f16g p16.5g Jan 22] strong gelding: modest handicapper at 5 yrs: well held in 2009: stays easy 2m: acts on polytrack and firm ground: often blinkered nowadays: tends to carry head high: ungenuine: fair hurdler. *T. Wall* **– §**

ARCHIPENKO (USA) 5 b.h. Kingmambo (USA) 125 – Bound (USA) (Nijinsky (CAN) 138) [2009 127: 8m* 8.9g^{6} 10d^{6} Apr 26] sturdy horse: high-class performer: won Al Fahidi Fort at Nad Al Sheba, Queen Elizabeth II Cup at Sha Tin and Summer Mile at Ascot in 2008: successful reappearance in Zabeel Mile at Nad Al Sheba in February, beating Vertigineux ¾ length: below best in Dubai Duty Free at Nad Al Sheba and Queen Elizabeth II Cup at Sha Tin: reported in July to have suffered slight fracture in near fetlock: stayed 1¼m: acted on soft and good to firm ground: usually blinkered/tongue tied in 2008/9: to stand at Lanwades Stud, Newmarket, fee £8,000. *M. F. de Kock, South Africa* **126**

ARCHITRAVE 2 ch.g. (May 10) Hernando (FR) 127 – White Palace 80 (Shirley Heights 130) [2009 8.1m 9m^{5} 8m^{3} p8.6g^{3} Oct 15] lengthy gelding: brother to useful 7f (at 2 yrs)/1¼m winner Portal and half-brother to several winners, including useful 1m/1¼m winner Ice Palace (by Polar Falcon): dam 1m winner: fair maiden: best effort when third in nursery at Wolverhampton (pulled hard in front): should stay 1¼m: sold 32,000 gns. *Sir Mark Prescott* **75**

ARCH REBEL (USA) 8 b.g. Arch (USA) 127 – Sheba's Step (USA) (Alysheba (USA)) [2009 109: 10d^{5} 10m^{3} Sep 19] well-made gelding: useful performer: better effort in 2009 when 4¾ lengths third to Prince Siegfried in listed race at Ayr: effective at 1¼m/1½m: acts on soft and good to firm ground: tried blinkered, in cheekpieces nowadays: tongue tied twice: often slowly away, and almost refused to race on reappearance: not to be trusted: fairly useful hurdler. *N. Meade, Ireland* **109 §**

ARCH WALKER (IRE) 2 ch.g. (Mar 13) Choisir (AUS) 126 – Clunie 84 (Inchinor 119) [2009 5g Apr 29] good-bodied gelding: 100/1, very green and well held in maiden at Pontefract: gelded. *Jedd O'Keeffe* **–**

ARCOLA (IRE) 3 ch.f. Nayef (USA) 129 – Ashbilya (USA) (Nureyev (USA) 131) [2009 60: 8g 8.1g 10f* 10g^{2} p11g^{3} 10f^{3} 12m^{6} p9.5g p12m Nov 21] strong filly: fair handicapper: won at Brighton in July: stays 1½m: acts on polytrack and firm ground: held up. *D. M. Simcock* **77**

ARCTIC CAPE 4 b.g. Cape Cross (IRE) 129 – Arctic Air 79 (Polar Falcon (USA) 126) [2009 89: 8m^{6} 9.2s* 9.8d^{6} 8.9d^{6} 8m^{3} 12v 10.2v Nov 4] tall, angular gelding: fairly useful handicapper: won at Hamilton in May: left M. Johnston after fifth start: stays 9f: acts on soft and good to firm ground: untrustworthy. *D. E. Pipe* **84 §**

ARCTIC COSMOS (USA) 2 b.c. (Jan 31) North Light (IRE) 126 – Fifth Avenue Doll (USA) (Marquetry (USA) 121) [2009 p8g^{4} 8g^{4} Oct 16] 47,000Y: big, lengthy colt: first foal: dam US 5.5f to 8.5f (including at 2 yrs) winner: fair form when fourth in maidens at Kempton and Redcar (still green and not knocked about): should stay 1¼m: remains capable of better. *J. H. M. Gosden* **68 p**

ARCTIC DESTINY (IRE) 2 b.c. (Apr 2) Trans Island 119 – Partytime (IRE) 91 (Tagula (IRE) 116) [2009 5m^{6} 6s 5.1g^{5} 5m^{5} Jun 24] quite good-topped colt: poor form in maidens last 2 starts. *K. R. Burke* **47**

ARCTIC FREEDOM (USA) 3 b.f. War Chant (USA) 126 – Polar Bird 111 (Thatching 131) [2009 75: 7.1m^{5} 7m p8.6g^{6} 7g^{6} 7f^{4} 8d p10.7g Nov 18] close-coupled filly: fair maiden: left E. Dunlop 25,000 gns before final start: should stay 1m: acts on polytrack: tried blinkered: none too straightforward. *Niall O'Callaghan, Ireland* **67**

ARCTIC (IRE) 2 gr.c. (Apr 15) Shamardal (USA) 129 – Shawanni 105 (Shareef Dancer (USA) 135) [2009 5g* 5v* 6v* 6m^{5} Oct 2] 9,000Y: big, well-made colt: half-brother to several winners, including smart 1¼m (including at 2 yrs and in UAE) to 2m winner Shanty Star (by Hernando) and 5-y-o Hinton Admiral: dam 2-y-o 7f winner (would have stayed 1¼m): smart form: won maiden at Bellewstown and listed race at the Curragh (by 5 lengths from Sole Power), both in July, and 6-runner Go And Go Round **116 +**

Mr R. A. Pegum's "Arctic"

Tower Stakes at the Curragh (beat Air Chief Marshal impressively by 4½ lengths, in control some way out) in August: firmer ground, below-form last of 5 to Awzaan in Middle Park Stakes at Newmarket final start, hanging right: will stay 7f+. *Miss T. A. M. Collins, Ireland*

ARCTIC WINGS (IRE) 5 b.g. In The Wings 128 – Arctic Hunt (IRE) (Bering 136) [2009 p14g⁶ p16g f14m Dec 5] rather leggy, dipped-backed gelding: fair handicapper in 2007: missed 2008: fairly useful hurdler, successful in January: little impact on Flat in 2009: tried blinkered. *A. W. Carroll* **–**

ARDENT PRINCE 6 b.g. Polar Prince (IRE) 117 – Anthem Flight (USA) (Fly So Free (USA) 122) [2009 62: p9.5g p8.6g* p7.1g² p9.5g p7g* p8.6g³ p8.6g p7g p8.6g p8.6m p8.6g p7.1g p7g⁶ p8g p7g p8.6g³ p7m⁵ Dec 30] tall gelding: modest handicapper: won at Wolverhampton in January and Lingfield in February: effective at 7f to 8.6f: acts on polytrack and good to firm going: tried in cheekpieces. *A. J. McCabe* **64**

ARDMADDY (IRE) 5 b.g. Generous (IRE) 139 – Yazmin (IRE) 94 (Green Desert (USA) 127) [2009 69: p12g³ p13g* p12m p12g⁵ p13g² p12g⁴ p16m⁴ Dec 30] workmanlike gelding: fair handicapper: won at Lingfield in February: stays 13f: acts on polytrack: usually blinkered. *G. L. Moore* **66**

ARE CAN (USA) 3 b. or br.c. Arch (USA) 127 – Golden Show (USA) (Theatrical 128) [2009 50: 10m 8m Aug 9] tall, close-coupled colt: little form since debut at 2 yrs: tried in cheekpieces: once withdrawn (reared over in paddock). *J. S. Wainwright* **–**

AREEDA (IRE) 2 b.f. (Mar 20) Refuse To Bend (IRE) 128 – Raindancing (IRE) 94 (Tirol 127) [2009 6m⁵ 6m⁶ Jul 10] 115,000Y: good-topped filly: closely related to 5-y-o Yossi and 1m/9.5f winner Ballare (by Barathea) and half-sister to 2 winners, including fairly useful 2000 2-y-o 5f winner Jack Spratt (by So Factual): dam 2-y-o 6f winner: better effort in maidens when sixth to Bella Swan at Newmarket, still in need of experience (edged right): will be suited by 1m+: looked open to further progress. *C. E. Brittain* **64 p**

AREEG (IRE) 2 b.f. (Mar 14) Doyen (IRE) 132 – Total Aloof 72 (Groom Dancer **–**
(USA) 128) [2009 7m 7.1m Sep 29] 34,000F, 56,000Y: stocky filly: half-sister to several winners, notably smart 6f/7f winner (including Dewhurst Stakes) Tout Seul (by Ali-Royal): dam 5f winner: green and well beaten in maidens: joined B. Hellier. *W. Jarvis*

ARES CHOIX 3 b.f. Choisir (AUS) 126 – Ares Vallis (IRE) 107 (Caerleon (USA) 132) **–**
[2009 90: 6m Aug 16] tall, lengthy filly: fairly useful performer at 2 yrs: tailed off in listed race at Pontefract only outing in 2009: speedy (usually front runner), raced only at 5f/6f: acts on any turf going: sold 35,000 gns in December. *P. C. Haslam*

ARFINNIT (IRE) 8 b.g. College Chapel 122 – Tidal Reach (USA) 68 (Kris S (USA)) **51**
[2009 67: p6g^{2} p6g p6g 5.7m^{5} 6m Jun 23] good-topped gelding: has a quick action: modest performer nowadays: stays 6f: acts on polytrack and firm going: wears headgear. *Mrs A. L. M. King*

ARGANIL (USA) 4 ch.g. Langfuhr (CAN) 124 – Sherona (USA) (Mr Greeley (USA) **112**
122) [2009 106p: f5m* p5g* 6m 5v^{4} 6d^{5} 5d^{2} 6m p5g* p6g^{5} Nov 21] smallish, strong gelding: smart performer: won handicap at Southwell and listed race at Lingfield (by ¾ length from Judd Street) in March and listed race at Dundalk in October: also ran well when neck second to Cheveton in handicap at Haydock: best at 5f: acts on all-weather and heavy going: usually races up with pace. *K. A. Ryan*

ARGAUM (IRE) 2 ch.c. (Mar 13) Medicean 128 – Poppy Carew (IRE) 110 (Danehill **73 p**
(USA) 126) [2009 p8g^{3} 8.3m p7.1g^{6} Nov 2] quite attractive colt: seventh foal: half-brother to 3 winners, including 2005 2-y-o 7f winner Suzy Bliss (stayed 1½m, by Spinning World) and 1½m winner Cutting Crew (by Diesis), both useful: dam, 7f (at 2 yrs) to 1½m winner, sister to smart 1¼m performer Leporello: fair form in maidens, shaping as though capable of better still final start: will be suited by 1¼m+. *W. R. Swinburn*

ARGENT AVIA 3 gr.f. Silver Patriarch (IRE) 125 – Mountain Bird 50 (Superlative **–**
118) [2009 7s 9.8m 8d Sep 7] first foal: dam sprint maiden: shown little in maidens. *M. Brittain*

ARGENTINE (IRE) 5 b.g. Fasliyev (USA) 120 – Teller (ARG) (Southern Halo **84**
(USA)) [2009 62: p6g^{4} f5g^{3} p6m^{5} f5g* f5g^{4} 5m^{4} 5g^{3} 5m* 6m* 5m* 5m^{2} 5m^{3} 5m* 5g 5m^{4} 6g 5g f5m^{3} p5.1g p6g Dec 12] strong, lengthy gelding: fairly useful handicapper: won at Southwell in March and, having left L. Lungo £2,200, Hamilton (3) and Carlisle in June: best at 5f: acts on all-weather and firm going: tried in cheekpieces/tongue tie, blinkered nowadays. *J. A. McShane*

ARGYLL 2 b.c. (Apr 4) Xaar 132 – Vitesse (IRE) 61 (Royal Academy (USA) 130) **59 d**
[2009 6m 6g 7g p7g 8g 8m 7m p6g Dec 7] leggy, close-coupled colt: modest maiden: below form after third start: may prove best short of 7f. *J. Pearce*

ARIADNES FILLY (IRE) 3 b.f. Xaar 132 – Christaleni 77 (Zilzal (USA) 137) [2009 **62**
67: 6m^{5} 5.1d p7g Jun 10] tall filly: modest maiden: needs further than 5f, and will be suited by 1m+: sold 6,000 gns in July, sent to Bahrain. *Mrs A. J. Perrett*

ARIEL BENDER 2 gr.g. (May 16) Needwood Blade 117 – Wandering Stranger 69 **–**
(Petong 126) [2009 5g^{5} 5g 5.1g 5m 6.1m^{6} 5s^{6} 5g Jul 25] unfurnished gelding: no form in maidens/nurseries: tried blinkered. *Peter Grayson*

ARIKINUI 4 b.f. Noverre (USA) 125 – Off The Blocks 55 (Salse (USA) 128) [2009 –: **54**
p8.6g^{3} p8.6g Feb 23] sturdy filly: modest maiden: stays 8.6f: raced on polytrack and good to soft ground. *K. R. Burke*

ARIZONA JOHN (IRE) 4 b.g. Rahy (USA) 115 – Preseli (IRE) 115 (Caerleon (USA) **86**
132) [2009 86: 8m 8.1m^{6} 7g 7.5g^{5} 6g 8f* 7.5m^{3} 8g^{3} 8m* 8m* 8m^{6} 8.3g^{5} p8.6g^{4} Dec 4] lengthy gelding: fairly useful ex-Irish performer: won seller at Redcar in July and, having been claimed from N. Wilson £6,000 after seventh start, handicaps there in August, and Yarmouth in September: stays 1m: acts on soft and firm going: has worn blinkers. *J. Mackie*

ARJEMIS 3 b.f. Hunting Lion (IRE) 115 – Kungfu Kerry (Celtic Swing 138) [2009 6d **64**
5m 7d^{4} 5m^{5} 5m^{2} 6d* 7m Sep 19] small filly: fourth foal: dam unraced half-sister to useful performer up to 1m Bazroy: modest performer: won maiden at Catterick in August: bled next time: may prove best at 6f: acts on good to firm and good to soft ground. *C. R. Wilson*

ARKELLION 2 b.g. (Feb 20) Mark of Esteem (IRE) 137 – Lovellian (Machiavellian **51**
(USA) 123) [2009 6g 7g^{5} 7m 6d Sep 15] compact gelding: left A. Haynes after debut: form only when well-held fifth in maiden at Chester. *P. D. Evans*

ARKEN LAD 2 b.g. (Apr 9) Arakan (USA) 123 – Object of Vertu (FR) (Kendor (FR) **60**
122) [2009 6g 7m p6g^{4} 6d* 7d^{3} p8m p6m^{6} Oct 31] rather leggy gelding: modest performer: won seller at Yarmouth in July: stays 7f: acts on good to soft going: in cheekpieces (only form) third to fifth starts. *D. Donovan*

ARLENE PHILLIPS 3 ch.f. Groom Dancer (USA) 128 – Careful Dancer (Gorytus **54**
(USA) 132) [2009 49: 7g p10g^3 10s^4 10g 14.1g 10m* p12g^6 p12g Oct 20] sparely-made filly: modest handicapper: won at Ffos Las in September: stays 1¼m: acts on polytrack and good to firm going, probably on soft. *R. Hannon*

ARLEQUIN 2 b.c. (Feb 16) Rock of Gibraltar (IRE) 133 – Fairy Dance (IRE) (Zafonic **77**
(USA) 130) [2009 7d 8m 8g* 8g Oct 23] close-coupled colt: first foal: dam once-raced half-sister to very smart performer up to 12.5f Dark Moondancer: fair performer: won maiden at Newcastle in September by ¾ length from Judiciary: respectable effort when mid-field in nursery at Doncaster: will stay 1¼m. *J. D. Bethell*

ARMOUR 2 b.c. (Feb 6) Azamour (IRE) 130 – Tenable (Polish Precedent (USA) 131) **74 p**
[2009 7d p6g* Sep 17] 20,000F: good sort: fourth foal: half-brother to fairly useful 1m/9.5f winner Milla's Rocket (by Galileo): dam unraced half-sister to very smart performer up to 13.4f Day Flight and to dam of high-class 1m/1¼m performer Phoenix Tower: better effort in maidens when winning at Wolverhampton by ¾ length from Barlaman, forced to wait for gap: should stay 7f+: sure to improve again. *M. J. Grassick, Ireland*

ARNIE GURU 2 ch.g. (Mar 19) Ishiguru (USA) 114 – Who Goes There 63 (Wolfhound **62**
(USA) 126) [2009 7m 7f^4 Sep 7] much better effort in maidens at Folkestone when 7 lengths fourth to Diam Queen, not knocked about. *M. J. Attwater*

AROMATIC 3 b.f. Medicean 128 – Red Garland (Selkirk (USA) 129) [2009 77p: 9.9f* **88**
p10g* 9.9m^5 10.4g 8.1d^4 Sep 16] rangy filly: has scope: fairly useful performer: won maiden at Salisbury and handicap at Lingfield in May: failed to build on those efforts after (blinkered, found little final outing): stays 1¼m: acts on polytrack and firm going: sold 20,000 gns. *J. H. M. Gosden*

AROUNDTHEBAY 3 b.f. Diktat 126 – Bayleaf 104 (Efisio 120) [2009 78: p6g* 7d **89**
6m* 7.1g^6 8.1m p6g p7g p8g Oct 29] rather sparely-made, unfurnished filly: fairly useful performer: won handicaps at Kempton in March and Folkestone in June: little impact in listed races/handicaps after: seems to stay 7f, but all 3 wins at 6f: acts on polytrack and good to firm ground. *H. J. L. Dunlop*

ARRABIATA 4 b.f. Piccolo 121 – Paperweight 77 (In The Wings 128) [2009 50: f7s **–**
Jan 4] good-topped filly: poor maiden: blinkered last 4 outings. *C. N. Kellett*

ARRIVA LA DIVA 3 ch.f. Needwood Blade 117 – Hillside Girl (IRE) 78 (Tagula **56**
(IRE) 116) [2009 –: 6d 7d 5m^2 5g* 5f^2 5m^3 5v Sep 4] compact filly: modest handicapper: won at Ayr in July: said to have finished distressed final outing: best at 5f: acts on firm ground. *J. J. Quinn*

ARRIVEDERLA (IRE) 3 b.f. Acclamation 118 – Alwiyda (USA) (Trempolino **89**
(USA) 135) [2009 p7g^3 7m* 7.1v* 8g^4 Jun 6] €70,000Y: rangy, useful-looking filly: sixth foal: half-sister to several winners, including French 1½m winner Qudrah (by Darshaan) and 4-y-o Keyala, both fairly useful: dam French 1½m winner: fairly useful form: won maiden at Lingfield and handicap at Haydock in May: likely to stay beyond 1m: acts on heavy and good to firm going. *H. J. L. Dunlop*

ARROGANCE 3 b.g. Josr Algarhoud (IRE) 118 – Rise 'n Shine 67 (Night Shift (USA)) **65**
[2009 65: 9.7g^5 9.9g^4 11m May 30] fair maiden: seems to stay 1¼m: acts on polytrack and good to soft going: sold 4,000 gns in July. *G. L. Moore*

ARRY'S ORSE 2 b.c. (Mar 23) Exceed And Excel (AUS) 126 – Georgianna (IRE) **72 p**
(Petardia 113) [2009 6m^5 Aug 21] £92,000 2-y-o: strong colt: fourth foal: half-brother to 3-y-o Future Gem: dam unraced out of half-sister to smart 1¼m performer Elegant Air: 11/2 and green, encouraging 4¾ lengths fifth to Businessman in maiden at York, slowly away and considerately handled: will do better. *B. Smart*

ART CONNOISSEUR (IRE) 3 b.c. Lucky Story (USA) 128 – Withorwithoutyou **121**
(IRE) 91 (Danehill (USA) 126) [2009 117: 7m 6m* 6m 5m 6d 6m Sep 27]

Overseas-trained runners enjoyed some notable successes at Royal Ascot, but they didn't win the biggest prize on offer at the meeting despite mounting a very strong challenge for it. The Golden Jubilee Stakes was worth £278,457 to the winner, and the betting was dominated by J J The Jet Plane and Sacred Kingdom representing South Africa and Hong Kong respectively. Neither managed even to reach a place as, for the fourth year running, the race went to one of the home-trained contingent, on this occasion 20/1-shot Art Connoisseur. Successful in the Coventry Stakes over the same course and distance twelve months earlier, Art Connoisseur returned to form somewhat out of the blue to win by a neck from one of the other overseas challengers Cannonball. Both first and second came from the back of the field in a race where the early pace wasn't strong, Art Connoisseur quickening to take over on the stand rail entering the final furlong and running on well. American-trained Cannonball finished two and a half lengths clear of third-placed Lesson In Humility, who in turn was followed home by J J The Jet Plane and Sacred Kingdom. Well back in the field was Kingsgate Native, who had also sprung a surprise—starting at 33/1—in the 2008 renewal.

Art Connoisseur had his problems between his two Royal Ascot victories. He was an impressive winner of a vintage renewal of the Coventry, runner-up Intense Focus and third-placed Lord Shanakill going on to finish first and second respectively in the Dewhurst Stakes. Art Connoisseur, however, failed to do himself justice in two subsequent appearances and was found to have suffered a small crack to his off-fore cannon bone after the second of those. He was stepped up to seven furlongs on his return in April to see if he could make a Guineas challenge but he failed to make an impact and then threw a splint, the recovery from which put his participation in the Golden Jubilee in some doubt, his exercise restricted to swimming for two weeks. In the light of Art Connoisseur's performances after the Golden Jubilee, it would seem he has had further troubles. Kept to sprint distances, Art Connoisseur failed to make the first ten in any of his four starts after Royal Ascot. His saddle slipped in the Nunthorpe Stakes, but there seemed no excuses for his disappointing performances in the July Cup, Sprint Cup and Diadem Stakes. Incidentally, Art Connoisseur was partnered in both the Nunthorpe and Sprint Cup by Hayley Turner, who wasn't without her own problems in the latest season. In 2008 Turner became the first woman to ride a hundred winners in a calendar year in Britain, but she reached only just over half that total in 2009 as a result of her having to miss over four months. It did look initially as though Turner would be sitting out the whole of the year, and part of 2010, after suffering head injuries in a fall on the gallops at Newmarket in early-March, after which she was informed by the BHA's chief medical advisor that she would not be allowed to apply for her licence until twelve months after her accident. With backing from Art Connoisseur's trainer Michael Bell and supporting evidence from two neurosurgeons, Turner appealed successfully against the decision and resumed race-riding in July.

Golden Jubilee Stakes, Ascot—Art Connoisseur and American challenger Cannonball have both come from off the pace and are clear of Lesson In Humility; J J The Jet Plane (noseband) takes fourth

Mr R. A. Green's "Art Connoisseur"

Art Connoisseur (IRE) (b.c. 2006)	Lucky Story (USA) (b or br 2001)	Kris S (b or br 1977)	Roberto
			Sharp Queen
		Spring Flight (b 1987)	Miswaki
			Coco La Investment
	Withorwithoutyou (IRE) (b 2001)	Danehill (b 1986)	Danzig
			Razyana
		Morningsurprice (ch 1985)	Future Storm
			Morning Has Broken

Art Connoisseur, a good-topped attractive colt, has been retired and is to stand at the Irish National Stud at a fee of €6,000. He is from the first crop of Lucky Story and much the best of his sire's produce so far. He is also the first foal of Withorwithoutyou, a fairly useful winner over seven furlongs at two but not so good at three when she was unsuccessful. Withorwithoutyou's second foal is a colt by Refuse To Bend named Boycott, who showed fair form at up to a mile for John Gosden but was still a maiden at the end of the year. The next dam Morningsurprice is an unraced half-sister to the dam of Oaks and Irish Derby winner Balanchine. Morningsurprice has bred two other winners, including Miss Pelling, who was successful at Warwick in June. Art Connoisseur, best at sprint distances, won on soft going on his debut but raced mainly on good or firmer and acted on firm. Held up, he travelled strongly though showed a tendency to hang right. *M. L. W. Bell*

ART DECO (IRE) 6 ch.h. Peintre Celebre (USA) 137 – Sometime (IRE) (Royal **100**
Academy (USA) 130) [2009 p10g^5 May 28] rather leggy, close-coupled horse: smart

performer at 3 yrs: met with minor setbacks after final outing that year, and has raced only twice since (bled sole outing in 2007): seemingly useful form when fifth in minor event at Lingfield on belated return: stays 1½m: acts on soft and good to firm going, probably on polytrack: well held over hurdles later in year. *C. R. Egerton*

ART DISCOVERY (IRE) 3 br.g. Indian Haven 119 – Lady Cinders (IRE) (Dance of Life (USA)) [2009 –: f7s² 10.1d 11.9d Oct 15] modest maiden: tried in blinkers (looked unwilling final outing): sold 800 gns. *M. H. Tompkins* **53**

ARTESIUM 3 ch.g. Haafhd 129 – Multicolour 64 (Rainbow Quest (USA) 134) [2009 59: 10.3g 7.9g⁵ p7g p7g p7f* p7m p8m p6g f7g f7g⁵ p7m Dec 30] modest handicapper: won at Lingfield in September: stays 1m: acts on all-weather and firm going: tried tongue tied/in cheekpieces. *Pat Morris* **58**

ARTEUS 3 b.g. Fantastic Light (USA) 134 – Enchanted 99 (Magic Ring (IRE) 115) [2009 –: 7m² 7.1v 7m² 7g⁴ p7g* p8g 7.5g 7d* p7g* p7.1g* p7.1g⁵ Dec 18] tall gelding: fairly useful performer: won maiden at Kempton in August and handicaps at Folkestone in October, Kempton in November and Wolverhampton (by 2¼ lengths from Autumn Blades) in December: stays easy 7f: acts on polytrack, good to firm and good to soft ground: in cheekpieces/blinkers last 5 starts: usually front runner. *Jane Chapple-Hyam* **93**

ARTE VIVA (USA) 2 ch.f. (Mar 18) Giant's Causeway (USA) 132 – Helsinka (FR) (Pennekamp (USA) 130) [2009 p7g² p7.1g⁴ 8g Oct 20] $500,000Y: second foal: dam, French 10.5f/11f winner, half-sister to Shamardal (by Giant's Causeway): fair maiden: in frame at Kempton (minor event) and Wolverhampton: bred to stay beyond 7f, but needs to settle. *G. A. Butler* **73**

ART EXCELLENCE 2 b.c. (Apr 25) Noverre (USA) 125 – Her Ladyship 119 (Polish Precedent (USA) 131) [2009 7m⁶ p8g* 7v Oct 24] 32,000Y: compact, quite attractive colt: brother to useful 2006 2-y-o 6f winner Truly Royal, closely related to fairly useful 6f (at 2 yrs)/7f winner Upper Class (by Fantastic Light) and half-brother to several winners, including useful French 1999 2-y-o 7f/1m winner Dignify (by Rainbow Quest): dam French 10.5f winner and second in Prix de Diane: won maiden at Kempton in October by head from Magnetic Force: fairly useful form when eleventh of 14 in Horris Hill Stakes at Newbury: likely to prove best up to 1m: sold 40,000 gns, sent to Serbia. *S. A. Callaghan* **83**

ART EXHIBITION (IRE) 4 ch.g. Captain Rio 122 – Miss Dilletante (Primo Dominie 121) [2009 67: f12g⁵ 16g May 19] fair performer at 3 yrs: fit from hurdling (fairly useful form for C. Mann), below form in 2009, racing freely in blinkers final outing: stays 1½m: acts on polytrack. *B. R. Millman* **57**

ARTFUL DODGER 2 b.c. (Mar 27) Josr Algarhoud (IRE) 118 – Artistic Belle (IRE) 73 (Orpen (USA) 116) [2009 p7.1g Nov 6] 50/1, always behind in maiden at Wolverhampton. *T. R. Gretton* **–**

ART FUND (USA) 3 b.g. Speightstown (USA) 124 – Kew Garden (USA) (Seattle Slew (USA)) [2009 65: p7g⁶ p6g⁶ p7g⁵ Jan 30] just modest performer in 2009: stays 6f: acts on polytrack: sold £1,200 in February. *G. L. Moore* **60**

ART GALLERY 5 ch.g. Indian Ridge 123 – Party Doll 108 (Be My Guest (USA) 126) [2009 –: f12g 17.2g 15.8g³ 13v 15.8g Oct 6] rangy gelding: poor maiden: left R. C. Guest after reappearance: stays 15.8f: tried blinkered/in cheekpieces: poor hurdler. *D. W. Thompson* **45**

ARTHUR'S EDGE 5 b.g. Diktat 126 – Bright Edge 102 (Danehill Dancer (IRE) 117) [2009 81: p8.6g 8.3g 7.1m* 7m³ 8m 7.1m⁵ p7.1g 6m² 6d* 6d* 6s² Nov 7] lengthy gelding: useful performer: won handicaps at Chepstow in July and Goodwood and Brighton in October: improved again when head second to Fullandby in listed event at Doncaster final start: has won at 7f/1m, best form at 6f: acts on polytrack, good to firm and soft ground: races prominently. *B. Palling* **101**

ARTHUR'S GIRL 4 b.f. Hernando (FR) 127 – Maid of Camelot 102 (Caerleon (USA) 132) [2009 103: 12d⁵ 10.3s Nov 7] workmanlike filly: useful performer at 3 yrs: well below form in 2009, tongue tied final start: stays 1½m: acts on firm going. *J. H. M. Gosden* **–**

ARTISTIC LICENSE (IRE) 4 b.f. Chevalier (IRE) 115 – Alexander Eliott (IRE) 73 (Night Shift (USA)) [2009 93: p6g² p6g³ p6g⁴ 5.7g² 6d 5.7g⁶ 6m⁴ p6g* 6d 6m⁴ 5.7m* 6m³ 6m³ 6g 6g 6g* 5.7m² 6m⁴ 6m p6g Nov 14] attractive filly: fairly useful handicapper: won at Lingfield in May, Bath in June and Goodwood in August: races mainly at 6f: acts on polytrack and good to firm going: often gets behind/finishes strongly. *M. R. Channon* **94**

ART JEWEL (IRE) 2 b.f. (Mar 6) Bertolini (USA) 125 – Ma N'Ieme Biche (USA) (Key To The Kingdom (USA)) [2009 p5g* 5m³ 5s p6g² Jul 7] €10,500F, £31,000Y: **70 §**

sturdy filly: half-sister to several winners, including useful 6f/7f winner A Very Good Year (later successful in Hong Kong, by Indian Ridge) and fairly useful Irish 6.5f winner Drifting Snow (by Danehill Dancer): dam, French maiden, sister to Cheveley Park/1000 Guineas winner Ma Biche: fair form: won maiden at Lingfield in May: failed to progress, beaten in claimer final start: should stay 6f: tried visored: ungenuine: sold 13,000 gns. *S. A. Callaghan*

ART MACHINE (USA) 2 ch.f. (Mar 15) Sky Mesa (USA) 116 – Grazia 111 (Sharpo 132) [2009 p7g^4 p6g^6 7m^6 Sep 28] seventh foal: half-sister to 3 winners, including useful miler Master of Arts (by Swain) and fairly useful Irish 7f (including at 2 yrs) winner Caprarola (by Rahy): dam, 6f (including at 2 yrs) winner, closely related to Halling: promise in minor event at Kempton and maiden at Wolverhampton first 2 starts: unsuited by track when well held in maiden at Brighton: should be suited by 1m: acts on polytrack: capable of better. *Sir Mark Prescott* **61 p**

ART MAN 6 b.g. Dansili 127 – Persuasion 79 (Batshoof 122) [2009 94: p10g^6 p8g^6 p8g p8g^4 p10g^3 p13g* p12g^3 Jun 24] big gelding: fairly useful handicapper: won at Lingfield in May: stays 13f: acts on polytrack, probably on firm going: waited with: joined J. Frost. *G. L. Moore* **85**

ART MARKET (CAN) 6 ch.g. Giant's Causeway (USA) 132 – Fantasy Lake (USA) (Salt Lake (USA)) [2009 73: p8g p7g^2 p7m^2 p7f^6 p7g^3 p8m^5 p7m^3 Nov 21] rangy gelding: fair handicapper: stays 1¼m: acts on polytrack and good to firm going: tried blinkered/ tongue tied, in cheekpieces last 3 outings. *Miss Jo Crowley* **67**

ARTREJU (GER) 6 ch.g. Perugino (USA) 84 – Art of Easter (GER) (Dashing Blade 117) [2009 82§: p8g^4 p8.6g p10g p9.5g^4 10.2m 9m 10m^2 9.9m^5 10g 10d 10f^4 8m^4 10.9m p8g p12g p10m p9.5g Dec 7] compact gelding: modest handicapper nowadays: left G. L. Moore after ninth start: stays 11f: acts on polytrack, soft and good to firm going: tried in headgear: ungenuine. *P. Butler* **63 §**

ART SCHOLAR (IRE) 2 b.c. (May 6) Pyrus (USA) 106 – Marigold (FR) 88 (Marju (IRE) 127) [2009 5.7g* 6f^2 6m Sep 19] €6,000Y, €16,000 2-y-o: sturdy colt: second foal: dam, Irish 1½m/13f winner who stayed 2m, half-sister to Derby runner-up The Great Gatsby: fairly useful form: easily best effort when winning maiden at Bath in August by 5 lengths from Filwa: in cheekpieces, looked reluctant final start: should be suited by 7f+. *G. L. Moore* **89**

ARTS GUILD (USA) 4 b.g. Theatrical 128 – Gilded Edge 94 (Cadeaux Genereux 131) [2009 83: 9g^2 Aug 18] sparely-made, plain gelding: fairly useful maiden: stays 1½m: acts on polytrack, soft and good to firm going: tried in cheekpieces. *W. J. Musson* **80**

ARTSU 4 b.g. Bahamian Bounty 116 – War Shanty 66 (Warrshan (USA) 117) [2009 85: 5m 6d^4 5g^2 5m^2 5g^4 5v 5s^3 5m^6 p6g Oct 1] tall, useful-looking gelding: fair handicapper: best at 5f/6f: acts on polytrack, good to firm and heavy going: tried in cheekpieces: usually held up: pulls hard: often finds little: ungenuine. *M. Dods* **83 §**

ART SUMMER 2 ch.f. (Feb 21) Compton Place 125 – Karminskey Park 71§ (Sabrehill (USA) 120) [2009 5.1m^4 5g^3 5.1g^2 6m^3 p5g Oct 2] modest maiden: pulled up lame final start: may have proved best at 5f: dead. *D. M. Simcock* **64**

ART VALUE 4 ch.g. Barathea (IRE) 127 – Empty Purse (Pennine Walk 120) [2009 –: p9.5g^2 p10g 11.9m^4 12m^5 14.1m^5 12.1m^2 11.5g 11.9m Aug 5] good-topped gelding: modest maiden handicapper: stays 1½m: acts on polytrack, yet to race on extremes of going on turf: in cheekpieces last 3 starts. *M. Wigham* **58**

ARTY CRAFTY (USA) 3 b.f. Arch (USA) 127 – Princess Kris 82 (Kris 135) [2009 52p: p10g* 11.1g* p10m* p12m^2 p12g* p13g Oct 29] rangy filly: fairly useful form: most progressive in 2009, winning minor event at Kempton, and handicaps at Hamilton and Kempton, all in September, and handicap at Lingfield in October: stiff task when well held in listed race at Lingfield final outing: stays 1½m: acts on polytrack, only turf outing on good going. *Sir Mark Prescott* **81**

ARWAAH (IRE) 3 b.f. Dalakhani (IRE) 133 – Sahool 109 (Unfuwain (USA) 131) [2009 8m^5 10m* 12m^5 10.3s Nov 7] tall, good-topped filly: first foal: dam, 1m (at 2 yrs)/ 1½m winner, closely related to dam of high-class 1¼m/1½m performer Maraahel: useful form: easily won maiden at Newbury in August: ran well when 4¼ lengths fifth to Ashalanda in Pride Stakes at Newmarket next time, pulling hard and shuffled back at vital stage: below form (but shaped well) in listed race at Doncaster final outing (faded in soft going): stayed 1½m: acted on good to firm going: visits Dansili. *M. P. Tregoning* **106**

ARYACODDINME (IRE) 2 b.c. (May 4) Pyrus (USA) 106 – Rainbow Pet (IRE) 65 (Spectrum (IRE) 126) [2009 5m 6f Jun 1] tailed off in sellers. *G. A. Harker* **–**

ASAAB (IRE) 2 b.f. (Mar 7) Refuse To Bend (IRE) 128 – Shalev (GER) (Java Gold (USA)) [2009 6m^6 6s Jul 17] 38,000F, 16,000Y: rather leggy filly: second foal: dam, Italian maiden, half-sister to dam of very smart miler Indian Ink: encouraging 7½ lengths sixth to Hafawa in maiden at Pontefract: well-backed favourite, well below that form on soft ground at Newbury next time: remains open to improvement. *C. E. Brittain* **54 p**

ASABA 2 b.f. (Mar 17) Desert Style (IRE) 121 – Hoh Hedsor (Singspiel (IRE) 133) [2009 6m Jul 2] deep-girthed filly: first foal: dam, little sign of ability, half-sister to useful winners Alzianah (5f/6f) and Return of Amin (6f/7f): 14/1 and better for race, tailed off in maiden at Newbury. *S. Kirk* **–**

ASAINT NEEDS BRASS (USA) 3 b. or br.g. Lion Hearted (USA) – British Columbia (Selkirk (USA) 129) [2009 84: p5m^6 p6f p6g p5g p7g p5m p6g Nov 11] tall, useful-looking gelding: fairly useful performer at 2 yrs: little impact in 2009, then gelded. *J. R. Best* **–**

ASAKUSA 3 b.f. Royal Applause 124 – Kiss And Don'tell (USA) (Rahy (USA) 115) [2009 –p: 9.7d p9.5g 8m f7g Jun 7] good-bodied filly: modest form: tried blinkered: sold 1,000 gns in July, sent to Greece. *H. R. A. Cecil* **53**

ASATEER (IRE) 3 b.g. Alhaarth (IRE) 126 – Catatonic (Zafonic (USA) 130) [2009 89: 10m 10.3m^6 8.3g^3 8.1g^2 Aug 26] tall, close-coupled gelding: fairly useful maiden at best: stays 1¼m: raced only on good/good to firm going: ungenuine: gelded, then sold 10,000 gns. *B. W. Hills* **84 d**

AS BRAVE AS YOU (IRE) 2 b.g. (Apr 2) Hawk Wing (USA) 136 – Scanno's Choice (IRE) 54 (Pennine Walk 120) [2009 5g 6m 7m 6d p9.5g^4 f8m^3 p8.6g^6 Nov 30] good-bodied gelding: modest maiden: stays 9.5f: acts on all-weather. *B. Ellison* **53**

ASCENDANT 3 ch.g. Medicean 128 – Ascendancy (Sadler's Wells (USA) 132) [2009 79p: 12g* p16g^4 14d* 14m* Sep 27] tall, good-topped gelding: useful form: not seen out till August in 2009, but much improved to win maiden at Catterick (awarded race) and handicaps at Haydock and Musselburgh (beat Spirit Is Needed by head, pair clear) following month: stays easy 2m: acts on polytrack, soft and good to firm ground: often front runner: sold 160,000 gns, joined J. Howard Johnson. *Sir Mark Prescott* **98**

ASHALANDA (FR) 3 gr.f. Linamix (FR) 127 – Ashaninka (USA) (Woodman (USA) 126) [2009 9g* 12m* 11g^2 12m* 10g^4 Dec 13] rather leggy filly: fifth foal: sister to French 7f winner (including at 2 yrs) Ashalina and half-sister to French 7.5f to 9f winner Asagild (by Gilded Time): dam, US 8.5f winner, out of half-sister to US Grade 1 1m winner Quiet American: smart performer: won maiden at Langon (only start for J-C. Rouget) and Prix de Malleret at Saint-Cloud (acted as pacemaker but held on by **118**

Pride Stakes, Newmarket—Ashalanda (right) leaves it late to deny the previous year's winner Crystal Capella; Saphira's Fire (stars) and High Heeled (black cap) are next

short neck from Terre du Vent) in June, and Pride Stakes at Newmarket (best effort, led last stride to beat Crystal Capella by short head) in October: creditable 3½ lengths fourth to Vision d'Etat in Hong Kong Cup at Sha Tin final start, always prominent: stays 1½m: acts on good to firm going. *A. de Royer Dupre, France*

ASHBRITTLE 2 b.g. (Apr 11) Rainbow Quest (USA) 134 – Cacsarca (GER) (Generous (IRE) 139) [2009 8.3v³ Nov 4] 25,000Y: seventh foal: half-brother to several winners, including 9-y-o Corriolanus: dam, German 11f/1½m winner, sister to smart German 1½m performer Catella: 16/1 and green, promising 7¾ lengths third to Burj Nahar in maiden at Nottingham, finishing strongly: will be suited by 1¼m+: sure to improve. *R. M. Beckett* **70 p**

ASHES SUMMER (IRE) 3 b.f. Rock of Gibraltar (IRE) 133 – Time Ahead 112 (Spectrum (IRE) 126) [2009 11.7g⁴ p12g⁵ Sep 21] 15,000Y: quite good-topped filly: second foal: half-sister to 4-y-o World Time: dam, 1¼m winner (second in Prix de Diane), half-sister to Musidora Stakes winner Time Away: fair form in maidens. *P. R. Webber* **70**

ASHKALARA 2 b.f. (Feb 15) Footstepsinthesand 120 – Asheyana (IRE) (Soviet Star (USA) 128) [2009 6g 7g 7m³ 7m Sep 18] 12,000Y: lengthy, unfurnished filly: first foal: dam unraced sister to high-class French miler Ashkalani: modest maiden: reportedly in season final outing: free-going sort, worth another try at 6f. *H. S. Howe* **59**

ASHMOLIAN (IRE) 6 b.g. Grand Lodge (USA) 125 – Animatrice (USA) 115 (Alleged (USA) 138) [2009 56: f14g⁵ f11g³ p12g Feb 14] workmanlike gelding: modest maiden handicapper: stays 15.4f: acts on all-weather and soft ground: tried in blinkers/cheekpieces. *Miss Z. C. Davison* **52**

ASHRAM (IRE) 3 ch.g. Indian Haven 119 – Tara's Girl (IRE) 95 (Fayruz 116) [2009 116: 8m 8.1m² 7m³ 7s² 8d p8g* 7m* 7m⁵ Oct 17] lengthy, heavy-topped gelding: smart performer: won minor event at Kempton in August and listed race at Newbury (by 2½ lengths from Huntdown, making all) in September: creditable fifth to Arabian Gleam in Challenge Stakes at Newmarket final outing: gelded after: stays 1m: acts on polytrack, soft and good to firm going: visored nowadays. *Saeed bin Suroor* **114**

ASIAN POWER (IRE) 4 ch.g. Bertolini (USA) 125 – Cynara 65 (Imp Society (USA)) [2009 79: p6g p5g⁵ Jan 22] good-topped gelding: fair handicapper: below form in 2009: effective at 5f to 7f: acts on polytrack and good to firm going. *P. J. O'Gorman* **63**

ASIAN TALE (IRE) 3 b.f. Namid 128 – Literary 79 (Woodman (USA) 126) [2009 75: p7g⁴ f7g 7.1g⁵ 7m May 24] leggy filly: fair handicapper: below form after reappearance, looking reluctant final outing: stays easy 7f: acts on polytrack, good to firm and good to soft ground. *P. D. Evans* **70**

ASK 6 b.h. Sadler's Wells (USA) 132 – Request 87 (Rainbow Quest (USA) 134) [2009 125: 14s* 12g* 12m³ 15.5d* Oct 25] **126**

If there was a sense of unfinished business about Ask's five-race campaign in 2008, then the deal was successfully concluded in 2009. Returning to the track for a fourth campaign, the six-year-old did all that could reasonably have been expected of him, winning three of his four starts and running an excellent race in defeat when third behind stable-companions Conduit and Tartan Bearer in the King George VI and Queen Elizabeth Stakes at Ascot in July. Ask's 2008 campaign

Emirates Airline Yorkshire Cup, York—Ask wins on his reappearance for the third year running; he hangs left as he draws clear of Blue Bajan (noseband) and Veracity

had begun promisingly, with a victory over a barely adequate trip in the Gordon Richards Stakes at Sandown, but he failed to win again. He didn't have the rub of green in the Prince of Wales's Stakes at Royal Ascot, the King George—not having a clear run in either—nor in the Prix de l'Arc, not that he would have won any of them even had everything gone without a hitch. Ask's sixth at Longchamp behind Zarkava after missing the break was still the pick of his efforts, the bare form as good as any of the performances he had produced to that point.

Ask's 2009 campaign proved largely free of the pitfalls that had befallen him in some of his races the previous year, and he managed to pick up two Group 1 events, enhancing his record significantly without improving markedly on his best form. Ask was started off this time at a mile and three quarters in the Emirates Airline Yorkshire Cup at York. He hadn't been raced beyond a mile and a half since winning the Ormonde Stakes at Chester on his four-year-old reappearance. Holding clearly the best form in the race, Ask was sent off 2/1 favourite and had little trouble seeing off rivals who usually race over further and who were almost without exception below form on the day to boot. Ask romped home by six lengths from 33/1-chance Blue Bajan; the seven behind Ask were hardly seen again in 2009, and none won a race, on the Flat at least.

The opposition in the Investec Coronation Cup at Epsom three weeks later looked altogether stronger and Ask was only fourth choice in the market in a field of eight. Youmzain, runner-up twice in the Arc, was favourite at 2/1 ahead of the previous year's Oaks winner Look Here and the progressive Duncan, winner of a handicap and a listed race in the spring, both at 9/2, with Ask a 5/1 chance. Another classic winner in the line-up was the 2008 Irish Derby winner Frozen Fire, bidding to redeem his reputation after being beaten in a farcical Ormonde Stakes. Buccellati, who had won the Ormonde, the Sheema Classic winner Eastern Anthem and the Lincoln winner Expresso Star made up the octet. If the Yorkshire Cup had proven something of a gift, Ask's victory in the Coronation Cup owed something to the way the race was run. It developed into a tactical affair, with Frozen Fire—Murtagh no doubt wishing to avoid the same criticism he had faced at Chester—setting the pace, though not at any great tempo, the race turning into something of a sprint in the straight, Ask being better placed as the race began in earnest than both Youmzain and, particularly, Look Here. That said, Ask showed plenty of resolution after hitting the front to get home by a nose and the same from Youmzain and Look Here, with Duncan a close fourth. The general view was that Ask was a fortunate winner and would struggle to beat those on another occasion.

Investec Coronation Cup, Epsom—it could hardly be closer as, from right to left, Ask, Youmzain and Look Here approach the line, with Duncan just behind them

Prix Royal-Oak, Longchamp—a second Group 1 victory for Ask, over the longest distance he has tackled to date; Schiaparelli makes him work for it

By the time it came to the King George VI and Queen Elizabeth Stakes at the end of July, the trio in the frame behind him at Epsom had all been seen out again and done little for the form. Ask looked very much his stable's third string in the field at Ascot, behind both Conduit and Tartan Bearer in the market, and even behind Look Here, despite her below-par effort in the Pretty Polly at the Curragh after Epsom. Ask acquitted himself really well, however, putting in a strong challenge in the final two furlongs and going down only by a head for second to Tartan Bearer, a length and three quarters behind Conduit.

Ask missed the Arc and waited instead for the Prix Royal-Oak at Longchamp later in October. Rather like the Yorkshire Cup, this looked a well-chosen target over a longer trip, the opposition hardly daunting for a race of Group 1 status. Ask was followed home by five-times Group 1 winner Schiaparelli, whose victories at that level had come in Germany and Italy. None of the seven others in the field had won a Group 1, not many having even contested one. Ask won by a length and a half but didn't have to run up to his previous best.

Ask is likely to be back in 2010, said to be being aimed at the Sheema Classic first of all, a race which has twice gone to a seven-year-old and which Ask's trainer Sir Michael Stoute failed by a nose to win in 2009 with Spanish Moon, a horse slightly inferior to Ask. Ask has won a pattern race on his reappearance in each of the last three campaigns, and has a good record fresh, though his Coronation Cup win and an unlucky second in the Canadian International as a four-year-old both came after only a three-week break. Fuller details of Ask's campaign that year, which also included a win in the Cumberland Lodge Stakes, appear in *Racehorses of 2007*, along with complete details of his pedigree.

Ask (b.h. 2003)	Sadler's Wells (USA) (b 1981)	Northern Dancer (b 1961)	Nearctic
			Natalma
		Fairy Bridge (b 1975)	Bold Reason
			Special
	Request (b 1997)	Rainbow Quest (b 1981)	Blushing Groom
			I Will Follow
		Highbrow (b 1985)	Shirley Heights
			Highclere

Since those details appeared, Ask's two-year younger brother Kensington Oval has made his debut. Also in the care of Stoute—appropriately enough, given the Barbadian connection—Kensington Oval won first time up at three years, in a mile and a quarter maiden at Sandown, but he has failed to score since, though showing fairly useful form when placed in handicaps in 2009. Kensington Oval subsequently made a couple of appearances for Jonjo O'Neill over hurdles (something mooted for Ask at a much earlier stage of his career) showing a little promise. Ask's half-sister Making Hay (by Dr Fong), foaled in 2007, has yet to reach the track. The dam Request had a colt by Motivator in 2008. At least two other relatively close members of the family did win races in 2009, Four Winds and Kingdom of Fife, sons of Fairy Godmother, a half-sister to Request. Both have their quirks, though showed smart form on their day, Kingdom of Fife winning the Zetland Gold Cup and finishing third in the Cumberland Lodge. More distantly, this is also the family of Ghanaati, the One Thousand Guineas winner, who, like Ask, has Highclere as his third dam on the distaff side. Ask seems unlikely to be raced much beyond fifteen and a half furlongs, the distance of the Royal-Oak. He ran poorly on his only start on heavy going but acts on any other. He wore a tongue strap twice at three, running well both times. Ask has developed physically as he has matured, and having been 'none too substantial' as a three-year-old, has made up into a lengthy, good-topped horse. *Sir Michael Stoute*

ASKAR TAU (FR) 4 b.g. Montjeu (IRE) 137 – Autriche (IRE) 104 (Acatenango (GER) 127) [2009 111p: 16g 16.4m* 18m* 20g^5 15.5d^6 Oct 25] tall, rather leggy, useful-looking gelding: smart performer: reportedly suffered setback in spring (when also gelded) and not seen out until July: further improvement when winning Weatherbys Insurance Lonsdale Cup at York (beat Drill Sergeant 1¼ lengths) in August and DFS Doncaster Cup (by neck from Darley Sun) in September: respectable staying-on fifth to Alandi in Prix du Cadran at Longchamp but below form in Prix Royal-Oak at same course final start: probably stays 2½m: acts on polytrack, good to firm and good to soft ground: quirky, can take time to wind up: visored last 4 starts. *M. P. Tregoning* **118**

ASK DAN (IRE) 3 b.g. Refuse To Bend (IRE) 128 – Bush Cat (USA) 93 (Kingmambo (USA) 125) [2009 66: 7.5m^4 8f 7.1m 7.1m^5 7m^5 7.9g* 8.3g^6 8d 9.3d^5 8.3s* 8.3s 8.3v^4 7v^2 7.2m^4 7.2g Oct 23] small, compact gelding: fair performer: won sellers at Carlisle (sold from B. Smart 6,500 gns) in July and Hamilton in August: stays 1m: acts on polytrack, heavy and good to firm ground: tried blinkered, wears cheekpieces nowadays: often makes running. *M. Dods* **66**

DFS Doncaster Cup, Doncaster—Askar Tau, an improved performer in headgear, collars the three-year-old Darley Sun as the grey Geordieland drops away

ASK FRANK (IRE) 2 b.g. (Feb 15) Hawk Wing (USA) 136 – Riva Royale 93 (Royal Applause 124) [2009 6m³ 5.9g* Jul 4] 10,000Y: first foal: dam 5f (at 2 yrs)/7f winner: marked improvement when winning maiden at Carlisle by 10 lengths from Lucky Rave: sold to race in Hong Kong, where renamed Let Me Fight. *G. A. Swinbank* **104**

ASK JENNY (IRE) 7 b.m. Marju (IRE) 127 – Waltzing Matilda (Mujtahid (USA) 118) [2009 67: p5g⁴ p5.1g p6g³ p5g 5m⁴ 5.1m 5f³ 5.7d² 5m⁴ 6g⁵ 5m⁴ 5.3d 5m⁴ 6f p5g⁴ p5m⁶ p6g² p6g* p6m* p5m⁵ p6g⁵ Dec 19] sturdy mare: fair handicapper: won at Lingfield in November/December: best at 5f/easy 6f: acts on polytrack, firm and good to soft going: tried in cheekpieces: held up: tough. *Pat Morris* **67**

ASK THE ORACLE 3 ch.g. Where Or When (IRE) 124 – Delphic Way 63 (Warning 136) [2009 p7.1g² p8g⁵ f8f³ p10m⁴ p12g Dec 7] fair maiden: stays 1¼m: raced only on all-weather. *H. Morrison* **69**

ASMODEA 4 b.f. Dr Fong (USA) 128 – Latina (IRE) (King's Theatre (IRE) 128) [2009 49: p8g⁶ p12g Feb 4] poor maiden: may prove best around 1m: raced on polytrack and good/good to firm going. *B. G. Powell* **–**

ASPECTOFLOVE (IRE) 3 b.f. Danetime (IRE) 121 – Rose Vibert (Caerleon (USA) 132) [2009 84p: 6m⁴ 7d 7m³ 8g* 9d⁴ 8m 8g* Oct 18] tall, workmanlike filly: smart performer: won handicap at Leopardstown in August and listed race at Naas (beat She's Our Mark by 2 lengths) in October: stays 9f: acts on polytrack and good to firm going, probably on heavy: has joined Godolphin: has joined Godolphin. *John M. Oxx, Ireland* **113**

ASPENDALE (IRE) 4 b.g. Docksider (USA) 124 – Ambria (ITY) (Final Straw 127) [2009 –: 8m May 28] no form: tried blinkered. *D. Carroll* **–**

ASPEN DARLIN (IRE) 3 b.f. Indian Haven 119 – Manuka Magic (IRE) (Key of Luck (USA) 126) [2009 110: 8f May 3] tall, leggy, angular filly: smart performer at 2 yrs: broke down halfway in 1000 Guineas at Newmarket on return (reportedly suffered tendon injury and retired): stayed 7f: acted on heavy and good to firm going: best form in cheekpieces: sold 110,000 gns in November. *A. Bailey* **–**

ASPIRATIONAL (IRE) 3 ch.g. Rainbow Quest (USA) 134 – Londonnetdotcom (IRE) 101 (Night Shift (USA)) [2009 –: 10.2g 12.1g⁶ 12s p9.5g³ p12.2g⁴ Dec 12] modest maiden: likely to prove best at 1½m+: form only on polytrack. *B. Palling* **64**

ASPRO MAVRO (IRE) 3 b.c. Spartacus (IRE) 107 – Alexia Reveuse (IRE) (Dr Devious (IRE) 127) [2009 65p: p8.6g² p8m 8.3g² 7s⁶ Nov 7] well-made colt: fairly useful maiden: stays easy 8.6f: acts on polytrack, probably on soft going: races prominently. *J. H. M. Gosden* **84**

ASRAAB (IRE) 2 b.c. (Feb 22) Oasis Dream 129 – Alexander Queen (IRE) 96 (King's Best (USA) 132) [2009 6g* Oct 30] €220,000Y: good sort: first foal: dam, Irish 2-y-o 5f winner, half-sister to 6-y-o Dandy Man: 6/4 favourite, won 16-runner maiden at Newmarket readily by head from Illustrious Prince, leading over 1f out: useful sprinting prospect. *Saeed bin Suroor* **90 p**

ASRAR 7 b.m. King's Theatre (IRE) 128 – Zandaka (FR) (Doyoun 124) [2009 42: 15v Oct 31] poor maiden handicapper: seems to stay 2¼m: acts on good to firm ground, probably on soft: tried in cheekpieces: often reluctant to race. *Miss Lucinda V. Russell* **–**

ASSABIYYA (IRE) 3 b.f. Cape Cross (IRE) 129 – Coretta (IRE) 118 (Caerleon (USA) 132) [2009 10f* 9.7m² 10.4m⁶ Sep 26] angular filly: fifth foal: half-sister to 3 winners, including useful 1¼m to 1½m (including minor US stakes) winner Shared Dreams (by Seeking The Gold) and fairly useful 9f (in UAE) and 1¾m winner Call Me George (by Rainbow Quest): dam, 9f to 1½m (including several US Grade 2s) winner, out of smart half-sister to Barathea and Gossamer: fairly useful performer: won maiden at Windsor in August: improved when second of 4 in handicap at Folkestone next time: tailed off final outing: stays 1¼m: has left Godolphin. *Saeed bin Suroor* **91**

ASSAIL 3 b.g. Bertolini (USA) 125 – Roofer (IRE) 80 (Barathea (IRE) 127) [2009 74p: f8g³ 10g p8g* p8g³ p10g⁴ Sep 2] lengthy gelding: fairly useful handicapper: won at Kempton in July: stayed 1¼m: acted on polytrack: dead. *H. Morrison* **84**

ASSENT (IRE) 3 b.f. Kheleyf (USA) 116 – Villafranca (IRE) (In The Wings 128) [2009 67: p6g² p7g⁶ 6.1g⁴ 6.1g⁴ May 25] close-coupled filly: fair maiden handicapper: well worth another chance at 7f: acts on polytrack, soft and good to firm going: held up. *B. R. Millman* **70**

ASSERTING 3 b.f. Reset (AUS) 124 – Appelone (Emperor Jones (USA) 119) [2009 51: 6s² 7.1m 6m* 5.9m⁵ Jun 15] modest handicapper: won at Ayr in June: will prove best at 5f/6f: acts on soft and good to firm going. *J. A. McShane* **63**

ASSET (IRE) 6 b.g. Marju (IRE) 127 – Snow Peak (Arazi (USA) 135) [2009 111: 6.5g^{4} 6g* 6g 7f* 7.1g^{4} 6m^{2} 6.5g 7g^{2} 6d^{6} 6m^{6} 7m^{6} Oct 17] tall, good-topped gelding: very smart performer: won handicap at Nad Al Sheba in February and listed race at Leicester (beat Regal Parade ½ length, hung badly right) in April: excellent ¾-length second to High Standing in Wokingham Stakes at Royal Ascot sixth start: respectable effort after only when second to Ordnance Row in Supreme Stakes at Goodwood, outbattled: has won at 1m, best at 6f/7f: acts on polytrack, soft and good to firm going: blinkered/visored: quirky and unreliable. *Saeed bin Suroor* **121 §**

ASTARTA (IRE) 2 b.f. (Apr 7) Green Desert (USA) 127 – Broken Romance (IRE) (Ela-Mana-Mou 132) [2009 5.2g^{6} 6m^{5} p6g^{3} Jul 8] 50,000Y: good-topped filly: half-sister to several winners, including 7f (at 2 yrs) to 2m winner Romantic Affair and 1½m/1¾m winner Gulf (both smart, by Persian Bold): dam unraced: fair form in maidens: will be suited by 7f+: sent to Germany. *P. F. I. Cole* **67**

ASTERRLINI (IRE) 2 b.f. (Apr 20) Refuse To Bend (IRE) 128 – Alithini (IRE) 75 (Darshaan 133) [2009 8m Sep 18] 15,000Y: fifth foal: dam, French 1½m winner, sister to Park Hill Stakes winner Discreet Brief: 25/1, not knocked about when tenth to Wigmore Hall in maiden at Newmarket: will be well suited by 1¼m+: should do better. *C. E. Brittain* **49 p**

ASTON BOY 4 ch.g. Dr Fong (USA) 128 – Hectic Tina 85 (Hector Protector (USA) 124) [2009 50: p11g p12.2g^{5} Apr 6] quite attractive gelding: poor maiden: stays 1½m: acts on polytrack. *M. Blanshard* **49**

ASTONISHMENT (IRE) 2 b.c. (Jan 22) Desert Style (IRE) 121 – Lucky Norwegian (IRE) (Almutawakel 126) [2009 6d 7m^{2} 7.1m^{4} 7d^{2} p7g* 7.1g^{2} 7m* 7m^{5} 6g^{4} 8g^{4} Oct 19] neat colt: first foal: dam, winning sprinter in Norway, half-sister to dam of 3-y-o Elusive Wave: fairly useful performer: won maiden at Kempton in August and nursery at Goodwood in September: creditable close fourth to Gallic Star in listed event at Pontefract final outing: effective at 7f/1m: acts on polytrack, good to firm and good to soft going: races prominently: sold 57,000 gns. *S. Kirk* **91**

ASTON LAD 8 b.g. Bijou d'Inde 127 – Fishki 36 (Niniski (USA) 125) [2009 55: 12.4s May 22] modest handicapper: well held only outing on Flat in 2009: was effective at 1½m to 2m: acted on soft ground: joined Mrs S. Humphrey: dead. *Micky Hammond* **–**

ASTORMFROMILLINOIS (USA) 6 ch.g. Illinois Storm (USA) – Sweetannie-annie (USA) (Marquetry (USA) 121) [2009 p7.1g Nov 16] well held in 6f maiden claimer on dirt at Santa Anita at 3 yrs for K. Mulhall: soundly beaten in seller on British debut. *George Baker* **–**

ASTRAL FLOWER 2 b.f. (Feb 26) Kalanisi (IRE) 132 – Arum Lily (USA) (Woodman (USA) 126) [2009 p8g^{5} p9.5g^{4} Nov 14] second foal: half-sister to 3-y-o Redwood: dam, French 1m/9f winner, out of Prix de Diane/Prix Vermeille winner Jolypha, herself sister to Dancing Brave: easily better effort in maidens when 2¾ lengths fourth to Powerful Melody at Wolverhampton: will stay 1¼m: should do better still. *Sir Michael Stoute* **67 p**

ASTROANGEL 5 b.m. Groom Dancer (USA) 128 – Nutmeg (IRE) 70 (Lake Coniston (IRE) 131) [2009 62§: 8g 7g^{4} 8m^{3} 8g^{2} 8f 8m^{5} 8g^{4} 13.8g Oct 17] neat, leggy mare: modest maiden handicapper: stays 1m: acts on polytrack, firm and good to soft going: tried in headgear (usually wears cheekpieces): ungenuine. *M. H. Tompkins* **60 §**

ASTROBRAVA 3 ch.f. Falbrav (IRE) 133 – Nutmeg (IRE) 70 (Lake Coniston (IRE) 131) [2009 58: 12.1m^{5} 10s^{5} 9.9m^{3} 8m^{6} f11g Aug 25] good-topped filly: modest maiden: may prove best short of 1¼m. *M. H. Tompkins* **55**

ASTRODIVA 3 b.f. Where Or When (IRE) 124 – Astromancer (USA) 62 (Silver Hawk (USA) 123) [2009 67p: 8d^{2} 10.1d^{2} 9.2g^{2} 14m^{3} 11.7g^{3} 10.3m^{3} p12m^{4} 12.4d^{2} Oct 13] fair maiden at best: in frame all 8 starts, but well below form last 4: stays 1¾m: acts on good to firm and good to soft going. *M. H. Tompkins* **78 d**

ASTRODONNA 4 ch.f. Carnival Dancer 123 – Mega (IRE) 66 (Petardia 113) [2009 83: 8d^{2} 8g^{6} p8g^{3} 7m 8m^{4} 8.1g^{6} 8s^{2} 8g* 8.5m^{6} p8g^{3} p8g^{6} Nov 13] sturdy filly: fair handicapper: won at Yarmouth in August: stays 8.6f: acts on polytrack, soft and good to firm going: usually held up. *M. H. Tompkins* **79**

ASTROLEO 3 ch.g. Groom Dancer (USA) 128 – Astrolove (IRE) (Bigstone (IRE) 126) [2009 47: f12g^{3} 12.1m^{3} f14g* 16v 14.1g^{3} p16m p16g^{5} f14m^{6} Nov 11] sturdy gelding: modest handicapper: won at Southwell in July: stays 2m: acts on all-weather and good to firm going, possibly unsuited by soft/heavy. *M. H. Tompkins* **57**

ASTROLIBRA 5 b.m. Sakhee (USA) 136 – Optimistic 90 (Reprimand 122) [2009 65: 10.2m^{4} 10f 10m^{5} 10.9g^{3} 11.9f^{4} 10g f11g* 12d^{4} 11.9d^{6} f11g^{5} f12f^{4} Dec 11] good-topped **67**

mare: fair handicapper: won apprentice event at Southwell in August: stays 1½m: acts on all-weather, firm and good to soft ground. *M. H. Tompkins*

ASTROMOON 2 b.f. (Mar 16) Beat Hollow 126 – Astromancer (USA) 62 (Silver **64 p** Hawk (USA) 123) [2009 8m 8d^6 Oct 27] second foal: dam 1¾m winner: better effort in maidens when 7¼ lengths sixth to Commissionaire at Yarmouth: travelling well: will be well suited by 1¼m+: open to further improvement. *M. H. Tompkins*

ASTRONOMER'S DREAM 2 ch.f. (Feb 18) Galileo (IRE) 134 – Danehill's Dream **56** (IRE) (Danehill (USA) 126) [2009 7d 7g p7g p8m Nov 4] smallish, close-coupled filly: first foal: dam, unraced sister to useful performer up to 1½m Summerland, out of half-sister to dam of Derby winner Dr Devious: modest maiden: too free in nursery final start: should be suited by 1¼m+. *E. F. Vaughan*

ASTRONOMICAL (IRE) 7 b.g. Mister Baileys 123 – Charm The Stars (Roi Danzig **73** (USA)) [2009 10.4g^5 12g^2 12g 10g 9.9f^2 12d 10m^2 10.2m* 10m 10.2g p12.2g^3 Nov 21] strong, close-coupled gelding: has a quick action: fair handicapper: off 3 years prior to return: won amateur event at Nottingham in September: stays 1½m: acts on polytrack, firm and good to soft ground: in cheekpieces last 5 starts. *R. Hollinshead*

ASTROPHYSICAL JET 2 b.f. (Feb 10) Dubawi (IRE) 129 – Common Knowledge **87** (Rainbow Quest (USA) 134) [2009 6.1g* 6m^3 7m^5 Oct 17] 42,000Y: big, strong filly: fourth foal: half-sister to 4-y-o Coin of The Realm: dam unraced sister to dam of 6-y-o Ask and half-sister to very smart middle-distance stayer Blueprint: won maiden at Nottingham in August by 3 lengths: fairly useful form when 4 lengths third to Distinctive in Firth of Clyde Stakes at Ayr and 8¼ lengths fifth to Music Show in Rockfel Stakes at Newmarket (again travelled well): should stay 1m+. *E. S. McMahon*

ASTROVENUS 2 ch.f. (Mar 4) Tobougg (IRE) 125 – Astrolove (IRE) (Bigstone (IRE) **50 p** 126) [2009 6g 7d Oct 27] third foal: half-sister to 3-y-o Astroleo: dam little form: outpaced in maidens at Yarmouth: will be well suited by 1¼m+: likely to do better. *M. H. Tompkins*

ASWAAQ (IRE) 3 b.f. Peintre Celebre (USA) 137 – Hureya (USA) 82 (Woodman **–** (USA) 126) [2009 74p: 8m^5 Aug 29] leggy filly: casily better effort in maidens 11 months apart when fifth at Leicester at 2 yrs: should stay 1m: sold 16,000 gns. *J. L. Dunlop*

ATABAAS ALLURE (FR) 3 b.f. Alhaarth (IRE) 126 – Atabaa (FR) (Anabaa (USA) **86** 130) [2009 87: 10g^5 14g^6 11d 8.5m^3 9g 9.8m Aug 15] strong, well-made filly: fairly useful handicapper: effective at 1m, barely at 1¾m: acts on polytrack, good to firm and good to soft going: often front runner. *M. Johnston*

ATACAMA CROSSING (IRE) 2 b.c. (Mar 25) Footstepsinthesand 120 – Endure **78** (IRE) (Green Desert (USA) 127) [2009 6g^2 6g* 7d 7m Sep 9] 38,000Y: quite good-topped colt: first foal: dam twice-raced half-sister to useful performer up to 1¼m Alexis: fair performer: won maiden at Leicester in May: soundly beaten in nurseries: stays 6f: sold 7,500 gns. *B. W. Hills*

ATACAMA SUNRISE 3 b.f. Desert Sun 120 – Top of The Morning 56 (Keen 116) **74** [2009 10.2g^5 10.1d^4 10g^6 11.8g 10.2g 9g* p8.6m^2 8g^3 8.1m 8g p10m* Dec 16] good-bodied filly: sixth foal: half-sister to 4-y-o Lady Longcroft and 5-y-o Brouhaha: dam, maiden, half-sister to useful 1¼m winner Whitefoot: fair performer: won handicap at Yarmouth in July and claimer at Lingfield in December: stays easy 1¼m: acts on polytrack: tried in cheekpieces: travels strongly held up. *J. Pearce*

AT A GREAT RATE (USA) 3 b.f. Arch (USA) 127 – Glia (USA) 110 (A P Indy **82** (USA) 131) [2009 62p: 10.2m* 11m^4 8.3m^4 10s^6 8g^3 8.5m^5 10d^4 Oct 21] compact filly: fairly useful performer: won maiden at Nottingham in April: held form afterwards, leaving H. Cecil before final outing: stays 1¼m: acts on soft and good to firm going: has finished weakly. *D. Sepulchre, France*

ATAKORA (IRE) 2 b.f. (Apr 7) King's Best (USA) 132 – Orinoco (IRE) 53 (Darshaan **60 p** 133) [2009 7s p7g 7m^6 Oct 1] sturdy, quite attractive filly: fourth foal: half-sister to 3 winners, including 6-y-o Bandama and fairly useful 1½m winner Intiquilla (by Galileo): dam once-raced half-sister to Irish Oaks winner Winona: some promise in maidens, and looks type to do better at 3 yrs: will be suited by 1¼m+. *Mrs A. J. Perrett*

ATASARI (IRE) 2 b.f. (Feb 18) Whipper (USA) 126 – Azra (IRE) 102 (Danehill **110** (USA) 126) [2009 5v^6 6v* 5v 6s^5 8m* 8s^2 7m^2 Oct 17] tall filly: half-sister to several winners, including 6-y-o Basra: dam Irish 2-y-o 5f to 7f winner: smart performer: won maiden at the Curragh in May and nursery at Gowran in September: improved when runner-up last 2 starts 6 days apart, in listed race at the Curragh (beaten ¾ length by Lady Lupus) and Rockfel Stakes at Newmarket (neck behind Music Show): stays 1m: acts on heavy and good to firm ground. *J. S. Bolger, Ireland*

ATEEB 3 b.g. Red Ransom (USA) – Design Perfection (USA) 105 (Diesis 133) [2009 59p: 10m^5 Apr 2] big, strong gelding: fair maiden: best effort sole outing at 3 yrs (fifth at Leicester, gelded after): stays 1¼m. *M. Johnston* **67**

AT FIRST SIGHT (IRE) 2 ch.c. (Apr 10) Galileo (IRE) 134 – Healing Music (FR) (Bering 136) [2009 7s^5 8s* Jul 10] €165,000F: third foal: dam, fairly useful French 2-y-o 7f winner, half-sister to smart French/US performer up to 1½m Fast And Furious: encouraging fifth to Kingsfort in maiden at the Curragh then landed odds in similar contest at Gowran by 4½ lengths from Cool Marble, always prominent: will stay beyond 1m: useful prospect. *A. P. O'Brien, Ireland* **83 p**

ATHAAKEEL (IRE) 3 b.f. Almutawakel 126 – Asaafeer (USA) (Dayjur (USA) 137) [2009 6g p6g* p6g 7m p6g^5 p6g* p6g Nov 11] 1,500 2-y-o: third foal: dam unraced sister to useful 1997 2-y-o sprinter Asfurah: fair performer: won sellers at Wolverhampton in June and Lingfield in October: should be suited by 7f: acts on polytrack, well held both turf outings. *R. A. Harris* **73**

ATHANIA (IRE) 3 ch.f. Fath (USA) 116 – Xania 32 (Mujtahid (USA) 118) [2009 78: p6g^4 8m^6 7.1v p7g^3 6f^6 7.6m* 8g 8m^5 8m Sep 18] workmanlike filly: fair handicapper: won at Chester in July: below form after: stays 7.6f: acts on polytrack, good to firm and good to soft going: visored 3 of last 4 starts (including for win). *A. P. Jarvis* **72**

ATHBOY AUCTION 4 b.f. Auction House (USA) 120 – Thabeh 57 (Shareef Dancer (USA) 135) [2009 57: p7g 7g 6g^4 7f^3 7m 10.2d 7m p6m^4 p7m Nov 29] smallish filly: modest maiden: barely stays 7f: acts on polytrack, good to firm and good to soft ground: usually tongue tied in 2009. *H. J. Collingridge* **54**

ATHEER DUBAI (IRE) 4 b.c. Dubai Destination (USA) 127 – Atheer (USA) 74 (Lear Fan (USA) 130) [2009 76§: p6g^2 p5g^5 p6g^3 May 27] sturdy colt: fair handicapper: effective at 5f to 7f: acts on polytrack and good to firm ground: effective with/without blinkers, tried in cheekpieces: possibly not straightforward: sold 5,500 gns in July, sent to Greece. *E. F. Vaughan* **74**

ATHENIAN GARDEN (USA) 2 b.f. (Apr 15) Royal Academy (USA) 130 – Webee (USA) (Kingmambo (USA) 125) [2009 p7.1g^6 8d^4 Oct 22] $150,000Y: third foal: half-sister to winner in USA by Real Quiet: dam ran 3 times in USA: better than result in maidens at Wolverhampton (very green, hampered) and Brighton (travelled well): capable of better. *H. R. A. Cecil* **77 p**

ATHERTON (IRE) 2 b.c. (Apr 10) Cadeaux Genereux 131 – Bibi Karam (IRE) 104 (Persian Bold 123) [2009 p6g f6g 6.1d Oct 15] rather leggy colt: well held in maidens. *J. G. Given* **–**

ATHLONE (IRE) 5 b.m. Montjeu (IRE) 137 – Almi Ad (USA) 78 (Silver Hawk (USA) 123) [2009 11.9g 10.9d^6 Jun 15] €10,000F, €40,000Y: fourth foal: dam, ran twice, out of half sister to Coronation Stakes winner Magic of Life: useful performer at best: successful in listed event at Milan in 2008 when trained by A. & G. Botti in Italy: well held in similar events in Britain in 2009: stays 11f: acts on soft and good to firm ground: has been blinkered. *L. M. Cumani* **–**

ATHWAAB 2 b.f. (Mar 2) Cadeaux Genereux 131 – Ahdaaf (USA) 84 (Bahri (USA) 125) [2009 5f^5 p6g p5g p6g* f6f^3 f5g^3 p5m^2 Dec 30] lengthy filly: first foal: dam, 7f winner (stayed 1m), out of useful sister to high-class sprinter Elnadim and close relative to Irish 1000 Guineas winner Mehthaaf: fair performer: won nursery at Kempton in September (left E. Dunlop 12,500 gns after): likely to prove best at 6f: acts on all-weather. *M. G. Quinlan* **71**

ATLAAL (USA) 2 ch.c. (Mar 23) Speightstown (USA) 124 – Deputy Maiden (USA) (Deputy Minister (CAN)) [2009 6m^2 6.1g^4 6m* Sep 25] $270,000Y, resold $410,000Y: small, attractive colt: third foal: half-brother to winner in USA by Vindication: dam unraced half-sister to Canadian Grade 3 7f winner Lemon Maid: fairly useful form in maidens: simple task, landed odds by 6 lengths at Haydock: had finished promising second to Quarrel at Ascot on debut: likely to do better. *M. A. Jarvis* **81 p**

ATLANTIC BEACH 4 ch.g. Kyllachy 129 – Amused 78 (Prince Sabo 123) [2009 72: 6m^4 6v^3 6m^2 6m^4 5m^6 6m Aug 8] fairly useful handicapper: left R. Fahey prior to final start: likely to stay 7f: acts on any going: tried blinkered/visored. *J. Hetherton* **80**

ATLANTIC GAMBLE (IRE) 9 b.g. Darnay 117 – Full Traceability (IRE) 53 (Ron's Victory (USA) 129) [2009 63: p9.5g Jan 7] lengthy gelding: modest performer: below form sole 9-y-o start: stays 1¾m: acts on all-weather and soft ground: wears cheekpieces: has bled: none too consistent. *K. R. Burke* **–**

ATLANTIC SPORT (USA) 4 b.c. Machiavellian (USA) 123 – Shy Lady (FR) 91 (Kaldoun (FR) 122) [2009 115: 8m^4 8d 7.1g^5 6d^6 Jun 27] tall, well-made colt: smart **113**

performer: creditable effort in 2009 only when 3¾ lengths fifth to Main Aim in John of Gaunt Stakes at Haydock: effective at 7f/1m: acts on soft and good to firm ground: often held up and travels strongly: sent to Germany. *M. R. Channon*

ATLANTIC STORY (USA) 7 b. or br.g. Stormy Atlantic (USA) – Story Book Girl (USA) (Siberian Express (USA) 125) [2009 101, a116: p8g⁴ p7g 7f³ 7m³ 7g⁶ 6m⁴ 6g³ 6m³ 6m³ 5m³ Sep 26] big, good-topped gelding: has a short, quick action: smart handicapper on all-weather, useful on turf: in frame 7 times in 2009, best effort when 2½ lengths fourth to Red Somerset at Lingfield on first outing: effective at 5f to 8.6f: acts on all-weather, firm and good to soft going: usually blinkered/tongue tied (finished weakly without latter seventh outing): often races prominently: consistent. *M. W. Easterby* **96 a108**

ATLANTIS STAR 2 b.c. (Feb 8) Cape Cross (IRE) 129 – Ladeena (IRE) 80 (Dubai Millennium 140) [2009 6g* 6.1m² 7m³ 7m Oct 3] 200,000Y: first foal: dam, 7f winner, out of Fillies' Mile winner Aqaarid: useful performer: won maiden at Pontefract in August by 6 lengths: much improved when ½-length third to Vale of York in listed race at Goodwood, pulling hard: tongue tied, well below form in sales race at Newmarket final start: stays 7f. *Saeed bin Suroor* **102**

ATOMIC TWISTER 2 b.f. (Apr 1) Dubawi (IRE) 129 – Lauren (GER) (Lightning (FR) 129) [2009 6m 6g Jun 15] 20,000F, 3,000Y, 7,000 2-y-o: leggy, light-framed filly: half-sister to several winners in Germany, including listed winners Lisieux (at 1m, by Sternkonig) and Laurel (at 11f, by Goofalik): dam German 1m (including at 2 yrs) and 11f winner: well beaten in maiden/seller. *P. F. I. Cole* **–**

A TOUCH OF LUCK 2 b.g. (Feb 26) Lucky Story (USA) 128 – Optimise (IRE) 69 (Danehill (USA) 126) [2009 5m 5s⁴ 6s May 22] small, sturdy gelding: poor form in maidens, then gelded: dead. *T. D. Easterby* **44**

ATTAINABLE 3 b. or br.f. Kalanisi (IRE) 132 – Balleta (USA) 87 (Lyphard (USA) 132) [2009 72p: p12g³ p12g⁶ Oct 22] quite attractive filly: fair maiden: off 11 months, below form both outings at 3 yrs: should stay at least 1¼m: raced only on polytrack and soft ground: sold 14,000 gns. *Mrs A. J. Perrett* **61**

ATTORNEY GENERAL (IRE) 10 b.g. Sadler's Wells (USA) 132 – Her Ladyship 119 (Polish Precedent (USA) 131) [2009 12v Oct 24] angular gelding: fairly useful winner at 3 yrs: well held on belated Flat return: fairly useful hurdler nowadays. *C. Gordon* **–**

AT WITS END 3 b.g. Orpen (USA) 116 – Pagan Princess 54 (Mujtahid (USA) 118) [2009 p8.6g⁴ p8.6g⁴ p9.5g* Oct 10] fourth foal: dam, maiden, half-sister to useful performer up to 1¾m Hambleden: progressive form in maidens at Wolverhampton, winning by neck from Burma Rock in October: stays 9.5f: open to further improvement. *J. A. R. Toller* **88 p**

AUBURN PLACE 2 ch.f. (Mar 18) Compton Place 125 – Barboukh 95 (Night Shift (USA)) [2009 p8m Oct 28] 26,000Y: half-sister to smart French 1¼m winner Barbola (by Diesis) and useful 1m/1¼m winner Tarboush (by Polish Precedent): dam, 1m winner who stayed 1¼m, out of half-sister to Old Vic: 25/1, slowly away and always behind in maiden at Kempton. *E. F. Vaughan* **–**

AUCTION BELLE 4 b.f. Auction House (USA) 120 – Island Colony (USA) (Pleasant Colony (USA)) [2009 47: f12d⁵ f11d p16.5g⁶ Jan 22] poor maiden. *R. Curtis* **47**

AUDACITY OF HOPE 2 b.c. (Feb 15) Red Ransom (USA) – Aliena (IRE) (Grand Lodge (USA) 125) [2009 5m³ 6m* 7d² 7.1g 7m* 7m* 7m⁴ 7v³ Oct 24] lengthy, useful-looking colt: has scope: sixth foal: dam French/US 2-y-o 7f/1m winner: useful performer: won maiden at Ripon in June and nurseries at Doncaster and Newmarket in September: good efforts when in frame in Somerville Tattersall Stakes at Newmarket and Horris Hill Stakes at Newbury (very close third to Carnaby Street, bit short of room close home): should stay 1m: acts on heavy and good to firm ground: tongue tied last 4 starts: capable of better still. *P. J. McBride* **103 p**

AUDEMAR (IRE) 3 ch.c. Exceed And Excel (AUS) 126 – Bathe In Light (USA) 72 (Sunshine Forever (USA)) [2009 78p: 6g⁶ p8g⁴ p7g* 7m p7g⁴ p8g⁴ p8g* p8f³ Oct 14] good-quartered colt: fairly useful handicapper: won at Kempton in August and October (beat Block Party 2½ lengths): stays 1m: acts on polytrack. *E. F. Vaughan* **94**

AUDRINNA (IRE) 2 b.f. (May 3) Oratorio (IRE) 128 – Zvezda (USA) (Nureyev (USA) 131) [2009 6m 6g² 5.8g a6g* a6g⁶ a8s⁴ a6.8g* Dec 13] good-bodied filly: fourth foal: dam, French maiden, sister to Dewhurst Stakes third Zentsov Street: claimed from M. Quinlan £7,000 after second in seller at Leicester (tongue tied): successful at Taby in maiden in October and minor event in December: stays 6.8f: acts on dirt. *C. Bjorling, Sweden* **53 +**

AUGUSTA GOLD (USA) 3 b. or br.c. Medaglia d'Oro (USA) 129 – Golden Gorse (USA) (His Majesty (USA)) [2009 67: p10g^5 f11g^2 f12g^2 a8g^2 7.5d 10.5d a11.5g^5 a10g^5 a4.8g^4 a10.5g* a14g* a11g^4 Nov 7] sturdy colt: fair performer: second in claimer and maiden at Southwell second/third starts before leaving N. Littmoden: won 2 minor events at Mons in October: stays 1¾m: acts on all-weather: usually blinkered. *Mme L. Braem, Belgium* **69**

AUGUST DAYS (IRE) 3 ch.f. Noverre (USA) 125 – Vitesse (IRE) 61 (Royal Academy (USA) 130) [2009 58: 5.1g^6 5.1m 6m 9g 8f 8.3d^6 9m Aug 27] lengthy filly: poor performer: best at 5f: acts on polytrack, good to firm and good to soft going: tried tongue tied. *J. Pearce* **42**

AUGUST GALE (USA) 4 b.g. Storm Cat (USA) – Lady Bonanza (USA) (Seeking The Gold (USA)) [2009 88d: p7.1g Mar 30] rather leggy, good-topped gelding: fairly useful form in maidens early in 2008 but has since lost way: tried blinkered: tongue tied on reappearance. *M. W. Easterby* **–**

AUGUSTUS JOHN (IRE) 6 gr.g. Danehill (USA) 126 – Rizerie (FR) 98 (Highest Honor (FR) 124) [2009 76: f11d^3 f12g^3 p12g^2 p12g^2 p13.9g* f14g^3 p16g^2 p16g 13.3g 12m^4 p12.2g^5 p12.2g^3 p13.9g^2 p13.9g^2 Dec 17] strong, useful-looking gelding: fair handicapper: claimed from S. Parr £6,000 fourth start: won at Wolverhampton (amateurs) in March: stays easy 2m, effective at much shorter: acts on all-weather and good to firm going: tried in headgear/tongue tie: held up: strong traveller. *R. Brotherton* **76**

AULD ARTY (FR) 3 b. or br.g. Dansili 127 – Provisoire (USA) (Gone West (USA)) [2009 79: p6g^2 p6g* p7g^3 p7g^6 6f 7g 7f 7m Aug 23] close-coupled gelding: fair performer: won maiden at Lingfield in January: well below form on turf last 4 starts: effective at 6f/7f: acts on polytrack, good to firm and good to soft going: in cheekpieces last 5 of 6 starts: temperament under suspicion: sold £7,200 in August. *T. G. Mills* **– a77**

AULTCHARN (FR) 2 b.c. (Mar 1) Kyllachy 129 – Nuit Sans Fin (FR) (Lead On Time (USA) 123) [2009 6.5g 8v^6 Oct 24] 60,000F, 120,000Y: rather unfurnished colt: sixth foal: half-brother to useful French 1m/10.5f winner Matin de Tempete (by Cardoun) and fairly useful 2001 2-y-o 6f winner Amour Sans Fin (by Kendor): dam once-raced half-sister to dam of 3-y-o Jukebox Jury: travelled well long way when 10 lengths sixth to Multames, better effort in maidens at Newbury: should continue to progress. *B. J. Meehan* **73 p**

AUNTIE CRAIK 5 b.m. Cotation – Mrs Poppyford (Mistertopogigo (IRE) 118) [2009 p8.6g Dec 7] first foal: dam well held in bumper: showed nothing in bumpers/maiden. *S. Gollings* **–**

AUNTIE MAME 5 b.m. Diktat 126 – Mother Molly (USA) 78 (Irish River (FR) 131) [2009 73: 10.2m^3 11.7f* May 31] lengthy mare: fair handicapper: won at Bath in May: stays easy 1½m: raced only on polytrack and good going or firmer (acts on firm). *D. J. Coakley* **72**

AUNT NICOLA 3 b.f. Reel Buddy (USA) 118 – Night Gypsy 74 (Mind Games 121) [2009 85: 7m^4 6d 6m 7.1m^6 7d 6.1g^2 6g^3 Aug 30] sturdy filly: fair performer nowadays: may prove best at 5f/6f: acts on fibresand and good to firm going. *M. L. W. Bell* **77**

AUNTY BETTY (IRE) 2 b.f. (Mar 29) Camacho 118 – Jina (IRE) 36 (Petardia 113) [2009 6m Aug 10] €8,500Y, resold £8,000Y: small filly: sixth foal: half-sister to Irish 2006 2-y-o 7f winner Heather Heath (by Tendulkar) and winner up to 7f in Italy by Indian Rocket: dam Irish maiden: 33/1, very green and well held in maiden at Windsor. *M. S. Tuck* **–**

AURA 4 b.f. Barathea (IRE) 127 – Finger of Light 89 (Green Desert (USA) 127) [2009 –: f11d Jan 8] leggy filly: little form: blinkered/tongue tied last 2 starts. *H. J. L. Dunlop* **–**

AURA OF CALM (IRE) 7 ch.g. Grand Lodge (USA) 125 – Perils of Joy (IRE) 83 (Rainbow Quest (USA) 134) [2009 –: 12g 14.1m 12d Jun 17] plain gelding: little form since 2007: stays 1¾m: acts on firm ground: usually tongue tied: tried blinkered. *Ronald O'Leary, Ireland* **–**

AUREATE 5 ch.g. Jade Robbery (USA) 121 – Anne d'Autriche (IRE) 75 (Rainbow Quest (USA) 134) [2009 92: p12.2g^3 f14g* 12g 12.3m^6 f12g* f12g^2 p12.2g* 11.5m 12v^3 13.1m p13.9g^4 Oct 29] big, rangy gelding: fairly useful performer: won handicap in January and claimer in May, both at Southwell, and amateur seller at Wolverhampton in June: stays 1¾m: acts on all-weather, heavy and good to firm going: sometimes races freely. *B. Ellison* **81 a92 d**

AURORA LIGHTS 2 ch.f. (Feb 1) Fantastic Light (USA) 134 – Sweet Revival 41 (Claude Monet (USA) 121) [2009 p5.1g Dec 26] 8,000Y: half-sister to several winners, **–**

notably US Grade 1 9f/1¼m winner Sweet Return (7.5f winner in Britain at 2 yrs, by Elmaamul): dam 1¼m winner: 20/1, inadequate test when well held in maiden at Wolverhampton. *R. A. Fahey*

AURORA SKY (IRE) 3 gr.f. Hawk Wing (USA) 136 – To The Skies (USA) 89 (Sky **76**
Classic (CAN)) [2009 73: 7g^{4} 7m^{4} 8.5g^{2} 7m^{5} p8g 7d^{5} Sep 3] fair maiden handicapper: stays 8.5f: acts on polytrack and good to firm ground. *J. Akehurst*

AURORIAN (IRE) 3 b.g. Fantastic Light (USA) 134 – Aurelia 80 (Rainbow Quest **90**
(USA) 134) [2009 93: 10s^{6} 10d^{5} 10.1g^{6} 8m 10m 11d 10g^{5} p10m^{4} p12m* Dec 4] tall gelding: fairly useful handicapper: won at Lingfield in December: stays easy 1½m: acts on polytrack and good to firm going. *R. Hannon*

AUSONIUS 3 b.g. Kyllachy 129 – Baileys Silver (USA) (Marlin (USA) 124) [2009 **66**
68p: 7d 7m p10g p10g^{2} Oct 24] good-bodied gelding: modest maiden: stays 1¼m: acts on polytrack: sold 10,000 gns. *L. M. Cumani*

AUSSIE BLUE (IRE) 5 b.g. Bahamian Bounty 116 – Luanshya 78 (First Trump 118) **73**
[2009 71: 8.3m 8f 8.5m 8d 7.9g^{2} 8g* 8m^{5} 8g^{2} 8.1s 8m^{6} 7.5g^{4} 8m^{2} 8m^{3} 8g p7.1g p8m Nov 4] strong gelding: good mover: fair handicapper: won at Redcar in June: best at 1m: acts on firm and good to soft ground: tried in headgear: often held up. *R. M. Whitaker*

AUSTRALIA DAY (IRE) 6 gr.g. Key of Luck (USA) 126 – Atalina (FR) (Linamix **107**
(FR) 127) [2009 102: p10g^{5} 10m* 10m^{3} 9.9g 10.3m^{4} 12m^{2} Sep 27] good-topped gelding: useful handicapper: won at Sandown (beat Wintercast by 2½ lengths) in June: in frame 3 of next 4 starts, ran creditably when third to Fanjura at same course: stays 1½m: acts on polytrack, unraced on extremes of going on turf: exuberant sort, usually forces pace: useful hurdler, successful in September. *P. R. Webber*

AUTHENTIC 4 ch.g. Pivotal 124 – Red Passion (USA) (Seeking The Gold (USA)) **92**
[2009 7m^{4} 7.5s 8d^{4} 7.5d^{6} 7.5m* 7.5g* 7.5m^{2} 8m Sep 19] 8,000 2-y-o: second foal: brother to fairly useful 6f winner Dramatic, also successful in Sweden: dam, tailed off only start, out of smart 7f/1m winner Lovers Knot: fairly useful performer: successful 3 times in Italy, including in handicaps at Milan in May and Varese in June: left M. Gaspirini in Italy and gelded, well supported but shaped as if amiss in handicap at Ayr: stays 1m: acts on good to firm and good to soft going: tracks leaders. *L. M. Cumani*

AUTOCRACY 2 b.c. (Apr 6) Green Desert (USA) 127 – Imperial Bailiwick (IRE) 104 **70**
(Imperial Frontier (USA) 112) [2009 5m 5s^{3} p6g^{3} Oct 15] strong, compact colt: closely related to 3-y-o Impressible and half-brother to several winners, notably 8-y-o Reverence and smart 6f (at 2 yrs) to 1m winner Helm Bank (by Wild Again): dam 2-y-o 5f (including Flying Childers Stakes) winner: best effort in maidens when ½-length third to I'malwaysright at Wolverhampton final start, travelling well: stays 6f. *W. J. Haggas*

AUTUMN BLADES (IRE) 4 ch.g. Daggers Drawn (USA) 114 – September Tide **91 §**
(IRE) 58 (Thatching 131) [2009 84: p7g^{4} p7g p8g^{2} f7g* f7g^{3} 7m^{2} f7g^{3} 7m^{4} 7m 7g 7.9m p7.1g^{3} 7s^{3} 7d^{4} p7g^{3} 6g p7.1g^{3} 7m* p7m^{3} 8g^{6} p7g^{2} p7g^{2} f7m^{3} p7g^{3} p7.1g^{2} p7.1g* p7f^{4} p7g* Dec 31] compact gelding: fairly useful performer: won handicap at Southwell in March, claimer at Brighton in September, and handicaps at Wolverhampton and Lingfield, both in December: effective at 7f/easy 1m: acts on all-weather, soft and good to firm going: often wears headgear, in cheekpieces of late: consistent, but no battler. *A. Bailey*

AUTUMN CHARM 4 ch.f. Reel Buddy (USA) 118 – Eurolink Cafe (Grand Lodge **42**
(USA) 125) [2009 58: p11g p13.3g f14g p12g 10.9d 8.3m f11m 15.8g^{4} f11g^{6} Aug 25] poor performer nowadays: probably stays 13.3f: acts on all-weather: tried in cheekpieces/visor: usually held up: possibly not straightforward. *Lucinda Featherstone*

AUTUMN HARVEST 5 b.g. Beat Hollow 126 – Welsh Autumn 107 (Tenby 125) **83**
[2009 12m^{6} 12d* 11.5m^{4} 12g^{6} Jun 6] bumper winner/modest maiden hurdler: fairly useful form on Flat: 66/1, won maiden at Thirsk in May: stays 1½m: tongue tied: quirky: joined Jonjo O'Neill. *A. J. McCabe*

AUTUMN MORNING (IRE) 3 b.f. Danetime (IRE) 121 – Soviet Maid (IRE) **60**
(Soviet Star (USA) 128) [2009 62: p8.6g^{5} p9.5g^{5} p8.6g p9.5g^{2} p8.6g^{5} p8.6g^{4} p8.6g 8.3g^{4} 8f 8.1g 8f^{4} 7.1m^{6} Jul 1] lengthy filly: modest performer: free-going sort, stays 9.5f: acts on polytrack and firm ground: often slowly away: visored final outing. *P. D. Evans*

AVA DOLL 2 b.f. (Mar 29) Statue of Liberty (USA) 115 – Foolish Gift (FR) 53 (Bara- **–**
thea (IRE) 127) [2009 8d 7g p8g Nov 14] 1,000F: second foal: dam placed at 1½m: no sign of ability in maidens. *J. R. Jenkins*

A VALLEY AWAY (IRE) 5 ch.m. City On A Hill (USA) 114 – Sharkiyah (IRE) 75 **–**
(Polish Precedent (USA) 131) [2009 –: f11s^{4} p11g Jan 10] little form in maidens/handicap. *Jane Chapple-Hyam*

AVA'S WORLD (IRE) 5 b.m. Desert Prince (IRE) 130 – Taibhseach (USA) 94 (Secreto (USA) 128) [2009 46: 5f^{6} 5g^{4} 6g^{6} Aug 4] small mare: little form in 2009: tried blinkered. *Peter Grayson* –

AVE 3 b.f. Danehill Dancer (IRE) 117 – Anna Amalia (IRE) (In The Wings 128) [2009 96p: 8m^{3} 8d* 10.4g^{2} 9.9g* 9.5m* 12m Oct 17] lengthy filly: has scope: smart performer: won handicap at Salisbury in July, listed race there in August and Denny Cordell Lavarack & Lanwades Stud Fillies Stakes at Gowran (beat Choose Me 1½ lengths) in September: well below form in Pride Stakes at Newmarket final outing: stays 10.4f: acts on polytrack, good to firm and good to soft going. *Sir Michael Stoute* **112**

AVEC MOI 2 b.f. (Apr 15) Reset (AUS) 124 – Pardon Moi 52 (First Trump 118) [2009 5.1m 5.2g^{4} p6g 5f p5g^{5} 6s 5.2d 5.2g^{4} 5m 6m f5g^{4} 6.1d^{6} f6g^{3} f6m^{5} p7g^{4} Nov 25] leggy filly: first foal: dam 6f winner, including at 2 yrs: poor and inconsistent maiden. *Mrs C. A. Dunnett* **47**

AVEN MAC (IRE) 3 ch.f. Indian Haven 119 – Anamara (IRE) 68 (Fairy King (USA)) [2009 54: 8.5m^{5} 8g 8m 9.8d^{2} 12.1g^{5} 12.4d^{6} 12g^{5} f12m Nov 6] leggy filly: poor maiden: stays 1½m: probably acts on heavy going: sometimes in cheekpieces: held up. *N. Bycroft* **46**

AVENUESNALLEYWAYS (IRE) 2 b.c. (Mar 28) Bertolini (USA) 125 – Princess Mood (GER) (Muhtarram (USA) 125) [2009 p6g Aug 24] €30,000F, £31,000Y: compact colt: fifth foal: half-brother to smart 6f/7f winner Kingsgate Prince (by Desert Sun), 3-y-o Captain Ramius and 5-y-o Smugglers Bay: dam German maiden: 25/1 and green, slowly away when 5 lengths seventh to dead-heaters Brick Red and Haadeeth in maiden at Kempton: likely to do better. *R. M. Beckett* **62 p**

AVEROO 4 br.g. Averti (IRE) 117 – Roo 97 (Rudimentary (USA) 118) [2009 71: p6g 7d 6m 6g 6s 6m^{2} 6m* 6m^{2} 7m* p7.1g^{4} 7m Oct 26] strong, useful-looking gelding: fair handicapper: won at Redcar in August and Leicester (apprentice event) in October: effective at 6f to 1m: acts on polytrack and good to firm going: held up: usually wears cheekpieces: has looked none too keen. *M. D. Squance* **68**

AVERROES (IRE) 2 ch.c. (May 1) Galileo (IRE) 134 – Shapely (USA) 81 (Alleged (USA) 138) [2009 7m^{4} 8.1d* 8g^{5} Sep 19] €70,000F, 100,000Y: close-coupled colt: half-brother to several winners, including fairly useful/unreliable 1m/1¼m winner Persuade (by Lure) and 5-y-o Dan Tucker: dam, 2-y-o 7f winner (only start), half-sister to dam of Prix de l'Arc de Triomphe winner Rail Link: fairly useful form: won maiden at Chepstow in August by 2¼ lengths from Comradeship: last of 5 in Prix des Chenes at Longchamp: stays 1m. *C. G. Cox* **85**

AVERTIS 4 b.g. Averti (IRE) 117 – Double Stake (USA) (Kokand (USA)) [2009 86: 8m^{3} f8g^{3} p7.1g p9.5g f8m^{3} p8m p7f f8f* f8g Dec 27] good-topped gelding: fairly useful handicapper: won at Southwell in December: stays 8.6f: acts on all-weather and good to firm ground: tried in headgear: tongue tied: often makes running. *Stef Liddiard* **86**

AVERTITOP 4 b.g. Averti (IRE) 117 – Lucayan Belle (Cadeaux Genereux 131) [2009 62: 7d Mar 31] close-coupled gelding: fair maiden at 2 yrs: below form all starts since: stays 7f: acts on good to firm going, probably on polytrack. *J. Gallagher* –

AVERTOR 3 b.g. Oasis Dream 129 – Avessia 65 (Averti (IRE) 117) [2009 6d^{2} 5g* 5d^{4} Jun 26] first foal: dam twice-raced sister/half-sister to very smart sprinters Avonbridge and Patavellian: fairly useful form: won maiden at Doncaster in June by 4½ lengths from She's In The Money, making all: said to have finished lame on handicap debut next time (has had knee problems): will prove best at 5f/6f. *R. Charlton* **85**

AVERTUOSO 5 b.g. Averti (IRE) 117 – First Musical 107 (First Trump 118) [2009 87: 6m 5g 5g^{5} 5d 5m^{2} 5d^{6} Oct 28] big, strong gelding: type to carry condition: fair handicapper nowadays: best at 5f: acts on firm and good to soft going: effective with or without visor: tried tongue tied: often slowly away. *B. Smart* **72**

AVERY 5 gr.g. Averti (IRE) 117 – Bandanna 98 (Bandmaster (USA) 97) [2009 –: p7.1g Jan 9] maiden: no form since 2007: tried blinkered. *R. J. Hodges* –

AVIATE 2 b.f. (Feb 24) Dansili 127 – Emplane (USA) 101 (Irish River (FR) 131) [2009 p8m* Nov 19] seventh foal: sister to smart French 2004 2-y-o 7f winner Early March and useful 2008 2-y-o 7f winner Wingwalker and half-sister to 3 winners: dam, 1m winner, sister to smart 1¼m performer Boatman: 7/4 favourite, promising debut when winning maiden at Kempton readily by length from Clairvoyance, slowly away and quickening to lead final 1f: useful prospect. *H. R. A. Cecil* **86 p**

AVISO (GER) 5 b.g. Tertullian (USA) 115 – Akasma (GER) (Windwurf (GER)) [2009 93: p10g f8g p8g^{6} 10.3g 8g Jul 31] big, rangy ex-German gelding: useful performer at best: just fair form in Britain: stays 1m: acts on soft and good to firm ground. *B. J. Curley* **75**

AVITUS 3 gr. or ro.g. Monsieur Bond (IRE) 120 – Top 74 (Shirley Heights 130) [2009 –: **65**
9.8m^3 9f^2 12.1g 12m 10m^2 Sep 24] stocky gelding: fair maiden: stays 1¼m: acts on firm
going. *Micky Hammond*

AVOCA DANCER (IRE) 6 ch.m. Compton Place 125 – Kashra (IRE) 95 (Dancing **62**
Dissident (USA) 119) [2009 70: f7d p6g f6g^3 f6g^4 p6g^5 p6g 6g p6g^3 7f* p7.1g^4 p7g 6g
7.6d 7.6m^6 7.1d^5 p7m^5 p7m^5 Oct 26] sturdy, lengthy mare: modest handicapper: left Gay
Kelleway £800 after fifth start: won at Lingfield in June: best around 7f nowadays: acts
on all-weather, firm and good to soft ground: wears headgear: held up. *Karen George*

AVOIR CHOISI (IRE) 3 ch.g. Choisir (AUS) 126 – Dolara (IRE) (Dolphin Street **71**
(FR) 125) [2009 67p: p8g^2 p7g* 8f^3 f7g 8m p11g^6 8m p9.5g 7.2g f7m Dec 15] tall,
lengthy gelding: fair performer: won maiden at Kempton in January: left P. Chapple-
Hyam 10,000 gns after sixth start, I. Semple after ninth: may prove best around 7f: acts
on polytrack and firm going. *N. Wilson*

AVON CALLED 2 b.f. (Jan 27) Avonbridge 123 – Bahawir Pour (USA) (Green Dancer **–**
(USA) 132) [2009 p8.6g Oct 2] 3,000F: half-sister to several winners, including 2002
2-y-o 7f winner Captain Saif (by Compton Place) and 1m winner Future's Dream (by
Bertolini), both useful: dam unraced: 33/1 and green, tailed off in maiden at Wolverhampton. *W. M. Brisbourne*

AVON CASTLE 2 b.f. (May 3) Avonbridge 123 – Castellina (USA) (Danzig Connec- **64**
tion (USA)) [2009 p5g p6m^6 p6g^2 p7g^6 Dec 31] half-sister to several winners, including
Irish 7-y-o Blaise Hollow and 2002 2-y-o 1m winner Blaise Castle (by Irish River), both
useful: dam, US 8.5f winner, half-sister to US Grade 1 1¼m winner Chelsey Flower:
modest maiden: best effort when neck second to Two Kisses at Wolverhampton: should
stay 7f: raced only on polytrack. *G. L. Moore*

AVONCREEK 5 b.g. Tipsy Creek (USA) 115 – Avondale Girl (IRE) 73 (Case Law 113) **47**
[2009 65: 6g 6.1f^6 6m 7.6m 6g 5.9d^6 6m^5 6m Sep 23] close-coupled, quite attractive
gelding: poor performer nowadays: best at 5f/6f: acts on polytrack, firm and good to soft
going: has worn cheekpieces. *B. P. J. Baugh*

AVONGATE 2 b.g. (Mar 29) Avonbridge 123 – Palacegate Episode (IRE) 111 **73**
(Drumalis 125) [2009 6m 5.7g 6d* 6m p6m Oct 28] £74,000Y: rather leggy gelding: half-
brother to 3 winners, including smart Scandinavian sprinter King Quantas (by Danehill)
and fairly useful 2002 2-y-o 6f winner Gilded Edge (by Cadeaux Genereux), and to dam
of very smart sprinter/miler Dutch Art: dam prolific 5f winner, including at 2 yrs: best
effort when winning maiden at Newbury in August by ½ length from Tasmeem: well
held in 2 nurseries, then gelded: likely to prove best at 5f/6f: acts on good to soft going.
R. Hannon

AVON GROUNDS 2 b.c. (Mar 24) Avonbridge 123 – Good Grounds (USA) (Alleged **–**
(USA) 138) [2009 6.1m 7m 7.1m^6 p5g Oct 21] small colt: well held in maidens/nursery:
tried in cheekpieces. *J. M. Bradley*

AVON KRYSTAL 2 b.f. (Feb 23) Avonbridge 123 – Kryssa 82 (Kris 135) [2009 6m **–**
5.1v^4 p6g 8m Sep 12] smallish filly: first foal: dam, 5f to 1m winner, from family of very
smart sprinter Avonbridge: well held in maidens/claimer. *R. Hannon*

AVON LADY 2 b.f. (Mar 18) Avonbridge 123 – Delightful Rhythm (USA) (Diesis 133) **69 p**
[2009 7f^6 8d* Oct 15] second foal: dam unraced half-sister to useful performer up to 1¾m
Pentatonic: better effort in maidens when winning at Brighton by neck from Harlestone
Times: stays 1m: should progress again. *J. R. Fanshawe*

AVONLINI 3 b.f. Bertolini (USA) 125 – Avondale Girl (IRE) 73 (Case Law 113) [2009 **42**
–: 7.1g^6 6.1m 7m p8.6g Sep 3] poor maiden. *B. P. J. Baugh*

AVON RIVER 2 ch.c. (Feb 12) Avonbridge 123 – Night Kiss (FR) 71 (Night Shift **82**
(USA)) [2009 5.1g p5g* 6g 7m* 7d 7g^3 7.1g 8m Sep 8] £21,000Y: lengthy colt: first foal:
dam 7f winner (including at 2 yrs): fairly useful performer: won maiden at Kempton in
May and minor event at Doncaster in June: creditable effort after only when third in
nursery at Salisbury: stays 7f: acts on polytrack and good to firm ground. *R. Hannon*

AVON ROCK 2 b.g. (Mar 18) Avonbridge 123 – Big Pink (IRE) (Bigstone (IRE) 126) **54**
[2009 6m 6.5g 7d Oct 22] good-topped gelding: form in maidens only when seventh to
Exceedingly Bold at Newbury second start: bred to stay 7f+: tongue tied. *J. W. Hills*

AVONROSE 2 b.f. (Apr 3) Avonbridge 123 – Loveleaves 93 (Polar Falcon (USA) 126) **85**
[2009 5f 6m* 6m^5 6f^2 6s^6 7.1g^2 6.5m 6m Oct 3] 20,000Y: tall filly: fourth foal: half-sister
to 5-y-o Lovelace: dam 1m winner: fairly useful performer: won maiden at Redcar in
May: good efforts in listed event at Cork and minor event at Haydock next 2 starts: stays
7f: acts on good to firm going (ran poorly on soft): races prominently. *M. Johnston*

AVONTUUR (FR) 7 ch.g. Kabool 119 – Ipoh (FR) (Funambule (USA) 118) [2009 70: **77**
f6g f7g 6.9g p7.1g* 6g^3 7g^2 5.9g^2 7g 6g^4 6g^4 6g^6 7m 6m^4 6m* 6g^2 6m 6d^3 7.2g Oct 23] lengthy gelding: fair handicapper: won at Wolverhampton in June and Newcastle in August: best at 6f/7f: acts on all-weather, heavy and good to firm going: has worn cheekpieces, back in blinkers last 5 starts. *Mrs R. A. Carr*

AVONVALLEY 2 b.f. (Feb 8) Avonbridge 123 – Piper's Ash (USA) 84 (Royal **74**
Academy (USA) 130) [2009 5.1g^3 5.1g^2 p5.1g^2 5.1g* 5m 5.1g^3 5.2m 5.7f^4 Aug 22] **a79**
4,000Y: lengthy, workmanlike filly: first foal: dam 2-y-o 5f winner: fair performer: won maiden at Chepstow in May: will stay 6f: best effort on polytrack. *M. S. Saunders*

AVOW (USA) 2 b.g. (May 7) Mingun (USA) 117 – Knoosh (USA) 113 (Storm Bird **69 §**
(CAN) 134) [2009 6d 7m 7g^3 7g 7g^5 p6g^3 7g p7.1g^2 p6m^2 Sep 26] big gelding: fair maiden: stays 7f: acts on polytrack, best turf effort on good going: usually blinkered: ungenuine: gelded after final start. *J. S. Moore*

AVRILO 3 ch.f. Piccolo 121 – Arctic High 62 (Polar Falcon (USA) 126) [2009 –: f8g^3 **62**
8d 5.7f 5f^4 5.1f^2 6f 5.2s^6 5.1g^2 5.1g^2 5m^4 5.1d^3 p5f^2 p5.1g^4 p5g^2 p6g p6g Nov 13] plain filly: modest maiden handicapper: best at 5f: acts on polytrack, firm and good to soft going. *M. S. Saunders*

AWAIT THE DAWN (USA) 2 b.c. (Mar 23) Giant's Causeway (USA) 132 – **99 p**
Valentine Band (USA) 104 (Dixieland Band (USA)) [2009 8s* 7m Sep 12] good-bodied colt: fifth foal: half-brother to smart French 1m (at 2 yrs)/9f winner Putney Bridge (by Mizzen Mast): dam, 1¼m winner, half-sister to smart French miler Multiplex and smart performer up to 1¾m Memorise out of sister to Irish Derby runner-up Deploy and half-sister to Warning and Commander In Chief: useful form: won maiden at Naas in July impressively by 4 lengths from Banyan Tree: well below that form when last of 7 to Poet's Voice in Champagne Stakes at Doncaster: will prove best at 1m+: acts on soft going: remains capable of better. *A. P. O'Brien, Ireland*

AWAKEN 8 b.m. Zafonic (USA) 130 – Dawna 106 (Polish Precedent (USA) 131) [2009 **51**
–: 9.9m 9.3m 10.1m^3 10f^4 9m 10.1m Aug 13] modest performer: stays 11f: acts on firm and good to soft going: held up. *Miss Tracy Waggott*

AWANI 3 b.f. Sakhee (USA) 136 – Hatton Gardens 96 (Auction Ring (USA) 123) [2009 **51**
10d 10v p12g^3 f11g p12m^6 Sep 30] 100,000Y: half-sister to several winners, including smart Irish 7f (at 2 yrs) and 12.5f winner Lime Gardens (by Sadler's Wells) and useful 7f (at 2 yrs) to 10.4f winner Ludgate (by Lyphard): dam, Irish 6f to 1m winner, half-sister to high-class 1m/1¼m performer Kooyonga: modest maiden: left Caroline Hutchinson in Ireland after second start: stays 1½m: acts on polytrack and good to soft going. *E. F. Vaughan*

AWASEEF (USA) 2 ch.f. (Mar 31) Haafhd 129 – Emtyazat (Gone West (USA)) [2009 **78**
p7g^3 p8m^2 Sep 16] first foal: dam unraced half-sister to very smart US Grade 1 1m winner Corinthian: placed in maidens at Kempton, odds on and better effort when ¾-length second to Wild Rose: stays 1m. *J. H. M. Gosden*

AWATUKI (IRE) 6 b.g. Distant Music (USA) 126 – Itkan (IRE) (Marju (IRE) 127) **64**
[2009 –, a91: 10g 9g 10d^3 p10m^5 p10m Dec 16] strong, workmanlike gelding: handicapper, just modest form in 2009: stays 11f: acts on polytrack, firm and good to soft ground. *J. R. Boyle*

AWE 5 b.g. Muhtarram (USA) 125 – Fleet of Light 94 (Spectrum (IRE) 126) [2009 8.1g **–**
Jun 22] no form. *Mrs N. S. Evans*

AWESOME ACT (USA) 2 ch.c. (Apr 17) Awesome Again (CAN) 133 – Houdini's **108**
Honey (USA) 84 (Mr Prospector (USA)) [2009 7d^2 7g^2 p7g^3 7m* 7m 8f^4 Nov 7] $240,000Y: well-made colt: fourth foal: dam, 1¼m winner (later won in USA), sister to 2000 Guineas runner-up Machiavellian and half-sister to very smart French performer up to 1¼m Exit To Nowhere: useful form: won maiden at Goodwood in October by 1¼ lengths from Morana: further improvement when 1½ lengths fourth to Pounced in Breeders' Cup Juvenile Turf at Santa Anita, taking strong hold but staying on well: will stay 1¼m: acts on polytrack and firm going. *J. Noseda*

AWESOME SURPRISE (USA) 3 b.f. Awesome Again (CAN) 133 – Native Roots **76**
(IRE) (Indian Ridge 123) [2009 8m^4 8.3m^2 7m^3 p8.6g* Sep 11] $400,000Y: attractive filly: fourth foal: sister to very smart 2004 2-y-o 6f to 8.5f (Breeders' Cup Juvenile) winner Wilko, stayed 1¼m, and half-sister to fairly useful 1¼m winner Aboriginie (by Street Cry): dam US 6.5f winner: fair performer: won maiden at Wolverhampton: should stay 1¼m: raced only on polytrack and good to firm going: sent to USA. *J. Noseda*

AWINNERSGAME (IRE) 3 b.g. Kyllachy 129 – Polish Descent (IRE) (Danehill **111**
(USA) 126) [2009 112: 7m^2 6d^3 6g^5 7m 6m* 6g Oct 10] close-coupled gelding: smart

performer: won 4-runner minor event at Yarmouth in September by 1¼ lengths from Global City: well held in pattern races at Ascot either side, but had run well when second to Ouqba in listed Free Handicap at Newmarket earlier: stays 7f: acts on firm and soft going: held up: tried visored. *J. Noseda*

A WISH FOR YOU 4 ch.f. Tumbleweed Ridge 117 – Peperonata (IRE) 91 (Cyrano de Bergerac 120) [2009 70d: p6g Jan 9] sturdy, lengthy filly: one-time fair performer: well held since early-2008: often wears blinkers/cheekpieces. *D. K. Ivory* **–**

AWSAAL 2 b.c. (Feb 9) Nayef (USA) 129 – Design Perfection (USA) 105 (Diesis 133) [2009 7g Oct 30] 280,000Y: well-made colt: third foal: half-brother to 4-y-o Capucci: dam 1¼m winner (ran twice), out of sister to high-class 1¼m performer Stagecraft: 14/1, mid-field in maiden at Newmarket, considerately handled once held: will stay at least 1m: should improve. *J. L. Dunlop* **65 p**

AWZAAN 2 br.c. (Feb 8) Alhaarth (IRE) 126 – Nufoos 110 (Zafonic (USA) 130) [2009 6g* 6m* 6m* 6m* Oct 2] **119 p**

Quantity rather than quality seems to be what matters for some breeders, who set great store by statistics based on progeny earnings or numbers of winners to gauge the merit of a stallion. The method is not so readily accepted for assessing the merits of trainers and jockeys, though prize money and/or numbers of winners still form the basis of seasonal tables. Mark Johnston's numerical domination of the trainers' table and his feat of passing the two-hundred-winner mark in October merited no shortage of praise but, if anything, the media seemed to underplay the feat, certainly compared to the exposure when jumps trainer Martin Pipe reached the same seasonal milestone for the first time in 1988/9. With year-round racing and a gradual expansion of the fixture list, there are considerably more races now than a couple of decades ago, which certainly provides some perspective for Henry Cecil's superb achievement in sending out eighty-nine horses to win one hundred and eighty races from four hundred and forty-five starts in Britain in 1987. His percentage of winners to runners was just over forty per cent and the tally included twenty-four of the ninety-nine British pattern races, including six Group 1s.

Mark Johnston's runners achieved a strike rate of just under eighteen per cent with his two hundred and sixteen winners which included five in British pattern races. These came from Awzaan (Mill Reef Stakes and Middle Park Stakes), Holberg (Queen's Vase), Jukebox Jury (Rose of Lancaster Stakes) and Shakespearean (Solario Stakes). The Derby Italiano and St Leger winner Mastery also started the year with Johnston before joining Godolphin. Jukebox Jury and Lady Jane Digby landed pattern races on foreign soil and Shakespearean won the Goffs Million Mile. These major victories were among five wins outside Britain and took Johnston's overall score to two hundred and twenty-one (over a hundred of them for Sheikh Mohammed's son, Sheikh Hamdan bin Mohammed). Johnston profited from the wider range of opportunities and from the fact that the momentum of his stable—one of the largest in Britain—was not interrupted by illness. For the purposes of comparison, champion trainer Sir Michael Stoute's team notched ninety-nine wins at a strike rate of twenty-three per cent and Richard Hannon's one hundred and eighty-eight wins yielded a ratio of winners to runners of just under fourteen per cent. Beating the record of one hundred and eighty-nine set by Hannon the year before, then reaching two hundred when Corsica won at Ayr, must have given Johnston a tremendous feeling of satisfaction, especially as it came with record 1, 2, 3 earnings for the stable of £2,607,701 at home and over £1m abroad, helped considerably, of course, by Shakespearean's richly-endowed sales race success. 'I certainly never thought about it at the start of the season,' said Johnston, 'when I set myself a target of one hundred and sixty-six to beat my previous best.' Mind you, Johnston's achievement is still a long way short of the world record set by American trainer Steve Asmussen in 2009 with six hundred and fifty wins from just under three thousand starts.

Exceptionally for a subsequent Group 1 winner, Awzaan started his career in a maiden at Hamilton, a track at which, incidentally, dual listed winner Layla's Hero also got off the mark. Among Johnston's other good two-year-olds from previous seasons, Shamardal won his first race at Ayr, Attraction her first at Nottingham and Kirklees his first at Catterick. Johnston has runners on virtually every course over the year and boasts the best record of any trainer at Hamilton

Dubai Duty Free Mill Reef Stakes, Newbury—Awzaan takes the step up in class in his stride and pulls away from Angel's Pursuit, Quarrel (grey) and Radiohead (right)

over the last five years. Despite this, Awzaan did not start favourite in the field of six. That position went to Paradise Spectre, who had finished fourth of five on his debut and ended the year still a maiden. Awzaan beat Paradise Spectre by a length and he was not the market leader on his next appearance either, going off 9/1 joint-seventh favourite of ten—all of whom had won last time—in a minor event at Newmarket in July. Awzaan certainly made an impression this time, winning by five lengths from Amary, his cause probably helped nonetheless by some of his opponents setting too strong gallop. As they dropped out, Awzaan came through from behind to lead a furlong out and draw clear in style.

One of the races Johnston has used before as a stepping-stone for one of his good juveniles is the Vintage Stakes at Goodwood, another course at which he has a superb record. Lucky Story and Shamardal both won the Vintage, but there was no Johnston contender this time, nor was there in the Richmond Stakes, Awzaan bypassing Goodwood and not being seen out again until more than ten weeks later in the Dubai Duty Free Mill Reef Stakes at Newbury. His absence from the course was reportedly on the explicit instructions of owner Hamdan Al Maktoum, who felt a break would be of benefit. Maintaining what was fast becoming a tradition, Awzaan again failed to start favourite in the seven-runner Mill Reef, sent off second choice behind 5/4-shot Radiohead who had a penalty for his win in the Norfolk Stakes, the only pattern win recorded by any of the runners (he had finished a creditable third in the Nunthorpe on his latest appearance). The other runners had all won, and Angel's Pursuit had also finished a close second in a listed race at Deauville, but it was not a vintage line-up for a Mill Reef. Awzaan took the step up in class in his stride. Waited with again, as Ascot and Chester winner Quarrel took them along, Awzaan produced a fine turn of foot to lead inside the final furlong and was fully in control as he held off the challenging Angel's Pursuit to win by a length and a quarter, with Radiohead below form in fourth.

On the face of it, despite the races being less than a fortnight apart the Middle Park Stakes is an obvious target for the winner of the Mill Reef. However, only four colts have completed the double—Habat in 1973, Formidable in 1977, Primo Valentino in 1999 and Dark Angel in 2007—while the filly Forest Flower, who won the 1986 Mill Reef, went on to be first past the post in the Cheveley Park Stakes. The Middle Park has been sponsored by Hamdan Al Maktoum's Shadwell Stud since 2002 and the closest the owner had come to winning it, with very few runners, since that date (he had won it with Fard in 1994 and Hayil in 1997) was with third-placed Tajdeef in 2007. Much like the Prix Morny, which also attracted a field of only five, there could be no complaints about the quality of those that lined up for the Middle Park. As in the Morny, there were no runners from Ballydoyle, but all of the quintet were pattern winners. In addition to Awzaan, Radiohead was turned out again, Poet's Voice had landed the Champagne Stakes, Showcasing had achieved a similarly impressive victory in the Gimcrack Stakes and Irish raider Arctic was unbeaten in three starts, including a smooth victory in the Group 3 Round Tower Stakes last time. Awzaan did not start favourite this time either, sent off as third choice behind Poet's Voice and Showcasing. Awzaan broke well but, as Poet's Voice led from Showcasing, Richard Hills eased him back to fourth. Two furlongs out, Awzaan produced his trademark turn of foot to take it up over a furlong out. Once in front, he tended to drift left—reports that he hung violently are wide of the mark—which didn't do Poet's Voice any favours, though it had no effect on the outcome. With Poet's Voice and Showcasing clearly held, Radiohead came from last to throw down the biggest challenge but Awzaan always had his measure and passed the post three quarters of a length to the good, with Showcasing a neck away third. Hills was suspended for a day for careless riding. Immediately after the Middle Park, Awzaan was quoted variously at between 7/1 and 14/1 for the Two Thousand Guineas; he had been on offer at 12/1 after the Mill Reef. By the end of the year, in the wake of St Nicholas Abbey's performance in the Racing Post Trophy, 12/1 was freely available about Awzaan.

Awzaan is something of a chip of the old block since his sire Alhaarth, also owned by Hamdan Al Maktoum, was also unbeaten in his first season, in the process proving himself the best of his generation when winning the Dewhurst. Alhaarth raced exclusively over seven furlongs at two and proved effective at middle distances at three and at four. He has had an in-and-out career at stud and has had only two other Group 1 winners, Haafhd, successful in the Two Thousand Guineas and Champion Stakes, and globe-trotting middle-distance performer Phoenix Reach, who notched big races in Canada, Hong Kong and Dubai. Alhaarth's Group 2 winners include the good middle-distance stayer Bandari—who was also trained by Mark Johnston—and smart sprinter Dominica. Awzaan's chances of staying a mile are quite good, though there is more speed on the dam's side. Awzaan is the first foal of Nufoos (as a point of interest, a number of other two-year-old Group 1 winners were also first foals, namely Arcano, Beethoven, Jan Vermeer, Rosanara, Siyouni and Special Duty; though there are more first foals in the thoroughbred population than second foals, and so on, this represents a remarkable concentration). Nufoos was trained by Johnston, following the well-tried practice of sending a mare's progeny to the person who trained her, which can and does reap dividends, though it is not followed by every large-scale owner-breeder. Nufoos was campaigned in typical style for one of Johnston's, having thirteen starts in two years and finishing out of the frame in only three of them.

Shadwell Middle Park Stakes, Newmarket—Awzaan, now at Group 1 level, remains unbeaten; Radiohead (rail) is much closer this time, while Showcasing (blaze) and Poet's Voice (left) are also in contention

Mr Hamdan Al Maktoum's "Awzaan"

Awzaan (br.c. Feb 8, 2007)	Alhaarth (IRE) (b 1993)	Unfuwain (b 1985)	Northern Dancer
			Height of Fashion
		Irish Valley (ch 1982)	Irish River
			Green Valley
	Nufoos (b 2002)	Zafonic (b 1990)	Gone West
			Zaizafon
		Desert Lynx (b 1993)	Green Desert
			Sweeping

Nufoos's wins came in a six-furlong maiden and a five-furlong nursery in her first season and she won a listed race at Warwick over seven furlongs at three, when she was also a close second in the Group 3 Chartwell Fillies' Stakes over the same trip. Nufoos, who has a yearling colt by Haafhd and a colt foal by Dubai Destination, proved she just about stayed a mile on her final appearance, though she herself comes from a family principally associated with speed. Awzaan's grandam Desert Lynx won at six furlongs at both three and four and foaled five other winners, three of whom scored over a mile and a quarter. The next dam, Sweeping, won at six furlongs but stayed nine and produced three other winners including the smart sprinter Watching, as well as a winner over two and a half miles by Sadler's Wells. Most of Sweeping's best relatives were sprinters, including her dam Glancing (Prix d'Arenberg), Bassenthwaite (the 1984 Middle Park Stakes winner) and Keen Hunter (Prix de l'Abbaye de Longchamp). On balance, with the most speedy elements some way back in his pedigree, coupled with the fact that he is not a headstrong type, Awzaan should get a mile and he makes more appeal than some in the list for the Two Thousand Guineas. A good-topped colt with the scope to train on, he looks the part and, whatever happens at Newmarket, he looks to have a bright future. *M. Johnston*

AXINIT (GER) 9 gr.g. Linamix (FR) 127 – Assia (IRE) (Royal Academy (USA) 130) [2009 –: p12m Sep 23] little recent form on Flat: often in cheekpieces/tongue tie. *E. J. Creighton* **–**

AXIOM 5 ch.h. Pivotal 124 – Exhibitor (USA) 68 (Royal Academy (USA) 130) [2009 100: 8.1m^2 8m^6 7g* 7.6m^4 7m^2 Sep 26] useful-looking horse: smart performer: won minor event at Goodwood in July: good efforts in frame next 2 starts, improved again when neck second of 28 to Advanced in valuable handicap at Ascot: stays 1m: acts on polytrack, soft and good to firm going: patiently ridden. *L. M. Cumani* **113**

AYE AYE DIGBY (IRE) 4 b.g. Captain Rio 122 – Jane Digby (IRE) 84 (Magical Strike (USA) 114) [2009 96: 6d^3 6g* 6d^2 6g^6 6g* 6m^4 6g^4 6m 6d^3 6g Oct 23] strong, quite attractive gelding: has a quick action: useful handicapper: won at Goodwood in May and Newmarket in July: good length third to Arthur's Edge at Goodwood penultimate start: effective at 6f/7f: acts on good to firm and good to soft going: tends to hang. *H. Candy* **100**

AYPEEYES (IRE) 5 b.g. King Charlemagne (USA) 120 – Habaza (IRE) 68 (Shernazar 131) [2009 88: p12.2g^4 p12g 10.2g* Apr 28] rather leggy gelding: fairly useful performer: won seller at Bath: respectable efforts in handicaps previously: stays 1½m: acts on polytrack, good to firm and good to soft ground: blinkered/visored last 6 starts: joined J. K. Price, won over hurdles in June, let down by attitude after. *A. King* **79**

AYRPASSIONATA 4 ch.f. Where Or When (IRE) 124 – Least Said (USA) (Trempolino (USA) 135) [2009 –: 9.2g^5 Jun 17] well held in maidens. *I. Semple* **–**

AY TAY TATE (IRE) 3 b.g. Catcher In The Rye (IRE) 115 – Vintage Belle (IRE) (Waajib 121) [2009 74: 8.3m 8g p6m 7v p9.5g^6 p9.5g Oct 23] strong, workmanlike gelding: modest maiden nowadays: left I. McInnes after reappearance: effective at 6f to 1m: acts on good to firm and good to soft going, probably on polytrack: tried visored. *D. Shaw* **55**

AZADAY (IRE) 2 b.f. (Mar 6) Azamour (IRE) 130 – Generous Lady 98 (Generous (IRE) 139) [2009 8m 8.3m 8g Oct 23] sturdy filly: half-sister to several winners, including very smart 7f (at 2 yrs) to 1½m winner (also second in St Leger) High Accolade (by Mark of Esteem) and 5-y-o Highland Legacy: dam Irish 1½m/1¾m winner: down the field and not unduly knocked about in maidens: will be suited by 1¼m+: type to do better in handicaps. *C. F. Wall* **54 p**

AZHARIA 3 b.f. Oasis Dream 129 – Presto Vento 103 (Air Express (IRE) 125) [2009 f6g^3 p7g^5 6m^4 p7g 6m 6m p7g^5 p7g p10m Nov 3] 62,000Y: sturdy, deep-girthed filly: second foal: half-sister to 5f (at 2 yrs)/6f winner Presto Levanter (by Rock of Gibraltar): dam 5f (at 2 yrs)/7f winner: fair maiden: left C. Brittain 7,800 gns after sixth start: may prove best up to 7f: tried in cheekpieces/blinkers. *R. Hannon* **65**

AZIF 2 ch.f. (Mar 8) Where Or When (IRE) 124 – Dance Away 94 (Pivotal 124) [2009 5m^5 5g* 5s^5 5g 5m 6g 6m^5 5m Sep 22] 1,000F, 5,000Y: small, leggy filly: second foal: dam, 5f winner, ran only at 2 yrs: fair form when winning maiden at Windsor in April: lost way after next start, including in nurseries: best effort at 5f on good ground: sold 1,000 gns. *Miss Gay Kelleway* **73 d**

AZIZI 2 b.c. (Jan 30) Haafhd 129 – Harayir (USA) 119 (Gulch (USA)) [2009 6g^4 p7g* 7m* 7m^2 8m* 8g^4 Oct 10] sturdy colt: half-brother to 3 winners, including smart 1¼m winner Izdiham and useful 1½m winner Moonjaz (both by Nashwan): dam 6f (at 2 yrs) to 1m (1000 Guineas) winner: useful performer: won maiden at Lingfield in July and nurseries at Newcastle in August and Doncaster (best effort, beat Baltimore Clipper 2¼ lengths, surging clear after hanging markedly left) in September: just respectable fourth to Morana in Autumn Stakes at Ascot final outing: stays 1m: acts on polytrack and good to firm going: held up. *W. J. Haggas* **109**

AZIZ (IRE) 3 b.c. Catcher In The Rye (IRE) 115 – Imposition (UAE) (Be My Guest (USA) 126) [2009 52: 12.6g May 4] good-topped colt: modest maiden at 2 yrs: well held only outing in 2009: probably stays 1m: often blinkered. *Miss D. Mountain* **–**

AZLAK (USA) 2 ch.c. (May 22) Shamardal (USA) 129 – Nasaieb (IRE) 89 (Fairy King (USA)) [2009 7g 7g 8.1g^6 8m^6 Sep 12] big, strong colt: modest form at best in maidens: well held in nursery at Doncaster (slowly away). *C. E. Brittain* **60**

AZMEEL 2 b.c. (Feb 14) Azamour (IRE) 130 – Best Side (IRE) 100 (King's Best (USA) 132) [2009 7.1g* 7m* 8g Sep 27] 60,000F, €65,000Y: strong, useful-looking colt: first foal: dam, Irish 7f (at 2 yrs)/1m winner, half-sister to 3-y-o Grand Ducal and 5-y-o Al Khaleej: impressive winner of maiden at Sandown in July and listed event at Newbury (beat Practitioner comfortably by 3½ lengths) in August: never better than mid-field in valuable sales race at the Curragh: should stay 1m: slowly away first/final outings: useful. *J. H. M. Gosden* **105**

AZURE MIST 4 ch.f. Bahamian Bounty 116 – Inquirendo (USA) 81 (Roberto (USA) **79**
131) [2009 76: 6g^3 6g^2 7m 6g^3 7f^3 7g 7g* Oct 20] sparely-made filly: fair handicapper:
won at Yarmouth in October: barely stays easy 1¼m, effective at much shorter: acts on
polytrack, firm and good to soft going: tough and consistent. *M. H. Tompkins*

AZYGOUS 6 ch.g. Foxhound (USA) 103 – Flag (Selkirk (USA) 129) [2009 71: 5m 5m **–**
Aug 16] neat gelding: fair handicapper at best: well held in 2009: best at 5f/6f: acts on
polytrack, firm and good to soft going: tried in headgear. *M. W. Easterby*

AZZEZ LIFE 2 br.g. (Apr 2) Avonbridge 123 – Glascoed (Adbass (USA) 102) [2009 **–**
5g 6.1g 6g 5m f6g Nov 17] close-coupled gelding: no form: tried blinkered. *R. C. Guest*

B

BAAHER (USA) 5 b.g. War Chant (USA) 126 – Raajiya (USA) 83 (Gulch (USA)) **67**
[2009 67d: 13.1d^2 16.1d 17.5m 16.1d Oct 13] fair maiden handicapper: stays 13f: acts on
polytrack and good to soft ground: tried in cheekpieces. *J. S. Goldie*

BAAN (USA) 6 ch.g. Diesis 133 – Madaen (USA) (Nureyev (USA) 131) [2009 74§: **72**
p14g^3 p16.5g^2 p16g^2 p16g^4 15g^3 p12.2g^6 16d* 16d* 16d^4 16.4d^5 p16.5g 18g^3 15.8s
Oct 27] small, good-topped gelding: fair handicapper: won at Yarmouth in July and
Thirsk in August: stays 2m: acts on all-weather, soft and good to firm going: has worn
headgear (in cheekpieces final 4 outings): quirky but reliable. *H. J. Collingridge*

BAARIQ 3 b.g. Royal Applause 124 – Second of May 72 (Lion Cavern (USA) 117) **78**
[2009 82: 8m 7d 7d p7.1m p8g^5 Oct 14] tall, good-topped gelding: fair handicapper: best
form at 7f: acts on polytrack and good to firm going: sold 3,200 gns. *P. W. Chapple-Hyam*

BABA GHANOUSH 7 ch.m. Zaha (CAN) 106 – Vrennan 74 (Suave Dancer (USA) **53**
136) [2009 46: p6g^3 p6g p8g p8g p7g p8g^3 p8g^3 p8g p8m Dec 6] modest performer: stays
1m: raced mainly on polytrack: wears headgear. *M. J. Attwater*

BABAJAGA (IRE) 2 ch.f. (Apr 18) Night Shift (USA) – Art Fair (Alzao (USA) 117) **–**
[2009 p6g 6s Jul 21] €20,000Y, 18,000 2-y-o: fourth foal: half-sister to 3 winners in Italy,
including 1m winner Last Samurai (by One Cool Cat): dam unraced out of Prix de Diane
winner Lypharita: well beaten in maidens: has flashed tail: sold 800 gns in October, sent
to Spain. *J. M. P. Eustace*

BAB AL SALAM (USA) 3 b.c. Seeking The Gold (USA) – Encandiladora (ARG) **111**
(Equalize (USA)) [2009 91p: 8.1g* p10f* 10.2m* 10m^3 p10m* Nov 3] good-topped colt:
smart handicapper: progressed to win at Sandown in August, Lingfield and Bath in
September, and Kempton (beat Waldvogel 3¼ lengths, travelling strongly) in November:
stays 1¼m: raced only on polytrack and good/good to firm going. *Saeed bin Suroor*

BAB AL SHAMS (IRE) 2 b.c. (Feb 13) Cape Cross (IRE) 129 – Shimna 62 (Mr **85 p**
Prospector (USA)) [2009 8m^2 7m Oct 3] 200,000Y: rangy colt: sixth foal: brother to 3-y-o
Black Eagle, closely related to useful 7f (at 2 yrs)/1m (in US) winner Santa Fe (by Green
Desert) and half-brother to smart 1m (at 2 yrs)/1¼m winner Hazeymm (by Marju) and
5-y-o Sahrati: dam, ran once in Ireland, half-sister to St Leger winner Shantou: 15/8,
promising debut when 2 lengths second to Rigidity (pair clear) in maiden at Yarmouth,
eased late: unsuited by drop in trip and poorly drawn in sales race at Newmarket: will be
suited by 1¼m+: useful prospect. *Saeed bin Suroor*

BAB AT THE BOWSTER (IRE) 2 b.f. (Mar 2) Footstepsinthesand 120 – Charm- **84**
ingly (USA) 62 (King of Kings (IRE) 125) [2009 6g^3 7f* 7.1g 7m* 7m* Oct 3] €25,000F,
€24,000Y: quite good-topped filly: second foal: half-sister to 3-y-o Full of Love: dam,
ran 3 times in Ireland, out of half-sister to top-class miler Zilzal: fairly useful performer:
won maiden at Brighton in August and nurseries at Chester in September and Newmarket
(further improvement, beat Cash Queen Anna by short head despite hanging markedly
left) in October: stays 7f: acts on firm ground: sold 115,000 gns. *W. J. Haggas*

BABEL 4 b.f. Xaar 132 – Day Star 77 (Dayjur (USA) 137) [2009 78: p5g p5g p5g^6 **54**
Mar 20] just modest performer in 2009: speedy, likely to prove best at 5f: acts on poly-
track and good to soft ground: usually races up with pace: sent to Syrian Arab Rebublic.
M. Wigham

BABILU 4 ch.f. Lomitas 129 – Creeking 65 (Persian Bold 123) [2009 76: 12d^3 12d **67**
11.9f^4 16.2v* Jul 24] big filly: fair performer: won claimer at Chepstow (joined D. Burchell £10,000) in July: stays 2m: acts on polytrack and heavy ground. *A. G. Newcombe*

BABYCAKES (IRE) 2 b.f. (Feb 2) Marju (IRE) 127 – Dark Rosaleen (IRE) (Darshaan **–**
133) [2009 8g p8g Nov 14] 90,000Y: third foal: half-sister to 4-y-o Rosaleen and 5-y-o
Rosbay: dam unraced: well held in maidens. *M. L. W. Bell*

BABY DOTTIE 2 ch.f. (Mar 19) Dr Fong (USA) 128 – Auntie Dot Com 70 (Tagula (IRE) 116) [2009 p6g^2 6m^2 6.5m^6 p5m^3 p7g^2 p7m^3 Oct 31] rather leggy filly: third foal: half-sister to 3-y-o Young Dottie: dam 2-y-o 5f winner: fair maiden: barely stays easy 7f: raced on polytrack/good to firm ground. *P. M. Phelan* **71**

BABY IS HERE (IRE) 3 b.f. Namid 128 – Attymon Lill (IRE) (Marju (IRE) 127) [2009 –: p12m^6 Nov 19] no form. *D. J. S. ffrench Davis* **–**

BABY JOSR 3 b.g. Josr Algarhoud (IRE) 118 – Bella Helena (Balidar 133) [2009 55: p6g* p6g^3 8.3g^5 7g^4 8s 9m p7g^2 p7g 8.1m p8m Sep 24] workmanlike gelding: modest handicapper: won at Wolverhampton in March: probably stays 1m: acts on polytrack, best turf effort on good ground: usually visored/tongue tied: sold £800. *I. A. Wood* **61 a64**

BABY JUDGE (IRE) 2 ch.g. (Feb 20) Captain Rio 122 – Darling Clementine (Lion Cavern (USA) 117) [2009 5g 6g 5g^4 5m 5m^5 f6m^5 f5g 6m f5g^6 5d^6 7g^3 7m* 8g 7m^3 7v^6 f6m f5g^4 f7g Dec 18] workmanlike gelding: modest performer: claimed from R. Harris £6,000 second start: won nursery at Yarmouth in September: should prove as effective at 6f as 7f: acts on good to firm going: tried blinkered: not straightforward. *M. C. Chapman* **62 §**

BABYLONIAN 2 b.f. (Mar 19) Shamardal (USA) 129 – Evil Empire (GER) 108 (Acatenango (GER) 127) [2009 6m^3 6g^2 6m^5 Jul 10] good-bodied filly: has scope: sixth foal: half-sister to smart 11f/1½m winner Counterpunch (by Halling) and useful 2006 2-y-o 1m/1¼m winner Empire Day (by Lomitas): dam German 7f to 1½m winner: fair form in maidens: will do better at 1m+. *M. Johnston* **66 p**

BABY QUEEN (IRE) 3 b.f. Royal Applause 124 – Kissing Time 79 (Lugana Beach 116) [2009 p6g p5.1m^5 6m 5.1m 5.1g* 5.1f* 5m 5d^6 5m Aug 9] 1,500 2-y-o: workmanlike filly: fourth foal: half-sister to 2005 2-y-o 7f winner Fun Time (by Fraam): dam, 5f (including at 2 yrs) winner, half-sister to smart sprinter Acclamation (by Royal Applause): fair handicapper: won at Nottingham in May and Bath in June: will prove best at 5f/6f: acts on firm going: often makes running. *B. P. J. Baugh* **69**

BABY ROCK 4 b.g. Selkirk (USA) 129 – Vanishing Point (USA) (Caller I D (USA)) [2009 75: 6m 6m 6d^3 Aug 28] big, leggy gelding: maiden: fair at 3 yrs: just modest form at best in 2009: raced only at 6f: acts on soft going. *C. F. Wall* **62**

BABY STRANGE 5 gr.g. Superior Premium 122 – The Manx Touch (IRE) 70 (Petardia 113) [2009 105: p6g^4 6f 6m* 6m^6 6m 6d 7g p6g^4 p7.1g f5g p6m^3 p7g Oct 21] leggy, useful-looking gelding: useful handicapper: won at Newcastle (by neck from Errigal Lad) in May, best effort in 2009: in-and-out form after: effective at 6f/7f: acts on polytrack, soft and good to firm going: tried visored (raced freely): usually held up: edgy sort, tends to sweat. *D. Shaw* **100**

BACK IN THE RED (IRE) 5 ch.g. Redback 116 – Fureur de Vivre (IRE) (Bluebird (USA) 125) [2009 79: f5g* f6g* f5g^3 f5g* f6g^4 p6m f5g^5 5.7f f6g Jul 7] strong gelding: fair performer: won seller and claimer in January, and handicap in February, all at Southwell: best at 5f/6f: acts on all-weather, firm and good to soft going: tried in cheekpieces, blinkered nowadays: usually front runner. *R. A. Harris* **77**

BACKLASH 8 b.m. Fraam 114 – Mezza Luna (Distant Relative 128) [2009 51: p11g^5 p12g p10g p12g Feb 19] poor performer: stays easy 1½m: acts on polytrack and soft going: tried tongue tied/in headgear: has been very slowly away. *A. W. Carroll* **45**

BACK ON 2 b.c. (Apr 16) Reset (AUS) 124 – Teal Flower (Pivotal 124) [2009 5m^4 p5g 7m Jun 20] leggy, close-coupled colt: little sign of ability in maidens. *G. C. Bravery* **–**

BACK TO PARIS (IRE) 7 b.g. Lil's Boy (USA) 109 – Alisco (IRE) (Shalford (IRE) 124§) [2009 p9.5g^5 Dec 19] useful handicapper at best: left E. Griffin, Ireland, and off over 2 years, just modest form in claimer on return: stays 1¼m: acts on firm and good to soft ground. *Paul Murphy* **50**

BADDAM 7 b.g. Mujahid (USA) 125 – Aude La Belle (FR) 81 (Ela-Mana-Mou 132) [2009 98: 16m^3 20m 21g 16.4m^4 15g^2 18m Sep 19] rather leggy, quite good-topped gelding: fairly useful performer nowadays (similar over hurdles): creditable efforts in 2009 only when in frame: stays 2¾m: acts on firm and soft going: tried in cheekpieces/visor/tongue strap. *Ian Williams* **90**

BADGE 3 b.g. Acclamation 118 – Be My Wish 80 (Be My Chief (USA) 122) [2009 5.7g^6 6d^3 May 16] easily better effort in maidens when third at Doncaster: dead. *R. Charlton* **75**

BADGE OF HONOUR 3 ch.g. Storming Home 128 – Loch Katrine (Selkirk (USA) 129) [2009 –: p8g^2 p10g^2 p8.6g* p10g* 12s 11d p12g Nov 18] fair performer: won maiden at Wolverhampton in February and handicap at Lingfield in March: left M. Johnston after: stays 1¼m: form only on polytrack: blinkered/tongue tied final start: usually leads. *Niall O'Callaghan, Ireland* **78 d**

BADIAT ALZAMAN (IRE) 3 b.f. Zamindar (USA) 116 – Fair Weather (IRE) 101 (Marju (IRE) 127) [2009 79: p7.1g^2 8.1g* 8.5g^5 8m 8m 9.9g^5 10.1m^6 p10g^2 Nov 13] rangy filly: useful performer: won maiden at Warwick in May: very good ½-length second to Tinshu in handicap at Lingfield final start: free-going sort, but stays 1¼m: acts on polytrack and good to firm ground: held up. *D. M. Simcock* **99**

BAD MOON RISING 4 ch.g. Piccolo 121 – Janette Parkes 39 (Pursuit of Love 124) [2009 43: p8g^2 p8g Mar 11] strong gelding: modest maiden: stays 1m: raced mostly on polytrack: in cheekpieces last 4 starts. *J. Akehurst* **51**

BA DREAMFLIGHT 4 b.g. Noverre (USA) 125 – Aunt Tate (Tate Gallery (USA) 117) [2009 65: p12g f12g 10.2f^3 11.6g 10.2g 9.9m^5 p10g^6 10m^5 Sep 12] rather leggy gelding: modest handicapper nowadays: stays 1½m: acts on all-weather, soft and good to firm going: tried visored/in cheekpieces: races handily: temperamental and unreliable. *H. Morrison* **52 §**

BADTANMAN 3 ch.c. Primo Valentino (IRE) 116 – Pearls (Mon Tresor 113) [2009 –: p5.1g^6 p5.1m^4 p5.1g^3 p5.1g p5.1g^3 5m 5g^4 5m^5 5m^6 5g^6 p5.1g 5s 5g p7g p5g^6 Nov 25] poor maiden handicapper: raced mainly at 5f: acts on polytrack and good to firm ground: tried visored, often blinkered: lazy. *Peter Grayson* **44**

BAGAMOYO 2 b.c. (Mar 17) Acclamation 118 – Queen of Silk (IRE) 93 (Brief Truce (USA) 126) [2009 6s* 6m^3 6m^2 p6m^2 Oct 7] sixth foal: brother to 4-y-o Pha Mai Blue and half-brother to 3 winners, including fairly useful 1m to 11.6f winner Brief Goodbye (by Slip Anchor): dam, Irish 2-y-o 1m winner, half-sister to smart Irish 7f/1m performer Tarry Flynn: fairly useful performer: won maiden at Doncaster in August: creditable efforts in minor events/nursery after: should be suited by 7f: acts on polytrack, soft and good to firm going. *J. R. Fanshawe* **92**

BAGBER 3 b.g. Diktat 126 – Torcross 96 (Vettori (IRE) 119) [2009 76p: p8g^3 10.2m^3 10m^4 12.4s^2 10m^2 12d^4 p11g^3 p12g* 9.9g* 10g^4 Oct 23] big, leggy gelding: fairly useful performer: won maiden at Kempton in August and claimer at Salisbury (claimed from H. Dunlop £30,000) in September: stays 1½m: acts on polytrack, soft and good to firm ground: races prominently: not straightforward. *P. Monteith* **83**

BAGGSY (IRE) 2 b.f. (Feb 24) Statue of Liberty (USA) 115 – Nisibis (In The Wings 128) [2009 p7g p7g^6 Nov 11] rather leggy filly: sixth foal: sister to 3-y-o State General and half-sister to 3 winners, including 4-y-o Bushy Dell: dam, maiden, half-sister to smart performer up to 9f Nijo: green and little impact in maidens at Kempton. *Miss J. Feilden* **53**

BA GLOBETROTTER 3 ch.g. Needwood Blade 117 – Generous Share 62 (Cadeaux Genereux 131) [2009 50: 8d^6 5.7f^3 5.1f^4 6m^6 7m 6g^3 Jul 5] angular gelding: poor maiden: seems effective at 6f to 1¼m: acts on polytrack, firm and good to soft going. *M. R. Channon* **48**

BAHAMA BAILEYS 4 ch.g. Bahamian Bounty 116 – Baileys Silver (USA) (Marlin (USA) 124) [2009 60: 6s 5m 6m 8g 10.1d Oct 27] tall gelding: modest performer in 2008: well held at 4 yrs: tried blinkered. *C. A. Dwyer* **–**

BAHAMARAMA (IRE) 4 ch.f. Bahamian Bounty 116 – Cole Slaw (Absalom 128) [2009 53: f6g p5.1m p5g Mar 20] modest performer in 2008: well held at 4 yrs: wears cheekpieces. *R. A. Harris* **–**

BAHAMIAN BABE 3 ch.f. Bahamian Bounty 116 – Baby Bunting 63 (Wolfhound (USA) 126) [2009 94: 5.1g^5 5m 5m* 5m 5g^4 5m 6m Oct 1] strong, good-bodied filly: fairly useful performer: won handicap at Leicester in June by neck from Lenny Bee: below form after: speedy, and best at 5f: acts on fibresand, soft and good to firm going: races prominently. *M. L. W. Bell* **92**

BAHAMIAN BALLAD 4 ch.f. Bahamian Bounty 116 – Record Time 69 (Clantime 101) [2009 56, a49: 5m^2 5m^4 5m 6d 5m^4 5m 5g Sep 30] good-topped filly: modest maiden handicapper: best at 5f/6f: acts on good to firm ground, probably on fibresand: tried blinkered, often visored. *J. D. Bethell* **54**

BAHAMIAN BALLET 7 ch.g. Bahamian Bounty 116 – Plie 75 (Superlative 118) [2009 85: 5m^2 5m 5g^3 5m^5 5m^2 5g^5 5d Aug 19] workmanlike gelding: fair handicapper nowadays, on long losing run: races mostly at 5f: acts on polytrack, good to firm and good to soft ground. *E. S. McMahon* **76**

BAHAMIAN BAY 7 b.m. Bahamian Bounty 116 – Moly 64 (Inchinor 119) [2009 57: f6s f7g^3 f6g Jan 29] quite good-topped mare: poor performer: stays easy 7f: acts on all-weather, best turf effort on good ground: visored last 2 starts: none too consistent. *M. Brittain* **46**

BAHAMIAN BLISS 4 b.f. Bahamian Bounty 116 – Fragrance (Mtoto 134) [2009 70: **67 d**
p6g^{4} 6m 5.5g^{6} p6g p6m p6g p7m^{6} Nov 29] angular filly: regressive handicapper: effective at 6f/7f: acts on polytrack: tried blinkered. *J. A. R. Toller*

BAHAMIAN BOLT 2 ch.g. (Apr 12) Bahamian Bounty 116 – Feeling Blue 60 **–**
(Missed Flight 123) [2009 6s Nov 7] 66/1, well held in maiden at Doncaster. *R. Bastiman*

BAHAMIAN CEILIDH 3 ch.f. Bahamian Bounty 116 – Crofters Ceilidh 101 **72 d**
(Scottish Reel 123) [2009 78: 5.2d^{4} 6m^{3} 5.7f^{3} p5g^{3} 5m^{5} p5.1g 5g p6g 5.1m 6m 10m Oct 6] good-topped filly: fair handicapper: well below form after fourth outing, leaving Tom Dascombe £3,500 after sixth one: barely stays 6f: acts on polytrack, firm and good to soft going. *B. N. Pollock*

BAHAMIAN KID 4 b.g. Bahamian Bounty 116 – Barachois Princess (USA) 62 **77**
(Barachois (CAN)) [2009 80: 7.1g 7.1g* 7.6g 7m^{6} 8.1m p7m p7.1g^{4} p6g^{3} p6m p7.1g^{2} Dec 26] useful-looking gelding: not a good walker: fair handicapper: won at Warwick in June: effective at 6f/7f: acts on polytrack and firm going: wears headgear: tends to hang. *R. Hollinshead*

BAHAMIAN LAD 4 b.g. Bahamian Bounty 116 – Danehill Princess (IRE) 62 (Dane- **80**
hill (USA) 126) [2009 72: f8g p6g* p6g* p5.1g^{6} p6g^{5} 6m 6f^{3} 6d 6m^{5} p6g* p6g p6m* p6g^{2} **a90**
p5g^{3} p6m^{2} p6m^{4} Dec 30] lengthy, quite attractive gelding: fairly useful handicapper, better on all-weather: won at Wolverhampton in February, March and September, and Kempton in October: effective at 5f/6f: acts on polytrack and firm going. *R. Hollinshead*

BAHAMIAN MOUSE (IRE) 3 ch.f. Bahamian Bounty 116 – Minnina (IRE) (In The **–**
Wings 128) [2009 7m^{5} 7.1m Sep 10] second foal: half-sister to 4-y-o Willridge: dam, ran once, out of useful 6f/7f performer Cheyenne Spirit: well beaten in maidens. *Andrew Turnell*

BAHAMIAN MUSIC (IRE) 2 b.f. (Feb 20) Bahamian Bounty 116 – Strings (Unfu- **85**
wain (USA) 131) [2009 7m^{3} 7d* p7.1g* 6.5m^{4} 7m Sep 27] 32,000Y: lengthy, unfurnished filly: second foal: half-sister to German/Belgian 9f (at 2 yrs)/11.5f winner Super Flight (by Exceed And Excel): dam unraced close relative to Poule d'Essai des Poulains winner Victory Note: fairly useful performer: won maiden at Newcastle in July and nursery at Wolverhampton in August: good fourth to In The Slips in nursery at Doncaster: seemed amiss final outing: will be suited by 1m: acts on polytrack, good to firm and good to soft going. *R. A. Fahey*

BAHAMIAN SUN (IRE) 2 ch.g. (Mar 12) Bahamian Bounty 116 – Firesteed (IRE) **–**
91 (Common Grounds 118) [2009 6s 8.1m Sep 10] strong gelding: tailed off in maidens, said to have had breathing problem latter outing: tongue tied. *Tom Dascombe*

BAHATI (IRE) 2 ch.f. (Apr 6) Intikhab (USA) 135 – Dawn Chorus (IRE) (Mukad- **85**
damah (USA) 125) [2009 6m* 7.1m 6g^{4} 6.5m^{6} Sep 10] 6,000Y: tall, angular filly: seventh foal: half-sister to several winners, including 7f (at 2 yrs) to 1¼m winner Solid Approach and 7f winner Dangle (by Desert Style), both useful in Ireland: dam unraced: fairly useful performer: won maiden at Newbury in May by ¾ length from Silver Symphony: creditable efforts in nurseries last 2 starts (slowly away both times): should stay 1m. *J. G. Portman*

BAHEEYA 3 ch.f. Almutawakel 126 – My American Beauty 93 (Wolfhound (USA) **61 ?**
126) [2009 –p: 10.3g 7g May 20] strong, good-bodied filly: seemingly best effort in maidens (modest form) when seventh at Goodwood final start: sold 5,000 gns. *C. E. Brittain*

BAHIANO (IRE) 8 ch.g. Barathea (IRE) 127 – Trystero (Shareef Dancer (USA) 135) **75**
[2009 91: p8g^{5} p8g 8m May 22] compact gelding: fair handicapper nowadays, on long losing run: stays 1m: acts on polytrack and firm going: held up: tried in cheekpieces. *C. E. Brittain*

BAHKOV (IRE) 3 ch.g. Bahamian Bounty 116 – Petrikov (IRE) (In The Wings 128) **62**
[2009 62p: 8s^{5} 6m^{4} 8.1g 8.3m^{6} 7.5m^{4} 7g^{3} 8d^{6} p6g^{6} Sep 25] compact gelding: modest maiden: left Tom Dascombe after fifth start: barely stays 1m: acts on good to firm ground. *Andrew Turnell*

BAHRAIN STORM (IRE) 6 b.g. Bahhare (USA) 122 – Dance Up A Storm (USA) **100**
(Storm Bird (CAN) 134) [2009 109: 12s 14s* p10.7g 18m Oct 17] tall gelding: smart hurdler: useful performer on Flat: won minor event at Galway in July (day after success in Galway Hurdle): better than bare result in Cesarewitch at Newmarket (Handicap, eighth of 32 to Darley Sun) final start, drawn wide and enduring rough race: probably stays 2¼m: acts on polytrack and any turf going: blinkered. *Patrick J. Flynn, Ireland*

BAHRAJ (USA) 2 b. or br.f. (Mar 22) Key of Luck (USA) 126 – Alattrah (USA) **75**
(Shadeed (USA) 135) [2009 6m^{4} 5g^{6} 5m^{4} 7g* 6g* Dec 13] fifth living foal: half-sister to

Italian 6.8f/1m winner Ghada (by Belong To Me): dam unraced sister to 1000 Guineas winner Shadayid: fair form: won nursery at Catterick in October and minor event at Dos Hermanas in December: sold from M. Johnston 7,000 gns in between: stays 7f: makes running. *A. Onaya, Spain*

BAIBARS (USA) 2 b. or br.c. (Feb 19) Gone West (USA) – Mombasa (USA) (Dynaformer (USA)) [2009 p7g Oct 21] $65,000Y, 40,000 2-y-o: tall colt: fifth foal: closely related to winner in USA by Grand Slam: dam French maiden out of half-sister to Breeders' Cup Mile winner Cozzene: 12/1 and backward, ran green and never in contention in maiden at Kempton: likely to improve. *G. A. Butler* **50 p**

BAILA ME (GER) 4 b.f. Samum (GER) 126 – Bandeira (GER) (Law Society (USA) 130) [2009 112: 10m^{2} 12m^{6} p13g* 12s Nov 7] useful-looking, lengthy filly: smart performer: off nearly 12 months prior to reappearance: back to best when winning listed race at Lingfield in October by 4 lengths from Rosika: creditable effort otherwise in 2009 only when 3¼ lengths second to Prince Siegfried in similar event at Ayr: stays 13f: acts on polytrack, good to firm and good to soft ground. *Saeed bin Suroor* **112**

BAILEYS CACAO (IRE) 3 b.f. Invincible Spirit (IRE) 121 – Baileys Cream 79 (Mister Baileys 123) [2009 104: 7s 7m^{2} 7m^{5} 8.5g^{4} Jun 6] strong, compact filly: useful performer: best effort in 2009 when nose second to San Sicharia in Chartwell Fillies' Stakes at Lingfield: stamina stretched when fourth to Eva's Request in Princess Elizabeth Stakes at Epsom final outing: stays 7f: acts on good to firm and good to soft going. *R. Hannon* **102**

BAILEYS RED 3 b.g. Diktat 126 – Red Ryding Hood 83 (Wolfhound (USA) 126) [2009 51: 10.1g p12g Jun 20] unfurnished gelding: maiden: modest at 2 yrs: no form in 2009: stays 8.5f. *J. G. Given* **–**

BAILEYS VISION 2 b.f. (Mar 2) Kyllachy 129 – Southern Psychic (USA) (Alwasmi (USA) 115) [2009 5.5f^{2} 6g^{2} 6f 6d^{4} p7g 7m^{5} 7g^{4} 6s Oct 27] tall filly: has scope: closely related to French 11f/1½m winner Oskar The Winner (by Pivotal) and half-sister to several winners, including smart 6f (at 2 yrs)/1m winner Rumpold (by Mister Baileys) and useful 7f (at 2 yrs) to 1¼m winner Wing Commander (by Royal Applause): dam sprint winner in USA: fair maiden: generally disappointing after first 2 starts: should stay 7f: acts on firm going: visored last 2 starts: unreliable. *M. Johnston* **65 §**

BAILIEBOROUGH (IRE) 10 b.g. Charnwood Forest (IRE) 125 – Sherannda (USA) (Trempolino (USA) 135) [2009 69: p8g^{5} p8.6g^{2} p9.5g^{6} 10.3m p8.6g Apr 4] quite good-topped gelding: modest performer nowadays: stays 10.4f: acts on polytrack, firm and good to soft going: sometimes wears headgear: none too consistent. *B. Ellison* **64**

BAIZICALLY (IRE) 6 ch.g. Galileo (IRE) 134 – Baize 95 (Efisio 120) [2009 –: 8.3g 10.4v^{5} 13m* 14g* 12.5m^{2} 11.5m 14g^{6} Jul 6] strong gelding: fair handicapper nowadays: won at Hamilton and Musselburgh within 3 days in June: stays 1¾m: acts on all-weather and firm going: often front runner nowadays: sold 8,000 gns, joined John Joseph Hanlon, Ireland. *G. A. Swinbank* **77**

BAJAN PARKES 6 b. or br.g. Zafonic (USA) 130 – My Melody Parkes 102 (Teenoso (USA) 135) [2009 89: 10.4g^{4} 12.3g 11.1v* 14d^{2} 14m 12g 12g^{4} 15v^{5} Oct 31] good-topped gelding: fairly useful handicapper: won at Hamilton in August: below form last 4 starts: stays 1¾m: acts on any turf going: tried in cheekpieces: often races prominently nowadays: none too consistent. *E. J. Alston* **86**

BAJAN PRIDE 5 b.g. Selkirk (USA) 129 – Spry 84 (Suave Dancer (USA) 136) [2009 72: f11g^{6} p8.6g^{6} p9.5g^{5} p9.5g^{4} 8.5m^{2} f8g^{6} f8f^{4} p8.6g^{5} f8f^{5} Dec 17] well-made gelding: modest performer nowadays: stays 11f: acts on all-weather, soft and good to firm going: tried in cheekpieces/visor. *R. A. Fahey* **64**

BAJAN TRYST (USA) 3 b. or br.g. Speightstown (USA) 124 – Garden Secrets (USA) (Time For A Change (USA)) [2009 77: p5g* p5g 6m 6m* 6m 5m 6g^{2} 6m Sep 10] useful-looking gelding: fairly useful performer: won maiden at Lingfield in March and handicap at Ripon in July: good effort after only when second in handicap on latter course: best kept to 5f/6f: acts on polytrack and good to firm ground: in cheekpieces last 3 starts: has hung left. *K. A. Ryan* **89**

BA JETSTREAM 2 b.g. (Apr 5) Monsieur Bond (IRE) 120 – Merch Rhyd-Y-Grug (Sabrehill (USA) 120) [2009 5m^{6} 6d 5.1g^{4} 6g^{3} 7d^{3} 7m p7g f8f Dec 12] useful-looking gelding: poor maiden: left M. Channon £6,000 after fifth start: stays 7f: acts on good to firm and good to soft going. *F. Jordan* **48**

BALAAGHA (USA) 3 b.f. Mr Greeley (USA) 122 – Echo Echo Echo (USA) (Eastern Echo (USA)) [2009 81p: 7m^{2} 7m* 7g^{2} 7g^{2} 8g^{2} 8m^{6} 8m Sep 26] big, strong filly: fluent mover: useful performer: won maiden at Chester in May: runner-up next 3 starts, best **101**

effort when beaten length by Strawberrydaiquiri in listed race at Ascot final occasion: unruly and unseated rider in stall final outing: stayed 1m: raced only on good/good to firm ground: was highly strung and often slowly away: visits Elnadim. *M. A. Jarvis*

BALAIS FOLLY (FR) 4 ch.g. Act One 124 – Bhima (Polar Falcon (USA) 126) [2009 **48**
53: p8g p7g p8m Oct 28] leggy gelding: poor maiden: stays 12.2f: acts on polytrack, good to firm and good to soft going: often wears headgear (not in 2009). *D. Haydn Jones*

BALATA 4 b.g. Averti (IRE) 117 – Manila Selection (USA) (Manila (USA)) [2009 78: **84**
p8g^3 p7g 7m^2 p7g^6 7m^4 6f p7g^5 7m* p7.1g^6 7m* 7g^2 8s^6 Dec 20] close-coupled gelding: fairly useful handicapper: better than ever when winning at Leicester and Folkestone in September: good second at York, then sold from B. R. Millman 13,500 gns: best at 7f: acts on all-weather, good to firm and good to soft going: genuine. *J. Maroto, Spain*

BALCARCE NOV (ARG) 4 b.c. Romanov (IRE) 119 – Rosada Fitz (ARG) (Fitzcar- **112**
raldo (ARG)) [2009 6.5g^2 7.5g^4 a9f 7.1s^4 8.1m* 7m^5 8m^2 7m 9m Oct 16] smallish, close-coupled colt: smart performer: won twice in Argentina (for J. Mayansky) in 2008, when also third in Grade 1: in frame in minor events at Nad Al Sheba first 2 starts in 2009, left H. Brown after next outing: won handicap at Haydock (beat Billy Dane by nose) in August: good ½-length second to Manassas in similar event at Doncaster, best effort after: seemingly best around 1m: acts on dirt and firm going: tongue tied in Dubai. *T. P. Tate*

BALDEMAR 4 b.g. Namid 128 – Keen Melody (USA) 60 (Sharpen Up 127) [2009 95: **97**
6m 5m 6m 6g* 6d 6d 6m* 7m 7g 6g Oct 23] quite good-topped gelding: has a quick, unimpressive action: useful handicapper: won in large fields at Epsom in June and, having left K. R. Burke after fifth start, Ayr in September: best at 6f: acts on good to soft and good to firm ground. *R. A. Fahey*

BALDUCCI 2 b.c. (Apr 9) Dansili 127 – Miss Meltemi (IRE) 100 (Miswaki Tern (USA) **80 p**
120) [2009 p8f^2 Dec 16] fifth foal: brother to useful 7f/1m winner (stays 1½m) Dont Dili Dali and 4-y-o Ada River, and half-brother to 2 winners: dam Italian 2-y-o 1m winner (third in Oaks d'Italia): well backed, encouraging ¾-length second to Valid Reason in maiden at Kempton, slowly away and looking likely winner over 1f out: sure to do better. *A. M. Balding*

BALERNO 10 b.g. Machiavellian (USA) 123 – Balabina (USA) 110 (Nijinsky (CAN) **48**
138) [2009 58: p7g^2 p8g p6g p7g p7g Feb 18] close-coupled gelding: poor performer nowadays: stays 1m: acts on all-weather, firm and soft going: tried in headgear/tongue tie: held up. *Mrs L. J. Mongan*

BALFOUR HOUSE 6 b.g. Wizard King 122 – Tymeera 62 (Timeless Times (USA) **–**
99) [2009 7f 8.1d Sep 4] no form: tried blinkered. *D. Burchell*

BALIERUS (GER) 2 b.c. (Mar 22) Singspiel (IRE) 133 – Brighella (GER) (Lomitas **63**
129) [2009 8m^6 8g a6f* Dec 11] rather leggy, lengthy colt: better effort in maidens for Saeed bin Suroor when sixth to Fareej at Newmarket: won similar event at Jebel Ali in December: effective at 6f, but bred to stay beyond 1m. *M. bin Shafya, UAE*

William Hill (Ayr) Bronze Cup Handicap, Ayr—in the first running of this event, the far side runners are in control, Baldemar, Ingleby Lady, Burnwynd Boy (No.26) and Esoterica the first four home

BALIGHA 4 ch.f. Alhaarth (IRE) 126 – Najmat Jumairah (USA) 56 (Mr Prospector (USA)) [2009 p8.6g 9m5 9.2g 6g5 May 23] 4,000 3-y-o: third living foal: dam, maiden who may have proved best at 1m/1¼m, closely related to winner up to 1¾m Sharaf Kabeer and half-sister to 1m/1¼m performer Kabool, both smart: modest maiden: seems to stay 9f (has taken strong hold): tried tongue tied. *G. A. Swinbank* **57**

BALIUS (IRE) 6 b.h. Mujahid (USA) 125 – Akhla (USA) 84 (Nashwan (USA) 135) [2009 122: 9m* 8.9g 10g a10g* 9.8g 10v5 Nov 8] very smart performer: won Jebel Hatta at Nad Al Sheba (by 1¼ lengths from Jay Peg) in March and (having left A. bin Huzaim after next outing) valuable Anatolia Trophy Stakes at Veliefendi (beat Dervis Aga 4½ lengths) in September: below best otherwise, though not entirely discredited when fifth to Voila Ici in Premio Roma on final start: stays 1¼m: acts on polytrack, heavy and good to firm ground: usually wears blinkers (not at Veliefendi): waited with. *Saeed bin Suroor* **120**

BALIYANA (IRE) 3 gr.f. Dalakhani (IRE) 133 – Balanka (IRE) 116 (Alzao (USA) 117) [2009 90: 8g* 8f Jun 19] tall, well-made filly: useful performer: much improved when winning Derrinstown Stud 1000 Guineas Trial at Leopardstown in May by 2½ lengths from Aaroness: tailed off in Coronation Stakes at Royal Ascot after: bred to have been suited by 1¼m/1½m: acted on good to soft going: stud. *John M. Oxx, Ireland* **108**

BALLACHULISH 2 b.g. (Feb 21) Kyllachy 129 – Romantic Drama (IRE) 65 (Primo Dominie 121) [2009 5g5 5m6 6m 6m 5.7m Sep 28] sturdy gelding: modest maiden: ran poorly last 2 starts: should stay 6f: sold 2,000 gns. *H. Candy* **61**

BALLADE DE LA MER 3 b.f. Ishiguru (USA) 114 – Riviere Rouge (Forzando 122) [2009 45: 10g 11.1d2 12.5m4 13.1d 12.5d5 Oct 28] modest maiden: stays 11f: acts on good to soft going. *A. G. Foster* **52**

BALLANTRAE (IRE) 3 b.f. Diktat 126 – Badawi (USA) 103 (Diesis 133) [2009 96: 7g6 Aug 14] tall, leggy, lengthy filly: useful performer at 2 yrs: well held in handicap at Newmarket sole outing in 2009: will stay 1m: acts on soft going. *M. L. W. Bell* **–**

BALLARINA 3 b.f. Compton Place 125 – Miss Uluwatu (IRE) 72 (Night Shift (USA)) [2009 –: 5m6 5g6 May 28] modest maiden: raced only at 5f: acts on good to firm ground. *E. J. Alston* **55**

BALLET DANCER (IRE) 3 b.f. Refuse To Bend (IRE) 128 – Showlady (USA) (Theatrical 128) [2009 77p: p9.5g* 9.9f3 p10g4 10.1g 8m Aug 6] tall filly: fair performer: won maiden at Wolverhampton in April: stays 1¼m: acts on polytrack and firm ground: reportedly had breathing problem fourth start, tongue tied next time: sold €24,000 in November. *M. A. Jarvis* **76**

BALLINTENI 7 b.g. Machiavellian (USA) 123 – Silabteni (USA) (Nureyev (USA) 131) [2009 100: p10g p8g 10g3 8.1f3 8.3m p12m4 10m5 9m Oct 16] leggy gelding: fairly useful handicapper nowadays: left D. Ivory after fourth start: needs good test at 1m, and stays 1½m: acts on polytrack, firm and soft going: tried tongue tied. *M. G. Quinlan* **92**

BALLODAIR (IRE) 2 b.g. (Apr 19) Antonius Pius (USA) 123§ – Vision of Dreams 93 (Efisio 120) [2009 6.1g2 6g* 6d2 6d 6m 6m Sep 25] €20,000Y, €42,000 2-y-o: sturdy gelding: first foal: dam 2-y-o 6f winner: fair performer: won maiden at Thirsk in June: no improvement in nurseries: may prove best up to 6f: acts on good to soft going: gelded after final start. *R. A. Fahey* **79**

BALLYALLA 3 b.f. Mind Games 121 – Molly Brown 95 (Rudimentary (USA) 118) [2009 90p: 8m5 7g 6m5 7m 8g4 9.7m3 p10m Oct 7] big, useful-looking filly: fairly useful performer: seems to stay 9.7f: acts on good to firm going: tried tongue tied. *R. Hannon* **83**

CGA Hungerford Stakes, Newbury—Balthazaar's Gift comes from well back and quickens away from Regal Parade, Plum Pudding (blaze) and Palace Moon (right)

BALLYCOMMON (USA) 2 b.g. (Apr 1) Roman Ruler (USA) 122 – Seth's Choice –
(USA) (Rahy (USA) 115) [2009 6m⁵ Jul 13] 11/8 favourite, ran green when fifth of 7 to Lord Aeryn in maiden at Ayr: dead. *K. A. Ryan*

BALLYCROY BOY (IRE) 4 b.g. Captain Rio 122 – Royal Baldini (USA) (Green –
Dancer (USA) 132) [2009 , a77: f6g^3 f7g^3 f6g* f7g^2 f6g^2 f7g^4 7s May 22] lengthy a70
gelding: fair performer: won seller at Southwell (left A. Bailey 6,000 gns) in February: stays 7f: best efforts on fibresand (well held on turf): tried in headgear (blinkered last 5 starts): possibly not straightforward. *Miss M. E. Rowland*

BALLYVONANE (USA) 2 b.c. (Mar 23) Strong Hope (USA) 120 – Wild Light 46
(USA) (Tabasco Cat (USA) 126) [2009 5g^4 6m p6g p6g^3 p6g p6m p7g^5 Nov 25] lengthy colt: poor maiden: stays 6f: acts on polytrack: blinkered last 4 starts. *L. A. Dace*

BALNAGORE 5 b. or br.g. Tobougg (IRE) 125 – Bogus Mix (IRE) 52 (Linamix (FR) 77
127) [2009 74: p10g* 10d p10g p11g^2 p11g* p11g 12m^3 p12m^6 Oct 12] tall gelding: a81
fairly useful handicapper on all-weather, fair on turf: won at Kempton in April and August (apprentices): stays 1½m: acts on polytrack and good to soft going: carries head awkwardly: often front runner: sold 23,000 gns. *J. L. Dunlop*

BALSHA (USA) 2 ch.f. (Feb 23) Mr Greeley (USA) 122 – Carefree Cheetah (USA) 66 53
(Trempolino (USA) 135) [2009 8m 8v p7g^6 Nov 18] $375,000Y: sixth foal: half-sister to winners in USA by War Chant and Tabasco Cat: dam, maiden (stayed 1¼m), sister to very smart sprinter/miler Arkadian Hero: modest form at best in maidens, not unduly knocked about final start. *E. A. L. Dunlop*

BALTHAZAAR'S GIFT (IRE) 6 b.h. Xaar 132 – Thats Your Opinion 48 (Last 121
Tycoon 131) [2009 112: 6.5g 6.5g^3 6.5g* a6f 7g^3 7m^2 7g^2 7m* 8g 7g^5 Oct 3] tall, good-topped horse: very smart performer: won handicap at Nad Al Sheba in February (left R. Simpson in UAE after next start) and CGA Hungerford Stakes at Newbury (back to best, came from poor position to beat Regal Parade 3 lengths) in August: best effort otherwise in 2009 when ½-length second to Finjaan in Betfair Cup at Goodwood seventh

HE Sheikh Sultan Bin Khalifa Al Nahyan's "Balthazaar's Gift"

outing: below form at Longchamp last 2 starts, in Prix du Moulin (started slowly, blindfold removed late) and Prix de la Foret: stays 7f: acts on good to firm and good to soft going, well held only outing on dirt: has worn cheekpieces/visor (not when successful): has run well when sweating: usually held up. *C. G. Cox*

BALTIC BEN (USA) 2 b.g. (May 1) Johannesburg (USA) 127 – Baltic Dip (IRE) 95 **–**
(Benny The Dip (USA) 127) [2009 8g 8d Oct 12] little impact in maidens at Salisbury, then gelded. *Eve Johnson Houghton*

BALTIMORE CLIPPER (USA) 2 b.c. (Feb 28) Mizzen Mast (USA) 121 – **88**
Resounding Grace (USA) (Thunder Gulch (USA) 129) [2009 7g^{6} p7.1g^{2} 8g^{2} 8m^{2} 8d^{5} Oct 12] $20,000F, 16,000Y: big colt: fourth foal: half-brother to 4-y-o Resounding Glory: dam, ran twice in France, half-sister to smart 1m/1¼m performer Flat Spin: fairly useful maiden: best effort when 2¼ lengths second to Azizi in nursery at Doncaster (hung left) penultimate start: stays 1m: acts on good to firm ground, found little on good to soft: has high head carriage. *P. F. I. Cole*

BALTIMORE JACK (IRE) 5 b.g. Night Shift (USA) – Itsibitsi (IRE) (Brief Truce **78**
(USA) 126) [2009 67: 7m^{3} 5.9g 8d^{5} 9m* 10m^{3} 10m* 10m* 10m^{3} 10.3g Oct 24] good-topped gelding: fair performer: won claimer at Redcar in August and handicaps at Pontefract (apprentices) and Redcar in September: effective at 7f to 1¼m: acts on polytrack, firm and soft going: sometimes blinkered: makes running/races prominently. *T. D. Walford*

BALTIMORE PATRIOT (IRE) 6 b.g. Tiger Hill (IRE) 127 – Berenice 100 (Groom **71**
Dancer (USA) 128) [2009 14g^{6} 14g 17d^{3} 14g^{2} 16g p13.9g^{3} p16.5g^{2} p13.9g^{4} Nov 30] fair handicapper: 3-time winner for Frau E. Mader in Germany in 2007: left Gerard Cully in Ireland after fifth outing: stays 17f: acts on polytrack and good to soft going. *R. Curtis*

BALWEARIE (IRE) 8 b.g. Sesaro (USA) 81 – Eight Mile Rock 76 (Dominion 123) **–**
[2009 10m Jul 13] sturdy gelding: one-time fair handicapper: off 27 months, slipped up sole start in 2009 (reportedly broke jaw): stays 13f: unraced on heavy going, acts on any other turf: often wears cheekpieces. *Miss L. A. Perratt*

BALZARINE 3 ch.f. Auction House (USA) 120 – Worsted 70 (Whittingham (IRE) **47**
104) [2009 7f 8.3g^{5} 8.1g p8g^{6} 7m Sep 21] sturdy filly: fourth foal: dam, sprint maiden, half-sister to 4-y-o Corrybrough: poor maiden: raced only at 7f/1m. *M. Blanshard*

BANANA REPUBLIC (IRE) 2 ch.c. (Mar 1) Danehill Dancer (IRE) 117 – Elite **70 p**
Guest (IRE) (Be My Guest (USA) 126) [2009 7s f8g^{2} 8.3g Oct 5] €60,000Y: big colt: brother to Irish 3-y-o Coat of Arms, closely related to 5f (at 2 yrs) to 7f winner Newton and 2005 2-y-o 6f/7f winner Amigoni (both useful in Ireland by Danehill), and half-brother to 2 winners in France, including useful 1¼m/1½m winner Hesiode (by Highest Honor): dam French 9f winner, half-sister to smart stayer Capal Garmon: fair form in maidens: head second at Southwell: type to improve at 3 yrs. *P. F. I. Cole*

BANCO BUSTO (IRE) 2 b.f. (May 1) Chineur (FR) 123 – Banco Solo (Distant **–**
Relative 128) [2009 p7g 7m Oct 6] 4,500Y: lengthy, angular filly: sixth foal: half-sister to several winners, including 3-y-o The Last Don: dam unraced sister to smart performer up to 1m My Branch, herself dam of Sprint Cup winner Tante Rose, and half-sister to smart middle-distance stayer/high-class hurdler Celestial Halo: looked awkward when well held in maidens at Kempton and Leicester. *H. S. Howe*

BANDAMA (IRE) 6 b.g. Green Desert (USA) 127 – Orinoco (IRE) 53 (Darshaan 133) **81**
[2009 97: 10m^{5} 12g p12g* p12g Nov 13] big, lengthy, good sort: fairly useful performer nowadays: won claimer at Kempton (left Mrs A. Perrett after, and gelded) in October: effective at 1¼m/1½m, should stay 1¾m: acts on polytrack, good to firm and good to soft going: tried in visor/cheekpieces. *John Joseph Hanlon, Ireland*

BANDANAMAN (IRE) 3 b.g. Danehill Dancer (IRE) 117 – Band of Angels (IRE) **65**
(Alzao (USA) 117) [2009 76: p8g 9f^{5} 8m^{5} Jun 5] lengthy gelding: fair maiden handicapper: should stay 1¼m: acts on soft and good to firm going: held up. *G. A. Swinbank*

BANDA SEA (IRE) 3 b.c. Tagula (IRE) 116 – Non Ultra (USA) 63 (Peintre Celebre **66**
(USA) 137) [2009 59: p7g^{2} p8m^{4} p8m Nov 19] sturdy colt: fair maiden, lightly raced: should stay 1m: acts on polytrack: tried in cheekpieces/blinkers: sold £3,000, sent to Germany. *P. J. Makin*

BANDEAR (IRE) 2 b.f. (Jan 29) Royal Applause 124 – Royals Special (IRE) 72 **67**
(Caerleon (USA) 132) [2009 p7.1g^{5} 7f^{3} 7m^{3} 7d 7m^{3} 6m Oct 1] 18,000F, 18,000Y: fourth foal: half-sister to 4-y-o Yes Mr President: dam, Irish maiden (stayed 1¼m), half-sister to high-class performers Distant Relative (miler) and Ezzoud (at 1¼m/1½m): fair maiden: stays 7f: acts on good to firm going: temperament under suspicion. *C. E. Brittain*

BANDEAU CHARMER 6 b.m. Band On The Run 102 – Fair Enchantress 64 (Enchantment 115) [2009 f12g^{6} Jul 14] no promise in bumpers/maiden/novice hurdles. *C. N. Kellett* –

BANDSTAND 3 b.g. Royal Applause 124 – Incise 89 (Dr Fong (USA) 128) [2009 f6g^{2} Dec 27] 42,000Y, £1,000 3-y-o: first foal: dam, 2-y-o 5f winner, half-sister to smart performer up to 7f Twilight Blues: 13/2, encouraging 4 lengths second to Poet's Place in maiden at Southwell: will improve. *B. Smart* **67 p**

BAN GARDA (IRE) 3 b.f. Daggers Drawn (USA) 114 – Lifeguard (IRE) (Desert Prince (IRE) 130) [2009 73p: 8.3m^{6} Aug 10] angular filly: fair form sole 2-y-o start (for N. Nevin in Ireland): still green when only sixth in maiden at Windsor on reappearance. *J. S. Moore* **56 +**

BANGED UP ABROAD (IRE) 2 b.c. (Apr 27) Royal Applause 124 – Annette Vallon (IRE) 92 (Efisio 120) [2009 p6g Sep 9] 66/1 and green, veered badly left at start when tailed off in maiden at Kempton. *M. G. Quinlan* –

BANKABLE (IRE) 5 b.h. Medicean 128 – Dance To The Top 107 (Sadler's Wells (USA) 132) [2009 122: 9g* 8.9g^{5} 10g^{3} 10m^{2} 8.1d* Sep 16] big, close-coupled, good-topped horse: smart performer: won handicap at Nad Al Sheba in February by ¾ length from Emmrooz: respectable 3 lengths third to Gloria de Campeao in Singapore International Cup at Kranji on third outing, then left M. de Kock: didn't need to be at best when winning listed race at Sandown in September by length from Ada River: stays 1¼m: acts on good to firm and good to soft ground, probably on firm: usually tongue tied in 2009: difficult in preliminaries before third start in 2008, sweated up sixth: waited with: joined H. Brown: reported in late-October to be suffering from a hoof problem. *G. L. Moore* **118**

BANKNOTE 7 b.h. Zafonic (USA) 130 – Brand (Shareef Dancer (USA) 135) [2009 108: 8m 7.5g^{6} Feb 19] smallish, quite good-topped horse: useful performer: below form in handicaps at Nad Al Sheba in 2009: stays 9.2f: acts on polytrack, good to firm and good to soft going. *A. M. Balding* **96**

BANKS AND BRAES 2 b.c. (Feb 26) Red Ransom (USA) – Bonnie Doon (IRE) (Grand Lodge (USA) 125) [2009 6.1g^{3} 7m^{5} 8m^{4} 8.3d Oct 12] smallish colt: fair maiden: only seventh in nursery at Windsor: stays 1m: acts on good to firm going. *R. Hannon* **69**

BANNABY (FR) 6 ch.h. Dyhim Diamond (IRE) 117 – Trelakari (FR) (Lashkari 128) [2009 115: 10d* 15.5s^{3} 14g^{6} 12g^{4} Aug 15] smart performer: won 4 times in 2008, notably Prix du Cadran at Longchamp: made winning reappearance in minor event at Madrid in April before creditable staying-on 1¼ lengths third to Americain in Prix Vicomtesse Vigier at Longchamp: below form afterwards, in Prix Maurice de Nieuil at Longchamp and Copa de Oro de San Sebastian: stays 2½m: acts on soft and good to firm ground: has been blinkered. *M. Delcher-Sanchez, Spain* **115**

BANTU 4 b. or br.f. Cape Cross (IRE) 129 – Lalindi (IRE) 80 (Cadeaux Genereux 131) [2009 80: 12.1m p11g 11.7g Sep 7] short-legged filly: maiden: fair form final 3-y-o start: well held in 2009: tried blinkered/visored/tongue tied: sold 20,000 gns. *J. H. M. Gosden* –

BANYAN TREE (IRE) 2 b.c. (Feb 27) Danehill Dancer (IRE) 117 – User Friendly 128 (Slip Anchor 136) [2009 8s^{2} 7s^{2} 8.5s* 8m^{4} 9s^{4} 10v Nov 14] closely related to useful Irish 1¼m/1½m winner Downtown and fairly useful Irish 8.5f winner Starspangled (both by Danehill) and half-brother to several winners, including smart Irish 1½m winner Two Miles West (by Sadler's Wells): dam won 5 Group 1s, including Oaks and St Leger: fairly useful performer: won maiden at Killarney in August, making all: creditable fourth in nursery at Gowran and listed race at Leopardstown (7½ lengths behind Mikhail Glinka): stiff task and not discredited in Criterium de Saint-Cloud final outing: should stay 1¼m: acts on soft and good to firm ground: has carried head very awkwardly. *A. P. O'Brien, Ireland* **93**

BAOLI 2 b.f. (Apr 25) Dansili 127 – Thorntoun Piccolo 64 (Groom Dancer (USA) 128) [2009 6g 7m 8v p7g Nov 14] 55,000Y: close-coupled filly: first foal: dam, maiden (stayed 7f), half-sister to smart performer up to 1m Vanderlin: modest maiden: should stay 1m. *R. Hannon* **55**

BARACONTI (IRE) 2 b.g. (Apr 6) Barathea (IRE) 127 – Continuous (IRE) 89 (Darshaan 133) [2009 7m^{5} p8.6g Oct 10] encouraging 3¾ lengths fifth to Cash Queen Anna at Redcar, better effort in maidens. *R. A. Fahey* **67**

BARAFUNDLE BOY 2 b.g. (Apr 1) Deportivo 116 – Barawin (FR) (Fijar Tango (FR) 127) [2009 6f 7m 6d p7m p7g Nov 18] rather leggy gelding: soundly beaten in maidens. *J. J. Bridger* –

BARALAKA 2 ch.g. (Feb 16) Barathea (IRE) 127 – Shakalaka Baby (Nashwan (USA) 135) [2009 p6g p6g^5 p7g Oct 9] 28,000Y: big, strong gelding: third foal: brother to 3-y-o Eastern Warrior: dam unraced half-sister to smart French sprinter Titus Livius: easily best effort in maidens when fifth at Kempton: not knocked about at Lingfield next time: gelded after: should stay 1m: capable of better. *Sir Mark Prescott* **75 p**

BARASTAR 2 b.g. (Apr 21) Sampower Star 118 – Barachois Princess (USA) 62 (Barachois (CAN)) [2009 6d 7.1m 6d^5 Jul 9] workmanlike gelding: modest form at best in maidens: gelded after. *J. R. Boyle* **53**

BARATARIA 7 ch.g. Barathea (IRE) 127 – Aethra (USA) 89 (Trempolino (USA) 135) [2009 62, a77: f8g^3 f8d^2 f8g^6 f8g^2 8.1v 7.9m 8d* 8m 8m 9.1g Oct 23] quite good-topped gelding: fair handicapper: won ladies event at Yarmouth in July: stays 1m: acts on fibre-sand and heavy going: has been slowly away: usually held up. *R. Bastiman* **78**

BARATHEA'S ACCLAIM 3 b.f. Acclamation 118 – Missbarathea (IRE) (Barathea (IRE) 127) [2009 p7g p8.6g^5 p8g p9.5g Oct 31] medium-sized filly: first foal: dam unraced: signs of a little ability: will be suited by return to 7f: tried tongue tied/in cheek-pieces. *P. R. Hedger* **–**

BARAWIN (IRE) 4 ch.f. Hawk Wing (USA) 136 – Cosabawn (IRE) 57 (Barathea (IRE) 127) [2009 87: p13.3g^4 f12g Jan 20] big, lengthy filly: fairly useful at 3 yrs: well held in 2009 (blinkered): stays 1¾m: acts on polytrack and soft ground: has shaped as though amiss/reportedly had breathing problem. *K. R. Burke* **–**

BARBARIAN 3 b.g. Noverre (USA) 125 – Love In The Mist (USA) 69 (Silver Hawk (USA) 123) [2009 70: p8g^2 8.3g^2 8.1g p8.6g^5 8d^2 8d^6 8m f11f^5 p8.6g^6 p8.6g^2 p8.6g^4 Dec 28] leggy gelding: fair maiden: left B. Hills 17,000 gns after fifth start: stays 8.6f: acts on polytrack and good to soft going: tried in headgear. *A. D. Brown* **77**

BARBEE (IRE) 3 ch.f. Night Shift (USA) – Barbizou (FR) (Selkirk (USA) 129) [2009 81d: 7.1g p7g Jun 10] sturdy filly: fairly useful performer early on at 2 yrs: lost way after (often shaping as if amiss), and well held in 2009: best at 5f/6f: acts on good to firm going: tried blinkered: sold 5,000 gns. *E. A. L. Dunlop* **–**

BARBEITO 3 b.f. Zaha (CAN) 106 – Tinta (Robellino (USA) 127) [2009 45: f7g^6 9g Jun 16] poor maiden: stays 8.6f: acts on all-weather: tried visored. *M. D. Squance* **35**

BARBIROLLI 7 b.g. Machiavellian (USA) 123 – Blushing Barada (USA) 53 (Blushing Groom (FR) 131) [2009 62: p12.2g^6 12d* p12g p12.2g* 10.9f^4 11.9m^6 11.5m^3 12.6d^6 12.1g^3 11m^3 12.6g^4 12d^5 12d 11.9m^6 12.1m* 12.3m^2 p12.2g^5 Dec 26] leggy gelding: modest handicapper: won at Folkestone (apprentices) in April, Wolverhampton (amateurs) in May and Beverley (selling event) in August: left W. M. Brisbourne £7,000 prior to final start: stays 12.6f: acts on polytrack, firm and soft going: tried visored/blinkered/tongue tied: usually held up: has found little. *W. B. Stone* **64**

BAR BLU (IRE) 4 b.f. Mull of Kintyre (USA) 114 – Ruwy 77 (Soviet Star (USA) 128) [2009 8.3m Jul 11] €2,000F, €11,000Y: sister to Irish 6-y-o Careless Abandon, and half-sister to 7f/1m winner Freya's Dream (by Danehill Dancer) and 8-y-o Jilly Why, both fairly useful: dam 1m winner: well beaten in bumper/seller (tongue tied). *G. A. Swinbank* **–**

BARCODE 3 b.f. Tobougg (IRE) 125 – Truly Madly Deeply (Most Welcome 131) [2009 56: p8.6g^2 p9.5m p10g Mar 24] rangy filly: modest performer: stays 8.6f: acts on polytrack (turf win on good ground): tried blinkered. *R. Hannon* **56**

BARI BAY 3 b.f. Bahri (USA) 125 – Sea Nymph (IRE) 85 (Spectrum (IRE) 126) [2009 –: p7g 7.1m p10g p12g^2 11.6d^4 11.9d^3 16m^4 p16f^5 Sep 10] modest maiden: left R. Beckett after fifth start: stays 2m: acts on polytrack, unraced on extremes of going on turf: tried in cheekpieces/blinkers. *J. W. Mullins* **59**

BARIOLO (FR) 5 b.g. Priolo (USA) 127 – La Bardane (FR) (Marignan (USA) 117) [2009 p12.2g^6 p13.9g Mar 2] fair handicapper: trained by F. Chappet in France in 2007, winning at Clairefontaine: stays 10.5f: acts on soft ground: usually blinkered in France. *Noel T. Chance* **66**

BARLAMAN (USA) 2 ch.c. (Apr 22) Langfuhr (CAN) 124 – Party Circuit (USA) (Kingmambo (USA) 125) [2009 p6g^4 p6g^3 p6g^2 p5.1m^3 p6g^2 Oct 15] $37,000Y, 130,000 2-y-o: good-bodied colt: first foal: dam US maiden: fair maiden: stays 6f: raced only on polytrack: tongue tied last 3 outings: signs of temperament: has left Godolphin. *Saeed bin Suroor* **70**

BARLEY BREE (IRE) 4 ch.f. Danehill Dancer (IRE) 117 – Aunty Mary 82 (Common Grounds 118) [2009 –p: 5m 5m 5g^6 5m Aug 13] lengthy filly: little form. *Mrs A. Duffield* **–**

BARLIFFEY (IRE) 4 b.g. Bahri (USA) 125 – Kildare Lady (IRE) (Indian Ridge 123) **81** [2009 81: 10f^4 10.1m^2 10m^5 8g^4 8m^3 8m p9.5g^3 Nov 12] good-topped gelding: fairly useful handicapper: stays 1¼m: acts on polytrack and firm ground: visored: often slowly away: not straightforward. *D. J. Coakley*

BARNES BRIDGE 4 ch.g. Zaha (CAN) 106 – Mo Stopher 47 (Sharpo 132) [2009 9m **–** p12g Jul 22] well held in maidens. *M. J. Attwater*

BARNEY MCGREW (IRE) 6 b.g. Mark of Esteem (IRE) 137 – Success Story 60 **115** (Sharrood (USA) 124) [2009 104: 6m^5 6m^2 6d^2 6d 6g^2 6d 5.4m* 5.6m 6m^2 Sep 19] rather leggy gelding: smart handicapper: better than ever in 2009, winning quite valuable event at York in August by neck from Hamish McGonagall: runner-up 4 other occasions, career-best effort when beaten head by Jimmy Styles in Ayr Gold Cup final start: best at 6f/7f: acts on polytrack, soft and good to firm going: edgy sort: has been early to post/ given trouble at start. *M. Dods*

BARNEZET (GR) 3 b.f. Invincible Spirit (IRE) 121 – Le Meridien (IRE) 67 (Magical **73** Wonder (USA) 125) [2009 73: p5g* p5.1g* p5m Dec 9] rather unfurnished filly: fair performer: won handicap at Lingfield in January and claimer at Wolverhampton (left R. Hannon £10,000) in March: raced only at 5f/6f: acts on polytrack and good to firm ground. *J. Pearce*

BARODINE 6 ch.g. Barathea (IRE) 127 – Granted (FR) 100 (Cadeaux Genereux 131) **62** [2009 –: p9.5g^5 p12g^4 p16g p10g^5 p9.5g^2 p9.5g* p9.5g^6 p8.6g^4 10m^5 8m^6 p8g^5 9.7m^4 8.1g^3 p8.6g^3 p13.9g^2 12.1v 11.9d^2 13.1f^2 p13.9g p12m p13.9g Dec 14] leggy, close-coupled gelding: has a round action: modest handicapper: won at Wolverhampton (apprentices) in March: stays 1¾m: acts on polytrack, firm and good to soft going: tried tongue tied/blinkered. *R. J. Hodges*

BARON DE'L (IRE) 6 ch.g. In The Wings 128 – Lightstorm (IRE) 58 (Darshaan 133) **108** [2009 108: 10s* 13s^4 10f 9d 14s 10s Sep 12] lengthy gelding: useful performer: won listed race at the Curragh (all 6 wins there) in April by neck from Estrela Brage: respectable fourth in similar event at Navan next time: below form after: best efforts at 1¼m: acts on heavy and good to firm ground, below form on polytrack: blinkered: best form ridden close up. *E. P. Harty, Ireland*

BARON OTTO (IRE) 3 b.g. Anabaa (USA) 130 – Marie Laurencin 75 (Peintre **61** Celebre (USA) 137) [2009 74p: 8m^5 p9.5g^4 7g 7g 7g 6.5f^3 Sep 13] good-bodied gelding: modest maiden: sold from W. Haggas 800 gns after third start: should stay 1m: blinkered last 2 starts in Britain. *K. Davies, Netherlands*

BARONOVICI (IRE) 4 b.g. Namid 128 – Allegrina (IRE) 70 (Barathea (IRE) 127) **59** [2009 65: 7m^5 7m^3 7.1m^6 6f May 11] strong, lengthy gelding: modest performer: stays easy 7f: probably acts on any going: often in visor/cheekpieces nowadays. *D. W. Barker*

BARONS SPY (IRE) 8 b.g. Danzero (AUS) – Princess Accord (USA) 115 (D'Accord **95** (USA)) [2009 95: 7.1m 6s^4 7m^5 7.1d 6g* 6.1m^2 6g^3 7m 7.1g^4 6d^4 6m^6 6m^6 Oct 5] lengthy gelding: useful handicapper: won at Warwick in June: in-and-out form after: winner at 8.6f, but best at 6f/7f nowadays: acts on polytrack, firm and soft going: tried tongue tied: has flashed tail: usually travels strongly. *R. J. Price*

BARONY (IRE) 3 ch.g. Swift Gulliver (IRE) 110 – Musical Flyer (IRE) (Prince of **–** Birds (USA) 121) [2009 p8.6g Dec 28] fifth foal: dam unraced: well held in maiden at Wolverhampton. *L. Smyth, Ireland*

BARQ (IRE) 2 br.c. (Apr 4) Green Desert (USA) 127 – Zaeema 93 (Zafonic (USA) **72 p** 130) [2009 p7.1g^3 Nov 13] fourth foal: half-brother to 3 winners, including useful 2007 2-y-o 6f winner Floristry (by Fasliyev) and 5-y-o Old Romney: dam, 2-y-o 7f winner on only start, out of Sun Chariot Stakes winner Talented: 4/1, 5½ lengths third to stable-companion Bronze Prince in maiden at Wolverhampton, not knocked about: will improve. *Saeed bin Suroor*

BARRALAND 4 b.g. Compton Place 125 – Dance Land (IRE) (Nordance (USA)) **–** [2009 78: 5g 5m Jun 20] neat gelding: fair handicapper in 2008: ran poorly both starts at 4 yrs: best at 5f: acts on polytrack and any turf going: tried visored: front runner/races prominently. *J. S. Goldie*

BARREQ (USA) 2 b.c. (Mar 30) Proud Citizen (USA) 122 – The Wrong Face (USA) **75 p** (Marlin (USA) 124) [2009 p7.1g^2 p7.1g^3 Dec 18] $45,000Y, 48,000 2-y-o: third foal: half-brother to winners in USA by Include and Harlan's Holiday: dam US 6.5f winner: green when placed in maidens at Wolverhampton, better effort when ½-length second to Saharia: will be suited by 1m: should still do better. *B. Smart*

BARRICADO (FR) 4 b.g. Anabaa (USA) 130 – Aube d'Irlande (FR) (Selkirk (USA) 129) [2009 80: 7g² p8g⁵ 7m* 8g⁵ 8d⁴ 8d 8m* 7g⁶ 8g 8s* 8s Nov 11] strong gelding: fairly useful performer: won handicap at Newcastle in May, ladies claimer at Clairefontaine (final start for E. O'Neill) in August and minor event at Nantes in October: effective around 7f, probably stays 1¼m: acts on polytrack, soft and good to firm going: visored/blinkered last 3 starts at 3 yrs: has hinted at temperament. *P. Monfort, France* **90**

BARSHIBA (IRE) 5 ch.m. Barathea (IRE) 127 – Dashiba 102 (Dashing Blade 117) [2009 113§: 9m⁴ 9f³ 12m⁵ 11.9m* 12g* 9.9d⁴ 12m⁴ 10m Oct 17] big, lengthy mare: poor walker: smart performer: formerly unreliable, but better than ever in 2009, winning bet365 Lancashire Oaks at Haydock (beat Fallen In Love 3¾ lengths) and listed race at Newmarket (by 3 lengths from Princess Taylor), both in July: held form after, fourth in Nassau Stakes at Goodwood (5 lengths behind Midday) and Yorkshire Oaks at York (beaten 3¼ lengths by Dar Re Mi), and 5 lengths seventh to Twice Over in Champion Stakes at Newmarket: free-going sort, though stays 1½m: acts on polytrack, firm and good to soft going: reportedly has impaired vision, and carries head awkwardly/hangs left: races prominently. *D. R. C. Elsworth* **116**

BARTER 3 ch.f. Daylami (IRE) 138 – Souk (IRE) 98 (Ahonoora 122) [2009 8.3f 9.9g 9.7m Jun 8] half-sister to several winners, including very smart stayer Golden Quest (by Rainbow Quest) and smart 1¼m/1½m winner Puce (by Darshaan), and to dam of Oaks winner Alexandrova: dam 7f winner (including at 2 yrs): fair form in maidens: bred to stay 1½m: type to do better in handicaps. *L. M. Cumani* **62 p**

BARTICA (IRE) 3 b.c. Tagula (IRE) 116 – More Risk (IRE) 82 (Fayruz 116) [2009 67: p8g p8g* p8g² Apr 21] big, strong colt: fair performer: won claimer at Lingfield in February: has won at easy 1m, may prove best at shorter: acts on polytrack and good to soft ground: in cheekpieces/blinkers in 2009. *R. Hannon* **71**

BARTON CHANCER 2 b.f. (Mar 4) Dubai Destination (USA) 127 – Lloc 79 (Absalom 128) [2009 5g p5g⁵ 5.2g⁶ May 29] lengthy filly: sister to 1¼m winner Gulf Coast and half-sister to 3 winners, including 5-y-o Luscivious and 6-y-o Cape of Storms: dam, 5f winner (including at 2 yrs), half-sister to July Cup winner Compton Place: no form in maidens/seller. *W. G. M. Turner* **–**

BARTON SANDS (IRE) 12 b.g. Tenby 125 – Hetty Green (Bay Express 132) [2009 64: p10g⁵ p9.5g p10g 11.5g May 20] neat gelding: modest performer: stays 1½m: acts on polytrack, firm and good to soft going: tried blinkered/visored: tongue tied: often held up, and needs good gallop. *Andrew Reid* **56**

BARWELL BRIDGE 3 b.g. Red Ransom (USA) – Sentimental Value (USA) 107 (Diesis 133) [2009 80: p10m² p9.5g² p10g* 9.9m² 10.4m* 12m³ 12g 12g⁴ 14m p12g⁴ 12m Sep 27] good-topped gelding: useful handicapper: won at Kempton in January and York in May: good third to Cosmic Sun in King George V Stakes at Royal Ascot: stays 1½m, stamina stretched at 1¾m: raced only on polytrack and good/good to firm ground: genuine: sold 80,000 gns, joined W. Greatrex, then gelded: won on hurdling debut in December. *S. Kirk* **97**

BARYNYA 3 ch.f. Pivotal 124 – Russian Rhythm (USA) 123 (Kingmambo (USA) 125) [2009 7s³ 8.3f³ 7m² Jul 11] rangy filly: has scope: first foal: dam 6f (at 2 yrs) to 1¼m winner, including 1000 Guineas and Nassau Stakes: fair form when placed in maidens, smooth-travelling ¾-length second to Shaws Diamond at York final start: should prove as effective at 1m as 7f. *Sir Michael Stoute* **77**

bet365 Lancashire Oaks, Haydock—
a first pattern-race success for Barshiba, who is clear of Fallen In Love

Mr J. C. Smith's "Barshiba"

BARZAN (IRE) 2 ch.c. (Mar 12) Danehill Dancer (IRE) 117 – Le Montrachet (Nashwan (USA) 135) [2009 6g³ 6m* 6g⁵ 7g 7m Oct 3] 80,000F, 100,000Y, £58,000 2-y-o: sturdy colt: third foal: half-brother to 2 winners, including fairly useful 1½m winner Baba Ganouge (by Desert Prince): dam unraced close relation to smart miler Gold Splash and to dam of Goldikova: fairly useful performer: landed odds in maiden at Brighton in May: best effort when fifth to Corporal Maddox in listed race at Epsom: off 3 months, seemed amiss final outing: should be suited by 7f+. *Tom Dascombe* **85**

BASALTICO (IRE) 5 b.h. Shantou (USA) 125 – Sfilza (Indian Ridge 123) [2009 111: 10g 14g 16m³ 12g⁶ 13.3m 13.4m⁴ 14.1s² 12g 16d Nov 3] good-topped, attractive horse: smart performer: trained by A. & G. Botti in 2008, winning 4 times in France/Italy, including listed race at Nantes: creditable efforts when in frame in 2009 (trained by H. Brown first 3 starts), in minor event at Nad Al Sheba (2¾ lengths third to Veracity), listed handicap at Chester (2¾ lengths fourth to Munsef) and minor event at Salisbury (dictated when nose second to The Betchworth Kid): seventh to Leica Ding in Group 3 Geelong Cup (Handicap) at Geelong penultimate start, staying on well after not clear run, but below form in Melbourne Cup at Flemington final start: stays 2m: acts on any going: tried tongue tied: to stay in Australia, and join L. Freedman. *L. M. Cumani* **113**

BASALT (IRE) 5 b.g. Rock of Gibraltar (IRE) 133 – Sniffle (IRE) 60 (Shernazar 131) [2009 92: p16.5g² p13m⁶ Nov 28] rather leggy gelding: has a round, unimpressive action: fairly useful handicapper: stays 2½m: acts on all-weather and any turf going: tried tongue tied. *T. J. Pitt* **84**

BASKERVILLE 6 b.g. Foxhound (USA) 103 – Miss Up N Go (Gorytus (USA) 132) [2009 82: 12.3g Aug 2] fairly useful performer at 5 yrs: well held sole start on Flat in 2009 (fair hurdler): stays 1¾m: acts on soft and good to firm going. *Mrs L. Williamson* **–**

BASLE 2 b.f. (Feb 25) Trade Fair 124 – Gibaltarik (IRE) 68 (Jareer (USA) 115) [2009 p6m² p6g* Oct 31] £15,000Y: half-sister to several winners, including 2-y-o 5f winners Patriot (useful in 1998, by Whittingham) and Queen's Victory (fairly useful in 2002, by Mujadil): dam 2-y-o 5f winner: encouraging efforts in maidens at Kempton (beaten nose by Cloud's End) and Wolverhampton (beat Valmina 2 lengths in 4-runner event): already fairly useful, and should progress. *Miss Gay Kelleway* **82 p**

BASQUE BEAUTY 4 b.f. Nayef (USA) 129 – River Cara (USA) 86 (Irish River (FR) 131) [2009 96: 8m 7m Jun 19] big, rangy filly: good walker/mover: useful performer at 3 yrs: well held in 2009: probably stays 1¼m: acts on soft and good to firm going. *W. J. Haggas* **–**

BASRA (IRE) 6 b.g. Soviet Star (USA) 128 – Azra (IRE) 102 (Danehill (USA) 126) [2009 91: p10g* p10g² p10g⁴ 10g⁵ 10f⁵ 9.9m⁵ 10.2m⁶ p10m² Dec 1] sturdy gelding: fairly useful handicapper: won at Lingfield in January: effective at 1m/1¼m: acts on polytrack, firm and good to soft going: tried in tongue tie/blinkers/cheekpieces: held up (often travels strongly). *Miss Jo Crowley* **87**

BASSINET (USA) 5 b.m. Stravinsky (USA) 133 – Berceau (USA) 105 (Alleged (USA) 138) [2009 84: p12g⁵ p12g* p12g p12g p13g² 12m 13m p12g Oct 9] lengthy, sparely-made mare: fairly useful handicapper: won at Lingfield in March: stays 13f: acts on polytrack, soft and good to firm ground: held up: sometimes finds little. *J. A. R. Toller* **82**

BATCHWORTH BLAISE 6 b.g. Little Jim – Batchworth Dancer 67 (Ballacashtal (CAN)) [2009 59: p7g⁶ p7g 7m 7m⁴ 7m 8m⁵ 7.6g 7f 7g 8g³ p7g p8m* p7m³ Dec 9] angular gelding: modest performer: won apprentice handicap at Lingfield in December: stays 8.3f: acts on polytrack, good to firm and good to soft ground: tried blinkered: often slowly away: held up: none too consistent. *E. A. Wheeler* **59**

BATEAU BLEU 2 b.g. (Feb 28) Auction House (USA) 120 – Fresh Look (IRE) 64 (Alzao (USA) 117) [2009 5m 6d 7m 10.2m* p8.6g⁴ Oct 9] sturdy, compact gelding: fair performer: best effort when winning nursery at Nottingham in September: stays 1¼m: acts on good to firm going, probably on polytrack: visored last 2 starts. *P. C. Haslam* **66**

BATELEUR 5 b.g. Fraam 114 – Search Party 78 (Rainbow Quest (USA) 134) [2009 75d: p6g⁶ p6g⁶ p6g² p6g⁵ 6g 6.1f² 6m² 6g⁶ 6f* 6m² 6f³ 6.1g³ 5.7f* 6d² 5.7m⁴ 6f 6m⁴ 5.7m⁵ 6g 6m Sep 14] good-topped gelding: fair handicapper: won at Folkestone and Bath in June: best at 6f: acts on polytrack, firm and good to soft going: tried visored: held up. *M. R. Channon* **72**

BATGIRL 2 ch.f. (Apr 18) Mark of Esteem (IRE) 137 – Serriera (FR) 51 (Highest Honor (FR) 124) [2009 7g 7g Oct 31] 11,000Y: small filly: second foal: dam, French/Irish maiden (stayed 1½m), half-sister to smart French 1¼m performer Sarrasin: well held in maidens at York and Newmarket. *John Berry* **–**

BATHWICK GINO 2 b.g. (Apr 20) Alamshar (IRE) 133 – Rockstine (IRE) 61 (Ballad Rock 122) [2009 5m⁶ 5.1m⁴ 7s 5.2g⁶ p7.1m⁴ p7.1g⁵ p6g⁵ p6m Sep 28] smallish gelding: temperamental maiden: left A. Haynes after third start: stays 6f: acts on polytrack and good to firm going: visored last 2 starts. *P. D. Evans* **58 §**

BATHWICK GOLD (IRE) 2 b.c. (Feb 14) Noverre (USA) 125 – Taalluf (USA) 82 (Hansel (USA)) [2009 6g 6g* 6m 6s Nov 7] small colt: fair performer: won maiden at Leicester in September: stiff tasks after, creditable effort in nursery final start: raced only at 6f: acts on soft going. *P. D. Evans* **67**

BATHWICK MAN 4 b.g. Mark of Esteem (IRE) 137 – Local Abbey (IRE) (Primo Dominie 121) [2009 –: 12.1v³ p16f² p16.5g Sep 12] close-coupled gelding: modest maiden on Flat: fairly useful form over hurdles, winning twice in summer: stays 2m: acts on polytrack and heavy going: tried visored/in cheekpieces/tongue tie last 3 starts. *D. E. Pipe* **60**

BATHWICK PURSUIT 3 b.g. Pursuit of Love 124 – Society Rose 88 (Saddlers' Hall (IRE) 126) [2009 57: 10d 7f⁵ p12g⁶ 8f⁵ 11.6m Jul 13] leggy gelding: poor maiden: should prove best short of 1½m. *P. D. Evans* **46**

BATHWICK XAARA 2 br.f. (Mar 18) Xaar 132 – Anapola (GER) (Polish Precedent (USA) 131) [2009 6m⁴ 6m⁴ 7m³ 6g p7g⁶ 6m⁶ p6f Oct 14] 800Y: compact filly: fourth foal: half-sister to 3-y-o Blazing Buck and German 9.5f winner Spectrana (by Spectrum): dam German 7f/1m winner: fair maiden: no improvement in nurseries: barely stays 7f: acts on polytrack and good to firm going. *J. G. Portman* **66**

BATTIMOORE (IRE) 3 b.f. Beckett (IRE) 116 – Silver Spoon (IRE) (College Chapel 122) [2009 –: 6s^{2} 7.1m 6g^{2} 7v p6g^{5} p6g p6m^{6} p7g^{4} p7.1g Dec 17] quite good-topped filly: modest maiden handicapper: left D. Loughnane, Ireland after sixth start: stays 7f: acts on polytrack and soft going. *I. W. McInnes* **57**

BATTLE 3 gr.g. Compton Place 125 – Molly Moon (IRE) 84 (Primo Dominie 121) [2009 71p: 6g^{4} 6m 5.1g^{3} 5.1d* 5.1m^{4} Sep 30] long-backed gelding: fair handicapper: won at Bath in August: raced only at 5f/6f: acts on good to firm and good to soft going: sold 8,000 gns. *H. Morrison* **78**

BATTLE HONOUR 2 b.g. (Feb 6) Mark of Esteem (IRE) 137 – Proserpine 95 (Robellino (USA) 127) [2009 7g Oct 30] unfurnished gelding: 50/1, down the field in maiden at Newmarket. *H. Candy* **62**

BATTLEMAIDEN (IRE) 2 br.f. (May 2) Shamardal (USA) 129 – Kirk 79 (Selkirk (USA) 129) [2009 6g^{6} 7g^{4} 6g^{2} p6f^{2} 6m^{6} Oct 1] 150,000Y, 125,000 2-y-o: fifth foal: closely related to useful 1¼m (including at 2 yrs) winner Natalie Jane (by Giant's Causeway) and half-sister to winner in Greece by Fasliyev: dam, 1m winner, closely related to smart performer up to 1¼m Carmelite House: fair maiden: respectable effort in nursery final start: bred to stay 1m: acts on polytrack and good to firm ground: has left Godolphin. *Saeed bin Suroor* **78**

BATTLE PAINT (USA) 5 b.h. Tale of The Cat (USA) 113 – Black Speck (USA) (Arch (USA) 127) [2009 103: p6g^{3} 7m Aug 21] big, strong, lengthy horse: smart performer, lightly raced: best effort for some time when 1¾ lengths third to Eisteddfod in minor event at Kempton, easily better effort in 2009: effective at 6f to 1m: acts on polytrack, raced only on good/good to firm ground on turf: tongue tied last 2 starts. *J. H. M. Gosden* **110**

BATTLE PLANNER (USA) 3 b.c. War Chant (USA) 126 – The Administrator (USA) (Afleet (CAN)) [2009 89p: 10g^{5} 12g^{2} 10s 12.1m^{3} p13.9g^{4} Oct 10] strong colt: fairly useful handicapper: left M. Johnston 9,000 gns after second start: should stay 1¾m: acts on fibresand and good to firm ground: in cheekpieces last 2 starts: possibly not straightforward. *I. Semple* **86**

BATTLE ROYAL (IRE) 3 b.c. Refuse To Bend (IRE) 128 – Style of Life (USA) (The Minstrel (CAN) 135) [2009 60p: 7d^{4} 8g^{4} 7m^{4} 8m a6.8g^{2} a8d* Dec 20] close-coupled colt: modest performer: sold from B. Smart £3,000 after fourth start: won minor event at Taby in December: stays 1m: acts on dirt and good to soft ground: often races freely. *Catharina Vang, Sweden* **57**

BATTLE STUDY (IRE) 2 b. or br.g. (Apr 5) Fath (USA) 116 – Osprey Point (IRE) (Entrepreneur 123) [2009 8d^{4} 7.5g^{2} p7.1g^{6} Nov 13] €1,000Y: tall, lengthy gelding: fifth foal: half-brother to winner in Italy by Choisir: dam unraced half-sister to Moyglare Stud Stakes winner Flutter Away: best effort in maidens when 6 lengths second to Namecheck at Beverley: in cheekpieces final start. *A. J. McCabe* **70**

BATTLING LIL (IRE) 5 b.m. Daggers Drawn (USA) 114 – Salva 73 (Grand Lodge (USA) 125) [2009 54: p8g Jan 18] big, good-topped mare: maiden: modest at 4 yrs: blinkered, well held sole outing in 2009: seems to stay 8.3f: acts on polytrack, yet to race on extremes of going on turf. *J. L. Spearing* **–**

BAUNAGAIN (IRE) 4 b.g. No Excuse Needed 123 – Manuka Honey (Mystiko (USA) 124) [2009 89: 6m^{2} 6m* 6g^{6} p6g p6f p5g f5g p7f^{3} p7g^{6} Dec 31] useful handicapper: career best when winning at Warwick in July: failed to repeat that form after: best form at 6f: acts on all-weather, good to firm and good to soft going. *P. W. Chapple-Hyam* **96**

BAVARIAN NORDIC (USA) 4 b.g. Barathea (IRE) 127 – Dubai Diamond (Octagonal (NZ) 126) [2009 87: 9.8d^{5} 12s^{5} 10.3d^{6} 12g^{5} 9.8g^{3} f8g^{4} 12v^{2} 10.4g Oct 9] strong, good-bodied gelding: has a round action: fairly useful handicapper: gelded after final start: stays 1½m: acts on fibresand and heavy going. *Mrs A. Duffield* **83**

BAVARICA 7 b.m. Dansili 127 – Blue Gentian (USA) 96 (Known Fact (USA) 135) [2009 75: p8g* p10g^{3} p10g^{2} p10g^{3} p8g p8g^{5} p8g* p8g^{6} p10g^{3} 10g^{3} p10g 10m 9m^{2} 9.7m^{3} 8.1g^{5} 9.7m^{3} 10g* 10g 10m 10.2m^{3} p8m^{2} p9.5g^{2} p9.5g^{3} Dec 14] rather leggy mare: fair handicapper: won at Lingfield in January (apprentices) and February, and Newmarket (amateurs) in July: effective at 1m/1¼m: acts on all-weather and firm ground: tough. *Miss J. Feilden* **75**

BAWAARDI (IRE) 3 b.g. Acclamation 118 – Global Trend (Bluebird (USA) 125) [2009 75p: 7d* 7s^{6} p7.1g^{6} p8.6g^{3} p8f^{2} p8.6g^{2} Dec 19] good-topped gelding: fairly useful handicapper: won maiden at Lingfield in September: left J. Gosden 17,000 gns after next outing: stays 8.6f: acts on polytrack, soft and good to firm ground: held up. *R. A. Fahey* **85**

BAWADI (USA) 3 b. or br.c. Medaglia d'Oro (USA) 129 – Chartreuse (CAN) (Danza- **88**
tore (CAN) 120) [2009 p10g* p12g^4 10m Sep 25] $50,000F, 170,000 2-y-o: tall, angular colt: half-brother to several winners in USA, including 1m minor stakes winner Unbridled Danz (by Unbridled's Song): dam Canadian 6.5f winner: fairly useful form: won maiden at Kempton in August: similar form after, still green in minor event at Ascot final start: effective at 1¼m/1½m: acts on polytrack: has joined M. bin Shafya in UAE. *Saeed bin Suroor*

BAWDSEY BANK 3 b.g. Tipsy Creek (USA) 115 – Busy (IRE) (In The Wings 128) **–**
[2009 7m 8.3g Oct 28] stocky gelding: well beaten in maidens. *John A. Harris*

BAYBERRY KING (USA) 6 b.g. Lear Fan (USA) 130 – Myrtle 96 (Batshoof 122) **–**
[2009 p8g Jan 11] robust gelding: lightly-raced maiden: well held sole outing in 2009. *Mrs A. M. Thorpe*

BAYBSHAMBLES (IRE) 5 b.g. Compton Admiral 121 – Payvashooz 78 (Ballacash- **79**
tal (CAN)) [2009 77: 5g 5m^2 5m^5 5d^5 5m^2 5m* 5m 5d 5m^4 5g 5m Oct 3] close-coupled gelding: fair handicapper: won at Beverley in July: best at 5f: acts on firm and soft going. *R. E. Barr*

BAYCAT (IRE) 3 b.g. One Cool Cat (USA) 123 – Greta d'Argent (IRE) 103 (Great **–**
Commotion (USA) 123) [2009 97d: 7s 6g 8m May 25] leggy, close-coupled gelding: useful early in career: has lost his way, well held in handicaps in 2009. *J. G. Portman*

BAY KNIGHT (IRE) 3 b.c. Johannesburg (USA) 127 – Sabeline (IRE) (Caerleon **94**
(USA) 132) [2009 7g 6m 5d* 5s 7v 6.3s^6 p7m* p6g* p7g Nov 18] €50,000F: closely related to winner in USA by Hennessy and half-brother to 3 winners abroad: dam unraced half-sister to high-class sprinter Tamarisk: fairly useful performer: won maiden at Tipperary in July (raced alone), and handicaps at Kempton in October and Dundalk (beat Copper Dock ¾ length) in November: stays easy 7f: acts on polytrack and good to soft ground. *W. McCreery, Ireland*

BAYLINI 5 gr.m. Bertolini (USA) 125 – Bay of Plenty (FR) (Octagonal (NZ) 126) [2009 **86**
91, a102: p10g^2 p10g^3 p10g^3 p8g p12g^2 p10g p11g^4 12f 12m^5 10m^2 10m^4 10f p10m^6 **a95**
Nov 28] tall, angular mare: useful handicapper on all-weather, fairly useful on turf: largely held form in 2009, best effort when fourth to Greylami at Kempton seventh outing: stays easy 1½m: acts on polytrack, good to firm and good to soft going. *Ms J. S. Doyle*

BAZART 7 b.g. Highest Honor (FR) 124 – Summer Exhibition (Royal Academy (USA) **–**
130) [2009 85: 14.1g^6 Jun 28] rangy gelding: fairly useful handicapper in 2008: fit from hurdling (fair form), well held sole Flat outing at 7 yrs (in cheekpieces): barely stays 1¾m: acts on soft and good to firm ground: often makes running. *B. J. Llewellyn*

BAZE MAC 2 b.f. (Feb 26) Needwood Blade 117 – Miss Maisey (IRE) (Entrepreneur **–**
123) [2009 5d 6g 5g 5.1s Nov 4] compact filly: third foal: half-sister to winner in Russia by Mujahid: dam unraced: no sign of ability: tried blinkered. *N. Bycroft*

BAZERGAN (IRE) 4 b.g. Machiavellian (USA) 123 – Lunda (IRE) 60 (Soviet Star **95**
(USA) 128) [2009 101: p8g^3 p11g^5 p11g 12g 9m^5 10.3f^3 9.9m* 10m^6 10.3m^5 10m Sep 19] strong, deep-girthed gelding: useful handicapper: won at Beverley in August, despite looking reluctant: stiffer tasks after: seems to stay 11f: acts on polytrack and firm going: usually wears cheekpieces (blinkered final start) and tongue tie: quirky. *C. E. Brittain*

BAZSHARANI 2 bl.f. (Feb 21) Auction House (USA) 120 – Ewenny 71 (Warrshan **61**
(USA) 117) [2009 5.1g^4 5.1m^2 6.1m^5 5m^6 p6g 5.7m 6.1s Oct 7] plain filly: sixth foal: half-sister to 3 winners, including useful 2005 2-y-o 6f/7f winner Johnny The Fish (by Most Welcome): dam 2-y-o 5f winner: maiden: well beaten last 4 starts, including in seller: raced at 5f/6f: acts on good to firm going. *P. D. Evans*

BEACH BOY (IRE) 2 ch.c. (Apr 28) Pearl of Love (IRE) 112 – Mermaid Beach (Slew **–**
O' Gold (USA)) [2009 f5g p6g p7.1g 5m Jul 16] no sign of ability in maidens/seller. *S. Wynne*

BEACH BUNNY (IRE) 4 b.f. High Chaparral (IRE) 132 – Miss Hawai (FR) (Peintre **114**
Celebre (USA) 137) [2009 112: 8g^3 8v^2 10d^2 10s^4 12s 9.5m^4 Sep 26] lengthy, useful-looking filly: smart performer: best efforts in 2009 when second at the Curragh in Tri Equestrian Stakes (beaten ½ length by Emily Blake) and Pretty Polly Stakes (short-headed by Dar Re Mi): effective at testing 1m to easy 1½m: acts on heavy and good to firm going: worth a try in headgear: usually held up. *Kevin Prendergast, Ireland*

BEACON LODGE (IRE) 4 b.c. Clodovil (IRE) 116 – Royal House (FR) 104 (Royal **119**
Academy (USA) 130) [2009 98: 6m 7.1g* 7.1g^2 8m* 8g^6 8g^3 8g^5 Oct 3] big, strong, good sort: very smart performer: reportedly suffered hairline fracture in 2008: improved in

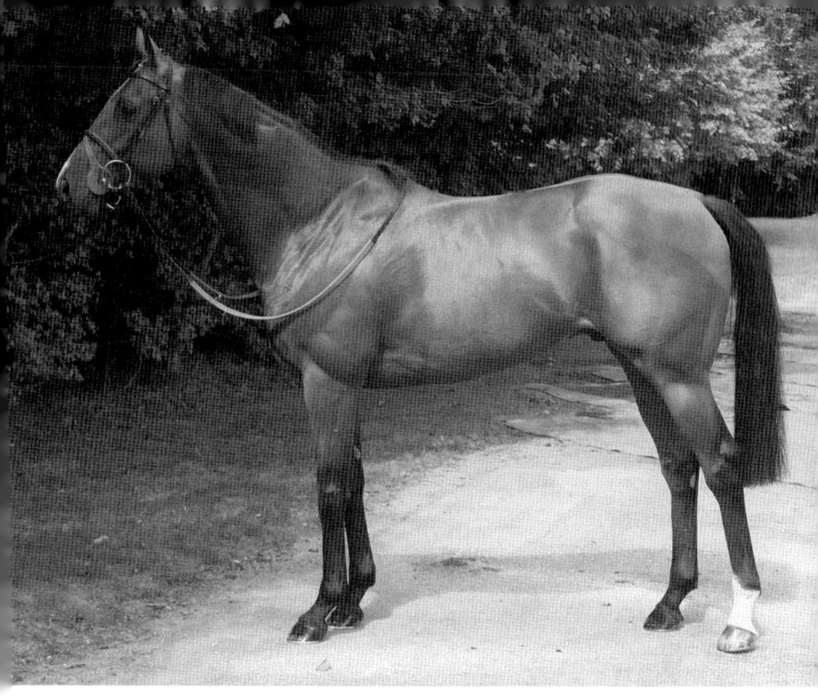

Mr and Mrs P. Hargreaves' "Beacon Lodge"

2009, winning listed race at Haydock (by ¾ length from Ordnance Row) in May and Prix du Chemin de Fer du Nord at Chantilly (hung left inside final 1f, beat Sahpresa 3 lengths) in June: good efforts otherwise when 2 lengths second to Main Aim in John of Gaunt Stakes at Haydock and 1½ lengths fourth (promoted to third) behind subsequently disqualified Delegator in Celebration Mile at Goodwood (poorly placed after slow start): respectable never-nearer fifth to Tamazirte in Prix Daniel Wildenstein at Longchamp final start: stays 1m: acts on good to firm and good to soft going. *C. G. Cox*

BE A DEVIL 2 ch.c. (Mar 28) Dubai Destination (USA) 127 – Devil's Imp (IRE) 84 **83**
(Cadeaux Genereux 131) [2009 5g p6g^6 p7.1g^5 p7.1g* p8.6g p7g^2 p7g^3 p7m^2 p8.6g^2 Dec 18] £35,000Y: angular colt: half-brother to several winners, notably smart 6f (at 2 yrs)/7f winner Miss Lucifer (by Noverre): dam, 6f and (at 2 yrs) 7f winner, half-sister to smart 1½m winners Amfortas and Legend Maker (latter dam of 1000 Guineas winner Virginia Waters): fairly useful performer: won nursery at Wolverhampton in October: progressive in similar company last 4 starts: stays 8.6f: acts on polytrack. *W. R. Muir*

BEA MENACE (USA) 3 b.f. Mizzen Mast (USA) 121 – Questonia 107 (Rainbow **93**
Quest (USA) 134) [2009 64: 7d 7m^2 p6g^5 6.1m 7g^5 7f* 7m^2 7m^3 8m* p7g* p7m^5 Oct 31] useful-looking filly: fairly useful performer: won handicap at Folkestone in July, and claimer at Pontefract and handicap at Kempton in October: stays 1m: acts on polytrack, unraced on heavy ground, acts on any other turf: tried blinkered: often front runner. *P. F. I. Cole*

BEAR TOBOUGGIE 2 b.f. (May 3) Tobougg (IRE) 125 – Brave Bear 69 (Bold Edge **58 p**
123) [2009 6s Nov 7] first foal: dam 5f winner: 16/1, 5 lengths seventh to Adventure Story in maiden at Doncaster: will improve. *G. A. Swinbank*

BEAT BABY (IRE) 2 ch.g. (Apr 5) Johannesburg (USA) 127 – Najiya 102 (Nashwan **63**
(USA) 135) [2009 6m 6m Aug 21] big, lengthy gelding: modest form in maidens at York, not given hard time. *J. Howard Johnson*

BEAT COMPANION 3 ch.c. Beat Hollow 126 – Comanche Companion 88 (Comanche Run 133) [2009 p10g 8d p10m^{4} Aug 8] sturdy, well-made colt: best effort in maidens (fair form) when fourth at Lingfield: stays 1¼m: acts on polytrack. *P. Howling* **69**

BEAT FASTER 3 b.f. Beat Hollow 126 – Supersonic 80 (Shirley Heights 130) [2009 52: 8.3m^{5} f8f^{5} p12g Nov 11] lengthy, angular filly: modest maiden: should stay 1¼m+: raced only on all-weather and good to firm ground. *J. G. Given* **51**

BEAT SEVEN 3 ch.f. Beat Hollow 126 – Twenty Seven (IRE) 75 (Efisio 120) [2009 102: 10m 8m 8.1m^{5} Jul 4] big, well-made filly: useful performer at 2 yrs: below form in 2009: stays 1m (failed to settle at 1¼m): acts on firm and good to soft going: sold £46,000 in December. *Miss Gay Kelleway* **90**

BEAT SURRENDER (FR) 2 b.c. (Feb 10) Bertolini (USA) 125 – Waking Redhead (USA) (Miswaki (USA) 124) [2009 6d* 7m 6v^{4} p6g^{6} 6g* Oct 18] €22,000F, €30,000Y: sturdy colt: fourth foal: half-brother to useful French 6f/7.5f winner Kerno (by Invincible Spirit): dam French 1m winner: useful performer: won maiden in July and nursery in October (blinkered, made all to beat Moonreach short head), both at Naas: should stay 7f: acts on good to soft going (well held in Acomb Stakes at York on good to firm). *G. M. Lyons, Ireland* **99**

BEAT THE BELL 4 b.g. Beat All (USA) 120 – Bella Beguine 78 (Komaite (USA)) [2009 103: p6g^{5} 6m^{4} 7m p6g^{3} p7g^{6} p6m^{6} p6g Dec 2] leggy gelding: useful performer: left A. Bailey after reappearance: third in handicap at Lingfield, only creditable effort at 4 yrs: best at 6f: acts on all-weather, unraced on extremes of going on turf: tried in cheekpieces. *J. A. Osborne* **95**

BEAT THE DEVIL 3 ch.g. Nayef (USA) 129 – Proud Titania (IRE) 103 (Fairy King (USA)) [2009 12g^{5} Aug 8] 33/1, well-held last in maiden at Newmarket. *T. R. George* **–**

BEAT THE ODDS 5 b.g. Beat Hollow 126 – Biodotis (Warning 136) [2009 10.5d^{5} 10d* p10g^{4} a8d^{2} Dec 20] winner of 5 races in Italy, including seller at Pisa in February (final start for D. Gambarota): in cheekpieces/tongue tie, poor form when fourth in claimer at Lingfield sole outing in Britain, then sold from F. Sheridan £2,200: stays 1¾m: acts on dirt, soft and good to firm going: has worn blinkers. *B. Bjorkman, Sweden* **?**

BEAT THE RUSH 2 b.g. (Mar 23) Tobougg (IRE) 125 – Rush Hour (IRE) (Night Shift (USA)) [2009 7d^{2} 7m^{5} 8d^{6} 8g* Oct 19] 10,000Y: good-topped gelding: fifth foal: brother to 2m winner/smart hurdler Bouggler and half-brother to fairly useful 6f (at 2 yrs)/7f winner Lincolneurocruiser (by Spectrum): dam unraced: fair performer: much improved when winning nursery at Pontefract by 2½ lengths from Dolphin Rock, strong at finish: will stay 1¼m: should progress further. *Miss J. A. Camacho* **78 p**

BEAT THE SHOWER 3 b.g. Beat Hollow 126 – Crimson Shower 61 (Dowsing (USA) 124) [2009 7d^{6} 8d f11g 14.1m^{5} 12s* 13.8v^{3} f12g^{6} Nov 17] 22,000F, 31,000Y: big, workmanlike gelding: modest performer: won handicap at Catterick in October: stays 13.8f: acts on heavy ground. *P. D. Niven* **64**

BEAUBRAV 3 b.g. Falbrav (IRE) 133 – Wavy Up (IRE) (Brustolon 117) [2009 58: p10g^{2} 12m^{4} 10d^{2} 10g^{6} 10.1g^{3} 10d^{2} 12m^{5} Aug 23] lengthy gelding: fair handicapper: stays 1½m: acts on polytrack and good to soft ground: tongue tied last 2 starts: joined M. Madgwick. *P. W. D'Arcy* **66**

BEAUCHAMP UNIQUE 6 b.m. Compton Admiral 121 – Beauchamp Jade 105 (Kalaglow 132) [2009 p12.2g 13m 7.9d Jul 26] smallish mare: fair performer in 2006: off almost 3 years, no form at 6 yrs: has worn cheekpieces/blinkers. *E. J. Cooper* **–**

BEAUCHAMP VICEROY 5 ch.g. Compton Admiral 121 – Compton Astoria (USA) (Lion Cavern (USA) 117) [2009 97: p12g^{5} p10g^{6} 8m^{6} p8g^{4} p8.6g* 7m f8g^{6} p8.6g p7.1g^{4} p7.1g^{2} p8m* p10g^{4} Nov 21] tall, close-coupled gelding: useful performer on all-weather, fair on turf: won seller at Wolverhampton (by 10 lengths) in July and handicap at Kempton in October: improved when 4 lengths fourth to Tranquil Tiger in listed race at Lingfield final start (dictated): stays easy 1½m: acts on polytrack, soft and good to firm going: often blinkered/tongue tied/in cheekpieces in 2009: probably not straightforward. *G. A. Butler* **78 a103**

BEAUCHAMP VIKING 5 b.g. Compton Admiral 121 – Beauchamp Jade 105 (Kalaglow 132) [2009 –: 8m 10.2f^{5} 10.2m Jun 13] raw-boned gelding: little form: tongue tied. *S. C. Burrough* **–**

BEAUCHAMP WIZARD 4 b.c. Compton Admiral 121 – Compton Astoria (USA) (Lion Cavern (USA) 117) [2009 81: 9g^{5} p7m 10m^{2} Oct 2] big, strong colt: fair performer, lightly raced: not sure to stay beyond 7f: acts on polytrack: tongue tied last 2 starts. *G. A. Butler* **72**

BEAUCHAMP WONDER 4 b.f. Compton Admiral 121 – Beauchamp Jade 105 (Kalaglow 132) [2009 70p: 17.2g^2 11s^3 Jul 17] lengthy filly: fair maiden handicapper, lightly raced: stays 17.2f: best effort on good ground. *G. A. Butler* **76**

BEAUCHAMP XENIA 3 b.f. Compton Admiral 121 – Beauchamp Jade 105 (Kalaglow 132) [2009 59p: 10g 12m^5 p12g^3 16g^6 Aug 29] workmanlike filly: fair maiden: stays 2m: acts on good to firm ground: tongue tied on debut. *H. Candy* **71**

BEAUCHAMP XERXES 3 ch.c. Compton Admiral 121 – Compton Astoria (USA) (Lion Cavern (USA) 117) [2009 8m^4 10.3m^4 11g^2 12f 10g 8.3m* 9m^2 p10m^4 p12m^3 p10g Nov 21] sturdy colt: sixth foal: brother to 4-y-o Beauchamp Wizard and 5-y-o Beauchamp Viceroy: dam unraced out of half-sister to Poule d'Essai des Pouliches winner Culture Vulture: useful performer: won maiden at Windsor in August: best efforts when placed in listed/minor events, including 3 lengths second to Alwaary at Goodwood and 3¾ lengths third to Once More Dubai at Kempton third/ninth starts: stays easy 1½m: acts on polytrack and good to firm going: tongue tied final outing. *G. A. Butler* **105**

BEAUCHAMP XIARA 3 b.f. Compton Admiral 121 – Beauchamp Buzz 85 (High Top 131) [2009 58p: 9.9f^4 p12g^2 12d Oct 11] close-coupled filly: fair form in maidens: looked uncomfortable on course/going in handicap at Goodwood final start: will stay 1¾m: acts on polytrack and firm going. *H. Candy* **76**

BEAUCHAMP YEOMAN 2 b.g. (May 9) Compton Admiral 121 – One Way Street 119 (Habitat 134) [2009 7g Oct 30] good-topped gelding: 100/1, well beaten in maiden at Newmarket: subsequently gelded. *H. Candy* **–**

BEAUCHAMP YORKER 2 ch.c. (Feb 6) Compton Admiral 121 – Compton Astoria (USA) (Lion Cavern (USA) 117) [2009 7m* Sep 19] well-made colt: brother to 3-y-o Beauchamp Xerxes, 4-y-o Beauchamp Wizard and 5-y-o Beauchamp Viceroy: dam unraced out of half-sister to Poule d'Essai des Pouliches winner Culture Vulture: 20/1, promising start when winning maiden at Newbury by head from Mufarrh (pair clear): will stay 1m: useful prospect. *H. Candy* **94 p**

BEAU FIGHTER 4 b.g. Tobougg (IRE) 125 – Belle de Jour 54 (Exit To Nowhere (USA) 122) [2009 70: 10d* 9.9m^6 11.9g^4 10.3d^3 Oct 24] close-coupled gelding: fair handicapper, lightly raced: won at Newbury in May: will stay 1½m: acts on good to soft ground: sold 20,000 gns, joined G. L. Moore. *C. F. Wall* **79**

BEAU JAZZ 8 br.g. Merdon Melody 98 – Ichor 52 (Primo Dominie 121) [2009 –: p7g p6g^6 p6g Nov 14] strong gelding: maiden: little form since 2006: tried in cheekpieces. *W. de Best-Turner* **–**

BEAUMONT BOY 5 b.g. Foxhound (USA) 103 – Play The Game 70 (Mummy's Game 120) [2009 58: 9m^4 9.1m^3 9m^6 8.3m^4 9.3m^3 7.1m Jun 19] leggy, close-coupled gelding: modest maiden: stays 9f: acts on soft and good to firm ground: wears cheekpieces/blinkers. *J. A. McShane* **52**

BEAUMONT PRINCESS (IRE) 3 b.f. Elusive City (USA) 117 – Pantera Piceno (IRE) (College Chapel 122) [2009 6m May 29] €13,000Y: third foal: dam Italian 7f winner: 33/1, always behind in maiden at Hamilton. *G. A. Swinbank* **–**

BEAUMONT'S PARTY (IRE) 2 b.c. (May 23) High Chaparral (IRE) 132 – Miss Champagne (FR) (Bering 136) [2009 7m^6 p7g^4 6g^5 Oct 30] €85,000 2-y-o: well-made, attractive colt: fourth foal: half-brother to useful 2008 2-y-o 7f winner Minor Vamp (by Hawk Wing) and Irish 2005 2-y-o 6f winner Play Misty For Me (by Danehill Dancer): dam unraced sister to useful French 6f/7f performer Stella Berine: fair form in maidens: should stay 1m. *R. Hannon* **77**

BEAUTIFUL BREEZE (IRE) 3 ch.g. Tobougg (IRE) 125 – Khayrat (IRE) (Polar Falcon (USA) 126) [2009 77: 7.5m^4 7.1m* 7.1f 8m^5 8.1m* Jul 1] sturdy gelding: fairly useful handicapper: won at Warwick in May and Chepstow in July: laboured efforts in between: will stay beyond 1m: acts on good to firm and good to soft going: sold 18,000 gns. *M. Johnston* **82**

BEAUTIFUL FILLY 3 b.f. Oasis Dream 129 – Royal Alchemist (USA) (Royal Academy (USA) 130) [2009 62p: p6g* 7d p6g p6g^2 p6m p7g^3 p7f^4 8m p7.1g* p7.1g^4 p8g Nov 21] fair performer: won maiden at Lingfield in April and handicap at Wolverhampton in October: stays 7f: acts on polytrack: often blinkered. *D. M. Simcock* **78**

BEAUTIFUL LADY (IRE) 4 b.f. Peintre Celebre (USA) 137 – Puteri Wentworth 88 (Sadler's Wells (USA) 132) [2009 77: 12d^5 13.1d May 18] leggy filly: fair handicapper at 3 yrs: well held in 2009: should stay 1¾m: acts on polytrack, firm and good to soft going: tried blinkered. *P. F. I. Cole* **–**

BEAUX YEUX 3 b.f. Cadeaux Genereux 131 – Cloud Hill (Danehill (USA) 126) [2009 –: f6s⁵ f6g³ f5g³ f6d⁴ f6g³ 5.9d 7v 7m f6m Nov 6] close-coupled filly: modest maiden: left P. Midgley prior to final start: stays 6f: acts on fibresand: tried in cheekpieces. *Miss A. Stokell* **54**

BEAVER PATROL (IRE) 7 ch.g. Tagula (IRE) 116 – Erne Project (IRE) 80 (Project Manager 111) [2009 113: 6.5g 6.5g 6m* 6m 7f⁴ 7m 6m 7m 6d 6m 7m Sep 12] strong, well-made gelding: smart performer at best: won minor event at Nad Al Sheba in February by 1¾ lengths from Lipocco: not discredited in listed race at Leicester (fourth to Asset) fifth start, but well below form otherwise in 2009: stays 7f: acts on polytrack, firm and soft going: usually blinkered/visored. *Eve Johnson Houghton* **113 d**

BEBENINE (IRE) 2 b.f. (Mar 21) Antonius Pius (USA) 123§ – Lady Fonic 77 (Zafonic (USA) 130) [2009 p5.1g⁴ 5m⁴ 5.1m 5g⁶ May 19] €8,000F, £2,200Y: close-coupled filly: first foal: dam, Irish maiden (stayed 1½m), out of half-sister to high-class performer up to 1½m Legal Case: modest form in maidens: bred to stay beyond 5f, but has looked all speed. *Pat Morris* **57**

BEBOPALULA (IRE) 2 gr.f. (Apr 8) Galileo (IRE) 134 – Pearl Bright (FR) 80 (Kaldoun (FR) 122) [2009 8g⁶ Oct 23] 44,000F, €80,000Y: fourth foal: half-sister to 4-y-o Berbice and a winner in Greece by Namid: dam 2-y-o 7f winner: 33/1 and green, very much caught the eye when 6½ lengths sixth of 21 to Modeyra in maiden at Doncaster, finishing well having been slowly away and hampered: sure to improve, possibly markedly. *B. W. Hills* **73 p**

BECAUSEWECAN (USA) 3 b.g. Giant's Causeway (USA) 132 – Belle Sultane (USA) (Seattle Slew (USA)) [2009 79: f8g² 12d* 11.9m⁶ 12g³ 11d⁴ p12g² 12m* Oct 16] strong, lengthy gelding: useful handicapper: won at Newmarket in June and October (further marked improvement when beating Hevelius a length): gelded after: stays 1½m: acts on all-weather, heavy and good to firm going: races prominently/makes running. *M. Johnston* **98**

BECKENHAM'S SECRET 5 b.g. Foxhound (USA) 103 – Berliese (IRE) (High Estate 127) [2009 56: p7g p8g⁵ p8g³ p8g p8g p7g⁵ 5.7m 10m 12m³ 10.2m Jun 13] smallish, close-coupled gelding: modest performer: stays 1½m: acts on polytrack, firm and good to soft going: has worn blinkers/visor: signs of temperament. *A. W. Carroll* **51**

BECKERMET (IRE) 7 b.g. Second Empire (IRE) 124 – Razida (IRE) 106 (Last Tycoon 131) [2009 116: p7.1g 6.1g⁵ 7m 6m 6m 6g² 6m 7g p7g² p6m⁵ p7.1g Nov 27] rather leggy, close-coupled gelding: just useful performer nowadays: best effort in 2009 when 2½ lengths fifth to Doncaster Rover in listed race at Chester second start: best at 6f/7f: acts on firm and good to soft going: front runner: tough, but none too consistent. *R. F. Fisher* **101**

BECKY QUICK (IRE) 4 b.f. Fantastic Light (USA) 134 – Private Bluff (USA) (Pine Bluff (USA)) [2009 –: 8.1g f6g 6s Aug 19] no form: tried blinkered. *Bruce Hellier* **–**

BECUILLE (IRE) 4 b.f. Redback 116 – Danz Danz (Efisio 120) [2009 72: p8g⁵ p9.5g p9.5g* p10g³ 10.2g 8d 9s* 9m p9.5m p9.5g³ p9.5g Nov 12] sturdy filly: fair handicapper: in-and-out form in 2009, won at Wolverhampton in April and Yarmouth in July: stays 1¼m: acts on polytrack, firm and soft going: blinkered last 5 starts: not straightforward. *B. J. Meehan* **79**

BEDARRA BOY 3 ch.g. Needwood Blade 117 – Roonah Quay (IRE) (Soviet Lad (USA)) [2009 p8g 7m 10f⁶ 10m³ p11g 12m 15.4m³ Sep 22] tall gelding: modest maiden: stays 15.4f: acts on good to firm ground: second in juvenile hurdle in October. *D. W. P. Arbuthnot* **58**

BED FELLOW (IRE) 5 b.g. Trans Island 119 – Moonlight Partner (IRE) 81 (Red Sunset 120) [2009 72d: 8.3m 12.1g⁵ 12.5m³ 12.5s⁵ 9m² 9m 9d² Oct 28] sturdy gelding: modest handicapper: left T. D. Barron after reappearance: stays 1½m: acts on polytrack and any turf going: tried visored/in cheekpieces: has bled: temperamental. *P. Monteith* **58 §**

BEDLOE'S ISLAND (IRE) 4 b.g. Statue of Liberty (USA) 115 – Scenaria (IRE) (Scenic 128) [2009 59: 5m* 6g⁴ 5g² 5d³ 5m² Sep 23] big gelding: fair handicapper: won at Redcar in June: may prove best at 5f: acts on good to firm and good to soft ground: saddle said to have slipped second outing. *N. Bycroft* **72**

BEDOUIN BLUE (IRE) 6 b.g. Desert Style (IRE) 121 – Society Fair (FR) (Always Fair (USA) 121) [2009 69: f11g f12g³ p12.2g p13.9g Mar 26] strong gelding: fair handicapper: stays 1½m: acts on all-weather and soft ground: tried in blinkers/cheekpieces. *A. J. Lidderdale* **65**

BEDOUIN STYLE (IRE) 3 b.g. Desert Style (IRE) 121 – Samaritan Woman (IRE) (Priolo (USA) 127) [2009 12.1g May 25] 50/1, very green when last in maiden at Chepstow. *Mrs A. M. Thorpe* –

BEES RIVER (IRE) 3 b.f. Acclamation 118 – Notley Park 71 (Wolfhound (USA) 126) [2009 74: 5.1g^3 p5.1g^5 5.1g^5 6f 5.1f^4 6d 5.3f^3 5m 5d^4 5g Sep 30] sparely-made filly: modest maiden handicapper at best in 2009: best at 5f: acts on polytrack, firm and good to soft going: tried visored. *A. P. Jarvis* 62 d

BEE STING 5 b.g. Selkirk (USA) 129 – Desert Lynx (IRE) 79 (Green Desert (USA) 127) [2009 95: 10.3m May 7] lengthy gelding: useful handicapper in 2008: little form over hurdles, and last sole Flat outing in 2009: stays 1½m: acts on polytrack and soft going, probably on good to firm: tried in headgear. *Mrs L. Williamson* –

BEE STINGER 7 b.g. Almaty (IRE) 113§ – Nest Egg (Prince Sabo 123) [2009 90: p9.5g p8g p10g^4 p10g^4 p8g* p8g^4 p10g^2 p8.6g p12m^2 p12.2g* p10m^6 Dec 16] workmanlike gelding: fairly useful performer: won handicap at Lingfield in March and, having left I. Wood £6,500 after sixth start and Heather Dalton after seventh, claimer at Wolverhampton in December (final start for B. Powell): stays 1½m: acts on polytrack and firm going: often wears headgear. *P. R. Hedger* 80

BEETHOVEN (IRE) 2 b.c. (Apr 2) Oratorio (IRE) 128 – Queen Titi (IRE) 108 (Sadler's Wells (USA) 132) [2009 6g^3 6f^2 7m^4 6.3s^3 6v^5 6g* 7s^3 6g^4 7g^6 7m* a8.5f^6 Nov 7] 117

Wrapping the two-year-olds he trains in cotton wool is anathema to Aidan O'Brien and he has reaped significant rewards from campaigning his best juveniles in line with the 'traditional' programme, exploiting the relative weakness of modern two-year-old racing. Holy Roman Emperor, Johannesburg, Oratorio, Rock of Gibraltar and Saratoga Springs all ran seven times in their first season, while Rumplestiltskin and Spartacus had six outings apiece. Between them, that septet won thirty-two races, fourteen of which were Group 1s. In the latest season Alfred Nobel started eight times and gained a Group 1 victory in the Phoenix Stakes. However, even he was trumped by a Ballydoyle two-year-old who set a record which will take some beating—Beethoven, who had his eleventh outing of the season in the Breeders' Cup Juvenile. It goes without saying that Beethoven, who enjoyed his day of days when gaining a last-gasp triumph in the Jumeirah Dewhurst Stakes, is an exceptionally tough colt, and a smart one, though his form hardly ranks him among the best two-year-olds his trainer has handled.

Beethoven's odds of 33/1 in the Dewhurst reflected his standing among the leading two-year-olds up to that point. He started the longest odds of any Group 1 winner from Ballydoyle in the trainer's thirteen-year stint there, ahead of 20/1-shots Classic Park in the 1997 Irish One Thousand Guineas and Black Minnaloushe in the 2001 Irish Two Thousand Guineas. Spartacus at 16/1 in the 2002 Phoenix Stakes had been the previous longest-priced winner of a Group 1 among the juveniles. Beethoven had been highly tried and, on the face of it, found wanting, with just one victory to his name, in an eleven-runner maiden at Leopardstown early in August on his sixth appearance. Even that win wasn't an easy one, since he was all out to hold on from Clashnacree by a head after making most of the running. Beethoven's runs in listed and pattern company had seen his finishing fourth to Big Audio in the Chesham Stakes at Royal Ascot, where he tended to hang, third behind Walk On Bye in the Anglesey Stakes at the Curragh after not having the best of luck in running, and fifth, four lengths behind Alfred Nobel, in the Phoenix Stakes at the Curragh again. Beethoven had also been placed in a maiden at York and a minor event at Naas and the probability that he was fully exposed seemed to be confirmed in three starts after his victory at Leopardstown. Two of those were Group 1s, the National Stakes at the Curragh and the Prix Jean-Luc Lagardere at Longchamp. Beethoven was sent off the outsider of the O'Brien contenders but ran well in the National, coming home ahead of stablemates Air Chief Marshal and Alfred Nobel when two lengths third of six to Kingsfort after being prominent from the outset. Beethoven matched that effort when under four lengths sixth of seven behind Siyouni in France, but he didn't run to the same form when fourth of twenty, two and three quarter lengths behind the winner Lucky General, when favourite for the Goffs Million Sprint at the Curragh in between the two pattern races. The six furlongs of the Goffs Million Sprint was possibly too

Jumeirah Dewhurst Stakes, Newmarket—
a 1,2,4 for Aidan O'Brien but not in the order expected as 33/1-shot Beethoven (visor) beats another son of Oratorio in Fencing Master (left) with Xtension (between first two) and Steinbeck (rail) next

sharp for Beethoven by this stage of his career, but, even with a visor applied for the first time in the Dewhurst, his chances beforehand looked pretty slim.

Ryan Moore had the mount on Beethoven at Newmarket, with stable-jockey Johnny Murtagh electing to ride Steinbeck, second favourite behind National Stakes runner-up Chabal despite not having run since a successful debut at Naas in May. Colm O'Donoghue was aboard the O'Brien 20/1-shot Fencing Master, winner of a maiden race at Dundalk six weeks earlier, and Sean Levey rode the rank outsider Lord High Admiral for the stable. There were four pattern winners among the ten other runners, Buzzword (Prix La Rochette), Dick Turpin (Richmond Stakes), Silver Grecian (Superlative Stakes) and Xtension (Vintage Stakes) but, in truth, this was not a Dewhurst with a lot of strength in depth. Steinbeck made the running at a strong gallop on the rail accompanied by Chabal's stable-companion Free Judgement, with Chabal close up racing a little too freely for his own good, and Beethoven not far behind. Fencing Master and Xtension were among those towards the rear. A number of riders were at work before halfway and, just over two furlongs out, Steinbeck was under pressure to keep ahead of Chabal. The field became bunched as Buzzword and, out wider, Fencing Master and Xtension also put in a challenge. After looking in trouble, ridden along and seemingly short of pace, Beethoven got his second wind and, switched right, started to make excellent progress approaching the final furlong. Chabal dropped out and Buzzword faltered, but Steinbeck, Fencing Master, Xtension and Beethoven all kept on strongly, with Xtension leading a hundred yards out before Beethoven on his inner and Fencing Master on his outer both closed the gap, with Beethoven taking a narrow advantage with fifty yards left. Running on with gusto, he held off Fencing Master by a neck with Xtension a nose away third and Steinbeck a neck back in fourth, the quartet a length and three quarters in front of Buzzword. A cracking finish, similar to 2008, when Intense Focus won by a nose, the same and half a length, and to 2001, when Rock of Gibraltar—O'Brien's only previous winner of the race—beat his stable-companions Landseer and Tendulkar by a short head and a head. The visor obviously made a difference to Beethoven, O'Brien revealing that its use was the idea of one of his sons, Joseph, who had told him earlier in the week: 'There's loads in there. Put a visor on him and maybe (it'll) sharpen him up a bit.' O'Brien also commented, rather obscurely, that 'Beethoven has been getting better with every run, even though his form figures don't suggest it.' That's an interesting line of thinking but not one which could really be squared with the form-book—at least not the way we read it. The Dewhurst form is itself not outstanding and there is probably more reason to be optimistic about the prospects of the second and fourth, who have plenty of scope and must have benefited from the experience. Fencing Master, in particular, looked green. Still, plenty of credit should go to Beethoven for winning. He did not win his only subsequent race, though, the Breeders' Cup Juvenile at Santa Anita. Unproven on the pro-ride surface and clearly some way short of the best of his generation—stable-companion

St Nicholas Abbey—Beethoven, who was visored again, started at just over 14/1. He was badly hampered on the first turn and left with an awful lot to do, but he recovered well to finish a respectable sixth, beaten less than three lengths, behind fellow European challenger Vale of York.

The Coolmore partners had an additional reason to be satisfied with the outcome of the Dewhurst since both the winner and runner-up are from the first crop of their young sire Oratorio. Coincidentally, another Coolmore sire, none other than the now-retired Sadler's Wells, did even better with two colts from his first crop in the 1988 Dewhurst Stakes—Prince of Dance and Scenic dead-heated for first. Oratorio, as resilient as one could wish to find, won the Prix Jean-Luc Lagardere and finished second to Shamardal in the Dewhurst before doing even better at three, winning the Eclipse and Irish Champion Stakes. Oratorio covered a large book of mares, one hundred and forty-four to be precise, and had around a hundred foals on the ground in his first crop. He didn't have anything like so many winners as some of the other first-season sires, with just eleven from almost fifty runners in Europe, but they did also include the useful Big Audio, on the mark in the Chesham Stakes and Stonehenge Stakes. The Coolmore partners frequently purchase progeny by their stallions and Beethoven changed hands for €260,000 at the Goffs Million Sale. Beethoven's dam Queen Titi was bred and owned by Aidan O'Brien's wife Ann Marie and the colt was bred by the couple in partnership under the name Whisperview Trading Ltd. So why 'sell' him at Goffs? The fact that he went through the Goffs sale-ring did, of course, guarantee entry to the Goffs Million races in the event of Beethoven's proving good enough.

Beethoven (IRE) (b.c. Apr 2, 2007)	Oratorio (IRE) (b 2002)	Danehill (b 1986)	Danzig
			Razyana
		Mahrah (b 1987)	Vaguely Noble
			Montage
	Queen Titi (IRE) (b 2002)	Sadler's Wells (b 1981)	Northern Dancer
			Fairy Bridge
		Litani River (ch 1986)	Irish River
			Luv Luvin'

In his toughness, Beethoven takes after Queen Titi—he is her first foal—as well as after Oratorio. Queen Titi won two of her thirteen races as a three-year-old, both at a mile, notably the Garnet Stakes, a listed event at Naas, on her final appearance. She is a sister to the smart seven- to nine-furlong filly Psalm, successful in the Concorde Stakes as a three-year-old in 2008, and is a close relative of the useful Ballydoyle three-year-old of the latest season, Trojan War. The grandam Litani River was a listed-placed maiden in France and very well related since her sister, Or Vision, foaled Group 1 winners Dolphin Street, Insight and Saffron Walden and a half-sister, Brigid, produced two of the same ilk in Sequoyah and Listen. Sequoyah has subsequently made a significant mark at stud by producing Henrythenavigator. There is enough stamina in the pedigree to suggest that Beethoven will stay at least a mile and a quarter. With several other potential Two Thousand Guineas candidates in the stable possessing much more scope for improvement, Beethoven is likely to find life tough as a three-year-old. His odds for the Guineas over the winter, with 33/1 freely available, accurately reflect his chance, taking everything into account. The Poule d'Essai des Poulains, a race which is invariably third choice for the O'Brien contenders behind the English and Irish equivalents, may be his classic target. Whatever his future he certainly doesn't look to be another Rock of Gibraltar in the making at this stage. *A. P. O'Brien, Ireland*

BEFORE THE WAR (USA) 2 ch.c. (Jan 21) El Corredor (USA) 123 – Adrenalin Running (USA) (A P Indy (USA) 131) [2009 p7g p7.1m^5 Nov 28] $165,000F, 55,000 2-y-o: second foal: half-brother to winner in USA by Toccet: dam US 7f winner out of half-sister to smart Irish/US middle-distance performer Phantom Breeze: green, similar form in maidens at Kempton and Wolverhampton: likely to do better. *L. M. Cumani* **61 p**

BEFORTYFOUR 4 b.g. Kyllachy 129 – Ivania 81 (First Trump 118) [2009 115: 5d^5 Jul 17] strong, close-coupled gelding: smart performer in 2008: better for run, faded when fifth to Nota Bene in minor event at Newmarket sole start at 4 yrs: speedy front runner, will prove best at 5f: acts on polytrack and good to firm ground: sold just £3,200 in December. *M. A. Jarvis* **97**

BE GRATEFUL (IRE) 2 b. or br.f. (May 15) Efisio 120 – Dwingeloo (IRE) 83 (Dancing Dissident (USA) 119) [2009 5m^5 p5.1m^5 5.1g^6 p7g Nov 14] seventh foal: sister to 6-y-o sprinter Miss Vegas and half-sister to 2 winners, including smart US Grade 3 1m winner Realt Na Mara: dam 2-y-o 5f winner: modest maiden: well held in nursery (caught wide throughout): should stay 6f. *H. Morrison* **59**

BEHIND BLUE EYES 3 b.g. Kyllachy 129 – Mamoura (IRE) 97 (Lomond (USA) 128) [2009 p8.6g 7g 10.2g Apr 28] little impact in seller/maidens: tried in cheekpieces/ visor. *Karen George* **–**

BEHKABAD (FR) 2 b.c. (Mar 21) Cape Cross (IRE) 129 – Behkara (IRE) 116 (Kris 135) [2009 6m* 7.5g* 8g* Sep 19] second foal: half-brother to smart French 1½m/13f winner Beheshtam (by Peintre Celebre): dam, French 1½m to 15f (Prix Hubert de Chaudenay) winner, out of Arc runner-up Behera: unbeaten in newcomers race at La Teste in July, minor event at Deauville in August and Prix des Chenes at Longchamp in September: beat Arasin for last 2 wins, by ¾ length final start, taking time to find stride but quickening to lead close home: will stay 1¼m: will progress further. *J-C. Rouget, France* **108 p**

BE INVINCIBLE (IRE) 2 b.c. (Mar 17) Invincible Spirit (IRE) 121 – Lupulina (CAN) (Saratoga Six (USA)) [2009 5m* 6d^3 7g Oct 24] €80,000Y: good-topped colt: brother to 4-y-o Legal Eagle and half-brother to several winners abroad: dam, German 7f winner, half-sister to smart stayer Poltarf: fair form: won maiden at Windsor in April: failed to build on that in minor event/nursery, off 5 months before final start: should stay 7f. *B. W. Hills* **79**

BE KIND 3 b.f. Generous (IRE) 139 – Aquavita 56 (Kalaglow 132) [2009 8.3m p12g^6 p12m p16.5g Oct 17] stocky filly: fourth foal: half-sister to 6-y-o Follow The Dream; dam 2m and hurdles winner: poor maiden: bred to be suited by 2m+: tried in cheekpieces. *Karen George* **47**

BELATED SILVER (IRE) 3 gr. or ro.g. Clodovil (IRE) 116 – Premier Place (USA) (Out of Place (USA)) [2009 80: p7g^4 8f^4 f7g^3 7.1v^6 p6g* 7m^3 Jul 3] deep-girthed gelding: fair performer: won claimer at Wolverhampton in June: stays 7f: acts on all-weather and soft going: sold 23,000 gns, sent to Qatar. *Tom Dascombe* **77**

BEL CANTOR 6 b.h. Largesse 112 – Palmstead Belle (IRE) 79 (Wolfhound (USA) 126) [2009 98, a80: 6m 6m^6 6g 6m 6m^3 6g p6g* p6g 6g 6g^4 6m^2 p6g 6m 6g 5.1m^2 6m 6.1m^2 6m 6d f5m* p6g^2 f5g^4 f5m Dec 15] leggy horse: fairly useful handicapper: won at Kempton (apprentices) in July and Southwell in November: effective at 5f to easy 7f: acts on all-weather and any turf going: often wears cheekpieces: usually front runner: none too consistent. *W. J. H. Ratcliffe* **87**

BELGOOREE 2 b.f. (Feb 8) Haafhd 129 – Ziggy Zaggy (Diktat 126) [2009 p7.1g Dec 4] 105,000F, 40,000Y: first foal: dam unraced half-sister to very smart 1¼m/1½m performer Imperial Dancer: 11/2, well held in maiden at Wolverhampton, weakening quickly. *J. G. Given* **–**

BELINSKY (IRE) 2 b.c. (Apr 12) Compton Place 125 – Westwood (FR) (Anabaa (USA) 130) [2009 5g^3 6m^6 f5g^3 f6g^4 p6g* Sep 2] quite attractive colt: fair performer: dropped in class, won seller at Lingfield in September: effective at 5f/6f: acts on all-weather: sold 12,500 gns. *S. A. Callaghan* **68**

BELLA CHARLIE (IRE) 2 b.c. (Mar 15) Pyrus (USA) 106 – Beseeching (IRE) 50 (Hamas (IRE) 125§) [2009 p7g p7m^6 f6d^6 Dec 29] 11,000Y: fifth foal: half-brother to 3 winners, including Irish 5-y-o Mojito Royale: dam, maiden, stayed 1¾m: best effort in maidens when sixth to Too Putra at Kempton, still green: faced plenty of kickback at Southwell next time: remains open to improvement. *M. G. Quinlan* **59 p**

BELLA FIGHETTA 3 b.f. Bertolini (USA) 125 – My Girl 39 (Mon Tresor 113) [2009 10.2d p8m^6 p7.1g^6 p6m^5 p5.1g Dec 4] 7,500Y: sturdy filly: fifth foal: sister to 2006 2-y-o 5f seller winner Danger Alley and half-sister to fairly useful 2002 2-y-o 5f winner Redding (by Puissance): dam sprint maiden: poor form in maidens: tried blinkered/in cheekpieces: withdrawn after giving trouble at stall intended debut. *Ms J. S. Doyle* **49**

BELLAHARRY (IRE) 2 b.f. (Apr 12) Lucky Story (USA) 128 – Saharan Song (IRE) 64 (Singspiel (IRE) 133) [2009 8.1d p7.1g^6 8.3g Oct 28] second foal: dam maiden (stayed 9.5f): no form, including in sellers. *Matthew Salaman* **–**

BELLA MEDICI 4 ch.f. Medicean 128 – Missouri 86 (Charnwood Forest (IRE) 125) [2009 68§: p16g Feb 11] sturdy filly: modest performer: stays 11.5f: acts on good to firm and good to soft going: has refused to race (no stalls), and one to treat with caution. *P. G. Murphy* **57 §**

BELLA ROWENA 3 b.f. Kyllachy 129 – Luxurious (USA) (Lyphard (USA) 132) [2009 75: 7m 7m Jun 27] leggy, close-coupled filly: fair form in maidens at 2 yrs: well held both starts in 2009: free-going sort: sent to France. *A. M. Balding* **–**

BELLA SWAN 2 ch.f. (Apr 29) Leporello (IRE) 118 – Lydia Maria 70 (Dancing Brave (USA) 140) [2009 6m^3 6m^2 6m* 7g^3 7m^4 Oct 2] well-made filly: closely related to very smart 1¼m to 1¾m winner Barolo (by Danehill) and half-sister to several winners, including Irish 7-y-o Propinquity: dam, maiden (stayed 1¼m), out of Nassau Stakes/ Yorkshire Oaks winner Connaught Bridge: fairly useful performer: won maiden at Newmarket in July by ¾ length from Water Biscuit: better effort in pattern company after when creditable 7¾ lengths fourth of 8 to Tabassum in Oh So Sharp Stakes at Newmarket: stays 7f. *W. R. Swinburn* **87**

BELLE BELLINO (FR) 4 b.f. Robellino (USA) 127 – Hoh Chi Min 103 (Efisio 120) [2009 68: 5.7g^6 5.1d Apr 28] smallish filly: fair performer at 3 yrs: well held in 2009: best around 6f: acts on heavy and good to firm ground. *R. M. Beckett* **–**

BELLE DES AIRS (IRE) 3 ch.f. Dr Fong (USA) 128 – Belle Reine (King of Kings (IRE) 125) [2009 86: 7d^4 6m^2 7d^2 6d^5 7g^3 7m* 7m^2 Sep 13] workmanlike filly: fairly useful handicapper: won at Epsom in September: also ran well when runner-up: stays 7f: acts on firm and good to soft going. *R. M. Beckett* **92**

BELLE EPONINE 2 b.f. (Feb 24) Fraam 114 – Red Ryding Hood 83 (Wolfhound (USA) 126) [2009 5g^6 6m 7m* f7g 7m a9.5g Oct 21] 1,000F, 6,000Y: fourth foal: half-sister to 5f winner (including at 2 yrs) Baileys Outshine (by Inchinor): dam 5f winner: modest performer: won seller at Redcar in June: not discredited in claimers in France last 2 starts: stays 9.5f: acts on all-weather and good to firm going. *E. J. O'Neill* **62**

BELLE NOVERRE (IRE) 5 b.m. Noverre (USA) 125 – Belle Etoile (FR) (Lead On Time (USA) 123) [2009 89: 6s 9m 10.7g 8.3g^4 a6g^5 p8g 7g p10.7g^4 p9.5g^6 Nov 14] lengthy, rather unfurnished mare: fair handicapper: left J. Bolger after second start: barely stays 10.7f: acts on polytrack, firm and good to soft going: usually wears cheekpieces: tried tongue tied: tends to carry head awkwardly. *Shaun Harley, Ireland* **78** **a75**

BELLE PARK 2 b.f. (May 26) Hamairi (IRE) 112 – Cape Siren (Warning 136) [2009 p5m 5.1g p8m p6g Dec 7] sixth foal: half-sister to winner in Sweden by Efisio: dam, no form, half-sister to dam of high-class stayer Septimus: signs of a little ability: bred to stay 1m. *Karen George* **–**

BELLES BEAU 2 b.f. (Feb 23) Fraam 114 – Victory Flip (IRE) 67 (Victory Note (USA) 120) [2009 p7.1g Dec 18] second foal: half-sister to 4-y-o My Mate Max: dam maiden: 33/1 and green, down the field in maiden at Wolverhampton. *R. Hollinshead* **–**

BELLE ZORRO 2 br.f. (Mar 25) Dr Fong (USA) 128 – Special Beat 65 (Bustino 136) [2009 p8m p8m p7g Oct 9] close-coupled filly: half-sister to several winners, notably 6-y-o Gee Dee Nen: dam 17f winner: green, outpaced over inadequate trips in maidens: will be suited by 1¼m+: capable of better. *M. L. W. Bell* **– p**

BELLINI ROSE (IRE) 2 b.f. (May 4) Bertolini (USA) 125 – Prospectress (USA) 87 (Mining (USA)) [2009 p5g* p7g^4 Nov 5] fifth foal: dam 7f to 1½m (US Grade 2 event) winner: fair form: won maiden at Lingfield in October: raced freely/hung left when last of 4 minor event there: may prove best short of 7f. *Tom Dascombe* **69**

BELL ISLAND 5 b.g. Dansili 127 – Thermal Spring 77 (Zafonic (USA) 130) [2009 83: p10g p13g* p13g* p16g^5 13.3m^4 14m^4 13m^6 11m^5 p13g* p13.9g^4 p12m Dec 9] rather leggy, lengthy gelding: fairly useful handicapper on all-weather, fair on turf: won at Lingfield in February, March and October: stays 2m: acts on polytrack, good to firm and good to soft ground: wears headgear: temperamental. *Lady Herries* **77 §** **a81 §**

BELLOMI (IRE) 4 br. or gr.g. Lemon Drop Kid (USA) 131 – Reina Blanca 102 (Darshaan 133) [2009 95: 7.1m 8.3g May 19] useful performer at 3 yrs: no show in 2009, including in seller: stays 7f: acts on firm and good to soft going. *A. G. Juckes* **–**

BELL'S OCEAN (USA) 2 b.f. (Mar 3) Proud Citizen (USA) 122 – Golden Train (USA) (Slew O' Gold (USA)) [2009 5m^2 6m^5 6m* 6f 7m^6 6g 6m p6g^3 6d^3 p6m^5 6g 6g Oct 19] $55,000Y: leggy filly: seventh foal: half-sister to 2 winners in USA: dam unraced out of Grade 1 8.5f winner By Land By Sea: fair performer: won 5-runner maiden at Newmarket in May: held form in nurseries until last 2 starts: stays 6f: acts on polytrack, good to firm and good to soft going. *J. Ryan* **68**

BELOW ZERO (IRE) 2 b.c. (Apr 20) Shamardal (USA) 129 – Chilly Start (IRE) (Caerleon (USA) 132) [2009 6g^3 5.7f* Jun 5] fifth foal: half-brother to 1¼m winner Oscar Snowman (by Selkirk) and Irish 3-y-o Haaf Ok, both fairly useful: dam unraced **94 p**

close relation of Lammtarra: favourite, much better effort in maidens when winning at Bath in June by 8 lengths from Six Diamonds, making all and allowed to coast final 1f: will stay 7f: useful colt in the making. *M. Johnston*

BEN 4 b.g. Bertolini (USA) 125 – Bold Byzantium (Bold Arrangement 127) [2009 66: **39**
p5m p6g p5.1g p5.1g Mar 30] sturdy gelding: just poor performer in 2009: best at 5f: acts on polytrack and firm going: usually visored (blinkered last 2 starts). *P. G. Murphy*

BENANDONNER (USA) 6 ch.g. Giant's Causeway (USA) 132 – Cape Verdi (IRE) **106**
126 (Caerleon (USA) 132) [2009 106: p7.1g^4 8m p7g^2 8s 8m* 7d^4 7m 8g 8g 8m^3 8g^2 p8.6g^3 p7g* p8f^4 Dec 20] good-topped gelding: useful performer: won handicap at Ripon (by ½ length from City of The Kings) in June and claimer at Lingfield (left R. Fahey £15,000 gns) in December: effective at 7f to 1¼m: acts on all-weather, heavy and good to firm going. *Mike Murphy*

BENAYOUN 5 b.g. Inchinor 119 – Sosumi 101 (Be My Chief (USA) 122) [2009 50: **47**
12m^6 Jun 3] well-made gelding: poor performer: stays 8.3f: acts on polytrack and soft going: blinkered last 2 starts. *B. J. Llewellyn*

BEN BACCHUS (IRE) 7 b.g. Bahhare (USA) 122 – Bodfaridistinction (IRE) 77 **50**
(Distinctly North (USA) 115) [2009 –, a58: p12g* p12g^5 p13.9g^5 p12g p11g^6 12d 11.9m **a58**
11.8m^3 p12g^6 12.6g^6 Jul 3] good-topped gelding: modest handicapper, better on all-weather: won apprentice event at Kempton in January: stays 1¾m: acts on all-weather and good to firm going: tried in blinkers. *P. W. Hiatt*

BENBAUN (IRE) 8 b.g. Stravinsky (USA) 133 – Escape To Victory (Salse (USA) 128) **122**
[2009 114: 5d 5m^2 5m^3 5g* 5m^2 5g^4 5g^4 Oct 4] big, useful-looking gelding: very smart performer: won Dubai Duty Free Millenium Millionaire Sapphire Stakes at the Curragh (seventh course success, beat Snaefell 2½ lengths) in June: best effort since 2007 when neck second to Borderlescott in Nunthorpe Stakes at York next time, headed only well inside final 1f: respectable length fourth to Total Gallery in Prix de l'Abbaye de Longchamp final start: effective at 5f/6f: acts on firm and good to soft going: blinkered/visored: usually races prominently. *K. A. Ryan*

BEN CHORLEY 5 gr.g. Inchinor 119 – Arantxa 77§ (Sharpo 132) [2009 101: 8m^5 **90**
10.4m Jul 11] handicapper, lightly raced: useful at 4 yrs: off 12 months, better effort in 2009 when fifth at Newcastle (withdrawn after unseating rider to post and running loose prior to intended reappearance): should stay 1¼m (pulled too hard when tried): acts on soft ground. *D. R. Lanigan*

BENCOOLEN (IRE) 4 b.g. Daylami (IRE) 138 – Jakarta (IRE) 79 (Machiavellian **99**
(USA) 123) [2009 99: 8m^2 10.1g 8m^3 10.4m 8.5g 8g 9s* 8g^3 9m Oct 3] good-topped gelding: useful handicapper: won at Goodwood (apprentices, beat Mountain Pride by ¾ length) in August: also ran well when in frame first/third starts: stays 10.9f: acts on firm and soft going: has worn visor/cheekpieces: often unruly at stall. *D. Nicholls*

BENDED KNEE 3 b.f. Refuse To Bend (IRE) 128 – Flavian 94 (Catrail (USA) 123) **83**
[2009 8f^2 7.1m^2 6g^3 7g* Oct 31] angular filly: third foal: half-sister to 2005 2-y-o 6f/7f winner Young Flavio (by Mark of Esteem) and winner up to 1½m in Scandinavia by Halling: dam, 6f (at 2 yrs)/7f winner, out of Musidora Stakes winner Fatah Flare: fairly useful performer: placed all starts prior to winning handicap at Newmarket, making virtually all: stays 7f: raced only on good ground or firmer. *H. Candy*

BENEDICTE (IRE) 3 b.f. Galileo (IRE) 134 – Rachelle (IRE) (Mark of Esteem (IRE) **77 +**
137) [2009 10m^6 10.3m* 10m 10.3s Nov 7] 210,000Y, 100,000 2-y-o: sturdy filly: fourth foal: half-sister to very smart 6f (including Middle Park Stakes) winner Amadeus Wolf (by Mozart) and fairly useful 7f/1m winner Always A Rock (by Rock of Gibraltar): dam, Italian 1m winner, out of Oaks d'Italia runner-up Rose Violet: fair performer: won maiden at Chester in September: out of depth in listed races last 2 starts (flattered first occasion): raced only at 1¼m: acts on good to firm going: sent to Italy. *M. Botti*

BENEDICT SPIRIT (IRE) 4 b.g. Invincible Spirit (IRE) 121 – Kathy Caerleon **81**
(IRE) (Caerleon (USA) 132) [2009 69, a82: f12s* p14g^5 f12d^3 f12g^2 f12g^2 10g^2 9.9m^2 10.4v 12m^2 p9.5g p12.2g^4 f12f^3 f11m^4 p9.5g^{5d} Dec 7] sturdy gelding: fairly useful performer: won handicap at Southwell in January: mostly creditable efforts after, claimed from M. Tompkins £16,000 after ninth start: disqualified after rider failed to draw correct weight final start: stays 1½m: acts on all-weather and good to firm going: consistent. *D. Burchell*

BENETTI (IRE) 3 ch.g. Kheleyf (USA) 116 – Assigh Lady (IRE) 83 (Great Commo- **–**
tion (USA) 123) [2009 42: 7f 5.1f Jun 5] lengthy gelding: maiden: poor at 2 yrs, no form in 2009: visored final outing. *M. Madgwick*

*Dubai Duty Free Millennium Millionaire Sapphire Stakes, the Curragh—
Benbaun records his seventh course success; the grey Snaefell is second with Inxile (right) third*

BENFLEET BOY 5 gr.g. Fasliyev (USA) 120 – Nicely (IRE) 94 (Bustino 136) [2009 83: 12m^2 12v Oct 24] useful-looking gelding: fair handicapper: stays 1½m: acts on polytrack, heavy and good to firm ground: often races prominently. *B. G. Powell* **79**

BENGAL TIGER 3 ch.g. Tagula (IRE) 116 – Floriana 61 (Selkirk (USA) 129) [2009 8m 8.1m^6 p12g^2 p12m* Sep 16] lengthy gelding: second foal: half-brother to 1½m seller winner Ericarrow (by Bollin Eric): dam, maiden, sister to smart performer up to 7f Border Music: useful form: further marked improvement when winning maiden at Kempton in September by 7 lengths from Buckie Boy, striding clear: stays 1½m: carried head awkwardly second/third starts: sold 30,000 gns. *A. M. Balding* **95**

BENGERS LASS (USA) 3 ch.f. Orientate (USA) 127 – Wiedniu (USA) 106 (Danzig Connection (USA)) [2009 p10m 8.3d 10.2g p12m^5 Nov 29] $9,000Y: sturdy filly: half-sister to several winners, including fairly useful Irish 7f (at 2 yrs)/1m winner Queen's Love (by Kingmambo): dam maiden (stayed 1m): well beaten in maidens: tried tongue tied. *R. Curtis* **–**

BENHEGO 4 ch.g. Act One 124 – Sadaka (USA) 77 (Kingmambo (USA) 125) [2009 80, a84: p16g* p16g* p16g^4 Mar 28] workmanlike gelding: fairly useful handicapper: won at Kempton in February and Lingfield in March: stays 2m: acts on polytrack, good to firm and good to soft ground (unraced on extremes): has hung: successful both starts over hurdles. *G. L. Moore* **87**

BENITEZ BOND 4 ch.g. Bahamian Bounty 116 – Triple Tricks (IRE) 70 (Royal Academy (USA) 130) [2009 –: 8g f8g^2 8m^6 p9.5g p9.5g^6 Sep 3] modest maiden: stays 1m: easily best effort on fibresand. *G. R. Oldroyd* **– a60**

BENLLECH 5 b.g. Lujain (USA) 119 – Four Legs Good (IRE) 58 (Be My Guest (USA) 126) [2009 105: 6g 6.5g^4 p7g p6g 6m 6m^2 6g^2 Jun 25] close-coupled gelding: has a rather round action: useful handicapper: back to best when runner-up at Redcar (beaten head by Johannes) and Warwick (neck behind Barons Spy) last 2 starts: effective at 5f to 7f: acts on polytrack and good to firm going: tongue tied once. *D. M. Simcock* **101**

BENNELONG 3 b.g. Bahamian Bounty 116 – Bundle Up (USA) (Miner's Mark (USA) 120) [2009 84: 8s^5 p8g^2 p8g^6 8m^4 7.1g^3 f8f* p8m^2 p8m^3 p8f^5 Dec 16] rangy gelding: fairly useful performer: won maiden at Southwell in October (left R. Beckett 15,000 gns after): good efforts in handicaps after when placed: stays easy 1m: acts on all-weather, soft and good to firm going: tried in cheekpieces. *G. L. Moore* **84**

BENNY THE BEAR 2 ch.g. (Apr 29) Rambling Bear 115 – Mitchelland 72 (Nam- **60**
aqualand (USA)) [2009 6m^3 6s^4 Aug 19] modest form in maidens at Newcastle and Hamilton. *James Moffatt*

BENOZZO GOZZOLI 3 ch.g. Medicean 128 – Star Precision 103 (Shavian 125) **65**
[2009 f8g^6 f8g p8g^4 9.7d p8.6g 8.5m 8.1d 10m^4 p16g^4 16g* p16g Nov 5] fair performer: much improved when winning handicap at Nottingham (by 9 lengths) in October: stays 2m: best effort on good ground. *H. Morrison*

BENRISH (IRE) 2 b.c. (Jan 31) Refuse To Bend (IRE) 128 – Miss Trish (IRE) 104 **81**
(Danetime (IRE) 121) [2009 6m^2 6g^2 7g^3 7s^4 Nov 3] £82,000Y: first foal: dam Irish 7f to 8.5f winner: fairly useful form: second in maidens at Ayr for B. Smart, then in frame in maiden and minor event at Maisons-Laffitte: stays 7f: acts on good to firm ground. *X. Nakkachdji, France*

BEN'S DREAM (IRE) 3 br.g. Kyllachy 129 – Kelso Magic (USA) 98 (Distant View **75**
(USA) 126) [2009 80p: p6g^5 5.7g^5 6f 5m^4 6g* 6m^4 6d p6m 6d^3 Oct 12] workmanlike gelding: fair handicapper: won at Warwick in July: will prove best kept to 5f/6f: acts on good to firm and good to soft going: tongue tied nowadays, also in cheekpieces final start: none too consistent. *A. M. Balding*

BENTLEY 5 b.g. Piccolo 121 – April Lee 70 (Superpower 113) [2009 70: 7m p6g 7d^6 **70**
8m 6d 6m p7.1g^5 p6g* p6g^4 p7m Dec 30] sturdy gelding: fair performer: won seller at Wolverhampton in December: best at 6f/7f: acts on all-weather, good to firm and good to soft going: sometimes visored: none too consistent. *J. G. Given*

BENTLEY BROOK (IRE) 7 ch.g. Singspiel (IRE) 133 – Gay Bentley (USA) (River- **80**
man (USA) 131) [2009 88: p12.2g^5 p16g^6 f12d^4 p16.5g^6 p16.5g* f14g^4 f14d Dec 29] workmanlike gelding: fairly useful handicapper: won at Wolverhampton in November: stays 16.5f: acts on all-weather, good to firm and good to soft going: tried blinkered/tongue tied. *R. Curtis*

BERBERI 3 ch.c. Bertolini (USA) 125 – Bird of Prey (IRE) 69 (Last Tycoon 131) [2009 –
8.1m Apr 25] 100/1 and tongue tied, green when tailed off in maiden at Haydock. *A. G. Newcombe*

BERBICE (IRE) 4 gr.g. Acclamation 118 – Pearl Bright (FR) 80 (Kaldoun (FR) 122) **85 §**
[2009 95§: 5.8s 7v 6m^5 7g 6.5s 6m^6 7f^2 p7g^2 p8m^2 p7g* p8m^5 Oct 26] tall, close-coupled gelding: fairly useful handicapper: runner-up 3 times prior to winning at Kempton in October: stays 7f: acts on polytrack, firm and good to soft going: tried tongue tied/in cheekpieces, blinkered last 3 starts: sometimes starts slowly: tends to hang/find little: ungenuine. *S. Donohoe, Ireland*

BERE DAVIS (FR) 4 gr.g. Verglas (IRE) 118 – Zerelda (Exhibitioner 111) [2009 85: **81**
7d^2 8m^3 8.5m^3 8m* 7.9m 7f^5 7m^4 8.1m^2 7.1m^6 8m 8m 7d^3 7.2g 8.1m^4 8.1m^5 9.1g^4 Oct 23] sturdy, close-coupled gelding: has a round action: fairly useful handicapper: won at Thirsk in May: left P. D. Evans prior to final start: stays 1m: acts on firm and good to soft ground: tried tongue tied/in headgear: front runner/races prominently: signs of temperament. *M. A. Barnes*

BERESFORD LADY 5 b.m. Presidium 124 – Coney Hills 35 (Beverley Boy 99) –
[2009 –: p8.6g^6 Jan 7] leggy mare: maiden: little form since 2007: has worn cheekpieces. *A. D. Brown*

BERGONZI (IRE) 5 ch.g. Indian Ridge 123 – Lady Windley (Baillamont (USA) 124) **84**
[2009 80: 13.8m^5 9.9m^6 11.5m^3 12.1m 15.8g* 13.8g^2 16.4m^6 14.1g^5 Oct 16] rangy gelding: fairly useful handicapper: won at Catterick in July: stays 2m: acts on polytrack, good to firm and good to soft going: tried in visor/cheekpieces/tongue strap. *J. Howard Johnson*

BERING DE LAURIERE (FR) 6 ch.g. Evening World (FR) 111 – Shenedova (FR) –
(Hellios (USA)) [2009 p13g f12g^4 Feb 12] fair form at best in bumpers for Jean-Rene Auvray: well held over hurdles for current handler, and no form in claimer/maiden on Flat. *B. G. Powell*

BERKALANI (IRE) 3 b.f. Ashkalani (IRE) 128 – Berkeley Hall 68 (Saddlers' Hall –
(IRE) 126) [2009 7.1d 10.2g Oct 21] second foal: sister to 4-y-o Just Jimmy: dam 6f winner: well held in seller/maiden. *P. D. Evans*

BERLING (IRE) 2 gr.c. (Mar 27) Montjeu (IRE) 137 – Danaskaya (IRE) 106 (Danehill **77**
(USA) 126) [2009 8g^6 8m^5 9d^3 Oct 11] 650,000Y: third foal: half-brother to useful 7f (in Ireland at 2 yrs)/1m (in USA) winner Kayd Kodaun (by Traditionally): dam, Irish 2-y-o 6f winner, closely related to smart Irish performer up to 1m Modeeroch: easily best effort in maidens when 3 lengths third to Ted Spread at Goodwood: should stay 1¼m: acts on good to soft going. *J. L. Dunlop*

BERMACHA 4 ch.f. Bertolini (USA) 125 – Machaera (Machiavellian (USA) 123) **53** [2009 75: p8.6g f8g^{5} 10g 8.1g f8g Nov 17] rather leggy, quite attractive filly: just modest performer nowadays: stays 8.6f: acts on polytrack and soft ground. *J. E. Long*

BERMONDSEY BOB (IRE) 3 b.g. Trans Island 119 – Tread Softly (IRE) 70 (Roi **50** Danzig (USA)) [2009 73: 6m 6f 7.6f 8.3m 7g^{4} 6m^{5} 6.1d* 6m^{5} 6d Oct 12] good-topped gelding: modest handicapper nowadays: won at Chepstow in September: best at 5f/6f: acts on soft and good to firm going: tried in cheekpieces: none too consistent. *J. L. Spearing*

BERMONDSEY GIRL 3 b.f. Bertolini (USA) 125 – Upend 120 (Main Reef 126) **69** [2009 7d^{5} 8m 7g^{6} 7g* p7.1g p7.1g 7g^{3} Oct 20] sturdy filly: half-sister to several winners, including useful 1m (at 2 yrs) to 1½m winner Al Azhar (by Alzao) and smart 1m winner Musicanna (by Cape Cross) and to dam of high-class sprinter Overdose: dam, 1¼m/1½m (St Simon Stakes) winner, half-sister to dam of high-class stayer/Champion Hurdle winner Royal Gait: fair performer: won handicap at Lingfield in July: should stay 1m: acts on polytrack, best turf effort on good ground: sold 35,000 gns. *C. F. Wall*

BERNABEU (IRE) 7 b.g. Mark of Esteem (IRE) 137 – Snow Ballet (IRE) (Sadler's **61** Wells (USA) 132) [2009 61: p12.2g^{5} p12g^{2} p12g^{4} p12g^{4} p12.2g^{5} p13.9g^{5} 11.9d^{5} f12m p12m^{5} Nov 27] modest performer: effective at 1¼m/1½m: acts on polytrack and soft ground: tried blinkered: usually races close to pace. *S. Curran*

BERNIE THE BOLT (IRE) 3 br.g. Milan 129 – Chaparral Lady (IRE) 81 (Broken **106** Hearted 124) [2009 53p: 10m^{5} 12.1g^{3} 14m^{3} 16g^{3} 14s* 14m^{3} 18m* Sep 19] workmanlike gelding: useful and progressive form: won maiden at Lingfield in August and handicap at Newmarket (beat Alanbrooke 4½ lengths, going away) in September: stays 2¼m: acts on soft and good to firm going. *A. M. Balding*

BERNIX 7 gr.g. Linamix (FR) 127 – Bernique (USA) (Affirmed (USA)) [2009 12d **–** 10.2m f8g^{4} f11m 8.5m 9.9g f8f f11m^{6} Dec 15] maiden: missed 2008: modest at best in **a56** 2009: should stay 1¾m: acts on fibresand and firm ground: tried tongue tied/in cheekpieces. *N. Tinkler*

BERRIEDALE 3 ch.f. Fraam 114 – Carradale 73 (Pursuit of Love 124) [2009 –: 10m^{5} **60** f11g 12.1m* 14m^{6} 12m^{4} 11.1s 12.5m Aug 7] neat filly: modest performer: won minor event at Beverley in May: stays 1½m: acts on good to firm going: won juvenile hurdle in September. *Mrs A. Duffield*

BERRYMEAD 4 br.f. Killer Instinct 111 – Mill End Quest 65 (King's Signet (USA) **62 §** 110) [2009 60: f6s f6g p6g^{6} p8.6m f8d 5.7g^{3} 6m 5g 5.7f^{6} 5f 5.3d* 5.3m^{5} 5.3f^{6} 6g^{4} **a50 §** 7g 5.3d^{5} 5g^{6} 5.3m 5.1s p6g^{5} f5f^{5} f5g Dec 22] neat filly: modest handicapper, better on turf: won at Brighton in June: best efforts at 5f/6f: acts on all-weather, firm and good to soft going: tried blinkered/in cheekpieces: usually slowly away: untrustworthy. *Miss A. Stokell*

BERRYNARBOR 4 b.f. Tobougg (IRE) 125 – River Art (USA) (Irish River (FR) 131) **53** [2009 57: p12.2g 11.7g 10.2m^{6} p12m Dec 6] smallish, sturdy filly: modest performer: stays 13f: acts on polytrack, good to firm and good to soft going. *A. G. Newcombe*

BERTBRAND 4 b.g. Bertolini (USA) 125 – Mi Amor (IRE) 47 (Alzao (USA) 117) **70 d** [2009 75: f5g^{2} f6g f6g p6g^{5} p5.1g* p6g^{4} p5.1g p6g 6m 5s^{2} 5.1s p6g f7f^{6} Dec 12] sturdy gelding: modest performer: won seller at Wolverhampton in June: below form after next start, leaving D. Flood after seventh: stays 6f: acts on all-weather and soft going: often blinkered/in cheekpieces: has hung. *I. W. McInnes*

BERTIE BACON 3 b.g. Bertolini (USA) 125 – Streaky (IRE) 63 (Danetime (IRE) **–** 121) [2009 9m Aug 27] unseated both starts in juvenile hurdles before last in seller on Flat debut (wore cheekpieces). *W. G. M. Turner*

BERTIE BLACK 2 b.g. (Mar 26) Bertolini (USA) 125 – Bella Chica (IRE) 95 **–** (Bigstone (IRE) 126) [2009 6d May 17] 33/1 and visored, tailed off in seller at Ripon. *N. Tinkler*

BERTIE BOO 4 b.g. Where Or When (IRE) 124 – Lucy Boo (Singspiel (IRE) 133) **–** [2009 –: f8g May 5] sparely-made gelding: little form. *G. J. Smith*

BERTIE BUCKLE (IRE) 2 b.g. (Apr 8) Bertolini (USA) 125 – Buckle (IRE) 77 **52** (Common Grounds 118) [2009 p6g p6g^{6} p6f Dec 13] modest maiden: best effort when sixth at Wolverhampton. *J. R. Gask*

BERTIE'S BIRTHDAY (IRE) 3 b.f. Elnadim (USA) 128 – Goldfinch 61 (Zilzal **50** (USA) 137) [2009 7.1f^{6} 6m May 30] €2,500Y: fourth foal: half-sister to winning sprinter in Italy by Titus Livius: dam maiden (stayed 1m): seemingly modest form in maidens only on debut. *Jonjo O'Neill*

BERTIE SMALLS 3 b.g. Xaar 132 – Largo (IRE) 94 (Selkirk (USA) 129) [2009 50: 10.2m 11.6d 9g^3 Jun 16] smallish gelding: modest maiden: best effort on good ground final start (blinkered): should stay 1¼m. *M. H. Tompkins* **55**

BERTIE SOUTHSTREET 6 b. or br.g. Bertolini (USA) 125 – Salvezza (IRE) 97 (Superpower 113) [2009 81: p5m^3 p6g^6 p7g p6g^5 6m* 6m^3 5m p6g^5 5.7g p6m* p6g* p6g^4 p5.1g* p5.1g^4 p6g^2 Dec 5] leggy gelding: fair performer: won claimer at Folkestone in June and, having left J. Boyle £5,000 after seventh start, handicaps (2) and claimer at Wolverhampton between August and October: best at 5f/6f nowadays: acts on polytrack, firm and soft going: wears headgear: races prominently. *Karen George* **74**

BERTIE VISTA 4 b.g. Bertolini (USA) 125 – Off Camera (Efisio 120) [2009 69: 8f f6g^5 7.5m 7m^4 p7.1g^3 7g^4 7.5g^5 p6m^5 7.2m 6g^3 Oct 16] tall, good-bodied gelding: modest maiden: stays 7f: acts on all-weather, soft and good to firm ground: often blinkered, tried in cheekpieces: none too consistent: sold £1,400. *T. D. Easterby* **63**

BERTOLIVER 5 b.g. Bertolini (USA) 125 – Calcavella 75 (Pursuit of Love 124) [2009 101: 5g 5m 5v 5.1g^3 5.1m^2 5m^2 5.2d 5.1m* 5d 5g p5.1g^5 p6m^4 p5m^3 Dec 30] good-topped gelding: fairly useful handicapper: best effort in 2009 when winning at Chester in August: left Tom Dascombe after next outing: best at 5f: acts on all-weather and good to firm ground: usually front runner. *S. C. Williams* **94**

BERT'S MEMORY 5 b.m. Bertolini (USA) 125 – Meg's Memory (IRE) 59 (Superlative 118) [2009 58: 12.1m^2 12d^4 12.1v 10m^5 13.8m Sep 19] workmanlike mare: modest performer: stays 1½m: acts on fibresand, firm and good to soft going: has worn cheekpieces/blinkers: has raced freely: none too consistent. *Jennie Candlish* **58**

BESPOKE BOY 4 b.g. Acclamation 118 – Milly Fleur 67 (Primo Dominie 121) [2009 –: p10g^4 f8g p9.5g 10.2g 12.1m^6 12.1v Jul 24] small, sturdy gelding: just modest performer nowadays: left P. Haslam after third outing: appears to stay 1¼m: acts on polytrack, best turf efforts on good ground: tried tongue tied/in cheekpieces. *Mrs N. S. Evans* **60**

BESSIE LOU (IRE) 3 b.f. Montjeu (IRE) 137 – Almond Mousse (FR) 109 (Exit To Nowhere (USA) 122) [2009 76p: 8.1g^2 10.3m^6 10.3g 8s 10.3m 8m p12.2g^6 Oct 15] sturdy filly: fair maiden: below form after reappearance: should stay 1¼m: acts on good to soft ground: tried in cheekpieces: sold 4,000 gns. *K. A. Ryan* **76 d**

BEST BIDDER (USA) 3 b.f. Mr Greeley (USA) 122 – Party Stripes (USA) (Candy Stripes (USA) 115) [2009 67: p7g 8.3m 10.2g 12.1m 11.8g 12.1m Jun 30] sparely-made filly: modest maiden: will prove best short of 1½m: unraced on extremes of going on turf. *Pat Morris* **52**

BEST IN CLASS 3 gr.g. Best of The Bests (IRE) 122 – Third Party 63 (Terimon 124) [2009 47: p8g^2 p8g* 8.3g^4 10m 9.9g 8.3m^6 p7g* p8g^4 p8g p10g* p10m Dec 9] leggy gelding: fairly useful performer: won maiden at Kempton in February, then handicaps at Lingfield in July and, having left Tom Dascombe, Kempton in November: stays 1¼m: acts on polytrack, best turf effort on good ground. *S. C. Williams* **85**

BEST INTENT 2 ch.f. (Apr 8) King's Best (USA) 132 – Hydro Calido (USA) 117 (Nureyev (USA) 131) [2009 7g Oct 31] lengthy, good-topped filly: half-sister to several winners, including smart Japanese performer up to 11f Shinko Calido (by Silver Hawk) and useful French 7f/1m winner Esperero (by Forty Niner): dam, French miler, half-sister to Machiavellian and Exit To Nowhere: 20/1 and backward, travelled comfortably long way when thirteenth to Revered in maiden at Newmarket: sure to improve. *M. A. Jarvis* **– p**

BEST ONE 5 ch.g. Best of The Bests (IRE) 122 – Nasaieb (IRE) 89 (Fairy King (USA)) [2009 86: 5.7g 5m^5 5.3m 5.7f 5.7m^3 5.3m^6 p6g p5g^6 5.3f 5.1m 6.1d 5m^5 p5m* p7.1g p5g p6g p5m^3 f5f* f5g^5 p5g^4 Dec 31] sturdy, quite attractive gelding: just fair handicapper at 5 yrs: won at Kempton in October and Southwell in December: best at 5f/6f: acts on all-weather, firm and soft ground: usually wears headgear: tried tongue tied. *R. A. Harris* **70**

BESTOWED 4 b.g. Kyllachy 129 – Granted (FR) 100 (Cadeaux Genereux 131) [2009 10m 9.8m 8m^4 8g 10.2g 11.6m 9.9m 9.8d^4 10m^3 p8.6g^4 p9.5g^2 p8.6g^4 p9.5g* p9.5g^3 Dec 28] rather leggy gelding: no show in bumpers: fair handicapper on Flat: claimed from M. Chapman £4,000 after ninth start: won at Wolverhampton in December: stays 1¼m: acts on polytrack, unraced on extremes of going on turf: visored last 2 outings. *P. D. Evans* **68**

BEST PROSPECT (IRE) 7 b.g. Orpen (USA) 116 – Bright Prospect (USA) (Miswaki (USA) 124) [2009 102§: f11g^4 10.2d 10.4m 8.9g 10.1d^3 10.3d 10.2v^2 10s^5 Aug 26] big, lengthy gelding: fairly useful handicapper nowadays (similar standard over hurdles): best efforts in 2009 when placed fifth/seventh starts: stays 1½m: acts on soft and good to firm going: usually tongue tied: travels strongly, but often finds little. *M. Dods* **84 §**

BEST SHOT 3 b.f. Xaar 132 – Xaymara (USA) (Sanglamore (USA) 126) [2009 p8g Apr 29] half-sister to French 2001 2-y-o 4.5f (stayed 7f) winner Extinguisher (by Zamindar) and 6-y-o Dream Theme, both useful: dam, French 1m winner, half-sister to dams of 1000 Guineas winner Wince and very smart US performer up to 1¼m Skimming: 16/1, far too green in maiden at Kempton: sold 1,200 gns, sent to Bahrain. *B. W. Hills* –

BEST SHOW (IRE) 2 b.c. (Mar 26) King's Best (USA) 132 – Showering (Danehill (USA) 126) [2009 7g^6 7f Sep 7] good-topped colt: modest form when sixth in maiden at Newmarket: pulled up next time: tongue tied: dead. *Mrs A. J. Perrett* 58

BEST TRIP (IRE) 2 b.g. (Mar 11) Whipper (USA) 126 – Tereed Elhawa 75 (Cadeaux Genereux 131) [2009 6s Nov 7] 1,500F, €40,000Y: fifth foal: half-brother to 6-y-o European Dream and 5f winner in Italy by Noverre: dam 2-y-o 6f winner: 40/1, signs of ability when down the field in maiden at Doncaster: should do better. *R. C. Guest* – p

BEST TUNE 3 b.f. King's Best (USA) 132 – Silver Rhapsody (USA) 115 (Silver Hawk (USA) 123) [2009 10m^4 11.9g^4 p11g^6 Jul 1] fourth foal: half-sister to winner in Italy by Diesis: dam 1¼m/1½m (Princess Royal Stakes) winner: modest form in maidens: should stay 1½m: sold 3,000 gns in December. *J. Noseda* 53

BESTY 2 ch.g. (Feb 17) Compton Place 125 – Petrovna (IRE) 78 (Petardia 113) [2009 6s 5m^4 6m^3 6g 5d* Oct 28] £18,000Y: lengthy, good-topped gelding: fifth foal: half-brother to 6-y-o Brunelleschi and 7f winner Mitzi Caspar (by Kirkwall): dam 2-y-o 5f winner: fair performer: improved when winning nursery at Musselburgh: gelded after: best effort at 5f: acts on good to soft ground: races prominently. *B. Smart* 76

BET NOIR (IRE) 4 b.f. King's Best (USA) 132 – Ivowen (USA) 104 (Theatrical 128) [2009 65: p13.9g p10g^4 p8g p8g p8g Apr 11] leggy, useful-looking filly: fair maiden at 3 yrs: poor in 2009: stays 1¾m: acts on polytrack. *A. W. Carroll* 41

BETONY (USA) 3 b.f. Elusive Quality (USA) – Cala (FR) 98 (Desert Prince (IRE) 130) [2009 p7.1g 7s^2 p7m^6 Aug 20] second foal: sister to 7f winner Top Draw: dam, 6f/7f winner, half-sister to several useful winners, including 6f/7f winner Badminton: best effort in maidens when second at Yarmouth: sold 8,000 gns. *M. L. W. Bell* 67

BETOULA 3 ch.f. Bertolini (USA) 125 – Pab's Choice 61 (Telsmoss 91) [2009 34: 5.7g Sep 7] poor maiden: raced only at 5f/6f. *Mrs A. L. M. King* –

BETSY THE BEST 3 ch.f. Best of The Bests (IRE) 122 – Dusty's Darling (Doyoun 124) [2009 –: f8s^4 Jan 1] no form: tried in cheekpieces/tongue strap. *R. Bastiman* –

BETTERAS BERTIE 6 gr.g. Paris House 123 – Suffolk Girl (Statoblest 120) [2009 61: f8s^2 f8s^3 f8g^5 f8g^3 8f* 8g 8m* 8g 8m 10m f8f Oct 21] strong, lengthy gelding: fair handicapper: won at Doncaster (apprentices) in May and Pontefract in June: stays 1m: acts on fibresand and firm going: tried visored: held up: often slowly away. *M. Brittain* 74

BETTER BE BLUE (IRE) 2 b.f. (Mar 10) Big Bad Bob (IRE) 118 – Ginger Lily (IRE) 68 (Lucky Guest 109) [2009 6.5s^6 8s^6 8v^3 7d 7g 7d^3 p8g^4 f7f Nov 24] €800Y: fourth foal: dam, 7f winner, out of half-sister to very smart 9f/1¼m winner Running Stag: fair maiden at best: below form in claimers last 5 starts, leaving Miss S. Collins in Ireland after second occasion: stays 1m: best efforts on heavy/soft going. *H. J. L. Dunlop* 67

BETTER IN TIME (USA) 3 b.f. City Place (USA) – Ineda Doll (USA) (Langfuhr (CAN) 124) [2009 67: 8.3m 8.3g Jul 6] medium-sized filly: fair maiden at 2 yrs: well held in 2009: sold 2,500 gns. *Jane Chapple-Hyam* –

BETTYS TOUCH 4 b.f. Lujain (USA) 119 – Fadaki Hawaki (USA) 60 (Vice Regent (CAN)) [2009 –: 5d^5 5g 5g Oct 6] close-coupled filly: poor maiden: best at 5f/6f: acts on good to soft ground: awkward ride. *K. G. Reveley* 37

BETWS Y COED (IRE) 3 br.f. Indian Haven 119 – Tommys Queen (IRE) (Ali-Royal (IRE) 127) [2009 53: p8.6g^6 p8.6g p8.6g^5 f8g^5 f8g^5 Feb 3] leggy filly: modest maiden: probably stays 9.5f: acts on all-weather: wears cheekpieces. *A. Bailey* 52

BEWDLEY 4 b.f. Best of The Bests (IRE) 122 – Garota de Ipanema (FR) (Al Nasr (FR) 126) [2009 41: f7g f6g p9.5g p8.6g Apr 4] maiden: little form in 2009: reportedly bled on reappearance. *R. E. Peacock* –

BEYONDA DREAM 3 b.f. And Beyond (IRE) 113 – Richenda 75 (Mister Baileys 123) [2009 10.9g p13.9g p12.2g p13.9g Dec 14] first foal: dam, maiden (stayed 1m), form only at 2 yrs: well held in maidens/handicap: tried in cheekpieces. *Lucinda Featherstone* –

BEYOND ATLOW 4 ch.g. And Beyond (IRE) 113 – Argostoli (Marju (IRE) 127) [2009 p9.5g p12.2g Dec 5] well held in maidens. *Lucinda Featherstone* –

Clipper Logistics' "Beyond Desire"

BEYOND DESIRE 2 b.f. (Apr 11) Invincible Spirit (IRE) 121 – Compradore 82 (Mujtahid (USA) 118) [2009 6g* 6m^2 6m^4 Sep 19] £55,000Y: smallish, sturdy filly: fourth foal: half-sister to 5-y-o Cherri Fosfate: dam, 5f (at 2 yrs) to 7f winner, half-sister to smart performer up to 14.6f Mazuna: 2/1 favourite, created good impression when winning maiden at Goodwood in July by 1¼ lengths from Nimue: again good speed when 3 lengths second to Lady of The Desert in Lowther Stakes at York next time: much better than bare form when fourth to Distinctive in Firth of Clyde Stakes at Ayr, first home on disadvantaged stand side: raced only at 6f: remains smart prospect. *M. A. Jarvis* **105 p**

BEYOND THE CITY (USA) 2 b.c. (Mar 6) Elusive Quality (USA) – Whats Doin (USA) (Relaunch (USA)) [2009 7.1m 7m 8m p8m^6 p5g Oct 21] rangy, attractive colt: modest form in maidens/nurseries: may prove best at 6f/7f: sold 3,000 gns. *R. Hannon* **55**

BIANCA CAPELLO 4 b.f. Medicean 128 – Totom 81 (Mtoto 134) [2009 57: p8.6g^5 10.9f May 12] leggy filly: modest maiden: should stay beyond 8.6f: acts on polytrack, best turf efforts on good ground: tried visored. *J. R. Fanshawe* **51**

BIBIANA BAY 2 b.f. (May 7) Leporello (IRE) 118 – Polisonne (Polish Precedent (USA) 131) [2009 p6g Dec 18] half-sister to 3 winners, including Irish 1m winner Disobey (by Machiavellian): dam, 2-y-o 5f winner in Belgium, close relative of Cheveley Park Stakes winner Regal Rose: 80/1, soundly beaten in maiden at Wolverhampton. *B. I. Case* **–**

BICKERSTEN 3 ch.g. Piccolo 121 – Niseem (USA) (Hennessy (USA) 122) [2009 59: p7g* p8g* 8f^6 8d^5 7s 9d p8g p8g^4 p8.6g^4 Dec 5] sturdy gelding: fair performer: won maiden in February and handicap in March, both at Lingfield: left M. Channon after fourth start: effective at 7f/1m: form only on polytrack: tried in cheekpieces. *C. Moore, Ireland* **74**

BICKSTA 3 b.f. Haafhd 129 – Premiere Dance (IRE) (Loup Solitaire (USA) 117) [2009 7s 7m 10m^3 10.3m p10g 10f^4 8.5m^4 p10g^6 f11g^6 f11f^6 Dec 17] 35,000Y: leggy filly: fourth foal: half-sister to smart 5f to 6.5f winner Prince Tamino (by Mozart) and French 1m/8.5f winner Sing Silence (by Sakhee): dam, French 7.5f winner, half-sister to Prix de la Foret winner Poplar Bluff: modest maiden: left E. Vaughan after eighth start: stays 11f: acts on all-weather and firm ground: tried blinkered/visored. *P. T. Midgley* **57**

BIDABLE 5 b.m. Auction House (USA) 120 – Dubitable 59 (Formidable (USA) 125) [2009 59: p8.6g p7g 7.1d^3 8.1m 8d p8.6g^2 p8.6g^2 p9.5g* p8.6g Dec 5] leggy mare: fair handicapper: won at Wolverhampton in November: stays 9.5f: acts on polytrack, soft and good to firm ground: tried tongue tied: none too consistent. *B. Palling* **65**

BID ART (IRE) 4 b.g. Hawk Wing (USA) 136 – Crystal Theatre (IRE) 72 (King's Theatre (IRE) 128) [2009 60: p10g p10g p10g Feb 11] smallish, sturdy gelding: regressive maiden: tried in cheekpieces. *Jamie Snowden* **–**

BIDEEYA (USA) 2 b. or br.f. (Apr 16) Dubawi (IRE) 129 – Menhoubah (USA) 107 (Dixieland Band (USA)) [2009 7g^2 7g 6f^6 p7g Oct 8] compact filly: second foal: half-sister to 3-y-o Morning Sir Alan: dam 6f (at 2 yrs) and 11f (Oaks d'Italia) winner: modest form in maidens: pulled too hard in nursery (in cheekpieces): should stay 1m. *C. E. Brittain* **61**

BID FOR GLORY 5 ch.h. Auction House (USA) 120 – Woodland Steps 86 (Bold Owl 101) [2009 101d: 8m 10d^6 8.5m p8.6g^2 p9.5g^3 p9.5g Oct 9] close-coupled, good-topped horse: has a quick action: just fair handicapper nowadays: stays 11f: acts on polytrack, soft and good to firm going: has worn cheekpieces/visor. *H. J. Collingridge* **76**

BID FOR GOLD 5 b.g. Auction House (USA) 120 – Gold And Blue (IRE) (Bluebird (USA) 125) [2009 74: 6m f7g 5.9m 6g^2 6g* 5.9g* 6v^4 6g^5 6d^4 7s 7s Nov 7] compact gelding: fair handicapper: won at Hamilton in June and Carlisle (apprentices) in July: seems best at 6f: acts on firm and soft going: below form in blinkers/cheekpieces: usually races prominently. *Jedd O'Keeffe* **79**

BIENHEUREUX 8 b.g. Bien Bien (USA) 125 – Rochea 67 (Rock City 120) [2009 68: f12s^3 f12g^3 f14g^6 11.9m^3 Apr 26] workmanlike gelding: modest handicapper nowadays: effective at 1½m to easy 2m: acts on all-weather, firm and soft going: sometimes wears headgear: usually tongue tied: held up. *Miss Gay Kelleway* **55**

BIGALO'S STAR (IRE) 3 b.g. Xaar 132 – Toi Toi (IRE) 82 (In The Wings 128) [2009 79: 12s 13.8m 12g Oct 17] sturdy gelding: fair form at 2 yrs: well held in 2009: tried in cheekpieces. *L. A. Mullaney* **–**

BIG APPLE BOY (IRE) 3 b.c. Statue of Liberty (USA) 115 – Go For Grace (IRE) 89 (Shalford (IRE) 124§) [2009 90: 8g^4 8d^2 8m^6 8m^4 6m* 6g Jul 8] strong, deep-girthed colt: useful handicapper: easily best effort when winning at Pontefract (made all, by 6 lengths) in June: unable to dominate, well beaten at Newmarket final start: best form (and both wins) at 6f: acts on soft and good to firm going. *Jedd O'Keeffe* **99**

BIG AUDIO (IRE) 2 b.c. (Feb 15) Oratorio (IRE) 128 – Tarbela (IRE) 68 (Grand Lodge (USA) 125) [2009 6m^4 6f^2 7m* 7m 7g^4 8m* Aug 21] 30,000F, £87,000Y: strong colt: type to carry condition: second foal: half-brother to 3-y-o Spiritual Healing: dam, Irish maiden (best at 7f), half-sister to dam of 2-y-o Arcano: useful performer: won listed events at Royal Ascot (Chesham Stakes, by short head from Emperor Claudius) in June and Salisbury (dictated, beat Dubai Miracle by head) in August: respectable fourth to Xtension in Vintage Stakes at Goodwood penultimate outing: stays 1m: sold 175,000 gns, joined Godolphin. *R. Hannon* **102**

BIG BAY (USA) 3 b.c. Horse Chestnut (SAF) 119 – Takipy (USA) (Persian Bold 123) [2009 8m^3 p8g^3 8g^2 8m 8.3g* p8m* Nov 26] $47,000Y, 22,000 2-y-o: deep-girthed colt: half-brother to winners in Japan by Housebuster and Marquetry: dam unraced half-sister to smart Irish 2004 2-y-o 5f/6f winner Damson: useful performer: won maiden at Nottingham in October and handicap at Kempton (improved when beating Chapter And Verse 1¾ lengths) in November: stays 8.3f: raced only on polytrack and good/good to firm going. *Jane Chapple-Hyam* **100**

BIG BOOM 4 ch.g. Cadeaux Genereux 131 – Kastaway 91 (Distant Relative 128) [2009 49: f7g^5 6s^2 6s^2 6s* 6g^4 Aug 5] fair handicapper: won at Leicester in July: stays 6f: raced on all-weather and good ground or softer on turf (best efforts on soft). *M. Quinn* **72**

BIG BOUND (USA) 3 b.c. Grand Slam (USA) 120 – Golden Cat (USA) 102 (Storm Cat (USA)) [2009 88p: p10g* 10m^2 10.3m^5 10m^3 10m 10m* 12g 10m Sep 25] big, lengthy colt: useful performer: won maiden at Lingfield in March and minor event at Leicester (by head from Libel Law) in July: creditable efforts in between when head second to Above Average in Classic Trial at Sandown and 3½ lengths third to Palavicini in listed race at Newmarket: not discredited in face of stiff tasks in pattern company last 2 starts: stays 1¼m: acts on polytrack and good to firm ground: sold 200,000 gns. *J. H. M. Gosden* **104**

BIG BUZZ (IRE) 2 b.g. (Apr 6) Redback 116 – Aphra Benn (IRE) 67 (In The Wings 128) [2009 8.1g Aug 6] €3,400F, 12,000Y: third foal: dam, maiden, half-sister to useful 7f to 1¼m winner Mezzogiorno: 33/1, slowly away and tailed off in maiden at Haydock: sold 800 gns, joined M. Ramadan in UAE. *Mrs L. Stubbs* **–**

BIGFANOFTHAT (IRE) 4 b.g. Rock of Gibraltar (IRE) 133 – Miss Salsa (USA) (Unbridled (USA) 128) [2009 –: p7g^5 7d^3 7g 6s^6 p7g 8g Aug 5] heavy-bodied gelding: fair performer: should stay 1m: raced on polytrack and good going or softer on turf: tried visored/blinkered/tongue tied: none too consistent. *M. D. Squance* **69**

BIG HANDS LYNCH (IRE) 2 b.c. (Apr 27) Hawkeye (IRE) 122 – Mrs Kanning 61 (Distant View (USA) 126) [2009 p8g p8g p8g Dec 7] strong colt: down the field in maidens at Lingfield. *J. R. Boyle* **–**

BIG NIGE (IRE) 3 br.g. Mull of Kintyre (USA) 114 – Queen's Quest (Rainbow Quest (USA) 134) [2009 69: 8m p10m^3 Dec 30] close-coupled gelding: fair maiden: good third at Lingfield final start: may prove best short of 1¼m: acts on polytrack. *J. Pearce* **71**

BIG NOISE 5 b.h. Lake Coniston (IRE) 131 – Mitsubishi Video (IRE) (Doulab (USA) 115) [2009 100: 7g* 7g^5 6.5m^5 7m 7m Oct 16] strong, good-topped horse: useful handicapper: won at Leicester (beat Woodcote Place by ½ length) in July: respectable efforts after: stays 1m: acts on polytrack, soft and good to firm ground: held up. *Dr J. D. Scargill* **100**

BIG ROBERT 5 b.h. Medicean 128 – Top Flight Queen 82 (Mark of Esteem (IRE) 137) [2009 106: 12g^3 10g^5 10g p12g^3 p11g p10.7g p12g p10.7g p10.7g Nov 20] stocky, well-made horse: useful performer: third in handicap at Nad Al Sheba (¾ length behind Gravitas) and listed race at Kempton (to Scintillo): left K. R. Burke after fifth start, below form after: stays 13f: acts on polytrack, soft and good to firm going: blinkered final outing: sometimes tongue tied in 2007: usually held up. *P. D. Deegan, Ireland* **99**

BIG SLICK (IRE) 4 ch.c. Rossini (USA) 118 – Why Worry Now (IRE) 75 (College Chapel 122) [2009 68: f7g 7d^3 7g Jul 8] strong colt: fair handicapper: seems to stay 7f: raced on good going or softer on turf. *M. Brittain* **65**

BIG SUR 3 ch.g. Selkirk (USA) 129 – Bombazine (IRE) 97 (Generous (IRE) 139) [2009 p7.1g p7g p8m^4 Nov 28] big gelding: half-brother to several winners, notably French/UAE 1m (at 2 yrs) to 1½m winner Gravitas (by Mark of Esteem) and 11f to 15.5f (in France) winner Armure (by Dalakhani), both smart: dam, 1¼m winner, half-sister to Barathea and Gossamer: progressive form in maidens, fourth at Lingfield: will be suited by 1¼m+: type to do better in handicaps. *T. Keddy* **68 p**

BIG TALK 2 b.c. (Apr 17) Selkirk (USA) 129 – Common Request (USA) (Lear Fan (USA) 130) [2009 8.1d 9d 8v Oct 24] well held in maidens. *S. Kirk* **–**

BIG WAVE BAY (IRE) 2 b.c. (Mar 12) Alamshar (IRE) 133 – Lady Pahia (IRE) 81 (Pivotal 124) [2009 7g^6 8d^4 7.2m Sep 18] modest form first 2 starts in maidens, fourth at Thirsk (hung left). *A. P. Jarvis* **59**

BIG WHITFIELD 3 b.g. Tobougg (IRE) 125 – Natalie Jay 88 (Ballacashtal (CAN)) [2009 10m^5 p9.5g 8.3g^5 Oct 28] lengthy gelding: fair form in maidens: bred to stay 1¼m. *M. Dods* **65**

BIJOU DAN 8 ch.g. Bijou d'Inde 127 – Cal Norma's Lady (IRE) 87 (Lyphard's Special (USA) 122) [2009 70: 15.8m^3 16m 15.8g* 14v 14.1m^5 12m* 15.8g^5 Jul 8] lengthy, good-bodied gelding: fair handicapper: won at Catterick in May and July: stays easy 15.8f: acts on all-weather, heavy and good to firm ground: effective with or without headgear: consistent: fair hurdler, successful twice in 2009/10. *G. M. Moore* **76**

BIKINI BABE (IRE) 2 b.f. (Apr 4) Montjeu (IRE) 137 – Zeiting (IRE) 105 (Zieten (USA) 118) [2009 6m 7.1m* 7m 7.1m^3 7g 7g^2 Sep 27] €150,000Y: lengthy filly: fifth foal: half-sister to 2005 2-y-o 6f winner Mutawajid (by Zafonic), French 2006 2-y-o 7f **101**

winner Zut Alors (by Pivotal), both useful, and 4-y-o Mohathab: dam 6f (in France at 2 yrs) to 8.5f (in US) winner: useful performer: won maiden at Sandown in June: best efforts when placed in listed race at same course and C. L. Weld Park Stakes at the Curragh (½-length second to Lady Springbank): will stay 1m: races prominently. *M. Johnston*

BILASH 2 gr. or ro.c. (Mar 8) Choisir (AUS) 126 – Goldeva 104 (Makbul 104) [2009 6m^3 6.1g^5 6m 5m Sep 17] small colt: fair maiden at best: likely to prove best at 5f/6f. *R. Hollinshead* **66**

BILBOA 4 b.g. Averti (IRE) 117 – Anita Marie (IRE) (Anita's Prince 126) [2009 60§: 5m 5.1d 6m 6.1g 5.7g 5.7g Sep 7] compact gelding: temperamental maiden: wears cheekpieces. *J. M. Bradley* **45 §**

BILLBERRY 4 gr.g. Diktat 126 – Elderberry (Bin Ajwaad (IRE) 119) [2009 64, a70+: p8g^3 p7g^2 p6g 7s^4 8g 6m^3 7f^2 p7m^6 p7m^5 p6g^4 p6g* p7m^6 p6f^5 Dec 21] big gelding: fair handicapper: won at Lingfield in November: effective at 6f to easy 1m: acts on polytrack, soft and good to firm going: tried in cheekpieces: tongue tied. *S. C. Williams* **79**

BILLICH 6 ch.h. Observatory (USA) 131 – Pomponette (USA) (Rahy (USA) 115) [2009 p12.2g Aug 10] good-topped horse: fairly useful handicapper in 2007: off 2 years, last in seller sole outing in 2009: stays 16.5f: acts on polytrack and firm going. *S. W. Hall* **–**

BILLIE JEAN 2 b.f. (Mar 15) Bertolini (USA) 125 – Factice (USA) 78 (Known Fact (USA) 135) [2009 5m 6g p6m f5f* Dec 17] £55,000 2-y-o: small filly: half-sister to several winners, notably 2000 Guineas winner Cockney Rebel (6f winner at 2 yrs, by Val Royal): dam Irish 2-y-o 5f winner: won nursery at Southwell, easily best effort: may prove best at 5f. *B. W. Hills* **65**

BILLIONAIRE BOY (IRE) 2 b.c. (Apr 16) Acclamation 118 – Shalwell (IRE) (Shalford (IRE) 124§) [2009 6g^5 Sep 30] 12/1, soundly beaten in maiden at Newcastle. *Pat Morris* **–**

BILLY BEETROOT (USA) 3 b.g. Rossini (USA) 118 – Grazia 111 (Sharpo 132) [2009 52p: 5.1g^2 5.1m^3 6d^2 5g^2 5m^3 5m^3 6g^2 5.3g* 6m* 5g^4 6m p6g^2 6m 6g 5.1d 5.1d^4 p6f^6 5.7g^3 p5.1g p6m p6g Dec 5] close-coupled gelding: fair performer: won handicap at Brighton and claimer at Folkestone (left S. C. Williams £6,000) 24 hrs apart in June: raced only at 5f/6f: acts on polytrack and good to firm going: tried blinkered/in cheekpieces: often tongue tied: weak finisher. *R. A. Harris* **67**

BILLY BOWMORE 4 b.g. Bahamian Bounty 116 – Shaieef (IRE) 66 (Shareef Dancer (USA) 135) [2009 69: f8g f8g 6m 7.5m^6 6d^6 Jun 17] rather leggy gelding: maiden: just modest at 4 yrs: stays 7.5f: acts on polytrack and good to firm ground: tried blinkered. *P. A. Kirby* **50**

BILLY CADIZ 4 b.g. Zilzal (USA) 137 – Faraway Moon 61 (Distant Relative 128) [2009 –: 6d 6g 7g Oct 17] compact gelding: no form. *N. Tinkler* **–**

BILLY DANE (IRE) 5 b.g. Fayruz 116 – Lomalou (IRE) (Lightning Dealer 103) [2009 92: 8.1m* 8.5m* 8.1v 8g^6 7g 8m 6.9g^2 8.1m^2 8g^2 8m^2 7g Oct 10] tall, lengthy gelding: useful handicapper: won at Haydock in April and Beverley in May: creditable efforts after when runner-up: barely stays 9f: acts on polytrack, firm and good to soft ground: effective with/without cheekpieces: usually front runner. *F. P. Murtagh* **95**

BILLY HOT ROCKS (IRE) 4 b.g. Intikhab (USA) 135 – Rock Abbey (IRE) (College Chapel 122) [2009 68: p7g f5g^5 f6g 7m Apr 1] fair performer in 2008: modest at best in 2009 (said to have had breathing problem final start): usually wears headgear nowadays. *Miss Gay Kelleway* **51**

BILLYONAIR 2 ch.g. (Feb 14) Auction House (USA) 120 – Westmead Tango 59 (Pursuit of Love 124) [2009 p6g p8g Nov 14] rather sparely-made gelding: well held in minor event/maiden at Lingfield. *W. de Best-Turner* **–**

BILLY RED 5 ch.g. Dr Fong (USA) 128 – Liberty Bound 85 (Primo Dominie 121) [2009 74§: p6g* p6g^6 6d p6g 5.3m^2 5.3f^2 5f 5m 5.3m* 5f^2 6d^6 f5g p6g^4 p6g* p6g* p6g^6 p6g p6m^2 p6m^2 Dec 6] lengthy gelding: fairly useful handicapper: won at Great Leighs in January, Brighton in June, Wolverhampton in September and Lingfield in October: best at 5f/6f: acts on polytrack, firm and good to soft going: blinkered (tried visored): races prominently/front runner. *J. R. Jenkins* **86**

BILLY'S BID 2 b.f. (Jan 29) Kyllachy 129 – Bajan Blue 59 (Lycius (USA) 124) [2009 5m 7.5m^5 7g Jul 16] £5,000Y: close-coupled filly: fourth foal: half-sister to 13f winner Storm Prospect (by Mujahid): dam 11.6f seller winner: well held in maidens. *I. W. McInnes* **–**

BILLY SIMMONDS 4 b.g. Man Among Men (IRE) – Lizzie Simmonds (IRE) 61 (Common Grounds 118) [2009 p7g 10m Sep 17] angular gelding: well held in maidens. *Miss J. Feilden* –

BILLY SMART (IRE) 3 ch.c. Exceed And Excel (AUS) 126 – Amber Tide (IRE) 75 (Pursuit of Love 124) [2009 58: 10.2m^5 8d f7g^4 8g 8.5g 10m Sep 12] good-bodied colt: modest maiden: left D. ffrench Davis prior to final start: likely to prove best short of 1¼m: tried blinkered (hung left)/tongue tied. *A. J. Lidderdale* **54**

BILLY THE GAS 4 b.g. Dr Fong (USA) 128 – Hawayah (IRE) 68 (Shareef Dancer (USA) 135) [2009 10m Jul 16] last in bumper/maiden. *N. Tinkler* –

BINANTI 9 b.g. Bin Ajwaad (IRE) 119 – Princess Rosananti (IRE) (Shareef Dancer (USA) 135) [2009 99: 7m^6 p7g p7.1g Jun 29] smallish, useful-looking gelding: useful handicapper at best: very much on downgrade: effective blinkered/visored or not. *P. R. Chamings* **70**

BIN END 3 b.g. King's Best (USA) 132 – Overboard (IRE) 73 (Rainbow Quest (USA) 134) [2009 76p: 10m* 10.4m^4 11m^2 May 21] useful-looking gelding: fairly useful performer: won maiden at Leicester in April: good efforts in handicaps next 2 starts, though looked unwilling on latter occasion (gelded after): will stay 1½m: unraced on extremes of going. *M. L. W. Bell* **89**

BINFIELD (IRE) 4 b.f. Officer (USA) 120 – Identify (IRE) 105 (Persian Bold 123) [2009 76: p8g^3 p8g 8m^6 8g^2 8m 9g^4 8m p8g 8.1m^3 8.3g p8m^6 f8g Nov 17] tall filly: fair handicapper: stays 1m: acts on polytrack and soft ground: none too consistent. *B. G. Powell* **77**

BINIOU (IRE) 6 b.g. Mozart (IRE) 131 – Cap Coz (IRE) 110 (Indian Ridge 123) [2009 98: 5d* 5g* 6d 5.1d* Aug 11] leggy gelding: smart performer: returned to form in 2009, winning handicaps at Thirsk in May and Newmarket in July, and minor event at Nottingham (comfortably by 2¼ lengths from Wi Dud) in August: had form at 7f, raced mainly at 5f/6f: acted on polytrack, soft and good to firm going: dead. *R. M. H. Cowell* **111**

BINNION BAY (IRE) 8 b.g. Fasliyev (USA) 120 – Literary 79 (Woodman (USA) 126) [2009 58, a65: p8g^6 p7g* p7g^3 p7g 7m^3 8m 9m 10m^3 p8g p10g^2 8.3m 8m 10d 7.6m 9g^6 p8m p10m p12g p10g* Dec 7] tall, useful-looking gelding: fair handicapper on all-weather, modest on turf: won at Kempton in February and Lingfield in December: stays 1¼m, effective at shorter: acts on all-weather and good to firm ground: wears headgear: held up (often slowly away). *J. J. Bridger* **56** **a65**

BIN SHAMARDAL (IRE) 2 ch.c. (Apr 7) Shamardal (USA) 129 – Lonely Ahead (USA) 97 (Rahy (USA) 115) [2009 7d Aug 1] good-topped colt: first foal: dam, 2-y-o 6f winner, out of 1000 Guineas winner Sayyedati: 20/1, 8¾ lengths ninth to Stags Leap in maiden at Goodwood: should do better. *B. W. Hills* **57 p**

BINTALALEUMYDARLIN (IRE) 2 b.f. (Mar 21) Refuse To Bend (IRE) 128 – Silly Game (IRE) (Bigstone (IRE) 126) [2009 7d 7.1s^4 7m 8g 8g^6 Oct 19] €34,000F, €26,000Y: angular filly: third foal: closely related to useful performer up to 13f Better Hand (by Montjeu), 7f winner at 2 yrs: dam Italian 2-y-o 7.5f winner (also won over jumps): modest maiden: needs to settle to stay 1m: sold 4,000 gns. *M. Johnston* **52**

BINT ALMATAR (USA) 2 b.f. (Jan 17) Kingmambo (USA) 125 – Firth of Lorne (IRE) 112 (Danehill (USA) 126) [2009 8.3m* 8g Oct 31] useful-looking filly: has scope: second foal: half-sister to 3-y-o Loch Linnhe: dam, French (at 2 yrs)/US 1m winner, out of 1000 Guineas runner-up/smart sprinter Kerrera: 2/1 favourite, won maiden at Nottingham in September by ½ length from Michevious Spirit: still green, well held in listed race at Newmarket: not certain to stay beyond 1m: joined H-A. Pantall, France. *Saeed bin Suroor* **75**

BINTALWAADI 2 b.f. (Mar 14) Barathea (IRE) 127 – Al Durrah (USA) (Darshaan 133) [2009 6.1v^2 Jul 30] third foal: half-sister to 1¼m/11f winner in Italy by Alhaarth: dam, unraced, out of useful sister to high-class sprinter Elnadim and close relative to Irish 1000 Guineas winner Mehthaaf: 9/1, in need of experience and not knocked about when 3 lengths second of 5 to Fairy Promises in maiden at Nottingham: should improve. *E. A. L. Dunlop* **67 p**

BINT DOYEN 2 br.f. (Jan 31) Doyen (IRE) 132 – Zonda 100 (Fabulous Dancer (USA) 124) [2009 7d* 7m Oct 17] useful-looking filly: half-sister to several winners, including smart miler Zoning (6f/7f winner at 2 yrs, by Warning) and 3-y-o Dialogue: dam 5f (at 2 yrs) to 8.5f (in USA) winner: 25/1, promising start when winning maiden at **82 p**

Folkestone by ¾ length from Old Money, off bridle over 2f out: still green when last in Rockfel Stakes at Newmarket 11 days later: bred to be suited by 1m+: will still do better. *C. E. Brittain*

BIRBONE (FR) 4 b.g. Sendawar (IRE) 129 – Labour of Love (USA) (Silver Deputy (CAN)) [2009 109: p10g^6 May 28] useful form in France at 3 yrs, winning minor event at Chantilly: in frame in 4 listed races after: left J-M. Beguigne, last in minor event at Lingfield only outing in 2009, carrying head awkwardly (gelded after): stays 1¼m: acts on good to soft going: has worn cheekpieces: races in touch: has left Godolphin. *Saeed bin Suroor* –

BIRDINTHEHAND (FR) 3 b.f. Nayef (USA) 129 – Bird In The Sky (CAN) (Sky Classic (CAN)) [2009 f11g^3 11.8m^2 11.6m^2 12.3d 12g* 11.5g^3 13m^3 14.5g 12s a12g Dec 29] lengthy, angular filly: fifth foal: half-sister to French 13.5f winner Alawal We Bas (by Alhaarth): dam, placed at 9f in US, half-sister to US Grade 1 9f winner Roanoke: fair performer: placed in maidens first 3 starts before sold from H. Cecil 11,500 gns: won similar event at Beaupreau in August: stays 13f: acts on fibresand and good to firm ground. *H-A. Pantall, France* 74

BIRD ON THE WIRE 2 ch. or ro.f. (Apr 29) Compton Place 125 – Pomponette (USA) (Rahy (USA) 115) [2009 p6g p6m p7g f6g Nov 17] sixth foal: half-sister to 7f winner Desert Daisy (by Desert Prince) and fairly useful 11.5f to 16.5f winner Billich (by Observatory): dam unraced half-sister to smart sprinter Blue Goblin: modest maiden: tried in cheekpieces. *W. G. M. Turner* 53

BIRKSIDE 6 ch.g. Spinning World (USA) 130 – Bright Hope (IRE) 84 (Danehill (USA) 126) [2009 95: 12.3m^5 12m 11.1m* 12.1m 11.5m^6 11.1m^2 13d^4 12g 12.5g* 14m^5 12.5m^3 p12.2g^5 12.5d^6 Oct 28] lengthy, well-made gelding: fairly useful performer at best nowadays: won claimers at Hamilton (left Ollie Pears £12,000) in May and Musselburgh in August: effective at 1¼m to 1¾m: acts on polytrack, firm and soft ground, well beaten on heavy: tried in cheekpieces/tongue tie. *Miss L. A. Perratt* 80 d

BIRTHDAY STAR (IRE) 7 b.g. Desert King (IRE) 129 – White Paper (IRE) (Marignan (USA) 117) [2009 –: f14m^6 Dec 5] close-coupled gelding: one-time fair performer: lightly raced and little form since 2007: tried blinkered/in cheekpieces. *Mrs L. C. Jewell* –

BISHAARA (IRE) 3 b.f. Alhaarth (IRE) 126 – Majmu (USA) 105 (Al Nasr (FR) 126) [2009 70p: p8g^6 Mar 16] promising fourth only 2-y-o start: easy to back, well held sole outing in 2009: should stay 1m: sold 20,000 gns in July, sent to USA. *J. H. M. Gosden* –

BISHOPBRIGGS (USA) 4 ch.g. Victory Gallop (CAN) 130 – Inny River (USA) (Seattle Slew (USA)) [2009 79: p6g p7g p6g p6g f5g p7m Dec 30] lengthy gelding: handicapper: just poor form at 4 yrs, leaving S. Parr after reappearance and J. Ryan before final outing: tried in tongue tie/cheekpieces. *M. G. Quinlan* 48

BISHOP ROCK (USA) 3 b.c. Vicar (USA) 120 – Rhumba Rage (USA) (Nureyev (USA) 131) [2009 62: p10g^5 9.7f 9.9g Jun 19] strong colt: modest maiden: may prove best short of 1¼m: best effort on polytrack: tried tongue tied. *M. H. Tompkins* 62

BITTER HONEY 2 b.f. (Apr 22) Reset (AUS) 124 – Piccolo Cativo 67 (Komaite (USA)) [2009 6v^4 5.1g 6s^3 6d^4 p6g p6g p6g^5 Dec 11] fourth foal: half-sister to 6-y-o Pitbull: dam 5f (including at 2 yrs) to 7.8f winner: modest maiden: stays 6f: acts on heavy going: looked awkward third outing. *Mrs G. S. Rees* 61 a55

BITTER MAN (IRE) 2 b.c. (Mar 25) Azamour (IRE) 130 – Savieres (IRE) 79 (Sadler's Wells (USA) 132) [2009 7.1m^3 Jun 12] €41,000F, 30,000Y: third foal: dam, Irish 11f winner, out of US Grade 1 9f winner Gravieres: 25/1, 4 lengths third to Bikini Babe in maiden at Sandown, needing the experience: will stay 1¼m. *M. R. Channon* 66

BIVOUAC (UAE) 5 b.g. Jade Robbery (USA) 121 – Tentpole (USA) 85 (Rainbow Quest (USA) 134) [2009 77: f7g 10.3m^6 10g^5 8.3m 9.9m^4 8.5m^6 8s 10m Sep 14] leggy gelding: fair handicapper: stays 1¼m: acts on polytrack and soft ground, probably on good to firm. *G. A. Swinbank* 68

BLACK ATTACK (IRE) 3 br.g. Invincible Spirit (IRE) 121 – Mughetta (Prince Sabo 123) [2009 80d: p5.1g Feb 16] compact gelding: maiden: has gone wrong way: gelded after only start in 2009: tried blinkered/visored. *Paul Green* –

BLACK BACCARA 2 b.f. (Mar 20) Superior Premium 122 – Areish (IRE) 66 (Keen 116) [2009 5d* Mar 31] third living foal: dam 1m to 1½m winner: 20/1, won maiden at Folkestone by head from Tom Folan, making virtually all: not seen out again: should stay 6f/7f. *P. S. McEntee* 69

totesport.com Dante Stakes, York—Black Bear Island (centre) gets up close home to thwart stable-companion Freemantle (right) with Sans Frontieres third

BLACK BEAR ISLAND (IRE) 3 b.c. Sadler's Wells (USA) 132 – Kasora (IRE) (Darshaan 133) [2009 100p: 10g³ 10.4g* 12g 12f³ 12g 10g² 8f⁶ 10f Nov 29] smallish colt: smart performer: won totesport.com Dante Stakes at York in May, coming from last to beat Freemantle by head: tenth of 12 in Derby at Epsom next time: placed after in King Edward VII Stakes at Royal Ascot (4¼ lengths third to Father Time) and Secretariat Stakes at Arlington (ridden more prominently than usual when head second to Take The Points, hanging into winner over 1f out): sold privately and left A. O'Brien in Ireland after: blinkered, only eighth in Hollywood Derby final outing: needs further than 1m, and should be suited by 1½m: raced only on good or firm going. *J. C. Canani, USA* **114**

BLACK BEAUTY 6 br.g. Diktat 126 – Euridice (IRE) 66 (Woodman (USA) 126) [2009 10.3m Mar 29] close-coupled gelding: one-time fairly useful handicapper: unraced on Flat in 2008 (fair hurdler/fairly useful chaser): only modest form sole Flat outing in 2009 (in cheekpieces): should stay 11f: acts on firm going, some promise on polytrack. *M. G. Quinlan* **57**

BLACK CLOUD 6 b.g. Cloudings (IRE) 112 – Dutch Czarina 45 (Prince Sabo 123) [2009 –: p16g 16.4m Jul 9] modest hurdler: no form on Flat. *G. P. Enright* **–**

BLACK DADDY 2 b.g. (Mar 5) Night Shift (USA) – Sareb (FR) (Indian Ridge 123) [2009 p5g⁶ 5.1m 7m 7g 6.1s³ Oct 7] compact gelding: modest maiden: likely to prove best at 5f/6f: acts on soft ground: sold 5,000 gns, sent to Greece. *R. Hannon* **55**

BLACK DAHLIA 4 br.f. Dansili 127 – South Rock 102 (Rock City 120) [2009 85: p8.6g³ 8m⁵ 10.3m 10d⁴ 12m³ 8g⁴ 9.3m⁶ 10.3d 13.8g 8m⁵ 8.3m* 8.1m² p7m³ p7g p7.1g* p7g* p7f⁵ Dec 16] well-made filly: useful handicapper: left A. McCabe after seventh start: won at Leicester in September and Wolverhampton and Kempton (improved when beating King's Colour by 6 lengths) in November: creditable fifth in listed race at Kempton final start: form at 1½m, possibly best around 7f: acts on polytrack, soft and good to firm going. *J. A. Glover* **100**

BLACK DRAFT 7 b. or br.g. Josr Algarhoud (IRE) 118 – Tilia 56 (Primo Dominie 121) [2009 –: p8g f6g p7g 7.1m p6f⁴ Dec 16] rather leggy gelding: form (modest) only on final start: stays 6f: acts on polytrack: tried blinkered/visored. *B. Forsey* **51**

BLACK EAGLE (IRE) 3 b.c. Cape Cross (IRE) 129 – Shimna 62 (Mr Prospector (USA)) [2009 8m^5 10.2d* p9.5g^2 p10g* a9f Dec 18] 200,000Y: good-topped colt: fifth foal: closely related to useful 7f (at 2 yrs)/1m (in USA) winner Santa Fe (by Green Desert) and half-brother to smart 1m (at 2 yrs)/1¼m winner Hazeymm (by Marju) and 5-y-o Sahrati: dam, ran once in Ireland, half-sister to St Leger winner Shantou: useful performer: won maiden at Nottingham in October and handicap at Lingfield (beat Bound By Honour by ¾ length) in November: left Saeed bin Suroor before well held in minor event at Jebel Ali final outing: bred to stay 1½m: acts on polytrack and good to soft ground. *A. bin Huzaim, UAE* **102**

BLACK FALCON (IRE) 9 ch.g. In The Wings 128 – Muwasim (USA) (Meadowlake (USA)) [2009 64§, a74§: f12s^3 f12g^4 f12g f12f f11g Dec 8] rather leggy, quite attractive gelding: modest performer nowadays: stays 1½m: acts on all-weather, firm and soft going: tried in headgear: ungenuine. *John A. Harris* **60 §**

BLACK JACARI (IRE) 4 b.g. Black Sam Bellamy (IRE) 121 – Amalia (IRE) 111 (Danehill (USA) 126) [2009 89: 14m^3 Jul 22] workmanlike gelding: fairly useful handicapper (similar standard over hurdles): stays 1¾m: acts on good to firm and good to soft ground: none too genuine: sold £21,000. *A. King* **86**

BLACK MOMA (IRE) 5 b.m. Averti (IRE) 117 – Sareb (FR) (Indian Ridge 123) [2009 70: 6m f5g 6m^4 5.1g^6 5m^6 Aug 19] close-coupled mare: just modest handicapper in 2009: best at 5f: acts on polytrack, firm and soft going: often races prominently. *J. R. Boyle* **51**

BLACK N BREW (USA) 3 b.g. Milwaukee Brew (USA) 122 – Natural Glow (USA) (Siphon (BRZ) 130) [2009 71: p10g^2 p11g^2 p10g^3 11.6m 7d^3 p8g^5 p10m* p12m^6 Dec 16] rather leggy gelding: fairly useful handicapper: won at Lingfield in December: effective at 7f to 11f: acts on polytrack, good to firm and good to soft going. *J. R. Best* **81**

BLACK NUN 3 b.f. Fasliyev (USA) 120 – Roxy (Rock City 120) [2009 63: p8.6g^6 p12.2g p12.2g 10.2v^6 Jul 17] lengthy, useful-looking filly: disappointing maiden: best efforts at 7f on polytrack: tried blinkered/visored. *S. Wynne* **53**

BLACK OR RED (IRE) 4 b.g. Cape Cross (IRE) 129 – Gentle Thoughts 73 (Darshaan 133) [2009 –, a61: p13.9g 17.2d^2 16g* 16s^2 p16g^4 15.8v p16.5g^6 16d^2 15v p16g^5 p16.5g* Dec 5] leggy gelding: fairly useful handicapper: won at Ffos Las in July and Wolverhampton in December: stays 17f: acts on polytrack and soft going: usually blinkered (not last 2 starts): tried tongue tied. *I. A. Wood* **86**

BLACK QUARTZ (FR) 2 b.c. (May 7) Danehill Dancer (IRE) 117 – Mirina (FR) (Pursuit of Love 124) [2009 6v^4 6d^2 7s* 7d* Aug 1] €200,000Y: big colt: sixth foal: half-brother to 3 winners in France, including useful 7f/1m winner Marine Bleue (by Desert Prince): dam, French 11f winner, half-sister to dam of Grand Prix de Saint-Cloud winner Mirio: progressive form: won maiden at the Curragh (made all) in July and nursery at Galway (idled, by short head from Corcovada, pair 8 lengths clear) in August: will stay 1m: already useful, and capable of better still. *A. P. O'Brien, Ireland* **107 p**

BLACK RAIN 4 b.g. Desert Prince (IRE) 130 – Antigua (Selkirk (USA) 129) [2009 85: 10s 10m 10d 8.3m 8.3m p12.2g* 10g Oct 19] workmanlike gelding: fairly useful handicapper: back to best when winning at Wolverhampton in October: stays 1½m: acts on polytrack and good to soft ground: tried tongue tied/visored: held up nowadays: sold 10,000 gns. *M. Wigham* **83**

BLACK RIVER FALLS (USA) 3 b.g. Fusaichi Pegasus (USA) 130 – La Lorgnette (CAN) (Val de L'Orne (FR) 133) [2009 12.4g^4 9.2g 9.2m^4 8.1s 9.9m^3 p12.2g 11.1g Sep 20] modest maiden: may prove best short of 1½m: acts on good to firm going: blinkered last 3 starts: probably not straightforward: sold £800. *I. Semple* **62**

BLACK SALIX (USA) 3 br.f. More Than Ready (USA) 120 – Woodman's Dancer (USA) (Woodman (USA) 126) [2009 54: 6.1m 8s 8m 8.3m Sep 30] smallish filly: poor maiden: best effort at 5f on good to soft going (on debut). *Mrs P. Sly* **46**

BLACK SAPPHIRE 2 b.f. (Mar 11) Motivator 131 – Esquiline (USA) (Gone West (USA)) [2009 7d^5 7g 8g Aug 29] €13,000Y, 15,000 2-y-o: lengthy, unfurnished filly: half-sister to 3 winners, notably 6f to 8.5f (including US minor stakes) winner Wixoe Express (by Anabaa) and French 11f winner Coppet (by Pennekamp), both useful: dam, maiden, out of half-sister to Arlington Million winner Mill Native: easily best effort in maidens when fifth at Newmarket: should stay 1m. *Miss Amy Weaver* **59**

BLACK SNOWFLAKE (USA) 2 b.c. (Feb 14) Elusive Quality (USA) – Black Escort (USA) 101 (Southern Halo (USA)) [2009 6m^2 6g* 7g* 8m^3 8.1v^3 8g^4 8g^5 Oct 19] $370,000Y: strong colt: second foal: dam, 4.5f (in France at 2 yrs) to 6f (in USA) winner, **95**

out of sister to smart sprinter King's Signet: useful performer: won maiden at Haydock and nursery at Goodwood (by neck from Gunner Lindley) in July: at least respectable efforts after, including when fourth of 5 to Behkabad in Prix des Chenes at Longchamp: should prove best at 7f/1m: acts on heavy and good to firm going: hung left final start. *Saeed bin Suroor*

BLACK SPIRIT (USA) 2 b.c. (Apr 2) Black Minnaloushe (USA) 123 – L'Extra Honor (USA) (Hero's Honor (USA)) [2009 7g* 7.1g^4 8m Sep 26] 68,000F, 62,000Y: well-made colt: half-brother to 3 winners, notably smart 6f (at 2 yrs) to 1m winner Majestic Roi (by Street Cry): dam, French 1½m winner (including listed race), half-sister to very smart 1¼m winner Montelimar: useful form: won minor event at Ascot in July by head from Prompter: still green, good 2½ lengths fourth to Shakespearean in Solario Stakes at Sandown next time: shaped as if amiss in Royal Lodge Stakes at Ascot final start: should stay 1m: tongue tied. *C. G. Cox* **99**

BLACK STOCKING 4 br.f. Dansili 127 – Mariette 35 (Blushing Scribe (USA) 107) [2009 8m^6 7f 7d^5 p8f^6 p9.5g^5 p9.5g^6 Nov 20] sturdy filly: sixth foal: half-sister to fairly useful 7f/1m winner Azreme (by Unfuwain): dam ran 3 times: modest maiden: left M. Wigham after debut: stays 9.5f: acts on polytrack, good to firm and good to soft going. *Rae Guest* **52**

BLACKSTONE VEGAS 3 ch.g. Nayef (USA) 129 – Waqood (USA) 75 (Riverman (USA) 131) [2009 66: 12.1s 11.1m^2 Jun 4] modest maiden: should stay 1½m: blinkered final start. *J. Howard Johnson* **59**

BLACKTOFT (USA) 6 b. or br.g. Theatrical 128 – Black Truffle (USA) (Mt Livermore (USA)) [2009 85: p10g^3 p8g^4 p8.6g* p10g* p9.5g* p12.2g^3 Feb 26] big, leggy gelding: fairly useful performer: successful in claimers at Wolverhampton (2) and Lingfield in February, claimed from S. C. Williams £8,000 after: stays 11f, effective at shorter: acts on all-weather and good to firm going: usually in headgear: fair hurdler, successful twice in 2009/10. *Evan Williams* **82**

BLACK TOR FIGARRO (IRE) 4 b.g. Rock of Gibraltar (IRE) 133 – Will Be Blue (IRE) (Darshaan 133) [2009 70: p12g p16g^5 Feb 24] close-coupled, leggy gelding: fair handicapper in 2008: well held at 4 yrs. *B. W. Duke* **–**

BLACKWATER FORT (USA) 3 b. or br.g. Doneraile Court (USA) – Clearwater (USA) (Seeking The Gold (USA)) [2009 66: 6f^4 6s 6d^4 7f p7m Aug 8] regressive maiden: should prove best at 5f/6f: acts on good to firm and good to soft going: tried visored/blinkered. *J. Gallagher* **52**

BLADE OF CLASS 2 b.f. (Apr 14) Needwood Blade 117 – Top of The Class (IRE) 69 (Rudimentary (USA) 118) [2009 f5g May 18] £1,000Y: second foal: dam 6f (at 2 yrs) to 10.5f winner: 50/1, very green in maiden at Southwell. *P. D. Evans* **–**

BLADE OF GLORY 2 ch.f. (May 24) Needwood Blade 117 – Jewel (IRE) 64 (Cyrano de Bergerac 120) [2009 6g p6g p7.1g^6 6g p7f Sep 10] £2,200Y: workmanlike filly: eighth foal: dam, sprint maiden, half-sister to smart 1996 2-y-o sprinter Deadly Dudley: no form, including in seller: tried visored/in cheekpieces. *A. J. McCabe* **–**

BLADES HARMONY 2 b.g. (May 18) Needwood Blade 117 – Yabint El Sham 83 (Sizzling Melody 117) [2009 f7g^4 Dec 22] £30,000Y: third foal: half-brother to fairly useful 2005 2-y-o 5f winner Nigella (by Band On The Run): dam 5f (including at 2 yrs)/6f winner: 17/2 and green, signs of ability when well-held fourth to Secretive in maiden at Southwell, very slowly away: should do better. *E. S. McMahon* **– p**

BLADES PRINCESS 3 ch.f. Needwood Blade 117 – Breezy Palms (Tragic Role (USA)) [2009 92: 5.1g 5g 5d^6 5d 5m p5.1g^6 Oct 10] leggy, attractive filly: fairly useful performer: likely to prove best kept to 5f: acts on polytrack and soft ground, promise on good to firm: tried blinkered/in cheekpieces. *E. S. McMahon* **81**

BLAISE TOWER 3 ch.g. Fantastic Light (USA) 134 – Blaise Castle (USA) 97 (Irish River (FR) 131) [2009 75p: p8g* p10g^4 9.9g 9.9m^3 11d Aug 1] rather leggy gelding: fairly useful handicapper: won at Kempton in January: stays 1¼m: acts on all-weather and good to firm going. *G. L. Moore* **84**

BLAKENEYS PET (IRE) 3 b.f. Celtic Swing 138 – Kathryn's Pet 92 (Blakeney 126) [2009 p12g Dec 31] third foal: sister to 1½m to 2m winner Celtic Carisma: dam 1½m to 1¾m winner: modest form in bumpers, soundly beaten in juvenile hurdles: tailed off in seller on Flat debut. *W. G. M. Turner* **–**

BLAKESHALL DIAMOND 4 gr.f. Piccolo 121 – Hi Hoh (IRE) (Fayruz 116) [2009 69d: p5.1g 5.3d 5f 5.3f 5.2g^6 6g^5 5m Sep 13] modest handicapper: raced at 5f/6f: acts on polytrack. *A. J. Chamberlain* **55**

BLAKESHALL QUEST 9 b.m. Piccolo 121 – Corniche Quest (IRE) 74 (Salt Dome (USA)) [2009 –, a66: f6d f5g^4 f6g^5 p6m f6g^4 f6g^2 f6g^4 Jun 7] compact mare: modest handicapper: best at 5f/6f: acts on all-weather (though successful only on fibresand), lightly raced on turf: visored/blinkered: usually forces pace: none too consistent. *R. Brotherton* **– a57**

BLAKEY'S BOY 2 b.g. (Feb 20) Hawk Wing (USA) 136 – Divine Grace (IRE) (Definite Article 121) [2009 7d* 7m^3 8g Oct 10] 24,000F, 40,000Y: tall, good-topped gelding: has scope: fourth foal: half-brother to smart German 6f/7f (including at 2 yrs) winner Electric Beat (by Shinko Forest) and 5f winner Divalini (by Bertolini): dam ran twice: fairly useful form: won maiden at Salisbury in July: still green, good 5½ lengths third to Azmeel in listed event at Newbury (sweated, hung right): last in Autumn Stakes at Ascot (found little, gelded after): should stay 1m: carries head high and clear signs of temperament. *J. L. Dunlop* **89**

BLANDFORD FLYER 6 b.g. Soviet Star (USA) 128 – Vento Del Oreno (FR) 67 (Lando (GER) 128) [2009 f14g Jan 27] smallish, well-made gelding: poor hurdler: little form on Flat since 2005 (unraced in 2007/8). *M. J. Gingell* **–**

BLAST 2 ch.f. (May 6) Avonbridge 123 – Pain Perdu (IRE) (Waajib 121) [2009 6s 6g p7g p6g^6 p7.1g Nov 2] 24,000Y: half-sister to several winners, including 5-y-o Tifernati and fairly useful 2002 2-y-o 7f winner Sister Bluebird (by Bluebird): dam French 1¼m winner: modest maiden: left D. Myerscough in Ireland after third start: stays 7f: acts on polytrack, probably on soft going: blinkered last 2 starts. *J. R. Gask* **59**

BLASTIE 4 b.g. Josr Algarhoud (IRE) 118 – Passerella (FR) (Brustolon 117) [2009 8m 8d 7m^4 9.9f 10m Sep 14] workmanlike gelding: modest form at best. *T. D. Walford* **54**

BLAZING BUCK 3 ch.g. Fraam 114 – Anapola (GER) (Polish Precedent (USA) 131) [2009 77: p9.5g^6 10.9g 8.3d 12.1g^4 10.2m^5 Sep 10] small gelding: modest performer nowadays: left H. Dunlop after reappearance: stays 1¼m: acts on good to firm and good to soft ground: successful over hurdles in November. *A. W. Carroll* **59**

BLAZING HEIGHTS 6 b.g. Compton Place 125 – Harrken Heights (IRE) (Belmez (USA) 131) [2009 81: 5m^4 5v 5g 5m^5 5g 5m^6 5g 5f^4 5g^3 5d 5m 5g 5m 5m 6g 5s Oct 27] dipped-backed gelding: fairly useful performer at 5 yrs: regressed in 2009: has won at 6f, best at 5f: acts on firm and soft going: sometimes in headgear: has been slowly away. *J. S. Goldie* **70 d**

BLESSED PLACE 9 ch.g. Compton Place 125 – Cathedra (So Blessed 130) [2009 75: 6m 6m 6m 5m p6g 5m^5 5.2s^2 5d* 5g^3 5g Aug 12] leggy gelding: fair handicapper: won apprentice event at Thirsk in July: effective at 5f/easy 6f: acts on all-weather, firm and soft going: tried blinkered/tongue tied/in cheekpieces: front runner. *D. J. S. ffrench Davis* **65**

BLESSING BELLE (IRE) 3 ch.f. Traditionally (USA) 117 – Kind of Loving 64 (Diesis 133) [2009 –: 8.3g* p10g^5 8s a7.5g^5 Dec 30] good-topped filly: fair performer: won seller at Hamilton in May: sold from M. Tompkins 7,500 gns after next start: best effort when fifth in claimer at Deauville final outing: should stay 1¼m. *Mme G. Rarick, France* **70**

BLINKA ME 2 b.c. (Jan 7) Tiger Hill (IRE) 127 – Easy To Love (USA) 86 (Diesis 133) [2009 6g^6 7g 7d 8m p10m^5 Nov 21] sturdy, lengthy colt: modest maiden: stays 1¼m: acts on polytrack: blinkered (best effort) final start. *M. H. Tompkins* **57**

BLISSFUL MOMENT (USA) 2 b. or br.c. (Mar 14) Dynaformer (USA) – Arabian Spell (IRE) 100 (Desert Prince (IRE) 130) [2009 8m^4 Oct 1] $380,000Y: good-bodied colt: first foal: dam, 1m winner, half-sister to 4-y-o Red Merlin: 5/1, very green when 4 lengths fourth to Fareej in maiden at Newmarket, soon niggled and strong at finish: will be suited by 1¼m+: sure to improve and win races. *Sir Michael Stoute* **78 p**

BLITZED 2 b.g. (Mar 26) Fantastic Light (USA) 134 – Broken Peace (USA) (Devil's Bag (USA)) [2009 7g^6 Oct 30] lengthy gelding: half-brother to several winners, including useful French 7.5f/1m winner Reverse Angle (by Spinning World) and 1½m winner Stormy Day (by Rainbow Quest): dam French 1m winner (including at 2 yrs): 125/1, encouraging 5½ lengths sixth to Quick Wit in maiden at Newmarket, late headway under hand riding: will stay 1m+: likely to improve. *G. L. Moore* **71 p**

BLIZZARD BLUES (USA) 3 ch.c. Mr Greeley (USA) 122 – Blush Damask (USA) 106 (Green Dancer (USA) 132) [2009 10g* 10.4g^3 Oct 9] well-made colt: fourth foal: half-brother to 2 winners, notably useful 5.5f (in France) to 9f (in Switzerland) winner Blue Damask (by Rahy): dam German 2-y-o 7f winner: useful form: blinkered, won maiden at Newmarket in July by ¾ length from Manifest, coltish beforehand and hanging **101**

badly left in front: improved when 2½ lengths third to Peligroso in minor event at York 3 months later, consenting to run on only late: temperament already under suspicion. *H. R. A. Cecil*

BLOCKLEY (USA) 5 b.g. Johannesburg (USA) 127 – Saintly Manner (USA) (St **72**
Jovite (USA) 135) [2009 66: p12.2g* p13.3g p13.9g^2 f14g* p13.9g* 16d^2 p16g^3 10g^6 10d 11.6m 16d^3 p16g p16.5g^2 Dec 5] fair handicapper: won at Wolverhampton in January, and Southwell and Wolverhampton in March: stays 2m: acts on all-weather, heavy and good to firm going: tried in headgear/tongue tie: signs of temperament. *Ian Williams*

BLOCK PARTY 3 b.c. Dansili 127 – Mylania 70 (Midyan (USA) 124) [2009 75p: 8m^4 **89**
8.1g^2 8.3g* 8g^3 7m p8g^2 p8f Oct 14] big colt: fairly useful performer: won maiden at Windsor in July: best efforts otherwise in 2009 when runner-up: stays 1m: acts on polytrack and good to firm ground: tried visored: no battler: sold 28,000 gns. *R. Charlton*

BLOW HOLE (USA) 4 ch.g. Mr Greeley (USA) 122 – Nevis (USA) (Cox's Ridge **–**
(USA)) [2009 82: 10m p8g Jul 18] rangy gelding: fairly useful maiden handicapper at 3 yrs: no form in 2009 (including over hurdles). *Paul Mason*

BLOWN IT (USA) 3 b. or br.g. More Than Ready (USA) 120 – Short Shadow (USA) **83**
(Out of Place (USA)) [2009 82: 6s^4 6g^3 6g^4 5g^5 6g 6f* 6d 5m^3 6d p6g^5 p6m^4 Nov 21] good-topped gelding: has a quick action: fairly useful handicapper: won at Ayr in August: effective at 5f/6f: acts on polytrack and firm going: tried blinkered/in cheekpieces: none too consistent. *I. Semple*

BLOW YOUR MIND 3 b.c. Mind Games 121 – Ashkernazy (IRE) 60 (Salt Dome **59**
(USA)) [2009 64: 6m 5m^6 5m 5g^6 Sep 21] good-topped colt: modest maiden: best at 5f: acts on good to firm going: tried blinkered/visored. *Karen McLintock*

BLUE AGAIN 2 b.f. (Mar 2) Leporello (IRE) 118 – Forever Blue (Spectrum (IRE) 126) **– p**
[2009 p7m Nov 26] first foal: dam unraced half-sister to smart performers up to 9f Putra Pekan and Sapphire Ring: 20/1, signs of ability when eighth to Bramshaw in maiden at Kempton, running green: bred to stay 1m: capable of better. *W. R. Swinburn*

BLUE ANGEL (IRE) 2 b.f. (Feb 27) Oratorio (IRE) 128 – Blue Cloud (IRE) 106 **99**
(Nashwan (USA) 135) [2009 p7g* 6g^2 7g 7g^4 8m^6 Sep 26] €34,000F, 32,000Y: sturdy filly: seventh foal: half-sister to 3 winners in France, including 7f (at 2 yrs) to 1¼m winner Bomber Pilot (by Numerous) and 13f winner Burning Fire (by Polish Precedent): dam, French 7f/1m winner (latter at 2 yrs), half-sister to high-class 7f to 1¼m performer Bigstone: useful performer: won maiden at Kempton in July: much improved last 2 starts, very close fourth to Sent From Heaven in Prestige Stakes at Goodwood then 4¼ lengths sixth to Hibaayeb in Fillies' Mile at Ascot: will be suited by 1¼m: acts on polytrack and good to firm ground. *R. Hannon*

BLUE AVON 2 b.f. (Feb 19) Avonbridge 123 – Blue Nile (IRE) 70 (Bluebird (USA) **56**
125) [2009 6g^6 7d 6m^2 7g Sep 14] close-coupled filly: half-sister to several winners, including 7f (at 2 yrs) to 2m winner Gone Too Far (by Reprimand): dam, 1¼m winner, half-sister to smart 1¼m performer Revelation: maiden: form only when second at Newcastle, dictating: should stay 7f: acts on good to firm going. *R. A. Fahey*

BLUE BAJAN (IRE) 7 b.g. Montjeu (IRE) 137 – Gentle Thoughts 73 (Darshaan 133) **114**
[2009 14s^2 12.3m^4 16m^4 Oct 17] tall, quite good-topped gelding: smart performer: fit from hurdling (very smart form), as good as ever when 6 lengths second to Ask in Yorkshire Cup at York on belated Flat return: off 4 months, below form in listed race at Chester and Jockey Club Cup at Newmarket after: stays 1¾m: acts on polytrack, soft and good to firm going: blinkered once: often sweats up/edgy: held up. *Andrew Turnell*

BLUEBARU 3 b.g. Bahamian Bounty 116 – Gina of Hithermoor (Reprimand 122) **–**
[2009 –: 6f Apr 17] plain gelding: no form: tried visored. *L. R. James*

BLUEBELL RIDGE (IRE) 4 b.f. Distant Music (USA) 126 – Miss Indigo 62 (Indian **69**
Ridge 123) [2009 72: p12m p12.2g* Jan 26] leggy filly: fair performer: won handicap at Wolverhampton (carried head high and hung left) in January: stays 13.8f: raced on polytrack and good going or firmer on turf: tried blinkered: sold 11,000 gns in February, sent to Saudi Arabia. *D. W. P. Arbuthnot*

BLUEBIRD CHARIOT 6 b.g. Bluebird (USA) 125 – Boadicea's Chariot (Comman- **41**
che Run 133) [2009 56?: 6f^5 7.1d 5.7g p7g^6 Nov 25] poor maiden. *J. M. Bradley*

BLUEBOK 8 ch.g. Indian Ridge 123 – Blue Sirocco (Bluebird (USA) 125) [2009 70: **71**
p5.1g p5m^6 p5g^3 p5.1g^3 p5g^5 p5g^4 p5g^2 p5.1g* p5g^2 5.3m^3 5.1m^5 5g p5g^3 5m^5 5.2m^6 5m p5g* p5g^3 5.1m^5 5d^6 5.1m^2 5m^5 p5g p5.1g^5 p5.1g p5.1g^4 p5m^4 Dec 6] compact gelding: fair handicapper: won at Wolverhampton in April and Lingfield in July: best at 5f: acts on polytrack and firm going: blinkered/tongue tied: tough. *J. M. Bradley*

BLUE BOND 2 ch.g. (Mar 31) Monsieur Bond (IRE) 120 – Azula 80 (Bluebird (USA) 125) [2009 5m p5.1g⁴ 5f⁶ 6d 7m⁶ 7s f6m⁶ p7.1g Aug 10] unfurnished gelding: poor maiden: tried in cheekpieces/blinkers. *P. T. Midgley* **42**

BLUE CELESTE 3 b.f. Sakhee (USA) 136 – Ellie Ardensky 100 (Slip Anchor 136) [2009 10.2g p10m⁶ Dec 9] 3,000Y: eighth foal: half-sister to several winners, including smart 1m and 14.6f winner Pole Star (by Polar Falcon) and 2004 2-y-o 1m winner Emile Zola (by Singspiel): dam 9f/1¼m winner: well held in maidens. *R. T. Phillips* **–**

BLUE CHARM 5 b.g. Averti (IRE) 117 – Exotic Forest 66 (Dominion 123) [2009 77: f7d² p7g³ p7.1g³ f6g² f7g³ 6m⁴ 8g* 8d 8.5g⁶ 7.5m⁴ 8.3g 8.5g³ 8.5m Jul 28] good-topped gelding: fair handicapper: left S. Kirk after third start: won at Pontefract in April: stays 8.5f: acts on all-weather, good to firm and good to soft ground: tried tongue tied: usually held up. *I. W. McInnes* **76**

BLUECROP BOY 5 b.g. Zaha (CAN) 106 – Pearl Dawn (IRE) 91 (Jareer (USA) 115) [2009 60: p16.5g⁶ Sep 12] modest maiden: below form sole start at 5 yrs: stays 1½m: acts on fibresand: tried in headgear. *D. J. S. ffrench Davis* **49 +**

BLUE DAGGER (IRE) 3 ch.g. Daggers Drawn (USA) 114 – Sports Post Lady (IRE) 72 (M Double M (USA)) [2009 64d: 8d Jul 24] sturdy, lengthy gelding: no form since debut at 2 yrs. *P. C. Haslam* **–**

BLUE DYNASTY (USA) 3 b.g. Dynaformer (USA) – Saudia (USA) 84 (Gone West (USA)) [2009 71: 11.8m⁶ 15g⁶ Jul 3] sturdy gelding: fair performer: should stay beyond 1½m: tried blinkered: lazy: sold 4,000 gns in October. *Mrs A. J. Perrett* **68**

BLUE EMIRATE 2 b.g. (Mar 21) Dubai Destination (USA) 127 – Dorinda Gray (IRE) (Docksider (USA) 124) [2009 6g³ 7m 6g Aug 31] compact gelding: well held in maidens/seller. *P. C. Haslam* **–**

BLUE GLOVE (IRE) 2 b.f. (Jan 11) Bertolini (USA) 125 – Red Shoe (Selkirk (USA) 129) [2009 p8m p7m p8m⁴ Dec 30] second foal: dam, unraced half-sister to smart French miler Barricade, out of sister to Dancing Brave: well held in maidens/claimer. *J. A. Osborne* **–**

BLUEGRASS LION (USA) 3 b. or br.g. Volponi (USA) 131 – Exactly Dixie (USA) (Dixie Brass (USA)) [2009 11.8g⁵ f12f Nov 24] better effort in maidens (modest form) when fifth at Leicester. *Paul Green* **56**

BLUE HILLS 8 br.g. Vettori (IRE) 119 – Slow Jazz (USA) 106 (Chief's Crown (USA)) [2009 66, a75: f14s⁵ f14g* f16g² f14g⁴ p13.9g⁶ p13.9g f12g⁴ p13.9g May 11] tall gelding: fair handicapper: won amateur event at Southwell in January: stays 2m: acts on all-weather, firm and good to soft going: wears headgear: races prominently. *P. W. Hiatt* **67**

BLUE JACK 4 b.g. Cadeaux Genereux 131 – Fairy Flight (IRE) 86 (Fairy King (USA)) [2009 88: 5.7g³ 5.7g² 6f 6m⁶ 5f* 5m⁵ 5g* 5g 5d* 5g* 5d 6m Sep 19] sturdy gelding: useful handicapper: progressed well in blinkers, winning at Sandown in June, Windsor and Goodwood in July, and Sandown (by length from Tony The Tap) in August: poor efforts last 2 starts, laboured in Ayr Gold Cup on latest: best at 5f/6f: acts on polytrack, firm and good to soft ground: tried tongue tied: usually held up: sold 65,000 gns. *W. R. Muir* **106**

BLUEJAIN 4 b.g. Lujain (USA) 119 – Belle of The Blues (IRE) (Blues Traveller (IRE) 119) [2009 92: p8.6g Jan 16] tall, useful-looking gelding: fairly useful handicapper at 3 yrs: broke down at Wolverhampton: stayed 1¼m: best form on polytrack: dead. *Miss Gay Kelleway* **–**

BLUE JET (USA) 5 b.g. Black Minnaloushe (USA) 123 – Clickety Click (USA) (Sovereign Dancer (USA)) [2009 63: 16m 12g⁶ 14.1m³ 14.1g² f14g 13.1d 14.1g 13.8m³ 15.8g⁶ Oct 6] leggy, close-coupled gelding: modest performer: stays 2m: acts on polytrack, good to firm and good to soft ground: tried in cheekpieces/visor: inconsistent, and one to treat with caution. *R. M. Whitaker* **54 §**

BLUE LYRIC 2 b.f. (Mar 10) Refuse To Bend (IRE) 128 – Powder Blue 64 (Daylami (IRE) 138) [2009 6g⁶ p6g³ 8g⁶ p7g* p7g* Dec 2] 58,000Y: first foal: dam twice-raced half-sister to dam of 3-y-o Fantasia out of Cheveley Park Stakes winner Blue Duster: fairly useful performer: much improved to win nurseries at Kempton in November and December: should stay 1m: acts on polytrack: capable of better still. *L. M. Cumani* **81 p**

BLUE MAIDEN 2 b.f. (Feb 24) Medicean 128 – Bluebelle 80 (Generous (IRE) 139) [2009 6m² 6g* 7g² 7m⁵ Oct 2] rather leggy filly: seventh foal: half-sister to Italian 10.5f/11f winner Doctor Kris (by Dr Fong): dam, 1½m winner, half-sister to useful German winner up to 11f (Preis der Diana) Centaine: useful performer: won maiden at Newmarket in July by ½ length from Mon Cadeaux: much improved when length second to Long Lashes in Sweet Solera Stakes there next time: off almost 2 months (had suffered foot **105**

problem), shaped as if in need of race when only fifth in Oh So Sharp Stakes at Newmarket: will be suited by 1m+. *P. J. McBride*

BLUE MONDAY 8 b.g. Darshaan 133 – Lunda (IRE) 60 (Soviet Star (USA) 128) [2009 119: 10d⁴ 10g⁴ Aug 15] rangy, attractive gelding: impresses in appearance: smart performer: changed hands 72,000 gns in May: not quite so good in 2009 but still finished fourth in listed race at Newbury (1½ lengths behind Crime Scene) and Prix Gontaut-Biron at Deauville (beaten 2 lengths by Crossharbour): seems to stay 2m: acts on any turf going: has run well when sweating. *R. Charlton* **111**

BLUE NEPTUNE 2 ch.c. (Feb 25) Compton Place 125 – Centre Court 74 (Second Set (IRE) 127) [2009 5m 5m⁶ p5.1m p5g* p5.1g p5.1g p5m³ p5m³ p5m⁶ Dec 30] neat colt: modest performer: won nursery at Kempton in October: raced only at 5f: acts on polytrack. *W. R. Muir* **62**

BLUE NOODLES 3 b.g. Reset (AUS) 124 – Gleam of Light (IRE) 81 (Danehill (USA) 126) [2009 63: f6d 6m³ 7m³ 6m⁵ 6s* 6d⁵ 5.9m² 6m³ 6g⁶ 7s² 7s³ 7.1d* p7.1g* 7d² Oct 15] leggy gelding: fair performer: won claimer at Newcastle in May and, after leaving D. Barker after eighth outing and claimed from Ollie Pears £6,000 eleventh start, seller at Chepstow and handicap at Wolverhampton in September: stays 7f: acts on polytrack, soft and good to firm ground: front runner/races prominently. *P. D. Evans* **78**

BLUE NYMPH 3 ch.f. Selkirk (USA) 129 – Blue Icon (Peintre Celebre (USA) 137) [2009 75p: p11g² f12g² 11.7g² p12m* f14g* Oct 18] big, lengthy filly: fairly useful form: runner-up 3 starts prior to winning maiden at Kempton in September and handicap at Southwell in October: stays 1¾m: acts on all-weather, raced only on good/good to soft going on turf: sold 68,000 gns, joined J. J. Quinn. *R. M. Beckett* **93**

BLUE RUM (IRE) 2 b.g. (Mar 9) Pyrus (USA) 106 – Secret Combe (IRE) 81 (Mujadil (USA) 119) [2009 5f³ 5m⁴ 6d⁵ 6.1s⁶ f6g Nov 17] tall gelding: modest maiden: will prove best at 5f/easy 6f: tried in cheekpieces. *P. C. Haslam* **50**

BLUES JAZZ 3 b.g. Josr Algarhoud (IRE) 118 – Belle of The Blues (IRE) (Blues Traveller (IRE) 119) [2009 p8m Sep 24] 33/1, signs of ability when well held in maiden at Kempton. *Miss Gay Kelleway* **–**

BLUE SKY BASIN 4 b.g. Desert Prince (IRE) 130 – Kimba (USA) (Kris S (USA)) [2009 115p: 7.5g a7f 6.5g³ a7g* 7m May 9] close-coupled gelding: useful handicapper: won at Jebel Ali in March by a head from Tasteyville, then left M. bin Shafya in UAE: lacklustre effort on British return in Victoria Cup at Ascot: best up to 7f: acts on polytrack/dirt, soft and good to firm going: races prominently: sold only £5,500 in October. *Saeed bin Suroor* **109**

BLUE SKY THINKING (IRE) 10 b.g. Danehill Dancer (IRE) 117 – Lauretta Blue (IRE) (Bluebird (USA) 125) [2009 78: f8d p9.5g Jan 9] tall, rather leggy gelding: has reportedly had joints pin fired: useful performer at best, lightly raced since 2007: well held in seller/claimer at 10 yrs. *K. R. Burke* **–**

BLUES MINOR (IRE) 4 b.g. Acclamation 118 – Narbayda (IRE) 68 (Kahyasi 130) [2009 74: p7.1g p7.1g 10.4g p8.6g Sep 5] quite attractive gelding: has a quick action: fair performer in 2008: well held at 4 yrs: blinkered 5 of last 6 starts. *M. Mullineaux* **–**

BLUE SPARKLE (IRE) 2 b.f. (Apr 12) Acclamation 118 – Westlife (IRE) 32 (Mind Games 121) [2009 6m³ 6f 7s³ Sep 3] €65,000F, €85,000Y: angular filly: fourth foal: half-sister to 5f winner Orpenlina (by Orpen) and 2007 2-y-o 6f seller winner Pearo (by Captain Rio): dam, maiden, half-sister to useful sprinter Pepperoni: fair maiden: third at Goodwood and Salisbury: may prove best at short of 7f. *Mrs A. J. Perrett* **65**

BLUE SPARTAN (IRE) 4 gr.g. Spartacus (IRE) 107 – Bridelina (FR) (Linamix (FR) 127) [2009 82: 8m Apr 29] leggy, lengthy gelding: fairly useful at 3 yrs: poorly drawn sole start in 2009 (gelded after): stays 9f: acts on soft ground: joined C. Mann, well held on hurdling debut. *B. J. Meehan* **–**

BLUE SPINNAKER (IRE) 10 b.g. Bluebird (USA) 125 – Suedoise (Kris 135) [2009 96: 10.2d 8.5m 9.9g⁶ 8.9d 8g 8.5m 8.3d⁶ 8s 10g Oct 19] sturdy gelding: useful handicapper at best: on downgrade: effective at 1m/1¼m: acts on any going: tried in blinkers/cheekpieces: held up. *M. W. Easterby* **76 d**

BLUE TANGO (IRE) 3 ch.c. Noverre (USA) 125 – It Takes Two (IRE) (Alzao (USA) 117) [2009 81: p10g⁴ p10g 11.6m 14g f14g³ 14g p12.2g* p12.2m p12m⁶ 10g Oct 19] good-topped colt: fair handicapper: enterprisingly ridden when winning at Wolverhampton in September: stays 1¾m: acts on all-weather and soft ground: blinkered last 5 starts: usually held up in 2009 (often pulls hard). *Mrs A. J. Perrett* **72**

BLUE TOMATO 8 b.g. Orpen (USA) 116 – Ocean Grove (IRE) 84 (Fairy King (USA)) [2009 98: p5.1g² f5g² p6g² p5.1g² p6g* p5.1m³ p6g* p5.1g³ 5m 6m⁵ 6f² p7g³ 5m* 5g* 6m 5g² 5d* 5g⁴ 5m 5m Sep 18] lengthy, useful-looking gelding: fairly useful performer: won claimers at Wolverhampton (2) in March, seller in May and handicap in June, both at Musselburgh, and seller at Hamilton (left D. Nicholls £3,500) in July: best at 5f/6f: acts on polytrack (probably on fibresand) and firm going: effective in cheekpieces or not: tried tongue tied: usually held up: has reportedly bled. *Miss L. A. Perratt* **87**

BLUE TURK 4 b.g. Where Or When (IRE) 124 – Pearly River 72 (Elegant Air 119) [2009 62: 7g⁶ p7g 7.6d² 8g p10m* p8m⁴ p12m p10m Nov 3] medium-sized gelding: fair handicapper: left G. Lyons in Ireland after second start: won at Kempton in September: stays 1¼m: acts on polytrack, best turf effort on good to soft going. *J. R. Boyle* **67**

BLUE WARRIOR (IRE) 4 b.g. Touch of The Blues (FR) 125 – Warrior Wings 81 (Indian Ridge 123) [2009 6f Jun 20] 25/1, tailed off in maiden at Lingfield: in blindfold, broke out of stall and ended up in lake at Kempton before intended debut. *J. R. Best* **–**

BLUE ZEPHYR 2 br.c. (Feb 21) Pastoral Pursuits 127 – Pippa's Dancer (IRE) 86 (Desert Style (IRE) 121) [2009 p5g⁵ Apr 4] first foal: dam, 5f/6f winner, half-sister to smart performer up to 7f Strahan: 14/1, 3¾ lengths fifth to Soccer in maiden at Lingfield, soon behind after slow start then going on well under considerate handling: wasn't seen out again. *W. R. Muir* **60**

BLUIE 2 b.g. (Feb 3) Ishiguru (USA) 114 – Flying Highest (Spectrum (IRE) 126) [2009 5g 6d⁴ 6d³ 6g* 6d* 6s* 6d⁴ 6m⁴ Sep 18] 5,000Y: big, good-topped gelding: first foal: dam, ran once, out of half-sister to very smart sprinter Bolshoi: fairly useful performer: won seller at Haydock in July and nurseries at Goodwood (beat Layla's Hero 1½ lengths) and Hamilton, both in August: will prove at least as effective at 5f as 6f: acts on soft and good to firm ground: sent to Hong Kong. *D. Nicholls* **85**

BLUSHING BERTIE 3 b.g. Bertolini (USA) 125 – Blushing Sunrise (USA) (Cox's Ridge (USA)) [2009 –: p8.6g Jun 22] well held in maidens. *J. W. Unett* **–**

BLUSHING DREAMER (IRE) 3 ch.f. Frenchmans Bay (FR) 118 – Second Dream (IRE) (Second Set (IRE) 127) [2009 –: p8.6g Dec 3] no form: tried blinkered/visored. *Miss N. A. Lloyd-Beavis* **–**

BLUSHING HEART 5 b.m. Observatory (USA) 131 – Navarazi (Arazi (USA) 135) [2009 62: f12g⁵ f12g Feb 1] workmanlike mare: modest performer: should stay 1½m: raced on fibresand and good going or softer: temperament under suspicion. *G. M. Moore* **54**

BLUSHING HILARY (IRE) 6 ch.m. City On A Hill (USA) 114 – Trinida (Jaazeiro (USA) 127) [2009 56: p12g Jan 22] sturdy mare: modest maiden handicapper: stayed 17f: acted on all-weather, good to soft and good to firm ground: usually wore headgear: had found little: modest hurdler: dead. *Mrs S. J. Humphrey* **–**

BLUSHING (IRE) 2 b.f. (Apr 14) Fasliyev (USA) 120 – Danseuse du Bois (USA) (Woodman (USA) 126) [2009 5.7f⁵ 6m⁴ p6g Aug 27] €14,000F, £40,000Y: compact filly: fifth foal: sister to 3-y-o Saucy Brown and half-sister to winners abroad by Danehill Dancer and Montjeu: dam, French maiden, out of useful half-sister to Poule d'Essai des Pouliches winner Danseuse du Soir: modest form first 2 starts in maidens: will be at least as effective at 5f as 6f. *B. J. Meehan* **56**

BLUSHING MAID 3 br.f. Namid 128 – Music Maid (IRE) 74 (Inzar (USA) 112) [2009 65: 5.7f⁴ 5.7f⁶ p6g⁶ 6m⁶ 5.7m⁶ p6g 6m⁶ p6f 6m Sep 29] lengthy filly: fair handicapper: stays 6f: acts on polytrack and firm going. *H. S. Howe* **65**

BLUSHING SOUL (USA) 3 ch.g. Perfect Soul (IRE) 122 – Kalimenta (USA) 54 (Rahy (USA) 115) [2009 74: p10.7g p12g Dec 31] lightly-raced maiden: little impact either start in 2009 (left J. Oxx, Ireland and modest form over hurdles for Miss P. Robson in between): stays 1m: raced only on polytrack: in blinkers/cheekpieces since debut: signs of temperament. *L. A. Dace* **69**

BLYTHE KNIGHT (IRE) 9 ch.g. Selkirk (USA) 129 – Blushing Barada (USA) 53 (Blushing Groom (FR) 131) [2009 119: p8g² 8m 8m⁶ 8g⁵ 8.1m 9.9g Jul 28] quite good-topped gelding: had a round action: smart performer at best, winning 8 races on Flat, including Lincoln Handicap at Redcar in 2006 and Diomed Stakes at Epsom in 2007 and 2008: not quite so good in 2009, best effort when seventh in Lincoln at Doncaster on second outing: had form up to 1½m, but was best at 7f to 8.5f later in career: acted on polytrack, firm and soft going: had worn headgear, though not since 2005: reportedly retired. *J. J. Quinn* **105**

BOARD MEETING (IRE) 3 b.f. Anabaa (USA) 130 – Bright Moon (USA) 123 (Alysheba (USA)) [2009 11g* 10.5d² 10.5m⁵ 10g* 12g³ 10g² Oct 4] big, lengthy, good-bodied filly: half-sister to several winners in France, notably very smart 1m to 10.5f (Prix de Diane) winner Bright Sky (by Wolfhound): dam, French 1½m/13.5f winner, dual winner of Prix de Pomone: smart performer: won minor event at Longchamp in April and Prix de Psyche Beachcomber Hotels Royal Palm at Deauville (by short head from Proportional) in August: good efforts at Longchamp last 2 starts, in Prix Vermeille (1¾ lengths behind demoted Dar Re Mi, promoted to third) and Prix de l'Opera (1½ lengths second to Shalanaya), staying on well both times: stays 1½m. *E. Lellouche, France* **116**

BOBAL GIRL 4 ch.f. Tobougg (IRE) 125 – Al Guswa 98 (Shernazar 131) [2009 57: p8g Jan 5] modest maiden: well held sole start in 2009: stays 1½m: best efforts on polytrack: tried blinkered/tongue tied. *M. D. Squance* **–**

BOBBIE SOXER (IRE) 3 br.f. Pivotal 124 – Fantasy Girl (IRE) 55 (Marju (IRE) 127) [2009 75: p7g² 6m² 6m* 6m⁴ 6m 6m 6.1g² 5.7m⁴ p6m Oct 12] leggy filly: fairly useful handicapper: won at Leicester in May: stays 7f: raced only on polytrack and good/good to firm going. *J. L. Dunlop* **90**

BOBBLE ROCK (IRE) 3 ch.c. Rock of Gibraltar (IRE) 133 – Torosay Spring 116 (First Trump 118) [2009 7f³ 7s⁶ 6m 8g p7m p11m Sep 30] little form: tried blinkered. *J. R. Best* **–**

BOBBY CHARLES 8 ch.g. Polish Precedent (USA) 131 – Dina Line (USA) 60 (Diesis 133) [2009 60+: 10d Jul 17] good-topped gelding: fairly useful handicapper at best: lightly raced in recent years, and just modest form sole start in 2009. *Dr J. D. Scargill* **63**

BOBBY MCGEE 2 b.f. (Mar 25) Captain Rio 122 – Al Kahina (Mark of Esteem (IRE) 137) [2009 6m⁶ Oct 1] 33/1 and green, signs of ability in maiden at Ayr: dead. *Jedd O'Keeffe* **–**

BOBBY'S DOLL 2 ch.f. (May 3) Needwood Blade 117 – Nine To Five 64 (Imp Society (USA)) [2009 6m⁶ p6g p6m⁴ p6m⁴ p7.1m⁵ Nov 28] close-coupled filly: fifth foal: half-sister to 2005 2-y-o 6f winner Trombone Tom (by Superior Premium): dam, 5f winner, ran only at 2 yrs: modest maiden: stays 6f. *T. T. Clement* **55**

BOBEACHWAY (IRE) 3 b.g. Chevalier (IRE) 115 – Miss Barcelona (IRE) 53 (Mac's Imp (USA) 116) [2009 8.1m 8m 9d⁵ May 17] lengthy gelding: fourth foal: brother to fairly useful 2007 2-y-o 6f winner Johar Jamal: dam, maiden (stayed 1¼m), half-sister to Rockfel Stakes winner Name of Love: modest form and not knocked about in maidens, but not seen out after May. *M. Dods* **54**

BOBERING 9 b.g. Bob's Return (IRE) 123 – Ring The Rafters (Batshoof 122) [2009 54: p10g p9.5g p9.5g⁶ p9.5g p9.5g p9.5g⁶ Dec 11] strong gelding: poor performer nowadays: best around 1¼m: acts on all-weather: usually held up. *B. P. J. Baugh* **46**

BOB GOES ELECTRIC (IRE) 2 br.c. (Feb 11) Camacho 118 – Gracious Gretclo 54 (Common Grounds 118) [2009 5g May 2] £19,000Y: half-brother to several winners, including 7-y-o Our Kes and 8-y-o Granston: dam maiden (stayed 6f): 6/1, beaten less than 10 lengths in maiden at Goodwood, early speed: not seen out again. *J. R. Best* **–**

BOBS DREAMFLIGHT 3 b.g. Royal Applause 124 – Millybaa (USA) 105 (Anabaa (USA) 130) [2009 80: p6g² 5g 6m 7m 6m² p6g p7g Nov 25] fairly useful handicapper: largely below form after reappearance: stays 6f: acts on polytrack, good to firm and good to soft ground. *D. K. Ivory* **81**

BOBSKI (IRE) 7 b.g. Victory Note (USA) 120 – Vivid Impression (Cure The Blues (USA)) [2009 82§: f7g⁶ p8g⁴ p8.6g³ p8g³ p8.6g² p8g 8.3m² 8m³ 8g Jun 4] good-topped gelding: fair performer: placed several times in varied company, then left Gay Kelleway prior to final start: effective at 6f to 8.3f: acts on polytrack and good to firm going: tried blinkered/tongue tied, often in cheekpieces: held up: ungenuine. *M. Keller, Germany* **72 §**

BOB STOCK (IRE) 3 b.g. Dubai Destination (USA) 127 – Red Rita (IRE) 97§ (Kefaah (USA) 124) [2009 65p: 8.1g² 8m 7g 8.3v p7m p8.6g³ Dec 5] strong, good-bodied gelding: fair maiden: first past post in handicap at Warwick in May (carried head awkwardly and hung right once hitting front, demoted): stays 8.6f: best effort on good ground: temperament under suspicion. *W. J. Musson* **69**

BOB'S YOUR UNCLE 6 br.g. Zilzal (USA) 137 – Bob's Princess 69 (Bob's Return (IRE) 123) [2009 68: 11.9m 16g³ p16g 16.4m⁶ 13.1f Aug 22] leggy gelding: modest handicapper: stays 2m: acts on polytrack, good to firm and good to soft going: sometimes hangs. *J. G. Portman* **59**

BODY GOLD (ARG) 6 b.g. Body Glove (ARG) – Aurifera (ARG) (Climber (USA)) –
[2009 12m 10.2d p12.2g Nov 13] good-bodied Argentinian-bred gelding: successful in maiden and Grade 2 Premio Eduardo Casey at Palermo in 2006: left Jorge Mayansky and gelded, tailed off in handicaps in Britain: stays 1½m: acts on dirt. *P. J. Makin*

BOFFIN 4 b.g. Kalanisi (IRE) 132 – Phi Beta Kappa (USA) 74 (Diesis 133) [2009 10m **54**
p12g^4 12m^6 11m^4 11.7g 10.2m p10m p8.6g p8.6g Dec 19] compact gelding: mid-field only start in bumper: modest maiden: stays 11f: acts on polytrack and good to firm ground: in cheekpieces last 3 starts. *Eve Johnson Houghton*

BOGA (IRE) 2 b.f. (Apr 10) Invincible Spirit (IRE) 121 – Miznapp (Pennekamp (USA) **63**
130) [2009 p5g^4 5.1m* 6d^3 5m^4 5.1m^5 7g p5g Aug 24] £24,000Y: close-coupled, sparely-made filly: fourth foal: half-sister to winner in USA by Montjeu: dam unraced half-sister to smart Irish 7f winner An Tadh: modest form at best: won seller at Bath in May: left M. Channon £10,000 after fourth start: likely to prove best at 5f/6f: acts on good to firm and good to soft going: one to treat with caution. *R. J. Hodges*

BOGSIDE THEATRE (IRE) 5 b.m. Fruits of Love (USA) 127 – Royal Jubilee (IRE) –
81 (King's Theatre (IRE) 128) [2009 102: 16m 12.1d 13.1m f14g^4 Oct 27] close-coupled mare: useful performer at 3/4 yrs: long way below form in 2009. *G. M. Moore*

BOGULA (IRE) 3 b.f. Tagula (IRE) 116 – Bobbydazzle 81 (Rock Hopper 124) [2009 **60**
10m^4 9.8m^4 10m 10m^4 9.9g 12.4d Oct 13] €15,500Y: close-coupled filly: fifth foal: half-sister to 3 winners, including 9.5f/1¼m winner Distiller (by Invincible Spirit) and Irish 5f winner Shinko Dancer (by Shinko Forest), both fairly useful: dam, 1m (including at 2 yrs) winner, half-sister to smart 7f performer Tumbleweed Ridge: modest maiden: stays 1¼m: acts on good to firm ground. *Mrs A. Duffield*

BOHOBE (IRE) 4 b.f. Noverre (USA) 125 – Green Life 63 (Green Desert (USA) 127) **65**
[2009 65: 6g^2 f6g 6m* 6.1m 6d* 6d 5.1d Aug 31] quite good-topped filly: fair handicapper: won at Salisbury (apprentice event) in June and Yarmouth (dead-heated) in July: stays 6f: acts on polytrack, good to firm and good to soft going: tried blinkered: sold 1,500 gns. *Rae Guest*

BOHO CHIC 3 b.f. Kyllachy 129 – Summer Lightning (IRE) 81 (Tamure (IRE) 125) **68**
[2009 66: p7m p6g 5.7g* 5.1m^6 6m* p6g p6g^2 Oct 20] neat filly: fair performer: won seller at Bath and handicap at Brighton in September: should prove best at 5f/6f: acts on polytrack, soft and good to firm going: has worn cheekpieces (including for both wins). *George Baker*

BOIS JOLI (IRE) 4 ch.f. Orpen (USA) 116 – Claba di San Jore (IRE) (Barathea (IRE) **75**
127) [2009 84: p11g^3 Feb 8] fairly useful performer: respectable third in claimer at Kempton sole start in 2009: stays 1½m: acts on polytrack and good to firm going. *M. Botti*

BOJANGLES ANDREWS 2 b.c. (Mar 10) Avonbridge 123 – Polished Up 51 (Polish **46**
Precedent (USA) 131) [2009 7g 6m^4 6m 6.1s 7m Oct 26] workmanlike colt: poor maiden: well held in nurseries: tried visored. *B. G. Powell*

BOLANDERI (USA) 4 ch.g. Seeking The Gold (USA) – Lilium 111 (Nashwan (USA) **82**
135) [2009 p10g^3 8.3g^3 10f^3 10m^3 11.6m^4 11.7f^5 10m* 8m^2 Sep 12] close-coupled gelding: twice-raced in bumpers, third on debut: fairly useful handicapper: won at Leicester (apprentices) in September: improved again when runner-up at Ffos Las: stays 1¼m: acts on good to firm going: pulled hard when blinkered sixth start. *Andrew Turnell*

BOLCKOW 6 b.g. Marju (IRE) 127 – Stamatina (Warning 136) [2009 61: f11g Aug 27] –
tall gelding: modest handicapper: stayed 1½m: acted on all-weather, firm and good to soft going: dead. *J. T. Stimpson*

BOLD ACCOUNT (IRE) 3 b. or br.g. Bold Fact (USA) 116 – Generate 66 (Generous **52**
(IRE) 139) [2009 71: p6g f6g^4 p5.1g f6g^5 6g f5g^3 6d f6m 6g Aug 4] small, strong gelding: fair performer at 2 yrs: regressed in 2009 (often in cheekpieces). *Garry Moss*

BOLD ADVENTURE 5 ch.g. Arkadian Hero (USA) 123 – Impatiente (USA) (Vague- **72**
ly Noble 140) [2009 76: p16.5g* p16g^2 p16.5g* p13.9g^2 p16g^6 p13.9g^6 14g^4 p13.9g p16.5g^5 p16.5g p13.9g Dec 17] good-bodied gelding: fair handicapper: won at Wolverhampton in February and March: stays 16.5f: acts on polytrack and soft going: held up. *W. J. Musson*

BOLD ALASKA (IRE) 6 b.g. Cape Cross (IRE) 129 – Dramatic Entry (IRE) 68 –
(Persian Bold 123) [2009 p8g p6g Nov 5] good-bodied gelding: fairly useful winner in 2006: off nearly 3 years, no sign of retaining ability in 2009 (said to have finished lame second occasion). *Peter Grayson*

BOLD ARGUMENT (IRE) 6 ch.g. Shinko Forest (IRE) – Ivory Bride 86 (Domynsky 110) [2009 77: p7g 6g 6m^{3} 6m* 5f 5m 6g 5.7m 5s Sep 3] big, lengthy gelding: fair handicapper: won at Windsor in June: best at stiff 5f/6f: acts on polytrack, firm and good to soft going: tried tongue tied/blinkered: has carried head awkwardly. *Mrs P. N. Dutfield* **75**

BOLD BOMBER 3 b.c. Kyllachy 129 – Latina (IRE) (King's Theatre (IRE) 128) [2009 52: 5m 8m 8f 6m 6g 5.9g^{4} 5.9d 9.9g f7m^{6} p8.6g Dec 3] modest maiden: seems to stay 1m: acts on fibresand and good to firm ground: tried blinkered. *Paul Green* **55**

BOLD CROSS (IRE) 6 b.g. Cape Cross (IRE) 129 – Machikane Akaiito (IRE) (Persian Bold 123) [2009 77: 7.1g* p8.6g^{6} 8.1v^{6} 8m^{2} 8.1m* 7.1d^{3} 8m* 7g^{4} 8g 8m^{4} 10.2m^{2} 7.1g 10.1m^{5} p8.6g Sep 12] leggy gelding: fairly useful handicapper: won at Chepstow in May and Haydock and Doncaster in June: effective at 7f to 1¼m: acts on polytrack, soft and good to firm ground: held up: genuine. *E. G. Bevan* **90**

BOLD DIKTATOR 7 b.g. Diktat 126 – Madam Bold (Never So Bold 135) [2009 8m^{3} 8.3m p8.6g Oct 17] strong gelding: fairly useful handicapper in 2007: off nearly 21 months, fair form on reappearance: well held after: stays 8.6f: acts on polytrack and firm going: effective with or without blinkers: usually races prominently. *R. M. Whitaker* **70**

BOLD DIVA 4 ch.f. Bold Edge 123 – Trina's Pet 65 (Efisio 120) [2009 50, a65: f6d^{5} p6g^{5} p7g p7g^{2} p7g^{4} p6g^{3} p8g^{4} p8g^{3} p7.1g^{4} p7.1g^{6} f7g^{2} f6g^{3} May 18] rather leggy filly: modest handicapper on all-weather, unraced on turf in 2009: effective at 6f to 1m: acts on all-weather: tried blinkered: visored: usually held up. *A. W. Carroll* **–** **a60**

BOLD HAWK 3 b.g. Mujahid (USA) 125 – Girl Next Door 58 (Local Suitor (USA) 128) [2009 –: 6.1f 6g 6.1g p6g Jul 8] strong gelding: poor maiden: in cheekpieces/blinkers last 3 starts. *Mrs C. A. Dunnett* **44**

BOLD HAZE 7 ch.g. Bold Edge 123 – Melody Park 104 (Music Boy 124) [2009 –: 6f May 11] big, good-bodied gelding: fair performer at best: little form since 2007: visored. *Miss S. E. Hall* **–**

BOLD INDIAN (IRE) 5 b.g. Indian Danehill (IRE) 124 – Desert Gift 69 (Green Desert (USA) 127) [2009 65§: p8.6g^{5} p9.5g 8.3m^{5} 8m^{6} 8m^{3} 9.2d^{5} 8.3s^{2} 7.5m^{3} 10m^{2} 10m^{2} 10m^{3} Oct 3] sturdy gelding: modest performer: claimed from I. Semple £3,000 after eighth start: stays 1¼m: acts on polytrack, firm and soft going: below form in cheekpieces: has hung/found little, and one to be wary of. *M. E. Sowersby* **63 §**

BOLDINOR 6 b.g. Inchinor 119 – Rambold 72 (Rambo Dancer (CAN) 107) [2009 65§: 5.7d 6.1g 6m 6m^{5} 6f^{3} 6d^{4} 6m^{3} 6.1d^{3} 6f^{2} 6m^{6} 6m Sep 28] close-coupled gelding: modest performer: best at 6f: acts on polytrack, firm and good to soft going: tried tongue tied: has looked hard ride, and not one to trust. *M. R. Bosley* **55 §**

BOLD MARC (IRE) 7 b.g. Bold Fact (USA) 116 – Zara's Birthday (IRE) 71 (Waajib 121) [2009 89: 7f 7m^{7} 8.1v^{4} 7m^{4} p8g^{3} 7.9m^{3} 7m* 7g 7.6g p7m^{1} p7g 7v^{6} Nov 3] smallish, good-bodied gelding: fairly useful handicapper on turf, fair on all-weather: won at Catterick in July: trained by K. R. Burke until after eighth start: seems better at 7f than 1m: acts on all-weather and any turf going: tried in headgear, not since 2006: usually front runner. *A. P. Jarvis* **89** **a79**

BOLD MINSTREL (IRE) 7 br.g. Bold Fact (USA) 116 – Ponda Rosa (IRE) 66 (Case Law 113) [2009 60: p5.1g Feb 9] good-bodied gelding: modest handicapper: said to have finished lame sole start in 2009: barely stays 5.7f: acts on polytrack, good to firm and good to soft going: tried visored: has bled: inconsistent. *M. Quinn* **–**

BOLD RING 3 ch.f. Bold Edge 123 – Floppie Disk 82 (Magic Ring (IRE) 115) [2009 59: p7g^{2} p7g 6m 7.1m 5m^{6} 6.1g 6f* 6m^{4} 6.1m^{6} 6d 6.1m* 6f^{3} 6m^{6} p5.1g^{4} p6g^{2} p6f p6g^{4} 6m^{3} p6g^{4} p6g^{4} p7.1g^{5} Oct 30] leggy filly: fair handicapper: won at Warwick in May and Nottingham in July: stays 7f: acts on polytrack and firm ground. *E. J. Creighton* **67**

BOLD ROSE 3 ch.f. Bold Edge 123 – Bowden Rose 100 (Dashing Blade 117) [2009 64: p6g^{5} p6g f5g* f5g 6.1g* 6.1g 6.1g 6d^{6} 5m 6.1v 6d f5f p7m* Dec 30] well-grown filly: fair handicapper: won at Southwell in February, Chepstow in May and Lingfield in December: stays 7f: acts on all-weather and heavy going: usually in cheekpieces: tried tongue tied. *M. D. I. Usher* **69**

BOLD TIE 3 ch.g. Bold Edge 123 – Level Pegging (IRE) 48 (Common Grounds 118) [2009 76p: 5f^{5} Jun 2] sturdy gelding: fair form, lightly raced: won maiden at 2 yrs: became unbalanced in handicap at Folkestone, only outing in 2009, then gelded: will prove best at 5f/6f. *R. Hannon* **68 +**

BOLLIN ANDREW 2 b.c. (May 14) Bollin Eric 125 – Bollin Roberta 75 (Bob's Return (IRE) 123) [2009 7m 7s 9m Sep 14] tall, good-topped colt: fifth foal: half-brother **– p**

to 5-y-o Bollin Freddie and 6-y-o Bollin Dolly: dam 7f/8.5f winner: down the field in maidens: bred to be well suited by 1¼m+: type to do better in handicaps. *T. D. Easterby*

BOLLIN DOLLY 6 ch.m. Bien Bien (USA) 125 – Bollin Roberta 75 (Bob's Return (IRE) 123) [2009 10m* 10m^2 10g* 10.2v^4 Nov 4] good-topped mare: fair handicapper: off 23 months, better than ever when winning at Redcar in August and Pontefract in October: effective at 1¼m, bred to stay further: acts on firm and good to soft ground: has been troublesome at stall: usually races prominently. *T. D. Easterby* **77**

BOLLIN FELIX 5 br.g. Generous (IRE) 139 – Bollin Magdalene 55 (Teenoso (USA) 135) [2009 99: 16m^5 12s^5 16.2g^2 16.4d^4 Jun 12] leggy, close-coupled gelding: useful handicapper: at least respectable efforts all starts in 2009, including when ¾-length second to Hits Only Vic at Haydock: should stay beyond 2m: has form on good to firm going, but goes particularly well on softer than good (acts on heavy): usually blinkered, visored last 2 starts. *T. D. Easterby* **95**

BOLLIN FRANNY 5 br.g. Bertolini (USA) 125 – Bollin Ann 72 (Anshan 119) [2009 62: p5g^5 p5.1g p6g^3 p6g^6 5f p6g^5 f6g 6g 6m^6 6m Sep 17] good-topped gelding: modest performer: said to have finished lame final start: was effective at 5f/6f: acted on polytrack and firm going: tried blinkered/in cheekpieces: raced prominently: was none too consistent: dead. *J. E. Long* **55**

BOLLIN FREDDIE 5 ch.g. Golden Snake (USA) 127 – Bollin Roberta 75 (Bob's Return (IRE) 123) [2009 56: 12.4s 9.9m* Jun 10] good-topped gelding: modest handicapper: won at Beverley: stays 1½m: acts on fibresand, heavy and good to firm ground. *A. J. Lockwood* **62**

BOLLIN GRETA 4 b.f. Mtoto 134 – Bollin Zola 90 (Alzao (USA) 117) [2009 77p: 12f^4 14m^4 14g^5 12d^3 12g* Jul 3] rangy filly: fair handicapper: won at Doncaster: stays 1¾m: acts on firm and soft going. *T. D. Easterby* **79**

BOLLIN JASMINE 2 b.f. (Apr 19) Silver Patriarch (IRE) 125 – Bollin Zola 90 (Alzao (USA) 117) [2009 7m Sep 23] tall, unfurnished filly: weak at present: half-sister to several winners, notably St Leger winner Bollin Eric (by Shaamit), successful from 1m (at 2 yrs) to 2m, and smart sprinter Bollin Joanne (by Damister): dam 5f (at 2 yrs) and 7f winner: 80/1, well beaten in maiden at Redcar: sold £2,100. *T. D. Easterby* **–**

BOLLIN JUDITH 3 b.f. Bollin Eric 125 – Bollin Nellie 98 (Rock Hopper 124) [2009 53p: 12.1m^4 12.1m^3 14.1m* 14g^3 12d^3 16g^6 14.1m^2 14.1g* 15v^2 Oct 31] leggy filly: fairly useful handicapper: won at Redcar in May and October: further progress when runner-up at Ayr final start: should be well suited by 2m+: acts on heavy and good to firm going. *T. D. Easterby* **82**

BOLLIN JULIE 2 b.f. (May 19) Bollin Eric 125 – Bollin Nellie 98 (Rock Hopper 124) [2009 8d 8.3v Nov 4] close-coupled filly: fourth foal: sister to 3-y-o Bollin Judith: dam 1¼m/1½m winner: better effort in maidens when seventh to Burj Nahar at Nottingham latter start, considerately handled: will be suited by 1¼m+: type to do better in handicaps. *T. D. Easterby* **53 p**

BOLLIN RACHEL 2 gr.f. (Apr 18) Silver Patriarch (IRE) 125 – Bollin Ann 72 (Anshan 119) [2009 7m Jun 20] smallish filly: sixth foal: half-sister to winning sprinters Bollin Billy (by Mind Games) and 5-y-o Bollin Franny: dam, 5f winner, half-sister to St Leger winner Bollin Eric and smart sprinter Bollin Joanne: 28/1, well beaten in maiden at Redcar: sold £1,600 in October. *T. D. Easterby* **–**

BOLLYWOOD (IRE) 6 ch.g. Indian Rocket 115 – La Fille de Cirque 49 (Cadeaux Genereux 131) [2009 55?: p12g Dec 31] compact gelding: modest performer at 5 yrs: well held sole start in 2009: tried blinkered/in cheekpieces. *J. J. Bridger* **–**

BOLLYWOOD STYLE 4 b.f. Josr Algarhoud (IRE) 118 – Dane Dancing (IRE) 68 (Danehill (USA) 126) [2009 p8g^4 p7g^2 p8g p7g* p7g^2 p6m^6 p7.1g Dec 11] fair handicapper, lightly raced (missed 2008): won at Lingfield in February: effective at 7f to easy 1¼m: raced only on polytrack. *J. R. Best* **66**

BOLODENKA (IRE) 7 b.g. Soviet Star (USA) 128 – My-Lorraine (IRE) 77 (Mac's Imp (USA) 116) [2009 105: p8.6g 8m 8.1m 7m 9.8d^2 8m 8s p7g^5 p8.6g^4 p9.5g Dec 26] leggy, useful-looking gelding: just fairly useful handicapper nowadays: easily best effort in 2009 when 7 lengths second to Distant Memories at Ripon: stays 1¼m: acts on polytrack, heavy and good to firm going: tried tongue tied: patiently ridden. *R. A. Fahey* **94**

BOLSHOI KING (IRE) 3 b.g. Fasliyev (USA) 120 – Nawaji (USA) 45 (Trempolino (USA) 135) [2009 8.3g 6m^6 6m Jun 29] good-topped gelding: tailed off all starts, in cheekpieces final outing: sold 2,500 gns, sent to Greece. *B. J. Meehan* **–**

BOLTON HALL (IRE) 7 b.g. Imperial Ballet (IRE) 110 – Muneera (USA) 67 (Green Dancer (USA) 132) [2009 –§: p13.9g^{6} p16.5g^{6} 12.1m 17.2m^{4} 16g 11.6m^{4} 10m Sep 12] strong, angular gelding: modest and ungenuine nowadays: stays 1½m: acts on polytrack and firm going: usually in tongue tie/cheekpieces: winning hurdler. *W. K. Goldsworthy* **51 §**

BOMBADERO (IRE) 2 b.c. (Mar 29) Sadler's Wells (USA) 132 – Fantasy Girl (IRE) 55 (Marju (IRE) 127) [2009 8g 8v^{4} Oct 24] compact colt: half-brother to several winners, including smart 7f (at 2 yrs) to 10.5f winner Big Bad Bob (by Bob Back): dam, maiden (stayed 1½m), half-sister to smart 1¼m/1½m performer Persian Lightning: much better effort in maidens at Newbury when 6 lengths fourth to Gardening Leave, best work late: will be suited by 1¼m+: will improve further. *J. L. Dunlop* **73 p**

BOMBARDIER WELLS 4 b.g. Red Ransom (USA) – Bow River Gold (Rainbow Quest (USA) 134) [2009 73: p10g* Feb 11] good-topped gelding: fair performer: won seller at Lingfield: stayed 1¼m: acted on polytrack: tried blinkered: joined R. York £1,100 in July: fell fatally on chasing debut in August. *C. J. Down* **67**

BOMBAY MIST 2 b.f. (Apr 13) Rambling Bear 115 – Paris Mist (Paris House 123) [2009 5f f5m Nov 11] £800Y: workmanlike filly: seventh foal: half-sister to winners abroad by Lujain and Bertolini: dam unraced: last in maidens nearly 7 months apart. *R. C. Guest* **–**

BOMBER BROWN (IRE) 3 b.g. Pyrus (USA) 106 – Secret of Gold (IRE) (Peintre Celebre (USA) 137) [2009 p8g p10g^{3} 8.3m^{4} 10.1g^{2} 9g* 10d^{3} p10m^{5} 11m^{4} 10.4g Oct 10] €16,000F, 11,000Y: leggy gelding: second foal: dam, ran once in Italy, out of half-sister to US Grade 1 1¼m winner Mi Selecto: fairly useful performer: won maiden at Yarmouth in July: stays 1¼m: acts on polytrack, unraced on extremes of going on turf: gelded after final start. *P. W. Chapple-Hyam* **83**

BOMBER COMMAND (USA) 6 b.g. Stravinsky (USA) 133 – Parish Manor (USA) **–**
(Waquoit (USA)) [2009 86, a99: p8g^{5} p7g 8m 7m 8g p8m^{6} 7m p8g^{2} p8g* p8g p8.6g^{6} **a95**
p8.6g Nov 13] big, workmanlike gelding: useful handicapper on all-weather, below form on turf in 2009: won at Kempton in September: stays 8.6f: acts on polytrack and good to firm ground: usually wears headgear: tried tongue tied: none too consistent nowadays. *J. W. Hills*

BOMBIE BOY 4 b.g. Tobougg (IRE) 125 – Waraqa (USA) 76 (Red Ransom (USA)) [2009 9.2g^{6} Jun 17] poor form in bumpers/over hurdles: well held in maiden at Hamilton on Flat debut. *K. W. Hogg, Isle of Man* **–**

BOMBINA 3 b.f. Lomitas 129 – Firebelly 86 (Nicolotte 118) [2009 85: 8m* 10.2g^{2} 8d^{4} 7d^{3} 8m^{5} 8f^{6} 8f^{4} 6f^{2} Dec 20] rather leggy, attractive filly: fairly useful performer: won handicap at Newmarket in May: creditable efforts most starts after, leaving P. Chapple-Hyam after fifth outing: may prove best up to 1m: acts on firm and good to soft going: suspect temperament, and has refused to enter stall. *Kathy Walsh, USA* **82**

BOM BOMS (IRE) 2 b.c. (Mar 25) Fayruz 116 – Mechilie 47 (Belmez (USA) 131) [2009 p5.1m p7.1g Oct 9] last in maidens at Wolverhampton: sold 1,000 gns, joined M. Ramadan in UAE. *Tom Dascombe* **–**

BO MCGINTY (IRE) 8 ch.g. Fayruz 116 – Georges Park Lady (IRE) (Tirol 127) [2009 92: f5s^{6} p5g^{4} f6g^{3} f5g^{5} p5.1g^{4} p5.1g^{3} p5g^{2} p5.1g^{2} 5m^{4} 5f^{4} 5m^{6} 6d 5m^{4} 5.1g^{5} 5m^{3} 5m^{5} p6g p5.1g f5m^{5} p5f^{5} f6d^{5} Dec 29] good-topped gelding: fairly useful handicapper: possibly best at 5f nowadays: acts on all-weather and any turf going: usually wears headgear. *R. A. Fahey* **85**

BONA FORTUNA 2 ch.g. (Feb 8) Mark of Esteem (IRE) 137 – Time Honoured 83 (Sadler's Wells (USA) 132) [2009 p7.1g p7.1g f8m Nov 6] 62,000Y: third foal: dam, 1m winner from 2 starts at 2 yrs, sister to smart 1½m winner Time Allowed out of top-class middle-distance performer Time Charter: very green when well held in maidens, then gelded: should stay at least 1m: likely to do better. *Sir Mark Prescott* **– p**

BONAMASSA 2 b.c. (May 1) Sulamani (IRE) 130 – Anastasia Venture 70 (Lion Cavern (USA) 117) [2009 p8g p8f Dec 16] well held in maidens: bred to be suited by 1¼m (dam best at 1m/1¼m). *M. J. Attwater* **–**

BONASERA (IRE) 2 b.f. (Mar 14) Kheleyf (USA) 116 – Jumlah (Unfuwain (USA) 131) [2009 5m^{5} 5m^{6} 7.2s^{6} 6d 6g f6g Oct 27] £800Y: first foal: dam unraced: no form. *A. Berry* **–**

BONDAGE (IRE) 2 b.g. (Apr 12) Whipper (USA) 126 – Shamah 96 (Unfuwain (USA) 131) [2009 7d^{5} p7m^{6} p8f^{6} Dec 16] €15,000F, €34,000Y, 30,000 2-y-o: fifth foal: half-brother to 4-y-o Daraahem and fairly useful 1m winner Safqa (by Singspiel): dam, **60 p**

1m winner, stayed 1¼m: similar form in maidens, not knocked about final start: should be suited by 1m+: type to make a better 3-y-o. *J. R. Fanshawe*

BOND CASINO 5 b.m. Kyllachy 129 – Songsheet 74 (Dominion 123) [2009 54: f14s f12d Mar 10] good bodied mare: modest handicapper in 2008: well held at 5 yrs: tried in cheekpieces/visor. *G. R. Oldroyd* –

BOND CITY (IRE) 7 b.g. Trans Island 119 – Where's Charlotte 53 (Sure Blade (USA) 130) [2009 104: 6s 6m^5 6g^5 7g p7.1g^2 6g 6g^6 6g p6g^3 7.2s p7.1g 6m 7g f6f 7s Oct 27] strong gelding: useful handicapper: in-and-out form in 2009, placed twice at Wolverhampton: effective at 5f to easy 7f: acts on polytrack, firm and soft going: tried in blinkers/cheekpieces. *G. R. Oldroyd* 97

BOND CRUZ 6 b.g. King's Best (USA) 132 – Arabis 88 (Arazi (USA) 135) [2009 –: p12m Nov 27] sturdy gelding: maiden: little form on Flat since 2005. *T. Keddy* –

BONDED (IRE) 2 b.c. (Apr 2) Oasis Dream 129 – Lovealoch (IRE) 108 (Lomond (USA) 128) [2009 8v p8.6g^3 p8f^3 Dec 16] 36,000F, 80,000 2-y-o: half-brother to several winners, including smart 2005 2-y-o 5f/6f winner Flashy Wings (by Zafonic) and French 10.5f winner Sagamartha (by Rainbow Quest): dam, 7f (at 2 yrs) to 9f winner, later successful in USA: similar form when third in maidens at Wolverhampton and Kempton (carried head awkwardly). *B. J. Meehan* 70

BOND FASTRAC 2 b.c. (Mar 21) Monsieur Bond (IRE) 120 – Kanisfluh 89 (Pivotal 124) [2009 p6g^5 6m* 6m^2 6m^5 Sep 9] £20,000Y: tall, close-coupled colt: second foal: dam Irish 2-y-o 6f/7f winner: useful performer: won maiden at Redcar in July by 2¼ lengths from Elusive Sue: best effort when short-head second to Yurituni in nursery at York: should be at least as effective at 5f as 6f. *G. R. Oldroyd* 96

BOND TOGETHER 2 ch.g. (Apr 28) Monsieur Bond (IRE) 120 – My Bonus 79 (Cyrano de Bergerac 120) [2009 5m p5.1g^2 p5.1g^3 6d 6d^5 Jul 20] close-coupled gelding: poor maiden: tried blinkered/visored: quirky. *P. D. Evans* 46

BONFIRE KNIGHT 2 b.c. (Feb 28) Red Ransom (USA) – Attune 102 (Singspiel (IRE) 133) [2009 p7.1g^2 6v^3 7g* 6m 8m^2 Aug 31] £38,000Y: first foal: dam 7f/1m winner: fairly useful performer: won maiden at Catterick in August: upped in trip, good 2¾ lengths second to Layali Al Andalus in nursery at Newcastle final start: needs further than 6f and stays 1m: acts on polytrack, heavy and good to firm ground: tongue tied first 3 starts: races prominently: capable of better still. *J. J. Quinn* 83 p

BONHEURS ART (IRE) 2 b.f. (Apr 23) Acclamation 118 – Anneliina 80 (Cadeaux Genereux 131) [2009 6g^4 6m^2 6m^5 6g^2 Oct 19] £90,000Y: lengthy filly: has fluent action: fifth foal: half-sister to 3 winners, including 3-y-o Rioliina and 5-y-o Cheap Street: dam maiden who stayed 7f: fair form in maidens and nursery: raced only at 6f on good/good to firm going: sold 16,500 gns. *B. W. Hills* 74

BONNE 4 b.f. Namid 128 – Jouet 71 (Reprimand 122) [2009 72: p7.1g 6d 6g 6g 6d Aug 1] tall, unfurnished filly: fair handicapper at 3 yrs: just modest in 2009: should prove best at 6f/7f: acts on good to soft ground: blinkered last 3 starts. *Miss J. R. Tooth* 57

BONNET O'BONNIE 5 br.m. Makbul 104 – Parkside Prospect 65 (Piccolo 121) [2009 47: f6g^2 f6g 6d Jul 15] modest maiden: stays 7f: acts on all-weather. *J. Mackie* 57

BONNIE BEA 3 b.f. Royal Applause 124 – Boojum 101 (Mujtahid (USA) 118) [2009 –: p8.6g^4 8.3d Oct 12] leggy, lengthy filly: well held in maidens. *B. I. Case* –

BONNIE BRAE 2 b.f. (Feb 26) Mujahid (USA) 125 – Skara Brae 49 (Inchinor 119) [2009 p8g 7d^2 Oct 22] fourth foal: half-sister to 2 winners, including 5-y-o Vogarth: dam, maiden, out of smart performer up to 1m Tahilla: better effort in maidens when 1¾ lengths second to Essexbridge at Brighton, still green: should be suited by 1m: open to further improvement. *G. G. Margarson* 66 p

BONNIE CHARLIE 3 ch.c. Intikhab (USA) 135 – Scottish Exile (IRE) 75 (Ashkalani (IRE) 128) [2009 111: p8g^5 7s^6 6m 7m^4 6m^4 6g^4 7m^2 Oct 16] strong, close-coupled colt: smart performer: mostly at least respectable efforts in 2009, and ran well in Bengough Memorial Stakes at Ascot (1½ lengths fourth to Royal Rock) and handicap at Newmarket (1½ lengths second to Esoterica) last 2 starts: stays 7f: unraced on firm going, acts on any other turf: sold 105,000 gns, joined W. Haggas. *R. Hannon* 110

BONNIE PRINCE BLUE 6 ch.g. Tipsy Creek (USA) 115 – Heart So Blue (Dilum (USA) 115) [2009 91§: 6s^2 6g^4 6g 6g 6g^3 6d* 6v^5 p6g^4 f6m^3 Nov 11] quite attractive gelding: fairly useful handicapper: won at Catterick in August: form at 1m, probably best at 6f: acts on all-weather, heavy and good to firm going: often blinkered: ungenuine. *D. Nicholls* 83 §

BON SPIEL 5 b.h. Singspiel (IRE) 133 – L'Affaire Monique 101 (Machiavellian (USA) 123) [2009 104: 12m^5 10g p10g 10.4m 9m^5 10.2d Oct 15] small horse: useful handicapper: creditable efforts at Nad Al Sheba early in year, including 7½ lengths seventh to Pompeyano on second start: below form after: seemingly effective at 1m to 1½m: acts on polytrack, heavy and good to firm going: once tongue tied. *L. M. Cumani* **103**

BONUS (IRE) 9 b.g. Cadeaux Genereux 131 – Khamseh 85 (Thatching 131) [2009 –, **– §**
a114: p7g^2 p6g^3 p8g^3 p8g^4 p7.1g^6 Mar 7] big, strong, angular gelding: smart performer **a111 §**
on all-weather, just useful on turf in recent years: won 10 races during career, including Phoenix Sprint Stakes at the Curragh in 2003: in frame first 4 starts in 2009, good 1¼ lengths second to Aeroplane in handicap at Kempton: finished weakly in listed race at Wolverhampton (subsequently found to have multiple fractures in a pastern and was put down): was effective at 5f, seemingly at easy 1m: acted on polytrack and firm going: often wore headgear: tried tongue tied: held up: was temperamental. *G. A. Butler*

BONZO 4 b.g. Where Or When (IRE) 124 – Making Memories (IRE) (Alzao (USA) 117) [2009 54: p13.3g Jan 15] modest maiden at 3 yrs: well held sole start in 2009 (blinkered): stays 1¾m: acts on polytrack. *P. Howling* **–**

BOO 7 b.g. Namaqualand (USA) – Violet (IRE) 77 (Mukaddamah (USA) 125) [2009 –, **56**
a98d: p12.2g^5 8.1d^6 p9.5g 10.2g^4 Oct 28] quite good-topped gelding: useful performer at **a73**
best (on polytrack): on downgrade: stays 1¼m: acts on polytrack and firm going: has worn headgear. *J. W. Unett*

BOOGIE DANCER 5 b.m. Tobougg (IRE) 125 – Bolero (Rainbow Quest (USA) 134) [2009 65: p8g Jan 10] good-topped mare: maiden, fair at best: lightly raced on Flat since 2007 (modest hurdler), and well held sole 5-y-o start. *H. S. Howe* **–**

BOOGIE DIVA 2 b.f. (Feb 14) Tobougg (IRE) 125 – Distant Diva 86 (Distant Relative 128) [2009 7m^3 7g^2 7m 7m^3 Oct 6] sturdy filly: third foal: half-sister to 3-y-o Imaginary Diva: dam 2-y-o 5f winner: fairly useful maiden: easily best effort when 3¼ lengths second to Pollenator at Newmarket: should be at least as effective at 6f as 7f: signs of temperament penultimate start. *M. Botti* **81**

BOOGIE WALTZER 2 b.f. (Feb 9) Tobougg (IRE) 125 – Upping The Tempo (Dunbeath (USA) 127) [2009 6d 7f^6 6s^5 p6g^4 5.1s^2 p5m^6 p5.1g^3 Dec 14] half-sister to fairly useful 9-y-o Hey Presto and winner in Turkey by Forzando: dam unraced half-sister to useful sprinter Up And At 'em: modest maiden: stays easy 6f: acts on polytrack and soft ground. *S. C. Williams* **56**

BOOKIEBASHER BABE (IRE) 4 b.f. Orpen (USA) 116 – Jay Gee (IRE) 93 (Second Set (IRE) 127) [2009 72: p8g^6 f8g^4 p8g f8g^6 p8.6g^4 f8g* f8g* 9g 9m^5 8d^2 8s 10d^5 p9.5m p8g Oct 11] leggy, lengthy filly: fair handicapper: won at Southwell in April and May: stays easy 1¼m: acts on all-weather and soft going: tried visored: none too consistent. *M. Quinn* **74**

BOOKIESINDEX BOY 5 b.g. Piccolo 121 – United Passion 74 (Emarati (USA) 74) **59 §**
[2009 68§, a84§: p5g^5 p5g p5.1g^6 5.1d 5m 5.1m 5.1d^3 p5.1g^2 p5m^2 p5m p5m Dec 9] **a75 §**
strong, good-topped gelding: fair handicapper on all-weather, modest on turf: best at 5f: acts on all-weather and soft going: often blinkered/visored: usually races prominently: temperamental. *J. R. Jenkins*

BOOKIESINDEX GIRL (IRE) 2 b.f. (Mar 16) Rakti 130 – Distant Valley 104 (Distant Relative 128) [2009 5.1f 6g f5g^6 p6g 6m f6g^4 f6m^6 f7g^2 f8f^3 p7g* Dec 31] £10,000 2-y-o: good-topped filly: second foal: half-sister to German 7f winner Harquahala (by High Chaparral): dam 6f/7f (at 2 yrs, including Rockfel Stakes) to 8.5f (US Grade 3) winner: modest performer: won nursery at Lingfield in December: barely stays 1m: acts on all-weather. *J. R. Jenkins* **57**

BOOK OF TRUTH (USA) 2 b. or br.c. (May 15) Truluck (USA) – Elise's Notebook (USA) (Notebook (USA)) [2009 7.1m 7.6d p7g 8m Sep 12] sturdy colt: maiden: form only on debut. *D. M. Simcock* **60 d**

BOOTLEG 3 b.g. Bahamian Bounty 116 – Asbo 66 (Abou Zouz (USA) 109) [2009 –p: 6s May 8] small, sturdy gelding: very green in maidens 8 months apart: sold £800, sent to Greece, and reportedly successful over 5f. *D. Nicholls* **?**

BOQUITO (IRE) 2 b.c. (Apr 12) Rahy (USA) 115 – Fantasia Girl (IRE) 101 (Caerleon (USA) 132) [2009 6g 6s^4 6.1g p8g* p8m* p8m^3 p8.6g^5 Oct 23] rather unfurnished colt: fourth foal: brother to 3-y-o Ra Junior: dam Irish 9f/1¼m winner (stayed 1½m): fair performer: won 2 nurseries at Kempton in September: likely to stay beyond 1m: acts on polytrack and soft going: reliable: sold 27,000 gns. *Miss Amy Weaver* **78**

BORASCO (USA) 4 ch.f. Stormy Atlantic (USA) – Seek (USA) (Devil's Bag (USA)) **83**
[2009 93: f6g^5 7d^5 7m p7.1g 7v p7.1g^2 f6g^5 p7.1g^5 Dec 19] lengthy filly: fairly useful handicapper: below form after reappearance: stays 7f: acts on all-weather, good to firm and good to soft going. *T. D. Barron*

BORDER ARTIST 10 ch.g. Selkirk (USA) 129 – Aunt Tate (Tate Gallery (USA) 117) **–**
[2009 57: 7f May 12] well-made gelding: modest performer: slipped up sole 10-y-o start: stays 8.5f: acts on all-weather, firm and good to soft going: tried in headgear: held up. *J. Pearce*

BORDERLESCOTT 7 b.g. Compton Place 125 – Jeewan 82 (Touching Wood (USA) 127) [2009 125: 5m^3 5v^2 5m^5 5.1m* 5g^4 5m* 5g^6 6g Dec 13] **123**

Borderlescott joined an illustrious band when he achieved the remarkably rare feat of winning the Nunthorpe Stakes for a second time. Not since 1981, when Sharpo gained the second of his three successive wins in the race, had a previous winner come back to score again. Sharpo was a top-class sprinter, though he was not so good as the three others who have won the race twice since the Second World War, Abernant, Royal Serenade and Right Boy. Right Boy, like Borderlescott, was unfashionably bred, bought cheaply and trained in Yorkshire when he won the Nunthorpe in 1958 and 1959. In all, he won sixteen of his twenty-nine races and got better with age, his final appearance coming when runner-up in the Portland Handicap, in which he failed by three quarters of a length to concede 32 lb to the winner. Abernant achieved a Timeform rating of 142, making him the highest-rated sprinter in the long history of these Annuals. All told, he won fourteen of his seventeen starts, when his victories, apart from his two in the Nunthorpe in 1949 and 1950, included the July Cup twice and the King's Stand Stakes. Abernant's trademark was blinding early speed and he finished second in the three races in which he met with defeat, including a narrow one in the Two Thousand Guineas before reverting to sprinting. Royal Serenade, rated 132, was successful in the Nunthorpe in 1951 and 1952, and was then transferred to the States where he won the Hollywood Gold Cup over a mile and a quarter as a five-year-old.

Genuine, tough and reliable he may be, but Borderlescott doesn't come close to matching the achievements of those names of the past, his second Nunthorpe win a particular credit to the small yard of Robin Bastiman. Borderlescott's first three starts in 2009 betrayed signs that perhaps he wasn't quite the same horse as the previous year. General rustiness seemed a mitigating circumstance for his third to Amour Propre in the Palace House Stakes at Newmarket in May; similar allowances could be made when he was a beaten favourite on heavy ground, a surface he hadn't previously encountered, behind Look Busy in the Temple Stakes at Haydock. There were, however, no excuses for Borderlescott's fifth in the King's Stand Stakes at Royal Ascot; he was well placed from the start and did best of that group, but could finish no closer than just over four lengths behind the winner Scenic Blast. A win finally followed in the listed toteswinger City Wall Stakes at Chester, the well-drawn Borderlescott starting favourite and winning by a length at level weights with Captain Gerrard, the form hardly representing a return to his very best but at least representing a step in the right direction, especially as

Coolmore Nunthorpe Stakes, York—back-to-back wins in the race (but on different courses) for Borderlescott as he leads late on to beat Benbaun (left); the two-year-old Radiohead (behind first 2) is next ahead of Tax Free (right) and Amour Propre (star on cap)

Borderlescott didn't have a clear run. Borderlescott had been second in the Temple Stakes before being beaten a nose in the City Wall the previous year. As in 2008, Borderlescott was sent to Goodwood where twelve months earlier he had run a gallant race in the Stewards Cup under 9-10. Borderlescott's Goodwood target in the latest campaign was the King George Stakes. He ended up a beaten favourite, finishing fourth behind Kingsgate Native, but definitely shaped as if retaining all his ability, the draw—he was isolated in the middle in stall 16—putting him at a disadvantage with the first three who were drawn 2, 1 and 3 respectively.

The field for the Coolmore-sponsored Nunthorpe, while short on quality, was certainly representative, with only the King's Stand runner-up Fleeting Spirit a significant absentee among the best British-trained sprinters. Kingsgate Native, Amour Propre, Look Busy and Captain Gerrard were among those Borderlescott encountered again. In all, fifteen of the sixteen runners were trained in Britain, the only overseas raider being the South African-trained Mythical Flight, who had cut little ice in the King's Stand. Kingsgate Native had won the Nunthorpe as a two-year-old in 2007 and started favourite ahead of Radiohead, a juvenile bidding to emulate him, and the three-year-old Amour Propre. Borderlescott was sent off fourth choice at 9/1. While the field was billed to all intents and purposes beforehand as a domestic one, the finish turned out more parochial still, very much a benefit for Yorkshire-trained horses. The eight-year-old former Abbaye winner Benbaun, now trained at Hambleton by Kevin Ryan, blazed a trail up the stand rail, with Borderlescott tracking the pace before coming through to catch Benbaun close home, winning by a neck. Ironically, Borderlescott was ridden for the first time by Ryan's stable-jockey Neil Callan, booked before the decision to run Benbaun was finalised. Radiohead took third, closely followed by another Yorkshire-trained runner Tax Free and Amour Propre, with Kingsgate Native only sixth. The form was almost on a par with the pick of Borderlescott's previous form.

York's Ebor meeting had been abandoned the previous year and the Nunthorpe switched to Newmarket, but with reduced prize money. As caricatures of Yorkshiremen go, the comments of Borderlescott's trainer after the latest Nunthorpe were a gift to the assembled Press: 'This is special because it's my home ground and this year I'll get the full percentage.' There were no problems with the weather at York in 2009 and the Nunthorpe was back at its rightful home, just eight miles away from Bastiman's yard at Wetherby.

Connections needed their passports for Borderlescott's last two starts in 2009, having to travel not just south of Sheffield but to France and then to Hong Kong. Borderlescott's second tilt at the Prix de l'Abbaye might well have resulted in his matching his third in 2008 had he not met serious trouble in running, in third place when running out of room and losing momentum, before ending up sixth behind Total Gallery, with Benbaun two places ahead. As in the previous year, the French authorities reportedly refused permission for Borderlescott to have a travelling companion, so he was kept in the horsebox until close to race time. Borderlescott's connections had turned down an invitation to Hong Kong in 2008 but they accepted this time, only for Borderlescott to finish down the field in the Hong Kong Sprint. Borderlescott might have run in the Ayr Gold Cup after the Nunthorpe—he has a good record in the top sprint handicaps—but a penalty for his win at York would have meant his carrying 10-4, and running off a BHA mark of 118. He would have needed to have shown form as good as Sharpo at his best to have won facing that task. Borderlescott stays in training and, as Benbaun showed in the latest season, age is not necessarily going to stand in the way of further success.

Borderlescott (b.g. 2002)	Compton Place (ch 1994)	Indian Ridge (ch 1985)	Ahonoora
			Hillbrow
		Nosey (b 1981)	Nebbiolo
			Little Cynthia
	Jeewan (b 1985)	Touching Wood (b 1979)	Roberto
			Mandera
		Adeebah (br 1980)	Damascus
			Transylvania

Full details of Borderlescott's pedigree appeared in *Racehorses of 2008* and there is little new to add. A yearling sister to Borderlescott was retained for 50,000 guineas at the Newmarket October Sales. The smallish, strong, close-coupled Borderlescott is effective at both five and six furlongs. He acts on any turf going and on polytrack. His win in the Nunthorpe was the twelfth of his career from forty-five starts and lifted his earnings to over the £620,000-mark. He was one of only four individual winners sent out by his stable in the latest season, the others including Singeur who won four times and fell just short in listed class on his final start. Singeur has a long way to go to match Borderlescott who is a very smart sprinter on his day, and as genuine as they come. *R. Bastiman*

BORDER OWL (IRE) 4 b.g. Selkirk (USA) 129 – Nightbird (IRE) 108 (Night Shift (USA)) [2009 88: 12m 8.1v^5 8f^3 8.9d 7m^5 8m 8g^5 f8g f8f^5 Dec 11] tall, angular gelding: fairly useful handicapper: below form after third start: stays 8.3f: acts on polytrack, firm and good to soft going: tried visored. *P. Salmon* **81 d**

BORDER PATROL 3 b.c. Selkirk (USA) 129 – Ffestiniog (IRE) 96 (Efisio 120) [2009 90P: 8s* 6d* 8.1m* 8s* 7g 8s^2 Nov 1] rangy, attractive colt: smart performer: won maiden at Newbury in April, listed races at same course and Sandown in May, and Solonaway Stakes at the Curragh (beat Poet by ½ length) in September: good 1½ lengths second to Zafisio in Prix Perth at Saint-Cloud final start: effective at 6f to 1m: acts on soft and good to firm ground (though missed several possible engagements during summer on firmer than good): always behind after not best of starts in Prix de la Foret at Longchamp on penultimate outing: held up and has a turn of foot. *R. Charlton* **119**

BORDER TALE 9 b.g. Selkirk (USA) 129 – Likely Story (IRE) 94 (Night Shift (USA)) [2009 –: p12.2g p13.9m 16.1d^2 13m^2 13m^2 12d^3 16.1d Sep 7] strong gelding: modest handicapper: stays 2m, effective at shorter: acts on all-weather, soft and good to firm going: tried visored/tongue tied/in cheekpieces: has had breathing problems: fair hurdler. *James Moffatt* **59**

Solonaway Stakes, the Curragh—
Border Patrol (right) has to battle quite hard as Poet rallies

BORN A DANCER (IRE) 2 b.f. (Apr 24) Danehill Dancer (IRE) 117 – Born Beautiful (USA) (Silver Deputy (CAN)) [2009 6m 6.5m Sep 25] 3,000Y: tall, good-bodied filly: seventh foal: closely related to fairly useful 7f (at 2 yrs)/1m winner Denver (by Danehill) and French 1m winner We Will Rock You (by Rock of Gibraltar), later successful in USA: dam unraced half-sister to dam of Cheveley Park winner Pas de Reponse and Poule d'Essai des Poulains winner Green Tune: slowly away and signs of ability in maiden at Newbury: stiff task in sales race at Ascot: should be suited by 7f/1m: probably capable of better. *J. W. Hills* **– p**

BORN ROMANTIC 3 b.f. High Chaparral (IRE) 132 – Maid For Romance 71 (Pursuit of Love 124) [2009 10d p10g Jun 17] fourth foal: dam once-raced half-sister to smart performers Lady In Waiting (up to 1½m) and Savannah Bay (stayer): green, well beaten in maidens. *H. J. L. Dunlop* **–**

BORN TO BE KING (USA) 3 b.c. Storm Cat (USA) – Quarter Moon (IRE) 120 (Sadler's Wells (USA) 132) [2009 97p: 8g^3 8m 10s^6 8m Jun 16] tall, lengthy colt: useful performer: generally used as pacemaker in 2009, easily best effort when 3½ lengths third to Recharge in 2000 Guineas Trial at Leopardstown: stays 1m: acts on good to firm and good to soft ground: carries head awkwardly: joined D. Selvaratnam in UAE. *A. P. O'Brien, Ireland* **105**

BORN TOBOUGGIE (GER) 4 b.f. Tobougg (IRE) 125 – Braissim (Dancing Brave (USA) 140) [2009 99: p8g* 8g^3 May 2] big, good-bodied filly: useful performer: improved when winning listed race at Kempton in April by 2½ lengths from Perfect Star: unable to dominate when below-form third in similar event at Goodwood (reportedly jarred up after): free-going sort, probably best around 1m: acts on polytrack and heavy going: signs of temperament: sold 120,000 gns in December, sent to Japan. *H. R. A. Cecil* **106**

BORN TO PERFORM 4 br.g. Theatrical 128 – My Hansel (USA) 98 (Hansel (USA)) [2009 12m 9.2m^5 9.3d^5 8s Aug 23] useful form when successful both outings in bumpers: modest maiden on Flat: should prove best at 1¼m+. *G. A. Swinbank* **59**

BORN WEST (USA) 5 b. or br.g. Gone West (USA) – Admirer (USA) (Private Terms (USA)) [2009 –: p13.9g p16.5g^3 p16g p16.5g Apr 6] stocky gelding: modest maiden handicapper nowadays: stays 2m: acts on polytrack: tried blinkered. *N. B. King* **60**

BORODINSKY 8 b.g. Magic Ring (IRE) 115 – Valldemosa 81 (Music Boy 124) [2009 49: 8.3m^6 7g 7f^6 Jul 2] heavy-topped gelding: poor performer: effective at 6f to 9f: acts on firm and soft going: tried visored/in cheekpieces. *R. E. Barr* **43**

BOROUJ (IRE) 7 ch.g. Unfuwain (USA) 131 – Amanah (USA) 100 (Mr Prospector (USA)) [2009 ?: p8.6g f12g Feb 19] lengthy gelding: fair handicapper in 2008: fit from hurdling, well beaten at 7 yrs: tried in cheekpieces/visor/tongue strap. *Joss Saville* **–**

BORROMEO (USA) 3 ch.g. Mr Greeley (USA) 122 – Luxury On The Lake (USA) (Salt Lake (USA)) [2009 8.1g 10f^6 11.8m^3 11.7f^2 Jun 24] close-coupled gelding: fair maiden: stays 11.8f: raced only on good ground or firmer: sold £9,000. *M. Johnston* **72**

BOSAMCLIFF (IRE) 4 b.f. Daylami (IRE) 138 – L'Animee (Green Tune (USA) 125) [2009 71: 6m^5 8.3m^6 8.1m^4 10m 8.3g^2 8d^3 10.2g^3 9.1v* f12f* f11m^5 Dec 5] fair handicapper: improved to win at Ayr in October and Southwell in November: stays 1½m: acts on fibresand, heavy and good to firm going. *P. D. Evans* **75**

BOSCAGE (USA) 4 b.g. Forestry (USA) 121 – Prospinsky (USA) (Mr Prospector (USA)) [2009 p8g* f8g* 8g^4 8s Apr 18] $475,000Y: tall, good-topped gelding: eighth foal: brother to winner in USA and half-brother to 3 winners there: dam, ran 3 times in US, out of US Grade 2 9f winner Nikishka, herself half-sister to US Grade 1 1¼m winner Ida Delia: useful performer: created good impression when winning maiden at Lingfield and handicap at Southwell (by 8 lengths) in March: well below form on turf subsequently (gelded after final start): likely to stay 1¼m. *M. Johnston* **–** **a98**

BOSS HOG 4 b.g. Key of Luck (USA) 126 – Dania (GER) (Night Shift (USA)) [2009 78: p7.1g^2 f7g* f8g^5 f7d^3 p7g 8m f7g^5 f7g 7f^5 7g 7.5g^5 7.1g 7.5g 5.9d^5 7.5m^6 8.5m^4 f8g^2 p7m Oct 26] fair performer on all-weather, modest on turf: won maiden at Southwell in February: left R. Curtis after fifth start: stays 1m: acts on all-weather (best efforts on fibresand): tried in cheekpieces/blinkers. *P. T. Midgley* **58** **a71**

BOSS'S DESTINATION 2 b.g. (Mar 28) Dubai Destination (USA) 127 – Blushing Sunrise (USA) (Cox's Ridge (USA)) [2009 5d^5 7d^5 Aug 10] 14,000F, €28,000Y: half-brother to 1m/9f winner Sharp Needle (by Mark of Esteem), later successful in USA, and 4-y-o Rosy Dawn: dam US 6.5f winner: better effort in maidens when 7½ lengths **62 p**

fifth to Our Joe Mac at Thirsk latter start, not unduly knocked about: capable of better. *G. A. Swinbank*

BOSSY KITTY 2 ch.f. (Mar 8) Avonbridge 123 – Between The Sticks 83 (Pharly (FR) **81**
130) [2009 5m 5.1m^{5} 5d 5m 5d^{3} 5m^{4} 5g^{2} 5m^{5} 6m 5d* 5d^{3} 5m* 6g* 6s Nov 7] £9,000Y: sturdy filly: half-sister to several winning sprinters, including 10-y-o Pic Up Sticks: dam 2-y-o 5f winner: fairly useful performer: won maiden at Ripon in September and nurseries at Ayr and York (dead-heated with Jeannie Galloway) in October: effective at 5f/6f: acts on good to soft and good to firm going, well held on soft final start. *N. Tinkler*

BOSTON BLUE 2 b.g. (Apr 17) Halling (USA) 133 – City of Gold (IRE) 91 (Sadler's **70**
Wells (USA) 132) [2009 p8g^{4} p8g^{5} Nov 14] 52,000Y: workmanlike gelding: sixth foal: brother to 2 winners, including 3-y-o Mabuya, and half-brother to winner in Japan by Sunday Silence: dam 7f (at 2 yrs) and 1½m winner: similar form when never nearer in maidens at Lingfield, then gelded: will stay 1¼m. *W. J. Knight*

BOSUN BREESE 4 b.g. Bahamian Bounty 116 – Nellie Melba 82 (Hurricane Sky **–**
(AUS)) [2009 93: p5.1g Nov 16] lengthy, rather hollow-backed gelding: fairly useful handicapper: well below form sole outing in 2009: best at 5f: acts on good to firm going: tried tongue tied: has been early to post. *T. D. Barron*

BOTANIST 2 b.c. (Apr 1) Selkirk (USA) 129 – Red Camellia 116 (Polar Falcon (USA) **88 p**
126) [2009 7m 8.1d^{2} 8.3m* Oct 13] good-topped colt: seventh foal: brother to smart 7f (at 2 yrs) to 1¼m winner Red Bloom and half-brother to 2 winners, including smart 1¼m to 13.4f winner Red Gala (by Sinndar): dam, 2-y-o 6f/7f (Prestige Stakes) winner, out of half-sister to Ibn Bey and Roseate Tern: fairly useful form in maidens: beaten a nose by Zeitoper at Sandown before winning at Leicester by 2¾ lengths from Protaras: stays 1m: tends to wander: should do better still. *Sir Michael Stoute*

BOTHAM (USA) 5 b. or br.g. Cryptoclearance (USA) – Oval (USA) (Kris S (USA)) **74**
[2009 61: 5m 8.3m* 6m^{2} 8g 7.2g^{6} 6g* 6f 6s* 5.9d^{2} 6m^{6} 9.2g 8m 7.2g* 7.2v Oct 31] good-topped gelding: fair handicapper: won at Hamilton in May (amateurs), July and August (apprentices) and Ayr in October: effective at stiff 6f to 8.3f: acts on all-weather, firm and soft ground: tried blinkered/tongue tied: held up. *J. S. Goldie*

BOTH ENDS BURNING (IRE) 2 ch.f. (Feb 20) Choisir (AUS) 126 – Giadamar **–**
(IRE) (Be My Guest (USA) 126) [2009 6m 7m Aug 9] €20,000F, £18,000 2-y-o: sixth foal: closely related to Irish 1¼m winner Can She Dance (by Danehill Dancer) and half-sister to 3 winners, including useful Irish 1m/1¼m winner Nopekan (by Sri Pekan): dam unraced half-sister to dam of very smart/high-class middle-distance performers Luso and Warrsan: well held in maidens at Redcar. *J. S. Wainwright*

BOTHWELL CASTLE (IRE) 2 b.g. (Apr 2) Captain Rio 122 – Majesty's Nurse **57**
(Indian King (USA) 128) [2009 6s 6g^{3} 6m^{4} 6.1s p8.6g Oct 9] heavy-bodied gelding: maiden: no impact in nurseries: mostly raced at 6f, stamina stretched at 8.6f: tried in cheekpieces. *P. C. Haslam*

BOTHY 3 ch.g. Pivotal 124 – Villa Carlotta 110 (Rainbow Quest (USA) 134) [2009 95p: **95**
8.5g* 11.1g^{6} 10.2d^{4} Oct 15] compact gelding: useful form, lightly raced: won maiden at Epsom in April: gelded and off 5 months, creditable fourth in handicap at Nottingham final start: stays 1¼m: acts on soft going: joined B. Ellison 60,000 gns, successful on hurdling debut in December. *R. M. Beckett*

BOTLEY BELL 2 b.f. (Jan 27) Imperial Dancer 123 – Curbridge Bell (Fraam 114) **53**
[2009 6m p7g 6.1m^{6} 6d 6d Jul 27] small filly: first foal: dam ran once: modest maiden: well below form in sellers last 2 starts (looked awkward in visor on latter): should stay 7f: acts on good to firm going. *M. R. Channon*

BOUGGIE DAIZE 3 b.f. Tobougg (IRE) 125 – Milly's Lass 79 (Mind Games 121) **63**
[2009 78: 8m 7m Jul 25] sturdy filly: maiden: fair at 2 yrs: below form in 2009: stays 7f: acts on soft and good to firm going. *C. G. Cox*

BOULD MOVER 2 b.c. (Apr 15) Kyllachy 129 – Maugwenna 85 (Danehill (USA) **104**
126) [2009 p5g^{4} 5d^{3} 5m* 5m* 5g^{5} 6g 5m^{2} 5g^{4} Oct 10] 3,000Y: compact colt: third foal: half-brother to 4-y-o Mac Dalia: dam 2-y-o 5f winner: useful performer: won maiden at Musselburgh in June and minor event at Beverley in July: improved efforts last 2 starts, length second to Sand Vixen in Flying Childers Stakes at Doncaster and 1½ lengths fourth to Our Jonathan in Cornwallis Stakes at Ascot: probably best at 5f: acts on good to firm going. *R. Curtis*

BOUND BY HONOUR (SAF) 6 b.g. Rambo Dancer (CAN) 107 – Child of Grace **103**
(SAF) (Only A Pound 93) [2009 8g^{4} 10g 12g 10m^{5} 10.4m 9m^{4} 10m 10.1m p10g^{2} p10m* p9.5g^{6} Dec 17] good-bodied gelding: won twice in South Africa in 2008, including

Grade 2 event at Turffontein: useful handicapper in 2009: ran at Nad Al Sheba for H. Brown first 4 starts: best effort in Britain when winning at Lingfield in November by length from The Cayterers: stays 1½m: acts on polytrack and soft going: usually blinkered: sometimes tongue tied. *G. L. Moore*

BOUND FOR STARDOM 2 b.f. (Mar 20) Royal Applause 124 – Liberty Bound 85 (Primo Dominie 121) [2009 5.7g Aug 28] third foal: sister to 3-y-o Boundless Applause and half-sister to 5-y-o Billy Red: dam, 5f winner, half-sister to smart sprinter Majestic Missile (by Royal Applause): 40/1 and green, well held in maiden at Bath. *W. S. Kittow* **–**

BOUNDLESS APPLAUSE 3 b.f. Royal Applause 124 – Liberty Bound 85 (Primo Dominie 121) [2009 –: 5.1f 6d³ 6.1g 6m⁴ 5.1d³ 6m* p6g p6m⁵ p6m Dec 16] modest handicapper: won at Yarmouth in September: stays 6f: acts on polytrack, good to firm and good to soft going: tried in cheekpieces. *I. A. Wood* **53**

BOUNDLESS PROSPECT (USA) 10 b.g. Boundary (USA) 117 – Cape (USA) (Mr Prospector (USA)) [2009 80: f8d³ p12.2g* f11g² f11g* 10g² 12v f12m³ f11g² f12f* Dec 17] lengthy gelding: fair performer: won claimer at Wolverhampton in January, seller at Southwell in March and handicap at Southwell in December: stays 1½m: acts on all-weather, firm and soft going: tried in headgear: held up (often races lazily). *P. D. Evans* **75**

BOUNTIFUL BAY 4 b.f. Bahamian Bounty 116 – My Preference (Reference Point 139) [2009 64: 6m p6g² p6g p6g p6m⁵ p6f Dec 21] leggy filly: modest maiden handicapper: stays 6f: best efforts on polytrack: sometimes tongue tied. *Matthew Salaman* **57**

BOUNTY BOX 3 b.f. Bahamian Bounty 116 – Bible Box (IRE) 93 (Bin Ajwaad (IRE) 119) [2009 88p: 5d³ 6g* 6m* 6m² 6m⁶ Oct 16] tall, good-bodied filly: useful performer: won handicaps at Newmarket in July and August: more improvement when neck second to Sea of Leaves there next time: drawn widest when only sixth in listed race on same course final start: will prove best at 5f/6f: acts on soft and good to firm going. *C. F. Wall* **104**

BOUNTY REEF 3 b.f. Bahamian Bounty 116 – Shaieef (IRE) 66 (Shareef Dancer (USA) 135) [2009 63: 10g 8m 7.6g⁵ 10.9g⁶ 10.2g 8m 7.1d⁴ 10.9m Sep 29] small, sparely-made filly: modest winner at 2 yrs: disappointing in 2009: stays 1m (possibly not 1¼m): acts on heavy and good to firm going: held up: tried visored. *P. D. Evans* **51**

BOURBON HIGHBALL (IRE) 4 b.g. Catcher In The Rye (IRE) 115 – Be Exciting (IRE) 88 (Be My Guest (USA) 126) [2009 65: p12.2g Jan 9] good-topped gelding: maiden: on downgrade: tried tongue tied/in cheekpieces. *P. C. Haslam* **–**

BOURNE 3 gr.g. Linamix (FR) 127 – L'Affaire Monique 101 (Machiavellian (USA) 123) [2009 8m⁴ 10f 10.9g⁴ p12g⁴ Oct 8] sturdy gelding: third foal: half-brother to 4-y-o Short Affair and 5-y-o Bon Spiel: dam, 1¼m winner, sister to smart performer up to 1¾m Whitewater Affair and half-sister to very smart 1½m performer Little Rock: fairly useful maiden: likely to stay beyond 1½m: raced only on polytrack and good ground or firmer: gelded after final start. *L. M. Cumani* **80**

BOURN FAIR 3 ch.f. Systematic 121 – Astelia (Sabrehill (USA) 120) [2009 53: p9.5g³ p9.5g f12m p12m p8.6g Dec 18] modest maiden handicapper: seems to stay 1½m: acts on all-weather: tried tongue tied. *P. J. McBride* **53**

BOURSE (IRE) 4 b.g. Dubai Destination (USA) 127 – Quarter Note (USA) 109 (Danehill (USA) 126) [2009 76: p9.5g p8.6g⁴ 8m⁶ 8f⁵ 9m⁵ 10.1s 8.3m 9.1g 8d⁴ 9g⁵ 10.1m⁵ 12.5s 12.5m⁶ Sep 14] compact gelding: fair performer: regressed in 2009: should stay 1¼m: acts on heavy and good to firm going: has worn cheekpieces/blinkers. *A. G. Foster* **68 d**

BOUVARDIA 3 b.f. Oasis Dream 129 – Arabesque 100 (Zafonic (USA) 130) [2009 88: 5.2d² 6.1m* 6m* 6m² Aug 16] well-made filly: useful performer: successful in handicaps at Nottingham and Newmarket (beat Akhenaten ½ length) in May: off 3 months, bit below form when 3½ lengths second to Mullein in listed race at Pontefract final start: would have proved best at 5f/6f: acted on soft and good to firm ground: possibly had her quirks (wandered badly at Nottingham): visits Champs Elysees. *H. R. A. Cecil* **103**

BOW BEAVER (USA) 2 b.c. (Jan 13) Vindication (USA) 122 – Miss Carolina (USA) (Unbridled (USA) 128) [2009 5g* 7m² 6g Sep 20] $50,000Y, 35,000 2-y-o: second foal: half-brother to winner in USA by Touch Gold: dam unraced daughter of US Grade 3 9f winner Ziggy's Act: fair form: well backed, won maiden at Carlisle in June: best effort when 3½ lengths second to Spying in minor event at Newcastle: stays 7f: made running first 2 starts. *J. Howard Johnson* **79**

BOWDER STONE (IRE) 4 b.g. Rock of Gibraltar (IRE) 133 – Ghita (IRE) 69 (Zilzal (USA) 137) [2009 86: 10.3g 12.3m May 8] rather leggy gelding: fairly useful handi- **–**

capper in 2008: well below form at 4 yrs (reportedly struck into on reappearance): stays easy 10.3f: acts on soft and good to firm going. *E. J. Alston*

BOWDLER'S MAGIC 2 b.c. (Mar 1) Hernando (FR) 127 – Slew The Moon (ARG) **77 p**
(Kitwood (USA) 119) [2009 8d p9.5g^2 p8.6g* Nov 21] third foal: half-brother to Irish 2007 2-y-o 1m winner Luz de La Luna (by Cozzene): dam Argentinian Group 1 1m winner: won maiden at Wolverhampton comfortably by 2 lengths from Oriental Scot, making all: stays 9.5f: still open to improvement. *M. Johnston*

BOWMAKER 2 b.g. (Apr 29) Dubawi (IRE) 129 – Viola Da Braccio (IRE) 58 (Vettori **84 p**
(IRE) 119) [2009 f6g* Oct 27] 62,000F, 20,000 2-y-o: second foal: half-brother to 3-y-o Sham Sheer: dam, maiden who stayed 12.5f, half-sister to dam of Rock of Gibraltar: 11/4, won maiden at Southwell easily by 7 lengths from Clear Ice: will stay 7f/1m: looks a useful prospect. *M. Johnston*

BOWSERS BEAU 3 br.g. Sakhee (USA) 136 – Shawahid (USA) (A P Indy (USA) **74**
131) [2009 9.9m^4 p8g^4 p12g^2 Oct 21] well-made gelding: second foal: dam unraced half-sister to 3-y-o Ghanaati: fair form in maidens: carried head awkwardly last 2 starts: stays 1½m: sold 35,000 gns. *M. P. Tregoning*

BOW TO NO ONE (IRE) 3 b.f. Refuse To Bend (IRE) 128 – Deadly Buzz (IRE) **94**
(Darshaan 133) [2009 10m^5 p8g^4 10m^3 10d 8m^4 11.1g^4 12m* p12g* p16m* Oct 31] €27,000Y: angular filly: second foal: dam unraced half-sister to useful French/US performer up to 1¼m Arabic Song: fairly useful handicapper: improved late in year, winning at Pontefract and Kempton (2) in October, by 10 lengths on final occasion: stays easy 2m: acts on polytrack, unraced on extremes of going on turf. *A. P. Jarvis*

BOX OFFICE 3 b.c. Storming Home 128 – Dream Ticket (USA) 73 (Danzig (USA)) **–**
[2009 97p: 8g^6 10g^2 Dec 24] well-made colt: useful winner at 2 yrs: well held in handicap at Newcastle in April, then sold from M. Johnston only 5,000 gns: second after in minor event at Doha: stays 1¼m. *T. Al Alawi, Qatar*

BOY BLUE 4 b.c. Observatory (USA) 131 – Rowan Flower (IRE) 67 (Ashkalani (IRE) **91**
128) [2009 89: 8m^5 8.1m^3 8d^4 7g 7d^3 8s^4 8s f8g 7s 7s Nov 7] sturdy colt: fairly useful handicapper: best efforts in 2009 when in frame: stays 1m: acts on soft and good to firm going. *P. Salmon*

BOYCOTT (IRE) 2 b.g. (Apr 6) Refuse To Bend (IRE) 128 – Withorwithoutyou (IRE) **65**
91 (Danehill (USA) 126) [2009 7m 7g 7m 7d p8m^4 p7g^3 Oct 8] well-made gelding: fair maiden: best efforts when in frame in nurseries at Kempton (subsequently gelded): stays 1m: acts on polytrack: blinkered last 4 starts: has finished weakly: front runner. *J. H. M. Gosden*

BOY DANCER (IRE) 6 ch.g. Danehill Dancer (IRE) 117 – Mary Gabry (IRE) (Kris **48**
135) [2009 66: 9.3m 7.5m 9.1g 8m 12.5s 9.9f 12g f8f^2 Nov 24] strong, stocky gelding: poor handicapper nowadays: stays 1¼m: acts on all-weather, good to firm and good to soft going: tried in cheekpieces. *J. J. Quinn*

BOY RACER (IRE) 4 br.g. Singspiel (IRE) 133 – Gombay Girl (USA) 82 (Woodman **–**
(USA) 126) [2009 75d: 7m 12.5d Oct 28] leggy, useful-looking gelding: regressive maiden. *C. J. Teague*

BOY THE BELL 2 b.g. (May 10) Choisir (AUS) 126 – Bella Beguine 78 (Komaite **70**
(USA)) [2009 p7.1g p6g^3 f6f^2 Dec 11] second foal: half-brother to 4-y-o Beat The Bell: dam, 6f winner, half-sister to dam of 6-y-o Moorhouse Lad: similar form when placed in maidens at Wolverhampton and Southwell: likely to prove best at 5f/6f. *J. A. Osborne*

BOZ 5 gr.h. Grand Lodge (USA) 125 – Dali's Grey (Linamix (FR) 127) [2009 99: 12f^3 **99**
14m^4 12m 12m 12m^3 14m^4 10m^5 14d 11g a10.5g^2 Dec 15] good-bodied horse: type to carry condition: useful performer: best efforts in 2009 when third to Hatton Flight in handicap at Newmarket and (having left L. Cumani after fourth start) when 3¼ lengths fourth to Ryan in listed race at Milan sixth start: stays 1¾m: acts on polytrack and firm going: effective with/without blinkers/visor: has raced lazily. *M. Gasparini, Italy*

BRADDOCK (IRE) 6 b.g. Pivotal 124 – Sedna (FR) (Bering 136) [2009 77: 6s^6 7g^3 7v **75**
6v 7d 7s 7s 6.3s^3 p6g^2 p6m^6 Oct 26] close-coupled gelding: fair handicapper: effective at 6f to 1m: acts on polytrack and heavy going: usually wears cheekpieces/blinkers/tongue strap: usually races close up. *S. Donohoe, Ireland*

BRADFORD (IRE) 2 b.c. (Feb 5) Pyrus (USA) 106 – Lypharden (IRE) (Lyphard's **69**
Special (USA) 122) [2009 6g^4 6d^2 p7.1g^4 7d^6 Jul 20] easily best effort in maidens when second at Newcastle: raced at 6f/7f: acts on good to soft going: tried visored. *K. R. Burke*

BRADS HOUSE (IRE) 7 b.g. Rossini (USA) 118 – Gold Stamp (Golden Act (USA)) [2009 12m 17.1m Sep 17] leggy gelding: fairly useful performer in 2005: fairly useful hurdler in 2006/7: off 2½ years, no promise on return. *J. G. M. O'Shea* **–**

BRAD'S LUCK (IRE) 3 ch.g. Lucky Story (USA) 128 – Seymour (IRE) 78 (Eagle Eyed (USA) 111) [2009 60p: $10.4v^4$ $10.3g^4$ 9.9f 10.3d 11.5s p12.2g p9.5g p16g $p16.5g^2$ Oct 17] rangy gelding: modest handicapper: stays 2m: acts on polytrack and good to firm going: signs of temperament. *M. Blanshard* **64**

BRAE HILL (IRE) 3 b.g. Fath (USA) 116 – Auriga 73 (Belmez (USA) 131) [2009 92: 6m 7m* 7d p7.1g $7m^2$ Sep 26] strong, lengthy gelding: useful handicapper: improved when winning at Chester (by 2¾ lengths from Cheviot) in June: creditable effort after only when length second to Desert Dreamer at same course: stays 7f: acts on soft and good to firm going: races prominently. *M. L. W. Bell* **100**

BRAGGADOCIO 2 br.g. (Apr 11) Fraam 114 – Brangane (IRE) (Anita's Prince 126) [2009 p6g Jul 8] 8/1, tailed off in maiden at Lingfield: gelded: sold £1,050. *P. Winkworth* **–**

BRAHMS AND MIST (FR) 9 b.g. River Mist (USA) 119 – Strabit (Stradavinsky 121) [2009 –: p12g Nov 13] no form over jumps: tailed off in seller/maiden. *D. J. S. ffrench Davis* **–**

BRAILLE 4 b.g. Bahamian Bounty 116 – Branston Gem 59 (So Factual (USA) 120) [2009 73: 5m 5g 5m 6g Aug 4] lengthy, workmanlike gelding: reportedly has only one eye: fair handicapper at 3 yrs: well held in 2009. *T. D. Walford* **–**

BRAMALEA 4 b.f. Whitmore's Conn (USA) 117 – Aster (IRE) (Danehill (USA) 126) [2009 78: $p9.5g^3$ $10.2g^3$ p10g $10.2f^2$ $10g^3$ $11.9s^2$ $10.2f^4$ $11s^2$ 10g $11.5s^4$ p10m $12d^3$ $11.5d^3$ p12.2g* $p12.2g^4$ Oct 3] lengthy filly: fair handicapper: in frame 12 times in 2009, winning at Wolverhampton in September: stays 1½m: acts on polytrack, soft and good to firm ground: once in cheekpieces (ran poorly): often front runner/races prominently (not last 2 starts). *B. W. Duke* **74**

BRAMBLEBERRY 2 b.f. (Apr 8) Cape Cross (IRE) 129 – Miss Satamixa (FR) 123 (Linamix (FR) 127) [2009 p5g* 5m $6.1g^5$ p5g* $p5m^5$ $5g^5$ Sep 22] compact filly: closely related to useful French 7f winner Man O Desert (by Green Desert) and half-sister to Irish 3-y-o Byzantine and fairly useful French 12.5f/13f winner Mister Wells (Sadler's Wells): dam French 5.5f to 1m (Prix Jacques le Marois) winner: fair performer, better on all-weather than turf: won maiden in June and minor event in August, both at Lingfield: speedy, likely to prove best at 5f: acts on polytrack: sold 32,000 gns. *Tom Dascombe* **62 a79**

BRAMSHAW (USA) 2 gr. or ro.c. (Jan 21) Langfuhr (CAN) 124 – Milagra (USA) (Maria's Mon (USA) 121) [2009 p7m* Nov 26] $130,000Y: third foal: half-brother to Canadian 2007 2-y-o 5f/6.5f minor stakes winner Bear Holiday (by Harlan's Holiday): dam US 6f winner: 8/1, promising debut when winning maiden at Kempton going away by ½ length from Count of Anjou, pulling hard early: useful performer in making. *Mrs A. J. Perrett* **80 p**

BRAMSHILL LADY (IRE) 2 gr. or ro.f. (Feb 24) Verglas (IRE) 118 – Jinx Johnson (IRE) 59 (Desert King (IRE) 129) [2009 $5g^4$ $5m^5$ 7m 7m Oct 26] €17,000F, £20,000Y: angular filly: first foal: dam, Irish 8.5f winner, half-sister to useful Italian performer up to 1m Morena Park: modest maiden: only seventh in nursery at Leicester: should stay 7f: tried tongue tied: said to have had irregular heartbeat third outing. *Pat Eddery* **61**

BRANANX (USA) 2 b.c. (Jan 28) Red Ransom (USA) – Shady Reflection (USA) 88 (Sultry Song (USA)) [2009 7g Oct 23] $110,000F, 50,000 2-y-o: compact colt: first foal: dam 1m winner, including at 2 yrs: 20/1, eighth in maiden at Doncaster, slowly away and late headway: should improve. *K. A. Ryan* **54 p**

BRANDERBURGO (IRE) 2 b.c. (Apr 24) High Chaparral (IRE) 132 – Farhad (Red Ransom (USA)) [2009 $6f^6$ $7.1m^3$ $7g^5$ $8m^3$ 8g $9s^3$ $8m^4$ 10d* Dec 23] close-coupled, deep-girthed colt: second foal: dam, Italian 7f/7.5f winner, half-sister to smart performers around 9f Singhalese and Docofthebay: fairly useful performer: in frame in listed races at Milan (final start for M. Botti) and Syracuse before winning minor event at Naples in December: stays 1¼m: acts on soft and good to firm ground: in cheekpieces fourth/fifth starts. *L. Riccardi, Italy* **87**

BRANDY BUTTER 3 ch.g. Domedriver (IRE) 128 – Brand (Shareef Dancer (USA) 135) [2009 p10g $p10g^6$ p12g $p12m^5$ $17.2g^4$ Oct 21] modest maiden: seemingly stays 17f: raced only on polytrack/good ground: often visored: joined D. Pipe 6,000 gns. *A. M. Balding* **59 ?**

BRANDYWELL BOY (IRE) 6 b.g. Danetime (IRE) 121 – Alexander Eliott (IRE) 73 (Night Shift (USA)) [2009 82: p6g p6g³ p5g* p5g³ p6g 5g p6g 5.1m 5g⁴ 5.2g² 5m 5.2m* 5m³ 5.1m⁶ 5.1m⁴ 5f 5g⁴ 5m⁵ 5s² 5m² 5m* 5m⁵ p5g² p5g⁴ 5.1g⁶ p6m p6m* p6f Dec 21] close-coupled gelding: fairly useful handicapper on all-weather, fair on turf: won at Lingfield (claimer) in February, Newbury in June, Goodwood (apprentices) in September and Lingfield in November: effective at 5f/6f: acts on polytrack, firm and soft going: tactically versatile: tough. *D. J. S. ffrench Davis* **73 a82**

BRANNAGH (USA) 2 gr.c. (Apr 19) Hennessy (USA) 122 – Green Room (USA) (Theatrical 128) [2009 6m³ p7g³ Oct 29] 105,000Y: well-made colt: second foal: half-brother to 3-y-o Lord Shanakill: dam unraced half-sister to US Grade 1 1¼m winner Spanish Fern: better effort in maidens when 1¼ lengths third to Fine Sight at Lingfield, edging left: likely to stay 1m: tongue tied: will improve again. *J. Noseda* **82 p**

BRASINGAMAN ERIC 2 b.c. (Mar 26) Bollin Eric 125 – Serene Pearl (IRE) 55 (Night Shift (USA)) [2009 5g⁴ 6g⁴ p7.1g⁶ Jul 7] modest form in maidens: hung left at Wolverhampton final start: bred to stay at least 1m. *Mrs G. S. Rees* **50**

BRASINGAMAN HIFIVE 4 b.f. High Estate 127 – Our Miss Florence (Carlitin 50) [2009 90: 8.1m 8.1v³ 8.1g⁵ 7.6g³ 8m p8.6g⁶ 8.3g Oct 28] leggy filly: fairly useful handicapper: stays 1m: acts on heavy going. *Mrs G. S. Rees* **84**

BRASSINI 4 gr.g. Bertolini (USA) 125 – Silver Spell 54 (Aragon 118) [2009 102: p7g 6g 7m³ 7g⁵ 7.1m* 7g Jun 26] close-coupled gelding: fairly useful handicapper: won at Sandown in June: pulled up amiss at Chester 13 days later: stayed 7f: acted on firm and soft ground: raced prominently: dead. *B. R. Millman* **94**

BRAVALTO 3 b.c. Falbrav (IRE) 133 – Bunty Boo 110 (Noalto 120) [2009 66: p7.1g⁶ Dec 12] best effort (fair form in maidens) on second outing at 2 yrs: shaped as though in need of only start in 2009: raced only at 6f/7f on polytrack and soft ground. *B. Smart* **52 +**

BRAVE AMBITION (IRE) 2 b.g. (Apr 28) Spartacus (IRE) 107 – I Want You Now (IRE) (Nicolotte 118) [2009 f5g 6m 7.5m f7g Nov 17] leggy gelding: no form in maidens/sellers, leaving Garry Moss after third start. *R. C. Guest* **–**

BRAVE BEAT 3 b.g. Beat Hollow 126 – Be Brave (FR) (Green Forest (USA) 134) [2009 p12g 12.1g 10m 15g Jul 3] little form: tried blinkered. *H. J. L. Dunlop* **–**

BRAVE BUGSY (IRE) 6 b.g. Mujadil (USA) 119 – Advancing (IRE) (Ela-Mana-Mou 132) [2009 68: 17.2d⁵ 17.2f² p16g⁶ 17.2m* Jul 16] fair form in bumpers/poor winning hurdler: fair handicapper on Flat: won at Bath: stays 17f: acts on firm going: visored last 3 starts. *A. M. Balding* **66**

BRAVE DEALER 3 ch.g. Falbrav (IRE) 133 – Sharp Terms (Kris 135) [2009 10d 10m⁶ 10d Jul 7] sturdy gelding: best effort in maidens (fair form) when sixth at Sandown: likely to stay 1½m: sold 4,500 gns in October. *R. Charlton* **63**

BRAVE DECISION 2 gr.g. (Feb 18) With Approval (CAN) – Brave Vanessa (USA) 62 (Private Account (USA)) [2009 p7.1g³ Dec 28] half-brother to 3 winners, including 1¼m winner Simiola (by Shaamit) and 1½m winner Imminent Victory (by Benny The Dip): dam, 6f winner (stayed 1m), sister to US Grade 2 winner around 1m Topicount: 25/1, length third to Capricornus in maiden at Wolverhampton, green before running on well: will stay at least 1m: open to improvement. *A. J. McCabe* **67 p**

BRAVE ENOUGH (USA) 2 b.c. (Apr 5) Yes It's True (USA) 116 – Courageous (USA) (Kingmambo (USA) 125) [2009 p7m p7.1g⁵ Dec 28] better effort in maidens when fifth to Capricornus at Wolverhampton, late headway. *M. A. Magnusson* **62**

BRAVE GHURKA 2 b.g. (Mar 30) Bahamian Bounty 116 – Wondrous Maid (GER) (Mondrian (GER) 125) [2009 7d 6d⁶ p7g⁵ p7m⁵ p7f Dec 20] tall, rather leggy gelding: fair maiden: best effort at 6f. *S. Kirk* **66**

BRAVEHEART MOVE (IRE) 3 b.g. Cape Cross (IRE) 129 – Token Gesture (IRE) 113 (Alzao (USA) 117) [2009 87p: 12.3m* 12g 12m* 14m 13g* Sep 20] big, strong gelding: type to carry condition: useful handicapper: largely progressive in 2009, winning at Chester in May, Pontefract in August and Hamilton (beat Merchant of Dubai by neck, taking time to pick up) in September: should stay 1¾m: acts on good to firm going: sold 150,000 gns, joined Jonjo O'Neill, then gelded. *Sir Mark Prescott* **101**

BRAVE KNAVE (IRE) 4 b.c. Averti (IRE) 117 – Recall (IRE) (Revoque (IRE) 122) [2009 45: 11.6m⁶ Jun 28] close-coupled colt: poor maiden: well held sole start in 2009: tried tongue tied. *B. De Haan* **–**

BRAVELY FOUGHT (IRE) 4 b.g. Indian Ridge 123 – Amazing Tale 80 (Shareef Dancer (USA) 135) [2009 87: 7f 10g* 10g* 9.9g p10.7g^{6} 9d^{5} 8s 8.5g p10g p12g^{3} Nov 27] lengthy gelding: useful handicapper: improved at 4 yrs, winning at Leopardstown in June and Fairyhouse in July: further progress when length third to Avanti Albert at Dundalk final start: effective at 9f to easy 1½m: acts on polytrack and good to soft going: tried blinkered/tongue tied: occasionally hangs left. *Miss S. J. Harty, Ireland* **106**

BRAVELY (IRE) 5 b.g. Rock of Gibraltar (IRE) 133 – Raghida (IRE) 102 (Nordico (USA)) [2009 79: 7m^{3} 7f^{4} 7s^{2} 7m^{2} 6g 7m^{6} 7m 5d* 5g 6m^{4} 5m 5m 5g^{2} 5.1g Oct 28] quite attractive gelding: fairly useful handicapper: won at Newcastle in July: effective from 5f to 7f: acts on firm and soft ground. *T. D. Easterby* **84**

BRAVE MAVE 4 gr.f. Daylami (IRE) 138 – Baalbek 76 (Barathea (IRE) 127) [2009 83: p12.2g 12m^{5} 11.8m p13g^{5} f12f Nov 24] leggy filly: fair handicapper: left W. Jarvis after third start: stays 1½m: acts on fibresand, soft and good to firm going: tried blinkered. *Jane Chapple-Hyam* **77**

BRAVE OPTIMIST (IRE) 4 b.f. Diktat 126 – Maine Lobster (USA) 71 (Woodman (USA) 126) [2009 –: p8.6g^{6} Feb 14] well held in maidens. *Paul Green* **–**

BRAVE PROSPECTOR 4 b.c. Oasis Dream 129 – Simply Times (USA) 64 (Dodge (USA)) [2009 106: 6m 6d 5.4m 6.5m* 6m 6g^{3} Oct 10] well-made colt: smart performer: better than ever when winning handicap at Doncaster in September by 1¼ lengths from Castles In The Air: good 1½ lengths third to Royal Rock in Bengough Memorial Stakes at Ascot final start: stays 6.5f: acts on firm and good to soft going: tongue tied. *P. W. Chapple-Hyam* **110**

BRAVO BELLE (IRE) 2 b.f. (Apr 6) Bertolini (USA) 125 – Dazilyn Lady (USA) 105 (Zilzal (USA) 137) [2009 6v^{5} Nov 3] €4,000 2-y-o: fifth foal: half-sister to 1m winner Mark of Love (by Mark of Esteem): dam 2-y-o 6f winner (stayed 1m): 33/1, well held in maiden at Catterick. *T. H. Caldwell* **–**

BRAVO BLUE (IRE) 2 b.f. (Apr 5) Mark of Esteem (IRE) 137 – Fantazia 100 (Zafonic (USA) 130) [2009 6m 7m^{6} 7g Oct 23] 9,000F, €7,500 2-y-o: leggy filly: fifth foal: half-sister to 1m/1¼m winner Bon Viveur (by Mozart): dam 1¼m/11f winner: soundly beaten in maidens/minor event. *T. H. Caldwell* **–**

BRAVO BRAVO 2 b.g. (Apr 10) Sadler's Wells (USA) 132 – Top Table 65 (Shirley Heights 130) [2009 8.1m Sep 11] 66/1 and very green, tailed off in maiden at Sandown: gelded. *Eve Johnson Houghton* **–**

BRAVO ECHO 3 b.c. Oasis Dream 129 – Bold Empress (USA) (Diesis 133) [2009 97P: 7d 7.1f^{3} 7m^{5} 8g* 8.1m^{3} p8f^{5} Dec 20] big, strong colt: type to carry condition: powerful galloper: fairly useful handicapper: won at Newmarket in July: creditable efforts both starts after, leaving J. Gosden 48,000 gns in between: should prove better at 1m than shorter: acts on polytrack and firm ground, poor efforts both starts on softer than good: has flashed tail under whip. *M. J. Attwater* **93**

BRAZILIAN BRUSH (IRE) 4 ch.g. Captain Rio 122 – Ejder (IRE) (Indian Ridge 123) [2009 73: p6g p6g p6g p5g^{6} 5g 6m 6.1g^{6} 5.7g p6m f6g^{6} Dec 8] well-made gelding: just modest performer in 2009: stays easy 7f: acts on polytrack, good to firm and good to soft ground: tried in cheekpieces: usually tongue tied. *J. M. Bradley* **51**

BREACH OF PEACE (USA) 3 b.f. Royal Academy (USA) 130 – Hasardeuse (USA) (Distant View (USA) 126) [2009 64p: p7g 8.3m^{6} 8m^{6} 9.7f^{5} Jun 2] quite attractive filly: fair maiden: stays 9.7f: acts on firm going: sold 14,000 gns in December. *R. Charlton* **71**

BREADSTICK 3 br.f. Diktat 126 – Poilane (Kris 135) [2009 70: 9.9g^{2} 9.9m 8.1g^{6} p8g^{4} 7.1d^{6} Sep 4] rangy filly: fair maiden: stays 1¼m: acts on polytrack: tried blinkered/tongue tied: sold £1,300. *H. Morrison* **73**

BREAKEVIE (IRE) 3 b.f. Mull of Kintyre (USA) 114 – Skehana (IRE) 69 (Mukaddamah (USA) 125) [2009 54: 6g^{4} 7.1m May 19] tall, good-topped filly: lightly-raced maiden: just poor form in 2009: should stay 7f. *R. A. Fahey* **45**

BREAKHEART (IRE) 2 b.g. (Jan 17) Sakhee (USA) 136 – Exorcet (FR) 78 (Selkirk (USA) 129) [2009 7m 8g^{2} Oct 21] strong gelding: half-brother to 6f winners Night Rocket and Dark Missile (both by Night Shift), latter smart: dam 6f winner out of smart sprinter Stack Rock: much better effort in maidens when 5 lengths second to Rasmy at Bath: gelded after: stays 1m. *A. M. Balding* **79**

BREATHLESS KISS (USA) 2 b.f. (Feb 9) Roman Ruler (USA) 122 – Crusading **69 +**
Miss Cox (USA) (Crusader Sword (USA)) [2009 5d* 6g^{6} Aug 31] $145,000F, $60,000 2-y-o: good-topped filly: half-sister to 3 winners in USA: dam US 2-y-o 7f winner: won minor event at Doncaster in July by ¾ length from High Spice: seemed amiss (hung right, reportedly lost action) in listed race at Ripon. *K. A. Ryan*

BREEZE OF THE AIR 2 ch.c. (Jan 25) Compton Place 125 – Dixieanna 81 (Night **56**
Shift (USA)) [2009 5.7f^{6} 6m^{6} 7d^{5} Jul 22] rather unfurnished colt: modest form in maidens: likely to prove best at 5f/6f: sold £4,200 in August. *M. R. Channon*

BRENDA DUKE 2 ch.f. (Mar 1) Bachelor Duke (USA) 122 – Fiina 68 (Most Welcome **43**
131) [2009 p7m 8.3g Oct 28] second foal: dam, Irish maiden, sister to smart German performer (best at 1½m) Flying Dream: better effort when eighth in seller at Nottingham latter start: bred to stay 1m+: very slowly away on debut. *J. G. Portman*

BRENIN TARAN 3 gr.g. Lujain (USA) 119 – Silver Chime 74 (Robellino (USA) 127) **91**
[2009 84: 5f* 5g 5g^{6} 5m^{4} 5.1m^{4} 6m p5g^{2} 5.7m^{2} 6m Sep 25] leggy, workmanlike gelding: fairly useful handicapper: won at Thirsk in April: good efforts when runner-up after: stays 5.7f: acts on polytrack and firm ground: in cheekpieces last 3 starts: has looked none too keen: gelded after final outing. *D. M. Simcock*

BRER RABBIT 3 b.f. Invincible Spirit (IRE) 121 – Red Rabbit 86 (Suave Dancer **66**
(USA) 136) [2009 66: p8g^{2} p8.6g* p10g p9.5g p9.5g^{6} 8.3g p9.5g p8.6m^{6} f8f Dec 17] attractive filly: fair handicapper: won at Wolverhampton in March: left B. Hills 2,000 gns after seventh start: stays 8.6f: acts on polytrack: not straightforward. *Seamus Fahey, Ireland*

BRETT VALE (IRE) 3 br.g. Sinndar (IRE) 134 – Pinta (IRE) (Ahonoora 122) [2009 **95**
p6g f6g^{5} p6g^{5} p7g p10g* 10d* 11.5s^{2} 10g* 10g^{5} p10f^{6} 12m* p9.5g p12g^{2} p16m* p12f^{3} Dec 19] €55,000Y: useful-looking gelding: half-brother to several winners, including 7-y-o Rain Stops Play: dam, Italian 7.5f winner (including listed race at 2 yrs), out of half-sister to high-class 9f/1¼m filly Timarida: progressed into a useful performer: won handicaps at Lingfield and Brighton in June and Sandown in August, claimer at Newmarket (left Sir Mark Prescott £40,000) in September and handicap at Kempton (beat Moonbeam Dancer 2¾ lengths) in December: stays 2m: acts on polytrack, good to firm and good to soft ground. *P. R. Hedger*

BRIANNSTA (IRE) 7 b.g. Bluebird (USA) 125 – Nacote (IRE) (Mtoto 134) [2009 61: **62**
p7g^{6} p7g^{4} f6g p6g^{3} 6d^{5} 6m^{2} 7m^{4} 6m 6m^{6} p6g* p7m^{3} p6g p6g p6m p6m Dec 16] lengthy, quite attractive gelding: modest performer: won handicap at Wolverhampton in October: stays easy 7f: acts on polytrack, soft and good to firm ground: often visored/blinkered: none too consistent. *J. E. Long*

BRIARY MAC 2 b.f. (Mar 10) Royal Applause 124 – Red May (IRE) 70 (Persian Bold **66**
123) [2009 6g^{2} 6s^{5} 6v^{4} Nov 3] 8,000F, £1,000Y: fifth foal: half-sister to 2 winners, including 6f (at 2 yrs)/7f winner Redeye Special (by Efisio): dam maiden (stayed 1½m): easily best effort in maidens when 4 lengths second to Coin From Heaven at Redcar: raced on soft/heavy going after. *N. Bycroft*

BRICK RED 2 ch.g. (Feb 24) Dubawi (IRE) 129 – Duchcov 101 (Caerleon (USA) 132) **88 p**
[2009 7m p6g* 7m^{6} 7d^{2} Oct 11] big, deep-girthed gelding: type to carry condition: fourth foal: half-brother to 3 winners, including fairly useful 5f (at 2 yrs)/1m winner Rescue Me (by Red Ransom) and 3-y-o Seek The Fair Land: dam 1¼m winner: progressive form: dead-heated with Haadeeth in maiden at Kempton in August: good nose second to Ransom Note in nursery at Goodwood: gelded after: will stay 1m: acts on polytrack, good to firm and good to soft ground: open to further improvement. *A. M. Balding*

BRIDEVIEW 3 ch.f. Kyllachy 129 – Dolce Piccata 88 (Piccolo 121) [2009 57: p6g 5.1f **–**
5g Jun 20] maiden: modest at 2 yrs: well held in 2009, left P. Prendergast in Ireland after reappearance: tried in cheekpieces/tongue tie. *Edgar Byrne*

BRIDGE NOTE (USA) 3 b.f. Stravinsky (USA) 133 – Myrtle 96 (Batshoof 122) **49**
[2009 f6g 6.1f May 8] $250,000Y: small filly: fifth foal: sister to high-class 6f/7f winner Soldier's Tale: dam, 2-y-o 7.5f winner, later successful in USA: poor form in maidens: sold 14,000 gns. *J. Noseda*

BRIDGE OF FERMOY (IRE) 4 b.g. Danetime (IRE) 121 – Banco Solo (Distant **61 d**
Relative 128) [2009 79: p7m^{5} f8g p7g^{6} p8g^{5} p8.6g p10g p10g^{6} p12g Oct 20] tall, lengthy gelding: fair performer at 3 yrs: regressed in 2009, leaving Gay Kelleway after fifth start: effective at 7f to 1¼m: acts on polytrack, soft and good to firm going: usually wears headgear/tongue tie. *D. C. O'Brien*

BRIDGE OF GOLD (USA) 3 b.c. Giant's Causeway (USA) 132 – Lady Doc (USA) (Doc's Leader (USA)) [2009 8s* 8.1m^4 p8g^4 Jun 25] $250,000Y: useful-looking colt: fifth foal: half-brother to several winners in US, including Grade 3 1m winner Lady Marlboro (by Smoke Glacken): dam US 6f to 8.5f winner: useful form: won maiden at Newbury in April: improved when 2¼ lengths fourth to Border Patrol in listed race at Sandown next time: missed break and well below form final start: raced only at 1m. *M. A. Magnusson* **97**

BRIDGE VALLEY 2 ch.g. (Mar 4) Avonbridge 123 – Go Between 91 (Daggers Drawn (USA) 114) [2009 6d^4 6m^5 7.1m^3 6.1v^2 5g* 6m^3 7d 6s Nov 7] 58,000F, £30,000Y: compact gelding: second foal: half-brother to 3-y-o Go Nani Go: dam, 6f (at 2 yrs)/7f winner, half-sister to smart Irish 5f to 1m winner Grecian Dancer: fair performer: won maiden at Sandown in August: well below form in nurseries last 2 starts: stays 6f: acts on heavy and good to firm going: gets behind: gelded after final start. *R. Hannon* **77**

BRIDGEWATER BOYS 8 b.g. Atraf 116 – Dunloe (IRE) 54 (Shaadi (USA) 126) [2009 78: p13.3g^2 p13.9g^3 p16.5g^4 p13g^6 p12g* p12.2g^2 f11g* p12.2g^3 12g 12.5m^2 12f^2 p12.2g 13g^2 18g 12m 13.8m^6 f11g 13.8m Sep 19] lengthy gelding: fair performer: won seller at Lingfield in February and claimer at Southwell (left P. D. Evans £6,000) in March: well below form last 5 starts: stays 13.8f: acts on all-weather, firm and soft ground: wears headgear: tried tongue tied: patiently ridden. *T. J. Pitt* **75 d**

BRIEF CANDLE 3 br.f. Diktat 126 – Bright Hope (IRE) 84 (Danehill (USA) 126) [2009 88p: 8m^5 9m 8.3m^5 8m Sep 25] sturdy filly: fairly useful handicapper: stays 8.3f: raced only on polytrack and good/good to firm ground: tongue tied last 6 starts: sold 4,000 gns. *W. R. Swinburn* **84**

BRIEF ENCOUNTER (IRE) 3 b. or br.g. Pyrus (USA) 106 – Just One Look 77 (Barathea (IRE) 127) [2009 90p: 7s^6 7m* 8m 8m* 8d^6 p8g^2 8m^5 9m 10g* Dec 24] rather leggy gelding: useful performer: won handicaps at York in May and Newmarket (beat Crackdown ¾ length) in July: good efforts after when 1¼ lengths second to Ashram in minor event at Kempton and fifth to Manassas in handicap at Doncaster: sold from A. Balding 140,000 gns, won minor event at Doha in December: stays 1¼m: acts on polytrack and good to firm ground: waited with. *I. Al Malki, Qatar* **106**

BRIEF LOOK 3 b.f. Sadler's Wells (USA) 132 – Half Glance 104 (Danehill (USA) 126) [2009 10m^2 f11g^2 p12g* p12f* 12m^3 14.1s Oct 12] first living foal: dam, 7f/1m (including May Hill Stakes at 2 yrs) winner who stayed 1¼m, half-sister to very smart 1½m/1¾m performer Tycoon (by Sadler's Wells): fairly useful performer: won maiden at Kempton in August and handicap at Lingfield in September: improved again when third in handicap at Newmarket: should stay 1¾m: acts on polytrack and good to firm ground, well below form on soft: sent to USA. *H. R. A. Cecil* **94**

BRIERTY (IRE) 3 b.f. Statue of Liberty (USA) 115 – Bridelina (FR) (Linamix (FR) 127) [2009 88: 7d 7f^2 8m^6 6g^4 5.4g* 6m^5 6.1g^5 6g p6m^5 p6g p7.1g Dec 18] sturdy filly: fairly useful handicapper: won at York in July: effective at 5.4f to 7f: acts on polytrack and firm going: tried visored. *D. Carroll* **85**

BRIERY BLAZE 6 b.m. Dansili 127 – Sabonis (USA) 68 (The Minstrel (CAN) 135) [2009 –: p6g p5.1g^5 p12.2g Feb 16] plain mare: one-time modest performer: little form since 2007: usually wears blinkers/cheekpieces. *T. Wall* **–**

BRIERY LANE (IRE) 8 ch.g. Tagula (IRE) 116 – Branston Berry (IRE) 86 (Mukaddamah (USA) 125) [2009 61: f5g p6g^6 p5.1g p6g 6m 6m^6 Jul 6] lengthy gelding: poor performer nowadays: effective at 5f to easy 7f: acts on polytrack, firm and soft going: tried in tongue tie, often wears cheekpieces: none too consistent. *J. M. Bradley* **48**

BRIGADOON 2 b.c. (Mar 2) Compton Place 125 – Briggsmaid 70 (Elegant Air 119) [2009 7g f7m^2 f5m^3 Dec 5] 3,000Y: half-brother to several fairly useful winners, including 9-y-o Cruise Director: dam won from 1½m to 2m: fair form in maidens: will stay 1m+. *W. Jarvis* **72 +**

BRIGHT FALCON 4 ch.g. Hawk Wing (USA) 136 – Cream Tease 99 (Pursuit of Love 124) [2009 76d: f7g 16m 21.6m 7.5m 8.3g 8f 8.3m 6d* 6m 7m Sep 16] good-topped gelding: modest performer: won apprentice seller at Ripon in June, left S. Parr after: effective at 6f to 1m: acts on good to soft going: often wears headgear/tongue strap. *J. Balding* **55**

BRIGHT SPARKY (GER) 6 ch.g. Dashing Blade 117 – Braissim (Dancing Brave (USA) 140) [2009 56: f11g* f12g 9.9m 14.1m^3 16d 15.8g p13.9g^2 Dec 14] big, good-topped gelding: modest handicapper: won amateur event at Southwell in February: stays 2m: acts on all-weather and good to firm ground: usually tongue tied/blinkered/visored: successful over fences in October. *M. W. Easterby* **57**

BRIGHT WIRE (IRE) 3 b.g. Elusive City (USA) 117 – Alinga (IRE) 91 (King's Theatre (IRE) 128) [2009 –: p7g^4 8g p10g 11.5m^6 p12g 11.7g 16g p12g Dec 31] big gelding: poor maiden: probably stays 1½m: tried visored. *M. Madgwick* **44**

BRILLIANA 3 b.f. Danehill Dancer (IRE) 117 – Streak of Silver (USA) 66 (Dynaformer (USA)) [2009 65p: 10m^3 10m^2 p10g^5 11.7m* 12m^2 Sep 9] tall, unfurnished filly: fairly useful form: very easy winner of maiden at Bath in August: good second in handicap at Epsom after: stays 1½m: acts on good to firm going. *D. R. Lanigan* **92**

BRING IT ON HOME 5 b.g. Beat Hollow 126 – Dernier Cri 63 (Slip Anchor 136) [2009 64: f12g^2 Feb 19] modest maiden: stays 13.3f: best efforts on good ground: tried blinkered: has shown signs of temperament: fair hurdler: joined Mrs S. Leech. *G. L. Moore* **64**

BRING SWEETS (IRE) 2 b.g. (Mar 19) Firebreak 125 – Missperon (IRE) 77 (Orpen (USA) 116) [2009 5m 5m^6 5g^6 7m Oct 26] leggy gelding: poor maiden. *B. Ellison* **41**

BRINK 2 b.f. (Apr 17) Powerscourt 126 – Fonage (Zafonic (USA) 130) [2009 p8.6g^5 7g^3 7.1d^2 Oct 28] 8,000 2-y-o: tall filly: fourth foal: half-sister to fairly useful 2006 2-y-o 5f/7.5f winner Zafonical Storm (by Aljabr): dam, US 6.5f/1m winner, half-sister to dam of Prix de l'Arc de Triomphe winner Rail Link: placed in maidens at Catterick and Musselburgh: should stay 1m+. *T. J. Pitt* **65**

BRINSCALL 2 b.f. (Feb 24) Lucky Story (USA) 128 – Happy Lady (FR) 72 (Cadeaux Genereux 131) [2009 5m^5 6v^3 6g^6 7.5m 6g^4 6g^2 7g^4 p6g^5 Dec 3] 1,700F, £26,000Y: unfurnished filly: sixth foal: half-sister to 3 winners, including 3-y-o Penny's Gift: dam, maiden, half-sister to smart performer up to 2m Rainbow Ways: fair maiden: left T. Easterby after fourth start: should stay 7f+: best efforts on good ground. *R. A. Fahey* **71**

BRISBANE (IRE) 2 b.g. (Feb 14) Kheleyf (USA) 116 – Waroonga (IRE) (Brief Truce (USA) 126) [2009 6d^4 6g^2 6m Jun 14] well-made gelding: easily best effort when length second to Niran in 5-runner minor event at Yarmouth: broke awkwardly final outing: sprint bred: gelded, sold £3,500 in December. *J. H. M. Gosden* **67**

BRISTOL DELAURIERE (FR) 5 b.g. Epistolaire (IRE) 118 – Shenedova (FR) (Hellios (USA)) [2009 p12m Sep 24] little encouragement in bumpers/maiden hurdle, and in maiden on Flat debut. *Miss N. A. Lloyd-Beavis* **–**

BROAD CAIRN 3 b.g. Green Desert (USA) 127 – Celtic Cross 100 (Selkirk (USA) 129) [2009 86p: 7d^3 8.1g* 7.1m 7.1m* 7.1g^3 7.1g* 7m p7g^4 Oct 11] quite attractive gelding: fairly useful performer: won maiden at Haydock in May, then handicaps at Sandown in July and Warwick in August: stays 1m: acts on polytrack and good to firm ground. *R. Charlton* **93**

BROAD TOWN GIRL 6 b.m. Woodborough (USA) 112 – Fortunes Course (IRE) 55 (Crash Course 128) [2009 42: 12.1g Jun 17] smallish mare: poor maiden: tried visored. *W. S. Coltherd* **–**

BROCKFIELD 3 ch.c. Falbrav (IRE) 133 – Irish Light (USA) 91 (Irish River (FR) 131) [2009 8m^4 8g 8m^5 8g^5 Aug 5] lengthy, good-topped colt: modest maiden: raced only at 1m on good/good to firm ground. *M. Brittain* **55**

BROCTUNE PAPA GIO 2 b.g. (Jan 27) Tobougg (IRE) 125 – Fairlie 70 (Halling (USA) 133) [2009 8g Oct 16] 150/1, well held in maiden at Redcar. *K. G. Reveley* **–**

BRODY'S BOY 2 ch.c. (Mar 23) Tumbleweed Ridge 117 – Raffelina (USA) (Carson City (USA)) [2009 6g Oct 30] lengthy colt: 150/1, always behind in maiden at Newmarket. *G. L. Moore* **–**

BROMHEAD (USA) 3 ch.g. Johannesburg (USA) 127 – Caramel Queen (NZ) (Turbulent Dancer (USA)) [2009 p7m^5 p10g* p10g^4 p8.6g^4 p8g^4 7f p8g 9s^5 10.1g 8g 7m p9.5g 11.8m 11.5g^3 10.1d Oct 27] fair performer: won maiden at Lingfield in January: left B. Meehan after sixth start: stays 11.5f: acts on polytrack: tongue tied after sixth start: often pulls hard. *Mrs C. A. Dunnett* **74 d**

BRONTE'S HOPE 5 ch.m. Gorse 116 – General Jane (Be My Chief (USA) 122) [2009 63: 6g^3 Apr 21] workmanlike mare: modest handicapper: best efforts at 6f: raced only on polytrack/good going: tried in cheekpieces: dead. *M. P. Tregoning* **58**

BRONZE BEAU 2 ch.g. (Mar 31) Compton Place 125 – Bella Cantata (Singspiel (IRE) 133) [2009 p5g^5 5m^4 5s^2 5d 5m^5 5d^2 5d^3 5g^2 5m^4 5g^3 p5.1g^6 Nov 2] 3,000Y: lengthy gelding: second foal: dam unraced half-sister to high-class 1¼m performer Stagecraft: fair maiden: raced only at 5f: acts on good to soft ground: has started very slowly/hung badly left: temperamental. *Mrs L. Stubbs* **77 §**

Hardwicke Stakes, Royal Ascot—a second successive Group 2 win for Bronze Cannon, who is about to overhaul Campanologist (left); Dansant is third

BRONZE CANNON (USA) 4 b. or br.c. Lemon Drop Kid (USA) 131 – Victoria Cross (IRE) 101 (Mark of Esteem (IRE) 137) [2009 111: p10g^3 p10g^3 12m* 12m* a12g^4 12g Sep 27] smallish, strong colt: has a quick, unimpressive action: very smart performer: much improved to win 3-runner stanjames.com Jockey Club Stakes at Newmarket (beat Casual Conquest 3 lengths) in May and Hardwicke Stakes at Royal Ascot (led close home to beat Campanologist ½ length) in June: below form in valuable event on dirt at Moscow and Preis von Europa at Cologne last 2 starts: stays 1½m: acts on polytrack and good to firm going: genuine. *J. H. M. Gosden* **123**

BRONZE PRINCE 2 b.c. (Feb 26) Oasis Dream 129 – Sweet Pea 94 (Persian Bold 123) [2009 p7.1g* Nov 13] 220,000Y: sixth foal: half-brother to useful 6f (at 2 yrs)/7f winner Scarlet Runner (by Night Shift) and fairly useful Irish 1½m winner Scent (by Groom Dancer): dam 1m winner: 7/4 on and tongue tied, won maiden at Wolverhampton readily by 1½ lengths from Cabal: should stay 1m: useful prospect. *Saeed bin Suroor* **91 p**

BROOKLANDS BAY (IRE) 2 b.g. (Apr 6) Pyrus (USA) 106 – Brooklands Time (IRE) 63 (Danetime (IRE) 121) [2009 p8.6g* Oct 17] €4,200Y, resold £10,000Y: second foal: dam, sprint maiden, half-sister to useful Irish/UAE performer up to 1m Cat Belling: 33/1, won maiden at Wolverhampton by ¾ length from Angelena Ballerina, leading over 1f out: open to improvement. *J. R. Weymes* **75 p**

BROOKLYN SPIRIT 3 ch.g. Cadeaux Genereux 131 – Serengeti Bride (USA) 91 (Lion Cavern (USA) 117) [2009 –: 10m* 12m 11m Oct 1] won maiden at Sandown in June, only form: shaped as if amiss both starts after: stays 1¼m: acts on good to firm ground. *C. G. Cox* **74**

BROOKSBY 3 b.f. Diktat 126 – Lovely Lyca 76 (Night Shift (USA)) [2009 77: p8g^6 9.9m p7g^5 8d^6 7g^3 8m^2 p7m^4 p8g^2 8.5m^4 p8f^5 10m p7g^3 p8m p10g Nov 14] big, good-bodied filly: fair performer: claimed from R. Hannon £6,000 eighth start: stays 1m: acts on polytrack, soft and good to firm going: tried visored, usually blinkered: temperamental. *L. A. Dace* **73 §**

BROOMFIELD BUDDY 3 b.f. Reel Buddy (USA) 118 – Tancred Arms 73 (Clantime 101) [2009 –: 7m Apr 22] well held in maidens. *D. W. Barker* **–**

BROOMIELAW 5 ch.g. Rock of Gibraltar (IRE) 133 – Peony 108 (Lion Cavern (USA) 117) [2009 10g* 10m 12s p12.2g^6 Nov 20] tall, close-coupled, good-topped gelding: useful handicapper, very lightly raced (missed 2008): impressive comeback to win at Newmarket in August by neck from Laaheb: not at best after: stays 1¼m (not 1½m): acts on polytrack and good to firm ground. *E. A. L. Dunlop* **104**

BROOTOMMITTY (IRE) 2 b.f. (Mar 15) Azamour (IRE) 130 – Polyandry (IRE) 99 (Pennekamp (USA) 130) [2009 7.2s^4 Aug 26] £20,000Y: fourth foal: half-sister to 3-y-o Cause For Applause: dam 6f (at 2 yrs in France) to 9f (in USA) winner: 10/1, well held in maiden at Ayr, slowly away. *I. Semple* **–**

BROTHER BARRY (USA) 4 b. or br.g. Forestry (USA) 121 – Saratoga Sugar (USA) (Gone West (USA)) [2009 70: f8g^4 7m^3 5m May 25] medium-sized, good-bodied gelding: fair maiden: best short of 1m: acts on fibresand and good to firm ground. *G. A. Swinbank* **66**

BROTHER CHA (IRE) 3 ch.c. Indian Ridge 123 – Sun On The Sea (IRE) 109 (Bering 136) [2009 7m 7.1m* Aug 20] sturdy colt: type to carry condition: poor mover: first foal: dam 1¼m winner: better effort in maidens (fair form) when winning at Chepstow in August by length from Luc Jordan, still green: bred to stay 1m: capable of further progress. *M. G. Quinlan* **79 p**

BROUGHTON BECK (IRE) 3 ch.g. Distant Music (USA) 126 – Mauras Pride (IRE) (Cadeaux Genereux 131) [2009 55p: p10g^6 p9.5g^4 Feb 23] modest maiden: stays easy 1¼m: raced only on all-weather. *R. F. Fisher* **59**

BROUGHTONS DAY 2 b.g. (Apr 2) Mujahid (USA) 125 – Rainy Day Song 61 (Persian Bold 123) [2009 6m^6 Aug 15] half-brother to several winners, including 3-y-o Rainy Night and 1m/1¼m winner Broughton Spirit (by Bishop of Cashel): dam, maiden, half-sister to dam of 1000 Guineas second Princess Ellen: 100/1, not knocked about when sixth to Arabian Pride in maiden at Newmarket: will be suited by 7f+: capable of better. *W. J. Musson* **50 p**

BROUGHTONS FLIGHT (IRE) 4 ch.f. Hawk Wing (USA) 136 – Aldburgh (Bluebird (USA) 125) [2009 70d: p10g^2 p10g^3 p10g Jan 28] strong, lengthy filly: modest maiden handicapper: stays 1¼m: acts on polytrack and good to firm going. *W. J. Musson* **62**

BROUGHTONS PARADIS (IRE) 3 b.f. Royal Applause 124 – Amankila (IRE) 62 (Revoque (IRE) 122) [2009 50: p10g^2 8m^3 12g^2 11.5m* p12.2g^6 11.6d^3 10g^2 p12m^6 p12f^5 Dec 21] close-coupled filly: fair handicapper: won at Yarmouth in August: stays 1½m: acts on polytrack, good to firm and good to soft going. *W. J. Musson* **72**

BROUGHTONS POINT 3 b.f. Falbrav (IRE) 133 – Glowing Reference (Reference Point 139) [2009 10.1g^6 p8.6g p9.5g p10g Dec 7] half-sister to several winners, including 1996 2-y-o 7f winner White Hot (by Weldnaas), later minor stakes winner in USA, and 9f to 12.5f winner Westgate Run (by Emperor Jones): dam unraced close relative to King Edward VII Stakes winner Private Tender: little form. *W. J. Musson* **–**

BROUGHTONS SILK 4 b.f. Medicean 128 – Soviet Cry (Soviet Star (USA) 128) [2009 57: 8.3g p7.1g p8.6g 8s 8g* 8g^6 10.1g^5 p8.6g^6 p8g Oct 21] leggy filly: modest performer: won selling handicap at Yarmouth in August, easily best effort: stays 1m: best effort on good ground (unraced on firmer than good): sold 2,500 gns. *W. J. Musson* **64**

BROUHAHA 5 b.g. Bahhare (USA) 122 – Top of The Morning 56 (Keen 116) [2009 65: p9.5g* p8.6g* p9.5g* p9.5g p10g* p11g p8.6g* 8m p10g^6 p8g^2 10g^4 8.3v 9g^2 10m^2 p9.5g p8.6g p9.5m^2 p9.5g Dec 17] big, well-made gelding: fairly useful handicapper, better on all-weather: won at Wolverhampton (4, maiden first occasion) and Kempton between January and April: in-and-out form after: stays 1¼m: acts on polytrack, good to firm and good to soft going: tried in cheekpieces/tongue tie: has been withdrawn having caused trouble at stall. *Tom Dascombe* **86 a93**

BROWN LENTIC (IRE) 3 b.c. Invincible Spirit (IRE) 121 – Indienne (IRE) 69 (Indian Ridge 123) [2009 –: p5g* p5g^5 p5g^5 p5.1g p5.1g Apr 25] strong colt: poor performer: won handicap at Lingfield in January: raced only at 5f/6f: acts on polytrack. *Miss J. Feilden* **49**

BRUNELLESCHI 6 ch.g. Bertolini (USA) 125 – Petrovna (IRE) 78 (Petardia 113) [2009 85d: p6g* p6g* 6m* 6m 6m^2 p6g 6g* 6m^5 5g p7g 7g Oct 31] strong, compact gelding: has a quick action: fairly useful handicapper: successful at Lingfield and Kempton in March, Windsor in April and Newmarket in August: below form after, shaping as if amiss last 2 starts: stays 6f: acts on polytrack, firm and soft going: tried visored, usually blinkered: has hung left. *P. L. Gilligan* **88**

BRUNETTE (IRE) 2 br.f. (Feb 27) Camacho 118 – Hidden Agenda (FR) 55 (Machiavellian (USA) 123) [2009 6m p7g^2 p7g^2 8.1g^4 8m 9m 10.2m Sep 30] 30,000Y: good-topped filly: seventh foal: half-sister to 3 winners, including useful winners around 9f Regal Agenda and Sting Like A Bee (both by Ali-Royal): dam, maiden (stayed 11f), out of smart 7f/1m performer Ever Genial: fair maiden on polytrack, modest on turf: well held in nurseries: should stay 1m+: acts on polytrack: sold 3,000 gns. *R. Hannon* **53 a68**

BRUNSTON 3 gr.g. High Chaparral (IRE) 132 – Molly Mello (GER) 106 (Big Shuffle (USA) 122) [2009 72p: 8g^2 9.9m* 11d^5 11m* 12m 11.9m^4 Jul 4] good-topped gelding: fairly useful handicapper: won at Salisbury and Goodwood in May: good fourth final start (gelded after): stays 1½m: acts on good to firm and good to soft going. *R. Charlton* **92**

BRUSHING 3 ch.f. Medicean 128 – Seasonal Blossom (IRE) (Fairy King (USA)) [2009 –: 6g* 7.2g^6 Sep 17] big, workmanlike filly: off 11 months and 50/1, won maiden at Yarmouth in August: stays 7f: raced only on good ground. *M. H. Tompkins* **70**

betchronicle.com Ormonde Stakes, Chester—Buccellati wins a farcically slowly-run three-runner contest after which Johnny Murtagh, rider of odds-on Frozen Fire, is jeered by punters; Scintillo finishes second

BRUT 7 b.g. Mind Games 121 – Champenoise 64 (Forzando 122) [2009 79, a–: 5m 5m 6m^5 5f^6 5m 5g^3 5g^5 Jun 17] lengthy, good-topped gelding: modest handicapper nowadays: stays easy 7f, races mostly at 5f/6f: acts on fibresand, firm and soft going: tried visored, usually wears cheekpieces: usually races up with pace. *D. W. Barker* **63**

BRUTON STREET (USA) 3 b. or br.g. Dynaformer (USA) – Fit For A Queen (USA) 81 (Fit To Fight (USA)) [2009 65p: 10g^3 10g^4 10.2g^3 12g^5 10.2s^3 10.3g^2 12v* Nov 3] strong gelding: fairly useful performer: won maiden at Catterick in November by 10 lengths from Outrageous Request: stays 1½m: raced only on good going or softer (acts on heavy). *J. H. M. Gosden* **90**

BRYNFA BOY 3 b.g. Namid 128 – Funny Girl (IRE) 78 (Darshaan 133) [2009 53: 6g 6.1f 5.1g 6g^5 5m^2 5m^5 p5.1g* Dec 11] tall gelding: fair handicapper: improved to win at Wolverhampton (maiden) in December: may prove best at 5f: acts on polytrack and firm ground: tried tongue tied: quirky. *P. W. D'Arcy* **71**

BUACHAILL DONA (IRE) 6 b.g. Namid 128 – Serious Contender (IRE) (Tenby 125) [2009 114: 6.5g 6g p6g* 6g^6 5m 5d^2 6d 5g^2 5.4m 5.6m 5g^6 Sep 22] sturdy, deep-girthed gelding: smart performer: won minor event at Kempton in April: good efforts after when runner-up in handicaps at Newcastle (beaten neck by Pavershooz in Gosforth Park Cup) and Ascot (went down by 1½ lengths to Group Therapy): below form last 3 outings (bled first occasion): best at 5f/easy 6f: acts on polytrack, firm and good to soft going: usually makes running/races prominently: none too reliable. *D. Nicholls* **111**

BUAIL ISTEACH (IRE) 4 b.f. Acclamation 118 – Its All Eurs (IRE) 67 (Barathea (IRE) 127) [2009 –: p7.1g p7g^6 p7g 7m^5 7m 6m 8g Jul 14] modest maiden: stays 7f: raced on polytrack and good/good to firm going: blinkered last 3 starts. *E. J. Creighton* **52**

BUBBELAS 2 b.f. (Feb 6) Pastoral Pursuits 127 – Arctic High 62 (Polar Falcon (USA) 126) [2009 5g 6g* 6d^5 7d^6 6g 6m^4 Sep 21] £6,000Y: third foal: half-sister to 2006 2-y-o 5f winner Triple Shadow (by Compton Place): dam 8.5f winner: fair form: won maiden at Pontefract in June by neck from Angelena Ballerina: failed to progress, including in nurseries: stays 6f: acts on good to soft going, probably on good to firm. *J. J. Quinn* **64**

BUBBER (IRE) 2 b.f. (Apr 28) Westerner 130 – Bubble N Squeak (IRE) 91 (Catrail (USA) 123) [2009 6s^6 f7g^4 p6g Dec 18] third foal: half-sister to 3-y-o Mr Freddy and 5-y-o Singleb: dam Irish 9f to 2m winner: modest form in maidens, not knocked about final start: will be suited by 1m+: should do better. *R. A. Fahey* **59 p**

BUBBLY BELLINI (IRE) 2 b.g. (Apr 17) Mull of Kintyre (USA) 114 – Gwapa (IRE) 84 (Imperial Frontier (USA) 112) [2009 6m^6 5m^4 7m^5 6g^5 p7.1m^6 p6m^2 p6g* p6g^2 f5g* f7d^2 Dec 29] fair performer: won claimer at Wolverhampton and (having left A. Bailey after next start) seller at Southwell, both in December: stays 7f: acts on all-weather, probably on good to firm going: in cheekpieces last 3 starts, tending to wander last 2: consistent. *George Baker* **73**

BUBBLY BRAVEHEART (IRE) 2 b.g. (Feb 24) Cape Cross (IRE) 129 – Infinity (FR) (Bering 136) [2009 p6g 7.1m^5 7.1m^6 7d 8g^6 p8.6g^2 8.3d p8g^4 p8.6g^2 p8.6g* **67**

p9.5g^{6} Dec 12] close-coupled gelding: fair performer: won seller at Wolverhampton in December: stays 8.6f: acts on polytrack and good to firm going: sometimes blinkered/in cheekpieces. *A. Bailey*

BUBSES BOY 3 ch.g. Needwood Blade 117 – Welcome Home 55 (Most Welcome 131) **62** [2009 –p: 9.7d^{3} f11g p10g^{4} 10g 10.1g^{4} 10.1g* 16g^{5} p11g p12m^{6} 12m^{4} p12m p10g Nov 14] good-topped gelding: modest performer: won claimer at Yarmouth (left M. Bell £5,000) in August: stays 1½m: acts on polytrack, good to firm and good to soft going: not straightforward. *P. Howling*

BUCCELLATI 5 ch.h. Soviet Star (USA) 128 – Susi Wong (IRE) (Selkirk (USA) 129) **119** [2009 118: 10g^{3} 13.4m* 12g 12g^{4} 12m^{3} 12g Dec 13] close-coupled, quite attractive horse: smart performer: won farcical 3-runner betchronicle.com Ormonde Stakes at Chester in May by 3 lengths from Scintillo, rather forced into making running in race that developed into 3f sprint: badly hampered and finished lame in Coronation Cup at Epsom next time (then off over 3 months): best effort after when good 2½ lengths third to Champs Elysees in Canadian International at Woodbine, tending to hang left: not discredited when ninth to Daryakana in Hong Kong Vase at Sha Tin final outing: effective at 1¼m to easy 13.4f: acts on any turf going: blinkered/visored nowadays: sometimes races freely/carries head awkwardly: often waited with. *A. M. Balding*

BUCK CANNON (IRE) 4 b.g. High Chaparral (IRE) 132 – Folgore (USA) 83 (Irish **–** River (FR) 131) [2009 55: p8g Jan 6] sturdy gelding: modest maiden: looked temperamental sole 4-y-o start: stays 1m: raced on polytrack and good ground. *P. M. Phelan*

BUCKED OFF (SAF) 5 b.g. Casey Tibbs (IRE) 110 – See Me Fly (SAF) (Caesour **100 §** (USA) 110) [2009 a8.5g^{6} 10g^{4} 10g^{5} a9g^{3} 12m 10g^{4} 8m^{4} 10g Oct 10] sturdy gelding: useful performer: raced in South Africa from 2006 to 2008, winning once (maiden at Kenilworth) from 17 starts: ran in handicaps in UAE first 4 starts in 2009, creditable efforts on last 3, including when 5 lengths third to Military Power at Jebel Ali (left H. Brown after): best effort in Britain when fourth in handicap at Ascot penultimate start: stays 1¼m: raced mainly on good going: has raced freely: carries head very high, and not one to trust: sold 14,000 gns, sent to Germany. *T. P. Tate*

BUCKIE BOY (IRE) 3 b.g. Bahri (USA) 125 – Woodren (USA) 91 (Woodman (USA) **86** 126) [2009 10m^{4} 10f^{2} 10g^{4} 10.1g^{3} p10m^{5} p12m^{2} p12m* p13g^{3} 16d Oct 28] 35,000Y: medium-sized gelding: fifth foal: half-brother to Swedish winner up to 1½m Wings of A Dove (by Hernando): dam, Irish 2m winner, out of half-sister to Assert, Bikala and Eurobird: fairly useful performer: won maiden at Kempton in September: creditable third in handicap next time (final start for H. Cecil): stays 13f: acts on polytrack and firm going: blinkered/visored first 5 starts: gelded after final outing. *J. S. Goldie*

BUCKLE UP 3 ch.g. Primo Valentino (IRE) 116 – Ambitious 98 (Ardkinglass 114) **43** [2009 –: p6g^{5} p7g 5.1d f7g^{6} 9g 8.3m^{6} 8.3d^{4} 7s Jul 29] rather leggy, workmanlike gelding: poor maiden: stays 1m: tried in cheekpieces. *D. K. Ivory*

BUDDHIST MONK 4 b.g. Dr Fong (USA) 128 – Circle of Light 102 (Anshan 119) **90 §** [2009 95: 10.3g^{6} 10.1d^{3} 12.3m^{3} 14m^{3} 14m^{5} 16.1d 12g 16.4m 10f* 10g* 10m^{2} 10.4m* Sep 25] tall gelding: fairly useful performer: won claimers at Brighton and Leicester and seller at Haydock, all in September: stays 1¾m: acts on polytrack, firm and good to soft going: in cheekpieces/visor/tongue tie last 7 starts: tricky ride (can find little): sold 18,000 gns. *Ian Williams*

BUDDY HOLLY 4 b.g. Reel Buddy (USA) 118 – Night Symphonie (Cloudings (IRE) **84 §** 112) [2009 86: f11g^{3} 12d^{4} 10d^{3} p10g* 10d^{4} 10m 10s^{6} p8g 12m^{2} p12m Oct 12] good- **a89 §** topped gelding: fairly useful handicapper: won apprentice event at Kempton in June: stays 1½m: acts on polytrack, good to firm and soft ground, probably on fibresand: tried visored: front runner nowadays: temperamental (has carried head awkwardly), and not one to rely on. *Pat Eddery*

BUDDY MARVELLOUS (IRE) 3 ch.g. Redback 116 – La Paola (IRE) 68 **–** (Common Grounds 118) [2009 54: p7g p6g Jan 28] maiden: modest at 2 yrs: has gone wrong way: best efforts at 5f on good/good to firm going: tried in cheekpieces/blinkers. *R. A. Harris*

BUDS DILEMMA 5 b.m. Anabaa (USA) 130 – Lady Thynn (FR) (Crystal Glitters **45** (USA) 127) [2009 36: f7g^{4} p8g Mar 11] workmanlike mare: poor maiden: seems to stay 1¼m: tried blinkered. *S. Gollings*

BUDVA 2 b.c. (Jun 17) Kylian (USA) – Danlu (USA) (Danzig (USA)) [2009 f8m f8f^{3} **64** f8m Dec 5] best effort when third in minor event at Southwell, awkward under pressure: gelded after final start. *H. Morrison*

BUFFETT 2 b.c. (Feb 4) Bertolini (USA) 125 – Batik (IRE) 93 (Peintre Celebre (USA) 137) [2009 6m[6] 7m[5] 6m[5] p8m[4] Sep 23] good-topped colt: first foal: dam, 1¼m/1½m winner, half-sister to smart performer up to 2m Bauer: progressive maiden: fourth in nursery at Kempton, not unduly knocked about: will be suited by 1¼m: capable of further improvement. *L. M. Cumani* **69 p**

BUGAKU 4 ch.g. Montjeu (IRE) 137 – Bryony Brind (IRE) 105 (Kris 135) [2009 10g* p10g[3] 10d 10g[6] p11g[4] 14.6m 12g Oct 10] good-bodied gelding: useful performer: won maiden at Sandown in May: often looked moody in handicaps after, best efforts when in frame: should stay 1½m: acts on polytrack, unraced on extremes of going on turf: tongue tied (said to have had breathing problem) final start: ungenuine. *Sir Michael Stoute* **95 §**

BUGSY'S BOY 5 b.g. Double Trigger (IRE) 123 – Bugsy's Sister (Aragon 118) [2009 78: 16g[2] Oct 8] sturdy gelding: fair handicapper: stays 2¼m: acts on polytrack and soft going: effective with or without cheekpieces: fairly useful hurdler. *George Baker* **78**

BULBERRY HILL 8 b.g. Makbul 104 – Hurtleberry (IRE) 87 (Tirol 127) [2009 46: f14g f16g[6] Apr 21] poor handicapper: stays 2m: acts on all-weather, lightly raced on turf: tried tongue tied. *R. W. Price* **44**

BULELLA 3 b.f. Makbul 104 – Bella Tutrice (IRE) 78 (Woodborough (USA) 112) [2009 62: f6s[3] Jan 4] modest maiden: stays 6f: acts on all-weather and good to soft going. *Garry Moss* **61**

BULLET DUCK (IRE) 2 br. or gr.f. (Apr 22) Redback 116 – Helibel (IRE) 73 (Pivotal 124) [2009 6m 6.1s Oct 7] 1,500Y: leggy filly: second foal: dam, sprint maiden, half-sister to smart performer up to 9f Pentecost: soundly beaten in maidens: sold 1,500 gns. *Tom Dascombe* **–**

BULLET MAN (USA) 4 b. or br.g. Mr Greeley (USA) 122 – Silk Tapestry (USA) 77 (Tank's Prospect (USA)) [2009 94p: 10.1d[6] 10.2d[6] 10m* 10m[2] 12m 10m Aug 29] neat gelding: fairly useful handicapper: won at Newmarket (dictated) in May: progressed again but looked rather awkward (slow to break/flashed tail under pressure) when runner-up at Pontefract: shaped as if amiss last 2 starts (gelded after): stays 1¼m: acts on polytrack, good to firm and good to soft ground. *L. M. Cumani* **94**

BULLET TRAIN 2 b.c. (Jan 28) Sadler's Wells (USA) 132 – Kind (IRE) 112 (Danehill (USA) 126) [2009 8d* Oct 27] first foal: dam, 5f to 7f winner, half-sister to high-class 1¼m to 1¾m performer Powerscourt (by Sadler's Wells): 2/1 favourite, highly promising when winning maiden at Yarmouth by short head from Lion Mountain (pair clear), travelling best, then looking green and coaxed home: should stay 1¼m: useful prospect. *H. R. A. Cecil* **86 p**

BULL MARKET (IRE) 6 b.g. Danehill (USA) 126 – Paper Moon (IRE) 92 (Lake Coniston (IRE) 131) [2009 84: p8.6g[3] p9.5g 12d p13.9g p8g p12.2g[2] Nov 21] big, strong gelding: fair handicapper nowadays: left Ian Williams after second start: stays 1½m: acts on all-weather and good to firm ground: free-going sort. *M. S. Tuck* **76**

BULWARK (IRE) 7 b.g. Montjeu (IRE) 137 – Bulaxie 110 (Bustino 136) [2009 108§: 16.4m[6] 21.7m[6] 14m 16g[5] 18m 16g p16.5g Nov 14] good-bodied gelding: has reportedly had breathing operation: just fairly useful handicapper in 2009, let down by temperament: stays 2¼m: acts on polytrack, firm and soft going: usually blinkered/visored: ungenuine. *Ian Williams* **84 §**

BUMBLE ROSE (IRE) 6 b.m. Kornado 120 – Bukowina (GER) (Windwurf (GER)) [2009 12.5m 10.1s[6] 9.2g 9.1m[5] 12.1g Jun 17] modest form in bumpers/let down by jumping over hurdles for Lucinda Russell: little form on Flat: often in cheekpieces. *A. G. Foster* **–**

BUNDLE UP 6 b.m. Diktat 126 – Bundle (Cadeaux Genereux 131) [2009 61: p11g 12m[6] 11.9g[6] p16.5g Oct 17] workmanlike mare: modest performer at 5 yrs: well held on Flat in 2009 (left P. D. Evans after second start), but won 3 times over hurdles (modest form). *J. L. Flint* **–**

BUNGIE 5 gr.g. Forzando 122 – Sweet Whisper 63 (Petong 126) [2009 51: p7.1g Jan 12] leggy, useful-looking gelding: modest performer: no show sole Flat outing in 2009: seems to stay 7f: acts on all-weather and good to soft ground: tried blinkered/visored. *Jennie Candlish* **–**

BUN OIR (USA) 2 b. or br.c. (May 9) Seeking The Gold (USA) – Fraulein 117 (Acatenango (GER) 127) [2009 7m 7g 7g 8.3d Oct 12] quite good-topped colt: modest form in maidens/nursery: should be suited by 1m. *R. Hannon* **61**

BUN PENNY 3 ch.f. Bertolini (USA) 125 – Mint Royale (IRE) 44 (Cadeaux Genereux 131) [2009 –: 7.5g 5.9m Jun 15] no form. *G. M. Moore* **–**

BUREAUCRAT 7 b.g. Machiavellian (USA) 123 – Lajna 88 (Be My Guest (USA) 126) [2009 97: 12g 14g 13.3m Aug 14] good-bodied gelding: fairly useful handicapper, including over jumps: stays 1½m: acts on good to firm ground: tried in cheekpieces: joined M. F. Harris. *P. J. Hobbs* **92**

BURGAU ROYAL 2 b.c. (Apr 9) Noverre (USA) 125 – Regal Ransom (IRE) (Anabaa (USA) 130) [2009 6g^4 6m^2 6m^2 Aug 29] smallish colt: fair form: best efforts when second in maiden at Lingfield and minor event at Windsor: was bred to stay 7f: withdrawn after unruly in stall intended second outing: dead. *M. R. Channon* **75**

BURGUNDY ICE (USA) 3 gr. or ro.f. Storm Cat (USA) – Cara Rafaela (USA) 117 (Quiet American (USA)) [2009 92p: 8.1m^2 8m 8m^3 p8f* f8f^2 Oct 21] good-topped filly: fluent mover: useful handicapper: won at Kempton in October: creditable second at Southwell week later: stays 1m, will prove as effective back at 7f: acts on all-weather and good to firm ground: reportedly had breathing problem at 2 yrs: has left Godolphin. *Saeed bin Suroor* **96**

BURJ NAHAR 2 b.c. (Mar 18) Shamardal (USA) 129 – Melikah (IRE) 116 (Lammtarra (USA) 134) [2009 8.3v* Nov 4] sturdy, attractive colt: fourth foal: half-brother to useful French 7f (at 2 yrs)/1¼m winner Valedictory (by Dubai Destination) and fairly useful 1¼m/11f winner Villarrica (by Selkirk): dam, 1¼m winner (placed in Oaks/Irish Oaks), half-sister to Galileo and Sea The Stars, out of Prix de l'Arc de Triomphe winner Urban Sea: 11/8 on, created most favourable impression when winning maiden at Nottingham by 3¾ lengths from Molon Labe, cruising clear final 2f: will be suited by 1¼m+: already useful, and sure to go on to much better things. *Saeed bin Suroor* **97 P**

BURMA ROCK (IRE) 3 b.g. Danehill Dancer (IRE) 117 – Burmese Princess (USA) 64 (King of Kings (IRE) 125) [2009 76: 7m^3 8g^4 7.1g^5 8.1m^4 p9.5g^2 p10m* Oct 26] stocky gelding: type to carry condition: fairly useful performer: improved to win handicap at Kempton in October, idling: gelded after: stays 1¼m: acts on polytrack, soft and good to firm ground. *L. M. Cumani* **87**

BURNBANK (IRE) 6 ch.g. Danehill Dancer (IRE) 117 – Roseau 75 (Nashwan (USA) 135) [2009 –: p12.2g Feb 14] lengthy gelding: fair maiden at 3 yrs: lightly raced and no recent form on Flat (thought to have gone lame sole start in 2009). *J. M. Jefferson* **–**

BURNBRAKE 4 b.g. Mujahid (USA) 125 – Duena (Grand Lodge (USA) 125) [2009 74: p8g^6 p10g^5 10d p8m^4 p8m^5 p8m Nov 4] strong gelding: fair handicapper: stays 1¼m: acts on polytrack, best efforts on turf on good ground: visored last 2 starts. *L. Montague Hall* **66**

BURNETT (IRE) 2 b.c. (Mar 20) Dynaformer (USA) – Secret Garden (IRE) 106 (Danehill (USA) 126) [2009 8d* 7v Oct 24] 165,000F, 460,000Y: third foal: half-brother to useful 2008 2-y-o 6f winner Weatherstaff (by Elusive Quality): dam, 7f to 8.5f (in USA) winner, out of half-sister to Gold Cup winner Gildoran: green, won maiden at Newcastle in October easily by 4 lengths from Pytheas: testing conditions, ran no sort of race in Horris Hill Stakes at Newbury (favourite) next time: should stay 1¼m: looked useful prospect on debut. *Saeed bin Suroor* **91 +**

BURNING INCENSE (IRE) 6 b.g. Namid 128 – Night Scent (IRE) 85 (Scenic 128) [2009 95: 5d 7d p7.1g^6 6d Oct 13] big, strong gelding: useful handicapper at best: on long losing run, and well below form in 2009: has worn blinkers/cheekpieces: sold 1,200 gns. *M. Dods* **–**

BURNING THREAD (IRE) 2 b.g. (Mar 8) Captain Rio 122 – Desert Rose (Green Desert (USA) 127) [2009 p6g Dec 3] 20/1, slowly away and always behind in maiden at Wolverhampton. *T. J. Etherington* **–**

BURNS NIGHT 3 ch.c. Selkirk (USA) 129 – Night Frolic 68 (Night Shift (USA)) [2009 7m^6 8.5m* 8.5m^3 8g^2 8.5g^4 8m 10.1m p9.5g^5 10g Oct 19] 210,000Y: sturdy, useful-looking colt: first foal: dam, 1m winner, half-sister to useful French/US performer up to 10.5f Miss Caerleona, herself dam of smart 1m/9f performer Karen's Caper: fairly useful performer: won maiden at Beverley in June: should stay 1¼m: acts on good to firm going: blinkered sixth start: temperament under suspicion: sold £11,000. *M. Johnston* **85**

BURNT CREAM 2 b.f. (Apr 9) Exceed And Excel (AUS) 126 – Basbousate Nadia 92 (Wolfhound (USA) 126) [2009 5d^4 5g^4 Sep 22] £7,000Y, £60,000 2-y-o: good-bodied filly: third foal: half-sister to 4-y-o Albaqaa: dam 2-y-o 5f winner: modest form when fourth in maiden/minor event (to Coolminx at Beverley, travelling well) over 4 months apart. *B. Smart* **61**

BURNWYND BOY 4 b.g. Tobougg (IRE) 125 – Cadeau Speciale 54 (Cadeaux Genereux 131) [2009 111?: 6m 7m 6g 6g 6g 6m^3 6g Sep 20] tall, good-topped gelding: smart **85**

performer at 3 yrs: fairly useful at best in 2009: stays 7f: acts on good to firm and good to soft going: tried in headgear: inconsistent: joined J. McShane. *D. Nicholls*

BURTONDALE BOY (IRE) 2 b.g. (Feb 9) Shinko Forest (IRE) – Irish Moss (USA) (Irish River (FR) 131) [2009 5m 5f 6m 5g f5g 5g Oct 6] workmanlike gelding: no form: tried in cheekpieces. *P. T. Midgley* **–**

BURY ST EDMUNDS 2 ch.c. (Feb 8) Zafeen (FR) 123 – Naivety 78 (Machiavellian (USA) 123) [2009 7d 5.1g^5 8.3m^4 7g f8m p9.5g Dec 12] poor maiden: stays 8.3f. *A. G. Newcombe* **41**

BURY TREASURE (IRE) 4 ch.g. Choisir (AUS) 126 – Future Treasure 88 (Habitat 134) [2009 58, a68: p10g f8g Feb 1] good-quartered gelding: fair handicapper on all-weather at 3 yrs: modest at best in 2009: stays 8.6f: acts on polytrack and good to soft ground: tried in cheekpieces. *Miss Gay Kelleway* **54**

BURZA 3 ch.f. Bold Edge 123 – Welcome Star (IRE) (Most Welcome 131) [2009 p8.6g* p8.6g^5 7m 8.3m^3 10m* 10s^5 10.2g 9g^3 8.3g Sep 14] smallish filly: third foal: dam unraced: fair performer: won maiden at Wolverhampton in February and handicap at Newbury in June: stays 1¼m: acts on soft and good to firm going. *J. Mackie* **78**

BUSCADOR (USA) 10 ch.g. Crafty Prospector (USA) – Fairway Flag (USA) (Fairway Phantom (USA)) [2009 –, a69: p9.5g^2 p9.5g p9.5g^5 p13.9g^4 p13.9g p12.2g^3 p9.5g^5 p12.2g^5 Apr 25] fair performer on all-weather, unraced on turf since 2006: stays easy 13.8f: acts on all-weather, had form on soft and good to firm ground earlier in career: reportedly finished lame sixth start: races prominently. *W. M. Brisbourne* **–** **a66**

BUSHMAN 5 gr.g. Maria's Mon (USA) 121 – Housa Dancer (FR) 109 (Fabulous Dancer (USA) 124) [2009 114: 10g 10.3m^6 8m 8d^5 8g* 8.1v^2 9m 8g^3 Oct 31] well-made gelding: smart performer: won minor event at Newmarket in August by 4 lengths from Kay Gee Bee: good efforts when placed in listed races after, 1½ lengths second to Confront at Haydock and ½-length third to Prince of Dance at Newmarket: raced at 1m/1¼m: acts on heavy and good to firm going. *D. M. Simcock* **112**

BUSH MASTER 2 b.g. (Feb 27) Hunting Lion (IRE) 115 – Patandon Girl (IRE) 66 (Night Shift (USA)) [2009 5m 6g p7g^2 6m^3 5g^2 7f^6 6m^4 p5g^2 5g p6f p5g^4 p7m p6m^6 Dec 6] 2,500F, £18,000Y: workmanlike gelding: second foal: dam 6f winner: fair maiden: left D. Ivory after debut, R. Hannon (sold 13,500 gns) after tenth start: stays 6f: acts on polytrack and good to firm ground: not straightforward. *J. R. Boyle* **73**

BUSHRANGER (IRE) 3 b.c. Danetime (IRE) 121 – Danz Danz (Efisio 120) [2009 119: 6v^4 6m 6d Sep 5] smallish, good-bodied colt: smart 2-y-o in 2008, winning 4 times, including Prix Morny at Deauville and Middle Park Stakes at Newmarket: below that level in 2009, in Greenlands Stakes at the Curragh (fourth to Utmost Respect, hanging left), Golden Jubilee Stakes at Royal Ascot (visored/sweating when eleventh behind Art Connoisseur, hanging right) and Sprint Cup at Haydock (ninth to Regal Parade): raced mainly at 6f: acted on firm going: to stand at Tally-Ho Stud, Co Westmeath, Ireland, fee €7,500. *David Wachman, Ireland* **105**

BUSH TUCKER (IRE) 2 b.c. (May 13) Choisir (AUS) 126 – Queen's Victory 93 (Mujadil (USA) 119) [2009 5m^2 p5g^2 5.1m* 6m^3 Sep 9] €23,000Y: strong colt: third foal: dam 2-y-o 5f winner: fairly useful performer: won maiden at Bath in August by 2½ lengths from Gooseberry Bush: good third to Radio City in nursery at Epsom, again free (also unbalanced on hill): may prove best at 5f: sent to Hong Kong, where renamed Horse Galore. *P. Winkworth* **86**

BUSHVELD (IRE) 3 b.c. Cape Cross (IRE) 129 – Gold Sunrise (USA) 108 (Forty Niner (USA)) [2009 86p: p10g^2 p8g^2 Jan 28] fairly useful performer: good second in handicaps both starts in 2009: barely stays 1¼m: acts on polytrack: sold £12,500 in August. *M. Johnston* **86**

BUSHY DELL (IRE) 4 br.f. King Charlemagne (USA) 120 – Nisibis (In The Wings 128) [2009 81: p13g 12.1g^5 p12.2g^5 12g 11.6m^5 p13.9g* p13.9g f14d^5 Dec 29] lengthy filly: fair performer: won handicap at Wolverhampton in September: stays 1¾m: acts on polytrack. *Miss J. Feilden* **76**

BUSINESS AS USUAL 2 b.c. (Feb 6) Invincible Spirit (IRE) 121 – Lesgor (USA) 106 (Irish River (FR) 131) [2009 7m* p8g^2 Oct 14] seventh foal: closely related to French 2002 2-y-o 7f winner Lavinia's Grace (by Green Desert) and half-brother to useful 2005 2-y-o 7f (stayed 13f) winner Guilia (by Galileo): dam French 1¼m winner: won maiden at Yarmouth in September by 2¼ lengths from Govern, with subsequent winners behind: similar form when second of 3 to Fareej in minor event at Lingfield: should stay 1¼m: capable of better. *M. A. Jarvis* **87 p**

BUSINESS CLASS (BRZ) 4 b.g. Thignon Lafre (BRZ) – Dioner (BRZ) (Rotioner (BRZ)) [2009 54p: f8g^3 7g^3 7s 7.5g 8m 7m^3 f8g* 9d^5 f8g^4 Nov 17] fair performer: won handicap at Southwell in September: stays 1m: acts on fibresand and good to soft going: gelded. *D. Nicholls* **72**

BUSINESSMAN 2 b.c. (Feb 12) Acclamation 118 – Venus Rising (Observatory (USA) 131) [2009 6m* 6g Aug 31] tall, angular colt: won maiden at York in August: reportedly suffered stress fracture to pelvis in listed race at Ripon: dead. *M. Johnston* **82**

BUSSELL ALONG (IRE) 3 b.f. Mujadil (USA) 119 – Waaedah (USA) 81 (Halling (USA) 133) [2009 55p: 7m 7m^3 9.8m^4 10.1d^3 Jul 21] modest maiden: should stay 1½m: acts on soft and good to firm going. *M. L. W. Bell* **52**

BUSTAN (IRE) 10 b.g. Darshaan 133 – Dazzlingly Radiant 81 (Try My Best (USA) 130) [2009 89: 8.1g^3 8.5m 10f 8.1m 8g 8g 9m Aug 27] strong gelding: fairly useful handicapper: creditable third at Sandown: below form after, including in seller: effective at 7f to 1½m: acts on polytrack, firm and soft going: blinkered (raced freely) once, in cheekpieces last 2 starts. *G. C. Bravery* **82 d**

BUSTARD BAY (IRE) 2 b.g. (Apr 15) Footstepsinthesand 120 – Toy Show (IRE) 86 (Danehill (USA) 126) [2009 5.1g^5 7d 7g^5 7g 6.1s Oct 7] deep-girthed gelding: modest maiden: no improvement in nurseries: stays 7f. *J. G. Given* **52**

BUSTER HYVONEN (IRE) 7 b.g. Dansili 127 – Serotina (IRE) 73 (Mtoto 134) [2009 99: p11g p16g Mar 28] well-made gelding: just fairly useful handicapper in 2009: stays easy 2m: raced on all-weather and good/good to firm going: can take good hold. *J. R. Fanshawe* **85**

BUTCH AND SUNDANCE 2 b.g. (Feb 25) Captain Rio 122 – Be My Wish 80 (Be My Chief (USA) 122) [2009 6g 6s* 7d^6 7g^2 6m 8m^3 8g Oct 23] £20,000Y: good-topped gelding: fifth foal: half-brother to 15.4f winner Himba (by Vettori): dam 6f/7f winner: fairly useful performer: won maiden at Yarmouth in July by short head from Kings Bayonet: ran well when placed in nurseries: stays 1m: acts on soft and good to firm ground: blinkered (ran poorly) fifth/final starts: sold 20,000 gns. *B. J. Meehan* **88**

BUTE STREET 4 b.g. Superior Premium 122 – Hard To Follow (Dilum (USA) 115) [2009 11.7m p9.5g p13.9g^3 p16.5g* p16.5g Oct 30] modest performer: won handicap at Wolverhampton in October: stays 2m: acts on polytrack. *R. J. Hodges* **58**

BUTSTILLITMOVES (IRE) 3 b.f. Galileo (IRE) 134 – Deuxieme (IRE) 74 (Second Empire (IRE) 124) [2009 p10g^6 Mar 19] €48,000Y, 48,000 2-y-o: first foal: dam, 6f winner, closely related to smart performer up to 9f King's County: 11/1, green in maiden at Kempton: sold 2,500 gns in July, sent to Greece. *J. H. M. Gosden* **56**

BUXTON 5 b.g. Auction House (USA) 120 – Dam Certain (IRE) 61 (Damister (USA) 123) [2009 85, a97: 6d^2 6g 7m 6g 7g 7g^6 6m^4 p6g^3 p7g p7m^5 p8g Oct 8] close-coupled gelding: fairly useful handicapper: good second on reappearance: below form after: effective at 6f to 1m: acts on polytrack, firm and good to soft ground: tried blinkered: tongue tied. *R. Ingram* **89 d**

BUY ON THE RED 8 b.g. Komaite (USA) – Red Rosein 97 (Red Sunset 120) [2009 80: 7m 7m^2 6g^3 5m 5m* 5.9g 5g^6 6g 5s^6 5g p5m* p5f^2 Dec 19] tall, quite good-topped gelding: fairly useful handicapper: won at Leicester (ladies) in June and Lingfield (seller) in December: form up to 7f, best at 5f nowadays: acts on polytrack and firm going: usually wears headgear: races prominently. *D. Nicholls* **81**

BUZZ BIRD 2 b.f. (Mar 27) Danbird (AUS) – Ashtaroute (USA) 60 (Holy Bull (USA) 134) [2009 7d 7m 6m 8m Sep 23] good-bodied filly: second foal: dam, maiden (stayed 1½m), half-sister to 6f/7f performer Sleeping Weapon and 1m/1¼m winner Glen Nevis, both smart: poor form in maidens/nursery. *T. D. Barron* **44**

BUZZWORD 2 b.c. (Apr 5) Pivotal 124 – Bustling 106 (Danehill (USA) 126) [2009 6m^2 6m* 6g^2 7.1g^2 7g* 7g^3 7m^5 8f^5 Nov 7] sturdy colt: type to carry condition: fourth foal: dam, French 9.5f (at 2 yrs) to 1½m winner, half-sister to grandam of 4-y-o Lush Lashes out of half-sister to Prix de l'Arc de Triomphe winner Saumarez: useful performer: won maiden at Windsor (easily) in July and Prix La Rochette at Longchamp (beat Siyouni 1½ lengths, making most) in September: creditable efforts after in Prix Jean-Luc Lagardere at Longchamp (2 lengths third to Siyouni), Dewhurst Stakes at Newmarket (2½ lengths fifth to Beethoven) and Breeders' Cup Juvenile Turf at Santa Anita (2½ lengths fifth to Pounced, staying on well): will be suited by 1¼m: acts on firm going. *Saeed bin Suroor* **109**

BY COMMAND 4 b.g. Red Ransom (USA) – Rafha 123 (Kris 135) [2009 96: 10m 10m^5 10d^4 10.2g^6 12s^3 10m^4 8.1g 8.3m 10.1d^3 p9.5g 9.9g^4 p10g^4 Oct 21] sturdy gelding: fairly useful performer: regressed gradually during 2009: stays 1¼m: acts on good to firm going: tried blinkered/in cheekpieces: has pulled hard: sold 10,500 gns, joined K. Ryan. *J. W. Hills* **80**

BY REQUEST 3 b.f. Giant's Causeway (USA) 132 – Approach 105 (Darshaan 133) [2009 8g 11.7g^6 Sep 7] strong filly: first foal: dam, 7.5f (at 2 yrs) to 1¼m winner, half-sister to very smart miler Aussie Rules, out of Nassau and Sun Chariot Stakes winner Last Second: better effort in maidens when sixth at Bath, not handling bend: bred to be suited by 1¼m+. *Sir Mark Prescott* **64**

BYRON BAY 7 b.g. My Best Valentine 122 – Candarela 41 (Damister (USA) 123) [2009 77d: f12g 16.1d 12.4s f8g* 8d 8d f8m^2 8d^3 8m^4 f8g^5 10g f7m Nov 12] tall, leggy gelding: modest handicapper nowadays, better on all-weather: won at Southwell in June: stays 1¼m: acts on any going, though best recent efforts on fibresand: tried in cheekpieces/visor: often makes running: sometimes looks awkward. *R. Johnson* **50 a62**

BY THE WIND (IRE) 3 b.g. Iron Mask (USA) 117 – Macha Rua (IRE) 57 (Eagle Eyed (USA) 111) [2009 f5g p5g p5.1g Aug 10] no form in maidens. *T. J. Etherington* **–**

C

CABAL 2 b.f. (Feb 16) Kyllachy 129 – Secret Flame 78 (Machiavellian (USA) 123) [2009 p7.1g^2 Nov 13] second foal: half-sister to 3-y-o Double Act: dam, 9f winner, closely related to dam of high-class miler Excellent Art: 7/1, promising 1½ lengths second to Bronze Prince in maiden at Wolverhampton: likely to improve. *Sir Michael Stoute* **77 p**

CABARET (IRE) 2 b.f. (May 4) Galileo (IRE) 134 – Witch of Fife (USA) 91 (Lear Fan (USA) 130) [2009 7m^2 7s* 7d* 8g Oct 4] €300,000Y: quite attractive filly: half-sister to 3 winners, notably smart Hong Kong performer up to 1m Ho Choi (by Pivotal), 6f winner in Britain at 2 yrs, and 5-y-o Drumfire: dam 2-y-o 6f/7f winner: useful performer: won maiden at the Curragh in June and Silver Flash Stakes at Leopardstown (by 4½ lengths from Alshahbaa, making all and clear over 1f out) in July: saddle seemed to slip when tailed off in Prix Marcel Boussac at Longchamp after 2½-month break (reportedly missed race previous week with slight allergy): should be suited by 1m. *A. P. O'Brien, Ireland* **105**

CABERNET SAUVIGNON 3 br.g. Dansili 127 – Halcyon Daze 82 (Halling (USA) 133) [2009 79p: 7.1m 8.3m^6 8m^2 8.5m^5 8f^3 p7g^6 8g p7.1g Dec 12] rangy, attractive gelding: fair maiden: left J. Hills 13,000 gns after fifth start: stays 1m: acts on polytrack, raced only on good ground or firmer on turf: tried blinkered/tongue tied. *Gordon Elliott, Ireland* **73**

CABOPINO (IRE) 4 ch.f. Captain Rio 122 – Fey Rouge (IRE) (Fayruz 116) [2009 58: f6g f5g^5 Feb 1] modest maiden: stays 7f: raced on all-weather and good ground: sold 2,000 gns. *K. R. Burke* **52**

CACTUS CURTSEY 3 b.f. Royal Applause 124 – Prairie Flower (IRE) (Zieten (USA) 118) [2009 7g^3 8d 8m^5 p6m 7g Aug 28] lengthy, useful-looking filly: has scope: first foal: dam useful French 1m (at 2 yrs) and 1½m winner (stayed 15f): modest maiden: seems to stay 1m: tried tongue tied. *J. R. Fanshawe* **54**

CACTUS KING 6 b.g. Green Desert (USA) 127 – Apache Star 96 (Arazi (USA) 135) [2009 90: p7g^5 p8g 10g^3 p10g^6 p12g Jun 6] big, strong gelding: fair performer at best in 2009: stays 1¼m: acts on polytrack, soft and good to firm ground: tried in cheekpieces/ blinkers: not straightforward. *P. M. Phelan* **76**

CADEAUX FAX 4 ch.g. Largesse 112 – Facsimile 67 (Superlative 118) [2009 –: 8.1m^5 8m 7s^4 8.1g^2 8.1m 7.1d* 7.1d^3 7m^2 p8m* 8.3g^5 Oct 19] fair handicapper: won at Chepstow in August and Kempton in October: stays 1m: acts on polytrack, good to firm and good to soft ground. *B. R. Millman* **74**

CADLEY ROAD (IRE) 2 b.c. (Mar 7) Elusive City (USA) 117 – Rouge Noir (USA) (Saint Ballado (CAN)) [2009 7m^3 7.1m* 7m^2 8g^6 7v^6 Oct 24] €110,000Y: third foal: half-brother to useful 2008 2-y-o 5f winner Light The Fire (by Invincible Spirit) and French 11.5f winner Blanc Sur Blanc (by Hold That Tiger): dam, US 6f winner, out of useful Italian miler Ardana: useful performer: won maiden at Sandown in July in good style by 2½ lengths from High Twelve: creditable efforts after, sixth to Carnaby Street in **98**

Horris Hill Stakes at Newbury (again made running) final start: barely stays 1m, and worth a try at 6f: acts on heavy and good to firm ground. *R. Hannon*

CADRE (IRE) 4 b.g. King's Best (USA) 132 – Desert Frolic (IRE) 94 (Persian Bold 123) [2009 96p: p7g 8m* 8.1m6 8m 8g4 8.1d3 7m Sep 26] tall gelding: useful performer: won handicap at Yarmouth (beat Tartan Gigha 3¼ lengths) in May: good 2¼ lengths third to Bankable in listed event at Sandown sixth start: stays 1m: acts on polytrack, good to soft and good to firm going: has joined Godolphin. *J. H. M. Gosden* **104**

CAERLAVEROCK (IRE) 4 br.g. Statue of Liberty (USA) 115 – Daziyra (IRE) (Doyoun 124) [2009 12.4g5 11.1g* 12d3 12g3 16.4d Jun 12] big gelding: fairly useful bumper winner: similar form on Flat: won maiden at Hamilton in May: should stay 1¾m: acts on good to soft going: blinkered last 2 starts: signs of temperament. *G. A. Swinbank* **86**

CAERUS (USA) 3 b.c. Greatness (USA) – Bellewood (USA) (Alydar (USA)) [2009 75: p8g 6g6 7m6 8m 7m3 a8g* a5.5g* 6g5 a8g2 a8g* a8g3 Nov 20] angular colt: fair performer: left W. Knight 9,000 gns after fifth start: won minor events at Ovrevoll in August and September and Taby in November: effective at 5.5f to 1m: acts on dirt/polytrack and good to firm going: tried visored. *K. E. Swartling, Norway* **65 a75**

CAFE FIORE (IRE) 3 b.f. Clodovil (IRE) 116 – Carpet Lover (IRE) 46 (Fayruz 116) [2009 54: f5d Jan 8] maiden: well beaten only start in 2009: stays 6f: acts on polytrack: tried visored/blinkered. *T. J. Pitt* **–**

CAFE GRECO 2 b.g. (Feb 13) Red Ransom (USA) – Mocca (IRE) 99 (Sri Pekan (USA) 117) [2009 7m2 7d4 p8m p7.1g5 p8m 8.3d4 Oct 12] sturdy gelding: first foal: dam 1m (at 2 yrs)/1¼m winner: fair maiden: no improvement in nurseries: should be suited by 1m+: acts on polytrack, good to firm and good to soft going: tried visored: got worked up and walked to post third start: sold 7,000 gns. *P. J. Makin* **71**

CAKE (IRE) 4 b.f. Acclamation 118 – Carpet Lady (IRE) 70 (Night Shift (USA)) [2009 98: 5.2s 5g* 5m2 5g 6d5 5m 5.4m 5m Sep 12] small, strong filly: useful handicapper: won at Goodwood in May by ½ length from Little Pete: good second to Piscean there next time: below form subsequently: best at 5f: acts on polytrack and good to firm going, probably on heavy. *R. Hannon* **100**

CAKE STAND 3 b.g. Haafhd 129 – Galette 94 (Caerleon (USA) 132) [2009 –: 7g 8m5 8s p7f6 7m p8f Oct 14] small, stocky gelding: modest maiden: stayed 1m: acted on polytrack and good to firm going: visored last 3 starts: dead. *J. A. R. Toller* **54**

CALABAZA 7 ch.g. Zaha (CAN) 106 – Mo Stopher 47 (Sharpo 132) [2009 65, a47: 6g 5m Jul 13] strong gelding: modest at 6 yrs: little form in 2009. *M. J. Attwater* **–**

CALAHONDA 3 ch.f. Haafhd 129 – Californie (IRE) (Rainbow Quest (USA) 134) [2009 91: 7s 6m5 p6g6 p6g 7g p7g4 f8g* Aug 25] rather leggy, attractive filly: fairly useful handicapper: dropped in weights, won at Southwell in August: effective at 6f to 1m: acts on all-weather, good to firm and good to soft going: tried in cheekpieces. *P. W. D'Arcy* **89**

CALALOO (IRE) 3 b.g. Dansili 127 – Maraami 83 (Selkirk (USA) 129) [2009 86: 8.3g 11.6g3 p12g3 p12.2g4 10.9g5 10m2 10m5 p12g 11.7g Oct 21] useful-looking gelding: fairly useful handicapper: stays 1½m: acts on polytrack, firm and soft ground: blinkered last 5 starts: sold 2,000 gns. *C. R. Egerton* **83**

CALATRAVA CAPE (IRE) 2 b. or br.f. (Feb 12) Cape Cross (IRE) 129 – Pershaan (IRE) 92 (Darshaan 133) [2009 7g5 7d 7m 8m6 8m2 Sep 24] unfurnished filly: second foal: half-sister 3-y-o Tinkerbelle: dam, 1½m winner (stayed 2m), half-sister to smart performer up to 1½m Persian Lightning: fair maiden: good second to In The Slips in nursery at Pontefract: will be suited by 1¼m+: should continue to progress. *J. L. Dunlop* **76 p**

CALCULATING (IRE) 5 b.g. Machiavellian (USA) 123 – Zaheemah (USA) 96 (El Prado (IRE) 119) [2009 85, a93: p16g6 p16g4 f14g4 p16g p16g5 p13.9g4 f14g2 f14g* 15.4g p13.9g3 16g3 16g p16g4 p16g2 p16g3 16d 12g* 14g3 p16g4 p13.9g* p16.5g3 f16m* f14d Dec 29] strong, attractive gelding: fair handicapper nowadays, better on all-weather: won at Southwell in March, Epsom in July, Wolverhampton in November and Southwell in December: stays 2m: acts on all-weather, good to firm and good to soft going: tried tongue tied/in cheekpieces: held up: signs of temperament. *M. D. I. Usher* **65 a76**

CALCULUS AFFAIR (IRE) 2 b.c. (Mar 10) Trans Island 119 – Where's Charlotte 53 (Sure Blade (USA) 130) [2009 p7m4 p7g5 Dec 31] 35,000F, 55,000Y: sixth foal: brother to 7-y-o Bond City and half-brother to 3 winners, including 6-y-o Quince: dam sprint maiden: better effort in maidens when encouraging fourth at Lingfield on debut: still green next time: remains open to improvement. *J. Noseda* **59 p**

CALDERCRUIX (USA) 2 ch.c. (May 25) Rahy (USA) 115 – Al Theraab (USA) 81 (Roberto (USA) 131) [2009 7m 7g 7g^3 Oct 23] $140,000Y: good-topped colt: closely related to French 1m winner Ebdaa (by Nashwan) and half-brother to several winners, including smart Irish 2004 2-y-o 1m winner Albert Hall (by Danehill), later successful in South Africa, and 9-y-o Flighty Fellow: dam 1m winner: easily best effort in maidens when third to Tamaathul at Doncaster: likely to stay 1m: should progress again. *T. P. Tate* **76 p**

CALDERMUD (IRE) 2 ch.c. (Jan 9) Chineur (FR) 123 – Dalal 63 (Cadeaux Genereux 131) [2009 6m^5 p6g Sep 9] well-made colt: better effort in maidens when fifth to Marcus Cicero at Windsor. *J. R. Best* **66**

CALDERS 2 b.f. (Apr 29) Monsieur Bond (IRE) 120 – Delicious 51 (Dominion 123) [2009 5m 6d 6m Aug 8] half-sister to 11-y-o Fantasy Believer: dam maiden (stayed 1¾m): well beaten in maidens/seller. *A. Berry* **–**

CALEDONIA PRINCESS 3 b.f. Kyllachy 129 – Granuaile O'Malley (IRE) 55 (Mark of Esteem (IRE) 137) [2009 82: 6m 7d p6g^6 f7g 6d p6g^5 p6g^5 p5.1g* p5m p5.1g Dec 4] strong filly: fair handicapper: won at Wolverhampton in November: effective at 5f/6f: acts on polytrack and good to soft going: effective blinkered or not. *R. Curtis* **77**

CALIFORNIA BRIGHT (IRE) 3 ch.f. Rock of Gibraltar (IRE) 133 – Woodyousmileforme (USA) (Woodman (USA) 126) [2009 10g 12g^3 Jun 5] 32,000F, €80,000Y: sixth foal: half-sister to French 9.5f winner Glad Eye (by Giant's Causeway) and winner in USA by A P Indy: dam, 1m/8.5f winner in USA, sister to Grand Criterium winner/very smart winner up to 1½m in USA Ciro: little solid form in maidens in Britain: sold 7,000 gns in July, subsequently won at 6f in Greece. *J. G. Given* **?**

CALLE VISTAMAR 2 ch.f. (May 24) Stage Pass 108 – Champagne Bubbleigh VII (Damsire Unregistered) [2009 p6g p7.1g Sep 19] non-thoroughbred filly: first foal: dam unraced: no show in claimer/seller (pulled up). *S. Wynne* **–**

CALLEY HO 3 b.g. Kyllachy 129 – Lucayan Belle (Cadeaux Genereux 131) [2009 70: 6m 8.3m Jul 11] rather leggy, close-coupled gelding: fair performer at 2 yrs: well beaten in 2009. *Mrs L. Stubbs* **–**

CALL FOR LIBERTY (IRE) 4 b.c. Statue of Liberty (USA) 115 – Give A Whistle (IRE) 100 (Mujadil (USA) 119) [2009 76: p7.1g 7g^5 7g^5 a5.5g a6g^3 Dec 27] strong, medium-sized colt: fair performer at 3 yrs: not at best in 2009, sold from B. Smart £2,000 after second start: best at 5f/6f: acts on dirt and good to firm going: tried blinkered. *C. von der Recke, Germany* **62**

CALLIGRAPHER (USA) 3 ch.g. Rahy (USA) 115 – Calista 108 (Caerleon (USA) 132) [2009 91p: 6m 6m^6 Jun 10] sturdy gelding: fairly useful performer, lightly raced: below best both starts in 2009, looking unwilling final outing: stays 6f: raced only on polytrack and good/good to firm going: sold 14,000 gns, sent to Bahrain. *M. A. Jarvis* **82**

CALLING BIRDS (IRE) 3 b.f. Royal Applause 124 – Jezyah (USA) 80 (Chief's Crown (USA)) [2009 –: p8g p10g^5 10.2g 10m 9m^6 p10g Jul 18] modest maiden: left J. Osborne after second start: stays 1¼m: acts on polytrack: tried in headgear. *Karen George* **51**

CALLING VICTORY (FR) 3 b.f. Vettori (IRE) 119 – Calling Card (Bering 136) [2009 p8.6g^2 p8.6g^2 10.1d^6 10d p10g Jun 6] €45,000Y: fourth foal: half-sister to Italian 9f/10.5f winner Daily Call (by Daylami): dam useful French 10.5f winner: fair form when runner-up in maidens first 2 starts: well held after: should stay 1¼m: acts on polytrack: tried blinkered: signs of temperament: sold 6,500 gns. *M. Botti* **65**

CALLISTO MOON 5 b.g. Mujahid (USA) 125 – Nursling (IRE) 57 (Kahyasi 130) [2009 80: p16g^4 f14g^5 14m* 14m* 16.4m^5 14m* 17.2m* 16d Oct 28] close-coupled gelding: fairly useful handicapper: improved in 2009, winning at Sandown and Musselburgh in June, Sandown in July and Bath in September: stays 17f: acts on polytrack and good to firm going: effective blinkered/in cheekpieces or not: front runner nowadays. *R. Curtis* **92**

CALLIS WOOD 3 br.f. Shinko Forest (IRE) – Meltonby 67 (Sayf El Arab (USA) 127) [2009 7m 9d May 17] leggy filly: seventh foal: dam 6f to 1m winner, including at 2 yrs: well held in maidens. *Ollie Pears* **–**

CALL IT ON (IRE) 3 ch.g. Raise A Grand (IRE) 114 – Birthday Present (Cadeaux Genereux 131) [2009 87: 10.4m 8d^3 10.4g^5 10m^3 10m^2 10m^6 10d^3 10.3g Oct 23] sturdy gelding: fairly useful handicapper: held form well in 2009, placed 4 times: stays 1¼m: acts on good to firm and good to soft going: consistent: gelded after final start. *M. H. Tompkins* **93**

CALL ME AL (IRE) 4 b.g. Alhaarth (IRE) 126 – Takarna (IRE) 70 (Mark of Esteem (IRE) 137) [2009 66: p16.5g 8.3m May 29] fair maiden handicapper: well beaten both starts in 2009: effective at 7f/1m: acts on polytrack. *J. J. Lambe, Ireland* –

CALL ME COURAGEOUS (IRE) 3 ch.g. Captain Rio 122 – Golden Concorde (Super Concorde (USA) 128) [2009 66: 8.1g 8f 6f 6m^4 6d^2 6m f6g 7.1d Sep 4] neat gelding: modest maiden: left A. Haynes after sixth start: stays 6f: acts on good to firm and good to soft going: tried visored/in cheekpieces. *R. A. Harris* **56**

CALL ME ROSY (IRE) 5 ch.m. Shinko Forest (IRE) – Fanciful (IRE) (Mujtahid (USA) 118) [2009 –: 7g^5 6m 6m Jun 30] sturdy, workmanlike mare: poor maiden handicapper: seemingly stays 7f: acts on polytrack. *B. Smart* **49**

CALL OF DUTY (IRE) 4 br.g. Storming Home 128 – Blushing Barada (USA) 53 (Blushing Groom (FR) 131) [2009 10.1d 6.9g 8d 7.9g^6 9.9m 13g^4 12.1s^2 12g^4 15.8v 9.9g Sep 22] modest handicapper nowadays: missed 2008: stays 13f: acts on polytrack and soft ground. *Mrs Dianne Sayer* **64**

CALL OF KTULU (IRE) 4 b.g. Noverre (USA) 125 – Yankee Dancer 62 (Groom Dancer (USA) 128) [2009 –: 8m 8m 7.5m Jul 3] of no account. *J. S. Wainwright* –

CALL OF THE KINGS 2 b.g. (Feb 16) Acclamation 118 – Surrey Down (USA) (Forest Wildcat (USA) 120) [2009 6m^4 p7g a7g* Dec 27] rather unfurnished gelding: better effort in maidens in Britain for R. Teal when fourth of 5 at Goodwood: stays 7f: blinkered second start: sold 1,200 gns, won similar event at Gran Canaria in December. *J. Martel, Spain* **57**

CALL TO ARMS (IRE) 2 br.g. (Jan 26) Shamardal (USA) 129 – Requesting (Rainbow Quest (USA) 134) [2009 6g^2 6m^3 6m^2 Sep 15] €33,000Y: good-topped gelding: sixth foal: half-brother to 3 winners, including useful 1m (at 2 yrs)/1¼m winner Dr Faustus (by Sadler's Wells) and 2005 2-y-o 6f winner Desert Flora (by Green Desert): dam unraced half-sister to very smart 1¼m performer Last Second (dam of Poule d'Essai des Poulains winner Aussie Rules) and to dams of Alborada, Albanova, Quarter Moon and Yesterday: fair maiden: best effort on debut: raced freely/looked awkward subsequently: bred to stay 1¼m: gelded after final start. *M. Johnston* **77**

CALL TO REASON (IRE) 2 ch.f. (Mar 22) Pivotal 124 – Venturi 103 (Danehill Dancer (IRE) 117) [2009 7g^2 Oct 31] big, rangy filly: second foal: half-sister to 3-y-o Cilium: dam, Irish 2-y-o 6f/7f winner, sister to smart French performer up to 1¼m Feels All Right: 14/1, promising ½-length second of 20 to Revered in maiden at Newmarket, quickening to challenge 1f out: sure to improve. *J. Noseda* **80 p**

CALM AND SERENE (USA) 2 b.f. (Mar 25) Quiet American (USA) – Charm Away (USA) (Silver Charm (USA) 132) [2009 8.3s 8d Oct 15] $25,000Y, 30,000 2-y-o: leggy, quite attractive filly: second foal: half-sister to winner in USA by Sky Mesa: dam, US 1m winner, closely related to 1996 US Grade 2 2-y-o 9f winner The Silver Move: showed a little ability in maidens at Nottingham and Brighton (too free). *Rae Guest* **50**

CALMDOWNMATE (IRE) 4 b.g. Danehill Dancer (IRE) 117 – Lady Digby (IRE) 96 (Petorius 117) [2009 87, a70: f5d* f5g^2 f5g f6g* 6m f5m* 5g 6m f6g^3 f6g^5 f5m Dec 15] strong, medium-sized gelding: fairly useful performer: won apprentice claimer in January and handicaps in February and May, all at Southwell: best at 5f/6f: acts on fibresand, good to firm and good to soft going: tried visored/blinkered. *Mrs R. A. Carr* **80**

CALM STORM (IRE) 2 b.c. (Feb 9) Whipper (USA) 126 – Dark Hyacinth (IRE) 65 (Darshaan 133) [2009 7g p6g^6 p6g^6 p8m 8.3d Oct 12] rather leggy colt: modest maiden: well held in nurseries, none too keen in visor final start: bred to be suited by 7f+: best effort on polytrack: sold 7,000 gns, sent to Kazakhstan. *J. Noseda* **62**

CALTIRE (GER) 4 b.g. Pentire 132 – Caluna (SWI) 102 (Lagunas) [2009 67: p12g^6 f12g^6 p10g Mar 18] lengthy, angular gelding: modest performer nowadays: probably stays 1½m: acts on polytrack and good to soft going: usually blinkered: held up: not straightforward. *M. G. Quinlan* **59**

CALYPSO BAY (IRE) 3 b.c. Galileo (IRE) 134 – Poule de Luxe (IRE) 75 (Cadeaux Genereux 131) [2009 10m^3 10.3m p10g^6 May 30] 65,000Y: sturdy colt: first foal: dam, 7f winner, half-sister to useful miler Squaw Dance: fairly useful maiden: standout effort when third to Sopranist at Newmarket on debut: looked awkward subsequently: raced only at 1¼m: acts on good to firm going. *J. Noseda* **89**

CALYPSO GIRL (IRE) 3 gr.f. Verglas (IRE) 118 – Clochette (IRE) 83 (Namaqualand (USA)) [2009 77: 7m 6g^5 6d 6f^5 6f 5m 6d 6.1d 5.7g Sep 7] angular filly: modest performer at 3 yrs: best at 5f/6f: acts on heavy going: tried visored. *P. D. Evans* **64**

CALYPSO PRINCE 3 ch.g. Lucky Story (USA) 128 – Eleonora d'Arborea 78 (Prince Sabo 123) [2009 –: p7.1g p5.1g p10g Feb 11] little form. *M. D. I. Usher* –

CALYPSO STAR (IRE) 2 ch.c. (Feb 26) Exceed And Excel (AUS) 126 – Reematna 75 (Sabrehill (USA) 120) [2009 6d6 p7g 8g p8m2 f8m2 Nov 11] €38,000F, 27,000Y: strong colt: sixth foal: brother to 3-y-o My Verse and half-brother to 3 winners, including useful 6f (at 2 yrs) to 9f (in UAE) winner Dahteer (by Bachir): dam, maiden (may have proven best at 7f/1m), half-sister to very smart 1½m performer Morshdi: fair maiden: easily best efforts when runner-up in nurseries: stays 1m: acts on all-weather. *R. Hannon* 70 +

CALZAGHE (IRE) 5 ch.g. Galileo (IRE) 134 – Novelette (Darshaan 133) [2009 78§: p12.2g5 f12g3 p12.2g4 p12.2g p12.2g4 12d p13g* 11.9m5 Apr 26] big, good-topped gelding: fair performer: left D. Nicholls £6,000 after second outing, F. Sheridan £3,000 after fifth: won handicap at Lingfield in April: should stay 2m: acts on polytrack, good to firm and good to soft ground: sometimes visored, tried tongue tied: quirky: fairly useful hurdler, completed hat-trick in November. *Jim Best* 74 §

CAMACHO FLYER (IRE) 2 b.g. (May 3) Camacho 118 – Despondent (IRE) 34 (Broken Hearted 124) [2009 5m 5m 5g 6f 5m4 f5g5 5d* 5m 5g6 5g Oct 17] neat gelding: fair performer at best: made all in maiden at Catterick in August: no form after: raced mainly at 5f: acts on good to soft and good to firm ground: tried in cheekpieces/visored/tongue tied: races prominently: inconsistent: gelded after final start. *P. T. Midgley* 66 ?

CAMBUSLANG (IRE) 2 b.c. (Apr 28) Chevalier (IRE) 115 – Zafine 67 (Zafonic (USA) 130) [2009 5m5 5g3 7.2g3 6d 6s 6g Sep 20] modest maiden: no form in nurseries: barely stays 7f: acts on good to firm going: tried in cheekpieces. *I. Semple* 58

CAME BACK (IRE) 6 ch.g. Bertolini (USA) 125 – Distant Decree (USA) (Distant View (USA) 126) [2009 96: f6s6 p6g4 f6g5 p5.1m5 p5.1g f5g Apr 27] workmanlike gelding: just fair performer in 2009: effective at 5f/6f: acts on all-weather, below form both starts on turf: usually races up with pace: gelded after final start. *Miss A. Stokell* 78

CAMELOT QUEEN 4 gr.f. Baryshnikov (AUS) – Guarded Expression 51 (Siberian Express (USA) 125) [2009 p8g p7.1g6 p8g 6m May 3] lengthy filly: sixth foal: half-sister to 3 winners, including fairly useful sprinters Jackie's Baby (also won at 2 yrs, by Then Again) and Musical Fair (by Piccolo): dam maiden: well held in maidens. *W. S. Kittow* –

totepool Winter Hill Stakes, Windsor—Campanologist (noseband) holds off Bankable (right) and Kingdom of Fife (visor) to justify favouritism in Windsor's feature race of the year

CAMERA SHY (IRE) 5 ch.g. Pivotal 124 – Shy Danceuse (FR) (Groom Dancer (USA) 128) [2009 60: 10.1g^3 10.1g* 11.8m* Jun 25] modest handicapper, lightly raced: won at Yarmouth (apprentices) and Leicester in June: stays 1½m: acts on polytrack and good to firm going: in cheekpieces once. *K. A. Morgan* **60**

CAMEROONEY 6 b.g. Sugarfoot 118 – Enkindle 39 (Relkino 131) [2009 52?: 7m^4 p8.6g^3 p9.5g f7f^6 f8g Dec 27] modest maiden: stays 1¼m: acts on all-weather and good to firm going. *B. Ellison* **56**

CAMILLA KNIGHT (IRE) 3 ch.f. Night Shift (USA) – Koukla Mou (Keen 116) [2009 p7g 7f Sep 8] 18,000Y: lengthy filly: fourth foal: sister to 2005 2-y-o 5f winner John Claude and half-sister to French/Belgian winner up to 7.5f All The More (by Ali-Royal): dam unraced: well held in maidens. *W. R. Swinburn* **–**

CAMOMILE 3 b.f. Xaar 132 – Pretty Davis (USA) (Trempolino (USA) 135) [2009 7g^5 6s^6 6g f7g Dec 18] 12,000F: half-sister to 3 winners, including 8.5f (at 2 yrs) to 15f winner Fait Le Jojo (by Pistolet Bleu) and 1½m to 2m winner Timing (by Alhaarth), both fairly useful: dam French 1¼m winner: well held in maidens (for K. Ryan)/minor event. *Miss Tracy Waggott* **–**

CAMPAIGNER 2 b.c. (Mar 27) Dansili 127 – Rosapenna (IRE) 84 (Spectrum (IRE) 126) [2009 6g 6m 7.1g p6g^6 p6g 7m p7m Oct 7] smallish colt: maiden: form only in nursery at Goodwood penultimate start (probably flattered). *J. W. Hills* **55 ?**

CAMPANOLOGIST (USA) 4 b.c. Kingmambo (USA) 125 – Ring of Music (Sadler's Wells (USA) 132) [2009 119: 10m 12m^2 12m 10.4m^2 10m* 11m^3 12m^2 10m Oct 17] tall, good-topped colt: impresses in appearance: smart performer: runner-up in Hardwicke Stakes at Royal Ascot (½ length behind Bronze Cannon) and Rose of Lancaster Stakes at Haydock (beaten 1¼ lengths by Jukebox Jury) prior to winning totepool Winter Hill Stakes at Windsor in August by ½ length from Bankable: also ran well after when length third to Doctor Freemantle in Dubai Duty Free Arc Trial at Newbury and 2¼ lengths second to Mawatheeq in Cumberland Lodge Stakes at Ascot: below form in Champion Stakes at Newmarket final start: stays 1½m: acts on polytrack and firm ground: usually races prominently. *Saeed bin Suroor* **119**

CAMPBELLS LAD 8 b.g. Mind Games 121 – T O O Mamma's (IRE) 50 (Classic Secret (USA) 91) [2009 12g May 23] big gelding: one-time fair performer: missed 2008: well held only start at 8 yrs: tried in cheekpieces/blinkers. *A. Berry* **–**

CAMPLI (IRE) 7 b.g. Zafonic (USA) 130 – Sept A Neuf (Be My Guest (USA) 126) [2009 –: p9.5g^2 p8.6g^5 7.1m^2 7m p7.1g* 7g^3 7.9m^6 7.9m^4 Jun 24] fair handicapper: won at Wolverhampton in April: has form at 1¾m, races at shorter nowadays (effective at 7f): raced on polytrack and good ground or firmer: versatile tactically. *B. Ellison* **78**

CAMPS BAY (USA) 5 b.g. Cozzene (USA) – Seewillo (USA) (Pleasant Colony (USA)) [2009 109: 12f^4 14g 14m 12m 12m^4 12m^4 12d Oct 24] rangy gelding: useful handicapper: not so good or genuine in 2009, best effort when 2¼ lengths fourth to Dansili Dancer at Doncaster on reappearance: stays 1¾m: acts on firm and good to soft going: tried blinkered/in cheekpieces: held up: moody. *Mrs A. J. Perrett* **100**

CANADIAN DANEHILL (IRE) 7 b.g. Indian Danehill (IRE) 124 – San Jovita (CAN) 71 (St Jovite (USA) 135) [2009 100: f5s^3 p5g p5.1g^2 p5.1g^3 f5m^6 p5.1g^3 5m* 5f^2 5m^6 5m* 5m* 5g 5g 5d p5.1g f5g^6 f5d^6 Dec 29] big, lengthy gelding: useful handicapper: won at Newmarket in May and Sandown and Newmarket (by head from Tabaret) in July: best at 5f: acts on all-weather, firm and soft going: wears cheekpieces: usually races prominently. *R. M. H. Cowell* **96**

CANARY GIRL 6 br.m. Primo Valentino (IRE) 116 – Cumbrian Concerto 44 (Petong 126) [2009 –: 7f^6 8.1g 7m Oct 26] no form since 2007. *G. Prodromou* **–**

CAN CAN STAR 6 br.h. Lend A Hand 124 – Carrie Can Can 73 (Green Tune (USA) 125) [2009 77: p11g^4 p12g^3 p10g* p10g* p10g^4 p8g^3 10.3g^5 p8g^4 10g^4 10g^4 10.3m p10g^6 10.2m* 10s^5 8.3f^3 10.2m^4 8.3m^2 p12g^3 10.1m^3 10g p10g^3 p10m^4 p8.6g^2 Dec 12] rather leggy horse: fairly useful handicapper: won at Lingfield in January and February, and Nottingham (apprentices) in July: numerous creditable efforts otherwise: effective at 1m to easy 13f: acts on polytrack and firm going: blinkered once: edgy sort, has sweated/raced freely: usually held up: tough and reliable. *A. W. Carroll* **89**

CANDILEJAS 3 b.f. Diktat 126 – Nacho Venture (FR) 88 (Rainbow Quest (USA) 134) [2009 66: 8.3g p12m p10g p8g Nov 18] modest maiden: best effort at 7f: raced only on polytrack and good ground: tried tongue tied/in cheekpieces. *R. J. Smith* **52**

CANDLE 6 b.m. Dansili 127 – Celia Brady 62 (Last Tycoon 131) [2009 98: p16g 14g f12g Aug 10] close-coupled, quite attractive mare: just fairly useful handicapper in 2009: stays 1¾m: acts on polytrack, soft and good to firm ground: fair winning hurdler. *T. R. George* **80**

CANDLESHOE (IRE) 2 b.f. (Apr 15) Danehill Dancer (IRE) 117 – Keepers Dawn (IRE) 103 (Alzao (USA) 117) [2009 6m^4 7d 6f^5 Aug 17] 50,000Y: compact filly: sixth foal: half-sister to 1¼m winner Keepers Knight (by Sri Pekan): dam 2-y-o 6f winner: fair maiden: best effort on debut: not knocked about final start: should stay 7f. *R. Hannon* **66**

CANDY ANCHOR (FR) 10 b.m. Slip Anchor 136 – Kandavu 87 (Safawan 118) [2009 50: 11.8m May 25] lengthy mare: modest maiden: slipped and fell only outing in 2009: stayed 1½m: acted on polytrack: formerly blinkered, tried tongue tied: dead. *R. E. Peacock* **–**

CANDYFLOSS GIRL 2 b.f. (Feb 9) Intikhab (USA) 135 – Annatalia 82 (Pivotal 124) [2009 6m 6m 5.7g^6 p6g^3 p5g* p6g^5 p6m^3 7m 7v Oct 24] 16,000 2-y-o: sturdy filly: second foal: dam, 2-y-o 5f winner, half-sister to smart sprinter Aahayson: fair performer: won nursery at Kempton in August: mostly creditable efforts after: stays 7f: acts on polytrack and good to firm ground: has flashed tail. *H. J. L. Dunlop* **65**

CANDY RIDE (IRE) 3 ch.f. Pivotal 124 – Mia Mambo (USA) (Affirmed (USA)) [2009 7s^5 8.3g^2 8.3g* 8.3m^2 9g* 10.3s Nov 7] lengthy filly: has scope: second foal: half-sister to winner in Greece by Gulch: dam unraced out of sister to Miesque: fairly useful performer: won maiden at Nottingham in June and handicap at Sandown in July: stiff task in listed race final start: should stay 1¼m: acts on good to firm going: signs of temperament. *E. A. L. Dunlop* **82**

CANDY ROSE 4 b.f. Tobougg (IRE) 125 – Cottage Maid (Inchinor 119) [2009 70: p8g 9m^6 7f^4 p7m p10g^6 Oct 21] angular filly: modest maiden: effective at 7f to 9f: acts on polytrack and good to firm going: tried in cheekpieces/tongue tie. *M. P. Tregoning* **60**

CANE CAT (IRE) 2 b. or br.f. (Apr 27) One Cool Cat (USA) 123 – Seven Wonders (USA) (Rahy (USA) 115) [2009 5m^5 5.1m^6 5.1g^4 5f p7g^6 6g^5 p6m^4 6.1s^3 6g^6 5.1s p6g^2 p6g Dec 14] €10,000Y: unfurnished filly: fifth foal: half-sister to fairly useful 5f (at 2 yrs) and 9.5f winner Connotation (by Mujahid) and 2 winners abroad: dam unraced half-sister to smart US 1¼m performer Boatman out of half-sister to Irish 1000 Guineas winner Al Bahathri: modest maiden: stays 6f: acts on polytrack and soft ground: front runner/races prominently. *A. W. Carroll* **54**

CANFORD CLIFFS (IRE) 2 b.c. (Feb 8) Tagula (IRE) 116 – Mrs Marsh (Marju (IRE) 127) [2009 6g* 6m* 6m^3 Aug 23] **122**

Two-year-olds have long been the backbone of Richard Hannon's stable which, for the third season running, sent out more juvenile winners than any other British-based yard, the latest campaign yielding a total prize money haul of more than £2,600,000 from this age group. That staggering sum included two particularly lucrative wins on Irish soil, one of them by prolific Lucky General, with the filly Full Mandate providing a one, two for the stable, in the Goffs Million Sprint at the Curragh in late-September, twelve months after Hannon-trained horses had landed both Million races under their previous format when there was a race for each of the sexes. Goffs will not be staging these very valuable prizes in 2010, but the Hannon stable will still have other fruitful sales races to aim at. The other win on Irish soil in the latest season came when Dick Turpin provided the stable with its sixth win in the Tattersalls Ireland Sale Stakes in August (run at Fairyhouse for the first time in 2009), and then there was bargain buy Monsieur Chevalier who made it seven wins for the Hannon stable in the Weatherbys Super Sprint at Newbury. In addition, Hannon also saddled outsiders to win three autumn two-year-old pattern races, Pollenator (14/1) in the May Hill at Doncaster, Sir Parky (33/1) in the Somerville Tattersall Stakes at Newmarket and Carnaby Street (14/1) in the Horris Hill at Newbury. In terms of merit, though, the stable's best two-year-old of 2009 was Canford Cliffs, who justified a huge home reputation when winning his first two starts, including a six-length win in the Coventry Stakes at Royal Ascot on the second occasion.

Ironically, the Coventry is one two-year-old race in which the Hannon yard doesn't have a particularly good record, its only previous win coming with Rock City back in 1989. Although Canford Cliffs failed to emulate his predecessor by winning again after Royal Ascot—Rock City went on to win both the July Stakes and Gimcrack Stakes—the chances are that he has already shown form of a significantly higher standard. Only one Coventry winner (Three Valleys in 2003) has scored by a wider margin than Canford Cliffs since Mill Reef romped home by eight lengths in the 1970 renewal, an impressive statement considering that such as Chief Singer, Sure Blade and Henrythenavigator have featured on the race's roll of honour in the interim. Canford Cliffs already had a wide-margin success to his name when he arrived at Royal Ascot, having landed the odds by seven lengths in an eight-runner maiden at Newbury in mid-May when the fact that he was one of seven newcomers in the field did not help in assessing the form. Canford Cliffs was clearly a smart prospect though, and was all the rage in the Coventry, sent off 7/4 favourite against twelve rivals. His supporters never had a moment's worry, Canford Cliffs making virtually all and, one by one, seeing off every rival that tried to make a race of it with him (perhaps significantly, both placed horses came from well off the pace). Canford Cliffs was still galloping on strongly at the finish and probably had more in hand than the bare result suggests, particularly as Richard Hughes (who also rode Three Valleys to his Coventry win) had the luxury of being able to take things easy late on. Connections clearly had big plans for Canford Cliffs but he fluffed his lines when managing only third of five behind Arcano in the Prix Morny at Deauville two months later. Canford Cliffs wasn't beaten far at Deauville in a bunched finish and the race was run in a course record time, but, even so, he didn't shape as if in the same form at Ascot. 'Something obviously went wrong,' was Hannon's verdict, whilst Hughes reported that the colt 'lugged left'. Nothing came to light afterwards, though the fact that Canford Cliffs wasn't seen again gives further support to the theory that he simply wasn't the same Canford Cliffs at Deauville.

The Coventry third and fourth, Rakaan (who hinted at temperament) and Moran Gra, may not have advertised the Royal Ascot form subsequently, but the

Coventry Stakes, Royal Ascot—six-length winner Canford Cliffs posts an excellent timefigure as trainer Richard Hannon lands his first Coventry success in twenty years; following him home are Xtension (breastgirth) and Rakaan (left)

Heffer Syndicate, Mrs Roy & Mrs Instance's "Canford Cliffs"

same cannot be said of runner-up Xtension, who went on to win the Vintage Stakes at Goodwood and then finished a close third in the Dewhurst. The excellent winning timefigure, equivalent to a rating of 122, for the Coventry suggests it would be unwise to underestimate Canford Cliffs' prospects for 2010 despite his subsequent Deauville disappointment. The aforementioned Chief Singer (who won the Coventry on his debut) is one particularly notable example of how a good horse can bounce back from a disappointing final outing at two. Chief Singer flopped in far more alarming fashion than Canford Cliffs on his only start (in the July Stakes) after the Coventry before developing into a top-notch three-year-old, winning twice at Group 1 level (July Cup and Sussex Stakes) after finishing runner-up to El Gran Senor in a very strong renewal of the Two Thousand Guineas. The latter race is the only British classic that Hannon has won during his long career, with the victories of Mon Fils (1973), Don't Forget Me (1987) and Tirol (1990) among those whose successes have helped to expand the Marlborough training establishment, which now operates two yards Everleigh and Herridge (used solely for two-year-olds). Hannon has also gone close in the Newmarket classic with Lucky Lindy in 1992 (runner-up at 50/1), Tamburlaine in 2001 (runner-up at 12/1) and Redback in 2002 (third at 25/1). Canford Cliffs is available at 12/1 at the time of writing for the 2010 Two Thousand Guineas—he was as short as 6/1 after his Coventry win—and boasts better form at this stage of his career than any of those previous Hannon-trained Guineas contenders. There is a stumbling block, though, in that he has to prove his stamina, having been raced only at six furlongs, and only on good ground or firmer.

The strong Canford Cliffs was described as a 'proper sprint-type two-year-old' by Timeform's paddock judge before his debut at Newbury, his physique presumably the prime attraction to the Hannon team. In truth, the £50,000 that Canford Cliffs fetched at the St Leger Yearling Sales in August 2008 didn't really look a bargain price tag, judged on pedigree. The 1996 Poule d'Essai des Poulains third Tagula wasn't a fashionable sire, and the unraced dam Mrs Marsh had produced just one foal previously, a 2005 Barathea colt called Zeeran, who had shown little form for Clive Brittain at the time and was disposed of for just £800 at the end of the year—after which, incidentally, he did go on in 2009 to win three times at around a mile in Sweden. Mrs Marsh herself is a half-sister to five winners, however, including the fillies Baltic Dip and Pina Colada, who were both successful at two for Hannon (Baltic Dip showing useful form) before being exported to the States where Pina Colada won twice at up to seven and a half furlongs and was placed in graded company. Another of Mrs Marsh's successful siblings, the fair mile and a quarter winner Triple Sharp (also a winning hurdler), has done well since being retired to the paddocks, producing a couple of useful two-year-old winners in Ellmau (later successful at up to eleven furlongs) and Nasri. However, the most notable performer on the bottom line of this pedigree is third dam Triple Tipple, a smart and prolific winner at around a mile for Luca Cumani in the early-'eighties prior to gaining further success in the States. Although Canford Cliffs' grandam Drei raced only once (when a promising fourth over a mile at three), Triple Tipple did enjoy success at stud, notably with the useful winning miler Triode (also trained by Cumani), who has since produced several above-average performers herself as a broodmare, including the one-time useful mile and a half winner Compton Commander.

Canford Cliffs (IRE) (b.c. Feb 8, 2007)	Tagula (IRE) (b 1993)	Taufan (b 1977)	Stop The Music
			Stolen Date
		Twin Island (ch 1989)	Standaan
			Jolly Widow
	Mrs Marsh (b 2001)	Marju (br 1988)	Last Tycoon
			Flame of Tara
		Drei (b 1991)	Lyphard
			Triple Tipple

The racing records of most of his antecedents give some hope that Canford Cliffs will stay further than sprint distances—his connections are confident he will last out a mile—but it won't prove a disaster if this keen-going sort does prove ideally suited by shorter after all. The consistent Rock City, for example, won twice in Group 3 races over seven furlongs as a three-year-old when he also finished a creditable fourth (behind stablemate Tirol) in the Two Thousand Guineas. *R. Hannon*

CANMOSS (USA) 3 ch.c. Maria's Mon (USA) 121 – Dance For Free (CAN) (Fly So Free (USA) 122) [2009 71: 12g^2 12.6g^5 14.1f^6 a12g^2 12d^2 a12g* 14.5d 12g 15d 12s Oct 28] big colt: fair performer: claimed from E. O'Neill €16,555 after fourth start: won claimer at Deauville in August: below form after: stays 1½m: acts on all-weather and firm going: usually wears cheekpieces/blinkers nowadays. *A. Bonin, France* 73

CANNONBALL (USA) 4 b. or br.g. Catienus (USA) 115 – No Deadline (USA) (Skywalker (USA)) [2009 5f^4 5.5g^2 5g^2 5m^6 6m^2 5.5f* 6.5f^3 6g Dec 13] compact gelding: second foal: brother to winner in USA: dam US 1m/8.5f winner: very smart performer: dropped back in trip in 2009, close second in Grade 3 events at Keeneland and Churchill Downs, and in Golden Jubilee Stakes at Royal Ascot (improved form, beaten neck by Art Connoisseur, closing strongly late): off 2½ months, won non-graded stakes at Saratoga in September by a neck from Silver Timber: respectable staying-on third to California Flag in Breeders' Cup Turf Sprint at Santa Anita before below form in Hong Kong Sprint at Sha Tin final start: has form up to 9f, but clearly effective at much shorter: acts on firm and good to soft going: blinkered on debut: has worn tongue tie. *Wesley A. Ward, USA* 122

CANONGATE 5 gr.g. Highest Honor (FR) 124 – Tremiere (FR) (Anabaa (USA) 130) [2009 10g 9g Aug 13] big gelding: useful handicapper at best: left R. Gibson in France, last both starts in 2009, then gelded: stays 1m: acts on heavy ground: failed to enter stall on intended reappearance. *Miss E. C. Lavelle* –

CANSILI STAR 2 b.g. (May 6) Dansili 127 – Canis Star (Wolfhound (USA) 126) [2009 6g^2 7.1s^4 6g^5 7m^2 7d^4 Oct 6] 105,000Y: fifth foal: half-brother to 5-y-o Jawaab: dam unraced half-sister to smart milers Guest Artiste and Inchmurrin, latter dam of smart 7f/1m performer Inchinor: fairly useful maiden: best effort when second to Astonishment 87 in nursery at Goodwood: gelded after final outing: stays 7f: acts on good to firm ground. *M. A. Jarvis*

CANTABILLY (IRE) 6 b.g. Distant Music (USA) 126 – Cantaloupe (Priolo (USA) 127) [2009 73: p10g p10g^6 p13.9m^4 p16.5g^5 Mar 13] close-coupled gelding: fair handicapper: stays 17f: acts on polytrack, firm and soft going. *R. J. Hodges* **68**

CANTON ROAD 3 b.g. Galileo (IRE) 134 – Welsh Diva 112 (Selkirk (USA) 129) [2009 58p: 11.8m^2 p12g^6 11m f11g^3 p12.2g Sep 5] fair maiden: regressed after reappearance, often finding little: stays 1½m: acts on good to firm going: tried blinkered/tongue tied: sold 2,500 gns. *P. F. I. Cole* **72 d**

CANUCATCHER (IRE) 3 b.f. Catcher In The Rye (IRE) 115 – Never Zal (Zilzal (USA) 137) [2009 –: f11g^4 Mar 19] sturdy filly: little form. *T. D. Walford* **–**

CANWINN (IRE) 3 b.c. Refuse To Bend (IRE) 128 – Born To Glamour (Ajdal (USA) 130) [2009 102: p8g^6 10.1g^6 8.1v 8m 8m^4 8m^3 8m 8s^2 Sep 5] angular colt: fairly useful handicapper: good efforts in frame 3 of last 4 starts: should stay beyond 1m: acts on soft and good to firm going: tried visored: tended to hang final start. *M. R. Channon* **93**

CANYON RANCH 3 b.c. Danehill Dancer (IRE) 117 – Model Queen (USA) 76 (Kingmambo (USA) 125) [2009 8m^4 8g 8m^2 Jul 6] lengthy, good-topped colt: fair form in maidens: best effort when second at Ripon, looking awkward: raced only at 1m on good/good to firm going: dead. *L. M. Cumani* **73**

CAOBA 5 b.m. Hernando (FR) 127 – Seeker 75 (Rainbow Quest (USA) 134) [2009 16g* 16g May 29] ex-French-trained mare: fairly useful hurdler: fair form on Flat, lightly raced: won handicap at Nottingham in May: stays 2m: wore cheekpieces final outing. *V. R. A. Dartnall* **74 +**

CAOL ILA (IRE) 2 b.f. (Apr 24) Invincible Spirit (IRE) 121 – Pink Cashmere (IRE) (Polar Falcon (USA) 126) [2009 p5.1g^5 6m p5.1m^6 p5g^6 p5.1g^3 f5f^4 Dec 17] 40,000Y: small filly: sister to 2006 2-y-o 6f winner Naayla, closely related to 6f (at 2 yrs)/7f winner Motu (by Desert Style) and half-sister to several winners, including useful 2004 2-y-o 5f winner Pike Bishop (by Namid): dam unraced half-sister to July Cup winner Owington: modest maiden: bred to be best at 5f/6f: acts on polytrack, promise on good to firm. *J. G. Given* **56**

CAPABLE GUEST (IRE) 7 b. or br.g. Cape Cross (IRE) 129 – Alexander Confranc (IRE) 73 (Magical Wonder (USA) 125) [2009 101§: p9.5g^4 8.5g 8.9g 10m^6 12g^4 10d^5 11.9f 13.3m^5 15.9m p12g^6 12m^3 12.4g* p12m 12v^3 12.5d^3 p13.9g^2 p13.9g^5 Nov 12] workmanlike gelding: fairly useful handicapper: generally regressive in 2009, much reduced mark when winning at Newcastle in September: stays 1¾m: acts on polytrack and any turf going: sometimes blinkered/visored: held up: moody. *M. R. Channon* **89 d**

CAPACITY (IRE) 2 b.c. (Feb 3) Cape Cross (IRE) 129 – Carry On Katie (USA) 109 (Fasliyev (USA) 120) [2009 6m^4 6g^5 6s^2 6.1g^2 Aug 2] unfurnished colt: second foal: dam 2-y-o 6f winner (including Lowther/Cheveley Park Stakes) who stayed 1m: fair maiden: best effort when runner-up in nursery at Chester final start: likely to be suited by 7f: acts on soft ground: sold £3,500 in December. *M. Johnston* **75**

CAPANIA (IRE) 5 br.m. Cape Cross (IRE) 129 – Gentle Papoose (Commanche Run 133) [2009 63: p7.1g Feb 9] sturdy mare: maiden: well beaten only start at 5 yrs: stays 8.6f: raced on all-weather and good to firm going: tried visored/in cheekpieces. *E. G. Bevan* **–**

CAPEABILITY (IRE) 3 b.g. Cape Cross (IRE) 129 – Mennetou (IRE) (Entrepreneur 123) [2009 87: p8g^2 p8.6g^2 10m^6 10m^6 8m 10.3g 10.2v p10g^2 p9.5g^5 Dec 3] useful-looking gelding: fairly useful maiden: not at best after third start: seems to stay 1¼m, but not short of speed: acts on polytrack and good to firm ground. *M. R. Channon* **88**

CAPE AMBER (IRE) 4 b.f. Cape Cross (IRE) 129 – Maramba 97 (Rainbow Quest (USA) 134) [2009 109: 9.9g^5 Aug 12] big, rangy filly: useful performer at 3 yrs: raced too freely in listed event at Salisbury only start in 2009, below form: was a free-going sort, best short of 1½m: acted on soft and good to firm ground: dead. *R. M. Beckett* **92**

CAPE BLANCO (IRE) 2 ch.c. (Apr 20) Galileo (IRE) 134 – Laurel Delight 104 (Presidium 124) [2009 7g* 7s* 7s* Aug 22] **110 p**

For the fourth year in a row the Tyros Stakes at Leopardstown in July was won by a son of Galileo, Cape Blanco following Teofilo, New Approach and Rip Van Winkle. In taking the latest renewal Cape Blanco showed a level of form that at least matched that which his immediate predecessors had achieved in the same race,

Galileo European Breeders' Fund Futurity Stakes, Fairyhouse—Cape Blanco (left) maintains his unbeaten record with a workmanlike victory over Mister Tee, King Ledley (noseband) and Marfach (cheekpieces)

and he leapt temporarily to the head of the Irish juvenile rankings as a result. His reign turned out to be short-lived, his form surpassed, among others, by a number of the fellow bluebloods in his own stable. That said, the unbeaten Cape Blanco remains a very smart prospect and, while it would be expecting too much for him even to get close to matching the exploits of New Approach and Rip Van Winkle, there are surely more pattern races to be won with him at three.

Cape Blanco faced just four opponents, including stablemate Kingdom of Munster, in the Korean Racing Authority Tyros Stakes, a race which had been promoted from listed to Group 3 status in 2007. Cape Blanco had looked very promising when winning a minor event at Fairyhouse the previous month on his debut, and duly stepped up considerably on that form when landing the odds at Leopardstown. Soon in front, Cape Blanco drew clear most impressively, after being ridden briefly over a furlong out, before being eased markedly near the line, value for double the three and a half lengths he had to spare over close-finishers Marfach and Perfect Symmetry. Both Teofilo and New Approach had followed up in the Group 2 Futurity Stakes and Cape Blanco did likewise, though not in the manner expected. The opposition to Cape Blanco looked no stronger than at Leopardstown—Marfach and Kingdom of Munster were again among his rivals in a seven-runner field—and he started at even shorter odds, 5/1-on in fact. Front-running tactics were employed once more, but this time Cape Blanco came under pressure two furlongs out and it was only well inside the final furlong that he managed to shake off the maiden Mister Tee, a length and a quarter the winning margin. The going seemed no softer than for the Tyros Stakes, but, according to Cape Blanco's rider Johnny Murtagh, the colt 'hated the ground and is definitely a fast-ground horse'. Cape Blanco, who wasn't seen out again, at least got an opportunity to show that he is not one to shirk the issue.

Cape Blanco (IRE) (ch.c. Apr 20, 2007)	Galileo (IRE) (b 1998)	Sadler's Wells (b 1981)	Northern Dancer
			Fairy Bridge
		Urban Sea (ch 1989)	Miswaki
			Allegretta
	Laurel Delight (ch 1990)	Presidium (b 1982)	General Assembly
			Doubly Sure
		Foudroyer (ch 1980)	Artaius
			Foudre

Cape Blanco has been raced solely at seven furlongs so far but he will stay a mile and possibly further still, even though his dam is a half-sister to the very smart sprinter Paris House and was all speed herself. Laurel Delight, trained like Paris House by Jack Berry, did virtually all of her racing at five furlongs and won four times. Cape Blanco, a €330,000 yearling, is Laurel Delight's eighth foal and fourth winner. Two of her other winners were also sprinters, Laurel Pleasure (by Selkirk) successful in Britain and Sweden and Spassky (by Emperor Jones) in Italy. The best of her offspring so far stayed eleven furlongs, Mr O'Brien (by Mukaddamah) showing very smart form at up to that trip in the States. With Cape Blanco's sire Galileo at least as much an influence for stamina as Mukaddamah, it would be no great surprise if middle distances proved within Cape Blanco's compass. *A. P. O'Brien, Ireland*

CAPE COBRA 5 ch.g. Inchinor 119 – Cape Merino 103 (Clantime 101) [2009 63§: 8m² p7.1g⁴ p7.1g p6g f5f Nov 24] fair handicapper: stays 1m: acts on polytrack, good to firm and good to soft going: sometimes blinkered: has given trouble at start: temperamental. *H. Morrison* **66 §**

CAPE COLONY 4 gr.c. Cape Town (IRE) 119 – Lucky Princess (Bijou d'Inde 127) [2009 93: p11g p12.2m p12g⁶ p12g⁵ 12g* 14m p12g⁴ Jun 24] good-topped colt: fairly useful handicapper: won at Doncaster in June: none too consistent otherwise: stays 1½m: acts on polytrack, good to firm and good to soft going: held up. *R. Hannon* **85**

CAPE DANCER (IRE) 5 b.m. Cape Cross (IRE) 129 – Yankee Dancer 62 (Groom Dancer (USA) 128) [2009 51: 10.1d⁶ Jun 6] sturdy, workmanlike mare: fluent mover: poor maiden: stays 1½m: acts on fibresand, firm and soft ground: tried in cheekpieces. *J. S. Wainwright* **47**

CAPE D'OR (IRE) 2 b.c. (Mar 31) Cape Cross (IRE) 129 – Sombreffe 71 (Polish Precedent (USA) 131) [2009 6m⁵ 7m³ Jun 27] 65,000F, 40,000Y, 100,000 2-y-o: neat colt: half-brother to several winners, including smart 1m (at 2 yrs)/1¼m (in Germany) winner Ransom O'War (by Red Ransom) and useful Irish 1m winner Madame Cerito (by Diesis): dam, 7f winner, closely related to smart performers up to 7f Russian Bond and Snaadee: similar form in maidens at Newmarket (second favourite, badly hampered) and Doncaster (8¼ lengths third to Layali Al Andalus): should stay 7f. *R. Hannon* **71**

CAPE EXPRESS (IRE) 4 b.g. Cape Cross (IRE) 129 – Lilissa (IRE) (Doyoun 124) [2009 80p: p12.2g* p11g³ 12.1d⁶ 10g⁴ Aug 14] useful handicapper, lightly raced: won at Wolverhampton (by 6 lengths) in January: excellent 1¼ lengths third to Greylami at Kempton next time: below form on turf after: stays 1½m: acts on polytrack. *M. A. Jarvis* **103**

CAPEFLY 4 b.f. Cape Cross (IRE) 129 – Patacake Patacake (USA) 67 (Bahri (USA) 125) [2009 –: p6g³ p6g Jan 24] neat filly: fair maiden, lightly raced: should stay 7f: acts on polytrack and firm going: tongue tied in 2009. *P. W. Chapple-Hyam* **69**

CAPE GREKO 7 ro.g. Loup Sauvage (USA) 125 – Onefortheditch (USA) 79 (With Approval (CAN)) [2009 –: 16s 10m p12m p16g⁶ p12m⁴ p16m Dec 1] tall, good-bodied gelding: modest handicapper nowadays: seems to stay 2m: acts on polytrack and firm ground: often visored. *B. G. Powell* **64**

CAPE HAWK (IRE) 5 b.g. Cape Cross (IRE) 129 – Hawksbill Special (IRE) (Taufan (USA) 119) [2009 101, a106: p8g 8.1g 8m³ 8m⁴ 8.3m⁶ 8g 9s⁴ 8.3m² 7m 8m⁵ 8d* Oct 11] strong, well-made gelding: useful handicapper: won at Goodwood in October: stays 1m: acts on polytrack, good to firm and good to soft ground: tried visored: sold 18,000 gns. *R. Hannon* **97**

CAPE KIMBERLEY 2 b.g. (May 3) Arakan (USA) 123 – Etoile Volant (USA) (Silver Hawk (USA) 123) [2009 f6g⁴ f6g⁵ 6d f5g⁶ f6g² f6m* p6m⁵ Nov 19] £10,000 2-y-o: first foal: dam unraced half-sister to useful performer up to 7f Ma Yoram out of sister to smart 7f/1m winner Rami: fair performer: improved to win nursery at Southwell in November: stays 6f: raced mostly on fibresand: gelded after final start. *J. G. Given* **75**

CAPE MARIEN (IRE) 3 b.f. Cape Cross (IRE) 129 – Marienbad (FR) (Darshaan 133) [2009 10m 11.6m* 11.5d p12m² p13.9g* p12m* p16.5g³ Oct 23] 100,000Y: big filly: half-sister to several winners, notably Prix de l'Arc de Triomphe winner Marienbard (by Caerleon): dam French 1m winner, including at 2 yrs: fairly useful form: won maiden at Windsor in June and handicaps at Wolverhampton and Kempton in October: stamina stretched final start: will prove best short of 2m: acts on polytrack and good to firm going: will still progress further. *D. R. Lanigan* **92 p**

CAPE MELODY 3 b.f. Piccolo 121 – Cape Charlotte (Mon Tresor 113) [2009 p7g 6m² 6m² 6m⁴ 6.1m* 7m⁶ 6g² 5g⁵ 6d⁴ 6d Oct 22] 8,000F, 16,000Y: big, useful-looking filly: **83**

second foal: dam unraced half-sister to useful sprinter Cape Merino, herself dam of very smart Hong Kong sprinter Cape of Good Hope: fairly useful handicapper: won at Chepstow in June: best form at 6f: acts on good to firm going. *H. Morrison*

CAPE OF LUCK (IRE) 6 b.g. Cape Cross (IRE) 129 – Fledgling 76 (Efisio 120) [2009 83, a58: p12g^4 p10g^3 p12g 10.2g 12m^4 10m May 22] smallish, well made gelding: modest handicapper nowadays: seemingly stays 1½m: acts on polytrack, good to firm and good to soft going: tongue tied once: sometimes wears cheekpieces/blinkers. *P. M. Phelan* **58**

CAPE OF STORMS 6 b.g. Cape Cross (IRE) 129 – Lloc 79 (Absalom 128) [2009 72: f6d^6 f6d^4 f6g^4 f6g^5 f6g* f7g^3 f6g^5 f7g^5 f6g* p6g f6g Dec 18] compact gelding: fair handicapper: won at Southwell in February and March: best at 6f/7f: acts on all-weather, lightly raced on turf: tried in headgear: usually races prominently. *R. Brotherton* **66**

CAPE QUARTER (USA) 3 b.g. Elusive Quality (USA) – June Moon (IRE) (Sadler's Wells (USA) 132) [2009 79P: f7m* Nov 12] useful-looking gelding: fair form in maidens 12 months apart (gelded in between): still green when winning at Southwell in November: will stay 1m: capable of better. *W. J. Haggas* **79 p**

CAPERCAILLIE (USA) 2 ch.f. (Apr 16) Elusive Quality (USA) – Silent Eskimo (USA) (Eskimo (USA)) [2009 5m* 5g* 5m^4 6g^4 6g Oct 10] $375,000Y: tall, useful-looking filly: has scope: sixth foal: half-sister to 3 winners in USA, including Silent Fusaichi (by Fusaichi Pegasus), 9f winner in France at 2 yrs: dam US Grade 2 8.5f winner: useful performer: won maiden in May and minor event in June, both at Musselburgh: at least respectable efforts when fourth in Queen Mary Stakes at Royal Ascot (7 lengths behind Jealous Again) and Cherry Hinton Stakes at Newmarket (beaten 6 lengths by Misheer): off 3 months, shaped as if amiss final outing: should prove better suited by 6f than 5f: acts on good to firm going. *M. Johnston* **95**

CAPE ROBERTO (IRE) 4 b.g. Cape Cross (IRE) 129 – Kalwada (USA) (Roberto (USA) 131) [2009 63: 10.1d Oct 27] compact gelding: modest maiden: well held only start at 4 yrs: stays 1m: acts on polytrack: has looked none too keen. *John Berry* **–**

CAPE ROCK 4 b.g. Cape Cross (IRE) 129 – Wildwood Flower 107 (Distant Relative 128) [2009 78: 7.1m* 6g^2 7g^3 7.1m^3 Aug 20] good-topped gelding: fairly useful handicapper: won at Chepstow in June: good placed efforts after: free-going sort, stays 7f: acts on polytrack, soft and good to firm going: in cheekpieces final start (reportedly bled). *W. J. Knight* **86**

CAPE ROYAL 9 b.g. Prince Sabo 123 – Indigo 86 (Primo Dominie 121) [2009 90: 5.3m 5m^6 5m^3 5f^2 5m^3 5g 5.1m^3 5.1v^2 5.1v^2 6f 5m^5 5m* 5m^2 5m^2 p5.1g 5m p5.1g 5.3d p5g^5 p5m^4 f5m^4 p5.1g p5m p5f^5 Dec 19] good-bodied gelding: type to carry plenty of condition: fairly useful handicapper on turf, fair on all-weather: won at Windsor in August: best at 5f: acts on all-weather and any turf going: blinkered/tongue tied: usually front runner: tough. *J. M. Bradley* **81 a73**

CAPE TRIBULATION 5 b.g. Hernando (FR) 127 – Gay Fantastic (Ela-Mana-Mou 132) [2009 94: 16.2g 12d Oct 24] good-bodied gelding: fairly useful performer on Flat at 4 yrs: shaped as if amiss in 2009: smart hurdler, in frame in Graded company in December: should stay 2m: raced on good/good to soft going. *J. M. Jefferson* **–**

CAPE VALE (IRE) 4 b.g. Cape Cross (IRE) 129 – Wolf Cleugh (IRE) 65 (Last Tycoon 131) [2009 96: 5m 6d^4 6g 5g^5 6m^2 6g* 6d^2 6m* 6m 5g^2 5d Oct 24] good-bodied, attractive gelding: useful handicapper: won at Ffos Las in July and Haydock in September: good second at Catterick penultimate start: effective at 5f/6f: acts on firm and good to soft going: front runner. *D. Nicholls* **98**

CAPISTRANO 6 b.g. Efisio 120 – Washita (Valiyar 129) [2009 56: f11g^4 f16g 8.3g^3 8.3g* Jun 17] close-coupled gelding: poor handicapper: left P. Mason after second start: won at Odense in June: stays 1¾m: acts on all-weather: has worn blinkers/cheekpieces. *M. Seisboll, Denmark* **47**

CAPITAL ATTRACTION (USA) 2 ch.c. (Feb 10) Speightstown (USA) 124 – Cecilia's Crown (USA) (Chief's Crown (USA)) [2009 8.3m^4 Oct 13] $105,000Y, 95,000 2-y-o: useful-looking colt: fourth foal: half-brother to winner in USA by Mineshaft: dam, US 5.5f (at 2 yrs) to 1m winner, placed in Grade 3 event at 2 yrs: 20/1, promising 5½ lengths fourth to Botanist in maiden at Leicester, wandering final 1f: should do better. *H. R. A. Cecil* **67 p**

CAPITALISE (IRE) 6 b.g. City On A Hill (USA) 114 – Prime Interest (IRE) (Kings Lake (USA) 133) [2009 69: p13.3g p16.5g p13g p13.9m^5 p16.5g^4 Mar 13] workmanlike **57**

gelding: modest handicapper nowadays: effective at 1½m to 2¼m: acts on polytrack and firm going: tried blinkered/tongue tied/in cheekpieces: held up: not straightforward. *Miss Gay Kelleway*

CAPITELLI (IRE) 3 b.f. Cape Cross (IRE) 129 – Dear Girl (IRE) 105 (Fairy King 76
(USA)) [2009 89: 9.9f^5 10g 10.2g^3 p12m^5 Nov 4] lightly-made filly: fair maiden: stays 1¼m: acts on polytrack and firm going: sold 4,000 gns. *R. Hannon*

CAPONE (IRE) 4 b.g. Daggers Drawn (USA) 114 – Order of The Day (USA) (Dayjur 96
(USA) 137) [2009 78: 7m 7g^6 6g* 6g* 6m^3 5.5d 7.2v^6 p6g^5 p6m^2 p6m^3 p6f* p6g^6 Dec 28] lengthy gelding: useful handicapper: won at Doncaster in July, Yarmouth in August and, having left G. Moss after sixth start, Kempton (improved when beating Vhujon ¾ length) in December: should stay 7f: acts on polytrack, good to firm and good to soft going: blinkered once: patiently ridden. *R. Curtis*

CAPO REGIME 3 ch.g. Captain Rio 122 – Ashtree Belle 87 (Up And At 'em 109) 69 §
[2009 69: 5.1m f6g* p6g 7.1m^3 7d 8g^5 8.1g^5 8m p7g^3 7m f8g^6 f6g^3 f7m Dec 15] lengthy gelding: fair performer: won claimer at Southwell in May: claimed from D. Nicholls £6,000 fourth start: stays 1m: acts on all-weather and good to firm going: often visored: hard ride. *P. Howling*

CAPPED FOR VICTORY (USA) 8 b.g. Red Ransom (USA) – Nazoo (IRE) 99 –
(Nijinsky (CAN) 138) [2009 58: f8s^6 p8.6g Apr 4] good-topped gelding: regressive maiden: tried blinkered/tongue tied. *W. Storey*

CAPRICORN RUN (USA) 6 br. or b.g. Elusive Quality (USA) – Cercida (USA) 106 §
(Copelan (USA)) [2009 113§: p8g^3 p8g^6 p7.1g^4 p7g* p7.1g^3 p7g* p8.6g p7g 6m 7m^3 6g^6 p7g^2 7f 6g 7m p6g^4 p7f Dec 16] well-made gelding: useful handicapper: won at Kempton and Lingfield in February: typically in-and-out form after, ran well when third at Newcastle (narrowly beaten by Mister Hardy) and runner-up at Lingfield (head behind Abbondanza): sold £65,000 after fourteenth start: probably best at 7f/1m nowadays: acts on all-weather and good to firm ground: usually wears headgear: often slowly away: one to treat with caution. *A. J. McCabe*

CAPRICORNUS (USA) 2 ch.c. (Feb 25) Rahy (USA) 115 – Silent Partner (USA) 70 p
(Capote (USA)) [2009 p8f^4 p7.1g* Dec 28] $65,000Y: seventh foal: brother to 2-y-o winner in USA and half-brother to 2 winners abroad: dam, US winner up to 8.5f (including at 2 yrs), half-sister to smart US Grade 3 1½m winner Lakeshore Road: fair form: won maiden at Wolverhampton by ½ length from Mnasikia, making all: will prove fully effective at 1m: should go on improving. *M. Johnston*

CAPRIO (IRE) 4 ch.g. Captain Rio 122 – Disarm (IRE) (Bahamian Bounty 116) [2009 90
82: f7d^2 p6g* p7.1m^2 f7g^2 p7g^3 f7g^2 f7g^5 6m* 6m^3 p6g 6d^5 7g^2 7d^2 7f^2 p7m p7.1g* Nov 27] useful looking gelding: fairly useful performer: won handicaps at Kempton (match) in February and, having left Tom Dascombe and rejoined former trainer after seventh start, Goodwood in May and Wolverhampton in November: effective at 6f/7f: acts on all-weather, firm and good to soft going: tried in blinkers/cheekpieces. *J. R. Boyle*

CAP ST JEAN (IRE) 5 b.g. Cape Cross (IRE) 129 – Karminiya (IRE) 58 (Primo 72
Dominie 121) [2009 72: f7s^2 f7g^2 f7g^4 p7.1g* f7d^2 p7.1g^6 f7g* f7g Jun 2] sturdy gelding: fair performer: won handicap at Wolverhampton in February and seller at Southwell in April: stays 9.5f: acts on all-weather and good to firm ground: wears cheekpieces: often slowly away/held up. *R. Hollinshead*

CAPTAIN BLAKE (IRE) 2 b. or br.g. (Mar 23) Captain Rio 122 – Green Flower –
(USA) 56 (Fappiano (USA)) [2009 p5g 5m 6.1g 8.1d 8m^6 8m Sep 23] rather leggy gelding: no form (left A. Haynes after second start). *P. D. Evans*

CAPTAIN BLUEBIRD (IRE) 2 ch.c. (May 1) Captain Rio 122 – Dolly Blue (IRE) 64
(Pennekamp (USA) 130) [2009 p6g^5 6g 6d^4 Aug 2] big colt: best effort in maidens when 9 lengths fourth to Quadrille at Newbury. *D. Donovan*

CAPTAIN BRADZ (USA) 3 ch.c. Diesis 133 – Garden Rose (IRE) 115 (Caerleon –
(USA) 132) [2009 –: f8s^2 f7d^6 p5.1g Jan 23] big colt: no solid form. *P. T. Midgley*

CAPTAIN BRILLIANCE (USA) 4 ch.c. Officer (USA) 120 – Bloomin Genius 111
(USA) (Beau Genius (CAN)) [2009 7m* 7m^2 7m 8m 8m^6 7d^3 Oct 24] big, good-topped colt: smart performer: missed 2008: won handicap at Newmarket in June: good efforts after when neck second to Plum Pudding in Bunbury Cup (handicap) at same track and 1¼ lengths third to Mia's Boy in minor event at Doncaster (visored): should stay 1m: raced only on good to firm and good to soft going. *J. Noseda*

CAPTAIN CAREY 3 b.g. Fraam 114 – Brigadiers Bird (IRE) (Mujadil (USA) 119) **81**
[2009 71+: p6g f5g* 5.1g* 5.2d^{6} 5g^{2} 5g^{5} 5d* 5.7f^{5} Aug 22] angular gelding: fairly useful handicapper: won at Southwell in March, Bath in April and Windsor in June: best form at 5f: acts on all-weather and good to soft going: sometimes slowly away. *M. S. Saunders*

CAPTAIN CASH 2 ch.g. (Mar 3) Kyllachy 129 – Fission 77 (Efisio 120) [2009 5m 6m 8d Aug 28] lengthy gelding: well held in maidens. *T. D. Easterby*

CAPTAIN CAVENDISH (IRE) 3 b.g. Captain Rio 122 – Fahan (IRE) 71 (Sri Pekan **–**
(USA) 117) [2009 63: f7g^{6} p7.1g p7.1g 7g p9.5g 7g Aug 28] modest performer at 2 yrs: well beaten at 3 yrs: wears headgear. *A. Bailey*

CAPTAIN CLINT (IRE) 2 b.g. (May 8) Captain Rio 122 – Lake Poopo (IRE) 79 **–**
(Persian Heights 129) [2009 6m 7g 7m f8m Nov 11] lengthy gelding: well held in maidens/nursery (tongue tied): subsequently gelded. *M. H. Tompkins*

CAPTAIN COOL (IRE) 2 ch.g. (Mar 23) Captain Rio 122 – Aiaie (Zafonic (USA) **52**
130) [2009 5m^{5} 5m 6m 7.5m^{6} 8.3m^{5} 8g 7d^{4} p7g^{3} p7g^{2} Dec 31] good-topped gelding: modest maiden: stays 7.5f: acts on polytrack, good to firm and good to soft going. *R. Hannon*

CAPTAIN DANCER (IRE) 3 ch.g. Danehill Dancer (IRE) 117 – Rain Flower (IRE) **79**
(Indian Ridge 123) [2009 83p: f7g 7s^{5} 7g^{6} Oct 23] attractive colt: fair performer, lightly raced: should prove best up to 7f: acts on soft going. *B. W. Hills*

CAPTAIN DUNNE (IRE) 4 b.g. Captain Rio 122 – Queen Bodicea (IRE) (Revoque **108**
(IRE) 122) [2009 106: 6g 5d^{2} 5g^{2} 5d 5g 5g^{6} 5.4m^{5} 5d^{6} 5.6m^{3} 5g* 6g Oct 10] lengthy, workmanlike gelding: useful handicapper: won minor event at Beverley in September: also ran well at 4 yrs when runner-up at Thirsk (beaten neck by Biniou) and Epsom ('Dash', short head behind Indian Trail): speedy front runner, very best form at 5f: acts on fibresand, soft and good to firm going. *T. D. Easterby*

CAPTAIN ELLIS (USA) 3 b.g. Five Star Day (USA) 120 – Adventure (USA) **84**
(Unbridled's Song (USA) 125) [2009 89: 8.1g^{3} 8.1f* 7m f8g Aug 27] big, strong, useful-looking gelding: fairly useful performer: won maiden at Haydock in July: trained by K. R. Burke prior to final start: free-going sort, stays easy 1m: acts on firm and soft going: tried in cheekpieces: sold 3,500 gns, sent to Switzerland. *A. P. Jarvis*

CAPTAIN FLACK 3 ch.g. Lucky Story (USA) 128 – Au Contraire § (Groom Dancer **65**
(USA) 128) [2009 –: p10g p12g* 14.1m p12.2g^{3} 14.1g^{4} Aug 30] tall gelding: fair performer: won seller at Lingfield in June: stays 1¾m: acts on polytrack: blinkered last 4 starts: not straightforward. *J. A. R. Toller*

CAPTAIN FLASHEART (IRE) 3 ch.g. Captain Rio 122 – Catfoot Lane 50 (Bats- **86 p**
hoof 122) [2009 51p: p5g^{5} p5g^{5} 7d 8s^{3} p8f* 7m* Sep 16] fairly useful form: much improved when winning handicaps at Kempton (apprentices) and Yarmouth (by 6 lengths) in September: stays 1m: acts on polytrack, soft and good to firm ground: likely to progress further. *S. C. Williams*

CAPTAIN GERRARD (IRE) 4 b.c. Oasis Dream 129 – Delphinus (Soviet Star **112**
(USA) 128) [2009 113: 6m 5v 5g 5m^{4} 5g 5m 5.1m^{2} 5m 5m^{6} 5.2m 5m 6g 5d^{6} Oct 24] smallish, strong colt: carried condition: smart performer: won Cornwallis Stakes at Ascot at 2 yrs and Palace House Stakes at Newmarket in 2008: none too consistent in 2009, best efforts when in frame in King's Stand Stakes at Royal Ascot (4 lengths fourth to Scenic Blast) and listed race at Chester (length second to Borderlescott): was best at 5f: acted on soft and good to firm going: tried blinkered: former front runner: to stand at Mickley Stud, Shropshire, fee £3,500. *B. Smart*

CAPTAIN IMPERIAL (IRE) 3 b.g. Captain Rio 122 – Imperialist (IRE) 93 (Imp- **71**
erial Frontier (USA) 112) [2009 75: 10g 12m 12g 12s 8d^{3} 7v^{5} p8.6g p12g p13.9g Nov 30] close-coupled gelding: fair performer: left T. Tate £5,600 after seventh start: seems to stay 8.6f: acts on all-weather and soft ground: twice pulled up in 2009. *R. Bastiman*

CAPTAIN JACKSPARRA (IRE) 5 b.g. Danehill (USA) 126 – Push A Venture 58 **87**
(Shirley Heights 130) [2009 98: 7m 7.1m^{2} f7g 7.1m f7g 9.3m^{2} 8.1m^{3} p8g* 7.6g p7.1g p8g^{5} Sep 9] dipped-backed gelding: useful at best, fairly useful in 2009: won claimer at Lingfield in July: barely stayed 9.3f: acted on all-weather and firm going: tried in cheek-pieces: was a free-going sort, usually raced prominently: was none too consistent: dead. *K. A. Ryan*

CAPTAIN KALLIS (IRE) 3 ch.g. Captain Rio 122 – Alicedale (USA) (Trempolino **66**
(USA) 135) [2009 66: f6g^{3} 6.1g^{2} 6f^{5} 5m^{5} f6g 6s^{3} 6g 6.1d Sep 4] compact gelding: fair

handicapper: free-going sort, but stays 7f: acts on fibresand, probably on soft going: tried visored: tongue tied last 4 starts: has looked hard ride. *D. J. S. ffrench Davis*

CAPTAIN MACARRY (IRE) 4 ch.g. Captain Rio 122 – Grannys Reluctance (IRE) **99** 63 (Anita's Prince 126) [2009 83: f7d^4 f7g^4 p7.1g* 7m^6 7.1m 7.5m* 8.5m^3 7g 8.5m^5 6.9g* 7m^2 p7.1g* 7m p7g* Oct 21] strong, sturdy gelding: useful handicapper: progressive in 2009, winning at Wolverhampton in February, Beverley in May, Carlisle in August, Wolverhampton in September and Kempton in October: effective at 7f/1m: acts on all-weather and firm going: visored: races prominently: sold 42,000 gns. *B. Smart*

CAPTAIN MAINWARING 4 b.g. Auction House (USA) 120 – Shalyah (IRE) 65 **62** (Shalford (IRE) 124§) [2009 67: p13g^3 p13.9g p12g 12m 10.1g^5 11.5g Jul 20] compact gelding: modest handicapper: stays 13f: acts on polytrack and soft going: in blinkers/cheekpieces at 4 yrs: races prominently. *N. P. Littmoden*

CAPTAIN OATS (IRE) 6 b.g. Bahhare (USA) 122 – Adarika (Kings Lake (USA) **60 ?** 133) [2009 10.2m^6 12.6d 10.2g^4 11.6f^6 8.1g^4 13.1g^2 Sep 7] angular gelding: modest maiden handicapper: possibly flattered from out of weights final start: stays 13f: acts on firm and good to soft going: tried in cheekpieces. *Mrs P. Ford*

CAPTAIN PEACHEY 3 b.c. Pursuit of Love 124 – Dekelsmary 61 (Komaite (USA)) **–** [2009 7.1m 6m 7d 5.1m^6 6m 5.7g Aug 6] sturdy colt: little sign of ability: tried blinkered. *B. R. Millman*

CAPTAIN RAMIUS (IRE) 3 b.c. Kheleyf (USA) 116 – Princess Mood (GER) **95** (Muhtarram (USA) 125) [2009 104: p8g 7m^6 May 23] sturdy colt: useful performer: unbeaten at 2 yrs: below form in listed events at Kempton and Newmarket in 2009: should stay 1m: acts on polytrack: has hung both ways under pressure. *S. A. Callaghan*

CAPTAINRISK (IRE) 3 b.g. Captain Rio 122 – Helderberg (USA) 79 (Diesis 133) **78** [2009 77: p8.6g^2 p8g^3 p7.1g* f7g^3 7.1m^5 8.1g^2 7g^5 Aug 12] fair handicapper: won at Wolverhampton in February: left M. Botti 20,000 gns prior to final start: gelded after: effective at 7f to 8.6f: acts on all-weather and good to firm going: often wears headgear: not straightforward. *Mrs C. A. Dunnett*

CAPTAIN ROYALE (IRE) 4 ch.g. Captain Rio 122 – Paix Royale (Royal Academy **63** (USA) 130) [2009 70: 8.5m f7g 7s f6g 6g^5 6m^4 6m^6 5s^2 5g* 5m^6 6g^5 5.1s Nov 4] strong, good-topped gelding: modest performer: won handicap at Hamilton in September: effective at stiff 5f, seems to stay 1m: acts on all-weather, good to firm and heavy going: tried visored, often in cheekpieces: has looked none too keen. *Miss Tracy Waggott*

CAPTAIN SACHIN (IRE) 2 b.g. (Mar 3) Captain Rio 122 – Belalzao (IRE) 71 **–** (Alzao (USA) 117) [2009 5g May 2] close-coupled gelding: 16/1 and very green, pulled up in maiden at Doncaster (veered left at start, rider lost irons). *T. J. Etherington*

CAPTAIN SCOOBY 3 b.g. Captain Rio 122 – Scooby Dooby Do 62 (Atraf 116) [2009 **78** 82: 6m^3 6m^3 6v^4 6d^3 6m^4 6g^5 5d* 6s^6 5m 6.1d Oct 15] good-topped gelding: fair handicapper: won at Carlisle in August: effective at 5f/6f: acts on soft and good to firm going: tried in cheekpieces/visor. *R. M. Whitaker*

CAPTAIN SIRUS (FR) 6 b.g. Fly To The Stars 124 – Zudika (IRE) (Ezzoud (IRE) **–** 126) [2009 –: 7m May 9] little form. *P. Butler*

CAPTAIN'S PARADISE (IRE) 2 b.f. (Apr 13) Rock of Gibraltar (IRE) 133 – **– p** Minnie Habit (Habitat 134) [2009 p6g 7d Jul 24] 115,000Y: half-sister to several winners, notably very smart 9f to 1½m winner Kutub (by In The Wings): dam Irish 9f winner: behind in maidens: likely to do better at 3 yrs. *Sir Mark Prescott*

CAPTAIN TEDDO 3 ch.c. Auction House (USA) 120 – Charlottevalentina (IRE) 80 **–** (Perugino (USA) 84) [2009 6m p7g 5.1m Sep 13] no sign of ability. *R. Ingram*

CAPTAIN WALCOT 3 b.g. Fantastic Light (USA) 134 – Princess Minnie (Mistertopogigo (IRE) 118) **56** [2009 63: p10g^5 p8.6g^6 Jan 25] good-topped gelding: modest maiden: best efforts at 1m: raced only on polytrack and good going or firmer: tried in cheekpieces, blinkered nowadays. *R. Hannon*

CAPUCCI 4 b.g. King's Best (USA) 132 – Design Perfection (USA) 105 (Diesis 133) **87** [2009 90: 8m^6 8.1m^5 8m^3 8.1m^6 p7.1g^2 6g^6 9.1d^5 8g 7.5g^4 p7.1g* 7g^5 Oct 17] robust gelding: fairly useful performer: won claimer at Wolverhampton in October: effective at 7f/1m: acts on polytrack, unraced on extremes of going on turf: often tongue tied, in cheekpieces last 2 starts: not straightforward: sold £12,500. *J. J. Quinn*

CARACAL 2 b.c. (Feb 9) Dubai Destination (USA) 127 – Desert Lynx (IRE) 79 (Green Desert (USA) 127) [2009 7.1m 7d^4 Jul 25] modest form in maidens at Warwick and Newcastle. *M. Johnston* **63**

CARACCIOLA (GER) 12 b.g. Lando (GER) 128 – Capitolina (FR) (Empery (USA) 128) [2009 112: 14m* 21.7m* 16g^4 Jul 30] **108**

'Brown Jack vies with Arkle for the title of the most popular horse ever to have raced in the British Isles,' wrote respected racing historians Roger Mortimer and Peter Willett in 1972, a view which was backed up by John Randall and Tony Morris in 'A Century of Champions' in late-1999, who described the gelding as 'the only Flat horse in the 20th century to make a significant impact on the non-racing British public'. Seven successive wins at Royal Ascot, including six victories in the marathon Queen Alexandra Stakes, largely explain why Brown Jack became such a favourite in the late-'twenties and early-'thirties, particularly as those Flat exploits all came after he had enjoyed notable success in his first and only campaign over hurdles when he won the second running of the Champion Hurdle at Cheltenham as a four-year-old. Brown Jack could not run in Royal Ascot's premier race, the Gold Cup, because geldings were ineligible to run in any championship event at that time (the rule banning the participation of geldings in the Gold Cup was only relaxed in 1986!). However, Brown Jack put up several notable performances against the leading entires of the period, his efforts suggesting he would have held his own in the Gold Cup—his length win in the 1931 Chester Cup, for example, coming from that year's Gold Cup winner Trimdon to whom Brown Jack was conceding 6 lb. Brown Jack was partnered by popular champion jockey Steve Donoghue for the vast majority of his Flat career and

Stowe Family Law LLP Grand Cup, York—Caracciola (right) becomes the oldest winner of a listed race in Britain as he gets the better of a good battle with Friston Forest

Queen Alexandra Stakes, Ascot—Caracciola surpasses the legendary Brown Jack to become Royal Ascot's oldest winner; behind him are Tyrrells Wood (left) and the grey Amerigo

chalked up plenty of other big-race wins away from Ascot, including the Ebor, Doncaster Cup and Goodwood Cup. An impressive overall record contributed to his unprecedented popularity, which resulted, after retirement, in 1934, in Brown Jack being made the subject of a biography published that year, as well as having a steam train named after him and a bronze statue by Sir Alfred Munnings commissioned at Ascot.

Royal Ascot has witnessed in recent years the performances of another record-breaking stayer, those of Yeats. However, the four-times Gold Cup winner wasn't the horse who claimed one of Brown Jack's Royal Ascot records in 2009. Fittingly, perhaps, that claim to fame fell to a gelding and in the very race which Brown Jack made his own, the Queen Alexandra Stakes, the latest renewal of which went to twelve-year-old Caracciola, who became the oldest-ever Royal Ascot winner—surpassing Brown Jack, who had claimed his final victory in the race at the age of ten. In common with Brown Jack, ex-German Caracciola began his career on British soil over jumps and had had twenty-three starts in that sphere—thirteen (including four wins) over hurdles and ten (two wins) over fences—before connections opted to put him back on the Flat in 2006. An uninspiring tenth of fifteen in a staying handicap at Ascot did not set the pulse racing but Caracciola has proved a model of consistency in three subsequent Flat campaigns, finishing out of the frame just twice from eleven starts (including in Ascot's Brown Jack Handicap in 2008) and winning four times (he has not won from thirteen starts over hurdles in the same period). Caracciola's Royal Ascot win isn't the only time he has belied his advanced years, either. His victory at 50/1 in the 2008 totesport.com Cesarewitch at Newmarket, when stepping up on his second the previous year as a ten-year-old twelve months earlier, made him the oldest winner in that race's 170-year history (Brown Jack was third under top weight in the 1929 renewal), whilst his 2009 reappearance win in the Stowe Family Law LLP Grand Cup at York in late-May saw him become the oldest horse to win a listed race, wresting that particular title from another durable stayer Further Flight, who was eleven when winning a listed handicap at Chester in 1997. With Dale Gibson standing in for regular jockey Eddie Ahern (claimed elsewhere that afternoon), there was a change of tactics for Caracciola's York win as he dictated matters to counter fears of a steady pace over the mile and three quarters before finding plenty under pressure to hold off the favourite Friston Forest by a short head.

Caracciola had nearly a mile further to cover when next seen in the Queen Alexandra, still Britain's longest Flat race despite having ninety-five yards shaved off it when Ascot's track was realigned in 2005. As usual, the long-standing event drew a mixed bag in terms of ability and attracted several who, like Caracciola, had been hurdling the previous winter, including his stable-companion Tasheba (the 100/30 favourite). Caracciola won despite having managed only sixth in the 2008 renewal and conceding weight all round in the latest one by virtue of a penalty for his York win. Reunited with Ahern, Caracciola showed the best finishing speed to win by two and a half lengths, chased home by Tyrrells Wood, Amerigo and Tasheba, a trio whose combined age was twelve! The Queen Alexandra was Henderson's last training success before a three-month ban on entries from his stable following the failing of a dope-test by one of the Queen's jumpers Moonlit Path during the 2008/9 National Hunt season. This meant Caracciola had to be switched to the nearby yard of Barry Hills (Further Flight's trainer) for his only subsequent outing in 2009, when he ran rather a flat race and managed only a well-beaten fourth of ten behind Schiaparelli in the Goodwood Cup (a race Brown Jack won in 1930). The Melbourne Cup and a very valuable Group 2 staying event in Japan were being mooted as possible end-of-season targets for Caracciola at the time, but Henderson finally reported in November that ideas of a foreign trip had been scrapped due to Caracciola not pleasing in his work.

The Goodwood Cup wasn't the first pattern race Caracciola had contested, as he had reached a similar standard during his career on the Flat in Germany for Peter Rau, overcoming a foot problem which sidelined him for eighteen months after his two-year-old debut to win five times at up to a mile and a half as a four-year-old before finishing unplaced in Group 3 company. It's doubtful whether Caracciola's subsequent exploits in Britain will have made much of an impact back in his native country but his namesake won't be forgotten there. The pioneering German racing driver Rudolf Caracciola was widely regarded as the greatest between the wars and won the European Drivers' Championship (forerunner of Formula One) a record three times. Caracciola isn't the only legendary racing driver to have been recognised in horseracing circles. Formula One's huge global impact (average televised audience 600m per grand prix) explains why horses named after its champions have tasted success all around the world. Senna was a prolific winner at up to a mile and a quarter in Germany, Mansell a winning sprinter in Italy, Surtees a successful export to the States, Rosberg a smart miler in the UAE and Raikkonen a winning stayer on the Flat/over hurdles in Ireland (Ascari, Fangio, Piquet and Prost were all also winners on British soil). Irish trainer Augustine Leahy enjoyed plenty of success when housing much of the grand prix grid for a period during the 'nineties, notably with the fairly useful hurdler/chaser Hakkinen (his successful stable companions included Irvine and Coulthard), but he drew a blank with Schumacher!

Caracciola (GER) (b.g. 1997)	Lando (GER) (b 1990)	Acatenango (ch 1982)	Surumu
			Aggravate
		Laurea (b 1983)	Sharpman
			Licata
	Capitolina (FR) (b 1984)	Empery (b 1973)	Vaguely Noble
			Pamplona
		Conquista (b 1978)	Caro
			Clementina

Caracciola isn't the only offspring of Capitolina (a mile- to mile-and-a-quarter winner in France) to have enjoyed his fair share of champagne moments, as all eleven of the dam's foals to reach the racecourse have won. Chief amongst these is Camp David (by Surumu), who was a smart and prolific winning stayer in

Germany during the mid-'nineties, though he was well held in the 1997 Gold Cup on his only Royal Ascot appearance. The majority of the others have also plied their trade on the Flat in Germany, including the listed winner Ceneketes (by Lagunas) and Caracciola's close relative Capitain Rodgers (by Laroche), who won seven times at up to a mile and a half for Rau. There have been several other winners away from Germany, however, notably Caracciola's sister Capitana, who developed into a fairly useful two-mile hurdler for his connections.

Rudolf Caracciola was dubbed 'Regenmeister' (rainmaster) for his prowess in wet conditions, but his equine namesake doesn't follow suit and has shown his very best form (including over jumps) on good going or firmer, his two record-breaking wins in 2009 coming on good to firm. Caracciola clearly stays very well, though he isn't a sluggard by any means and has put up his best performances at the minimum trip so far over jumps. Retirement apparently isn't yet on the cards, with Henderson reporting that Caracciola is due to carry on as a teenager on the Flat in 2010. *B. W. Hills*

CARAMELITA 2 b.f. (Apr 14) Deportivo 116 – Apple of My Eye 70 (Fraam 114) **69**
[2009 6m^{5} 6m^{5} 6d^{2} 6m^{4} p6m^{3} f5g^{3} Dec 8] first foal: dam, 2-y-o 6f winner, half-sister to useful performers up to 1m Spitfire and Fruit of Glory: fair maiden: effective at 5f/6f: ridden prominently. *J. R. Jenkins*

CARANBOLA 3 br.f. Lucky Story (USA) 128 – Ladywell Blaise (IRE) 63 (Turtle **72**
Island (IRE) 123) [2009 90: 5f^{6} 6d^{6} 6m 6m 6g 6d 6m^{3} 6d^{5} 5m^{2} 5g Sep 21] leggy, lengthy filly: just fair handicapper nowadays: will prove best kept to 5f/6f: acts on soft and good to firm going. *M. Brittain*

CARA'S REQUEST (AUS) 4 gr.g. Urgent Request (IRE) 120 – Carahill (AUS) **83**
(Danehill (USA) 126) [2009 79: 8.1v 8.3m^{5} 6m^{5} 7g 7s^{3} 7.2v Oct 31] compact gelding: fairly useful performer: left L. Cumani after second start: gelded after final one: likely to prove best up to 1m: acts on soft and good to firm ground: temperament firmly under suspicion. *D. Nicholls*

CARAVAN OF DREAMS (IRE) 3 b.f. Anabaa (USA) 130 – Smart 'n Noble (USA) **62**
(Smarten (USA)) [2009 74: p7g^{5} Jan 28] sturdy filly: fair maiden in 2008: below form only start at 3 yrs: stays 1m: raced only on polytrack and good ground or firmer on turf. *M. A. Jarvis*

CARBON HOOFPRINT 3 b.g. Green Tune (USA) 125 – Salome's Attack 90 **90**
(Anabaa (USA) 130) [2009 p8g^{3} p8g^{2} 8g^{3} 10m^{6} 8m^{2} 8m^{2} 8d* 8f^{2} 8m^{6} p7g^{5} f7m^{4} Nov 12] 15,000Y: lengthy gelding: second foal: half brother to fairly useful 2007 2-y-o 6f winner (stays 1¼m) Double Attack (by Peintre Celebre): dam, French 7.5f (at 2 yrs) to 9.5f winner, half-sister to very smart stayer Double Honour and to dam of 3-y-o Cavalryman: fairly useful performer: won handicap at Bath in August: stays 1m: acts on all-weather, firm and good to soft going: claimed £13,000 final start, and sent to USA. *P. J. Makin*

CARBON PRINT (USA) 4 ch.g. Johannesburg (USA) 127 – Caithness (USA) **62**
(Roberto (USA) 131) [2009 47: 10g 9.9g 10d^{4} 10s^{5} 10.1g Aug 30] quite attractive gelding: modest maiden: stays 1¼m: raced on good going or softer: held up. *P. R. Webber*

CARCINETTO (IRE) 7 b.m. Danetime (IRE) 121 – Dolphin Stamp (IRE) (Dolphin **104**
Street (FR) 125) [2009 96: p6g^{5} p6g^{5} p6g 5.7g* 7.1m^{3} 7f^{2} 7f^{3} 5.1g 5.1m 6.1m^{2} 6d^{4} 7m* 6m^{6} 6m 7m 6.1g^{4} 6m^{6} 7.6m* 7g 7m 7.6m^{3} 6m^{4} 7m^{6} p8g^{4} p8.6g p7g^{2} p7g^{5} p8m p7f Dec 16] angular mare: useful performer, improved again in 2009: won handicap at Bath in April, minor event at Leicester (by 7 lengths from Qalahari) in June and handicap at Chester (beat Lowther a neck) in August: also placed twice in listed races: stays 1m: acts on polytrack and firm ground, below form on softer than good: tried in headgear: versatile regards tactics. *P. D. Evans*

CARDENIO (USA) 3 b. or br.f. Proud Citizen (USA) 122 – Divine Diva (USA) **49**
(Theatrical 128) [2009 6f 6g 6m p7f p8f Oct 14] $32,000Y, £32,000 2-y-o: third foal: half-sister to 2 winners, including 2007 2-y-o 6f winner Eager Diva (by More Than Ready): dam, ran once in USA, sister to US Grade 3 8.5f winner Sing For Free: poor maiden. *J. R. Gask*

CARDINAL 4 ch.c. Pivotal 124 – Fictitious 100 (Machiavellian (USA) 123) [2009 p8g **66**
6m 6g^{5} 6v^{2} 7.6d^{4} 6.1d^{5} 7m p6g Nov 13] plain colt: fair maiden: stays 6f: acts on polytrack and heavy ground, probably on good to firm: tried tongue tied. *R. A. Harris*

CARDINAL JAMES (IRE) 5 br.g. Bishop of Cashel 122 – Dilwara (IRE) (Lashkari **55**
128) [2009 p11g^{5} Feb 25] poor hurdler: 4/1, 5¼ lengths fifth to Soul Singer in maiden at Kempton, carried left in straight. *Miss Tor Sturgis*

CARDOSSI 2 ch.f. (Feb 26) Dr Fong (USA) 128 – English Harbour 81 (Sabrehill **–**
(USA) 120) [2009 8g Oct 20] fourth foal: half-sister to winner in Greece by Nashwan: dam, 1¼m winner, half-sister to high-class 1¼m/1½m performer Environment Friend: 33/1 and green, always behind in maiden at Yarmouth. *M. L. W. Bell*

CARIAD COCH 2 b.f. (Feb 9) Reset (AUS) 124 – Silly Mid-On (Midyan (USA) 124) **37**
[2009 5m^{5} f5g 6v p5.1m p6m Sep 28] seventh foal: half-sister to 5-y-o Tobago Reef: dam once-raced half-sister to smart 1¼m to 2m winner Sarangani: poor form, including in seller. *Mrs L. Stubbs*

CARIBBEAN CORAL 10 ch.g. Brief Truce (USA) 126 – Caribbean Star 81 (Soviet **73**
Star (USA) 128) [2009 89: p5g^{3} p5g^{4} p5g 6d 5.7m^{2} 6g^{2} 5.1g^{4} 6g^{3} 6m^{3} 5.7m* 6m* 6m^{2} 5.3f 5.3f^{2} 5.1m^{4} 5g^{3} 5.3m^{6} Sep 28] strong gelding: fair performer: won sellers at Bath and Brighton in June: effective at 5f/easy 6f: acts on polytrack and any turf going: tried in visor/cheekpieces: tends to carry head awkwardly, but is reliable. *A. B. Haynes*

CARIBOU ISLAND 2 b.c. (Mar 1) Dansili 127 – Lake Nipigon (Selkirk (USA) 129) **57**
[2009 7m^{5} Aug 5] €160,000Y: first foal: dam unraced half-sister to Irish sprinter Blue Dream and 1m/9f performer Equity Princess, both useful: 9/2, fifth to Jutland in maiden at Brighton (not unduly knocked about), then left Godolphin. *Saeed bin Suroor*

CARIOCA (IRE) 2 br.f. (Apr 30) Rakti 130 – Cidaris (IRE) (Persian Bold 123) [2009 **72**
7g^{4} 7g^{6} Aug 8] €95,000F: sturdy filly: seventh foal: half-sister to 3 winners, including useful 5f (at 2 yrs) and 1m winner Irony (by Mujadil): dam, ran once at 2 yrs in Ireland, out of sister to 2000 Guineas winner Mystiko: fair form in maidens at Doncaster (fourth to Clarietta) and Newmarket (sixth to Eolith, not knocked about). *M. Botti*

CARLCOL GIRL 2 b.f. (Mar 17) Where Or When (IRE) 124 – Capstick (JPN) (Mach- **–**
iavellian (USA) 123) [2009 7d 7d p7.1g 8m^{5} 8.3d 7d Oct 27] leggy filly: second foal: dam unraced: no form: tried visored/in cheekpieces. *Mrs C. A. Dunnett*

CARLETON 4 b.g. Hunting Lion (IRE) 115 – Canadian Capers 70 (Ballacashtal **83**
(CAN)) [2009 94: 6g^{5} 6d 6m^{6} 6g^{4} p7.1g^{4} p7.1g^{3} Jul 13] big, strong gelding: usually takes the eye: fairly useful handicapper: shaped well several times at 4 yrs, but on lengthy losing run: stays 7f: acts on polytrack, firm and good to soft going: tends to get behind. *W. J. Musson*

CARLITOS SPIRIT (IRE) 5 ch.g. Redback 116 – Negria (IRE) (Al Hareb (USA) **88**
123) [2009 90: p7g^{5} 7m 8.1g 7m^{5} 7m^{3} 7.6f* 8d 7.1m^{5} p8g^{6} p8g^{5} p7m Sep 23] lengthy gelding: fairly useful handicapper: won at Lingfield in June: stays 1m: acts on polytrack, firm and soft going: tried blinkered: not straightforward, tends to wander: joined I. McInnes. *B. R. Millman*

CARLTON MAC 4 ch.g. Timeless Times (USA) 99 – Julie's Gift (Presidium 124) **51**
[2009 51: 12d 15.8g* 12.1m 15.8v 12.1g^{6} Sep 22] small gelding: modest performer: won seller at Catterick in August: stays 15.8f: acts on heavy ground: often in headgear. *N. Bycroft*

CARLTON SCROOP (FR) 6 ch.g. Priolo (USA) 127 – Elms Schooldays (Emarati **68**
(USA) 74) [2009 54: p11g* p16g^{3} p12g^{2} p16.5g^{2} p12g p12g* Mar 18] stocky gelding: fair handicapper: won at Kempton in January and Lingfield in March: effective at 11f to 2m: acts on polytrack and good to firm ground: blinkered. *J. Jay*

CARMELA MARIA 4 b.f. Medicean 128 – Carmela Owen (Owington 123) [2009 71: **67**
10.1d p10g 12m^{2} 10.9d^{3} 10g^{5} 11.9f^{5} 11s^{5} 9.7m^{6} 10.1g^{2} p12.2g^{2} 13.8m^{6} Sep 19] sturdy filly: fair handicapper: claimed from S. C. Williams £6,000 after penultimate start: stays 1½m: acts on polytrack, good to soft and good to firm going: races prominently: in cheek-pieces last 3 starts. *M. E. Sowersby*

CARMENERO (GER) 6 b.g. Barathea (IRE) 127 – Claire Fraser (USA) (Gone West **78**
(USA)) [2009 85: p7g^{6} 7g^{4} p7g^{4} 7g^{5} 6d* p7.1g 7.5f p7m^{4} p6g^{6} 6d^{5} p7m p6g Dec 12] sturdy, close-coupled gelding: fair performer: won seller at Brighton (left W. Muir 11,500 gns) in August: stays 1m: acts on polytrack and firm going: held up: effective in cheek-pieces or not. *C. R. Dore*

CARNABY STREET (IRE) 2 b.c. (Feb 3) Le Vie Dei Colori 126 – Prodigal Daugh- **104**
ter (Alhaarth (IRE) 126) [2009 6.1m 6g^{2} 6g 6m^{2} 6.5m 6d* 7v* Oct 24] €30,000F, £50,000Y: good-bodied colt: first foal: dam unraced daughter of useful Irish 6f/7f

Noodles Racing's "Carnaby Street"

performer Shallow Ground: useful performer: won maiden at Goodwood (readily) and totesport Horris Hill Stakes at Newbury (beat Pleasant Day a short head, rallying gamely), both in October: also ran well when neck second to Midnight Martini in sales race at York fourth start: will stay 1m: acts on heavy and good to firm ground. *R. Hannon*

CARNACKI (USA) 2 b.c. (Feb 18) Ghostzapper (USA) 137 – Guana (FR) (Sillery (USA) 122) [2009 p7f Sep 10] 12/1, badly in need of experience when last in maiden at Kempton: sold 2,500 gns. *J. Noseda* –

CARNAVAL COURT (IRE) 2 b.f. (Mar 28) Saffron Walden (FR) 123 – Bellagio Princess 58 (Kris 135) [2009 6g 6.1g^4 8.1d p8m 7.1m p8m^2 Oct 12] tall filly: second foal: sister to 3-y-o Foundation Room: dam, maiden (should have stayed 1m), out of half-sister to Coronation Stakes winner Balisada: modest maiden: stays 1m: acts on polytrack: tried visored/blinkered: sold £750. *A. M. Balding* **63**

CARNIVAL DREAM 4 b.f. Carnival Dancer 123 – Reach The Wind (USA) (Relaunch (USA)) [2009 49: p7.1g p8.6m 7m 7.9g^4 9.3m 8m^3 8m 8m^4 7m^2 6s^2 7m^6 7.2m p8.6g p6g* p7.1m Nov 28] leggy, close-coupled filly: modest performer: won handicap at Wolverhampton in November: probably stays 1m: acts on polytrack, firm and soft ground: often wears blinkers/cheekpieces. *H. A. McWilliams* **63**

CARNIVAL FAIR 4 b.f. Carnival Dancer 123 – Testament (Darshaan 133) [2009 8m 12.5m^5 12.4g 8f 11.8m p12.2g Nov 9] 4,000 2-y-o: second foal: half-sister to winner in Greece by Pivotal: dam, ran once, closely related to smart middle-distance stayer Sacrament: well held in 2 bumpers: little form on Flat: left R. Fahey after fourth start: tried tongue tied/visored. *S. Wynne* –

CARNIVAL TIME (IRE) 2 ch.g. (Feb 23) Captain Rio 122 – Latest (IRE) (Bob Back (USA) 124) [2009 6g 6.1g Aug 13] good-topped gelding: well beaten in maidens at Windsor and Chepstow (blinkered): subsequently gelded. *C. G. Cox* –

CARNIVORE 7 ch.g. Zafonic (USA) 130 – Ermine (IRE) 86 (Cadeaux Genereux 131) [2009 88: p7.1g p8.6g* p7g⁶ 7s² 7m 7.9m 7g* p7.1g⁶ p7f⁵ Dec 21] tall gelding: fairly useful performer: won claimer at Wolverhampton in February and apprentice handicap at Redcar in September: effective at 7f to 8.6f: acts on polytrack, firm and good to soft going: tried tongue tied: sometimes finds little. *T. D. Barron* **85**

CAROLE OS (IRE) 4 b.f. Catcher In The Rye (IRE) 115 – Kuda Chantik (IRE) 53 (Lashkari 128) [2009 –: p8g Mar 1] little form since 2007. *S. W. Hall* –

CARPE DIEM 4 b.g. Stravinsky (USA) 133 – Spare That Tree (USA) (Woodman (USA) 126) [2009 61: 8.5m⁴ 8.3m 7.5m² 7.9m³ 8m f8g⁶ 7.9g 8d⁴ 9.8d 8.5m Sep 16] strong gelding: modest maiden handicapper: stays 8.4f: acts on firm ground: tried visored/in cheekpieces. *R. A. Fahey* **60**

CARRAGOLD 3 b.c. Diktat 126 – Shadow Roll (IRE) 79 (Mark of Esteem (IRE) 137) [2009 6m⁴ 6d⁶ 7.5m³ 8m⁵ 8.5m² p9.5g⁵ p12.2g Dec 12] workmanlike colt: modest maiden: stays 9.5f: acts on polytrack, yet to race on extremes of going on turf. *M. Brittain* **60**

CARRAZARA (IRE) 3 b.f. Namid 128 – Carrozzina 70 (Vettori (IRE) 119) [2009 p10g⁶ 10s 8.1g 5.1g 7g Jun 20] leggy filly: third foal: sister to 4-y-o Solent Ridge: dam 2-y-o 7f winner: no form: tried blinkered. *Edgar Byrne* –

CARR HALL (IRE) 6 b.g. Rossini (USA) 118 – Pidgeon Bay (IRE) 66 (Perugino (USA) 84) [2009 12d⁶ 12m* 8.5f⁵ p13.9m p12m⁴ p13.9g⁴ p12g⁵ Dec 31] tall gelding: modest handicapper: won at Les Landes in August: left Mrs J. Le Brocq in Jersey after fourth start: probably best short of 1¾m: acts on polytrack, firm and good to soft going: tried blinkered. *B. G. Powell* **60**

CARRIES LASS 2 br.f. (Apr 7) Auction House (USA) 120 – Carranita (IRE) 111 (Anita's Prince 126) [2009 5g 5.7f⁶ 6g⁶ 6g Jul 4] leggy filly: sixth foal: dam 5f/6f winner, including at 2 yrs: poor form in maidens/sellers: tried blinkered: not straightforward. *J. A. Osborne* **36**

CARRY ON CLEO 4 ch.f. First Trump 118 – Classy Cleo (IRE) 102 (Mujadil (USA) 119) [2009 59: p9.5g p9.5g p9.5g p9.5g⁶ Feb 17] compact filly: poor performer nowadays: stays 1¼m: acts on polytrack and heavy ground: wears visor/blinkers, tried tongue tied. *A. Berry* **36**

CARSINGTON 5 ch.m. And Beyond (IRE) 113 – Nutmeg Point (Nashwan (USA) 135) [2009 10.4g May 29] half-sister to winners in Italy by Zilzal and Halling: dam unraced half-sister to very smart middle-distance performer John French: poor form in bumpers/maiden at Haydock (seventh of 10). *Lucinda Featherstone* **47**

CARSON'S SPIRIT (USA) 5 ch.g. Carson City (USA) – Pascarina (FR) (Exit To Nowhere (USA) 122) [2009 72: 7m Jul 3] good-topped gelding: fair handicapper, very lightly raced nowadays: well beaten in claimer only start at 5 yrs: stays 1m: acts on soft and good to firm going: blinkered once: not straightforward. *J. R. Gask* –

CARTE DIAMOND (USA) 8 ch.g. Theatrical 128 – Liteup My Life (USA) (Green Dancer (USA) 132) [2009 109: 12m⁶ p16g³ 18.7m 16.1d 12m f14g³ Oct 27] tall gelding: one-time smart performer: form in 2009 only when 3¾ lengths third to Keenes Day in handicap at Lingfield on second start: was effective at 1½m to easy 2m: acted on polytrack, soft and good to firm going: tried blinkered: refused to race fourth 7-y-o outing: inconsistent: reportedly retired. *B. Ellison* **102 §**

CARTE D'ORO (IRE) 3 b.f. Medaglia d'Oro (USA) 129 – Prospectress (USA) 87 (Mining (USA)) [2009 –: 10.2g 10m⁵ 9.9f⁵ 9.9g 10f⁴ Sep 2] lengthy filly: modest maiden: stays 1¼m: acts on firm going. *R. M. Beckett* **64**

CARTER 3 b.g. Reset (AUS) 124 – Cameo Role (GER) 78 (Acatenango (GER) 127) [2009 59: 8.1m 8.3g⁴ 10.3g* 10.3g 10s⁵ 11.1g⁶ p10g⁶ p12m² Oct 26] workmanlike gelding: fair handicapper: won at Chester in June: stays 1½m: acts on polytrack, best turf efforts on good going. *W. M. Brisbourne* **66**

CARTOON 3 br.f. Danehill Dancer (IRE) 117 – Elfin Laughter 76 (Alzao (USA) 117) [2009 –p: 8.3m* Apr 20] tall filly: fairly useful form, lightly raced: won maiden at Windsor only start at 3 yrs by neck from Strawberrydaiquiri: stays 1m: acts on good to firm going: sold 70,000 gns in December. *M. A. Jarvis* **81**

CARTOONIST (IRE) 6 ch.g. Fruits of Love (USA) 127 – Verusa (IRE) (Petorius 117) [2009 p12g Jan 18] no longer of any account. *M. Mullineaux* **–**

CARVED EMERALD 4 b.f. Pivotal 124 – Emerald Peace (IRE) 103 (Green Desert (USA) 127) [2009 85: a7.5g a7g^5 8g^6 p7m p6m^5 p6g Oct 24] fairly useful performer: left R. Gibson in France after third start: stays 1m: acts on all-weather: has been blinkered. *D. R. C. Elsworth* **88**

CASABLANCA MINX (IRE) 6 b.m. Desert Story (IRE) 115 – Conspire (IRE) 81 (Turtle Island (IRE) 123) [2009 65: p8.6g^6 p10g p12.2g* f12d 12m 11.5m 9m^4 10.2g^2 11.5g^4 11.9d^5 12.1m^5 p9.5g^6 p9.5g p12.2g^5 p13.9g Dec 14] lengthy mare: modest handicapper: won at Wolverhampton (amateurs) in February: left Gay Kelleway after eleventh start: stays 13f: acts on polytrack, firm and soft ground: blinkered/visored: has been tongue tied: held up: hard ride. *A. G. Juckes* **60 §**

CASANOVA KID 2 b.c. (Apr 19) Pastoral Pursuits 127 – Dust 61 (Green Desert (USA) 127) [2009 5.1m^6 p6g 6f^6 5g p6m Nov 21] strong colt: no form in maidens. *E. J. Creighton* **–**

CASCATA (IRE) 3 b.f. Montjeu (IRE) 137 – Leaping Water (Sure Blade (USA) 130) [2009 80p: p9.5g^4 9.9m^6 9.8m^2 12m^4 Sep 19] well-made filly: fairly useful handicapper: good efforts in frame last 2 starts: stays 1½m: acts on polytrack and good to firm ground. *L. M. Cumani* **86**

CASEWICK STAR 2 ch.f. (Apr 5) Reset (AUS) 124 – Be My Tinker 75 (Be My Chief (USA) 122) [2009 5.2d Jul 27] third foal: dam 5f/6f winner: 25/1, last in maiden at Yarmouth. *P. W. D'Arcy* **–**

CASEY'S REBEL (IRE) 2 b.f. (May 19) Antonius Pius (USA) 123§ – Agent Scully (IRE) 66 (Simply Great (FR) 122) [2009 6.1v^4 7d 7m Sep 1] €3,000 2-y-o: small filly: half-sister to 1m winner Spot The Subbie (by Tagula) and Irish 8.5f winner Annie's Dream (by Lahib): dam Irish 10.5f winner: well beaten in maiden/sellers. *M. G. Quinlan* **–**

CASHELGAR (IRE) 3 b.c. Anabaa (USA) 130 – Tropical Barth (IRE) (Peintre Celebre (USA) 137) [2009 10.5g* 10m^2 10g^4 Jul 26] €55,000Y: lengthy, good-topped colt: second foal: half-brother to French 1½m winner Time To Go (by High Chaparral): dam French 9.5f winner: smart performer: won minor event at Saint-Cloud in May: much improved when ½-length second to Glass Harmonium in listed Hampton Court Stakes at Royal Ascot next time: not at best when fourth to Debussy in Prix Eugene Adam at Maisons-Laffitte final start: stays 10.5f: best effort on good to firm going. *A. de Royer Dupre, France* **118**

CASH IN THE ATTIC 3 b.f. Auction House (USA) 120 – Aziz Presenting (IRE) 86 (Charnwood Forest (IRE) 125) [2009 61d: p8.6g^2 f8g^6 p8g p8g^4 7.1m^4 8f^6 8f^5 7s Jul 29] angular filly: modest maiden: stays 8.6f: acts on polytrack, soft and good to firm ground. *M. R. Channon* **55**

CASHLEEN (USA) 3 ch.f. Lemon Drop Kid (USA) 131 – Radu Cool (USA) (Carnivalay (USA)) [2009 73+: p9.5g 6m 8.3m 7m 6.1m^5 7m^6 Aug 13] strong, well-made filly: fair handicapper: bred to stay 1m: acts on good to firm going: tried blinkered/in cheekpieces: sold £5,500 in December. *K. A. Ryan* **66**

CASH ON (IRE) 7 ch.g. Spectrum (IRE) 126 – Lady Lucre (IRE) 73 (Last Tycoon 131) [2009 75§: p12.2g^5 p13g^4 p16g 11.5g May 20] good-topped gelding: fair handicapper: stays 1¾m: acts on polytrack and good to firm ground: tried in visor (reluctant to race)/cheekpieces: one to treat with caution. *Karen George* **67 §**

CASH QUEEN ANNA (IRE) 2 b.f. (Feb 26) Dr Fong (USA) 128 – Cashel Queen (USA) 69 (Kingmambo (USA) 125) [2009 6s^3 7m^2 7m^2 7m* 7m^2 Oct 3] €50,000Y: lengthy filly: second foal: dam, maiden (stayed 1¼m), out of Prix de Diane winner Caerlina: fairly useful performer: landed odds in maiden at Redcar in September: good short-head second to Bab At The Bowster in nursery at Newmarket subsequent outing: will stay 1m: acts on soft and good to firm going: carries head awkwardly: sent to USA. *B. W. Hills* **80**

CASILDA (IRE) 4 b.f. Cape Cross (IRE) 129 – Koniya (IRE) (Doyoun 124) [2009 95: p10g^3 9f^2 10m 10m^6 Sep 19] leggy filly: useful performer: seemed to run very well when 1¼ lengths second of 4 to Heaven Sent in Dahlia Stakes at Newmarket (dictated): well held in patern/listed company after: stays 1½m: acts on polytrack, firm and soft going: sent to Australia. *A. M. Balding* **104 ?**

CASINO NIGHT 4 ch.f. Night Shift (USA) – Come Fly With Me (Bluebird (USA) 125) [2009 77: f11d^5 f8g 8m^2 7.1m 8.1m 9m 8.5g^4 6.9g 9m^3 8.3m^4 9.2d^2 11.5d^3 9.2s* **82**

9.2v^{4} 9.1d^{4} 8g 12.4g^{6} 10.4g Oct 9] strong filly: fairly useful handicapper: left R. Johnson after tenth outing: won at Hamilton in August: stays 11.5f: acts on polytrack, heavy and good to firm going: has worn cheekpieces: reliable. *F. P. Murtagh*

CASSIDY K 2 ch.f. (Mar 7) Zafeen (FR) 123 – Alizar (IRE) 62 (Rahy (USA) 115) [2009 **54**
5m^{3} 6d^{2} 6m^{5} 6m^{3} 7.5m^{3} 7g 7v Nov 3] €2,700F: second foal: dam 5f/6f (including at 2 yrs) winner: modest maiden: left J. Howard Johnson after sixth outing: stays 7.5f: acts on good to firm and good to soft going. *D. W. Thompson*

CASSIQUE LADY (IRE) 4 b.f. Langfuhr (CAN) 124 – Palacoona (FR) 105 (Last **105**
Tycoon 131) [2009 98: 8g 11.9g^{3} 10.9d* 14d^{2} 14.6m Sep 10] good-topped filly: useful performer: won listed race at Warwick in June by ½ length from Princess Taylor: good 1½ lengths second to Sevenna in Lillie Langtry Stakes at Goodwood, easily better effort after: stays 1¾m: has won on firm ground, but raced mainly on good or softer nowadays (acts on good to soft): patiently ridden. *Mrs L. Wadham*

CASTANEOUS (IRE) 5 b.g. Lahib (USA) 129 – Witchy Native (IRE) (Be My Native **68**
(USA) 122) [2009 68+: p12.2g* p12g 10d 12d 10m Jun 24] fair performer: won maiden at Wolverhampton in January easily by 8 lengths: well held after: stays 1½m: tried blinkered/in cheekpieces/tongue tied. *P. J. Rothwell, Ireland*

CASTANO 5 br.g. Makbul 104 – Royal Orchid (IRE) 74 (Shalford (IRE) 124§) [2009 **67 §**
77: 6g^{3} 6.1g^{3} 7m^{6} 7f p7g^{4} 6s 6.1m^{4} p6g* 6.1s^{5} 7m^{5} f7m Nov 12] sturdy, workmanlike gelding: fair handicapper: won at Wolverhampton in September: best at 6f/7f: acts on all-weather and any turf going: tried visored, effective with or without cheekpieces: ungenuine. *B. R. Millman*

CASTELLINA 5 ch.m. Medicean 128 – Protectorate 91 (Hector Protector (USA) 124) **54**
[2009 10.2g^{2} p10g 14.1g p9.5g Oct 10] fairly useful performer in France, successful 5 times: left J-C. Rouget after final 4-y-o start: just modest in 2009, claimed from P. Hobbs £5,000 after reappearance: stays 10.5f: acts on polytrack and heavy going: tried tongue tied. *E. J. Creighton*

CASTER SUGAR (USA) 3 b.f. Cozzene (USA) – Only Royale (IRE) 121 (Caerleon **87**
(USA) 132) [2009 72: 6.1g^{3} 7m p7g^{4} 8.1g^{5} 8m* 8.5g* 9g^{6} 10f^{2} 10f* 11m* Oct 1] close-coupled filly: fairly useful handicapper: steadily progressive in 2009, winning at Salisbury and Epsom in July, Brighton in September and Goodwood in October: stays 11f: acts on firm going. *R. Hannon*

CASTING COUCH (IRE) 3 b.f. Royal Applause 124 – McQueenie (IRE) 77 (Dane- **73**
hill (USA) 126) [2009 60: 7m^{4} 7m 7.1m^{3} 7.1m Sep 10] unfurnished filly: fair maiden: below form after reappearance: should stay 1m: acts on good to firm going: sold 2,000 gns. *B. W. Hills*

CASTLEBURY (IRE) 4 b.g. Spartacus (IRE) 107 – La Vie En Rouge (IRE) (College **70**
Chapel 122) [2009 71: 8g^{4} 9.2s^{5} 8d 7d^{4} 6d 10g* 8.3s^{4} 8m^{5} Aug 9] close-coupled gelding: fair handicapper: won at Pontefract in July: stays 1¼m: acts on good to firm ground: tried blinkered. *G. A. Swinbank*

CASTLECARRA (IRE) 4 b.g. Mull of Kintyre (USA) 114 – Sketch Pad 78 (Warning **55 d**
136) [2009 5m^{3} 6g^{6} 5d 5s p9.5g f6g Dec 8] modest form on debut: regressive subsequently: tried blinkered/tongue tied. *J. Hetherton*

CASTLEFISH (IRE) 5 b.g. Carrowkeel (IRE) 106 – Haven Island (IRE) (Revoque **–**
(IRE) 122) [2009 8f 6.1d Sep 4] no form. *D. Burchell*

CASTLE MYTH (USA) 3 b. or br.g. Johannesburg (USA) 127 – Castlemania (CAN) **70**
(Bold Ruckus (USA)) [2009 54: 7.1m f11g p9.5g^{3} 8d 10.3g 10s 8d p9.5g^{2} p9.5g^{4} p8.6g* f8f^{5} p8.6g^{3} p9.5g Dec 28] fair performer: improved when winning handicap at Wolverhampton in November: stays 9.5f: acts on polytrack: held up: blinkered/tongue tied later in 2009: none too consistent. *B. Ellison*

CASTLES IN THE AIR 4 b.g. Oasis Dream 129 – Dance Parade (USA) 107 (Gone **100**
West (USA)) [2009 79: 6m 6s* 6g^{6} 7m^{2} 8g 7m* 7g p7.1g^{2} 6.5m^{2} 7m Sep 26] rather leggy, quite attractive gelding: useful handicapper: won at Hamilton in May and Ascot (ladies event) in July: good efforts after when second at Wolverhampton (behind Leahurst) and Doncaster (to Brave Prospector): best at 6f/7f: acts on polytrack, firm and soft going: tried visored (wandered): often races prominently. *R. A. Fahey*

CAST OF STARS (IRE) 2 b.g. (Feb 28) Nayef (USA) 129 – Scarpe Rosse (IRE) 88 **66**
(Sadler's Wells (USA) 132) [2009 8.1d 9d^{5} p10m^{2} Dec 9] €13,000Y, £30,000 2-y-o: fourth foal: dam, 1¼m winner, half-sister to smart 7f to 1¼m winner Brilliant Red, out of sister to Rainbow Quest: fair form in maidens: stays 1¼m. *R. M. Beckett*

CASUAL CONQUEST (IRE) 4 b.g. Hernando (FR) 127 – Lady Luck (IRE) 71 **123**
(Kris 135) [2009 119: 12m^2 10.5v* 10s^3 10s* 10d Sep 5]

The decision to keep Casual Conquest in training at four was rewarded with two lucrative wins at pattern level, including a record-equalling fifth win in the Tattersalls Gold Cup for his trainer Dermot Weld. But it wasn't all plain sailing, by any means, and there were some disappointing efforts too. Casual Conquest had an excuse for his well-held seventh of nine behind Sea The Stars in the Irish Champion Stakes at Leopardstown in September—subsequently found to have mucus on the lungs—but, on more than one occasion, he failed to see out his race so well as expected, the fitting of a tongue strap for much of the season hinting at a possible physical problem. That Leopardstown flop is nonetheless the only time Casual Conquest has finished out of the first three in nine career starts, though, as a four-year-old, he failed to improve significantly on his three-year-old form when placed in both the Epsom Derby (after being supplemented for £75,000) and the Irish Derby (when runner-up to Frozen Fire).

Rustiness after a ten-month absence, plus firmer ground than ideal, seemed plausible explanations for Casual Conquest's failure to land the odds in a three-runner renewal of the Jockey Club Stakes at Newmarket in May, but his second to Bronze Cannon was still slightly disappointing, particularly as his task had been made easier by main market rival Spanish Moon refusing to enter the stalls. The fact that Casual Conquest was fitted with a tongue strap and dropped in trip (from a mile and a half to a mile and a quarter) for the remainder of the campaign suggests that lack of sharpness might not have been the sole reason he was found wanting in the latter stages of the Jockey Club Stakes. The changes paid an immediate dividend in the Tattersalls Gold Cup at the Curragh later in May, Ireland's first Group 1 race of the season for older horses. The field was slightly smaller than usual (seven runners is the average over the past twenty years) but four of the five looked closely matched on their three-year-old form. Weld's other runner Famous Name shaded favouritism from Thewayyouare, with Casual Conquest third choice at 11/4, despite the fact stable jockey Pat Smullen remained loyal to him. Casual Conquest drew clear inside the final two furlongs, after gradually stepping things up from the front, to beat Famous Name by five and a half lengths, with the filly Lush Lashes a further length and three quarters away in third. This fifth Tattersalls win for Weld matched the record in the race held by Vincent O'Brien, who died (aged ninety-two) eight days after the latest renewal.

The globe-trotting exploits of the Weld stable are well documented and the Arlington Million and the Prix de l'Arc de Triomphe were mentioned as possible big-race targets for Casual Conquest straight after his Tattersalls Gold Cup win. As it was, he never left home soil for his three remaining outings. Starting at odds on

Tattersalls Gold Cup, the Curragh—a record-equalling fifth win in the race for trainer Dermot Weld as Casual Conquest makes all to beat stable-companion Famous Name

(conceding weight all round) he managed only third to She's Our Mark in the Meld Stakes at Leopardstown in July, not finding so much as expected after leading over a furlong out. Casual Conquest resumed winning ways in the Royal Whip Stakes back at the Curragh the following month, winning in workmanlike fashion by a length and a quarter from his only serious rival Curtain Call. Revealingly perhaps, Casual Conquest was fitted with blinkers for the first time in the Irish Champion next time, when he was sent off at 16/1 in a field dominated by leading three-year-olds. Casual Conquest wasn't seen out again after the Irish Champion, reportedly suffering a 'slight setback' while connections were considering a tilt at either the Arc or the Joe Hirsch Turf Classic at Belmont Park.

Casual Conquest (IRE) (b.g. 2005)	Hernando (FR) (b 1990)	Niniski (b 1976)	Nijinsky
			Virginia Hills
		Whakilyric (b 1984)	Miswaki
			Lyrism
	Lady Luck (IRE) (ch 1996)	Kris (ch 1976)	Sharpen Up
			Doubly Sure
		Latest Chapter (ch 1989)	Ahonoora
			Irish Edition

Casual Conquest's family has served connections very well down the years. The 1990 Belmont Stakes winner Go And Go, who remains the only European-trained winner of any of North America's Triple Crown races, was a half-brother to Casual Conquest's unraced grandam Latest Chapter, who has proved a profitable source of winners for Moyglare Stud, producing seven winners to date, six of them trained by Weld. The best of this sextet was the smart Social Harmony, a prolific winner at five furlongs to a mile, whilst Artist's Tale showed useful form when claiming two wins (at seven furlongs and a mile) as a three-year-old in 2006. Casual Conquest's dam Lady Luck won over a mile on the second of just two career starts for Weld and has also done well as a broodmare with four winners from as many runners to date. In addition to Casual Conquest, she has produced a useful miler in Elusive Double (by Grand Lodge) and a pair of fairly useful performers at up to nine furlongs in Media Asset (by Polish Precedent) and Moving Heart (by Anabaa). Lady Luck's two-year-old colt Aided And Abetted (by Danehill Dancer) is also in training with Weld but has yet to reach the racecourse, while her 2008 colt by Desert Style is named A Word Apart. The fitting of headgear has been a recurring theme in the racing careers of most of the names mentioned—Go And Go's historic Belmont Stakes win came in a first-time visor—so it is arguably not so surprising that Casual Conquest ended up being tried in blinkers. Casual Conquest possesses more stamina than most in his immediate family, though it should be noted that his great grandam is a half-sister to the dam of the Weld-trained Melbourne Cup winner Media Puzzle. Casual Conquest might well be worth another try at around a mile and a half, even though all four of his wins have come over shorter. Tall and close coupled, with a quick action, Casual Conquest made a winning debut on good to firm ground on his sole two-year-old appearance, but subsequent events have suggested he may be ideally suited by good ground or softer (he acts well on heavy). He is effective held up or making the running. Unusually for a colt who had recently won a Group 1 event, Casual Conquest was gelded at the end of the year. *D. K. Weld, Ireland*

CASUAL GARCIA 4 gr.g. Hernando (FR) 127 – Frosty Welcome (USA) 105 (With Approval (CAN)) [2009 84: 16m 16m^6 21g 17.1m^4 15.8d 16m^6 Sep 13] leggy gelding: just fair handicapper in 2009: stays 2m: acts on polytrack and good to firm ground: usually blinkered: front runner: ungenuine: joined N. Gifford, fair winning hurdler. *Sir Mark Prescott* **75 §**

CATAI 5 b.h. Mark of Esteem (IRE) 137 – China 74 (Royal Academy (USA) 130) [2009 p12.2g Feb 16] successful 3 times in varied company in 2008 for M. Gasparini in Italy: poor form over hurdles, and well beaten on British Flat debut in amateur handicap at Wolverhampton: stays 1½m: acts on firm ground. *P. Monteith* **–**

CATALAN BAY (AUS) 5 b.m. Rock of Gibraltar (IRE) 133 – Kim Angel (AUS) (Serheed (USA)) [2009 p6g^2 p7.1m^4 6g^2 6d 7d^5 7.1m^4 6m^6 Sep 17] strong mare: winner of 3 of her 13 races in Australia: beaten 2¾ lengths when fourth/sixth in Group 2s second/third starts in 2008 when trained by L. Freedman: fairly useful handicapper in Britain, **81**

often finding less than seemed likely: had form at 1¼m in Australia, but raced at 6f/7f in Britain: acts on polytrack, unraced on extremes on turf: tried visored/tongue tied/ blinkered. *J. R. Gask*

CATALINA SUNRISE (USA) 3 ch.f. Malibu Moon (USA) – Jealous Forum (USA) **84**
(Open Forum (USA)) [2009 p8g a9.5g a9.5g* Dec 18] third foal: dam, Canadian 4.5f (at 2 yrs) to 8.5f winner, half-sister to very smart US Grade 1 7f winner Trippi: green on debut for L. Cumani: easily best effort when winning minor event at Deauville by ½ length from Darbaza: stays 9.5f: raced only on all-weather. *J. E. Pease, France*

CATAWOLLOW 2 b.f. (Feb 24) Beat Hollow 126 – Catalonia (IRE) 76 (Catrail (USA) **47**
123) [2009 6m 8.3v f8m Dec 5] £2,000Y: plain, sturdy filly: third foal: dam, 7f winner, half-sister to smart performer up to 2m The Glow-Worm: poor form in maidens: should stay 1m+. *R. C. Guest*

CATBELLS (IRE) 2 ch.f. (Apr 22) Rakti 130 – Moonbi Ridge (IRE) 102 (Definite **72**
Article 121) [2009 6m^2 6.1m^5 6g 6m^6 7m Oct 3] €30,000Y: rather leggy filly: third foal: half-sister to useful Swedish sprinter Exhibition (by Invincible Spirit), 6f winner in Britain at 2 yrs: dam Irish 1¼m/1½m winner: fair maiden: should be suited by 7f+: none too reliable. *A. Bailey*

CATCHANOVA (IRE) 2 b.c. (Mar 3) Catcher In The Rye (IRE) 115 – Head For The **64**
Stars (IRE) (Head For Heights 125) [2009 6g 5.7g 6m^6 p7m^3 p8m Nov 4] angular colt: modest maiden: should stay 1m: tongue tied last 3 starts. *Eve Johnson Houghton*

CATCHER OF DREAMS (IRE) 3 b.c. Catcher In The Rye (IRE) 115 – No Islands **–**
(Lomond (USA) 128) [2009 59: 9.1v Oct 31] modest maiden in 2008: seemingly amiss only start at 3 yrs. *A. G. Foster*

CATCH KEY (IRE) 3 b.f. Key of Luck (USA) 126 – Catch Me 75 (Rudimentary **53**
(USA) 118) [2009 7m^6 7.5m^4 7.5g 9.9m^4 Jul 4] workmanlike filly: half-sister to 7-y-o Game Lad and 1¼m winner Pay Attention (by Revoque): dam, 2-y-o 7f/7.5f winner, half-sister to smart performer up to 9f Missile: modest maiden: should stay 1¼m (met trouble final start): raced only on good/good to firm going. *T. D. Easterby*

CATCHMEIFYOUCAN (FR) 3 b.g. Marju (IRE) 127 – Catch Us (FR) (Selkirk **66**
(USA) 129) [2009 10m 10g p10m^6 10g Oct 19] sturdy gelding: has fluent action: fair maiden: raced only at 1¼m (worth a try at shorter): acts on polytrack: tried blinkered. *C. G. Cox*

CATCHPENNY 3 b.f. Piccolo 121 – Noble Penny 64 (Pennekamp (USA) 130) [2009 **56**
6s^3 5d^3 p6m^5 f7g f6m^2 p7.1m Nov 28] 1,000F: first foal: dam, maiden, effective at 7f/ 1m: modest maiden: stays 6f: acts on all-weather and soft ground: tried in cheekpieces. *K. A. Ryan*

CATEGORICAL 6 b.g. Diktat 126 – Zibet 90 (Kris 135) [2009 74: 16m Apr 13] leggy **66**
gelding: fair handicapper, lightly raced on Flat nowadays: stays 2m: acts on fibresand and soft going: has joined Lucinda Russell. *K. G. Reveley*

CATE WASHINGTON 6 b.m. Superior Premium 122 – Willisa 67 (Polar Falcon **–**
(USA) 126) [2009 p6g p6g p7g 10.1g 11.7f May 31] of little account nowadays. *Mrs L. Williamson*

CATHERINE (IRE) 3 ch.f. Modigliani (USA) 106 – Jillians Pride (IRE) (Persian **60**
Mews 116) [2009 –: 8s^4 7v 7d 6.5d f7m p6g Nov 13] good-topped filly: modest maiden: below form after reappearance: stays 1m: best effort on soft going. *M. L. Fagan, Ireland*

CATHERINES CALL (IRE) 2 b.f. (May 19) Captain Rio 122 – It's Academic 73 **45**
(Royal Academy (USA) 130) [2009 p6g^6 Sep 4] €1,000Y: half-sister to several winners, including fairly useful 5f/6f winner Strathclyde (by Petong): dam 6f/7f winner: 25/1, sixth to Ferris Wheel in maiden at Kempton, slowly away. *D. Donovan*

CAT HUNTER 2 b.f. (Mar 9) One Cool Cat (USA) 123 – Eoz (IRE) 86 (Sadler's Wells **69**
(USA) 132) [2009 p6g^5 7.1m^3 p7g* 8g Oct 31] 2,500F: smallish, leggy filly: third foal: half-sister to French 11.5f winner Generoz (by Cadeaux Genereux): dam 1½m winner: fair form: won maiden at Lingfield in October: stiff task/seemed amiss final start: should be suited by 1m+: acts on polytrack. *Mrs A. J. Perrett*

CATIVO 3 b.f. Deportivo 116 – Catriona 75 (Bustino 136) [2009 –: 8.1g 7g p6m^5 p8m^5 **48**
p7g p7f Dec 21] strong filly: poor maiden: tongue tied after reappearance. *B. R. Millman*

CATIVO CAVALLINO 6 ch.g. Bertolini (USA) 125 – Sea Isle 73 (Selkirk (USA) **72**
129) [2009 85: p7g^5 p6g^4 p7g^3 6d^3 6g^2 p7m^6 7.6m^3 p6g* p7m^3 p7g^5 Nov 18] lengthy

gelding: fair handicapper nowadays: won at Kempton in September: stays 7f: acts on polytrack, firm and soft ground: tried in cheekpieces. *J. E. Long*

CAT JUNIOR (USA) 4 b. or br.c. Storm Cat (USA) – Luna Wells (IRE) 119 (Sadler's **121**
Wells (USA) 132) [2009 117: a8f p6m^3 7g^3 7m^2 7g^4 Oct 3] well-made colt: very smart performer: best efforts at 4 yrs when placed in Supreme Stakes at Goodwood (unlucky length third to Ordnance Row) and Park Stakes at Doncaster (neck second to Duff, best of those in main group) on third/fourth starts: below form when fourth to Varenar in Prix de la Foret at Longchamp final outing: best at 7f/1m: acts on firm ground: effective with or without tongue tie. *B. J. Meehan*

CAT SIX (USA) 5 b.m. Tale of The Cat (USA) 113 – Hurricane Warning (USA) **–**
(Thunder Gulch (USA) 129) [2009 12.1m f12g Jul 27] angular mare: regressive maiden. *T. Wall*

CAUCUS 2 b.c. (Feb 19) Cape Cross (IRE) 129 – Maid To Perfection 102 (Sadler's **76 p**
Wells (USA) 132) [2009 7d 7m 7m^4 Sep 1] neat colt: fourth foal: half-brother to 3-y-o Queen of Pentacles and Irish 5-y-o Perfect Reward: dam 7f (at 2 yrs) to 1¼m winner: progressive form in maidens, strong-finishing fourth to Markazzi at Leicester: will be well suited by 1m+: will do better still. *J. L. Dunlop*

CAUGHT IN PARADISE (IRE) 4 b.g. Catcher In The Rye (IRE) 115 – Paradis **– §**
(Bijou d'Inde 127) [2009 53§: p8g Jan 6] rather leggy gelding: modest performer in 2008: well held sole start at 4 yrs: tried in blinkers/cheekpieces/tongue tie: ungenuine. *D. W. Thompson*

CAUGHT ON CAMERA 3 b.f. Red Ransom (USA) – Colorsnap (Shirley Heights **61**
130) [2009 58p: p10g 9m^4 12g 10.1m^3 Aug 13] compact filly: modest maiden: stays 1¼m: acts on good to firm ground, probably on polytrack. *M. L. W. Bell*

CAUSE FOR APPLAUSE (IRE) 3 b.f. Royal Applause 124 – Polyandry (IRE) 99 **59**
(Pennekamp (USA) 130) [2009 –: f8s* f8g f8g^4 f8g^4 8g p8.6g^5 p9.5g f7f Dec 12] smallish filly: modest performer: won seller at Southwell in January: left B. Smart after fourth outing: stays 8.6f: acts on all-weather: sometimes visored, including for win. *R. Craggs*

CAUSEWAY COAST (USA) 2 b. or br.f. (Apr 2) Giant's Causeway (USA) 132 – **–**
Manda Island (USA) 81 (Dynaformer (USA)) [2009 8g Oct 23] 28,000Y: first foal: dam, 1m winner, half-sister to smart 7f winner Capistrano Day, out of US Grade 1 9f winner Alcando: 20/1, very green when in rear in maiden at Doncaster. *P. W. Chapple-Hyam*

CAUSEWAY KING (USA) 3 ch.g. Giant's Causeway (USA) 132 – A P Petal (USA) **62**
(A P Indy (USA) 131) [2009 73?: p8g p11g^5 12m Aug 23] tall gelding: modest maiden: stays 11f: acts on polytrack: won juvenile hurdle in November. *A. King*

CAUSTIC WIT (IRE) 11 b.g. Cadeaux Genereux 131 – Baldemosa (FR) (Lead On **59**
Time (USA) 123) [2009 70d: 6g^6 6m^5 6.1g* 6f^5 6m 5.7m^4 6.1g 6s 5.7m Aug 16] leggy, quite good-topped gelding: modest handicapper nowadays: won at Chepstow (apprentices) in May: best at 5f/6f: acts on all-weather, firm and soft going: effective with or without cheekpieces. *M. S. Saunders*

CAVALRY GUARD (USA) 5 ch.g. Officer (USA) 120 – Leeward City (USA) **61 §**
(Carson City (USA)) [2009 74d: p7g^4 p8g^6 p7g^4 p7g^3 p8g^3 p7g p8g^5 8.3m^2 7f 7g 8.3m p8g p7g^2 p8g p7g^2 p7m^3 Dec 30] good-topped gelding: modest handicapper: stays 8.3f: acts on polytrack and good to firm going: usually wears headgear: temperamental. *T. D. McCarthy*

CAVALRYMAN 3 b.c. Halling (USA) 133 – Silversword (FR) 102 (Highest **130**
Honor (FR) 124) [2009 10d^4 10s^2 10g* 12g* 12g* 12g^3 Oct 4]

Andre Fabre's 'new start', having sold the larger of his stables to Sheikh Mohammed in August 2008, turned out to be something of the proverbial curate's egg. With one hundred and eighteen individual runners, fewer than in many of his championship seasons during a twenty-one-year reign as France's top trainer, Fabre came third in the latest table of domestic earnings behind Jean-Claude Rouget and Alain de Royer Dupre. The good parts of Fabre's season included the development of Cavalryman, who trained on into the best of his age in France, and Cutlass Bay, who promised to do almost as well before injury intervened. Of those parts which failed to live up to expectations, perhaps the most notable was the lack of achievement by the two-year-olds. This was the age group on which most emphasis was supposed to be placed, with a view to identifying the stable's horses—among those owned by Sheikh Mohammed—which could make a mark for Godolphin in their classic season. Fabre's general record is much better with three-year-olds and upwards than with juveniles. In the last ten years, for example, he has trained the winners of four Group 1 races for two-year-olds, all of them in the two end-of-season prizes the Criterium International and Criterium de Saint-Cloud, while garnering thirty Group 1s with horses aged three and above. This trend was followed in the latest season, Fabre saddling only two two-year-old winners in listed or pattern company for Sheikh Mohammed, Zanzibari in the Prix de Cabourg and Colonial in the Prix Roland de Chambure. By comparison, Saeed bin Suroor's two-year-olds won seven pattern events, including three in France, with Buzzword, Passion For Gold and Zeitoper. Some of the promising, lightly-raced two-year-old winners trained by Fabre may well make a mark—Wedding March is still one to watch out for despite her defeat in the Prix Marcel Boussac—but whether the first year of this particular experiment can be regarded as a success must be debatable.

There is no debate, however, to be had about Cavalryman, a perfect example of Fabre's expertise at bringing on relatively late-developing three-year-olds, a skill exhibited with such as Subotica, Carnegie, Sagamix, Hurricane Run and Rail Link, none of whom contested a listed or pattern race at two (three of them did not run at that age) and all of whom went on to win the Prix de l'Arc de Triomphe. Cavalryman, who will join Saeed bin Suroor at four, ran twice as a juvenile without setting the world alight, finishing a close fourth in a newcomers event at Longchamp in September then decisively beating eight opponents in a minor event at Saint-Cloud the following month. Cavalryman wasn't a fast starter as a three-year-old, though he was an early starter, his reappearance coming in a listed race at Saint-Cloud in March, in which he started third favourite and finished just over a length behind Allybar in fourth, going on well at the end. More than six weeks later he joined Cutlass Bay in the Prix Greffulhe at Saint-Cloud again. Frankie Dettori was on Cutlass Bay, who started favourite, with Cavalryman only fifth of eight in the betting. Cavalryman improved again, leading briefly over a furlong out and keeping on to go down by half a length to Cutlass Bay.

The first two in the Greffulhe looked types to keep on the right side but Cutlass Bay wasn't seen again, an announcement made in August that he was out for the season, though his problems, which had probably surfaced earlier in the summer, were not specified. Either way, the mantle of developing into the best three-year-old in Fabre's yard, and also into the best horse owned by Sheikh Mohammed anywhere in the northern hemisphere, fell on Cavalryman. He proceeded to win his next three races, starting with what looked the relatively straightforward task of giving weight all round to six rivals in the Prix Matchem at Saint-Cloud at the beginning of June. Straightforward or not, Cavalryman impressed tremendously with the style of his victory, making the running to land the odds with consummate ease by six lengths from Cirrus des Aigles. Fabre did not have a runner in the Prix du Jockey Club, a race he has won just once (with Peintre Celebre in 1997), and Cavalryman made his next appearance in the

Juddmonte Grand Prix de Paris, Longchamp—Maxime Guyon produces Cavalryman (No.2) to beat foreign raiders Age of Aquarius (blaze), Mastery (No.5) and Freemantle (rail)

Juddmonte Grand Prix de Paris at Longchamp in mid-July. Fabre had trained nine previous winners of the Grand Prix in its various guises, seven of them between 1991 and 1999, with the roll of honour including Subotica, Peintre Celebre and Rail Link. Five of Cavalryman's seven opponents were trained outside France, the strength of the home based middle-distance three-year-old colts weakened further by the enforced retirement of Prix du Jockey Club winner Le Havre with a tendon injury. The five overseas raiders at Longchamp were not out of the top drawer either, with Derby Italiano winner Mastery, third in the Queen's Vase on his latest appearance, representing Godolphin and a Ballydoyle quartet being led by Lingfield Derby Trial winner Age of Aquarius, who had finished seventh in the Derby. The two other French contenders were the fourth and twelfth in the Prix du Jockey Club, Beheshtam (who started odds on) and Wajir. Cavalryman took closer order turning for home, responded well under pressure to deprive Age of Aquarius of the lead a furlong out and galloped on strongly to win by a length and a half, with Mastery two lengths behind Age of Aquarius in third. Beheshtam finished sixth. This was, surprisingly, the first Group 1 victory for the owner/trainer combination of Sheikh Mohammed and Fabre in more than ten years, since Gracioso in the 1999 Prix Lupin to be precise. The partnership had been represented by at least one better colt in the interim, that colt being Doyen who did not win a Group 1 until he joined Godolphin.

The Grand Prix de Paris—still the only European Group 1 event run in the evening after its switch to Bastille Day in 2005—was Cavalryman's first race at a mile and a half and the trip clearly suited him. He certainly looked worth aiming at the Prix de l'Arc de Triomphe, given his rate of progress and his trainer's splendid record with horses of his type. The Prix Niel is Fabre's first choice as a preparatory race for his Arc three-year-olds; the timing is right, three weeks before the main event, and it is run over same the course and distance as the Arc itself. Fabre's nine previous Prix Niel winners included the five colts mentioned above, plus Trempolino, who all went on to win the Arc, though Subotica had to wait a year after being forced to miss the Arc as a three-year-old after developing a rash (Fabre's other Arc winner Peintre Celebre was most unlucky in the Niel after being boxed in). By the time of the latest Qatar Prix Niel the ownership of Cavalryman and several other pattern-class horses had been transferred from Sheikh Mohammed to Godolphin SNC, which stands for Societe en Nom Collectif. This is a French form of general partnership and Godolphin SNC horses carry beige colours rather than the royal blue used by the British-based arm of the operation. Cavalryman was ridden for the first time in the Niel by Frankie Dettori, who had taken over from Maxime Guyon, Fabre's young first-choice jockey who impressed with his riding through the year. There were four other runners including Cavalryman's stable-companion Claremont, winner of the Prix du Lys and ridden by Guyon, and Beheshtam trying his luck again. Cavalryman looked in marvellous shape, though his demeanour was a shade languid in the preliminaries. In a steadily-run affair—the slowest of the three big races on Longchamp's 'day of Arc trials'—Cavalryman wore down the leader Aizavoski in the final furlong and held off Beheshtam by half a length for a workmanlike victory.

While it could be assumed that his trainer had left something to work on, the form shown by Cavalryman in the Niel put him still well short of the standard set by the leading middle-distance three-year-olds and he looked to have a lot on his plate in the Prix de l'Arc de Triomphe, for which he was supplemented at a cost of €100,000. Beheshtam was the only other French-trained three-year-old colt in the line-up. Cavalryman started 17/1 sixth favourite and surpassed himself, soon handy after being drawn widest of all and keeping on really well for third after initially looking a little one paced when ridden along to hold his position three furlongs out. He finished a head behind the strong-finishing Youmzain who in turn was two lengths adrift of Sea The Stars. Those behind Cavalryman included Conduit, Dar Re Mi, Fame And Glory and Stacelita, the form representing Cavalryman's best performance by some way and providing plenty of reason for Sheikh Mohammed to feel optimistic about his prospects in the top open-aged middle distance races in 2010. The Sheikh's unwillingness to bid for yearlings by Coolmore sires, whose record of getting horses who excel over middle distances is second to none, has contributed to Godolphin's struggling to remain a force in recent years in the best events at a mile and a quarter and a mile and a half. Since the likes of Doyen, Dubai Millennium, Fantastic Light, Grandera, Kutoob, Mamool, Marienbard, Moon Ballad, Sakhee, Street Cry and Sulamani earlier in the century, Godolphin has had precious few contenders, with no three-year-olds among them, capable of making their mark in the top Group 1 events over these distances. Cavalryman is the highest-rated middle-distance three-year-old with a Godolphin connection since Lammtarra, who was rated 134 after winning the Arc in 1995. In between, Central Park has been the only three-year-old Group 1 winner over a mile and a quarter or a mile and a half among the colts, his win coming in the 1998 Derby Italiano. By comparison, Ballydoyle has had around twenty in the same period. Cavalryman, a strong, well-made individual who has the appearance of a colt who will train on well, has raced only on good going or softer, so it remains to be seen how he handles firm, the more so since such conditions place more emphasis on speed than on stamina, which seems Cavalryman's strong suit.

Cavalryman (b.c. 2006)	Halling (USA) (ch 1991)	Diesis (ch 1980)	Sharpen Up
			Doubly Sure
		Dance Machine (b 1982)	Green Dancer
			Never A Lady
	Silversword (FR) (b 1993)	Highest Honor (gr 1983)	Kenmare
			High River
		Silver Cobra (bl or br 1986)	Silver Hawk
			Copperhead

Godolphin S.N.C.'s "Cavalryman"

Cavalryman's success, and that of Cutlass Bay, emphasised Halling's merit as a stallion. He has been at Dalham Hall in Newmarket for the last three years after a spell in the United Arab Emirates, where he covered significantly smaller books. Cavalryman is his first Group 1 winner and, along with Cutlass Bay, Queen's Vase winner Holberg and smart handicapper Opinion Poll, from a crop of only forty-five; Halling's crop of foals in the last two years—the first crops since his return to Darley—have topped seventy. Halling's sojourn in the United Arab Emirates did not compromise his stallion career in the sense that he was still able to get good horses, but the larger numbers of foals—and hence runners—he should achieve in Europe should help to boost his tally of major winners and his reputation among commercial breeders. Cavalryman, Cutlass Bay, Holberg and Opinion Poll have all shown more stamina than Halling seemed to possess, his own major victories coming at a mile and a quarter. Cavalryman's dam Silversword was lightly raced but won at a mile and a half and put up her best effort when third, promoted to second, in a moderate renewal of the Prix du Royaumont over that distance. Silversword was clearly thought to have plenty of stamina, her final outing being over a mile and three quarters, though she finished well beaten. Silversword had not been notably successful as a broodmare before Cavalryman came along: from seven previous foals, she produced minor winners by Theatrical and Jade Robbery and a three-parts sister to Cavalryman called Finity (by Diesis) who won at seven furlongs as a two-year-old in Ireland and finished third in the C. L. Weld Park Stakes over the same trip. Darley weeded out Silversword in November 2007 when she fetched €35,000, her purchasers selling the filly she was carrying by sprinter Exceed And Excel for only €25,000 as a foal at Goffs (the same filly fetched 110,000 guineas as a yearling at Tattersalls in the latest season, Silversword herself going through the ring again in December, making €100,000 at Deauville, a good price for a mare aged sixteen). Cavalryman's grandam Silver Cobra, whose other foals included Goodwood Cup runner-up Double Honour (a full sister to Silversword), was a sister to the smart Silver Ending, winner of the Grade 1 Pegasus Handicap. Cavalryman's great grandam Copperhead was a half-sister to the dam of Magnificient Style, successful in the Musidora Stakes and an excellent broodmare who is the dam of champion juvenile filly Playful Act, whose main success came in the Fillies' Mile, and Group 2 winners Echoes In Eternity and Percussionist. Playful Act set a world record price for a broodmare at the time when purchased for $10,500,000 on behalf of Sheikh Mohammed at Keeneland in 2007. *A. Fabre, France*

CAVENDISH 5 b.g. Pursuit of Love 124 – Bathwick Babe (IRE) 71 (Sri Pekan (USA) 117) [2009 80: p13.9g Sep 25] leggy gelding: fair handicapper at best: well held only start at 5 yrs: stays 2m: acts on polytrack and soft ground: tried visored, usually blinkered: races prominently. *J. M. P. Eustace* **–**

CAVENDISH ROAD (IRE) 3 b.g. Bachelor Duke (USA) 122 – Gronchi Rosa (IRE) (Nashwan (USA) 135) [2009 72d: 7m* 8.1g 7m4 7f* 7f3 8f* 8m 8m3 p8g3 Oct 26] sturdy gelding: fair handicapper: won at Folkestone in April, and Brighton in June and August: stays 1m: acts on polytrack and firm going: tried blinkered/tongue tied (at 2 yrs). *W. R. Muir* **79**

CAVE OF THE GIANT (IRE) 7 b.g. Giant's Causeway (USA) 132 – Maroussie (FR) 115 (Saumarez 132) [2009 14.1g5 Jun 28] leggy, close-coupled gelding: fair maiden at best on Flat, lightly raced: well held only start at 7 yrs: tried blinkered. *T. D. McCarthy* **–**

CAVIAR 2 gr.f. (Jan 26) Thunder Gulch (USA) 129 – Cozzene'saffair (USA) (Black Tie Affair 128) [2009 6g3 6m p6g6 Jul 8] 40,000F, 45,000Y: sturdy filly: fourth foal: half-sister to winners in USA by Open Forum and Valid Expectations: dam US 1m/8.5f winner: fair maiden: best effort on debut: raced at 6f: sold £4,000 in October. *R. Hannon* **66**

CAVITIE 3 b.g. Teofilio (IRE) 93 – Kirriemuir 51 (Lochnager 132) [2009 50: p6g6 6.1f 5g2 f5g2 6g6 p6f Oct 14] well-made gelding: modest maiden: likely to prove best at 5f/6f. *Andrew Reid* **54**

CAWDOR (IRE) 3 b.g. Kyllachy 129 – Dim Ots 92 (Alhijaz 122) [2009 77+: 5.7g2 6m3 5m2 7m 6m 6.1d* Oct 15] rather leggy gelding: fairly useful handicapper: gelded, improved when winning at Nottingham in October: best at 5f/6f: acts on soft and good to firm going: tried blinkered: sold 8,500 gns, joined Mrs L. Stubbs. *H. Candy* **88**

CAYMAN FOX 4 ch.f. Cayman Kai (IRE) 114 – Kalarram (Muhtarram (USA) 125) [2009 81: 5g 5m5 5g* 5m2 5d3 5m5 p5.1g2 5g p5.1g4 p5.1g2 p5.1g2 p5.1g4 p5.1g6 Dec 4] lengthy filly: fair performer: won claimer at Hamilton in June: best at 5f: acts on polytrack and soft going: in eyeshields of late: speedy front runner. *James Moffatt* **72**

CAYMAN SKY 3 b.g. Fantastic Light (USA) 134 – Comme Ca (Cyrano de Bergerac 120) [2009 69: p10g6 10.2g4 11.6g3 11.6m6 11m4 14m2 11.6g 11.5s p12m3 11.6d p12g3 p12m4 Oct 26] sturdy gelding: fair maiden handicapper: stayed 1¾m: acted on polytrack and good to firm going, well below form on softer than good: blinkered after debut: dead. *R. Hannon* **69**

CAYO COSTA (IRE) 2 ch.f. (May 1) Kheleyf (USA) 116 – Tropical Paradise (USA) (Manila (USA)) [2009 8.3g Oct 28] sixth foal: half-sister to 3 winners, including 6f (including at 2 yrs, later in South Africa) winner Close To Paradise (by Clodovil): dam unraced half-sister to 1987 US Grade 1 2-y-o 8.5f winner Antiqua: 33/1, very green when well held in seller at Nottingham. *A. J. McCabe* **–**

CECIL'S GIFT 2 b.f. (Feb 15) Act One 124 – Poyle Jenny 32 (Piccolo 121) [2009 6g 5.1g5 f5g Jul 7] smallish filly: first foal: dam maiden: poor form in sellers. *W. G. M. Turner* **40**

CECILY 3 b.f. Oasis Dream 129 – Odette 72 (Pursuit of Love 124) [2009 87p: p6g3 p6g5 p5g4 f5g6 p5g3 p6g2 6g4 p6g* p5g4 5m4 p6g3 p5g4 p6g Dec 2] good-topped filly: fairly useful handicapper: won at Wolverhampton in April: effective at 5f/6f: acts on polytrack and good to firm ground: blinkered last 3 starts: races prominently. *Sir Mark Prescott* **88**

CECILY PARSLEY 3 b.f. Fantastic Light (USA) 134 – Salim Toto 107 (Mtoto 134) [2009 12m5 11.7g 11.7m6 p12g Oct 2] good-topped filly: second foal: half-sister to fairly useful 1½m winner Touchdown (by Singspiel): dam 1¼m/1½m winner: poor maiden: raced only around 1½m: tongue tied on debut. *H. Morrison* **49**

CECINA MARINA 6 b.m. Sugarfoot 118 – Chasetown Cailin 59 (Suave Dancer (USA) 136) [2009 50: f11g 13.8m3 14.1m p13.9g 11.1v2 9.9g 10.9m 12g3 12s5 Oct 27] lightly-made mare: modest maiden: stays 1½m: acts on heavy and good to firm going: tried in cheekpieces. *Mrs K. Walton* **50**

CEEDWELL 2 ch.f. (Mar 17) Exceed And Excel (AUS) 126 – Muja Farewell 94 (Mujtahid (USA) 118) [2009 5m* 5m* 5m3 6g6 8.3g5 Sep 7] £65,000Y: strong filly: fourth foal: half-sister to 5-y-o Nabra: dam 5f winner (including at 2 yrs): useful performer: won maiden at Carlisle in May and minor event at Catterick (landed odds by 5 lengths from Tillys Tale) in June: again strong at finish when good 7 lengths third to Jealous Again in Queen Mary Stakes at Royal Ascot: below best last 2 starts when sixth to Misheer in Cherry Hinton Stakes at Newmarket (looked laboured, final start for B. Smart) and fifth of 7 to Green Rock in listed race at Craon: should stay 6f: possibly not straightforward. *E. Libaud, France* **95**

CEILIDH HOUSE 2 ch.f. (Mar 10) Selkirk (USA) 129 – Villa Carlotta 110 (Rainbow Quest (USA) 134) [2009 8.3s* Oct 7] strong filly: fifth foal: sister to 5-y-o Shela House and half-sister to 3-y-o Bothy and fairly useful 1¼m winner Villa Sonata (by Mozart): dam, 1¼m/1½m winner, half-sister to smart US 9f/1¼m performer Battle of Hastings: 11/4, created excellent impression when winning maiden at Nottingham by 4 lengths from Life And Soul, slowly away and green before forging down outside to take control 1f out: will be suited by 1¼m: useful prospect. *R. M. Beckett* **84 p**

CELEBRIAN 2 b.f. (Mar 29) Fasliyev (USA) 120 – Triplemoon (USA) 77 (Trempolino (USA) 135) [2009 7d p7g p8m Nov 19] lengthy filly: third foal: dam 1½m/1¾m winner: modest form in maidens: tongue tied final outing. *W. R. Swinburn* **57**

CELENDINE 2 b.f. (Mar 2) Oratorio (IRE) 128 – Affaire d'Amour 100 (Hernando (FR) 127) [2009 6g Sep 21] €45,000Y: third foal: half-sister to 1½m winner Sangfroid (by With Approval): dam, 15f/2m winner, sister to smart performer up to 1¾m Foreign Affairs: 20/1, seventh of 8 in maiden at Hamilton, inadequate trip and considerately handled: will stay 1¼m+: should do better. *G. A. Swinbank* **58 p**

CELESTIAL DREAM (IRE) 3 b.f. Oasis Dream 129 – Lochangel 119 (Night Shift (USA)) [2009 64+: 6f2 p5g* 5.1f3 Jun 5] fair form: won on handicap debut at Lingfield in May: likely to prove best at 5f: acts on polytrack and firm going, probably on soft: travels strongly: sold 18,000 gns in November. *A. M. Balding* **69**

CELESTIAL GIRL 2 b.f. (Apr 14) Dubai Destination (USA) 127 – Brightest Star 77 (Unfuwain (USA) 131) [2009 p7.1g Dec 28] fourth foal: closely related to 3-y-o King's **49 p**

Starlet: dam, lightly-raced maiden (shaped like a stayer), half-sister to Oaks winner Lady Carla: 11/1, needed experience in maiden at Wolverhampton: will progress. *H. Morrison*

CELESTIAL TRYST 2 b.f. (Feb 5) Tobougg (IRE) 125 – Celestial Welcome 96 (Most Welcome 131) [2009 5m 7g* 8g⁶ 7d Oct 11] £22,000Y: sturdy filly: fourth foal: half-sister to fairly useful 2005 2-y-o 7f winner Startori (by Vettori) and 7-y-o Shekan Star: dam, 7f to 1½m winner, half-sister to smart performer up to 1½m Snowstorm: fair performer: won maiden at Doncaster in July (wandered): failed to progress in listed race at Deauville and nursery at Goodwood (soon struggling): should stay 1m+. *G. M. Moore* **76**

CELLARMASTER (IRE) 8 ch.g. Alhaarth (IRE) 126 – Cheeky Weeky (Cadeaux Genereux 131) [2009 –: p16g Jan 16] angular, useful-looking gelding: lightly raced and no recent form on Flat. *Mark Gillard* **–**

CELTIC CARISMA 7 b.m. Celtic Swing 138 – Kathryn's Pet 92 (Blakeney 126) [2009 16.1d⁶ 14.1m 16.1d² 17.1m⁶ 16.1d⁴ Sep 7] strong mare: modest handicapper: unraced on Flat in 2007/8: stays 17f: acts on firm and good to soft ground: held up. *K. G. Reveley* **54**

CELTIC CHANGE (IRE) 5 br.g. Celtic Swing 138 – Changi (IRE) (Lear Fan (USA) 130) [2009 86: 8m² 9m 8.9d 7.9m⁶ 8.1g* 8.5m* 8m⁶ 8g² 8g 8m Oct 3] good-topped gelding: fairly useful handicapper: better than ever in 2009, winning at Haydock and Beverley in July: best form around 1m: acts on soft and good to firm ground: usually wears headgear, also tongue tied of late: races prominently. *M. Dods* **90**

CELTIC CHARLIE (FR) 4 ch.c. Until Sundown (USA) – India Regalona (USA) (Dehere (USA) 121) [2009 –: p12f Oct 14] maiden: no form since 2007. *P. M. Phelan* **–**

CELTIC COMMITMENT 3 gr.c. Mull of Kintyre (USA) 114 – Grey Again 63 (Unfuwain (USA) 131) [2009 71: p8g⁵ Jan 21] leggy colt: fair maiden at 2 yrs: well held in claimer only start in 2009: stays 9f: acts on polytrack and good to soft going. *R. Hannon* **–**

CELTICELLO (IRE) 7 b. or br.g. Celtic Swing 138 – Viola Royale (IRE) 90 (Royal Academy (USA) 130) [2009 81: p12g Feb 18] leggy gelding: fairly useful performer at best: well below form only Flat start at 7 yrs: stays easy 1¾m: acts on soft going and polytrack: tried in cheekpieces: sold £8,000, joined Paul Murphy in April: fair hurdler. *P. D. Evans* **55**

CELTIC GOLD (USA) 5 b.g. Elusive Quality (USA) – Fortune (IRE) 80 (Night Shift (USA)) [2009 63: p12m* p10g⁶ p12g⁵ p12g⁶ 10f² Apr 25] sturdy gelding: fair performer: won maiden at Lingfield in January: stays 1½m: raced on polytrack and firm going: tried tongue tied: sold £6,000. *Andrew Turnell* **73**

CELTIC LASS 3 b.f. Celtic Swing 138 – Nsx 74 (Roi Danzig (USA)) [2009 p10g⁶ 10m Jul 20] rather leggy filly: sixth foal: half-sister to 1½m/1¾m winner Peak of Perfection (by Deploy), 7f winner Camberley and 1¼m winner Shahzan House (latter 2 by Sri Pekan), all useful: dam 2-y-o 5f winner: signs of ability in maidens at Kempton and Windsor. *M. A. Jarvis* **–**

CELTIC LYNN (IRE) 4 br.f. Celtic Swing 138 – Sheryl Lynn (Miller's Mate 116) [2009 82: 7s* 7m⁵ 8d⁵ 7g³ 8.3s⁶ 7d Sep 6] smallish filly: fairly useful handicapper: won at Newcastle in May: should stay 1m: acts on soft and good to firm going: usually held up. *M. Dods* **83**

CELTIC RANSOM 2 b.c. (Feb 10) Red Ransom (USA) – Welsh Valley (USA) 64 (Irish River (FR) 131) [2009 7m 6.5g p7m Oct 26] useful-looking colt: showed ability in maidens at Newbury: caught wide final outing. *J. W. Hills* **57**

CELTIC REBEL (IRE) 3 b.g. Bahri (USA) 125 – Farjah (IRE) (Charnwood Forest (IRE) 125) [2009 62: p6g⁴ f5g 5m Apr 22] good-topped gelding: modest maiden handicapper: raced only at 5f/6f: acts on polytrack: sold 2,000 gns. *S. A. Callaghan* **57**

CELTIC SOVEREIGN (IRE) 3 b.g. Celtic Swing 138 – Penny Ha'penny 84 (Bishop of Cashel 122) [2009 p7f* Dec 21] 26,000Y: second foal: half-brother to 4-y-o Half A Crown: dam, 5f winner, half-sister to smart sprinter Celtic Mill (by Celtic Swing): 20/1, promising debut when winning maiden at Kempton in December readily by 1½ lengths from Peponi: likely to improve. *M. G. Quinlan* **84 p**

CELTIC SPIRIT (IRE) 6 ch.g. Pivotal 124 – Cavernista 75 (Lion Cavern (USA) 117) [2009 102: p12g⁵ 12g Apr 22] leggy gelding: useful handicapper on all-weather, lightly raced on turf nowadays: creditable fifth on reappearance: too much to do only other start at 6 yrs: stays 13.3f: acts on polytrack and soft going: tried blinkered/in cheekpieces. *G. L. Moore* **– a97**

CELTIC STEP 5 br.g. Selkirk (USA) 129 – Inchiri 108 (Sadler's Wells (USA) 132) **83 d**
[2009 85: 8.9d 8v^3 7g 8s f8g^5 7.2v^4 f8g^3 p8.6g^3 f8f^2 Dec 12] big gelding: fairly useful handicapper: below form after second start: best around 1m: acts on all-weather, heavy and good to firm going: tried blinkered/in cheekpieces: carries head high. *P. D. Niven*

CELTIC SULTAN (IRE) 5 b.g. Celtic Swing 138 – Farjah (IRE) (Charnwood Forest **99**
(IRE) 125) [2009 111d: 6g 7.6m 7g* 7f^2 7f 7g^2 7m 7g 7.6m 6.5m 7m^4 7m^3 7g 7s Nov 7] sturdy, useful-looking gelding: just useful handicapper at 5 yrs: won at Catterick in May: stays 7.6f: acts on firm going: front runner. *T. P. Tate*

CENTENARY (IRE) 5 b.g. Traditionally (USA) 117 – Catherinofaragon (USA) **42**
(Chief's Crown (USA)) [2009 54: 16.1d 14.1m Jun 20] neat gelding: poor handicapper nowadays: stays 2m: acts on polytrack, firm and good to soft going: sometimes wears headgear. *M. W. Easterby*

CENTENEROLA (USA) 4 b.f. Century City (IRE) 124 – Lady Angharad (IRE) 95 **–**
(Tenby 125) [2009 77d: f8s Jan 4] big, strong filly: regressive handicapper: tried blinkered/visored: sold 11,000 gns in December. *D. Shaw*

CENTENNIAL (IRE) 4 gr.c. Dalakhani (IRE) 133 – Lurina (IRE) 111 (Lure (USA) **110**
131) [2009 115: 12s^2 14s^6 20m 16g 15.5g Sep 13] angular colt: has a round action: smart performer: creditable 1½ lengths second to Enroller in John Porter Stakes at Newbury on reappearance: well below form after in Yorkshire Cup at York, Gold Cup at Royal Ascot, Goodwood Cup and Prix Gladiateur at Longchamp: stays 1½m: acts on soft and good to firm going: usually blinkered/visored. *J. H. M. Gosden*

CENTIGRADE (IRE) 2 gr.g. (Feb 16) Verglas (IRE) 118 – American Queen (FR) **99 p**
(Fairy King (USA)) [2009 6g^4 7.1g* 8m* Sep 19] €36,000Y, resold €42,000Y, 67,000 2-y-o: good-topped gelding: seventh foal: half-brother to Irish 4-y-o American Princess and winner in Holland by Halling: dam, French maiden, closely related to very smart French middle-distance performer Antheus: most progressive: won maiden at Warwick (readily by ¾ length from Start Right) in August and nursery at Ayr (beat Aquarian Spirit ¾ length in impressive fashion, coming from last to first) in September (gelded after): will stay 1¼m+: already useful, and type to go on improving. *W. J. Haggas*

CENTIME 2 b.f. (Apr 27) Royal Applause 124 – Argent du Bois (USA) (Silver Hawk **57**
(USA) 123) [2009 7d 8g Oct 23] fifth foal: sister to 2 winners, notably smart US Grade 1 1m to 1¼m winner Ticker Tape, 6.5f/7f winner in Britain at 2 yrs, and half-sister to 2 winners: dam French maiden who stayed 1m: down the field in maidens at Salisbury (modest form) and Doncaster. *B. J. Meehan*

CENTURIO 2 b.c. (Mar 30) Pivotal 124 – Grain of Gold 74 (Mr Prospector (USA)) **84 p**
[2009 8.1d^3 8g^2 Oct 8] 90,000Y: tall, angular colt: fourth foal: half brother to 2 winners, including fairly useful 9.5f winner Gold Prospect (by Rainbow Quest): dam, 1¼m winner, out of Irish/Yorkshire Oaks winner Pure Grain: shaped well when placed in maidens at Sandown (3¼ lengths third to Zeitoper) and Newbury (7 lengths second to Kalypso King, plenty left at finish): sure to improve again. *R. Charlton*

CEREAL KILLER (IRE) 2 br.c. (Mar 5) Xaar 132 – Snap Crackle Pop (IRE) 87 **70 p**
(Statoblest 120) [2009 5m 7m 6d^4 Oct 11] 16,000Y: good-topped colt: half-brother to several winners, including 8-y-o Handsome Cross and useful 6f (at 2 yrs) to 1m winner Sharp Nephew (by Dr Fong): dam 2-y-o 5f winner: easily best effort in maidens when 5¾ lengths fourth to Carnaby Street at Goodwood, going on at finish: should stay 7f: should do better still. *R. Hannon*

CEREMONIAL JADE (UAE) 6 b.g. Jade Robbery (USA) 121 – Talah 87 (Danehill **–**
(USA) 126) [2009 –, a115: p6g^5 p7.1g* 7m p7g^3 p6g p7f^3 Dec 16] good-topped gelding: **a112**
smart performer on all-weather, lightly raced on turf nowadays: won listed race at Wolverhampton in March by head from Vitznau: creditable third to Dohasa in similar event at Kempton final start: races mainly at 6f/7f: acts on polytrack and firm going: has won in cheekpieces: tongue tied: versatile regarding tactics. *M. Botti*

CERITO 3 ch.g. Bahamian Bounty 116 – Pascali 61 (Compton Place 125) [2009 93: 6d **90**
p5g^4 p6g^6 p5g Nov 25] rather leggy gelding: fairly useful handicapper: best at 5f: acts on polytrack, firm and good to soft going. *J. R. Boyle*

CERTAIN JUSTICE (USA) 11 gr.g. Lit de Justice (USA) 125 – Pure Misk 55 **–**
(Rainbow Quest (USA) 134) [2009 75: f7d Jan 8] rather leggy gelding: fair handicapper: well held only start at 11 yrs: effective at 6f to 1m: acts on all-weather, soft and good to firm going: tried in blinkers/cheekpieces: held up. *Stef Liddiard*

CERTIFIABLE 8 b.g. Deploy 131 – Gentle Irony 65 (Mazilier (USA) 107) [2009 54: p8g Jan 18] modest handicapper: well beaten only start in 2009: effective at 7f/1m: acts on polytrack, lightly raced on turf: tried in cheekpieces/visor: front runner. *Miss Z. C. Davison* –

CESARE 8 b.g. Machiavellian (USA) 123 – Tromond 94 (Lomond (USA) 128) [2009 124: 8m^2 8m^5 8g^3 8g^5 p8.6g^4 Sep 17] deep-girthed gelding: very smart performer at best: creditable 1½ lengths second to Paco Boy in Queen Anne Stakes at Royal Ascot on reappearance: disappointing after, including when sixth (promoted to fifth) in Celebration Mile at Goodwood on penultimate start: stays 1m: acts on polytrack, firm and soft going: held up: third on hurdling debut in December. *J. R. Fanshawe* **123 d**

CHABAL (IRE) 2 b.c. (Feb 10) Galileo (IRE) 134 – Vagary (IRE) (Zafonic (USA) 130) [2009 7d* 7s^2 7m Oct 17] **114 p**

It could hardly be described as Chabalmania, a word used to convey the popularity in France of Sebastien Chabal, but the first appearance in Britain of the colt named after the famous rugby union player did spark plenty of interest. Not only was Chabal attempting to give trainer Jim Bolger a fourth consecutive victory in the Dewhurst Stakes, but just a few days before the race it was reported that he had been bought by Sheikh Mohammed and would be joining Godolphin afterwards. Bolger, perhaps somewhat mischievously, had been quoted as saying that the colt represented his best chance of a Dewhurst winner in the last five years, but Chabal, who started favourite, failed by a long way to follow in the footsteps of the Bolger-trained trio Teofilo, New Approach and Intense Focus. On ground firmer than he had encountered on his two previous starts, Chabal raced freely up with the pace and was just about the last to come off the bridle. However, his

Lady O'Reilly and Mrs J. S. Bolger's "Chabal"

exertions took their toll in the later stages and he dropped away somewhat tamely to finish tenth of fifteen behind Beethoven, already beaten when his rider dropped his whip a furlong out.

Chabal had made an eye-catching debut in a maiden at Leopardstown in September. Second favourite in a fourteen-runner field, he raced a bit freely in mid-division but quickened well to lead over a furlong out and kept on strongly to win by a length and a quarter from close-finishers Behtarini and Dynasty, both of whom had had the benefit of a previous run. Just a week later Chabal was stepped up markedly in class in the National Stakes at the Curragh, a race won by both Teofilo and New Approach, that pair having had three runs under their belt going into it. Despite his relative lack of experience, Chabal went very close to emulating them, finding plenty off the bridle and going down only by a neck to another relatively inexperienced runner who was also sold to Godolphin in the autumn, the once-raced maiden winner Kingsfort. In third place, almost two lengths behind Chabal, was Beethoven, doing best of the three runners from Ballydoyle. Chabal looked a most promising colt going into the Dewhurst and, although his reputation took a knock at Newmarket, he could well resume his progress on his return and remains the type to win pattern races in 2010.

Chabal (IRE) (b.c. Feb 10, 2007)	Galileo (IRE) (b 1998)	Sadler's Wells (b 1981)	Northern Dancer
			Fairy Bridge
		Urban Sea (ch 1989)	Miswaki
			Allegretta
	Vagary (IRE) (gr 2002)	Zafonic (b 1990)	Gone West
			Zaizafon
		Vadsagreya (gr 1992)	Linamix
			Vadsa

Chabal was prominent in the Two Thousand Guineas and Derby betting before the Dewhurst. While he will stay at least a mile, a mile and a half may prove beyond him. That will apply all the more so if he doesn't become more amenable to restraint. Chabal's sire Galileo is an influence for stamina but his dam Vagary (whose first foal he is) is from a family whose most prominent members have been milers. Vagary is an unraced Zafonic mare out of Vadsagreya, a winner at seven furlongs (at two) and a mile in France. Vadsagreya has also produced a winner to Galileo, in the form of the Chesham Stakes runner-up Global Genius, and she is also the grandam of the smart five-furlong performer Spin Cycle. Vadsa, the great grandam of Chabal, won at nine furlongs in France. As well as producing no fewer than thirteen winners of her own at stud, Vadsa is also the grandam of the Breeders' Cup Mile winner Val Royal and the very smart French miler Vahorimix, and great grandam of the Prix d'Ispahan and Queen Anne Stakes winner Valixir. Chabal, a lengthy, angular colt, acts on soft going. *J. S. Bolger, Ireland*

CHACHAMAIDEE (IRE) 2 b.f. (Jan 29) Footstepsinthesand 120 – Canterbury Lace **95**
(USA) (Danehill (USA) 126) [2009 6m* 6f^3 7g^6 6m^5 Aug 20] 130,000F, 135,000Y: strong, useful-looking filly: third foal: half-sister to 4-y-o Maybe I Will: dam unraced sister to smart Irish 2002 2-y-o 1m winner Chevalier and half-sister to 1000 Guineas winner Virginia Waters: useful performer: won maiden at Lingfield in June: good 3¾ lengths third to Habaayib in Albany Stakes at Royal Ascot: not discredited in pattern races after: bred to stay at least 7f (raced too freely when tried): acts on firm going. *H. R. A. Cecil*

CHADWELL SPRING (IRE) 3 b.f. Statue of Liberty (USA) 115 – Cresalin (Coquelin **79**
(USA) 121) [2009 68: p8.6g^3 p8.6g 8.1g 7g^3 7m^6 9m* 8m^6 p10m 8.5m* 8m^4 8.5m Oct 3] good-topped filly: fair handicapper: won at Lingfield in July and Epsom in September: stays 9f: acts on polytrack and good to firm going: tried in cheekpieces: inconsistent. *Miss J. Feilden*

CHAIN OF EVENTS 2 ch.g. (Apr 28) Nayef (USA) 129 – Ermine (IRE) 86 (Cadeaux **76 +**
Genereux 131) [2009 7s^3 8m Sep 10] 85,000Y: neat gelding: sixth foal: brother to smart 11f winner Top Lock (stayed 1½m) and half-brother to 2 winners, including 7-y-o Carnivore: dam, 1m winner, half-sister to very smart 1¼m/1½m winner Border Arrow: fair form in maidens at Newbury (third to Emerald Commander) and Doncaster (subsequently gelded): will stay 1¼m+. *B. W. Hills*

CHAIN OF OFFICE 2 ch.f. (Jan 23) Mark of Esteem (IRE) 137 – Lady Mayor (Kris 135) [2009 7g^6 8m* 8g Oct 20] sturdy filly: third foal: half-sister to 4-y-o To Be Or Not To Be: dam unraced sister to useful 1¼m performer Lord Mayor: fair form: won maiden at Ffos Las in September by length from Cheetah, making all: pulled too hard in nursery at Yarmouth: stays 1m. *W. J. Haggas* **75**

CHAIRMAN PAT (USA) 2 ch.c. (May 18) Proud Citizen (USA) 122 – Sejm's Lunar Star (USA) (Sejm (USA)) [2009 6m p7g^5 7g^2 7f^5 8m 7m^6 8.3d Oct 15] $57,000Y, £24,000 2-y-o: rather leggy colt: fifth foal: half-brother to winners in USA by Harlan's Holiday and Dixie Union: dam US 8.5f winner (including at 2 yrs): fair maiden: no improvement in nurseries: should stay 1m: acts on polytrack and good to firm going. *Tom Dascombe* **70**

CHALENTINA 6 b.m. Primo Valentino (IRE) 116 – Chantilly Myth 81 (Sri Pekan (USA) 117) [2009 –: p7g^3 p6g^4 p7g^5 p7g p6g Mar 16] lengthy mare: poor performer: best at 6f/7f: acts on polytrack, firm and good to soft going: tried blinkered: has bled. *J. E. Long* **47**

CHALICE WELCOME 6 b.g. Most Welcome 131 – Blue Peru (IRE) 48 (Perugino (USA) 84) [2009 58: p10g* p9.5g^2 p10g^6 p10g^2 10f* 10m 11.5g 10m 11.5m* 10m^6 p12m* Dec 9] lengthy gelding: fair handicapper: improved through 2009, winning at Lingfield in January, Brighton in May, Yarmouth in September and Lingfield in December: stays 1½m: acts on polytrack and firm ground: tried blinkered/visored: held up. *N. B. King* **78**

CHALK HILL BLUE 3 b.f. Reset (AUS) 124 – Golubitsa (IRE) (Bluebird (USA) 125) [2009 62: 10.2m p10g^6 8.1g 11.6m 10.2g Jul 23] leggy filly: modest maiden: stays easy 1¼m: acts on polytrack and good to soft going: tried blinkered. *Eve Johnson Houghton* **53**

CHALLENGING (UAE) 3 b.f. Halling (USA) 133 – Small Change (IRE) 96 (Danzig (USA)) [2009 50: 8.5g 9.9m Jul 4] close-coupled filly: poor maiden: stayed 7f: acted on heavy ground: dead. *M. W. Easterby* **46**

CHAMPAGNE ALL DAY 3 ch.g. Timeless Times (USA) 99 – Miss Ceylon 75 (Brief Truce (USA) 126) [2009 6g Oct 16] small gelding: 200/1, always behind in maiden at Redcar. *S. P. Griffiths* **–**

CHAMPAGNE COCKTAIL (IRE) 8 b.g. Dushyantor (USA) 123 – Kunuz (Ela-Mana-Mou 132) [2009 f12g^3 p16g Jun 17] maiden: unraced on Flat for nearly 4 years, modest form in 2009: stays 2m: acts on fibresand: tried blinkered. *R. J. Price* **55**

CHAMPAGNE FIZZ (IRE) 3 gr.f. King Charlemagne (USA) 120 – Silver Moon (Environment Friend 128) [2009 68: 7g^6 7.6g 9.9g^6 p12g^3 p12g p11f* Dec 16] rather leggy filly: fair performer: won maiden at Kempton in December: stays 1½m: acts on polytrack, unraced on extremes of going on turf. *Miss Jo Crowley* **65**

CHAMPAGNE FUTURE 3 b.f. Compton Place 125 – Jade Pet 90 (Petong 126) [2009 –: 6m^3 5.7g* 5s^2 May 15] well-made filly: fairly useful form: won maiden at Bath in April: good second to Sloop Johnb in handicap at York next time: will prove best at 5f/6f: acts on soft ground. *W. R. Swinburn* **81**

CHAMPAGNELIFESTYLE 2 b.f. (Jan 26) Montjeu (IRE) 137 – White Rose (GER) 105 (Platini (GER) 126) [2009 7d* 7m Oct 17] 140,000F: rangy filly: has scope: third foal: closely related to useful French/German 1¼m winner Promesse de L'Aube (by Galileo): dam, 2-y-o 7f (Prix Miesque) winner who stayed 11f, closely related to smart German St Leger winner Win For Us: 9/1, most promising when winning maiden at Newmarket in July by 1¼ lengths from Qaraaba, leading on bridle over 2f out and strong at finish: firmer ground and gone in coat, well held in Rockfel Stakes there: will be well suited by 1m+: remains a smart prospect. *B. W. Hills* **93 p**

CHAMPAGNE SHADOW (IRE) 8 b.g. Kahyasi 130 – Moet (IRE) 72 (Mac's Imp (USA) 116) [2009 68: p14g^4 p12g^3 Jun 27] modest performer nowadays: effective at 1½m to 16.5f: acts on polytrack and soft going: formerly blinkered, usually in cheek-pieces nowadays: temperamental. *J. Pearce* **59**

CHAMPAGNE STYLE (USA) 2 ch.c. (Apr 29) Lion Heart (USA) 124 – Statute (USA) (Verzy (CAN)) [2009 7.1g^2 p7g^2 8m* Oct 16] $100,000Y, $100,000 2-y-o: close-coupled colt: fifth foal: half-brother to 3 winners in US: dam US 6f winner: useful form: much improved to win muddling 5-runner minor event at Newmarket in October by 3¾ lengths from Kalypso King, off bridle early: stays 1m. *B. J. Meehan* **101**

CHAMPAIN SANDS (IRE) 10 b.g. Green Desert (USA) 127 – Grecian Bride (IRE) **71**
(Groom Dancer (USA) 128) [2009 75, a57: 8f 8m^{2} 8m^{4} 7.9m^{2} 8f* 7.9m 7.9m 7m 8g 8f **a–**
7.5f Aug 29] smallish gelding: fair handicapper, better on turf: won at Thirsk in June: best
at 7f/1m: acts on all-weather, firm and good to soft going: tried visored/blinkered/tongue
tied: held up. *E. J. Alston*

CHAMPION GIRL (IRE) 3 b.f. Captain Rio 122 – Sea of Serenity (USA) (Conquis- **50**
tador Cielo (USA)) [2009 74?: 6.1g p8.6g 7d^{4} p8.6m 7.1d Sep 4] workmanlike filly:
modest maiden: stays 7f: acts on soft going: tried blinkered. *D. Haydn Jones*

CHANDIKA 3 b.f. Exceed And Excel (AUS) 126 – Jitterbug (IRE) (Marju (IRE) 127) **69**
[2009 6m 6m^{6} 6m^{5} 5m^{3} 5g^{2} 5.1d^{6} 5m^{6} p5m* Nov 3] £20,000 2-y-o: neat filly: fourth foal:
half-sister to 3 winners, including 4-y-o Horatio Carter: dam unraced: fair handicapper:
in cheekpieces, won at Kempton in November: may prove best at 5f: acts on polytrack
and good to firm ground. *C. G. Cox*

CHANDRAYAAN 2 ch.g. (Mar 19) Bertolini (USA) 125 – Muffled (USA) 67 (Miza- **60**
aya 104) [2009 7d 7.6d p7.1g^{5} 7s 6d^{4} p6m* p7g Oct 8] lengthy gelding: fair performer **a65**
on all-weather, modest on turf: best effort when winning nursery at Wolverhampton in
September: stays 7f: acts on polytrack and good to soft ground: visored last 3 outings,
very slowly away final one: sold 6,500 gns. *E. A. L. Dunlop*

CHANGINGOFTHEGUARD (IRE) 3 b.c. Montjeu (IRE) 137 – Miletrian (IRE) **118**
113 (Marju (IRE) 127) [2009 80p: 10.3m^{2} 10v^{3} 10g* 12.9m* 14m^{2} 14.6m^{6} Sep 12]
lengthy, good-topped colt: smart performer: excellent progress in 2009, winning maiden
at Navan and Ulster Derby Handicap at Down Royal, both in June: very good head second
to Sesenta in Ebor Handicap at York (slowly away, stormed home once in clear) then
respectable sixth to Mastery in St Leger at Doncaster final start: stays 1¾m: acts on good
to firm going, promise on heavy: sold privately and joined D. Hayes in Australia: reported
in late-October to have suffered an abscess in near-hind hoof: taken out of Melbourne
Cup Nov 3 after considered to be lame by race stewards. *A. P. O'Brien, Ireland*

CHANGING SKIES (IRE) 4 b.f. Sadler's Wells (USA) 132 – Magnificient Style **95**
(USA) 107 (Silver Hawk (USA) 123) [2009 107: 10.4g^{4} 9d* 9d^{2} Oct 24] lightly-
made filly: useful performer: 10½ lengths fourth of 5 to Crystal Capella in Middleton
Stakes at York on reappearance, then left B. Meehan: won allowance race at Belmont
in September: stays 1½m: yet to race on heavy ground, probably acts on any other.
W. I. Mott, USA

CHANGING THE GUARD 3 b.g. King's Best (USA) 132 – Our Queen of Kings **93**
(Arazi (USA) 135) [2009 p5g* p6g^{2} p7.1g^{2} p7.1g* p8g^{3} 7.5m^{2} 7.1v^{5} 10.4g* 10m^{5} 9.9g
Jul 30] 130,000F, £6,500 2-y-o: smallish gelding: half-brother to several winners, notably
smart 6f (at 2 yrs) to 1m (Sun Chariot Stakes) winner Spinning Queen (by Spinning
World): dam unraced half-sister to Fanmore (high class) and Labeeb (very smart), both
best up to 1¼m: fairly useful performer: won maiden at Great Leighs in January and
handicaps at Wolverhampton in March and York in June: will stay beyond 10.4f: acts on
polytrack and good to firm ground: effective with/without visor: reliable. *R. A. Fahey*

CHANNEL CROSSING 7 b.g. Deploy 131 – Wave Dancer 76 (Dance In Time **46**
(CAN)) [2009 74: 10m 10m^{4} 11.8m^{3} 11.8m 11.9d 11.9d Oct 22] sturdy gelding: just poor
performer nowadays: stays 1½m: acts on all-weather, soft and good to firm ground: tried
in cheekpieces: races prominently. *S. Wynne*

CHANROSSA (IRE) 3 b.f. Galileo (IRE) 134 – Palacoona (FR) 105 (Last Tycoon **72**
131) [2009 –: 10g^{5} 10m^{6} 11.6m 12g^{5} p11g^{5} p12m p10g^{2} p10g p10g^{2} p10g^{2} p12m p10m^{2}
Dec 30] lengthy filly: fair maiden handicapper: stays 11f: acts on polytrack, unraced on
extremes of going on turf: in cheekpieces last 3 starts. *E. A. L. Dunlop*

CHANTILLY CREME (USA) 2 b.f. (Apr 7) Johannesburg (USA) 127 – Creme de **99**
La Creme (FR) (Vettori (IRE) 119) [2009 5g* 5m^{5} 5g^{2} 6d* 7g 8m Sep 26] leggy,
attractive filly: first foal: dam, maiden in France/USA, half-sister to useful French miler
Via Milano: useful performer: won minor event at Longchamp in May and listed race at
La Teste (by ¾ length from Virginia Hall) in August: creditable efforts in between when
fifth to Jealous Again in Queen Mary Stakes at Royal Ascot and length second to Dolled
Up in Prix du Bois at Chantilly: stiff task in Fillies' Mile at Ascot final start: should prove
best short of 1m: acts on good to firm and good to soft ground. *R. Gibson, France*

CHANTILLY DANCER (IRE) 3 b.f. Danehill Dancer (IRE) 117 – Antiguan Jane **57**
71 (Shirley Heights 130) [2009 61: f8g^{5} f8g^{6} p8g^{6} p10g 8d^{4} 8m^{5} 10.1g^{4} 9g* 10.1g^{6}

10.1m^5 Sep 16] close-coupled filly: modest performer: won seller at Yarmouth in June: stays 1¼m: acts on good to firm and good to soft going: tried visored. *M. Quinn*

CHANTILLY JEWEL (USA) 4 b.f. Century City (IRE) 124 – Betty's Star (USA) (Pentelicus (USA)) [2009 f6g p7.1g f6g^4 f5g^5 p6g^5 6g^5 5m^2 5.5g 5.2s^4 5.2s p5f* p5g^6 p6g^4 p6g f5f Dec 11] $60,000Y, resold $40,000Y: lengthy filly: third foal: closely related to winning US sprinter by Langfuhr and half-sister to US minor sprint stakes winner Cherokee Jewel (by Cherokee Run): dam winning US sprinter (third in Grade 3 at 2 yrs): fair performer: won maiden at Lingfield in September: best at 5f/6f: acts on polytrack, soft and good to firm going: wears headgear: none too consistent. *R. M. H. Cowell* **66**

CHANTILLY PASSION (FR) 8 b.g. Double Trigger (IRE) 123 – Chantilly Fashion (FR) (Northern Fashion (USA) 114) [2009 10.1m Jun 25] modest form in bumpers: tailed off in seller at Newcastle on Flat debut. *B. Storey* **–**

CHANTILLY PEARL (USA) 3 b. or br.f. Smart Strike (CAN) 121 – Cataballerina (USA) (Tabasco Cat (USA) 126) [2009 71p: 8m 6.9m^4 10f^6 8m^2 8m^5 p8.6g^4 p9.5g^2 p10g Nov 25] fair handicapper: stays 9.5f: raced only on polytrack and going firmer than good. *J. G. Given* **74**

CHANTILLY TIFFANY 5 ch.m. Pivotal 124 – Gaily Royal (IRE) (Royal Academy (USA) 130) [2009 115: 7m 8v 8m^4 7g p8g^3 7m^4 7s^6 Oct 25] lengthy mare: smart performer at 4 yrs: only useful nowadays: best effort at 5 yrs when 4¾ lengths fourth to Spacious in Windsor Forest Stakes at Royal Ascot third start: best form at 7f: acts on polytrack, soft and good to firm ground: twice blinkered at 3 yrs: sold 320,000 gns, joined J. Gosden. *E. A. L. Dunlop* **103**

CHAPERNO (USA) 2 b. or br.c. (Jan 26) More Than Ready (USA) 120 – Timeless Forest (USA) (Forestry (USA) 121) [2009 6m^2 6d^2 6m* 7g 6m^3 p6g^6 6g^2 p6g* Oct 26] $120,000Y: lengthy colt: first foal: dam, US maiden, out of US Grade 2 8.5f winner Biding Time: useful performer: won maiden at York in July and minor event at Lingfield (best effort, by short head from Ongoodform, confidently ridden) in October: stays 7f: acts on polytrack and good to firm ground: tried visored: sometimes finds little. *Saeed bin Suroor* **97**

CHAPTER AND VERSE (IRE) 3 gr.g. One Cool Cat (USA) 123 – Beautiful Hill (IRE) 74 (Danehill (USA) 126) [2009 80: 10m* 10.3m^4 10g^6 8m* 8g 8.1m p8f^4 p10m^3 p8m^2 p8.6g^2 Nov 27] compact gelding: fairly useful performer: won maiden at Pontefract in April and handicap at Ripon in August: left B. Hills 24,000 gns after seventh start: stays 1¼m: acts on polytrack and good to firm ground. *Mike Murphy* **92**

CHAPTER (IRE) 7 ch.g. Sinndar (IRE) 134 – Web of Intrigue 66 (Machiavellian (USA) 123) [2009 56§: p12g 10.2g May 5] rather leggy gelding: temperamental handicapper: well held at 7 yrs: wears headgear: one to avoid. *Mrs A. L. M. King* **– §**

CHARDONNAY 2 br.f. (Apr 16) Piccolo 121 – Icy 44 (Mind Games 121) [2009 6m^3 p7.1g* Oct 9] big, lengthy filly: fourth foal: dam, sprint maiden, ran only at 2 yrs: better effort in maidens (very green on debut) when winning at Wolverhampton by ¾ length from Serafina's Flight: stays easy 7f: likely to do better still. *G. A. Swinbank* **71 p**

CHARDONNAY STAR (IRE) 2 b.f. (Apr 20) Bertolini (USA) 125 – Coup de Coeur (IRE) (Kahyasi 130) [2009 5d 6v f7g Nov 17] €9,000Y: workmanlike filly: fourth foal: dam unraced: no form in maidens. *C. J. Teague* **–**

CHARGER 3 b.g. Rock of Gibraltar (IRE) 133 – Ruthless Rose (USA) (Conquistador Cielo (USA)) [2009 10m^4 10g 9.9m^4 10.2s 11.9d* Oct 15] compact gelding: type to carry condition: closely related to 3 winners, notably smart 2000 2-y-o 6f (including Cheveley Park) winner Regal Rose (by Danehill), and half-brother to several winners, notably smart stayer Regal Flush (by Sakhee): dam, ran twice, half-sister to high-class miler Shaadi: fairly useful performer: won maiden at Brighton in October: stays 1½m: acts on good to firm and good to soft going: sold 20,000 gns, joined P. Stafford, Ireland. *J. Noseda* **80**

CHARGING INDIAN (IRE) 3 b.g. Chevalier (IRE) 115 – Kathy Tolfa (IRE) (Sri Pekan (USA) 117) [2009 82: p7g 8d 6g 7.2g p8m 12.4d^5 f11f* f12m^4 f12f^5 f11g^4 Dec 18] strong gelding: fair handicapper: left D. Lanigan £1,800 after third outing: won at Southwell in October: stays 11f: acts on all-weather and soft going: in cheekpieces last 4 starts: none too genuine. *P. T. Midgley* **76**

CHARISMATIC LADY 3 ch.f. Bertolini (USA) 125 – Norcroft Lady 85 (Mujtahid (USA) 118) [2009 44: 8.3f^6 10.1m^5 10f^3 12v 10.1g^5 7m 8m 8g Oct 20] unfurnished filly: regressive maiden: left M. Botti after fifth start: stays 1¼m: acts on firm going: tried blinkered. *Jane Chapple-Hyam* **67 d**

CHARITY BELLE (USA) 3 b.f. Empire Maker (USA) 129 – Sweet Charity (USA) (A P Indy (USA) 131) [2009 10.1m* 10m^4 10g^2 10m* 12.5g^5 12m Oct 17] big, rangy filly: third foal: half-sister to winners abroad by Coronado's Quest and Lemon Drop Kid: dam, US 1m winner, out of US Grade 1 1m/1¼m winner Banker's Lady: useful performer: won maiden at Newcastle in May and Darley Prix de la Nonette at Deauville (beat Article Rare ½ length) in August: also ran well when second to Hollow Green in handicap at Ffos Las and fifth to Daryakana in Prix de Royallieu at Longchamp: folded tamely in Pride Stakes at Newmarket final outing: barely stays 12.5f: raced only on good/ good to firm going: makes running. *J. H. M. Gosden* **107**

CHARITY FAIR 2 ch.f. (Feb 28) Bahamian Bounty 116 – Be Most Welcome (Most Welcome 131) [2009 5s^6 5m 5m^5 6m 6d 6m^6 7m 6d^3 7m 8m 6g 7.1d^4 7.2v^4 Oct 31] £3,000Y: sparely-made filly: second foal: closely related to winner in Denmark by Touch of The Blues: dam unraced: poor maiden: stays 7f: acts on good to firm and good to soft going: has started slowly: tried in cheekpieces. *A. Berry* **45**

CHARLES BEAR 2 br.f. (Mar 23) Needwood Blade 117 – Zamyatina (IRE) 76 (Danehill Dancer (IRE) 117) [2009 p7.1g p6g^4 Dec 18] second foal: dam unreliable 6f (at 2 yrs)/7f winner: better effort (modest form) in maidens at Wolverhampton when fourth. *E. S. McMahon* **55**

CHARLES DARWIN (IRE) 6 ch.g. Tagula (IRE) 116 – Seymour (IRE) 78 (Eagle Eyed (USA) 111) [2009 91§: p6g^4 p6g^6 6f 6v 6m^6 7.6f^3 8.1m 7.6d 6m p6g* p6g^5 p6g Nov 11] well-made gelding: fair handicapper nowadays: won at Wolverhampton in September: best at 6f: acts on polytrack, firm and soft going: tried in blinkers/cheekpieces: held up: unreliable. *M. Blanshard* **71 §**

CHARLES PARNELL (IRE) 6 b.g. Elnadim (USA) 128 – Titania (Fairy King (USA)) [2009 90: f6s^2 5g 6d f6g^5 f6g 5.9d^3 6d^5 p7.1g^2 p6g^6 p6g^5 p6g^5 p7.1g^6 Dec 12] leggy gelding: fairly useful performer on all-weather, fair on turf: left M. Dods £4,000 after tenth outing: effective at 5f to 7f: acts on all-weather and any turf going: tried in headgear: held up. *S. P. Griffiths* **65 a89**

CHARLESTON 8 ch.g. Pursuit of Love 124 – Discomatic (USA) (Roberto (USA) 131) [2009 p14g p13g p12g^6 Mar 4] sturdy gelding: lightly raced and little form on Flat since 2004. *R. Rowe* **–**

CHARLEVOIX (IRE) 4 b.f. King Charlemagne (USA) 120 – Cayman Sound 72 (Turtle Island (IRE) 123) [2009 78: 8d^5 8g* 8m^4 8.1g Jun 18] rather leggy filly: fair handicapper: won at Yarmouth in April: will stay 1¼m: acts on polytrack and good to firm ground. *C. F. Wall* **75**

CHARLIE ALLNUT 4 b.g. Desert Style (IRE) 121 – Queen of Africa (USA) (Peintre Celebre (USA) 137) [2009 68: p7.1g p6g f7g^3 f6g^3 7m p7.1g Nov 20] tall, good-topped gelding: modest maiden nowadays: best at 6f/7f: acts on fibresand and good to soft going: wears headgear. *S. Wynne* **52**

CHARLIE BEAR 8 ch.h. Bahamian Bounty 116 – Abi 84 (Chief's Crown (USA)) [2009 51§: f16d p12g f11g^4 p11g f11g^6 12d Apr 9] tall horse: modest handicapper: stays 11f: acts on all-weather, firm and good to soft ground: tried in cheekpieces/blinkers: often slowly away: unreliable. *Miss Z. C. Davison* **53 §**

CHARLIE BE (IRE) 4 ch.g. King Charlemagne (USA) 120 – Miriana (IRE) (Bluebird (USA) 125) [2009 52: 10.2g 7f Aug 18] maiden: well held at 4 yrs. *Mrs P. N. Dutfield* **–**

CHARLIE COOL 6 ch.h. Rainbow Quest (USA) 134 – Tigwa 68 (Cadeaux Genereux 131) [2009 a8f 9d 10g 10g* 10g^4 8g^6 10.4m 8m 10.4d^2 10m 10.2d p9.5g p9.5m^6 Nov 28] lengthy, good-topped horse: missed 2008: useful handicapper at best nowadays: won at Nad Al Sheba in February for D. Selvaratnam: trained by J. Gosden next start only (sold 22,000 gns): regressive after: effective at 1m/1¼m: acts on polytrack, good to firm and good to soft going: tried in headgear: sometimes tongue tied: held up: quirky. *Mrs R. A. Carr* **106 d**

CHARLIE DELTA 6 b.g. Pennekamp (USA) 130 – Papita (IRE) 77 (Law Society (USA) 130) [2009 79: 7.1g 6m 6m^6 6.1m 5.1m 7.1d^4 7.1d^2 8m 7m p6f* f7m p7g^3 p7.1g^5 p7m^6 p6g* p6m^4 Dec 30] close-coupled gelding: fair handicapper: won at Kempton in October and Wolverhampton in December: best at 6f/7f: acts on all-weather, heavy and good to firm going: wears headgear. *R. A. Harris* **70**

CHARLIE FARNSBARNS (IRE) 5 b.g. Cape Cross (IRE) 129 – Lafleur (IRE) 75 (Grand Lodge (USA) 125) [2009 120: 8.9g 10g^5 12m^4 9.9m^3 8.3m^5 8.1v^6 9m* **113**

9m4 Oct 16] good-topped gelding: smart performer: won minor event at Newbury in September by length from Beauchamp Xerxes: had earlier run well when 4 lengths fifth to Tartan Bearer in Gordon Richards Stakes at Sandown and when 2¼ lengths third to Tranquil Tiger in listed race at Goodwood second/fourth starts: met trouble when fourth to Steele Tango in Darley Stakes at Newmarket on final start: has form at 1¼m, all wins at 9f or shorter: acts on soft and good to firm going: blinkered once (ran poorly): has been early to post: tends to hang: sold 65,000 gns. *B. J. Meehan*

CHARLIE GREEN (IRE) 4 b.g. Traditionally (USA) 117 – Saninka (IRE) 82 (Doyoun 124) [2009 –: p12.2g Dec 17] lengthy gelding: little form: tried visored/tongue tied. *Paul Green* –

CHARLIE OXO 4 br.g. Puissance 110 – Aegean Mist 63 (Prince Sabo 123) [2009 p7.1g Nov 20] workmanlike gelding: last in maidens. *B. P. J. Baugh* –

CHARLIE SMIRKE (USA) 3 b.g. Gulch (USA) – Two Altazano (USA) 115 (Manzotti (USA)) [2009 71: p10g6 8.3m 10s6 10d p7g3 p8f2 p8f2 Dec 20] lengthy, rather unfurnished gelding: fair maiden: gelded after reappearance: stays 1m: acts on polytrack: tried blinkered. *G. L. Moore* 68

CHARLIE TIPPLE 5 b.g. Diktat 126 – Swing of The Tide 75 (Sri Pekan (USA) 117) [2009 91: 8m2 8m5 8d 8.1g2 8m 8m 9.1d 8m3 8.3m5 Oct 26] big, good-topped gelding: fairly useful handicapper: good second at Haydock on fourth outing: stays easy 1¼m: acts on any going: blinkered once, wears cheekpieces: not entirely straightforward. *T. D. Easterby* 89

CHARLIE TOKYO (IRE) 6 b.g. Trans Island 119 – Ellistown Lady (IRE) (Red Sunset 120) [2009 98§: 12s 10.3f5 10.3g3 12g 10d3 10s* 10.4d4 10g 10.4g 10g2 Oct 23] good-bodied gelding: good walker: fairly useful handicapper nowadays: won at Leicester in August: effective at 9f to 1½m: acts on polytrack, heavy and good to firm going: blinkered/visored: temperamental (often finds little). *R. A. Fahey* 93 §

CHARLIETOO 3 b.g. King Charlemagne (USA) 120 – Ticcatoo (IRE) 60 (Dolphin Street (FR) 125) [2009 6m2 p7.1g p7.1g 7m 6.1g p5.1g Sep 3] lengthy gelding: fair maiden at best: second in seller at Leicester (left R. Hollinshead £6,000) on debut: regressed after: will prove best at 5f/6f: acts on good to firm going. *E. G. Bevan* 67 d

CHARLOTTE GREY 5 gr.m. Wizard King 122 – Great Intent (Aragon 118) [2009 55: f6s* f7g* f6g2 f7g Feb 19] tall, leggy mare: fair handicapper: won twice at Southwell in January: effective at 5f to 7f: acts on all-weather and firm ground: races up with pace. *P. J. McBride* 66

CHARLOTTE POINT (USA) 3 b.f. Distorted Humor (USA) 117 – Skygusty (USA) (Skywalker (USA)) [2009 81: p8g2 8m* 8.3m* 8g2 p8g3 8m p8m 10g Oct 19] lengthy filly: fairly useful handicapper: won at Goodwood in May and Nottingham in June: best around 1m: acts on polytrack and good to firm going: often makes running: reared leaving stall sixth outing. *P. F. I. Cole* 89

CHARLOTTESOMETIMES (USA) 2 b. or br.f. (Feb 6) Dehere (USA) 121 – Alexander Charlote (IRE) 77 (Titus Livius (FR) 115) [2009 p7.1g6 6g4 5g6 Jul 27] 4,000 2-y-o: lengthy filly: first foal: dam US 8.5f winner: signs of ability in maidens: bred to stay 1m: likely to do better in handicaps. *D. M. Simcock* – p

CHARMAXJOANNE 2 ch.f. (Apr 8) Lucky Story (USA) 128 – Dance of The Swans (IRE) 69 (Try My Best (USA) 130) [2009 5m 7m4 p8.6g Dec 3] £3,500Y: fifth foal: half-sister to fairly useful 2003 2-y-o 5f winner Peters Choice (by Wolfhound) and 5f (including at 2 yrs)/6f winner Sandgate Cygnet (by Fleetwood): dam 2-y-o 5f winner: form only when fourth in claimer at Newcastle. *P. C. Haslam* 43

CHARMEL'S LAD 4 ch.g. Compton Place 125 – Fittonia (FR) 66 (Ashkalani (IRE) 128) [2009 64§: p7g f6g4 f6g5 p7.1g5 Mar 23] lengthy, useful-looking gelding: modest maiden: stays 7f: acts on all-weather and good to soft going: tried visored/in cheekpieces: often tongue tied: irresolute: sold £800, joined A. Dickman. *W. R. Swinburn* 61 §

CHARMINAMIX (IRE) 6 gr.g. Linamix (FR) 127 – Cheeky Charm (USA) 56 (Nureyev (USA) 131) [2009 98: 10g p10.7g5 12.9m 9.9g 10.4m6 p10.7g2 p12g Nov 27] lengthy, workmanlike gelding: fairly useful handicapper: respectable sixth at York: stays 1½m: acts on polytrack and good to firm going: held up. *A. J. Martin, Ireland* 93

CHARMING ESCORT 5 ch.g. Rossini (USA) 118 – Iktizawa (Entrepreneur 123) [2009 65: p8g6 p7g Jan 10] big, workmanlike gelding: modest performer nowadays: stays 1m: raced on polytrack and good to soft going: tried visored. *T. T. Clement* 52

totesport.com November Handicap, Doncaster—a fourth win in the race for trainer John Gosden as Charm School (right) weaves through late to beat Hillview Boy and Ella (noseband), the last-named a daughter of the 1999 winner Flossy

CHARM SCHOOL 4 b.g. Dubai Destination (USA) 127 – Eve 81 (Rainbow Quest (USA) 134) [2009 110: 8m 8s 7g4 10.1g5 p11g* 10m5 9m 12s* Nov 7] sturdy gelding: smart handicapper: won at Kempton in September and Doncaster (totesport.com November Handicap, improved further when beating Hillview Boy by 1¾ lengths): stays 1½m: acts on polytrack, soft and good to firm going: blinkered (moody) once: held up: sent to UAE. *J. H. M. Gosden* **114**

CHARPOY COBRA 2 b.f. (Feb 2) Mark of Esteem (IRE) 137 – Duena (Grand Lodge (USA) 125) [2009 7g p8m6 p8g3 8g Oct 20] 3,000Y: good-topped filly: sixth foal: half-sister to 3 winners, including 3-y-o King of Defence and 4-y-o Burnbrake: dam unraced half-sister to useful 6f/7f performer Presto Vento: fair maiden: always behind in nursery: will prove best up to 1m. *J. A. R. Toller* **65**

CHARTIST 4 ch.g. Choisir (AUS) 126 – Sareb (FR) (Indian Ridge 123) [2009 93§: 7m5 7.1m4 6g 6g 5d 5d 6.1s Oct 7] strong, rangy gelding: fairly useful handicapper at best, regressive: left D. Nicholls prior to final start: free-going sort, very best efforts at 5f: acts on polytrack, good to firm and good to soft going: tried visored: ungenuine. *B. P. J. Baugh* **81 §**

CHASCA (IRE) 3 b.f. Namid 128 – Daganya (IRE) 104 (Danehill Dancer (IRE) 117) [2009 p6g* p6g4 6m* 5g 6g6 p6g5 6d a8g5 Dec 27] smallish filly: second foal: dam, Irish 6f winner (including at 2 yrs), sister to Irish 5-y-o Snaefell: fair performer: won maiden at Lingfield in March and handicap at Folkestone in April: sold from Mrs A. Perrett 2,000 gns before final start: stays 6f: acts on polytrack and good to firm going. *F. Ramirez, Spain* **72**

CHASE END 3 ch.f. Arkadian Hero (USA) 123 – Sestina (FR) 86 (Bering 136) [2009 p6g6 p6g Jan 21] second foal: dam maiden (stayed 7f): little impact in maidens at Great Leighs (slowly away) and Wolverhampton. *J. M. P. Eustace* **–**

CHASING AMY 3 b.f. Namid 128 – Inspiring (IRE) (Anabaa (USA) 130) [2009 61: 6.1m 6g p8.6g p7g p7f6 p6m Sep 28] angular filly: modest maiden: best form at 6f, will prove at least as effective at 5f: acts on polytrack, soft and good to firm going: tried blinkered. *M. G. Quinlan* **54**

CHASING STARS 4 ch.f. Observatory (USA) 131 – Post Modern (USA) (Nureyev (USA) 131) [2009 7m 7g4 8s Nov 4] fourth living foal: half-sister to useful 1½m winner Risk Taker (by Rainbow Quest) and 1m/8.6f winner Postmaster (by Dansili): dam unraced sister to Oaks winner Reams of Verse and half-sister to dam of 3-y-o Midday: useful performer: won 3 times in 2008, including listed race at Saint-Cloud: in rear in Chartwell Fillies' Stakes at Lingfield on reappearance: easily best effort in 2009 **103**

when close fourth to demoted As de Trebol in Prix du Palais-Royal at Longchamp: off 5 months after: raced only at 7f/1m: probably acts on any ground: has had tongue tied. *Mme C. Head-Maarek, France*

CHATANOOGACHOOCHOO 4 ch.f. Piccolo 121 – Taza (Persian Bold 123) [2009 69: 10m 8.1m^{2} 7.1v^{6} 8g^{4} 8m 9g^{3} p12g^{4} p8.6g^{4} p9.5g^{1} p12.2g^{1} Dec 17] leggy filly: fair maiden handicapper: stays 1¼m: acts on polytrack and good to firm going: tends to race freely. *M. Hill* **71**

CHAT DE LA BURG (USA) 2 ch.c. (Feb 26) Johannesburg (USA) 127 – Catsuit (USA) (Sir Cat (USA) 118) [2009 6m^{2} p5g* Oct 22] $130,000Y: quite attractive colt: first foal: dam US 6f (including at 2 yrs)/6.5f winner: won maiden at Kempton by ¾ length from La Fortunata, leading near finish: will stay 7f: should improve again. *J. R. Best* **78 p**

CHAT DE SOIE (IRE) 2 b.f. (Mar 15) Barathea (IRE) 127 – Margay (IRE) 98 (Marju (IRE) 127) [2009 7g 7m^{5} 7.5f^{4} p8m 9m^{4} Sep 23] €12,000Y: fourth foal: half-sister to fairly useful French 2007 2-y-o 6f winner Pull The Plug (by Pulpit) and a winner in USA by Hennessy: dam 7f (in Ireland at 2 yrs)/1m (in USA) winner: modest maiden: stays 9f: acts on firm ground. *J. S. Moore* **57**

CHATEAUNEUF (IRE) 3 b.f. Marju (IRE) 127 – Night Eyes (IRE) (Night Shift (USA)) [2009 52: 8m^{6} 8.3m^{6} 8.3v^{5} p10g^{5} p12m^{5} p9.5g Nov 13] angular filly: modest maiden: left B. Hills 2,500 gns after fifth start: stays easy 1½m: acts on polytrack and good to firm ground: tried in cheekpieces. *W. M. Brisbourne* **59**

CHATEAU ZARA 2 b.f. (Feb 8) Zaha (CAN) 106 – Glensara (Petoski 135) [2009 p7g Oct 24] sixth foal: half-sister to 3 winners, including useful 6f (including at 2 yrs)/7f winner Chateau Nicol (by Distant Relative) and fairly useful 6f/7f winner Hypocrisy (by Bertolini): dam unraced: 22/1, always rear in maiden at Kempton. *C. G. Cox* **–**

CHATTERSZAHA 3 ch.f. Zaha (CAN) 106 – Chatter's Princess (Cadeaux Genereux 131) [2009 65§: f6g p5.1g p7g 5.2d Oct 27] well-made filly: ungenuine maiden: visored once. *C. Drew* **– §**

CHAUSSINI 2 b.f. (Feb 14) Dubawi (IRE) 129 – Miss Chaussini (IRE) 76 (Rossini (USA) 118) [2009 6g 6m^{3} 6m^{2} 6g Oct 30] 10,000Y: smallish filly: first foal: dam, Irish 7f winner, out of sister to very smart French sprinter Tenue de Soiree: progressive form in maidens, 4 lengths second to Inler at Newmarket: last in listed race on same course (said to have finished lame) subsequent outing: likely to stay 7f: acts on good to firm going. *J. A. R. Toller* **80**

CHEAM FOREVER (USA) 3 b.g. Exchange Rate (USA) 111 – Many Charms (USA) (St Jovite (USA) 135) [2009 71: p7g^{3} 6f f7g 8d* 8m* 8f^{3} 8.5m^{3} 8.1m* 8.1m^{4} Oct 5] rangy gelding: fairly useful handicapper: won at Pontefract in July, Brighton in August and Warwick (visored) in September: stays 1m: acts on polytrack, firm and good to soft ground: front runner/races prominently: has looked awkward. *R. Charlton* **85**

CHEAP STREET 5 ch.g. Compton Place 125 – Anneliina 80 (Cadeaux Genereux 131) [2009 76, a62: p7g 6g 7g^{2} 7.1d^{6} 7.1d^{5} Sep 4] smallish gelding: modest handicapper nowadays: effective at 6f/7f: acts on firm and good to soft ground: tried blinkered. *J. G. Portman* **61**

CHEAP THRILLS 3 ch.f. Bertolini (USA) 125 – Licence To Thrill 83 (Wolfhound (USA) 126) [2009 71p: p6g* p6g^{3} 7.1f^{2} 7m* 7d^{3} 7m p7.1g^{5} p7m p6g p6g^{3} p6g^{6} f6g* f6d^{4} Dec 29] useful-looking filly: fair performer: won maiden at Lingfield in January, handicap at Newmarket in May and claimer at Southwell in December: stays 7f: acts on all-weather, firm and good to soft ground. *J. A. Osborne* **79**

CHECKLOW (USA) 4 b.g. Street Cry (IRE) 130 – Comstock Queen (USA) (Silver Hawk (USA) 123) [2009 93: p8g^{2} p8g^{5} 10.4m^{2} 10m 8.9g 10g Oct 10] big, strong gelding: useful handicapper: best effort when second to Moonquake at York on third start: disappointing after: should stay 1½m: acts on polytrack and firm ground: tried visored/in cheekpieces: suspect temperament, has given trouble at stall: joined J. Howard Johnson. *J. Noseda* **98**

CHECK THE ANCHOR (IRE) 2 ch.g. (Feb 16) Observatory (USA) 131 – Fleet River (USA) 93 (Riverman (USA) 131) [2009 6m 9m 7m Sep 23] tall gelding: no sign of ability in maidens at Redcar. *N. Tinkler* **–**

CHECK UP (IRE) 8 b.g. Frimaire – Melons Lady (IRE) (The Noble Player (USA) 126) [2009 66§: p12g Feb 7] good-topped gelding: ungenuine handicapper: well beaten only start at 8 yrs: stays 1½m: acts on soft ground: tried in cheekpieces. *J. L. Flint* **– §**

CHEEKY CRUMPET 3 b.f. Mind Games 121 – Woore Lass (IRE) 75 (Persian Bold 123) [2009 6m 6f Apr 17] leggy filly: second foal: dam 6f (at 2 yrs) and 1m winner: well-held last in maidens. *A. Berry* –

CHEERFULLY 2 br.f. (Jan 27) Sadler's Wells (USA) 132 – Light of Morn 99 (Daylami (IRE) 138) [2009 7g Oct 31] useful-looking filly: first foal: dam, 11.5f winner, half-sister to smart 1½m/1¾m winner Moments of Joy, out of Yorkshire Oaks/Prix Vermeille winner My Emma, herself half-sister to St Leger and Gold Cup winner Classic Cliche: 8/1 and very green, mid-field in maiden at Newmarket, not knocked about: will be suited by 1¼m+: capable of better. *J. H. M. Gosden* **53 p**

CHEERS BIG EARS (IRE) 3 br.c. Kheleyf (USA) 116 – Grey Galava 64 (Generous (IRE) 139) [2009 p7.1g⁶ 7m⁴ 6g p6g³ Oct 26] modest maiden: bred to stay 1m: raced only on polytrack and good/good to firm going: sold 7,500 gns. *J. R. Best* **58**

CHEERS FOR THEA (IRE) 4 gr.f. Distant Music (USA) 126 – Popiplu (USA) (Cozzene (USA)) [2009 61: 9.9m 9.9m² 10.2m³ 10d⁵ 9.9m³ 12v⁴ 11.5g⁴ p9.5g³ p8.6g* 8m p8.6m* Sep 28] fair handicapper, better on all-weather: improved when winning twice at Wolverhampton in September: stays 1¼m: acts on polytrack, soft and good to firm going: blinkered/tongue tied last 4 starts. *T. D. Easterby* **65 + a76**

CHEERY CAT (USA) 5 b. or br.g. Catienus (USA) 115 – Olinka (USA) (Wolfhound (USA) 126) [2009 71: f6g 7m⁴ 7.5m 7m 8d 7.1g⁵ 6m⁴ 7m⁵ p6g* p7m p6g³ p6m Dec 10] rather leggy, close-coupled gelding: modest handicapper: left D. Barker after sixth start: won apprentice event at Lingfield in October: effective at 6f/7f: acts on polytrack, good to firm and good to soft going: usually in cheekpieces, tried visored. *J. Balding* **56**

CHEETAH 2 b.f. (May 4) Tiger Hill (IRE) 127 – Kassiyra (IRE) (Kendor (FR) 122) [2009 8m² 8g³ Oct 23] third foal: half-sister to 5-y-o Speed Ticket: dam, French 1½m winner, half-sister to smart French stayer Kassani, out of half-sister to Derby winner Kahyasi: better effort in maidens when 2¼ lengths third to Modeyra at Doncaster: will be suited by 1¼m+: should continue to progress. *L. M. Cumani* **82 p**

CHEETAH BEETAH 3 ch.f. Compton Place 125 – Scylla 50 (Rock City 120) [2009 6s 6s⁶ 6m 8d p6g 5.1d⁶ Aug 31] 8,500Y: seventh foal: half-sister to fairly useful 2003 2-y-o 5f to 7f winner Stealthelimelight (by Royal Applause): dam, maiden, half-sister to smart sprinter Northern Goddess: no form: left M. Halford in Ireland after third start. *H. S. Howe* –

CHEF DE CAMP (FR) 6 gr.g. Smadoun (FR) 111 – Jolie Cheftaine (FR) (Chef de Clan II (FR)) [2009 p10g⁶ Jan 10] won 11.5f non-thoroughbred event in French Provinces at 4 yrs for G. Macaire: 100/1, tailed off in claimer at Lingfield. *M. R. Hoad* –

CHELSEA MORNING (USA) 2 ch.f. (Feb 8) Giant's Causeway (USA) 132 – Binya (GER) 106 (Royal Solo (IRE) 113) [2009 7g³ Jul 10] $200,000Y: second foal: dam, 7f (in France) to 11f (US Grade 3) winner, half-sister to US Grade 1 9f/1¼m winner Sabin: 10/3 and green, 4½ lengths third to Middle Club in maiden at Newbury, soon off bridle: should stay 1m+: sure to do better. *B. W. Hills* **78 p**

CHENIN (IRE) 3 b.f. Statue of Liberty (USA) 115 – Baltic Beach (IRE) (Polish Precedent (USA) 131) [2009 p6g p5g 5m p5.1g f5m p5.1g⁶ p5f⁵ Sep 4] third foal: half-sister to fairly useful 5f (including at 2 yrs) winner Glenviews Youngone (by Namid): dam unraced: poor maiden: tried blinkered. *Peter Grayson* **42**

CHERISH THE MOMENT (IRE) 3 b.c. Galileo (IRE) 134 – Belleclaire (IRE) (Bigstone (IRE) 126) [2009 80p: 10m³ 10g 12g 10m² 11.5m³ 12d⁴ Oct 11] smallish, close-coupled colt: fair maiden: stays 1½m: acts on heavy and good to firm going: tried in cheekpieces: temperamental: sold 15,000 gns. *B. W. Hills* **76 §**

CHERRIES ON TOP (IRE) 4 ch.g. Elnadim (USA) 128 – Easy Going (Hamas (IRE) 125§) [2009 46: 7g May 5] lengthy gelding: poor maiden in 2008: refused to race only outing at 4 yrs: best left alone. *D. Nicholls* **– §**

CHERRI FOSFATE 5 b.g. Mujahid (USA) 125 – Compradore 82 (Mujtahid (USA) 118) [2009 76: 8f⁵ 7m Jun 16] close-coupled gelding: fair handicapper, lightly raced at 5 yrs: stays 10.5f: acts on all-weather, firm and soft going: often wears headgear. *D. Carroll* **74**

CHERRY BEE 2 b. or gr.f. (Jan 31) Acclamation 118 – Norfolk Lavender (CAN) 80 (Ascot Knight (CAN) 130) [2009 5m² 5d⁴ 6m² 6s³ 8.3m* Aug 24] €35,000Y: leggy filly: half-sister to several winners, including useful 1m (including at 2 yrs) to 1½m winner Celtic Mission (by Cozzene) and fairly useful 7f (including at 2 yrs)/1m winner In The Pink (by Indian Ridge): dam, 1m/8.5f (latter minor US stakes) winner, out of 1000 **75**

Guineas winner Nocturnal Spree: fair performer: best effort when winning nursery at Windsor: stays 8.3f: acts on soft and good to firm going: races prominently. *M. Johnston*

CHERRY BELLE (IRE) 3 b.f. Red Ransom (USA) – Pondicherry (USA) 64 (Sir Wimborne (USA) 118) [2009 59§: 8m 10.3g 10.9g 10m6 Sep 21] leggy filly: just poor form in 2009: best form at 7f/1m: acts on any turf going: usually visored: ungenuine. *P. D. Evans* **44 §**

CHERRY PLUM 3 ch.f. Medicean 128 – Putuna 98 (Generous (IRE) 139) [2009 p8g p8.6g4 Feb 26] sixth foal: half-sister to 4-y-o My Aunt Fanny and 7-y-o Kingsholm: dam 8.5f/1¼m winner: always behind in maidens at Kempton (green) and Wolverhampton (last of 4). *A. M. Balding* **–**

CHESHIRE LADY (IRE) 2 b.f. (Apr 6) Marju (IRE) 127 – Kiris World 107 (Distant Relative 128) [2009 5.1g6 5.1g Jul 4] £22,000 2-y-o: third foal: dam Italian sprinter: little impact in maidens at Chester and Nottingham. *W. M. Brisbourne* **–**

CHESHIRE PRINCE 5 br.g. Desert Prince (IRE) 130 – Bundle Up (USA) (Miner's Mark (USA) 120) [2009 92: 10.3m* 10m 12g 10d2 10g2 10.4m 13.4m6 10m 12m 10.9m6 Oct 5] close-coupled gelding: useful handicapper: won at Chester (fourth course success) in May: good second at Newbury and Newmarket after: stays easy 13.4f: acts on any going: sometimes pulls hard: usually races up with pace: joined N. King £30,000, won over hurdles in November. *W. M. Brisbourne* **97**

CHESHIRE ROSE 4 ch.f. Bertolini (USA) 125 – Merch Rhyd-Y-Grug (Sabrehill (USA) 120) [2009 76: f5g5 f5g6 p5.1g2 5m 5d6 6d3 5.1d3 f5g5 5m p5.1g p5g5 p5.1g Nov 14] angular filly: fair handicapper: left T. D. Barron 2,100 gns after fifth start: stays 6f: acts on all-weather and soft going: tried blinkered/tongue tied, often in cheekpieces later in 2009: none too consistent. *A. M. Hales* **71**

CHEVETON 5 ch.g. Most Welcome 131 – Attribute 69 (Warning 136) [2009 103: f5g* 5.2s5 5m2 5g3 5d 5m3 6g 5g5 6m 5d* 6g2 5d Oct 24] stocky gelding: useful handicapper: won at Southwell in March and Haydock (beat Arganil by neck) in September: good 1¾ lengths second to Kaldoun Kingdom at York penultimate start: best at 5f/6f: acts on all-weather, best turf efforts on good going or softer: races close up. *R. J. Price* **104**

CHEVEYO (IRE) 3 br.g. Celtic Swing 138 – La Catalane (IRE) (Marju (IRE) 127) [2009 7m3 8.7m5 8g4 p6g2 p6g4 8s p6g2 p8g p7f Dec 21] €85,000F: second foal: dam unraced half-sister to smart Irish performer up to 7f Bezelle and smart performer up to 1m Iftiraas: fairly useful maiden on all-weather, fair on turf: left G. Lyons in Ireland prior to final start: likely to prove best at 6f/7f: acts on polytrack and good to firm ground. *Pat Morris* **73 a80**

CHEVIOT (USA) 3 b.g. Rahy (USA) 115 – Camlet 94 (Green Desert (USA) 127) [2009 94p: 6m2 6m3 7m2 Jun 27] good-bodied gelding: type to carry condition: fairly useful handicapper: speedy, but stays 7f: winner on polytrack, best efforts on good/good to firm ground: in cheekpieces last 2 starts. *M. A. Jarvis* **91**

CHEYENNE CHANT 2 ch.f. (Feb 27) Singspiel (IRE) 133 – Apache Song (USA) (Dynaformer (USA)) [2009 f7f5 p7.1g p8.6g Nov 21] 18,000F: sixth foal: half-sister to 2 winners in France, including 1m to 11.5f winner Apache Legend (by Perugino): dam, French 9f winner, half-sister to smart French 1m/1¼m performers Android and Art Moderne: green, well held in maidens: likely to flourish at 1¼m+. *Sir Mark Prescott* **– p**

CHEYENNE RED (IRE) 3 br.g. Namid 128 – Red Leggings 84 (Shareef Dancer (USA) 135) [2009 f6g4 6d4 6d4 5m2 6m3 5d2 6s* 5f3 6s4 6g* 6.1d2 Oct 15] 17,500F, 12,000Y: small gelding: sixth foal: half-brother to winner in Greece by Bahhare: dam, 2-y-o 7f winner, later stayed 1¼m: fair performer: steadily progressive throughout 2009, winning maiden in August and handicap in September, both at Hamilton: will stay 7f: acts on soft and good to firm going. *M. Dods* **78**

CHIA (IRE) 6 ch.m. Ashkalani (IRE) 128 – Motley (Rainbow Quest (USA) 134) [2009 69, a77: p9.5g p9.5g p9.5g p9.5g Dec 28] leggy mare: just modest handicapper in 2009: stays easy 1½m: acts on all-weather and firm ground: tried visored, usually in cheekpieces nowadays. *D. Haydn Jones* **63**

CHIBERTA KING 3 b.g. King's Best (USA) 132 – Glam Rock 102 (Nashwan (USA) 135) [2009 61: 11.6m* 12m* 12m2 12g 12g2 14m2 12m Sep 27] big, strong gelding: useful handicapper: won at Windsor in April and Newmarket in May: good efforts when runner-up 3 times after (to Cosmic Sun in King George V Stakes at Royal Ascot first occasion): stays 1¾m: acts on good to firm going: usually races close up. *A. M. Balding* **97**

CHICAGO COP (IRE) 3 b.g. Fasliyev (USA) 120 – Sassari (IRE) 76 (Darshaan 133) [2009 90+: p7g Apr 11] useful-looking gelding: fairly useful winner at 2 yrs: well beaten only start in 2009: will prove best at 5f/6f: sold £9,000 in May. *D. Nicholls* –

CHICAMIA 5 b.m. Kyllachy 129 – Inflation 68 (Primo Dominie 121) [2009 8.5m 10g p9.5g p16.5g p8.6g Dec 14] close-coupled mare: poor maiden: missed 2008: seems to stay 1¼m: acts on polytrack, good to firm and good to soft ground: tried in cheekpieces/blinkers. *M. Mullineaux* **48**

CHICANE 2 b.f. (Jan 18) Motivator 131 – Wosaita 70 (Generous (IRE) 139) [2009 p7.1g^4 Nov 14] half-sister to several winners, including useful 7f (at 2 yrs)/1m winner Whazzis (by Desert Prince): dam, third at 1½m from 3 starts, half-sister to Prix de Diane winner Rafha, herself dam of very smart sprinter Invincible Spirit: 20/1 and green, 9¾ lengths fourth to Huroof in maiden at Wolverhampton, keeping on not knocked about: bred to be well suited by 1¼m+: should improve. *W. J. Haggas* **65 p**

CHICHA MORADA (USA) 2 b.f. (May 16) Tale of The Cat (USA) 113 – Unbridled Charmer (USA) (Unbridled (USA) 128) [2009 p7g^6 Jul 15] $35,000Y: tall, angular filly: third foal: half-sister to a winner in USA by Tiznow: dam US 1m winner: 20/1, travelled well then ran green and not knocked about when sixth to Sent From Heaven in maiden at Kempton: sure to improve. *D. M. Simcock* **62 p**

CHICHEN DAAWE 3 b.f. Daawe (USA) 103 – Chichen Itza (Shareef Dancer (USA) 135) [2009 8.5m^5 6d^5 7d^5 8.5m^3 8m 10.1m^2 10m* 9.9g^5 10g^4 p13.9g Nov 2] close-coupled filly: third foal: sister to 6-y-o Daaweitza: dam unraced: modest handicapper: won at Ffos Las in September: stays 1¼m: acts on good to firm ground. *B. Ellison* **59**

CHICHI (IRE) 2 b.f. (Mar 26) Tomba 119 – Chiffon 70§ (Polish Precedent (USA) 131) [2009 p7m p7g Dec 31] second foal: dam, unreliable 7f winner, half-sister to smart performer up to 10.4f Johannian: well held in maidens. *R. Hannon* –

CHICHINA (USA) 2 b.f. (May 4) Afleet Alex (USA) 128 – St Aye (USA) 90 (Nureyev (USA) 131) [2009 6g 7.1m p8.6g Oct 17] $35,000Y: third foal: half-sister to 4-y-o Naomh Geileis and a winner in USA by Fusaichi Pegasus: dam, US 8.5f winner, half-sister to dam of high-class 1¼m performer Oratorio: signs of ability in maidens: should stay 1¼m: likely to do better. *M. Johnston* **– p**

CHICITA BANANA 2 b.f. (Feb 2) Danehill Dancer (IRE) 117 – Night Frolic 68 (Night Shift (USA)) [2009 5m 5.1g* 5f^2 5s 6f p7g^3 5.5g^3 p6m Sep 24] 60,000Y: leggy filly: second foal: half-sister to 3-y-o Burns Night: dam, 1m winner, half-sister to useful French/US performer up to 10.5f Miss Caerleona, herself dam of smart 1m/9f performer Karen's Caper: fair performer: won maiden at Bath in April: creditable third in nurseries: stays easy 7f: acts on polytrack and firm ground: sold 9,000 gns. *George Baker* **69**

CHICORA (USA) 3 b.f. Congaree (USA) 127 – Old Money (AUS) (Old Spice (AUS)) [2009 7m^5 p8g^3 9.9g^6 10m^3 10.3m 8.1g^2 Aug 21] big, lengthy filly: has scope: first live foal: dam 7f (in USA) to 1½m (Australian Group 1) winner: fair maiden: should stay beyond 1m: sold 7,500 gns, sent to Saudi Arabia. *J. H. M. Gosden* **70**

CHIC SHANIQUE (USA) 3 b. or br.f. Dynaformer (USA) – Toll Order (USA) (Loup Sauvage (USA) 125) [2009 64: 8s p10g 12.1m^2 p12g^5 11.5g Jul 20] angular filly: modest maiden: stays 1½m: acts on polytrack and good to firm ground. *Tom Dascombe* **61**

CHIEF EDITOR 5 b.g. Tomba 119 – Princess Zara (Reprimand 122) [2009 116: 5.2s* 5m May 2] big, strong, well-made gelding: smart performer: better than ever when winning handicap at Newbury in April by ½ length from Sohraab: suffered heart attack in Palace House Stakes at Newmarket: was effective at 5f/6f: acted on all-weather, soft and good to firm going: dead. *M. A. Jarvis* **118**

CHIEF EXEC 7 b.g. Zafonic (USA) 130 – Shot At Love (IRE) 79 (Last Tycoon 131) [2009 –, a81: 7d p7g p7.1g* p7g^2 7.6g^6 p7.1g^4 p8g p7.1g^2 p7.1g^3 p7g^5 p7.1g^4 p7.1g^4 Dec 18] leggy gelding: fairly useful handicapper on all-weather, modest on turf: won at Wolverhampton in July: best up to 1m: acts on polytrack and firm ground: wears headgear: held up (sometimes slowly away). *J. R. Gask* **54 a82**

CHIEF OF TEN 2 ch.c. (Feb 25) Doyen (IRE) 132 – Fudge (Polar Falcon (USA) 126) [2009 8.3v p8g Nov 14] rangy colt: well held in maidens: sold £800. *D. R. Lanigan* –

CHIEF RED CLOUD (USA) 3 b. or br.g. Cherokee Run (USA) 122 – Pertuisane (Zamindar (USA) 116) [2009 –: 7.5m^4 p8g* p8g^4 8.1g^4 p6g^3 p7.1g^5 p7.1g Oct 1] **72**

workmanlike gelding: fair handicapper: won at Kempton in June: trained by K. R. Burke until after third start: stays 1m: acts on polytrack. *A. P. Jarvis*

CHIEF WREN (USA) 2 b.f. (Feb 12) Elusive Quality (USA) – Sea Gift (USA) 84 (A P Indy (USA) 131) [2009 p8m⁶ Dec 4] first foal: dam, 1¼m winner (only start), half-sister to useful performer up to 1m Bicoastal out of US Grade 3 9f winner Ocean Queen: 33/1, showed some ability when mid-field in maiden at Lingfield: should improve. *E. F. Vaughan* **48 p**

CHIFAH 2 b.f. (Mar 7) Choisir (AUS) 126 – Danifah (IRE) 77 (Perugino (USA) 84) [2009 5m f5g⁶ 6.1g⁶ May 25] £5,000Y: leggy filly: first foal: dam 5f (at 2 yrs) to 1m winner: poor maiden: tried in claimer. *P. D. Evans* **44**

CHIFF CHAFF 5 ch.m. Mtoto 134 – Hen Harrier 94 (Polar Falcon (USA) 126) [2009 65: p13.9g³ 15.8m p16.5g 16d Jul 27] sturdy mare: modest handicapper: free-going sort, but stays 2m: acts on polytrack, soft and good to firm going. *C. R. Dore* **62**

CHILD OF OUR TIME (IRE) 2 b.f. (Feb 18) Oratorio (IRE) 128 – Shariyfa (FR) (Zayyani 119) [2009 7m 8g Oct 20] £21,000Y: rather leggy filly: sixth foal: half-sister to winner in Italy by Eagle Eyed and winner in USA by Dixieland Band: dam unraced half-sister to dam of high-class miler Sendawar: better effort in maidens when eighth to Principal Role at Yarmouth latter start. *P. W. Chapple-Hyam* **66**

CHILEAN FIZZ 2 b.f. (Mar 31) Domedriver (IRE) 128 – Alter Ego 84 (Alzao (USA) 117) [2009 6m 5g⁵ 5g⁴ 5d Aug 26] €4,500Y: third foal: dam 2-y-o 7f winner: poor form in maidens/seller. *Mrs A. Duffield* **45**

CHILL OUT CHARLEY 2 b.g. (May 18) Cyrano de Bergerac 120 – We're Joken 62 (Statoblest 120) [2009 5g 6m Jun 27] medium-sized gelding: tailed off in maidens. *J. J. Bridger* **–**

CHILLY FILLY (IRE) 3 b.f. Montjeu (IRE) 137 – Chill Seeking (USA) 102 (Theatrical 128) [2009 82: p12g² 12m* Apr 18] good-topped filly: fair performer: won maiden at Doncaster in April: stays 1½m: acts on polytrack, soft and good to firm going: quirky (has hung/raced freely). *M. Johnston* **80**

CHIMBONDA 3 ch.c. Dr Fong (USA) 128 – Ambonnay 89 (Ashkalani (IRE) 128) [2009 70, a66: p6g p6g² f5g p5g⁴ f5g⁵ 5.1m 5m⁶ 8.3g 5m⁵ 5g Jun 17] sturdy colt: regressive maiden: best at 5f/6f: acts on all-weather and soft ground: tried in headgear/tongue tie: often front runner. *S. Parr* **55 d**

CHINA BAY 2 b.f. (Feb 1) Reset (AUS) 124 – Kathryn Janeway (IRE) 71 (In The Wings 128) [2009 p5.1g⁶ f5g⁵ 6g p8m⁶ Oct 28] £1,000Y: leggy filly: first foal: dam maiden (stayed 11.7f): poor form in maidens/seller: left Tom Dascombe after third start. *P. M. Phelan* **38**

CHINA LILY (USA) 2 b. or br.f. (Mar 23) Street Cry (IRE) 130 – Lil Lisa Can (USA) (Lil's Lad (USA) 121) [2009 7.5m⁶ p7.1g Oct 1] $85,000Y, resold $75,000Y, 75,000 2-y-o: close-coupled, attractive filly: first foal: dam, US 6.5f winner, out of half-sister to high-class US filly up to 9f Hidden Lake: sixth to Silent Secret in maiden at Beverley: shaped as if amiss subsequent start: has left Godolphin. *Saeed bin Suroor* **54**

CHINCHON (IRE) 4 b.c. Marju (IRE) 127 – Jarama (IRE) (Hector Protector (USA) 124) [2009 113: 10s³ 10d⁴ 12m² 11f⁴ 10g² 10m* Sep 25] first foal: dam French 9.5f winner who stayed 11f: smart performer: won minor event at Longchamp in 2008 and La Coupe de Maisons-Laffitte (beat Putney Bridge ¾ length) in September: in frame all previous outings in 2009, best efforts in Queen Elizabeth II Cup at Sha Tin (fourth to Presvis), Grand Prix de Chantilly (beaten a head by Scintillo) and listed race at Longchamp (short-neck second to Mundybash): effective at 1¼m and stays 1½m, at least in steadily-run race: acts on heavy and good to firm going: has worn cheekpieces, including last 2 starts. *C. Laffon-Parias, France* **118**

CHINCOTEAGUE (IRE) 3 b.f. Daylami (IRE) 138 – Blue Water (USA) 104 (Bering 136) [2009 11.7g³ 10.2m² Sep 28] fifth foal: half-sister to 3 winners, including 1m to 1½m winner Indian Creek and 7f (at 2 yrs)/1m winner Desert Dew (both smart by Indian Ridge): dam French 1¼m/1½m winner: fair form when placed in maidens at Bath, 2 lengths second to Tanfidh: should stay 1½m: capable of further improvement. *B. J. Meehan* **75 p**

CHINESE DEMOCRACY (USA) 2 b.f. (May 5) Proud Citizen (USA) 122 – Double's Lass (USA) (Mr Leader (USA)) [2009 5g⁶ 6m 5.1m⁴ p5g⁵ Oct 21] $60,000Y: leggy filly: half-sister to several winners in US, including Grade 3 1m winner Spotsgone **58 ?**

(by Bright Launch): dam US 2-y-o 5.5f/6f winner: modest maiden: off 4 months, bumped start when respectable fifth in nursery at Kempton. *P. F. I. Cole*

CHINESE PROFIT 4 b.g. Acclamation 118 – Tancholo (So Factual (USA) 120) [2009 –: 7m^2 8g p8g p10g 7m f8f Dec 12] plain gelding: modest maiden: little impact after reappearance: stays 7f: acts on good to firm going: tried in cheekpieces. *G. C. Bravery* **57 d**

CHINESE WHITE (IRE) 4 gr.f. Dalakhani (IRE) 133 – Chiang Mai (IRE) 113 (Sadler's Wells (USA) 132) [2009 112: 9.5v^2 10g^3 9.5g* 9v* 10s* 10d Oct 25] close-coupled filly: smart performer: successful at Gowran in listed race in August and at the Curragh in Dance Design Stakes (beat Latin Love 4½ lengths) later in month and Irish National Stud Blandford Stakes (by 2 lengths from Roman Empress) in September: favourite, ran poorly in Premio Lydia Tesio at Rome final start: has form at 1½m, but best at 9f/1¼m: acts on heavy and good to firm going: tongue tied last 2 starts in 2008. *D. K. Weld, Ireland* **117**

CHINK OF LIGHT 2 ch.c. (Feb 27) Dr Fong (USA) 128 – Isle of Flame (Shirley Heights 130) [2009 8.3v Nov 4] 65,000Y: brother to useful 9f (at 2 yrs) to 2m winner Kindling and half-brother to several winners, including smart French 9f/1¼m winner Thattinger (by Salse) and useful 1½m to 2m winner Dorothy's Friend (by Grand Lodge): dam unraced: 14/1 and green, mid-field in maiden at Nottingham, late headway: will be suited by 1¼m+: will improve. *A. M. Balding* **55 p**

CHINOISE (IRE) 2 b.f. (Apr 27) Chineur (FR) 123 – Grey Pursuit (IRE) 63 (Pursuit of Love 124) [2009 6g^5 p7g Jul 15] €2,000Y: rather leggy filly: second foal: dam Irish sprint maiden: better effort when fifth in seller at Windsor. *P. M. Phelan* **43**

CHINTZ (IRE) 3 b.f. Danehill Dancer (IRE) 117 – Gold Dodger (USA) (Slew O' Gold (USA)) [2009 112p: 7g 8v^5 8f 9s^6 9v^4 8s 8g Oct 18] tall, lengthy filly: useful performer: creditable effort in 2009 only when seventh to Border Patrol in Solonaway Stakes at the Curragh sixth outing: well held in Coronation Stakes at Royal Ascot third start: barely stays 1m: acts on soft ground: in cheekpieces last 3 starts: free-going sort. *David Wachman, Ireland* **100**

CHIN WAG (IRE) 5 b.g. Iron Mask (USA) 117 – Sweet Chat (IRE) (Common Grounds 118) [2009 69: 8g^3 9.1g 6g^5 6s 6f^6 8m Aug 31] workmanlike gelding: modest performer nowadays: stays 9f: acts on polytrack, good to firm and good to soft going: often in headgear: held up. *J. S. Goldie* **54**

Irish National Stud Blandford Stakes, the Curragh—
Chinese White notches up her hat-trick as she beats Roman Empress in this Group 2 contest

CHIP N PIN 5 b.m. Erhaab (USA) 127 – Vallauris 94 (Faustus (USA) 118) [2009 46: 12m Jul 1] strong mare: maiden handicapper, lightly raced on Flat nowadays: well held sole start at 5 yrs: stays 1½m: acts on firm ground: tried blinkered. *T. D. Easterby* –

CHIPOLINI (IRE) 3 b.g. Bertolini (USA) 125 – Chimere (FR) (Soviet Lad (USA)) [2009 57?: 5m 5m f7g 6d^5 5m Jul 3] leggy gelding: poor maiden: stays 6f: acts on good to firm and good to soft going: tried visored/blinkered. *D. Carroll* 44

CHIPS O'TOOLE (IRE) 2 b.c. (Mar 24) Fasliyev (USA) 120 – Miss Megs (IRE) 81 (Croco Rouge (IRE) 126) [2009 5.7g^3 6d^2 5.1m^3 5.5g 6m* 5g^2 p6m^6 6g^4 Oct 30] 30,000Y: good-bodied colt: second foal: half-brother to 3-y-o Golden Pool: dam Irish 9f/11f winner: useful performer: won nursery at Goodwood (by neck from Gouray Girl) in October: good ½-length second to The Only Boss in minor event at Catterick next time: free-going sort, raced only at 5f/6f: acts on polytrack, good to firm and good to soft going. *B. J. Meehan* 95

CHJIMES (IRE) 5 b.g. Fath (USA) 116 – Radiance (IRE) 54 (Thatching 131) [2009 84: p5g* p6g^3 p5g* p5g* p5.1g^4 p5g^6 5v 6d^6 5g p5m^3 p5.1g^6 p5.1g^3 p5g^6 p5g p5.1g^6 p5m^5 Dec 30] close-coupled gelding: has a round action: fairly useful handicapper on all-weather, fair on turf: won at Lingfield in January, February and March: has won at 7f, best at 5f/6f: acts on all-weather and soft ground: tried visored: held up: signs of temperament. *C. R. Dore* 75 a92

CHOC'A'MOCA (IRE) 2 b.g. (Apr 5) Camacho 118 – Dear Catch (IRE) 69 (Bluebird (USA) 125) [2009 5m 7s 6s Oct 27] workmanlike gelding: well held in maidens: tried blinkered. *I. W. McInnes* –

CHOCK A BLOCK (IRE) 3 gr.c. Dalakhani (IRE) 133 – Choc Ice (IRE) 115 (Kahyasi 130) [2009 99p: 11g^5 10.3g^3 12m* 12v Oct 24] lengthy, good-quartered colt: smart form: best effort when winning slowly-run 4-runner listed race at Newmarket in October by short head from Drill Sergeant, idling: stays 1½m: acts on good to firm ground, well held in St Simon Stakes at Newbury on heavy. *Saeed bin Suroor* 114

CHOCOLATE CARAMEL (USA) 7 b.g. Storm Creek (USA) – Sandhill (BRZ) (Baynoun 128) [2009 97: p12.2g^4 f14d Dec 29] tall gelding: fairly useful performer: below form both starts in 2009: stays 2¼m: acts on polytrack, firm and soft ground: tried blinkered. *R. A. Fahey* 69

CHOCOLATE COOKIE (IRE) 2 b.f. (Apr 19) Desert Style (IRE) 121 – Back At de Front (IRE) 70 (Cape Cross (IRE) 129) [2009 6g^3 5.2d 5g^3 7m^4 5.7g^4 p7f^3 p5.1g^2 p6m^2 p7g* Nov 18] €10,000Y: lengthy, unfurnished filly: first foal: dam 6f winner, including at 2 yrs: fair performer: left R. Hannon after seventh start: won claimer at Lingfield: stays easy 7f: acts on polytrack and good to soft going. *J. R. Boyle* 67

CHOCOLICIOUS (IRE) 3 b. or br.f. Captain Rio 122 – Queenfisher 101 (Scottish Reel 123) [2009 68: f7g^4 6m* p7.1g^3 6m* 6s^3 6g* May 26] workmanlike filly: fair performer: won seller at Leicester and apprentice claimer at Redcar, both in April, and claimer at Leicester in May: likely to prove best at 5f/6f: acts on all-weather, soft and good to firm ground: visored last 5 starts: sold £2,500 in October. *B. Smart* 78

CHOICE 2 b.f. (Feb 12) Azamour (IRE) 130 – Poise (IRE) 93 (Rainbow Quest (USA) 134) [2009 8g^6 Oct 20] first foal: dam, 1¼m winner, out of half-sister to dam of Daylami and Dalakhani: 12/1 and green, 6 lengths sixth to Principal Role in maiden at Yarmouth: will be suited by 1¼m+: sure to do better. *Sir Michael Stoute* 71 p

CHOIR SOLO 2 b.f. (Feb 27) Medicean 128 – Choirgirl 106 (Unfuwain (USA) 131) [2009 8g Oct 20] fifth foal: half-sister to fairly useful 1½m winners Chord and Choral Festival (both by Pivotal): dam, 2-y-o 7f winner (stayed 1¼m), half-sister to very smart 1m/1¼m performer Chorist: 33/1 and blinkered, well held in maiden at Yarmouth: sold 2,000 gns, sent to Hungary. *J. H. M. Gosden* –

CHOISEAU (IRE) 4 b.g. Choisir (AUS) 126 – Little Linnet 75 (Be My Guest (USA) 126) [2009 85: f6g^4 7g^2 Jul 31] good-bodied gelding: fairly useful performer, lightly raced: good efforts both starts at 4 yrs: stays 7f: acts on fibresand and good to firm going: sold only 2,000 gns in October, sent to Greece. *Pat Eddery* 90

CHOISHARP (IRE) 3 b.c. Choisir (AUS) 126 – Ballea Queen (IRE) (College Chapel 122) [2009 69: f6g^6 5m^4 5.1m^2 6g^3 6m^2 6m^3 5.2g* Aug 30] fair handicapper: won at Yarmouth in August: may prove best at 5f: acts on good to firm going: tried blinkered, including for win. *M. Botti* 74

CHOOKIE AVON 2 ch.g. (Mar 28) Avonbridge 123 – Lady of Windsor (IRE) 73§ (Woods of Windsor (USA)) [2009 6d 6g^6 p7.1g^6 p8.6g^3 Nov 21] fair form at best in maidens: stays 7f. *I. Semple* **65**

CHOOKIE HAMILTON 5 ch.g. Compton Place 125 – Lady of Windsor (IRE) 73§ (Woods of Windsor (USA)) [2009 71: f12s^2 p13.9g^4 12.4m 13g* 11.5m* 13.1g* 13d^2 13.8g^5 10s p13.9g 13g^6 p13.9g^3 p12.2g* p12.2g* p13m^5 Nov 28] lengthy, angular gelding: fairly useful handicapper: revitalised at 5 yrs, winning at Hamilton and Carlisle in May, Ayr in June and Wolverhampton (2) in November: stays 1¾m: acts on all-weather, good to firm and good to soft ground: tried in headgear. *I. Semple* **88**

CHOOKIE HEITON (IRE) 11 br.g. Fumo di Londra (IRE) 108 – Royal Wolff (Prince Tenderfoot (USA) 126) [2009 71d: p6g^5 p6g 5g^6 6m 5.9m Jun 15] strong, lengthy gelding: one-time smart performer, only modest nowadays: best at 5f/6f: acts on polytrack, firm and good to soft going: tried in cheekpieces. *I. Semple* **62**

CHOOSY FLOOSY 3 b.f. Lend A Hand 124 – In The Stocks 59 (Reprimand 122) [2009 8.1g^5 p8.6g 8.3m 11.9d p10g Dec 7] chunky filly: third foal: half-sister to 5.7f winner Hawridge Miss (by Piccolo): dam 1m to 11.5f winner: modest maiden: best effort at 8.3f on good to firm going. *Pat Eddery* **50**

CHORAL FESTIVAL 3 b.f. Pivotal 124 – Choirgirl 106 (Unfuwain (USA) 131) [2009 83p: f12g* 11.9g p12f Dec 21] unfurnished filly: fair performer: won maiden at Southwell in July: left Sir Mark Prescott 8,000 gns after next start: stays 1½m: acts on fibresand and soft going. *J. J. Bridger* **76**

CHORAL SERVICE 3 ch.g. Pivotal 124 – Choir Mistress (Chief Singer 131) [2009 –p: 8.3g 8g^4 10.9g^3 Jun 25] tall, rather leggy gelding: fair form: much improved when third on handicap debut at Warwick: will stay 1½m: sold 16,000 gns. *W. J. Haggas* **78**

CHOREE (IRE) 3 ch.f. Choisir (AUS) 126 – Reem Al Fala (Green Desert (USA) 127) [2009 6m^6 6g^4 5m Jun 16] €50,000F, €30,000Y: close-coupled filly: third foal: dam unraced half-sister to dam of 6-y-o Balthazaar's Gift: poor form in maidens. *T. D. Easterby* **37**

CHOREOGRAPHY 6 ch.g. Medicean 128 – Stark Ballet (USA) (Nureyev (USA) 131) [2009 88: 6g 5m 7m 7g 7f^6 6d 7f^6 6m^5 7f* 8m 7d Oct 6] leggy gelding: fair handicapper nowadays: won at Brighton in September: stays 1m: acts on any turf going: often wears headgear. *Jim Best* **78**

CHORUS BOY 2 ch.c. (May 11) Kyllachy 129 – Dame Jude 76 (Dilum (USA) 115) [2009 6m 6m 7d^6 p8g^5 f7f^6 Nov 24] smallish colt: modest maiden: stays 1m: blinkered last 3 starts. *G. G. Margarson* **53**

CHOSEN FOREVER 4 b.g. Choisir (AUS) 126 – Forever Bond (Danetime (IRE) 121) [2009 76: 5.9m f8m 6m p7.1m^6 p8.6g^3 p9.5g* p9.5g* Dec 28] big, strong, lengthy gelding: fair handicapper: won twice at Wolverhampton in December: stays 9.5f: acts on polytrack, best turf efforts on good going: tried in cheekpieces. *G. R. Oldroyd* **73**

CHOSEN ONE (IRE) 4 ch.g. Choisir (AUS) 126 – Copious (IRE) (Generous (IRE) 139) [2009 73: 6d 6.1g 6g 6g 5g^3 5.1d^4 5s^2 f5m p6f^3 Dec 13] compact gelding: fair handicapper: effective at 5f/6f: acts on polytrack, heavy and good to firm going. *B. Smart* **69**

CHOSEN SON (IRE) 3 b. or br.g. Kheleyf (USA) 116 – Choice Pickings (IRE) (Among Men (USA) 124) [2009 74: p5g p6m p5g p7f^4 p7m p5g^3 p5m f5m p5g^3 Nov 25] fair maiden: should prove best at 5f/6f: raced mainly on polytrack: tongue tied last 2 starts. *P. J. O'Gorman* **69**

CHRIS'S JEM 3 b.f. Makbul 104 – Royal Orchid (IRE) 74 (Shalford (IRE) 124§) [2009 p6g 6d^2 5m* 5m^5 5s p5g^6 5f^5 p6m Sep 30] sturdy filly: sixth foal: sister to 5-y-o Castano and half-sister to 2 winners, including fairly useful 5f/6f winner Maddie's A Jem (by Emperor Jones): dam, maiden, half-sister to smart performer up to 1m Ho Leng: fair performer: won maiden at Folkestone in April: stays 6f: acts on polytrack, good to firm and good to soft going. *J. R. Jenkins* **65**

CHRISTINA ROSSETTI 3 b.f. Falbrav (IRE) 133 – First Exhibit (Machiavellian (USA) 123) [2009 p8g^3 7m Apr 16] 25,000Y: lengthy filly: has scope: third foal: half-sister to 4-y-o Prime Exhibit and winner in USA by Johannesburg: dam, unraced half-sister to smart 1½m/1¾m winner Moments of Joy, out of Yorkshire Oaks and Prix Vermeille winner My Emma: fair form in maidens: sold 800 gns in December. *J. H. M. Gosden* **68**

CHRISTMASCAMETWICE 3 b.f. Monsieur Bond (IRE) 120 – My Poppet (Mid- **61**
yan (USA) 124) [2009 p6g^3 p6g^6 p6g 5.7f May 13] 4,000Y: fourth foal: dam, maiden,
half-sister to high-class sprinter Kyllachy: modest maiden: went wrong way after debut.
J. A. Osborne

CHRISTMAS CARNIVAL 2 ch.c. (Mar 10) Cadeaux Genereux 131 – Ellebanna 69 **75**
(Tina's Pet 121) [2009 7m^5 p8.6g^3 Oct 10] 70,000Y: sturdy colt: brother to 1m winner
City Bonus and half-brother to several winners, including 6-y-o Ours and smart 7f/1m
winner Mine (by Primo Dominie): dam, 5f (including at 2 yrs) winner, half-sister to very
smart sprinter Bolshoi: fair form in maidens at Newbury and Wolverhampton (third to
Start Right). *B. J. Meehan*

CHRISTMAS COMING 2 b.c. (Mar 18) Cape Cross (IRE) 129 – Aunty Rose (IRE) **64**
103 (Caerleon (USA) 132) [2009 p7m^4 p8f p7m^2 Dec 16] modest maiden: in frame at
Kempton and Lingfield: should stay 1m (pulled hard when tried at trip). *D. R. C. Elsworth*

CHRISTOPHERS QUEST 4 b.g. Forzando 122 – Kaprisky (IRE) (Red Sunset 120) **–**
[2009 68: 8g 8.3g Oct 19] good-bodied gelding: regressive maiden: last both starts in
2009, then gelded. *Miss N. A. Lloyd-Beavis*

CHRISTOPHER WREN (USA) 2 ch.c. (Feb 28) D'Wildcat (USA) 118 – Ashley's **80 p**
Coy (USA) (Country Pine (USA)) [2009 p7g^3 p8g 7m^3 8.3d* Oct 12] $25,000F:
well-made colt: fourth foal: half-brother to winner in USA by Groomstick: dam US 1m to
1½m winner: fairly useful form: much improved when winning nursery at Windsor by
2¼ lengths from Wild Rockette: should be suited by 1¼m+: acts on good to soft going:
open to further improvement. *J. R. Best*

CHUSHKA 2 ch.f. (Mar 10) Pivotal 124 – Ravine 81 (Indian Ridge 123) [2009 6m^4 6m^4 **65**
Sep 14] £75,000Y: rather leggy filly: sixth foal: half-sister to 3 winners, including smart
2004 2-y-o 6f (July Stakes) winner Captain Hurricane (by Desert Style) and 7f winner
Nelly's Glen (by Efisio): dam, 6f/7f winner, half-sister to 1000 Guineas second Niche:
fourth in maidens at Redcar, better effort on debut: should be suited by 7f. *B. Smart*

CIAN ROONEY (IRE) 2 b.g. (Apr 25) Camacho 118 – Exponent (USA) (Exbourne **66**
(USA) 125) [2009 5m 5m^4 5g* 6m Aug 8] €47,000Y: closely related to smart sprinter
Drayton (by Danetime), 5f winner in Ireland at 2 yrs, and half-brother to fairly useful 5f
(at 2 yrs)/6f winner Exponential (by Namid): dam unraced: fair performer: won maiden
at Pontefract in July, making all: poor effort in nursery: gelded after: should be suited by
6f. *Mrs A. Duffield*

CIARA EILE (IRE) 9 b.m. Victory Note (USA) 120 – Graceful Resign 77 (Most **54**
Welcome 131) [2009 –: 12d^4 14.1m May 25] quite good-topped ex-Irish mare: modest
handicapper: stays 1½m: acts on soft and good to firm going: twice blinkered at 4 yrs.
D. Carroll

CIGALAS 4 ch.g. Selkirk (USA) 129 – Langoustine (AUS) 117 (Danehill (USA) 126) **73 d**
[2009 91: 8m 7.1m 9m 8g^4 8g^5 8g 7g 9.2g Sep 21] tall, good-topped gelding: has fluent
action: fairly useful performer at best: on downgrade: probably stays 1m: acts on good to
soft ground. *Mrs J. C. McGregor*

CILIUM (IRE) 3 b.f. War Chant (USA) 126 – Venturi 103 (Danehill Dancer (IRE) 117) **94**
[2009 8g^2 8s^3 7d 8g* 9v^5 7m p10.7g 8g Oct 18] first foal: dam, Irish 2-y-o 6f/7f winner,
sister to smart French performer up to 1¼m Feels All Right: fairly useful performer: won
maiden at Leopardstown in August: good fifth to Chinese White in Dance Design Stakes
at the Curragh next time: well held after, including in listed race at Doncaster: stays 9f:
acts on heavy ground. *Andrew Oliver, Ireland*

CILL RIALAIG 4 gr.f. Environment Friend 128 – Pang Valley Girl (Rock Hopper 124) **98**
[2009 11.8m^4 p12g^3 12m^3 9.9m* 9.9m^2 10.1m* 10m^6 10g* 10v^6 10.3s Nov 7] quite
good-topped filly: first foal: dam once-raced half-sister to 5-y-o Sohraab and useful 7f/
1m performer Pango: dual bumper winner: useful handicapper on Flat: progressive, won
at Salisbury in June, Epsom in August and Ascot (beat Espiritu by short head) in October:
best efforts at 1¼m: acts on good to firm ground, below form on soft/heavy last 2 starts.
H. Morrison

CILS BLANCS (IRE) 3 b.f. Barathea (IRE) 127 – Immortelle (Arazi (USA) 135) **62**
[2009 8.1m^6 8.1g 7s* 7.1g^3 f7m^5 Nov 12] 45,000F: leggy filly: sixth foal: half-sister to
1½m winner Corker (by Grand Lodge) and winner in Greece by Generous: dam unraced
half-sister to Poule d'Essai des Pouliches winner Danseuse du Soir: modest performer:
won maiden at Thirsk in August: best efforts at 7f: acts on soft going. *B. Smart*

Blue Square Brigadier Gerard Stakes, Sandown—Italian import Cima de Triomphe (grey) lowers the colours of Conduit (left) in a muddling renewal; Stotsfold (blaze) is third

CIMA DE TRIOMPHE (IRE) 4 gr.c. Galileo (IRE) 134 – Sopran Londa (IRE) 104 (Danehill (USA) 126) [2009 121: 10.5g^6 10m* 10m^4 10g^4 12d 10g Oct 31] good-bodied colt: smart performer: won Blue Square Brigadier Gerard Stakes at Sandown (finished strongly to beat Conduit, who gave 7 lb, by nose) in May: respectable efforts when fourth to Sea The Stars in Eclipse Stakes at Sandown next time and ninth of 11 to Scenic Shot in Mackinnon Stakes at Flemington final outing, racing too keenly in blinkers: stays 1½m: acts on firm and good to soft ground: has had tongue tied: held up: has rejoined B. Grizzetti in Italy. *L. M. Cumani* **115**

CINDY INCIDENTALLY 3 ch.f. Shinko Forest (IRE) – Bayrami 39 (Emarati (USA) 74) [2009 –: p5.1g^6 p5.1g^4 p5g 5.1g 5.1m 6m^3 7g^2 6m^6 7v p7.1g Sep 25] poor maiden: seems to stay 7f: acts on polytrack and good to firm going: tried in cheekpieces, blinkered of late. *Miss Gay Kelleway* **49**

CINEMATIC (IRE) 6 b.g. Bahhare (USA) 122 – Eastern Star (IRE) (Sri Pekan (USA) 117) [2009 72+: p10g^2 p10g 10.2m p10g^5 Apr 29] tall, leggy gelding: fair handicapper: stays 1¼m: acts on polytrack, firm and good to soft going. *J. R. Boyle* **75**

CIPHER 3 b.g. Reset (AUS) 124 – Subtle Charm (Machiavellian (USA) 123) [2009 6m 8g* 8d^3 Jun 27] second foal: dam lightly-raced half-sister to Oaks winner Snow Bride, herself dam of Lammtarra: fairly useful form: standout effort when winning maiden at Redcar in June by 4½ lengths from Luc Jordan: well held in handicap next time: stays 1m: sold 26,000 gns in July. *M. Johnston* **85**

CIRCLE DANCE (IRE) 4 b. or br.g. Namid 128 – Rivana 79 (Green Desert (USA) 127) [2009 79: p5g^2 p5g^3 p5.1g^3 f5g^6 p6g^5 p5.1m* 5g p5g 6m^5 5m f6g 6s^3 6g^3 6s 6m^4 5.1g f7g Dec 8] tall gelding: fair performer: won maiden at Wolverhampton in March: left D. Shaw prior to final start: effective at 5f, should stay 7f: acts on all-weather, firm and soft going: tried in cheekpieces, usually visored. *Miss M. E. Rowland* **69**

CIRCUIT DANCER (IRE) 9 b.g. Mujadil (USA) 119 – Trysinger (IRE) (Try My Best (USA) 130) [2009 76: 5m 5g^5 5f 6.1g^6 6m^5 Jun 30] tall gelding: modest handicapper nowadays: effective at 5f to easy 7f: acts on polytrack, firm and soft going: tried in cheekpieces at 5 yrs: reportedly bled final start. *D. Nicholls* **63**

CIRCUMVENT 2 ch.g. (Feb 22) Tobougg (IRE) 125 – Seren Devious (Dr Devious (IRE) 127) [2009 f6g* p7g^2 7m* 8d* 9d^2 Oct 18] second foal: half-brother to 3-y-o Seradim: dam unraced half-sister to Lingfield Derby Trial winner Saddler's Quest: useful performer: won maiden at Southwell in August, 4-runner minor event at Leicester in September and 4-runner Prix Thomas Bryon at Saint-Cloud (beat Silver Grey 1½ lengths) in October: good short-neck second of 5 to Zeitoper in Prix de Conde at Longchamp final start: will be suited by 1¼m. *P. F. I. Cole* **104**

CIRCUS CLOWN (IRE) 4 b.g. Vettori (IRE) 119 – Comic (IRE) 87 (Be My Chief (USA) 122) [2009 59: 11.1g^{6} Sep 21] maiden handicapper: below form only start at 4 yrs: stays 11f: visored once. *P. Monteith* **–**

CIRCUS GIRL (IRE) 2 ch.f. (May 19) Bertolini (USA) 125 – Blew Her Top (USA) (Blushing John (USA) 120) [2009 p7g^{5} Nov 11] 13,000F: half-sister to 3 winners including 2005 2-y-o 6f winner Musical High (by Mozart), later successful at 1m in USA, and useful 5f (in France at 2 yrs) to 8.5f winner Arabic Song (by Alhaarth): dam unraced half-sister to US Grade 1 9f/1¼m winner Life At The Top: 11/1, shaped with promise when 9½ lengths fifth of 14 to Mass Rally in maiden at Kempton: should improve. *R. M. Beckett* **54 p**

CIRRUS DES AIGLES (FR) 3 b.g. Even Top (IRE) 127 – Taille de Guepe (FR) (Septieme Ciel (USA) 123) [2009 a10g^{2} a8g* a8g^{2} a10g^{2} a9.5g^{2} 8d^{2} 10g* 10.5s* 10g^{2} 12g^{2} 10g^{3} 10g^{3} 10d* 12m^{2} 10g* 12d* 12g^{5} Dec 13] fourth foal: half-brother to fairly useful French 6f to 1m winner Mesnil des Aigles (by Neverneyev): dam unraced: smart performer: thrived on busy campaign, winning maiden at Cagnes-sur-Mer in January, 2 minor events at Longchamp in May, listed race at Le Lion-d'Angers in August, Prix du Prince d'Orange at Longchamp (beat World Heritage ¾ length) in September and Prix du Conseil de Paris (had to wait for gap before bursting clear to beat Makt by 6 lengths, looked nearer 4) in October: good length fifth to Daryakana in Hong Kong Vase at Sha Tin final start: stays 1½m: acts on all-weather, probably on heavy and good to firm going: remarkably tough and consistent. *Mme C. Barande Barbe, France* **119**

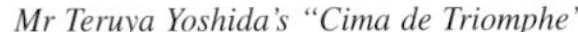

Mr Teruya Yoshida's "Cima de Triomphe"

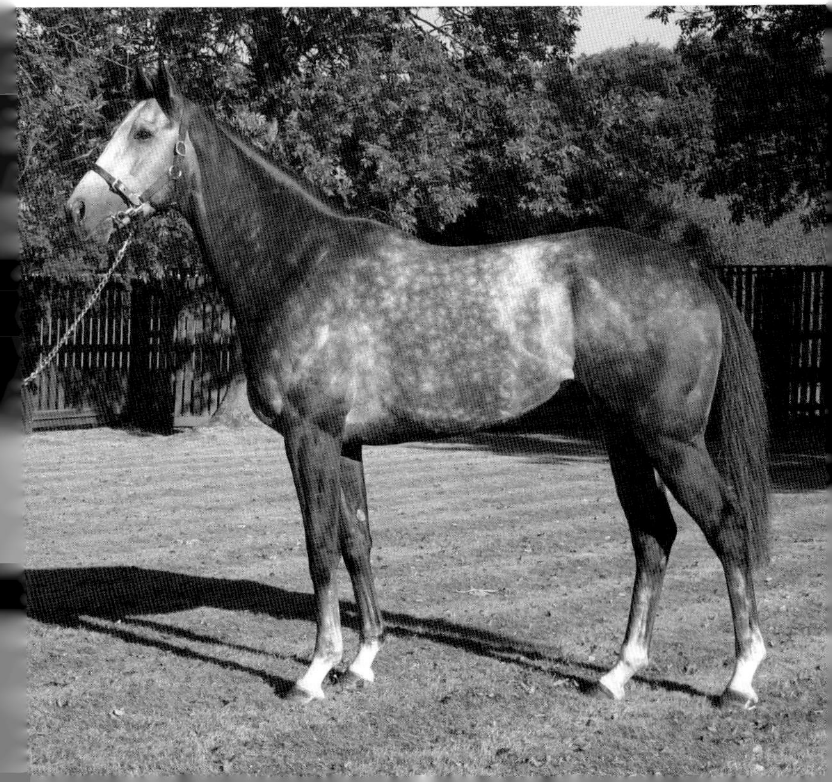

CITIZENSHIP 3 b.g. Beat Hollow 126 – Three More (USA) (Sanglamore (USA) 126) **86** [2009 77?: p7.1g^{6} p9.5g* 10m^{5} 12.3m^{5} 11.8g* 12.5g^{4} 14s^{4} 11d^{2} 11.9g^{2} 10.4g^{6} 12v^{2} 12s Nov 5] sturdy gelding: fairly useful handicapper: won at Wolverhampton in February and Leicester in May: stays 12.5f, not 1¾m: acts on polytrack, heavy and good to firm going: blinkered once, tried tongue tied. *Ian Williams*

CITRUS STAR (USA) 2 b.g. (Jan 25) Broken Vow (USA) 117 – Twist A Lime (USA) **106** (Copelan (USA)) [2009 6.1g^{2} 5m* 5g* 6d^{3} Oct 24] 35,000 2-y-o: well-made gelding: seventh foal: half-brother to several winners in North America, including Canadian 2000 Grade 2 2-y-o 1m winner Speed Gun (by Demaloot Demashoot): dam US 5f (at 2 yrs) to 7f winner: quickly progressed into useful performer, winning maiden at Pontefract in September and nursery at Windsor (by 3¼ lengths from Felsham) in October: creditable ½-length third to Layla's Hero in listed event at Doncaster: gelded after: bred to stay beyond 6f: acts on good to firm and good to soft going. *C. F. Wall*

CITY DANCER (IRE) 3 b.f. Elusive City (USA) 117 – Calypso Dancer (FR) 61 **104** (Celtic Swing 138) [2009 89p: 5m^{3} 5.1m^{3} 5g^{4} 5g^{5} 5m^{6} 5m^{2} 6.1g^{3} 6m 5m 6g^{6} Sep 20] useful performer: several good efforts in 2009 without winning, particularly when third to Doctor Parkes in handicap at Chester on second start: placed in listed races at Ayr and Chester after: best at 5f: acts on polytrack, good to firm and good to soft ground. *A. Berry*

CITY FOR CONQUEST (IRE) 6 b.m. City On A Hill (USA) 114 – Northern Life **55 §** (IRE) (Distinctly North (USA) 115) [2009 59: f6g^{6} 6m^{4} f6g^{5} 7m^{6} 6m^{5} 7m^{6} 5m 6g Jul 23] compact mare: modest handicapper: stays 6f: acts on all-weather, firm and soft going: tried in headgear: temperamental. *John A. Harris*

CITY GOSSIP (IRE) 2 b.f. (Apr 1) Shinko Forest (IRE) – Lady At War (Warning 136) **56** [2009 p6g^{5} p6g 8.3g^{4} f7m^{4} f7f^{2} Dec 17] modest form in maidens/sellers. *M. G. Quinlan*

CITY LEADER (IRE) 4 gr.c. Fasliyev (USA) 120 – Kanmary (FR) 117 (Kenmare **118** (FR) 125) [2009 115: 11m^{4} 9.8g 10m^{5} 10v^{4} Nov 8] tall, good sort: smart performer: lightly raced in 2009, best effort when 2¾ lengths fifth to Twice Over in Champion Stakes at Newmarket: respectable fourth to Voila Ici in Premio Roma at Rome on final outing: stays 1½m: acts on good to firm and good to soft going: blinkered last 2 starts. *B. J. Meehan*

CITY OF ROME (IRE) 2 b.c. (Apr 4) Elusive City (USA) 117 – Marain (IRE) (Marju **48** (IRE) 127) [2009 7.1m 6.1v^{5} 7m 8g Sep 7] sturdy colt: poor maiden: well held in nursery. *R. Hannon*

CITY OF THE KINGS (IRE) 4 b.g. Cape Cross (IRE) 129 – Prima Volta 80 (Primo **101** Dominie 121) [2009 98: 8m^{2} 9d* 8m* 8g 8g 8.1m 7g 8.3m Oct 26] well-made gelding: useful handicapper: better than ever when winning at Ripon in June and York (beat Webbow by nose) in July: below form after: stays 1¼m, effective at shorter: acts on polytrack, good to firm and good to soft going. *G. A. Harker*

CITYSCAPE 3 ch.c. Selkirk (USA) 129 – Tantina (USA) 115 (Distant View (USA) **111** 126) [2009 113p: 7s^{2} 8m May 2] tall, useful-looking colt: smart performer: creditable length second to Vocalised in Greenham Stakes at Newbury on reappearance: beat only one home in 2000 Guineas at Newmarket (reportedly finished sore on foreleg and hindleg) next time, and not seen out again: should stay 1¼m: acts on soft and good to firm going: stays in training. *R. Charlton*

CITY STABLE (IRE) 4 b.g. Machiavellian (USA) 123 – Rainbow City (IRE) 85 **64** (Rainbow Quest (USA) 134) [2009 88: p13.9g f12g^{3} p12g^{6} p12g^{6} 12m 12m Jul 23] rather leggy gelding: just modest form in 2009: likely to stay 2m: acts on all-weather, good to firm and good to soft going: has hung right. *M. Wigham*

CITY STYLE (USA) 3 b.g. City Zip (USA) 112 – Brattothecore (CAN) (Katahaula **111** County (CAN)) [2009 6.5g* 7.5g* 7.1g^{3} 8g^{4} Oct 31] first foal: dam Canadian 5f to 8.5f winner, including at 2 yrs: smart performer: trained by Cheryl Asmussen in USA at 2 yrs, winning maiden claimer at Lone Star Park and valuable non-graded stakes at Louisiana Downs: won minor events at Nad Al Sheba in February and March (beat Liberation 1¾ lengths): in frame in listed races after, at Haydock (3 lengths third to Beacon Lodge) and Newmarket (hung badly when fourth to Prince of Dance): stays 8.5f: acts on dirt and firm going. *Saeed bin Suroor*

CITY VAULTS GIRL (IRE) 2 b.f. (Apr 20) Oratorio (IRE) 128 – Uriah (GER) 109 **73** (Acatenango (GER) 127) [2009 6m^{3} 6m^{3} 7g^{5} 8g^{4} 8g^{3} Oct 20] close-coupled filly: third foal: closely related to fairly useful 2008 2-y-o 6f winner Uramazin (by Danehill Dancer), later 1m winner in Hong Kong, and half-sister to 4-y-o Unleashed: dam German 11f/ 1½m winner: fair performer: good third in nursery at Yarmouth final start: will stay 1¼m. *R. A. Fahey*

CITY WELL 6 b.g. Sadler's Wells (USA) 132 – City Dance (USA) (Seattle Slew (USA)) [2009 –: p13.9g p16.5g Oct 1] lengthy, good-topped gelding: lightly raced and no form since 2006. *Mrs L. J. Young* **–**

CLADDAGH 2 b.g. (Mar 28) Dubai Destination (USA) 127 – Ring of Love 77 (Magic Ring (IRE) 115) [2009 9m^{6} f8f^{3} f8d^{4} Dec 29] strong, good-bodied gelding: best effort in maidens when third at Southwell: stays 1m. *M. Johnston* **65**

CLAIMANT (IRE) 2 b.g. (Apr 4) Acclamation 118 – Between The Winds (USA) (Diesis 133) [2009 7s 7g Jul 24] strong gelding: poor form in maidens at Newbury and York (gelded after). *Miss J. R. Tooth* **49**

CLAIRVOYANCE (IRE) 2 b.f. (Feb 18) Shamardal (USA) 129 – Crystal View (IRE) 96 (Imperial Ballet (IRE) 110) [2009 p8m^{2} Nov 19] £80,000Y: first foal: dam, Irish 2-y-o 7f/1m winner, half-sister to useful Irish 7f to 1¼m performer Miss Trish: 6/1, encouraging length second to Aviate in steadily-run maiden at Kempton, getting first run on winner: bred to stay 1¼m: capable of better. *J. H. M. Gosden* **75 p**

CLANACHY 3 b.f. Kyllachy 129 – Antonia's Dream 70 (Clantime 101) [2009 9g 8d 7m 5m 5m^{4} Sep 27] 5,000Y: fifth foal: dam, maiden (ran only at 5f at 2 yrs), half-sister to smart performer up to 8.5f Jo Mell: poor maiden. *A. G. Foster* **39**

CLAN PIPER 2 b.c. (Apr 25) Exceed And Excel (AUS) 126 – Song of Skye 84 (Warning 136) [2009 5.2s 6m^{4} 6.1g Aug 14] useful-looking colt: modest form at best in maidens: sold 2,000 gns in October. *J. H. M. Gosden* **50**

CLARIETTA 2 b. or br.f. (Apr 6) Shamardal (USA) 129 – Claxon 110 (Caerleon (USA) 132) [2009 7m 7g* 7d* 8m^{5} 8g^{3} Oct 31] sturdy, lengthy filly: sixth foal: half-sister to smart 7f (at 2 yrs) to 11.5f winner Cassydora (by Darshaan) and 1¼m winners Circle of Love (by Sakhee) and Classic Remark (by Dr Fong), both at least fairly useful: dam, 1m (including at 2 yrs) and 1¼m (Premio Lydia Tesio) winner, half-sister to smart 1¼m winner Bull Run: useful performer: won maiden at Doncaster in July and nursery at Newmarket (beat Audacity of Hope ¾ length) in August: ran well when 4¼ lengths fifth to Pollenator in May Hill Stakes at Doncaster and 4½ lengths third to Timepiece in listed event at Newmarket: likely to stay 1¼m: acts on good to firm and good to soft going. *J. L. Dunlop* **96**

CLASH CITY ROCKER 3 bl.g. Needwood Blade 117 – Wandering Stranger 69 (Petong 126) [2009 7d Jul 24] 16/1, well held in maiden at Thirsk. *G. A. Swinbank* **–**

CLASHNACREE (IRE) 2 b. or br.c. (Mar 13) Footstepsinthesand 120 – Miss Moore (IRE) 51 (Tagula (IRE) 116) [2009 6v^{2} 6g^{2} 5m 6g^{2} Aug 6] €60,000F, €70,000Y: attractive colt: third foal: dam, Irish 8.5f winner, half-sister to useful performer up to 1¼m Unconditional Love: fairly useful maiden: second at the Curragh and Leopardstown in May and Leopardstown (tongue tied, beaten head by Beethoven) in August: started slowly when well held in listed contest at Royal Ascot: may prove best at 5f/6f: travels strongly: sent to Hong Kong, where renamed Mr Vigorous. *T. Stack, Ireland* **91**

CLASS ATTRACTION (IRE) 5 b.m. Act One 124 – She's All Class (USA) (Rahy (USA) 115) [2009 9.5d^{2} 9.8g* 10d^{4} 8s^{4} 8m^{5} 9.9g Aug 30] half-sister to several winners, including useful French 9f/1¼m winner She Ann (by Anabaa) and fairly useful 6f (at 2 yrs) to 8.5f winner Flint River (by Red Ransom): dam, US 6f (at 2 yrs) and 8.3f winner, sister to useful Irish 1996 2-y-o sprinter Raphane: useful performer: winner of 3 races, including minor event at Longchamp in June: good fifth to Grey Soldier in listed handicap at Deauville but then always behind (slowly away) in similar event at Goodwood final outing: stays 1¼m: acts on all-weather, good to firm and good to soft ground: has had tongue tied. *J. E. Hammond, France* **104**

CLASSICALLY (IRE) 3 b.g. Indian Haven 119 – Specifically (USA) (Sky Classic (CAN)) [2009 88p: 10.3g^{3} 10m 10m 10d p8.6g^{3} p8g* p8g^{4} Oct 22] tall gelding: fairly useful performer: won maiden at Kempton in October: stays 1¼m: acts on polytrack and heavy going: sold 24,000 gns. *R. Charlton* **83**

CLASSICAL PIECE (USA) 2 b.g. (May 15) Brahms (USA) 118 – Nueva (USA) (Jade Hunter (USA)) [2009 p7m p7g^{4} 6s Nov 7] modest form in maidens: should stay 1m. *Mrs D. J. Sanderson* **63**

CLASSICAL RHYTHM (IRE) 4 ch.g. Traditionally (USA) 117 – Golden Angel (USA) (Slew O' Gold (USA)) [2009 72, a62: 10.2g^{6} 11.7g^{4} 10g^{6} f12g 11.6m 12g 10g 10g^{4} 11.9m^{2} 12m^{3} 11.6m Aug 29] tall gelding: fair handicapper: not so good after second start: stays 1½m: acts on polytrack, good to firm and good to soft ground: tried blinkered. *J. R. Boyle* **69 d**

CLASSIC BLUE (IRE) 5 b.m. Tagula (IRE) 116 – Palace Blue (IRE) (Dara Monarch 128) [2009 66: 8.1g 10.2g^5 10g f8g Dec 27] compact mare: just poor handicapper in 2009: stays 1½m: acts on polytrack: tried tongue tied. *Ian Williams* **45**

CLASSIC COLORI (IRE) 2 b.c. (Mar 23) Le Vie Dei Colori 126 – Beryl 77 (Bering 136) [2009 6g* 7v Oct 24] €55,000Y: good-topped colt: sixth foal: half-brother to several winners, including useful US 1m winner Vauquelin (by Xaar) and fairly useful 5f (at 2 yrs) to 9f (in Ireland) winner Glenmuir (by Josr Algarhoud): dam 1½m winner: very noisy beforehand, unruly stall and withdrawn on intended debut: well-backed favourite, won maiden at Windsor in July in good style by 1½ lengths from Dubai Set: similar form when 5 lengths eighth to Carnaby Street in Horris Hill Stakes at Newbury: should stay 1m: already useful, and remains open to further improvement. *Tom Dascombe* **96 p**

CLASSIC CONTOURS (USA) 3 b.g. Najran (USA) – What's Up Kittycat (USA) (Tabasco Cat (USA) 126) [2009 70p: 7.1m 9.9m^5 12.1s* 12.1m* 12.1g^2 12m^3 12.3m^4 14.1m^3 14s^4 14.1m^4 Sep 14] sturdy gelding: fair handicapper: won at Hamilton and Beverley in May: stays 1¾m: acts on soft and good to firm ground: consistent. *J. J. Quinn* **77**

CLASSIC DANCER 4 b.f. Groom Dancer (USA) 128 – Versatility 61 (Teenoso (USA) 135) [2009 –: 15.8g Aug 4] no sign of ability. *Jane Chapple-Hyam* **–**

CLASSIC DESCENT 4 b.g. Auction House (USA) 120 – Polish Descent (IRE) (Danehill (USA) 126) [2009 98: 7m p7g^6 7m p7g Oct 21] strong, lengthy gelding: fairly useful handicapper nowadays: should stay 1m: best efforts on good ground: tongue tied last 2 starts: sold 5,000 gns, then gelded. *P. J. Makin* **83**

CLASSIC LEGEND 4 b.f. Galileo (IRE) 134 – Lady Lahar 106 (Fraam 114) [2009 96: 8m 8m 8m^5 10.4g* 10g^6 Jul 21] compact filly: fairly useful handicapper: won at Haydock in July: effective at 1m to 1½m: acts on polytrack and good to firm ground. *B. J. Meehan* **93**

CLASSIC PORT (FR) 5 gr.h. Slickly (FR) 128 – Portella (GER) 109 (Protektor (GER) 120) [2009 106: 8f^6 Jun 24] strong horse: useful performer at best: reportedly underwent stem cell treatment for tendon injury after 4 yrs: last only start in 2009: stays 8.6f: acts on polytrack and firm going. *J. R. Best* **–**

CLASSIC PUNCH (IRE) 6 b.g. Mozart (IRE) 131 – Rum Cay (USA) 75 (Our Native (USA)) [2009 107§: 14g 12g^2 12m 12m* 12g^3 12m 10g^2 11.6m^3 12m^4 Oct 2] big, rangy gelding: useful performer: won minor event at Ripon (beat Hobby by 6 lengths) in April: creditable 3¼ lengths second to Ajhar in similar race at Newmarket in August: stays 1½m: acts on soft and good to firm ground: makes running: irresolute. *D. R. C. Elsworth* **108 §**

CLASSIC VINTAGE (USA) 3 b.c. El Prado (IRE) 119 – Cellars Shiraz (USA) (Kissin Kris (USA) 122) [2009 95p: 10m^6 11.9v 12f* 12m^3 12g* 14m^6 14g^4 12g Oct 10] tall colt: useful performer: won handicaps at Salisbury in June and Goodwood (beat State Banquet 2¾ lengths) in July: also ran well when fourth to Mourilyan in listed race **103**

Racing UK Heritage Handicap, Goodwood—a quite valuable prize for the locally-trained Classic Vintage, who is chased home by outsiders State Banquet (hooped cap) and Becausewecan

at Goodwood on seventh start: barely stays 1¾m: acts on firm and soft going: waited with. *Mrs A. J. Perrett*

CLASS IS CLASS (IRE) 3 b.g. Montjeu (IRE) 137 – Hector's Girl 99 (Hector Protector (USA) 124) [2009 87p: 8g* 10m³ 12m² 10m⁴ 12g Oct 10] strong, lengthy gelding: useful performer: won maiden at Yarmouth in May: improved form in handicaps next 3 starts, very good efforts when second to Whispering Gallery at York and fourth to Almiqdaad in John Smith's Stakes at Newbury: stays 1½m: acts on good to firm ground, probably on heavy: held up: gelded after final start. *Sir Michael Stoute* **107**

CLASSLIN 2 b.f. (Mar 21) Bertolini (USA) 125 – Class Wan 74 (Safawan 118) [2009 6f 5.4d⁵ 6m 5m Oct 1] fourth foal: half-sister to 4-y-o Killer Class: dam 2-y-o 5f/6f winner: no form, including in nursery. *J. S. Goldie* **–**

CLAYTON FLICK (IRE) 2 b.c. (May 9) Kheleyf (USA) 116 – Mambodorga (USA) (Kingmambo (USA) 125) [2009 p8g 7f 6g p5.1g p8.6g⁶ f7m² Dec 15] compact colt: modest maiden: stays 7f: acts on fibresand. *A. B. Haynes* **52**

CLEAR HAND 3 b.g. Lend A Hand 124 – Miss Maisey (IRE) (Entrepreneur 123) [2009 53: p10g 8m 6.1v⁶ 6m 6m⁴ 6.1g³ 6.1d 7m Sep 21] compact gelding: modest maiden: may prove best at 6f/7f: blinkered nowadays. *B. R. Millman* **52**

CLEAR ICE (IRE) 2 gr.g. (Mar 16) Verglas (IRE) 118 – Mynu Girl (IRE) (Charnwood Forest (IRE) 125) [2009 6g⁵ 5.9m⁵ 6g⁴ 5m 6m 6m f5g² f6g² f5m* f6g² f7f⁵ f6f* p6f Dec 19] €32,000F, €12,000Y: second foal: dam, no form in Ireland, half-sister to 5-y-o Vitznau and smart performer up to 2m Riddlesdown: fair performer on all-weather, modest on turf: won maiden in November and nursery in December, both at Southwell: stays 6f: acts on fibresand. *D. Nicholls* **63 a76**

CLEARING HOUSE 4 ch.g. Zamindar (USA) 116 – Easy Option (IRE) 115 (Prince Sabo 123) [2009 58: f12g p7f p7m Oct 7] modest maiden at 3 yrs: well held in 2009. *R. W. Price* **–**

CLEAR REEF 5 b.h. Hernando (FR) 127 – Trinity Reef 80 (Bustino 136) [2009 93: p12.2g⁶ p14g² f12g⁵ p12g⁴ p12g⁵ p12g³ 14v* 16.2g 12m 14.8g² 12g⁵ 16.1g 14v⁵ p16.5g* p16g³ f14d* Dec 29] tall, angular horse: fairly useful handicapper: won at Haydock in May, Wolverhampton in November (awarded race) and Southwell in December: stays easy 16.5f: acts on all-weather and any turf going: usually in cheekpieces. *Jane Chapple-Hyam* **93**

CLEAR SAILING 6 b.g. Selkirk (USA) 129 – Welsh Autumn 107 (Tenby 125) [2009 88: f8d² p10g* f8g² f8g² p8.6g⁴ p9.5g⁶ 10g p8.6g³ f8g² p8.6g* Dec 4] big, strong gelding: fairly useful performer: won seller at Great Leighs in January and claimer at Wolverhampton in December: stays 1¼m: acts on all-weather and good to soft ground: wears cheekpieces: front runner: carries head high (wears net muzzle). *Ollie Pears* **82**

CLEAVER 8 ch.g. Kris 135 – Much Too Risky 87 (Bustino 136) [2009 88§: 16s³ 16g² 16.4d³ 16d⁶ 14.6g Oct 23] leggy, quite good-topped gelding: fairly useful handicapper: stays 2m: acts on polytrack and heavy ground: usually held up: ungenuine. *Lady Herries* **88 §**

CLEISTHENES (USA) 3 b.g. Pleasantly Perfect (USA) 130 – Do The Mambo (USA) (Kingmambo (USA) 125) [2009 6f* 8f⁵ 8.5f⁶ 6.5f² 6.5f² 6f Nov 22] $25,000Y, £50,000 2-y-o: fifth foal: half-brother to 4-y-o Jack Dawkins and 2005 2-y-o 7f/1m winner Manbala (by Linamix), both useful: dam unraced: 2/1-on, won maiden at Brighton in May by 6 lengths from Celestial Dream: left W. Haggas after: second in 2 allowance races at Santa Anita in October: should stay 7f+: raced only on firm going. *J. W. Sadler, USA* **86**

CLERICAL (USA) 3 b.g. Yes It's True (USA) 116 – Clerical Etoile (ARG) (The Watcher (USA)) [2009 57: p5g³ 6m p5g⁵ 5.2g⁵ p6f⁴ p7m² p8g⁵ p7g Dec 2] good-topped gelding: modest maiden: stays 7f: acts on polytrack: tried visored, often in cheekpieces. *R. M. H. Cowell* **58**

CLERK'S CHOICE (IRE) 3 b.g. Bachelor Duke (USA) 122 – Credit Crunch (IRE) 51 (Caerleon (USA) 132) [2009 80: 7d³ 10g³ 9m* 10m 10.3m² 10.1m⁴ 11.8m³ Oct 6] sturdy gelding: fairly useful handicapper: won at Sandown in June: tailed off final outing: stays 1¼m: acts on all-weather, soft and good to firm ground: patiently ridden: has joined M. Banks. *W. Jarvis* **91**

CLEVELAND 7 b.g. Pennekamp (USA) 130 – Clerio 108 (Soviet Star (USA) 128) [2009 58§, a69§: f6g⁶ f6g² Feb 20] lengthy gelding: fair performer: stays 7f: acts on fibresand and good to firm going: no easy ride. *R. Hollinshead* **68 §**

CLEVER MOLLY (IRE) 2 b.f. (Feb 23) Mull of Kintyre (USA) 114 – Mother Molly (USA) 78 (Irish River (FR) 131) [2009 5d 5.9g⁵ 5g² 5.9g⁶ 5d⁴ 5g³ 6g f5g Sep 29] **61**

lengthy filly: half-sister to 5-y-o Auntie Mame and a winner in Greece by Tobougg: dam, temperamental maiden, best effort at 6f at 2 yrs: modest maiden: best at 5f: acts on good to soft going: sold £3,000. *E. J. Alston*

CLEVER OMNEYA (USA) 3 ch.f. Toccet (USA) 118 – Clever Empress (Crafty Prospector (USA)) [2009 6d p5.1g p6m p6m⁵ Dec 9] $125,000Y, 55,000 2-y-o: fifth foal: half-sister to 3 winners, including smart UAE sprinter Terrific Challenge (by Royal Academy), earlier successful in North America, and 1m (at 2 yrs)/11.5f winner Regal Connection (by Deputy Commander): dam ran once in USA: poor form in maidens. *J. R. Jenkins* **46**

CLIENTELE (USA) 3 b. or br.g. Mr Greeley (USA) 122 – Pracer (USA) 106 (Lyphard (USA) 132) [2009 11.1g⁴ 8g* 8.3m 7.1g² p8.6g⁴ 7.2m p8.6g Oct 16] $45,000Y: closely related to winner in USA by Gone West and half-brother to 3 winners, including 5-y-o King of The Beers: dam 1¼m to 1½m winner in France/Italy, including Premio Lydia Tesio: fairly useful performer: won maiden at Pontefract in July: amiss last 2 starts: stays 8.6f: raced only on polytrack and good/good to firm ground: free-going sort, races prominently: sold £6,000. *M. Johnston* **90**

CLIFTON BRIDGE 2 b.g. (Feb 10) Avonbridge 123 – Ambitious 98 (Ardkinglass 114) [2009 p6f⁵ p5.1g* Dec 26] 21,000F: fourth foal: closely related to 2006 2-y-o 5f winner Camissa (by Averti): dam 5f/6f winner: much better effort in maidens when winning at Wolverhampton by 1¼ lengths from Praesepe: should stay 6f: capable of further improvement. *R. M. Beckett* **77 p**

CLIFTON DANCER 4 b.f. Fraam 114 – Crofters Ceilidh 101 (Scottish Reel 123) [2009 98: 7.5d³ 8g 7f 7g Jul 29] quite good-topped filly: useful performer: creditable third in handicap at Nad Al Sheba on reappearance: below form after (covered by Sleeping Indian after second start, but failed to get in foal): stays 7.5f: acts on soft and good to firm going: sold 30,000 gns in November. *Tom Dascombe* **95**

CLIFTON ENCORE (USA) 2 b.f. (Feb 14) War Chant (USA) 126 – Theatrical Pause (USA) (Theatrical 128) [2009 5.1g Oct 21] $15,000F: first foal: dam unraced half-sister to smart sprinter Country Reel out of useful half-sister to top-class sprinter Anabaa: 3/1 and green, down the field in maiden at Bath: likely to improve. *Tom Dascombe* **– p**

CLIFTON KID (IRE) 2 b.g. (Apr 3) Danbird (AUS) – Flossytoo 66 (Royal Applause 124) [2009 f7g⁶ Dec 22] 33/1 and green, tailed off in maiden at Southwell. *R. C. Guest* **–**

CLIMATE (IRE) 10 ch.g. Catrail (USA) 123 – Burishki 49 (Chilibang 120) [2009 69: p9.5g p8g⁵ p8m⁶ p8.6g p9.5g p8.6g* p9.5g Dec 28] strong, compact gelding: modest performer nowadays: won handicap at Wolverhampton in December: stays easy 1¼m: acts on all-weather and any turf going: usually in headgear: held up. *P. D. Evans* **64**

CLINCHER 3 b.f. Royal Applause 124 – Clincher Club 77 (Polish Patriot (USA) 128) [2009 6g⁵ p5.1g p6g Nov 16] 90,000Y: neat filly: seventh foal: half-sister to several winners, including smart 2004 2-y-o 6f winner Henrik (by Primo Dominie) and fairly useful 6f (at 2 yrs) and 1m winner Spritzeria (by Bigstone): dam, 5f (at 2 yrs) and 7.5f winner, half-sister to smart sprinter Paradise Isle: signs of ability in maidens, not knocked about: bred to prove best at 5f/6f: sold 5,000 gns. *J. A. Osborne* **–**

CLINGING VINE (USA) 3 b. or br.f. Fusaichi Pegasus (USA) 130 – Nemea (USA) 71 (The Minstrel (CAN) 135) [2009 60: p8g Jan 17] leggy filly: modest maiden: best effort at 7f: sold 5,000 gns in February. *R. Hannon* **51**

CLIPPERDOWN (IRE) 8 b.g. Green Desert (USA) 127 – Maroussie (FR) 115 (Saumarez 132) [2009 –: 9.7m p10g² p12g³ p10g² 11.5g³ 10m 10s 9m 9m² p10g⁵ p9.5g Oct 10] big, strong, well-made gelding: fair performer at best nowadays: stays 1¼m: acts on polytrack and firm ground: tongue tied: tried in cheekpieces/blinkers. *E. J. Creighton* **72**

CLIPPITY CLOP (IRE) 3 b.g. Clodovil (IRE) 116 – Son Chou 63 (Cyrano de Bergerac 120) [2009 f8g* 10.2g 14.1m 10m⁴ 8.1m⁶ p9.5g p12.2g Oct 15] fair performer: won maiden at Southwell in March: best effort at 1m on fibresand: sold 5,200 gns, joined M. Ramadan in UAE. *J. A. Osborne* **70**

CLOCKMAKER (IRE) 3 b.c. Danetime (IRE) 121 – Lady Ingabelle (IRE) 71 (Catrail (USA) 123) [2009 8s² Apr 18] €46,000F, 130,000Y: well-made colt: second foal: dam, maiden (best around 1¼m), half-sister to smart performer up to 7f Mister Links: 7/2, 1¾ lengths second to Bridge of Gold in maiden at Newbury, forced to switch before staying on strongly: not seen out again. *J. H. M. Gosden* **88**

CLOPF (IRE) 8 b.g. Dr Massini (IRE) 117 – Chroma (IRE) (Supreme Leader 123) [2009 77: 16g* 20m p17g⁵ 14s 16g⁴ 16s Nov 5] smart hurdler/useful chaser: fairly useful **92 §**

handicapper on Flat: won at Leopardstown in May: well below form at Royal Ascot next time: stays 2m, not 2½m: acts on polytrack, soft and good to firm going: tried blinkered: sometimes slowly away: weak finisher. *A. Heffernan, Ireland*

CLOSE ALLIANCE (USA) 3 b.c. Gone West (USA) – Shoogle (USA) 86 (A P Indy **97**
(USA) 131) [2009 96p: p9g 8m^{6} 10m^{4} a9f^{6} a9f^{3} Sep 6] good-topped colt: useful performer: creditable fourth to Your Old Pal in listed race at Newmarket on third outing, then left J. Gosden: stays 1¼m: acts on polytrack and good to firm going: blinkered final outing. *R. J. Frankel, USA*

CLOUDESLEY (IRE) 3 b.g. Trans Island 119 – Decatur (Deploy 131) [2009 65: p7g^{6} **75**
8m^{2} 8s^{2} 9m^{3} 9.9f^{6} p8m^{2} 10g^{6} 10m^{6} Oct 13] compact gelding: fair maiden: should stay 1¼m: acts on polytrack, soft and good to firm going: tried in cheekpieces/visor: sold 10,500 gns. *A. M. Balding*

CLOUD'S END 2 b.f. (Apr 13) Dubawi (IRE) 129 – Kangra Valley 56 (Indian Ridge **83 p**
123) [2009 6.1m^{3} p6m* Oct 12] sturdy filly: half-sister to several winners, notably very smart 5f to 1m winner (including 6f at 2 yrs) Airwave (by Air Express) and useful 2004 2-y-o 6f winner Reqqa (by Royal Applause): dam 2-y-o 5f winner: won maiden at Kempton by nose from Basle, making most: sure to progress again. *W. J. Haggas*

CLOUDY CITY (USA) 2 b. or br.g. (Feb 20) Giant's Causeway (USA) 132 – Mambo **75**
Slew (USA) (Kingmambo (USA) 125) [2009 7.1g^{6} 8.1g^{4} 8g^{3} Aug 29] $50,000Y: useful-looking gelding: first foal: dam US Grade 3 1m (at 2 yrs)/9f winner: progressive form in maidens: third to Notorize at Goodwood (carried head high, gelded after): should stay beyond 1m. *M. Johnston*

CLOUDY START 3 b.c. Oasis Dream 129 – Set Fair (USA) (Alleged (USA) 138) **109**
[2009 95+: 7s 7g^{3} 7g* p8g* 8m^{2} 8g 7.6m^{4} Sep 12] tall colt: useful performer: won handicap at Epsom and minor event at Kempton (beat Set The Trend 3¾ lengths), both in June: also ran well when ¾-length second to Spring of Fame in minor event at Newmarket: stays 1m: acts on polytrack and good to firm ground: sold 45,000 gns. *H. R. A. Cecil*

CLOVIS 4 b.g. Kingmambo (USA) 125 – Darling Flame (USA) 101 (Capote (USA)) **72 §**
[2009 76§: p10g* p10g^{5} p10g^{5} 11.9g^{6} p12g 10.2m 10.2f^{2} 10g^{6} 10g 11.7g* p12m^{6} Sep 23] tall, lengthy gelding: fair performer: won maiden at Kempton in February and seller at Bath (sold from N. Mulholland 4,200 gns) in August: probably stays 1½m: acts on all-weather, firm and good to soft ground: usually in blinkers/cheekpieces: tried tongue tied: held up: ungenuine. *Andrew Turnell*

CLOWANCE 4 b.f. Montjeu (IRE) 137 – Freni (GER) (Sternkoenig (IRE) 122) [2009 **117**
107: 14s^{2} 15.5d^{4} Oct 25] rangy filly: smart performer: suffered injury and missed second half of 2008: excellent ½-length second to Alandi in Irish St Leger at the Curragh on return in September, coming with strong late run to almost get on terms in final 1f: not discredited when keeping-on 6 lengths fourth to Ask in Prix Royal-Oak at Longchamp next time: should stay 2m: acts on soft going: edgy type, thoroughly mulish at stalls at Longchamp. *R. Charlton*

CLOWANCE HOUSE 3 ch.g. Galileo (IRE) 134 – Corsican Sunset (USA) 102 **95**
(Thunder Gulch (USA) 129) [2009 88p: 11s^{3} 12m* 12m^{3} 16f 14m^{3} 14m^{6} Sep 12] useful-looking gelding: useful performer: won maiden at Salisbury in May: better form after, third in handicap at Newmarket and seventh in Queen's Vase at Royal Ascot third/fourth starts: stays 2m: acts on any going: races prominently. *R. Charlton*

CLUB TAHITI 3 b.f. Hernando (FR) 127 – Freni (GER) (Sternkoenig (IRE) 122) **92**
[2009 87p: 10m 8d^{4} 9g^{3} Jul 29] rather leggy filly: fairly useful form, lightly raced: good efforts in handicaps at Newbury and Goodwood last 2 starts, not seen to best effect either occasion: bred to be suited by 1¼m/1½m: acts on soft ground. *R. Charlton*

CLUELESS 7 b.g. Royal Applause 124 – Pure (Slip Anchor 136) [2009 76d: f12g^{6} **– §**
Mar 22] big, lengthy gelding: one-time useful performer: regressive at 6 yrs, and well held sole start on Flat in 2009: tried blinkered/in cheekpieces: tends to hang: one to treat with caution. *G. A. Charlton*

CLUMBER PLACE 3 ch.f. Compton Place 125 – Inquirendo (USA) 81 (Roberto **62**
(USA) 131) [2009 67: p8g 7.5m^{6} 8.3m 10.2g^{6} 8s 7.1m* Sep 14] modest handicapper: won at Musselburgh in September: stays 7f: acts on soft and good to firm going. *R. C. Guest*

CLUMBER PURSUITS 2 ch.f. (Apr 9) Pastoral Pursuits 127 – Inquirendo (USA) 81 **–**
(Roberto (USA) 131) [2009 6m 6m Aug 29] £800Y: closely related to 4-y-o Azure Mist and half-sister to several winners, including 3-y-o Clumber Place: dam 1½m winner: well held in maidens. *S. A. Harris*

CLUNY 3 b.f. Celtic Swing 138 – Muschana 100 (Deploy 131) [2009 –p: 9.7m[3] 10.1m[4] 12f[4] 11.6d p12m Oct 26] fair maiden: should stay 1½m: acts on good to firm ground. *J. R. Fanshawe* **65**

C'MON YOU IRONS (IRE) 4 b.g. Orpen (USA) 116 – Laissez Faire (IRE) (Tagula (IRE) 116) [2009 84: p7m[2] p7g[4] p6g[4] p7g[4] 6m 6f[2] 6m* 6g* 6v* 6g 6g 6d[5] Oct 6] neat gelding: fairly useful handicapper: completed hat-trick at Windsor (2) and Pontefract in June/July: effective at 6f/7f: acts on polytrack and any turf going: tried blinkered: races close up. *M. R. Hoad* **84**

CNOC MOY (IRE) 5 b.g. Mull of Kintyre (USA) 114 – Ewar Sunrise 67 (Shavian 125) [2009 p16g[5] Feb 8] lengthy gelding: fairly useful handicapper: bit below best only outing on Flat since 2007: stays 2m: acts on polytrack and firm going. *O. Sherwood* **78**

COASTAL PATH 5 b.h. Halling (USA) 133 – Coraline (Sadler's Wells (USA) 132) [2009 121: 12g[2] 15.5s May 17] tall, imposing horse: smart performer: won his first 6 starts, including Prix de Barbeville and Prix Vicomtesse Vigier at Longchamp in 2008: shorter trip, creditable staying-on 2 lengths second to Magadan (rec. 7 lb) in Prix d'Hedouville at Longchamp on reappearance: disappointing in Prix Vicomtesse Vigier at Longchamp next time: reported in July to have been retired due to injury: stayed 2½m: won on soft ground, but best efforts on good: to stand at Haras de Saint-Voir, France (and at Haras de La Monnerie in alternate years), fee €3,500. *A. Fabre, France* **119**

COBO BAY 4 b.g. Primo Valentino (IRE) 116 – Fisher Island (IRE) 59 (Sri Pekan (USA) 117) [2009 104: 8m 8s 10.1g 9d[4] 8g[2] 8.3v* 7d[3] 8.1m 7s Nov 7] tall, good-topped gelding: useful handicapper: won at Nottingham (beat Jack Cool by 1½ lengths) in July: good placed efforts either side: stays 8.3f: acts on polytrack and heavy going: usually wears headgear: races up with pace. *K. A. Ryan* **100**

COBOS 3 b.f. Royal Applause 124 – Darya (USA) (Gulch (USA)) [2009 66: 8d 10g 10f[6] p8g Jul 15] strong, lengthy filly: maiden: little form at 3 yrs. *Ms E. L. McWilliam* **–**

COCKNEY CLASS (USA) 2 gr. or ro.c. (Mar 14) Speightstown (USA) 124 – Snappy Little Cat (USA) (Tactical Cat (USA) 116) [2009 7g[3] 7g[3] Jul 31] $145,000Y, $70,000 2-y-o: first foal: dam US 6f (including at 2 yrs)/1m winner: third in minor events in small fields at Ascot (to Black Spirit) and Newmarket (beaten just over 10 lengths by Poet's Voice, not knocked about): already fairly useful, and capable of better. *B. J. Meehan* **82 p**

COCKNEY COLONEL (USA) 2 b. or br.g. (Feb 21) Dixie Union (USA) 121 – Kristina's Wish (USA) (Smart Strike (CAN) 121) [2009 5m 6d Jul 20] tall, unfurnished gelding: well beaten in maiden/seller, then gelded. *E. J. Creighton* **–**

COCKTAIL PARTY (IRE) 3 b.f. Acclamation 118 – Irish Moss (USA) (Irish River (FR) 131) [2009 64: 6.1g 6d 8s 5.9d 5.1d[2] 5.1d 5m[4] 6g p5m[5] p5g[4] p6m[3] Dec 10] unfurnished filly: modest handicapper: should prove best at 5f/6f: acts on polytrack, soft and good to firm going: tongue tied of late: ungenuine. *J. W. Hills* **58 §**

COCO L'ESCARGOT 5 b.m. Slip Anchor 136 – Dafne 68§ (Nashwan (USA) 135) [2009 56: p11g[6] Jan 6] smallish, sturdy mare: modest maiden at 4 yrs: last sole start in 2009: should stay 1¾m: acts on good to soft going: visored nowadays: sent to Saudi Arabia. *J. R. Jenkins* **–**

COCONUT MOON 7 b.m. Bahamian Bounty 116 – Lunar Ridge (Indian Ridge 123) [2009 79: 5g 5m p5.1g 5m 5m 5g 5m 6d[4] 6s 6f[4] 5g 6m 5v Nov 3] smallish mare: regressive handicapper: stays 6f: acts on polytrack, firm and soft going: tried blinkered. *A. Berry* **54**

COCONUT SHY 3 b.f. Bahamian Bounty 116 – Lets Be Fair 94 (Efisio 120) [2009 88: f6g[4] f6g[3] Jul 27] tall, close-coupled filly: fair performer: raced only at 5f/6f: acts on heavy going: tongue tied. *G. Prodromou* **74**

CODA AGENCY 6 b.g. Agnes World (USA) 123 – The Frog Lady (IRE) 52 (Al Hareb (USA) 123) [2009 74: p16g p16g* p16g p16g Sep 4] strong gelding: fair handicapper: won at Kempton in June: stays 17f: acts on all-weather and good to firm ground. *D. W. P. Arbuthnot* **74**

CO DEPENDENT (USA) 3 ch.c. Cozzene (USA) – Glowing Breeze (USA) (Southern Halo (USA)) [2009 75p: p9.5g p8g[3] p8.6g[2] Feb 27] sturdy colt: fair maiden: stays 8.6f: raced only on polytrack since debut. *J. A. Osborne* **70**

COEUR BRULE (FR) 3 b.g. Polish Summer 120 – Sally's Cry (FR) (Freedom Cry 132) [2009 46: 9.9m p16m Sep 16] poor maiden. *Edgar Byrne* **–**

COEUR COURAGEUX (FR) 7 b.g. Xaar 132 – Linoise (FR) 108 (Caerwent 123) [2009 61: p7g p8.6g 7d Apr 13] tall, rather leggy gelding: one-time useful performer: modest at best nowadays: best at 7f/1m: acts on polytrack, best turf form on good going: sometimes tongue tied, tried in cheekpieces. *M. D. Squance* **58**

COEUR DE LIONNE (IRE) 5 b.g. Invincible Spirit (IRE) 121 – Lionne (Darshaan 133) [2009 96: 9.8d^6 10.3d 12g* 12s 12m p10m^3 p13m^2 p12.2g^6 Dec 11] sturdy, useful-looking gelding: useful handicapper on all-weather, fairly useful on turf: won at Newmarket in August: stays 1½m: acts on polytrack, good to firm and good to soft going: tried in cheekpieces. *E. A. L. Dunlop* **86 a95**

COGNAC BOY (USA) 3 b. or br.g. Hennessy (USA) 122 – City Sleeper (USA) (Carson City (USA)) [2009 62: p8g^5 p7g* p7g^4 p8g^5 p7g^4 7f f7g p6g 8f^2 8g^4 7m^3 7.1d Aug 31] smallish, strong, quite attractive gelding: modest performer: won claimer at Lingfield (left R. Hannon £5,000) in January: stays easy 1m: acts on polytrack and firm ground: usually wears headgear nowadays: sold £850, sent to Qatar. *A. B. Haynes* **63**

COILED SPRING 3 b.g. Observatory (USA) 131 – Balmy 89 (Zafonic (USA) 130) [2009 84: 10.2g^3 12d^4 May 16] strong gelding: fair maiden: stays 1¼m: acts on good to firm going: sold 35,000 gns in July, and gelded. *Mrs A. J. Perrett* **78**

COILL GLAS (IRE) 4 b.g. Green Desert (USA) 127 – Forest Express (AUS) (Kaaptive Edition (NZ)) [2009 70p: p8.6g^3 Jan 7] twice-raced maiden: fair form on debut, well held sole start at 4 yrs: should stay beyond 1m: raced on polytrack. *W. J. Haggas* **–**

COIN FROM HEAVEN (IRE) 2 b.f. (Apr 25) Invincible Spirit (IRE) 121 – Capital Gain (FR) (Bluebird (USA) 125) [2009 6m^3 6g* 6g Oct 30] €87,000F: compact filly: third foal: dam, Italian maiden, sister to useful 7f/1m performer Holly Blue: fairly useful form: won maiden at Redcar in October by 4 lengths: stiff task, good seventh to Queen's Grace in listed event at Newmarket next time: should stay 7f. *R. A. Fahey* **86**

COIN OF THE REALM (IRE) 4 b.g. Galileo (IRE) 134 – Common Knowledge (Rainbow Quest (USA) 134) [2009 87: 12g^4 12g* 12m 12g Oct 10] good-bodied gelding: useful handicapper: improvement in 2009, winning at Epsom in June: well held after: will stay 1¾m: raced on polytrack and good to soft going. *G. L. Moore* **95**

COJO (IRE) 2 b.f. (Mar 15) Rock of Gibraltar (IRE) 133 – Love Excelling (FR) (Polish Precedent (USA) 131) [2009 6m^6 7d^2 p8.6g^5 Oct 29] 115,000Y: third foal: half-sister to Irish 4-y-o Angels Story: dam once-raced half-sister to Oaks winner Love Divine, herself dam of St Leger winner Sixties Icon: easily best effort in maidens when short-head second to Qaraaba at Salisbury: should stay 1m+: sold 11,000 gns. *B. J. Meehan* **74**

COLANGNIK (USA) 3 b.f. Sky Classic (CAN) – Rainbow Strike (USA) (Smart Strike (CAN) 121) [2009 74p: 10d 9.9m p10m^6 p12m p10g p8g^6 p10g p10g Nov 14] tall filly: fair maiden handicapper, regressive: stays 1¼m: best efforts on polytrack: visored last 2 starts. *J. R. Best* **67 d**

COLD MOUNTAIN (IRE) 7 b.g. Inchinor 119 – Streak of Silver (USA) 66 (Dynaformer (USA)) [2009 55+: 18g^3 Aug 13] compact gelding: fairly useful hurdler/fair chaser: modest maiden on Flat (lightly raced): stays 2¼m: tried in cheekpieces/blinkers/tongue tie. *J. W. Mullins* **57**

COLD QUEST (USA) 5 b.g. Seeking The Gold (USA) – Polaire (IRE) 108 (Polish Patriot (USA) 128) [2009 100: 10.4m 10.4m 9.8d 9.2g^6 9m^6 7.2g Oct 23] strong gelding: one-time useful handicapper: very much on downgrade: tried in cheekpieces. *Miss L. A. Perratt* **–**

COLD TURKEY 9 b.g. Polar Falcon (USA) 126 – South Rock 102 (Rock City 120) [2009 95: p10g p12g p10g^6 p10g^6 p12g p16g^3 Apr 21] sturdy gelding: just fair handicapper nowadays: effective at 1½m to easy 2¼m: acts on polytrack, firm and soft ground: held up. *G. L. Moore* **75**

COLEORTON CHOICE 3 ch.c. Choisir (AUS) 126 – Tayovullin (IRE) 65 (Shalford (IRE) 124§) [2009 88: 5f^2 6m^4 6g^5 6g* 6g f6f^6 p6m Nov 3] workmanlike colt: fairly useful handicapper: won at Ayr in May: effective at 5f/6f: acts on any turf going: tongue tied last 2 starts: none too consistent. *K. A. Ryan* **90**

COLEORTON DANCER 7 ch.g. Danehill Dancer (IRE) 117 – Tayovullin (IRE) 65 (Shalford (IRE) 124§) [2009 77§: 5.9m 6.1g Jun 11] leggy, quite good-topped gelding: modest handicapper nowadays, on long losing run: stays easy 7f: acts on all-weather, heavy and good to firm going: tried blinkered/in cheekpieces: one to treat with caution. *K. A. Ryan* **54 §**

COLEPEPER 2 b.c. (Jan 28) Cape Cross (IRE) 129 – Autumn Wealth (IRE) 108 **94**
(Cadeaux Genereux 131) [2009 6s^{2} 7s 6m* 6g^{5} Oct 9] 115,000Y: smallish colt: first foal: dam 1¼m/1½m winner: fairly useful performer: won maiden at Catterick in September by 5 lengths from Johannesgray, making all: creditable fifth in nursery at York: should be suited by 7f+: acts on good to firm ground, shaped well on soft on debut. *M. Johnston*

COLIN STAITE 3 b.g. Superior Premium 122 – Downclose Duchess 49 (King's Signet **–**
(USA) 110) [2009 –: f7d Jan 8] no sign of ability. *R. Brotherton*

COLLATERAL DAMAGE (IRE) 6 b.g. Orpen (USA) 116 – Jay Gee (IRE) 93 **104**
(Second Set (IRE) 127) [2009 93: 8m^{4} 8.1g^{2} 8m 8.9d 7.9m 8.5m^{5} 8g^{3} 8m^{4} 8s* 8g* 8g* 8m* f8g^{3} 8v* 7s* Nov 7] big, strong gelding: useful handicapper: thrived in second half 2009, winning 6 of last 7 starts at Ayr (3), Redcar (2) and Doncaster (by ¾ length from Mia's Boy): effective at 7f to 1½m: acts on fibresand, heavy and good to firm ground: tongue tied nowadays: tried blinkered: tough. *T. D. Easterby*

COLLEGE LAND BOY 5 b.g. Cois Na Tine (IRE) 101 – Welcome Lu 45 (Most **–**
Welcome 131) [2009 52: 9.9g Sep 22] stocky, compact gelding: modest maiden at 4 yrs: well held sole start in 2009: stays 1¼m: acts on firm and good to soft going: tried visored. *A. Kirtley*

COLOMBARD (IRE) 4 b.g. Almutawakel 126 – Searching Star 63 (Rainbow Quest **59**
(USA) 134) [2009 75: 7m p6g 6.1f^{4} 7m^{6} p7.1g 8m^{6} 7g^{4} p6g^{3} 6m^{6} p7.1g^{6} p6g^{2} p5g^{5} p6g^{2} p6g^{4} p6m^{4} p5m^{4} p6m^{4} p6g^{3} p5g Dec 31] sturdy gelding: modest handicapper nowadays: should stay 1m: acts on polytrack and firm ground: often blinkered/visored: tried tongue tied. *Pat Morris*

COLONEL CARTER (IRE) 2 br.c. (Mar 18) Danehill Dancer (IRE) 117 – Pina **82**
Colada 77 (Sabrehill (USA) 120) [2009 7m^{3} 8.3s^{4} Oct 7] 45,000F, €50,000Y: good-topped colt: third foal: dam, 5f (at 2 yrs) and 7.5f (in USA) winner, half-sister to dam of 2-y-o Canford Cliffs: better effort in maidens when 1½ lengths third to Critical Moment at Newbury: ran in snatches on soft ground. *B. J. Meehan*

COLONEL FLAY 5 ch.g. Danehill Dancer (IRE) 117 – Bobbie Dee 93 (Blakeney 126) **81**
[2009 81: 14.1m* 14m^{5} 14.1g^{2} 14.1m^{3} 14.1m^{3} 12m^{5} p12g^{5} Oct 26] good-topped gelding: fairly useful handicapper: won at Nottingham in May: stays 1¾m: acts on polytrack and good to firm ground: travels strongly: held up. *Mrs P. N. Dutfield*

COLONEL HENRY 2 br.g. (Mar 23) Imperial Dancer 123 – Spark of Life 63 (Rain- **–**
bows For Life (CAN)) [2009 p8f Dec 16] 50/1, slowly away and always behind in maiden at Kempton. *S. Dow*

COLONEL MAK 2 br.g. (Feb 1) Makbul 104 – Colonel's Daughter 61 (Colonel **94**
Collins (USA) 122) [2009 6m 6m^{3} 6m* 6d^{2} 6d* 6g^{3} 6m^{4} 6m^{3} 6m^{6} 6d^{5} Oct 24] £5,500Y: small, sturdy gelding: third foal: half-brother to 2006 2-y-o 5f seller winner Dotty's Daughter (by Forzando): dam, sprint maiden, half-sister to US Grade 3 6.5f winner Shuffling Kid: fairly useful performer: won maiden in June and nursery in July, both at Hamilton: creditable fifth to Layla's Hero in listed event at Doncaster final start: gelded after: likely to prove best at 5f/6f: acts on good to soft and good to firm going. *D. H. Brown*

COLONEL MUNRO (IRE) 2 b.c. (Feb 22) Azamour (IRE) 130 – Zooming (IRE) **–**
(Indian Ridge 123) [2009 p8.6g Oct 1] 16/1, tailed off in claimer at Wolverhampton. *D. Nicholls*

COLONEL SHERMAN (USA) 4 b. or br.c. Mr Greeley (USA) 122 – Spankin 'n **–**
Fannin (USA) (Lear Fan (USA) 130) [2009 65: p10m* p10g^{2} p12g^{3} p8g^{3} 8.3g 10.1s **a71**
p8.6g f12f p9.5g^{6} f12g Dec 22] tall colt: fair handicapper: won at Lingfield in January: claimed from L. Dace £12,000 fourth start, little impact after: stays 13f: acts on polytrack, below form on turf: front runner. *P. A. Kirby*

COLONIAL (IRE) 2 b.c. (Apr 25) Cape Cross (IRE) 129 – Elizabeth Bay (USA) 116 **108**
(Mr Prospector (USA)) [2009 5d^{2} 6g* 7g* 7g^{6} Sep 6] half-brother to several winners, including smart 6f (including at 2 yrs) to 9f (US Grade 3) winner Bayeux (by Red Ransom) and useful 7f (at 2 yrs) and 1m (in USA) winner Jahaam (by Danzig): dam, French/US 1m/9f performer, out of US Grade 1 9f/1¼m winner Life At The Top: useful form: won minor event at Chantilly (by 5 lengths) in June and listed race at Longchamp (in good style, by 2½ lengths from American Nizzy) in July: well below form in Prix La Rochette at Longchamp final start: will stay 1m. *A. Fabre, France*

COLORUS (IRE) 6 b.g. Night Shift (USA) – Duck Over 72 (Warning 136) [2009 76: **84**
f5d p5g f5g^{3} f5g^{4} p5g^{6} f5g^{2} f5m* 5m f5g^{2} f5m^{5} 5m* 5d 5m 5.1m 5.2m* 5m 5m^{6} 5.3d f5g* f5m p5.1g^{2} f5g^{3} f5m^{2} f5d Dec 29] stocky, good sort: fairly useful handicapper:

won at Southwell in March, Windsor (apprentices) in July, Yarmouth in September and Southwell in October: best at 5f: acts on fibresand, good to firm and good to soft going: wears headgear: races prominently: none too consistent. *W. J. H. Ratcliffe*

COLOURFUL MOVE 4 b.c. Rainbow Quest (USA) 134 – Flit (USA) 72 (Lyphard (USA) 132) [2009 68: f12s^{4} p16g^{3} p16g* 15m^{4} 16g p16g^{2} 16g p16g p16.5g^{4} p16g^{3} f14m^{3} p13.9g^{3} Dec 14] fair handicapper: won at Kempton in April: stays 2m: acts on all-weather and good to firm going: often races prominently. *P. G. Murphy* **68**

COLOUR OF MONEY 4 br.g. Kyllachy 129 – Euridice (IRE) 66 (Woodman (USA) 126) [2009 50: p7g* p7.1g^{5} p8g^{4} p7.1g Jun 5] stocky gelding: fair handicapper: won at Lingfield in March: stays 1m: acts on polytrack: tried in cheekpieces: sold 6,000 gns. *S. A. Callaghan* **66**

COLOURSOFTHEGLEN (IRE) 2 ch.c. (Feb 26) Le Vie Dei Colori 126 – Gertie Laurie (Lomond (USA) 128) [2009 6v^{2} 7f^{2} p7.1g* 7g^{2} 7g^{5} 8f Nov 28] €14,000Y: leggy colt: fifth foal: half-brother to 4-y-o Discanti and German 8.5f/9.5f winner Lucky Desert (by Desert Style): dam unraced half-sister to dam of Arc runner-up Leggera: fairly useful performer: won maiden at Wolverhampton in June: good efforts in nurseries next 2 starts, then left Tom Dascombe: stiff task, seventh of 8 in Grade 3 Generous Stakes at Hollywood final outing: stays 7f: acts on polytrack, probably on any turf going. *E. Truman, USA* **86**

COLOUR TROOPER (IRE) 4 ch.g. Traditionally (USA) 117 – Viola Royale (IRE) 90 (Royal Academy (USA) 130) [2009 77: 11.7g^{5} 10g^{5} 11.6m 10g Jul 10] compact gelding: fair handicapper: stays 11.6f: raced on polytrack and good/good to firm going: tried in blinkers/cheekpieces: sold £7,000, joined D. Pipe. *P. Winkworth* **76**

COMADOIR (IRE) 3 ch.c. Medecis 119 – Hymn of The Dawn (USA) 73 (Phone Trick (USA)) [2009 79: p5g* p5g^{3} p6g^{4} p6g p7g^{6} 7.6f^{5} p6m* p6g p6g^{6} p6g p6m^{6} Dec 6] rather leggy, useful-looking colt: fairly useful performer: successful at Lingfield in maiden in January and handicap in July: likely to prove best at 5f/6f: acts on polytrack and any turf going: tried blinkered. *Miss Jo Crowley* **84**

COME AND GO (UAE) 3 b.g. Halling (USA) 133 – Woven Silk (USA) 104 (Danzig (USA)) [2009 82: 7m 10m^{5} 8g^{5} 8m^{6} 6m^{2} 6s 6m^{2} 7d Aug 26] leggy gelding: fair handicapper: stays 1¼m, seemingly effective at 6f: acts on firm and good to soft going. *G. A. Swinbank* **79**

COME APRIL 5 b.m. Singspiel (IRE) 133 – So Admirable (Suave Dancer (USA) 136) [2009 12m 10g Oct 19] good-topped, attractive mare: fair 1¼m winner at 3 yrs: missed 2008, well held in 2009: sold £3,800. *P. R. Webber* **–**

COMEDY ACT 2 b.g. (Mar 15) Motivator 131 – Comic (IRE) 87 (Be My Chief (USA) 122) [2009 7m^{5} 7m p8m Aug 8] 72,000Y: sixth foal: half-brother to high-class Hong Kong 1m to 1½m winner Viva Pataca (by Marju), also 6f to 8.5f winner in Britain at 2 yrs as Comic Strip: dam, 1¼m/11.5f winner, half-sister to smart US 1m/1¼m performer Brave Act: form in maidens only at Leicester on debut: bred to do lot better at 1¼m+. *Sir Mark Prescott* **55 p**

COMEDY HALL (USA) 2 b.c. (Feb 1) Valid Expectations (USA) – Comedy At The Met (USA) (Metfield (USA)) [2009 6g^{5} f6g^{2} 5v* 6m 6m* Oct 5] strong colt: third foal: dam, US 6f/7f winner, half-sister to very smart US sprinter/miler Kela: useful performer: won maiden at Catterick in September and nursery at Warwick (resumed progress, beat Ongoodform ½ length, pair clear) in October: likely to stay 7f+: acts on fibresand, heavy and good to firm ground. *M. Johnston* **98**

COMEINTOTHESPACE (IRE) 7 b.g. Tagula (IRE) 116 – Playa Del Sol (IRE) (Alzao (USA) 117) [2009 –: p12g^{4} p9.5g p12g^{5} f11g p13g 10.2g^{6} 11.9m 10.4g p8g Jun 24] quite good-topped gelding: modest performer: stays easy 1½m: acts on all-weather and any turf going: tried blinkered/in cheekpieces. *R. A. Farrant* **50**

COME ON BUCKERS (IRE) 3 ch.g. Fath (USA) 116 – Deerussa (IRE) (Jareer (USA) 115) [2009 61: p6g 7f^{5} p6g^{3} 6m^{2} 6.1m f6g^{6} 7s^{6} 8m p7g^{2} p7f^{5} p6f* p6g^{5} p6g p5g^{6} p5g^{2} p5m Nov 3] sturdy gelding: fair performer: won handicap at Kempton in September: effective at 5f to 7f: acts on all-weather, soft and good to firm going: tried in headgear: front runner/races prominently. *E. J. Creighton* **65**

COME ON SAFARI (IRE) 2 b.g. (Feb 17) Antonius Pius (USA) 123§ – Calypso Dancer (FR) 61 (Celtic Swing 138) [2009 6g 5.7g^{4} 7m* p8g^{5} Nov 18] €65,000F, £30,000Y: compact gelding: second foal: half-brother to 3-y-o City Dancer: dam, French 5f winner, out of sister to smart 1¼m performer Leporello: fair performer: won maiden at **79**

Folkestone in August: stays 7f: acts on good to firm going, probably on polytrack: gelded after final start. *P. Winkworth*

COME ON TOBY 3 b.g. Piccolo 121 – Fleeting Moon 70 (Fleetwood (IRE) 107) **–**
[2009 –: p8g Mar 14] close-coupled gelding: no sign of ability. *Miss Amy Weaver*

COMING BACK 3 ch.f. Fantastic Light (USA) 134 – Return (USA) 99 (Sadler's Wells **89**
(USA) 132) [2009 65p: p10g* 9.9f^{2} 10m^{5} Jun 23] rangy filly: fairly useful form: won maiden at Kempton in March: excellent second in handicap at Salisbury next time: ran as if amiss final start: stayed 1¼m: acted on polytrack and firm going: visits Three Valleys. *J. H. M. Gosden*

COMMANCHE RAIDER (IRE) 2 b.g. (Feb 8) Tale of The Cat (USA) 113 – **75 p**
Alsharq (IRE) 72 (Machiavellian (USA) 123) [2009 5m^{4} 5g* Oct 6] first foal: dam, 7f winner, half-sister to Rockfel Stakes winner Sayedah: better effort in maidens 4½ months apart when winning at Catterick by 4 lengths from Il Forno: will stay 6f: likely to improve further. *M. Dods*

COMMANDER WISH 6 ch.g. Arkadian Hero (USA) 123 – Flighty Dancer (Pivotal **73 d**
124) [2009 76: 5g^{3} 6m 5m 5g 5g 5m 5m 5m^{6} 5m p6g 6g 5s^{6} 5.1s^{6} p5g^{6} p5m Dec 6] stocky gelding: fair handicapper early in 2009: on downgrade: best at 5f: acts on polytrack, soft and good to firm going: usually in cheekpieces: has been tongue tied: held up. *Lucinda Featherstone*

COMMANDINGPRESENCE (USA) 3 b. or br.f. Thunder Gulch (USA) 129 – **65**
Sehra (USA) (Silver Hawk (USA) 123) [2009 72p: p8g p7g^{3} p8g p8g p7g 7.1m p7g^{6} 10m 10m p7f 7d^{3} p6m^{4} p7m p7m^{5} p8m^{6} p6m^{3} p6m^{6} p6m Dec 16] lengthy filly: fair maiden: left B. Meehan 4,600 gns after second start, Ms J. Doyle after ninth: probably stays 1m: acts on polytrack, good to firm and good to soft ground: tried in headgear/tongue tie. *J. J. Bridger*

COMMAND MARSHAL (FR) 6 b.g. Commands (AUS) – Marsakara (IRE) (Turtle **63**
Island (IRE) 123) [2009 82: p16.5g^{6} p16m^{6} Dec 30] modest handicapper nowadays: stays 2m: acts on good to soft going: fair hurdler, won twice in October. *M. J. Scudamore*

COMMANDO SCOTT (IRE) 8 b.g. Danetime (IRE) 121 – Faye 79 (Monsanto (FR) **73**
121) [2009 7.1m 6s 7g 7.9m p7.1g^{2} 6v^{5} 8g^{5} p7.1g^{4} 8s Sep 5] good-topped gelding: missed 2008: fair handicapper nowadays: stays 1m: acts on polytrack and any turf going (all wins on good or softer): tried blinkered. *I. W. McInnes*

COMMISSIONAIRE 2 b.c. (Apr 20) Medicean 128 – Appointed One (USA) (Danzig **90 p**
(USA)) [2009 8d* Oct 27] seventh foal: brother to fairly useful 1m winner Officer (later successful up to 1¼m in France) and half-brother to several winners, notably smart 7f (at 2 yrs)/1m (including in US) winner Battle Chant (by Coronado's Quest): dam, US 1m minor stakes winner, sister to smart miler Emperor Jones and closely related to top-class 1985 2-y-o Bakharoff: 11/1, highly promising when winning maiden at Yarmouth by 1¼ lengths from Longliner, slowly away and quickening from last to lead final 1f: useful prospect. *J. H. M. Gosden*

COMMON DIVA 3 ch.f. Auction House (USA) 120 – Vida (IRE) 70 (Wolfhound **79**
(USA) 126) [2009 75: p8.6g^{3} p8.6g* p8.6g^{4} p8.6g* p8g p8.6g* p7.1g^{3} p9.5g^{6} 8g^{2} 8s^{6} 8d^{5} 8.3m^{5} p8.6g^{3} p7.1g Oct 10] fair performer: won handicaps in January and February, and claimer in March, all at Wolverhampton: effective at 7f to easy 9.5f: acts on polytrack and good to firm going: races prominently: consistent: sold £2,200, sent to Sweden. *A. J. McCabe*

COMPETITOR 8 b.g. Danzero (AUS) – Ceanothus (IRE) 61 (Bluebird (USA) 125) **–**
[2009 –, a68d: p10g^{6} p12g^{5} p10g^{5} Feb 18] modest performer on all-weather nowadays, **a59**
little recent form on turf: stays 1½m: acts on polytrack: wears headgear: has suffered breathing problems (sometimes tongue tied)/run as if amiss. *J. Akehurst*

COMPLETE FRONTLINE (GER) 4 ch.g. Tertullian (USA) 115 – Carola Rouge **–**
(Arazi (USA) 135) [2009 66: 8f 9m May 19] angular gelding: maiden: fair at 3 yrs: well held in 2009: stays easy 1m: acts on polytrack, firm and soft ground: tried in cheekpieces/visor. *K. R. Burke*

COMPRIMARIO (IRE) 3 b.g. Montjeu (IRE) 137 – Soubrette (USA) (Opening **–**
Verse (USA) 126) [2009 12m^{6} May 3] rangy gelding: 9/1, more temperament than ability in maiden at Salisbury: joined N. Twiston-Davies, won juvenile hurdle in December. *J. L. Dunlop*

COMPTON BLUE 3 b.c. Compton Place 125 – Blue Goddess (IRE) 94 (Blues Travel- **81**
ler (IRE) 119) [2009 70p: 6.1g 6.1g^{4} p6g^{6} 8.1g* p8g 7g 8m 8.3g^{2} 8.3g* Oct 19] well-made colt: fairly useful handicapper: won at Sandown in August and Windsor in October (blinkered): stays 8.3f: best efforts on good ground. *R. Hannon*

COMPTON CHARLIE 5 b.g. Compton Place 125 – Tell Tale Fox (Tel Quel (FR) 125) [2009 67: 12d 11.5m 12.1m Jul 1] leggy gelding: fair handicapper at best: well held in 2009: tried in cheekpieces. *J. G. Portman* **–**

COMPTON CLASSIC 7 b.g. Compton Place 125 – Ayr Classic 74 (Local Suitor (USA) 128) [2009 77: p6g p6g^{7} p5g p6g^{3} p6g^{2} p6g^{2} p6g p6g^{2} p6g* p6g^{1} p6g 5.7g^{2} 5.1d 5s^{3} p6m 5.1d^{6} p5m Nov 3] good-bodied gelding: fair handicapper, better on all-weather: left Tom Dascombe after third start: won at Kempton in April: effective at 5f/6f: acts on polytrack, heavy and good to firm going: wears headgear: tried tongue tied: free-going sort. *J. R. Boyle* **71 a78**

COMPTON FALCON 5 ch.g. Peintre Celebre (USA) 137 – Lesgor (USA) 106 (Irish River (FR) 131) [2009 73: p12.2g^{3} p11g Sep 2] rangy gelding: modest maiden handicapper nowadays: left G. Butler after reappearance: seems to stay 2m: acts on polytrack, soft and firm going: tried visored/blinkered/tongue tied: held up: not straightforward. *H. Candy* **55**

COMPTON FORD 3 ch.g. Compton Place 125 – Coffee Time (IRE) 88 (Efisio 120) [2009 58: 5m^{3} 5m* 5m^{2} 5g^{5} 5m^{4} 5m^{6} 5d p5.1g^{4} 5g^{5} Aug 3] good-topped gelding: fair handicapper: won at Catterick in April: best at sharp 5f: acts on good to firm and good to soft going (probably on polytrack): tried in headgear: not straightforward: sold £3,200. *M. Dods* **73**

COMPTON LAD 6 b.g. Compton Place 125 – Kintara (Cyrano de Bergerac 120) [2009 40: 5m May 19] maiden: poor at 5 yrs: last sole start in 2009. *D. A. Nolan* **–**

COMPTON PARK 2 ch.c. (Feb 3) Compton Place 125 – Corps de Ballet (IRE) 92 (Fasliyev (USA) 120) [2009 p7m Nov 26] 15/2, badly in need of experience in maiden at Kempton. *W. J. Knight* **–**

COMPTON ROSE 4 ch.f. Compton Place 125 – Benjarong 50 (Sharpo 132) [2009 72: 5.1m 5.1m 6m 6.1d 5.1m Sep 10] lengthy filly: maiden handicapper: well held at 4 yrs. *H. Candy* **–**

COMPTON'S ELEVEN 8 gr.g. Compton Place 125 – Princess Tara 85 (Prince Sabo 123) [2009 94: p7g^{5} p7g^{2} p6g^{2} 7f 7m 7.1m^{5} 7m 7m 7f^{4} 7.1d^{6} 7g^{5} 7.2g^{2} 7g^{5} 7m 7m^{2} 7g 7g^{6} 7m 7m^{5} 7.2g^{3} Oct 23] good-topped gelding: fairly useful handicapper: not quite so good at 8 yrs: effective at 6f/7f: acts on polytrack, firm and soft going: held up: sometimes carries head high/edges left. *M. R. Channon* **82**

COMPTONSPIRIT 5 ch.m. Compton Place 125 – Croeso Cynnes 70 (Most Welcome 131) [2009 76: p6g 5m^{2} 5m 5.1m^{4} 5v^{5} 5m^{6} 6m^{3} 5.5g^{4} 5g 5m^{3} 5m^{5} 6m^{2} 5g^{4} Sep 30] workmanlike mare: fair handicapper: effective at 5f/6f: acts on polytrack, firm and soft ground: effective with/without cheekpieces. *B. P. J. Baugh* **71**

COMPTON WAY 2 b.c. (Feb 28) Compton Place 125 – Never Away 53 (Royal Applause 124) [2009 6g 6s Nov 7] well-made colt: down the field in maidens. *B. W. Hills* **–**

COMRADE COTTON 5 b.g. Royal Applause 124 – Cutpurse Moll 76 (Green Desert (USA) 127) [2009 67: p7g p7g^{4} p7g p8g^{4} 6d 8.3m^{3} 10f^{3} 10m^{2} 11.8m* 10.2m p8g Jun 10] lengthy gelding: fair handicapper: won apprentice event at Leicester in May: stays 11.8f: acts on polytrack, firm and soft going: often wears headgear: usually held up. *J. Ryan* **66**

COMRADESHIP (IRE) 2 ch.c. (Feb 15) Dubawi (IRE) 129 – Friendlier (Zafonic (USA) 130) [2009 8g 8.1d^{2} 8m^{6} 8.3s^{5} 8d^{6} f8m^{2} f8m* Nov 11] 110,000Y: big, strong colt: third foal: half-brother to 4-y-o Foolin Myself: dam unraced half-sister to Oaks and St Leger winner User Friendly: fairly useful performer: good efforts in blinkers at Southwell last 2 starts, though again found less than seemed likely and just held on when winning nursery: should be as least as effective at 7f as 1m: acts on fibresand and good to soft ground: sold £22,000. *J. H. M. Gosden* **85**

CON ARTIST (IRE) 2 b.c. (Apr 20) Invincible Spirit (IRE) 121 – Hoodwink (IRE) (Selkirk (USA) 129) [2009 f8m^{3} p8g* Nov 14] 42,000F, 40,000Y, 75,000 2-y-o: third foal: half-brother to useful German 2008 2-y-o 6f winner Muriel (by Fath) and a winner in Greece by Kalanisi: dam unraced half-sister to Irish Oaks winner Margarula: better effort in maidens in November when winning at Lingfield by 1¾ lengths from Fatanah, dictating and hard driven. *Saeed bin Suroor* **87**

CONCLUSIVE 3 b.g. Selkirk (USA) 129 – Never A Doubt 107 (Night Shift (USA)) [2009 –: p7g 7m 7m p8g^{5} Jun 25] strong gelding: modest maiden: stays 1m: form only on polytrack: tried in cheekpieces: sold 4,500 gns. *R. M. Beckett* **53**

CONCORDE KISS (USA) 2 b.f. (May 1) Harlan's Holiday (USA) 124 – Saraa Ree (USA) 102 (Caro 133) [2009 p8m p8.6g[5] f8d Dec 29] half-sister to several winners, notably high-class performer up to 11f in USA Sarafan (by Lear Fan), 6f to 1m winner in Britain at 2 yrs: dam, 7f winner, out of sister to Irish River: modest form at best in maidens. *S. Kirk* **52**

CONDUIT (IRE) 4 ch.c. Dalakhani (IRE) 133 – Well Head (IRE) (Sadler's Wells (USA) 132) [2009 130: 10m[2] 10m[3] 12m* 12g[4] 12f* 12f[4] Nov 29] **130**

The latest edition of the King George VI and Queen Elizabeth Stakes, which carried total prize money of £1m in the first year of sponsorship by Betfair, was a notable triumph for Ballymacoll Stud. The stud, on a three-hundred-acre estate in County Meath, Ireland, keeps around twenty mares nowadays and has a similar number of horses in training, all of whom continue to carry the pale blue colours first made famous by the Sobell and Weinstock horses. Michael Sobell (later knighted) and his son-in-law Arnold (later Lord) Weinstock acquired Ballymacoll in 1960 after the death of the legendary Dorothy Paget, the purchase price of £250,000 including approximately one hundred and thirty horses, mostly fillies and broodmares.

Miss Paget, who died at the age of only fifty-four, owned Golden Miller, who won the Cheltenham Gold Cup five times, and had the largest string of racehorses in Britain in her heyday. She had become one of the richest women in the world when inheriting part of the fortune of her grandfather the American sportsman, politician and businessman William C. Whitney (the Whitney millions also benefited racing in Britain through the patronage of Dorothy Paget's cousin Jock Whitney, owner of another pre-war chasing 'great' Easter Hero). Dorothy Paget first established a name for herself on the Flat by spending huge sums on fashionably-bred yearlings, but she enjoyed greater success after building up a considerable broodmare band (when she bred the winners of sixty-two races in 1948 it prompted one writer to record that 'Never before in British turf history have so many races been won in a single season by horses all bred by the same person').

Dorothy Paget did not purchase Ballymacoll Stud until 1946 and her wartime, home-bred Derby winner Straight Deal was not moved there from Miss Paget's Elsenham Stud in Essex until 1953. Miss Paget never actually visited Ballymacoll and it failed to provide her with an outstanding horse during her lifetime. Michael Sobell and the Weinstocks (Lord Weinstock's son Simon, who died at the age of forty-four, became a partner in Ballymacoll with his father in 1974) began to reap rewards from Ballymacoll from the late-'sixties onwards. One of the first major winners was the popular Reform, so undersized as a yearling that he was not included in the draft sent to the sales by his breeders because it was thought he might be a bad advertisement for the stud! He won five of his six starts at two and, holding no classic engagements, took the St James's Palace, the Sussex, the Queen Elizabeth II and the Champion Stakes in the course of a searching programme at three. Reform was a great grandson of the Hyperion mare Coventry Belle, one of two original Dorothy Paget mares upon which much of Ballymacoll's success has been founded.

Coventry Belle's most notable descendants also include North Light, the second of two Derby winners in Ballymacoll's Sobell/Weinstock era, following Troy who also won the Irish Derby, King George and what is now the International at York. Another descended from Coventry Belle is Golan, the second winner of the King George VI and Queen Elizabeth Stakes bred by Ballymacoll (the Weinstock colours were also carried to success in the King George by the four-year-old Ela-Mana-Mou, the year after Troy, but he had been purchased for £500,000 at the end of his three-year-old campaign by a partnership involving Airlie Stud and members of the Weinstock family). The latest King George field included two home-bred four-year-olds in the Ballymacoll colours, the 2008 Derby runner-up Tartan Bearer, another from the Coventry Belle family, and the 2008 St Leger winner Conduit, who comes from the family of Ballymacoll's other noted foundation mare, the Phalaris mare Jamaica, whose high-class descendants—through her daughter Solana, who was moved to Ballymacoll after Miss Paget's acquisition—include Oaks and St Leger winner Sun Princess and her half-brother the Coronation Cup winner and St Leger runner-up Saddlers' Hall, as well as the Irish Two

Thousand Guineas and Champion Stakes winner Spectrum, who is a half-brother to Conduit's dam (and also the sire of Tartan Bearer).

Conduit won one of the strongest St Legers for years—his thirteen rivals included Irish Derby winner Frozen Fire and Oaks winner Look Here—and he followed up to crown his three-year old campaign with a top-class performance to win the Breeders' Cup Turf at Santa Anita. Conduit had always been well thought of, but he hadn't taken up any of the big-race entries made for him as a two-year-old, getting off the mark on the all-weather at Wolverhampton on the last of three starts as a juvenile. He progressed hand-over-fist as a three-year-old, however, after winning a handicap by six lengths at Epsom on Derby Day, his stable running Chester Vase winner Doctor Fremantle and Dee Stakes winner Tajaaweed in the Derby, as well as Tartan Bearer who had won the Dante. Conduit ended the campaign the highest-rated horse in his stable and the highest-rated of the European-trained three-year-olds that remained in training, Tartan Bearer not being seen out again after a below-par third in the Irish Derby (there had been a plan to bring him back for the Champion Stakes but connections had eventually decided against it).

Conduit and Tartan Bearer were both seen out twice in the latest season before the King George, Tartan Bearer reeling in Pipedreamer in fine style, hitting the front very late, in the Gordon Richards Stakes at Sandown and then coming a good second to Vision d'Etat in the Prince of Wales's Stakes at Royal Ascot. Conduit probably wasn't so versatile as Tartan Bearer in terms of his distance requirements but he too had both his outings before the King George over a mile and a quarter, a trip almost certainly short of his optimum. The Brigadier Gerard Stakes at Sandown, in which Conduit had to concede 7 lb all round, was falsely run and, in going down by a nose to Cima de Triomphe (with Pipedreamer a close fifth), Conduit provided plenty of encouragement for his chances in the top mile and a half races later in the season. Even with a pacemaker charged with ensuring a very strong gallop, Conduit couldn't get near the outstanding three-year-olds Sea The Stars and Rip Van Winkle in the Coral-Eclipse, a race which his trainer has won five times with maturing older horses, a group with which his patient approach has yielded rich dividends down the years.

Three of the Stoute-trained Eclipse winners beat Derby winners at Sandown, Erhaab finishing only third behind Ezzoud in 1994, while Benny The Dip and Authorized came second to Pilsudski and Notnowcato in 1997 and 2007 respectively. Ezzoud and Pilsudski were both sent next to Ascot for the King George, the latter finishing second to Swain in a renewal dominated by older horses while the former's challenge lasted only a few strides, jinking and unseating his rider soon after the start. The King George was won by Derby runner-up King's Theatre in Ezzoud's year (Erhaab finished down the field, looking unlikely to play a part in the finish before he was badly hampered by the riderless Ezzoud in the home straight). Another of the Stoute-trained Eclipse winners, Opera House in 1993, followed up in the King George (with Commander In Chief, winner of the

*King George VI and Queen Elizabeth Stakes (Sponsored by Betfair), Ascot—
a famous result for Sir Michael Stoute as Conduit is chased home by stable-companions
Tartan Bearer (No.5) and Ask (almost hidden); Alwaary is a good fourth ahead of Golden Sword*

Derby at both Epsom and the Curragh, third), but the general make-up of the King George field has undergone a significant change since the 'nineties. For most of its history, the King George has been an eminently worthy championship attracting both the leaders of the classic generation and the best of the previous season's middle-distance horses that have stayed in training. In the 'nineties, for example, there were at least three three-year-olds in the King George line-up most years; seven Derby winners took part and five of the editions were won by three-year-olds and five by older horses.

The last Derby winner successful in the King George was Galileo in 2001, the last time the race attracted a field that could truly be regarded as vintage. The Irish Derby winner Alamshar was the last three-year-old to win, in 2003 which was also the last year the race was contested by the Epsom Derby winner (Kris Kin who came third). In the five runnings between 2003 and the latest edition, only two three-year-olds contested the King George, the Irish Derby third Tycoon in 2004 and the Oaks winner Eswarah in 2005 (when the race was run at Newbury). The Eclipse, by contrast, has attracted three of the last five Derby winners, though it is far too early to conclude that the Sandown race is assuming the traditional mantle of the King George as the most important midsummer clash of the generations. The 2008 Derby winner New Approach might well have run in the King George had he not been sidelined by injury and the choice of the Eclipse rather than the King George for Sea The Stars was said to have been dictated by his missing the Irish Derby a week before Sandown because of connections' fears over the prospect of soft ground at the Curragh. Had Sea The Stars contested the Irish Derby, and come through that race unscathed, there would have been a fairly good chance, given the prevailing good to firm conditions, of his being seen at Ascot. Though the King George wasn't on the agenda at the time, Oxx said after the Derby—when nominating the Irish Derby as the next race—that Sea The Stars was 'a summer horse and he will be kept going over the summer.' After the Eclipse, Oxx confirmed that 'had he run in the Irish Derby we would probably have aimed him at the King George, but missing the Curragh and going to Sandown changed the situation, in terms of the time we have between upcoming races.'

Needless to say, had Sea The Stars appeared in the King George he would have started at odds on and his presence would have been a much needed shot in the arm for the race, though the on-course attendance of 26,232 was still just above that for the previous year (the latest King George day programme included a new big race for purebred Arabians and was also augmented by an after-racing concert by Supergrass). The new five-year contract with Betfair, after the race had been run for two years without a backer, represents a fresh opportunity to consider ideas for restoring the King George to its former glories. Increasing the prize money is clearly going to be a key factor and Ascot has announced its intention to raise the King George's total prize fund eventually to £1.5m. Even with the rise in 2009, however, the first prize for the King George of £567,700 was still some way short of the £709,625 for the Derby, while, with the fall in the value of sterling, it was dwarfed by the £2,096,881 on offer for the Prix de l'Arc de Triomphe, now the world's most valuable race on turf. The King George figured in joint-sixtieth place in a list of the world's most valuable races in 2009 produced by the International Racing Bureau (Britain's richest race, the Derby, fell from thirteenth the previous year to forty-second). A bonus scheme, possibly involving up to 10,000,000 dollars (which would be the joint-richest prize in world racing with the Dubai World Cup), is one of the proposals being considered for the King George, with the aim of enticing more overseas challengers to Ascot. *Racehorses* has consistently raised the idea of the King George succeeding the St Leger and being promoted as the third leg of a 'modern' triple crown in Britain, supported by a bonus scheme, but horizons now seem broader, the aim to establish the King George as one of the major events on the global scene (though right-handed Ascot might be said to be 'the wrong way round' for the Americans). Ascot has a much better record than any other British course for attracting overseas challengers to its big races, the King George, for example, having had runners finish in the first three from North America (Hard Buck) and Japan (Heart's Cry) in the last six years. Both horses had earlier contested the Dubai Sheema Classic—the world's richest turf race at the time—and that might be a race to include in plans for a proposed King George

Emirates Airline Breeders' Cup Turf, Santa Anita—Conduit becomes the first British-trained horse to claim successive Breeders' Cup wins; Presious Passion (blinkers), Dar Re Mi (right) and Conduit's stable-companion Spanish Moon (left) complete the frame

bonus, while the Prix de l'Arc de Triomphe and the Breeders' Cup Turf or Classic are other events said to be already in the frame.

The classic generation returned to the latest King George after a three-year absence, though Golden Sword (five-length runner-up in the Irish Derby) and Alwaary (a good third, promoted to second, behind Doctor Fremantle in the Princess of Wales's Stakes) were not particularly notable representatives of their age group. A third three-year-old Rockhampton started at 125/1 and fulfilled the role of Ballydoyle pacemaker, as he had in the Irish Derby. Golden Sword was the principal challenger from Ballydoyle, which also ran Frozen Fire after winning the two previous editions with four-year-olds Dylan Thomas and Duke of Marmalade, both of whom started short-priced favourites. Those two successes had stretched the winning run of favourites in the King George to five and Conduit, who started at 13/8 (with Tartan Bearer 7/2 second favourite), made it six. Travelling well, held up as usual, Conduit moved through to challenge with two furlongs to go and drew away to win by a length and three quarters and a head from Tartan Bearer and the Coronation Cup winner Ask, the second and third slightly impeded by Conduit who edged right after hitting the front. A stewards' inquiry left the placings unaltered but Conduit's rider Ryan Moore picked up a harsh-looking three-day ban for careless riding as a result of Conduit's failing to keep straight, while Tartan Bearer's rider Michael Kinane, left short of room when tightened up by Conduit, was cautioned for using his whip improperly down the shoulder. Those were the only two blemishes on a red-letter day for the Sir Michael Stoute yard which produced a feat unique in the history of the King George by sending out the first three home. It was only the fourth time a trainer had achieved a one, two, three in a Group 1 Flat race in Britain since the pattern designation was introduced in 1971. Saeed bin Suroor trained the first three in the Eclipse in 1998 and Aidan O'Brien did the same in the 2001 Dewhurst and the 2007 St James's Palace (O'Brien has also achieved the feat five times in Ireland and once in France). Conduit, Tartan Bearer and Ask were followed home by Alwaary and Golden Sword, with Look Here and Frozen Fire in sixth and seventh, both below the form they had shown in the Coronation Cup when third and fifth behind Ask. One bizarre footnote to the King George was provided when a twenty-six-year-old gambling addict from Rochdale was found guilty at Bolton Crown Court in January 2010 of sending threats to the owners of Conduit before Ascot, warning them that if the horse ran in the King George it would be killed (he was given a suspended prison sentence after telling the court he had no intention of carrying out the threat which was an attempt to have the horse withdrawn because he had forgotten to place a bet on the horse on behalf of a syndicate and faced a £55,000 payout if it won).

The prize money won by Conduit, Tartan Bearer and Ask in the King George went a long way to securing a tenth domestic trainers' title for Sir Michael Stoute. Conduit and Ask were Stoute's only Group 1 winners in Britain in the latest season, but Ask (Prix Royal-Oak) and Spanish Moon (Grand Prix de Saint-Cloud), won Group 1s in France, and Conduit went on to win a second Breeders' Cup Turf at Santa Anita. Among the stable's other pattern winners was the high-class stayer Patkai who carried the Ballymacoll colours to success in the Sagaro Stakes at Ascot before finishing second at the Royal meeting to Yeats in the Gold Cup. Ballymacoll Stud was also responsible for the stable's only Royal Ascot winner, Glass Harmonium (whose dam is closely related to Conduit) in the latest Hampton Court Stakes.

Before tackling the Breeders' Cup Turf, Conduit had his sights set on the Prix de l'Arc de Triomphe, a race in which the Sobell/Weinstock/Ballymacoll horses have recorded a string of notable efforts without so far yielding a victory. Homeric, Troy, Ela-Mana-Mou and Sun Princess were all placed in the days when most of the Ballymacoll horses were trained by Dick Hern. Pilsudski was placed in successive years for Stoute, since when Golan has been beaten a short head for third and Islington and North Light have narrowly failed to make the frame. Conduit emulated Golan, finishing fourth (a head behind third-placed Cavalryman) to Sea The Stars, getting closer to him than in the Eclipse, staying on well in the last two furlongs and beaten a little over two lengths. While there was much speculation about whether or not Sea The Stars would go on to the Breeders' Cup, Conduit's ticket to Santa Anita had already been booked and paid for. The Breeders' Cup Turf has become something of a benefit for European runners and Conduit's second victory—emulating the double achieved by Ballydoyle with High Chaparral—took

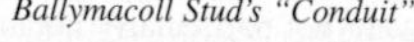

Ballymacoll Stud's "Conduit"

the score to fourteen and a half victories for Europe and eleven and a half to North America (including the dead-heat in 2003, when High Chaparral achieved his second victory). Unlike the previous year, Conduit ran on lasix, permitted medication in the States—but not in Europe—which is ostensibly used on horses who have bled in the lungs. However, application of the rules is permissive and most European trainers adopt a 'when in Rome . . .' approach to medication with their challengers for America's top races. It is, however, always laudable when use of lasix is shunned by the visitors, as it was at the latest Breeders' Cup most notably by Ballydoyle (though the only one of its runners at the meeting to start on lasix, Man of Iron, was its only winner).

The latest Emirates Airline Breeders' Cup Turf was not a vintage renewal and the field of seven was the smallest in the race's history. Conduit started at odds on and won in workmanlike fashion, briefly stumbling and becoming unbalanced after improving between horses rounding the home turn before catching front-running Presious Passion inside the final furlong to win by half a length, with European runners Dar Re Mi, Spanish Moon and Red Rocks third, fourth and fifth. Conduit's was one of a record six victories at the Breeders' Cup meeting for European-trained challengers, the successes of Conduit, Midday, Pounced and Vale of York bringing the number of British-trained Breeders' Cup winners to twenty, a total which now includes five by Conduit's trainer, four of them in the Breeders' Cup Turf (Pilsudski in 1996 and Kalanisi in 2000 preceding Conduit's two wins) and the other with Islington in the Filly & Mare Turf. Conduit had the final race of his career in Japan at the end of November, running a creditable fourth in the Japan Cup, and he has been retired to Shigeyuki Okada's Big Red Farm, where the stallion roster also includes Dubai World Cup winner Roses In May and Dubai Sheema Classic winner Stay Gold.

Conduit (IRE) (ch.c. 2005)	Dalakhani (IRE) (gr 2000)	Darshaan (b 1981)	Shirley Heights
			Delsy
		Daltawa (gr 1989)	Miswaki
			Damana
	Well Head (IRE) (b 1989)	Sadler's Wells (b 1981)	Northern Dancer
			Fairy Bridge
		River Dancer (b 1983)	Irish River
			Dancing Shadow

The good-topped, attractive Conduit had his pedigree fully examined in *Racehorses of 2008* and, as Conduit was his unraced dam's last foal and had to be fostered, there is virtually nothing to add, except perhaps to mention that the very smart Glass Harmonium is out of the mile and a half winner Spring Symphony, a sister to Well Head's Great Voltigeur winner Hard Top who came fifth in the St Leger (Spring Symphony and Hard Top are by Darshaan, the sire of Conduit's sire Dalakhani). The grandam River Dancer is best known as the dam of Spectrum, while the great grandam Dancing Shadow, a half-sister to Sun Princess and Saddlers' Hall, is also the dam of Ballerina, a Ballymacoll discard who became dam of the 2000 St Leger winner Millenary. Another member of the family sold by Ballymacoll, Well Head's half-sister Ballet Shoes, went on to produce the 2000 Irish Oaks and Yorkshire Oaks winner Petrushka. Millenary's sister Head In The Clouds was represented on the racecourse in the latest season by the Irish Oaks runner-up Roses For The Lady, a daughter of Sadler's Wells, who has played a significant role in the family's success down the years, both as a sire and, with Conduit, as a broodmare sire. Conduit's considerable achievements over a mile and a half far outweighed his St Leger victory, though he stands out as one of the best modern-day winners of the final classic. It is worth recording that there hasn't been a more highly rated winner of the St Leger since 1987 when it was won by Reference Point, coincidentally the last St Leger winner who also won a King George (though Reference Point won his as a three-year-old). No St Leger winner had gone on to success in the King George as a four-year-old since Alcide—a short head runner-up in the Gold Cup on his previous start—in 1959, though the 1973 St Leger winner Bustino went down narrowly to Grundy at Ascot in 1974 in a King George dubbed the 'race of the century.' The patiently-ridden Conduit, who was unraced on soft or heavy going, had a tendency to edge right in a finish but was reliable and, except on his racecourse debut, never finished out of the frame. *Sir Michael Stoute*

Nayef Joel Stakes, Newmarket—Nayef's son Confront is an appropriate winner of this contest; he is chased home by Rio de La Plata (left), Forgotten Voice (No.4) and Donativum

CONFESSIONAL 2 b.g. (May 3) Dubawi (IRE) 129 – Golden Nun 108 (Bishop of Cashel 122) [2009 6g 5m 5d³ 5m² 6m p6g² 6v* Nov 3] £30,000Y: good-topped gelding: first foal: dam 5f/6.5f winner (including at 2 yrs): fairly useful performer: easily landed odds in maiden at Catterick, hanging right: effective at 5f/6f: acts on polytrack, heavy and good to firm going: tried blinkered: tricky ride/pulls hard. *T. D. Easterby* **80**

CONFIDE IN ME 5 b.g. Medicean 128 – Confidante (USA) 95 (Dayjur (USA) 137) [2009 55: 8g² 9.7m* 10.2g² 9.1g⁴ p8g⁵ 10g p8g⁶ p8.6m⁵ 7m⁵ p8.6g* p8g p8.6g⁴ p8m⁵ Nov 29] workmanlike gelding: fair handicapper: won at Folkestone in June and Wolverhampton in October: stays 1¼m: acts on polytrack and good to firm ground: often in cheekpieces/blinkers in 2009: usually tongue tied. *G. A. Butler* **66**

CONFIDENTIALITY (IRE) 5 b.m. Desert Style (IRE) 121 – Confidential 60 (Generous (IRE) 139) [2009 92: p10g* p8.6g⁵ p12g 10.3m⁶ p10g⁴ 10g⁶ 10g p10.7g p8g⁵ p10m* p9.5g² Dec 26] good-topped mare: fairly useful handicapper, better on all-weather: won at Lingfield in January and, having been trained by Edward Lynam in Ireland sixth to ninth outings, December: stays easy 1½m: acts on polytrack, best turf efforts on good ground: held up. *M. Wigham* **84 a93**

CONFRONT 4 b.g. Nayef (USA) 129 – Contiguous (USA) (Danzig (USA)) [2009 98+: 9m* 8.5g² 10m⁴ 8m² 8m² 7m* 8.1v* 8m* 8g⁶ Dec 13] big, good-topped gelding: smart performer: thrived in 2009, winning handicap at Newmarket in May, listed races at York in August and Haydock (by 1½ lengths from Bushman) in September and Nayef Joel Stakes at Newmarket (beat Rio de La Plata ½ length) in October: runner-up earlier in Diomed Stakes at Epsom (to Mac Love), Summer Mile at Ascot (behind Aqlaam) and Sovereign Stakes at Salisbury (beaten 1½ lengths by Mac Love): ran well when 1½ lengths sixth to Good Ba Ba in Hong Kong Mile at Sha Tin final start, staying on well from rear: should stay 1¼m: acts on heavy and good to firm ground: usually races prominently. *Sir Michael Stoute* **119**

CONFUCHIAS (IRE) 5 b.h. Cape Cross (IRE) 129 – Schust Madame (IRE) 46 (Second Set (IRE) 127) [2009 109: 6.5g 6g⁶ 6.5g⁵ 6m⁶ 6m 6g 6g 7s⁴ p7g³ f6m⁴ f6g² Dec 18] rather leggy, attractive horse: useful performer: left K. R. Burke after fourth start: best at 6f/7f nowadays: acts on all-weather, heavy and good to firm going: tried in cheekpieces. *Pat Eddery* **99**

CONFUCIUS FORTUNE (IRE) 2 gr.g. (Mar 22) Verglas (IRE) 118 – Duck Over 72 (Warning 136) [2009 6g p7m* Sep 30] 20,000Y: close-coupled filly: sixth foal: half-brother to 6-y-o Colorus and Hong Kong 7f winner Pocket Money (by Namid): dam maiden (stayed 1m): much better effort in maidens when winning at Kempton by 1¼ lengths from Indian Valley: stays 7f: sent to Hong Kong. *J. R. Boyle* **81 +**

CONISTON WOOD 3 b.f. Needwood Blade 117 – Litewska (IRE) 86 (Mujadil (USA) 119) [2009 52: f8g^5 5m Apr 13] maiden: well held at 3 yrs: tried blinkered. *M. W. Easterby* –

CONJECTURE 7 b.g. Danzig (USA) – Golden Opinion (USA) 127 (Slew O' Gold (USA)) [2009 73: 6m^2 6g^5 6m^6 6d 5g^4 6d^6 6m 6m Aug 29] fair handicapper: effective at 5f/6f: acts on polytrack, firm and soft going: tried blinkered/visored: tends to edge left: usually races up with pace. *R. Bastiman* **66**

CONNIPTION (IRE) 2 b.f. (Feb 26) Danehill Dancer (IRE) 117 – Showbiz (IRE) 89 (Sadler's Wells (USA) 132) [2009 6s* 6s^5 6m^5 6g^4 Oct 30] 225,000Y: rangy filly: first foal: dam, Irish 2-y-o 7f winner, half-sister to smart Scandinavian performer at 6f to 1m Hanzano, out of unraced sister to Irish 1000 Guineas winner Trusted Partner: useful performer: won maiden at Newbury in July: best effort when 2¾ lengths fourth to Queen's Grace in listed race at Newmarket final start: raced only at 6f: acts on soft ground: veered right second outing: sold 130,000 gns, sent to USA. *B. J. Meehan* **94**

CONNOR'S CHOICE 4 b.g. Bertolini (USA) 125 – Susan's Dowry 74 (Efisio 120) [2009 82d: 7f 6m* 6.1d^2 p6m p7.1g* p7m^2 Nov 21] neat gelding: has round action: fair performer: won seller at Lingfield in August and handicap at Wolverhampton in October: stays 7f: acts on polytrack, soft and good to firm going: tried blinkered. *Andrew Turnell* **73**

CONNY NOBEL (IRE) 5 gr.g. Marju (IRE) 127 – Beauharnaise (FR) (Linamix (FR) 127) [2009 p12.2g^3 Feb 16] modest maiden: missed 2008: stays 2¼m, effective at much shorter: acts on polytrack and soft going, probably on firm: tried in visor/cheekpieces/tongue tie: ungenuine. *C. Roberts* **53 §**

Mr K. Abdulla's "Confront"

CONO ZUR (FR) 2 b.c. (May 29) Anabaa (USA) 130 – Alaskan Idol (USA) (Carson City (USA)) [2009 7m* 7v Nov 3] €20,000Y: fourth foal: half-brother to French 2007 2-y-o 9f winner Alaskan Way (by Giant's Causeway) and a winner in USA by Hennessy: dam, ran once in France, half-sister to Breeders' Cup Classic winner Arcangues: looked promising when winning maiden at Newcastle (made all to beat Unshakable Will 3 lengths) in August: favourite, tailed off in nursery on heavy ground at Catterick: bred to stay 1m. *M. Johnston* **79**

CONQUISTO 4 ch.g. Hernando (FR) 127 – Seal Indigo (IRE) 93 (Glenstal (USA) 118) [2009 97: 12d^5 12g* 12g^5 14v 13.1m^4 12s p13m Nov 28] close-coupled gelding: fairly useful handicapper: won at Doncaster in July: left C. Cox 55,000 gns after fifth start: free-going sort, but stays 1½m: acts on soft and good to firm ground: held up. *S. Gollings* **94**

CONRY (IRE) 3 ch.g. Captain Rio 122 – Altizaf 66 (Zafonic (USA) 130) [2009 78: 7.2d^4 6v 6.7m^4 7.5g* 6s^6 7d* 7m^4 p7m^4 p8g 7s* 7v^2 Nov 3] close-coupled gelding: fairly useful handicapper: won at Tipperary in June and, having left Caroline Hutchinson after fifth start and rejoined former trainer, Catterick in August and October: stays 7.5f: acts on polytrack, heavy and good to firm going: tried in cheekpieces. *Pat Morris* **94**

CONSEQUENCE 3 br. or gr.g. Paris House 123 – Scrutinize (IRE) (Selkirk (USA) 129) [2009 –: 7d 7m^6 Aug 8] little form. *A. Dickman* **–**

CONSEQUENTIAL 2 b.f. (Mar 4) Pivotal 124 – Thirteen Tricks (USA) 77 (Grand Slam (USA) 120) [2009 7g^6 p8.6g^2 Dec 11] 22,000Y: well-made filly: second foal: dam, 1¼m winner, out of half-sister to Breeders' Cup Sprint runner-up Mr Greeley: better effort when 2½ lengths second of 4 to Mister Angry in minor event at Wolverhampton, travelling best most of way: open to further improvement. *D. M. Simcock* **71 p**

CONSIDER YOURSELF (USA) 2 gr. or ro.f. (Jan 22) Afleet Alex (USA) 128 – Champagne Royale (USA) (French Deputy (USA) 118) [2009 7g 8m Sep 18] $110,000Y: big filly: first foal: dam 6.5f/8.5f winner in North America: still green, much better effort in maidens when seventh to Golden Aria at Newmarket, not knocked about: open to further improvement. *M. L. W. Bell* **66 p**

CONSTANT CHEERS (IRE) 6 b.g. Royal Applause 124 – Juno Marlowe (IRE) 100 (Danehill (USA) 126) [2009 90: 9.7m^4 p10g^5 10.1d* 10.2m^5 10.1m^4 9.9m^5 Sep 12] sturdy gelding: fairly useful handicapper: won at Epsom in July: flattered when last of 5 in Select Stakes (acted as pacemaker) at Goodwood final start: stays 1½m: acts on polytrack, good to soft and good to firm ground: sometimes wears cheekpieces/visor: races prominently. *W. R. Swinburn* **85**

CONSTANT CONTACT 2 b.c. (Apr 18) Passing Glance 119 – Floriana 61 (Selkirk (USA) 129) [2009 7.1m 7f^5 7m* 7m^2 Oct 3] rather unfurnished colt: third foal: half-brother to 1½m (seller) and 12.5f (in Germany) winner Ericarrow (by Bollin Eric) and 3-y-o Bengal Tiger: dam, maiden (stayed 1¼m), sister to smart 5f to 7f performer Border Music: fairly useful performer: much improved to win maiden at Epsom in August by 2 lengths from Cash Queen Anna: good short-head second to Lord Aeryn in nursery there next time: likely to be suited by 1m. *A. M. Balding* **91**

CONSULT 2 ch.g. (Feb 28) Dr Fong (USA) 128 – Merle (Selkirk (USA) 129) [2009 f7g^6 p8g p7g Nov 11] 65,000F, €75,000Y: tall gelding: second foal: dam unraced half-sister to very smart stayer Solo Mio: always behind in maidens: likely to do better over 1¼m+. *Sir Mark Prescott* **– p**

CONTEMPLATE 3 ch.f. Compton Place 125 – Billie Blue 63 (Ballad Rock 122) [2009 –: f7g^6 8d 7m 7m^2 7g Oct 20] lengthy filly: modest maiden: clear best effort at 7f on good to firm going: blinkered last 2 starts. *Dr J. D. Scargill* **55**

CONTEST (IRE) 5 b.h. Danehill Dancer (IRE) 117 – Mala Mala (IRE) 104 (Brief Truce (USA) 126) [2009 110: p6g* 6.5g 6g^6 6g^5 6m^4 5.5d^2 6m* 5m 5g^3 6g 5g 6m^2 7g 5.5d Oct 6] lengthy, useful-looking horse: smart performer at best: won minor event at Lingfield in January (only start for D. Simcock) and listed race at Chantilly in April by 2½ lengths from Mariol: best effort afterwards when second to same rival in Prix de Meautry at Deauville twelfth start: effective at 5f/6f: acts on polytrack, firm and soft going: usually blinkered nowadays, tried in cheekpieces/tongue tie. *C. Theodorakis, France* **112**

CONTRACT CATERER (IRE) 2 b.c. (Mar 18) Azamour (IRE) 130 – Nawaji (USA) 45 (Trempolino (USA) 135) [2009 6v^4 7m^2 7m* 7g^4 8m* Sep 8] good-topped colt: closely related to fairly useful but ungenuine 9.7f winner Noticeable (by Night Shift) and half-brother to 2 fairly useful winners, including 7f (at 2 yrs) to 1¼m winner Press Express (by Entrepreneur): dam, maiden who stayed 13f, sister to smart performer up to **87**

1½m Triarius: fairly useful performer: won maiden at Catterick in July and nursery at Goodwood (by neck from Flying Destination) in September: stays 1m: acts on good to firm ground: races prominently. *Pat Eddery*

CONTRADA 4 b.g. Medicean 128 – Trounce (Barathea (IRE) 127) [2009 74: p12g Apr 1] rangy gelding: fair handicapper: well held only start at 4 yrs: stays 1¼m: acts on good to soft going: tried blinkered: signs of temperament. *J. A. B. Old* **–**

CONTRARY (IRE) 2 ch.f. (Mar 4) Mark of Esteem (IRE) 137 – Crystal Gaze (IRE) (Rainbow Quest (USA) 134) [2009 p7g 7s* Oct 30] strong filly: second foal: dam unraced sister to useful 1¼m/1½m winner and smart hurdler Desert Quest: some promise in maiden at Kempton for E. Dunlop: won similar event at Moulins following month by length from Compton Effect: will stay 1m: likely to progress again. *E. J. O'Neill* **79 p**

CONTREDANSE (IRE) 2 br.f. (Apr 16) Danehill Dancer (IRE) 117 – Ahdaab (USA) 73 (Rahy (USA) 115) [2009 7m 7m p8m³ Nov 19] 200,000Y: sturdy filly: fifth foal: sister to 3 winners, including 3-y-o Set Sail and smart Canadian performer up to 1¼m Callwood Dancer, and closely related to useful 5f (at 2 yrs) to 9f (in US) winner Walklikeanegyptian (by Danehill): dam, maiden (stayed 1¼m), half-sister to Queen Elizabeth II Stakes winner Maroof: fair maiden: not clear run when third at Kempton: may stay beyond 1m: sold 135,000 gns. *B. J. Meehan* **73**

CONVALLARIA (FR) 6 b.m. Cape Cross (IRE) 129 – Scarlet Davis (FR) (Ti King (FR) 121) [2009 67: p7g² p8g p7g⁴ p7g⁵ p7.1g p7g Jul 15] workmanlike mare: modest handicapper: best form at 7f: acts on polytrack and good to soft ground: usually blinkered: tried tongue tied: has hung. *C. F. Wall* **64**

CONVERTI 5 b.g. Averti (IRE) 117 – Conquestadora 98 (Hernando (FR) 127) [2009 56: 15m⁵ 16d Jul 18] leggy gelding: modest performer: stays 15f: acts on polytrack and good to firm going: blinkered at 5 yrs: fair hurdler. *H. J. Manners* **58**

CONVINCE (USA) 8 ch.g. Mt Livermore (USA) – Conical 63 (Zafonic (USA) 130) [2009 –: p7.1g³ p6g* p7g³ f6g* p6g⁴ 7s* 7.1m⁵ 7g² 6g 7g⁵ 6.1d² p6g⁶ p7m f6g⁵ f7f* Dec 12] tall, close-coupled gelding: fair handicapper: won at Kempton (minor event) in January, Southwell in March, Brighton in May and, having left K. Prendergast after twelfth start, Southwell (dead-heated) in December: best at 6f/7f: acts on all-weather, firm and soft ground: sometimes wears headgear: has carried head awkwardly. *J. L. Flint* **71**

CONVITEZZA 3 b.f. Domedriver (IRE) 128 – Condoleezza (USA) 78 (Cozzene (USA)) [2009 8m⁶ 8g 10m⁵ 8m⁶ 7g 7g Oct 23] £1,000 2-y-o: rather leggy filly: second foal: sister to 4-y-o Indy Driver: dam 1¾m winner: poor maiden. *M. E. Sowersby* **–**

CONVIVIAL SPIRIT 5 b.g. Lake Coniston (IRE) 131 – Ruby Princess (IRE) 70 (Mac's Imp (USA) 116) [2009 51, a69: p8g Jan 31] strong, workmanlike gelding: fair performer, on long losing run: below form in seller only start at 5 yrs: stays easy 8.6f: acts on polytrack and firm going: tongue tied: tried in visor/cheekpieces: sometimes races freely. *E. F. Vaughan* **–**

COOKIE GALORE 2 ch.f. (Mar 30) Monsieur Bond (IRE) 120 – Ginger Cookie 47 (Bold Edge 123) [2009 5g⁶ 6g f6g⁴ 6.1d p5g³ Oct 21] £1,000Y: workmanlike filly: first foal: dam, maiden (stayed 7f), half-sister to useful miler Peculiarity: poor maiden: stays 6f: acts on all-weather. *J. A. Glover* **47**

COOK'S ENDEAVOUR (USA) 3 b.g. Gone West (USA) – Weekend In London (USA) (Belong To Me (USA)) [2009 85p: 8m 7d 7m³ 6d³ 7m 7d p7.1g 8m² 7g f7m⁶ Nov 12] big, good-topped gelding: has plenty of scope: fair handicapper: stays 1m: acts on fibresand, firm and soft going: tried in cheekpieces: races prominently. *K. A. Ryan* **79**

COOL ART (IRE) 3 b.g. One Cool Cat (USA) 123 – Fee Faw Fum (IRE) (Great Commotion (USA) 123) [2009 83: p7g p7g p7g⁴ 6g 6g⁶ 5m⁶ f6g p6g p7g⁴ 6g 6g Oct 23] attractive gelding: fair performer, regressive: claimed from S. Callaghan £15,000 third start, Peter Grayson £6,000 after ninth: stays 7f: acts on polytrack and good to firm going: often blinkered. *J. S. Wainwright* **78 d**

COOL BARANCA (GER) 3 b.f. Beat Hollow 126 – Cool Storm (IRE) 58 (Rainbow Quest (USA) 134) [2009 8g 7.8g² 8d⁴ 9.2g³ 9.1g* 8v² Oct 31] ex-German filly: third foal: dam, ran once, half-sister to Derby second Walk In The Park out of Irish 1000 Guineas winner Classic Park: fairly useful form: left P. Schiergen after second in minor event at Bad Harzburg second start: won claimer at Ayr in October: good second in handicap there final start: will prove best at 1¼m+: raced only on good going or softer (acts on heavy). *P. Monteith* **83**

COOL EBONY 6 br.g. Erhaab (USA) 127 – Monawara (IRE) 73 (Namaqualand (USA)) [2009 83: p8g 8.1g^5 8.3m^6 8.3m* Aug 9] sturdy gelding: fairly useful handicapper: won apprentice event at Windsor in August: stays 9f: acts on firm and soft going: tried in cheekpieces. *P. J. Makin* **81**

COOLE DODGER (IRE) 4 ch.g. Where Or When (IRE) 124 – Shining High 90 (Shirley Heights 130) [2009 80§: 9.8d 7.9g 7.5m^6 p7g 9.9m^6 8.3s^3 8.5m^3 f8g Sep 29] rather leggy gelding: modest performer nowadays: stays 8.5f: acts on polytrack, soft and good to firm going: ungenuine. *B. Ellison* **61 §**

COOLELLA (IRE) 2 gr.f. (Mar 2) Verglas (IRE) 118 – Tianella (GER) 74 (Acatenango (GER) 127) [2009 6v 5.9g^3 f6g^6 6d p8.6g^6 Sep 19] €5,000Y, resold £8,000Y: third foal: dam maiden (stayed 1½m): maiden, modest form at best: should stay 7f+. *J. R. Weymes* **51**

COOL FASHION (IRE) 4 b.f. Orpen (USA) 116 – Fun Fashion (IRE) 64 (Polish Patriot (USA) 128) [2009 48: 5f 5.9g Jun 1] poor maiden: best form at 5f/6f: wears headgear nowadays. *Ollie Pears* **–**

COOL HAND JAKE 3 b.g. Storming Home 128 – Monawara (IRE) 73 (Namaqualand (USA)) [2009 76: p8g* 8.3m^6 p8.6g* p8g* p8g p8g^3 p10m Sep 23] close-coupled gelding: fairly useful performer: won maiden at Kempton in January, and handicaps at Wolverhampton and Kempton in June: stays 8.6f: best efforts on polytrack: tongue tied last 2 starts (gelded after). *P. J. Makin* **85**

COOL JUDGEMENT (IRE) 4 b.g. Peintre Celebre (USA) 137 – Sadinga (IRE) 85 (Sadler's Wells (USA) 132) [2009 105: 14.1m^2 May 3] strong, useful-looking gelding: useful handicapper: good 2¼ lengths second to Woolfall Treasure at Salisbury, only start at 4 yrs: stayed 1¾m: acted on soft and good to firm ground: retired. *M. A. Jarvis* **105**

COOL KITTEN (IRE) 2 b.f. (Apr 11) One Cool Cat (USA) 123 – Zoom Lens (IRE) 65 (Caerleon (USA) 132) [2009 6m 7m 8d^6 Oct 15] 30,000Y: compact filly: half-sister to several winners, including smart 7f/1m winner (including at 2 yrs) Atlantis Prince (by Tagula) and 3-y-o Perfect Shot: dam maiden (stayed 1½m): poor form in maidens. *W. J. Knight* **47**

COOL LIBBY (IRE) 3 br.f. One Cool Cat (USA) 123 – Cosabawn (IRE) 57 (Barathea (IRE) 127) [2009 60?: 8.1g 8f^6 10.1d 8.5f Aug 31] close-coupled filly: poor maiden: should stay beyond 1m. *A. B. Haynes* **45**

COOL MADAM 3 b.f. Ishiguru (USA) 114 – Face The Judge (USA) 59 (Benny The Dip (USA) 127) [2009 –: p6g p5.1g^5 f6d 10.2g Apr 28] little form. *D. Flood* **–**

COOLMINX (IRE) 2 b.f. (Mar 25) One Cool Cat (USA) 123 – Greta d'Argent (IRE) 103 (Great Commotion (USA) 123) [2009 5.4d* 5g* 6g^2 Oct 10] €13,000F, €25,000Y: unfurnished filly: second foal: sister to 3-y-o Baycat: dam, 8.5f (at 2 yrs) to 1½m winner, half-sister to smart stayer Winged d'Argent: useful form: won maiden at York and minor event at Beverley, both in September: good 2¼ lengths second to Layla's Hero in listed event at York subsequent outing, clear briefly: stays 6f: type to make an even better 3-y-o. *R. A. Fahey* **95 p**

COOLNAHARAN (IRE) 9 b.g. Blues Traveller (IRE) 119 – Alma Assembly (General Assembly (USA)) [2009 10.2m^2 p12.2g^6 p10.7f 9.1v p9.5g* p9.5g^6 p9.5g* Dec 11] modest performer: won minor event in November and handicap in December, both at Wolverhampton: stays 10.7f: acts on polytrack and firm going: in cheekpieces last 3 starts. *L. Smyth, Ireland* **66**

COOLREE STAR (IRE) 2 ch.g. (Apr 13) Kheleyf (USA) 116 – Amount 80 (Salse (USA) 128) [2009 5m 6d* 6d^5 p6g 6m^2 6g 6g* 6s p6m^2 p6m Dec 4] workmanlike gelding: second foal: dam, 7f (at 2 yrs) to 9f (in France) winner, half-sister to smart performer up to 1¼m Protectress: fair performer: won seller at Yarmouth (left W. Muir 10,000 gns) in July and nursery at Windsor in October: will stay 7f: acts on good to firm and good to soft going. *J. A. Glover* **79**

COOL SANDS (IRE) 7 b.g. Trans Island 119 – Shalerina (USA) (Shalford (IRE) 124§) [2009 44, a80: f6d f7g^5 5.9m f6g f6g f6g p6g p6g^5 f6g^2 p6g^3 f6g^3 p6f^2 Dec 21] strong gelding: fair handicapper: was best at 6f: acted on all-weather, well held on turf after 2006: visored: was usually held up: raced lazily: dead. *J. G. Given* **– a65**

COOL SONATA (IRE) 3 b.f. One Cool Cat (USA) 123 – Sonatina 103 (Distant Relative 128) [2009 49: f8g Jan 20] compact filly: maiden: well beaten only start at 3 yrs: stays 7f: acts on fibresand. *M. Brittain* **–**

COOL STRIKE (UAE) 3 b.g. Halling (USA) 133 – Velour 94 (Mtoto 134) [2009 65: 10m 11m^{2} 11.7m* 12.3m^{3} 12m* 14g^{5} Jul 28] good-topped gelding: useful handicapper: improved to win at Bath in June and Newmarket in July: should be suited by 1¾m+: acts on good to firm going, promise on polytrack: visored of late. *A. M. Balding* **97**

COOL VALENTINE 2 b.c. (Feb 14) One Cool Cat (USA) 123 – Miss Mirasol 92 (Sheikh Albadou 128) [2009 p6g^{2} 6d^{4} 5.7g^{6} 7.1g* 8m^{4} p8m^{4} Sep 30] 11,000F, 13,000Y: second foal: half-brother to 4-y-o Dark Prospect: dam 2-y-o 6f winner: fairly useful performer: won nursery at Sandown (beat Astonishment 2¼ lengths) in August: stays 1m: acts on polytrack and good to firm going: carried head awkwardly final start: sold 68,000 gns, sent to Denmark. *A. M. Balding* **80**

COOPER ISLAND KID (USA) 3 b. or br.g. Arch (USA) 127 – Raven Quiver (USA) (Old Trieste (USA) 122) [2009 65?: 11.6m f8g 11.5d 16v Jul 30] leggy gelding: modest maiden handicapper. *P. W. D'Arcy* **55**

COOPERMAN 3 b.g. Sulamani (IRE) 130 – Minibule (FR) 73 (Funambule (USA) 118) [2009 10.3g 10.1m^{4} 10g 12m 12g Jul 15] tall gelding: little form. *P. T. Midgley* **–**

COORDINATED CUT (IRE) 2 b.c. (Feb 14) Montjeu (IRE) 137 – Apache Star 96 (Arazi (USA) 135) [2009 8m* 8d Oct 24] 325,000Y: rangy colt: half-brother to several winners, including useful 2001 2-y-o 6f winner Sahara Desert (by Green Desert) and smart 1¼m (including in UAE) winner Wild Savannah (by Singspiel): dam 7f (at 2 yrs) to 9f winner: highly promising when landing odds in maiden at Doncaster in September by 1¼ lengths from Tactician, idling: still very green (worked up beforehand) when well-held tenth in Racing Post Trophy on same course: will stay 1¼m: has joined M. Bell: has scope, and type to make even better 3-y-o. *P. W. Chapple-Hyam* **94 p**

COPPERBEECH (IRE) 3 b.f. Red Ransom (USA) – Aynthia (USA) 104 (Zafonic (USA) 130) [2009 105p: 9.9m^{6} p10m^{3} 10m 11.8m^{2} 10.3s^{3} Nov 7] quite attractive filly: creditable efforts when placed in 2009, 2 lengths third to Queen of Pentacles in listed event at Doncaster final start: stays 1½m: acts on polytrack, soft and good to firm going. *Saeed bin Suroor* **101**

COPPER DOCK (IRE) 5 b.g. Docksider (USA) 124 – Sundown 71 (Polish Precedent (USA) 131) [2009 90: p5g^{3} p6g^{6} 5m 5g 5d 5g p6g^{5} p5g^{4} 5m p7f p7g^{3} p6g* p6g^{2} p6g* Nov 27] sturdy gelding: useful handicapper: improved towards end of 2009, winning at Dundalk in October and November (beat Tellelle by ½ length): effective at 5f to easy 7f: acts on polytrack and good to firm going: tried in blinkers/cheekpieces/tongue tie: usually travels strongly: held up. *T. G. McCourt, Ireland* **107**

COPPER KING 5 ch.g. Ishiguru (USA) 114 – Dorissio (IRE) 75 (Efisio 120) [2009 68: p7g p8g f8d^{5} p7.1g f7g^{4} p8g* p8g p8g^{5} p8g Nov 18] good-bodied gelding: modest handicapper: won at Lingfield in June: stays 1m: acts on polytrack, good to firm and good to soft ground: tried in cheekpieces/visor/tongue tie. *Miss Tor Sturgis* **54**

COPPER PENNY 2 b.f. (Mar 31) Dansili 127 – Makara (Lion Cavern (USA) 117) [2009 7g Aug 8] 70,000Y: fourth foal: sister to fairly useful French 6.5f and (including at 2 yrs) 1m winner Asque and half-sister to Irish 4-y-o Fourpenny Lane: dam unraced half-sister to useful French sprinter Tayseer: 18/1, showed some ability when down the field in maiden at Newmarket, not knocked about. *D. R. Lanigan* **52**

COPPER SOVEREIGN 7 ch.g. Compton Place 125 – Lady Kitty (Petong 126) [2009 6m 7f p8g Oct 11] no sign of ability. *Jamie Poulton* **–**

COPPERWOOD 4 ch.g. Bahamian Bounty 116 – Sophielu 80 (Rudimentary (USA) 118) [2009 62: p8g^{3} p7g^{6} p8g^{3} p8.6g 7g^{6} p7m^{2} p7m^{6} p7m* Nov 29] lengthy gelding: fair handicapper: won at Kempton in November: barely stays 1m: acts on polytrack: tried blinkered. *M. Blanshard* **68**

CORALAMBER (IRE) 2 gr.f. (Feb 5) Monsieur Bond (IRE) 120 – Silver Sun 83 (Green Desert (USA) 127) [2009 5m 6f^{6} f5g 5m^{5} Jul 1] eighth foal: sister to 3-y-o Deckchair and half-sister to 2 winning sprinters: dam, 9f winner, half-sister to smart stayer Tioman Island: poor maiden: should stay 6f. *Garry Moss* **35**

CORAL POINT (IRE) 3 ch.g. Hawkeye (IRE) 122 – Green Crystal 57 (Green Dancer (USA) 132) [2009 –: 11.6d^{5} Jun 8] big, good-topped gelding: first form when fifth in maiden at Windsor, then gelded. *S. Curran* **59**

CORAL SHORES 4 b.f. Carnival Dancer 123 – Leading Role 90 (Cadeaux Genereux 131) [2009 70: f8g^{6} p10g f11g^{4} p10g^{5} f11g^{5} p13g^{5} 11.9m^{4} 10.9f* 11.9m^{3} 11.7f^{3} 10.9d* 11.9m^{4} 11.5m 9.9g^{5} p9.5g f11m^{3} Dec 5] good-topped filly: fair handicapper: won at **70**

Warwick in May and June: stays 1½m: acts on all-weather, firm and soft going: visored: races prominently. *P. W. Hiatt*

CORDELL (IRE) 4 b.g. Fasliyev (USA) 120 – Urgele (FR) 102 (Zafonic (USA) 130) [2009 95: p8g[5] 8s 8m 7g 10m 8.1g[6] 8d* 8.5m 7m p8g p7g 8g Oct 20] strong, rangy gelding: useful performer on all-weather, fair on turf: won claimer at Brighton (left R. Hannon £16,000) in August: inconsistent otherwise: stays 9f: acts on polytrack and good to firm going. *R. Ingram* **79 a100**

CORDIALITY 2 b.g. (Mar 14) Kingsalsa (USA) 118 – Peace 85 (Sadler's Wells (USA) 132) [2009 p8m 8.3s f8m Dec 5] useful-looking gelding: modest form at best in maidens: left J. Fanshawe 6,000 gns after second outing: should stay 1¼m. *P. G. Murphy* **60**

CORDOBA 3 b.f. Oasis Dream 129 – Spanish Sun (USA) 119 (El Prado (IRE) 119) [2009 p11g* Jul 1] well-made filly: second foal: dam, 7f (at 2 yrs) and 1½m (Ribblesdale Stakes) winner from 3 starts, sister to 5-y-o Spanish Moon: 5/2, won maiden at Kempton by ¾ length from Blue Nymph: would have stayed 1½m: visits Rail Link. *Sir Michael Stoute* **77**

CORKING (IRE) 4 b.f. Montjeu (IRE) 137 – Scanno's Choice (IRE) 54 (Pennine Walk 120) [2009 61: f14s p13.9g 17.2d* 17.2f May 31] sturdy filly: modest handicapper: won amateur event at Bath in May: stays 17f: acts on soft going: races prominently: tried blinkered. *J. L. Flint* **63**

CORLOUGH MOUNTAIN 5 ch.g. Inchinor 119 – Two Step 60 (Mujtahid (USA) 118) [2009 77d: p12g* p12g[6] p12.2g* p13.9g[6] 11.9m 7m 10f 10.9m p12g p16m Dec 1] workmanlike gelding: modest handicapper: won amateur events at Kempton in January and Wolverhampton in February: barely stays 2m: acts on polytrack and heavy ground: tried in cheekpieces/tongue tie. *P. Butler* **57**

CORNISH BARONESS 2 b.f. (May 31) Reset (AUS) 124 – Milady Lillie (IRE) 65 (Distinctly North (USA) 115) [2009 8.3m Sep 1] 800F: sixth foal: half-sister to 2005 2-y-o 6f seller winner Savannah Pride (by Namid): dam, 7f winner, out of Irish 1000 Guineas runner-up Millingdale Lillie: 50/1, always behind in maiden at Leicester. *R. Hannon* **–**

CORNISH BEAU (IRE) 2 ch.c. (Feb 23) Pearl of Love (IRE) 112 – Marimar (IRE) (Grand Lodge (USA) 125) [2009 7d[5] 7m[3] 8.1d[6] f8m[2] Nov 6] fair maiden: placed at Folkestone and Southwell (nursery): likely to stay 1¼m: acts on fibresand and good to firm going. *M. H. Tompkins* **69**

CORNISH CASTLE (USA) 3 ch.g. Mizzen Mast (USA) 121 – Rouwaki (USA) (Miswaki (USA) 124) [2009 65: 10.3g 8.3m* 8.3m* 8m[4] 9.8m 8g[4] Jun 30] good-bodied gelding: fair handicapper: won at Nottingham (2) in April: stays 8.3f: raced only on good/good to firm going: tried blinkered: held up: sold £1,500, joined Joss Saville. *T. D. Walford* **76**

CORNUS 7 ch.g. Inchinor 119 – Demerger (USA) (Distant View (USA) 126) [2009 90: p7g p7.1g* p6g* p7.1g[5] p7.1m[3] p6g p8.6g[6] 7m 7m[3] 6f* 7m 6m[4] 6d 7g[6] 7g p7.1g 7d[5] 6m[6] 7g p7.1g[6] f6g Dec 18] smallish, sturdy gelding: fairly useful handicapper: won at Wolverhampton in January, Lingfield in February and Thirsk in April: left A. McCabe after fourteenth start: stays 7f: acts on polytrack and any turf going: usually blinkered: held up. *J. A. Glover* **83**

CORONADO'S GOLD (USA) 8 ch.g. Coronado's Quest (USA) 130 – Debit My Account (USA) (Classic Account (USA)) [2009 63: 15.8m 12.4m 15.8g 9.9g[3] May 23] modest handicapper: stays 15.8f: acts on soft and good to firm going: tried in cheekpieces: none too consistent. *B. Ellison* **60**

CORONARIA 2 b.f. (Mar 15) Starcraft (NZ) 128 – Anthos (GER) 91 (Big Shuffle (USA) 122) [2009 6g Jul 25] good-bodied filly: 13/2, returned injured when last in maiden at York: dead. *W. J. Haggas* **–**

CORPORAL MADDOX 2 b.c. (Mar 30) Royal Applause 124 – Noble View (USA) 68 (Distant View (USA) 126) [2009 5.1m[4] 5g* 6g* 5g[3] 7g[3] 6m[6] 7g* 6d[6] Oct 24] 47,000F, £40,000Y: good-topped colt: fourth foal: brother to 5-y-o Silver Hotspur and half-brother to 3-y-o Aegean Shadow: dam, maiden, half-sister to Poule d'Essai des Pouliches winner Houseproud: useful performer: won maiden at Hamilton in May and listed race at Epsom (by neck from Walkingonthemoon) in June and, having left K. R. Burke after fourth start, A. Jarvis after sixth, minor event at Ascot (best effort, beat Quadrille by head) in October: also ran well when third to Xtension in Vintage Stakes at Goodwood fifth outing: may prove best up to 7f: best efforts on good ground. *H. R. A. Cecil* **104**

CORRIB (IRE) 6 b.m. Lahib (USA) 129 – Montana Miss (IRE) 80 (Earl of Barking (IRE) 119) [2009 63: f12g^6 f11g^4 11.7f 10.2m^4 12.1m^4 10g^3 10m^3 11.9d p9.5g^5 p9.5g^5 Dec 18] leggy mare: modest handicapper: stays 1½m: acts on polytrack, best turf efforts on good going or firmer. *B. Palling* **55**

CORRIOLANUS (GER) 9 b.g. Zamindar (USA) 116 – Caesarea (GER) (Generous (IRE) 139) [2009 68+: p10g^3 p10g p12g^6 10.2g^4 12d* May 15] strong, close-coupled gelding: fair performer nowadays: won apprentice handicap at Newbury in May: stays 1½m: acts on polytrack, firm and good to soft going: tried in blinkers/cheekpieces (including at Newbury). *A. M. Balding* **75**

CORR POINT (IRE) 2 b.g. (Feb 10) Azamour (IRE) 130 – Naazeq 80 (Nashwan (USA) 135) [2009 p7.1g p7g p7m Nov 26] €50,000Y, 55,000 2-y-o: half-brother to several at least fairly useful winners, notably smart 7f to 9f (in USA) winner Tamweel (by Gulch): dam, 10.5f winner, sister to smart performer up to 2½m Shaya: down the field in maidens at Wolverhampton and Kempton (2), pulling hard final start: gelded after: bred to be suited by 1m+: capable of better. *J. A. Osborne* **– p**

CORRYBROUGH 4 ch.c. Kyllachy 129 – Calamanco 71 (Clantime 101) [2009 118: p6m^5 6d Sep 5] big, strong colt: smart performer at best: reportedly suffered stress fractures above his knees in April: below form on belated return, seventh to Regal Parade in Sprint Cup at Haydock final start: was effective at stiff 5f/6f: raced only on polytrack and good/good to soft going: held up, and took time to warm to task: reportedly fractured a sesamoid and severely damaged a tendon on gallops in October: dead. *H. Candy* **103**

CORSICA (IRE) 2 b.c. (Feb 11) Cape Cross (IRE) 129 – Cedar Sea (IRE) (Persian Bold 123) [2009 8.1g^2 8d^5 8.1m^5 8g* Oct 23] 20,000Y, 48,000 2-y-o: lengthy colt: third foal: dam, French 1m winner, half-sister to Coventry Stakes winner Cd Europe: fairly useful performer: won maiden at Ayr in October, not fully extended: raced only at 1m: acts on good to firm going: said to have been distressed second start. *M. Johnston* **80**

CORTON CHARLEMAGNE (IRE) 3 b.f. King Charlemagne (USA) 120 – Teller (ARG) (Southern Halo (USA)) [2009 68: p7g 6f^2 6g^5 5m* 5m* 5g^3 5f* 5m^5 5.1m^5 Sep 30] lengthy, angular filly: fairly useful handicapper: won at Windsor and Newcastle in August and Folkestone in September: may prove best at 5f: acts on polytrack and firm ground. *Rae Guest* **80**

CORUM (IRE) 6 b.g. Galileo (IRE) 134 – Vallee Des Reves (USA) (Kingmambo (USA) 125) [2009 76: 15m Jul 9] strong, good-bodied gelding: fair handicapper at 5 yrs: well held sole start on Flat in 2009: seems to stay easy 2m: acts on polytrack and good to firm going: usually wears cheekpieces: successful 3 times over hurdles later in 2009, joined D. Pipe 12,000 gns after first occasion. *Mrs K. Waldron* **–**

COSIMO 3 ch.g. Medicean 128 – Flight Soundly (IRE) 78 (Caerleon (USA) 132) [2009 86p: 10f^5 11.6g^4 10m^2 10.2g^5 Jul 4] good-topped gelding: fair maiden: stays 11.6f: acts on polytrack and firm going: visored last 2 starts: sold 18,000 gns, sent to Saudi Arabia. *Sir Michael Stoute* **76**

COSIMO DE MEDICI 2 b.g. (Mar 5) Medicean 128 – Wish 79 (Danehill (USA) 126) [2009 p5g^6 p6m^5 p6f Dec 13] 70,000F, 55,000Y, 800 2-y-o: fifth foal: half-brother to 3 winners, including Irish 5f/6.7f winner Wildwish (by Alhaarth) and French 5.5f winner Antinea (by Royal Applause): dam, 2-y-o 6f winner, out of smart performer up to 1m Dazzle: green and not knocked about when showing ability in 3 maidens: remains likely to progress. *H. Morrison* **63 p**

COSMEA 4 b.f. Compton Place 125 – St James's Antigua (IRE) 79 (Law Society (USA) 130) [2009 87: 10f* 10m^4 9.9g 12m^3 12m^4 Sep 18] sturdy filly: fairly useful handicapper: won at Sandown (dead-heated) in June: stays 1½m: acts on firm ground. *A. King* **87**

COSMIC 3 b.g. Nayef (USA) 129 – Urania 66 (Most Welcome 131) [2009 9m 9.8m Apr 25] big, strong gelding: last in maidens at Redcar and Ripon. *T. D. Easterby* **–**

COSMIC DESTINY (IRE) 7 b.m. Soviet Star (USA) 128 – Cruelle (USA) (Irish River (FR) 131) [2009 79: p5g p5g p6g 5.3m^5 5g^5 5.3m^3 5m^3 5f^5 5.3m^4 5.3f 5m^4 5m 5.3m 5.3d p6g p5m Dec 6] smallish mare: fair handicapper: best up to 5.5f: acts on polytrack, firm and good to soft going: held up: none too consistent. *E. F. Vaughan* **69**

COSMIC ORBIT 2 b.c. (Mar 13) Royal Applause 124 – Susquehanna Days (USA) 68 (Chief's Crown (USA)) [2009 7m^5 7d^5 Jul 25] quite good-topped colt: modest form in maidens at Redcar (green) and Newcastle (better effort, not unduly knocked about): should be suited by at least 1m: joined R. Curtis. *K. R. Burke* **58**

King George V Stakes (Heritage Handicap), Ascot—maiden Cosmic Sun springs a 66/1 surprise as he holds off fellow pacesetters Chiberta King (noseband) and Barwell Bridge (rail)

COSMIC SUN 3 b.g. Helissio (FR) 136 – Cosmic Case 66 (Casteddu 111) [2009 85: 10.4m 12.5g 12m* 11.9m³ 12m* 12g⁴ 14m⁴ 14.6m³ Sep 11] sturdy gelding: useful handicapper: much improved in 2009, winning at Royal Ascot (66/1, King George V Stakes, by 1¼ lengths from Chiberta King) in June and York (beat Lochiel ¾ length) in July: good efforts last 2 starts, third to Nanton in Mallard Stakes at Doncaster on final outing: stays 14.6f: acts on heavy and good to firm going: genuine. *R. A. Fahey* **102**

COSMOPOLITAN 4 ch.f. Cadeaux Genereux 131 – Parisian Elegance 90 (Zilzal (USA) 137) [2009 93p: 8m* 8m* 8g 8d* 7g 8m Sep 26] strong, lengthy filly: useful performer: won maiden at Goodwood and handicap at Newmarket in June and handicap at Newbury in July: generally highly tried otherwise: stays 1m: acts on heavy and good to firm going: races prominently: sent to Japan. *J. H. M. Gosden* **98**

COSSACK PRINCE 4 b.g. Dubai Destination (USA) 127 – Danemere (IRE) 90 (Danehill (USA) 126) [2009 78: p12g p12g* p12g 12m* 12m² 9.9m⁴ 12m 11.5d p10f Dec 20] big, rangy gelding: fair performer: won claimer at Kempton in February and handicap at Goodwood in May: below form after next start: stays 15f: acts on polytrack and good to firm ground: tried in cheekpieces: front runner. *Mrs L. J. Mongan* **79**

COTE D'ARGENT 6 b.g. Lujain (USA) 119 – In The Groove 127 (Night Shift (USA)) [2009 –: 12.4s³ 12d 16.1d⁴ 13.1g² Jun 19] tall, leggy gelding: fair handicapper: stays 13f: acts on soft ground: joined C. Down. *L. Lungo* **71**

COTILLION 3 b.g. Sadler's Wells (USA) 132 – Riberac 110 (Efisio 120) [2009 10d² 10m⁶ 12g² 12g⁵ 10.2s² 12v⁴ Nov 3] tall gelding: fourth foal: half-brother to fairly useful 1m winner Montrachet (by Singspiel) and 1½m winner Emilion (by Fantastic Light): dam 5f (at 2 yrs) to 1¼m winner: fairly useful maiden: runner-up 3 times, tending to wander: stays 1½m: acts on soft going: said to have had breathing problem fourth start. *W. J. Haggas* **84**

COTSWOLDS 4 br.g. Green Desert (USA) 127 – Valley of Gold (FR) 117 (Shirley Heights 130) [2009 –: 7g* 7.5g 8.1f⁵ 8.3m³ 8.5m* Jul 3] lengthy gelding: fairly useful performer: won maiden at Catterick in May and handicap at Beverley in July: stays 8.5f: acts on good to firm going: signs of temperament: sent to Switzerland. *M. Johnston* **85**

COTSWOLD VILLAGE (AUS) 3 b.f. Hawk Wing (USA) 136 – Scenic Bold Dancer (AUS) (Scenic 128) [2009 p10g Nov 18] first foal: dam unraced: no show in maiden. *M. R. Bosley* **–**

COTTAM BREEZE 4 b.f. Diktat 126 – Flower Breeze (USA) 75 (Rahy (USA) 115) [2009 7.5m Jun 10] no sign of ability: tried in cheekpieces. *J. S. Wainwright* **–**

COTTONFIELDS (USA) 3 gr. or ro.g. Maria's Mon (USA) 121 – Known Romance (USA) (Known Fact (USA) 135) [2009 7d 10f p10g⁵ Aug 14] lengthy gelding: fair maiden: best effort on debut: should stay 1¼m: signs of temperament. *Mrs H. S. Main* **65 ?**

COTTON TOP (IRE) 2 b.f. (Apr 6) Fath (USA) 116 – Common Cause 87 (Polish Patriot (USA) 128) [2009 7.1m³ p7.1g 7g p8.6g Dec 3] rather leggy filly: sixth foal: half-sister to 3 winners, including 6-y-o Wovoka: dam, 11.5f/1½m winner, out of half-sister to smart French/US performer up to 1¼m Kirkwall: best effort when third in maiden at Warwick on debut: should stay 1m. *M. R. Channon* **59**

COULD IT BE MAGIC 2 b.c. (Apr 16) Dubai Destination (USA) 127 – Lomapamar 76 (Nashwan (USA) 135) [2009 5m^{6} 6g^{3} 7.5m^{5} 6.1g^{2} p6g^{5} 6s^{5} p7m^{3} p7m Dec 6] lengthy colt: second foal: dam, 1¼m winner, half-sister to very smart middle-distance stayer Mons: fair maiden: stays 7.5f: acts on good to firm going: in cheekpieces last 5 starts *W. G. M. Turner* **72**

COUNCELLOR (FR) 7 b.g. Gilded Time (USA) – Sudden Storm Bird (USA) (Storm Bird (CAN) 134) [2009 84, a97: f8s* p7.1g^{2} p8g^{5} p7g^{4} p7.1g 8m 7m^{6} 7g^{2} 7m Jun 12] big, strong gelding: useful performer on all-weather, fair on turf: won handicap at Southwell in January: best at 7f/1m: acts on all-weather, good to firm and good to soft ground: tongue tied: has awkward head carriage. *Stef Liddiard* **77 a97**

COUNT BERTONI (IRE) 2 b.c. (Mar 3) Bertolini (USA) 125 – Queen Sceptre (IRE) 97 (Fairy King (USA)) [2009 6s^{2} 6m^{6} 7.2g^{5} 7.2m^{4} 7g^{3} f7f^{4} 7v^{2} Nov 3] €52,000Y: strong colt: half-brother to 9-y-o Minority Report and 4-y-o North Parade: dam 5f (at 2 yrs) to 1m (in USA) winner: maiden: fairly useful form on debut, below that subsequently (left T. Tate after third start): likely to stay 1m: acts on heavy going: blinkered (well held) penultimate outing: not straightforward. *S. Gollings* **82 §**

COUNT CEPRANO (IRE) 5 b.g. Desert Prince (IRE) 130 – Camerlata (Common Grounds 118) [2009 94: p6g^{4} p6g^{2} p6g^{2} p6g^{6} p7g^{4} p7.1g^{6} p6g^{6} 7m 6m p7g 7.5m^{5} 8.3g^{3} 8.3m 7s 8s^{6} 8.3s f8g 7m Sep 16] compact gelding: fairly useful handicapper, on downgrade: effective at 6f to 9f: acts on polytrack, soft and good to firm going: tried in cheekpieces: held up. *C. R. Dore* **86 d**

COUNT COUGAR (USA) 9 b.g. Sir Cat (USA) 118 – Gold Script (USA) (Seeking The Gold (USA)) [2009 –, a70: f5g f5f Nov 24] sturdy gelding: poor mover: regressive handicapper: tried in blinkers/cheekpieces. *S. P. Griffiths* **–**

COUNTDOWN 7 ch.g. Pivotal 124 – Quiz Time 90 (Efisio 120) [2009 92: 6f 7m^{5} p7g 7m 7d Sep 6] close-coupled gelding: fairly useful handicapper: left M. Squance after fourth start: effective at 6f to 7.6f: acts on polytrack and any turf going: has been blinkered/visored: held up. *R. A. Fahey* **80**

COUNTENANCE 3 ch.g. Medicean 128 – Glamorous (Sanglamore (USA) 126) [2009 10m 9d^{3} p8g^{4} 10.3d p10g Oct 14] compact gelding: fair maiden: best effort at 1m on polytrack: sold 8,000 gns. *W. J. Haggas* **66**

COUNTENANCE DIVINE 2 ch.f. (Mar 15) Pivotal 124 – Sundari (IRE) 103 (Danehill (USA) 126) [2009 7g Oct 31] third foal: dam 2-y-o 6f and 1m winner: 13/2 and backward, promising 7 lengths seventh to Revered in maiden at Newmarket, travelling strongly and not knocked about once held: sure to do better. *B. W. Hills* **64 p**

COUNTESS COMET (IRE) 2 b.f. (Apr 8) Medicean 128 – Countess Sybil (IRE) 73 (Dr Devious (IRE) 127) [2009 8.3d^{4} Oct 15] neat filly: fifth foal: half-sister to 2 winners abroad, including Italian winner up to 1¼m by Mister Baileys: dam Irish 1¾m winner: 25/1 and backward, encouraging fourth to Saboteur in maiden at Nottingham: should stay 1¼m: capable of better. *R. M. Beckett* **61 p**

COUNTESS ZARA (IRE) 3 b.f. Xaar 132 – Lochridge 110 (Indian Ridge 123) [2009 68: p7g 8g^{5} 7m^{5} 6f^{4} Jun 24] good-bodied filly: fair maiden handicapper: stays 1m: acts on firm and good to soft going, below form on polytrack: visored/blinkered last 3 starts: sold 4,000 gns, sent to Bahrain. *A. M. Balding* **66**

COUNT LUCIEN 3 b.c. Danehill Dancer (IRE) 117 – Paquita (IRE) 90 (Sadler's Wells (USA) 132) [2009 10g^{4} 10m 8.1m^{5} Jul 23] tall, attractive colt: fair maiden: barely stays 1¼m: found little all starts: sold 5,000 gns in October, sent to Germany. *J. H. M. Gosden* **68**

COUNT OF ANJOU (USA) 2 b. or br.c. (Feb 8) Lion Heart (USA) 124 – Woodmaven (USA) (Woodman (USA) 126) [2009 6.5g^{5} 8v p7m^{2} Nov 26] $95,000F, €140,000Y: useful-looking colt: third foal: half-brother to Irish 3-y-o Roof Fiddle: dam, ran twice in USA, half-sister to 1000 Guineas runner-up Arch Swing: fair maiden: best effort when ½-length second to Bramshaw at Kempton: likely to prove suited by 6f: acts on polytrack. *R. Hannon* **74**

COUNT OF TUSCANY (USA) 3 b.c. Arch (USA) 127 – Corsini 88 (Machiavellian (USA) 123) [2009 77p: 12g^{2} 9.9m^{3} p12g* Oct 21] big, strong, lengthy colt: fairly useful form: won maiden at Kempton (by 6 lengths) in October: stays 1½m: acts on polytrack and good to firm going: sold 65,000 gns. *Mrs A. J. Perrett* **85**

COUNT ON GUEST 3 ch.g. Fantastic Light (USA) 134 – Countess Guest (IRE) 59 (Spectrum (IRE) 126) [2009 68: 10.1d^{5} 11.6g 10.1m 8.3m 12f 8m^{2} 8f 7g 7m Sep 15] smallish gelding: modest maiden: stays 1¼m: acts on good to firm ground: tried blinkered: tongue tied last 4 starts. *G. G. Margarson* **64**

COUNT PARIS (USA) 3 ch.c. Pivotal 124 – Dearly 107 (Rahy (USA) 115) [2009 82: p6g p7g^4 Apr 21] rather leggy colt: fair performer: will stay 1m: acts on polytrack and heavy going. *M. Johnston* **72**

COUNTRYCRAFT 2 b.g. (Apr 14) Pastoral Pursuits 127 – Turn Back 73 (Pivotal 124) [2009 5m Jul 4] 66/1 and very green, soon outpaced in maiden at Beverley. *Miss S. E. Hall* **–**

COUNTRYMANS DREAM 2 b.g. (Apr 17) Mark of Esteem (IRE) 137 – Lateralle (IRE) (Unfuwain (USA) 131) [2009 5g 5g^5 5.9m 7.5m 8m Sep 23] no form. *J. R. Weymes* **–**

COUNTRY PRINCESS (FR) 2 b.f. (Feb 12) Country Reel (USA) 113 – Millefiori (USA) (Machiavellian (USA) 123) [2009 5.1g 5m^4 6m May 15] €55,000Y: second foal: dam, French 6.5f/1m winner, out of useful 2-y-o 6f/7f winner Lovely Millie: again well backed, best effort in maidens when fourth at Windsor: drawn wide all starts. *R. M. Beckett* **56 +**

COUNTRY ROAD (IRE) 3 b.c. Montjeu (IRE) 137 – Souffle 105 (Zafonic (USA) 130) [2009 10.3s 10.9g^3 10.2d^6 p11g^5 Oct 22] 180,000F: sixth foal: closely related to winner in USA by El Prado: dam, 1¼m winner (stayed 2m), half-sister to Grand Prix de Paris winner Grape Tree Road and smart stayer Windsor Castle: fairly useful maiden: standout effort on second start: bred to stay 1½m+, though needs to learn to settle: raced on polytrack/good ground or softer: quirky (veered violently left second/fourth outings): sold 16,000 gns, joined David Easterby. *P. W. Chapple-Hyam* **81**

COUNTRYSTYLE LASS (IRE) 3 b.f. Kheleyf (USA) 116 – Davis Rock 71 (Rock City 120) [2009 8.3g 8.3g^4 8.3m p7f 7m Sep 28] workmanlike filly: fourth foal: dam 6f (at 2 yrs) to 1m winner: poor maiden. *P. Winkworth* **46**

COUNTRYWIDE CITY (IRE) 3 b.g. Elusive City (USA) 117 – Handy Station (IRE) 55 (Desert Style (IRE) 121) [2009 80: 6m 5.7f 5m Jun 28] compact gelding: fairly useful performer in 2008: well beaten at 3 yrs. *Jane Southcombe* **–**

COUNTRYWIDE COMET (IRE) 4 b.g. Desert Style (IRE) 121 – Darzao (IRE) (Alzao (USA) 117) [2009 49: p7m p8.6g f8g p9.5g^4 p8g p8g Mar 11] good-topped gelding: poor performer: stays 9.4f: acts on all-weather and good to firm ground: tried in cheekpieces/blinkers. *P. Howling* **44**

COUNTRYWIDE ICE (IRE) 2 gr.g. (Apr 25) Verglas (IRE) 118 – Samaritan Woman (IRE) (Priolo (USA) 127) [2009 5m f5g 5m f5g 5s^4 6m 6s^5 6g Aug 31] good-bodied gelding: temperamental maiden: very close fourth in nursery at Haydock: little form otherwise: should be suited by 6f+: blinkered/in cheekpieces last 5 starts: one to treat with caution. *K. A. Ryan* **50 §**

COUNTRYWIDE JAIME (IRE) 3 b.f. Danetime (IRE) 121 – Naraina (IRE) (Desert Story (IRE) 115) [2009 –: p5g^5 p5g^6 p8m Dec 6] little impact in maidens (for S. Callaghan)/handicap. *M. Wigham* **–**

COUNTRYWIDE SUN 7 b.g. Benny The Dip (USA) 127 – Sundae Girl (USA) 75 (Green Dancer (USA) 132) [2009 14m May 19] smallish, close-coupled gelding: modest performer in 2004: well beaten both Flat starts since. *A. C. Whillans* **–**

COUNT TREVISIO (IRE) 6 b.g. Danehill (USA) 126 – Stylish (Anshan 119) [2009 p7g^6 p8g p9.5g^3 p12.2m^6 p9.5g^4 p8.6g^5 8m May 30] lengthy gelding: fairly useful handicapper nowadays: stays 1¼m: acts on polytrack and firm going: tried in cheekpieces: tail flasher. *J. R. Gask* **85**

COUP DE TORCHON (FR) 4 b.f. Namid 128 – Tashtiyana (IRE) (Doyoun 124) [2009 61: 7.6g Jul 25] maiden: modest in 2008: last sole 4-y-o outing: best effort at 7f on good to firm ground. *J. A. Osborne* **–**

COURAGEOUS (IRE) 3 ch.c. Refuse To Bend (IRE) 128 – Bella Bella (IRE) 95 (Sri Pekan (USA) 117) [2009 103: 7m 7m^3 7m 8g 7d Oct 24] good-topped colt: useful performer: best effort at 3 yrs when 4½ lengths third to Alyarf in listed race at Newmarket: stays 1m: acts on soft and good to firm going. *B. Smart* **96**

COURSE DE DIAMANTE (IRE) 3 b.f. Galileo (IRE) 134 – Desert Bluebell 83 (Kalaglow 132) [2009 8.3f 9.9m^6 10m^4 11.6m^5 Jun 29] good-topped filly: half-sister to several winners, including 1m (at 2 yrs) to 9f (in USA) winner Desert Mirage (by Caerleon) and 6f (in USA) and 1m winner Roses In The Snow (by Be My Guest), both useful: dam, maiden who probably stayed 1¾m, sister to dam of Tenby: fair maiden: best effort when fourth at Newbury: should stay beyond 1¼m: sold €14,000 in November. *D. R. Lanigan* **78**

COURT DRINKING (USA) 2 ch.c. (Mar 22) Alke (USA) 118 – Royal Forum (USA) (Open Forum (USA)) [2009 p6g^6 Dec 3] 7/1 and very green, down the field in maiden at Wolverhampton. *J. R. Best* **45**

COURT GOWN (IRE) 2 b.f. (Feb 5) Zafeen (FR) 123 – Silk Law (IRE) 80 (Barathea (IRE) 127) [2009 7g^2 7m* Aug 29] £20,000Y: good bodied filly: fourth foal: half-sister to 4-y-o Lady Sorcerer and 2005 2-y-o 1¼m winner Ms Rainbow Runner (by Josr Algarhoud): dam, 2-y-o 6f/7f winner, out of Fillies' Mile second Jural: won minor event at Redcar by ¾ length from Al Naouwee (pair clear): should stay 1m: sent to USA: capable of further improvement. *E. S. McMahon* **75 p**

COURT MASTERPIECE 9 b.h. Polish Precedent (USA) 131 – Easy Option (IRE) 115 (Prince Sabo 123) [2009 7m^3 7g^5 8g 7m 10.4d^3 9m^4 Sep 27] lengthy, angular horse: showed traces of stringhalt: one-time high-class performer: went to stud in Ireland in 2008 (proved subfertile): smart form when ½-length third to Regal Parade in minor event at York on reappearance: regressed after, beaten in claimers last 2 starts: was effective at 7f/easy 1m: acted on polytrack, good to firm and good to soft going, probably on soft: usually held up: to stand at Norton Grove Stud, Malton, N. Yorkshire. *J. J. Quinn* **111 d**

COURT PRINCESS 6 b.m. Mtoto 134 – Fairfields Cone (Celtic Cone 116) [2009 11.7g p12m^5 p11g p16g^4 p16m* p16m Dec 30] half-sister to several winners at 1½m+, including useful Court Shareef (by Shareef Dancer) and fairly useful Kaluana Court (by Batshoof): dam, lightly raced on Flat, winning hurdler up to 2¾m: little form over hurdles for C. Longsdon: fair performer on Flat: improved when winning handicap at Lingfield in December: stays 2m: raced on polytrack and good going. *George Baker* **71**

COURT WING (IRE) 3 b.f. Hawk Wing (USA) 136 – Nicely (IRE) 94 (Bustino 136) [2009 p7g 8.3f 9.9m May 21] 9,000F: leggy filly: fourth foal: half-sister to 5-y-o Benfleet Boy and 6-y-o Supsonic: dam, 1m (at 2 yrs) and 2m winner, out of half-sister to very smart 9f to 1½m performer Terimon: no sign of ability. *George Baker* **–**

COUSIN CHARLIE 3 b.g. Choisir (AUS) 126 – Michelle Ma Belle (IRE) 90 (Shareef Dancer (USA) 135) [2009 69: p7g Jan 14] rather leggy gelding: maiden: well beaten only start at 3 yrs. *S. Kirk* **–**

COVER DRIVE (USA) 6 br.g. Giant's Causeway (USA) 132 – Woodland Orchid (IRE) 64 (Woodman (USA) 126) [2009 83d: p12g p10g^6 Jan 22] tall gelding: useful handicapper at best (winner in UAE): became temperamental: stayed 1½m: tried tongue tied/in headgear: sometimes sweated: dead. *Christian Wroe* **– §**

COVERT AMBITION 4 ch.c. Singspiel (IRE) 133 – Super Tassa (IRE) 118 (Lahib (USA) 129) [2009 105p: p10g* 10m^2 10d^2 14.1s^6 Sep 3] big, strong, good sort: smart performer: won handicap at Kempton in June: better efforts after when runner-up in listed events at Sandown (4 lengths behind Kirklees) and Newbury (beaten length by Crime Scene): ran as if amiss final start: should be suited by 1½m+: acts on polytrack, good to firm and good to soft going. *Saeed bin Suroor* **114**

COVERT MISSION 6 b.m. Overbury (IRE) 116 – Peg's Permission (Ra Nova 83) [2009 70: p12.2g^5 12s^4 Oct 27] modest handicapper: stays 13.9f: acts on polytrack, soft and good to firm going. *P. D. Evans* **60**

COYOTE CREEK 5 b.g. Zilzal (USA) 137 – High Barn 72 (Shirley Heights 130) [2009 90: 10.1d 12d^2 12d Jun 12] good-bodied gelding: fairly useful handicapper: barely stays 1¾m: acts on good to firm and good to soft ground: often in headgear: races up with pace: sold 800 gns in October. *E. F. Vaughan* **88**

COZY TIGER (USA) 4 gr.g. Hold That Tiger (USA) 117 – Cozelia (USA) (Cozzene (USA)) [2009 78p: p11g^6 Jan 28] big, leggy gelding: fair maiden: below form only start in 2009: stays 11.6f: raced on polytrack and good to soft going: strong traveller: held up. *W. J. Musson* **60**

CRACKDOWN (IRE) 3 b.c. Refuse To Bend (IRE) 128 – Whitefoot 103 (Be My Chief (USA) 122) [2009 94: 8m* 8m 8.1m^2 8m^2 7m 8g Jul 31] good-topped colt: has scope: useful handicapper: won at Ripon in April by ¾ length from dead-heaters Mutamaashi and Firebet: excellent second in competitive events at Sandown (beaten a head by Acrostic) and Newmarket (went down by ¾ length to Brief Encounter) in July: well below form last 2 starts: stays 1m: acts on good to firm and good to soft going: front runner: sent to UAE. *M. Johnston* **108**

CRACKENTORP 4 b.g. Generous (IRE) 139 – Raspberry Sauce 65 (Niniski (USA) 125) [2009 96p: 12m^2 12m 10.9m^2 Oct 5] strong, attractive gelding: useful handicapper: very good efforts when runner-up at Goodwood (¾ length behind Red Merlin) and Warwick (beaten ¾ length by Alcalde): below form at Royal Ascot in between: stays 1½m: acts on polytrack and good to firm going: sold 57,000 gns. *R. M. Beckett* **101**

CRACKING LASS (IRE) 2 b.f. (Feb 18) Whipper (USA) 126 – Lady From Limerick (IRE) 61 (Rainbows For Life (CAN)) [2009 6s 6m 7s* 6m^5 7m Oct 3] €76,000F, 35,000Y: smallish, close-coupled filly: fourth foal: half-sister to 3 winners, including useful 6f (including at 2 yrs)/7f winner Tagula Sunrise (by Tagula): dam sprint maiden: fairly useful performer: won maiden at Thirsk in September: best effort when fifth to Society Rock in valuable sales race at Newmarket: will stay 1m: acts on soft and good to firm going. *R. A. Fahey* **84**

CRAGGANMORE CREEK 6 b.g. Tipsy Creek (USA) 115 – Polish Abbey (Polish Precedent (USA) 131) [2009 –, a60: f11g^2 p12.2g^5 f12d^2 f11g^4 f12g 10m^6 11.5g 11.5g^6 f11m p16g p16m Dec 1] tall gelding: modest handicapper: stays 2m: acts on all-weather: usually in headgear. *D. Morris* **–** **a52**

CRAG PATH 3 b.f. Celtic Swing 138 – Juvenilia (IRE) 55 (Masterclass (USA) 116) [2009 p8g^4 p10g^3 9.7d p8.6g Apr 25] half-sister to 3 winners, including fairly useful 6f/7f winner Riquewihr (by Compton Place) and 6f winner Cool Tiger (by Vettori): dam third at 7f both starts: modest maiden: stays 1¼m: acts on polytrack. *D. R. C. Elsworth* **62**

CRAICATTACK (IRE) 2 ch.g. (Mar 10) Arakan (USA) 123 – Jack-N-Jilly (IRE) 43 (Anita's Prince 126) [2009 6m 6m^2 6m* 5m^6 5.3m^3 6s 6m^3 6m p7.1g^5 Dec 26] €4,000Y: compact gelding: half-brother to 2001 2-y-o 5f/7f winner Strandiam (by Darnay) and Italian 6f/7f winner by Rossini: dam, placed in 5f/6f sellers, ran only at 2 yrs: fair performer: won maiden at Brighton in June: good third in nursery at Newbury seventh start: gelded prior to final outing: stays 6f: acts on good to firm going, possibly not soft. *J. S. Moore* **78**

CRAIGHALL 2 b.f. (Apr 8) Dubawi (IRE) 129 – Craigmill 85 (Slip Anchor 136) [2009 8g Oct 23] 55,000Y: half-sister to several winners, including smart 1m winner Castleton and useful 1¼m winner Craigstown (both by Cape Cross): dam, 7f winner, half-sister to smart dam of very smart performers Invermark (stayer) and Craigsteel (stayed 1¾m): 100/1 and green, eighth of 21 to Modeyra in maiden at Doncaster, missing break and late headway: should stay 1¼m: sure to improve. *D. M. Simcock* **62 p**

CRANWORTH BLAZE 5 b.m. Diktat 126 – Julietta Mia (USA) 72 (Woodman (USA) 126) [2009 47: 5f 5m 7g 6d 10d Oct 22] lengthy mare: poor maiden: left T. Etherington after fourth start: seems to stay 9f: acts on polytrack and firm ground: tried blinkered. *A. G. Newcombe* **43**

CRAZY BOLD (GER) 6 ch.g. Erminius (GER) 111 – Crazy Love (GER) (Presto) [2009 f11g^5 10.2d^5 Aug 11] winner of 3 races in Germany, including handicaps at Dortmund and Cologne in 2008 for U. Stoltefuss: just poor form on Flat in Britain (won twice over hurdles in May): stays 1¼m: acts on sand, raced on good ground or softer on turf. *A. W. Carroll* **49**

CRAZY CHRIS 4 b. or br.f. Ishiguru (USA) 114 – Ellopassoff 69 (Librate 91) [2009 p8g^2 10.3m^4 10.2g^5 p10g* Nov 25] third foal: dam 1m/1¼m winner: bumper winner for P. Payne: fairly useful form on Flat: left Tom Dascombe, best effort when winning handicap at Kempton in November: stays 1¼m: acts on polytrack. *B. Palling* **83**

CRAZY COLOURS 3 ch.g. Dalakhani (IRE) 133 – Eternity Ring (Alzao (USA) 117) [2009 50: p8g^4 p9.5g^6 Jan 26] fair maiden: stays 9.5f: raced only on polytrack: blinkered/in cheekpieces since debut: races lazily. *Jane Chapple-Hyam* **65**

CREACHADOIR (IRE) 5 b.h. King's Best (USA) 132 – Sadima (IRE) 103 (Sadler's Wells (USA) 132) [2009 126: 8.9g Mar 28] strong, rangy horse: high-class performer in 2007 (trained first half of year by J. Bolger) and 2008 (ran only twice, but won Lockinge Stakes at Newbury): reportedly suffered condylar fracture of off-fore after: beat only one home in Dubai Duty Free at Nad Al Sheba on only outing in 2009, fading: was best at 1m, probably on good/good to firm ground: to stand at Haras du Logis, France, fee €4,500. *Saeed bin Suroor* **–**

CREATIVE (IRE) 4 b.g. Acclamation 118 – Pride of Pendle 80 (Grey Desire 115) [2009 61: 6d^5 p6g^2 5g^2 f6g 6g^6 6m^4 5g^2 5m^4 Jun 19] sturdy gelding: fair maiden: effective at 5f, barely stays 7f: acts on firm and good to soft ground: sometimes visored/blinkered: sold 5,500 gns. *M. H. Tompkins* **67**

CREDENTIAL 7 b.g. Dansili 127 – Sabria (USA) (Miswaki (USA) 124) [2009 63: 10.1g 10.1g^4 11.5g^2 f11m* 12.1m 10.2d^6 Aug 11] sturdy gelding: modest handicapper: won apprentice event at Southwell in July: stays 1½m: acts on fibresand, good to firm and good to soft ground: tried in cheekpieces: front runner. *John A. Harris* **59**

CREDIT SWAP 4 b.g. Diktat 126 – Locharia 91 (Wolfhound (USA) 126) [2009 89: p6g p6g^5 6d 6m^4 7m^2 p7g 7m^5 8g* 8g* 8g* 8m^2 8m^3 Sep 27] lengthy gelding: progressed **102**

into useful handicapper in 2009, winning at Newbury, Ascot (beat Foolin Myself by 1½ lengths, pair clear) and Newmarket, all in July: creditable efforts when placed at Newmarket and Ascot last 2 starts: better at 1m than shorter: acts on polytrack, firm and soft going: held up: consistent. *M. Wigham*

CREESE 2 b.f. (Jan 25) Halling (USA) 133 – Why Dubai (USA) 93 (Kris S (USA)) [2009 7m* Aug 23] first foal: dam, 2-y-o 7f winner, out of sister to US Grade 1 9f/9.5f winner Awe Inspiring: 20/1, promising when winning maiden at Folkestone by neck from Hibaayeb (subsequent Group 1 winner), finishing strongly in centre: should stay 1m+: sure to go on to better things. *H. R. A. Cecil* **88 p**

CREEVY (IRE) 2 b.f. (Apr 29) Trans Island 119 – Kilbride Lass (IRE) (Lahib (USA) 129) [2009 7m p7.1g^5 8.1d 7g 7.1m^2 8g f8m^6 p7g^6 p10m^4 p8.6g^6 Dec 17] compact filly: modest maiden: should stay 1m: acts on good to firm going. *S. Kirk* **58**

CRESHENDO 3 b.g. Kyllachy 129 – Dry Wit (IRE) 68 (Desert Prince (IRE) 130) [2009 77: p6g p7g 5.7f^5 5.1g May 26] fair form when winning 6f maiden on good to soft going only start at 2 yrs: below that form in 2009: tried in headgear. *R. M. Beckett* **59**

CRIDDA BOY 3 ch.g. Mark of Esteem (IRE) 137 – Second Affair (IRE) 85 (Pursuit of Love 124) [2009 8.1m 10d 7m Jun 9] leggy gelding: no sign of ability. *A. G. Newcombe* **–**

CRIMEA (IRE) 3 b.g. Kheleyf (USA) 116 – Russian Countess (USA) 104 (Nureyev (USA) 131) [2009 5m* 5g^6 5m* p5g Nov 1] 120,000Y: lengthy, well-made gelding: half-brother to several winners, including smart 7f (at 2 yrs) and 11.5f winner Crown of Light (by Mtoto) and useful 7f and 8.5f winner Romanzof (by Kris): dam French 2-y-o 1m winner: fairly useful form: won maiden at Thirsk in June and handicap at Hamilton in July: form only on good to firm going: gelded after final start. *M. Johnston* **94**

CRIME SCENE (IRE) 6 b.g. Royal Applause 124 – Crime (USA) (Gulch (USA)) [2009 111: a10f^5 12d* 12m 12g^2 12m^6 10d* 12g 12g^6 16d^2 Nov 3] tall gelding: smart performer: better than ever in 2009, winning handicap at Nad Al Sheba (by 1¼ lengths from Engrupido) in January and, having left M. bin Shafya after fourth start, listed race at Newbury (beat Covert Ambition by length, dictating) in July: blinkered, excellent ¾-length second of 23 to Shocking in Melbourne Cup at Flemington final start: effective at 1¼m to 2m: acts on good to firm and good to soft going: has run well when sweating: sometimes tricky ride: last on all 3 starts at Goodwood, including twice at 6 yrs. *Saeed bin Suroor* **118**

Shadwell Beech House Stud Stakes (Steventon), Newbury—Ahmed Ajtebi drives home Crime Scene ahead of Godolphin's first string Covert Ambition (No.3); Traffic Guard (No.10) and Blue Monday are next

CRIME WRITER (USA) 3 b.g. Elusive Quality (USA) – Larrocha (IRE) 116 (Sadler's Wells (USA) 132) [2009 6m³ 7.5m² 7.2g* 7g 7g³ 7.1m⁶ 9.8g Aug 3] close-coupled gelding: seventh foal: closely related to useful 11f winner Western Adventure (by Gone West) and half-brother to 3 winners, notably very smart 9f to 1½m winner Razkalla (by Caerleon): dam, 1¼m and 1½m winner and third in Prix Vermeille, half-sister to Ardross: fairly useful performer: won maiden at Ayr in June: should be suited by 1m+: raced only on good/good to firm ground: sold £9,000, sent to Kuwait. *M. Johnston* **84**

CRIMSON FERN (IRE) 5 ch.m. Titus Livius (FR) 115 – Crimada (IRE) (Mukaddamah (USA) 125) [2009 104: p5g⁵ 5.2s 5.1g² 5m⁶ 5g Jun 6] lengthy, angular mare: useful handicapper: best effort at 5 yrs when nose second to Look Busy in listed race at Bath: pulled up in 'Dash' at Epsom final start (bled): strong traveller, best at 5f/6f: acts on polytrack, soft and good to firm going: versatile regarding tactics. *M. S. Saunders* **102**

CRIMSON FLAME (IRE) 6 b.g. Celtic Swing 138 – Wish List (IRE) 98 (Mujadil (USA) 119) [2009 –: p8.6g⁴ Dec 28] smallish, lightly-made gelding: very lightly raced nowadays: off 21 months, poor form sole 6-y-o start: should stay beyond 1m: acts on polytrack and firm ground: tried visored. *M. S. Tuck* **46**

CRIMSON MIST 3 b.g. Red Ransom (USA) – Lavinia Fontana (IRE) 116 (Sharpo 132) [2009 6d f6g⁶ 7d Jul 24] well-made gelding: poor form in maidens. *J. J. Quinn* **46**

CRIMSON MITRE 4 b.c. Bishop of Cashel 122 – Pink Champagne (Cosmonaut) [2009 73: f12g⁴ 12d p12g f14g² f12g* f12g 11.8m⁴ f12f⁵ Dec 17] sturdy colt: fair handicapper, better on all-weather: won at Southwell in July: stays 1¾m: acts on fibresand, good to firm and good to soft ground: tends to race freely up with pace. *J. Jay* **69 a77**

CRIMSON RIBBON (USA) 3 b.f. Lemon Drop Kid (USA) 131 – Victoria Cross (IRE) 101 (Mark of Esteem (IRE) 137) [2009 p9.5g³ 12m* 10.1m 10g⁵ p13g⁶ p10g Nov 13] compact filly: third foal: sister to 4-y-o Bronze Cannon and half-sister to fairly useful 2006 2-y-o 7f winner Valiance (by Horse Chestnut): dam, 7f winner who probably stayed 1¼m, out of smart performer up to 1¾m Glowing With Pride: fairly useful performer: won maiden at Newmarket in May: best effort when sixth in listed race at Lingfield fifth start: stays 13f: acts on polytrack and good to firm going. *J. H. M. Gosden* **92**

CRIMSON SKY (IRE) 3 b.c. Montjeu (IRE) 137 – Park Crystal (IRE) (Danehill (USA) 126) [2009 10s 10g* Oct 7] €575,000Y: third foal: dam unraced half-sister to Derby second Walk In The Park, out of Irish 1000 Guineas winner Classic Park: left debut form well behind when readily winning 23-runner maiden at Navan in October by 3 lengths from Chapter Nine, coming from some way off pace and going clear in final 1f: likely to stay 1½m: open to considerable improvement. *A. P. O'Brien, Ireland* **91 P**

CRIPSEY BROOK 11 ch.g. Lycius (USA) 124 – Duwon (IRE) 55 (Polish Precedent (USA) 131) [2009 70: 10m 12d⁶ 14.1m⁵ 14.6m⁴ 14.1m³ 14.1f⁴ 12g 14.1m 12.1m 14.1g⁶ 12.4d Oct 13] tall gelding: modest handicapper at best nowadays: effective at 1¼m, probably stays 2m: acts on firm and good to soft going: tried blinkered: formerly tongue tied: waited with. *K. G. Reveley* **62 d**

CRITERION 4 b.g. Dr Fong (USA) 128 – Film Script 105 (Unfuwain (USA) 131) [2009 85: p16g⁶ 16s 18g 16m p10m f8g⁴ Dec 27] tall gelding: fair handicapper nowadays: below form after reappearance: stays 2m: acts on polytrack, firm and good to soft going: tried in visor/cheekpieces: ungenuine. *Ian Williams* **77 §**

CRITICAL MOMENT (USA) 2 b.c. (Mar 1) Aptitude (USA) 128 – Rouwaki (USA) (Miswaki (USA) 124) [2009 7g³ 7m* 7v⁵ Oct 24] rangy colt: fourth foal: half-brother to 3-y-o Cornish Castle and 4-y-o Rattan: dam, US maiden, half-sister to US Grade 1 9f/1¼m winner Flute: progressive form: won maiden at Newbury in September by nose from Lay Claim: good 2¼ lengths fifth to Carnaby Street in Horris Hill Stakes at same course, strong at finish: will be suited by 1m: acts on heavy and good to firm ground: already useful, and capable of bettter still. *B. W. Hills* **98 p**

CRITICAL PATH (IRE) 3 b.f. Noverre (USA) 125 – Elemental 82 (Rudimentary (USA) 118) [2009 p8g⁴ 8g³ 10.1m* 10d⁶ 10d⁴ p10g⁵ Nov 13] sparely-made filly: third foal: half-sister to 2 winners, including 6f (including in Ireland at 2 yrs and in USA) winner Sovine (by Xaar): dam, maiden (stayed 1½m), half-sister to smart miler Safawan: fairly useful performer: best effort when winning maiden at Epsom in July: stays 1¼m: acts on polytrack, good to firm and good to soft going. *A. M. Balding* **81**

CRITICIZE (USA) 3 b.g. Mizzen Mast (USA) 121 – Euphonize (USA) (Seattle Slew (USA)) [2009 7d² 7.1g⁴ p8g⁴ Sep 8] tall gelding: third living foal: half-brother to US 6f winner Dulcet Tone (by Empire Maker): dam unraced daughter of smart French/US performer up to 1m Euphonic, herself closely related to Danehill: fair maiden: easily best effort on debut: sold 8,500 gns. *R. Charlton* **79**

CROCODILE BAY (IRE) 6 b.g. Spectrum (IRE) 126 – Shenkara (IRE) 79 (Night **75 d**
Shift (USA)) [2009 95d: f6s^2 f7g^2 f6g^5 f8g 6d^4 f7g 7.5m^6 8.3m 7.5m f7g^4 7.5g Aug 12]
good-topped, attractive gelding: has a quick action: useful handicapper at 5 yrs: on
downgrade: effective at 6f to 8.6f: acts on all-weather, soft and good to firm going: often
blinkered: none too consistent. *John A. Harris*

CROCUS ROSE 3 b.f. Royal Applause 124 – Crodelle (IRE) (Formidable (USA) 125) **84**
[2009 –: 10m^6 p11g^5 12g^3 14v^2 14.1m* p16g^3 14.6g* Oct 23] angular filly: fairly useful
handicapper: won at Salisbury in August and Doncaster in October: stays easy 2m: acts
on polytrack, heavy and good to firm going. *H. J. L. Dunlop*

CROESO CUSAN 4 b.f. Diktat 126 – Croeso Croeso 100 (Most Welcome 131) [2009 **68**
71: 8.1g 8d^6 10.2g 8.1d^4 8d 9.1v^2 10.2v^5 Nov 4] fair handicapper: stays 9f: acts on heavy
ground: inconsistent. *J. L. Spearing*

CROESO YNOL 3 ch.f. Medicean 128 – Croeso Croeso 100 (Most Welcome 131) **44**
[2009 6m 6g 7.1m^4 6.1d^6 7m^6 Sep 16] second foal: half-sister to 4-y-o Croeso Cusan:
dam 5f/6f winner: poor maiden: stays 7f. *J. L. Spearing*

CROFT BRIDGE 2 ch.g. (Apr 22) Avonbridge 123 – Aahgowangowan (IRE) 88 **53**
(Tagula (IRE) 116) [2009 5d 5s^5 6g p5.1g Oct 3] sturdy gelding: modest maiden: should
stay 6f: acts on soft going. *M. Dods*

CROISULTAN (IRE) 3 ch.c. Refuse To Bend (IRE) 128 – Zoudie 79 (Ezzoud (IRE) **104**
126) [2009 98: 6v^6 5.8s^2 5.8v* 7g 5g^3 5v 6s^4 5s^4 6s^4 7g Sep 27] good-topped colt: useful
performer: won 3-runner minor event at Navan in May by 3½ lengths from Sugar Free:
well beaten in listed race at Epsom (hung) next time: good efforts after when fourth, in
listed contests at Fairyhouse and Tipperary, and Phoenix Sprint Stakes at the Curragh
(2 lengths behind Girouette): best at 5f/6f: acts on polytrack and heavy going: tried
blinkered. *Liam McAteer, Ireland*

CROIX ROUGE (USA) 7 b.g. Chester House (USA) 123 – Rougeur (USA) (Blushing **68**
Groom (FR) 131) [2009 p12m^6 p16g p11f^6 Dec 16] smallish, good-topped gelding: raced
mainly in Spain since 2 yrs, winning 8 races at Mijas: off 19 months, fair form in Britain
in 2009: stays 13f: acts on polytrack/sand: tried blinkered. *R. J. Smith*

CROON 7 b.g. Sinndar (IRE) 134 – Shy Minstrel (USA) (The Minstrel (CAN) 135) **–**
[2009 11.6m p12m Oct 7] close-coupled gelding: one-time fairly useful handicapper:
unraced on Flat in 2008: well held at 7 yrs: tried in cheekpieces. *Andrew Turnell*

CROSBY JEMMA 5 ch.m. Lomitas 129 – Gino's Spirits 98 (Perugino (USA) 84) **–**
[2009 50: p8.6g Jan 19] modest maiden: well held sole 5-y-o start: should stay 1¼m:
raced only on polytrack and good ground or firmer. *M. E. Sowersby*

CROSSBOW CREEK 11 b.g. Lugana Beach 116 – Roxy River 38 (Ardross 134) **85**
[2009 92: p16g^6 p12.2g 11.5m 11.6f^5 12m* 14.1s^5 Oct 12] rangy, good-bodied gelding:
useful hurdler/smart chaser in his prime: fairly useful handicapper on Flat: won amateur
event at Ascot in September: stays 2m: acts on polytrack, good to firm and good to soft
ground: dropped out. *M. G. Rimell*

CROSSHARBOUR 5 b.h. Zamindar (USA) 116 – Docklands (USA) (Theatrical 128) **120**
[2009 119: 10g* 12g^3 Sep 13] big, well-made horse: very smart performer: won La Coupe
and Prix du Conseil de Paris, both at Longchamp, in 2008: reportedly suffered stress
fracture before successful reappearance in Prix Gontaut-Biron Hong Kong Jockey-Club
at Deauville in August by neck from Adelar, leading before home turn: ran well but found
less than seemed likely/wandered when 1¼ lengths third of 4 to Spanish Moon in Prix
Foy at Longchamp final start: effective at 1¼m/1½m: acted on soft and good to firm
going: to stand at French National Stud, Cercy la Tour, fee €1,300. *A. Fabre, France*

CROSS KEY (IRE) 2 b.f. (Apr 7) Trans Island 119 – Cayman Sunrise (IRE) 68 **55**
(Peintre Celebre (USA) 137) [2009 5v^4 6g^4 5d^5 Aug 19] third foal: half-sister to winning
sprinter in Italy by Indian Lodge: dam, maiden (stayed 1¼m), out of US Grade 3 9f
winner Sum: modest form in maidens, not knocked about second start: should stay 7f+.
R. A. Fahey

CROSS OF LORRAINE (IRE) 6 b.g. Pivotal 124 – My-Lorraine (IRE) 77 (Mac's **60**
Imp (USA) 116) [2009 69: 5g 6.1g 8d 7.5m^6 8m 7.5g 7.2s 7.5m^4 Aug 30] compact
gelding: modest handicapper nowadays: stays 7.5f: acts on all-weather, heavy and good
to firm ground: blinkered. *J. Wade*

CROSS REEF 4 b.f. Cape Cross (IRE) 129 – Mureefa (USA) 73 (Bahri (USA) 125) **64 d**
[2009 p7g 10m p9.5g^6 8.1g 11.7f f8g p8.6g 7.1v 7d Sep 15] 1,200 3-y-o: good-bodied
filly: second foal: half-sister to useful 1m (at 2 yrs) to 1¼m winner Habalwatan (by In
The Wings): dam ran twice (second at 1¼m): regressive maiden: may prove best short of
9.5f: best efforts on polytrack: tried in cheekpieces/visor. *R. A. Harris*

CROSS SECTION (USA) 3 b. or br.f. Cape Cross (IRE) 129 – Demure (Machiavellian (USA) 123) [2009 76p: 7m^5 6g^6 p7m^4 p8.6g^2 p8f^4 Dec 20] fair maiden: stays 8.6f: acts on polytrack: tried in cheekpieces. *E. F. Vaughan* **67**

CROSS THE BOSS (IRE) 2 b.g. (Jan 10) Cape Cross (IRE) 129 – Lady Salsa (IRE) (Gone West (USA)) [2009 7g Oct 23] 100/1, very green when well held in maiden at Doncaster. *P. C. Haslam* **–**

CROSS THE LINE (IRE) 7 b.g. Cape Cross (IRE) 129 – Baalbek 76 (Barathea (IRE) 127) [2009 71, a89: p8g^2 p8g^3 Apr 1] big gelding: fair handicapper: stays 1m: acts on polytrack, soft and good to firm ground: tried visored: usually held up: finds little. *A. P. Jarvis* **79**

CROWDED HOUSE 3 ch.c. Rainbow Quest (USA) 134 – Wiener Wald (USA) (Woodman (USA) 126) [2009 124p: 10.4g 12g^6 Jun 6] big, strong colt: impresses in appearance: very smart performer in 2008 when highest rated 2-y-o, winning Racing Post Trophy at Doncaster: didn't go on as expected at 3 yrs, only eighth behind Black Bear Island in Dante Stakes at York (scoped badly afterwards) before shaping with more encouragement when 8 lengths sixth to Sea The Stars in Derby at Epsom, quickening sharply from rear only to run into trouble/hang down camber: not seen after: should prove best at 1¼m/1½m: raced only on polytrack and good/good to firm going: usually waited with. *B. J. Meehan* **111 +**

CROWN AFFAIR (IRE) 3 b.f. Royal Applause 124 – Alyousufeya (IRE) 75 (Kingmambo (USA) 125) [2009 –: p7.1g^4 p8g^4 p8g 9m p8g Aug 15] workmanlike filly: modest maiden: seems to stay 1m: acts on polytrack, no form on turf. *J. W. Hills* **56**

CROWN CHOICE 4 b.g. King's Best (USA) 132 – Belle Allemande (CAN) (Royal Academy (USA) 130) [2009 78: p7g* p7g* 7m p7g 8g Oct 31] rangy, attractive gelding: useful performer: won maiden and handicap (much improved when beating Woodcote Place by 3¾ lengths) at Kempton in April: disappointing after: raced at 7f/1m: acts on polytrack: tongue tied final start. *W. R. Swinburn* **100**

CROWN (IRE) 2 b.f. (Mar 14) Royal Applause 124 – Bolivia (USA) (Distant View (USA) 126) [2009 5.1g^5 5m 5g* 5m* 5m 6g^5 7.1m^5 6.1m^4 7m Oct 2] 50,000F: lengthy filly: second foal: dam unraced half-sister to smart performers up to 1½m Bal Harbour and Bequeath: fairly useful performer: won maiden and minor event (4 ran, by 1¼ lengths from Red Avalanche), both at Windsor in May: creditable efforts after only when fifth in Cherry Hinton Stakes at Newmarket and listed event at Sandown: stays 7f: raced only on good/good to firm going: sold 18,000 gns. *R. Hannon* **86**

CROY (IRE) 4 b.f. Elnadim (USA) 128 – Flower Fairy (FR) (Fairy King (USA)) [2009 f6g f8g^5 Feb 10] fourth foal: half-sister to 1¼m winner King Halling (by Halling): dam unraced half-sister to smart French/US performer up to 10.5f Golden Arches: well held in maidens at Southwell (said to have finished lame second occasion). *S. Parr* **–**

CRUCIFORM (IRE) 3 b. or br.g. Cape Cross (IRE) 129 – Tshusick 81 (Dancing Brave (USA) 140) [2009 –: 7m Aug 28] good-topped ex-Irish-trained gelding: well held in maidens. *D. Nicholls* **–**

CRUIKADYKE 3 b.c. Kyllachy 129 – Shoshone (Be My Chief (USA) 122) [2009 88: 8.1m^6 8.1v 8.3g 10m^3 10.1g^6 8m* p8g 8m Sep 16] big, useful-looking colt: fairly useful performer: won claimer at Salisbury in July: stays 1m: acts on firm and good to soft going: sold £6,500, sent to Sweden. *P. F. I. Cole* **85**

CRUISE CONTROL 3 b.g. Piccolo 121 – Urban Dancer (IRE) 89 (Generous (IRE) 139) [2009 –: p6g^6 8.3g 7.1v 6.1g p8.6g p7.1g Sep 25] modest maiden: well beaten after reappearance. *R. J. Price* **53 d**

CRUISE DIRECTOR 9 b.g. Zilzal (USA) 137 – Briggsmaid 70 (Elegant Air 119) [2009 79: p13g p12.2g^3 f14g^4 Mar 3] heavy-topped gelding: fair performer: stays 1¾m: acts on all-weather, soft and good to firm going: fair hurdler, won in November. *Ian Williams* **72**

CRUNCHED 2 b.c. (Mar 12) Dubai Destination (USA) 127 – Amica 86 (Averti (IRE) 117) [2009 7s^5 8g^4 7.5m^3 p8.6g* Oct 31] £12,500Y: quite attractive colt: first foal: dam 6f (at 2 yrs) to 8.5f winner: fair performer: won 4-runner maiden at Wolverhampton: stays 8.6f: acts on polytrack and good to firm ground. *M. L. W. Bell* **72**

CRUSHING (IRE) 2 b.g. (Feb 23) Kheleyf (USA) 116 – Filmgame (IRE) 53 (Be My Guest (USA) 126) [2009 5m^4 6d^2 5m^6 6m 7m^5 p7g p5.1g p6g p8.6g^5 Dec 17] strong gelding: fair maiden: best effort second start, left T. D. Barron after fourth: stays 6f: acts on good to firm and good to soft going: tried in cheekpieces. *A. J. McCabe* **66**

CRUSH (IRE) 3 b.c. Kheleyf (USA) 116 – Premier Amour 111 (Salmon Leap (USA) 131) [2009 p7.1g^6 Apr 3] 7/1, slowly away and always behind in maiden at Wolverhampton: sent to Saudi Arabia. *D. M. Simcock* –

CRUX 7 b.g. Pivotal 124 – Penny Dip 86 (Cadeaux Genereux 131) [2009 53: 7m 7g^6 8.3m^6 9m^3 8d^3 8m Jun 30] rather leggy gelding: modest maiden: stays 9f: acts on polytrack, good to firm and good to soft ground. *R. E. Barr* 58

CRY ALOT BOY 6 ch.g. Spinning World (USA) 130 – Intellectuelle (Caerleon (USA) 132) [2009 p8g^6 10.4v^2 8g^6 10.4m^2 10.2m^6 10s* p10g^2 p10m^6 p10m Dec 16] workmanlike gelding: fair bumper winner: fairly useful handicapper on Flat: won at Leicester in July: stays 1¼m: unraced on firm going, acts on any other and polytrack: often slowly away/races freely. *K. A. Morgan* 83

CRY FOR THE MOON (USA) 3 b.g. Street Cry (IRE) 130 – Kafaf (USA) 78 (Zilzal (USA) 137) [2009 75: 12g* 14g^3 14.1f^3 14m^4 12m 12m^6 15m^5 Sep 29] lengthy gelding: fairly useful handicapper: won at Pontefract in April: stays 1¾m: acts on firm going: not straightforward: sold 35,000 gns, joined J. Culloty in Ireland, then gelded. *Mrs A. J. Perrett* 85

CRY OF FREEDOM (USA) 3 b.g. Street Cry (IRE) 130 – Tustarta (USA) 105 (Trempolino (USA) 135) [2009 96: p8g^5 10m Apr 15] strong gelding: useful performer at 2 yrs: well below form both starts in 2009: should stay 1m: acts on good to firm and good to soft going: tried blinkered. *M. Johnston* –

CRY OF TRUTH (IRE) 3 b.f. Danetime (IRE) 121 – Clandolly (IRE) 89 (Burslem 123) [2009 7m^6 7m 6m^4 6m Jun 3] €36,000Y, £1,000 2-y-o: sister to fairly useful 5f to 7f winner Abientot and half-sister to 3 winners, including Irish 6f/7f winner Clanboyo (by Marju): dam Irish 5f winner: modest maiden: raced only at 6f/7f on good to firm going. *D. W. Barker* 54

CRYSTAL B GOOD (USA) 3 b. or br.f. Successful Appeal (USA) 118 – Unbridled Run (USA) (Unbridled (USA) 128) [2009 p6g^6 p6g 7m^4 8g 6f^4 6g^2 p6g p6g Dec 31] leggy filly: second foal: half-sister to winner in USA by Tale of The Cat: dam US maiden half-sister to Kentucky Derby runner-up Tejano Run: modest maiden: stays 7f: raced only on polytrack and good going or firmer. *J. R. Best* 58

CRYSTAL BRIDGE 2 b.f. (Feb 12) Avonbridge 123 – Heaven-Liegh-Grey 90 (Grey Desire 115) [2009 5.1g 5.1m^6 5m p8.6g p8.6g Dec 19] £2,000Y: half-sister to several winners, including fairly useful 1m/9f winner French Connection (by Tirol): dam best at 5f: soundly beaten in maidens: tried in cheekpieces. *Mrs L. Williamson* –

CRYSTAL CAPELLA 4 b.f. Cape Cross (IRE) 129 – Crystal Star 100 (Mark of Esteem (IRE) 137) [2009 116: 10.4g* 10g^5 12m^2 Oct 17] good-bodied filly: smart performer: further progress when winning totepool Middleton Stakes at York in May by 119

totepool Middleton Stakes, York—
Crystal Capella (blaze) just gets the better of Dar Re Mi in a grandstand finish

short head from Dar Re Mi: off 5 months after: better effort on return when short-head second to Ashalanda in Pride Stakes at Newmarket final start: stays 1½m: yet to race on heavy going, acts on any other turf and polytrack. *Sir Michael Stoute*

CRYSTAL CROWN (IRE) 5 b.g. Grand Lodge (USA) 125 – Top Crystal (IRE) **–** (Sadler's Wells (USA) 132) [2009 67: 8m May 22] well-made gelding: maiden, lightly raced: well held sole 5-y-o start: stays 1¼m: tried tongue tied. *B. G. Powell*

CRYSTAL FEATHER 3 ch.f. Monsieur Bond (IRE) 120 – Prince's Feather (IRE) 77 **68** (Cadeaux Genereux 131) [2009 –p: f7g^3 f7g^3 p10g^6 p8.6g* 10.1g^6 9m* 9.8g^3 Aug 31] leggy filly: fair performer: won minor event at Wolverhampton in May and handicap at Yarmouth in August: stays 1¼m: acts on all-weather and good to firm going. *E. F. Vaughan*

CRYSTAL GALE (IRE) 2 gr.f. (Jan 17) Verglas (IRE) 118 – Mango Groove (IRE) 67 **71** (Unfuwain (USA) 131) [2009 6m^3 6m 7g^3 8g^3 8.1d^5 Sep 4] 18,000Y: workmanlike filly: first foal: dam, maiden (raced only at 1¼m), out of May Hill Stakes winner Solar Crystal: fair maiden: stays 1m: acts on good to firm ground. *W. J. Knight*

CRYSTAL GLASS 2 b.g. (Apr 27) Exceed And Excel (AUS) 126 – Cumbrian Crystal **–** 69 (Mind Games 121) [2009 7g 6s f7g^6 Nov 17] well beaten in maidens: subsequently gelded. *T. D. Easterby*

CRYSTALLIZE 3 b.g. Bertolini (USA) 125 – Adamas (IRE) 75 (Fairy King (USA)) **68** [2009 64: p8g 7.1m^6 7m^5 p7.1g* 7g* 7.1g^4 7m^4 6g p7.1g p7m^4 p7m^6 p7.1g^4 Dec 11] strong gelding: fair handicapper: won at Wolverhampton and Yarmouth, both in May: stays 1m: acts on polytrack and soft going. *A. B. Haynes*

CRYSTAL MOMENTS 3 b.f. Haafhd 129 – Celestial Choir 94 (Celestial Storm **96** (USA) 132) [2009 85: p6g^2 6f 5m 6g^2 6g^5 6g^4 p6g^4 7v* 6s Nov 7] attractive filly: useful performer: won handicap at Newbury in October: stays 7f: acts on polytrack and any turf going. *E. A. L. Dunlop*

CRYSTAL PRINCE 5 b.g. Marju (IRE) 127 – Crystal Ring (IRE) 83 (Kris 135) [2009 **–** 79: 11.6g Jun 15] strong, good-bodied gelding: maiden handicapper: well held only start in 2009: best short of 1½m: acts on good to firm going: tried blinkered/in cheekpieces. *C. E. Longsdon*

CRYSTANY (IRE) 4 b.f. Green Desert (USA) 127 – Crystal Music (USA) 114 **96** (Nureyev (USA) 131) [2009 98: 6d 6.1m^5 6m^6 Jun 12] sturdy, compact filly: useful performer: creditable fifth to Lesson In Humility in listed race at Nottingham, best effort in 2009: stays 7f: acts on polytrack and good to firm going: sometimes slowly away: blinkered final outing. *E. A. L. Dunlop*

CUCCINELLO (IRE) 6 b.m. Makbul 104 – Costa Verde 77 (King of Spain 121) **–** [2009 9m Jun 6] of no account. *K. W. Hogg, Isle of Man*

CUCKOO ROCK (IRE) 2 b.g. (Apr 1) Refuse To Bend (IRE) 128 – Ringmoor Down **–** 113 (Pivotal 124) [2009 7.1m 8.1m Sep 10] well held in maidens. *J. G. Portman*

CUIS GHAIRE (IRE) 3 b.f. Galileo (IRE) 134 – Scribonia (IRE) (Danehill (USA) **113** 126) [2009 106: 8f^2 8v 7m Oct 17] strong, sturdy filly: smart performer: best effort when 1½ lengths second to Ghanaati in 1000 Guineas at Newmarket, racing to fore but becoming unbalanced in Dip: excuses both starts after, in Irish 1000 Guineas at the Curragh (heavy ground) and Challenge Stakes at Newmarket (off nearly 5 months, wintry in coat): stayed 1m: acted on firm going: hung left fourth outing at 2 yrs: visits Sea The Stars. *J. S. Bolger, Ireland*

CULLYBACKEY (IRE) 4 ch.f. Golan (IRE) 129 – Leitrim Lodge (IRE) 64 (Classic **55** Music (USA)) [2009 57p: 8.5m 9.1g^6 12.1g p6g^5 p7m p6m^6 Nov 26] modest maiden: left G. A. Swinbank after third start: stays 9f: acts on good to soft ground: tried blinkered. *J. R. Boyle*

CULTIVAR 2 b.c. (Mar 9) Xaar 132 – New Orchid (USA) 106 (Quest For Fame 127) **77 p** [2009 7m^3 7m^6 Sep 1] big, deep-girthed colt: second foal: half-brother to 4-y-o African Rose: dam, 1¼m winner, half-sister to Dewhurst winner Distant Music: better effort in maidens when 5½ lengths third to Pounced (subsequent Grade 2 winner) at Newbury, slowly away: jinked under pressure final start: remains capable of better. *B. W. Hills*

CULTURED PRIDE (IRE) 2 ch.f. (Apr 5) King's Best (USA) 132 – Cultured Pearl **77** (IRE) 72 (Lammtarra (USA) 134) [2009 6m 6g* 6m^5 7d^5 8m^3 6.5m Sep 25] 18,000Y: good-topped filly: fifth foal: sister to fairly useful 2005 2-y-o 6f winner Culture Queen and half-sister to 3 winners, including 1½m/1¾m winner Pearl's A Singer (by Spectrum): dam, maiden (should have stayed 1¼m), out of smart miler Culture Vulture: fair performer: won maiden at Goodwood in June: creditable third in nursery at same course: stays 1m: acts on good to firm going. *R. Hannon*

CUMANA BAY 3 b.f. Dansili 127 – Mayaro Bay 108 (Robellino (USA) 127) [2009 72p: p7g^2 8m^2 7m* 8.3g^2 8g* 7g^6 7m^5 8.3f^2 7m p7g^5 Oct 29] sturdy filly: fairly useful handicapper: won at Newbury in May and Newmarket in June: held form well otherwise: stays 1m: unraced on heavy going, acts on any other turf and polytrack. *R. Hannon* **90**

CUMBRIAN GOLD (USA) 3 ch.g. Gilded Time (USA) – Brackenber (USA) (Lycius (USA) 124) [2009 –: f8g Feb 3] well held all starts: tried visored: signs of temperament. *B. Smart* **–**

CUMBRIAN KNIGHT (IRE) 11 b.g. Presenting 120 – Crashrun (Crash Course 128) [2009 –, a69: f16d f14g Jan 27] fair handicapper in 2008: well held at 11 yrs: stays 16.5f: acts on all-weather, best turf effort on good ground: usually amateur ridden: modest hurdler. *J. M. Jefferson* **–**

CUMULUS NIMBUS 2 ch.c. (Mar 12) Muhtathir 126 – Supreme Talent (Desert King (IRE) 129) [2009 7g* 7.5g^2 7.1g 7.1d^3 7m^3 Oct 13] €70,000Y: sturdy colt: second foal: dam, French 1m/1¼m winner, closely related to smart Irish 2000 2-y-o 6f/7f winner Honours List: fairly useful performer: won maiden at Lingfield in July: ran creditably after when placed in minor events: will stay 1m. *R. Hannon* **86**

CUNNING PLAN (IRE) 2 ch.c. (Feb 24) Bachelor Duke (USA) 122 – Madamaa (IRE) 88 (Alzao (USA) 117) [2009 7m 6g^6 Oct 20] very green in maidens at Goodwood and Yarmouth (better effort) 3 weeks apart. *P. W. Chapple-Hyam* **51**

CUPID'S GLORY 7 b.g. Pursuit of Love 124 – Doctor's Glory (USA) 91 (Elmaamul (USA) 125) [2009 92: 9.9g^5 p9.5g p12m Nov 26] rather lengthy, good-bodied gelding: fairly useful handicapper: below form after reappearance: stays 11.5f: acts on polytrack, soft and good to firm going: tried blinkered/in cheekpieces. *G. L. Moore* **84**

Mrs J. S. Bolger & Mr D. H. Dobson's "Cuis Ghaire"

CURACAO 3 b.g. Sakhee (USA) 136 – Bourbonella (Rainbow Quest (USA) 134) [2009 69: p11g² p12g³ 11m⁵ 12d* 14.1m* 14g³ f16g⁴ 16m³ Sep 30] strong gelding: fairly useful handicapper: won at Salisbury (2) in July: barely stays 2m: acts on polytrack, good to firm and good to soft going. *Mrs A. J. Perrett* **88**

CURLEW (IRE) 3 b.g. Cape Cross (IRE) 129 – Billbill (USA) (Storm Cat (USA)) [2009 8.3m Jun 30] 5/4, shaped as if badly in need of run when last in maiden at Hamilton: sold £3,500, joined F. Hollis. *M. Johnston* **–**

CURTAIN CALL (FR) 4 b.c. Sadler's Wells (USA) 132 – Apsara (FR) (Darshaan 133) [2009 116: 10v* 9.3s⁶ 12m⁴ 10.4g⁴ 10s² p12m Sep 5] strong, close-coupled colt: smart performer: won High Chaparral EBF Mooresbridge Stakes at the Curragh in May by 3 lengths from Famous Name, idling/hanging left: good efforts after when 3 lengths fourth to Spanish Moon in Grand Prix de Saint-Cloud and 1¼ lengths second to Casual Conquest in Royal Whip Stakes at the Curragh on third/fifth outings: put down after rupturing tendons in September Stakes at Kempton: needed good test at 1¼m, and stayed 1½m: acted on heavy and good to firm ground. *L. M. Cumani* **118**

CURTAINS 2 b.f. (Feb 8) Dubawi (IRE) 129 – Voile (IRE) 102 (Barathea (IRE) 127) [2009 5.3m³ 5.1m³ 6m² 6g*dis 6f⁵ 6g⁴ Jun 27] £26,000 2-y-o: first foal: dam 2-y-o 6f winner: fairly useful performer: first past post in maiden at Brighton (disqualified after failing dope test) in June: better form both starts after, fifth to Habaayib in Albany Stakes at Royal Ascot and fourth to Jira in listed event at Newmarket: likely to stay 7f. *S. Dow* **89**

CUSTODY (IRE) 3 b.g. Fusaichi Pegasus (USA) 130 – Shahtoush (IRE) 120 (Alzao (USA) 117) [2009 87: 10.9g⁵ 9.9m⁶ p12m³ 10.2s Oct 7] good-topped gelding: just fair maiden at 3 yrs: stays 11f: acts on polytrack and heavy going: often in headgear: has found little: one to treat with caution: sold 7,000 gns. *Sir Michael Stoute* **79 §**

CUT AND THRUST (IRE) 3 b.g. Haafhd 129 – Ego 107 (Green Desert (USA) 127) [2009 74: p7g* p8g⁶ p8g² p8g 7d p7f Dec 21] lengthy, useful-looking gelding: fairly useful handicapper: won at Kempton in January: left M. Jarvis 5,000 gns prior to final start: stays 1m: acts on polytrack, lightly raced on turf: usually in cheekpieces. *M. Wellings* **80**

CUTE ASS (IRE) 4 b.f. Fath (USA) 116 – John's Ballad (IRE) (Ballad Rock 122) [2009 94: 5m² Jun 3] small, sturdy filly: useful handicapper: creditable second only start at 4 yrs: speedy, and best at 5f: acts on good to firm and good to soft going: visored once: sold 33,000 gns in December, reportedly in foal to Dubai Destination. *K. R. Burke* **99**

CUTHBERT (IRE) 2 ch.c. (Mar 29) Bertolini (USA) 125 – Tequise (IRE) 97 (Victory Note (USA) 120) [2009 6m³ 6d² 7g⁴ 6.1d 7d⁶ 7m³ p7m p7m⁵ p7g* Dec 31] €11,000F, 11,000Y: first living foal: dam Irish 1m/1¼m winner: fair performer: improved when winning maiden at Lingfield in December: should stay 1m: acts on polytrack, good to firm and good to soft ground: blinkered seventh/eighth starts. *W. Jarvis* **73**

CUTLASS BAY (UAE) 3 b.c. Halling (USA) 133 – Dunnes River (USA) 84 (Danzig (USA)) [2009 10s* 10s* May 12] fourth foal: brother to smart 7f (including at 2 yrs) to 1½m (King Edward VII Stakes) winner Boscobel and half-brother to smart 2005 2-y-o 1m winner Crested (by Fantastic Light), later smart 1m/9f winner in USA: dam, 1m winner on only start, out of smart French/US 1m/9f performer Elizabeth Bay: unbeaten in maiden at Argentan at 2 yrs, minor event at Fontainebleau in March and Prix Greffulhe at Saint-Cloud (beat stable-companion Cavalryman ½ length, leading over 1f out) in May: will stay 1½m: looked set to do better still but reportedly injured in training in August and missed rest of year. *A. Fabre, France* **113 +**

CUTS BOTH WAYS (USA) 2 b.g. (Apr 3) Johannesburg (USA) 127 – Wise Investor (USA) (Belong To Me (USA)) [2009 6m⁴ p7m 8.1d 7m³ Oct 26] modest maiden: stays 7f: tried blinkered: possibly not straightforward. *P. F. I. Cole* **52**

CUT THE CACKLE (IRE) 3 b.f. Danetime (IRE) 121 – Alexander Anapolis (IRE) 94 (Spectrum (IRE) 126) [2009 86: 5g⁶ p6g² 6m⁶ 6m 5g⁴ 6g² p6g⁵ p6g⁵ Nov 5] good-topped filly: fairly useful handicapper: best at 5f/easy 6f: acts on polytrack, good to firm and good to soft going. *P. Winkworth* **83**

CWMNI 3 b.f. Auction House (USA) 120 – Sontime 65 (Son Pardo 107) [2009 55: p7g⁶ f7g⁴ p10g 7f⁴ 7.1m 6.1g 5.7g* 6.1d 6.1d Sep 4] modest performer: won seller at Bath in July: stays 7f: acts on polytrack. *B. Palling* **56**

CWM RHONDDA (USA) 4 b.f. Gulch (USA) – Frayne (USA) (Red Ransom (USA)) [2009 64: p8g 8.3m⁵ 10.1m* 10.1g* 12m⁴ 10.1g* 9.8m⁵ 10.1m Sep 16] tall filly: fairly useful handicapper: won at Yarmouth in May (2) and July: best around 1¼m: acts on soft and good to firm going: tried tongue tied. *P. W. Chapple-Hyam* **80**

CYAN EYED 2 b.f. (Mar 11) Orpen (USA) 116 – Morale (Bluebird (USA) 125) [2009 **67**
7s 6.5m p5g^{2} Oct 22] 22,000F, £30,000Y: sturdy, lengthy filly: sixth foal: sister to fairly useful 2005 2-y-o 5f winner Clare Hills and half-sister to 2 winners, including useful Irish 9.5f winner Hoffman (by Dr Devious): dam French maiden: fair form: second in claimer at Kempton: should stay 7f: sold 8,500 gns. *Tom Dascombe*

CYBER SPACE 5 b.g. Medicean 128 – Coyaima (GER) 100 (Night Shift (USA)) **58**
[2009 p8g p7.1g 10.1g p10g^{4} Aug 1] compact gelding: modest maiden: stays 1¼m: raced on polytrack and good ground. *B. J. McMath*

CYBORG 5 ch.g. Halling (USA) 133 – Ciboure 74 (Norwick (USA) 125) [2009 79: **87**
11.6g^{4} 12m^{5} 12m^{3} 12m^{3} 13.3g* 16d^{5} 12g^{3} 14.8g^{5} p12m^{4} Oct 12] big, rangy gelding: fairly useful handicapper: won at Newbury in July: stays 2m: acts on polytrack and good to firm ground: sold 36,000 gns, joined Charles Byrnes, Ireland. *D. R. C. Elsworth*

CYFLYMDER (IRE) 3 b.g. Mujadil (USA) 119 – Nashwan Star (IRE) 68 (Nashwan **100**
(USA) 135) [2009 75: p7g* p7g 6.1m^{4} 7.1f* 7m* 7.1m* 8.1g^{2} 7m^{4} 7.1g^{3} 7.6m^{2} 7d 7s Nov 7] smallish gelding: useful handicapper: much improved in 2009, winning at Lingfield in March, Sandown and Newmarket in June, and Sandown (by length from Maswerte) in July: several good efforts after: stays 1m: acts on polytrack, firm and soft going: badly hampered and unseated rider early on penultimate outing: reliable. *R. Hannon*

CYFRWYS (IRE) 8 b.m. Foxhound (USA) 103 – Divine Elegance (IRE) (College **46**
Chapel 122) [2009 55: p8g^{6} p7g p7.1g 7.1g 8.1g May 26] close-coupled mare: poor performer nowadays: stays easy 1m: acts on all-weather, good to firm and good to soft ground: sometimes visored/in cheekpieces: tried tongue tied: usually races prominently: carries head high. *B. Palling*

CYGNET 3 b.c. Dansili 127 – Ballet Princess (Muhtarram (USA) 125) [2009 85p: **92 p**
10.1m^{2} Sep 16] good-bodied colt: fairly useful form in just 3 races: best effort when second in handicap at Yarmouth, only outing at 3 yrs, still green and finishing strongly: will stay 1½m: type to progress in 2010. *L. M. Cumani*

CYGNET COMMITTEE (IRE) 2 gr.f. (Mar 4) Kheleyf (USA) 116 – Forest Light **49**
(IRE) 69 (Rainbow Quest (USA) 134) [2009 5d 7m 6g 5g^{5} 6m^{4} 7m^{3} 6g^{4} 5m 6.1s 7g^{6} 7d Oct 27] €6,500Y, £15,000 2-y-o: sturdy, lengthy filly: third foal: dam 12.6f winner: poor maiden: stays 7f: acts on good to firm going: tried in cheekpieces, usually blinkered. *J. S. Wainwright*

CYRIL THE SQUIRREL 5 b.g. Cyrano de Bergerac 120 – All Done (Northern State **–**
(USA) 91) [2009 58: p10g May 4] lengthy, angular gelding: maiden: well held sole 5-y-o start: stays 1½m: raced on polytrack: tried in cheekpieces/blinkers. *Karen George*

D

DAAWEITZA 6 ch.g. Daawe (USA) 103 – Chichen Itza (Shareef Dancer (USA) 135) **91**
[2009 93: 10.3g 8m 7m 8.1g^{6} 7.5g^{3} 7m 8m^{2} 7.9m^{2} 7.9g^{4} 6g 6g^{5} 7.6g 10m* 8g^{5} p9.5g 8m^{2} **a80**
10.2d 8.3m^{4} p12.2g^{5} p16.5g^{3} f12f^{3} Dec 12] sturdy gelding: fairly useful handicapper, better on turf: won ladies event at Redcar in August: good efforts when in frame after: stays 16.5f, effective at much shorter: acts on all-weather, firm and soft going: effective with/without headgear. *B. Ellison*

DABBERS RIDGE (IRE) 7 b.h. Indian Ridge 123 – Much Commended 100 (Most **83 d**
Welcome 131) [2009 109d: p7.1g 8m 7.1m^{4} 7d f7g 7g* p7.1g^{3} 7f* 9m^{6} 8m p8g^{6} p7g^{4} 7.2v f7m p7m^{5} p9.5g Dec 11] rather leggy horse: fairly useful performer: won claimers in June and July (apprentices), both at Redcar: well below form after: best up to 7.6f: acts on firm and soft going: tried in cheekpieces/blinkers: usually held up: not an easy ride. *I. W. McInnes*

DA BOMBER (IRE) 4 b.g. Tagula (IRE) 116 – Talahari (IRE) (Roi Danzig (USA)) **57**
[2009 58: 8.1v 8.1g 7.9m p9.5g p8.6g Dec 14] tall gelding: modest maiden: may prove best around 1m. *J. W. Unett*

DADDY COOL 5 b.g. Kyllachy 129 – Addicted To Love 73 (Touching Wood (USA) **–**
127) [2009 –: p5m Jan 9] sturdy gelding: no form since 2007: tried in headgear. *W. G. M. Turner*

DADDY'S GIFT (IRE) 3 b.f. Trans Island 119 – Lady Corduff (IRE) 78 (Titus Livius (FR) 115) [2009 84: p6g^{2} p6g* 7s 6m 6m^{3} 6m^{5} 6m 7m^{5} 7m^{6} p6m p6g p8g^{3} p6g* Dec 2] big, workmanlike filly: useful handicapper: improved to win at Kempton in March and December: best at 6f: acts on polytrack, soft and good to firm going: visored ninth outing: tactically versatile. *R. Hannon* **95**

DADO MUSH 6 b.g. Almushtarak (IRE) 122 – Princess of Spain (King of Spain 121) [2009 –, a83: f8g 8.1m p9.5g f8g f12f^{3} f8f Dec 17] just modest handicapper nowadays: seemingly stays 1½m: best efforts on fibresand: tried visored, usually wears cheekpieces. *T. T. Clement* **– a55**

DAFEEF 2 b.c. (Feb 13) Medicean 128 – Almahab (USA) (Danzig (USA)) [2009 6g^{2} 6m* Aug 29] smallish, strong colt: second foal: half-brother to 3-y-o Mutamaashi: dam unraced half-sister to 3-y-o Almiqdaad and smart 6f/7f performer Munaddam: promising both starts in maidens, winning at Newmarket comfortably by 3¼ lengths from Lean Machine despite pulling hard and veering right: should stay 7f/1m: already useful, and capable of better still. *Saeed bin Suroor* **97 p**

DAFT LAD 2 b. or br.c. (Mar 26) Danbird (AUS) – Stolen Melody 74 (Robellino (USA) 127) [2009 5m 5d f5g 5m 5g 6g Aug 31] close-coupled colt: poor maiden: visored last 3 starts. *L. A. Mullaney* **45**

DAGGERMAN 4 ch.g. Daggers Drawn (USA) 114 – Another Mans Cause (FR) (Highest Honor (FR) 124) [2009 68?: p12.2g f12g p8g Feb 25] small gelding: maiden: well held in 2009. *R. Curtis* **–**

DAHAAM 2 b.c. (Mar 4) Red Ransom (USA) – Almansoora (USA) 78 (Bahri (USA) 125) [2009 7.1g^{2} p8g^{2} p8f* Oct 14] good-topped colt: first foal: dam, 2-y-o 7f winner, half-sister to dam of Breeders' Cup Filly & Mare Turf winner Lahudood, out of useful close relative to Nayef and half-sister to Nashwan and Unfuwain: fairly useful form: made all in maiden at Kempton by ½ length from Robust Wish: barely stays 1m: hung right second start: has left Godolphin. *Saeed bin Suroor* **80**

DAHAKAA 2 ch.c. (Feb 22) Bertolini (USA) 125 – Dorrati (USA) (Dubai Millennium 140) [2009 5m^{3} p6g* Aug 10] good-bodied colt: first foal: dam unraced half-sister to smart performer up to 1¼m Baharah out of Ribblesdale Stakes winner Bahr: fairly useful form: favourite, won maiden at Wolverhampton by 1¼ lengths from Wellmarked, making all but wayward (swerved badly right/flashed tail): sold £6,000 in December. *M. A. Jarvis* **81**

DAHAMA 3 b.f. Green Desert (USA) 127 – Darling Flame (USA) 101 (Capote (USA)) [2009 66: f7g^{4} 6g Jun 16] short-backed filly: fair maiden at 2 yrs: well held both outings in 2009, upset in stall latter occasion (tongue tied). *C. E. Brittain* **–**

DAHES (IRE) 2 b.c. (Apr 6) Azamour (IRE) 130 – Delphie Queen (IRE) 104 (Desert Sun 120) [2009 6m^{5} 7.5g a6f^{3} Dec 11] €45,000Y, £27,000 2-y-o: small, sturdy colt: first foal: dam 6f (in Ireland at 2 yrs)/7f winner: modest form in maidens at Hamilton and, having left B. Smart after next start, Jebel Ali: should stay 7f. *A. Al Raihe, UAE* **56**

DAILY DOUBLE 3 gr.g. Needwood Blade 117 – Coffee To Go (Environment Friend 128) [2009 63: p7g^{5} p7g^{5} p8g* 10g^{3} p8g^{6} 8.5g 10m p10g 8f^{2} Jun 24] modest performer: won claimer at Lingfield in March: claimed to join Mrs H. Manners final start: stays 1m: acts on polytrack and firm ground: tried blinkered: usually held up. *D. K. Ivory* **63**

DAILY PLANET (IRE) 3 ch.g. Titus Livius (FR) 115 – Flattering News (USA) 77 (Pleasant Colony (USA)) [2009 38§: 7f Jul 23] stocky gelding: temperamental maiden: said to have bled when pulled up only outing in 2009: tried visored/in cheekpieces. *B. W. Duke* **– §**

DAISY BROWN 2 b.f. (Apr 8) Exceed And Excel (AUS) 126 – Hazy Heights 56 (Shirley Heights 130) [2009 5g^{5} 6m 5g^{2} 5m^{4} 5g^{6} 5m^{6} 6.1s Oct 7] £3,000Y: plain filly: fifth foal: half-sister to 4-y-o Fortunella: dam 1m winner: modest maiden: should stay 6f: acts on good to firm going. *N. Tinkler* **50**

DAISY MOSES (IRE) 3 br.f. Mull of Kintyre (USA) 114 – Starring (FR) 74 (Ashkalani (IRE) 128) [2009 70: 5m 7.1v p6g f6g^{6} Jul 14] fair performer at best: should stay 6f: acts on good to soft going: sold 1,500 gns in October. *D. Nicholls* **70 d**

DAISYS FANTASY 4 br.f. Diktat 126 – Double Fantasy 83 (Mind Games 121) [2009 f8g^{6} Feb 10] second foal: dam 2-y-o 5f winner: 33/1, tailed off in maiden at Southwell (very green). *S. Parr* **–**

DAJEN 3 b.c. Kyllachy 129 – Eau Rouge 77 (Grand Lodge (USA) 125) [2009 6s 6g p7g^{6} p7m^{4} Nov 21] 28,000Y: good-bodied colt: fourth foal: dam 5f winner: fair form in maiden/handicap last 2 starts: stays 7f: best efforts on polytrack. *D. M. Simcock* **71**

DAKIYAH (IRE) 5 b.m. Observatory (USA) 131 – Darariyna (IRE) 80 (Shirley Heights 130) [2009 89: 11.6g4 9g p12g* 12g3 14m6 p12m5 Nov 29] workmanlike mare: fairly useful handicapper: won at Kempton in June: stays 1½m: acts on polytrack and soft ground: usually wears cheekpieces. *Mrs L. J. Mongan* **89**

DAKOTA HILLS 3 ch.g. Danehill Dancer (IRE) 117 – Karla June (Unfuwain (USA) 131) [2009 73: p7g p6g Nov 25] tall, angular gelding: maiden: off 11 months and gelded, little impact in 2009: stays 6f: acts on polytrack and firm going. *J. R. Best* **63**

DALAROSSIE 4 br.g. Kyllachy 129 – Damalis (IRE) 106 (Mukaddamah (USA) 125) [2009 71: 5m 5f 5m6 6d3 6g5 6m 5m6 5m2 5g 5g2 5g4 a6g4 Dec 13] quite attractive gelding: modest handicapper: sold from E. Alston £1,800 before final start: stays 6f: acts on polytrack, firm and good to soft going: often races prominently: tried blinkered (ran poorly): possibly not straightforward. *Madeleine Smith, Sweden* **64**

DALEPAK FLYER (IRE) 3 ch.c. Noverre (USA) 125 – Hartstown House (IRE) 83 (Primo Dominie 121) [2009 56: p6g5 p7.1g4 7.1m f6g p6g Jun 29] smallish colt: modest maiden handicapper: stays easy 7f: acts on polytrack and firm going: tried blinkered/in cheekpieces: sold 2,500 gns in July. *Paul Mason* **59**

DALESWAY 3 b.g. Muhtarram (USA) 125 – Si Si Si (Lomitas 129) [2009 –: 8d3 8m6 Aug 16] leggy gelding: fair maiden: shaped as though amiss latter start in 2009: bred to stay 1¼m+: sold £800. *R. A. Fahey* **69**

DALLOOL 8 b.g. Unfuwain (USA) 131 – Sardonic 105 (Kris 135) [2009 60+: p16g3 Feb 24] lightly raced on Flat since 2004 (modest hurdler/poor chaser): modest form when third in handicap at Lingfield sole start in 2009: stays 2m: acts on polytrack and good to soft ground: visored/tongue tied in 2006. *P. M. Phelan* **60**

DALMUNZIE (IRE) 3 ch.f. Choisir (AUS) 126 – Berenice (ITY) (Marouble 116) [2009 6g 8g Jun 9] 29,000F, 42,000Y: half-sister to several winners, including Irish 6f winner (including at 2 yrs) Berenica (by College Chapel) and 6f (in Ireland at 2 yrs) to 11f (in Italy) winner The Bomber Liston (by Perugino), both useful: dam unraced: well held in maidens at Catterick and Redcar. *J. J. Quinn* **–**

DALRADIAN (IRE) 3 b.g. Dansili 127 – Aethra (USA) 89 (Trempolino (USA) 135) [2009 78: p8g* 7s 8.1g2 8m6 p8g* 8.1m p8m3 Jul 15] big, strong gelding: useful performer on all-weather, fairly useful on turf: won maiden in March and handicap in May, both at Lingfield: creditable close third to Tudor Key in minor event at same course final start (gelded after): stays 1m: acts on polytrack, best turf effort on good ground: often travels strongly held up. *W. J. Knight* **82 a96**

DALRYMPLE (IRE) 3 ch.g. Daylami (IRE) 138 – Dallaah 94 (Green Desert (USA) 127) [2009 p8.6g6 p12g 10g* 11.6m 10m5 10m 7g6 p12g 9m 10d6 11.9d p12m Nov 27] smallish gelding: modest performer: left J. Osborne prior to winning claimer at Windsor (left N. King) in April: well below form last 6 starts, leaving Ian Williams after first occasion (gelded after third): stays 1¼m: acts on polytrack and good to firm ground: tried visored: tongue tied last 2 outings: modest form in juvenile hurdles. *M. Madgwick* **58 d**

DALTABAN (FR) 5 b.g. Rainbow Quest (USA) 134 – Daltaiyma (IRE) (Doyoun 124) [2009 –: 18g 15.8s f8g f12f6 Dec 11] lengthy ex-French-trained gelding: well held on Flat in Britain (fair but moody juvenile hurdler in 2007/8): tried blinkered/visored. *P. Salmon* **–**

DAMANIYAT GIRL (USA) 3 ch.f. Elusive Quality (USA) – Dabaweyaa 118 (Shareef Dancer (USA) 135) [2009 93p: 7m2 7m5 8m 7.1g2 8m4 8g2 8m 6m* Oct 16] tall, useful-looking filly: useful performer: dropped in trip, improved when winning listed race at Newmarket in October by head from Vitoria, quickening well to lead final 1f: may prove best at 6f: acts on polytrack and good to firm going (unraced on softer than good): blinkered last 5 starts: joined E. Harty in USA. *W. J. Haggas* **108**

DAMASCUS GOLD 5 b.h. Thowra (FR) – Damasquiner 56 (Casteddu 111) [2009 69: 11m 16d Oct 11] workmanlike horse: maiden: well held in 2009: usually wears cheekpieces/blinkers. *Miss Z. C. Davison* **–**

DAME ANOUSKA (IRE) 3 b.f. Exceed And Excel (AUS) 126 – True Joy (IRE) (Zilzal (USA) 137) [2009 7m2 8d4 8s5 9d2 9.8f5 7f2 a9g2d 8s* Nov 13] seventh foal: half-sister to several winners, notably useful 7f to 9f winner Nans Joy (by In The Wings): dam once-raced half-sister to Green Desert: fair performer: second in maiden at Catterick on debut, only start in Britain: held form in France afterwards, winning women jockeys claimer at Maisons-Laffitte (wore cheekpieces) in November: stays 9f: acts on all-weather and any ground on turf. *E. J. O'Neill* **76**

DAME SHANAKILL (USA) 2 ch.f. (Feb 24) Mr Greeley (USA) 122 – Innovate (USA) (Relaunch (USA)) [2009 p7m Oct 26] $125,000Y: fourth foal: half-sister to 3 winners in USA: dam US 8.5f/9f winner: 12/1 and green, down the field in maiden at Kempton: should improve. *H. R. A. Cecil* **– p**

DAMETIME (IRE) 3 b.f. Danetime (IRE) 121 – Fee Eria (FR) (Always Fair (USA) 121) [2009 72: p6g^{6} 7.5v p6g^{6} 6.1g* p6g* 6m 6g^{2} 6s^{6} 6s 6.3s p6g^{4} p5.1g p5g Oct 16] tall filly: fairly useful handicapper: won at Chepstow in May and Lingfield in June: good second at Ayr seventh outing: best at 5f/easy 6f: acts on polytrack and soft going: usually tongue tied: races close up. *D. Loughnane, Ireland* **82**

DAMIEN (IRE) 3 gr.c. Namid 128 – Miss Shaan (FR) (Darshaan 133) [2009 109: p7g^{4} 6m^{6} 6g^{3} 6g Jul 8] compact colt: useful performer: not so good in 2009, best effort when third to Danehill Destiny in listed race at Haydock: missed second half of season with foot problem: should stay 7f: acts on soft and good to firm ground. *B. W. Hills* **98**

DAMIETTA (USA) 2 b.f. (May 23) More Than Ready (USA) 120 – Dixie Eyes Blazing (USA) 56 (Gone West (USA)) [2009 6g^{3} p7g* 7m 6.5m Sep 10] 40,000 2-y-o: good-topped filly: half-sister to several winners, including 2006 2-y-o 7f winner Greyt Big Stuff (by Aljabr) and 1m winner Johnny Reb (by Danehill): dam, ran twice, out of sister to smart dam of Zafonic: fair performer: won maiden at Kempton in August: likely to stay 1m: acts on polytrack: has left Godolphin. *Saeed bin Suroor* **76**

DAMIKA (IRE) 6 ch.g. Namid 128 – Emly Express (IRE) (High Estate 127) [2009 109: 5g 7f 7d 6g 6m^{6} 6d 7.2m^{4} 7m^{3} Sep 26] strong, good-topped gelding: just fairly useful handicapper in 2009: several respectable efforts: effective at stiff 5f to 7f: acts on any turf going: usually held up. *R. M. Whitaker* **94**

DAMINI (USA) 3 b.f. Seeking The Gold (USA) – Dalisay (IRE) 76 (Sadler's Wells (USA) 132) [2009 76: 8.3m 8f^{3} 8.5f^{3} 8.5f^{4} Dec 20] compact filly: fair maiden: left Sir Michael Stoute after reappearance: probably stays 1m: acts on firm going: blinkered final outing. *N. D. Drysdale, USA* **68**

DAN BUOY (FR) 6 b.g. Slip Anchor 136 – Bramosia (Forzando 122) [2009 p16.5g Nov 30] tall gelding: fairly useful maiden: in cheekpieces, well held only Flat outing in 2009: stays 12.6f: acts on soft going. *R. C. Guest* **–**

DANCEALOT LADY (USA) 2 b.f. (Jan 20) Theatrical 128 – Guadaira (IRE) (Grand Lodge (USA) 125) [2009 6.1v p6g 7m^{6} 8g Sep 7] $9,000F: first foal: dam lightly raced in USA: no form in maidens/nursery. *P. Winkworth* **–**

DANCE AND DANCE (IRE) 3 b.c. Royal Applause 124 – Caldy Dancer (IRE) 97 (Soviet Star (USA) 128) [2009 68: p6g^{3} f6g^{2} p7g^{2} p7g* f7g^{6} 7m^{2} 7.5f 7m^{5} p7f* p7g^{2} p7.1g p8g^{3} Nov 25] fairly useful performer: steadily progressive in 2009, winning maiden at Lingfield in February and handicap at Kempton in October: stays 1m: acts on polytrack and good to firm going. *E. F. Vaughan* **94**

DANCE CARD 4 b.f. Cape Cross (IRE) 129 – Dance On 93 (Caerleon (USA) 132) [2009 –: 8g^{4} 7m* 7.2g 6d Oct 13] fair performer, lightly raced: won maiden at Newcastle in August: stays 7f: acts on good to firm going, below form (hung) on good to soft final start: tongue tied in 2009. *A. G. Foster* **77**

DANCE CLUB (IRE) 3 b.f. Fasliyev (USA) 120 – Two Clubs 111 (First Trump 118) [2009 68: 8s 6m^{2} 7m* 7m^{4} p7.1g Sep 18] small filly: fair handicapper: won at Yarmouth in August: should stay 1m: acts on good to firm going: tends to race close up: sold 32,000 gns. *W. Jarvis* **71**

DANCE EAST 2 b.f. (Jan 30) Shamardal (USA) 129 – Russian Dance (USA) 93 (Nureyev (USA) 131) [2009 6m Aug 24] second foal: dam, 2-y-o 6f winner, closely related to Racing Post Trophy/Dante Stakes winner Saratoga Springs: 14/1 and very green, always behind in maiden at Windsor: should do better. *J. Noseda* **– p**

DANCE FOR JULIE (IRE) 2 b.f. (Feb 17) Redback 116 – Dancing Steps (Zafonic (USA) 130) [2009 6m^{3} 6m^{2} 5m^{2} 6s* 6g^{6} Sep 20] £14,000Y: lengthy, quite attractive filly: third foal: dam unraced sister to useful UAE winner up to 1¼m Seeking The Prize: fair performer: won maiden at Thirsk in September: ran poorly in nursery (slowly away) final outing: effective at 5f/6f: acts on soft and good to firm ground: usually races prominently. *P. C. Haslam* **75**

DANCE GDANSK (IRE) 3 b.c. Fasliyev (USA) 120 – Tordasia (IRE) (Dr Devious (IRE) 127) [2009 p12m p12m p12g p16m^{5} p16.5g Dec 5] poor maiden. *M. Blanshard* **46**

DANCEINTOTHELIGHT 2 gr.g. (Feb 22) Dansili 127 – Kali 83 (Linamix (FR) 127) [2009 8.5m^{5} 8.3g^{6} 8d^{4} 8g^{2} Oct 23] 95,000F: second foal: dam 7f winner: progressive form in maidens, second at Ayr: stays 1m: acts on good to soft going: flashed tail penultimate start (gelded after). *K. A. Ryan* **77**

DANCELECTIC (IRE) 3 b.c. Barathea (IRE) 127 – Sheer Spirit (IRE) 86 (Caerleon (USA) 132) [2009 –: 10.2g Apr 28] no form: tongue tied. *D. R. Lanigan* –

DANCE ON BY (IRE) 2 b.f. (Apr 20) Sadler's Wells (USA) 132 – Kasora (IRE) (Darshaan 133) [2009 7d Oct 26] sister to several winners, notably 1m (Racing Post Trophy) to 1½m (Derby and Breeders' Cup Turf) winner High Chaparral and 3-y-o Black Bear Island, and half-sister to 2 winners in Ireland: dam unraced daughter of high-class French 1m/1¼m winner and Arc third Kozana: 5/1 and blanketed for stall entry, 7 lengths ninth to What A Charm in maiden at Leopardstown, held up and late headway without being at all knocked about: sure to do much better. *A. P. O'Brien, Ireland* **63 P**

DANCER IN DEMAND (IRE) 4 ch.g. Danehill Dancer (IRE) 117 – Sought Out (IRE) 119 (Rainbow Quest (USA) 134) [2009 71p: p12g² Apr 15] sturdy gelding: lightly-raced maiden: best effort (fair form) when 2 lengths second to It's Dubai Dolly at Kempton sole start in 2009: will be suited by 1¾m. *Sir Michael Stoute* **79**

DANCER'S LEGACY 4 ch.g. Nayef (USA) 129 – Blond Moment (USA) (Affirmed (USA)) [2009 86d: 8g 10.1d 10m 8.1g⁶ 8.5m 8f⁴ 7f⁵ p10m³ 9.7s⁴ Oct 6] attractive gelding: just modest handicapper in 2009, leaving E. Dunlop after reappearance: stays easy 1¼m: acts on polytrack and firm going: tried visored/in cheekpieces: formerly tongue tied: not straightforward. *J. R. Boyle* **61**

DANCE SAUVAGE 6 ch.g. Groom Dancer (USA) 128 – Peace Dance (Bikala 134) [2009 54: 14m 16.1d 17.2g 11.1v⁴ Aug 19] tall gelding: maiden handicapper: well held in 2009. *B. Storey* –

DANCE SOCIETY 3 b.g. Mull of Kintyre (USA) 114 – Gracious Imp (USA) (Imp Society (USA)) [2009 53p: 6m⁵ 7.1g Jun 6] good-topped gelding: maiden: blinkered, just poor form in 2009. *T. D. Easterby* **41**

DANCE THE STAR (USA) 4 b. or br.c. Dynaformer (USA) – Dance The Slew (USA) (Slew City Slew (USA)) [2009 97: p10g⁶ 12f p12g⁴ p11g² 12m⁴ 12m p12.2g² p12.2g³ Dec 11] tall, attractive colt: useful handicapper: best efforts at 4 yrs when in frame: should stay beyond 1½m: acts on polytrack and good to firm ground (unraced on softer than good): held up. *D. M. Simcock* **99**

DANCE WITH CHANCE (IRE) 2 b.f. (Feb 17) Kalanisi (IRE) 132 – Persian Lass (IRE) 103 (Grand Lodge (USA) 125) [2009 p7g 7g Oct 31] smallish filly: third foal: dam, 1¼m winner, out of smart French 10.5f and 12.5f winner Noble Tiara: down the field in maidens at Lingfield and Newmarket. *W. R. Swinburn* –

DANCING AGAIN 3 ch.f. Reel Buddy (USA) 118 – Batchworth Breeze (Beveled (USA)) [2009 8.3g 6g p5.1g p5g Nov 5] chunky filly: second foal: dam, little form, sister to smart sprinter Dancing Mystery: soundly beaten in maidens. *E. A. Wheeler* –

DANCING DAVID (IRE) 2 b.c. (May 3) Danehill Dancer (IRE) 117 – Seek Easy (USA) (Seeking The Gold (USA)) [2009 8d² 8g* 8d⁴ Oct 24] rangy colt: fifth foal: half-brother to 3 winners, including useful 11f (in USA) and 1½m winner Ordination (by Fantastic Light): dam unraced half-sister to US Grade 2 1m winner Conserve: progressed quickly into useful 2-y-o, won maiden at Newbury (by 2¾ lengths from Tamaathul) in October, then 6½ lengths fourth to St Nicholas Abbey in Racing Post Trophy at Doncaster: will stay 1¼m: smart prospect. *B. J. Meehan* **105 p**

DANCING DEANO (IRE) 7 b.g. Second Empire (IRE) 124 – Ultimate Beat (USA) (Go And Go) [2009 77: p7.1g⁵ p8.6g² p8.6g² p8.6g⁴ f7d⁶ p7.1g Mar 23] good-topped gelding: fair performer: stays 8.6f: has form on good to firm and good to soft ground, races mainly on all-weather nowadays: formerly visored: races prominently. *R. Hollinshead* **77**

DANCING DUO 5 b.m. Groom Dancer (USA) 128 – Affaire Royale (IRE) 95 (Royal Academy (USA) 130) [2009 57: f8s⁶ p8g² p7.1g p8g p8.6m² 7g Apr 30] attractive mare: modest handicapper: stays 8.6f: acts on all-weather and good to soft going: visored: often held up: not entirely straightforward (has given trouble at start). *D. Shaw* **57**

DANCING FREDDY (IRE) 2 b.c. (Apr 12) Chineur (FR) 123 – Majesty's Dancer (IRE) (Danehill Dancer (IRE) 117) [2009 p5.1g² 5g² 5.1g* 5g³ 5m 6f⁶ 5g p5.1g⁵ 6m p5.1g³ 5d² 6s Nov 7] £15,000 2-y-o: stocky colt: third foal: dam maiden half-sister to useful miler Dancal: fairly useful performer: won maiden at Nottingham in May: creditable second in nursery at Musselburgh penultimate start: best efforts at 5f: acts on polytrack and good to soft ground: worth a try in headgear. *J. G. Given* **83**

DANCING GHOST (IRE) 3 gr.f. Verglas (IRE) 118 – Ghost Dance (IRE) (Lure (USA) 131) [2009 7g f12m Nov 11] €16,000Y: tall, unfurnished filly: third foal: half-sister to 1m winner in Hong Kong by Pivotal: dam useful French 9f to 10.5f winner: well held in maiden/claimer. *Jane Chapple-Hyam* –

DANCING JEST (IRE) 5 b.m. Averti (IRE) 117 – Mezzanine (Sadler's Wells (USA) 132) [2009 67: 8g 10.1m^2 10.1m^2 10m* 8.3m^2 9.7m^5 8m 8.3m Sep 21] smallish, good-bodied mare: fair handicapper: won at Leicester in June: stays 1¼m: acts on firm going: makes running/races prominently. *Rae Guest* **71**

DANCING LYRA 8 b.g. Alzao (USA) 117 – Badaayer (USA) 105 (Silver Hawk (USA) 123) [2009 71: p10g f11g^2 f12g^6 f11g^2 9m^5 f12g* 12d^5 f14g^4 12d^4 Jul 15] small, compact gelding: has a quick action: fair handicapper: won at Southwell in June: stays 13f: acts on all-weather, heavy and good to firm going: tried tongue tied: usually held up. *R. A. Fahey* **69**

DANCING MAITE 4 ch.g. Ballet Master (USA) 92 – Ace Maite (Komaite (USA)) [2009 75: p7.1g^4 p7.1g^3 p6g* 6f^2 8m 6m* 7g 7g^4 6g* 6g^4 6m 6m 6m^5 f6g^6 p7.1g Dec 3] fairly useful handicapper: improved in first half of 2009, winning at Wolverhampton in April, Newmarket (apprentices) in May and York in June: below form after: best form at 6f: acts on all-weather, firm and soft ground: races close up. *S. R. Bowring* **92**

DANCING POPPY 2 b.f. (Mar 3) Kyllachy 129 – Broughtons Motto 75 (Mtoto 134) [2009 6g^5 7.1m^3 p7.1g 7m p6m^6 Oct 12] 16,000Y: tall, close-coupled filly: fourth foal: half-sister to 3-y-o Emeebee and 5-y-o Medicea Sidera: dam 5f (at 2 yrs) to 1¼m winner: modest maiden: best form at 6f: acts on polytrack: sold £1,500. *M. R. Channon* **55**

DANCING QUEEN (IRE) 2 ch.f. (Feb 15) Danehill Dancer (IRE) 117 – Elauyun (IRE) (Muhtarram (USA) 125) [2009 7g^6 8m^5 8.1m^2 Sep 26] 58,000F, €50,000Y: tall filly: has scope: fourth foal: dam unraced half-sister to Eclipse/Irish Champion Stakes winner Oratorio: fair form in maidens: second to Zahoo at Haydock (dictated, edged right): stays 1m. *M. A. Magnusson* **73**

DANCING RED DEVIL (IRE) 2 b.f. (Mar 8) Desert Style (IRE) 121 – Mannsara (IRE) (Royal Academy (USA) 130) [2009 5.1m* 5.1m^5 5v^5 6m^5 6s Aug 22] €13,000Y: sixth foal: half-sister to 3 winners, including 3-y-o Russian George and 6-y-o Manzila: dam, French maiden, half-sister to smart French miler Massigann: fair performer: won minor event at Chester in June: failed to progress, blinkered final start: should stay 6f: acts on good to firm ground, probably on heavy. *Paul Green* **73**

DANCING RHYTHM 4 b.g. Piccolo 121 – Will You Dance 83 (Shareef Dancer (USA) 135) [2009 –: p8g 8g 8m 6m^5 5f May 12] robust gelding: modest maiden: seemed to stay 1m: dead. *M. S. Saunders* **64**

DANCING STORM 6 b.m. Trans Island 119 – Stormswell 56 (Persian Bold 123) [2009 71: 8.3m 8.1g^6 8.1g^5 10g 8m^4 8m 8.1m^6 8d Oct 22] lengthy mare: modest handicapper nowadays: best around 1m: has form on polytrack/firm going, possibly best on softer than good: tried in cheekpieces (well held). *W. S. Kittow* **61**

DANCING WAVE 3 b.f. Baryshnikov (AUS) – Wavet 64 (Pursuit of Love 124) [2009 55: f6d* f7g^2 f7g^2 f7g^2 p6g^6 7.5m f6g^3 7.5m^3 10.4m^6 7g 6m^4 5g* 5m^2 5m f6m 6m 6g^2 f6g f5g Dec 22] strong, lengthy filly: fair performer: won claimer at Southwell in January and handicap at Redcar in June: effective at 5f to 7.5f: acts on fibresand, soft and good to firm ground: often front runner, though has raced lazily. *M. C. Chapman* **68** **a60**

DANCING WELCOME 3 b.f. Kyllachy 129 – Highland Gait 63 (Most Welcome 131) [2009 –: p5g^3 p6g p6g 5g^4 6.1g^6 5.7f p6g^2 p5.1g^3 6d^5 6m^2 6.1g^2 6m^4 7.1d^4 7m p6m^2 p7m* f6g^2 p7g* p7m^3 p7.1g p7.1g Dec 28] modest handicapper: won at Kempton and Lingfield, both in November: stays 7f: acts on all-weather, good to firm and good to soft going: blinkered nowadays. *J. M. Bradley* **71**

DANCING WIZARD 5 ch.g. Dancing Spree (USA) – Magic Legs 54 (Reprimand 122) [2009 56: p9.5g Mar 26] maiden, very lightly raced: well held sole outing in 2009: stays 7f: raced on polytrack. *Norma Twomey* **–**

DANCOURT (IRE) 3 b.g. Cadeaux Genereux 131 – Stage Struck (IRE) 83 (Sadler's Wells (USA) 132) [2009 77p: p8g^2 9m^2 8g* 10m* 10.4m^4 Aug 8] good-bodied gelding: useful handicapper: won at Newmarket and Sandown (beat Press The Button 4 lengths) in July: should stay beyond 1¼m: acts on polytrack and good to firm going: sold 40,000 gns in October, joined Godolphin. *Sir Michael Stoute* **99**

DANDARRELL 2 b.g. (Mar 31) Makbul 104 – Dress Design (IRE) 84 (Brief Truce (USA) 126) [2009 6s^5 f7g^2 Nov 17] fair form in maidens at Doncaster and Southwell (9 lengths second to Solicitor, refusing to settle). *Miss J. A. Camacho* **65**

DANDEREK 3 ch.g. Fantastic Light (USA) 134 – Maureena (IRE) (Grand Lodge (USA) 125) [2009 p11f^4 Dec 16] half-brother to 5-y-o Alfresco and 11.6f winner Dancing Dik (by Diktat): dam unraced: hinted at ability in 3-y-o bumper: modest form when 4 lengths fourth to Champagne Fizz in maiden at Kempton, outpaced: will be suited by 1½m. *R. A. Fahey* **61**

DANDINO 2 br.c. (Mar 25) Dansili 127 – Generous Diana 90 (Generous (IRE) 139) [2009 8d 8.3g² Oct 28] fifth foal: dam 9f/1¼m winner who stayed 1½m: much better effort in maidens when 4 lengths second to Psychic Ability at Nottingham: will be suited by 1¼m. *J. G. Given* **77**

DANDY MAN (IRE) 6 b.h. Mozart (IRE) 131 – Lady Alexander (IRE) 112 (Night Shift (USA)) [2009 121: 5m 5g 5m 5g⁵ 5m 5m* 5m⁴ 5m⁴ Oct 1] small, strong horse: very smart performer at his peak, successful in Palace House Stakes at Newmarket (in 2006) and 3 listed races: just smart in 2009, winning 3-runner minor event at Leicester in September by 1¼ lengths from Peace Offering: several other creditable efforts, including when fifth to Kingsgate Native in Audi Stakes at Goodwood: was best at 5f: had won on good to soft going, best efforts on good or firmer (acted on firm): usually tongue tied: tried blinkered (ran poorly): usually raced up with pace: to stand at Ballyhane Stud, Co Carlow, Ireland, fee €4,500. *Saeed bin Suroor* **110**

DANE COTTAGE 2 ch.f. (Jan 22) Beat Hollow 126 – Lady Soleas (Be My Guest (USA) 126) [2009 5g Oct 19] second foal: dam unraced out of useful sprinter Farhana: 33/1 and green, well held in maiden at Windsor. *Miss Gay Kelleway* **–**

DANEHILL DESTINY 3 b.f. Danehill Dancer (IRE) 117 – Comeraincomeshine (IRE) 67 (Night Shift (USA)) [2009 101: 7s³ 6g* 6m⁶ 6s⁶ Sep 13] well-made filly: useful performer: 3¼ lengths third to Lahaleeb in Fred Darling Stakes at Newbury prior to winning listed race at Haydock in May by 1½ lengths from Doncaster Rover: below form after, going off too fast in Renaissance Stakes at the Curragh final start: was effective at 6f/7f: acted on soft ground, possibly not on firmer than good: tried blinkered: tongue tied in 2009: visits Pivotal. *W. J. Haggas* **104**

DANEHILL INTELLECT (IRE) 2 ch.f. (May 5) Danehill Dancer (IRE) 117 – Intellectuelle (Caerleon (USA) 132) [2009 p7g⁶ 8.3m⁴ Sep 1] sturdy filly: sister to Irish 1¼m winner Strike One and half-sister to 3 winners, including fairly useful 2007 2-y-o 6f winner Montaquila (by Hawk Wing) and 6-y-o Cry Alot Boy: dam, French 1m winner, half-sister to smart French performer up to 10.5f Audacieuse and useful stayer Lord Jim: better effort in maidens when 4 lengths fourth to Quiet at Leicester, again given considerate ride: should stay 1¼m: capable of further improvement. *G. A. Butler* **67 p**

DANEHILL'S PEARL (IRE) 3 b.f. Danehill Dancer (IRE) 117 – Mother of Pearl (IRE) 113 (Sadler's Wells (USA) 132) [2009 7s* 10d⁵ 10m⁶ 10d* Jul 25] 165,000F: tall filly: fifth foal: half-sister to 3 winners, including useful 1m to 1½m (latter in UAE) winner Pearly King (by Kingmambo): dam, 2-y-o 7f/1m winner (stayed 1½m), closely related to Irish 2000 Guineas winner Turtle Island: useful form: won maiden at Newbury in April and listed race at Vichy (best effort when beating Flash Dance by length) in July: stays 1¼m: best efforts on ground softer than good. *Tom Dascombe* **103**

DANEHILLSUNDANCE (IRE) 5 b.g. Danehill Dancer (IRE) 117 – Rosie's Guest (IRE) (Be My Guest (USA) 126) [2009 97: p6g⁶ 7.5g 8m 7m 10.2g³ 8.5m* 8.5m 8.3g⁵ 10g Oct 19] tall, leggy gelding: fairly useful handicapper nowadays: left S. Parr after reappearance: won at Beverley in July: seemed amiss final start: effective at 7f to 1¼m: acts on polytrack, firm and good to soft going: tongue tied last 6 starts: often held up. *D. H. Brown* **82**

DANETIME LILY (IRE) 5 b.m. Danetime (IRE) 121 – Millie's Lily (IRE) 74 (Distinctly North (USA) 115) [2009 83: 5g 5g* 5d⁵ 5m⁵ 5v 5s⁴ Aug 9] good-topped mare: fairly useful handicapper: improved when winning at Down Royal in June: best at 5f: best efforts on good going or firmer (some promise on polytrack): in cheekpieces last 4 starts: tongue tied on reappearance: usually races close up: tough and game. *Ms Joanna Morgan, Ireland* **85**

DANETIME PANTHER (IRE) 5 b.g. Danetime (IRE) 121 – Annotate (Groom Dancer (USA) 128) [2009 83: 8.3g 10s 10g³ 12m⁵ Jun 9] tall gelding: fair handicapper: stays 1¼m: acts on all-weather, good to firm and good to soft going: tried blinkered, in cheekpieces last 2 starts: often held up: successful over hurdles in July/August. *Ian Williams* **77**

DANGER MULALLY 2 b.g. (Jan 29) Governor Brown (USA) 104 – Glittering Image (IRE) (Sadler's Wells (USA) 132) [2009 6m 7m⁵ 7.1m* 7d p8g p8m p8m* Dec 9] £16,000Y: leggy gelding: fifth foal: half-brother to fairly useful Irish 2006 2-y-o 8.5f winner Miss Josiey Wales (later 1m winner in USA by Val Royal) and 4-y-o Focail Eile: dam unraced out of smart performer up to 1¼m Noora Abu: fair performer: won maiden at Warwick in July and nursery at Kempton in December: stays 1m: acts on polytrack and good to firm going: tongue tied last 2 starts. *A. M. Balding* **75**

DANGEROUS MIDGE (USA) 3 b.c. Lion Heart (USA) 124 – Adored Slew (USA) (Seattle Slew (USA)) [2009 10m 9.9g* 10.2g^3 10.3m* Sep 11] $120,000Y: tall, good-bodied colt: sixth foal: half-brother to several winners, including fairly useful French 7.5f to 1¼m winner Silver Traffic (by Carson City): dam, useful French/US 1m/1¼m winner: useful form: won maiden at Salisbury in June and minor event at Doncaster (improved when beating Lady Artemisia 1¼ lengths) in September: will stay 1½m: acts on good to firm ground: open to further progress. *B. J. Meehan* **99 p**

DANIELLA DE BRUIJN (IRE) 2 b.f. (Jan 22) Orpen (USA) 116 – Ardent Lady 79 (Alhaarth (IRE) 126) [2009 5.1m^4 5.2m^4 6v* 6.1m^2 6g^4 6m^5 p8.6g* p7m^4 p8m^3 p9.5g Oct 29] £16,000Y: lengthy filly: third foal: half-sister to 2008 2-y-o 5f winner First Choice (by Choisir): dam 9f winner: fair performer: won maiden at Haydock in May and claimer at Wolverhampton in October: stays 1m: acts on polytrack, heavy and good to firm ground. *A. B. Haynes* **73**

DANIEL THOMAS (IRE) 7 b.g. Dansili 127 – Last Look (Rainbow Quest (USA) 134) [2009 83: 8.1m 8.1m p8g p10m p8m^2 p8g^4 p8m^3 p8m p9.5g^5 p8.6g* Dec 28] good-topped gelding: has a quick action: fair performer nowadays: won apprentice seller at Wolverhampton in December: stays 9f: acts on polytrack, soft and good to firm going: in cheekpieces/visor last 6 starts: held up (often slowly away). *Mrs A. L. M. King* **75**

DANIES BOY (IRE) 3 b.c. Elusive City (USA) 117 – Daniela Samuel (USA) (No Robbery) [2009 p7g^4 p7g^3 7.1m^3 7f* May 14] unfurnished colt: half-brother to 3 winners, notably smart 1m winner Prince Arthur (by Fairy King): dam Italian 5f to 1m winner: fair performer: won claimer at Salisbury in May: likely to prove best up to 7f: sent to Saudi Arabia. *R. Hannon* **73**

DANI'S GIRL (IRE) 6 b. or br.m. Second Empire (IRE) 124 – Quench The Lamp (IRE) (Glow (USA)) [2009 100: 8m 10.5m 10g 11d^3 12m^5 12m 10.1m p16m* Dec 30] quite good-topped mare: fairly useful handicapper nowadays: left P. Fahy in Ireland after fourth start: won at Kempton in December: stays easy 2m: acts on polytrack and any turf going: blinkered once: fairly useful hurdler. *P. M. Phelan* **90**

DANISH ART (IRE) 4 b.g. Danehill Dancer (IRE) 117 – Lady Ounavarra (IRE) (Simply Great (FR) 122) [2009 83: p7.1g f6g^6 f7g f7g 7g p7.1g^6 8.5m^5 Sep 16] smallish gelding: one-time fairly useful performer: just modest form at best in 2009: stays easy 7f: acts on polytrack and good to firm ground. *M. W. Easterby* **57**

DANNIOS 3 b.c. Tobougg (IRE) 125 – Fleuve d'Or (IRE) (Last Tycoon 131) [2009 67p: 8.1g 8.3m 10d Aug 7] fair maiden at 2 yrs: well beaten in handicaps in 2009: blinkered final outing. *L. M. Cumani* **–**

DANNY'S CHOICE 2 ch.f. (Feb 25) Compton Place 125 – Pie High 96 (Salse (USA) 128) [2009 5f^2 5.1g* 5g^6 6f* 6.5m Sep 25] £65,000Y: smallish, good-quartered filly: third foal: half-sister to 2007 2-y-o 1m winner Crosstar (by Cape Cross): dam, 7f winner (including at 2 yrs), half-sister to smart sprinter Leap For Joy: fairly useful performer: won maiden at Nottingham in July and minor event at Folkestone in September: best effort when sixth to Piccadilly Filly in listed event at Deauville: effective at 5f/6f. *R. M. Beckett* **88**

DANSANT 5 b.h. Dansili 127 – La Balagna (Kris 135) [2009 118: p10g^2 a10f^6 p10g* 12m^3 13.3m^5 Aug 15] tall, good-topped horse: smart performer, better on all-weather: won listed race at Kempton in March by ½ length from Kandidate: creditable efforts otherwise in 2009 when placed in similar event at Lingfield (½-length second to Suits Me) and Hardwicke Stakes at Royal Ascot (3½ lengths third to Bronze Cannon): effective at 1¼m to 1¾m: acts on polytrack, good to firm and good to soft going (possibly not on soft): travels strongly waited with, and has good turn of foot: has hung but reliable. *G. A. Butler* **112 a116**

DANSE ON WOOD 3 b.c. Dansili 127 – Woodwin (IRE) 97 (Woodman (USA) 126) [2009 10m 12m p12g^2 p16g p12g Oct 22] 65,000Y: deep-girthed colt: sixth foal: half-brother to several fairly useful performers, including Irish 7-y-o Star Wood and 1m winner Coppice (by Rainbow Quest): dam, Irish 1m winner, half-sister to smart Irish 1¼m winner Fracas: fair maiden: easily best effort when runner-up third outing: well held in handicaps after: stays 1½m: raced only on polytrack and good to firm ground: sold 6,000 gns. *J. Noseda* **74**

DANSILI DANCER 7 b.g. Dansili 127 – Magic Slipper 97 (Habitat 134) [2009 106: p12g^3 12f^4 12f* 12m^6 11.9m 14m 12m^4 Sep 27] strong, close-coupled gelding: useful handicapper: won at Doncaster in May by 1½ lengths from Meethaaq: had earlier run well when fourth to Hatton Flight at Newmarket: best effort after when respectable fourth **108**

to Record Breaker at Ascot final start: stays 1¾m: acts on polytrack and firm going (promise on good to soft earlier in career): well beaten only start in cheekpieces. *C. G. Cox*

DANSILVER 5 b.g. Dansili 127 – Silver Gyre (IRE) 65 (Silver Hawk (USA) 123) **67**
[2009 67: p12.2g^{2} p12g^{3} p16.5g* Jan 22] strong gelding: fair handicapper: won at Wolverhampton in January: stays 16.5f: acts on polytrack, soft and firm going: tried in cheekpieces. *A. W. Carroll*

DANSIMAR 5 gr.m. Daylami (IRE) 138 – Hylandra (USA) (Bering 136) [2009 14.6g^{5} **65**
17.2d^{3} May 18] good-topped mare: fair maiden handicapper: stays 2¼m: acts on polytrack, good to firm and good to soft ground: useful hurdler. *Miss Venetia Williams*

DANTARI (IRE) 4 b.c. Alhaarth (IRE) 126 – Daniysha (IRE) 76 (Doyoun 124) [2009 **70**
71: p13g^{6} 15m^{3} 16g^{6} Jul 21] fair maiden, lightly raced on Flat: stays 15f: acts on polytrack and good to firm ground, probably on soft: tried blinkered: fairly useful hurdler, successful in October. *Evan Williams*

DANTE DEO (USA) 3 b.f. Proud Citizen (USA) 122 – Best Feature (USA) (El Gran **62**
Senor (USA) 136) [2009 59p: p9.2g^{6} p7.1g 8m 7.5m^{5} 7.5m* 8f^{6} 8s May 22] close-coupled filly: modest performer: won handicap at Beverley in May: should be suited by 1m+: acts on all-weather and good to firm going (well held on soft): sold £3,500 in July. *T. D. Barron*

DAN TUCKER 5 b.g. Dansili 127 – Shapely (USA) 81 (Alleged (USA) 138) [2009 76: **66**
p12g^{4} Mar 19] close-coupled gelding: fair handicapper: barely stayed 1¾m: acted on polytrack, firm and good to soft ground: had worn blinkers: usually held up: won over hurdles in April, but fell week later: dead. *Jim Best*

DANUBE (IRE) 2 b.f. (Jan 24) Montjeu (IRE) 137 – Darabela (IRE) 84 (Desert King **59 p**
(IRE) 129) [2009 8.3m^{5} Sep 1] sturdy, attractive filly: third foal: half-sister to 3-y-o Doncosaque: dam, Irish 7f winner, half-sister to smart stayer Darasim out of half-sister to 4-y-o Dar Re Mi: 7/2 and very green, encouraging 7¼ lengths fifth to Quiet in maiden at Leicester: should be suited by 1¼m+: should improve. *H. R. A. Cecil*

DANUM DANCER 5 ch.g. Allied Forces (USA) 123 – Branston Dancer (Rudimentary **73**
(USA) 118) [2009 –: 6g 6s^{3} f5g^{5} f5m f6g^{4} f6g* f7m f6d Dec 29] rather leggy, lengthy gelding: fair handicapper: won at Southwell in December: effective at 5f/6f: acts on fibresand, firm and soft going: sometimes blinkered. *N. Bycroft*

DANVILLA 2 b.f. (Feb 9) Dansili 127 – Newtown Villa (Spectrum (IRE) 126) [2009 **–**
p8g Oct 9] first foal: dam twice-raced daughter of useful 1½m winner New Abbey: 100/1, slowly away and tailed off in maiden at Lingfield. *P. R. Webber*

DANZADIL (IRE) 3 b.f. Mujadil (USA) 119 – Changari (USA) 90 (Gulch (USA)) **54**
[2009 59: 6d p6g 5m 7g^{3} p7m 8m p6g^{4} Oct 26] angular filly: modest maiden handicapper: stays 7f: acts on polytrack, good to firm and good to soft ground: sold 1,500 gns. *R. A. Teal*

DANZATRICE 7 b.m. Tamure (IRE) 125 – Miss Petronella (Petoski 135) [2009 76: **76**
16m^{2} 14m 16m* 16.4d^{6} 16.1m 16.2m^{6} 16s^{3} 16.1g^{2} 16d^{5} 16.4d^{4} 17.5m^{2} 18g 15v Oct 31] lengthy mare: fair handicapper: won at Ripon in May: stays 17.5f: acts on soft and good to firm going: ridden patiently: quirky, but consistent. *C. W. Thornton*

DANZIG FOX 4 b.g. Foxhound (USA) 103 – Via Dolorosa (Chaddleworth (IRE) 103) **59**
[2009 67: p6g 7.6m^{5} 8s 6d p7.1g 12s Oct 27] modest handicapper nowadays: gelded after reappearance: stays 7.5f: acts on good to firm ground: tried blinkered/in cheekpieces. *M. Mullineaux*

DANZILI BAY 7 b.h. Dansili 127 – Lady Bankes (IRE) 69 (Alzao (USA) 117) [2009 **–**
73: 6m May 9] small, sturdy horse: fair handicapper in 2008: ran as if needing sole outing in 2009: best at 5f/6f: acts on firm and soft going. *A. W. Carroll*

DANZOE (IRE) 2 b.g. (Mar 27) Kheleyf (USA) 116 – Fiaba 66 (Precocious 126) [2009 **79**
5.2m^{2} 6g^{2} 6d^{6} 6d* 6m^{4} 5g 5m 7.1m^{5} 7d Oct 11] unfurnished gelding: fair performer: won maiden at Ripon in June: below form in nurseries last 4 starts: stays 6f: acts on good to firm and good to soft ground: sold 9,000 gns, and gelded. *D. Donovan*

DAPHNE DU MAURIER (IRE) 2 b.f. (Mar 1) Arakan (USA) 123 – Butter Knife **– §**
(IRE) (Sure Blade (USA) 130) [2009 6m 6f^{5} 5d 7.1m Sep 14] €3,000Y: sparely-made filly: closely related to 1¼m winner Uncle Cent (by Peintre Celebre) and half-sister to 2 winners, including 2006 2-y-o 5f/6f winner Gold Spirit (by Invincible Spirit), both useful: dam unraced half-sister to high-class performer up to 1½m Ace and very smart performer up to 1¼m Hawkeye: no form, including in seller: temperamental. *I. Semple*

totesport.com Chester Cup (Heritage Handicap)—a fourth win in the race for trainer Barry Hills as Daraahem (right) just shades Ajaan (blinkers) with Halla San (hooped cap) third and Desert Sea fourth in a typically competitive renewal

DARAAHEM (IRE) 4 ch.g. Act One 124 – Shamah 96 (Unfuwain (USA) 131) [2009 105: 18.7m* May 6] big, strong gelding: useful handicapper: improved when winning totesport.com Chester Cup sole outing in 2009, travelling well and finding plenty to hold Ajaan by neck: injured a suspensory after: stayed 18.7f: acted on good to firm and good to soft going: retired. *B. W. Hills* **109**

DARAIYM (IRE) 4 b.g. Peintre Celebre (USA) 137 – Dararita (IRE) (Halo (USA)) [2009 61: p16.5g^5 15.8m* 18m* 21.6m^6 Apr 20] smallish, lengthy gelding: modest handicapper: won at Catterick and Pontefract in April: stays 2¼m (stretched by 21.6f final outing): acts on polytrack and good to firm ground. *Paul Green* **61**

DARCEY 3 ch.f. Noverre (USA) 125 – Firozi 63 (Forzando 122) [2009 79: 7m^5 6.9m^3 7d 6m^2 7m* 6m* 7v^3 8m* p8m^6 8.1m^3 p7g 8g Oct 30] neat filly: fairly useful performer: won sellers at Newcastle and Ripon (apprentices) in August, and claimer at Yarmouth (left R. Fahey) in September: stays 1m: acts on soft and good to firm going (ran poorly on heavy): shaped as if amiss third outing. *Miss Amy Weaver* **81**

DARCY'S PRIDE (IRE) 5 b. or br.m. Danetime (IRE) 121 – Cox's Ridge (IRE) (Indian Ridge 123) [2009 72: 5m 5m* 6m 5g^4 5m 5m 5m^3 5g 5m 5m^2 5m* 6m 5m^4 5g 5m^3 p5.1g Nov 6] quite good-topped mare: modest handicapper nowadays: won at Redcar in April and, having left D. Barker after sixth start, Newcastle in August: best at 5f: acts on any turf going: tongue tied nowadays: often races prominently: none too consistent. *P. T. Midgley* **64**

DAREDEVIL DAN 3 b.g. Golden Snake (USA) 127 – Tiempo 50 (King of Spain 121) [2009 –: 10.1d^3 10.1m^3 13g 11.9d^3 Oct 15] compact gelding: fair maiden: may prove best short of 13f for time being: waited with (slowly away third outing). *M. H. Tompkins* **71**

DAREH (IRE) 3 b.f. Invincible Spirit (IRE) 121 – Delage (Bellypha 130) [2009 72: p6g^2 6s May 4] modest maiden at 3 yrs: likely to stay 1m: sold 3,500 gns. *M. Johnston* **64**

DAR ES SALAAM 5 ch.g. King's Best (USA) 132 – Place de L'Opera 98 (Sadler's Wells (USA) 132) [2009 86: 12g^6 10.1d 12g^3 10d 10g^6 14.6g Oct 23] well-made gelding: fairly useful handicapper: left J. Goldie prior to final start: should stay 1¾m: acts on firm and soft ground: won over hurdles in November. *James Moffatt* **82**

DARFOUR 5 b.g. Inchinor 119 – Gai Bulga 110 (Kris 135) [2009 67: 9.1m² 8g⁴ 10m⁵ 8m 8.3s⁶ 7.1m⁶ Sep 14] lengthy, workmanlike gelding: just modest handicapper in 2009: well below form last 4 starts: probably stays 1¼m: acts on firm ground: tried in cheekpieces, visored last 2 starts: sold £6,500 in October. *J. S. Goldie* **63**

DARING DREAM (GER) 4 ch.c. Big Shuffle (USA) 122 – Daring Action (Arazi (USA) 135) [2009 72: p8g⁴ p7g⁵ p8g 8g³ 8f² 7.2s* 6m⁴ 6d 7.2g⁶ Oct 23] leggy, workmanlike colt: fair handicapper: left A. P. Jarvis, won at Ayr in August: effective at 6f to 1m: acts on polytrack, soft and firm ground: sometimes visored. *J. S. Goldie* **76**

DARING RACER (GER) 6 ch.g. Big Shuffle (USA) 122 – Daring Action (Arazi (USA) 135) [2009 68: 10m⁴ 9m³ 8.5m⁵ 10g⁶ 10.1m⁵ Aug 20] lengthy gelding: just modest handicapper in 2009: stayed 15.4f: acted on polytrack, good to firm and good to soft going: wore cheekpieces: joined Tim Vaughan: dead. *Mrs L. J. Mongan* **60**

DARK CAMELLIA 4 b.f. Olden Times 121 – Miss Mirror 77 (Magic Mirror 105) [2009 70: p6g⁵ 7f⁵ 8g p6g p7.1g⁵ p7m p8.6g⁶ p8m* p8m p7m Nov 29] tall filly: fair performer on all-weather, poor on turf: won maiden at Kempton in November: stays 1m: acts on polytrack: tried blinkered: usually tongue tied: travels strongly: held up. *H. J. L. Dunlop* **42 a68**

DARK DESERT 3 b.c. Best of The Bests (IRE) 122 – Dune Safari (IRE) 63 (Key of Luck (USA) 126) [2009 45: p8.6g⁵ Jan 16] poor maiden: stays 8.6f: acts on polytrack. *A. G. Newcombe* **44**

DARK ECHOES 3 bl.g. Diktat 126 – Calamanco 71 (Clantime 101) [2009 63?: 8.3d⁵ 8d 8s⁵ 11.5s⁵ 10.3d 8.3v⁵ f7g⁴ Oct 18] workmanlike gelding: modest maiden: stays 1m: acts on good to soft ground: blinkered final start. *Jedd O'Keeffe* **57**

DARK ENERGY 5 br.g. Observatory (USA) 131 – Waterfowl Creek (IRE) 88 (Be My Guest (USA) 126) [2009 76: 12g⁴ p16.5g p13.9g⁶ p13.9g⁵ p12m Dec 9] small gelding: fair handicapper: trained by R. Harris second start only: stays 1¾m: acts on polytrack and soft going: usually tongue tied nowadays: held up: fair winning hurdler. *M. J. Scudamore* **66**

DARK EYES (IRE) 2 b.f. (Apr 21) Camacho 118 – Sherkova (USA) (State Dinner (USA)) [2009 5.7g* 6m³ p7g⁵ 7m³ 8g Oct 31] smallish filly: half-sister to several winners, including 1m winner Russian Party (by Lycius) and 2m winner Norma's Lady (by Unfuwain): dam unraced half-sister to Prix de Diane winner Lady In Silver: fairly useful performer: won maiden at Bath in July: ran creditably after only when third in nursery at Newmarket: stays 7f: acts on good to firm going: races freely. *D. J. Coakley* **83**

DARK LANE 3 b.g. Namid 128 – Corps de Ballet (IRE) 92 (Fasliyev (USA) 120) [2009 85: 6g* 6m 5d² 6g 5d⁵ 6g 6m³ 6m Sep 18] leggy gelding: fairly useful handicapper: won at Haydock in May: left T. D. Barron after fourth start: may prove best at 6f: acts on good to firm and good to soft going: tried in cheekpieces. *R. A. Fahey* **89**

DARK MISCHIEF 3 b.g. Namid 128 – Syrian Queen 82 (Slip Anchor 136) [2009 98p: 6m* 6m⁵ 6g 6m⁵ 7d p6f³ 6m* Sep 15] good-topped gelding: useful performer: won handicap at Newmarket in April and minor event at Haydock (improved when beating Silaah by length, making all) in September: should stay 7f: acts on polytrack and good to firm ground: sent to Hong Kong, where renamed Kelly's Horse. *H. Candy* **101**

DARK MOMENT 3 gr.g. Spartacus (IRE) 107 – Dim Ofan 80 (Petong 126) [2009 62?: 7.1m* 7g 8.3g⁴ 7.1g* 6m* 6s* 7.1m 7g⁶ Oct 17] well-made gelding: fairly useful handicapper: won at Musselburgh in June, and on same course, Newcastle and Hamilton all in August: should stay 1m: acts on soft and good to firm going: in cheekpieces last 5 starts: has looked temperamental (refused to race second outing). *A. Dickman* **80**

DARK OASIS 3 b.g. Dubai Destination (USA) 127 – Silent Waters (Polish Precedent (USA) 131) [2009 62: p8.6g² p9.5m 9.9m 8.3g² 9.8m² 11.6m³ 12m 10d 16.2g³ 16v⁶ 14.1g f16g⁵ Aug 27] leggy gelding: modest maiden: left K. Ryan after fifth start: stays 2m: acts on all-weather and good to firm ground: often in blinkers/cheekpieces for previous stable: won 2 juvenile hurdles in October. *M. C. Chapman* **62**

DARK PLANET 6 ch.g. Singspiel (IRE) 133 – Warning Shadows (IRE) 113 (Cadeaux Genereux 131) [2009 58: f8s f12d 12.4m 10.1g 12g May 5] strong gelding: modest at 5 yrs: well held in 2009: usually wears cheekpieces/visor. *D. W. Thompson* **–**

DARK PROSPECT 4 b.g. Nayef (USA) 129 – Miss Mirasol 92 (Sheikh Albadou 128) [2009 88: 10.1d 10g* p10g⁵ 10d² 9.9g 10.3m⁴ 10.2s³ 10g Oct 19] big, good-topped gelding: fairly useful handicapper: won at Leicester in May: mostly at least respectable efforts after: stays 1¼m: acts on polytrack, firm and soft going: has worn cheekpieces, blinkered last 2 starts: front runner/races prominently: sold 40,000 gns. *M. A. Jarvis* **93**

totesport.com Cesarewitch (Heritage Handicap), Newmarket—'handicap good thing' Darley Sun provides up-and-coming trainer David Simcock with his biggest win to date; runner-up Mamlook (striped cap) is placed for the second year running, ahead of Sereth and Dayia (right)

DARK QUEST 3 b.f. Rainbow Quest (USA) 134 – Pure Grain 121 (Polish Precedent (USA) 131) [2009 10s 12m4 12.1m5 10d2 14s3 Aug 7] unfurnished filly: half-sister to several winners, including smart 7f (at 2 yrs) and 10.5f winner Goncharova (by Gone West) and useful 1¼m winner Grain of Truth (by Gulch), later successful in USA: dam 7f (Prestige Stakes at 2 yrs) to 1½m (Irish/Yorkshire Oaks) winner: fair form in maidens: stays 1½m: acts on good to firm and good to soft going: twice found little. *J. L. Dunlop* **75**

DARK RANGER 3 b. or br.g. Where Or When (IRE) 124 – Dark Raider (IRE) 77 (Definite Article 121) [2009 48: p8g3 p8g* p8.6g3 10.2d3 p10g* 10.3g2 9.9m3 8g p8g p10g5 p8f4 Dec 13] leggy gelding: fair performer: won handicap at Lingfield in March and minor event there in May (gelded after): stays 10.3f: acts on polytrack and good to firm going. *T. J. Pitt* **65**

DARK TARA 4 br.f. Diktat 126 – Karisal (IRE) 80 (Persian Bold 123) [2009 –: p6g p7.1g* f6g5 p8g Oct 30] tall, quite good-topped filly: fair handicapper: won at Wolverhampton in January: left R. Fahey after next outing: effective at 6f/7f: acts on polytrack, soft and good to firm going: tried in blinkers/cheekpieces/tongue tie: temperament under suspicion. *John Joseph Hanlon, Ireland* **65**

DARK VELVET (IRE) 3 b.f. Statue of Liberty (USA) 115 – Lovingit (IRE) 62 (Fasliyev (USA) 120) [2009 61: 7.1f 7g 6v 8.3s5 6s f7g p7.1g Dec 17] maiden: well held in 2009: tried blinkered/in cheekpieces. *E. J. Alston* **–**

DARLEY STAR 4 gr.f. King's Best (USA) 132 – Amellnaa (IRE) 86 (Sadler's Wells (USA) 132) [2009 64: p10g6 p11g f11g Mar 22] rather leggy filly: modest handicapper: stays 1¼m: acts on polytrack and good to firm going: in cheekpieces 2 of 3 starts in 2009: often races prominently. *R. A. Harris* **54**

DARLEY SUN (IRE) 3 b.c. Tiger Hill (IRE) 127 – Sagamartha (Rainbow Quest (USA) 134) [2009 67+: p11g6 14.1f* 14g4 14m* 14.1f2 16g* 18m2 18m* Oct 17] useful-looking colt: smart performer: one of the most improved 3-y-os of 2009, winning handicaps at Nottingham in May, Haydock in June, Ascot in July and Newmarket (9/2 favourite, readily beat Mamlook by 5 lengths in totesport.com Cesarewitch, forging clear once finding full stride) in October: also ran well when neck second to Askar Tau in Doncaster Cup seventh outing: suited by 2m+: acts on firm going: type to go on and win pattern races in 2010 when he will be with Saeed bin Suroor. *D. M. Simcock* **114 p**

DARLING BUDS 2 b.f. (Mar 26) Reel Buddy (USA) 118 – Its Another Gift 64 (Primo Dominie 121) [2009 p6g f6f6 p6g5 Dec 18] sister to useful 2007 2-y-o 6f winner Reel Gift (later successful in Greece) and half-sister to useful 2-y-o 5f winners Gifted Gamble (in 2004, by Mind Games) and Scented Present (in 2006, by Foxhound): dam sprint maiden: modest form at best in maidens. *K. A. Ryan* **54**

DAR RE MI 4 b.f. Singspiel (IRE) 133 – Darara 129 (Top Ville 129) [2009 119: 10.4g² 10d* 12m* 12g⁵ 12g⁵ 12f³ Nov 7] **124**

'Daylight robbery in Vermeille', 'Dar Re Mi disqualified in French farce', 'Dar Re Mi victime d'un hold up' . . . sections of the British and French Press were united in their condemnation of British-trained Dar Re Mi's demotion by the Longchamp stewards to fifth place after she had passed the post first in the Qatar Prix Vermeille in September. A section of the Longchamp crowd made their feelings known at the time by booing as the post-race presentations were made to the connections of the promoted favourite Stacelita, whose unbeaten record was preserved by the stewards' decision. The frustration of Dar Re Mi's connections—an emotional Lady Lloyd-Webber confessed to being 'really pissed off, so sorry for the mare'—was at least partly understandable. Dar Re Mi was deprived of a prestigious race in which she was clearly the winner on merit, a race she would certainly have kept had it taken place in Britain or Ireland.

The rules on interference differ among some major racing jurisdictions, sometimes causing confusion that does the sport's image no good at all. The rules of racing in general need harmonising, given the growing ambition for global promotion of racing and of the betting on its showcase events. A universal ban on drug use is the most important pre-requisite if the potential global betting audience is to have full confidence in the integrity of the sport. Compared to that particular mountain, however, harmonising the rules on interference is no more than a molehill and it would be amazing if international agreement could not be reached provided the major nations set about the job with a will. FIFA, football's world governing body, has over two hundred member countries which use the same *Laws of the Game*. There have been universal rules for football since the 1870s. France Galop president Edouard de Rothschild acknowledged the 'need to move fast as France and other countries cannot continue with different rules. It is unthinkable that a jockey, in the middle of the home straight, should have to consider whether he can make a move because he is in France or Britain. The level of adrenalin is too high.' He might have added that having different rules also adds an avoidable element of risk to betting, as some uninitiated British punters who backed Dar Re Mi discovered to their cost, most betting firms in Britain settling on the official result (those who backed Stacelita, of course, were able to breathe a sigh of relief, though some bookmakers, including Paddy Power and Skybet, paid out on both as a goodwill gesture).

Audi Pretty Polly Stakes, the Curragh—Dar Re Mi (No.2) is pushed close by outsider Beach Bunny (noseband) in a muddling race; favourite Look Here is a below-par third

Darley Yorkshire Oaks, York—Dar Re Mi claims the scalp of another Epsom Oaks winner in Sariska (left); Roman Empress and Barshiba (right) follow them home

Dar Re Mi had progressed well as a three-year-old, winning in listed and Group 3 company, and her latest appearance in the Prix Vermeille followed a good second to Zarkava in the same race twelve months earlier (she had also finished second to Lush Lashes in the Yorkshire Oaks at three). Dar Re Mi was trained principally for an autumn campaign at four, brought along steadily and not quite at her best when beaten a short head at odds on by Crystal Capella in the Middleton Stakes at York in May on her reappearance. But she arrived at Longchamp in the form of her life, having broken her Group 1 duck in a tactical Audi Pretty Polly Stakes at the Curragh in June when she was sent for home in earnest over three furlongs out and held the persistent challenge of 25/1-shot Beach Bunny by a short head (with the previous year's Oaks winner Look Here and Lush Lashes third and fourth). Dar Re Mi drifted right, forcing the runner-up off a true line, the result of the subsequent stewards' inquiry presumably music to the ears of her connections —and backers—on this particular occasion. Dar Re Mi also hit the right note in the Darley Yorkshire Oaks nearly two months later. Her second Group 1 victory came at the expense of the latest Oaks winner Sariska, who had gone on to complete the Anglo-Irish Oaks double in facile style. Odds-on Sariska was undoubtedly below her best at York—found to be in season afterwards—but Dar Re Mi's performance at least emphasised her gameness and her own reliability as she responded to Sariska's challenge in the last two furlongs to win by three quarters of a length.

Dar Re Mi was the only British-trained contender in the twelve-runner Vermeille and she stood out in the paddock, starting 2/1 second favourite behind the odds-on Prix de Diane winner Stacelita. Stacelita was coupled in the betting with her pacemaker Volver, who fulfilled her role until allowing Stacelita to slip through on the rail a furlong and a half out. Stacelita effectively stole a march on Dar Re Mi, who had to be switched across to the rail herself as Stacelita's pacemaker dropped back (Dar Re Mi's connections argued that the manoeuvre by Volver's jockey constituted team tactics and initiated the problems that followed). Dar Re Mi ran on gamely to collar Stacelita in the final strides but, in the process, she was deemed to have interfered with fifth-placed Soberania, who missed out on fourth by a short neck. If a runner in France fails to obtain its best possible placing (and therefore maximum prize money) because of interference, the horse responsible for the interference must be placed behind it, draconian compared to Britain, for example, where no winner can lose a race unless any interference it caused has 'improved' its own position.

The connections of Dar Re Mi appealed against the disqualification but the general view expressed in the British media beforehand that there had been 'minimal' contact between Dar Re Mi and Soberania was wide of the mark; the head-on film of the race was not readily available to racegoers on the day—France Galop is to ensure in future that replays of the race are shown from each viewpoint—but it showed that Dar Re Mi gave Soberania a considerable bump when switched right. Soberania's rider gave evidence to the appeal that the ground he lost did not cost him fourth place, but the Longchamp stewards' decision was upheld.

It was hard to find anyone, though, who disagreed with the immediate post-race summing-up of Stacelita's jockey Christophe Lemaire that 'Everyone knows Dar Re Mi was the best today.' Dar Re Mi's connections also had a point about the part played by Volver, whose rider was arguably lucky not to face disciplinary action. That said, in the context of the strict but crystal clear French rules, it has to be said that the Longchamp stewards seemed to have good grounds for disqualifying Dar Re Mi. When Dar Re Mi and Stacelita renewed rivalry three weeks later over the same course and distance in the Prix de l'Arc de Triomphe, Dar Re Mi confirmed the Vermeille form when finishing two places ahead of Stacelita, the pair fifth and joint-seventh respectively behind Sea The Stars, Dar Re Mi going second again briefly inside the final furlong. Dar Re Mi rounded off a good year with a creditable effort at the Breeders' Cup, stable jockey Jimmy Fortune (who will be riding freelance in 2010) losing the ride to Frankie Dettori when Dar Re Mi finished third to the Arc third Conduit in the Turf, a race chosen instead of the Filly & Mare Turf because its mile and a half suits Dar Re Mi ideally.

Dar Re Mi (b.f. 2005)	Singspiel (IRE) (b 1992)	In The Wings (b 1986)	Sadler's Wells
			High Hawk
		Glorious Song (b 1976)	Halo
			Ballade
	Darara (b 1983)	Top Ville (b 1976)	High Top
			Sega Ville
		Delsy (b 1972)	Abdos
			Kelty

The big, strong, attractive Dar Re Mi, an easy mover who did well physically from three to four, will make a fine replacement for her retired dam Darara at Watership Down Stud, though she is set to stay in training for another season,

Lord Lloyd-Webber's "Dar Re Mi"

presumably partly in the expectation of making it third time lucky in the Prix Vermeille, a race that Darara herself won as a three-year-old before coming sixth in the vintage Arc won by Dancing Brave. Darara and her illustrious half-brother Darshaan are descended on the dam's side from the celebrated Boussac mare Tourzima whom the Aga Khan—who purchased fifty-six mares and foals from the Boussac bloodstock empire when it was dispersed in 1978/9—describes as his 'rock, just as Mumtaz Mahal was for my grandfather.' The Boussac mares have served the Aga Khan's studs very well but Darara herself—a small, lightly-made individual—was sent to the December Sales as an eleven-year-old and Watership Down paid 470,000 guineas for her. She soon repaid her purchase price, the Shirley Heights foal she was carrying—the subsequent smart mile and a half performer Kilimanjaro—making 500,000 guineas as a yearling and two Sadler's Wells colts that followed in the next four years, Prix du Jockey Club third Rhagaas and Diaghilev, fetching 500,000 guineas and 3,400,000 guineas respectively as yearlings. The smart Diaghilev was sold privately out of Ballydoyle as a three-year-old and became a Group 1 winner in Hong Kong under the name of River Dancer. Another earlier son of Sadler's Wells, the smart middle-distance performer Darazari, became a Group 1 winner in Australia. Darara was barren for four years before ending a long wait for her first fillies when producing the fair middle-distance maiden Evita (by Selkirk) and, at the age of twenty-two, Dar Re Mi. Darara was barren again to Pivotal the year after producing Dar Re Mi but her final foal became her tenth winner when the two-year-old colt Rewilding (by Tiger Hill) won a minor event at Maisons-Laffitte for Sheikh Mohammed and Andre Fabre in November. He was his dam's third colt to be sold for 500,000 guineas as a yearling and must have good prospects of proving smart himself. The game and genuine Dar Re Mi, who usually races close up, has yet to race on soft or heavy going but probably acts on any other. She is sometimes bandaged behind. *J. H. M. Gosden*

DARSHONIN 2 ch.g. (Mar 21) Pivotal 124 – Incheni (IRE) 100 (Nashwan (USA) 135) [2009 6m 7m Oct 3] backward and green, seventh to Pastoral Player in maiden at Newbury: tailed off in sales race at Newmarket (gelded after). *J. Noseda* **56**

DART 5 br.m. Diktat 126 – Eilean Shona 102 (Suave Dancer (USA) 136) [2009 75: f14s^2 f14g^5 14v 17.1g^5 f14g^4 f14m f14m^2 f14g* Dec 22] good-topped mare: fair handicapper: left J. Fanshawe 6,500 gns after fourth outing: dropped in weights, won at Southwell in December: stays 2m: raced mostly on all-weather: tried tongue tied. *Mrs S. Lamyman* **72**

D'ARTAGNANS DREAM 3 b.g. Cyrano de Bergerac 120 – Kairine (IRE) (Kahyasi 130) [2009 67: 9.7m 8.5g 8g 8.1d^6 p8.6g^6 p12g^2 p12g^4 p12m Oct 26] fair maiden: stays easy 1½m: acts on polytrack and good to soft going: tried in cheekpieces, blinkered last 4 starts: held up (sometimes slowly away). *G. D. Blake* **67**

DARWIN'S DRAGON 3 ch.g. Royal Dragon (USA) 118 – Darwinia (GER) (Acatenango (GER) 127) [2009 70: 8.3g 8m f7g 7.1m p8g Jun 25] smallish gelding: modest maiden: below form after reappearance: stays 1m: tried blinkered: sold 3,500 gns in July, sent to Greece. *P. F. I. Cole* **64 d**

DARYAINUR (IRE) 2 br.f. (Mar 26) Auction House (USA) 120 – Maylan (IRE) 47 (Lashkari 128) [2009 7m 8.3m p8g Oct 26] compact filly: third foal: dam maiden (stayed 1¼m): well beaten in maidens. *W. de Best-Turner* **–**

DARYAKANA (FR) 3 ch.f. Selkirk (USA) 129 – Daryaba (IRE) 121 (Night Shift (USA)) [2009 12d* 13.5g* 12g* 12.5g* 12g* Dec 13] **120 p**

In a year of ups and downs for Christophe Lemaire, whose season has been documented in the essay on Rosanara, losing the opportunity to partner the unbeaten Daryakana will be one of his main regrets. Injury forced him to miss out when due to ride her for the first time in the Prix de Royallieu; and he was suspended when Daryakana signed off for the season in the Hong Kong Vase. The suspension was incurred at the Japan Cup meeting where Lemaire enjoyed one of his many big-race victories in 2009, winning the feature race on Vodka.

Daryakana was not seen out until July but she made up for lost time, winning three races before the Qatar Prix de Royallieu at Longchamp in October, her victories coming in a newcomers race at Clairefontaine, a minor event at Deauville and a listed contest at Chantilly. It did not look the most competitive renewal of the Group 2 Royallieu, and was even less competitive with the favourite

Qatar Prix de Royallieu, Longchamp—Gerald Mosse replaces the sidelined Christophe Lemaire as Daryakana maintains her unbeaten record in good style; Peinture Rare is second

Plumania not at her best, but second favourite Daryakana, patiently and confidently ridden by Gerald Mosse, won quite impressively by two and a half lengths from Peinture Rare. Two and a half months later, Mosse repeated his Royallieu tactics in the Group 1 Cathay Pacific Hong Kong Vase at Sha Tin, dropping Daryakana out last then bringing her wide into the straight. Two furlongs out, Daryakana had only one of her twelve rivals behind her, but she still managed to maintain her unbeaten record against more battle-hardened types than she had encountered previously. Daryakana's strong run took her to the front on the line, a short head the margin of victory over the favourite Spanish Moon. It was a very smart performance and Daryakana may well continue her improvement as a four-year-old when, rare for one of her owner's fillies, she remains in training. If she progresses again she will certainly be one to reckon with in the top middle-distance events in Europe in 2010 when, all being well, Christophe Lemaire will finally get the opportunity to ride her.

Daryakana (FR) (ch.f. 2006)	Selkirk (USA) (ch 1988)	Sharpen Up (ch 1969)	Atan
			Rocchetta
		Annie Edge (ch 1980)	Nebbiolo
			Friendly Court
	Daryaba (IRE) (b 1996)	Night Shift (b 1980)	Northern Dancer
			Ciboulette
		Darata (b 1988)	Vayrann
			Darazina

Daryakana's dam Daryaba, also owned by the Aga Khan and trained by Alain de Royer Dupre, was of a similar standard to her daughter but reached that level in even quicker time. Daryaba, raced only as a three-year-old, won three of her five starts, including the Prix de Diane on her third and Prix Vermeille on her fourth. She then lined up for the Arc as fourth choice in the betting, but she finished down the field and it was reported that she had bled a little subsequently and returned with mucus in her lungs. Daryakana is Daryaba's fifth foal and fourth winner, the pick of her previous produce the smart French middle-distance

Cathay Pacific Hong Kong Vase, Sha Tin—
Daryakana (right, noseband) makes it five wins out of five as she pounces late to win from fellow European raiders Spanish Moon (left) and strong-finishing Kasbah Bliss (second right)

performer Daramsar (by Rainbow Quest), winner of the 2006 Prix du Conseil de Paris. Daryaba is the best of several winners produced by Darata, who won a listed race at Longchamp before being placed in the Prix de Royaumont and Prix Minerve and finishing fourth in the Prix de Royallieu. The next dam Darazina won over an extended mile and a quarter. Daryakana, who stays thirteen and a half furlongs, has raced only on good ground since making her debut on good to soft. *A. de Royer Dupre, France*

DARYAL (IRE) 8 b.g. Night Shift (USA) – Darata (IRE) (Vayrann 133) [2009 11.6g Jul 6] good-topped gelding: fairly useful handicapper on Flat, very lightly raced: blinkered, well held sole start in 2009: stays 1¾m: acts on firm and soft ground. *G. L. Moore* –

DASH BACK (USA) 4 b.f. Sahm (USA) 112 – Nadwah (USA) 107 (Shadeed (USA) 135) [2009 53: 7g 7.2d² p7g² 7m 7m* 7s 7d 6g⁵ 7d 8g p7g 8m 8.5g p6g² p6g⁴ p7.1g* p6g⁴ Dec 7] lengthy filly: fairly useful handicapper: won at Cork in June and Wolverhampton in December: best around 7f: acts on polytrack, good to firm and good to soft going: often held up. *Adrian McGuinness, Ireland* 84

DASHEENA 6 b.m. Magic Ring (IRE) 115 – Sweet And Lucky (Lucky Wednesday 124) [2009 71d: p6g p7.1g⁶ p7.1g a6g⁶ a6g⁶ a6.8g⁴ a8g a6.8s Jun 13] angular mare: just modest handicapper in 2009: left A. McCabe after third start: stays 1m: acts on all-weather, firm and good to soft going: wears headgear (in cheekpieces last 3 starts in Britain): tried tongue tied: usually waited with. *Charlotte Sjogren, Sweden* 52

DASHER REILLY (USA) 8 b.g. Ghazi (USA) – Kutira (USA) (Dixieland Band (USA)) [2009 –: f16g p16.5g Jan 22] well held on Flat: tried blinkered. *A. Sadik* –

DASHING DANIEL 4 gr.g. Zamindar (USA) 116 – Etienne Lady (IRE) 67 (Imperial Frontier (USA) 112) [2009 52: 8g 6m 7.6g Jun 26] maiden: well held in 2009, in cheekpieces final start. *N. J. Vaughan* –

DASHING DOC (IRE) 2 ch.g. (Feb 7) Dr Fong (USA) 128 – Dashiba 102 (Dashing Blade 117) [2009 p6g 7m³ 7m⁴ 7g⁴ 7d³ 8g* 8m⁴ Sep 15] good-topped gelding: fourth foal: brother to useful 2005 2-y-o 1m winner Doctor Dash and half-brother to 5-y-o Barshiba: dam 9f/1¼m winner: fair performer: won maiden at Newmarket in August: should stay beyond 1m: acts on good to firm and good to soft going: gelded after final start. *D. R. C. Elsworth* 79

DATABASE (IRE) 2 ch.c. (Mar 31) Singspiel (IRE) 133 – Memory Green (USA) (Green Forest (USA) 134) [2009 8g³ 8g* Oct 21] 78,000Y: rather unfurnished colt: seventh foal: half-brother to 3 winners, including smart 1m (at 2 yrs)/1¼m winner Dr Greenfield and useful 1m and (at 2 yrs) 8.6f winner Forgery (both by Dr Devious): dam, won around 1¼m in US, out of sister to Glint of Gold: promising both starts in maidens, winning at Bath by ¾ length from Whistleinthewind: will be suited by 1¼m: has left Godolphin: should improve again. *Saeed bin Suroor* 84 p

DAUNTSEY PARK (IRE) 2 ch.c. (Feb 17) Refuse To Bend (IRE) 128 – Shauna's Honey (IRE) 88 (Danehill (USA) 126) [2009 6g 7.1m p8f p7g⁶ Nov 14] strong colt: modest maiden: best effort when sixth in nursery at Lingfield: should stay at least 1m. *Miss Tor Sturgis* 58

DAVANA 3 b.f. Primo Valentino (IRE) 116 – Bombay Sapphire (Be My Chief (USA) 122) [2009 –: 6.1f 8.3g^6 8.3d^3 p9.5g^5 p12.2g^6 p8.6m^3 f8f^3 p8.6g^5 Dec 19] modest maiden: stays 8.6f: acts on all-weather. *W. J. H. Ratcliffe* **53**

DAVAYE 5 b.m. Bold Edge 123 – Last Impression 69 (Imp Society (USA)) [2009 5d May 15] leggy, quite good-topped mare: one-time fair performer: missed 2008: well beaten sole start at 5 yrs. *K. R. Burke* **–**

DAVE DIAMOND 3 b.g. Deportivo 116 – Blossoming (Vague Shot 108) [2009 8.3m Jul 11] tailed off in seller at Nottingham. *P. D. Evans* **–**

DAVENPORT (IRE) 7 b.g. Bold Fact (USA) 116 – Semence d'Or (FR) (Kaldoun (FR) 122) [2009 82: f8s^3 p9.5g f11g^5 Feb 3] leggy, close-coupled gelding: fair handicapper nowadays: stays 11f: acts on all-weather and soft going (below form on firmer than good): wears cheekpieces nowadays: sometimes slowly away: held up. *B. R. Millman* **71**

DAVIDS CITY (IRE) 5 b.g. Laveron 111 – Irelands Own (IRE) (Commanche Run 133) [2009 p13.9g^5 p13.9m p12.2g Dec 7] modest form in bumpers for Gordon Elliott in Ireland: similar level on Flat in sellers/claimer. *G. A. Harker* **53**

DAVIDS MARK 9 b.g. Polar Prince (IRE) 117 – Star of Flanders (Puissance 110) [2009 59: p6g^5 p6g* p6g^2 p6g p6g 6g^4 6.1f 6m^6 p6g^6 p6g p6m^4 p6f Dec 21] compact gelding: modest handicapper: won at Lingfield in January: barely stays 7f: acts on all-weather, firm and soft going: tried in headgear/tongue tie: held up. *J. R. Jenkins* **59**

DAVIDS MATADOR 3 b.g. Dansili 127 – Mousseline (USA) (Barathea (IRE) 127) [2009 73: 8.1g^6 9.9g 7.6f^6 8d^6 7m^6 p7g^5 p6f^5 7m p6g^5 Oct 23] compact gelding: fair maiden handicapper: below form after reappearance (gelded following third outing): stays 1m: yet to race on extremes of going on turf: tried in blinkers/cheekpieces: sold 2,500 gns. *Eve Johnson Houghton* **73**

DAWNBREAK (USA) 2 ch.f. (Mar 10) Distorted Humor (USA) 117 – Dawn Princess (USA) (Polish Numbers (USA)) [2009 p7g* 7m^6 7m^2 Oct 13] $270,000Y, $560,000 2-y-o: tall, attractive filly: fifth foal: half-sister to several winners in USA: dam, US 6f to 1m (including at 2 yrs) winner, out of half-sister to Breeders' Cup Juvenile Fillies winner Countess Diana: fairly useful form: won maiden at Lingfield in September: best effort when 4 lengths second to Hafawa in minor event at Leicester, dictating: will stay 1m. *Saeed bin Suroor* **87**

DAWN STORM (IRE) 4 ch.g. City On A Hill (USA) 114 – Flames (Blushing Flame (USA) 109) [2009 p9.5g p12.2g^5 p16.5g^3 f14g^3 Dec 22] modest maiden: stays 16.5f: raced on all-weather: tried in cheekpieces/blinkers. *J. L. Spearing* **58**

DAWN WIND 4 b.f. Vettori (IRE) 119 – Topper (IRE) (Priolo (USA) 127) [2009 50: p12.2g^6 p11g^3 p12.2g^3 p12.2g 17.2g 8d Jul 27] tall, narrow filly: modest maiden handicapper, better on all-weather: stays 11f: acts on polytrack and good to firm going: usually wears headgear: tongue tied first 5 starts in 2009. *I. A. Wood* **–** **a55**

DAWSON CREEK (IRE) 5 ch.g. Titus Livius (FR) 115 – Particular Friend 88 (Cadeaux Genereux 131) [2009 74: p7g p7m 7.6m p10g^6 p7m p8m Dec 9] good-bodied gelding: modest handicapper: stays easy 1m: acts on polytrack and soft ground: has worn cheekpieces/blinkers: tried tongue tied. *B. Gubby* **59**

DAYANARA (USA) 3 b. or br.f. Action This Day (USA) 121 – Dana Did It (USA) (Wagon Limit (USA) 122) [2009 8.3g p8g 11.7g p12g^6 p12g^6 Oct 20] $50,000Y: rather leggy filly: first foal: dam, US 6f winner from 2 starts, half-sister to US Grade 2 7f winner Proper Gamble: modest maiden: stays easy 1½m: blinkered final start: sold 1,000 gns, joined Mrs S. Leech. *C. G. Cox* **56**

DAY CARE 8 gr.g. Daylami (IRE) 138 – Ancara 109 (Dancing Brave (USA) 140) [2009 54: p12g^2 p10.7g^3 p13.9g^2 Nov 2] big gelding: modest maiden handicapper: stays easy 1¾m: acts on polytrack: tried blinkered/in cheekpieces/tongue tied. *R. McGlinchey, Ireland* **62**

DAYIA (IRE) 5 br.m. Act One 124 – Masharik (IRE) 93 (Caerleon (USA) 132) [2009 85: 15.4g^3 p16g^2 16.2g^5 p13.9g* 18m^4 16d^2 Oct 28] tall, leggy mare: useful bumper winner: fairly useful handicapper on Flat: won at Wolverhampton in October: creditable efforts after at Newmarket (Cesarewitch) and Musselburgh: stays 2¼m: acts on polytrack, good to soft and good to firm ground. *J. Pearce* **94**

DAY IN DUBAI 3 b.f. Dubai Destination (USA) 127 – Pazzazz (IRE) (Green Desert (USA) 127) [2009 –: 6m^6 6f 5m 7g 6m 7d 6g p10g^5 Nov 1] lengthy filly: little form. *J. J. Bridger* **–**

DAY OF THE EAGLE (IRE) 3 b.g. Danehill Dancer (IRE) 117 – Puck's Castle 92 (Shirley Heights 130) [2009 8d 9.9m^3 9.9m^5 8g^3 8g* Oct 30] €100,000Y: lengthy gelding: half-brother to 3 winners, including 5f winner (including at 2 yrs) Emerald Peace (by Green Desert) and Irish 1½m winner Down Mexico Way (by Sadler's Wells), both useful: dam, 1m winner (ran only at 2 yrs), half-sister to Cheveley Park Stakes winner Embassy: fairly useful form: steadily progressive, and won apprentice handicap at Newmarket in October (hung left, gelded after): should stay beyond 1m: unraced on extremes of going. *L. M. Cumani* **84**

DAYS OF PLEASURE (IRE) 4 b.g. Fraam 114 – Altizaf 66 (Zafonic (USA) 130) [2009 69: p12g Jan 17] fair performer at 3 yrs: last only start on Flat in 2009 (successful over hurdles in March): stays 1m: raced solely on all-weather. *C. Gordon* **–**

DAYS OF THUNDER (IRE) 4 b.g. Choisir (AUS) 126 – Grazina (Mark of Esteem (IRE) 137) [2009 8.1g f6g 7s 10m p9.5g Dec 19] no form. *B. R. Summers* **–**

DAZAKHEE 2 ch.f. (Mar 31) Sakhee (USA) 136 – Ziya (IRE) (Lion Cavern (USA) 117) [2009 6f^4 7d 6m 6d f8m^5 Nov 11] tall filly: fourth foal: half-sister to winner in Greece by Singspiel: dam unraced half-sister to Greenham Stakes winner who stayed 1½m Zayyani: modest maiden: fifth in nursery at Southwell: should stay beyond 1m: acts on fibresand: in cheekpieces fourth start. *P. T. Midgley* **50**

DAZED AND AMAZED 5 b.g. Averti (IRE) 117 – Amazed 58 (Clantime 101) [2009 91: 5.7g* 6g^4 5g 5.7f^4 5m 5d 5.2d^5 5m^4 p6g Oct 9] compact, well-made gelding: fairly useful handicapper: won at Bath in April: largely below form otherwise in 2009: best at 5f/easy 6f: acts on polytrack, good to firm and good to soft going: tried blinkered/tongue tied. *R. Hannon* **91**

DAZEEN 2 b.g. (Feb 23) Zafeen (FR) 123 – Bond Finesse (IRE) 61 (Danehill Dancer (IRE) 117) [2009 6g 5m^2 6m^5 5d^2 6m^4 Aug 28] tall gelding: fair maiden: probably stays 6f: acts on good to firm going, probably on good to soft: has raced freely. *P. T. Midgley* **73**

DAZINSKI 3 ch.g. Sulamani (IRE) 130 – Shuheb 93 (Nashwan (USA) 135) [2009 67: 12.1g^5 12d^3 14.1s^2 14.1m^3 15.9m* 16g^3 16m* 16g Oct 30] angular gelding: useful handicapper: won at Chester in August and Nottingham (beat Ermyn Lodge by 2 lengths) in September: shaped as if amiss final start: likely to stay beyond 2m: acts on soft and good to firm going. *M. H. Tompkins* **95**

DAZZLING BAY 9 b.g. Mind Games 121 – Adorable Cherub (USA) 58 (Halo (USA)) [2009 91§: 6m 6m^6 6m^2 6m^3 6g 6m Aug 31] big, rather leggy gelding: has a round action: fairly useful handicapper: stays 6f: acts on polytrack and firm ground: often blinkered: has been reluctant to post/slowly away: often held up: unreliable. *T. D. Easterby* **83 §**

DAZZLING BEGUM 4 br.f. Okawango (USA) 115 – Dream On Me 60 (Prince Sabo 123) [2009 58: p12.2g^4 f12g f12g^2 f12g^2 f12g^6 f12d^3 p13.9g f12g 11.9m^6 11.5g 14.1g^3 12m^3 f14g* 16d^4 12.1g^5 13.1d p16.5g^3 15.4m* p13.9g^6 p16.5g f14m p12.2g* f14g^5 Dec 22] plain filly: modest handicapper: won at Southwell in July, Folkestone in September and Wolverhampton in December: stays 16.5f: acts on all-weather, soft and good to firm ground: often in headgear in 2009: ridden patiently. *J. Pearce* **60**

DAZZLING COLOURS 4 b.c. Oasis Dream 129 – Dazzle 116 (Gone West (USA)) [2009 p7g 8.3g p7.1g 6m 10.1g Jul 20] strong, well-made colt: maiden: missed 2008: little form at 4 yrs: visored last 2 starts. *T. T. Clement* **–**

DAZZLING LIGHT (UAE) 4 b. or br.f. Halling (USA) 133 – Crown of Light 112 (Mtoto 134) [2009 77: 9m^3 12.5m^2 11.1g^3 12m^2 14m* 11.5m^5 12m^4 12m 16.4d 13.1m^3 13.4m^2 13.1m^4 16d^5 Oct 28] useful-looking filly: fairly useful handicapper: won at Musselburgh in May: stays 2m: acts on good to firm and good to soft ground. *J. S. Goldie* **85**

DEACON BLUES 2 b.c. (Feb 19) Compton Place 125 – Persario 96 (Bishop of Cashel 122) [2009 6.1s^5 6m* Oct 26] sturdy, good-quartered colt: first foal: dam, 6f/7f winner, sister to smart miler Heretic and closely related to smart 7f/1m performer Warningford: heavily supported, better effort in maidens when winning at Leicester in October readily by 1¼ lengths from Rolling Hills, racing keenly and in control final 2f: useful prospect. *J. R. Fanshawe* **83 p**

DEAD CAT BOUNCE (IRE) 3 b.c. Mujadil (USA) 119 – Where's Charlotte 53 (Sure Blade (USA) 130) [2009 50p: p8g p8g^6 p9.5m p10g^2 8d 9.8m 8m^4 May 19] rather leggy colt: modest maiden: stays 1¼m: best efforts on polytrack: in blinkers/cheekpieces last 4 starts, when also tongue tied: possibly not straightforward. *J. Pearce* **57** **a63**

DEADLINE (UAE) 5 ch.g. Machiavellian (USA) 123 – Time Changes (USA) (Danzig (USA)) [2009 –: f8g^5 f11g^6 Mar 17] workmanlike gelding: just poor handicapper in 2009: **49**

stays 1¼m: acts on all-weather, firm and good to soft going: tried in cheekpieces: fair hurdler, joined Mrs A. Thorpe £4,200 in June, successful twice after. *P. T. Midgley*

DEADLY ENCOUNTER (IRE) 3 br.g. Lend A Hand 124 – Cautious Joe 73 (First Trump 118) [2009 90d: 7.1v^5 7.1m* 7m^6 7.1m^4 7d^4 Jul 30] tall, leggy gelding: fairly useful handicapper: won at Haydock in June: said to have been struck into behind final start: worth a try at 1m: unraced on firm going, acts on any other. *R. A. Fahey* **87**

DEADLY SECRET (USA) 3 b.g. Johannesburg (USA) 127 – Lypink (USA) 107 (Lyphard (USA) 132) [2009 97: 7m 8.1v 8g^2 8m 8.1g^5 8m Aug 16] angular gelding: useful handicapper: creditable effort in 2009 only when 1¼ lengths second to Roman Republic at Doncaster: stays 1m: acts on firm and good to soft going: often races prominently. *R. A. Fahey* **96**

DEAD WOMANS PASS (IRE) 2 b.f. (Feb 13) High Chaparral (IRE) 132 – Pedicure (Atticus (USA) 121) [2009 6m 7g 5.4d 7.1m 7.1d^5 Oct 28] €25,000Y: rather leggy filly: third foal: sister to French 1¼m winner High Perfection: dam, French maiden, closely related to smart performer up to 7f Diableneyev: poor maiden: should be as effective at 6f as 7f. *N. Wilson* **39**

DEAL (IRE) 2 b.f. (Apr 25) Invincible Spirit (IRE) 121 – Desert Order (IRE) (Desert King (IRE) 129) [2009 5g^3 5.5f^3 5d* 5m^5 6s^3 6m 5.2m Aug 14] neat filly: fourth foal: dam unraced half-sister to smart Irish performer up to 1m Beckett: fairly useful performer: won maiden at Warwick in June: ran creditably in listed races next 2 starts, including third to Duplicity at Newbury: effective at 5f/6f: acts on soft and good to firm going. *R. Hannon* **84**

DEAN IARRACHT (IRE) 3 b.g. Danetime (IRE) 121 – Sirdhana 79 (Selkirk (USA) 129) [2009 67: 7g^3 f7g^6 7g^3 8m^4 7m 8.1s^4 9.3d^3 10s 8s 8m^5 8.3v^4 p9.5g^3 Dec 4] sturdy gelding: fair maiden handicapper: left M. Dods before penultimate outing: stays 9.3f: acts on soft and good to firm going: tried in headgear: tongue tied once: usually held up. *Miss Tracy Waggott* **72**

DEAR MAURICE 5 b.g. Indian Ridge 123 – Shamaiel (IRE) 113 (Lycius (USA) 124) [2009 93: 9.9g^4 9.8d^3 8.1v 8g^4 10.2g^4 8.3m^2 8.3f^6 8m^3 p9.5g^3 p10g Oct 22] well-made gelding: fairly useful handicapper: stays 9.5f: acts on polytrack and good to firm going: tried in headgear: usually held up: sometimes finishes weakly. *E. A. L. Dunlop* **84**

DEAR MR FANTASY (IRE) 2 b.c. (Mar 21) Kingsalsa (USA) 118 – Heart Ofthe Matter (Rainbow Quest (USA) 134) [2009 p6g^5 6m 7g p7.1m* p7.1g p8m p8.6g Oct 9] modest performer: won claimer at Wolverhampton in August: should stay 1m: acts on polytrack: sold 3,500 gns. *J. W. Hills* **59**

DEAUVILLE FLYER 3 b.g. Dubai Destination (USA) 127 – Reaf (In The Wings 128) [2009 7m^6 8m 12.4g^3 12m* 12d^3 14m^4 14v* 16.4d^2 14.6g^3 Oct 23] 45,000Y: unfurnished gelding: first foal: dam unraced sister to smart stayer Boreas: fairly useful handicapper: progressed steadily in 2009, winning at Doncaster in June and Haydock in July: gelded after final start: stays 2m: acts on heavy and good to firm going. *T. D. Easterby* **88**

DEAUVILLE POST (FR) 2 b.c. (Apr 6) American Post 121 – Loyola (FR) (Sicyos (USA) 126) [2009 7.1m 7g^4 7.1g^2 8g^3 Aug 28] €25,000Y: tall colt: half-brother to several winners abroad, including French 5f to 11f winner Lady of Shanghai (by Septieme Ciel): dam, French 7.5f winner, closely related to smart French performer up to 1m Boreale: progressive form, doing particularly well when 1¼ lengths third to Whippers Love in nursery at Newmarket: stays 1m. *R. Hannon* **88**

DEAUVILLE VISION (IRE) 6 b.m. Danehill Dancer (IRE) 117 – Alexia Reveuse (IRE) (Dr Devious (IRE) 127) [2009 108: 8s 8v^3 10s* 9g 9s^5 10s^4 9v^6 Aug 30] tall, rather leggy mare: smart performer: won listed race at the Curragh in June by 2½ lengths from She's Our Mark: well below form after: stayed 1¼m: went well on ground softer than good: usually in cheekpieces, blinkered sixth start: reportedly in foal to Kheleyf. *M. Halford, Ireland* **110**

DEBDENE BANK (IRE) 6 b.m. Pivotal 124 – Nedaarah 83 (Reference Point 139) [2009 70: p8g^5 p9.5g^6 p8g 10.9m 11.5g^2 f12g 10d^2 p8.6m^3 p13.9g^2 p12g^3 p13.9g^6 Nov 30] good-topped mare: fair maiden handicapper: stays 13.8f: acts on polytrack, good to firm and good to soft ground: consistent. *Mrs Mary Hambro* **70**

DEBORD (FR) 6 ch.g. Sendawar (IRE) 129 – Partie de Dames (USA) (Bering 136) [2009 –§: p16g 15.4m^6 Aug 6] strong gelding: little form since 2007: tried blinkered: unreliable. *Jamie Poulton* **– §**

DEBUSSY (IRE) 3 b.c. Diesis 133 – Opera Comique (FR) 100 (Singspiel (IRE) 133) [2009 70p: p10g* 10.1g* 12.3m^3 12g 12f 10g* 10m^6 Aug 16] strong colt: smart performer: won maiden at Lingfield in March, minor event at Epsom (beat Midday readily by 1¼ lengths) in April and Prix Eugene Adam at Maisons-Laffitte (by ½ length from World Heritage) in July: creditable efforts most other starts, including when third to Golden Sword in Chester Vase, eighth to Sea The Stars in Derby at Epsom and fifth (demoted to sixth after edging left) behind Sri Putra in Prix Guillaume d'Ornano at Deauville: effective at 1¼m/1½m: raced only on polytrack and good going or firmer: tried in cheekpieces (well held) fifth outing: often makes running. *J. H. M. Gosden* **114**

DECAMERON (USA) 4 br.g. Theatrical 128 – Morning Pride (IRE) 113 (Machiavellian (USA) 123) [2009 94: 8.1g^5 7f f8g 10m^5 p8m^4 p8g p7.1g Dec 26] good-bodied gelding: fairly useful handicapper: not so good in 2009: left Sir Michael Stoute 22,000 gns and gelded after second outing: stays 1m: acts on polytrack and good to firm going: tried visored (looked reluctant)/in cheekpieces. *R. A. Harris* **82**

DECEMBER 3 b.g. Oasis Dream 129 – Winter Solstice 104 (Unfuwain (USA) 131) [2009 –p: 8s 10m p10g^3 p12g^5 p12f^6 Dec 21] stocky gelding: fair maiden: stays easy 1½m: acts on polytrack and good to firm ground: tongue tied second start (left Sir Michael Stoute 6,000 gns after). *Mrs C. A. Dunnett* **68**

DECEMBER DRAW (IRE) 3 br.g. Medecis 119 – New York (IRE) 72 (Danzero (AUS)) [2009 86p: 8.3g^3 9g^5 8.3g^3 p8g p10m^6 Dec 9] fairly useful handicapper: stays 1¼m: raced only on polytrack and good ground: in cheekpieces final start. *W. J. Knight* **87**

DECENCY (IRE) 2 b.f. (May 18) Celtic Swing 138 – Siem Reap (USA) (El Gran Senor (USA) 136) [2009 p6g 6g p6g Nov 9] €40,000F: rather leggy filly: fifth foal: sister to useful Irish 2007 2-y-o 6f winner Irish Jig, later successful in Hong Kong, and half-sister to winner in Spain by Revoque: dam, unraced, out of smart Irish sprinter Sunset Reigns: signs of ability when down the field in maidens: type to do better in handicaps. *E. A. L. Dunlop* **46 p**

DECHIPER (IRE) 7 b. or br.g. Almutawakel 126 – Safiya (USA) (Riverman (USA) 131) [2009 70: 12.4m^5 10.1g^5 12.4s* 16.1d 11.5m^2 10.1d* 10.1d^2 11.5d 10g^6 8m 8m^4 12d 12.4g^4 16.1d 18g^4 Oct 19] lengthy, deep-girthed gelding: fair handicapper: won at Newcastle (all 5 wins there) in May and June: effective at 1¼m to 2m: acts on soft and good to firm going: tried in cheekpieces: waited with. *R. Johnson* **76**

DECIDER (USA) 6 ch.g. High Yield (USA) 121 – Nikita Moon (USA) (Secret Hello (USA)) [2009 –, a76: p5.1g f5g^3 p5.1g^6 p5.1g^3 p5g^6 p5.1m^3 f5g^4 f5g^2 f5m^4 f5g f5g p5.1g^2 p5.1g f6g^4 p5.1g^5 5.1d 5m^3 p5.1g* p6g^3 p5.1g^4 p5.1g* p6g p5.1g^2 p5m^2 p5f^4 Dec 19] rangy gelding: fair performer on all-weather, modest on turf: won handicap at Wolverhampton in September and seller there in November: best at 5f/6f: acts on all-weather and firm going: often blinkered/in cheekpieces: races prominently: none too consistent. *R. A. Harris* **55 + a73**

DECIMUS MERIDIUS (IRE) 2 ch.c. (Feb 8) Danehill Dancer (IRE) 117 – Simaat (USA) 72 (Mr Prospector (USA)) [2009 7g^3 8d 8.3g Sep 20] modest form in maidens, best effort on debut: should be suited by 1m+. *J. Howard Johnson* **60**

DECISION 3 b.g. Royal Applause 124 – Corinium (IRE) 116 (Turtle Island (IRE) 123) [2009 81: 10.2g^2 10d^2 10.4g^4 10m^2 12g^3 10.3m 10m 10g* Oct 19] smallish, compact gelding: fairly useful performer: won handicap at Windsor in October: stays 1½m: acts on soft and good to firm ground: tried in cheekpieces: front runner/races prominently: sold 30,000 gns, then gelded. *C. G. Cox* **87**

DECKCHAIR 3 b.f. Monsieur Bond (IRE) 120 – Silver Sun 83 (Green Desert (USA) 127) [2009 61: p5g^3 p6g^5 p5g^4 p6g^4 p7g p6g* 5m^5 p6g 6d 7m^4 7m^5 p7g p6m^5 Nov 26] close-coupled filly: modest performer: won seller at Wolverhampton in March: left H. Collingridge after ninth start: stays 7f: acts on polytrack and good to firm going: visored. *S. Curran* **59**

DECORATIVE (IRE) 2 b.f. (Feb 16) Danehill Dancer (IRE) 117 – Source of Life (IRE) (Fasliyev (USA) 120) [2009 6g* Aug 30] 130,000Y: first foal: dam unraced half-sister to 4-y-o Forgotten Voice (by Danehill Dancer), out of half-sister to Breeders' Cup Classic winner Arcangues: 11/4 favourite, created most favourable impression when winning maiden at Yarmouth easily by 4 lengths from Battlemaiden, travelling strongly and stretching away for pressure: bred to stay 1m: looks a smart prospect. *M. A. Jarvis* **96 P**

DECORUM (USA) 3 b.c. Dynaformer (USA) – Shy Greeting (ARG) (Shy Tom (USA)) [2009 78p: 10.1m^3 11d^3 p12.2g^2 13g^5 11.9d^2 a12g^4 a12g^4 Dec 29] good sort: fairly useful maiden: sold from J. Gosden 16,000 gns after fifth start (blinkered): stays 1½m: acts on polytrack, good to firm and good to soft ground: usually tongue tied: irresolute. *F. Vermeulen, France* **83 §**

DECREE ABSOLUTE (USA) 2 b. or br.g. (Feb 15) Orientate (USA) 127 – Midriff (USA) (Naevus (USA)) [2009 6m* 6m^2 7d 7.1m Sep 29] $9,000Y, £20,000 2-y-o: medium-sized gelding: fifth foal: brother to winner in USA: half-brother to 2 winners, including 5-y-o Nordic Light: dam US 6f winner: fair form: won maiden at Salisbury in June: only form subsequently when good second of 4 to Jack My Boy in minor event at Pontefract: stays 6f: gelded after final start. *Miss J. R. Tooth* **73**

DEDANTE 3 br. or gr.f. One Cool Cat (USA) 123 – Cloridja (Indian Ridge 123) [2009 62: p5g^6 p5g^6 f5g 6d Jul 20] lengthy, angular filly: modest maiden: refused to race final outing: free-going sort, raced mostly at 5f: acts on all-weather and firm going: usually blinkered in 2009: races up with pace: one to treat with caution. *D. K. Ivory* **49 §**

DEE CEE ELLE 5 b.m. Groom Dancer (USA) 128 – Missouri 86 (Charnwood Forest (IRE) 125) [2009 –: p16.5g 11.7f^5 p16.5g^3 Aug 10] close-coupled mare: modest handicapper on Flat in 2009: stays 16.5f: acts on all-weather and good to firm ground: tried in cheekpieces: modest hurdler. *D. Burchell* **57**

DEELY PLAZA 2 b.g. (Apr 18) Compton Place 125 – Anchorage (IRE) 86 (Slip Anchor 136) [2009 6m p6g^4 7m^4 8.3d^5 8g^4 Oct 19] 20,000F, 40,000Y: lengthy, quite attractive gelding: half-brother to several winners, including 1997 2-y-o 7f winner Red Leggings (by Shareef Dancer) and 2m winner Lord Alaska (by Sir Harry Lewis), both fairly useful, and to dam of 3-y-o Sayif: dam 1½m winner: fair maiden: should stay 1¼m: acts on polytrack, good to firm and good to soft going: sold 9,000 gns, joined J. Glover and gelded. *R. Hannon* **71**

DEEP WINTER 4 ch.f. Pivotal 124 – Russian Snows (IRE) 113 (Sadler's Wells (USA) 132) [2009 91: 8m^2 8g^3 9m 10.4m 10.4g Jul 25] strong, angular filly: fairly useful performer: creditable efforts when placed first 2 outings, third to Waky Love in listed event at Hanover latter occasion: below form after: stayed 10.2f: acted on polytrack, firm and soft going: stud. *R. A. Fahey* **94**

DEFECTOR (IRE) 3 b.g. Fasliyev (USA) 120 – Rich Dancer 70 (Halling (USA) 133) [2009 73: 6g^5 7g 6m^3 f6g^2 6d f6g^4 p6g p7m* f7g^5 p7m^2 p7g^3 p7m^3 p7g p7m^5 p7.1g^3 p7m* Dec 30] lengthy gelding: fairly useful handicapper: won at Kempton in September and December: stays 7f: acts on all-weather and good to firm going: tried blinkered/in cheekpieces. *W. R. Muir* **83**

DEFI (IRE) 7 b.g. Rainbow Quest (USA) 134 – Danse Classique (IRE) 94 (Night Shift (USA)) [2009 54: 9m^6 9.1g 7.9g 7.1m 8g 8s Aug 27] good-bodied gelding: has a moderate, quick action: poor performer: stays 9f: acts on polytrack and firm going: tried in cheekpieces, usually in blinkers/tongue tie at 7 yrs: often races prominently. *D. A. Nolan* **49**

DEFINIGHTLY 3 b. or br.g. Diktat 126 – Perfect Night 79 (Danzig Connection (USA)) [2009 102: 6m 7.1v^6 6g Jun 13] sturdy, lengthy gelding: just fairly useful form at best in 2009: gelded after final start: stays 7f: acts on soft going. *R. Charlton* **85**

DEIRDRE 2 b.f. (Mar 5) Dubawi (IRE) 129 – Dolores 111 (Danehill (USA) 126) [2009 p7g^5 8d* Oct 13] attractive filly: fourth foal: half-sister to 4-y-o Duncan and smart stayer Samuel (by Sakhee): dam 1m winner: better effort in maidens when winning at Newcastle readily by 3¼ lengths from Anaya, dictating: should stay 1¼m: open to further improvement. *J. H. M. Gosden* **79 p**

DELEGATOR 3 b.c. Dansili 127 – Indian Love Bird (Efisio 120) [2009 116p: 8m* 8m^2 8v 8m^2 8g*^{dis} 8m^3 8f^5 Nov 7] **125**

Godolphin ended up having a particularly good year after a sticky period —one that is in danger of becoming habitual—following its annual spring relocation from Dubai to Newmarket. The bulk of Godolphin's winners came in the second half of the year, the most important victories including those of Mastery in the St Leger and Vale of York in the Breeders' Cup Juvenile. There were thirteen Group/Grade 1 victories (nine of them in the USA)—a number bettered only in 1999 (18), 2001 (15) and 2002 (16)—among the record 202 races won around the globe (at a strike rate of 27%). It could still be claimed with partial justification, though, that Godolphin fell short at the very highest level, in that it did not have a 'flagship horse' to match Daylami, Fantastic Light and Grandera in 1999, 2001 and 2002 respectively. 'You can't judge us because we didn't win the Guineas or the Derby or we didn't take Royal Ascot by storm . . . some people imagine that every horse we run has to be a superstar, but that's not realistic,' is how racing manager Simon Crisford counters such claims.

Godolphin's attempts to procure a ready-made, potential 'flagship horse' during the course of the season included the private purchase of two colts who made their mark in both the Two Thousand Guineas and the St James's Palace Stakes. Evasive, sixth (after an interrupted preparation) and then fourth in those two races, joined Godolphin from Sir Michael Stoute after Royal Ascot and Delegator, runner-up in both events, left Brian Meehan in another high profile summer transfer. Evasive made only one more appearance, when a beaten favourite in the Hungerford Stakes at Newbury, but Delegator raised hopes when winning the totesport.com Celebration Mile at Goodwood on his first run for Godolphin, though they took a knock when he was subsequently beaten convincingly by Rip Van Winkle and Zacinto in the Queen Elizabeth II Stakes and managed only fifth in the Breeders' Cup Mile. Worse was to follow when Delegator was stripped of the Celebration Mile at an inquiry finally held by the Disciplinary Panel of the BHA in December after he failed a dope test at Goodwood. Analysis had confirmed the presence of methylprednisolone, a prohibited substance. 'Delegator was treated with an anti-inflammatory which took longer to clear his system than we thought, it was one of those things,' was how Simon Crisford explained it. Godolphin have had a classic winner—Noverre in the 2001 Poule d'Essai des Poulains—disqualified in similar circumstances involving methylprednisolone. With Delegator, the sources of the substance were two injections of Depo-Medrone into Delegator's forelegs on July 13th. The Celebration Mile was on August 29th, Godolphin's veterinary surgeon having advised a withdrawal period for the drug of forty-two days. Delegator's case illustrated that nothing is cut and dried when it comes to the risks of using banned race-day substances in training. Saeed bin Suroor was fined £750 and told that horses in his care would be the subject of examination and sample testing over the next twelve months.

Godolphin's "Delegator"

The purchase of Delegator may still pay dividends when he returns to action as a four-year-old. There are no plans to race him in Dubai, where he is being wintered, and his training will be geared to a European programme. Although he has established himself as a high-class miler, he will also be given the chance to show what he can do at shorter trips and, all being well, could make a big name for himself as a sprinter-miler. Delegator had made a very favourable impression when beaten a length and a half into fifth (with Rip Van Winkle also turning in an eye-catching performance in seventh) in the Dewhurst on the last of three outings at two. As a stablemate of the season's top two-year-old and leading home-trained classic hope Crowded House, Delegator was a 33/1-shot for the Two Thousand Guineas before reports of sparkling home work in the spring coincided with his being heavily backed for Newmarket. Looking to have done plenty of work, he romped home in the banshahousestables.com Craven Stakes over the course and distance in April, quickening smartly after being confidently ridden (held up last) to win by two and three quarter lengths from Sans Frontieres. Crowded House had already had his reappearance postponed until the Dante and Delegator, said by his trainer to be 'primed with both barrels', started 3/1 favourite on Two Thousand Guineas day. He found only Sea The Stars too good for him, going down by a length and a half despite hanging badly left at one stage, with Gan Amhras third and Rip Van Winkle, who had had a setback in his preparation, fourth (Delegator and Evasive were the only British-trained runners in the first six).

Well below his best on heavy ground when eighth of nine in the Irish Two Thousand Guineas, Delegator arguably improved on his Newmarket form at Royal Ascot, where he ran the Irish Guineas winner Mastercraftsman to a neck in the St James's Palace Stakes, getting his nose in front a hundred yards out, after again showing a good turn of foot, and only being run out of it close home. It was over two months before Delegator was seen again, under the Godolphin banner in the Celebration Mile at the end of August. He landed the odds by a length and a half and a head from Zacinto and Ordnance Row, again showing that speed is his principal asset as Frankie Dettori extricated him from a pocket at just the right time to unleash an irresistible run in a race turned into something of a sprint by a steady early gallop. When Delegator tackled the Queen Elizabeth II Stakes, Rip Van Winkle's rider Johnny Murtagh ensured that the emphasis was firmly on stamina, sending his mount for home fully three furlongs out after the Prix du Moulin winner Aqlaam had been forced to set a particularly strong gallop from the start to deny Rip Van Winkle the lead. Delegator managed only third of four in the end, beaten by a length and a quarter and three and a quarter, eased when it was clear he had no more to give in a race that turned into a gruelling test at the trip. Delegator didn't come up to expectations behind Goldikova in the Breeders' Cup Mile at Santa Anita where Zacinto (also in the Mile) and Rip Van Winkle (Classic) also ran some way below their Queen Elizabeth II Stakes form.

Delegator (b.c. 2006)	Dansili (b 1996)	Danehill (b 1986)	Danzig
			Razyana
		Hasili (b 1991)	Kahyasi
			Kerali
	Indian Love Bird (b 1999)	Efisio (b 1982)	Formidable
			Eldoret
		Indian Love Song (b 1983)	Be My Guest
			Indian Bird

Delegator, a strong individual who did well physically from two to three, is by the high-class miler Dansili, who has sired an Arc winner in Rail Link and is also the sire of Zacinto, among others. Dansili sires winners over a wide range of distances, though the average distance of races won by his progeny is around nine furlongs. Delegator's dam Indian Love Bird was an unraced sister to the smart six- and seven-furlong performer Tomba, who won the Prix de la Foret and Royal Ascot's Cork And Orrery Stakes (now the Golden Jubilee), and was also placed three times in the Sprint Cup at Haydock. Delegator's grandam Indian Love Song is also the dam of the Prix du Jockey Club winner Holding Court, whose sire Hernando is a noted influence for stamina (Efisio, the sire of Indian Love Bird and Tomba, was an influence for speed). Delegator is the third foal out of Indian Love Bird and her only winner so far; she had a two-year-old filly by Oasis Dream who was not in training, while a year-younger half-brother by Haafhd died as a foal. Another half-sister to Indian Love Bird, the now-deceased Language of Love, is the dam of the Celebration Mile third Ordnance Row, who carries the original colours sported by Delegator, those of small owner-breeder Mrs Poilin Good, whose Boxhedge Hall Stud is in Cheshire. Mrs Good's joy at Delegator's Two Thousand Guineas performance was sadly tempered when her smart five-year-old Chief Editor (by Tomba, whom she also bred) died from a heart attack in the Palace House Stakes, the race straight after the Guineas. Delegator should not be inconvenienced by being dropped back in trip as a four-year-old, and when tackling a mile he will probably be suited by conditions that put the emphasis on speed (he acts well on good to firm going and ran his worst race on heavy in the Irish Guineas). He is waited with to make the most effective use of his good turn of foot. *Saeed bin Suroor*

DELORIA 2 ch.f. (Apr 7) Mark of Esteem (IRE) 137 – Denica (IRE) (Night Shift (USA)) [2009 6m² 6m* p6g⁵ 7m 6m⁶ 6g Oct 19] leggy filly: second foal: half-sister to 3-y-o Equipe de Nuit: dam unraced sister to useful German performer up to 1m Denice: fair performer: won maiden at Salisbury in July: below form in nurseries last 3 starts, poor effort in blinkers final one: should be suited by 7f+: acts on polytrack and good to firm going: sold 4,000 gns. *Eve Johnson Houghton* **69**

DELTA SKY (IRE) 2 ch.f. (Apr 4) Refuse To Bend (IRE) 128 – Delta Blues (IRE) (Digamist (USA) 110) [2009 7m 7g p6g⁵ p7g Dec 31] £9,000 2-y-o: leggy filly: half-sister to several winners, including 2001 2-y-o 7f winner Cop My Gator (by Danehill Dancer): dam ran once at 2 yrs in Ireland: poor form in maidens/nursery. *Miss Amy Weaver* **49**

DEMEANOUR (USA) 3 ch.f. Giant's Causeway (USA) 132 – Akuna Bay (USA) 88 (Mr Prospector (USA)) [2009 69p: p10g² 10g³ 10.2g⁴ p12g³ p11g⁴ p9.5g² p9.5g³ p12g³ a12d* Dec 26] good-bodied filly: fair handicapper: sold from E. Dunlop 26,000 gns before winning at Taby in December: stays easy 1½m, effective at shorter: acts on dirt/polytrack: tried in visor/cheekpieces. *Lars Bexell, Sweden* **77**

DEMOCRATE 4 b.c. Dalakhani (IRE) 133 – Aiglonne (USA) 108 (Silver Hawk (USA) 123) [2009 110: 10m 10g Aug 14] second foal: half-brother to French 2006 2-y-o 1m winner Apophis (by Rainbow Quest): dam, French 9f to 1½m winner, half-sister to dam of smart French 1¼m performer Germance: smart performer at 3 yrs, winning Prix Hocquart at Longchamp: left A. Fabre and tongue tied, well below form in listed race at Sandown and minor event at Newmarket in 2009: left Godolphin after: will stay 1½m: sent to UAE. *Saeed bin Suroor* **–**

DEMOLITION 5 ch.g. Starborough 126 – Movie Star (IRE) (Barathea (IRE) 127) [2009 87: 10.3m³ 12.1m* 9.8m⁵ 12.1m 12g⁵ 12g* 9.8g² 9.9m³ 12s⁴ 10g* 13.1m² 10.4g⁴ Oct 9] lengthy gelding: useful performer: improved in 2009, winning handicap at Beverley in April, claimer at York in July and handicap at Ayr in September: will stay 13f: acts on soft and good to firm ground: in cheekpieces nowadays. *N. Wilson* **97**

DEMONSTRATIVE (USA) 2 b.g. (Apr 10) Elusive Quality (USA) – Loving Pride (USA) 105 (Quiet American (USA)) [2009 6g 6g³ 7m² 7m³ f7g⁴ 7.2v⁶ Oct 31] third foal: dam French 2-y-o 6f/1m (Prix d'Aumale) winner: fair maiden: good third in nursery at Chester fourth outing: stays 7f: acts on good to firm ground: slowly away last 2 outings: subsequently gelded. *M. Johnston* **72**

DENCOLSTINA 2 b.f. (Mar 11) Lujain (USA) 119 – Buthaina (IRE) 71 (Bahhare (USA) 122) [2009 5m p6g 7m⁵ Aug 13] first foal: dam, 1m winner, half-sister to useful 7f winner Slugger O'Toole: no form. *Joss Saville* **–**

DENICES DESERT 3 b.f. Green Desert (USA) 127 – Denice 106 (Night Shift (USA)) [2009 p8.6g 10.2m⁴ 10.2g p8g Nov 18] 100,000Y: fourth foal: dam German 2-y-o 5f winner and second in German 1000 Guineas: modest maiden: blinkered final start: sold 800 gns. *M. Botti* **53**

DEN MASCHINE 4 b.g. Sakhee (USA) 136 – Flamingo Flower (USA) (Diesis 133) [2009 p9.5g⁵ 9m 9.8m⁴ 12m² p12g⁴ 12d² 10.1m p12.2g Sep 5] workmanlike gelding: found little in bumper for K. Ryan: modest maiden: claimed from Ollie Pears sixth start: stays 1½m: raced on polytrack, good to firm and good to soft going: tried tongue tied/in cheekpieces. *B. N. Pollock* **62**

DEN'S BOY 4 b.g. Josr Algarhoud (IRE) 118 – Den's-Joy 85 (Archway (IRE) 115) [2009 –: 8s⁶ 8.1g Jun 22] compact gelding: no form. *S. Curran* **–**

DEN'S GIFT (IRE) 5 gr. or ro.g. City On A Hill (USA) 114 – Romanylei (IRE) 106 (Blues Traveller (IRE) 119) [2009 91: p8g* 8.3g 7g^3 7.1d^2 7m^4 8g^5 7m^5 p8m^2 p8m^2 Dec 30] sturdy gelding: useful handicapper: won at Lingfield in January: good second to Falcativ there penultimate outing: stays 1m: acts on polytrack, good to firm and good to soft ground: blinkered: races prominently/makes running: consistent. *C. G. Cox* **95**

DENTON DIVA 3 b.f. Tobougg (IRE) 125 – Seeking Utopia 76 (Wolfhound (USA) 126) [2009 64: f6g^4 f6g^2 7.1m f6g^4 6s^3 f6g^6 Aug 25] fair performer: effective at 6f/7f: acts on fibresand and heavy going: tried in cheekpieces/visor: often races close up: sold £800 in October. *M. Dods* **66**

DENTON (NZ) 6 b.g. Montjeu (IRE) 137 – Melora (NZ) (Sir Tristram 115) [2009 f8g p10g* 10.2d* p9.5g* 11.7g Oct 21] workmanlike New Zealand-bred gelding: lightly raced in Australia for L. Freedman, runner-up at Cranborne and Geelong in 2008: fairly useful handicapper in Britain: won at Lingfield and Nottingham in August and Wolverhampton in October: stays 1½m: acts on polytrack and good to soft ground: tongue tied in 2009 (said to have had breathing problem final start). *J. R. Gask* **78**

DENTON RYAL 2 b.f. (Feb 23) Trade Fair 124 – My Valentina 84 (Royal Academy (USA) 130) [2009 p7.1g 8g Oct 20] seventh foal: dam, 2-y-o 7f winner, half-sister to smart sprinter Averti: down the field in maidens at Wolverhampton and Yarmouth (seemingly modest form). *S. W. James* **58 ?**

DEORA DE 2 b.f. (Jan 22) Night Shift (USA) – Photo Flash (IRE) 76 (Bahamian Bounty 116) [2009 7d Oct 12] £115,000Y: fourth foal: sister to Irish 4-y-o Deal Breaker and half-sister to useful 2008 2-y-o 5f/6f (Richmond Stakes) winner Prolific (by Compton Place): dam, 1m winner, half-sister to smart miler Atlantis Prince: 66/1, tailed off in maiden at Salisbury: sold 28,000 gns. *E. A. L. Dunlop* **–**

DEO VALENTE (IRE) 4 b.g. Dubai Destination (USA) 127 – Pack Ice (USA) (Wekiva Springs (USA) 123) [2009 82: 8m 7.6f p8g 7.1d p6g p6g^3 5.1s p6g p6m Dec 10] leggy gelding: just modest maiden nowadays: stays 1m: acts on polytrack, good to firm and good to soft ground: tried in cheekpieces, blinkered/tongue tied last 4 outings. *J. M. Bradley* **59**

DEPORTISTA 3 ch.f. Deportivo 116 – Wadenhoe (IRE) 69 (Persian Bold 123) [2009 p6g 7m p9.5g p8g p8.6g^4 p9.5g Dec 19] third foal: half-sister to 11f/1½m winner An Scaribh (by Where Or When): dam 2-y-o 7f winner: poor form. *J. A. Pickering* **49**

DEPORTMENT 3 b.f. Barathea (IRE) 127 – Tina Heights 79 (Shirley Heights 130) [2009 10.3s^3 10m^5 10.1m^2 10.1d* Oct 27] big filly: sixth foal: closely related to Irish 4-y-o Bashkirov and half-sister to smart 7f/1m (including at 2 yrs) winner who stayed 1½m Summitville (by Grand Lodge) and Irish 6-y-o Worldly Wise: dam, 1¼m winner on only start, half-sister to useful stayer Life of Riley: fairly useful form: improved when winning handicap at Yarmouth in October by 1¾ lengths from Racing Hero: likely to be suited by 1½m+: acts on good to firm and good to soft going: sold 34,000 gns: useful prospect. *J. R. Fanshawe* **90 p**

DEPOSER (IRE) 3 b.g. Kheleyf (USA) 116 – Bezant (IRE) 51 (Zamindar (USA) 116) [2009 96: p9g p8g^2 10.3m^4 8.5g^3 7m^2 Jun 17] big, strong gelding: smart performer: improvement in 2009, markedly so when placed last 2 starts, 1¾ lengths third to Mac Love in Diomed Stakes at Epsom and ½-length second to Ouqba in Jersey Stakes at Royal Ascot (gelded after): best short of 10.3f: acts on polytrack, good to firm and good to soft going: often front runner (tends to race freely): sent to Hong Kong. *J. R. Best* **118**

DERAAYA (IRE) 4 b.f. Mujahid (USA) 125 – Hawafiz (Nashwan (USA) 135) [2009 p7g^5 p6g^3 p6g Jun 24] third foal: closely related to 6-y-o Markab and half-sister to fairly useful French 1½m winner Raml (by In The Wings): dam, French 7.5f (at 2 yrs)/1m winner, out of half-sister to very smart 1m/1¼m performer Zaahi: maiden: fairly useful form for F. Head in France at 3 yrs (sold 9,000 gns): fair in Britain in 2009: likely to stay 1m: raced on polytrack and good ground or softer. *K. A. Morgan* **78**

DERBAAS (USA) 3 b.c. Seeking The Gold (USA) – Sultana (USA) (Storm Cat (USA)) [2009 101: 9m^5 8.1v^3 8m^4 8.1v^3 8s Oct 12] big, close-coupled colt: useful performer: good efforts when third at Haydock in quite valuable handicap (beaten 3¼ lengths by Desert Creek) and listed race (3¼ lengths behind Confront): stays 1m: unraced on firm going, acts on any other: quirky: sent to UAE. *E. A. L. Dunlop* **108**

DERBY DESIRE (IRE) 5 b.m. Swallow Flight (IRE) 124 – Jaldi (IRE) 75 (Nordico (USA)) [2009 –: p9.5g Nov 13] of little account. *D. G. Duggan, Ireland* **–**

DERRINGBAY (IRE) 3 b.g. Mull of Kintyre (USA) 114 – Rustle In The Wind 70 (Barathea (IRE) 127) [2009 –: p9.2g^3 p10g 8.3m 10m 8m 6m 9g a10.8g^2 a9g^2 a9g a9.5g **63**

a7.5g⁵ Dec 30] lengthy, unfurnished gelding: modest maiden: sold from M. Tompkins 4,200 gns after sixth start: stays 10.8f: best efforts on all-weather: blinkered last 2 starts in Britain. *Mme G. Rarick, France*

DER ROSENKAVALIER (IRE) 3 gr.g. Captain Rio 122 – Brooks Masquerade (Absalom 128) [2009 –: 6g[6] 6m May 30] no form: left A. Balding 5,000 gns in July. *A. M. Balding* –

DERVAL (IRE) 2 b.f. (Mar 22) One Cool Cat (USA) 123 – Sagrada (GER) (Primo Dominie 121) [2009 6s 5g 5d Sep 1] €10,000Y: good-bodied filly: sixth foal: half-sister to 3 winners abroad, including smart Hong Kong 5f to 1m winner Sunny Sing (by Sri Pekan), 6f winner in Britain at 2 yrs as Sacred Nuts: dam German 7f winner: well held in maidens: tongue tied (said to have had breathing problem) final start. *K. A. Ryan* –

DESCARGO 5 ch.m. Delta Dancer – Secret Miss 55 (Beveled (USA)) [2009 p6g Dec 19] modest maiden at 3 yrs: off over 2½ years, no promise sole outing in 2009: bred to be suited by 7f+: acts on polytrack. *C. R. Dore* –

DESDAMONA (IRE) 3 b.f. Desert Style (IRE) 121 – Tattymulmona Queen (USA) 46 (Royal Academy (USA) 130) [2009 –: 8.3g 9.8m 9.3g 9.8m 12.1m Jul 28] little sign of ability: tongue tied fourth start. *A. Berry* –

DESERT AISLING (IRE) 2 gr.f. (Mar 4) Verglas (IRE) 118 – Desert Sprite (IRE) 62 (Tagula (IRE) 116) [2009 5g 7.1m 8g p9.5g[6] f8m Nov 11] leggy filly: first foal: dam, Irish sprint maiden, half-sister to useful Irish performer up to 1½m Jakarta Jade and 4-y-o Cadre: poor maiden. *Edgar Byrne* **45**

DESERT AUCTION (IRE) 2 b.c. (Apr 16) Desert Style (IRE) 121 – Double Gamble 76 (Ela-Mana-Mou 132) [2009 p5g[3] p5g[3] 5m* 5m* 6g 5m 6m[4] 5.2d 7d* 8m[6] 7m[5] 7m[6] 7g[5] Oct 24] €24,000Y: close-coupled colt: third foal: half-brother to winner in Greece by Gorse: dam 1½m winner: fairly useful performer: won maiden at Folkestone in April, minor event at Goodwood in May and nursery at Newbury in August: should stay 1m: acts on good to soft and good to firm going, early promise on polytrack: tough and consistent. *R. Hannon* **89**

DESERT BEN (IRE) 6 b.g. Desert Prince (IRE) 130 – Benefits Galore (IRE) 70 (Brief Truce (USA) 126) [2009 71: 7g 6d[3] 7g 6d 8m 6m 5s[5] 5g[3] p8g[4] p5g* Nov 25] strong gelding: fair handicapper: left C. Grant after seventh outing: back to form after, winning at Dundalk in November: effective at 5f to easy 1m: acts on polytrack, firm and soft going: often in headgear: tried tongue tied. *Peter Casey, Ireland* **73**

DESERT BUMP 3 b.f. Medicean 128 – Greenfly (Green Desert (USA) 127) [2009 69: p7.1g* p8g[2] Feb 7] fair form: won maiden at Wolverhampton in January: good second in claimer at Lingfield next time: stays 1m: raced only on polytrack. *E. F. Vaughan* **70**

DESERT CREEK (IRE) 3 ch.c. Refuse To Bend (IRE) 128 – Flagship 84 (Rainbow Quest (USA) 134) [2009 87p: 8.3g* 8.1v* 8m 8m[5] Jul 25] smallish colt: useful handicapper: much improved in 2009, winning at Windsor and Haydock (Betfred Silver Bowl, beat Set The Trend 1¼ lengths) in May: below form in quite valuable events at Ascot after (lame behind following latter race): bred to stay 1¼m: best form on good ground or softer (acts on heavy). *Sir Michael Stoute* **100**

Betfred Silver Bowl (Heritage Handicap), Haydock—the gambled-on Desert Creek (No.15) copes well with unseasonably heavy ground to provide apprentice Louis-Philippe Beuzelin with his biggest win to date; Set The Trend, switched to the turf, runs well to be second

DESERT DESTINY 9 b.g. Desert Prince (IRE) 130 – High Savannah 77 (Rousillon (USA) 133) [2009 79: 8.3g 10.1d^{4} 9m 13.8m* 14m^{2} 14.1f^{5} 14g^{5} Jul 6] leggy, useful-looking gelding: fair performer: won seller at Catterick in June: stays easy 1¾m: acts on firm going, probably on soft: tried visored/tongue tied/in cheekpieces: usually held up. *C. Grant* **74**

DESERT DREAMER (IRE) 8 b.g. Green Desert (USA) 127 – Follow That Dream 90 (Darshaan 133) [2009 83, a92: p7g* p7.1g^{3} p7g^{3} p7g* p7g* 6m^{3} 6m^{2} 6m^{2} 7.5m 7.1m* 7g^{2} 7m^{5} 7.1d^{4} 7g* 7m^{2} 7.1m 7m 7m^{6} 7.1g^{4} 7m^{6} p7.1g p7m 7m* p7g^{6} p7g p7g p7g p7g p7g^{2} p7.1g^{2} p7.1g^{6} p7g^{3} Dec 31] smallish, good-topped gelding: fairly useful performer: won claimer at Kempton in January, 2 sellers at Lingfield (left Tom Dascombe after latter) in March, and handicaps at Warwick in May and Chester in June and September: effective at 6f/7f: acts on all-weather, firm and good to soft ground: tried in blinkers/cheekpieces/tongue tie: held up: tough. *P. D. Evans* **92**

DESERT DUST 6 b.g. Vettori (IRE) 119 – Dust 61 (Green Desert (USA) 127) [2009 –, a38: p6g^{5} f6g f5f f5g^{6} Dec 22] modest handicapper: probably best at 5f: acts on all-weather: often wears headgear. *H. J. Collingridge* **–** **a51**

DESERT FAIRY 3 b.f. Tobougg (IRE) 125 – Regal Fairy (IRE) (Desert King (IRE) 129) [2009 –: 10.3m 9.9m^{5} p12g^{6} p9.5g^{6} p12.2g^{3} p12.2g^{5} p8.6g^{4} Dec 18] lengthy filly: modest maiden: stays 1½m: acts on polytrack. *J. W. Unett* **52**

DESERT FALLS 3 b.g. Pyrus (USA) 106 – Sally Traffic 57 (River Falls 113) [2009 88: 5f^{4} 6.1m 6m^{4} 6m^{3} 6m^{5} 6s 6m^{3} 7.5f^{2} 7m p7.1g Nov 12] good-topped gelding: fairly useful performer: effective at 5f to 7.5f: acts on polytrack, unraced on heavy going (acts on any other turf): tried tongue tied: races up with pace. *R. M. Whitaker* **85**

DESERT FEVER 3 b.g. Dubai Destination (USA) 127 – Gaijin 97 (Caerleon (USA) 132) [2009 61p: 7.1m^{6} 10m 10g 10.3d^{6} Jul 16] big, rangy gelding: modest form: probably flattered third start: should stay 1m+: has joined N. Twiston-Davies. *B. W. Hills* **51 +**

DESERT FOREST (IRE) 2 b.g. (Feb 14) Desert Style (IRE) 121 – Mine Hostess (IRE) (Shernazar 131) [2009 6f 6g^{2} 7m^{2} 7d^{2} 7m^{4} 8g Oct 16] 9,000F, £16,000Y: good-bodied gelding: brother to useful Irish miler Desert Trail and half-brother to Irish 9.5f to 1½m winner Liffeydale (by Ajraas): dam unraced: fair maiden: seemed amiss last 2 starts, in cheekpieces final one: stays 7f: acts on good to firm and good to soft going. *J. Howard Johnson* **72**

DESERT HAWK 8 b.g. Cape Cross (IRE) 129 – Milling (IRE) 89 (In The Wings 128) [2009 62: p12.2g p12.2g^{5} p12g^{4} p10g p12.2g^{2} p9.5g* p9.5g^{6} p9.5g^{5} p9.5g p12.2g^{3} 11.8m^{4} 10.1g 10.9g 12d 10.1g^{5} 12.3m p9.5g p12f p13.9g p12m p12.2g Dec 7] stocky gelding: modest handicapper: won at Wolverhampton in February: stays 1½m: acts on polytrack, firm and soft going: tried blinkered/visored: held up: not straightforward. *W. M. Brisbourne* **57**

DESERT HUNTER (IRE) 6 b.g. Desert Story (IRE) 115 – She-Wolff (IRE) 104 (Pips Pride 117) [2009 53: 7m 8.5m 7.9g* 7.5m 8m^{2} 8v^{5} 8s Aug 23] good-topped gelding: modest handicapper: won at Carlisle (apprentices) in June: stays 8.5f: acts on polytrack, good to firm and good to soft going. *Micky Hammond* **59**

DESERT ICON (IRE) 3 b.g. Desert Style (IRE) 121 – Gilded Vanity (IRE) 83 (Indian Ridge 123) [2009 81: p6g 6g^{6} 6g^{2} 6s 6m^{6} p6f 6m Sep 25] angular gelding: poor mover: fairly useful handicapper: raced only at 6f: acts on good to firm and good to soft going: races up with pace. *W. J. Knight* **87**

DESERT KISS 4 b.f. Cape Cross (IRE) 129 – Kiss And Don'tell (USA) (Rahy (USA) 115) [2009 72: 8d^{4} 8.1g p8g* 8m* 8g^{2} 8.3f^{4} 8.1m*^{dis} Sep 11] leggy filly: fairly useful handicapper, lightly raced: first past post at Kempton (apprentices) in June, Ascot in July and Sandown (disqualified after rider weighed in light) in September: raced around 1m: acts on polytrack and good to firm going. *W. R. Swinburn* **92**

DESERT LARK 4 ch.g. Sakhee (USA) 136 – Oyster Catcher (IRE) 105 (Bluebird (USA) 125) [2009 –: p8g p12g^{2} p9.5g^{4} p10g Feb 22] lengthy gelding: modest maiden: stays easy 1½m: acts on polytrack. *K. A. Ryan* **56**

DESERT LEADER (IRE) 8 b.g. Green Desert (USA) 127 – Za Aamah (USA) (Mr Prospector (USA)) [2009 63: p12.2g p12.2g p12.2g^{4} 12.3m p12.2g p12.2m Sep 28] good sort: modest handicapper: stays 1½m: acts on all-weather: sometimes slowly away. *W. M. Brisbourne* **56**

DESERT LIAISON 2 b.f. (Feb 20) Dansili 127 – Toffee Nosed 97 (Selkirk (USA) 129) [2009 7g Aug 8] 50,000F, €200,000Y: well-made filly: fifth foal: half-sister to **64 p**

winner in Belgium by Desert Prince: dam 7f winner: 6/1, promising seventh to Tabassum in maiden at Newmarket, travelling smoothly and not knocked about: sure to do better. *J. Noseda*

DESERT LIGHT (IRE) 8 b.g. Desert Sun 120 – Nacote (IRE) (Mtoto 134) [2009 59: p6g p6g p6g^6 p5.1g p5.1g^5 p5g^2 Feb 12] sturdy gelding: modest performer: effective at 5f to 7f: acts on all-weather, good to firm and good to soft ground: visored: held up: tends to hang/race lazily. *D. Shaw* **53**

DESERT LORD 9 b.g. Green Desert (USA) 127 – Red Carnival (USA) 109 (Mr Prospector (USA)) [2009 112: 5d 5g Jun 6] lengthy, good-topped gelding: successful in Prix de l'Abbaye at Longchamp in 2006: hasn't won since, and tailed off in handicaps in 2009: front runner, best at bare 5f: acts on polytrack, firm and good to soft going: blinkered. *K. A. Ryan* **–**

DESERT LOVER (IRE) 7 b.g. Desert Prince (IRE) 130 – Crystal Flute (Lycius (USA) 124) [2009 49: p7.1g p8.6g f8g p9.5g^3 8.1g^6 7.6m 11.9m Aug 5] close-coupled gelding: modest performer: left R. Price prior to final start: stayed 9.5f: acted on all-weather, probably on good to soft going: sometimes wore cheekpieces/visor/tongue tie: dead. *A. M. Hales* **51**

DESERT MILE (IRE) 6 b.m. Desert Style (IRE) 121 – Maiskaya (IRE) 69 (Mark of Esteem (IRE) 137) [2009 86: 8m 8g^6 10g 8.5g^6 9d f8g p7.1g f7m Dec 15] fair handicapper: left Edward Lynam in Ireland after fifth start: well held after: stays 9f: acts on sand/polytrack, soft and firm going: in cheekpieces (ran respectably) third outing: sometimes slowly away: often held up. *Ollie Pears* **78 d**

DESERT OPAL 9 ch.g. Cadeaux Genereux 131 – Nullarbor (Green Desert (USA) 127) [2009 80: p5g^6 p5.1g p5.1g^4 p5g^4 Feb 10] leggy, good-topped gelding: just modest handicapper in 2009: best at 5f nowadays: acts on polytrack, heavy and good to firm going: wears cheekpieces/blinkers. *C. R. Dore* **60**

DESERT PARTY (USA) 3 b.c. Street Cry (IRE) 130 – Sage Cat (USA) (Tabasco Cat (USA) 126) [2009 109: a7g* a8f* a9f^2 a10s May 2] $425,000Y, $2,100,000 2-y-o: fourth foal: half-brother to 3 winners, including fairly useful 7f winner Cleide da Silva (by Monarchos): dam US 6f winner: smart performer: won twice in 2008, including Grade 2 Sanford Stakes at Saratoga: reportedly had filling in a leg after final start that year, then left E. Harty in USA: successful at Nad Al Sheba in 2009 in minor event (by ½ length) in January and UAE 2000 Guineas (impressively by 4¾ lengths) in February, both from Regal Ransom: 5/2-on, went down by ½ length to same rival in UAE Derby there next time: below form in Kentucky Derby at Churchill Downs final outing (subsequently found to have a chip in near-fore ankle and underwent surgery): stays 9f: acts on polytrack/dirt: tongue tied. *Saeed bin Suroor* **115**

DESERT PHANTOM (USA) 3 b.c. Arch (USA) 127 – Junkinthetrunk (USA) (Top Account (USA) 115) [2009 101: 6s Nov 7] well-made colt: useful form at 2 yrs: well below form in listed race at Doncaster only outing in 2009: should be suited by 7f/1m: acts on soft going. *D. M. Simcock* **–**

DESERT POPPY (IRE) 2 b.f. (Apr 14) Oasis Dream 129 – Flanders (IRE) 110 (Common Grounds 118) [2009 p6f^6 5.7m^2 p5m* p5.1g^2 p5.1g^2 Nov 13] 32,000Y: sixth foal: closely related to German 7f winner Farbenspiel (by Desert Prince) and half-sister to several winners, including useful French/US 7f/1m (including at 2 yrs) winner Louvain (by Sinndar): dam 5f (including at 2 yrs) winner: fair performer: won maiden at Kempton in October: good second in nurseries after: should be suited by 6f: acts on polytrack: not straightforward. *W. R. Swinburn* **79**

DESERT PRIDE 4 b.g. Desert Style (IRE) 121 – Dalu (IRE) 72 (Dancing Brave (USA) 140) [2009 78: p6g^3 7.1g^4 p6g 6.1m^3 6.1m^5 6m^4 p6m^6 5.7g^5 5.1s Nov 4] fair maiden handicapper: should stay 7f: acts on polytrack and firm going: visored of late: tongue tied once: ridden patiently. *W. S. Kittow* **69**

DESERT RAT (IRE) 5 b.g. Desert Sun 120 – Virtue Rewarded (IRE) (Darshaan 133) [2009 –: p10g^4 Feb 22] smallish, strong gelding: fair handicapper at best: poor form sole start on Flat in 2009: should stay 1¼m: acts on soft and good to firm ground: usually in headgear. *Tim Vaughan* **45**

DESERT RECLUSE (IRE) 2 ch.c. (Feb 10) Redback 116 – Desert Design (Desert King (IRE) 129) [2009 p7g p7.1g p7g Dec 31] £14,000Y: first foal: dam unraced out of half-sister to dam of Arc winner Rail Link: not knocked about in maidens: likely to do better. *Pat Eddery* **– p**

DESERT SAGE 2 ch.f. (Mar 24) Selkirk (USA) 129 – Prairie Flower (IRE) (Zieten (USA) 118) [2009 8.3s² Oct 7] strong filly: second foal: dam useful French 1m (at 2 yrs) to 1½m winner (stayed 15f): 22/1 and green, promising ½-length second to Anhar in maiden at Nottingham, slowly away and finishing well: will be suited by 1¼m: sure to improve. *R. M. Beckett* **75 p**

DESERT SEA (IRE) 6 b.g. Desert Sun 120 – Sea of Time (USA) (Gilded Time (USA)) [2009 99: p16g* 18.7m⁴ 16.4m* 14m 14.6m Sep 11] compact gelding: useful performer: won handicap at Kempton in March and listed race at Sandown (beat Victoria Montoya by length) in July: creditable effort otherwise in 2009 only when fourth to Daraahem in Chester Cup in between: effective at 1¾m to 18.7f: acts on polytrack, good to firm and good to soft going: usually held up. *D. W. P. Arbuthnot* **104**

DESERT STREAK (FR) 3 b.c. Green Desert (USA) 127 – Niner's Home (USA) (Forty Niner (USA)) [2009 63: 10f p7g* p7.1g² p6g⁴ p7m 7d⁶ a6f⁴ Dec 12] good-bodied colt: fair handicapper: left H. Dunlop, won at Lingfield in August: left C. Cox after fifth start: not sure to stay beyond 7f: best efforts on polytrack/dirt: in cheekpieces fourth/fifth outings. *R. Simpson, UAE* **75**

DESERT STRIKE 3 b.g. Bertolini (USA) 125 – Mary Jane 77 (Tina's Pet 121) [2009 80: p5g* p5g⁵ 5g³ 5f² 5m⁵ 5.1m 6g⁵ p6g Nov 11] rangy gelding: fair handicapper: won at Great Leighs (dead-heated with Lady Vivien) in January: may prove best at 5f: acts on polytrack and firm ground: in cheekpieces final outing: nervous type, and one to treat with caution. *P. F. I. Cole* **77 §**

DESERT VISION 5 b.g. Alhaarth (IRE) 126 – Fragrant Oasis (USA) 113 (Rahy (USA) 115) [2009 77: f11g 8s p12.2g 10.3g 10.2v p12.2g* p9.5g* p9.5g² p9.5g* f11g² Dec 27] long-backed, workmanlike gelding: fairly useful handicapper on all-weather, fair on turf: improved late in year, and won at Wolverhampton in November and December (2): good second at Southwell final outing: stays easy 1½m: acts on all-weather: usually tongue tied: blinkered/visored last 5 starts. *M. W. Easterby* **68 a94**

DESIRE TO EXCEL (IRE) 3 b.g. Desert Style (IRE) 121 – Sanpala (Sanglamore (USA) 126) [2009 85d: 7.1m* f7g 7m* 8.5m* 8.5g* Jul 30] strong, good-bodied gelding: fairly useful performer: won maiden at Musselburgh in April and handicaps at Leicester in June and Beverley and Goodwood in July: stayed 8.5f: acted on good to firm going: blinkered (below form) once: usually forced pace: dead. *P. F. I. Cole* **85**

DE SOTO 8 b.g. Hernando (FR) 127 – Vanessa Bell (IRE) (Lahib (USA) 129) [2009 12.6m⁴ 14s⁴ Aug 7] one-time useful hurdler, fairly useful chaser nowadays (won in August): tongue tied, fair form at best in maidens on Flat in 2009: will need 2m+. *P. R. Webber* **65**

DESPERATE DAN 8 b.g. Danzero (AUS) – Alzianah 102 (Alzao (USA) 117) [2009 81: p5.1g³ f5g p5.1m* p5.1m* p5g⁵ p5.1g* p5.1g* p5.1g² p5.1g² p5.1g² 5m⁴ 6g 5.7f* 5.7f² 5.7m 5m 5.1m* 6d³ 5g⁵ 6g 5.7m 5.1m* p6g⁴ p5.1g⁴ p5.1g⁴ p6m² Nov 26] quite good-topped gelding: fairly useful performer: won claimers/sellers at Wolverhampton in February, March (2) and April, and handicaps/claimer at Bath in May, July and September: effective at 5f/6f: acts on all-weather, firm and soft going: wears headgear (usually visored): travels strongly held up, and sometimes finds little. *A. B. Haynes* **87**

DESTINATION AIM 2 b.c. (Feb 19) Dubai Destination (USA) 127 – Tessa Reef (IRE) (Mark of Esteem (IRE) 137) [2009 7d⁴ 7g* Aug 14] deep-girthed colt: second foal: dam, useful French 1m/9f winner, out of sister to Miesque: promising efforts in maidens, winning at Newmarket by 2¾ lengths from Get A Grip, soon prominent and gradually getting on top: will be suited by 1m: sure to do better still. *Saeed bin Suroor* **89 p**

DESTINATIONUNKNOWN (USA) 3 b.f. Arch (USA) 127 – Private Funds (USA) (Private Terms (USA)) [2009 p7g⁵ f8g⁵ p8g⁶ 8f May 11] $72,000F, $50,000Y: third foal: half-sister to winners in USA by Boundary and Changeintheweather: dam US 1m/8.5f winner: modest maiden: left W. Haggas prior to final outing: stays 1m: acts on all-weather: tried blinkered/in cheekpieces. *A. J. McCabe* **58**

DESTINY BLUE (IRE) 2 b.c. (Mar 24) Danehill Dancer (IRE) 117 – Arpege (IRE) (Sadler's Wells (USA) 132) [2009 p8g⁴ Nov 14] fourth foal: closely related to useful French 1¼m/11f winner Beau Vengerov (by Danehill) and half-brother to winner in Japan by Fasliyev: dam unraced sister to smart performer up to 1½m Crimson Tide out of half-sister to Derby winner Shahrastani: 40/1, 7¼ lengths fourth to Rumoush in maiden at Lingfield, travelling well fair way and not knocked about once held. *J. A. Osborne* **67**

DESTINY RULES 2 br.f. (Feb 4) Endoli (USA) 108 – Up The Order (Forzando 122) [2009 6m Oct 5] small filly: first foal: dam no form: 33/1, missed break and always behind in maiden at Warwick. *John Berry* **–**

DESTINY'S DANCER 2 b.f. (Apr 2) Dubai Destination (USA) 127 – Cybinka 107 (Selkirk (USA) 129) [2009 6d^5 6m^6 6m^5 Aug 22] £7,000Y: workmanlike filly: sixth foal: half-sister to 4-y-o Young Ivanhoe: dam, 7f winner (including at 2 yrs), out of half-sister to Kris and Diesis: unplaced but shaped with some promise in maidens: should stay 7f: capable of better. *P. C. Haslam* **– p**

DESTINYS DREAM (IRE) 4 b.f. Mull of Kintyre (USA) 114 – Dream of Jenny 73 (Caerleon (USA) 132) [2009 74: 12.4m^4 9.9m^4 12f* 10g^4 10.1d^6 7.9m 10.1d^6 12.3m^3 12.3g* 12v 13.4m^5 10m Oct 3] smallish, sturdy filly: fair handicapper: won at Thirsk in April and Chester in August: stays 1½m: acts on firm going, below form all starts on softer than good: often held up. *Miss Tracy Waggott* **78**

DEUCE 3 ch.f. Where Or When (IRE) 124 – Justbetweenfriends (USA) 85 (Diesis 133) [2009 67: 10m 11.8m^2 14m 12m p12.2g^2 p12g^2 16g* 16m^2 p13.9g^3 p16.5g^5 p16.5g Oct 23] lengthy filly: fair handicapper: won at Nottingham in August: stays 2m: acts on polytrack and good to firm going: blinkered nowadays: temperamental: sold 13,000 gns. *Eve Johnson Houghton* **75 §**

DEUTSCHLAND (USA) 6 b.g. Red Ransom (USA) – Rhine Valley (USA) 101 (Danzig (USA)) [2009 13g* p17g* 14m 18m^5 Sep 11] good-bodied gelding: fairly useful hurdler/smart chaser, runner-up in Galway Hurdle in July: useful performer on Flat: won handicaps at Navan (apprentices) in June and Dundalk in July: best effort when close eighth to Sesenta in Ebor at York third start: well-held last of 5 in Doncaster Cup final outing: stays 17f: acts on polytrack, heavy and good to firm ground: tried in cheekpieces. *W. P. Mullins, Ireland* **108**

DEVASSA 2 b.f. (Mar 28) Reel Buddy (USA) 118 – Signs And Wonders 75§ (Danehill (USA) 126) [2009 5.1m^6 5.1g^3 5.1g^2 5m^4 p5.1g p5g Oct 22] fifth foal: half-sister to 4-y-o King's Wonder and 2004 2-y-o 5f winner Wonderful Mind (by Mind Games): dam, 1¼m winner, sister to dam of Queen Mary winners Romantic Liason and Romantic Myth: modest maiden: will be suited by 6f+: acts on good to firm ground, possibly not on polytrack. *C. G. Cox* **60**

DEVELOP U 2 b.g. (Apr 8) Mutazayid (IRE) – Verdura 63 (Green Desert (USA) 127) [2009 8.3g p10m p8.6g^5 Dec 3] poor form in sellers/claimer. *W. G. M. Turner* **43**

DEVER DREAM 2 b.f. (Feb 19) Medicean 128 – Sharplaw Venture 95 (Polar Falcon (USA) 126) [2009 6m^5 Sep 18] second foal: dam, 2-y-o 5f/6.5f winner (stayed 1m), half-sister to high-class performer up to 1m Firebreak: 33/1, encouraging 2½ lengths fifth to Side Glance in maiden at Newmarket, fading late: sold 13,000 gns: capable of better. *W. J. Haggas* **68 p**

DEVIANT WAYS 3 b.f. Celtic Swing 138 – Khwezi (Bering 136) [2009 p8g Apr 28] second foal: dam unraced: tailed off in maiden at Lingfield. *S. Kirk* **–**

DEVIL TO PAY 3 b.g. Red Ransom (USA) – My Way (IRE) (Marju (IRE) 127) [2009 66p: 10.2g 9.9g* 12m^2 14.1m^2 14g 14.6g Oct 23] good-topped gelding: fairly useful handicapper: won at Goodwood in May: better form when second after: stays 1¾m: acts on good to firm going: waited with: joined A. King 45,000 gns and gelded. *J. L. Dunlop* **85**

DEVIL YOU KNOW (IRE) 3 b.g. Elusive City (USA) 117 – Certainly Brave 77 (Indian Ridge 123) [2009 5.1d^4 6.1f* 6g^4 p6g* 6g^2 6m^4 5d 6g 5.2m^4 Sep 15] 48,000F, 60,000Y: good-bodied gelding: second foal: dam, Irish maiden who stayed 7f, out of Cheveley Park Stakes winner Dead Certain: fairly useful performer: won maiden at Nottingham in May and handicap at Kempton in June: free-going sort, raced only at 5f/6f: acts on polytrack and firm going: tongue tied last 2 outings: not straightforward: sold 7,000 gns. *D. R. C. Elsworth* **86**

DEVINIUS (IRE) 4 ch.f. Choisir (AUS) 126 – Vampress (IRE) 57 (Marju (IRE) 127) [2009 71: 7d^4 7d 10d^3 8g 7.1m p9.5g^6 Oct 23] close-coupled filly: modest handicapper at best in 2009: free-going sort, but stays 1m: acts on soft ground: ridden patiently. *G. A. Swinbank* **63**

DEVOLUTION (IRE) 11 b.g. Distinctly North (USA) 115 – Election Special 78 (Chief Singer 131) [2009 f11g Apr 27] very lightly raced and little form on Flat since 2003. *Miss C. Dyson* **–**

DEVON DIVA 3 b.f. Systematic 121 – General Jane (Be My Chief (USA) 122) [2009 54: p8.6g 10.2g Oct 21] maiden: well held in 2009. *J. F. Panvert* **–**

DEVOTED TO YOU (IRE) 2 b.f. (Mar 24) Danehill Dancer (IRE) 117 – Alleged Devotion (USA) (Alleged (USA) 138) [2009 7s^3 6d^3 7s* 7g^2 Aug 6] tall filly: has scope: closely related to useful Irish performer up to 1¼m (7f winner at 2 yrs) Altius and fairly **99**

useful 1m winner Classira (both by Danehill) and half-sister to several winners, including useful Irish 1¼m/1½m winner Royal Devotion (by Sadler's Wells): dam unraced half-sister to Oaks/Irish Derby winner Balanchine: useful performer: much improved when winning maiden at Galway in July by 9 lengths from Brushed Aside, leading 2f out: good 1¾ lengths second to Lillie Langtry in Debutante Stakes at Leopardstown, leading briefly under pressure 1f out, but edging right: will stay 1m/1¼m. *A. P. O'Brien, Ireland*

DEVOTEE (USA) 3 ch.f. Elusive Quality (USA) – Danuta (USA) 108 (Sunday Silence **103**
(USA)) [2009 a8f a9f* 8f a8s^{3} a10f a6s^{6} a8f^{6} Nov 13] strong, useful-looking filly: second foal: half-sister to French 9.8f winner Lady Middleton (by Kingmambo): dam 1m (including in USA at 2 yrs)/9f (UAE Oaks) winner: useful performer: won listed UAE Oaks at Nad Al Sheba in February by 1¼ lengths from Earth Living: well below form after, including when last of 13 finishers in 1000 Guineas at Newmarket: left Saeed bin Suroor after fifth outing: stays 9f: acts on dirt: often tongue tied: suffered irregular heartbeat on reappearance. *T. Albertrani, USA*

DEVOTION TO DUTY (IRE) 3 b.c. Montjeu (IRE) 137 – Charmante (USA) 88 **87**
(Alydar (USA)) [2009 –p: 10m^{4} 10.3m 10.4g* 12s^{6} 12g Oct 10] big, strong colt: fairly useful performer: won maiden at Haydock in May: should be suited by 1½m: acts on good to firm going: sold 16,000 gns. *B. W. Hills*

DEYAS DREAM 3 b.f. Clodovil (IRE) 116 – Dream On Deya (IRE) (Dolphin Street **60**
(FR) 125) [2009 79: p7g 8.5g^{6} 7.1f 7m^{6} Jun 14] good-topped filly: maiden: just modest form at 3 yrs: probably stays 7f: acts on polytrack and soft going: suspect temperament. *A. M. Balding*

DHAAWIAH (USA) 3 b.f. Elusive Quality (USA) – Huja (IRE) 102 (Alzao (USA) **85**
117) [2009 p8g^{2} p7m* p7g Sep 5] second foal: dam, 2-y-o 7f winner, sister to high-class 1¼m/1½m performer Maraahel: fairly useful form: won maiden at Lingfield in August: below form in handicap at Kempton next time: stays 1m: raced only on polytrack: has left Godolphin. *Saeed bin Suroor*

DHAN DHANA (IRE) 2 b.f. (Apr 12) Dubawi (IRE) 129 – Kylemore (IRE) (Sadler's **51 p**
Wells (USA) 132) [2009 p7g p7m 7g Oct 31] 52,000Y: rather leggy filly: sixth foal: half-sister to 4-y-o Annabelle's Charm and fairly useful 2008 2-y-o 7f winner Purple Sage (by Danehill Dancer): dam, ran twice in Ireland, sister to Racing Post Trophy winner Aristotle and Canadian International winner Ballingarry and half-sister to high-class 1m/ 9f performer Starborough and to dam of 2-y-o St Nicholas Abbey: clear signs of ability when down the field in maidens, not knocked about at Newmarket final start: likely to be suited by 1m+: capable of better. *W. J. Haggas*

DHANIA (IRE) 3 b.g. Gulch (USA) – Novograd (USA) (Gentlemen (ARG) 136) [2009 **74 d**
75p: p8.6g^{4} 8.5g^{4} 10m 8.1g 11.6m^{2} 10.1g^{3} 11.6m^{3} 12m^{3} p12g 11.9d^{2} Oct 15] tall gelding: fair maiden: below form after second outing: free-going sort, but stays 1½m: acts on good to firm and good to soft ground: visored/blinkered nowadays. *R. A. Teal*

DHAULAR DHAR (IRE) 7 b.h. Indian Ridge 123 – Pescara (IRE) 108 (Common **104**
Grounds 118) [2009 109: 7m^{3} 7f 7m 7m 7g^{6} 7.6m 7m 7m 7g^{4} 7s Nov 7] leggy, quite attractive horse: useful handicapper: creditable efforts in 2009 only when 3¼ lengths third of 27 to Swift Gift in Victoria Cup at Ascot and sixth to Jeninsky in quite valuable event at Newmarket: best at 6f/7f nowadays: acts on polytrack, firm and soft going: held up. *J. S. Goldie*

DHERGHAAM (IRE) 2 b.c. (May 9) Exceed And Excel (AUS) 126 – Alnasreya **81**
(IRE) 80 (Machiavellian (USA) 123) [2009 6m^{3} 6m 6g^{2} Oct 20] lengthy, useful-looking colt: second foal: dam, 1m winner from 3 starts, half-sister to Chilean Grade 1 11f winner Fontanella Borghese: fairly useful maiden: length second to Rule of Nature at Yarmouth (again travelled well). *E. A. L. Dunlop*

DHHAMAAN (IRE) 4 b.g. Dilshaan 119 – Safe Care (IRE) (Caerleon (USA) 132) **61**
[2009 74d, a82d: p7.1g p7.1g f7g p6g^{4} p6g p8.6g^{3} p7.1g p6m p7.1g 6m f7g p8.6g Dec 14] sturdy gelding: just modest performer at best in 2009: stays 7f: acts on polytrack and good to firm ground: tried visored, usually blinkered: tried tongue tied: often front runner. *Mrs R. A. Carr*

DHUSHAN 3 b.g. Rainbow Quest (USA) 134 – Abyaan (IRE) 106 (Ela-Mana-Mou **89**
132) [2009 11s^{4} 12.1g* 16f 13m 9.9f Aug 29] big, well-made gelding: fifth foal: half-brother to 2005 2-y-o 1m winner Botteen and Irish 5-y-o Elyaadi (both fairly useful, by Singspiel): dam, 1¼m winner who stayed 12.5f, sister to dam of very smart 1m/9f winner Autumn Glory: fairly useful performer: won maiden at Chepstow in May:

disappointing upped in class subsequently: gelded after final start: should prove best beyond 1½m. *M. A. Jarvis*

DIABOLICAL (USA) 6 ch.h. Artax (USA) 126 – Bonnie Byerly (USA) (Dayjur **117**
(USA) 137) [2009 119: a6f^{3} a6f^{3} 6g^{3} 6m^{6} Jun 20] good-bodied horse: smart performer: creditable third in Golden Shaheen at Nad Al Sheba (to Big City Man) and KrisFlyer International Sprint at Kranji (3¾ lengths behind Sacred Kingdom) second/third starts: better than result when sixth in Golden Jubilee Stakes at Royal Ascot final outing: had won at 8.5f, seemed best at 6f/7f: acted on dirt, firm and good to soft going: wore bandages: to stand at A & A Ranch, New Mexico, USA, fee $3,500. *Saeed bin Suroor*

DIALECT 3 b.f. Diktat 126 – Welsh Autumn 107 (Tenby 125) [2009 79: 8.3m 8g Oct 8] **–**
sturdy filly: fair winner at 2 yrs: well held in handicaps in 2009: should be suited by 1m+: sold 2,500 gns. *Mrs A. J. Perrett*

DIALOGUE 3 b.c. Singspiel (IRE) 133 – Zonda 100 (Fabulous Dancer (USA) 124) **78**
[2009 91: 10d 10.1g 10m^{5} 12m^{6} 10m Oct 3] close-coupled, useful-looking colt: just fair handicapper in 2009, leaving M. Johnston £17,000 prior to final outing: stays 8.6f: acts on polytrack: has reportedly had breathing problem. *G. A. Harker*

DIAMOND AFFAIR (IRE) 2 b.f. (Feb 11) Namid 128 – Subtle Affair (IRE) 96 **52**
(Barathea (IRE) 127) [2009 5g^{6} 5m^{3} f5g^{2} 5.1g^{4} 5g 5.2d f5g 5m 5g Oct 6] £2,200 2-y-o: leggy filly: first foal: dam, 11f/11.5f winner, half-sister to smart performer up to 2m Lochbuie: regressive maiden: raced only at 5f: acts on fibresand and good to firm going: tried tongue tied: front runner/races prominently: not straightforward. *M. G. Quinlan*

DIAMOND BLADE 3 ch.g. Needwood Blade 117 – Branston Gem 59 (So Factual **71**
(USA) 120) [2009 –: f6g^{2} 6m^{3} 5g^{3} 6m^{2} 6g 5s^{4} 5m^{5} 5.9d^{6} 6g^{4} 6m* f6g* f6g* Dec 8] lengthy, good-bodied gelding: fair handicapper: won at Redcar in September, then Southwell in November and December: raced only at 5f/6f: acts on fibresand and good to firm going: in cheekpieces last 4 starts: races prominently. *T. D. Easterby*

DIAMOND DAISY (IRE) 3 b.f. Elnadim (USA) 128 – Charlotte's Dancer (Kris 135) **82**
[2009 59: 7.1m^{2} p8.6g^{2} 8d^{3} 7.1m^{4} 6.9g^{4} 7.5m* 8d* 8m^{3} 8s^{6} 8m^{2} 8.1m^{6} Sep 29] deep-girthed filly: fairly useful handicapper: improved to win at Beverley in July and Thirsk in August: further progress when second at Pontefract tenth start: stays 8.6f: acts on polytrack, good to firm and good to soft ground. *Mrs A. Duffield*

DIAMOND DEE 3 ch.f. Deploy 131 – Diamond Swan (Colonel Collins (USA) 122) **47**
[2009 7m^{6} p10g May 28] good-topped filly: second foal: dam unraced: poor form in maidens: modest form in juvenile hurdles. *M. D. I. Usher*

DIAMOND DUCHESS (IRE) 2 ch.f. (Mar 20) Dubawi (IRE) 129 – Tarakana (USA) **76**
101 (Shahrastani (USA) 135) [2009 6.1m^{4} 7g^{3} 8.1g* 8m^{5} 8g^{3} p8m^{3} 10.2m Sep 30] €80,000F, 34,000Y: sturdy filly: half-sister to several useful winners, including Irish 1m (at 2 yrs) to 1½m winner Tarakala (by Doyoun) and 4-y-o Always Bold: dam Irish 9f winner (stayed 1½m): fair performer: won maiden at Haydock in August: good third in nurseries fifth/sixth starts: should be suited by 1¼m+. *D. R. Lanigan*

DIAMOND FIRE (IRE) 5 b.g. King Charlemagne (USA) 120 – Diamond Sun (Primo **63**
Dominie 121) [2009 62: 8m^{5} 7m^{2} 8g 5s^{4} 8v a6g^{3} 7d 7.2m^{5} 5g^{4} 5g p6g* p7g^{2} Nov 26] modest handicapper: won at Wolverhampton (apprentices) in November: effective at 5f to 1m: acts on polytrack/sand and good to firm going: often blinkered: tongue tied 3 of last 4 starts: tends to finish weakly. *Adrian McGuinness, Ireland*

DIAMOND JOHNNY G (USA) 2 b.c. (Feb 6) Omega Code (USA) – My Dancin **76 ?**
Girl (USA) (Sun War Dancer (USA)) [2009 p6g^{2} 5m^{6} 6m Jul 9] $21,000F: compact colt: second foal: dam US 6f winner, including at 2 yrs: fair form: second to Swilly Ferry in maiden at Lingfield: subsequently sixth to Radiohead in Norfolk Stakes at Royal Ascot and well-held tenth in July Stakes at Newmarket. *J. R. Best*

DIAMOND JO (IRE) 3 b.f. Johannesburg (USA) 127 – Still As Sweet (IRE) 89 (Fairy **–**
King (USA)) [2009 –: 7m 9.3d Jul 26] well held in maidens. *Pat Morris*

DIAMOND LASS (IRE) 4 b.f. Rock of Gibraltar (IRE) 133 – Keralba (USA) (Sheikh **72 d**
Albadou 128) [2009 7f^{3} f8g 9.9g 9.8m^{5} 9.1g^{2} 10m 8m 10g p8.6g^{5} Nov 14] rather leggy filly: fair maiden handicapper: below form after reappearance: stays 9.8f: acts on firm ground. *R. A. Fahey*

DIAMOND LAURA 2 bl. or gr.f. (Mar 10) Lucky Story (USA) 128 – Erracht 76 **82**
(Emarati (USA) 74) [2009 5g^{2} 5g^{2} p5.1g* 5s^{4} 5g p6g* 5g* 6.1g* 6s^{2} 6.1m^{3} p6g^{2} p6m Sep 26] £4,000Y: unfurnished filly: second foal: half-sister to 3-y-o Agnes Love: dam 5f (including at 2 yrs)/6f winner: fairly useful performer: won maiden at Wolverhampton in

May, claimers at Wolverhampton and Beverley (left P. D. Evans £13,000) in July and nursery at Chester in August: below form in claimers last 2 starts: raced only at 5f/6f: acts on polytrack and soft ground, probably on good to firm: sold £13,000. *Mrs R. A. Carr*

DIAMOND PAULA (IRE) 3 b.f. Spartacus (IRE) 107 – Balgren (IRE) (Ballad Rock 122) [2009 7.1g⁶ p8.6m Aug 21] €6,000Y: seventh foal: half-sister to several winners, including fairly useful 1m winner Diamond Yas (by Mull of Kintyre): dam unraced: slowly away in maidens. *P. D. Evans* **–**

DIAMOND SURPRISE 3 b.f. Mark of Esteem (IRE) 137 – Lucky Dip 68 (Tirol 127) [2009 64: f6g² f6g² f6g* f8d³ p6g p8m Nov 3] lightly-made filly: fair performer: won handicap at Southwell in February (left R. Curtis after next start): stays 6f: acts on fibresand and good to soft ground. *R. J. Smith* **68**

DIAMOND TWISTER (USA) 3 b.c. Omega Code (USA) – King's Pact (USA) (Slewacide (USA)) [2009 72: p6g³ p8g⁴ p10g* p10g² 9.9m⁶ p12g⁴ p12g⁶ 10m⁵ 9.9g⁵ 12m 7.6f² 8.3g 10.3d a7.5g² p8g⁴ 7f⁶ p9.5g p8m² p10m p8g p10g⁵ Nov 25] useful-looking colt: fairly useful performer: won maiden at Lingfield in February: effective at 7.5f to easy 1½m: acts on polytrack and firm going: usually tongue tied. *J. R. Best* **80**

DIAM QUEEN (GER) 2 b.f. (Feb 4) Lando (GER) 128 – Dance Solo 66 (Sadler's Wells (USA) 132) [2009 7f* p8.6g² p8g* Nov 18] 80,000Y: first foal: dam, maiden (placed up to 11f in Germany), half-sister to high-class miler Excellent Art: fairly useful form: won maiden at Folkestone in September and nursery at Lingfield (still green, beat Nave cosily by ½ length) in November: will be suited by 1¼m: type to go on improving. *L. M. Cumani* **93 p**

DIANA'S CHOICE (SAF) 5 b.m. Windrush (USA) – Fly To The Stars (SAF) (Desert Team (USA) 114) [2009 a6g³ 6g* 6.5g* a6f⁴ 6m⁴ 6m 7m Jul 25] smart performer: 5-time winner (including 2 Grade 3s) in South Africa for Riaan Van Reenen: won 2 handicaps at Nad Al Sheba in February (second one by ½ length from Munaddam): below form after, including in Britain last 3 starts (tongue tied final one): stays 7f, races mainly at shorter: acts on soft going. *M. F. de Kock, South Africa* **115**

DIANE'S CHOICE 6 ch.m. Komaite (USA) – Ramajana (USA) (Shadeed (USA) 135) [2009 87: 5.7d⁵ 5.1g 5.2g⁶ 5m p5.1g³ p6g³ 5.3g 5.1g² 5.1d* 5m f5g p6g 6m³ 6m⁴ 5.7g⁴ p7m⁴ p8g⁴ f6g p7m⁵ Dec 30] rangy mare: handicapper, just modest at 6 yrs: won at Bath in August: best at 5f/easy 6f: acts on polytrack and any turf going: usually wears headgear: tried tongue tied: held up: none too consistent. *Miss Gay Kelleway* **63**

DIAPASON (IRE) 3 b.f. Mull of Kintyre (USA) 114 – Suaad (IRE) 88 (Fools Holme (USA)) [2009 66p: 7m³ 7g* 8.3m 7g 8.3g 8m p7.1g⁶ p7.1g* Dec 28] rangy filly: fairly useful form: won maiden at Leicester in July and handicap at Wolverhampton in December: may prove best up to 7f: acts on polytrack. *Tom Dascombe* **80**

DICE (IRE) 3 b.c. Kalanisi (IRE) 132 – Rain Dancer (IRE) (Sadler's Wells (USA) 132) [2009 65p: 7g² 10.2d 9.7f⁶ 11.9m* 14g² 12d⁶ p13.9g² 15m² Oct 5] good-topped colt: fairly useful handicapper: won maiden event at Brighton in July: good efforts when runner-up after: stays 15f: acts on polytrack and good to firm going: held up: not straightforward: sold 42,000 gns. *L. M. Cumani* **84**

DICEY AFFAIR 3 b.f. Medicean 128 – Lucky Dice (Perugino (USA) 84) [2009 72: p7g p6g 7g⁴ 7f 7.1d 7m p7g⁶ 8d⁶ 8d p6m⁶ p7m⁴ Dec 30] rather leggy filly: maiden handicapper, just modest in 2009: stays 7f: acts on polytrack: tried in cheekpieces, tongue tied last 5 starts. *G. L. Moore* **59**

DICHOH 6 b.g. Diktat 126 – Hoh Dancer 66 (Indian Ridge 123) [2009 –, a92: p8.6g* p8.6g² p8.6g* p8g* p8g p7g 8.1m² p11g 8.1g 8d⁵ p8g² 8g* p7g* 8d⁴ p8g³ p8m⁶ p8g⁴ Dec 7] heavy-topped gelding: fairly useful performer on all-weather, fair on turf: won claimers at Wolverhampton and Lingfield in January (left M. Jarvis 17,000 gns) and March (2, left F. Sheridan £1,000 after latter) and, having left Rae Guest after fifth start, handicap at Salisbury in September and claimer at Lingfield in October: stays 8.6f: acts on all-weather: in headgear nowadays: tried tongue tied: quirky. *M. Madgwick* **69 a89**

DICKIE DEANO 5 b.g. Sooty Tern 79 – Chez Bonito (IRE) 49 (Persian Bold 123) [2009 –: p10g Feb 22] no form. *J. M. Bradley* **–**

DICKIE LE DAVOIR 5 b.g. Kyllachy 129 – Downeaster Alexa (USA) (Red Ryder (USA)) [2009 90, a82: f5g f6g⁵ 6m 6f f5g⁴ 6g³ 6g⁵ 6m⁴ p7.1g⁵ 5m² 6d* 5m 6v p6m³ 7d 5m f6g⁵ f5f⁴ p6g⁶ f6g Dec 8] good-topped gelding: fair handicapper nowadays, better on turf: won at Pontefract in July: left John Harris after sixteenth start: probably best at 6f/7f: acts on all-weather, soft and good to firm going: sometimes in headgear: held up, and takes time to warm to task. *R. C. Guest* **79 a65**

Richmond Stakes, Goodwood—
Dick Turpin (second right) pulls clear of Buzzword (rail) and Stargaze (fourth left) in a rough race

DICK TURPIN (IRE) 2 b.c. (Apr 30) Arakan (USA) 123 – Merrily 73 (Sharrood (USA) 124) [2009 6d* 6g* 6g* 6s* 7g^5 7m^6 Oct 17] €12,000F, €26,000Y: good-topped colt: seventh foal: half-brother to 3 winners, including fairly useful Irish 5f winner Lady Schmuck (by Clodovil): dam, sprint maiden, half-sister to useful 5f winner Deep Finesse: smart performer: successful first 4 starts, in maiden at Windsor in June, minor event at Salisbury and Richmond Stakes at Goodwood (beat Buzzword 3 lengths, having given trouble at stall) in July and valuable sales race at Fairyhouse (beat In Some Respect easily by 1½ lengths) in August: below form in Prix Jean-Luc Lagardere at Longchamp (shuffled back at crucial stage) and Dewhurst Stakes at Newmarket (threatened briefly over 1f out) last 2 starts: may well prove best short of 7f: acts on soft going. *R. Hannon* **111**

DICTATION 7 b.m. Diktat 126 – Monaiya (Shareef Dancer (USA) 135) [2009 46: p9.5g Jan 23] poor handicapper: stayed 10.7f: acted on polytrack, heavy and good to firm ground: in cheekpieces once, usually blinkered: dead. *Mrs Valerie Keatley, Ireland* **–**

DIDDUMS 3 b.g. Royal Applause 124 – Sahara Shade (USA) 79 (Shadeed (USA) 135) [2009 82: 6m^4 p6g 7m p7.1g 6m^5 6m^3 6g* 6m^5 6m p6g^6 p6g^6 p6g p7g p6g p6g Dec 31] leggy gelding: fair handicapper: won at Goodwood in August: left J. Hills 6,000 gns after tenth start: effective at 6f/7f: acts on polytrack and good to firm going: twice blinkered: usually held up. *P. S. McEntee* **75**

DIEGO RIVERA 4 b.g. Orpen (USA) 116 – Manuka Too (IRE) 68 (First Trump 118) [2009 71: p8g^6 p8g^4 p8g p7.1g* p8g 7.1g p7.1g p7.1g^3 p7.1g^6 6g Oct 19] useful-looking gelding: fair handicapper: won at Wolverhampton in April: likely to prove best at 7f: tried visored: suspect temperament: sold 7,000 gns. *P. J. Makin* **74**

DIE HAARD 3 ch.g. Haafhd 129 – Decision Maid (USA) 105 (Diesis 133) [2009 –: p7g Oct 2] little form. *J. R. Gask* **–**

DIES SOLIS 2 ch.c. (Apr 10) Exceed And Excel (AUS) 126 – Rose of America 81 (Brief Truce (USA) 126) [2009 7.2m^5 6m^5 7.2v^6 Oct 31] not knocked about in maidens at Ayr, best effort when fifth to Unshakable Will on debut. *I. Semple* **55**

DIG DEEP (IRE) 7 b.g. Entrepreneur 123 – Diamond Quest (Rainbow Quest (USA) 134) [2009 90: 5m 6g 5g^4 5m^4 6m 7.1g 7.1m* 7.5f p7.1g p6g^5 f6f^2 Nov 24] well-made gelding: fairly useful handicapper: won at Chepstow in August: stays 7f: acts on all-weather, firm and soft ground: often tongue tied: held up. *J. J. Quinn* **82**

DIGGERATT (USA) 3 gr. or ro.f. Maria's Mon (USA) 121 – Miss Exhilaration (USA) (Gulch (USA)) [2009 77: 7.1v 6m^5 7m^2 8m^6 7.5g^6 7.9g* 8m* p8g^3 7.5m^5 p8g^3 p8m Sep 30] close-coupled filly: fairly useful performer: won claimers at Carlisle and Redcar within 7 days in August: stays 1m: acts on polytrack, heavy and good to firm going: in cheekpieces last 2 starts. *R. A. Fahey* **78**

DIGGER DEREK (IRE) 3 b.g. Key of Luck (USA) 126 – Carson Dancer (USA) 52 (Carson City (USA)) [2009 81: f8g^4 9.9m^5 12.3m 10.3m^3 9.3d^6 9.9g 10s^4 8m^4 p8g Oct 11] neat gelding: just fair handicapper in 2009, gelded after third start: should stay 1¼m: acts on soft and good to firm going. *R. A. Fahey* **69**

DIGIT 3 ch.f. Reel Buddy (USA) 118 – Compact Disc (IRE) 48 (Royal Academy (USA) **43**
130) [2009 67: 6f 6m^{3} 8.3d 7v Sep 4] workmanlike filly: fair winner at 2 yrs: just poor form in claimers/seller in 2009: stays 7f: acts on good to firm and good to soft going: none too resolute. *B. Smart*

DIGITAL 12 ch.g. Safawan 118 – Heavenly Goddess (Soviet Star (USA) 128) [2009 87: **77 d**
5g^{5} 6m^{4} 6g^{5} 5.3m^{4} 5g 5m 6g 5.1m^{3} 5.1v^{6} 5f 5m Aug 16] workmanlike gelding: handicapper: on downgrade in 2009: races mostly at 5f/6f nowadays: acts on any turf going: sometimes visored: tends to get behind. *M. R. Channon*

DIJEERR (USA) 5 b.h. Danzig (USA) – Sharp Minister (CAN) (Deputy Minister **113**
(CAN)) [2009 113: 7.5d 8g a8f* a8f 8.3m^{5} 7.6m* Sep 12] sturdy horse: smart performer: won minor events at Nad Al Sheba (beat Tiz Now Tiz Then 2¼ lengths) in February and, having left M. bin Shafya after fourth start, Chester (4 ran, beat Cyflymder ¾ length) in September: stays 9f: acts on dirt, soft and good to firm going: visored: tongue tied last 4 starts: races prominently: has left Godolphin. *Saeed bin Suroor*

DIKTALINA 3 b.f. Diktat 126 – Oiselina (FR) 95 (Linamix (FR) 127) [2009 61: 11.6g **61 §**
12m p12g^{2} 11.6m* p12g^{4} 11.5g^{5} 13.1d 13.8m^{2} 16.1g p12g Oct 20] tall filly: modest performer: won seller at Windsor in July: stays 13.8f: acts on polytrack and good to firm ground: often forces pace: one to treat with caution: sold 10,000 gns, joined Mrs A. Thorpe. *W. R. Muir*

DIKTARAM 3 b.g. Diktat 126 – Aries (GER) 79 (Big Shuffle (USA) 122) [2009 –: **–**
f11g^{5} 12.5m^{6} 12.1s p12g f14g Jul 14] little form: tried visored/in cheekpieces. *J. R. Weymes*

DIKTATORSHIP (IRE) 6 b.g. Diktat 126 – Polka Dancer 93 (Dancing Brave (USA) **55**
140) [2009 55: p13.9g^{2} p12.2g^{3} p12.2g^{3} p16.5g^{5} p13.9g^{6} Dec 14] good-topped gelding: modest handicapper: stays 1¾m: acts on all-weather, soft and good to firm going: tried in headgear/tongue tie, effective without. *Jennie Candlish*

DIKTAT QUEEN 3 b.f. Diktat 126 – Sakura Queen (IRE) 52 (Woodman (USA) 126) **77**
[2009 7m^{6} 7.1m* 8g 8g Oct 21] close-coupled filly: half-sister to several winners, including 1m to 1¼m winner Son of Thunder (by Dr Fong) and 1½m winner Reine Cerise (by Shareef Dancer): dam, maiden who stayed 1¼m, half-sister to dam of Rock of Gibraltar: fair form when winning maiden at Chepstow in September: said to have bled final start: should stay 1m+: acts on good to firm ground: sold £3,100, sent to Sweden. *Rae Guest*

DILLENDA 3 b. or br.f. Lend A Hand 124 – Samadilla (IRE) 83 (Mujadil (USA) 119) **–**
[2009 55: 7.5m 7g Jun 9] strong, close-coupled filly: has round action: maiden: well below form in handicaps in 2009. *T. D. Easterby*

Tattersalls Ireland Sale Stakes, Fairyhouse—a change of venue but yet another big pay-day for Richard Hannon's stable, as Dick Turpin (centre) becomes his stable's sixth winner of this race; In Some Respect (right) is second

DILLI DANCER 4 b.f. Dansili 127 – Cup of Kindness (USA) (Secretariat (USA)) **69 d** [2009 6m^5 6m^4 6d^6 7g p7m^4 p5.1g p6f^5 Oct 14] half-sister to 9.5f/1¼m winner Cup of Love (by Behrens) and several winners in USA: dam unraced half-sister to very smart 6f/7f performer Iktamal and smart French 1½m performer First Magnitude: fair form only when fifth in maiden on debut: stays 7f: best effort on good to firm ground. *G. D. Blake*

DIMAIRE 2 b.f. (Mar 12) Kheleyf (USA) 116 – Dim Ots 92 (Alhijaz 122) [2009 p6g **65** p7.1g 5.7g^6 5m^2 f5g^2 5.1g^4 f5m^3 p5.1g^2 Dec 14] £3,000Y: seventh foal: half-sister to 7f and 9.4f winner How's Things (by Danzig Connection) and 3-y-o Cawdor: dam 5f (at 2 yrs) and 6f winner: fair maiden: best efforts at 5f: acts on fibresand and good to firm going. *D. Haydn Jones*

DIMAN WATERS (IRE) 2 br.g. (May 3) Namid 128 – Phantom Waters 79 (Pharly **68** (FR) 130) [2009 6v^5 6m^4 6.1d 5.1s^6 Nov 4] tall, good-topped gelding: fair form: creditable sixth in nursery at Nottingham, leading: should stay 7f: acts on soft and good to firm going: looked awkward after lay-off third start. *E. J. Alston*

DIMASHQ 7 b.m. Mtoto 134 – Agwaas (IRE) (Rainbow Quest (USA) 134) [2009 65, **60** a–: 12g 16m^6 14m^5 13m^6 12d* 12m^5 12d* 12g 13g^5 12.1m^3 13.8g^2 12s f14m Nov 11] **a–** sparely-made mare: modest performer: won ladies handicap at Ripon in June and claimer at Catterick in July: effective at 1½m to 2m: acts on firm and good to soft ground (no form on all-weather): none too consistent. *P. T. Midgley*

DIMINUTO 5 b.m. Iron Mask (USA) 117 – Thicket 87 (Wolfhound (USA) 126) [2009 **51** 84d: f5g p7.1g p6g p6g^6 f6g p6g Mar 24] small mare: just modest at best in 2009: stays 6f: acts on all-weather, firm and soft going: often forces pace: not straightforward. *M. D. I. Usher*

DINGAAN (IRE) 6 b.g. Tagula (IRE) 116 – Boughtbyphone 62 (Warning 136) [2009 **89** 92, a95: 7m 7g 7.1m^3 7g^4 8g^2 8m* 8f^4 8m^6 8m Oct 1] tall gelding: fairly useful handicapper: won at Bath in July: stays 1m: acts on polytrack, firm and good to soft going: sometimes in headgear: quirky. *A. M. Balding*

DINKIE SHORT 2 b.g. (Feb 28) Reset (AUS) 124 – Spring Sunrise 59 (Robellino **52** (USA) 127) [2009 7.1g 8g^6 7m^6 p8.6g p7m Oct 7] maiden: seemed flattered second start: worth a try at 6f: blinkered final outing. *W. R. Muir*

DINKY DEB 2 ch.f. (Apr 29) Captain Rio 122 – Debinnair (FR) (Wolfhound (USA) **–** 126) [2009 p5g p5.1g^6 5.2g May 29] small, leggy filly: sixth foal: half-sister to French 7.5f (including at 2 yrs) to 9f winner Vicalex (by Cape Cross): dam French 2-y-o 6f winner: well held, including in seller. *D. K. Ivory*

DINKYS DIAMOND (IRE) 2 b.g. (Apr 15) Modigliani (USA) 106 – Along Came **58 ?** Molly (Dr Fong (USA) 128) [2009 6d 7d^6 6g^5 7.2m Sep 18] close-coupled gelding: maiden: form only when fifth to Makbullet at Ripon. *B. Ellison*

DINNER DATE 7 ch.g. Groom Dancer (USA) 128 – Misleading Lady (Warning 136) **65** [2009 80: p8g^4 p8g p8g 10.1d 10.1m 8g 10g 10.1g^3 10m^3 p10m^2 p8m* p8m^3 p8m* p10m **a79** Dec 9] rather leggy, quite attractive gelding: fair handicapper, better on all-weather: won at Kempton in October and November: effective at 1m to easy 1½m: acts on polytrack and good to firm going: travels strongly held up. *T. Keddy*

DIRAR (IRE) 4 b.g. King's Best (USA) 132 – Dibiya (IRE) 102 (Caerleon (USA) 132) **109** [2009 99: 14g^2 18m p10.7g^5 p12.2g* Dec 11] quite good-topped gelding: useful performer (also winning hurdler): won handicap at Wolverhampton in December easily by 1¾ lengths from Mister New York: stays 1¾m: acts on polytrack, good to firm and good to soft going. *Gordon Elliott, Ireland*

DIRECTA'S DIGGER (IRE) 5 b.g. Daggers Drawn (USA) 114 – Chita Rivera 61 **–** (Chief Singer 131) [2009 83: 14g May 29] small, close-coupled gelding: fairly useful handicapper: in cheekpieces, well held sole start in 2009: stays 2¼m: acts on good to firm going: visored in 2008. *M. J. Scudamore*

DIRECT DEBIT (IRE) 6 b.g. Dansili 127 – Dimple (Fairy King (USA)) [2009 86: **75** p8.6g p7.1g^5 p10g 10.2g 8d^3 7.1m 8m^4 8m Jul 6] lengthy, quite attractive gelding: fair handicapper: stayed easy 1¼m: acted on polytrack, good to firm and good to soft going: tried in cheekpieces: dead. *M. Wellings*

DIRECTOR'S CHAIR 4 b.g. Catcher In The Rye (IRE) 115 – Capegulch (USA) **73 §** (Gulch (USA)) [2009 72§: p10g 10.3m* 10.1m 10m^4 10d 8.5m p12g^6 Nov 18] tall, angular gelding: fair handicapper: won amateur event at Doncaster in March: stays 11f: acts on all-weather and good to firm going: tried blinkered/in cheekpieces: races close up: irresolute: sold £4,000. *Miss J. Feilden*

DIRECTORSHIP 3 br.c. Diktat 126 – Away To Me (Exit To Nowhere (USA) 122) **84** [2009 87: 10d 8.1m* 8g^6 10m^6 10d Oct 12] well-made colt: fairly useful performer: won maiden at Sandown in July: may prove best short of 1¼m: acts on soft and good to firm going. *P. R. Chamings*

DIRICULOUS 5 b.g. Diktat 126 – Sheila's Secret (IRE) 97 (Bluebird (USA) 125) **99** [2009 112: p6g^3 6s p6g^6 6g 6g^3 6g p6f^5 p6g f6f Oct 21] workmanlike gelding: useful form at best in 2009, often looking laboured: effective at 5f/6f: acts on all-weather, firm and good to soft going: blinkered/in cheekpieces last 5 starts. *T. G. Mills*

DISCANTI (IRE) 4 ch.g. Distant Music (USA) 126 – Gertie Laurie (Lomond (USA) **82** 128) [2009 84p: 5f^3 f5g^6 5d 5m^3 5m^6 5m^4 5g^5 5g* 5m 5g Oct 9] strong, long-backed gelding: fairly useful handicapper: won at Beverley in August: speedy, raced mostly at 5f: best efforts on good going or firmer (acts on firm): tried tongue tied: often held up. *T. D. Easterby*

DISHDASHA (IRE) 7 b.g. Desert Prince (IRE) 130 – Counterplot (IRE) 91 (Last **77** Tycoon 131) [2009 p13.3g* p12g^2 p12g* p12g^4 Mar 16] strong, workmanlike gelding: fair handicapper: progressive in 2009, winning at Great Leighs in January and Kempton in February: stays 13.3f: acts on polytrack, raced only on good ground or firmer on turf: tongue tied at 7 yrs: held up: fairly useful hurdler/chaser, successful in April/July. *Mrs A. M. Thorpe*

DISPOL ANTONIO (IRE) 2 b.g. (Jan 22) Antonius Pius (USA) 123§ – Brief Fairy **52** (IRE) (Brief Truce (USA) 126) [2009 6d 6m 7m 7.5m^5 7d^5 7d^6 Jul 31] rather leggy gelding: modest maiden: seems to stay 7.5f: visored last 4 starts: sold £4,000. *P. T. Midgley*

DISPOL DIVA 3 b.f. Deportivo 116 – Kingston Rose (GER) (Robellino (USA) 127) **69** [2009 58: f8g^4 f8g^6 f11g* 12m^2 12.1m* 12g^5 12.1s^3 12.1g^6 12m 9.9m^2 12g^3 12d^5 Jul 31] tall, leggy filly: fair performer: won claimer at Southwell in March and handicap at Beverley in April: stays 1½m: acts on fibresand and any turf going: visored. *P. T. Midgley*

DISPOL FAY (IRE) 2 b.f. (May 6) Fayruz 116 – Hever Rosina 63 (Efisio 120) [2009 **– p** 5g 6s f5m f5m Dec 5] €6,500Y: sixth foal: sister to 5f (including at 2 yrs) winner Shank On Fourteen and half-sister to 2 winners, including 6f (at 2 yrs) to 1m winner Tequila Sheila (by Raise A Grand), both fairly useful: dam 6f winner: signs of ability in minor event/maidens: capable of better. *P. T. Midgley*

DISPOL GRAND (IRE) 3 b.g. Raise A Grand (IRE) 114 – Hever Rosina 63 (Efisio **73** 120) [2009 67: f5g^3 f5g^2 5m^6 5m^2 5m^4 5m^3 5g* 5m^2 5d* 5d^4 5.4g^5 5m^4 5d 5m^4 6d 5m^6 Aug 31] good-bodied gelding: fair handicapper: won at Ayr in May and Newcastle in June: raced only at 5f/6f: acts on fibresand, soft and good to firm going. *P. T. Midgley*

DISPOL KABIRA 2 b.f. (Mar 13) Kheleyf (USA) 116 – Abir 73 (Soviet Star (USA) **57 §** 128) [2009 5m 5m^6 5s* 6d^6 6m^6 6f^4 7d 6s^6 5m 5g 6.1s 7g 7m Oct 26] £2,000Y: angular filly: seventh foal: half-sister to 3 fairly useful winners, including Irish 2002 2-y-o 7f winner Bond (by Lahib) and 4-y-o Gala Casino Star: dam, maiden (best around 7f), half-sister to smart performer up to 1¾m Ranin: easily best effort when winning maiden at Hamilton in May: left P. Midgley after seventh start: should stay 6f: acts on soft going, probably on firm: ungenuine. *D. W. Thompson*

DISPOL KEASHA 2 ch.f. (Feb 12) Kheleyf (USA) 116 – Easy Mover (IRE) 77 **75** (Bluebird (USA) 125) [2009 5m^2 5m* 5s^6 5g^4 Jun 6] £16,000Y: sturdy filly: first foal: dam, 2-y-o 7f winner, stayed 1¼m: fair form: won maiden at Musselburgh in May: creditable fourth to Capercaillie in minor event at same course: raced at 5f: acts on good to firm going: front runner. *T. D. Barron*

DISPOL KYLIE (IRE) 3 b.f. Kheleyf (USA) 116 – Professional Mom (USA) **75** (Spinning World (USA) 130) [2009 82: f5g 5f 5m^4 5d^3 5m^4 5d^4 5d 5s^5 5m^3 5v^5 Sep 4] big, leggy filly: just fair handicapper at 3 yrs: raced only at 5f: acts on soft and good to firm ground: tried in cheekpieces (well held): sometimes makes running. *P. T. Midgley*

DISTANT DREAMER (USA) 3 ch.f. Rahy (USA) 115 – Khazayin (USA) 74 (Bahri **–** (USA) 125) [2009 6d 6m^5 7d f7f Dec 12] $47,000Y: fourth foal: half-sister to 3 winners, including useful performer up to 1¼m Jaish (by Seeking The Gold), 6f winner at 2 yrs, and fairly useful 11f winner Jawaaneb (by Kingmambo) who stayed 2m: dam, maiden (stayed 1¼m), sister to Arc winner Sakhee: well held in maidens/handicap. *Rae Guest*

DISTANT MEMORIES (IRE) 3 b.g. Falbrav (IRE) 133 – Amathia (IRE) 105 (Darshaan 133) [2009 86p: 11.9v^2 10.4g 9.8v* 9.8d* 10d^2 Oct 26] tall gelding: progressed **109** into useful performer in 2009, winning handicaps at Ripon in July and September (by 7 lengths from Bolodenka): good 2 lengths second to Raise Your Heart in listed race at Leopardstown final outing: seems best around 1¼m: acts on heavy going: races prominently. *T. P. Tate*

DISTANT PLEASURE 5 b.m. Diktat 126 – Our Pleasure (IRE) (Lake Coniston (IRE) 131) [2009 66: 8d⁶ 8.1g 8v 7.2s⁶ 7.2g Oct 23] leggy mare: handicapper, just modest in 2009: stays 1m: acts on heavy and good to firm going: in cheekpieces last 2 starts. *M. Dods* **55**

DISTANT SUN (USA) 5 b.g. Distant View (USA) 126 – The Great Flora (USA) (Unaccounted For (USA) 124) [2009 84, a93: 6g 8m 6d 5m 5g⁴ 5m* 6m 5d³ Oct 28] leggy gelding: fair handicapper nowadays: won at Musselburgh in September: best up to 7f: acts on polytrack, soft and good to firm going: tried in cheekpieces: has looked difficult ride. *Miss L. A. Perratt* **78**

DISTANT VISION (IRE) 6 br.m. Distant Music (USA) 126 – Najeyba 80 (Indian Ridge 123) [2009 51: p5.1g 6g 5f² 5m⁴ 5.9g³ 5m 5.9m 5m⁴ 5g² 6m p5.1g⁵ Oct 17] angular mare: modest maiden: best at 5f: acts on good to firm and good to soft ground: often in headgear in 2009: tried tongue tied. *H. A. McWilliams* **54**

DI STEFANO 2 b.g. (Mar 4) Bahamian Bounty 116 – Marisa (GER) (Desert Sun 120) [2009 5.2s⁴ 5g⁴ 5m* 5m³ 5m² 6m 6g³ 6.5m 6g⁵ Sep 30] £60,000Y: sturdy gelding: second foal: half-brother to useful 2008 2-y-o 5f/6f winner Smokey Storm (by One Cool Cat), later 7.5f winner in Denmark: dam unraced: fairly useful performer: won maiden at Ripon in June: best efforts when placed in listed events, third to Hold Your Colour at Ripon seventh start: stays 6f: acts on good to firm ground: visored seventh/eighth starts: ungenuine: gelded after final start. *M. R. Channon* **94 §**

DISTINCTIVE 2 b.f. (Jan 24) Tobougg (IRE) 125 – Blue Azure (USA) 67 (American Chance (USA) 117) [2009 6g³ 6m* 6m* 7m Oct 17] neat filly: first foal: dam lightly-raced maiden who should have stayed beyond 1m: useful performer: won maiden at Redcar in August and Laundry Cottage Stud Firth of Clyde Stakes at Ayr (significant improvement, beat Midnight Martini 3¾ lengths, well on top on favoured far side) in September: ran poorly in Rockfel Stakes at Newmarket final start: should be suited by 7f+. *B. Smart* **100**

DISTINCTIVE IMAGE (USA) 4 b.c. Mineshaft (USA) 132 – Dock Leaf (USA) (Woodman (USA) 126) [2009 83: p12.2m* p12g² p12g² 12f p12.2g⁴ 11.8d⁴ 12.3g² f12g* Aug 10] attractive colt: useful handicapper on all-weather, fairly useful on turf: won at Wolverhampton in March and Southwell (by 8 lengths): further significant improvement when beating Kensington Oval in August for latter success: stays 1½m: acts on all-weather, best turf effort on good going: held up: has joined G. Butler. *R. Hollinshead* **85 a100**

DISTINCTLY GAME 7 b.g. Mind Games 121 – Distinctly Blu (IRE) 70 (Distinctly North (USA) 115) [2009 92: p6g⁵ p6g⁴ p6g* p6g⁴ p6g² p6g⁴ p6g³ p6g Apr 16] tall, quite good-topped gelding: fairly useful handicapper: won at Lingfield in January: free-going sort, effective at 5f/6f: acts on all-weather, good to firm and good to soft going: tried in cheekpieces/blinkers, tongue tied of late. *K. A. Ryan* **84**

DITZY DIVA 3 b.f. Imperial Dancer 123 – Runs In The Family 69 (Distant Relative 128) [2009 –: 10.9g Aug 31] good-quartered filly: last in maidens. *B. G. Powell* **–**

DIVERTIMENTI (IRE) 5 b.g. Green Desert (USA) 127 – Ballet Shoes (IRE) 75 (Ela-Mana-Mou 132) [2009 84: p7g⁴ p8g p7g* p7g⁶ p7.1g⁴ 7g p7g p7.1g⁶ p10g⁴ p8m p12g f5g³ Dec 22] sturdy gelding: fair handicapper: won at Lingfield (apprentices) in January: below form after: best at 6f/7f: acts on all-weather and good to firm ground: usually wears blinkers/cheekpieces. *S. R. Bowring* **73**

DIVINATORE 3 b.g. Sakhee (USA) 136 – Divina Mia 66 (Dowsing (USA) 124) [2009 –: p8g⁴ p9.5g² 8.3f² 11d 10m 11.6m⁴ p8m⁵ p10m⁵ Dec 10] rather leggy gelding: fair maiden: should be suited by 1¼m+: acts on polytrack and firm going: tried in cheekpieces. *D. Haydn Jones* **71**

DIVINE FORCE 3 b.g. Bertolini (USA) 125 – Malcesine (IRE) 46 (Auction Ring (USA) 123) [2009 p7g⁵ p7.1g² p7g⁵ p6g³ f6d⁶ 6.1m p6m 6g⁵ p7g² p6m* Dec 1] half-brother to several winners by Komaite, including useful sprinters Castelletto and Final Dynasty: dam 1m seller winner: fair handicapper: left J. Osborne and gelded after fifth start: won at Lingfield in December: raced only at 6f/7f: best efforts on polytrack. *M. Wigham* **76**

DIVINE SPIRIT 8 b.g. Foxhound (USA) 103 – Vocation (IRE) 74 (Royal Academy (USA) 130) [2009 85: 5m 5d² 5v 5g⁵ 5m⁶ 5d 5g 5g 5g p5.1g p5.1g 5s Oct 27] smallish, good-bodied gelding: just fair handicapper in 2009: stays 6f: acts on polytrack and any turf going: has worn cheekpieces/blinkers: held up. *M. Dods* **78**

DIVINE WHITE 6 ch.m. College Chapel 122 – Snowy Mantle 54 (Siberian Express (USA) 125) [2009 –: f6g³ f6g f6g² f6g 6.1g 7.6d 7g 6m⁴ 6g f6d Dec 29] lengthy, leggy mare: modest maiden: best at 6f/7f: acts on all-weather and firm going, probably on heavy: tried in headgear: signs of temperament. *G. P. Enright* **51**

DIXEY 4 br.f. Diktat 126 – Hoh Dancer 66 (Indian Ridge 123) [2009 98: p8g³ p7g 7.1m¹ p7.1g 7.6g² p8g⁴ 7.2m 8.3m⁵ 7v² 7s Nov 7] rangy filly: useful handicapper: good efforts when second at Chester and Newbury (neck behind Crystal Moments): free-going sort, but stays 7.6f: acts on polytrack, heavy and good to firm ground: in cheekpieces last 2 outings: forces pace. *M. A. Jarvis* **98**

DIXIE BRIGHT (USA) 2 b. or br.g. (Apr 8) Dixie Union (USA) 121 – Tell Me Now (USA) (A P Indy (USA) 131) [2009 5g p6g* 6g⁵ p7.1g p7g p6m p8.6g 7m² Oct 26] $105,000Y: good-topped gelding: third foal: half-brother to fairly useful Irish 2007 2-y-o 7f winner Greek Mythology (by Mr Greeley): dam unraced half-sister to smart 7f performer Wind Cheetah and to dam of Prix de Diane winner Confidential Lady: fair performer at best: won maiden at Wolverhampton in June: form otherwise only when second in nursery at Leicester: stays 7f: acts on polytrack and good to firm ground: tried blinkered/visored: hung left throughout third outing: unreliable: sold 6,500 gns after final start. *J. G. Given* **74 §**

DIXI HEIGHTS 2 b.f. (Feb 5) Golan (IRE) 129 – Ninfa of Cisterna (Polish Patriot (USA) 128) [2009 p5g⁶ 6g⁶ 6s³ 5.5g 6.1s Oct 7] tall filly: sixth foal: half-sister to 3 winners, including 6-y-o Mr Garston: dam, Italian 5f/6f (including at 2 yrs) winner, out of half-sister to Poule d'Essai des Poulains winner Victory Note: modest maiden: little impact in nurseries: stays 6f: acts on soft going. *J. R. Boyle* **54**

DIZZINESS (USA) 2 b.f. (Mar 30) Stormy Atlantic (USA) – Danzante (USA) 107 (Danzig (USA)) [2009 6d⁶ Jun 26] close-coupled filly: half-sister to several winners, including smart 1m (at 2 yrs)/9f (US Grade 1) winner Monzante (by Maria's Mon) and useful French 1996 2-y-o 7f winner Alpha Plus (by Mr Prospector): dam, 6.5f (in France at 2 yrs) to 8.5f (in USA) winner, half-sister to Breeders' Cup Classic winner Skywalker: 7/2 and green, shaped better than result when 2 lengths sixth to Emma Dora in maiden at Newmarket: will stay 7f+: capable of better. *R. Charlton* **58 p**

DJALALABAD (FR) 5 b.m. King's Best (USA) 132 – Daraydala (IRE) 108 (Royal Academy (USA) 130) [2009 62: p7.1g* 8.3m p7.1g⁵ 7m⁶ 8f 7m p7.1g⁴ p8g p8.6g⁵ 7m p7m⁶ p8m³ p8g⁴ p7m p8g³ p8m p7.1g⁶ Dec 17] leggy mare: modest handicapper, better on all-weather: won at Wolverhampton in March: likely to prove best at 6f/7f: acts on polytrack, good to firm and good to soft ground: tried visored, in cheekpieces nowadays: tongue tied: held up: none too reliable. *Mrs C. A. Dunnett* **52 a64**

DJANGO REINHARDT 3 b.g. Tobougg (IRE) 125 – Alexander Ballet 86 (Mind Games 121) [2009 57p: p6g 6d p6f Sep 10] maiden: no form in 2009. *J. R. Gask* **–**

DO BE BRAVE (IRE) 3 ch.g. Kheleyf (USA) 116 – Fear Not (IRE) 64 (Alzao (USA) 117) [2009 60: p7g f7g p8g 10m Jul 15] rather leggy gelding: modest maiden: well below form last 3 starts. *Paul Mason* **56**

DOBRAVANY (IRE) 5 b.g. Danehill Dancer (IRE) 117 – Eadaoin (USA) (King of Kings (IRE) 125) [2009 65d: p8.6g p9.5g p8g⁵ p8g² p9.5g³ 11.5g⁵ Jul 2] useful-looking gelding: modest performer: left Adrian McGuinness in Ireland after second start: stays 1¼m: acts on polytrack, soft and good to firm going: usually wears headgear: unreliable. *K. A. Morgan* **57 §**

DOC JONES (IRE) 3 ch.g. Docksider (USA) 124 – Quick Return (Polish Precedent (USA) 131) [2009 68: p7.1g⁵ 6.1f⁴ 7.1f² 7f* p6g 7.6m⁴ 6m⁵ 6d² 7m⁵ 5.1m p7.1g³ 5.7g⁵ 5.7m⁵ Sep 13] workmanlike gelding: fair performer: won maiden at Thirsk in June: should stay 1m: acts on polytrack, firm and good to soft going: often makes running. *P. D. Evans* **79**

DOCOFTHEBAY (IRE) 5 ch.g. Docksider (USA) 124 – Baize 95 (Efisio 120) [2009 111: p8.6g³ 10g 10g p10g 8m 8.3m³ 8g³ 8g⁵ 8m 9m Oct 3] sturdy, compact gelding: just useful performer nowadays: best efforts in 2009 when third in minor event at Nottingham and totesport Mile (Handicap) at Goodwood (beaten 3 lengths by Laa Rayb) sixth/seventh starts: gelded after final outing: best around 1m: acts on all-weather, firm and good to soft going: tried in blinkers/cheekpieces: held up (sometimes slowly away): ungenuine. *J. A. Osborne* **100 §**

DOCTOR CRANE (USA) 3 b.g. Doneraile Court (USA) – Sharons Song (USA) (Badger Land (USA)) [2009 92?: 10m⁴ 10m* May 24] quite attractive gelding: good mover with a long stride: useful handicapper: improved in 2009, winning at Newmarket in May by ¾ length from Hyades: gelded after: stays 1¼m: acts on good to firm ground: races prominently. *J. H. M. Gosden* **100**

Princess of Wales's Blue Square Stakes, Newmarket—Doctor Fremantle gets the better of the almost-hidden Schiaparelli (who is demoted a place for causing trouble when hanging right) and Alwaary (dark sleeves, striped cap)

DOCTOR DELTA 4 b.c. Dr Fong (USA) 128 – Delta Tempo (IRE) (Bluebird (USA) 125) [2009 51: f8g^4 p8.6g p9.5g^4 f12g 12m Jun 3] good-topped colt: poor maiden handicapper: stays 1½m: acts on all-weather. *M. Brittain* **49**

DOCTOR DINO (FR) 7 ch.h. Muhtathir 126 – Logica (IRE) 81 (Priolo (USA) 127) [2009 123: 12g Mar 28] good-topped horse: very smart performer at best: won Man o'War Stakes at Belmont in 2007, and Hong Kong Vase at Sha Tin in 2007 and 2008: found to have tendon injury when only eighth to Eastern Anthem in Dubai Sheema Classic at Nad Al Sheba sole start in 2009: stayed 1½m: acted on firm and soft going: held up: tremendously reliable and was a credit to his connections: to stand at Haras du Mesnil, France, fee €3,000. *R. Gibson, France* **110**

DOCTOR FREMANTLE 4 b.c. Sadler's Wells (USA) 132 – Summer Breeze 101 (Rainbow Quest (USA) 134) [2009 116p: 10.3m* 12m 12m* 11m* 10m Oct 17] sturdy colt: very smart performer: won extrabet.com Huxley Stakes at Chester in May, Princess of Wales's Blue Square Stakes at Newmarket (by ½ length from demoted Schiaparelli) in July and Dubai Duty Free Arc Trial at Newbury (beat Look Here by nose, coming from last place in steadily-run affair) in September: seemed amiss in Champion Stakes at Newmarket final start: stays 1½m: unraced on extremes of going: often races freely: held up: sold privately, and to join L. Freedman in Australia. *Sir Michael Stoute* **123**

DOCTOR HILARY 7 b.g. Mujahid (USA) 125 – Agony Aunt 81 (Formidable (USA) 125) [2009 88d: p6g p6g Dec 7] strong gelding: on downgrade at 6 yrs, and well held both starts in 2009: tried blinkered/tongue tied, visored nowadays. *A. B. Haynes* **–**

DOCTOR OF MUSIC (IRE) 3 ch.g. Dr Fong (USA) 128 – Sublime Beauty (USA) 93 (Caerleon (USA) 132) [2009 7d 8d^6 8.3g 9.9g Sep 22] poor form. *B. Smart* **45**

DOCTOR PARKES 3 b.g. Diktat 126 – Lucky Parkes 108 (Full Extent (USA) 113) [2009 83: 5.1m* 5g 5m^4 5g* 5m Sep 26] strong gelding: fairly useful handicapper: won at Chester in May and Ripon in August: best at 5f: acts on good to firm going: usually races prominently. *E. J. Alston* **91**

DOCTOR ZHIVAGO 2 b.c. (Mar 5) Shamardal (USA) 129 – Balalaika 108 (Sadler's Wells (USA) 132) [2009 f8m* Dec 5] 150,000Y: seventh foal: half-brother to 3 winners, including very smart 7f to 1¼m winner Alkaadhem (by Green Desert) and useful 1m/1¼m winner Lookalike (by Rainbow Quest): dam, 9f winner who stayed 1½m, sister to high-class 1¼m performer Stagecraft: 3/1, shaped with considerable promise when winning maiden at Southwell by 2 lengths from Master Leon, getting hang of things late and plenty to spare: will stay 1¼m: useful prospect. *M. Johnston* **75 P**

DODAA (USA) 6 b.g. Dayjur (USA) 137 – Ra'a (USA) 106 (Diesis 133) [2009 77: f5s p5.1g^5 p5.1g p5g^6 p5.1g^5 p5g^3 f5g f5g Dec 22] workmanlike gelding: just modest performer nowadays: effective at 5f/6f: acts on all-weather and firm going: tried blinkered: speedy front runner. *N. Wilson* **57**

DOGGERBANK (IRE) 3 b.f. Oasis Dream 129 – Discreet Brief (IRE) 113 (Darshaan 133) [2009 10m^2 12.6m* 13g^2 12m* Aug 13] well-made filly: second foal: half-sister to useful 1¼m winner Secret Dancer (by Sadler's Wells): dam, 1¼m and 14.6f (Park Hill Stakes) winner, out of half-sister to Yorkshire Oaks winner Key Change: soon progressed into useful performer, winning maiden at Warwick in July and handicap at Salisbury (beat Lyceana 3 lengths) in August: stays 13f: should continue to improve. *H. R. A. Cecil* **95 p**

DOHASA (IRE) 4 b.g. Bold Fact (USA) 116 – Zara's Birthday (IRE) 71 (Waajib 121) [2009 117: 6g³ 6.5g³ 6m³ 7s² 6m 7m² 7m p7g* 7g* 7.5m² p7f* Dec 16] big, well-made gelding: smart performer: won minor events at Dundalk and the Curragh in September, and listed race at Kempton (beat Dunelight by a head) in December: also ran well when ¾-length second to Duff in Concorde Stakes at Tipperary penultimate start: stays 7.5f: acts on polytrack, firm and soft going: blinkered once at 2 yrs: usually held up. *G. M. Lyons, Ireland* **115**

DOLLAR EXPRESS (USA) 3 ch.g. Broken Vow (USA) 117 – Feminine (USA) (Tale of The Cat (USA) 113) [2009 p7g⁶ p7g⁶ p8.6g⁴ p12g⁴ f12g⁴ Mar 27] modest maiden: stays easy 1½m: raced only on all-weather: joined E. Tuer £4,800 in April, then gelded. *J. Noseda* **63**

DOLLED UP (IRE) 2 b.f. (May 11) Whipper (USA) 126 – Belle de Cadix (IRE) 82 (Law Society (USA) 130) [2009 5g² 5.5g³ 6d* 5g* 5.5g³ 6m⁴ 5.5g² 6s³ Nov 3] half-sister to several winners, including fairly useful 2005 2-y-o 7f winner In A Flash (by Night Shift), later successful in USA, and useful French/US performer up to 8.5f Zeiting (by Zieten): dam Irish 13f winner: useful performer: won maiden at Saint-Cloud in June and Prix du Bois at Chantilly (by length from Chantilly Creme) in July: good efforts next 2 starts when 1¾ lengths third to Special Duty in Prix Robert Papin at Maisons-Laffitte and keeping-on close fourth of 5 to Arcano in Prix Morny at Deauville: below best last 2 starts when placed behind Sorciere in Prix d'Arenberg at Chantilly and Our Jonathan in muddling Criterium de Maisons-Laffitte: stays 6f: acts on good to firm and good to soft ground. *R. Collet, France* **109**

DOLLY NO HAIR 4 ch.g. Reel Buddy (USA) 118 – Champagne Grandy 84 (Vaigly Great 127) [2009 72d: 9.1m⁶ 8m 8m 8d 7.2m f7g⁶ f6m Nov 6] tall gelding: maiden: little form in 2009, leaving D. Barker after second start: tried in headgear/tongue tie. *N. Wilson* **–**

Mr K. Abdulla's "Doctor Fremantle"

DOLLY PENROSE 4 b.f. Hernando (FR) 127 – Mistinguett (IRE) 77 (Doyoun 124) [2009 90: 16m³ 16m⁵ 16.2g 14g² 13.1m² 15.9m⁴ 14s* 14d 16g⁶ 16d⁶ 14.6m⁶ 18m² 12g Oct 30] leggy filly: fairly useful handicapper: won at Haydock in July: mostly creditable efforts otherwise: barely stays 2¼m: acts on heavy and good to firm going: visored last 3 starts: often travels strongly held up: joined C. Down, fairly useful form over hurdles. *M. R. Channon* **90**

DOLLY WILL DO 2 b.f. (Mar 26) Bahamian Bounty 116 – Desert Flower (Green Desert (USA) 127) [2009 5.1g 5.1m⁵ 5m p6m 5.7g 8.1d Aug 31] £400Y: fifth foal: half-sister to 1½m winner Fleetfoot Mac (by Fleetwood) and 5-y-o Papa's Princess: dam unraced sister to smart 1991 2-y-o 5f winner Magic Ring: poor maiden. *N. P. Mulholland* **43**

DOLORES ORTIZ (IRE) 3 b.f. High Chaparral (IRE) 132 – Ma N'Ieme Biche (USA) (Key To The Kingdom (USA)) [2009 8m 8.3g 10f 10.1g 8m Aug 6] rangy filly: closely related to Irish 1½m winner Mabel (by In The Wings) and half-sister to several winners, including useful 6f/7f winner A Very Good Year (later successful in Hong Kong, by Indian Ridge): dam, French maiden, sister to Cheveley Park/1000 Guineas winner Ma Biche: modest maiden: visored (shaped as though amiss) final start: best effort at 1m on good ground: sold £800 in August. *S. C. Williams* **58**

DOLPHIN ROCK 2 b.g. (Mar 1) Mark of Esteem (IRE) 137 – Lark In The Park (IRE) 57 (Grand Lodge (USA) 125) [2009 6g p6g³ 6g⁵ f7g⁴ p7.1g² 7m⁴ p8.6g⁶ 8.3d³ 8g² Oct 19] £1,600Y: stocky gelding: first foal: dam 1m winner: fair maiden: good placed efforts in nurseries last 2 starts (gelded after final one): stays 8.3f: acts on polytrack and good to soft going. *Mrs G. S. Rees* **73**

DOMADA 4 ch.f. Domedriver (IRE) 128 – Estimada 64 (Mark of Esteem (IRE) 137) [2009 f7d 8.1v May 22] 2,400Y: first foal: dam, second at 11.5f on only start, out of useful 1¼m/1½m performer Gisarne: tailed off in seller/maiden (tongue tied in latter). *W. J. H. Ratcliffe* **–**

DOME ROCKET 3 b.g. Domedriver (IRE) 128 – Sea Ridge 65§ (Slip Anchor 136) [2009 81: p11g⁵ 9.9g⁴ p9.5g* 10.9g² 10.1g* 9.9g p10m 10.2s Oct 7] angular gelding: fairly useful performer: won claimer at Wolverhampton in June and handicap at Epsom in July: should stay 11f: acts on soft going: in cheekpieces last 4 starts: signs of temperament: sold 12,000 gns. *W. J. Knight* **86**

DOMESDAY (UAE) 8 b.g. Cape Cross (IRE) 129 – Deceive 100 (Machiavellian (USA) 123) [2009 –: 10.1g⁴ 8g 10.2m Sep 30] good-topped gelding: poor maiden: barely stays 9.5f: acts on polytrack and good to firm ground: tried in visor/cheekpieces. *T. T. Clement* **46**

DOMINATION 2 b.g. (Feb 7) Motivator 131 – Soliza (IRE) 93 (Intikhab (USA) 135) [2009 9d⁴ 8v f8m⁶ Nov 6] first foal: dam, Irish 1¼m winner, half-sister to smart performers up to 1½m Salford Mill and Ovambo: best effort in maidens when 4¼ lengths fourth to Ted Spread at Goodwood: possibly unsuited by ground subsequently: will be suited by 1¼m+: gelded after final start: remains likely to do better. *H. Morrison* **74 p**

DO MORE BUSINESS (IRE) 2 b.g. (Feb 28) Dubai Destination (USA) 127 – Tokyo Song (USA) (Stravinsky (USA) 133) [2009 5m* 7m 7g p5g⁵ p6g⁴ 6d⁶ Sep 15] fair performer: awarded seller at Goodwood in May: creditable effort after only when fourth in nursery at Kempton: may prove best at 5f/6f: acts on polytrack and good to firm going: inconsistent. *P. M. Phelan* **69**

DOM POLSKI 3 b.g. Polish Precedent (USA) 131 – Camerlata (Common Grounds 118) [2009 p7.1g⁴ p7g⁴ p7g⁵ p8.6g p8g³ Oct 8] sturdy gelding: third foal: half-brother to 5-y-o Count Ceprano: dam unraced half-sister to Middle Park Stakes winner Primo Valentino: fair maiden: stays 1m: raced only on polytrack: tongue tied after debut: sold £3,000. *W. R. Swinburn* **75**

DONA ALBA (IRE) 4 b.f. Peintre Celebre (USA) 137 – Fantastic Fantasy (IRE) 85 (Lahib (USA) 129) [2009 99: 10.1g³ 10m⁴ 12m 9.9g 10.4m⁵ Aug 18] close-coupled filly: useful handicapper: good 3 lengths third to Duncan at Epsom on reappearance: respectable efforts at best after: stays 1¼m: acts on firm going (once raced on softer than good): often held up. *J. L. Dunlop* **97**

DONAIR 2 ch.c. (Mar 16) Nayef (USA) 129 – Darwinia (GER) (Acatenango (GER) 127) [2009 7m 8.3g Oct 28] leggy colt: well held in maidens at Leicester (green, not knocked about) and Nottingham: will be suited by 1¼m. *P. F. I. Cole* **–**

DONARD LODGE (IRE) 4 b.f. Elnadim (USA) 128 – Knockatotaun 65 (Spectrum (IRE) 126) [2009 59: p6g⁶ p7.1g 6.3g⁵ p6g⁶ p7g Nov 26] poor handicapper nowadays: left J. Balding after second start: stays easy 7f: raced mostly on polytrack: tried in cheekpieces: often tongue tied: tends to get behind. *Patrick Martin, Ireland* **49**

DONATIVUM 3 gr.g. Cadeaux Genereux 131 – Miss Universe (IRE) 99 (Warning 136) **118** [2009 111p: 7m^4 7m^5 8g* 8d^5 8m^5 8m^4 7m^3 Oct 17] angular gelding: smart performer: won listed race at Deauville in July by short neck from Polarix: improved efforts at Newmarket last 2 starts, in Joel Stakes (1¾ lengths fourth to Confront) and Challenge Stakes (again looked awkward when length third to Arabian Gleam): effective at 7f/1m: acts on firm and good to soft going: held up. *Saeed bin Suroor*

DON CARLOS (GER) 2 b.c. (Mar 17) Galileo (IRE) 134 – Dapprima (GER) 107 **102 p** (Shareef Dancer (USA) 135) [2009 7g^3 7d* 10v^4 Nov 14] 220,000F, 300,000Y: closely related to useful German 8.5f winner Davidoff (by Montjeu), stays 1½m, and half-brother to several winners abroad, including smart German 6f (at 2 yrs) to 9f winner Denaro (by Dashing Blade): dam, German 7f (at 2 yrs) and 1m winner, second in 10.5f Prix de Flore: landed odds in maiden at Leopardstown in October by ½ length from Legendary Lad, making most: 9¼ lengths fourth to Passion For Gold in Criterium de Saint-Cloud final start, challenging under 2f out: stays 1¼m: should improve further. *A. P. O'Brien, Ireland*

DONCASTER ROVER (USA) 3 b.g. War Chant (USA) 126 – Rebridled Dreams **108** (USA) (Unbridled's Song (USA) 125) [2009 99: p7g 6g^2 6m* 6d^3 6.1g* 6s Aug 16] well-made gelding: has scratchy action: smart performer: left S. Parr after reappearance: won minor event at Haydock in July and listed race at Chester (beat Sohraab ½ length) in August: stays 6f: acts on good to firm and good to soft going: held up. *D. H. Brown*

DONCOSAQUE (IRE) 3 b.c. Xaar 132 – Darabela (IRE) 84 (Desert King (IRE) 129) **87** [2009 72+, a86: p10m^3 p10g^3 p8g^4 p10g* p8.6g^3 10m^6 9.9m^3 10g 10m^5 8.3g^6 Jun 22] close-coupled colt: fairly useful handicapper: won at Lingfield in February: stays 1¼m: acts on polytrack and good to firm going. *P. Howling*

DONGOLA (IRE) 2 b.f. (Mar 9) Xaar 132 – Laura Margaret (Persian Bold 123) [2009 **–** 5g Apr 27] 8,000F, 5,500Y: good-topped filly: half-sister to several winners, including fairly useful 1m to 1½m winner Yankeedoodledandy (by Orpen): dam Italian 2-y-o 9.5f winner: 25/1 and backward, slowly away and well held in maiden at Windsor (said to have finished lame). *P. Winkworth*

DONNA ELVIRA 2 b.f. (Jan 18) Doyen (IRE) 132 – Impatiente (USA) (Vaguely **73** Noble 140) [2009 8d^2 p8m Oct 28] 20,000Y: closely related to several winners, including useful stayers Busy Lizzie and Eminence Grise (both by Sadler's Wells), and half-sister to 3 winners, including 2002 2-y-o 1m winner Flake (by Zilzal): dam, French maiden, out of US Grade 1 9f/1¼m winner Sangue: much better effort in maidens when neck second to Flaming Miracle at Salisbury, strong at finish: beaten long way out on polytrack (at Kempton): will be suited by 1½m+. *R. Hannon*

DONNY BOWL 4 b.c. Presidium 124 – Perpetuo 81 (Mtoto 134) [2009 6m^6 7m **–** Oct 13] well beaten in maiden/seller. *I. W. McInnes*

DON PELE (IRE) 7 b.g. Monashee Mountain (USA) 115 – Big Fandango (Bigstone **76** (IRE) 126) [2009 80: f6s* f5d^2 p6g^6 p6g^3 f6g^4 p5g^4 p5g* p6g* p6g^3 f6g^2 p6g^5 6g^5 6g^3 5.2m 6g f6g 6g^4 6s^4 5.7m p6g^5 p6g^6 p6g^3 f5g p6g^4 Dec 31] good-bodied gelding: fair performer nowadays: won claimer at Southwell in January, handicap at Lingfield in February and seller at Wolverhampton in March: trained twelfth start only by J. Pearce: effective at 5f/6f: acts on all-weather, heavy and good to firm going: wears cheekpieces/ blinkers. *R. A. Harris*

DON PICOLO 4 b.g. Bertolini (USA) 125 – Baby Come Back (IRE) (Fayruz 116) **–** [2009 56: f7g Feb 10] sturdy gelding: modest performer: well held sole start in 2009: stays 1m: acts on fibresand: usually blinkered. *R. Curtis*

DON PIETRO 6 b.g. Bertolini (USA) 125 – Silver Spell 54 (Aragon 118) [2009 79: **78** p10g^4 p8g^3 f7g^6 p8.6g^2 p10g^4 p9.5g^5 8m^2 10.2g* 10d^4 8f* Aug 22] tall gelding: fair performer: won seller at Bath in July and handicap there in August: stays 1¼m: acts on polytrack and any turf going: often in headgear: headstrong. *R. Curtis*

DON STEFANO 2 b.g. (Mar 29) Deportivo 116 – Molly Music 62 (Music Boy 124) **–** [2009 f8g Aug 27] 28/1, tailed off in maiden at Southwell. *W. G. M. Turner*

DONTBUGTHEBUNNY (USA) 2 ch.f. (Jan 26) Theatrical 128 – Stravinia (USA) **46** (Stravinsky (USA) 133) [2009 6m^4 8.3m^2 p7.1g^5 p9.5g f8m^5 f7g^3 Nov 17] 20,000Y: first foal: dam unraced: poor maiden plater: should be suited by 1¼m+: sold 1,800 gns. *George Baker*

DON'T PANIC (IRE) 5 ch.g. Fath (USA) 116 – Torrmana (IRE) (Ela-Mana-Mou 132) **§§** [2009 113: 8m 8m Apr 29] strong gelding: smart performer at 4 yrs: refused to race final outing that year and on both appearances in 2009: served ban from racing after BHA inquiry in May: won over hurdles for R. Hodges in November: very much one to treat with caution. *P. W. Chapple-Hyam*

DONTPAYTHEFERRYMAN (USA) 4 ch.g. Wiseman's Ferry (USA) 102 – Expletive Deleted (USA) (Dr Blum (USA)) [2009 62: p11g² p12.2g³ f11g³ 10g³ 11.1s³ 12.5s³ p13.9g p12f⁶ Oct 14] modest maiden handicapper: left P. D. Evans after second outing, A. Dickman after third, R. Fahey after seventh: likely to be suited by 1¾m+: acts on all-weather and soft going: tried in cheekpieces: has worn tongue tie: fairly useful winning hurdler. *B. Ellison* **60**

DONTRISKIT 3 ch.f. Bertolini (USA) 125 – Risky Valentine 68 (Risk Me (FR) 127) [2009 p7g Jan 14] fourth foal: half-sister to 6f/7f winner Mister Elegant (by Fraam) and 4-y-o Zeffirelli: dam 5f (at 2 yrs)/6f winner: 100/1, last in maiden at Kempton. *J. L. Spearing* **–**

DON'T STOP ME NOW (IRE) 4 b.f. Catcher In The Rye (IRE) 115 – Persian Flower (Persian Heights 129) [2009 64: 16m* 10.5m 10g 14g⁶ 15.9m 16g p16g³ Oct 14] rather leggy filly: fair handicapper: won at Musselburgh in April, then left J. Howard Johnson: stays 2m: acts on polytrack and good to firm going: in cheekpieces last 2 starts. *John Joseph Hanlon, Ireland* **75**

DON'T TELL MARY (IRE) 2 b.f. (Mar 15) Starcraft (NZ) 128 – Only In Dreams 78 (Polar Falcon (USA) 126) [2009 5.1f* 5g* 5m 5g 7v⁶ Oct 24] £32,000Y: tall, angular filly: seventh foal: half-sister to 3 winners, including 2003 2-y-o 5f/6f winner Cape Fear (by Cape Cross) and 3-y-o Exceptional Art, both smart: dam 2-y-o 7f winner: fairly useful performer: won maiden at Bath and listed race at Beverley (by 4 lengths from The Hermitage) in May: well below form after, off nearly 4 months before penultimate start: should be suited by 6f+. *Tom Dascombe* **94**

DONTUWISHITWERESO 3 b.g. Kyllachy 129 – Prospering 50 (Prince Sabo 123) [2009 f6d² f6g* p6g f7g 6g 8g f6g⁵ p6m⁵ p7.1g⁵ f6d⁴ Dec 29] won maiden at Southwell in March: below form after: best effort at 6f on fibresand: tried visored. *P. W. D'Arcy* **65**

DOON HAYMER (IRE) 4 b.g. Barathea (IRE) 127 – Mutige (Warning 136) [2009 79: 9.2m³ 9.2d* 9.2s⁴ 9.2v 9.1d⁶ Aug 27] useful-looking gelding: fairly useful handicapper: won at Hamilton in July: below form after: best up to 9.2f: acts on heavy and good to firm going: sometimes visored, wore cheekpieces final outing. *I. Semple* **81**

DOONIGAN (IRE) 5 b.g. Val Royal (FR) 127 – Music In My Life (IRE) 59 (Law Society (USA) 130) [2009 –: f11g 17.2d May 18] tall gelding: maiden: little form since 2007: tried in headgear. *G. Brown* **–**

DORBACK 2 ch.c. (Apr 3) Kyllachy 129 – Pink Supreme 70 (Night Shift (USA)) [2009 6m* 6.1d⁶ 5g² 6g 6g⁵ Oct 30] 22,000F, £54,000Y: good-topped colt: second foal: half-brother to 3-y-o Time For Old Time: dam sprint maiden: useful performer: won maiden at Windsor (by 1½ lengths from Buzzword) in June: often better than result after, including when good fifth to Rum King in minor event at Newmarket: stays 6f: acts on good to firm ground. *H. Candy* **95**

DORIC ECHO 3 b.g. Bertolini (USA) 125 – Latour 79 (Sri Pekan (USA) 117) [2009 81: 7.1m⁵ 7m 7g 7.1g⁵ 8s⁴ 8g³ f7g 7g Oct 16] good-topped gelding: fair handicapper: stays 1m: acts on heavy and good to firm going: in cheekpieces penultimate outing: sold £7,000. *B. Smart* **77**

DORIC LADY 4 b.f. Kyllachy 129 – Tanasie (Cadeaux Genereux 131) [2009 86: 6g⁴ 6m* 6m⁴ 5g* 6g 5g 5m 6d p6g* Nov 14] workmanlike filly: fairly useful handicapper: won at Leicester in May, Doncaster in July and Lingfield in November: should prove best at 5f/6f: acts on polytrack, soft and good to firm ground: held up (sometimes slowly away). *J. A. R. Toller* **91**

DORMER FLEET 2 b.c. (Feb 11) Kyllachy 129 – Petong's Pet (Petong 126) [2009 p7m 6.1d* 7d 6s Nov 7] second foal: dam unraced sister to Champagne Stakes winner Petardia: easily best effort when winning maiden at Nottingham in October: well held in nurseries: may prove best at 6f: sold £4,000. *J. H. M. Gosden* **73**

DORN DANCER (IRE) 7 b.m. Danehill Dancer (IRE) 117 – Appledorn 99 (Doulab (USA) 115) [2009 85: f6g 7m 6m 6d 5.9m 8m 6d⁶ 7d p7.1g p7.1g 7g Oct 17] good-topped mare: handicapper, fair at best in 2009: left D. Barker after sixth outing: best at 5f/6f: best efforts on good going or softer: tried blinkered/in cheekpieces: patiently ridden (sometimes gets behind). *W. M. Brisbourne* **69**

DO THE DEAL (IRE) 3 ch.f. Halling (USA) 133 – Cairns (UAE) 107 (Cadeaux Genereux 131) [2009 67: 7m⁴ 9.3g⁵ 8m p6g p10.7g³ p10.7g⁵ p8g Nov 27] fair maiden: left J. J. Quinn after third outing: stays 10.7f: acts on polytrack, good to firm and good to soft going: tried in cheekpieces, blinkered last 3 starts. *D. M. Leigh, Ireland* **67**

DO THE STRAND (IRE) 3 b.c. Galileo (IRE) 134 – Aiming Upwards (Blushing Flame (USA) 109) [2009 8s 10g⁴ 10.3s* Aug 1] €47,000Y: sturdy colt: fourth foal: closely related to Italian 7.5f winner Asmera (by Montjeu) and half-brother to 7f (and up to 1¼m in Channel Islands) winner Top Level (by Fasliyev): dam unraced: progressive form in maidens, fairly useful effort when winning at Doncaster in August by ½ length from Troopingthecolour: will stay 1½m+: should improve further. *B. W. Hills* **93 p**

DOT'S DELIGHT 5 b.m. Golden Snake (USA) 127 – Hotel California (IRE) 58 (Last Tycoon 131) [2009 53: p10g p13.9g* f11m 11.9d⁴ 13.1f⁴ Aug 22] good-topped mare: modest performer: won handicap at Wolverhampton in July: stays 1¾m: acts on all-weather, good to firm and good to soft going: tried blinkered/in cheekpieces. *M. G. Rimell* **56**

DOUBLE ACT 3 b.g. Where Or When (IRE) 124 – Secret Flame 78 (Machiavellian (USA) 123) [2009 82: p8.6g* p8g* p8g³ Feb 14] tall, attractive gelding: fairly useful performer: won claimers at Wolverhampton and Kempton (left J. Noseda £15,000) in January: stays 8.6f: acts on polytrack: tongue tied: no form in juvenile hurdles, sold £750 in July. *Evan Williams* **81**

DOUBLE BANDED (IRE) 5 b.g. Mark of Esteem (IRE) 137 – Bronzewing 103 (Beldale Flutter (USA) 130) [2009 97: 18.7m 16.2g 14m⁶ 13.1m⁶ 15.9m² 18m⁴ Sep 19] leggy, sparely-made gelding: fairly useful handicapper: left Ian Williams after fourth outing: stays easy 2m: acts on polytrack, firm and good to soft going: tried in cheekpieces: has run well when sweating: travels strongly, but weak finisher: sold £1,600. *K. A. Ryan* **91 §**

DOUBLE BILL (USA) 5 b. or br.g. Mr Greeley (USA) 122 – Salty Perfume (USA) (Salt Lake (USA)) [2009 –, a79: p7.1g³ Dec 28] big, strong gelding: fair handicapper: off 14 months, respectable third at Wolverhampton: effective at 5f to 7f: acts on all-weather, had form on good to firm ground at 3 yrs: tried in cheekpieces/blinkers. *P. F. I. Cole* **– a68**

DOUBLE CARPET (IRE) 6 b.g. Lahib (USA) 129 – Cupid Miss (Anita's Prince 126) [2009 75: p6g p6g 6g p6g⁶ 6g Jul 23] angular gelding: handicapper, just modest form in 2009: stays 6f: acts on all-weather and soft ground. *G. Woodward* **– a59**

DOUBLE EXPOSURE 5 b.g. Double Trigger (IRE) 123 – Last Night's Fun (IRE) (Law Society (USA) 130) [2009 p11g 14m³ Oct 1] lightly-raced maiden: little form. *Jamie Poulton* **–**

DOUBLE FORTUNE 2 b.f. (Mar 16) Singspiel (IRE) 133 – Four-Legged Friend 101 (Aragon 118) [2009 p8f Dec 16] half-sister to several winners, including fairly useful 1m (including at 2 yrs)/1¼m winner Herr Trigger (by Sharrood): dam 2-y-o 5f winner: 100/1, well held in maiden at Kempton. *Jamie Poulton* **–**

DOUBLE MOON 3 b.g. Makbul 104 – Emoona (FR) (Linamix (FR) 127) [2009 9.9g 7.1g⁴ 7.1g 10.1g⁶ Aug 5] well-made gelding: poor maiden. *George Baker* **49**

DOUBLE ROLLOVER 2 b.c. (Mar 29) Fantastic Light (USA) 134 – Princess Miletrian (IRE) 80 (Danehill (USA) 126) [2009 7d 7.6d 7g p7.1m⁵ p7f 8m Sep 17] smallish, lengthy colt: poor maiden plater: usually in headgear: sold 1,000 gns, sent to Italy. *W. R. Muir* **39**

DOUBLE SPECTRE (IRE) 7 b.g. Spectrum (IRE) 126 – Phantom Ring 62 (Magic Ring (IRE) 115) [2009 75: p14g³ 11.7m⁶ 11.7f 12m 16g³ 15.4m p12m Oct 28] smallish, close-coupled gelding: fair handicapper: probably stays 2m, effective at much shorter: acts on polytrack, firm and good to soft going: blinkered final start: often held up. *Jean-Rene Auvray* **70**

DOUBLE VALENTINE 6 ch.m. Primo Valentino (IRE) 116 – Charlottevalentina (IRE) 80 (Perugino (USA) 84) [2009 –, a65: p7g³ p8g p8g p9.5g⁵ p10g⁶ p8g 8g p8m p7m p7g⁵ Nov 25] stocky mare: modest performer: below form after reappearance: stays 1m: acts on polytrack and good to firm going: waited with: blinkered last 2 starts. *R. Ingram* **– a61 d**

DOUBLE WHAMMY 3 b.g. Systematic 121 – Honor Rouge (IRE) 96 (Highest Honor (FR) 124) [2009 10f 11.7g⁵ 11.5m⁵ Sep 2] tall, angular gelding: fair form in maidens: likely to stay at least 2m. *Jamie Poulton* **65**

DOUBLY GUEST 5 b.m. Barathea Guest 117 – Countess Guest (IRE) 59 (Spectrum (IRE) 126) [2009 16.4m³ 16g² 15.9m⁶ Sep 12] workmanlike mare: has a round action: fair handicapper: left N. Henderson after reappearance and B. Hills £12,000 prior to final start: stays 17f: acts on firm and soft going: tried in cheekpieces: waited with: fairly useful but irresolute hurdler. *Tim Vaughan* **79**

DOUBNOV (FR) 6 gr.g. Linamix (FR) 127 – Karmitycia (FR) (Last Tycoon 131) [2009 110: 12s p10m 10g p12m* p12f Dec 19] sturdy gelding: smart performer for Saeed **82**

bin Suroor in 2008 (sold 16,000 gns): just fairly useful in 2009, winning seller at Lingfield in November: stays 1½m: acts on polytrack, heavy and good to firm going: in cheekpieces last 2 starts. *Ian Williams*

DOUBTFUL SOUND (USA) 5 b.g. Diesis 133 – Roam Free (USA) (Unbridled (USA) 128) [2009 98: p6g* p5g4 p5.1g3 p6g6 f5g p5.1g6 Nov 16] strong, lengthy gelding: useful handicapper: won at Lingfield in January by 2¼ lengths from Little Edward: good efforts after only on third/final starts: effective at 5f to 7f: acts on all-weather and good to firm going: usually blinkered/in cheekpieces nowadays. *R. Hollinshead* **101**

DOUCHKETTE (FR) 3 b.f. Califet (FR) 126 – Douchka (FR) (Fijar Tango (FR) 127) [2009 8.3g 8d Jul 17] good-topped filly: third foal: dam French 13f winner: unplaced in hurdle at Compiegne for F. Belmont in France: well beaten in maidens. *John Berry* **–**

DOVE COTTAGE (IRE) 7 b.g. Great Commotion (USA) 123 – Pooka 65 (Dominion 123) [2009 83: 10g5 10g4 10.2m 10.9g4 12m2 12s* 11.7g Oct 21] close-coupled gelding: fairly useful handicapper: won at Folkestone in October: below form otherwise in 2009: stays 1½m: acts on polytrack, firm and soft going: tried in cheekpieces: front runner/races prominently. *W. S. Kittow* **83**

DOVEDON ANGEL 3 b.f. Winged Love (IRE) 121 – Alexander Star (IRE) 68 (Inzar (USA) 112) [2009 –: p10g5 12v p12.2g4 p10g3 p11f2 Dec 16] leggy filly: modest maiden: stays easy 11f: acts on polytrack. *Miss Gay Kelleway* **60**

DOVEDON DIVA 2 b.f. (Feb 22) Generous (IRE) 139 – Alexander Star (IRE) 68 (Inzar (USA) 112) [2009 8.3d 7d 6s Nov 7] compact, workmanlike filly: third foal: dam 5f winner: little impact in maidens, though showed modest form at Doncaster final start: has hung/pulled hard. *T. Keddy* **52**

DOVEDON EARL 3 b.g. Millkom 124 – Syrian Flutist 59 (Shaamit (IRE) 127) [2009 p10m p12m4 Nov 29] seemingly modest form in second of 2 maidens at Kempton. *T. Keddy* **62 ?**

DOVEDON HERO 9 ch.g. Millkom 124 – Hot Topic (IRE) (Desse Zenny (USA)) [2009 69: 10.3m f12g May 18] sturdy gelding: fair performer at best: below form both starts in 2009: stays 2m: acts on all-weather and firm going: tried blinkered/in cheekpieces: held up. *P. J. McBride* **–**

DOVE (IRE) 4 b.f. Sadler's Wells (USA) 132 – Golden Digger (USA) 66 (Mr Prospector (USA)) [2009 10d* p13g Oct 29] smallish filly: useful form in 2-y-o maidens: missed 2008: better effort in 2009 when comfortably winning maiden at Pontefract in July: should stay 1½m: acts on good to soft going. *J. H. M. Gosden* **82 +**

DOVE MEWS 3 b.f. Namid 128 – Flying Fulmar 83 (Bahamian Bounty 116) [2009 87: 6m 6m 6d6 7g4 7g2 p6m Sep 16] lengthy filly: has a round action: just fair at 3 yrs, tending to find little: likely to prove best at 5f/6f: acts on soft and good to firm going: sold 4,000 gns. *M. L. W. Bell* **68**

DOWER GLEN 2 b.f. (Apr 12) Camacho 118 – Aimee's Delight 85 (Robellino (USA) 127) [2009 5m5 5s2 5g 5m3 5m5 5g3 5f4 5s6 5m Sep 16] £12,500Y: compact filly: second foal: dam, 5f (at 2 yrs) to 8.3f winner, out of half-sister to July Cup winner Compton Place: modest maiden: will prove best at 5f: acts on soft and good to firm ground: tried blinkered: becoming temperamental. *I. Semple* **57**

DOWLLEH 5 b.g. Noverre (USA) 125 – Al Persian (IRE) (Persian Bold 123) [2009 –: 6d Sep 7] good-topped gelding: handicapper, no form since 2007: tried in cheekpieces. *G. Brown* **–**

DOWNHILLER (IRE) 4 ch.g. Alhaarth (IRE) 126 – Ski For Gold 76 (Shirley Heights 130) [2009 106: p16g 16m* 18.7m May 6] neat gelding: useful handicapper: won at Ripon in April readily by ½ length from Wells Lyrical: respectable seventh to Daraahem in Chester Cup 11 days later (suffered leg injury, then gelded after): should stay 2¼m: acts on polytrack, firm and soft going. *J. L. Dunlop* **106**

DOWNHILL SKIER (IRE) 5 ch.g. Danehill Dancer (IRE) 117 – Duchy of Cornwall (USA) 83 (The Minstrel (CAN) 135) [2009 61: p7g* p7.1g* p7.1g6 p7g4 p7g2 p7.1g2 p7.1g4 f8d3 f8g p8.6g4 p7.1g* p7.1g 6d* 6f6 7.2s 6.1s p6g4 p7.1g4 p7m5 Nov 21] lengthy gelding: fair handicapper: won at Kempton and Wolverhampton in January, Wolverhampton in April and Thirsk in July: stays 8.6f: acts on all-weather and good to soft going: tried blinkered: held up. *W. M. Brisbourne* **74**

DOWNING STREET (IRE) 8 b.g. Sadler's Wells (USA) 132 – Photographie (USA) (Trempolino (USA) 135) [2009 81: 14f4 16.4m Aug 21] big gelding: handicapper: just fair in 2009: stays 2m: unraced on extremes of going: in headgear nowadays: tried tongue tied: fair hurdler, successful in April (has bled over jumps). *Jennie Candlish* **72**

DOWNSTREAM 3 b.f. Marju (IRE) 127 – Sister Moonshine (FR) 99 (Piccolo 121) [2009 51: p6g Jan 12] leggy filly: maiden: shaped as if amiss only outing in 2009: stays 7f: tried blinkered/tongue tied. *D. M. Simcock* –

DOWNTOOBUSINESS 2 b.g. (Mar 7) Desert Sun 120 – Mariette 35 (Blushing Scribe (USA) 107) [2009 7.1m p7g p8g Aug 24] poor maiden. *Karen George* 48

DOYENNE DREAM 2 b.f. (Apr 18) Doyen (IRE) 132 – Cribella (USA) 71 (Robellino (USA) 127) [2009 8d Oct 27] closely related to useful 1¼m winner Ruby Wine (by Kayf Tara) who stayed 1½m: dam 1½m winner: 100/1, well held in maiden at Yarmouth: bred to be suited by 1¼m+. *J. M. P. Eustace* –

DRACO BOY 2 gr.g. (Apr 24) Silver Patriarch (IRE) 125 – Miss Tehente (FR) (Tehente (FR)) [2009 6g 7.1g p7g Oct 9] soundly beaten in maidens. *Andrew Turnell* –

DRAGONESSA (IRE) 2 b.f. (Mar 30) Red Ransom (USA) – Principessa 74 (Machiavellian (USA) 123) [2009 6m p6g p7g 6d* p6m 6.1s² 5.1s Nov 4] small filly: second foal: dam, maiden (stayed 11.7f), sister to smart French sprinter Titus Livius: modest performer: won nursery at Lingfield in September: should stay 7f: acts on soft ground: races prominently. *B. Palling* 58

DRAGON FLAME (IRE) 6 b.g. Tagula (IRE) 116 – Noble Rocket (Reprimand 122) [2009 75: f5g 5.2g* 5m⁶ 5g³ 5.1v 5.2g Aug 30] angular gelding: fairly useful handicapper: won at Yarmouth in May: below form after: best around 5f: acts on soft going: effective with or without visor: often front runner: sold 1,500 gns. *M. Quinn* 80

DRAGON SLAYER (IRE) 7 ch.g. Night Shift (USA) – Arandora Star (USA) (Sagace (FR) 135) [2009 81: 10.3m 10.1d 10.2f⁵ 11.5g³ 10m⁵ 10.1g⁶ 10.2g⁶ 9s² 10.1g* 10g² 10m 9g⁴ 10.2m⁵ 10.2g* Oct 28] rather leggy, close-coupled gelding: fair handicapper: won at Yarmouth (apprentices) in July and Nottingham (ladies event) in October: best at 1¼m nowadays: acts on all-weather, soft and good to firm ground: tried in cheekpieces: free-going sort. *John A. Harris* 74

DRAMATIC JEWEL (USA) 3 b.g. Diesis 133 – Seeking The Jewel (USA) (Seeking The Gold (USA)) [2009 8.1g p10g⁶ p12g p10m⁴ p9.5g³ Oct 3] $40,000Y: lengthy gelding: third foal: dam, US 1m winner, out of close relation to US Grade 1 9f winner Dramatic Gold: fair maiden: stays 1¼m: acts on polytrack: sold £4,000. *J. W. Hills* 71

DRAMATIC SOLO 4 ch.f. Nayef (USA) 129 – Just Dreams 85 (Salse (USA) 128) [2009 76: p16g* p13.9g⁶ p16g⁴ p13g³ 18m⁴ 16m³ 12m⁴ 13m* 14g³ 14.1f³ 14.1m⁵ 14g* 12m³ 14m³ 14.1g³ Oct 16] quite good-topped filly: fair handicapper: won at Lingfield in January and Musselburgh in May and August (both apprentice events, trained by K. R. Burke prior to latter occasion): stays easy 2m: acts on polytrack and firm ground: visored/blinkered nowadays: free-going front runner. *A. P. Jarvis* 76

DRAWNFROMTHEPAST (IRE) 4 ch.g. Tagula (IRE) 116 – Ball Cat (FR) (Cricket Ball (USA) 124) [2009 p6g⁴ 6d 6m⁶ 7f 6.5m 6m p6m⁴ p6g⁴ p6g⁴ p6g⁴ Nov 14] sturdy gelding: useful handicapper: missed 2008: best effort at 4 yrs when sixth to High Standing at Goodwood third outing: raced mainly at 5f/6f: acts on polytrack and good to firm going: often tongue tied in 2009: gelded after final start. *J. A. Osborne* 97

DRAWN GOLD 5 b.g. Daggers Drawn (USA) 114 – Gold Belt (IRE) 61 (Bellypha 130) [2009 74: p9.5g p12.2g² 12m⁴ 14g 12.6d* 12.3m⁴ 11.9g² 12.3m³ 12m 16g⁴ᵈ p13.9g⁶ p13.9g³ Nov 30] workmanlike gelding: fair handicapper: won amateur event at Warwick in June: stays 12.6f: acts on polytrack, firm and good to soft ground. *R. Hollinshead* 70

DR BRASS 4 b.g. Dr Fong (USA) 128 – Tropical Heights (FR) (Shirley Heights 130) [2009 82: p10g p12.2g 11.6g Apr 27] lengthy gelding: has quick action: fairly useful handicapper at 3 yrs, well held in 2009: often wears blinkers/cheekpieces. *B. N. Pollock* –

DREAM CATCH ME (IRE) 3 b.f. Xaar 132 – Dancerette (Groom Dancer (USA) 128) [2009 p6g⁴ p6g³ p5g⁶ 6m Apr 30] 2,000 2-y-o: half-sister to winner in Japan by Singspiel: dam French 11f winner: modest form only on debut: will be suited by 7f+. *J. R. Boyle* 56

DREAMCOAT 3 ch.c. Pivotal 124 – Follow A Dream (USA) 90 (Gone West (USA)) [2009 –p: 8s⁴ 7d³ 8.3g Jun 11] big, strong colt: fair form in maidens: stays 1m: acts on soft ground: sold £22,000 in August. *J. H. M. Gosden* 76

DREAM DATE (IRE) 3 b.f. Oasis Dream 129 – Femme Fatale 102 (Fairy King (USA)) [2009 70: p7g* p7.1g* a6.5g³ 7g a6g a6g a6.5g⁵ Jul 11] quite attractive filly: fair performer: made all in handicaps at Lingfield and Wolverhampton in January: sold from W. Haggas 27,000 gns, best effort after when third in minor event at Mijas next outing: stays 7f: acts on polytrack/sand: tongue tied 4 of last 5 starts in Britain: re-sold 8,000 gns in November. *J. L. Eyre, Spain* 78

Sky Bet City of York Stakes, York—the judge is unable to separate Confront (left) and the grey Dream Eater; Royal Confidence (right) is third, just ahead of Secret Society (behind dead-heaters)

DREAM DESERT (IRE) 4 ch.c. Elnadim (USA) 128 – Bravo Dancer 87 (Acate- **91**
nango (GER) 127) [2009 93: p11g^{3} 12g^{6} 10.3m 10.1g 12m Jun 28] good-topped colt: fairly useful handicapper: stayed 1½m, possibly better at shorter: acted on polytrack and firm going: dead. *M. R. Channon*

DREAM EATER (IRE) 4 gr.c. Night Shift (USA) – Kapria (FR) 103 (Simon du **117**
Desert (FR) 116) [2009 117: 7.1m^{2} 8.1g^{2} 8d 8m^{5} 7g^{4} 8m^{4} 7g^{4} 7m* 8g^{2} 6m Sep 27] big, strong, good-bodied colt: smart performer: dead-heated with Confront in listed race at York in August: good second otherwise in 2009 in Mile at Sandown (beaten ¾ length by Paco Boy) and very valuable Topkapi Trophy at Veliefendi (beaten head by Pressing) second/penultimate starts: stays 1m: acts on polytrack and firm going: tongue tied: often pulls too hard. *A. M. Balding*

DREAM EXPRESS (IRE) 4 b.g. Fasliyev (USA) 120 – Lothlorien (USA) 80 **76 §**
(Woodman (USA) 126) [2009 82: p7.1g 7f 7s^{3} 7s 7m 7g 7.5m* 6g* 7d^{4} 6f^{3} p7.1g^{5} p6g^{4} p6g 6m^{6} 6d^{6} p7m p6g^{5} p8m p7.1g Dec 11] rangy gelding: just fair performer at 4 yrs: won seller at Beverley and claimer at Ayr in July: claimed from M. Dods £10,000 tenth start: effective at 6f to 7.5f: acts on polytrack, soft and firm going: tried in headgear/tongue tie: tricky ride (often pulls hard). *P. Howling*

DREAM HUNTRESS 3 ch.f. Dubai Destination (USA) 127 – Dream Lady (Benny **69**
The Dip (USA) 127) [2009 65: p10g p8.6g 8d^{2} 8d^{5} p8.6g p8m^{3} Dec 9] fair performer: left B. Meehan after reappearance: should stay 1¼m: acts on polytrack and good to soft ground. *J. W. Hills*

DREAM IN BLUE 4 b.g. Oasis Dream 129 – Blue Birds Fly 78 (Rainbow Quest **61**
(USA) 134) [2009 p11g^{2} p13g^{2} p12.2g^{2} 18m 17.2m^{6} 15.8g 12g f12f^{4} p12.2g^{6} f11m* **a71**
f11g^{3} Dec 27] fair performer on all-weather, modest on turf: left J. Osborne after sixth outing (trained on fourth start only by Mrs S. Smith): won seller at Southwell in December: stays 13f: acts on all-weather: tried in cheekpieces/blinkers/tongue tie. *J. A. Glover*

DREAM IN WAITING 3 b.f. Oasis Dream 129 – Lady In Waiting 113 (Kylian **84**
(USA)) [2009 88: 10.4g p8.6g^{3} Oct 29] good-bodied filly: fairly useful performer: stays 8.6f: acts on polytrack, soft and good to firm going. *B. J. Meehan*

DREAM LODGE (IRE) 5 ch.g. Grand Lodge (USA) 125 – Secret Dream (IRE) **113**
(Zafonic (USA) 130) [2009 103: 8m 8m^{3} 9m 8g 8g* 10f 8d* 8g^{4} 10.4m^{4} 8.9m^{2} 10m^{5} 8m^{4} Oct 3] good-topped gelding: smart performer: left J. Given after fourth start: improved after, winning handicap at Redcar in June and minor event at Doncaster (by nose from Perks) in July: creditable efforts after when in frame, including when length second to Palavicini in Strensall Stakes at York tenth outing: stays 10.4f: acts on polytrack, firm and good to soft going: tried visored: races prominently. *R. A. Fahey*

DREAM MOUNTAIN 6 b.g. Mozart (IRE) 131 – Statua (IRE) 98 (Statoblest 120) **–**
[2009 f14g p12g p16g Apr 1] useful-looking gelding: handicapper: well below form in 2009: tried in cheekpieces/visor. *Ms J. S. Doyle*

DREAM NUMBER (IRE) 2 ch.f. (Apr 26) Fath (USA) 116 – Very Nice (Daylami (IRE) 138) [2009 5.1g^5 5m^3 5.7m^3 p6f^5 7m* p7.1g Nov 9] second foal: half-sister to 3-y-o Seek N' Destroy: dam, unraced, out of half-sister to very smart 1¼m performer One So Wonderful: fair performer: won nursery at Leicester in October: found nothing (reportedly lost a shoe) final start: stays 7f. *W. R. Muir* **71**

DREAM OF FORTUNE (IRE) 5 b.g. Danehill Dancer (IRE) 117 – Tootling (IRE) (Pennine Walk 120) [2009 85: p9.5g^3 p10g^3 p9.5g* p9.5g^2 p10g^4 10g^6 12m p9.5g p8g^4 p10g p12m^3 p10m^3 p10m^3 p10f* Dec 20] quite attractive gelding: fairly useful handicapper: won at Wolverhampton in February and Kempton in December: seems to stay 1½m: acts on polytrack and good to firm going: tried blinkered: usually tongue tied. *M. G. Quinlan* **84**

DREAM OF GERONTIUS (IRE) 2 b.f. (Apr 9) Oratorio (IRE) 128 – Shades of Rosegold (IRE) (Bluebird (USA) 125) [2009 5.1g p5g^3 6m 7m Sep 1] €41,000F, £21,000Y: sturdy filly: fourth foal: dam, maiden, half-sister to useful 1m/1¼m performer Alexis: flattered when third in maiden at Kempton: showed nothing otherwise: should stay 6f+: tried blinkered (none too keen). *R. Hannon* **–**

DREAM OF OLWYN (IRE) 4 b.f. Nayef (USA) 129 – Jam (IRE) (Arazi (USA) 135) [2009 79: 10.2f* 10.4g^2 10.2v Nov 4] angular filly: fair handicapper: won at Nottingham in May: stays 10.4f: acts on polytrack, firm and soft going: travels strongly close up. *J. G. Given* **78**

DREAMONANDON (IRE) 3 b.g. Val Royal (FR) 127 – Boley Lass (IRE) 93 (Archway (IRE) 115) [2009 58p: 9.9m^6 8d 8.3g Jun 17] workmanlike gelding: modest maiden: stayed 1¼m: best effort on good to firm going: dead. *G. A. Swinbank* **62**

DREAM ON CONNIE 3 b.g. Cape Cross (IRE) 129 – Fantasize 99 (Groom Dancer (USA) 128) [2009 8m p10g^5 10m 8.3g 8.5g^6 9.9g^5 10m 10.1m^3 10m p10g Oct 24] sturdy gelding: fair maiden: stays 1¼m: acts on polytrack: tried visored/in cheekpieces: often tongue tied. *W. J. Knight* **69**

DREAM RAINBOW 4 b.g. Oasis Dream 129 – Bint Zamayem (IRE) 95 (Rainbow Quest (USA) 134) [2009 66: 6d p7.1g 7g Aug 14] sturdy gelding: maiden: no form in 2009: tried visored/tongue tied. *Joss Saville* **–**

DREAMS JEWEL 9 b.g. Dreams End 93 – Jewel of The Nile 35 (Glenstal (USA) 118) [2009 66: p16g^3 f14g 16.4g p13.9g Nov 30] angular gelding: modest handicapper nowadays: stays 2m: acts on all-weather and soft going: held up: fair hurdler, won in October. *C. Roberts* **61**

DREAMSPEED (IRE) 2 b.c. (Mar 12) Barathea (IRE) 127 – Kapria (FR) 103 (Simon du Desert (FR) 116) [2009 7.1m* 7g 8m^5 8m^5 Sep 26] 62,000F: well-made colt: fourth foal: half-brother to 3 winners, notably 4-y-o Dream Eater: dam French 1¼m/10.5f winner: fairly useful performer: won maiden at Sandown in July: upped in grade and better form after, fifth to Joshua Tree in Royal Lodge Stakes at Ascot final outing: should stay 1¼m. *A. M. Balding* **93**

DREAM SPINNER 2 b.g. (Apr 29) Royal Applause 124 – Dream Quest 102 (Rainbow Quest (USA) 134) [2009 7.1m^4 7.1m^5 7f^4 8m p8m^6 10m^3 Oct 5] fifth foal: half-brother to fairly useful 1½m/13f winner Nando's Dream (by Hernando): dam, 1¼m winner who stayed 1½m, sister to smart German 1½m performer Baroon and half-sister to smart sprinters Struggler and Vision of Night: fair maiden: stays 1¼m: acts on polytrack and good to firm going: gelded after final start. *J. L. Dunlop* **70**

DREAM STREET ROSE (USA) 4 b. or br.f. Yankee Victor (USA) 121 – Dixie Fine (USA) (L'Emigrant (USA) 129) [2009 p8.6g Apr 25] 14,000Y, 800 3-y-o: closely related to winner in USA by Saint Ballado and half-sister to French 7.5f winner Vassar (by Royal Academy): dam, US 6.5f to 8.3f winner, half-sister to dam of Dolphin Street and Saffron Walden: tongue tied, said to have had breathing problem when tailed off in seller at Wolverhampton. *K. R. Burke* **–**

DREAM THEME 6 b.g. Distant Music (USA) 126 – Xaymara (USA) (Sanglamore (USA) 126) [2009 97: 7m f7g^3 6g^2 5f May 11] big, good-bodied gelding: just fair form at best in 2009, often missing break badly: effective at 6f/7f: acts on all-weather, probably on any turf going: often slowly away: tried visored: waited with. *D. Nicholls* **75 §**

DREAMWALK (IRE) 3 b.g. Bahri (USA) 125 – Celtic Silhouette (FR) (Celtic Swing 138) [2009 80: 10.2g^2 10.1m* 10.1g 10m^4 10.2g^4 11.7f^2 9.9m 10m* Oct 2] strong gelding: fairly useful performer: won maiden at Yarmouth in May and handicap at Newmarket (2 ran) in October: will be suited by 1½m: acts on firm ground: visored last 4 starts: sold 16,000 gns, joined R. Curtis. *R. M. Beckett* **85**

DREAM WIN 3 b.c. Oasis Dream 129 – Wince 117 (Selkirk (USA) 129) [2009 82P: 8d^{5} Apr 13] well-made colt: shaped really well in maiden at 2 yrs: failed to build on that in similar event at Yarmouth in April: should stay at least 1m: sold 10,000 gns in October. *Sir Michael Stoute* **59**

DREAMY EYED (IRE) 2 b.f. (Jun 1) Shamardal (USA) 129 – Misty Eyed (IRE) 112 (Paris House 123) [2009 6m 7s p5m p5g Oct 21] €18,000Y: compact filly: second foal: dam 2-y-o 5f winner, including Molecomb Stakes: easily best effort when seventh to Desert Poppy in maiden at Kempton third start, well placed. *Mrs P. N. Dutfield* **55**

DRESSED TO DANCE (IRE) 5 b.m. Namid 128 – Costume Drama (USA) (Alleged (USA) 138) [2009 95: p7g^{4} p6g^{3} p6g^{6} p7.1g^{5} 5.7m* 7m^{4} 6g^{3} 6f^{4} 5.7g^{2} 7f 6.1m^{2} 6m 6d Oct 12] big, strong mare: just fairly useful at best in 2009: won seller at Bath (left P. D. Evans 7,200 gns) in May: best at 6f/7f: acts on polytrack and any turf going: blinkered/visored: held up: sold 4,500 gns. *R. A. Harris* **82**

DREWS LANE 2 b.f. (Mar 3) Forzando 122 – Emerald Dream (IRE) 47 (Vision (USA)) [2009 7g^{6} 7d 8.3m^{6} 7m Sep 1] seventh foal: sister to fairly useful 5f (at 2 yrs) to 1¼m (in UAE) winner Cotosol and half-sister to 7f (at 2 yrs)/1m winner Whatatodo (by Compton Place): dam maiden who stayed 1¼m: poor maiden plater: tried tongue tied/in cheekpieces. *W. G. M. Turner* **35**

DR FINLEY (IRE) 2 ch.g. (Mar 10) Dr Fong (USA) 128 – Farrfesheena (USA) 89 (Rahy (USA) 115) [2009 7s^{4} 7.6d^{2} 7f^{4} 8d^{3} Oct 15] useful-looking gelding: fourth foal: half-brother to fairly useful 8.6f winner House of Lords (by Doneraile Court) and 6f/7f winner Blackmalkin (by Forest Wildcat): dam maiden (stayed 1m): fair maiden: should stay 1m: gelded after final start. *M. L. W. Bell* **77**

DRIFT AND DREAM 2 b.f. (May 4) Exceed And Excel (AUS) 126 – Sea Drift (FR) 72 (Warning 136) [2009 5.2g* 6g^{5} 5m^{2} 5d^{2} Sep 16] sixth foal: half-sister to fairly useful 6f/7f winner Ocean Gift (by Cadeaux Genereux) and Italian 7.5f winner Janjira (by Montjeu): dam, 7f winner, half-sister to dam of Middle Park Stakes winner Dark Angel: fair performer: won maiden at Yarmouth in June: good second in nurseries at Sandown last 2 starts: should stay 6f: acts on good to firm and good to soft going. *C. F. Wall* **73**

DRIFTING GOLD 5 ch.m. Bold Edge 123 – Driftholme 27 (Safawan 118) [2009 79: p5m^{3} p5g* p5.1g^{5} p5.1g^{5} p5g^{4} p5.1g^{4} 5g 5.3m* 5.3m^{2} 5g^{2} p6g^{5} 5m 5m p5.1g Oct 15] angular mare: fairly useful handicapper: won at Kempton in January and Brighton in April: best at 5f/6f: acts on polytrack and good to firm going: wears headgear. *C. G. Cox* **82**

DRILL SERGEANT 4 br.g. Rock of Gibraltar (IRE) 133 – Dolydille (IRE) 108 (Dolphin Street (FR) 125) [2009 113: 10g 14g 16m 12m^{2} 10.1g 12m^{3} 12.1d^{3} 12f^{3} 12g^{2} 12m* 11.9m^{5} 14m^{6} 14g^{3} 16.4m^{2} 18m^{4} 12m 12m^{2} 12v^{5} Oct 24] big, leggy gelding: smart performer: won Duke of Edinburgh Stakes (Handicap) at Royal Ascot by 1¼ lengths **113**

*Duke of Edinburgh Stakes (Heritage Handicap), Ascot—
the sole win of a busy campaign for the notably tough Drill Sergeant;
Record Breaker (right), Martyr (left) and Young Mick (black sleeves, partially hidden) fill the frame*

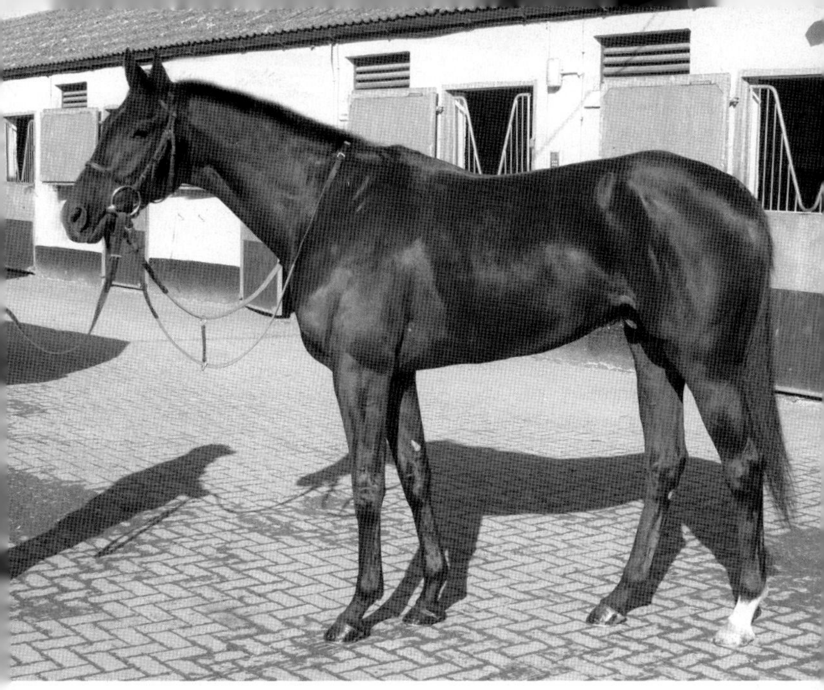

Mr J. Barson's "Drill Sergeant"

from Record Breaker: placed on 8 other occasions in 2009, including when 1¼ lengths second to Askar Tau in Lonsdale Cup at York on fourteenth start: stays 2m: acts on any going: front runner/races prominently: tough. *M. Johnston*

DRINKING BUDDY 2 ch.g. (Mar 15) Reel Buddy (USA) 118 – Tancred Arms 73 **50**
(Clantime 101) [2009 6v^5 7d^5 6m^3 7g^4 6g^2 6m^6 6.1s 8g 7m Oct 26] strong gelding: modest maiden: left K. Ryan after fourth start: stays 7f: acts on heavy and good to firm going: tried tongue tied. *D. W. Thompson*

DRIVEN (IRE) 4 b.g. Domedriver (IRE) 128 – Wonderful World (GER) (Dashing **80**
Blade 117) [2009 68: 8m* p8g^2 8m^5 8m^3 8.5m 7f^3 p7m 8m 7d Oct 15] useful-looking gelding: fairly useful handicapper: won at Brighton in April: well below form last 3 starts: stays 1m: acts on polytrack and firm ground: often races freely: sold 5,500 gns, sent to Greece. *Mrs A. J. Perrett*

DRIZZI (IRE) 8 b.g. Night Shift (USA) – Woopi Gold (IRE) (Last Tycoon 131) [2009 **–**
72: f14g Dec 22] fair performer: well held sole outing in 2009: stays 1¾m: acts on all-weather and good to firm ground: tried in cheekpieces/tongue tie: has bled. *Jim Best*

DR JAMESON (IRE) 3 b.g. Orpen (USA) 116 – Touraneena (Robellino (USA) 127) **77**
[2009 80: 8.5m^3 7.5m* 8m^5 10.3m 8.1m^5 p9.5g^6 p8.6g f8f^3 Dec 17] useful-looking gelding: fair performer: won maiden at Beverley in May: should stay 1¼m: acts on soft and good to firm going: blinkered/visored last 2 starts. *R. A. Fahey*

DR LIGHT (IRE) 5 b.g. Medicean 128 – Allumette (Rainbow Quest (USA) 134) **–**
[2009 60: f11g^5 p12.2g Feb 16] maiden handicapper: well below form in 2009. *M. A. Peill*

DR LIVINGSTONE (IRE) 4 b.g. Dr Fong (USA) 128 – Radhwa (FR) (Shining Steel **98**
123) [2009 93: 10m^2 10m^6 p11g^5 10v^2 Oct 24] good-topped gelding: useful handicapper: very good efforts in 2009 when runner-up, beaten ¾ length by Rainbow Peak at Newbury final start: stays 1¼m: acts on polytrack, heavy and good to firm going: sometimes races freely. *C. R. Egerton*

Kennet Valley Thoroughbreds IV's "Drumfire"

DR MATHIAS 2 b.g. (Mar 26) Dubai Destination (USA) 127 – Herminoe 83 (Rainbow Quest (USA) 134) [2009 8g 8m* p8.6g p8.6g Oct 23] fair form: best effort when winning claimer at Ffos Las (left W. Muir £12,000) in September: should stay 1¼m: acts on good to firm ground. *P. D. Evans* **66**

DR MCFAB 5 ch.g. Dr Fong (USA) 128 – Barbera 54 (Barathea (IRE) 127) [2009 –: p13.9m 10.9f³ 11.5m 9m Aug 27] good-topped gelding: maiden handicapper: form in 2009 (modest) only when third: stays 10.9f: acts on polytrack and firm ground: tried visored/in cheekpieces. *Miss Tor Sturgis* **54**

DROGBA (ARG) 4 b.c. Lucky Roberto (USA) 118 – Gattara (ARG) (Potrillazo (ARG)) [2009 p8f⁶ Dec 19] third foal: dam Argentinian 1m winner: champion 2-y-o colt in Peru, winning 3 of 4 starts at Monterrico in 2008, last of them Grade 3 event (by 5½ lengths): left A. Olivares, off 18 months and visored, 3½ lengths last of 6 to Jaroslaw in minor event at Lingfield on British debut, held up: stays 7f. *M. Botti* **92 ?**

DROMBEG PRIDE (IRE) 5 b.g. High Account (USA) 65 – Proserpina (Most Welcome 131) [2009 –: p16g Jan 16] good-topped gelding: little form. *G. P. Enright* **–**

DROMORE (IRE) 2 ch.g. (Feb 17) Traditionally (USA) 117 – Try To Catch Me (USA) (Shareef Dancer (USA) 135) [2009 p7g 7m* 8m 8g Oct 23] 14,000Y: tall, good-topped gelding: closely related to high-class 7f (at 2 yrs) to 1½m winner Storming Home (by Machiavellian) and half-brother to several winners: dam French miler: fair performer: won maiden at Salisbury in August: creditable effort when mid-field in nursery at Doncaster final start: gelded after: stays 1m: acts on good to firm going. *A. M. Balding* **76**

DROP THE HAMMER 3 b.f. Lucky Story (USA) 128 – Paperweight 77 (In The Wings 128) [2009 66: 10.1d⁶ 12.1g 12.1m³ 14g* f14m⁵ 16g³ 16.4d 16.1g 14.1g Oct 16] modest performer: won handicap at Haydock in July: stays 2m: acts on heavy and good to firm going: usually races prominently. *T. P. Tate* **63**

DRUBINCA 2 b.g. (Feb 27) Dubai Destination (USA) 127 – Racina 103 (Bluebird (USA) 125) [2009 6g 7m 7.1m5 Sep 29] useful-looking gelding: well held in maidens: gelded. *S. C. Williams* –

DRUMADOON BAY (IRE) 5 b.g. Marju (IRE) 127 – Mythical Creek (USA) (Pleasant Tap (USA)) [2009 61: 7.9g 8m4 10.1d 7.1g6 Jul 6] sturdy, workmanlike gelding: maiden: modest form at 5 yrs only when fourth at Musselburgh second start: best effort at 8.5f on good going. *G. A. Swinbank* 52

DRUMBEAT (IRE) 3 b.c. Montjeu (IRE) 137 – Maskaya (IRE) 92 (Machiavellian (USA) 123) [2009 108: 9m2 10.3m3 8v6 10.5g 12g 9.5s2 8s2 Jul 22] deep-girthed colt: useful performer: several creditable efforts in 2009 (often highly tried), including when placed in listed race at Newmarket (2 lengths second to Redwood), Dee Stakes at Chester (beaten 2 heads when third to South Easter) and minor event at Naas (1¾ lengths second to Firey Red) on first/second/final starts: should stay 1½m: acts on heavy and good to firm going: quirky. *A. P. O'Brien, Ireland* 106

DRUM DRAGON 3 b.f. Beat Hollow 126 – Qilin (IRE) 94 (Second Set (IRE) 127) [2009 69p: 6m p8.6g2 8.3m* 8.5g6 10.4v3 10.1d4 12m6 12g* p12m4 p12m6 Nov 26] tall, unfurnished filly: fairly useful performer: won maiden at Hamilton in June and claimer at Catterick in October: stays 1½m: acts on polytrack, heavy and good to firm going: headstrong. *M. H. Tompkins* 80

DRUMFIRE (IRE) 5 b.h. Danehill Dancer (IRE) 117 – Witch of Fife (USA) 91 (Lear Fan (USA) 130) [2009 110: 10m3 10m4 12m2 12m 9.9g* 12g4 10m Aug 29] big, lengthy horse: smart performer: better than ever in 2009, winning quite valuable handicap at Goodwood (beat Sweet Lightning by ½ length) in July: creditable efforts otherwise when fourth in Brigadier Gerard Stakes at Sandown (to Cima de Triomphe) and Glorious Stakes at Goodwood (behind Illustrious Blue) second/sixth outings: effective at 1¼m/1½m: acts on firm and soft going: held up: sold 50,000 gns. *M. Johnston* 115

DRUMHALLAGH (IRE) 4 b.g. Barathea (IRE) 127 – Nashua Song (IRE) (Kahyasi 130) [2009 58: p13.9m 10.9m Apr 13] leggy gelding: maiden, lightly raced: well below form both starts in 2009: tried blinkered. *Tom Dascombe* –

DRUM MAJOR (IRE) 4 b.g. Sadler's Wells (USA) 132 – Phantom Gold 119 (Machiavellian (USA) 123) [2009 74: p12m4 p13g 13.3m2 11.6g5 p16g 11.5s5 14.1m Aug 21] sturdy gelding: fair handicapper: stays 13.3f: acts on polytrack, soft and good to firm ground: tried blinkered. *G. L. Moore* 75

DRUMPELLIER (IRE) 2 ch.f. (Mar 8) Rakti 130 – Early Memory (USA) 83 (Devil's Bag (USA)) [2009 5m4 5m6 5m6 6d5 f5g4 6v* 6.1d 6g4 Aug 14] £800Y: good-topped filly: sixth foal: half-sister to Irish 4-y-o Final Flashback: dam, Irish 7f winner, sister to high-class US performer up to 1¼m Twilight Agenda: modest performer: dead-heated in seller at Ripon in July: creditable fourth in nursery at Catterick final start: should stay beyond 6f: acts on heavy ground. *P. T. Midgley* 60

DRUNKEN SAILOR (IRE) 4 b.g. Tendulkar (USA) 114 – Ronni Pancake 56 (Mujadil (USA) 119) [2009 88: 10m5 10g 12.9m2 12g2 12s* 12g* 14s6 10m2 Sep 19] sparely-made gelding: useful handicapper: won at Galway in July and Gowran in August: improved further when 1¼ lengths second to Almiqdaad in John Smith's Stakes at Newbury final outing: stays 1¾m: acts on polytrack, soft and good to firm going: wears cheekpieces/blinkers: sometimes tongue tied: game and consistent: has joined L. Cumani. *Paul Flynn, Ireland* 107

DRUSSELL (IRE) 3 b.g. Orpen (USA) 116 – Cahermee Queen (USA) 65 (King of Kings (IRE) 125) [2009 p12.2g* 15.9m 14.1g p10g p10m Oct 26] 10,000Y, 5,000 2-y-o: third foal: half-brother to winner in USA by Danehill Dancer: dam once-raced half-sister to US Grade 2 winners Esteemed Friend (7f) and Badouizm (9f): fair form: raced only in Britain, and won maiden at Wolverhampton in March: stays 1½m: best efforts on polytrack. *S. Donohoe, Ireland* 72

DR WINTRINGHAM (IRE) 3 b.f. Monsieur Bond (IRE) 120 – Shirley Collins 76 (Robellino (USA) 127) [2009 68: 6g 5.1g3 5.1f3 6d5 6m3 6g3 6d2 8.1g* 8.3m4 8m4 8g p7m2 Nov 29] sturdy, lengthy filly: fair handicapper: left J. S. Moore after fifth start: won at Chepstow in August: stays 8.3f: acts on polytrack, firm and good to soft going: held up for current yard. *Karen George* 72

DRY SPEEDFIT (IRE) 4 b.g. Desert Style (IRE) 121 – Annmary Girl (Zafonic (USA) 130) [2009 73d: 8.3m Jul 11] lengthy, angular gelding: has a quick action: regressive form, well held only outing in 2009: refused to race final 3-y-o start: tried blinkered/visored. *Micky Hammond* – §

DUALAGI 5 b.m. Royal Applause 124 – Lady Melbourne (IRE) 76 (Indian Ridge 123) [2009 71: p6g 6m 5.7f^2 6m* 6f p6g^3 f6g^4 6d^6 6s^5 6m^3 6m^3 6m^4 5.7g Oct 21] good-topped mare: fair handicapper: won at Salisbury in May: effective at 5f/6f: acts on all-weather, soft and good to firm going: tried in cheekpieces: usually held up: attitude under suspicion. *M. R. Bosley* **68**

DUAR MAPEL (USA) 3 b.g. Lemon Drop Kid (USA) 131 – Pitchacurve (USA) (Defrere (USA)) [2009 75?: p8.6g^3 8.3g 10m 11.7m^6 12.3g^3 11.8g*^{dis} 12g* 10s a12g Dec 18] neat gelding: fair performer: left Paul Mason after fourth start: first past post in maiden at Saint-Galmier (disqualified) in September and minor event at Lyon Parilly in October: stays 1½m: acts on all-weather: usually blinkered in Britain (looked reluctant in visor final start there). *N. Bertran de Balanda, France* **79**

DUBAI BOUNTY 2 ch.f. (Jan 27) Dubai Destination (USA) 127 – Mary Read 100 (Bahamian Bounty 116) [2009 p8.6g* Dec 26] 50,000Y: first foal: dam, 5f winner, ran only at 2 yrs: 11/4, won 4-runner minor event at Wolverhampton by neck from Lovers Causeway, edging ahead final 1f: will improve. *G. A. Butler* **71 p**

DUBAI CREEK (IRE) 3 b.g. Cape Cross (IRE) 129 – Humilis (IRE) 98 (Sadler's Wells (USA) 132) [2009 10.1m^5 p9.5g^5 Oct 10] 290,000Y: first foal: dam Irish 1¼m winner: fair form in maidens, still green when fifth to At Wits End at Wolverhampton latter outing: sold £11,000, joined D. McCain Jnr. *M. Johnston* **68**

DUBAI CREST 3 b.g. Dubai Destination (USA) 127 – On The Brink 88 (Mind Games 121) [2009 81: 9.9m* 10f^2 10.1g 12m 11d 10m* 9.9f^6 10.2m^4 10m^6 10.9m^5 10g Oct 19] good-topped gelding: fairly useful handicapper: won at Beverley in April and Windsor in August: stays 1¼m: acts on polytrack, firm and soft going: blinkered once (hung left): gelded after final start. *Mrs A. J. Perrett* **93**

DUBAI DIVA 3 b.f. Dubai Destination (USA) 127 – Marine City (JPN) 77 (Carnegie (IRE) 129) [2009 62p: f11g^4 12s p16g* p16.5g^4 f16m Dec 15] fair performer: won handicap at Lingfield in November: stays 2m: acts on all-weather. *C. F. Wall* **72**

DUBAI DYNAMO 4 b.g. Kyllachy 129 – Miss Mercy (IRE) 62 (Law Society (USA) 130) [2009 100: p8g* p8g 8m 8m 8s Oct 12] stocky gelding: type to carry condition: useful handicapper: won at Kempton (beat Tartan Gigha 1¾ lengths) in April: well below form after: stays 1m: acts on all-weather, firm and good to soft going: tried blinkered: untrustworthy: sold 6,000 gns. *P. F. I. Cole* **100 §**

DUBAI ECHO (USA) 3 b. or br.g. Mr Greeley (USA) 122 – Entendu (USA) (Diesis 133) [2009 67p: 10m^2 9.2g^4 9.8m* 10.1m^4 Jul 2] strong gelding: fairly useful performer: won maiden at Ripon in June: stays 1¼m: acts on good to firm going: sold 24,000 gns, sent to USA. *Sir Michael Stoute* **85**

DUBAI GEM 3 b.f. Fantastic Light (USA) 134 – Reflectance 56 (Sadler's Wells (USA) 132) [2009 8m^6 9.9m^5 8m^5 Jun 5] 30,000Y: close-coupled filly: first foal: dam once-raced daughter of smart French sprinter Spain Lane: fair form in maidens at Goodwood. *Jamie Poulton* **70**

DUBAI HILLS 3 b.g. Dubai Destination (USA) 127 – Hill Welcome 52 (Most Welcome 131) [2009 83: 6m^4 6g 6g Aug 31] strong gelding: just fair form at best at 3 yrs: should stay 7f: acts on soft and good to firm going. *B. Smart* **74**

DUBAI LEGEND 3 ch.f. Cadeaux Genereux 131 – Royal Future (IRE) (Royal Academy (USA) 130) [2009 83: 6m* 6m 6.1g^5 6g 6.1d Oct 15] leggy, attractive filly: just fair performer in 2009: won maiden at Salisbury in May: well worth a try at 1m: acts on good to firm going: sold £800. *D. M. Simcock* **77**

DUBAI MEDIA (CAN) 2 b.f. (Mar 30) Songandaprayer (USA) 118 – Forty Gran (USA) (El Gran Senor (USA) 136) [2009 7g p7g^4 Oct 29] $250,000Y: tall, good-topped filly: fifth foal: half-sister to smart 2008 2-y-o 6f and 8.5f (US Grade 1 event) winner and Breeders' Cup Juvenile runner-up Square Eddie (by Smart Strike) and 3 winners in Canada: dam US 2-y-o 1m winner: fair form in maidens at Newmarket (green) and Lingfield (fourth to Padmini): should stay 1m. *D. M. Simcock* **72**

DUBAI MEYDAN (IRE) 4 b.g. High Chaparral (IRE) 132 – Miss Golden Sands 80 (Kris 135) [2009 86: p8g p7f p7g^3 p7m* Oct 28] well-made gelding: fairly useful performer: better than ever when winning handicap at Kempton in October: should stay 1m: acts on polytrack: tried blinkered: held up. *Miss Gay Kelleway* **91**

DUBAI MIRACLE (USA) 2 ch.c. (Jan 31) Consolidator (USA) 121 – East Cape (USA) (Mr Prospector (USA)) [2009 p6g^4 p7g^3 p7g* 8m^2 8m Sep 26] $75,000Y, 46,000 2-y-o: sixth foal: closely related to 2 winners in USA by Forestry and half-brother to 3 **98**

winners abroad by Royal Anthem: dam unraced close relative to US Grade 1 9f winner West By West: useful performer: won maiden at Lingfield in July: much improved when head second to Big Audio in listed event at Salisbury, hanging right off bridle: stiff task, seemed amiss in Royal Lodge Stakes at Ascot final start: stays 1m: acts on polytrack and good to firm going. *D. M. Simcock*

DUBAI PETAL (IRE) 4 b.f. Dubai Destination (USA) 127 – Out of Egypt (USA) (Red Ransom (USA)) [2009 77: p12m Jan 9] strong, lengthy, dipped-backed filly: fair handicapper, better on turf: below form sole start in 2009: stays 1¾m: acts on polytrack, firm and soft going: held up: has raced lazily. *J. S. Moore* – **a64**

DUBAI PHANTOM (USA) 2 b.g. (Mar 21) Arch (USA) 127 – Sharp Apple (USA) (Diesis 133) [2009 8.1m p8m5 p8.6g3 Oct 17] 16,000Y: compact gelding: progressive form in maidens, third to Brooklands Bay at Wolverhampton (forced wide): gelded after: should stay 9f: blinkered first 2 starts. *D. M. Simcock* **68**

DUBAI SET 2 ch.c. (Mar 19) Reset (AUS) 124 – Bint Makbul 65 (Makbul 104) [2009 6g4 6m3 6g2 5.7g2 6m* 6d3 6s* Nov 7] lengthy colt: second foal: brother to 3-y-o Saxford: dam 7f winner: fairly useful performer: won maiden at Lingfield in August and nursery at Doncaster (beat Gouray Girl by head) in November: will probably stay 7f: acts on soft and good to firm going: races prominently: genuine. *R. Hannon* **92**

DUBAI STORMING 3 b.g. Storming Home 128 – Tropical Breeze (IRE) (Kris 135) [2009 –: p10g5 p11g* p12.2g* p10g4 p12g5 p11g Sep 5] good-topped gelding: fairly useful performer: won maiden at Kempton in February and handicap at Wolverhampton in March: stays 1½m: raced only on polytrack: blinkered on debut: held up: sold 3,000 gns. *E. A. L. Dunlop* **81**

DUBAI'S TOUCH 5 b.h. Dr Fong (USA) 128 – Noble Peregrine (Lomond (USA) 128) [2009 110: 8.3m4 8.9g 8m 8g* 8g 8g Aug 8] strong horse: useful form in 2009 only when winning handicap at Ascot in July by 3 lengths from One Way Or Another: stays 1¼m: acts on polytrack, firm and soft going: blinkered last 3 starts: not entirely straightforward. *M. Johnston* **105**

DUBAI TO BARNSLEY 4 b.g. Superior Premium 122 – Oakwell Ace 57 (Clantime 101) [2009 64: p6g f6g 5m4 5m2 5m4 5d4 5g5 p7.1g p6g Nov 20] modest performer: left Garry Moss after second outing: below form last 5 starts: best at 5f: acts on all-weather, soft and good to firm going: tried in cheekpieces. *D. A. Nolan* **64 d**

DUBAI TSUNAMI 3 gr.f. Fantastic Light (USA) 134 – Citrine Spirit (IRE) 76 (Soviet Star (USA) 128) [2009 –: p8.6g Jun 22] close-coupled filly: no form: signs of temperament. *E. A. L. Dunlop* –

DUBARA REEF (IRE) 2 ch.g. (May 22) Dubawi (IRE) 129 – Mamara Reef 71 (Salse (USA) 128) [2009 7s 8.1m p7.1g Nov 20] close-coupled gelding: soundly beaten in maidens. *Paul Green* –

DUBAWI HEIGHTS 2 b.f. (Feb 11) Dubawi (IRE) 129 – Rosie's Posy (IRE) 86 (Suave Dancer (USA) 136) [2009 6m 6g5 6m3 6.5m2 7m2 7m6 Oct 17] 62,000F, 72,000Y: compact filly: third foal: half-sister to useful 6f (at 2 yrs)/1m winner Generous Thought (by Cadeaux Genereux): dam, 2-y-o 5.7f winner, half-sister to Sprint Cup winner Tante Rose: useful maiden: very good placed efforts in Lowther Stakes at York (5¼ lengths third to Lady of The Desert) and valuable sales races at Ascot (½-length second of 27 to Shamandar) and Newmarket (2¼ lengths second to Lillie Langtry): well below form in Rockfel Stakes at Newmarket final outing: stays 7f: races prominently: sold 75,000 gns, sent to USA. *S. A. Callaghan* **96**

DUBAWI KING 2 b.g. (Apr 15) Dubawi (IRE) 129 – Laughing Girl (USA) 85 (Woodman (USA) 126) [2009 8.3s 8.3g Oct 28] good-bodied gelding: soundly beaten in maidens at Nottingham. *N. Tinkler* –

DUBAWI PHANTOM 2 ch.c. (Mar 2) Dubawi (IRE) 129 – Anna Amalia (IRE) (In The Wings 128) [2009 6m5 7.1m6 7g2 7g* 7.1g3 8g6 7v Oct 24] 42,000Y: rather leggy colt: second foal: half-brother to 3-y-o Ave: dam, French 1½m winner, out of Park Hill Stakes winner Anna of Saxony: useful performer: won maiden at Epsom in July: easily best effort when 1½ lengths third to Shakespearean in Solario Stakes at Sandown: should stay 1m (pulled too hard when tried): possibly unsuited by heavy ground: blinkered fifth/sixth starts. *D. M. Simcock* **102**

DUBBURG (USA) 4 ch.g. Johannesburg (USA) 127 – Plaisir Des Yeux (FR) 105 (Funambule (USA) 118) [2009 77: p8g 10f6 10m5 10d p9.5g6 p12.2g3 10.2v Nov 4] useful-looking gelding: fair performer: stays 1½m: acts on polytrack, soft and good to firm going: tried blinkered: waited with. *W. J. Musson* **68**

DFS Park Stakes, Doncaster—Irish raider Duff (nearside) goes one better than in the 2007 renewal as he claims the second of three pattern-race wins in 2009; also involved in a close finish are Cat Junior (quartered cap), Arabian Gleam (far side) and Ouqba (striped cap)

DUCAL DAISEY 3 b.f. Shahrastani (USA) 135 – Jimgareen (IRE) 66 (Lahib (USA) 129) [2009 11.7g Aug 28] 2,000Y: third foal: dam, maiden, stayed 9f: well beaten in seller at Bath. *A. B. Haynes* –

DUCAL DESTINY 2 b.c. (Jan 10) Reset (AUS) 124 – Lucky Thing (Green Desert (USA) 127) [2009 5m[5] 6g[5] Jun 9] soundly beaten in maidens. *J. R. Weymes* –

DUCAL REGANCY DUKE 5 gr.g. Bertolini (USA) 125 – Fun Run (USA) (Skip Away (USA) 134) [2009 –: 7m 14.1g[6] 14.1m 9g[4] 9.3d 9g 5.9d Aug 19] little form: in headgear in 2009. *C. J. Teague* –

DUCAL REGANCY RED 5 ch.m. Bertolini (USA) 125 – One For Jeannie 68 (Clantime 101) [2009 60d: f5g f5m[6] Mar 22] poor performer: best at 5f: acts on all-weather and good to soft ground: races up with pace. *C. J. Teague* 46

DUCHESS DORA (IRE) 2 b.f. (Apr 17) Tagula (IRE) 116 – Teodora (IRE) 93 (Fairy King (USA)) [2009 5m[3] 5g* 5m[2] 5g* 5m* 5m[5] 6g[6] Oct 10] €17,000F, £15,500Y: lengthy, unfurnished filly: sixth foal: sister to fairly useful 2007 2-y-o 7f winner Fadhb Ar Bith and half-sister to 2 winners, including 2005 2-y-o 1m winner Prince of Love (by Fruits of Love): dam unreliable 2-y-o 6f winner: useful performer: won maiden at Catterick in May and nurseries at Sandown and Beverley (by neck from Gertmegalush) in August: well below form in listed events last 2 starts: should stay 6f (raced freely when tried): acts on good to firm ground: races prominently. *J. J. Quinn* 95

DUCHESS OF ALBA 4 b.f. Compton Place 125 – Marie La Rose (FR) (Night Shift (USA)) [2009 8.1g 8m p12g Sep 21] 18,500Y: good-bodied filly: half-sister to 3 winners, including French 1m (at 2 yrs)/1¼m winner Contemporary Art (by Blushing Flame): dam, French 1¼m winner, out of half-sister to Prix Ganay winner Vert Amande and Prix Vermeille winner Indian Rose: well held in maidens: tongue tied final start. *G. C. Bravery* –

DUCHESS OF DOOM (IRE) 3 b.f. Exceed And Excel (AUS) 126 – Tallahassee Spirit (THA) (Presidential (USA)) [2009 48: 7m p8.6g 10.1m Sep 16] poor maiden: left S. Callaghan after second start. *C. Gordon* 36

DUCHESS RAVEL (IRE) 2 br.f. (Mar 12) Bachelor Duke (USA) 122 – Bolero Again (IRE) 76 (Sadler's Wells (USA) 132) [2009 5m[3] Jun 29] 20,000Y: first foal: dam, 1¼m winner, out of US Grade 1 9f winner Gravieres: 5/1, encouraging 5¼ lengths third to Virginia Hall in maiden at Windsor, green before staying on: likely to stay 1m+: sure to improve. *R. Hannon* 66 p

DUDLEY 2 ch.g. (Apr 28) Compton Place 125 – Just A Glimmer 93 (Bishop of Cashel 122) [2009 6m 6g 5.7g Jul 31] lengthy gelding: no form in maidens: gelded after final start. *J. G. Portman* –

DUDLEY DOCKER (IRE) 7 b.g. Victory Note (USA) 120 – Nordic Abu (IRE) 60 (Nordico (USA)) [2009 82, a89: p7g^6 p7.1g^4 p7.1g f8g 9m^6 8.1g^4 8m^5 8g^4 p9.5g^5 Dec 7] leggy gelding: fair handicapper nowadays, better on all-weather: left C. Dore after fourth outing, T. Clement after eighth: stays 8.6f: acts on all-weather and firm ground: effective in headgear or not: held up: quirky. *D. C. O'Brien* **69 a76**

DUELLIST 2 b.c. (Mar 4) Dubawi (IRE) 129 – Satin Flower (USA) 115 (Shadeed (USA) 135) [2009 f6d^4 Dec 29] half-brother to several winners, including 1998 2-y-o 6f (including Middle Park Stakes) winner Lujain (by Seeking The Gold) and 7f (at 2 yrs)/1½m winner Lilium (by Nashwan), both smart: dam 7f (Jersey Stakes)/1m winner who stayed 9f: 13/8 favourite, 4¾ lengths fourth to Exearti in maiden at Southwell, not knocked about: will stay 7f: likely to improve. *M. Johnston* **64 p**

DUFF (IRE) 6 b.g. Spinning World (USA) 130 – Shining Prospect (Lycius (USA) 124) [2009 118: p6g^2 6m 7m* 6m 5m 7m* 7.5m* 8g Dec 13] sturdy, dipped-backed gelding: very smart performer: won Ballycorus Stakes at Leopardstown (by neck from Dohasa) in June, DFS Park Stakes at Doncaster (raced alone, rallied to beat Cat Junior a neck) in September and Coolmore Stud Home of Champions Concorde Stakes at Tipperary (by ¾ length from Dohasa) in October: best at 6f to 1m: acts on polytrack, good to firm and good to soft going: has got on toes beforehand: usually races up with pace (held up when below form in Hong Kong Mile at Sha Tin final start). *Edward Lynam, Ireland* **122**

DUGATTI 3 b.c. Bertolini (USA) 125 – Go Polar 89 (Polar Falcon (USA) 126) [2009 7.1m 5.1d Apr 28] workmanlike colt: well held in maidens. *Mike Murphy* **–**

DUKE OF BOTHWELL (USA) 3 ch.g. Hennessy (USA) 122 – Crooked Wood (USA) 93 (Woodman (USA) 126) [2009 p5.1g 6s^5 7m 7.2m Oct 1] form only on second start. *R. A. Fahey* **46**

DUKE OF BURGUNDY (FR) 6 b.g. Danehill (USA) 126 – Valley of Gold (FR) 117 (Shirley Heights 130) [2009 12g^6 10.9g^2 8d^2 10.2s^6 Oct 7] sold unraced from Saeed bin Suroor 14,000 gns in October 2006: fairly useful bumper performer: similar form in maidens only when when runner-up at Warwick second start: stays 1¼m: raced on good ground or softer. *Jennie Candlish* **82**

DUKE OF MILAN (IRE) 6 ch.g. Desert Prince (IRE) 130 – Abyat (USA) (Shadeed (USA) 135) [2009 63: p6g^2 p7g^2 p7g^2 p7g 8m^6 7d^3 6m^4 p7g^2 7g^2 5.7g^5 7f^2 7g 7g^6 8d Oct 11] angular gelding: fair performer: left G. Bravery after fourth start, sold from T. Dascombe £4,000 after tenth: effective at 5f to easy 7f: acts on polytrack, firm and good to soft going: tried in headgear (visored last 4 starts): travels strongly held up, but finds little. *Klaus Wilhelm, Germany* **68**

DUKE OF NORMANDY (IRE) 3 gr.g. Refuse To Bend (IRE) 128 – Marie de Bayeux (FR) 109 (Turgeon (USA) 123) [2009 64: p7g^4 p7g^6 p9.5g^4 p9.5m^2 p8g^3 p9.5g^2 9.9m 8.1g 10.3g^4 10.4s 10.3g 10.1g p8.6g p9.5g^6 p9.5g Nov 13] leggy gelding: fair maiden handicapper at best: left M. Johnston £10,000 after sixth start: stays 9.5f: acts on polytrack: in cheekpieces/tongue tie final outing: signs of temperament (races freely). *B. P. J. Baugh* **69 d**

DUKE OF RAINFORD 2 gr.g. (Feb 4) Bahamian Bounty 116 – Night Haven 99 (Night Shift (USA)) [2009 5.1m 5m p5g^3 5s* 6d 5m^6 p5g^3 5m p5.1g f5f Dec 17] modest performer: dead-heated in nursery at Haydock in July: left Ian Williams after sixth start, D. Nicholls after eighth: should stay 6f (pulled hard when tried): acts on polytrack, soft and good to firm going: tried blinkered/tongue tied: possibly not straightforward. *M. Herrington* **53**

DUKE OF URBINO 3 ch.g. Medicean 128 – Nefeli (First Trump 118) [2009 f7g^4 f6d^5 8.3g 6d Aug 27] modest maiden: gelded after second start: acts on fibresand: tried in cheekpieces. *K. A. Ryan* **53**

DUKES ART 3 b.c. Bachelor Duke (USA) 122 – Creme Caramel (USA) 88 (Septieme Ciel (USA) 123) [2009 79p: 8d^4 8g^4 p8g 7g* 7d* p7g^2 p7g Oct 24] smallish colt: useful performer: won maiden at Doncaster and handicap at Yarmouth, both in July: improved markedly when nose second to Audemar in handicap at Kempton next start: stays 1m: acts on polytrack and good to soft ground. *J. A. R. Toller* **96**

DULCE DOMUM 3 b.f. Dansili 127 – Enclave (USA) (Woodman (USA) 126) [2009 –: f8g^5 p9.5g^3 10m f12g 12.1m^5 p12g^6 10f^5 16.2g^6 Jul 20] poor maiden: stays 1½m: acts on all-weather and good to firm ground: tried visored. *A. B. Haynes* **46**

DULCIE 3 b.f. Hernando (FR) 127 – Dulcinea 73 (Selkirk (USA) 129) [2009 78: 9.9m 14s^{3} 16.1g^{3} f16g^{2} 16.4d* 16g Oct 30] good-bodied filly: fairly useful handicapper: won at York in September: stays 2m: acts on fibresand and soft ground: waited with. *M. H. Tompkins* **87**

DUNASKIN (IRE) 9 b.g. Bahhare (USA) 122 – Mirwara (IRE) (Darshaan 133) [2009 102: 14.1m^{4} 18.7m 12.1d^{5} 12m^{6} 12g f12g^{6} p13.9g^{6} f14g^{2} f11m^{2} f14d^{6} Dec 29] smallish, workmanlike gelding: fairly useful performer nowadays: probably stays 1¾m: acts on all-weather, heavy and good to firm going: tried visored/in cheekpieces: often front runner. *B. Ellison* **92**

DUNCAN 4 b.c. Dalakhani (IRE) 133 – Dolores 111 (Danehill (USA) 126) [2009 107p: 10.1g* 12m* 12g^{4} 12m 10.4m^{3} Aug 8] rather leggy colt: very smart performer: left J. Dunlop, improved in 2009, winning handicap at Epsom in April and listed race at Ascot (by 3¾ lengths from Starfala) in May: good efforts when in frame after in Coronation Cup at Epsom (length fourth to Ask) and Rose of Lancaster Stakes at Haydock (2¼ lengths third to Jukebox Jury): effective at 1¼m/1½m: unraced on extremes of going: pulled too hard fourth start. *J. H. M. Gosden* **120**

DUNDRY 8 b.g. Bin Ajwaad (IRE) 119 – China's Pearl (Shirley Heights 130) [2009 76: p12g^{2} p13g^{4} Feb 10] big, good-topped gelding: fair handicapper: effective at 1½m to 2m: acts on all-weather, soft and good to firm ground: wears cheekpieces. *G. L. Moore* **78**

DUNEEN DREAM (USA) 4 ch.g. Hennessy (USA) 122 – T N T Red (USA) (Explosive Red (CAN) 119) [2009 58: p9.5g p9.5g p12.2g p12f^{5} p13.9g^{4} Dec 14] lengthy gelding: modest handicapper: stays easy 1½m: acts on polytrack: tried tongue tied: signs of temperament at 3 yrs. *Mrs N. S. Evans* **54**

DUNELIGHT (IRE) 6 ch.h. Desert Sun 120 – Badee'a (IRE) (Marju (IRE) 127) [2009 115: p8m^{6} p7f^{2} Dec 16] strong, good sort: good walker: smart performer: off 16 months, better for return when head second to Dohasa in listed race at Kempton: free-going sort, best at 7f/1m: acts on polytrack and firm going: tried blinkered, visored nowadays: front runner. *C. G. Cox* **112**

DUNES QUEEN (USA) 3 b.f. Elusive Quality (USA) – Queen's Logic (IRE) 125 (Grand Lodge (USA) 125) [2009 68p: p6g* 7m^{5} 6s^{5} 5g^{4} May 27] lengthy, angular filly: fairly useful form: won maiden at Kempton in March: very good fifth to Fantasia in Nell Gwyn Stakes at Newmarket next time: stayed 7f: acted on polytrack and good to firm going: stud. *M. R. Channon* **84**

DUNFISHIN (IRE) 2 ch.c. (Apr 24) Chineur (FR) 123 – Sisal (IRE) 84 (Danehill (USA) 126) [2009 p7.1g Dec 28] 50/1, tailed off in maiden at Wolverhampton. *M. S. Tuck* **–**

DUNGANNON 2 b.g. (Apr 16) Monsieur Bond (IRE) 120 – May Light 62 (Midyan (USA) 124) [2009 6g^{5} Jun 22] 10,000Y: brother to 1m winner in Scandinavia and half-brother to 3 winners, notably very smart 6f winner Bygone Days (by Desert King): dam maiden (stayed 7f): 16/1 and green, eye-catching 4 lengths fifth to Palisades Park in maiden at Windsor, soon well behind and finishing best (gelded after): likely to stay 7f: sure to improve. *A. M. Balding* **65 p**

DUNN'O (IRE) 4 b.g. Cape Cross (IRE) 129 – Indian Express 61 (Indian Ridge 123) [2009 92: 8m 8.1g* 7.6m^{6} 8.1m* 8m 8g^{6} 7.6m 7m^{3} 8.1m Sep 25] big, good-bodied gelding: useful handicapper: better than ever in 2009, winning at Sandown in April and May (beat Axiom by ½ length): stays 1m: acts on good to firm and good to soft going: forces pace. *C. G. Cox* **104**

DUNWHINNY 2 b.g. (Mar 17) Tobougg (IRE) 125 – Possibility 59 (Robellino (USA) 127) [2009 p6g p7.1g 7s Jul 14] leggy gelding: well held in maidens. *P. W. D'Arcy* **–**

DUPLICITY 2 b.c. (Jan 14) Cadeaux Genereux 131 – Artful (IRE) (Green Desert (USA) 127) [2009 p7g^{4} 7.1m^{2} 6s* 6s^{5} Oct 12] strong colt: first foal: dam, French 7.5f winner, half-sister to smart Irish 2008 2-y-o 7f winner Chintz, out of half-sister to smart French performers up to 1½m Prospect Wells and Prospect Park: useful performer: improved to win listed race at Newbury in July by length (value extra) from Hearts of Fire: off 3 months, not discredited when fifth to Eightfold Path in Prix Eclipse at Chantilly: should stay 7f: acts on soft ground. *R. Hannon* **93**

D'URBERVILLE 2 b.g. (Feb 17) Auction House (USA) 120 – Laser Crystal (IRE) 67 (King's Theatre (IRE) 128) [2009 6m 6m 7f^{5} 8m p7g p7g^{4} p7g^{6} Dec 31] sturdy gelding: modest maiden: left R. Ingram after second start: stays 7f: acts on polytrack and firm going. *J. R. Jenkins* **59**

DURGAN 3 b.c. Dansili 127 – Peryllys 67 (Warning 136) [2009 74: 7d^4 7.1f p7f^6 Dec 21] compact colt: fair maiden: raced only at 7f. *Mrs L. C. Jewell* **74**

DURHAM EXPRESS (IRE) 2 b.g. (Mar 10) Acclamation 118 – Edwina (IRE) 63 (Caerleon (USA) 132) [2009 5d^3 5g* 5g^4 Oct 17] €22,000Y: tall gelding: half-brother to several winners, notably very smart 7f (at 2 yrs) to 9f (in UAE) winner Seihali (by Alzao) and 5-y-o Rebel Duke: dam, maiden (should have stayed beyond 6f), half-sister to useful sprinter Roger The Butler: fair form: won maiden at Redcar in September: good fourth to The Only Boss in minor event at Catterick: will be suited by 6f: type to do better still at 3 yrs. *M. Dods* **72 p**

DURHAM REFLECTION (IRE) 2 b.g. (Feb 23) Pastoral Pursuits 127 – Opari (IRE) (Night Shift (USA)) [2009 6d^5 6m^6 7d^5 6m^2 6s^3 7g^5 7.1m* Sep 14] €18,000F, £26,000Y: seventh foal: half-brother to useful French 2003 2-y-o 5.5f winner La Lola (by Zafonic) and 7f/1m winner Lii Najma (by Medicean): dam French 2-y-o 6f winner: fair performer: best effort when winning seller at Musselburgh: stays easy 7f: acts on soft and good to firm going: tried in cheekpieces: front runner/races prominently. *J. Howard Johnson* **76**

DURHAM TOWN (IRE) 2 b.g. (Mar 26) Arakan (USA) 123 – Southern Spectrum (IRE) (Spectrum (IRE) 126) [2009 5g 5m^4 p7g 6g^6 7g^6 Aug 12] tall gelding: modest maiden: should stay 7f: acts on good to firm ground: not straightforward. *D. K. Ivory* **59**

DURING THE WAR (USA) 2 b.g. (May 1) Lion Heart (USA) 124 – Carson's Star (USA) (Carson City (USA)) [2009 p7f 7.1m p7m^5 Nov 27] useful-looking gelding: best effort in maidens when seventh to Thrust Control at Warwick second start (left L. Cumani 7,000 gns and gelded after). *C. A. Dwyer* **60**

DUSHSTORM (IRE) 8 b.g. Dushyantor (USA) 123 – Between The Winds (USA) (Diesis 133) [2009 75: p8.6g Jan 7] smallish gelding: fair performer in 2008: well below form sole 8-y-o start: stays easy 1½m: acts on polytrack and good to soft ground: effective in cheekpieces or not. *R. J. Price* **49**

DUSK 4 b.g. Fantastic Light (USA) 134 – Dark Veil (USA) 96 (Gulch (USA)) [2009 77: p12g^3 p12.2g^5 10.9d 10.1g Jul 20] sturdy gelding: fair maiden: barely stays 1¾m: acts on all-weather, good to firm and good to soft ground: blinkered: held up: none too genuine (weak finisher): modest winning chaser for Evan Williams later in year. *Mrs S. J. Humphrey* **68**

DUSTER 2 b.g. (Mar 5) Pastoral Pursuits 127 – Spring Clean (FR) 89 (Danehill (USA) 126) [2009 p7g^2 f6g^2 p7.1g^5 6g Oct 19] 9,000F: second foal: dam Irish 2-y-o 6f winner: fair maiden: respectable effort in nursery: stays 7f: acts on all-weather. *H. Morrison* **71**

DUSTRY (IRE) 3 b.c. Chevalier (IRE) 115 – Church Mice (IRE) 82 (Petardia 113) [2009 73: p8g p8g 8.3m^5 10.4g 8d 7.1d Sep 4] good-topped colt: fair handicapper: well below form after second start: stays 6f: acts on polytrack and good to soft going: blinkered last 2 starts. *R. Hannon* **70 d**

DUSTY SPIRIT 2 b.c. (May 18) Invincible Spirit (IRE) 121 – Dusty Dazzler (IRE) 102 (Titus Livius (FR) 115) [2009 p5g^6 5d 5.1m^4 p5f 5m^3 5m^2 p5g^4 5.1g* 6s Nov 7] good-topped colt: second foal: dam 5f (including at 2 yrs)/6f winner: fair performer: won maiden at Bath in October: should stay 6f: acts on good to firm going, below form on polytrack. *W. G. M. Turner* **78 a57**

DUTIFUL 2 ch.c. (Jan 24) Dubawi (IRE) 129 – Pelagia (IRE) 77 (Lycius (USA) 124) [2009 7m 8d^6 6m p7g p7g^3 p7.1m* p7m Dec 6] compact colt: fair form: improved to win nursery at Wolverhampton in November: should stay 1m+: acts on polytrack. *M. R. Channon* **66**

DUTY AND DESTINY (IRE) 2 b.f. (Apr 18) Montjeu (IRE) 137 – Swilly (USA) (Irish River (FR) 131) [2009 7d^4 7g^4 10.2m^2 p8.6g^2 Nov 12] 180,000Y: tall, lengthy filly: fifth foal: sister to 5-y-o Mississippian: dam, ran twice in France, half-sister to useful dam of smart Italian 1m/1¼m performer Distant Way: fairly useful maiden: good second to Nafura in nursery at Wolverhampton final start: stays 1¼m: acts on polytrack and good to firm going: has been ponied to start/unruly in stall: sold 18,000 gns. *B. J. Meehan* **82**

DUTY FREE (IRE) 5 b.g. Rock of Gibraltar (IRE) 133 – Photographie (USA) (Trempolino (USA) 135) [2009 92: p12g 11.7g Apr 28] good-topped gelding: handicapper: just fair form in 2 starts in 2009: stays 1¾m: raced on polytrack and good going or firmer: tried in cheekpieces: fair form over hurdles. *C. R. Egerton* **70**

DVINSKY (USA) 8 b.g. Stravinsky (USA) 133 – Festive Season (USA) (Lypheor 118) **77**
[2009 70+, a92: p6g^{2} p6g* p6g^{5} p7g^{4} p6g p6g p6g^{5} p7g^{2} p6g^{2} 6m^{2} p6g^{5} p7g^{6} 6m^{5} p6g 6g **a95**
p7g 6m^{2} p6g^{6} 6f p6g^{4} 6m^{2} p6g p7g^{5} p6m^{2} p6g p7m* p6g^{6} p6g p6g^{5} p6m^{4} p6m^{6} p7f^{6} p6m^{3} Dec 30] compact gelding: useful handicapper on all-weather, fair on turf: won at Great Leighs in January and, having dropped in weights, Kempton in October: effective at 6f/7f: acts on polytrack, firm and soft going: tried tongue tied/in headgear, blinkered nowadays: races prominently: tough. *P. Howling*

DYLANESQUE 2 b.f. (Mar 3) Royal Applause 124 – Ventura Highway (Machiavellian **79**
(USA) 123) [2009 6m 6m* 7m^{6} 7g Oct 24] good-bodied filly: third foal: half-sister to smart 9f (in Ireland at 2 yrs)/11.5f (Lingfield Derby Trial) winner Alessandro Volta (by Montjeu): dam unraced daughter of smart miler Hyabella, herself half-sister to high-class 1¼m performer Stagecraft: fair performer: still green when winning maiden at Yarmouth in September: below form in nurseries after: should stay 7f+. *M. A. Jarvis*

DYNAMIC DRIVE (IRE) 2 b.c. (Feb 1) Motivator 131 – Biriyani (IRE) 71 (Danehill **60**
(USA) 126) [2009 p8f^{6} Oct 14] first foal: dam, maiden (best effort at 6f at 2 yrs), half-sister to very smart performer up to 10.5f Mister Monet and Moyglare Stud Stakes/Irish 1000 Guineas winner Tarascon: 25/1, 7½ lengths sixth to Dahaam in maiden at Kempton: should stay 1¼m. *W. R. Swinburn*

DYNAMIC IDOL (USA) 2 b. or br.c. (Mar 30) Dynaformer (USA) – El Nafis (USA) **60 p**
73 (Kingmambo (USA) 125) [2009 f8m^{4} Dec 5] $250,000Y: fourth foal: half-brother to smart 7f/1m (including at 2 yrs) winner Nasheej (by Swain) and a winner in USA by Delaware Township: dam, 2-y-o 1m winner, out of sister to Seattle Dancer, close relative of Lomond and half-sister to Seattle Slew: 11/8 favourite, 8 lengths fourth to Doctor Zhivago in maiden at Southwell, failing to handle bend: should improve. *M. A. Magnusson*

DYNAMO DAVE (USA) 4 b.g. Distorted Humor (USA) 117 – Nothing Special **58**
(CAN) (Tejabo (CAN)) [2009 50: p8g^{3} p8g^{6} p8g p8g^{4} p7g p10g 10.2g 10f 11.5g 10.2m 10d^{5} 10.2f^{6} 8f^{6} 6f* 6d p6g^{4} 6m 6g 6m 5m p7g* p7m p7m^{3} Dec 30] good-topped gelding: modest performer: won seller at Folkestone in July and apprentice handicap at Lingfield in November: best up to 1m: acts on polytrack and firm going: often in headgear: tried tongue tied: none too reliable. *M. D. I. Usher*

DYNASTY 2 b.c. (Mar 30) Danehill Dancer (IRE) 117 – Dash To The Top 116§ **97 p**
(Montjeu (IRE) 137) [2009 6s^{2} 7d^{3} 7m p6g* Oct 30] 300,000Y: big colt: first foal: dam temperamental 1m (at 2 yrs)/1¼m winner who stayed 1½m: placed in maidens (looked awkward) and eighth from poor draw in sales race at Newmarket before landing odds in maiden at Dundalk by 2½ lengths from One Set, awkward leaving stall and again carrying head high and wandering markedly: will stay 1m: useful already and can do better if temperament holds. *A. P. O'Brien, Ireland*

DYNA WALTZ 2 b.f. (Feb 14) Dynaformer (USA) – Valentine Waltz (IRE) 116 (Be **101 p**
My Guest (USA) 126) [2009 7d^{3} 7g^{2} p8g* 8m^{5} Sep 26] good-bodied filly: fifth foal: dam, 7f (including at 2 yrs) and 1m (Poule d'Essai des Pouliches) winner, out of half-sister to top-class sprinter/miler Last Tycoon: won maiden at Kempton (made running) in August: much improved when 3¼ lengths fifth to Hibaayeb in Fillies' Mile at Ascot, closing gradually having raced wider than ideal: stays 1m: acts on polytrack and good to firm ground: already useful, and likely to do better still. *J. H. M. Gosden*

DZESMIN (POL) 7 b.g. Professional (IRE) 73 – Dzakarta (POL) (Aprizzo (IRE)) **86**
[2009 94: f11g^{5} 12m^{6} 14m^{6} 16.1m^{5} Jun 25] angular gelding: fairly useful handicapper: stays 2m: acts on polytrack, heavy and good to firm going: often wears cheekpieces: held up. *R. A. Fahey*

E

EAGER TO BOW (IRE) 3 b.g. Acclamation 118 – Tullawadgeen (IRE) (Sinndar **–**
(IRE) 134) [2009 52: 8.1g 7m^{6} Jul 6] lengthy, rather unfurnished gelding: modest at 2 yrs: well held in handicaps in 2009: blinkered final outing. *P. R. Chamings*

EAGLE NEBULA 5 ch.g. Observatory (USA) 131 – Tarocchi (USA) (Affirmed **69**
(USA)) [2009 74: p7g p7g p7g 10.1g^{4} p11g p9.5g* p10m^{2} p16g^{2} p12m^{5} Dec 9] workmanlike gelding: fair handicapper: won at Wolverhampton in September: will prove best short of 2m: acts on polytrack and good to soft ground: tried visored: ridden patiently: temperament under suspicion. *B. R. Johnson*

Dubai Sheema Classic - Sponsored By Nakheel, Nad Al Sheba—
Eastern Anthem shows further improvement stepped up to Group 1 company and completes his hat-trick; Spanish Moon (right) and Purple Moon (blaze) run him very close

EARLSMEDIC 4 ch.g. Dr Fong (USA) 128 – Area Girl 76 (Jareer (USA) 115) [2009 90: 6m5 6m* 6m 6m 5m4 6m 6.1m 6m4 p6g3 p6m* p6m* p6g5 Dec 28] useful handicapper: won at Yarmouth in May and Kempton (2) in November: best form at 6f: acts on polytrack, heavy and good to firm going: often visored: usually races up with pace: carries head high. *S. C. Williams* **99**

EARLY DART 2 b.f. (Feb 16) Auction House (USA) 120 – Cozette (IRE) 49 (Danehill Dancer (IRE) 117) [2009 p8.6g Dec 11] third foal: sister to 2006 2-y-o 5f winner Autumn Storm: dam lightly-raced maiden who should have stayed 1¼m+: 50/1 and reluctant to load, pulled herself up soon after start in minor event at Wolverhampton: one to be wary of. *A. Berry* **– §**

EARLY GIRL 4 b.f. Compton Place 125 – Reciprocal (IRE) 88 (Night Shift (USA)) [2009 p11g f8g4 Feb 10] second foal: dam 9f winner: soundly beaten in maidens. *P. D. Evans* **–**

EARLY MORNING RAIN (IRE) 3 b.f. Rock of Gibraltar (IRE) 133 – Honorine (IRE) 89 (Mark of Esteem (IRE) 137) [2009 7f 6m Aug 8] first foal: dam, 1m/1¼m winner, half-sister to smart performers Desert Dew (up to 1¼m) and Indian Creek (up to 1½m): well held in maidens: wore eyecover latter start. *Rae Guest* **–**

EARMARK 6 b.g. Halling (USA) 133 – Earlene (IRE) 111 (In The Wings 128) [2009 p8f4 8g 10v 7s p9.5g2 Oct 17] modest maiden: left James McAuley prior to final outing: stays 9.5f: acts on polytrack: in cheekpieces for previous yard. *Seamus Fahey, Ireland* **64**

EASTERLY BREEZE (IRE) 5 b.g. Green Desert (USA) 127 – Chiang Mai (IRE) 113 (Sadler's Wells (USA) 132) [2009 79: p8g p12.2g p12.2m4 p9.5g6 p12m4 p13.9m3 Nov 28] tall, good-topped gelding: fair maiden: left P. Deegan in Ireland after reappearance, M. Tuck after second outing: stays easy 1¾m: acts on polytrack and good to firm ground: tried in cheekpieces, blinkered last 5 starts (also tongue tied last 4). *Mrs L. J. Young* **68**

EASTERN ANTHEM (IRE) 5 b.h. Singspiel (IRE) 133 – Kazzia (GER) 121 (Zinaad 114) [2009 115: 10g* 12g* 12g* 12g6 20m5 12g3 12d2 12g2 Sep 27] leggy, quite good-topped horse: very smart performer: reportedly had wind operation prior to reappearance: improved early in year, winning 2 handicaps at Nad Al Sheba in February and 15-runner Dubai Sheema Classic there (led on line to beat Spanish Moon by nose, overcoming slow start) in March: left M. bin Shafya and returned to former trainer, below form next 2 starts: placed in Group 1 events in Germany last 3 starts, back to best when 3 lengths second to Getaway in Grosser Preis von Baden at Baden-Baden and nose second to Jukebox Jury in Preis von Europa at Cologne: effective at 1¼m to 1¾m: acts on soft and good to firm going, probably on heavy: usually tongue tied: patiently ridden. *Saeed bin Suroor* **123**

EASTERN ARIA (UAE) 3 b. or br.f. Halling (USA) 133 – Badraan (USA) (Danzig (USA)) [2009 p8g2 f8g* p8.6g3 p10g* 10d p10g2 9.9m* 10.3g2 10.1m* 10m 11d* 10m4 9.9f* 10.3m2 12g* 10m4 Oct 17] angular filly: second foal: sister to fairly useful 2007 2-y-o 7f winner Harlem Shuffle: dam, UAE 6f/7f winner, out of US Grade 3 2-y-o 8.5f winner Gold Sunrise: developed into a useful performer: won maiden at Southwell in **108**

totesportcasino.com Heritage Handicap, Beverley—the tough and genuine Eastern Aria gains the sixth of her seven wins; Honimiere (partially obscured) and Eastern Empire are next to finish

February, handicaps at Lingfield in March, Goodwood in June, Epsom in July, and Goodwood then Beverley in August, and listed race at Saint-Cloud (beat Superstition 2 lengths) in September: respectable fourth to Lahaleeb in E. P. Taylor Stakes at Woodbine final outing: stays 1½m: acts on all-weather, firm and good to soft going: often front runner/races prominently: tough and genuine. *M. Johnston*

EASTERN EMPIRE 3 b.g. Dubai Destination (USA) 127 – Possessive Artiste 73 (Shareef Dancer (USA) 135) [2009 58: p7g³ 8m* 8m* 8m 8g⁶ 8m⁴ 9.9f³ Aug 29] well-made gelding: useful performer: won maiden and handicap at Goodwood in May: creditable third to Eastern Aria in handicap at Beverley final start: stays 1¼m: acts on firm ground: sent to Hong Kong. *J. W. Hills* **96**

EASTERN GIFT 4 ch.g. Cadeaux Genereux 131 – Dahshah 77 (Mujtahid (USA) 118) [2009 92, a83: p8g⁵ 8m 7.6m 7m 10.2g 8d 10f² 9m² 8.5m² 8.5m³ p8g p8.6g p7m⁶ p7.1g f8g p7.1g⁶ p9.5g² p7.1g⁵ Dec 28] lengthy gelding: fairly useful handicapper: stays 1¼m: acts on polytrack, soft and firm ground: tried in cheekpieces/visor: usually held up. *Miss Gay Kelleway* **80**

EASTERN HILLS 4 b.g. Dubai Destination (USA) 127 – Rainbow Mountain 71 (Rainbow Quest (USA) 134) [2009 82: 8d 7m 6g³ 5.9g³ 7m 7g 6g⁶ 7.2g 6.1s² 7g⁴ 7.2g⁴ 10.2v⁵ Nov 4] fair handicapper: should stay 1m: acts on soft ground: tried visored: none too consistent: gelded after final start. *J. S. Wainwright* **77**

EASTERN WARRIOR 3 ch.g. Barathea (IRE) 127 – Shakalaka Baby (Nashwan (USA) 135) [2009 73: 8.1m² 7.1v² 8.3g² 8m* 8.1m⁵ 8.1g⁶ 8.5m⁵ 8g³ Oct 21] lengthy gelding: fairly useful performer: won maiden at Ripon in July: stays 1m: acts on heavy and good to firm ground. *J. W. Hills* **82**

EASTFIELDS LAD 7 b.g. Overbury (IRE) 116 – Honey Day (Lucky Wednesday 124) [2009 f7g f6g Feb 20] close-coupled gelding: no solid form: tried blinkered. *S. R. Bowring* **–**

EAST OF THE SUN (IRE) 3 ch.g. Dr Fong (USA) 128 – Arabis 88 (Arazi (USA) 135) [2009 10.4v⁵ 12m 12g 16d 7s Nov 9] good-topped gelding: modest maiden: sold from T. Tate £1,000 after fourth start: blinkered final outing. *G. Verheye, Belgium* **53**

EASTWELL SMILES 5 br.g. Erhaab (USA) 127 – Miss University (USA) (Beau Genius (CAN)) [2009 p13g⁵ p16g 15.4g⁵ 16.4m Jun 8] handicapper: missed 2008, and just modest at 5 yrs: stays 15f: acts on polytrack: in cheekpieces final outing: tongue tied in 2007. *R. T. Phillips* **60**

EASY TARGET (FR) 4 ch.c. Danehill Dancer (IRE) 117 – Aiming 76 (Highest Honor (FR) 124) [2009 104: 6.5g a8f a6f 9g* 9g^5 7d 8g* p8g^6 Aug 14] compact colt: useful performer: won minor event at Saint-Malo in May and claimer at Maisons-Laffitte (left X Nakkachdji €11,399) in July: creditable 3 lengths sixth to Musleh in handicap at Kempton final start: stays 9f: acts on polytrack, heavy and good to firm going: blinkered third start. *G. L. Moore* **95**

EASY TERMS 2 b.f. (Apr 30) Trade Fair 124 – Effie (Royal Academy (USA) 130) [2009 6g May 20] fifth foal: half-sister to fairly useful 2006 2-y-o 6f winner Lakshmi (by Efisio), later successful in Saudi Arabia: dam unraced half-sister to useful 7f/1m performers Kootenay and Jay Gee's Choice: 11/1 and green, seventh to La Pantera in maiden at Goodwood: not seen out again. *B. R. Millman* **56**

EASY WONDER (GER) 4 b.f. Royal Dragon (USA) 118 – Emy Coasting (USA) 78 (El Gran Senor (USA) 136) [2009 67: p6g p7g p5g^6 p6g^4 p6g^4 6m f6g^3 5.7m 6m p6g^6 p6m p8.6g p7m^4 Dec 30] compact filly: modest handicapper: probably best up to 7f nowadays: acts on all-weather and any turf going: usually in cheekpieces/blinkers. *I. A. Wood* **54**

EAU GOOD 5 ch.g. Cadeaux Genereux 131 – Girl's Best Friend 89 (Nicolotte 118) [2009 85: f7d Jan 2] angular gelding: fairly useful handicapper at best: blinkered once: held up: dead. *G. J. Smith* **–**

EBERT 6 b.g. Polish Precedent (USA) 131 – Fanfare 89 (Deploy 131) [2009 83: p13.3g^3 p12g^3 f12g^3 f12g^4 Feb 6] strong gelding: just modest form in 2009: barely stays 1½m: acts on all-weather and firm ground: tried blinkered/in cheekpieces: nervy sort. *R. A. Fahey* **59**

EBIAYN (FR) 3 b.g. Monsun (GER) 124 – Drei (USA) 67 (Lyphard (USA) 132) [2009 79p: 8s^3 p8g^3 12g^4 10.1m^4 Oct 3] well-made gelding: fairly useful maiden: gelded after second outing: should stay 1½m: acts on polytrack, soft and good to firm ground: sold 30,000 gns, joined A. King. *M. A. Jarvis* **83**

EBONY BOOM (IRE) 2 b.c. (Feb 7) Boreal (GER) 126 – Elegant As Well (IRE) (Sadler's Wells (USA) 132) [2009 7s p7m^4 8.5m^2 p8g^3 Nov 1] first foal: dam, unraced, out of half-sister to high-class 1m/1¼m performer Archipenko: fair form when placed in maidens at Epsom and Lingfield (third to Sowaylm): will be suited by 1¼m+: well held on soft ground on debut: should do better still at 3 yrs. *H. R. A. Cecil* **79 p**

EBONY EYES 3 br.f. King's Best (USA) 132 – Qui Liz (USA) (Benny The Dip (USA) 127) [2009 9g^6 9m^3 10.1m^5 p10m^6 p11g* p12m^3 p12m* Nov 21] second foal: half-sister to winner abroad by Rock of Gibraltar: dam unraced half-sister to William Hill Futurity winner Bakharoff and smart miler Emperor Jones: fairly useful handicapper: improved to win at Kempton in September and November: stays 1½m: acts on polytrack: usually held up. *W. J. Knight* **86**

EBORBRAV 3 b.g. Falbrav (IRE) 133 – Eboracum (IRE) 87 (Alzao (USA) 117) [2009 –: 10.1s^5 12d May 16] workmanlike gelding: no solid form in maidens. *T. D. Easterby* **–**

EBRAAM (USA) 6 b.g. Red Ransom (USA) – Futuh (USA) 95 (Diesis 133) [2009 101, a108: p6g p5g^5 p5g^3 p6g* p7g f5g^3 5g^5 6m 6m 5m 5.2d^3 5g^4 5g 6d p6m^3 p6g* p6g^2 p5m^2 p6g^2 Dec 28] well-made gelding: useful performer on all-weather, fairly useful on turf in 2009: won handicap at Wolverhampton in February and claimer there in November (left P. Howling): runner-up last 3 starts, good efforts when beaten 2¼ lengths by Jaconet in listed race at Lingfield and head by Imprimis Tagula in handicap at Wolverhampton (claimed from Mike Murphy in between): best at 5f/6f: acts on all-weather, firm and good to soft ground: strong traveller: tongue tied final outing. *S. Curran* **89 a108**

ECHO DANCER 3 br.g. Danehill Dancer (IRE) 117 – Entail (USA) 97 (Riverman (USA) 131) [2009 57p: f8g* 8m p8.6g p10g^6 f8g^2 8g f11g p8.6g Dec 3] strong, well-made gelding: fair performer: won maiden at Southwell in January: left S. Callaghan £7,500 after sixth start: stays 1m: best efforts on fibresand, promise on turf. *T. Wall* **70**

ECHO FOREST 3 b.g. Mark of Esteem (IRE) 137 – Engulfed (USA) 72 (Gulch (USA)) [2009 35: 9m 11.6m Jul 13] workmanlike gelding: little form. *J. R. Best* **–**

ECLIPSED (USA) 2 ch.c. (Mar 3) Proud Citizen (USA) 122 – Kamareyah (IRE) 80 (Hamas (IRE) 125§) [2009 7d 6d Oct 12] sturdy colt: backward, well held in maidens at Folkestone and Windsor. *J. R. Best* **–**

ECOLE D'ART (USA) 8 b.g. Theatrical 128 – Colour Chart (USA) 122 (Mr Prospector (USA)) [2009 –§: 8m^5 10.5m 17.5m* Sep 18] fair hurdler: just similar level on Flat nowadays: won handicap at Ayr in September: stays 17.5f: acts on soft and good to firm ground: reportedly blind in left eye (wore eyecover earlier in career): often slowly away (sometimes markedly so): not to be trusted. *J. J. Lambe, Ireland* **78 §**

EDAS 7 b.g. Celtic Swing 138 – Eden (IRE) 88 (Polish Precedent (USA) 131) [2009 72: f11g* f11g^{3} f11g^{2} 12.5m^{3} 12g^{2} 12m^{4} f12g^{3} 13m^{3} 11.5d^{4} 13v^{6} 10m^{2} 12.4d 9d* Oct 28] good-topped gelding: fair handicapper: won at Southwell in January and, after leaving J. J. Quinn fifth start, R. C. Guest after sixth and R. Harris after seventh, amateur event at Musselburgh in October: stays 13f: acts on all-weather and any turf going: tried in cheekpieces/visor: reliable. *T. A. K. Cuthbert* **76**

EDDIE BOY 3 b.g. Tobougg (IRE) 125 – Maristax 74 (Reprimand 122) [2009 69p: f11g^{3} 8.3m 9.9g 10.3d 9g^{4} Aug 18] useful-looking gelding: just modest at best at 3 yrs: should stay 1m+: acts on soft going: visored final outing: sold £2,200. *M. L. W. Bell* **56**

EDEN PARK 3 ch.f. Tobougg (IRE) 125 – Aegean Flame 86 (Anshan 119) [2009 61: 5.1m f6g May 18] rangy filly: maiden: well held both starts in 2009. *M. Dods* **–**

EDE'S 9 ch.g. Bijou d'Inde 127 – Ballagarrow Girl 66 (North Stoke 130) [2009 p16g Nov 11] lengthy gelding: maiden: fair hurdler in 2008. *P. M. Phelan* **–**

EDE'S DOT COM (IRE) 5 b.g. Trans Island 119 – Kilkee Bay (IRE) 61 (Case Law 113) [2009 67: p8g^{3} p8g^{3} p6g p8g p12m 8d^{2} p7m* Oct 28] sturdy gelding: fair performer: won minor event at Kempton in October: stays 1m: acts on polytrack, good to firm and good to soft going. *P. M. Phelan* **66**

EDGE CLOSER 5 b.h. Bold Edge 123 – Blue Goddess (IRE) 94 (Blues Traveller (IRE) 119) [2009 117: 6m 6m 6m^{3} 6d^{6} Jul 18] lengthy, angular horse: just useful in 2009, best efforts when seventh to Tax Free in listed race at Newmarket on reappearance and third to J J The Jet Plane in listed race at Windsor: well below form other 2 starts (said to have had breathing problem final outing): raced mainly at 6f: acts on polytrack, soft and good to firm ground: sometimes tongue tied: races prominently. *R. Hannon* **101**

EDGE END 5 ch.g. Bold Edge 123 – Rag Time Belle 34 (Raga Navarro (ITY) 119) [2009 45: p6g^{6} p5.1g p6g Nov 20] close-coupled gelding: modest maiden: likely to prove best at 5f/6f: acts on polytrack and good to firm ground: tried in headgear. *P. D. Evans* **51**

EDGEFOUR (IRE) 5 b.m. King's Best (USA) 132 – Highshaan (Pistolet Bleu (IRE) 133) [2009 –: p12m^{6} Sep 24] seemingly modest form on Flat (lightly raced): fair hurdler. *B. I. Case* **51 ?**

EDGEWATER (IRE) 2 b.g. (Feb 28) Bahamian Bounty 116 – Esteemed Lady (IRE) 96 (Mark of Esteem (IRE) 137) [2009 6m 6m^{4} p7g^{3} p7g^{2} 8.1m^{4} 6m* p7g^{4} p6m* Dec 30] 60,000Y: strong, attractive gelding: second foal: half-brother to 3-y-o Sleepy Blue Ocean: dam, in frame both starts around 6f at 2 yrs, half-sister to useful performers Revenue (up to 7f) and La Mottie (up to 9f): fairly useful performer: won nurseries at Pontefract in October (subsequently left B. Meehan 24,000 gns) and Lingfield in December: stays easy 7f: raced only on polytrack and good to firm going. *J. Akehurst* **85**

EDGEWORTH (IRE) 3 b.g. Pyrus (USA) 106 – Credibility 65 (Komaite (USA)) [2009 56: p7g^{4} p7g^{2} 8g^{4} 8.3m^{3} 8.3m 8.3m* 8m* 8.5g^{5} 8g^{6} 8.3g* 8m p8f 7g^{6} Oct 31] leggy gelding: fairly useful handicapper: won at Windsor and Newmarket in June, and Leicester in September: shaped well final start (poorly placed): stays 8.5f: acts on polytrack and good to firm ground. *B. G. Powell* **81**

EDINBURGH KNIGHT (IRE) 2 b.c. (Mar 3) Selkirk (USA) 129 – Pippas Song 75 (Reference Point 139) [2009 6m Aug 15] brother to fairly useful 2001 2-y-o 1m winner Shanty and half-brother to 7f to 8.6f winner Night Air and 5f to 7f winner (including at 2 yrs) Nightbird (both useful, by Night Shift): dam, 1½m winner, half-sister to dam of 2000 Guineas winner Footstepsinthesand: 15/2, very green when last in maiden at Newmarket: should be suited by 7f+: probably capable of better. *P. W. D'Arcy* **– p**

EDITH'S BOY (IRE) 3 ch.g. Trans Island 119 – My Ramona 65 (Alhijaz 122) [2009 69: p5g^{3} p5g^{4} p6g^{3} p6g^{2} p6g^{4} 5g^{3} 5.1d^{5} 5m^{2} p5m* 5.3d^{2} p5m* p5f Dec 19] good-quartered gelding: fair performer: won maiden at Kempton in September and handicap at Lingfield in November: best around 5f: acts on polytrack, good to firm and good to soft ground: races prominently nowadays. *S. Dow* **77**

ED'S A RED 2 b.f. (Mar 14) Auction House (USA) 120 – Gracious Imp (USA) (Imp Society (USA)) [2009 6m^{4} 6.1m^{6} 6m Sep 15] half-sister to 3 winners, including 6f (at 2 yrs)/7f winner Sophies Symphony (by Merdon Melody): dam little form: tailed off all starts. *A. Berry* **–**

ED'S PRIDE (IRE) 3 b.c. Catcher In The Rye (IRE) 115 – Queenliness (Exit To Nowhere (USA) 122) [2009 38: p8.6g^{4} p9.5g^{4} f8g^{5} f7d^{5} Mar 10] tall colt: poor maiden: stays 9.5f: acts on all-weather: wears cheekpieces/blinkers. *K. A. Ryan* **49**

EDWARD LEAR 2 b.c. (May 15) Refuse To Bend (IRE) 128 – Darrery 98 (Darshaan 133) [2009 p8f 7g Oct 17] quite attractive colt: pulled hard when well held in maidens at Lingfield and Catterick: sold 1,800 gns. *E. F. Vaughan* –

EDWARD LONGSHANKS (USA) 2 b.c. (Jan 24) More Than Ready (USA) 120 – Amour Mio (USA) (Private Terms (USA)) [2009 7m 9m 8d Oct 13] well-made colt: green, well held in maidens: sold 2,500 gns. *T. P. Tate* –

EDWARD WHYMPER 2 ch.g. (Jan 15) Bahamian Bounty 116 – Sosumi 101 (Be My Chief (USA) 122) [2009 6m 6g 6s p7g 7g² 8.3d³ p7g⁵ p7g² p8m² Dec 1] big, good-topped gelding: fourth foal: half-brother to 3 winners, including 4-y-o Tevez and 5-y-o Benayoun: dam, 2-y-o 5f winner (stayed 1¼m), out of half-sister to Compton Admiral and Summoner: fair maiden: best efforts when placed in nurseries: stays 8.3f: acts on polytrack and good to soft going. *M. H. Tompkins* **70**

EENY MAC (IRE) 2 ch.g. (Apr 27) Redback 116 – Sally Green (IRE) 79 (Common Grounds 118) [2009 5g 7d 7.5g Aug 12] close-coupled gelding: behind in maidens (signs of ability final start, gelded after). *N. Bycroft* –

EFFERVESCE (IRE) 2 ch.f. (Apr 7) Galileo (IRE) 134 – Royal Fizz (IRE) (Royal Academy (USA) 130) [2009 p7.1g⁵ Nov 14] 220,000F, 280,000Y: half-sister to 3 winners, including 4-y-o Hitchens: dam, French 2-y-o 6.5f winner, half-sister to smart Hong Kong performer up to 1¼m Floral Pegasus: 7/2 and green, 11½ lengths fifth to Huroof in maiden at Wolverhampton, slowly away and poorly positioned, then keeping on not knocked about: likely to improve. *Sir Michael Stoute* **60 p**

EFFICIENCY 3 b.f. Efisio 120 – Trounce (Barathea (IRE) 127) [2009 86p: p7g 7d⁶ p8g 8d 10d p9.5g p8m Nov 29] smallish, stocky filly: just fair form at best in 2009: stays 1m: raced only on polytrack and going softer than good on turf: has twice refused at stall. *M. Blanshard* **75**

EFFIGY 5 b.g. Efisio 120 – Hymne d'Amour (USA) 58 (Dixieland Band (USA)) [2009 82: 8.3m 8.3m² 8m³ 8.3m² 8g³ 8g³ 9s³ 8m² 8m² 8d⁶ Oct 11] lengthy gelding: fairly useful handicapper: probably best around 1m: acts on polytrack, soft and good to firm going: travels smoothly: reliable. *H. Candy* **87**

EFFORT 3 ch.g. Dr Fong (USA) 128 – Party Doll 108 (Be My Guest (USA) 126) [2009 97: p6g⁶ 8.1m a7f⁶ a6g⁶ a5f a5f Dec 18] useful-looking gelding: handicapper: just fairly useful form on reappearance: subsequently below par, leaving M. Johnston after second start: stays 6f: acts on polytrack, firm and soft going. *A. bin Huzaim, UAE* **86**

EFIDIUM 11 b.g. Presidium 124 – Efipetite 54 (Efisio 120) [2009 73: 7m 7.5m 9m⁵ 8g³ 8m 7f² 7.5m⁵ 6.9d³ 8m⁵ 8d 7g 9.9g³ 10.9m 10.2m⁴ 12.4d 7m Oct 26] small gelding: fair handicapper: stays 1¼m: acts on fibresand, firm and soft going: tried blinkered: held up. *N. Bycroft* **68**

EFISIO PRINCESS 6 br.m. Efisio 120 – Hardiprincess (Keen 116) [2009 72: f6g* f7g⁴ 6s 6g⁴ 5.1g 6d* f6m⁴ p6f Dec 13] good-topped mare: fair handicapper: won at Southwell in January and Windsor in October: will prove best at 5f/6f: acts on fibresand and soft ground: usually front runner. *J. E. Long* **73**

EFISTORM 8 b.g. Efisio 120 – Abundance 62 (Cadeaux Genereux 131) [2009 95: f5g⁴ f5g 5g* 5m² 5m⁵ 5v⁶ 5g* 5g³ 5f³ 5m 5m⁵ 5m 6.1m Sep 26] smallish, quite good-topped gelding: fairly useful handicapper: bit below best in 2009, but successful at Windsor in April and Musselburgh in July: probably best at 5f nowadays: acts on all-weather, firm and soft ground: tried in cheekpieces: held up (sometimes gets behind). *C. R. Dore* **87**

EFORETTA (GER) 7 ch.m. Dr Fong (USA) 128 – Erminora (GER) (Highest Honor (FR) 124) [2009 f16d f12g⁴ f12g⁵ f14g⁴ f16g³ f16g* p16g* 16g⁴ May 29] close-coupled mare: fair handicapper: missed 2008: won at Southwell in April and Kempton in May: stays 2¼m: acts on all-weather and firm ground: tried in blinkers/cheekpieces. *A. W. Carroll* **66**

EGYPTIAN LORD 6 ch.g. Bold Edge 123 – Calypso Lady (IRE) 88 (Priolo (USA) 127) [2009 58§: f5g 5g f5f f5g Dec 22] workmanlike gelding: showed nothing but temperament in 2009: tried visored, blinkered of late: one to avoid. *Peter Grayson* **§§**

EGYPTOLOGY (IRE) 2 ch.g. (Mar 29) Shamardal (USA) 129 – Golden Digger (USA) 66 (Mr Prospector (USA)) [2009 8d p7.1g⁶ p7g⁵ Nov 18] modest form in maidens, fading from prominence: gelded after: bred to be suited by 1m+. *M. Johnston* **64**

EIGHTDAYSAWEEK 3 b.f. Montjeu (IRE) 137 – Figlette (Darshaan 133) [2009 –p: 10.2g⁶ f11g* f11g² 11m f14m⁴ 10.2g f11g* p16f p13.9g⁴ p9.5g⁵ f11g⁴ p7.1g f11g⁵ f11g³ Dec 18] well-made filly: modest performer: won handicap at Southwell in April and claimer there in August (left S. Kirk): stays 11f: probably best on fibresand: tried in cheekpieces: has looked awkward: none too consistent. *A. J. McCabe* **–** **a64**

EIGHTEENFIFTY 5 ch.g. Hernando (FR) 127 – Colleville 97 (Pharly (FR) 130) [2009 p12.2g* p13.9g³ 16g p16g² Aug 17] useful bumper winner: only fair on Flat, very lightly raced: won maiden at Wolverhampton in February: trained prior to final start by N. Henderson: stays 2m. *B. W. Hills* **77**

EIGHTFOLD PATH (USA) 2 b.c. (Feb 1) Giant's Causeway (USA) 132 – Divine Proportions (USA) 125 (Kingmambo (USA) 125) [2009 6g* 7g³ 6s* Oct 12] first foal: dam, 5f (at 2 yrs) to 10.5f winner, including Poule d'Essai des Pouliches and Prix de Diane, half-sister to high-class performer up to 1m Whipper: progressive form: won newcomers race at Deauville in August and Prix Eclipse at Chantilly (made all, held on by head from Irish Cat) in October: 3½ lengths third to Buzzword in Prix La Rochette at Longchamp in between: bred to stay at least 1m: likely to make a smart 3-y-o. *P. Bary, France* **104 p**

EIGHT HOURS 2 b.g. (Feb 8) Bahamian Bounty 116 – Alchimie (IRE) (Sri Pekan (USA) 117) [2009 5m p5.1g* 6m 6d² 6d* 6m Sep 18] compact gelding: fair performer: won maiden at Wolverhampton in April and nursery at Ripon in September: stays 6f: acts on polytrack and good to soft ground: blinkered final start (ran poorly, gelded after). *R. A. Fahey* **65**

EIJAAZ (IRE) 8 b.g. Green Desert (USA) 127 – Kismah 111 (Machiavellian (USA) 123) [2009 72: 12d 9.8m⁶ 10m² 10.1d 13.8g⁶ 10m³ 10m 13.8v Nov 3] quite attractive gelding: fair handicapper: effective at 1¼m to 1¾m: acts on polytrack and any turf going: tried in cheekpieces/visor: has awkward head carriage: held up. *G. A. Harker* **73**

EIMEAR'S PRIDE (IRE) 9 b.g. Sri Pekan (USA) 117 – Elinor Dashwood (IRE) 61 (Fools Holme (USA)) [2009 16m Jun 29] maiden: very lightly raced and no form since 2004: blinkered only outing in 2009. *D. Loughnane, Ireland* **–**

EISTEDDFOD 8 ch.g. Cadeaux Genereux 131 – Ffestiniog (IRE) 96 (Efisio 120) [2009 111: p6g* p6g² 6m 6s² p6m⁴ f7g⁴ Dec 22] lengthy, good-quartered gelding: smart performer: won minor event at Kempton in March by neck from Hogmaneigh: creditable ¾-length second to Zidane in minor event at Doncaster fourth outing, best other effort: effective at 6f/7f: yet to race on heavy going, acts on any other turf and polytrack: tried in cheekpieces/blinkers/tongue tie. *P. F. I. Cole* **111**

EI TANNIOLA (IRE) 4 b.f. Dr Massini (IRE) 117 – Academic Accuracy 70 (Environment Friend 128) [2009 f7g 8.3g May 19] first foal: dam maiden (stayed 7f): no sign of ability in bumper/maiden hurdle for M. Gingell, and in sellers on Flat (wore cheekpieces). *G. J. Smith* **–**

EJAAB 2 b. or br.g. (Feb 24) Kyllachy 129 – Whittle Woods Girl 80 (Emarati (USA) 74) [2009 5f⁴ 6d* p6g³ 7d Sep 6] £60,000Y: good-bodied gelding: half-brother to several winners, including 5f/6f winner High Esteem (by Common Grounds) and 7f winner Zagala (by Polar Falcon): dam, 6f winner, sister to useful 6f/7f performer Emerging Market and half-sister to smart performer up to 7f Atraf: fairly useful form: won maiden at Catterick in July: much better effort in nurseries after when respectable third at Kempton: stays 6f: acts on polytrack and good to soft going: sold 5,500 gns. *W. J. Haggas* **80**

EJEED (USA) 4 b.g. Rahy (USA) 115 – Lahan 117 (Unfuwain (USA) 131) [2009 64: 7m 6f p6g p7m⁶ p8m p8g⁴ p8f⁶ Dec 20] lengthy gelding: lightly-raced maiden, just modest in 2009: will stay 1¼m+: tried in cheekpieces. *Miss Z. C. Davison* **60**

EKTIMAAL 6 ch.g. Bahamian Bounty 116 – Secret Circle (Magic Ring (IRE) 115) [2009 93: 8.3m⁶ p7g p8.6g⁴ p7f⁶ p6g* p6g⁵ p7.1g p6f⁵ Dec 21] tall, good-topped gelding: fairly useful handicapper: won at Lingfield in November: effective at 6f to 1m: acts on polytrack and good to firm going: tongue tied prior to 2009: travels strongly. *E. A. L. Dunlop* **88**

ELAALA (USA) 7 ch.m. Aljabr (USA) 125 – Nufuth (USA) (Nureyev (USA) 131) [2009 58: 16g⁵ May 19] neat mare: modest handicapper, very lighty raced on Flat since 2005 (fair hurdler, successful in June): stays 1¾m: acts on fibresand and good to soft going. *B. D. Leavy* **54**

ELA GORRIE MOU 3 b.f. Mujahid (USA) 125 – Real Flame (Cyrano de Bergerac 120) [2009 –: 8.3f 9g⁴ 8.3v⁵ 8g* 8m* Sep 12] strong, useful-looking filly: fair performer: much improved to win handicaps at Yarmouth in August and Ffos Las in September: stays 9f: acts on good to firm ground. *T. T. Clement* **76**

EL AMEEN 3 b.c. Haafhd 129 – Gracious (Grand Lodge (USA) 125) [2009 7g³ 8m³ 7m² 7m² p8g Oct 14] 60,000F: strong colt: first foal: dam, unraced, out of half-sister to smart sprinter Paradise Isle: fair maiden: should be suited by 1m: blinkered final outing: raced only on polytrack and good/good to firm going: often makes running: sold 12,000 gns. *M. Johnston* **76**

ELATION (IRE) 2 b.f. (Mar 1) Cape Cross (IRE) 129 – Attraction 125 (Efisio 120) **79 p** [2009 p6m^4 p7m* Dec 16] first foal: dam 5f/6f (Queen Mary Stakes/Cherry Hinton Stakes) to 1m (including 1000 Guineas) winner: better effort in maidens when winning at Lingfield by 4½ lengths from Freddie's Girl, making all: will stay 1m: open to further improvement. *M. Johnston*

EL BRAVO 3 ch.g. Falbrav (IRE) 133 – Alessandra 101 (Generous (IRE) 139) [2009 **81** p7g p10g^4 p12g^2 p12g^3 p12.2g* 11.6m^2 11d^6 14g^5 May 21] good-topped gelding: seventh foal: half-brother to 3 winners, including 7-y-o Alessano: dam, 1½m winner (would have stayed further), closely related to Park Hill Stakes winner Casey: fairly useful performer: won maiden at Wolverhampton in April: should stay 1¾m: acts on polytrack and good to firm ground. *G. L. Moore*

ELDALIL 2 br.f. (Apr 6) Singspiel (IRE) 133 – White House 84 (Pursuit of Love 124) **51 p** [2009 p7g^6 Sep 4] 85,000F: fifth foal: half-sister to 1¼m winner Bronze Star (by Mark of Esteem) and 4-y-o Madam President: dam, 1¼m winner, half-sister to smart middle-distance performers Little Rock, Short Skirt and Whitewater Affair: 7/1, not knocked about when 8½ lengths sixth to Eolith in minor event at Kempton: bred to be well suited by 1m+: sure to improve. *Sir Michael Stoute*

EL DECECY (USA) 5 b.g. Seeking The Gold (USA) – Ashraakat (USA) 105 (Danzig **87** (USA)) [2009 94: p6g^6 p6g^5 p5.1g^2 p8g^3 7m 8m^3 7m* 7m^6 6m* 10.3g 10.3m 6g 7m* 8m 7.1m* 7.5m 5g 9.2d^5 Jul 17] tall, sparely-made gelding: fairly useful performer: not so good in 2009, though won sellers at Redcar and Brighton in April, Redcar in May and Chepstow in June: effective at 6f to 1½m: acts on polytrack, firm and soft going: sometimes wears headgear: tried tongue tied: often front runner: none too consistent. *S. Parr*

EL DIEGO (IRE) 5 b.g. Sadler's Wells (USA) 132 – Goncharova (USA) 112 (Gone **84** West (USA)) [2009 80: f12d* p12.2g* f14g^2 p12g^6 p12g Oct 9] fairly useful handicapper, lightly raced: won at Southwell (maiden) and Wolverhampton in January: stays 1¾m: acts on all-weather and good to firm going. *J. R. Gask*

ELEANORA DUSE (IRE) 2 b.f. (Mar 19) Azamour (IRE) 130 – Drama Class (IRE) **82 p** 102 (Caerleon (USA) 132) [2009 p7g^6 7m p8m* Nov 19] quite good-topped filly: sixth foal: half-sister to 3 winners, including smart 7f (at 2 yrs)/1¼m winner Scottish Stage (by Selkirk) and 3-y-o Namibian Orator: dam, 1¼m winner, out of sister to high-class performer up to 1¼m Prince of Dance: easily best effort in maidens when winning at Kempton in November easily by 3½ lengths from Inner Angel, soon disputing: should be suited by 1¼m+: got worked up in preliminaries and ran poorly second start: likely to do better still. *Sir Michael Stoute*

ELEANOR ELOISE (USA) 5 b.m. Minardi (USA) 119 – Javana (USA) (Sandpit **47** (BRZ) 129) [2009 61: p7g p5.1g^4 6f 7d^4 7.6m Aug 15] maiden handicapper, just poor in 2009: stays 7f: acts on polytrack: tried in blinkers/cheekpieces. *J. R. Gask*

ELECTIONEER (USA) 2 b.g. (Jan 14) Elusive Quality (USA) – Secret Charm (IRE) **81** 109 (Green Desert (USA) 127) [2009 5.7f^4 5m* 5m Aug 15] first foal: dam, 7f (at 2 yrs)/1m winner, half-sister to Oaks third Relish The Thought: fairly useful form: won maiden at Beverley (by 1¼ lengths from Trinder) in July: disappointing in nursery at Newmarket (subsequently gelded): bred to stay at least 7f. *M. Johnston*

ELECTRIC CITY (IRE) 2 b.f. (Mar 9) Elusive City (USA) 117 – Accell (IRE) 56 **65** (Magical Wonder (USA) 125) [2009 p7g 6g^3 6d^4 p7.1g^6 Sep 11] £1,800 2-y-o: half-sister to 2 winners, notably smart French 2004 2-y-o 1m winner Guillaume Tell (by Rossini): dam, Irish 8.5f/1½m winner, out of sister to 2000 Guineas winner Tap On Wood: fair maiden: third to Taajub at Newmarket: respectable effort in nursery final start: should stay 7f. *M. G. Quinlan*

ELECTRIC FEEL 2 b.f. (Apr 5) Firebreak 125 – Night Gypsy 74 (Mind Games 121) **99** [2009 6m* 6f^6 6g^3 7m^2 7v* Oct 24] £28,000Y, £36,000 2-y-o: small, sparely-made filly: fifth foal: half-sister to 3-y-o Aunt Nicola and 6-y-o Safari Mischief: dam 2-y-o 5f winner: useful performer: won maiden at Newmarket in May and listed race at Newbury (by 1¼ lengths from Za Za Zoom) in October: also ran well when 4 lengths second to Tabassum in Oh So Sharp Stakes at Newmarket: stays testing 7f: acts on heavy and good to firm going. *M. Botti*

ELECTRIC WARRIOR (IRE) 6 b.g. Bold Fact (USA) 116 – Dungeon Princess **80 d** (IRE) 62 (Danehill (USA) 126) [2009 97: p7g^2 p8g* p8g* f7g^5 p7g p8g f8f p7.1g p7.1g p7.1g^6 p8.6g Dec 28] strong, lengthy gelding: fairly useful performer: won 2 claimers at Lingfield in February, leaving K. R. Burke £12,000 after latter: largely out of sorts after: possibly best around 1m nowadays: acts on all-weather, firm and soft going. *C. R. Dore*

ELECTROLYSER (IRE) 4 gr.c. Daylami (IRE) 138 – Iviza (IRE) 105§ (Sadler's **104** Wells (USA) 132) [2009 104p: 12s^4 16.1d^5 16m* 18m Oct 17] lengthy colt: useful performer, lightly raced: won listed event at Ascot (beat Oasis Knight ¾ length) in September: struggled from wide draw in Cesarewitch at Newmarket final outing: stays 2m: acts on polytrack, soft and good to firm going. *C. G. Cox*

ELEGANT DANCER (IRE) 2 ch.f. (Apr 18) Choisir (AUS) 126 – Sofistication **54** (IRE) 68 (Dayjur (USA) 137) [2009 5m^4 5m 5.1g^3 May 19] rather leggy filly: second foal: half-sister to 3-y-o Rio Cobolo: dam 7f winner: modest form at best in maidens. *Paul Green*

ELEMENTS (IRE) 3 b.f. Rock of Gibraltar (IRE) 133 – Ghita (IRE) 69 (Zilzal (USA) **54** 137) [2009 –: 8.1v^6 7d^6 8.3v 7v p8.6g 9.1g Oct 23] maiden, modest form at best: bred to stay 1¼m: raced only on polytrack and good going or softer. *E. J. Alston*

ELEVATE BAMBINA 3 b.f. Spartacus (IRE) 107 – Miri (IRE) (Sillery (USA) 122) **–** [2009 –: p7g^6 Feb 13] sturdy filly: little sign of ablity. *A. Berry*

ELEVATE BOBBOB 3 b.g. Observatory (USA) 131 – Grandma Lily (IRE) 88 **–** (Bigstone (IRE) 126) [2009 f8g p8.6g f7g p12.2g f7g Dec 18] little form: visored final outing. *A. Berry*

ELHAMRI 5 b. or br.g. Noverre (USA) 125 – Seamstress (IRE) 72 (Barathea (IRE) **91** 127) [2009 98: 5.2s 5g^4 5.1m 5g p5g 5g 5g Aug 12] small, strong gelding: useful handicapper at best: well below form after second start: probably best at 5f: acts on polytrack and good to firm going. *S. Kirk*

ELIE SHORE 2 b.f. (Apr 28) Tobougg (IRE) 125 – Mitsuki 91§ (Puissance 110) [2009 **44** 7m^5 8.3g p8.6g 8g p8.6g Dec 3] third foal: dam 5f/6f winner, including at 2 yrs: poor maiden: stays 8.6f: acts on polytrack: visored last 3 starts. *P. C. Haslam*

ELIJAH PEPPER (USA) 4 ch.g. Crafty Prospector (USA) – Dovie Dee (USA) **76** (Housebuster (USA)) [2009 69: 6m* 6m^6 6m^5 6f^5 6m^3 7d 6m 6m p6g^5 Dec 12] leggy gelding: fair handicapper: won at Thirsk in May: stays 6f: acts on polytrack, good to firm and good to soft going: tried blinkered. *T. D. Barron*

ELIOT (GER) 3 b.c. Tiger Hill (IRE) 127 – Esposita (GER) (Sternkoenig (IRE) 122) **118** [2009 11d^4 11d^2 11g^5 12g^4 12g* 12g^3 Sep 27] first foal: dam, German 9f to 11f winner, half-sister to very smart German performer up to 1½m Egerton: smart performer: 1¾ lengths fourth to Wiener Walzer in Deutsches Derby at Hamburg fourth outing: simple task in minor event at Hoppegarten in August (won by 12 lengths) before best effort when 2½ lengths third to Jukebox Jury in Preis von Europa at Cologne final start: stays 1½m: raced only on good/good to soft ground. *T. Mundry, Germany*

ELISIARIO (IRE) 4 b.g. Clodovil (IRE) 116 – Kahla (Green Desert (USA) 127) [2009 **82** 77: p7g^2 f7g* f7g* p8g^2 p7g^6 8d Jul 17] rather leggy gelding: fairly useful performer: improved to win maiden in March and handicap in April, both at Southwell: stays 1m: acts on all-weather, well beaten both turf starts. *J. R. Boyle*

ELITE LAND 6 b.g. Namaqualand (USA) – Petite Elite 47 (Anfield 117) [2009 76: **75** 12g^4 13g^5 12m^4 12d^3 13.8m* Sep 19] close-coupled gelding: fair handicapper: won at Catterick (third win from 4 starts at track) in September: stays 13.8f: acts on fibresand, firm and soft going: tried blinkered/in cheekpieces: fair hurdler. *B. Ellison*

ELIZABELLE (IRE) 2 b.f. (May 14) Westerner 130 – Jus'chillin' (IRE) 60 (Elbio **63 p** 125) [2009 7m 7d^3 p7g 7d Sep 3] €35,000Y: stocky filly: seventh foal: half-sister to 3-y-o Orizaba and 5f (at 2 yrs) and 1m (in Spain) winner Robbo's Rocket (by Perugino): dam sprint maiden: modest form given insufficient test in maidens/nursery: should be well suited by 1m+: remains capable of better. *R. Hannon*

ELIZABETH'S QUEST 4 b.f. Piccolo 121 – Reina 24 (Homeboy 114) [2009 –: f7g **–** p10g Nov 5] angular filly: maiden handicapper: well beaten in cheekpieces both starts in 2009. *Miss N. A. Lloyd-Beavis*

ELIZA DOOLITTLE 3 b.f. Royal Applause 124 – Green Supreme (Primo Dominie **67** 121) [2009 6s^6 6g^4 p6g^6 6g^4 p7m* Oct 26] 140,000Y: half-sister to several winners, notably smart sprinters Fire Up The Band (by Prince Sabo) and Strike Up The Band and Sampower Star (both by Cyrano de Bergerac): dam unraced: fair performer: improved in handicaps last 2 starts, winning at Kempton in October: stays 7f: acts on polytrack. *J. R. Fanshawe*

ELKHORN 7 b.g. Indian Ridge 123 – Rimba (USA) 82 (Dayjur (USA) 137) [2009 73: **60** p6g^3 p6g 6.1g p6g 6m^3 6m^4 6g^5 6m^2 6m 6m^2 6d^4 6m^6 6m^3 6g^3 Oct 20] leggy gelding: modest handicapper nowadays: best at stiff 5f/easy 6f: acts on polytrack, firm and good to soft going: wears headgear: held up: reliable. *Miss J. A. Camacho*

ELK TRAIL (IRE) 4 ch.g. Captain Rio 122 – Panpipes (USA) 69 (Woodman (USA) 126) [2009 83: f8s^{4} f8d^{4} f12g^{3} 10.2v^{6} Nov 4] well-made gelding: maiden handicapper, just fair form in 2009: stays 1¼m: acts on fibresand and firm going: tried blinkered: usually races prominently. *Mrs P. Sly* **72**

ELLA 5 b.m. Pivotal 124 – Flossy 107 (Efisio 120) [2009 94p: f12g 9.8d^{4} 10.2d^{3} 12s^{3} Nov 7] good-topped mare: useful handicapper, lightly raced: good efforts when placed, 4¼ lengths third to Charm School in November Handicap at Doncaster final start: stays 1½m: raced only on good going or softer on turf (acts well on heavy), below form on all-weather: free-going sort, tends to race prominently. *G. A. Swinbank* **98**

ELLA GRACE (USA) 2 b. or br.f. (Apr 8) Broken Vow (USA) 117 – Shy Swan (USA) (Nureyev (USA) 131) [2009 6m^{4} 6s 6m 8m^{2} 10.2m^{4} Sep 30] $13,000F, €25,000Y, 30,000 2-y-o: good-topped filly: half-sister to 3 winners abroad, including German 8.5f to 11.5f winner Silver Swan (by Silver Hawk): dam US maiden: fair maiden: best effort when second to Fantastic Pick in nursery at Redcar: stays 1m (raced freely at 1¼m): acts on good to firm going. *R. A. Fahey* **67**

ELLA WOODCOCK (IRE) 5 b.g. Daggers Drawn (USA) 114 – Hollow Haze (USA) 90 (Woodman (USA) 126) [2009 89: 12.4g^{3} 8s 8m 9.2g 13.4m^{6} 8g^{3} p9.5g p8.6g^{5} p8.6g^{6} p8.6g^{2} p9.5g* p9.5g^{5} Dec 18] good-topped gelding: fair handicapper: left C. Grant after reappearance: won at Wolverhampton in December: stays 10.3f: acts on polytrack and good to firm ground: often in cheekpieces/blinkers: tongue tied once: quirky. *E. J. Alston* **75**

ELLBEEDEE (IRE) 2 b.f. (Feb 20) Dalakhani (IRE) 133 – Tochar Ban (USA) 83 (Assert 134) [2009 8g Oct 23] €75,000Y: half-sister to several winners, including US Grade 2 1m winner Uncharted Haven (by Turtle Island) and useful 2003 2-y-o 7f winner Torinmoor (by Intikhab) who stayed 1¼m: dam 1¼m winner: 20/1, looked and ran as if needing race when mid-field in 21-runner maiden at Doncaster: should improve. *M. A. Jarvis* **55 p**

ELLEMUJIE 4 b.g. Mujahid (USA) 125 – Jennelle 97 (Nomination 125) [2009 97: 8.1g^{4} 8m^{5} 8.1f* 8m 8.1m 8g 8.1g 10m^{4} 8m^{5} 8m 9m p10g^{6} Oct 22] good-topped gelding: useful handicapper: won at Sandown in June by length from Mujood: below that level after: effective at 7f to 1¼m: acts on polytrack and firm going: edgy sort: held up (sometimes slowly away). *D. K. Ivory* **99**

ELLEN VANNIN (IRE) 2 ch.f. (Mar 31) Tagula (IRE) 116 – Felin Special (Lyphard's Special (USA) 122) [2009 6m^{6} 7.1g p7.1g 6g Oct 19] half-sister to several winners, including 5f (at 2 yrs) to 7f winner Bon Ami (by Paris House) and Irish 7f and 1¼m winner Frosty Wind (by Forest Wind), both useful: dam Irish 2-y-o 6f winner: modest form in maidens/nursery: stays 7f: acts on polytrack. *Eve Johnson Houghton* **53**

EL LIBERTADOR (USA) 3 br.g. Giant's Causeway (USA) 132 – Istikbal (USA) (Kingmambo (USA) 125) [2009 53p: 8.1m^{4} p8g^{4} 8.3m^{3} 9g 8.1m^{4} 7m 8.3g^{4} 8g^{2} p8g^{3} p8m^{5} Nov 19] good-topped gelding: fair handicapper: stays 1m: acts on polytrack and good to firm going: tongue tied once. *E. A. Wheeler* **77**

ELLIES IMAGE 2 b.f. (Feb 20) Lucky Story (USA) 128 – Crown City (USA) 56 (Coronado's Quest (USA) 130) [2009 6m p7.1g 7m p8.6g Sep 11] second foal: dam maiden (stayed 1m): well held in maidens. *B. P. J. Baugh* **–**

ELLIES INSPIRATION 4 b.f. Puissance 110 – Star View Lady (Precocious 126) [2009 6m 8.1v 8.1g May 29] angular filly: fourth foal: dam unraced: well held in maidens: dead. *M. Mullineaux* **–**

ELLIPTICAL (USA) 3 b.g. Arch (USA) 127 – Citidance Missy (USA) (Citidancer (USA)) [2009 73: 9.9g* 10.1g 8d* 7m^{3} p8m^{6} 10.2d Oct 15] good-bodied gelding: useful performer: won maiden at Goodwood in May and handicap at Salisbury (beat Rafiqa ½ length) in July: should stay 1¼m: acts on good to firm and good to soft going: well below form in cheekpieces/tongue tie final start: gelded after. *G. A. Butler* **95**

ELLIWAN 4 b.g. Nayef (USA) 129 – Ashbilya (USA) (Nureyev (USA) 131) [2009 77d: p10g^{6} f12d* f11g^{3} f11g^{4} 12.4s f8f Nov 24] well-made gelding: modest handicapper nowadays: won apprentice event at Southwell in March: stays 1½m: acts on all-weather and firm ground: blinkered in 2009: tried tongue tied: has looked hard ride. *M. W. Easterby* **64**

ELLMAU 4 ch.g. Dr Fong (USA) 128 – Triple Sharp 80 (Selkirk (USA) 129) [2009 90: p10g 10.3g 10.3m^{4} 10.3m^{4} 10.2s* 12d^{4} Oct 24] useful-looking gelding: fairly useful handicapper: left A. McCabe, won at Nottingham in October by head from Watergate: barely stays 1½m: acts on fibresand, firm and soft ground: free-going sort, races prominently. *E. S. McMahon* **93**

ELLMOLLELL 2 b.f. (Apr 3) Piccolo 121 – Runs In The Family 69 (Distant Relative 128) [2009 5g 5f p6g 5g^5 6.5m p7.1g p8.6g f8f Dec 11] £11,500Y: sturdy filly: sister to useful 5f and (including at 2 yrs) 6f winner Angel Sprints and half-sister to 2 winners in Italy: dam 5f to (at 2 yrs) 6f winner: poor maiden: best efforts on polytrack. *S. Kirk* **46**

EL LOCO UNO (USA) 3 ch.c. Fusaichi Pegasus (USA) 130 – La Vida Loca (IRE) 102 (Caerleon (USA) 132) [2009 8m^2 p8g^5 p8g* 8.3m 7s Aug 9] quite attractive colt: third foal: half-brother to winner in USA by Cherokee Run: dam, Irish 2-y-o 5f winner (later 1m winner in USA), half-sister to smart performer up to 1½m Crimson Tide out of half-sister to Derby winner Shahrastani: fairly useful performer: won maiden at Lingfield in June: poor efforts both starts in handicaps after: stays 1m. *H. R. A. Cecil* **88**

ELMFIELD GIANT (USA) 2 ch.g. (May 19) Giant's Causeway (USA) 132 – Princess Atoosa (USA) (Gone West (USA)) [2009 6d 7.5m^6 7m^2 f8g^4 Aug 27] $105,000Y: good-topped gelding: fifth foal: closely related to a winner in Japan by Storm Cat and half-brother to 2 winners in USA by A P Indy: dam unraced out of high-class 1m/1¼m winner Kooyonga: best effort in maidens when 2½ lengths second to Right Step at Newcastle: should stay 1m: gelded after final start. *R. A. Fahey* **77**

ELMS SCHOOL STORY 3 b.f. Lucky Story (USA) 128 – Elms Schoolgirl 79 (Emarati (USA) 74) [2009 10.9g Aug 31] third foal: half-sister to 7f to 1¼m winner Elms Schoolboy (by Komaite): dam 1¼m/1½m winner: signs of ability in maiden at Warwick: should improve. *Miss Venetia Williams* **– p**

ELNA BRIGHT 4 b.g. Elnadim (USA) 128 – Acicula (IRE) 96 (Night Shift (USA)) [2009 90: p8g^3 8g* 8.3g^6 7.6m 8.3m^5 7m* 7g^4 7m^2 p8g^2 7m 8.1g^3 8m^2 8m* 10.1m p10m^4 p7g* p8f Dec 20] tall, deep-girthed gelding: has a quick, unimpressive action: useful performer: won minor event at Bath in April, claimer at Salisbury in June and, having been claimed from P. D. Evans £17,000 after eleventh start, handicaps at Ascot in September and Lingfield (better than ever when beating Jonny Mudball 1½ lengths) in November: effective at 7f/1m: acts on polytrack and firm going: held up, usually travels strongly. *B. R. Johnson* **101**

ELNAWIN 3 b.c. Elnadim (USA) 128 – Acicula (IRE) 96 (Night Shift (USA)) [2009 112+: p7g^2 6m^5 6d^5 May 15] compact colt: useful performer: best effort in listed races in 2009 when 3½ lengths fifth to Border Patrol at Newbury final start: worth a try at 5f: acts on polytrack, good to firm and good to soft ground. *R. Hannon* **109**

ELOISE 3 ch.f. Hernando (FR) 127 – Eternelle 90 (Green Desert (USA) 127) [2009 p12g^5 f11g 12.1g f11g* p16f^6 Sep 10] second foal: sister to Spanish 7.5f winner Sassicaia: dam, 9.4f winner, half-sister to high-class German performer up to 1½m Caitano: modest form: improved when winning handicap at Southwell in August: stays 11f: raced only on all-weather and good ground: blinkered last 2 starts: sold 3,500 gns. *Sir Mark Prescott* **56**

EL POTRO 7 b.g. Forzando 122 – Gaelic Air 65 (Ballad Rock 122) [2009 67: 6m^5 5.1d 6.1g 5.1s p7g p6g^5 f6d Dec 29] sturdy gelding: handicapper, just modest form in 2009: effective at 5f/6f: acts on all-weather and any turf going: tried blinkered. *J. R. Holt* **56**

EL PRESIDENTE (IRE) 4 b.g. Daylami (IRE) 138 – Todi (IRE) (Spinning World (USA) 130) [2009 93: p10.7s^5 8s 10.1m Sep 16] fairly useful performer: sold £21,000 and left M. Halford in Ireland prior to final start: stays easy 10.7f: acts on polytrack and soft ground: usually in cheekpieces/blinkers nowadays: sometimes slowly away. *N. B. King* **88**

ELSIE JO (IRE) 3 b.f. Catcher In The Rye (IRE) 115 – Joy St Clair (IRE) (Try My Best (USA) 130) [2009 46p: p7g^2 p7g^3 p6g Mar 13] good-topped filly: modest maiden, lightly raced: stays 7f: acts on polytrack. *M. Wigham* **58**

ELSIE'S ORPHAN 2 br.f. (May 8) Pastoral Pursuits 127 – Elsie Plunkett 92 (Mind Games 121) [2009 p6f p5m^6 Oct 7] fifth foal: half-sister to fairly useful 2006 2-y-o 5f winner Eliza May (by Kyllachy) and 3-y-o Lady Vivien: dam 2-y-o 5f winner: modest form in maidens at Kempton, sixth to Desert Poppy (forced wide): bred to prove best at 5f/6f: capable of better. *P. R. Chamings* **60 p**

ELSPETH'S BOY (USA) 2 b. or br.c. (Mar 30) Tiznow (USA) 133 – Miss Waki Club (USA) (Miswaki (USA) 124) [2009 p7.1g* Nov 2] $11,000F: brother to a winner in USA and half-brother to several winners, including French 4.5f to 1m winner Six Acts (by Night Shift) and fairly useful 2003 2-y-o 6f winner King Carnival (by King of Kings): dam US 4.5f/5f winner: 33/1, created favourable impression when winning maiden at Wolverhampton by 1¼ lengths from Music Maestro, green before leading final 1f: will stay 1m: likely to improve. *J. R. Best* **90 p**

ELTHEEB 2 gr.c. (Apr 24) Red Ransom (USA) – Snowdrops (Gulch (USA)) [2009 7g 7d 8.3s 8d^3 Oct 22] 150,000Y: tall, close-coupled colt: first foal: dam US 1m/9f winner, including Grade 3 events: fair maiden: easily best effort when 2½ lengths third to Tertiary at Brighton: stays 1m. *J. L. Dunlop* **75**

ELUSIVE AWARD (USA) 2 b.c. (Mar 10) Elusive Quality (USA) – Victoria Cross (IRE) 101 (Mark of Esteem (IRE) 137) [2009 7g* p7g* 8d Oct 24] 7,000Y: good-topped colt: fourth foal: half-brother to 3 winners, notably 4-y-o Bronze Cannon: dam, 7f winner who probably stayed 1¼m, out of smart performer up to 1¾m Glowing With Pride: useful form: won maiden at Leopardstown in August and minor event at Dundalk (beat Miracle Match by head) in September: shaped as if amiss in Racing Post Trophy at Doncaster: should stay 1m. *Andrew Oliver, Ireland* **101**

ELUSIVE DREAMS (USA) 5 ch.g. Elusive Quality (USA) – Bally Five (USA) (Miswaki (USA) 124) [2009 70: p6g p6g p6g^2 p6g a6.8g* a6.8s^4 a6g* a6.8g* a6.8d* Dec 19] sturdy gelding: modest handicapper: sold from P. Howling £3,500 after fourth start: won at Taby in May, June, July and December: stays 1m, raced at shorter nowadays: acts on polytrack/dirt, good to firm and good to soft ground: often visored (including last 2 outings in Britain): held up (sometimes slowly away). *B. Bjorkman, Sweden* **63**

ELUSIVE FAME (USA) 3 b.g. Elusive Quality (USA) – Advancing Star (USA) 115 (Soviet Star (USA) 128) [2009 92p: 6m 7d 6m^5 7g 6m f6g* f6g^6 f7g* p7g^6 p8g p7.1g p8g p8.6g p7.1g f8g* p8m f8f^3 f8m^6 f8g^3 Dec 27] strong gelding: fairly useful handicapper on all-weather, fair on turf: won at Southwell in July, August and November: stays 1m: acts on all-weather: usually blinkered, tried visored: none too consistent. *M. Johnston* **69 a81**

ELUSIVE GLEN (IRE) 3 b.c. Elusive City (USA) 117 – Glenarff (USA) (Irish River (FR) 131) [2009 f8g^5 8.5m Apr 23] modest form in maidens only on debut: pulled up second outing (reportedly damaged a fetlock). *M. Johnston* **55**

ELUSIVE HAWK (IRE) 5 b. or br.g. Noverre (USA) 125 – Two Clubs 111 (First Trump 118) [2009 –, a81: p6g^2 7d^2 7m^6 f6g^3 f6g* 6d f6f^5 f5m Dec 15] close-coupled gelding: fairly useful handicapper on all-weather, fair on turf: won at Southwell in July: best at 6f/7f: acts on fibresand and good to soft going. *B. J. Curley* **78 a82**

ELUSIVE MUSE 3 ch.g. Exit To Nowhere (USA) 122 – Dance A Dream 115 (Sadler's Wells (USA) 132) [2009 8m^5 8.1g^6 12g^4 14.1m Aug 29] modest form only when fifth in maiden on debut. *M. Dods* **57**

ELUSIVE PIMPERNEL (USA) 2 b. or br.c. (Feb 14) Elusive Quality (USA) – Cara Fantasy (IRE) 84 (Sadler's Wells (USA) 132) [2009 7g* 7m* 8d^2 Oct 24] **116 p**

It seemed ironic that, after waiting such a long time for a first pattern-race success in Britain, Windflower Overseas Holdings Inc should enjoy a second just three days after their first. Elusive Pimpernel broke the ice in the Acomb Stakes at York's August meeting and his half-brother and stablemate Palavicini followed suit in the Strensall Stakes. The pair are the latest in a long line of at least useful performers Windflower have had in training with John Dunlop over the years, though only Big Bad Bob (in Germany in 2003) had been successful in a European pattern race before the latest season.

Elusive Pimpernel created such a favourable impression on his only start before York that he was sent off second favourite in a ten-runner field for the Watch The Last 2 Races On Racing UK Acomb Stakes. His credentials were based on accounting for fourteen rivals at Newmarket six weeks earlier in what is traditionally one of the best two-year-old maidens of the season. Elusive Pimpernel, a 12/1-shot that day, ran on strongly once he realized what was required and led close home to win by half a length from Timely Jazz, with fellow newcomers Poet's Voice and Emerald Commander third and fourth. Poet's Voice and Emerald Commander reopposed at York, both having been successful in the meantime, Poet's Voice starting favourite at 7/4, with Elusive Pimpernel at 7/2. Elusive Pimpernel came out on top again, despite leaving his finishing effort even later this time. Flat out in last for much of the way as Poet's Voice set a strong pace, Elusive Pimpernel was brought wide in the straight and finished very strongly, along with Emerald Commander, as the leader began to flag. Emerald Commander got to the front well inside the final furlong, but Elusive Pimpernel collared him in the final strides to win by a head, with Poet's Voice half a length back in third. It looked an above-average renewal of the Acomb at the time, and by season's end the form had been boosted several times, including by Poet's Voice, who won the Champagne

Watch The Last 2 Races On Racing UK Acomb Stakes, York—Elusive Pimpernel finishes very strongly out wide and overhauls Emerald Commander (centre) and Poet's Voice

Stakes, and by fifth-placed Vale of York, who won the Breeders' Cup Juvenile. Elusive Pimpernel himself did the Acomb form no harm on his only subsequent start, though he lost his unbeaten record in the Racing Post Trophy at Doncaster. He was no match for the impressive St Nicholas Abbey, who beat him by three and three quarter lengths, but Elusive Pimpernel beat the rest decisively, showing in the process that he is as effective on good to soft going as he is on good to firm. The step up to a mile suited Elusive Pimpernel as well, though he would have benefited from a stronger gallop as he was once again doing his best work late on.

Elusive Pimpernel (USA) (b. or br.c. Feb 14, 2007)	Elusive Quality (USA) (b 1993)	Gone West (b 1984)	Mr Prospector
			Secrettame
		Touch of Greatness (b 1986)	Hero's Honor
			Ivory Wand
	Cara Fantasy (IRE) (b 2000)	Sadler's Wells (b 1981)	Northern Dancer
			Fairy Bridge
		Gay Fantasy (b 1981)	Troy
			Miss Upward

Elusive Pimpernel is by the sprinter-miler Elusive Quality, who won two Grade 3 handicaps in the States as a five-year-old, including the Poker Handicap at Belmont, where he broke the world record for a mile on turf. Elusive Quality is responsible for top-class performers on each side of the Atlantic in Raven's Pass and Smarty Jones, both of whom won at up to a mile and a quarter, and Elusive Pimpernel will stay at least that far. Palavicini (by Giant's Causeway) is a free-running sort but is fully effective at a mile and a quarter and wasn't far below his best when tried at a mile and a half. Given that Elusive Pimpernel is a more relaxed individual than his half-brother, there is a good chance that a mile and a half will prove to be within his compass. Elusive Pimpernel is the second foal of Cara Fantasy, who gained both of her wins at a mile and a half, in a maiden and a handicap at Leicester as a three-year-old, and also ran well over an extended mile and three quarters the following season. She is a half-sister to several other Dunlop-trained winners who have carried the now-familiar red and yellow halved silks, including the useful performers Lucky Guest, Fantasy Hill and Son of Sharp Shot. Elusive Pimpernel's grandam Gay Fantasy is an unraced sister to the dam of Derby winner Oath. A big, strong colt who should make up into an even better three-year-old, Elusive Pimpernel may not have the speed required to win a Guineas and taking in the Dante on the way to the Derby may be a better option. A slight doubt about Epsom proving ideal for Elusive Pimpernel is raised by his round action, though that is not something to consider until he shows himself to be worth his place in the line-up. *J. L. Dunlop*

ELUSIVE RONNIE (IRE) 3 b.g. One Cool Cat (USA) 123 – Elusive Kitty (USA) 73 (Elusive Quality (USA)) [2009 61: p6g^5 p6g p5g^3 p6g^5 p7g^3 7d^4 6m 6m p7f p5g* p6g^2 p6m^2 p6m p6g Dec 31] sturdy gelding: fair performer on all-weather, modest on turf: won handicap at Kempton in November: stays easy 7f: acts on polytrack and good to firm going: wears cheekpieces/blinkers. *R. A. Teal* **53 a68**

ELUSIVE STYLE (IRE) 3 b.f. Elusive City (USA) 117 – Brooklands Lodge (USA) 67 (Grand Lodge (USA) 125) [2009 7m 8g 7g^3 8.3v 10m 5v Nov 3] €3,600Y, £5,000 2-y-o: first foal: dam, maiden (stayed 1½m), sister to useful Irish 1½m performer Piranesi: poor form. *S. P. Griffiths* **44**

ELUSIVE SUE (USA) 2 b. or br.f. (Jan 31) Elusive Quality (USA) – Show Me The Stage (USA) (Slew The Surgeon (USA)) [2009 5d 5m^{2} 6m^{2} 6m 6m* Sep 15] $80,000Y: rather leggy filly: fifth foal: closely related/half-sister to several winners in USA: dam US Grade 3 winning sprinter: fair performer: won maiden at Haydock in September: stays 6f: got worked up before running poorly fourth start. *R. A. Fahey* **76**

ELUSIVE TRADER (USA) 2 b. or br.c. (May 3) Elusive Quality (USA) – Kumari Continent (USA) 114 (Kris S (USA)) [2009 p5g^{2} p6g^{3} 5m* Sep 16] $55,000Y, 160,000 2-y-o: useful-looking colt: fourth foal: dam US Grade 2 9f winner: similar form all 3 starts, winning maiden at Beverley readily: should stay 7f. *R. Hannon* **75**

ELUSIVE WARRIOR (USA) 6 b.g. Elusive Quality (USA) – Love To Fight (CAN) (Fit To Fight (USA)) [2009 78: f7s^{3} f7d^{4} f7g^{4} f7g f6g^{4} 7m f7g^{6} f7m^{2} f7m^{2} Dec 15] rangy gelding: just fair at 6 yrs: best at 6f/7f: acts on all-weather and firm ground: wears cheekpieces: often front runner. *A. J. McCabe* **– a70**

ELUSIVE WAVE (IRE) 3 b.f. Elusive City (USA) 117 – Multicolour Wave (IRE) (Rainbow Quest (USA) 134) [2009 107: 7g* 8m* 8f^{4} 8d^{2} 8g Sep 6] **120**

Not only were both winners of the fillies' classics in France trained by Jean-Claude Rouget and ridden by Christophe Lemaire, but they also raced in the same colours. The orange, large royal blue spots belong to Martin Schwartz, who made his fortune trading stocks, futures and options and wrote *Pit Bull: Lessons From Wall Street's Champion Day Trader*. Schwartz would also be better qualified than most to give lessons on purchasing racehorses, judged on the success he has enjoyed with Elusive Wave and Stacelita. The former won the Poule d'Essai des Pouliches seven months after Schwartz had paid €660,000 for her at the Arc Sale; while he purchased a half share in Stacelita shortly before she won the Prix de Diane.

Schwartz is Elusive Wave's third owner. The filly first changed hands, moved from Richard Hannon to Rouget, after making an impressive winning debut in a two-year-old maiden at Goodwood. She was bought by Marc de Chambure who aimed her at a listed race named in memory of his father. Elusive Wave landed the Prix Roland de Chambure at Longchamp before going on to complete her hat-trick in the Prix du Calvados at Deauville. On her final start at two, which came the day after the Arc Sale, Elusive Wave showed further improvement to finish runner-up to Proportional in the Prix Marcel Boussac at Longchamp. Elusive Wave had one run between the Marcel Boussac and the Pouliches, making all to win the Prix Imprudence at Maisons-Laffitte in April by two lengths from Entre Deux Eaux. Elusive Wave went to Longchamp with better credentials than most in the eleven-runner field and was one of only three at single-figure odds on the pari-mutuel, impressive Nell Gwyn winner Fantasia a short-priced favourite ahead of Proportional, who had finished third behind Elusive Wave's stablemate Tamazirte on her reappearance in the Prix de la Grotte. Front-running tactics were again

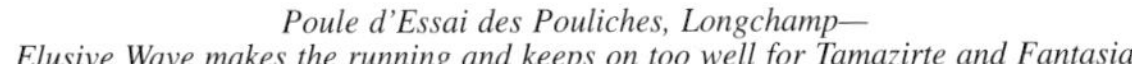
Poule d'Essai des Pouliches, Longchamp—
Elusive Wave makes the running and keeps on too well for Tamazirte and Fantasia

employed on Elusive Wave with Lemaire allowed to dictate matters. Asked to quicken in the straight, she responded well and held on to win by half a length from Tamazirte, with Fantasia and Proportional third and fourth. Elusive Wave failed to give her running when chasing a strong pace on very firm ground in the Coronation Stakes at Royal Ascot on her next start, but then finished a good second to Goldikova in the Prix Rothschild at Deauville, where she was ridden with more restraint than usual, no match for the winner but pulling three lengths clear of the remainder. Things didn't go so well for Elusive Wave afterwards and her season ended on a low note. Favourite for the Prix du Moulin de Longchamp, Elusive Wave banged her nose as her stall opened and then refused to race. Elusive Wave, who appeared most genuine previously, subsequently passed a stalls test before she was due to contest the Prix de la Foret at the beginning of October. However, she reportedly wasn't well in the lead up to the Foret and had to be scratched. She is set to return to action in 2010.

Elusive Wave (IRE) (b.f. 2006)	Elusive City (USA) (b 2000)	Elusive Quality (b 1993)	Gone West
			Touch of Greatness
		Star of Paris (b or br 1995)	Dayjur
			Liturgism
	Multicolour Wave (IRE) (b 1998)	Rainbow Quest (b 1981)	Blushing Groom
			I Will Follow
		Echoes (b 1987)	Niniski
			Equal Honor

Elusive Wave's sire Elusive City was a smart two-year-old who won the Prix Morny, though he wasn't at all straightforward, often proving troublesome in the preliminaries. Elusive Wave's dam Multicolour Wave, who didn't show much in a couple of runs on the Flat in France, was sold for only 11,500 guineas at the December Sales in 2001. She was looking a bargain even before her fourth foal Elusive Wave began to make a name for herself, her previous offspring Million Waves (by Mull of Kintyre), Million Spirits (by Invincible Spirit) and Photophore (by Clodovil) all fairly useful winners by that time, the first two in Ireland and the last-named in France. Multicolour Wave's remarkable run was continued by Wealdmore Wave, her two-year-old colt by Oratorio who won a maiden at Navan in April. The well-bred Multicolour Wave, a half-sister to four winners and also to the dam of the 2008 Queen Mary winner Langs Lash, is a daughter of the Prix Corrida winner Echoes. Elusive Wave, a tall, rather unfurnished filly who should stay beyond a mile, acts on good to firm and good to soft going. *J-C. Rouget, France*

ELVIRA MADIGAN 2 b.f. (Jan 24) Sakhee (USA) 136 – Santa Isobel 94 (Nashwan (USA) 135) [2009 p8m^4 p8m^3 p8f^3 Dec 16] fourth foal: half-sister to 2 winners, including 4-y-o Isabelonabicycle: dam 1¼m winner: fair maiden: bred to be suited by 1¼m+: raced only on polytrack. *A. M. Balding* **74**

EMAIL EXIT (IRE) 2 ch.c. (Apr 12) Titus Livius (FR) 115 – Christoph's Girl 50 (Efisio 120) [2009 5g 6s 6m 5g 6.1s^4 a9.5g a9.5g^3 Dec 24] good-topped colt: modest maiden: sold from C. Wall 4,200 gns after fifth start: stays 9.5f: acts on all-weather at Deauville and soft going. *Mme G. Rarick, France* **54**

EMBRA (IRE) 4 b.g. Monashee Mountain (USA) 115 – Ivory Turner (Efisio 120) [2009 79p: 5m 5.9m 5m p6m^3 6g p5m^3 p6g f5f^2 Nov 24] strong-quartered gelding: fair handicapper nowadays: should prove best at 5f/6f: raced on polytrack and good/good to firm going: none too consistent. *T. J. Etherington* **67**

EMBSAY CRAG 3 b.g. Elmaamul (USA) 125 – Wigman Lady (IRE) 64 (Tenby 125) [2009 71: 7.5m^4 8m^6 8.5g^5 10.3g* 12.3m^5 10.4s^2 11.9g^4 10.3m* 12m^4 10.4g^3 10.3g Oct 23] smallish gelding: fairly useful handicapper: won at Chester in June and August: stays 1½m: acts on soft and good to firm going: usually races prominently: has raced keenly/missed break: consistent. *Mrs K. Walton* **88**

EMEEBEE 3 b.g. Medicean 128 – Broughtons Motto 75 (Mtoto 134) [2009 75p: p8g 7g^3 p7.1g^3 Nov 12] fairly useful performer: best efforts when third in handicaps: should be suited by 1m. *W. J. Musson* **83**

EMERALDA 3 b.f. Desert Prince (IRE) 130 – Edouna (FR) (Doyoun 124) [2009 10.2m^6 10.2g Apr 28] third foal: half-sister to 6-y-o Enthusius: dam French 1¼m/1½m winner: down the field in maidens. *Pat Eddery* **51**

EMERALD COMMANDER (IRE) 2 b.c. (Mar 22) Pivotal 124 – Brigitta (IRE) (Sadler's Wells (USA) 132) [2009 7g^4 7s* 7m^2 8.1v* 8s^2 Nov 1] 40,000Y, £72,000 2-y-o: **115**

strong colt: fifth foal: half-brother to 2007 2-y-o 7f winner Albaraari (by Green Desert): dam, French 9.5f/10.5f winner, sister to Racing Post Trophy winner Commander Collins and closely related to Breeders' Cup Sprint winner Lit de Justice and 2000 Guineas/ Derby third Colonel Collins; smart performer: won maiden at Newbury in July and listed race at Haydock (beat Nideeb readily by 2½ lengths) in September: best effort when head second to Elusive Pimpernel in Acomb Stakes at York in between: sold privately and left R. Hannon before respectable 4 lengths second to Jan Vermeer in Criterium International at Saint-Cloud (flashed tail) final start: stays 1m: unraced on firm going, acts on any other. *Saeed bin Suroor*

EMERALD GIRL (IRE) 2 b.f. (Jan 7) Chineur (FR) 123 – Faypool (IRE) (Fayruz 116) [2009 5.9m³ 5m² 5m* 5g³ 6g⁵ 6g* 6g⁴ Oct 9] €5,000Y, €9,000 2-y-o: unfurnished filly: half-sister to several winners, including 2001 2-y-o 7f winner Mr Blue Sky (by Blues Traveller) and 2004 2-y-o 5f winner Dane's Castle (by Danetime), both fairly useful: dam, maiden in Switzerland, half-sister to smart sprinter Croft Pool: fair performer: won maiden at Beverley in July and nursery at Hamilton in September: will be well suited by 7f: raced only on good/good to firm ground. *R. A. Fahey* **76 +**

EMERALD GLADE (IRE) 2 b.f. (Apr 2) Azamour (IRE) 130 – Woodland Glade 72 (Mark of Esteem (IRE) 137) [2009 6g⁶ 7d 6m 7.5m⁵ Sep 16] 16,000Y: tall, angular filly: has scope: second foal: dam, ran 3 times (stayed 1m), half-sister to smart sprinter Baron's Pit: best effort in maidens when fifth to Silent Secret at Beverley: will be suited by 1m+: type to make better 3-y-o. *T. D. Easterby* **55 p**

EMERALD HAWK (IRE) 3 b. or br.c. Hawk Wing (USA) 136 – Fabulous Pet (Somethingfabulous (USA)) [2009 10m 7g 7.5m 11.6d 18g⁵ Oct 19] sturdy colt: well held in varied company: trained by S. Parr on debut: visored/blinkered last 3 starts. *D. H. Brown* **–**

EMERALD ROCK (CAN) 4 b.g. Johannesburg (USA) 127 – Classic Jones (CAN) (Regal Classic (CAN)) [2009 p9.5g⁴ p8g⁶ p9.5g⁴ p12.2g 10g⁵ Oct 16] big, rangy gelding: fair maiden: trained by N. Vaughan first 3 outings (gelded after): should be suited by 1½m: acts on polytrack: in cheekpieces last 2 starts. *Tom Dascombe* **65**

EMERALDS SPIRIT (IRE) 2 b.f. (Jan 28) Rock of Gibraltar (IRE) 133 – Spiritual Air 93 (Royal Applause 124) [2009 5g⁶ 6g 7d⁶ 5g⁶ 8m⁵ Sep 24] 23,000Y: close-coupled filly: second foal: half-sister to 3-y-o Andean Margin: dam, 2-y-o 6f winner (stayed 1m), half-sister to useful sprinter Mystical Land: maiden: disappointing after debut. *J. R. Weymes* **56 d**

EMERALD WILDERNESS (IRE) 5 b.g. Green Desert (USA) 127 – Simla Bibi 69 (Indian Ridge 123) [2009 105: p12g² p11g* 9m⁶ 10m 10g* Jul 25] tall, sparely-made gelding: useful handicapper, better on all-weather: won at Kempton (beat John Terry by neck) in February and Newmarket in July: free-going sort, but stays 1½m: acts on polytrack, good to firm and good to soft ground: effective blinkered or not. *A. King* **98** **a106**

EMILY BLAKE (IRE) 5 b.m. Lend A Hand 124 – Kirri (IRE) (Lycius (USA) 124) [2009 110: 6s² 5d 7v* 8v* 8g⁶ Jun 28] medium-sized mare: smart performer: won Oratorio EBF Athasi Stakes (by 1¾ lengths from Mad About You) and Tri Equestrian Stakes (by ½ length from Beach Bunny), both at the Curragh in May: below form in listed race there final outing: effective at 6f to 1m: acts on polytrack and heavy going: usually races close up: sometimes carries head awkwardly: reportedly in foal to Invincible Spirit. *J. C. Hayden, Ireland* **115**

EMILY HARLEY (IRE) 3 b.f. Sulamani (IRE) 130 – Princess Bankes 44 (Vettori (IRE) 119) [2009 a7.5g 7.8g 9s 11g 14.5d³ a12g 15g⁶ 17.2g⁵ Oct 21] first foal: dam, maiden (stayed 1½m), half-sister to useful sprinter Danzili Bay: modest maiden: left E. Danel in France prior to final start: stays 15f: acts on good to soft ground. *W. G. M. Turner* **56**

EMIRATES CHAMPION 3 b.c. Haafhd 129 – Janaat 74 (Kris 135) [2009 91p: 11.1g⁵ 10g* Oct 23] useful form: off 5 months and tongue tied, much improved when winning handicap at Ayr in October impressively by 6 lengths from Charlie Tokyo: stays 1¼m: raced only on polytrack and good going: smart prospect. *Saeed bin Suroor* **106 p**

EMIRATESDOTCOM 3 b.g. Pivotal 124 – Teggiano (IRE) 108 (Mujtahid (USA) 118) [2009 9m 8d 8g 15.4m Sep 22] angular gelding: poor form. *M. Johnston* **42**

EMIRATES DREAM (USA) 2 b.c. (Feb 18) Kingmambo (USA) 125 – My Boston Gal (USA) 108 (Boston Harbor (USA) 122) [2009 7m* 7g⁴ 8g³ 8m³ Oct 16] $850,000Y: strong, lengthy colt: second foal: dam US Grade 2 7f and (at 2 yrs) 8.5f winner: useful performer: won maiden at York in July: much better form at Longchamp next 2 starts, fourth to Buzzword in Prix La Rochette then very good 1½ lengths third of 5 to Behkabad in Prix des Chenes (headed only well inside final 1f): seemed to go off too hard when **104**

below form in minor event at Newmarket final start: stays 1m: looks type to train on well. *Saeed bin Suroor*

EMIRATES HILLS 2 b.f. (Apr 4) Dubawi (IRE) 129 – Starstone (Diktat 126) [2009 6g5 7g 6f* 6.5m 6m Sep 21] 55,000Y: small filly: first foal: dam unraced half-sister to high-class 6f/7f performers Goodricke and Pastoral Pursuits: fair performer: won maiden at Windsor in August: creditable seventh in nursery at Doncaster next time: should stay 7f: visored (weakened tamely) final start. *E. F. Vaughan* **76**

EMIRATES ROADSHOW (USA) 3 ch.g. Distorted Humor (USA) 117 – Just A Bird (USA) (Storm Bird (CAN) 134) [2009 95p: 8.3g2 8g3 8m 10m 8.5m2 9g Aug 30] strong, rangy gelding: fairly useful handicapper: placed 3 times in 2009 (also seventh in Britannia Stakes at Royal Ascot): gelded after fourth outing: stays 8.5f: raced only on good/good to firm going: races prominently. *Saeed bin Suroor* **93**

EMIRATES SPORTS 3 b.c. King's Best (USA) 132 – Time Saved 89 (Green Desert (USA) 127) [2009 97p: p8g* 7.1m5 8m3 Aug 8] close-coupled colt: fairly useful performer, lightly raced: won handicap at Kempton (by short head from Nice To Know) in July: respectable efforts after: will stay 1¼m: both wins on polytrack: has left Godolphin. *Saeed bin Suroor* **94**

EMIRATES WORLD (IRE) 3 b.g. Exceed And Excel (AUS) 126 – Enrich (USA) 103 (Dynaformer (USA)) [2009 72: p7g* p7g5 f7g5 Mar 22] strong, well-made gelding: fair performer: left Saeed bin Suroor and gelded, improved when winning maiden at Lingfield in January: stays 1m: acts on polytrack: tried visored: sold £7,500 in April. *M. Johnston* **72**

EMMA DORA (IRE) 2 b.f. (Apr 14) Medaglia d'Oro (USA) 129 – My Girl Lisa (USA) (With Approval (CAN)) [2009 6m 6g5 6d* 6g6 8g p8m 8.3d5 7d6 p8.6g6 Nov 12] £17,000 2-y-o: small, leggy filly: third foal: half-sister to winners in USA by Point Given and Sky Mesa: dam US 5f winner, including at 2 yrs: modest performer: best effort when winning maiden at Newmarket in June: stays 6f: acts on good to soft going: temperament under suspicion. *D. R. C. Elsworth* **64**

EMMA JEAN LASS (IRE) 2 b.f. (Jan 17) Choisir (AUS) 126 – Enlisted (IRE) 83 (Sadler's Wells (USA) 132) [2009 p5g2 5m6 5.1g4 5.7g2 6m 6d p6g3 f6g Dec 27] 11,000F, £12,000Y: smallish filly: half-sister to several winners, including 6-y-o Mull of Dubai: dam 1¼m winner: modest maiden: left J. S. Moore after sixth start: stays 5.7f: acts on polytrack, best turf efforts on good ground. *P. D. Evans* **64**

EMMROOZ 4 b.c. Red Ransom (USA) – Nasmatt 96 (Danehill (USA) 126) [2009 9g2 8.3m2 Jun 3] well-made, attractive colt: useful performer: missed 2008: improved in 2009, second in handicap at Nad Al Sheba (beaten ¾ length by Bankable) and minor event at Nottingham (went down by 1¼ lengths to Khateeb): stays 9f: acts on good to firm and good to soft going: has joined D. Selvaratnam in UAE. *Saeed bin Suroor* **109**

EMOTIVE 6 b.g. Pursuit of Love 124 – Ruby Julie (Clantime 101) [2009 13v5 Aug 24] leggy gelding: handicapper: well held sole Flat start in 2009: tried blinkered/in cheekpieces: poor hurdler. *F. P. Murtagh* **–**

EMPEROR CLAUDIUS (USA) 2 b.c. (Jan 11) Giant's Causeway (USA) 132 – Virginia Waters (USA) 116 (Kingmambo (USA) 125) [2009 6g3 6m* 7m2 7m6 7m6 Sep 12] $35,000Y: smallish colt: first foal: dam 7f (at 2 yrs)/1m (1000 Guineas) winner: useful performer: won maiden at Fairyhouse in June: good short-head second to Big Audio in listed Chesham Stakes at Royal Ascot: below form in Superlative Stakes at Newmarket and Champagne Stakes at Doncaster last 2 starts: should stay 1m. *A. P. O'Brien, Ireland* **102**

EMPEROR COURT (IRE) 5 ch.h. Singspiel (IRE) 133 – Tarquina (USA) (Niniski (USA) 125) [2009 90: p9.5g p10g p10g5 10.4m* 9.9m4 10m3 10.1m5 p8g3 p8.6g5 Oct 16] tall horse: fairly useful handicapper: won at Haydock in June: should stay 1½m: acts on polytrack and firm going: front runner: consistent: sold 26,000 gns in October, sent to Sweden. *P. J. Makin* **92**

EMPEROR'S WELL 10 ch.g. First Trump 118 – Catherines Well 99 (Junius (USA) 124) [2009 66: 8.3m 8g 8.5m 8m 8m 7.9g2 8.5m4 9.9g5 p8.6g5 p9.5g3 Oct 29] well-made gelding: just modest handicapper in 2009: stays 1¼m: acts on all-weather, heavy and good to firm going: tried visored, often blinkered. *M. W. Easterby* **57**

EMPIRE SEEKER (USA) 4 b.g. Seeking The Gold (USA) – Lady From Shanghai (USA) (Storm Cat (USA)) [2009 –: p10g p11g 8.1g p10g6 Aug 1] sturdy gelding: modest maiden: could prove best at 1m: tried in cheekpieces. *Mrs H. S. Main* **56**

EMPOWERED (IRE) 4 b.c. Fasliyev (USA) 120 – Funsie (FR) (Saumarez 132) [2009 91p: p9.5g2 10.3g* 12.3m* May 8] compact colt: has a quick action: useful form: **96**

won handicaps at Doncaster (apprentices) and Chester (dead-heated with Red Merlin, doing well after looking green when that rival swept by over 2f out), both in May: stays 1½m: acts on polytrack and good to firm going: sold 25,000 gns in December. *W. J. Haggas*

EMPRESS LEIZU (IRE) 2 b.f. (Apr 14) Chineur (FR) 123 – Silk Point (IRE) **50**
(Barathea (IRE) 127) [2009 8g p8g p8m p8.6g* Dec 7] 12,500Y: fourth foal: half-sister to 2 winners, including 5-y-o All of Me: dam unraced out of smart performer up to 1¼m Scimitarra: modest form: won claimer at Wolverhampton (claimed £5,000) in December, dictating: stays 8.6f: acts on polytrack. *E. A. L. Dunlop*

EMPRESSOFBOOGIE 2 b.f. (May 1) Tobougg (IRE) 125 – Akhira 90 (Emperor **52**
Jones (USA) 119) [2009 6m^{4} 6s^{4} 7.1m^{5} p8.6g Oct 1] 10,500Y: unfurnished filly: fourth living foal: half-sister to useful 5f winner (including at 2 yrs) Empress Jain (by Lujain) and 4-y-o Another Decree: dam, 7f winner, out of half-sister to smart 6f/7f performer Danehill Dancer: modest maiden: well held in seller/claimer last 2 starts: should stay 7f. *M. Dods*

EMULOUS 2 b.f. (Apr 28) Dansili 127 – Aspiring Diva (USA) (Distant View (USA) **84 P**
126) [2009 7s* Oct 12] fourth foal: sister to useful French 2005 2-y-o 5f/5.5f winner Daring Diva and half-sister to 2 winners, including 4-y-o Striking Spirit: dam, fairly useful French 5f/6.5f winner (latter at 2 yrs), out of US Grade 2 8.5f winner Queen of Song: 10/1, won 28-runner maiden at the Curragh by length from Dance Hall Girl, challenging on bridle 1f out and not at all hard pressed to assert: should stay 1m: open to considerable improvement and type to make her mark in pattern company. *D. K. Weld, Ireland*

ENACT 3 b.f. Kyllachy 129 – Constitute (USA) 85 (Gone West (USA)) [2009 82p: 6m^{2} **104**
7m 7.1v 6g 7d^{5} 6.1g* 7s^{2} 6m^{2} 6m^{3} Oct 16] rather leggy, attractive filly: useful performer: much improved when winning handicap at Nottingham in August by 2¾ lengths from Bobbie Soxer: good placed efforts after, 1¼ lengths third to Damaniyat Girl in listed race at Newmarket on final occasion: may prove best at 6f: acts on soft and good to firm going: stays in training. *Sir Michael Stoute*

ENCIRCLED 5 b.m. In The Wings 128 – Ring of Esteem (Mark of Esteem (IRE) 137) **95**
[2009 86, a96: p12g^{6} p12g^{2} 10.3m^{3} p10g 11.6m^{5} p12m Oct 12] sturdy mare: useful performer: best efforts in 2009 when placed in handicaps at Kempton and Doncaster: well below form after: stays 1½m: acts on polytrack, good to firm and good to soft ground (not on soft): travels strongly held up. *J. R. Jenkins*

ENCOMPASSING (IRE) 2 b.c. (Feb 22) Montjeu (IRE) 137 – Sophisticat (USA) 117 **92 p**
(Storm Cat (USA)) [2009 7.5m^{2} 6g^{2} Oct 18] fourth foal: half-brother to smart French 1m/8.5f winner Sefroua (by Kingmambo) and Irish 3-y-o Pursuit of Glory: dam, 6f (at 2 yrs) and 1m (Coronation Stakes) winner, out of multiple US Grade 1 winner Serena's Song: much better effort when 1¼ lengths second to Utrillo in minor event at Tipperary: again odds on, seemed unsuited by drop in trip: should stay 1m+: capable of better. *A. P. O'Brien, Ireland*

ENCORE BELLE 4 b.f. Beat Hollow 126 – Rada's Daughter 107 (Robellino (USA) **62**
127) [2009 64: p10g^{6} 10.9m^{3} 10m^{6} 10.2m 11.7f^{6} 9.7m 10.2g^{6} Jul 23] medium-sized filly: modest maiden: should stay 1½m: acts on good to firm and good to soft going: visored final outing. *Mouse Hamilton-Fairley*

ENDEAVOURED (IRE) 3 b.g. Peintre Celebre (USA) 137 – Addaya (IRE) (Persian **–**
Bold 123) [2009 47: 11.9d Oct 15] well held in maidens/seller (wore blinkers/tongue tie in latter). *D. Carroll*

ENDERBY SPIRIT (GR) 3 gr.c. Invincible Spirit (IRE) 121 – Arctic Ice (IRE) 82 **108**
(Zafonic (USA) 130) [2009 101: 6m^{4} 6m^{2} 6d^{6} 6m* 6g^{3} 6d 6m 6g Oct 10] tall colt: useful performer: won handicap at Haydock in July by neck from Servoca: good length third to Total Gallery in quite valuable similar event at Newmarket 4 days later, but below form after: speedy, will prove best at 5f/6f: unraced on extremes of going. *B. Smart*

EN FUEGO 2 b.c. (Mar 16) Firebreak 125 – Yanomami (USA) 71 (Slew O' Gold **79 +**
(USA)) [2009 6m 7d^{3} Oct 27] 8,000F, £32,000Y: close-coupled colt: half-brother to several winners, including fairly useful 5f (including at 2 yrs)/6f winner Mirasol Princess (by Ali-Royal) and 6f/7f winner (including at 2 yrs) Fractured Foxy (by Foxhound): dam 6f winner: easily better effort in maidens when close third to London Stripe at Yarmouth, bumped at start and racing freely close up: probably a sprinter. *P. W. Chapple-Hyam*

ENGLAND (IRE) 2 b.c. (Feb 17) Bertolini (USA) 125 – Radha (Bishop of Cashel 122) **50**
[2009 6g^{5} 5m^{5} 6m^{6} Jun 27] sturdy colt: modest form in minor event/maidens. *N. P. Littmoden*

ENGLISH ARCHER 6 b.g. Rock City 120 – Fire Sprite 83 (Mummy's Game 120) [2009 14.1m 12.1v 16d 16.1d 9.9g Sep 22] leggy gelding: handicapper: no form in 2009: tried in cheekpieces/tongue tie. *A. Kirtley* –

ENGLISH CITY (IRE) 6 ch.h. City On A Hill (USA) 114 – Toledana (IRE) (Sure Blade (USA) 130) [2009 56: 14g³ 13.1d⁵ Aug 27] sturdy horse: modest performer, very lightly raced on Flat since 2006: stays 1¾m: best on good going or firmer: tried in cheekpieces: fairly useful hurdler. *Mrs L. B. Normile* 57 +

ENGULF (IRE) 2 b.c. (Mar 2) Danehill Dancer (IRE) 117 – All Embracing (IRE) 82 (Night Shift (USA)) [2009 6m⁵ Aug 15] €260,000Y: second foal: dam, 7f winner, half-sister to smart 1¼m performer Highdown: 7/1 and very green, 9 lengths fifth to Arabian Pride in maiden at Newmarket, slowly away and hanging left: will stay 7f: should improve. *W. J. Haggas* 53 p

ENHANCING 3 b.f. Hawk Wing (USA) 136 – Enhance (Entrepreneur 123) [2009 65: 10.3g p7.1g³ 8s⁶ 7g p7.1g 7m p9.5g⁴ Oct 15] sturdy filly: modest maiden: left A. McCabe after third start: stays 9.5f: tried in cheekpieces/visor/tongue tie: sold £800, sent to Belgium. *J. A. Glover* 59

ENJOYMENT 2 b.f. (Apr 19) Dansili 127 – Have Fun (Indian Ridge 123) [2009 7g⁴ 7g Aug 5] workmanlike filly: fourth foal: half-sister to Irish 4-y-o Nice Dream: dam, French 7.5f/11f winner, out of close relative/half-sister to US Grade 1 9f winners Corrazona and Thirty Six Red: encouraging 2¾ lengths fourth to Celestial Tryst in maiden at Doncaster: raced freely/finished tamely (reportedly injured pelvis) next time. *M. L. W. Bell* 67

ENJOY THE MOMENT 6 b.g. Generous (IRE) 139 – Denial (Sadler's Wells (USA) 132) [2009 101: 17.2m⁶ 18m Oct 17] sturdy gelding: useful handicapper, lightly raced since 2007: better effort in 2009 when 8 lengths sixth to Callisto Moon at Bath on reappearance: stays 2¾m: acts on soft and good to firm going: held up. *J. A. Osborne* 96

ENLIGHTENMENT (IRE) 9 b.g. Presenting 120 – Shaiybaniyda 74 (He Loves Me 120) [2009 p13g* 12g Jul 21] fairly useful hurdler/useful chaser: fair form when winning maiden at Lingfield in February on belated Flat debut: stays 13f: acts on polytrack. *Evan Williams* 74

ENLIST 5 b.g. Beat Hollow 126 – Dawna 106 (Polish Precedent (USA) 131) [2009 p9.5g³ p9.5g⁶ Apr 4] well beaten at 3 yrs for A. Fabre in France (no encouragement over hurdles for Mary Meek): fair form in maidens on Flat in 2009: should be suited by 1¼m+: raced on polytrack in Britain. *A. J. Lidderdale* 68

ENROLLER (IRE) 4 b.c. Marju (IRE) 127 – Walk On Quest (FR) (Rainbow Quest (USA) 134) [2009 110: 12s* 12m⁴ 12m⁶ 16g⁵ 16.4m⁵ 12g⁶ 12v Oct 24] good-bodied colt: smart performer: won Dubai Tennis Championships Stakes (John Porter) at Newbury in April by 1½ lengths from Centennial: best effort after when 5 lengths sixth to Jukebox Jury in Preis von Europa at Cologne sixth outing: stays 2m, effective at 1½m given good test: acts on firm ground, all wins on softer than good. *W. R. Muir* 112

ENSIGN'S TRICK 5 b.m. Cayman Kai (IRE) 114 – River Ensign 63 (River God (USA) 121) [2009 63§: 8g Oct 20] smallish, strong mare: regressive form: well held sole start in 2009: unreliable. *W. M. Brisbourne* – §

ENSNARE 4 b.g. Pivotal 124 – Entrap (USA) 106 (Phone Trick (USA)) [2009 p8g p10g⁴ p9.5g⁶ p8.6g* 9.1g* 10m 8.3m p8m* p8g² p8.6g⁶ Dec 4] 10,500 3-y-o: medium-sized gelding: first foal: dam 6f winner (including at 2 yrs): fairly useful handicapper: left A. Hales, won at Wolverhampton in June, Ayr in July and Kempton in November: should stay 1¼m: acts on polytrack. *Ian Williams* 81

ENTHUSIUS 6 b.g. Generous (IRE) 139 – Edouna (FR) (Doyoun 124) [2009 p14g⁵ 11.6m 16m 16d Oct 11] lengthy gelding: poor handicapper: stays 2m: acts on polytrack: tried blinkered. *G. L. Moore* 49

ENTICEMENT 3 b.f. Montjeu (IRE) 137 – Ecoutila (USA) (Rahy (USA) 115) [2009 102p: 10.4m³ 12m 10m* 10.5s Oct 28] lengthy filly: useful performer: won listed race at Newmarket in October by short head from Pachattack: creditable efforts otherwise in 2009, including when 7¼ lengths third to Sariska in Musidora Stakes at York on reappearance: should be suited by 1½m: acts on soft and good to firm going. *Sir Michael Stoute* 102

ENTREAT 3 ch.f. Pivotal 124 – River Saint (USA) 73§ (Irish River (FR) 131) [2009 62p: 10m³ 9.9f³ 11.9g⁵ p10g³ 9.7m* 10d³ 8.1m Sep 25] big filly: fairly useful performer: improved when winning maiden at Folkestone in August: stays 1¼m: acts on polytrack, firm and good to soft going: visored last 3 starts. *Sir Michael Stoute* 87

EOLITH 2 ch.f. (Apr 22) Pastoral Pursuits 127 – Evening Guest (FR) (Be My Guest (USA) 126) [2009 7g* p7g* Sep 4] third foal: half-sister to Irish 4-y-o Eventide: dam, 99 p unraced, out of close relative to very smart German 1¼m/11f performer Epalo: won maiden at Newmarket (by short head and 2¾ lengths from Pollenator and Hibaayeb, both subsequent pattern-race winners) in August and minor event at Kempton (beat Arte Viva comfortably by length, showing good turn of foot): should be suited by 1m: already useful, and should do better still. *W. J. Knight*

EPIC (IRE) 2 b.g. (May 25) Celtic Swing 138 – Needwood Epic 61 (Midyan (USA) 124) [2009 7m⁶ p7g⁵ 7.5m* p8.6g³ p8.6g p8.6g³ Dec 18] €20,000Y: big gelding: seventh foal: half-brother to several winners, including smart 7f (at 2 yrs)/1m winner Yasoodd (by Inchinor) and useful French 1m (including at 2 yrs)/1¼m winner Gript (by First Trump): dam 1¾m winner: fair performer: won maiden at Beverley in September: good third in nursery at Wolverhampton next time: will be suited by 1¼m: acts on polytrack and good to firm ground. *M. Johnston* **77**

EPIC ODYSSEY 4 ch.g. Dubai Destination (USA) 127 – Royal Gift (Cadeaux Genereux 131) [2009 93: p6g² p6g* p6g³ 6g May 28] strong, lengthy gelding: fairly useful performer: won claimer at Kempton (left J. Boyle £12,000) in February: claimed from J. Gask £9,000 after next start: effective at 5f to easy 7f: acts on polytrack, firm and good to soft going: tried in cheekpieces: usually races close up. *L. Smyth, Ireland* **84**

EPIDAURIAN KING (IRE) 6 b.g. King's Best (USA) 132 – Thurayya (Nashwan (USA) 135) [2009 71: p11g⁵ p9.5g⁶ p12g² p12.2g⁵ 9.9m 7.5m 12g⁶ May 23] fair handicapper: free-going sort, though seemingly stays easy 1½m (effective at much shorter): acts on polytrack: has been visored: held up. *D. Shaw* **64**

EPSOM SALTS 4 b.g. Josr Algarhoud (IRE) 118 – Captive Heart (Conquistador Cielo (USA)) [2009 81: 15.4g 16g 16.4m⁴ 11.6g 12m* 13.3g⁵ 11.9f⁴ 12m* 12m³ 12m* 18m³ 12m Oct 3] medium-sized gelding: fairly useful handicapper: better than ever in 2009, winning at Epsom in July, August (ladies event) and September (jump jockeys event): effective at 1½m, seemingly stays 2¼m: acts on polytrack and good to firm going: usually held up. *P. M. Phelan* **85**

EQUIANO (FR) 4 b.c. Acclamation 118 – Entente Cordiale (IRE) 72 (Ela-Mana-Mou 132) [2009 121: 6m² 6m 5m 5m 6m 5g 5m 6d⁵ 5g Oct 4] well-made colt: very smart performer at 3 yrs, winning King's Stand Stakes at Royal Ascot (reportedly found to have stress fracture of tibia after final outing): disappointing in 2009, just useful form when ½-length second to Tax Free in listed race at Newmarket on reappearance: best at 5f/6f: acts on any going: blinkered fourth/fifth outings: usually races prominently/makes running. *B. W. Hills* **109**

EQUININE (IRE) 3 ch.f. Namid 128 – Goldilocks (IRE) (Caerleon (USA) 132) [2009 70: 7m³ 7g 7s³ p7g² 6g* 6m² p7m p6g Nov 12] rather leggy filly: fair performer: won maiden at Redcar in September: left B. Hills prior to final start: stays 7f: acts on polytrack and good to firm going, probably on soft. *Peter Grayson* **78**

EQUINITY 3 b.f. Ishiguru (USA) 114 – Notable Lady (IRE) 95 (Victory Note (USA) 120) [2009 60?: f5g⁶ p6g 5.3f⁴ 5g 6m* 6m p6g p6m⁵ p6m p6m² Dec 30] workmanlike filly: modest handicapper: won at Folkestone in August: best efforts at 6f: acts on polytrack and good to firm going: tongue tied nowadays: none too consistent. *J. Pearce* **53**

EQUIPE DE NUIT 3 ch.c. Sulamani (IRE) 130 – Denica (IRE) (Night Shift (USA)) [2009 80: p7g⁶ 10.4m 10.1g 10m⁶ 9.7f³ 10.1m² 9g³ 10.1g⁴ p8g⁴ 8m⁵ 7m* 6m 7m Oct 13] close-coupled, workmanlike colt: fair performer: won seller at Leicester in September: stays 1¼m: acts on polytrack and firm going, unraced on softer than good: makes running. *S. C. Williams* **76**

EQUULEUS PICTOR 5 br.g. Piccolo 121 – Vax Rapide 80 (Sharpo 132) [2009 88: 5m 5d⁴ 5v* 5d* 5m⁵ 5g⁶ 5d 5d 5g³ 5g⁴ 5d f5g² f5d³ Dec 29] tall gelding: useful handicapper: won at Haydock in May and York (beat Kay Two 1½ lengths) in June: best at 5f: acts on fibresand and heavy going: often front runner. *J. L. Spearing* **96**

EREBUS (IRE) 2 b.c. (Apr 4) Fasliyev (USA) 120 – Velvet Slipper 50 (Muhtafal (USA)) [2009 6d p7m p7.1g⁶ Dec 28] angular colt: modest form in maidens: stays 7f. *S. Kirk* **61**

EREEFORD 3 b.g. Ishiguru (USA) 114 – Miss Twiddles (IRE) (Desert King (IRE) 129) [2009 f5g⁶ f7g Apr 23] well held in maidens at Southwell. *M. W. Easterby* **–**

ERFAAN (USA) 2 b. or br.c. (Jan 13) Forest Camp (USA) 114 – Look For Good (USA) (Unbridled's Song (USA) 125) [2009 6m 7g Jul 8] good-bodied, attractive colt: fair form in well-contested maidens at Newbury and Newmarket (eighth to Elusive Pimpernel): sold 8,000 gns in October. *B. W. Hills* **65**

ERGO (FR) 5 br.h. Grand Lodge (USA) 125 – Erhawah (Mark of Esteem (IRE) 137) [2009 55: p8.6g* p8.6g* 7m² 8.3g* 8g⁵ 10.1d⁴ 8.1s 8m p8.6g⁴ Sep 12] fair handicapper: won at Wolverhampton in February and March, and Hamilton (jump jockeys event) in May: stays 1¼m: acts on polytrack, good to firm and good to soft going: wears headgear. *James Moffatt* **77**

ERINJAY (IRE) 3 b.g. Bachelor Duke (USA) 122 – Quinella (Generous (IRE) 139) [2009 p5.1g p8f* Dec 20] €3,000F, €6,000Y, £7,000 2-y-o: sixth foal: closely related to 7-y-o Surwaki: dam twice-raced half-sister to very smart middle-distance stayer Banket and to dam of Pentire: off 9½ months, better effort when winning maiden at Kempton in December by 3½ lengths from Charlie Smirke, always prominent and staying on well: will stay 1¼m: should continue to progress. *M. Wigham* **75 p**

ERMINE AND VELVET 3 ch.f. Nayef (USA) 129 – Ermine (IRE) 86 (Cadeaux Genereux 131) [2009 7s⁴ p8g 7d² 7g² 7.1g 8m 7m² 8m Sep 26] 40,000Y: leggy filly: fifth foal: sister to smart 11f winner Top Lock and half-sister to 2 winners, including 7-y-o Carnivore: dam, 1m winner, half-sister to very smart 1¼m/1½m winner Border Arrow: fairly useful maiden: stays 1m: acts on good to firm and good to soft going: often races prominently. *C. E. Brittain* **87**

ERMINE GREY 8 gr.g. Wolfhound (USA) 126 – Impulsive Decision (IRE) 71 (Nomination 125) [2009 69: p8g⁵ p10g⁵ 8.5g⁵ f8g 8.1d³ p9.5g⁴ Oct 10] rather leggy gelding: fair handicapper: stays 1¼m: acts on all-weather and any turf going: tried in headgear: waited with, and sometimes takes strong hold. *S. Gollings* **68**

ERMINE SEA 6 b.g. Rainbow Quest (USA) 134 – Bint Pasha (USA) 126 (Affirmed (USA)) [2009 16m³ 20m 16g⁶ 15g⁵ Aug 26] angular, quite attractive gelding: fairly useful handicapper: third to Judgethemoment at Ascot, below form after: stays 2m: acts on polytrack, good to firm and good to soft going: tried in blinkers/cheekpieces. *Miss H. C. Knight* **93**

ERMYN EXPRESS 2 b.f. (Jan 31) Selkirk (USA) 129 – Aymara 85 (Darshaan 133) [2009 p7g p8m p6m³ p8f⁴ Dec 20] sixth foal: half-sister to 6-y-o Adage: dam 1½m winner: modest maiden: should stay at least 1m. *P. M. Phelan* **58**

ERMYN LODGE 3 b.c. Singspiel (IRE) 133 – Rosewood Belle (USA) 70 (Woodman (USA) 126) [2009 59: p12g* 11.6g² 14.1f⁵ p16g³ 14g² 14g* p16g² 16m² Sep 30] tall colt: fairly useful handicapper: won at Kempton in March and Sandown in August: further progress when runner-up next 2 starts: stays 2m: acts on polytrack and firm going: has raced lazily, travelled better in visor last 4 starts. *P. M. Phelan* **84**

ERMYNTRUDE 2 b. or br.f. (Feb 20) Rock of Gibraltar (IRE) 133 – Ruthie 72 (Pursuit of Love 124) [2009 p8g⁵ 8d p8m⁴ p7m Dec 6] second foal: dam 2-y-o 7.5f winner: modest form in maidens. *P. M. Phelan* **52**

ERNIES KEEP 3 ch.g. Young Ern 120 – Croeso Cynnes 70 (Most Welcome 131) [2009 –: 9m 9.8m 11.1m⁵ 12.1m 15.8g 14.1m 12.4d Sep 7] small gelding: little form, including in juvenile hurdles: tried in cheekpieces. *W. Storey* **–**

ERRIGAL LAD 4 ch.g. Bertolini (USA) 125 – La Belle Vie 73 (Indian King (USA) 128) [2009 89: 6m² 7g⁵ 7.2g 6m² 6d⁶ 6d⁵ 6d⁶ 6m Aug 31] tall, good-topped gelding: fairly useful handicapper: left K. Ryan £14,000 before final start: effective at 6f/7f: acts on good to firm and good to soft going: often blinkered/in cheekpieces: usually races prominently. *J. Balding* **90**

ERROL FLYNN (IRE) 3 b. or br.g. Danehill Dancer (IRE) 117 – Warusha (GER) (Shareef Dancer (USA) 135) [2009 8m 8.1g 10f 11.7g p10g Oct 11] well-made gelding: type to carry condition: poor maiden: left J. Noseda after debut, R. Harris prior to final start: tried blinkered/in cheekpieces/tongue tied: unwilling. *B. G. Powell* **47 §**

ERTIYAAD 2 b.f. (Mar 10) Sakhee (USA) 136 – Asawer (IRE) 110 (Darshaan 133) [2009 p7g Nov 11] first foal: dam, 1¼m winner who stayed 1½m, out of sister to high-class miler Mukaddamah: 14/1, in need of experience when mid-field in maiden at Kempton: sure to improve. *Sir Michael Stoute* **– p**

ESAAR (USA) 2 b.c. (Mar 24) Mr Greeley (USA) 122 – Al Desima 93 (Emperor Jones (USA) 119) [2009 7m³ 7m² Oct 2] $500,000Y: useful-looking colt: has scope: has a fluent action: fifth foal: closely related to 3-y-o Rublevka Star and Irish 4-y-o Qeyaada and half-brother to 2 winners, including 6-y-o Altilhar: dam, 2-y-o 7f winner, later smart up to 1¼m in USA: promising efforts in well-contested maidens at Newbury and Newmarket (still green, ½-length second to Swiss Cross, again travelling best only to edge left): should stay 1m: already useful, and sure to improve again. *B. W. Hills* **96 p**

ESCAPE ARTIST 2 gr.g. (Mar 23) Act One 124 – Free At Last 115 (Shirley Heights 130) [2009 7m 7.5m 7.5g^6 Aug 12] 52,000Y: tall, attractive gelding: has scope: half-brother to several winners, including 8-y-o Mikado and smart 1¼m/1½m performer in Britain/USA Coretta (by Caerleon): dam, 2-y-o 7f winner (later won up to 11f in USA), half-sister to Barathea and Gossamer: green and not knocked about in maidens (gelded after final start): will be suited by 1m+: sort to do better in handicaps. *T. D. Easterby* **– p**

ESCAPE WALL 8 ch.g. Kirkwall 118 – Island Escape (IRE) 63 (Turtle Island (IRE) 123) [2009 p8g Oct 11] no form over hurdles or in seller on Flat debut. *R. J. Hodges* **–**

ESEEJ (USA) 4 ch.g. Aljabr (USA) 125 – Jinaan (USA) 72 (Mr Prospector (USA)) [2009 69: p12g^6 f11g^4 p12g^2 p12.2g* f12g* p12g 12g 11.6m^2 12m p10m^6 f11g* 16g p13.9g^4 p12.2g f11g^4 Dec 27] big gelding: has powerful action: fairly useful handicapper: won at Wolverhampton in February and Southwell in March and October: stays 1½m: acts on all-weather and good to firm ground: front runner: none too consistent. *P. W. Hiatt* **84**

ESOTERICA (IRE) 6 b.g. Bluebird (USA) 125 – Mysterious Plans (IRE) (Last Tycoon 131) [2009 86: 7.1m^6 7.1m 8d^5 8g* 7.2m* 7g^5 8m 7m 7m 7.6m^5 7.2s^6 6m^4 7m 7m* Oct 16] useful-looking gelding: useful handicapper: won at Ayr in May and June, and Newmarket (further improvement, beat Bonnie Charlie 1½ lengths) in October: best at 7f/1m: acts on firm and soft going: usually wears headgear: tactically versatile: reliable. *J. S. Goldie* **101**

ESPECIALLY SPECIAL (IRE) 3 b.f. Exceed And Excel (AUS) 126 – Super Trouper (FR) 64 (Nashwan (USA) 135) [2009 81+: 5g^6 p6g p7.1g^4 p7g p5g^4 p5.1g p5m^4 p5f Dec 19] tall, useful-looking filly: just fair performer nowadays: left S. Kirk 4,000 gns after fifth outing: stays easy 7f: acts on polytrack. *Peter Grayson* **71**

ESPERO (IRE) 3 b.g. Celtic Swing 138 – Zota (IRE) 27 (Barathea (IRE) 127) [2009 58: 8.1g^2 9g^6 p7g^3 p7.1g^2 p8.6g* p8.6g* Oct 29] tall gelding: fairly useful performer: won maiden in September and, having been gelded, handicap in October, both at Wolverhampton: stays 8.6f: acts on polytrack. *R. A. Farrant* **90**

ESPIRITU (FR) 3 b.g. Dansili 127 – Red Bravo (USA) (Red Ransom (USA)) [2009 89p: 7m^5 8g^2 7.5m* 8m^4 7m 8m^3 8m 8m 10g^2 Oct 10] strong, attractive gelding: fluent mover: smart performer: won maiden at Beverley in June: much better form in frame in competitive handicaps at Ascot after, particularly when short-head second to Cill Rialaig: suited by 1¼m: acts on good to firm and good to soft ground: visored/in cheekpieces of late: held up: temperamental: sold 200,000 gns, joined Godolphin. *J. Noseda* **110 §**

ESPRESSO STEPS (USA) 3 b. or br.f. Medaglia d'Oro (USA) 129 – Walk On Gold (USA) (Seeking The Gold (USA)) [2009 p6g p8m^6 p7.1g Dec 12] $35,000Y: fourth foal: half-sister to winner in USA by Joyeux Danseur: dam, ran once in USA, sister to smart French sprinter and closely related to US Grade 1 9f/1¼m winner Marquetry: well held in maidens. *P. Howling* **–**

ESPRIT DE MIDAS 3 b.g. Namid 128 – Spritzeria 81 (Bigstone (IRE) 126) [2009 66p: f7g* f7g* f7g* f6g^6 6g* f6m^6 Dec 5] rangy gelding: has scope: fairly useful handicapper, winning 3 times at Southwell within 11 days in February and at Leicester in May: off 6½ months prior to final outing: effective at 6f/7f: acts on fibresand: races prominently. *K. A. Ryan* **94**

ESPY 4 b.g. Piccolo 121 – Running Glimpse (IRE) 84 (Runnett 125) [2009 82: 5.7g p6g 6m 5g^6 5.7f^2 5.3f^3 5.1m 5.2s^4 5f^2 5m p6g^3 p6g^4 6d p6g^6 p6g^2 Dec 7] workmanlike gelding: fair handicapper: left S. Kirk prior to final start: best at 5f/easy 6f: acts on polytrack, firm and good to soft going. *I. W. McInnes* **75**

ESSEXBRIDGE 2 b.c. (Feb 1) Avonbridge 123 – Aonach Mor (Anabaa (USA) 130) [2009 7m^4 p7g^2 7d* Oct 22] 21,000F, £22,000Y: fifth foal: half-brother to 1m seller winner Mercari (by Bahamian Bounty): dam unraced: progressive form in maidens, winning at Brighton by 1¾ lengths from Bonnie Brae: should stay 1m. *R. Hannon* **76**

ESTATE 7 b.g. Montjeu (IRE) 137 – Fig Tree Drive (USA) 94 (Miswaki (USA) 124) [2009 81: p16m Dec 10] close-coupled gelding: fairly useful handicapper at best: well held only Flat outing in 2009: stays 16.5f: acts on polytrack, soft and good to firm ground: tried blinkered/tongue tied: fair hurdler nowadays. *D. E. Pipe* **–**

ESTEEM DANCER 3 ch.g. Mark of Esteem (IRE) 137 – Lake Diva 70 (Docksider (USA) 124) [2009 49: p7g^4 p7.1g f8g Mar 11] poor maiden. *J. G. Given* **–**

ESTEEM LORD 3 ch.g. Mark of Esteem (IRE) 137 – Milady Lillie (IRE) 65 (Distinctly North (USA) 115) [2009 53: p8g p8g^2 p8g^2 7m 8m p8g Jun 24] sturdy gelding: fair maiden: stays 1m: acts on polytrack and good to firm going. *Jamie Poulton* **64**

ESTEEM MACHINE (USA) 5 b.g. Mark of Esteem (IRE) 137 – Theme (IRE) (Sadler's Wells (USA) 132) [2009 99: p7g p7g^5 6d 5f^4 5m 5m^2 6g* 6m 6g 6m p6m^4 6g^4 p7g^5 p8m^6 Dec 1] strong, lengthy gelding: fairly useful handicapper: won at Newmarket in July: below form otherwise in 2009: effective at 5f to easy 7f: acts on polytrack, good to firm and good to soft going: tried visored: held up: sold £5,300. *R. A. Teal* **93**

ESTEJO (GER) 5 b.h. Johan Cruyff 118 – Este (GER) (The Noble Player (USA) 126) [2009 113: 10m^6 10m 10m* 9.8g 10v Nov 8] strong, rangy horse: smart performer: comfortably won minor event at Milan in September: creditable 2½ lengths sixth to Selmis in Premio Presidente della Repubblica at Rome on reappearance but well beaten otherwise, in Prince of Wales's Stakes at Royal Ascot, Prix Dollar at Longchamp and Premio Roma (won race in 2008) at Rome: effective at 1¼m/1½m: acts on firm and soft ground. *Ralf Rohne, Germany* **113**

ESTONIA 2 b.f. (Feb 5) Exceed And Excel (AUS) 126 – Global Trend (Bluebird (USA) 125) [2009 6m Aug 15] useful-looking filly: has scope: second foal: half-sister to 3-y-o Bawaardi: dam unraced half-sister to smart French/US sprinter/miler Night Chapter: 11/2 and backward, tenth of 11 in maiden at Newbury, slowly away and hampered over 1f out: type to do better. *J. H. M. Gosden* **– p**

ESUVIA (IRE) 2 b.f. (May 3) Whipper (USA) 126 – Aoife (IRE) 83 (Thatching 131) [2009 6s^3 p6g^2 f6f* Dec 11] 20,000Y: half-sister to several winners, including smart sprinter Resplendent Glory (by Namid) and 6-y-o Matuza: dam, 6f winner, half-sister to smart sprinter Funny Valentine: best effort in maidens when winning at Southwell, travelling strongly: raced only at 6f: very much type to do better still. *B. Smart* **75 p**

ETAIN (IRE) 5 b.m. Alhaarth (IRE) 126 – Brogan's Well (IRE) (Caerleon (USA) 132) [2009 74: p10m Nov 3] good-topped mare: handicapper: well held sole start in 2009: stays 1½m: acts on polytrack and soft going: tried in cheekpieces: temperament under suspicion. *Mrs Lawney Hill* **–**

ETERNAL INSTINCT 2 b.f. (May 9) Exceed And Excel (AUS) 126 – Glenhurich (IRE) 59 (Sri Pekan (USA) 117) [2009 5m* 5s 5g 6f 5g* 5.2d 5s^3 6m 6.5m 6m 5d^4 Oct 28] £22,000Y: tall, unfurnished filly: third foal: half-sister to 4-y-o Glenluji: dam 1m winner: fair performer: won maiden at Haydock in April and nursery at Musselburgh in July: best at 5f: acts on soft and good to firm going: usually held up. *J. S. Goldie* **77**

ETERNAL OPTIMIST (IRE) 4 b.f. Bahri (USA) 125 – Shore Lark (USA) (Storm Bird (CAN) 134) [2009 67: p6g Feb 23] tall filly: modest maiden: well below form only outing in 2009: stays 8.6f: acts on polytrack, soft and good to firm going: tried in cheekpieces/visor. *Paul Green* **–**

ETHICS GIRL (IRE) 3 b.f. Hernando (FR) 127 – Palinisa (FR) 106 (Night Shift (USA)) [2009 –: 7g^6 9.3g^2 10g 8.1m* 10.2g^5 9g* 9.9f 9.7f^4 12m^2 p12.2g^3 p13g^3 p9.5m^3 Nov 28] close-coupled filly: fairly useful handicapper: won at Chepstow in July and Sandown in August: good placed efforts last 4 starts: stays 13f: acts on polytrack and firm going: ridden patiently. *John Berry* **85**

ETOILE D'OR (IRE) 5 ch.m. Soviet Star (USA) 128 – Christeningpresent (IRE) (Cadeaux Genereux 131) [2009 –: f12g Feb 10] workmanlike mare: modest performer in 2007: well held both Flat starts since: stays 11.5f: acts on soft and good to firm going: joined T. Vaughan £2,200 in April, won over hurdles in November. *M. J. Gingell* **–**

ETON FABLE (IRE) 4 b.g. Val Royal (FR) 127 – Lina Story (Linamix (FR) 127) [2009 79: p10g^2 p12g^3 12m* 10.1d^5 14.6g^3 14m 17.1g 12g 11.9f* 12m^2 Aug 16] workmanlike gelding: fairly useful handicapper: won at Pontefract in April and Brighton in August: ran well final start: effective at 1¼m to 1¾m: acts on polytrack, firm and soft going: tried visored, in cheekpieces in 2009: forces pace. *W. J. H. Ratcliffe* **87**

ETON RIFLES (IRE) 4 b.g. Pivotal 124 – Maritsa (IRE) 59 (Danehill (USA) 126) [2009 92p: 7d^3 6v* 6d^3 7d^2 6d^3 6g* Sep 20] useful performer: won handicap at Haydock in May and minor event at Hamilton (beat Beckermet by length) in September: likely to prove best up to 7f: raced only on good going or softer (acts on heavy): often forces pace. *J. Howard Johnson* **100**

ETRUSCAN (IRE) 4 b.g. Selkirk (USA) 129 – Maddelina (IRE) 54 (Sadler's Wells (USA) 132) [2009 8.3d^2 12v^4 f11f^5 Dec 17] good-topped gelding: fairly useful form: missed 2008: best effort when fourth in ladies handicap at Newbury second start: stays 1½m: acts on heavy going. *C. Gordon* **84**

ETTRICK MILL 3 ch.g. Selkirk (USA) 129 – Milly-M (Cadeaux Genereux 131) [2009 f8g p8g^5 10.1m^5 9.2g^4 Sep 21] clear best effort in maidens on second start. *M. Johnston* **66**

EUREKA MOMENT 4 b.f. Alhaarth (IRE) 126 – Burn Baby Burn (IRE) (King's Theatre (IRE) 128) [2009 73: p13.3g⁴ p12.2g² p13g⁴ Feb 4] tall, leggy filly: fair performer: stays 1¾m: acts on all-weather and good to firm going: tried blinkered: not straightforward: sold 8,500 gns. *E. A. L. Dunlop* **68**

EUROCELEB (IRE) 4 ch.f. Peintre Celebre (USA) 137 – Eurobird 118 (Ela-Mana-Mou 132) [2009 76: f12d³ p13.9g Jan 19] rangy filly: fair maiden at 3 yrs: below form in 2009: should stay at least 1¾m: acts on polytrack: wore cheekpieces final outing: has awkward head carriage and one to treat with caution. *H. Morrison* **57 §**

EUROPEAN DREAM (IRE) 6 br.g. Kalanisi (IRE) 132 – Tereed Elhawa 75 (Cadeaux Genereux 131) [2009 –: 8s 8.1v 8.3v⁶ Nov 4] close-coupled gelding: smart in 2007: well held on Flat since: usually wears cheekpieces: waited with: fairly useful hurdler. *R. C. Guest* **–**

EUROTANZ (IRE) 3 b.f. Danehill Dancer (IRE) 117 – Eurostorm (USA) 104 (Storm Bird (CAN) 134) [2009 68p: 8d⁶ 10m⁴ 10d⁴ 8g⁵ p9.5g Sep 17] leggy filly: fair maiden: stays 1¼m: acts on polytrack, good to firm and good to soft ground: refused to enter stall intended second outing: sold 1,200 gns. *H. Morrison* **68**

EUSTON SQUARE 3 b.g. Oasis Dream 129 – Krisia (Kris 135) [2009 67p: 7m³ p7g³ 7m³ 7m* p7g⁶ Oct 21] good-bodied gelding: type to carry condition: fairly useful performer: won maiden at Leicester in October: likely to be suited by 1m: acts on polytrack and good to firm going: sold 25,000 gns, then gelded. *J. H. M. Gosden* **86**

EVASIVE 3 ch.c. Elusive Quality (USA) – Canda (USA) 100 (Storm Cat (USA)) [2009 112p: 8m⁶ 8m⁴ 7m⁶ Aug 15] strong, deep-girthed colt: smart performer: improved when 4½ lengths sixth to Sea The Stars in 2000 Guineas at Newmarket (interrupted preparation) and 3½ lengths fourth to Mastercraftsman in St James's Palace Stakes at Royal Ascot first 2 starts: left Sir Michael Stoute, below-form sixth in Hungerford Stakes at Newbury final outing: may prove ideally suited by 7f: acts on heavy and good to firm going. *Saeed bin Suroor* **116**

EVA'S REQUEST (IRE) 4 ch.f. Soviet Star (USA) 128 – Ingabelle 108 (Taufan (USA) 119) [2009 108: 8g³ 9g 8m 8g* 8.5g* 8m³ 8g 8d⁵ 8g* 10d* 8f Nov 22] **115**

For the second successive year Mick Channon's yard fared less well than might have been expected on the home front, though, in terms of prize money won overall, the 2009 season turned out to be its most successful yet. The stable's success owed much to the overseas exploits of Eva's Request, Halicarnassus, Lahaleeb and Youmzain. The five races won by the first three were worth almost £900,000 in total, a figure greater than the first prize money earned by the rest of the Channon string in winning one hundred and eight races in Britain. Youmzain didn't win a race in 2009 but he was the biggest single earner for the yard thanks mainly to his second in the Arc which accounted for the bulk of the £1m or so that he earned in place money during the season. Lahaleeb was the next biggest contributor with her victory in the E. P. Taylor Stakes at Woodbine, but both Eva's Request and Halicarnassus made sizeable contributions, winning two races apiece including one each at Veliefendi in Turkey. Eva's Request also had a couple of victories to her name in Britain, and, while nothing like so valuable, they helped to take her winning earnings for the year to over £343,000.

It would have been difficult for anyone who saw Eva's Request make her two-year-old debut to imagine that she would go on to do so well. A 10/1-shot for a fillies maiden at Nottingham in June 2007, she looked nothing out of the ordinary in the paddock and didn't show much in the race itself, beating only two home. Yet, by the end of September that year, Eva's Request had won two races including the C. L. Weld Park Stakes at the Curragh. Further improvement came at three, when she won a listed handicap at Ascot, and she continued to progress at four, beginning her latest campaign at Nad Al Sheba, where she gave her better performance when third in the Group 3 Cape Verdi. Eva's Request then ran five times in Britain, winning a listed race at Goodwood in May and the Princess Elizabeth Stakes (Sponsored by Investec) at Epsom in June, the latter by a length from French challenger Alnadana, who handled the gradients nothing like so well as the winner.

Back on her travels, Eva's Request ran as well as could be expected at the time when fifth to Goldikova in the Prix Rothschild at Deauville. She then needed only to perform to a similar level to justify favouritism in the France Galop Istanbul Trophy at Veliefendi. A valuable event for fillies and mares, the Istanbul Trophy attracted one other challenger from Britain, the three-year-old Damaniyat Girl, and

Premio Lydia Tesio Shadwell, Rome—Eva's Request (right) steps up in trip and crowns a fine season; also involved in the photo finish are, from left to right, Night Magic, Les Fazzani and Nashmiah

the pair finished first and second, separated by a length. Next stop was Italy and the Group 1 Premio Lydia Tesio Shadwell at Rome, where Eva's Request was one of five British challengers in a fifteen-runner field which also included the Irish-trained Chinese White, who started favourite. Eva's Request was very patiently ridden and saw the trip out well on her first attempt over as far as a mile and a quarter; brought wide into the straight, she got up near the line to win by a head from the German Oaks winner Night Magic. British runners occupied the next four places, Les Fazzani and Nashmiah close up in third and fourth. It was a career high from Eva's Request, who went on to Japan but could finish only tenth in the Mile Championship at Kyoto. Her final appearance of the year came at the December Sales, where she was sold for 525,000 guineas to take up broodmare duties in the States, reportedly set to visit Smart Strike.

Eva's Request (IRE) (ch.f. 2005)	Soviet Star (USA) (b 1984)	Nureyev (b 1977)	Northern Dancer
			Special
		Veruschka (b 1967)	Venture VII
			Marie d'Anjou
	Ingabelle (b 1984)	Taufan (b 1977)	Stop The Music
			Stolen Date
		Bodelle (ch 1975)	Falcon
			Shade

Eva's Request, a €150,000 yearling, is the eighth individual winner produced by her dam Ingabelle, who died in 2008, and they include her full sister Soviet Belle, the winner of a six-furlong maiden at the Curragh at two. The best of Ingabelle's produce before Eva's Request were also Irish-trained fillies, Wild Bluebell (by Bluebird), who won the Concorde Stakes at Tipperary, and Priory Belle (by Priolo), successful in the Moyglare Stud Stakes at the Curragh. Ingabelle herself won the Phoenix Sprint Stakes and is a daughter of Bodelle, a winner both on the Flat, at up to thirteen furlongs, and over hurdles in Ireland. Bodelle is one of the many winners produced by Shade, a fairly useful performer who also stayed thirteen furlongs. A mile and a quarter would probably have proved the limit for the leggy Eva's Request, a tough and genuine sort who was effective either waited with or racing close to the pace. She acted on polytrack, good to firm and good to soft ground. *M. R. Channon*

EVELITH REGENT (IRE) 6 b.g. Imperial Ballet (IRE) 110 – No Avail (IRE) 73 (Imperial Frontier (USA) 112) [2009 72: 12g^5 May 23] lengthy, sparely-made gelding: fairly useful bumper winner: fair maiden: well held in seller sole start in 2009: barely stays 1½m: yet to race on extremes of going: headstrong front-runner. *G. A. Swinbank* –

EVELYN MAY (IRE) 3 b.f. Acclamation 118 – Lady Eberspacher (IRE) 68 (Royal Abjar (USA) 121) [2009 84: p5g^4 5g 6g^3 5f^3 6m 5.1g^6 6g^6 p5g* 5m p6g^4 Nov 5] tall filly: has scope: fairly useful handicapper on all-weather, fair on turf: won at Kempton in September: may prove best at 5f: acts on polytrack, raced only on good going or firmer on turf. *B. W. Hills* **75 a85**

EVEN BOLDER 6 ch.g. Bold Edge 123 – Level Pegging (IRE) 48 (Common Grounds **84**
118) [2009 90: p5.1g^3 5m 5f 5.7m 5m 5m^3 5.2d^6 5g 5g^6 5f 5m^6 5m* 5g* 5.3d p6g^2 p5g p6m Dec 6] strong, workmanlike gelding: fairly useful handicapper: won apprentice events at Goodwood and Ascot in October: best at 5f/easy 6f: acts on polytrack, firm and good to soft ground: tried in cheekpieces. *E. A. Wheeler*

EVENING GLOW 2 b.f. (Apr 18) Fantastic Light (USA) 134 – Kartuzy (JPN) 82 **–**
(Polish Precedent (USA) 131) [2009 p7g 6m Sep 15] smallish filly: third foal: dam, 11.5f winner, half-sister to Arc winner Marienbard: last in maidens at Kempton and Yarmouth: bred to be suited by 1¼m+. *C. E. Brittain*

EVENING SUNSET (GER) 3 b.f. Dansili 127 – Evening Promise 108 (Aragon 118) **73**
[2009 63: 8.5g 8.1g^6 8d^5 8s^3 8.1g^4 9m^3 8.3g* 8g 8m^4 10f^2 p10g^4 Oct 14] big, workmanlike filly: fair handicapper: won at Hamilton in July: left M. Channon after ninth start: stays 1¼m: acts on polytrack, unraced on heavy ground, acts on any other: fair winner of 2 juvenile hurdles. *M. G. Quinlan*

EVENING TALE (IRE) 2 b.f. (Mar 12) Rock of Gibraltar (IRE) 133 – Wondrous **70**
Story (USA) 91 (Royal Academy (USA) 130) [2009 p7g p7.1g^3 Nov 14] 100,000F, €75,000Y: useful-looking filly: second foal: dam, 2-y-o 7f winner who stayed 8.5f, half-sister to smart 1½m performer Theatre Script: easily better effort in maidens when 6½ lengths third to Huroof at Wolverhampton, making running and again racing freely (edged left): should stay 1m: sold 6,000 gns. *B. J. Meehan*

EVENS AND ODDS (IRE) 5 ch.g. Johannesburg (USA) 127 – Coeur de La Mer **112**
(IRE) 87 (Caerleon (USA) 132) [2009 106: 6m^3 6f* 7m 6m 6d^2 6m^4 Sep 19] lengthy, useful-looking gelding: smart handicapper: better than ever in 2009, winning quite valuable event at Newmarket in May by 3¼ lengths from Thebes: good efforts in frame in Stewards' Cup at Goodwood (length second to Genki) and Ayr Gold Cup (1½ lengths fourth to Jimmy Styles) last 2 starts: has form at 7f, all wins at 5f/6f: acts on all-weather, firm and good to soft going: used to wear blinkers/cheekpieces: tried tongue tied. *D. Nicholls*

EVENSTORM (USA) 4 ch.f. Stephen Got Even (USA) 125 – Summer Wind Storm **41**
(USA) (Storm Cat (USA)) [2009 56: p7g Feb 11] rather sparely-made filly: modest maiden handicapper: stays easy 7f: has raced only on polytrack and good/good to firm ground: edgy sort. *B. Gubby*

EVERAARD (USA) 3 ch.g. Lion Heart (USA) 124 – Via Gras (USA) (Montbrook **76**
(USA)) [2009 64p: p8g^5 7.1m^3 8.3g^3 8.1g* 8.5g^3 8s 10g^4 9.9f^3 10d 12m^2 10g^4 p10g^2 p12g^5 Oct 22] good-quartered gelding: fair handicapper: awarded race at Warwick in May: stays 1½m: acts on polytrack and firm going: sold 19,000 gns, joined Mrs K. Walton, then gelded. *D. R. C. Elsworth*

EVER A GENT 2 b.g. (Mar 29) Gentleman's Deal (IRE) 114 – Mill End Quest 65 **46**
(King's Signet (USA) 110) [2009 f8f^6 f8m^6 f7f^6 Dec 11] poor form in maidens. *M. W. Easterby*

EVER CHEERFUL 8 b.g. Atraf 116 – Big Story 50 (Cadeaux Genereux 131) [2009 **69**
75: p7g^4 p7g^3 p7g^2 p7g^3 p7g^6 p7g p7g^2 p7m p7.1g p7g^4 p7g Dec 7] workmanlike gelding: fluent mover: fair handicapper: effective at 5f to easy 7f: acts on all-weather, firm and soft going: tried tongue tied/visored, wears cheekpieces: races up with pace. *A. B. Haynes*

EVERGREEN DANCER (IRE) 2 b.c. (Mar 16) Noverre (USA) 125 – Persea (IRE) **55**
64 (Fasliyev (USA) 120) [2009 6s^4 6g 6g p6g 7d 6d Sep 15] lengthy colt: modest maiden: down the field in nurseries, finishing weakly (visored final start): stays 6f: sold £2,000. *J. R. Best*

EVER SO BOLD 2 b.g. (Jan 26) Reset (AUS) 124 – Bold Byzantium (Bold Arrange- **73**
ment 127) [2009 5m^5 5g 5m^3 5g^4 7d^4 7d^5 p7.1g p7g* p7.1g^4 p7m^4 Nov 27] rather leggy gelding: fourth foal: half-brother to 4-y-o Ben and 6.5f/1m winner in Spain by Josr Algarhoud: dam lightly-raced half-sister to smart sprinter Daring Destiny: fair performer: much improved in blinkers last 3 starts, winning nursery at Kempton in October: stays 7f: acts on polytrack, probably on good to soft and good to firm going. *W. R. Muir*

EVERYBODY KNOWS 4 b.g. King's Best (USA) 132 – Logic 94 (Slip Anchor 136) **90**
[2009 84: p7g^2 p7g^5 8.3m* 8m Jun 27] fairly useful handicapper, lightly raced: won at Windsor in May: free-going sort, effective at 7f to 1¼m: acts on polytrack, good to firm and good to soft going: forces pace: gelded after final start. *Miss Jo Crowley*

EVERYMAN 5 gr.g. Act One 124 – Maid To Dance 62 (Pyramus (USA) 78) [2009 67: **57**
p9.5g^5 p10g f11g^5 p12g^4 10.2m^5 p12g^4 p11g^6 p8.6g^5 10.2g^3 11.6g^6 Jul 27] big gelding: modest performer: stays 1½m: acts on polytrack and soft going: tried in blinkers/visor. *A. W. Carroll*

EVERYMANFORHIMSELF (IRE) 5 b.g. Fasliyev (USA) 120 – Luisa Demon **106**
(IRE) (Barathea (IRE) 127) [2009 104: 6m 5m^3 5g^2 6m^2 5m^2 6g 6m* 6m 5.6m^2 6m **a98**
6m^6 7g^2 p7g^3 Nov 21] big, strong gelding: has quick action: useful handicapper: won at
Haydock in August and placed 7 times in 2009: effective at 5f to 7f: acts on soft and good
to firm going: usually wears headgear. *K. A. Ryan*

EVERYNIGHT (IRE) 3 b.g. Rock of Gibraltar (IRE) 133 – Rasana 74 (Royal Acad- **90**
emy (USA) 130) [2009 81p: 10.3g* 10m 8.1m^6 8.3g^4 8m^3 p10f^5 8m Sep 16] good-bodied
gelding: fairly useful performer: won maiden at Doncaster in March: stays 10.3f: acts on
good to firm going: wore cheekpieces final start (unseated leaving stall). *M. Botti*

EVERYTHING 4 bl.f. Namid 128 – Flight Sequence 88 (Polar Falcon (USA) 126) **–**
[2009 71: f6d^6 Jan 8] well-grown filly: fair performer at best: well below form only start
in 2009: best efforts at 6f: acts on fibresand, soft and good to firm going: tried in cheekpieces. *P. T. Midgley*

EVETTE 4 b.f. Loup Solitaire (USA) 117 – La Scarlet (FR) (Highest Honor (FR) 124) **–**
[2009 –: p10g^6 p7g Feb 18] leggy filly: poor maiden. *H. J. Collingridge*

EVIANNE 5 b.m. Lugana Beach 116 – Folk Dance (USA) (Bertrando (USA) 127) [2009 **–**
45: 8.1m 10g 8d^6 8f Sep 2] poor maiden: tried blinkered. *P. W. Hiatt*

EVIDENT PRIDE (USA) 6 b.g. Chester House (USA) 123 – Proud Fact (USA) 108 **75**
(Known Fact (USA) 135) [2009 100: p12g* p12g p11g^5 p11g 9.7m^6 8.5m p12f^3 12s^6 **a94**
p12g^4 p13m^3 p12f^6 Dec 19] strong, lengthy gelding: fairly useful handicapper on
all-weather, fair on turf: won at Lingfield in January: stays easy 13f: acts on polytrack,
probably on good to firm ground: tried visored: held up: tends to edge left. *B. R. Johnson*

EVNA (USA) 3 ch.f. Grand Slam (USA) 120 – Our Josephina (USA) (Tale of The Cat **72**
(USA) 113) [2009 8.1g 8g f5m* 5s^3 6m Aug 6] deep-girthed filly: fair form: won maiden
at Southwell in July: likely to have proved best at 5f/6f: best effort on fibresand: dead.
R. A. Fahey

EXCEED ELEGANCE (IRE) 3 b.f. Exceed And Excel (AUS) 126 – Colleen (IRE) **64**
(Sadler's Wells (USA) 132) [2009 –: 6g 5g^5 p5.1g^5 5d^2 6g^3 5d^5 p6g p7g p6g^2 p5.1g^6 p6f
Dec 21] good-topped filly: modest maiden: stays 6f: acts on polytrack and good to soft
going: tried tongue tied. *D. Shaw*

EXCEEDINGLY BOLD 2 b.c. (Mar 12) Exceed And Excel (AUS) 126 – Grey Pearl **89**
97 (Ali-Royal (IRE) 127) [2009 6m^2 6g^3 6.5g* 7v Oct 24] £20,000Y: close-coupled
colt: second foal: half-brother to 3-y-o Sakhee's Pearl: dam 6f/7f winner: fairly useful
performer: won maiden at Newbury in October by 3½ lengths from Strictly Dancing: stiff
task, ran at least as well when ninth to Carnaby Street in Horris Hill Stakes there: may
prove best up to 7f. *Miss Gay Kelleway*

EXCEEDINGLY GOOD (IRE) 3 ch.f. Exceed And Excel (AUS) 126 – Ikan (IRE) **61**
98 (Sri Pekan (USA) 117) [2009 71: 6g^4 6m 6m 5m^5 Aug 30] strong, good-topped filly:
modest maiden: should prove best at 5f/6f: best effort on good to firm going: visored final
outing, then sold £800. *B. Smart*

EXCEED POWER 2 ch.f. (Mar 17) Exceed And Excel (AUS) 126 – Israar (Machia- **53**
vellian (USA) 123) [2009 6f 6g 5.1m^5 5m p5g^4 p5g p5g^4 Oct 21] 23,000Y: lengthy, rather
unfurnished filly: first foal: dam, unraced, out of half-sister to Phoenix Stakes winner
Pharaoh's Delight, herself grandam of Breeders' Cup Turf winner Red Rocks: modest
maiden: should stay 6f: acts on polytrack: tongue tied last 3 starts: possibly not straightforward. *D. M. Simcock*

EXCEEDTHEWILDMAN 2 b.c. (Mar 9) Exceed And Excel (AUS) 126 – Naomi **76**
Wildman (USA) (Kingmambo (USA) 125) [2009 6m^3 7m^3 6.5g p8g^6 p7m* p7m^4 p7f^3
Dec 19] £16,000Y: tall colt: third foal: half-brother to 3-y-o Sherman McCoy: dam ran 4
times: fair performer: won nursery at Lingfield in November: should stay 1m: acts on
polytrack and good to firm ground: in cheekpieces last 3 starts. *J. S. Moore*

EXCELLENT DAY (IRE) 2 b.f. (Apr 15) Invincible Spirit (IRE) 121 – Tosca (Be **75**
My Guest (USA) 126) [2009 6m 5m^2 5g* Aug 6] €50,000F, 50,000Y: good-topped filly:
half-sister to 2007 2-y-o 5f winner Dalkey Girl (by Raise A Grand), later useful up to
1½m in Scandinavia, and 1½m/1¾m winner Tilla (by Bin Ajwaad): dam unraced: fair
form in maidens, winning at Sandown by head from More Lashes: should stay 6f+.
M. R. Channon

EXCELLENT GUEST 2 b.c. (Feb 22) Exceed And Excel (AUS) 126 – Princess **84**
Speedfit (FR) 77 (Desert Prince (IRE) 130) [2009 6g^4 6g^4 7g^3 6m* 6m Aug 18] strong
colt: third foal: half-brother to 2 winners, including 3-y-o Imperial Guest: dam, 1m
winner, half-sister to smart French/UAE performer up to 12.5f Sibling Rival: fairly useful

form in maidens: won 4-runner event at Yarmouth in August by 4 lengths from Serhaal, making all: ran poorly in nursery at York: stays 7f. *G. G. Margarson*

EXCELLENT SHOW 3 ch.f. Exceed And Excel (AUS) 126 – Quiz Show 82 (Primo Dominie 121) [2009 82: 6m 5m³ 5m⁵ 5g³ 5.1m³ 5g p5g² p5m* Dec 30] compact filly: fairly useful handicapper: changed owners £6,500 before penultimate start: won at Kempton in December: worth another try at 6f: acts on polytrack, good to firm and good to soft ground. *B. Smart* **89**

EXCELLENT THOUGHT 2 b.f. (Mar 24) Exceed And Excel (AUS) 126 – Amiata 89 (Pennekamp (USA) 130) [2009 5d⁵ 5m² 6d³ 5.1g² p5.1g² p6m³ Nov 19] 17,000F, €36,000Y, 130,000 2-y-o: first foal: dam, Irish 5f winner, out of half-sister to smart miler Inchmurrin (dam of Inchinor): fair maiden: effective at 5f/6f: acts on polytrack, good to firm and good to soft going: consistent. *W. J. Haggas* **73**

EXCELLENT VISION 2 b.c. (Feb 26) Exceed And Excel (AUS) 126 – Classic Vision 59 (Classic Cliche (IRE) 128) [2009 6g⁴ 6g³ Oct 9] 90,000F, 120,000Y, 190,000 2-y-o: second foal: half-brother to 4-y-o Farsighted: dam, 6f/1m winner, closely related to 7f/1m performer Yeast and half-sister to sprinter Orientor, both smart: promise in maidens, still green when 5 lengths third to Walvis Bay at York, slowly away and late headway: will do better. *B. Smart* **70 p**

EXCELLERATOR (IRE) 3 ch.f. Exceed And Excel (AUS) 126 – Amsicora (Cadeaux Genereux 131) [2009 95: 6m³ 5m 5m f5g² Oct 27] leggy filly: useful performer: improved when nose second to Rowe Park in minor event at Southwell final outing: speedy, will prove best at 5f/6f: acts on fibresand and good to firm going: visored (out of depth in Nunthorpe Stakes) second start: tongue tied in 2009. *George Baker* **101**

EXCELLING (IRE) 2 b.f. (Feb 5) Exceed And Excel (AUS) 126 – Nojoom (IRE) (Alhaarth (IRE) 126) [2009 5.1g 5g* 5.2m p5f⁴ 6.5m Sep 25] 5,000Y: sturdy filly: first foal: dam, ran twice, out of half-sister to Eclipse/Irish Champion Stakes winner Oratorio: fairly useful performer: won maiden at Lingfield in July by 5 lengths: well below form last 2 starts: should stay 6f+. *P. J. Makin* **82**

EXCELSIOR ACADEMY 3 b.g. Montjeu (IRE) 137 – Birthday Suit (IRE) 94 (Daylami (IRE) 138) [2009 71: 10.2g⁵ 12.6g³ 14g 14.1s* p16g⁴ 13g⁴ 11.9g* Aug 6] well-made gelding: fairly useful handicapper: won at Yarmouth in June and Haydock in August: stays 2m: acts on polytrack and soft going: tried blinkered: not straightforward. *B. J. Meehan* **83**

EXCEPTIONAL ART 3 ch.g. Exceed And Excel (AUS) 126 – Only In Dreams 78 (Polar Falcon (USA) 126) [2009 90p: 7g² 7.1v* p8g⁶ 5m* Aug 29] good-topped gelding: smart performer, lightly raced: won handicap at Haydock (by 1¾ lengths from Leahurst) in May and, having left P. Chapple-Hyam 41,000 gns, listed race at Beverley (beat Sohraab by head, getting up final strides) in August: should stay 1m: acts on heavy and good to firm going: sent to Hong Kong. *D. Nicholls* **108**

EXCITABLE (IRE) 3 b.f. Exceed And Excel (AUS) 126 – Kalwada (USA) (Roberto (USA) 131) [2009 60?: 5g³ 5m⁴ 5m p5g⁴ 5d 5g Oct 6] leggy filly: modest maiden: will prove best at 5f: acts on polytrack: in cheekpieces final start. *Mrs D. J. Sanderson* **52**

EXCLAMATION 4 br.g. Acclamation 118 – Summer Siren (FR) (Saint Cyrien (FR) 128) [2009 95: 6m⁴ 6f³ 6d 6m f5g³ p6g⁶ Nov 14] big, lengthy gelding: useful performer, lightly raced: best effort in 2009 when 1½ lengths fourth to Tax Free in listed race at Newmarket on reappearance: should prove best at 5f/6f: acts on fibresand, firm and good to soft ground. *B. J. Meehan* **106** **a100**

EXCUSEZ MOI (USA) 7 b.g. Fusaichi Pegasus (USA) 130 – Jiving 69 (Generous (IRE) 139) [2009 114d: f5s⁵ f7g⁶ p7g² f5g⁴ p6g 7m 7.1m* 6g⁵ 6m* 6s 5g* 6m⁴ 6m 6d⁴ 6d⁵ 6g³ 6m 6d 6.5m 6g 5d² 7s⁶ Nov 7] tall gelding: useful performer in 2009, winning handicaps at Musselburgh in April and Ripon in May, and minor event at Beverley later in May: several creditable efforts after, including when 2 lengths third to Knot In Wood in Sky Bet Dash (Handicap) at York sixteenth outing: effective at 5f to 7f: acts on polytrack, dirt, soft and good to firm going: often in headgear/tongue tie: held up, sometimes slowly away: often gives trouble before start. *Mrs R. A. Carr* **102**

EXEARTI 2 b.f. (Feb 23) Exceed And Excel (AUS) 126 – Graffiti Girl (IRE) 67 (Sadler's Wells (USA) 132) [2009 p6m p6g⁵ f6f³ f7g³ f6d* Dec 29] third foal: half-sister to fairly useful 2008 2-y-o 5f winner Zezao (by Fasliyev) and French 1¼m winner Orient Celebrity (by Peintre Celebre): dam, maiden (stayed 1½m), out of sister to smart 1994 2-y-o Sri Pekan: fair performer: left Paul Mason after debut: best effort when winning maiden at Southwell, making all: may prove best at 6f: raced on all-weather. *A. J. McCabe* **69**

William Hill Lincoln (Heritage Handicap), Doncaster—the favourite Expresso Star is clear of Zaahid, Flipando (second right), Mia's Boy (far rail) and Huzzah (check sleeves)

EXECUTION (IRE) 2 b.c. (Mar 7) Alhaarth (IRE) 126 – Headrest (Habitat 134) [2009 p7.1g p7g^4 7d^6 p8g p8m^6 p8.6g^3 8.3d a7.5g* a8g^2 a9.5g^2 Dec 24] lengthy colt: modest performer: sold from E. Dunlop 9,000 gns after seventh start (blinkered): won maiden at Mons in November: stays 9.5f: acts on all-weather and good to soft going: not straightforward (has flashed tail). *N. Minner, Belgium* **61**

EXEMPLARY 2 b.c. (Mar 19) Sulamani (IRE) 130 – Epitome (IRE) 71 (Nashwan (USA) 135) [2009 f8g^4 p8.6g^3 10.2m* Sep 28] fourth foal: half-brother to 3 winners in France, including useful 1½m winners Synopsis (by In The Wings) and Epic Similie (by Lomitas): dam, maiden who stayed 1½m, out of high-class 6f/7f performer Proskona: progressive form in maidens, still green when winning at Bath by 2 lengths from Duty And Destiny: will be suited by 1½m+: open to further improvement. *M. Johnston* **85 p**

EX GRACIA 3 ch.f. Efisio 120 – Action de Grace (USA) (Riverman (USA) 131) [2009 6d 7s Aug 1] half-sister to French winners Acke (at 1¼m/1½m, by Loup Solitaire) and Action Bleue (at 1m, by Fasliyev): dam, French maiden, sister/half-sister to smart French 1m/1¼m performers Android and Art Moderne: well beaten in maidens. *K. A. Ryan* **–**

EXGRAY (IRE) 2 gr.f. (Mar 31) Exceed And Excel (AUS) 126 – Mrs Gray 61 (Red Sunset 120) [2009 5m^2 5m* 5.5d^5 7d^2 a7.5g* Dec 24] £42,000Y: half-sister to several winners, including useful 6f (at 2 yrs) to 1m (US minor stakes) winner Steelaninch (by Inchinor) and fairly useful 7f (at 2 yrs) to 1¼m winner Anuvasteel (by Vettori): dam 2-y-o 7f winner: fairly useful performer: won maiden at Hamilton in June (final start for B. Smart) and minor event at Deauville (all-weather) in December: stays 7.5f: in cheekpieces last 2 starts. *X. T. Demeaulte, France* **80**

EXISTENTIALIST 2 b.f. (Apr 27) Exceed And Excel (AUS) 126 – Owdbetts (IRE) 69 (High Estate 127) [2009 5g^3 5m* 5g 5m^3 5.2d 5.2m 5.7f^5 p6g* 6m Oct 5] £19,000Y: rather unfurnished filly: half-sister to several winners, including smart sprinter Ratio (by Pivotal) and useful 5f to (in UAE) 1¼m winner Rochdale (by Bertolini): dam 7f (at 2 yrs) and 1¼m winner: fair performer: won maiden at Windsor in May and weak claimer at Wolverhampton (claimed from J. Portman £13,000) in September: stays easy 6f: acts on polytrack and good to firm ground: inconsistent. *A. E. Price* **78**

EXIT SMILING 7 ch.g. Dr Fong (USA) 128 – Away To Me (Exit To Nowhere (USA) 122) [2009 96, a72: f8g* f8g^4 8m 9.8m^4 8.5m^4 8.5m^6 8d^2 8m 9d^2 8.5m^3 8.5m^2 8g* 8m^5 8g^5 8g^4 Sep 17] big, good-topped gelding: fairly useful handicapper: won at Southwell in February and Pontefract in August: stays 9f: acts on all-weather, heavy and good to firm going: tried visored/blinkered: sometimes races freely. *P. T. Midgley* **91 a81**

EXOPUNTIA 3 b.f. Sure Blade (USA) 130 – Opuntia (Rousillon (USA) 133) [2009 –: 6g^2 6.1m 6m 7g 8m Sep 23] rangy filly: modest maiden: should stay 7f: tried in cheekpieces: not straightforward. *R. M. Whitaker* **59**

EXOTIC BEAUTY 2 b.f. (Feb 23) Barathea (IRE) 127 – Lady Dominatrix (IRE) 112 (Danehill Dancer (IRE) 117) [2009 5g^3 6f^2 5.1m* 6g 6m* 6g^4 5m 6m Oct 3] €75,000Y: compact filly: third foal: half-sister to fairly useful 2007 2-y-o 5f winner Janina (by Namid) and 3-y-o Mattamia: dam 5f (including at 2 yrs)/6f winner: useful performer: won minor events at Bath in June and Ripon (easily best effort, made all to beat Hafawa by short head) in August: ran poorly after: effective at 5f/6f: acts on good to firm going: visored final start: sold 27,000 gns. *M. R. Channon* **96**

EXPENSIVE DINNER 3 ch.f. Dr Fong (USA) 128 – Reservation (IRE) 78 (Common **59**
Grounds 118) [2009 –: 6g^6 p7g Aug 14] big, workmanlike filly: modest form at best in maidens: dead. *E. F. Vaughan*

EXPENSIVE LEGACY 2 ch.f. (Mar 6) Piccolo 121 – American Rouge (IRE) (Grand **48**
Lodge (USA) 125) [2009 7m p7g 7m 7.1m^6 8g p10m^6 Nov 21] medium-sized filly: fourth foal: dam unraced: poor maiden: stays 1¼m. *H. J. L. Dunlop*

EXPENSIVE PROBLEM 6 b.g. Medicean 128 – Dance Steppe (Rambo Dancer **75**
(CAN) 107) [2009 8g^6 8.3m* 10.1d^6 8.5m p7m Oct 12] close-coupled gelding: won 3 times in Spain, including twice in 2008: returned to Britain, fair form when winning handicap at Windsor in June: below form after: probably best at 1m/9f: acts on polytrack/sand and good to firm ground: visored once at 2 yrs. *R. J. Smith*

EXPLORATOR (IRE) 2 b.c. (Mar 12) Whipper (USA) 126 – Certainly Brave 77 **53**
(Indian Ridge 123) [2009 p7m p7g^4 Dec 31] better effort in maidens when fourth at Lingfield, still very green. *George Baker*

EXPRESSIVE 3 b.f. Falbrav (IRE) 133 – Exclusive 115 (Polar Falcon (USA) 126) **81**
[2009 p7.1g^2 p8g^3 p8.6m^2 p8.6g^2 p9.5m* Sep 28] sixth foal: half-sister to 7f/1m winner Chic (by Machiavellian) and 6f (at 2 yrs) to 9f (including Celebration Mile) winner Echelon (by Danehill), both very smart: dam, 7f (at 2 yrs)/1m (Coronation Stakes) winner, half-sister to 2000 Guineas winner Entrepreneur: fairly useful performer: won handicap at Wolverhampton in September: stays 9.5f: raced only on polytrack. *Sir Michael Stoute*

EXPRESSO STAR (USA) 4 b.c. War Chant (USA) 126 – Caffe Latte (IRE) 118 **113**
(Seattle Dancer (USA) 119) [2009 109p: 8m* 10.3m^3 12g 8s Nov 1] good-topped colt: smart performer: justified favouritism in William Hill Lincoln (Handicap) at Doncaster in March by 2½ lengths from Zaahid, asserting quickly over 2f out: just respectable efforts at best in pattern company after, ½-length third to Doctor Fremantle in Huxley Stakes at Chester second outing: off 5 months before final start: effective at 1m/1¼m: seems to act on any going. *J. H. M. Gosden*

EXPRESS WISH 5 b.h. Danehill Dancer (IRE) 117 – Waffle On 89 (Chief Singer 131) **109**
[2009 116: 7s 7g 7g^5 7m 7g^4 6m^5 Sep 12] good-topped horse: useful performer: best efforts in 2009 when fifth in Lennox Stakes (beaten 3¼ lengths by Finjaan) and fourth in Supreme Stakes (3½ lengths behind Ordnance Row) at Goodwood third/fifth starts: best at 7f: acts on polytrack, firm and soft ground: once visored/tongue tied. *J. Noseda*

EXTRACURRICULAR (USA) 3 ch.f. Thunder Gulch (USA) 129 – Frans Lass **61**
(USA) (Shanekite (USA)) [2009 p8g^5 p8.6g^4 p10g^5 10.1d^6 8m^4 p7g Aug 24] $17,000F, 30,000Y: sturdy filly: sister to winner in USA and half-sister to several winners there: dam US 6.5f (including at 2 yrs)/7f winner: modest maiden: left M. Botti after fifth start: best effort at 1m on polytrack. *S. Gollings*

EXTRATERRESTRIAL 5 b.g. Mind Games 121 – Expectation (IRE) 59 (Night **104**
Shift (USA)) [2009 102: p8.6g 8m^2 p8g^3 8s* 8g 8.1m 8g 8m 8m* Sep 19] lengthy gelding: useful handicapper: won at Newbury (Dubai Duty Free Spring Cup, by ¾ length from Arabian Spirit) in April and Ayr in September: further progress when beating Billy Dane 1¾ lengths for latter success: best at 7f/1m: acts on polytrack, heavy and good to firm going: has worn blinkers/cheekpieces: held up. *R. A. Fahey*

EXTREME GREEN 2 ch.f. (Feb 20) Motivator 131 – Ventura (IRE) 91 (Spectrum **–**
(IRE) 126) [2009 7.1m 8d Oct 22] tall filly: has scope: fourth foal: half-sister to 11f winner Cedar Mountain (by Galileo), later smart up to 1¾m in USA, and French 9f/1¼m winner Lakuta (by Pivotal): dam, Irish 1m winner, out of close relation to Generous: very green and no impact in maidens at Warwick and Brighton: bred to be suited by 1¼m+: sold 2,000 gns. *A. M. Balding*

EXTREMELY SO 3 ch.f. Kyllachy 129 – Antigua (Selkirk (USA) 129) [2009 58: **68**
p12g^6 12.1m 10.1g^2 10.3m^6 10.1g^2 10g 12m^4 11.5g* p12g^2 p16m^3 Dec 1] tall filly: fair performer: won seller at Yarmouth in October: stays 2m: acts on polytrack and good to firm going. *P. J. McBride*

EXTREME PLEASURE (IRE) 4 b.f. High Chaparral (IRE) 132 – Height of Passion **–**
(Shirley Heights 130) [2009 72: 14.6m 11.5m 18g Aug 13] maiden: largely well held in handicaps in 2009. *W. J. Knight*

EXTREME WARRIOR (IRE) 2 ch.g. (Jan 25) Dubawi (IRE) 129 – Extreme Beauty **83**
(USA) 89 (Rahy (USA) 115) [2009 6m 6m* 6m^4 7d^5 Jul 18] 140,000Y: well-made gelding: first foal: dam, 6f (at 2 yrs)/7f winner, half-sister to very smart US Grade 1 1¼m winner Go Between: fairly useful performer: won maiden at Newmarket in June by 2¼ lengths from Black Snowflake: just respectable efforts in minor events after, then gelded: should stay 7f: blinkered after debut. *D. R. Lanigan*

EYE FOR THE GIRLS 3 ch.g. Bertolini (USA) 125 – Aunt Ruby (USA) 67 (Rubiano (USA)) [2009 –: 8s 8m 7g 6f^5 6m^6 6d* 8.1g p7f 7m^3 8d Oct 15] angular gelding: has only one eye: modest handicapper: won at Yarmouth in July: stays 7f: acts on good to firm and good to soft going. *M. R. Channon* **60**

EYE OF ETERNITY 2 b.f. (Feb 1) Oratorio (IRE) 128 – Eyeq (IRE) 106 (Cadeaux Genereux 131) [2009 7d Oct 27] first foal: dam Danish miler: 66/1, always behind in maiden at Yarmouth. *Rae Guest* **–**

EYES LIKE A HAWK (IRE) 3 b. or br.f. Diktat 126 – Mexican Hawk (USA) 98 (Silver Hawk (USA) 123) [2009 57p: 6m^5 7s^5 7.6m^4 p8f Sep 10] modest maiden: said to have bled final outing: should be suited by 1m: tongue tied in 2009. *Tom Dascombe* **62**

EYESORE 3 b.f. Reel Buddy (USA) 118 – Segretezza (IRE) 48 (Perugino (USA) 84) [2009 –: 14.1m f7g Dec 18] no form. *S. A. Harris* **–**

EZDEYAAD (USA) 5 b.g. Lemon Drop Kid (USA) 131 – August Storm (USA) (Storm Creek (USA)) [2009 90: 8m 7.9m^5 7.2m^2 8.1m* 8.1g^3 8m 8g^5 8g^6 8.1m^3 7g^5 Oct 9] sturdy gelding: fairly useful handicapper: won at Haydock in June: changed owners £25,000 after seventh start: stays 1m: acts on firm and soft ground: usually travels well up with pace: withdrawn having bolted to post prior to intended reappearance. *G. A. Swinbank* **88**

EZDIYAAD (IRE) 5 b.h. Galileo (IRE) 134 – Wijdan (USA) 101 (Mr Prospector (USA)) [2009 107: 12s^6 9m 10g^5 11.8m^3 Oct 26] big, rangy horse: useful performer: creditable efforts last 2 starts, in handicap at Ascot (4¾ lengths fifth to Cill Rialaig) and minor event at Leicester (¾-length third to Once More Dubai): probably best at 1m/1¼m: acts on heavy and good to firm ground: carries head high and best treated with caution. *M. P. Tregoning* **103 §**

F

FAASEL (IRE) 8 b.g. Unfuwain (USA) 131 – Waqood (USA) 75 (Riverman (USA) 131) [2009 16.2g 13.1m Jun 20] smart but ungenuine hurdler/chaser: lightly raced on Flat, useful performer in 2004, well held both starts since: stays 2m: acts on heavy and good to firm ground: often blinkered. *N. G. Richards* **– §**

FABLED DANCER (IRE) 3 ch.g. Choisir (AUS) 126 – Age of Fable (IRE) (Entrepreneur 123) [2009 7d 8m^5 8d Sep 7] modest form in maidens: raced only at 7f/1m on good to firm and good to soft going. *E. J. Alston* **56**

FABREZE 4 ch.g. Choisir (AUS) 126 – Impulsive Decision (IRE) 71 (Nomination 125) [2009 101: 6g Jul 10] big, strong gelding: useful performer in 2008: off a year, well held sole outing in 2009 (aggravated an old leg injury): gelded after: will prove best at 5f/6f: acts on polytrack. *P. J. Makin* **–**

FAINTLY HOPEFUL 4 b.g. Marju (IRE) 127 – Twilight Patrol 96 (Robellino (USA) 127) [2009 55: p7m p6g p6g^4 p6g 6m Aug 15] leggy gelding: modest maiden: should stay 7f: raced on polytrack and going softer than good: often in cheekpieces in 2009. *R. A. Teal* **51**

FAIR ALONG (GER) 7 b.g. Alkalde (GER) – Fairy Tango (FR) (Acatenango (GER) 127) [2009 91: 18m Oct 17] rather leggy, quite good-topped gelding: winning chaser/smart hurdler, won Grade 2 in October: lightly raced on Flat in recent years, well held in Cesarewitch only start in 2009: stays 2¼m: acts on all-weather, good to firm and good to soft going: tried in cheekpieces/blinkers. *P. J. Hobbs* **–**

FAIR BUNNY 2 b.f. (Mar 4) Trade Fair 124 – Coney Hills 35 (Beverley Boy 99) [2009 5.4d 6m 5g^3 6g^4 6g^6 5d^6 f6g* p6g^6 f6f^6 Dec 11] tall filly: seventh foal: half-sister to 3-y-o Fitzolini and 8-y-o Fitzwarren: dam maiden (stayed 7f): fair performer: won nursery at Southwell in November: stays 6f: acts on fibresand. *A. D. Brown* **65**

FAIRLY HONEST 5 br.g. Alhaarth (IRE) 126 – Miller's Melody 86 (Chief Singer 131) [2009 60: p10g^6 p9.5g^5 p8.6g^6 f8g p8g* p8g^5 p8g^3 7m 8s^5 8m^5 8f^4 Jul 5] leggy, close-coupled gelding: modest performer: won minor event at Kempton in February: best at 1m/1¼m: acts on polytrack, firm and good to soft ground: blinkered once. *P. W. Hiatt* **58**

FAIRMILE 7 b.g. Spectrum (IRE) 126 – Juno Marlowe (IRE) 100 (Danehill (USA) 126) [2009 104: 12m^4 10.3m^4 p10g^2 12m^5 10.1d* 12g^5 p8.6g^6 p12.2g Nov 20] tall gelding: has a quick action: useful performer in 2009: won minor event at Epsom in July: creditable fourth in Huxley Stakes at Chester (beaten 1¾ lengths by Doctor Fremantle) second start: left Ian Williams after sixth appearance: best at 1¼m: acts on polytrack, firm and soft going: tried in cheekpieces/blinkers: tongue tied last 4 outings: held up and travels well. *George Baker* **103**

FAIR NELLA 2 b.f. (May 15) Trade Fair 124 – Zanella (IRE) 87 (Nordico (USA)) [2009 6m^{6} 5.7g^{4} 6f^{6} Aug 17] £10,000Y: compact filly: half-sister to several winners, including 2006 2-y-o 6f winner La Roca (by Rock of Gibraltar) and 1½m/1¾m winner Zalimar (by Montjeu), both fairly useful: dam Irish 2-y-o 1m winner: modest maiden: should stay 7f. *J. G. Portman* **61**

FAIR PASSION 2 b.f. (Mar 12) Trade Fair 124 – United Passion 74 (Emarati (USA) 74) [2009 p5g^{6} p5.1g^{3} Nov 2] third foal: half-sister to 5-y-o Bookiesindex Boy: dam 5f winner: better effort in maidens when 1¾ lengths third to Tartufo Dolce at Wolverhampton, forced wide and going on at finish: likely to be suited by 6f. *D. Shaw* **68**

FAIRPLAYTOMYSELF 4 ch.f. Ballet Master (USA) 92 – Over The Moon 64 (Beveled (USA)) [2009 10.9g p8.6g^{6} 10.2m^{5} p9.5g p8.6m^{4} p8m p8.6g^{2} Dec 19] second foal: dam 7f to 11f winner: modest maiden: stays 8.6f: raced on polytrack and good/good to firm going: signs of temperament. *P. W. Hiatt* **55**

FAIR TRADE 2 ch.c. (Feb 2) Trade Fair 124 – Ballet 61 (Sharrood (USA) 124) [2009 8m^{2} Oct 16] 80,000Y: tall colt: has scope: half-brother to several winners, including smart 1m (at 2 yrs)/1¼m winner Island Sound (by Turtle Island) and useful 1¼m and 11.6f winner Serge Lifar (by Shirley Heights): dam, maiden, half-sister to May Hill winner Satinette: 40/1, most promising head second to Invincible Soul in maiden at Newmarket, missing break and finishing best: should stay 1¼m: sure to do better. *D. R. C. Elsworth* **95 p**

FAIRY FLIGHT (USA) 2 b. or br.f. (Apr 26) Fusaichi Pegasus (USA) 130 – La Barberina (USA) (Nijinsky (CAN) 138) [2009 p8.6g^{5} p8m* Dec 4] $130,000Y, $150,000 2-y-o: sister to useful US 7f (at 2 yrs)/8.5f winner Ex Caelis and half-sister to 2 winners abroad: dam, placed at 11f in France, closely related to US Grade 1 8.5f winner Fantastic Look: better effort in maidens 2 weeks apart when winning at Lingfield by ½ length from Leaving Alone, showing good turn of foot: should improve again. *W. J. Knight* **80 p**

FAIRY PROMISES (USA) 2 ch.f. (Feb 17) Broken Vow (USA) 117 – Fairy Glade (USA) (Gone West (USA)) [2009 6.1m 6.1v* 7.1d^{4} 7m Oct 2] well-made filly: third foal: dam unraced half-sister to very smart US performer up to 1¼m Skimming: fair performer: won maiden at Nottingham in July: stiffer tasks and similar form after: should prove suited by 7f+. *Pat Eddery* **75**

FAIRYS IN A STORM (IRE) 2 gr.f. (Mar 10) Choisir (AUS) 126 – Fidra (IRE) 66 (Vettori (IRE) 119) [2009 5m 6d 6g^{5} May 28] €2,000Y: unfurnished filly: first foal: dam lightly-raced maiden (should have stayed 1¼m): little form in maidens/seller. *P. T. Midgley* **–**

FAIRYWATER GREY (IRE) 2 gr.f. (Apr 1) Swift Gulliver (IRE) 110 – Chilling 62 (Chilibang 120) [2009 p5g p6g 7g Jul 18] rather leggy filly: sixth foal: dam, 5f to 1¼m (in Ireland) winner, half-sister to smart performer up to 1¾m Hannibal Lad: well beaten in maidens. *J. J. Bridger* **–**

FAITED TO PRETEND (IRE) 2 b.f. (Apr 10) Kheleyf (USA) 116 – Lady Moranbon (USA) (Trempolino (USA) 135) [2009 p7g p7g Nov 11] €27,000F, £31,000Y: leggy filly: sister to 3-y-o Muraweg, closely related to useful 9.5f/1¼m winner Diego Cao (by Cape Cross) and half-sister to several winners, including 5-y-o Sweet Gale: dam French 9f/1¼m winner: green in maidens, better effort when seventh to Padmini at Lingfield on debut. *M. L. W. Bell* **61**

FAITH AND REASON (USA) 6 b.g. Sunday Silence (USA) – Sheer Reason (USA) 110 (Danzig (USA)) [2009 76: 14.1m^{6} 16.4m 10.1g 10m^{6} Jul 22] good-bodied gelding: modest handicapper in 2009: should stay 1½m: acts on polytrack and firm going: tried in headgear/tongue strap: fair hurdler: joined C. Grant. *B. J. Curley* **60**

FAITHFUL DUCHESS (IRE) 2 b.f. (Apr 22) Bachelor Duke (USA) 122 – Portelet 91 (Night Shift (USA)) [2009 6m 6g^{4} p6g Sep 18] 60,000Y: deep-girthed filly: half-sister to several winners, including 3-y-o Splendorinthegrass, very smart 6f/7f (including at 2 yrs) winner Etlaala and smart 7f/1m winner Selective (all by Selkirk): dam 5f winner: easily best effort in maidens when fourth to Decorative at Yarmouth: should stay 7f. *E. A. L. Dunlop* **70**

FAITHFUL ONE (IRE) 2 b.f. (Mar 8) Dubawi (IRE) 129 – Have Faith (IRE) 87 (Machiavellian (USA) 123) [2009 7s^{2} p7g^{2} 7m^{2} 7v Oct 24] compact filly: second foal: half-sister to winner abroad by Cape Cross: dam, 2-y-o 7f winner, half-sister to Nassau Stakes winner Favourable Terms: runner-up in maidens first 3 starts, best effort when 2 lengths behind Marie de Medici (pair clear) at Leicester third occasion: soundly beaten in listed event on heavy going final outing: will be suited by 1m. *D. R. Lanigan* **92**

FAITHFUL RULER (USA) 5 b. or br.g. Elusive Quality (USA) – Fancy Ruler (USA) (Half A Year (USA) 130) [2009 81: p9.5g³ p10g⁴ p9.5g³ p8.6g* p8g 8.3d³ 9.1d² 8g* 8.1m f8g 8v⁵ p10m⁴ p9.5g⁵ Dec 17] good-bodied gelding: useful handicapper: better than ever in 2009, winning at Wolverhampton in March and Ayr (beat Spirit of A Nation 3 lengths) in September: may prove best around 1m: acts on all-weather and good to soft ground. *R. A. Fahey* **95**

FAITH JICARO (IRE) 2 b.f. (Mar 4) One Cool Cat (USA) 123 – Wings To Soar (USA) 67 (Woodman (USA) 126) [2009 6m² 6g² Jul 14] 10,000F: third foal: half-sister to Irish 3-y-o Spinning Wings: dam, maiden (stayed 1¼m), out of dual Yorkshire Oaks winner Only Royale: second in maidens at Haydock (better effort, beaten 3 lengths by Jeanie Johnston) and Brighton (wandered): should stay 7f+. *Mrs L. Williamson* **81**

FAJITA 3 b.c. Lahib (USA) 129 – La Fija (USA) 49 (Dixieland Band (USA)) [2009 66: 8.3g⁶ 8.1g 8.3m² 7g² 8d* 8.3g⁴ 8g³ 8g⁶ 7g* 7m³ 8m⁴ 8m⁴ Oct 1] lengthy colt: fair performer: won claimers at Newmarket in June and August: stays 1m: acts on good to firm and good to soft going: in cheekpieces/blinkers last 4 starts: sold 15,000 gns. *G. L. Moore* **77**

FAJR (IRE) 7 b.g. Green Desert (USA) 127 – Ta Rib (USA) 116 (Mr Prospector (USA)) [2009 116d: p8g p8.6g⁶ p7g⁶ Feb 4] strong, good-bodied gelding: just useful handicapper in 2009: creditable 4 lengths sixth to Capricorn Run at Kempton final start: stays 1m: acts on polytrack, soft and good to firm ground: usually wears headgear: tried tongue tied: held up. *Miss Gay Kelleway* **96**

FALAHILL 2 ch.c. (Apr 26) Selkirk (USA) 129 – Felucca 94 (Green Desert (USA) 127) [2009 8g Oct 8] angular colt: 50/1, tailed off in maiden at Newbury. *R. Hannon* **–**

FALAKEE 2 b.c. (Feb 9) Sakhee (USA) 136 – Sakhya (IRE) (Barathea (IRE) 127) [2009 7g Oct 23] first foal: dam, ran once, out of sister to Shirley Heights: 12/1, shaped as if in need of race when down the field in maiden at Doncaster: should improve. *P. W. Chapple-Hyam* **– p**

FALASTEEN (IRE) 2 ch.g. (Mar 27) Titus Livius (FR) 115 – Law Review (IRE) 63 (Case Law 113) [2009 5d* 5m³ 6m⁵ 5d⁴ 5.1m* Sep 26] £40,000Y: stocky gelding: seventh foal: brother to fairly useful 2003 2-y-o 5f/6f winner Latin Review and 4-y-o Opus Maximus, and half-brother to useful 6f (at 2 yrs) to 9f winner Layazaal (by Mujadil): dam, maiden (stayed 1m), half-sister to top-class sprinter Lake Coniston: fairly useful performer: won maiden at York in June and nursery at Chester (beat Yurituni ½ length) in September: likely to prove best at 5f: acts on good to firm and good to soft going: makes running. *D. Nicholls* **94**

FALCATIV 4 b.g. Falbrav (IRE) 133 – Frottola 109 (Muhtarram (USA) 125) [2009 98p: 11.5m* 12f⁵ 11.9m 10g⁵ p8m* p8f* Dec 20] good-bodied, attractive gelding: useful handicapper: won at Yarmouth in May and, having left L. Cumani 8,000 gns (gelded), Lingfield and Kempton (improved again when beating Aeroplane ¾ length) in December: effective at 1m to 1½m: acts on polytrack and good to firm going. *M. Botti* **102**

FALCOLNRY (IRE) 4 b.f. Hawk Wing (USA) 136 – Fear And Greed (IRE) 106 (Brief Truce (USA) 126) [2009 86: p6g Jan 11] strong, lengthy filly: fairly useful performer: heavily backed, ran poorly in handicap sole start in 2009: may prove best up to 7f: acts on good to firm ground. *E. F. Vaughan* **–**

FALCON FLIGHT (IRE) 2 b.c. (Mar 31) Montjeu (IRE) 137 – Elegant As Always (USA) 80 (Nashwan (USA) 135) [2009 8d³ Oct 21] sixth foal: closely related to fairly useful Irish 1½m winner Born For Glory (by Sadler's Wells): dam twice-raced half-sister to high-class 1m/1¼m performer Archipenko: 33/1, encouraging 7½ lengths third to stable-companion Flying Cross in maiden at Navan, patiently ridden and green under pressure: will be suited by 1¼m+: will do better. *A. P. O'Brien, Ireland* **80 p**

FALCON ROCK (IRE) 4 b.g. Hawk Wing (USA) 136 – Champaka (IRE) (Caerleon (USA) 132) [2009 7.1f³ 8.3d² p10g² 10g* 11.6f² 10m² 12m² Sep 12] tall gelding: useful handicapper: ran twice for J. Hammond in France at 3 yrs: won at Windsor in July by length from Wing Play: runner-up all starts after, good ½-length second to Precision Break at Doncaster final occasion: stays 1½m: acts on polytrack, probably on any turf going: tried in cheekpieces: tricky ride: sent to USA. *S. A. Callaghan* **97**

FALCON'S TRIBUTE (IRE) 7 b.m. Beneficial 117 – Early Storm (IRE) (Glacial Storm (USA) 127) [2009 10m 8.3m³ Sep 30] workmanlike mare: winning hurdler: modest novice chaser for P. Beaumont: similar form in maidens on Flat. *P. Salmon* **59**

FALDAL 3 br.f. Falbrav (IRE) 133 – Tidal 94 (Bin Ajwaad (IRE) 119) [2009 88p: 10g* 9.9m 12g Jul 14] lengthy, angular filly: fairly useful performer: won handicap at Ponte- **88**

fract in April: stiff tasks and not discredited in listed races after: probably stays 1½m: acts on polytrack, raced only on good/good to firm ground on turf. *Tom Dascombe*

FALLEN IDOL 2 b.c. (Mar 18) Pivotal 124 – Fallen Star 112 (Brief Truce (USA) 126) [2009 p7f* Sep 10] fourth foal: half-brother to 3-y-o Fallen In Love and fairly useful 1½m winner Star of Gibraltar (by Rock of Gibraltar): dam, 7f/1m winner, half-sister to very smart miler Fly To The Stars: 4/1, most promising debut when winning maiden at Kempton by ½ length from Golden Shaheen, taking time to assert: will be suited by 1m+: will improve. *J. H. M. Gosden* **94 p**

FALLEN IN LOVE 3 b.f. Galileo (IRE) 134 – Fallen Star 112 (Brief Truce (USA) 126) [2009 77p: 9.9m² 10m³ 11.9m² 12d² 12m⁶ Aug 20] angular, quite attractive filly: useful performer: improved in 2009, placed in listed races at Goodwood and Newbury, Lancashire Oaks at Haydock (3¾ lengths second to Barshiba) and listed event at Newbury (length second to Polly's Mark): worth a try at 1¾m: acts on good to firm and good to soft going. *J. L. Dunlop* **104**

FALLING ANGEL 2 b.f. (Apr 24) Kylian (USA) – Belle Ile (USA) 67 (Diesis 133) [2009 6g² 6m² 6f Jun 19] half-sister to several winners, including fairly useful 1m winner Woolly Bully (by Robellino): dam, 1m winner, out of US Grade 1 1¼m winner Bonne Ile: second in maidens at Goodwood (2¼ lengths behind La Pantera) and York (beaten neck by Sweet Sonnet but should have won, rider taking things easy final 1f): soundly beaten in Albany Stakes at Royal Ascot: should stay 7f/1m. *P. F. I. Cole* **79**

FALPIASE (IRE) 7 b.g. Montjeu (IRE) 137 – Gift of The Night (USA) (Slewpy (USA)) [2009 12g Jun 13] tall, angular gelding: fairly useful maiden on Flat: stayed 2m: acted on polytrack and good to firm going: tried blinkered: was none too genuine: fair hurdler, broke down in July: dead. *J. Howard Johnson* **80**

FAME AND GLORY 3 b.c. Montjeu (IRE) 137 – Gryada 93 (Shirley Heights 130) [2009 109p: 10d* 10g* 12g² 12g* 10d² 12g⁶ 10m⁶ Oct 17] **133**

Derby fame and glory for the colt of that name came at the Curragh, rather than at Epsom. Fame And Glory's impressive victory in the Dubai Duty Free Irish Derby gave his trainer Aidan O'Brien a seventh success in the race, surpassing the six saddled by his great namesake and predecessor at Ballydoyle. It was Vincent O'Brien who transformed Ballydoyle from a County Tipperary farm—'When we moved here in 1951, the first job was to make gaps in the fences for the horses to work'—into one of the most influential training operations in racing history. He sent out a long line of champions, won twenty-seven Irish classics in all and sixteen in Britain, including the Derby six times, three of those—with Sir Ivor, Nijinsky and Roberto—in five runnings between 1968 and 1972. In a poll of *Racing Post* readers in 2003, Vincent O'Brien was voted the greatest of the racing greats with Lester Piggott—who rode many of O'Brien's big winners (including four of his Derby winners)—in second place. O'Brien, who answered Gabriel's final summons on June 1st at the age of ninety-two, always said that doing his 'bit for the Irish bloodstock industry' gave him more satisfaction than any of his training feats, a point developed in more detail in the essay on Sixties Icon in *Racehorses of 2006*.

The expansion of the Coolmore stud empire was built on O'Brien's achievements at Ballydoyle with North American bloodlines, the stud career of the great Sadler's Wells ultimately the richest dividend from O'Brien's perspicacity in being one of the first to identify that the Northern Dancer line would prove so commercially successful. The latest fields for the Derby and Irish Derby owed much to the O'Brien legacy, the progeny of Sadler's Wells and his sons well represented, as they usually are nowadays at Epsom and the Curragh. Ballydoyle and Coolmore are now largely under the stewardship of O'Brien's son-in-law John Magnier, who was responsible for appointing Aidan O'Brien to take over at Ballydoyle. Like Vincent, who had a string of Cheltenham winners and is the only trainer to have won three consecutive Grand Nationals, Aidan made a smooth transition from the jumping world to the Flat and has proved a more than worthy successor, handling a much larger string and keeping Ballydoyle at the forefront of British and Irish racing. The current master of Ballydoyle took less time than his predecessor to win all ten British and Irish classics (only British trainer Dick Hern has also compiled a full set) and he now needs only five more to match Vincent O'Brien's Irish classic total and two more to match his British total.

Derrinstown Stud Derby Trial Stakes, Leopardstown—Fame And Glory wins impressively from Mourayan and Fergus McIver (blinkers) and goes to the head of the Derby betting

Six of the seven Aidan O'Brien-trained Irish Derby winners also ran at Epsom, Galileo and High Chaparral completing the double, while Dylan Thomas, Soldier of Fortune and Frozen Fire improved out of all recognition between Epsom and the Curragh. Dylan Thomas ran away with the Irish Derby by three and a half lengths after coming third to Sir Percy in a blanket finish at Epsom, Soldier of Fortune improved from fifth at Epsom to first at the Curragh and Frozen Fire from eleventh, though he had seemed not to act on the course at Epsom. Like his three immediate predecessors on the Irish Derby roll of honour, Fame And Glory had previously been part of a multiple entry representing Ballydoyle in the Derby at Epsom, a race seemingly assured of the continuing backing of John Magnier and his investment partners Michael Tabor and Derrick Smith. 'In Vincent's time, the Derby was the centre of the year, it was *the* race,' said Magnier. 'Maybe it has lost some of its gloss, but it is the race where all the qualities of a colt are tested . . . we run those we feel are entitled to run, it's a chance for them to prove themselves.' After a battalion of Ballydoyle colts had auditioned for a place, six eventually made the line-up for the latest renewal: Rip Van Winkle (the mount of Ballydoyle's number-one Johnny Murtagh) had finished fourth in the Two Thousand Guineas, Black Bear Island had won the Dante at York, Golden Sword and Masterofthehorse had come first and second in the Chester Vase, Age of Aquarius had won the Derby Trial at Lingfield and Fame And Glory, who started 9/4 favourite ahead of the Two Thousand Guineas winner Sea The Stars and Rip Van Winkle, had followed the route to Epsom taken by Galileo and High Chaparral, among others, maintaining his unbeaten record in the P. W. McGrath Memorial Ballysax Stakes at Leopardstown in April and the Derrinstown Stud Derby Trial (by five lengths) over the same course the following month, penalised in both for his Group 1 win in the Criterium de Saint-Cloud and conceding weight all round.

O'Brien's personal supervision of his runners in the saddling boxes at Epsom resulted in them entering the parade ring after the signal for jockeys to mount had been given. The apologetic trainer was fined £840 at a subsequent inquiry, the stewards reportedly 'taking a dim view'—which was still better than the view that the paying public and the worldwide TV audience had had to settle for. Ballydoyle's massed ranks went on to fill second, third, fourth and fifth in a clean sweep for Ireland behind Sea The Stars, with Fame And Glory, beaten a length and three quarters, coming out best, though only a neck, a nose and a short head in front of Masterofthehorse, Rip Van Winkle and Golden Sword. Golden Sword and Age of Aquarius had opened up a clear lead after a steady first three furlongs, the early pace leading to some expressions of surprise that Ballydoyle had allowed the race to develop into one that seemingly played to the strengths of Sea The Stars (and Rip Van Winkle) and not to those of Fame And Glory whom some felt would have been suited by a flat-out gallop all the way. O'Brien summed up the situation later by saying 'What happened at Epsom happened. It wasn't the plan and it just worked out that way. All our horses went there to run on their merits and Sea The Stars was that bit too good for them.'

Prospects of an eagerly-anticipated rematch between Fame And Glory and Sea The Stars in the Irish Derby were quashed by the late defection of Sea The Stars following heavy rain on the Friday night, though the going dried out in the next thirty-six hours which made the absence of Sea The Stars all the more disappointing. The half dozen from Ballydoyle—in an eleven-runner line-up without a single overseas challenger—also included Masterofthehorse and Golden Sword, but, in a strongly-run encounter, Fame And Glory (ridden by Murtagh this time) left them all standing, producing a fine turn of foot after being settled much further off the pace than the eventual second and third Golden Sword—who was sent on well over three furlongs out—and Mourayan. Stretching clear in tremendous style over the final furlong once he had collared Golden Sword, Fame And Glory won by five lengths and a length, with Masterofthehorse ten lengths further back in fourth. Fame And Glory's winning margin was the second-widest of the seven winners from Ballydoyle under Aidan O'Brien. Soldier of Fortune won by nine, though wide-margin victories in the Irish Derby are by no means so rare as you might think for a major classic. St Jovite, the last before Fame And Glory to win the Irish Derby after finishing second at Epsom, won by twelve (from Derby winner Dr Devious), the biggest winning margin since the Irish Derby became recognised as an event of world-wide importance in the 'sixties. The official winning margin recorded by Sinndar was the same as that for Soldier of Fortune, while Shahrastani and Assert were returned as eight-length winners and Zagreb as a six-length winner. Fame And Glory's sire Montjeu, who was trained in France, also won the race by five.

John Magnier observed at the end of the season that, had it not been for Sea The Stars, Ballydoyle would have cleaned up, collecting the Eclipse with Rip Van Winkle, the International with Mastercraftsman and the Derby and the Irish Champion with Fame And Glory, instead of them all coming second to Sea The Stars. On the other side of the coin, Ballydoyle probably had good reason to be thankful that Sea The Stars at least missed the Irish Derby, for which he would have been odds on. Judged on the bare form, there wasn't a great deal to choose between the respective Derby-winning performances at Epsom and the Curragh of Sea The Stars and Fame And Glory, though there was clearly more to come from the Epsom winner as he demonstrated next time at Sandown (the Eclipse form was franked when Rip Van Winkle won the Sussex and third-placed Conduit the King George VI and Queen Elizabeth Stakes).

While Sea The Stars continued with a summer campaign, Fame And Glory was given a break before being brought back to take on Sea The Stars at Leopards-

*Dubai Duty Free Irish Derby, the Curragh—
the field is well strung out as Fame And Glory gives Aidan O'Brien his seventh victory in the race; his stable-companions Golden Sword and Masterofthehorse are split by the blinkered Mourayan*

town in early-September, where Mastercraftsman was also in the five-strong Ballydoyle challenge. As with the Irish Derby, there were doubts beforehand about the participation of Sea The Stars because of fears over soft ground. Fortunately, Leopardstown avoided the worst of the rain—which led to several meetings being lost at around the same time—and the Irish Champion Stakes was able to live up to its name. Confirmed a definite runner only a couple of hours before, Sea The Stars produced the best performance of his career to beat Fame And Glory and Mastercraftsman by two and a half lengths and the same, the first three drawing well clear. Fame And Glory's own performance was good enough to have won most recent renewals of the race, though he couldn't respond when tackled by Sea The Stars after being sent to the front early in the home straight to ensure the race was a thorough test. The rest of Fame And Glory's season was an anti-climax as he managed only sixth behind Sea The Stars in the Arc, never really threatening, and was then a long way below his best when a beaten favourite in the Champion Stakes at Newmarket, a target that in hindsight, in the words of his trainer, 'was probably a mistake so soon after the Arc.'

Fame And Glory (b.c. 2006)	Montjeu (IRE) (b 1996)	Sadler's Wells (b 1981)	Northern Dancer
			Fairy Bridge
		Floripedes (b 1985)	Top Ville
			Toute Cy
	Gryada (b 1993)	Shirley Heights (b 1975)	Mill Reef
			Hardiemma
		Grimpola (br 1982)	Windwurf
			Gondel

Fame And Glory, a big, quite good-looking colt, is the third Irish Derby winner sired by Montjeu, following Hurricane Run and Frozen Fire (he has also sired two Epsom Derby winners, Motivator and Authorized, from his first five three-year-old crops in the northern hemisphere, while his record also boasts two winners of the Australian Derby, Nom du Jeu and Roman Emperor). Fame And Glory's dam Gryada, a fairly useful two-year-old who didn't train on, made a good start as a broodmare at Plantation Stud, producing the useful Guaranda (by Acatenango), a winner at a mile and a quarter and a mile and a half (and now the dam of the Group 3 winner Gravitation), and the smart middle-distance stayer Grampian (by Selkirk) in her first two years. Gryada's record stood at four winners from as many runners when she was moved on at the 2005 December Sales after Lady Howard de Walden had sold Plantation Stud and much of the stock to Dermot and Perle O'Rourke. Gryada made 160,000 guineas in foal to Montjeu. Returned to the same sale the following year—in foal to Sadler's Wells this time—Gryada changed hands for 180,000 guineas, while her Montjeu colt foal (Fame And Glory) realised 190,000 guineas, joining Ballydoyle/Coolmore, who also bought the Sadler's Wells offspring (now named Rain Forest) for 200,000 guineas two years later. Fame And Glory's year-older sister Yummy Mummy maintained her dam's good record at stud when winning at a mile and a quarter at Sligo as a three-year-old, showing fairly useful form. She was sold (in foal to Dalakhani) at the December Sales in 2009 for 460,000 guineas. Gryada's own dam Grimpola was acquired by Plantation Stud from Germany where she won the Schwarzgold-Rennen (at the time that country's version of the One Thousand Guineas). Gryada's sire Shirley Heights sired Lord Howard de Walden's Derby winner Slip Anchor, who was also out of a German mare, Sayonara, who came second in the Preis der Diana (German Oaks). Grimpola was twice covered by Slip Anchor, one of the produce being the useful out-and-out stayer Gondolier and the other an unraced mare called Gonfalon, who was returned to Germany where she produced the Deutschlandpreis and Preis von Europa winner Gonbarda and two other pattern winners. Fame And Glory, who is effective at a mile and a quarter and a mile and a half, stays in training. It may be worth bearing in mind that the going for the Champion Stakes at Newmarket was firmer than he had previously encountered, and his best efforts have come on good or softer (he acts on heavy). *A. P. O'Brien, Ireland*

FAME IS THE SPUR 2 ch.f. (Mar 8) Motivator 131 – Subya 107 (Night Shift (USA)) **74 +**
[2009 7s 6.5m Sep 25] 30,000Y: tall, leggy filly: half-sister to several winners, notably 1¼m/1½m winner Villa Carlotta (by Rainbow Quest) and US Grade 2 9.5f/1¼m winner

Battle of Hastings (by Royal Applause), both smart: dam 5f (at 2 yrs) to 1¼m winner: encouraging seventh to Pipette in maiden at Salisbury on debut: stiff task, mid-field in sales race at Ascot: will be well suited by 1¼m. *J. W. Hills*

FAMOUS (IRE) 2 gr.f. (Feb 13) Danehill Dancer (IRE) 117 – Starlight Dreams (USA) (Black Tie Affair 128) [2009 6s^2 6d^4 7g* 7g^5 7v^2 8g^4 Sep 27] €1,000,000Y: seventh foal: sister to 3-y-o Mastercraftsman, closely related to US Grade 3 1m winner Genuine Devotion (by Rock of Gibraltar) and half-sister to 2004 2-y-o 6f seller winner Nordhock (by Luhuk): dam, US 1m winner, out of close relative to dam of Sakhee: useful performer: won maiden at Leopardstown in July by 3½ lengths from Rosa Muscosa: in frame at the Curragh last 2 starts, in Moyglare Stud Stakes (excellent 2½ lengths second to Termagant) and Goffs Million Mile (close fourth to Shakespearean): should prove at least as effective at 1m as 7f: acts well on heavy going: usually races close up. *A. P. O'Brien, Ireland* **104**

FAMOUS NAME 4 b.c. Dansili 127 – Fame At Last (USA) 98 (Quest For Fame 127) [2009 121: 10v^2 10.5v^2 8g* 9s* 8s* 8g^2 9.8g^3 Oct 3] good-topped colt: very smart performer: easy winner of listed race in June, Keeneland International Stakes (by 2 lengths from Staying On) in July and Desmond Stakes (by 4½ lengths from Three Rocks, going clear from over 1f out) in August, all at the Curragh: creditable efforts after at Longchamp when 1½ lengths second to Aqlaam in Prix du Moulin and third, beaten 2 necks by Pipedreamer, in Prix Dollar: effective at 1m/1¼m: acts on heavy ground: visored/blinkered once each: travels strongly held up. *D. K. Weld, Ireland* **123**

Desmond Stakes, the Curragh—Famous Name easily completes a course hat-trick

FAN CLUB 5 ch.g. Zamindar (USA) 116 – Starfan (USA) 101 (Lear Fan (USA) 130) [2009 48: f6s f5g f8g 9.3m 16g 12m 16.5s 9.2d Jul 17] lengthy, good-topped gelding: poor performer: stays 1m: acts on good to firm ground: formerly blinkered. *Mrs R. A. Carr* –

FANCY FOOTSTEPS (IRE) 4 gr.f. Noverre (USA) 125 – Fancy Intense (Peintre Celebre (USA) 137) [2009 79: p8g* 8d 8.3d 7m³ p8g³ p8g* p8g⁴ p8g p8g⁶ Oct 8] rather leggy filly: fairly useful handicapper: won at Kempton in January and August: stays 1m: acts on polytrack and good to firm going: sold 15,000 gns, sent to Kazakhstan. *C. G. Cox* 84

FANCY SET (IRE) 3 b.f. Reset (AUS) 124 – Crafty Fancy (IRE) 91 (Intikhab (USA) 135) [2009 f6g 7d f6g May 1] first foal: dam, 2-y-o 5f winner who stayed 1m, half-sister to smart performer up to 1½m Come On Jonny: well held all 3 starts, including in a seller: tried blinkered. *D. J. S. ffrench Davis* –

FANCY STAR 2 b.c. (Mar 23) Starcraft (NZ) 128 – Lorien Hill (IRE) 78 (Danehill (USA) 126) [2009 7s 7d Aug 1] strong, useful-looking colt: soundly beaten in maidens at Newbury and Goodwood (saddle reportedly slipped). *B. W. Hills* –

FANDANGO BOY 8 b.g. Victory Note (USA) 120 – Dancing Chimes (London Bells (CAN) 109) [2009 71§: p10g³ p9.5g p9.5g p9.5g 8m 8g 6m 7g p8g p12g² p8g* p7g* p8.6g⁵ Dec 7] fairly useful handicapper: left D. Carroll after fourth start: won at Dundalk twice in November: effective at 7f to easy 1¼m: acts on polytrack and firm going: tried in cheekpieces: unreliable. *J. P. Broderick, Ireland* 80 §

FANDITHA (IRE) 3 ch.f. Danehill Dancer (IRE) 117 – Splendid (IRE) (Mujtahid (USA) 118) [2009 81: p8g² 8.1g⁴ 8m⁶ 8d⁴ 9g 9g 8.1d³ 11m* 10g³ 12g³ Oct 30] good-topped filly: fairly useful handicapper: won at Goodwood in September: stays 11f: acts on polytrack, good to firm and good to soft ground: signs of temperament (resented blinkers sixth start). *R. Hannon* 93

FANGFOSS GIRLS 3 ch.f. Monsieur Bond (IRE) 120 – Bond Shakira 54 (Daggers Drawn (USA) 114) [2009 68: p5g² p6g⁶ p5g⁶ 5.1g⁵ 5g⁶ Apr 21] small filly: regressive form in 2009, leaving L. Wells prior to fourth start: stays 6f: acts on polytrack and good to soft going. *G. L. Moore* 65

FANJURA (IRE) 4 b.g. Marju (IRE) 127 – Accelerating (USA) 76 (Lear Fan (USA) 130) [2009 92: 8g² 8s⁵ 10.3m 8.9g 10m* 10g* 10m* 10.3m³ 9.9m³ Sep 23] well-made, attractive gelding: smart performer: improved in 2009, winning handicaps at Sandown and Ascot in July, and Sandown (beat Antinori by neck) in August: below-par third to Twice Over in listed race at Goodwood final start: stays 1¼m: acts on soft and good to firm ground: tactically versatile: sold 210,000 gns, to join L. Freedman in Australia. *B. W. Hills* 111

FANTASIA 3 b.f. Sadler's Wells (USA) 132 – Blue Symphony 73 (Darshaan 133) [2009 111p: 7m* 8m³ 10.5m 7m* 8m⁶ Oct 3] strong, lengthy filly: type to carry condition: smart performer: reported in February to have changed owners: won Leslie Harrison Memorial 116

Japan Racing Association Sceptre Stakes, Doncaster—
Fantasia lands the odds in good style from Shamwari Lodge and Say No Now (third left)

Nell Gwyn Stakes at Newmarket (by 7 lengths from Damaniyat Girl) in April and listed event at Doncaster (quickened smartly to beat Shamwari Lodge 2 lengths) in September: creditable effort otherwise when 2 lengths third to Elusive Wave in Poule d'Essai des Pouliches at Longchamp: should stay beyond 1m: acts on good to firm and good to soft going: possibly best fresh: has joined J. Sheppard in USA. *L. M. Cumani*

FANTASTICAL 3 b.f. Fantastic Light (USA) 134 – First Musical 107 (First Trump 118) [2009 p8g[4] p8g 8g May 28] 22,000Y: fifth foal: half-sister to 5-y-o Avertuoso and 5.7f winner Casterossa (by Rossini): dam 2-y-o 5f/6f winner: modest form in maidens only on debut. *C. E. Brittain* **60**

FANTASTIC CUIX (FR) 2 gr.f. (Feb 18) Fantastic Light (USA) 134 – Cuixmala (FR) (Highest Honor (FR) 124) [2009 8g p8m[4] Nov 19] seventh foal: half-sister to smart French 1¼m to 15.5f winner Mont Rocher (by Caerleon) and useful French 1¼m to 15f winner Yayo (by Petit Loup): dam unraced half-sister to Montjeu: better effort in maidens when 2¼ lengths fourth to Aviate at Kempton, wide and not knocked about late: will be suited by 1½m+: said to have hit head on stall on debut: will do better. *L. M. Cumani* **72 p**

FANTASTIC DUBAI (USA) 3 b.c. Storm Cat (USA) – Shy Lady (FR) 91 (Kaldoun (FR) 122) [2009 64p: p7g* p7g[2] 6s[2] 6m[2] Jun 12] $400,000Y: good-topped colt: sixth foal: half-brother to very smart miler Zafeen (by Zafonic), 4-y-o Atlantic Sport and useful 2001 2-y-o 6f/7f winner Ya Hajar (by Lycius): dam useful German 2-y-o 5f/6f winner: fairly useful form: won maiden at Lingfield in March: better efforts when runner-up in handicaps 3 starts after: stays 7f: acts on polytrack, soft and good to firm going: has joined M. Al Muhain in UAE. *M. R. Channon* **82**

FANTASTIC FRED (IRE) 3 br.g. Fantastic Light (USA) 134 – Luxury Launch (USA) (Seeking The Gold (USA)) [2009 41: p8.6g* p8.6g* p9.5g[6] p8g[2] p8g 10m May 7] modest performer: won 2 handicaps at Wolverhampton in January: stays 8.6f: acts on polytrack. *J. A. Osborne* **61**

FANTASTIC MORNING 5 ch.g. Fantastic Light (USA) 134 – Gombay Girl (USA) 82 (Woodman (USA) 126) [2009 –: 11.6g 9.9m p12m p12g Oct 20] angular, well-made gelding: no form in 2009: tried blinkered/in cheekpieces. *F. Jordan* **–**

FANTASTIC PICK 2 b.g. (Feb 12) Fantastic Light (USA) 134 – Umlilo 64 (Mtoto 134) [2009 6d[6] 7m 6g 8g* 8m* 10.2m[2] 8g Oct 19] 18,000Y: sturdy gelding: first foal: dam, maiden, half-sister to smart performers up to 1½m Sir George Turner and Tissifer: fairly useful performer: won nurseries at Bath and Redcar (easily) in September: said to have finished distressed final start: should stay 1½m: acts on good to firm ground: sold 25,000 gns, sent to USA. *B. J. Meehan* **80**

FANTASTIC PRINCE 2 ch.g. (Feb 20) Cadeaux Genereux 131 – Fantaisiste 103 (Nashwan (USA) 135) [2009 6g 6m[2] 6m[3] 6g 7m[5] Sep 10] 50,000Y: big, lengthy gelding: first foal: dam, 6f winner (including at 2 yrs), out of sister/half-sister to smart performers up to 1½m Moon Solitaire and Germano: maiden: placed at Newmarket and Ayr: no comparable form, awkward in blinkers final start: should stay 7f: probably not straightforward. *P. F. I. Cole* **72**

FANTASTIC STRIKE (IRE) 2 b.c. (Apr 25) Noverre (USA) 125 – Hariya (IRE) 99 (Shernazar 131) [2009 6m[5] 5.9g 6m[2] 8g[4] Sep 7] €30,000F, 5,000Y: tall colt: third foal: half-brother to fairly useful French 9f to 10.5f winner Himariya (by Marju): dam, Irish 1¼m winner, half-sister to smart Irish/US performer up to 1¼m Harghar: fair maiden: fourth to Fantastic Pick in nursery at Bath, no room 2f out and finishing strongly: likely to stay 1¼m: capable of better. *M. Johnston* **74 p**

FANTASY BELIEVER 11 b.g. Sure Blade (USA) 130 – Delicious 51 (Dominion 123) [2009 85: 5m 6m 6m 5m[4] 5m[4] 6d[2] Jul 9] sturdy gelding: handicapper, just fair in 2009: effective at 5f to 7f: acts on any going: sometimes hangs/carries head awkwardly: waited with. *J. J. Quinn* **71**

FANTASY EXPLORER 6 b.g. Compton Place 125 – Zinzi (Song 132) [2009 96: 6m 6f 5g p6g* p5g[2] p5.1g[3] p6m[2] Nov 19] good-topped gelding: useful handicapper: won at Kempton in October: improved when ½-length second to Earlsmedic there final outing: best at 5f/easy 6f: acts on polytrack, firm and good to soft going: tried in cheekpieces (ran well). *J. J. Quinn* **101**

FANTASY FIGHTER (IRE) 4 b.g. Danetime (IRE) 121 – Lady Montekin (Montekin 125) [2009 65§: p6g[3] p6g p6g p5g 6s p6f[3] p6g[5] p6g* p6g* p5.1g p6g[2] Dec 12] fair handicapper: better than ever when winning at Wolverhampton and Lingfield in November: best at 6f: acts on all-weather: tried visored: irresolute (often flashes tail). *J. J. Quinn* **40 § a69 §**

Britannia Stakes (Heritage Handicap), Royal Ascot—Fareer (right) is produced late and comes off best in a very close finish with Secret Society, Mirrored (left) and Espiritu (visor)

FANTASY GLADIATOR 3 b.g. Ishiguru (USA) 114 – Fancier Bit (Lion Cavern (USA) 117) [2009 70+: 5m^5 5d^3 6g^2 f6g* p6m* Sep 24] fairly useful performer: improved when winning maiden at Southwell in August and handicap at Kempton in September: will stay 7f: acts on all-weather, best turf effort on good ground. *R. M. H. Cowell* **84**

FANTASY LAND (IRE) 3 ch.f. Danehill Dancer (IRE) 117 – Wondrous Story (USA) 91 (Royal Academy (USA) 130) [2009 7s 7m^3 7g^3 8m p6g^6 7g 7m 7m p6g Sep 25] €130,000Y: lengthy filly: first foal: dam, 2-y-o 7f winner who stayed 8.5f, half-sister to smart 1½m performer Theatre Script: fair form only when third in maidens: stays 7f: tried blinkered: tongue tied after debut: temperament under suspicion. *B. J. Meehan* **73 d**

FANTASY PRINCESS (USA) 4 ch.f. Johannesburg (USA) 127 – Fantasy 80 (Cadeaux Genereux 131) [2009 85: 9g p9.5m p12g f8g^4 Oct 27] tall, angular filly: handicapper, just fair in 2009: stays easy 1¼m: acts on all-weather, soft and good to firm ground: tongue tied last 3 starts, also in cheekpieces second occasion: sold 9,000 gns. *G. A. Butler* **78**

FANTASY RIDE 7 b.h. Bahhare (USA) 122 – Grand Splendour 79 (Shirley Heights 130) [2009 64, a71: p12g^2 p12.2g^2 p12g p12g^5 9.7d 10.1m^6 10.1g^2 10.1g^2 10.1g^4 p9.5g^4 p12f p12g p13.9g^2 p12m p12.2g^3 p12m^4 p12g^4 Dec 31] rather leggy horse (not a gelding as in previous Annuals): has a markedly round action: modest performer: stays 1¾m: acts on polytrack, soft and good to firm ground: tried blinkered: held up: has looked reluctant under pressure. *J. Pearce* **61**

FANTINO 3 b.g. Shinko Forest (IRE) – Illustre Inconnue (USA) (Septieme Ciel (USA) 123) [2009 68p: 8.1g 8.3g^5 8.3m^5 8g 10m^2 11.8m* 11.5m 14.1g 10g Oct 19] workmanlike gelding: fair handicapper: won at Leicester in September: stays 1½m: raced only on good/good to firm going. *J. Mackie* **71**

FANUNALTER 3 b.g. Falbrav (IRE) 133 – Step Danzer (IRE) 105 (Desert Prince (IRE) 130) [2009 8m^2 10.5d p8g* 8.1m^2 8m p8.6g^3 Nov 13] strong, useful-looking gelding: first foal: dam, Italian 7.5f (at 2 yrs) to 1¼m winner, second in Oaks d'Italia: useful performer: had first 2 starts in Italy: won maiden at Kempton in August: further improvement when placed in handicaps after, 2¼ lengths third to Stand Guard at Wolverhampton final outing (gelded after): should stay 1¼m: acts on polytrack and good to firm going: has been tongue tied. *M. Botti* **102**

FARADAY (IRE) 6 b.g. Montjeu (IRE) 137 – Fureau (GER) (Ferdinand (USA)) [2009 60: p10g Feb 9] modest performer: well below form only start in 2009: stays 1½m: acts on polytrack, good to soft and good to firm ground: tried blinkered. *N. P. Mulholland* **–**

FARAWAY SOUND (IRE) 3 b.g. Distant Music (USA) 126 – Queen Consort 69 (Diesis 133) [2009 81d: 6m^6 5v^6 Sep 4] good-topped gelding: just modest form at 3 yrs: should prove best at 5f: acts on firm ground: tried in cheekpieces/visor. *P. C. Haslam* **62**

FARDYIEH 2 b.f. (Feb 21) King's Best (USA) 132 – Injaaz 99 (Sheikh Albadou 128) [2009 6g 6m^2 p6g* 6.5m 6g Oct 8] 28,000Y: strong filly: second foal: half-sister to fairly useful 2007 2-y-o 6f winner Classic Fortune (by Royal Applause): dam 6f (including at 2 yrs)/7f winner: progressive in maidens, winning at Kempton in September: well below form in nursery final start: should stay 7f: acts on polytrack and good to firm ground. *C. E. Brittain* **82**

FAREEHA 4 b.f. King's Best (USA) 132 – Shatarah 79 (Gulch (USA)) [2009 52: p8.6g Oct 30] sturdy filly: modest maiden: below form sole outing in 2009: stays easy 1¼m: seems to act on polytrack and good to firm going. *J. Mackie* –

FAREEJ (USA) 2 b.c. (Mar 12) Kingmambo (USA) 125 – Adonesque (IRE) 106 (Sadler's Wells (USA) 132) [2009 8m* p8g* Oct 14] close-coupled, useful-looking colt: fifth foal: brother to useful French 1m winner Bergamask and half-brother to useful 2006 2-y-o 6f winner Alderney (by Elusive Quality): dam, Irish 9f/1¼m winner, half-sister to smart 6f/7f performer Danehill Dancer: made promising start, winning maiden at Newmarket (green, beat William Van Gogh 2¼ lengths) and 3-runner minor event at Lingfield (by 2¼ lengths from Business As Usual, quickening clear final 1f), both in October: stays 1m: will continue to progress. *Saeed bin Suroor* **93 p**

FAREER 3 ch.c. Bahamian Bounty 116 – Songsheet 74 (Dominion 123) [2009 92: 7s^3 7.6m* 8.1v^5 8m* Jun 18] lengthy colt: progressed into a useful handicapper, winning at Chester in May and Britannia Stakes at Royal Ascot (by head from Secret Society, dropped out before well-timed run to get up close home) in June: suffered from minor soundness problems after: stays 1m: acts on soft and good to firm ground. *E. A. L. Dunlop* **107**

FAREHAM TOWN 2 ch.f. (May 13) Cape Town (IRE) 119 – Fareham § (Komaite (USA)) [2009 p6g p7.1g^3 p6g Dec 18] second foal: dam temperamental maiden: easily best effort in maidens at Wolverhampton when 7¼ lengths third to Lady of Akita. *S. Kirk* **51**

FARLEIGH 3 b.f. Trans Island 119 – Medway (IRE) 60 (Shernazar 131) [2009 67p: 8.3g* 8d^3 8.1g^6 Aug 13] smallish filly: fair form: won maiden at Windsor in May: bred to be suited by 1¼m+: raced only on polytrack and good/good to soft going. *A. M. Balding* **78**

FARLEIGH HOUSE (USA) 5 b.g. Lear Fan (USA) 130 – Verasina (USA) 83 (Woodman (USA) 126) [2009 8.3m^5 10m 10m^6 p11g p8.6g^2 9.7m^3 p9.5g* p8.6g^2 Oct 16] rather leggy, lengthy gelding: ran in allowance races for B. Cecil in USA in 2008, second 3 times (gelded after): fairly useful handicapper on return to Britain, winning at Wolverhampton in October: stays easy 9.7f: acts on polytrack, firm and good to soft going: tried blinkered (in USA). *Sir Mark Prescott* **92**

FARLEY STAR 5 b.m. Alzao (USA) 117 – Girl of My Dreams (IRE) 51 (Marju (IRE) 127) [2009 96: 8.3m^3 7v^4 Oct 24] useful-looking mare: useful handicapper: shaped well both starts in 2009, 3¼ lengths fourth to Crystal Moments at Newbury: stays 9.8f: acts on polytrack, heavy and good to firm ground: held up. *M. G. Quinlan* **97**

FARMER GILES (IRE) 2 b.c. (Feb 4) Danroad (AUS) 112 – Demeter (USA) 79 (Diesis 133) [2009 5m^6 5f^2 5f^3 5d* 6m p5g^4 5m 7m^3 7m^4 8g Oct 23] €19,500Y, resold £46,000Y: useful-looking colt: fifth foal: half-brother to 3-y-o Pyrrha and fairly useful 1½m winner Alrafidain (by Monsun): dam, ran once, out of Irish 1000 Guineas winner Nicer: fairly useful performer: won maiden at Ripon (by 6 lengths) in June: ran well after only when in frame in nurseries at Doncaster and Ascot eighth/ninth starts: stays 7f: acts on good to firm and good to soft going: has shown signs of temperament: sold 28,000 gns. *M. L. W. Bell* **90**

FARMERS DREAM (IRE) 2 b.f. (May 5) Antonius Pius (USA) 123§ – Beucaire (IRE) 88 (Entrepreneur 123) [2009 6.5g 6m p6m^6 Nov 4] angular filly: third foal: dam, Irish 9f winner, out of Irish 1000 Guineas winner Tarascon: sixth at Kempton, only form in maidens: should stay beyond 6f. *J. L. Spearing* **46**

FARMERS WISH (IRE) 2 b.f. (Mar 6) Val Royal (FR) 127 – Farmers Swing (IRE) (River Falls 113) [2009 6m^4 6m^2 6.1v* 6m* 7m^6 6g^2 6g^5 p6m^4 6s Nov 7] 8,000F: neat filly: fourth foal: half-sister to 3 winners, including 5-y-o Northern Dare and 6-y-o Valentino Swing: dam, Norwegian 8.5f winner, half-sister to useful performer up to 1m Scarteen Fox: fairly useful performer: won maiden at Chepstow in July and minor event at Haydock in August: in frame in nurseries at Hamilton and Kempton: stays 6f: acts on polytrack, heavy and good to firm going: front runner. *J. L. Spearing* **83**

FARNCOMBE (IRE) 3 ch.f. Where Or When (IRE) 124 – Promenade 87 (Primo Dominie 121) [2009 7s 7g^3 6g^3 p7g^6 p9.5g^3 p10g* p10g^5 p12g Dec 7] 20,000Y: well-made filly: first foal: dam 2-y-o 5f winner, out of half-sister to Irish 2000 Guineas winner Wassl: fair performer: won claimer at Lingfield (left M. Tregoning £6,000) in November: stays 1¼m: acts on polytrack and soft ground. *R. A. Harris* **68**

FARNE ISLAND 6 ch.g. Arkadian Hero (USA) 123 – Holy Island 81 (Deploy 131) [2009 59: 10m^2 10.1g^4 9.2m^5 Jun 30] sturdy gelding: modest handicapper: stays 11f: acts on polytrack, firm and soft going. *Micky Hammond* **59**

FAR 'N WIDE 3 ch.f. Rainbow Quest (USA) 134 – Raspberry Sauce 65 (Niniski (USA) 125) [2009 12m May 15] sixth foal: half-sister to 4-y-o Crackentorp and fairly useful 1¼m to 13f winner Boot 'N Toot (by Mtoto): dam 1m to 11.6f winner: well held in maiden at Newmarket. *W. J. Haggas* –

FARRIERS GATE 3 ch.f. Lomitas 129 – Mountain Stream (FR) (Vettori (IRE) 119) [2009 –: p8g p6g Mar 1] angular filly: no form: tried blinkered. *M. E. Rimmer* –

FARSIGHTED 4 b.f. Where Or When (IRE) 124 – Classic Vision 59 (Classic Cliche (IRE) 128) [2009 –: p7g p10g Jan 16] small filly: regressive handicapper: tried blinkered. *J. M. P. Eustace* –

FAR VIEW (IRE) 2 b.c. (Feb 19) Oasis Dream 129 – Night Mirage (USA) 80 (Silver Hawk (USA) 123) [2009 p7g Nov 18] 10/1 and tongue tied, slowly away and badly in need of experience when tailed off in maiden at Kempton. *J. W. Hills* –

FASCILE 2 b.g. (Apr 20) Forzando 122 – Frankie Fair (IRE) 73 (Red Sunset 120) [2009 5m Apr 20] neat gelding: 100/1 and bit backward, always behind in maiden at Windsor: sold £500, joined M. Scudamore. *E. J. Creighton* –

FASETTE 2 b.f. (Feb 23) Fasliyev (USA) 120 – Londonnet (IRE) 74 (Catrail (USA) 123) [2009 6g Jun 6] 1,000Y: good-topped filly: third foal: half-sister to French 1¼m winner Horseguard (by Beat Hollow): dam once-raced half-sister to useful performer up to 1¼m Keld: 33/1, last in maiden at Doncaster, very slowly away. *M. H. Tompkins* –

FASHIONABLE GAL (IRE) 2 b.f. (Feb 10) Galileo (IRE) 134 – Fashion 84 (Bin Ajwaad (IRE) 119) [2009 7.5m Sep 16] big, lengthy filly: fifth foal: half-sister to fairly useful 1m winner Scot Love (by Dansili) and 2006 2-y-o 7f seller winner Disco Queen (by Night Shift): dam, 1m (at 2 yrs)/1¼m winner, closely related to Oaks d'Italia winner Bright Generation: 25/1, ninth in maiden at Beverley: bred to be suited by 1¼m+: will do better. *Sir Mark Prescott* **– p**

FASHION ICON (USA) 3 ch.f. Van Nistelrooy (USA) 108 – Los Altos (USA) (Robin Des Pins (USA) 119) [2009 56: p6g⁵ f5g⁵ p5.1g³ p6g⁴ f5g² 5m² 5m 5m⁴ 5g⁴ f5g Jun 2] compact filly: modest maiden: best at 5f: acts on all-weather and good to firm going: tried blinkered (looked awkward). *T. D. Barron* **62**

FASHION INSIDER (USA) 2 b. or br.f. (Apr 15) Indian Charlie (USA) 126 – Shahalo (USA) (Halo (USA)) [2009 7g⁴ p8m² Dec 4] $460,000Y: sturdy, attractive filly: sister to smart US Grade 2 winners Bwana Charlie (6f) and My Pal Charlie (9f) and half-sister to 2 winners in USA, including Grade 3 8.5f winner Bwana Bull (by Holy Bull): dam, ran twice in USA, half-sister to useful 7f/1m performer Neuwest: fair form in maidens, neck second to Gifted Apakay at Lingfield: should prove at least as effective at 7f as 1m: sent to USA: should improve again. *B. J. Meehan* **76 p**

FASILIGHT 2 b.f. (Jan 16) Fasliyev (USA) 120 – Rajmata (IRE) 66 (Prince Sabo 123) [2009 5.2m⁵ 6m² p7g³ 7g p7.1g⁶ p6g p5.1g* a8g³ Nov 28] 10,000Y: angular filly: third foal: half-sister to 3-y-o Tobond: dam, sprint maiden, half-sister to useful sprinters King of Russia and Fast Heart: fair performer: won seller at Wolverhampton in October, final start for M. Botti: probably stays 1m: acts on polytrack and good to firm going. *Mme L. Braem, Belgium* **67**

FASLIYANNE (IRE) 3 b.f. Fasliyev (USA) 120 – Happy Memories (IRE) (Thatching 131) [2009 71d: p5.1g f5g² f5g⁴ p5g³ 5m* 5m² 5m² 5m³ 5.1g⁶ 5g² 5m 5m² 5m⁵ 5.1m 5g f5g Dec 22] sturdy filly: fair handicapper on turf, modest on all-weather: won at Catterick in April: best at 5f: acts on all-weather and good to firm ground: usually wears headgear: tried tongue tied: races close up: has found little. *K. A. Ryan* **70 a54**

FAST ELAINE (IRE) 2 ch.f. (May 5) Bahamian Bounty 116 – Miss A Note (USA) (Miswaki (USA) 124) [2009 5g 6m 8.3m 8m Sep 17] €1,000Y, €5,200 2-y-o: third foal: half-sister to winner in Greece by High Chaparral: dam, US 6.5f winner, half-sister to Canadian Grade 3 2-y-o 8.5f winner Skip Code: no form, including in seller. *Mrs L. C. Jewell* –

FAST FREDDIE 5 b.g. Agnes World (USA) 123 – Bella Chica (IRE) 95 (Bigstone (IRE) 126) [2009 67, a82: p5.1g f5g p5g⁶ 6m⁶ 5.3m 5.5g² 7m⁴ 5.5f² 7m² 5.5d⁴ 7m⁴ 5f⁶ Aug 31] lengthy, good-topped gelding: fair handicapper on all-weather, modest on turf: left S. Parr after fifth start, then second in handicaps at Les Landes: stays 7f: acts on polytrack (below form both starts on fibresand) and good to soft going, seemingly on firm: tried blinkered/tongue tied. *Mrs A. Malzard, Jersey* **62 a67**

FAST LIVING 4 b.g. Fasliyev (USA) 120 – Fairy Contessa (IRE) 63 (Fairy King (USA)) [2009 f6g⁵ p6g Sep 25] poor form in maiden/seller: left Ms E. McWilliam after debut. *A. M. Hales* **47**

FASTNET STORM (IRE) 3 br.g. Rock of Gibraltar (IRE) 133 – Dreams 88 (Rainbow Quest (USA) 134) [2009 82: 8g 10.4m 9.8m* 10m* 9.9g 10.3m³ 10.1m⁶ 10.2d* 8g³ Oct 31] workmanlike gelding: useful handicapper: won at Ripon and Pontefract in June, and Nottingham (beat Gala Casino Star by neck) in October: stays 10.3f: acts on soft and good to firm going: front runner/races prominently. *T. P. Tate* **98**

FASTRAC BOY 6 b.g. Bold Edge 123 – Nesyred (IRE) 75 (Paris House 123) [2009 59: p5g Jan 5] lengthy gelding: modest handicapper: well held sole start in 2009: best at 5f: acts on polytrack and firm going: tried tongue tied. *J. R. Best* **–**

FATAL ATTRACTION 4 b.f. Oasis Dream 129 – Millyant 114 (Primo Dominic 121) [2009 p5g^4 5m^4 5g^3 5d^6 p5.1g^6 p5.1g^3 Oct 17] 170,000Y, 3,000 3-y-o: half-sister to 3 winning sprinters, including useful Millybaa (by Anabaa) and fairly useful Millinsky (by Stravinsky): dam, 5f performer, half-sister to very smart sprinter Prince Sabo: fair form in maidens only on second/third starts: should be suited by 6f: acts on polytrack and good to firm ground. *Rae Guest* **65**

FATANAH (IRE) 2 b.f. (Apr 5) Green Desert (USA) 127 – Wijdan (USA) 101 (Mr Prospector (USA)) [2009 8m p8g^2 Nov 14] tall, useful-looking filly: has plenty of scope: closely related to smart 7f/1m (later US Grade 2 1¼m) winner Makderah (by Danehill) and half-sister to several winners, including smart 1m winner Oriental Fashion (by Marju) and 5-y-o Ezdiyaad: dam, 1m and 10.4f winner, closely related to Nayef and half-sister to Nashwan and Unfuwain: very green, encouraging efforts in maidens at Newmarket and Lingfield (1¾ lengths second to Con Artist): type to do better still at 3 yrs. *M. P. Tregoning* **76 p**

FAT BOY (IRE) 4 ch.g. Choisir (AUS) 126 – Gold Shift (USA) (Night Shift (USA)) [2009 118: 5m 5g 6m Aug 29] strong, stocky gelding: smart performer at best, well below form in 2009 (gelded after final start): should prove best at 6f: acts on polytrack, good to firm and good to soft going: tried tongue tied: formerly front runner: has joined D. Nicholls. *P. W. Chapple-Hyam* **–**

FAT CHANCE 3 gr.f. Linamix (FR) 127 – Hymenee (USA) (Chief's Crown (USA)) [2009 54p: 7m 10m 9.8m Jul 6] leggy filly: no form in 2009: tried blinkered. *Rae Guest* **–**

FATEFUL ATTRACTION 6 b.m. Mujahid (USA) 125 – Heavens Above (FR) (Pistolet Bleu (IRE) 133) [2009 49, a78d: p16g^6 p12g^3 p11g Feb 25] leggy mare: modest maiden, no recent form on turf: stays 1½m: acts on all-weather and firm going: usually wears headgear: sometimes tongue tied: held up: none too consistent. *I. A. Wood* **–** **a51**

FATHER FIGURE (USA) 3 gr.g. Mizzen Mast (USA) 121 – Family (USA) (Danzig (USA)) [2009 8d^5 10g p10m p13g Oct 11] lengthy gelding: third foal: dam unraced sister to Danehill: fair form first 2 starts in France in 2009: left D. Smaga 25,000 gns and gelded, well held both starts in Britain: may prove best at 1m: acts on good to soft going. *Heather Dalton* **74 d**

FATHER TIME 3 b.c. Dansili 127 – Clepsydra 78 (Sadler's Wells (USA) 132) [2009 92P: 10s^3 11.5m^3 10m^2 12f* 12m^3 14.6m^4 a14f^6 Nov 6] heavy-bodied colt: smart performer: improved when winning King Edward VII Stakes at Royal Ascot impressively by 4 lengths from Your Old Pal, showing good turn of foot and still strong at finish: in frame most other starts, creditable efforts in Great Voltigeur Stakes at York (5¾ lengths third to Monitor Closely) and St Leger at Doncaster (3½ lengths fourth to Mastery) fifth/ **117 §**

King Edward VII Stakes, Royal Ascot—
a seventh success in the race—and a seventy-first at the Royal meeting—for trainer Henry Cecil as Father Time shows a good turn of foot to account for Your Old Pal (rail), Black Bear Island and Free Agent

Mr K. Abdulla's "Father Time"

sixth outings: stays 14.6f: acts on polytrack, firm and soft going, well held in Breeders' Cup Marathon on pro-ride at Santa Anita final outing: held up: nervy sort, looks awkward under pressure (tends to hang): ungenuine. *H. R. A. Cecil*

FATHEY (IRE) 3 ch.g. Fath (USA) 116 – Christoph's Girl 50 (Efisio 120) [2009 70: 6s[5] 6m[5] 5.9m 6m[2] 6.9d[2] 6.9g 6s 7.2s 7.1m[4] 8g[6] 7m[5] Oct 13] sturdy gelding: fair handicapper: stays 7f: acts on heavy and good to firm going: tried blinkered: usually races prominently: signs of temperament (once refused at stall). *R. A. Fahey* **72**

FATHOM FIVE (IRE) 5 b.g. Fath (USA) 116 – Ambria (ITY) (Final Straw 127) [2009 108: 5g* 5d 5m[6] 5m 5d[5] 5g[3] 5d Oct 24] strong, compact gelding: useful handicapper: won at Epsom (beat Wotashirtfull ¾ length) in April: largely below form after: best at 5f: acts on soft ground: often up with pace: possibly not straightforward (has hung). *C. F. Wall* **100**

FATHSTA (IRE) 4 b.g. Fath (USA) 116 – Kilbride Lass (IRE) (Lahib (USA) 129) [2009 103: 6m[6] p7g[5] 7.6m[3] 7g[2] 7.6g 7m p7g[6] p7g[4] p6g[2] p6m* Dec 10] stocky, compact gelding: useful handicapper: left D. Nicholls after sixth start: won at Kempton in December by 1¾ lengths from Bahamian Lad: best at 6f/7f: yet to race on heavy going, acts on polytrack and any other turf: strong-travelling sort. *D. M. Simcock* **100**

FAULT 3 b.g. Bahamian Bounty 116 – Trundley Wood 66 (Wassl 125) [2009 91: p5g* 5.1m[6] 5g[3] 5m 6g 5m 5m p6f 5.1m[2] 5.1m[5] p5g p5.1g[6] p6g* p7.1g[3] p6g[5] p7g[6] Nov 18] smallish, well-made gelding: fairly useful performer at best: won handicaps at Kempton in April (beat Affluent ½ length) and, having dropped long way in weights, in October **99 d**

(dead-heated with Hellbender): stays 7f: acts on polytrack, good to firm and good to soft going: tried in headgear: usually tongue tied. *Stef Liddiard*

FAVORITE WOODS 2 b.c. (Feb 18) Sakhee (USA) 136 – South Club Hill (Danehill (USA) 126) [2009 p8f⁶ a7.5g⁵ a9.5g Dec 30] sold from W. Haggas 6,500 gns after debut: best effort when fifth in claimer at Deauville. *Mlle S. Houben, France* **66**

FAVOURING (IRE) 7 ch.g. Fayruz 116 – Peace Dividend (IRE) (Alzao (USA) 117) [2009 43: 7.5m f6g Jul 27] sturdy gelding: well below form in 2009: blinkered/visored. *M. C. Chapman* **–**

FAVOURITE GIRL (IRE) 3 b.f. Refuse To Bend (IRE) 128 – Zuccini Wind (IRE) (Revoque (IRE) 122) [2009 107: 7s 6.1m⁶ 6g³ 7.1g 6m 6g 5m 6m 6m⁵ 5g 7s Oct 27] smallish, angular filly: useful performer: easily best effort in 2009 when 4 lengths third to Swiss Diva in quite valuable handicap at York third start: best efforts in strongly-run events over straight 6f: unraced on firm going, acts on any other: tried blinkered. *T. D. Easterby* **97 d**

FAVOURS BRAVE 3 b.g. Galileo (IRE) 134 – Tuning 114 (Rainbow Quest (USA) 134) [2009 72p: 10m⁴ p12g³ 14.1f 14m⁴ f11g⁴ p12.2g f11f Oct 21] close-coupled gelding: fair maiden at best in 2009, leaving J. Gosden 28,000 gns after fourth start (gelded after next outing): should stay 1¾m: acts on polytrack and good to firm going. *Mrs S. Lamyman* **75**

FAWLEY GREEN 2 b.g. (Mar 11) Shamardal (USA) 129 – Wars (IRE) 60 (Green Desert (USA) 127) [2009 6m 5.7f² 6m⁴ 5m⁴ 7d Oct 11] £30,000Y: fourth foal: half-brother to 3 winners, including 5-y-o Heroes and fairly useful 7f winner Usk Poppy (by Mark of Esteem): dam, maiden who stayed 7f, sister to very smart 7f to 9f performer Gabr: fair maiden: failed to progress after second at Bath: stays 5.7f: acts on firm going. *W. R. Muir* **70**

FAYRE BELLA 2 ch.f. (Apr 10) Zafeen (FR) 123 – Hollybell 87§ (Beveled (USA)) [2009 7g Oct 31] workmanlike filly: third foal: half-sister to 3-y-o Miss Holybell: dam 5f (at 2 yrs)/6f winner: 150/1, tailed off in maiden at Newmarket. *J. Gallagher* **–**

FAZBEE (IRE) 3 b.f. Fasliyev (USA) 120 – Kelpie (IRE) 86 (Kahyasi 130) [2009 86: 7m⁶ 7g⁴ 10g⁴ p12g⁵ 10m⁴ p11g⁵ 7m 8.5m² 8m⁶ p8.6g p6m⁴ p6f⁶ Dec 13] leggy, lengthy filly: fairly useful performer: probably stays 1½m: acts on polytrack and good to firm going, probably on firm and soft: tried in cheekpieces/visor: usually held up. *P. W. D'Arcy* **81**

FAZZA 2 ch.g. (Feb 23) Sulamani (IRE) 130 – Markievicz (IRE) 73 (Doyoun 124) [2009 6g 6.1m² p5g⁵ 6g p7f² p7g* Dec 31] £8,500Y: close-coupled gelding: half-brother to 3 winners, including Irish 5-y-o Surrey Spinner and 1¼m to 2m winner Paarl Rock (by Common Grounds): dam Irish 6.5f winner: fair performer: won maiden at Lingfield: will be suited by 1m+: best form on polytrack. *D. W. P. Arbuthnot* **73**

FEAR NOTHING 2 ch.c. (Feb 11) Exceed And Excel (AUS) 126 – Galatrix 72 (Be My Guest (USA) 126) [2009 p5.1g⁶ 5m³ 5g⁵ Oct 6] 32,000F, £38,000 2-y-o: half-brother to 2 winners, notably very smart 6f/7f winner Royal Millennium (by Royal Academy): dam, 1m winner, half-sister to Croco Rouge and to dam of Sleepytime, Ali-Royal and Taipan: easily best effort in maidens when 2¾ lengths third to Magical Macey at Haydock (hung left). *E. S. McMahon* **72**

FEASIBLE 4 ch.g. Efisio 120 – Zoena 67 (Emarati (USA) 74) [2009 71: 10.2m 8m⁴ p8g² p8g² p8g² 8.3m 8m Sep 13] good-bodied gelding: fair maiden handicapper: should stay beyond 1m: acts on polytrack, firm and good to soft going: tried blinkered: usually races close up. *J. G. Portman* **70**

FEATHERED CROWN (FR) 3 ch.c. Indian Ridge 123 – Attractive Crown (USA) 105 (Chief's Crown (USA)) [2009 a8f⁶ 10m² 10.1m* f14g⁵ Oct 18] well-made colt: fifth foal: half-brother to useful French 1m/1¼m winner Basemah (by Lemon Drop Kid): dam, Irish 6f (at 2 yrs) and 1m winner, later won in USA: fairly useful form: trained on debut by R. Simpson in UAE: best effort when winning maiden at Epsom in October: stays 1¼m: acts on good to firm going. *H. R. A. Cecil* **85**

FEATHERWEIGHT (IRE) 3 ch.f. Fantastic Light (USA) 134 – Dancing Feather 72 (Suave Dancer (USA) 136) [2009 85: 10m* 10g⁶ 10s 10f³ 9.9m* 9.9s⁴ 12g² Oct 30] leggy filly: has fluent action: fairly useful performer: won maiden at Windsor in May and handicap at Goodwood in September: good second in handicap at Newmarket final start: stays 1½m: acts on polytrack, firm and soft going. *B. W. Hills* **89**

FEDERAL RESERVE 2 ch.g. (Feb 26) Central Park (IRE) 123 – Attlongglast (Groom Dancer (USA) 128) [2009 p7g 7f Aug 18] well held in maidens. *M. Madgwick* **–**

FEELIN FOXY 5 b.m. Foxhound (USA) 103 – Charlie Girl 70 (Puissance 110) [2009 84: 5m⁵ 5m 5g² 5d⁴ 5f³ 5m* 5.5g² 5d* 5d² 5d² 6.1g 5d³ 5m² p5.1g² p5.1g⁶ p5.1g* f5m⁴ p5g⁶ Nov 25] tall mare: fairly useful handicapper: better than ever in 2009, winning at Lingfield in June, Doncaster in July and Wolverhampton in October: speedy, best at 5f: acts on all-weather, firm and soft going: has worn visor: races close up. *J. G. Given* **91**

FEELING FAB (FR) 3 b.f. Refuse To Bend (IRE) 128 – Les Planches (Tropular) [2009 98: 8.1m⁴ 8m⁴ 7m 8.3m³ 7m p7g³ 7m⁴ p7g⁵ 8m* 10g⁴ Dec 24] big, lengthy filly: fairly useful performer: won handicap at Musselburgh in September: left M. Johnston 30,000 gns before final outing: effective at 7f/1m: acts on polytrack and good to firm going: free-going sort, usually front runner: not straightforward: sold 30,000 gns in October, sent to Bahrain. *J. Al Ghazali, Qatar* **93**

FEELING FRAGILE (IRE) 2 b.g. (Feb 17) Fasliyev (USA) 120 – Boutique (Selkirk (USA) 129) [2009 5.7g p7.1g⁴ p7.1g⁶ p7m² Dec 10] 3,500Y: second foal: dam, French maiden, out of Irish Oaks winner Bolas: best effort in maidens when ½-length second to Prince of Sorrento at Kempton, making running: races freely and will prove at least as effective at 6f as 7f. *Pat Eddery* **71**

FEELING FRESH (IRE) 4 b.c. Xaar 132 – Oh'cecilia (IRE) 95 (Scenic 128) [2009 70: 5g³ 6m* 8.1v³ 6f³ Aug 8] sturdy colt: fair handicapper: won apprentice race at Hamilton in July: effective at 6f to testing 1m: acts on all-weather and any turf going: tried visored: held up: lazy sort. *Paul Green* **68**

FEELING (IRE) 5 b.g. Sadler's Wells (USA) 132 – La Pitie (USA) (Devil's Bag (USA)) [2009 –: 10m⁴ p9.5g⁴ Dec 11] useful-looking gelding: maiden: just poor form on Flat since 2007 (modest winning hurdler): tried blinkered/visored. *D. Burchell* **48**

FEELING PECKISH (USA) 5 ch.g. Point Given (USA) 134 – Sunday Bazaar (USA) (Nureyev (USA) 131) [2009 –, a50: 14.1m⁶ 16.2m⁴ 16d Aug 10] sturdy gelding: poor maiden, including over hurdles/fences: stays 2m: best form on fibresand: tongue tied of late. *M. C. Chapman* **47**

FEELING STYLISH (IRE) 3 b.f. Desert Style (IRE) 121 – No Hard Feelings (IRE) 86 (Alzao (USA) 117) [2009 42: 6f 7.5m f6g⁴ f7g 10g⁵ 9.8m⁶ 7s⁶ Aug 9] neat filly: poor maiden: seems to stay 1¼m. *N. Tinkler* **41**

FEEL THE MAGIC (IRE) 2 b.f. (Mar 24) Cadeaux Genereux 131 – Triple Green 69 (Green Desert (USA) 127) [2009 p6g p8g p7g p7g⁶ p8.6g⁶ p6g⁵ f6m p7g Dec 31] 15,000F: half-sister to 3 winners, including 5-y-o Titan Triumph and fairly useful 1m (at 2 yrs) to 1½m winner Fair Gale (by Storming Home): dam, maiden who stayed 1m, half-sister to smart 1¼m/1½m performer Talented: poor maiden: may prove best at 6f: raced only on all-weather. *S. Kirk* **47**

FEET OF FURY 3 b.f. Deportivo 116 – Fury Dance (USA) (Cryptoclearance (USA)) [2009 59p: 7m⁴ p7g 7.1f⁶ 7m 6g⁴ 7m⁵ 8d p9.5g⁴ Oct 3] tall, workmanlike filly: modest maiden handicapper: stays 9.5f: acts on polytrack and good to firm ground. *W. M. Brisbourne* **60**

FEISTY'S BROTHER 2 b.c. (Feb 26) Dubawi (IRE) 129 – Hawait Al Barr 100 (Green Desert (USA) 127) [2009 6g 7m⁶ Jun 19] no show in maiden/seller: sold 7,000 gns, sent to Greece. *D. M. Simcock* **–**

FELDAY 3 b.g. Bahamian Bounty 116 – Monaiya (Shareef Dancer (USA) 135) [2009 91: 7s⁴ 6m 6g⁴ 6m 7g* 7m 7s³ f6m* Dec 5] strong, lengthy gelding: type to carry condition: useful handicapper: won at York in October and Southwell (beat Ingleby Arch ½ length) in December: likely to prove best at 6f/7f: acts on fibresand and soft ground: races prominently. *H. Morrison* **100**

FELICIA 4 b.f. Diktat 126 – Gracia 78 (Linamix (FR) 127) [2009 56: p10g 10m p10g⁴ p12m³ p12g p12g p12m p10g² Dec 7] neat filly: modest maiden: stays 1½m: acts on polytrack: races prominently. *J. E. Long* **57**

FELL PACK 5 b.g. Lake Coniston (IRE) 131 – All On 68 (Dunbeath (USA) 127) [2009 55p: 9.9m⁵ 12.1m⁴ 10.1s* 12m⁵ 10.1d⁵ 12d 10g⁴ 12.1g 15.8d⁵ 13.8m⁴ Sep 19] big, lengthy gelding: modest handicapper: won at Newcastle in May: stayed 1½m: acted on soft ground, probably on good to firm: tried in cheekpieces: dead. *J. J. Quinn* **63**

FELSHAM 2 br.c. (Mar 19) Kyllachy 129 – Border Minstral (IRE) 69 (Sri Pekan (USA) 117) [2009 5g³ p5m* 5g² 6s³ Nov 7] 26,000Y: angular colt: third foal: half-brother to 5-y-o Oldjoesaid: dam, 2-y-o 6f winner, half-sister to smart performer up to 1¼m Mountain Song: fair performer: won maiden at Kempton in September: good efforts in nurseries after, third to Dubai Set at Doncaster: will prove best at 5f/6f: will do better still. *H. Candy* **79 p**

FEMME DE FER 3 b.f. Hamas (IRE) 125§ – Ajeebah (IRE) (Mujtahid (USA) 118) [2009 6m^2 6g^3 5.7g^5 p5.1g^2 p5m^3 p5m^3 p5f Dec 19] fourth foal: sister to useful 2001 2-y-o 5f/6f winner Shukran and half-sister to 1¼m winner Golden Dynasty (by Erhaab): dam, ran 3 times, half-sister to useful performer up to 1¼m Cape Grace: fair maiden handicapper: free-going sort, likely to prove best at 5f: acts on polytrack. *C. G. Cox* **79**

FENCING MASTER 2 b.c. (Apr 25) Oratorio (IRE) 128 – Moonlight Dance (USA) 111 (Alysheba (USA)) [2009 p7g* 7m^2 Oct 17] **116 p**

The strength in depth of Ballydoyle's latest prospective classic crop is highlighted in the ante-post markets for the 2010 Two Thousand Guineas and Derby, in which Aidan O'Brien is responsible, at the time of writing, for nearly half the horses in the top dozen in the betting on each of the races. The progressive Fencing Master features in both lists—20/1 for Newmarket and 25/1 for Epsom—and appeals as the sort who will do very well at three. He has already emulated his sire Oratorio by finishing runner-up in the Dewhurst Stakes at Newmarket, where he was beaten a neck by stable-companion Beethoven (also by Oratorio) as O'Brien saddled three of the first four home in a bunched finish. Fencing Master's performance was all the more meritorious in that, together with fourth-placed stable-companion Steinbeck, he was the least experienced runner in a field of fifteen, having had only one previous outing. Oratorio, by the way, had already chalked up six runs (including four wins) by the same stage of his career, while Beethoven's Newmarket run was his tenth of the campaign. After suffering interference at the start, 20/1-shot Fencing Master looked green, racing out wide for most of the way and barely ever on the bridle, before staying on strongly and failing by a neck to get the better of Beethoven (who started at 33/1), with a nose and a neck the distances back to Xtension and Steinbeck, the latter the choice of O'Brien's stable-jockey Johnny Murtagh (Colm O'Donoghue had the mount on Fencing Master). Murtagh had ridden Fencing Master when he had made a successful debut in a fourteen-runner median auction maiden on the polytrack at Dundalk six weeks before the Dewhurst, needing a fair bit of riding to get the better of the favourite Moonreach by a neck.

Inexperience might not be the only explanation for the style of Fencing Master's two displays to date, as his sire was quite a lazy sort (tried in a visor at one stage), for all that he proved tough during a racing career with O'Brien in which he gained his most important victories in the Eclipse Stakes and the Irish Champion Stakes after reaching the frame in the Two Thousand Guineas at both Newmarket and the Curragh. A similar schedule may well be on the cards for Fencing Master who seems sure to come into his own with another winter under his belt, particularly over a mile and a mile and a quarter.

Fencing Master (b.c. Apr 25, 2007)	Oratorio (IRE) (b 2002)	Danehill (b 1986)	Danzig
			Razyana
		Mahrah (b 1987)	Vaguely Noble
			Montage
	Moonlight Dance (USA) (b 1991)	Alysheba (b 1984)	Alydar
			Bel Sheba
		Madelia (ch 1974)	Caro
			Moonmadness

First-season sire Oratorio may look a good stallion prospect but he certainly cannot take all the credit for the promising start the strong, sturdy Fencing Master has made. Fencing Master cost €400,000 as a yearling and hails from an excellent family, being one of six winners so far out of his dam Moonlight Dance, among them the 2004 Prix de Diane runner-up Millionaia (by Peintre Celebre) and two other useful or better performers at around a mile and a quarter in France, Memoire (by Sadler's Wells) and Maitre du Jeu (by another Danehill stallion Rock of Gibraltar), as well as the smart French miler Memory Maker (by Lure). Moonlight Dance herself was a smart performer at up to a mile and quarter and won the Prix Saint-Alary, a race Fencing Master's high-class grandam Madelia also won, along with the Poule d'Essai des Pouliches and the Prix de Diane (despite breaking down on her near-fore). Madelia produced four other winners, notably the Dante Stakes winner Claude Monet, who failed to stay in the Derby. Oratorio also failed to stay in the Derby and Moonlight Dance didn't last home when a short-priced favourite taking on the colts in the Prix du Jockey Club (then still run over a mile and a half), though her half-brother Marignan had been a strong-finishing runner-up in the same race two years earlier. There's no guarantee that Fencing Master himself will stay the Derby trip, though it would occasion no surprise to see him allowed to take his chance at Epsom given that O'Brien has saddled a total of twenty-seven runners in the last five renewals of the Derby. A mile and a quarter is unlikely to pose any problem for Fencing Master, however, and, a winner on polytrack, his Dewhurst effort suggests he handles firmish ground well on turf (all six of Oratorio's career wins came on firm/good to firm going). *A. P. O'Brien, Ireland*

FENELLA ROSE 2 b.f. (May 9) Compton Place 125 – Xtrasensory 96 (Royal **73**
Applause 124) [2009 5.1f^2 5g 5g^3 6m* 6g Oct 10] 10,000Y: sturdy, lengthy filly: third foal: half-sister to fairly useful 2008 2-y-o 5f/6f winner Tishtar (by Kyllachy) and 7f (at 2 yrs)/1m winner Redsensor (by Redback): dam 2-y-o 6f winner: fair performer: won maiden at Epsom (dictated, hung left) in September: stays 6f: acts on good to firm going: visored last 2 starts: sold 1,500 gns, sent to Germany. *S. C. Williams*

FENNERS (USA) 6 ch.g. Pleasant Tap (USA) – Legal Opinion (IRE) (Polish Precedent **60**
(USA) 131) [2009 69: p12.2g^4 13m^2 12.1g^2 13.1g^5 12g^5 12.1g^4 15.8d^3 14.1g^3 13.8m^4 p13.9g 15.8g Oct 6] sturdy gelding: modest handicapper: stays 15.8f: acts on polytrack, firm and good to soft going: sometimes in headgear: tried tongue tied: often races lazily, and has hung badly right. *M. W. Easterby*

FEN SPIRIT (IRE) 3 b.f. Invincible Spirit (IRE) 121 – Irinatinvidio (Rudimentary **80**
(USA) 118) [2009 89p: p7g p6m^5 p6f Dec 21] tall filly: fairly useful handicapper: best at 6f: acts on polytrack. *J. H. M. Gosden*

FERGUS MCIVER (IRE) 3 b.c. Sadler's Wells (USA) 132 – Danelissima (IRE) 107 **114**
(Danehill (USA) 126) [2009 87p: 10s* 10d^2 12v^2 10g^3 8v^5 14d^4 8.5d Aug 18] smart performer: won maiden at the Curragh in April: much better form after when in frame at Leopardstown in Ballysax Stakes (length second to Fame And Glory) on second start, Derrinstown Stud Derby Trial (5½ lengths third behind same rival) and listed race (2½ lengths fourth to Profound Beauty): effective at 1¼m to 1¾m: acts on soft going: in cheekpieces/blinkers in 2009: tongue tied final start: carries head high/tends to hang left. *J. S. Bolger, Ireland*

FERNANDO TORRES 3 b.g. Giant's Causeway (USA) 132 – Alstemeria (IRE) 103 **75**
(Danehill (USA) 126) [2009 8.1g^5 8g 8.3m^4 8m^6 8s p7g* p8m^3 p8f^3 p7m^2 Dec 30] good-bodied gelding: fair handicapper: left D. Nicholls, won at Kempton in November: stays easy 1m: acts on polytrack: wore cheekpieces final start. *Matthew Salaman*

FERN HOUSE (IRE) 7 b.g. Xaar 132 – Certain Impression (USA) (Forli (ARG)) **50 §**
[2009 59§: p6g 9.9m 7.5m 6m 7.9g^5 8m^4 7.1g 6.9d 5f^3 5.1m 5.1d^4 5m 5m 5s Oct 27] modest handicapper: effective at 5f to 7f: acts on polytrack, firm and good to soft going: has worn headgear: temperamental. *Bruce Hellier*

FERRIS WHEEL (IRE) 2 b.f. (Mar 10) One Cool Cat (USA) 123 – Saffron Crocus **75**
83 (Shareef Dancer (USA) 135) [2009 6m^4 p6g* 7m Sep 18] €22,000Y: leggy filly: closely related to fairly useful Irish 2002 2-y-o 6f winner Catoffle (later won abroad, by Catrail) and half-sister to several winners, notably smart 7f (at 2 yrs) to 1½m (US Grade 3) winner Boule d'Or (by Croco Rouge): dam Irish 1½m/13f winner: best effort when winning maiden at Kempton in September by 2¼ lengths from Alice Alleyne: should stay 7f/1m. *P. F. I. Cole*

FESKO 3 b.f. Shinko Forest (IRE) – Young Sue 76 (Local Suitor (USA) 128) [2009 83p: **88**
f6g* p7.1g^3 f6g^2 7.1g 8d^4 8.3m 8m* 8g^3 8m 8v 8s 8.3s^5 7d 6g* 6g^3 6m f6g^2 Oct 18] good-topped filly: fairly useful handicapper: won at Southwell in February, Thirsk in June and Leicester in September: effective at 6f to easy 1m: acts on all-weather, good to firm and good to soft going: often makes running/races prominently: quirky: sold £15,000. *M. Johnston*

FESTIVAL DREAMS 4 ch.g. Largesse 112 – Bright Spangle (IRE) 67 (General **47**
Monash (USA) 107) [2009 54: p11g^5 Jan 10] modest maiden, lightly raced: seems to stay easy 2m: modest hurdler, successful twice in 2009/10. *Miss J. S. Davis*

FESTOSO (IRE) 4 b.f. Diesis 133 – Garah 107 (Ajdal (USA) 130) [2009 102: p8g^6 **102**
6v* 7g^6 6d^5 7m^3 6g 6s Nov 7] sturdy filly: useful performer: won listed race at Haydock in May by 1¼ lengths from Pusey Street Lady: well below form 3 of last 4 starts: effective at 6f/7f: unraced on firm going, acts on any other turf: blinkered last 3 starts: usually held up: sold 460,000 gns. *H. J. L. Dunlop*

FETCHING 2 b.f. (Apr 3) Zamindar (USA) 116 – Esplanade 77 (Danehill (USA) 126) **58 p**
[2009 p7g^6 Nov 11] second foal: sister to 4-y-o Seasider: dam, 1¼m winner, sister to

useful French/US performer up to 1m Kithira and half-sister to smart French performer up to 1½m Tenuous: 10/1, shaped well when 10 lengths sixth to Mass Rally in maiden at Kempton, closing under considerate handling: will stay 1m+: sure to improve. *B. W. Hills*

FEUDAL (IRE) 3 b.c. Xaar 132 – Noble Rose (IRE) 113 (Caerleon (USA) 132) [2009 61p: f6g p8g 8m a10g^{2} a8g a8g^{6} a12g* a12g^{4} 14d^{6} a10g^{6} a12d Dec 26] modest performer: sold from M. Johnston £1,600 after second start: upped in trip, won maiden at Taby in September: stays 1½m: acts on dirt. *Carlos Figueroa, Sweden* **58 +**

FEVER TREE 2 b.f. (Feb 2) Trade Fair 124 – Spielbound (Singspiel (IRE) 133) [2009 p7.1g p8g^{6} Dec 7] first foal: dam unraced half-sister to useful performer up to 1¾m Windsor Boy: better effort when sixth in maiden at Lingfield. *P. J. Makin* **52**

FIANCEE (IRE) 3 b.f. Pivotal 124 – Name of Love (IRE) 105 (Petardia 113) [2009 7s 8d Jul 17] compact filly: seventh foal: half-sister to 9.5f winner Almavara (by Fusaichi Pegasus) and winner in USA by Lemon Drop Kid: dam, 7f winner (including Rockfel Stakes), ran only at 2 yrs: modest form in maidens only on debut: sold 3,500 gns in December. *R. Charlton* **59**

FIBS AND FLANNEL 2 ch.g. (Mar 20) Tobougg (IRE) 125 – Queens Jubilee 71 (Cayman Kai (IRE) 114) [2009 5s^{5} 5d^{6} 6d^{4} 6m Aug 22] sturdy gelding: modest form when not unduly knocked about in 3 maidens: stiff task final start (gelded after): stays 6f: acts on good to soft going. *T. D. Easterby* **58**

FIDDLERS FORD (IRE) 8 b.g. Sadler's Wells (USA) 132 – Old Domesday Book 93 (High Top 131) [2009 64: p16.5g^{5} Jan 29] strong, good-bodied gelding: modest handicapper, lightly raced: stays 2¼m: acts on polytrack and good to firm going: tried in visor/cheekpieces. *T. Keddy* **–**

FIDLER BAY 3 b.g. Falbrav (IRE) 133 – Fiddle-Dee-Dee (IRE) (Mujtahid (USA) 118) [2009 p10g May 28] green in maiden at Lingfield. *H. Candy* **–**

FIEFDOM (IRE) 7 br.g. Singspiel (IRE) 133 – Chiquita Linda (IRE) (Mujadil (USA) 119) [2009 85: 7m 7.5m^{4} p8g^{2} p8g^{5} p7g^{5} 7g^{3} 7m p7g p7.1g p7g^{6} p8g^{3} 7.5g p8g^{5} p8.6g^{6} p7.1g^{6} p8m^{6} p8m Nov 29] compact gelding: has a quick action: fairly useful handicapper at best: below form later in 2009: stays 8.6f: acts on polytrack, firm and soft going: tried in cheekpieces/blinkers: has hung left: held up. *I. W. McInnes* **80**

FIELD DAY (IRE) 2 br.f. (Mar 15) Cape Cross (IRE) 129 – Naval Affair (IRE) 101 (Last Tycoon 131) [2009 7g* Oct 31] well-made filly: fifth foal: closely related to winner in Japan by Green Desert and half-sister to fairly useful 1m/1½m winner (stayed 2m) War At Sea (by Bering): dam, 2-y-o 7f winner who should have stayed 1½m, half-sister to smart 1m/1¼m winner King Adam: 14/1, promising when winning maiden at Newmarket by 1½ lengths from Scorn, running on strongly: will be suited by at least 1¼m: will go on to better things. *B. J. Meehan* **85 p**

FIELD ELECT 2 b.g. (Feb 25) Zafeen (FR) 123 – Princess Carranita (IRE) (Desert Sun 120) [2009 6.1v Jul 17] 25/1, refused to race in maiden at Nottingham: broke out of stall and withdrawn later in July. *Garry Moss* **– §**

FIELDER (IRE) 4 b.g. Catcher In The Rye (IRE) 115 – Miss Garuda 94 (Persian Bold 123) [2009 –: p11g^{3} p12g Apr 1] fair maiden, lightly raced: should stay 1½m: acts on polytrack. *J. G. Portman* **71**

FIELD FANTASY 3 ch.f. Bold Edge 123 – Princess Carranita (IRE) (Desert Sun 120) [2009 –: p5g^{6} p5.1g^{4} f5g 6f^{6} 6d 6g f7g Jun 2] leggy filly: poor maiden: blinkered final outing. *Garry Moss* **44**

FIELD OF DREAM 2 b.c. (Mar 14) Oasis Dream 129 – Field of Hope (IRE) 119 (Selkirk (USA) 129) [2009 5m* 5.5d* 7m Sep 8] sixth foal: half-brother to several winners, including very smart performer up to 1¼m Olympian Odyssey (by Sadler's Wells), 7f winner at 2 yrs: dam French/Italian 7f (Prix de la Foret)/1m (including at 2 yrs) winner: fairly useful form: won both starts in Italy for B. Grizzetti, maiden at Milan (by 5 lengths) in May and listed race at Rome (by length from Golden Acclamation) in June: off 3 months and very easy to back, soundly beaten in listed race at Goodwood: should stay 7f: acts on good to firm and good to soft going. *L. M. Cumani* **93**

FIERY LAD (IRE) 4 b.g. Mull of Kintyre (USA) 114 – Forget Paris (IRE) (Broken Hearted 124) [2009 117: 10g^{2} 10g^{3} 12m^{6} 10s^{6} 9g^{2} 10d^{6} p10.7g^{2} Oct 2] heavy-topped gelding: smart performer: placed in handicaps at Nad Al Sheba in February: creditable effort after only when short-head second to Shreyas in listed race at Leopardstown fifth outing: stays 10.7f: acts on polytrack and firm going, possibly not on softer than good: tried blinkered: held up/travels well: reportedly sold, and has joined L. Cumani. *G. M. Lyons, Ireland* **117**

FIFER (IRE) 3 b.f. Soviet Star (USA) 128 – Fife (IRE) 95 (Lomond (USA) 128) [2009 –: 7.5m 6g Jul 5] no sign of ability. *Pat Morris* –

FIFTH AMENDMENT 3 ch.g. Presidium 124 – Lady Magician (Lord Bud 121) [2009 66: 6f 5g 7.2g^5 7.9g 6g^6 6d Aug 27] leggy gelding: fair maiden: form in 2009 only on third outing: stays 7f: acts on soft going. *A. Berry* **65**

FIFTH ZAK 5 b.g. Best of The Bests (IRE) 122 – Zakuska 96 (Zafonic (USA) 130) [2009 56: f11s f12g f8g^6 Feb 5] maiden: well held in 2009: tried in cheekpieces. *S. R. Bowring* –

FIFTY CENTS 5 ch.g. Diesis 133 – Solaia (USA) 110 (Miswaki (USA) 124) [2009 89: p8.6g Jan 2] good-topped gelding: fairly useful performer, very lightly raced: pulled up amiss sole start in 2009: stays 1m: acts on soft and good to firm ground. *M. F. Harris* –

FIFTYFOURTH STREET 3 ch.g. Central Park (IRE) 123 – Retaliator 80 (Rudimentary (USA) 118) [2009 6m 6g^4 f5m^4 6m^5 Aug 14] stocky, round-barrelled gelding: fair maiden: stays 6f: acts on good to firm ground: tongue tied last 3 starts, then gelded. *P. J. Makin* **73**

FIFTY (IRE) 4 b.f. Fasliyev (USA) 120 – Amethyst (IRE) 111 (Sadler's Wells (USA) 132) [2009 78: 7f^4 6m p7g 8m^6 7.6g^3 p8g Aug 5] angular filly: fair handicapper: stays 7f: acts on good to firm ground: ungenuine. *R. Hannon* **66 §**

FIFTY MOORE 2 b.g. (Mar 24) Selkirk (USA) 129 – Franglais (GER) (Lion Cavern (USA) 117) [2009 6g Jun 13] strong, deep-girthed gelding: 10/1 and green, well held in maiden at York, slowly away: gelded after. *Jedd O'Keeffe* –

FIGARO FLYER (IRE) 6 b.g. Mozart (IRE) 131 – Ellway Star (IRE) 104 (Night Shift (USA)) [2009 83: p6g p5.1g^3 f5g^3 p6g^5 p5g^4 p6g^3 f5g* p6g^5 5m^5 f6g^6 5.2s f5g^2 f5g^2 p5.1g^4 f5m^6 p6g^6 p6f Dec 13] sturdy gelding: fair handicapper: won at Southwell in April: effective at 5f to easy 7f: acts on all-weather and firm going, not on softer than good. *P. Howling* **77**

FIGHT CLUB (GER) 8 b.h. Lavirco (GER) 125 – Flaming Song (IRE) (Darshaan 133) [2009 104d: 9m Oct 3] sturdy horse: one-time smart performer: well held in Cambridgeshire at Newmarket sole outing in 2009: stays 11f: acts on soft ground: tried blinkered. *Evan Williams* –

FIGHTING BRAVE (USA) 2 br.c. (Feb 23) Storm Cat (USA) – Get Lucky (USA) (Mr Prospector (USA)) [2009 p7f* p7g^5 Oct 9] $2,000,000Y: half-brother to several winners in US, including smart 7f (including at 2 yrs)/1m (Grade 2) winner Girolamo, 1996 Grade 3 2-y-o 8.5f winner Accelerator and Grade 2 1m winner Daydreaming, all by A P Indy: dam, US Grade 3 8.5f winner, sister to Breeders' Cup Juvenile winner Rhythm: 3/1, won maiden at Dundalk by 1¾ lengths from Keraloun: better form when 2½ lengths fifth to Mister Tee in listed race there 5 days later, still green and running on only late: will stay at least 1m: should improve again. *A. P. O'Brien, Ireland* **97 p**

FIGHTING TALK (IRE) 2 ch.c. (Feb 21) Shamardal (USA) 129 – Slap Shot (IRE) 115 (Lycius (USA) 124) [2009 7m Sep 23] 85,000Y: strong colt: second foal: half-brother to 6f (in Germany) and 7f (at 2 yrs) winner Samara Valley (by Dalakhani): dam, Italian 5f/6f winner (including at 2 yrs), runner-up in Prix de l'Abbaye: 9/1, looked and ran as if needing race when seventh to Cash Queen Anna in maiden at Redcar, hampered/eased: will do better. *M. Johnston* **66 p**

FILEMOT 4 ch.f. Largesse 112 – Hickleton Lady (IRE) 64 (Kala Shikari 125) [2009 64: 5.1d May 18] angular filly: poor maiden nowadays: should stay 6f: acts on good to soft ground. *John Berry* **43**

FILIBUSTER 2 b.g. (Mar 30) Tobougg (IRE) 125 – Blinding Mission (IRE) 70 (Marju (IRE) 127) [2009 8m Oct 1] unfurnished gelding: 150/1, last in maiden at Newmarket. *Mrs C. A. Dunnett* –

FILLIGREE (IRE) 4 b.f. Kyllachy 129 – Clunie 84 (Inchinor 119) [2009 94: 6f 6m^6 5.7f* 5.7m 6m^2 6g 6m^4 5.7m* 6m 6m p6m^5 Nov 3] sturdy filly: fairly useful handicapper: won at Bath in June and September: best at 5f/6f: acts on firm and good to soft going. *Rae Guest* **93**

FILM FESTIVAL (USA) 6 ch.g. Diesis 133 – To Act (USA) (Roberto (USA) 131) [2009 83: 10.3g 14m^5 12m May 30] good-topped gelding: handicapper, just fair form in 2009: barely stays 1¾m: acts on firm and soft going. *B. Ellison* **76**

FILM SET (USA) 3 b. or br.c. Johar (USA) 130 – Dippers (USA) 86 (Polish Numbers (USA)) [2009 91: 7.1v 8.3m^3 p8m^2 7.1g^6 a7.5g^4 a7.5g^3 Dec 29] compact colt: useful **97**

performer: good short-head second to Tudor Key in minor event at Lingfield third start: below form afterwards, sold from Saeed bin Suroor 6,000 gns after next outing: stays 8.3f: acts on polytrack, soft and good to firm going: tongue tied in Britain at 3 yrs. *F. Vermeulen, France*

FILUN 4 b.g. Montjeu (IRE) 137 – Sispre (FR) (Master Willie 129) [2009 71: p12g^2 p12g* p12g 12d 11.6g^6 11m 12.1v 10s^3 p12.2m^5 11.8m p12m Sep 24] rangy, attractive gelding: fair handicapper: won at Kempton in March: stays easy 1½m: acts on polytrack, good to firm and good to soft ground: tried blinkered/in cheekpieces. *A. Middleton* **74**

FILWA (IRE) 2 b.f. (Apr 23) Invincible Spirit (IRE) 121 – Capessa (IRE) (Perugino (USA) 84) [2009 5.1m^5 6f^2 5.7g^2 6g 6g^2 Oct 19] €22,000Y, £20,000 2-y-o: rather unfurnished filly: first foal: dam Italian 7f (at 2 yrs) to 11f winner: fair maiden: runner-up 3 times: should stay 7f: sent to Qatar. *B. J. Meehan* **74**

FINAL ANSWER 2 b.c. (Mar 10) Kyllachy 129 – Valandraud (IRE) (College Chapel 122) [2009 5m* Jul 23] £32,000Y: compact colt: fourth foal: half-brother to Italian 5f (including at 2 yrs) winner Rio Ther (by Bertolini): dam unraced out of half-sister to sprinters Prince Sabo (very smart) and Millyant (smart): 7/2, won maiden at Sandown by 1¼ lengths from Excellent Day, making all in good style: joined J. Moore in Hong Kong: useful sprinting prospect. *E. S. McMahon* **89 p**

FINAL BID (IRE) 6 b.g. Mujadil (USA) 119 – Dusky Virgin 62 (Missed Flight 123) [2009 f8s f8g Jan 15] fair winning hurdler: maiden on Flat, no form in 2009: tried blinkered. *A. Berry* **–**

FINAL DRIVE (IRE) 3 b.g. Viking Ruler (AUS) – Forest Delight (IRE) 58 (Shinko Forest (IRE)) [2009 61: 10.1d 7g^4 p7g^5 p7g^6 p10g p8g* p7m* Nov 4] good-topped gelding: fair handicapper: won at Lingfield and Kempton within 4 days in November: stays 1m: acts on polytrack: often slowly away. *E. J. Creighton* **73**

FINAL OVATION (IRE) 2 b.g. (Mar 20) Acclamation 118 – Last Gasp (Barathea (IRE) 127) [2009 5g^4 5m^2 6d 5m 5s^4 5m^2 5g Oct 6] sturdy, good-quartered gelding: fair maiden: best efforts at 5f on good to firm ground. *J. J. Quinn* **69**

FINAL QUEST (IRE) 6 ch.m. King Charlemagne (USA) 120 – Tuscaloosa (Robellino (USA) 127) [2009 –: p9.5g Nov 13] modest maiden in 2005: well held both Flat starts since: tried blinkered. *P. J. McKenna, Ireland* **–**

FINAL RHAPSODY 3 b.f. Royal Applause 124 – Rivers Rhapsody 104 (Dominion 123) [2009 69p: 5.7f 6.1g p6g Jun 4] fair form in 2008: well held at 3 yrs. *J. A. Geake* **–**

FINAL SALUTE 3 b.g. Royal Applause 124 – Wildwood Flower 107 (Distant Relative 128) [2009 79: f7g^2 6s p7f f6d Dec 29] strong gelding: fair performer: well below form after reappearance: stays 7f: acts on fibresand, probably on soft going: best efforts when visored. *B. Smart* **78**

FINAL SON 4 b.g. Fourstars Allstar (USA) 122 – Dulzie 56 (Safawan 118) [2009 8.3g 10.4v^4 p12g^5 f8g p10g Sep 9] close-coupled gelding: modest maiden: should stay 1½m: acts on polytrack and heavy ground. *A. P. Jarvis* **57**

FINAL TUNE (IRE) 6 ch.g. Grand Lodge (USA) 125 – Jackie's Opera (FR) (Indian Ridge 123) [2009 77: f8g Feb 20] angular gelding: fair handicapper, very lightly raced since 2007: stays easy 9.5f: acts on all-weather, firm and good to soft going. *Miss M. E. Rowland* **–**

FINAL TURN 2 b.c. (Apr 17) Kyllachy 129 – Eveningperformance 121 (Night Shift (USA)) [2009 p6g^5 p5.1g^6 Dec 26] modest form in maidens at Lingfield and Wolverhampton. *H. Candy* **50**

FINAL VERSE 6 b.g. Mark of Esteem (IRE) 137 – Tamassos 67 (Dance In Time (CAN)) [2009 103: 8m^2 8m 8m 10d 8m 9.9s p9.5g f7m p8m* p10m p8m Dec 30] good-topped, attractive gelding: has a quick action: useful handicapper: good second to Ace of Hearts at Newmarket on reappearance: below best after, though won at Lingfield in November: stays 9.5f: acts on polytrack, soft and good to firm going: edgy sort: held up. *Matthew Salaman* **99 d**

FINAL VICTORY 3 ch.g. Generous (IRE) 139 – Persian Victory (IRE) (Persian Bold 123) [2009 76p: 12g^3 12.4s* p12g* 12f^3 14m^2 14m^3 14m 12m^3 p12.2g Nov 13] 4,000Y: strong, lengthy gelding: fairly useful performer: won maiden at Newcastle in May and handicap at Kempton in June: good efforts after when placed: stays 1¾m: unraced on heavy ground, acts on any other turf going and polytrack: gelded after final start. *A. M. Balding* **93**

Betfair Cup (Lennox), Goodwood—
Finjaan quickens between Balthazaar's Gift (right) and Regal Parade (left)

FINCH FLYER (IRE) 2 ch.c. (Apr 22) Indian Ridge 123 – Imelda (USA) (Manila (USA)) [2009 5m p7g 8d⁶ Oct 22] form in maidens only when 10 lengths sixth to Tertiary at Brighton. *G. L. Moore* **54**

FINE ART COLLECTOR (IRE) 3 ch.g. Choisir (AUS) 126 – New Foundation (IRE) 89 (College Chapel 122) [2009 7f⁵ p8m p7.1g Oct 1] quite good-topped gelding: not knocked about in maidens: may prove best up to 7f. *G. L. Moore* **55 +**

FINE LACE (IRE) 2 b.f. (Jan 27) Barathea (IRE) 127 – Fine Detail (IRE) 93 (Shirley Heights 130) [2009 7.6d p8g 8.1m p8.6g* 8.3d⁵ p8m p10m³ p8.6g⁵ Dec 18] 9,000Y: close-coupled, sparely-made filly: half-sister to several winners, including useful 1m/1¼m winners Fashionable (by Nashwan) and Artistic Style (by Anabaa): dam, 1½m winner only start, half-sister to very smart French performer up to 12.5f De Quest and US Grade 1 9f/1¼m winner Wandesta: fair performer: won nursery at Wolverhampton in October: stays 1¼m: acts on polytrack. *D. J. S. ffrench Davis* **65**

FINE RULER (IRE) 5 b.g. King's Best (USA) 132 – Bint Alajwaad (IRE) (Fairy King (USA)) [2009 72: p8g³ p8g² p8g⁶ p8g² p8g⁶ p8.6g p7f p8m p7.1g p8m p8m* p8.6g⁴ p8m⁴ Nov 29] tall, leggy gelding: fair handicapper: won at Kempton in October: stays 9.7f: acts on polytrack and good to firm going: races freely held up. *M. R. Bosley* **70**

FINE SIGHT 2 b.c. (Feb 13) Cape Cross (IRE) 129 – Daring Aim 89 (Daylami (IRE) 138) [2009 6g⁶ 7.1s² 7g² 8.3g² p7g* Oct 29] useful-looking colt: second foal: half-brother to 3-y-o Highland Glen: dam, 1½m winner, half-sister to Oaks runner-up Flight of Fancy, out of smart performer up to 13.3f Phantom Gold: fairly useful performer: thrice runner-up in maidens before winning similar event at Lingfield by ½ length from Shamir: should prove suited by 1m+: acts on polytrack, probably on soft going. *R. Hannon* **86**

FINE SILK (USA) 3 ch.f. Rahy (USA) 115 – Meiosis (USA) 98 (Danzig (USA)) [2009 7.2g 7m⁴ 7m⁵ Aug 28] fourth foal: sister to useful sprinter (including at 2 yrs) League Champion and smart performer up to 1m Rahiyah, 6f winner at 2 yrs: dam, 7f winner, out of high-class French sprinter/miler Golden Opinion: modest form in maidens: worth a try at 6f: sold 6,000 gns in December. *B. Smart* **58**

FINEST RESERVE (IRE) 2 b.c. (Apr 10) Royal Applause 124 – Red Bandanna (IRE) 80 (Montjeu (IRE) 137) [2009 7.1g 7m 8m^2 8m^2 Sep 24] 90,000Y: strong colt: first foal: dam, Irish maiden (stayed 9.5f), half-sister to smart performer up to 1¼m winner Foodbroker Fancy: fair maiden: runner-up at Goodwood and Pontefract (beaten 6 lengths by Musaafer): stays 1m. *M. R. Channon* **73**

FINE THE WORLD 5 b.m. Agnes World (USA) 123 – Fine Honor (FR) (Highest Honor (FR) 124) [2009 p9.5g p9.5g 8m^5 12f 10m^5 7d^4 8.5m^6 10f* Aug 31] third foal: dam French 1¼m winner: left G. Ham after second start: won handicap at Les Landes in August: stays 1¼m: acts on firm going. *Mrs J. L. Le Brocq, Jersey* **51**

FINE TOLERANCE 3 b.f. Bertolini (USA) 125 – Sashay 72 (Bishop of Cashel 122) [2009 –: 8m p10g 10m^2 11.6g^3 p10g^4 p10m 11.9d^6 p12.2g p12m^3 Dec 6] leggy, lengthy filly: modest maiden: left J. Boyle after seventh start: stays 1½m: acts on polytrack and good to firm ground. *Miss S. L. Davison* **61**

FINISHED ARTICLE (IRE) 12 b.g. Indian Ridge 123 – Summer Fashion 84 (Moorestyle 137) [2009 50: p8g Jan 11] workmanlike gelding: modest performer: inadequate trip only outing in 2009: stays 1¾m: acts on polytrack, firm and good to soft going: tried blinkered/tongue tied. *Mrs D. Thomas* **–**

FINJAAN 3 b.c. Royal Applause 124 – Alhufoof (USA) 100 (Dayjur (USA) 137) [2009 116: 8m 7g* 6d Sep 5] leggy, close-coupled colt: has a quick action: very smart performer: best effort in 2009 when winning Betfair Cup (Lennox) at Goodwood in July by ½ length from Balthazaar's Gift, quickening through once switched: will prove best up to 7f (non-stayer in 2000 Guineas at Newmarket on reappearance): acts on good to firm ground, well below form in Sprint Cup at Haydock on good to soft final outing. *M. P. Tregoning* **122**

FINNEGAN MCCOOL 3 b.g. Efisio 120 – Royal Jade 82 (Last Tycoon 131) [2009 80: 5g 5m 6g^6 7m^6 5.7m^4 6m p7g* p7g Oct 22] medium-sized gelding: fairly useful performer: won handicap at Lingfield in October by neck from King of Defence: below form next time: stays 7f: acts on polytrack and good to firm ground: in cheekpieces of late: inconsistent: sold 14,000 gns. *R. M. Beckett* **80**

FINNEGANS RAINBOW 7 ch.g. Spectrum (IRE) 126 – Fairy Story (IRE) 80 (Persian Bold 123) [2009 –: 10g^6 p9.5g Dec 19] big gelding: maiden: no form since 2007: tried blinkered. *M. C. Chapman* **–**

FINNEY HILL 4 b.f. Mark of Esteem (IRE) 137 – Ringing Hill 88 (Charnwood Forest (IRE) 125) [2009 78: 10.2g^2 9.9s^3 10.2g* 12g Oct 30] smallish, workmanlike filly: fairly useful performer: won maiden at Bath in October: should be suited by 1½m: acts on soft ground: sold 5,000 gns. *H. Candy* **83**

FINSBURY 6 gr.g. Observatory (USA) 131 – Carmela Owen (Owington 123) [2009 69: 5.9g^2 6m^3 6g^6 7.1g^6 6m 7g^4 7.1m 7.2m* 6d^6 7.2v Oct 31] medium-sized gelding: fair handicapper: won at Ayr in October: effective at 6f to 1m: acts on polytrack, good to firm and good to soft ground: tried visored: held up: quirky. *J. S. Goldie* **69**

FIN VIN DE LEU (GER) 3 b.g. Dr Fong (USA) 128 – Fairy Queen (IRE) 116 (Fairy King (USA)) [2009 79p: p8g^3 f12g* p12g^2 p12g 12.5g 12m 15.8g^3 12g 16.2g* 15.9m^4 16.4d p13.9g^2 17.2m^2 p13.9g^6 f14g^3 Oct 18] rangy gelding: fairly useful performer: won maiden at Southwell in March and handicap at Beverley in August: stays 17f: acts on all-weather and good to firm going: makes running: tends to carry head awkwardly: sold 16,000 gns. *M. Johnston* **85**

FIRE AND RAIN (FR) 6 b.g. Galileo (IRE) 134 – Quatre Saisons (FR) (Homme de Loi (IRE) 120) [2009 20m Jun 16] strong, good-bodied gelding: has a quick action: very lightly raced on Flat since 2006: useful chaser, successful 4 of last 6 starts. *Miss E. C. Lavelle* **–**

FIRE AND STONE (IRE) 2 b.g. (Mar 11) Hawk Wing (USA) 136 – Shinkoh Rose (FR) 67 (Warning 136) [2009 6m 6g^3 7m^4 7d 8.3d Oct 12] rather leggy gelding: modest maiden: below form in nurseries last 2 starts: stays 7f: acts on good to firm going: has looked awkward: sold 2,500 gns. *Tom Dascombe* **64**

FIREBACK 2 b.g. (May 9) Firebreak 125 – So Discreet (Tragic Role (USA)) [2009 6g^6 7g 7m^6 Sep 19] useful-looking gelding: best effort in maidens when 7 lengths sixth to Beauchamp Yorker at Newbury final start (gelded after): shapes as though will stay 1m. *A. M. Balding* **69**

Blue Square Heritage Handicap, Newmarket—third win in a row for the thriving Firebet; it's close for the minor placings between, from right to left, Roman Republic, Class Is Class and Mister Dee Bee

FIREBET (IRE) 3 b.c. Dubai Destination (USA) 127 – Dancing Prize (IRE) 99 (Sadler's Wells (USA) 132) [2009 84: 8m² 7m² 8.3g* 8m* 10m* 12g² 10.1m* Aug 31] well-made colt: smart performer: left Mrs A. Duffield after second outing: much improved after, winning handicaps at Nottingham and Ayr in June, Newmarket (valuable event, best effort when beating Roman Republic 1¾ lengths) in July and minor event at Epsom (landed odds) in August: creditable 1¾ lengths second to Harbinger in Gordon Stakes at Goodwood sixth start: stays easy 1½m: acts on good to firm and good to soft going: reportedly sold privately, and has joined Godolphin. *R. A. Fahey* **115**

FIREFLASH (IRE) 2 b.c. (Mar 15) Noverre (USA) 125 – Miss Langkawi 76 (Daylami (IRE) 138) [2009 6m 6m 7s 10m Oct 5] stocky colt: soundly beaten in maidens: tried in cheekpieces. *Mrs A. Duffield* **–**

FIREFLY MUSTIQUE 2 b.c. (Apr 18) Oasis Dream 129 – My Ballerina (USA) 94 (Sir Ivor (USA) 135) [2009 6m⁴ 7m 8d Oct 27] good-bodied colt: well held in maidens. *George Baker* **–**

FIREHAWK 2 b.g. (Feb 18) Firebreak 125 – Distinctly Blu (IRE) 70 (Distinctly North (USA) 115) [2009 6d⁵ 7m⁶ p8.6g⁶ Oct 2] leggy gelding: modest form in maidens first 2 starts: not bred to need 1m: gelded after final start. *J. G. Portman* **56**

FIRE KING 3 b.g. Falbrav (IRE) 133 – Dancing Fire (USA) (Dayjur (USA) 137) [2009 –: 9.7m⁴ 8g⁴ 10m* 10g⁵ 10d 8f² 8d⁴ p8m 8g⁶ 8d p10g⁴ p8m Nov 29] workmanlike gelding: fair handicapper: won at Lingfield in July: stays 1¼m: acts on firm and good to soft ground: tried visored/in cheekpieces: none too consistent. *J. A. Geake* **68**

FIRE ME GUN 3 b.f. Reel Buddy (USA) 118 – Manderina (Mind Games 121) [2009 –: p9.5g p9.5g f14g⁶ Jul 14] no form. *M. Mullineaux* **–**

FIRENZA BOND 4 b.g. Captain Rio 122 – Bond Stasia (IRE) 54 (Mukaddamah (USA) 125) [2009 66: p5.1g³ p5.1g⁶ 5.3m May 22] tall gelding: fair performer: claimed from G. Oldroyd after reappearance: below form subsequently: raced at 5f: acts on polytrack and good to soft going: tried blinkered/in cheekpieces. *D. Flood* **66**

FIRE RAISER 2 b.g. (Feb 5) Firebreak 125 – Mara River 86 (Efisio 120) [2009 p6m⁵ 5g Oct 19] rather leggy gelding: better effort when fifth in claimer at Kempton (bandaged). *A. M. Balding* **61**

FIRESIDE 4 b.g. Dr Fong (USA) 128 – Al Hasnaa (Zafonic (USA) 130) [2009 –: 8m 7g 6.5g⁵ 10s⁵ 8.5s* Nov 8] good-topped gelding: useful at 2 yrs: lightly raced and just fair form since: sold from M. Jarvis 13,000 gns after second start in 2009: won minor event at Krefeld in November: stays 8.5f: acts on soft and good to firm going. *Frau N. Bach, Germany* **79**

FIRESTORM (IRE) 5 b.g. Celtic Swing 138 – National Ballet (Shareef Dancer (USA) 135) [2009 –: 15m 13.8m 15.8g 12.4d Oct 13] close-coupled gelding: maiden: little form since 2 yrs: tried blinkered/in cheekpieces. *C. W. Fairhurst* **–**

FIRETAIL 2 b.f. (Jan 18) Selkirk (USA) 129 – Snow Goose 111 (Polar Falcon (USA) 126) [2009 8.3v p8m Nov 19] lengthy, unfurnished filly: second foal: dam, 6f (at 2 yrs) to **–**

1m winner, sister to smart performer up to 1¼m Merry Merlin and half-sister to smart stayer Dusky Warbler: soundly beaten in maidens. *M. L. W. Bell*

FIRETRAP 2 b.g. (May 10) Firebreak 125 – Amber Mill 96 (Doulab (USA) 115) [2009 5g 5.9g4 5g4 5d2 6g3 6d5 Aug 27] fair maiden: stays 6f: visored (raced freely, below form) final start. *Mrs A. Duffield* **65**

FIRE UP THE BAND 10 b.g. Prince Sabo 123 – Green Supreme (Primo Dominie 121) [2009 98d: p7.1g6 p5.1g p5.1m 5g 5d Jul 22] lengthy, good-topped gelding: shadow of former self: tried visored. *A. Berry* **–**

FIREWALKER 4 b.f. Bertolini (USA) 125 – Crystal Canyon 59 (Efisio 120) [2009 52: p5.1g4 p5.1g f5g p5.1g Apr 4] modest maiden: will prove best at 5f/6f: acts on polytrack, good to firm and good to soft ground: blinkered/in cheekpieces in 2009. *P. T. Dalton* **50**

FIRSAAN (IRE) 3 b.g. Haafhd 129 – Walayef (USA) 105 (Danzig (USA)) [2009 61: 8m f12f Nov 24] ex-Irish maiden: no form in 2009. *J. R. Norton* **–**

FIRST AVENUE 4 b.g. Montjeu (IRE) 137 – Marciala (IRE) (Machiavellian (USA) 123) [2009 105: 12g 12s Nov 7] big, lengthy gelding: handicapper: well below useful best both starts on Flat in 2009 (fairly useful hurdler): stays 1½m: acts on soft and good to firm going: wears cheekpieces: races up with pace: quirky. *G. L. Moore* **–**

FIRST BAY (IRE) 3 b.g. Hawk Wing (USA) 136 – Montmartre (IRE) 98 (Grand Lodge (USA) 125) [2009 9.3d3 9.2v3 9.2g3 Sep 20] first foal: dam, 7f (at 2 yrs) to 1¼m winner, half-sister to smart miler Rebel Rebel: fairly useful form in maiden/claimers: well worth a try at 1¼m: acts on heavy going. *J. Howard Johnson* **85**

FIRST BLADE 3 ch.g. Needwood Blade 117 – Antonias Melody 86 (Rambo Dancer (CAN) 107) [2009 48: f5g3 f6g6 8.3d 6.1m2 f6m* f6g5 p5.1g* p7.1g4 5.1m3 f5g6 5s3 Oct 27] big, lengthy gelding: fair handicapper: won at Southwell in July and Wolverhampton in August: effective at 5f to 7f: acts on all-weather, soft and good to firm going: blinkered of late: sometimes slowly away. *S. R. Bowring* **70**

FIRST CAT 2 b.g. (Mar 5) One Cool Cat (USA) 123 – Zina La Belle (Mark of Esteem (IRE) 137) [2009 6m p7g p7g6 8m* 8d3 9m2 Sep 18] first foal: dam, Italian 1m/9.5f winner, half-sister to smart 2000 2-y-o Honours List: blind in one eye: fairly useful performer: won nursery at Salisbury in August: good efforts after, neck second to Lethal Combination in nursery at Newmarket: stays 9f: acts on good to firm and good to soft going. *R. Hannon* **89**

FIRST CITY 3 b.f. Diktat 126 – City Maiden (USA) (Carson City (USA)) [2009 87p: 7m3 8m 8m5 7g 8g 7m5 8.3m4 Oct 13] strong filly: useful performer: highly tried early in year, third to Fantasia in Nell Gwyn Stakes at Newmarket: best efforts on last 2 starts, 2¾ lengths fifth to Golden Stream in listed race at Ascot and 4¾ lengths fourth to Moonlife in minor event at Leicester: probably stays 1m: yet to race on firm going, acts on any other: tends to carry head high. *D. M. Simcock* **96**

FIRST FANDANGO 2 b.c. (Mar 7) Hernando (FR) 127 – First Fantasy 97 (Be My Chief (USA) 122) [2009 8g6 8v5 Oct 24] 30,000Y: good-topped colt: fifth foal: half-brother to 1m winner Infatuate (by Inchinor) and 3-y-o Sitwell: dam, 1¼m winner, out of half-sister to Melbourne Cup winner Jeune: green, similar form in maidens at Newbury, hanging left when fifth to Gardening Leave: will be suited by 1¼m+: capable of better. *J. W. Hills* **72 p**

FIRST HAND 3 b.f. Act One 124 – Strong Hand 99 (First Trump 118) [2009 –: f8g5 f7g f11g 12.1g Sep 22] well held in varied company: tried blinkered. *M. W. Easterby* **–**

FIRST IN COMMAND (IRE) 4 b.g. Captain Rio 122 – Queen Sigi (IRE) (Fairy King (USA)) [2009 98: 6s 5d 5.8s 6v 6m* 6m2 6v 6m3 5.1m4 5m4 6g Sep 27] fairly useful handicapper: won at Doncaster in June: best around 6f: acts on soft and good to firm ground: tongue tied: usually held up, and tends to find little. *D. Loughnane, Ireland* **88**

FIRST IN SHOW 4 b.f. Zamindar (USA) 116 – Rose Show (Belmez (USA) 131) [2009 53: p7g4 Jan 10] poor maiden: stays 8.6f: raced only on polytrack since debut: blinkered sole 4-y-o start: often tongue tied. *A. M. Balding* **48**

FIRST INSTANCE 2 b.c. (Feb 24) Cape Cross (IRE) 129 – Court Lane (USA) 81 (Machiavellian (USA) 123) [2009 6d 8.1d5 p7g4 Oct 14] well-made colt: fifth foal: closely related to smart 2003 2-y-o 5f winner Holborn (by Green Desert) and half-brother to 2006 2-y-o 7f winner Show Trial (by Jade Robbery): dam, 6f (at 2 yrs) to 1m winner, out of Cherry Hinton winner Chicarica: easily best effort in maidens when fifth to Zeitoper at Sandown: seems to stay 1m: sold £2,000. *M. Johnston* **79**

FIRST IN THE QUEUE (IRE) 2 b.c. (Mar 9) Azamour (IRE) 130 – Irina (IRE) 91 (Polar Falcon (USA) 126) [2009 8.1d 8.1m^2 8.3g 8g^3 p8.6g* Nov 6] 30,000Y: rather leggy colt: fourth foal: half-brother to useful Irish/US 7f to 9f winner Icemancometh (by Marju) and fairly useful 7f (including at 2 yrs) winner Imperial Lucky (by Desert Story): dam Irish 7f/1m winner: fairly useful performer: best effort in maidens when winning at Wolverhampton: will stay 1¼m: acts on polytrack and good to firm ground. *S. Kirk* **83**

FIRST MAID 3 br.f. First Trump 118 – Angel Maid (Forzando 122) [2009 p12g 12.1g 11.7g p12m p13.9g Oct 29] 1,000Y: first foal: dam well beaten: little form in varied company. *A. B. Haynes* **–**

FIRST ORDER 8 b.g. Primo Dominie 121 – Unconditional Love (IRE) 104 (Polish Patriot (USA) 128) [2009 93: f5s^2 p6g^4 f5g^4 5.7g^5 p5.1g^5 5m^2 5g 5m^5 5m^3 p5g^5 5m 5m 6s 6d 5g p5.1g f5g^4 p5.1g^4 p5.1g p6g^2 Dec 19] big, strong gelding: fairly useful handicapper: well below form after tenth start: effective at 5f/6f: acts on all-weather, firm and good to soft ground: visored: tactically versatile: has looked tricky ride. *Miss A. Stokell* **89 d**

FIRST POST (IRE) 2 b.g. (Apr 12) Celtic Swing 138 – Consignia (IRE) 67 (Definite Article 121) [2009 8g 8v Oct 24] green, always behind in maidens at Bath and Newbury. *D. Haydn Jones* **–**

FIRST SERVICE (IRE) 3 ch.c. Intikhab (USA) 135 – Princess Sceptre (Cadeaux Genereux 131) [2009 64p: p7g^4 p7.1g* Nov 20] good-topped colt: progressive form in maidens, winning at Wolverhampton in November: raced only at 7f on polytrack and good ground: should improve further. *R. Charlton* **80 p**

FIRST SPIRIT 3 ch.f. First Trump 118 – Flaming Spirt 78§ (Blushing Flame (USA) 109) [2009 –: p12g^3 p12g 10g^5 11.6m^6 11.6g 12m p12g* 11.6d^3 p12g^3 p12g 10.9g^3 Jul 3] sturdy filly: modest performer: won seller at Lingfield in May: stays 1½m: acts on polytrack and good to soft ground: in cheekpieces last 5 starts. *J. S. Moore* **58**

FIRST SWALLOW 4 ch.g. Bahamian Bounty 116 – Promise Fulfilled (USA) 90 (Bet Twice (USA)) [2009 68: 5m^6 5m 5g 5d^3 6d 5.9d 5s^6 6g^2 5.1s^5 f5f* f6g^4 f5g^2 Dec 22] big gelding: has scope: fair handicapper: left R. Fahey after seventh start: won at Southwell in November: good second there final start: stays 6f: acts on fibresand, soft and good to firm ground: tried in cheekpieces: tongue tied last 5 starts. *D. H. Brown* **72**

FIRST TERM 2 b.f. (Mar 2) Acclamation 118 – School Days 77 (Slip Anchor 136) [2009 6g^5 6m^4 Aug 24] £44,000Y: useful-looking filly: has scope: second foal: dam 1m winner: modest form in maidens at Goodwood (better effort, fifth to Beyond Desire) and Windsor (favourite): should stay 7f. *R. Hannon* **64**

FIRST TO CALL 5 ch.g. First Trump 118 – Scarlett Holly 81 (Red Sunset 120) [2009 85: p10m p12m p16m^4 Dec 10] strong, good-bodied gelding: handicapper, lightly raced: just fair form in 2009: stays 1½m: acts on all-weather, best turf effort on good ground: tried tongue tied. *P. J. Makin* **77**

FISADARA 3 b.f. Nayef (USA) 129 – Success Story 60 (Sharrood (USA) 124) [2009 56p: 10s 10m^2 10.2g 11.7f* 11.5m^6 10m^4 12f Sep 7] leggy filly: fair performer: won maiden at Bath in June, then left B. Hills 22,000 gns: stays 1½m: acts on firm going. *Jane Chapple-Hyam* **69**

FISH CALLED JOHNNY 5 b.g. Kyllachy 129 – Clare Celeste 73 (Coquelin (USA) 121) [2009 57: f7s p7.1g a6g^4 a6g^3 a8g^3 a8g 10.5g* 10g^4 8g^2 12g^2 9g 8g a8s a10g Dec 6] close-coupled gelding: modest performer nowadays: sold from A. Berry £800 after second start: won handicap at Gothenburg in June: stays 1½m: acts on heavy and good to firm going, probably on polytrack/dirt: tried tongue tied: usually blinkered of late: none too straightforward. *Catharina Vang, Sweden* **57**

FISHFORCOMPLIMENTS 5 b.g. Royal Applause 124 – Flyfisher (USA) (Riverman (USA) 131) [2009 102§: 7m^2 7m 7g^2 6m* 6m 6d 6d 8m 9.2v^2 6m 7m 7s p7.1g p6m^5 p6f^3 Dec 21] big, leggy gelding: useful handicapper: won at Hamilton in June by 3 lengths from Vhujon: below form after: probably best at 6f/7f nowadays: acts on soft and good to firm going: sometimes wears headgear: unreliable. *R. A. Fahey* **104 d**

FISTRAL 5 b.g. Piccolo 121 – Fayre Holly (IRE) 57 (Fayruz 116) [2009 55: f12g^5 12.4s 11.8m^5 15m^2 14.6m 12m 16d^3 14.1g 16.1d^6 Sep 7] lengthy gelding: modest handicapper: stays 2m: acts on fibresand, good to firm and good to soft going: tried in blinkers/cheekpieces. *P. D. Niven* **59**

FITOLINI 4 ch.f. Bertolini (USA) 125 – Miss Fit (IRE) 87 (Hamas (IRE) 125§) [2009 –§: p5.1g p6g p5.1g Feb 9] strong, lengthy filly: handicapper: no form since 2007: one to avoid. *Mrs G. S. Rees* **– §**

FITZ 3 b.g. Mind Games 121 – Timoko (Dancing Spree (USA)) [2009 44: 7g^5 7.6m^5 p7g^3 p7f* f8g 8d^5 Oct 15] workmanlike gelding: modest handicapper: won at Lingfield in September (gelded after): stays 7.6f: acts on polytrack: in cheekpieces final start. *Matthew Salaman* **63**

FITZ FLYER (IRE) 3 b.c. Acclamation 118 – Starry Night 89 (Sheikh Albadou 128) [2009 96: f5d* Dec 29] well-made colt: useful performer, very lightly raced: improved when winning handicap at Southwell by nose from Rebel Duke only start in 2009: effective at 5f/6f: acts on fibresand, soft and good to firm going. *D. H. Brown* **101 +**

FITZOLINI 3 b.g. Bertolini (USA) 125 – Coney Hills 35 (Beverley Boy 99) [2009 69: 6g^6 f7g 5.9m 7g 5.9g 6d^6 p8.6g* p8g^6 p9.5g^2 p8.6g^6 Dec 14] strong gelding: modest handicapper: won at Wolverhampton in November: stays easy 8.6f: acts on polytrack and heavy going: usually wears cheekpieces, tried visored. *A. D. Brown* **61**

FITZWARREN 8 b.g. Presidium 124 – Coney Hills 35 (Beverley Boy 99) [2009 –: p6g^5 7g 7.5g 5.9g 7.5m 6m 9.9g^2 10g 9d p10g^5 Dec 7] small gelding: handicapper, modest at best in 2009: stays 1¼m: acts on firm and good to soft going: usually wears headgear: tongue tied last 4 starts. *A. D. Brown* **50**

FIULIN 4 ch.c. Galileo (IRE) 134 – Fafinta (IRE) (Indian Ridge 123) [2009 115: 14.1m* 14s^5 16.4m^5 13.3m^6 14.6m Sep 11] big, strong colt: smart performer: won listed event at Nottingham in April by 6 lengths from The Betchworth Kid: well below form after, in cheekpieces final outing: stays 2m: acts on good to firm and good to soft going, probably on polytrack: sold 280,000 gns, joined Evan Williams. *M. Botti* **113**

FIUNTAS (IRE) 6 b.g. Lil's Boy (USA) 109 – Scarpetta (USA) 75 (Seattle Dancer (USA) 119) [2009 f5g^4 f6g Feb 20] maiden: lightly raced and just modest form since 2005: tried in cheekpieces/tongue tie. *Shaun Harley, Ireland* **60**

FIVE A SIDE 5 b.g. Lomitas 129 – Fifth Emerald 54 (Formidable (USA) 125) [2009 p12.2g Jan 12] sturdy, close-coupled gelding: well held sole outing on Flat in 2009 (modest hurdler): tried blinkered. *Evan Williams* **–**

FIVE CENTS 2 b.c. (Mar 5) Exceed And Excel (AUS) 126 – Native Nickel (IRE) (Be My Native (USA) 122) [2009 7m^3 7m* 6m^5 7d^5 Oct 11] 92,000 2-y-o: good-quartered colt: half-brother to winners abroad by Agnes World and Key of Luck: dam unraced half-sister to useful sprinter Orpsie Boy: fairly useful form: won maiden at Epsom in September: better effort in nurseries when creditable fifth at Haydock third start: stays 7f, will prove at least as effective at 6f: has left Godolphin. *Saeed bin Suroor* **79**

FIVEFOLD (USA) 2 b. or br.c. (Mar 25) Hennessy (USA) 122 – Calming (USA) 71 (Wild Again (USA)) [2009 p7g p7g^2 p7.1g p7m^2 p7m^3 p8m^4 Dec 9] $80,000F, 24,000Y: fourth foal: half-brother to French winner around 1m Mezzo Forte (by Stravinsky): dam, US 1m winner, half-sister to smart US miler Chinese Dragon: fair maiden: in frame in nurseries last 3 starts: stays 1m: raced only on polytrack. *J. Akehurst* **79**

FIVEFOOTNUMBERONE (IRE) 3 b.g. Acclamation 118 – Longueville Legend (IRE) 93 (Cajun Cadet 93) [2009 86: 6m 6m^5 6.1m^4 5g* 5m^6 5g^6 5s^6 5g^2 5s^4 5m p5.1g^3 5v^6 Nov 3] lengthy gelding: has scope: fluent mover: fairly useful handicapper: won at Haydock in May: best at 5f: acts on polytrack and any turf going: often in headgear (not for wins). *J. J. Quinn* **82**

FIVE GOLD RINGS (IRE) 3 ch.f. Captain Rio 122 – Metisse (IRE) 68 (Indian Ridge 123) [2009 p5.1g^2 p6g* p6g 6f p5g Oct 24] €56,000F, €55,000Y: first foal: dam, Irish sprint maiden, sister to smart Irish sprinter Timote: fair form when winning maiden at Lingfield in February: well held after: stays 6f: acts on polytrack: sold 3,000 gns, joined M. Hazell. *J. A. Osborne* **68**

FIVEONTHREEFORJD 4 br.g. Compton Admiral 121 – Patrician Fox (IRE) 67§ (Nicolotte 118) [2009 –: f8f Dec 12] tailed off in maiden/seller 15 months apart. *W. J. H. Ratcliffe* **–**

FIVE STAR JUNIOR (USA) 3 b.g. Five Star Day (USA) 120 – Sir Harriett (USA) (Sir Harry Lewis (USA) 127) [2009 76: p6g* p6g* p6g* p6g* p7g^5 p6g^2 6m^4 6f^4 6m^3 6g^4 6m^4 6m^4 p6g^3 p6g Dec 28] useful performer, better on all-weather: thrived early in 2009, winning maiden at Kempton and handicaps at Lingfield (2) and Wolverhampton in January/February: good ½-length second to Daddy's Gift in handicap at Kempton 2 outings later: mainly respectable efforts after: effective at 5f to 7f: acts on polytrack and good to firm ground. *Mrs L. Stubbs* **97** **a103**

FIVE WISHES 5 b.m. Bahamian Bounty 116 – Due West 56 (Inchinor 119) [2009 72: 8.3g 12g May 23] smallish, strong mare: fair performer: well below form both starts in 2009: tried visored, usually wears blinkers: not entirely straightforward. *G. A. Harker* **–**

FIXATION 5 ch.g. Observatory (USA) 131 – Fetish 85 (Dancing Brave (USA) 140) [2009 11.6g 16m⁵ Jul 15] lengthy gelding: modest maiden in 2007: below form in handicaps both starts since: stays 1¼m: not straightforward. *Mrs L. C. Jewell* **–**

FIZZLEPHUT (IRE) 7 b.g. Indian Rocket 115 – Cladantom (IRE) 70 (High Estate 127) [2009 67: p5g⁶ p5.1g p5g² p5.1m* f5m⁵ p6g p5g⁴ p5.1g p5g 5.1d⁶ 6m³ 5f⁴ 5.1g p5g p5.1g⁶ 5g 5.1m Sep 13] lengthy gelding: modest handicapper: won at Wolverhampton in February: best form at 5f: acts on all-weather and good to firm going: often wears headgear: has flashed tail: none too consistent. *Miss J. R. Tooth* **63**

FLAG OF GLORY 2 b.g. (Feb 11) Trade Fair 124 – Rainbow Sky 79 (Rainbow Quest (USA) 134) [2009 7d 8.3d⁶ 8d Oct 27] compact gelding: modest form in maidens last 2 starts (gelded after final one). *C. F. Wall* **53**

FLAGSTONE (USA) 5 ch.g. Distant View (USA) 126 – Navarene (USA) (Known Fact (USA) 135) [2009 59: p7.1g p9.5g Jan 30] sturdy gelding: maiden, lightly raced: no form in 2009: tried tongue tied. *Ian Williams* **–**

FLAM 4 b.f. Singspiel (IRE) 133 – Delauncy (Machiavellian (USA) 123) [2009 74: p12m p13g Feb 21] rather leggy, lengthy filly: maiden handicapper: well below form both outings in 2009: stays 1½m: acts on polytrack and good to firm going: tried in cheekpieces. *A. M. Hales* **–**

FLAMBEAU 2 b.f. (Mar 2) Oasis Dream 129 – Flavian 94 (Catrail (USA) 123) [2009 7d⁵ Oct 12] fourth foal: half-sister to 3 winners, including 3-y-o Bended Knee: dam, 6f (at 2 yrs)/7f winner, out of Musidora Stakes winner Fatah Flare: 14/1, encouraging 2½ lengths fifth to Qaraaba in maiden at Salisbury, drawn wide and not having hard race: likely to improve. *H. Candy* **67 p**

FLAMBOYANT RED (IRE) 3 ch.g. Redback 116 – Flamboyant (Danzero (AUS)) [2009 –: p6g³ p6g p6g⁴ p5g 7g Jun 16] useful-looking gelding: poor maiden: should stay 7f+: tongue tied last 2 starts: signs of temperament. *Miss Gay Kelleway* **46**

FLAME CREEK (IRE) 13 b.g. Shardari 134 – Sheila's Pet (IRE) (Welsh Term 126) [2009 70, a82d: f12d 16g 13.3m 16.5s⁵ 14.1s⁵ Jul 14] tall gelding: veteran handicapper: no form in 2009: tried tongue tied. *E. J. Creighton* **–**

FLAME OF GIBRALTAR (IRE) 3 b.f. Rock of Gibraltar (IRE) 133 – Spirit of Tara (IRE) 106 (Sadler's Wells (USA) 132) [2009 10m² 10m* 12m² 12g⁴ 12m³ 10.1m⁵ 12m p13g⁵ Oct 29] €900,000Y: deep-girthed filly: seventh foal: half-sister to high-class 1m to 11.5f winner Echo of Light (by Dubai Millennium), smart 9f to 1½m winner Akarem and useful Irish 1m/9f winner Multazem (both by Kingmambo): dam, Irish 1½m winner, sister to Salsabil and half-sister to Marju: useful performer: won maiden at Lingfield in June: much better efforts after in Ribblesdale Stakes at Royal Ascot (4 lengths second to Flying Cloud) and listed race at York (4 lengths third to Tanoura): stays 1½m: best efforts on good to firm going. *H. R. A. Cecil* **101**

FLAME OF HESTIA (IRE) 3 ch.f. Giant's Causeway (USA) 132 – Ellen (IRE) (Machiavellian (USA) 123) [2009 56p: 8m³ 8.1f² Jul 2] leggy filly: fair form in maidens: placed in 2009 at Newmarket and Haydock (suffered minor injury to off-fore fetlock): will prove suited by 1¼m+. *J. R. Fanshawe* **70**

FLAMESTONE 5 b.g. Piccolo 121 – Renee 55 (Wolfhound (USA) 126) [2009 60: p6g² p6g* p6g p6g⁴ p6g⁴ p8g⁴ p7g² p6g³ 8f p8g Jun 24] close-coupled gelding: modest performer: won minor event at Kempton in January: effective at 6f to 1m: acts on polytrack, good to firm and good to soft ground: tried in blinkers/cheekpieces: held up. *A. E. Price* **53**

FLAMING BLAZE 3 b.g. Tobougg (IRE) 125 – Catch The Flame (USA) (Storm Bird (CAN) 134) [2009 f7g⁶ 9d 8f⁶ Jul 2] well held in maidens/seller (tongue tied). *P. C. Haslam* **–**

FLAMING CAT (IRE) 6 b. or br.g. Orpen (USA) 116 – Brave Cat (IRE) (Catrail (USA) 123) [2009 –: 7f Jul 2] tall gelding: little form: tried in cheekpieces. *F. Watson* **–**

FLAMING MIRACLE 2 ch.c. (Mar 14) Firebreak 125 – Sukuma (IRE) 55 (Highest Honor (FR) 124) [2009 6m p6g⁶ 6m⁵ 8m² 8.3m² 8m⁶ p8.6g² 8d* Oct 12] workmanlike colt: second foal: dam maiden (stayed 1m): fairly useful performer: won maiden at Salisbury: stays 1m: acts on polytrack, good to firm and good to soft going: has been slowly away/finished weakly: sold 35,000 gns. *A. M. Balding* **80**

FLAMINGO FANTASY (GER) 4 ch.c. Fantastic Light (USA) 134 – Flamingo Road (GER) 118 (Acatenango (GER) 127) [2009 14.6g* 16g* 12g* 12d² 12g Aug 16] €58,000Y: third foal: half-brother to German 1¼m/1½m winner Flamingo Rainbow (by Rainbow Quest): dam German 10.5f/11f (including Preis der Diana) winner: smart **118**

performer: improved in 2009, winning listed race at Mulheim and Betty Barclay-Rennen at Baden-Baden (by ½ length from Ruten) in May, and Hansa-Preis at Hamburg (by 2 lengths from Getaway) in June: creditable ¾-length second to Getaway in Deutschland-Preis at Dusseldorf before running poorly in Rheinland-Pokal at Cologne final start: effective at 1½m to 2m: acts on good to soft ground. *W. Hickst, Germany*

FLAMING RUBY 3 b.f. Hunting Lion (IRE) 115 – Floral Spark 69 (Forzando 122) [2009 45: p5.1g⁶ f5g f8g Mar 26] small filly: poor form. *N. Tinkler* **–**

FLAMSTEED (IRE) 3 b.c. Clodovil (IRE) 116 – Nautical Gem (IRE) (Alhaarth (IRE) 126) [2009 68: p6g³ p6g³ p5g* p6g² p6g³ 6g² p6g⁵ 5m 6s⁴ 6m⁴ p7g⁴ p6g Oct 20] fair performer: won maiden at Lingfield in February: will prove best at 5f/6f: acts on polytrack, best turf effort on good going: sold 3,000 gns. *M. Quinn* **74**

FLANDERS FIELDS 4 b.g. Galileo (IRE) 134 – Vimy Ridge (FR) (Indian Ridge 123) [2009 p12g Jan 24] better effort in maidens in France at 3 yrs for A. Fabre when sixth at Compiegne latter occasion: sold 26,000 gns and gelded, tailed off in similar event on British debut: stays 1½m: sold £1,800 in October, resold £800 in November. *G. L. Moore* **–**

FLANEUR 2 b.g. (Mar 3) Chineur (FR) 123 – Tatanka (IRE) (Lear Fan (USA) 130) [2009 5.1m 6v⁵ 5m³ 6d³ 6d* 6m² 6m 7m 6g³ 6s⁵ Nov 7] 17,000F, £7,000Y: close-coupled gelding: fourth foal: half-brother to 4-y-o Tasheba: dam unraced out of half-sister to Coronation Cup winner Be My Native: fairly useful performer: won nursery at Newcastle in July: good efforts in similar events last 2 starts (subsequently gelded): stays 6f well: acts on soft and good to firm ground: blinkered after debut: races prominently. *T. D. Easterby* **80**

FLANNEL (IRE) 3 gr.g. Clodovil (IRE) 116 – La Captive (IRE) 68 (Selkirk (USA) 129) [2009 57: 10.1d 10m 11m 10.3d f12g 14.1g Aug 14] big gelding: modest maiden: should stay 1½m: acts on good to firm going. *J. R. Fanshawe* **59**

FLAPJACK 2 b.f. (Apr 28) Trade Fair 124 – Inya Lake 101 (Whittingham (IRE) 104) [2009 5g⁶ 5.3m⁴ 5.5m³ 6m⁶ 5g⁵ 7d⁵ p5g p6g⁴ p6m 6.1s Oct 7] £10,000Y: compact filly: seventh foal: half-sister to 3 winning sprinters, notably 5-y-o Jimmy Styles: dam 5f winner, including at 2 yrs: fair form in maidens second/third starts, well below that level after: stays 5.5f: acts on good to firm going: sold 2,500 gns. *R. Hannon* **65 d**

FLAPPER (IRE) 3 b.f. Selkirk (USA) 129 – Pure Spin (USA) (Machiavellian (USA) 123) [2009 61p: 8m⁴ 8g⁴ 10.3m 8g* 8g* 8m 8.1d² 8m 8g⁵ Oct 30] leggy, close-coupled filly: fairly useful handicapper: won at York (apprentices) in July and Newmarket in August: best around 1m: acts on polytrack, good to firm and good to soft going. *J. W. Hills* **80**

FLASH FOR FREEDOM (USA) 2 b.c. (Feb 26) Essence of Dubai (USA) 118 – Isathriller (USA) (Buckaroo (USA)) [2009 6m p6g p7g p7g p8m Dec 1] no form in maidens/nurseries. *J. R. Best* **–**

FLASHGUN (USA) 3 b.c. Lemon Drop Kid (USA) 131 – Tolltally Light (USA) (Majestic Light (USA)) [2009 64: p9.5g 8.3d⁴ 8d Jun 26] good-bodied colt: modest maiden: stays 8.3f: raced only on ground softer than good on turf, no form on polytrack. *M. G. Quinlan* **51**

FLASH MCGAHON (IRE) 5 b.g. Namid 128 – Astuti (IRE) 84 (Waajib 121) [2009 104: 5m 6m⁶ 5m 5d⁶ 5m⁶ f5m Dec 15] tall, good-topped ex-Irish gelding: just fairly useful handicapper nowadays: effective at 5f/6f: acts on polytrack, good to firm and good to soft going: tried blinkered/in cheekpieces. *D. Nicholls* **86**

FLASHY LOVER (IRE) 2 b.f. (Mar 11) Trans Island 119 – Irish Lover (USA) (Irish River (FR) 131) [2009 6m 6m⁶ 6m⁵ 6v³ 7d* Aug 7] €8,000Y: angular filly: fifth foal: half-sister to 2 winners, including Irish 5-y-o Frutti Tutti: dam, Italian 1¼m winner, half-sister to smart Flashy Wings and to dam of 3-y-o Darley Sun: modest performer: won seller at Newmarket: stays 7f: acts on good to firm and good to soft ground: sold €5,200. *M. R. Channon* **54**

FLASHY MAX 4 b.g. Primo Valentino (IRE) 116 – Be Practical 83 (Tragic Role (USA)) [2009 56: 7.5m 8f 7.5m 7.6g 10.1m Aug 13] workmanlike gelding: handicapper: no form in 2009: tried in cheekpieces. *Jedd O'Keeffe* **–**

FLASHY PHOTON 4 b.g. Compton Place 125 – Showboat (USA) (Theatrical 128) [2009 77: p7g 6m 6s 7g⁴ 7g 6.1s 6g Oct 20] compact gelding: handicapper, just modest at best in 2009: should prove well suited by 7f: best efforts on good ground: blinkered final outing. *H. Candy* **59**

FLAWED GENIUS 4 b.g. Fasliyev (USA) 120 – Talented 112 (Bustino 136) [2009 **96 §** 103: p8.6g^6 p7g 8m^6 7f^6 8m* 7.6m 10m 8m 8g* 8m^3 8s 8m^4 8g^6 p7.1g 8m 9m p7g Nov 25] strong, well-made gelding: useful performer at best: won handicap at Thirsk in May and claimer at Doncaster in July: looked most temperamental after, refusing to race last 3 outings: stays 1m: acts on polytrack and firm going: tried visored/in cheekpieces: often tongue tied: banned from racing from starting stalls at BHA inquiry in December. *K. A. Ryan*

FLAWLESS DIAMOND (IRE) 3 ch.f. Indian Haven 119 – Mystery Hill (USA) 72 **52** (Danehill (USA) 126) [2009 54: p7g^2 p7.1g^5 p7g^3 Jan 23] well-made filly: modest performer: stays 7f: acts on polytrack and heavy going: wears blinkers/cheekpieces: none too consistent. *J. S. Moore*

FLAXEN LAKE 2 b.g. (Apr 10) Sampower Star 118 – Cloudy Reef 57 (Cragador 110) **71** [2009 5m^6 5m^3 p5.1m^4 p5.1g^3 p5.1g^6 f6f^4 Dec 11] lengthy gelding: half-brother to several winners, including 5f/6f winner Gilded Cove and 5f (at 2 yrs)/7f winner Ochre Bay (both fairly useful by Polar Prince): dam maiden (raced only around 5f): fair maiden: should stay 6f: tried in cheekpieces. *R. Hollinshead*

FLEETING ECHO 2 b.f. (Feb 4) Beat Hollow 126 – Sempre Sorriso 52 (Fleetwood **89** (IRE) 107) [2009 5g^5 p5g* 6m^4 6g* 6g^3 6d 6g^2 p6m^3 Oct 28] smallish filly: second foal: dam, maiden (stayed 1m), out of smart 7f/1m performer Ever Genial: fairly useful performer: won maiden at Kempton in June and nursery at Lingfield in July: good placed efforts behind Freeforaday in nurseries at Newbury and Kempton last 2 starts: likely to stay 7f: acts on polytrack, best turf form on good going. *R. Hannon*

FLEETING SPIRIT (IRE) 4 b.f. Invincible Spirit (IRE) 121 – Millennium Tale **124** (FR) (Distant Relative 128) [2009 122: 5m^2 6m* 6d^2 5g^2 a6f Nov 7]

Fleeting Spirit finally managed a Group 1 win, in the Darley July Cup at Newmarket in the middle of the summer, arguably as strong a championship sprint as any run in Britain all year. She remained in form for rather longer than she had as a three year old and took the runner-up spot in three other Group 1 events, going down by a neck, half a length and three quarters of a length. The fact that had she repeated her July Cup form she would have had a record of four Group 1 wins out of four only reinforced the feeling of 'what might have been' that has followed her throughout her career. Fleeting Spirit wasn't far off the best of a mediocre bunch of British-trained sprinters on the form of her Newmarket run, but the comparison with Lochsong, the last filly to dominate the colts and geldings in the top sprints, prompted by Fleeting Spirit's July Cup effort, couldn't be sustained after her subsequent efforts. For the second year running there was a scattering of 'if onlys': a slight setback kept Fleeting Spirit out of the Nunthorpe at York, as it had in 2008, and there was a further, though less serious contretemps with the stalls and the authorities before and after the Prix de l'Abbaye at Longchamp.

The July Cup drew an intriguing mix of established sprinters from around the globe—the veteran Australian gelding Takeover Target, the South African representative J J The Jet Plane, the French-trained African Rose, who had won the Sprint Cup at Doncaster the previous year—as well as the high-class miler Paco Boy. Paco Boy had won the Queen Anne Stakes at Royal Ascot the previous month (the fourth in that race Main Aim was also in the field), while the winners of the two Group 1 sprints at Royal Ascot were also among the thirteen lining up on the July course. The only three-year-old in the July Cup line-up, Art Connoisseur, had won the Golden Jubilee, while the Australian-trained Scenic Blast had won the King's Stand Stakes. Fleeting Spirit reappeared in the King's Stand, a race in which she had started favourite after an impressive return in the Temple Stakes at Haydock the previous year, beaten three quarters of a length into third behind Equiano and Takeover Target on that occasion. She met defeat by the same margin in 2009, Scenic Blast starting 11/4 favourite with Fleeting Spirit next best at 7/2. Scenic Blast was by no means all out at Royal Ascot and, with the return to six furlongs regarded as not sure to suit Fleeting Spirit, she was sent off at 12/1 in the July Cup. Scenic Blast was a short-priced favourite at 11/8. Only Paco Boy (9/2) and J J The Jet Plane (13/2), beaten favourite in the Golden Jubilee, started at shorter odds than Fleeting Spirit, with Art Connoisseur sent off the same odds as her.

In contrast to several of her rivals, everything went as well as it could for Fleeting Spirit in the July Cup. Those who raced up with the pace dominated,

Darley July Cup, Newmarket—Fleeting Spirit gains a deserved Group 1 win, though she veers off a true line in front, hampering runner-up Main Aim; J J The Jet Plane (right) finishes third in a strong, international field

Takeover Target and Main Aim taking turns in front, with Fleeting Spirit travelling typically smoothly close by. Approaching the final furlong, Fleeting Spirit was asked to go to the front under just hand riding and looked in control before veering both ways when ridden more firmly, hampering Main Aim and the keeping-on King's Apostle. Fleeting Spirit was never in much danger of losing the race as she would have won anyway, having a length and a quarter to spare over runner-up Main Aim at the line. J J The Jet Plane took third, ahead of Paco Boy, who came from a hopeless position for fourth, King's Apostle probably denied that placing by the interference he suffered. Art Connoisseur was in nothing like the same form as at Ascot, while Scenic Blast was even more disappointing and later reported to have swallowed his tongue. His compatriot Takeover Target suffered a career-ending injury. Fleeting Spirit was ridden at Newmarket by Tom Queally, gaining the second of five wins in Group 1/Grade 1 races during the year, having come in for the mount on Art Connoisseur at Ascot due to Jamie Spencer's suspension.

Forced to miss the Nunthorpe, Fleeting Spirit was next seen in the Sprint Cup at Haydock nearly two months later. By that time the form of the July Cup had taken a knock or two, the second and third well held in the Lennox Stakes at Goodwood though Paco Boy had run well, albeit back at a mile, and King's Apostle had gone on to Group 1 success in the Prix Maurice de Gheest at Deauville. The Sprint Cup dented the July Cup form further when Main Aim and J J The Jet Plane finished last and next to last. Fleeting Spirit herself went close to justifying favouritism at Haydock, just outstayed, on ground softer than she had previously encountered, by the 2008 Ayr Gold Cup winner Regal Parade after leading on the bridle. With the Wokingham winner High Standing in third and the winner appearing to show by some way his best form, the overall form of the Sprint Cup fell a little short of what might be expected at this level. Back at five furlongs, the Abbaye seemed to offer a good opportunity for Fleeting Spirit to confirm herself as Europe's best sprinter, but she failed by a neck to overhaul the three-year-old Total Gallery after starting slowly. With little more than two and a half lengths covering the first eight home, all but one of them trained in Britain, the form again looked a little short of the norm for a Group 1 sprint. Fleeting Spirit has the highest rating in this Annual of any of those that ran in the Abbaye and the Sprint Cup and she is rated higher than any of the British-trained runners in the King's Stand, though, even with the sex allowance, she couldn't manage a win in any of them.

Fleeting Spirit looks set to return for a further campaign in the top British sprints, though she is reportedly unlikely to go for the Abbaye again, her trainer reportedly unhappy with the French starter's unhelpfulness after Fleeting Spirit's misfortune the previous year, when her stall malfunctioned resulting in a rerun at the end of the day's card. Fleeting Spirit is reportedly also unlikely to be sent for the Breeders' Cup in 2010. She failed to show to advantage in the Turf Sprint as a three-year-old and an ambitious tilt at the Sprint itself, on pro-ride at Santa Anita, was also a failure, Fleeting Spirit managing only seventh of the nine runners behind Dancing In Silks, never able to go the pace from the outside draw.

Fleeting Spirit (IRE) (b.f. 2005)	Invincible Spirit (IRE) (b 1997)	Green Desert (b 1983)	Danzig
			Foreign Courier
		Rafha (b 1987)	Kris
			Eljazzi
	Millennium Tale (FR) (b 1996)	Distant Relative (b 1986)	Habitat
			Royal Sister II
		The Bean Sidhe (b 1983)	Corvaro
			Whiskey Mountain

There is little to add to details previously given of Fleeting Spirit's pedigree. Her year-younger brother, named Jackstown Road when in training with Noseda, was renamed Spanish Tale and ran twice in Spain in 2009. A filly foal, also by Invincible Spirit, was offered at the Newmarket December Sales and bought back at 105,000 guineas. A half-sister by Verglas had been sold at the same sale the previous year for 95,000 guineas. One of Fleeting Spirit's half-sisters, Je Ne Suis Pas La, a durable performer in the French Provinces where she won ten times from one hundred and six starts at up to eleven furlongs, added to her record at stud when Kutubia gained victories at Angouleme and La Teste in 2009. Fleeting Spirit, a compact, attractive filly, is effective at five and six furlongs and on firm and good to soft going, though softish ground at the longer trip stretches her stamina. She is a strong traveller and traded significantly shorter in running on Betfair at some stage

The Searchers' "Fleeting Spirit"

of all her defeats in 2009, being matched at a low of 1.03, just .02 off the minimum price, in the Sprint Cup. As she showed in the July Cup, and to a lesser extent at Ascot, she isn't always a straightforward ride once off the bridle. *J. Noseda*

FLEETING STAR (USA) 3 gr. or ro.f. Exchange Rate (USA) 111 – Disperse A Star **87**
(USA) (Dispersal (USA)) [2009 89P: 7g^6 p7.1g 6m^2 6f* 6m Sep 19] close-coupled filly: has a quick, unimpressive action: fairly useful handicapper: won at Brighton in August: stays 6f: acts on polytrack and firm going: visored last 3 starts. *J. Noseda*

FLEETWOOD FLAME 4 ch.f. Fleetwood (IRE) 107 – Barden Lady 54 (Presidium **–**
124) [2009 –: 10.9m 9g 12d Jul 22] showed little in maidens/handicap. *W. M. Brisbourne*

FLEETWOODSANDS (IRE) 2 b.g. (May 3) Footstepsinthesand 120 – Litchfield **–**
Hills (USA) (Relaunch (USA)) [2009 6m Jun 25] 18/1 and tongue tied, tailed off in maiden at Hamilton. *P. C. Haslam*

FLEUR DE LION (IRE) 3 ch.f. Lion Heart (USA) 124 – Viburnum (USA) (El Gran **71**
Senor (USA) 136) [2009 50: p8.6g^6 p7g^5 p7g p9.5m^4 p12g p12g f11g 10s^3 p10g^6 8f 10.2v^4 10.2g^4 11.9m* 11.9f 10m^5 p9.5g^2 11.6d p10g^6 p12m^2 p12f* p12f^4 Dec 21] rather leggy, attractive filly: fair performer: won selling handicap at Brighton in August and claimer at Kempton in December: stays 1½m: acts on polytrack, soft and good to firm going: tried blinkered: none too consistent. *S. Kirk*

FLEURISSIMO 3 ch.f. Dr Fong (USA) 128 – Agnus (IRE) (In The Wings 128) [2009 **78**
79p: 10s^2 Apr 17] good-topped filly: fair form in maidens: will stay 1½m: raced only on good going or softer. *J. L. Dunlop*

FLEURON 3 b. or br.f. Diktat 126 – Forthwith 104 (Midyan (USA) 124) [2009 –: p7g **–**
p7g Feb 11] little form in polytrack maidens. *P. Howling*

FLEXIBLE FRIEND (IRE) 5 b.h. Danehill (USA) 126 – Ripple of Pride (IRE) 93 **–**
(Sadler's Wells (USA) 132) [2009 –: 12.1m 16.2v Jul 24] maiden: lightly raced and no form since 2007 (including over hurdles): tried blinkered/tongue tied. *B. J. Llewellyn*

FLIGHTY FELLOW (IRE) 9 ch.g. Flying Spur (AUS) – Al Theraab (USA) 81 **65**
(Roberto (USA) 131) [2009 7g^3 8.5f^5 9m* 9d 8.5d^6 10m^6 p8.6m^5 p9.5g^6 Dec 18] big, lengthy gelding: fair handicapper: won 4-runner event at Les Landes in July: modest form at best in Britain in 2009, leaving Mrs J. Le Brocq in Jersey prior to final outing: stays 9f: acts on polytrack, firm and soft ground: usually wears headgear: no easy ride (tends to wander). *B. G. Powell*

FLIPACOIN 4 b.f. Josr Algarhoud (IRE) 118 – Eclectic (Emarati (USA) 74) [2009 –: **–**
p8g 10g^5 Apr 8] strong filly: no form. *S. Dow*

FLIPANDO (IRE) 8 b.g. Sri Pekan (USA) 117 – Magic Touch (Fairy King (USA)) **103**
[2009 101: p8g^2 p8.6g* 8m^3 9m^4 8g^6 10m 8.9g 8m^2 8.1f^2 8.1m^4 8m 8g 8m 8m f8g Oct 18] tall gelding: useful handicapper: won at Wolverhampton in March: good placed efforts otherwise, including when 3¾ lengths third to Expresso Star in Lincoln at Doncaster third outing: well below form last 5 starts: stays 10.4f: acts on polytrack, firm and soft ground: held up: tends to hang. *T. D. Barron*

FLIP FLOP (IRE) 2 b.f. (May 5) Footstepsinthesand 120 – Dame Alicia (IRE) 94 **85**
(Sadler's Wells (USA) 132) [2009 6m^2 p7g^4 6d* 8g^5 Oct 31] €30,000Y: rather leggy filly: third foal: half-sister to fairly useful Irish 1½m winner Lady Alicia (by Hawk Wing): dam, Irish 9f winner, closely related to smart miler Century City: fairly useful performer: won maiden at Folkestone in October: stiff task, good fifth to Timepiece in listed event at Newmarket (raced freely): stays 1m. *B. W. Hills*

FLIPPING 2 br.g. (Jan 30) Kheleyf (USA) 116 – Felona 92 (Caerleon (USA) 132) [2009 **80**
6.1m 6s* 6.1d^4 7m^4 p8.6g^5 8g p8g p8.6g^2 Dec 7] £12,000Y: fifth foal: half-brother to 9f winner Reem One (by Rainbow Quest) and winner abroad by Mtoto: dam, 9f/1¼m winner from 3 starts, half-sister to smart but untrustworthy performer up to 1m Aramram: fairly useful performer: won maiden at Haydock in July: creditable efforts in nurseries fifth/sixth starts: stays 8.6f: acts on polytrack and soft ground. *W. S. Kittow*

FLIRTY (IRE) 3 b.f. Lujain (USA) 119 – Fifth Edition 66 (Rock Hopper 124) [2009 –: **54**
f6s^6 7g 10s 9g p12.2g 13.8m^3 p12g 11.5g p12m^4 f14g Dec 22] modest maiden: stays 13.8f: acts on polytrack and good to firm going. *Rae Guest*

FLODDEN FIELD 3 ch.g. Selkirk (USA) 129 – Sister Bluebird 94 (Bluebird (USA) **64**
125) [2009 –: 10m^5 p9.5g Oct 15] maiden: modest form only on reappearance. *P. W. Chapple-Hyam*

FLOODLIT 3 b.f. Fantastic Light (USA) 134 – Westerly Air (USA) 80 (Gone West – (USA)) [2009 88p: 11.5m 12m Aug 13] fairly useful maiden winner only 2-y-o start: shaped as if amiss both starts in 2009: should be suited by 1m+. *J. H. M. Gosden*

FLOODS OF TEARS 3 br.f. Lucky Story (USA) 128 – Lady Natilda 64 (First Trump – 118) [2009 62d: f6g^4 f7g^6 p8g 7.5m 10g 6m 8.3g Oct 28] sturdy filly: maiden: form only on debut at 2 yrs: left D. Flood prior to final outing: tried blinkered. *I. W. McInnes*

FLOOR SHOW 3 ch.g. Bahamian Bounty 116 – Dancing Spirit (IRE) 72 (Ahonoora **88** 122) [2009 78p: 7g* 7d^2 7.1m 7m Jul 25] big, useful-looking gelding: has plenty of scope: fairly useful handicapper: won at Newcastle in April: best effort when second at Doncaster next time: has form at 7f, may prove ideally suited by return to shorter: acts on good to soft going: sold 10,000 gns in October, then gelded. *E. S. McMahon*

FLORA'S PRIDE 5 b.m. Alflora (IRE) 120 – Pennys Pride (IRE) 76 (Pips Pride 117) **62** [2009 11.1g^6 10.4v 10.1m^5 8g^4 8m^5 10f^5 10m 14.1g 10m^5 10m^5 10m^4 10g^3 12s^2 Oct 27] lengthy mare: second foal: dam, 1¼m/bumper winner, half-sister to useful 1¼m/1½m performer Penny A Day: modest maiden: should be suited by 1½m+: acts on soft and good to firm going. *K. G. Reveley*

FLORA TREVELYAN 3 b.f. Cape Cross (IRE) 129 – Why So Silent (Mill Reef **92** (USA) 141) [2009 85p: p8g^2 8.1g* 10g^2 10m Oct 16] good-topped filly: fairly useful performer: readily landed odds in maiden at Sandown in August: better than result both starts after: stays 1¼m: raced only on polytrack and good/good to firm ground. *W. R. Swinburn*

FLORENSKY (IRE) 2 br.c. (Mar 27) Sinndar (IRE) 134 – White Star (IRE) 108 **67** (Darshaan 133) [2009 8m^4 8d^6 Oct 28] good-topped colt: better effort in maidens when 3½ lengths sixth to Jupiter Fidius at Musselburgh, gaining under considerate handling: will be suited by 1¼m+: has left Godolphin, and sent to UAE. *Saeed bin Suroor*

FLORENTIA 3 ch.f. Medicean 128 – Area Girl 76 (Jareer (USA) 115) [2009 66p: p7g **75** f5m^3 f6g p7g^3 p7.1g^3 8m* 9.7s* p8.6g^3 p10g p9.5g^3 Dec 7] useful-looking filly: fair handicapper: won at Bath in September and Folkestone in October: stays 9.7f: acts on polytrack, soft and good to firm going. *Sir Mark Prescott*

FLORENTINE RULER (USA) 2 b.c. (Apr 3) Medicean 128 – Follow That Dream **68 p** 90 (Darshaan 133) [2009 8.3g^6 Oct 28] sixth foal: half-brother to 8-y-o Desert Dreamer and German 1m/1¼m performer Point Pleasant (by Grand Lodge): dam, 1½m winner, half-sister to high-class 1¼m/1½m winner Storming Home: 14/1 and green, encouraging 7¾ lengths sixth to Psychic Ability in maiden at Nottingham, slowly away and not knocked about: will stay 1¼m: sure to improve. *H. R. A. Cecil*

FLORES SEA (USA) 5 ch.g. Luhuk (USA) 114 – Perceptive (USA) (Capote (USA)) **85** [2009 79: f7g^2 f7g f8g^2 f7g* f7g^2 7.1m^3 7.1m f7g^4 9m^2 f7m^7 p8.6g^5 f8g Dec 27] lengthy gelding: fairly useful handicapper: won at Southwell in March: stays 1m: acts on all-weather, firm and soft going: often in cheekpieces/blinkers. *T. D. Barron*

FLORIO VINCITORE (IRE) 2 b.g. (Apr 24) High Chaparral (IRE) 132 – Salome's **75** Attack 90 (Anabaa (USA) 130) [2009 6g^2 7m p6g* f6m^2 6d^6 f8g^2 8.3g^6 7m^6 Sep 18] £2,000Y: lengthy gelding: third foal: half-brother to 3-y-o Carbon Hoofprint and 2007 2-y-o 6f winner Double Attack (by Peintre Celebre): dam, French 7.5f (at 2 yrs) to 9.5f winner, half-sister to very smart stayer Double Honour and to dam of 3-y-o Cavalryman: fair performer: won maiden at Lingfield in July: has raced freely, but should stay 1¼m: acts on all-weather. *E. J. Creighton*

FLOTATE (USA) 2 b. or br.f. (Mar 24) Orientate (USA) 127 – Flo Jo (USA) (Graus- **51** tark) [2009 p7g p6g 7f Sep 7] $27,000Y: close-coupled filly: half-sister to several winners in USA: dam US 6f winner: form in maidens only when mid-field at Kempton on debut. *Jane Chapple-Hyam*

FLOTATION (USA) 2 b. or br.f. (Apr 7) Chapel Royal (USA) 110 – Storm Dove **59 p** (USA) 108 (Storm Bird (CAN) 134) [2009 7g Oct 31] good-topped filly: half-sister to several winners, including fairly useful 2000 2-y-o 7f winner Good Standing (by Distant View) and Irish 4-y-o Cruel Sea: dam, 6f (at 2 yrs) and 7f winner, out of smart French performer up to 1¼m Daeltown: 33/1 and green, 8¼ lengths seventh to Field Day in maiden at Newmarket, slowly away and late headway: should improve. *B. W. Hills*

FLOUNCING (IRE) 2 b.f. (Feb 21) Barathea (IRE) 127 – Man Eater 74 (Mark of **78 p** Esteem (IRE) 137) [2009 p7g^3 8d^2 p7m^2 Oct 31] €22,000Y: useful-looking filly: third foal: dam sprint maiden: fair placed form in maidens, second to Totally Ours at Kempton (pulled hard) final start: may prove best up to 7f: capable of better. *W. J. Haggas*

FLOW CHART (IRE) 2 b.g. (Feb 5) Acclamation 118 – Free Flow (Mujahid (USA) 125) [2009 5m^{4} 5m^{3} 5g 6m^{3} 6g^{6} 7g 5m^{6} f6g* Dec 27] £800Y: lengthy gelding: first foal: dam unraced: fair performer: won nursery at Southwell: stays 6f: acts on fibresand and good to firm going: tried blinkered (including for win). *T. D. Barron* **72**

FLOWERBUD 4 b.f. Fantastic Light (USA) 134 – Maidment 112 (Insan (USA) 119) [2009 53: p11g^{5} p12g^{5} 12.6d p16g 13.1f Aug 22] maiden: modest form in 2009 only on reappearance: left Ms J. Doyle after second outing: probably stays 13f. *G. A. Ham* **56**

FLOWING CAPE (IRE) 4 b.g. Cape Cross (IRE) 129 – Jet Lock (USA) (Crafty Prospector (USA)) [2009 85: p7.1g* p6g* p8.6g^{5} p7g^{3} p8.6g p7g f6m^{5} f7g^{6} p6g^{4} Dec 28] lengthy, good-topped gelding: useful handicapper: won twice at Wolverhampton in February, beating Methaaly by ½ length for latter success: probably stays 8.6f, though not short of speed: acts on polytrack and good to firm ground, yet to race on ground softer than good: tried in cheekpieces, tongue tied final outing. *R. Hollinshead* **99**

FLUTE MAGIC 3 b.g. Piccolo 121 – Overcome (Belmez (USA) 131) [2009 72: p7.1g 6f 7.1g 6d^{5} 7d 6.1g p6g^{6} p9.5g Oct 3] workmanlike gelding: maiden, just modest form at 3 yrs: stays 7f: acts on firm and good to soft going: tried in headgear/tongue tie. *W. S. Kittow* **61**

FLY BUTTERFLY 3 ch.f. Bahamian Bounty 116 – Aconite 52 (Primo Dominie 121) [2009 52: 6.1g 5.1f 8m Jun 13] quite good-topped filly: maiden: no form at 3 yrs: tried blinkered. *M. R. Channon* **–**

FLY BY NELLY 3 b.f. Compton Place 125 – Dancing Nelly 52 (Shareef Dancer (USA) 135) [2009 60: 7m^{2} 7m^{3} 7m^{2} 7m 7.6g p7m^{2} p7.1g p7f^{4} Dec 21] leggy filly: fair maiden handicapper: stays 7f: raced only on polytrack and good/good to firm ground. *H. Morrison* **70**

FLYINFLYOUT 2 b.f. (Mar 31) Fath (USA) 116 – Hana Dee 72 (Cadeaux Genereux 131) [2009 6g^{4} 6m^{5} 5.7f* 6f 6g 5.1m^{5} 7g 7g p7g 8g p6m Sep 28] 2,000F: good-topped filly: second foal: half-sister to 3-y-o Screaming Brave: dam, maiden (stayed 2m), sister to smart 1m/1¼m performer Chrysander and half-sister to smart performer up to 1m Millennium Force: fair performer: won maiden at Bath in May: regressed in nurseries: best efforts around 6f: acts on firm going. *M. R. Channon* **70**

FLYING APPLAUSE 4 b.g. Royal Applause 124 – Mrs Gray 61 (Red Sunset 120) [2009 84: f8g p9.5g^{4} f11g^{6} p8g 8.3m* 10f 8.3g^{6} 6g 6.1g* 5.1m^{2} 6g^{6} 5.1v^{5} 6m Aug 8] leggy, close-coupled gelding: fair handicapper: won at Nottingham in April and June: effective at stiff 5f to 1¼m: acts on polytrack and good to firm going: in blinkers/tongue tie of late: usually front runner. *S. R. Bowring* **75**

FLYING BANTAM (IRE) 8 b.g. Fayruz 116 – Natural Pearl (Petong 126) [2009 82d: 6m 7m^{6} 8.1g^{6} 8m f8g 8d Aug 10] small, well-made gelding: just modest form in 2009: tried in cheekpieces, blinkered final outing. *J. R. Norton* **53**

FLYING CLOUD (IRE) 3 b.f. Storming Home 128 – Criquette 104 (Shirley Heights 130) [2009 10g* 10.5d* 12m* 10d^{6} Oct 25] angular filly: sister to useful 1m (at 2 yrs) to 11f winner Captain Webb, closely related to fairly useful Irish 2004 2-y-o 7f winner Hestia (by Machiavellian) and half-sister to 2 winners, including useful French 7f/1m winner Open Offer (by Cadeaux Genereux): dam, 7f (at 2 yrs) and 9f (in UAE) winner, half-sister to top-class miler Markofdistinction: useful performer: won newcomers race at Longchamp in April, Prix Cleopatre at Saint-Cloud in May and, having left A. Fabre in France, Ribblesdale Stakes at Royal Ascot (showed good turn of foot to beat Flame of Gibraltar 4 lengths): reportedly returned lame there and off 4 months before creditable 2¾ lengths sixth to Eva's Request in Premio Lydia Tesio at Rome final start: stays 1½m: acts on good to firm and good to soft going. *Saeed bin Suroor* **109**

Ribblesdale Stakes, Royal Ascot—
a welcome change of fortune for Godolphin after a disappointing start to the season;
Flying Cloud keeps her unbeaten record, with Flame of Gibraltar and Uvinza (rail) second and third

FLYING CLOUD (USA) 3 ch.f. Giant's Causeway (USA) 132 – St Francis Wood (USA) 95 (Irish River (FR) 131) [2009 –p: p8g 8g p12g Jun 25] tall filly: poor form in maidens/minor event. *B. J. Meehan* **45**

FLYING CROSS (IRE) 2 b.c. (May 7) Sadler's Wells (USA) 132 – Ramruma (USA) 123 (Diesis 133) [2009 8g⁴ 8d* Oct 21] fifth foal: dam 1½m winner (including Oaks) and second in St Leger: confirmed promise when landing odds in maiden at Navan by 3½ lengths from Brazilian Beauty, still green (head high) but eventually finishing strongly: will be suited by 1¼m/1½m: smart prospect. *A. P. O'Brien, Ireland* **98 P**

FLYING DESTINATION 2 ch.g. (Apr 26) Dubai Destination (USA) 127 – Fly For Fame (Shaadi (USA) 126) [2009 6m 7.1g⁴ 7.1g 8m² p8m⁵ Sep 30] compact gelding: seventh foal: half-brother to several winners, including fairly useful Irish 1½m/13f winner Fire Finch (by Halling): dam, useful French 1¼m (at 2 yrs)/1½m winner, out of smart French performer around 1¼m Fly Me: fair maiden: creditable efforts in nurseries last 2 starts, subsequently gelded: sure to be suited by 1¼m+. *W. J. Knight* **75**

FLYING DOCTOR 6 b.g. Mark of Esteem (IRE) 137 – Vice Vixen (CAN) (Vice Regent (CAN)) [2009 p16.5g Jan 22] tall, close-coupled gelding: fair hurdler: lightly-raced maiden on Flat. *N. G. Richards* **–**

FLYING GAZEBO (IRE) 3 b.g. Orpen (USA) 116 – Grand Summit (IRE) (Grand Lodge (USA) 125) [2009 8.1g 8m⁶ 8d⁴ 8.1d⁵ p12m Dec 9] modest maiden: best efforts second/third starts. *J. S. Moore* **55**

FLYING GOOSE (IRE) 5 ch.g. Danehill Dancer (IRE) 117 – Top of The Form (IRE) 79 (Masterclass (USA) 116) [2009 86d: p12g 16.2v Jul 24] sturdy, good-topped gelding: well below form both starts in 2009: tried blinkered/in cheekpieces: wayward: sold £700, sent to Greece. *R. A. Harris* **– §**

FLYING INDIAN 4 ch.f. Hawk Wing (USA) 136 – Poppadam 87 (Salse (USA) 128) [2009 66: f5d f5g⁶ f6g p5g⁵ Feb 12] strong filly: poor performer nowadays: stays 6f: acts on polytrack, soft and good to firm going: in headgear nowadays. *J. Balding* **41**

FLYING LADY (IRE) 3 b.f. Hawk Wing (USA) 136 – Lady Nessa (USA) (Al Nasr (FR) 126) [2009 81: p8g⁵ p8g p8.6g² p8g³ p10g* 10g² p9.5g⁵ p8.6g⁶ Apr 25] tall, rather leggy filly: fair performer: won seller at Lingfield in March: best form up to 8.6f: acts on polytrack and good to firm going: temperamental. *M. R. Channon* **73 §**

FLYING PHOEBE 3 b.f. Sakhee (USA) 136 – Altaweelah (IRE) 104 (Fairy King (USA)) [2009 10.1m 10.3m⁵ 12g 9.9m⁴ 12.1g³ 12.5m 11.5g Oct 20] €25,000Y, 19,000 2-y-o: fifth foal: half-sister to fairly useful 2003 2-y-o 7f winner Qasirah (by Machiavellian): dam, 10.5f/1½m winner, half-sister to smart performer up to 2m Lost Soldier Three: modest maiden: stays 1½m: raced only on good/good to firm ground. *Mrs L. Stubbs* **56**

FLYING RIVER (IRE) 3 b.f. Bachelor Duke (USA) 122 – Suzuran (Generous (IRE) 139) [2009 –: p8g p8.6g⁵ 9f³ 10.5f* 9.5g⁵ 7g 8.5g 9f⁴ Oct 4] poor performer: left Tom Dascombe after second start: won minor event at Duindigt in June: stays 10.5f: acts on firm ground. *J. H. Smith, Holland* **49**

FLYING SILKS (IRE) 3 b.g. Barathea (IRE) 127 – Future Flight 85 (Polar Falcon (USA) 126) [2009 67+: 6g⁴ 7m 8.1s³ 8g* p8g⁵ 8d⁶ 8.3v Nov 4] quite attractive gelding: fair handicapper: easily best effort when winning at Pontefract in August: stays 1m: acts on polytrack and soft ground. *J. R. Gask* **74**

FLYING SQUAD (UAE) 5 b.g. Jade Robbery (USA) 121 – Sandova (IRE) 101 (Green Desert (USA) 127) [2009 78: p12.2g f8g p8g⁶ p8g f8g⁵ p12.2m 10.9g f12m⁴ Nov 12] fair performer: regressive after reappearance: stays 1½m: acts on all-weather: tried tongue tied. *M. F. Harris* **75 d**

FLYING STATESMAN (USA) 2 b.g. (Jan 26) Johannesburg (USA) 127 – Insomnie (USA) (Seattle Slew (USA)) [2009 6g² 6m* 6m Jun 16] $50,000Y: well-made gelding: second foal: closely related to winner in USA by Hennessy: dam unraced half-sister to US Grade 2 9f winner Distilled: fairly useful form in maidens first 2 starts, making all when winning at Ayr in June by 1½ lengths from Layali Al Andalus (subsequent runner-up in Group 2): well held in Coventry Stakes at Royal Ascot (hung right, returned lame): subsequently gelded. *R. A. Fahey* **86**

FLYING VALENTINO 5 b.m. Primo Valentino (IRE) 116 – Flying Romance (IRE) 68 (Flying Spur (AUS)) [2009 83: p6m p8.6g³ 8.3m⁶ 8m 10m³ 8.3m* 8g³ 8m 8.3f p7.1g Oct 30] narrow mare: fairly useful handicapper: won at Windsor in June: best around 1m: acts on polytrack, good to firm and good to soft ground: none too consistent. *Ian Williams* **86**

FLY IN JOHNNY (IRE) 4 b.g. Fasliyev (USA) 120 – Goodness Gracious (IRE) 93 (Green Desert (USA) 127) [2009 62d: p7g p6g^3 p6g 8m 7m 5f^6 6m 5.2s 6g p6g Jul 22] sturdy gelding: modest maiden: stays 1m: acts on polytrack, firm and good to soft going: often in headgear: irresolute. *J. J. Bridger* **52 §**

FLYNN'S ISLAND (IRE) 3 b.g. Trans Island 119 – Cappuccino (IRE) (Mujadil (USA) 119) [2009 7m 7m 8m 8s 10g 7.1m 7.9g^5 Jul 4] strong gelding: maiden, modest form at best: should be suited by 1m+: blinkered/visored last 3 starts. *M. Dods* **51**

FLY SILCA FLY (IRE) 2 b.f. (Feb 18) Hawk Wing (USA) 136 – Nevis Peak (AUS) (Danehill (USA) 126) [2009 5.2g^5 6m^2 7m 6f^2 5v* 6d^6 6m* 6.1m^2 Aug 21] 8,000F, £30,000Y: good-topped filly: second living foal: dam unraced: fairly useful performer: won maiden at Ripon in July and nursery at Windsor in August: good 4 lengths second to Walk On Water in minor event at Chester final start: should prove best at 5f/6f: acts on heavy and good to firm ground. *M. R. Channon* **84**

FLY WITH THE STARS (USA) 4 ch.g. Fusaichi Pegasus (USA) 130 – Forest Key (USA) (Green Forest (USA) 134) [2009 62: 9s 18g Aug 13] tall gelding: maiden, lightly raced: should stay 1¼m: tried tongue tied. *A. B. Haynes* **–**

FOCAIL EILE 4 b.g. Noverre (USA) 125 – Glittering Image (IRE) (Sadler's Wells (USA) 132) [2009 67: p8.6g^2 p8.6g* 8m 8.3g^4 8.3v* 8.3s* 8.3d^4 8s p8m Nov 3] long-backed gelding: fairly useful performer: left E. McMahon after reappearance: won maiden at Wolverhampton in January and, having left Gay Kelleway after fourth outing, handicaps at Nottingham in July and Leicester in August: stays 9.5f: acts on polytrack and heavy going. *J. Ryan* **81**

FOCHABERS 2 b.g. (Apr 15) Dr Fong (USA) 128 – Celtic Cross 100 (Selkirk (USA) 129) [2009 p8g p8g^4 f8d^5 Dec 29] easily best effort in maidens when 3¾ lengths fourth to Hidden Glory at Lingfield: bred to stay 1¼m+. *R. Charlton* **66**

FOL HOLLOW (IRE) 4 b.g. Monashee Mountain (USA) 115 – Constance Do (Risk Me (FR) 127) [2009 102: 5m* 5d* 5m^6 5g 6m^4 5m* 5v 5m^4 6d 5g^4 5.4m^3 5m^3 6m 5m^4 Sep 26] strong, compact gelding: useful handicapper: won at Beverley and Naas in April, and Beverley (beat Everymanforhimself ¾ length) in June: largely creditable efforts after, including when fourth to Judge 'n Jury in Hong Kong Sprint at Ascot eighth outing: best at 5f/easy 6f: acts on good to firm and good to soft going: usually up with pace. *D. Nicholls* **104**

FOLIO (IRE) 9 b.g. Perugino (USA) 84 – Bayleaf 104 (Efisio 120) [2009 88: p10g* p10g* p10g^4 p10g^3 10.3g p10g^6 10m 10g 10d^6 Jun 8] rather leggy, useful-looking gelding: fairly useful handicapper: won at Great Leighs and Lingfield in January: below form on turf after: best around 1¼m: unraced on heavy ground, acts on any other turf and polytrack: usually held up. *W. J. Musson* **63 a83**

FOLK TUNE (IRE) 6 b.h. Danehill (USA) 126 – Musk Lime (USA) 97 (Private Account (USA)) [2009 12m^6 13.1m Sep 19] useful winner (3 times) at 7.5f/1m in France for J-C. Rouget in 2006: fairly useful 2m/2½m winning hurdler for Ferdy Murphy prior to well beaten both Flat starts in 2009: successful over fences in October. *J. J. Quinn* **–**

FOLLETTA (IRE) 2 b.f. (Jan 29) Le Vie Dei Colori 126 – Finnine (USA) (Zafonic (USA) 130) [2009 6g^4 6m^4 6g 6d^2 6m 7g^5 p8m p8g^2 7d Oct 22] £5,000Y: sturdy filly: second foal: half-sister to Italian 2007 2-y-o 7f winner Starviet (by Soviet Star): dam unraced out of useful close relative to smart sprinter Dancing Dissident: fair maiden: stays 1m: acts on polytrack and good to soft ground: tried in cheekpieces: moody, and needs treating with caution: sold 5,000 gns. *R. Hannon* **67 §**

FOL LIAM 3 b.g. Observatory (USA) 131 – Tide of Fortune (Soviet Star (USA) 128) [2009 78: 10.3m 10.4m f7g^3 p6g p7.1g^5 8.3g p6g^5 p7.1g^3 Sep 5] workmanlike gelding: fair performer: largely below form in 2009, claimed from Ian Williams £5,500 after third start: stays 7f: acts on polytrack, good to firm and good to soft going: usually held up. *A. J. McCabe* **70**

FOLLOW THE DREAM 6 b.m. Double Trigger (IRE) 123 – Aquavita 56 (Kalaglow 132) [2009 p12.2g^6 p12g^6 p12g 11.5g p12g^5 p13.9g^6 16g^3 18g* p16.5g^2 p16.5g^2 f14g* Dec 8] second foal: dam 2m and hurdles winner: fair handicapper: won at Chepstow in August and Southwell in December: stays 2¼m: raced on all-weather and good going: held up: signs of temperament. *Karen George* **69**

FOLLOW THE FLAG (IRE) 5 ch.g. Traditionally (USA) 117 – Iktidar 80 (Green Desert (USA) 127) [2009 81: f8g^5 p8.6g^3 p8.6g* p9.5g 7m^4 p7.1g 8m^2 8f^6 8m 8m 8.3d 8.3g^2 f8g^3 p8.6g p7.1g^5 8.3m^2 10m* 10m^4 p12.2g^2 p9.5m p12f^5 Dec 19] heavy-topped gelding: fairly useful handicapper: won at Wolverhampton (apprentices) in March and Redcar in October: stays 1¼m: acts on polytrack and firm going: tried in blinkers, often wears cheekpieces nowadays. *A. J. McCabe* **85**

FOLLOW YOUR SPIRIT 4 b.g. Compton Place 125 – Ymlaen (IRE) 84 (Desert Prince (IRE) 130) [2009 52: f7g 7.1g May 5] plain gelding: maiden: well held in 2009: tried in cheekpieces. *B. Palling* –

FOLLY BRIDGE 2 b.f. (Jan 28) Avonbridge 123 – Jalissa 83 (Mister Baileys 123) [2009 6g³ 6f* 7g³ Sep 30] 44,000F: workmanlike filly: first foal: dam, 6f winner who stayed 1m, half-sister to smart performer up to 1½m Vintage Premium: fairly useful form in maidens, third to Mon Cadeaux at Salisbury prior to winning at Lingfield in September by 2½ lengths from Quaestor: respectable third to Fremont in minor event at Salisbury (travelled well long way) final start: may prove best short of 7f. *R. Charlton* **83**

FOLLY LODGE 5 ch.m. Grand Lodge (USA) 125 – Marika 103 (Marju (IRE) 127) [2009 92: f8g² 7m 7g 8d* 8d 8g Jul 24] strong, good-bodied mare: has a fluent action: fairly useful performer: won handicap at Doncaster in July: stays 1¼m: acts on all-weather, heavy and good to firm ground. *R. M. Beckett* **92**

FOLSOMPRISONBLUES (IRE) 3 br.c. Mull of Kintyre (USA) 114 – Prosaic Star (IRE) 81 (Common Grounds 118) [2009 83p: 7s 7m⁶ May 2] useful-looking colt: fairly useful form: not discredited in face of stiff task when seventh to Vocalised in Greenham Stakes at Newbury on reappearance: last in handicap next time: probably stays 7f: tongue tied in 2009: sold 6,000 gns in July. *E. J. O'Neill* **88**

FOL WIZARD 2 ch.g. (Apr 27) Piccolo 121 – Go Go Girl 74 (Pivotal 124) [2009 6g 7m Jun 19] compact gelding: well beaten in claimer/seller (gelded after). *P. C. Haslam* –

FOND 2 br.f. (Mar 13) Makbul 104 – Favour 82 (Gothenberg (IRE) 117) [2009 6m⁵ 7g Oct 16] leggy filly: first foal: dam, 6f (including at 2 yrs) winner, half-sister to useful 6f/7f performer Onlytime Will Tell: no form in seller/claimer. *Ollie Pears* –

FONDANT FANCY 3 b.f. Falbrav (IRE) 133 – Foodbroker Fancy (IRE) 113 (Halling (USA) 133) [2009 –p: 10.2g³ 10.2g⁵ 8.3g 7g Jul 25] close-coupled filly: fair maiden: will prove best at 1¼m+: raced only on good/good to firm going: has hinted at temperament: sold 5,500 gns in December. *H. J. L. Dunlop* **70**

FONGOLI 3 b.f. Dr Fong (USA) 128 – Darmagi (IRE) 80 (Desert King (IRE) 129) [2009 56: 10.2g 10s² 11.5m⁴ 16v Jul 30] good-bodied filly: modest maiden handicapper: probably stays 11.5f: acts on polytrack, heavy and good to firm going: often visored: fair juvenile hurdler, twice successful in July. *B. G. Powell* **54**

FONG'S ALIBI 3 b.f. Dr Fong (USA) 128 – Alchemy (IRE) (Sadler's Wells (USA) 132) [2009 73: p8g* p10g⁵ 9.9m 8.3m 10m* 12m⁵ 10m² 10.2g⁵ 10d 9g* 10f³ Sep 2] tall filly: fair performer: won handicap at Lingfield in February, seller at Leicester in June and claimer at Nottingham in August: stays 1¼m: acts on polytrack, heavy and good to firm going: in cheekpieces nowadays. *J. S. Moore* **75**

FONTERUTOLI (IRE) 2 gr.c. (Apr 22) Verglas (IRE) 118 – Goldendale (IRE) (Ali-Royal (IRE) 127) [2009 6m³ 6m² 7m² Jun 27] €45,000Y: third foal: half-brother to winners in Italy by Stravinsky and Distant View: dam, placed only start in USA, half-sister to US Grade 2 1m/9f winner Sweet Ludy and Italian sprinter Late Parade, both smart: fair form when runner-up in 2 maidens at Doncaster, beaten 7 lengths by Layali Al Andalus final start: stays 7f. *M. Botti* **75**

FONTLEY 2 b.f. (Mar 26) Sadler's Wells (USA) 132 – Horatia (IRE) 106 (Machiavellian (USA) 123) [2009 7s 7.1d* 7v⁴ Oct 24] fifth foal: closely related to fairly useful 7f/1m (including in UAE) winner Muzdaher (by Danzig): dam, 1¼m winner (later Grade 3 9f winner in USA), out of smart half-sister to top-class miler Markofdistinction: best effort when winning minor event at Sandown in September by head from Spa's Dancer: respectable fourth to Electric Feel in listed race at Newbury: sure to be suited by 1m+: remains open to improvement. *Eve Johnson Houghton* **80 p**

FOOLIN MYSELF 4 b.c. Montjeu (IRE) 137 – Friendlier (Zafonic (USA) 130) [2009 10s⁴ 9m 10.1g 8.9g 8g² f8g* p8.6g⁶ 7m Oct 16] big, strong colt: useful handicapper, lightly raced: had setback and missed 2008 (left B. Hills): best effort when winning at Southwell in August by 7 lengths from Xpres Maite: effective at 1m/1¼m: acts on fibresand and soft ground, below form all starts on good to firm: lost action and pulled up on third outing: blinkered last 3 starts. *M. L. W. Bell* **105**

FOOLS GOLD 4 b.g. Ishiguru (USA) 114 – Sally Green (IRE) 79 (Common Grounds 118) [2009 79: f7g³ 8.3m f8g⁵ p8g p7g Jul 22] deep-girthed gelding: fair handicapper, no recent form on turf: probably best at 7f: acts on all-weather: often races prominently: none too consistent. *Paul Mason* **75**

FOOTSIE (IRE) 2 b.f. (Apr 16) Footstepsinthesand 120 – Marlene-D 57 (Selkirk (USA) 129) [2009 7m 8g Oct 23] leggy, close-coupled filly: sixth foal: half-sister to 4-y-o General Eliott, 2004 2-y-o 6f/7f winner Shanghai Lily (by King's Best) and 7f (at 2 yrs)/ 1m winner Eden Rock (by Danehill), latter 2 useful: dam, Irish 9f winner, half-sister to smart stayer Arden: better effort when ninth to Lillie Langtry in sales race at Newmarket on debut. *J. G. Given* **63**

FOOTSTEPSOFSPRING (FR) 2 b.c. (Feb 27) Footstepsinthesand 120 – Moon West (USA) (Gone West (USA)) [2009 5f^{6} 6m^{2} 5m^{2} 5g* 6m 6g^{4} 6.1m^{3} p7g^{4} 6m^{6} 6g^{6} Sep 30] 72,000F: strong colt: type to carry condition: first foal: dam, fairly useful French 1m winner, closely related to smart milers Dupont, Pacino and Moon Dazzle: fairly useful performer: won maiden at Windsor in June: held form well in minor events after: stays 7f: acts on polytrack and good to firm going: sold 18,000 gns. *R. Hannon* **86**

FORBIDDEN (IRE) 6 ch.g. Singspiel (IRE) 133 – Fragrant Oasis (USA) 113 (Rahy (USA) 115) [2009 77: p8.6g^{3} p8.6g* p8.6g^{2} p8g^{6} 8.5s p8g 8.3m* 8.1g 8g^{2} 8m^{2} 8.5s 8g^{2} p8g^{4} 9.8g p8g^{5} 9.7m p8.6g^{5} p8.6g^{6} Oct 17] fair performer: won seller at Wolverhampton in February and apprentice handicap at Nottingham in May: best at 1m: acts on polytrack and good to firm going, well below form on soft: tried blinkered/in cheekpieces: tongue tied: usually held up. *D. Loughnane, Ireland* **78**

FORBIDDEN PARADISE (IRE) 2 ch.f. (Mar 5) Chineur (FR) 123 – Villa Nova (IRE) 55 (Petardia 113) [2009 5m^{2} 8f* a8.5f 8f^{6} Nov 29] 5,000Y: unfurnished filly: seventh foal: half-sister to several winners, including 1¼m winner Six of Diamonds (by Redback) and 5f (at 2 yrs) to 8.5f (in UAE) winner Prince of Denmark (by Danetime), both useful: dam, Irish maiden, best at 1m/9f: short-head second to Sheka in maiden at Ripon on debut, finishing strongly from well back: left K. R. Burke and off 4 months, won maiden at Del Mar in August by a nose: much stiffer tasks after, far from discredited when sixth to The Mailet in Grade 3 Miesque Stakes at Hollywood final outing: should stay 9f: acts on firm going. *D. E. Hofmans, USA* **92**

FORCED OPINION (USA) 4 gr.c. Distant View (USA) 126 – Kinetic Force (USA) (Holy Bull (USA) 134) [2009 60: p8g^{6} 9m p9.5g Oct 23] maiden: well held in 2009. *K. A. Morgan* **–**

FORCE GROUP (IRE) 5 b.g. Invincible Spirit (IRE) 121 – Spicebird (IRE) 67 (Ela-Mana-Mou 132) [2009 88: 12g^{5} 12d^{6} 14m^{4} 12m 12g^{3} 12m^{6} 12d^{2} 14d^{4} p13.9g 11.7g^{5} p13g^{2} p12.2g^{6} p10m^{6} Nov 21] close-coupled, good-topped gelding: just fair handicapper at 5 yrs: stays 1½m: acts on heavy and good to firm going: blinkered last 5 starts. *M. H. Tompkins* **79**

FORCE TRADITION (IRE) 4 ch.g. Traditionally (USA) 117 – Kind of Loving 64 (Diesis 133) [2009 59: f12s^{4} p16g 10g 8g Jul 12] medium-sized gelding: modest maiden: sold from M. Tompkins £800 after second start: seems to stay 1½m: acts on fibresand: tried blinkered. *Frau A. Schwarzenbeck, Germany* **57**

FOREIGN INVESTMENT (IRE) 3 ch.f. Desert Prince (IRE) 130 – Muneera (USA) 67 (Green Dancer (USA) 132) [2009 p6g^{4} p7.1g* p8g p8.6g* 7m^{2} p8.6g 7.1m^{6} 8.1g^{3} 7.1v^{4} Jul 24] €4,500Y: fifth foal: half-sister to 2 winners, including 7-y-o Bolton Hall: dam twice-raced sister to useful German miler Huambo: fair performer: won maiden in February and handicap in April, both at Wolverhampton: stays 8.6f: acts on polytrack and good to firm ground. *P. D. Evans* **71**

FOREIGN KING (USA) 5 b.g. Kingmambo (USA) 125 – Foreign Aid (USA) (Danzig (USA)) [2009 69: p12g Jan 6] sturdy gelding: modest performer: well below form sole start in 2009: effective from 1½m to 2m: acts on polytrack and good to firm going: fair hurdler. *J. W. Mullins* **–**

FOREIGN RHYTHM (IRE) 4 ch.f. Distant Music (USA) 126 – Happy Talk (IRE) 74 (Hamas (IRE) 125§) [2009 61§: 6g 5g 6d 5m* 5m^{5} 5m 5g 6s^{6} 5m 6m^{4} 6m 6m^{6} 5g^{6} 5s Oct 27] rather leggy, close-coupled filly: modest handicapper: won apprentice event at Beverley in June: best at 5f/6f: acts on soft and good to firm going: tried tongue tied/ visored/in cheekpieces: ungenuine (often gets behind). *N. Tinkler* **56 §**

FOREST CROWN 2 b.f. (Apr 1) Royal Applause 124 – Wiener Wald (USA) (Woodman (USA) 126) [2009 5f^{3} p5m^{4} p6m* Nov 4] sister to useful 6f winner (including at 2 yrs) Riotous Applause and half-sister to several winners, notably 3-y-o Crowded House and 5-y-o Heron Bay: dam, US maiden, out of close relative to Storm Cat: fair form in maidens, winning at Kempton in good style by length from Mutafajer: stays 6f: capable of better still. *R. M. Beckett* **79 p**

FOREST DANE 9 b.g. Danetime (IRE) 121 – Forest Maid (Thatching 131) [2009 82: p6g[5] p6g[3] p6g[2] 6f[6] 5m 5.7m[2] p6g[4] 6m[3] 6m[6] 5.3d p6g[3] p6g[2] p6g[3] p6f[4] p6g[5] Dec 31] smallish, good-topped gelding: fair handicapper nowadays: effective at 5f to 7f: acts on polytrack and firm going: held up. *Mrs N. Smith* **76**

FOREST RUNNER 2 b.c. (Mar 21) Pivotal 124 – Tiriana (Common Grounds 118) [2009 7.1m[2] Sep 10] 240,000F: brother to smart 6f/7f (including at 2 yrs) winner/Irish 1000 Guineas runner-up Penkenna Princess, closely related to fairly useful 6f/7f winner Divine Power (by Kyllachy) and half-brother to 3 winners, including 8-y-o Salut Saint Cloud: dam French maiden (stayed 1m): 9/1, promising 3¼ lengths second to Hunting Tartan (pair clear) in maiden at Chepstow, merely pushed out: sure to progress. *Saeed bin Suroor* **78 p**

FORETHOUGHT 2 b.f. (Mar 26) Lujain (USA) 119 – Flourish (Selkirk (USA) 129) [2009 7g 8m 8m 8g Oct 16] sixth foal: sister to fairly useful 2006 2-y-o 6f winner Non Compliant and half-sister to several winners, including useful 2007 2-y-o 6f winner Bobs Surprise (by Bertolini): dam unraced half-sister to useful 1¼m performer Forthwith: fair maiden: best effort on debut: not bred to need 1m. *P. Howling* **66**

FOREVER CHANGES 4 gr.f. Bertolini (USA) 125 – Days of Grace 79 (Wolfhound (USA) 126) [2009 56: p6g p6g p5g p7m Dec 30] modest maiden handicapper: stays 6f: form only on polytrack: tried in cheekpieces. *L. Montague Hall* **52**

FOREVER'S GIRL 3 b.f. Monsieur Bond (IRE) 120 – Forever Bond (Danetime (IRE) 121) [2009 56: p6g* p5.1g[4] f5g[3] f5g[4] 6m 5m[5] p6g[5] p5.1g[6] p5.1g* p5.1g* Nov 30] fair handicapper: improved at 3 yrs, winning at Wolverhampton in January and November (2): effective at 5f/6f: acts on all-weather, little form on turf. *G. R. Oldroyd* **–** **a74**

FORGET (IRE) 2 b.f. (Mar 27) Tiger Hill (IRE) 127 – Wajina 112 (Rainbow Quest (USA) 134) [2009 p5g[3] 5.5f May 12] quite good-topped filly: fourth foal: half-sister to French 10.5f/11.5f winner Huaca (by Thunder Gulch): dam, French 10.5f winner who stayed 15.5f, sister to St Leger winner Nedawi: better effort in maidens when third to Art Jewel at Lingfield: bred to need 1¼m+. *C. E. Brittain* **57**

FORGET IT 4 b.g. Galileo (IRE) 134 – Queens Way (FR) (Zafonic (USA) 130) [2009 74: 16d Oct 11] big, angular gelding: fair maiden handicapper: well held sole start in 2009 (gelded after): stays 17f: acts on polytrack and soft going: fair form over hurdles. *G. L. Moore* **–**

FORGOTTEN ARMY (IRE) 2 b.c. (Feb 13) Arakan (USA) 123 – Brioney (IRE) 70 (Barathea (IRE) 127) [2009 7d 7.1g 7m* Sep 18] modest form in maidens, winning weak event at Newmarket by neck from Verdant: should stay 1m. *M. H. Tompkins* **58 +**

Royal Hunt Cup (Heritage Handicap), Royal Ascot—Forgotten Voice comfortably justifies favouritism on his turf debut; Huzzah, Mia's Boy and Nanton come next as the stand-side runners dominate

Mrs Susan Roy's "Forgotten Voice"

FORGOTTEN VOICE (IRE) 4 b.g. Danehill Dancer (IRE) 117 – Asnieres (USA) (Spend A Buck (USA)) [2009 p8g* p8g* 8m* 8d^4 8g^4 8.9m^5 8m^3 10m Oct 17] big, strong gelding: smart performer: missed 2008: won handicaps at Kempton in April and May, and Royal Ascot (25-runner Hunt Cup, beat Huzzah 2¼ lengths) in June: in-and-out form in better company after, creditable efforts only in Sussex Stakes at Goodwood (7½ lengths fourth to Rip Van Winkle) and Joel Stakes at Newmarket (length third to Confront) fifth/seventh outings: stays 1m: acts on polytrack and good to firm ground: gelded after final start. *J. Noseda* **116**

FORICHERFORPOORER 2 ch. or gr.f. (Mar 31) Where Or When (IRE) 124 – Bridal Path 75 (Groom Dancer (USA) 128) [2009 6d 6m 5g^6 7d 6m Aug 8] 6,000Y: first foal: dam, 2-y-o 5f winner, closely related to smart performer up to 1¼m Cupid's Glory: no sign of ability: visored in seller final start. *N. Tinkler* **–**

FOR LIFE (IRE) 7 b.g. Bachir (IRE) 118 – Zest (USA) (Zilzal (USA) 137) [2009 77: 6d p6g* 5m^6 p6g^6 p6m p6m Dec 6] strong, lengthy gelding: fairly useful handicapper: easily best effort in 2009 when winning at Lingfield in May: speedy, but stays 7f: acts on all-weather and firm ground: has worn visor/cheekpieces: front runner: has looked temperamental. *J. E. Long* **81**

FORMATION (USA) 4 ch.g. Van Nistelrooy (USA) 108 – Miss Valedictorian (USA) (With Approval (CAN)) [2009 93§: p8g^2 p10g* p10g* f11g^3 p12g^3 p10g^2 p10g^5 May 1] strong, good-bodied gelding: useful handicapper: better than ever in 2009, winning at Lingfield in January and February, beating Ace of Hearts by head for latter success: good length second to Press The Button at Kempton sixth start: stays 1¼m: acts on polytrack (well held on fibresand) and good to soft going, yet to race on extremes: flashes tail and reportedly resents whip: consistent but best treated with caution: sold 55,000 gns in July, sent to Saudi Arabia. *J. R. Boyle* **98 §**

FORMAX (FR) 7 gr.g. Marathon (USA) 116 – Fortuna (FR) (Kaldoun (FR) 122) [2009 **92 +**
97: 12g 18.7m May 6] lightly-made gelding: useful handicapper: plenty to do both starts in 2009: stays 1¾m: acts on soft and good to firm going: held up: consistent. *M. P. Tregoning*

FORMIDABLE GUEST 5 b.m. Dilshaan 119 – Fizzy Treat 79 (Efisio 120) [2009 68: **73**
p9.5g^2 p9.5g* p9.5g* p10g^2 p10g^4 p9.5g^3 p9.5g^4 p10g^3 p10g^5 p9.5g Dec 14] big mare: fair handicapper: won at Wolverhampton in January and February: effective at 9.5f to 1½m: acts on polytrack: tried visored (found little): held up: reliable. *J. Pearce*

FORMULA (USA) 3 b. or br.g. Stormin Fever (USA) 116 – Misty Gallop (USA) **75**
(Victory Gallop (CAN) 130) [2009 88: 7m 8.3g^2 10m^3 7g^4 p8.6g* p8m^5 p10m^3 p12g^4 **a85**
p10g Oct 22] tall gelding: has plenty of scope: fairly useful performer on all-weather, fair on turf: won maiden at Wolverhampton in August: stays 1½m: acts on polytrack and good to firm going. *R. Hannon*

FORREST FLYER (IRE) 5 b.g. Daylami (IRE) 138 – Gerante (USA) (Private **74**
Account (USA)) [2009 64: 14m^5 12.4s* 13m^3 14.6m 12.5m* 13.1g* 12g^6 12.1s 14s^5 17.5m 15v Oct 31] tall, close-coupled gelding: fair handicapper: improved in 2009, winning at Newcastle in May, Musselburgh in June and Ayr in July: stays 13f: acts on soft and good to firm going: tried visored: often front runner. *I. Semple*

FORREST STAR 4 ch.f. Fraam 114 – Starfleet 66 (Inchinor 119) [2009 57: 6g 6m 7.1g **–**
6f f6g f8g Dec 27] maiden handicapper: well held in 2009, leaving Miss L. Perratt after fourth start. *M. Johnston*

FORSHOUR 2 ch.g. (May 5) Forzando 122 – Sharoura 90 (Inchinor 119) [2009 p7.1g^2 **64**
7d^3 p8.6g 8g Oct 19] good-topped gelding: modest form in maidens first 2 starts, third to Our Joe Mac at Thirsk: well held in nursery final outing: stays 7f. *E. S. McMahon*

FORT CHURCHILL (IRE) 8 b.g. Barathea (IRE) 127 – Brisighella (IRE) (Al Hareb **58**
(USA) 123) [2009 79: p16.5g 12.5m^6 p9.5g^3 12g^3 May 5] big, good-topped gelding: just modest at 8 yrs: stays 1½m: acts on polytrack, firm and soft going: tried in cheekpieces, usually blinkered/tongue tied: claimed to join Jim Best £5,000 final start. *B. Ellison*

FORTE DEI MARMI 3 b.g. Selkirk (USA) 129 – Frangy 77 (Sadler's Wells (USA) **86**
132) [2009 76p: 9g* 9m Jun 13] close-coupled gelding: fairly useful form: won handicap at Goodwood in May: took strong hold when disappointing next time: suffered minor injury after, and gelded: will be suited by 1¼m/1½m. *L. M. Cumani*

FORTEZZA 3 b.f. Efisio 120 – Donna Anna (Be My Chief (USA) 122) [2009 6d 6d 6g **52**
Aug 12] third foal: half-sister to 5-y-o Northern Fling: dam, no form, sister to smart 1m/1¼m performer Donna Viola and half-sister to dam of July Cup winner Frizzante (by Efisio) and smart sprinter Zidane: modest form in maidens. *C. F. Wall*

FORTHE MILLIONKISS (GER) 5 b.h. Dashing Blade 117 – Forever Nice (GER) **107 §**
(Greinton 119) [2009 112: 8d 8.1g^5 a8.7g 8g^4 8s 8.5s^6 8v* a9.5g Dec 10] fourth foal: half-brother to German 6.5f (at 2 yrs) to 1m winner Forever Free (by Platini): dam German 6f (at 2 yrs) to 1m winner: smart performer in 2008, winning 3 times, including Grosser Preis der Sparkasse Hannover: thoroughly inconsistent and just useful at best in 2009, though won minor event at Saint-Cloud in November: only other form when fifth to Paco Boy in Sandown Mile and fourth to Earl of Fire in Hamburger Meile at Hamburg: best around 1m: acts on heavy and good to firm ground: unreliable. *Uwe Ostmann, Germany*

FORTINA'S BOY (USA) 3 ch.c. Mr Greeley (USA) 122 – Really Quick (USA) (In **63**
Reality) [2009 8d p8g 8f^5 p7f p6g p6g Nov 21] good-topped colt: modest maiden: best efforts at 1m: acts on polytrack: tried tongue tied. *W. R. Swinburn*

FORTUITOUS (IRE) 5 ch.g. Tobougg (IRE) 125 – Shallop 55 (Salse (USA) 128) **40**
[2009 –: f7g^6 p9.5g Jan 22] poor form: tried visored. *S. Gollings*

FORTUNATE BID (IRE) 3 ch.g. Modigliani (USA) 106 – Mystery Bid (Auction **79**
Ring (USA) 123) [2009 64: 7.1m 8.3g* 8.1s^5 8m^2 8m^4 8m 8.3g p8.6g Oct 30] stocky gelding: fair performer: improved to win handicap at Windsor in July (left B. Hills 8,500 gns after): should stay beyond 1m: acts on good to firm ground: usually front runner/races prominently. *Mrs L. Stubbs*

FORTUNATE FLAME 3 b.g. Key of Luck (USA) 126 – Candescent (Machiavellian **71 d**
(USA) 123) [2009 f8g^2 7m^4 p7.1g^3 f7g^5 7m 8.3s^6 p7.1g p9.5g Oct 15] fair maiden: gelded after fourth start, below form subsequently: stays 1m: acts on all-weather: tried visored: sold £2,000. *K. A. Ryan*

FORTUNATE ISLE (USA) 7 ch.g. Swain (IRE) 134 – Isla Del Rey (USA) 103 **72**
(Nureyev (USA) 131) [2009 –: 8m^5 9.9m 9.3m Jun 15] angular gelding: handicapper, lightly raced on Flat since 2007: will prove best beyond 1m: has worn cheekpieces: modest hurdler. *R. A. Fahey*

FORTUNELLA 4 b.f. Polish Precedent (USA) 131 – Hazy Heights 56 (Shirley Heights **59**
130) [2009 65: f14s^2 f16g f11g p12.2g May 11] rather leggy filly: modest handicapper: well below form after reappearance in 2009: stays 1¾m: form only on fibresand: in cheekpieces/visor nowadays. *Miss Gay Kelleway*

FORTUNE POINT (IRE) 11 ch.g. Cadeaux Genereux 131 – Mountains of Mist **– §**
(IRE) 80 (Shirley Heights 130) [2009 55§: p10g^5 Feb 10] strong, angular gelding: lightly raced on Flat in recent years (poor hurdler): tried in headgear/tongue tie: unreliable. *A. W. Carroll*

FORTUNES OF FIRE 2 ch.g. (Mar 2) Avonbridge 123 – Lucky Arrow 60 (Indian **94 p**
Ridge 123) [2009 6d* Sep 7] 5,000F, £10,000Y: sixth foal: half-brother to fairly useful/ungenuine 1¾m to 2¼m winner Whispering Death (by Pivotal) and winner in Greece by Dansili: dam ran once: 40/1, highly promising when winning maiden at Newcastle by length from Aalsmeer, soon prominent: should stay 7f+: useful prospect. *G. A. Swinbank*

FORTUNI (IRE) 3 b.g. Montjeu (IRE) 137 – Desert Ease (IRE) 94 (Green Desert **99 p**
(USA) 127) [2009 80p: p12g* 12v^4 Jul 18] tall gelding: useful form: upped in trip, significant improvement when winning handicap at Lingfield in May by 4 lengths from Sehoy: heavy ground, poor effort in similar event on turf debut only other start in 2009 (gelded after): likely to stay beyond 1½m: acts on polytrack: remains open to further improvement. *Sir Mark Prescott*

FORTY THIRTY (IRE) 3 b.g. Poliglote 121 – Ciena (FR) (Gold Away (IRE) 125) **60**
[2009 71: p11g^5 p11g^6 p8.6g 10m^4 7d^3 Aug 7] sturdy gelding: maiden, modest form at 3 yrs: left M. Channon prior to final outing: stays 1¼m: acts on polytrack and heavy ground: signs of temperament: won juvenile hurdles in August/September. *Miss S. West*

FORWARD FELINE (IRE) 3 b.f. One Cool Cat (USA) 123 – Ymlaen (IRE) 84 **75**
(Desert Prince (IRE) 130) [2009 75: p7.1g^5 p6g^2 7d 6.1g^6 6.1m 6.1s 6s p6g p7.1g* Dec 12] smallish, good-bodied filly: fair handicapper: won at Wolverhampton in December: stays 7f: acts on polytrack, soft and good to firm ground: tried in cheekpieces/visor: tactically versatile. *B. Palling*

FORWARD PLANNING (USA) 3 ch.f. Orientate (USA) 127 – Casa's Kids (USA) **55**
(Theatrical 128) [2009 7d 7m^4 8.3m Sep 30] $75,000Y, 90,000 2-y-o: tall filly: second foal: dam, US 1m/8.5f winner, sister to US Grade 3 8.5f winner Sing For Free: modest form at best in maidens: worth a try at 6f: sold £800, sent to Sweden. *M. Johnston*

FORZARZI (IRE) 5 b.g. Forzando 122 – Zarzi (IRE) (Suave Dancer (USA) 136) **61**
[2009 64: p8.6g 7m^6 7.5m 6.9g 8.3m^4 7.9m^5 7.9g Jul 4] modest handicapper: stays 8.6f: acts on polytrack and good to firm going: often in cheekpieces: none too consistent. *H. A. McWilliams*

FOSSGATE 8 ch.g. Halling (USA) 133 – Peryllys 67 (Warning 136) [2009 74: 16m **63**
12m 12.1m^6 12.1m^3 12g* 12.1v^5 12.1m^3 9.9g^6 Sep 22] angular gelding: modest handicapper: won at Ripon in August: stays 1½m: acts on polytrack, firm and soft going: tried in headgear (blinkered last 4 starts): tends to hang right. *J. D. Bethell*

FOUNDATION ROOM (IRE) 3 ch.f. Saffron Walden (FR) 123 – Bellagio Princess **91**
58 (Kris 135) [2009 84: 7.6m^3 8.1v 7.1g^5 Jun 25] sturdy filly: fairly useful performer: ran respectably in listed race at Warwick final start: should stay 1m: acts on soft and good to firm going: refused to enter stall intended final outing (July): sold 11,000 gns in December. *A. M. Balding*

FOUR KICKS (IRE) 3 b.f. Pyrus (USA) 106 – Dynamo Minsk (IRE) 62 (Polish Pre- **58**
cedent (USA) 131) [2009 7m 8.5d^6 7s 8.5s 5s 7.1m Sep 14] second foal: dam maiden (stayed 9f): modest maiden: stays 8.5f. *Muredach Kelly, Ireland*

FOURLANENDS 2 ch.c. (Mar 1) Dubawi (IRE) 129 – Nova Cyngi (USA) (Kris S **–**
(USA)) [2009 6s Sep 5] good-bodied colt: 28/1 and drawn wide, well held in maiden at Thirsk (very green, hung). *N. Wilson*

FOUR MIRACLES 5 b.m. Vettori (IRE) 119 – North Kildare (USA) (Northjet 136) **87**
[2009 96: 16m^6 14.1m^4 May 9] angular mare: fairly useful handicapper: stays 2¼m: acts on fibresand, firm and good to soft going: waited with: reliable. *M. H. Tompkins*

FOUR MIRRORS (CAN) 3 b.g. Gulch (USA) – Solarity (CAN) (Ascot Knight **63 d**
(CAN) 130) [2009 8g 8m^4 8d 8.5s p10g p8f Oct 14] modest maiden: well below form after second outing, leaving D. Myerscough in Ireland prior to final start: stays 1m: tongue tied 4 of 5 starts after debut, also in cheekpieces/blinkers last 2 outings. *C. R. Dore*

FOURPENNY LANE 4 b.f. Efisio 120 – Makara (Lion Cavern (USA) 117) [2009 **110**
110: 5.8s 5v 7d 7m^4 7g^5 p6g^5 p6g^3 7d p7f* p6g^2 8g p8g* p8g* Nov 13] good-topped filly: smart performer: back to best when successful at Dundalk in handicap and minor event

(drew 7 lengths clear of Clodova) in October and listed race (beat San Sicharia ½ length) in November: stays easy 1m: acts on polytrack, soft and good to firm going: tried in cheekpieces/blinkers: blanketed for stall entry (sometimes slowly away). *Ms Joanna Morgan, Ireland*

FOUR TEL 5 gr.g. Vettori (IRE) 119 – Etienne Lady (IRE) 67 (Imperial Frontier (USA) 112) [2009 70: 7g⁵ 7.6g⁵ p8m p9.5g Oct 9] fair handicapper, lightly raced: trained by N. Vaughan until after second outing: should stay 1m: acts on polytrack. *Tom Dascombe* **68**

FOURTH DIMENSION (IRE) 10 b.g. Entrepreneur 123 – Isle of Spice (USA) 74 (Diesis 133) [2009 77: 11.7m 14.1m May 19] sturdy gelding: handicapper: well held in 2009: stays 2m: acts on firm and soft ground. *Miss T. Spearing* **–**

FOURTH GENERATION (IRE) 2 ch.g. (Feb 7) Kris Kin (USA) 126 – Merewood Lodge (IRE) (Grand Lodge (USA) 125) [2009 7s 8g² Oct 16] big, lengthy gelding: first foal: dam unraced half-sister to useful sprinter Boast: gelded and off 6 weeks, easily better effort in maidens when short-head second to Medicinal Compound at Redcar, still learning. *G. A. Swinbank* **79 +**

FOURTOWNS FLYER (IRE) 5 b.g. Danetime (IRE) 121 – Music Khan (Music Boy 124) [2009 6s 6g p5.1g* p5.1g³ Nov 14] €8,000Y: half-brother to several winners, including fairly useful 1m winner Compromiznotension (by Key of Luck): dam French 6f/1m winner: fair form: won maiden at Wolverhampton in October: good third in handicap there next time (said to have finished lame): may prove best at 5f/6f: acts on polytrack: in cheekpieces last 2 starts: tongue tied 3 of 4 outings. *L. Smyth, Ireland* **79**

FOUR WINDS 3 b.g. Red Ransom (USA) – Fairy Godmother 113 (Fairy King (USA)) [2009 110p: 10s² 8m* 10m⁶ 8d⁴ 8.5d² Aug 18] strong, rangy gelding: useful performer: good 1¾ lengths second to High Heeled in minor event at Newbury before winning similar race at Newmarket in May by 2 lengths from Patrician's Glory: respectable efforts in listed contests after, blinkered when 1¾ lengths second to Poet at Killarney: needs good test at 1m, and should stay 1½m: acts on soft and good to firm going: tends to hang (markedly so at Killarney): sold 21,000 gns in October. *M. L. W. Bell* **109**

FOXHAVEN 7 ch.g. Unfuwain (USA) 131 – Dancing Mirage (IRE) 83 (Machiavellian (USA) 123) [2009 112: 11.6f* 11.7g² Oct 21] smallish, sturdy, lengthy gelding: well below smart best both outings in 2009, though won claimer at Windsor in August: best at 1¼m/1½m: acts on firm and soft going: often visored: races prominently: genuine. *P. R. Chamings* **90 +**

FOXHOLES LODGE 4 b.f. Nasheyt – Duxford Lodge (Dara Monarch 128) [2009 f5m 8m Aug 16] first foal: dam little worthwhile form: last in maidens. *J. D. Bethell* **–**

FOXTROT ALPHA (IRE) 3 b.f. Desert Prince (IRE) 130 – Imelda (USA) (Manila (USA)) [2009 72: 8m p7g² p7g 7g p6g³ 6d p8m Nov 4] sparely-made filly: fair handicapper: effective at 6f/7f: acts on polytrack, good to firm and good to soft going. *P. Winkworth* **69**

FOXTROT BRAVO (IRE) 3 b.g. Noverre (USA) 125 – Standcorrected (Shareef Dancer (USA) 135) [2009 –: f7g⁶ p10g⁶ p8g² 8g⁶ p8m p8m p8.6g p8m⁵ Dec 6] modest maiden: left P. Winkworth after second start: stays 1m: acts on polytrack. *Miss S. L. Davison* **61**

FOXTROT CHARLIE 3 b.g. Lucky Story (USA) 128 – Holy Smoke 83 (Statoblest 120) [2009 73: 8.3m 10g² 8.3m p10g* p10m Sep 26] tall gelding: fair handicapper: won at Kempton in September: stays 1¼m: acts on polytrack: often blinkered. *P. Winkworth* **77**

FOXTROT DELTA (IRE) 2 ch.c. (May 12) Namid 128 – Tarziyana (USA) 76 (Danzig (USA)) [2009 p6g p8m⁶ p7g Oct 9] smallish colt: modest form in maidens: should stay 1m: sold 8,000 gns, sent to Spain. *P. Winkworth* **57**

FOXTROT FOXTROT 2 b.g. (Mar 4) Royal Applause 124 – Darmagi (IRE) 80 (Desert King (IRE) 129) [2009 6m p8g p7g Oct 9] rather leggy gelding: well held in maidens: sold 2,800 gns, sent to Greece. *P. Winkworth* **–**

FOXY MUSIC 5 b.g. Foxhound (USA) 103 – Primum Tempus 49 (Primo Dominie 121) [2009 89: p5.1g⁶ f5g 5v⁴ 5g 5m² 5.1m 5s Jul 17] tall, leggy gelding: fairly useful handicapper: best at sharp 5f: acts on any ground: tried blinkered at 2 yrs: front runner: tends to hang. *E. J. Alston* **84**

FRAAMTAAZTIIC 2 b.f. (Apr 8) Fraam 114 – Dahlawise (IRE) 76 (Caerleon (USA) 132) [2009 6m⁶ p8g p6g Oct 20] £5,800Y: lengthy, unfurnished filly: half-sister to several winners, including fairly useful Irish 2008 2-y-o 5f winner Emily Dickinson (by Kyllachy) and 5f/6f winner Dahlidya (by Midyan): dam 2-y-o 6f winner: soundly beaten in minor event/maidens. *R. J. Hodges* **–**

FRANALI (IRE) 3 b.f. Kheleyf (USA) 116 – Christeningpresent (IRE) (Cadeaux Genereux 131) [2009 44: 15.8g Aug 4] poor maiden. *R. F. Fisher* –

FRANCESCA CONTI (IRE) 2 b.f. (Apr 19) Atraf 116 – Gentian Blue (IRE) (Tirol 127) [2009 5m May 9] £1,000 2-y-o: sixth foal: dam German 7.5f winner: 14/1, last in seller at Thirsk. *K. R. Burke* –

FRANCESCO (FR) 5 gr.g. Kaldounevees (FR) 118 – Mount Gable (Head For Heights 125) [2009 –: 16m[5] Apr 3] well held on Flat in Britain (winning hurdler). *Mrs L. B. Normile* –

FRANCHESCA'S GOLD 3 b.f. Monsieur Bond (IRE) 120 – Anita Marie (IRE) (Anita's Prince 126) [2009 52: p5m p7g p9.5g p11f[6] Dec 16] rather leggy filly: poor maiden: will prove best short of 11f. *Jane Southcombe* 45

FRANCIS ALBERT 3 b.g. Mind Games 121 – Via Dolorosa (Chaddleworth (IRE) 103) [2009 5g 6d p5.1g 5m[2] 5m Sep 23] modest performer: raced only at 5f/6f: acts on good to firm ground. *M. Mullineaux* 63

FRANCIS WALSINGHAM (IRE) 3 b.g. Invincible Spirit (IRE) 121 – Web of Intrigue 66 (Machiavellian (USA) 123) [2009 65p: p7g[4] 7d 6m* 6g[4] 6d[4] 5g[5] 6g Sep 30] sturdy gelding: fair performer: won maiden at Ripon in June: effective at 6f/7f: acts on polytrack, good to firm and good to soft ground: gelded after final start. *H. Morrison* 77

FRANCO IS MY NAME 3 b.g. Namid 128 – Veronica Franco 90 (Darshaan 133) [2009 9.9m p12m p11g[6] p10g* Nov 14] fourth foal: half-brother to 2005 2-y-o 7f winner Veronica's Girl (by Desert Prince) and Italian 1¼m winner Verothea (by Barathea): dam 1½m to 2m winner: fair form: much improved to win handicap at Lingfield in November, idling: stays 1¼m: acts on polytrack: open to further progress. *P. R. Hedger* 73 p

FRANKIE FALCO 3 b.g. Bollin Eric 125 – Marsh Marigold 65 (Tina's Pet 121) [2009 f12f[5] Dec 12] well beaten in bumper and in maiden on Flat debut. *G. Fierro* –

FRANKI J 2 ch.f. (Apr 16) Barathea (IRE) 127 – Whassup (FR) (Midyan (USA) 124) [2009 p8.6g p7.1g p8.6g p7g[5] Dec 31] 12,500F, 5,000Y: third foal: closely related to Irish 4-y-o Inquisitive Look: dam, placed up to 10.5f in France out of May Hill Stakes winner Bright Crocus: modest form on debut: well beaten after. *D. Donovan* 56

FRANKSALOT (IRE) 9 ch.g. Desert Story (IRE) 115 – Rosie's Guest (IRE) (Be My Guest (USA) 126) [2009 65: p7g p7.1g Jan 23] tall, close-coupled gelding: handicapper, well held both starts in 2009: blinkered/in cheekpieces nowadays. *I. W. McInnes* –

FRANK STREET 3 ch.g. Fraam 114 – Pudding Lane (IRE) 64 (College Chapel 122) [2009 81: 5.7g[3] 7.1g 6m May 25] good-quartered gelding: maiden, just fair at 3 yrs: likely to prove best at 7f+: acts on good to soft going. *Eve Johnson Houghton* 69

FRATELLINO 2 ch.c. (Apr 14) Auction House (USA) 120 – Vida (IRE) 70 (Wolfhound (USA) 126) [2009 5m* 5m[4] 5.1m 5m* 5g[4] 5m[5] 6g[4] 5m[2] 5.1m[4] 5g Oct 10] £2,200Y: small, sturdy colt: sixth foal: brother to 3-y-o Common Diva and 2 winners abroad: dam, Irish sprint maiden, half-sister to Ebor winner Mudawin: useful performer: won maiden at Beverley in April and minor event at York in May: best effort when neck second of 22 to Strike The Tiger in listed Windsor Castle Stakes at Royal Ascot: off over 3 months, soon off bridle last 2 starts: usually speedy front runner, raced mainly at 5f: raced only on good/good to firm ground. *A. J. McCabe* 96

FRAVIA 3 b.f. Bertolini (USA) 125 – Alizar (IRE) 62 (Rahy (USA) 115) [2009 p6g[5] 6d[5] Mar 31] 3,500F, 2,000Y: first foal: dam 5f/6f (including at 2 yrs) winner: well held in maidens. *B. J. McMath* –

FREDA'S ROSE (IRE) 5 b.m. Rossini (USA) 118 – African Scene (IRE) 31 (Scenic 128) [2009 8m[4] 9.8m[5] 8d[2] 10m[4] 10m[6] p9.5g Oct 29] smallish mare: third foal: dam Irish maiden: signs of ability in bumpers/poor form over hurdles: modest maiden on Flat: left O. Brennan prior to final outing: stays 9.7f: acts on good to firm and good to soft going. *J. Mackie* 57

FREDDIE BOLT 3 b.c. Diktat 126 – Birjand 99 (Green Desert (USA) 127) [2009 –: 7m Sep 14] tailed off in maidens. *F. Watson* –

FREDDIE'S GIRL (USA) 2 b. or br.f. (Feb 20) More Than Ready (USA) 120 – Carib Gal (USA) (Awesome Again (CAN) 133) [2009 p6g 6m 5.7g[3] 6m p7m[2] Dec 16] $45,000F, £9,000 2-y-o: neat filly: first foal: dam US maiden: fair maiden: second at Lingfield final outing: stays 7f: acts on polytrack. *Stef Liddiard* 65

FRED KENNET 4 ch.g. Kadastrof (FR) 86 – Evaporate 51 (Insan (USA) 119) [2009 f11g Aug 10] fair form in bumpers/winning hurdler: well held on Flat debut. *M. Salaman* –

FREE AGENT 3 b.g. Dr Fong (USA) 128 – Film Script 105 (Unfuwain (USA) 131) **107** [2009 101p: 11g^4 12f^4 13m^4 14.1s^3 14m^4 Oct 1] tall gelding: good walker: powerful mover: useful performer: had bone chip removed from near-hind hock after final 2-y-o outing: in frame all starts in 2009, best efforts in listed race at Goodwood (fourth to Alwaary), King Edward VII Stakes at Royal Ascot (6½ lengths fourth to Father Time) and minor event at Salisbury (close third to The Betchworth Kid) first/second/fourth outings: stays 1¾m: acts on soft and good to firm going: blinkered last 2 starts, gelded after running as though amiss final one. *R. Hannon*

FREEDOM FIRE (IRE) 3 b.g. Alhaarth (IRE) 126 – Feel Free (IRE) 86 (Generous **70** (IRE) 139) [2009 –: 8.3g^4 10.1g^4 11.5d^4 p10m^4 p8m^3 Oct 12] strong gelding: fair maiden: stays 1¼m: acts on polytrack, unraced on going firmer than good on turf: sold 20,000 gns, joined G. L. Moore. *J. M. P. Eustace*

FREEDOM FLYING 6 b.m. Kalanisi (IRE) 132 – Free Spirit (IRE) (Caerleon (USA) **–** 132) [2009 –: 12.5m Apr 12] rather leggy, lengthy mare: well beaten in maidens on Flat: tried in cheekpieces: modest hurdler. *Joss Saville*

FREEDOM PASS (USA) 2 b.f. (Jan 14) Gulch (USA) – Bold Desire 58 (Cadeaux **54 p** Genereux 131) [2009 p7g^4 Nov 18] 55,000F, 32,000 2-y-o: first foal: dam, ran twice, sister to useful performer up to 7f Irresistible: 10/1, slowly away when fourth of 9 to Khanivorous in maiden at Kempton: will improve. *J. A. R. Toller*

FREE FALLING 3 ch.f. Selkirk (USA) 129 – Free Flying 52 (Groom Dancer (USA) **58** 128) [2009 59p: p8.6g p10g p8g 8.3f^5 9.7m^5 p12g p10g f14g^6 Dec 22] good-topped filly: modest maiden: left L. Cumani after third start: should stay 1¼m: acts on polytrack: tried blinkered, in cheekpieces/tongue tie last 3 starts. *A. J. Lidderdale*

FREEFORADAY (USA) 2 ch.c. (Jan 17) Freefourinternet (USA) 117 – All My **100** Yesterdays (USA) (Wild Again (USA)) [2009 5g^6 5m^2 6f^4 5m* 6m^4 6g* p6m* Oct 28] $6,000F: compact colt: second foal: half-brother to winner in US by Greatness: dam US 2-y-o 1m winner: useful performer: most progressive to win nurseries at Folkestone in September and Newbury and Kempton (beat Gouray Girl by length) in October: will be suited by 7f: acts on polytrack and good to firm going. *J. R. Best*

FREE FOR ALL (IRE) 2 br.c. (Feb 12) Statue of Liberty (USA) 115 – Allegorica **81 p** (IRE) (Alzao (USA) 117) [2009 6m^6 6.5g^3 Oct 8] €26,000F: strong colt: fifth foal: half-brother to Irish 5-y-o Miss Gorica and fairly useful 5f (at 2 yrs) to 1m winner Celtic Spa (by Celtic Swing): dam Italian 5f (at 2 yrs) to 7.5f winner: promising in maidens, 1¾ lengths third to Noafal at Newbury, hanging right: likely to stay 1m: very slowly away on debut: should improve again. *S. Kirk*

FREE GRAIN 2 b.f. (May 9) Sakhee (USA) 136 – All Grain 102 (Polish Precedent **73** (USA) 131) [2009 7s^6 7g Oct 31] fifth foal: half-sister to fairly useful 7f/1m winner Granary (by Singspiel): dam, 12.6f winner, sister to Irish/Yorkshire Oaks winner Pure Grain: 16/1, promising 3¼ lengths sixth to Kithonia in maiden at Salisbury, considerately handled: shaped as if amiss at Newmarket: will be well suited by 1m+. *J. L. Dunlop*

FREEING 3 b.f. Dansili 127 – Sweeping 104 (Indian King (USA) 128) [2009 55p: 6g^6 **55** 6m^3 p7g Nov 18] modest maiden: should stay beyond 6f. *J. A. R. Toller*

FREE JUDGEMENT (USA) 2 b.c. (Feb 25) Vindication (USA) 122 – South Bay **111** Cove (CAN) (Fusaichi Pegasus (USA) 130) [2009 6v^5 7s^2 6g p8g* p7g^4 7m 7d* Oct 26] $100,000F, €50,000Y: neat, attractive colt: first foal: dam Canadian 2-y-o 4.5f to 6f winner, including minor stakes: smart performer: won maiden at Dundalk and J. R. A. Killavullan Stakes at Leopardstown (readily by 2 lengths from Lord High Admiral, leading over 1f out) in October: better than result when 5½ lengths eighth to Beethoven in Dewhurst Stakes at Newmarket sixth start, drawn wide yet up with pace long way: effective at 7f/easy 1m: acts on polytrack, soft and good to firm going. *J. S. Bolger, Ireland*

FREEMANTLE 3 b.c. Galileo (IRE) 134 – Patacake Patacake (USA) 67 (Bahri (USA) **114** 125) [2009 105p: 10.4g^2 10m^5 12g^4 8g 10d Dec 27] big, good sort: smart performer: ran well when in frame in Dante Stakes at York (head second to stable-companion Black Bear Island) and Grand Prix de Paris (3¾ lengths fourth to Cavalryman): left A. O'Brien in Ireland, and off 5 months (renamed Straight Forward), below form in handicaps at Sha Tin last 2 starts: will prove best at 1½m+: acts on heavy going: usually races prominently (forced too strong a pace at Ascot second outing). *A. S. Cruz, Hong Kong*

FREEPRESSIONIST 3 ch.f. Compton Place 125 – Sophielu 80 (Rudimentary (USA) **64** 118) [2009 73: p6g 6m^4 6.1g^5 5m^5 6d f6m^5 p6g p6g^5 6m Sep 28] lengthy filly: handicapper, just modest at 3 yrs: best at 5f/6f: acts on polytrack: tried blinkered: none too consistent: sold 800 gns. *R. A. Teal*

FREE TUSSY (ARG) 5 br.g. Freelancer (USA) – Perlada (ARG) (Cipayo (ARG)) **87**
[2009 95d: p7g^4 p7g p7g^6 p10g* p10g p10g* 11.9f 10.1d^2 12m^3 10.2m^2 12m^4 p10g* p10m* Nov 21] leggy gelding: fairly useful handicapper nowadays: won at Lingfield in April, June and October, and Kempton in November: stays 1½m: acts on dirt/polytrack, good to firm and good to soft going: blinkered (usually tongue tied). *G. L. Moore*

FREGATE ISLAND (IRE) 6 gr.g. Daylami (IRE) 138 – Briery (IRE) 66 (Salse **93**
(USA) 128) [2009 93: 16m^6 May 9] tall, angular gelding: fairly useful performer: below form sole start in 2009: stays 2m: acts on polytrack and good to firm going: races prominently: consistent. *A. G. Newcombe*

FREMEN (USA) 9 ch.g. Rahy (USA) 115 – Northern Trick (USA) 131 (Northern **90**
Dancer) [2009 102: p8g* p8g^2 p8g^3 p8g^4 8.3m* 8.5m^6 8.1g^2 7.1m* 8.3s* 9m^3 Sep 14] big, lengthy gelding: fairly useful performer: won handicap at Lingfield in March, sellers at Hamilton in June and Musselburgh in August, and claimer at Hamilton later in August: effective at 7f to easy 9f: acts on polytrack and any turf going: usually held up (often slowly away). *D. Nicholls*

FREMONT (IRE) 2 b.c. (Feb 25) Marju (IRE) 127 – Snow Peak (Arazi (USA) 135) **100**
[2009 6m* 6m 6.5m^4 7g* Sep 30] 48,000F: tall colt: fourth foal: brother to 6-y-o Asset: dam French 7.5f/1m winner: won maiden at Goodwood in May and minor event at Salisbury (5 ran, easily by 2½ lengths from Side Glance, hanging left) in September: better form when fourth to Swilly Ferry in sales race at Doncaster penultimate start: stays 7f: already useful. *R. Hannon*

FRENCH APPLAUSE (IRE) 3 b.g. Royal Applause 124 – A Ma Guise (USA) **84**
(Silver Hawk (USA) 123) [2009 9d^2 8g^2 7g^5 Jul 3] 25,000F, 31,000Y: big, strong gelding: first foal: dam, French (at 2 yrs)/US 7f winner, out of US Grade 3 8.5f winner Traces of Gold: fairly useful form in maidens: will be suited by return to 1m+. *T. P. Tate*

FRENCH ART 4 ch.g. Peintre Celebre (USA) 137 – Orange Sunset (IRE) 99 (Roanoke **75**
(USA)) [2009 85: 8m 8d 8m^6 8m 8.1s 8s 8m^6 10m^4 8m^2 p8m^2 8.3g^2 9d^4 p8m* p8m^4 Dec 9] smallish, sturdy, quite attractive gelding: fair handicapper: won at Kempton in November: best around 1m: acts on polytrack, soft and good to firm ground: in cheek-pieces last 2 outings: reportedly had breathing problem sixth start. *N. Tinkler*

FRENCH CONNEXION (IRE) 2 b.f. (Mar 16) Chineur (FR) 123 – Hunzy (IRE) **54**
(Desert King (IRE) 129) [2009 p5g^6 5.1g 5.1g^3 5.1m^3 6f 6g 5.2d 7f^6 p7g p6m^4 Sep 26] €4,000Y: small filly: third foal: half-sister to Italian 5f (at 2 yrs) to 9f winner Dynamic Power (by Namid): dam, Italian 6f and (at 2 yrs) 7.5f winner, half-sister to very smart Irish hurdler Hurricane Fly: modest maiden: stays 6f: acts on polytrack, best turf efforts on good going: has hung right: inconsistent. *J. S. Moore*

FRENCH FANTASY 2 ch.f. (May 1) Cadeaux Genereux 131 – Footlight Fantasy **– p**
(USA) 68 (Nureyev (USA) 131) [2009 8g p7g p6g Nov 9] lengthy filly: sister to fairly useful 7f winners Hatch (later successful up to 8.5f in USA) and Leading Role (at 2 yrs in 1999) and half-sister to several winners, including useful 7f/1m winner Unscrupulous (by Machiavellian): dam 7f winner out of top-class miler Milligram: very green and well held in maidens: pulled hard last 2 starts, hung right final one: type to do better in time. *H. Morrison*

FRENCH HOLLOW 4 b.g. Beat Hollow 126 – Campaspe 79 (Dominion 123) [2009 **73**
12v^3 p12g^4 p12.2g^2 Dec 5] fourth foal: dam 1½m/1¾m winner: fairly useful form in bumpers, winning in June: best effort in maidens when second to Inflammable at Wolverhampton: stays 1½m: raced only on polytrack and heavy going. *T. J. Fitzgerald*

FRENCH SEVENTYFIVE 2 b.g. (Feb 25) Pursuit of Love 124 – Miss Tun (Komaite **66**
(USA)) [2009 6m 7m^4 6m^6 Aug 5] well-made gelding: easily best effort in maidens when fourth to Layali Al Andalus at Doncaster: hung badly left at Newcastle final start: stays 7f. *T. D. Walford*

FRENCH WIND 2 b.c. (Mar 16) Cadeaux Genereux 131 – Blast (USA) (Roar (USA) **–**
116) [2009 p7.1g Dec 18] well held in maiden at Wolverhampton. *Pat Eddery*

FREQUENCY 2 b.c. (May 16) Starcraft (NZ) 128 – Soundwave (Prince Sabo 123) **79 p**
[2009 6.1s p6g^2 Oct 20] 13,000Y: second foal: half-brother to 3-y-o Sloop Johnb: dam unraced half-sister to very smart sprinter Airwave: easily better effort in maidens when 1¾ lengths second to Oil Strike at Lingfield, still green: open to further improvement. *E. A. L. Dunlop*

FREYA'S FLIGHT (IRE) 3 ch.f. Viking Ruler (AUS) – Polish Saga 59 (Polish **53**
Patriot (USA) 128) [2009 6d^6 7.5m^5 f6g Dec 27] €3,000Y: seventh foal: half-sister to several winners, including useful 9f/1¼m winner James Caird (by Catrail): dam maiden (best at 6f): modest form in maidens. *K. A. Ryan*

FRIENDS HOPE 8 ch.m. Docksider (USA) 124 – Stygian (USA) 73 (Irish River (FR) **79**
131) [2009 83: f8g^5 p12.2g^4 p11g^5 f11d^2 f11g^6 8g^5 f8g^6 12m^4 f11m Dec 15] sturdy mare: fair performer: stays 1½m: acts on all-weather, firm and soft going. *R. Curtis*

FRIGHTNIGHT (IRE) 3 ch.c. Night Shift (USA) – Scared (Royal Academy (USA) **–**
130) [2009 p8.6g^6 p9.5g Mar 5] little form in maidens (tongue tied latter occasion). *A. B. Haynes*

FRILL A MINUTE 5 b.m. Lake Coniston (IRE) 131 – Superfrills 54 (Superpower **–**
113) [2009 –: 6.9d 6m 7g 7v Nov 3] workmanlike mare: of no account. *Miss L. C. Siddall*

FRINGE SUCCESS (IRE) 2 b.f. (Mar 24) Selkirk (USA) 129 – Stage Struck (IRE) **61 p**
83 (Sadler's Wells (USA) 132) [2009 7g p8.6g^6 Oct 29] well-made filly: half-sister to several winners, including smart 9f/1¼m winner Stage Gift (by Cadeaux Genereux) and 3-y-o Dancourt: dam, 1½m winner, sister to high-class performer up to 1¼m Prince of Dance out of Oaks/St Leger winner Sun Princess: easily better effort in maidens when 10 lengths eighth to Pollenator at Newmarket on debut: still green at Wolverhampton, losing position 3f out: will be suited by 1¼m+: capable of better. *Sir Michael Stoute*

FRISBEE 5 b.m. Efisio 120 – Flying Carpet 76 (Barathea (IRE) 127) [2009 76: 6d 5.1g^2 **74**
p6g Nov 6] fair performer, lightly raced: left C. Teague after reappearance: should prove best at 5f/6f: raced only on all-weather and good/good to soft ground. *D. W. Thompson*

FRISTON FOREST (IRE) 5 ch.h. Barathea (IRE) 127 – Talented 112 (Bustino 136) **115**
[2009 105: 14g* 14m^2 16.1d^3 14m 16g^6 12s^4 Nov 7] good-topped ex-French horse: smart performer: left A. Fabre, won handicap at Nad Al Sheba in February by nose from stable-companion Veracity: good efforts in Britain after when in frame in Northumberland Plate at Newcastle (2¾ lengths third to Som Tala) and November Handicap at Doncaster (fourth to Charm School): effective at 1½m to 2m: acts on firm and soft ground. *Saeed bin Suroor*

FROGNAL (IRE) 3 b.g. Kheleyf (USA) 116 – Shannon Dore (IRE) 81 (Turtle Island **94**
(IRE) 123) [2009 94: 6m p6f^6 6m^4 7m^3 7m^3 Oct 16] lengthy, angular gelding: fairly useful handicapper: effective at 6f/7f: acts on polytrack and good to firm going (unraced on softer than good): usually held up: sold 20,000 gns. *B. J. Meehan*

FROMSONG (IRE) 11 b.g. Fayruz 116 – Lindas Delight 54 (Batshoof 122) [2009 76, **74**
a97: p6g^4 p5g^3 p5g^6 p5g^3 p5g^3 p6g 6g^5 6m^5 5.7d^4 p5g^3 5m^5 5m^6 5f 5s p6m^2 p6m p6g **a85**
p5.1g^5 p5m^3 p5f* Dec 19] tall, angular gelding: fairly useful handicapper on all-weather, fair on turf: not at best later in 2009, but won at Lingfield in December: best at 5f/easy 6f: acts on polytrack, firm and soft going: has worn cheekpieces, including last 2 starts: tried tongue tied: usually races close up. *D. K. Ivory*

FROMTHEBEGINNING 3 b.g. Lomitas 129 – Zacchera 82 (Zamindar (USA) 116) **59**
[2009 69p: p10g 8.3m^5 May 11] just modest maiden in 2009: headstrong, and worth a try at 7f: bolted to post second outing, gelded after. *D. R. C. Elsworth*

FRONTLINE BOY (IRE) 2 b.c. (Apr 16) One Cool Cat (USA) 123 – Diamant (IRE) **66**
(Bigstone (IRE) 126) [2009 7d 6m^6 6m^3 6m Oct 5] close-coupled colt: fair form in maidens: pulled hard when well held in nursery final start: should stay 7f. *A. P. Jarvis*

FRONT RANK (IRE) 9 b.g. Sadler's Wells (USA) 132 – Alignment (IRE) 98 (Alzao **60**
(USA) 117) [2009 63: p12.2g^4 12d 13m 16d^2 13v^3 16.1d^3 12.4d^3 Oct 13] strong, good-bodied gelding: modest handicapper: stays 2m: acts on fibresand and any turf going: often front runner: fair hurdler, successful in August. *Mrs Dianne Sayer*

FROSTED 3 ch.f. Dr Fong (USA) 128 – Arctic Air 79 (Polar Falcon (USA) 126) [2009 **65**
61p: p9.5g^4 Apr 25] useful-looking filly: fair form when fourth in maiden at Wolverhampton sole start in 2009: sold 17,000 gns in December. *J. H. M. Gosden*

FROSTY'S GIFT 5 ch.m. Bold Edge 123 – Coughlan's Gift 70 (Alnasr Alwasheek **43**
117) [2009 50: p8g^6 p9.5g 7m Jun 9] workmanlike mare: poor maiden: should stay at least 9.5f: raced only on polytrack and going firmer than good. *J. C. Fox*

FROZEN FIRE (GER) 4 b.c. Montjeu (IRE) 137 – Flamingo Sea (USA) (Woodman **115 §**
(USA) 126) [2009 122: 13.4m^3 12g^5 12m Jul 25] lengthy colt: won Irish Derby at the Curragh in 2008: best effort in 2009 (just smart form) when 4 lengths fifth to Ask in Coronation Cup at Epsom second start: weakened quickly when well held in King George VI and Queen Elizabeth Stakes at Ascot next time: should stay beyond 1½m: acts on good to firm and good to soft going: blanketed for stall entry (has got worked up/proved uncooperative in preliminaries): tends to hang/carry head awkwardly, and is one to treat with caution: sold privately after final outing, and joined M. de Kock. *A. P. O'Brien, Ireland*

FROZEN POWER (IRE) 2 b.c. (Feb 17) Oasis Dream 129 – Musical Treat (IRE) 98 (Royal Academy (USA) 130) [2009 6g^4 6m* 7g* 7g* 8m 8g Oct 19] 500,000Y: useful-looking colt: fifth foal: half-brother to 3 winners, notably very smart Irish 6f (at 2 yrs) to 1m (including 1000 Guineas) winner Finsceal Beo (by Mr Greeley) who stayed 10.5f: dam 7f winner (stayed 1¼m and later won in Canada): useful performer: won maiden at Epsom in July and nursery at Salisbury and listed race at Deauville (beat Boltcity 2 lengths) in August: well beaten in Royal Lodge Stakes at Ascot (held when badly hampered) and listed event at Pontefract (seemed amiss) after: should stay 1m: raced only on good/good to firm ground. *Saeed bin Suroor* **108**

FUEL CELL (IRE) 8 b.g. Desert Style (IRE) 121 – Tappen Zee (Sandhurst Prince 128) [2009 –: 7.5g Aug 12] compact gelding: ran only 3 times on Flat after 2007: tried in headgear/tongue strap: signs of temperament: fair hurdler at best: dead. *I. W. McInnes* **–**

FUISSE (FR) 3 b.c. Green Tune (USA) 125 – Funny Feerie (FR) (Sillery (USA) 122) [2009 107: 10d^3 8d* 10.5g^2 Jun 7] fifth foal: half-brother to 2 winners in France, notably smart 1m (at 2 yrs, when also won Criterium de Saint-Cloud) to 10.5f (Prix Noailles) winner Full of Gold (by Gold Away): dam useful French hurdler: very smart performer: successful in newcomers race at Deauville and minor event at Longchamp at 2 yrs: improved to win listed race at Maisons-Laffitte in May by 6 lengths from Diableside: good 1½ lengths second to Le Havre in Prix du Jockey Club at Chantilly final start, leading under 2f out before hanging right and headed inside final 1f: stays 10.5f: raced only on good ground or softer. *Mme C. Head-Maarek, France* **120**

FUJIN DANCER (FR) 4 ch.c. Storming Home 128 – Badaayer (USA) 105 (Silver Hawk (USA) 123) [2009 77: 9.9m^4 10g^6 p8.6g^2 p10m^2 Dec 16] strong colt: fair performer: claimed from R. Fahey £8,000 third start: stays 10.4f: acts on polytrack and good to firm ground: tried blinkered. *K. A. Ryan* **77**

FULFILMENT (IRE) 3 ch.f. Alhaarth (IRE) 126 – Noble Dane (IRE) 79 (Danehill (USA) 126) [2009 8d p8.6g p9.5g Oct 10] 46,000Y: lengthy filly: sixth foal: half-sister to fairly useful 1½m to 17.2f winner Let It Be (by Entrepreneur) and winner in Sweden by Domedriver: dam, 2-y-o 1m winner (stayed 1½m), sister to smart but ungenuine performer up to 1¼m Amrak Ajeeb: modest form in maidens: bred to be suited by 1¼m+: should do better. *W. J. Musson* **53 p**

FULFORD 4 ch.g. Elmaamul (USA) 125 – Last Impression 69 (Imp Society (USA)) [2009 64: f6d f6g 6g 6g 8.1v 6m f6g Dec 8] workmanlike gelding: modest handicapper: best at 6f: acts on all-weather, soft and good to firm going: tried visored. *M. Brittain* **53**

FULHAM BROADWAY (IRE) 3 ch.c. Exceed And Excel (AUS) 126 – Lomalou (IRE) (Lightning Dealer 103) [2009 90p: p6g^2 Jun 17] useful form: shaped well when ¾-length second to Mac's Power in handicap at Kempton sole outing in 2009, poorly drawn and shuffled back early: suffered tendon injury after: should prove best at 5f/6f. *E. F. Vaughan* **97**

FULLANDBY (IRE) 7 b.g. Monashee Mountain (USA) 115 – Ivory Turner (Efisio 120) [2009 111: 5.2s^3 6f 5g^2 5g 6d 5g 5m 5.6m 6m^5 7g 5d^4 p6m* 6s* p6g Nov 21] strong, good-bodied gelding: carries condition: still useful: won handicap at Kempton and listed race at Doncaster (beat Arthur's Edge by head) in November: creditable efforts otherwise in 2009 only when placed: effective at stiff 5f to 7f: acts on polytrack, soft and good to firm going: tried blinkered: held up. *T. J. Etherington* **108**

FULLBACK (IRE) 3 ch.g. Redback 116 – Feet of Flame (USA) 59 (Theatrical 128) [2009 94: a7g a8f p8g p8g^2 8m^4 10d^4 p8g p10f^4 Sep 4] strong gelding: fairly useful performer: best efforts in 2009 when in frame in minor events at Lingfield fourth/final starts (gelded after): barely stays 1¼m: acts on polytrack and good to firm ground. *J. S. Moore* **94**

FULL BLUE 3 b. or gr.f. Falbrav (IRE) 133 – Miss University (USA) (Beau Genius (CAN)) [2009 –: 10m 12g 14.1g Aug 14] no form. *S. C. Williams* **–**

FULL MANDATE (IRE) 2 b.f. (Apr 7) Acclamation 118 – Dani Ridge (IRE) 92 (Indian Ridge 123) [2009 5f^4 6m* 6m^2 7g 6g^2 8f Nov 29] €60,000Y: well-made filly: third foal: half-sister to 2008 2-y-o 6f winner Danidh Dubai (by Noverre) and 5f winner (including at 2 yrs) Ridge Wood Dani (by Invincible Spirit), both fairly useful: dam, 6f winner, sister to useful 7f/1m performer Blomberg: useful performer: won maiden at Newbury in July by 1¼ lengths from Deloria, making virtually all: good second in Princess Margaret Stakes (beaten 1½ lengths by Lady of The Desert) at Ascot and valuable Goffs Million Sprint (beaten 1¾ lengths by Lucky General) at the Curragh: sold from R. Hannon 150,000 gns after: will prove best at 5f/6f (pulled up in Grade 3 Miesque Stakes at Hollywood at 1m): pulled much too hard fourth outing. *J. M. Cassidy, USA* **98**

FULL OF LOVE (IRE) 3 b.f. Hawk Wing (USA) 136 – Charmingly (USA) 62 (King **88**
of Kings (IRE) 125) [2009 57: 8m* p8.6g* 8d^2 8d^3 9g^2 10g Oct 8] leggy filly: has round action: fairly useful performer: won maiden at Newcastle and handicap at Wolverhampton, both in April: good placed efforts next 3 starts: stays 9f: acts on polytrack, unraced on extremes of ground on turf. *B. W. Hills*

FULL OF NATURE 3 ch.f. Monsieur Bond (IRE) 120 – Secret Circle (Magic Ring **77**
(IRE) 115) [2009 77: 9.9f^4 p10g 10d 8d^3 8.3f p10m^4 9.7m^4 12f^5 p9.5g^6 Oct 2] strong filly: fair handicapper: stays 1¼m: acts on polytrack, firm and good to soft ground: often slowly away: signs of temperament. *S. Kirk*

FULL SPEED (GER) 4 b.g. Sholokhov (IRE) 121 – Flagny (FR) (Kaldoun (FR) 122) **92**
[2009 92: 10.3g* 10m 10g 10.4m 10.3m^3 12m^5 12g Oct 10] strong gelding: type to carry condition: fairly useful handicapper: won at Chester in June: creditable effort after only when third in minor event at Doncaster: stays 1½m: acts on soft and good to firm going: often travels strongly: sold 28,000 gns. *G. A. Swinbank*

FULL TOSS 3 b.g. Nayef (USA) 129 – Spinning Top 105 (Alzao (USA) 117) [2009 **97**
101: p8g 10.3s p8g 8.1m^6 10m^3 p10m* p9.5g^4 f11g* f14d^4 Dec 29] smallish, strong gelding: useful performer: won claimer at Lingfield (left R. Hannon £12,000) and handicap at Southwell, both in December: barely stays 1¾m: acts on all-weather and good to firm ground. *P. D. Evans*

FULL VICTORY (IRE) 7 b.g. Imperial Ballet (IRE) 110 – Full Traceability (IRE) 53 **76**
(Ron's Victory (USA) 129) [2009 90d: 7.1g^5 8d* 8.1g 8.1g^4 8.3v^3 8.3v^4 p8.6g 8.3g^3 8g^6 Oct 21] good-topped gelding: just fair handicapper in 2009, winning at Bath in May: stays 9f: acts on all-weather, heavy and good to firm going: tried in blinkers/cheekpieces: often hangs left. *R. A. Farrant*

FUNDAY 3 b.f. Daylami (IRE) 138 – Morina (USA) (Lyphard (USA) 132) [2009 10f^3 **93**
10m* 10.1g^3 12m^4 10.1m^2 12m* 12m^3 Oct 2] good-topped filly: sister to useful hurdler Pigeon Island and half-sister to several winners, including very smart 6f (at 2 yrs) to 1½m winner Mons and smart 1¼m winner Inforapenny (both by Deploy): dam French 11f winner: fairly useful performer: won maiden at Lingfield in June and handicap at Epsom in September: far from discredited when third of 4 to Chock A Block in listed race at Newmarket final outing: stays 1½m: acts on good to firm going. *G. L. Moore*

FUN IN THE SUN 5 ch.g. Piccolo 121 – Caught In The Rain 66 (Spectrum (IRE) 126) **55**
[2009 60: p7g^2 f8g p7g* p7g p8g^5 p7g^4 7m 7g^4 7m Aug 23] modest performer: won **a64**
handicap at Lingfield in February: best around 7f: acts on polytrack, heavy and good to firm ground: tried visored/blinkered. *A. B. Haynes*

FUNKY MUNKY 4 b.g. Talaash (IRE) 110 – Chilibang Bang 68 (Chilibang 120) **70**
[2009 f8g^5 7.1m 8m^5 8m 8d* 9.2g^6 p8.6m Sep 28] seventh foal: dam 5f (at 2 yrs) to 7f winner: fair handicapper, lightly raced: best effort when winning selling event at Thirsk in August: stays 1m: acts on good to soft ground. *G. A. Swinbank*

FUNKY TOWN (IRE) 7 b.g. Anshan 119 – Dance Rhythm (IRE) (Dancing Dissident **–**
(USA) 119) [2009 54: p12g p8g 12d Apr 9] maiden: no form in 2009. *J. Akehurst*

FURMAGIATT 5 b.g. In The Wings 128 – Sumingasefa (Danehill (USA) 126) [2009 **§§**
f12g Mar 27] fair form in bumpers: refused to race in maiden at Southwell. *Mrs S. Leech*

FURMIGADELAGIUSTA 5 ch.h. Galileo (IRE) 134 – Sispre (FR) (Master Willie **114**
129) [2009 107: 12m^3 12s* 12m* 14m Jul 11] good-topped horse: smart performer: further progress in 2009, winning handicap at York in May and listed race at Pontefract (beat Drumfire 2½ lengths, quickening clear final 1f) in June: shaped as if amiss final outing: stays 1¾m: acts on polytrack, soft and good to firm ground: consistent. *K. R. Burke*

FURNACE (IRE) 5 b.g. Green Desert (USA) 127 – Lyrical Dance (USA) (Lear Fan **110**
(USA) 130) [2009 102: 8m^2 7.5g 8m* a5g 8g May 14] leggy, quite attractive gelding: smart performer: best effort in 2009 when winning minor event at Nad Al Sheba in February by ¾ length from Kachgai (left M. bin Shafya after next start): went off too fast in handicap at York back in Britain: effective at 7f/1m: acts on polytrack, good to firm and good to soft going. *Saeed bin Suroor*

FUSAICHI FLYER (USA) 2 b. or br.g. (Mar 31) Fusaichi Pegasus (USA) 130 – **68 p**
Songbook (Singspiel (IRE) 133) [2009 p7.1g^6 p7.1g^2 p7.1g Dec 28] first foal: dam unraced half-sister to smart Irish 7f/1m winner Two-Twenty-Two out of sister to Irish 1000 Guineas winner Trusted Partner: fair maiden: best effort when eye-catching second to Playboy Blues at Wolverhampton: will stay 1m: remains open to improvement. *R. Charlton*

FUSENAM 2 b.g. (Mar 17) Refuse To Bend (IRE) 128 – Namat (IRE) 93 (Daylami (IRE) 138) [2009 8d^6 8d p9.5g Nov 14] fair maiden: gelded, easily best effort when seventh at Wolverhampton final start: will stay 1¼m+. *Miss J. A. Camacho* **65**

FUTURE GEM 3 b.f. Bertolini (USA) 125 – Georgianna (IRE) (Petardia 113) [2009 40: 6f 6m 5g* 5g^5 5m 6g^2 6d^2 5m^5 5.9d* 6d* 5v^2 6g^2 7g Oct 16] close-coupled filly: fair performer: improved to win maiden at Catterick in May, then handicaps at Carlisle and Ayr in August: best at 5f/6f: acts on heavy going: in cheekpieces nowadays: sold £3,000. *A. Dickman* **71**

FUTURE REGIME (IRE) 2 b.f. (Feb 10) Xaar 132 – Sadalsud (IRE) (Shaadi (USA) 126) [2009 p5.1m 6s p6g^3 p5.1g^5 p5.1g^5 Dec 26] €20,000F, £50,000Y: seventh foal: half-sister to 3 winners, notably 4-y-o Ancien Regime: dam Italian 5f (at 2 yrs)/1m winner: modest maiden: stays 6f: form only on polytrack. *Pat Morris* **56**

FUTURIST 2 b.c. (Mar 9) Halling (USA) 133 – Crystal Gazing (USA) 114 (El Gran Senor (USA) 136) [2009 7m 10.2m^3 10m* Oct 5] rangy colt: half-brother to several winners, including smart UAE sprinter Conroy (by Gone West) and fairly useful Irish 1¼m winner Dark Veil (by Gulch): dam 6f/7f winner (including Rockfel and Nell Gwyn Stakes) and third in 1000 Guineas: progressive form in maidens, winning at Pontefract by 1½ lengths from Indochina, eased markedly: stays 1¼m: has joined A. bin Huzaim in UAE: type to do better still at 3 yrs. *Saeed bin Suroor* **84 p**

FUZZY CAT 3 b.g. Nayef (USA) 129 – Curfew 102 (Marju (IRE) 127) [2009 –p: 7d 10.1d 8.3m^5 f6m^2 5.9d f6g* 6g p6f^3 Dec 21] modest handicapper: won at Southwell in August: worth a try at 5f: acts on all-weather: usually blinkered. *T. D. Barron* **59**

FYELEHK (IRE) 3 b.g. Kheleyf (USA) 116 – Opalescent (IRE) (Polish Precedent (USA) 131) [2009 59: p8g^4 p6g^4 p5.1g^4 p6g* 6m^5 6.1m^3 6f* 6g* 6m^3 5.7m p6g 6d* a7g^3 Dec 5] neat gelding: fair performer: progressed steadily in 2009, winning minor event at Kempton in April then handicaps at Folkestone (apprentices) and Epsom in July, and Windsor in October: left B. R. Millman before final start: will prove best at 5f/6f: acts on polytrack, firm and good to soft going: tongue tied once at 2 yrs: races prominently. *Mme L. Braem, Belgium* **78**

FYODOR (IRE) 8 b.g. Fasliyev (USA) 120 – Royale Figurine (IRE) 107 (Dominion Royale 112) [2009 109: p6g 5m f5g^6 6f p6g^2 6m 5.1g^6 6m 5.7m^6 5.1m p6g^6 p6g p6g Oct 10] tall, good-topped gelding: one-time smart performer: deteriorated considerably in 2009 (claimed from C. Dore £6,000 after fifth start), and showed plenty of temperament: was best at 5f/6f: acted on all-weather and firm going (not at best on softer than good): sometimes wore headgear: held up: dead. *P. D. Evans* **81 d**

FYODOROVICH (USA) 4 b.g. Stravinsky (USA) 133 – Omnia (USA) 85 (Green Dancer (USA) 132) [2009 –§: 8m 9m 7d 5.9m 8m^4 7.5m 8m 6m 8d^6 8d Sep 7] useful-looking gelding: modest handicapper at best in 2009: stays 1m: acts on good to firm ground: often visored/blinkered: ungenuine: gelded after final start. *J. S. Wainwright* **53 §**

G

GABRIEL'S SPIRIT (IRE) 2 b.c. (Apr 13) Invincible Spirit (IRE) 121 – Over Rating 74 (Desert King (IRE) 129) [2009 6g 6m^4 7.1g Aug 31] form in maidens only when 8 lengths fourth to Arabian Pride at Newmarket: should stay 7f. *Miss Amy Weaver* **56**

GADITANA 3 b.f. Rainbow Quest (USA) 134 – Armeria (USA) 79 (Northern Dancer) [2009 10.2g Oct 21] sister to several at least useful winners, notably Racing Post Trophy winner and St Leger second Armiger: dam, 1¼m winner, half-sister to Park Hill winner I Want To Be: well held in maiden at Bath: sold 92,000 gns. *Pat Eddery* **–**

GADOBOUT DANCER 2 b.f. (Apr 20) Tobougg (IRE) 125 – Delta Tempo (IRE) (Bluebird (USA) 125) [2009 7.5g 7.5m 8.3m Sep 30] workmanlike filly: half-sister to 3 winners, including 7f to 9.4f winner Paso Doble (by Dancing Spree): dam unraced: soundly beaten in maidens: tried in cheekpieces. *I. W. McInnes* **–**

GAELIC ROSE (IRE) 3 b.f. King Charlemagne (USA) 120 – Harry's Irish Rose (USA) (Sir Harry Lewis (USA) 127) [2009 46: 10.2g 10m p12g^5 Jun 20] sturdy filly: poor maiden. *S. Kirk* **46**

GAIA PRINCE (USA) 4 b. or br.g. Forestry (USA) 121 – Castlebrook (USA) (Montbrook (USA)) [2009 76: 9.7m^3 10m^2 12f^3 14m Jun 13] tall gelding: fairly useful maiden handicapper: may prove best up to 1¼m: acts on firm ground, yet to race on softer than good. *Mrs A. J. Perrett* **85**

GAILY NOBLE (IRE) 3 b.c. One Cool Cat (USA) 123 – Dream Genie (Puissance **87**
110) [2009 80: p8.6g* p10g^2 9.9m^2 8m^5 8.1f^2 10f^4 p8g^5 9.2g^4 p9.5g* p8.6g^4 p8.6g^4
p8.6g^6 f8m Dec 15] rather leggy colt: fairly useful performer: successful at Wolverhampton in maiden in February and claimer in October: stays easy 1¼m: acts on polytrack and firm ground: often front runner. *A. B. Haynes*

GAINSHARE 4 b.g. Lend A Hand 124 – Red Shareef (Marju (IRE) 127) [2009 72: p6g^5 **64**
f6g^5 p6g^3 Feb 26] quite good-topped gelding: just modest handicapper in 2009: stays 6f: acts on polytrack and good to soft ground: edgy sort, often takes keen hold: none too consistent. *Mrs R. A. Carr*

GALA CASINO STAR (IRE) 4 ch.g. Dr Fong (USA) 128 – Abir 73 (Soviet Star **95**
(USA) 128) [2009 93: p8g 10.3m^4 9.9g^5 8.1m^2 9d^3 8m^6 8v^4 8s^2 8m^3 10.4m 8g^2 10.2d^2
p8.6g^3 Nov 27] tall gelding: useful handicapper: several good placed efforts in 2009: stays 1¼m: acts on polytrack and any turf going: tried blinkered/visored: consistent. *R. A. Fahey*

GALACHIYA 2 ch.f. (Mar 6) Gulch (USA) – Empress Anna (IRE) (Imperial Ballet **68**
(IRE) 110) [2009 6g Jul 24] 34,000Y: first foal: dam, US 1m winner, out of smart 5f winner Cutlers Corner: 33/1, seventh of 9 to Walk On Water in maiden at Ascot, green and awkward. *C. E. Brittain*

GALA EVENING 7 b.g. Daylami (IRE) 138 – Balleta (USA) 87 (Lyphard (USA) 132) **95**
[2009 –, a101: p16g^2 18.7m 20m^4 Jun 16] strong, quite attractive gelding: useful handicapper, lightly raced: creditable efforts in 2009 when in frame, at Kempton (1½ lengths second to Desert Sea) and Ascot Stakes at Royal Ascot (fourth to Judgethemoment): barely stays 2½m: acts on polytrack and good to firm going: held up. *J. A. B. Old*

GALA SUNDAY (USA) 9 b.g. Lear Fan (USA) 130 – Sunday Bazaar (USA) (Nureyev **66**
(USA) 131) [2009 69: 10.2m 10m 10.2m 9.9g 10m* 9.9m^2 9.9m 10m^5 10.9m^6 10g^5
Oct 16] smallish, well-made gelding: fair handicapper: won ladies event at Pontefract in June: best at 1¼m: acts on polytrack, firm and soft going: usually blinkered/tongue tied. *M. W. Easterby*

GALATIAN 2 ch.g. (Apr 15) Traditionally (USA) 117 – Easy To Imagine (USA) **71**
(Cozzene (USA)) [2009 7m 6.5g^4 6m^5 Oct 26] 3,000Y: strong gelding: third foal: half-brother to 4-y-o Tangerine Trees and 5-y-o Masai Moon: dam unraced sister to useful stayer Hiddensee out of smart performer up to 1m Zarani Sidi Anna: progressive form in maidens, fifth to Deacon Blues at Leicester (hung right under pressure): should stay 7f. *B. R. Millman*

GALEOTA (IRE) 7 b.g. Mujadil (USA) 119 – Refined (IRE) 95 (Statoblest 120) [2009 **98 ?**
116: 6.1m 5d^6 6s 5.1m Sep 13] strong, good-topped gelding: one-time smart performer: well below best in 2009, including in claimer: best at 5f/6f: acts on firm and soft going: wore cheekpieces once at 2 yrs. *R. Hannon*

GALIENT (IRE) 6 b.g. Galileo (IRE) 134 – Endorsement 107 (Warning 136) [2009 **–**
91: 20m Jun 16] tall, good-topped gelding: fluent mover: very lightly raced on Flat nowadays: below form sole start in 2009: tried in cheekpieces: fairly useful hurdler at best. *N. J. Henderson*

GALILEAN MOON 3 b.f. Galileo (IRE) 134 – Fascinating Rhythm 85 (Slip Anchor **80**
136) [2009 10m^6 12.1m^3 12g* 12m^5 p13.9g Sep 11] 320,000Y: fifth foal: half-sister to useful 1¼m/1½m winner Pentatonic (by Giant's Causeway): dam, 2-y-o 1m winner who disappointed both 3-y-o starts, out of Fillies' Mile runner-up Pick of The Pops: fairly useful performer: won maiden at Newmarket in July, best effort: should be well suited by 1¾m: raced only on polytrack and good/good to firm going. *Sir Michael Stoute*

GALIOTTO (IRE) 3 b.g. Galileo (IRE) 134 – Welsh Motto (USA) (Mtoto 134) [2009 **60**
10m^6 10m 11.8m^6 11.5g^2 11.5m^2 p12.2g^5 p13.9g^3 Oct 2] close-coupled gelding: modest maiden handicapper: stays 13.9f: raced only on polytrack and good/good to firm going. *C. F. Wall*

GALLAGHER 3 ch.c. Bahamian Bounty 116 – Roo 97 (Rudimentary (USA) 118) **112**
[2009 117: 7m^4 7m* 8d 7m^5 Aug 15] useful-looking colt: smart performer: not quite so good in 2009: fourth to Ouqba in Jersey Stakes at Royal Ascot before winning minor event at Newbury in July by 2 lengths from Plum Pudding: below form after (reportedly sustained minor injury final outing): stays 7f: acts on good to firm going (ran poorly on good to soft): travels strongly, but sometimes finds little. *B. J. Meehan*

GALLANT EAGLE (IRE) 2 ch.c. (Apr 12) Hawk Wing (USA) 136 – Generous **81**
Gesture (IRE) 86 (Fasliyev (USA) 120) [2009 6m^4 6g^6 6m^4 7f^3 p7.1g* Sep 18] €20,000F: second foal: dam, 6f winner, closely related to smart miler Harvest Queen: fairly useful

performer: won nursery at Wolverhampton by ½ length from Kinky Afro: stays 7f: acts on polytrack and good to firm going. *S. Kirk*

GALLANTRY 7 b.g. Green Desert (USA) 127 – Gay Gallanta (USA) 112 (Woodman (USA) 126) [2009 101: p8g^6 p8.6g^6 p7g* p8.6g* p7g^6 7f 8m^5 7g 7g^2 p8m 7.1g p7.1g^5 p7.1g^5 p8.6g p7g p7g^4 p7.1g p7.1g p8m^5 Dec 30] strong gelding: useful handicapper: won at Lingfield and Wolverhampton in February: stays 8.6f: acts on polytrack and firm going, well held on softer than good: held up (often slowly away). *P. Howling* **95**

GALLEGO 7 br.g. Danzero (AUS) – Shafir (IRE) 68 (Shaadi (USA) 126) [2009 77, a–: 11.7g 10.2f^6 10m^5 10f 10m 7f* 8m* 10d 8d^2 8.1m^6 10.2m^6 Sep 30] strong, close-coupled gelding: fair handicapper: won amateur events at Salisbury in June and July: effective at 7f to 1¼m: acts on polytrack, firm and good to soft going: tried blinkered/visored: usually slowly away: held up. *R. J. Price* **77**

GALLEY SLAVE (IRE) 4 b.g. Spartacus (IRE) 107 – Cimeterre (IRE) 49 (Arazi (USA) 135) [2009 –§: p10g f12g^3 10.3s Aug 1] unreliable maiden: little form on Flat since 2 yrs. *M. C. Chapman* **– §**

GALLIC STAR (IRE) 2 b.f. (Feb 4) Galileo (IRE) 134 – Oman Sea (USA) 81 (Rahy (USA) 115) [2009 6m 6m* 7.1m^4 7g^5 8m^4 8g* Oct 19] 68,000F, €130,000Y: close-coupled filly: second foal: dam, 2-y-o 6f winner from 3 starts, sister to 6-y-o Racer Forever: useful performer: won maiden at Leicester in June and listed event at Pontefract (beat Tominator a short head) in October: better form when fifth to Long Lashes in Sweet Solera Stakes at Newmarket and 3¾ lengths fourth to Pollenator in May Hill Stakes at Doncaster fourth/fifth starts: likely to stay beyond 1m. *M. R. Channon* **98**

GALPIN JUNIOR (USA) 3 ch.g. Hennessy (USA) 122 – Reluctant Diva (Sadler's Wells (USA) 132) [2009 99: 6m^6 6m f6f Oct 21] just fairly useful performer at best in 2009, sixth in listed race at Goodwood on belated reappearance: may prove best at 5f/6f: raced only on fibresand and good to firm going: tongue tied at 3 yrs, also blinkered final outing: sold 6,500 gns, then gelded. *B. J. Meehan* **91**

GAMBLING JACK 4 b.g. First Trump 118 – Star of Flanders (Puissance 110) [2009 58: p7g^4 p8.6g 6m^6 8.1g 6m^6 Jun 1] tall, lengthy gelding: modest maiden: barely stays 7f: acts on polytrack, firm and soft ground: tried blinkered/tongue tied. *A. W. Carroll* **52**

GAMBLING QUEEN 2 b.f. (Apr 30) Zafeen (FR) 123 – Pure Speculation 80 (Salse (USA) 128) [2009 6m Jun 23] tall, angular filly: second foal: half-sister to useful 2008 2-y-o 5f winner Doughnut (by Acclamation): dam, 2-y-o 7f winner, half-sister to useful performer up to 1¼m The Judge: 25/1 and green, well held in maiden at Newbury. *Mrs P. Sly* **–**

GAMEDOR (FR) 4 ch.g. Kendor (FR) 122 – Garmeria (FR) (Kadrou (FR) 126) [2009 a12g^3 a12g^5 12g^5 17d* 13d^4 15.5d 13g 12d^3 11g p13g Oct 11] fifth foal: half-brother to French 6f (at 2 yrs)/7.5f winner Brown Fox (by Polar Falcon): dam French 9f to 11f winner: fair performer: won minor event at Nimes in March: left J-M. Capitte €20,000 and off 6 months, well held in handicap at Lingfield final start: stays 17f: acts on good to soft ground: tried blinkered. *G. L. Moore* **75**

GAMEGEAR 4 br.f. Tomba 119 – Princess of Hearts 61 (Prince Sabo 123) [2009 f7g f8g Mar 17] second foal: dam ungenuine 7f (at 2 yrs)/1m seller winner: well held in maidens at Southwell (blinkered latter occasion). *S. R. Bowring* **–**

GAME LAD 7 b.g. Mind Games 121 – Catch Me 75 (Rudimentary (USA) 118) [2009 91: 7m 7d^4 7d 7d f7g Sep 29] big, lengthy gelding: fair handicapper nowadays: all wins at 7f, but stays 1m: has form on any going, but probably best on good or softer nowadays (4 of 5 wins on soft/heavy): tongue tied: held up. *T. D. Easterby* **76**

GAME ROSEANNA 3 b.f. Mind Games 121 – Rosy Sunset (IRE) (Red Sunset 120) [2009 59: 10.4s^3 10.3g^6 13.8m^6 11.5g^6 Oct 20] close-coupled filly: modest maiden: stays 10.4f: acts on soft going. *W. M. Brisbourne* **59**

GAMES (IRE) 8 b.g. Lord Americo – Anns Run (Deep Run 119) [2009 6v p8g p5f 7m 14d 17.8s^6 f14g Dec 22] one-time fair hurdler/chaser: no form on Flat, left P. Rothwell in Ireland prior to final start: often slowly away, and is ungenuine. *C. N. Kellett* **– §**

GAME STALKER (USA) 3 b. or br.c. Elusive Quality (USA) – Windsharp (USA) 123 (Lear Fan (USA) 130) [2009 10.2g^4 9.7m* Sep 22] sixth foal: closely related to Breeders' Cup Turf winner Johar (by Gone West) and half-brother to US Grade 1 9f winner Dessert (by Storm Cat): dam US Grade 1 1¼m/1½m winner: much improved to win maiden at Folkestone in September easily by 2¾ lengths from Naheell, making most but still green: stays 9.7f: has joined M. bin Shafya in UAE. *Saeed bin Suroor* **82**

Mrs J. S. Bolger's "Gan Amhras"

GAMESTERS LADY 6 br.m. Almushtarak (IRE) 122 – Tycoon Tina 61 (Tina's Pet 121) [2009 70: p12.2g⁶ f11d* f12d⁴ p13.9g⁶ 12m 11.7f 10m³ 12.3g 11m⁶ 10.2g⁶ 10.4g p9.5g Aug 10] sturdy mare: fair handicapper: won at Southwell in February: stays 1½m: acts on all-weather, soft and firm going: tried in cheekpieces/blinkers: unreliable. *W. M. Brisbourne* **65 §**

GAN AMHRAS (IRE) 3 b.c. Galileo (IRE) 134 – All's Forgotten (USA) 81 (Darshaan 133) [2009 108p: 8m³ 12g 12g⁶ 7g Sep 27] leggy colt: very smart performer: much improved when 2¼ lengths third to Sea The Stars in 2000 Guineas at Newmarket, racing handily: well below form after, at Epsom in Derby, then at the Curragh in Irish Derby and minor event (favourite), finding little both times: bred to stay at least 1¼m: acts on good to firm going. *J. S. Bolger, Ireland* **122**

GANDALF 7 b.g. Sadler's Wells (USA) 132 – Enchant 92 (Lion Cavern (USA) 117) [2009 14s 14.1m⁵ p16g* 16g Oct 8] good-topped gelding: fairly useful handicapper: left James Burns in Ireland after reappearance: won at Kempton in September: stays 2m: acts on polytrack and good to firm going: has looked none too keen. *Miss Amy Weaver* **80**

GAP PRINCESS (IRE) 5 b.m. Noverre (USA) 125 – Safe Care (IRE) (Caerleon (USA) 132) [2009 79: 5m³ 5m³ 7.1m 7f² 7.2m⁶ 6d² 5m* 6d p6g⁵ p6g* Dec 7] leggy mare: fairly useful performer: won claimer at Hamilton in June (left R. Fahey £8,000 after) and handicap at Wolverhampton in December: effective at 5f to 7f: acts on polytrack and firm ground, probably on good to soft: held up. *G. A. Harker* **81**

GARDENING LEAVE 2 b.c. (Mar 31) Selkirk (USA) 129 – Misty Waters (IRE) (Caerleon (USA) 132) [2009 8g 8v* 10v⁶ Nov 14] €24,000Y: seventh foal: half-brother to 3 winners in Japan: dam unraced sister to useful Irish 9f/1¼m winner Fantasia Girl: progressive form: made all when winning maiden at Newbury in October by 3½ lengths from Prince of Dreams (awkward head carriage): stiff task, not discredited when sixth to Passion For Gold in Criterium de Saint-Cloud: stays 1¼m. *A. M. Balding* **93 +**

GARDEN PARTY 5 b.g. Green Desert (USA) 127 – Tempting Prospect 95 (Shirley Heights 130) [2009 82: p8.6g^2 f8g^6 p8.6g^3 p8g^2 8m^3 8.5g^4 10m^4 8.5f* 9d^3 12m^3 12f^3 Aug 31] lengthy gelding: just fair form in 2009, leaving R. Harris after fourth start: won handicap at Les Landes in June: seems to stay 1½m: acts on polytrack and firm going: often in headgear: moody. *T. J. Bougourd, Jersey* **67**

GARLOGS 6 b.g. Hunting Lion (IRE) 115 – Fading (Pharly (FR) 130) [2009 86: p5.1g f5g f5g f5m Mar 22] close-coupled gelding: fairly useful handicapper in 2008: well held at 6 yrs: tried blinkered/visored. *R. Hollinshead* **–**

GARNICA (FR) 6 gr.g. Linamix (FR) 127 – Gueridia (IRE) (Night Shift (USA)) [2009 117: 7.1g^4 7.1g 6g 7d 7s Nov 7] strong, well-made gelding: just useful form in 2009, best effort when 6¾ lengths fourth to Beacon Lodge in listed race at Haydock: best at 6f/7f: has form on good to firm ground, all wins on good or softer (acts on heavy). *D. Nicholls* **102**

GARRA MOLLY (IRE) 4 b.f. Nayef (USA) 129 – Aminata 98 (Glenstal (USA) 118) [2009 77: p9.5m^2 p9.5g^4 10m Aug 15] lengthy filly: fair maiden handicapper: stays 1¾m: acts on polytrack and soft going: sold 28,000 gns, reportedly in foal to Dr Fong. *G. A. Swinbank* **70**

GARSTANG 6 ch.g. Atraf 116 – Approved Quality (IRE) 66 (Persian Heights 129) [2009 71: f6g p5g* p6g p5g* 5d^6 5s^3 p5g^2 p5m^2 5m p5.1g^4 p5.1g^2 p5g^3 Oct 9] rather leggy, workmanlike gelding: fairly useful handicapper on all-weather, fair on turf: better than ever in 2009, won at Kempton in April and June: in frame 6 of last 7 starts: effective at 5f to easy 7f: acts on polytrack, firm and soft ground: usually blinkered. *J. Balding* **70 a86**

GARTER KNIGHT 3 b.g. Mark of Esteem (IRE) 137 – Granted (FR) 100 (Cadeaux Genereux 131) [2009 p10g p8.6g^6 p7g 8.3m^4 10m^2 10g 10.2g^2 8.3v^3 Nov 4] fifth foal: half-brother to 3 winners, including 4-y-o Bestowed and 5-y-o Perfect Star: dam 1m winner who stayed 9f: fair maiden: left M. Bell 11,000 gns and off 4 months after fifth start: stays 1¼m: best effort on good ground: held up. *Mrs P. Sly* **73**

GARTER STAR 4 b.f. Mark of Esteem (IRE) 137 – Palace Affair 113 (Pursuit of Love 124) [2009 p7g^6 6m May 21] sturdy filly: second foal: half-sister to 5-y-o April Fool: dam, 5f to 7f winner (including 6f at 2 yrs), half-sister to high-class sprinter Sakhee's Secret: better effort in maidens when sixth at Lingfield. *H. Morrison* **56**

GASAT (IRE) 8 b.h. Marju (IRE) 127 – Pechenga (Nureyev (USA) 131) [2009 ?: p10g^2 p13g p10g^2 p12g^3 p10g* p10g^2 10.2g^2 10m 10m 9m^4 p10g p12g Oct 8] sturdy horse: fair performer: left F. Sheridan after reappearance: won seller at Lingfield in March: below form last 5 starts: stays 1½m: acts on all-weather, good to firm and good to soft ground: tried tongue tied: races prominently: sold £4,000, sent to Qatar. *A. B. Haynes* **74**

GASELEE (USA) 3 b.f. Toccet (USA) 118 – Vingt Et Une (FR) (Sadler's Wells (USA) 132) [2009 p9.2g^4 p10g p8g p12g^4 9g* 8.5m^2 10.2g^4 12d^2 f11f^2 Oct 21] $95,000Y: close-coupled filly: seventh foal: half-sister to several winners, including 1½m winners Sayadaw (smart) and Year Two Thousand (useful) (both by Darshaan): dam, French 1¼m winner, sister to very smart 1m to 1½m performer Johann Quatz and half-sister to Prix du Jockey Club winner Hernando: fair performer: won maiden at Musselburgh in July: in frame in handicaps after: stays 1½m: acts on fibresand, good to firm and good to soft going: races prominently. *Rae Guest* **77**

GASPARILLA (IRE) 2 b.f. (Mar 20) Fath (USA) 116 – Tazmeera (IRE) 76 (Priolo (USA) 127) [2009 5m^3 5m^5 5m^3 6.1d^5 p5.1m^6 6g^5 p6g 5m f5g Sep 29] £800Y: angular filly: first foal: dam, Irish 2-y-o 1m winner, out of half-sister to Prix du Jockey Club winner Top Ville: poor maiden: stays 6f: acts on good to firm and good to soft going: usually races prominently. *A. J. McCabe* **43**

GASSIN 3 b.g. Selkirk (USA) 129 – Miss Riviera Golf 106 (Hernando (FR) 127) [2009 70: 8.3g* 8.1g^5 8.3v 8g p7.1g* p7g^3 p7.1g* Oct 23] sturdy gelding: fairly useful performer: won maiden at Nottingham in June and handicaps at Wolverhampton (2) in October: stays 8.3f: acts on polytrack: strong-travelling sort: visored last 3 starts: sold 18,000 gns. *M. L. W. Bell* **85**

GAYANULA (USA) 4 b.f. Yonaguska (USA) 112 – Betamillion Bock (USA) (Bet Twice (USA)) [2009 67: f14s^3 f12g^2 f12g f12g^4 f12g^6 Jun 2] modest handicapper: stays 1¾m: best efforts on fibresand: in cheekpieces last 2 starts. *Miss J. A. Camacho* **63**

GAY MIRAGE (GER) 2 b.f. (Apr 3) Highest Honor (FR) 124 – Geminiani (IRE) 106 (King of Kings (IRE) 125) [2009 8.3v^6 Nov 4] attractive filly: third foal: half-sister to 4-y-o Amerigo: dam, 2-y-o 7f winner who stayed 1¼m, closely related to smart 2004 2-y-o sprinter Damson: 12/1, encouraging sixth to Burj Nahar in maiden at Nottingham, not knocked about once beaten: will improve. *M. A. Jarvis* **59 p**

GAZAMALI (IRE) 2 b.c. (Apr 4) Namid 128 – Frond 85 (Alzao (USA) 117) [2009 5m 5m⁶ 7g Oct 17] unfurnished colt: green and little impact in minor event/maidens, off 6 months prior to final start. *G. A. Harker* **–**

GAZBOOLOU 5 b.g. Royal Applause 124 – Warning Star 104 (Warning 136) [2009 79: p8g² p8g⁴ p7.1g² 7m 7m³ 7.1g⁶ 8.3m p7.1g² p8g p7m³ p7m Oct 12] sturdy gelding: fairly useful handicapper on all-weather, fair on turf: effective at 7f/1m: acts on polytrack and firm ground. *David Pinder* **73 a81**

GEARBOX (IRE) 3 br.g. Tillerman 123 – Persian Empress (IRE) 51 (Persian Bold 123) [2009 8.3g⁶ Aug 14] workmanlike gelding: 10/1, well held in maiden at Nottingham: had been withdrawn (moved badly to start) prior to intended debut. *R. Hannon* **–**

GEE DEE NEN 6 b.g. Mister Baileys 123 – Special Beat 65 (Bustino 136) [2009 100: p16g⁵ 16g 16.4m Aug 21] close-coupled, good-topped gelding: just fairly useful handicapper in 2009: stays 2m: acts on polytrack, soft and good to firm going: visored once at 3 yrs: fairly useful hurdler, joined G. L. Moore after final start. *Jim Best* **93**

GEE GINA 3 b.f. Hunting Lion (IRE) 115 – La Thuile 46 (Statoblest 120) [2009 –: 5m 5g⁴ 5m⁴ 5m² 5m⁵ 5m* Aug 30] fair handicapper: won at Beverley in August: raced mainly at 5f: acts on good to firm ground. *P. T. Midgley* **66**

GEE MAJOR 2 b.g. (Feb 26) Reset (AUS) 124 – Polly Golightly 84 (Weldnaas (USA) 112) [2009 6g 6.1s Oct 7] well held in maidens 3 months apart, leaving N. Vaughan in between: gelded after final start. *Tom Dascombe* **–**

GEESE A LAYING (IRE) 3 b.f. Elusive City (USA) 117 – King of All (IRE) (King of Clubs 124) [2009 f6g p5g⁵ p5g Mar 25] €41,000Y: fourth foal: half-sister to useful 2004 2-y-o 6f winner Haunting Memories (by Barathea) and fairly useful 2007 2-y-o 5f winner Regal Rhythm (by Namid): dam, Italian 6f to 7.5f winner (including at 2 yrs), out of sister to high-class miler Noalcoholic: little form. *J. A. Osborne* **–**

GEEZERS COLOURS 4 b.g. Fraam 114 – Konica 57 (Desert King (IRE) 129) [2009 –, a95: p7g 6g 7g 6d⁶ p8g² p7g p7.1g³ Dec 26] good-topped gelding: just fair performer in 2009: trained by K. R. Burke first 4 starts, by A. Jarvis for fifth one: stays easy 1m: acts on polytrack, little solid form on turf: often races prominently: said to have finished lame fourth outing. *J. R. Weymes* **74**

GELERT (IRE) 4 b.c. Acclamation 118 – Game Leader (IRE) 72 (Mukaddamah (USA) 125) [2009 52: p5.1g⁶ 5f 5m 5m 5m 5m 5g⁵ Jul 16] poor maiden: left P. Grayson after third start: raced mostly at 5f: acts on all-weather and heavy going: tried tongue tied, usually blinkered. *A. Berry* **43**

GEMS STAR 3 b.g. Elmaamul (USA) 125 – Slipperose 72 (Persepolis (FR) 127) [2009 48: 6m 6s 7.1g⁴ 5.9d Aug 19] big, good-topped gelding: poor maiden: likely to prove best at 7f+. *J. J. Quinn* **48**

GENARI 6 b.g. Generous (IRE) 139 – Sari 83 (Faustus (USA) 118) [2009 p16.5g Nov 14] big, good-topped gelding: fairly useful handicapper in 2007: not clear run only Flat outing since: effective at 1m to 11f: acts on fibresand, firm and good to soft ground: tried blinkered/tongue tied: fair hurdler. *Gordon Elliott, Ireland* **–**

GENE AUTRY (USA) 2 b. or br.c. (Mar 16) Zavata (USA) 111 – Total Acceptance (USA) (With Approval (CAN)) [2009 7s⁴ 7g⁴ 6m* Aug 10] $5,000Y, resold £20,000Y: good-quartered colt: fourth foal: half-brother to winners in USA by Smoke Glacken and Out of Place: dam ran twice in USA: fairly useful form in maidens: won at Windsor by ¾ length from Bonheurs Art, taking while to get on top: stays 7f: likely to do better still. *R. Hannon* **81 p**

GENERAL ELIOTT (IRE) 4 b.g. Rock of Gibraltar (IRE) 133 – Marlene-D 57 (Selkirk (USA) 129) [2009 114: 8m*dis 8.5g 9m⁵ 9m 8.3v³ p10g p8f³ Dec 19] big, leggy, close-coupled gelding: smart performer: first past post in listed race at Ascot (beat Perfect Stride by nose) in April, but failed dope test and disqualified: respectable effort after only when third to Alexandros in minor event at Nottingham fifth start: best around 1m: acts on heavy and good to firm going: tried blinkered/in cheekpieces. *P. F. I. Cole* **114 d**

GENERAL FEELING (IRE) 8 b.g. General Monash (USA) 107 – Kamadara (IRE) (Kahyasi 130) [2009 70: p10g² p8g* p8g* p10g³ p12g⁶ 8.3m 8.5m⁵ p8g⁴ 9.1g 9.3m p8.6m p10m Dec 16] good-bodied gelding: fair handicapper on all-weather, modest on turf: won twice at Lingfield in January: largely below form after, leaving S. Mason after sixth start, D. Nicholls after tenth: stays 1¼m: acts on polytrack, firm and soft going: has worn blinkers/tongue tie/cheekpieces: often slowly away. *Ollie Pears* **59 a75**

GENERAL SAM (USA) 3 ch.g. Trippi (USA) 121 – Milagro Blue (USA) (Cure The Blues (USA)) [2009 p7m p7g p10g Jan 30] little form in 3 maidens at Lingfield: sold £800, then gelded. *R. Hannon* –

GENERAL TING (IRE) 4 b.c. Daylami (IRE) 138 – Luana 101 (Shaadi (USA) 126) [2009 86p: p12f 16g 14.1g^4 Oct 16] fair handicapper: let down by attitude in 2009: stays 1¾m: acts on polytrack, good to firm and good to soft going: hangs left: sold 8,000 gns. *Sir Mark Prescott* 77 §

GENERAL TUFTO 4 b.g. Fantastic Light (USA) 134 – Miss Pinkerton 104 (Danehill (USA) 126) [2009 58: f8s^4 f11d^6 f8g^3 p12.2g^3 f12g* f8g* f8g* f8g^2 f8d^4 f11g* f12g^5 f11g^2 10.2m 9.8m^5 8g 10.2f^3 10.1m^3 12d 9.9g* 11.5g 9.9m^5 8.3m^6 10d^5 f8m^6 9.9m^3 9m^2 10.2d^3 10m 10m^3 11m 10.2g 10.2v f8f^3 f11g^3 f8f* f8f f8g Dec 27] sturdy gelding: fair handicapper: won at Southwell in February (3) and March (including 2 apprentice events), Beverley (ladies) in May and Southwell in December: stays 1½m: acts on all-weather, firm and good to soft going: tried in headgear, blinkered nowadays: sometimes hangs left: very tough. *C. Smith* 75

GENERAL ZHUKOV 3 b.g. Largesse 112 – Hickleton Lady (IRE) 64 (Kala Shikari 125) [2009 56: 8d p8g 8.3m 10g* May 26] useful-looking gelding: fair form: won handicap at Leicester in May: stays 1¼m: held up. *J. M. P. Eustace* 73

GENEROSO (USA) 2 b.c. (Feb 11) Gone West (USA) – Kentucky Rose (FR) 110 (Hernando (FR) 127) [2009 6m 7m^6 8.3g Oct 28] soundly beaten in maidens/seller: bred to stay 1m+. *S. C. Williams* –

GENEROUS LAD (IRE) 6 b.g. Generous (IRE) 139 – Tudor Loom (Sallust 134) [2009 75: p13g p12g p12g^2 11.9m 10f^5 11.5g 10.1g^5 12m^3 12m^6 10.1g 10m Sep 12] leggy gelding: modest handicapper nowadays: stays 1½m: acts on polytrack and firm going: tried blinkered, usually in cheekpieces. *A. B. Haynes* 60

GENEROUS STAR 6 ch.g. Generous (IRE) 139 – Elegant Dance 71 (Statoblest 120) [2009 68: p13.3g^3 p16.5g^4 p13.9m^2 15.4g Apr 21] modest maiden handicapper: stayed 16.5f: acted on polytrack: tried in cheekpieces, tongue tie: dead. *J. Pearce* 64

GENEVA GEYSER (GER) 3 b.g. One Cool Cat (USA) 123 – Genevra (IRE) 107 (Danehill (USA) 126) [2009 77p: p7g^5 8g 8.1f^5 10m* 12f^3 10f* 9.9g 10m* 10.3m p12.2g Oct 17] big gelding: fairly useful handicapper: won at Redcar in May and July, and Newbury (awarded race) in August: lost action and pulled up final outing (gelded after): should stay beyond 1¼m: acts on polytrack and firm going: blinkered third start: often looks uncooperative: best when able to dominate. *J. M. P. Eustace* 94

GENKI (IRE) 5 ch.g. Shinko Forest (IRE) – Emma's Star (ITY) (Darshaan 133) [2009 106: 6m^5 6m 6m^2 7m^4 6d* 6m 6s^3 Oct 11] good-topped gelding: smart performer: injured at 4 yrs: won bluesquare.com Stewards' Cup at Goodwood in August by length from Evens And Odds, asserting final 1f: below form in Ayr Gold Cup and listed race at the Curragh after: probably best at 6f: acts on soft and good to firm going: tends to get on toes: usually held up (wasn't at Goodwood). *R. Charlton* 113

GENTLE BEAT (IRE) 2 b.g. (Jan 25) Whipper (USA) 126 – Soft (USA) (Lear Fan (USA) 130) [2009 5f^3 5g 6m^6 5g^3 6f^5 7d 5m 7.1m^4 Sep 14] 26,000F, 25,000Y: close-coupled gelding: second foal: dam unraced sister to smart performer up to 1¼m Comfy: fair maiden: third at Thirsk and Haydock: well below form after: should stay 6f: acts on firm going: in cheekpieces last 2 starts: sold £3,000. *T. D. Easterby* 71

GENTLE GURU 5 b.m. Ishiguru (USA) 114 – Soft Touch (IRE) 78 (Petorius 117) [2009 98: 5.1g 6v 6g 6g^6 6g 5g^6 5g^4 6d^5 p7m p6g p6g* p6g p6f f6d^3 Dec 29] good-topped mare: just fair handicapper nowadays: won at Kempton in November: effective at 5f to 7f: acts on polytrack, heavy and good to firm going: held up. *R. T. Phillips* 79

bluesquare.com Stewards' Cup (Heritage Handicap), Goodwood—visibility is sadly restricted for one of the season's traditionally great spectacles; Genki holds off Evens And Odds (check sleeves), Knot In Wood (partially obscured by winner) and Markab (left)

Blue Square Henry II Stakes, Sandown—Geordieland has the measure of Patkai, though the runner-up would have finished closer but for being hampered

GEOFFDAW 4 b.g. Vettori (IRE) 119 – Talighta (USA) 62 (Barathea (IRE) 127) [2009 84: p6g^{6} p7g p7g^{3} p6g^{5} p6g^{5} 6g 7g^{5} 6d^{6} Aug 7] rather leggy gelding: just modest performer nowadays: stays 7f: acts on all-weather and good to firm going: usually in cheekpieces/visor: temperamental. *P. D. Evans* **63 §**

GEOJIMALI 7 ch.g. Compton Place 125 – Harrken Heights (IRE) (Belmez (USA) 131) [2009 88: 6m 6d Oct 13] heavy-topped gelding: fairly useful handicapper in 2008: in cheekpieces when encouraging ninth at Newcastle, latter 2009 outing: probably best at 6f/7f nowadays: acts on polytrack, firm and soft going: usually gets behind, and best in well-run race. *J. S. Goldie* **68 +**

GEORDIE DANCER (IRE) 7 b.g. Dansili 127 – Awtaar (USA) 67 (Lyphard (USA) 132) [2009 52§: p6g Feb 17] good-bodied gelding: modest performer: well held only outing in 2009: usually in headgear. *A. Berry* **– §**

GEORDIELAND (FR) 8 gr.h. Johann Quatz (FR) 120 – Aerdee (FR) (Highest Honor (FR) 124) [2009 121: 16.4m* 20m^{3} 18m^{3} Sep 11] strong, close-coupled horse: very smart performer: better than ever when winning Henry II Stakes at Sandown in May by 5 lengths from Patkai: disappointing third both subsequent starts, 18½ lengths behind Yeats in Gold Cup at Royal Ascot then 3¼ lengths behind Askar Tau in Doncaster Cup: stays 2½m: acts on any turf going: tried blinkered: has bled: held up: travels strongly, but usually finds little. *J. A. Osborne* **122 §**

GEORGE ADAMSON (IRE) 3 b.g. Where Or When (IRE) 124 – Tactile (Groom Dancer (USA) 128) [2009 7.5m^{5} 10.4v 8g 7.1m^{5} Jun 29] tall gelding: poor maiden: should be suited by 1m. *G. A. Swinbank* **49**

GEORGE BAKER (IRE) 2 b.g. (Apr 13) Camacho 118 – Petite Maxine 70 (Sharpo 132) [2009 5f 5g^{3} 5m 7m 6m^{3} p7f^{5} p6m^{6} p8m Oct 12] £31,000Y: unfurnished gelding: half-brother to several winners, including 5f (including at 2 yrs)/6f winner Pipadash (by Pips Pride) and 2005 2-y-o 7f winner Under My Thumb (by Desert Style), both fairly useful: dam maiden (stayed 7f): fairly useful maiden, well below best after third outing: should stay at least 6f: acts on good to firm going: in cheekpieces last 3 starts: ridden second to fourth outings by George Baker. *George Baker* **81 d**

GEORGE BENJAMIN 2 b.g. (Mar 15) Trade Fair 124 – Unchain My Heart 70 (Pursuit of Love 124) [2009 5d^{2} 6m^{3} 6g^{3} 7d^{2} 7.2m^{2} 6g^{2} Oct 9] £4,000Y: compact gelding: third foal: half-brother to 6f winner Calloff The Search (by Piccolo): dam 7f/1m winner: fair maiden: stays 7f: acts on good to firm and good to soft going. *D. Nicholls* **75**

GEORGEBERNARDSHAW (IRE) 4 b.c. Danehill Dancer (IRE) 117 – Khamseh 85 (Thatching 131) [2009 113: 7s 5d 6v 7m³ 6.3g 7s² 6s³ 8s³ 10.4m⁴ Aug 18] big, lengthy, angular colt: smart performer: creditable efforts in 2009 only when 1½ lengths third to Duff in Ballycorus Stakes at Leopardstown and 1¼ lengths second to Three Rocks in Minstrel Stakes at the Curragh fourth/sixth starts: effective at 6f to easy 1m: acts on heavy and good to firm going: tends to carry head high: unreliable. *A. P. O'Brien, Ireland* **113 §**

GEORGE REX (USA) 3 b. or br.g. Johannesburg (USA) 127 – Royal Linkage (USA) (Linkage (USA)) [2009 70: 8m 7g Jun 16] leggy gelding: fair maiden at 2 yrs: well held in 2009: sold 800 gns. *B. J. Meehan* **–**

GEORGE THE BEST (IRE) 8 b.g. Imperial Ballet (IRE) 110 – En Retard (IRE) 97 (Petardia 113) [2009 –§: f6g 5m 5s Aug 24] workmanlike gelding: no form since 2007: tried visored: ungenuine. *Micky Hammond* **– §**

GEORGE THISBY 3 b.g. Royal Applause 124 – Warning Belle (Warning 136) [2009 7m² 7.1m⁴ 6m³ 6f² f6g* 6m² 7m⁶ 6.1d Oct 15] 20,000Y: lengthy gelding: seventh foal: half-brother to several winners, including useful 2001 2-y-o 7f winner Desert Warning (by Mark of Esteem) and fairly useful 7f winner Siren Sound (by Singspiel): dam unraced half-sister to high-class 1¼m performer Stagecraft: fairly useful performer: won maiden at Southwell in July: ran well in handicaps at Newbury next 2 starts: stays 7f: acts on fibresand and firm ground. *B. R. Millman* **80**

GEORGIE BEE 3 b.f. Ishiguru (USA) 114 – Light of Aragon 41 (Aragon 118) [2009 52: 6m 7.5m⁶ p8.6g⁴ 8m⁴ 8m³ 9.9g⁴ 9.9m 8m f8g Nov 17] close-coupled filly: modest maiden: left D. Carroll after third outing: probably stays 1¼m: acts on good to firm ground: tried blinkered. *T. D. Walford* **56**

GEORGINA MACRAE 3 b.f. Bahamian Bounty 116 – Sadly Sober (IRE) 70 (Roi Danzig (USA)) [2009 p7g p7g p7g Mar 18] 25,000Y: half-sister to 2 winners, including useful 7f/1m winner Ettrick Water (by Selkirk): dam, maiden (stayed 1¼m), half-sister to smart performer up to 1½m Overbury: outpaced in maidens at Lingfield. *A. M. Balding* **46**

GERTMEGALUSH (IRE) 2 b.g. (Apr 29) One Cool Cat (USA) 123 – Aiming Upwards (Blushing Flame (USA) 109) [2009 5m⁴ 5m* 5m⁴ 6d 5m* 5g 5m 5m² 6m³ 6g Oct 9] leggy gelding: fifth foal: half-brother to 3 winners, including 3-y-o Do The Strand: dam unraced out of half-sister to dam of Derby winner Oath: fairly useful performer: claimed from Tom Dascombe £6,000 on debut: won seller at Thirsk in May and nursery at York in July: will prove best at 5f/6f: acts on good to firm ground: blinkered last 3 outings: sometimes slowly away: quirky and one to treat with caution. *J. D. Bethell* **86 §**

GERTRUDE BELL 2 ch.f. (Mar 8) Sinndar (IRE) 134 – Sugar Mill (FR) (Polar Falcon (USA) 126) [2009 8m³ p8g³ 8g² Oct 23] third foal: dam useful French 1¼m winner: fairly useful form when placed in maidens, ½-length second of 21 to Modeyra at Doncaster: will be well suited by 1¼m+. *J. H. M. Gosden* **87**

GESSABELLE 2 b.f. (May 5) Largesse 112 – Palmstead Belle (IRE) 79 (Wolfhound (USA) 126) [2009 5g 6g 6m f5g 6.1s Oct 7] sister to 3 winners, including 5-y-o Lazy Darren and 6-y-o Bel Cantor: dam 2-y-o 5f winner: no form in varied company: usually tongue tied: has looked awkward. *P. S. McEntee* **–**

GET A GRIP (IRE) 2 b.c. (Mar 15) Royal Applause 124 – Landela 64 (Alhaarth (IRE) 126) [2009 7g² p8g* Sep 21] €35,000Y, 34,000 2-y-o: angular colt: first foal: dam twice-raced half-sister to smart/very smart French performers up to 1½m Kalabar and Zambezi Sun: better effort in maidens when winning at Kempton by 2½ lengths from Dahaam, travelling strongly: will stay beyond 1m: sent to USA: likely to improve further. *J. A. R. Toller* **88 p**

GETAWAY (GER) 6 b.h. Monsun (GER) 124 – Guernica (Unfuwain (USA) 131) [2009 127: 12g² 12d* 12g² 12d* 12g Oct 4] **127**

Leading German owner-breeder Baron Georg von Ullmann has enjoyed considerable success in recent seasons with horses he has transferred from Germany to be trained by Andre Fabre. His 2004 Deutsches Derby winner Shirocco made the move to France as a four-year-old, winning the Breeders' Cup Turf at the end of that season and counting the Coronation Cup among his successes at five. Even more successful was Manduro, who developed into a top-class five-year-old in 2007 when unbeaten in five pattern races, including the Prince of Wales's Stakes and Prix Jacques le Marois, and seemed well on course for the Arc until sustaining an injury when winning his trial, the Prix Foy. As a result, the same owner's Getaway, who had been with Fabre since the beginning of his racing career as a

Grosser Mercedes-Benz Preis von Baden, Baden-Baden—Getaway returns to his best to win the most important race for three-year-olds and upwards in Germany; he is clear of Eastern Anthem (noseband), Youmzain (right) and Deutches Derby winner Wiener Walzer

three-year-old and had progressed into a very smart stayer, was supplemented for the Arc and emerged with plenty of credit on his first try in top middle-distance company, staying on to be beaten just over a length and a half into fourth behind Dylan Thomas.

That effort promised plenty for Getaway's five-year-old season and, when he was an impressive winner of the Jockey Club Stakes at Newmarket on his reappearance the following spring, it looked only a matter of time before he became his owner's third son of Monsun in as many seasons to make his mark at Group 1 level. In the event, his only subsequent win that year came in another Group 2, the Grand Prix de Deauville, and he failed even to make the frame in four attempts in Group 1 company, including when seeming not to handle the track at Epsom as a short-priced favourite for the Coronation Cup and when finishing a never-nearer eighth to Zarkava in a second attempt at the Arc. With his limitations seemingly exposed against the best mile and a half horses, Getaway was expected to be returned to staying company in 2009, even though he had been a disappointing favourite put back up in trip in the Prix Royal-Oak on his final outing.

However, it was over a mile and a half that Getaway finally won a Group 1, though not in France for Andre Fabre, but back in his homeland where he became Germany's highest-rated horse of the year in the hands of the von Ullmann family's private trainer Jens Hirschberger. Getaway progressed with each of his first four starts in Germany, ultimately coming right back to the sort of high-class form he had shown when winning the Jockey Club Stakes. He made his reappearance at Hamburg at the end of June in the Hansa-Preis in which he went down by two lengths to a race-fit and improving four-year-old Flamingo Fantasy. Three weeks later in the Group 1 Deutschland-Preis at Dusseldorf, on slightly better terms, Getaway turned the tables on Flamingo Fantasy, beating him by three quarters of a length after finding a gap on the rail approaching the final furlong. The previous year's Deutsches Derby winner Kamsin finished fourth behind Getaway at both Hamburg and Dusseldorf but Getaway found the latest winner of that race, his own stable-companion Wiener Walzer, a much tougher rival in the Rheinland-Pokal at Cologne. Filling the first two places throughout, Getaway and Wiener Walzer engaged in a duel for most of the straight, with Getaway looking like proving the stronger until the three-year-old rallied to win by a short head.

Despite his reverse at Cologne, Getaway started favourite when meeting Wiener Walzer again in Germany's top race, the Grosser Mercedes-Benz Preis von Baden at Baden-Baden in September. Godolphin's Eastern Anthem, third behind the stablemates at Cologne, renewed rivalry, along with Youmzain who had finished in front of Getaway in each of the two previous Arcs. The previous year's winner Kamsin was there again, the field of six completed by outsider Adelar. Getaway came right back to his best with a stylish win, travelling well in third, as Wiener

Walzer took them along in single file for a long way, before quickening decisively over a furlong out after the field had bunched when coming wide into the straight. Getaway passed the post three lengths clear of Eastern Anthem, with Youmzain another half length back in third, ahead of a disappointing Wiener Walzer, Kamsin and Adelar.

Getaway went into his third Arc at the top of his form but he failed to make much of an impact at Longchamp, though he might have finished in about the same position as the year before with a better run. Reunited with Stephane Pasquier for the first time since the previous season's Coronation Cup (Olivier Peslier had ridden him in his first two Arcs), Getaway was in mid-division when his jockey unsuccessfully went for a gap on the rails up Sea The Stars's inner shortly after the home turn. He was staying on again when meeting further trouble in the final furlong, Pasquier eventually easing him to pass the post thirteenth of the nineteen runners.

Getaway (GER) (b.h. 2003)	Monsun (GER) (br 1990)	Konigsstuhl (br 1976)	Dschingis Khan
			Konigskronung
		Mosella (b 1985)	Surumu
			Monasia
	Guernica (b 1994)	Unfuwain (b 1985)	Northern Dancer
			Height of Fashion
		Greenvera (ch 1989)	Riverman
			Greenway

Getaway's pedigree has been discussed in the last two editions of *Racehorses*. To summarise, he is out of a half-sister to the dual Gold Cup winner Royal Rebel and comes from the same family, established by the Wertheimers in France, as Goldikova. Closer up, Getaway's smart sister Guadalupe, who won the Oaks d'Italia and was second in the Yorkshire Oaks, is now the dam of the four-year-old filly Guantana, who showed smart form for Getaway's connections over eleven furlongs in the latest season, winning two listed races and beaten a nose in a Group 3 at Bremen. Although stoutly bred and campaigned as a stayer early on, Getaway's best form is at a mile and a half and, while he was often ridden from behind in France, he travelled well closer to the pace in his latter races in Germany. Raced only on good or good to soft ground in the last couple of seasons, he has proven effective on good to firm and also won on soft going earlier in his career. A big, angular, heavy-topped horse, Getaway has proven typical of his sire in reaching his peak as an older horse. He looks set to stay in training as a seven-year-old. *J. Hirschberger, Germany*

GETCARTER 3 b.c. Fasliyev (USA) 120 – Pourquoi Pas (IRE) 109 (Nordico (USA)) **88**
[2009 69: 8.3m^3 8m^5 7m^6 7g* 6m* 6g 6m^3 p6g* p7.1g Nov 12] tall, leggy colt: fairly useful handicapper: won at Salisbury (apprentices) and Newbury within 3 days in August, and Kempton in September: best at 6f/7f: acts on polytrack and good to firm ground. *R. Hannon*

GHAAYER 3 b.g. Nayef (USA) 129 – Valthea (FR) (Antheus (USA) 122) [2009 –: 8s **?**
a7.5s a8.5g^2 Dec 27] good-topped gelding: sold from M. Tregoning 5,500 gns after reappearance: first form in maidens when second at Dortmund final start: stays 8.5f: acts on sand. *C. von der Recke, Germany*

GHAILL FORCE 7 b.g. Piccolo 121 – Coir 'a' Ghaill 38 (Jalmood (USA) 126) [2009 **–**
–: 10m May 30] little form since 2007: tried in headgear/tongue tie. *P. Butler*

GHANAATI (USA) 3 b.f. Giant's Causeway (USA) 132 – Sarayir (USA) 104 (Mr **122**
Prospector (USA)) [2009 93p: 8f* 8f* 8g^3 8m^2 Oct 3]

When Sheikh Mohammed changed the name of the two-year-old Yaazer to Dubai Millennium, in the belief that the horse might be good enough to win the 2000 Dubai World Cup, there were plenty who thought he was tempting providence. But Dubai Millennium lived up to all the exalted expectations, duly running away with the Dubai World Cup as a four-year-old, in the process establishing himself as an early prime candidate for the title 'horse of the decade'. Sea The Stars came along in the last year of the first decade of the new millennium to earn a share of that title, in a year that produced another notable example of Maktoum optimism paying off after an eleventh-hour decision over a name change. Sheikh Hamdan

stanjames.com 1000 Guineas Stakes, Newmarket—Ghanaati, with just two runs in all-weather maidens under her belt, makes a winning turf debut; Cuis Ghaire, Super Sleuth (blaze), Heart Shaped (partially obscured by runner-up), Rainbow View (right) and Penny's Gift (left) follow her home

had reportedly applied in the States for the name Algaawia ('beauty') for the 2008 two-year-old filly out of Sarayir—'a mare he really treasures'—but particularly high hopes must have been held for her after she had wintered in Dubai before her two-year-old season. The name Ghanaati, meaning 'my love' in Arabic, was registered in the States in April and with Weatherbys in late-May. According to Sheikh Hamdan's jockey Richard Hills, son of the trainer, 'it was the first time Sheikh Hamdan had changed a horse's name, so he'd clearly seen something he liked.' The name Algaawia was later given to a filly out of Nafisah who ran only once in Ireland.

While the pre-season signals before her three-year-old campaign from Weatherdown House couldn't have been stronger—'she's wintered well and has an outstanding chance' was the message from the trainer—to most outside her stable Ghanaati was an unknown quantity in the stanjames.com One Thousand Guineas. For a start, she had never run on turf, her two-year-old campaign comprising two ordinary maidens on the polytrack at Kempton, the second of which—in late-October —she won impressively by six lengths, showing fairly useful form. Ghanaati was somewhat reluctant to go into the stalls that day and had to pass a stalls test afterwards. She looked sure to improve at three but her stable had had a relatively quiet year in 2008, without a single pattern winner, and few gave Ghanaati serious consideration for the classics. A gallop by her before racing on the first day of the Craven meeting attracted little attention, with media interest focussed on One Thousand Guineas winter favourite Rainbow View and Cheveley Park winner Serious Attitude also exercising on the Newmarket course in separate gallops the same morning. When Fantasia, in the same ownership as Rainbow View, ran away with the Nell Gwyn that afternoon it was taken as a further boost for Rainbow View's chances, especially as it soon became apparent that Fantasia would be going instead for the Poule d'Essai des Pouliches. Barry Hills, who won the 1978 One Thousand Guineas with Enstone Spark, has been fighting throat cancer but his stable had a good start to the latest season, making the headlines when sending out the 3,000th winner of the trainer's career in April and when recording his 300th success at Newmarket in the course of a treble on Nell Gwyn day.

Ghanaati was sent off at 20/1 on Guineas day in a market dominated by Rainbow View who started at 11/8-on—the first odds-on favourite since Bosra Sham in 1996—with 8/1-shot Serious Attitude and leading Irish-trained challenger 12/1-shot Cuis Ghaire the only others at shorter than 14/1 (six of the fourteen runners started at odds between 33/1 and 100/1). Ghanaati and Cuis Ghaire were among those who raced prominently from the start in a One Thousand Guineas run on firm going and with a strong wind behind the runners. Ghanaati got on top of Cuis Ghaire two furlongs out and was in control throughout the final furlong, showing signs of her inexperience when edging left but beating Cuis Ghaire by a length and a half, with a further length and a quarter back to the fast-finishing Fred Darling runner-up Super Sleuth, who did best of those who had run in the spring trials. The Ballydoyle challenger Heart Shaped, Rainbow View, who was niggled along in mid-division at halfway, and Penny's Gift finished just behind Super

Sleuth, with Serious Attitude only seventh. The Timeform computer timefigure for Ghanaati, equivalent to a timerating of 116, backed up the assessment of the form as well up to standard for the race, though, at the time, the absence of Fantasia and the below-par effort of Rainbow View (racing for the first time on firm going) counted against the likelihood of its proving conclusive as a guide to the respective merits of the classic fillies at a mile.

The second and third in the One Thousand Guineas were both well beaten on heavy going behind Again in the Irish One Thousand Guineas, in which the change in ground probably accounted for the return to form of Fred Darling winner Lahaleeb who improved from tenth at Newmarket to second at the Curragh. Rainbow View went on from Newmarket to Epsom, where she finished fourth to Sariska in the Oaks. Ghanaati and Heart Shaped didn't appear between the Guineas and the Coronation Stakes, in which they were joined, in a strong field, by Rainbow View, Lahaleeb and the winners of the Irish and French One Thousand Guineas, Again and Elusive Wave, the latter joined by a second French-trained challenger, the Prix de Sandringham runner-up Reggane, while the Irish challenge also included the Aga Khan's Baliyana who had won the One Thousand Guineas Trial at Leopardstown. Ghanaati started 2/1 favourite, with Elusive Wave at 4/1, Rainbow View at 13/2, Baliyana 15/2, Again 8/1, Reggane 9/1, Heart Shaped 12/1 and Lahaleeb 16/1. One of the rank outsiders Chintz, a stable-companion of Again, ensured a strong gallop until Ghanaati strode to the front on the bridle two furlongs out and quickly went clear to win by two lengths and two and a quarter from Reggane and Rainbow View, both of whom came from well back, the latter short of room and only getting a clear run approaching the final furlong. Elusive Wave, Lahaleeb and Heart Shaped completed the first six, with an eleven-length gap back to seventh-placed Again, whose flop was put down to the firm going.

Ghanaati's victory in the Coronation Stakes—on the day her trainer was discharged from hospital—was one of the performances of the Royal meeting and it established her as the top three-year-old filly in Europe over the trip, as she followed in the footsteps of Russian Rhythm and Attraction who landed the One Thousand Guineas/Coronation Stakes double in 2003 and 2004 (Attraction also won the Irish Guineas in between while Russian Rhythm went on to complete her own treble in fillies' races when winning the Nassau at Goodwood). The Coronation Stakes was overdue for elevation to Group 1 long before it was finally granted that status in 1988, but before the successes of Russian Rhythm, Attraction and Ghanaati no winner of the One Thousand Guineas had actually gone on to win the Coronation since One In A Million was awarded the race on the disqualification of first-past-the-post (and winner on merit) Buz Kashi in 1979, in the days when Group 1 winners carried a penalty and when stewards had no option but to relegate winners whose riders were found guilty of causing interference by careless riding. The previous Hills-trained One Thousand Guineas winner Enstone Spark, incidentally, fell in the 1978 Coronation, while neither of the stable's Irish One Thousand Guineas winners, Nicer nor Hula Angel, distinguished themselves in the Coronation, the 2005 One Thousand Guineas runner-up Maids Causeway the only previous Coronation winner for Hills.

Ghanaati's Goodwood target was the Sussex Stakes, rather than the Nassau Stakes, and she started 2/1 second favourite behind Rip Van Winkle in a vintage

Coronation Stakes, Royal Ascot—in a cracking renewal, Ghanaati has burst clear of Reggane, Rainbow View (light colours), Elusive Wave (rail), Lahaleeb (right) and Heart Shaped

edition. Rip Van Winkle recorded the best performance in the Sussex for thirty years, winning from the Queen Anne winner Paco Boy who convincingly beat the rest. Ghanaati travelled strongly for a long way before lugging right towards the rail when it came to the crunch, eventually managing third, six and a half lengths behind the winner. She returned home sore behind after the Sussex and her only other racecourse appearance before retirement came over two months later in the Sun Chariot Stakes at Newmarket, by which time she had gone in her coat and had been clipped. Ghanaati still ran fairly well, finishing second to the French four-year-old Sahpresa, but she was almost certainly past her best, keeping on gamely but unable to repel the winner inside the final furlong after making hard work of passing another four-year-old Spacious to take the lead.

The good-topped Ghanaati is an imposing filly with plenty of size about her and will make a valuable addition to her owner's broodmare band. She visits Dansili in 2010. In common with the rest of the Maktoum family's studs, Shadwell has not used any of the Coolmore or Ashford Stud stallions since relations turned particularly frosty in the middle of the decade. Ghanaati's dam Sarayir visited Giant's Causeway at Ashford in 2005—the year classic winners Footstepsinthe-sand and Shamardal came from his first crop—just before the final parting of the ways, the mating resulting in Ghanaati. Shamardal and the aforementioned Maids Causeway were both out of mares by sons of Mr Prospector, and Ghanaati is out of a mare by Mr Prospector himself, in common with another of Giant's Causeway's best offspring, the high-class American miler Aragorn. Ghanaati's dam Sarayir was a useful racemare, successful in the listed Oh So Sharp Stakes at Newmarket at two and in the Virginia Stakes, a listed rated stakes over a mile and a quarter at

Mr Hamdan Al Maktoum's "Ghanaati"

Newcastle at three, and she was very well bred, closely related to Nayef and a half-sister to Nashwan and Unfuwain. Among the other siblings of Sarayir were two winning sisters Bashayer, the grandam of the 2007 Breeders' Cup Filly & Mare Turf winner Lahudood, and Wijdan, the dam of Group 2 winners in the States and in Italy respectively, Makderah and Oriental Fashion.

Ghanaati's grandam Height of Fashion, originally owned and bred by the Queen, was sold to Sheikh Hamdan as a three-year-old for a sum understood to be over £1m. She had won the Acomb, the May Hill and the Fillies' Mile at two and continued her unbeaten run the next year in the Lupe Stakes and the Princess of Wales's Stakes before the change of ownership. Height of Fashion was then well beaten in both the King George and the Yorkshire Oaks, but she more than made amends at stud, becoming one of the most successful mares of the modern era, breeding eight winners, all of them rated at least 100. Height of Fashion's second foal Unfuwain was the best middle-distance three-year-old of his generation; her third Nashwan won the Two Thousand Guineas, Derby, Eclipse and King George; and her twelfth and final foal Nayef won the Champion Stakes, Dubai Sheema Classic, Juddmonte International and Prince of Wales's Stakes. Unfuwain, Nashwan and Nayef all went on to sire Group 1 winners themselves, while Height of Fashion's daughters are still making a valuable contribution to the continuing success of Shadwell. Sarayir's contribution to that success had, at one time, seemed somewhat disappointing, given the excellent chances she had been given (the first four stallions she visited were Sadler's Wells, A P Indy, Storm Cat and Danzig). Three of her first five foals were winners, though none of them had been better than fairly useful. All that changed in the latest season, though, when Sarayir was represented not only by Ghanaati, but also by Mawatheeq (the result of a second visit to Danzig) whose career took off as a four-year-old, after he had been lightly raced, and yielded an impressive win in the Cumberland Lodge Stakes at Ascot and a good second in the Champion Stakes at Newmarket, with the promise of even better things at five if he maintains his progress.

Ghanaati, by the way, is by no means the first from her female line to distinguish herself in the One Thousand Guineas. Her great grandam Highclere carried the royal colours to victory in 1974 (before going on to win the Prix de Diane), while her fifth dam Hypericum won the race in 1946 and her sixth dam Feola was second in 1936. Sarayir herself contested the 1997 Guineas, finishing ninth to Sleepytime. Another One Thousand Guineas winner, Pebbles in 1984, was from the same family, her fourth dam Above Board a half-sister to Hypericum (Sheikh Hamdan's 1990 One Thousand Guineas, Oaks and Irish Derby winner Salsabil is a descendant of another branch of the family from a half-sister to Feola).

Ghanaati (USA) (b.f. 2006)	Giant's Causeway (USA) (ch 1997)	Storm Cat (b or br 1983)	Storm Bird
			Terlingua
		Mariah's Storm (b 1991)	Rahy
			Immense
	Sarayir (USA) (b 1994)	Mr Prospector (b 1970)	Raise A Native
			Gold Digger
		Height of Fashion (b 1979)	Bustino
			Highclere

Ghanaati was never raced beyond a mile, though she gave the impression she would have got a mile and a quarter given the opportunity (her trainer said in a pre-season interview that she would 'get a mile and a quarter standing on her head and we may think of the Oaks further down the line'). Ghanaati acted on firm ground and never encountered going softer than good on turf. Her victory on polytrack was an illustration of how far racing on Britain's all-weather tracks has progressed since it was first introduced to provide cover for winter jumps fixtures lost to the weather. The first all-weather fixture took place on October 30th 1989 at Lingfield which staged twelve races, including five divisions of a claimer and three divisions of a maiden for three-year-olds and older horses (the third division of the maiden was won by a 7/1-shot ridden by Richard Hills, whose twin brother Michael also rode a winner on the card). The all-weather's image of staging only low-quality racing has taken time to shake off but Ghanaati is now the third classic winner in Britain—following St Leger winners Lucarno and Conduit—to gain her first victory in a maiden on an artificial surface. *B. W. Hills*

GHANEEMA (USA) 3 b.f. Forestry (USA) 121 – Unify (USA) (Farma Way (USA)) [2009 8.1g² Aug 13] $500,000Y: tall filly: seventh foal: closely related to fairly useful 7.5f winner Arcadius (by Giant's Causeway) and half-sister to winner in USA by Danzig: dam, US 1m winner, half-sister to smart performers Bernstein (at 6f/7f) and Della Francesca (up to 1½m): 4/1, promising ½-length second to Mezenah in maiden at Sandown, not given hard time but responding well, only outing: visits Dubawi. *M. P. Tregoning* **82**

GHAZWAH 2 b.f. (Jan 21) Shamardal (USA) 129 – Bahja (USA) 76 (Seeking The Gold (USA)) [2009 6m⁴ 7d² p7g³ 6g Oct 30] well-made, attractive filly: first foal: dam twice-raced daughter of Poule d'Essai des Pouliches winner Valentine Waltz: fair maiden: placed at Goodwood and Kempton: should stay 1m. *J. H. M. Gosden* **68**

GHEED (IRE) 4 b.f. Cape Cross (IRE) 129 – Hareer 81 (Anabaa (USA) 130) [2009 57: p12.2g p8f Dec 20] well-made filly: lightly-raced maiden: little impact in 2009: tongue tied 2 of 3 starts. *K. A. Morgan* **47**

GHIMAAR 4 b.g. Dubai Destination (USA) 127 – Charlecote (IRE) (Caerleon (USA) 132) [2009 105: 12g 10s⁵ 12m 16s* 14s⁴ 12v⁴ 12d⁴ Sep 16] leggy gelding: smart performer: won amateur handicap at Galway in July under 12-0 by 2½ lengths from Evening Rushour: respectable efforts at best otherwise: below form in Duke of Edinburgh Stakes at Royal Ascot third outing: stays 2m: acts on any turf going (some promise on polytrack): tried blinkered, including on last 2 starts: usually held up: sold 60,000 gns. *D. K. Weld, Ireland* **110**

GHOST DANCER 5 ch.g. Danehill Dancer (IRE) 117 – Reservation (IRE) 78 (Common Grounds 118) [2009 82: p7.1g 7.1g 7m 6.1g³ 6.1g 5m⁶ 6d 5.7g⁴ 6m² 6g⁴ 6g* 6m² 6m² 6.1s⁶ p6g³ p6g Nov 1] good-topped gelding: fair handicapper: won at Warwick in August: has won over 1m, races mainly at 6f: acts on polytrack, firm and good to soft going: in cheekpieces nowadays. *J. M. Bradley* **79**

GHOST (IRE) 2 b.g. (Feb 11) Invincible Spirit (IRE) 121 – Alexander Phantom (IRE) (Soviet Star (USA) 128) [2009 6m⁴ 6g² 6g³ 6m⁵ Sep 24] 52,000Y: useful-looking gelding: first foal: dam, unraced, out of half-sister to dam of Grand Criterium/Dante Stakes winner Tenby: easily best effort in maidens when 1¼ lengths second to Mr David at Newmarket: bred to stay beyond 6f, though has looked headstrong: temperamental and not one to trust (gelded after final start). *B. W. Hills* **84 §**

GHOSTWING 2 gr.g. (Mar 19) Kheleyf (USA) 116 – Someone's Angel (USA) (Runaway Groom (CAN)) [2009 5g³ 6m* 6m⁵ 6g⁵ 6m 6.5m 6g Oct 10] £75,000Y: sturdy gelding: second foal: dam, lightly-raced maiden, out of half-sister to very smart sprinter Nabeel Dancer: fairly useful performer: left Mrs A. Duffield after debut: won maiden at Ayr in June: looked awkward when creditable fifth in July Stakes at Newmarket and Richmond Stakes at Goodwood: well below form after: will be suited by 7f: tried in cheekpieces: ungenuine: sold 12,000 gns, then gelded. *R. A. Fahey* **92 §**

GHUFA (IRE) 5 b.g. Sakhee (USA) 136 – Hawriyah (USA) 103 (Dayjur (USA) 137) [2009 69: p9.5g* f12g³ p10g³ p8g⁴ f11g² 12g 10m⁶ 10.2g p12.2g* p12m⁵ p12g³ p13.9g³ p12.2g* p9.5g* p12g² Dec 31] good-bodied gelding: fair performer, better on all-weather: won apprentice handicap in February and sellers/claimer in September and December (2), all at Wolverhampton: stays 1½m: acts on all-weather, soft and good to firm going: in cheekpieces once. *George Baker* **65 a75**

GIANT SEQUOIA (USA) 5 ch.g. Giant's Causeway (USA) 132 – Beware of The Cat (USA) (Caveat (USA)) [2009 10.2g 11.5g f12g⁶ 12.1v p11m* p12g* p12m³ p10g p10m* Dec 10] fairly useful performer: left K. J. Burke after second start, A. Chamberlain after fourth: improved after, winning minor event at Kempton in September and handicaps at Lingfield in October and Kempton in December: stays 1½m: acts on polytrack: tongue tied nowadays. *Jane Chapple-Hyam* **83**

GIANTS PLAY (USA) 2 b.f. (Jan 17) Giant's Causeway (USA) 132 – Playful Act (IRE) 113 (Sadler's Wells (USA) 132) [2009 p7g² 8g⁴ Oct 23] $850,000Y: sturdy filly: first foal: dam, Fillies' Mile and Lancashire Oaks winner, sister to very smart performer up to 1¾m Percussionist: still green, better effort in maidens when 3 lengths fourth of 21 to Modeyra at Doncaster, gaining gradually: will be suited by 1m+: should improve again. *Sir Michael Stoute* **80 p**

GIANT STRIDES 3 b.f. Xaar 132 – Brandish (Warning 136) [2009 62: p6g⁴ p9.2g⁵ Jan 13] tall filly: modest maiden: should be suited by 1m+: raced only on all-weather. *P. D. Evans* **60**

GIBB RIVER (IRE) 3 ch.g. Mr Greeley (USA) 122 – Laurentine (USA) (Private Account (USA)) [2009 76p: 11s⁶ 12m² 12.1g² 16f 12d² 14s² 14m⁵ Aug 21] big, good-topped gelding: fairly useful maiden: seems to stay 2m: acts on firm and soft going: blinkered penultimate start. *P. W. Chapple-Hyam* **85**

GIBRALTAR BLUE (IRE) 2 ch.f. (Apr 7) Rock of Gibraltar (IRE) 133 – Holly Blue 107 (Bluebird (USA) 125) [2009 6s* 6g 7m^4 Oct 17] €75,000Y: useful-looking filly: sixth foal: half-sister to winners abroad by Royal Applause and Fantastic Light: dam 1m winner: won maiden at Fairyhouse in August by neck from Dynasty, coming from well back: better form in sales race at the Curragh and Rockfel Stakes at Newmarket (7 lengths fourth to Music Show, delayed in run and still last 1½f out): will stay 1m: slowly away all starts: already useful, and will improve further. *T. Stack, Ireland* **98 p**

GIBRALTAR LASS (USA) 2 ch.f. (Jan 7) Concerto (USA) 114 – Mango Lassie (USA) (Montreal Red (USA) 117) [2009 p6g p5.1m^6 Nov 28] sturdy filly: first foal: dam US 5.5f (including at 2 yrs)/6f winner: poor form in maidens. *H. J. Collingridge* **49**

GIBSON SQUARE (USA) 3 b.g. Gilded Time (USA) – Beyond The Fence (USA) (Grand Slam (USA) 120) [2009 –: p8.6g^6 12.1g 11.5m 10f Jun 30] strong gelding: little form: tried visored/tongue tied. *S. C. Williams* **–**

GIDDYWELL 5 b.m. Ishiguru (USA) 114 – Understudy 60 (In The Wings 128) [2009 61: p9.5g* p9.5g^3 p8.6m^3 p9.5g p8.6g p9.5g Apr 24] modest handicapper: won at Wolverhampton in January: stays 1½m, effective at shorter: acts on all-weather and any turf going: wears cheekpieces. *R. Hollinshead* **61**

GIFTED APAKAY (USA) 2 ch.f. (Apr 1) Leroidesanimaux (BRZ) 127 – Sentimental Gift (USA) (Green Dancer (USA) 132) [2009 p8f^3 p7g p8m* Dec 4] $75,000Y, 20,000 2-y-o: half-sister to several winners in North/South America, including Argentinian Grade 1 1¼m winner Alexine (by Runaway Groom): dam unraced: easily best effort in maidens when winning at Lingfield gamely by neck from Fashion Insider: will stay 1¼m. *E. A. L. Dunlop* **77**

GIFTED HEIR (IRE) 5 b.g. Princely Heir (IRE) 111 – Inzar Lady (IRE) (Inzar (USA) 112) [2009 66d: p8.6g 8g^5 10.1g 8d 8f^2 8m^2 10.1g^6 p9.5g^3 p8.6g* p8g p10g^3 p8.6g p8.6m p9.5g Dec 11] small gelding: fair handicapper: won at Wolverhampton (apprentices) in October: best at 1m/1¼m: acts on polytrack and firm going: tried in headgear: inconsistent. *A. Bailey* **64**

GIFTED LEADER (USA) 4 b.g. Diesis 133 – Zaghruta (USA) (Gone West (USA)) [2009 72: 10m^5 12m 14g* 12g^2 12g 12m 14.6g Oct 23] well-made gelding: fairly useful handicapper: won at Haydock in May: good ¾-length second to Mull of Dubai in ladies race at York next time: below form after: stays 1¾m: unraced on extremes of ground. *Ian Williams* **92**

GIFT HORSE 9 ch.g. Cadeaux Genereux 131 – Careful Dancer (Gorytus (USA) 132) [2009 93: 6m 6f 6d^2 6g* 5.1g 7g 5.7m 6d 7g^4 7.2s 7f^4 6.1m Sep 10] lengthy, angular gelding: fairly useful performer nowadays: won claimer at Ayr (left D. Nicholls £8,000) in May: has won at 1m, best at shorter: acts on polytrack and any turf going: usually wears visor/cheekpieces: tried tongue tied: held up. *P. D. Evans* **81**

GIFT OF LOVE (IRE) 2 b.f. (Apr 8) Azamour (IRE) 130 – Spot Prize (USA) 108 (Seattle Dancer (USA) 119) [2009 7d Jul 17] good-topped filly: half-sister to several winners, including smart 1½m to 15f winner Gold Medallist (by Zilzal) and useful 7f (at 2 yrs) and 1¼m winner Premier Prize (by Selkirk): dam, 2-y-o 5f winner, fourth in Oaks: 20/1 and very green, down the field in maiden at Newmarket: bred to be suited by 1¼m+. *D. R. C. Elsworth* **–**

GIGANTICUS (USA) 6 ch.g. Giant's Causeway (USA) 132 – Shy Princess (USA) 117 (Irish River (FR) 131) [2009 106: p7g^5 7m 7m 7m^4 7f* 7m 7m 7m^5 7m Oct 16] rangy gelding: useful handicapper: won 29-runner Buckingham Palace Stakes at Royal Ascot in June by 1¾ lengths from Al Muheer: creditable effort otherwise only when fifth of 28 to Advanced in valuable event at same track penultimate start: best at 7f: acts on firm going: sold 40,000 gns, sent to USA. *B. W. Hills* **106**

GILDED AGE 3 b.g. Cape Cross (IRE) 129 – Sweet Folly (IRE) 109 (Singspiel (IRE) 133) [2009 p10g^5 9m^2 12.4g* 12s p12g^4 10m^5 10.2g^2 12d^5 11m^4 Sep 23] tall gelding: has scope: second foal: closely related to fairly useful 7f winner Frivolous (by Green Desert): dam, French 10.5f winner, closely related to Earl of Sefton Stakes winner Apprehension and half-sister to smart performer up to 1m Kissing Cousin: fairly useful performer: landed odds in maiden at Newcastle in April: good second in handicap at Nottingham seventh start (left M. Johnston 40,000 gns after): stays 1½m: acts on good to soft ground. *A. King* **80**

GILLBURG (USA) 2 ch.g. (Jan 29) Johannesburg (USA) 127 – Bourbon Ball (USA) (Peintre Celebre (USA) 137) [2009 5.1m^3 5.1m^6 6g^5 6m^2 6d^2 6.1d^2 6s* 6d^2 7m^5 6m p6g^2 p7m Nov 27] lengthy, angular gelding: first foal: dam, US 7f winner, half-sister to 5-y-o Malt Or Mash: fair performer: won maiden at Hamilton in August: ran creditably when **77**

second in nursery/claimer after: stays 6f: acts on soft and good to firm going: usually in cheekpieces/blinkers: has pulled hard/looked awkward. *K. A. Ryan*

GILT EDGE GIRL 3 ch.f. Monsieur Bond (IRE) 120 – Tahara (IRE) (Caerleon (USA) 132) [2009 72: p5g^2 5.1d* 6m* 5g^3 6m^5 5g^3 p5.1g* Nov 16] compact, attractive filly: useful performer: won maiden at Nottingham in April, then handicaps at Windsor in May and Wolverhampton (beat Ivory Silk 1½ lengths) in November: should prove best at 5f/6f: acts on polytrack, soft and good to firm going. *C. G. Cox* **99**

GINGER GREY (IRE) 2 gr.g. (Apr 3) Bertolini (USA) 125 – Just In Love (FR) (Highest Honor (FR) 124) [2009 6m^5 6s^2 6g^3 7m 5m p6g^2 6g^2 6g^3 7m^6 8g^5 7.1m^2 p7.1g^3 7d^3 Oct 22] good-topped gelding: fair maiden: effective at 6f/7f: acts on polytrack, good to firm and good to soft going: sometimes blinkered/in cheekpieces: consistent: sold 15,000 gns, then gelded. *S. A. Callaghan* **65**

GINGER JACK 2 ch.g. (Feb 14) Refuse To Bend (IRE) 128 – Coretta (IRE) 118 (Caerleon (USA) 132) [2009 f8g 8g^5 Sep 30] better effort in maidens (very slowly away on debut, gelded after) when 9¼ lengths fifth to Arlequin at Newcastle: has left Godolphin. *Saeed bin Suroor* **55**

GINGER TED (IRE) 2 ch.g. (Apr 12) Fath (USA) 116 – Estertide (IRE) (Tagula (IRE) 116) [2009 5.1m 5.1d^4 6g^5 f5g 6.1v* 6d 6.1d* 6d Sep 5] €2,000F, £1,600Y: compact gelding: fifth foal: dam unraced: fair performer: won nurseries at Nottingham in July and August: stays 6f: acts on heavy going: tried blinkered/in cheekpieces (not when successful): inconsistent. *R. C. Guest* **79**

GINGKO LADY (USA) 4 ch.f. Mr Greeley (USA) 122 – Highland Tide (USA) (Highland Blade (USA)) [2009 42: p6g p8g f8g p8g^6 Apr 2] poor maiden: tried in cheekpieces/visor: sold 2,500 gns. *J. R. Boyle* **49**

GINOBILI (IRE) 3 b.g. Fasliyev (USA) 120 – Imperial Graf (USA) (Blushing John (USA) 120) [2009 96: 6.1m^5 5g^6 5g 5g 5m^6 5.7m p6m* 7m p6g Oct 24] tall gelding: useful performer at best: won claimer at Kempton (left Stef Liddiard 6,000 gns) in September: best at 5f/6f: acts on polytrack, soft and good to firm going: wears blinkers/cheekpieces: has joined M. Scudamore. *Andrew Reid* **96 d**

GIOACCHINO (IRE) 4 b.g. Rossini (USA) 118 – Gareyba (IRE) (Fairy King (USA)) [2009 63: 6.1g^4 6m f6g* 5.7m^6 6d^2 6.1m 6d p6m 6.1d Aug 31] modest handicapper: won at Southwell in June: stays 6f: acts on fibresand and any turf going: tried in cheekpieces/tongue tie. *R. A. Harris* **63**

GIO PONTI (USA) 4 b.c. Tale of The Cat (USA) 113 – Chipeta Springs (USA) (Alydar) [2009 a9f^5 8f* 10d* 11f* 10g* 12s^2 a10f^2 Nov 7] closely related/half-brother to several winners in USA: dam US 1m/8.5f winner: top-class performer: improved into the best performer on turf in US in 2009, winning 4 Grade 1s in a row, namely Frank E. Kilroe Mile Handicap at Santa Anita (by a nose from Ventura) in March, Manhattan Handicap at Belmont (beat Marsh Side 1½ lengths) in June, Man o'War Stakes at Belmont (going away by 1¾ lengths from Musketier) in July and Arlington Million (beat Just As Well 1¼ lengths) in August: second on last 2 starts, in Joe Hirsch Turf Classic at Belmont (odds-on, went down by 1¾ lengths to Interpatation, quickening to lead entering straight, but tiring in soft ground) and Breeders' Cup Classic (best effort, beaten a length by Zenyatta, leading 1f out but caught in final 50 yards): effective at 1m and should prove fully effective over easy 1½m: acts on pro-ride, firm and good to soft going: held up. *C. Clement, USA* **130**

GIPTAR (IRE) 2 b.g. (Mar 6) Kheleyf (USA) 116 – Titania (Fairy King (USA)) [2009 5g^6 f6g^3 Oct 27] €30,000F, 5,000Y, £8,500 2-y-o: seventh foal: half-brother to 3 winners, including 6-y-o Charles Parnell: dam unraced: well backed/slowly away in maidens, better effort when 8¼ lengths third to Bowmaker at Southwell, last off bridle: gelded after, then sent to USA: will improve further. *E. F. Vaughan* **63 p**

GITANO HERNANDO 3 ch.c. Hernando (FR) 127 – Gino's Spirits 98 (Perugino (USA) 84) [2009 90p: 10.3m* 10.3m^2 p8.6g* a9f* Oct 10] **124**

Ambitious plans to run Gitano Hernando in the Belmont Stakes in the spring were thwarted by a setback, but all came good in the end when he claimed several notable scalps in the Grade 1 Goodwood Stakes at the Oak Tree meeting at Santa Anita in October. Before his trip to California, Gitano Hernando had not even won a pattern race, managing three victories from six starts in varied company in Britain, his most recent outing having seen him land a class 3 conditions race at Wolverhampton. Some transition from the West Midlands to the West Coast of America!

Gitano Hernando ran three times as a two-year-old and, after being beaten at Nottingham and Brighton, he got off the mark in a maiden over an extended nine furlongs at Wolverhampton after the end of the turf season, showing fairly useful form with the promise of better to come. He changed hands after Wolverhampton, coming into the ownership for his three year old campaign of Team Valor International, which is based in Kentucky and has had a fair bit of success over the years with horses acquired from somewhat unlikely sources, winning the Dubai Duty Free at Nad Al Sheba with the Zimbabwean-bred mare Ipi Tombe and finding the Kentucky Derby runner-up Captain Bodgit in the racing backwater of Maryland.

Gitano Hernando's three-year-old career started off with an impressive win in a handicap at Doncaster's Lincoln meeting, looking a handicapper to follow. However, with the Belmont Stakes challenge on the horizon, he was stepped up in class in the Group 3 Dee Stakes at Chester in early-May. He might well have made a successful start in pattern company but for meeting interference on the home turn, his finishing run just too late as he went down by a head to South Easter in a four-way photo finish. There was greater misfortune to come, as Gitano Hernando was reportedly badly jarred up afterwards and was forced to miss the Belmont. It wasn't until September that he returned to the track, when, facing smart older opposition Cesare, Mia's Boy and Foolin Myself at Wolverhampton, he scored with something to spare after travelling well all the way, his winning margin of two lengths over Mia's Boy not doing him full justice. The form looked well up to the standard required for a tilt at a listed event, or even another Group 3, but connections already had their eyes on the Goodwood Stakes, a challenge that looked ambitious to say the least.

Heading the line-up at Santa Anita was Mine That Bird, winner of the Kentucky Derby and placed in both the Preakness and the Belmont. The other three-year-old in the field Chocolate Candy had been runner-up in the Santa Anita Derby. The older horses included Colonel John, winner of the Santa Anita Derby and the Travers Stakes at three, Richard's Kid, who had won the Pacific Classic on his most recent start, with Colonel John and another of the Goodwood Stakes runners the Grade 2 winner Parading behind him, Tiago, winner of the Goodwood in 2007 and third to Raven's Pass in the 2008 Breeders' Cup Classic, and Monzante, a Grade 1 handicap winner in 2008; in all there were five Grade 1 winners. In a race that wasn't run at a flat-out gallop by any means, Gitano Hernando stalked the pace, and was able to quicken through when a gap came into the straight, showing a better turn of foot than Colonel John, with Richard's Kid finishing late for third, the distances a neck and three quarters of a length. Chocolate Candy came fifth and Mine That Bird sixth. The win opened up the option to run Gitano Hernando at the Breeders' Cup, though it would have cost 250,000 dollars to enter at that stage. However, connections decided to wait for the spring and a trip to Dubai, with the Dubai World Cup itself said to be the target. The placed horses in the Goodwood Stakes went on to finish fifth and sixth in the Breeders' Cup Classic back at Santa Anita and Gitano Hernando would have needed to improve again to have had a chance against Zenyatta. Gitano Hernando's win in the Goodwood Stakes provided his young trainer Marco Botti, in his fourth season based at Newmarket, with his biggest win to date and was a first major winner for jockey Kieren Fallon since his return to the saddle in September.

Goodwood Stakes, Santa Anita—Gitano Hernando provides trainer Marco Botti with his most high profile success; Colonel John (noseband) and Richard's Kid (left) are close behind

The good-topped Gitano Hernando was one of two winners at the highest level in 2009 for his sire Hernando, Casual Conquest winning the Group 1 Tattersalls Gold Cup. Hernando is an influence for stamina and there may well be more to come from Gitano Hernando as a four year old, particularly when he is stepped up to a mile and a half. Gitano

Gitano Hernando (ch.c. 2006)	Hernando (FR) (b 1990)	Niniski (b 1976)	Nijinsky
			Virginia Hills
		Whakilyric (b 1984)	Miswaki
			Lyrism
	Gino's Spirits (ch 1996)	Perugino (b 1991)	Danzig
			Fairy Bridge
		Rising Spirits (ch 1985)	Cure The Blues
			Mrs McArdy

Hernando's dam Gino's Spirits improved with age and racing too. She won three times in Britain, showing marked improvement on her eighteenth start to land the listed John Musker Stakes at Yarmouth. She followed that with a second in the then-Group 2 Sun Chariot Stakes before winning a Grade 3 handicap in America the following year. She was sold for 550,000 dollars at Keeneland towards the end of 2001. Gitano Hernando is her fourth foal, the first three being the Swedish mile and a half winner Eclipse Park (by Rainbow Quest), the modest maiden hurdler Crosby Jemma (by Lomitas) and the once-raced maiden Ginos Destination (by Dubai Destination). Her fifth foal, the two-year-old Dr Fong filly India Spirit, won twice from twelve starts in Italy in 2009. Gitano Hernando's grandam Rising Spirits looked promising when winning a Naas maiden for Dermot Weld at two before being sent to the States, where she, like her daughter and grandson, also won (a claimer over seven furlongs). She has produced a hotch-potch of runners in a fairly lengthy career at stud, the pick of the others apart from Gino's Spirit including the three-year-old seven-furlong winner Rising Kheleyf. The third dam Mrs McArdy won the 1977 One Thousand Guineas, a rare classic winner for the north, being trained by Mick Easterby; only Attraction, trained by Mark Johnston, has taken the prize up the A1 since. Mrs McArdy was another fruitful producer at stud, all seven of her foals to reach the racecourse being successful, much the best of them the smart mile- to mile-and-a-quarter winner Citidancer. Her unraced foals included the dam of the champion 1998 Japanese two-year-old colt Admire Cozzene. Gitano Hernando, as stated, will be at least as effective at a mile and a half as at around a mile and a quarter (the Goodwood Stakes is nine furlongs). He acts on polytrack/pro-ride and on good to firm going. It is perhaps appropriate that he has gone on his travels to earn his reputation, 'gitano' meaning gypsy in both Spanish and Italian. *M. Botti*

GIULIETTA DA VINCI 2 b.f. (Feb 5) Mujahid (USA) 125 – Gennie Bond 73 (Pivotal 124) [2009 6m^6 7m^5 7d* 7d 7d 6g^5 p8g* p8.6g^4 f7m^5 Dec 15] £1,800Y: sturdy filly: first foal: dam, maiden, barely stayed 1m: fair performer: won maiden at Leicester in July and claimer at Lingfield (claimed from R. Hannon £8,000) in November: stays 1m: acts on polytrack and good to soft ground. *N. Tinkler* **71**

GIVE (IRE) 3 b.f. High Chaparral (IRE) 132 – Generous Gesture (IRE) 86 (Fasliyev (USA) 120) [2009 55: p8.6g^6 p10g p9.5m Feb 25] sparely-made filly: poor maiden: stays 9f: yet to race on extremes of going: wears cheekpieces. *R. A. Harris* **47**

GIVEN A CHOICE (IRE) 7 b.g. Trans Island 119 – Miss Audimar (USA) (Mr Leader (USA)) [2009 78, a89: p10m Nov 21] big, strong gelding: good mover: fairly useful performer on all-weather, fair on turf: below form sole start at 7 yrs: stays 1½m: acts on polytrack, good to firm and good to soft ground: tried visored, wears cheekpieces nowadays: has raced freely: held up. *J. Pearce* **–**

GIVE US A SONG (USA) 3 b. or br.g. Songandaprayer (USA) 118 – Mama G (USA) (Prospector's Bid (USA)) [2009 70: p8g p7g^6 p7g^4 7m p8g p8m p7.1g Dec 26] well-grown gelding: modest handicapper nowadays: gelded after third start: stays 1m: acts on polytrack: tried in cheekpieces. *J. S. Moore* **61**

GIZMONDO 6 ch.g. Lomitas 129 – India Atlanta (Ahonoora 122) [2009 68: p10g^6 Jan 11] fair handicapper: blinkered, well held only Flat outing in 2009: should stay 1½m: acts on polytrack and firm ground: fair hurdler. *G. L. Moore* **–**

GLADIATORUS (USA) 4 b.c. Silic (FR) 125 – Gmaasha (IRE) (Kris 135) [2009 7.5g* 8g* 8.9g* 8m^6 8m 8g^5 8d* 8f Nov 7] **128**

Sea The Stars's dominance of the season in Europe was so complete that it was easy to forget that he was not the only horse with a claim to being the world's best at some stage during 2009. Gladiatorus topped the global rankings in the early part of the year after an impressive hat-trick at Nad Al Sheba. While Sea The Stars's claims to the title grew ever stronger as the season progressed, those of Gladiatorus receded at a similar rate, however, his once tall reputation taking some hefty knocks in Europe's top mile races before being at least partially restored with a runaway victory in the Premio Vittorio di Capua in October.

Gladiatorus raced in Dubai in the colours of Sheikh Mohammed's youngest son, Sheikh Mansoor, for the stable of Mubarak bin Shafya who was in his first season as a trainer of thoroughbreds after starting out as a handler of endurance horses. Gladiatorus made a successful reappearance in a seven and a half furlong handicap on the first day of the Dubai International Carnival, making the running and winning unchallenged from a field that included the previous season's Dubai Duty Free winner Jay Peg. Front-running became Gladiatorus's trademark and he followed up impressively over a mile in the Group 2 Al Fahidi Fort in February, beating a smart field with another zestful display, passing the post full of running five and three quarter lengths clear of Hunting Tower. Whilst already showing form that suggested he would be capable of making his mark at Group 1 level, the Dubai Duty Free on the Dubai World Cup card promised to be a stern test. The slightly longer trip was a concern, while the field he faced looked the strongest of any event on the card, the World Cup included. Among his fifteen rivals were Jay Peg, Archipenko, an unlucky third the year before and now favourite, the high-class Japanese mare Vodka (fourth in 2008), America's leading miler on turf Kip Deville, another much improved dual winner at the Carnival in Presvis, the previous season's top European seven-furlong performer Paco Boy, and a three-strong challenge from Godolphin which included Group 1 winners Creachadoir and Lady Marian. None of them managed to keep up with Gladiatorus, however, as he quickly established a clear lead, with Vodka in turn racing clear of the rest in second. Still a long way in front turning for home, Gladiatorus showed no signs of stopping in the straight, the only one to make any kind of impression being Presvis who had had to be dropped out in rear from a wide draw. Presvis finished well but Gladiatorus still had three and a quarter lengths to spare at the line, with Godolphin's apparent third string, Alexandros, another who finished well, a further two lengths back in third. Presvis went on to gain consolation in Hong Kong next time, and others further down the field, including eighth-placed Paco Boy, left their efforts in the Duty Free well behind later in the year.

The Duty Free raised not only the profile of Gladiatorus, but that of his jockey too. Ahmed Ajtebi went on to complete a double for the bin Shafya stable in the card's other major turf race, the Dubai Sheema Classic, in which he brought Eastern Anthem from off the pace to lead on the line in a three-way photo finish. Ajtebi is a Dubaian national (a nephew of Saeed Manana, a successful owner in Britain) and, as a 'home-grown' rider, his big-race successes must have given particular pleasure, including on a personal level, to Sheikh Mohammed, who, by all accounts, was instrumental in promoting Ajtebi's career on horseback. Ajtebi gained experience in Ireland (with John Oxx), Australia (where he enjoyed his first winner, in 2004—celebrating too wildly in the view of the stewards who fined him for his histrionics) and South Africa (riding a number of winners for Mike de Kock) as well as at home in Dubai. Ajtebi's childhood career in camel racing (he outgrew the weight limit in his mid-teens) received plenty of coverage in the Press

Dubai Duty Free Sponsored By Dubai Duty Free, Nad Al Sheba—Ahmed Ajtebi is already celebrating as front-running Gladiatorus wins virtually unchallenged from Presvis and Alexandros

Premio Vittorio di Capua, Milan—Ajtebi can afford to look round as Gladiatorus again makes all; Win For Sure is his nearest pursuer

though it had little relevance compared to his horseracing achievements. Ajtebi was champion apprentice in Dubai in 2007/8 and had spells in Britain in 2007 and 2008, riding sixteen winners, including Regal Parade in the Buckingham Palace Stakes at the Royal meeting, his very first ride at Ascot. A visa irregularity cut short his stay in Britain in 2008, but back in Dubai he went on to become the first Dubaian jockey to ride out his claim (notching up seventy winners), though he was still entitled to a 3-lb claim when riding in Britain in the latest season.

By the time of his next race, when favourite for the Queen Anne Stakes at Royal Ascot, Gladiatorus had rejoined Godolphin (he had been with Saeed bin Suroor for his three-year-old season but had not raced), but Ajtebi still kept the ride, with Frankie Dettori partnering the stable's other runner Alexandros. Gladiatorus showed nothing like his Dubai form, never able to get away from his field and going out tamely, eased down in sixth behind Paco Boy. Dettori replaced Ajtebi on Gladiatorus in the Prix Jacques le Marois at Deauville, but he ran another dismal race, missing the break and dropping out with two furlongs to go after tracking the pace rather than being forced up to take the lead, eventually beating only Goldikova's pacemaker. With Ajtebi back on board, Gladiatorus blazed off in front in the Prix du Moulin but couldn't find any extra when headed a furlong out, still running his best race since Dubai in finishing fifth behind Aqlaam, beaten four and a half lengths by the winner. Gladiatorus was back to something near his best next time in the Premio Vittorio di Capua at Milan, pulling away again in the final furlong to win by four and a half lengths from Win For Sure to give Godolphin its fifth winner of the race since 1999. Sent to Santa Anita for the Breeders' Cup Mile, Gladiatorus was harried for the lead by two of his rivals and beat only two home.

Prior to his abortive three-year-old campaign and his sudden rise to prominence in Dubai, Gladiatorus had been a useful and prolific winner as a two-year-old in Italy. He won six of his nine starts there, including four listed events, and was runner-up on two other occasions, notably when beaten half a length by Scintillo in the Gran Criterium at Milan. Dettori was in the saddle on that occasion, so his rider may well have had a part to play in Gladiatorus's joining Godolphin not long afterwards. Two million dollars was reportedly the sum that changed hands, though, whether or not that was the exact figure, it is safe to say that it dwarfed the 8,000 dollars that Gladiatorus made as a yearling.

Silic, the sire of Gladiatorus, won the 1999 Breeders' Cup Mile but he has had only small crops and was covering in California in the latest season at just 3,500 dollars. Gladiatorus comes from a top family on the distaff side, the Irish One Thousand Guineas winner and One Thousand Guineas runner-up Al Bahathri being his grandam. Like her grandson, Al Bahathri was an habitual front runner and her short-head defeat at Newmarket came only after she was collared in the last stride. Al Bahathri's unraced daughter Gmaasha had the best possible opportunities at stud to begin with, visiting Danzig, Mr Prospector and Storm Cat in her first three years, but the results were disappointing, although the Mr Prospector colt Sinan did eventually win a couple of minor races in the States after finishing in mid-field in two maidens in Britain as a two-year-old for Godolphin. Gmaasha was eventually culled from the Shadwell broodmare band and it was not until her tenth foal,

Gladiatorus came along, that she had her second winner. A third soon followed, though, and another good one, again in Italy, when My Sweet Baby (by Minardi) won the latest Premio Regina Elena (Italian 1000 Guineas) for Gladiatorus's original trainer Riccardo Menichetti. Gmaasha's latest runner, the two-year-old colt Stendardo (by Castledale), failed to make the frame in four starts for the same stable at Rome in the autumn. As for Al Bahathri, she proved a much more successful broodmare for Sheikh Hamdan than Gmaasha. Her successes at stud included Gmaasha's full sister Hasbah, runner-up in the Coronation Stakes (another race Al Bahathri won), the Greenham and Challenge Stakes winner Munir, and best of all, the Two Thousand Guineas and Champion Stakes winner Haafhd. Al Bahathri had her final foal in 2005 and is reported to be thriving in retirement in the company of another classic-winning former member of the Shadwell broodmare band who produced a classic winner of her own, the One Thousand Guineas and Oaks winner Midway Lady (dam of 2005 Oaks winner Eswarah). Gladiatorus was one of three European Group 1 winners added to the family's score in 2009, the other two descending from Al Bahathri's full sister Chain Fern. Her grandson Lord Shanakill won the Prix Jean Prat, while her great grandson Hearts of Fire initiated a notable family double when winning the Gran Criterium at Milan just before Gladiatorus's success later on the card. Chain Fern is also the dam and grandam respectively of two Grade 1 winners in the States over a mile and a quarter, Spanish Fern (Yellow Ribbon Stakes) and Heatseeker (Santa Anita Handicap).

Gladiatorus (USA) (b.c. 2005)	Silic (FR) (b 1995)	Sillery (b 1988)	Blushing Groom
			Silvermine
		Balletomane (b 1988)	Sadler's Wells
			Franconia
	Gmaasha (IRE) (ch 1989)	Kris (ch 1976)	Sharpen Up
			Doubly Sure
		Al Bahathri (ch 1982)	Blushing Groom
			Chain Store

Godolphin's "Gladiatorus"

The big, rangy Gladiatorus had been under consideration for the Arlington Million in the summer but was ruled out with a corn in a foot. Whether he would have proven as effective at Arlington over a mile and a quarter must be doubted given his exuberant nature which seemed to make even a mile look too far for him on occasions in the latest season. He certainly wouldn't have enjoyed an uncontested lead at Arlington, with the trailblazing American gelding Presious Passion also in the field, and, whatever trip he races at in future, being able to settle into a comfortable rhythm in front is probably going to be as crucial as any factor in Gladiatorus's winning more races. The way he races, it would be interesting to see Gladiatorus tried at a bit shorter than a mile at some stage. He acts on good to firm and good to soft ground. *Saeed bin Suroor*

GLAMOROSO (IRE) 4 b.g. Mull of Kintyre (USA) 114 – Tuneful 89 (Pivotal 124) [2009 50: p8g[3] p9.5g 9m 12.1m 9.8d 12.1g Sep 22] sturdy gelding: poor maiden: stays 1m: acts on polytrack. *A. Kirtley* **47**

GLAMOROUS SPIRIT (IRE) 3 b.f. Invincible Spirit (IRE) 121 – Glamorous Air (IRE) (Air Express (IRE) 125) [2009 84: p5g[2] 6g[3] 5g[5] p5g* 5g[5] 5m 5.1m* 5d 5.1m p5m* Dec 1] unfurnished filly: fairly useful performer: won handicaps at Kempton in May and Chester in July, then claimer at Lingfield in December: raced only at 5f/6f: acts on polytrack, soft and good to firm going: front runner: none too consistent. *R. A. Harris* **93**

GLAMOUR PROFESSION (IRE) 2 ch.f. (Apr 28) Captain Rio 122 – Kriva 69 (Reference Point 139) [2009 5m 7g[6] 8m p7g[6] Oct 8] €14,000F, €28,000Y: seventh foal: sister to 3-y-o Midnight Cruiser and half-sister to several winners, including useful Scandinavian performer up to 2m Peruginos Flyer (by Perugino): dam 17f winner: modest maiden: sixth in nursery at Kempton: has looked awkward: sold 1,500 gns. *R. Hannon* **53**

GLAN LADY (IRE) 3 b.f. Court Cave (IRE) – Vanished (IRE) 77 (Fayruz 116) [2009 60: f6d[2] f6g[3] p6g f6g[5] f7d f6g 10m 10m Jun 18] modest performer: left J. Spearing after reappearance and little form after next start, refusing to race final outing: stays 7f: acts on fibresand and soft going: blinkered/in cheekpieces nowadays: often slowly away. *G. J. Smith* **52 §**

GLAN Y MOR (IRE) 2 b.f. (Mar 24) Mark of Esteem (IRE) 137 – Molly Mello (GER) 106 (Big Shuffle (USA) 122) [2009 7s Sep 3] third foal: half-sister to 3-y-o Brunston and 7f winner Molly Ann (by Medicean): dam useful German 7f winner, including at 2 yrs: 25/1, well beaten in maiden at Salisbury, swishing tail repeatedly and finding little. *F. J. Brennan* **–**

GLASS HARMONIUM (IRE) 3 gr.c. Verglas (IRE) 118 – Spring Symphony (IRE) 94 (Darshaan 133) [2009 88p: 8m[5] 10.4g[6] 10m* 9m[4] 9m[2] Oct 16] useful-looking colt: smart performer: significant improvement at 3 yrs, winning listed Hampton Court Stakes at Royal Ascot in June by ½ length from Cashelgar, staying on strongly: creditable head second to Steele Tango in Darley Stakes at Newmarket final outing: will be well suited by 1½m: raced only on good/good to firm ground. *Sir Michael Stoute* **116**

GLASSHOUGHTON 6 b.g. Dansili 127 – Roseum 102 (Lahib (USA) 129) [2009 91: 5m 5d[6] 6m[3] 6g 5d 5m p7.1g 6d Oct 13] smallish, angular gelding: just fair handicapper at best in 2009: best at 5f/6f: acts on heavy and good to firm going: has worn cheekpieces/blinkers: sold £1,800. *M. Dods* **76**

GLASS OF RED (IRE) 2 gr.f. (Mar 20) Verglas (IRE) 118 – Embassy Belle (IRE) 82 (Marju (IRE) 127) [2009 5g 6.1m[6] p7g 8.3g* Oct 28] €50,000Y: lengthy filly: first foal: dam Irish 7f/8.5f winner: off 3 months, easily best effort when winning seller at Nottingham: stays 8.3f: finished weakly third start: sold 10,000 gns, sent to USA. *R. M. Beckett* **67**

GLEAMING SPIRIT (IRE) 5 b.g. Mujadil (USA) 119 – Gleam (Green Desert (USA) 127) [2009 73: 5g 5d 5d 5.2d p5.1g p5m[6] Dec 1] strong gelding: handicapper: little form in 2009: visored/blinkered. *Peter Grayson* **–**

GLENCAIRN STAR 8 b.g. Selkirk (USA) 129 – Bianca Nera 107 (Salse (USA) 128) [2009 5d 6m f5f Nov 24] good sort: fairly useful at best: off over 2 years, no form in 2009: tried in cheekpieces. *F. Watson* **–**

GLENCALVIE (IRE) 8 ch.g. Grand Lodge (USA) 125 – Top of The Form (IRE) 79 (Masterclass (USA) 116) [2009 88: p8g p7g[5] p8g p7g p8g 7m 7.6f Jun 20] strong, well-made gelding: fairly useful handicapper in 2008: on downgrade: stays 8.3f: acts on polytrack and firm going: wears visor/cheekpieces: temperament under suspicion. *J. Akehurst* **71 d**

Hampton Court Stakes, Royal Ascot—Glass Harmonium hangs right and Cashelgar is short of room as the pair pull clear of Monitor Closely

GLEN LASS 2 ch.f. (Feb 3) Zafeen (FR) 123 – Welcome Aboard 68 (Be My Guest **63**
(USA) 126) [2009 5.2s^{6} 5g 7.5m^{6} 7s^{3} 7d^{2} 8m^{3} p8m p10m p8.6g^{2} p9.5g* p8.6g* p8m* Dec 30] 1,000Y: strong filly: third foal: half-sister to 11f winner in Italy by Medicean: dam, 1m winner, out of half-sister to 1000 Guineas winner On The House: modest performer: left J. S. Moore £5,000 after sixth start: won claimers at Wolverhampton (2) and Kempton in December: stays 9.5f: acts on polytrack, good to firm and soft going: tried in cheekpieces, blinkered last 4 starts: signs of temperament. *J. Pearce*

GLENLINI 3 b.f. Bertolini (USA) 125 – Glenhurich (IRE) 59 (Sri Pekan (USA) 117) **68**
[2009 52: 5m^{2} 5g^{5} Jul 6] easily best effort when second in maiden at Musselburgh: well beaten in seller on same course next time. *J. S. Goldie*

GLENLUJI 4 b.g. Lujain (USA) 119 – Glenhurich (IRE) 59 (Sri Pekan (USA) 117) **55**
[2009 –: 5s 5m^{5} 5m 6d 5g 5g 7.2m 7.2g^{5} 9.1v Oct 31] modest handicapper: stays 7.2f: acts on good to firm ground: held up. *J. S. Goldie*

GLEN MOLLY (IRE) 3 b.f. Danetime (IRE) 121 – Sonorous (IRE) 98 (Ashkalani **97**
(IRE) 128) [2009 95p: 7.1g^{3} 7d^{2} 7m^{4} 7g* 7g 7v 7s Nov 7] unfurnished filly: useful handicapper: won at Newmarket in August by 2¼ lengths from Imaam: below form after: stays 7f: best effort on good going. *B. W. Hills*

GLENMUIR (IRE) 6 b.g. Josr Algarhoud (IRE) 118 – Beryl 77 (Bering 136) [2009 **79**
81: 7g^{3} 10g 8s 8g^{4} Sep 3] tall, lengthy gelding: fair handicapper: left Gordon Elliott in Ireland prior to final outing: best at 7f to 9.5f: acts on firm and soft going: tried blinkered: tongue tied once: tends to look none too keen. *J. J. Quinn*

GLENRIDDING 5 b.g. Averti (IRE) 117 – Appelone (Emperor Jones (USA) 119) **85**
[2009 81: p9.5g 8f^{6} 8.5g 8.1g 7.6g* 7g* 7.6m^{2} 7g 7.6g 7d* 8s p7.1g p8.6g 7s 7s Nov 7] tall gelding: fairly useful handicapper: won at Chester and Thirsk (5 days apart) in June and Thirsk in August: well below form after: stays easy 9.5f: acts on polytrack, firm and good to soft ground: tried blinkered, usually in cheekpieces: front runner. *J. G. Given*

GLEN SHIEL (USA) 2 ch.g. (Feb 2) Whywhywhy (USA) 115 – Staffin 93 (Salse **79**
(USA) 128) [2009 6s^{6} 5d^{2} 6m* Sep 12] $20,000Y, resold 50,000Y: sixth foal: half-brother

to 2 winners in USA by Tactical Advantage and Songandaprayer: dam, 2-y-o 7f winner, half-sister to dam of smart sprinter Sir Gerry: progressive in maidens, winning at Ffos Las by ½ length from Stefanki, rallying: gelded after: should stay 7f. *M. Johnston*

GLIMPSE OF LIGHT (IRE) 3 b.f. Passing Glance 119 – Sankaty Light (USA) 55 (Summer Squall (USA)) [2009 69: p5g f6g Apr 27] maiden: just modest form in 2009 (gave trouble stall second occasion): will stay 7f: raced only on all-weather. *A. M. Balding* **52**

GLOBAL 3 ch.g. Bahamian Bounty 116 – Tuppenny Blue 49 (Pennekamp (USA) 130) [2009 78: p7g⁴ 9.9m* 8.1g* 8g* 9m 8f⁵ 8d 8.3f⁴ 9g 8m 7s Oct 12] medium-sized gelding: fairly useful handicapper: won at Salisbury, Chepstow and Goodwood within 9 days in May: struggled badly after: has won at 1¼m, best at 1m: acts on polytrack and good to firm going: blinkered final outing: sold 18,000 gns, then gelded. *R. Hannon* **93 d**

GLOBAL CITY (IRE) 3 b.c. Exceed And Excel (AUS) 126 – Victory Peak (Shirley Heights 130) [2009 99: 6m⁴ 6m⁵ 6m* 6g 6d 6m² 6g p6g* Nov 14] strong, good sort: smart performer: won handicap at Haydock (beat White Shift 2¼ lengths) in June and minor event at Lingfield (by neck from Son of The Cat) in November: 1¼ lengths second to Awinnersgame in minor event at Yarmouth, only creditable effort in between: best efforts at 6f: acts on polytrack and good to firm going: tongue tied. *Saeed bin Suroor* **110**

GLOBAL CONQUEST (IRE) 3 b.f. Captain Rio 122 – Triphibious 69 (Zafonic (USA) 130) [2009 6m² 7f² 7g⁴ 7s⁴ p7.1g² p10g* Oct 14] €4,500F, €500Y, 800 2-y-o: leggy filly: third foal: half-sister to 2007 2-y-o 5f seller winner My Sheilas Dream (by Acclamation), later successful in Greece: dam, temperamental maiden, out of sister to smart 1¼m/1½m performer Talented: fairly useful form: won handicap at Lingfield in October: stays 1¼m: acts on polytrack and firm going: sold 9,000 gns. *Pat Eddery* **83**

GLOBAL STRATEGY 6 b.g. Rainbow Quest (USA) 134 – Pleasuring 68 (Good Times (ITY)) [2009 p16g Feb 8] strong gelding: one-time fairly useful handicapper: poor hurdler nowadays, and tailed off on belated Flat return. *O. Sherwood* **–**

GLOBAL TRAFFIC 5 br.g. Generous (IRE) 139 – Eyes Wide Open 44 (Fraam 114) [2009 66: f14g p16.5g Feb 20] strong gelding: modest handicapper: little form in 2009, pulled up amiss final outing: usually wears blinkers/visor. *R. Ford* **–**

GLOBAL VILLAGE (IRE) 4 b.g. Dubai Destination (USA) 127 – Zelding (IRE) 108 (Warning 136) [2009 p6g⁴ 7g⁶ 5.1d⁵ 7g² p6g³ p7g* p7g* 7g⁵ 8.3m³ Aug 9] sturdy gelding: fair handicapper: won twice at Kempton in July: stays 1m: acts on polytrack and good to firm ground: gelded after final start. *Miss D. Mountain* **73**

GLORIA DE CAMPEAO (BRZ) 6 b.h. Impression (ARG) – Audacity (BRZ) (Clackson (BRZ)) [2009 118?: a8g⁵ a9f⁴ a9f* a10f² 10g* 10g Aug 8] very smart performer: better than ever when winning handicap at Nad Al Sheba (by 4¼ lengths from Art of War) in February and Singapore Airlines International Cup at Kranji (beat strong-finishing Presvis by a head, leading after 6f and just holding on) in May: far from discredited when 14 lengths second to Well Armed in Dubai World Cup at Nad Al Sheba in between, chasing leaders and battling on well: well below form in Arlington Million final start: stays 1¼m: acts on dirt and heavy going. *P. Bary, France* **123**

GLORIOUS DREAMS (USA) 3 b. or br.f. Honour And Glory (USA) 122 – Crissy Aya (USA) (Saros 120) [2009 76: p6g 5s 6d 6g Jul 4] workmanlike filly: fair form when winning maiden on debut at 2 yrs: no form since: tried in cheekpieces. *T. J. Pitt* **–**

GLOUCESTER 6 b.g. Montjeu (IRE) 137 – Birdlip (USA) (Sanglamore (USA) 126) [2009 –: p10g⁴ 11.6m* 11.9m* 11.6g³ 12g⁶ 13.3m⁴ 12m Sep 25] strong gelding: fairly useful handicapper (similar level over hurdles): won at Windsor and Haydock in June: stays 13.2f: acts on polytrack and good to firm ground: tried in blinkers/cheekpieces/ tongue tie. *M. J. Scudamore* **84**

GLOWING (IRE) 4 b.f. Dansili 127 – Brightest (Rainbow Quest (USA) 134) [2009 93: p8g* 9g⁴ 7g* 7m Sep 26] tall, lengthy filly: useful performer: won minor event at Dundalk in April and Irish Stallion Farms EBF Brownstown Stakes at Fairyhouse (improved to beat Luminous Eyes by short head) in July: left Charles O'Brien in Ireland, last in listed race at Ascot (said to have lost a front shoe): effective from 7f to 1¼m: acts on polytrack and firm ground: tongue tied in 2008: has looked none too keen: sent to USA. *L. M. Cumani* **108**

GLOWING PRAISE 3 ch.g. Fantastic Light (USA) 134 – Beading 82 (Polish Precedent (USA) 131) [2009 81p: 9m⁶ 8.3m* 8d⁴ 8m⁴ 7m 8.1m⁴ 8m* Sep 25] strong gelding: fairly useful handicapper: won at Leicester in June and Ascot (beat Satwa Laird ½ length) in September: headstrong sort, though stays 8.3f: acts on soft and good to firm going: refused to enter stall intended reappearance. *E. S. McMahon* **90**

GLOW STAR (SAF) 5 ch.g. Muhtafal (USA) – Arctic Glow (SAF) (Northern Guest (USA)) [2009 7.5g 7.5g^5 a7g^6 8g 7g 7m p7g^3 p8m^3 Dec 4] sturdy gelding: useful performer: trained by M. Miller in South Africa in 2008, winning 3 times: ran in UAE for H. Brown first 3 starts: good third in handicap at Lingfield final outing: stays 1m: acts on polytrack, dirt and soft going: blinkered in UAE. *G. L. Moore* **98**

GO ALONE (IRE) 3 b.g. Elusive City (USA) 117 – Ya Ya (IRE) (Royal Academy (USA) 130) [2009 p7.1g 9d 6m* 7m^6 6g^2 6g^4 6g Aug 5] €80,000Y, 18,000 2-y-o: second foal: dam unraced half-sister to useful Irish performer up to 1m The Bower: fair performer: won maiden at Redcar in May: stays 6f: acts on good to firm going. *G. A. Swinbank* **72**

GO AMWELL 6 b.g. Kayf Tara 130 – Daarat Alayaam (IRE) (Reference Point 139) [2009 69: 15.4g 18g^3 16g p16g^4 p16g^5 Jul 8] modest handicapper: stays 21.6f: acts on all-weather, soft and good to firm going: tried visored: patiently ridden. *J. R. Jenkins* **64**

GOBAMA 2 br.f. (Apr 21) Dr Fong (USA) 128 – Chine 100 (Inchinor 119) [2009 7m* 7m^3 7m 7g^3 p7.1g^6 Nov 9] 2,000F: tall, leggy filly: fifth foal: half-sister to 2 winners, including ungenuine 9f winner Red Chairman (by Red Ransom), stayed 2m: dam French/US 8.5f to 1¼m winner: fair performer: won maiden at Salisbury in July: good efforts in nurseries last 2 starts: bred to stay 1m+, but needs to learn to settle. *J. W. Hills* **74**

GOBLIN 8 b.g. Atraf 116 – Forest Fantasy 61 (Rambo Dancer (CAN) 107) [2009 55: f16d^4 p12g Feb 7] sturdy, lengthy gelding: poor performer nowadays: stays 1½m: acts on all-weather and firm ground: tried in cheekpieces. *D. E. Cantillon* **48**

GO BLUE CHIP 2 br.g. (Apr 14) More Than Ready (USA) 120 – Bon Vivant (USA) (Salt Lake (USA)) [2009 6m p6f Dec 13] well held in maidens. *H. Candy* **–**

GODDESS OF LIGHT (IRE) 2 b.f. (Mar 26) Chineur (FR) 123 – Blues Over (IRE) (Sri Pekan (USA) 117) [2009 5.1g^6 p6f^4 p6g^3 p6g^2 p5m* Nov 28] €1,500Y: half-sister to winner in Norway by Redback: dam ran 3 times: fair performer: improved when winning nursery at Lingfield in November: may prove best at 5f/6f: acts on polytrack. *D. Loughnane, Ireland* **75**

GODFREY STREET 6 ch.g. Compton Place 125 – Tahara (IRE) (Caerleon (USA) 132) [2009 91: p5g* p5.1g^2 f5g^6 p5.1g^5 5.1g^4 5.1m^2 f5g^6 p5.1g 5v^3 f5m f5g^4 Dec 27] strong, compact gelding: fairly useful performer: won handicap at Great Leighs in January: below form after: best at 5f: acts on all-weather, heavy and good to firm going: wears blinkers/cheekpieces: often front runner. *A. G. Newcombe* **81 d**

GO FORTH NORTH (USA) 2 ch.f. (Mar 23) North Light (IRE) 126 – Witch Tradition (USA) (Holy Bull (USA) 134) [2009 7f^3 7m^4 7d^4 Jul 27] second foal: half-sister to winner in USA by Sligo Bay: dam US 6f/6.5f winner: modest form in maidens: green on debut, not clear run both starts after. *M. L. W. Bell* **62 +**

GO FREE 8 b.g. Easycall 115 – Miss Traxdata (Absalom 128) [2009 –: 14.1m Aug 21] lightly raced and little form on Flat in recent years: tried visored. *J. G. M. O'Shea* **–**

GO GO GREEN (IRE) 3 b.c. Acclamation 118 – Preponderance (IRE) 85 (Cyrano de Bergerac 120) [2009 90: 5g 5d^4 5g^5 6g 6v^6 5m 5m* 5g^4 5g* p5g Nov 1] angular colt: useful handicapper: won at Pontefract (3 wins from 3 starts) in September and October (beat Taurus Twins 2¾ lengths): often front runner, best at 5f/6f: acts on polytrack, soft and good to firm ground: tried tongue tied. *D. H. Brown* **96**

GOING FOR GOLD 3 b.f. Barathea (IRE) 127 – Flash of Gold 76 (Darshaan 133) [2009 62p: 10m^3 11.9f* 11.9g^3 12m^4 p12g^5 Oct 8] tall, attractive filly: fairly useful handicapper: won at Haydock in July: likely to stay beyond 1½m: acts on polytrack and firm going: reliable. *R. Charlton* **84**

GOING FRENCH (IRE) 2 ch.c. (Mar 17) Frenchmans Bay (FR) 118 – Easy Going (Hamas (IRE) 125§) [2009 6m^2 f5g^3 5.7f^3 7.5m^2 6g^2 7g p6m^2 f5m^4 Dec 5] rather leggy colt: fourth foal: half-brother to 2006 2-y-o 5f winner Going Straight (by Princely Heir): dam unraced half-sister to smart sprinter Easycall: fair maiden: likely to prove best at 5f/6f: acts on all-weather and good to firm going. *R. Curtis* **71**

GOJERI (IRE) 2 ch.g. (Apr 7) Choisir (AUS) 126 – Lady Elysees (USA) (Royal Academy (USA) 130) [2009 6.1d 6g^6 Oct 30] 35,000F, 26,000Y: sturdy, attractive gelding: second foal: dam unraced half-sister to US Grade 3 8.5f winner Gone For Real: much better effort in maidens when 4½ lengths sixth to Asraab at Newmarket: will be suited by 7f: should progress further. *M. A. Jarvis* **72 p**

GOLD AGAIN (USA) 4 b.f. Touch Gold (USA) 127 – Miss Insync (USA) (Miswaki (USA) 124) [2009 63p: p6g^6 p7g p7.1g Jun 22] angular filly: modest maiden: stays 7f: raced on polytrack and good to soft going: tried tongue tied/visored: sold 6,200 gns. *W. R. Swinburn* **62**

GOLDAN JESS (IRE) 5 b.g. Golan (IRE) 129 – Bendis (GER) (Danehill (USA) 126) **57** [2009 –: 12.6g² 13g⁶ 14.1m² 14.1g⁵ 15.8g² Oct 6] neat gelding: modest maiden: stays 2m: acts on heavy and good to firm ground: tried blinkered/visored: fair hurdler. *P. A. Kirby*

GOLD BUBBLES (USA) 2 b.f. (Feb 21) Street Cry (IRE) 130 – Well Revered (USA) **97** (Red Ransom (USA)) [2009 6d* 6g² 6d³ 7g⁴ 6m⁶ 7v⁶ Aug 30] $90,000Y: good-topped filly: first foal: dam, ran twice in USA, half-sister to smart 1¼m/1½m performer Fahal: useful performer: won maiden at Leopardstown in April by 2½ lengths from Air Chief Marshal: in frame in minor event at Naas, listed race at the Curragh and Debutante Stakes at Leopardstown (2¼ lengths fourth to Lillie Langtry) next 3 starts: well below best in Lowther Stakes at York (drawn wide) and Moyglare Stud Stakes at the Curragh (heavy ground) last 2 outings: stays 7f: acts on good to soft ground: in blinkers/cheekpieces last 3 starts. *J. S. Bolger, Ireland*

GOLD CRUSHER (USA) 2 b.g. (Mar 4) Johannesburg (USA) 127 – Compressed **63** (USA) (Green Forest (USA) 134) [2009 6m⁴ f6m³ p6g⁶ Aug 24] good-topped gelding: modest form in minor events/maiden: sold 3,500 gns and gelded. *R. M. H. Cowell*

GOLD DIAMOND (USA) 2 b.g. (Apr 11) Seeking The Gold (USA) – Dubai **65 d** Diamond (Octagonal (NZ) 126) [2009 7m⁶ 7g 7g⁴ 7d 6g 7d f6m Nov 11] good-bodied gelding: fair maiden at best: well below form in nurseries last 4 starts, blinkered final one: stays 7f: acts on good to firm going: sold £2,800. *M. Johnston*

GOLDEN ARIA (IRE) 2 b.f. (May 7) Rakti 130 – Yellow Trumpet 75 (Petong 126) **84** [2009 6m⁴ 7s³ 8m* Sep 18] €32,000F, €30,000 2-y-o: tall, good-topped filly: fifth foal: half-sister to 3 winners, including useful Irish 5f winner (including at 2 yrs) City of Tribes (by Invincible Spirit) and 3-y-o Silverglas: dam, 2-y-o 5f winner, half-sister to smart 7f performer Naahy: progressive in maidens, winning by ½ length from Timepiece at Newmarket (took good hold): should be at least as effective at 7f as 1m. *R. Hannon*

GOLDEN BISHOP 4 ch.g. Medicean 128 – Hen Harrier 94 (Polar Falcon (USA) 126) **–** [2009 77: p9.5g Jan 9] good-bodied gelding: fair performer: stays 11.5f: acts on polytrack, good to firm and good to soft ground: breaks blood vessels (including when tailed off sole start in 2009). *R. A. Fahey*

GOLDEN BUTTON (IRE) 4 ch.f. Trans Island 119 – Velvet Appeal (IRE) 101 **80** (Petorius 117) [2009 7g² p8.6m* 8.5m⁶ p9.5m³ 10.4g⁶ Oct 9] €42,000Y: sturdy filly: half-sister to several winners, including 7f winner Craiova (by Turtle Island) and 1m (including at 2 yrs) winner The Illies (by Fasliyev), both useful: dam Irish 1m winner: fairly useful performer: won maiden at Wolverhampton in August: likely to prove best around 1m: acts on polytrack: sold 27,000 gns. *Sir Mark Prescott*

GOLDEN DESERT (IRE) 5 b.g. Desert Prince (IRE) 130 – Jules (IRE) 76 (Danehill **112** (USA) 126) [2009 99: 7m³ 7f⁶ 7g 7m² 7m² 6g* 7m* 7m 6g 7d Oct 24] strong, lengthy gelding: improved into a smart handicapper: won at Goodwood in August and September (beat Noble Citizen by length): below form last 2 starts, in Bengough Memorial Stakes at Ascot and well-contested minor event at Doncaster: effective at 6f/7f: acts on polytrack and firm going: effective visored or not: tactically versatile. *T. G. Mills*

GOLDEN DESTINY (IRE) 3 ch.f. Captain Rio 122 – Dear Catch (IRE) 69 (Bluebird **103** (USA) 125) [2009 86: 7d 6m³ 5m* 5g* 5.7f* 5.7m* Sep 13] good-topped filly: useful handicapper: in cheekpieces, much improved when winning at Sandown (2) and Bath (2) from July to September, beating Brenin Taran by neck on latter course for final success: best at 5f/6f: acts on firm and soft going: makes running/races prominently. *P. J. Makin*

GOLDEN DIXIE (USA) 10 ch.g. Dixieland Band (USA) – Beyrouth (USA) (Alleged **76** (USA) 138) [2009 94: 5.7g f5g⁴ 5m⁴ 6m² 6m 6m 5.7m³ 6.1g* 6g⁴ 6d⁵ 6g 5g⁵ 5s⁵ 5.7g 6m⁴ 6d p6g p6g p6g f5f⁶ f6g⁵ f5f⁶ p6f³ Dec 21] good-bodied gelding: just fair handicapper nowadays: won at Chepstow in June: largely below form after: best at 5f/6f: acts on polytrack, firm and good to soft going: tried in cheekpieces. *R. A. Harris*

GOLDEN EMPEROR (IRE) 2 ro.g. (Apr 7) Antonius Pius (USA) 123§ – Lily Shing **57** Shang 73 (Spectrum (IRE) 126) [2009 6m 7.1s³ p8.6g⁴ Oct 2] modest maiden: in frame at Musselburgh and Wolverhampton, considerately handled: should stay 1m+: sold 6,000 gns. *G. A. Swinbank*

GOLDEN FLIGHT (IRE) 3 ch.g. Hawk Wing (USA) 136 – Cassilis (IRE) (Persian **64** Bold 123) [2009 59: 7g⁵ 8.1g⁴ p8.6g 8f⁵ Jul 5] big, leggy gelding: modest maiden: likely to be suited by 1¼m: acts on firm going: sold 7,000 gns. *J. W. Hills*

GOLDEN FUTURE 6 b.g. Muhtarram (USA) 125 – Nazca (Zilzal (USA) 137) [2009 **60** f11g f7g⁵ 8d⁵ 10.2g 12d⁵ 11.5g* f11g⁶ 12.4d³ p16.5g 13.8g³ Oct 17] modest handicapper: left M. Murphy in Ireland and off over 2½ years prior to reappearance: first win at Carlisle in August: stays 1½m: acts on fibresand, firm and good to soft going: tried in cheekpieces/blinkers/tongue tie. *P. D. Niven*

GOLDEN GAMES (IRE) 3 b.f. Montjeu (IRE) 137 – Ski For Gold 76 (Shirley Heights 130) [2009 57p: 10.2m 12.6g 14.1m^2 14g^2 12m^4 Aug 19] fair maiden handicapper: left J. Dunlop 14,000 gns prior to final start: stays 1¾m: acts on good to firm ground. *D. C. O'Brien* **70**

GOLDEN GATES (IRE) 2 b.g. (Feb 10) Key of Luck (USA) 126 – Golden Anthem (USA) 93 (Lion Cavern (USA) 117) [2009 10m^4 Oct 5] €18,000Y: first foal: dam, 2-y-o 5f winner, half-sister to smart 7f/1m winner Fong's Thong: 50/1, 4¾ lengths fourth to Futurist in maiden at Pontefract, green before late headway: will do better. *Mrs A. Duffield* **68 p**

GOLDEN GROOM 6 b.g. Groom Dancer (USA) 128 – Reine de Thebes (FR) 67 (Darshaan 133) [2009 12m* Jun 2] rather leggy gelding: fair handicapper: successful last 3 starts, leaving C. Fairhurst and off 21 months prior to winning at Ripon in June sole outing in 2009: stays 2m: acts on good to firm and good to soft going: races prominently: reliable. *P. Beaumont* **65**

GOLDEN KISS 3 b.f. Golden Snake (USA) 127 – Kiss Me Again (IRE) 80 (Cyrano de Bergerac 120) [2009 –: 7m 9d May 17] no form. *Paul Murphy* **–**

GOLDEN PENNY 4 b.g. Xaar 132 – Dog Rose (SAF) (Fort Wood (USA) 117) [2009 84: 7.1m 9m^6 7s* 7.9m 8g 8g 7.2v f8f f8f Dec 17] lengthy, good-topped gelding: has round action: fairly useful handicapper: easily best effort in 2009 when winning at Newcastle in May: left A. G. Foster after sixth start: stays 1m: acts on all-weather, firm and soft going: blinkered final outing. *M. Dods* **84**

GOLDEN PIPPIN 2 b.f. (Mar 20) Medicean 128 – Surf The Net 91 (Cape Cross (IRE) 129) [2009 6m 6g^5 7g p7g p8g p7.1g Nov 2] compact filly: second foal: dam 2-y-o 6f winner (stayed 1m): poor maiden: should stay 1m. *R. Hannon* **43**

GOLDEN POOL (IRE) 3 b.f. Danetime (IRE) 121 – Miss Megs (IRE) 81 (Croco Rouge (IRE) 126) [2009 57: 7m^6 f7g 6d a8g^3 a5.5g^5 a8g^3 a5.5g^3 a8g* a5.5g^2 a8g^2 a8g^2 a8g* Nov 27] angular filly: modest performer: sold from S. Callaghan 2,000 gns after third start: won maiden in October and minor event in November, both at Ovrevoll: stays 1m: acts on dirt/polytrack. *Cathrine Witso Slettemark, Norway* **56**

GOLDEN PROSPECT 5 b.g. Lujain (USA) 119 – Petonellajill 73 (Petong 126) [2009 78: p8g^4 p8g p7.1g 6g^5 6m 7g* 7f^5 7f^3 7.6g 8f^6 7g 8f* p7.1g^3 7m^5 p7.1g^5 p8.6g p7m p7m p8.6g^2 p7.1g p7.1g^6 Dec 28] good-topped gelding: fair handicapper: won at Brighton in June and September (apprentices): left J. Hills £8,000 after fifteenth start: stays 1m: acts on polytrack, firm and good to soft going: tried in cheekpieces, blinkered last 3 starts: held up. *Miss J. R. Tooth* **65**

GOLDEN RING 3 b.c. Hawk Wing (USA) 136 – Farhana 109 (Fayruz 116) [2009 10m 10m 8m Jun 20] big, heavy-topped colt: well held in maidens at Newmarket: sold £3,600. *P. J. O'Gorman* **–**

GOLDEN ROCK (IRE) 3 ch.g. Rock of Gibraltar (IRE) 133 – Sister Golden Hair (IRE) (Glint of Gold 128) [2009 10m^5 10m^6 10g^2 12s 10g 10.2v Nov 4] €190,000F, 92,000 2-y-o: well-made gelding: half-brother to several winners, including useful 7f (in Ireland at 2 yrs)/1m winner Alexis (by Alzao), later successful in Canada: dam German 2-y-o 1m winner: fairly useful maiden: runner-up at Windsor: little impact in handicaps after: stays 1¼m: best effort on good ground: tried visored. *R. Charlton* **77**

GOLDEN ROSIE (IRE) 3 ch.f. Exceed And Excel (AUS) 126 – Kelsey Rose 97 (Most Welcome 131) [2009 74: 7m^5 7m^3 6g^6 6d Oct 12] close-coupled, good-topped filly: fair handicapper: regressive form in 2009: should prove best at 5f/6f: acts on good to soft going: has hung right: wore a hood second/third starts: sold 13,500. *B. W. Hills* **67**

GOLDEN RUN 6 b.m. Commanche Run 133 – Goldengirlmichelle (IRE) 41 (Project Manager 111) [2009 p9.5g Apr 20] modest hurdler: well held in claimer at Wolverhampton on Flat debut. *R. Hollinshead* **–**

GOLDEN SHAHEEN (IRE) 2 b.g. (Feb 11) Invincible Spirit (IRE) 121 – Cheeky Weeky (Cadeaux Genereux 131) [2009 7.2s^2 p7f^2 7m p7g* Oct 21] 125,000F, 150,000Y: well-made gelding: brother to fairly useful 2006 2-y-o 6f winner Pretty Majestic and half-brother to several winners, including 8-y-o Cellarmaster: dam French maiden (stayed 1½m): fairly useful performer: won maiden at Kempton by 3½ lengths from Warning Song, dictating: subsequently gelded: likely to stay at least 1m: acts on polytrack: visored last 2 starts. *Saeed bin Suroor* **90**

GOLDEN SQUARE 7 ch.g. Tomba 119 – Cherish Me 88 (Polar Falcon (USA) 126) [2009 56d: p8g p8g p10g^3 p8g^3 p10g p8g p7g Nov 25] workmanlike gelding: modest performer: stays 1¼m: acts on all-weather, firm and good to soft ground: tried in headgear: no battler. *A. W. Carroll* **52**

Virgin Money Chester Vase, Chester—an Aidan O'Brien 1,2 but not in the order the market predicted; Golden Sword makes all while Masterofthehorse finishes strongly out wide ahead of Debussy, Sight Unseen and Saptapadi

GOLDEN STREAM (IRE) 3 b.f. Sadler's Wells (USA) 132 – Phantom Gold 119 (Machiavellian (USA) 123) [2009 97p: 10f^6 8m^2 7.1g* 7g 8m^3 7m* 6g Oct 10] good-topped filly: has a fluent action: useful performer: won listed races at Warwick (by 1½ lengths from Damaniyat Girl) in June and Ascot (beat Red Dune by length) in September: below form in 6f Bengough Memorial Stakes at Ascot final outing: should stay beyond 1m: raced only on good going or firmer: tactically versatile. *Sir Michael Stoute* **107**

GOLDEN SWORD 3 b.c. High Chaparral (IRE) 132 – Sitara 74 (Salse (USA) 128) [2009 88p: 10.5g^4 12.3m* 12g^5 12g^2 12m^5 Jul 25] tall, useful-looking colt: has scope: very smart performer: 25/1, improved form when winning Virgin Money Chester Vase in May by 2 lengths from Masterofthehorse: best efforts when 2¼ lengths fifth to Sea The Stars in Derby at Epsom and 5 lengths second to Fame And Glory in Irish equivalent at the Curragh: possibly feeling effects of busy campaign when respectable fifth to Conduit in King George VI and Queen Elizabeth Stakes at Ascot final start: will stay at least 1¾m: acts on soft and good to firm going: usually races up with pace: has joined M. de Kock. *A. P. O'Brien, Ireland* **122**

GOLDEN TIGER 2 br.c. (Jan 14) Kyllachy 129 – Roxy (Rock City 120) [2009 f7g^2 Dec 22] 12,000F, £16,000Y, £2,600 2-y-o: seventh foal: half-brother to 7f (including 2-y-o seller) winner Night Kiss (by Night Shift): dam unraced half-sister to Irish 1000 Guineas runner-up Goodnight Kiss: 5/1, encouraging 3 lengths second to Secretive in maiden at Southwell: should improve. *T. P. Tate* **67 p**

GOLDEN WATERS 2 b.f. (Mar 24) Dubai Destination (USA) 127 – Faraway Waters 102 (Pharly (FR) 130) [2009 8g^5 Sep 30] seventh foal: half-sister to smart 1m (at 2 yrs)/ 1¼m winner Something Exciting (by Halling), second in Oaks: dam, 2-y-o 6f winner who stayed 1½m, half-sister to smart performer up to 1¾m Gower Song: 33/1, 2½ lengths fifth to Spoken in maiden at Salisbury: will stay 1¼m: should do better. *Eve Johnson Houghton* **66 p**

GOLD EXPRESS 6 b.g. Observatory (USA) 131 – Vanishing Point (USA) (Caller I D (USA)) [2009 81: 6g^6 p7g 7m p6g^3 6m 6m^4 p8g* 8.3m* 8.1g Aug 21] big, strong gelding: fairly useful handicapper: won at Kempton and Windsor in July: eased as if amiss at Sandown final start: stays 8.3f: acts on polytrack, good to firm and good to soft ground: held up: travels strongly. *P. J. O'Gorman* **90**

GOLD FIX (IRE) 2 b.f. (Apr 4) Fath (USA) 116 – Gold Blended (IRE) 59 (Goldmark (USA) 113) [2009 6m 7g 6s 7d^2 7m^3 7g* p7.1m^6 7d* 7m^2 p8.6g^2 7g^6 Oct 17] small filly: second foal: half-sister to 3-y-o Wilbury Star: dam, winning Irish hurdler, half-sister to smart performer up to 13.4f Compton Bolter: fair performer: won seller at Catterick in August and nursery at Epsom in September: stays 8.6f: acts on polytrack, soft and good to firm going: sold €5,000. *M. R. Channon* **67**

GOLDIKOVA (IRE) 4 b.f. Anabaa (USA) 130 – Born Gold (USA) (Blushing Groom (FR) 131) [2009 129: 9.3s 8g* 8d* 8m* 7g^3 8f* Nov 7] **133**

The 'seventies and 'eighties saw the emergence in France of four rattling good racemares, contemporaries Allez France and Dahlia, rated 136 and 135 respectively by Timeform, and, a decade later, Triptych and Miesque, both rated 133. Allez France was kept in training for four seasons and her thirteen victories included eight Group 1 events; the extraordinarily hardy and much travelled Dahlia, whom Allez France beat all seven times they met, stayed in training even longer and won ten Group/Grade 1s in four different countries, though one of those ten was achieved after she had been transferred permanently to the States (the Canadian International that she won in 1974 was a strong edition but officially carried only Grade 2 status then). Like Dahlia, Triptych was a particularly durable racemare and most of her forty-one races were in Group 1 company, her record including nine Group 1 wins by the time she was retired as a six-year-old.

The two-years-younger Miesque never met Triptych in racecourse competition, Miesque doing nearly all her racing at a mile while Triptych was raced mostly at middle distances. The curtain came down on their careers on the same November afternoon in 1988 when both contested races at the Breeders' Cup. Triptych's fourth in the Turf was overshadowed by Miesque's second victory in the Breeders' Cup Mile, which gave her a tenth Group 1 victory, a record for a European-trained filly or mare since the pattern was introduced. That illustrious quartet could be joined in the next season by the miler Goldikova, who emulated Miesque in the latest season by winning her second successive Breeders' Cup Mile, a victory which brought her Group 1 total to seven wins.

The latest season was the thirty-ninth in the history of the European pattern and there were more opportunities for horses to earn 'black type' than ever before, with 392 races designated Group 1, 2 or 3. The growth in the number of pattern races has been particularly noticeable over the last decade, one of the areas of expansion being the number of Group 1s now open to older fillies and mares. Three of the Group 1s won by Goldikova—the Falmouth Stakes and two editions of the Prix Rothschild—are relatively new creations, following a radical overhaul of the pattern system relating to fillies and mares which saw the Falmouth, the Prix d'Astarte (now Rothschild), the Matron, the Pretty Polly, the Sun Chariot and the Premio Lydia Tesio all elevated to Group 1 in 2004 (the Prix Jean Romanet was upgraded in 2009). This particular extension of the pattern was designed to encourage owners and breeders to keep their fillies and mares in training in Europe after

Etihad Airways Falmouth Stakes, Newmarket—the first of four Group/Grade 1s in the season for Goldikova who doesn't need to be at her best to take care of Heaven Sent (blaze), Spacious (left) and Rainbow View

Prix Rothschild (formerly Prix d'Astarte), Deauville—Goldikova wins for the second year running; Poule d'Essai des Pouliches winner Elusive Wave is clear of the rest, Proviso (fourth left) coming through for third ahead of Sahpresa and Eva's Request (rail)

the age of three, rather than pack them off to stud or transfer them to North America where there are more opportunities.

The total number of Group 1s in Europe in all categories in 2009 was eighty-five, compared to seventy-one in 1988, Miesque's final season, and seventy-three in 1998. Clashes between top fillies and top colts have traditionally added interest to the open championship races in Europe, in contrast to America where a full Grade 1 programme for four-year-old fillies and mares has been in place for very much longer and has led largely to fillies and mares not taking on the colts. The undefeated Zenyatta became the first mare to win the Breeders' Cup Classic, stretching her run to fourteen consecutive victories, the other thirteen in races restricted to her own sex including the previous year's Breeders' Cup Ladies Classic. Zenyatta's epic win at Santa Anita, which overshadowed the others on the day, including that of Goldikova, put her one in front of another legendary American racemare, the undefeated Personal Ensign who, coincidentally, had her final race on the same Breeders' Cup card that featured the farewells of Miesque and Triptych, Personal Ensign contesting the Breeders' Cup Distaff (now Ladies Classic) in which she got the better of a battle royal with Winning Colors. Eight of Dahlia's and seven of Miesque's ten Group 1 victories were achieved in open company, by the way, as were eight of Triptych's nine.

Goldikova's own Group 1 tally would almost certainly have been even higher by now, but for her being foaled in the same year as another outstanding French filly, the unbeaten Zarkava, behind whom Goldikova was placed in both the Poule d'Essai des Pouliches and the Prix de Diane. Zarkava matched Allez France by winning France's top two-year-old race for fillies, the Prix Marcel Boussac (known as the Criterium des Pouliches when Allez France won it), and three of the historic championship events in France for three-year-old fillies, the Poule d'Essai des Pouliches, Prix de Diane and Prix Vermeille (restricted to three-year-olds until 2004 when it was first opened to four-year-olds). Zarkava went one better than Allez France as a three-year-old in the Prix de l'Arc de Triomphe, earning a Timeform rating of 133 (Allez France ended her three-year-old season with a rating of 132, achieving her 136 as a four-year-old when undefeated in five races—all against colts—her three Group 1s including the Prix de l'Arc). The financial pressure on an owner to retire a top-class filly at the end of her three-year-old days has never been so great as with a top colt whose reputation and stud value has been established by classic success or victory in one or more of the great open-aged championship events. It has nevertheless always been a matter for regret that so many top horses are retired without having the chance to realise their fullest potential. Had her owner decided to test Zarkava at four, there is, of course, no guarantee that she would have trained on—what her trainer described as her 'strong spirit' probably played a small part in the decision to retire her—but at risk would have been the value of one foal, not, as with a top colt, the whole of one season's stud fees.

As it was, Zarkava's retirement left the way clear for Goldikova to assume the mantle she had been denied by Zarkava as a three-year-old, that of Europe's best filly. Her main target was a second Breeders' Cup Mile at Santa Anita, the first course that has staged the Breeders' Cup in successive years. Goldikova's European campaign got off to a disappointing start when she managed only seventh of nine, starting a short-priced favourite, in the Prix d'Ispahan at Longchamp in May, the soft going possibly a factor (she had been beaten on heavy on her reappearance at three). Goldikova had gone from strength to strength as a three-year-old once her clashes with Zarkava were out of the way, beating members of her own sex in the Prix Chloe at Maisons-Laffitte and in the Prix Rothschild at Deauville before maintaining her good run with victories against the colts in the Prix du Moulin at Longchamp and in the Breeders' Cup Mile. Goldikova resumed winning ways after her setback in the d'Ispahan, taking the Etihad Airways Falmouth Stakes at Newmarket in July (showing the best speed and then doing no more than necessary in front to win from Heaven Sent and Spacious) and the Prix Rothschild (impressively from the Poule d'Essai des Pouliches winner Elusive Wave with the runners-up in the Irish Guineas and the Coronation Stakes also in the strong field). There was only a fortnight between the Prix Rothschild and Goldikova's principal European objective, the Prix du Haras de Fresnay-le-Buffard - Jacques le Marois over the same course and distance. Odds-on Goldikova and her pacemaker Only Green were the only fillies in the nine-strong line-up which included the Poule d'Essai des Poulains winner Silver Frost, the Prix d'Ispahan winner Never On Sunday and the Dubai Duty Free winner Gladiatorus. The last-named was joined from Britain by the Lockinge winner Virtual and by Aqlaam, who was on the comeback trail and had gained his first win of the year in the Summer Mile at Ascot. Goldikova was brilliant, taking over on the bridle two furlongs out and quickening right away when shaken up to win by six lengths and five from Aqlaam and Virtual. Silver Frost, Never On Sunday and Gladiatorus all performed well below their best but the official margin of Goldikova's victory—though the distance looked to be around five lengths, rather than the six returned—hadn't been equalled since another four-year-old filly Lianga put up a similarly spectacular performance to brush aside a smart field in 1975 (Northjet won by five from a top-class one in 1981). Goldikova's winning time of 1m 33.50sec smashed Spinning World's race record time by almost a second, though, contrary to reports, it was not inside the official course record—a scarcely believable 1m 33.20sec set by Gay Style in the 1974 Prix d'Astarte.

There have been few better performances by a filly at a mile in Timeform's experience than Goldikova's in the Jacques le Marois. Those that might arguably rank at least as highly can be counted on the fingers of one hand. The estimable Petite Etoile was never off a tight rein in the 1959 Sussex Stakes, winning 'very easily indeed' according to *Racehorses* which rated her 134 after an undefeated

*Prix du Haras de Fresnay-le-Buffard - Jacques le Marois, Deauville—
a breathtaking performance from Goldikova, one of the best by a filly at a mile in
Timeform's long experience; Aqlaam easily takes care of the remainder, who are headed by Virtual*

TVG Breeders' Cup Mile, Santa Anita—another authoritative display as Goldikova ends 2009 as she did 2008 and takes her career total of Group/Grade 1 wins to seven; Courageous Cat (blaze), Justenuffhumor and Court Vision (blinkers) fill the next three places

campaign in which she won top races at a mile to a mile and a half. French-trained Hula Dancer, rated 133, was beaten only once in a nine-start career and numbered a six-length win in the Prix du Moulin among a series of outstanding performances which also included a very easy win in the Jacques le Marois before a brilliant performance in the Champion Stakes at Newmarket, all as a three-year-old. Lianga also earned a rating of 133 and was equally at home at a mile or over sprint distances, winning the July Cup, Prix de l'Abbaye and Haydock Sprint Cup in the same season as the Jacques le Marois. Also in the argument is the very fine mile- to mile-and-a-quarter performer Rose Bowl, a year-younger contemporary of Lianga (the pair were virtually inseparable in a three-way photo-finish to the 1975 Sussex Stakes in which they were just touched off by Two Thousand Guineas winner Bolkonski). Rose Bowl won successive editions of the Queen Elizabeth II Stakes in fine style (rated 133 after her first win) and she also won a Champion Stakes (from five-year-old Allez France). And then there is Miesque who won both her editions of the Breeders' Cup Mile very decisively—by three and a half lengths the first time and by four lengths the second—and was a champion by any standards. Winner of both the One Thousand Guineas and the Poule d'Essai des Pouliches, she was the first to win the Prix Jacques le Marois twice and also won the Prix du Moulin, building up a record of twelve wins from sixteen starts and only once finishing worse than second.

Goldikova cannot now finish her career with a record for consistency to match that of Miesque—it currently stands at ten wins from fifteen starts (her five defeats including finishing third twice and unplaced once). Goldikova is not much the worse for that and she stays in training with a good chance of going one better than Miesque by winning a third Breeders' Cup Mile. Her second victory in the race followed a setback in the Prix de la Foret at Longchamp, where, starting at long odds on, she was narrowly beaten into third after crossing from a wide draw to race a little more prominently than usual, her rider reporting 'she was off today . . . in the last two and a half furlongs I had nothing in my hands, she was flat.' Goldikova has suffered four of her five defeats at Longchamp where she has won only once, probably no more than coincidence since two of the defeats were by Zarkava, but something worth recording nonetheless. If anything ailed Goldikova in the Foret, it didn't seem to concern her trainer unduly ('Did she use herself too much early on?' was his post-race comment). Freddie Head, who rode Miesque in all her races, stuck by his opinion—expressed after the Jacques le Marois—that Goldikova was 'superior to Miesque'.

'I think she is better than last year, in better condition and she has travelled better . . . I am very confident,' Head reported before the Breeders' Cup Mile (in which Goldikova, who had raced drug free the year before, ran on lasix). Goldikova was the clear pick on form in what proved no better than an average renewal of the Mile for which the going was firm, as it had been twelve months earlier. The race itself was plain sailing for Goldikova, who gave her rider Olivier Peslier an arm-chair ride. The early pace was very strong—if anything too strong—and Goldikova was dropped in behind this time from a wide draw (her starting position had raised concerns beforehand). Once she began her finishing run on the outside in the home straight, Goldikova always looked likely to peg back the leaders and eventually won with something in hand by half a length from the progressive three-year-old Courageous Cat. Goldikova's win was the eleventh for Europe in twenty-six runnings, but Barathea's success in 1994 remains the only one by a British challenger following the eclipse of the latest three-pronged attack, Delegator managing fifth, Gladiatorus only ninth, after being one of the trailblazers, and Zacinto all but pulled up. Goldikova, who won the female turf horse of the year Eclipse Award, is the fourth dual winner of the Mile—following Miesque, Lure and Da Hoss—and the fifth of her sex to win it, four of those having been Europeans (Ridgewood Pearl and Six Perfections were successful between Miesque and Goldikova).

Goldikova (IRE) (b.f. 2005)	Anabaa (USA) (b 1992)	Danzig (b 1977)	Northern Dancer
			Pas de Nom
		Balbonella (b or br 1984)	Gay Mecene
			Bamieres
	Born Gold (USA) (ch 1991)	Blushing Groom (ch 1974)	Red God
			Runaway Bride
		Riviere d'Or (b 1985)	Lyphard
			Gold River

The extended pedigree of the close-coupled Goldikova was dealt with in detail in *Racehorses of 2008* but there are some updates. Her sire Anabaa died from peritonitis after an operation for colic in July, Goldikova's dam having been one of eighty-five mares who visited him in what turned out to be his final season. Anabaa's remarkable story is recounted fully in the essay on him in *Racehorses of 1996* but, to recap, he was affected by a spinal injury and diagnosed as a 'wobbler' as a two-year-old. Anabaa seemed unlikely to make the racecourse and his owner Sheikh Maktoum Al Maktoum gave him away to Alec Head, the father of Anabaa's trainer Criquette Head. Alec Head hoped that the well-bred Anabaa (by Danzig out of a Group 1 winner) might recover sufficiently to carry out duties as a teaser at Haras du Quesnay. Anabaa confounded the prognosis of the vets and eventually raced for the Head family as a three-year-old (after being offered back to Sheikh Maktoum). His development at four into Europe's undisputed champion sprinter (ridden by Goldikova's trainer) earned him a place at the Haras du Quesnay in his own right and he made a fine start to his stallion career with Amonita winning the Prix Marcel Boussac and another member of his first crop, Anabaa Blue, going on to success in the Prix du Jockey Club. In the end, Anabaa didn't live up to the loftiest expectations raised by his first crop, though he became a fixture in the list of leading French sires and also enjoyed success in Australia. Goldikova's dam Born Gold eventually won at a mile in the French Provinces as a four-year-old after proving disappointing for Criquette Head at three. Born Gold's sister Gold Splash was a much better racemare, winning the Marcel Boussac and the Coronation Stakes, but the fortunes of the two have been reversed at stud. While Gold Splash has produced only three winners, none of them above listed level, Born Gold has bred ten winners so far, the latest of them her Green Tune two-year-old Ocean Seven, who won a nine-furlong newcomers race at Fontainebleau in November by five lengths. Born Gold has had two other pattern winners besides Goldikova, the smart Gold Sound (by Green Tune) successful in the nine-furlong Prix de Guiche and the useful Gold Round (by Caerleon), who won the Prix Cleopatre over an extended mile and a quarter. The respective achievements at stud of Born Gold and Gold Splash illustrate that a filly's racing record is not necessarily a reliable guide to her prospects as a broodmare. When Goldikova herself is eventually retired, there is also bound to be discussion about whether a mare's stud prospects are prejudiced by racing her beyond the age of three. This is perhaps a topic for another time but, among the top racemares mentioned earlier in this essay, Dahlia bred four Group/Grade 1 winners, Personal Ensign three and Miesque two, while Lianga is the great grandam of champion sire Danehill Dancer, and Rose Bowl the grandam of Sprint Cup winner Iktamal (Petite Etoile was barren more often than not at stud but Zarkava is among her descendents; Triptych, carrying her first foal, died after being struck by a truck in her paddock). Goldikova is best at a mile and acts on firm and good to soft ground. She is genuine but has a tendency to be mulish at the stalls (as she was in the latest season before the Falmouth and the Jacques le Marois, and a little less so at the Breeders' Cup start). She usually tracks the pace and has a fine turn of foot. *F. Head, France*

GOLD MAHA 3 b.f. Diktat 126 – Westwood (FR) (Anabaa (USA) 130) [2009 8d 10.9m4 10.4g5 14m4 10m 13.8m Sep 19] leggy filly: modest maiden: left M. Channon 3,000 gns after fourth start: stays 10.9f: unraced on extremes of going. *M. E. Sowersby* **59**

GOLD PARTY 2 ch.c. (Apr 24) Bahamian Bounty 116 – West River (USA) (Gone West (USA)) [2009 6m5 7f p9.5g p7m3 f8d2 Dec 29] half-brother to several winners, including 3-y-o Sparkaway and 8-y-o Nero West: dam ran once: fair maiden: left Tom Dascombe after second start: best effort when length second at Southwell: stays 1m: acts on all-weather: in eyeshields/tongue tie last 2 starts. *K. McAuliffe* **67**

GOLD ROCK (FR) 4 b.c. Anabaa (USA) 130 – Golden Sea (FR) (Saint Cyrien (FR) 128) [2009 p8g5 p10g5 p6g4 p9.5g Mar 30] ex-French colt: fairly useful 7f winner at 2 yrs for F. Head: trained by H-A. Pantall in 2008: well held at 4 yrs, including in claimers. *A. W. Carroll* **–**

GOLD RULES 2 ch.c. (Jan 26) Gold Away (IRE) 125 – Raphaela (FR) (Octagonal (NZ) 126) [2009 6m 6s 6m2 Aug 22] £31,000Y: good-topped colt: third foal: brother to French 1½m winner Radieuse: dam French 11.5f winner: easily best effort in maidens when 3½ lengths second to Tasmeem at Ripon: will be suited by 1m+: likely to do better still. *L. M. Cumani* **82 p**

GOLD STORY 2 ch.g. (Mar 31) Lucky Story (USA) 128 – Incatinka 63 (Inca Chief (USA)) [2009 6s6 6m5 6m 7g4 Sep 3] angular gelding: modest maiden: fourth in nursery at Redcar: stays 7f. *B. Ellison* **53**

GOLDTREK (USA) 2 b.f. (Mar 5) Medallist (USA) 117 – Traipse (USA) (Digression (USA) 116) [2009 8g p8g6 p8m6 Dec 4] $90,000Y: compact filly: third foal: half-sister to winner in USA by Include: dam US 1m/8.5f winner: modest form when sixth in maidens at Lingfield (pulled hard). *R. Charlton* **63**

GOLIATHS BOY (IRE) 3 ch.g. Medecis 119 – Green Belt (FR) (Tirol 127) [2009 95: 7.6m 10.1g 10.4g 8.1g2 10.3m5 10.3m2 9.9s2 Oct 12] leggy gelding: fairly useful handicapper: creditable efforts last 4 starts: stays 1¼m: acts on heavy and good to firm ground. *R. A. Fahey* **91**

GO MAN GO (IRE) 7 b.g. Courtship 88 – Rose of Summer (IRE) (Taufan (USA) 119) [2009 11.1g Jul 16] no sign of ability in bumper/over hurdles/in maiden on Flat. *B. Storey* **–**

GOMRATH (IRE) 2 b.c. (Jan 28) Lomitas 129 – Diner de Lune (IRE) (Be My Guest (USA) 126) [2009 7d Aug 1] 110,000Y: rangy colt: sixth foal: half-brother to 4-y-o Tyrrells Wood and French 6.5f winner Sara Luna (by Mark of Esteem): dam, French 2-y-o 7f/1m winner, half-sister to several at least smart winners, including Irish Oaks winner Moonstone: 25/1 and backward, 5¼ lengths seventh to Stags Leap in maiden at Goodwood: will be well suited by 1¼m+: will progress. *M. R. Channon* **67 p**

GO NANI GO 3 b.c. Kyllachy 129 – Go Between 91 (Daggers Drawn (USA) 114) [2009 87: 5m Aug 20] smallish, stocky colt: fairly useful performer at 2 yrs: well held sole outing in 2009: free-going sort, best at 5f: acts on good to soft ground. *B. Smart* **–**

GONE HUNTING 3 b.g. Hunting Lion (IRE) 115 – Arasong 76 (Aragon 118) [2009 89: p7g3 p6g* f6g6 p7g p6g 6g p6m Dec 30] strong, close-coupled gelding: fairly useful performer: won claimer at Wolverhampton (left W. Turner £11,000) in January: below form after, leaving Peter Grayson prior to final outing: stays 6f: acts on polytrack and soft ground: tried blinkered: often tongue tied. *J. Pearce* **86**

GONE'N'DUNNETT (IRE) 10 b.g. Petardia 113 – Skerries Bell 71 (Taufan (USA) 119) [2009 60§: p6g p6g5 f6g 7g 5.3f 5.3m 5.2s6 5.2s2 6g Aug 5] strong gelding: poor handicapper nowadays: best at 5f/6f: acts on all-weather, firm and soft going: wears headgear: has hung left: one to leave alone. *Mrs C. A. Dunnett* **48 §**

GOOD AGAIN 3 ch.f. Dubai Destination (USA) 127 – Good Girl (IRE) 100 (College Chapel 122) [2009 85: p8g* 8m4 8m* 8.1v4 8m6 7g 8m* Oct 5] sturdy filly: useful handicapper: won at Lingfield in April, Ascot in May and Pontefract (beat Truism 1½ lengths, travelling strongly and finding plenty) in October: stays 1m: unraced on firm going, acts on any other and polytrack: held up. *G. A. Butler* **104**

GOOD BA BA (USA) 7 b.g. Lear Fan (USA) 130 – Elle Meme (USA) (Zilzal (USA) 137) [2009 127: 8g* 7g² 8d⁴ 8m 8g³ 8g* Dec 13] high-class performer: successful at Sha Tin in Citi Stewards' Cup (for second year running, beat Fellowship 1¾ lengths) in January and, having left A. Schutz after third start, Cathay Pacific Hong Kong Mile (for third year in a row, by ½ length from Happy Zero, leading close home) in December: placed there in between in Queen's Silver Jubilee Cup (¾-length second to Egyptian Ra) and International Mile Trial (1½ lengths third to Fellowship): best at 7f/1m: acts on good to firm going: wears tongue tie: usually held up. *D. Cruz, Hong Kong* **126**

GOOD BUY DUBAI (USA) 3 gr.g. Essence of Dubai (USA) 118 – Sofisticada (USA) (Northern Jove (CAN)) [2009 54p: p10g⁴ p10g² p12g⁴ p12g* 12.1m⁶ 11.6g* 14.1f 12m³ p10g³ p10g³ p12g⁶ p12g⁵ 12s⁴ 11.6d p12g⁴ Oct 20] useful-looking gelding: fair handicapper: won at Kempton and Windsor in April: stays 1½m: acts on polytrack and good to firm ground: tried tongue tied, visored final outing: races lazily, and is unreliable. *J. R. Best* **64 §**

GOODBYE CASH (IRE) 5 b.m. Danetime (IRE) 121 – Jellybeen (IRE) 72 (Petardia 113) [2009 74d: 6m* 6m 6g 6m 7g* 7f³ 7f³ 7m* 8s⁵ 7.1d 8f⁵ 7m⁴ 7m⁴ p7.1g⁶ p7m² p7g p7m² p7.1g⁵ p7.1g⁵ p7.1g Dec 26] small, leggy mare: fair performer: won handicap at L'Ancresse (Guernsey) in May, seller at Brighton in July and handicap at Folkestone in August: effective at 6f/7f: acts on all-weather, heavy and good to firm going: tried in cheekpieces. *P. D. Evans* **68**

GOODBYE EARL (IRE) 2 b.f. (Mar 8) Bertolini (USA) 125 – Begine (IRE) (Germany (USA) 124) [2009 5m⁶ 5.1m⁴ 5s 5g² 5g 5g⁶ 5g³ 5.1m⁴ 5d² 5s⁴ 5m⁶ 5d⁵ 5d 5m Sep 14] €4,700Y: sparely-made filly: fifth foal: half-sister to 7f to 11f winner Tancredi (by Rossini): dam unraced half-sister to dam of smart sprinter Eastern Purple: fair maiden: raced only at 5f: acts on soft and good to firm going: has hung right: races prominently: not one to trust. *A. Berry* **69 §**

GOODBYE MR BOND 9 b.g. Elmaamul (USA) 125 – Fifth Emerald 54 (Formidable (USA) 125) [2009 97: 8m 8.1m 9.8d 8.9d 7.9m 8.1g³ 9.2s⁵ 8g Aug 5] strong, lengthy gelding: just fair handicapper in 2009: needs good test at 1m nowadays, and stays 1¼m: acts on fibresand and any turf going: visored (raced freely) once: waited with. *E. J. Alston* **72**

GOOD CAUSE (IRE) 8 b.g. Simply Great (FR) 122 – Smashing Pet (Mummy's Pet 125) [2009 57: 10g Aug 5] workmanlike gelding: modest maiden: well held only outing in 2009: dead. *Mrs S. Lamyman* **–**

GOOD EFFECT (USA) 5 ch.g. Woodman (USA) 126 – River Dreams (USA) (Riverman (USA) 131) [2009 78: p12g 11.9g³ p13g 11.9m 11.7f 12m⁴ p13.9g Sep 17] strong, useful-looking gelding: modest handicapper nowadays: left C. Morlock 6,000 gns after sixth start: barely stays 1½m: acts on polytrack and good to soft going: tried in cheekpieces/visor/tongue tie: usually waited with: has hung: one to avoid. *Tim Vaughan* **60 §**

GOOD FOR HER 3 b.f. Rock of Gibraltar (IRE) 133 – Tyranny 97 (Machiavellian (USA) 123) [2009 72: 8m⁶ 7g³ 8m⁴ Aug 5] close-coupled filly: fair maiden: stays 1m: unraced on ground softer than good: has raced freely. *J. L. Dunlop* **69**

GOOD GORSOON (USA) 4 b.c. Stravinsky (USA) 133 – Alwaysinbloom (USA) (Unbridled (USA) 128) [2009 92: 6m 5.1m⁶ 6d 5m p5g³ 5m 6g⁴ 5d 5f 6m 6m* p6g p5g Oct 22] quite good-topped colt: fairly useful handicapper: won at Newmarket in September: effective at 5f/easy 6f: acts on polytrack and firm going: free-going sort, sometimes finds little: none too consistent: sold 12,000 gns. *B. W. Hills* **93**

GOOD HUMOURED 3 b.g. Rock of Gibraltar (IRE) 133 – Humouresque 110 (Pivotal 124) [2009 61p: p7.1g⁴ p8g p6m⁵ f6g p10g³ Oct 24] sturdy gelding: fair maiden: stays 1¼m: raced only on all-weather: sold 5,500 gns. *Sir Mark Prescott* **67**

GOODISON GOAL (IRE) 2 b.f. (Mar 17) Trade Fair 124 – Chantilly (FR) (Sanglamore (USA) 126) [2009 7.1m 6m p6g⁶ f6g⁶ p7.1m p7g³ Dec 31] €14,000F, £8,000Y: seventh foal: half-sister to 4-y-o Jebel Tara: dam unraced half-sister to dam of 3-y-o Harbinger: modest maiden: third in nursery final start: likely to stay 1m: acts on all-weather. *Pat Morris* **52**

GOODISON PARK 2 ch.f. (Jan 27) Big Shuffle (USA) 122 – Perfect Dream 72 (Emperor Jones (USA) 119) [2009 7m 7m⁴ 8d Oct 13] third foal: half-sister to 5-y-o Perlachy: dam Irish maiden (stayed 1½m): gradual improvement, 9 lengths eighth to Deirdre in maiden at Newcastle final start. *A. G. Foster* **59**

GOOD KARMA (IRE) 5 b.g. Shernazar 131 – Kayrava (Irish River (FR) 131) [2009 p9.5g Oct 23] poor maiden hurdler: well held on Flat debut. *P. J. Rothwell, Ireland* **–**

GOOD QUEEN BEST 3 b.f. Best of The Bests (IRE) 122 – Spring Sunrise 59 –
(Robellino (USA) 127) [2009 46: 7.6d 8d Aug 28] leggy filly: poor maiden. *B. De Haan*

GOODWOOD DIVA 2 ch.f. (Mar 11) Kyllachy 129 – Donna Vita 85 (Vettori (IRE) **49**
119) [2009 6g 7f p7g Oct 20] 17,000Y: second foal: dam, 2-y-o 7f winner, half-sister to useful performer up to 2m Sentinel: poor form in maidens: seemed amiss final start: sold 1,500 gns. *J. L. Dunlop*

GOODWOOD MAESTRO 2 b.g. (Mar 4) Piccolo 121 – Madurai 71 (Chilibang 120) **85**
[2009 6m* p6m^5 7g Oct 24] brother to fairly useful 1999 2-y-o 6f winner Maestersinger and half-brother to winner in Czech Republic by First Trump: dam 6f winner: fairly useful form when winning maiden at Goodwood (by ¾ length from Footstepsofspring, travelling strongly) in May: off 5 months, well below form in minor event/nursery, then gelded: stays 6f. *J. L. Dunlop*

GOODWOOD STARLIGHT (IRE) 4 br.g. Mtoto 134 – Starring (FR) 74 (Ashka- **89**
lani (IRE) 128) [2009 100: 10.1g 10m 12m 14g 9.9m^6 12m^6 9.9m^6 9.7m^6 12g^4 11.7g Oct 21] lightly-made gelding: fairly useful handicapper nowadays: stays 1½m: acts on polytrack, soft and good to firm going: tongue tied last 5 outings: sold £6,200. *G. L. Moore*

GOOGOOBARABAJAGAL (IRE) 3 b.g. Almutawakel 126 – Shamah 96 (Unfu- **58**
wain (USA) 131) [2009 58: 12m^5 12.1g^4 11.6g 14.1g^3 16g 15.4m^5 Sep 22] strong gelding: modest maiden handicapper: stays 2m: acts on good to firm ground: blinkered final outing. *W. S. Kittow*

GOOLAGONG (IRE) 2 b.f. (Mar 23) Giant's Causeway (USA) 132 – Maroochydore **67 p**
(IRE) 98 (Danehill (USA) 126) [2009 7.1g^4 Aug 21] 105,000Y: rangy filly: has scope: second foal: dam, Irish 2-y-o 6f/7f winner, half-sister to smart Hong Kong 1m/1¼m performer Bowman's Crossing: 7/2, 4 lengths fourth to Private Story in maiden at Sandown, travelling smoothly but no extra after 2f out: should do better. *R. M. Beckett*

GOOSEBERRY BUSH 2 b.f. (Feb 17) Tobougg (IRE) 125 – Away To Me (Exit To **68**
Nowhere (USA) 122) [2009 5g 6g 5.1m^2 5.1g 6.5m 5g^6 Oct 19] 4,000Y: well-made filly: half-sister to several winners, including 3-y-o Directorship and 7-y-o Exit Smiling: dam unraced: fair maiden: stays 6.5f: best efforts on good to firm going. *P. J. Makin*

GOOSE GREEN (IRE) 5 b.g. Invincible Spirit (IRE) 121 – Narbayda (IRE) 68 **72**
(Kahyasi 130) [2009 61: 10.9f 10m* 10g^4 10.2m* 10m* 10g^5 10g Jul 25] neat gelding: fair handicapper: won at Brighton in May, Bath in June and Brighton in July: stays 1¼m: acts on polytrack and any turf going: often held up. *R. J. Hodges*

GORDON FLASH 2 ch.c. (Mar 20) Alhaarth (IRE) 126 – Goslar 92 (In The Wings **62**
128) [2009 6m 8.1g^5 8.5d^3 9m^5 Sep 18] good-topped colt: modest maiden: should be suited by 9f+: acts on good to soft going. *R. Hannon*

GORDONSVILLE 6 b.g. Generous (IRE) 139 – Kimba (USA) (Kris S (USA)) [2009 **92**
88: 14m* 12s 12.1m^5 13.1m* 12m^4 16g^3 16.4m^5 13g^3 14m^4 18m^6 16d* Oct 28] tall gelding: fairly useful handicapper: won at Musselburgh in April, Ayr in June and Musselburgh in October: effective at 1½m to 2¼m: acts on polytrack and any turf going: held up: consistent. *J. S. Goldie*

GORDY BEE (USA) 3 b.c. More Than Ready (USA) 120 – Honoria (USA) 103 **77**
(Danzig (USA)) [2009 85: 10f^2 8d 8d 7g^3 Aug 29] compact colt: fair maiden: stays 1¼m: acts on firm and good to soft ground. *Pat Eddery*

GORE HILL (IRE) 3 ch.g. Exceed And Excel (AUS) 126 – Eschasse (USA) (Zilzal **57 +**
(USA) 137) [2009 –: 6m^3 5m 5.9m 7.5d* 7g 7g a6g 8d a8g Dec 13] modest performer: sold from K. R. Burke 3,000 gns after third start: won minor event at Klampenborg in August: left Jessica Long in Sweden after seventh outing: stays 7.5f: acts on good to soft going. *Goran Westerlund, Sweden*

GOSFORTH PARK 3 ch.c. Generous (IRE) 139 – Love And Kisses 70 (Salse (USA) **62**
128) [2009 10m^4 12m^6 12.4g^2 12s^6 14.1m^6 14m^3 12m^5 14v^4 12.4d^5 Oct 13] workmanlike colt: modest maiden handicapper: will be suited by 2m+: acts on heavy and good to firm ground. *M. Brittain*

GOSPEL SPIRIT 4 b.g. Cool Jazz 116 – Churchtown Spirit (Town And Country 124) –
[2009 10g p8f Dec 20] close-coupled gelding: fair form in bumpers, little show over hurdles: no form in maidens on Flat. *J. R. Jenkins*

GO SUNSHINE (IRE) 3 b.g. Tagula (IRE) 116 – Taoveret (IRE) (Flash of Steel 120) –
[2009 p7.1g p7.1g Apr 24] tongue tied, well held in maidens at Wolverhampton. *F. Sheridan*

GOSWICK 3 ch.f. Bertolini (USA) 125 – Holy Island 81 (Deploy 131) [2009 9.8m^{5} 9d 10.1m 12.1m 12d^{6} 12.5s 9.8g 8d^{6} Sep 7] big, workmanlike filly: modest maiden: stays 1¼m: acts on good to soft going. *Micky Hammond* **50**

GOT FLASH (FR) 3 b.g. Xaar 132 – Wild Flush (USA) (Pine Bluff (USA)) [2009 46: f7g^{4} f8g^{6} f8g Apr 23] neat gelding: modest maiden: should stay 1m: raced only on all-weather. *E. J. O'Neill* **56**

GO TO DUBAI 2 b.f. (Apr 5) Dubai Destination (USA) 127 – Black Belt Shopper (IRE) 82 (Desert Prince (IRE) 130) [2009 f5g^{5} 6g^{4} 7m^{2} 7.5m^{2} 7d^{4} Jul 22] 24,000F, 4,500Y: fourth foal: half-sister to 6f winner Exit Strategy (by Cadeaux Genereux) and a winner in Japan by Medicean: dam 2-y-o 6f winner: modest maiden: stays 7.5f: races prominently: sold 1,500 gns in October. *M. W. Easterby* **53**

GOURAY GIRL (IRE) 2 b.f. (May 10) Redback 116 – Brillano (FR) 75 (Desert King (IRE) 129) [2009 p6g* 6m^{2} p6m^{2} 6s^{2} Nov 7] 3,000Y, €24,000 2-y-o: third foal: sister to 4-y-o Sarah Park: dam 2-y-o 7f winner: fairly useful form: won maiden at Wolverhampton in September: good efforts when runner-up in nurseries, beaten head by Dubai Set at Doncaster final start: will be suited by 7f+: acts on polytrack, soft and good to firm ground. *W. R. Swinburn* **93**

GOVENOR ELIOTT (IRE) 4 ch.g. Rock of Gibraltar (IRE) 133 – Lac Dessert (USA) 91 (Lac Ouimet (USA)) [2009 –: 8.5m^{6} 10g p7.1g^{5} f6g Dec 8] rather leggy gelding: fair maiden at 2 yrs: little form since: blinkered once. *A. J. Lockwood* **–**

GOVERN 2 b.c. (Mar 25) Empire Maker (USA) 129 – Imroz (USA) 99 (Nureyev (USA) 131) [2009 7m^{2} 7d^{3} p7g Oct 29] sturdy colt: seventh foal: half-brother to 3 winners, including fairly useful 1¼m winner Posteritas (by Lear Fan) and 2002 2-y-o 7f winner Apex Star (by Diesis), later successful abroad: dam, 6f (at 2 yrs)/7f winner, out of Prix du Moulin winner and Oaks runner-up All At Sea: fairly useful form when placed in maidens at Yarmouth and Folkestone (third to Bint Doyen): tailed off at Lingfield: raced only at 7f. *H. R. A. Cecil* **80**

GOVERNMENT (IRE) 8 b.g. Great Dane (IRE) 122 – Hidden Agenda (FR) 55 (Machiavellian (USA) 123) [2009 56d: f8s f7s^{5} f8s f6g f8g^{5} f8g^{5} f7g f7g Mar 3] well-made gelding: poor performer: stays 1m: acts on fibresand and firm going: tried in blinkers: has bled: often makes running/races prominently. *M. C. Chapman* **47**

GOWER 5 b.g. Averti (IRE) 117 – Alashaan 73 (Darshaan 133) [2009 65: p6g p5.1g p6g p6g^{5} 5.1m 6.1f 5g f6g p6g^{3} f6g f5g^{5} Dec 22] rather leggy, close-coupled gelding: modest performer: best at 5f/easy 6f: acts on polytrack and good to soft going: sometimes in headgear: none too consistent. *R. J. Price* **53**

GOWER SOPHIA 2 b.f. (Apr 15) Captain Rio 122 – Hollow Quaill (IRE) 82 (Entrepreneur 123) [2009 5m^{2} 5m^{3} 5d^{3} 5m 5m^{4} f5g p6m^{2} 5g^{2} p5.1g^{5} 6v^{2} f5m p5.1g^{4} Dec 14] rather leggy filly: second foal: dam, Irish 1m winner, out of half-sister to Breeders' Cup Turf winner Northern Spur and high-class stayer Kneller: modest maiden: stays easy 6f: acts on polytrack, probably on good to firm going: tried blinkered, often visored: races prominently. *M. Brittain* **64**

GOWER VALENTINE 3 b.f. Primo Valentino (IRE) 116 – Mania (IRE) (Danehill (USA) 126) [2009 88: 5g 5g 5.9m 6d^{4} 6m^{2} 7g Oct 16] medium-sized filly: fairly useful handicapper: second at Leicester: below form otherwise: should prove best at 5f/6f: acts on good to firm ground: edgy sort. *D. Nicholls* **80**

GO WIN GIRL 2 gr.f. (Mar 29) Mark of Esteem (IRE) 137 – Grey Again 63 (Unfuwain (USA) 131) [2009 6g Jun 30] sixth foal: half-sister to 1m to 11f winner River Logic and French 5.5f (at 2 yrs) to 1½m winner Yeva Winner (both by Fasliyev): dam, 7f (at 2 yrs) to 11f winner, half-sister to smart performer up to 1½m Alost and to dam of very smart sprinter Pipalong: 50/1, tailed off in maiden at Thirsk. *P. C. Haslam* **–**

GOZOME (IRE) 5 ch.g. Golan (IRE) 129 – Schonbein (IRE) 60 (Persian Heights 129) [2009 p8.6g p8.6g 10m Apr 2] no form in maidens. *D. G. Bridgwater* **–**

GRA ADHMHAR (IRE) 2 b.g. (Feb 15) Mull of Kintyre (USA) 114 – Enya (Orpen (USA) 116) [2009 p8f^{6} Dec 20] 11/2, down the field in maiden at Kempton. *D. J. Coakley* **–**

GRACEANDGRATITUDE 2 b.f. (Apr 19) Royal Applause 124 – Shararah 87 (Machiavellian (USA) 123) [2009 5f p5g^{6} p6g p5m^{6} Dec 10] third foal: sister to 6f and (in Qatar) 1m winner Regal Veil and half-sister to 3-y-o Itsher: dam 6f winner: modest form at best: should stay 6f. *S. C. Williams* **53**

GRACECHURCH (IRE) 6 b.g. Marju (IRE) 127 – Saffron Crocus 83 (Shareef Dancer (USA) 135) [2009 72: p10g 8.1g 11.7f 10.2f^{4} 10.2f^{2} 10.2f^{3} 8g^{5} 10m p10m p8.6g **61**

Oct 15] leggy, useful-looking gelding: just modest handicapper in 2009: was best at 1¼m: acted on polytrack, firm and soft going: often held up: sometimes sweated: won over hurdles in August: dead. *R. J. Hodges*

GRACEFUL DESCENT (FR) 4 b.f. Hawk Wing (USA) 136 – Itab (USA) 71 (Dayjur (USA) 137) [2009 77: 10m^2 9.9m^2 9.9g^2 10.4g^2 11.1v* 12.5m^2 9.1g^2 Oct 23] good-topped filly: fair performer: won claimer at Hamilton in August (left R. Fahey after): should be suited by 1¾m: acts on polytrack, heavy and good to firm going: none too keen under pressure penultimate start. *J. S. Goldie* **77**

GRACE JICARO 2 ch.f. (Mar 6) Firebreak 125 – Anita In Wales (IRE) (Anita's Prince 126) [2009 5m 5m^5 5m 5g^5 5.3m^5 5m^5 5.1g Oct 21] sparely-made filly: fifth foal: dam ran once on Flat and twice over hurdles: poor maiden: blinkered (looked reluctant) final outing. *Mrs L. Williamson* **43**

GRACELIGHTENING 2 b.f. (Apr 27) Reset (AUS) 124 – Monica Geller 86 (Komaite (USA)) [2009 6.1v^5 8d^3 p8.6g^5 Sep 11] close-coupled filly: second foal: dam 1m (including at 2 yrs)/9f winner: best effort in maidens when third to Jibrrya at Thirsk: stays 1m: acts on good to soft going. *Paul Green* **65**

GRACE O'MALLEY (IRE) 3 b.f. Refuse To Bend (IRE) 128 – Lionne (Darshaan 133) [2009 85P: 10d^6 12m* 12v^4 10d Oct 26] tall, unfurnished filly: useful performer: won Kerry Group Noblesse Stakes at Cork in June by short head from Tanoura: creditable 11½ lengths fourth to Sariska in Irish Oaks at the Curragh, much better effort after: should prove as effective at 1¼m as 1½m: acts on heavy and good to firm ground. *D. K. Weld, Ireland* **107**

GRACIE'S GAMES 3 b.f. Mind Games 121 – Little Kenny 50 (Warning 136) [2009 58: p6g p6f^4 p8g p6g p8.6g Dec 19] leggy filly: modest maiden handicapper: should be suited by 7f+. *R. J. Price* **52**

GRACIE'S GIFT (IRE) 7 b.g. Imperial Ballet (IRE) 110 – Settle Petal (IRE) (Roi Danzig (USA)) [2009 58: f6g* p7.1g^3 7g^2 f7g* 6g f7m^6 p6g^2 Dec 19] compact gelding: fair handicapper: won at Southwell in March and May: stays 1m: acts on all-weather, heavy and good to firm going: tried in cheekpieces: usually held up. *R. C. Guest* **66**

GRACIOUS MELANGE 2 b.f. (Feb 20) Medicean 128 – Goodness Gracious (IRE) 93 (Green Desert (USA) 127) [2009 p8f* Dec 16] £58,000Y: third foal: dam, 2-y-o 7f winner, half-sister to smart performer up to 1m Flat Spin: 12/1 and green, won maiden at Kempton by 2 lengths from Tiger Star, quickening to lead over 1f out: will progress. *M. Botti* **83 p**

GRAIL KNIGHT 4 ch.g. Carnival Dancer 123 – Nashkova (Nashwan (USA) 135) [2009 –: 10.1m^6 14m 14m May 19] little form. *A. G. Foster* **–**

GRAMERCY (IRE) 2 b.c. (Mar 17) Whipper (USA) 126 – Topiary (IRE) (Selkirk (USA) 129) [2009 p6g^4 p7.1g^5 p6g* Nov 9] €72,000F, €52,000Y: second foal: dam, French 9f winner, half-sister to useful French performer up to 10.5f Top Toss: progressive form in maidens at Wolverhampton, on final start beating Goddess of Light easily by 2¼ lengths: should prove as effective at 7f as 6f: likely to progress further. *M. L. W. Bell* **79 p**

GRAMS AND OUNCES 2 b.c. (Jan 27) Royal Applause 124 – Ashdown Princess (IRE) (King's Theatre (IRE) 128) [2009 7g p8.6g^3 p8f^3 Dec 20] sturdy colt: modest maiden: third at Wolverhampton (seller) and Kempton: stays 8.6f. *Miss Amy Weaver* **64**

GRANAKEY (IRE) 6 b.m. Key of Luck (USA) 126 – Grand Morning (IRE) 77 (King of Clubs 124) [2009 –: p5m^6 p6g Nov 27] lightly raced and just poor form since 2007: stays 1m: raced on all-weather (best form on fibresand). *Ian Williams* **46**

GRANARY GIRL 7 b.m. Kingsinger (IRE) 94 – Highland Blue 55 (Never So Bold 135) [2009 66: 10.2m* 11.5g^2 10.2g^3 10.2m^5 12d 12g Jul 31] leggy mare: fair handicapper: won at Nottingham in May: stays 1½m: acts on all-weather and firm going: held up. *J. Pearce* **66**

GRANDAD BILL (IRE) 6 ch.g. Intikhab (USA) 135 – Matikanehanafubuki (IRE) (Caerleon (USA) 132) [2009 77: 14m 13g^6 14m^3 12d^2 12.5m^3 14g^3 12.5s^2 12d* 12.5m^2 12.4d^6 Oct 13] rather leggy gelding: poor mover: fair handicapper: won apprentice event at York in September: stays 1¾m: acts on heavy and good to firm going: consistent. *J. S. Goldie* **69**

GRAND ART (IRE) 5 b.g. Raise A Grand (IRE) 114 – Mulberry River (IRE) (Bluebird (USA) 125) [2009 81: 10m^6 12g* 12d^3 12m* 12m* 12g 12m^4 12m^3 16.2m^4 16.4g 12g^3 12m^5 12.1m^2 14m^2 Sep 14] well-made gelding: fairly useful handicapper: won at Catterick (claimer, claimed from J. Howard Johnson £6,000), Newmarket (ladies) and York (amateurs) in May: good efforts when runner-up last 2 starts: stays 2m, effective at shorter: acts on good to firm and good to soft ground: held up: sold £12,000. *P. T. Midgley* **83**

GRAND COURT (IRE) 6 b.m. Grand Lodge (USA) 125 – Nice One Clare (IRE) 117 (Mukaddamah (USA) 125) [2009 –: p8.6g Jan 19] lightly raced and little form since 2006: tried in cheekpieces. *George Baker* **–**

GRAND DIAMOND (IRE) 5 b.g. Grand Lodge (USA) 125 – Winona (IRE) 120 (Alzao (USA) 117) [2009 73: 7.1m^5 7.1m^5 8f 8m^2 10m^4 8m 8g^4 8m^2 8g^3 7.1m^3 9d Oct 28] good-bodied gelding: fair handicapper: effective at 7f to 1¼m: acts on polytrack, good to firm and good to soft going: usually wears cheekpieces: consistent. *J. S. Goldie* **73**

GRAND DUCAL (IRE) 3 b.c. Danehill Dancer (IRE) 117 – Mood Swings (IRE) 77 (Shirley Heights 130) [2009 97: 10v* 10d^4 12g Oct 4] useful-looking colt: smart performer: much improved when winning Airlie Stud Gallinule Stakes at the Curragh in May by head from Alaivan, leading close home: off over 3 months, creditable 14 lengths fourth to Sea The Stars in Irish Champion Stakes at Leopardstown next time, but acted as pacemaker behind same rival in Prix de l'Arc de Triomphe at Longchamp final start: should stay 1½m: probably acts on any going. *A. P. O'Brien, Ireland* **116**

GRANDE CAIMAN (IRE) 5 ch.g. Grand Lodge (USA) 125 – Sweet Retreat (Indian Ridge 123) [2009 96, a110: p12g^2 p11g p12g 14.1m^4 May 3] leggy gelding: useful handicapper: creditable effort in 2009 only when ½-length second to Evident Pride at Lingfield: seemed amiss next 3 starts, then gelded: effective at 1½m to 2m: acts on polytrack, good to firm and good to soft going: tried in cheekpieces, wears blinkers nowadays. *R. Hannon* **–** **a109**

GRANDE SAGGIO 2 gr.c. (Mar 30) Cape Cross (IRE) 129 – Success Story 60 (Sharrood (USA) 124) [2009 8.3v^2 Nov 4] 77,000F, 120,000Y: sturdy, well-made colt: half-brother to several winners, including 6-y-o Barney McGrew and useful 1¼m/1½m winner Film Script (by Unfuwain): dam 1¼m winner: 4/1, encouraging 2¼ lengths second to Green Lightning in maiden at Nottingham: will stay 1¼m: sure to improve. *M. Botti* **79 p**

GRAND EXIT 3 b.f. Exit To Nowhere (USA) 122 – Little Feat (Terimon 124) [2009 p12m Sep 30] second foal: dam bumper winner: tailed off in maiden at Kempton. *A. J. McCabe* **–**

GRAND HONOUR (IRE) 3 gr.g. Verglas (IRE) 118 – Rosy Dudley (IRE) 72 (Grand Lodge (USA) 125) [2009 83: p7.1g^5 p7.1g^3 p7.1g^2 p7g^2 p7g p7g 7.1m 8m p6g^5 p7g^4 7g^6 p8f p7m Dec 30] small, close-coupled gelding: fair handicapper: best at 7f: acts on polytrack, good to firm and good to soft going: held up. *P. Howling* **76**

GRAND MARY (IRE) 2 ch.f. (Apr 27) Kyllachy 129 – Magic Sister 63 (Cadeaux Genereux 131) [2009 5.1g 7d Sep 15] 115,000F, 88,000Y: fourth foal: half-sister to smart 1m winner (including Falmouth Stakes) Rajeem (by Diktat): dam, maiden (stayed 7f), sister to Prix Morny winner Hoh Magic: signs of ability in maidens at Bath and Lingfield (travelled well out wide, not knocked about): probably capable of better. *P. F. I. Cole* **– p**

GRAND OPERA (IRE) 6 b.g. City On A Hill (USA) 114 – Victoria's Secret (IRE) 70 (Law Society (USA) 130) [2009 92: p8.6g^4 p8g* p9.5g Dec 17] angular, good-topped gelding: useful handicapper: better than ever when winning at Dundalk in November: respectable efforts at Wolverhampton otherwise: effective at 7f to 9.5f: unraced on heavy going, acts on any other turf and on polytrack/sand: sometimes blinkered/tongue tied, in cheekpieces last 2 starts: fairly useful hurdler. *Gordon Elliott, Ireland* **96**

GRAND PALACE (IRE) 6 b.g. Grand Lodge (USA) 125 – Pocket Book (IRE) 60 (Reference Point 139) [2009 74: p5.1g^4 f6d p6g* f5g^3 p6g* p6g^3 p6g p6g^6 p6g p6g p6g p6g^5 p6g p6m^5 p6m^2 p5g^2 Dec 31] fair handicapper: won at Wolverhampton in January and Kempton in February: below form after next start, leaving D. Shaw after eighth: best at 5f/6f: acts on all-weather: visored: usually held up. *H. J. Evans* **74**

GRAND PASSION (IRE) 9 b.g. Grand Lodge (USA) 125 – Lovers' Parlour 83 (Beldale Flutter (USA) 130) [2009 –, a109: p12g^5 p11g^3 p11g p10g p10g 12m 8g Sep 3] good-bodied gelding: useful handicapper on his day, mostly keeps to all-weather nowadays: creditable efforts in handicaps first 2 starts, narrow third to Emerald Wilderness at Kempton latter occasion: well held after: stays 11f: acts on polytrack, firm and soft going: held up. *C. F. Wall* **–** **a105**

GRAND PERE 3 b.g. Monsieur Bond (IRE) 120 – Ejay 48 (Emperor Jones (USA) 119) [2009 p8.6g^5 9m 8.3g 10f Aug 3] rather leggy gelding: poor maiden. *P. D. Evans* **49**

GRAND SEFTON 6 br.g. Pivotal 124 – Nahlin (Slip Anchor 136) [2009 p10g Mar 18] rangy gelding: little form nowadays, including over hurdles. *N. R. Mitchell* **–**

GRAND STITCH (USA) 3 b. or br.g. Grand Slam (USA) 120 – Lil Sister Stich (USA) (Seattle Bound (USA)) [2009 71: 6d May 22] good-bodied gelding: fair maiden at 2 yrs: well held only outing in 2009. *D. Carroll* **–**

GRAND VALUE (USA) 4 b.f. Grand Slam (USA) 120 – Privyet Nadya (USA) (Cure The Blues (USA)) [2009 62: p12.2g Feb 16] rather leggy, useful-looking filly: modest maiden handicapper: last sole outing in 2009: stays 7f: acts on soft and good to firm going: races prominently. *R. Ford* **–**

GRAND VISTA 5 b.g. Danehill (USA) 126 – Revealing 106 (Halling (USA) 133) [2009 110: 7.5d 7.5m 6g a5g^6 a6g p8m 7g Jul 29] stocky gelding: smart performer at best: won twice at 2 yrs in France when trained by A. Fabre: good placed efforts at Nad Al Sheba in handicap and listed race early in 2008: just fairly useful form at best for H. Brown in UAE early in 2009, then well held both starts in Britain, very reluctant to leave stall on final outing (gelded after): stays 1m: acts on soft and good to firm ground: sometimes very slowly away: often tongue tied. *G. L. Moore* **92**

GRAND VIZIER (IRE) 5 b.g. Desert Style (IRE) 121 – Distant Decree (USA) (Distant View (USA) 126) [2009 81, a95: 8.3d p8g* 8d p8g^5 p8f^6 Dec 20] sturdy gelding: useful handicapper on all-weather, fairly useful at best on turf: won at Kempton in June by ¾ length from Brouhaha: likely to stay 1¼m: acts on polytrack, yet to race on extremes of going on turf. *C. F. Wall* **– a96**

GRAND ZAFEEN 2 ch.f. (Jan 26) Zafeen (FR) 123 – Majestic Desert 113 (Fraam 114) [2009 5m* 5m^2 5m 5m^2 Jul 3] sturdy filly: first foal: dam 5f (at 2 yrs) to 7f (including Fred Darling Stakes) winner who stayed 1m: fairly useful performer: won maiden at Pontefract in April: runner-up in minor events at Goodwood (best effort, beaten neck by Desert Auction) and Beverley (bumped leaving stall and raced freely): should stay 6f/7f: slowly away third outing (Queen Mary Stakes). *M. R. Channon* **83**

GRANGE CORNER 4 ch.f. First Trump 118 – Blennerville (IRE) (General View) [2009 –: f11s^5 p12.2g f8g^5 May 5] little form. *Garry Moss* **–**

GRANITE GIRL 2 b.f. (Feb 2) Kyllachy 129 – Native Ring (FR) (Bering 136) [2009 6m^3 8g^6 Oct 20] sixth foal: half-sister to winner in Greece by Zafonic: dam French 10.5f winner: better effort in maidens when 4½ lengths sixth to Hymnsheet at Yarmouth. *P. J. McBride* **70**

GRANNY MCPHEE 3 b.f. Bahri (USA) 125 – Allumette (Rainbow Quest (USA) 134) [2009 77: p7.1g 6m^6 7m^4 10f 7m 10m^4 p9.5g* Oct 3] tall filly: fair handicapper: won at Wolverhampton in October: stays 9.5f: acts on polytrack and good to firm ground: reluctant to leave stall and unseated rider fourth outing: none too consistent. *A. Bailey* **71**

GRANSKI (IRE) 3 b.g. Alhaarth (IRE) 126 – Purple Haze (IRE) 103 (Spectrum (IRE) 126) [2009 67: 10m^4 9.9m 12m 8d 10g^4 10s p10.7g p10.7g Nov 26] rangy gelding: fair maiden: below form after reappearance, leaving R. Hannon 8,000 gns after fifth outing: stays 1¼m: acts on good to firm and good to soft going: tried blinkered/in cheekpieces. *D. M. Fogarty, Ireland* **71 d**

GRANSTON (IRE) 8 gr.g. Revoque (IRE) 122 – Gracious Gretclo 54 (Common Grounds 118) [2009 93: 10.3g^2 10.3m^2 9.8m* 10.3f^4 8.9g 9.9m^2 9.8d 10g^6 9m Oct 3] leggy, quite good-topped gelding: useful handicapper: won at Ripon in May: in-and-out form after: stays 1¼m: acts on polytrack, firm and soft going: tried in visor/cheekpieces: rarely knuckles down for pressure: unreliable. *J. D. Bethell* **95 §**

GRANT ME A WISH 3 ch.g. Timeless Times (USA) 99 – Baby Be (Bold Arrangement 127) [2009 6g Oct 16] small gelding: tailed off in maiden at Redcar. *S. P. Griffiths* **–**

GRASP 7 b.g. Kayf Tara 130 – Circe 73 (Main Reef 126) [2009 –: 16.4m^5 16g Jul 21] close-coupled gelding: lightly raced and little form on Flat since 2007: tried in tongue tie, often visored/blinkered. *P. D. Evans* **–**

GRATUITOUS (IRE) 5 b.g. Rudimentary (USA) 118 – Accell (IRE) 56 (Magical Wonder (USA) 125) [2009 p12.2g Feb 16] compact gelding: modest maiden handicapper in 2007: well held only outing on Flat since: best effort at 1m on good going. *L. McHugh, Ireland* **–**

GRAVITATION 4 b.f. Galileo (IRE) 134 – Guaranda 97 (Acatenango (GER) 127) [2009 112: 11.9g 16.4m^5 Jul 4] rangy filly: smart performer in 2008: well held in listed races at Haydock and Sandown in 2009: stays 2m: acts on firm going (possibly unsuited by soft). *W. Jarvis* **–**

GRAYCLIFFE (IRE) 3 gr.g. Val Royal (FR) 127 – Popiplu (USA) (Cozzene (USA)) [2009 61p: p8g p9.5m^6 p10g* 10.2m p12g^3 11.8g p12g 12.5g^5 Aug 11] fair handicapper: won at Kempton in April: stays 1½m: acts on polytrack. *Pat Morris* **66**

GRAYLYN RUBY (FR) 4 b.g. Limnos (JPN) 124 – Nandi (IRE) (Mujadil (USA) 119) [2009 74, a83: p12.2g 12m^5 12.4s^6 11.5g* 12m^5 12g^2 p12.2m^6 11.5m 12.4g 11.8m^3 Oct 13] smallish, leggy gelding: fair handicapper: won at Yarmouth in May: stays 1¾m: acts on polytrack, best turf efforts on good ground: gelded after final start. *J. Jay* **78**

GRAYMALKIN (IRE) 2 gr.c. (Apr 16) Singspiel (IRE) 133 – Pearl Grey 98 (Gone **88**
West (USA)) [2009 7.1m^6 8.1m* p8.6g^4 Oct 15] rather leggy colt: second foal: half-brother to fairly useful French 7.5f winner Pearling (by Cape Cross): dam 2-y-o 5f/6f winner: still green, won maiden at Haydock in September by ½ length from Start Right: only fourth in nursery at Wolverhampton: stays 1m: has joined M. bin Shafya in UAE. *Saeed bin Suroor*

GRAZE ON AND ON 4 ch.f. Elmaamul (USA) 125 – Laena 72 (Roman Warrior 132) **–**
[2009 –: 16g Jun 30] tall filly: modest winning hurdler: little form on Flat: tried in cheekpieces. *J. J. Quinn*

GRAZEON GOLD BLEND 6 ch.g. Paris House 123 – Thalya (Crofthall 110) [2009 **89**
91: 6m 6g 6m* 6m^2 6m^4 6m 8s^5 7.5m^2 7g^6 Oct 9] big gelding: fairly useful handicapper: won at Ripon in June: stays 7f: acts on firm and soft going: effective visored/in cheekpieces or not. *J. J. Quinn*

GREAT ART (IRE) 3 b.c. One Cool Cat (USA) 123 – Passe Passe (USA) 78 (Lear Fan **75**
(USA) 130) [2009 85p: 7g^4 7m* 8g 7g Oct 23] heavy-topped, attractive colt: fair performer: jarred a knee only outing at 2 yrs: won maiden at Catterick in September: bred to stay 1m+: unraced on extremes of going: sold 19,000 gns. *P. W. Chapple-Hyam*

GREAT BOUNDER (CAN) 3 b.g. Mr Greeley (USA) 122 – Jo Zak (USA) (Vilzak **65**
(USA)) [2009 64: p11g 12m p12.2g p8.6g p9.5g^2 f8f^2 p7g p7.1g^6 Dec 28] fair maiden: left J. R. Best prior to final start: stays 9.5f: acts on all-weather. *A. B. Haynes*

GREAT CHARM (IRE) 4 b.g. Orpen (USA) 116 – Briery (IRE) 66 (Salse (USA) **84**
128) [2009 96: p7g 6m 6m 6g p6g f6g^3 p6g^3 f6f* Nov 24] big gelding: fairly useful handicapper nowadays: left M. Bell, won at Southwell in November: stays 7f: acts on all-weather, firm and soft going. *E. J. Alston*

GREAT INTRIGUE (IRE) 2 b.g. (Jan 13) Azamour (IRE) 130 – Bakewell Tart (IRE) **67 +**
92 (Tagula (IRE) 116) [2009 6m 6d 6m^5 Oct 1] 50,000 2-y-o: small, sturdy gelding: second foal: dam, 2-y-o 7f winner, sister to useful 7f winner Macaroon: best effort in maidens when 7½ lengths seventh to Arcano at Newbury on debut: better than result both starts after, gelded before final one: should stay 7f+. *J. S. Moore*

GREAT KNIGHT (IRE) 4 b.g. Acclamation 118 – Wild Vintage (USA) (Alysheba **66**
(USA)) [2009 66: p6g^4 p6m* f6g^6 6.1f p7.1g^5 p6g* p6g^5 6d p6g^5 6m p6m Aug 21] good-topped gelding: fair handicapper: won at Wolverhampton in February and June: best at 6f: acts on all-weather, firm and good to soft going: tried blinkered/visored: has hung: often finishes weakly: sold 1,000 gns, joined John Joseph Hanlon in Ireland. *S. Kirk*

GREAT QUEST (IRE) 7 b.m. Montjeu (IRE) 137 – Paparazzi (IRE) 68 (Shernazar **59**
131) [2009 p13.9g 13g 14g^4 17.1m 16.1d Sep 7] modest handicapper: stays 17f: acts on soft and good to firm going: tried blinkered/in cheekpieces: held up. *James Moffatt*

GREAT VIEW (IRE) 10 b.g. Great Commotion (USA) 123 – Tara View (IRE) (Wassl **66**
125) [2009 75: 11.7m^5 12m 12.1m^4 12.1v Aug 4] lengthy gelding: fair handicapper: barely stays 15f: acts on all-weather and any turf going: wears headgear: held up. *Mrs A. L. M. King*

GREAT WESTERN (USA) 3 b.c. Gone West (USA) – Pleasant Temper (USA) **–**
(Storm Cat (USA)) [2009 51: 10.2d Apr 28] close-coupled colt: modest maiden at 2 yrs: well held only outing in 2009: should prove best up to 1m: sent to Saudi Arabia. *P. F. I. Cole*

GREEK ENVOY 5 br.g. Diktat 126 – South Shore 102 (Caerleon (USA) 132) [2009 **–**
97: 12d Oct 24] rangy, useful-looking gelding: one-time useful performer: off nearly 12 months, pulled up in handicap at Doncaster sole outing in 2009: stays 1½m: acts on soft ground: not straightforward. *T. P. Tate*

GREEK KEY (IRE) 2 ch.c. (Jan 31) Selkirk (USA) 129 – Doohulla (USA) 100 **61**
(Stravinsky (USA) 133) [2009 7.1g 7s p7m^6 7f 7.1m^5 6g Oct 19] tall, useful-looking colt: fair maiden: stays 7f: acts on polytrack and good to firm going: tends to race freely/hang: sold 8,500 gns. *M. L. W. Bell*

GREEK SECRET 6 b.g. Josr Algarhoud (IRE) 118 – Mazurkanova 63 (Song 132) **64**
[2009 60: p7g^6 6g 7m 5m* 6m 6m^5 5.1d p6g^6 p7.1m p6f^6 p5g* Dec 31] leggy gelding: modest handicapper: won at Beverley in July and Lingfield in December: effective at 5f/6f: acts on polytrack, firm and soft going: often in cheekpieces/blinkers: held up: none too genuine. *J. O'Reilly*

GREEK THEATRE (USA) 4 ch.g. Smoke Glacken (USA) 120 – Theatre Flight **59**
(USA) 83 (Theatrical 128) [2009 70: f8f^4 Dec 12] tall gelding: fair handicapper at 3 yrs: below form only outing in 2009: stays 1m: acts on polytrack and good to firm going: has raced freely. *P. S. McEntee*

GREEN AGENDA 3 b.g. Anabaa (USA) 130 – Capistrano Day (USA) 110 (Diesis 133) [2009 –p: p7g* p8g* f8g^2 7.1m* 8f* p8g^4 8d^4 8g^3 8m 8g 8d^2 8.5m p8g 8.5g^6 10.1d^5 Oct 27] stocky gelding: type to carry condition: fairly useful handicapper: won at Lingfield and Kempton in March, then Musselburgh and Thirsk in April: below form last 4 starts: likely to prove best up to 1m: acts on all-weather, firm and good to soft ground: usually races prominently. *M. Johnston* **81**

GREEN ARMY 2 b.c. (Feb 12) Sulamani (IRE) 130 – Dowhatjen 86 (Desert Style (IRE) 121) [2009 8g Oct 16] 66/1, very green when well held in maiden at Redcar. *M. R. Channon* **–**

GREENBELT 8 b.g. Desert Prince (IRE) 130 – Emerald (USA) (El Gran Senor (USA) 136) [2009 –: f12g^3 f12g^2 12.4s f12g^4 12.4d^4 f11g^3 Oct 27] modest handicapper: stays 1½m: acts on all-weather and heavy going: tried in cheekpieces: consistent. *G. M. Moore* **60**

GREEN BERET (IRE) 3 b.g. Fayruz 116 – Grandel (Owington 123) [2009 98p: 6g* 6m^5 5.1m^5 5m^2 5m^4 5g^3 5m^5 Aug 20] good-bodied gelding: useful handicapper: won at Brighton in April by 3 lengths from Flamsteed: best efforts after when placed at Newmarket and Goodwood (close third to Noble Storm): effective at 5f/6f: unraced on extremes of going: visored final outing: sent to UAE. *J. H. M. Gosden* **103**

GREEN COMMUNITY (USA) 2 gr. or ro.f. (Mar 11) El Prado (IRE) 119 – Dreams (USA) (Silver Hawk (USA) 123) [2009 6s^4 p7.1g^4 8.1d^3 7g^6 Sep 14] $160,000Y: fifth foal: sister to smart US 8.5f/9f winner Elysium Fields and half-sister to winner in USA by Tale of The Cat: dam, US 8.5f/9.5f winner, half-sister to US Grade 3 9f winner My Girl Jeannie: fair maiden: stays 1m. *E. F. Vaughan* **67**

GREEN DAY PACKER (IRE) 5 br.g. Daylami (IRE) 138 – Durrah Green 79 (Green Desert (USA) 127) [2009 p13.3g^6 12m Jul 1] small, sturdy gelding: maiden: just poor form in 2009: should stay 13f: acts on polytrack and good to firm ground: tried tongue tied. *P. C. Haslam* **43**

GREEN DYNASTY (IRE) 3 ch.g. Giant's Causeway (USA) 132 – Rose Gypsy 114 (Green Desert (USA) 127) [2009 70p: p8g^6 p8g^5 p8.6g^4 8.3d 10g 10.3g 8.3m^4 Jun 30] modest maiden: should be suited by 1¼m: blinkered final outing: needs treating with caution: sold 3,000 gns in July. *M. Johnston* **64**

GREEN EARTH (IRE) 2 b.c. (Apr 15) Cape Cross (IRE) 129 – Inchyre 102 (Shirley Heights 130) [2009 7m 7.1g 7f^3 7g^6 7.1m* 8.3d 7d Oct 22] 45,000Y: lengthy, attractive colt: half-brother to 3 winners, including 1¼m/1½m winner Inchiri (by Sadler's Wells) and 9.5f to 11f winner Whirly Bird (by Nashwan), both useful: dam, 1m winner (stayed 1½m), half-sister to smart performer up to 1m Inchinor: fair performer: won nursery at Warwick in September: should be suited by 1m+: acts on good to firm going. *Mrs A. J. Perrett* **77**

GREEN ENDEAVOUR (CAN) 3 b.g. Forestry (USA) 121 – Zuri Ridge (USA) (Cox's Ridge (USA)) [2009 –: p12g 10m Jul 6] little form: blinkered final outing: sold 2,500 gns. *Mrs A. J. Perrett* **–**

GREEN ENERGY 2 b.g. (Mar 27) Rainbow Quest (USA) 134 – Carambola (IRE) 100 (Danehill (USA) 126) [2009 6.5g 8g Oct 21] tall gelding: well beaten in maidens, then gelded. *Mrs A. J. Perrett* **–**

GREEN FOR LUCK (IRE) 2 b.c. (Mar 29) Key of Luck (USA) 126 – Kasota (IRE) 72 (Alzao (USA) 117) [2009 6g 7m^6 8m^3 10m Oct 5] compact colt: modest maiden: left T. Tate after second start: should be suited by 1¼m+. *S. Gollings* **64**

GREENISLAND (IRE) 3 b.f. Fasliyev (USA) 120 – Green Castle (IRE) 101 (Indian Ridge 123) [2009 77: 8d^3 8s 8m 7g* 8g^3 7g 6m 7m^3 p8g Oct 29] close-coupled filly: useful performer: 66/1, back to form when winning handicap at Newmarket in July: creditable efforts after only when third in listed races at Ascot, beaten 3 lengths by Strawberrydaiquiri then 1¼ lengths by Golden Stream: stays 1m: acts on polytrack, good to firm and good to soft going: front runner/races prominently. *H. Morrison* **100**

GREEN LAGONDA (AUS) 7 gr.g. Crown Jester (AUS) – Fidelis (AUS) (John's Hope (AUS)) [2009 73: p6g^5 p5g^5 p5g^5 p5.1m^3 p5.1g^2 p6g^5 p5.1g 5.1d^3 5.7m p5.1g^3 6g 5.1g^2 6f 5m^3 5.1g^3 5f* 5.1m^4 5.1m 5.3d^2 5.3f* 5.1m^6 p6g 5.1m* 5.1m^2 p5.1g 5.3d^3 Oct 15] lengthy gelding: fair performer: left Stef Liddiard £6,000 after fifteenth start: improved after, winning handicaps at Folkestone in July and Brighton in August and claimer at Bath in September: best at 5f/6f: acts on polytrack, firm and good to soft ground: tried in cheekpieces: tough. *P. D. Evans* **76**

GREEN LIGHTNING (IRE) 2 b.c. (Jan 19) Montjeu (IRE) 137 – Angelic Song (CAN) (Halo (USA)) [2009 7.2m^{6} 8.3m^{6} 8.3v* Nov 4] 70,000Y: big, good-topped colt: closely related/half-brother to several winners, including very smart Irish 1m (at 2 yrs) to 1½m (Grade 1 in US) winner Sligo Bay and smart Irish 8.5f (at 2 yrs) and 13.3f winner Wolfe Tone (both by Sadler's Wells): dam unraced sister to American champions Glorious Song (older female, dam of Singspiel) and Devil's Bag (2-y-o): progressive in maidens, winning at Nottingham very easily by 2¼ lengths from Grande Saggio, making all: will be suited by 1¼m+: acts on heavy ground: will improve further. *M. Johnston* **84 p**

GREEN MANALISHI 8 b.g. Green Desert (USA) 127 – Silca-Cisa 93 (Hallgate 127) [2009 111: p5g 5.1m^{5} 5d 5.1m 5m 5.4m 5.6m^{4} 6m^{3} 5m* 6g^{4} p5g^{5} p5g* p6g^{4} p6g Nov 21] sturdy gelding: smart performer on all-weather, just useful on turf in 2009: won handicaps at Haydock in September and Lingfield (back to very best when beating Fantasy Explorer 1¼ lengths) in November: best at 5f/easy 6f: acts on polytrack and firm going: tried blinkered: in cheekpieces last 8 starts. *K. A. Ryan* **102 a112**

GREEN MOON (IRE) 2 b.c. (Feb 16) Montjeu (IRE) 137 – Green Noon (FR) 112 (Green Tune (USA) 125) [2009 8g 8v^{4} Oct 24] sturdy colt: first foal: dam French 2-y-o 7f/1m (Prix d'Aumale) winner who stayed 1¼m: much better effort in maidens at Newbury when 6½ lengths fourth to Multames, nearest finish: will stay 1¼m: should improve again. *H. J. L. Dunlop* **81 p**

GREEN ONIONS 3 b.g. Royal Applause 124 – Tremiere (FR) (Anabaa (USA) 130) [2009 71: p6g* p6g p5.1g^{3} f5g^{4} 5m^{6} 5g^{2} 5d^{6} 5.2s f6g p6g f6g p8m p6f Dec 16] fair performer: won maiden at Great Leighs in January: left D. ffrench Davis after ninth outing: best at 5f/6f: acts on all-weather and good to firm going, possibly not on softer than good: tried in cheekpieces/blinkered: often front runner. *A. J. Lidderdale* **70**

GREENORE GORDON 2 ch.g. (Apr 3) Namid 128 – Approaching Storm (IRE) 88 (Entrepreneur 123) [2009 5g 5.7g Jul 23] well held in maidens 3½ months apart (gelded in between). *M. S. Saunders* **–**

GREEN PARK (IRE) 6 b.g. Shinko Forest (IRE) – Danccini (IRE) 78 (Dancing Dissident (USA) 119) [2009 96: 8m 5d 6m 5d^{3} 6g^{4} 5m^{6} 5m 6m 5g^{3} 6g^{5} 5m^{3} 5.1v^{6} p6g* p6g 5g p6g f6m p6m^{6} p5.1g* Dec 5] useful-looking gelding: fairly useful handicapper: won at Wolverhampton in October and December: best at 5f/6f: acts on all-weather and any turf going: usually blinkered: patiently ridden. *D. Carroll* **84**

GREEN PASSION (USA) 3 b. or br.g. Forestry (USA) 121 – Date Stone (USA) (Forty Niner (USA)) [2009 –: p9.5g^{3} p10g^{6} 10m Oct 3] fair maiden: off over 8 months, shaped as if needing race on handicap debut at Redcar final outing (gelded after): stays 1¼m. *M. Johnston* **70 +**

GREEN POPPY 3 b.f. Green Desert (USA) 127 – Vimy Ridge (FR) (Indian Ridge 123) [2009 66: 6f^{6} 8g 7m^{5} 5m 5g^{3} p5.1g Oct 17] smallish, compact filly: modest maiden: left Eve Johnson Houghton after third outing: probably best at 5f: acts on firm ground. *B. Smart* **59**

GREEN SHOOTS 2 b.f. (Feb 20) Reset (AUS) 124 – Cryptogam 73 (Zamindar (USA) 116) [2009 6.1m 6m p5.1g 8g Oct 16] third foal: dam, maiden (stayed 1½m), out of half-sister to St Leger winner Toulon: no form. *M. E. Sowersby* **–**

GREEN SPIRIT (IRE) 3 b.g. Invincible Spirit (IRE) 121 – Randonneur (IRE) 91 (Red Sunset 120) [2009 7m 6m Apr 20] stocky, compact gelding: tailed off in maidens. *Pat Morris* **–**

GREENSWARD 3 b.g. Green Desert (USA) 127 – Frizzante 121 (Efisio 120) [2009 91: 7m^{6} 7.1m^{2} 7.1m^{4} Jul 10] sturdy gelding: fairly useful handicapper: may prove best at 6f: raced only on good/good to firm ground: waited with: gelded after final start. *B. J. Meehan* **87**

GREEN VELVET 4 b.f. Iron Mask (USA) 117 – Scarlett Ribbon 104 (Most Welcome 131) [2009 59: p5g^{4} p6g^{3} p5g* p6g* 5.3m 5m^{4} 6m^{2} 6m^{5} p6m^{2} Dec 1] good-bodied filly: fair handicapper: won twice at Lingfield in March (5 days apart): effective at 5f/6f: acts on polytrack and good to firm ground. *P. J. Makin* **71**

GREEN WADI 4 b.g. Dansili 127 – Peryllys 67 (Warning 136) [2009 80: p12m^{3} p10m Dec 9] well-made gelding: fairly useful handicapper: stays 1½m: acts on polytrack, firm and soft going. *G. L. Moore* **83**

GREENWICH MEANTIME 9 b.g. Royal Academy (USA) 130 – Shirley Valentine 104 (Shirley Heights 130) [2009 99: p16g^{3} p16g^{6} 14.5d^{2} a12g* 12m^{2} 12g^{3} 13d^{5} 12s^{5} a12g^{2} a12g^{5} a12g Dec 20] sturdy gelding: fairly useful performer: creditable third in **88 d**

handicap at Kempton on reappearance: left A. King after next start: below best (mainly in claimers) in France afterwards, though made all at Deauville in August (female jockeys, claimed from E. O'Neill €14,200): trained next 2 starts by F. Chappet: stays 18.7f: acts on all-weather, good to firm and good to soft going: tried in cheekpieces. *Mme C. Barande Barbe, France*

GREENWICH VILLAGE 6 b.g. Mtoto 134 – D'Azy 91 (Persian Bold 123) [2009 **84** 87: p16g* p16g^{3} 14g Jun 19] small gelding: fairly useful handicapper: won at Kempton in January: stays 2m: acts on polytrack and firm ground: has raced freely: sold 14,000 gns in July. *W. J. Knight*

GREMLIN 5 b.g. Mujahid (USA) 125 – Fairy Free (Rousillon (USA) 133) [2009 70: **64** p12.2g^{2} Jun 22] tall, leggy gelding: has a quick action: left A. King £5,000 prior to only Flat outing in 2009 (just modest form, claimed £6,000): stays 1½m: acts on polytrack, firm and good to soft going: tried blinkered (wandered). *I. W. McInnes*

GRETHEL (IRE) 5 b.m. Fruits of Love (USA) 127 – Stay Sharpe (USA) (Sharpen Up **55 §** 127) [2009 66§: 9.8m^{6} 9.9m 8.3g 10d^{6} 10.4g^{6} 8m^{5} 9.2g^{2} 9m^{4} 8m^{5} 9.9m 10.4v^{6} 7.9g^{5} 8.5m 12.5s^{6} 9.9f 12.4d 12.5m 11.9d 10m^{6} 12.5m^{6} 12g Oct 17] leggy, plain mare: modest handicapper: stays easy 12.5f: acts on heavy and good to firm going: sometimes races freely: unreliable. *A. Berry*

GREY BOY (GER) 8 gr.g. Medaaly 114 – Grey Perri 103 (Siberian Express (USA) **83 d** 125) [2009 82: p8g 8.3g^{4} p7g* 8m 7m^{3} 7m^{6} p7g^{3} 8.1g^{4} 8g 7g 6m 6.1s p7m^{6} 8g^{5} p8m^{6} p8g^{6} p7f Dec 13] tall gelding: fairly useful handicapper: won at Kempton in April: largely below form after: stays 1m: acts on polytrack, firm and good to soft going: often travels strongly. *A. W. Carroll*

GREY BUNTING 2 gr.c. (May 7) Oasis Dream 129 – Ribbons And Bows (IRE) 91 (Dr **67 p** Devious (IRE) 127) [2009 6.5g^{6} p7m^{4} Oct 26] 65,000F, 70,000Y: good-topped colt: second foal: half-brother to 3-y-o Time Medicean: dam 6f (at 2 yrs) and 9.5f winner (stayed 1½m) out of half-sister to very smart performer up to 1½m Terimon: similar form in maidens at Newbury and Kempton (not unduly knocked about, fourth to Prizefighting): will stay 1m: should improve. *B. W. Hills*

GREY COMMAND (USA) 4 gr.c. Daylami (IRE) 138 – Shmoose (IRE) 106 (Caer- **70** leon (USA) 132) [2009 75: 7s 10.1d 11.5m^{5} 10.1d^{2} 12d 12d^{4} 10.1d^{6} 9.9f^{6} 10m^{5} 10m p9.5g^{2} Dec 11] sturdy, close-coupled colt: fair maiden handicapper: stays 10.3f: acts on polytrack, firm and soft going: inconsistent. *M. Brittain*

GREYFRIARSCHORISTA 2 ch.c. (Feb 18) King's Best (USA) 132 – Misty **59 p** Heights 105 (Fasliyev (USA) 120) [2009 7g^{4} Aug 4] €8,000Y: first foal: dam Irish 7.5f (at 2 yrs)/9.5f winner: 9/2, 1¾ lengths fourth to Bonfire Knight in maiden at Catterick, soon close up: will stay at least 1m: likely to improve. *M. Johnston*

GREY GARTH (IRE) 2 gr.g. (Apr 29) Verglas (IRE) 118 – Again Royale (IRE) **–** (Royal Academy (USA) 130) [2009 6d^{6} Jun 27] big, strong gelding: 20/1 and green, well held in maiden at Newcastle. *J. D. Bethell*

GREY GRANITE (IRE) 3 gr.c. Dalakhani (IRE) 133 – Royal Ballerina (IRE) 117 **83** (Sadler's Wells (USA) 132) [2009 74p: 12m^{5} 10.4v* May 21] lengthy colt: fairly useful form: won maiden at Haydock in May by 7 lengths from Cry Alot Boy, making all: not seen out again: bred to be suited by 1½m: acts on heavy going. *W. Jarvis*

GREY GURKHA 8 gr.h. Kasakov – Royal Rebeka (Grey Desire 115) [2009 65: 8.3m **–** 7.5m f8m 8d 7.5g 8.5m p8m Nov 29] modest handicapper at 7 yrs: little form in 2009. *I. W. McInnes*

GREYLAMI (IRE) 4 gr.g. Daylami (IRE) 138 – Silent Crystal (USA) 94 (Diesis 133) **99** [2009 96: p11g^{4} p11g* 10.1g 12s 10m^{2} 12m 10m^{3} 9m^{3} 10m^{2} 9m Oct 3] good-topped gelding: useful handicapper: won Rosebery Stakes at Kempton in March by head from Sweet Lightning: good placed efforts 4 times after: stays 11f: acts on polytrack, good to firm and soft going: travels strongly held up (best in well-run race). *T. G. Mills*

GREYSTOKE PRINCE 4 gr.g. Diktat 126 – Grey Princess (IRE) 92 (Common **61** Grounds 118) [2009 80: p7g p7.1g 7m^{5} p7g 7m p7m p7.1g f6g p7g p10g^{4} p8m^{2} p6m^{5} Dec 16] leggy gelding: just modest handicapper nowadays: left W. Swinburn 3,500 gns after seventh start: stays 7f: acts on polytrack: sometimes in cheekpieces/blinkers: often tongue tied, including last 5 starts. *P. S. McEntee*

GRIMES FAITH 6 b.g. Woodborough (USA) 112 – Emma Grimes (IRE) 54 (Nordico **79** (USA)) [2009 76: f5d^{4} f5g^{2} f6g^{2} f5g* f5g* p5g^{6} p5.1g^{3} f5g* f5m* 6g^{6} 5.1d 5d 5g p6g^{6} 6g 5s 5v^{4} p5.1g p6g f5g Dec 27] good-topped gelding: fair performer: won seller and claimer in February and handicap and seller in March, all at Southwell: off 4 months, below form after, leaving K. Ryan after eighteenth start: best at 5f/6f: acts on all-weather and any turf going: wears blinkers/cheekpieces. *R. C. Guest*

GRIPSHOLM CASTLE (USA) 3 b. or br.f. Dynaformer (USA) – Randaroo (USA) 117 (Gold Case (USA)) [2009 10m* 10.1m^4 10.4m* 10m Oct 16] €260,000Y: deep-girthed filly: first foal: dam US Grade 2 7f/1m winner: useful form: won maiden at Newmarket in May and handicap at Haydock (off 3 months, improved to beat Presbyterian Nun 7 lengths) in September: dull in coat, well below form in listed race on former course final outing: will be suited by 1½m: joined B. Cecil in USA. *H. R. A. Cecil* **107**

GRIS DE GRIS (IRE) 5 gr.h. Slickly (FR) 128 – Deesse Grise (FR) (Lead On Time (USA) 123) [2009 116: 8d* 8d^2 9.3s^2 7g^5 9.8g^2 10d^3 10g* 8g Dec 13] third foal: half-brother to French 7.5f/1¼m winner Efisia (by Efisio): dam, French 5.5f (at 2 yrs) to 1m winner, half-sister to dam of very smart sprinter Pipalong: very smart performer: successful in 2008 in listed races at Cagnes-sur-Mer and Saint-Cloud, and Prix du Muguet at Saint-Cloud: left J-M. Capitte after sixth start that year: won Prix Edmond Blanc at Saint-Cloud (by 2 lengths from Alnadana) in March and listed race at Marseilles Borely (beat Capitaine Courage 1½ lengths) in November: at least creditable efforts in between, including when second in Prix du Muguet at Saint-Cloud (¾ length behind Vertigineux), Prix d'Ispahan at Longchamp (beaten a length by Never On Sunday) and Prix Dollar at Longchamp (went down by a neck to Pipedreamer): fair tenth to Good Ba Ba in Hong Kong Mile at Sha Tin final start: stays 1¼m: acts on all-weather and heavy ground: has worn cheekpieces: usually races prominently: reliable. *A. de Royer Dupre, France* **120**

GRISSOM (IRE) 3 b.g. Desert Prince (IRE) 130 – Misty Peak (IRE) 83 (Sri Pekan (USA) 117) [2009 72: 5m^4 5m^3 5s 6g* 6m 6s^5 6d^3 6d^5 6f^4 6s* 5m^2 6.1m 7s^2 7.2v^2 7v^4 Nov 3] smallish gelding: fairly useful handicapper: won at Ayr in June and August: good efforts when runner-up after: effective at 5f to 7f: acts on heavy and good to firm going: tried tongue tied: races prominently. *A. Berry* **88**

GRITSTONE 2 b.g. (Mar 15) Dansili 127 – Cape Trafalgar (IRE) 88 (Cape Cross (IRE) 129) [2009 7.5g^2 7.2m^4 7m Oct 3] small gelding: second foal: dam 2-y-o 5f/6f winner: similar form in maidens/sales race (gelded after): should stay 1m *R. A. Fahey* **71**

GRIZEDALE (IRE) 10 ch.g. Lake Coniston (IRE) 131 – Zabeta (Diesis 133) [2009 65§: p6g p7g 7f p7g^6 p7g^5 7g Aug 29] strong gelding: modest handicapper nowadays: stays 1m: acts on polytrack and any turf going: usually wears tongue tie/cheekpieces: held up: one to avoid. *M. J. Attwater* **52 §**

GROOVE MASTER 2 b.g. (May 5) Tobougg (IRE) 125 – Magic Mistress 89 (Magic Ring (IRE) 115) [2009 7s 8.1d 10.2m^5 Sep 28] modest form at best in maidens: bred to stay 1¼m. *A. King* **52**

GROSS PROPHET 4 b.g. Lujain (USA) 119 – Done And Dusted (IRE) 75 (Up And At 'em 109) [2009 86: 10.2g* 12m^3 10m^4 10.3m^2 p11g^5 12m 10m^2 p10g Nov 1] workmanlike gelding: fairly useful performer: won claimer at Chepstow in May: largely respectable efforts after, leaving Tom Dascombe after fifth start: shaped as if amiss final outing: probably stays 1½m: acts on polytrack, soft and good to firm ground. *A. J. Lidderdale* **84**

GROUND PATROL 8 b.g. Ashkalani (IRE) 128 – Good Grounds (USA) (Alleged (USA) 138) [2009 54: 10.2f May 31] good-topped gelding: modest performer in 2008: well held only outing in 2009: stays 1½m: acts on polytrack, firm and good to soft going: tried in headgear/tongue tie. *N. R. Mitchell* **–**

GROUP CAPTAIN 7 b.g. Dr Fong (USA) 128 – Alusha 88 (Soviet Star (USA) 128) [2009 –: p12g 12g^5 12g^6 p16g^3 12m 13m* 12g 15.5s^3 12.5v Nov 24] lengthy gelding: useful performer: left H. Collingridge after fifth outing: won minor event at Chateaubriant in September: stays 2m: acts on polytrack, firm and soft going: held up: not straightforward. *A. Fracas, France* **96**

GROUP LEADER (IRE) 3 ch.g. Noverre (USA) 125 – Stem The Tide (USA) (Proud Truth (USA)) [2009 –: 8.3v^3 8.3g^4 p9.5g 10.1d 8.3v Nov 4] fair maiden: soundly beaten in handicaps last 3 starts: stays 8.3f: best effort on good going: tried visored. *J. R. Jenkins* **71**

GROUP THERAPY 4 ch.g. Choisir (AUS) 126 – Licence To Thrill 83 (Wolfhound (USA) 126) [2009 –: 5m 5g 5g^5 5m 5m^2 5m 5g* 5m 5.6m 5m Oct 1] good-topped gelding: smart performer: improved for new yard in 2009, winning handicap at Ascot in August by 1½ lengths from Buachaill Dona: tame efforts after, including in listed races: raced mainly around 5f: acts on firm going. *N. P. Littmoden* **112**

GROVE VIEW STAR 4 ch.g. Auction House (USA) 120 – Gracious Imp (USA) (Imp Society (USA)) [2009 68: p10.7g 12.9d^{4} p12g^{5} p12g^{4} p9.5g^{3} p11f Dec 16] modest maiden handicapper: left G. M. Lyons in Ireland after fourth start: stays 13f: acts on polytrack and heavy ground: often blinkered/tongue tied. *Pat Morris* **64**

GRUDGE 4 b.g. Timeless Times (USA) 99 – Envy (IRE) (Paris House 123) [2009 78: 5g^{3} 5d^{4} 5f 5d^{2} 5g p5.1g p5.1g^{2} 5s^{5} p5.1g^{2} p5.1g* f5g^{2} Dec 27] compact gelding: fair handicapper: left D. Barker after return: won at Wolverhampton in November: raced only at 5f: acts on all-weather, soft and good to firm going: tried in cheekpieces: front runner/ races prominently: hangs left. *Ollie Pears* **77**

GUARINO (GER) 5 b.g. Acatenango (GER) 127 – Global World (GER) (Big Shuffle (USA) 122) [2009 10m^{6} Jul 3] ex-German gelding: won maiden at Dortmund at 2 yrs: in frame in minor events at Cologne, Chantilly and Compiegne all 3 starts in 2007: left P. Schiergen and off almost 2 years, possibly amiss in listed race at Sandown on British debut: stays 11f: acts on good to soft ground. *G. L. Moore* **–**

GUERTINO (IRE) 4 ch.g. Choisir (AUS) 126 – Isana (JPN) (Sunday Silence (USA)) [2009 94: 6m 5g^{5} p6g 5g 7s Oct 27] tall, good-topped gelding: fluent mover: fairly useful performer at best: left B. Smart £1,800 before just fair form on belated return: stays 6f: acts on firm and good to soft going: tried blinkered. *C. J. Teague* **77**

GUESSWORK 2 ch.f. (Feb 6) Rock of Gibraltar (IRE) 133 – Show Off 56 (Efisio 120) [2009 5.2g^{4} 6.1g^{4} p5g 5d^{6} Sep 16] tall, leggy filly: has scope: half-sister to several winners, including fairly useful 2005 2-y-o 6f winner Bling (by Mark of Esteem) and 7f winner Bluff (by Bluebird): dam sprint maiden (ran only at 2 yrs): maiden: form only when fourth at Newbury (minor event) and Nottingham: should be as effective at 5f as 6f: tried in cheekpieces: sold £800. *W. Jarvis* **65**

GUEST BOOK (IRE) 2 b.c. (Apr 10) Green Desert (USA) 127 – Your Welcome (Darshaan 133) [2009 6m^{6} 7.1m* 7m^{2} Sep 27] sturdy, good-bodied colt: third foal: dam French maiden (stayed 1½m): won maiden at Chepstow in September by ½ length from Viking Dancer, idling markedly: creditable 2 lengths second to Pleasant Day in nursery at Ascot: will stay 1m: useful prospect. *M. Johnston* **88 p**

GUEST CONNECTIONS 6 b.g. Zafonic (USA) 130 – Llyn Gwynant 115 (Persian Bold 123) [2009 81: 6m^{6} 5m 6g* 6m^{3} 6s 5g 5m Oct 3] tall, leggy, attractive gelding: fair handicapper nowadays: won at Hamilton in May: effective at 5f to 7f: acts on soft and good to firm going: tried blinkered, visored nowadays: held up: often difficult in stall. *D. Nicholls* **74**

GUESTOFTHENATION (USA) 3 b. or br.g. Gulch (USA) – French Flag (Darshaan 133) [2009 87: 10f^{4} 11m p12.2g^{3} 12d 11d Aug 1] well-made, attractive gelding: fair handicapper: in and out form in 2009: stays 1½m: acts on polytrack and heavy going: blinkered final outing. *M. Johnston* **79**

GUGA (IRE) 3 b.g. Rock of Gibraltar (IRE) 133 – Attitre (FR) 105 (Mtoto 134) [2009 61p: p6g^{6} 7.1m 6m f8g* f12g^{2} 8m^{5} Aug 6] stocky gelding: fair performer: won handicap at Southwell in July: good second in similar event there next time: claimed £6,000 after final start (gelded after): stays 1½m: acts on fibresand: has joined Dr R. Newland. *George Baker* **70**

GUIDECCA TEN 2 b.c. (Feb 14) Peintre Celebre (USA) 137 – Silver Rhapsody (USA) 115 (Silver Hawk (USA) 123) [2009 8.1g^{4} 8.3g^{3} Oct 5] useful-looking, rather leggy colt: fair form in maidens at Sandown and Windsor: would have been suited by 1¼m+: dead. *A. M. Balding* **77**

GUILDED WARRIOR 6 b.g. Mujahid (USA) 125 – Pearly River 72 (Elegant Air 119) [2009 96: p7g^{3} 7m 7g^{6} 8.3m^{4} 7m^{2} 7.1g^{2} 7g 7m 8.3m Oct 26] sturdy gelding: useful handicapper: good second at Epsom and Sandown fifth/sixth starts: effective at 7f/1m: acts on polytrack and any turf going: tried visored: forces pace. *W. S. Kittow* **96**

GUILDENSTERN (IRE) 7 b.g. Danetime (IRE) 121 – Lyphard Abu (IRE) 78 (Lyphard's Special (USA) 122) [2009 66: p7g^{6} p7g* p7.1g* p7g^{6} p7.1g^{2} p7.1m^{6} p6g^{2} p6g^{3} p7.1g^{3} p7g p7.1g 8m 8d p7.1g f6g^{3} p6g^{3} p7.1g^{4} p6m p7m^{6} p7.1g^{3} f6g f7m p7.1g^{4} Dec 28] well-made gelding: fair handicapper: won at Kempton and Wolverhampton in January: effective at 6f/7f: acts on all-weather, good to firm and good to soft going: tried in visor/cheekpieces: formerly tongue tied: held up. *P. Howling* **76**

GUILIN (IRE) 3 b.f. Giant's Causeway (USA) 132 – Chantress 99 (Peintre Celebre (USA) 137) [2009 –: p12g 10g p10g 10.1g 12.1g^{4} 14.1g^{4} 16g^{5} Aug 29] modest maiden: stays 2m: best efforts on good ground: tried blinkered. *P. F. I. Cole* **55**

GUISEPPE VERDI (USA) 5 ch.g. Sky Classic (CAN) – Lovington (USA) (Afleet **67** (CAN)) [2009 p10g* 11m^5 p10g^3 p12m p9.5g^2 Dec 28] strong, lengthy gelding: fair performer nowadays: off almost 2 years prior to winning seller at Lingfield in July: probably stays 11f: acts on polytrack and good to firm ground. *Miss Tor Sturgis*

GULF OF AQABA (USA) 3 b. or br.g. Mr Greeley (USA) 122 – Ocean Jewel (USA) **60** (Alleged (USA) 138) [2009 10.4m^5 10.3m^5 10g 9.9g^4 Jul 20] big, unfurnished gelding: modest maiden: worth a try at 1½m+: gelded and has joined D. Pipe. *M. Johnston*

GULF PRESIDENT 3 b.c. Polish Precedent (USA) 131 – Gay Minette (IRE) (Peintre **66** Celebre (USA) 137) [2009 61p: p8.6g^3 p10g^4 11d 8.1g 10g^5 p8.6g^3 11.1d 12f^3 Jul 23] lengthy colt: fair maiden: stays 1½m: acts on polytrack, firm and good to soft going: effective visored or not: temperament under suspicion: sold £5,000, then joined Tim Vaughan. *M. R. Channon*

GULF PUNCH 2 b.f. (Jan 23) Dubawi (IRE) 129 – Fruit Punch (IRE) 73 (Barathea **52** (IRE) 127) [2009 5.5f^5 6m^5 p7g^4 p6g^3 f7g^6 7d^4 7.5m p7.1m 7d 8g 7g 8m 7.1m Sep 29] 35,000F: fourth foal: half-sister to winner in Greece by Fantastic Light: dam, French 1½m winner, out of half-sister to Riverman: modest maiden: left R. Hannon £5,000 after fourth start: stays 7f: acts on polytrack (soon off bridle on fibresand), firm and good to soft going: tried in cheekpieces. *M. F. Harris*

GULNAZ 4 b.f. Tobougg (IRE) 125 – Hymn Book (IRE) 65 (Darshaan 133) [2009 54: **49** f11m^4 11.5g 12.4d 12s f12f^6 Nov 24] poor maiden: left Mrs G. Rees after second start: stays 11f: form only on fibresand. *C. J. Teague*

GUMND (IRE) 2 b.c. (Feb 1) Selkirk (USA) 129 – Surval (IRE) 91 (Sadler's Wells **68 p** (USA) 132) [2009 7.1m p7g^6 Jun 24] 85,000Y: third foal: dam, 10.5f winner, half-sister to Park Hill Stakes winner Delilah: better effort in maidens when sixth to Invincible Prince at Kempton, pulling hard and still green: should stay 1m+: should do better still. *C. E. Brittain*

GUNDAROO 2 b.f. (Feb 22) Oasis Dream 129 – Encore My Love 68 (Royal Applause **64** 124) [2009 6d^5 6.1m^2 6.1v^3 6g^6 Aug 26] useful-looking filly: fourth foal: half-sister to fairly useful 2006 2-y-o 5f/6f winner Prospect Place (by Compton Place): dam, ran once, half-sister to leading 1989 2-y-o (successful at 6f to 1m) Be My Chief: modest maiden: only sixth in nursery: signs of temperament. *J. L. Dunlop*

GUNFIGHTER (IRE) 6 ch.g. Machiavellian (USA) 123 – Reunion (IRE) 108 (Be **§§** My Guest (USA) 126) [2009 91§: p7.1m Feb 25] big, rangy gelding: fairly useful handicapper at best: has refused to race last 4 outings, leaving R. Johnson prior to only appearance in 2009: tried in cheekpieces: thoroughly temperamental, and was banned from racing on Flat for a second time at BHA inquiry in March. *R. A. Farrant*

GUN FOR SALE (USA) 4 b.g. Quiet American (USA) – Do The Hustle (USA) **54** (Known Fact (USA) 135) [2009 –: p8g^2 8g^3 7m 7.6g^5 8m^4 p8m Sep 24] big, well-made gelding: modest maiden: stays 1m: acts on polytrack, best effort on turf on good going: tried tongue tied: suspect attitude. *P. J. Makin*

GUNNADOIT (USA) 4 b. or br.g. Almutawakel 126 – Gharam (USA) 108 (Green **–** Dancer (USA) 132) [2009 64: p13.9g Feb 7] good-bodied gelding: modest performer at 3 yrs: well held sole start in 2009: stays 1½m: acts on polytrack and good to soft going: tried in blinkers/cheekpieces: held up. *N. B. King*

GUNNER BE LUCKY (IRE) 6 b.g. Key of Luck (USA) 126 – Iolanta (IRE) 77 **–** (Danehill (USA) 126) [2009 8.1m Jul 1] tailed off in bumper at Stratford and claimer at Chepstow. *B. Palling*

GUNNER LINDLEY (IRE) 2 ch.c. (Feb 9) Medicean 128 – Lasso 58 (Indian Ridge **91** 123) [2009 6m^4 6g^2 7.1s* 7g^2 7m^5 8m Sep 12] 19,000Y: useful-looking colt: first foal: dam, 7f winner, out of half-sister to very smart 7f/1m performer Rebecca Sharp: fairly useful performer: won maiden at Haydock in July: good second to Black Snowflake in maiden at Haydock and nursery at Goodwood: should stay 1m: acts on soft ground. *B. W. Hills*

GUNSLINGER (FR) 4 b.g. High Chaparral (IRE) 132 – Gamine (IRE) 69 (High **84** Estate 127) [2009 10.2s* p12m^3 f11g^5 Dec 22] ex-French gelding: closely related to French 11.5f winner Gare du Nord (by In The Wings) and half-brother to 3 winners in France, including useful 1¼m winner Grand Opening (by Desert King): dam, maiden who stayed 1¾m, out of half-sister to Saddlers' Hall and Sun Princess: fairly useful performer: sold from E. Lellouche €38,000 and off 11 months, won maiden at Nottingham in October: stays 1½m: acts on polytrack and heavy ground. *M. J. Scudamore*

GURTAVALLIG (IRE) 4 ch.f. Starborough 126 – Alcadia (IRE) 91 (Thatching 131) [2009 6f^{6} 6m^{5} Jun 2] sixth foal: half-sister to useful Irish 2005 2-y-o 5f winner Cappa Brack (by Danehill Dancer): dam Irish 7f winner: tailed off in maidens. *T. J. Pitt* **–**

GURTEEN DIAMOND 3 b.f. Kyllachy 129 – Precious 65 (Danehill (USA) 126) [2009 56+: p6g^{3} p6g^{2} f6g^{3} p6g p6g* p6g^{3} 6m^{5} p7m Oct 12] fair performer: left N. Vaughan and off 7 months after fourth start: won maiden at Wolverhampton in September: below form last 2 starts: raced mostly at 6f on polytrack: wore eyecover first 4 outings. *P. D. Evans* **75**

GUTO 6 b.g. Foxhound (USA) 103 – Mujadilly 43 (Mujadil (USA) 119) [2009 78: f5g p5g f5g^{3} f5m^{2} f5g^{4} 5.1m f5g* f5m^{6} 5v^{6} f6g^{2} 5.2s^{2} 6s^{4} 5.1d* f5g* 6s^{6} 5m* f5g 5.3d f5m p6m Nov 28] quite good-topped gelding: fairly useful performer: won claimer at Southwell in April and handicaps at Nottingham and Southwell in August and Ayr in September: below form after: best at 5f/easy 6f: acts on all-weather, heavy and good to firm going: occasionally in blinkers/cheekpieces. *W. J. H. Ratcliffe* **83**

GWENLLIAN (IRE) 2 b.f. (Mar 29) Royal Dragon (USA) 118 – Desiraka (Kris 135) [2009 6s Nov 7] fifth foal: half-sister to German 1m winner Destyne (by Sternkoenig): dam, German 7f/7.5f winner, half-sister to smart German performer up to 1½m Dickens: 16/1, down the field in maiden at Doncaster. *J. L. Hassett, Ireland* **–**

GWERTHYBYD 3 b.f. Auction House (USA) 120 – Minette 55 (Bishop of Cashel 122) [2009 58: p8.6g^{6} p9.5g 8f^{3} Jun 24] modest maiden: may prove best up to 8.6f: acts on polytrack, probably on firm ground: often races freely. *B. Palling* **51**

GWILYM (GER) 6 b.g. Agnes World (USA) 123 – Glady Rose (GER) (Surumu (GER)) [2009 77: p5.1g p5m^{2} p5g p5.1g* p5.1g^{5} p5.1g^{4} p6m^{4} 6g^{3} 5.1m 6m^{3} 6m^{6} 5m^{4} 5f^{3} 6m* 5m p6g* p6g^{4} p6m Nov 21] compact gelding: fairly useful handicapper: won at Wolverhampton in January, Lingfield in August and Wolverhampton in October: effective at 5f/6f: acts on polytrack and firm going: tried in blinkers/cheekpieces. *D. Haydn Jones* **80**

GWYNEDD (IRE) 2 br.f. (Mar 21) Bertolini (USA) 125 – Bethesda 91 (Distant Relative 128) [2009 6m^{2} 5f* 6.1m 6m Aug 10] £28,000Y: good-topped filly: fifth foal: half-sister to 3-y-o Masamah and 2006 2-y-o 5f winner Fluttering Rose (by Compton Place): dam, winner around 6f, half-sister to Middle Park winner Fard: fair performer: won maiden at Lingfield in June: pulled too hard in nurseries after: likely to prove best at 5f: acts on firm going. *E. S. McMahon* **73**

GWYRE (IRE) 3 b.f. Mull of Kintyre (USA) 114 – Boadicea (Celtic Swing 138) [2009 10.1d 10m^{3} 10.1d^{4} 14.1m Aug 29] €12,000Y: second foal: dam French 2-y-o 8.5f winner: modest maiden: stays 1¼m: unraced on extremes of going. *T. D. Easterby* **54**

GYPSY BOY (USA) 2 b. or br.c. (Feb 15) Dixie Union (USA) 121 – Think Fast (USA) (Crafty Prospector (USA)) [2009 p6g^{5} p7g^{4} Sep 5] rather leggy colt: similar form in maiden and minor event at Kempton: will stay 1m. *R. Curtis* **68**

GYPSY JAZZ (IRE) 2 b.f. (Apr 29) Antonius Pius (USA) 123§ – Dawn's Folly (IRE) 47 (Bluebird (USA) 125) [2009 5.9m^{3} 6.1m p6g 6.1s* Oct 7] £1,000Y: workmanlike filly: sixth foal: closely related to fairly useful 2008 2-y-o 5f winner Fool Me (by Mull of Kintyre) and 5f (including at 2 yrs) winner Red Eagle (by Eagle Eyed) and half-sister to fairly useful 2002 2-y-o 6f/7f winner Love Is Blind (by Ali Royal): dam Irish maiden (probably stayed 7f): fair performer: easily best effort when winning nursery at Nottingham, though again looked awkward: raced only at 6f: acts on soft ground. *Jennie Candlish* **66**

H

HAADEETH 2 b.g. (Feb 25) Oasis Dream 129 – Musical Key 71 (Key of Luck (USA) 126) [2009 p6g* 6m^{2} 6g^{6} Oct 30] £80,000Y: well-made gelding: third foal: half-brother to 3-y-o Key Signature: dam, sprint maiden, half-sister to smart sprinter Volata: progressive form: won maiden at Kempton (dead-heated with Brick Red) in August: beaten short head in nursery at Newbury, then 2 lengths sixth to Rum King in minor event at Newmarket (well backed, went freely): raced only at 6f: likely to do better still. *M. P. Tregoning* **93 p**

HAAFHDS DELIGHT (IRE) 3 b.f. Haafhd 129 – Twitcher's Delight (Polar Falcon (USA) 126) [2009 –: p9.5g^{6} Feb 14] little sign of ability. *W. M. Brisbourne* **–**

HAAFHD TIME (IRE) 3 b.f. Haafhd 129 – Amusing Time (IRE) 104 (Sadler's Wells (USA) 132) [2009 –p: 10s 12m³ 12.1m⁶ p12g* 14.1m p11g* p11g⁴ p10g⁶ p12m Sep 30] sturdy filly: fair performer: split a pastern after only 2-y-o run: improved to win minor event at Kempton in June and handicap there in August: should stay 1¾m: acts on polytrack and good to firm ground. *Tom Dascombe* **67**

HAAJES 5 ch.g. Indian Ridge 123 – Imelda (USA) (Manila (USA)) [2009 102: f7g p5g p5.1g* f6g³ p5g⁶ p6g⁵ 6m 5.1m⁵ 5d⁶ 5g 5m³ 5d 6m³ 5v² 6g² 5m 5m* 6m 6d Oct 11] compact gelding: useful handicapper: won at Wolverhampton in February and, having left S. Parr after eighth start, Ffos Las in September: good efforts otherwise when placed: effective at 5f/6f: acts on all-weather, heavy and good to firm going: tried blinkered/visored: tongue tied: often races lazily. *J. Balding* **95**

HAAKIMA (USA) 3 b. or br.f. Dixieland Band (USA) – Be Fair (BRZ) (Fast Gold (USA)) [2009 79: p8g* 7s 8m p8g Oct 8] tall, leggy filly: fair performer: won maiden at Kempton in March: below form after: stays 8.5f: acts on polytrack, unraced on extremes of turf going. *C. E. Brittain* **67**

HAARTH SOVEREIGN (IRE) 5 b.g. Alhaarth (IRE) 126 – Summer Queen 80 (Robellino (USA) 127) [2009 86: p12g* 12.1m 14m² p16g⁵ 14d⁶ p13.9g Oct 9] rangy gelding: fairly useful handicapper: won at Kempton in April: stays 15f: acts on polytrack, firm and soft going: tried in cheekpieces: tongue tied last 4 outings: sold £11,000. *W. R. Swinburn* **86**

HAASEM (USA) 6 b.g. Seeking The Gold (USA) – Thawakib (IRE) 108 (Sadler's Wells (USA) 132) [2009 79: p7g p8g⁴ 8m p7.1g⁴ Dec 28] sturdy gelding: just modest handicapper at 6 yrs: best at 7f/1m: acts on polytrack and good to firm going: usually visored nowadays: waited with: tends to carry head awkwardly under pressure. *J. R. Jenkins* **63**

HAASHED (USA) 3 ch.g. Mr Greeley (USA) 122 – Guerre Et Paix (USA) (Soviet Star (USA) 128) [2009 93P: p9g Mar 18] very promising winner of maiden at Lingfield on only outing at 2 yrs: favourite, last in valuable minor event at Kempton sole start in 2009: gelded after. *M. Johnston* **–**

HAATHEQ (USA) 2 b.c. (Apr 30) Seeking The Gold (USA) – Alshadiyah (USA) 102 (Danzig (USA)) [2009 7s 7g 7m⁵ Sep 23] good-topped colt: fourth foal: closely related to fairly useful 6f/7f winner Badweia (by Kingmambo) and half-brother to useful 2006 2-y-o 6f winner Wid (by Elusive Quality): dam, 2-y-o 6f winner, out of 1000 Guineas winner Shadayid: progressive form in maidens, fifth to Workforce at Goodwood (raced freely): should be at least as effective at 6f as 7f: likely to do better still. *J. L. Dunlop* **72 p**

HABAAYIB 2 b.f. (Mar 4) Royal Applause 124 – Silver Kestrel (USA) (Silver Hawk (USA) 123) [2009 5m³ 5.1f* 6f* 6g² 6m Oct 2] 130,000Y: well-made, attractive filly: second foal: dam, US 7f winner, out of US Grade 2 6.5f winner Salty Perfume, herself half-sister to Middle Park/Dewhurst Stakes second Green Perfume: useful performer: won maiden at Nottingham in May and 22-runner Albany Stakes at Royal Ascot (significant improvement, beat Lillie Langtry readily by 1¼ lengths) in June: reportedly in season when just respectable 3¼ lengths second to Misheer in Cherry Hinton Stakes at Newmarket: off 3 months (reportedly suffered ringworm), tailed off in Cheveley Park Stakes there final start: will prove best up to 7f: acts on firm going. *E. A. L. Dunlop* **108**

HABSHAN (USA) 9 ch.g. Swain (IRE) 134 – Cambara 97 (Dancing Brave (USA) 140) [2009 96: 8m³ 8.1f⁶ 8g 8g Jul 24] smallish, good-topped gelding: fairly useful handicapper nowadays: stays 8.6f: acts on polytrack, good to firm and good to soft going: held up (travels well). *C. F. Wall* **88**

HACHI 2 ch.f. (Apr 5) Kyllachy 129 – Milly-M (Cadeaux Genereux 131) [2009 5m 5m⁵ 6g² 6g³ 6d p6g Sep 4] 7,500F, €15,000Y: angular filly: fifth foal: half-sister to fairly useful 2006 2-y-o 7f winner Mimisel (by Selkirk) and 6f winner Conrad (by Royal Applause): dam unraced daughter of smart 5f performer Millyant: modest maiden: stays 6f: tried blinkered. *J. L. Spearing* **50**

HADAF (IRE) 4 b.c. Fasliyev (USA) 120 – Elhida (IRE) 99 (Mujtahid (USA) 118) [2009 91: 5m 5m 5g 5m Aug 29] compact colt: just fair handicapper in 2009: best at 5f: acts on polytrack and good to firm going: sold 10,000 gns, sent to Bahrain. *M. P. Tregoning* **73**

HADA MEN (USA) 4 b.g. Dynaformer (USA) – Catchy (USA) (Storm Cat (USA)) [2009 85: 12f* 11.8d³ 14.1d² 16.4m 14d Sep 15] stocky gelding: fairly useful handicapper, lightly raced: won at Folkestone in June: should stay 2m: unraced on soft/heavy going, acts on any other turf and polytrack: sold 10,000 gns, joined Miss T. Jackson. *L. M. Cumani* **85**

HAFAWA (IRE) 2 b.f. (Mar 6) Intikhab (USA) 135 – Banaadir (USA) 50 (Diesis 133) [2009 6m* 6m² 7m* Oct 13] strong, lengthy filly: fifth foal: half-sister to 3 fairly useful winners around 9f, including 3-y-o Hukba: dam, ran 3 times, out of Prix Saint-Alary winner Treble: won maiden at Pontefract in June and minor event at Leicester (beat Dawnbreak in good style by 4 lengths, edging right) in October: likely to stay 1m: already useful, and capable of better still. *M. Johnston* **99 p**

HAIL BOLD CHIEF (USA) 2 b.g. (Feb 18) Dynaformer (USA) – Yanaseeni (USA) (Trempolino (USA) 135) [2009 p8.6g 8.3g⁵ Oct 28] $80,000Y: fourth foal: half-brother to French 1m winner Falcon Dive (by Diesis): dam, US 1¼m winner, sister to very smart German 1¼m/1½m performer Germany: better effort in maidens when fifth to Psychic Ability at Nottingham, repeatedly denied clear run and eased when held (gelded after): should stay 1¼m. *G. A. Swinbank* **77**

HAIL CAESAR (IRE) 3 gr.c. Montjeu (IRE) 137 – Alabastrine 56 (Green Desert (USA) 127) [2009 103: 8g⁴ 10d⁴ 10g⁴ 8v 10m⁴ 12f 9.5s* 12g Jul 14] quite good-topped colt: useful performer: won minor event at Gowran in July by 4½ lengths from Drumbeat: creditable efforts otherwise in 2009 when fourth in 2000 Guineas Trial, Ballysax Stakes and Derby Trial at Leopardstown (8 lengths behind Fame And Glory) earlier in year: pacemaker in Grand Prix de Paris at Longchamp final start: stays 1¼m: acts on heavy and good to firm going: blinkered last 2 starts: sometimes carries head awkwardly: has joined T. Walsh. *A. P. O'Brien, Ireland* **104**

HAIL PROMENADER (IRE) 3 b.c. Acclamation 118 – Tribal Rite 95 (Be My Native (USA) 122) [2009 83: 8.3g⁵ p8g⁶ 7.1m² 7.1m⁶ 7m² 7.1g² 7g Oct 9] tall colt: fairly useful handicapper: best efforts when runner-up at Salisbury and Sandown fifth/sixth starts: may prove best at 1m: acts on polytrack, firm and soft going. *B. W. Hills* **91**

HAIRSPRAY 2 ch.f. (Feb 21) Bahamian Bounty 116 – Quickstyx 72 (Night Shift (USA)) [2009 6m⁴ 6m* 6g⁵ 6g 6g* 5.2m⁶ 6m 5g Oct 10] close-coupled filly: second foal: half-sister to 2008 2-y-o 5.8f (in Sweden) to 7.5f winner Blusher (by Fraam): dam, 1m winner (stayed 1¼m), half-sister to smart performer up to 1¼m Red Fort: fairly useful performer: won maiden at Lingfield in May and minor event at Newmarket (by neck from Blue Angel) in July: below form after: likely to stay 7f: raced only on good/good to firm ground: sometimes slowly away, markedly so final outing. *M. R. Channon* **90**

HAIRS VITAL (IRE) 2 b.g. (Feb 23) Pearl of Love (IRE) 112 – Blue Banner (IRE) 84 (Grand Lodge (USA) 125) [2009 5m⁴ 6s⁴ 6g⁵ 5g f5g⁵ f8g⁵ a6.5g Dec 23] €30,000F, £16,000Y: first foal: dam, Irish 2-y-o 5f winner, stayed 7f: fair maiden: best efforts second/third starts: best form at 6f: acts on soft going, below form on all-weather: tried blinkered. *E. J. O'Neill* **73 d**

HAJAR (USA) 3 gr. or ro.g. Rahy (USA) 115 – Laiyl (IRE) 85 (Nureyev (USA) 131) [2009 8m³ 9.2m* Jun 25] unfurnished gelding: sixth foal: half-brother to 3 winners, notably very smart 6f (in France at 2 yrs) to 1m winner Layman (stayed 1¼m, by Sunday Silence): dam, 1¼m winner from 2 starts, out of Irish Oaks winner Alydaress, herself half-sister to Cheveley Park Stakes winners Park Appeal (dam of Cape Cross) and Desirable (dam of Shadayid): fair form in maidens, winning at Hamilton in June: sold 8,000 gns in July. *M. Johnston* **71**

HAJJAAN (USA) 2 b.c. (Mar 21) Mr Greeley (USA) 122 – Danzig Island (USA) (Danzig (USA)) [2009 6g³ Oct 30] $400,000Y: lengthy, unfurnished colt: half-brother to several winners in USA, including Grade 3 1m winner High Strike Zone (by Smart Strike): dam unraced half-sister to very smart performer up to 1¼m Sharrood: 16/1, promising length third to Asraab in maiden at Newmarket, travelling strongly and not unduly knocked about: sure to improve. *J. L. Dunlop* **83 p**

HAJMAH (IRE) 3 ch.f. Singspiel (IRE) 133 – Midnight Line (USA) 114 (Kris S (USA)) [2009 10m³ 11.7g* 11.6g⁵ p12g Oct 26] sturdy filly: fifth foal: half-sister to 3 winners, including useful 1¼m winner Moon Quest (by Rainbow Quest): dam 7f (at 2 yrs) to 1½m (Grade 2 in USA) winner and third in Oaks: fairly useful form: won maiden at Bath in September: stays 11.6f: acts on good to firm ground: joined M. Al Subouse in UAE. *Saeed bin Suroor* **85**

HAJOUM (IRE) 3 b.c. Exceed And Excel (AUS) 126 – Blue Iris 105 (Petong 126) [2009 80: 6m² 6g* p6g² p6m⁴ Nov 3] lengthy, angular colt: useful performer: won maiden at Windsor in October: better form when in frame in handicaps after: raced only at 6f: best efforts on polytrack: tried tongue tied. *Saeed bin Suroor* **95**

HALAAK (USA) 3 br.f. Harlan's Holiday (USA) 124 – Henderson Band (USA) (Chimes Band (USA) 117) [2009 55+: f6s² f5d* p6g⁴ 5.1f⁶ 6m⁵ 5m³ 5.3f² 6f² 6g³ p5g⁴ **67**

p6g 5.3m^2 f5g^3 Oct 18] compact filly: fair handicapper: won at Southwell in January: effective at 5f/6f: acts on all-weather and firm going: usually blinkered: held up: reliable. *D. M. Simcock*

HALAM BANKES 2 b.c. (May 3) Lucky Owners (NZ) 122 – Grace Bankes 44 (Efisio 120) [2009 5.5d^5 7d^6 5.5d* 6g 7m^3 6g p6g Nov 16] won claimer at Saint-Malo in August: left E. Danel in France, well held in claimer at Wolverhampton final start: stays 5.5f. *W. G. M. Turner* **61**

HALCYON DANCER 3 ch.f. Reset (AUS) 124 – Volitant (Ashkalani (IRE) 128) [2009 7.2g^4 6d^6 7d^3 6m^6 6g^3 p6g^6 Sep 25] lengthy filly: second foal: half-sister to 6f winner in Japan by Observatory: dam unraced half-sister to smart sprinter Volata: modest maiden: stays 7f, should prove effective at shorter. *M. Dods* **62**

HALCYON PRINCESS (IRE) 3 b.f. Barathea (IRE) 127 – Serene Princess (USA) 85 (Louis Quatorze (USA) 125) [2009 –: 8g^5 8.5s^6 8m 8.1d p9.5g p11m Sep 30] maiden: fair form only on reappearance (left Mrs J. Harrington in Ireland £1,600 after next start): stays 1m: in cheekpieces last 2 outings. *D. G. Bridgwater* **67 d**

HALDIBARI (IRE) 5 b.g. Kahyasi 130 – Haladiya (IRE) (Darshaan 133) [2009 59: p12.2g^6 21.6m^2 17.1g^3 17.1m 17.1m Sep 17] good-topped gelding: modest maiden, lightly raced: stays 21.5f: acts on good to firm ground: unreliable. *S. Lycett* **64 §**

HALF A CROWN (IRE) 4 b.c. Compton Place 125 – Penny Ha'penny 84 (Bishop of Cashel 122) [2009 60: f6g 5m 5.9g 5m 5m^6 6m 6s^3 6m 5d* 5m^4 5.1d 6g* Oct 23] lengthy, workmanlike colt: fair handicapper: left D. Barker after fifth start: improved after to win at Newcastle (maiden) in September and Ayr in October: likely to prove best at 5f/6f: acts on good to soft ground: in headgear since 4-y-o reappearance: tried tongue tied: has finished weakly. *M. Dods* **67**

HALF SISTER (IRE) 2 b.f. (May 14) Oratorio (IRE) 128 – Fifty Five (IRE) (Lake Coniston (IRE) 131) [2009 6m Aug 15] 48,000Y: good-topped filly: sixth foal: half-sister to 2 winners abroad, including French 6.5f winner Fix (by Orpen): dam, French 1¼m winner, half-sister to George Washington and Grandera: 14/1, backward and very green, tailed off in maiden at Newbury: bred to be well suited by 7f+. *R. Hannon* **–**

HALFWAY HOUSE 3 b.g. Dubai Destination (USA) 127 – Zanzibar (IRE) 113 (In The Wings 128) [2009 62p: 11.6g 10g 10f* 12f* 11.9f^2 12m^6 12m^4 p12g^3 Oct 8] good-topped gelding: fairly useful handicapper: improved to win at Brighton in June and Folkestone in July: stays 1½m: acts on polytrack and firm going: held up: sold 8,000 gns. *M. L. W. Bell* **87**

HALFWAY THERE 2 b.f. (Feb 11) Ishiguru (USA) 114 – Hi Ho Silca 56 (Atraf 116) [2009 p8.6g Dec 19] second foal: dam twice-raced half-sister to useful Irish 1998 2-y-o sprinter Camargo: 25/1 and green, tailed off in maiden at Wolverhampton. *J. G. Given* **–**

HALICARNASSUS (IRE) 5 b.h. Cape Cross (IRE) 129 – Launch Time (USA) (Relaunch (USA)) [2009 117§: 10g* 12g 10m^4 p10g^4 p10g^6 9.8m* 10g^6 10.3m 10m^2 9.9m^2 12m^2 10f 10m^5 10.4g 12g^3 13.3m^2 12g* 11m^5 12m^4 12v Oct 24] tall, rather leggy horse: smart performer: won handicap at Nad Al Sheba (beat Bruges ¾ length) in February, minor event at Ripon in April and very valuable Bosphorus Cup at Veliefendi (by ½ length from Pan River) in September: several respectable efforts otherwise in 2009, including when 3½ lengths second to Kite Wood in Geoffrey Freer Stakes at Newbury on sixteenth start: stays 13f: acts on firm ground, tailed off on heavy: tried visored: sometimes sweats: moody, and not one to trust. *M. R. Channon* **113 §**

HALING PARK (UAE) 3 b.f. Halling (USA) 133 – Friendly (USA) (Lear Fan (USA) 130) [2009 8g 7m 7s 9.7m^4 p10g 10m^6 8d p11f^5 Dec 16] €15,000Y: sturdy filly: fourth foal: sister to 4-y-o Hawk Mountain and half-sister to 1¼m and 13.3f winner Garrulous (by Lomitas): dam unraced out of close relation to 1½m performers Assatis (high class) and Warrshan (smart): modest maiden: bred to stay 1½m+: acts on polytrack and good to firm going: tried in cheekpieces. *G. L. Moore* **55**

HALJAFERIA (UAE) 3 ch.g. Halling (USA) 133 – Melisendra (FR) (Highest Honor (FR) 124) [2009 78p: p8g^3 p10g^3 12m^4 12m* 12s 12m^5 16f 13g Jul 25] lengthy, angular gelding: fair performer: won maiden at Thirsk in May: will stay 1¾m: acts on polytrack and good to firm ground, below form on soft. *D. R. C. Elsworth* **79**

HALLA SAN 7 b.g. Halling (USA) 133 – St Radegund 85 (Green Desert (USA) 127) [2009 102: p11g 18.7m^3 14m^3 21.7m Jun 20] tall gelding: has a quick action: useful performer: good third in Chester Cup (Handicap) (½ length behind Daraahem) second outing: below best otherwise in 2009: stays 2¼m: acts on soft and good to firm going: useful hurdler. *R. A. Fahey* **103**

HALLINGDAL BLUE (UAE) 3 b.f. Halling (USA) 133 – Blue Melody (USA) 103 (Dayjur (USA) 137) [2009 –: 11.5g p11g a8g a12g³ 12g a12g a11.5g a12g a8g³ Nov 29] small, angular filly: poor maiden: sold from H. Cecil 800 gns after second start: stays 1½m: acts on dirt: tried blinkered. *Cathrine Witso Slettemark, Norway* **?**

HALLINGDAL (UAE) 4 b.f. Halling (USA) 133 – Saik (USA) (Riverman (USA) 131) [2009 88: p8g² p7.1g* p6g⁵ p7g p8g 8.3m 7g 8.3d³ 8.3g³ 8.3m⁶ 8g⁵ 10m 9g 8.1g³ 9m⁴ 9.7m* 8d 9.9m⁵ p9.5m² p10m⁴ p10g p10g⁶ p12m p10m⁴ p10f² Dec 20] good-topped filly: fairly useful handicapper on all-weather, fair on turf: won at Wolverhampton in February and, having left Ms J. Doyle after sixth start, Folkestone in August: stays 1¼m: acts on polytrack, good to firm and good to soft going: held up (sometimes slowly away). *J. J. Bridger* **76 a82**

HALLING GAL 3 b.f. Halling (USA) 133 – Saik (USA) (Riverman (USA) 131) [2009 8g⁵ 9g* Jun 19] 25,000Y: well-made filly: sixth foal: sister to 4-y-o Hallingdal and half-sister to 3 winners, including fairly useful 7f winner Wistman (by Woodman): dam unraced close relative to dam of Prix de l'Arc de Triomphe runner-up Mubtaker: fairly useful form: better effort in maidens at Goodwood when successful in June by head from Queen Eleanor: not sure to stay much beyond 9f. *W. R. Muir* **85**

HALLSTATT (IRE) 3 ch.c. Halling (USA) 133 – Last Resort 116 (Lahib (USA) 129) [2009 p10g* p10g⁵ 10.4g³ 10.3m² 10.1g² 10m⁶ Jul 23] fifth foal: brother to Irish 5-y-o Abroad and half-brother to smart US performer up to 1m Rebellion (by Mozart): dam 7f winner, including Challenge Stakes: fairly useful performer: won maiden at Lingfield in May: better form when placed in handicaps after: raced only around 1¼m: acts on polytrack and good to firm going: joined Evan Williams £16,000 after final start. *M. Johnston* **85**

HALLUCINATING 2 b.g. (Apr 10) Oasis Dream 129 – Follow Flanders 92 (Pursuit of Love 124) [2009 6g Oct 30] sturdy gelding: 100/1 and backward, in rear in maiden at Newmarket: dead. *H. Candy* **–**

HALSION CHALLENGE 4 b.g. King's Best (USA) 132 – Zaynah (IRE) (Kahyasi 130) [2009 44: p8g⁴ p8g² p7g³ p8g⁴ Feb 19] modest maiden: stays 1m: acts on polytrack: tried in cheekpieces: tongue tied nowadays. *J. R. Best* **54**

HALSION CHANCER 5 b.g. Atraf 116 – Lucky Dip 68 (Tirol 127) [2009 –, a97: p10g³ p8g² p8g⁴ 7m* 6m⁶ 6g⁶ p6g p7g Sep 8] lengthy gelding: fairly useful handicapper: won at Lingfield in June: below form after: effective from 7f to easy 1¼m: acts on polytrack and good to firm going. *J. R. Best* **82 a86**

HALTELA (IRE) 2 b.g. (Apr 5) Namid 128 – Quivala (USA) (Thunder Gulch (USA) 129) [2009 5m 6g* 6g⁴ 6m⁵ 8g⁴ 6g 7g Oct 24] tall gelding: has scope: third foal: half-brother to fairly useful 2007 2-y-o 5f winner Kersaint and 2008 2-y-o 6f winner Sweet Smile (both by Catcher In The Rye): dam, French 1m winner, out of smart sister to Prix de Diane winner Caerlina: fairly useful performer: won maiden at York in June: best effort when fourth to Simenon in minor event at Ayr fifth start: stays 1m: in headgear last 4 starts: has hung left: sold £10,000. *K. A. Ryan* **86**

HALYARD (IRE) 2 b.c. (Feb 13) Halling (USA) 133 – Brindisi 103 (Dr Fong (USA) 128) [2009 7.1m 7d⁵ Sep 15] smallish, good-bodied colt: modest form in maidens at Sandown and Lingfield: will be suited by 1m. *W. R. Swinburn* **61**

HAMAASY 8 b.g. Machiavellian (USA) 123 – Sakha 109 (Wolfhound (USA) 126) [2009 –, a67: f7d² f6d² f7g⁵ f7g² f7g⁶ f6g f7d f6g³ f6g f7g 5.7g 6f p8.6g Sep 25] quite attractive gelding: fair performer on all-weather: below form later in 2009, leaving R. Harris after tenth outing: best at 6f/7f: acts on fibresand (lightly raced on turf nowadays): tried tongue tied/visored, often in cheekpieces in 2009. *G. A. Ham* **– a65**

HAMBLEDON HILL 3 ch.g. Selkirk (USA) 129 – Dominica 115 (Alhaarth (IRE) 126) [2009 75: 8.1g⁵ 9.9m⁵ 9.9f p11g⁴ 13g 11m³ Aug 14] lengthy, unfurnished gelding: fair maiden: stays 11f: acts on polytrack, good to firm and good to soft going. *R. Hannon* **70**

HAMBLETON 2 b.c. (Feb 8) Monsieur Bond (IRE) 120 – Only Yours 113 (Aragon 118) [2009 5g f6g⁶ Sep 29] easily better effort in maidens 5 months apart when sixth to Amenable at Southwell, though seemed ill at ease on surface. *B. Smart* **52 +**

HAMISH MCGONAGALL 4 b.g. Namid 128 – Anatase (Danehill (USA) 126) [2009 107: 5m⁴ 5g⁴ 5m⁴ 5g⁴ 5d³ 5m² 5.4m² 5m⁶ 5d 5m 6g 5d Oct 24] big, strong, lengthy gelding: useful handicapper: in frame first 7 starts in 2009, runner-up in valuable events at Ascot (½ length behind Judge 'N Jury) and York (neck second to Barney McGrew): below form after: best at 5f: unraced on extremes of going: travels strongly close up. *T. D. Easterby* **108**

HAMLOOLA 2 b.f. (Apr 29) Red Ransom (USA) – Dusty Answer 97 (Zafonic (USA) 130) [2009 6s^3 Nov 7] 210,000Y: fourth foal: half-sister to useful French 10.5f winner Counterclaim (by Pivotal): dam, 2-y-o 7f winner, half-sister to US Grade 2 9f winner Spotlight out of smart performer up to 1½m Dust Dancer: 15/2, length third to Adventure Story in maiden at Doncaster, very green and nearest finish: will stay 1m: sure to improve. *W. J. Haggas* **74 p**

HAMMER 4 b.g. Beat Hollow 126 – Tranquil Moon 70 (Deploy 131) [2009 76: p12m^2 p12g^4 p12.2g^6 11.6g 15m^6 May 9] lengthy, angular gelding: fair maiden: stays 13.3f: acts on polytrack, soft and good to firm going: temperament under suspicion. *R. T. Phillips* **70**

HAMMER OF THE GODS (IRE) 9 ch.g. Tagula (IRE) 116 – Bhama (FR) (Habitat 134) [2009 –, a79: p6g Feb 18] strong gelding: poor mover: fair handicapper on all-weather in 2008: well below form sole start in 2009: usually wears headgear/tongue tie. *G. C. Bravery* **50**

HAMOODY (USA) 5 ch.g. Johannesburg (USA) 127 – Northern Gulch (USA) (Gulch (USA)) [2009 6g 6g^5 6g^2 6m Sep 10] strong, lengthy gelding: fluent mover: useful form in allowance races in USA in 2008: left Jenine Sahadi and returned to former trainer before reappearance: fairly useful form at 5 yrs, runner-up in handicap at Goodwood: stays 6.5f: acts on polytrack and firm going: sold 25,000 gns, then gelded. *P. W. Chapple-Hyam* **93**

HANBELATION (USA) 2 b. or br.f. (Feb 25) Malibu Moon (USA) – Baldellia (FR) (Grape Tree Road 122) [2009 p6m Nov 29] $150,000Y: third foal: half-sister to 2 winners in France including 9.5f winner Bodegon (by Diesis): dam useful French 1m (including at 2 yrs) winner: 20/1, pulled hard when behind in maiden at Kempton. *E. F. Vaughan* **–**

HANBRIN BHOY (IRE) 5 b.g. Cape Cross (IRE) 129 – Sea of Stone (USA) 71 (Sanglamore (USA) 126) [2009 77: p10g Apr 29] workmanlike gelding: lightly-raced handicapper: well held sole start in 2009: should stay 1¼m: acts on polytrack, firm and soft going. *R. Dickin* **–**

HANDCUFF 3 br.g. Lend A Hand 124 – Peruvian Jade 76 (Petong 126) [2009 60: 5.1g^4 5.1g 6f 7m 8.3d^5 7s^5 6.1g 5.1d 5m 5g 5g Sep 30] smallish gelding: modest maiden: left J. Gallagher £1,100 after seventh start: best effort at 5f: acts on polytrack and soft going: tried in headgear: sold £800. *I. Semple* **52**

HAND PAINTED 3 b.g. Lend A Hand 124 – Scarlett Holly 81 (Red Sunset 120) [2009 75p: p6g 6f^3 6s* 6d* 6g^2 6m^2 7m* 6g^5 Sep 14] strong gelding: fairly useful handicapper: won at Brighton in May and June, and Folkestone in August: stays 7f: acts on firm and soft going: usually races prominently: gelded after final start. *P. J. Makin* **82**

HANDSINTHEMIST (IRE) 4 b.f. Lend A Hand 124 – Hollow Haze (USA) 90 (Woodman (USA) 126) [2009 53: f5m^2 f5g* f5g* 5m^6 f5g^5 f5g^5 5m^5 5m 5g^5 5d^6 f5f^3 Dec 11] tall, leggy filly: modest handicapper: won twice at Southwell in March: should stay 6f: acts on all-weather, firm and good to soft going: formerly in cheekpieces, tried visored. *P. T. Midgley* **61**

HANDSOME CROSS (IRE) 8 b.g. Cape Cross (IRE) 129 – Snap Crackle Pop (IRE) 87 (Statoblest 120) [2009 85: 5m^4 5g^3 5g 5m p5.1g p5.1g p5m^5 p6g* Dec 31] strong gelding: fairly useful handicapper: not so good later in year, though still won at Lingfield in December: stays easy 6f: acts on polytrack, firm and good to soft going: visored last 2 starts. *W. J. Musson* **82 d**

HANDSOME FALCON 5 b.g. Kyllachy 129 – Bonne Etoile 94 (Diesis 133) [2009 84: 8m^5 8.5m^2 8.5m^2 8.9d 8d^6 8.5m^4 8.5m^2 8.3d^2 8s 8.1m^2 p8.6g* 7g p9.5g^5 Oct 31] big, angular gelding: fairly useful handicapper: better than ever when winning at Wolverhampton in October: should stay 1¼m: acts on polytrack, soft and good to firm going. *R. A. Fahey* **90**

HANNAH GREELEY (USA) 2 b. or br.f. (Feb 4) Mr Greeley (USA) 122 – Miss Hannah (USA) (Deputy Minister (CAN)) [2009 p7f 8.3s Oct 7] $120,000Y: first foal: dam US 7f winner: well held in maidens. *J. R. Boyle* **–**

HANNICEAN 5 ch.g. Medicean 128 – Hannah's Music 85 (Music Boy 124) [2009 80: p10g^4 10.2g 10m 12d p8.6g Nov 16] strong, lengthy gelding: fair handicapper: left R. Price prior to final start: stays 1¼m: acts on soft and good to firm going: tried tongue tied: sold £1,100, joined Ian Williams. *N. B. King* **75**

HANOVERIAN BARON 4 b.g. Green Desert (USA) 127 – Josh's Pearl (IRE) 103 (Sadler's Wells (USA) 132) [2009 98: 7f 7f p7.1g^4 f6g 10d* 9.9s* Oct 12] good-topped gelding: fairly useful handicapper nowadays: left D. Nicholls and dropped in weights prior to winning at Sandown in September and Salisbury in October: stays 1¼m: acts on polytrack, soft and good to firm going: tried blinkered. *A. G. Newcombe* **86**

Betfair Gordon Stakes, Goodwood—Harbinger briefly heads the St Leger betting following victory over northern raider Firebet (noseband)

HANSOMIS (IRE) 5 b.m. Titus Livius (FR) 115 – Handsome Anna (IRE) 67 (Bigstone (IRE) 126) [2009 62: 6m² 5.9g* 5.9m* 6m² 6m² 5.9g 7m³ 6m 7m 6m⁴ 6m 6d Oct 13] leggy, quite attractive mare: fair handicapper: won twice at Carlisle in June: effective at 6f/7f: acts on heavy and good to firm ground: tried in cheekpieces. *B. Mactaggart* **73**

HANSON'D (IRE) 2 ch.c. (May 5) Pivotal 124 – Dinka Raja (USA) (Woodman (USA) 126) [2009 6m⁴ 7.2m* 8d Oct 24] 57,000 2-y-o: well-made colt: seventh foal: half-brother to 3 winners, notably useful 2003 2-y-o 6f (including Cheveley Park Stakes) winner Carry On Katie (by Fasliyev): dam, French 1m winner from 2 starts, out of half-sister to very smart fillies up to 1¼m Grise Mine and Kostroma: won maiden at Ayr in September by 6 lengths from George Benjamin: good 10 lengths seventh to St Nicholas Abbey in Racing Post Trophy at Doncaster: stays 1m: acts on good to firm and good to soft going: already useful. *K. A. Ryan* **95 +**

HANTA YO (IRE) 3 ch.g. Alhaarth (IRE) 126 – Tekindia (FR) (Indian Ridge 123) [2009 55p: 6f p5.1g Aug 10] maiden: just poor form at 3 yrs. *J. R. Gask* **43**

HAPPY AND GLORIOUS (IRE) 3 ch.f. Refuse To Bend (IRE) 128 – Wondrous Joy 98 (Machiavellian (USA) 123) [2009 –: p7.1g⁶ p9.5m 8g⁵ 10m p8g Aug 15] attractive filly: maiden: modest form only on reappearance. *J. W. Hills* **52**

HAPPY ANNIVERSARY (IRE) 3 b.f. Intikhab (USA) 135 – Happy Story (IRE) 74 (Bigstone (IRE) 126) [2009 86: 7m³ 7m² 7g² 8.1g⁴ 8m⁵ 8d 7s⁵ Nov 7] leggy filly: fairly useful handicapper: effective at 6f to easy 1m: acts on soft and good to firm going: reliable. *Mrs D. J. Sanderson* **88**

HAPPY DUBAI (IRE) 2 ch.c. (Apr 4) Indian Ridge 123 – Gentle Wind (USA) (Gentlemen (ARG) 136) [2009 6f² 6d³ 7s³ 7m³ Sep 23] €8,000F: strong colt: second foal: dam, US 5f winner, half-sister to very smart French/US performer up to 1½m Talloires: fair maiden: stays 7f: acts on firm and soft ground: tried tongue tied/visored: joined A. Al Raihe in UAE. *B. Smart* **75**

HAPPY FOREVER (FR) 3 b.f. Dr Fong (USA) 128 – Happyanunoit (NZ) 122 (Yachtie (AUS)) [2009 83: p6g³ p6g⁴ p6g⁴ 7m³ Jun 14] leggy filly: fair performer: stays 7f: acts on polytrack, good to firm and good to soft going: signs of temperament: sold 27,000 gns in July. *M. Botti* **78**

HAPPY MOOD 2 b.f. (May 1) Piccolo 121 – Love And Kisses 70 (Salse (USA) 128) [2009 7g Oct 31] sturdy, good-bodied filly: fourth foal: dam, 1¾m winner, half-sister to dam of very smart performer up to 12.5f in France/US Dark Moondancer out of high-class sprinter Soba: 100/1 and green, well held in maiden at Newmarket. *G. L. Moore* **–**

HARALD BLUETOOTH (IRE) 4 b.c. Danetime (IRE) 121 – Goldthroat (IRE) 79 (Zafonic (USA) 130) [2009 92: p8.6g* p8g* Jan 21] strong colt: type to carry condition: useful handicapper, lightly raced: further improvement in 2009, winning at Wolverhampton and Kempton (by neck from Ocean Legend, pulled up lame after line): stays 8.6f: acts on polytrack, soft and good to firm going: held up. *D. M. Simcock* **97**

HARBINGER 3 b.c. Dansili 127 – Penang Pearl (FR) 106 (Bering 136) [2009 8m² 10.3m* 12g* 12m 12v³ Oct 24] 180,000Y: big, well-made colt: fifth foal: half-brother to 6-y-o Penang Cinta and 2004 2-y-o 5f winner Penang Sapphire (by Spectrum): dam 1m/9f winner: smart performer: won maiden at Chester in May and Betfair Gordon Stakes at Goodwood (beat Firebet 1¾ lengths, overcoming false test with something to spare) in July: tongue tied, creditable 6¼ lengths third to High Heeled in St Simon Stakes at Newbury final outing: stays 1½m: acts on heavy and good to firm ground: shaped as though amiss in Great Voltigeur Stakes at York fourth outing. *Sir Michael Stoute* **118**

HARBOUR BLUES 4 ch.c. Best of The Bests (IRE) 122 – Lady Georgia 94 (Arazi (USA) 135) [2009 92: 5.7g⁴ p6g² 6g May 2] lengthy, useful-looking colt: fairly useful performer: will prove best at 5f/6f: acts on polytrack and soft ground, probably on good to firm: tongue tied: usually makes running. *A. W. Carroll* **85**

HARCAS (IRE) 7 br.g. Priolo (USA) 127 – Genetta (Green Desert (USA) 127) [2009 61: 15.8m⁴ 15.8g⁵ 16m 12m 14.1m* 14m⁶ 13.8m Sep 19] sturdy gelding: fair handicapper: won Redcar in August: stays 2m: acts on good to firm going: usually wears headgear: races up with pace. *M. Todhunter* **67**

HARDANGER (IRE) 4 b.c. Halling (USA) 133 – Naughty Nell 89 (Danehill Dancer (IRE) 117) [2009 68: 8.3m 6.9d 7v p8f⁵ Oct 14] quite good-topped colt: maiden, well held in 2009. *T. J. Fitzgerald* **–**

HARD BALL 3 b.g. Pivotal 124 – Miss Pinkerton 104 (Danehill (USA) 126) [2009 72: p10g 8m 8s 11.6d 10.1d 8.3v f7f* Dec 12] tall, quite attractive gelding: modest handicapper: won at Southwell in December: stays 8.3f: acts on fibresand and heavy going: visored last 2 starts. *M. Quinn* **59**

HARD LUCK STORY 3 b. or br.g. Lucky Story (USA) 128 – Howards Heroine (IRE) 70§ (Danehill Dancer (IRE) 117) [2009 66: 9m⁴ 12m³ 8.3g⁴ 12.5m Sep 14] maiden, just modest at 3 yrs: should stay 1¼m: acts on heavy going: tried in cheekpieces: one to treat with caution. *I. Semple* **62 §**

HARLECH CASTLE 4 b.g. Royal Applause 124 – Ffestiniog (IRE) 96 (Efisio 120) [2009 91: 5m 6f 6m³ 6v 6g² 6m⁵ f6g p6g p7g p6m³ p6g f6d* Dec 29] smallish, good-topped gelding: fairly useful handicapper: left P. Cole after seventh start: won at Southwell in December: effective at 6f/7f: acts on all-weather, firm and soft going: often blinkered: none too consistent. *J. R. Boyle* **89**

HARLEQUINN DANSEUR (IRE) 4 b.g. Noverre (USA) 125 – Nassma (IRE) 95 (Sadler's Wells (USA) 132) [2009 –: 11.9f* 11.9m⁵ 12m⁶ May 24] rather leggy gelding: modest performer: 8 lb out of handicap, won at Brighton in May: stays 1½m: acts on firm going: tried visored/blinkered/tongue tied. *N. B. King* **55**

HARLESTONE GOLD 4 b.g. Golden Snake (USA) 127 – Harlestone Lady (Shaamit (IRE) 127) [2009 66: 11.8m Apr 2] useful-looking gelding: maiden, raced only 3 times: fair form at 3 yrs: well held only outing in 2009. *J. L. Dunlop* **–**

HARLESTONE SNAKE 3 b.g. Golden Snake (USA) 127 – Harlestone Lady (Shaamit (IRE) 127) [2009 68p: 9.9g 11m³ 14m* 14g⁶ p16g Sep 5] leggy gelding: fairly useful handicapper: won at Goodwood in June: suffered fatal injury at Kempton in September: would have stayed 2m: acted on good to firm going. *J. L. Dunlop* **80**

HARLESTONE TIMES (IRE) 2 b.c. (Feb 12) Olden Times 121 – Harlestone Lady (Shaamit (IRE) 127) [2009 7g 7g⁴ 8m³ 8d² Oct 15] third foal: half-brother to 3-y-o Harlestone Snake: dam unraced sister to smart stayer Harlestone Grey: fair maiden: placed at Ffos Las and Brighton: will be suited by 1¼m+: type to do better. *J. L. Dunlop* **73 p**

HARLEY FERN 3 b.f. Primo Valentino (IRE) 116 – Its All Relative 90 (Distant Relative 128) [2009 –: p9.5g Nov 6] no form in maidens. *M. E. Rimmer* **–**

HAROLDINI (IRE) 7 b.g. Orpen (USA) 116 – Ciubanga (IRE) (Arazi (USA) 135) [2009 –, a77: f7d⁵ f8g⁵ f7g⁵ f7g² p7.1g⁵ f8g⁶ f8g f7g² f7g³ f8g⁶ p7.1g p8.6g Jul 13] lengthy gelding: fair handicapper: effective at 7f/1m: acts on all-weather (best efforts on fibresand), good to firm and good to soft going: wears headgear. *J. Balding* **– a68**

HARRIET'S GIRL 3 ch.f. Choisir (AUS) 126 – Harriet (IRE) (Grand Lodge (USA) **82**
125) [2009 74: 6m 7.1m^3 6.9m^5 6m^6 8g^2 8.1g* 8m 8.3g^3 8.3g 8g^3 Oct 30] tall filly: fairly useful handicapper: trained by K. R. Burke prior to winning at Haydock in August: stays 1m: acts on good to firm going: usually held up. *A. P. Jarvis*

HARRISON GEORGE (IRE) 4 b.g. Danetime (IRE) 121 – Dry Lightning 63 **102**
(Shareef Dancer (USA) 135) [2009 98: 6m^4 6s^2 7f 6m 6g^2 6g^5 7g^3 6d^6 7.2m* 7g^5 Oct 10] good-topped gelding: useful handicapper: better than ever when winning at Ayr in September by 2 lengths from Osteopathic Remedy: mostly creditable efforts otherwise in 2009 (gelded after final start): effective at 6f/7f: acts on polytrack, heavy and good to firm going: reliable. *R. A. Fahey*

HARRISON'S FLYER (IRE) 8 b.g. Imperial Ballet (IRE) 110 – Smart Pet 77 (Pet- **45 §**
ong 126) [2009 66: p7g p7.1g p7.1g 7d^6 7.1m^6 6.1g^6 6.1d^5 6.1m^6 Sep 10] good-topped gelding: handicapper, just poor form in 2009: stays easy 7f: acts on all-weather, firm and soft ground: wears headgear (often in cheekpieces): temperamental. *J. M. Bradley*

HARRIS TWEED 2 b.c. (Feb 2) Hernando (FR) 127 – Frog 84 (Akarad (FR) 130) **64 p**
[2009 p7g p7.1g^5 Nov 6] good-topped colt: seventh foal: half-brother to 3 winners, including 2m/17f winner Froglet (by Shaamit) and 7f (at 2 yrs)/to 1½m winner Vale de Lobo (by Loup Sauvage), both fairly useful: dam 1¼m/1½m winner: shaped well given inadequate test in maidens, plenty to do and finishing strongly when fifth to Sea of Heartbreak at Wolverhampton: will be suited by 1½m: sure to do better still. *Sir Mark Prescott*

HARRY AFRICA (IRE) 3 b.g. Catcher In The Rye (IRE) 115 – Brave Dance (IRE) **–**
(Kris 135) [2009 –: 10m Jul 8] ex-Irish gelding: well held in maidens/seller (tried visored). *Mrs S. Leech*

HARRY DAYS (IRE) 3 b.c. Alhaarth (IRE) 126 – Blushing Minstrel (IRE) 85 **69**
(Nicholas (USA) 111) [2009 7m 10s p8.6g^4 Nov 14] seemingly best effort in maidens when fourth at Wolverhampton, having run of things. *P. J. Lally, Ireland*

HARRY PAGET (IRE) 2 gr.c. (Apr 1) Starcraft (NZ) 128 – True Love (Robellino **–**
(USA) 127) [2009 7.6d 9m 9d Oct 11] well-grown colt: well held in maidens. *J. R. Best*

HARRY PATCH 3 b.g. Lujain (USA) 119 – Hoh Dancer 66 (Indian Ridge 123) [2009 **91 +**
97p: p6g^3 May 1] strong, rangy gelding: useful winner of both starts at 2 yrs: unsuited by track when 1½ lengths third to Swiss Diva in handicap at Lingfield on sole outing in 2009: should prove best kept to 5f/6f: acts on soft ground. *M. A. Jarvis*

HARRY THE HAWK 5 b.g. Pursuit of Love 124 – Elora Gorge (IRE) (High Estate **83**
127) [2009 80: 10.1d^2 12d 10.3d^5 12g* 13.8g^4 12v Sep 4] quite good-topped gelding: fairly useful handicapper: won at Doncaster in July: stays 13.8f: acts on heavy and good to firm ground: strong traveller, sometimes finds little. *T. D. Walford*

HARRY UP 8 ch.g. Piccolo 121 – Faraway Lass 94 (Distant Relative 128) [2009 81, **69**
a97: f5s^4 p5.1g* p5.1g* p5.1g p5g^5 p5.1g* p5.1m^4 p5.1g^5 p5.1g^2 p5.1g* p5.1g* **a93**
5.7m^4 5g^5 p5g p5.1g Dec 5] strong gelding: fairly useful on all-weather, fair on turf: won claimers at Wolverhampton in January (2), February, April and May (tenth course success, left K. Ryan £12,000): left Andrew Reid after thirteenth outing: speedy, best at 5f: acts on all-weather, firm and soft ground: tried blinkered, wears cheekpieces: front runner. *M. J. Scudamore*

HARTING HILL 4 b.g. Mujahid (USA) 125 – Mossy Rose 78 (King of Spain 121) **67**
[2009 60: p9.5g p10g^4 10g^5 14.1m^6 p10g p8.6g^4 p7g* Dec 2] short-backed gelding: fair performer: won minor event at Kempton in December: effective at 7f to 11f: best efforts on polytrack. *M. P. Tregoning*

HARTLEY 3 b.g. Lucky Story (USA) 128 – Arctic Song (Charnwood Forest (IRE) 125) **108**
[2009 95: 7m^2 7m^3 8d^2 Aug 1] lengthy, good-topped gelding: useful performer: marked improvement in 2009, placed all 3 starts, best effort when head second to comfortable winner Zacinto in listed race at Goodwood last occasion: stays 1m: unraced on extremes of going: races prominently: sent to Hong Kong, where renamed Royal Panache. *J. D. Bethell*

HART OF GOLD 5 b.g. Foxhound (USA) 103 – Bullion 85 (Sabrehill (USA) 120) **72 d**
[2009 76: p6g^2 p6g^2 p6g^4 p6g^3 p6g^4 6g 6m^4 p6g^3 6m^3 5.3f^4 6m 7d^4 5m 6.1m p6g p6g^6 p6m^6 p6f p7m^2 Dec 30] good-bodied gelding: fair handicapper: below form in second half of year: best at 5f/6f: acts on polytrack, firm and soft ground: wears blinkers/cheekpieces. *R. A. Harris*

HARTSHEAD 10 b.g. Machiavellian (USA) 123 – Zalitzine (USA) 98 (Zilzal (USA) 137) [2009 85: 6.9d6 8g 7m3 8m 8s5 10m Sep 23] tall, leggy gelding: handicapper, just fair form in 2009: stays 1m: acts on firm and good to soft ground: usually waited with: none too reliable. *W. Storey* **77**

HARTY BOY (USA) 3 ch.g. Stravinsky (USA) 133 – Peanut Gallery (USA) (Mister Baileys 123) [2009 p8g4 p8g4 p8g4 p8.6g6 p7.1g 8.3m 8.1g6 p8g6 p9.5g p12m Dec 6] fair maiden: left M. Bell after third outing: subsequently went wrong way (left Mrs S. Leech after seventh start): best at 1m: acts on polytrack: tried in headgear/tongue tie. *Jim Best* **68 d**

HARVEST DANCER (IRE) 2 ch.c. (Apr 3) Danehill Dancer (IRE) 117 – Autumnal (IRE) 104 (Indian Ridge 123) [2009 7m4 Aug 14] rather leggy, lengthy colt: fourth foal: dam 5f (at 2 yrs)/6f winner: 7/1, encouraging 1½ lengths fourth to Najd in maiden at Newbury, leading 1f out: will improve. *B. J. Meehan* **83 p**

HARVEST SONG (IRE) 3 b.g. Sadler's Wells (USA) 132 – La Mouline (IRE) 103 (Nashwan (USA) 135) [2009 –p: 12d May 16] leggy gelding: well held in maidens. *Sir Michael Stoute* **–**

HASANPOUR (IRE) 9 b.g. Dr Devious (IRE) 127 – Hasainiya (IRE) 109 (Top Ville 129) [2009 66: 21.6m Apr 20] tall, useful-looking gelding: fair performer: stays 2m: acts on heavy and good to firm going: formerly blinkered. *K. J. Burke* **65**

HASSADIN 3 ch.g. Reset (AUS) 124 – Crocolat 77 (Croco Rouge (IRE) 126) [2009 63: p10g p10g 12.1m 11.5m5 14d3 11.9f4 Aug 18] poor maiden handicapper: seems to stay 1¾m: acts on polytrack: tried in cheekpieces/visor/tongue strap. *A. B. Haynes* **49**

HASTY (IRE) 2 b.f. (Apr 12) Invincible Spirit (IRE) 121 – Saramacca (IRE) 54 (Kahyasi 130) [2009 6g5 6m2 p7g2 7f* 6.5m5 7m3 Oct 2] €21,000Y, resold €95,000Y: smallish, attractive filly: sixth foal: sister to 2 winners, including 3-y-o Invincible Miss and half-sister to 2 winners, including 6-y-o Rajeh: dam Irish 1½m winner: fairly useful performer: won maiden at Folkestone in July by length from Pollenator: creditable efforts after, 6¾ lengths third to Tabassum in Oh So Sharp Stakes at Newmarket: stays 7f: acts on firm going: races prominently. *B. W. Hills* **90**

HATCH A PLAN (IRE) 8 b.g. Vettori (IRE) 119 – Fast Chick 93 (Henbit (USA) 130) [2009 68d: p11g6 p12g5 p10g2 p12g p9.5g6 10.2g5 11.7f5 10.2f2 10.2f* 10.2m3 11m* 10m 10d p11f Dec 16] leggy, workmanlike gelding: fair handicapper: won at Bath in June and Newbury (apprentices) in July: stays 1½m: acts on polytrack, best turf efforts on good going or firmer: tried in cheekpieces. *Mouse Hamilton-Fairley* **65**

HATHAAL (IRE) 10 b.g. Alzao (USA) 117 – Ballet Shoes (IRE) 75 (Ela-Mana-Mou 132) [2009 11.5m Jun 4] good-topped gelding: has a short, unimpressive action: missed 2008: no form in 2009, including over hurdles: tried blinkered/visored/tongue tied. *Jim Best* **–**

HATHAWAY (IRE) 2 ch.f. (Feb 21) Redback 116 – Finty (IRE) (Entrepreneur 123) [2009 5d5 6m6 7.1m p6g Dec 18] 3,700Y: compact filly: third foal: sister to 4-y-o Ocean Glory: dam unraced: modest form in maidens. *W. M. Brisbourne* **54**

HATMAN JACK (IRE) 3 ch.g. Bahamian Bounty 116 – Mary Hinge 100 (Dowsing (USA) 124) [2009 61: p6g4 p6g4 p7g 5.1g 10.2g 8f p7g3 p6g* p6g5 p7g p6g p6g6 Dec 31] fair performer: won handicap at Lingfield in August: likely to prove best at 6f/7f: acts on polytrack: twice in cheekpieces, including at Lingfield: none too consistent. *B. G. Powell* **67**

HATTA DIAMOND (IRE) 3 ch.c. Pivotal 124 – Moonshell (IRE) 117 (Sadler's Wells (USA) 132) [2009 p9.5g5 p8.6g* 9.7g6 10g4 9.8m6 10f3 9.3g5 10g Dec 24] sixth foal: half-brother to smart 1¾m winner Alunissage (by Rainbow Quest) and fairly useful 1¼m winner Moonsprite (by Seeking The Gold): dam, 1m (at 2 yrs) and 1½m (Oaks) winner, sister to Doyen: fair form: won maiden at Wolverhampton in March: good efforts in handicaps after when in frame: left M. Johnston 14,000 gns after sixth start: will stay 1½m: acts on polytrack and firm going: blinkered last 2 outings: temperament under suspicion. *R. Al Jehani, Qatar* **77**

HATTA FORT 4 b.c. Cape Cross (IRE) 129 – Oshiponga 72 (Barathea (IRE) 127) [2009 6.5g6 6.5g* 6m2 6m 6m6 8.5g 8g5 Sep 3] strong colt: smart performer: trained at 2 yrs by M. Channon: ran in USA in 2008, winning optional claimer at Saratoga and Grade 3 Perryville Stakes at Keeneland: improved again in 2009, winning handicap at Nad Al Sheba in February by short head from Imbongi: good 1¼ lengths second to J J The Jet Plane in Al Quoz Sprint on same course next time: respectable effort after only when sixth to Utmost Respect in Duke of York Stakes at York: stays 7f: acts on synthetic surfaces, firm and good to soft going: tongue tied in 2009, also blinkered final outing. *Saeed bin Suroor* **114**

Call Stan James 08000 351135 Stakes (Heritage Handicap), Newmarket—the genuine handicapper Hatton Flight completes a hat-trick, winning from Redesignation (stripes), Boz (dark colours) and Dansili Dancer (far side)

HATTON FLIGHT 5 b.g. Kahyasi 130 – Platonic 79 (Zafonic (USA) 130) [2009 94: p12g* 12g* 12f* 12m 11.9m 12.3m^5 Sep 12] leggy gelding: useful handicapper: further progress in 2009, winning at Lingfield and Epsom in April and Newmarket (quite valuable event, by 1¼ lengths from Redesignation) in May: well below form after: best around 1½m: acts on polytrack and firm ground: tried in cheekpieces, wears blinkers nowadays: free-going sort: genuine. *A. M. Balding* **104**

HAULAGE LADY (IRE) 3 b.f. Xaar 132 – Blue Mantle (IRE) 79 (Barathea (IRE) 127) [2009 61: 8s^6 8s 9.3g^6 7.9g^4 9.3d Jul 26] big, workmanlike filly: maiden: just poor form in 2009: in cheekpieces last 3 starts: wayward. *Karen McLintock* **44 §**

HAUNTING 3 b.f. Beat Hollow 126 – Broken Spectre 65 (Rainbow Quest (USA) 134) [2009 12g 12.4d Oct 13] £1,600 3-y-o: fifth foal: dam, ran twice, sister to Racing Post Trophy winner/St Leger runner-up Armiger: well held in maidens. *A. G. Foster* **–**

HAVELOCK FLYER 2 b.c. (Mar 19) Mujahid (USA) 125 – Dragon Flyer (IRE) 105 (Tagula (IRE) 116) [2009 5m 6d 5g Jul 8] smallish colt: well beaten in maidens/seller: tongue tied first 2 starts. *C. Grant* **–**

HAVE MORE 2 ch.f. (Mar 9) Haafhd 129 – For More (FR) (Sanglamore (USA) 126) [2009 6f p7g 7m Aug 23] quite attractive filly: fifth foal: half-sister to 3 winners, including useful 1½m/2m winner Junior (useful, by Singspiel) and 7-y-o Humble Opinion: dam, French 9f to 12.5f winner, also successful over hurdles: well held in maidens: sold £1,800. *B. J. Meehan* **–**

HAVING A BALL 5 b.g. Mark of Esteem (IRE) 137 – All Smiles 41 (Halling (USA) 133) [2009 54, a67: p8g^5 p8g* f8g p8m^5 p8m^2 8.3g^6 p8m^2 p8m Nov 21] smallish gelding: fair handicapper on all-weather, modest on turf: won at Kempton in April: stays 1m: acts on all-weather and soft going: held up. *P. D. Cundell* **53 a72**

HAWAANA (IRE) 4 b.g. Bahri (USA) 125 – Congress (IRE) 86 (Dancing Brave (USA) 140) [2009 80: p8g* p7g^6 8.3m^6 p8g^5 p8g^4 8.3m^4 p8g* p8m^4 p8g p8m^5 p10m^4 Dec 9] good-topped gelding: fairly useful handicapper: won at Kempton in March and, having left Eve Johnson Houghton after sixth start, Lingfield in October: stays 1¼m: acts on polytrack, good to firm and good to soft going. *Miss Gay Kelleway* **89**

HAWAASS (USA) 4 b.g. Seeking The Gold (USA) – Sheroog (USA) 77 (Shareef Dancer (USA) 135) [2009 95p: 10m^2 10.1g Apr 22] big, good-topped gelding: useful handicapper, very lightly raced: further improvement when ¾-length second to Ladies Best at Pontefract on reappearance, better effort in 2009 (gelded after final outing): will stay 1½m: acts on good to firm going. *M. Johnston* **97**

HAWKEYETHENOO (IRE) 3 b.g. Hawk Wing (USA) 136 – Stardance (USA) (Rahy (USA) 115) [2009 57: 8s^4 p8.6g^3 8.3g^5 8g^2 8.5m* f8m 5.9g^6 6s^3 5m* 5m^2 5g* 5d^4 Oct 28] good-topped gelding: fairly useful handicapper: won at Beverley (apprentices) in July and, having left M. Easterby after eighth start and gelded, Musselburgh in September and Ayr in October: has won at 8.5f, may prove best at 5f/6f: acts on soft and good to firm going: effective with/without blinkers/visor: tried tongue tied: signs of temperament. *J. S. Goldie* **81**

HAWKIT (USA) 8 b.g. Silver Hawk (USA) 123 – Hey Ghaz (USA) (Ghazi (USA)) [2009 81d: 8.3g 9m 10g^2 10m 11.1s^4 12.1s^3 10s^6 12.4d^2 11.1g^5 12.4d^4 9.1g^5 9.1v^2 Oct 31] quite good-topped gelding: handicapper, just fair in 2009: stays 1½m: acts on all-weather, heavy and good to firm going: tried tongue tied: held up. *P. Monteith* **65**

HAWKLEAF FLIER (IRE) 3 b.f. Hawk Wing (USA) 136 – Flyleaf (FR) (Persian Bold 123) [2009 54: 7.5m 10.2d^5 8f 10g^6 7.9g^3 7m Aug 14] smallish, angular filly: poor maiden: stays 1¼m: blinkered last 2 starts. *T. D. Easterby* **48**

HAWK MOUNTAIN (UAE) 4 b.g. Halling (USA) 133 – Friendly (USA) (Lear Fan (USA) 130) [2009 79p: 14.6g* 14m^4 16.4d^2 14.6m* 16.4g^2 16.4m^4 14.6m^5 Sep 11] strong gelding: fairly useful handicapper: improved in 2009, winning at Doncaster in May and June: ran well when in frame at York next 2 starts: stays 16.4f: acts on soft and good to firm going: reliable. *J. J. Quinn* **94**

HAWKSBURY HEIGHTS 7 ch.g. Nashwan (USA) 135 – Gentle Dame 75 (Kris 135) [2009 p13.9g Dec 14] fair maiden at best: well held both Flat outings since 2006: stays 11f: acts on good to firm ground: modest hurdler. *J. J. Lambe, Ireland* **–**

HAWK'S EYE 3 br.g. Hawk Wing (USA) 136 – Inchiri 108 (Sadler's Wells (USA) 132) [2009 66: 10m^2 9.9m 8m^3 8d^3 10f* 10m* Aug 27] workmanlike gelding: fairly useful handicapper: left E. Vaughan 12,500 gns, improved to win at Windsor and Lingfield within 11 days in August: stays 1¼m: acts on firm and good to soft going: held up: not straightforward. *M. F. de Kock, South Africa* **87**

HAWKSPRING (IRE) 3 b.c. Hawk Wing (USA) 136 – Katavi (USA) 56 (Stravinsky (USA) 133) [2009 63: f6s^4 f7d* p10g p8.6g^3 f8g^2 f7g^2 p7g^2 f6g^4 p8g* f8d^2 p8.6g f8g^5 f7g^6 Mar 22] fair performer: won sellers at Southwell in January and Lingfield in February: best at 7f/1m: raced only on all-weather: effective with/without cheekpieces/visor: wears tongue tie: usually races prominently. *S. Parr* **75**

HAWKSTAR EXPRESS (IRE) 4 b.g. Hawk Wing (USA) 136 – Band of Angels (IRE) (Alzao (USA) 117) [2009 53: p8g p13.3g^4 Jan 15] strong gelding: poor maiden: stays 1¼m: acts on polytrack and good to soft ground: tried in headgear/tongue tie. *J. R. Boyle* **46**

HAWRIDGE KING 7 b.g. Erhaab (USA) 127 – Sadaka (USA) 77 (Kingmambo (USA) 125) [2009 88: 11.6g^6 14v^6 15g^5 14f* 14m^4 15.9m^2 16m^5 15m^4 14.1s^4 16g^2 Oct 30] quite good-topped gelding: fairly useful handicapper: won at Haydock in July: stays 2m: acts on polytrack, firm and good to soft ground: tried visored: held up. *W. S. Kittow* **87**

HAWRIDGE STAR (IRE) 7 b.g. Alzao (USA) 117 – Serenity 98 (Selkirk (USA) 129) [2009 81: 16d^4 14.6g Oct 23] close-coupled gelding: fair performer: not at best in 2009: stays 1¾m: acts on soft and good to firm ground: tried visored: none too consistent. *W. S. Kittow* **69**

HAYEK 2 b.c. (Jan 30) Royal Applause 124 – Salagama (IRE) 89 (Alzao (USA) 117) [2009 7d 6m p7g Oct 14] good-bodied colt: easily best effort in maidens when tenth to Al Zir at Newmarket on debut: stays 7f. *W. Jarvis* **65**

HAY FEVER (IRE) 3 b.g. Namid 128 – Allergy 99 (Alzao (USA) 117) [2009 77: p8g 6m^4 7m p6m^2 p7g 7m Oct 26] good-topped gelding: fair maiden: in-and-out form in 2009: best at 5f/6f: acts on polytrack, good to firm and good to soft going: tried blinkered. *Eve Johnson Houghton* **67**

HAYLEY'S GIRL 3 b.f. Deportivo 116 – Eurolink Artemis 75 (Common Grounds 118) [2009 45: 6d 7m p5.1g p6m p5m Dec 9] angular filly: little form at 3 yrs: tried blinkered. *S. W. James* **–**

HAYZOOM 2 b.c. (Mar 6) Anabaa (USA) 130 – Green Swallow (FR) 107 (Green Tune (USA) 125) [2009 8d^5 Oct 27] 80,000Y: second foal: dam, French 2-y-o 6f/7f (Prix du Calvados) winner, half-sister to useful French/US performer up to 1½m Green Girl: 10/1 and green, encouraging 5¼ lengths fifth to Bullet Train in maiden at Yarmouth, soon off bridle and staying on late: should improve. *P. W. Chapple-Hyam* **71 p**

HAZELRIGG (IRE) 4 b.g. Namid 128 – Emma's Star (ITY) (Darshaan 133) [2009 81: 5d 5g³ p6g³ 7g 7.2v Oct 31] rangy gelding: has scope: fairly useful handicapper: should stay 7f: acts on polytrack, soft and good to firm going: in cheekpieces last 3 outings. *T. D. Easterby* **80**

HAZY DANCER 3 b.f. Oasis Dream 129 – Shadow Dancing 110 (Unfuwain (USA) 131) [2009 81p: 11.4m⁶ 12m p12g⁵ p12g⁴ p12m Nov 4] compact filly: fair performer: stays 1½m: acts on polytrack: tried tongue tied. *M. P. Tregoning* **76**

HAZYTOO 5 ch.g. Sakhee (USA) 136 – Shukran 99 (Hamas (IRE) 125§) [2009 76§: p7g³ p7g 6m* 6m 6m p7m Dec 4] lengthy gelding: fairly useful handicapper: won at Warwick in May: effective at 6f to 1m: acts on polytrack and firm ground: tried in cheekpieces: temperamental. *P. J. Makin* **80 §**

HEADACHE 4 b.g. Cape Cross (IRE) 129 – Romantic Myth 105 (Mind Games 121) [2009 59: p8g f8g⁴ p8.6g⁵ p8.6g⁵ p7m² p6g⁴ p7g³ p7m f7f* f7g Dec 18] smallish gelding: modest handicapper: won at Southwell in December: may prove best at 7f: acts on all-weather: in blinkers last 6 starts: tongue tied: races prominently. *B. W. Duke* **63**

HEAD DOWN 3 b.g. Acclamation 118 – Creese (USA) (Diesis 133) [2009 88?, a67: p7m³ p6g² p8g³ p7g² p7g* 7.1f² 7.1m³ 7m 7.1m³ 8m⁴ p8g* p8g p8m Dec 30] well-made gelding: fairly useful performer: won maiden at Lingfield in March and claimer at same track (left R. Hannon £12,000) in August: effective at 7f to 8.6f: acts on polytrack and firm ground. *Mrs L. C. Jewell* **88**

HEAD FIRST 3 b.f. Dansili 127 – Break Point (Reference Point 139) [2009 8d 8.1g⁵ 8m p11m p9.5g⁴ p9.5g* p8.6g⁴ p9.5g⁴ Dec 28] compact filly: modest handicapper: won at Wolverhampton in November: stays 9.5f: acts on polytrack. *W. Jarvis* **64**

HEADFORD VIEW (IRE) 5 b.m. Bold Fact (USA) 116 – Headfort Rose (IRE) 76 (Desert Style (IRE) 121) [2009 97p: 7f⁴ 7d* 7m p6g 8v 8m³ p7f⁵ Oct 4] workmanlike mare: useful handicapper: better than ever when winning at the Curragh in June by short head from Hallie's Comet: creditable efforts last 2 starts, length third to Ahla Wasahl in listed handicap at Ascot former occasion: probably best at 7f/1m: acts on polytrack, firm and good to soft going: wears cheekpieces: held up: has won 4 times at Dundalk. *J. Halpin, Ireland* **102**

HEAD HUNTED 2 b.g. (Jan 22) Dubai Destination (USA) 127 – Tropical Breeze (IRE) (Kris 135) [2009 8.3v⁴ Nov 4] second foal: half-brother to 3-y-o Dubai Storming: dam unraced: 20/1, promising 8¼ lengths fourth to Burj Nahar in maiden at Nottingham, eye-catching headway under considerate handling: will stay 1¼m: sure to improve. *E. A. L. Dunlop* **70 p**

HEADING EAST (IRE) 3 ch.g. Dubai Destination (USA) 127 – Nausicaa (USA) (Diesis 133) [2009 74: p8.6g⁵ 10.4s⁶ 8g 10m Aug 9] lengthy gelding: fair maiden at 2 yrs: well held in 2009: tried in cheekpieces. *K. A. Ryan* **–**

HEADING TO FIRST 2 b.c. (Apr 11) Sulamani (IRE) 130 – Bahirah 71 (Ashkalani (IRE) 128) [2009 7f⁴ 7g Jul 8] lengthy colt: has scope: has a low action: fifth foal: closely related/half-brother to winners abroad by Sulamani and Polish Precedent (2): dam, 9.4f winner who stayed 1½m, half-sister to very smart stayer San Sebastian, Oaks runner-up Noushkey and to dam of high-class 1½m performer Alkaased: plenty of promise in maidens at Lingfield and Newmarket (tenth to Elusive Pimpernel), travelling strongly both times: bred to stay 1¼m+. *C. E. Brittain* **63**

HEADLINE ACT 3 ch.c. Dalakhani (IRE) 133 – Daring Miss 113 (Sadler's Wells (USA) 132) [2009 86p: 10m⁴ p12g* 12.3m 12m⁴ 13g Jul 25] leggy colt: fairly useful handicapper: won at Kempton in April: stays 1½m: acts on polytrack, soft and good to firm going: held up: sold 42,000 gns in October, joined J. Culloty in Ireland. *J. H. M. Gosden* **86**

HEAD TO HEAD (IRE) 5 gr.g. Mull of Kintyre (USA) 114 – Shoka (FR) 86 (Kaldoun (FR) 122) [2009 58: f6s³ f6g* f6g⁵ p5g² f6g f5g p5g f6g² 6d p6g p5m³ p6m⁶ p5g² p6m⁴ f5f² Dec 11] modest handicapper: won at Southwell in January: best at 5f/6f: acts on all-weather and soft going: wears blinkers/cheekpieces/tongue tie. *A. D. Brown* **60**

HEAD TO KERRY (IRE) 9 b.g. Eagle Eyed (USA) 111 – The Poachers Lady (IRE) (Salmon Leap (USA) 131) [2009 –: f12s⁶ Jan 6] lengthy gelding: very lightly raced and little form on Flat in recent years (modest maiden hurdler): tried in cheekpieces/tongue tie. *D. J. S. ffrench Davis* **–**

HEARTHSTEAD MAISON (IRE) 5 b.g. Peintre Celebre (USA) 137 – Pieds de Plume (FR) (Seattle Slew (USA)) [2009 119: 9d⁵ 10m Feb 26] close-coupled gelding: **115**

smart performer: creditable 3½ lengths fifth to Third Set in handicap at Nad Al Sheba, better effort there in 2009: barely stayed 11f: acted on polytrack and firm going, possibly not on softer than good: often made running: dead. *M. Johnston*

HEART OF DUBAI (USA) 4 b.c. Outofthebox (USA) 118 – Diablo's Blend (USA) (Diablo (USA)) [2009 72d: 12f 9.8m^5 8.5m 10.1s May 22] tall colt: fair performer at best: regressive since mid-2008: tried in cheekpieces. *Micky Hammond* **52**

HEART OF TUSCANY 3 b.f. Falbrav (IRE) 133 – Zarma (FR) (Machiavellian (USA) 123) [2009 59: 10.2g^5 12m 9.7m^6 p12g^6 11.9m Aug 5] modest maiden: stays 1¼m: in cheekpieces last 2 starts: held up. *W. J. Knight* **59**

HEARTSEASE 3 b.f. Pursuit of Love 124 – Balsamita (FR) (Midyan (USA) 124) [2009 54: 10.2m^3 9.9g 8f^6 8.1g 9m^2 10.2g 10s^6 Aug 7] fair maiden handicapper: best effort when runner-up fifth start: stays 1¼m: acts on good to firm ground. *J. G. Portman* **66**

HEART SHAPED (USA) 3 ch.f. Storm Cat (USA) – Twenty Eight Carat (USA) (Alydar (USA)) [2009 109: 7g^2 8f^4 8f^6 7g^5 6s 8d Sep 5] tall, leggy filly: useful performer: best effort in 2009 when 2¾ lengths fourth to Ghanaati in 1000 Guineas at Newmarket: just fair efforts at best after, sixth to same filly in Coronation Stakes at Royal Ascot and fifth to Glowing in Brownstown Stakes at Fairyhouse: was best at 1m: acted well on firm going: often found little: visits Galileo. *A. P. O'Brien, Ireland* **109**

HEARTS OF FIRE 2 b.c. (Apr 22) Firebreak 125 – Alexander Ballet 86 (Mind Games 121) [2009 5m* 5m^4 5g^2 5m^5 6s^2 7m* 7d* 8d* Oct 11] **118**

Two-year-olds capable of winning pattern races are an extremely rare sight on a racecourse in March but the historic Brocklesby Stakes, the opening two-year-old race of the latest British Flat season, was won by a colt who went on to record one of the best performances by a juvenile in Europe in the Gran Criterium at Milan in October. The Brocklesby is now a class 4 event—it was downgraded from class 3 (or class C as it was then) in 1998—and its standard tends not to vary much nowadays. There have, though, been some notable winners down the years,

williamhill.com - Play Poker Brocklesby Conditions Stakes, Doncaster—Hearts of Fire wins the first two-year-old race of the British season

Gran Criterium, Milan—going from strength to strength,
Hearts of Fire (left) provides Pat Eddery with his first Group 1 win as a trainer;
another British-based raider Vale of York (noseband) chases him home, the pair five lengths clear

headed by the outstandingly fast Deep Diver who won it in 1971 and trained on into a champion sprinter at three when he was the highest-rated horse to race over any distance in Europe. The Bill O'Gorman-trained pair Brondesbury and Provideo won the Brocklesby in 1982 and 1984 respectively, the former a brilliantly speedy juvenile whose other wins included the Norfolk Stakes at Royal Ascot and the latter voted Horse of the Year after equalling a long-standing record for the number of wins by a two-year-old (the Brocklesby had also been the starting point for The Bard whose nineteenth-century achievement of sixteen victories Provideo equalled). Mind Games, sire of the dam of the latest Brocklesby winner Hearts of Fire, has been the best-known name on the Brocklesby's roll of honour since Provideo. Mind Games won the 1994 edition and trained on to establish himself as a very smart sprinter at both three and four. Horses beaten in the Brocklesby who went on to considerably better things include fourth-placed Cawston's Clown in the 'seventies and third-placed Muchea in the 'nineties.

The latest Brocklesby attracted a field of nineteen—a predictably mixed bag on pedigree and looks—but the race turned out to be an above-average renewal. Hearts of Fire, a 12/1-shot, raced on the favoured stand side (a strong wind made things difficult for those further out) and won going away from Archers Road and Swilly Ferry, both of whom also held their form and went on to establish themselves as useful two-year-olds, the last-named returning to Doncaster to win the valuable sales event staged at the St Leger meeting. Hearts of Fire developed differently from his more illustrious Brocklesby-winning predecessors. He didn't improve on his Brocklesby form until stepped up in trip in July, Archers Road turning the tables on him in the Brian Yeardley Continental Two-Year-Old Trophy at Beverley on his third outing and his fifth at 25/1 in the Windsor Castle Stakes at Royal Ascot then suggesting he was fully exposed. On his first outing over six, however, Hearts of Fire was beaten only a length by Duplicity in the listed Rose Bowl Stakes at Newbury. Stepped up further in trip afterwards, Hearts of Fire gained a first victory since the Brocklesby in the listed Prix Francois Boutin over seven at Deauville in August, when he led home a one, two, three for British-trained runners, winning by five lengths and a length and a half from Cadley Road and Walkingonthemoon. There was no looking back now, Hearts of Fire graduating successfully to minor pattern company when landing the odds in the Zukunfts-Rennen (formerly run as the Maurice-Lacroix Trophy) at Baden-Baden in September and then completing a lucrative overseas hat-trick when patiently ridden and getting up to win the Gran Criterium, Italy's top two-year-old event, by a neck from the Royal Lodge third Vale of York (who went on to win the Breeders' Cup Juvenile at Santa Anita on his next start). The Gran Criterium was another one, two, three for British-trained challengers, with the Vintage Stakes runner-up Mata Keranjang finishing five lengths further behind Vale of York in third and the rest well strung out. The victories of Hearts of Fire at Baden-Baden and Milan provided eleven-times champion jockey Pat Eddery with his first pattern winner and his first Group 1 winner respectively as a trainer. He trains a string of around forty-five in Buckinghamshire and the latest season was his fourth since taking out a licence.

Hearts of Fire (b.c. Apr 22, 2007)	Firebreak (b 1999)	Charnwood Forest (b or br 1992)	Warning
			Dance of Leaves
		Breakaway (b 1985)	Song
			Catherine Howard
	Alexander Ballet (b 1999)	Mind Games (b 1992)	Puissance
			Aryaf
		Dayville (b 1994)	Dayjur
			Chain Fern

The close-coupled Hearts of Fire went through the sale-ring both as a foal (6,000 guineas) and as a yearling (£13,000), his lack of physical scope and an uncommercial pedigree probably counting against him. Firebreak, the sire of Hearts of Fire, was bought by Godolphin for 525,000 guineas at the end of his two-year-old campaign (in which the Mill Reef was among four wins); he did well in the royal blue colours, three more seasons' racing yielding, among others, two wins in the Godolphin Mile and one in the Hong Kong Mile. Firebreak was still in training at six but was unable to race, so when he was found a place at stud he had been out of the limelight for some time (Hearts of Fire is one of thirty-six foals from his first crop). Hearts of Fire's yearling brother may end up racing for Godolphin too in due course, as he was a 100,000-guinea purchase by John Ferguson at Newmarket in October. Hearts of Fire is the third foal out of the Irish five-furlong winner Alexander Ballet, the only other one to reach the racecourse being the modest at best Django Reinhardt (by Tobougg). Hearts of Fire's grandam Dayville was a fairly useful sprinter (whose other winners include the useful sprinting filly Day By Day) and his great grandam Chain Fern is an unraced sister to Irish One Thousand Guineas winner Al Bahathri. Chain Fern built up a fine record as a broodmare, her best offspring being the American Grade 1 (Yellow Ribbon Stakes) mile-and-a-quarter winner Spanish Fern, while her unraced daughters Rusty Back and Green Room produced, respectively, the Santa Anita Handicap winner Heat-seeker and the latest Prix Jean Prat winner Lord Shanakill (this is also the family of Gladiatorus). Hearts of Fire is well suited by seven furlongs and a mile, and he acts on soft and good to firm going. Whatever he achieves at three, he must already have fulfilled the wildest dreams of the members of the Pat Eddery Racing syndicate which owns him. *Pat Eddery*

HEATHYARDS JUNIOR 3 b.g. Beat All (USA) 120 – Heathyards Lady (USA) 76 (Mining (USA)) [2009 p9.5g^{6} p9.5g^{5} p8.6g* Dec 7] half-brother to 9-y-o Heathyards Pride: dam 6f to 8.5f winner: easily best effort in maidens at Wolverhampton when beating Cross Section ½ length in December: should be suited by 1¼m+: open to further improvement. *R. Hollinshead* **73 p**

HEATHYARDS PRIDE 9 b.g. Polar Prince (IRE) 117 – Heathyards Lady (USA) 76 (Mining (USA)) [2009 82: p12.2g^{2} p12.2g^{2} Jan 29] leggy gelding: fairly useful handicapper: effective at 11f to easy 2m: acts on all-weather and firm ground: held up: reliable. *R. Hollinshead* **86**

HEAVEN 4 ch.f. Reel Buddy (USA) 118 – Wedgewood Star 74 (Bishop of Cashel 122) [2009 84: 5m 5.7f^{4} 5.1m 5f 5m 5.7g^{6} Sep 7] compact filly: just fair handicapper at 4 yrs: best at 5f: acts on polytrack and firm ground: held up (often got behind in 2009). *P. J. Makin* **73**

HEAVENLY ENCOUNTER 4 b.f. Lujain (USA) 119 – Inchcoonan 81 (Emperor Jones (USA) 119) [2009 –: p6g p5g Feb 12] little form: tried visored. *K. R. Burke* **–**

HEAVENLY SAINT 4 b.f. Bertolini (USA) 125 – Heavenly Glow (Shavian 125) [2009 –: 8.1m 8m 8.1m 10.2m 10m^{5} p7.1g^{6} p8g p8.6g Oct 30] leggy filly: poor performer: stays 1¼m: acts on polytrack and good to firm going: tried in cheekpieces. *C. Roberts* **48**

HEAVENLY STELLA (USA) 4 b. or br.f. Wild Wonder (USA) 117 – Nijivision (USA) (Superoyale (USA)) [2009 8g Aug 31] $23,000Y: workmanlike filly: eighth foal: half-sister to several winners in USA: dam US 6f (including at 2 yrs)/7f winner: favourite, lost action when well beaten in bumper: plenty to do in maiden at Ripon later in month: will do better. *G. A. Swinbank* **– p**

HEAVEN OR HELL (IRE) 3 b.g. Jammaal 121 – Adjasalma (USA) (Lear Fan (USA) 130) [2009 62: 8.1d^5 10m^6 Sep 12] poor performer nowadays: stays 6f: acts on soft going: tried visored. *P. D. Evans* **47**

HEAVEN SENT 6 ch.m. Pivotal 124 – Heavenly Ray (USA) 97 (Rahy (USA) 115) [2009 116: 9f* 8m^2 8g^2 9.9d 8d^2 8m^5 Oct 3] quite good-topped mare: smart performer: won stanjames.com Dahlia Stakes at Newmarket in May for second successive year, beating Casilda 1¼ lengths: also good second in Windsor Forest Stakes at Royal Ascot (beaten length by Spacious), Falmouth Stakes at Newmarket (½ length behind Goldikova) and Matron Stakes at Leopardstown (went down by 2 lengths to Rainbow View): was effective at 1m/1¼m: acted on polytrack, firm and good to soft going: visits Dansili. *Sir Michael Stoute* **116**

HEBRIDEAN (IRE) 4 b.g. Bach (IRE) 121 – Delphinium (IRE) 58 (Dr Massini (IRE) 117) [2009 116: 9m 10g^4 p12m^6 Nov 29] smallish gelding: smart performer at 3 yrs (useful juvenile hurdler in 2008/9 for P. Nicholls): not so good in 2009, best effort when fourth to Laaheb in listed race at Newmarket: stays 1½m: acts on soft and good to firm going: held up. *L. M. Cumani* **106**

Cheveley Park Stud's "Heaven Sent"

HECTOR'S HOUSE 3 b.g. Tobougg (IRE) 125 – Thrasher 80 (Hector Protector (USA) 124) [2009 69: 10m^5 10.4v^6 8.5m^6 12d Jul 24] good-topped gelding: modest maiden: should stay 1m: acts on heavy ground: sold £1,000, fair winning juvenile hurdler for Evan Williams. *M. Dods* **60**

HECTOR SPECTRE (IRE) 3 gr.c. Verglas (IRE) 118 – Hallcardia 104 (Halling (USA) 133) [2009 p7g p7g^3 p8.6g^3 8.5g 10m^2 11.5s 8f^5 9m^6 p8.6g* 8.1d p9.5g^5 p8m **68**
10d* p10g^2 p10g^5 p12m^3 p12f^4 p10m^2 Dec 30] €115,000Y: first foal: dam 7f (at 2 yrs)/ 1¼m winner: fair performer: left B. Meehan £4,000 after fifth start: won handicaps at Wolverhampton in July and, having left K. Prendergast, Brighton (selling event) in October: stays 1½m: acts on polytrack, good to firm and good to soft ground: effective with/without visor. *P. D. Evans* **a74**

HEDGEROW (IRE) 2 b.f. (Apr 2) Azamour (IRE) 130 – Miss Childrey (IRE) 97 (Dr Fong (USA) 128) [2009 7d^5 7m 6g^4 Sep 30] 21,000Y: tall filly: second foal: dam Irish 2-y-o 5f/6f winner: modest form in maidens, set plenty to do final start: will stay 1m. *A. Dickman* **51 +**

HEKAAYA (IRE) 3 b.f. Kheleyf (USA) 116 – Victoria Regia (IRE) 90 (Lomond (USA) 128) [2009 52: p7g 8g p6g Sep 12] neat filly: maiden: poor form in 2009: stays 6f: acts on polytrack: tried visored. *M. P. Tregoning* **42**

HELAKU (IRE) 2 b.c. (Apr 10) Rakti 130 – Saibhreas (IRE) 83 (Last Tycoon 131) [2009 8m 9d Oct 11] modest form when down the field in maidens at Newmarket (green) and Goodwood: should stay 1¼m. *R. Hannon* **52**

HELIEORBEA 3 b.g. Reset (AUS) 124 – Rendition 95 (Polish Precedent (USA) 131) [2009 7.5m^3 7.5m^2 9g^3 7m^2 6s* p7.1g^6 8m f8g^6 8m^4 Oct 5] 23,000F, 34,000Y: tall gelding: fourth foal: dam, 7f winner, half-sister to US Grade 1 9f winner Jovial: fair performer: won maiden at Hamilton in August: stays 7.5f: acts on polytrack, soft and good to firm going: tried in cheekpieces: fair winning juvenile hurdler. *T. D. Easterby* **78**

HELIGOLAND 2 b.f. (Mar 16) Trade Fair 124 – Fine Frenzy (IRE) 68 (Great Commotion (USA) 123) [2009 5.7g p8m p7.1g p8.6g Nov 30] leggy filly: second foal: dam 2-y-o 5f winner: poor maiden. *A. G. Newcombe* **43**

HELIODOR (USA) 3 b.c. Scrimshaw (USA) – Playing Footsie (USA) (Valiant Nature **103**
(USA) 118) [2009 92: 9m^3 10m^6 10m^5 10d^6 12g^6 p12m^6 p10m* 12v^4 Oct 24] good-topped colt: useful performer: improved when winning well-contested minor event at Kempton in September by neck from Wasan: at least respectable efforts other starts, including when sixth in Gordon Stakes at Goodwood on fifth start and fourth to High Heeled in St Simon Stakes at Newbury: stays 1½m: acts on polytrack and good to firm ground: once blinkered. *R. Hannon* **a108**

HELLBENDER (IRE) 3 ch.g. Exceed And Excel (AUS) 126 – Desert Rose (Green **–**
Desert (USA) 127) [2009 67+: f6s^2 p6g* p6g^2 p7.1g^3 7.1v^5 7d 6g p6g^2 p6g^3 p6g^3 p6g* p7g* p7g^6 p7.1g^6 Dec 3] strong gelding: fairly useful handicapper on all-weather, little form on turf in 2009: won at Lingfield in January, Kempton in October and Lingfield in November: effective at 6f/7f: tactically versatile. *S. Kirk* **a87**

HELLENIO 2 b.c. (May 17) Cape Cross (IRE) 129 – Llia 94 (Shirley Heights 130) [2009 7d 7m^4 p8g 7f^5 p8m 7.1m^3 7d Oct 27] smallish, narrow colt: modest maiden: probably stays 1m: acts on polytrack and good to firm ground. *S. C. Williams* **62**

HELLO SUNSHINE 3 b.g. Deportivo 116 – Full English (Perugino (USA) 84) [2009 6f 5.1d 6.1f 7s p5.1g Aug 17] compact gelding: little form. *T. J. Pitt* **–**

HELPING HAND (IRE) 4 b.g. Lend A Hand 124 – Cardinal Press (Sharrood (USA) 124) [2009 69: p6g f5g 5f 5m 6m 5g 6m^5 5.7g^2 p5.1g Sep 19] rather leggy gelding: handicapper, just modest at 4 yrs: stays 6f: acts on all-weather and good to firm going: often forces pace. *R. Hollinshead* **60**

HELPMERONDA 3 b.f. Medicean 128 – Lady Donatella 57 (Last Tycoon 131) [2009 61: p8.6g^3 p9.5g f7g^5 p9.5g Dec 28] maiden: little form at 3 yrs: left S. Callaghan after third start: tried blinkered. *W. M. Brisbourne* **–**

HEL'S ANGEL (IRE) 3 b.f. Pyrus (USA) 106 – Any Dream (IRE) 81 (Shernazar 131) [2009 66: 8d* 8.5g^6 7g 8m* 8.5m^6 8.5g^2 8m^4 7m^5 8.3g 8.5g^3 Sep 22] close-coupled filly: fair handicapper: won at Thirsk in May and Pontefract in June: will stay 1¼m: acts on good to firm and good to soft ground (yet to race on extremes). *Mrs A. Duffield* **78**

HELVETIO 7 b.g. Theatrical 128 – Personal Love (USA) 103 (Diesis 133) [2009 –: p13.9g p13.9g^5 Mar 27] well-made gelding: lightly raced and little form on Flat since 2006: tried blinkered: joined D. Pipe. *Micky Hammond* **–**

HENDERSYDE (USA) 4 ch.g. Giant's Causeway (USA) 132 – Cimmaron Lady **98**
(USA) (Grand Slam (USA) 120) [2009 88: p12g* 14m* 16.1d^4 16g^5 14.1m^5 16m Sep 26]
rather leggy gelding: useful handicapper: won at Kempton in April and Newmarket in
May: further progress when fourth to Som Tala in Northumberland Plate at Newcastle:
bit below form after: stays 2m: acts on polytrack, good to firm and good to soft ground:
often tongue tied. *W. R. Swinburn*

HENNESSY ISLAND (USA) 4 ch.g. Hennessy (USA) 122 – Heavenly Dawn (USA) **46**
(Holy Bull (USA) 134) [2009 65: p7g p11g 8m 7s^6 May 27] maiden: just poor form in
2009: raced at 7f/1m, mainly on all-weather: tried in cheekpieces. *T. G. Mills*

HENRY HAVELOCK 2 ch.c. (Apr 29) Noverre (USA) 125 – Burmese Princess **–**
(USA) 64 (King of Kings (IRE) 125) [2009 7.5g^6 8.3s 8d Oct 28] tall, close-coupled colt:
soundly beaten in maidens. *C. Grant*

HENRY HOLMES 6 b.g. Josr Algarhoud (IRE) 118 – Henrietta Holmes (IRE) 61 **44**
(Persian Bold 123) [2009 p10g^5 Jun 20] maiden: poor form only Flat outing since 2007:
stays 13f: raced only on polytrack. *Mrs L. Richards*

HENRY SAN (IRE) 2 ch.c. (Feb 13) Exceed And Excel (AUS) 126 – Esclava (USA) **79**
(Nureyev (USA) 131) [2009 7.1g^5 8.1d^4 8.3g^4 Oct 5] strong, stocky colt: half-brother to
ungenuine 1¼m winner Croix de Guerre (by Highest Honor) and 3 winners in Japan:
dam, third at 1¼m in France, out of Prix de Diane winner Escaline: fair form in maidens,
fourth at Sandown (to Zeitoper) and Windsor (to Mont Agel): stays 1m. *A. King*

HERAWATI 3 b.g. Celtic Swing 138 – Lady of Jakarta (USA) (Procida (USA) 129) **–**
[2009 –: 10m Apr 7] lengthy, leggy gelding: tailed off in maidens. *T. D. Easterby*

HERBERT CRESCENT 4 b.g. Averti (IRE) 117 – With Distinction 59 (Zafonic **67 §**
(USA) 130) [2009 80: p8g* p8.6g^4 p8g 8.5m 7s p8.6m p7.1g^4 p7.1g^2 p8.6g^2 p8.6g^2 p9.5g
f8f^6 Dec 17] stocky gelding: just fair handicapper in 2009: won apprentice event at
Lingfield in January: stays 8.6f: acts on polytrack, soft and good to firm ground: tried in
blinkers/cheekpieces: unreliable. *Ollie Pears*

HERECOMESBELLA 3 b.f. Lujain (USA) 119 – Blushing Belle 74 (Local Suitor **55**
(USA) 128) [2009 43: p8.6g^4 p9.5g^3 p9.5m^4 p10g^4 10m^4 8.3g^5 7g^5 7.5m 8.3d Jul 22] tall
filly: modest maiden early in 2009: well below form last 3 starts, leaving Stef Liddiard
after first of them: will prove best short of 9.5f: best form on polytrack: usually blinkered.
P. G. Murphy

HERE COMES DANNY 3 b.g. Kyllachy 129 – Clarice Orsini (Common Grounds **78**
118) [2009 –: p5g^6 p6g* f6d^5 7m p7.1g^6 Oct 2] strong gelding: fair performer: heavily
backed, easily best effort when winning maiden at Wolverhampton in February: gelded
prior to final outing: should prove best at 5f/6f: acts on polytrack: sold 3,500 gns, sent to
Greece. *M. Wigham*

HERECOMETHEGIRLS 3 b.f. Falbrav (IRE) 133 – Always On My Mind 91 **61**
(Distant Relative 128) [2009 8.3v^6 8.1g^4 p8.6g^6 p8g^6 p8.6g p9.5g^5 Nov 13] sixth foal:
half-sister to several winners, including useful 7f winner (including at 2 yrs) Just Like A
Woman (by Observatory) and fairly useful 7f/1m winner Dr Thong (by Dr Fong): dam, 6f
winner, half-sister to smart 6f/7f performer Red Carpet: modest maiden: worth a try at
1¼m: form only on polytrack. *M. L. W. Bell*

HEREFORD BOY 5 ch.g. Tomba 119 – Grown At Rowan 75 (Gabitat 119) [2009 88: **74**
5g 5g^2 5m^5 p5g 5m 5.1m p6g^3 p7m p8m 6d^2 p7m* p7m p8m* p7f^4 Dec 21] strong
gelding: fair handicapper: won at Kempton in October and November: stays 1m: acts on
polytrack, firm and soft ground: usually wears blinkers/cheekpieces: held up. *D. K. Ivory*

HERE NOW AND WHY (IRE) 2 br.c. (Feb 2) Pastoral Pursuits 127 – Why Now 81 **87**
(Dansili 127) [2009 5m^2 5m* 5m* 5m 5.2d^5 5g 5m^3 5m 5g Oct 5] sturdy colt: first
foal: dam, 5f/6f winner, out of half-sister to very smart miler Greensmith: fairly useful
performer: won maiden at Ripon in April and minor event at Thirsk in May: creditable
efforts after only when fifth in Super Sprint at Newbury and third in nursery at Musselburgh: raced only at 5f: acts on good to firm and good to soft going: usually races up with
pace. *K. A. Ryan*

HERITAGE COAST (USA) 4 b.f. Dynaformer (USA) – Bristol Channel 113 **84**
(Generous (IRE) 139) [2009 84: 9.9m^4 12m^3 10m^2 10.3m* 9.9s p10m p12.2g Nov 16]
chunky filly: type to carry condition: fairly useful performer: landed odds in maiden at
Chester in August: will stay beyond 1½m: acts on polytrack and good to firm going,
promise on soft: often races prominently: sold 17,000 gns. *H. Morrison*

HERMIONE'S MAGIC 3 ch.f. Systematic 121 – Eleonor Sympson 50 (Cadeaux Genereux 131) [2009 78p: 8m^3 8f* 9f 8f^5 8f* 8f^3 Dec 3] useful performer: left P. McBride after reappearance: won optional claimers at Del Mar in August and Santa Anita in October: ran creditably final outing: will stay 1¼m: acts on firm going. *Kathy Walsh, USA* **102**

HERNANDO'S BOY 8 b.g. Hernando (FR) 127 – Leave At Dawn (Slip Anchor 136) [2009 75: 15.8v 13.8m 15.8g^5 13.8g^4 Oct 17] rather lightly-made, workmanlike gelding: fair handicapper: below best in 2009: stays 1¾m: acts on soft and good to firm going. *K. G. Reveley* **65**

HEROES 5 b.g. Diktat 126 – Wars (IRE) 60 (Green Desert (USA) 127) [2009 88: 8s* 10d^5 10m^5 Jul 29] good-topped gelding: fairly useful performer: won claimer at Brighton in May: effective at 7f/1m: acts on polytrack, soft and good to firm going: tried visored, in cheekpieces nowadays: tongue tied final outing. *Tim Vaughan* **88**

HERON BAY 5 b.h. Hernando (FR) 127 – Wiener Wald (USA) (Woodman (USA) 126) [2009 107: 9m 10m 12m 10d^4 12g^3 p11g 12d Oct 24] strong, close-coupled horse: useful handicapper: best efforts in 2009 at Redcar (Zetland Gold Cup, eighth behind Kingdom of Fife), Newbury and Ascot (length third to Press The Button) second, fourth and fifth starts: stays 1¾m: acts on polytrack, good to firm and good to soft going: held up. *C. F. Wall* **100**

HERONWAY (IRE) 7 b.g. Heron Island (IRE) 116 – French Willow (IRE) (Un Desperado (FR) 125) [2009 p13.9g Nov 27] no encouragement over hurdles: tailed off in maiden at Wolverhampton on Flat debut. *W. J. Greatrex* **–**

HERRBEE (IRE) 4 b.g. Mark of Esteem (IRE) 137 – Reematna 75 (Sabrehill (USA) 120) [2009 52d: p8.6g Jan 19] good-bodied gelding: regressive maiden: tried in cheekpieces. *J. L. Spearing* **–**

HERRERA (IRE) 4 b.f. High Chaparral (IRE) 132 – Silk (IRE) (Machiavellian (USA) 123) [2009 73: 12.4m* 12f 16.2g* 16m^6 16.4d^5 13.1g^6 16.4g 12.1v* p12g^4 14.6g Oct 23] angular filly: fair handicapper: won at Newcastle in April, Beverley in May and Hamilton in August: stays 2m: acts on soft and good to firm going. *R. A. Fahey* **79**

HERSCHEL (IRE) 3 br.g. Dr Fong (USA) 128 – Rafting (IRE) 87 (Darshaan 133) [2009 79+: p8g 9g 12m^4 Jun 11] useful-looking gelding: fair handicapper: stays 1½m: acts on polytrack, good to firm and good to soft going: signs of temperament: gelded, won juvenile hurdle in June: sold 10,000 gns in October. *G. L. Moore* **77**

HE'S A HUMBUG (IRE) 5 b.g. Tagula (IRE) 116 – Acidanthera 81 (Alzao (USA) 117) [2009 94: 6m 5m 6s 7s 7m 7g* 6g 5m f6f p7.1g Dec 5] rangy, good sort: just fair handicapper nowadays: won at Catterick in July: stays 7f: acts on all-weather, soft and good to firm ground: usually in headgear: inconsistent. *J. O'Reilly* **77**

HE'S COOL (IRE) 4 b.g. Viking Ruler (AUS) – Miss Progressive (IRE) 52 (Common Grounds 118) [2009 63: p8f^6 p6g 16d p16.5g* f14m Nov 11] modest handicapper: left G. Lyons after second start: won at Wolverhampton in October: stays 2m: acts on polytrack: in cheekpieces last 2 starts. *Aidan Anthony Howard, Ireland* **64**

HE'S INVINCIBLE 2 b.g. (Mar 22) Invincible Spirit (IRE) 121 – Adamas (IRE) 75 (Fairy King (USA)) [2009 6m^6 6.1g 6g^5 Jul 10] modest form in maidens, fifth to Trailblazing at Ascot: met with setback after, then gelded: likely to be suited by 7f. *B. J. Meehan* **62**

HESLINGTON 2 ch.c. (Mar 9) Piccolo 121 – Spice Island 68 (Reprimand 122) [2009 5m 5.1m^5 5m^2 f5g* Sep 29] 3,500Y: good-bodied colt: fourth foal: half-brother to 2007 2-y-o 5f winner Ginger Pickle (by Compton Place): dam 2-y-o 6f winner: fair performer: off over 5 months, won nursery at Southwell: may prove best at 5f. *M. Brittain* **74**

HETTIE HUBBLE 3 ch.f. Dr Fong (USA) 128 – White Rabbit 99 (Zilzal (USA) 137) [2009 51: 7g 6m 6d 7.9g^6 6m^3 8.3s^3 6s^2 8.3v^2 6d^4 7v^4 Sep 4] workmanlike filly: modest maiden: stays 1m: acts on heavy and good to firm ground. *D. W. Thompson* **59**

HEUREUX (USA) 6 b.g. Stravinsky (USA) 133 – Storm West (USA) (Gone West (USA)) [2009 73: 6s^5 7.1m 8.3m^3 6.8s* 8g* 6g* 6.8g* 6s^6 Oct 16] good-topped gelding: fairly useful performer: left J. H. Johnson before winning 4 times at Ovrevoll in August/September: effective at 6f to 1m: acts on firm and soft going: often blinkered/visored, tried in cheekpieces: has had breathing problem. *Jens Erik Lindstol, Norway* **89**

HEVELIUS 4 b.g. Polish Precedent (USA) 131 – Sharp Terms (Kris 135) [2009 99p: 10.3f^2 11.9m^6 12m 12m^2 12s Nov 7] sturdy gelding: type to carry plenty of condition: useful performer, lightly raced: gelded after second outing: best efforts when runner-up at Doncaster and Newmarket: not at best in competitive events otherwise in 2009: stays 1½m: acts on firm and good to soft ground. *W. R. Swinburn* **97**

HEY PRESTO 9 b.g. Piccolo 121 – Upping The Tempo (Dunbeath (USA) 127) [2009 53: 7f p8g 9.9m Jun 28] strong, good-topped gelding: no form in 2009: tried blinkered/in cheekpieces. *R. Rowe* –

HEY UP DAD 3 b.g. Fantastic Light (USA) 134 – Spanish Quest (Rainbow Quest (USA) 134) [2009 72p: 8.1m⁵ 10.4v 12f⁵ 8.1g⁶ 8d⁴ 10.3d 9.8d⁵ 8m Sep 18] close-coupled gelding: regressive form in 2009: should be suited by further than 1m: acts on heavy going: tried in blinkers/cheekpieces/tongue tie: seems ungenuine: sold £1,500. *M. Dods* 67 d

H HARRISON (IRE) 9 b.g. Eagle Eyed (USA) 111 – Penrose (IRE) 75 (Wolfhound (USA) 126) [2009 85, a70: p7.1g⁶ p7g³ p7.1g 7m⁵ 7f 7g⁶ 7.1m 7s 6g 7.6g² 7.6m 7g 7.1m 7m 7m p7m p8g p7.1g Dec 17] smallish gelding: fairly useful handicapper at best, winner of 14 of his 145 races: regressed in 2009: stayed 7.6f: acted on polytrack, firm and good to soft going: tried in cheekpieces/blinkers: carried head high: reportedly retired. *I. W. McInnes* 71

HIBAAYEB 2 b.f. (Apr 20) Singspiel (IRE) 133 – Lady Zonda 95 (Lion Cavern (USA) 117) [2009 7g³ 7m² 8m² 8m* Sep 26] 110

Clive Brittain has sent out the winners of nearly forty different Group 1s and Grade 1s across the globe but the Meon Valley Stud Fillies' Mile at Ascot is the only Group 1 he has won more than twice. He didn't have much subsequent success with his first two winners, Ivanka (1992) fracturing her pelvis early the following year and Teggiano (1999) joining Godolphin, for whom she finished second once from two starts. The third member of Brittain's triumvirate, Hibaayeb, is following Teggiano in moving to Godolphin.

Brittain is renowned for supposedly tilting at windmills and Hibaayeb's form figures before she lined up at Ascot at the end of September might have suggested she was another to add to the list in this particular race. Besides his two winners, Brittain had had ten runners in the Fillies' Mile since its elevation to Group 1 status in 1990 and seven of them were maidens. Four of the ten, including the unraced filly Wadlia in 2007, started at 100/1 and three of them at 50/1. Hibaayeb was a maiden but had better credentials than her predecessors. Her three runs had brought three places: third of twelve behind Eolith and Pollenator in a maiden at Newmarket at the start of August, when she had a relatively hard race for a debutante; a neck second of thirteen behind Creese in a similar event at Folkestone at the end of the same month; and second place in the May Hill Stakes at Doncaster in mid-September. The form in the May Hill, Hibaayeb's first outing

Meon Valley Stud Fillies' Mile, Ascot—
supplemented Hibaayeb (centre) rewards her connections by winning from Lady Darshaan (third right), giving 75-y-o trainer Clive Brittain his first Group 1 win in over three years; You'll Be Mine (third left) shapes well in third place and becomes winter favourite for the Oaks

Mr Mohammed Al Nabouda's "Hibaayeb"

over a mile, represented considerable improvement. Starting the complete outsider at 40/1 in a field of seven, Hibaayeb had odds-on Seta beaten seventy-five yards out but couldn't cope with Pollenator, whose finishing effort clinched victory by half a length. The May Hill was run at a rather muddling pace and Hibaayeb, who wandered in the closing stages, profited from being ridden prominently and having a better run than some so, even though Pollenator was not among her rivals in a less than vintage Fillies' Mile just over a fortnight later, the decision to supplement Hibaayeb at a cost of £20,000 was still a bold one. Among the races for juvenile fillies in Britain, the Fillies' Mile is second to none as a guide to the future, with four of the last eight winners having gone on to win at least one Group 1 at three. The latest edition lacked an obvious high-class prospect of the calibre of the previous year's winner Rainbow View. The favourite was Long Lashes, bought privately by Godolphin after her first start and beaten on heavy ground in the Moyglare Stud Stakes after landing the Sweet Solera Stakes. Next came Ballydoyle's well-bred Leopardstown maiden winner You'll Be Mine and the Prestige Stakes runner-up Mudaaraah. The winner of that race in a blanket finish, Sent From Heaven, was at 8/1, along with Hibaayeb, while Cherry Hinton Stakes third Lady Darshaan, stepping up in trip,was 9/1. There were three others, Chantilly Creme from France, successful in the Criterium du Bequet, a listed event in the Provinces, but last of twelve in the Prix du Calvados on her most recent appearance, and a pair of Kempton maiden winners Dyna Waltz and Blue Angel, the latter fourth in the Prestige Stakes. The tactics employed on Hibaayeb were similar to those in the May Hill and, in a race in which none of the runners coming from off the pace proved able to take a hand in the finish, the tactics of staying in touch were ideal. This time, though, nothing was able to peg Hibaayeb back. Sent From Heaven made the running from Lady Darshaan and Hibaayeb but, when the leader came under pressure just over a furlong out, her pursuers challenged on either side, Hibaayeb managing to squeeze through on the rail to take it up. Hibaayeb drifted left once through, impeding Sent From Heaven, and her rider Neil Callan then accidentally struck Lady Darshaan across the head with his whip. Hibaayeb galloped on strongly to triumph by three quarters of a length with You'll Be Mine (the filly with arguably the most potential of all the runners) keeping on to finish a length and half away third. Hibaayeb had to survive a lengthy stewards' inquiry. Given the trouble in running that some of the beaten runners encountered, coupled with the fact that the first eight horses were covered by not much more than five lengths, there is some reason to regard the form of the Fillies' Mile as possibly none too reliable. Hibaayeb was quoted at 25/1 for both the fillies' classics after her win.

Hibaayeb (b.f. Apr 20, 2007)	Singspiel (IRE) (b 1992)	In The Wings (b 1986)	Sadler's Wells
			High Hawk
		Glorious Song (b 1976)	Halo
			Ballade
	Lady Zonda (b 1999)	Lion Cavern (ch 1989)	Mr Prospector
			Secrettame
		Zonda (br 1988)	Fabulous Dancer
			Oh So Hot

Hibaayeb will need to improve again to hit the jackpot in the best races at three. As a lengthy, good-topped filly with only four runs behind her, there is every chance she will do so, though her victory in the Fillies' Mile suggested she might prove short of speed against such as Special Duty in the One Thousand Guineas. If Hibaayeb takes after her sire Singspiel, winner of such as the Japan Cup and Dubai World Cup, she will certainly be suited by middle distances. Singspiel had an excellent year, with Dar Re Mi and Eastern Anthem also winning Group 1 races. Both those are fully effective at a mile and a half, though the speed on the distaff side of Hibaayeb's pedigree means it is not possible to offer a cast-iron guarantee that she'll stay that trip. Her dam Lady Zonda, by the sprinter-miler Lion Cavern, was a useful handicapper, scoring at seven furlongs and a mile. She has produced one other winner, May Meeting (by Diktat), who ran twice at two in Ireland, where she won a maiden and was a close second in the listed Rochestown Stakes, both at around six furlongs, before running four times without success in the States the following year. One of Lady Zonda's other offspring is Hibaayeb's three-year-old brother Kattar, who has shown only modest form in six starts. Next up are a yearling colt by Halling bought by Mark Johnston for 80,000 guineas at Tattersalls in October and a filly foal by Refuse To Bend. Lady Zonda is a half-sister to Zoning, a smart performer at up to a mile. Her dam Zonda won over six furlongs at two and five furlongs at three and was out of Oh So Hot. The last-named never ran but was a sister to two good fillies in Roussalka, winner of a Coronation Stakes and two editions of the Nassau Stakes, and the One Thousand Guineas runner-up Our Home. She was also a half-sister to the exceptional Fillies' Mile and fillies' triple crown winner Oh So Sharp. Roussalka is third dam of Group 1 winners Ameerat and Collier Hill, and Oh So Sharp became the dam of a Group 1 scorer, Rosefinch, and the grandam of Shantou, successful in the St Leger. This is a fine family and Hibaayeb may add further lustre to it. *C. E. Brittain*

HIBIKI (IRE) 5 b.g. Montjeu (IRE) 137 – White Queen (IRE) 86 (Spectrum (IRE) 126) [2009 12m* Aug 31] quite attractive gelding: fairly useful performer, lightly raced on Flat: won amateur handicap at Epsom (in cheekpieces) sole outing in 2009: will stay 1¾m: acts on soft and good to firm ground: usually held up: useful hurdler. *P. J. Hobbs* **88**

HICCUPS 9 b.g. Polar Prince (IRE) 117 – Simmie's Special 75 (Precocious 126) [2009 87: 7m 7g^4 7g 7m^2 7g 7.9d^4 6.9g 6m^5 Aug 5] tall gelding: fair handicapper nowadays: stays 7f: acts on any turf going: has worn visor/cheekpieces: usually waited with: temperamental. *M. Dods* **79 §**

HI DANCER 6 b.g. Medicean 128 – Sea Music (Inchinor 119) [2009 63: f16d* p12.2g 13m* 10m^5 Jun 29] useful-looking gelding: fair handicapper: better than ever in 2009, winning at Southwell (amateurs) in January and Hamilton (ladies) in June: effective at 13f to 2m: acts on fibresand, firm and good to soft ground: fair hurdler. *P. C. Haslam* **77**

HIDDEN BRIEF 3 b.f. Barathea (IRE) 127 – Hazaradjat (IRE) 82 (Darshaan 133) **98**
[2009 76P: 10m^2 11.4m^4 10m* 10.3s^6 a9.5g^3 Dec 9] rangy filly: useful performer: landed odds in maiden at Newbury in June: good efforts otherwise in 2009, particularly when promoted third to Savoie in listed race at Deauville (all-weather) final outing: stays 11.4f: acts on soft and good to firm going: makes running. *M. A. Jarvis*

HIDDEN CITY (IRE) 2 b.c. (Apr 4) Elusive City (USA) 117 – Lizanne (USA) **–**
(Theatrical 128) [2009 6d 6g 6d Jul 27] well held in sellers: tried tongue tied/in cheek-pieces. *J. S. Moore*

HIDDEN DOOR (IRE) 4 b.f. Montjeu (IRE) 137 – Yaselda 82 (Green Desert (USA) **61**
127) [2009 72: p8g 10m 7m p8.6g 10.1m^2 11.9d 10.1d^5 Oct 27] rather leggy filly: just modest performer at 4 yrs: left Jane Chapple-Hyam 4,500 gns after second outing: stays 1¼m: acts on polytrack and good to firm going: none too consistent. *G. Prodromou*

HIDDEN FIRE 2 b.f. (May 3) Alhaarth (IRE) 126 – Premier Prize 106 (Selkirk (USA) **52**
129) [2009 7d Oct 12] third foal: dam, 7f (at 2 yrs)/1¼m winner, half-sister to smart stayer Gold Medallist: 33/1, very green when eleventh in maiden at Salisbury: will be suited by 1m+. *D. R. C. Elsworth*

HIDDEN GLORY 2 b.g. (Feb 5) Mujahid (USA) 125 – Leominda 67 (Lion Cavern **81**
(USA) 117) [2009 7m^4 p7g^2 p8g* Dec 7] 26,000Y: big, useful-looking gelding: third foal: half-brother to 2 winners abroad, including French 1m winner Athara (by Forzando): dam, sprint maiden, half-sister to dam of smart performers Franklins Gardens (stayer) and Polar Ben (up to 1m): fairly useful form: odds on, won maiden at Lingfield by 3 lengths from Spice Fair: stays 1m. *Pat Eddery*

HIDDEN HORSE 5 b.m. Fasliyev (USA) 120 – Hopping Higgins (IRE) 103 (Brief **–**
Truce (USA) 126) [2009 p7g Jan 21] fourth foal: dam Irish 2-y-o 5f winner: has shaped as if amiss in bumper/maiden. *M. R. Channon*

HIERARCH (IRE) 2 b.c. (May 9) Dansili 127 – Danse Classique (IRE) 94 (Night **58 p**
Shift (USA)) [2009 6m^5 Jul 26] €48,000Y, €50,000 2-y-o: rangy colt: sixth foal: half-brother to 7-y-o Defi and Irish 1½m winner Dazzling Dancer (by Nashwan), both fairly useful: dam, Irish 7f winner, half-sister to Irish/Yorkshire Oaks and Prix de l'Opera winner Petrushka: 9/2, very green when 8½ lengths fifth to Quarrel in maiden at Ascot: should be suited by 7f+: likely to do better. *R. Hannon*

HI FLING 3 b.c. Oasis Dream 129 – Crafty Buzz (USA) (Crafty Prospector (USA)) **66**
[2009 60: p8g 9.9m 11.5s p12g* 11.5d 11.5g^6 12m Aug 23] lengthy, good-bodied colt: fair handicapper: won at Lingfield in June: stays 1½m: acts on polytrack: blinkered last 4 starts: sold £800, sent to Sweden. *B. J. Meehan*

HIGGY'S RAGAZZO (FR) 2 b.c. (Mar 21) Sinndar (IRE) 134 – Super Crusty (IRE) **86 p**
(Namid 128) [2009 8.1d^5 8.1m* Sep 10] €44,000Y: first foal: dam, French 11.5f winner, out of half-sister to very smart French 1½m performer Shawanda (by Sinndar): better effort in maidens at Chepstow when winning comfortably by a length from First In The Queue: will be suited by 1¼m+: will continue to improve. *R. Hannon*

HIGH ACHIEVED 3 b.f. Dansili 127 – Achieve (Rainbow Quest (USA) 134) [2009 **76 p**
6m* 6.1g^3 Aug 14] 85,000F, 300,000Y: third foal: half-sister to winner in Greece by Zamindar: dam unraced sister to Derby winner Quest For Fame: fair form: won maiden at Salisbury in July: good third in handicap at Nottingham next time: will be suited by 7f/1m: will improve again. *P. W. Chapple-Hyam*

HIGH AMBITION 6 b.g. High Estate 127 – So Ambitious (Teenoso (USA) 135) **87**
[2009 7m 8m 10.1d* 12g* 12m^3 f11g Oct 18] tall gelding: fairly useful handicapper: missed 2008: won at Newcastle in June and Pontefract in August: stays 1½m: acts on polytrack, firm and good to soft ground: tried visored: held up. *R. A. Fahey*

HIGHAMS PARK (IRE) 3 ch.f. Redback 116 – Miss Caoimhe (IRE) (Barathea (IRE) **–**
127) [2009 –: f11g 12.1g 16v^4 18g 16g Aug 29] no form. *J. G. Portman*

HIGHCLIFFE BRIDGE (IRE) 2 b.f. (Mar 5) Avonbridge 123 – Peig Sayers (IRE) **51**
58 (Royal Academy (USA) 130) [2009 5.1f^6 6.1g^5 6f^3 7s^3 7m^3 7s* 7g 7g p8g 7g Sep 14] leggy filly: eighth foal: half-sister to 1½m/2m winner Tharua (by Indian Danehill): dam, Irish maiden (best at 1m at 2 yrs), closely related to very smart stayer Assessor: modest performer at best: won selling nursery at Yarmouth (left P. D. Evans 5,600 gns) in July: stays 1m: acts on firm and soft going: blinkered last 2 starts. *N. P. Littmoden*

HIGH COMEDY 2 b.c. (Mar 15) Exceed And Excel (AUS) 126 – Ecstatic 94 **74**
(Nashwan (USA) 135) [2009 6.1s^4 6g Oct 20] big, useful-looking colt: fifth foal: dam, 2-y-o 6f winner who stayed 9f, out of half-sister to very smart 6f to 1m performer Pursuit of Love: better effort in maidens when fourth at Nottingham: bit said to have slipped through mouth final start: joined M. Al Subouse in UAE. *Saeed bin Suroor*

Mr and Mrs Steven Jenkins' "High Heeled"

HIGH CONSTABLE 2 b.c. (Mar 31) Shamardal (USA) 129 – Abbey Strand (USA) 78 (Shadeed (USA) 135) [2009 p7.1g^3 Dec 5] half-brother to several winners, notably very smart 7f (at 2 yrs) to 9f (Dubai Duty Free) winner Right Approach (by Machiavellian): dam 1m winner: 2/1 on, encouraging effort when close third to Saharia in maiden at Wolverhampton, green under pressure: bred to be suited by 1m+: will improve. *R. Charlton* **74 p**

HIGH CROSS (IRE) 3 b.f. Cape Cross (IRE) 129 – Overruled (IRE) 91 (Last Tycoon 131) [2009 f8g^4 f8g^2 f11g^4 p9.5m* p10g^3 p9.5g^2 12g Apr 29] sturdy, lengthy filly: half-sister to several winners, including smart Irish 7f (at 2 yrs) to 1½m (Irish Oaks) winner Vintage Tipple (by Entrepreneur) and 5-y-o Record Breaker: dam, 1m (at 2 yrs)/ 1¼m winner (stayed 1¾m), half-sister to smart performer up to 1½m Overbury: fair performer: won handicap at Wolverhampton in March: stays 1¼m: form only on all-weather. *Sir Mark Prescott* **78**

HIGH CURRAGH 6 b.g. Pursuit of Love 124 – Pretty Poppy 67 (Song 132) [2009 94: 6m* 6g^4 6m^2 6d 6m^5 6m 5m 5g^3 f6g^5 6g^2 7.5g^3 7d p6m p6g 8g 15s a7.5g Dec 19] strong, lengthy gelding: fluent mover: fairly useful performer: won handicap at Ripon in April: regressive form after third start, claimed from K. Ryan £7,000 after fifteenth outing: effective at stiff 5f to 7f: acts on polytrack and any turf going: often wears headgear: races up with pace. *E. J. O'Neill* **88 d**

HIGHEST ESTEEM 5 b.g. Mark of Esteem (IRE) 137 – For More (FR) (Sanglamore (USA) 126) [2009 76: p16.5g^{2} Apr 6] good-topped gelding: fair handicapper, lightly raced: fit from hurdling (successful in February), creditable second only Flat start in 2009: stays easy 16.5f: acts on polytrack: wears cheekpieces. *G. L. Moore* **71**

HIGH FIVE SOCIETY 5 b.g. Compton Admiral 121 – Sarah Madeline 48 (Pelder (IRE) 125) [2009 60: f8d^{6} f8g p9.5g* p9.5g^{2} f8d 8g* 10g p9.5g Sep 18] close-coupled gelding: fair performer: won minor event at Wolverhampton in February and handicap at Yarmouth in May: barely stays 10.5f: acts on polytrack and good to soft going: tried in cheekpieces, wears blinkers nowadays: tongue tied. *S. R. Bowring* **67**

HIGHGATE CAT 3 b.g. One Cool Cat (USA) 123 – Angry Bark (USA) 62 (Woodman (USA) 126) [2009 p7g^{5} p7g^{6} 7d 7.1g Jun 18] rangy gelding: fair maiden: raced only at 7f. *B. R. Millman* **65**

HIGH HEELED (IRE) 3 b.f. High Chaparral (IRE) 132 – Uncharted Haven (Turtle Island (IRE) 123) [2009 90: 10s* 10.4m^{4} 12g^{3} 11.9m^{3} 10.4g* 9.9d^{5} 12m^{4} 12v* Oct 24] useful-looking filly: smart performer: won minor event at Newbury in April, listed race at York in July and St Simon Stakes at Newbury (beat Tastahil 6 lengths, getting to front easily 2f out before forging clear) in October: also ran well when 2½ lengths third to Sariska in Oaks at Epsom third outing: stays 1½m: acts on polytrack, best turf efforts on good or softer going (acts on heavy): sold 600,000 gns, joined J. Gosden. *B. W. Hills* **118**

HIGH HOLBORN (IRE) 2 b.g. (Mar 18) Danehill Dancer (IRE) 117 – Wedding Morn (IRE) 62 (Sadler's Wells (USA) 132) [2009 7g 7g^{5} 7m 8m Sep 8] sturdy gelding: modest maiden: should stay 1m+: has looked difficult ride. *B. J. Meehan* **64**

HIGH IMPORTANCE (USA) 2 b.c. (Mar 6) Arch (USA) 127 – Music Lane (USA) (Miswaki (USA) 124) [2009 p7g^{4} 7d^{3} Oct 22] $260,000Y: brother to 2 winners abroad, closely related to winner in USA by Kris S and half-brother to 2 winners by Silver Hawk, including useful 1¼m winner Light Scent: dam, US 6f winner, half-sister to US Grade 1 winner up to 1½m Hawkster: fair form in maidens at Lingfield and Brighton (possibly unsuited by track/ground): remains capable of better. *J. Noseda* **75 p**

HIGHKINGOFIRELAND 3 b. or br.g. Danehill Dancer (IRE) 117 – Lucky Date (IRE) 91 (Halling (USA) 133) [2009 7m 9.8m^{4} 9d* 9m 12m^{6} 10.4s^{4} 10.3d 10.2v^{3} Nov 4] 35,000Y: neat gelding: second foal: half-brother to fairly useful French 7.5f to 10.5f (including 1m at 2 yrs) winner Rava (by Nayef): dam 2-y-o 7f winner: fair performer: best effort when winning maiden at Ripon in May: trained until after sixth start by K. R. Burke: likely to prove best up to 1¼m: acts on heavy and good to firm going. *A. P. Jarvis* **73**

HIGHLAND BRIDGE 2 b.c. (Feb 3) Avonbridge 123 – Reciprocal (IRE) 88 (Night Shift (USA)) [2009 p8g p7g^{3} Nov 18] much better effort in maidens when 5 lengths third to Khanivorous at Kempton. *D. R. C. Elsworth* **61**

HIGHLAND GLEN 3 b.g. Montjeu (IRE) 137 – Daring Aim 89 (Daylami (IRE) 138) [2009 60p: 10m* 11.9v^{6} 12m^{6} p12g* 11.8m* Oct 6] rangy gelding: useful performer: progressed, winning maiden at Lingfield in May then handicaps at Kempton (by length from Ottoman Empire) in September and Leicester (reluctant to enter stall when beating Souter Point ½ length in 3-runner event) in October: likely to stay 1¾m: acts on polytrack and good to firm going: has joined Saeed bin Suroor. *Sir Michael Stoute* **104**

HIGHLAND HARVEST 5 b.g. Averti (IRE) 117 – Bee One (IRE) 81§ (Catrail (USA) 123) [2009 90: 8m 8m 7g p7g 6g* 5d 6d^{2} 6g 6m 6d p7g^{6} Nov 11] close-coupled gelding: fair handicapper: won at Brighton in July: probably best at 6f/7f nowadays: acts on polytrack, soft and good to firm ground: not straightforward. *Jamie Poulton* **79**

HIGHLAND HOMESTEAD 4 b.g. Makbul 104 – Highland Rossie 67 (Pablond 93) [2009 72: p16g p16g Nov 11] close-coupled gelding: handicapper: well held in 2009: stays easy 2m: acts on all-weather, soft and good to firm going: tried blinkered. *M. R. Hoad* **–**

HIGHLAND JEWEL (IRE) 2 b.f. (May 1) Azamour (IRE) 130 – Raysiza (IRE) (Alzao (USA) 117) [2009 7s 7d Oct 12] sixth foal: half-sister to several winners, including fairly useful 2007 2-y-o 6f winner Highland Daughter (by Kyllachy) and useful Slovakian stayer Ryan (by Generous): dam useful Italian 7.5f/9f winner: modest form in maidens at Salisbury: will be suited by 1m+. *C. G. Cox* **58**

HIGHLAND KNIGHT (IRE) 2 b.c. (Feb 16) Night Shift (USA) – Highland Shot 91 (Selkirk (USA) 129) [2009 8.3m Oct 13] good-topped colt: second foal: dam, 7f to 8.5f winner, half-sister to stayer Grey Shot, 7f performer Opera Cape and sprinter Night Shot **56**

(by Night Shift), all smart: 100/1 and green, 10¼ lengths eighth to Botanist in maiden at Leicester (tongue tied). *A. M. Balding*

HIGHLAND LASSIE (IRE) 3 b.f. Oasis Dream 129 – Arlesiana (USA) (Woodman (USA) 126) [2009 8m 8.3g^6 8.3g^2 8m p9.5g Sep 3] 160,000Y: leggy filly: fourth foal: half-sister to 2 winners, including French 10.5f winner Empreinte Celebre (by Peintre Celebre): dam, ran once in France, closely related to very smart performer up to 1¼m Miswaki Tern: fair maiden: best effort on third start: should stay beyond 1m. *B. J. Meehan* **66**

HIGHLAND LEGACY 5 ch.g. Selkirk (USA) 129 – Generous Lady 98 (Generous (IRE) 139) [2009 101: 16g^4 14v 18m 12s Nov 7] good-topped gelding: fairly useful handicapper nowadays: should stay beyond 2m: has won on good to firm going, better form on softer than good: held up: visored last 3 starts. *M. L. W. Bell* **94**

HIGHLAND LOVE 4 b.g. Fruits of Love (USA) 127 – Diabaig 76 (Precocious 126) [2009 77: 10.2f 10.4g p12.2m^3 12v^5 p12.2g Sep 19] good-bodied gelding: fair handicapper: likely to prove best up to 1¼m: acts on polytrack, heavy and good to firm ground: joined Jedd O'Keeffe. *J. T. Stimpson* **68**

HIGHLAND QUAICH 2 ch.c. (Apr 8) Compton Place 125 – Bee One (IRE) 81§ (Catrail (USA) 123) [2009 p8g^6 p7g* p7g^4 p7f^6 Dec 20] sturdy colt: fourth foal: closely related to 3-y-o Highland River and half-brother to 5-y-o Highland Harvest: dam temperamental sprint maiden: fair performer: won maiden at Kempton in October: creditable efforts in nurseries: stays 7f: raced only on polytrack. *D. R. C. Elsworth* **71**

HIGHLAND RIVER 3 b.g. Indian Creek 119 – Bee One (IRE) 81§ (Catrail (USA) 123) [2009 66: 8.3m 8.5g 10g 11.6m p8m^4 p8g p9.5g p7.1g f8g Dec 27] good-bodied gelding: fair handicapper on all-weather, modest on turf: left D. Elsworth after sixth start: free-going sort, will prove best up to 1m: acts on polytrack: visored once. *A. Sadik* **55 a65**

HIGHLAND SONG (IRE) 6 ch.g. Fayruz 116 – Rose 'n Reason (IRE) (Reasonable (FR) 119) [2009 55: f6g^2 p7.1g^6 Feb 9] well-made gelding: modest performer: effective at 5f/6f: acts on all-weather, soft and good to firm going: tried in cheekpieces. *R. F. Fisher* **52**

HIGHLAND STARLIGHT (USA) 3 ch.f. Dixieland Band (USA) – Fran's Flash (USA) (Star de Naskra (USA)) [2009 65: 7g^6 7f p8.6g^6 8g p8f Oct 14] lengthy filly: modest maiden, sporadic form: seems to stay 8.6f: signs of temperament. *C. G. Cox* **59**

HIGHLAND STORM 3 b.g. Storming Home 128 – Real Emotion (USA) (El Prado (IRE) 119) [2009 84§: 10.2d^4 12m 11.6g^6 10.9g^2 10.4g^5 16g Aug 18] big, good-topped gelding: just fair handicapper at 3 yrs: claimed from George Baker £6,000 fourth outing: stays 1½m: acts on heavy and good to firm going: tried in headgear: temperamental. *B. N. Pollock* **74 §**

HIGHLAND WARRIOR 10 b.g. Makbul 104 – Highland Rowena 59 (Royben 125) [2009 84: p5g^6 5m 5m 5m 5m 5d 5m* 5g* 5g 5d^5 5.1d 5g 5g^5 5g Oct 27] big, leggy gelding: fair handicapper: won apprentice race at York and amateur event at Doncaster in July: below form after: races mainly at 5f: acts on any turf going: tried in cheekpieces: held up. *P. T. Midgley* **79**

HIGHLY ACCLAIMED 3 b.f. Acclamation 118 – Ebba 88 (Elmaamul (USA) 125) [2009 42p: 6m^6 6m 7.5m f6g^5 f8g^4 8d 6s 5.9d^3 5s^4 Aug 26] angular filly: modest maiden: stays 6f: acts on fibresand, soft and good to firm ground: in cheekpieces/visor last 4 starts. *Mrs A. Duffield* **56**

HIGHLY REGAL (IRE) 4 b.g. High Chaparral (IRE) 132 – Regal Portrait (IRE) 57 (Royal Academy (USA) 130) [2009 60§: p8g* p8g* p8g* f8g* p8g^3 p8g* 8m^5 p8g^3 8.1m 7g p8g* p7g^5 f8m^5 p8g Nov 25] lengthy gelding: fairly useful handicapper on all-weather, fair on turf: won at Kempton (3) in January/February, Southwell in March and Kempton in April and September: best form at 1m: acts on all-weather and soft ground: tried in cheekpieces/tongue strap, blinkered in 2009: quirky. *R. A. Teal* **76 a87**

HIGH MORNING 3 br.f. Cape Cross (IRE) 129 – Joharra (USA) (Kris S (USA)) [2009 8.3f 8.1g 7f Jun 24] 30,000Y: lengthy, good-topped filly: second foal: sister to fairly useful 1¼m winner Caprivi: dam, maiden who stayed 9f, half-sister to very smart performer up to 1¼m Equerry and Breeders' Cup Juvenile Fillies winner Tempera: little form in maidens: tongue tied final outing: sold 3,500 gns in December. *D. M. Simcock* **–**

HIGH 'N DRY (IRE) 5 ch.m. Halling (USA) 133 – Sisal (IRE) 84 (Danehill (USA) 126) [2009 74§: p10g Apr 4] workmanlike mare: fair handicapper: well held sole outing in 2009: stays 1¼m: acts on polytrack, unraced on extremes of going on turf: usually wears cheekpieces: ungenuine. *M. A. Allen* **– §**

HIGH OFFICE 3 b.g. High Chaparral (IRE) 132 – White House 84 (Pursuit of Love 124) [2009 77p: 9m^{3} 9.9m^{2} 9.8m^{4} Jun 2] rather leggy gelding: fairly useful maiden: will stay 1½m: acts on polytrack, soft and good to firm going. *R. A. Fahey* **81**

HIGH ON A HILL (IRE) 2 b.c. (Apr 12) Val Royal (FR) 127 – Blue Kestrel (IRE) 70 (Bluebird (USA) 125) [2009 p8f p8g 8d^{3} f8m^{4} Nov 6] lengthy colt: fair maiden: third at Salisbury, best effort: should stay beyond 1m. *S. Kirk* **69**

HIGH POINT (IRE) 11 b.g. Ela-Mana-Mou 132 – Top Lady (IRE) 83 (Shirley Heights 130) [2009 73: 16g May 29] lengthy, leggy gelding: fair handicapper: lightly raced since 2007, and well held sole outing all 11 yrs: tried visored. *G. P. Enright* **–**

HIGH PROFIT (IRE) 5 ch.g. Selkirk (USA) 129 – Spot Prize (USA) 108 (Seattle Dancer (USA) 119) [2009 66: 6m^{6} 8g^{5} 8.5m 9.1g p12.2g^{4} 12m Jul 1] maiden, lightly raced on Flat: just modest form in 2009: should stay 1¼m/1½m: acts on polytrack: tried in cheekpieces/visor. *James Moffatt* **59**

HIGH RANSOM 2 b.f. (Mar 15) Red Ransom (USA) – Shortfall 103 (Last Tycoon 131) [2009 8v Oct 24] 52,000Y: fifth foal: sister to useful 9f/1½m winner Contraband (also smart 2m chaser) and half-sister to fairly useful winners up to 13f Fall In Line (by Linamix) and Parachute (by Hector Protector): dam, won around 1¼m, half-sister to dam of 4-y-o Overdose: 16/1, staying-on seventh to Gardening Leave in maiden at Newbury: will be suited by 1¼m+: open to improvement. *M. A. Jarvis* **56 p**

HIGH RESOLUTION 2 ch.g. (Mar 9) Haafhd 129 – Individual Talents (USA) 77 (Distant View (USA) 126) [2009 7m 7.1m 7g p7.1m^{3} p7.1g^{3} 8m^{2} p8.6g 6g Oct 23] modest maiden: claimed from S. C. Williams £5,000 sixth start (selling nursery): should be suited by 1¼m+. *Miss L. A. Perratt* **55**

HIGH RIDGE 10 ch.g. Indian Ridge 123 – Change For A Buck (USA) 83 (Time For A Change (USA)) [2009 52: p6m f6g Nov 17] big, lengthy gelding: handicapper: no form in 2009: wears cheekpieces/blinkers. *J. L. Flint* **–**

HIGH ROLLING 2 b.g. (Apr 8) Fantastic Light (USA) 134 – Roller Girl (Merdon Melody 98) [2009 6d 7.5m^{6} 5g^{3} 6s^{4} 7g^{3} 8m^{5} Sep 23] good-topped gelding: fair maiden: third in nursery at Redcar fifth start, best effort: stays 7f. *T. D. Easterby* **68**

HIGH SEVERA (IRE) 3 b.c. High Chaparral (IRE) 132 – Severa (GER) (Kendor (FR) 122) [2009 11s 9.2g^{3} 8.1v* 8.3g^{5} 10m 8s^{6} Aug 26] fifth foal: half-brother to winner in Greece by Mujadil: dam German 7f/7.5f winner: fairly useful performer: won maiden at Haydock in May: trained prior to final start by K. R. Burke: should prove best at 1¼m+: acts on heavy ground: sold 5,000 gns in October. *A. P. Jarvis* **81**

HIGH SPICE (USA) 2 b.f. (Feb 13) Songandaprayer (USA) 118 – Erin Moor (USA) (Holy Bull (USA) 134) [2009 5f* 5m^{6} 5m 5d^{2} 6m 5m^{4} p5.1g^{3} p6m^{5} Oct 28] $110,000Y: deep-girthed filly: fourth foal: half-sister to winners in USA by Lemon Drop Kid and Forestry: dam, US 2-y-o 7f/1m winner, out of half-sister to US Grade 1 winners Willa On The Move (8.5f) and Will's Way (up to 1¼m): fairly useful performer: won maiden at Newmarket (beat Radiohead 1¼ lengths) in May: creditable efforts in nurseries last 2 starts: stays 6f: acts on polytrack and firm going, probably on good to soft. *R. M. H. Cowell* **82**

HIGH STANDING (USA) 4 b. or br.g. High Yield (USA) 121 – Nena Maka (Selkirk (USA) 129) [2009 95: 6g* 6m* 6m* 6d* 6d^{3} 6m^{4} Sep 27] tall gelding: has a round action: smart performer: most progressive early in 2009, winning handicaps at Doncaster and **117**

Wokingham Stakes (Heritage Handicap), Royal Ascot—the highly drawn runners dominate as High Standing proves too strong for joint top weights Asset (rail) and Rock of Rochelle

Goodwood in May, Wokingham Stakes (Handicap) at Royal Ascot (by ¾ length from Asset) in June and Shadwell Stakes (Hackwood) at Newbury (beat Prime Defender 1¼ lengths) in July: respectable efforts after, in Sprint Cup at Haydock (2½ lengths third to Regal Parade) and Diadem Stakes at Ascot (3 lengths fourth to Sayif): best at 6f/7f: acts on polytrack, good to firm and good to soft going: held up: has sharp turn of foot. *W. J. Haggas*

HIGH TENSILE 3 b.f. Diktat 126 – Shifty Mouse 44 (Night Shift (USA)) [2009 –: 8g 8.3g Aug 14] no form in maidens. *J. G. Given* –

HIGHTIME HEROINE (IRE) 3 b.f. Danetime (IRE) 121 – Esterlina (IRE) 95 (Highest Honor (FR) 124) [2009 6m³ 7m² 6d³ 6s² 6m* 6g² p7.1m² p7g p7g³ Nov 5] €45,000F, 135,000Y: good-topped filly: third foal: half-sister to useful 7f (at 2 yrs)/1m winner Redolent (by Redback) who stayed 1¼m: dam, Irish 1m winner, out of close relation to Fillies' Mile winner/Oaks third Leap Lively: fairly useful performer: won maiden at Yarmouth in August: placed in handicaps 3 of 4 starts after, good effort final occasion: should stay 1m: acts on polytrack and good to firm ground. *J. Noseda* **89**

HIGH TRAIL (IRE) 2 b.f. (Mar 7) Acclamation 118 – Set Trail (IRE) 76 (Second Set (IRE) 127) [2009 p7m Sep 24] sixth foal: half-sister to 3 winners, including 1¼m winner Forehand (by Lend A Hand) and 2002 2-y-o 8.5f winner Toro Bravo (by Alhaarth): dam 2-y-o 7f winner: 50/1, well held in claimer at Kempton. *Rae Guest* –

HIGH TWELVE (IRE) 2 b.c. (Mar 30) Montjeu (IRE) 137 – Much Faster (IRE) 113 (Fasliyev (USA) 120) [2009 7.1m² 8.1g* 8m⁴ 7m Oct 17] 380,000Y: rangy colt: second foal: half-brother 3-y-o Sugar Free: dam French 2-y-o 5f/5.5f (Prix Robert Papin) winner: useful performer: easily landed odds in maiden at Sandown in August: best effort when 4¼ lengths fourth to Joshua Tree in Royal Lodge Stakes at Ascot, slowly away and not knocked about when meeting trouble final 1f: stiffish task (also very early to post), seemed to lack for speed when only twelfth in Dewhurst Stakes at Newmarket final outing: will stay beyond 1m. *J. H. M. Gosden* **104 +**

HIGHWAY CODE (USA) 3 b.g. Street Cry (IRE) 130 – Fairy Heights (IRE) 110 (Fairy King (USA)) [2009 10m 10.1g 9.3d Jul 26] modest form in maidens: sold £14,000 in August and joined R. Lee. *M. Johnston* **52**

HIGHWAY MAGIC (IRE) 3 ch.c. Rainbow Quest (USA) 134 – Adultress (IRE) (Ela-Mana-Mou 132) [2009 70?: 12m⁶ 8d Jul 27] workmanlike colt: maiden: well held in 2009. *A. P. Jarvis* –

HILBRE COURT (USA) 4 b. or br.g. Doneraile Court (USA) – Glasgow's Gold (USA) (Seeking The Gold (USA)) [2009 76+, a88: p10g f8g³ f8g* p9.5g f8g² f8g f8g* 8.1v 8m 10g p8.6g f8f³ f8m⁶ f8g³ f8f f8f* f8g² Dec 27] rather leggy gelding: fairly useful handicapper: won at Southwell in February, April and December: stays 1¼m: acts on all-weather, little recent form on turf: tried blinkered, often in cheekpieces. *B. P. J. Baugh* – **a82**

HILBRE POINT (USA) 3 b.g. Giant's Causeway (USA) 132 – Lady Carla 122 (Caerleon (USA) 132) [2009 –p: 7m 8.5g 11d 10.2d May 18] sturdy gelding: has reportedly had problems with corns: little form: blinkered final outing, then gelded. *B. J. Meehan* –

HILL BILLY ROCK (IRE) 6 b.g. Halling (USA) 133 – Polska (USA) 103 (Danzig (USA)) [2009 78: f14s⁵ 13m⁵ Jun 4] strong gelding: just modest handicapper in 2009, leaving G. A. Swinbank after reappearance: will stay 2m: acts on soft and good to firm going: possibly not straightforward. *Mrs S. C. Bradburne* **61**

HILL CROSS (IRE) 3 b.g. Barathea (IRE) 127 – Darayna (IRE) (Shernazar 131) [2009 –: 12.1m 14.1m May 25] compact gelding: little form. *K. G. Reveley* –

HILL OF CLARE (IRE) 7 br. or b.m. Daylami (IRE) 138 – Sarah-Clare 67 (Reach 122) [2009 48: 10.2g 8.1g 16.2v² 18g⁶ 16d Oct 11] sparely-made mare: modest and inconsistent maiden: stays 2¼m: acts on polytrack, heavy and good to firm going: tried tongue tied. *G. H. Jones* **53**

HILL OF LUJAIN 5 b.g. Lujain (USA) 119 – Cinder Hills 72 (Deploy 131) [2009 54: p6g p7.1g p8.6m⁶ 10.9f May 12] sturdy gelding: regressive handicapper: wore cheekpieces final start. *Ian Williams* **45**

HILL OF MILLER (IRE) 2 b.g. (Apr 28) Indian Ridge 123 – Roshani (IRE) 79 (Kris 135) [2009 6g³ 5.9g 6.1v⁴ p6g 6s⁶ 6m⁶ 5.7m⁶ p6m² p6m⁴ p6g⁵ p5m Dec 30] €17,000Y: fifth foal: half-brother to useful 1m/1¼m winners Zayn Zen and Zaafran (both by Singspiel): dam, 1m/1¼m winner, out of half-sister to Oh So Sharp: fair maiden: needs to settle to stay beyond 6f: acts on polytrack, soft and good to firm going. *Rae Guest* **71**

HILLSIDE LAD 3 b.g. Tobougg (IRE) 125 – Cumbrian Concerto 44 (Petong 126) **70 §**
[2009 76: p6g 6f^{6} 5m^{4} 5m^{3} p6g 6d* 5.1g^{4} 6m 7.1d Sep 4] fair handicapper: won at Salisbury in July: best at 5f/6f: unraced on soft/heavy going, acts on polytrack and any other turf: visored/in cheekpieces last 5 starts: temperamental: sold £1,500, sent to Qatar. *R. M. Beckett*

HILLTOP ALCHEMY 3 ch.g. Zaha (CAN) 106 – Saferjel (Elmaamul (USA) 125) **–**
[2009 8m 9g p12m p12m p8m Oct 28] good-bodied gelding: no form: tried visored. *J. R. Jenkins*

HILLTOP ARTISTRY 3 b.c. Polish Precedent (USA) 131 – Hilltop 45 (Absalom **69**
128) [2009 –: 8.1g^{4} 8s 8.1g^{3} 8d^{3} Jul 7] workmanlike colt: fair maiden: stays 1m: acts on good to soft ground. *S. W. James*

HILLTOP LEGACY 6 b.m. Danzig Connection (USA) – Hilltop 45 (Absalom 128) **60**
[2009 –: p6g p7g 6g^{4} 6s 7g^{6} Aug 5] modest maiden: stays 7f: best efforts on good ground. *J. R. Jenkins*

HILL TRIBE 2 b.f. (Mar 12) Tiger Hill (IRE) 127 – Morning Queen (GER) (Konigs- **78 p**
stuhl (GER)) [2009 6g 6m^{5} 7m^{3} Aug 23] 47,000Y: tall, good-bodied filly: half-sister to several winners, including 1¼m (at 2 yrs) to 2¼m winner Love Brothers (by Lomitas) and French 1m (at 2 yrs) to 11.5f winner Moonrise (by Grand Lodge): dam, German 1m winner, sister to very smart German 11f/1½m performer Monsun: progressive form in maidens, 1¼ lengths third to Creese at Folkestone: will be well suited by 1m+: sold 30,000 gns: type to do better still at 3 yrs. *J. R. Best*

HILLVIEW BOY (IRE) 5 b. or br.g. Bishop of Cashel 122 – Arandora Star (USA) **103**
(Sagace (FR) 135) [2009 9.2g* 10g^{2} 12g^{3} 12m 10.3s* 10m 10g^{3} 12d^{2} 12s^{2} Nov 7] tall gelding: fairly useful bumper winner: useful handicapper on Flat: won at Hamilton (maiden) in May and Doncaster in August: good placed efforts last 3 starts, particularly when 1¾ lengths second to Charm School in November Handicap at Doncaster final outing: stays 1½m: acts on soft and good to firm ground: usually held up. *J. S. Goldie*

HIMALYA (IRE) 3 b.g. Danehill Dancer (IRE) 117 – Lady Miletrian (IRE) 103 **110**
(Barathea (IRE) 127) [2009 109: 7m^{6} 5m^{6} 6g^{3} p6g^{3} p7f^{4} Dec 16] rangy, good sort: has scope: smart performer: reportedly very sick after latter start at 2 yrs: not seen out in 2009 until September: in frame in listed races last 2 starts, at Lingfield and Kempton (close fourth to Dohasa): should stay 1m: acts on polytrack and firm ground: sometimes ponied to start. *J. Noseda*

HINDFORD OAK SIOUX 3 b.f. Green Card (USA) 110 – Sharp Susy (Beveled **–**
(USA)) [2009 56: 10.2v 7.1g Aug 11] maiden: no form in 2009. *Mrs L. Williamson*

HINDU KUSH (IRE) 4 b.c. Sadler's Wells (USA) 132 – Tambora 75 (Darshaan 133) **109 d**
[2009 111: 12m^{5} 13s^{2} 18.7m 14g* 20m^{6} 12s^{5} 14g 13.4m 14v 13g 12g f14g^{6} Oct 18] smallish colt: useful performer: won listed event at Leopardstown in May by length from Alandi: had also run well when 3½ lengths second to same rival in similar event at Navan: below form in second half of year: stays 15f: acts on firm and good to soft going: often front runner: sometimes looks awkward under pressure: sold 32,000 gns. *D. Nicholls*

HINT OF HONEY 3 ch.f. King Charlemagne (USA) 120 – Jugendliebe (IRE) (Persian **61**
Bold 123) [2009 –: p6g^{4} f7g p7g^{4} p6g f6g 6f f8g* Dec 27] modest handicapper: won at Southwell in December: stays 1m: acts on all-weather. *A. G. Newcombe*

HINTON ADMIRAL 5 b.g. Spectrum (IRE) 126 – Shawanni 105 (Shareef Dancer **88**
(USA) 135) [2009 105d: 7.1m 7d 6g* May 29] good-topped gelding: just fairly useful at 5 yrs: won claimer at Yarmouth in May: effective from 6f to 1¼m: acts on polytrack and good to firm going: tried in cheekpieces. *R. A. Fahey*

HIP HIP HOORAY 3 ch.f. Monsieur Bond (IRE) 120 – Birthday Belle 70 (Lycius **72**
(USA) 124) [2009 73: p8g^{5} 8.3g 10m^{3} 9g^{2} 9.9m 8.3m* 10g^{5} 9g^{5} 8.1g^{4} p9.5g^{5} 9.9m p10m 10g p8g Oct 14] workmanlike filly: fair handicapper: won at Windsor in June: effective at 1m/1¼m: acts on all-weather, good to firm and good to soft going: in cheekpieces last 3 outings: held up. *L. A. Dace*

HIPPODROME (IRE) 7 b.g. Montjeu (IRE) 137 – Moon Diamond (Unfuwain (USA) **–**
131) [2009 –: f14g f11g Mar 22] good-bodied gelding: little form on Flat since 2005: tried in headgear: fair hurdler, successful in April. *John A. Harris*

HIPPOLYTUS 4 ch.g. Observatory (USA) 131 – Pasithea (IRE) 101 (Celtic Swing **83**
138) [2009 80: 7s 10.4g* 10.2m^{4} 9.2s^{2} 9.2v^{6} 9.8d^{5} Sep 1] strong, lengthy gelding: fairly useful handicapper: won apprentice event at Haydock in June: stays 10.4f: acts on heavy and good to firm ground: sold £10,000. *J. J. Quinn*

John Smith's Extra Smooth Silver Cup Stakes (Handicap), York—
Hits Only Vic gets up late to beat Warringah (white face) and Magicalmysterytour (noseband)

HISARONU (IRE) 3 b.f. Stravinsky (USA) 133 – Journey of Hope (USA) 95 (Slew O' **75**
Gold (USA)) [2009 8d^{5} p9.5g^{2} Apr 25] €16,000Y: sixth foal: closely related to 2 winners, including useful Irish 1¼m winner Dream To Dress (by Theatrical), later successful in USA, and half-sister to 2 winners, including Irish 1½m winner Anticipated Move (by Silver Hawk): dam, Irish 2-y-o 6f winner who stayed 1m, later successful in USA: fair form in maidens. *H. R. A. Cecil*

HI SHINKO 3 b.g. Shinko Forest (IRE) – Up Front (IRE) 61 (Up And At 'em 109) **84**
[2009 73: 6d* 6m^{6} 6f 5f* 5m^{6} 6g^{4} 5.1g^{3} 7d^{2} 7m^{3} 7d* 7m^{2} 7m^{5} 7s Oct 12] close-coupled gelding: fairly useful performer: improved at 3 yrs, winning maiden at Folkestone in March and handicaps on same course in June and at Epsom in September: stays 7f: acts on firm and good to soft going: blinkered third outing: races prominently. *B. R. Millman*

HI SPEC (IRE) 6 b.m. Spectrum (IRE) 126 – Queen of Fibres (IRE) 65 (Scenic 128) **55**
[2009 55: p8.6g p8g p8.6g f8g 7g p8m^{3} p9.5g^{3} p9.5g Dec 11] modest performer: stays 8.6f: acts on sand, polytrack and soft ground: wears headgear: has looked reluctant. *Miss M. E. Rowland*

HISTORICAL GIANT (USA) 4 ch.g. Giant's Causeway (USA) 132 – Onima (USA) **51**
(Jade Hunter (USA)) [2009 47: p10g p12g^{5} Feb 7] big, strong gelding: modest maiden, lightly raced: stays 1½m: acts on polytrack: signs of temperament. *E. F. Vaughan*

HISTORY LESSON 3 ch.c. Golan (IRE) 129 – Once Upon A Time 77 (Teenoso **93**
(USA) 135) [2009 85p: 9.7m* 10.1g^{4} 12f^{4} 11.6m* 12m 10m 10d^{2} 10.3g^{3} Oct 23] close-coupled colt: fairly useful performer: won maiden at Folkestone in April and handicap at Windsor in July: stays 11.6f: acts on polytrack, good to firm and good to soft going: often makes running: sold 22,000 gns, joined A. Jones. *R. Hannon*

HITCHENS (IRE) 4 b.g. Acclamation 118 – Royal Fizz (IRE) (Royal Academy **110**
(USA) 130) [2009 110: 6f* 6m 5m^{6} 5g 5d 6d 6m^{6} 6m 6m* 6g^{3} 6g^{5} Oct 23] good-topped gelding: useful performer: won minor event at Thirsk (by 3 lengths from Knot In Wood) in April and handicap at Haydock (beat Prohibit by short head) in September: best form at 6f: acts on polytrack and firm going. *T. D. Barron*

HITCHES DUBAI (BRZ) 4 ch.g. A Good Reason (BRZ) – Orquidea Vermelha (BRZ) (Lucence (USA)) [2009 –: 6g^4 5m* 6f Aug 8] fair form only when winning maiden at Beverley in July: best effort at 5f: raced on good going or firmer. *D. Nicholls* **73**

HITS ONLY CASH 7 b.g. Inchinor 119 – Persian Blue 64 (Persian Bold 123) [2009 73: p8.6g^3 8g^4 8.1g^2 p8.6g p8.6g p8g* p9.5g^6 8s^6 p8.6g p9.5g* p10m p9.5g Oct 17] close-coupled gelding: fair handicapper: won at Kempton in August and Wolverhampton in September: stays 9.5f: acts on polytrack, probably on good to firm ground: tried blinkered, usually in cheekpieces: held up. *J. Pearce* **70**

HITS ONLY JUDE (IRE) 6 gr.g. Bold Fact (USA) 116 – Grey Goddess 117 (Godswalk (USA) 130) [2009 84, a90: f7g^2 6g f6g^2 f6g^2 6d^4 5g^4 6m 6s f7g^2 p7.1g f8m^4 Dec 15] sturdy, close-coupled gelding: fairly useful handicapper on all-weather, fair on turf: stays 1m: acts on all-weather (best recent efforts on fibresand), soft and good to firm going: tried blinkered/visored. *D. Carroll* **71** **a84**

HITS ONLY TIME 4 ch.g. Bertolini (USA) 125 – South Wind 62 (Tina's Pet 121) [2009 54: 6m 12.1m 9.9m Jul 14] strong gelding: maiden: well held in 2009. *D. Carroll* **–**

HITS ONLY VIC (USA) 5 b.g. Lemon Drop Kid (USA) 131 – Royal Family (USA) (Private Terms (USA)) [2009 100: 16.2g* 16.1d 14m* 14m^3 14v Sep 5] workmanlike gelding: smart handicapper: further progress in 2009, winning at Haydock in May and York (listed event, beat Warringah by short head) in July: better still when length third to Sesenta in Ebor at York: stays 2m: unraced on firm ground, acts on any other: waited with: a credit to connections. *D. Carroll* **110**

HIT THE SWITCH 3 b.g. Reset (AUS) 124 – Scenic Venture (IRE) (Desert King (IRE) 129) [2009 70: f6d^4 p7g 8s 6.1g 6v 7.1m^6 9.9g 10.3g 12g 14v f6g f8f* p8g^5 f7g^3 f8g* f8g^6 Dec 27] good-bodied gelding: fair handicapper: won at Southwell in November/December: effective at 6f to 1m: acts on fibresand and heavy going: tried in cheekpieces. *Pat Morris* **68**

HOBBY 4 b.f. Robellino (USA) 127 – Wydah (Suave Dancer (USA) 136) [2009 100: 12m^2 10.9d^5 14m Jul 11] close-coupled filly: just fairly useful performer at best in 2009: stayed 1½m: acted on firm and soft going: tried in cheekpieces: raced prominently: stud. *R. M. Beckett* **93**

HOBOOB (USA) 3 ch.f. Seeking The Gold (USA) – Bint Salsabil (USA) 110 (Nashwan (USA) 135) [2009 54p: 10m Apr 24] good-bodied filly: modest form in maidens: sold 25,000 gns in December. *J. L. Dunlop* **59**

HOBSON 4 b.g. Choisir (AUS) 126 – Educating Rita 64 (Emarati (USA) 74) [2009 74: 7g* 8.1g^4 7f^3 7g^2 7f^2 6m^5 7g^5 7g^5 7m* 8m^5 7d^6 Oct 6] fairly useful handicapper: won at Yarmouth in April and Leicester in September: free-going sort, stays 7f: acts on polytrack, firm and good to soft going: tried blinkered: often makes running. *Eve Johnson Houghton* **80**

HOGMANEIGH (IRE) 6 b.g. Namid 128 – Magical Peace (IRE) 80 (Magical Wonder (USA) 125) [2009 112: p6g^2 5m 5v^6 5g 6m 6m 6g Oct 10] strong, close-coupled gelding: smart performer: good neck second to Eisteddfod in minor event at Kempton on reappearance: respectable effort after only when seventh in Ayr Gold Cup sixth outing (first start after leaving S. C. Williams): effective at 5f/6f: raced mainly on good ground or softer (acts on heavy): held up. *J. S. Goldie* **110**

HOH HOH HOH 7 ch.g. Piccolo 121 – Nesting 47 (Thatching 131) [2009 110: p6g 6m 5.1m* 5m^2 5g^3 5m 5.1m^3 6.1g^6 5m 5m Sep 26] good-topped gelding: smart performer: won minor event at Nottingham in April: back to very best when placed next 2 outings, in Palace House Stakes at Newmarket (2½ lengths second to Amour Propre) and listed event at Haydock (close third behind Ialysos): below form after: best at 5f nowadays: acts on firm and good to soft going: often slowly away. *R. J. Price* **114**

HOHROD 3 ch.g. Tipsy Creek (USA) 115 – Agara (Young Ern 120) [2009 f6g 6d 8.3g f8g Dec 18] little sign of ability in maidens/handicap. *John A. Harris* **–**

HOLBECK GHYLL (IRE) 7 ch.g. Titus Livius (FR) 115 – Crimada (IRE) (Mukaddamah (USA) 125) [2009 97: 5.2s Apr 17] good-topped gelding: useful handicapper: well below form sole outing in 2009 (blindfold still on when stall opened): best at 5f/6f: acts on polytrack and firm going: tried blinkered, sometimes wears cheekpieces. *A. M. Balding* **–**

HOLBERG (UAE) 3 b.c. Halling (USA) 133 – Sweet Willa (USA) (Assert 134) [2009 87p: 11.8f* 11.1g^3 16f* Jun 19] leggy colt: smart performer: much improved in 2009, **117**

Queen's Vase, Royal Ascot—
a fifth win in nine years in this race for trainer Mark Johnston as Holberg relishes the step up in trip; Yankee Doodle (right), subsequent St Leger winner Mastery (left) and Tactic (striped cap) come next

winning 3-runner handicap at Leicester in April and Queen's Vase at Royal Ascot (beat Yankee Doodle 4 lengths, surging clear): well suited by 2m: acts on all-weather, firm and good to soft going: reported in July to have sustained an injury, then joined Godolphin. *M. Johnston*

HOLDEN EAGLE 4 b.c. Catcher In The Rye (IRE) 115 – Bird of Prey (IRE) 69 (Last Tycoon 131) [2009 83: 10s 10.2g³ 12g 12m 10.9g³ 12m⁵ p12g⁵ Oct 21] big colt: fairly useful maiden handicapper: barely stays 1½m: acts on good to firm and good to soft ground: races freely held up. *A. G. Newcombe* **83**

HOLD FIRE 5 b.m. Lear Spear (USA) 124 – Kahyasi Moll (IRE) 35 (Brief Truce (USA) 126) [2009 –: 8.1g 10m 10g Jun 22] no solid form: tried blinkered. *A. W. Carroll* **–**

HOLD ME 2 ch.f. (Apr 9) Hold That Tiger (USA) 117 – Sultry Lass (USA) (Private Account (USA)) [2009 p8.6g⁶ 7m Oct 6] half-sister to several minor winners in USA: dam, US 8.5f winner, half-sister to Musidora Stakes winner Cassis and to dam of Breeders' Cup Juvenile Fillies winner Storm Song: easily better effort in maidens when sixth to Sejanus at Wolverhampton: sold 3,000 gns. *H. R. A. Cecil* **56**

HOLD ON TIGER (IRE) 2 ch.c. (Mar 5) Acclamation 118 – Our Juliette (IRE) (Namid 128) [2009 6m 5.9m² 6d* 6m⁵ 5g⁶ Oct 17] €20,000Y, £16,000 2-y-o: first foal: dam unraced half-sister to smart performer up to 1¾m Salsalino: fair performer: won maiden at Ayr in August: stays 6f: acts on good to firm and good to soft going. *I. Semple* **73**

HOLD THE BUCKS (USA) 3 b.g. Hold That Tiger (USA) 117 – Buck's Lady (USA) (Alleged (USA) 138) [2009 72: p8.6g* p8g³ p8.6g⁴ p8g² p8.6g² p8g⁴ p10g 10g⁴ p8g* 9.9g⁵ p8g p10g³ Oct 2] workmanlike gelding: fair performer: won claimers at Wolverhampton in January and Kempton in April: stays 1¼m: acts on polytrack and good to soft going: sometimes in cheekpieces: probably not straightforward (tends to race lazily), but is consistent. *J. S. Moore* **72**

HOLD THE STAR 3 b.f. Red Ransom (USA) – Sydney Star 91 (Machiavellian (USA) 123) [2009 55p: 9.7d p9.5g p7.1g² 7g 8f p8.6m⁶ p12.2g f7m p7.1g⁴ p8.6g p7.1g⁴ p8.6g⁶ Dec 28] rangy filly: has scope: fair maiden: left E. Vaughan £1,200 after seventh outing: best up to 1m: acts on polytrack: tried blinkered/visored: held up. *Miss A. Stokell* **66**

HOLD YOUR COLOUR (IRE) 2 br. or gr.g. (Mar 25) Verglas (IRE) 118 – Azia (IRE) 71 (Desert Story (IRE) 115) [2009 6m^6 6m* 6g* Aug 31] €38,000F, £30,000Y: good-bodied gelding: second foal: brother to 3-y-o Taste The Wine: dam, Irish 2-y-o 7f winner, stayed 1½m: progressive form: off 3 months (gelded), won sales race (by 4 lengths from Exceedingly Bold) and listed event (beat Skylla by length) at Ripon in August: will be well suited by 7f+: joined A. Millard in Hong Kong, where renamed Supreme Fay Fay: already useful, and capable of better still. *B. J. Meehan* **100 p**

HOLIDAY COCKTAIL 7 b.g. Mister Baileys 123 – Bermuda Lily 78 (Dunbeath (USA) 127) [2009 84: 12s 10.4g Oct 9] quite good-topped gelding: handicapper: well below form both starts on Flat in 2009: tried visored/tongue tied, effective with/without cheekpieces: fair hurdler. *J. J. Quinn* **–**

HOLKHAM 2 ch.g. (Apr 2) Beat Hollow 126 – Spring Sixpence 60 (Dowsing (USA) 124) [2009 6g^5 7g p6g^5 Sep 17] little form. *N. P. Littmoden* **–**

HOLLINS 5 b.g. Lost Soldier (USA) 103 – Cutting Reef (IRE) 105 (Kris 135) [2009 72: 10d* 10g^4 10s 12g Oct 10] has round action: fairly useful handicapper: easily best effort when winning at Pontefract in July: stays 13.8f: acts on good to soft going: won over hurdles in December. *Micky Hammond* **82**

HOLLOW GREEN (IRE) 3 b.f. Beat Hollow 126 – Three Greens (Niniski (USA) 125) [2009 65: 10m* 12m 12.1g 11.6d* 10m^6 11.6m* 11.6m^2 10m^5 10g* 11.6g* 10m^6 10s* 10.3m^3 12m^4 10g 10.3g 12g 10.3s Nov 7] angular filly: improved into a fairly useful performer: won claimers (2) and handicap at Windsor in May/June, then handicaps at Ffos Las and Windsor in July, and Ayr in August: stays 1½m: unraced on firm going, acts on any other turf: tried visored: patiently ridden. *P. D. Evans* **90**

HOLLOW JO 9 b.g. Most Welcome 131 – Sir Hollow (USA) (Sir Ivor (USA) 135) [2009 –, a75: p6g* p7g p6g^6 p5g* p5g^3 p6g* p6g p6g 6f p6g^4 p6m^4 f6g^5 f5g^4 p6g^2 Dec 31] strong, lengthy gelding: fair handicapper: won at Kempton (2) and Lingfield in January/February: best at 5f/6f: acts on all-weather, little recent form on turf: tried tongue tied/in cheekpieces, usually visored nowadays. *J. R. Jenkins* **–** **a69**

HOLLYWOOD GEORGE 5 b.g. Royal Applause 124 – Aunt Tate (Tate Gallery (USA) 117) [2009 56: p8g Jan 11] modest performer at 4 yrs: well held sole outing in 2009 (gelded after): wears cheekpieces (tried blinkered). *Miss M. E. Rowland* **–**

HOLOKO HEIGHTS 4 br.g. Pivotal 124 – Treble Heights (IRE) 107 (Unfuwain (USA) 131) [2009 p8g p7.1g p7g 10.9m^4 p12g^3 12.4s^3 15m* Jun 3] fair performer: in cheekpieces, won handicap at Ayr in June: will stay 2m: acts on polytrack, soft and good to firm ground: no easy ride: joined Tim Vaughan, won novice hurdle in November. *N. J. Vaughan* **71**

HOLYFIELD WARRIOR (IRE) 5 b.g. Princely Heir (IRE) 111 – Perugino Lady (IRE) 75 (Perugino (USA) 84) [2009 61: p8g* p9.5g^2 f12g^3 Dec 22] fair handicapper: returned from long absence to win at Lingfield in November: stays 9.5f: acts on polytrack: tried in cheekpieces. *R. J. Smith* **66**

HOLYROOD 3 b.g. Falbrav (IRE) 133 – White Palace 80 (Shirley Heights 130) [2009 78p: 10.1d* 10d^3 12.5g 12g Aug 8] big, lengthy gelding: fairly useful performer: won maiden at Yarmouth in April: stays 1¼m: raced only on good/good to soft ground: tried visored: sold 17,000 gns in October. *Sir Michael Stoute* **87**

HOME 4 b.g. Domedriver (IRE) 128 – Swahili (IRE) 76 (Kendor (FR) 122) [2009 70§: p12g p13.9g^2 p13g^6 p16g^5 14.1m p16g p13.9g^3 Dec 14] small, close-coupled gelding: modest handicapper: barely stays easy 2m: acts on all-weather, unraced on extremes of going on turf: has worn cheekpieces, visored final start: tongue tied last 4 outings. *C. Gordon* **63**

HOME ADVANTAGE 2 b.c. (May 11) Beat Hollow 126 – Houseproud (USA) 115 (Riverman (USA) 131) [2009 8.3d Oct 15] sturdy colt: closely related to fairly useful 11.5f winner Ballet Suite (by Sadler's Wells) and half-brother to 2 winners, including useful 6.5f to 7.5f (including at 2 yrs and in US) winner Imperial President (by Known Fact): dam French 5.5f (at 2 yrs) and 1m (Poule d'Essai des Pouliches) winner: 12/1, very green when down the field in maiden at Nottingham: bred to stay 1¼m: capable of better. *R. Charlton* **– p**

HOME BEFORE DARK 3 b.g. Bertolini (USA) 125 – Compton Girl (Compton Place 125) [2009 44: 7.1m 6v 7m^6 10m Sep 23] workmanlike gelding: maiden, no form at 3 yrs. *R. M. Whitaker* **–**

HOMEBRED STAR 8 ch.g. Safawan 118 – Celtic Chimes (Celtic Cone 116) [2009 p12g p10g^4 10m 11.5m Sep 15] poor performer: missed 2008: stays 1¼m: acts on polytrack: has worn cheekpieces/blinkers. *G. P. Enright* **46**

HONEST BROKER (IRE) 2 b.c. (May 17) Trade Fair 124 – Kashra (IRE) 95 (Dancing Dissident (USA) 119) [2009 6g^4 7g 7.2v^3 p7.1g^4 f8f^3 Dec 12] good-topped colt: modest maiden: in frame in nurseries last 2 starts: stays 1m: acts on all-weather and heavy going. *M. Johnston* **63**

HONEST QUALITY (USA) 3 b.f. Elusive Quality (USA) – Honest Lady (USA) 119 (Seattle Slew (USA)) [2009 105: 8m^6 7.1g Jun 25] smallish, sturdy filly: well below form both starts at 3 yrs: stayed 7f: acted on good to firm going: visits Dansili. *H. R. A. Cecil* **–**

HONEST VALUE (IRE) 4 b.g. Chevalier (IRE) 115 – Sensimelia (IRE) 68 (Inzar (USA) 112) [2009 57: p5.1g* Jan 29] workmanlike gelding: modest performer: visored, won apprentice minor event at Wolverhampton sole outing at 4 yrs: effective at 5f/6f: acts on polytrack and firm ground: tried in cheekpieces: often finds little. *Mrs L. C. Jewell* **52**

HONEY BERRY (IRE) 3 ch.f. Captain Rio 122 – Daggers At Dawn (IRE) (Daggers Drawn (USA) 114) [2009 p6g^6 p5g 6m 5g^6 6m^6 6m^6 Jul 1] €15,500F, 7,500Y: strong, lengthy filly: first foal: dam unraced out of half-sister to high-class miler Second Set: poor maiden: stays 6f: visored last 3 starts. *Pat Morris* **45**

HONIMIERE (IRE) 3 b.f. Fasliyev (USA) 120 – Sugar (Hernando (FR) 127) [2009 73p: 8m^4 7g^4 9.3m* 8d^3 9.9g* 9.9m* 8.3s^4 9.9f^2 10m* 10m Oct 16] good-topped filly: improved into a useful performer: successful in handicaps at Carlisle in June, Beverley (2) in July and Newmarket (beat Pachattack 2½ lengths, making all) in September: gone in coat, below form in listed race on last-named course final outing: stays 1¼m: acts on firm and soft going: has awkward head carriage, but seems genuine: usually races prominently. *G. A. Swinbank* **99**

HONKEY TONK TONY (IRE) 4 b.c. On The Ridge (IRE) 115 – Lisa's Girl (IRE) (Distinctly North (USA) 115) [2009 –: p9.5g p12g p7g Oct 29] medium-sized colt: little form: tried blinkered/in cheekpieces. *Luke Comer, Ireland* **–**

HONORABLE ENDEAVOR 3 b.g. Law Society (USA) 130 – Lilac Dance (Fabulous Dancer (USA) 124) [2009 53+: p8.6g^2 p10g 14.1s^4 15.4m^2 14.1g p16m^2 p12g^4 p16.5g^5 f14m Dec 5] fair maiden handicapper: stays 2m: acts on polytrack, soft and good to firm going: visored/in cheekpieces nowadays: not one to trust. *E. F. Vaughan* **66 §**

HONOR IN PEACE (USA) 2 b.c. (Mar 21) Peace Rules (USA) 124 – Jeanne's Honor (USA) (Honour And Glory (USA) 122) [2009 p4.5f^3 a5f* 7m a6s^4 p7f^6 5f a6f* Nov 19] $62,000Y: good-bodied colt: first foal: dam, Canadian 6.5f winner, out of US Grade 1 8.5f winner Jeanne Jones: fairly useful performer: won maiden in May (by 5 lengths) and claimer in November (by 8¼ lengths), both at Churchill Downs: shaped as if amiss in listed Chesham Stakes at Royal Ascot third outing (reportedly had a temperature about 2 weeks before): stays 6f: acts on dirt: blinkered first 3 starts, also tongue tied at Royal Ascot. *Wesley A. Ward, USA* **92**

HONOURED (IRE) 2 ch.g. (Feb 11) Mark of Esteem (IRE) 137 – Traou Mad (IRE) 107 (Barathea (IRE) 127) [2009 p7.1g f7g p8g Nov 25] well held in maidens. *Sir Mark Prescott* **–**

HONOURS STRIDE (IRE) 3 b.f. Red Ransom (USA) – Dance Parade (USA) 107 (Gone West (USA)) [2009 72: 9.9m^2 10.3m* Jun 14] tall filly: fairly useful and progressive form: won handicap at Doncaster in June by short head from Nice Time: would have been suited by 1½m: stud. *Sir Michael Stoute* **81**

HOOF IT 2 b.g. (Mar 28) Monsieur Bond (IRE) 120 – Forever Bond (Danetime (IRE) 121) [2009 6m^4 7g^4 6m* Aug 5] 6,000F, £14,000Y: big, strong gelding: third foal: brother to 3-y-o Forever's Girl and half-brother to 4-y-o Chosen Forever: dam unraced half-sister to smart sprinter Ratio: fair form: won maiden at Newcastle by 1½ lengths from Blue Avon, idling: will be as effective at 5f as 6f. *M. W. Easterby* **72**

HOOLIGAN SEAN 2 ch.g. (Apr 26) Ishiguru (USA) 114 – Sheesha (USA) (Shadeed (USA) 135) [2009 6d^6 7f^2 Sep 7] 5,000F, £23,000Y: rather leggy gelding: brother to 3-y-o Shangani and half-brother to 3 winners by Aragon, including 7-y-o Seamus Shindig and fairly useful 7f winner Shebeen: dam once-raced close relative to smart stayer Samraan: much better effort in maidens when ½-length second to Diam Queen (pair clear) at Folkestone. *H. Candy* **79**

HOPEFUL LADY 3 b.f. Elmaamul (USA) 125 – Tennessee Star (Teenoso (USA) 135) [2009 8g 7.5m^4 7g 9.9m 7m Sep 15] first foal: dam unraced: no form. *I. W. McInnes* **–**

HOPE'N'REASON (USA) 2 b. or br.f. (Feb 5) Stormy Atlantic (USA) – La Bataille (USA) (Out of Place (USA)) [2009 p6m 5g Aug 6] 9,000Y: stocky filly: first foal: dam, placed at 1m in US on only start, out of US Grade 1 2-y-o 7f winner Contredance: well held in maidens at Lingfield and Sandown. *D. M. Simcock* –

HORATIO CARTER 4 b.g. Bahamian Bounty 116 – Jitterbug (IRE) (Marju (IRE) 127) [2009 87: 7m* 7d² 7g³ 7f 7d* 7m 8g 6d 6m Sep 19] strong, good-topped gelding: useful handicapper: further progress in 2009, winning at Thirsk in May and Newcastle (beat Osteopathic Remedy by short head) in June: good efforts otherwise when placed at Newcastle and Catterick: best efforts at 7f: acts on soft going: usually wears cheekpieces: races prominently. *K. A. Ryan* 99

HORSEFORD HILL 5 b.g. In The Wings 128 – Love of Silver (USA) 110 (Arctic Tern (USA) 126) [2009 93: 18m Oct 17] tall gelding: fairly useful handicapper in 2008: won over hurdles in April/May for N. Henderson: well held in Cesarewitch sole outing on Flat in 2009 (blinkered): stays 15f: acts on polytrack, good to firm and good to soft going. *Miss J. R. Tooth* –

HORSERADISH 2 b.g. (Mar 21) Kyllachy 129 – Lihou Island 89 (Beveled (USA)) [2009 6g² f6g² 6.1d* Oct 15] 12,000Y: attractive gelding: third foal: dam 2-y-o 6f winner: fair form: landed odds in maiden at Nottingham by 1½ lengths from Silk Street, pushed clear at halfway: subsequently gelded: raced only at 6f. *M. L. W. Bell* 78

HORSESHOE REEF (AUS) 6 b.g. Encosta de Lago (AUS) – Christies Beach (AUS) (Naturalism (NZ)) [2009 p10g² p12g p13.9g⁵ f11g³ 11.6m p10g 11m³ 12g Jul 21] won handicap at Sandown (Australia) early in 2008: third 3 of 5 other starts that year, leaving M. Price after final outing: best effort in similar events in Britain on first outing: stays 15.5f: acts on polytrack, soft and good to firm ground: tried in cheekpieces: modest form on hurdling debut for G. L. Moore, joined Jamie Snowden after. *J. R. Gask* 82

HORSLEY WARRIOR 3 b.c. Alhaarth (IRE) 126 – Polish Lake (Polish Precedent (USA) 131) [2009 72p: 10m f11g² 12m p12.2g Jun 29] strong colt: fair maiden: stays 11f. *E. S. McMahon* 69

HOSANNA 3 b.f. Oasis Dream 129 – Rada's Daughter 107 (Robellino (USA) 127) [2009 71: 8g 6g 6s 7.1g⁶ 5m 5m 5m² Oct 1] sturdy filly: maiden, just modest at 3 yrs: best at 5f/6f: acts on polytrack and good to firm going: tried blinkered. *J. Barclay* 53

HOSS CARTWRIGHT (IRE) 2 b.g. (Apr 1) High Chaparral (IRE) 132 – Her Grace (IRE) (Spectrum (IRE) 126) [2009 7m⁴ 7d² 7s* Aug 9] €25,000Y: first foal: dam unraced half-sister to Irish Oaks winner Vintage Tipple: fair form in maidens: second to Bahamian Music (pair clear, best effort) at Newcastle then won at Leicester by neck from King's Parade, dictating: will be suited by 1m+. *J. Howard Johnson* 76

HOT CHILLI 2 gr.f. (Feb 25) Verglas (IRE) 118 – Hot And Spicy 75 (Grand Lodge (USA) 125) [2009 p7m Sep 30] first foal: dam, Irish maiden (stayed 1¼m), half-sister to Oaks d'Italia winner Zanzibar: 33/1, behind in maiden at Kempton. *J. R. Fanshawe* –

HOT DIAMOND 5 b.g. Desert Prince (IRE) 130 – Panna 106 (Polish Precedent (USA) 131) [2009 86: 12g Jun 6] sturdy gelding: handicapper: very lightly raced on Flat in recent seasons, and well held sole outing in 2009: will stay 2m: acts on good to firm and good to soft ground: held up (usually slowly away): fairly useful hurdler, good third in valuable event in May. *P. J. Hobbs* –

HOT FORM 2 b.f. (Mar 19) Dr Fong (USA) 128 – Hot Tin Roof (IRE) 112 (Thatching 131) [2009 p6g⁶ Oct 20] fifth foal: half-sister to Irish 7f winner Maggie The Cat (by Fasliyev): dam 6f/7f winner: 12/1, 9½ lengths sixth to Oil Strike in maiden at Lingfield: bred to stay 7f: sold 800 gns. *M. Botti* –

HOTGROVE BOY 2 b.g. (Mar 11) Tobougg (IRE) 125 – Tanwir 76 (Unfuwain (USA) 131) [2009 7.1s⁶ 8g 8d Oct 13] no form. *A. G. Foster* –

HOTHAM 6 b.g. Komaite (USA) – Malcesine (IRE) 46 (Auction Ring (USA) 123) [2009 94: 5m 6m 5v 5m 6g 6d 5g³ 6g² 6g⁴ 5g* 5s⁵ 5d² 6d⁵ 6g* 6m² 6m 5g² 5g* 6g⁴ Oct 23] lengthy, quite attractive gelding: useful handicapper: won at Pontefract in July, Redcar in September and Pontefract in October: good fourth at Doncaster final outing: effective at 5f/6f: acts on polytrack and any turf going. *N. Wilson* 97

HOT PROSPECT 2 b.c. (Mar 12) Motivator 131 – Model Queen (USA) 76 (Kingmambo (USA) 125) [2009 7g² 8.1m* 8g⁶ Oct 19] 230,000Y: well-made colt: fifth foal: closely related to useful French 10.5f/1½m winner Mount Helicon (by Montjeu) who stayed 15f and half-brother to 2 winners, including 5-y-o Regal Parade: dam, 7.5f winner, out of half-sister to dam of Zafonic: second to Vale of York in maiden at York before 102 p winning similar event at Sandown in September by 2 lengths from Morana, making all: worked up in preliminaries, pulled hard when only sixth in listed event at Pontefract: bred to stay 1¼m+: already useful, and remains capable of better still. *M. A. Jarvis*

HOT PURSUITS 2 br.f. (Jan 29) Pastoral Pursuits 127 – Perfect Partner (Be My Chief (USA) 122) [2009 6g p6g^3 p6g^3 7m 5g* Oct 19] 7,000F, £500Y: close-coupled filly: fifth foal: half-sister to 6f seller winner Molly Dancer (by Emarati) and a winner abroad by Medicean: dam unraced half-sister to smart sprinter Funfair Wane: fair performer: won maiden at Windsor: likely to prove best at 5f/6f: acts on polytrack, best turf effort on good ground. *H. Morrison* **78**

HOT ROD MAMMA (IRE) 2 ch.f. (Feb 3) Traditionally (USA) 117 – Try The Air (IRE) (Foxhound (USA) 103) [2009 6g 5.1m^5 5g^6 5g^4 6m 6v^3 f5m Nov 11] second foal: dam, little form, half-sister to high-class 1¼m/1½m performer Storming Home: poor maiden: raced only at 5f/6f: signs of temperament. *A. Berry* **49**

HOT SPARK 2 b.c. (May 9) Firebreak 125 – On The Brink 88 (Mind Games 121) [2009 6d^6 p6g^2 Oct 3] £13,000Y: third foal: half-brother to 3-y-o Dubai Crest: dam, 2-y-o 5f winner, half-sister to useful sprinters Eastern Romance, Blue Tomato and Sea Hunter: much better effort in maidens (fair form) when 3¼ lengths second to Never The Waiter at Wolverhampton, good speed. *K. A. Ryan* **76 +**

HOUDA (IRE) 2 ch.f. (Feb 28) Trans Island 119 – Islandagore (IRE) 97 (Indian Ridge 123) [2009 6f p7g Aug 14] 17,000F, £15,000Y: angular filly: fifth foal: sister to 3-y-o Island Sunset and half-sister to 3 winners, including 7f (at 2 yrs)/1m winner Right Ted (by Mujadil): dam Irish 7f winner from 2 starts (stayed 9f): down the field in maidens at Windsor (poor form) and Kempton (failed to settle). *J. G. Portman* **46**

HOUDELLA 3 b.f. Josr Algarhoud (IRE) 118 – Norbella (Nordico (USA)) [2009 –: 8.1g 6g May 19] well held in maidens. *B. W. Hills* **–**

HOUNDS DITCH 2 b.g. (Mar 30) Avonbridge 123 – Pudding Lane (IRE) 64 (College Chapel 122) [2009 5m^4 f6g Sep 29] better effort in maidens when 3¼ lengths fourth to Morgans Choice at Ffos Las: still green next time (gelded after). *Eve Johnson Houghton* **59**

HOURI (IRE) 4 b.f. Alhaarth (IRE) 126 – Witching Hour (IRE) 88 (Alzao (USA) 117) [2009 79: 10f 10.2m 10m 12.1m^5 10g Oct 16] sturdy filly: handicapper, just modest form at 4 yrs: should stay 1½m: acts on good to firm ground: usually wears headgear: tried tongue tied. *J. T. Stimpson* **50**

HOUSE OF FRILLS 2 b.f. (Mar 15) Paris House 123 – Frilly Front 82 (Aragon 118) [2009 5m* 5m^3 Jul 3] third foal: dam 5f winner, including at 2 yrs: won seller at Redcar in April: good third to Bould Mover in minor event at Beverley: likely to be best at 5f/6f. *T. D. Barron* **69 +**

HOUSE OF RULES 2 b.g. (Apr 30) Forzando 122 – Bramble Bear 72 (Beveled (USA)) [2009 6m^6 f6g 6g^6 Oct 19] compact gelding: easily best effort in maidens when sixth to Distinctive at Redcar on debut: raced only at 6f. *Julie Camacho* **59**

HOUSE POINT 2 b.f. (Mar 10) Pivotal 124 – Lighthouse 92 (Warning 136) [2009 6m Oct 16] 52,000Y: sturdy filly: has round action: sixth foal: sister to 3-y-o Point of Light and half-sister to 3 winners, including 2004 2-y-o 5f winner All For Laura (by Cadeaux Genereux), now dam of 2-y-o Misheer: dam, 1m winner, half-sister to Middle Park Stakes winner First Trump: 66/1, eighth in maiden at Newmarket, considerately handled: will stay 7f+: capable of better. *S. C. Williams* **59 p**

HOUSE RED (IRE) 2 b.g. (Apr 11) Antonius Pius (USA) 123§ – Cindy's Star (IRE) 68 (Dancing Dissident (USA) 119) [2009 5m 6m^5 6g 6m^6 7m* p8.6g^3 Nov 12] €22,000F, €50,000Y: neat gelding: half-brother to several winners, including fairly useful Irish 2000 2-y-o 7f winner Ducky Divey (by Elbio), later successful in Hong Kong, and 1m winner Faith Healer (by Key of Luck): dam 1m winner: fair performer: won nursery at Leicester in October: stays 8.6f: acts on polytrack and good to firm going. *B. W. Hills* **72**

HOVERING HAWK (IRE) 2 b.f. (Mar 10) Hawk Wing (USA) 136 – Cause Celebre (IRE) 80 (Peintre Celebre (USA) 137) [2009 p7.1g p7m Dec 10] second foal: dam, won around 1¼m/11f, out of half-sister to top-class French miler Bellypha: well held in maidens: bred to be suited by 1m+. *B. W. Hills* **–**

HOWARD 3 ch.c. Haafhd 129 – Dolores 111 (Danehill (USA) 126) [2009 74p: 10m 10m 8.3m^4 7g^5 Jun 16] strong, compact colt: fair maiden: should stay 1¼m: temperament under suspicion (looked moody in cheekpieces final start). *J. L. Dunlop* **74**

HOWARDS PRINCE 6 gr.g. Bertolini (USA) 125 – Grey Princess (IRE) 92 (Common Grounds 118) [2009 43: 5m 5f 5m 5g 5d⁶ 5s 5g Sep 21] close-coupled gelding: no form in 2009: has worn cheekpieces/blinkers: tried tongue tied. *D. A. Nolan* –

HOWARDS TIPPLE 5 b.g. Diktat 126 – Grey Princess (IRE) 92 (Common Grounds 118) [2009 69: 6g 5m² 5g⁴ 6m⁵ 6m 6g 5f 5s⁴ 5g Sep 21] modest performer nowadays: best at stiff 5f/6f: acts on polytrack and any turf going: usually wears visor/cheekpieces: none too consistent. *I. Semple* 60

HOWARDS WAY 4 b.g. Bertolini (USA) 125 – Love Quest (Pursuit of Love 124) [2009 59: 5d Sep 7] modest maiden, lightly raced: well held sole start at 4 yrs: should be suited by 7f: acts on good to firm going. *D. A. Nolan* –

HOWDIGO 4 b.g. Tobougg (IRE) 125 – Woodrising 64 (Nomination 125) [2009 97: 10m 15m³ 9m p12m² 12d Oct 24] rather leggy gelding: fairly useful handicapper: best effort at 4 yrs when second at Kempton: effective at 1½m to 15f: acts on polytrack, soft and good to firm going: sold 55,000 gns, later won at 1½m in Bahrain. *J. R. Best* 94

HOWDOYALIKEMENOW (IRE) 2 ch.f. (Feb 6) Captain Rio 122 – Berenice (ITY) (Marouble 116) [2009 6m 7g 6d 7.1m Sep 14] lengthy filly: half-sister to several winners, including Irish 6f winner (including at 2 yrs) Berenica (by College Chapel) and 6f (in Ireland at 2 yrs) to 11f (in Italy) winner The Bomber Liston (by Perugino), both useful: dam unraced: no form: blinkered (none too keen) last 2 starts. *K. A. Ryan* –

HOW MANY TIMES (IRE) 4 b.f. Okawango (USA) 115 – Blu Tu Miami (USA) (Robin Des Pins (USA) 119) [2009 68: p8g Mar 16] ex-Irish maiden, lightly raced: well held sole outing in 2009: usually in cheekpieces. *J. R. Gask* –

HOW'S SHE CUTTIN' (IRE) 6 ch.m. Shinko Forest (IRE) – Magic Annemarie (IRE) 75 (Dancing Dissident (USA) 119) [2009 99: f5s³ Jan 1] good-topped mare: useful handicapper in 2008: not discredited only outing in 2009: speedy, was effective at 5f/6f: acted on fibresand and any turf going: often blinkered/visored: probably not straightforward, but was consistent: covered by Teofilio in spring. *T. D. Barron* 93

HUBBLE SPACE 2 ch.f. (Apr 25) Observatory (USA) 131 – Double Stake (USA) (Kokand (USA)) [2009 p7g⁶ p8m p8.6g⁴ p8.6g Dec 17] sixth foal: half-sister to 4-y-o Avertis and 1m winner Miss Marauder (by Mujahid): dam US 6f to 9f minor stakes winner: modest maiden: stays 8.6f: raced only on polytrack. *M. Botti* 54

HUCK FINN (NZ) 9 b.g. Foxbay (NZ) – Reckless Spirit (NZ) (Straight Strike (USA)) [2009 p10g p16g⁶ p12g Feb 7] 1m winner in New Zealand earlier in career: of little account over jumps nowadays: modest form in handicaps on Flat: tried in cheekpieces. *M. Madgwick* 52

HUCKING HEAT (IRE) 5 b.g. Desert Sun 120 – Vltava (IRE) 73 (Sri Pekan (USA) 117) [2009 68, a88: p9.5g⁶ f12g³ p9.5g⁴ p9.5g 10.4g⁴ 10.2m⁶ p12.2g 9.9m⁵ 10.4g⁵ p8.6g⁶ p9.5g⁵ p9.5g⁴ Dec 4] sturdy gelding: just fair handicapper at 5 yrs: stays 1½m: acts on all-weather, firm and good to soft going: usually wears headgear: none too consistent. *R. Hollinshead* 76

HUCKING HERO (IRE) 4 b.g. Iron Mask (USA) 117 – Selkirk Flyer (Selkirk (USA) 129) [2009 79: p8g² p10g⁴ p8g a4s⁴ a10s⁶ p10g⁴ p8g⁴ p12g³ 10.1d⁶ p10g⁴ 10m³ 10d⁵ 10.1d⁵ 11.8m⁶ p13.9g* p13g⁶ p12.2g p16g⁵ Nov 25] fair performer: left J. R. Best £7,000 and gelded after twelfth outing: won seller at Wolverhampton in October: barely stays easy 1¾m: acts on polytrack and firm going: tried in headgear: sometimes slowly away: joined Tim Vaughan. *J. R. Boyle* 78

HUDOO 2 ch.f. (Apr 27) Halling (USA) 133 – Zarara (USA) (Manila (USA)) [2009 p7.1g* Oct 30] 90,000Y: sixth foal: closely related to very smart 1¼m (at 2 yrs) to 1¾m winner All The Good (by Diesis) and half-sister to winner in Italy by Daylami: dam unraced half-sister to Oaks winner Ramruma: 9/4, promising when winning maiden at Wolverhampton by head from Madame Excelerate, green and getting up close home: will be suited by 1¼m+: sure to improve. *Saeed bin Suroor* 73 p

HUFF AND PUFF 2 b.c. (Mar 2) Azamour (IRE) 130 – Coyote 91 (Indian Ridge 123) [2009 7g⁵ Oct 30] 70,000Y: attractive colt: fifth foal: half-brother to 3-y-o Oh Goodness Me and useful 1¼m/1½m winner Eradicate (by Montjeu): dam, 1m winner, out of Falmouth/Nassau Stakes winner Caramba: 50/1 and green, 4½ lengths fifth to Quick Wit in maiden at Newmarket, getting behind and awkward when first ridden: will be suited by 1¼m+: sure to improve. *Mrs A. J. Perrett* 74 p

HUGS DESTINY (IRE) 8 b.g. Victory Note (USA) 120 – Embracing 91 (Reference Point 139) [2009 61: 14m May 1] sturdy gelding: modest handicapper in 2008: well held only outing in 2009: stays 1¾m (not 2m): acts on polytrack, firm and good to soft going: tried blinkered/in cheekpieces: tongue tied: usually front runner. *M. A. Barnes* –

HUKBA (IRE) 3 b.f. Anabaa (USA) 130 – Banaadir (USA) 50 (Diesis 133) [2009 89p: 10s^6 9d^2 10.3m^3 a9.5g* 9m^3 10.5g^6 10d Oct 15] useful-looking filly: fairly useful performer: sold from E. Dunlop 25,000 gns after third start: won minor event at Deauville in August: stays 10.5f: acts on all-weather, good to firm and good to soft ground. *F. Vermeulen, France* **81**

HULCOTE ROSE (IRE) 2 b.f. (Feb 21) Rock of Gibraltar (IRE) 133 – Siksikawa (Mark of Esteem (IRE) 137) [2009 7g p6m^3 p6g* Oct 21] €95,000Y: good-topped filly: fourth foal: half-sister to US 8.5f winner Sweet Love (by Barathea): dam, ran once, half-sister to high-class Fanmore (up to 1¼m) and very smart Labeeb (best at 1m/9f): fair performer: won maiden at Kempton by length from Merton Matriarch, again travelling well: bred to stay beyond 6f. *S. Kirk* **70 +**

HUM AGAIN (IRE) 2 b.c. (Feb 6) Marju (IRE) 127 – Kazatzka 62 (Groom Dancer (USA) 128) [2009 7m Aug 13] 66/1, well held in maiden at Salisbury. *J. S. Moore* **–**

HUMBLE OPINION 7 br.g. Singspiel (IRE) 133 – For More (FR) (Sanglamore (USA) 126) [2009 95: p12.2m^3 p12g^4 p10g^4 20m 12g^6 10.3s 10m^5 9.9m^3 10m Sep 18] useful-looking gelding: useful handicapper: good efforts when in frame on all-weather first 3 starts: below form after: stays 1½m: acts on polytrack and firm going: blinkered last 2 outings: fairly useful form over hurdles. *A. King* **95 d**

HUMIDOR (IRE) 2 b.g. (May 1) Camacho 118 – Miss Indigo 62 (Indian Ridge 123) [2009 6g 6d^2 6m^3 Oct 26] 14,000Y: well-made gelding: fifth foal: half-brother to 3 winners, including 3-y-o Keep Dancing and 4-y-o Bluebell Ridge: dam maiden half-sister to useful performer up to 1½m Musetta: fair form when placed in maidens at Windsor and Leicester (again pulled hard): subsequently gelded. *R. Charlton* **78**

HUMOUROUS (IRE) 7 b.g. Darshaan 133 – Amusing Time (IRE) 104 (Sadler's Wells (USA) 132) [2009 14m^6 11.5m 14g Aug 11] well-made gelding: of little account nowadays (including over hurdles): blinkered last 2 outings: tongue tied. *B. Storey* **–**

HUMUNGOUS (IRE) 6 ch.g. Giant's Causeway (USA) 132 – Doula (USA) (Gone West (USA)) [2009 109: 10.3m 10m 9d^5 Jun 18] tall gelding: just fairly useful form in 2009: best at 1m/1¼m: acts on polytrack, firm and good to soft going: usually blinkered/in cheekpieces: held up: moody nowadays, and one to treat with caution. *C. R. Egerton* **89 §**

HUNTDOWN (USA) 3 ch.c. Elusive Quality (USA) – Infinite Spirit (USA) 108 (Maria's Mon (USA) 121) [2009 106: 7g^2 7m^5 7m^2 7m Oct 3] good-bodied colt: smart performer: improved when 1¼ lengths second to Imbongi in Criterion Stakes at Newmarket on reappearance: respectable efforts at best in listed races after: stays 7f: raced only on good/good to firm going. *Saeed bin Suroor* **112**

HUNTERVIEW 3 ch.g. Reset (AUS) 124 – Mount Elbrus 106 (Barathea (IRE) 127) [2009 83p: f8g* 8m^4 7.6m^6 8g^6 p8m^5 10.1m^2 12d* Oct 24] big, lengthy gelding: useful handicapper: won at Southwell in March and Doncaster (beat Hillview Boy 1¾ lengths) in October: stays 1½m: acts on all-weather, heavy and good to firm ground: blinkered last 3 starts: joined D. Pipe 95,000 gns. *M. A. Jarvis* **101**

HUNTING COUNTRY 4 b.g. Cape Cross (IRE) 129 – Steeple (Selkirk (USA) 129) [2009 99: p12g^6 10.2d a9.8f a9f^6 Nov 20] quite attractive gelding: fairly useful handicapper: left M. Johnston after second start: stays 1½m: acts on all-weather and good to firm going. *A. bin Huzaim, UAE* **89**

HUNTINGFORTREASURE 2 b.g. (Apr 20) Pastoral Pursuits 127 – Treasure Trove (USA) 62 (The Minstrel (CAN) 135) [2009 7.2m^2 7g^2 Oct 17] 5,000F: tall gelding: half-brother to several winners, notably very smart German 6f to 1m winner Toylsome (by Cadeaux Genereux): dam, maiden who stayed 7f, half-sister to useful 5f (Queen Mary Stakes) to 1m (US Grade 2 event) winner Dance Parade: runner-up in maidens at Ayr and Catterick (still green): likely to improve. *M. Dods* **76 p**

HUNTING HAZE 6 b.g. Foxhound (USA) 103 – Second Affair (IRE) 85 (Pursuit of Love 124) [2009 59: 15.8g 14.1m 12d 12g 10g 12s Oct 27] maiden handicapper: no form in 2009: tried in cheekpieces, blinkered last 2 starts. *A. Crook* **–**

HUNTING TARTAN 2 b.c. (Mar 1) Oasis Dream 129 – Delta (Zafonic (USA) 130) [2009 7.1m* 7m Oct 1] big, well-made colt: type to carry condition: second foal: half-brother to 3-y-o Sampi: dam, useful French 1m winner, out of half-sister to very smart performer up to 1½m Eltish and smart sprinter Forest Gazelle: good impression when winning maiden at Chepstow in September easily by 3¼ lengths from Forest Runner: similar form when eighth of 9 in Somerville Tattersall Stakes at Newmarket, not knocked about: should stay 1m: type to make useful 3-y-o. *J. H. M. Gosden* **93 p**

HUNTING TOWER 5 b.g. Sadler's Wells (USA) 132 – Fictitious 100 (Machiavellian (USA) 123) [2009 12.9d^{2} 13.1m^{5} 13.1m^{2} Oct 1] leggy gelding: fairly useful performer: stays 13f: acts on polytrack, good to firm and good to soft ground: fairly useful hurdler, successful 4 times in 2009/10. *J. J. Lambe, Ireland* **90**

HUNT THE BOTTLE (IRE) 4 b.c. Bertolini (USA) 125 – Zanoubia (USA) 94 (Our Emblem (USA) 114) [2009 69§: p6g p6g^{6} p8.6g^{5} p9.5g^{3} p9.5g^{6} p9.5g f6g 8d May 22] good-topped, quite attractive colt: handicapper, just modest at 4 yrs: stayed 9.5f: acted on polytrack and good to soft going: tried in blinkers/cheekpieces: was ungenuine: dead. *M. Mullineaux* **56 §**

HURAKAN (IRE) 3 gr.g. Daylami (IRE) 138 – Gothic Dream (IRE) 113 (Nashwan (USA) 135) [2009 84p: 11m 10d p10g^{2} p8g* p10m^{3} p10m^{5} p12f p10f^{4} Dec 20] lengthy gelding: fairly useful performer: claimed from Mrs A. Perrett £12,000, back to best when winning handicap at Lingfield in November: stays 1¼m: acts on polytrack and good to firm going. *P. D. Evans* **82**

HURFORHARMONY (IRE) 6 b.m. Orpen (USA) 116 – Zolba (IRE) 56 (Classic Secret (USA) 91) [2009 49: p12.2g^{5} p8.6g^{6} Jan 22] poor maiden: probably stays 1¾m. *Adrian McGuinness, Ireland* **49**

HURLINGHAM 5 b.g. Halling (USA) 133 – Society (IRE) 73 (Barathea (IRE) 127) [2009 85: 10.3g 10.2d^{4} 12d^{6} 12m^{2} 11.5m 10.3d 10.2v^{4} 9.9m^{6} 12s^{6} 10.4g f8m Nov 6] tall, quite attractive gelding: fairly useful handicapper: stays 13f: acts on all-weather, heavy and good to firm ground: tried blinkered/in cheekpieces: tongue tied once: often looks none too keen. *M. W. Easterby* **85**

HUROOF (IRE) 2 ch.f. (Feb 24) Pivotal 124 – Esloob (USA) 106 (Diesis 133) [2009 7g^{2} 7m^{4} p7.1g* Nov 14] leggy filly: third live foal: dam, 7f (at 2 yrs) and 1¼m winner, out of Yorkshire Oaks winner Roseate Tern: off 3 months and in cheekpieces, best effort in maidens when landing odds by 6 lengths at Wolverhampton: encouraging second to Tabassum at Newmarket on debut: will stay 1m: useful prospect. *Saeed bin Suroor* **87 p**

HURRICANE COAST 10 b.g. Hurricane Sky (AUS) – Tread Carefully 51 (Sharpo 132) [2009 68: f6s^{3} p6g^{3} f8g* p8.6g p8.6m^{5} p5.1g^{6} f6g p6g p12.2g f6g^{6} 8.3m May 29] tall gelding: modest handicapper at 10 yrs: won apprentice event at Southwell in January: was effective at 6f to 1m: acted on all-weather, firm and soft going: often wore headgear: tried tongue tied: held up: was quirky: dead. *D. Flood* **61**

HURRICANE HYMNBOOK (USA) 4 b.g. Pulpit (USA) 117 – April Squall (USA) (Summer Squall (USA)) [2009 107d: 8.1f 8.3m^{5} Jun 28] lengthy gelding: lightly-raced handicapper: not knocked about either start in 2009: stays 1m: raced only on polytrack and good going or firmer (acts on firm). *Stef Liddiard* **81 +**

HURRICANE SPIRIT (IRE) 5 b.h. Invincible Spirit (IRE) 121 – Gale Warning (IRE) (Last Tycoon 131) [2009 104: 7f 6g^{5} 6g p6g p7g p8g* p8g^{4} Oct 9] big, well-made horse: handicapper: just fairly useful in 2009, though won at Kempton in September: effective at 6f to 1m: acts on polytrack, good to firm and good to soft going. *J. R. Best* **92**

HURRICANE THOMAS (IRE) 5 b.g. Celtic Swing 138 – Viola Royale (IRE) 90 (Royal Academy (USA) 130) [2009 63: 9.9g^{4} 12m^{4} 12.1g^{4} 10m^{4} 9.9m 13g* 12g 12.4d^{6} 9.9g* 10.9m^{2} 12.4d 10.2g Oct 28] big, good-topped gelding: fair handicapper: won amateur events at Musselburgh in July and Beverley in September: effective at 1¼m to 1¾m: acts on polytrack, soft and good to firm going: tried in cheekpieces/visor. *R. A. Fahey* **65**

HURSTPIERPOINT (IRE) 4 b.f. Night Shift (USA) – Double Gamble 76 (Ela-Mana-Mou 132) [2009 57: p10g Aug 1] smallish filly: modest maiden: below form sole Flat start in 2009 (poor maiden hurdler): stays 1¼m: acts on polytrack and good to firm going: none too consistent. *M. G. Rimell* **–**

HUSTLE (IRE) 4 ch.g. Choisir (AUS) 126 – Granny Kelly (USA) 60 (Irish River (FR) 131) [2009 93: p9.5g^{5} p8g 6d^{5} 7m^{4} 7m* 7g 7f p7.1g 8.3v^{6} 8m^{5} p6g^{5} 8m^{4} p7m^{3} p7g p7.1g^{6} p7m^{5} p7f^{5} Dec 13] good sort: fairly useful handicapper: dead-heated at Newmarket in May: below form after: effective at 6f to 1¼m: acts on polytrack, good to firm and good to soft ground: tried in headgear/tongue tie. *Miss Gay Kelleway* **93**

HUYGENS 2 b.c. (Apr 25) Zafeen (FR) 123 – Lindfield Belle (IRE) 78 (Fairy King (USA)) [2009 5.7f^{5} 7m* p8m^{3} Dec 9] 74,000F, 55,000Y: half-brother to several winners, notably very smart 5f (including at 2 yrs)/6f winner Baltic King and useful Irish 2007 2-y-o 6f winner Domingues (both by Danetime): dam 2-y-o 5f winner: fairly useful form: won maiden at Folkestone in June by 2¾ lengths from Astonishment: off 6 months, good head third to Danger Mulally in nursery at Kempton, travelling strongly: stays 1m: open to further improvement. *D. J. Coakley* **86 p**

HUZZAH (IRE) 4 b.c. Acclamation 118 – Borders Belle (IRE) 96 (Pursuit of Love 124) [2009 107: 8m5 8s 8m2 8.1m4 8g 8m 8m 8s Oct 12] strong colt: useful handicapper: creditable efforts in 2009 only in Lincoln at Doncaster (4½ lengths fifth to Expresso Star), Royal Hunt Cup at Royal Ascot (2¼ lengths second to Forgotten Voice) and quite valuable event at Sandown (fourth to Acrostic): stays 1m: acts on polytrack, soft and good to firm going. *B. W. Hills* **105**

HYADES (USA) 3 b. or br.c. Aldebaran (USA) 126 – Lingerie (Shirley Heights 130) [2009 86p: 11s5 8g* 10m2 8m6 9.9g6 p8g6 Aug 24] strong, good sort: useful performer: won maiden at Yarmouth in April: good efforts all starts after, including when sixth in handicaps at Royal Ascot (to Fareer in Britannia Stakes) and Goodwood (behind Roman Republic) fourth/fifth outings: stays 1¼m: acts on polytrack and good to firm going: sold 55,000 gns in October. *H. R. A. Cecil* **98**

HYDE LEA FLYER 4 b.g. Hernando (FR) 127 – Sea Ridge 65§ (Slip Anchor 136) [2009 85: p8.6g2 8m 8.3d 8m p8.6g p8.6g p8.6g5 p8.6g4 Dec 7] big, lengthy gelding: fairly useful handicapper: gelded after reappearance: below best after: stays 9.5f: acts on polytrack and good to soft going: races freely. *E. S. McMahon* **83**

HYDRANT 3 b.g. Haafhd 129 – Spring 112 (Sadler's Wells (USA) 132) [2009 69: f11f3 Dec 17] strong, good-bodied gelding: fair maiden: stays 11f: acts on fibresand: no form over hurdles. *P. Salmon* **74**

HYMNSHEET 2 b.f. (May 2) Pivotal 124 – Choir Mistress (Chief Singer 131) [2009 8g* Oct 20] sister to very smart 1m/1¼m winner Chorist and half-sister to several winners, including useful 1998 2-y-o 7f winner Choirgirl (stayed 1¼m, by Unfuwain): dam unraced half-sister to smart middle-distance stayer Sacrament: 10/3, promising when winning maiden at Yarmouth readily by length from Thousandkissesdeep: will stay 1¼m: sure to improve. *Sir Michael Stoute* **84 p**

HYPER VIPER (IRE) 4 b.g. Atraf 116 – Double Letter (IRE) (M Double M (USA)) [2009 16.1m Jun 25] strong, compact gelding: maiden: no show only Flat start in 2009: tried in cheekpieces, often blinkered. *C. Grant* **–**

HYPNOSIS 6 b.m. Mind Games 121 – Salacious (Sallust 134) [2009 89: 5m5 5g3 5m2 5m 5m3 f5g 5g Oct 17] leggy mare: fairly useful performer: effective at 5f/6f: acts on fibresand, firm and soft going. *N. Wilson* **87**

HYPNOTIC 7 ch.g. Lomitas 129 – Hypnotize 103 (Machiavellian (USA) 123) [2009 66: 8m* 8m 7f4 7.6m 8f2 p8.6m f7m Nov 12] leggy gelding: fair handicapper: won at Brighton in June: stays 1m: acts on polytrack and any turf going: tried blinkered/visored/tongue tied: sold £400. *Jim Best* **69**

HYPNOTIC GAZE (IRE) 3 b.g. Chevalier (IRE) 115 – Red Trance (IRE) 79 (Soviet Star (USA) 128) [2009 48: p8.6g3 p8.6g4 8.3m4 8.1g5 8v3 9.3d2 10.3g5 Aug 2] compact gelding: fair maiden handicapper: stays 9.3f: acts on polytrack, heavy and good to firm ground: tried in cheekpieces. *J. Mackie* **72**

HYPNOTIST (UAE) 3 b.g. Halling (USA) 133 – Poised (USA) (Rahy (USA) 115) [2009 60p: p8.6g3 p10g3 p7g2 8m5 10m6 10.9g 10.1g5 9g6 8.3m4 7g4 Oct 23] good-bodied gelding: fair maiden handicapper: gelded after sixth outing: stays easy 1¼m: acts on polytrack and good to firm ground: tried in cheekpieces. *C. E. Brittain* **77**

HYPNOTIZED (USA) 2 b.c. (Mar 9) Elusive Quality (USA) – Delighted (IRE) 74 (Danehill (USA) 126) [2009 7m5 p7g5 p7g* Nov 18] $110,000Y: tall colt: has scope: third foal: brother to useful 2008 2-y-o 6f winner Absent Pleasure: dam, ran 3 times, half-sister to smart French 1¼m/1½m performers Crimson Quest and Hijaz: progressive form in maidens, winning at Kempton by 2½ lengths from Vaultage: likely to stay 1m: type to progress further. *M. L. W. Bell* **86 p**

HYSTERICAL LADY 3 b.f. Choisir (AUS) 126 – Royal Mistress (Fasliyev (USA) 120) [2009 80: f6g* 5m3 6m* 5d6 5d4 5m5 p6g Oct 9] fair performer: won maiden at Southwell in March and handicap at Thirsk in May: stays 6f: acts on fibresand, good to firm and good to soft going: sold 8,000 gns. *D. Nicholls* **77**

I

IACHIMO 3 ch.g. Sakhee (USA) 136 – Latin Review (IRE) 87 (Titus Livius (FR) 115) [2009 57+: p5g* p5.1g 5.1g 5m3 5d5 5g 5d3 5m6 5g Aug 26] sturdy gelding: modest handicapper: won at Lingfield in March: likely to prove best at 5f: acts on polytrack, good to firm and good to soft ground: tried visored/in cheekpieces. *A. P. Jarvis* **57**

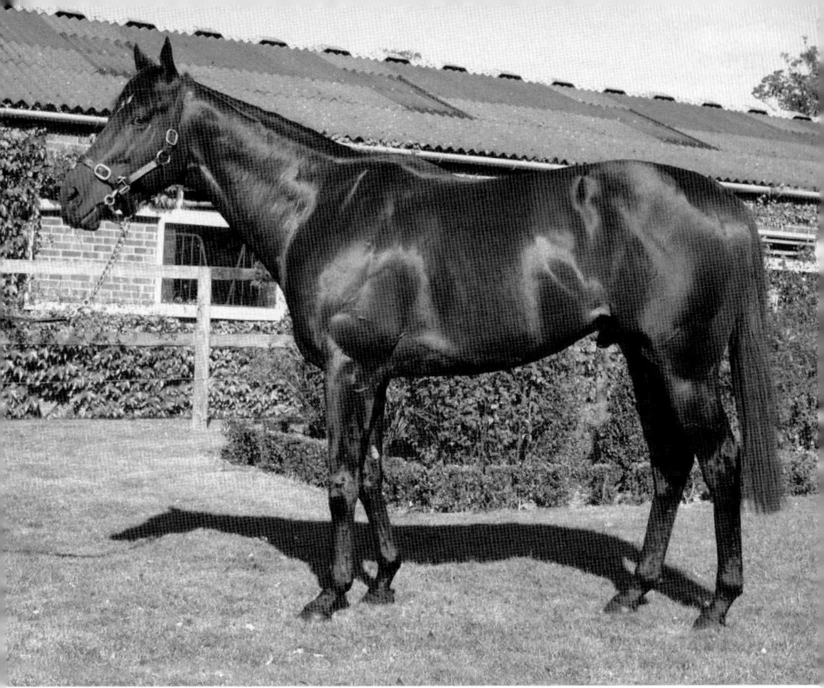

Mrs M. Marinopoulos' "Ialysos"

IALYSOS (GR) 5 br.h. So Factual (USA) 120 – Vallota (Polish Precedent (USA) 131) [2009 a5s* a7s* 5g* 6m 5m* 5g 5m Aug 21] sturdy horse: first foal: dam unraced half-sister to 1¼m and 12.5f winner Ismaros and 6f (at 2 yrs)/7f winner Epagris, both useful: smart performer: unbeaten in 7 races in Greece (including first 2 starts in 2009) for G. Kassis, all at Markopoulou: continued to thrive in Britain, winning listed race at Haydock (beat Anglezarke by neck) in May and Coral Charge (Sprint) at Sandown (by ½ length from Triple Aspect, relishing uphill finish after under pressure halfway) in July: below form in King George Stakes at Goodwood and Nunthorpe Stakes at York (unsuited by increased emphasis on speed) last 2 starts: successful at 7f in Greece, campaigned as sprinter in Britain (but needs good test at 5f): acts on sand, raced only on good/good to firm ground on turf. *L. M. Cumani* **118**

I AM THAT (IRE) 2 b.c. (Apr 2) Statue of Liberty (USA) 115 – Victory Again (IRE) 55 (Victory Note (USA) 120) [2009 5d* 6m^4 p6m^3 Oct 7] smallish colt: first foal: dam, Irish maiden, half-sister to smart performer up to 8.5f Little White Lie: fair performer: won maiden at Carlisle in August: better form when in frame in minor events: will be suited by 7f: sold 17,000 gns. *S. A. Callaghan* **76**

I AM THE MAN 4 b.g. Auction House (USA) 120 – Sally Gardens 60 (Alzao (USA) 117) [2009 p10m^2 Dec 9] 2,500F, 16,500Y: third foal: dam, 2-y-o 7f seller winner, granddaughter of Yorkshire Oaks winner Sally Brown: 11/1, encouraging length second to Pyrus Time in maiden at Lingfield, travelling comfortably long way following slow start: capable of better. *B. J. McMath* **74 p**

IASIA (GR) 3 b.f. One Cool Cat (USA) 123 – Alanis (Warning 136) [2009 76p: 8m^5 7g 7.1m* 7m 7g^2 7m^6 6m^5 p7g Nov 18] good-bodied filly: useful performer: won handicap at Warwick in July: seemingly improved when mid-field in listed races at Doncaster and Newmarket sixth/seventh starts: stays 1m: acts on polytrack and good to firm going. *Jane Chapple-Hyam* **100**

IBBETSON (USA) 4 b. or br.g. Street Cry (IRE) 130 – Object of Virtue (USA) **62**
(Partner's Hero (USA)) [2009 79: 8m^5 8m 8.3g^6 Oct 5] tall gelding: modest maiden: stays 1¼m: acts on polytrack (best effort) and good to soft going: sold £5,000, joined Mrs A. Thorpe. *W. R. Swinburn*

IBMAB 2 ch.g. (Mar 1) Deportivo 116 – Kilmovee 59 (Inchinor 119) [2009 5g^6 6g 6d^3 **66**
7g* 7m^2 p7f 7d Oct 27] rather leggy gelding: fair performer: won claimer at Yarmouth in August: stays 7f: tried tongue tied: seemed amiss final outing: sold 3,000 gns. *Mrs L. Stubbs*

IBN HIYYAN (USA) 2 gr. or ro.g. (Apr 9) El Prado (IRE) 119 – Lovely Later (USA) **57**
(Green Dancer (USA) 132) [2009 7.2g 8g p8f Oct 14] form in maidens only when last of 8 at Newmarket second start: gelded after final outing. *M. Johnston*

IBROX (IRE) 4 b.g. Mujahid (USA) 125 – Ling Lane (Slip Anchor 136) [2009 71: **80**
f11d^2 f12g* f14g^6 f12g 10g* 13.1g 10.4g^3 11.1v^4 11.9d f11g* f12f^4 Dec 12] good-topped gelding: fairly useful handicapper: won at Southwell (maiden) in January, Ayr in June and Southwell in October: effective at 1¼m/1½m: acts on fibresand and heavy ground: in cheekpieces last 2 starts. *A. D. Brown*

ICE AND FIRE 10 b.g. Cadeaux Genereux 131 – Tanz (IRE) 79 (Sadler's Wells (USA) **–**
132) [2009 –, a52: f16g^5 16d Apr 14] quite good-topped gelding: modest handicapper at 9 yrs: below form in 2009: stays 16.5f: acts on all-weather, little recent form on turf: wears headgear: tends to edge right: none too consistent. *J. T. Stimpson*

ICE ATTACK (IRE) 3 gr.f. Verglas (IRE) 118 – Little Whisper (IRE) 95 (Be My Guest **–**
(USA) 126) [2009 51p: f6g^5 5g^4 5.3g^5 Jun 7] maiden: little form in 2009: tried visored. *Pat Morris*

ICE BELLINI 4 ch.f. Erhaab (USA) 127 – Peach Sorbet (IRE) 77 (Spectrum (IRE) **67**
126) [2009 70: p14g^2 p13.9m^6 12.4s^4 11.9f^5 May 12] workmanlike filly: fair handicapper: stays 1¾m: acts on all-weather and heavy ground: visored/blinkered nowadays: joined Jim Best £7,800. *Miss Gay Kelleway*

ICE COOL LADY (IRE) 2 gr.f. (Feb 8) Verglas (IRE) 118 – Cafe Creme (IRE) **73**
(Catrail (USA) 123) [2009 5g^6 p5.1g^6 6f^4 6d 7f* 7m^4 p7g Nov 13] €15,000Y: tall, leggy filly: third foal: half-sister to 3-y-o Parisian Art and 4-y-o Red Expresso: dam unraced half-sister to Cheveley Park Stakes winner Seazun: fair performer: won nursery at Lingfield in September: likely to stay 1m: acts on firm ground: has looked hard ride. *W. R. Swinburn*

ICE DIVA 2 b. or gr.f. (Feb 24) Verglas (IRE) 118 – La Coqueta (GER) (Kris 135) [2009 **73**
7m 8g^5 p8.6g^2 Nov 6] 20,000F, 8,500Y: tall, good-bodied filly: fourth foal: dam unraced half-sister to high-class German 1½m performer Lavirco: similar form in maidens last 2 starts, doing too much from the front when runner-up at Wolverhampton: stays 8.6f. *P. W. D'Arcy*

ICELANDIC 7 b.g. Selkirk (USA) 129 – Icicle 104 (Polar Falcon (USA) 126) [2009 **113**
117: p5g^4 6v^3 6m^6 5d^2 6s^3 6g 6s^6 Nov 7] strong gelding: smart performer: in-and-out form in 2009, best efforts when placed in Greenlands Stakes at the Curragh (3¼ lengths third to Utmost Respect) and minor event at Newmarket (length second to Nota Bene): effective at stiff 5f to 1m: acts on all-weather, soft and good to firm ground: tongue tied. *F. Sheridan*

ICEMAN GEORGE 5 b.g. Beat Hollow 126 – Diebiedale 58 (Dominion 123) [2009 **68**
69: f8d^3 f11g^4 10.3m^4 p12g 10.1m^5 10.1m 10.1g^2 10m* 10.1g^3 10d* 10d 10m Aug 15] compact gelding: fair handicapper: won at Newbury (amateur event) in June and Newmarket in July: stays easy 1½m: acts on all-weather, good to firm and good to soft going: usually in headgear. *D. Morris*

ICE PLANET 8 b.g. Polar Falcon (USA) 126 – Preference (Efisio 120) [2009 93d: f6g^5 **65**
f7g^5 6g^5 6g^3 6m 6.1s Oct 7] useful-looking gelding: just fair performer nowadays: best around 6f: acts on firm and soft ground: has been bandaged fore joints. *Mrs R. A. Carr*

I CERTAINLY MAY 4 b.g. Royal Applause 124 – Deep Ravine (USA) 50 (Gulch **50 d**
(USA)) [2009 60: p8g^2 p10g p8g p8g 9m 10.1g Jul 30] quite good-topped gelding: modest maiden handicapper on all-weather, little recent form on turf: stays easy 1¼m: acts on polytrack: tried blinkered, often wears cheekpieces. *S. Dow*

ICESOLATOR (IRE) 3 b.g. One Cool Cat (USA) 123 – Zinnia (Zilzal (USA) 137) **107**
[2009 98: p7g p8g^3 7s^3 8.3m^3 7g Nov 22] leggy, close-coupled gelding: has a quick action: useful performer: improved in 2009, good third in Greenham Stakes at Newbury (beaten 2½ lengths by Vocalised) and listed race at Windsor (2¼ lengths behind Ordnance Row) third/fourth starts: left R. Hannon and renamed Regency Winner, below form in

handicap at Sha Tin final outing: stays 8.3f: acts on polytrack, soft and good to firm going. *D. E. Ferraris, Hong Kong*

ICE VIKING (IRE) 2 b.c. (May 6) Danehill Dancer (IRE) 117 – Maddelina (IRE) 54 **68** (Sadler's Wells (USA) 132) [2009 6g^5 6.1g^5 7.1g^6 p7.1g^5 7m 8.3d^6 Oct 15] tall colt: fair maiden: should stay 1m: acts on polytrack. *J. G. Given*

I CONFESS 4 br.g. Fantastic Light (USA) 134 – Vadsagreya (FR) (Linamix (FR) 127) **87** [2009 84: p7g 6m^6 7m^5 7m^3 p8g* 7m^5 7.1d^5 p7g* 7g 8g 7.6g^5 7m^2 8f^5 p7g^3 p8.6g^3 p7.1g^4 6.1m^5 p7g p7g p6g^6 p7g^5 p8m^4 p7m^6 p7f^3 p7f^5 Dec 21] useful-looking gelding: fairly useful handicapper: won at Lingfield in May and June: stays easy 8.6f: acts on polytrack and any turf going: tried visored, usually blinkered: front runner/races prominently: tough. *P. D. Evans*

IDEALISM 2 b.c. (Jan 29) Motivator 131 – Fickle 95 (Danehill (USA) 126) [2009 8.3d **– p** Oct 15] 100,000Y: strong, lengthy colt: fourth foal: half-brother to 2 winners, including useful 1m/9f (Dahlia Stakes) winner Tarfah (by Kingmambo): dam, 1m/1¼m winner, half-sister to useful French performer up to 13.5f Faru: 10/1, well held in maiden at Nottingham (very green): bred to be suited by 1¼m+: looks sort to do better. *J. H. M. Gosden*

IDLE POWER (IRE) 11 b. or br.g. Common Grounds 118 – Idle Fancy 79 (Mujtahid **81** (USA) 118) [2009 93: 7m p6g^5 7m p7g^4 7g p7m^3 6d* 6d^2 6d^6 p7m Oct 31] close-coupled **a72** gelding: fairly useful handicapper on turf, fair on all-weather: won at Epsom in September: effective at 6f/7f: acts on polytrack, firm and soft going: used to wear blinkers/cheekpieces: races prominently. *J. R. Boyle*

IFATFIRST (IRE) 6 b.g. Grand Lodge (USA) 125 – Gaily Grecian (IRE) (Ela-Mana- **73** Mou 132) [2009 58: 11.1m* 13.1g^4 13.1g^2 11.5d^5 12.5m^6 14s^6 14m* 14m^3 14.1g Oct 16] fair handicapper: won at Hamilton in June and Musselburgh in September: stays 1¾m: acts on polytrack and good to firm going: tried blinkered: sold £5,000. *J. S. Goldie*

IFFY 8 b.g. Orpen (USA) 116 – Hopesay 84 (Warning 136) [2009 9m^5 p12m p12g^5 p10m **56** Nov 3] workmanlike gelding: fairly useful handicapper in 2005: just modest form on return to Flat in 2009 (fair hurdler/chaser for R. Lee): stays 1¼m: acts on all-weather and good to firm going. *A. B. Haynes*

IF I WERE A BOY (IRE) 2 b.f. (Feb 22) Invincible Spirit (IRE) 121 – Attymon Lill **75** (IRE) (Marju (IRE) 127) [2009 6m^3 7.1g^5 p6f^3 7d^6 p8.6g^2 p8.6g^5 p8g^3 p8m^5 p8m^5 p8.6g* Dec 19] 55,000Y: second foal: dam, little form in Ireland, out of close relative to Saddlers' Hall and half-sister to Sun Princess: fair performer: won maiden at Wolverhampton by 5 lengths: stays 8.6f: acts on polytrack and good to firm ground: tried in cheekpieces (including for win). *S. Kirk*

IF ONLY 3 ch.g. Monsieur Bond (IRE) 120 – La Belle Dominique 76 (Dominion 123) **64** [2009 p7g^3 p7.1g 7d^5 f6g^4 f6g^5 p7g^6 p6f^2 6m^4 Sep 28] modest maiden: stays 7f: acts on all-weather and good to firm ground: tried blinkered: often races freely. *J. Jay*

IF YOU KNEW SUZY 4 b.f. Efisio 120 – Sioux 76 (Kris 135) [2009 –: f12g^2 p8.6g^5 **73 d** 7m f8g^4 f8g^3 10d f8f f6g^6 Dec 27] fair maiden: on downgrade, left G. A. Swinbank after sixth start: best short of 1½m: acts on all-weather: sometimes tongue tied: looks a weak finisher. *R. E. Barr*

IGNATIEFF (IRE) 2 b.g. (Apr 15) Fasliyev (USA) 120 – Genial Jenny (IRE) 70 **82** (Danehill (USA) 126) [2009 5m^5 5.1m^5 5m^2 5f^4 5.2g^2 5m^3 5g 5s* 5g* 5m^5 Sep 14] 10,000Y: good-topped gelding: half-brother to 3 winners, including Irish 4-y-o Indiana Girl: dam Irish 9f winner: fairly useful performer: won maiden at Thirsk and nursery at Musselburgh in August: raced only at 5f: acts on soft and good to firm going: tried in cheekpieces: races up with pace. *Mrs L. Stubbs*

IGNEOUS 3 ch.g. Lucky Story (USA) 128 – Double Top (IRE) (Thatching 131) [2009 **46** 49: 7.1m 9.3d 8m^5 8d Sep 7] leggy gelding: poor maiden: seems to stay 1m: tried blinkered/in cheekpieces. *D. W. Thompson*

IGNITION 7 ch.m. Rock City 120 – Fire Sprite 83 (Mummy's Game 120) [2009 46: **51** p6g^4 Jan 6] leggy, close-coupled mare: modest performer: stays 9f: acts on polytrack, firm and good to soft going: effective with or without cheekpieces. *A. Kirtley*

IGOTIM 3 b.g. Umistim 119 – Glistening Silver 58 (Puissance 110) [2009 –: 8.3m p7g **–** Jun 4] angular gelding: little form. *J. Gallagher*

IGOYOUGO 3 b.g. Millkom 124 – Club Oasis (Forzando 122) [2009 54: 5m^2 5f* **85** 5m* 5m^4 5.1m^2 5d* Oct 28] leggy, close-coupled gelding: fairly useful handicapper: improved through 2009, winning at Ayr and Newcastle in August, and Musselburgh in October: speedy, but should stay 6f: acts on firm and good to soft ground: races prominently. *G. A. Harker*

IGUACU 5 b.g. Desert Prince (IRE) 130 – Gay Gallanta (USA) 112 (Woodman (USA) 126) [2009 –: 7.1m^{5} f6g^{5} 7m^{3} 6.1g^{6} 6.1m 9m^{2} 10.2g* p8.6g 11.9d^{4} 10.2g^{6} f12m^{3} p10g^{2} p12m* p13.9g Dec 14] compact, quite attractive gelding: modest handicapper: won at Nottingham (ladies) in July and Kempton in December: stays 1½m: acts on all-weather, good to firm and good to soft going: tried blinkered. *George Baker* **63**

IKE QUEBEC (FR) 4 ch.g. Dr Fong (USA) 128 – Avezia (FR) (Night Shift (USA)) [2009 79: p7g p7g^{3} p7g p8.6g Mar 20] stocky gelding: just modest handicapper in 2009: stays easy 7f: acts on polytrack (lightly raced on turf): often blinkered/visored: usually races prominently. *J. R. Boyle* **60**

IKETI (GR) 3 b.f. Filandros (GR) – Eldora (FR) (Highest Honor (FR) 124) [2009 p10g^{3} 10s 10.9g 10g Oct 19] big, deep-girthed filly: first foal: dam French 1¼m winner: form only when third in maiden on debut, though hampered next 2 starts: raced only around 1¼m: best effort on polytrack: returned to Greece. *Jane Chapple-Hyam* **64**

ILDIKO (USA) 2 b.f. (Feb 20) Yes It's True (USA) 116 – Eternity 77 (Suave Dancer (USA) 136) [2009 p8g 8g 8.3v Nov 4] good-topped filly: seventh foal: half-sister to several winners, including 5-y-o Sagredo and fairly useful 13f/1¾m winner Artless (by Aptitude): dam, 11f/1½m winner, half-sister to Fillies' Mile winner Tessla: showed ability on first of 3 starts in maidens: bred to be suited by 1¼m+: type to do better at 3 yrs. *Sir Mark Prescott* **64 p**

ILE ROYALE 4 b.f. Royal Applause 124 – Island Destiny 79 (Kris 135) [2009 53§: 6m^{4} 6g^{5} 6f Jun 30] rather leggy filly: poor and irresolute maiden: stays 1m: acts on polytrack and good to firm going: sometimes blinkered/visored. *W. S. Kittow* **49 §**

IL FORNO 2 b.g. (Feb 8) Exceed And Excel (AUS) 126 – Fred's Dream 67 (Cadeaux Genereux 131) [2009 6g^{2} 6d^{4} 5.1g^{2} p6g^{5} 7m 5g^{2} Oct 6] £23,000Y: good-topped gelding: fourth foal: half-brother to 3-y-o What A Fella: dam maiden (stayed 1m): fair maiden: below form after third start: stays 6f. *D. Nicholls* **74**

IL GRANDE ARDONE 4 b.c. Dr Fong (USA) 128 – Bombalarina (IRE) (Barathea (IRE) 127) [2009 84: f12g a10s 10s^{3} Mar 15] fairly useful performer at best: well below form in 2009, leaving F. Sheridan 22,000 gns after reappearance: stays 1½m: acts on all-weather/sand and heavy ground: in cheekpieces/tongue tie in Britain. *C. von der Recke, Germany* **–**

ILIE NASTASE (FR) 5 b.g. Royal Applause 124 – Flying Diva 100 (Chief Singer 131) [2009 8m 7.6m 8.1v^{4} 8m^{5} p8g^{5} 7m 8v^{2} 8s 10.4m p9.5g p9.5g a9.5g Dec 19] big, lengthy gelding: useful performer: winner of 4 minor events in France for R. Gibson (sold 27,000 gns and gelded after 2008): mostly at least respectable efforts in 2009, leaving D. Nicholls after ninth start, D. Simcock prior to final outing: barely stays 10.4f: acts on all-weather, heavy and good to firm going: tried blinkered/in cheekpieces: not straightforward. *E. J. O'Neill* **95**

ILKLEY 2 b.f. (Feb 7) Fantastic Light (USA) 134 – Zakuska 96 (Zafonic (USA) 130) [2009 8.3m 7s^{5} 7.5g Sep 22] workmanlike filly: half-sister to 2 winners, including fairly useful 6f to 8.6f winner Barzak (by Barathea): dam, 1¼m winner from 3 starts, closely related to US Grade 1 9f winner Link River: form in maidens only when fifth at Thirsk. *M. W. Easterby* **42**

I'LLDOIT 2 br.g. (Feb 15) Tamayaz (CAN) 121 – Club Oasis (Forzando 122) [2009 7.5g Aug 12] small gelding: 50/1 and on edge, slowly away and always in rear in maiden at Beverley. *G. A. Harker* **–**

ILLICIT 4 b.g. Oasis Dream 129 – Daring Miss 113 (Sadler's Wells (USA) 132) [2009 10g p8.6g p13.9g p10g Nov 25] smallish, lengthy gelding: fair maiden for A. Fabre in France at 3 yrs: limited encouragement in 2009, leaving Paul Mason after reappearance: stays 11f: raced only on polytrack and good/good to soft ground: tried tongue tied/in cheekpieces. *J. R. Holt* **–**

ILLUMINATIVE (USA) 3 b.g. Point Given (USA) 134 – Pretty Clear (USA) 89 (Mr Prospector (USA)) [2009 p8.6g^{2} p8g^{2} p9.5g* Oct 23] $30,000Y: third foal: half-brother to 7f winner (including at 2 yrs) Prince of Charm (by Mizzen Mast) and a winner in USA by Empire Maker: dam, 6f winner, sister to high-class miler Distant View: fair form in polytrack maidens: landed odds at Wolverhampton by 7 lengths (carried head awkwardly): shapes as though will be suited by 1¼m: sold 27,000 gns. *J. H. M. Gosden* **78**

ILLUSIVE SPIRIT (IRE) 3 b.g. Clodovil (IRE) 116 – Poker Dice (Primo Dominie 121) [2009 8m p8g^{5} 8g^{6} 8m 8.3v* 8g Oct 8] 60,000Y: sturdy gelding: fifth foal: half-brother to 2 winners, including Irish 7-y-o Cheddar Island: dam unraced: fair performer: won maiden at Nottingham in July: likely to stay beyond 1m: acts on polytrack and heavy ground: sold 2,000 gns, sent to Norway. *J. H. M. Gosden* **71**

Coutts Glorious Stakes, Goodwood—
course specialist Illustrious Blue (No.6) overhauls long-time leader Warringah

ILLUSTRIOUS BLUE 6 b. or br.h. Dansili 127 – Gipsy Moth 99 (Efisio 120) [2009 114: 9.9m4 12m3 12m6 12g* 12g5 12m 12v Oct 24] close-coupled horse: has a rather round action: smart performer: as good as ever when winning Coutts Glorious Stakes at Goodwood (sixth course success) in July, beating Warringah by neck: respectable efforts at best otherwise in 2009: stays 1½m: acts on polytrack, firm and soft going: effective visored or not: held up. *W. J. Knight* **115**

ILLUSTRIOUS PRINCE (IRE) 2 b.c. (Mar 26) Acclamation 118 – Sacred Love (IRE) 69 (Barathea (IRE) 127) [2009 p7g5 6g2 Oct 30] 72,000Y: big, heavy-bodied colt: third foal: brother to 3-y-o Mastoora: dam, maiden (should have stayed at least 1¼m), out of sister to very smart French 1½m performer De Quest: much better effort in maidens when head second to Asraab at Newmarket, rallying: will stay 7f: should improve again. *J. Noseda* **86 p**

IL PORTICO 2 b.g. (Apr 6) Zafeen (FR) 123 – Diddymu (IRE) 66 (Revoque (IRE) 122) [2009 7s 6.1g6 8m Sep 13] well-made gelding: poor form in maidens, then gelded. *M. R. Channon* **49**

ILSTON LORD (IRE) 2 b.c. (Mar 5) One Cool Cat (USA) 123 – Canouan (IRE) 94 (Sadler's Wells (USA) 132) [2009 6g6 8g 8m5 Sep 13] unfurnished colt: modest form in maidens: will stay 1¼m+: sold 15,000 gns. *M. P. Tregoning* **64**

IMAAM 3 ch.c. Pivotal 124 – Khulood (USA) 103 (Storm Cat (USA)) [2009 78: 7d* 8.1m5 8d5 7g2 7s* Aug 9] sturdy colt: fairly useful performer: progressed steadily in 2009, winning maiden at Folkestone in March and handicap at Leicester in August: stays 1m: acts on soft and good to firm ground: sold 30,000 gns. *J. L. Dunlop* **90**

I'M AGENIUS 6 b.m. Killer Instinct 111 – I'm Sophie (IRE) 64 (Shalford (IRE) 124§) [2009 –: f8d f7d Mar 10] workmanlike mare: maiden: little form since 2007: left R. Curtis prior to final start: suspect temperament. *D. Burchell* **–**

IMAGINARY DIVA 3 b.f. Lend A Hand 124 – Distant Diva 86 (Distant Relative 128) [2009 70: p5g f5g 6d4 5.1m2 5.2g3 5.3g3 5m3 5s3 5m5 p5.1g4 5m4 5.2d6 Oct 27] compact filly: fair handicapper: stays 6f: acts on all-weather, soft and good to firm ground: tried visored. *G. G. Margarson* **65**

I'MALWAYSRIGHT (IRE) 2 b.g. (Apr 6) Namid 128 – Tashyra (IRE) 59 (Tagula (IRE) 116) [2009 5m2 p6g p5g2 p6g4 5.2g p5g2 p6g* p5.1g Oct 30] £14,000 2-y-o: useful-looking gelding: second foal: half-brother to winner in Greece by Acclamation: dam sprint maiden: fair performer: won maiden at Wolverhampton in October: stays 6f: acts on polytrack: tried blinkered: gelded after final start. *D. R. C. Elsworth* **71**

IMBONGI (SAF) 5 ch.h. Russian Revival (USA) 125 – Garden Verse (SAF) (Foveros 121) [2009 6.5g[2] 8g[4] 9m[4] 8d[6] 7g* 8m[3] Jul 11] close-coupled horse: smart performer: won Grade 2s at Turffontein and Greyville (2) in 2008: excellent efforts in Grade 1s at Clairwood after, notably when ¾-length second to Dancer's Daughter in Gold Challenge: as good as ever in 2009, winning John Bovington Memorial Criterion Stakes at Newmarket in June by 1¼ lengths from Huntdown: creditable efforts otherwise in handicap (short-head second to Hatta Fort) and Jebel Hatta (1½ lengths fourth to Balius) at Nad Al Sheba on first/third starts, and in Summer Mile at Ascot (length third to Aqlaam): effective at 6.5f to 9f: acts on good to firm ground. *M. F. de Kock, South Africa* **119**

IMCO SPIRIT (IRE) 3 b.g. Invincible Spirit (IRE) 121 – Treasure Hope (IRE) (Treasure Kay 114) [2009 79p: p7f[2] p7g* p8g[3] 7.6m[5] 7g 8f[4] a8.5f[5] Nov 6] compact gelding: fairly useful performer: won maiden at Dundalk in April: left G. Lyons in Ireland after fifth outing: stays easy 1m: acts on polytrack and firm going: blinkered (raced freely, bit below form at Chester) fourth outing. *P. Gallagher, USA* **93**

I'M IN THE PINK (FR) 5 b.g. Garuda (IRE) 116 – Ahwaki (FR) (River Mist (USA) 119) [2009 10m 12m[4] 10.2g[3] 10.2g[6] 10.4g* 10.3g[2] 10.2g[4] 10.3m 12.3g[3] 12m 10.2v* Nov 4] sturdy gelding: twice-raced in maiden points in 2008: well held in bumper (for R. Price): fairly useful handicapper: won at Haydock (ladies event) in May and Nottingham in November: stays 1½m: acts on heavy ground. *P. D. Evans* **82**

IMJIN RIVER (IRE) 2 b.c. (Mar 12) Namid 128 – Lady Nasrana (FR) (Al Nasr (FR) 126) [2009 6m 5.4d[6] 7m f6g* p6m* p6m[3] Nov 26] €4,000F, €7,000Y: good-topped colt: fifth foal: brother to 4-y-o More Time Tim and half-brother to 3-y-o Rio Royale: dam, Belgian 2-y-o 5f winner, half-sister to US Grade 1 9f/1¼m winner Janet: fairly useful performer: won nurseries at Southwell in October and Kempton (idled) in November: should stay 7f: acts on all-weather. *M. H. Tompkins* **83**

IMMACULATE RED 6 ch.g. Woodborough (USA) 112 – Primula Bairn 77 (Bairn (USA) 126) [2009 p11f Dec 16] compact gelding: little form since 2006: tried blinkered. *C. Roberts* **–**

I'MNEVERWRONG (IRE) 2 ch.f. (Feb 16) Compton Place 125 – Anthyllis (IRE) (Night Shift (USA)) [2009 6m[3] 8f[6] 6f[5] Nov 20] 10,000Y, £20,000 2-y-o: third foal: half-sister to useful 7f winner in France Topkapi Diamond (by Acclamation): dam, Irish maiden, sister to US Grade 2 1½m winner Plicck: fair form in maidens, leaving D. Elsworth after debut: stays 1m. *J. M. Cassidy, USA* **72**

IM OVA ERE DAD (IRE) 6 b.g. Second Empire (IRE) 124 – Eurolink Profile 74 (Prince Sabo 123) [2009 92: 8.3m[2] p8.6g[5] May 18] workmanlike gelding: fairly useful handicapper: stays 9f (refused to settle at 1¼m): acts on all-weather and firm ground: held up. *D. E. Cantillon* **89**

IMPECCABLE GUEST (IRE) 6 b.m. Orpen (USA) 116 – Perfect Guest (What A Guest 119) [2009 f12g May 1] leggy mare: modest maiden in 2006: fair form over hurdles later that year and in 2007: off 2 years, no form in 2 runs at 6 yrs (first over hurdles). *J. Mackie* **–**

IMPERIAL ANGEL (IRE) 3 gr.f. Tagula (IRE) 116 – New Deal 76 (Rainbow Quest (USA) 134) [2009 45: 12.1m 14.1m 8.3g Jun 17] poor form: tried blinkered. *D. Carroll* **–**

IMPERIAL DELIGHT 2 b.g. (Jan 29) Royal Applause 124 – Playgirl (IRE) 77 (Caerleon (USA) 132) [2009 6d[4] 6d[3] 6g Oct 30] 38,000F: compact gelding: third foal: dam, ran 3 times (second at 1¼m), half-sister to smart 9f/1¼m performer Stage Gift, out of sister to high-class performer up to 1¼m Prince of Dance: best effort in maidens when ¾-length third to Za Za Zoom at Windsor: gelded after final start: should be suited by 7f+. *H. Candy* **76 +**

IMPERIAL DJAY (IRE) 4 b.g. Dilshaan 119 – Slayjay (IRE) 94 (Mujtahid (USA) 118) [2009 72: p7.1g f6g[5] p6g[3] p6m[2] f6g p7g p7.1g[5] p7.1g[6] p7.1g[3] 7f[4] p8.6g 7g 6v[6] 6m[6] 6.1d Sep 4] workmanlike gelding: modest maiden handicapper nowadays: left G. Smith after eighth start: acts on polytrack and good to soft going: tried in headgear/tongue tie: has finished weakly. *J. R. Holt* **61**

IMPERIAL ECHO (USA) 8 b.g. Labeeb 124 – Regal Baby (USA) (Northern Baby (CAN) 127) [2009 80d: 7.1m[6] 6.9g[4] 6m[3] 6d[5] 7m 7.2m[4] Oct 1] leggy, quite good-topped gelding: modest performer nowadays: stays 7f: acts on any turf going, probably on polytrack: tried blinkered/visored: usually held up. *T. D. Barron* **58**

IMPERIAL GUEST 3 ch.g. Imperial Dancer 123 – Princess Speedfit (FR) 77 (Desert Prince (IRE) 130) [2009 103: 8m 8m 6d 6f[5] 6g 6g[6] 6m[3] Jul 20] angular gelding: just fairly useful form in 2009 (gelded after final start): best at 6f: acts on good to firm going: ungenuine. *G. G. Margarson* **91 §**

IMPERIAL HARRY 6 b.g. Alhaarth (IRE) 126 – Serpentara 75 (Kris 135) [2009 p12g p12g* p12.2g p12g³ p12g 12g 10g p12m Sep 23] tall gelding: fair handicapper: won at Kempton in January: left D. Pipe after fifth start, well held subsequently: stays 1½m: acts on polytrack, firm and good to soft going: has carried head awkwardly/pulled hard: tried visored/in cheekpieces. *Jean-Rene Auvray* **79**

IMPERIAL HOUSE 3 b.c. Imperial Dancer 123 – Cotton House (IRE) 107 (Mujadil (USA) 119) [2009 7m⁶ 6g* 6d 8s 7g³ p7g p6g⁶ Dec 5] 22,000F, 45,000Y: strong, useful-looking colt: third foal: dam 5f (at 2 yrs)/6f winner: fair performer: won maiden at Redcar in June: left M. Channon 6,000 gns prior to final start: stays 7f: acts on polytrack and good to firm ground: tried blinkered (tends to race lazily). *R. A. Harris* **73**

IMPERIAL SKYLIGHT 3 gr.g. Imperial Dancer 123 – Sky Light Dreams (Dreams To Reality (USA) 113) [2009 66: p7.1g³ p7g² f7g⁴ p7g* p7g² p7g² p7g⁶ 7m 7m 7.1g⁶ 6g 6f⁶ p7m 7m p6g⁶ 7m⁴ 7m p7g⁴ p7m p7m p8m⁴ p7.1g⁵ p7m⁶ Dec 30] smallish, leggy gelding: fair handicapper on all-weather, modest on turf: won at Kempton in February: stays 1m: acts on polytrack, good to firm and good to soft ground: tried visored: none too consistent. *M. R. Channon* **59 a68**

IMPERIAL SWORD 6 b.g. Danehill Dancer (IRE) 117 – Hajat 64 (Mujtahid (USA) 118) [2009 69: p7.1g 5m* 6g² 6s⁴ 5v* 5m 5m 5d⁶ 5.9g 6g⁶ 6d² 6f* 6m 6g Oct 23] close-coupled, dipped-backed gelding: has a quick action: fair handicapper: won apprentice events at Ripon in April, Haydock in May and Ayr in August: effective at 5f to 7f: acts on fibresand and any turf going: blinkered: usually claimer ridden: often gets behind/races lazily. *T. D. Barron* **72**

IMPERIAL WARRIOR 2 ch.g. (Feb 19) Imperial Dancer 123 – Tribal Lady 80 (Absalom 128) [2009 6m⁶ 6m³ 6m 7g 6g f7f³ Oct 21] workmanlike gelding: fair maiden: stays 7f: acts on good to firm going, probably on fibresand: usually slowly away. *H. Morrison* **68**

IMPERIUM 8 b.g. Imperial Ballet (IRE) 110 – Partenza (USA) (Red Ransom (USA)) [2009 67: p12g* p12g³ p13g p10g³ p12g³ 8.1g⁵ 12m⁴ 10g⁶ 7g 10.2m p12m p7m p8m⁴ p8.6g p12m Dec 9] leggy gelding: fair handicapper: won at Kempton in January: stays easy 1½m: acts on all-weather, firm and soft going: effective with/without headgear: tried tongue tied: usually held up. *Jean-Rene Auvray* **65**

IMPLICATION 3 b.f. Pivotal 124 – Insinuation (IRE) 70 (Danehill (USA) 126) [2009 –p: 8m² 8.3m p8.6g² p8g² 8m 8g² p8.6g² 8d* p8g⁶ 8g⁶ f8g³ Oct 27] big filly: fairly useful performer: won maiden at Newcastle in September: should prove as effective at 7f as 1m: acts on polytrack, good to firm and good to soft ground: sold 16,000 gns. *E. A. L. Dunlop* **81**

IMPOSING 3 b.c. Danehill Dancer (IRE) 117 – On Fair Stage (IRE) 103 (Sadler's Wells (USA) 132) [2009 89p: 10m² Apr 16] lengthy, useful-looking colt: useful form, lightly raced: improved when short-head second to Perpetually in handicap at Newmarket on only outing in 2009: will stay 1½m. *Sir Michael Stoute* **99**

IMPRESSIBLE 3 b.f. Oasis Dream 129 – Imperial Bailiwick (IRE) 104 (Imperial Frontier (USA) 112) [2009 65+: 5.1m² 5m* 5s³ 5g* 5m² 5.1m* 5.1m 5s* 5m 5m⁵ 5m² Sep 26] small, strong filly: improved into useful handicapper in 2009, winning at Haydock in April, Carlisle and Chester in June, and Hamilton in August: good second to Green Manalishi at Haydock final start: likely to prove best at 5f: acts on soft and good to firm going, promise on polytrack: front runner/races prominently. *E. J. Alston* **95**

IMPRIMIS TAGULA (IRE) 5 b.g. Tagula (IRE) 116 – Strelitzia (IRE) (Bluebird (USA) 125) [2009 84: p7.1g⁴ f6g* p6g² p7.1g² f5g* f6g* 6g⁶ 6m⁶ p7g² f7g* 7.2g⁴ p7.1g⁵ 6m³ f6g p6g² 5g f5g p6g⁶ f6g⁴ f6m* p6m* p7f² f7g* p6g* Dec 28] big, strong gelding: useful performer on all-weather, lightly raced and just fair on turf: had very successful 2009, winning handicap in February, claimers in March, April and June and handicap in November, all at Southwell: marked improvement in December to win handicaps at Lingfield, Southwell (beat Ingleby Arch 9 lengths) and Wolverhampton (by a head from Ebraam): has won at 5f, best at 6f/7f: acts on all-weather and good to firm going: tried blinkered, visored nowadays. *A. Bailey* **71 a107**

IMPROMPTU 5 b.g. Mujadil (USA) 119 – Pie In The Sky (Bishop of Cashel 122) [2009 78: p6g³ p7g Apr 4] smallish gelding: fair handicapper: stays 6f: acts on firm and soft going, probably on polytrack: said to have bled final starts at 4/5 yrs. *P. G. Murphy* **68**

IMPROPER (USA) 3 b.g. Northern Afleet (USA) 117 – Bare It Properly (USA) (Proper Reality (USA)) [2009 –: 8.1g 10m 11.9d 14.1m p7g Oct 8] leggy gelding: little form. *Mouse Hamilton-Fairley* **–**

IMPURE THOUGHTS 4 b.g. Averti (IRE) 117 – Blooming Lucky (IRE) 40 (Lucky Guest 109) [2009 p9.5g Nov 20] well held in maidens in 2007: left J. R. Best and off 2 years, bolted before start when tailed off on return. *D. W. Thompson* –

I'M SUPER TOO (IRE) 2 b.g. (Apr 6) Fasliyev (USA) 120 – Congress (IRE) 86 (Dancing Brave (USA) 140) [2009 5.9g 6s^2 7.5m^5 Sep 16] €10,000Y: workmanlike gelding: half-brother to several winners, including useful Irish 7.5f (at 2 yrs)/1¼m winner Royal Intrigue (by Royal Applause) and 4-y-o Hawaana: dam, 2-y-o 1m winner, sister to very smart 6f/7f performer Cherokee Rose: best effort in maidens when 1¾ lengths second to Dance For Julie at Thirsk: should stay at least 7f. *G. A. Swinbank* **71**

INCA SLEW (IRE) 3 ch.g. City On A Hill (USA) 114 – Con Dancer (Shareef Dancer (USA) 135) [2009 52: p8.6g^6 p9.5g 12.1m Jun 10] modest maiden: stays 8.6f: tried in headgear: quirky. *P. C. Haslam* **54**

INCA SOLDIER (FR) 6 br.g. Intikhab (USA) 135 – Chrysalu 102 (Distant Relative 128) [2009 67: p6g^2 p6g 7d p8g^6 7g 6m Aug 29] sturdy gelding: fair handicapper: below form after reappearance, leaving R. C. Guest after fourth start: probably best short of 1m nowadays: acts on all-weather and firm ground: held up: none too consistent. *S. A. Harris* **65**

INCENDO 3 ch.g. King's Best (USA) 132 – Kindle (Selkirk (USA) 129) [2009 75p: 8.3d^6 8m^6 p12g^2 12g^4 10m^5 11.5m^2 p12g* Oct 8] close-coupled gelding: fairly useful handicapper: tongue tied, improved last 2 starts, and barely off bridle when winning at Kempton in October: stays 1½m: acts on polytrack and good to firm going: patiently ridden: hung right second outing: quirky. *J. R. Fanshawe* **85 +**

INCHANDO (FR) 5 ch.h. Hernando (FR) 127 – Nordican Inch 108 (Inchinor 119) [2009 10g 10m f8g 12.1v^5 12.1v^2 18g^2 Aug 13] maiden: lightly raced for A. Fabre in France at 2/3 yrs (in frame in maidens/claimer): left J. Bertran de Balanda €7,000 and off 11 months before reappearance: modest form in Britain: stays 2¼m: acts on heavy going. *A. W. Carroll* **63**

INCH LODGE 7 ch.h. Grand Lodge (USA) 125 – Legaya 94 (Shirley Heights 130) [2009 68, a82d: p10g p10g* p10g^2 p11g^3 p11g 9m p10g p11g* p12m 12m p12m^4 p12m f12g^4 p12m^4 p11f^3 Dec 16] good-topped horse: fair handicapper, better on all-weather: won at Lingfield in February and Kempton (apprentice event) in September: stays 1½m: acts on all-weather and firm going: usually tongue tied. *Miss D. Mountain* **–** **a70**

INCHNADAMPH 9 b.g. Inchinor 119 – Pelf (USA) 79 (Al Nasr (FR) 126) [2009 97: p16g 18.7m^6 16.4d 16g^5 16.4g^3 16.4m 18m 16d^4 Oct 28] tall, workmanlike gelding: useful handicapper at best: stays 18.7f: acts on firm and soft going: tongue tied: has run well when sweating: travels strongly. *T. J. Fitzgerald* **95**

INCHPAST 8 ch.g. Inchinor 119 – Victor Ludorum (Rainbow Quest (USA) 134) [2009 82: 14.1g^6 18g^4 16g* 16m* 18m^6 16d p16g^4 16m^3 18m^6 Sep 19] workmanlike gelding: fair handicapper: won at Goodwood in May and Ripon in June: stays 21f: acts on polytrack and firm ground: blinkered. *M. H. Tompkins* **75**

INCOMPARABLE 4 ch.g. Compton Place 125 – Indian Silk (IRE) 74 (Dolphin Street (FR) 125) [2009 79: p6g^6 p5g^2 p5.1g^2 f5g^2 p5.1g* p5g^4 p5.1g^3 5d 6m^2 6g^6 5m* 5m^4 5g Oct 9] big, strong gelding: fairly useful handicapper: won at Wolverhampton in February and, having left A. McCabe after seventh start, Doncaster in September: effective at 5f/6f: acts on all-weather and good to firm ground: tried blinkered/in cheekpieces: usually front runner (slowly away final outing). *J. A. Glover* **91**

INCONSPICUOUS MISS (USA) 3 b. or br.f. War Chant (USA) 126 – Orissa (USA) (Devil's Bag (USA)) [2009 63: p8.6g 7m 7g p9.5g* p12m p9.5g p10g^3 f12m p10g Nov 25] fair performer: won handicap at Wolverhampton in September: stays 9.5f: acts on all-weather: tried tongue tied/in cheekpieces: none too consistent: sold 8,200 gns. *George Baker* **72**

INCY WINCY 3 b.g. Zahran (IRE) 77 – Miss Money Spider (IRE) 65 (Statoblest 120) [2009 –: p9.5g^5 p8g^5 f8g^6 7d^5 p7g p8m p9.5g Dec 11] leggy, unfurnished gelding: poor maiden: tried in cheekpieces/blinkers. *J. M. Bradley* **42**

INDEPENDENT JAMES (IRE) 3 b.g. Singspiel (IRE) 133 – Massomah (USA) 90 (Seeking The Gold (USA)) [2009 p8g^5 7d 8d 14.1m 10.2v^5 Jul 17] little form, including in seller (visored). *S. C. Williams* –

INDIANA FOX 6 b.m. Foxhound (USA) 103 – Ridgewood Ruby (IRE) 77 (Indian Ridge 123) [2009 –: p10m p12g Jan 16] smallish mare: little form on Flat: tried blinkered. *B. G. Powell* –

INDIAN ART (IRE) 3 b.c. Choisir (AUS) 126 – Eastern Ember 85 (Indian King (USA) 128) [2009 88: 7s 7m^5 p6g^2 7m 6m^2 7m* 7.1m^2 p8g p7g^5 7s Oct 12] good-topped, **94** **a85**

attractive colt: has a quick, unimpressive action: fairly useful performer, better on turf: won claimer at Salisbury in July: stays 7f: acts on polytrack and good to firm going: visored once (worked up): suspect temperament. *R. Hannon*

INDIAN DAYS 4 ch.c. Daylami (IRE) 138 – Cap Coz (IRE) 110 (Indian Ridge 123) [2009 106: 10g 10.3m^5 10m 10f^6 12m^4 12g p12m^3 12.3m^3 12m Sep 27] strong, useful-looking colt: useful performer: several creditable efforts in 2009 (often highly tried), including 4¾ lengths fourth to Doctor Fremantle in Princess of Wales's Stakes at Newmarket and 5¼ lengths third to Kirklees in September Stakes at Kempton fifth/seventh starts: stays 1½m: acts on polytrack, firm and good to soft going. *J. G. Given* **108**

INDIAN DIVA (IRE) 4 b.f. Indian Danehill (IRE) 124 – Katherine Gorge (USA) (Hansel (USA)) [2009 86: f7g* p8.6g^5 p7.1g f7d^4 f7g 8m f7g 6s 6m Aug 22] workmanlike filly: fairly useful performer: won handicap at Southwell in January: left R. Curtis £5,000 after fourth start: out of sorts after: best form at 7f: acts on all-weather and good to soft going: effective with or without blinkers: has been tongue tied (including at Southwell): reluctant to race eighth outing. *P. T. Midgley* **86 d**

INDIAN PIPE DREAM (IRE) 7 br.g. Indian Danehill (IRE) 124 – Build A Dream (USA) (Runaway Groom (CAN)) [2009 14m Sep 26] strong, lengthy gelding: useful performer in 2005 for J. Gosden: fairly useful hurdler since for D. Pipe, but no form in 2009 for current yard, including on Flat return. *S. Gollings* **–**

INDIAN SKIPPER (IRE) 4 b.g. Indian Danehill (IRE) 124 – Rosy Lydgate 53 (Last Tycoon 131) [2009 82: 10m^2 8m^2 8.9d 8m^5 6d^4 6m* 6m^6 6m 7m^2 f6m^3 f8f^4 f7g^5 Dec 22] leggy, workmanlike gelding: fairly useful performer: won handicap at Folkestone in August: claimed from M. Tompkins £6,000 ninth start: barely stays 1½m, effective at much shorter: acts on polytrack, soft and good to firm going: usually in cheekpieces/blinkers. *R. C. Guest* **82**

INDIAN STORY (IRE) 3 b.f. Indian Ridge 123 – Law Tudor (IRE) (Law Society (USA) 130) [2009 p7g Feb 11] half-sister to several winners in Italy, including useful 6f to 1m winner (including at 2 yrs) Love Roi (by Roi Danzig): dam Italian 10.5f winner: 25/1, well held in maiden at Lingfield. *G. C. Bravery* **–**

INDIAN TONIC (IRE) 3 b.f. Tiger Hill (IRE) 127 – Wellspring (IRE) 88 (Caerleon (USA) 132) [2009 74: 8d 7m^5 8.3g^6 p8m^5 8g Oct 20] leggy filly: fair maiden: stays 8.3f: acts on polytrack, unraced on extremes of going on turf: sold 3,000 gns, sent to Hungary. *W. Jarvis* **66**

INDIAN TRAIL 9 ch.g. Indian Ridge 123 – Take Heart 84 (Electric 126) [2009 111d: f6g^4 5g^3 6m 5m^4 5g* 5d^6 5d^5 5m 5m^5 5d^4 6g 5.4m 5m^4 Aug 31] big, strong gelding: useful handicapper: won Investec 'Dash' at Epsom in June by short head from Captain Dunne: creditable efforts after when fifth at Ascot and fourth at Goodwood ninth/tenth starts: has won at 7f, best at 5f/6f on good ground or firmer: usually blinkered/visored: usually held up: no easy ride. *D. Nicholls* **95**

Investec 'Dash' (Heritage Handicap), Epsom—
the visored Indian Trail swoops late to catch Captain Dunne (left) and Strike Up The Band (stars)

INDIAN VALLEY (USA) 2 b.f. (Apr 25) Cherokee Run (USA) 122 – Shade Dance (USA) (Nureyev (USA) 131) [2009 7.5m² p7m² 7v Oct 24] $72,000Y: half-sister to several winners abroad including French 1m winner Haute Danse (by Lear Fan): dam unraced half-sister to very smart 7.5f to 1¼m winner Equerry and Breeders' Cup Juvenile Fillies winner Tempera: similar form when runner-up in maidens at Beverley and Kempton: stiff task/met trouble in listed race at Newbury: stays 7f. *Rae Guest* **73 +**

INDIAN VIOLET (IRE) 3 b.g. Indian Ridge 123 – Violet Spring (IRE) 32 (Exactly Sharp (USA) 121) [2009 7m p8g 7m 8.3m² 8g⁴ 8m⁴ 8.1d 8m⁵ Sep 28] 155,000Y: tall gelding: has scope: fourth foal: closely related to fairly useful 6f and (at 2 yrs) 7f winner Violet Ballerina (by Namid) and half-brother to useful 2003 2-y-o 6f (Richmond Stakes) winner Carrizo Creek (by Charnwood Forest), later 1m winner in Hong Kong: dam Irish 2m winner: fair maiden: worth a try at 1¼m: acts on good to firm going: signs of temperament: sold £5,000. *P. F. I. Cole* **72**

INDICIBLE (FR) 5 ch.g. Dyhim Diamond (IRE) 117 – Caslon (FR) (Deep Roots 124) [2009 92: p12.2g 11.9f Aug 6] stocky gelding: fairly useful handicapper at 4 yrs: well held in 2009: stays 1½m: acts on polytrack and good to soft going: has shaped as if amiss. *A. King* **–**

INDIGO BELLE (IRE) 3 b.f. Mull of Kintyre (USA) 114 – Frances Canty (USA) (Lear Fan (USA) 130) [2009 –: f11g⁶ 10.1d 10m 7.9g 15.8g⁶ Aug 4] little form. *Mrs A. Duffield* **–**

INDIGO INK 2 b.f. (Apr 30) Rock of Gibraltar (IRE) 133 – Blue Indigo (FR) (Pistolet Bleu (IRE) 133) [2009 7m 8.3g³ p8g p7m⁶ Dec 9] unfurnished filly: sixth foal: half-sister to 1m (at 2 yrs) to 9f (US Grade 3 event) winner Genre (by Orpen): dam, French maiden (placed up to 12.5f), out of half-sister to Breeders' Cup Classic winner Arcangues: left S. Callaghan, form only when third in seller at Nottingham: stays 8.3f. *Miss Amy Weaver* **56**

INDOCHINA 2 b.g. (Apr 2) Sulamani (IRE) 130 – Lane County (USA) (Rahy (USA) 115) [2009 8.5d⁵ 9m⁴ 10m² Oct 5] lengthy, good-topped gelding: second foal: half-brother to fairly useful 2008 2-y-o 1m winner Red Spider (by Red Ransom): dam unraced out of US Grade 1 9f winner Link River: easily best effort in maidens when 1½ lengths second to Futurist at Pontefract, dictating: gelded after: stays 1¼m. *M. Johnston* **74**

INDONESIA 7 ch.g. Lomitas 129 – Idraak (Kris 135) [2009 86: 14m⁶ 17.1g 16.1m Jun 25] strong, useful-looking gelding: fair handicapper: lightly raced nowadays: stays 17f: acts on good to firm and good to soft ground: sold £1,200. *T. D. Walford* **71**

INDY DRIVER 4 ch.g. Domedriver (IRE) 128 – Condoleezza (USA) 78 (Cozzene (USA)) [2009 82: p8.6g⁵ 10.2m² 10m⁴ p12.2g⁶ 10m⁴ 8.3g 7.6g* 8.5m* 8m⁵ 7m⁶ 8d p8m² p10m³ p9.5g Dec 26] good-bodied gelding: fairly useful handicapper: won at Lingfield in July and Epsom in August: left J. Fanshawe 12,000 gns after twelfth start: best up to 1¼m: acts on all-weather and good to firm ground: tried visored, in cheekpieces nowadays. *Matthew Salaman* **85**

INFAMOUS ANGEL 3 b.f. Exceed And Excel (AUS) 126 – Evangeline (Sadler's Wells (USA) 132) [2009 101: 7s 8g⁴ 7m⁶ 8.5g⁶ 6m 7g Jul 31] well-made filly: useful performer: best effort in 2009 (often highly tried) when sixth to San Sicharia in Chartwell Fillies' Stakes at Lingfield third start: stays 7f: acts on good to firm going: sold 270,000 gns in December. *R. Hannon* **96**

INFANTA (IRE) 2 b.f. (Mar 27) Cape Cross (IRE) 129 – Maria Isabella (USA) 96 (Kris 135) [2009 7.1d³ Oct 28] sixth foal: closely related to 7f winner Viscountess (by Green Desert) and half-sister to smart French 9f/9.5f winner Utrecht (by Rock of Gibraltar): dam, 2-y-o 1m winner, half-sister to Bosra Sham, Hector Protector and Shanghai: 5/4 favourite but very green, 7 lengths third to Tatiana Romanova in maiden at Musselburgh, late headway under hand riding: sure to improve. *Saeed bin Suroor* **56 p**

INFINITE PATIENCE 4 b. or br.f. High Chaparral (IRE) 132 – Idma 67 (Midyan (USA) 124) [2009 63d: p10g Jul 18] strong, rangy filly: maiden: regressive at 3 yrs, and well held in seller sole start in 2009: tried blinkered/in cheekpieces: has looked reluctant. *T. D. McCarthy* **– §**

INFINITY BOND 4 b.g. Forzando 122 – Bond Girl (Magic Ring (IRE) 115) [2009 69: 7s 7.1m⁴ 7.1m² 7.1m⁶ Jun 19] well-made gelding: fair handicapper: stays 7f: acts on good to firm ground. *G. R. Oldroyd* **71**

INFINITY WORLD 2 b.f. (Apr 29) Lucky Story (USA) 128 – Musical Refrain (IRE) (Dancing Dissident (USA) 119) [2009 7m 6m p7.1g³ p6g⁶ Dec 18] sixth foal: half-sister to fairly useful Irish 5f/6f winner Ms Victoria (by Fasliyev): dam, Italian maiden, half-sister to very smart 6f/7f performer Monsieur Bond: modest form in maidens: likely to prove best up to 7f. *G. R. Oldroyd* **57**

INFIRAAD 3 ch.c. Haafhd 129 – Razzle (IRE) 68 (Green Desert (USA) 127) [2009 77p: 7m* 7m* 7m 8g Oct 31] well-made colt: useful performer: reportedly had a knee chip removed after sole 2-y-o start: highly progressive in the spring, winning maiden and handicap at Newmarket, latter by 4 lengths from Firebet: down the field after in Jersey Stakes at Royal Ascot (shaped as if amiss) and handicap at Newmarket (off 4 months, possibly needed run). stays 7f: raced only on good/good to firm going. *B. W. Hills* **105 +**

INFLAMMABLE 3 b.f. Montjeu (IRE) 137 – Flame Valley (USA) 112 (Gulch (USA)) [2009 76p: f11f^4 p16m^4 f12f^3 p13.9g^2 p12.2g* Dec 5] attractive filly: fair performer: won maiden at Wolverhampton in December: barely stays 1¾m: acts on all-weather and heavy going. *Sir Mark Prescott* **70**

IN FOOTLIGHTS (USA) 3 b.c. Elusive Quality (USA) – Triple Act (USA) 66 (Theatrical 128) [2009 8m* 10m^5 Jul 16] good-bodied colt: first foal: dam, US 1m winner, half-sister to very smart US Grade 1 1m winner Corinthian: 5/2 favourite, readily won maiden at Newmarket in June: last in minor event at Leicester next time: stays 1m. *Saeed bin Suroor* **84**

INFORMAL AFFAIR 3 b.g. Makbul 104 – Fontaine Lady 41 (Millfontaine 114) [2009 8m 12g 12g^5 Aug 14] well held in maidens. *J. D. Bethell* **–**

INGENUE 3 b.f. Hernando (FR) 127 – I Do 81 (Selkirk (USA) 129) [2009 10m p12g 11.7g 13.8m 15.4m 15.8g* p16g^2 p16.5g^6 Nov 16] sturdy filly: second foal: dam, 2-y-o 7f winner, half-sister to useful performer up to 1¼m Oblige: modest handicapper: won at Catterick in October: left Sir Mark Prescott after next outing: stays 2m: raced only on polytrack and good/good to firm ground: blinkered last 5 starts. *P. Howling* **64**

INGLEBY ARCH (USA) 6 b.g. Arch (USA) 127 – Inca Dove (USA) (Mr Prospector (USA)) [2009 95: f6g* f6g^4 6m 6g 6d^5 6v^2 6m^6 6g 6d^3 f6g 6g p7.1g^5 6d^3 f6g* f6f* f6m^2 f7g^2 Dec 22] strong, well-made gelding: useful handicapper on all-weather, fairly useful on turf: won at Southwell in February and October (2): as good as ever when beating Nightjar 1¼ lengths for latest success: best at 6f: acts on fibresand, heavy and good to firm going: tried blinkered/visored: has high head carriage: tactically versatile. *T. D. Barron* **83** **a101**

INGLEBY LADY 3 ch.f. Captain Rio 122 – Petra Nova 51 (First Trump 118) [2009 6m* 6m^6 6g^4 5m* 5d^3 6m* 6m 6m^2 Sep 18] 15,000F, 24,000Y: stocky, well-made filly: fourth foal: sister to 4-y-o Mey Blossom and half-sister to 7.5f winner Paris Heights (by Paris House) and 1m seller winner Tafilah (by Foxhound): dam sprint maiden: useful performer: won maiden at Pontefract in April, and handicaps at Redcar in June and August: good second to Baldemar in handicap at Ayr final start: best kept to 5f/6f: acts on good to firm ground. *T. D. Barron* **102**

INGLEBY PRINCESS 5 br.m. Bold Edge 123 – Bob's Princess 69 (Bob's Return (IRE) 123) [2009 74: 6m 6f^5 6m 5.9g^4 5.9m 6m^3 6m^6 6d^2 f7g^5 6s^5 8g^5 8d^4 10m^4 7.2m^6 9.1g^6 f7m* f8g^4 f7g^4 Dec 8] leggy, angular mare: fair performer: won claimer at Southwell in November: stays 1m: acts on fibresand and any turf going: tried blinkered/in cheekpieces. *T. D. Barron* **67**

INGLEBY SPIRIT 2 b.g. (Feb 25) Avonbridge 123 – Encore du Cristal (USA) 82 (Quiet American (USA)) [2009 5m 6v* 6m^3 7g f8g^3 8m^4 Sep 19] 31,000F, 25,000Y: tall gelding: fourth foal: half-brother to 5-y-o Norman The Great: dam 1¼m winner: fairly useful performer: won maiden at Haydock (by 8 lengths) in May: mostly creditable efforts after: stays 1m: acts on heavy and good to firm ground: gelded after final start. *R. A. Fahey* **82**

INGLEBY STAR (IRE) 4 b.g. Fath (USA) 116 – Rosy Scintilla (IRE) (Thatching 131) [2009 69: 5v 5m 5m^4 5g* 5m^2 5g* 5d^2 5g* 5g^4 5m 5m^6 5g 5d f5m^6 Dec 15] chunky, deep-girthed gelding: fair handicapper: won at Ayr (2, amateur event first occasion) and Musselburgh, all in July: raced at 5f: acts on fibresand, good to soft and good to firm ground: tried blinkered, usually wears cheekpieces nowadays: has hung left. *N. Wilson* **78**

INHERITOR (IRE) 3 b.g. Kheleyf (USA) 116 – Miss Devious (IRE) 51 (Dr Devious (IRE) 127) [2009 85: 8.1f^4 7m^3 8m^3 7.1m^5 6.9g* 7m^6 7m 7g p7.1g^2 p8.6g* Dec 12] good-topped gelding: fairly useful handicapper: won at Carlisle in August and Wolverhampton in December: stays easy 8.6f: acts on polytrack and good to firm going. *B. Smart* **92**

INHIBITION 3 br.f. Nayef (USA) 129 – Spurned (USA) 91 (Robellino (USA) 127) [2009 68p: p12g* 11.5m^6 11.5d^4 13m^6 Jul 9] lengthy filly: has scope: useful performer: won maiden at Kempton in April: improved next 2 starts, fourth in listed race at Le Lion-d'Angers latter occasion: below form in Bahrain Trophy at Newmarket final start: stays 1½m: acts on polytrack, unraced on extremes of ground on turf. *A. M. Balding* **96**

INIS BOFFIN 3 b.f. Danehill Dancer (IRE) 117 – Windmill 71 (Ezzoud (IRE) 126) [2009 –: p7.1g^3 p8.6g* 10.2g 8.1g^2 11.6m 10s 8m^2 10m^5 Aug 27] close-coupled filly: fairly useful handicapper: won at Wolverhampton in May: stays 8.6f: acts on polytrack and good to firm going: tends to hang left: none too consistent. *S. Kirk* **81**

INITTOWINIT 2 ch.f. (May 1) Trade Fair 124 – Moly (FR) (Anabaa (USA) 130) [2009 7f p7.1g 7m Sep 1] fourth foal: dam useful French 2-y-o 1m winner: well held in maidens/seller (blinkered). *W. R. Muir* **–**

INKA DANCER (IRE) 7 ch.m. Intikhab (USA) 135 – Grannys Reluctance (IRE) 63 (Anita's Prince 126) [2009 57: p6g^6 p7.1g^2 p6g^4 p7g p6g^3 p7.1g 8.1g May 4] small mare: modest handicapper: effective at 6f/7f: acts on polytrack, firm and good to soft going: has hung right: none too consistent. *B. Palling* **57**

INLER (IRE) 2 br.c. (Feb 7) Red Ransom (USA) – Wedding Gift (FR) 108 (Always Fair (USA) 121) [2009 6m* Oct 16] €30,000F, £55,000Y: strong colt: type to carry condition: seventh foal: half-brother to 3 winners, including 6.5f and (at 2 yrs) 1m winner Wana Doo (by Grand Slam) and 7f/1m winner Sky Gift (by Stravinsky), both fairly useful in France: dam French 2-y-o 7f/1m winner who stayed 10.5f: evens favourite, very good impression when winning maiden at Newmarket by 4 lengths from Chaussini, going strongly up with pace and merely pushed out: should stay 1m: smart prospect. *J. R. Best* **98 P**

INLOVINGMEMORY (IRE) 2 br. or gr.f. (Mar 9) Dubai Destination (USA) 127 – Oiselina (FR) 95 (Linamix (FR) 127) [2009 6f^2 Jun 1] unfurnished filly: half-sister to several winners, including fairly useful 2005 2-y-o 1m winner Salute The General (by Mark of Esteem), who stayed 1½m, and 3-y-o Diktalina: dam, French 10.5f winner, half-sister to smart French performer up to 12.5f Oiseau Rare: 12/1, 1¼ lengths second to Anjomarba in seller at Thirsk (claimed £6,000, joined P. D. Evans), off bridle before halfway: should stay at least 1m. *R. A. Fahey* **61**

INNACTUALFACT 3 b.f. Lujain (USA) 119 – Alzianah 102 (Alzao (USA) 117) [2009 65: p10m^5 p10g* p11g^6 p10g^6 8.3m p10g p10g p12g p10g p12m Dec 9] small filly: fair handicapper: won at Lingfield in January: largely below form after: stays 1¼m: acts on polytrack and soft ground: in cheekpieces/blinkers last 4 starts. *L. A. Dace* **65 d**

INNER ANGEL 2 ch.f. (Feb 12) Motivator 131 – Sea Angel (Nashwan (USA) 135) [2009 p8m^3 p8m^2 Nov 19] 24,000Y: first foal: dam, French 10.5f/1½m winner, sister to useful 7f/1m winner Noisette, out of close relation to US Grade 1 9f/1¼m winner Sabin: similar form when placed in maidens at Kempton, second to Eleanora Duse: should be suited by 1¼m+: capable of better. *M. Botti* **73 p**

INNER VOICE (USA) 6 gr.g. Cozzene (USA) – Miss Henderson Co (USA) (Silver Hawk (USA) 123) [2009 60: p16.5g Feb 20] modest handicapper at 5 yrs: well held in 2009 (including over hurdles): should stay 2m: acts on good to soft going: blinkered. *J. J. Lambe, Ireland* **–**

INN FOR THE DANCER 7 b.g. Groom Dancer (USA) 128 – Lady Joyce (FR) (Galetto (FR) 118) [2009 55: p12g^5 p12.2g^5 p13.9g^6 12.1v Jul 24] workmanlike gelding: modest maiden handicapper, lightly raced nowadays: stays easy 1¾m: acts on polytrack and firm going: tried in cheekpieces: held up: said to have bled third outing. *J. C. Fox* **52**

INN SWINGER (IRE) 3 b.f. Makbul 104 – Sheik'n Swing 73 (Celtic Swing 138) [2009 37: p6g p6g Jan 17] poor maiden: form only at 5f/6f. *W. G. M. Turner* **39**

INPURSUITOFFREEDOM 2 b. or br.f. (Feb 3) Pastoral Pursuits 127 – Quilt 53 (Terimon 124) [2009 7g^3 p8.6g^5 Oct 17] sixth foal: half-sister to 2 winners, including fairly useful 1¼m to 1¾m winner Quarrymount (by Polar Falcon): dam maiden (stayed 1¼m): easily better effort in maidens 2 months apart when 3¾ lengths third to Destination Aim at Newmarket: should stay 1m. *P. J. McBride* **66**

INQUEST 4 b.g. Rainbow Quest (USA) 134 – Katy Nowaitee 112 (Komaite (USA)) [2009 79: p10g^3 p10g^2 p10g^6 Feb 18] fair maiden: appears to stay 1½m: raced only on polytrack and good going or softer: sold £5,000. *Mrs A. J. Perrett* **66**

INQUISITRESS 5 b.m. Hernando (FR) 127 – Caribbean Star 81 (Soviet Star (USA) 128) [2009 58, a65: p8g p10m^4 p8g^5 p12g p8g^5 p10g^6 p10g^5 p10g^5 p10g* 10m^6 p11g 8d^4 9.7s^5 8d^6 p8m* p8g^4 p8g^6 p10g^4 p8m^6 p10g^3 p7m Dec 30] small, workmanlike mare: modest handicapper: won at Lingfield (apprentices) in August and Kempton in October: stays 1¼m: acts on polytrack and good to firm going: tried in blinkers: unreliable. *J. J. Bridger* **54 a60**

IN SECRET 3 b.f. Dalakhani (IRE) 133 – Conspiracy 98 (Rudimentary (USA) 118) [2009 –P: 8m 7m^3 8m^3 10m 10m^2 10d 10.2g^2 p10g p10m^2 f12f^2 Dec 12] sturdy filly: fair maiden: should stay 1½m: acts on good to firm ground: ungenuine. *J. L. Dunlop* **77 §**

INSHAALLAH 2 ch.g. (Apr 6) Doyen (IRE) 132 – Lake Diva 70 (Docksider (USA) 124) [2009 8.3d 8.3g f7g^5 Nov 17] compact gelding: best effort in maidens when fifth to Solicitor at Southwell: gelded after: should stay 1m+. *J. G. Given* **55**

INSIDE KNOWLEDGE (USA) 3 gr. or ro.g. Mizzen Mast (USA) 121 – Kithira 106 (Danehill (USA) 126) [2009 59: f5g 8.3m f8g 10.3g^3 14v^6 12s Oct 27] smallish gelding: modest maiden handicapper: should stay 1½m: best efforts on good ground: tried in cheekpieces. *G. Woodward* **55**

INSIDE STORY (IRE) 7 b.g. Rossini (USA) 118 – Sliding (Formidable (USA) 125) [2009 80: p7g^4 p7.1g^4 p7.1g f8g^2 p8g^4 p9.5g^5 f11g* f12d^5 9.9m 8.3g^3 8m* 7.9g^3 8m^4 8.1s^6 7g 8s^5 8.3g 8.1d^6 p8.6m p8m^6 p10m p9.5g Dec 28] rather leggy gelding: fair handicapper: won at Southwell in February and Goodwood in May: stays 11f: acts on all-weather, firm and good to soft ground: blinkered: often slowly away in 2009: signs of temperament. *C. R. Dore* **76**

INSIDE TRACK (IRE) 2 b.g. (Feb 27) Bertolini (USA) 125 – True Crystal (IRE) 94 (Sadler's Wells (USA) 132) [2009 7.1g 8.1d^2 p8m^2 8d^5 p7m^6 p7g^6 p8.6g^3 p7m^3 f7f* Dec 17] 9,000Y: sturdy gelding: fourth foal: dam, 1¼m winner who stayed 1½m, out of Lancashire Oaks winner State Crystal: fair performer: claimed from B. Meehan £3,000, then won 4-runner maiden at Southwell: stays 1m: acts on all-weather and good to soft going: blinkered last 4 starts: has found little. *P. T. Midgley* **78**

INSIDE TRADE (IRE) 3 b.g. Xaar 132 – Azolia (IRE) (Alzao (USA) 117) [2009 8s 8m^6 7m p8g^6 9m p8m p7m p7m Nov 4] good-bodied gelding: poor maiden: left R. Beckett after fifth start: probably stays 9f: tried visored/tongue tied. *N. P. Mulholland* **48**

INSIGNIA (IRE) 7 b.g. Royal Applause 124 – Amathea (FR) (Exit To Nowhere (USA) 122) [2009 p12g Feb 7] maiden: well held only Flat start in 2009: tried in cheekpieces/visor. *Mrs A. M. Thorpe* **–**

INSOLENCE (USA) 3 b.f. Mr Greeley (USA) 122 – Brianda (IRE) (Alzao (USA) 117) [2009 8m^5 8.3g^3 10.1m^4 10.2g^3 p9.5g^2 10.2g^4 p9.5g^3 p9.5g* Nov 14] $350,000Y: sturdy filly: fourth foal: closely related to winner in USA by Gone West and half-sister to fairly useful French 1m winner Anoush (by Giant's Causeway): dam French/US 1m/1¼m winner (placed in Grade 2 events): fairly useful performer: won handicap at Wolverhampton in November: stays 1¼m: acts on polytrack and good to firm ground: has looked reluctant. *Sir Michael Stoute* **82**

IN SOME RESPECT (IRE) 2 b.c. (Mar 9) Indian Haven 119 – Burnin' Memories (USA) (Lit de Justice (USA) 125) [2009 5g^3 6g^2 6v^4 6s^2 p6g^4 6d* Sep 22] €10,000Y: tall, close-coupled colt: second foal: half-brother to Irish 3-y-o Glebe Queen: dam 7.5f (including at 2 yrs) to 8.5f (including minor stakes) winner in USA: useful performer: had to work very hard to land odds in maiden at Fairyhouse: best efforts when in frame behind Alfred Nobel in Railway Stakes (1¼ lengths second) and Phoenix Stakes (3½ lengths fourth) at the Curragh second/third starts, and when fourth to Love Lockdown in Sirenia Stakes at Kempton: should be suited by 7f: acts on polytrack and heavy going: sent to Hong Kong, where renamed Dragon Fighter. *Andrew Oliver, Ireland* **100**

INSPAINAGAIN (USA) 5 ch.g. Miswaki (USA) 124 – Counter Cat (USA) (Hennessy (USA) 122) [2009 81: f5m 6m Jun 27] attractive gelding: fairly useful handicapper at 4 yrs: well held in 2009: likely to prove best at 5f: acts on heavy and good to firm going: sold 2,500 gns. *Paul Mason* **–**

INSPECTOR CLOUSEAU (IRE) 4 gr.g. Daylami (IRE) 138 – Claustra (FR) 91 (Green Desert (USA) 127) [2009 84: 12m^4 10g 12.3g^2 14.6m^5 12.3m 12g* 13.4m Sep 26] close-coupled gelding: fair handicapper: won amateur event at Catterick in August: stays 1½m: acts on good to firm and good to soft going: usually makes running. *T. P. Tate* **79**

INSPIRINA (IRE) 5 b.g. Invincible Spirit (IRE) 121 – La Stellina (IRE) 100 (Marju (IRE) 127) [2009 82: 12.3g^4 10m^6 12.3m* 10.3m^5 12m* 12g 12.3g^4 12m^4 12g^4 10.3d^2 Oct 24] good-bodied gelding: type to carry condition: fair handicapper: won at Chester and Epsom in July: stays 1¾m: acts on polytrack, firm and soft ground: sometimes slowly away: refused to race sixth outing. *R. Ford* **74**

INSTALMENT 3 b.g. Cape Cross (IRE) 129 – New Assembly (IRE) 99 (Machiavellian (USA) 123) [2009 88: 6m* 7m 6m^4 Jul 4] good-topped gelding: useful performer: won handicap at Salisbury in May by neck from Timeteam: poor efforts after, in Jersey Stakes at Royal Ascot and minor event at Haydock: effective at 6f/7f: acts on good to firm and good to soft going: has shown signs of temperament: sold 25,000 gns, sent to Saudi Arabia. *R. Hannon* **104**

IN STEP 3 b.f. Montjeu (IRE) 137 – Heart's Harmony (Blushing Groom (FR) 131) [2009 55: p9.5g4 p10g Jan 17] modest maiden: should stay 1¼m: raced only on all-weather and good ground: tried blinkered (has hung): sold 2,500 gns in February. *W. J. Haggas* **51**

INSTRUCTOR 8 ch.g. Groom Dancer (USA) 128 – Doctor's Glory (USA) 91 (Elmaamul (USA) 125) [2009 –: 10m Jul 29] good-topped gelding: easy mover: one-time fairly useful handicapper, little form since 2007. *C. A. Mulhall* **–**

INTABIH (USA) 4 b. or br.c. More Than Ready (USA) 120 – Lookaway Dixieland (USA) (Dixieland Band (USA)) [2009 91: f8g* 8m p10g 8.5g5 10m6 Jun 22] useful-looking colt: fairly useful handicapper: won at Southwell in March: creditable effort after only when fifth at Epsom: effective at 1m/1¼m: acts on all-weather, best turf effort on good ground: sold 36,000 gns. *C. E. Brittain* **92**

INTAVAC BOY 8 ch.g. Emperor Fountain 112 – Altaia (FR) 90 (Sicyos (USA) 126) [2009 –: 12.1m 9.9m 10g 12s p12.2g Dec 12] sparely-made gelding: little form since 2007: tried visored/in cheekpieces. *S. P. Griffiths* **–**

INTEGRATION 9 b.g. Piccolo 121 – Discrimination 72 (Efisio 120) [2009 –: f11g Feb 3] smallish, quite attractive gelding: long-standing maiden on Flat: little form since 2007 (including over hurdles). *Miss M. E. Rowland* **–**

INTEGRIA 3 b.g. Intikhab (USA) 135 – Alegria 94 (Night Shift (USA)) [2009 72: 6.1g 7m p6g3 7s5 p8m* p7.1g p8g Oct 22] useful-looking gelding: fair handicapper: won at Kempton in September: stays 1m: acts on polytrack and soft going: blinkered last 5 starts: sold 11,000 gns, joined Venetia Williams. *J. M. P. Eustace* **72**

INTENSE 3 b.f. Dansili 127 – Modesta (IRE) 105 (Sadler's Wells (USA) 132) [2009 94p: 8m* 7m p8g Oct 29] strong, close-coupled filly: useful performer, lightly raced: improved to win handicap at Newmarket in September by 1¼ lengths from Credit Swap: disappointing after, in listed race at Lingfield on final outing: stayed 1m: acted on good to firm and good to soft ground: visits Zamindar. *B. W. Hills* **99**

INTENSE FOCUS (USA) 3 b.c. Giant's Causeway (USA) 132 – Daneleta (IRE) 101 (Danehill (USA) 126) [2009 117: 8g2 8m5 Jun 16] neat colt: smart performer: won Dewhurst Stakes (blanket finish) at Newmarket at 2 yrs: notch below that form in 2009, length second to Recharge in Leopardstown 2000 Guineas Trial and, after 3-month break, 5 lengths fifth to Mastercraftsman in St James's Palace Stakes at Royal Ascot (hung both ways under pressure): stayed 1m: acted on firm and good to soft going: usually blinkered/visored, also often tongue tied: raced prominently: to stand at Ballylinch Stud, Co Kilkenny, Ireland. *J. S. Bolger, Ireland* **114**

INTERACTIVE (IRE) 6 b.g. King's Best (USA) 132 – Forentia 89 (Formidable (USA) 125) [2009 73, a78: p6g5 p6g* p7g2 p7g2 p7g6 7m 6.1m3 6m6 p6g6 p6g p7.1g p6g Nov 21] tall gelding: fair performer, better on all-weather: won seller at Kempton in January: below form after fifth start, sold from Andrew Turnell £2,000 after ninth: effective at 6f/7f: acts on polytrack and good to firm ground: tried visored. *D. Burchell* **76**

INTERAKT 2 b.f. (Feb 24) Rakti 130 – Amelie Pouliche (FR) (Desert Prince (IRE) 130) [2009 7m5 7m2 7m3 7m4 8.1m3 8m5 Sep 15] 1,700F: rather unfurnished filly: first foal: dam, French 1m winner, half-sister to useful French 1½m winner Deflagration: fair maiden: stays 1m. *M. R. Channon* **69**

INTERCHOICE STAR 4 b.g. Josr Algarhoud (IRE) 118 – Blakeshall Girl 64 (Piccolo 121) [2009 –: p7.1g3 p6g2 f6g5 p6g 7m3 8.1g p10g p9.5g p9.5g3 p7.1m4 p8.6g4 p8.6g6 Dec 28] modest maiden handicapper: stays 9.5f: acts on polytrack and good to firm going: tried in cheekpieces. *R. Hollinshead* **60**

INTERDIAMONDS 3 b.f. Montjeu (IRE) 137 – Interpose (Indian Ridge 123) [2009 9.8m2 12m2 10.3m* 12s2 12m 14m2 14s2 14v6 f12g2 Sep 29] tall, deep-girthed filly: fairly useful performer: won maiden at Doncaster in June: creditable efforts in handicaps after when runner-up: stays 1¾m: acts on fibresand, soft and good to firm going: races up with pace. *M. Johnston* **84**

INTEREST FREE 2 b.f. (Jan 29) Kyllachy 129 – Holly Hayes (IRE) (Alzao (USA) 117) [2009 6m Sep 14] 5,000F, £7,000Y: compact filly: second foal: dam, ran twice, out of sister to Prix Saint-Alary winner Fitnah: 50/1, 10¼ lengths eighth to Secret Queen in maiden at Redcar, prominent to halfway. *T. D. Easterby* **52**

INTERLACE 2 ch.f. (Feb 7) Pivotal 124 – Splice 114 (Sharpo 132) [2009 6g p6f* 7g p6m5 Nov 26] sister to 2 winners, including smart 6f (including at 2 yrs)/7f (in UAE) winner Feet So Fast, closely related to 6f and (at 2 yrs) 7f winner Rise (by Polar Falcon), and half-sister to 3 winners, including smart 2004 2-y-o 6f winner (including Lowther **78**

Stakes) Soar (by Danzero): dam 5f (at 2 yrs)/6f winner: fair performer: best effort when winning maiden at Kempton in September: should stay 7f: acts on polytrack: blinkered (never going well) final start: seemed amiss third outing. *Sir Mark Prescott*

INTERNATIONALDEBUT (IRE) 4 b.g. High Chaparral (IRE) 132 – Whisper Light (IRE) 74 (Caerleon (USA) 132) [2009 103: p6g f7g^5 p10g^4 p10g p8g^3 p8g^3 p8g p7.1g^6 p10g 6m 5.1m 7.6m^5 5g* 5g^5 5m^5 6g 6m^3 12m 6m^5 6d 6m p7g Oct 11] well-made, attractive gelding: good walker: has a round action: useful handicapper: won at York (beat Everymanforhimself short head) in May: also ran well when in frame: well below form last 5 starts, leaving S. Parr after third occasion: effective at 5f to 8.6f: acts on polytrack, soft and good to firm going: tried tongue tied: held up. *J. Balding* **99**

INTERSKY CHARM (USA) 5 ch.g. Lure (USA) 131 – Catala (USA) (Northern Park (USA) 107) [2009 90d: 10.2m f12g^6 7.9m* 7.9m^5 7.9g^3 8m^3 8m 8m p9.5g* Oct 9] strong, heavy-topped gelding: fair handicapper: won at Carlisle in June and Wolverhampton in October: best at 1m/1¼m: acts on all-weather, good to firm and good to soft going: tried in cheekpieces/visor: sold £7,500, joined Mrs S. Bradburne. *R. M. Whitaker* **76**

INTERSKY MUSIC (USA) 6 b.g. Victory Gallop (CAN) 130 – Resounding Grace (USA) (Thunder Gulch (USA) 129) [2009 12.1v^6 Jul 24] leggy gelding: fair hurdler: modest maiden on Flat, lightly raced: may prove best short of 1½m. *Jonjo O'Neill* **54**

INTER VISION (USA) 9 b.g. Cryptoclearance (USA) – Fateful (USA) 90 (Topsider (USA)) [2009 102: 5d 6m 6m 6d 6m^6 6d 7m^6 7m^6 6g^4 6v^4 7.5g^2 5g^5 7s^5 7v Nov 3] tall gelding: fairly useful handicapper nowadays: effective at 5f to 7.4f: acts on polytrack and any turf going: in cheekpieces once: held up. *A. Dickman* **85**

INTHAWAIN 3 b.f. Bertolini (USA) 125 – Ambassadress (USA) (Alleged (USA) 138) [2009 61: p8.6g^4 f6g^2 f6d^2 7.1m^5 f6g^2 6m^6 6s 5m^6 f6m f6g f6g Dec 8] modest maiden: best at 5f/6f: acts on fibresand, soft and good to firm going. *N. Wilson* **63**

IN THE MOOD (IRE) 3 ch.f. Hawk Wing (USA) 136 – Grecian Glory (IRE) 88 (Zafonic (USA) 130) [2009 63: 7d^4 8g^2 p8g 8g Oct 30] rangy, deep-girthed filly: fair maiden: stays 1m: raced only on polytrack and good/good to soft ground: slowly away last 2 outings. *W. Jarvis* **72**

IN THE SLIPS (USA) 2 b.f. (Mar 23) More Than Ready (USA) 120 – Tjinouska (USA) 86 (Cozzene (USA)) [2009 p7g 6f 6f^3 6.5m* 8m* 8f^2 Nov 29] sturdy filly: fourth foal: half-sister to 3 winners, including 3-y-o Straits of Hormuz: dam, 1½m winner, half-sister to dam of Melbourne Cup winner Delta Blues: useful performer: won nurseries at Doncaster and Pontefract in September: left P. Cole, very good ½-length second to The Mailet in Grade 3 Miesque Stakes at Hollywood, staying on well after short of room: will stay 1¼m: acts on firm going. *J. Mullins, USA* **104**

INTIKAMA (IRE) 3 ch.f. Intikhab (USA) 135 – Really Gifted (IRE) (Cadeaux Genereux 131) [2009 71: 8.3g^6 9s^4 10g^5 10.1m^3 f11g^5 11.5g 10.1d Oct 27] workmanlike filly: fair maiden: below form after second start: should stay 1¼m: acts on soft going: tried in cheekpieces/blinkers/tongue tie: sold 5,800 gns. *M. H. Tompkins* **70 d**

INTIMAR (IRE) 3 b.f. Intikhab (USA) 135 – Genetta (Green Desert (USA) 127) [2009 a6.5g^6 a8.8s^3 8.1g^4 p12g p11f Dec 16] €5,000Y, €4,000 2-y-o: compact filly: half-sister to several winners, including 1m (at 2 yrs) and 11f winner Raybaan (by Flying Spur) and 6f (at 2 yrs) to 1m winner Tiber Tiger (by Titus Livius), both fairly useful: dam, French maiden, out of half-sister to top-class performer up to 1½m Kalaglow: better of first 2 starts at Mijas when sixth on debut: little form in maidens/handicap in Britain. *R. J. Smith* **41**

INTOLERABLE (IRE) 3 b.g. Intikhab (USA) 135 – Institutrice (IRE) 87 (College Chapel 122) [2009 5.1d^4 5.1m^3 6f* p7g p7g Oct 9] €12,000Y, resold €26,000Y: good-topped gelding: fourth foal: half-brother to 3 winners, including useful 6f (at 2 yrs)/7f winner Postgraduate (by Almutawakel) and 5f winner (including at 2 yrs) Bella Tutrice (by Woodborough): dam Irish maiden who seemed to stay 1¼m: fair performer: easily best effort when winning maiden at Lingfield in June: should stay 7f: acts on firm going: sold 800 gns, sent to Greece. *R. M. Beckett* **78**

INTO MAC 3 b.g. Shinko Forest (IRE) – Efipetite 54 (Efisio 120) [2009 6m Jun 26] 100/1, well beaten in maiden at Doncaster, then gelded. *N. Bycroft* **–**

INTO MY ARMS 3 gr.f. Kyllachy 129 – True Love (Robellino (USA) 127) [2009 –: 8g Apr 21] poor form. *M. S. Saunders* **41**

INTO THE LIGHT 4 b.g. Fantastic Light (USA) 134 – Boadicea's Chariot (Commanche Run 133) [2009 75: 11.6m^4 p12.2g^5 11.8m^2 11.8m^6 Jul 16] close-coupled gelding: fair maiden: stays 1¾m: acts on polytrack and good to firm ground: blinkered/visored last 2 starts. *E. S. McMahon* **75**

INTREPID JACK 7 b.h. Compton Place 125 – Maria Theresa (Primo Dominie 121) [2009 119: 6.5g4 6m 6m 6m2 6m 7m4 6m 6g6 5.4m4 5.6m 6m Sep 19] strong, lengthy horse: smart performer: not quite so good in 2009, best effort when length fourth to Hatta Fort in handicap at Nad Al Sheba: just respectable efforts at best after, including when in frame in listed race at Windsor (4 lengths second to J J The Jet Plane) and handicap at York (fourth to Barney McGrew) fourth/ninth starts: effective at testing 5f to 7f: acts on polytrack, soft and good to firm going: tried visored/blinkered: held up: sent to USA. *H. Morrison* **113**

INVASIAN (IRE) 8 ch.g. Desert Prince (IRE) 130 – Jarrayan 64 (Machiavellian (USA) 123) [2009 95: 10s* f11g p10g 10.1s* 11.8m* 12g3 Jul 24] close-coupled, quite attractive gelding: fairly useful performer: won handicap at Newbury in April, and claimers at Yarmouth and Leicester in July: stays 1½m: acts on polytrack, soft and good to firm ground: tried tongue tied: sometimes races freely: usually forces pace: none too consistent. *P. W. D'Arcy* **90**

INVENTION (USA) 6 b.g. Lear Fan (USA) 130 – Carya (USA) (Northern Dancer) [2009 –: 11.7g2 p13g6 16g5 May 29] angular, quite attractive gelding: has a quick, unimpressive action: fair handicapper nowadays: will prove fully effective at 2m: acts on polytrack, good to firm and good to soft ground: tried visored: tongue tied in 2009. *Miss E. C. Lavelle* **72**

INVENTOR (IRE) 4 b.g. Alzao (USA) 117 – Magnificent Bell (IRE) (Octagonal (NZ) 126) [2009 107: p12m5 12g Oct 10] strong, short-backed gelding: useful performer: off 11 months, creditable 6¾ lengths fifth to Kirklees in September Stakes at Kempton, easily better effort in 2009: should stay 1¾m: acts on polytrack, good to firm and good to soft going: sold 15,000 gns, successful hurdling debut for D. McCain Jnr. *B. J. Meehan* **105**

INVINCIBLE FORCE (IRE) 5 b.g. Invincible Spirit (IRE) 121 – Highly Respected (IRE) 57 (High Estate 127) [2009 102: f6g4 8m 6m 5.1m 7.6m 6v* 7.6g* 6m 7m6 7g Oct 10] close-coupled gelding: useful handicapper: won at the Curragh (beat Daring Man by 1¾ lengths) in July and Chester (by length from Dixey) in August: below form othwerwise in 2009: best at 5f to 7.6f: acts on all-weather and any turf going: tried visored: blinkered: versatile regarding tactics (often makes running). *Paul Green* **102**

INVINCIBLE HEART (GR) 3 b.g. Invincible Spirit (IRE) 121 – Flamingo Bay (IRE) 77 (Catrail (USA) 123) [2009 96: 7m2 6.1m* 6m6 7g Dec 19] smallish, sturdy gelding: useful performer: won on handicap debut at Chester in May: left Jane Chapple-Hyam, gelded and off 7 months before final outing (tongue tied): best form at 6f: acts on soft and good to firm going. *C. Fownes, Hong Kong* **97**

INVINCIBLE HERO (IRE) 2 b.c. (Mar 24) Invincible Spirit (IRE) 121 – Bridelina (FR) (Linamix (FR) 127) [2009 p7f 7m3 Sep 18] better effort in maidens when ¾-length third to Forgotten Army at Newmarket, pulling hard in front: tongue tied. *J. Noseda* **56**

INVINCIBLE ISLE (IRE) 3 b.f. Invincible Spirit (IRE) 121 – Ile de France (ITY) (Danehill (USA) 126) [2009 9.7d2 p8g6 7m* 7d2 7g5 6.1g3 6g 6m* p7.1m4 f6g5 Oct 18] tall filly: has scope: third foal: half-sister to 2 winners in Italy, including 7.5f (at 2 yrs)/ 8.5f winner Fidias (by Almutawakel): dam, ran 3 times in France, half-sister to useful Italian performer up to 1½m Oxford Line: fairly useful performer: won maiden at Doncaster in June and handicap at Pontefract in September: effective at 6f/7f: acts on all-weather, good to firm and good to soft going. *H. R. A. Cecil* **89**

INVINCIBLE JOE (IRE) 4 b.g. Invincible Spirit (IRE) 121 – Abbey Park (USA) 71 (Known Fact (USA) 135) [2009 95: 5v 10v 8s 8g 7s p8g Oct 14] useful performer in 2008: below form at 4 yrs: effective at 7f to easy 8.5f: acts on good to firm and good to soft going: tried blinkered, sometimes in cheekpieces (including for both wins): sometimes slowly away. *John Joseph Hanlon, Ireland* **72**

INVINCIBLE LAD (IRE) 5 b.g. Invincible Spirit (IRE) 121 – Lady Ellen 67 (Horage 124) [2009 96: 5m 5g* 5f3 5m 5d3 5.1m6 5m 5m6 f5g* f6f3 5d Oct 24] strong gelding: useful handicapper on all-weather, fairly useful on turf: won at Leicester in May and Southwell (improved again) in September: good third at latter course penultimate start: speedy, best at 5f/easy 6f: acts on all-weather, soft and good to firm going: ran poorly only try in cheekpieces. *E. J. Alston* **91** **a98**

INVINCIBLE MISS (IRE) 3 b.f. Invincible Spirit (IRE) 121 – Saramacca (IRE) 54 (Kahyasi 130) [2009 65+: p7.1g2 p8.6g3 p7.1g* Apr 24] fair performer: won seller at Wolverhampton in April: may prove best short of 8.6f: raced mainly on polytrack. *M. Wigham* **65**

INVINCIBLE PRINCE (IRE) 2 b.g. (Feb 10) Invincible Spirit (IRE) 121 – Forest Prize 77 (Charnwood Forest (IRE) 125) [2009 p7g* 7m 8d5 8m5 Oct 16] £45,000Y: compact gelding: fourth foal: half-brother to 7f winner Polish Prize (by Polish Precedent): dam, 2-y-o 6f winner (stayed 1¼m, became unreliable), half-sister to high-class 6f/7f performer Somnus: form only when winning maiden at Kempton in June by ½ length from Hasty: stays 7f: acts on polytrack: blinkered final start (looked reluctant, gelded after). *R. M. Beckett* **– a86**

INVINCIBLE SOUL (IRE) 2 b.c. (May 7) Invincible Spirit (IRE) 121 – Licorne 93 (Sadler's Wells (USA) 132) [2009 7d 7m 7m3 8m* Oct 16] €35,000F, €160,000Y: compact colt: half-brother to useful 1¼m winner Dabus (by Kris): dam, 1¼m/1½m winner, half-sister to Yorkshire Oaks winner Catchascatchcan, herself dam of very smart miler Antonius Pius: most progressive in maidens, useful form when winning at Newmarket by head from Fair Trade (edged right): should stay 1¼m: acts on good to firm ground. *R. Hannon* **95**

INVISIBLE MAN 3 ch.c. Elusive Quality (USA) – Eternal Reve (USA) 116 (Diesis 133) [2009 85p: 7m4 p8g4 8m* 8m 7m4 8g* 8m* 9m Sep 12] strong colt: has fluent action: useful performer: won maiden/handicap at Newmarket in May/July and handicap at Pontefract (beat Kaolak by neck, again travelling strongly) in August: said to have finished lame final start: should stay 9f: acts on polytrack and good to firm going. *J. H. M. Gosden* **99**

INXILE (IRE) 4 b.g. Fayruz 116 – Grandel (Owington 123) [2009 112: 6m5 5d* 5m3 5f* 5g3 5g3 5m5 5m5 Oct 1] strong, compact gelding: smart performer: won listed races at Naas (by ½ length from Reverence) in April and June (by length from Miss Gorica): also first past post in Prix de Saint-Georges at Longchamp (beat Mood Music ¾ length) in between, but demoted (caused interference): just respectable efforts after: effective at 5f/6f: acts on firm and soft going: sometimes early to post: usually forces pace. *D. Nicholls* **113**

Woodlands Stakes, Naas—Adrian Nicholls drives Inxile (No.2) to the first of two listed wins on Irish soil in 2009; fellow raider Reverence is second with Le Cadre Noir (partially hidden by Reverence) third

IPSWICH LAD 2 ch.c. (Apr 9) Halling (USA) 133 – Poised (USA) (Rahy (USA) 115) [2009 8.1m^5 8m^4 p8g^3 p10m^3 Dec 9] €46,000Y: fifth foal: brother to useful 2007 2-y-o 6f/7f winner Gothenburg: dam, ran twice in France, sister to Noverre and closely related to Arazi: fair maiden: stays 1m: visored (looked lazy) final start. *A. M. Balding* **70**

IPTKAAR (USA) 2 br.f. (Feb 21) Dixie Union (USA) 121 – Low Tolerance (USA) (Proud Truth (USA)) [2009 6s^3 7m^4 6m 7m Oct 3] 52,000Y: leggy filly: closely related/half-sister to several winners in USA: dam US Grade 3 8.5f winner: modest form in frame in maidens: probably flattered when seventh to Society Rock in sales race at Newmarket third start: will probably stay 1m. *C. E. Brittain* **63 +**

IRELAND DANCER (IRE) 5 ch.g. Trans Island 119 – Come Dancing 48 (Suave Dancer (USA) 136) [2009 –: p8.6g Nov 21] maiden: no form since 2007 (including over hurdles). *John Berry* **–**

IRISH BALLAD 7 b.g. Singspiel (IRE) 133 – Auenlust (GER) (Surumu (GER)) [2009 64: p16g^6 p16g^4 p16g^2 p16g* p16g^4 p13g Apr 19] neat gelding: modest handicapper: won at Lingfield in March: amiss final start: stays 16.5f: acts on polytrack and firm going: tried tongue tied: often races prominently. *S. Dow* **64**

IRISH BAY (IRE) 6 b.g. Brief Passing (IRE) – Echo Bay (IRE) (Barry's Run (IRE) 48) [2009 59: p6g Nov 16] smallish gelding: modest maiden, very lightly raced. *Luke Comer, Ireland* **–**

IRISH EYES 2 b.g. (Feb 5) Mark of Esteem (IRE) 137 – Diabaig 76 (Precocious 126) [2009 7d 7s Sep 5] stocky gelding: last in maidens, then gelded. *Jedd O'Keeffe* **–**

IRISH HEARTBEAT (IRE) 4 b.g. Celtic Swing 138 – She's All Class (USA) (Rahy (USA) 115) [2009 87: 8s 5.8s^6 6.3g^3 7m^2 6v^4 5s^3 5s* 6g^4 6g Oct 10] useful handicapper: in frame 4 times in 2009 before winning at the Curragh in September by short head from Siodull: not at all discredited last 2 starts: effective at 5f, seemingly at 9f: acts on soft and good to firm ground: in cheekpieces last 3 outings: often races up with pace: sold 65,000 gns. *D. Myerscough, Ireland* **97**

IRISH JUGGER (USA) 2 ch.g. (Apr 14) Johannesburg (USA) 127 – Jinny's Gold (USA) (Gold Fever (USA) 119) [2009 6m^3 7g^5 6m^5 Aug 15] $220,000Y: second foal: half-brother to winner in Canada by Golden Missile: dam US 1m (at 2 yrs)/8.5f winner: best effort when 5½ lengths fifth to Missionaire in maiden at Newmarket second start (trained by K. R. Burke): sold 4,500 gns, then gelded. *A. P. Jarvis* **70**

IRISH MUSIC (IRE) 4 b.g. Namid 128 – Kelly's Tune 63 (Alhaarth (IRE) 126) [2009 68: 6m^5 5.2d^4 p5m^2 p6m^2 p6g Dec 19] compact gelding: fair maiden: effective at 5f to 7f: acts on polytrack, unraced on extremes of going on turf. *A. P. Jarvis* **70**

IRISH PEARL (IRE) 4 b.f. Statue of Liberty (USA) 115 – Helen Wells (IRE) 72 (Sadler's Wells (USA) 132) [2009 99: f5s^6 p6g Jan 8] lengthy filly: useful handicapper in 2008: below form both starts at 4 yrs, finishing weakly: speedy, effective at 5f/6f: acts on all-weather and heavy ground: sold 9,000 gns, sent to Saudi Arabia. *K. R. Burke* **85**

IRISH SAINT (IRE) 3 ch.g. Kheleyf (USA) 116 – Tarifana (IRE) 100 (Dr Devious (IRE) 127) [2009 57p: p12.2m p9.5g 7.5m 8f 6g Aug 5] maiden: modest at 2 yrs: little form in 2009: tried visored. *T. J. Pitt* **–**

IRISH STREAM (USA) 11 ch.g. Irish River (FR) 131 – Euphonic (USA) 113 (The Minstrel (CAN) 135) [2009 47: p10g^4 10.2g 10.9f May 12] big gelding: modest handicapper, lightly raced on Flat nowadays: shaped as though on downgrade in 2009: stays 10.7f: acts on polytrack, soft and good to firm going: tried in headgear (visored last 2 starts): tends to carry head awkwardly. *B. G. Powell* **50**

IRON CONDOR 2 b.g. (Feb 26) Tobougg (IRE) 125 – Coh Sho No 59 (Old Vic 136) [2009 7d^4 7g^4 p7m^3 8g Oct 23] fair form at best in maidens: tailed off in nursery: will be suited by 1¼m+. *J. M. P. Eustace* **68**

IRON HAGUE (IRE) 8 b.g. Among Men (USA) 124 – Conditional Sale (IRE) (Petorius 117) [2009 11.8m May 25] modest form over jumps: little form on Flat since 2006 (lightly raced): has worn headgear/tongue tie. *O. Brennan* **–**

IRON MAN OF MERSEY (FR) 3 b.g. Poliglote 121 – Miss Echo § (Chief Singer 131) [2009 –: 10.2g 6m 10g 8.1s p7f 8m 8g Sep 30] close-coupled gelding: regressive maiden: bred to stay 1½m: best efforts on good ground: tried blinkered. *A. W. Carroll* **58 d**

IRON MASTER 3 b. or gr.g. High Chaparral (IRE) 132 – Blushing Queen (IRE) 75 (Desert King (IRE) 129) [2009 10g 8m 11.6m^5 p8m Nov 28] little form in maidens: tried tongue tied. *J. J. Bridger* **–**

IRON MAX (IRE) 3 b.g. Iron Mask (USA) 117 – Starisa (IRE) (College Chapel 122) **48** [2009 –: 6g^5 6d 6m f7f Dec 12] neat gelding: poor maiden: left N. Vaughan prior to final start: best effort at 6f. *Tom Dascombe*

IRON OUT (USA) 3 b.g. Straight Man (USA) 115 – Fit Fighter (USA) (Fit To Fight **91** (USA)) [2009 57: f6g^2 p7.1g^4 p7.1g^4 10g f7g^2 6m 7m* f8g^2 f8g^3 8g^6 f7g^2 p7g^4 7m^2 p8f^4 7g^2 7m^2 8.3v^2 f8g^2 p9.5g* p9.5g* p10m p9.5g^3 Dec 26] sparely-made gelding: fairly useful performer: won seller at Leicester in June and 2 handicaps at Wolverhampton (amateurs second occasion) in December: stays 9.5f: acts on all-weather, heavy and good to firm going: consistent. *R. Hollinshead*

IRON VELVET (USA) 2 b.g. (Feb 11) Dubawi (IRE) 129 – Not For Turning (USA) **76** (Deputy Minister (CAN)) [2009 6.1m 6m^2 7g 6g* 6d 7m^6 Sep 19] well-made gelding: second foal: dam unraced half-sister to very smart US Grade 1 9f winner Pike Place Dancer and smart US Grade 2 9f winner Petionville: fair performer: won nursery at Catterick in August: should stay at least 7f: acts on good to firm going: seemed amiss penultimate start, gelded after final one. *M. Johnston*

ISABELLA GREY 3 gr.f. Choisir (AUS) 126 – Karsiyaka (IRE) (Kahyasi 130) [2009 **92** 86: 8s^4 8.1v 7g Jun 5] tall filly: fairly useful performer, lightly raced: best effort when fourth to Nashmiah in listed race at York on reappearance: folded tamely after: stays 1m: acts on soft going, returned jarred up sole start on good to firm. *K. A. Ryan*

ISABELLA ROMEE (IRE) 3 gr.f. Bahri (USA) 125 – Silver Clasp (IRE) (Linamix **57** (FR) 127) [2009 61: f8g^6 7g 6m Aug 15] smallish, angular filly: modest maiden: probably best at 6f: tried in cheekpieces. *Jane Chapple-Hyam*

ISABELLA'S FANCY 4 br.f. Captain Rio 122 – Princess of Spain (King of Spain 121) **57 d** [2009 59: f7d f7g^3 f8g^6 f8d 7m 8m 7.1d^6 Sep 4] leggy filly: modest performer: below form after second start: best efforts at 6f/7f: acts on fibresand and good to firm ground: tried visored/blinkered. *A. G. Newcombe*

ISABELONABICYCLE 4 b.f. Helissio (FR) 136 – Santa Isobel 94 (Nashwan (USA) **78** 135) [2009 74: p12.2g^2 15.4g* 15m^3 16g^6 14.6m^2 p16g* 16d 14.1m Aug 13] big filly: fair handicapper: won at Folkestone in April and Kempton in July: stays 2m: acts on polytrack and good to firm ground: quirky. *A. M. Balding*

ISABEL'S PET 3 b.f. Lucky Story (USA) 128 – Perle d'Azur 91 (Mind Games 121) **–** [2009 p6g Nov 16] third foal: dam 2-y-o 6f winner: 50/1, well held in maiden at Wolverhampton. *Karen George*

ISDAAR (IRE) 2 b.g. (Feb 2) Invincible Spirit (IRE) 121 – Kildare Lady (IRE) (Indian **65** Ridge 123) [2009 6g 8.1m^4 8.3m^5 8d Oct 22] compact gelding: fair form in maidens second/third starts: stays 1m: acts on good to firm going: blinkered (found little) final outing: sold 10,000 gns, sent to Greece. *J. H. M. Gosden*

I SEE NICE SEA 3 b.f. Miesque's Son (USA) 117 – North Sea (IRE) 60 (Selkirk **–** (USA) 129) [2009 8.3f^5 8g 10m^6 12d 8.5m Sep 16] good-bodied filly: first foal: dam, maiden (should have stayed 1¼m), out of half-sister to smart performer up to 1¼m King Adam: little form: left L. Cumani after second start: tried in cheekpieces/blinkers. *Ollie Pears*

ISHE A LORD 2 b.g. (Mar 30) Ishiguru (USA) 114 – Lady Killer (IRE) 76 (Daggers **54** Drawn (USA) 114) [2009 5m^2 p6m^5 p6g p6g Dec 7] modest maiden plater. *W. G. M. Turner*

ISHE MAC 3 b.f. Ishiguru (USA) 114 – Zacinta (USA) (Hawkster (USA)) [2009 79: **88** 7m* 7m^6 7m 6d* 6g Aug 31] compact filly: fairly useful performer: won maiden in May and handicap in August, both at Thirsk: stays 7f: acts on good to firm and good to soft going: game. *N. Bycroft*

ISHETOO 5 b.g. Ishiguru (USA) 114 – Ticcatoo (IRE) 60 (Dolphin Street (FR) 125) **105** [2009 106: 6m^5 6s 5m* 5g^6 5d 6m 5m^3 6m^5 6m 5m 6d 5.6m^5 5g^3 5g Oct 17] strong gelding: useful handicapper: won sportingbet.com Sprint at York (beat Peak District by neck) in May: sixth at Musselburgh and third in valuable event at Ascot, only creditable efforts after: stays 6f, though very best efforts at 5f: acts on heavy and good to firm going: tried in cheekpieces, visored final start. *A. Dickman*

ISHIADANCER 4 b.f. Ishiguru (USA) 114 – Abaklea (IRE) (Doyoun 124) [2009 68: **86** 7m* 7.2s^2 f7g^3 7g^2 7.2g* 7.2v^6 p7.1g^4 p7.1g Dec 18] fairly useful performer: won maiden at Redcar in July and handicap at Ayr in October: stays 7f: acts on all-weather, soft and good to firm going: often makes running. *E. J. Alston*

ISHIBEE (IRE) 5 b.m. Ishiguru (USA) 114 – Beauty (IRE) 74 (Alzao (USA) 117) **57** [2009 54: p6g^3 p6g p6g^6 p5g^2 p5g 7m 7f^5 7m 6m^5 5m^6 7f^3 6m^4 7.6d^5 6m* 6m 7m 5m p7m **a54**

p6m^4 p7m Nov 4] sturdy mare: modest handicapper: ended long losing run at Folkestone in August: barely stays 7f: acts on polytrack, firm and soft going: wears cheekpieces/visor: held up: none too consistent. *J. J. Bridger*

ISHIPINK 2 ch.f. (Feb 10) Ishiguru (USA) 114 – Christmas Rose (Absalom 128) [2009 5.1d^4 5.7f^5 5.1g Aug 28] £12,000Y: fifth foal: half-sister to 3 winners, including fairly useful 6f winner Snow Wolf (by Wolfhound): dam twice-raced half-sister to Gimcrack Stakes winner Bannister: no form. *R. J. Hodges* **–**

ISHISMART 5 ch.m. Ishiguru (USA) 114 – Smartie Lee 66 (Dominion 123) [2009 15.8g^3 p12.2g^2 p12.2g Nov 21] strong mare: modest maiden, lightly raced on Flat (fair hurdler): stays 15.8f: raced only on polytrack and good/good to soft ground. *R. Hollinshead* **53**

ISHTAR GATE (USA) 2 b. or br.c. (Mar 30) Gone West (USA) – Sometime (IRE) (Royal Academy (USA) 130) [2009 7m* 7g 8.5m^5 Oct 3] $230,000Y: tall, close-coupled colt, unfurnished at present: sixth foal: half-brother to 6-y-o Art Deco and 7f (at 2 yrs)/11f winner Manyana (by Alzao) and Irish winner around 1¼m winner Vincenzio Galilei (by Galileo), both useful: dam unraced sister to Sleepytime and Ali-Royal and half-sister to Taipan: won maiden at Leicester in June by head from Contract Caterer: down the field in Vintage Stakes at Goodwood and minor event (had been off 3 months, tailed off) at Epsom: should stay 1m+. *P. F. I. Cole* **84**

ISINTSHELOVELY (IRE) 6 ch.m. Broken Hearted 124 – Sarah Blue (IRE) (Bob Back (USA) 124) [2009 11.8g Sep 14] fairly useful bumper winner: modest hurdler: 14/1, little promise in maiden on Flat debut. *B. G. Powell* **–**

ISITCOZIMCOOL (IRE) 4 b.g. Shinko Forest (IRE) – Hazarama (IRE) 91 (Kahyasi 130) [2009 p7g 6s 6g Jun 20] fair form in bumpers (signs of temperament): little form in claimer/maidens: tried in cheekpieces. *D. E. Cantillon* **–**

IS IT TIME (IRE) 5 b.m. Danetime (IRE) 121 – Ishaam 76 (Selkirk (USA) 129) [2009 67: p7g 5.2m Jun 23] workmanlike mare: fair handicapper in 2008: well held at 5 yrs: effective at 5f to 7f: acts on all-weather and good to firm going: sold £550. *Mrs P. N. Dutfield* **–**

ISLAND CHIEF 3 b.g. Reel Buddy (USA) 118 – Fisher Island (IRE) 59 (Sri Pekan (USA) 117) [2009 71d: 8s 7.1m^2 8s 7.1m* 7.1g^3 7.5m^3 6.9g^2 8g* 8s 8g 7g^4 7m Oct 26] close-coupled gelding: fairly useful handicapper: returned to form, and won at Musselburgh in May and July: stays 1m: acts on soft and good to firm ground: usually in cheekpieces/blinkers: often front runner/races prominently. *K. A. Ryan* **82**

ISLAND EXPRESS (IRE) 2 b.c. (Mar 22) Chineur (FR) 123 – Cayman Expresso (IRE) 79 (Fayruz 116) [2009 5d 5m^2 5g^6 5.5m 5g^6 6f 6m^5 Jun 3] sturdy colt: modest maiden: left J. S. Moore £6,000 after second start: will prove best at 5f/6f: acts on firm going: tried in cheekpieces. *Miss A. Stokell* **50**

ISLAND LEGEND (IRE) 3 b.g. Trans Island 119 – Legand of Tara (USA) (Gold Legend (USA)) [2009 p5g^3 6.1f p5.1g* 6d p5g^4 p6g p5.1g^6 Oct 9] €2,000F, 2,500Y: big, lengthy gelding: fourth foal: dam unraced: fair performer: won maiden at Wolverhampton in August: will prove best at 5f/6f: acts on polytrack, no form on turf. *J. M. Bradley* **– a74**

ISLAND MUSIC (IRE) 4 b.f. Mujahid (USA) 125 – Ischia 64 (Lion Cavern (USA) 117) [2009 74: 7s 9m 10.1d^3 10g 10m^6 8.3m^5 8.5g^2 9.8m^6 10m p8.6g^4 9d^6 p8.6g Nov 14] close-coupled filly: fair handicapper: stays 1¼m: acts on polytrack and heavy ground: sometimes in cheekpieces. *J. J. Quinn* **70**

ISLAND SUNSET (IRE) 3 ch.f. Trans Island 119 – Islandagore (IRE) 97 (Indian Ridge 123) [2009 80p: 8.1g* Jul 3] fairly useful form: successful on both starts, including 4-runner handicap at Haydock in July, at work in rear some way out: stays 1m: acts on polytrack. *W. R. Muir* **85**

ISLAND VISTA 4 b.f. Montjeu (IRE) 137 – Colorvista (Shirley Heights 130) [2009 92: 12d p12g Jun 24] rather leggy filly: fairly useful performer at 3 yrs: tailed off both starts in 2009: stays 1½m: acts on polytrack and good to firm going. *M. A. Jarvis* **–**

ISLE DE MAURICE 7 b.g. Sinndar (IRE) 134 – Circe's Isle (Be My Guest (USA) 126) [2009 p16g^6 p16m^2 Dec 1] quite good-topped gelding: fair handicapper: very lightly raced on Flat in recent years (fair but ungenuine hurdler for Mrs D. Grissell): stays 2m: acts on polytrack: blinkered nowadays. *G. L. Moore* **67**

ISLE OF ELLIS (IRE) 2 b.g. (Apr 20) Statue of Liberty (USA) 115 – Fable 37 (Absalom 128) [2009 5m p5.1g Apr 16] leggy gelding: well held in minor event/maiden: subsequently gelded. *A. J. McCabe* **–**

ISPHAHAN 6 b.g. Diktat 126 – Waltzing Star (IRE) (Danehill (USA) 126) [2009 97: 8.1g6 8m 8m 8g5 8g4 8.1g2 7m5 8m p8m Nov 28] lengthy gelding: fairly useful handicapper: creditable effort in 2009 only when runner-up at Sandown: best at 7f/1m: acts on polytrack, firm and good to soft ground: often wears cheekpieces/visor: signs of temperament. *A. M. Balding* **92**

ISSABELLA GEM (IRE) 2 b.f. (Feb 10) Marju (IRE) 127 – Robin (Slip Anchor 136) [2009 7d Oct 12] €43,000Y: fifth foal: half-sister to 3 winners, notably 1m (at 2 yrs) to 1½m winner London Express (by King Charlemagne): dam unraced half-sister to very smart performer up to 1¾m Top Class: 25/1, 6¾ lengths eighth to Thrill in maiden at Salisbury: should stay 1¼m+. *C. G. Cox* **71**

ISSHE A LADY 3 b.f. Ishiguru (USA) 114 – Lady Killer (IRE) 76 (Daggers Drawn (USA) 114) [2009 p6g Feb 24] first foal: dam 2-y-o 5f winner: 16/1, well held in maiden at Lingfield. *W. G. M. Turner* **–**

ISTIDLAAL 2 ch.c. (Mar 17) Singspiel (IRE) 133 – On A Soapbox (USA) 119 (Mi Cielo (USA)) [2009 8m Oct 1] 200,000Y: lengthy colt: has scope: second foal: half-brother to very smart 9.5f to 2m winner Soapy Danger (by Danzig): dam US Grade 1 1½m winner: 8/1 and green, down the field in maiden at Newmarket: will be suited by 1¼m+: likely to do better. *Sir Michael Stoute* **58 p**

ISTIQDAAM 4 b.g. Pivotal 124 – Auspicious 103 (Shirley Heights 130) [2009 80: p7.1g6 6m5 6g4 6g 6g 7v5 9.1v6 p7m* p7.1g2 p7.1g* Dec 11] compact gelding: fairly useful performer: won handicaps at Kempton in November and Wolverhampton in December: effective at 7f/1m: acts on polytrack, best turf effort on good ground: blinkered last 4 starts. *M. W. Easterby* **82**

ITAINTEASYBEINGME 3 ch.g. Lucky Story (USA) 128 – Concubine (IRE) 76 (Danehill (USA) 126) [2009 60: 6d5 8.5g 7g2 8s5 8.3g Jul 6] sturdy gelding: modest maiden handicapper: stays 1m: acts on soft and good to firm ground. *J. R. Boyle* **60**

ITALIAN DAME 3 b.f. Bertolini (USA) 125 – Soyalang (FR) (Alydeed (CAN) 120) [2009 8d 6m 6g5 Sep 3] 2,000Y: third foal: half-sister to 6f winner Orotund (by Orpen): dam, French maiden, stayed 10.5f: little form in maidens/seller. *J. R. Turner* **–**

ITALIANO 10 b.g. Emperor Jones (USA) 119 – Elka (USA) (Val de L'Orne (FR) 133) [2009 9.3m 12.1m6 12d Jul 15] fair hurdler at best/maiden chaser: well held in 3 claimers on Flat, leaving P. Beaumont prior to final start: blinkered last 2 outings: dead. *Mrs Marjorie Fife* **–**

ITALIAN TOM (IRE) 2 b.c. (Mar 25) Le Vie Dei Colori 126 – Brave Cat (IRE) (Catrail (USA) 123) [2009 5f5 5.1g* p5g6 5.2g2 p5g* 5d* 6g p5.1g p5.1g6 p6m4 f5g* f5g4 Dec 18] €13,000F, €11,500Y, £36,000 2-y-o: smallish colt: sixth foal: half-brother to fairly useful 2007 2-y-o 5f winner (stayed 1m) Eileen's Violet (by Catcher In The Rye) and winner in Italy by Revoque: dam unraced: fairly useful performer: won seller at Chepstow in June and nurseries at Kempton (first run after leaving S. Callaghan) and Sandown in September and Southwell in December: probably stays 6f: acts on all-weather and good to soft ground. *R. A. Harris* **81**

ITCANBEDONE AGAIN (IRE) 10 b.g. Sri Pekan (USA) 117 – Maradata (IRE) 68 (Shardari 134) [2009 p9.5g Aug 10] tall, good-topped gelding: modest performer in 2007: no show only outing since. *J. W. Unett* **–**

ITHBAAT (USA) 3 b. or br.c. Arch (USA) 127 – Annul (USA) (Conquistador Cielo (USA)) [2009 85P: 8g2 8m* 8m 9m4 12m2 Jul 2] rangy, good sort: fairly useful handicapper: won maiden at Yarmouth in May: good second in handicap at Newbury final start: stays 1½m: raced only on good/good to firm going: sold 150,000 gns. *J. H. M. Gosden* **92**

ITHINKBEST 3 b.g. King's Best (USA) 132 – Monturani (IRE) 112 (Indian Ridge 123) [2009 65p: 8.5g5 8.3g2 10m3 8.1m3 8m* p8.6g* Oct 16] tall gelding: useful performer: won maiden at Pontefract and handicap at Wolverhampton (beat Farleigh House by neck), both in October: should stay 1¼m: acts on polytrack and good to firm ground (unraced on softer than good). *Sir Michael Stoute* **95**

ITLAAQ 3 b.c. Alhaarth (IRE) 126 – Hathrah (IRE) 113 (Linamix (FR) 127) [2009 77p: 8m 9.9g* 11d5 p12g2 Oct 8] attractive colt: fairly useful handicapper: won at Goodwood in May: good second at Kempton final start: stays 1½m: acts on polytrack and soft going: held up. *J. L. Dunlop* **93**

IT MUST BE LOVE 3 b.f. Piccolo 121 – True Bird (IRE) 63 (In The Wings 128) [2009 7g5 10.4v May 21] 2,000Y: lengthy, unfurnished filly: fifth foal: half-sister to winner in Spain by Vettori: dam maiden who stayed 2m: last in minor event/maiden. *D. Flood* **–**

IT'S A DATE 4 b.g. Kyllachy 129 – By Arrangement (IRE) 60 (Bold Arrangement 127) [2009 86: 12m2 12m* 14m6 11.8d* 13.3m Aug 14] useful-looking gelding: good walker: **90**

fairly useful handicapper: won at Salisbury in June and Leicester in July: may prove best around 1½m: acts on soft and good to firm going. *A. King*

IT'S A DEAL (IRE) 2 b.f. (Mar 19) Indian Haven 119 – Gold And Blue (IRE) (Bluebird (USA) 125) [2009 6g p7g p7g 7f[6] Sep 8] €17,000F, £8,000Y: sturdy filly: half-sister to several winners, including 5f winner Jodeeka (by Fraam) and 6f (including at 2 yrs) to 9f winner Blue Star (by Whittingham), both useful: dam lightly-raced Irish maiden: poor form in maidens/nursery. *P. Winkworth* **38**

ITS ALRIGHT (IRE) 2 b.f. (Feb 12) King's Best (USA) 132 – Lightwood Lady (IRE) 84 (Anabaa (USA) 130) [2009 5m* Apr 16] €8,000Y: first foal: dam, Irish 6f winner, out of half-sister to 2000 Guineas winner Pennekamp and Irish 2000 Guineas winner Black Minnaloushe: 7/1, won maiden at Newmarket by 1½ lengths from Mijas Playa: reportedly had a chip removed after: will stay 6f. *A. Bailey* **83**

IT'S A MANS WORLD 3 b.g. Kyllachy 129 – Exhibitor (USA) 68 (Royal Academy (USA) 130) [2009 71: p8g[4] p6g[2] p7g[6] p7g[5] p7.1g[5] 10.2d 8s[6] p6g[2] 6.1m 6s[2] 5.9g* 6m[3] Aug 28] good-bodied gelding: fair handicapper: left P. McBride £6,000 second start, S. Dow £6,000 after fourth: won at Carlisle in August: effective at 6f to 1m: acts on polytrack and good to firm ground: visored of late. *K. M. Prendergast* **71**

ITSAWINDUP 5 b.g. Elnadim (USA) 128 – Topwinder (USA) (Topsider (USA)) [2009 57: p13.3g p12g[3] p10g* p12g[6] p10g[5] 12d Apr 9] close-coupled gelding: modest performer: won handicap at Kempton in February: stays 1½m: acts on polytrack: tried visored: tongue tied. *Miss S. West* **54**

ITS BEYOND ME 5 ch.g. And Beyond (IRE) 113 – Hand On Heart (IRE) 62 (Taufan (USA) 119) [2009 7.9g Jun 1] tailed off both starts in bumpers, and in claimer on Flat debut (saddle said to have slipped). *F. P. Murtagh* **–**

IT'S DUBAI DOLLY 3 ch.f. Dubai Destination (USA) 127 – Betrothal (IRE) (Groom Dancer (USA) 128) [2009 82?: p12g* p12g 12m 10d* p11g 12m 10.3s Nov 7] leggy filly: fairly useful performer: won maiden at Kempton in April and handicap at Newbury in August: effective at 1¼m/1½m: acts on polytrack and soft going: unreliable. *A. J. Lidderdale* **80 §**

ITSHER 3 br.f. Diktat 126 – Shararah 87 (Machiavellian (USA) 123) [2009 56: p6g[5] p7g[3] 7g[6] 6d[4] 6d[2] 6f[2] 6f* 6g* 5.3f* Jul 5] fair handicapper: improved to win at Brighton (2) and Leicester in June/July: effective at 5f/6f: acts on polytrack, firm and good to soft ground: blinkered last 5 starts: signs of temperament: sold 25,000 gns. *S. C. Williams* **76**

ITSHIM 3 b.g. Ishiguru (USA) 114 – Sumitra 56 (Tragic Role (USA)) [2009 –: p5g* p5.1g* p7g* 6f a8.5f[4] p6f a6.5f* a6.5f a6f[2] a6f[2] Dec 15] angular gelding: fair performer: improved in February, winning minor event at Kempton, and handicaps at Wolverhampton and Lingfield: left S. C. Williams after: trained by J. Sadler next 3 starts: won optional claimer at Zia Park in October: winner at 7f, may well prove best at 5f/6f: acts on dirt/polytrack: tongue tied last 4 starts in Britain. *H. Dominguez, USA* **74**

IT'S JOSR 4 b.g. Josr Algarhoud (IRE) 118 – It's So Easy 63 (Shaadi (USA) 126) [2009 66: 8.3m 10d[5] 8.1g 8.1d 10.2m p12f[2] p12g[2] Oct 20] close-coupled gelding: fair handicapper: stays 1½m: acts on all-weather and good to soft going: wears headgear: none too consistent. *I. A. Wood* **65**

ITS MOON (IRE) 5 b.m. Tobougg (IRE) 125 – Shallat (IRE) 59 (Pennekamp (USA) 130) [2009 70: 15.8g[6] May 5] smallish, workmanlike mare: fair handicapper: stamina possibly stretched sole start in 2009: stays 1¾m: acts on soft and good to firm ground: in blinkers/visor last 4 starts: races prominently: sold £2,300. *T. D. Walford* **–**

IT'S MY DAY (IRE) 4 ch.g. Soviet Star (USA) 128 – Ezana (Ela-Mana-Mou 132) [2009 73: p10g[5] p10g p10g[3] p10g 11.9m 11.6m 10f[5] 10f[6] Aug 18] leggy gelding: fair handicapper: out of sorts after third start: should stay 1½m: acts on polytrack and firm going: tried in cheekpieces/visor: wayward. *C. Gordon* **70 d**

ITSTHURSDAYALREADY 2 b.g. (Apr 5) Exceed And Excel (AUS) 126 – Succinct 104 (Hector Protector (USA) 124) [2009 5m[2] 5.1g* 5m 5.2d 6m 5.5g[5] p7.1g[2] Dec 26] 18,000Y: close-coupled gelding: second foal: half-brother to fairly useful 2008 2-y-o 7f winner Starry Sky (by Oasis Dream): dam, 1¼m winner, out of half-sister to smart 7f/1m performer Ardkinglass: fair performer: won maiden at Chester in June: good second in nursery at Wolverhampton: stays 7f: acts on polytrack and good to firm ground. *J. G. Given* **74**

ITSY BITSY 7 b.m. Danzig Connection (USA) – Cos I Do (IRE) (Double Schwartz 128) [2009 55: f11g 10m 10.1g 12g[6] 12.1m Aug 13] modest handicapper: stays 1¼m: raced only on all-weather and good/good to firm ground: sometimes in cheekpieces: inconsistent. *W. J. Musson* **–**

ITWASONLYAKISS (IRE) 2 b.f. (Apr 13) Exceed And Excel (AUS) 126 – Reem **74**
One (IRE) 79 (Rainbow Quest (USA) 134) [2009 5m^{5} 5g^{2} 5m 6m^{2} Jul 20] €26,000Y:
lengthy, angular filly: second foal: dam, 9f winner, stayed 1½m: fair maiden: runner-up at
Sandown and Windsor: may prove best at 5f/6f. *J. W. Hills*

IVER BRIDGE LAD 2 b.c. (Feb 10) Avonbridge 123 – Flutonia (FR) 66 (Ashkalani **109**
(IRE) 128) [2009 5g^{2} 5m^{3} p6g* 5m* 5g p6g^{2} 5.1m^{6} 5g^{3} 7v^{4} Oct 24] 8,000F, 1,000Y:
compact colt: third foal: dam 1¼m winner: useful performer: won maiden at Kempton in
June and listed race at Sandown (beat Di Stefano ½ length) in July: best effort when close
third to Our Jonathan in Cornwallis Stakes at Ascot eighth start: effective at 5f and stays
7f: acts on polytrack, heavy and good to firm going. *J. Ryan*

IVOR NOVELLO (IRE) 3 b.g. Noverre (USA) 125 – Pearly Brooks 77 (Efisio 120) **51**
[2009 –: 6m^{4} p6g 8f^{5} May 11] compact gelding: modest maiden: best effort at 6f: acts on
good to firm ground. *G. A. Swinbank*

IVORY JAZZ 2 b.c. (May 9) Dubai Destination (USA) 127 – Slow Jazz (USA) 106 **69**
(Chief's Crown (USA)) [2009 p7.1g 6s^{3} Jul 21] much better effort in maidens when 1¼
lengths third to Butch And Sundance at Yarmouth: should stay 7f. *D. K. Ivory*

IVORY LACE 8 b.m. Atraf 116 – Miriam 59 (Forzando 122) [2009 90, a84: 8.3g 8m **79**
7m^{3} 7m 7g^{3} 7m^{3} 8g^{3} 7m^{5} 7f^{4} 7f* 7m^{4} 7m p7m p8g^{4} p8m Nov 28] rather leggy mare: fair
handicapper nowadays: won at Brighton in August: effective at 7f/1m: acts on polytrack,
firm and soft going: tried in blinkers/cheekpieces: held up. *S. Woodman*

IVORY SILK 4 b.f. Diktat 126 – Ivory's Joy 109 (Tina's Pet 121) [2009 94: p5g^{2} 5m^{2} **82**
5m 5.2d 5m^{5} p5.1g^{3} 5g^{5} p5.1g^{2} p6g^{6} Dec 2] lengthy filly: fairly useful handicapper, better **a94**
on all-weather: creditable efforts in 2009 when placed: effective at 5f/6f: acts on poly-
track, unraced on extremes of going on turf: usually in blinkers. *J. R. Gask*

IVY THE TERRIBLE 3 b.f. Bahamian Bounty 116 – Emerald Fire 86 (Pivotal 124) **–**
[2009 6g 7.1g Jun 25] 24,000Y: small filly: first foal: dam, 6f (including at 2 yrs) winner,
from family of very smart/high-class sprinters Pastoral Pursuits and Goodricke (both by
Bahamian Bounty): well beaten in maidens. *Dr J. D. Scargill*

IZAAJ (USA) 2 ch.c. (Jan 15) Giant's Causeway (USA) 132 – Miss Coronado (USA) **82**
(Coronado's Quest (USA) 130) [2009 5f^{3} 6m* 7m Jun 20] useful-looking colt: first foal:
dam, US Grade 2 8.5f winner, half-sister to smart performer up to 9f Karen's Caper:
easily best effort when winning maiden at Yarmouth in May by length from Rock of
Love: said to have had a breathing problem in Chesham Stakes at Royal Ascot: should
stay 7f: tongue tied: has joined M. bin Shafya in UAE. *Saeed bin Suroor*

IZUIZORIZUAIN'T (IRE) 2 ch.f. (Feb 21) Johannesburg (USA) 127 – Justly Royal **55**
(USA) (Royal Academy (USA) 130) [2009 5g^{2} 5m^{3} 7m^{6} 7m^{4} 6.1s^{4} 7g^{3} 7m f7f^{4} p8.6g
Dec 3] 10,000Y: leggy filly: first foal: dam US 1m winner out of Oaks d'Italia winner
Bright Generation: modest maiden: stays 7f: acts on soft and good to firm ground: tried
blinkered: looks hard ride. *K. A. Ryan*

IZZIBIZZI 4 b.f. Medicean 128 – Sleave Silk (IRE) 58 (Unfuwain (USA) 131) [2009 **75**
92: 8m 8d 8g^{4} 7.2g^{5} p7m^{5} p8g Oct 26] leggy, lengthy filly: just fair handicapper nowadays: stays 1m: acts on polytrack and heavy ground: in cheekpieces last 4 starts: sold
4,000 gns. *E. A. L. Dunlop*

IZZI MILL (USA) 3 gr. or ro.f. Lemon Drop Kid (USA) 131 – Lets Get Cozzy (USA) **75**
(Cozzene (USA)) [2009 77: 7.1m^{2} 6m^{4} 7.5g 7d^{2} 7m 7.1m^{3} p6g^{5} 6d Oct 12] angular filly:
fair maiden: stays 7f: acts on polytrack, good to firm and good to soft going: free-going
sort. *D. R. C. Elsworth*

IZZY LOU (IRE) 3 ch.f. Spinning World (USA) 130 – High Spot 73 (Shirley Heights **–**
130) [2009 68: p8.6g 8.3g Jul 16] lengthy filly: maiden: fair form on 2-y-o debut:
disappointing since: sold 7,000 gns in December. *K. A. Ryan*

J

JABAL TARIQ 4 ch.c. Rock of Gibraltar (IRE) 133 – Sueboog (IRE) 109 (Darshaan **90**
133) [2009 88: 10m^{5} 9.9g^{3} p12g^{2} 12m 12g^{4} p11g^{6} 12m^{5} 10m Sep 25] big, strong colt:
fairly useful handicapper: best efforts when in frame second/third starts: stays 1½m: acts
on polytrack and good to soft ground: usually races up with pace: temperament under
suspicion. *B. W. Hills*

JABROOT (IRE) 3 ch.f. Alhaarth (IRE) 126 – Walesiana (GER) (Star Appeal 133) [2009 p10g^4 12m^5 f12g^3 12g Jul 31] well-made filly: closely related to 2 winners by Unfuwain, notably Musidora/Nassau Stakes winner Zahrat Dubai, and half-sister to 3 winners, including 1½m winner Warluskee (by Dancing Brave): dam German 6f (at 2 yrs) to 1m (Group 2) winner: best effort in maidens when third at Southwell: in cheekpieces, said to have finished distressed on handicap debut later in month: stays 1½m: sold €20,000 in November. *M. A. Jarvis* **71**

JACHOL (IRE) 3 b.g. Bachelor Duke (USA) 122 – Restiv Star (FR) 108 (Soviet Star (USA) 128) [2009 –p: 8m^2 9.9g 10.1g^2 12g^3 10s^3 p12.2g^2 Sep 11] good-topped gelding: modest maiden handicapper: stays 1½m: acts on polytrack, soft and good to firm going: tried in cheekpieces: sold 11,000 gns. *W. J. Haggas* **64**

JACK COOL (IRE) 3 b.c. One Cool Cat (USA) 123 – Rachrush (IRE) (Sadler's Wells (USA) 132) [2009 57p: 10m 7m 7g* 7m^4 8.3v^2 7g f8f Oct 21] well-made colt: fairly useful performer: won maiden at Yarmouth (by 12 lengths) in June: improved again when runner-up in handicap at Nottingham: stays 1m: acts on heavy ground: said to have finished lame final start: sold 16,500 gns. *P. W. Chapple-Hyam* **90**

JACK DAWKINS (USA) 4 b.g. Fantastic Light (USA) 134 – Do The Mambo (USA) (Kingmambo (USA) 125) [2009 105: 8.1g 10.3f* 10m 8g^5 10.4m Aug 18] good-topped gelding: useful performer: won handicap at Doncaster in May by nose from Hevelius (pair clear): below form otherwise in 2009: effective at 1m/1¼m: unraced on heavy going, acts on any other and polytrack: held up: sold 44,000 gns, then gelded. *H. R. A. Cecil* **101**

JACKDAY (IRE) 4 b.g. Daylami (IRE) 138 – Magic Lady (IRE) (Bigstone (IRE) 126) [2009 64: 16.2g^3 16m^2 16.1m^4 16g^2 16s^4 16.2g^2 16d^2 17.1m^4 15.8g* 15.8s^4 Oct 27] strong, lengthy gelding: fair handicapper: won at Catterick in October: stays 2m: acts on soft and good to firm ground: has run well sweating: consistent. *T. D. Easterby* **74**

JACK GALVIN (IRE) 3 b.g. Danetime (IRE) 121 – Tumbleweed Pearl 96 (Aragon 118) [2009 6g^6 p5.1g Oct 17] €65,000F, 62,000Y: medium-sized gelding: half-brother to useful 2006 2-y-o 5f (Queen Mary Stakes) winner Gilded (by Redback) and 6f winner Jasmine Pearl (by King of Kings): dam, 6f winner (including at 2 yrs), half-sister to smart 7f performer Tumbleweed Ridge: signs of ability in maidens: bred to prove best at 5f/6f: capable of better. *J. R. Gask* **– p**

JACKIE DANNY 2 b.f. (Apr 1) Mujahid (USA) 125 – Baileys Applause 59 (Royal Applause 124) [2009 5g 5m^5 5.2g^4 May 29] small filly: second foal: half-sister to 2008 2-y-o 5f seller winner Royal Raider (by Piccolo): dam 5f winner: poor form in maiden/seller last 2 starts. *C. A. Dwyer* **48**

JACKIE KIELY 8 ch.g. Vettori (IRE) 119 – Fudge (Polar Falcon (USA) 126) [2009 70, a81: f12g f12g^4 10.9m^3 f11g^3 10.9f^5 11.5g f12g^2 12.6d^2 12.1m 16.2v p12.2g f12m^2 f12g^3 f14m^3 f12g^2 Dec 22] leggy gelding: modest performer: stays 2m, all wins at shorter: acts on all-weather, firm and soft going: in cheekpieces last 4 starts: tongue tied: usually held up. *R. Brotherton* **64**

JACK JUNIOR (USA) 5 b. or br.g. Songandaprayer (USA) 118 – Ra Hydee (USA) (Rahy (USA) 115) [2009 105: 7.5g a8.5f^4 a10f p7g p8g^6 8m p7.1g 8g 10.4d 9.2g^5 p7.1g^4 Oct 3] leggy, rather lightly-made gelding: useful handicapper: creditable 1¼ lengths fourth to Roman's Run at Nad Al Sheba second start: well below form after fifth start, including in claimers: stays 9f: acts on dirt/polytrack, good to firm and good to soft going: tried blinkered. *D. Nicholls* **105 d**

JACK KANE 2 ch.c. (Mar 17) Ishiguru (USA) 114 – Armada Grove 75 (Fleetwood (IRE) 107) [2009 7m Aug 14] 50/1, well held in maiden at Newcastle. *J. A. McShane* **–**

JACK LUEY 2 b.c. (Feb 24) Danbird (AUS) – Icenaslice (IRE) 78 (Fayruz 116) [2009 5m^4 5m^6 5d^3 5v^5 5m^5 6.1d^5 6s^3 5.1s^4 f6m* Nov 12] rather leggy colt: fair performer: good fourth in nursery at Nottingham prior to winning seller at Southwell (rider lost iron): stays 6f: acts on fibresand, soft and good to firm going: in cheekpieces last 3 starts: races prominently. *L. A. Mullaney* **68**

JACK MY BOY (IRE) 2 b.c. (Jan 28) Tagula (IRE) 116 – Bobanlyn (IRE) 76 (Dance of Life (USA)) [2009 5m^3 5m* 6d* 6g 6m* 7m^6 6m^6 6d 6m 6g^3 6s^4 Nov 7] €17,000Y: lengthy colt: has scope: half-brother to fairly useful Irish performer up to 2m Great Guns (by Deploy), 9f winner at 2 yrs, and winner up to 1½m in Italy by Kris: dam 6f (at 2 yrs) to 1½m winner: fairly useful form: won maiden at Beverley in April and minor events at Newcastle in May and Pontefract in June: creditable efforts in nurseries last 2 starts: should stay 7f: acts on soft and good to firm ground: unreliable. *P. D. Evans* **83 §**

JACK O'LANTERN 2 b.g. (Apr 9) Shamardal (USA) 129 – Bush Cat (USA) 93 (Kingmambo (USA) 125) [2009 7g³ Oct 23] 95,000Y: strong gelding: third foal: half-brother to fairly useful 2007 2-y-o 1m winner Meer Kat (by Red Ransom) and 3-y-o Ask Dan: dam, 2-y-o 7f winner (stayed 11.4f), out of sister to smart 6f/7f performer Nicholas: 10/1, promising 3¼ lengths third to Rashaad in maiden at Doncaster, always prominent: likely to be suited by 1m+: sold 34,000 gns, then gelded: should progress. *J. H. M. Gosden* **79 p**

JACK RACKHAM 5 ch.g. Kyllachy 129 – Hill Welcome 52 (Most Welcome 131) [2009 80: f6d² f6s⁵ 6m 6m² 6m p6f³ Dec 13] strong, sturdy gelding: type to carry condition: fair handicapper: stays 6f: acts on all-weather and firm going: visored. *B. Smart* **76**

JACK'S HOUSE (IRE) 3 b.g. Danetime (IRE) 121 – Groupetime (USA) 69 (Gilded Time (USA)) [2009 52: f7d³ f7g⁵ 6g⁴ 6g 7.1m 6s 7m⁵ Sep 15] modest maiden: claimed from Jane Chapple-Hyam £5,000 after third outing: seems to stay 8.6f: acts on polytrack, best turf effort on good going: tried in cheekpieces, usually tongue tied: none too consistent. *Julie Camacho* **48**

JACOBITE PRINCE (IRE) 3 b.g. Chevalier (IRE) 115 – Kind Gesture (IRE) 46 (Alzao (USA) 117) [2009 68: 8.5g 7g 8d 10.1s⁶ 10.1g p10g Sep 8] lengthy, good-topped gelding: fair maiden at 2 yrs: badly lost way in 2009: tried in cheekpieces/blinkers. *M. H. Tompkins* **55 d**

JACONET (USA) 4 ch.f. Hussonet (USA) – Radiant Rocket (USA) (Peteski (CAN) 125) [2009 83: p6g* 5m* 5m* 5g 6m³ 5m 6g³ p6g* p6f* 5.6m 5m p6g* Nov 21] good-quartered filly: smart performer on all-weather, useful on turf: had fine year, winning handicaps at Wolverhampton in March, Musselburgh and Redcar in April, Wolverhampton in August and Lingfield (best effort beat Street Power by 5 lengths) in September, and listed race at Lingfield (by 2¼ lengths from Ebraam) in November: effective at 5f/6f: acts on polytrack and good to firm going (well held on soft): blinkered: front runner. *T. D. Barron* **98 a112**

JACQUELINE QUEST (IRE) 2 b.f. (Mar 1) Rock of Gibraltar (IRE) 133 – Coquette Rouge (IRE) 93 (Croco Rouge (IRE) 126) [2009 6m² 7m* 7v Oct 24] €60,000Y: good-topped, attractive filly: first foal: dam, Irish 1½m/17f winner, half-sister to smart performer up to 1½m Regime: promising efforts in maidens at Newbury (neck second to Queen's Grace) and Chester, landing odds by 9 lengths in latter in September: pulled too hard in listed race at Newbury: should be suited by 1m+: remains a useful prospect. *H. R. A. Cecil* **93 p**

JADALEE (IRE) 6 b.g. Desert Prince (IRE) 130 – Lionne (Darshaan 133) [2009 85: p13g⁵ 14v p16g⁴ p11g⁶ 14.8g* f12g⁵ p16g² p13.9g* p13.9g⁶ p13g² p13g⁵ Nov 1] tall, leggy gelding: fairly useful handicapper nowadays: won at Newmarket in July and Wolverhampton in September: stays 2m: acts on polytrack and firm going: wears cheekpieces/tongue tie: ridden more prominently nowadays: joined D. Pipe. *G. A. Butler* **85**

JAFARU 5 b.g. Silver Hawk (USA) 123 – Rafha 123 (Kris 135) [2009 71§: p13g³ 11.9m* 11.5m² p16g² 11.9m³ 11.9g³ f11m⁵ Jul 21] stocky gelding: fair handicapper: won at Brighton in May: stays 2m, effective at shorter: acts on polytrack, soft and good to firm going: usually blinkered/in cheekpieces: difficult ride, and is ungenuine: successful over hurdles in September: sold £500. *G. L. Moore* **65 § a69 §**

JAFIR (USA) 3 ch.c. Speightstown (USA) 124 – Day Mate (USA) (Dayjur (USA) 137) [2009 8.3d Oct 12] $210,000Y: tall, good-topped colt: half-brother to 3 winners in USA, notably smart Grade 2 9f winner Tap Day (by Pleasant Tap): dam, US 9f winner, half-sister to US Grade 2 9f/1½m winner Fairy Garden: 13/2, slowly away and green before late headway in maiden at Windsor (seventh of 14): will do better. *B. J. Meehan* **59 p**

JAGGER 9 gr.g. Linamix (FR) 127 – Sweetness Herself 106 (Unfuwain (USA) 131) [2009 96: p16g⁶ 14.1m⁵ p12.2g⁵ May 18] smallish, quite attractive gelding: just fairly useful handicapper nowadays: stays 2¼m: acts on polytrack, firm and good to soft going: sometimes wears cheekpieces: tried tongue tied: edgy type. *G. A. Butler* **85**

JAGO (SWI) 6 b.g. Brief Truce (USA) 126 – Jariyah (USA) (It's The One (USA)) [2009 77: p10g p13g p12.2g p9.5g⁴ 10d May 15] tall gelding: fair handicapper: free-going sort, but stays 13f: acts on polytrack, unraced on going firmer than good on turf: tried in cheekpieces. *A. M. Hales* **66**

JAIRZIHNO 2 b.c. (Feb 26) Royal Applause 124 – Polish Belle (Polish Precedent (USA) 131) [2009 6m* 6g³ 7g⁶ 8.3m⁴ p8m² 7d³ Oct 11] €50,000Y: unfurnished colt: fifth foal: half-brother to Italian 7.5f to 8.5f winner San Aerdna (by Red Ransom): dam unraced close relation to smart sprinter Danehurst: fairly useful performer: won maiden at Leicester in June: good efforts in nurseries last 2 starts: stays 1m: acts on polytrack, good to firm and good to soft going: sold 62,000 gns, sent to USA. *J. R. Best* **85**

JAKE THE SNAKE (IRE) 8 ch.g. Intikhab (USA) 135 – Tilbrook (IRE) 78 (Don't Forget Me 127) [2009 87: p8g* p7g* p8g³ p7g³ p8g* p8g³ p8g* p8g² p7g³ 7m⁵ p7g³ p8g⁴ 8g³ Jul 31] big, strong gelding: type to carry condition: fairly useful performer: won claimers at Kempton (3) and Lingfield between January and April: effective at stiff 6f to 1m: acts on polytrack, good to firm and good to soft going: possibly not straightforward (often slowly away): ridden by 5-lb claimer Amy Baker in 2009. *A. W. Carroll* **87**

JALAMID (IRE) 7 b.g. Danehill (USA) 126 – Vignelaure (IRE) 74 (Royal Academy (USA) 130) [2009 52: p13.9g 9m Apr 12] big, strong gelding: poor performer: probably stayed 1½m: acted on good to firm and good to soft going: tried blinkered: usually tongue tied: poor form over hurdles: fell fatally on chasing debut in June. *M. A. Barnes* **49**

JAMAAHIR (USA) 6 b.g. Bahri (USA) 125 – Elrehaan 96 (Sadler's Wells (USA) 132) [2009 p12.2g Jan 9] rather leggy, useful-looking gelding: has a round action: fair maiden in 2007: unraced at 5 yrs, and well held on return: tried tongue tied. *George Baker* **–**

JAMARJO (IRE) 2 b.g. (Apr 19) Marju (IRE) 127 – Athlumney Lady 98 (Lycius (USA) 124) [2009 6.1v² 7s p8.6g⁶ Nov 21] good-topped gelding: best effort in maidens when second to Running Mate at Nottingham: should stay 1m. *S. Gollings* **63**

JAMARY (IRE) 2 b. or br.f. (Mar 26) Grand Reward (USA) 112 – Datsdawayitis (USA) (Known Fact (USA) 135) [2009 p7g Jun 17] €49,000F, 20,000Y: closely related to 2 winners in USA by Crowning Storm and half-sister to several winners in USA, including dam of very smart 1¼m/1½m performer Cherry Mix: dam US 6f/7f winner: 10/1, virtually pulled up in maiden at Kempton having travelled well to home turn (said to have finished distressed). *C. E. Brittain* **–**

JAMES BARRYMORE 2 b.c. (Mar 16) Fraam 114 – Nine Red 63 (Royal Applause 124) [2009 p8m⁶ p7.1g³ p8g⁴ 7f³ 7m² p7.1g⁵ p8.6g Dec 17] leggy, unfurnished colt: first foal: dam, maiden (stayed 7f), half-sister to smart 6f/7f winner Snow Kid, out of smart 5f/6f winner Sarcita: fair maiden: stays 1m: acts on polytrack and firm ground: free-going sort. *R. Hannon* **74**

JAMES POLLARD (IRE) 4 ch.g. Indian Ridge 123 – Manuetti (IRE) 86 (Sadler's Wells (USA) 132) [2009 66: 8.3m⁶ p8g 6m p10m Sep 23] lengthy gelding: fair maiden handicapper: left D. Elsworth 7,000 gns prior to final start: stays 1¼m: acts on polytrack and good to firm going: pulls hard. *B. J. Llewellyn* **61**

JAMES STREET (IRE) 6 b.g. Fruits of Love (USA) 127 – Humble Mission (Shack (USA) 118) [2009 42: f7g 7.2g 6s Aug 12] quite good-topped gelding: no form in 2009: usually wears headgear. *Peter Grayson* **–**

JAMIESON GOLD (IRE) 6 b.g. Desert Style (IRE) 121 – Princess of Zurich (IRE) (Law Society (USA) 130) [2009 87§: 10m 9.2m 9.1g 9g⁶ 7.1m² 8g² 8s⁵ 8s 7.1m 8m⁵ Oct 1] useful-looking gelding: one-time useful winner: modest nowadays: stays 1¼m: acts on soft and good to firm going: often blinkered/in cheekpieces: moody and unreliable. *Miss L. A. Perratt* **64 §**

JANEIRO (IRE) 2 b.g. (Apr 27) Captain Rio 122 – Aspired (IRE) 57 (Mark of Esteem (IRE) 137) [2009 f5g⁴ 5g³ p6g² 6m² p6g 7d* 7g⁵ Aug 12] €8,000Y: first foal: dam, ran twice, half-sister to useful winner around 1¼m First Fantasy, out of half-sister to Melbourne Cup winner Jeune: fairly useful performer: won maiden at Yarmouth in July: stays 7f: acts on polytrack, good to firm and good to soft going: visored (ran poorly) fifth start: has pulled hard/looked awkward ride: sent to Hong Kong, where renamed Home With Glory. *Tom Dascombe* **87**

JANE OF ARC (FR) 5 ch.m. Trempolino (USA) 135 – Aerleon Jane 89 (Caerleon (USA) 132) [2009 61: 9m⁴ 14m 13m⁴ 12.5m⁴ 13m⁵ Jun 25] good-bodied mare: poor performer: best around 1½m: acts on good to firm and good to soft ground: usually wears cheekpieces (visored last time): races prominently. *J. S. Goldie* **48**

JANE'S PAYOFF (IRE) 4 b.f. Danetime (IRE) 121 – Alimony (IRE) 77 (Groom Dancer (USA) 128) [2009 72: p5g p5g Jul 22] angular filly: fair handicapper at 3 yrs: below form in 2009: best effort at 5f: tongue tied final outing. *Mrs L. C. Jewell* **61**

JANSHE GOLD 4 ch.f. Bertolini (USA) 125 – Rekindled Flame (IRE) (Kings Lake (USA) 133) [2009 59d: 8g⁵ 10.9f May 12] rather leggy filly: modest maiden: stays 1m. *J. G. Portman* **51**

JANUARY 6 gr.g. Daylami (IRE) 138 – Noushkey 118 (Polish Precedent (USA) 131) [2009 89: p8.6g⁶ a10s a7g p8g p10.7g Nov 13] lengthy, good-topped gelding: fair winning hurdler: fairly useful performer on Flat: stays 8.6f: acts on polytrack, best turf effort on good going: usually tongue tied: held up: signs of temperament. *T. M. Walsh, Ireland* **81**

JAN VERMEER (IRE) 2 b.c. (Feb 6) Montjeu (IRE) 137 – Shadow Song (IRE) (Pennekamp (USA) 130) [2009 7s[4] 8m* 8s* Nov 1] **119 p**

French race planners have had little cause to regret their decision to introduce a new race, the Criterium International at Saint-Cloud, as part of a shake-up of that country's two year old pattern races in 2001. The Group 1 contest for colts and fillies, run over a mile in late-October/early-November, effectively replaced the Grand Criterium run earlier in the autumn at Longchamp, that race reduced in trip as it was merged with the Prix de la Salamandre over the same track, ultimately to become the Prix Jean-Luc Lagardere. It is debatable whether the change of track or the later place in the calendar has made much of a contribution to the success of the new race, but it is fair to say that the Criterium International has so far unearthed plenty more future stars than its predecessor had succeeded in doing in its final years. The first three winners at Saint-Cloud—Act One, Dalakhani and Bago—went on to land eight more Group 1 races between them, the two last-named winning successive editions of the Prix de l'Arc de Triomphe. Subsequent winners of the Criterium International admittedly haven't enjoyed quite the same level of success as that trio, though 2006 winner Mount Nelson did return from injury to win the Eclipse Stakes at Sandown as a four-year-old. Mount Nelson was the first winner of the Criterium International trained outside France, though the contest has since lived up to its name by being won twice more by foreign raiders, Zafisio in 2008 and Jan Vermeer in 2009, the latter for Mount Nelson's trainer Aidan O'Brien.

The Criterium International was the final outing in a three-race campaign for Jan Vermeer, one which didn't start until mid-September when he finished a promising fourth behind Crystal Gal and Free Judgement in a seven-furlong maiden at the Curragh. Jan Vermeer looked in need of the experience that day and was a different proposition when making all to beat the well-bred Behtarini by two and a half lengths in similar company on firmer going at Gowran later in the month, seeing out the mile very well. The promotion to Group 1 company at Saint-Cloud five weeks later represented a significant step-up in class, however, his six rivals including Rosanara, sent off a warm favourite following her win in the Prix Marcel Boussac on her previous start. Jan Vermeer wasn't the choice of stable-jockey Johnny Murtagh either; he chose to ride Midas Touch, who had managed only third behind his stable companion in the aforementioned race at Gowran. Presumably the much softer ground at Saint-Cloud was one factor in Murtagh's decision to side with Midas Touch, who had won his next start impressively on soft. However, it was clear from an early stage that front-running Jan Vermeer was not at all incon-

*Criterium International, Saint-Cloud—
a third Group 1 two-year-old prize in just over a fortnight for Aidan O'Brien as Jan Vermeer keeps on strongly to beat Emerald Commander; Marcel Boussac winner Rosanara (noseband) is only third ahead of Midas Touch and Prizefighting (far side)*

venienced by the conditions. His jockey Colm O'Donoghue—Seamus Heffernan had been on board for both of the colt's previous starts—brought the field wide into the straight and Jan Vermeer kept on very strongly under pressure to forge clear, beating recent Godolphin purchase Emerald Commander by four lengths, with a below-par Rosanara a further length and a half away in third, closely followed by Midas Touch. It was O'Brien's third Group 1 two-year-old prize in the space of just over two weeks, following the successes of Beethoven in the Dewhurst Stakes at Newmarket and St Nicholas Abbey in the Racing Post Trophy at Doncaster.

Coolmore has unquestionably had the upper hand in its battles with fierce rival Godolphin in recent years, so it must be particularly galling for the latter that Jan Vermeer is the first foal out of one of its own cast-offs (Coolmore also snapped up her second foal, a yearling filly by Galileo, for 280,000 guineas in October). The dam Shadow Song carried Sheikh Mohammed's colours to victory in a three-year-old maiden over eleven furlongs at Segre in the French Provinces in 2005 on the last of her six starts for Alex Pantall, before being bought on behalf of Coolmore for 74,000 guineas later that summer. Shadow Song was one of eight winners out of the unraced Evening Air, the best of Shadow Song's siblings being half-sister Midnight Air, who won the 1991 May Hill Stakes at Doncaster when a leading two-year-old for Henry Cecil. Midnight Air has since been a success at stud, her best representative being Midnight Line, who won the May Hill herself in 1997 prior to finishing third in the following year's Oaks (also for Cecil). Evening Air is also the grandam of several other above-average performers, including two performers at different ends of the stamina spectrum, Imperial Beauty being a smart sprinter who won the 2001 Prix de l'Abbaye, whilst the Italian-based Silly Game picked up her black type by winning a fifteen-furlong listed newcomers hurdle for three-year-old fillies at Merano in 2002. Jan Vermeer's great grandam Nellie Forbes, who won once from just two starts (a two-year-old maiden over a mile at Leopardstown) for Vincent O'Brien, was a half-sister to America's champion three-year-old colt of 1976 Bold Forbes, winner of the Kentucky Derby and Belmont Stakes.

Jan Vermeer (IRE) (b.c. Feb 6, 2007)	Montjeu (IRE) (b 1996)	Sadler's Wells (b 1981)	Northern Dancer
			Fairy Bridge
		Floripedes (b 1985)	Top Ville
			Toute Cy
	Shadow Song (IRE) (b 2002)	Pennekamp (b 1992)	Bering
			Coral Dance
		Evening Air (br 1982)	J O Tobin
			Nellie Forbes

The big, useful-looking Jan Vermeer, who takes his name from the seventeenth-century Dutch painter, is around 12/1 second favourite in the 2010 Derby ante-post market at the time of writing. His sire Montjeu has now amassed seven Derby wins around the globe since retiring to stud in 2001—Motivator (2005 Derby), Hurricane Run (2005 Irish Derby), Authorized (2007 Derby), Nom du Jeu (2008 Australian Derby), Frozen Fire (2008 Irish Derby), Roman Emperor (2009 Australian Derby) and Fame And Glory (2009 Irish Derby). Jan Vermeer's Saint-Cloud form was amongst the best seen from a two-year-old in 2009 and he appeals very much as the sort who will do even better at three, particularly when tackling longer trips. Ironically, the biggest obstacle to Derby glory looks likely to be another son of Montjeu in his own stable, the Racing Post Trophy winner St Nicholas Abbey, who is just 2/1 in some places for Epsom. *A. P. O'Brien, Ireland*

JA ONE (IRE) 3 b.f. Acclamation 118 – Special Dancer (Shareef Dancer (USA) 135) **74**
[2009 63p: 9.9m^3 9.7f 11.6g^4 14g^4 16g^5 p16g* p16g^2 Oct 24] big, lengthy filly: has scope: fair handicapper: won at Lingfield in October: stays easy 2m: acts on polytrack and good to firm ground. *B. W. Hills*

JAPURA (USA) 5 ch.g. Giant's Causeway (USA) 132 – Exchange Place (USA) **57**
(Affirmed (USA)) [2009 –: p9.5g^5 p13.9g^6 p12g Feb 14] modest maiden nowadays: likely to prove best up to 1½m: raced on polytrack and good to soft ground: tried in cheekpieces. *T. J. Pitt*

JAQ'S SISTER 3 b.f. Bertolini (USA) 125 – Polly Golightly 84 (Weldnaas (USA) 112) **53**
[2009 –: p7.1g^3 p8.6g^6 p7.1g 8m p8g Dec 2] modest maiden: stays 7f: acts on polytrack: tried blinkered. *M. Blanshard*

JARGELLE (IRE) 3 b.f. Kheleyf (USA) 116 – Winter Tern (USA) (Arctic Tern (USA) 126) [2009 104: a7g⁴ 6.5g⁵ 5m² 5m⁶ 5g 5m³ 5m² Aug 31] angular filly: useful performer: unsuitable trip in UAE first 2 starts for E. Martins: back to form in handicaps at York and Epsom (short-head second to Siren's Gift) last 2 starts: best at 5f: raced only on good/ good to firm ground on turf. *K. A. Ryan* **104**

JAROSLAW (SAF) 6 b.g. Jallad (USA) 89 – Dacha (SAF) (Russian Fox (USA)) [2009 p7g⁴ p8f* Dec 19] useful performer: won 4 times in South Africa, including handicap at Vaal in 2008: probably best effort when fourth to J J The Jet Plane in Grade 2 handicap there next time: left Ernst Oertel and off a year, better effort in minor events in Britain when winning at Lingfield in December by neck from Ace of Hearts: has won at 1¼m, but effective at much shorter: acts on polytrack/dirt. *D. M. Simcock* **98 +**

JARRAH BAY 3 b.f. Mark of Esteem (IRE) 137 – Wannaplantatree 72 (Niniski (USA) 125) [2009 –: 8.1m Jul 10] leggy filly: little form. *J. G. M. O'Shea* **–**

JARROW (IRE) 2 ch.c. (Mar 29) Shamardal (USA) 129 – Wolf Cleugh (IRE) 65 (Last Tycoon 131) [2009 6s² p6g* p7m³ Nov 27] 95,000F, 190,000Y: half-brother to several winners, notably high-class sprinter Moss Vale (by Shinko Forest) and 4-y-o Cape Vale: dam, ran 3 times, half-sister to smart sprinter King's College: won maiden at Lingfield (by 4½ lengths from Picnic Party) in November: seemed not to stay when tried at 7f there: useful sprinting prospect. *M. Johnston* **92 p**

JARVO 8 b.g. Pursuit of Love 124 – Pinkie Rose (FR) (Kenmare (FR) 125) [2009 63: p9.5g⁶ p9.5g 10m 9.9m 9.9m 8.5m Aug 13] sturdy gelding: modest handicapper in 2008: out of sorts at 5 yrs: tried in tongue tie, usually wears headgear. *I. W. McInnes* **42**

JASER 4 ch.c. Alhaarth (IRE) 126 – Waafiah 57 (Anabaa (USA) 130) [2009 100: 8s 10d⁶ 10.3s p8g Sep 21] big, good-bodied colt: has a quick, unimpressive action: just fairly useful handicapper in 2009 (reportedly treated for spinal problem during winter 2008/9): stays 1¼m: yet to race on heavy going but acts on any other turf and polytrack: has hung under pressure: sold 4,000 gns. *P. W. Chapple-Hyam* **93**

JASLYN (IRE) 3 b. or br.f. Pyrus (USA) 106 – Ruby Julie (Clantime 101) [2009 47: f6d⁶ Jan 2] poor maiden: stays 1m: acts on polytrack and heavy ground. *J. R. Weymes* **–**

JASMENO 2 b.f. (Jan 23) Catcher In The Rye (IRE) 115 – Jasmick (IRE) 96 (Definite Article 121) [2009 8m 8d⁴ Oct 12] £1,200Y: second foal: dam 1½m/1¾m winner: better effort in maidens when 3½ lengths fourth to Flaming Miracle at Salisbury, closing late: will be suited by 1¼m+. *H. Morrison* **62**

JASMINE SCENT (IRE) 2 ch.f. (Feb 7) Namid 128 – Sky Galaxy (USA) 84 (Sky Classic (CAN)) [2009 5m 6g Jun 15] good-topped filly: first living foal: dam, 2-y-o 6f winner, half-sister to 5-y-o Mount Hadley: well beaten in maiden/seller at Windsor. *J. A. Osborne* **–**

JASPER CLIFF 3 b.g. Lucky Owners (NZ) 122 – Catmint 85 (Piccolo 121) [2009 –: 10g 12m 8.1g 9m Jun 22] close-coupled gelding: little sign of ability: tried blinkered. *Mark Gillard* **–**

JAWAAB (IRE) 5 ch.g. King's Best (USA) 132 – Canis Star (Wolfhound (USA) 126) [2009 86: 8m⁴ 10m³ 12m 10g⁶ 10.9g* 10.3d⁵ Oct 24] compact gelding: fairly useful handicapper: won at Warwick in August: stays 1¼m: acts on polytrack, soft and good to firm going: tried in cheekpieces: usually patiently ridden. *Mark Buckley* **84**

JAWAAHER (USA) 3 b.f. Empire Maker (USA) 129 – Winsome (Kris 135) [2009 p7.1g³ p7g 8m Apr 4] $47,000Y, 70,000 2-y-o: fifth foal: half-sister to 2 winners abroad, including French 11.5f winner For Criquette (by Barathea): dam, useful French 10.5f/ 11f winner, out of smart half-sister to top-class miler Markofdistinction: modest maiden: should stay 1m. *M. Johnston* **62**

JAY ELL THE TRIER (IRE) 5 br.g. Talkin Man (CAN) 120 – Killoughey Pride (IRE) (Top of The World 103) [2009 p13g Feb 11] fair form in bumper: well held in novice hurdles and on Flat debut. *Tim Vaughan* **–**

JAY GEE WIGMO 4 b.g. First Trump 118 – Queen of Shannon (IRE) 76 (Nordico (USA)) [2009 55: 8.1g 8f p8g 11.6m⁴ 8.1m 8f Aug 22] stocky gelding: modest maiden handicapper at 4 yrs: below form in 2009. *A. W. Carroll* **–**

JAYYID (IRE) 4 b.g. Daylami (IRE) 138 – Mellow Jazz 86 (Lycius (USA) 124) [2009 59: p10g Feb 11] maiden: modest form first 2 starts at 3 yrs: well held since: tried tongue tied. *C. E. Brittain* **–**

JAZACOSTA (USA) 3 ch.g. Dixieland Band (USA) – Dance With Del (USA) (Sword Dance) [2009 87: p8g 9.9m 8m 8m^2 8g 8.3g 8m p10g Oct 14] strong gelding: fair handicapper nowadays: stays 1m: acts on good to firm and good to soft going: tried in cheekpieces/blinkers: temperamental: sold 12,000 gns, then gelded. *Mrs A. J. Perrett* **75 §**

JAZRAWY 7 b.g. Dansili 127 – Dalila di Mare (IRE) (Bob Back (USA) 124) [2009 –: f11m^2 f12g Dec 22] short-backed, deep-girthed gelding: modest performer, lightly raced in recent years: stays 1¾m: acts on all-weather, firm and good to soft going: tried tongue tied. *A. J. McCabe* **63**

JAZZ AGE (IRE) 2 b.c. (May 15) Shamardal (USA) 129 – Tender Is Thenight (IRE) (Barathea (IRE) 127) [2009 8g^4 p8.6g p8f^5 Dec 16] easily best effort in maidens when 4¾ lengths fourth to Database at Bath (blinkered): left J. Gosden 15,000 gns after. *J. A. Glover* **72 d**

JEALOUS AGAIN (USA) 2 b.f. (Feb 1) Trippi (USA) 121 – Chi Sa (CAN) (Bold Ruckus (USA)) [2009 p4.5f* a5g^2 5m* Jun 17] **119**

Royal Ascot provided enough memorable races to satisfy the most discerning of judges. In terms of impressive winning performances, Yeats, Canford Cliffs and Scenic Blast all well and truly dominated their rivals, but it's a moot point whether any of that trio had their respective races won quite so far out as Jealous Again in the Queen Mary Stakes. With the added significance of the winner's being trained in the United States, the Queen Mary is a strong candidate to be regarded as one of the most remarkable races of the season on more than one level. There were no American-trained challengers at the Royal meeting between the 1928 Horse of the Year Reigh Count, runner-up in the 1929 Gold Cup after winning the Coronation Cup, and Mighty Beau, who came fifth in the King's Stand Stakes in 2005. Jealous Again's trainer Wesley Ward deserves credit for identifying an opportunity to put one over on the locals in a sphere of racing in which they were likely to prove vulnerable to an American challenge, namely two-year-old racing in the first part of the season under conditions which put the emphasis firmly on speed. Ward deserves even more credit for actually bringing his innovative and bold plan to a successful conclusion. A champion and Eclipse Award-winning apprentice rider, Ward turned to training twenty years ago after his own personal rise in the weights. He is not perennially one of the leaders of his profession in the United States in terms of money won or victories gained—his 2008 tally was ninety-four wins from three hundred and sixty starts for earnings of more than 2,200,000 dollars—but he has built up a reputation for training fast, precocious two-year-olds. The American graded stakes system provides few opportunities for such horses, with no Grade 1 races over shorter than seven furlongs and only one Grade 2 over six furlongs or shorter, that being the Sanford Stakes. It is not much better with the juvenile Grade 3s. The Debutante Stakes and Schuylerville Stakes over six furlongs are the only such events restricted to fillies; the Kentucky Juvenile at Churchill Downs, the solitary five-furlong graded race for any age group, is open to both sexes. Royal Ascot's two-year-old programme, with the Group 2 Coventry Stakes, Norfolk Stakes and Queen Mary Stakes, the Group 3 Albany Stakes and the listed Windsor Castle Stakes, clearly made an impression on Ward.

The Ward raiding party, if one can call it such, consisted of two-year-olds Aegean (Albany Stakes), Jealous Again, Strike The Tiger (Windsor Castle Stakes), Yogaroo (Norfolk Stakes) and Honor In Peace (seven-furlong Chesham Stakes) plus the four-year-old Cannonball (King's Stand Stakes and Golden Jubilee Stakes). Jealous Again had had two runs, hacking up in a ten-runner maiden special weight on polytrack at Keeneland at the start of April before going down by a length and a quarter to Aegean in the Kentucky Juvenile Stakes on dirt at the end of the month. Jealous Again showed blistering speed on both occasions and it was this particular quality which proved crucial at Ascot. Alacrity from the gate is the norm in American racing, especially in sprints, as many a European jockey and horse has found. In an interview later in the year in the *Blood-Horse*, Ward revealed: 'We do a lot of gate work. My horses are in a gate 40 or 50 times before they ever run so that they are used to the rattling around and used to having other horses in there with them. They're just very, very relaxed in the gate because of that, because they have been so well schooled and educated, that when the gate opens, more often than not, they're leaving and running.' Such a training regime, with its particular

Queen Mary Stakes, Royal Ascot—American challenger Jealous Again puts up an exhilarating performance to provide trainer Wesley Ward and jockey John Velazquez (who last rode at the Royal meeting—for Godolphin—in 2000) with a second winner of the week; Misheer and Ceedwell (rail) fill the places as Lady of The Desert (striped sleeves) fades into sixth

concentration on starting, would be virtually unthinkable in Europe, although the way Ward's horses left the gate at the Royal meeting proved its value, at least for them. Ward started out training in California but is based nowadays in Florida in the winter and at Keeneland, then Saratoga and Monmouth Park, at the height of summer. Around three weeks before Royal Ascot, he worked several of his contenders between races at a meeting on turf at River Downs in Ohio. Jealous Again and Aegean, for example, worked together over three furlongs in 34.8sec, a pretty fast time, with Ward telling reporters: 'I think we got exactly what we came for. By letting us work between races, the horses got a race-day experience and all proved up to the task.'

By the time Jealous Again lined up against twelve rivals for the Queen Mary, the Ward stable had already had a winner, Strike The Tiger. A comfortable winner of a maiden claiming race at Churchill Downs on his only start, he started at 33/1 in the Windsor Castle Stakes and made all, holding on gamely by a neck from Fratellino. After Ward's post-race claim that 'I thought I would save my best runner for the weakest race and that is Aegean in the Albany Stakes', Jealous Again started at 13/2 in the Queen Mary. The market was headed by Capercaillie, successful in two races at Musselburgh, Hamilton winner Rose Blossom, smooth Hilary Needler Trophy winner Don't Tell Mary and Lady of The Desert, who had won at Leicester on her only start. Most of the other runners had won, notably Misheer in the listed Marygate Stakes at York and the Longchamp winner Chantilly Creme, the only other overseas challenger. None of them got a look in as Jealous Again, drawn perfectly on the rail, burst out of the stalls and soon led at full tilt, her rider John Velazquez later revealing 'When the doors opened I yelled at her to make sure she got out.' Lady Royal Oak, on the far side, also started very quickly but, in less than a furlong, Jealous Again was nearly three lengths clear of those drawn nearest to her, including Misheer, Ceedwell and Lady of The Desert. After two furlongs, Lady Royal Oak was still showing speed and both Lady of The Desert and Misheer had managed to draw a little closer to Jealous Again, the latter coming under pressure as most of the other runners were left toiling. Lady of The Desert was given a reminder two and a half furlongs out but there was no sign of Jealous Again's starting to weaken, as Lady Royal Oak soon did. The hopes of Jealous Again's nearest pursuers quickly evaporated when Velazquez asked her to quicken with over a furlong to go. He got an immediate response as she doubled her advantage to six lengths and there was only one horse in it in the last hundred yards, Misheer staying on to chase home Jealous Again, five lengths behind, with Ceedwell getting third on the line, two lengths further back. Lady of The Desert finished more than ten lengths behind in sixth with the runners strung out like washing at the end, the field more reminiscent of that for a two-mile race run on soft going rather than a two-year-old race on good to firm at five furlongs.

Jealous Again's exhilarating performance was the best for at least thirty years in the Queen Mary Stakes, a race which has been won by such as Marling,

Lyric Fantasy, Queen's Logic and Attraction in that period. The timefigure was first class too, converting to a rating of 119. By the end of the season, no two-year-old filly in Europe had matched Jealous Again's performance at Royal Ascot and the beaten horses had themselves done plenty to advertise the form—Misheer won the Cherry Hinton Stakes and finished second in the Cheveley Park Stakes, Lady of The Desert won the Princess Margaret Stakes and the Lowther Stakes and finished third in the Cheveley Park, and fifth-placed Chantilly Creme ran second in the Prix du Bois and won the listed Criterium du Bequet. After Jealous Again's victory, Ward told the media: 'In America we train for speed and the reason I came over here was that I thought the others in the race here are trained to go on for next year. Your horses are bred to go longer and ours are bred for speed, and it worked out.' It didn't work out with Ward's other juvenile runners, Yogaroo managing only ninth in the Norfolk Stakes, Aegean ninth in the Albany Stakes, while Honor In Peace finished last in the Chesham Stakes. Cannonball did not run to his best in the King's Stand Stakes, though he put in a very smart performance when beaten only a neck by Art Connoisseur in the Golden Jubilee Stakes. In line with the old saying that a prophet is not without honour save in his own country, Ward's achievement received very little coverage in the sporting pages of the non-trade press in America, confirmation perhaps of how far the sport has fallen in the public consciousness there.

There were a couple of twists in the tail in the story of Jealous Again. A week after the Queen Mary, Ward announced that he planned to give the filly a rest to get over her race before targeting the Cheveley Park Stakes. That plan did not remain for long, with Sheikh Mohammed purchasing Jealous Again in July for an undisclosed sum, and the following week it was announced that she had joined Godolphin. Possible targets such as the Nunthorpe Stakes and Cheveley Park Stakes went by without her, but she then appeared in the five-day entries for the Cornwallis Stakes at Ascot in October, and she seemed an intended runner under a penalty. Saeed bin Suroor reported: 'She's been working very well and I'm happy so far with her. The filly has a good turn of foot and I'm looking to see a good run from her.' However, Jealous Again wasn't declared for the race with Suroor noting: 'We don't have any specific alternative plan, but she's in a lot of other races, so we have options before the end of the season.' However, no more was heard about her.

The second twist arrived with a two-page spread in the *Racing Post* in mid-August. The feature gave details of nine positive tests since 2003 for the bronchodilator clenbuterol on horses trained by Ward in America, plus one for using the stimulant phentermine (similar to amphetamine) and its metabolite hydroxyphentermine. The latest positive for excessive clenbuterol, on Notonthesamepage after he won at Gulfstream Park in Florida early in January, led to Ward's licence being suspended by the stewards for fifteen days, the punishment not coming into force until after Royal Ascot. Had the ban been imposed any earlier, Ward's English adventure could have been jeopardised. There was, by the way, no question of any of the trainer's Royal Ascot runners failing tests, the trainer having signed a declaration required by the *Rules of Racing* that none of his runners had received prohibited substances (including clenbuterol) 'except when prescribed by a veterinary surgeon' and the tests on his horses coming up clear. However, Ward did tell the *Racing Post*: 'I train every horse on clenbuterol and the majority of trainers, all the top trainers, train all their horses on it. It is not an illegal drug and it is wonderful for keeping horses' airways clean.' So evidently Jealous Again, Strike The Tiger, Cannonball and the others, had all received clenbuterol at some stage. Moreover, when asked in the *Racing Post* interview 'Even though you ran those horses over there without the medication, now that they're back over here, I guess they would be running on the meds we use here,' Ward replied: 'Yeah. I put them on the butazolidin for the race and then I'll also administer just a small dose of lasix.'

Bronchodilators such as clenbuterol, salbuterol and ipratropium all assist breathing but are illegal if found in tests on race days in America, as they are in other countries. In February, Paco Boy was disqualified from third in the 2008 Prix du Moulin after salbuterol was found in his sample and in 2006 Deep Impact was disqualified from third in the Prix de l'Arc de Triomphe after being treated with a nasal spray containing ipratropium. Clenbuterol was designed to free the respiratory system so horses could breathe more easily when exercising. However, in the longer term, it has the same effect as steroids (which are banned from both training and racing), building muscle and bringing a sheen to the coat. Horses are apparently more active on the drug, which can reportedly make them difficult. One apparent consequence of this has been an increase in positive tests in the States for the tranquiliser acepromazine, which makes particularly lively horses easier to handle. As a point of interest, the pop star Britney Spears is said to have become addicted to clenbuterol, reportedly initially believing it would help her lose weight and tone her body. Acknowledged possible side effects in humans using the drug include shaking, insomnia, sweating, increased blood pressure and nausea. Whatever the implications for the racehorses themselves and for those who bet on them, and whatever the samples taken after races may or may not reveal, the whole issue of drugs and their use in training gives cause for concern about the way the sport is perceived in an age when so many other global sports are being forced to address their own problems with performance-enhancing drugs.

Jealous Again (USA) (b.f. Feb 1, 2007)	Trippi (USA) (b 1997)	End Sweep (b 1991)	Forty Niner
			Broom Dance
		Jealous Appeal (b or br 1983)	Valid Appeal
			Jealous Cat
	Chi Sa (CAN) (b 1992)	Bold Ruckus (b or br 1976)	Boldnesian
			Raise A Ruckus
		Sinister Spinster (b or br 1981)	Sinister Purpose
			Spin To Win

R. Abrams, R. Brewer, M. Dutko and W. Ward's "Jealous Again"

The good-topped Jealous Again fetched 30,000 dollars at the Ocala sale in Florida in August 2008. Predictably, she doesn't have a patrician pedigree. Her sire Trippi stood in Florida until his sale to South Africa in 2008. He won at nine furlongs but was better over shorter, his principal successes coming in the seven-furlong Vosburgh Stakes and Tom Fool Handicap. Trippi tends to be an influence for speed but he has yet to have a Grade 1 winner. Jealous Again's dam Chi Sa won twice at around a mile in Canada and has produced four other winners, including another couple by Trippi in America and Japan. Jealous Again's grandam Sinister Spinster won ten races in Canada including the Ontario Matron Handicap over eight and a half furlongs and finished second in the Canadian Oaks. The daughter of a minor stakes winner, she foaled four other winners besides Chi Sa. On balance, Jealous Again's pedigree possesses enough stamina to suggest that she might prove effective at seven furlongs or even a mile, and she was quoted at 20/1 for the One Thousand Guineas part of the way through the summer. Any ideas of her staying a mile, though, can safely be scotched. What she displayed at two, and will always be her main asset provided she trains on, was blinding speed. The advantages she had at Royal Ascot will be less significant against mature rivals who have established themselves as specialist sprinters, but there seems little point in aiming Jealous Again at anything other than sprinting, preferably over five furlongs. Penalties for her Queen Mary Stakes win may well make things a little more difficult in Group 2 and 3 races. At the time of writing, however, it seems likely that Jealous Again will be sent back to America for her three-year-old career, rather than being seen in races such as the Temple Stakes and King's Stand, which would have given her the chance to repeat her electrifying Queen Mary performance. *Wesley A. Ward, USA*

JEANIE JOHNSTON (IRE) 2 b.f. (Mar 29) One Cool Cat (USA) 123 – Bahamamia 92 (Vettori (IRE) 119) [2009 6v^2 6m* 6g^2 6m^5 6m 6g Oct 30] €13,500Y: lengthy, good-bodied filly: second foal: sister to 3-y-o Marine Boy: dam, French 2-y-o 7.5f winner, half-sister to smart German miler Accento: fairly useful performer: won maiden at Haydock (by 3 lengths from Faith Jicaro) in June: ran creditably after when neck second to Jira in listed race at Newmarket and 4½ lengths fifth to Lady of The Desert in Princess Margaret Stakes at Ascot (final outing for K. R. Burke): will prove as effective at 5f as 6f: acts on good to firm ground: not straightforward. *A. P. Jarvis* **91**

JEAN JEANNIE 2 b.f. (Apr 4) Giant's Causeway (USA) 132 – Moon Dazzle (USA) 114 (Kingmambo (USA) 125) [2009 6m 7g Aug 1] 70,000Y: first foal: dam, 1m/9f winner, half-sister to smart milers Dupont and Pacino: better effort in maidens when seventh to Seta at Newmarket latter outing, too free in front: bred to stay 1m: sent to South Africa. *W. J. Haggas* **58**

JEANNIE GALLOWAY (IRE) 2 b.f. (Jan 18) Bahamian Bounty 116 – Housekeeper (IRE) 97 (Common Grounds 118) [2009 6m^6 7g^2 7m^3 6g* 6g* Oct 9] £3,500Y: lengthy, angular filly: has a round action: fourth foal: half-sister to Belgian 1m/10.5f winner Postsprofit (by Marju): dam, 5f to 1m (including in US) winner, half-sister to smart 1m/1¼m performer Polar Prince: fairly useful performer: left A. Foster, improved to win maiden at Ayr in September and nursery at York (dead-heated with Bossy Kitty) in October: should be at least as effective at 7f as 6f. *R. A. Fahey* **82**

JEANNIE (IRE) 3 b.f. Acclamation 118 – Sara Luna (IRE) (Mark of Esteem (IRE) 137) [2009 7m p6g p5.1g Oct 17] €3,000F, €6,000Y, £15,000 2-y-o: second foal: dam, French 6.5f winner, out of half-sister to smart/very smart fillies up to 1½m Cerulean Sky, L'Ancresse and Moonstone: well held in maidens/claimer. *A. Bailey* **–**

JEBEL ALI (IRE) 6 b.g. Fruits of Love (USA) 127 – Assertive Lass (USA) (Assert 134) [2009 67, a82: p10g^5 May 12] tall gelding: fair performer: stays 1½m: acts on polytrack, good to firm and good to soft ground: sometimes wears headgear. *B. Gubby* **70**

JEBEL TARA 4 b. or ch.g. Diktat 126 – Chantilly (FR) (Sanglamore (USA) 126) [2009 85d: f7g^4 f8g^5 8.3m^4 8f* 8g^3 8.5m^4 7.9m 7d 8m^5 10m Jul 29] lengthy, good-topped gelding: fair handicapper: won at Thirsk in April: stays 8.3f: acts on fibresand, soft and firm going: blinkered/tongue tied. *A. D. Brown* **74**

JECZMIEN (POL) 6 b.g. Fourth of June (USA) 82 – Jetka (POL) (Five Star Camp (USA)) [2009 p16g Jan 21] ex-Polish gelding: won 1m minor event at Ebreichsdorf (Austria) in 2007 when trained by K. Ziemianski: well held only outing on Flat in Britain: modest form over hurdles. *N. J. Gifford* **–**

Garbutt & Elliott Stakes (Nursery), York—Jeannie Galloway (far side) dead heats with Bossy Kitty (No.10) to provide jockey Dale Gibson with a final winner before his retirement twenty-four hours later

JEDI 3 ch.g. Pivotal 124 – Threefold (USA) 99 (Gulch (USA)) [2009 82p: 10m^5 12.3m^3 11d Aug 1] strong, compact gelding: fairly useful handicapper: good efforts first 2 starts: off 3 months, below form final start (held up/not knocked about), gelded after: stays 1½m: acts on soft and good to firm ground: remains capable of better. *Sir Michael Stoute* **89 p**

JEER (IRE) 5 ch.g. Selkirk (USA) 129 – Purring (USA) 79 (Mountain Cat (USA)) [2009 100: 10.3g 10.2d 10.3m^5 10m^4 10d^6 9.8d^3 10m^3 p10m^3 p9.5g^6 p12m^3 Dec 16] rather leggy, useful-looking gelding: has a quick, unimpressive action: just fair handicapper nowadays: seems to stay easy 1½m: acts on polytrack, heavy and good to firm going: tried blinkered: tongue tied 4 of last 5 starts. *M. W. Easterby* **76**

JEHU 2 b.c. (Mar 28) Antonius Pius (USA) 123§ – Chalosse (Doyoun 124) [2009 6g^5 6g^2 7m* 7m 7d* 7d^5 7.1g^4 8m^5 8m^3 7m^3 p7m^2 7g^6 7g^4 Oct 16] 24,000Y: unfurnished colt: sixth foal: half-brother to French 2004 2-y-o 5.5f to 1m winner Faussaire (by Fasliyev) and 1¼m and (in Spain) 1½m winner Challis (by Barathea), both fairly useful: dam, French maiden who stayed 1½m, closely related to high-class French performer up to 10.5f Creator: fairly useful performer: won maiden at Thirsk in June and nursery at Catterick in July: below form after eighth start, looking wayward: stays 1m: acts on polytrack, good to firm and good to soft going: tried visored: one to treat with caution: sold 19,000 gns, sent to Serbia. *M. R. Channon* **81 §**

JELLY BEAN 2 ch.f. (Mar 1) Observatory (USA) 131 – Grandma Lily (IRE) 88 (Bigstone (IRE) 126) [2009 6m 7g Jul 16] good-topped filly: second foal: dam, 5f to 7f winner, half-sister to useful performer up to 13f Masafi: better effort in maidens when 10½ lengths seventh to Clarietta at Doncaster (raced freely) latter start. *K. A. Ryan* **48**

JELLY MO 4 b.f. Royal Applause 124 – Flawless 107 (Warning 136) [2009 61: 10.2m^5 12.6g^5 10.1g^6 10.1m Aug 13] leggy filly: modest performer: stays 1¼m: acts on polytrack, good to firm and good to soft going: tried in cheekpieces. *W. M. Brisbourne* **55**

JELLYTOT (USA) 6 b.m. Minardi (USA) 119 – Dounine (Kaldoun (FR) 122) [2009 51: 6d 7.5g Aug 12] neat mare: one-time fair performer: on downgrade: tried blinkered. *I. W. McInnes* **–**

JEMIMAVILLE (IRE) 2 b.f. (Jan 29) Fasliyev (USA) 120 – Sparkling Isle 66 (Inchinor 119) [2009 6f 7g Oct 31] lengthy filly: fifth foal: sister to smart Spanish/French 6f (at 2 yrs) to 1m winner Trip To The Moon: dam maiden best at 6f/7f at 2 yrs: well held in maidens. *G. C. Bravery* **–**

JENINSKY (USA) 4 ch.f. Stravinsky (USA) 133 – Don't Ruffle Me (USA) (Pine Bluff (USA)) [2009 94: 7.1m^6 7g* 7g* 8d Oct 18] big, workmanlike filly: useful performer: won handicaps at Doncaster in July and Newmarket (further improvement, beat Signor Peltro ½ length) in August: best at 6f/7f: acts on polytrack, soft and good to firm ground. *Rae Guest* **99**

JENNEROUS BLUE 2 br.f. (Feb 12) Generous (IRE) 139 – Jennelle 97 (Nomination 125) [2009 p7g p8f p8g^6 p8.6g^4 Nov 30] fourth foal: half-sister to 3 winners, including 4-y-o Ellemujie: dam 5f winner, including at 2 yrs: modest maiden: stays 8.6f: raced only on polytrack. *D. K. Ivory* **52**

JENNIE JEROME (IRE) 4 br.f. Pivotal 124 – Colourfast (IRE) 88 (Spectrum (IRE) 126) [2009 87: 8m 11m 10.2v^2 p10m^4 Nov 21] angular filly: fairly useful performer: well held in listed races in Italy first 2 starts in 2009 for V. Valiani: ran respectably on return to Britain: stays 1¼m: acts on polytrack and heavy ground. *C. F. Wall* **83**

JENNY POTTS 5 b.m. Robellino (USA) 127 – Fleeting Vision (IRE) 79 (Vision (USA)) [2009 8m^5 8.5m^4 12d^6 9.2g* Jun 17] 10,000Y: compact mare: sixth foal: half-sister to 13f winner Bay Hawk (by Alhaarth) and 2m winner Killing Joke (by Double Trigger): dam, Irish 1½m to 2¼m winner, out of half-sister to St Leger winner Snurge: modest form in bumpers/winning hurdler: fair form on Flat: won at Hamilton on handicap debut, going right away final 1f: bred to be suited by 1¼m+: remains capable of better. *L. Lungo* **77 p**

JENNY SOBA 6 b.m. Observatory (USA) 131 – Majalis 79 (Mujadil (USA) 119) [2009 70: 12.6d^4 10.2m 12d^6 12g^2 12.4d^5 12s^5 10.3s p13.9g p12m p13.9g^5 Dec 14] small mare: modest handicapper: effective at 1¼m to 1¾m: acts on all-weather and any turf going: tried visored/in cheekpieces: held up: none too consistent. *Lucinda Featherstone* **64**

JENNY'S PRIDE (IRE) 3 ch.f. Fath (USA) 116 – Softly (IRE) 70 (Grand Lodge (USA) 125) [2009 p8.6g^5 8.3m^5 7s* 8.3v^6 7m 10m f7g^4 Dec 18] €2,000Y: close-coupled filly: third foal: dam, 1¼m winner, granddaughter of Oaks winner Diminuendo: modest performer: won seller at Leicester in July: likely to prove best up to 7f: acts on fibresand and soft ground. *John A. Harris* **60**

JEREMIAH (IRE) 3 ch.g. Captain Rio 122 – Miss Garuda 94 (Persian Bold 123) [2009 73: f7g^4 6g^2 f6g 6m 6f 7g p6g^6 7d* 7g^4 p8m^6 7m p7m Nov 21] medium-sized gelding: fair performer on turf, modest on all-weather: won maiden handicap at Brighton in August: stays 7f: acts on polytrack, firm and good to soft going: tried in cheekpieces/ visor. *J. G. Portman* **74** **a63**

JERONIMO JOE 3 ch.g. Primo Valentino (IRE) 116 – Yanomami (USA) 71 (Slew O' Gold (USA)) [2009 –: 10m 10.9g* p12.2g 10.1d^5 10m^2 10m^6 Oct 6] smallish, strong gelding: modest performer: won seller at Warwick in July: stays 11f: acts on good to firm going: sold £4,200. *A. B. Haynes* **63**

JERUSALEM (IRE) 3 ch.g. Indian Haven 119 – Wilrock (IRE) (Docksider (USA) 124) [2009 f6g^3 p8g 5.8g^4 a10g* 8g Jul 16] third in maiden at Southwell on debut: sold from A. Bailey 2,200 gns after next start (day later): won minor event at Taby in July: stays 1¼m: acts on dirt: blinkered. *Madeleine Smith, Sweden* **55**

JESSE JAMES (IRE) 3 b.g. King's Best (USA) 132 – Julie Jalouse (USA) 103 (Kris S (USA)) [2009 86p: p8g^2 8m^2 8.3f* 8m^4 Sep 13] good-bodied gelding: fairly useful performer: won maiden at Windsor in August: creditable fourth on handicap debut next time: will stay 1¼m: acts on polytrack and firm going, unraced on softer than good: refused at stall intended debut: sold 62,000 gns, then gelded. *J. H. M. Gosden* **94**

JESSICA HAYLLAR (USA) 2 b.f. (Feb 26) Arch (USA) 127 – Pearl Pride (USA) 71 (Theatrical 128) [2009 6d 6g^4 5m^5 6d^2 6m 6g^3 Oct 19] 33,000 2-y-o: first foal: dam, maiden, sister to smart performer up to 1¼m Playapart: fair maiden: runner-up in seller at Yarmouth (left M. Bell £5,000) and third in nursery at Windsor: bred to be suited by 7f+ (has raced freely): acts on good to soft going: sold 6,000 gns. *G. L. Moore* **66**

JESSICA WIGMO 6 b.m. Bahamian Bounty 116 – Queen of Shannon (IRE) 76 (Nordico (USA)) [2009 54, a66: p8g p7g p6g* p8g^4 p7g^5 p6g^3 p7g^5 p7.1g p8g 7.6d Aug 1] good-bodied mare: modest handicapper nowadays: won at Kempton in February: stays easy 1m: acts on polytrack and good to firm going: held up. *A. W. Carroll* **–** **a62**

JET D'EAU (FR) 3 b.f. Numerous (USA) – La Fontainiere (IRE) (Kaldoun (FR) 122) **101** [2009 93: 6m^5 7g^5 7m 8m 7v p7g Nov 21] well-made filly: useful performer: trained in France at 2 yrs, winning twice: good fifth first 2 starts in 2009, in handicap at Newmarket (3 lengths behind Bounty Box) and Supreme Stakes at Goodwood (beaten 5 lengths by Ordnance Row): below form in handicaps after: stays 1m: acts on firm and good to soft going: blinkered: temperament under suspicion. *G. L. Moore*

JETHRO BODINE (IRE) 3 b.g. Fath (USA) 116 – John's Ballad (IRE) (Ballad Rock **61** 122) [2009 49: 5m^5 5m* 5m^4 Apr 22] big, workmanlike gelding: modest handicapper: won at Redcar in April: effective at 5f/6f: acts on good to firm ground: in cheekpieces in 2009. *W. J. H. Ratcliffe*

JEU D'ESPRIT (IRE) 6 b.m. Montjeu (IRE) 137 – Cielo Vodkamartini (USA) (Con- **–** quistador Cielo (USA)) [2009 p16g Jul 8] fair handicapper in 2007: unraced on Flat in 2008 (fair form over hurdles): saddle slipped and pulled up only outing in 2009 (said to be lame): stays 1½m: acts on all-weather and heavy going. *Mrs L. J. Mongan*

JEUNOPSE (IRE) 3 b.f. Hawk Wing (USA) 136 – Innocence 73 (Unfuwain (USA) **66** 131) [2009 51p: 7.5g^5 8.3m^2 11.1g^5 12g^2 11g* 10.5s^6 12g Nov 28] leggy filly: fair performer: left B. Smart after third start: won maiden at Mont-de-Marsan in October: stays 1½m: acts on good to firm ground: blinkered final start. *X. T. Demeaulte, France*

JEWELLED 3 b.f. Fantastic Light (USA) 134 – Danemere (IRE) 90 (Danehill (USA) **78** 126) [2009 9.9g^5 9.7m^5 9.9g^5 10v^4 9.7m^5 8d^2 8m^5 8m^2 8.3g^3 p7.1g Nov 12] third foal: half-sister to 4-y-o Cossack Prince: dam 2-y-o 6f winner: fair maiden: best form around 1m: acts on good to firm and good to soft ground. *J. W. Hills*

JEWELLED DAGGER (IRE) 5 b.g. Daggers Drawn (USA) 114 – Cappadoce (IRE) **89** (General Monash (USA) 107) [2009 99, a–: p7g^5 7.1m^2 8d^5 7.2m^4 7.2g^6 6.9g 8g Aug 31] angular gelding: fairly useful handicapper: well below form after second start: effective at 7f to 9.8f: acts on polytrack, firm and good to soft going: tried visored: blinkered: makes running: modest form over hurdles: joined Lucinda Russell. *I. Semple*

JEWELLED REEF (IRE) 3 b.f. Marju (IRE) 127 – Aqaba 65 (Lake Coniston (IRE) **64** 131) [2009 62: 8.3m 9.9g 8f^2 8m^5 7m 8.1m^3 8m 6.1g^5 7.1d 7.1m^4 8m^3 8m^3 8d 10g Oct 19] quite attractive filly: modest maiden handicapper: stays 1m: acts on good to firm ground: sold 5,500 gns. *Eve Johnson Houghton*

JEZZA 3 b.g. Pentire 132 – Lara (GER) 103 (Sharpo 132) [2009 p10m p8.6m^6 p8g p12g **54** p13.9g^5 p12m^3 Dec 9] workmanlike gelding: modest maiden: stays 1¾m: raced only on polytrack. *Karen George*

JHINGA PALAK (IRE) 3 b.f. Fath (USA) 116 – Livius Lady (IRE) (Titus Livius **–** (FR) 115) [2009 75?: p6g 8.1g 7.1m Jul 1] workmanlike filly: seemingly fair form when fifth in valuable sales race at the Curragh at 2 yrs: well held otherwise, leaving P. D. Evans after reappearance: should stay 7f: tried tongue tied. *Mrs K. Waldron*

JIBRRYA 2 b.c. (Jan 25) Motivator 131 – Takarna (IRE) 70 (Mark of Esteem (IRE) 137) **82 p** [2009 8.1g^5 8d* Aug 28] 140,000Y: attractive colt: fourth foal: dam, ran 3 times in Ireland (second at 1m at 2 yrs), half-sister to smart performers up to 1½m Takarian and Takali: much better effort in maidens when winning at Thirsk by neck from Manhattan Fox: will be suited by 1¼m: open to further progress. *M. R. Channon*

JIGAJIG 2 ch.g. (May 10) Compton Place 125 – Eau Rouge 77 (Grand Lodge (USA) **–** 125) [2009 5m 6m^6 5d 5m 5g Oct 6] close-coupled gelding: no form: tried visored: signs of temperament. *N. Wilson*

JIGGALONG 3 ch.f. Mark of Esteem (IRE) 137 – Kalamansi (IRE) (Sadler's Wells **66** (USA) 132) [2009 –: 6g^2 5.5g 6.1m^6 8d^3 8m^2 p8g^3 p11g p12m p8m p8g p12f* f12g^4 Dec 22] fair handicapper: claimed from Jane Chapple-Hyam £7,000 sixth start, left R. Ingram after eighth: won at Kempton in December: stays 1½m: acts on polytrack, good to firm and good to soft ground: held up. *Jim Best*

JILL LE BROCQ 3 b.f. Reset (AUS) 124 – Our Krissie 65 (Kris 135) [2009 6m^4 6d **64** 6d^5 7.9g^2 Aug 3] modest maiden: best effort when blinkered at 7.9f: dead. *M. Dods*

JILLOLINI 3 br. or gr.f. Bertolini (USA) 125 – Someone's Angel (USA) (Runaway **40** Groom (CAN)) [2009 –: 6f^5 6d 5m^5 Jun 19] leggy filly: poor maiden: raced only at 5f/6f. *T. D. Easterby*

JILLY WHY (IRE) 8 b.m. Mujadil (USA) 119 – Ruwy 77 (Soviet Star (USA) 128) **76** [2009 84d, a65: p6g 5m 5m^4 7.6g^3 5g^6 5g^4 6d^2 5.1v* 6m^6 5d^4 5d 7m 5.1d^5 5.1g^4 p6g **a–** Nov 13] workmanlike mare: fair handicapper nowadays: won at Nottingham in July: effective at 5f, barely at 7f: acts on all-weather, best turf efforts on good going or softer (though has won on good to firm): tried visored, usually blinkered. *Paul Green*

William Hill (Ayr) Gold Cup (Heritage Handicap), Ayr—Frankie Dettori claims his first Ayr Gold Cup win as Jimmy Styles (cheekpieces) edges out Barney McGrew (No.5), 2008 fourth Knot In Wood and Evens And Odds; Tombi is first home on the stand side

JIMINOR MACK 6 bl.m. Little Jim – Copper Trader 53 (Faustus (USA) 118) [2009 54: p10g^6 p10g^6 p9.5g^5 p12g^6 f11g^3 p12g 10.1g 10.1g^3 10.2d^3 Aug 11] close-coupled mare: modest maiden: stays 1¼m: acts on all-weather and soft going: usually wears headgear: sometimes slowly away: none too consistent. *W. J. H. Ratcliffe* **52**

JIM MARTIN 4 b.g. Auction House (USA) 120 – Folly Finnesse 80 (Joligeneration 111) [2009 73: 9.2m 9.2v^4 10g 9.1v Oct 31] modest performer nowadays: stays 1¼m: acts on heavy going. *Miss L. A. Perratt* **60**

JIMMY DEAN 4 b.g. Ishiguru (USA) 114 – Sister Sal 74 (Bairn (USA) 126) [2009 58: p7.1g Jan 12] lengthy gelding: maiden: modest at 3 yrs: well held sole start in 2009: best efforts at 7f: acts on polytrack and firm ground: wears headgear/tongue tie. *M. Wellings* **–**

JIMMY RYAN (IRE) 8 b.g. Orpen (USA) 116 – Kaysama (FR) (Kenmare (FR) 125) [2009 5g 5m 6g^3 5.1g Oct 28] lengthy, quite good-topped gelding: smart performer in 2005: off over 4 years, fair form in 2009: best at 5f: raced only on good/good to firm going: has been early to post. *T. D. McCarthy* **69**

JIMMY STYLES 5 ch.g. Inchinor 119 – Inya Lake 101 (Whittingham (IRE) 104) [2009 103: 6m^2 6m* 6m 6m^5 6d 6m^4 6m^3 6.5m^3 6m* 6g^5 Oct 10] strong gelding: smart performer: improved in 2009, winning handicaps at Newmarket (by 1¾ lengths from Everymanforhimself) in May and Ayr (beat Barney McGrew by head in 26-runner William Hill (Ayr) Gold Cup) in September: respectable 3½ lengths equal-fifth to Royal Rock in Bengough Memorial Stakes at Ascot final start: stays 6.5f: acts on firm going: tried in cheekpieces (including last 2 starts). *C. G. Cox* **112**

JIMMY THE POACHER (IRE) 2 gr.g. (Mar 13) Verglas (IRE) 118 – Danish Gem (Danehill (USA) 126) [2009 7m^6 7g^4 7m^3 7d p7.1g Oct 16] fair maiden: best effort when close third to Ransom Note at Chester: will probably stay 1m: acts on good to firm ground: gelded after final start. *T. D. Easterby* **66**

JIMWIL (IRE) 3 b.g. One Cool Cat (USA) 123 – Vulnerable (Hector Protector (USA) 124) [2009 69: 6m^3 6d 6.1m 7g* 5.9m^5 7.1m^4 8m 7d p7.1g 6m 7m^6 7g^2 Oct 16] unfurnished gelding: fairly useful handicapper: improved when winning at Redcar in June: stays 7f: acts on firm and good to soft ground: usually blinkered, wore cheekpieces final start: often slowly away/none too keen: one to treat with caution. *M. Dods* **80 §**

JINKSY MINX 2 b.f. (Apr 4) Piccolo 121 – Medway (IRE) 60 (Shernazar 131) [2009 7f p8m Dec 4] 7,000F: half-sister to several winners, including 6-y-o Missoula and fairly useful 1½m winner Settlement Craic (by Ela-Mana-Mou): dam, 1½m winner, half-sister to very smart Hong Kong performer up to 1½m Indigenous: well held in maidens at Lingfield over 5 months apart, green. *Miss Suzy Smith* **–**

JINTO 2 ch.g. (Feb 12) Halling (USA) 133 – Sweet Willa (USA) (Assert 134) [2009 p8g p8g f8m^4 Nov 6] modest form at best in maidens: bred to stay well (brother to 3-y-o Holberg). *R. M. H. Cowell* **59**

JIRA 2 b.f. (Apr 13) Medicean 128 – Time Saved 89 (Green Desert (USA) 127) [2009 5m^4 6m* 6f 6g* 6m^4 7g 6s^4 6m^3 7m^5 Oct 3] 110,000Y: tall, lengthy filly: has scope: fifth foal: closely related to smart 7f (at 2 yrs) to 1½m winner Plea Bargain (by Machiavellian) and half-sister to useful 2007 2-y-o 7f winner Dubai Time (by Dubai Destination) and 3-y-o Emirates Sports: dam, 1¼m winner, out of top-class 1¼m/1½m performer Time Charter: useful performer: won maiden at Leicester and listed event at Newmarket (by neck from Jeanie Johnston) in June: ran well after when in frame in Princess Margaret Stakes at Ascot, listed event at Salisbury and sales race at Newmarket (third to Society Rock): should stay 7f: acts on soft and good to firm ground. *C. E. Brittain* **95**

J J THE JET PLANE (SAF) 5 b.g. Jet Master (SAF) – Majestic Guest (SAF) (Northern Guest (USA)) [2009 a5.5f^6 6m* 6m* 6m^4 6m^3 7g 6d 6m^4 5.2m^3 6m Sep 27] big, rangy gelding: very smart performer: dropped in trip, much improved when winning last 5 starts in South Africa in 2008 for L. Houdalakis, including Grade 1s at Turffontein, Scotsville and Clairwood: won Al Quoz Sprint at Nad Al Sheba (beat Hatta Fort 1¼ lengths) in February and listed race at Windsor (by 4 lengths from Intrepid Jack) in June: in frame in Golden Jubilee Stakes at Royal Ascot (below-par fourth to Art Connoisseur) and July Cup at Newmarket (1¾ lengths third to Fleeting Spirit) next 2 starts: mainly below form subsequently, leaving M. de Kock after sixth outing, though not discredited when ¾-length third to Strike The Deal in World Trophy at Newbury penultimate start: winner at 7f, but probably best at 5f/6f: acts on soft and good to firm going: blinkered final outing: tends to get on toes: usually races prominently. *R. Hannon* **121**

JOANNADARC (USA) 3 ch.f. Johannesburg (USA) 127 – Game Player (USA) (Drumalis 125) [2009 73: p7g^4 p7g^3 p7g^6 p10g^6 Apr 8] just modest maiden at 3 yrs: may prove best around 1m: acts on polytrack (unraced on turf). *S. A. Callaghan* **55**

JOAN'S LEGACY 2 b.f. (Mar 10) Piccolo 121 – Cc Canova (Millkom 124) [2009 6s 6m 5g^5 p7m Oct 26] close-coupled filly: fourth foal: half-sister to winner abroad by Best of The Bests: dam unraced half-sister to useful 6f/7f performer Marbella Silks: best effort in maidens when fifth to Bridge Valley at Sandown. *J. C. Fox* **52**

JOBEKANI (IRE) 3 b.g. Tagula (IRE) 116 – Lyca Ballerina 76 (Marju (IRE) 127) [2009 67: 8.3m 8.1g^3 8f 10.3g^6 10.3g 9g^5 p9.5g^3 p9.5g p9.5g Dec 19] lengthy gelding: fair maiden: probably stays 10.3f: acts on polytrack, good to firm and good to soft going: tried in cheekpieces: often held up. *Mrs L. Williamson* **65**

JOBE (USA) 3 b.g. Johannesburg (USA) 127 – Bello Cielo (USA) (Conquistador Cielo (USA)) [2009 99: p8g 6m^3 6s* 6g^6 7m 7d 6m Aug 15] good sort: useful performer: won minor event at Hamilton in May by 1¼ lengths from Able Master: creditable third to Total Gallery in listed race at Ascot on previous start: below form last 4 outings: best at 6f: acts on soft and good to firm going: tried tongue tied/in cheekpieces. *K. A. Ryan* **96**

JO'BURG (USA) 5 b.g. Johannesburg (USA) 127 – La Martina 100 (Atraf 116) [2009 86d: p8g 10.2m^4 10m* 9.9m^2 9.7m^2 10g* 10m^2 9.9m^5 10.1m^5 Oct 3] small, strong, good-bodied gelding: fairly useful handicapper: won at Newmarket (amateurs) in May and Newbury in July: stays 1¼m: acts on polytrack, firm and soft going: tried blinkered: not straightforward and suited by waiting tactics. *Lady Herries* **86**

JOCHESKI (IRE) 5 b.g. Mull of Kintyre (USA) 114 – Ludovica (Bustino 136) [2009 69: f12g Jan 13] fair handicapper: lightly raced on Flat in recent years: well held sole outing in 2009, though won over hurdles in September (fair form): stays 1¾m: acts on polytrack, firm and soft ground: tried visored. *A. G. Newcombe* **–**

JODAWES (USA) 2 b. or br.c. (Feb 19) Burning Roma (USA) 113 – Venetian Peach (USA) (Desert Wine (USA)) [2009 p7g^4 Dec 31] $12,500F: half-brother to 3 winners in USA: dam US 6f (including at 2 yrs)/6.5f winner: 8/1, encouraging fourth to Cuthbert in maiden at Lingfield: should improve. *J. R. Best* **56 p**

JOE CASTER 3 b.c. Makbul 104 – Oedipus Regina (Fraam 114) [2009 96: p7g p6g p6g 5g^6 p7.1g Jun 29] close-coupled colt: fairly useful performer: effective at 5f/6f: acts on polytrack and heavy going: takes strong hold. *J. M. P. Eustace* **84**

JOE JO STAR 7 b.g. Piccolo 121 – Zagreb Flyer (Old Vic 136) [2009 64: p8.6g* p10g² 9.1m* 9.9m² 12d* 11.5m 12m Aug 16] neat gelding: fairly useful handicapper: left B. Baugh, much improved in 2009 (also useful hurdler), won at Wolverhampton in January, and Ayr and York (by 7 lengths) in June, last 2 both apprentice events: stays 1½m: acts on polytrack, firm and good to soft ground: won in cheekpieces earlier in career: travels strongly. *R. A. Fahey* **85**

JOEL THE MOLE 2 ch.g. (Feb 22) Reel Buddy (USA) 118 – Fly South (Polar Falcon (USA) 126) [2009 6g⁶ 6m 6g Aug 31] workmanlike gelding: no form in claimer/sellers, looking awkward. *D. Nicholls* **–**

JOE PACKET 2 ch.c. (Feb 21) Joe Bear (IRE) 109 – Costa Packet (IRE) (Hussonet (USA)) [2009 6m⁵ 6m² 7.6d⁴ 7m² 6m⁵ Sep 19] quite good-topped colt: first foal: dam ran once: fair maiden: creditable fifth in nursery at Newbury: stays 7f. *J. G. Portman* **78**

JOE RUA (USA) 2 b. or br.c. (Feb 16) Johannesburg (USA) 127 – Red Tulle (USA) 66 (A P Indy (USA) 131) [2009 6m 6d⁶ 8.3g p7g p8m Dec 9] lengthy, angular colt: little form in maidens/nurseries: tried visored. *J. Ryan* **–**

JOHANNESGRAY (IRE) 2 gr.g. (Apr 18) Verglas (IRE) 118 – Prepare For War (IRE) (Marju (IRE) 127) [2009 6m² Sep 19] €26,000F, £10,000Y: third foal: dam, ran once, out of close relation of smart 2-y-o sprinter Mujadil/half-sister to high-class 1½m performer Fruits of Love: 8/1, 5 lengths second to Colepeper in maiden at Catterick, travelling strongly long way and not unduly knocked about once held: subsequently gelded: capable of better. *D. Nicholls* **79 p**

JOHANNES (IRE) 6 b.g. Mozart (IRE) 131 – Blue Sirocco (Bluebird (USA) 125) [2009 89: 6g* 6g² 6m* 7m 6g* 6m* 5.6m 6m 6g 6g³ Oct 23] good-topped gelding: useful handicapper: back to best in 2009, winning at Catterick in May, Redcar in June, Goodwood in July and Ripon (beat Red Cape 2¼ lengths) in August: creditable third to Servoca at Doncaster final start: has form at 7f, best at 6f: acts on good to firm and good to soft going: tongue tied (ran as if amiss) once. *R. A. Fahey* **103**

JOHANN ZOFFANY 3 b.c. Galileo (IRE) 134 – Belle Allemande (CAN) (Royal Academy (USA) 130) [2009 83p: 10s⁶ 10g* 10g* 12m 10d* 10d⁴ Sep 5] attractive colt: smart performer: won maiden at Naas and handicap at Leopardstown in May, and handicap at the Curragh (beat Ebashan 2½ lengths under 9-10) in June: not run of race in King George V Stakes (Handicap) at Royal Ascot fourth start: not discredited when 9½ lengths fourth to Poet in Kilternan Stakes at Leopardstown final start: should stay 1½m: acts on good to soft going: often makes running. *A. P. O'Brien, Ireland* **111**

Kilmacud Handicap, Leopardstown—trainer's son Joseph O'Brien rides his first winner as Johann Zoffany (right) justifies favouritism from Chebona Bula

JOHN CHARLES (IRE) 7 b.g. Fraam 114 – Norwegian Queen (IRE) (Affirmed (USA)) [2009 11s Jul 17] fair performer in 2006: tailed off only Flat start since (modest hurdler): sold £10,000, joined Jim Best. *B. De Haan* –

JOHN DILLON (IRE) 5 ch.g. Traditionally (USA) 117 – Matikanehanafubuki (IRE) (Caerleon (USA) 132) [2009 –: p13.3g^{5} f12g 12.1m Jul 28] big, strong gelding: just modest handicapper in 2009: stays 1½m: acts on soft and good to firm ground: tried blinkered, usually visored. *P. C. Haslam* 61

JOHN FORBES 7 b.g. High Estate 127 – Mavourneen (USA) (Dynaformer (USA)) [2009 10.1d 16.2m 12g^{2} 14g^{5} 13v^{2} 13.1d* 15.8v^{3} p16.5g* p16.5g^{2} 15v^{4} Oct 31] strong gelding: fairly useful handicapper: unraced on Flat in 2007/8: won at Ayr in August and Wolverhampton in October: seems to stay 2¼m: acts on polytrack, heavy and good to firm ground: tried blinkered: fairly useful hurdler (won in November). *B. Ellison* 80

JOHN KEATS 6 b.g. Bertolini (USA) 125 – Nightingale (Night Shift (USA)) [2009 87: 6v 6m^{3} 6m^{5} 6f^{2} 6g 6d^{4} 6g^{4} 6d 6m^{3} 6m^{3} 7.1m^{3} 6m^{3} 6d 7.2g Oct 23] sturdy, lengthy gelding: fair handicapper nowadays: stays 7f: acts on firm and good to soft going: tried in blinkers/cheekpieces: has shown temperament (tends to get behind): sold £800, sent to Sweden. *J. S. Goldie* 77

JOHNMANDERVILLE 3 b.g. Kheleyf (USA) 116 – Lady's Walk (IRE) (Charnwood Forest (IRE) 125) [2009 79: 8m 8g* 7m 8g 8g^{2} 8m 8.5m^{6} 8.1m^{6} p9.5g^{2} Oct 15] big, strong gelding: has stringhalt: fairly useful performer: won handicap at Newcastle in April: stays 1m: acts on polytrack and good to firm going: in cheekpieces last 2 starts: usually front runner/races prominently: tends to hang right: none too consistent: sold 16,000 gns. *A. P. Jarvis* 86

JOHNNY FRIENDLY 4 b.g. Auction House (USA) 120 – Quantum Lady 79 (Mujadil (USA) 119) [2009 69: p8g^{5} p7.1g 7m 9.8m^{6} 7m 8m^{4} May 28] big, workmanlike gelding: modest performer nowadays: stays 1m: acts on polytrack, soft and good to firm going: tried visored: front runner/races prominently. *K. R. Burke* 60

JOHNNYLEARY (IRE) 2 ch.g. (Mar 20) Fayruz 116 – Forgren (IRE) (Thatching 131) [2009 5.1m 6v May 21] well-grown gelding: well held in maidens at Chester and Haydock. *D. Nicholls* –

JOHNNY ROCKET (IRE) 4 ch.g. Viking Ruler (AUS) – Karen Blixen (Kris 135) [2009 10.1s^{3} 12d 12.4s^{6} May 22] workmanlike gelding: well beaten in bumper: easily best effort in maidens when third at Newcastle on debut: stays 1¼m. *K. A. Ryan* 74

JOHN POTTS 4 b.g. Josr Algarhoud (IRE) 118 – Crown City (USA) 56 (Coronado's Quest (USA) 130) [2009 58: p9.5g^{3} p9.5g^{2} p9.5g^{5} p9.5g p9.5g 10.1g p9.5g^{6} p9.5g^{3} p9.5g Dec 28] big, good-topped gelding: modest maiden handicapper: stays 9.5f: acts on polytrack, no form on turf: often in cheekpieces. *B. P. J. Baugh* – a55

JOHNSTON'S BABY (IRE) 7 b.m. Bob Back (USA) 124 – Mirror of Flowers (Artaius (USA) 129) [2009 p8.6g^{4} p12.2g^{3} f8g^{6} f11g p8.6g^{2} 10.2m^{2} 9m^{3} 9.3m^{4} 10.2g^{4} 9.3m^{3} 10.3m^{6} 10g p9.5g Aug 17] well held in bumper/maiden hurdle for M. O'Brien in Ireland: fair maiden on Flat: should stay 1½m: raced only on all-weather and good/good to firm ground. *E. J. Alston* 66

JOHNSTON'S GLORY (IRE) 5 b.m. Desert Sun 120 – Clos de Tart (IRE) (Indian Ridge 123) [2009 75: 6f^{3} 6g^{4} 6m 5.9m 6m Jul 29] sturdy mare: modest performer: best at 5f/6f: acts on polytrack, firm and good to soft ground: tried blinkered, usually in cheekpieces nowadays: often finds little: refused to race last 2 outings and one to avoid. *E. J. Alston* 64 §

JOHNSTOWN LAD (IRE) 5 b.g. Invincible Spirit (IRE) 121 – Pretext (Polish Precedent (USA) 131) [2009 96: p6g^{6} 5d 5v 5.7m^{5} 5g^{4} 5d 5.7g* 6m^{3} 5d^{5} p6g p6g^{2} p6m^{5} p5.1g^{4} Dec 5] sturdy gelding: fairly useful handicapper: left Niall Moran, won at Bath in September: best at 5f/6f: acts on polytrack, firm and good to soft going: tongue tied: tried blinkered/in cheekpieces. *D. Loughnane, Ireland* 91

JOHN TERRY (IRE) 6 b.g. Grand Lodge (USA) 125 – Kardashina (FR) (Darshaan 133) [2009 97§, a101§: p10g^{5} p12g^{6} p10g p11g^{2} p11g^{6} 12m^{2} 12m May 30] big, good sort: useful handicapper: runner-up at Kempton and Newmarket: stays 1½m: acts on polytrack, good to firm and good to soft going: tried in cheekpieces: usually races close up: temperamental. *Mrs A. J. Perrett* 95 §

JOINEDUPWRITING 4 b.g. Desert Style (IRE) 121 – Ink Pot (USA) 73 (Green Dancer (USA) 132) [2009 72: 9.8m* 9.3m^{2} 9.8m* 10m 9.8g Aug 3] smallish, strong gelding: fair performer: won seller in May and handicap in June, both at Ripon: stays easy 1¼m: acts on firm and good to soft going. *R. M. Whitaker* 67

JOIN UP 3 b.g. Green Desert (USA) 127 – Rise 84 (Polar Falcon (USA) 126) [2009 56: **62**
p7.1g 7g 6m 7.1m^4 8d^6 10d^3 10.1m^4 9.9m p10g^5 p10g p9.5g p8.6g^3 p8g^2 p8m*
p9.5g^2 p9.5g^2 Dec 28] close-coupled gelding: modest handicapper: won at Lingfield in
December: effective at 1m/1¼m: acts on polytrack and good to firm ground, probably on
good to soft: tried in cheekpieces/visor. *W. M. Brisbourne*

JOJESSE 5 ch.g. Compton Place 125 – Jodeeka 97 (Fraam 114) [2009 57: f7d 6f 9m **–**
8m 7.9g p7m p8.6g p12.2g Dec 12] workmanlike gelding: little impact in 2009, leaving
G. A. Swinbank after reappearance: tried blinkered. *W. Storey*

JOKERS WILD 2 b.c. (Jan 20) Compton Place 125 – Lady Hibernia (Anabaa (USA) **–**
130) [2009 p7g p6m Nov 28] well beaten in maidens. *A. M. Balding*

JOLIES DEE 4 br.f. Diktat 126 – Jolies Eaux 73 (Shirley Heights 130) [2009 –: p12m **–**
Jan 9] last in maidens at Lingfield. *J. R. Jenkins*

JOLLY RANCH 3 gr.f. Compton Place 125 – How Do I Know 91 (Petong 126) [2009 **63**
54+: p5.1g* p5.1g^4 5m^6 p5.1g 5.1g p5.1g^3 p5.1g^2 p5g^3 p5m^2 Dec 6] narrow filly: modest
performer: won maiden at Wolverhampton in January: speedy, may prove best at 5f: acts
on polytrack: races prominently. *A. G. Newcombe*

JONNIE SKULL (IRE) 3 b.g. Pyrus (USA) 106 – Sovereign Touch (IRE) (Pennine **75**
Walk 120) [2009 62: p8g^3 p8.6g^5 f8g^2 f7g^2 p12.2g^2 f8g^3 p12.2g^3 f11g^4 7g 8d^4 8s f8g^3 8m^6
8f^5 p7g* p7f^3 7m^2 p7.1g 7m p7m p12m f7g* f8f^4 f8g^2 Dec 18] compact gelding: fair
performer: left D. Elsworth £3,800 after second start: won minor event at Kempton in
August and handicap at Southwell in December: best efforts at 7f/1m: acts on all-weather
and good to firm going: tried blinkered, usually visored/tongue tied: races prominently.
P. S. McEntee

JONNY EBENEEZER 10 b.g. Hurricane Sky (AUS) – Leap of Faith (IRE) 65 **59**
(Northiam (USA)) [2009 67: 6m^4 5m^5 May 29] tall gelding: modest performer nowadays:
effective at 5f to 7f: acts on all-weather, soft and good to firm going: often wears headgear. *D. Flood*

JONNY LESTERS HAIR (IRE) 4 b.g. Danetime (IRE) 121 – Jupiter Inlet (IRE) **77**
(Jupiter Island 126) [2009 83: 7f^6 7.1m^6 7.5g^6 7m^3 7m^4 p7.1g^6 f7g 6d 7.2g^2 7.2v^5 Oct 31]
fair handicapper nowadays: stays 7.5f: acts on soft and good to firm going. *T. D. Easterby*

JONNY MUDBALL 3 b.c. Oasis Dream 129 – Waypoint 95 (Cadeaux Genereux 131) **104 p**
[2009 6g^4 p7g* p7g^2 Nov 21] 50,000Y: well-made colt: seventh foal: half-brother to 3
winners, including useful 2002 2-y-o 5f/5.5f (Prix Robert Papin) winner Never A Doubt
(by Night Shift): dam, 6f/7f winner, half-sister to very smart sprinter Acclamation: useful
form: won maiden at Lingfield in October by 5 lengths: good 1½ lengths second to Elna
Bright in handicap on same course, travelling strongly, still clear over 1f out: should
prove as effective at 6f as 7f: capable of further progress. *Tom Dascombe*

JONNY NO EYEBROWS 2 b.g. (Apr 1) Auction House (USA) 120 – She's **– §**
Expensive (IRE) 35 (Spectrum (IRE) 126) [2009 p6g p6g Dec 14] well held in seller at
Lingfield: refused to race next time, subsequently gelded. *I. A. Wood*

JONQUILLE (IRE) 4 ch.f. Rock of Gibraltar (IRE) 133 – Moonlight Wish (IRE) **50**
(Peintre Celebre (USA) 137) [2009 –: p9.5g f14g p13.9g^5 11.7m 14.1m May 25] smallish
filly: modest maiden: left R. Ford after second start: stays 1¾m: acts on polytrack: blinkered last 3 starts. *T. J. Pitt*

JORDAN'S LIGHT (USA) 6 gr. or ro.g. Aljabr (USA) 125 – Western Friend (USA) **65**
(Gone West (USA)) [2009 62: 8.3g 12.1s* 12.1v^3 12.4d 15.8g f12g Nov 17] tall
gelding: fair handicapper: won at Hamilton in August: left P. Monteith after fourth start:
stays 1½m: acts on all-weather, soft and good to firm going: sometimes visored: modest
hurdler/chaser, claimed £6,000 and joined P. D. Evans in December. *T. J. Pitt*

JORDAURA 3 br.c. Primo Valentino (IRE) 116 – Christina's Dream 74 (Spectrum **91**
(IRE) 126) [2009 70p: p6g* p6g p6g 5.7g^2 6g^4 p6g^4 6.1d^4 7g^2 7s* Nov 7] sturdy colt:
fairly useful handicapper: won at Kempton in April and Doncaster (apprentices) in November: stays 7f: acts on polytrack, soft and good to firm going: held up. *W. R. Swinburn*

JORD (IRE) 5 b.m. Trans Island 119 – Arcevia (IRE) 85 (Archway (IRE) 115) [2009 **55**
53, a80d: f7g f8g^3 p7.1g^3 p7.1g^3 p7.1g* p7.1g^2 p6g* f8g^3 8f^5 p7.1g 6d^4 8m^4 p5.1g p7m **a75**
p7.1g^2 f8g p6g^3 p7.1g^6 f6g^6 Dec 18] leggy, plain mare: fair handicapper on all-weather,
modest on turf: won at Wolverhampton in March and April: left A. McCabe after ninth
start: effective at 6f to easy 1¼m: acts on all-weather, good to firm and good to soft
ground: tried in cheekpieces: races up with pace. *J. A. Glover*

JORDI ROPER (IRE) 4 ch.g. Traditionally (USA) 117 – Xema (Danehill (USA) 126) **60**
[2009 56: f11s^3 f6d* f8g^2 f6g^2 f6g^4 f8g^6 f7g f8d^6 Mar 10] stocky gelding: modest per-

former: won handicap at Southwell in January: stays 9.5f, effective at much shorter: acts on all-weather: tried in blinkers/cheekpieces/tongue tie: sometimes races lazily. *S. Parr*

JOSEPH HENRY 7 b.g. Mujadil (USA) 119 – Iris May 87 (Brief Truce (USA) 126) **103**
[2009 97: 6m p7g 7g* 8g 7f 6m 6.3g^{6} 7m^{4} 8g 6m 6m 7g Oct 10] well-made gelding: useful handicapper: won at Naas in April by 5 lengths from Enigma Code: creditable efforts after when sixth to Mountain Coral at the Curragh and fourth to Plum Pudding in Bunbury Cup at Newmarket: winner at 1m, better at 6f/7f: acts on any going on turf: tried blinkered: usually races close up. *D. Nicholls*

JOSEPHINE MALINES 5 b.m. Inchinor 119 – Alrisha (IRE) 90 (Persian Bold 123) **56**
[2009 58: p9.5g 8d^{6} 8d^{2} 8.5m^{5} 8s^{3} Aug 27] rather leggy, lightly-made mare: modest performer: stays 1¼m: acts on soft and good to firm going: in cheekpieces nowadays: modest winning hurdler. *Mrs A. Duffield*

JOSHUA TREE (IRE) 2 b.c. (Mar 8) Montjeu (IRE) 137 – Madeira Mist (IRE) **115 p**
80 (Grand Lodge (USA) 125) [2009 7s* 8s^{2} 8m* Sep 26]

Running To Stand Still, a track from U2's seminal album *The Joshua Tree*, is a phrase which could justifiably be applied to the subsequent performances of most of the winners of the Royal Lodge Stakes at Ascot between 1996 and 2008, the years when the race fell to Benny The Dip and Jukebox Jury respectively. Only two of those successful in between, Admiralofthefleet and City Leader, managed to add to their victory in the following year. Admiralofthefleet at least fared better than Aidan O'Brien's first two winners of the race, Royal Kingdom and Mutinyonthebounty. Nonetheless, given that Admiralofthefleet was the best Royal Lodge winner for some years when he triumphed in 2006, it was disappointing that victory in the Dee Stakes turned out to be the highlight of his three-year-old season. O'Brien will be hoping for better from Joshua Tree, who provided the trainer with a fourth victory, one which was somewhat unexpected judged by the betting.

Joshua Tree and Mikhail Glinka were the Ballydoyle representatives in the ten-runner Juddmonte Royal Lodge Stakes, the latter the choice of stable number-one Johnny Murtagh and a 9/1-shot, with Colm O'Donoghue on board 12/1-shot Joshua Tree. The pair had similar profiles, having finished second in a nursery after making a successful debut in a maiden. Joshua Tree's maiden was at Gowran in August, the same one in which his stablemate, the 2008 Irish Derby winner Frozen Fire, had made a winning start as a two-year-old. Joshua Tree justified favouritism by a short head in a race in which all nine of his rivals were also newcomers; and he then went on to show better form when second to Puncher Clynch, beaten three quarters of a length, in a nursery at Listowel, despite not looking entirely at ease on the sharp track and also meeting some trouble. There was trouble aplenty to be found in the Royal Lodge too, though not this time by Joshua Tree who was brought wide in the straight as the field bunched and then went on to cause problems himself by veering right after sweeping to the front approaching the final furlong. Joshua Tree did appear the winner on merit, by a length and a quarter from close-finishers Waseet and Vale of York, and after a stewards' inquiry the placings remained unaltered. The form was just about on a par with that shown in the race by Admiralofthefleet and there should be further improvement to come from Joshua

Juddmonte Royal Lodge Stakes, Ascot—Joshua Tree shows much improved form despite veering right; Waseet (blaze) and Vale of York (noseband) chase him home

Tree, though there are several others, including some from his own yard, who look stronger contenders for the classics.

Joshua Tree (IRE) (b.c. Mar 8, 2007)	Montjeu (IRE) (b 1996)	Sadler's Wells (b 1981)	Northern Dancer Fairy Bridge
		Floripedes (b 1985)	Top Ville Toute Cy
	Madeira Mist (IRE) (b 1999)	Grand Lodge (ch 1991)	Chief's Crown La Papagena
		Mountains of Mist (b 1992)	Shirley Heights Magic of Life

By the time Joshua Tree reached the sale-ring in October 2008, his dam's first foal Storm Mist (by Giant's Causeway) had made three appearances and shown very little, yet Joshua Tree still fetched 360,000 guineas. Not that Joshua Tree didn't have plenty to recommend him otherwise, being a sturdy, attractive son of Montjeu from a very good family. His dam Madeira Mist, who finished fourth in a maiden at the Curragh on her only start at two, went on to win eight races at up to nine furlongs in North America, including a Grade 3. Madeira Mist is a half-sister to several winners including Misty Heights, a useful Irish performer at up to a mile and a quarter. Joshua Tree's grandam Mountains of Mist, a mile and a quarter winner, is a half-sister to the Lowther Stakes winner Enthused out of the Coronation Stakes winner Magic of Life. Joshua Tree's first two starts were on soft ground and it's a possibility, though we wouldn't want to put it any stronger, that the good to firm conditions he encountered at Ascot played a part in the much improved form he showed. *A. P. O'Brien, Ireland*

JOSH YOU ARE 6 b.g. Josr Algarhoud (IRE) 118 – Cibenze 74 (Owington 123) [2009 60, a81: p12.2g f11g p16g p13.9m 15.8g 11.5g May 28] tall gelding: handicapper: lost way in 2009, reportedly bled fourth outing: stays 2m: acts on polytrack, firm and good to soft going: signs of temperament. *Ian Williams* **67 d**

JOSIAH BARTLETT (IRE) 3 b.g. Invincible Spirit (IRE) 121 – Princess Caraboo (IRE) (Alzao (USA) 117) [2009 59: p9.5g p8.6g^{5} p7g* p8g^{2} p7g^{4} p7.1g p5.1g 7m 5m 6d^{5} 6f^{5} p5.1g p8m p7m p6g^{2} p7m^{6} f6g p8.6g p7m Dec 30] sturdy gelding: modest performer: left J. Hills 2,800 gns, won handicap at Lingfield in February: left P. McEntee after eleventh start: stays easy 8.6f: acts on all-weather: has worn blinkers/visor/tongue tie. *Ian Williams* **64**

JOSPHIEL (IRE) 4 b.f. Okawango (USA) 115 – Indian Honey (Indian King (USA) 128) [2009 63: 5m 6f^{4} 6g^{3} 6m^{3} 6g 6m Jul 1] lengthy filly: modest maiden: stays 7f, worth another try at 5f: acts on good to firm and good to soft going: blinkered last 4 starts (looked awkward final one): one to be wary of. *A. Berry* **64 §**

JOSR'S MAGIC (IRE) 5 b.g. Josr Algarhoud (IRE) 118 – Just The Trick (USA) 48 (Phone Trick (USA)) [2009 –, a69: p10m p8m p8g^{2} p7g^{4} p8m Dec 9] strong, compact gelding: type to carry condition: good mover: fair handicapper: effective at 7f to 1½m: acts on all-weather, had form on good to firm ground earlier in career: tried blinkered/ visored. *T. E. Powell* **– a67**

JOSS STICK 4 b.g. Josr Algarhoud (IRE) 118 – Queen's College (IRE) 57 (College Chapel 122) [2009 72: p6g^{6} p6g* p5g^{3} f5g^{6} p6g p6g^{6} p6g^{5} p6g^{2} p5g 6m^{2} 5.1m^{4} 5.1g^{5} 5.3d 6m^{3} 5.3g* 5.3d p5g^{6} 5.3f 5m 6g^{2} p6m 5m 6g p6g p7m Nov 4] lengthy gelding: fair handicapper: won at Lingfield (apprentices) in January and, having left R. Harris, Brighton in July: out of sorts last 5 starts: effective at 5f/6f: acts on polytrack and firm ground: tried in blinkers/cheekpieces/tongue tie. *J. J. Bridger* **67**

JOUNCE (USA) 2 ch.f. (Feb 11) Gone West (USA) – Shoogle (USA) 86 (A P Indy (USA) 131) [2009 p7.1g^{2} Nov 14] sixth foal: sister to 3-y-o Close Alliance, closely related to fairly useful French 1m winner Cross Purposes (by Distant View) and half-sister to 4-y-o Moral Duty: dam, 2-y-o 7f winner (stayed 1¼m), sister to high-class US performer up to 1½m Aptitude: 10/1, encouraging 6 lengths second to Huroof in maiden at Wolverhampton, staying on: bred to stay 1m+: should improve. *J. H. M. Gosden* **72 p**

JOURY 2 b.f. (Apr 2) Oratorio (IRE) 128 – Contradictive (USA) (Kingmambo (USA) 125) [2009 p7.1g Sep 25] fourth foal: dam unraced half-sister to smart French performer up to 10.5f Gracioso: 20/1, considerately handled when tailed off in maiden at Wolverhampton: bred to stay 1¼m. *S. A. Callaghan* **–**

JOYEAUX 7 b.m. Mark of Esteem (IRE) 137 – Divine Secret (Hernando (FR) 127) [2009 76: 5g 5d^{4} 5m 6m 5m^{3} 5m^{5} 6d 5s^{5} 5m^{2} 5m^{4} 5g 5g^{6} 6m^{5} 5.1d^{2} 5s^{4} p6g^{4} p6g^{5} Nov 27] **69**

leggy mare: fair handicapper: best at 5f/6f: acts on all-weather, firm and soft ground: effective visored or not: held up: quirky. *Ollie Pears*

JOZAFEEN 2 ch.f. (Apr 11) Zafeen (FR) 123 – Faithful Beauty (IRE) (Last Tycoon 131) [2009 6m 5.9g² 7.1s² 6.5m 6.1d² Oct 15] half-sister to 2008 2-y-o 7.5f winner Ubi Ace (by First Trump) and several winners abroad: dam unraced half-sister to useful sprinter Masha-Il: modest maiden: stays 7f: acts on soft going: signs of temperament. *R. Bastiman* **60**

JUBAIL (IRE) 2 ch.c. (Feb 17) Redback 116 – Daneville (IRE) (Danetime (IRE) 121) [2009 7m Aug 13] 22/1, 8¾ lengths tenth to Dromore in maiden at Salisbury. *A. King* **49**

JUBILANT NOTE (IRE) 7 b.g. Sadler's Wells (USA) 132 – Hint of Humour (USA) 93 (Woodman (USA) 126) [2009 76: 10.2g May 26] good-topped gelding: useful hurdler/chaser: fair handicapper on Flat: below form sole start in 2009: stays 1¾m: acts on polytrack and probably any turf going: usually blinkered (visored last 2 starts): tongue tied once in 2006. *M. D. Murphy, Ireland* **–**

JUBILEE JUGGINS (IRE) 3 b.c. Clodovil (IRE) 116 – Alleged Touch (USA) (Alleged (USA) 138) [2009 75: f5g⁵ Mar 11] leggy colt: fair performer at 2 yrs: below form sole start in 2009: best efforts at 5f, bred to stay further: acts on soft ground: tried blinkered. *N. P. Littmoden* **60**

JUDD STREET 7 b.g. Compton Place 125 – Pudding Lane (IRE) 64 (College Chapel 122) [2009 113: 6g³ 6g* 6m⁶ p5g² 5.1m³ 5g⁴ 6m* 6m 5m⁵ 6d p6m² 6d Sep 5] sturdy, close-coupled gelding: smart performer: as good as ever in 2009, winning handicap at Nad Al Sheba (beat Instant Recall by neck) in February and listed race at Salisbury (by nose from Palace Moon) in June: ran creditably after when fifth to Ialysos in Sprint Stakes at Sandown and 1½ lengths second to Ancien Regime in minor event at Lingfield: effective at 5f/easy 6f: acts on polytrack, raced mostly on good ground or firmer on turf (below form all 4 outings on going softer than good): blinkered/visored: travels strongly. *Eve Johnson Houghton* **113**

JUDGE 'N JURY 5 ch.g. Pivotal 124 – Cyclone Connie 98 (Dr Devious (IRE) 127) [2009 117: p5g³ 5.5d⁶ 5d⁵ 5m 5m 5g⁶ 5m⁴ 5m* 5g³ 6m 5v² 5.6m 5d Oct 24] stocky gelding: useful performer: won quite valuable handicap at Ascot in July by ½ length from Hamish McGonagall: in-and-out form after, ran creditably when third to Group Therapy in handicap at Ascot and length second to Reverence in Flying Five Stakes at the Curragh: best at 5f: acts on all-weather, heavy and good to firm ground: tongue tied: usually ridden prominently/travels strongly. *R. A. Harris* **109**

JUDGETHEMOMENT (USA) 4 br.c. Judge T C (USA) – Rachael Tennessee (USA) (Matsadoon (USA)) [2009 94: p16g* 16m* 20m* 16.4m⁴ 16g 16.4m 18m 16g Oct 30] smallish, stocky colt: useful handicapper: thrived in first half of 2009, winning at Kempton in April, and Ascot in May and June, last-named Ascot Stakes (beat Sesenta ½ length): lost way after: stays 2½m: acts on polytrack and firm going: tried in cheekpieces. *Jane Chapple-Hyam* **103**

Ascot Stakes (Handicap), Royal Ascot—a third win of the campaign for Judgethemoment (left), who holds off Sesenta and Royal Rationale (blinkers) with Gala Evening fourth

JUDICIARY (IRE) 2 b.c. (May 1) Invincible Spirit (IRE) 121 – Theory of Law (Generous (IRE) 139) [2009 8g^{2} 8m f8m* Nov 6] €22,000Y, 95,000 2-y-o: tall colt: has plenty of scope: brother to useful Italian 7.5f (at 2 yrs) to 11f winner Paint In Green, closely related to winner in Spain by Desert Prince and half-brother to French 6f winner Celtibero (by Celtic Swing): dam, French 11f winner, half-sister to Prix Morny winner Charge d'Affaires: progressive form in maidens, winning at Southwell by head from Comradeship, rallying: will probably stay 1¼m: should continue to improve. *Saeed bin Suroor* **85 p**

JUICY PEAR (IRE) 2 b.g. (Feb 15) Pyrus (USA) 106 – Cappadoce (IRE) (General Monash (USA) 107) [2009 p7.1g^{3} p7.1g p7g^{2} Nov 11] £45,000Y: third living foal: half-brother to 2 winners by Daggers Drawn, including 5-y-o Jewelled Dagger: dam ran once in France: placed in maidens at Wolverhampton and Kempton (4 lengths second to Mass Rally): will stay 1m. *M. L. W. Bell* **75 +**

JUKEBOX JURY (IRE) 3 gr.c. Montjeu (IRE) 137 – Mare Aux Fees (Kenmare (FR) 125) [2009 115: 9g 10m^{6} 10.4m* 12m^{4} 12.5m* 12g* 12m^{2} Oct 17] **123**

At the height of its popularity the weekly BBC television programme Jukebox Jury, which had its main run from 1959 to 1967, attracted audiences of around 12,000,000. The show involved four celebrities—or five on the occasion when The Rolling Stones were the guests in 1964—listening to and judging whether new pop record releases would be a hit or a miss. The decision led to a bell being sounded for a hit and a raspberry-sounding hooter for a miss, sounds which became as well known as almost any in Britain. At the start of the latest season a panel voting on whether Jukebox Jury the racehorse would be a hit or a miss would almost certainly have resulted in the bell being sounded. He had enjoyed a good two-year-old campaign, with victory in the Royal Lodge Stakes and second to Crowded House in the Racing Post Trophy the highlights, and he looked sure to improve when he got middle distances at three. Jukebox Jury endured one or two hiccups along the way, his reappearance delayed until near the end of June, but there is no doubting that by the end of the season his three-year-old campaign had been a resounding hit. He won pattern events in Britain, France and Germany and ran a fine race in defeat in the Canadian International. He proved himself the best horse in Mark Johnston's stable, and Awzaan and others may have their work cut out to displace him as the yard's standard bearer in the next season.

Jukebox Jury never gave the impression he would have enough speed for the Two Thousand Guineas but Johnston originally hoped to run him in that race, for which he was quoted at 40/1 in January. However, in early-February the colt had to be sent to Newmarket to be operated on for a wound in a fetlock that would not heal. No sooner had he begun cantering again in mid-March than he suffered a suspected stress fracture of a tibia. Both the Two Thousand Guineas and the Derby went by without him and he reappeared in the Prix Daphnis over nine furlongs at Longchamp, for which he was supplemented. Allowing for the problems he had had, and for the fact that he was giving weight all round over an inadequate trip, Jukebox Jury still seemed to merit a raspberry, rather than a ding, for his run here. After being reluctant at the stalls, he was rather slowly away, raced freely out wide and was unable to make any impression once pushed along on the home turn, coming last of seven behind Golden Century. In all probability, he needed the run and much better followed twelve days later in the Coral-Eclipse at Sandown, where Jukebox Jury started at 50/1 and finished a far from disgraced sixth of ten to Sea The Stars. Jukebox Jury would have been out of his depth against Sea The Stars whatever the trip, and the opposition in the totepool Rose of Lancaster Stakes at Haydock in early-August, headed by Hardwicke Stakes runner-up Campanologist and Coronation Cup fourth Duncan, was somewhat less demanding, though the Rose of Lancaster field was still strong for a Group 3 event. Jukebox Jury got back on the winning trail, giving every indication that he would improve again tried over further, outpaced initially in the straight before catching Campanologist inside the final furlong and beating him by a length and a quarter.

Jukebox Jury ran twice more in August, stepped up in trip. He did not run to form in the Great Voltigeur Stakes at York, finishing over eight lengths fourth of seven to Monitor Closely, but less than a fortnight later he won the Lucien Barriere Grand Prix de Deauville. As reported in *Racehorses of 2008*, Johnny Murtagh expressed doubts about Jukebox Jury's temperament after riding him twice, and Jukebox Jury had looked ungainly under pressure at York. He also tends to hang and lose concentration on occasions. He showed all of this at Deauville, not looking to have his mind fully on the job in the early stages, when he hung on the first bend and needed a slap on the neck to make him concentrate as they crossed the all-weather track. Before halfway Kasbah Bliss, successful in the Prix Gladiateur the year before, had taken over at the head of affairs from Jukebox Jury, who, however, regained the lead with a furlong and a half to go. Running on strongly, he held on resolutely by a nose from Pouvoir Absolu.

Jukebox Jury didn't need to reproduce his best form to win at Deauville but he certainly needed to in his next race four weeks later in the Preis von Europa at Cologne, for which he was supplemented. Over the preceding thirty years, three-year-olds and older horses had won an equal number of editions, but a change in the German weight-for-age scale meant that Jukebox Jury and the three other members of the classic crop in a field of ten were 2 lb worse off with their elders than their counterparts had been the year before. There were three other British challengers, each of whom was attempting to become the twelfth British-trained winner of the Preis von Europa in the same period. They were: the favourite Eastern Anthem, placed in two Group 1 races in Germany since winning the Dubai Sheema Classic; Bronze Cannon, successful in the Jockey Club Stakes and Hardwicke Stakes; and Enroller, fourth in the Hardwicke but out of form since. The home defence was led by the third and fourth in the Deutsches Derby, Toughness Danon and Eliot, and Poseidon Adventure, runner-up in the race in both 2007 and 2008. Jukebox Jury settled in behind front-running Enroller until turning for home, where the other runners began bunching behind. Jukebox Jury responded well when asked to quicken, hitting the front with more than two furlongs to go, and, although Eastern Anthem took second a furlong and a half out and made ground throughout the final furlong, Jukebox Jury always looked like just holding on under strong pressure and got home by a nose, with Eliot the best of the home-trained runners in third, two and a half lengths away. The stewards were busy dealing with whip offences after the race, fining Jukebox Jury's rider Royston Ffrench, winning his first Group 1 race, €250 for excessive use and Frankie Dettori €400 for a similar thing on the runner-up, while Karoly Kerekes on fourth-placed Poseidon Adventure received a one-day ban. Jukebox Jury earned £90,090 (at prevailing exchange rates) for his victory but that didn't make him the biggest winner of the afternoon for his stable, since Shakespearean picked up exactly ten times that amount for winning the Goffs Million Mile at the Curragh. Not a bad day's work for the trainer.

Lucien Barriere Grand Prix de Deauville, Deauville—
the grey Jukebox Jury is all out to beat Pouvoir Absolu (No.2), Kasbah Bliss (No.3) and Ideal World

Preis von Europa, Cologne—another lucrative win on foreign soil for Jukebox Jury as he provides regular jockey Royston Ffrench with his first Group 1 win; fellow British raider Eastern Anthem (noseband) is second

The Preis von Europa was another hard race for Jukebox Jury but it represented a marginally improved effort and he repeated the form in the Canadian International at Woodbine nearly three weeks later without managing to win. Sent off third favourite behind dual Grade 1 winner Champs Elysees and the Northern Dancer Turf Stakes winner Just As Well, Jukebox Jury soon took closer order after being a little slowly into his stride and was ridden along vigorously to take over in front early in the straight. He had most of his rivals beaten but Champs Elysees came on the outside to lead fifty yards from home and beat Jukebox Jury half a length, with Jukebox Jury two lengths clear of fellow British runner Buccellati in third. Jukebox Jury must have every chance of emulating his latest campaign at four, given the choice of Group 1 races spread across Europe at around a mile and a half, a trip which suits him ideally. He may find it hard to hit the jackpot in the top events in Britain but that won't be for want of trying on his part—as already mentioned, he is not short of determination in a finish.

Jukebox Jury (IRE) (gr.c. 2006)	Montjeu (IRE) (b 1996)	Sadler's Wells (b 1981)	Northern Dancer
			Fairy Bridge
		Floripedes (b 1985)	Top Ville
			Toute Cy
	Mare Aux Fees (gr 1988)	Kenmare (gr 1975)	Kalamoun
			Belle of Ireland
		Feerie Boreale (gr 1981)	Irish River
			Skelda

A good-bodied colt, Jukebox Jury has raced only on good going or firmer. His pedigree was analysed in detail in last year's Annual but there are just a few details to add. Belle Allure, Jukebox Jury's four-year-old half-sister, added another stakes race to her tally when landing the Grade 3 Athenia Stakes over an extended mile at Belmont Park in October. Their dam Mare Aux Fees, a winner at a mile and a quarter, has proved well worth the €30,000 she fetched at Deauville in December 2004 as a sixteen-year-old. She had an unraced two-year-old colt named Le Larron (by High Chaparral) in training with Alain de Royer Dupre in the latest season and her yearling colt by Hurricane Run was knocked down to Jukebox Jury's trainer for just €100,000 at Deauville in August. This sum was not much more than a third of the €270,000 Johnston paid for Jukebox Jury at the same venue two years before. *M. Johnston*

JULIE MILL (IRE) 3 b.f. Apprehension 112 – Ann's Mill 57 (Pelder (IRE) 125) [2009 –: p12g p8m p10g p8m Nov 19] lightly-made filly: little form. *R. A. Teal* **–**

JULIENAS (IRE) 2 b.c. (Feb 28) Cape Cross (IRE) 129 – Dora Carrington (IRE) 106 (Sri Pekan (USA) 117) [2009 p7g4 Oct 21] rangy colt: fourth foal: half-brother to 4-y-o Lytton: dam, 2-y-o 6f winner (including Cherry Hinton Stakes), half-sister to Middle Park winner Primo Valentino: 20/1 and very green, 4 lengths fourth to Golden Shaheen in maiden at Kempton, running on well when shaken up and nearest finish: sure to do better. *W. R. Swinburn* **77 p**

JUL'S LAD (IRE) 3 b.g. Modigliani (USA) 106 – Woodenitbenice (USA) (Nasty And 65 §
Bold (USA)) [2009 66: p8.6g^{2} p7.1g^{3} 9.9m 10.3g p8.6g p8.6g f8f Dec 17] maiden: fair form in 2009 only on reappearance: left M. Mullineaux after fifth start: stays 8.6f: acts on polytrack and good to soft going: tried in cheekpieces/blinkers: temperamental. *D. Carroll*

JULY JASMINE (USA) 3 b.f. Empire Maker (USA) 129 – Camanoe (USA) 63 (Gone 103
West (USA)) [2009 87p: 11.5m^{2} 12m^{5} 11.9m 9.9g^{3} Aug 30] good-topped filly: has a round action: useful performer: generally progressive in various company, second to Midday in listed race at Lingfield and fifth to Flying Cloud in Ribblesdale Stakes at Royal Ascot before best effort when length third to Nashmiah in listed handicap at Goodwood: stays 1½m: unraced on extremes of going: joined W. Mott in USA. *Sir Michael Stoute*

JUMAANA (IRE) 3 b.f. Selkirk (USA) 129 – Weqaar (USA) 83 (Red Ransom (USA)) 63
[2009 63: 9.9f 11.5s^{4} 10f^{3} Jul 5] good-bodied filly: modest maiden: stays 11.5f: acts on soft and good to firm ground: free-going sort: sold 7,000 gns. *J. L. Dunlop*

JUMBAJUKIBA 6 b.g. Barathea (IRE) 127 – Danseuse du Soir (IRE) 121 (Thatching 116
131) [2009 121: 7s^{6} 5.8s* 6v^{2} 8g^{2} 7s^{5} 8s^{5} 8.5g^{2} Oct 17] big gelding: smart performer: won listed race at Navan in April by 1¾ lengths from Croisultan: second in Greenlands Stakes (beaten 2½ lengths by Utmost Respect) and listed race (5 lengths behind Famous Name) next 2 starts, both at the Curragh: below form after: best at testing 5.8f to 1m: yet to race on firm going, acts on any other: blinkered (except when in cheekpieces final start): usually leads, and often gets clear: none too consistent. *Mrs J. Harrington, Ireland*

JUNG (USA) 3 b. or br.g. Stroll (USA) 119 – Witching Well (IRE) (Night Shift (USA)) –
[2009 –: 6d p6g Oct 10] no form: tried tongue tied/blinkered. *J. R. Gask*

JUPITER FIDIUS 2 b.c. (Apr 11) Haafhd 129 – Kyda (USA) 78 (Gulch (USA)) [2009 78 +
5f^{5} 7g^{6} 8d* Oct 28] 50,000F, 40,000Y: close-coupled colt: third foal: half-brother to 5-y-o Nota Liberata: dam 11f winner: easily best effort in maidens when winning at Musselburgh by 1¼ lengths, with bit to spare, from Taste The Victory: will stay 1¼m: acts on good to soft ground. *Mrs K. Walton*

JUST A MONKEY 2 ch.c. (Apr 23) Auction House (USA) 120 – Wedgewood Star 74 –
(Bishop of Cashel 122) [2009 6m 8.3m Aug 24] sturdy colt: well beaten in maiden/seller. *R. Curtis*

JUST BOND (IRE) 7 b.g. Namid 128 – Give Warning (IRE) (Warning 136) [2009 92: 91
f8s^{5} p8.6g^{3} p8.6g^{3} p8g p8.6g^{2} p9.5g^{5} p8.6g^{4} p8.6g^{4} 8m* 7.1m^{5} 8.1m^{2} 8m 8m* 8g p8.6g^{5} 8.1m 8m p9.5g^{6} p9.5g^{5} p9.5m* p8.6g^{3} p8.6g^{4} p9.5g Dec 26] smallish gelding: fairly useful handicapper: won at Musselburgh in April, Redcar in August and Wolverhampton in November: stays 9.5f: acts on polytrack, firm and good to soft ground: tried in cheekpieces/visor: usually held up: sometimes hangs right/finds little. *G. R. Oldroyd*

JUST CALL ME DAVE (USA) 3 b.g. Gneiss (USA) 110 – Proud Future (USA) –
(Proud Birdie (USA)) [2009 12g 10.9g 11.8g p16.5g f8f Nov 24] little form. *Paul Green*

JUSTCALLMEHANDSOME 7 ch.g. Handsome Ridge 121 – Pearl Dawn (IRE) 91 69
(Jareer (USA) 115) [2009 56+, a86: p8.6g^{4} p8g p8.6g^{2} p10g 8.1g^{3} 8.3m^{4} 8m^{6} 8.1g^{5} 8.5m^{5} a82
p7.1g p8m^{6} p8.6g^{5} p8m p8.6g* p8.6g^{3} Dec 19] lengthy, angular gelding: fairly useful handicapper on all-weather, fair on turf: won at Wolverhampton in December: stays 8.6f: acts on all-weather, soft and good to firm ground: visored: usually claimer ridden: tough. *D. J. S. ffrench Davis*

JUST CRYSTAL 5 b.m. Polar Prince (IRE) 117 – Grandads Dream (Never So Bold –
135) [2009 –: 7s^{5} 7m May 26] close-coupled mare: modest maiden in 2007: well held since. *B. P. J. Baugh*

JUST DAN 3 b.g. Best of The Bests (IRE) 122 – Scapavia (FR) (Alzao (USA) 117) 45
[2009 57: 14.1m 10.9g^{4} f14g^{4} 12.1m f11g 13.8m Sep 19] poor maiden: should stay 1¼m: in cheekpieces last 2 starts. *R. Hollinshead*

JUST DENNIS 5 b.g. Superior Premium 122 – Sweets (IRE) (Persian Heights 129) –
[2009 –: p12.2g p12.2g Mar 20] little form in bumpers, on Flat or over hurdles. *D. G. Bridgwater*

JUST FIVE (IRE) 3 b.g. Olmodavor (USA) 117 – Wildsplash (USA) (Deputy Minister 82
(CAN)) [2009 54: f8g* f8g^{4} f8g* f7g^{2} 8s* 7m 7.5m* 8.5g* p8.6g Oct 29] workmanlike gelding: fairly useful handicapper: much improved in 2009, winning at Southwell in February and March, Newcastle in May and Beverley in July (claimer) and September: stays 8.5f: acts on fibresand, soft and good to firm ground: tried tongue tied. *M. Dods*

JUST FOR MARY 5 b.g. Groom Dancer (USA) 128 – Summer Dance 86 (Sadler's Wells (USA) 132) [2009 79d: 7g 6s 7.2v4 7d6 6s 6m4 5d* 5v* 5g2 7d 5s2 5s5 5s Sep 12] useful handicapper: won at the Curragh in June and July: good second at Ayr and Tipperary after: seems best at testing 5f: acts on polytrack and any turf going: often blinkered in 2008: tongue tied on reappearance: often slowly away/comes from behind. *D. Loughnane, Ireland* **95**

JUST JIMMY (IRE) 4 b.g. Ashkalani (IRE) 128 – Berkeley Hall 68 (Saddlers' Hall (IRE) 126) [2009 63: p8g2 p8g3 p7g4 p7.1g* p8.6g6 p7g5 p7.1g 7m 8.1g 8.1g 7.1m4 6.1g2 6.1m 7.1d p8g2 8d p7m4 p8.6g* p8.6g5 p8.6g* p7.1g* Dec 28] angular gelding: fair handicapper: won at Wolverhampton in February and, having been trained fourteenth start only by K. Prendergast, November and December (2): stays 8.6f: acts on polytrack and soft ground: tried visored/tongue tied: tough and genuine. *P. D. Evans* **69**

JUST JOEY 5 b.m. Averti (IRE) 117 – Fly South (Polar Falcon (USA) 126) [2009 74: p6g p6g6 5.7g2 5m 5m 5m 5m 5.3f4 5.3m4 5.3g6 5f 5m6 5d Aug 26] sturdy mare: modest handicapper nowadays: stays 5.7f: acts on firm and good to soft going: blinkered/visored. *J. R. Weymes* **63**

JUST LIKE SILK (USA) 3 b.g. Elusive Quality (USA) – Ocean Silk (USA) 119 (Dynaformer (USA)) [2009 65p: p8g5 p10.7g3 p12g4 9.9g2 9.9m2 10d5 12m* Aug 15] good-bodied gelding: fairly useful handicapper: generally progressive, and won lady amateurs event at Newbury (tongue tied) in August by 4 lengths (gelded after): stays 1½m: acts on polytrack and good to firm going. *G. A. Butler* **94**

JUST LILLE (IRE) 6 b.m. Mull of Kintyre (USA) 114 – Tamasriya (IRE) (Doyoun 124) [2009 98: 9.8m3 10g6 9.8m2 9.8d4 8g2 12.1m2 8.3m* 11.9m 10m3 8.3s2 15g* 14.6m 13g4 18m3 Oct 5] sturdy mare: useful performer: won minor event at Hamilton in June and handicap at Warwick in August: several good efforts otherwise, including fourth in handicap at Hamilton penultimate start: effective at 1m to 15f: acts on firm and good to soft ground: wears cheekpieces: usually races prominently: reliable. *Mrs A. Duffield* **98**

JUST MANDY (IRE) 2 ch.f. (Feb 18) Noverre (USA) 125 – Unicamp 84 (Royal Academy (USA) 130) [2009 5.1m3 Jul 11] €16,000Y, £19,000 2-y-o: fifth foal: half-sister to 3 winners, including useful Irish 7f (at 2 yrs) to 13f winner Kempes (by Intikhab) and 5-y-o Smarty Socks: dam 2-y-o 6f winner: 10/3, 2¾ lengths third to Social Grace in maiden at Chester, getting hang of things late: will be suited by 6f+: should improve. *R. A. Fahey* **56 p**

JUST MOSSIE 4 ch.g. Ishiguru (USA) 114 – Marinsky (USA) 63 (Diesis 133) [2009 64: p9.5g Apr 24] sturdy gelding: modest maiden: stays 9.5f: acts on all-weather: often wears cheekpieces: modest hurdler. *W. G. M. Turner* **–**

JUST MUSTARD (USA) 3 gr. or ro.g. Johannesburg (USA) 127 – After All (IRE) 64 (Desert Story (IRE) 115) [2009 65p: p8g6 7m 6s4 7g Jul 4] smallish gelding: modest maiden: will prove best up to 7f: sold 6,000 gns, sent to Qatar. *G. A. Butler* **59**

JUST OBSERVING 6 ch.g. Observatory (USA) 131 – Just Speculation (IRE) 86 (Ahonoora 122) [2009 p10g2 p9.5g6 p9.5g p12g6 f12g3 10.3m 12.5m5 10.2m5 9.9m5 10m4 Jun 19] strong, close-coupled gelding: fair handicapper: below form after reappearance: stays 1½m: acts on polytrack, firm and good to soft going: tried visored: often in cheekpieces: has looked tricky ride: modest hurdler. *P. T. Midgley* **76 d**

JUSTONEFORTHEROAD 3 b.g. Domedriver (IRE) 128 – Lavinia's Grace (USA) 66 (Green Desert (USA) 127) [2009 68: 8.1m3 9f3 8m5 7m* p7m 7s Oct 12] close-coupled gelding: fair performer: left N. Vaughan, won maiden at Redcar in September: stays 9f: acts on firm going: gelded after final outing. *R. A. Fahey* **79**

JUST OSCAR (GER) 5 b.g. Surako (GER) 114 – Jade Chequer 71 (Green Desert (USA) 127) [2009 61: f7g5 7.1f5 7m2 7f 8.1g 7.6g 7.6m 15.8g5 Aug 4] workmanlike gelding: modest maiden: best up to 1m: acts on polytrack, firm and soft going: tried in headgear: not one to trust. *W. M. Brisbourne* **61**

JUST PICKLES 4 b.g. Piccolo 121 – Tenderetta (Tender King 123) [2009 7m 9m Apr 12] well held in bumper, and in sellers on Flat. *G. A. Swinbank* **–**

JUST SAM (IRE) 4 b.f. Mull of Kintyre (USA) 114 – Strawberry Sands 74 (Lugana Beach 116) [2009 63: 7m2 7s3 8.5m 6m* 6m 7.5m4 6d 6m* 6m* 6m 6g 6m2 6m* 6d Oct 13] workmanlike filly: fair handicapper: improved in 2009, winning at Redcar in May (amateurs), July, August and September: best at 6f: acts on polytrack, good to firm and good to soft going: tried visored: often front runner: reportedly in season tenth start. *R. E. Barr* **77**

JUST SERENADE 10 ch.m. Factual (USA) 108 – Thimbalina 63 (Salmon Leap (USA) 131) [2009 f14g p12g Feb 7] workmanlike mare: maiden handicapper: first races of any kind for nearly 5 years, well held on Flat in 2009: tried in headgear. *Mrs Lawney Hill* –

JUST SPIKE 6 ch.g. Cayman Kai (IRE) 114 – Grandads Dream (Never So Bold 135) [2009 63: 6g 6m 8.1m p8.6g^4 Oct 30] modest handicapper: stays 8.6f: acts on polytrack, firm and good to soft going. *B. P. J. Baugh* 52

JUST THE LADY 3 b.f. Ishiguru (USA) 114 – Just Run (IRE) 45 (Runnett 125) [2009 76: p5g* p5g^3 f5g^4 f5g^2 p6g f5g^6 p5g^6 p5.1g^5 Apr 6] lengthy filly: modest performer nowadays: won claimer at Kempton in January: best at 5f: acts on all-weather, soft and good to firm going: often front runner. *D. Nicholls* 62

JUST THE TONIC 2 ch.f. (May 10) Medicean 128 – Goodwood Blizzard 97 (Inchinor 119) [2009 6m^3 6m^5 7m^2 7d^4 7g 7d 6m^2 p7g 6g^3 5m^4 8m^6 Sep 23] 10,000Y: sparely-made filly: sixth foal: half-sister to several winners, including 3-y-o Snow Bay and 5-y-o Smirfy's Silver: dam 2-y-o 6f/7f winner: modest maiden: claimed from M. Channon £6,000 ninth start: best up to 7f: acts on good to firm and good to soft going: usually races prominently. *Mrs Marjorie Fife* 62

JUST TIMMY MARCUS 3 ch.g. Ishiguru (USA) 114 – Grandads Dream (Never So Bold 135) [2009 p6g* p6g* 6s 6m^6 7g p6g p7.1g^6 p7.1g^4 p7.1g^2 p7.1g^3 p7.1g^4 p7.1g^3 Dec 28] fourth foal: half-brother to 6-y-o Just Spike: dam unraced: fair performer: won maiden in February and handicap in March, both at Wolverhampton: stays 7f: acts on polytrack: tried in cheekpieces. *B. P. J. Baugh* 72

JUTLAND 2 b.g. (Feb 12) Halling (USA) 133 – Dramatique (Darshaan 133) [2009 7m^4 7.1m^6 7m* 7.1g^6 Aug 22] strong gelding: first foal: dam, French 10.7f winner, half-sister to useful UAE sprinter Conceal: progressive in maidens, winning at Brighton in August by 1½ lengths from Luminous Star, making virtually all: below form in nursery at Sandown (slowly away), subsequently gelded: will be suited by 1m. *M. Johnston* 80

JUWIREYA 2 b.f. (Mar 26) Nayef (USA) 129 – Katayeb (IRE) (Machiavellian (USA) 123) [2009 8m Sep 8] second foal: half-sister to 3-y-o Tahkeem: dam once-raced half-sister to high-class 1½m performer White Muzzle and dam of Dubai World Cup winner Almutawakel: 25/1, very green when well held in maiden at Goodwood. *M. P. Tregoning* –

K

KAABARI (USA) 3 b. or br.f. Seeking The Gold (USA) – Cloud Castle 119 (In The Wings 128) [2009 p7g* 7m 7m^3 9g 7s^5 12d 8m 7m^2 7m^5 Oct 3] neat filly: seventh foal: closely related to 9.7f winner Samdaniya (by Machiavellian) and half-sister to French 1½m winner Reverie Solitaire (by Nashwan) and 6f (at 2 yrs) to 1½m winner Queen's Best (by King's Best), latter 2 smart: dam, won Nell Gwyn Stakes and second in Prix Vermeille, half-sister to Luso, Warrsan and Needle Gun: fairly useful form: won maiden at Lingfield in March: creditable second in handicap at Folkestone eighth start: flattered in listed race final outing: should be well suited by 1m+: acts on polytrack and good to firm going. *C. E. Brittain* 89

KABEER 11 ch.g. Unfuwain (USA) 131 – Ta Rib (USA) 116 (Mr Prospector (USA)) [2009 –, a98: f7d^6 f7g^6 f8g^6 p7.1g^5 p8g p8.6g Mar 23] big, lengthy gelding: fair handicapper on all-weather, lightly raced and little recent form on turf: best up to 1m: acts on all-weather: tried in cheekpieces: usually tongue tied (not last 3 starts). *A. J. McCabe* – a65

KABIS AMIGOS 7 ch.g. Nashwan (USA) 135 – River Saint (USA) 73§ (Irish River (FR) 131) [2009 77d: p7m p7.1g^2 p7.1g p7.1g^3 p7g^5 p7.1g* p7.1g^3 p7.1g^5 p7.1g 7.1m^2 7.1m^5 7.5m* 8m^3 7m^6 7.5g^6 Aug 12] tall, leggy gelding: fair performer: won claimer at Wolverhampton in March and, having left S. Mason after ninth start, handicap at Beverley in June: stayed 1m: acted on all-weather, firm and good to soft going: wore headgear: formerly tongue tied: dead. *Ollie Pears* 79

KABOUGG 3 b.f. Tobougg (IRE) 125 – Karameg (IRE) 90 (Danehill (USA) 126) [2009 –: 8.3g f12m p13.9g Nov 27] no form. *A. J. McCabe* –

KAHAIL (USA) 2 b.c. (May 5) Rahy (USA) 115 – Al Ihsas (IRE) 99 (Danehill (USA) 126) [2009 6m 6g^5 6m^5 p6g^5 Aug 10] sturdy colt: modest form in maidens: may well be as effective at 5f as 6f: acts on polytrack and good to firm going: tongue tied after debut: sent to Qatar. *Miss D. Mountain* 60

Coral Sprint Trophy (Heritage Handicap), York—the favourite Kaldoun Kingdom (centre) follows up his Ayr Silver Cup win with a career-best effort; behind him are Cheveton (large star on cap), Hitchens (second left), Green Manalishi (cheekpieces) and Wi Dud (right)

KAHFRE 2 ch.g. (Feb 24) Peintre Celebre (USA) 137 – Minerva (IRE) (Caerleon (USA) 132) [2009 8m 8.3s p8g^5 Oct 26] well-made gelding: fifth foal: half-brother to 3 winners, including fairly useful 1¼m/1½m winner Valrhona (by Spectrum) and 3-y-o Maverin: dam, unraced, closely related to US Grade 2 11f winner Sword Dance: improved gradually in maidens, fifth to Treasure Town at Lingfield (gelded after): will be well suited by 1¼m+: should do better. *E. A. L. Dunlop* **65 p**

KAI BROON (IRE) 2 b.c. (May 17) Marju (IRE) 127 – Restiv Star (FR) 108 (Soviet Star (USA) 128) [2009 7d 6f^3 6d^5 Aug 27] modest form at best in maidens: soon ridden along (also hung left) final start: should be suited by 1m+. *Miss Lucinda V. Russell* **50**

KAIJAI (IRE) 3 b.f. Trans Island 119 – Consultant Stylist (IRE) (Desert Style (IRE) 121) [2009 –: 10g p11g 11.6m 9m Aug 27] angular filly: little sign of ability: tried visored: tongue tied in 2009. *Mrs L. C. Jewell* **–**

KAIKOURA 3 br.f. High Chaparral (IRE) 132 – Landowska (USA) (Langfuhr (CAN) 124) [2009 –: 7m 12d 7g^5 Jul 3] neat filly: little form, leaving T. Easterby prior to final start. *G. Woodward* **–**

KAI MER (IRE) 4 b.f. Captain Rio 122 – No Shame 56 (Formidable (USA) 125) [2009 –: f8g p9.5g Feb 13] no form: tried in cheekpieces. *Julie Camacho* **–**

KAI MOOK 2 b. or gr.f. (Apr 5) Littletown Boy (USA) – Beenaboutabit 68 (Komaite (USA)) [2009 p5m 7d p7.1g^2 p7f* p7f^5 Dec 20] first foal: dam maiden (best form at 6f): fair performer: won minor event at Lingfield in December: ran creditably in nursery following day: stays 7f: raced mainly on polytrack. *R. Ingram* **73**

KAISER WILLIE (IRE) 3 b.g. Xaar 132 – Miss Bellbird (IRE) (Danehill (USA) 126) [2009 48: p8g 10.2g 10g Jul 26] big, good-topped gelding: maiden, little form: gelded after second start in 2009: tried tongue tied. *B. W. Duke* **–**

KAJIMA 2 b.g. (Apr 2) Oasis Dream 129 – Mambo Mistress (USA) (Kingmambo (USA) 125) [2009 7m^5 7.1m^5 7g Oct 30] 74,000F, 82,000Y: third foal: half-brother to fairly useful French 8.5f winner Bestofthem (by Stormin Fever) and a winner in USA by Peace Rules: dam unraced: fair form in maidens: should stay 1m: gelded after final start. *R. Hannon* **72**

KAKAPUKA 2 br.c. (Mar 8) Shinko Forest (IRE) – No Rehearsal (FR) (Baillamont (USA) 124) [2009 5f 5.1g^3 5.7g^5 p6g 5m^4 6m^6 Oct 5] 18,000F: half-brother to several winners, notably smart 7f (at 2 yrs) to 1½m winner Jelani (by Darshaan): dam, French 8.5f/1¼m winner, out of half-sister to Miesque: fair maiden: well below form in nurseries fourth/final starts: should stay 6f. *Mrs A. L. M. King* **71**

KAKATOSI 2 br.c. (Mar 21) Pastoral Pursuits 127 – Ladywell Blaise (IRE) 63 (Turtle Island (IRE) 123) [2009 7g Oct 30] £25,000Y: third foal: half-brother to 3-y-o Caran- **67 p**

bola and German 7f/1m winner Lukian (by Orpen): dam 6f/7f winner: 66/1 and green, ninth in maiden at Newmarket, hampered early and some headway: should improve. *A. M. Balding*

KALAHARI DESERT (IRE) 2 b.g. (Apr 24) Captain Rio 122 – Sally Traffic 57 (River Falls 113) [2009 5s^4 5d^4 5.4d^4 5m f5g^5 6.1d^3 f6g^4 Oct 27] small gelding: modest maiden: stays 6f: acts on fibresand and good to soft going, probably on good to firm: races prominently: gelded after final start. *R. M. Whitaker* **61**

KALAM DALEEL (IRE) 2 gr.c. (Apr 26) Clodovil (IRE) 116 – Three Days In May 70 (Cadeaux Genereux 131) [2009 5f^3 6s* 7.1g^6 Aug 26] €65,000Y: second living foal: dam, 6f winner, half-sister to useful performer up to 1m Crazee Mental: easily best effort when landing odds in 4-runner maiden at Brighton in May by 15 lengths: still looked green final outing: will prove best up to 7f: remains open to improvement. *M. R. Channon* **91 p**

KALASAM 5 ch.g. Noverre (USA) 125 – Spring Sixpence 60 (Dowsing (USA) 124) [2009 76: 10.3m 10g 10.4v^3 9.2m^3 8m^3 8m^6 9.9m^3 8s^4 10g 10m^4 12d^6 11.9d Sep 15] smallish, strong gelding: fair handicapper: stays 1½m: acts on polytrack, heavy and good to firm ground: tried blinkered. *M. W. Easterby* **71**

KALDOUN KINGDOM (IRE) 4 b.g. King's Best (USA) 132 – Bint Kaldoun (IRE) 82 (Kaldoun (FR) 122) [2009 104: 5g 5m 6m 6g^4 6d^2 6m* 6g* Oct 10] compact gelding: has a scratchy action: useful handicapper: won at Ayr (25-runner William Hill (Ayr) Silver Cup, by neck from Lowther) in September and at York (Coral Sprint Trophy, beat Cheveton by 1¾ lengths) in October: gelded after: best at 6f: acts on heavy and good to firm going: held up. *R. A. Fahey* **108**

KALEO 5 ch.g. Lomitas 129 – Kazoo 108 (Shareef Dancer (USA) 135) [2009 p8g^6 10.1g 10m^6 12g 10.1d^2 9s^5 10.1m* 10.1m^3 10d* 10.1m* Oct 3] useful in Germany for A. Wohler, winning maiden at Bremen at 2 yrs: fairly useful form in Britain in 2009: won claimers at Epsom in August and Lingfield in September, and handicap at Epsom in October: stays 1¼m: acts on good to firm and good to soft ground: often makes running. *S. Dow* **88**

KALHAN SANDS (IRE) 4 b.g. Okawango (USA) 115 – Night Spirit (IRE) 78 (Night Shift (USA)) [2009 77: 7g 7s^6 7d 6d 5g^3 6m^5 5f^5 5.1m 5m p8.6g Oct 23] smallish, strong gelding: fair performer: stays 7f: acts on polytrack and soft ground: none too consistent. *J. J. Quinn* **67**

KALLIGAL 4 br.f. Kyllachy 129 – Anytime Baby 56 (Bairn (USA) 126) [2009 74, a45: p5g^4 5m^6 5.3d^2 5.3m 6g 5.1g 5m 6f^4 Sep 2] smallish, useful-looking filly: maiden handicapper, just modest at 4 yrs: stays 6f: acts on soft and good to firm ground: tried in cheekpieces/blinkers: unreliable. *R. Ingram* **59 §**

KALONI (IRE) 3 b.f. Kalanisi (IRE) 132 – Santarene (IRE) 46 (Scenic 128) [2009 78: 12.4s^4 10.2g^3 10.2g* 10s^4 9.8m* 10.1m 10m^5 Oct 16] good-topped filly: fairly useful performer: won handicaps at Nottingham in July and Ripon in August: ran well in listed races last 2 outings: worth another try at 1½m: acts on polytrack, soft and good to firm going. *Mrs P. Sly* **96**

KALYPSO KING (USA) 2 ch.c. (Apr 14) Giant's Causeway (USA) 132 – Kalypso Katie (IRE) 117 (Fairy King (USA)) [2009 6m^3 6m^3 8g* 8m^2 Oct 16] $45,000Y: small, leggy colt: fourth foal: half-brother to winner in USA by Thunder Gulch: dam, 1m (at 2 yrs)/1¼m (Musidora Stakes) winner, also runner-up in Oaks: useful performer: much improved when winning maiden at Newbury in October impressively by 7 lengths from Centurio, making all: just respectable second to Champagne Style in minor event at Newmarket, going off hard in front: will stay 1¼m: remains capable of better still. *R. Hannon* **105 p**

KAMANJA (UAE) 3 b.f. Red Ransom (USA) – Nasmatt 96 (Danehill (USA) 126) [2009 60p: p7m^4 f6g^3 p7g^3 p8g p8g 7m 7f p6g^6 p7g^5 p7g^6 p8.6g p10m^4 Dec 30] modest maiden: left M. Jarvis 4,000 gns after second start: stays 7f: form only on all-weather: tried in cheekpieces: held up. *M. J. Attwater* **57**

KAMES PARK (IRE) 7 b.g. Desert Sun 120 – Persian Sally (IRE) (Persian Bold 123) [2009 94d: f12s 12.1m^4 11.5g 12.5s p12g^3 p12.2g^3 p12m* p12.2g* Dec 26] lengthy, good-bodied gelding: just fair handicapper nowadays: left I. McInnes after reappearance: won at Kempton and Wolverhampton in December: stays 1¾m: acts on polytrack, soft and good to firm going: tried in blinkers/cheekpieces: held up (often slowly away): ungenuine. *R. C. Guest* **70 §**

KAMMAAN 3 b.f. Diktat 126 – Qasirah (IRE) 97 (Machiavellian (USA) 123) [2009 83p: p6g^2 p7.1g^5 8g^3 7d* 7.6m^6 6.9g^3 Aug 3] good-bodied filly: fairly useful form: improved when winning maiden at Newcastle in June: shaped well when third in handicap at Carlisle final outing: barely stays 1m: acts on good to soft going. *M. A. Jarvis* **85**

KAMSIN (GER) 4 br.c. Samum (GER) 126 – Kapitol (GER) 112 (Winged Love (IRE) 121) [2009 124: 12g* 11g5 12g4 12d4 12d5 Sep 6] strong, lengthy colt: very smart performer in 2008: not quite so good in 2009 (never had ideal conditions), though made all in Gerling-Preis at Cologne (beat Dwilano 1¼ lengths) in April: best effort after when 2¾ lengths fourth to Flamingo Fantasy in Hansa-Preis at Hamburg third start: only fifth of 6 to Getaway in Grosser Preis von Baden final outing (had won race in 2008): stays 1½m: goes well on soft/heavy ground: effective held up/making running. *P. Schiergen, Germany* **117**

KANACE 2 ch.c. (Apr 4) Pastoral Pursuits 127 – Pendulum 82 (Pursuit of Love 124) [2009 p5.1g p6g p5.1m Sep 28] no form in maidens at Wolverhampton. *Ian Williams* **–**

KANAF (IRE) 2 b.c. (Feb 9) Elnadim (USA) 128 – Catcher Applause 45 (Royal Applause 124) [2009 6.1g3 Jun 11] €20,000F, £50,000Y: third foal: dam, ran twice in Ireland, out of useful 1m winner Pfalz: 28/1, encouraging length third to Aerodynamic in maiden at Nottingham, slowly away and meeting trouble, not unduly knocked about: should improve. *E. A. L. Dunlop* **83 p**

KANDIDATE 7 b.h. Kabool 119 – Valleyrose (IRE) (Royal Academy (USA) 130) [2009 113: p10g6 f11g* p10g4 p10g p10g2 8.1g 10f 10.4m 10.4m p12m 10m Sep 19] strong, good-topped horse: had a quick action: impressed in appearance: smart performer at his best, successful 10 times, including 2 Group 3 events, and in handicap at Southwell in February: best effort in 2009 when ½-length second to Dansant in listed race at Kempton: out of sorts later in year: stayed easy 1½m: acted on all-weather/dirt and firm going: tried blinkered: formerly tongue tied: to stand at Haras de la Rousseliere, France, fee €1,500, live foal. *C. E. Brittain* **100 a112**

KANGRINA 7 b.m. Acatenango (GER) 127 – Kirona 107 (Robellino (USA) 127) [2009 70: f16g5 p16.5g Jan 22] big, good-bodied mare: handicapper: just poor form on Flat in 2009 (poor hurdler): stays 1½m: acts on all-weather and good to firm going. *George Baker* **49**

KANKAN PRINCE (IRE) 2 b.c. (Mar 7) Arakan (USA) 123 – Risanda (Kris 135) [2009 5.2g Aug 12] 12/1, slowly away and always behind in seller at Yarmouth. *M. G. Quinlan* **–**

KANNON 4 b.f. Kyllachy 129 – Violet (IRE) 77 (Mukaddamah (USA) 125) [2009 72: p8.6g5 p7g p8g p7.1g 7m 7m p8.6g6 12s f6g Dec 18] sturdy filly: handicapper: modest form in 2009 only on return: left I. McInnes prior to final start: stays 8.6f: acts on polytrack, soft and good to firm ground: tried visored/in cheekpieces. *A. J. McCabe* **57**

KANPAI (IRE) 7 br.g. Trans Island 119 – David's Star (Welsh Saint 126) [2009 70: 17.1m Sep 17] angular gelding: fair handicapper at best on Flat, well held only outing in 2009: useful hurdler/fairly useful winner over fences: effective with/without visor: dead. *J. G. M. O'Shea* **–**

KANSAI SPIRIT (IRE) 3 ch.c. Sinndar (IRE) 134 – Daanat Nawal (Machiavellian (USA) 123) [2009 78: 10g3 10f3 p12f Sep 4] good-topped colt: fairly useful maiden: said to have finished lame on handicap debut final start: stays 1¼m: acts on polytrack and firm going. *J. H. M. Gosden* **83**

KANSAS GOLD 6 b.g. Alhaarth (IRE) 126 – Star Tulip 99 (Night Shift (USA)) [2009 65: p9.5g a6g* a6g2 a6.8g 6m* 8g3 6.8g2 6g3 6g 7d a6g Oct 22] well-made gelding: modest handicapper: sold from J. Mackie £1,200 after reappearance: won at Taby in April and Gothenberg in June: stays 9.5f: acts on polytrack/dirt and firm going: blinkered for current stable, formerly tried visored/in cheekpieces. *Catharina Vang, Sweden* **?**

KAOLAK (USA) 3 b. or br.c. Action This Day (USA) 121 – Cerita (USA) (Magesterial (USA) 116) [2009 81+: p8g p8g4 8.3m4 8m4 10m 12d5 8.5g4 10g2 8g* 8m2 9g* 8m* 10.3m5 9m Oct 3] big, workmanlike colt: useful handicapper: much improved to win at Newmarket and Goodwood (twice, beat Truism by nose second occasion) in August/September: best at 1m/9f: acts on polytrack and good to firm going: usually visored: front runner. *J. Ryan* **103**

KAPELAD JUNIOR (IRE) 2 gr.g. (Apr 1) Clodovil (IRE) 116 – Prosaic Star (IRE) 81 (Common Grounds 118) [2009 5.7g 6m* p6g5 6d 6.1s p7.1g6 f7g6 Nov 17] small, sturdy gelding: modest performer: won seller at Redcar in August: stays easy 7f: acts on polytrack and good to firm ground: blinkered (below form) final start. *Pat Eddery* **57**

KAPPALYN (IRE) 4 b.f. Marju (IRE) 127 – Miss Tardy (JPN) (Lammtarra (USA) 134) [2009 50: p7g p6g May 20] sparely-made filly: maiden: no form in 2009: raced at 6f/7f. *J. R. Boyle* **–**

KAPSILIAT (IRE) 3 b.f. Cape Cross (IRE) 129 – Kootenay (IRE) 109 (Selkirk (USA) 129) [2009 56p: 8m^3 9g^4 p10g^4 10m Aug 9] rangy filly: has scope: fair maiden: stays 1¼m: acts on polytrack: sent to USA. *J. Noseda* 76

KAPTAIN KIRKUP (IRE) 2 ch.c. (Jan 20) Captain Rio 122 – Aquatint (Dansili 127) [2009 6s* 6m* 6d* 6d^6 6m^2 Oct 3] £15,000Y: strong colt: first foal: dam unraced half-sister to useful 9f and 1½m winner Marani, out of close relation to St Leger winner Toulon: useful performer: won first 3 starts, namely maiden in May and minor event in June, both at Newcastle, and nursery at Haydock in July: creditable efforts after, 4 lengths second to Lucky Like in listed race at Redcar: should stay 7f: acts on soft and good to firm going: reliable. *M. Dods* 95

KARABURAN (GER) 5 ch.g. Samum (GER) 126 – Kimora (GER) (Dashing Blade 117) [2009 –: 13.1d Aug 27] ex-German gelding: maiden: no form for current stable, including over hurdles: tried visored. *P. Monteith* –

KARAKA JACK 2 ch.c. (Mar 11) Pivotal 124 – Mauri Moon 104 (Green Desert (USA) 127) [2009 6m^4 7m 7g* f7f* Oct 21] 150,000Y: strong colt: fourth foal: brother to fairly useful 2007 2-y-o 7f winner Shamayel and half-brother to 2 winners, including 2008 2-y-o 1m winner Kiwi Moon (by Nayef): dam, 6f (at 2 yrs) to 1m winner, half-sister to useful French 1¼m performer All Glory: most progressive, winning maiden at York and nursery at Southwell (not extended, beat Stef And Stelio 8 lengths) in October: stays 7f: already useful, and open to further improvement. *M. Johnston* 96 p

KARAMOJO BELL 2 b.c. (Apr 13) Selkirk (USA) 129 – Shabby Chic (USA) 114 (Red Ransom (USA)) [2009 8g^5 8m^6 10m Oct 5] well-made colt: best effort in maidens when sixth to Coordinated Cut at Doncaster: broke down next time: dead. *T. P. Tate* 73

KARASHAR (IRE) 4 b.g. Kalanisi (IRE) 132 – Karaliyfa (IRE) 89 (Kahyasi 130) [2009 71: p7g p13g^4 p13.9g Nov 20] compact colt: fair maiden: stays 1¾m: acts on polytrack and soft ground: fair hurdler. *Evan Williams* 74

KARATE QUEEN 4 b.f. King's Best (USA) 132 – Black Belt Shopper (IRE) 82 (Desert Prince (IRE) 130) [2009 60: 6m 6m 8f Jul 2] close-coupled filly: maiden: no form in 2009: tried tongue tied. *R. E. Barr* –

KARGALI (IRE) 4 gr.c. Invincible Spirit (IRE) 121 – Karliyka (IRE) (Last Tycoon 131) [2009 111p: 7s^3 8d* 10v 10s^4 Jun 6] tall, lengthy colt: smart performer: best effort when winning listed race at Leopardstown in April by 1¼ lengths from Three Rocks: found to have suffered a quarter crack after third outing: may prove best short of 1¼m: acts on heavy ground: wears tongue tie: sold €51,000, joined Luke Comer, Ireland. *John M. Oxx, Ireland* 113

KARGAN (IRE) 4 b.g. Intikhab (USA) 135 – Karkiyla (IRE) (Darshaan 133) [2009 66: p8.6g^3 p8.6g^2 7.1m^2 7g^3 7.1m^4 7.1m^4 7.2g* 7.1g^3 8.5m^3 8.1d* 10d^5 Sep 16] sturdy gelding: fair handicapper: improved in 2009, winning at Ayr in July and, having left A. G. Foster after eighth start, Chepstow in September: stays 1m: acts on polytrack, soft and good to firm going: held up. *R. A. Farrant* 76

KARKY SCHULTZ (GER) 4 gr.g. Diktat 126 – Kazoo 108 (Shareef Dancer (USA) 135) [2009 68d: p12g p11g* 10.9g^2 p16g 11.5g^3 Jul 20] leggy gelding: fair handicapper: won at Kempton in June: stays 11.5f: acts on polytrack and soft going: tried blinkered: has looked hard ride: fair form over hurdles. *J. M. P. Eustace* 68

KARMEI 4 b.g. Royal Applause 124 – Lafite 100 (Robellino (USA) 127) [2009 60: p9.5g^3 p9.5g p8.6m 11.5g 10.2m^5 10.9d^6 12m Jun 26] smallish, robust gelding: maiden handicapper: just poor in 2009: stays 9.5f: acts on polytrack and firm going. *R. Curtis* 48

KARMEST 5 ch.m. Best of The Bests (IRE) 122 – Karmafair (IRE) (Always Fair (USA) 121) [2009 79: p12.2g p12.2g^3 f11g^3 12m 9.2g 12d f12g Jul 27] good-topped mare: fair handicapper: stays 1½m: acts on all-weather and soft ground: tried visored/ blinkered: has carried head awkwardly. *A. D. Brown* 71

KAROUSH (USA) 4 b. or br.c. Gone West (USA) – Victorica (USA) (Exbourne (USA) 125) [2009 84: 8.3f^4 Aug 17] strong, rangy colt: maiden: fairly useful form at 3 yrs: better than result sole start in 2009: should be suited by 1m: sent to Saudi Arabia. *Sir Michael Stoute* 68 +

KARTA (IRE) 3 br.f. Diktat 126 – Echo River (USA) 101 (Irish River (FR) 131) [2009 f7g^6 f8g^2 7g^4 9d 8.5g^2 8.5g^2 7s^5 7.5g^3 8s Nov 13] second foal: half-sister to 5-y-o Ravi River: dam 2-y-o 6f/7f winner: fair maiden: sold from M. Johnston 6,500 gns after third start: stays 8.5f: resold €7,500 after final outing. *H-A. Pantall, France* 73

Qatar Prix Gladiateur, Longchamp—Kasbah Bliss (No.2) produces a strong late burst to claim a second successive win in this Group 3; Pointilliste fills the runner-up spot

KASAA ED 3 b.f. Marju (IRE) 127 – Muwajaha 87 (Night Shift (USA)) [2009 68p: 6m 6m 9.3g Jun 1] strong filly: regressive form in maidens: best effort at 7f on good to soft going: nervous sort, attended by stable hand at outing. *M. Johnston* **51**

KASBAH BLISS (FR) 7 b.g. Kahyasi 130 – Marital Bliss (FR) (Double Bed (FR) 121) [2009 118: 15.5g 12.5m³ 15.5g* 20g² 12g³ Dec 13] strong, workmanlike gelding: top-class staying hurdler: very smart performer on Flat: reportedly finished distressed in Prix de Barbeville at Longchamp on return to Flat in April, but back to form when winning Qatar Prix Gladiateur at Longchamp in September for second successive year, beating Pointilliste by ¾ length, denied clear run for much of straight: good efforts last 2 starts, short-head second to Alandi in Prix du Cadran at Longchamp (more to do than winner) and close third to Daryakana in Hong Kong Vase at Sha Tin, staying on well both times: finds 1½m a minimum and stays 2½m: acts on heavy and good to firm going: usually held up, and has good turn of foot. *F. Doumen, France* **122**

KASBAN 5 b.g. Kingmambo (USA) 125 – Ebaraya (IRE) 82 (Sadler's Wells (USA) 132) [2009 84: 14m 13.3m 16.4m* 16g⁴ 21g Jul 29] compact gelding: fairly useful handicapper: won at Folkestone in June: stays 2m: acts on soft and good to firm ground: in cheekpieces/tongue tie last 3 starts. *Ian Williams* **80**

KASHIMIN (IRE) 4 b.g. Kyllachy 129 – Oh So Misty (Teenoso (USA) 135) [2009 88: 6g³ 6g³ 6m⁵ 6m 6g⁵ 7g p7.1g² 7v p7.1g Dec 3] lengthy gelding: fairly useful handicapper: stays 7f: acts on polytrack, good to firm and good to soft ground: tried blinkered. *G. A. Swinbank* **88**

KASHMINA 4 ch.f. Dr Fong (USA) 128 – Lady Melbourne (IRE) 76 (Indian Ridge 123) [2009 67§: 11.7m 10g* 10m p10g p12m⁵ p16m Dec 30] sturdy, lengthy filly: fair handicapper: won at Windsor in June: stays 1½m: acts on polytrack, firm and soft going: fair winning hurdler. *Miss S. West* **70**

KASHUBIAN QUEST 3 b.g. Rainbow Quest (USA) 134 – Kartuzy (JPN) 82 (Polish Precedent (USA) 131) [2009 10.2d Oct 15] 20,000Y: good-bodied gelding: 80/1, very backward when in rear in maiden at Nottingham: sold £800. *D. R. Lanigan* **–**

KASPIRIT (IRE) 2 b.f. (Apr 14) Invincible Spirit (IRE) 121 – Kathy Kab (IRE) (Intikhab (USA) 135) [2009 5m² 5.2m* 5.5d³ 6m² 5m² 5m 5g* 6d 6g Nov 22] €34,000Y: second foal: dam, Italian maiden, half-sister to useful Italian sprinters Kathy College and Kathy Pekan: fairly useful performer: won maiden at Yarmouth in May and (having left M. Wigham after good third in listed race at Rome) minor event at Milan in September: well held last 2 starts: best around 5f: acts on good to firm and good to soft ground. *G. Colella, Italy* **88**

KASSUTA 5 b.m. Kyllachy 129 – Happy Omen (Warning 136) [2009 –: 8m^{2} 8s^{3} 8m^{3} p9.5g 8d^{3} Oct 22] compact mare: modest performer: stays 1m: acts on polytrack, heavy and good to firm going: formerly in headgear: difficult ride. *R. M. H. Cowell* **56**

KATCHMORE (IRE) 2 br.g. (Mar 1) Catcher In The Rye (IRE) 115 – One For Me 62 (Tragic Role (USA)) [2009 8.1m p9.5g p7g^{2} Dec 31] best effort in maidens when 2¼ lengths second to Cuthbert at Lingfield: should stay beyond 7f. *Jean-Rene Auvray* **66**

KATEHARI (IRE) 2 b.f. (Feb 2) Noverre (USA) 125 – Katariya (IRE) 58 (Barathea (IRE) 127) [2009 7g 6m* 5.7m^{6} 6m^{3} Oct 1] €9,500F, 38,000Y: sturdy filly: first foal: dam twice-raced half-sister to 4-y-o Katiyra: fairly useful performer: won maiden at Windsor in August by neck from Flip Flop: very good 1¼ lengths third to Chips O'Toole in nursery at Goodwood: should be suited by 7f+. *A. M. Balding* **80**

KATE SKATE 2 ch.f. (Apr 14) Mark of Esteem (IRE) 137 – Saristar 93 (Starborough 126) [2009 5.1g^{6} 5m 5.1m^{2} 5m^{*dis} 6f p6g^{6} 8m^{6} p7m^{5} p6f Oct 14] leggy filly: first foal: dam 5f (at 2 yrs)/6f winner: fair performer: first past post in seller at Goodwood in May (claimed from P. Cole £13,000, subsequently failed dope test and disqualified): below form after: best efforts at 5f: acts on good to firm going. *Miss Gay Kelleway* **65**

KATE THE GREAT 3 b.f. Xaar 132 – Ros The Boss (IRE) 80 (Danehill (USA) 126) [2009 79: 6g 5m Jun 13] leggy filly: shaped as though amiss both starts in 2009. *C. G. Cox* **–**

KATHANIKKI GIRL (IRE) 3 b.f. Tagula (IRE) 116 – Tenalist (IRE) 69 (Tenby 125) [2009 –: p8.6g 8m 7m Jun 25] little sign of ability. *Mrs L. Williamson* **–**

KATHINDI (IRE) 2 ch.c. (Mar 21) Pearl of Love (IRE) 112 – Turfcare Flight (IRE) 64 (Mujadil (USA) 119) [2009 p6g^{3} p7g^{3} 6m p8m^{3} p7g^{3} Dec 31] sturdy colt: fair maiden: bred to stay beyond 1m: acts on polytrack. *J. S. Moore* **68**

KATHLEEN COX (IRE) 4 ch.f. Alhaarth (IRE) 126 – Gintilgalla (IRE) (Grand Lodge (USA) 125) [2009 –: p9.5g Nov 13] maiden: little form. *D. Loughnane, Ireland* **–**

KATHLEEN FRANCES 2 b.f. (Feb 16) Sakhee (USA) 136 – Trew Class 99 (Inchinor 119) [2009 8d Oct 27] first foal: dam 1¼m winner: 100/1 and very green, 7½ lengths seventh to Bullet Train in maiden at Yarmouth, late headway: should stay 1¼m. *M. H. Tompkins* **61**

KATIE GIRL 3 b.f. Makbul 104 – Katie Komaite 54 (Komaite (USA)) [2009 –: p8.6g^{5} 9d^{6} 9.2g 10.3g^{6} 12g 12d^{4} 9.9g f11g^{6} 12.4d 15.8g p9.5g^{4} p8.6g Dec 14] small filly: modest maiden handicapper: stays 1¼m: acts on good to soft ground: in cheekpieces of late: quirky and none too consistent. *Mrs G. S. Rees* **52**

KATIE KINGFISHER 5 b.m. Fraam 114 – Sonic Sapphire 67 (Royal Academy (USA) 130) [2009 46: f11g p10g Feb 18] poor maiden: stays 1¾m: acts on all-weather: in cheekpieces/blinkers nowadays. *T. T. Clement* **43**

KATIE THE HATTER (IRE) 3 b.f. Celtic Swing 138 – Kathleen's Dream (USA) (Last Tycoon 131) [2009 p7g p8f Dec 20] €16,000F, 15,000Y: tall filly: seventh foal: half-sister to useful 6f (in France at 2 yrs) to 8.5f (in US) winner Castor Troy (by Ali-Royal): dam unraced: modest form in polytrack maidens. *Mike Murphy* **62**

KATIYRA (IRE) 4 b.f. Peintre Celebre (USA) 137 – Katiykha (IRE) 117 (Darshaan 133) [2009 118: 10d^{5} 9.9d^{6} Aug 1] lengthy, angular filly: smart at 3 yrs: just useful form both starts in 2009, in Pretty Polly Stakes at the Curragh (3½ lengths fifth to Dar Re Mi) and Nassau Stakes at Goodwood (sixth to Midday): best efforts at 1¼m: acts on soft going: sometimes blanketed for stall entry. *John M. Oxx, Ireland* **108**

KATTAR 3 ch.c. Singspiel (IRE) 133 – Lady Zonda 95 (Lion Cavern (USA) 117) [2009 62+: 10m^{6} 9.7m^{4} 8.5g^{4} Jul 30] attractive colt: modest maiden at 2 yrs: well held in handicaps in 2009: tried tongue tied. *D. M. Simcock* **–**

KATYA KABANOVA 3 b.f. Sadler's Wells (USA) 132 – Kiftsgate Rose (FR) (Nashwan (USA) 135) [2009 10.3s p12g^{6} 11.8g Sep 14] 85,000F: second foal: dam unraced half-sister to smart French performer up to 12.5f Kentucky Rose: no form in maidens. *J. R. Fanshawe* **–**

KATY'S SECRET 2 b.f. (Feb 23) Mind Games 121 – Katy O'Hara 76 (Komaite (USA)) [2009 p6g^{2} p6g Dec 18] first foal: dam 2-y-o 5f/6f winner: much better effort in maidens at Wolverhampton when ¾-length second to Wellmarked. *W. Jarvis* **69**

KAVACHI (IRE) 6 b.g. Cadeaux Genereux 131 – Answered Prayer (Green Desert (USA) 127) [2009 94: 8m^{4} 10.1g 10m^{2} 8.1m^{3} 8.9g* 8m 8g 10m 10g Oct 10] workmanlike gelding: useful handicapper: better than ever when winning at York (beat Albaqaa by neck) in June: below form after: stays 1¼m: acts on firm and soft going: held up. *G. L. Moore* **97**

KAVAK 2 ch.c. (Apr 12) Dubawi (IRE) 129 – Kelang (Kris 135) [2009 7m^4 7s^6 p8m* **94 p**
Aug 8] 36,000 2-y-o: compact, useful-looking colt: half-brother to several winners abroad, including useful French/Italian 1m/1¼m winner Bukat Timah (by Inchinor): dam ran once in Italy: easily best effort in maidens when winning at Lingfield impressively by 4½ lengths from Navy List: stays 1m: acts on polytrack (promise on good to firm going/ well held on soft): hung left first/final starts: sent to Hong Kong, where renamed Outdoor Pegasus: useful prospect. *M. Botti*

KAVALOTI (IRE) 5 b.g. Kahyasi 130 – Just As Good (FR) (Kaldounevees (FR) 118) **84**
[2009 p16g^4 p16g^2 p16g^2 p16g* p16g* p16g Jul 1] good-topped gelding: fairly useful handicapper: won twice at Kempton in April: stays 2m: acts on polytrack, raced only on good going or softer on turf: usually blinkered nowadays. *G. L. Moore*

KAYAK (SAF) 7 b.g. Western Winter (USA) 116 – Donya (SAF) (Elliodor (FR) 114) **84**
[2009 96, a103: p8g Jan 17] tall gelding: fairly useful handicapper: just respectable effort sole start in 2009: stays 1½m: acts on all-weather, soft and good to firm going: tried blinkered: races prominently: not straightforward. *D. M. Simcock*

KAYCEEBEE 3 b.g. Cyrano de Bergerac 120 – Twice Upon A Time 79 (Primo Domi- **33**
nie 121) [2009 56: 5.1g 5.1f^6 Jun 5] sturdy gelding: poor maiden: free-going sort, best kept to 5f/6f: tried blinkered. *R. M. Beckett*

KAYF ARAMIS 7 b.g. Kayf Tara 130 – Ara (Birthright) [2009 80: 18g* 16g^5 20m^6 **95**
Jun 16] plain gelding: useful handicapper: won at York in May by 13 lengths from Rose Bien, coasting home: just respectable efforts after at Goodwood and Royal Ascot: stays 21f well: acts on soft and good to firm ground: tried in cheekpieces: races prominently: consistent: useful hurdler, joined N. Twiston-Davies. *Miss Venetia Williams*

KAYFIAR (USA) 3 ch.c. Lion Heart (USA) 124 – Ivor Jewel (USA) (Sir Ivor (USA) **63**
135) [2009 64: 9.9g^6 12m^6 10m 10s Aug 7] workmanlike colt: modest maiden: should stay 1¼m: tried blinkered. *P. F. I. Cole*

KAY GEE BE (IRE) 5 b.g. Fasliyev (USA) 120 – Pursuit of Truth (USA) 69 (Irish **99**
River (FR) 131) [2009 103: 9m^3 10m 8m^3 8m^5 8g^2 8m 8m^6 9m Oct 3] tall, good-topped gelding: useful performer: in-and-out form in 2009, best efforts when runner-up in minor event at Newmarket and sixth in handicap at Doncaster: stays 9f: yet to race on firm going, acts on any other turf and polytrack. *W. Jarvis*

KAYSTAR RIDGE 4 b.g. Tumbleweed Ridge 117 – Kayartis 57 (Kaytu 112) [2009 **64 d**
66: p6g^2 p6g p6g f6g p6g 6g 8g^3 p9.5g 10.1m^6 Sep 16] workmanlike gelding: modest handicapper: below form after reappearance: should stay 7f: acts on polytrack: tried in cheekpieces, often blinkered/tongue tied: none too consistent. *D. K. Ivory*

KAY TWO (IRE) 7 ch.g. Monashee Mountain (USA) 115 – Tricky 66 (Song 132) **93**
[2009 97, a81: 5d^5 5d^2 5m 5v^4 5.1m^3 5m 5g Oct 10] neat gelding: fairly useful handi- **a–**
capper, better on turf: reportedly bled final 2 starts in 2009: best at 5f: acts on all-weather and any turf going: tried blinkered: wears cheekpieces: races prominently. *R. J. Price*

KAZBOW (IRE) 3 b.g. Rainbow Quest (USA) 134 – Kasota (IRE) 72 (Alzao (USA) **81**
117) [2009 –p: 9.9m p12.2g^2 p12.2g^2 p12m^2 p12m* Nov 29] good-bodied gelding: fairly useful form: runner-up in handicaps prior to landing odds in maiden at Kempton in November: will be well suited by 1¾m+: acts on polytrack: races prominently. *L. M. Cumani*

KEELUNG (USA) 8 b.g. Lear Fan (USA) 130 – Miss Universal (IRE) 107 (Lycius **–**
(USA) 124) [2009 82: 13g 17.1g Jun 8] lengthy, good-topped gelding: fairly useful handicapper at best: well held in 2009: tried in cheekpieces: dead. *R. Ford*

KEEN AS MUSTARD 4 ch.g. Keen 116 – Dark Dolores 49 (Inchinor 119) [2009 **44**
p9.5g p8g^5 p8.6g p8.6g^5 8g 10f^6 10.2m Jun 3] poor maiden: stays 1¼m. *M. D. I. Usher*

KEEN BIDDER 2 ch.c. (Feb 24) Auction House (USA) 120 – Lady-Love 70 (Pursuit **80**
of Love 124) [2009 6v 6g 7m^4 7g* 7d^4 7d^4 7g^4 7m^3 8g^3 Oct 23] £11,000Y, resold £18,000Y: sturdy colt: fourth foal: brother to 5-y-o Party Palace and half-brother to 6-y-o Moody Tunes: dam 2-y-o 5f winner: fairly useful performer: won nursery at Newmarket (flashed tail) in July: good third to Antoniola in similar event at Doncaster final start: will stay 1¼m+: acts on good to firm and good to soft going: sold 40,000 gns, sent to USA. *D. M. Simcock*

KEENES DAY (FR) 4 gr.g. Daylami (IRE) 138 – Key Academy 103 (Royal Academy **102**
(USA) 130) [2009 101: p16g* 20m 16.1d 16g^4 13.4m^5 17.2m^4 16m^4 18m Oct 17] tall, good-bodied gelding: useful performer: won handicap at Lingfield in April: best effort when 1½ lengths fourth to Electrolyser in listed race at Ascot seventh start: stays 2m: acts on all-weather and good to firm going (seemingly not good to soft). *M. Johnston*

KEENES ROYALE 2 b.f. (Apr 15) Red Ransom (USA) – Kinnaird (IRE) 113 (Dr Devious (IRE) 127) [2009 7g 7m 8.3v^6 Nov 4] tall, good-topped filly: first foal: dam 6f (at 2 yrs) to 1¼m (Prix de l'Opera) winner: modest form in maidens: bred to stay 1¼m: tongue tied last 2 starts: remains open to improvement. *P. C. Haslam* **51 p**

KEEN WARRIOR 9 gr.g. Keen 116 – Briden (Minster Son 130) [2009 f11g Feb 20] fair hurdler: well held in maiden at Southwell on Flat debut. *Mrs S. Lamyman* **–**

KEEP DANCING (IRE) 3 ch.f. Distant Music (USA) 126 – Miss Indigo 62 (Indian Ridge 123) [2009 67: p5g^3 5.1m^6 5.1d^3 6.1g 5m^4 5.5g* 6g^5 5m^6 p6g 6g Oct 19] rather leggy filly: fair performer: easily best effort when winning handicap at Warwick in July: may prove best at 6f: acts on polytrack, soft and good to firm ground: in cheekpieces nowadays. *A. M. Balding* **77**

KEEPHOLDIN (IRE) 4 b.g. King's Best (USA) 132 – Dafariyna (IRE) 71 (Nashwan (USA) 135) [2009 p12m p11g Oct 22] no form over hurdles: well held in maidens. *N. P. Mulholland* **–**

KEEP ICY CALM (IRE) 3 br.f. One Cool Cat (USA) 123 – Alazima (USA) 64 (Riverman (USA) 131) [2009 66: p6g^6 p5g^4 Jan 16] modest maiden: stays 6f: raced only on polytrack: tried blinkered: sent to South Africa. *W. J. Haggas* **59**

KEEP RINGING (USA) 3 b. or br.f. More Than Ready (USA) 120 – No Knocks (USA) (A P Indy (USA) 131) [2009 p6g^6 p7g^3 p8.6g* p8g^4 Apr 15] $50,000Y, resold €70,000Y: second foal: half-sister to winner in USA by Fusaichi Pegasus: dam unraced half-sister to Kentucky Derby winner Go For Gin and high-class US performer up to 1¼m Pleasant Tap: fair performer: won maiden at Wolverhampton (dead-heated) in March: stays 8.6f: raced only on polytrack: held up: sent to South Africa. *W. J. Haggas* **76**

KEEPSGETTINGBETTER (IRE) 4 b.g. Modigliani (USA) 106 – Adua (IRE) 76 (Kenmare (FR) 125) [2009 68: p8.6g^5 p9.5g Feb 9] maiden: just modest form in 2009: stays 8.6f: raced on polytrack: tried blinkered. *J. R. Gask* **60**

KEEP SILENT 2 gr.f. (Mar 11) Largesse 112 – Not A Word (Batshoof 122) [2009 6m 6m Oct 26] close-coupled filly: fifth foal: sister to Scandinavian sprinter Not Secret and 1m winner Milton's Keen: dam unraced: well held in maidens. *W. J. H. Ratcliffe* **–**

KEEPTHEBOATAFLOAT (USA) 3 b.g. Fusaichi Pegasus (USA) 130 – The Perfect Life (IRE) 106 (Try My Best (USA) 130) [2009 85: a7g 7.5g p9g 12m^2 10.1m^4 Aug 20] neat gelding: fairly useful performer at best: trained by K. R. Burke prior to final outing: stays 7f: acts on polytrack: tried blinkered. *A. P. Jarvis* **85 d**

KEFALONIA (USA) 3 gr. or ro.f. Mizzen Mast (USA) 121 – Zante 108 (Zafonic (USA) 130) [2009 p8g^2 9m^5 p8.6g^4 p10m* Aug 8] third living foal: dam, 1m (including in USA)/1¼m winner, out of half-sister to champion 1997 2-y-o Xaar: fair form in maidens: best effort when winning at Lingfield in August: stays 1¼m: acts on polytrack: sold 7,500 gns in December. *B. W. Hills* **72**

KEIBLA SPIRIT 3 b.f. Auction House (USA) 120 – Rave On (ITY) 73 (Barathea (IRE) 127) [2009 6m p7m^4 7f^6 p6m p7m p7m Dec 9] lengthy, angular filly: third foal: sister to 7f winner Hit The Roof: dam, maiden, half-sister to useful Italian performer up to 1¼m Lady Bi: maiden: modest form only on second start: stays 7f. *R. Ingram* **53**

KEISHA KAYLEIGH (IRE) 6 b.m. Almutawakel 126 – Awtaar (USA) 67 (Lyphard (USA) 132) [2009 82: p9.5g 8m^4 9m^3 f12g^5 9.9g^5 10.1m* 10.1d^3 9g^4 10s^3 9.1d* Aug 27] leggy mare: fair performer: won seller at Newcastle in June and handicap at Ayr in August: stays 1¼m: acts on polytrack, soft and good to firm ground: formerly wore headgear: held up (often slowly away). *B. Ellison* **78**

KEITHSHAZEL (IRE) 2 b.f. (Feb 15) Fasliyev (USA) 120 – La Poterie (FR) (Bering 136) [2009 5d 5.1g f5g 7g Oct 16] small filly: first foal: dam French maiden half-sister to smart US Grade 1 9f winner Sicy d'Alsace: no form: left Garry Moss after third start. *R. C. Guest* **–**

KELAMON 5 b.g. Keltos (FR) 132 – Faraway Moon 61 (Distant Relative 128) [2009 85: p5.1g^4 6m 6m 5g 6m p6m f6g Nov 17] small, sturdy gelding: fair handicapper: well below form after reappearance: effective at 5f to easy 7f: acts on all-weather, heavy and good to firm going: tongue tied once. *S. C. Williams* **77 d**

KELEYF BYON BELIEF (IRE) 2 ch.f. (Apr 21) Kheleyf (USA) 116 – Carrozzina 70 (Vettori (IRE) 119) [2009 p8g 8m 7d Oct 26] fourth foal: half-sister to 4-y-o Solent Ridge: dam 2-y-o 7f winner: well held in maidens, leaving Edgar Byrne after second start. *J. C. McConnell, Ireland* **–**

KELLYS EYE (IRE) 2 b.g. (Mar 15) Noverre (USA) 125 – Limit (IRE) 69 (Barathea (IRE) 127) [2009 6d^{4} 6m^{2} 6g^{5} Oct 19] 24,000Y: compact gelding: first foal: dam temperamental 2-y-o 7f winner: best effort in maidens when 6 lengths second to Amitola at Ayr: should stay 7f+: gelded after final start. *B. Smart* **73**

KENAAYA (FR) 3 b. or br.f. Monsun (GER) 124 – Jindy's Dream (USA) (A P Indy (USA) 131) [2009 10m Jun 11] €300,000Y: first foal: dam, ran twice in France, out of US Grade 2 6f/7f winner J J'sdream: 7½ lengths seventh to Hidden Brief in maiden at Newbury, outpaced: sold €16,000. *J. H. M. Gosden* **67**

KENAI 4 ch.g. Arkadian Hero (USA) 123 – Hicklam Millie 49 (Absalom 128) [2009 64: p9.5g p6g^{5} Mar 26] sturdy gelding: maiden: well held both starts in 2009: tried in blinkers/cheekpieces. *W. K. Goldsworthy* **–**

KENDALEWOOD 3 b.g. Viking Ruler (AUS) – Wilsonic 78 (Damister (USA) 123) [2009 10.2m 10g 10.1d May 15] no show in maidens. *T. D. Walford* **–**

KENSEI (IRE) 2 ch.g. (Apr 29) Peintre Celebre (USA) 137 – Journey of Hope (USA) 95 (Slew O' Gold (USA)) [2009 7m^{3} 7.6d^{5} p7m^{2} p8.6g^{6} Oct 23] €65,000F: rather leggy gelding: closely related to 2 winners, including useful Irish 1¼m winner Dream To Dress (by Theatrical), later successful in USA, and half-sister to 2 winners, including Irish 1½m winner Anticipated Move (by Silver Hawk): dam 6f (at 2 yrs in Ireland) to 8.5f (in USA): fair maiden: below form in nursery, gelded after: will stay 1¼m+. *R. M. Beckett* **72**

KEN'S GIRL 5 ch.m. Ishiguru (USA) 114 – There's Two (IRE) 85 (Ashkalani (IRE) 128) [2009 72: 7.1g 7m^{5} 7m^{2} 7m^{2} 7.1v^{2} 7.1m 7m^{6} 6d Oct 12] tall, leggy mare: fair handicapper: best at 7f nowadays: acts on polytrack and any turf going: tried in cheekpieces: front runner. *W. S. Kittow* **78**

KENSINGTON (IRE) 8 b.g. Cape Cross (IRE) 129 – March Star (IRE) 109 (Mac's Imp (USA) 116) [2009 81: p8g^{5} p7.1g^{3} p7.1g p8g f7g^{3} p7.1g^{3} p7.1g^{2} f7g^{5} 6g p7.1g^{5} f6m p7.1g^{5} p7f^{3} p7m Dec 30] leggy gelding: fairly useful handicapper: left P. D. Evans after ninth start: best at 7f nowadays: acts on all-weather, firm and good to soft ground: often wears headgear. *A. J. McCabe* **80**

KENSINGTON OVAL 4 b.g. Sadler's Wells (USA) 132 – Request 87 (Rainbow Quest (USA) 134) [2009 91p: 10m^{3} 12g^{3} f12g^{2} Aug 10] strong, well-made gelding: fairly useful performer: good placed efforts in handicaps all starts in 2009: stays 1½m: acts on fibresand, good to firm and good to soft going: joined Jonjo O'Neill, little impact over hurdles. *Sir Michael Stoute* **93**

KENSWICK 2 b.f. (Jan 14) Avonbridge 123 – The Jotter 99 (Night Shift (USA)) [2009 6.1d^{4} 6m^{6} p6g Nov 9] 14,000Y: seventh foal: half-sister to several winners, including useful 1999 2-y-o 6f winner Final Row (by Indian Ridge), later successful in USA, and fairly useful 7f/1m winner Out For A Stroll (by Zamindar): dam 2-y-o 5f/6.5f winner: easily best effort in maidens when fourth at Nottingham. *Pat Eddery* **59**

KENTAVR'S DREAM 6 b.m. Robellino (USA) 127 – Very Good (Noalto 120) [2009 –: p10g Jan 13] small, leggy mare: little form. *P. Howling* **–**

KENTUCKY BOY (IRE) 5 b.g. Distant Music (USA) 126 – Delta Town (USA) (Sanglamore (USA) 126) [2009 64: f14g 18m^{6} Apr 7] good-bodied gelding: lightly-raced handicapper: well held in 2009: stays 17f: acts on polytrack and soft ground: tried in cheekpieces. *Jedd O'Keeffe* **–**

KENTUCKY LAKES 3 b.g. Generous (IRE) 139 – Inya Lake 101 (Whittingham (IRE) 104) [2009 7m 7.5m^{6} 10.1d 8d Jul 7] poor form. *Jedd O'Keeffe* **48**

KENYAN CAT 2 br.f. (May 10) One Cool Cat (USA) 123 – Nairobi (FR) (Anabaa (USA) 130) [2009 6g^{3} 7.1m^{4} 6m^{3} Oct 26] 16,000Y: third foal: dam, French maiden, out of half-sister to dam of smart 2-y-o sprinters Bint Allayl (in 1998) and Kheleyf (in 2003): steadily progressive in maidens, third to easy winner Miss Zooter at Leicester final start: should stay 7f. *George Baker* **67 +**

KERCHAK (USA) 2 b.c. (Feb 22) Royal Academy (USA) 130 – Traude (USA) (River Special (USA)) [2009 7.1g^{6} 7m^{6} 6m^{3} 6m^{6} Oct 16] $46,000F, 32,000Y: sturdy colt: fourth foal: half-brother to winner in USA by Real Quiet: dam, ran once in USA, out of half-sister to dam of Caerleon: best effort in maidens when length third to Side Glance at Newmarket: should stay 7f: seemed not to handle Epsom second start. *W. Jarvis* **78**

KEROLAD (IRE) 2 ch.g. (Apr 17) Kyllachy 129 – Absolute Precision (USA) (Irish River (FR) 131) [2009 6g 7m 6m 7g 8.3s^{2} Aug 1] sturdy gelding: no sign of ability, beaten 25 lengths in match (gelded after). *N. Wilson* **–**

KERRYS REQUIEM (IRE) 3 b.f. King's Best (USA) 132 – Moonlight Wish (IRE) (Peintre Celebre (USA) 137) [2009 91: 6m 6m^5 6m^2 5m^6 6m^3 6d^2 6g^3 6g 5g 5m^5 5.7m^6 6g^2 6d Oct 11] quite attractive filly: fairly useful handicapper: raced only at 5f/6f: acts on good to firm and good to soft going: ungenuine. *M. R. Channon* **94 §**

KERSIVAY 3 b.g. Royal Applause 124 – Lochmaddy (Selkirk (USA) 129) [2009 83: 7.1m^3 7m* 6.1m^6 6m^4 6.9g^6 p7.1g p7.1g^2 7m^5 p7.1g^5 p6m^3 Nov 28] good-topped gelding: fairly useful performer: won maiden at Catterick in April: left D. Barker after fourth start: stays easy 7f: acts on polytrack and good to firm going. *Ollie Pears* **81**

KESSRAA (IRE) 3 b.g. Kheleyf (USA) 116 – Safe Care (IRE) (Caerleon (USA) 132) [2009 –: 7f^2 7s^4 8m^5 8m^2 10.1m^3 Sep 9] well-made gelding: fair maiden: should stay 1¼m: acts on firm going. *M. R. Channon* **71**

KESTREL CROSS (IRE) 7 b.g. Cape Cross (IRE) 129 – Lady Rachel (IRE) 75 (Priolo (USA) 127) [2009 –: p10g^5 p10g^3 p9.5g Feb 7] sturdy, close-coupled gelding: one-time useful handicapper: just fair in 2009: broke down at Wolverhampton: stayed 1¼m: acted on polytrack, firm and good to soft going: tried blinkered: tongue tied in 2009: dead. *A. W. Carroll* **76**

KEVKAT (IRE) 8 br.g. Dushyantor (USA) 123 – Diamond Display (IRE) 96 (Shardari 134) [2009 98: p10g 10d 11.7f^3 Aug 22] leggy gelding: handicapper, just fair form on Flat in 2009: effective at 10.7f to 1¾m: acts on polytrack, good to firm and good to soft going: fairly useful hurdler. *D. E. Pipe* **75**

KEY ART (IRE) 2 b.c. (Mar 20) Kheleyf (USA) 116 – Gift of Spring (USA) (Gilded Time (USA)) [2009 5m^4 5.1g^2 6g^5 5g^2 5m^2 p5g^4 p5g^4 a7.5g^2 Nov 14] €100,000F, €100,000Y: attractive colt: second foal: brother to fairly useful Irish 5f (at 2 yrs)/6f winner Vegas Baby: dam French maiden (stayed 1½m): fair maiden: sold from J. Noseda 11,000 gns before final start: stays 7.5f: acts on polytrack and good to firm ground. *N. Minner, Belgium* **71**

KEY BREEZE 2 b.c. (Mar 15) Exceed And Excel (AUS) 126 – Cayman Sound 72 (Turtle Island (IRE) 123) [2009 6f^5 6m^5 p5g^4 Aug 1] useful-looking colt: has scope: best effort in maidens when fifth to Alrasm at Doncaster on debut: sold 11,000 gns in October. *J. H. M. Gosden* **67**

KEY DECISION (IRE) 5 br.g. Key of Luck (USA) 126 – Adalya (IRE) (Darshaan 133) [2009 79, a74: f11g* p10.7g^6 11.7d^5 12v 12m 10s^5 8s 9g p7g 12m 10s* Oct 11] sturdy gelding: fair performer: won maiden at Southwell in February and apprentice handicap at the Curragh in October: probably best at 1¼m/easy 1½m: acts on fibresand, soft and good to firm going: sometimes tongue tied. *Shaun Harley, Ireland* **77**

KEY LIGHT (IRE) 2 b.f. (Jan 28) Acclamation 118 – Eva Luna (IRE) 106 (Double Schwartz 128) [2009 p6m^4 p6m* Nov 29] €58,000F, €47,000Y: half-sister to 5f winner Burma Tiger (by Indian Ridge) and 7f winner National Swagger (by Giant's Causeway), both useful in Ireland: dam Irish 2-y-o 5f/6f winner (including Phoenix Stakes): better effort in maidens at Kempton when beating Zubova a head: likely to prove best at 5f/6f. *J. W. Hills* **73**

KEY OF FORTUNE (IRE) 3 b.f. Key of Luck (USA) 126 – Alaynia (IRE) 77 (Hamas (IRE) 125§) [2009 –: p9.5g^5 p12.2m^6 p12.2g^5 10.2m 12.1m^5 12.1g 11.5g^5 Aug 3] modest maiden handicapper: stays 1½m: acts on polytrack and good to firm ground. *Jennie Candlish* **63**

KEY REGARD (IRE) 3 b.g. Key of Luck (USA) 126 – Disregard That (IRE) (Don't Forget Me 127) [2009 p10g^2 p12g* p12g^3 p12g p12m^3 p12m^5 p13.9m* Nov 28] €75,000Y: brother to several winners, notably smart Irish/French sprinter Miss Emma and 4-y-o Redesignation, and half-brother to 2 winners: dam unraced: fair performer: won maiden at Lingfield in February and, having left J. Osborne (gelded) after third outing (modest form in juvenile hurdles for C. Mann), claimer at Wolverhampton in November: stays 1¾m: raced only on polytrack. *P. F. I. Cole* **77**

KEY SIGNATURE 3 b.f. Dansili 127 – Musical Key 71 (Key of Luck (USA) 126) [2009 90: 7s 7d 7.1f^5 7.1m 7g^3 7g 7.1g 8d^2 Oct 11] big, good-topped filly: fairly useful handicapper: stays 1m: acts on polytrack, firm and soft going: blinkered last 4 outings: sold 15,000 gns, sent to Saudi Arabia. *Pat Eddery* **88**

KEYS OF CYPRUS 7 ch.g. Deploy 131 – Krisia (Kris 135) [2009 91: 7g^5 7.9m 8v* 8s 7d 8g^4 f8f 7.2v* Oct 31] fairly useful handicapper: won at Ripon in July and Ayr in October: stays 1m: best form on going softer than good (unbeaten in 3 races on heavy): tried tongue tied: usually races prominently. *D. Nicholls* **86**

KEYTA BONITA (IRE) 2 b.f. (Feb 16) Denon (USA) 121 – Miss Corinne (Mark of Esteem (IRE) 137) [2009 6d^4 7d 7g^2 6m^2 7.5m^4 7m Oct 3] 3,500Y: unfurnished filly: first foal: dam, Italian 7.5f to 1½m winner, out of sister to dam of Derby winner Sir Percy: fair maiden: bred to stay 1¼m+: acts on good to firm going: sold 5,500 gns, sent to Czech Republic. *M. G. Quinlan* **66**

KEY TO LOVE (IRE) 3 b.f. Key of Luck (USA) 126 – Ski For Me (IRE) 88 (Barathea (IRE) 127) [2009 72, a64: p7.1g^6 5.1m 6.1g p6g Oct 26] leggy filly: just poor form in handicaps at 3 yrs: best at 5f/6f: acts on polytrack and soft going: tried in cheekpieces. *A. J. Chamberlain* **48**

K'GARI (USA) 3 ch.g. Fusaichi Pegasus (USA) 130 – To Act (USA) (Roberto (USA) 131) [2009 –: 8g 10.1m p13.9g^6 p16.5g* p16.5g Dec 5] modest performer: improved to win handicap at Wolverhampton in November: stays 16.5f: acts on polytrack: blinkered last 3 outings. *B. Ellison* **60**

KHAJAALY (IRE) 2 b.c. (Mar 16) Kheleyf (USA) 116 – Joyfullness (USA) (Dixieland Band (USA)) [2009 p8g^5 Oct 8] 38,000F, 140,000Y: fifth foal: half-brother to 3 winners, including fairly useful Irish 1m winner Song In My Heart (by Spartacus) and 6f/7f winner Contented (by Orpen): dam unraced daughter of US Grade 1 2-y-o 8.5f winner Arewehavingfunyet: 16/1 and green, encouraging 2 lengths fifth to Art Excellence in maiden at Kempton, running on: should improve. *E. A. L. Dunlop* **67 p**

KHANIVOROUS 2 b.g. (Apr 28) Dubai Destination (USA) 127 – Bright Edge 102 (Danehill Dancer (IRE) 117) [2009 5m^4 p5g^4 p7g* p8m^5 Dec 9] 72,000F: well-made gelding: third foal: half-brother to fairly useful 2007 2-y-o 5f winner Edge of Light (by Xaar) and 5-y-o Arthur's Edge: dam 6f winner, including at 2 yrs: fair performer: won maiden at Kempton in November: raced lazily but showed similar form in nursery there: stays 1m. *J. R. Boyle* **76**

KHANJAR (USA) 9 ch.g. Kris S (USA) – Alyssum (USA) (Storm Cat (USA)) [2009 11m Jun 23] sturdy, attractive gelding: handicapper: missed 2008: well held on return: stays easy 2m: acts on all-weather/dirt and firm going: sometimes visored/in cheekpieces. *J. Pearce* **–**

KHAN TENGRI (IRE) 3 gr.g. Sadler's Wells (USA) 132 – Ela Athena 119 (Ezzoud (IRE) 126) [2009 85p: p9.5g^2 p12g^6 10m Apr 24] big gelding: disappointing maiden: should be suited by 1¼m/1½m: tried blinkered: wayward: sold 29,000 gns in July, joined Patrick Brady in Ireland. *M. P. Tregoning* **66 §**

KHATEEB (IRE) 4 b.c. King's Best (USA) 132 – Choc Ice (IRE) 115 (Kahyasi 130) [2009 107: 10m^4 8.3m* 10f 8g* 8m^4 8m Oct 2] strong, close-coupled colt: smart performer: improved in 2009, winning minor event at Nottingham (by 1¼ lengths from Emmrooz) in June and listed race at Pontefract (beat Orizaba 1¾ lengths) in July: below form after in Sovereign Stakes at Salisbury and Joel Stakes at Newmarket: best at 1m: acts on polytrack and firm going: tongue tied. *M. A. Jarvis* **115**

KHATTAAB (USA) 2 b. or br.c. (Apr 12) Dixie Union (USA) 121 – Jemima 100 (Owington 123) [2009 6m* 7m^6 Oct 1] $200,000Y: rather leggy colt: fourth foal: half-brother to winners in USA by Rock of Gibraltar and A P Indy: dam, 2-y-o 5f/6f (including Lowther Stakes) winner, later 8.5f winner in USA: won maiden at Haydock in August by 7 lengths from Durham Reflection: again travelled strongly when under 4 lengths sixth to Sir Parky in Somerville Tattersall Stakes at Newmarket: may prove as effective at 6f as 7f: already useful, and open to more improvement. *B. W. Hills* **96 p**

KHAYAR (IRE) 3 b.c. Refuse To Bend (IRE) 128 – Khatela (IRE) 91 (Shernazar 131) [2009 54p: 10g^6 12m^4 11.5d 11.5g^3 14.1m^2 14.1m 16.1g^3 15m* Oct 5] good-topped colt: fair handicapper: won at Warwick in October: stays 2m: acts on good to firm going: tried tongue tied: joined Eric McNamara, Ireland. *M. H. Tompkins* **71**

KHAZARA 2 ch.f. (Apr 9) Starcraft (NZ) 128 – Mystery Lot (IRE) 87 (Revoque (IRE) 122) [2009 p8m 8.3d 8g Oct 21] leggy filly: first foal: dam 1¼m and hurdles winner: well held in maidens. *A. King* **–**

KHELEY (IRE) 3 b.f. Kheleyf (USA) 116 – Namesake (Nashwan (USA) 135) [2009 54: p6g* p6g^2 p6g* p5.1g* p6g 5v* p6g p5g^3 p6g p6f^4 Dec 13] workmanlike filly: fair performer: won seller at Wolverhampton, and handicaps at Kempton and Wolverhampton in January and apprentice handicap at Catterick in September: stays 6f: acts on polytrack and heavy going. *W. M. Brisbourne* **77**

KHESKIANTO (IRE) 3 b.f. Kheleyf (USA) 116 – Gently (IRE) (Darshaan 133) [2009 59: f7g* 7.5m^6 f6g^5 7.5m^2 7.1f^3 8.5g 6m^4 6m 8.5m^2 7d^5 6.1g 8m^3 8.3g^5 f8g 7m^2 7m f7m f7g f8g^5 Dec 18] leggy filly: fair performer: won seller at Southwell in **66**

February (left M. Botti 3,500 gns after): reportedly had breathing problem fourteenth start: best up to 8.5f: acts on all-weather, firm and good to soft going: not straightforward. *M. C. Chapman*

KHEYLIDE (IRE) 3 ch.g. Kheleyf (USA) 116 – Jayzdoll (IRE) (Stravinsky (USA) 133) [2009 79: 5m^6 5m^2 5m* 6v 5.2g^5 5m^4 5m^5 5m^3 5d 5m 5g 6m 5g^5 5m^6 5g^3 p5.1g Oct 17] strong, lengthy gelding: fair handicapper: awarded race at Newmarket in May: best at 5f: acts on polytrack and good to firm going (possibly not on softer than good): in cheekpieces/visor last 5 starts: held up (sometimes gets behind). *Mrs D. J. Sanderson* **73**

KHOR DUBAI (IRE) 3 b.c. Kheleyf (USA) 116 – Dievotchkina (IRE) (Bluebird (USA) 125) [2009 104: 8m^6 7g^6 7m^3 7m^3 7d p7g* 7.1g^2 p8.6g^3 p7g* Nov 18] useful-looking colt: smart performer: successful at Kempton in handicap in August (by neck from Penitent) and minor event in November (beat Carcinetto 3¼ lengths): also ran well when 2¼ lengths third to Gitano Hernando in minor event at Wolverhampton eighth start: stays 8.6f: acts on polytrack and good to firm ground: visored nowadays: has left Godolphin. *Saeed bin Suroor* **110**

KHUN JOHN (IRE) 6 b.g. Marju (IRE) 127 – Kathy Caerleon (IRE) (Caerleon (USA) 132) [2009 p12.2g^5 p10g^2 11.6m p12g 10.1s^3 10g p9.5g Oct 9] rangy gelding: fair performer: left V. Dartnall after second outing: stays easy 1¼m: acts on polytrack and good to firm ground: waited with. *W. J. Musson* **79**

KIAMA BAY (IRE) 3 b.g. Fraam 114 – La Panthere (USA) (Pine Bluff (USA)) [2009 52p: 7.5m 8.3g* Jun 17] tall gelding: much improved when winning handicap at Hamilton in June: suffered twisted joint after: will stay 1¼m. *J. J. Quinn* **70**

KICKAHEAD (USA) 7 b.g. Danzig (USA) – Krissante (USA) (Kris 135) [2009 p8g^4 8f p8g p12m^4 Dec 9] sturdy gelding: modest maiden handicapper on Flat, lightly raced: stays 1½m: acts on polytrack, good to firm and good to soft going: tried tongue tied: fairly useful hurdler, successful 3 times in 2009/10. *Ian Williams* **59**

KIDLAT 4 b.g. Cape Cross (IRE) 129 – Arruhan (IRE) 87 (Mujtahid (USA) 118) [2009 81: p10g^6 p10g^2 p10g^2 11.8m^5 10s 10m 10.2g* 10f^3 10d^5 10g^5 12m 10m^6 p10g Oct 22] big, good-topped gelding: fairly useful handicapper: won at Chepstow in May: said to have had breathing problem final start: stays 1¼m: acts on polytrack and firm ground: tongue tied. *B. G. Powell* **86**

KIDNAP (IRE) 2 b.c. (Mar 30) Desert Style (IRE) 121 – Rosalia (USA) 66 (Red Ransom (USA)) [2009 p6g p6g Dec 14] well beaten in maiden/seller. *M. G. Quinlan* **–**

KIDSON (USA) 3 b. or br.g. Lemon Drop Kid (USA) 131 – Solo (USA) (Halo (USA)) [2009 –: 11m 14.1s^2 16.2g^2 16v^3 Jul 30] modest maiden handicapper: stays 2m: acts on soft ground: gelded after final outing. *George Baker* **58**

KIELTY'S FOLLY 5 gr.g. Weet-A-Minute (IRE) 106 – Three Sweeties (Cruise Missile) [2009 51: p9.5g^2 p8g^2 p8g^6 8.1g^5 9.1g^5 8.3g p9.5g^2 p8.6g^5 p8.6g* Dec 19] close-coupled gelding: modest handicapper: won at Wolverhampton in December: stays easy 9.5f: acts on polytrack and soft going. *B. P. J. Baugh* **61**

KIHO 4 b.g. Dashing Blade 117 – Krim (GER) (Lagunas) [2009 66: 12g^6 p12g 15m^5 12d 17.2f^3 14m^3 15m^4 Jul 9] tall, leggy gelding: modest maiden handicapper: stays 17f: acts on firm ground: blinkered last 4 outings: temperament firmly under suspicion. *Eve Johnson Houghton* **64**

KILBURN 5 b.g. Grand Lodge (USA) 125 – Lady Lahar 106 (Fraam 114) [2009 p8g^2 p8g* p7g^3 8.3m 8m^6 May 30] strong, stocky gelding: type to carry condition: fair handicapper: missed 2008: won at Lingfield in March: may prove best short of 1m: acts on polytrack and good to firm ground: tried in cheekpieces. *A. J. Lidderdale* **78**

KILDANGAN GIRL 2 b.f. (Mar 19) Refuse To Bend (IRE) 128 – Paola Maria (Daylami (IRE) 138) [2009 6m^5 6s^6 p6g p7.1g Sep 3] second foal: dam unraced out of half-sister to Derby winner Oath and high-class performer up to 10.5f Pelder: well held in maidens/claimer. *W. R. Muir* **–**

KILDARE SUN (IRE) 7 b.g. Desert Sun 120 – Megan's Dream (IRE) 56 (Fayruz 116) [2009 82: p9.5g p9.5g^3 p9.5g^3 10.2m^5 8f^3 8m^3 8.3g^2 8f^2 8m^3 7.6g 8s 8.3m p8.6g^5 p9.5g* Oct 15] well-made gelding: fair handicapper: won at Wolverhampton in October: effective at 1m/1¼m: acts on polytrack and firm ground: visored/in cheekpieces nowadays. *J. Mackie* **78**

KILKENNY BAY 3 b.f. Tobougg (IRE) 125 – Miss Arizona (IRE) (Sure Blade (USA) 130) [2009 60: 8m May 16] maiden: well held sole start in 2009. *W. Jarvis* **–**

KILLER CLASS 4 ch.f. Kyllachy 129 – Class Wan 74 (Safawan 118) [2009 72: 5g 5s 5d 5g^5 5g 5m^3 5s Oct 27] small, workmanlike filly: fair handicapper: raced mainly at 5f: acts on any turf going. *J. S. Goldie* **68**

KILLUSTY FANCY (IRE) 2 b.c. (Mar 31) Refuse To Bend (IRE) 128 – Crafty Fancy (IRE) 91 (Intikhab (USA) 135) [2009 6d 7g 7s^3 p7.1g Sep 18] form only when 3¼ lengths third to Hoss Cartwright in maiden at Leicester. *D. J. S. ffrench Davis* **60**

KILMANSECK 2 b.g. (Apr 12) Royal Applause 124 – Corndavon (USA) 95 (Sheikh Albadou 128) [2009 6m 7.1g 6m 7.1m^2 6.1s Oct 7] sturdy, good-bodied gelding: easily best effort in maidens when length second to Landowner at Warwick: poorly drawn when well held in nursery final start: stays 7f: acts on good to firm ground. *Eve Johnson Houghton* **65**

KILMEENA DREAM 5 b.m. Foxhound (USA) 103 – Kilmeena Glen (Beveled (USA)) [2009 p6g 7m 6g Jun 18] sturdy mare: missed 2008: little form. *J. C. Fox* **–**

KILMEENA MAGIC 7 b.m. Fumo di Londra (IRE) 108 – Kilmeena Lady (Inca Chief (USA)) [2009 53: p12g Oct 8] maiden: lightly raced on Flat since 2007, and well held sole start at 7 yrs: tried in cheekpieces: modest winning hurdler. *J. C. Fox* **–**

KILMUN 3 b.g. Zamindar (USA) 116 – Didicoy (USA) 104 (Danzig (USA)) [2009 6g 8.3m 6g p7m f7g Dec 18] strong, deep-girthed gelding: no form: tried blinkered. *K. A. Ryan* **–**

KILSYTH (IRE) 3 b.f. Marju (IRE) 127 – Easter Song (USA) (Rubiano (USA)) [2009 –: f8g Feb 15] little form. *S. Parr* **–**

KILT ROCK (IRE) 2 ch.g. (Feb 4) Giant's Causeway (USA) 132 – Eliza (USA) 118 (Mt Livermore (USA)) [2009 6m^6 7m 6m p6m^2 p6g* p7.1g^5 Oct 16] 50,000 2-y-o: neat gelding: closely related to 3 winners abroad by Storm Cat and half-brother to 3 winners, including useful Irish 2006 2-y-o 5f/7.5f winner Country Song (by Fusaichi Pegasus): dam US Grade 1 8.5f winner, including Breeders' Cup Juvenile Fillies: fair performer: landed odds in nursery at Kempton in October: should stay 7f: acts on polytrack: gelded after final start. *T. G. Mills* **71**

KIMBERLEY DOWNS (USA) 3 gr.g. Giant's Causeway (USA) 132 – Fountain Lake (USA) (Vigors (USA)) [2009 84p: p9.5g* 12.3m^6 12m 14m 16m* 14.1s Oct 12] deep-girthed gelding: fairly useful handicapper: won at Wolverhampton in April and Ascot (beat Woolfall Treasure 4½ lengths) in September: stays 2m: acts on polytrack and good to firm ground: visored last 2 starts: sold 27,000 gns, then gelded. *M. Johnston* **93**

KIMBERLEY ROCKS (IRE) 3 b.f. Intikhab (USA) 135 – Kalimar (IRE) (Bigstone (IRE) 126) [2009 8m 8.3g^5 8.3g^3 p8g 8d p9.5g Sep 17] €65,000Y: good-bodied filly: fourth foal: half-sister to winner around 1½m Tibouchina (by Daylami) and 5-y-o Kindlelight Blue: dam, ran once in France, closely related to dam of smart stayer Kasthari: modest maiden: stays 1m: best efforts on good ground: bled on debut. *R. M. Beckett* **62**

KINA JAZZ 3 b.f. Kyllachy 129 – Tapas En Bal (FR) (Mille Balles (FR) 124) [2009 51: p6g^4 p6g p6g^5 p5.1m^6 8d p6g Nov 20] modest maiden: left M. Rimmer after fourth start, M. Botti after fifth: best effort at 6f on polytrack: tried blinkered/visored. *J. Ryan* **55**

KINDEST 3 b.f. Cadeaux Genereux 131 – Star Profile (IRE) 100 (Sadler's Wells (USA) 132) [2009 8.3m 8.3g^5 8.3g^4 8.3m^5 8.1s* 8.3v^2 8g^2 Aug 8] 40,000Y: good-topped filly: half-sister to several winners, including useful 11f/1½m winner Without A Trace (by Darshaan): dam, Irish 2-y-o 6f winner, closely related to smart Irish sprinter Lady Alexander (dam of 6-y-o Dandy Man): fairly useful handicapper: won at Haydock in July: raced only around 1m: acts on heavy going (below form both starts on good to firm). *C. F. Wall* **83**

KIND HEART 3 b.f. Red Ransom (USA) – Portorosa (USA) (Irish River (FR) 131) [2009 77p: 12d^4 10.4g^3 f11g^4 10m* 10m^2 Oct 6] tall filly: fair performer: won claimer at Redcar (left Sir Mark Prescott 13,000 gns) in September: stays 1½m: acts on all-weather, good to firm and good to soft going: claimed £6,000 and joined D. McCain Jnr after final start: won juvenile hurdle in October. *P. Howling* **77**

KINDLELIGHT BLUE (IRE) 5 gr.g. Golan (IRE) 129 – Kalimar (IRE) (Bigstone (IRE) 126) [2009 85: p10g^5 Mar 18] tall, leggy gelding: fairly useful handicapper at 4 yrs: just fair form only outing in 2009: stays 1¼m (not 1½m): acts on polytrack and good to firm ground. *N. P. Littmoden* **76**

KINETIC ART (IRE) 4 b.g. Mull of Kintyre (USA) 114 – Sylviani (Ashkalani (IRE) 128) [2009 13.8g^6 10.4m Sep 25] stocky gelding: modest form in bumpers: tailed off both Flat outings: dead. *R. M. Whitaker* **–**

KINETIX 3 gr.f. Linamix (FR) 127 – Kalambara (IRE) (Bluebird (USA) 125) [2009 8.3f^2 10m^2 10.1m^2 11.7g^2 p12g^3 p12g^3 Nov 13] 90,000F, 175,000Y: lengthy filly: second foal: dam, French 9.5f winner from 2 starts, half-sister to top-class 1¼m/1½m performer Kalanisi and high-class 1m/1¼m performer Kalaman: fair maiden: should stay 1½m: raced only on polytrack and good ground or firmer (acts on firm). *J. H. M. Gosden* **78**

KINGAROO (IRE) 3 b.g. King Charlemagne (USA) 120 – Lady Naomi (USA) (Distant View (USA) 126) [2009 59: f8g^2 p8.6g^4 f8g^3 f8g^2 p7.1g 8.3m 10g f8m f7g 10.1g^3 10.2g Oct 28] workmanlike gelding: fair handicapper: regressive form in 2009, leaving Garry Moss prior to final start: stays 8.6f: acts on all-weather, probably on good to firm going: tried in cheekpieces. *G. Woodward* **67 d**

KING BATHWICK (IRE) 4 b.g. Golan (IRE) 129 – Princess Sabaah (IRE) 90 (Desert King (IRE) 129) [2009 70: p8g Jan 5] workmanlike gelding: maiden: blinkered, well beaten sole start in 2009: tried tongue tied. *A. B. Haynes* **–**

KING CHARLES 5 b.g. King's Best (USA) 132 – Charlecote (IRE) (Caerleon (USA) 132) [2009 107: 9m^6 12s^6 10m 10m^4 10d* 10g^5 12g 10m 10g 10.1m^4 12m^5 10v Oct 24] strong, close-coupled gelding: useful handicapper: best effort in 2009 when winning at Newbury in July by ¾ length from Cheshire Prince: stays 1½m: acts on polytrack, firm and good to soft going: tried in cheekpieces, blinkered last 3 starts: sold 40,000 gns, sent to UAE. *E. A. L. Dunlop* **101**

KING COLUMBO (IRE) 4 ch.g. King Charlemagne (USA) 120 – Columbian Sand (IRE) (Salmon Leap (USA) 131) [2009 87: 8g^5 10m^3 10m^4 8m^6 8d* 8d^4 8g^5 8g 8m^2 7m 7g Oct 31] strong gelding: fairly useful handicapper: won at Newmarket in June: stays 1¼m: acts on polytrack, good to firm and good to soft ground: tried visored: races prominently: suspect temperament. *Miss J. Feilden* **80**

KING DE LUNE (FR) 7 ch.g. Muhtathir 126 – Eclipse de Lune (USA) (Shahrastani (USA) 135) [2009 p13.9m^3 p16.5g^6 Mar 13] successful 3 times up to 14.5f in France for J-L. Guillochon: better effort in handicaps in Britain (modest form) when third: should stay 2m. *C. E. Longsdon* **64**

KINGDOM OF FIFE 4 b.g. Kingmambo (USA) 125 – Fairy Godmother 113 (Fairy King (USA)) [2009 94: 10.3m^2 10m* 10.4m^2 10m^3 12m^3 Sep 27] good-bodied gelding: smart performer: much improved in 2009, winning totesuper7 Zetland Gold Cup (Handicap) at Redcar (beat Nanton by 2½ lengths) in May: good efforts after, 2¾ lengths second to Sirvino in John Smith's Cup (Handicap) at York, ¾-length third to Campanologist in Winter Hill Stakes at Windsor and 2½ lengths third to Mawatheeq in Cumberland Lodge Stakes at Ascot: effective at 1¼m/1½m: acts on good to firm and good to soft going, yet to race on extremes: visored first 4 starts in 2009: has raced freely. *Sir Michael Stoute* **113**

KINGDOM OF LIGHT 2 gr.c. (Apr 19) Exceed And Excel (AUS) 126 – Silver Chime 74 (Robellino (USA) 127) [2009 5g^2 6g* 5m 5m^2 5s^6 6m 6m^4 Oct 3] 34,000F, £100,000Y: well-made colt: second foal: half-brother to 3-y-o Brenin Taran: dam 6f winner: useful performer: won maiden at Haydock in May: best effort when under 5 lengths fourth to Lucky Like in listed race at Redcar: likely to prove at least as effective at 5f as 6f: acts on good to firm ground: seemed amiss third outing, creditable effort in tongue tie next time: races prominently. *J. Howard Johnson* **97**

totesuper7 Zetland Gold Cup (Heritage Handicap), Redcar—a triumph in the royal colours for visored front runner Kingdom of Fife, who turns the race into a procession

KING FERNANDO 6 gr.g. Silver Patriarch (IRE) 125 – Kastelruth (Midyan (USA) **?**
124) [2009 a12.5g^{6} a12.5g a12.5g^{4} a12.5g^{6} 10.8s^{5} 12v^{5} a11g* 12g^{5} 12m^{3} 12d Jun 18] winner of 7 races, including amateur minor event at Sonsbeck in April: left S. Smrczek in Germany, showed little in ladies handicap on British debut: stays 1¾m: acts on sand, heavy and good to firm ground: usually blinkered. *P. Beaumont*

KING FINGAL (IRE) 4 b.g. King's Best (USA) 132 – Llia 94 (Shirley Heights 130) **87**
[2009 89: 12m^{4} 12g^{2} 11.5m 12m 12.3g^{5} 12s^{5} 12g Oct 10] lengthy gelding: fairly useful handicapper: stays 1½m: acts on firm and soft ground: tried tongue tied: sold £10,000. *J. J. Quinn*

KING GABRIEL (IRE) 7 b.g. Desert King (IRE) 129 – Broken Spirit (IRE) (Slip **49**
Anchor 136) [2009 p12g^{5} p11g^{5} Feb 25] tall gelding: fair hurdler: maiden on Flat: just poor form in 2009: should stay 1½m: acts on polytrack and soft ground: tried tongue tied. *Andrew Turnell*

KING IN WAITING (IRE) 6 b.g. Sadler's Wells (USA) 132 – Ballerina (IRE) 88 **70**
(Dancing Brave (USA) 140) [2009 8.1g^{6} 10.1d^{5} 10d 12g 16s 12g 16.1d^{5} p16.5g^{2} 18g^{5} Oct 10] well-made gelding: fair handicapper: stays 2¼m: acts on polytrack, heavy and good to firm going: tried blinkered/visored: tongue tied of late: held up: fair hurdler, successful in October. *J. Hetherton*

KING JOCK (USA) 8 b.g. Ghazi (USA) – Glen Kate 118 (Glenstal (USA) 118) [2009 **110**
115, a89+: 7.5d^{4} 8g 7.5g^{3} 8m^{6} 8g 7.6m 8s 7.5m^{6} Oct 4] lengthy, good-topped gelding: **a–**
smart on turf, fairly useful at best on dirt: respectable 1½ lengths third to Summit Surge in handicap at Nad Al Sheba on third outing: left A. Manuel, UAE after next start: below form back in Ireland after, including in pattern races last 2 starts: effective at 7f/1m: acts on any turf going: usually held up: none too consistent. *R. J. Osborne, Ireland*

KING KENNY 4 ch.g. Lomitas 129 – Salanka (IRE) 68 (Persian Heights 129) [2009 **76 d**
81: p8.6g p5.1g p7.1g^{4} 7m 7m 6g 8.5g^{3} 9m^{4} 8.5d 8.5f^{4} Aug 31] neat gelding: fair performer in 2009: left S. Parr after sixth outing, below form at Les Landes after: free-going sort, effective at 6f to 9.5f: acts on polytrack, firm and soft ground: tried visored/tongue tied: temperament under suspicion. *Mrs A. Malzard, Jersey*

KING OF AXUM (IRE) 2 b.c. (Feb 9) Soviet Star (USA) 128 – Ezana (Ela-Mana- **77**
Mou 132) [2009 5g* 5m^{4} 6g^{3} 6d 7.5g Dec 13] €27,000F, 6,000Y: lengthy, good-topped colt: type to carry condition: brother to 4-y-o It's My Day and half-brother to several winners, notably smart Irish 7f (at 2 yrs) to 1½m winner Ebaziya (dam of 3 Group 1 winners, including Gold Cup winner Enzeli), by Darshaan: dam French 11.5f winner: fair performer: won maiden at Doncaster in May: sold from M. Johnston 15,000 gns and off over 5 months, far from discredited in listed race at Pisa final start: should stay 1m+. *Ernesto Tasende, Italy*

KING OF CADEAUX (IRE) 4 br.g. Cadeaux Genereux 131 – Purple Haze (IRE) **–**
103 (Spectrum (IRE) 126) [2009 52: p8.6g f6g Mar 3] modest handicapper at 3 yrs: below form in 2009: stays 7f: acts on polytrack: wears blinkers/cheekpieces. *M. A. Magnusson*

KING OF CHARM (IRE) 6 ch.g. King Charlemagne (USA) 120 – Pumpona (USA) **–**
(Sharpen Up 127) [2009 55: p6g Jan 3] modest performer at 5 yrs: shaped as though amiss sole outing in 2009: stays easy 7f: acts on polytrack and firm ground: often blinkered: tried tongue tied. *M. Hill*

KING OF CONNACHT 6 b.g. Polish Precedent (USA) 131 – Lady Melbourne (IRE) **67**
76 (Indian Ridge 123) [2009 62: 10.9m p9.5g^{4} 10.2m* 10.1m^{3} 10.2m^{4} 11m 10d 9m^{4} p9.5g^{2} p9.5g* 8g p9.5g p9.5g^{4} p9.5g^{4} p9.5g p9.5g* p9.5g^{6} p9.5g^{6} Dec 28] workmanlike gelding: fair handicapper: won at Bath in May and Wolverhampton in August and December: stays 1¼m: acts on polytrack, soft and good to firm ground: wears cheekpieces/visor: usually held up. *M. Wellings*

KING OF DALYAN (IRE) 4 ch.g. Desert Prince (IRE) 130 – Fawaayid (USA) 92 **–**
(Vaguely Noble 140) [2009 f8g Feb 5] of no account. *Miss Tracy Waggott*

KING OF DEFENCE 3 ch.g. Kyllachy 129 – Duena (Grand Lodge (USA) 125) [2009 **76**
63p: 7m^{3} 7m p7g^{2} p7m* p7g p7m^{2} p7m Dec 30] sturdy gelding: fair handicapper: won at Kempton in October: raced only at 7f: acts on polytrack and good to firm going. *M. A. Jarvis*

KING OF DIXIE (USA) 5 ch.g. Kingmambo (USA) 125 – Dixie Accent (USA) **112**
(Dixieland Band (USA)) [2009 115: p8g* 8m^{5} p8g* 8m^{5} May 30] big, strong gelding: smart performer: easily won minor events at Kempton in March and Lingfield (by 2¼ lengths from Fullback) in May: below form in listed races otherwise: gelded after final start: stays easy 1m: raced on polytrack and good to firm ground: edgy sort (once withdrawn after breaking through stall). *W. J. Knight*

KING OF EDEN (IRE) 3 b.g. Royal Applause 124 – Moonlight Paradise (USA) 111 (Irish River (FR) 131) [2009 6m5 6d4 8d 6s 6g5 6s Oct 27] modest maiden: stays 6f: acts on good to soft going. *E. J. Alston* **54**

KING OF LEGEND (IRE) 5 b.g. King Charlemagne (USA) 120 – Last Quarry 52 (Handsome Sailor 125) [2009 66: p8.6g* p8.6g3 f8g2 p8.6g 8.3m 8g* 8m4 9.2d6 9g p8.6m p8m2 p8m p10m Nov 21] medium-sized gelding: fair handicapper on all-weather, modest on turf: won at Wolverhampton in January and Ayr (apprentices) in June: left A. G. Foster after tenth start: stays 8.6f: acts on all-weather and good to firm ground: tried in cheekpieces: tongue tied sixth to tenth starts in 2009. *D. Morris* **62 a69**

KING OF REASON 2 b.c. (Apr 14) King's Best (USA) 132 – Sheer Reason (USA) 110 (Danzig (USA)) [2009 p6g3 6m4 6m3 Jul 23] good-topped colt: seventh foal: closely related to Italian 2008 2-y-o 7.5f winner La Brunetta (by Dubai Destination) and half-brother to 3 winners, including 6-y-o Faith And Reason: dam, French 2-y-o 6f winner, out of half-sister to dam of Fantastic Light: easily best effort in maidens when close third to Frozen Power at Epsom final start: should be suited by 7f. *D. M. Simcock* **79**

KING OF RHYTHM (IRE) 6 b.g. Imperial Ballet (IRE) 110 – Sharadja (IRE) (Doyoun 124) [2009 84§: 8.3g 6.9g3 6g6 5m 7.5m 7.9m 9.1g p9.5g4 p8.6g3 f7g* Dec 18] sturdy, workmanlike gelding: just modest performer nowadays: won minor event at Southwell in December: stays 1¼m, effective at shorter: acts on all-weather, heavy and good to firm going: tried in headgear (blinkered at Southwell). *D. Carroll* **64**

KING OF ROME (IRE) 4 b.c. Montjeu (IRE) 137 – Amizette (USA) (Forty Niner (USA)) [2009 116: 8m 12m3 12g p12m 11m6 p10m 8g Oct 31] strong, deep-girthed ex-Irish-trained colt: smart performer: creditable length third to Front House in Dubai City of Gold at Nad Al Sheba: below form in Britain last 4 starts, including in pattern/handicap company: stays 1½m: acts on firm and soft going: tried blinkered/tongue tied. *M. F. de Kock, South Africa* **116**

KING OF SPARTA (USA) 4 b.c. Van Nistelrooy (USA) 108 – Selling Sunshine (USA) (Danzig (USA)) [2009 52: 10g 12.1m Jul 3] strong colt: maiden handicapper: well held in 2009. *T. J. Fitzgerald* **–**

KING OF SWORDS (IRE) 5 b.g. Desert Prince (IRE) 130 – Okey Dorey (IRE) 96 (Lake Coniston (IRE) 131) [2009 77: 5m 5.1m2 5v 5f 5g6 5d 5d 5m 5.1m 6d 5g* 5m* 5m2 5m* 5m2 5g6 5g Oct 19] smallish gelding: fair handicapper: won at Pontefract (2) in August and Beverley in September: effective at 5f/6f: acts on any turf going: in cheekpieces of late. *N. Tinkler* **79**

KING OF THE BEERS (USA) 5 gr. or ro.g. Silver Deputy (CAN) – Pracer (USA) 106 (Lyphard (USA) 132) [2009 64: p10g3 f8g2 p11g3 p9.5g f8d4 f11g* p10g f12g2 f11g6 10.2m 10.2m 12.1m p8.6g f11m3 f12g5 f11g4 p12m Oct 7] strong gelding: fair handicapper: won at Southwell (apprentices) in March: stays 1½m: acts on all-weather, little recent form on turf: tried blinkered, usually wears cheekpieces: races lazily. *R. A. Harris* **– a69**

KING OF THE MOORS (USA) 6 b.g. King of Kings (IRE) 125 – Araza (USA) (Arazi (USA) 135) [2009 82: 9.9m3 10f5 9.2s3 8.3g6 7g3 8m 8.3m 8m 8d 8s3 9m* 10g3 9m* 8.3g3 10m 10.2v p8.6g f8f5 Dec 17] close-coupled gelding: fair performer: won claimers (2) at Musselburgh in September: stays 1¼m: acts on soft and good to firm going: has worn cheekpieces, blinkered of late: often forces pace: has looked awkward/pulled hard. *R. C. Guest* **76**

KING OF WANDS 3 b.c. Galileo (IRE) 134 – Maid To Treasure (IRE) 77 (Rainbow Quest (USA) 134) [2009 83p: 12g* 14g2 14.1f* 14m* 14g5 Aug 29] rather leggy colt: useful form: won maiden at Folkestone in April, and handicaps at Salisbury in June and Sandown (much improved, beat Final Victory by 8 lengths) in July: not discredited when 7 lengths fifth to Mourilyan in listed race at Goodwood final outing: likely to stay beyond 1¾m: acts on firm ground: remains open to further improvement. *J. L. Dunlop* **105 p**

KING OF WINDSOR (IRE) 2 b.g. (May 9) Intikhab (USA) 135 – Kismah 111 (Machiavellian (USA) 123) [2009 6g4 6m2 p6g5 Oct 15] €9,000Y: seventh foal: brother to 3-y-o Suruor and half-brother to several winners, including useful 7f/1m winner Tahirah (by Green Desert): dam 1m winner on both starts: fairly useful form: in frame in maidens at Salisbury, odds on when 1½ lengths second to Theladyinquestion: disappointing at Wolverhampton: gelded after: should stay 7f/1m. *R. M. Beckett* **87**

KING OLAV (UAE) 4 ch.g. Halling (USA) 133 – Karamzin (USA) (Nureyev (USA) 131) [2009 90: p10g* p11g2 p11g 9.9g2 12m 10m 10.4g5 12d p10m2 Nov 4] tall, angular gelding: useful handicapper: won at Lingfield in February: good second at Kempton final start: stays 11f: acts on polytrack and good to soft going. *A. W. Carroll* **97**

KING O'THE GYPSIES (IRE) 4 b.c. Sadler's Wells (USA) 132 – Love For Ever (IRE) (Darshaan 133) [2009 101: 12f May 30] rather leggy colt: useful performer: probably unsuited by ground in handicap at Doncaster sole Flat start in 2009: should stay 1¾m: acts on good to soft ground: fair form over hurdles. *J. Howard Johnson* **–**

KING PIN 4 b.g. Pivotal 124 – Danehurst 118 (Danehill (USA) 126) [2009 7m 7s 7m^2 7d^2 8m* 8.3m^3 8m 7g Sep 3] fair performer: won handicap at Redcar in June: stays 1m: acts on good to firm ground: held up. *Miss Tracy Waggott* **67**

KING RED 5 ch.h. King's Best (USA) 132 – Pearl Barley (IRE) 79 (Polish Precedent (USA) 131) [2009 p12g^4 p13.9g* p13.9g* Dec 17] 20,000F: third foal: half-brother to 6f winner Perfect Solution (by Entrepreneur): dam, Irish 6.5f winner, half-sister to high-class 7f/1m performer Nayyir and very smart performer up to 14.6f Highest: fairly useful form in bumpers, successful in February: progressive on Flat, winning maiden in November and handicap in December, both at Wolverhampton: will stay 2m: raced on polytrack: likely to continue progressing. *Tom Dascombe* **84 p**

KINGS ACE (IRE) 3 b.g. King's Best (USA) 132 – Full Cream (USA) 86 (Hennessy (USA) 122) [2009 61: f6g* 7m f6g 7g^3 6g 6d^2 6g p6g p7m^4 p8.6g^4 p7m^6 p9.5g Dec 19] strong, lengthy gelding: modest handicapper: won at Southwell in April: stays 8.6f: acts on all-weather, good to firm and good to soft going: sometimes visored. *A. P. Jarvis* **61**

KING'S ALCHEMIST 4 b.g. Slickly (FR) 128 – Pure Gold 88 (Dilum (USA) 115) [2009 63d: p10m Jan 9] tall, close-coupled gelding: maiden handicapper, regressive form on Flat: stays 1¼m: acts on soft ground: tried visored: modest hurdler. *M. D. I. Usher* **–**

KINGS APHRODITE 2 gr.g. (Apr 10) Reset (AUS) 124 – Arctic Queen (Linamix (FR) 127) [2009 5.1m 5.3m 6m May 21] modest form at best in maidens: bit said to have slipped final start (gelded after). *Miss Gay Kelleway* **53 +**

KING'S APOSTLE (IRE) 5 b.h. King's Best (USA) 132 – Politesse (USA) (Barathea (IRE) 127) [2009 119: 5m 6m^2 6m 6m^5 6.5g* Aug 9] **121**

A Group 1 is intended to provide the ultimate test—or, at least, form part of a series which, singly or together, play their part in determining a contemporary champion. The system isn't perfect by any means, nor can it ever be made so. The standard varies, with the make-up of the fields dependent on all sorts of variables beyond the control of the individual courses staging the races. The latest running of the Prix Maurice de Gheest at Deauville in August provided an example of a Group 1 that fell short of the ideal. Three of the twelve runners had won a Group 1 before, but two of those, Naaqoos and Serious Attitude, had won their championship races as two-year-olds, the Prix Jean-Luc Lagardere and a substandard Cheveley Park respectively. Their more recent efforts perhaps better reflected how they might perform in the Maurice de Gheest: Naaqoos had finished third, demoted to sixth, in the Poule d'Essai des Poulains on his latest start, Serious Attitude, on favourable terms, had won a Group 3 for fillies and mares, the Summer Stakes at York. The third Group 1 winner in the Maurice de Gheest line-up was African Rose, winner of the 2008 Sprint Cup (run at Doncaster when Haydock was abandoned). She had also finished second behind Marchand d'Or in the 2008 Maurice de Gheest (Marchand d'Or had been kept in training but had not been seen since the spring). Like Naaqoos and Serious Attitude, however, African Rose had yet to make the same impression in the latest season but, nonetheless, the trio headed the market, which, it should be said, was where they belonged, given the paucity of the opposition. The principals from the King's Stand, the July Cup and the Golden Jubilee (barring the third there Lesson In Humility) were conspicuous by their absence in a field in which, with one exception, none of the others had won above Group 3, four having won at that level, including Mariol and Tiza, tenth and eighth respectively in the Maurice de Gheest the previous year, and two at listed level, including the frustrating Asset, whose form when runner-up in the Wokingham was, in theory, a match for most of his rivals at Deauville. There was a Group 2 winner in the field in the shape of five-year-old King's Apostle.

King's Apostle had won six of his twenty-one career starts before he contested the Maurice de Gheest. Five of his wins had come in his three year-old season, in which, after winning a maiden at Lingfield on polytrack, he worked his way up the handicap, winning four times, his final success coming at York off a BHA mark of 91. A six-race campaign at four saw King's Apostle placed in both the Wokingham at Royal Ascot and the Stewards' Cup at Goodwood. In the

Prix Maurice de Gheest, Deauville—King's Apostle secures his biggest win; Mariol (far side), Lesson In Humility (No.8), Varenar (nearest camera) and Sayif are next

Stewards' Cup, his last run in a handicap, he failed by a head to beat his stable-companion Conquest, with Borderlescott a close third. Borderlescott, who emerged a 6-lb better horse at the weights than King's Apostle, won the Nunthorpe on his next start, making the transition from top handicapper to Group 1 performer. King's Apostle didn't fly quite so high but he ended his four-year-old campaign with a win in the Group 2 John Guest Diadem Stakes at Ascot, in which, visored for the first time, he prevailed by a neck in a finish in which a length and a half covered the first six home. King's Apostle's fourth year began with an encouraging run over an inadequate five furlongs in the Palace House Stakes at Newmarket which was followed by an excellent second in the Duke of York Stakes at York, in which he emerged the equal at the weights of the ill-fated winner Utmost Respect. The form was the best shown at up to that point by King's Apostle and entitled him to a crack at Group 1 company. However, with a visor fitted again, he failed to land a blow in the Golden Jubilee at Royal Ascot and was only fifth in the July Cup at Newmarket, though he suffered some interference, but for which he might have finished a place closer.

King's Apostle did, however, go on to add a Group 1 win to his record in the Maurice de Gheest. African Rose was found to have broken a blood vessel and was retired afterwards, Asset missed the break and ran well below his Ascot form, Serious Attitude was seemingly disadvantaged by racing in a stand-side group and also ran a long way below her best, and Naaqoos, who had missed a race earlier in the summer because of coughing, ran well below form after leading the stand side group (he wasn't seen again in 2009). King's Apostle's best was more than enough to see off the outsider Mariol by half a length, with Lesson In Humility one of three hard on the heels of the first two.

King's Apostle didn't get another chance after the Maurice de Gheest, meeting with a setback later in the month which forced his retirement, but his form was at least given something of a boost by others later in the year. Mariol picked up a Group 3 win, only his second success in twenty-nine attempts at listed or pattern level, the fourth Varenar won the Group 1 Prix de la Foret, the fifth Sayif went on to land the Diadem, while the sixth Dunkerque was another to pick up a Group 3 win. Nonetheless, the latest Maurice de Gheest did not represent genuine Group 1 form, King's Apostle's performance rated at the end of the season behind not only his own effort in the Duke of York but behind the best runs of both Sayif (in the Diadem) and Asset (Wokingham).

King's Apostle (IRE) (b.h. 2004)	King's Best (USA) (b 1997)	Kingmambo (b 1990)	Mr Prospector
			Miesque
		Allegretta (ch 1978)	Lombard
			Anatevka
	Politesse (USA) (ch 2000)	Barathea (b 1990)	Sadler's Wells
			Brocade
		Embassy (b 1995)	Cadeaux Genereux
			Pass The Peace

The well-made King's Apostle is to stand at Klawervlei Stud in South Africa. He was a third European Group 1 winner for his sire King's Best, now based in France, though he is not so good as the other pair, the milers, Proclamation and Creachadoir. King's Apostle is the first foal of his unraced dam Politesse. Her second and third foals are both by Hawk Wing and have yet to race; the second Pure Perfection was sold for only 10,000 guineas at the Newmarket December Sales. Politesse's fourth foal, a yearling colt by Cape Cross, was bought back for 320,000 guineas at Newmarket in October. Both King's Apostle's grandam Embassy and his great grandam Pass The Peace won the Cheveley Park and both became the leading two-year-old filly of their year. Embassy won three of her four starts as a two-year-old when with David Loder but she failed to run at three after joining Godolphin. The Michael Bell-trained Pass The Peace, in contrast, did well as a three-year-old, winning the Fred Darling and finishing second in the Pouliches. Embassy has produced three fairly useful winners in Britain, as well as three other foals of racing age who, like Politesse, have failed to make it to the racecourse. The pick of Embassy's winners, who all won at around seven furlongs to a mile, was Grosvenor Square who also went on later to win in the States. Pass The Peace produced another smart filly besides Embassy in Tarfshi, winner of the Pretty Polly Stakes at the Curragh. King's Apostle was best at around six furlongs. Except for one run at two on firm going, he did all his racing on either polytrack or good/good to firm going on turf. He took a fair hold in his races and could produce a good turn of foot, though the fact that he was twice tried in a visor was indicative of a slight quirkiness in his attitude at times. *W. J. Haggas*

KING'S APPROACH (IRE) 2 gr.c. (Feb 12) Fasliyev (USA) 120 – Lady Georgina 88 (Linamix (FR) 127) [2009 5.1m^{3} 5f* 6m^{3} 6g 6g^{5} 7g 6g 5m^{6} p6m^{6} Oct 7] €15,000F, €40,000Y: sturdy colt: first foal: dam 7f winner (stayed 9f): fair performer: won maiden at Leicester in April: well below form last 4 starts: stays 6f: acts on firm going. *R. Hannon* **75 d**

KINGS BAYONET 2 ch.g. (Feb 17) Needwood Blade 117 – Retaliator 80 (Rudimentary (USA) 118) [2009 6s^{2} 6m p7.1g* Sep 25] £11,000Y: sixth foal: half-brother to 3 winners, including 6-y-o King's Revenge: dam 6f (including at 2 yrs)/7f winner: best effort when winning maiden at Wolverhampton cosily by length from Robust Wish: gelded after: stays 7f. *H. R. A. Cecil* **86 +**

KING'S CAPRICE 8 ch.g. Pursuit of Love 124 – Palace Street (USA) 103 (Secreto (USA) 128) [2009 94: p7g 7g 7m Jun 12] rather leggy gelding: has a round action: handicapper: fairly useful at 7 yrs: well below form in 2009: tried visored: tongue tied. *J. A. Geake* **–**

KING'S CHORISTER 3 ch.g. King's Best (USA) 132 – Chorist 120 (Pivotal 124) [2009 62: p8.6g f8g p8.6g 10.2m^{6} 10.2d^{6} 10m^{3} p12g^{3} 12.1m 9.8m^{3} 10.1d* 8d^{2} 12.1m^{6} Jul 28] workmanlike gelding: fair performer: won seller at Yarmouth in July: stays 1¼m: acts on polytrack, good to firm and good to soft ground: tried blinkered/visored: tongue tied nowadays: signs of temperament. *Miss Gay Kelleway* **65**

KING'S COLOUR 4 b.g. King's Best (USA) 132 – Red Garland (Selkirk (USA) 129) [2009 73: p7g^{3} p8g^{6} p12g^{4} 7m^{4} 7g* 7m* p8g^{5} p7m^{2} p7g* p7g^{2} Nov 25] good-topped gelding: fairly useful handicapper: much improved in 2009, winning at Goodwood in August, Epsom in September and Lingfield in November: effective at 7f/1m: raced on polytrack and good/good to firm going. *B. R. Johnson* **93**

KING'S COUNSEL (IRE) 3 ch.g. Refuse To Bend (IRE) 128 – Nesaah's Princess (Sinndar (IRE) 134) [2009 52: 9.2m^{3} 10d^{5} 10.3g^{4} 10m^{2} 10m 8d^{6} 12.4d p12.2m^{6} Sep 28] good-bodied gelding: fair maiden: stays 1¼m: acts on soft and good to firm going: tried visored: fair form in juvenile hurdles. *J. Hetherton* **65**

KINGSDALE ORION (IRE) 5 b. or br.g. Intikhab (USA) 135 – Jinsiyah (USA) 98 (Housebuster (USA)) [2009 94: p9.5g[6] 10.3g[3] 8m 12m 12s 12g 11.5m[3] 10.1d* p11g[3] 9.8v[5] f12g[3] 10s[4] 12s[3] Sep 5] close-coupled gelding: fairly useful handicapper: won at Newcastle in June: stays 1½m: acts on all-weather and good to firm ground, all wins on softer than good (acts on heavy): tried in cheekpieces/blinkers/tongue strap. *B. Ellison* **84**

KINGS DESTINY 3 b.g. Dubai Destination (USA) 127 – Jalousie (IRE) 108 (Barathea (IRE) 127) [2009 86p: 10m* 12.3m[4] 12.5g[2] 12v* 14v[4] 12g[2] 12s Nov 7] big, well-made gelding: type to carry condition: useful handicapper: won at Leicester in April and Ripon (beat Lady Artemisia 2¼ lengths in 4-runner race) in July: good 3½ lengths second to Opinion Poll in quite valuable event at Ascot sixth outing: likely to prove best short of 1¾m: acts on polytrack, heavy and good to firm ground: raced bit too freely when below form in November Handicap at Doncaster final outing. *M. A. Jarvis* **108**

KINGSDINE (IRE) 2 b.c. (Feb 17) King's Best (USA) 132 – Lunadine (FR) (Bering 136) [2009 6s 7m[5] 8.1d Aug 31] form in maidens only when 7¾ lengths fifth to Many A Slip at Salisbury: should stay 1m. *M. S. Saunders* **61**

KING'S FABLE (USA) 6 b.g. Lear Fan (USA) 130 – Fairy Fable (IRE) 95 (Fairy King (USA)) [2009 70: p13.9g p10g 11.6m[2] p12.2g[5] p12m[6] Sep 24] sturdy gelding: modest handicapper nowadays: stays 13f: acts on polytrack and heavy going: usually in cheekpieces: waited with (slowly away): carries head high, and not straightforward. *Karen George* **60**

KINGSFORT (USA) 2 b. or br.c. (Mar 20) War Chant (USA) 126 – Princess Kris 82 (Kris 135) [2009 7s* 7s* Sep 12] **115 p**

Feste's line in *Twelfth Night*, 'For the rain it raineth every day', would have struck a depressing chord with racegoers and racing professionals in Britain and Ireland during what passed for summer. May, June and August had above-average rainfall while July was the wettest on record in many places. One location in Galway had over three feet of rain in those four months and it was the norm for the going across Ireland in particular to be unseasonably testing. Some Irish meetings were cancelled, others rescheduled, but, of the one hundred and twenty-four which took place between the start of May and the end of September (a much drier month once the first week had passed), seventy-nine carried the words soft or heavy in the going assessment and only nineteen were able to justifiably include the word firm, nearly all of them good to firm. The Curragh suffered especially badly—certainly compared with Leopardstown—with their nineteen meetings through the year having five designated as taking place on heavy, ten on soft, two on good to soft and two on good. This almost inevitably had an impact, particularly on two-year-old racing with most of the best events for first-season runners contested on that course. Competitive races on soft or heavy tend to take significantly more out of immature horses, especially those involved in finishes in which maximum effort is demanded, than in races on firmer going, possibly part of the explanation for the fact that there was only one runner from Britain, Long Lashes, in the three Irish Group 1 races for juveniles. None of this, however, detracts from the achievement of Kingsfort in winning the ladbrokes.com Vincent O'Brien National Stakes at the Curragh in mid-September on only his second start. He is a bright prospect.

A leggy, useful-looking colt, Kingsfort didn't look anywhere near the finished article physically at the Curragh. His only previous appearance had come a while earlier, in a well-contested twelve-runner maiden race on the same course at the end of June in which Aidan O'Brien, Jim Bolger, John Oxx and Dermot Weld also had runners. Kingsfort was second choice in the market behind O'Brien's Viscount Nelson and made a very favourable impression. After being waited with, he readily made ground from three furlongs out, led with a furlong and a half to go and was in no danger from that point, keeping on well to beat Stunning View by two lengths with Viscount Nelson four and a half lengths away third. Kingsfort had a reported setback after his victory but, in mid-August, his trainer Kevin Prendergast revealed—perhaps predictably—that the colt would be targeted at the National Stakes then possibly at the Racing Post Trophy.

With the habitual dominance of Aidan O'Brien and the other big guns among the Irish trainers, the members of the profession who operate on a smaller scale sometimes have a hard time making their presence felt. However, Kevin Prendergast, son of the legendary Paddy, has enjoyed his share of big-race successes, since first taking out a licence in the 'sixties. He has won eight classics: the Two Thousand Guineas with Nebbiolo in 1977, the Irish Two Thousand Guineas with Northern Treasure in 1976, the Irish One Thousand Guineas with Pidget in 1972 and Arctique Royale in 1981, and the Irish St Leger four times—with Pidget again, Conor Pass in 1973 and Oscar Schindler in 1996 and 1997. Prendergast had not won the National Stakes before, though, and by the time the race arrived another Group 1 had been added, Termagant providing him with a fourth victory in the Moyglare Stud Stakes a fortnight earlier.

The National Stakes is a much better guide to the future than the other Irish Group 1 event open to juvenile colts, the Phoenix Stakes, and in fact it has proved a better guide to the classics than any Group 1 in Europe. The latest renewal lacked strength in depth with only six lining up, though in the last twenty years there has been only one renewal—in 1996—with a field in double figures. There have been seven runners or fewer eleven times in that period. Half the latest field was trained by Aidan O'Brien, attempting an eighth win in the race. The contenders from Ballydoyle were short-priced favourite Alfred Nobel, successful in the Phoenix Stakes, the runner-up in that race Air Chief Marshal, and the Anglesey Stakes third Beethoven. Kingsfort was second choice in the betting at 9/4 with the Jim Bolger-trained Chabal, successful in a maiden at Leopardstown on his debut seven days earlier, third in the market at 9/2 and once-raced maiden Senior the rank outsider. The gallop set by Air Chief Marshal on the rail from Beethoven was not end-to-end and Kingsfort was always moving strongly close behind the leaders on the outside, with Alfred Nobel also seemingly going well towards the back. Kingsfort was sent on over a furlong out but Alfred Nobel appeared still full of running, a situation which changed in a matter of strides as he found nothing under pressure, hanging in the process. With Beethoven just keeping on at one pace it was left to Chabal, who had come under strong pressure before Kingsfort went on, to provide the strongest challenge. Kingsfort never really looked like being caught although he had only a neck to spare at the line as Chabal closed, the runner-up having had more to do after being blocked in his run by Kingsfort over a furlong out. Beethoven was a further length and three quarters behind in third, with Alfred Nobel last, just over a further length and a half away.

ladbrokes.com Vincent O'Brien National Stakes, the Curragh—Kingsfort (noseband) makes it two wins out of two; Chabal (left) chases him home and, like the winner, joined Godolphin later in the year; Beethoven (centre) is third with Air Chief Marshal fourth

Norman Ormiston's "Kingsfort"

Kingsfort (USA) (b. or br.c. Mar 20, 2007)	War Chant (USA) (b 1997)	Danzig (b 1977)	Northern Dancer
			Pas de Nom
		Hollywood Wildcat (b 1990)	Kris S
			Miss Wildcatter
	Princess Kris (b 1990)	Kris (ch 1976)	Sharpen Up
			Doubly Sure
		As You Desire Me (gr 1977)	Kalamoun
			Royal Saint

This may not have been the strongest renewal of the National Stakes in recent times—Beethoven showed improved form in a visor to win the Dewhurst Stakes later in the autumn with Chabal tenth—but there is no denying the promise of the winner. Kingsfort was generally made 8/1 favourite for the Two Thousand Guineas (from 16/1), with Prendergast confirming that that race would probably be on the agenda though Kingsfort would not run again at two. In the event, agent Anthony Stroud purchased Kingsfort soon afterwards for an unspecified sum on behalf of Sheikh Mohammed. Chabal followed soon afterwards and both colts will be trained by Saeed bin Suroor at three. Kingsfort should train on and strengthen Godolphin's team for the classics, though that may not necessarily be in the Derby because of the distance. Kingsfort's sire War Chant was superbly bred, by Danzig out of multiple Grade 1 winner Hollywood Wildcat, and lived up to his pedigree on the track at least, landing the Breeders' Cup Mile. So far he has not matched his racing achievements at stud, his fee having fallen from 75,000 dollars when he retired to 12,500 dollars in 2010. Kingsfort is his first Group 1 or Grade 1 scorer from six crops to race, though his first crop included Karen's Caper, beaten a short head in the Coronation Stakes. The distaff side of Kingsfort's pedigree is very much European. Kingsfort, who cost just €36,000 at the Goffs Sportsmans Yearling Sale, is the fourth winner out of Princess Kris, who was successful in a maiden event over a mile at Bath. The best of her earlier winners was Prince Arch (by Arch), who won the Grade 1 Gulfstream Park Handicap over eleven furlongs. Three-year-old filly Arty Crafty (also by Arch) won four races, three of them handicaps, at a mile and a quarter to a mile and a half in the space of twenty-four days in the autumn. Princess Kris's yearling filly by Good Reward was sold to John Ferguson on behalf of Sheikh Mohammed for €220,000 at Goffs in September. Kingsfort's grandam As You Desire Me was a smart performer who won two listed races at around a mile in France and stayed a mile and a quarter. The best of her nine winners at stud was Intimate Guest, winner of the May Hill Stakes, while another of her daughters is the grandam of Donativum, winner of the Breeders' Cup Juvenile Turf for Godolphin in 2008. As You Desire Me was well bred, out of Fred Darling Stakes winner and Coronation Stakes runner-up Royal Saint, a sister to triple classic-winning filly Altesse Royale. Royal Saint was a splendid broodmare too, breeding eight winners headed by good middle-distance stayer Classic Example, successful in the King Edward VII Stakes and third in the Irish Derby and the St Leger. There is enough stamina in the pedigree, and enough encouragement from the way he races, to suggest Kingsfort will stay a mile and a quarter. He wasn't the best two-year-old trained in Ireland, and several in Britain had better form, but the strong probability that he will improve when he fills to his frame at three should help him to bridge the gap. *Kevin Prendergast, Ireland*

KINGS GAMBIT (SAF) 5 ch.g. Silvano (GER) 126 – Lady Brompton (SAF) (Al Mufti (USA) 112) [2009 9g^5 9g^4 12m^5 12g 10.4g^3 13.3m 10.3g^4 10.4g^5 Oct 9] compact gelding: smart performer: progressed well for L. Wild in South Africa in 2008, winning 4 times, including South African Classic and South African Derby: creditable efforts in 2009 at Nad Al Sheba in handicap and Dubai City of Gold (fifth to Front House) then, having left H. Brown after fourth start, in York Stakes at York (1¾ lengths third to Kirklees) and minor event at Doncaster on second/third/fifth and seventh outings: stays 1½m: acts on dirt, soft and good to firm going: tried tongue tied. *T. P. Tate* **114**

KINGSGATE CASTLE 4 b.g. Kyllachy 129 – Ella Lamees 61 (Statoblest 120) [2009 76: p6g^5 6m 6g p7g p7g^6 6d p6g 6m^4 6d^2 p7.1g^4 6m p6g^2 p7g^2 8d p6f* p6f^2 Dec 21] tall gelding: fair performer: won minor event at Kempton in December: effective at 6f/7f: acts on polytrack, good to firm and good to soft going: blinkered/visored nowadays. *Miss Gay Kelleway* **71**

KINGSGATE CHOICE (IRE) 2 b.c. (Mar 4) Choisir (AUS) 126 – Kenema (IRE) 88 (Petardia 113) [2009 p6g^3 p6g* Nov 27] €9,500F, £60,000Y: fifth foal: half-brother to winner in Greece by Monashee Mountain: dam Irish 5f/6.5f winner: better effort in maidens at Wolverhampton when winning by ¾ length from Esuvia, racing very freely: may prove best up to 6f: open to further improvement. *J. R. Best* **80 p**

KINGSGATE NATIVE (IRE) 4 b.g. Mujadil (USA) 119 – Native Force (IRE) 82 (Indian Ridge 123) [2009 124: 6m 5g* 5m^6 Aug 21] **124**

Lot number 405 at the latest Tattersalls October Yearling Sales was always likely to attract plenty of interest as the bay filly in question—who was bought for 320,000 guineas by one of Richard Hannon's owners Julie Wood (flush from recent success in the Goffs Million Sprint)—is the only living foal produced by the ill-fated George Washington. Retired to Coolmore at the end of his three-year-old career for a fee of €60,000, the 2006 Two Thousand Guineas winner George Washington soon had his stallion duties aborted because of fertility problems and was returned to the track, making the frame three times in Group 1 company prior to his demise in the 2007 Breeders' Cup Classic. George Washington is certainly not the first high profile horse to have been a flop at stud, probably the most notable example being the great American champion of the mid-'nineties Cigar (winner of the inaugural Dubai World Cup in 1996), who proved infertile. Italian firm Assicurazioni Generali S.p.A paid out a reputed €25m insurance claim to Cigar's then-owners (Coolmore had a 75% stake) and, having taken possession of Cigar as part of that settlement, sent him to see out his retirement in the Hall of Champions section at Kentucky Horse Park.

That luxury retirement home is a far cry from the fate which befell some other big-race winners who struggled at stud. The 1994 Irish Champion Stakes winner Cezanne, for example, was still racing at the age of twelve—finishing eighth in a handicap hurdle at Wincanton—having failed as a stallion after the end of his racing days for Godolphin. Henry Candy's prolific pattern-winning sprinter Gorse suffered the indignity of finishing tailed-off last of twelve in an all-weather event at Southwell on his return to action (aged eleven) after becoming infertile during a short-lived spell at stud. Fellow sprinter Galeota fared better at first, winning three times at listed level after being bought back from an insurance company when infertile at stud, whilst controversial gelding Endless Summer—whose win in the 2000 Richmond Stakes was expunged five years later when it emerged he had been ineligible to run in that two-year-old contest—is another who won several times (albeit at a much lower level) during a lengthy sprinting career after having to be retired from stud duties. Tamarisk failed to win again in a varied career—which included two brief spells racing in the States and another successful insurance claim by Coolmore—after his victory in the 1998 Haydock Park Sprint Cup, but he subsequently regained fertility and was able to resume stud duties in 2003.

The 2006 Sussex Stakes winner Court Masterpiece had only three foals in his first crop in 2009 but, after a return to action in the latest season (including runs in claimers on his last two starts), he is to be given another chance at stud in 2010. Unfortunately, the same hopes cannot be entertained for another stud reject Kingsgate Native, who was gelded in December 2009 after further extensive tests revealed that the very smart sprinter was 'totally infertile'. That news is clearly a blow to Cheveley Park Stud, who purchased the stud rights to Kingsgate Native at the end of his two-year-old career, the highlight of which was his win against older horses in the Nunthorpe Stakes at York. Another Group 1 success followed at three in the Golden Jubilee Stakes at Royal Ascot, which prompted *Racehorses of 2008* to predict that this strong, lengthy colt would prove 'popular with commercial breeders'. However, after none of his first twenty mares tested in foal, Cheveley Park decided to return Kingsgate Native to the track with Sir Michael Stoute (he had previously been trained by John Best). Repeat wins in the Golden Jubilee (reportedly twisted a joint when thirteenth of fourteen) and the Nunthorpe (disappointing sixth behind Borderlescott) proved beyond him, but Kingsgate Native did win the Group 3 Audi Stakes (King George) at Goodwood in late-July with a performance that ranks amongst his very best. Sent off the 7/1 third choice in a field of seventeen, Kingsgate Native was ridden with a little more restraint than previously before bursting clear under Ryan Moore inside the final furlong to beat Total Gallery by two and three quarter lengths, with a further length and a half back to Inxile and the favourite Borderlescott. Although Kingsgate Native returned an impressive timefigure at Goodwood, it is also fair to say that he was probably favoured by the draw and Borderlescott comprehensively reversed the placings at York, where Kingsgate Native was sent off favourite to improve further on his record in the Nunthorpe—he was also third in the 2008 renewal (which was rerouted to Newmarket following York's abandonment).

Kingsgate Native (IRE) (b.g. 2005)	Mujadil (USA) (b 1988)	Storm Bird (b 1978)	Northern Dancer
			South Ocean
		Vallee Secrete (b 1977)	Secretariat
			Midou
	Native Force (IRE) (b 1998)	Indian Ridge (ch 1985)	Ahonoora
			Hillbrow
		La Pellegrina (b 1993)	Be My Guest
			Spanish Habit

Kingsgate Native's pedigree has been discussed in previous editions of *Racehorses* but, to recap, he is the second foal out of Native Force, who won a Sandown maiden over a mile at three. Native Force's four other foals to date have all been female, with the two out of this quartet to see a racecourse both successful, the seven-furlong selling handicap winner Assumption (by Beckett) and the fairly useful two-year-old Vanishing Grey (by Verglas), who won once from seven starts in the latest campaign for Brian Meehan. Native Force's next two foals both went under the hammer later in 2009, her yearling by Kodiac fetching 60,000 guineas at the same sale which featured the George Washington filly, whilst her Cape Cross foal was sold for double that amount at the same venue's December Foal Sales some seven weeks later. The most notable performer in this family before Kingsgate Native was also a filly, the 1994 One Thousand Guineas winner Las Meninas, who was a half-sister to Kingsgate Native's disappointing grandam La Pellegrina. Third dam Spanish Habit produced another classic winner in the form of Spanish Run, who won the Dansk St Leger in 1990, though he was very much the exception to the rule in this speedy family. Kingsgate Native's sire Mujadil is also an influence for speed, his best representative before Kingsgate Native being the aforementioned Galeota who was badly out of sorts in the latest season and ended up in claiming company. In common with his two pattern-winning sons, Mujadil was a precocious sort who did very well at two (he won the 1990 Cornwallis Stakes) and would also appear to have experienced problems of his own at stud of late, his returns from mares covered by him dipping into single figures on occasions in recent years.

Kingsgate Native is the first leading sprinter trained by Stoute since the likes of Marwell, Green Desert and Ajdal in the 'eighties. He isn't in quite the same league as that trio, but he should continue to pay his way. He has raced only on good or firmer to date. *Sir Michael Stoute*

KINGSGATE STORM (IRE) 3 gr.g. Mujadil (USA) 119 – In The Highlands (Petong 126) [2009 81?: p5g^4 7d 6m 6m^5 5m 6m p6g p7m^3 Oct 26] big, well-made gelding: just modest maiden at 3 yrs: gelded after reappearance: stays 7f: acts on polytrack. *J. R. Best* **60**

KING'S HEAD (IRE) 6 b.g. King's Best (USA) 132 – Ustka 60 (Lomond (USA) 128) [2009 100: p11g* p12g^5 9.8d 13.1m 14m 13.1m^3 10g^6 Oct 23] useful-looking gelding: fairly useful performer nowadays: won claimer at Kempton in February: left G. L. Moore £15,000 after next start: largely below form after: stays 13f: acts on polytrack and good to firm going: often wears cheekpieces. *Miss L. A. Perratt* **83**

KINGSHILL PRINCE 3 b.g. Mark of Esteem (IRE) 137 – Trefoil (FR) (Blakeney 126) [2009 69p: 8d 8.1g p8g Jun 25] strong gelding: maiden: no form in 2009. *W. J. Musson* **–**

KINGSHOLM 7 ch.g. Selkirk (USA) 129 – Putuna 98 (Generous (IRE) 139) [2009 77: p8.6g 10.3m 8m 9.9m 9.9g^6 10g 9.1g Oct 23] leggy gelding: has a quick action: fair performer at 6 yrs: little form in 2009: tried in cheekpieces. *N. Wilson* **–**

KING'S ICON (IRE) 4 b.g. King's Best (USA) 132 – Pink Sovietstaia (FR) (Soviet Star (USA) 128) [2009 76: 7.5m^6 7g^4 8.3g^2 8.1g^3 8m* 8g^2 p9.5g^2 p8.6g^2 p7.1g^2 Sep 11] good-bodied gelding: fair handicapper: won at Yarmouth in August: stays 9.4f: acts on polytrack and good to firm ground: tried in headgear: usually held up: not straightforward. *M. Wigham* **72**

KING'S JESTER (IRE) 7 b.g. King's Best (USA) 132 – Scent of Success (USA) 84 (Quiet American (USA)) [2009 7.2m^5 p7.1m p8.6g p9.5g^4 Dec 19] modest performer on Flat nowadays: left J. J. Lambe after reappearance: stays easy 9.5f: acts on polytrack and heavy ground: tried blinkered/in cheekpieces/tongue tied. *L. Smyth, Ireland* **57**

KING'S KAZEEM 4 b.f. King's Best (USA) 132 – Kazeem 73 (Darshaan 133) [2009 65: p10g^5 11.6m Jun 29] sturdy filly: maiden: little form in 2009: should stay 1¼m: acts on good to firm going: sold 800 gns. *G. L. Moore* **–**

KING'S LA MONT (IRE) 3 b.c. King's Best (USA) 132 – La Leuze (IRE) (Caerleon (USA) 132) [2009 70p: 10m^3 12m^5 10.2d 8.1g 10f^5 12f^6 10m Sep 28] rangy colt: fair maiden: below form after reappearance in 2009: should be suited by 1½m: acts on good to firm ground: tongue tied last 2 starts, also in cheekpieces final one: signs of temperament. *Mrs A. J. Perrett* **70**

KINGS MAIDEN (IRE) 6 b.m. King's Theatre (IRE) 128 – Maidenhair (IRE) (Darshaan 133) [2009 43: 10.1g^2 p13.9g* 12.4s^2 14.1m^4 12v^2 Jul 17] fair handicapper, lightly raced: won at Wolverhampton in May: probably stays 1¾m: acts on heavy and good to firm ground: held up. *James Moffatt* **72**

KINGSMAITE 8 b.g. Komaite (USA) – Antonias Melody 86 (Rambo Dancer (CAN) 107) [2009 60, a70: f7g^3 p6g* f7g f6g^4 f6g^3 f6g^3 f7g 6g^3 7m^6 f7g f6g* f6g p7.1g p7.1g^4 f7g p6g f8f Dec 12] workmanlike gelding: fair handicapper on all-weather, modest on turf: won at Wolverhampton (amateurs) in January and Southwell in June: effective at 6f to 1m: acts on all-weather and good to firm ground: usually wears blinkers/visor: formerly tongue tied: none too consistent. *S. R. Bowring* **52 a75**

KING'S MAJESTY (IRE) 7 b.g. King's Best (USA) 132 – Tiavanita (USA) (J O Tobin (USA) 130) [2009 68: p13g^3 p13g^2 p13g^2 11.9g^4 p12g Dec 31] close-coupled gelding: fair performer: stays 13f: acts on polytrack, good to firm and good to soft ground: tried in cheekpieces. *A. M. Hales* **70**

KING'S MASQUE 3 b.g. Noverre (USA) 125 – Top Flight Queen 82 (Mark of Esteem (IRE) 137) [2009 p8g4 p8g p8g5 10.9g6 10.1d4 8m p8m* 8d4 Oct 22] 14,000Y: good-topped gelding: fourth foal: half-brother to 3 winners, including 4-y-o Anne of Kiev and 5-y-o Big Robert: dam, 1¼m winner, half-sister to smart performer up to 1¾m Sacrament: fair performer on all-weather, modest on turf: won claimer at Kempton in September: should stay 1¼m: acts on polytrack and good to soft ground: sold 11,000 gns in October. *W. R. Muir* **63 a74**

KING'S MIRACLE (IRE) 3 ch.f. King's Best (USA) 132 – Pretty Sharp 64 (Interrex (CAN)) [2009 p6g p7.1g4 p8f Dec 20] 50,000Y: half-sister to several winners, notably smart 5f (at 2 yrs) to 7f winner Twilight Blues (by Bluebird): dam maiden (best at 7f at 2 yrs) who became temperamental: modest form in polytrack maidens. *J. R. Gask* **55**

KINGS 'N DREAMS 2 b.g. (Mar 23) Royal Applause 124 – Last Dream (IRE) 80 (Alzao (USA) 117) [2009 6.5g 6s4 p7m4 Nov 26] rather unfurnished gelding: half-brother to several winners, including 4-y-o Prairie Storm and useful French 8.5f winner Last Cry (by Peintre Celebre): dam, Irish 1½m winner, half-sister to Grand Criterium winners Lost World and Fijar Tango, latter also high class up to 1½m: best effort in maidens when fourth to Adventure Story at Doncaster: should stay 7f/1m: gelded after final start. *D. K. Ivory* **73**

KINGS OF LEO 2 b.f. (Jan 19) Compton Place 125 – Mrs Brown 60 (Royal Applause 124) [2009 5g5 5g* 5.1m 5.1m3 5m2 p5g 5.1m2 5g p6m p6m6 p5m4 p5m3 Dec 30] £13,000Y: sturdy filly: second foal: dam, maiden who probably stayed 1¼m, half-sister to useful Italian 2004 2-y-o sprinter Shifting Place: fairly useful performer: won maiden at Warwick in May: good second in nursery at Bath seventh start: left R. Hannon and below form after: best at 5f: acts on polytrack and good to firm ground. *J. R. Boyle* **82**

KINGS ON THE ROOF 3 b.c. King Charlemagne (USA) 120 – Stylish Clare (IRE) 77 (Desert Style (IRE) 121) [2009 –: p6g p7g4 p6g4 7m4 f7g 6d p8g Aug 5] modest maiden: stays 7f: acts on polytrack and good to firm going: tried in cheekpieces. *G. C. Bravery* **50**

KING'S PARADE 2 b.c. (Feb 12) Dynaformer (USA) – Bay Tree (IRE) 100 (Daylami (IRE) 138) [2009 7s2 7.1g3 p8.6g5 Oct 10] 220,000Y: first foal: dam, 2-y-o 6f/7f winner who stayed 1¼m, half-sister to Sprint Cup winner Tante Rose: fair form in maidens: should stay 1¼m. *Sir Michael Stoute* **72**

KINGSPARK BOY (IRE) 2 b.g. (Feb 4) Tillerman 123 – Malacca (USA) (Danzig (USA)) [2009 8m Sep 13] 33/1, tailed off in maiden at Ffos Las, looking awkward. *W. K. Goldsworthy* **–**

KINGS POINT (IRE) 8 b.h. Fasliyev (USA) 120 – Rahika Rose 91 (Unfuwain (USA) 131) [2009 101: 8m 7m 8m6 7.6m4 8m 8m 7d 7m 7m 9m4 8m4 Sep 23] strong, compact horse: unimpressive mover: useful performer: generally on downgrade in 2009 after fourth in quite valuable handicap at Chester on fourth outing: has won at 9f, recent best over 7f: acts on any going: tried in headgear: usually races prominently. *D. Nicholls* **96 d**

KING'S RANSOM 6 b.g. Daylami (IRE) 138 – Luana 101 (Shaadi (USA) 126) [2009 83: p8g5 p10g6 p8g 10.3m3 8m 10m 9m6 p11g Sep 2] rather leggy gelding: fair handicapper: stays 1½m: acts on all-weather, soft and good to firm going: tried in blinkers/cheekpieces: front runner. *S. Gollings* **73**

KING'S REALM (IRE) 2 ch.g. (Mar 30) King's Best (USA) 132 – Sweet Home Alabama (IRE) 56 (Desert Prince (IRE) 130) [2009 p8g 8.1m6 8.3s Oct 7] 47,000Y: workmanlike gelding: second foal: dam, Irish maiden (stayed 8.5f), half-sister to top-class miler Proclamation (by King's Best): modest form last 2 starts in maidens: type to do much better at 3 yrs. *Sir Mark Prescott* **57 p**

KING'S REVENGE 6 br.g. Wizard King 122 – Retaliator 80 (Rudimentary (USA) 118) [2009 10.2m6 11.6m6 12d p12.2m5 Sep 28] good-topped gelding: fairly useful performer on Flat in 2006 (similar form over hurdles since): just fair form in 2009, leaving A. King £18,000 after third outing: barely stays 1½m: acts on polytrack: tried blinkered. *S. Lycett* **69**

KING'S SABRE 3 ch.g. King's Best (USA) 132 – Lightsabre 63 (Polar Falcon (USA) 126) [2009 87?: p7g4 7g 7m p7g2 7m 7g4 p7.1g 7m2 p7g2 p6g 7m 5v5 p5.1g f6g6 p5.1g f5f f7g2 Dec 18] rather leggy gelding: fair maiden: claimed from W. Muir £6,000 ninth start: should stay 1m: acts on all-weather and good to firm ground: often blinkered/in cheekpieces: one to treat with caution. *R. C. Guest* **68 §**

KING'S SALUTE (USA) 3 b.c. Kingmambo (USA) 125 – Imperial Gesture (USA) 124 (Langfuhr (CAN) 124) [2009 10d p11g* p13m* Nov 28] second foal: dam, US/UAE 7f (including at 2 yrs) to 9f (Grade 1) winner, half-sister to US Grade 1 8.5f (at 2 yrs)/9f **97 p**

winner Sardula: useful and progressive form: trained on debut by A. Fabre in France: won maiden at Kempton in October and handicap at Lingfield in November, latter by 2½ lengths from Coeur de Lionne: stays 13f: acts on polytrack: will go on progressing. *M. Johnston*

KING'S SIREN (IRE) 3 b.f. King's Best (USA) 132 – Blue Siren 113 (Bluebird (USA) 125) [2009 77p: 8m 7m May 30] strong filly: fair performer at 2 yrs: well held in 2009. *A. M. Balding* **–**

KING'S SONG (IRE) 3 ch.c. Indian Ridge 123 – Alleluia 117 (Caerleon (USA) 132) [2009 73p: 10.3s^{6} p9.5g* 10m^{4} Sep 18] strong colt: fair handicapper: won at Wolverhampton in September: will be suited by 1½m+: acts on polytrack and good to firm ground: should progress further at 4 yrs. *Sir Michael Stoute* **79 p**

KING'S STARLET 3 b.f. King's Best (USA) 132 – Brightest Star 77 (Unfuwain (USA) 131) [2009 75p: p8g* 10d^{6} 8m 8.1m^{4} 7g 8.1g^{6} 7m 6m Oct 16] attractive filly: fairly useful performer: won maiden at Kempton in April: several good efforts in better company after, including when 3¼ lengths seventh to Summer Fete in Oak Tree Stakes at Goodwood fifth outing: should stay beyond 1m: bit appeared to slip through mouth second outing: temperament under suspicion (pulls hard). *H. Morrison* **94**

KINGSTON ACACIA 2 b.f. (Feb 9) King of Roses (AUS) – Derartu (AUS) (Last Tycoon 131) [2009 p7g p7f^{6} 8g p7g^{2} Nov 14] rather leggy filly: fourth foal: dam Australian 7f/1m winner: modest maiden: visored, creditable second in nursery at Lingfield: stays 7f. *A. M. Balding* **63**

KINGSTON FOLLY 2 gr.g. (Jun 4) Septieme Ciel (USA) 123 – Napapijri (FR) 58 (Highest Honor (FR) 124) [2009 p8g^{5} Dec 7] first foal: dam maiden (stayed 1m): 25/1, better than bare result when 6¼ lengths fifth to Hidden Glory in maiden at Lingfield, travelling strongly until final 1f: should improve. *A. B. Haynes* **60 p**

KINGS TOPIC (USA) 9 ch.g. Kingmambo (USA) 125 – Topicount (USA) (Private Account (USA)) [2009 74: p10g^{2} p9.5g p10g p10g* p10g p9.5g p10g^{5} p10g p10m^{6} Dec 4] deep-bodied gelding: fair handicapper: won apprentice event at Lingfield in March: stays 1¼m: acts on polytrack: tried blinkered, often in cheekpieces in 2009: has bled: lazy, and one to treat with caution. *A. B. Haynes* **71 §**

KINGS TROOP 3 ch.g. Bertolini (USA) 125 – Glorious Colours 54 (Spectrum (IRE) 126) [2009 89: 7s^{5} 8.1g 8s^{6} p8m p10g^{5} Nov 18] good-topped gelding: handicapper, just fair at 3 yrs: left H. Cecil prior to final outing: stays 1¼m: best efforts on good to soft going: tried blinkered. *A. King* **72**

KING SUPREME (IRE) 4 b.c. King's Best (USA) 132 – Oregon Trail (USA) (Gone West (USA)) [2009 86: p12g^{2} p10g^{4} 10g* 9.9g^{6} 11.6g^{2} 12m 12f^{2} 12m^{3} 11.6m^{3} 10.4s* 10.1g^{5} p11g p11g^{6} 11.7g^{4} p13g* Nov 1] close-coupled, good-bodied colt: fairly useful performer: won handicap at Brighton in April, claimer at Haydock in July and handicap at Lingfield in November: effective at 1¼m to 13f: acts on polytrack, firm and soft going: usually blinkered: consistent. *R. Hannon* **88**

KING'S WARRIOR (FR) 2 b.c. (Feb 4) King's Best (USA) 132 – Save Me The Waltz (FR) (Halling (USA) 133) [2009 7g^{4} Oct 30] €7,000F, €75,000Y: good-topped colt: second foal: dam, French 11f winner, half-sister to useful dam of very smart performer up to 1½m Best Name (by King's Best): 16/1, promising 4¼ lengths fourth to Quick Wit in maiden at Newmarket: will stay 1¼m+: will improve. *G. L. Moore* **74 p**

KINGSWINFORD (IRE) 3 b.g. Noverre (USA) 125 – Berenica (IRE) 101 (College Chapel 122) [2009 91: 6g 6g 7m^{6} 5.1m^{6} 6g^{4} 5.2d^{2} 6m^{2} 6s^{2} 7.2s^{2} 6.1m^{3} p6g^{5} 7s^{3} 6g* 7v^{3} 7s Nov 7] leggy gelding: fairly useful performer: won claimer at Windsor in October: stays 7f: acts on polytrack, heavy and good to firm going: visored once: consistent. *P. D. Evans* **86**

KING'S WONDER 4 ch.g. King's Best (USA) 132 – Signs And Wonders 75§ (Danehill (USA) 126) [2009 94: 7g* 7g p6m 7g^{5} 7m^{6} p7g^{5} Oct 11] tall, rather leggy gelding: useful handicapper: won at Goodwood in May: largely below form after: stays 7f: acts on polytrack and good to firm ground: free-going front runner: sold 16,500 gns. *W. R. Muir* **97**

KINIAN (USA) 2 ch.c. (Feb 3) Langfuhr (CAN) 124 – Back It Up (USA) (Mt Livermore (USA)) [2009 7f Sep 7] 33/1 and backward, well held in maiden at Folkestone. *J. R. Best* **–**

KINIGI (IRE) 3 gr.f. Verglas (IRE) 118 – Kamalame (USA) (Souvenir Copy (USA) 113) [2009 62: f7g^{3} f8g f7g^{5} 8g f6g* f6m 7s f6g 5.7g^{4} 7m^{4} p6g^{3} p6g^{3} f5f^{5} f6g^{3} f7f^{3} p6f^{4} Dec 21] fair performer: won claimer at Southwell in July: effective at 5f, should stay 1m: acts on all-weather and soft ground: in cheekpieces later in 2009. *R. A. Harris* **65**

KINKY AFRO (IRE) 2 b.f. (Apr 24) Modigliani (USA) 106 – Feet of Flame (USA) **72** 59 (Theatrical 128) [2009 6m p8m^4 8g^5 p7.1g^2 7m Oct 3] €16,000Y: strong filly: fifth foal: half-sister to fairly useful 2007 2-y-o 7f winner Orpen Fire (by Orpen) and 3-y-o Fullback: dam maiden (stayed 1¼m): fair maiden: good ½-length second to Gallant Eagle in nursery at Wolverhampton: stays 7f: acts on polytrack, possibly unsuited by good to firm going. *J. S. Moore*

KINOUT (IRE) 4 b.g. Invincible Spirit (IRE) 121 – Kinn (FR) (Suave Dancer (USA) **57** 136) [2009 78: f6s^4 f6d f6g f6g^6 Mar 22] good-topped, quite attractive gelding: has a round action: just modest form in 2009: will prove best at 5f/6f: acts on all-weather and any turf going: tried in cheekpieces/blinkers: often front runner. *K. A. Ryan*

KINSMAN (IRE) 12 b.g. Distant Relative 128 – Besito 79 (Wassl 125) [2009 –, a52: **–** p8g^6 p8g* p8g^6 p8g^5 p8g p8g Nov 1] leggy, useful-looking gelding: modest on all- **a55** weather, unraced on turf since 2005: won minor event at Great Leighs in January: stays 1¼m: acts on all-weather: wears headgear: tried tongue tied: held up. *T. D. McCarthy*

KINSYA 6 ch.g. Mister Baileys 123 – Kimono (IRE) (Machiavellian (USA) 123) [2009 **91** 95: 8.3m^4 8.1m 8g^2 8g f8g 8g 8d^4 Oct 11] strong, close-coupled gelding: fairly useful handicapper: effective at 7f to 1¼m: acts on polytrack, soft and good to firm going: held up. *M. H. Tompkins*

KINTYRE BAY 2 gr. or br.g. (Feb 6) Mull of Kintyre (USA) 114 – Dim Ofan 80 **–** (Petong 126) [2009 6s 6g Oct 19] lengthy, good-topped gelding: backward, well held in maidens. *T. D. Barron*

KIPCHAK (IRE) 4 b. or br.g. Soviet Star (USA) 128 – Khawafi 86 (Kris 135) [2009 **83** 67: p8.6g^4 p8g* p8g* f8g^3 p7.1g^4 p8g* 6m^5 7m* 6f^3 7g 6d p7g* p7g^4 7m 7m^3 8m 7s 6m 7f^3 7.1g^5 7g p6g 6d^6 f6f^3 p6g^6 p7.1g* f7m^3 p7m^6 Dec 30] fairly useful performer: won seller in January, handicap in February, seller in March (left C. Brittain 5,400 gns) and claimer (left A. McCabe £10,000) in May, all at Lingfield, and handicaps at Redcar in April and Wolverhampton in December: effective at 6f to 1m: acts on all-weather and firm going: in cheekpieces nowadays: front runner/races prominently: has looked awkward, but is tough. *C. R. Dore*

KIRIBATI KING (IRE) 4 b.g. Kalanisi (IRE) 132 – Everlasting (Desert King (IRE) **79** 129) [2009 88: 16s^6 18g 17.1g^6 16.4g^4 Jul 25] big gelding: fair handicapper nowadays: stays 17f: acts on good to firm ground, all wins on softer than good (acts on heavy): visored final start: joined C. Mann. *M. R. Channon*

KIRKBY'S GEM 2 b.f. (Feb 22) Firebreak 125 – Just A Gem (Superlative 118) [2009 **53** 5.9m 5.9g 5g^5 5d^6 5d^6 5d^3 5m 5g Oct 6] lengthy, unfurnished filly: half-sister to 7f/1m winner Flash Ram (by Mind Games): dam unraced sister to Oaks third Pearl Angel: modest maiden: probably best at 5f: none too consistent. *A. Berry*

KIRKIE (USA) 4 b. or br.g. Gulch (USA) – Saleela (USA) 85 (Nureyev (USA) 131) **51 §** [2009 –, a72: p8.6g p6m f11g p8.6g^5 Dec 18] maiden handicapper: left S. Parr prior to final start (only form): stays 8.6f: acts on all-weather: tried in headgear/togue tie: one to treat with caution (has refused to race). *T. J. Pitt*

KIRKLEES (IRE) 5 b.h. Jade Robbery (USA) 121 – Moyesii (USA) (Diesis 133) **123** [2009 115: 9m^3 10g* a10m^4 12g 10m* 10.4g* p12m* 12d Oct 17] big, strong horse: very

totesport.com September Stakes, Kempton—Kirklees makes it three out of three in Britain in 2009, conceding weight all round and winning from All The Aces (striped cap)

smart performer: won handicap at Nad Al Sheba (beat Hattan 3¼ lengths) in February, listed race at Sandown and Sky Bet York Stakes (comfortably by 1¼ lengths from Allied Powers) in July, and totesport.com September Stakes at Kempton (beat All The Aces ¾ length) in September: below form in Caulfield Cup (Handicap) final start: stays 1½m: acts on polytrack, firm and good to soft ground. *Saeed bin Suroor*

KIRK MICHAEL 5 b.g. Selkirk (USA) 129 – Pervenche (Latest Model 115) [2009 –: p7g^6 7m^2 7m^2 Jun 12] leggy, useful-looking gelding: fairly useful handicapper: raced only at 7f: acted on polytrack and good to firm going: dead. *H. Candy* **92**

KIRKSON 3 ch.g. Selkirk (USA) 129 – Viva Maria (Hernando (FR) 127) [2009 –: 7.1m 10m 8m^2 9g^5 10.9g^5 Jul 3] rather leggy gelding: modest maiden: stays 1m: acts on good to firm ground: tried blinkered: temperamental. *P. W. Chapple-Hyam* **63 §**

KIRSTY'S BOY (IRE) 2 ch.g. (Apr 6) Tagula (IRE) 116 – Mayfair 82 (Green Desert (USA) 127) [2009 p5g 5g* 5g^3 5m 6g^6 5.2d 6m 6m p7g^2 p7m* p8m^2 Dec 30] smallish, close-coupled gelding: eighth foal: half-brother to winner in Greece by Fleetwood: dam, 2-y-o 6f winner, sister to smart 1991 2-y-o sprinter Magic Ring: fair performer: won maiden at Goodwood in May and claimer at Lingfield in December: stays 7f: acts on polytrack and good to soft going: blinkered once: suspect temperament. *J. S. Moore* **76**

KIRSTYS LAD 7 b.g. Lake Coniston (IRE) 131 – Killick 69 (Slip Anchor 136) [2009 65: p9.5g^6 p8.6g p8.6g^3 p8.6g p12.2g^6 9.9g^2 12.3g 12.6d p8.6g 10g p8.6g p8.6g p9.5g^6 p9.5g^3 p9.5g p8.6g^3 Dec 19] good-bodied gelding: modest handicapper: stays easy 1½m: acts on polytrack and good to firm going: tried blinkered. *M. Mullineaux* **61**

KISS A PRINCE 3 b.g. Fraam 114 – Prancing 98 (Prince Sabo 123) [2009 –: p7g^3 p7g^2 p7g* 7m f7g p7g^3 p8g* p8g 8g^4 Oct 30] quite good-topped gelding: fair handicapper: won at Lingfield in March and August: stays 1m: acts on polytrack. *D. K. Ivory* **76**

KISS 'N TELL 3 ch.f. Sakhee (USA) 136 – Time For Tea (IRE) 73 (Imperial Frontier (USA) 112) [2009 8.1g Aug 13] lengthy filly: half-sister to several fairly useful winners, including 8-y-o Trifti: dam maiden (stayed 1¼m): tailed off in maiden at Sandown. *G. L. Moore* **–**

KITE WOOD (IRE) 3 b.c. Galileo (IRE) 134 – Kite Mark 58 (Mark of Esteem (IRE) 137) [2009 114p: 10.4g^5 12g 13m* 13.3m* 14.6m^2 Sep 12] big, strong colt: very smart performer: won Bahrain Trophy at Newmarket (by 2½ lengths from Tactic) in July and CGA Geoffrey Freer Stakes at Newbury (beat Halicarnassus readily by 3½ lengths) in August: favourite, good ¾-length second to stable-companion Mastery in St Leger at Doncaster final start, leading over 2f out: reportedly underwent treatment on ankles after: will stay 2m: unraced on extremes of going: has sweated/got on toes beforehand: races prominently. *Saeed bin Suroor* **121**

KITHONIA (FR) 2 b.f. (Jan 1) Sadler's Wells (USA) 132 – Ratukidul (FR) 79 (Danehill (USA) 126) [2009 7s* Sep 3] first foal: dam, 2-y-o 7f winner, half-sister to very smart French/US performer (best at 1m/1¼m) Johann Quatz (by Sadler's Wells) and Prix du Jockey Club winner Hernando: 15/8 favourite, promising when winning maiden at Salisbury readily by 2¼ lengths from Lady Slippers, green and drifting left when clear: will be well suited by 1¼m+: useful prospect. *H. R. A. Cecil* **90 p**

KIT KAT 2 b.g. (Jan 16) One Cool Cat (USA) 123 – Tanda Tula (IRE) (Alhaarth (IRE) 126) [2009 7.1m 7d p7.1g Aug 17] well beaten in maidens. *George Baker* **–**

KITTY ALLEN 3 br.f. One Cool Cat (USA) 123 – Aly McBe (USA) (Alydeed (CAN) 120) [2009 52: p7.1g p6g^5 p5g Mar 12] close-coupled filly: maiden: poor form in 2009: tried blinkered. *C. N. Kellett* **37**

KIWI BAY 4 b.g. Mujahid (USA) 125 – Bay of Plenty (FR) (Octagonal (NZ) 126) [2009 92: 6m 6g 6d^5 7g^3 7.2g^2 7.9m 7g^5 7m 7m^2 8m^4 8m* 7g^3 8.3g^2 7s^2 Nov 7] tall gelding: useful handicapper: in excellent form late in 2009, winning at Pontefract in September: further improvement after, including when second in apprentice event at Doncaster final start: stays 8.3f: acts on polytrack, soft and good to firm going: often held up. *M. Dods* **97**

KIYARI 3 b.f. Key of Luck (USA) 126 – Ashford Castle (USA) (Bates Motel (USA)) [2009 64: p8.6g* p10g^2 p9.5g^4 p10g^5 Apr 8] sturdy filly: type to carry condition: modest performer: won claimer at Wolverhampton in January: stays 1¼m: raced only on polytrack since debut. *M. Botti* **64**

KLADESTER (USA) 3 ch.g. Van Nistelrooy (USA) 108 – Longing To Dance (USA) (Nureyev (USA) 131) [2009 65: 7m^6 8d May 16] good-topped gelding: handicapper: well below form both starts at 3 yrs: tongue tied. *B. Smart* **–**

KLEIO 2 b.f. (Apr 2) Sadler's Wells (USA) 132 – Colza (USA) 89 (Alleged (USA) 138) [2009 p8m Dec 4] sister to smart French 1m (at 2 yrs) to 11.5f (Lingfield Derby Trial) winner Linda's Lad and half-sister to 3 winners abroad, including useful French miler Ulterior Motives (by Selkirk): dam, 2-y-o 1m winner, half-sister to dam of Prix de l'Arc de Triomphe winner Rail Link: 11/2 and green, down the field in maiden at Lingfield: should improve. *H. R. A. Cecil* **– p**

KLOOF 3 b.c. Cape Cross (IRE) 129 – Ravine 81 (Indian Ridge 123) [2009 p8g^4 8d^4 p7.1g 7m^2 8g^6 p7.1g^3 p7.1m 8m^4 6g Oct 16] 110,000Y: leggy colt: fifth foal: closely related to smart 2004 2-y-o 6f (July Stakes) winner Captain Hurricane (by Desert Style) and half-brother to 2 winners, including 7f winner Nelly's Glen (by Efisio): dam, 6f/7f winner, half-sister to 1000 Guineas second Niche: fair maiden: left J. Gosden 16,000 gns after fourth start: stays 1m: acts on polytrack and good to firm going: sent to Bahrain. *K. A. Ryan* **79**

KLYNCH 3 b.g. Kyllachy 129 – Inchcoonan 81 (Emperor Jones (USA) 119) [2009 80, a88: p6g 6g^3 6g 6g 6s* 6g 6d^3 6g p6g p6g Oct 2] close-coupled gelding: fairly useful handicapper: won at Haydock in July: below form after: effective at 5f/6f: acts on polytrack, firm and good to soft going: usually blinkered: held up: suspect attitude: sold 7,500 gns in October. *B. J. Meehan* **89**

KNAVESMIRE (IRE) 3 b.f. One Cool Cat (USA) 123 – Caribbean Escape (Pivotal 124) [2009 91: 7m 6m 6m 7g 7g Oct 9] tall filly: little impact in handicaps in 2009. *M. Brittain* **–**

KNEESY EARSY NOSEY 3 ch.f. Compton Place 125 – Evie Hone (IRE) 69 (Royal Academy (USA) 130) [2009 55: f8g^6 f8g p9.5g^3 p12.2m p9.5m 5.7f 10d 8g^3 6m^5 12.1m 8m^6 6m Aug 22] strong filly: modest performer at best: stays 9.5f: acts on all-weather: tried visored/in cheekpieces: none too consistent. *Miss A. Stokell* **39 a53**

KNIGHTFIRE (IRE) 2 b.g. (Mar 26) Invincible Spirit (IRE) 121 – The Castles (IRE) 95 (Imperial Ballet (IRE) 110) [2009 p5g^6 5g^5 5.7f p7.1m^2 f7g^2 Dec 18] good-quartered gelding: modest maiden: runner-up in nurseries at Wolverhampton and Southwell: stays easy 7f. *W. R. Swinburn* **58**

KNIGHT'S VICTORY (IRE) 3 b.g. Cape Cross (IRE) 129 – Diminuendo (USA) 126 (Diesis 133) [2009 f11g^6 9.8m* 9.8d Sep 1] good-topped gelding: half-brother to 3 winners, notably smart 1998 2-y-o 7f/1m winner (stayed 1½m) Calando (by Storm Cat): dam won Oaks: fair form: best effort when winning maiden at Ripon in August (still green): well beaten on handicap debut there next time: will be suited by 1½m: sold £3,500, joined Michael Smith. *M. Johnston* **76**

KNOCKBACK (IRE) 2 b.g. (Apr 28) Redback 116 – Knockanure (USA) 82 (Nureyev (USA) 131) [2009 5.7g p7g 6m^6 8.3d p8g p7g Nov 25] good-topped gelding: maiden: modest form at best. *P. R. Chamings* **50**

KNOCKDOLIAN (IRE) 2 b.c. (Feb 4) Montjeu (IRE) 137 – Doula (USA) (Gone West (USA)) [2009 8m 8v^3 Oct 24] strong colt: fifth foal: half-brother to 3 winners, including 6-y-o Humungous and French 1½m winner Ambitious Genes (by Grand Lodge): dam, US 1m winner, out of Breeders' Cup Juvenile Fillies winner Phone Chatter: better effort in maidens when 5¾ lengths third to Gardening Leave at Newbury: will be suited by 1¼m/1½m: will do better still. *R. Charlton* **73 p**

KNOCKENDUFF 2 b.f. (May 2) Oratorio (IRE) 128 – Sewards Folly 70 (Rudimentary (USA) 118) [2009 6m^4 6m^6 7d^3 7d^6 8m^4 p8g p8m^3 8m Sep 23] 130,000F, 75,000Y: lengthy filly: fifth foal: half-sister to 3-y-o Sayif and useful 2005 2-y-o 5f (Cornwallis Stakes)/6f winner Hunter Street (by Compton Place), later 7f winner in Italy: dam disappointing maiden: modest maiden: stays 1m: acts on polytrack and good to firm going: none too consistent: sold 52,000 gns. *M. R. Channon* **62**

CGA Geoffrey Freer Stakes, Newbury—Kite Wood warms up for the St Leger with a wide-margin win over Halicarnassus (second left) and Godolphin second string Age of Reason (third left)

Sky Bet Dash (Heritage Handicap), York—
smart handicappers Knot In Wood (white face) and Barney McGrew (noseband) fight out a photo finish

KNOCK THREE TIMES (IRE) 3 b.f. Hernando (FR) 127 – Tawoos (FR) 104 (Rainbow Quest (USA) 134) [2009 –: 8m[6] 8.3g[5] 9d 11.1m 8f 12d 14.1m[4] 14.1m[6] 16.1d Sep 7] modest maiden: stays 1¾m: acts on good to firm and good to soft ground: won juvenile hurdle in October. *W. Storey* **52**

KNOTGARDEN (IRE) 3 b.f. Dr Fong (USA) 128 – Eilean Shona 102 (Suave Dancer (USA) 136) [2009 10.3m[4] Jun 27] fifth foal: half-sister to 5-y-o Dart and 9.7f winner Penny Wedding (by Pennekamp): dam, 9f (at 2 yrs) to 2m winner, stayed 2¾m: encouraging fourth to Interdiamonds in maiden at Doncaster: will improve. *J. R. Fanshawe* **63 p**

KNOT IN WOOD (IRE) 7 b.g. Shinko Forest (IRE) – Notley Park 71 (Wolfhound (USA) 126) [2009 115: 6m[3] 6m[3] 6f[2] 6m 6v 6m 6d* 6d[4] 6g* 6d[3] 6m[3] 6m 6g 6s Nov 3] sturdy gelding: smart performer: won freebets.co.uk Chipchase Stakes at Newcastle (by 1¼ lengths from Ancien Regime) in June and Sky Bet Dash (Handicap) at York (by head from Barney McGrew) in July: good third in Stewards' Cup at Goodwood (1¾ lengths behind Genki) and Ayr Gold Cup (beaten a length by Jimmy Styles) next 2 starts: below form after: best form at 6f: acts on polytrack and any turf going: tried in blinkers/cheekpieces: reliable. *R. A. Fahey* **117**

KNOW BY NOW 3 b.g. Piccolo 121 – Addicted To Love 73 (Touching Wood (USA) 127) [2009 p7g[3] p8g[2] p7.1g 10m[4] 7.9g 8m 8m Sep 17] 52,000Y: half-brother to several winners, including fairly useful 5f winner Daddy Cool (by Kyllachy) and 7f/1m winner Unchain My Heart (by Pursuit of Love): dam 1¼m to 1¾m winner: fair form first 2 starts: went wrong way after: stays 1m: tried blinkered: sold £3,200 in October. *T. P. Tate* **75 d**

KNOWLEDGEABLE 2 b.g. (Feb 22) Reset (AUS) 124 – Belle's Edge (Danehill Dancer (IRE) 117) [2009 6.1g 7m 7.1m 7m[4] Oct 26] small gelding: poor maiden: likely to stay 1m. *B. Palling* **42**

KNOW NO FEAR 4 b.g. Primo Valentino (IRE) 116 – Alustar 71 (Emarati (USA) 74) [2009 81: p5g[4] p5g p5.1g[6] p5.1g[5] p6m 6d p5.1g 5m p5.1g p7m p7f Dec 16] tall, lengthy gelding: fair handicapper: left D. Shaw after eighth start: raced mostly at 5f: acts on polytrack, heavy and good to firm going. *A. J. Lidderdale* **76**

KOCHANSKI (IRE) 3 ch.f. King's Best (USA) 132 – Ascot Cyclone (USA) 93 (Rahy (USA) 115) [2009 –p: f8g[4] p10g[4] p12.2m* p12g 12.1m[2] 12m[3] 12.1s[5] f11g 11.8m[4] 14m[5] 12m 12.1m* 11.9m 12.1m[2] 12d[5] p12.2g Sep 11] angular filly: modest handicapper: won at Wolverhampton in February and Beverley (selling event) in July: left M. Johnston after fourteenth outing: stays 1½m: acts on polytrack and good to firm ground: none too consistent. *J. R. Weymes* **64**

KOKKOKILA 5 b.m. Robellino (USA) 127 – Meant To Be 84 (Morston (FR) 125) **70** [2009 74: 16d^{4} 12m^{5} p16g 12.1v^{6} 16d* 16g^{4} Oct 28] sturdy mare: fair handicapper: won jump jockeys event at Goodwood in October: stays 2m: acts on soft and good to firm ground: often in cheekpieces in 2009. *Lady Herries*

KOMREYEV STAR 7 b.g. Komaite (USA) – L'Ancressaan 67 (Dalsaan 125) [2009 **55** 60: f8s f8g f8g^{2} p9.5g^{6} f8g^{5} f8g 8.1d^{4} 8.3g f8f f8f^{6} f8f^{6} Dec 17] sturdy gelding: modest handicapper: stays 9.5f: acts on all-weather and any turf going: effective with/without cheekpieces: tried tongue tied: has reportedly bled. *R. E. Peacock*

KONA COAST 2 b.c. (Jan 24) Oasis Dream 129 – Macadamia (IRE) 115 (Classic **102** Cliche (IRE) 128) [2009 6g^{6} 7m^{5} 7f* 6m 7m^{2} Oct 3] 85,000Y: good-topped colt: second foal: dam, 1m (including at 2 yrs, and Falmouth Stakes)/1¼m winner, half-sister to smart performers Pistachio (sprinter) and Azarole (miler): useful performer: won maiden at Brighton in September: in cheekpieces, much improved when neck second to Oasis Dancer in sales race at Newmarket, rallying despite rider losing whip: will stay 1m: blinkered first 2 starts. *J. H. M. Gosden*

KONKA (USA) 3 ch.f. Johannesburg (USA) 127 – Defining Style (USA) (Out of Place **–** (USA)) [2009 –: f6g^{6} 8g^{6} Apr 8] no sign of ability: tried tongue tied. *E. F. Vaughan*

KOO AND THE GANG (IRE) 2 b.g. (Feb 22) Le Vie Dei Colori 126 – Entertain 56 **70** (Royal Applause 124) [2009 5m f5g^{2} f5g* 5g f5g p5.1g Oct 30] €13,000Y: compact gelding: first foal: dam, 6f winner, half-sister to useful performer up to 1¼m Deal Fair: fair performer: won maiden at Southwell in May: off nearly 4 months, well below form in nurseries last 2 starts: likely to stay 6f: acts on fibresand. *B. Ellison*

KOOKIE 2 b.f. (Feb 6) Makbul 104 – Breakfast Creek 63 (Hallgate 127) [2009 5v 6m^{6} **49** 7m 7m^{5} 7g Sep 3] leggy filly: half-sister to 3 winning sprinters, including 6f winner Game Flora (by Mind Games): dam 2-y-o 5f winner: poor maiden. *R. E. Barr*

KOOL KATIE 4 b.f. Millkom 124 – Katie Komaite 54 (Komaite (USA)) [2009 59: **59** 8.1v 10.4g 10.3m^{2} 9.9f 9.2g 10m 10g^{4} 9.1v p9.5g^{2} p9.5g Nov 30] smallish, stocky filly: modest maiden handicapper: stays 1¼m: acts on all-weather and firm ground: none too consistent: sold £3,200, sent to Belgium. *Mrs G. S. Rees*

KORALEVA TECTONA (IRE) 4 b.f. Fasliyev (USA) 120 – Miss Teak (USA) 95 **81** (Woodman (USA) 126) [2009 81: 7m 7m^{4} 7m 7m^{4} 6m^{6} 7g* 7g^{5} 7d 7m 7g Oct 31] big, lengthy filly: fairly useful handicapper: won at Epsom in July: stays 7f: acts on soft and good to firm going. *Pat Eddery*

KOSTAR 8 ch.g. Komaite (USA) – Black And Amber 45 (Weldnaas (USA) 112) [2009 **89** 95: 6m 6m 6g Aug 29] good-topped gelding: handicapper, just fairly useful form at 8 yrs: best at 6f/7f: acts on polytrack, firm and good to soft ground: in cheekpieces final start. *C. G. Cox*

KRIS KIN LINE (IRE) 3 ch.c. Kris Kin (USA) 126 – Shell Garland (USA) 80 **78** (Sadler's Wells (USA) 132) [2009 70p: 9.9g^{3} p12g* 14m Jul 10] fair form: won maiden at Lingfield in June: should stay 1¾m: sold £4,000 in October. *Sir Michael Stoute*

KRISTALLO (GER) 4 ch.g. Lando (GER) 128 – Key West (GER) (In The Wings 128) **68** [2009 11.6g^{4} 15g^{3} 15m Jul 9] placed in minor event at Hanover and maiden at Halle on last 2 starts in 2008 (sold from P. Rau in Germany 17,000 gns and gelded after): fair form in handicaps in Britain: stays 15f. *P. R. Webber*

KRISTEN JANE (USA) 2 ch.f. (Jan 21) Forest Wildcat (USA) 120 – British **49** Columbia (Selkirk (USA) 129) [2009 5d^{4} 5m 6d 5m^{6} 6g^{4} 5m 6g Oct 23] $17,000Y, £19,000 2-y-o: fourth foal: closely related to 3-y-o Asaint Needs Brass and half-sister to 2 winners, including 6f (at 2 yrs)/9f (in USA) winner Crumbs of Comfort (by Pulpit): dam, French maiden, half-sister to useful performer up to 1¼m Heart of Darkness: poor maiden: effective at 5f/6f: acts on good to firm and good to soft going. *Miss L. A. Perratt*

KRISTOPHER JAMES (IRE) 3 ch.g. Spartacus (IRE) 107 – Ela Alethia (Kris 135) **64** [2009 61: f8g f11g^{5} 10.3g^{3} 9m 10.4s^{5} 10.3g 10.1m^{4} 10s p10g p10g^{4} p9.5g* Oct 29] modest handicapper: won at Wolverhampton in October: stays 10.3f: acts on all-weather and good to firm ground. *W. M. Brisbourne*

KRONFUL 2 b.f. (Mar 5) Singspiel (IRE) 133 – Albahja 111 (Sinndar (IRE) 134) [2009 **63 p** 7.5f^{3} Aug 29] first foal: dam 1½m winner: 3/1 and green, 6¼ lengths third to Saafia in maiden at Beverley, soon off bridle and nearest finish: will be well suited by 1¼m+: sure to do better. *M. A. Jarvis*

KRUGERRAND (USA) 10 ch.g. Gulch (USA) – Nasers Pride (USA) (Al Nasr (FR) **72 §** 126) [2009 78§: p10g p12g^{6} p12g^{2} p12g^{2} p9.5g^{3} 11.6m^{2} May 7] big, lengthy gelding: fair performer: stays easy 1½m: acts on polytrack, firm and soft going: tried tongue tied: held up: ungenuine. *W. J. Musson*

KRYMIAN 2 gr.g. (Apr 9) Bahamian Bounty 116 – Kryena 72 (Kris 135) [2009 7.1g p8.6g² 8.3s Oct 7] well-made gelding: first foal: dam maiden (should have stayed 1¼m): easily best effort in maidens when length second to Miss Starlight at Wolverhampton: gelded after final start: stays 8.6f, should prove as effective at 7f. *Sir Michael Stoute* **85**

KRYSANTHE 2 b.f. (Mar 6) Kyllachy 129 – Aegean Magic 76 (Wolfhound (USA) 126) [2009 p6g p7g Nov 11] 9,000Y: third foal: half-sister to 3-y-o Sills Vincero: dam 6f winner: well held in maidens at Kempton. *J. A. Geake* **–**

KUANYAO (IRE) 3 b.g. American Post 121 – Nullarbor (Green Desert (USA) 127) [2009 –: 6m 6m* 7g³ 7m³ p7g² p7g* p7m* p7.1g* Dec 12] sturdy gelding: fairly useful handicapper: won at Salisbury in July, Lingfield in October, Kempton in November and Wolverhampton in December: stays 7f: acts on polytrack and good to firm going. *P. J. Makin* **81**

KUDU COUNTRY (IRE) 3 gr.g. Captain Rio 122 – Nirvavita (FR) (Highest Honor (FR) 124) [2009 79: 12s⁴ 12d⁶ 14m 14.1d³ 14v⁴ Sep 5] workmanlike gelding: fair handicapper: seems to stay 1¾m: unraced on firm going, acts on any other: often forces pace: won juvenile hurdles in November/December. *T. P. Tate* **79**

KUMBESHWAR 2 b.g. (Feb 19) Doyen (IRE) 132 – Camp Fire (IRE) 81 (Lahib (USA) 129) [2009 6g 7m⁶ 7m* 7g⁵ 7g³ 7v* Nov 3] lengthy, unfurnished gelding: third foal: half-brother to 2007 2-y-o 6f winner Night Robe (by Robellino): dam, 2-y-o 6f winner who stayed 1m, out of half-sister to Irish 2000 Guineas winner Flash of Steel: fairly useful performer: won maiden at Chester in September and nursery at Catterick in November: should stay 1m: acts on heavy and good to firm going: races prominently. *P. D. Evans* **82**

KUMMEL EXCESS (IRE) 2 ch.f. (Apr 30) Exceed And Excel (AUS) 126 – Ipanema Beach 67 (Lion Cavern (USA) 117) [2009 p5m p6g⁴ f5m² p5m⁴ p5.1g* Dec 14] €22,000F, 19,000Y: close-coupled filly: fourth foal: half-sister to 3 winners, including 6-y-o Lethal: dam 1m/8.5f winner: fair performer: won maiden at Wolverhampton: should be suited by 6f. *George Baker* **66**

KUNTE KINTEH 5 b.g. Indian Lodge (IRE) 127 – Summer Siren (FR) (Saint Cyrien (FR) 128) [2009 72: 6m 9.1v Oct 31] lengthy gelding: handicapper: well held both starts in 2009. *D. Nicholls* **–**

KURTANELLA 2 b. or br.f. (Mar 11) Pastoral Pursuits 127 – Aconite 52 (Primo Dominie 121) [2009 5m² 5.2g* 6f 6g p6g* 7m³ 7m⁴ 7m⁵ Oct 3] £20,000Y: compact filly: second foal: dam, sprint maiden, half-sister to useful sprinter Power Lake: fairly useful performer: won minor event at Newbury in May and nursery at Kempton in August: creditable efforts in nurseries after: stays 7f: acts on polytrack and good to firm going. *R. Hannon* **85**

KWAMI BISCUIT 2 ch.g. (May 11) Clerkenwell (USA) 113 – Singer On The Roof 62 (Chief Singer 131) [2009 7d⁵ 7d 6g Aug 31] close-coupled gelding: poor form in sellers/claimer. *G. A. Harker* **41**

KYBER 8 ch.g. First Trump 118 – Mahbob Dancer (FR) (Groom Dancer (USA) 128) [2009 70, a–: 15m⁵ 13.1g⁵ 16m⁴ 14g⁴ Aug 11] handicapper, just modest form on Flat in 2009: stays 2m: acts on polytrack, soft and good to firm going: fair hurdler. *J. S. Goldie* **57 a–**

KYLEENE 3 b.f. Kyllachy 129 – Mrs Nash 66 (Night Shift (USA)) [2009 73p: 6g² p7.1g* Aug 10] fair form: won handicap at Wolverhampton in August by a head from Desert Streak: will be suited by 1m: acts on polytrack: should improve again. *J. Noseda* **79 p**

KYLE (IRE) 5 ch.g. Kyllachy 129 – Staylily (IRE) (Grand Lodge (USA) 125) [2009 85: 5g³ f5g⁵ 6v p7g p6g⁵ 6v 6d* 6f⁶ 6m⁴ p6g 5m 5m 5m⁵ p5.1g p5g⁴ p6g⁴ p5f³ f6d Dec 29] strong, lengthy gelding: has a short, choppy action: fairly useful handicapper: dead-heated at Yarmouth in July: best at 6f/7f: acts on polytrack, firm and good to soft ground: tried in cheekpieces: usually held up. *C. R. Dore* **84**

KYLE OF BUTE 3 ch.g. Kyllachy 129 – Blinding Mission (IRE) 70 (Marju (IRE) 127) [2009 58: 7m 6.1m 8m³ 7m⁴ 7f⁴ 10d⁴ 10.1g⁵ 10f² 10d² 10m⁵ 10m* 10g⁵ 10.2g⁵ Oct 28] good-quartered gelding: fair performer: won seller at Leicester (left J. Dunlop 5,200 gns) in October: stays 1¼m: acts on firm and good to soft ground: tried blinkered/visored: gelded after final start. *B. P. J. Baugh* **71**

KYLLACHY KING 3 b.g. Kyllachy 129 – Baileys Dancer 90 (Groom Dancer (USA) 128) [2009 10m 10m Jun 13] strong gelding: down the field in maidens: sold 4,000 gns in July, sent to Greece. *Mrs A. J. Perrett* **–**

KYLLACHY STAR 3 b.g. Kyllachy 129 – Jaljuli 107 (Jalmood (USA) 126) [2009 83: p6g⁵ p7g⁴ 6g 7m* 7.1m* 8m⁶ 7d⁶ 7s³ 8v 7.2m⁵ p7g* 7s Nov 7] small, close-coupled geld- **101**

ing: useful handicapper: won at York in May, Sandown in June and Lingfield (beat Spirit of Sharjah by a length) in October: stays 1m: acts on polytrack, soft and good to firm going: consistent: gelded after final start. *R. A. Fahey*

KYLLACHY STORM 5 b.g. Kyllachy 129 – Social Storm (USA) (Future Storm **81**
(USA)) [2009 69: 6m^3 5.1m* 5.7d* 5.7f^5 5.7m^2 6g 5.7m^3 5g 5.7m^2 5.7g 5.7m^6 p6g **a67**
Oct 20] compact gelding: fairly useful handicapper: won twice at Bath in May: effective at 5f/6f: acts on soft and firm going: tried blinkered. *R. J. Hodges*

KYLLADDIE 2 ch.g. (Mar 14) Kyllachy 129 – Chance For Romance 81 (Entrepreneur **74**
123) [2009 6g^4 6d* 6m^4 6d^3 6d^5 p7.1g^5 p7.1g^3 p6g^4 Dec 17] £10,000Y: sturdy gelding: second foal: dam, 2-y-o 5.7f winner, half-sister to Queen Mary winners Romantic Myth and Romantic Liason: fair performer: won maiden at Ripon in May: left T. Tate £8,500 after fifth start: creditable efforts in nurseries at Wolverhampton after: stays easy 7f: acts on polytrack and good to soft going. *S. Gollings*

KYOATEE KILT 2 ch.c. (Apr 12) Kyllachy 129 – Oatey 68 (Master Willie 129) [2009 **54**
p6g p5.1g p7g^5 p8.6g^5 p10m^5 p7g Dec 31] modest form in maidens/nursery: stays 8.6f: tried blinkered. *P. F. I. Cole*

KYZER CHIEF 4 b.g. Rouvres (FR) 117 – Payvashooz 78 (Ballacashtal (CAN)) [2009 **74**
69: 5m^5 5m* 5g 5m^6 5g 5m^2 5d^5 5d^4 5m 5d^6 5m 5m^4 5m 5m^5 Oct 3] good-topped gelding: fair handicapper: won at Ripon in April: best at 5f/6f: yet to race on extremes of going: tried in cheekpieces: races prominently. *R. E. Barr*

L

LA ADELITA (IRE) 3 b.f. Anabaa (USA) 130 – Aiming 76 (Highest Honor (FR) 124) **–**
[2009 94: 7v Oct 24] strong filly: fairly useful performer at 2 yrs: well held only start in 2009: should prove best short of 1m: raced only on good ground or softer. *M. L. W. Bell*

LAAFET 4 b.g. Royal Applause 124 – Golden Way (IRE) 94 (Cadeaux Genereux 131) **76**
[2009 7s* 8.3d^5 p10g p8.6g^3 Dec 12] 70,000Y, £5,000 3-y-o: fourth foal: half-brother to very smart 1m to 1¼m winner (including US Grade 1 8.5f event) Ashkal Way (by Ashkalani): dam 1¼m winner: offered little in bumper: fair form on Flat: won maiden at Yarmouth in July: stays 8.6f: acts on polytrack and soft ground. *K. A. Morgan*

LAAHEB 3 b.g. Cape Cross (IRE) 129 – Maskunah (IRE) (Sadler's Wells (USA) 132) **118 p**
[2009 10m 10.1g* 10d* 10g^2 10m* 10g* Oct 31] 200,000Y: strong, well-made gelding: powerful galloper: fifth foal: half-brother to fairly useful 7f winner Guarantia (by Selkirk): dam unraced close relative of Nell Gwyn Stakes winner Cloud Castle (stayed 1½m) and half-sister to Luso, Warrsan and Needle Gun: smart and progressive form: won maiden at Yarmouth and handicap at Newmarket in July, handicap at Pontefract (by 4 lengths) in September and listed race at Newmarket (beat Prince Siegfried by length) in October: will stay 1½m: unraced on extremes of going: will improve further and make his mark in pattern company. *M. A. Jarvis*

Dalby Screw-Driver Handicap, Pontefract—
a one-sided affair as the progressive Laaheb claims the third of four wins in 2009

totesport Mile (Heritage Handicap), Goodwood—first-time blinkers work the oracle on Laa Rayb as he springs a 25/1 surprise; Spectait comes widest of all to claim second

LAA RAYB (USA) 5 b.g. Storm Cat (USA) – Society Lady (USA) 75 (Mr Prospector (USA)) [2009 118: 8m² 8.3m⁶ 7.1g 8.3m³ 7m 8g* 8m³ 8m 8.1d⁴ Sep 16] big, lengthy gelding: smart performer: easily best effort in 2009 when winning totesport Mile (Handicap) at Goodwood in July by 2¼ lengths from Spectait: respectable 4¼ lengths third to Mac Love in Sovereign Stakes at Salisbury next time: stays 1m: acts on fibresand, firm and good to soft going: blinkered last 4 starts: has given trouble at stall: untrustworthy. *M. Johnston* **116 §**

LAAZIM (USA) 3 b.g. Seeking The Gold (USA) – Lindy Wells (USA) (A P Indy (USA) 131) [2009 8g 8g 8g² 7g⁵ 12g³ 8m⁶ 8m² p8f Oct 14] $350,000Y: first foal: dam, ran twice in USA, half-sister to 4-y-o Cat Junior out of Prix Saint-Alary winner Luna Wells, herself half-sister to high-class performer up to 1¼m Linamix: fairly useful performer: left A. Fabre in France after fourth start: below form after: stays 1m (seemingly not 1½m): best efforts in blinkers: sold £7,500. *M. Johnston* **87 d**

LA BELLE DANE 3 b.f. Danetime (IRE) 121 – Lindfield Belle (IRE) 78 (Fairy King (USA)) [2009 7m May 8] 85,000F, 260,000Y: quite good-topped filly: sister to very smart 5f (including at 2 yrs)/6f winner Baltic King and useful Irish 2007 2-y-o 6f winner Domingues and half-sister to several winners: dam 2-y-o 5f winner: well held in maiden at Lingfield. *J. Noseda* **–**

LA BELLE JOANNIE 4 b.f. Lujain (USA) 119 – Sea Clover (IRE) 77 (Ela-Mana-Mou 132) [2009 –: 8.1g 8f³ 8.3m³ p10g 7s² 6.1d 7.1d² p10m f7m⁵ f8g Nov 17] leggy filly: modest maiden: stays easy 1¼m: acts on all-weather, firm and good to soft ground. *S. Curran* **55**

LABISA (IRE) 3 b.f. High Chaparral (IRE) 132 – Damiana (IRE) (Thatching 131) [2009 67: 8.3m² 7.5m² 7.1f* 7g⁴ 6v p7.1g⁶ p7.1g² p7m⁴ p6f⁵ Dec 20] lengthy filly: fairly useful handicapper: won at Warwick in May: effective at 6f to 8.6f: acts on polytrack and firm ground: held up: suspect temperament. *H. Morrison* **80**

LABRETELLA (IRE) 2 b.f. (Mar 21) Bahamian Bounty 116 – Known Class (USA) (Known Fact (USA) 135) [2009 5.2d⁶ 6g 7g 7g f8m³ f7f³ f8m³ f8g Dec 18] 22,000F, 8,000Y: good-topped filly: half-sister to several winners, including 4-y-o Royal Applord: dam US maiden: modest maiden: left M. Tompkins after third start, M. Dods after fourth: stays 1m: acts on fibresand. *D. W. Thompson* **55**

LA BRIGITTE 3 ch.f. Tobougg (IRE) 125 – Bardot (Efisio 120) [2009 88: 5g⁶ 5g² p6g Oct 30] leggy filly: fairly useful performer: left A. McCabe, improved when runner-up in handicap at Ripon: effective at 5f/6f: acts on fibresand and heavy ground: edgy sort, and often awkward under pressure. *J. A. Glover* **92**

LA CAPRIOSA 3 ch.f. Kyllachy 129 – La Caprice (USA) 84 (Housebuster (USA)) [2009 62: f6s* f5d³ f6g⁵ f6g² f5g* f6g³ p5.1g⁵ f6g* p6g p5.1g² 5m* 6m² 5m⁶ p5.1g² 5d⁵ 5g² 5s* 5m³ 6d³ 5m³ 6.1d 5.1g⁵ p5m Nov 3] strong filly: fair performer: won handicap and 2 claimers at Southwell from January to March, claimer at Beverley in April and, having left A. McCabe after fourteenth start, handicap at Doncaster in August: raced only at 5f/6f: acts on all-weather, soft and good to firm going: in cheekpieces final outing: usually forces pace. *J. A. Glover* **74**

LA COLUMBINA 4 ch.f. Carnival Dancer 123 – Darshay (FR) 87 (Darshaan 133) [2009 81: 10.3g 10m⁶ 9m 9.8d 11.8m f12f⁶ Dec 17] leggy filly: fairly useful at 3 yrs: well held in 2009, leaving G. Harker prior to final start: tried in headgear. *H. J. Evans* **–**

LA CORTEZANA 5 ch.m. Piccolo 121 – Blushing Belle 74 (Local Suitor (USA) 128) [2009 –: 10m Aug 9] sturdy mare: little form: dead. *A. P. Jarvis* –

LA COVETA (IRE) 4 b.f. Marju (IRE) 127 – Colourful Cast (IRE) 93 (Nashwan (USA) 135) [2009 86: 8.3m p8g^6 8m^4 8g^3 10g* 10.4g 10.2m f8g^6 Oct 27] close-coupled filly: fairly useful handicapper: won at Leicester in July: stays 1¼m: acts on good to firm ground: tried blinkered: has looked hard ride: sold 26,000 gns, sent to Saudi Arabia. *B. J. Meehan* **86**

LA CREME (IRE) 3 b.f. Clodovil (IRE) 116 – Dawiyda (IRE) (Ashkalani (IRE) 128) [2009 7s 8.1g^5 May 4] 19,000F, €100,000Y: unfurnished filly: first foal: dam unraced out of half-sister to Darshaan: better effort in maidens (fair form) when seventh at Newbury on debut. *M. R. Channon* **70**

LACROSSE 3 b.g. Cape Cross (IRE) 129 – La Sky (IRE) 107 (Law Society (USA) 130) [2009 p10g^4 p10g^3 10m^6 12g Jul 24] well-made gelding: half-brother to several winners, notably Oaks winner Love Divine (by Diesis, now dam of St Leger winner Sixties Icon): dam, 1¼m winner (probably stayed 1¾m), closely related to Champion Stakes winner Legal Case: fair maiden: stays 1½m: acts on polytrack: wore cheekpieces final start (gelded after). *M. A. Jarvis* **70**

LA DE TWO (IRE) 3 ch.c. Galileo (IRE) 134 – Firecrest (IRE) 107 (Darshaan 133) [2009 103p: p9.5g* Nov 6] neat colt: useful form when second to Kite Wood (Monitor Closely third) in maiden at Doncaster sole start at 2 yrs: left B. Hills and off 13 months, won similar event at Wolverhampton in November easily by 8 lengths from Warren Bank: will stay at least 1¼m: remains open to improvement. *Saeed bin Suroor* **103 p**

LA DI DA 2 b.f. (Apr 7) Oratorio (IRE) 128 – So Admirable (Suave Dancer (USA) 136) [2009 8g^4 Oct 23] £27,000Y: fourth foal: half-sister to 2 winners, including 5-y-o Come April: dam unraced sister to Eclipse winner Compton Admiral and half-sister to Queen Elizabeth II Stakes winner Summoner: 20/1 and green, encouraging 5¼ lengths fourth to Corsica in maiden at Ayr: will stay 1¼m: should improve. *I. Semple* **62 p**

LADIES BEST 5 b.g. King's Best (USA) 132 – Lady of The Lake 104 (Caerleon (USA) 132) [2009 102§: 10m* 10.1g^4 12.1d^4 10.4m^5 14m 10g 12s p12.2g Dec 11] good-bodied gelding: has a quick action: useful handicapper: won at Pontefract in April: creditable effort next time, but largely below form after: effective at 1¼m/1½m: acts on good to firm and good to soft going: tried in cheekpieces/tongue tie: ungenuine (often hangs): promise on hurdling debut. *B. Ellison* **97 §**

LADIES DANCING 3 b.g. Royal Applause 124 – Queen of Dance (IRE) (Sadler's Wells (USA) 132) [2009 p10g* p10g^3 12m p12.2g p9.5g^4 f11g^5 Dec 18] 34,000F, 55,000Y, £7,000 2-y-o: half-brother to several winners, including useful 1m to 1½m winner (including in Scandinavia) Tawoos (by Rainbow Quest) and fairly useful 1m (including at 2 yrs) to 1¼m winner Habanero (by Cadeaux Genereux): dam French 2-y-o 7f winner: fair form: won maiden at Lingfield in February: stays 1¼m: acts on polytrack. *J. A. Osborne* **77 d**

LA DIOSA (IRE) 3 b.f. Dansili 127 – El Divino (IRE) (Halling (USA) 133) [2009 76: p8.6g* p9.5g* p12.2m^5 f11g^5 p8g 11.5m p9.5g Oct 3] compact filly: fair performer: won sellers at Wolverhampton in January/February: well below form after third start, leaving George Baker after fourth one: stays easy 1½m: acts on polytrack and soft ground: signs of temperament. *Mrs S. Lamyman* **66**

LADY AMBERLINI 4 ch.f. Bertolini (USA) 125 – Deco Lady 65 (Wolfhound (USA) 126) [2009 68: p7.1g^4 8.3m p7.1g^6 p6g p7.1g p6m Oct 31] plain, angular filly: modest maiden: stays 1m: acts on polytrack (well held on turf): in cheekpieces final start. *C. R. Dore* **64**

LADY ANNE NEVILL 5 b.m. Nomadic Way (USA) 104 – Prudent Pet 65 (Distant Relative 128) [2009 12d 10.1m 10m 16g 12.1m^6 11.5g 16d Sep 1] angular mare: half-sister to 2 winners, including 6-y-o The Thrifty Bear: dam 7f (at 2 yrs) and 1m winner: poor maiden handicapper: stays 1½m: unraced on extremes of going: blinkered final outing. *C. W. Fairhurst* **47**

LADY ARTEMISIA (IRE) 3 b.f. Montjeu (IRE) 137 – Crimson Glory 75 (Lycius (USA) 124) [2009 10g 9.9f^2 10.1m^2 12m* 12v^2 14d^5 10.3m^2 10.2s^6 Oct 7] 26,000Y: quite attractive filly: fifth foal: closely related to fairly useful Irish 1½m winner Rebel Rover (by In The Wings): dam, 8.5f winner, closely related to very smart 1m/1¼m filly Crimplene: useful performer: won maiden at Newbury in June: best effort when 5 lengths fifth to Sevenna in Lillie Langtry Stakes at Goodwood sixth start: stays 1¾m: acts on any ground. *M. L. W. Bell* **98**

LADY ASHEENA 4 gr.f. Daylami (IRE) 138 – Star Profile (IRE) 100 (Sadler's Wells (USA) 132) [2009 –: f11g^{6} p12g* Feb 19] modest performer, lightly raced: won apprentice handicap at Kempton in February: stays 1½m: raced on all-weather. *J. Jay* **58**

LADY ASPEN (IRE) 6 b.m. Elnadim (USA) 128 – Misty Peak (IRE) 83 (Sri Pekan (USA) 117) [2009 58: p8g^{2} p7g p8.6g* p8.6g^{6} p8.6g^{6} 10.9m 10m^{4} 10.2f May 13] lengthy, angular mare: modest performer: won maiden at Wolverhampton in January: stays 1¼m: acts on polytrack, soft and good to firm going: tried blinkered/in cheekpieces: tongue tied in 2009. *Ian Williams* **58**

LADY AVON 2 ch.f. (Apr 7) Avonbridge 123 – Lady Filly 92 (Atraf 116) [2009 5.1g Aug 6] first foal: dam 2-y-o 5f winner: 20/1 and very green, well held in seller at Bath. *W. G. M. Turner* **–**

LADY BAHIA (IRE) 8 b.m. Orpen (USA) 116 – Do The Right Thing 71 (Busted 134) [2009 66: p5g^{6} f5g p5g^{3} Feb 9] big, good-topped mare: has a short, unimpressive action: just modest handicapper in 2009: best at 5f: acts on all-weather and firm going: blinkered: quirky. *Peter Grayson* **52 §**

LADY BLUESKY 6 gr.m. Cloudings (IRE) 112 – M N L Lady 85 (Polar Falcon (USA) 126) [2009 7.2g^{6} 7d^{6} 9.3d^{6} Jul 26] angular mare: useful form in bumpers: inadequate test in maidens on Flat: will be suited by 1½m+. *A. C. Whillans* **62**

LADY BRICKHOUSE 2 b.f. (Apr 9) Choisir (AUS) 126 – Music Maid (IRE) 74 (Inzar (USA) 112) [2009 6m 7m p6g f5m^{5} f6g^{4} Dec 27] good-topped filly: second foal: half-sister to 3-y-o Blushing Maid: dam 7f (including at 2 yrs)/1m winner: poor maiden: stays 6f: acts on fibresand. *M. D. Squance* **49**

LADY BRORA 4 b.f. Dashing Blade 117 – Tweed Mill 88 (Selkirk (USA) 129) [2009 83: 8g^{3} f8g^{2} 9g p10g 9g^{4} 10m^{4} 10g Oct 19] angular filly: fair handicapper: stays 1¼m: acts on all-weather, soft and good to firm going. *A. M. Balding* **77**

LADY BUCKET 2 b.f. (Feb 25) Avonbridge 123 – Heart of India (IRE) (Try My Best (USA) 130) [2009 5m 5.1g^{4} 7g 5d 5m f6m Nov 12] £12,000Y: half-sister to 3 winners, including Irish 6f (including at 2 yrs) winner King of Russia (by Common Grounds) and 2003 2-y-o 5f winner Fast Heart (by Fasliyev) both useful: dam unraced half-sister to very smart sprinter Bolshoi: no form: tried visored. *Paul Green* **–**

LADY CALIDO (USA) 4 b. or br.f. El Prado (IRE) 119 – Hydro Calido (USA) 117 (Nureyev (USA) 131) [2009 p10g 12.1m p9.5g* Aug 10] tall filly: fair form: missed 2008: blinkered, much improved when winning handicap at Wolverhampton in August: should have been suited by 1½m: sold 230,000 gns in December, reportedly in foal to Oasis Dream. *Sir Mark Prescott* **68**

LADY CAVENDISH (IRE) 2 ch.f. (Mar 30) Indian Haven 119 – Madame Marjou (IRE) 72 (Marju (IRE) 127) [2009 p8g^{6} p8.6g p8g 8.3g^{5} f8m p10m Nov 21] sturdy filly: first foal: dam, maiden (stayed 1¼m), out of half-sister to Coronation Cup winner Quiet Fling: modest maiden: stays 8.6f: tried in cheekpieces. *A. Bailey* **57**

LADY CHAMPAGNE 3 b.f. Zaha (CAN) 106 – Slavonic Dance (Muhtarram (USA) 125) [2009 p8.6g Dec 7] third foal: half-sister to 2006 2-y-o 7f seller winner Slavonic Lake (by Lake Coniston): dam unraced: well beaten in 3-y-o bumper (for P. McBride) and maiden at Wolverhampton on Flat debut. *Miss J. Feilden* **–**

LADY CHARLEMAGNE 4 b.f. King Charlemagne (USA) 120 – Prospering 50 (Prince Sabo 123) [2009 45: p8g p8g Jan 22] poor form: tried blinkered/visored. *N. P. Littmoden* **–**

LADY CHRISTIE 2 b.f. (Feb 5) Tobougg (IRE) 125 – Atnab (USA) 64 (Riverman (USA) 131) [2009 7s p7g Oct 20] half-sister to 3 winners, including useful French 9.5f (at 2 yrs) to 15f winner Grey Mystique (by Linamix) and fairly useful 2006 2-y-o 1m winner Millestan (by Invincible Spirit): dam, 1½m winner, out of half-sister to 1000 Guineas winner Fairy Footsteps and St Leger winner Light Cavalry: well held in maidens: bred to be suited by at least 1¼m. *M. Blanshard* **–**

LADY COMPTON 2 ch.f. (Apr 29) Compton Place 125 – Bright Spells 93 (Salse (USA) 128) [2009 5g 5d 6m 5g Oct 6] 1,300F, £2,700Y: workmanlike filly: half-sister to several winners, including 4-y-o Sunny Spells and Irish 1½m to 13f winner Stutter (by Polish Precedent): dam 2-y-o 6f winner: poor maiden: well held in nursery. *R. Bastiman* **44**

LADY DARSHAAN (IRE) 2 b.f. (Feb 10) High Chaparral (IRE) 132 – Diary (IRE) (Green Desert (USA) 127) [2009 6g^{3} 5m* 6g^{3} 8m^{2} Sep 26] £24,000 2-y-o: angular filly: third foal: half-sister to 3-y-o Total Gallery: dam, Greek 7f winner, half-sister to useful performer up to 1¾m Sunday Symphony: useful performer: won minor event at Windsor **109**

in June: much improved after, third to Misheer in Cherry Hinton Stakes at Newmarket and ¾-length second to Hibaayeb in Fillies' Mile at Ascot, in latter hit by winning rider's whip final 1f: stays 1m: acts on good to firm going. *J. S. Moore*

LADY DEAUVILLE (FR) 4 gr.f. Fasliyev (USA) 120 – Mercalle (FR) 108 (Kaldoun (FR) 122) [2009 115: 10s 10v^6 10.9d^4 9s^6 Jul 12] good-topped filly: smart at 3 yrs: below that level in 2009, best effort when sixth in Mooresbridge Stakes at the Curragh second outing: stays 1¼m: best on ground softer than good (acts on heavy): has joined Andrew Oliver in Ireland. *R. Curtis* **97**

LADY DINSDALE (IRE) 3 b.f. Refuse To Bend (IRE) 128 – Lady Digby (IRE) 96 (Petorius 117) [2009 –: 6s 6.1m 6d 8m 9.9m 8.3m p7g p7m p6m^6 Dec 9] workmanlike filly: little form: tried blinkered. *T. Keddy* **–**

LADY DRAC (IRE) 3 gr.f. Hawk Wing (USA) 136 – Cause Celebre (IRE) 80 (Peintre Celebre (USA) 137) [2009 81p: 10f^5 8.3m Jun 28] tall filly: just modest form at 3 yrs: signs of temperament. *B. W. Hills* **54**

LADY DUNHILL (IRE) 3 br.f. High Chaparral (IRE) 132 – Ribbon Glade (UAE) (Zafonic (USA) 130) [2009 48: f6s^3 f8g^3 f8g^3 f11g 8m Aug 9] modest maiden: should stay 11f: acts on fibresand. *E. W. Tuer* **54**

LADY FAS (IRE) 6 b.m. Fasliyev (USA) 120 – Lady Sheriff 90 (Taufan (USA) 119) [2009 55: p6g p8g Jan 10] smallish mare: maiden: well below form both outings in 2009 (amiss latter occasion). *A. W. Carroll* **–**

LADY FLORENCE 4 gr.f. Bollin Eric 125 – Silver Fan (Lear Fan (USA) 130) [2009 50: p7g^3 10m 7d^2 8m^2 8f* 8f* p8g^5 7.5g^2 8m 7f* 8m^4 7f 7f^6 7.5g 7d^3 8d^2 7m^4 p9.5g f12g Dec 22] workmanlike filly: fair performer: won seller in June and handicaps in July and August, all at Brighton: best at 7f/1m: acts on polytrack, firm and soft going: usually makes running. *A. B. Coogan* **70**

LADY FRANCESCA 3 b.f. Montjeu (IRE) 137 – Purring (USA) 79 (Mountain Cat (USA)) [2009 83: 8.5g^2 8g^2 8g^6 10m^2 10.5g p8.6g* 8m 9d^3 Oct 18] neat filly: useful performer: won maiden at Wolverhampton in September: best efforts in listed races on second and last 2 starts, including when 2¼ lengths second to Eva's Request at Goodwood and 2 lengths third to Lungwa at Longchamp: should be suited by 1¼m: acts on polytrack, good to firm and good to soft ground: sold 200,000 gns. *W. R. Muir* **98**

LADY GEM 3 b.f. Captain Rio 122 – Cosmic Song 58 (Cosmonaut) [2009 53: p6g^6 Jan 22] leggy filly: modest maiden at 2 yrs: in cheekpieces, signs of temperament sole start in 2009: should stay 7f: raced only on all-weather and going softer than good. *D. H. Brown* **–**

LADY HESTIA (USA) 4 b.f. Belong To Me (USA) – Awtaan (USA) 77 (Arazi (USA) 135) [2009 53p: 12d^2 11.9m* 14.1g* p16g^6 17.2m* 14.1g Oct 16] fair handicapper: won at Brighton in April, Yarmouth in August and Bath in September: stays 17f: acts on good to firm going. *M. P. Tregoning* **74**

LADY HETHERINGTON 2 b.f. (Apr 23) Kyllachy 129 – Silver Top Hat (USA) (Silver Hawk (USA) 123) [2009 p7g p7g p8m^6 Nov 19] rather leggy filly: fourth foal: dam, French/US maiden, half-sister to smart French/US performer up to 9f Elizabeth Bay: best effort in maidens when sixth to Eleanora Duse at Kempton: may prove best short of 1m. *Jamie Poulton* **60**

LADY HOPEFUL (IRE) 7 b.m. Lend A Hand 124 – Treble Term 66 (Lion Cavern (USA) 117) [2009 49§: p6g p5.1g p5.1g^6 p5g^2 5m 5m Jun 8] good-topped mare: poor performer: stays easy 7f: acts on all-weather, firm and good to soft ground: wears headgear: usually slowly away, and not one to trust. *Peter Grayson* **49 §**

LADY JANE DIGBY 4 b.f. Oasis Dream 129 – Scandalette (Niniski (USA) 125) [2009 85+: f8s^3 p10g* p10g^2 p10g^5 p10g* 12.1d^2 10.3g^2 10.9d^3 10.1m* 11g* Aug 23] raw-boned filly: smart performer: improved in 2009, winning handicaps at Lingfield in January and May, listed race at Newcastle (by 5 lengths from Syvilla) in June and Walther J. Jacobs-Stutenpreis at Bremen (by nose from Guantana) in August: stays 1½m: acts on all-weather, good to firm and good to soft going: consistent. *M. Johnston* **110**

LADY JINKS 4 ch.f. Kirkwall 118 – Art Deco Lady 51 (Master Willie 129) [2009 63: 11.7m 11.9m 11.7f^2 12m^5 12.1m^2 17.2m^5 11.6m^5 13.1f Aug 22] leggy filly: modest handicapper: stays 1½m: acts on polytrack, soft and firm going: tried blinkered: tail flasher: sold £550 and joined Miss J. Davies, fair form over hurdles. *R. J. Hodges* **59**

LADY KINGSTON 3 ch.f. Kyllachy 129 – Ash Moon (IRE) 92 (General Monash (USA) 107) [2009 –: p6g Mar 27] no form. *K. R. Burke* **–**

LADY LAM 3 b.f. Slip Anchor 136 – Tamara 83 (Marju (IRE) 127) [2009 p8g 7.1g^{5} 8.1m Jul 23] angular filly: poor form. *George Baker* **44**

LADY LAUREM 2 b.f. (Feb 25) Avonbridge 123 – Majestic Diva (IRE) (Royal Applause 124) [2009 5g 5s 5m Sep 18] first foal: dam unraced: no form in varied company. *D. A. Nolan* **–**

LADY LEFROY (IRE) 2 b.f. (Apr 16) Oratorio (IRE) 128 – Dos Talas (USA) (You And I (USA) 118) [2009 6m^{6} 6g 5v^{3} 7m 7m^{5} 8m^{4} p8m^{5} 7.2v Oct 31] close-coupled filly: modest maiden: probably stayed 1m: acted on heavy and good to firm going: became lazy (blinkered final start): dead. *R. A. Fahey* **56**

LADY LION 2 b.f. (Mar 6) Hunting Lion (IRE) 115 – Miss Brookie 70 (The West (USA) 107) [2009 5g 5f* 5m^{5} p5.1g^{5} 5m^{6} May 25] first foal: dam 2-y-o 5f winner: poor performer: won claimer at Thirsk in April: raced only at 5f: acts on firm going: withdrawn after causing trouble at stall on intended debut: looked unwilling in cheekpieces final outing. *W. G. M. Turner* **48**

LADY LLANOVER 9 ch.m. Halling (USA) 133 – Francia 59 (Legend of France (USA) 124) [2009 53: p12g p12g Feb 4] workmanlike mare: maiden: no form in 2009: tried in visor/cheekpieces. *P. D. Evans* **–**

LADY LONGCROFT 4 ch.f. Tobougg (IRE) 125 – Top of The Morning 56 (Keen 116) [2009 65: p9.5g^{2} f8g^{2} f12g* f11d^{3} f11g p9.5g Dec 28] modest performer: won maiden at Southwell in February: free-going sort, but stays 1½m: raced on all-weather and good to soft ground. *J. Pearce* **63**

LADY LU 3 b.f. Lujain (USA) 119 – Noble Story 61 (Last Tycoon 131) [2009 48: p6g Apr 22] lengthy, angular filly: poor form. *P. F. I. Cole* **–**

LADY LUACHMHAR (IRE) 3 b.f. Galileo (IRE) 134 – Radhwa (FR) (Shining Steel 123) [2009 10g^{4} 9d* 10.4s* 11d^{3} 12g^{6} Oct 10] 55,000F, €220,000Y: unfurnished filly: fourth foal: half-sister to 4-y-o Dr Livingstone: dam useful French 2-y-o 5f/7f winner: fairly useful form: won maiden at Ripon in May and, having left Mrs A. Duffield, apprentice handicap at Haydock in July: took strong hold both starts after: may prove best up to 10.4f: raced only on good ground or softer. *R. A. Fahey* **91**

LADY LUBE RYE (IRE) 2 b.f. (Apr 6) Catcher In The Rye (IRE) 115 – Lady Lucia (IRE) 51 (Royal Applause 124) [2009 5m 5m^{4} 5m* 5g 6d^{6} 5s^{3} 5g^{4} 5g^{4} 6m 6d^{6} Aug 27] €10,000Y: second foal: half-sister to useful 2008 2-y-o 5f winner Mullionmileanhour (by Mull of Kintyre): dam sprint maiden: fair performer: won maiden at Redcar in April: ran creditably when in frame in nurseries after: best at 5f: acts on soft and good to firm ground: usually races prominently. *N. Wilson* **65**

LADY LUPUS (IRE) 2 b.f. (May 4) High Chaparral (IRE) 132 – Lady Icarus (Rainbow Quest (USA) 134) [2009 8s 7g^{5} 8g^{4} 8s* Oct 11] seventh foal: half-sister to useful Irish 7f/1m winner Mystical Lady (by Halling): dam unraced close relative to smart milers Sharman and Hazaam out of high-class miler Sonic Lady: useful form: best effort when winning listed race at the Curragh in October by ¾ length from Atasari (subsequent Group 2 runner-up), soon niggled along: will be suited by 1¼m: likely to improve further. *A. P. O'Brien, Ireland* **100 p**

LADY MARIAN (GER) 4 b.f. Nayef (USA) 129 – La Felicita (Shareef Dancer (USA) 135) [2009 125: 8.9g 8d 10m^{2} 10s^{4} 10g^{6} 10d^{5} Oct 25] well-made filly: trained by W. Baltromei in Germany in 2008, wins included Prix de l'Opera at Longchamp: just smart form in 2009, easily best effort when short-head second to Alpine Rose in Prix Jean Romanet at Deauville: below par otherwise, including in Prix de l'Opera and Premio Lydia Tesio at Rome last 2 starts: needed at least 1¼m, but untried beyond 11f: acted on good to firm and good to soft ground (possibly not on soft): usually held up: stud. *Saeed bin Suroor* **119**

LADY MAYA 4 br.f. Prince Sabo 123 – Monte Mayor Lady (IRE) (Brief Truce (USA) 126) [2009 –: 10g 11.6g 14.1m Aug 21] workmanlike filly: little form: tried visored: dead. *Paul Henderson* **–**

LADY MEG (IRE) 3 b.f. Spartacus (IRE) 107 – Carna (IRE) 60 (Anita's Prince 126) [2009 –: 8.1g^{5} 7.1m 7m Sep 21] no form. *B. Palling* **–**

LADY MICKLEGATE (USA) 3 b.f. Johar (USA) 130 – Crimson Native (USA) (The Name's Jimmy (USA)) [2009 58p: p7g^{4} 7g^{5} 7m 9.9m p7g Oct 14] fair maiden: largely regressive, and refused to race final outing: stays 7f: acts on polytrack: one to be wary of: sold 800 gns. *J. R. Best* **75 d**

LADY NAVARA (IRE) 2 b.f. (Apr 21) Trans Island 119 – Changari (USA) 90 (Gulch (USA)) [2009 5s 6m 7g Jul 23] 3,500Y: close-coupled filly: second foal: dam, 2-y-o 5f **–**

winner, out of smart French 2-y-o 5f winner Danzari: well beaten in maidens: sold £1,500 in October. *M. Brittain*

LADY NORLELA 3 b.f. Reset (AUS) 124 – Lady Netbetsports (IRE) 76 (In The Wings 128) [2009 47: p6g⁶ 8.5m 8g 8.3v³ Aug 24] poor maiden: left R. Hannon after reappearance: likely to stay 1¼m: acts on heavy going: tongue tied last 2 starts. *T. J. Fitzgerald* **47**

LADY OAKSEY 3 b.f. Tobougg (IRE) 125 – Silk Law (IRE) 80 (Barathea (IRE) 127) [2009 10g 12.1g f12g⁵ 12.1v 9.9g Aug 12] useful-looking filly: third foal: half-sister to 4-y-o Lady Sorcerer and 1¼m winner Miss Rainbow Runner (by Josr Algarhoud): dam 2-y-o 6f/7f winner: seemingly modest maiden: stays 1½m: acts on fibresand. *W. S. Kittow* **62 ?**

LADY OF AKITA (USA) 2 ch.f. (Apr 25) Fantastic Light (USA) 134 – Chancey Squaw (USA) (Chief's Crown (USA)) [2009 p8g⁵ p7.1g* Dec 4] sister to Japanese Group 3 1¼m winner Jalisco Light and half-sister to 3 winners, notably top-class Japanese 1m/1¼m performer Agnes Digital (by Crafty Prospector): dam, US 1m winner, half-sister to Royal Lodge Stakes winner Royal Kingdom: better effort in maidens when winning at Wolverhampton by 1¼ lengths from Kai Mook: will be suited by 1¼m: open to further improvement. *J. H. M. Gosden* **70 p**

LADY OF GARMORAN (USA) 2 b. or br.f. (Feb 10) Mr Greeley (USA) 122 – Poetically (CAN) (Silver Deputy (CAN)) [2009 7d Oct 12] $235,000Y: fourth foal: half-sister to German 6f to 8.5f winner Cheeky Jack (by A P Indy): dam, Canadian 5.5f to 8.5f winner (including at 2 yrs), half-sister to smart US Grade 1 9f winner Citronnade: 40/1, well held in maiden at Salisbury. *P. F. I. Cole* **–**

LADY OF NAMID (IRE) 2 ch.f. (Mar 7) Namid 128 – Princess Killeen (IRE) (Sinndar (IRE) 134) [2009 7m Aug 23] first foal: dam, ran once, half-sister to Cheveley Park/Coronation Stakes winner Indian Ink: 100/1, slowly away and always behind in maiden at Folkestone. *R. Curtis* **–**

LADY OF THE DESERT (USA) 2 ch.f. (Mar 12) Rahy (USA) 115 – Queen's Logic (IRE) 125 (Grand Lodge (USA) 125) [2009 5g* 5m⁶ 6m* 6m* 6m³ Oct 2] **115**

Queen's Logic was always going to be a hard act to follow. The outstanding two-year-old filly of 2001 won all four of her starts including the Queen Mary, Lowther and Cheveley Park, races that her fourth foal Lady of The Desert also contested in the latest season. Lady of The Desert won the Lowther, putting up a performance bettered only by Queen Mary winner Jealous Again (with Lady of The Desert sixth) and Cheveley Park winner Special Duty (with Lady of The Desert third) among those of her age and sex who raced in Europe in 2009. It is to be hoped that Lady of The Desert does not emulate her dam in at least one way. Queen's Logic was favourite for the One Thousand Guineas after her scintillating victory in the Cheveley Park, but, after maintaining her unbeaten record in the Fred Darling Stakes on her reappearance, she wasn't seen out again.

Lady of The Desert gained the first of three successes as a two-year-old in a maiden at Leicester on her debut but ran only twice at five furlongs. She was stepped up to six after the Queen Mary at Royal Ascot, where she paid the price for taking on the all-the-way winner, still second entering the final furlong. There was nothing of Jealous Again's calibre in the Princess Margaret Abu Dhabi Stakes at Ascot in July, and Lady of The Desert justified favouritism in good style by a length and a half from Full Mandate, moving to the front on the bridle two furlongs out

Jaguar Cars Lowther Stakes, York—a fourth win in the last nine renewals for owner Jaber Abdullah as Lady of The Desert (striped sleeves) pulls clear of Beyond Desire and Dubawi Heights

and quickening clear before idling. Lady of The Desert also started favourite in both of her subsequent races. The first of those was the Jaguar Cars Lowther Stakes at York in August, when she won by three lengths from Beyond Desire. Lady of The Desert was even more impressive than at Ascot, producing a sharp burst of speed to settle matters when shaken up approaching the final furlong. There was no finishing kick from Lady of The Desert, however, in the Cheveley Park Stakes at Newmarket, in which she possibly took too much out of herself by racing freely. She was still the only one to make a race of it with the winner entering the Dip, but then tired badly, drifting left as she did so and losing second to Misheer late on, the pair two and three quarter lengths adrift of Special Duty.

Lady of The Desert (USA) (ch.f. Mar 12, 2007)	Rahy (USA) (ch 1985)	Blushing Groom (ch 1974)	Red God
			Runaway Bride
		Glorious Song (b 1976)	Halo
			Ballade
	Queen's Logic (IRE) (ch 1999)	Grand Lodge (ch 1991)	Chief's Crown
			La Papagena
		Lagrion (ch 1989)	Diesis
			Wrap It Up

Lady of The Desert's sire Rahy was effective at a mile and Queen's Logic seemed likely to stay at least that far, but Lady of The Desert herself looks all about speed, with six furlongs probably going to prove her optimum trip. Queen's Logic's other foals to reach the racecourse are both winners, the useful Go On Be A Tiger (by Machiavellian) over a mile in Britain at two and at six furlongs at Jebel Ali in March, and Dunes Queen (by Elusive Quality) in a six-furlong maiden at Kempton in the same month. Queen's Logic isn't the best produce of her dam, the middle-distance maiden Lagrion. That honour goes to Dylan Thomas, whose six Group 1 victories included an Irish Derby and an Arc. Lagrion is a sister to Middle Park runner-up Pure Genius and a daughter of an unraced half-sister to the Lingfield Oaks Trial winner Gift Wrapped. Lady of The Desert is owned, like her dam and siblings, by Jaber Abdullah, though, unlike them, she hasn't started her racing career with Mick Channon. In a physical sense, Lady of The Desert is similar to Queen's Logic only in colour. Lady of The Desert is a compact individual somewhat lacking in scope, whereas her dam was lengthy and quite attractive. Lady of The Desert has been accompanied by a pony on the way to the start, a growing custom with some of the runners from her stable, and she has raced only on good to firm ground since her debut, when it was good. *B. J. Meehan*

LADY PACHA 2 b.f. (Mar 18) Dubai Destination (USA) 127 – St Radegund 85 (Green Desert (USA) 127) [2009 7g 8.5m^6 7m Sep 26] seventh foal: half-sister to several winners, including useful 7.5f to 9f winner Rhadegunda (by Pivotal) and 7-y-o Halla San: dam, 7f winner, out of 1000 Guineas and Sussex Stakes winner On The House: well held in maidens. *T. J. Pitt* **–**

LADY PATTERN (IRE) 2 gr.f. (Apr 2) Verglas (IRE) 118 – Patteness (FR) (General Holme (USA) 128) [2009 5g 6f^3 6m* 6m 6g^6 7.1g^5 p6g^3 p6m^3 p6f^5 Oct 14] 9,000Y: angular filly: seventh foal: sister to 3-y-o Lady Rusty and half-sister to 2 winners, including useful Irish 7.5f (at 2 yrs) to 1½m winner Pantarez (by Saumarez): dam, French 7.5f to 1½m winner, half-sister to Park Hill Stakes winner Alexander Three D and US Grade 1 winner up to 1¼m Golden Apples: fairly useful form on turf, just fair on all-weather: won maiden at Newbury (by 2¼ lengths from Blue Maiden) in June: should stay 7f: acts on polytrack and good to firm going. *P. W. D'Arcy* **81 a68**

LADY PICOLA 3 b.f. Piccolo 121 – Sukuma (IRE) 55 (Highest Honor (FR) 124) [2009 p7.1g Sep 25] 800Y: first foal: dam maiden (stayed 1m): soundly beaten in maiden at Wolverhampton: sold 800 gns, sent to Bahrain. *Tom Dascombe* **–**

LADY PILOT 7 b.m. Dansili 127 – Mighty Flyer (IRE) (Mujtahid (USA) 118) [2009 81: 15.8g^4 14.1m^2 17.2f^4 15.4m Sep 22] workmanlike mare: just modest handicapper in 2009: stays 16.5f: races mainly on all-weather nowadays, acts on firm going: tried in headgear: fairly useful hurdler/fair chaser. *Jim Best* **64**

LADY RANGALI (IRE) 4 b.f. Danehill Dancer (IRE) 117 – Promising Lady 91 (Thunder Gulch (USA) 129) [2009 89: 7g 8g^3 8m^3 8m^6 8.5m^2 9.8v^6 Jul 18] leggy filly: fairly useful performer: stays 8.5f: yet to race on firm going, acts on any other turf: below form in cheekpieces fourth outing: has awkward head carriage, but is genuine: sold 16,000 gns in November. *Mrs A. Duffield* **89**

LADY ROMANOV (IRE) 6 br.m. Xaar 132 – Mixremember (FR) (Linamix (FR) 127) [2009 12.1v 10d 12m p12m p16m Dec 1] tall mare: modest handicapper at best nowadays (missed 2008): stays 1½m: acts on all-weather, probably on heavy going: tried in cheekpieces/visor. *P. Butler* **64 d**

LADY ROSE ANNE (IRE) 4 b.f. Red Ransom (USA) – Surval (IRE) 91 (Sadler's Wells (USA) 132) [2009 –: 12m 10g⁴ 12g 12g 10m Aug 9] fair maiden: left Mrs J. Harrington in Ireland after third start: needs to settle to stay 1½m. *T. D. Barron* **67**

LADY ROYAL OAK (IRE) 2 b.f. (Mar 5) Exceed And Excel (AUS) 126 – Enclave (USA) (Woodman (USA) 126) [2009 5.1m³ 5m p5g³ Aug 7] 11,000Y, £42,000 2-y-o: sturdy filly: sixth foal: half-sister to 1¼m winner Paradise Walk (by Sakhee): dam, ran twice in France, half-sister to smart performer up to 1¼m Comfy: fair maiden: third at Nottingham and Lingfield (tongue tied): will prove best at easy 5f. *M. Botti* **67**

LADY RUSTY (IRE) 3 gr.f. Verglas (IRE) 118 – Patteness (FR) (General Holme (USA) 128) [2009 73: 9g 10s p11g² p11g⁵ p16g⁶ 12d³ Oct 11] angular filly: fair handicapper: stays 1½m: acts on polytrack and soft going. *P. Winkworth* **76**

LADY SALAMA 3 b.f. Fasliyev (USA) 120 – Change of Heart (IRE) 59 (Revoque (IRE) 122) [2009 63: f8g⁴ f8d⁵ 7.1m p8.6g 8m May 19] good-topped filly: modest performer: likely to prove best short of 1m: acts on fibresand and soft going: tried visored. *K. R. Burke* **61**

LADY'S ART (FR) 3 gr.f. Verglas (IRE) 118 – Calithea (IRE) 55 (Marju (IRE) 127) [2009 p8g⁴ 8d 9.9m⁵ p10g p8f* Oct 14] fifth foal: sister to 3 winners, including useful French 1m (at 2 yrs) to 10.5f winner Chill and fairly useful Irish 9f winner Camouflage: dam, maiden (stayed 8.5f), half-sister to useful sprinter Blackheath: fair form: visored, won minor event at Kempton: stays 1m: acts on polytrack: sold 14,000 gns, joined S. Wattel in France. *E. F. Vaughan* **63**

LADY SLIPPERS (IRE) 2 ch.f. (Mar 11) Royal Academy (USA) 130 – Woodland Orchid (IRE) 64 (Woodman (USA) 126) [2009 7s² 7.1m⁴ 6m Oct 26] sister to useful 6f (including Coventry Stakes at 2 yrs)/7f winner Cd Europe and half-sister to 3 winners, including 6-y-o Cover Drive: dam, Irish maiden, half-sister to smart Irish performer up to 1m D'Anjou: best effort in maidens when second to Kithonia at Salisbury: should stay 1m: acts on soft going. *H. J. L. Dunlop* **65**

LADY SORCERER 4 b.f. Diktat 126 – Silk Law (IRE) 80 (Barathea (IRE) 127) [2009 77, a70: 12g p12g⁶ p16g 11.5g⁴ p11g⁴ 16d⁶ 13.1d⁴ 13.8m 10.1d² Oct 27] leggy, close-coupled filly: modest handicapper nowadays: stays 1¾m: acts on polytrack and soft going, probably on heavy: visored 5 of last 6 starts: has hung right. *A. P. Jarvis* **60**

LADY SPLODGE 5 b.m. Mark of Esteem (IRE) 137 – La Victoria (GER) (Rousillon (USA) 133) [2009 p9.5g Mar 5] modest form in maidens in 2007: off 16 months, pulled too hard in similar event at Wolverhampton. *George Baker* **–**

LADY SPRINGBANK (IRE) 2 gr.f. (Mar 27) Choisir (AUS) 126 – Severa (GER) (Kendor (FR) 122) [2009 6m³ 6m* 6f³ 7.1m⁶ 7g* Sep 27] £25,000 2-y-o: good-bodied filly: sixth foal: half-sister to 3-y-o High Severa and winner in Greece by Mujadil: dam German 7f/7.5f winner: useful performer: won maiden at Doncaster in June and, having left K. R. Burke, C. L. Weld Park Stakes at the Curragh (much improved to beat Bikini Babe ½ length, edging right) in September: stays 7f. *P. D. Deegan, Ireland* **102**

LADY'S PURSE 2 b.f. (Jan 29) Doyen (IRE) 132 – Jetbeeah (IRE) 95 (Lomond (USA) 128) [2009 7s Sep 3] 20,000Y: half-sister to several winners, including useful performer up to 1m Dazilyn Lady (by Zilzal), 6f winner at 2 yrs, and useful 1¼m winner Simondiun (by Hernando), who stayed 1¾m: dam 1m winner: 8/1, slowly away and always towards rear in maiden at Salisbury: bred to stay 1¼m+: has left Godolphin. *Saeed bin Suroor* **–**

LADY TRISH 3 b.f. Red Ransom (USA) – Artifice 80 (Green Desert (USA) 127) [2009 –: p7.1g p7g p6m Dec 16] well held in maidens/handicap. *C. A. Dwyer* **–**

LADY VALENTINO 5 b.m. Primo Valentino (IRE) 116 – Mystery Night (FR) (Fairy King (USA)) [2009 63: 8.3g 10m² 10.2m 11.8m⁴ 10m³ p12.2g⁵ p9.5g Sep 12] modest maiden: stays easy 1½m: acts on polytrack, firm and soft ground: tongue tied last 3 starts: reportedly had breathing problem final outing. *B. D. Leavy* **61**

LADY VALIANT 2 ch.f. (Apr 16) Dr Fong (USA) 128 – Protectorate 91 (Hector Protector (USA) 124) [2009 p7g³ p7g⁵ Jul 1] workmanlike filly: fourth foal: half-sister to 5-y-o Castellina: dam, 5f (at 2 yrs)/6f winner who stayed 1m, out of half-sister to Irish Oaks winner Possessive Dancer: better effort in maidens at Kempton when fifth to Blue Angel. *R. M. Beckett* **59**

LADY VIVIEN 3 b.f. Kyllachy 129 – Elsie Plunkett 92 (Mind Games 121) [2009 60: p5g* p5.1g* 5.1m 5m[6] 5d 6m[5] f5g p5.1g[5] p5.1g Oct 2] modest handicapper: won at Great Leighs (dead-heated) and Wolverhampton in January: raced only at 5f/6f: acts on polytrack: tried tongue tied. *D. H. Brown* **64**

LADY WILLA (IRE) 2 b.f. (Feb 25) Footstepsinthesand 120 – Change Partners (IRE) 79 (Hernando (FR) 127) [2009 7s p7g[6] Sep 21] workmanlike filly: second foal: dam 1½m winner: similar form in maidens, 5 lengths sixth to Muwakaba at Kempton: will be well suited by 1m+. *B. W. Hills* **68**

LADY ZENA 3 b.f. Mind Games 121 – Alustar 71 (Emarati (USA) 74) [2009 –p: f6g[3] f5g[5] 6g Jul 5] close-coupled filly: poor form: blinkered last 2 starts: dead. *M. W. Easterby* **38**

LADY ZOE (IRE) 2 b.f. (Mar 9) Chineur (FR) 123 – Petarga 87 (Petong 126) [2009 5d p5m p5.1g Oct 3] €3,800 2-y-o: fifth foal: half-sister to 3 winners by Compton Place, including 7f winner Special Place: dam 5f (including at 2 yrs)/6f winner: no form in maidens/seller: visored and tongue tied final outing. *D. Donovan* **–**

LA ESTRELLA (USA) 6 b.g. Theatrical 128 – Princess Ellen 114 (Tirol 127) [2009 94: f12s* p13.3g* p11g[2] p12.2m[4] Mar 4] lengthy, useful-looking gelding: fairly useful performer: won claimers at Southwell and Great Leighs in January: effective at 11f to 1¾m: acts on all-weather and good to firm going: tried blinkered: held up. *D. E. Cantillon* **94**

LA FORTUNATA 2 b.f. (Apr 10) Lucky Story (USA) 128 – Phantasmagoria 75 (Fraam 114) [2009 5.1f[3] 5g[3] 5f[3] 5.1m[4] 5g[5] 5m[3] p5m[2] p5g[2] Oct 22] close-coupled filly: first foal: dam in frame at 7f on only 2 starts: fair maiden: likely to prove best at 5f: acts on polytrack and firm going: free-going front runner. *J. R. Jenkins* **72**

LAGAN HANDOUT 3 gr.g. Lend A Hand 124 – Due To Me 58 (Compton Place 125) [2009 64d: p6g[5] 8.1g p7.1g May 18] modest maiden: form only at 5f/easy 6f: acts on good to soft going. *C. Gordon* **53**

LA GIFTED 3 b.f. Fraam 114 – Aileen's Gift (IRE) (Rainbow Quest (USA) 134) [2009 –: p7g[3] 8m[4] 7.1m[5] 8.1g[4] p7.1g 8f[4] 7m 8.3g 6v 6m 6.1g p7g* p7.1g* 7m* p7g[5] p8m[5] p7m p7g* p7.1g* p7.1g* p7.1g[5] p7.1g Dec 5] sturdy filly: fair handicapper: won at Lingfield, Wolverhampton and Catterick in September, Lingfield (apprentices) and Wolverhampton in October and Wolverhampton again in November: stays 1m, all wins around 7f: acts on polytrack and good to firm ground: tough. *M. R. Channon* **79**

LAGO INDIANO (IRE) 2 b.c. (Mar 1) Namid 128 – My Potters (USA) (Irish River (FR) 131) [2009 p6g[3] p6m[3] Nov 4] half-brother to several winners, including very smart 7f (at 2 yrs) and 1½m (Irish Oaks) winner Winona (by Alzao) and fairly useful 11.5f winner Gold Quest (by Rainbow Quest): dam, Irish 1m winner, half-sister to champion US sprinter My Juliet: similar form when third in maidens at Lingfield and Kempton: will stay 7f+: open to improvement. *Mrs A. J. Perrett* **74 p**

LAHALEEB (IRE) 3 b.f. Redback 116 – Flames (Blushing Flame (USA) 109) [2009 111: 7s* 8f 8v[2] 8f[5] 8d 8s[5] 10m* Oct 17] **121**

European challengers have enjoyed great success over the years in one of Canada's richest races, the E. P. Taylor Stakes for fillies and mares, which takes place in October on the turf course at Woodbine. Renamed—it was formerly known as the Nettie Stakes—in 1981 to honour the man who owned Windfields Farm and was a founder of the Jockey Club of Canada, it has been won on no fewer than twenty-one occasions since by European runners. Ten of those have come from Britain, Ivor's Image setting the ball rolling in 1986 when it was a Grade 2 race. Nowadays it has Grade 1 status and is worth around £360,000 to the winner, so it was no great surprise to see the British out in force for the latest renewal of this mile and quarter event.

British stables provided four of the eight runners and there was another British-trained winner, though the outcome was very different to the one predicted by the market. In betting order, the British representatives were Rainbow View, Look Here, Eastern Aria and Lahaleeb, and it was the complete outsider in the field who came out on top. Starting at 44.4/1 and tackling a distance beyond a mile for the first time, Lahaleeb showed improved form and won by a length and three quarters from Rainbow View, with Eastern Aria taking fourth and Look Here finishing a disappointing seventh. Ridden for the first time by William Buick, the joint-champion apprentice in Britain in 2008, who will be riding as first jockey to John Gosden in 2010, Lahaleeb was switched wide to challenge in the straight, took

E. P. Taylor Stakes Presented By Emirates Airline, Woodbine—
a 1,2 for British challengers as Lahaleeb causes a 44/1 upset, beating the favourite Rainbow View

the lead over a furlong out and was always in control from thereon, despite drifting markedly left.

Lahaleeb had been campaigned only at seven furlongs and a mile before Woodbine, all four of her wins coming at the former trip. They included the Rockfel Stakes on her final appearance at two and the Dubai Duty Free Stakes (Fred Darling) at Newbury in April on her return. In the latter Lahaleeb edged right and flashed her tail under pressure but still found plenty to peg back Super Sleuth very late on to win by a head. Lahaleeb's next five races after the Fred Darling were all at a mile, and she showed her form only in the second of them, when runner-up in the Irish One Thousand Guineas at the Curragh. Although battling on gamely after taking up the running two furlongs out, Lahaleeb was collared late on by Again and beaten a neck. Lahaleeb wasn't disgraced on her final outing at the trip when returned to the Curragh for the Solonaway Stakes. Lahaleeb finished fifth to Border Patrol but left the impression she would have been a clear third had she obtained a clear run.

Lahaleeb (IRE) (b.f. 2006)	Redback (ch 1999)	Mark of Esteem (b 1993)	Darshaan
			Homage
		Patsy Western (ch 1986)	Precocious
			Western Air
	Flames (b 1998)	Blushing Flame (b 1991)	Blushing Groom
			Nearctic Flame
		Dancing Debut (b 1993)	Polar Falcon
			Exclusive Virtue

Lahaleeb, a €40,000 foal who fetched 70,000 guineas as a yearling, is the best representative so far of her sire the Two Thousand Guineas third Redback, and has already achieved better form than her sire. Redback's first seven seasons at stud were spent in Ireland, but in November it was reported that he had been sold to stand at Haras de Victot in Normandy. Lahaleeb is the fourth foal out of her dam Flames and her second winner, after the fairly useful performer at up to a mile Precocious Star (by Bold Fact). A two-year-old full-sister to Lahaleeb named Pink Flames has had one run to date, showing a little promise in a maiden at Thirsk. The next dam Dancing Debut, out of a half-sister to Two Thousand Guineas winner Entrepreneur and Coronation Stakes winner Exclusive, was a lightly-raced maiden whose winners include the useful fillies Dance Partner and Kindlelight Debut. Lahaleeb seemed unsuited by the very firm going in both the One Thousand Guineas at Newmarket and Coronation Stakes at Royal Ascot, yet she showed in both the Rockfel and E. P. Taylor that good to firm didn't inconvenience her at all. Neither did the mud in the Irish One Thousand, while Lahaleeb has won twice on soft. The rather leggy Lahaleeb was sold for 1,000,000 guineas at the December Sales and will reportedly continue to race at four, starting off at the Dubai Carnival meeting. *M. R. Channon*

LAID BARE 2 b.f. (Mar 14) Barathea (IRE) 127 – Lady Eberspacher (IRE) 68 (Royal Abjar (USA) 121) [2009 8g p7m Oct 31] fifth foal: half-sister to 2005 2-y-o 5.7f winner Indian Lady (by Namid) and 3-y-o Evelyn May: dam sprint maiden: well held in maidens. *Mrs P. N. Dutfield* **–**

LAIRY (IRE) 2 ch.g. (Apr 10) Fath (USA) 116 – Akebia (USA) (Trempolino (USA) 135) [2009 5m^4 6d^3 6s^3 7s^6 6.1v^3 6.1d 5.5g p6g 6d^2 7.1m 5.1s p5m^5 f6m^5 Dec 15] small gelding: modest maiden: left D. Nicholls after second start: stays 6f: acts on good to soft ground: unreliable. *M. F. Harris* **53 §**

LAISH YA HAJAR (IRE) 5 ch.g. Grand Lodge (USA) 125 – Ya Hajar 106 (Lycius (USA) 124) [2009 78: 10.2g^4 9m^4 10.2m* Jun 12] heavy-topped gelding: fairly useful handicapper: better than ever when winning at Chepstow in June: stays 10.8f: acts on polytrack and firm ground: all wins when dictating. *P. R. Webber* **81**

LAJIDAAL (USA) 2 b.c. (Apr 11) Dynaformer (USA) – Tayibah (IRE) 81 (Sadler's Wells (USA) 132) [2009 8.1m Sep 11] fourth foal: half-brother to 3-y-o Alsahil: dam, second at 11.7f on only start, half-sister to smart performer up to 1¼m Makderah out of close relative to Nayef and half-sister to Nashwan and Unfuwain: 25/1, very green and always behind in maiden at Sandown: will be suited by 1¼m+: should do better. *M. P. Tregoning* **– p**

LAKE CHINI (IRE) 7 b.g. Raise A Grand (IRE) 114 – Where's The Money 87 (Lochnager 132) [2009 75: 5m 5m^4 5d 5g^3 5g^6 5.1d^2 5s^3 5m^5 f5g Oct 18] strong, good sort: has a round action: modest handicapper nowadays: stays easy 7f, races at 5f nowadays: acts on polytrack, heavy and good to firm going, below form on fibresand: wears cheekpieces/ blinkers. *M. W. Easterby* **63**

LAKE KALAMALKA (IRE) 3 b.f. Dr Fong (USA) 128 – Lady of The Lake 104 (Caerleon (USA) 132) [2009 60p: 9.7d^2 10.2g* 11.6m p12g^6 p16g^6 12m^3 12m^6 p12m Sep 30] close-coupled filly: fair handicapper: won at Bath in April: worth a try at 1¾m: acts on polytrack, good to firm and good to soft going: sold 3,000 gns. *J. L. Dunlop* **73**

LAKEMAN (IRE) 3 b.g. Tillerman 123 – Bishop's Lake 87 (Lake Coniston (IRE) 131) [2009 87: 7.5m^5 8d f7g^4 7m^5 6d^5 6.9g f7g^5 8s* 8g Sep 3] workmanlike gelding: fairly useful handicapper: won at Musselburgh in August: below form otherwise: stays 1m: acts on heavy going: tried visored (tailed off). *B. Ellison* **82**

LAKE NAKURU 2 ch.f. (Mar 14) Bahamian Bounty 116 – Social Storm (USA) (Future Storm (USA)) [2009 6m p6g^6 6f Aug 17] close-coupled filly: fifth foal: half-sister to 4-y-o Stevie Thunder and 5-y-o Kyllachy Storm: dam US 7f/8.5f winner, including at 2 yrs: no form in maidens/seller. *H. S. Howe* **–**

LAKE POET (IRE) 6 ch.h. Galileo (IRE) 134 – Lyric 58 (Lycius (USA) 124) [2009 100, a–: p10g^5 10m^4 10.1g^2 10.1g^2 a12g Jul 18] leggy, close-coupled horse: useful performer on turf, fairly useful at best on all-weather: good second in handicaps at Epsom last 2 starts in Britain for C. Brittain, beaten 2½ lengths by Duncan then ¾ length behind Seeking The Buck: well held in valuable event at Moscow final outing: stays 1½m: acts on firm and soft going: tried blinkered. *Y. Musayev, Russia* **105 a84**

LAKE SABINA 4 b.f. Diktat 126 – Telori 72 (Muhtarram (USA) 125) [2009 70: p5m p5g p6g^5 p7g p6g p6g 6m 8f May 12] neat filly: just modest maiden nowadays: stays 6f: acts on polytrack, heavy and good to firm going. *M. R. Hoad* **51**

LAKE WAKATIPU 7 b.m. Lake Coniston (IRE) 131 – Lady Broker 54 (Petorius 117) [2009 p13.9g Mar 26] lengthy mare: fair performer in 2006: no form on Flat since: fair hurdler, won in May. *R. Ford* **–**

LA MARSEILLAISE (IRE) 3 ch.f. Medicean 128 – Saturnalia (Cadeaux Genereux 131) [2009 7s 7m^3 p7g^2 p7.1m p7g^2 Oct 26] sturdy filly: second foal: dam, little form, sister to very smart German 6f to 1m performer Toylsome: fairly useful maiden: likely to stay 1m: acts on polytrack and good to firm ground: sold 21,000 gns, sent to USA. *B. W. Hills* **82**

LAMBENCY (IRE) 6 b.m. Daylami (IRE) 138 – Triomphale (USA) (Nureyev (USA) 131) [2009 64: 6m 6d 5g 6m Sep 23] quite good-topped mare: poor handicapper nowadays: effective at 5f to 7f: acts on polytrack, firm and soft going: tried in cheekpieces: often held up. *J. S. Goldie* **49**

LAMBOURN GENIE (UAE) 3 b.g. Halling (USA) 133 – Mystery Play (IRE) 104 (Sadler's Wells (USA) 132) [2009 54: 12.1g 11.7m 8.5m^4 10.1g^6 Jul 20] workmanlike gelding: just poor maiden at 3 yrs: should stay 1m+. *Tom Dascombe* **47**

LAMBRINI LACE (IRE) 4 br.f. Namid 128 – Feather 'n Lace (IRE) 73 (Green Desert (USA) 127) [2009 65: 7.2s^4 6d^6 6g p6g p8.6g f6d Dec 29] good bodied filly: modest handicapper nowadays: worth dropping back to 5f: acts on polytrack and heavy ground: visored/in cheekpieces last 3 starts. *Mrs L. Williamson* **58**

LAMH ALBASSER (USA) 2 ch.g. (Mar 10) Mr Greeley (USA) 122 – Madame Boulangere 100 (Royal Applause 124) [2009 6g^4 7m* 7m* 7m^4 7.1g^3 6.5m^6 7g^4 Oct 10] $450,000Y: lengthy, good-bodied gelding: fluent mover: third foal: dam 6f/6.5f winner, including at 2 yrs: useful performer: won maiden at Redcar in June and nursery at Newmarket in July: ran creditably after only when sixth to Swilly Ferry in sales race at Doncaster: stays 7f: acts on good to firm going: in cheekpieces last 2 starts, pulling hard final one: joined A. bin Huzaim in UAE. *Saeed bin Suroor* **94**

LAMINKA 3 b.f. Intikhab (USA) 135 – Lamees (USA) (Lomond (USA) 128) [2009 p8.6g^5 p8g 8m May 16] smallish filly: half-sister to several winners, including smart 7f (at 2 yrs)/1¼m winner Francesco Guardi (by Robellino): dam unraced: little form. *G. C. Bravery* **–**

LANA'S CHARM 3 b.f. Lend A Hand 124 – Eljariha 71 (Unfuwain (USA) 131) [2009 51: p5g^5 p6g^6 6g^5 p7f p6g Oct 23] modest maiden: well below form last 3 starts: tried tongue tied. *P. J. Makin* **57**

LANCASTER LAD (IRE) 4 b.c. Piccolo 121 – Ruby Julie (Clantime 101) [2009 64: f8g^4 p8g 8.1g 7g^3 8m 8f 8m 7m^5 Sep 28] good-bodied colt: modest performer: best around 1m: acts on all-weather and firm going: tried blinkered, usually in cheekpieces: often races freely held up. *A. B. Haynes* **52**

LANCETTO (FR) 4 b.g. Dubai Destination (USA) 127 – Lanciana (IRE) (Acatenango (GER) 127) [2009 102: 12g 12.1d 12v 10d Oct 26] useful at 3 yrs in Germany: well below form in 2009, leaving K. R. Burke prior to final outing: stays 1¼m: best efforts on good going. *James J. Hartnett, Ireland* **72**

LAND HAWK (IRE) 3 br.c. Trans Island 119 – Heike (Glenstal (USA) 118) [2009 74p: p7g^5 p8g^5 7m^5 9.8g^5 p8.6g^3 8.1m^3 Sep 29] close-coupled colt: fair maiden handicapper: stays 1m: acts on polytrack and good to firm going. *J. Pearce* **74**

LANDIKHAYA (IRE) 4 ch.g. Kris Kin (USA) 126 – Montana Lady (IRE) 83 (Be My Guest (USA) 126) [2009 64: p7g p12g Jan 18] stocky gelding: just poor form in 2009: seems best at 1m/1¼m: acts on polytrack, good to firm and good to soft ground: usually wears headgear. *D. K. Ivory* **46**

LAND 'N STARS 9 b.g. Mtoto 134 – Uncharted Waters 68 (Celestial Storm (USA) 132) [2009 100: p16g p16g Apr 21] leggy, close-coupled gelding: one-time smart performer: on downgrade, well beaten in handicaps in 2009 (blinkered): said to have bled final outing. *Jamie Poulton* **–**

LAND OF PLENTY (IRE) 2 b.f. (Apr 30) Azamour (IRE) 130 – Bring Plenty (USA) 100 (Southern Halo (USA)) [2009 8.1g 7.2s 7.1m p8.6g^2 p9.5g^5 Dec 12] 25,000Y: fourth foal: half-sister to winner in Italy by Stravinsky: dam, 2-y-o 6f winner, out of smart performer up to 1¼m Alcando: poor maiden: left M. Johnston after third start: stays 8.6f. *E. A. L. Dunlop* **45**

LANDOFTHEFOURONES (USA) 3 b.c. Aldebaran (USA) 126 – Cuanto Es (USA) (Exbourne (USA) 125) [2009 8d^5 8.3v^4 8m^2 p8.6g^4 Sep 11] well-made colt: sixth foal: closely related to 5-y-o Seeking The Buck and half-brother to winner in USA by Louis Quatorze: dam, US 6f to 8.5f winner, half-sister to smart US Grade 1 1¼m winner Honey Ryder: fair maiden: stays 1m: acts on good to firm and good to soft going: sold 10,000 gns. *D. R. Lanigan* **72**

LANDOWNER 2 b.c. (May 5) Shamardal (USA) 129 – Rentless (Zafonic (USA) 130) [2009 7f^4 7.1m* 8g* 7d^2 Oct 27] €280,000Y: attractive colt: fourth foal: half-brother to 5-y-o Riggins and winners in Italy by King's Best and Hawk Wing: dam, Italian 7f (at 2 yrs) to 1m winner, sister to useful 1¼m/1½m winner Yawmi: useful performer: won maiden at Warwick in September and nursery at Pontefract (much improved, beat Mason Hindmarsh a neck, pair 15 lengths clear) in October: below form on good to soft ground final start: stays 1m: has wandered: joined A. bin Huzaim in UAE. *Saeed bin Suroor* **94**

LANDUCCI 8 b.g. Averti (IRE) 117 – Divina Luna 96 (Dowsing (USA) 124) [2009 70, a85: p7m^6 p8g^2 p8g p7g^4 p7g^4 p8g* 8.3m^6 p7g^5 8s^4 7g* 6m^4 7g^3 8f^4 8.1m* Aug 20] big, close-coupled gelding: fair performer, better on all-weather: claimed from J. Hills £6,000 **70** **a77**

after first start: won handicaps at Kempton (fifth win there) in April and Chepstow in August, and seller at Brighton (sixth success there) in June: effective at 7f/1m: acts on polytrack, firm and soft going: usually wears headgear: tried tongue tied: sometimes edges left: none too consistent. *S. Curran*

LANGFORD DECOIT (IRE) 3 b.c. Peintre Celebre (USA) 137 – Litchfield Hills **59**
(USA) (Relaunch (USA)) [2009 10g 12m^6 12.1g^4 11.5s 11.6g Jun 22] modest maiden: tailed off in handicaps last 2 starts: stays 1½m: has joined Tim Vaughan. *M. R. Channon*

LANGHAM HOUSE 4 ch.g. Best of The Bests (IRE) 122 – Dafne 68§ (Nashwan **60**
(USA) 135) [2009 65: p7g^3 Jan 10] good-topped gelding: modest performer: stays 7f: acts on polytrack, firm and good to soft going: tried visored: has looked awkward. *J. R. Jenkins*

LANGLAND BAY 3 b.f. Diktat 126 – Dodo (IRE) 90 (Alzao (USA) 117) [2009 p6g^6 **61**
7m 7m^5 f7g p7.1g p8m Nov 4] lengthy, angular filly: seventh foal: half-sister to 3 winners, including 7-y-o Nota Bene and smart 6f (including at 2 yrs)/7f winner Tarjman (by Cadeaux Genereux): dam, 6f winner, out of very smart but temperamental sprinter Dead Certain: modest form only on first 2 starts: has had breathing problem. *W. R. Muir*

LANG SHINING (IRE) 5 ch.g. Dr Fong (USA) 128 – Dragnet (IRE) 72 (Rainbow **102**
Quest (USA) 134) [2009 110: 8g 10m 8m^4 9.9g^6 10m 8m Sep 19] leggy, close-coupled gelding: useful handicapper: best effort in 2009 when 2¾ lengths fourth to City of The Kings at York: stays 1¼m: acts on soft and good to firm ground: often worked up in preliminaries: acted as pacemaker second outing, but normally held up: sold 20,000 gns and gelded. *Sir Michael Stoute*

LANIZZA 2 ch.g. (Mar 26) Alhaarth (IRE) 126 – Cerulean Sky (IRE) 114 (Darshaan **–**
133) [2009 7m p7m Aug 20] neat gelding: well held in maidens, gelded in between: tried blinkered: sold 5,000 gns, sent to Bahrain. *E. A. L. Dunlop*

LANSDOWNE PRINCESS 7 b.m. Cloudings (IRE) 112 – Premier Princess 45 (Hard **40**
Fought 125) [2009 16.2v^6 Jul 24] poor maiden hurdler/chaser: poor form in claimer at Chepstow on Flat debut. *G. A. Ham*

LA PANTERA 2 b.f. (Jan 28) Captain Rio 122 – Pantita 74 (Polish Precedent (USA) **86**
131) [2009 5m^3 6g* 6m 6g p7.1g^3 Nov 9] 3,000F: angular filly: second foal: dam, maiden (stayed 1¼m), half-sister to dam of 6-y-o Mariol: fairly useful performer: won maiden at Goodwood in May: ran creditably in nurseries after only when third at Wolverhampton (very slowly away): stays 7f: acts on polytrack. *R. Hannon*

LAPINA (IRE) 5 ch.m. Fath (USA) 116 – Alpina (USA) 69 (El Prado (IRE) 119) [2009 **63**
73: p13.3g^2 p12.2g^6 p13g^5 12d^6 15g^4 15g^5 Jul 3] lengthy mare: fair handicapper on **a71**
all-weather, modest on turf: stays 2m: acts on polytrack, firm and good to soft ground: wears headgear: held up: probably not straightforward. *A. Middleton*

LA POLKA 3 ch.f. Carnival Dancer 123 – Indubitable 87 (Sharpo 132) [2009 10m p10g **69**
11.7g^6 16g^4 16g Aug 29] lengthy filly: half-sister to 3 winners, including 11f/1½m winner Gold Ring (by Groom Dancer) and 1¼m winner Cugina (by Distant Relative), both useful: dam 1¼m winner: fair maiden handicapper: stays 2m. *H. Morrison*

LA PRECIOSA 4 b.f. Arrasas (USA) 100 – Morning Star 58 (Statoblest 120) [2009 **–**
p8.6g f11f Dec 17] first foal: dam 2-y-o 5f winner: tailed off in bumper/maidens: tried in cheekpieces. *I. W. McInnes*

L'ARCO BALENO (IRE) 3 b.f. Catcher In The Rye (IRE) 115 – Rainbow Java (IRE) **58**
(Fairy King (USA)) [2009 p6g^3 f7g^3 p7g 8.3m 7g p10g Jun 6] modest maiden: should stay beyond 7f: acts on all-weather: sold 3,500 gns. *S. A. Callaghan*

LAREHAAN (USA) 2 b. or br.f. (Feb 21) Smarty Jones (USA) 134 – Wendy Vaala **–**
(USA) (Dayjur (USA) 137) [2009 6m Jul 10] $140,000F: unfurnished filly: half-sister to winners in USA/Russia by Gone West and Gulch: dam unraced half-sister to Irish Oaks winner Alydaress and Cheveley Park Stakes winners Park Appeal (dam of Cape Cross) and Desirable (dam of Shadayid): 11/1, very green when down the field in maiden at Newmarket: sold 4,500 gns in December. *B. W. Hills*

LARGEM 3 b.g. Largesse 112 – Jem's Law (Contract Law (USA) 108) [2009 59: 8.3v **64**
p12g^5 p12.2g* p12g^4 Oct 2] good-topped gelding: modest form: won handicap at Wolverhampton in September: should stay 1¾m: acts on polytrack. *J. R. Jenkins*

LARKHAM (USA) 3 b. or br.g. Action This Day (USA) 121 – La Sarto (USA) **94**
(Cormorant (USA)) [2009 76: p8.6g* 10g* 9.9m^3 10m*^{dis} 10m^4 Sep 24] tall, leggy gelding: fairly useful form: first past post in maiden at Wolverhampton in April and handicaps at Leicester in May and Newbury (disqualified after failing dope test) in August: will stay 1½m: raced only on polytrack and good/good to firm going: sold 10,000 gns. *R. M. Beckett*

LARKRISE STAR 2 b.f. (Mar 27) Where Or When (IRE) 124 – Katy Ivory (IRE) 68 (Night Shift (USA)) [2009 6d^5 p7g^4 p7g^4 Jul 15] workmanlike filly: sixth foal: sister to 4-y-o A Dream Come True and half-sister to 6f/7f winner in Italy by Pivotal: dam maiden who stayed 1m: modest form in maidens: should stay 1m. *D. K. Ivory* **63**

LA ROSA NOSTRA 4 ch.f. Dr Fong (USA) 128 – Rose Quantas (IRE) (Danehill (USA) 126) [2009 10.3m^2 10g^5 10f^6 12m^2 p12.2g^3 10.4v 8f^6 10m^6 p9.5g^4 Oct 9] workmanlike filly: fair handicapper: stays 1½m: acts on polytrack and good to firm going, possibly unsuited by heavy: tried in cheekpieces/tongue tie: usually races prominently: sold 10,000 gns. *W. R. Swinburn* **79**

LASSARINA (IRE) 3 b.f. Sakhee (USA) 136 – Kalanda (Desert King (IRE) 129) [2009 96p: 7s^5 7g^3 Jul 25] good-bodied filly: useful performer: fifth to Lahaleeb in Fred Darling Stakes at Newbury and, after 3-month break, good 3 lengths third to Pyrrha in handicap at Newmarket: may prove best up to 7f: sold 50,000 gns in November. *B. W. Hills* **102**

LASSO THE MOON 3 b.g. Sadler's Wells (USA) 132 – Hotelgenie Dot Com 107 (Selkirk (USA) 129) [2009 95: 11s 12m^2 10d^4 10.1g^3 12m 10m Jul 9] strong gelding: fairly useful maiden handicapper: effective at 1¼m/1½m: acts on soft and good to firm ground: moody (looked unwilling final outing, though said to have finished lame): gelded after. *M. R. Channon* **81**

LAST FLIGHT (IRE) 5 b.m. In The Wings 128 – Fantastic Fantasy (IRE) 85 (Lahib (USA) 129) [2009 21g Jul 29] tall mare: fairly useful handicapper: progressive in 2007: fit from hurdling (fairly useful form), well held on Flat return: stays 2¼m: acts on soft and good to firm going: visored/blinkered nowadays. *P. Bowen* **–**

LASTKINGOFSCOTLAND (IRE) 3 b.g. Danehill Dancer (IRE) 117 – Arcade (Rousillon (USA) 133) [2009 7.5v* 6.7d^2 7v^6 7v^2 p7g 9d f8m Dec 15] useful performer: won maiden at Tipperary in April: below form after next start, leaving Charles O'Brien in Ireland prior to final appearance: should stay 1m: acts on heavy going: slowly away first 3 outings. *G. C. Bravery* **99 d**

LAST OF THE LINE 4 b.g. Efisio 120 – Dance By Night 84 (Northfields (USA)) [2009 57, a79: f7g p8g^6 Feb 14] neat gelding: fair performer at best: well held in seller/claimer in 2009: usually in headgear. *B. N. Pollock* **–**

LAST OF THE RAVENS 2 b.f. (Feb 25) Zaha (CAN) 106 – Eccentric Dancer 47 (Rambo Dancer (CAN) 107) [2009 f7g^5 f6d Dec 29] seventh foal: sister to 1m seller winner Raven Rascal and half-sister to 2 winners, including 6f winner College Queen (by Lugana Beach): dam maiden who stayed 9.4f: little impact in maidens at Southwell. *J. F. Coupland* **–**

LAST ORDERS (IRE) 2 gr.c. (Apr 27) Bertolini (USA) 125 – Sassania (IRE) 78 (Persian Bold 123) [2009 5m^5 5.2m 6d Jul 20] well beaten in maidens/seller. *M. G. Quinlan* **–**

LASTROAROFDTIGER (USA) 3 b.g. Cherokee Run (USA) 122 – Innocent Affair (IRE) (Night Shift (USA)) [2009 63p: p8.6g* 7g p8g^5 8.1g p7.1g^6 p6g p7g Dec 31] fairly useful performer: won maiden at Wolverhampton (dead-heat) in March: trained by K. R. Burke until fifth start, left A. Jarvis and gelded prior to final outing: stays 8.6f: form only on polytrack. *J. R. Weymes* **– a81**

LASTROSEOFSUMMER (IRE) 3 ch.f. Haafhd 129 – Broken Romance (IRE) (Ela-Mana-Mou 132) [2009 8.3g^6 p12.2g Dec 5] 50,000Y: closely related to useful 1¾m winner Zurbaran and half-sister to several winners, including smart 7f (at 2 yrs) to 2m winner Romantic Affair (by Persian Bold): dam unraced: better effort in maidens on debut: should be suited by 1½m+. *Rae Guest* **58**

LAST SOVEREIGN 5 b.g. Pivotal 124 – Zayala (Royal Applause 124) [2009 83: p7g* 7m^2 8.3m 8d^3 7g^6 7g^4 6g^3 7d^4 p7m 6d^4 Oct 6] sturdy gelding: fairly useful handicapper: won at Kempton in February: largely creditable efforts after: stays 1m: acts on polytrack, soft and good to firm ground: effective with/without cheekpieces. *Jane Chapple-Hyam* **88**

LAST THREE MINUTES (IRE) 4 b.g. Val Royal (FR) 127 – Circe's Isle (Be My Guest (USA) 126) [2009 90: 8m^4 8d p8g* 8.9g^3 8g^6 10g^6 Jul 24] useful-looking gelding: fairly useful handicapper: won at Lingfield in May: better than bare result after, especially at York (unlucky third to Kavachi): probably stays 1¼m: acts on polytrack, soft and good to firm going: held up. *E. A. L. Dunlop* **93**

LA SYLVIA (IRE) 4 b.f. Oasis Dream 129 – Hawas 93 (Mujtahid (USA) 118) [2009 97: 5.1g 6.1m 6d* 6s^4 Nov 19] smallish filly: useful performer: ran in listed events in 2009, winning at Baden-Baden (by 1¾ lengths from Bella Platina) in September: stays 6f: acts on polytrack, soft and good to firm going: sold 78,000 gns. *E. J. O'Neill* **102**

LATANSAA 2 b.c. (Apr 21) Indian Ridge 123 – Sahool 109 (Unfuwain (USA) 131) [2009 8v³ Oct 24] second foal: half-brother to 3-y-o Arwaah: dam, 1m (at 2 yrs)/1½m winner, closely related to dam of high-class 1¼m/1½m performer Maraahel: 12/1, promising 5¾ lengths third to Multames in maiden at Newbury, travelling strongly up with pace long way and not given hard race once held: will stay 1¼m: sure to improve. *M. P. Tregoning* **83 p**

LATERLY (IRE) 4 b.g. Tiger Hill (IRE) 127 – La Candela (GER) (Alzao (USA) 117) [2009 105: 12s 11.9m 10.4m 10.4m³ 10.4m 10m p12.2g³ p12.2g⁵ p9.5g Dec 17] well-made gelding: useful handicapper: creditable third at Haydock (quite valuable event) in August and, having left T. Tate 57,000 gns, Wolverhampton in November: stays 1½m: acts on polytrack, soft and good to firm going: usually front runner. *S. Gollings* **98**

LATHAAT 2 b. or br.f. (Jan 17) Dubai Destination (USA) 127 – Khulood (USA) 103 (Storm Cat (USA)) [2009 6m May 30] third foal: half-sister to fairly useful 2007 2-y-o 5f winner Kashoof (by Green Desert) and 3-y-o Imaam: dam, 6f (at 2 yrs)/7f (Nell Gwyn Stakes) winner, half-sister to July Cup winner Elnadim and Irish 1000 Guineas winner Mehthaaf: 15/2, slowly away and ran green when behind in maiden at Lingfield: not seen out again. *J. L. Dunlop* **–**

LATIN SCHOLAR (IRE) 4 ch.g. Titus Livius (FR) 115 – Crimada (IRE) (Mukaddamah (USA) 125) [2009 83: 10.2g* p11g⁴ 9g⁵ 10.9g Aug 31] big, raw-boned gelding: fairly useful handicapper: won at Chepstow in June: failed to build on that after: likely to stay 1½m: acts on good to firm going. *A. King* **83**

LATIN TINGE (USA) 3 gr. or ro.f. King Cugat (USA) 122 – Southern Tradition (USA) (Family Doctor (USA)) [2009 85p: p8g⁵ 10g 11m⁶ p10m 10g p9.5g Oct 15] tall, rather unfurnished filly: fairly useful handicapper: may prove best up to 1¼m: acts on polytrack, probably on soft ground: blinkered final outing (looked awkward). *P. F. I. Cole* **80**

LA TOYA J (IRE) 2 b.f. (May 8) Noverre (USA) 125 – Bevel (USA) (Mr Prospector (USA)) [2009 p7g p7m³ p7g⁵ Dec 31] €24,000 2-y-o: closely related to 1½m winner Heavenly Bay and 1½m/1¾m winner Beldon Hill (both fairly useful, by Rahy) and half-sister to 2 winners, including 1¼m winner Payola (by Red Ransom): dam French 1m winner: left Edgar Byrne, best effort in maidens when third to Prince of Sorrento at Kempton: likely to be suited by 1m+: remains open to improvement. *R. Curtis* **57 p**

LAUBERHORN 2 b.g. (Apr 4) Dubai Destination (USA) 127 – Ski Run 112 (Petoski 135) [2009 7d 8.1m Sep 10] behind in maidens. *Eve Johnson Houghton* **–**

LAUDATORY 3 b.g. Royal Applause 124 – Copy-Cat 60 (Lion Cavern (USA) 117) [2009 78p: p7g* 7m⁴ 8m³ 8.1m 7g⁴ p8g⁴ p8g⁴ p8m² 8m⁶ Oct 5] tall, leggy gelding: fairly useful handicapper: gelded, won at Kempton in April: largely creditable efforts after: stays easy 1m: acts on polytrack and good to firm going: tried tongue tied: reliable: sold £23,000. *W. R. Swinburn* **93**

LAUGHING BOY (IRE) 3 b.g. Montjeu (IRE) 137 – Mala Mala (IRE) 104 (Brief Truce (USA) 126) [2009 10m⁴ 10d⁴ 10f² 10m³ 8m f11g Oct 18] 100,000F: attractive gelding: fourth foal: half-brother to several winners, notably smart sprinter Contest (by Danehill Dancer): dam, Irish 5f winner, half-sister to very smart 1¼m performer Mister Monet and Irish 1000 Guineas winner Tarascon: fairly useful maiden: well below form in handicaps last 2 starts: stays 1¼m: acts on firm going: sold 18,000 gns. *L. M. Cumani* **80**

LAUGHTER (IRE) 4 b.f. Sadler's Wells (USA) 132 – Smashing Review (USA) (Pleasant Tap (USA)) [2009 87p: 10.3g⁵ 10.1m Jun 25] lengthy filly: fairly useful performer, very lightly raced: off 13 months, towards rear in handicap/listed race in 2009: bred to stay 1½m: sold 45,000 gns in December. *Sir Michael Stoute* **86**

LAURA LAND 3 b.f. Lujain (USA) 119 – Perdicula (IRE) (Persian Heights 129) [2009 12m 10.3m⁶ 10.9g p10g Oct 11] 4,000Y: half-sister to 3 winners, including useful 1¼m winner Markovitch (by Mark of Esteem): dam, German winner around 1¼m, half-sister to Derby winner High-Rise: modest form. *W. M. Brisbourne* **53**

LAURA'S LADY (IRE) 3 b.f. Namid 128 – Catapila (USA) 72 (Tactical Cat (USA) 116) [2009 6f* 6m⁵ 7m⁴ 7.9g³ Jul 4] €8,500F: first foal: dam, Irish maiden (third at 6f at 2 yrs), out of half-sister to Preakness Stakes winner Corporate Report: modest form: won maiden at Redcar in May: failed to build on that after: stays 7f: held up. *G. A. Swinbank* **57**

LAUREL CREEK (IRE) 4 b.g. Sakura Laurel (JPN) – Eastern Sky (AUS) (Danehill (USA) 126) [2009 83: p12.2g* p16.5g* 16g 16m⁵ p17g⁶ 16g Aug 6] useful handicapper: won at Wolverhampton in February and March: tongue tied, well held final outing (gelded after): stays 16.5f: acts on polytrack and good to firm going: held up. *M. J. Grassick, Ireland* **97**

LAURELDEAN DESERT 2 b.f. (May 8) Green Desert (USA) 127 – Heady (Rousillon (USA) 133) [2009 5m^6 6m 6g^5 p7g Nov 14] 105,000F: lengthy, good-quartered filly: closely related to 7.5f/1m winner in Italy by Desert Prince and half-sister to several winners, notably very smart but ungenuine 7f/1m performer Salselon (by Salse): dam unraced half-sister to top-class miler Markofdistinction: easily best effort when fifth in maiden at Yarmouth: should stay 7f. *R. A. Fahey* **60**

LAURELDEANS BEST (IRE) 3 b.f. King's Best (USA) 132 – Vanishing River (USA) (Southern Halo (USA)) [2009 8g^3 p8.6g^3 p12.2g^3 Dec 5] second foal: dam, ran once in France, half-sister to very smart performers Vetheuil (effective at 1m) and Verveine (stayed 1½m) and to dams of Group 1 winners Maids Causeway, Vespone and Vallee Enchantee: third in maidens, better than bare result all starts: should be suited by 1½m+. *R. A. Fahey* **68**

LAURELDEAN SPIRIT (IRE) 2 br.f. (Mar 16) Whipper (USA) 126 – Mise (IRE) (Indian Ridge 123) [2009 7m^2 7d^4 7m^3 Sep 12] €85,000F, €150,000Y: tall filly: has scope: third foal: half-sister to smart 6f (at 2 yrs, Lowther Stakes)/1m (Falmouth Stakes) winner Nahoodh (by Clodovil) and 3-y-o Silver Games: dam unraced half-sister to smart French performer up to 1½m Not Just Swing: maiden: failed to progress after promising neck second to Emirates Dream at York: raced only at 7f: possibly quirky. *R. A. Fahey* **71**

LAUREN'S KITTY (IRE) 2 b.f. (Mar 15) One Cool Cat (USA) 123 – Home Comforts (Most Welcome 131) [2009 7d Oct 12] half-sister to several winners, including 1m winner Croft (by Mull of Kintyre): dam ran twice in Ireland: 100/1, last in maiden at Salisbury. *J. C. Fox* **–**

LAURIE GROVE (IRE) 3 b.g. Danehill Dancer (IRE) 117 – Fragrant (Cadeaux Genereux 131) [2009 83p: p8.6g^2 p8g^4 10m 8m^4 7s p8.6g^2 p9.5m p7f p10m^3 Dec 30] tall gelding: fairly useful handicapper: creditable efforts in 2009 only when runner-up: stays 8.6f: raced mostly on polytrack and good to firm ground: tried in cheekpieces. *T. G. Mills* **90**

LAVA LAMP (GER) 2 b.c. (May 11) Shamardal (USA) 129 – La Felicita (Shareef Dancer (USA) 135) [2009 6g^6 6.1g^2 7.1m^4 6m^3 6m^5 6s Nov 7] 55,000F, 60,000Y: sturdy colt: sixth foal: half-brother to 3 winners abroad, notably 4-y-o Lady Marian: dam German 1m winner: fair maiden: poor efforts last 2 starts, leaving M. Johnston £6,500 in between: should stay 7f+: acts on good to firm going: temperament under suspicion. *G. A. Harker* **77**

LAVA STEPS (USA) 3 b.c. Giant's Causeway (USA) 132 – Miznah (IRE) 102 (Sadler's Wells (USA) 132) [2009 63: 11.9m^4 10m f12f^2 f12f* Dec 12] well-made colt: fair performer: left P. Cole 2,500 gns after second start: won maiden at Southwell in December: stays 1½m: acts on fibresand. *P. T. Midgley* **77**

LA VERTE RUE (USA) 3 b.f. Johannesburg (USA) 127 – Settling In (USA) (Green Desert (USA) 127) [2009 74: p7g^5 5.5f 9d^6 8.5d* 7m^2 8.5f^6 Aug 31] modest performer nowadays: left J. Osborne after return: won handicap at Les Landes in August: stays 8.5f: acts on all-weather, good to firm and good to soft going. *Mrs A. Malzard, Jersey* **64**

LA VILLE LUMIERE (USA) 2 b.f. (Apr 26) Rahy (USA) 115 – La Sylphide (SWI) 110 (Barathea (IRE) 127) [2009 p6g^6 8.3m^3 8m^5 8g Oct 20] well-made filly: fifth foal: sister to fairly useful French 1½m winner La Seine and half-sister to 2 winners, including US Grade 2 11f winner Expansion (by Maria's Mon): dam, French 1¼m/10.5f (Prix Penelope) winner, closely related to 6-y-o Purple Moon/half-sister to high-class 1¼m performer Vespone: fair maiden: best effort when third at Leicester: should stay 1¼m: joined H-A. Pantall in France. *Saeed bin Suroor* **68**

LA VOILE ROUGE 4 ch.g. Daggers Drawn (USA) 114 – At Amal (IRE) (Astronef 116) [2009 p7.1g 6g Jul 31] tall, deep-bodied gelding: fairly useful at 2 yrs: off almost 2 years, just fair form in 2009: stays 7f. *R. M. Beckett* **75**

LAW AND ORDER 3 b.g. Lear Spear (USA) 124 – Sarcita 111 (Primo Dominie 121) [2009 60: 7.1m^6 7m 9m p10g Sep 9] good-topped gelding: modest maiden: not so good at 3 yrs: in cheekpieces final outing. *Miss J. R. Tooth* **50**

LAW OF ATTRACTION (IRE) 2 b.g. (Mar 5) Invincible Spirit (IRE) 121 – Karatisa (IRE) 93 (Nishapour (FR) 125) [2009 6g 6.1v^3 Jul 17] sturdy, quite attractive gelding: much better effort in maidens when 7¾ lengths third to Running Mate at Nottingham (gelded after). *J. R. Gask* **49 +**

LAW OF THE JUNGLE (IRE) 3 b.f. Catcher In The Rye (IRE) 115 – Haut Volee (Top Ville 129) [2009 69p: 7.2d^6 8g 10m 10g 8g^4 p8m^5 p9.5g^3 Dec 28] fair maiden: left David Wachman in Ireland after fifth start: seems to stay easy 9.5f: acts on polytrack and good to soft going: tried in cheekpieces. *Tom Dascombe* **66**

Sheikh Hamdan bin Mohammed Al Maktoum's "Layali Al Andalus"

LAWYER TO WORLD 5 gr.g. Marju (IRE) 127 – Legal Steps (IRE) (Law Society (USA) 130) [2009 –: f12g^5 f12g^5 16d 10.1g 10.2g Jul 4] angular gelding: modest performer: stays 1½m: acts on all-weather, well held on turf in 2009: often in headgear. *Mrs C. A. Dunnett* **– a51**

LAYALI AL ANDALUS 2 b.c. (Mar 7) Halling (USA) 133 – Lafite 100 (Robellino (USA) 127) [2009 6m^2 7m* 8m* 7m^5 8g^2 10v Nov 14] 60,000Y: rangy colt: fifth foal: dam, 1m/1¼m winner, half-sister to very smart 1¼m/1½m performer Imperial Dancer: smart performer: won maiden at Doncaster (by 7 lengths) in June and nursery at Newcastle (easily under 9-7, by 2¾ lengths from Bonfire Knight) in August: good ¾-length second to St Nicholas Abbey in Beresford Stakes at the Curragh: ran poorly fourth (sweating) and final starts: should stay 1¼m: races close up: withdrawn lame at start of Prix de Conde at Longchamp on intended sixth outing. *M. Johnston* **110**

LAY CLAIM (USA) 2 b. or br.c. (Apr 24) Seeking The Gold (USA) – Promptly (IRE) 88 (Lead On Time (USA) 123) [2009 7m^2 7g^4 p7g^4 Oct 29] attractive colt: closely related to smart 2003 2-y-o 7f/1m winner Fantastic View (by Distant View) and half-brother to several winners, including 3-y-o Weald Park: dam, 6f and (US minor stakes) 1m winner, out of Nell Gwyn Stakes winner Ghariba: maiden: failed to progress after promising nose second to Critical Moment at Newbury, finishing tamely both subsequent starts. *Sir Michael Stoute* **87**

LAYER CAKE 3 b.c. Monsieur Bond (IRE) 120 – Blue Indigo (FR) (Pistolet Bleu (IRE) 133) [2009 71: p8g^6 6.1m p8.6g^2 p8.6g^2 p10m p8.6m^5 8.1g^3 p8f^2 p8m^3 8m^5 p8g^6 Oct 22] attractive colt: fair maiden: stays 8.6f: acts on polytrack, probably on good to firm going: patiently ridden: signs of temperament, but consistent: sold 17,000 gns. *J. W. Hills* **74**

LAYLA'S BOY 2 ch.g. (Mar 2) Sakhee (USA) 136 – Gay Romance 71 (Singspiel (IRE) 133) [2009 6g^4 7.2g^2 7d^2 7m p8.6g^4 8.3g^4 8d^3 Oct 12] 17,000Y: first living foal: dam, 7f winner, closely related to high-class US 1m/9f performer Hawksley Hill and half-sister to dam of 8-y-o Benbaun: fair maiden: stays 8.6f: acts on polytrack and good to soft ground. *R. A. Fahey* **76**

LAYLA'S DANCER 2 b.c. (May 2) Danehill Dancer (IRE) 117 – Crumpetsfortea (IRE) (Henbit (USA) 130) [2009 7s* 8g^{4} Oct 23] 60,000Y, 130,000 2-y-o: good-bodied colt: seventh foal: brother to 3-y-o Prohibition, closely related to useful Irish 2005 2-y-o 7f winner James Joyce (by Danehill) and half-brother to 3 winners, including useful French 2001 2-y-o 6.5f/7f winner Contemporary (by Alzao): dam unraced: won maiden at Thirsk in September: better form when 1¼ lengths fourth to Antoniola in nursery at Doncaster, still green and finishing well: stays 1m: sure to progress again. *R. A. Fahey* **89 p**

LAYLA'S HERO (IRE) 2 b.g. (Mar 5) One Cool Cat (USA) 123 – Capua (USA) (Private Terms (USA)) [2009 6g^{4} 5g* 6d^{2} 6m* 6m 6d* 6g* 6d* Oct 24] £9,000Y: good-topped gelding: fourth foal: half-brother to Irish 7f winner Decarl (by Bluebird) and 5f/6f winner (including at 2 yrs) Alizar (by Rahy): dam unraced: smart performer: won maiden at Hamilton in July, nurseries at Haydock in August and September and listed races at York (beat Coolminx 2¼ lengths, travelling strongly) and Doncaster (gamely by head from Singeur) in October: will stay 7f: acts on good to firm and good to soft ground. *D. Nicholls* **111**

LAYLA'S LAD (USA) 2 b.c. (May 28) Dixieland Band (USA) – Requesting More (USA) (Norquestor (CAN)) [2009 p6g^{6} p7.1g p5.1m^{4} f7g^{5} Dec 18] modest maiden: stays 7f: raced only on all-weather. *R. A. Fahey* **62**

LAYLA'S LEXI 2 b.f. (Feb 22) Reset (AUS) 124 – Tricoteuse (Kris 135) [2009 5v^{3} 5m Sep 16] 1,200F, £20,000Y: tall filly: third foal: half-sister to 5-y-o Riguez Dancer and French 2008 2-y-o 9f winner Boudin (by Peintre Celebre): dam unraced: much better effort in maidens when 7 lengths third to Comedy Hall at Catterick: should be suited by 7f+. *D. Nicholls* **62 +**

LAYLA'S PRINCE (IRE) 2 b.g. (Mar 15) Statue of Liberty (USA) 115 – Nihonpillow Mirai (IRE) 48 (Zamindar (USA) 116) [2009 6m^{6} 6g Oct 9] €33,000F, £25,000Y: compact gelding: second foal: dam, Irish maiden (stayed 7f), out of smart performer up to 10.5f Ala Mahlik: green and not unduly knocked about when behind in maidens at Ripon and York: likely to do better. *D. Nicholls* **– p**

LAYLINE (IRE) 2 b.g. (Apr 22) King's Best (USA) 132 – Belle Reine (King of Kings (IRE) 125) [2009 8.1d* 8.5m^{3} 8g Oct 23] third foal: half-brother to 3-y-o Belle des Airs: dam unraced half-sister to smart miler Smart Enough: fairly useful performer: won maiden at Chepstow in September: better form when 1¾ lengths third to Zeitoper in minor event at Epsom: stays 8.5f: got worked up before final start. *R. M. Beckett* **93**

Coral Rockingham Stakes, York—one of five wins for bargain buy Layla's Hero (stars), who wins from Coolminx (noseband) and Never The Waiter

LA ZAMORA 3 b.f. Lujain (USA) 119 – Love Quest (Pursuit of Love 124) [2009 6m³ 6g² 5m* 5f⁵ 5m* 5g⁵ 5m 5s³ 5m Sep 18] 3,000F, 4,200Y: sturdy filly: second foal: dam unraced: fairly useful performer: won maiden at Musselburgh in May and handicap at Newmarket in June: in-and-out form after: stays 6f: acts on firm and soft going. *T. D. Barron* **87**

LAZY DARREN 5 b.g. Largesse 112 – Palmstead Belle (IRE) 79 (Wolfhound (USA) 126) [2009 10.3m Jun 5] close-coupled gelding: fairly useful handicapper in 2007: fit from hurdling, not knocked about at Doncaster only Flat outing since: stays easy 1¼m: acts on polytrack, firm and good to soft going: tried blinkered/visored (tailed off): held up and difficult ride (has hung left). *C. Grant* **71 +**

LEADENHALL LASS (IRE) 3 ch.f. Monsieur Bond (IRE) 120 – Zest (USA) (Zilzal (USA) 137) [2009 68: 6m⁵ p6g 6f³ 5m⁴ 5g⁴ 6m³ 6m* 7m² 7s Oct 12] lengthy filly: fairly useful handicapper: won at Epsom in September: stays 7f: acts on firm going: tried in cheekpieces, visored last 4 outings: races prominently. *P. M. Phelan* **82**

LEADER OF THE LAND (IRE) 2 ch.c. (Feb 12) Halling (USA) 133 – Cheerleader 84 (Singspiel (IRE) 133) [2009 8.3v p8g f8f⁴ Dec 12] lengthy colt: modest form in maidens: still green, improved when 5¾ lengths fourth to Sweet Child O'Mine at Southwell: bred to stay 1¼m. *D. R. Lanigan* **62**

LEADING EDGE (IRE) 4 gr.f. Clodovil (IRE) 116 – Ja Ganhou (Midyan (USA) 124) [2009 81: p6g² p6g⁵ p7.1g³ p6g² 5.7g⁵ 6s p6m 6m 6d³ 6g⁴ p6g³ p6g⁵ p6g* p6f Dec 20] workmanlike filly: fair handicapper: won at Wolverhampton in November: stays easy 7f: acts on polytrack, firm and soft ground: held up: sometimes gets behind. *M. R. Channon* **75**

LEAF HOLLOW 3 ch.f. Beat Hollow 126 – Lauren (GER) (Lightning (FR) 129) [2009 –: 10d⁵ Sep 15] no form. *M. Madgwick* **–**

LEAHURST (IRE) 3 gr.g. Verglas (IRE) 118 – Badee'a (IRE) (Marju (IRE) 127) [2009 56p: p7.1g* 7.1v² p7.1g* Sep 3] progressive form: won maiden in April and handicap (beat Castles In The Air 2¼ lengths, always travelling strongly) in September, both at Wolverhampton: likely to stay 1m: acts on polytrack and heavy going: smart prospect. *J. Noseda* **109 p**

LEAN BURN (USA) 3 b.g. Johannesburg (USA) 127 – Anthelion (USA) (Stop The Music (USA)) [2009 7.1d⁵ 8.3d p9.5g Nov 6] quite attractive gelding: modest maiden: best effort on second start: wears tongue tie. *A. G. Newcombe* **58**

LEANDROS (FR) 4 br.g. Invincible Spirit (IRE) 121 – Logjam (IRE) (Royal Academy (USA) 130) [2009 109: 6.5g² 6.5g⁶ 7.5g⁴ 6m 7.6m 7f* 6g² 7m p6g 8f a6f³ 6.5f² Dec 26] well-made gelding: smart performer: best efforts when in frame behind Munaddam then Swop in handicaps at Nad Al Sheba first/third outings: won minor event at Naas in June by head from Three Rocks: below form after next start, leaving G. Lyons in Ireland after ninth outing and P. Gallagher, USA after tenth: stays 7.5f: acts on polytrack, firm and good to soft ground: tried in cheekpieces, effective with/without blinkers. *M. Puype, USA* **112**

LEAN MACHINE 2 b.c. (Mar 21) Exceed And Excel (AUS) 126 – Al Corniche (IRE) 62 (Bluebird (USA) 125) [2009 7m² 7d² 6m² 6m⁴ Sep 12] 70,000Y: rather leggy colt: half-brother to 3 winners, including useful 1999 2-y-o 6f/1m winner Whyome (by Owington) and 6f (at 2 yrs)/9f winner Lady Kinvarrah (by Brief Truce): dam 2-y-o 5f winner who stayed 1¾m: fairly useful maiden: runner-up first 3 starts, beaten 3¼ lengths by Dafeef at Newmarket third occasion: seemed amiss final outing: stays 7f: makes running: hung right second start. *R. Hannon* **83**

LEARO DOCHAIS (USA) 3 b.g. Mutakddim (USA) 112 – Brush With The Law (USA) (Broad Brush (USA)) [2009 76: p7g⁶ 6m⁵ 7g* 7d³ 8.3m p7g⁶ p7g Dec 31] workmanlike gelding: fairly useful form: won maiden at Lingfield in July: below that level in handicaps after: should stay 1m: best effort on good going. *M. A. Jarvis* **82**

LEAVING ALONE (USA) 2 ch.f. (Apr 28) Mr Greeley (USA) 122 – Spankin' (USA) (A P Indy (USA) 131) [2009 7d⁶ p8m³ p8m² p7m⁵ Dec 16] $150,000Y, 120,000 2-y-o: fifth foal: closely related to French 7f/1m winner Mezel (by Grand Slam) and winner in USA by Came Home: dam unraced half-sister to very smart US performer up to 1½m Flag Down: fair maiden: placed at Kempton and Lingfield: stays 1m. *R. Hannon* **76**

LECEILE (USA) 3 b.f. Forest Camp (USA) 114 – Summerwood (USA) (Boston Harbor (USA) 122) [2009 73p: 10.1d* 10.2g* 9.9g² Aug 30] fairly useful form, lightly raced and progressive: won maiden at Newcastle in May and handicap at Nottingham in August: good second to Nashmiah in listed handicap at Goodwood next time, worn down close home: stays 1¼m: acts good to soft ground: twice withdrawn at start after reappearance when refusing to enter stall: front runner. *W. J. Haggas* **92**

LE CHIFFRE (IRE) 7 br.g. Celtic Swing 138 – Implicit View 63 (Persian Bold 123) –
[2009 79: p8m p8g Dec 7] tall gelding: fair handicapper at 6 yrs: soundly beaten both
starts in 2009: tried in blinkers, wears cheekpieces nowadays. *Miss S. West*

LE CORVEE (IRE) 7 b.g. Rossini (USA) 118 – Elupa (IRE) 98 (Mtoto 134) [2009 74: **58**
10.2m 10.2g 10.1m 11.5m^6 10.9g^4 12.1m^5 12.6g^3 13.1f^6 Aug 22] well-made gelding:
modest handicapper nowadays: stays 1½m: acts on polytrack and firm ground: sometimes slowly away: held up: has bled: fair hurdler, won in October. *A. W. Carroll*

LEDGERWOOD 4 b.g. Royal Applause 124 – Skies Are Blue 70 (Unfuwain (USA) –
131) [2009 64: f6g 9m Jun 22] quite attractive gelding: modest performer at best: no form
in 2009: often in cheekpieces/blinkers. *A. J. Chamberlain*

LEELU 3 b.f. Largesse 112 – Strat's Quest 65 (Nicholas (USA) 111) [2009 70: p8.6g 7m –
9.9f f8g^5 p10g p8g^2 f6g p8g^3 p7g* p7m^3 p7g^3 p7m^4 Nov 29] leggy filly: fair performer **a66**
on all-weather: won maiden at Kempton in October: may prove best at 6f/7f: acts on
all-weather, no form in 2 races on turf: front runner/races prominently. *D. W. P. Arbuthnot*

LEES ANTHEM 2 b.g. (Mar 7) Mujahid (USA) 125 – Lady Rock 65 (Mistertopogigo **75 d**
(IRE) 118) [2009 5m 5g^3 5g 5m 5m f5g^4 5g f6g Oct 27] well-made gelding: maiden:
regressed after debut, when would have been second but for crashing through rail: best
at 5f: acts on good to firm going, probably on fibresand: tried visored: one to treat with
caution. *C. J. Teague*

LEFTONTHESHELF (IRE) 3 ch.f. Namid 128 – Corryvreckan (IRE) 70 (Night **78**
Shift (USA)) [2009 83: 7f^4 6g^2 6g^3 6g^5 5.7g 6m p5.1g^3 Oct 29] leggy filly: fair performer:
best at 5f/6f: acts on polytrack and firm going: often in cheekpieces: weak finisher.
Miss T. Spearing

LEGAL EAGLE (IRE) 4 b.g. Invincible Spirit (IRE) 121 – Lupulina (CAN) (Sara- **86**
toga Six (USA)) [2009 84: p6g^2 5m^2 6d^2 6v 6m* 6m^5 6m 5.1m^3 5g^3 5s^2 5m 6m 5d 5m^3
6.1m p6g^2 5g^6 f5m^5 Nov 6] good-topped gelding: fairly useful performer: won claimer at
Hamilton (left D. Nicholls £12,000) in June: placed 5 times in handicaps after: effective
at 5f/6f: acts on polytrack, soft and good to firm going (below form on heavy): tried
blinkered (well held). *Paul Green*

LEGAL LEGACY 3 ch.g. Beat Hollow 126 – Dan's Delight (Machiavellian (USA) **87**
123) [2009 56p: 6m^4 7.1m* 7.1g* 7m* 6.9g^2 7m^4 7g Oct 9] fairly useful handicapper:
won at Musselburgh in May and at same course and Doncaster in June: rare poor effort at
York final outing: bred to stay 1m: acts on good to firm going: strong traveller. *M. Dods*

LEGAL LOVER (IRE) 7 b.g. Woodborough (USA) 112 – Victoria's Secret (IRE) 70 **61**
(Law Society (USA) 130) [2009 f7g f8g 8.1g 10m f8g Jul 27] sturdy gelding: missed
2008: modest handicapper nowadays: stays 8.6f: acts on all-weather, good to firm and
good to soft going: tried in cheekpieces: races prominently. *R. Hollinshead*

LEGENDARY GUEST 4 b.g. Bahamian Bounty 116 – Legend of Aragon 67 (Aragon – §
118) [2009 69§: f6g^6 7m 7m Apr 13] compact gelding: fair handicapper at 3 yrs: no form
in 2009: often visored/in cheekpieces: temperamental: has joined D. Pipe. *D. W. Barker*

LEGEND OF GREECE (IRE) 3 b.g. Danetime (IRE) 121 – Lodema (IRE) (Lycius –
(USA) 124) [2009 –: 8.3m 10.9g 9.7m^4 11.9d^6 Oct 15] good-topped gelding: well held in
maidens. *Mrs N. Smith*

LEGION D'HONNEUR (UAE) 4 b.g. Halling (USA) 133 – Renowned (IRE) (Dars- **83**
haan 133) [2009 78: 13g^3 18g^5 May 14] good-bodied gelding: fairly useful handicapper,
lightly raced: should stay at least 2m: acts on good to firm and good to soft going.
L. Lungo

LEGISLATE 3 b.c. Dansili 127 – Shining Water 111 (Kalaglow 132) [2009 79p: p8g* **96**
10m^3 10d 10m^3 9.8d^6 8m^2 Oct 1] compact colt: useful performer: won maiden at Lingfield in March: good ¾-length second to Proponent in handicap at Newmarket final
outing: stays 1¼m: acts on polytrack and good to firm going: often front runs: sent to
Saudi Arabia. *B. W. Hills*

LEGNANI 3 b.f. Fasliyev (USA) 120 – Top Sauce (Hector Protector (USA) 124) [2009 –
75: 9.8m 7s Aug 9] fair maiden at 2 yrs for Edward Lynam in Ireland: no form in sellers
in Britain: should stay 1m+: tried tongue tied/in cheekpieces/visor. *George Baker*

LE HAVRE (IRE) 3 b.c. Noverre (USA) 125 – Marie Rheinberg (GER) (Surako **124**
(GER) 114) [2009 106: 7g* 8m^2 10.5g* Jun 7]

Since the Prix du Jockey Club was reduced in trip to an extended ten furlongs in 2005, Vision d'Etat in 2008 is the only winner whose racing career has lasted beyond the summer of his three-year-old season, let alone continued at four.

Prix du Jockey Club, Chantilly—
the highlight of a memorable afternoon for trainer-jockey combination Jean-Claude Rouget and Christophe Lemaire as Le Havre beats Fuisse (centre) and Westphalia (striped cap)

Shamardal and Darsi each had only one more start after their wins at Chantilly, Shamardal winning the St James's Palace Stakes (run that year at York) before sustaining an injury on the eve of the Eclipse, and Darsi finishing fifth in the Irish Derby. 2007 winner Lawman managed two more outings, winning the Prix Jean Prat before running poorly in the Prix Jacques le Marois. As for the latest Prix du Jockey Club winner, Le Havre, he was not seen out again at all, his retirement announced early in July after he suffered tendon problems. Le Havre was not the only runner unable to improve his record after the 'French Derby'. Runner-up Fuisse was not seen out again either, and the third, Westphalia, was below form on his only subsequent outing. Although the field of seventeen managed just four wins subsequently, a listed race and three Group 3s, enough of the runners ran well in defeat, notably fourth-placed Beheshtam (runner-up in the Prix Niel and showing similar form in the Arc), to make Le Havre's performance at Chantilly the best in the race since Dalakhani in 2003.

Le Havre made a winning reappearance in the Prix Djebel at Maisons-Laffitte, a race in which many a French-trained classic hope has begun his three-year-old season. At the time, though, rather than improving his own classic prospects, Le Havre's win seemed to be viewed more as having inflicted damage on those of the runner-up, Naaqoos, the second favourite for the Two Thousand Guineas. As a result of his odds-on defeat—he went down by a head—Naaqoos was rerouted and joined Le Havre in the Poule d'Essai des Poulains at Longchamp where he again started favourite. Le Havre, however, had clearly benefited just as much from his reappearance and had Naaqoos behind him again, the pair second and third past the post (Naaqoos was subsequently demoted). Le Havre finished two lengths behind the winner Silver Frost, keeping on at the same pace from mid-division after not seeing much daylight up the straight.

With none of the trials for the Prix du Jockey Club revealing an outstanding candidate, the Poulains looked like being the key preparatory race. Silver Frost started favourite to emulate Shamardal, who had completed the French classic double four years earlier, while Westphalia, chief among four candidates from the Aidan O'Brien stable and promoted to third at Longchamp (unlucky not to have finished second instead of Le Havre), was also prominent in the betting. Despite his showing in the Poulains, and the fact that his trainer had won the three preceding races on the card (including both Group 3 contests with Le Havre's rider Christophe Lemaire), Le Havre was sent off at odds of nearly 12/1. Among those also preferred to him in the betting were Fuisse and Beheshtam, both listed winners last time out, the latter supplemented and unbeaten in two starts. The two British-trained runners looked to face stiffer tasks, though Parthenon, making his debut for Godolphin, was still improving, and Zafisio was already a Group 1 winner after taking the Criterium International at Saint-Cloud the previous autumn. Le Havre had started favourite for the Criterium International, after winning a newcomers race at Clairefontaine and a minor event at Saint-Cloud on his first two starts, but finished only seventh on soft ground at Saint-Cloud in a field which also included Silver Frost, Fuisse and another in the Jockey Club line-up Calvados Blues, all of whom had finished in front of Le Havre.

Patiently ridden in a truly-run race and enjoying a clearer run this time, Le Havre improved again. The leaders came back to the main field early in the straight, as Le Havre made progress up the inner, finding a gap to go second a furlong out and then keeping on up the rail to lead halfway through the final furlong. Fuisse, who took over when the leaders faded, was left rather isolated in the centre of the track, hanging right before Le Havre took his measure, and was beaten a length and a half, with the same distance back to Westphalia in third and the never-dangerous Beheshtam in fourth. Calvados Blues and Silver Frost, who proved less effective at the longer trip, completed the first six home. The Prix du Jockey Club had previously been a frustrating race for trainer Jean-Claude Rouget who has had a series of top-six finishes in the last ten years or so with colts that have won their trials only to fall a little short in the Jockey Club, though Literato's second in 2007 had seen the stable getting closer to the bull's-eye. For a yard that had had no previous success in the French classics, the stable's change of fortunes was remarkable in the latest season, with Le Havre's success sandwiched by those of Elusive Wave and Stacelita in the fillies' classics. Had Le Havre been fit to pursue the rest of his campaign, it was said that the Prix Jacques le Marois would probably have been his next race.

Le Havre (IRE) (b.c. 2006)	Noverre (USA) (b 1998)	Rahy (ch 1985)	Blushing Groom
			Glorious Song
		Danseur Fabuleux (b 1982)	Northern Dancer
			Fabuleux Jane
	Marie Rheinberg (GER) (b 2002)	Surako (b or br 1993)	Konigsstuhl
			Surata
		Marie d'Argonne (ch 1981)	Jefferson
			Mohair

Unlike most of the other leading French trainers, Jean-Claude Rouget does not rely heavily on major owner-breeders for his success, although he trains a small number of the Aga Khan's horses. Many of his best horses have been judicious purchases at the sales, not all of them for big sums. Coroner, third in the 2003 Prix du Jockey Club, was a 19,000-guinea purchase and Literato, who went on to win the Champion Stakes, was bought for €40,000, though Le Havre was a more expensive buy, costing €100,000 at Deauville as a yearling. His dam's second foal, Rainfall Shadow (a colt by Night Shift), won a minor event at Marseilles in the autumn, also for Rouget, while her yearling filly by Peintre Celebre was sold for €500,000 at Deauville in August. Their unraced dam, Marie Rheinberg, is by the Deutsches Derby runner-up Surako, but the grandam Marie d'Argonne had been mated with some much more illustrious stallions earlier in her lengthy stud career, among them Sadler's Wells and Nureyev. Much her best foal resulted from being covered by Nureyev in her very first year at stud, the mating resulting in the high-class sprinter-miler Polar Falcon. He himself proved an inspired acquisition by Cheveley Park Stud owner David Thomson at the end of his three-year-old season as the following year he won the Lockinge Stakes and Sprint Cup. Nearly twenty years later, that purchase is still paying dividends in no uncertain terms through Cheveley Park's top stallion Pivotal, a son of Polar Falcon. Le Havre's grandam Marie d'Argonne was useful in France, successful at a mile and a quarter and third in the Prix Penelope, before going on to win a couple of minor stakes in the States where she was also third in Grade 2 company. Marie d'Argonne, incidentally, was bred by Francois Mathet, much better known for his success as a trainer, which included six wins in the Prix du Jockey Club between 1965 and 1979, a joint record in the twentieth century. Marie d'Argonne was a half-sister to a still better filly in Marie de Litz, whose wins included the Prix de Pomone, the pair of them out of an unraced daughter of the Oaks third Imberline. Le Havre comes from just the third crop of his sire, the Sussex Stakes winner Noverre (who would also have been a French classic winner himself but for failing a dope test after the Poule d'Essai des Poulains). Noverre had little opportunity to prove himself at stud before his export to India in 2008. Le Havre's own stud career begins at the Haras de la Cauviniere, near Lisieux in Normandy (about thirty miles south of the channel port he is named after), at a fee of €5,000 live foal. *J-C. Rouget, France*

LEITZU (IRE) 2 b.f. (Jan 14) Barathea (IRE) 127 – Ann's Annie (IRE) 78 (Alzao **74**
(USA) 117) [2009 7d p8g^{6} 8.1d* 9m^{4} 10.2m^{5} Sep 30] tall, good-bodied filly: fifth foal: closely related to Irish 5-y-o Galianna and 6-y-o Sgt Schultz and half-sister to 1¾m winner Red River Rock (by Spectrum): dam, Irish 2-y-o 1m winner, half-sister to smart performer up to 1m Pipe Major: fair performer: won maiden at Chepstow in August: should stay 1¼m+: acts on good to firm and good to soft going. *M. R. Channon*

LEKITA 4 b.f. Kyllachy 129 – Tender Moment (IRE) 78 (Caerleon (USA) 132) [2009 **74**
80: 7m^{5} p7g Jun 17] sturdy filly: fair handicapper nowadays: stays 8.3f: acts on polytrack and good to firm ground: tried in cheekpieces: sold 9,000 gns, sent to Greece. *W. R. Swinburn*

LELEYF (IRE) 2 b.f. (Mar 17) Kheleyf (USA) 116 – Titchwell Lass 57 (Lead On Time **78**
(USA) 123) [2009 p5g* 5m* 5s 5g^{3} 6f 5m^{5} 6.1m^{5} 5.2d 6d 7m^{6} 5.5g* 6d^{6} 5m^{4} p5.1g^{2} 5.1m 5g^{4} p5.1g^{6} Oct 16] €7,200F, €35,000Y: angular filly: half-sister to several winners, including fairly useful 2004 2-y-o 5f winner Sundance (by Namid) and 8-y-o Louisiade: dam 1¼m winner: fair performer: won maiden at Lingfield in March, minor event at Salisbury in May and nursery at Warwick in August: best efforts up to 5.5f: acts on polytrack and good to firm ground. *M. R. Channon*

LEMON N SUGAR (USA) 4 b.f. Lemon Drop Kid (USA) 131 – Altos de Chavon **94+**
(USA) (Polish Numbers (USA)) [2009 80: f6s* p6g^{3} p6g* 6m* 6g^{4} p6g* Oct 9] big, good-bodied filly: fairly useful performer: won maiden at Southwell in January and handicaps at Lingfield in May, Goodwood in June and Lingfield in October: stays 7f: acts on all-weather and good to firm going: sold 25,000 gns, sent to Saudi Arabia. *J. Noseda*

L'ENCHANTERESSE (IRE) 2 ch.f. (Feb 24) Kyllachy 129 – Enchant 92 (Lion **71**
Cavern (USA) 117) [2009 6d^{3} 6g^{2} 5.1v^{3} 6m^{2} 7m 6g^{3} Oct 16] 55,000Y: good-topped filly: has scope: sixth foal: half-sister to 3 winners, including smart winner around 7f (including in UAE) Polar Magic (by Polar Falcon) and 7-y-o Gandalf: dam, 7f winner who stayed 1¼m, closely related to smart performer up to 1m Dazzle: fair maiden: best efforts when runner-up at York and Epsom: stays 6f: acts on good to firm going: pulled hard penultimate start: sold 16,000 gns, joined D. O'Neill in USA. *M. L. W. Bell*

LEND A GRAND (IRE) 5 br.g. Lend A Hand 124 – Grand Madam 66 (Grand Lodge **70**
(USA) 125) [2009 83: p7g^{2} p7g^{4} p7g p7g p8g^{2} p8.6g^{5} 8m May 25] smallish gelding: fair handicapper nowadays: may prove best around 1m: acts on polytrack and soft ground (well held on good to firm): tried blinkered: held up. *Miss Jo Crowley*

LEND A LIGHT 3 b.c. Lend A Hand 124 – No Candles Tonight 74 (Star Appeal 133) **–**
[2009 62?: p7g Feb 24] close-coupled colt: maiden: little form since debut. *I. W. McInnes*

LENKIEWICZ 2 gr.f. (Apr 13) Oratorio (IRE) 128 – Philadelphie (IRE) (Anabaa **79**
(USA) 130) [2009 5f^{6} 7m^{5} 7s^{5} 6.5m^{3} 8d Oct 12] sturdy filly: first foal: dam, useful French 1¼m winner, out of half-sister to smart French 7f performer Poplar Bluff: fair maiden: good 2¾ lengths third to Shamandar in sales race at Ascot: should stay 1m (pulled hard when tried): acts on soft and good to firm going. *B. R. Millman*

LENNIE BRISCOE (IRE) 3 b.g. Rock of Gibraltar (IRE) 133 – Tammany Hall (IRE) **65**
66 (Petorius 117) [2009 73p: p10g 10.2g^{6} 9.9g 8m 8f^{6} 7m^{3} 8m^{6} f8g Sep 29] good-topped, attractive gelding: fair maiden: may prove best at 1m: acts on good to firm ground: tried blinkered: none too consistent. *S. Kirk*

LENNY BEE 3 gr. or ro.g. Kyllachy 129 – Smart Hostess 101 (Most Welcome 131) **91**
[2009 p5g^{2} p5g* p5g^{2} 6g^{2} 5m^{2} 5m^{6} 5.1m^{3} 5.4g^{4} 5m* 5m^{3} 5m^{6} Sep 26] 30,000Y: workmanlike gelding: first foal: dam, 5f/6f winner, half-sister to smart sprinter Smart Predator: fairly useful performer: won maiden at Kempton in April and handicap at Newmarket in August: good third in similar event at Goodwood next time: effective at 5f/6f: raced only on polytrack and good/good to firm going. *D. H. Brown*

LEOBALLERO 9 ch.g. Lion Cavern (USA) 117 – Ball Gown 98 (Jalmood (USA) 126) –
[2009 8s 7.1m Jun 12] tall gelding: fairly useful handicapper in 2006: off almost 3 years, well beaten in 2009: tried in cheekpieces/blinkers: usually tongue tied. *K. M. Prendergast*

LEOCORNO (IRE) 3 br.f. Pivotal 124 – Highland Gift (IRE) 95 (Generous (IRE) 139) [2009 84P: 9g* 12m^{4} 12m^{2} 10m Oct 16] tall, attractive filly: has scope: useful form: won handicap at Sandown in May: further improvement when in frame after in Ribblesdale Stakes at Royal Ascot (fourth to Flying Cloud) and listed Galtres Stakes at York (½-length second to Tanoura): unsuited by drop in trip/steady pace in listed race at Newmarket final outing: best at 1½m: raced only on good/good to firm ground. *Sir Michael Stoute* **108**

LEONALDO (USA) 4 b.g. Silver Deputy (CAN) – Electric Talent (USA) (Capote (USA)) [2009 p8g^{3} p8.6g^{2} p7g^{4} p8.6g^{5} p7.1g Sep 12] $30,000Y: sixth foal: half-brother to several winners abroad, including French 9f/9.5f winner Electric Cove (by Spinning World): dam, French maiden, sister to US Grade 2 7f winner Looie Capote and half-sister to US Grade 2 1m winner Fast Catch: fairly useful performer: won newcomers race at Bordeaux and minor event at Tarbes in 2008 for J-C. Rouget: left Rupert Pritchard-Gordon in France prior to reappearance: in frame first 3 starts in 2009: off 6 months, tailed off final outing: stays 8.6f: acts on polytrack and soft ground: tried in cheekpieces. *J. R. Gask* **84**

LEONID GLOW 4 b.f. Hunting Lion (IRE) 115 – On Till Morning (IRE) 73 (Never So Bold 135) [2009 87: 6m 7m 6d^{3} 6g 6g^{3} 7m^{5} 7m^{4} 7m^{2} 7.2g^{2} p7.1g^{6} 6d^{2} 7.2v 7s Nov 7] fairly useful handicapper: placed 5 times in 2009: effective at 6f/7f: acts on good to firm and good to soft going: strong-travelling sort, usually held up. *M. Dods* **84**

LEOPARD HILLS (IRE) 2 b.g. (Feb 3) Acclamation 118 – Sadler's Park (USA) (Sadler's Wells (USA) 132) [2009 6d^{4} 7m^{6} 6d^{6} Jul 22] leggy gelding: easily best effort when 1¾ lengths fourth to Jack My Boy in minor event at Newcastle: should be suited by 7f+. *J. Howard Johnson* **65**

LEO THE LION (IRE) 3 b.g. Sulamani (IRE) 130 – Sail Away (GER) (Platini (GER) 126) [2009 p11g^{3} p11g^{4} p12g* 12g Apr 29] fair form: won maiden at Lingfield in February: shaped as if amiss final outing (gelded after): stayed 1½m: acted on polytrack: dead. *M. Johnston* **67**

LE PETIT VIGIER 3 b.f. Groom Dancer (USA) 128 – Fallujah (Dr Fong (USA) 128) [2009 52: f8g^{4} f8g^{2} f8g^{3} f7g^{6} f8g^{6} Mar 31] leggy filly: modest maiden handicapper: stays 1m: raced only on fibresand and going softer than good: tongue tied. *P. Beaumont* **50**

LEPTIS MAGNA 5 ch.g. Danehill Dancer (IRE) 117 – Dark Eyed Lady (IRE) 82 (Exhibitioner 111) [2009 71: p8g p8g 8d Oct 22] sturdy gelding: modest handicapper nowadays: left T. Powell after second start: stays 8.3f, probably not 1¼m: acts on soft ground, probably on polytrack: held up: nervy sort, often sweats. *R. H. York* **61**

LE REVE ROYAL 3 ch.f. Monsieur Bond (IRE) 120 – Bond Royale 89 (Piccolo 121) [2009 61: 6s 8d 7d^{3} f8g 10.3d p6g p8.6g Dec 19] angular filly: modest maiden handicapper: stays 7f: acts on soft ground: tried in cheekpieces/visor. *G. R. Oldroyd* **61**

LES FAZZANI (IRE) 5 b.m. Intikhab (USA) 135 – Massada 106 (Most Welcome 131) [2009 107: 10g^{6} 11.9g^{2} 12m 12d* 10d^{3} 10.3s^{4} p12m* Nov 29] workmanlike mare: smart performer: won valuable handicap at Leopardstown (by 1¼ lengths from Cruel Sea) in September and listed race at Kempton (by length from Mooakada) in November: good third (beaten 2 heads) to Eva's Request in Premio Lydia Tesio at Rome in between: stays 1½m: acts on polytrack and heavy going. *K. A. Ryan* **114**

LESLEY'S CHOICE 3 b.g. Lucky Story (USA) 128 – Wathbat Mtoto 88 (Mtoto 134) –
[2009 80: p6g^{5} p5g^{2} f5g^{2} p5g* f6g^{3} p5g^{6} 5m 5m 5d^{6} 6d 5f^{6} f5g^{2} f6g f5m* p5g* f5g* Dec 8] close-coupled gelding: useful handicapper on all-weather, fair at best on turf: won at Kempton in March and Southwell (2, beat Equuleus Pictor ¾ length latter occasion) and Kempton in November/December: best at 5f: acts on all-weather, best turf form on good going: in headgear later in 2009: often front runner. *R. Curtis* **a96**

LESLINGTAYLOR (IRE) 7 b.g. Orpen (USA) 116 – Rite of Spring 86 (Niniski (USA) 125) [2009 72: p12.2g^{5} p12.2g^{4} 12d^{4} Sep 6] good-topped gelding: fair on Flat nowadays, useful hurdler/chaser: stays 1¾m: acts on polytrack, soft and good to firm going. *J. J. Quinn* **77**

LESOTO DIAMOND (IRE) 7 b.m. Darnay 117 – Fallon (IRE) 66 (Arcane (USA)) [2009 81: p10.7g^{4} 16g^{6} 12m* 13g 12g 10g^{6} 12d p12g^{5} p10.7g^{4} p16m^{6} Dec 10] sturdy, lengthy mare: fairly useful handicapper: won at Fairyhouse in June: effective from 1¼m to 1¾m: acts on polytrack and firm going, probably not good to soft. *P. A. Fahy, Ireland* **86**

LESSING (FR) 4 b.f. Orpen (USA) 116 – Lady Morgane (IRE) (Medaaly 114) [2009 **103** 103: 7.5d^2 7.5m 6.5g 7d* 7g^5 8m^2 Aug 31] €28,000Y: strong, lengthy filly: first foal: dam fairly useful French 4.5f (at 2 yrs) to 7.5f winner: useful performer: won twice in Spain at 2 yrs and listed race at Deauville (final start for Y. Durepaire) on reappearance in 2008: trained remainder of 3-y-o season by R. Gibson and first 3 outings in 2009 (all at Nad Al Sheba) by X. Nakkachdji, best effort there when second in handicap on reappearance: won minor event at Maisons-Laffitte in May and creditable second (beaten nose by Murcielago) in similar event at Chantilly final outing: not seen to best effect when fifth to Summer Fete in Oak Tree Stakes at Goodwood on penultimate start, crowded out against rail: stays 1m: acts on all-weather, heavy and good to firm ground. *X. Demeaulte, France*

LESSON IN HUMILITY (IRE) 4 b.f. Mujadil (USA) 119 – Vanity (IRE) 75 (That- **115** ching 131) [2009 112: 6.1m* 6m* 6m^3 6m^2 6.5g^3 6m^4 Aug 30] lengthy, good-topped filly: smart performer: won listed race at Nottingham in May by 2¼ lengths from Carcinetto and Ballyogan Stakes at Leopardstown in June by 1¾ lengths from San Sicharia: good placed efforts next 3 starts, in Golden Jubilee Stakes at Royal Ascot (third to Art Connoisseur), Summer Stakes at York (head second to Serious Attitude, last run for K. R. Burke) and Prix Maurice de Gheest at Deauville (close third to King's Apostle): below best when fourth in Goldene Peitsche at Baden-Baden final outing: best around 6f: unraced on heavy going, acts on any other turf: sometimes early to post: races prominently: tends to hang/flash tail, but is genuine and consistent. *A. P. Jarvis*

LETHAL 6 ch.g. Nashwan (USA) 135 – Ipanema Beach 67 (Lion Cavern (USA) 117) **76** [2009 84: f6s^3 f7g* f6g^6 p6g^6 f6g* 6d* f7g^6 7s f7g^6 5.7m^5 6g p6g^2 p6g^2 p7g^5 p5g^4 p6m^3 p6g^2 p6m* p6f^6 Dec 13] good-topped gelding: fair performer: won seller in January and claimer in March, both at Southwell, and claimers at Yarmouth in April and, having been claimed from R. Fahey £5,000 ninth outing and left Andrew Reid after sixteenth, Kempton in November: stays easy 7f: acts on all-weather and good to soft going: forces pace. *M. J. Scudamore*

LETHAL COMBINATION (USA) 2 b.g. (Feb 12) Broken Vow (USA) 117 – Yard **91** (USA) (Boundary (USA) 117) [2009 6g 7g^3 p7m* 8m^6 9m* Sep 18] $110,000Y: tall gelding: has scope: first foal: dam, placed all 3 starts at 2 yrs in USA, out of half-sister to very smart 1m/1¼m winner and Oaks runner-up All At Sea: fairly useful performer: won maiden at Lingfield in August and nursery at Newmarket (much improved, beat First Cat a neck) in September: stays 9f: acts on polytrack and good to firm ground: sold 100,000 gns, sent to USA. *W. J. Haggas*

LETHAL GLAZE (IRE) 3 gr.g. Verglas (IRE) 118 – Sticky Green 75 (Lion Cavern **102** (USA) 117) [2009 81: 11.6g* 16f 11.9m^5 14s* p12g* 14m 12g 16g^5 Oct 30] good-topped gelding: useful handicapper: won at Windsor in May, Haydock (by 6 lengths) in July and Kempton (beat Becausewecan by head) in August: respectable efforts after: stays 1¾m: unraced on heavy going, acts on any other and polytrack. *R. Hannon*

LETHAM ISLAND (IRE) 5 b.m. Trans Island 119 – Common Cause 87 (Polish **– §** Patriot (USA) 128) [2009 16g Jul 25] tall mare: fair handicapper in 2007: fit from chasing and in cheekpieces, moody display at Lingfield on belated return to Flat: should stay 1½m: acts on all-weather, unraced on extremes of going on turf: races prominently: not one to trust: sold £4,500, joined Tim Vaughan. *R. M. Stronge*

LET IT ROCK (IRE) 2 b.f. (Feb 1) Noverre (USA) 125 – Green Life 63 (Green Desert **53** (USA) 127) [2009 5.1f May 8] £38,000Y: sister to 4-y-o Bohobe and half-sister to several winners, including 3-y-o Zuzu and fairly useful 2002 2-y-o 7f/1m winner Agilis (by Titus Livius): dam Irish maiden (stayed 7f): 10/1, seventh in maiden at Nottingham, green and not knocked about. *K. R. Burke*

LE TOREADOR 4 ch.g. Piccolo 121 – Peggy Spencer 77 (Formidable (USA) 125) **99** [2009 88+: 5m^5 5m^3 5m^2 5d 5m* 5g* 5d^5 5m 5.1m^2 5m^3 5.1m^6 5m* p5.1g* 6g 5g Oct 17] big, strong gelding: useful handicapper: won at Ayr and Thirsk in June, Leicester in September and Wolverhampton (beat Garstang by neck) in October: reportedly bled final outing: best form at 5f: acts on polytrack and any turf going: often tongue tied, also in cheekpieces last 5 starts: forces pace. *K. A. Ryan*

LETS GET CRACKING (FR) 5 b. or gr.h. Anabaa Blue 122 – Queenhood (FR) **–** (Linamix (FR) 127) [2009 p8.6g Jan 2] rather leggy, useful-looking horse: fair performer at 2 yrs: no form since (missed 2008). *A. E. Jones*

LETS MOVE IT 2 b.c. (Feb 25) Piccolo 121 – Park Star 68 (Gothenberg (IRE) 117) **48** [2009 p6g p5g p5.1m f5f^3 p5m Dec 30] poor maiden: visored last 3 starts. *D. Shaw*

LETS ROLL 8 b.g. Tamure (IRE) 125 – Miss Petronella (Petoski 135) [2009 87: 14m **75 d** 14m 14m^5 16.2m^2 16.2m^5 14g^5 16d^6 17.5m^5 16.1d 16g^5 Oct 28] leggy, close-coupled gelding: one-time useful handicapper, not won since 2006: on downgrade: stays 17.5f: acts on heavy and good to firm going: held up. *C. W. Thornton*

LET THEM EAT CAKE 2 b.f. (Mar 12) Danehill Dancer (IRE) 117 – Lady Adnil (IRE) (Stravinsky (USA) 133) [2009 7m^6 p8.6g f7g^3 Oct 18] modest maiden: should have stayed 1m: dead. *R. A. Fahey* **56**

LEULAHLEULAHLAY 3 ch.g. Dr Fong (USA) 128 – Fidelio's Miracle (USA) 108 (Mountain Cat (USA)) [2009 66: p11g^4 12g^2 p12f^3 p16m^5 Dec 30] leggy gelding: fair maiden: stays 1½m: left M. Johnston £15,000 after second start (moody and regressive over hurdles for current yard): tried in cheekpieces. *Evan Williams* **77 d**

LEVERAGE (IRE) 3 b.c. Xaar 132 – She Looks On High (USA) 71 (Secreto (USA) 128) [2009 6m^2 6g* 6m^2 p7f p7g^4 Oct 24] €15,000Y: half-brother to several winners in Italy: dam, ran twice (would have been suited by 1m+), half-sister to smart German miler Life's Luck: fairly useful performer: won maiden at Newbury in July: good second in handicap at Warwick next time: looked awkward final outing: should be suited by 7f: acts on good to firm going: sold 16,000 gns. *L. M. Cumani* **90**

LEVIATHAN 2 b.c. (Feb 19) Dubawi (IRE) 129 – Gipsy Moth 99 (Efisio 120) [2009 6m* 6m^5 7g^3 7d 7g* Oct 24] £22,000Y: close-coupled, good-quartered colt: sixth foal: half-brother to several winners, including 4-y-o Mullein and 6-y-o Illustrious Blue: dam, 5f winner (including at 2 yrs), half-sister to useful 1m winner Heavenly Whisper: fairly useful performer: won maiden at Hamilton in June and nursery at Doncaster (improved again, beat Yaa Wayl ½ length despite idling/hanging right) in October: stays 7f: acts on good to firm ground. *T. P. Tate* **93**

LEVITATION (IRE) 3 b.f. Vettori (IRE) 119 – Uplifting 77 (Magic Ring (IRE) 115) [2009 –: 8.1g^6 8m^2 10s 8g p10g^6 p8.6g^4 p8.6g* Dec 28] compact filly: fair performer: won maiden at Wolverhampton in December: stays 8.6f: acts on polytrack and good to firm going. *W. S. Kittow* **79**

LEWYN 2 b.f. (Mar 25) Exceed And Excel (AUS) 126 – Panoramic View (Polar Falcon (USA) 126) [2009 5m 5d^3 5m^4 5m^2 f5g^3 p5.1g* 5d p5.1g p5.1g Nov 13] 10,500F, 19,000Y: attractive filly: second foal: dam unraced half-sister to useful performers Craft Fair (up to 1¼m) and Kassiopeia (up to 1½m): fair performer: won nursery at Wolverhampton in October: raced only at 5f: acts on all-weather, good to firm and good to soft going: tried blinkered/visored: front runner/races prominently. *K. A. Ryan* **68**

LEXI'S LAYLA (IRE) 2 ch.f. (Apr 19) Kheleyf (USA) 116 – Woodstamp (IRE) 88 (Woodborough (USA) 112) [2009 6s^2 5.1v^2 5.7g p5g^3 Oct 22] €5,200Y, £27,000 2-y-o: second foal: dam Irish 7f winner: placed 3 of 4 starts in maidens, third to Chat de La Burg at Kempton: stays 6f: seemed amiss third start. *D. M. Simcock* **67**

LEXLENOS (IRE) 3 ch.f. Intikhab (USA) 135 – Blazing Glory (IRE) (Glow (USA)) [2009 77p: p7g^2 8f^6 9f^3 10f^3 9f 9f^2 a8.5f^2 a8.5f^3 Nov 28] progressed into a useful performer: second in handicap at Kempton on first outing, then left D. Elsworth: plenty more improvement in graded company at Hollywood next 3 starts, running very well when 3¾ lengths third to Gozzip Girl in American Oaks on fourth outing: below that form after, including in optional claimers: seems suited by 1¼m: acts on polytrack and firm going: blinkered final outing: held up. *P. Gallagher, USA* **107**

LEYTE GULF (USA) 6 b.g. Cozzene (USA) – Gabacha (USA) (Woodman (USA) 126) [2009 69: f14g 16d^5 14g* 16d p13.9g* p13.9g^2 p13.9g^5 p13.9g* p13.9g^2 f14g^3 Dec 8] strong gelding: fair handicapper: won at Haydock in August and Wolverhampton in September and November: stays 2m: acts on all-weather, raced mainly on good ground or softer on turf: travels strongly held up. *C. C. Bealby* **73**

LHASHAN 3 b.f. Green Desert (USA) 127 – Society Lady (USA) 75 (Mr Prospector (USA)) [2009 7g p6g Sep 12] strong filly: sister to 1998 2-y-o 5f/6f (Queen Mary/ Lowther Stakes) winner Bint Allayl and 5f (at 2 yrs) to 7f (Jersey Stakes) winner Kheleyf (both smart) and closely related/half-sister to several winners, including 5-y-o Laa Rayb: dam lightly-raced half-sister to smart US performer up to 8.5f Time Bandit: well held in maidens at Newmarket and Wolverhampton: sent to UAE. *M. A. Jarvis* **–**

L'HIRONDELLE (IRE) 5 b.g. Anabaa (USA) 130 – Auratum (USA) 93 (Carson City (USA)) [2009 85: p8g^3 p8g* p8g 7m 8f^4 p8g p8g^5 p8m^4 p7f* Dec 21] fairly useful handicapper: won at Lingfield in January and Kempton in December: effective at 7f/1m: acts on polytrack: races prominently: refused to race on debut. *M. J. Attwater* **93**

L'HOMME DE NUIT (GER) 5 b.g. Samum (GER) 126 – La Bouche (GER) 105 (In The Wings 128) [2009 76: p16g^3 Nov 5] well-made gelding: fair handicapper: stays 16.5f: raced mainly on polytrack: tried blinkered (looked unwilling), in cheekpieces last 3 starts (also tongue tied only outing in 2009): fair form over hurdles. *G. L. Moore* **75**

totescoop6 Stakes (Heritage Handicap), Haydock—
progressive three-year-old Libel Law shows smart form switched to handicap company;
the grey Nanton (obscured by winner) finishes second, Laterly third and Dancourt (pale colours) fourth

LIBANO (IRE) 3 b.c. Indian Ridge 123 – Daniela Grassi (Bound For Honour (USA)) [2009 7.5m* 7.5g* 8d* 8s^6 8.5g^5 7s* Nov 5] brother to Irish 7-y-o Slapper and half-brother to Italian 9f winner Ultra Dimidium (by Dr Devious): dam Italian 1m and (at 2 yrs) 8.5f winner: very smart performer: won minor event in March, listed race in April and Premio Parioli Memorial Lorenzo Brogi (by 4 lengths from Sottone, making all) later in April, all at Rome, leaving L. Polito in Italy after: shaped well next 2 starts then won listed race at Leopardstown in November by 2 lengths from Rayeni, soon in front and quickening clear 2f out: stays 1m: acts on soft and good to firm ground: tongue tied second/third starts. *D. K. Weld, Ireland* **121**

LIBEL LAW 3 ch.c. Kingmambo (USA) 125 – Innuendo (IRE) 110 (Caerleon (USA) 132) [2009 72p: 10m* 10.3m^6 10m^2 10.4m* Aug 8] good-topped colt: smart form, progressive: won maiden at Windsor in April and valuable totescoop6 Stakes (Handicap) at Haydock in August by 2¼ lengths from Nanton, in control 2f out: sixth to South Easter in Dee Stakes at Chester and head second to Big Bound in minor event at Leicester in between: headstrong, and may prove best around 1¼m: raced only on good/good to firm going: should make mark back in pattern company. *M. A. Jarvis* **112 p**

LIBERALLY (IRE) 4 b.f. Statue of Liberty (USA) 115 – Specifically (USA) (Sky Classic (CAN)) [2009 86: 10s^6 9.8d^4 10.2g* 10.5g 10g^6 Oct 8] useful-looking filly: fairly useful handicapper: won at Nottingham in July: stays 1¼m: acts on good to soft ground: sent to USA. *B. J. Meehan* **87**

LIBERATE 6 ch.g. Lomitas 129 – Eversince (USA) (Foolish Pleasure (USA)) [2009 96: 20m Jun 16] rangy gelding: fairly useful handicapper, lightly raced on Flat since 2006 (well held sole start at 6 yrs): stays 2½m: acts on all-weather and firm going: in cheekpieces last 2 outings: has wandered under pressure: useful hurdler. *P. J. Hobbs* **–**

LIBERATION (IRE) 3 b.c. Refuse To Bend (IRE) 128 – Mosaique Bleue (Shirley Heights 130) [2009 112: 7.5g^2 10m 8g^6 Oct 31] rangy colt: smart performer at 2 yrs for M. Johnston: only useful form in 2009: off 6 months, mid-field in handicap at Newmarket final outing: may prove best short of 1¼m: acts on soft and good to firm going: has hung. *Saeed bin Suroor* **99**

LIBERTINO (IRE) 2 ch.c. (Mar 19) Bertolini (USA) 125 – Villafranca (IRE) (In The Wings 128) [2009 6m^5 6m^2 p7g^4 Nov 18] sturdy, close-coupled colt: similar form in maidens last 2 starts, fourth to Hypnotized at Kempton, weakening: may prove best at 5f/6f. *B. J. Meehan* **68**

LIBERTY BEAU (IRE) 3 b.g. Statue of Liberty (USA) 115 – La Shalak (IRE) 79 (Shalford (IRE) 124§) [2009 59: p10g^3 Jan 17] modest maiden: likely to stay 1½m: raced only on polytrack. *D. R. C. Elsworth* **55**

LIBERTY DIAMOND 3 br.f. Needwood Blade 117 – Take Liberties 110 (Warning 136) [2009 74: 6m 6g May 15] fair maiden at 2 yrs: well held both starts in 2009: should prove best at 5f/6f: acts on heavy ground. *K. R. Burke* **–**

LIBERTY ESTELLE (IRE) 3 gr.f. Statue of Liberty (USA) 115 – Bella Estella (GER) (Sternkoenig (IRE) 122) [2009 –: p7.1g 10.3m May 6] angular filly: no form. *P. D. Evans* –

LIBERTY ISLAND (IRE) 4 b.g. Statue of Liberty (USA) 115 – Birthday (IRE) (Singspiel (IRE) 133) [2009 65: p6g p5g^2 p5g^3 5g* 5g^3 5g^4 p5g* p6g^5 p5.1g* p5g^2 p6g Nov 27] big gelding: fairly useful handicapper: won at Down Royal in June, Dundalk in July and Wolverhampton in October: best at 5f: acts on polytrack: tried blinkered: usually up with pace: game and consistent. *W. McCreery, Ireland* 84

LIBERTY LADY (IRE) 2 b.f. (Feb 16) Statue of Liberty (USA) 115 – Crossed Wire 77 (Lycius (USA) 124) [2009 p5m^2 p5.1m^2 p6f^6 Dec 13] second foal: dam, 15f winner, sister to useful 5.7f to 7.5f winner Roman Maze: runner-up in maidens at Kempton (beaten neck by Felsham) and Wolverhampton (beaten 5 lengths by Youcanalwaysdream): should be suited by 6f+. *D. Donovan* 62

LIBERTY LODGE (IRE) 3 b.g. Statue of Liberty (USA) 115 – Lady Justice 67 (Compton Place 125) [2009 –: f11g^5 7.5m May 12] no form: pulled up (reportedly lame) final outing. *G. A. Swinbank* –

LIBERTY POWER (IRE) 2 b.g. (Mar 19) Statue of Liberty (USA) 115 – Shaydeylaydeh (IRE) 53 (Shaddad (USA) 75) [2009 5.1g^6 Jul 4] 33/1, green and always behind in maiden at Nottingham (gelded after). *Garry Moss* –

LIBERTY SEEKER (FR) 10 ch.g. Machiavellian (USA) 123 – Samara (IRE) 108 (Polish Patriot (USA) 128) [2009 –: 12.6d 16g Jun 30] angular gelding: little form on Flat since 2006: tried in cheekpieces: fair hurdler, won in August. *John A. Harris* –

LIBERTY SHIP 4 b.g. Statue of Liberty (USA) 115 – Flag (Selkirk (USA) 129) [2009 73: p5.1g^3 f5g^6 5.1m^2 5g* 5d^5 5g^2 5d^2 5m^2 Jul 4] good-bodied gelding: fair handicapper: won at Catterick in May: effective at 5f/6f: acts on all-weather, firm and soft going: in cheekpieces/blinkers: tongue tied: has looked quirky, but is consistent. *J. D. Bethell* 77

LIBERTY SQUARE (USA) 2 ch.c. (Mar 14) Street Cry (IRE) 130 – Gracious Hope (USA) (Rahy (USA) 115) [2009 7m 8.3s^4 8g^4 Oct 21] $280,000Y: well-made colt: third foal: half-brother to winner in USA by Candy Ride: dam US maiden: fair form in maidens: tongue tied first/final starts: has left Godolphin. *Saeed bin Suroor* 72

LIBERTY TRAIL (IRE) 3 b.g. Statue of Liberty (USA) 115 – Karinski (USA) (Palace Music (USA) 129) [2009 66: 7.1m^2 7.1g 7.2g^2 8.3m^3 7.1g 6f^2 6s* 6g^6 6m^5 7g* 7.2v p7.1g p6g^6 Nov 21] fair performer: won maiden at Hamilton in August and handicap at Redcar in October: stays 8.3f: acts on polytrack, firm and soft going: tried in cheekpieces/blinkers: front runner. *I. Semple* 80

LIBERTY VALANCE (IRE) 4 b.g. Statue of Liberty (USA) 115 – Tabdea (USA) 106 (Topsider (USA)) [2009 79d: p7g^5 p7g^2 p7g^3 p7g p6g^5 p8g Jun 24] stocky gelding: modest handicapper nowadays: left S. Kirk prior to final start: effective at 6f/7f: acts on polytrack and good to firm going: tongue tied: weak finisher. *P. M. Phelan* 62

LIBRE 9 b.g. Bahamian Bounty 116 – Premier Blues (FR) 35 (Law Society (USA) 130) [2009 68: 9.7d 8.1g 8g^5 7g^3 8m^5 8.1m 8d 8.1g^6 8.1d^2 p9.5g^5 p10m p9.5g p9.5g^3 p9.5g p8.6g^2 p9.5g^6 Dec 28] small, leggy gelding: modest handicapper nowadays: stays 1¼m: acts on polytrack and any turf going: tried in blinkers/tongue tie/cheekpieces: held up: has hung left. *F. Jordan* 62

LICENCE TO TILL (USA) 2 b.c. (Feb 12) War Chant (USA) 126 – With A Wink (USA) (Clever Trick (USA)) [2009 5m 6d^3 5m^2 5m^3 p7m* p7.1g^3 Dec 26] $130,000Y: brother to winner in USA and half-brother to 3 winners there by Dixieland Band: dam US Grade 2 1¼m winner: fairly useful form: much improved when winning maiden at Lingfield in December by 8 lengths from Christmas Coming: respectable third in nursery at Wolverhampton final start: likely to stay 1m: acts on polytrack, probably on good to firm going: may still do better. *M. Johnston* 88 +

LIEBELEI (USA) 2 b. or br.f. (Feb 11) Royal Academy (USA) 130 – Part With Pride (USA) (Executive Pride 127) [2009 7g p7.1g 8g Oct 21] $85,000Y: angular filly: half-sister to several winners, including US Grade 3 8.5f/9f winner Happy Trails (by Peaks And Valleys): dam US 7f to 9f winner: well held in maidens. *H. J. L. Dunlop* –

LIEU DAY LOUIE (IRE) 2 b.g. (Mar 31) Bahamian Bounty 116 – Nebraska Lady (IRE) 87 (Lujain (USA) 119) [2009 5d 5g^2 5g 6g^4 5d^5 Oct 28] modest maiden: stays 6f: gelded after final start. *N. Wilson* 61

LIEUTENANT PIGEON 4 ch.g. Captain Rio 122 – Blue Velvet 100 (Formidable (USA) 125) [2009 82: p6g f6g^6 p6g p6g^6 Jul 22] well-made gelding: modest handicapper nowadays: stays 6f: acts on all-weather and good to soft going: tried blinkered. *Paul Mason* 54

LIFE AND SOUL (IRE) 2 b.c. (Feb 21) Azamour (IRE) 130 – Way For Life (GER) (Platini (GER) 126) [2009 7m 8.3s² p8g² Oct 26] 115,000Y: lengthy, attractive colt: fourth foal: closely related to German 2004 2-y-o 7f winner Winning Time (by Night Shift) and half-brother to smart 7f (in Ireland) to 1½m (in Hong Kong) winner Mr Medici (by Medicean) and useful German 1m/8.5f winner Viapervita (by Spectrum): dam German 7f (at 2 yrs)/1m winner: similar form when runner-up in maidens at Nottingham and Lingfield: likely to stay 1¼m. *Mrs A. J. Perrett* **77**

LIFE'S CHALLENGE (USA) 3 ch.f. Mr Greeley (USA) 122 – Danse du Diable (IRE) (Sadler's Wells (USA) 132) [2009 8m* 10m³ f8f p8f Dec 16] €75,000Y, 340,000 2-y-o: half-sister to several winners in France, including useful performer up to 1m Wicked Clutch (by Arctic Tern), 6f winner at 2 yrs: dam French 11.5f winner: fairly useful form: won maiden at Pontefract in August: similar form when third in handicap at Sandown next time: stays 1¼m: acts on good to firm going. *M. Johnston* **84**

LIFETIME ENDEAVOUR 5 b.g. Aragon 118 – Musical Star 54 (Music Boy 124) [2009 –: 6m 6g 6f 7m 10m Jun 19] little form. *R. E. Barr* **–**

LIGHT DUBAI (IRE) 3 b.f. Fantastic Light (USA) 134 – Seeking A Way (USA) 78 (Seeking The Gold (USA)) [2009 65p: p10g² 10s³ 9.7m² 9.9f 12.5g⁵ 9.2g⁴ 10g⁴ Jul 21] rangy filly: fair maiden: stays 12.5f: unraced on heavy going, probably acts on any other and polytrack. *M. R. Channon* **75**

LIGHTERMAN 2 ch.g. (Apr 11) Firebreak 125 – Manuka Too (IRE) 68 (First Trump 118) [2009 6g 7d 7g Aug 2] soundly beaten in maidens. *E. J. Alston* **–**

LIGHT FROM MARS 4 gr.g. Fantastic Light (USA) 134 – Hylandra (USA) (Bering 136) [2009 89: 8.3g* 8.1g² 8.1m 8m 7g³ 8.1g³ 8.1m² 7g* 7d⁶ Oct 24] good-topped gelding: useful handicapper: won at Windsor in April and York (improved to beat Everymanforhimself 2¾ lengths) in October: below form in minor event at Doncaster final outing: stays 1m: acts on good to firm ground. *B. R. Millman* **109**

LIGHTHEARTED (FR) 3 ch.f. Fantastic Light (USA) 134 – My Heart's Deelite (USA) (Afternoon Deelites (USA) 122) [2009 p6g² p6g⁴ 7m* 8g⁶ p7g 7m Jun 27] rather leggy filly: second foal: half-sister to winner in Italy by Johannesburg: dam US 5f (at 2 yrs)/6f winner: fair performer: ran twice in Italy at 2 yrs for V. Valiani: won handicap at Lingfield in May: below form last 2 starts, hanging left second occasion: best effort at 7f: acts on good to firm going: sold 5,000 gns in July. *C. G. Cox* **70**

LIGHT NIGHTS (IRE) 2 b.f. (Feb 7) Acclamation 118 – Grecian Grail (IRE) (Rainbow Quest (USA) 134) [2009 7.5f 6v⁶ f7g Nov 17] €20,000Y: second foal: dam, ran twice in France, out of very smart French performer up to 1¼m Grecian Urn: well held in maidens/seller. *T. D. Easterby* **–**

LIGHT SLEEPER 3 b.c. Kyllachy 129 – Snoozy (Cadeaux Genereux 131) [2009 75p: 8.1g⁴ p7.1g³ p7g⁵ Dec 2] sturdy colt: fair maiden, lightly raced: worth a try at 6f: acts on polytrack and soft going. *P. W. Chapple-Hyam* **75**

LIGHT THE CITY (IRE) 2 b.g. (Apr 14) Fantastic Light (USA) 134 – Marine City (JPN) 77 (Carnegie (IRE) 129) [2009 8m⁶ Sep 17] 33/1, very backward when well held in maiden at Yarmouth: sold £3,700, then gelded. *C. E. Brittain* **–**

LIGHT THE LIGHT (IRE) 4 ch.f. King Charlemagne (USA) 120 – Saana (IRE) (Erins Isle 121) [2009 64: p7m⁶ p7g 7d Jun 10] maiden: just poor form in 2009, leaving Rae Guest after second start: stays 1m: visored final outing (tailed off). *M. D. Squance* **49**

LIGHT THE WAY 2 b.c. (Mar 18) Fantastic Light (USA) 134 – Monteleone (IRE) (Montjeu (IRE) 137) [2009 7m 7f⁵ 7m p7g⁶ p6m³ p5m Dec 10] modest maiden: bred to stay beyond 7f, but is headstrong: tried tongue tied/blinkered. *P. J. Makin* **55**

LIKE FOR LIKE (IRE) 3 ch.f. Kheleyf (USA) 116 – Just Like Annie (IRE) 65 (Mujadil (USA) 119) [2009 72: 5.1g 5.1f⁵ 6d⁴ 8f 7.1m² 5.1g⁶ 8d 5.7g p5g Nov 18] leggy filly: modest performer nowadays: stays 7f: acts on polytrack, good to firm and good to soft going. *R. J. Hodges* **60**

LILAC MOON (GER) 5 b.m. Dr Fong (USA) 128 – Luna de Miel (Shareef Dancer (USA) 135) [2009 75: p10g 10.4g⁴ 10m⁵ p12.2g³ p10m Dec 10] good-bodied mare: fair handicapper: left N. Vaughan after second start: stays 1½m: acts on polytrack and firm going (unraced on softer than good): often races prominently/makes running. *Tom Dascombe* **71**

LILAC WINE 6 ch.m. Dancing Spree (USA) – Stay With Me Baby 67 (Nicholas Bill 125) [2009 59: p12g p12g⁵ 17.2d p16.5g⁴ 14.1m⁶ 16m⁶ Sep 2] modest maiden: stays 16.5f: acts on polytrack: tried in headgear: none too consistent. *D. J. S. ffrench Davis* **54**

*Tattersalls Timeform Fillies' 800, Newmarket—
Lillie Langtry lands the odds in this very valuable sales event; Dubawi Heights is second*

LILEO (IRE) 2 b.g. (Mar 31) Galileo (IRE) 134 – Jabali (FR) (Shirley Heights 130) **65 p** [2009 7d^4 Oct 27] half-brother to several winners in France, including useful 1¼m to 1½m winner Far From Old (by Vettori): dam twice-raced half-sister to very smart French stayer Floripedes, herself dam of Montjeu: 12/1, encouraging 5¾ lengths fourth to London Stripe in maiden at Yarmouth, very green and considerately handled (gelded after): bred to be well suited by 1½m: should improve. *L. M. Cumani*

LILLEPUT 4 b.f. High Estate 127 – A Little Hot (Petong 126) [2009 p6g p8g 10g^6 **–** 11.7f^4 11m^6 11.6m p8g Nov 1] angular filly: half-sister to 1¼m winner Dangerous Beans (by Bluegrass Prince): dam sprint maiden: little form: left Ms J. Doyle after second start. *E. A. Wheeler*

LILLIE LANGTRY (IRE) 2 b. or br.f. (Feb 27) Danehill Dancer (IRE) 117 – Hoity **106** Toity (Darshaan 133) [2009 6g^2 6f* 6f^2 7g* 7v^3 7m* 8f Nov 6] 70,000F, 230,000Y: attractive filly: has scope: third foal: dam unraced half-sister to useful 1m winner Sweet Emotion, out of half-sister to very smart 6f/7f performers Lead On Time and Great Commotion: useful performer: won Coolmore Stud Fillies' Sprint Stakes at Naas (by 2½ lengths from Kitty Kiernan) in June, Debutante Stakes at Leopardstown (by 1¾ lengths from Devoted To You) in August and Tattersalls Timeform Fillies' 800 at Newmarket (by 2¼ lengths from Dubawi Heights) in October: respectable third to Termagant in Moyglare Stud Stakes at the Curragh: favourite, reportedly suffered small fracture in a knee when eighth in Breeders' Cup Juvenile Fillies' Turf at Santa Anita final outing: should stay 1m: acts on firm ground. *A. P. O'Brien, Ireland*

LILLIE LE QUESNE 6 b.m. Desert Prince (IRE) 130 – Bathe In Light (USA) 72 **–** (Sunshine Forever (USA)) [2009 12.1g May 25] little form in maidens at 2 yrs: well held only outing since. *Jane Southcombe*

LILLY BE (IRE) 6 ch.m. Titus Livius (FR) 115 – Mystery Hill (USA) 72 (Danehill **81** (USA) 126) [2009 75§: p5g* p5g^2 5g^6 5g^3 p5g p5g p5g p5.1g Dec 5] sturdy mare: fairly useful handicapper: won at Dundalk in April: best at 5f/easy 6f: acts on sand/polytrack and firm going, probably on soft: wears cheekpieces/blinkers: races close up. *P. Magnier, Ireland*

LILLY BLUE (IRE) 3 b.f. Hawk Wing (USA) 136 – Holly Blue 107 (Bluebird (USA) **63** 125) [2009 65: p12g^6 9.7d^5 12m^5 9.9g 8g p9.5g^2 p12g 7g^5 8d^5 p8.6g Nov 2] sparely-made filly: modest maiden handicapper: claimed from M. Channon £6,000 after sixth outing: may prove best short of 1½m: acts on polytrack, soft and good to firm going. *R. Brotherton*

LILLY GROVE 4 b.f. Mtoto 134 – Armada Grove 75 (Fleetwood (IRE) 107) [2009 **62 p** 50?: p9.5g^6 p9.5g^2 Oct 23] modest form in maidens: may prove best short of 9.5f: remains open to improvement. *G. A. Swinbank*

LILLY ROYAL (IRE) 3 b.f. Tillerman 123 – Ervedya (IRE) (Doyoun 124) [2009 8.1m 8.3v² 7.1m⁶ 10.2s⁴ 11.9d⁵ 8.3v Nov 4] €5,700Y: seventh foal: half-sister to several winners, including fairly useful 7f (at 2 yrs)/7.5f (in France) winner Chauntry Gold (by Desert Style) and 9.4f to 1½m winner Cyber Babe (by Persian Bold): dam ran once: fair maiden: stays 1¼m: acts on heavy going: none too consistent. *B. Palling* **70**

LILYANNABANANA 2 ch.f. (Feb 11) Avonbridge 123 – Bundle (Cadeaux Genereux 131) [2009 5f 6g 6d² 7m⁶ Sep 12] 10,000F: fifth foal: half-sister to fairly useful 1¼m winner Top Gear (by Robellino) and 6-y-o Bundle Up: dam unraced: trained by A. Haynes on debut: form in maidens only when short-head second to Hold On Tiger at Ayr: should stay 7f: not straightforward. *P. D. Evans* **61**

LILY EVA 3 ch.f. Definite Article 121 – Avanindra (Zamindar (USA) 116) [2009 p8.6g p10m Dec 30] first foal: dam unraced: well held in maidens. *D. Donovan* **–**

LILY IN THE POND 2 br.f. (Feb 10) Kyllachy 129 – Tidal 94 (Bin Ajwaad (IRE) 119) [2009 p7m⁴ p8m p7g Dec 31] €12,500Y: second foal: half-sister to 3-y-o Faldal: dam 1¼m/1½m winner: modest form in maidens on polytrack. *Miss Gay Kelleway* **58**

LILY JICARO (IRE) 3 ch.f. Choisir (AUS) 126 – Mourir d'Aimer (USA) (Trempolino (USA) 135) [2009 59: 7.1m p7.1g 6m³ 6d 7.1m 5.3g² 6m 5.3d 5.9d 6m p5m 7g Oct 16] leggy filly: modest maiden: likely to prove best at 6f: best efforts on good going: tried visored: inconsistent. *Mrs L. Williamson* **58**

LILY LENOR (IRE) 2 b.f. (Jan 1) Bertolini (USA) 125 – Mosaique Beauty (IRE) 77 (Sadler's Wells (USA) 132) [2009 5m 5m 5m⁴ 6g Jun 13] £12,000Y: sturdy filly: first foal: dam, Irish 13f winner, sister to smart 1¼m/1½m performer Subtle Power: form only when 4¼ lengths fourth to Maidtorun in maiden at Beverley: should stay 6f. *B. Ellison* **50**

LILY LILY 2 b.f. (Feb 13) Efisio 120 – Bel Tempo (Petong 126) [2009 p8.6g⁶ p9.5g f8f² f8g* Dec 18] second living foal: dam twice-raced half-sister to high-class 7f/1m performer Le Vie dei Colori (by Efisio): modest form: won maiden at Southwell: stays 1m: acts on fibresand: blinkered last 2 starts. *K. McAuliffe* **60**

LILYMAY 9 b.m. Sovereign Water (FR) – Maysimp (IRE) (Mac's Imp (USA) 116) [2009 11.9f⁵ 14g Aug 7] leggy mare: little form. *B. P. J. Baugh* **–**

LILY OF THE NILE (UAE) 3 ch.f. Halling (USA) 133 – Covet (Polish Precedent (USA) 131) [2009 –: 12.1g 10m 10m Sep 21] no form: tried visored/in cheekpieces. *J. G. Portman* **–**

LILY RIO (IRE) 2 b. or br.f. (Apr 19) Marju (IRE) 127 – Jinsiyah (USA) 98 (Housebuster (USA)) [2009 8.1m 7d Oct 12] good-bodied filly: half-sister to several winners, including smart sprinter Indian Maiden (by Indian Ridge) and 5-y-o Kingsdale Orion: dam, 7f winner, out of half-sister to Kentucky Derby winner Winning Colors: very green when well held in maidens. *W. R. Muir* **–**

LILY WOOD 3 ch.f. Central Park (IRE) 123 – Lady Castanea (Superlative 118) [2009 8.3g p8.6g p8.6g⁶ Dec 14] second foal: dam unraced: modest form in maidens last 2 starts. *J. W. Unett* **53**

LIMELIGHT (USA) 4 gr.f. Dalakhani (IRE) 133 – Last Second (IRE) 121 (Alzao (USA) 117) [2009 54: p13.3g² p12g³ p16g⁶ f11g² Mar 22] modest maiden: stays 1¾m, probably not 2m: acts on all-weather, good to firm and good to soft ground: tried blinkered, in cheekpieces final outing: signs of temperament. *Sir Mark Prescott* **53**

LINBY (IRE) 4 b.g. Dr Fong (USA) 128 – Dubious (Darshaan 133) [2009 56: 12m 12.1m Jul 3] leggy gelding: modest performer at 3 yrs: well held in 2009: stays 1½m: acts on good to firm and good to soft ground. *Miss Tor Sturgis* **–**

LINDORO 4 b.g. Marju (IRE) 127 – Floppie (FR) (Law Society (USA) 130) [2009 97: 7f⁶ 7d⁶ p7.1g⁴ 7.1g p7g⁶ 7m* f7m p6g Dec 5] lengthy, quite attractive gelding: useful handicapper: won at Epsom in October: left W. Swinburn 13,000 gns, well held both starts after (saddle slipped first occasion): likely to stay 1m: acts on polytrack, good to firm and good to soft ground: tried in headgear/tongue tie. *M. G. Quinlan* **98 d**

LINDY HOP (IRE) 3 b.f. Danehill Dancer (IRE) 117 – Healing Music (FR) (Bering 136) [2009 61: 6m⁶ 7.1g⁵ p7g⁶ p7m⁶ p8m f8g⁶ p8.6g⁵ Dec 28] rangy filly: fair maiden: left W. Swinburn £18,000 after fifth start: should stay 1m: acts on polytrack. *K. A. Ryan* **68**

LION MOUNTAIN 2 b.c. (Apr 18) Tiger Hill (IRE) 127 – Cal Norma's Lady (IRE) 87 (Lyphard's Special (USA) 122) [2009 8d² Oct 27] 80,000F: half-brother to several winners, including useful 5f/6f (including Cheveley Park Stakes) winner Donna Blini (by Bertolini): dam 2-y-o 6f/7f winner (stayed 1¼m): 7/2, promising short-head second to Bullet Train (pair clear) in maiden at Yarmouth, soon prominent and battling: should stay 1¼m: should improve. *Saeed bin Suroor* **85 p**

LION ROAD (USA) 3 ch.g. Lion Heart (USA) 124 – Elusive Road (USA) (Elusive Quality (USA)) [2009 9.2g 11.9d Oct 15] well held in maidens at Hamilton (very green, missed break) and Brighton. *A. B. Haynes* –

LIQUID ASSET (FR) 2 ch.g. (Feb 4) Refuse To Bend (IRE) 128 – Lilyfoot (IRE) (Sanglamore (USA) 126) [2009 7.1m² 7g Jul 8] good-topped gelding: better effort in maidens when 3¼ lengths second to Bikini Babe at Sandown: will stay 1m+. *A. M. Balding* 68

LISAHANE BOG 2 b.c. (Mar 2) Royal Applause 124 – Veronica Franco 90 (Darshaan 133) [2009 7.1g p7f 8g 9d p7g* p7g* p7m* Dec 6] half-brother to 3-y-o Franco Is My Name, 2005 2-y-o 7f winner Veronica's Girl (by Desert Prince) and Italian 1¼m winner Verothea (by Barathea): dam 1½m to 2m winner: fair performer: won nurseries at Lingfield and Kempton in November and Lingfield in December: will stay 1m+: best form on polytrack: in cheekpieces last 4 starts. *P. R. Hedger* 71

LISBON LION (IRE) 4 br. or gr.g. Mull of Kintyre (USA) 114 – Ludovica (Bustino 136) [2009 65: f12g³ 12.4d⁴ 12s⁶ Oct 27] strong, good-bodied gelding: modest maiden: left N. Vaughan after reappearance: stays 1¾m, effective at shorter: acts on heavy going. *James Moffatt* 63

L'ISLE JOYEUSE 2 b.f. (Feb 21) Compton Place 125 – Sabalara (IRE) 61 (Mujadil (USA) 119) [2009 5.7g 5m⁵ 5.1g p5g Oct 11] second foal: dam maiden (stayed 7f): well held in maidens. *P. Winkworth* –

LIS PENDENS 2 b.g. (May 7) Tobougg (IRE) 125 – In Good Faith (USA) 74 (Dynaformer (USA)) [2009 8.1d 9d p9.5g Nov 14] well held in maidens. *W. R. Muir* –

LISTEN CAREFULLY (IRE) 5 ch.m. Lil's Boy (USA) 109 – Join The Party (Be My Guest (USA) 126) [2009 –: p12.2g p12s p8g 5.8s 6d 7d Jun 10] no form, left P. Rothwell in Ireland after fourth start: tried in cheekpieces. *Pat Morris* –

LISTILLO (USA) 2 ch.g. (Feb 20) More Than Ready (USA) 120 – Dowry (USA) (Belong To Me (USA)) [2009 6g⁶ 5f⁴ p6g² p6g² 5g² 5g² p5g 5.5g p5.1g² a7.5g a6.5g³ Dec 23] £24,000 2-y-o: close-coupled gelding: first foal: dam US 8.5f winner: fair but temperamental maiden: runner-up 5 times, including in nursery: left H. Dunlop after ninth outing: best at 5f/6f: acts on all-weather: tried visored (looked mulish): irresolute. *Mrs J. Bidgood, France* 74 §

LITENUP (IRE) 3 b.f. Trans Island 119 – Common Cause 87 (Polish Patriot (USA) 128) [2009 54: f8g² p8g p10g² p10g p12m p8f p10m⁴ Dec 30] close-coupled filly: modest maiden: stays 1¼m: acts on all-weather: tongue tied last 3 starts: none too consistent. *A. J. Lidderdale* 59

LITEUP MY WORLD (USA) 3 ch.g. Hennessy (USA) 122 – Liteup My Life (USA) (Green Dancer (USA) 132) [2009 64p: 7.5m⁵ 6m Jul 29] modest maiden: will need at least 1m: raced only on polytrack and good to firm going. *B. Ellison* 61

LITHAAM (IRE) 5 ch.g. Elnadim (USA) 128 – Elhida (IRE) 99 (Mujtahid (USA) 118) [2009 67: f5g⁶ p5.1g⁵ p5g⁴ f5g p5.1g 5m³ 5.3f 5.3g³ 5.2s⁶ 5.3d⁶ 5.1g* 5.1m⁴ 5.1d* p5.1g⁴ 5.1m* 5m³ 5m p5.1g 5.3d⁵ p5.1g* f5m⁵ p5.1g⁶ p5m⁵ p5m² p5f² Dec 19] big, strong gelding: fair handicapper: won at Nottingham and Chepstow (apprentices) in August, Chepstow in September and Wolverhampton in October: best at 5f: acts on all-weather, good to firm and good to soft going: wears cheekpieces: tough. *J. M. Bradley* 79

LITTLE ARROWS (IRE) 3 b.c. Danehill Dancer (IRE) 117 – Lovers Walk (USA) 50 (Diesis 133) [2009 83: 7v 6g 5g⁵ p5g³ p6g 8s p7.1g² Oct 31] fairly useful handicapper: stays 7f: acts on polytrack and good to soft going: usually in blinkers/cheekpieces: signs of temperament. *W. McCreery, Ireland* 82

LITTLE BILLIE 3 b.f. Efisio 120 – Kembla 59 (Known Fact (USA) 135) [2009 10.2d Oct 15] workmanlike filly: half-sister to 3 winners, including useful French 7f to 8.5f winner Quit Rent (by Fairy King): dam 5.7f (at 2 yrs) to 1¼m (in Italy) winner: always behind in maiden at Nottingham: sold £800. *Mike Murphy* –

LITTLE BLACKNUMBER 3 b.f. Superior Premium 122 – The Synergist (Botanic (USA)) [2009 57: p6g⁶ p8g⁶ Feb 27] poor maiden: stays 7f: acts on polytrack. *R. Hannon* 43

LITTLE BONES 4 ch.f. Tobougg (IRE) 125 – City Gambler 74 (Rock City 120) [2009 55: 6m Aug 22] smallish filly: modest maiden: tailed off in seller only outing in 2009: stays 7f: acts on good to firm ground, probably on polytrack: tried tongue tied. *J. F. Coupland* –

LITTLE BRAZILIEN 2 ch.f. (Apr 24) Kyllachy 129 – Girl From Ipanema 106 (Salse (USA) 128) [2009 5g⁴ 5.7g⁴ 5.7g p5g³ 5.1g³ 7.1m 7v Nov 14] compact filly: half-sister to several winners, including useful 1m/1¼m winner Wondrous Joy (by Machiavellian) and 61 fairly useful 1m (at 2 yrs)/1¼m winner Mr Tambourine Man (by Rainbow Quest): dam 7f (at 2 yrs)/1m winner: modest maiden: blinkered when third at Kempton (nursery) and Bath: sold from P. Cole 3,000 gns after sixth start (looked reluctant): best at 5f: acts on polytrack. *Mme G. Rarick, France*

LITTLE BUDDY 2 ch.g. (Apr 6) Reel Buddy (USA) 118 – Little Kenny 50 (Warning 136) [2009 6.1m 7.1m 6.1m Sep 30] workmanlike gelding: tailed off in maidens. *R. J. Price* **–**

LITTLE CALLA (IRE) 3 ch.f. Indian Ridge 123 – Queen of Palms (IRE) 104 (Desert Prince (IRE) 130) [2009 57: 7m² 6d f5m Jul 21] angular filly: modest maiden: stays 7f: acts on polytrack and good to firm ground: sold 1,000 gns. *E. A. L. Dunlop* **59**

LITTLE CARMELA 5 gr.m. Beat Hollow 126 – Carmela Owen (Owington 123) [2009 73: p14g* p12.2g⁴ p13.9g⁵ p16g⁶ 13.1d⁶ 14.1g² p13.9g p13g⁴ p16g⁵ p16m p12m p13.9g² Dec 14] strong mare: fair handicapper: won at Great Leighs in January: stays 2m: acts on polytrack, good to firm and good to soft ground: in cheekpieces/visor last 4 starts. *S. C. Williams* **69**

LITTLEDODAYNO (IRE) 6 b.m. Mujadil (USA) 119 – Perfect Welcome (Taufan (USA) 119) [2009 73: p6g p6g⁴ p6g Mar 18] smallish, leggy, close-coupled mare: fair handicapper: shaped as if amiss final outing: effective at 5f to 7f: acts on polytrack and firm going, probably on soft: tried in cheekpieces: held up. *M. Wigham* **67**

LITTLE EDEN (IRE) 4 b.g. Piccolo 121 – Paradise Eve 81 (Bahamian Bounty 116) [2009 62: f5g 5.1m 6.1f May 8] modest handicapper: should stay 6f: acts on fibresand and good to soft ground. *T. D. Barron* **51**

LITTLE EDWARD 11 gr.g. King's Signet (USA) 110 – Cedar Lady (Telsmoss 91) [2009 101: p6g² p5g³ p5g² p6g p5.1g* p6g 5m⁵ 6m May 30] angular gelding: useful performer: won handicap at Wolverhampton in March: below form after: effective at 5f/6f: acts on polytrack, firm and good to soft going: tried in cheekpieces: held up. *R. J. Hodges* **99**

LITTLE FINCH (IRE) 4 b.f. Acclamation 118 – Hard To Lay (IRE) 60 (Dolphin Street (FR) 125) [2009 44§: p10g Oct 21] strong filly: poor and untrustworthy performer: usually wears headgear. *Denis P. Quinn, Ireland* **– §**

LITTLE FIRECRACKER 4 b.f. Cadeaux Genereux 131 – El Hakma 94 (Shareef Dancer (USA) 135) [2009 60d: p9.5g Feb 13] close-coupled filly: modest winner early in 2008: mostly well held on Flat since: tried blinkered/in cheekpieces: sold £1,000, joined N. King, modest hurdler (won in November). *Miss M. E. Rowland* **–**

LITTLE GARCON (USA) 2 b.g. (Mar 17) Bernstein (USA) 115 – Demure (Machiavellian (USA) 123) [2009 6m p6g p6g* Oct 23] £55,000 2-y-o: half-brother to 3 winners, notably 7f (including at 2 yrs)/1m winner Il Warrd (by Pivotal) and 6f (at 2 yrs) to 1m winner Coy (by Danehill), both smart: dam unraced half-sister to smart 6f/7f performer Diffident: easily best effort in maidens when winning at Wolverhampton by 1¼ lengths from Confessional: subsequently gelded: should stay 7f/1m: will improve further. *M. Botti* **80 p**

LITTLE KNICKERS 4 b.f. Prince Sabo 123 – Pants 78 (Pivotal 124) [2009 71: p8g p7g⁵ p7g Apr 1] compact filly: modest handicapper in 2009: best up to 7f: acts on polytrack, raced only on good ground or softer on turf: blinkered. *E. J. Creighton* **55**

LITTLE LOST (IRE) 3 b.f. Tagula (IRE) 116 – Prima Marta (Primo Dominie 121) [2009 p6g p5.1m p5g⁵ p5f p5.1g Oct 9] £3,500 2-y-o: fourth foal: dam unraced: poor maiden: left J. Osborne after third start: tried in cheekpieces. *Karen George* **47**

LITTLE MEADOW (IRE) 2 b.f. (Apr 9) Antonius Pius (USA) 123§ – Cresalin (Coquelin (USA) 121) [2009 7m p8m f8g⁵ Dec 18] half-sister to 3-y-o Chadwell Spring and 2 winners abroad: dam, Irish 1¼m/11f winner, half-sister to dam of 1000 Guineas winner Las Meninas: poor form in maidens. *Miss J. Feilden* **49**

LITTLE MISS GINGER 5 ch.m. Whittingham (IRE) 104 – Miss Tress (IRE) 67 (Salse (USA) 128) [2009 p5.1g Jan 25] £700 4-y-o: second foal: dam maiden (stayed 1m): showed nothing in maiden at Wolverhampton: sold £600 in February. *P. S. McEntee* **–**

LITTLEMISSSUNSHINE (IRE) 4 b.f. Oasis Dream 129 – Sharp Catch (IRE) 98 (Common Grounds 118) [2009 74: 5m 5.1d⁴ 5.3f³ 5.1m* 5m⁵ p5m⁴ p5f³ p5m⁴ Dec 30] neat filly: fluent mover: fair handicapper: won at Chepstow in August: raced around 5f: acts on polytrack, soft and firm going: wears cheekpieces: tried tongue tied: reliable. *J. S. Moore* **76**

LITTLE OZ (IRE) 2 br.f. (Apr 7) Red Ransom (USA) – Australie (IRE) 114 (Sadler's Wells (USA) 132) [2009 8m⁶ 8g 8.3v⁴ Nov 4] first foal: dam, French 1m (at 2 yrs) to 10.5f **71**

winner (stayed 12.5f), half-sister to 4-y-o Forgotten Voice out of half-sister to Breeders' Cup Classic winner Arcangues: easily best effort in maidens when 5 lengths sixth to Golden Aria at Newmarket: will stay 1¼m. *E. A. L. Dunlop*

LITTLE PANDORA 5 b.m. Komaite (USA) – Little Talitha (Lugana Beach 116) [2009 –: f7g 7d 6d 6d 5s Aug 24] little form: tried tongue tied. *L. R. James*

LITTLE PERC (IRE) 2 ch.c. (Mar 14) Pearl of Love (IRE) 112 – Bitter Sweet 67 (Deploy 131) [2009 5g 5.1m May 6] tailed off in maiden and seller (blinkered). *G. L. Moore* **–**

LITTLE PERISHER 2 b.c. (Mar 13) Desert Sun 120 – Sasperella (Observatory (USA) 131) [2009 5.2s 5.3m^2 5m^3 5m* 6g^6 5m 5m^6 5.1m^6 6m^4 6m 6m 6g^5 6m 6g p6m* p7.1g p6g^5 Nov 16] stocky colt: first foal: dam unraced: fairly useful performer: won maiden at Ascot in May: below best after seventh start, though won claimer at Kempton in October: stays easy 6f: acts on polytrack and good to firm going: tried visored: unreliable. *A. P. Jarvis* **85 §**

LITTLE PETE (IRE) 4 ch.g. City On A Hill (USA) 114 – Full Traceability (IRE) 53 (Ron's Victory (USA) 129) [2009 95: 5g 5g^2 5m^3 5g 6m 5m^5 5d 6g p5.1g^5 p6m^2 p6g p6g^3 p6m Dec 10] lengthy gelding: useful handicapper: largely below form after third start, leaving A. Balding after tenth: stays easy 6f: acts on polytrack, soft and good to firm going: tried in cheekpieces/visor/tongue tie. *I. W. McInnes* **97**

LITTLE PRUDENCE 3 ch.f. Generous (IRE) 139 – Redgrave Devil (Tug of War 117) [2009 10m^3 12.1m^4 12.6m^5 11.6m^5 16g Aug 29] small filly: half-sister to Irish 1¼m winner Red Piper (by Emarati): dam fair hurdler: fair maiden: probably stays 2m. *R. M. Beckett* **73**

LITTLE RICHARD (IRE) 10 b.g. Alhaarth (IRE) 126 – Intricacy 65 (Formidable (USA) 125) [2009 69: p12m^3 p12g^4 p12.2g p13.9g^3 p12.2g^6 p13.9g p12.2g^4 p12.2g^2 Dec 26] small, workmanlike gelding: fair handicapper: effective at 1½m to 16.5f: raced on polytrack nowadays: wears cheekpieces: reliable. *M. Wellings* **67**

LITTLE ROCOCOA 4 b.g. Killer Instinct 111 – Little Kenny 50 (Warning 136) [2009 –: p8.6g f11g Mar 17] workmanlike gelding: little sign of ability: tried tongue tied. *R. J. Price* **–**

LITTLE ROXY (IRE) 4 b.f. Dilshaan 119 – Brunswick (Warning 136) [2009 p11g p11g Feb 8] half-sister to 2 winners, including fairly useful 5f/6f winner Simpsons Mount (by Tagula): dam unraced: well held in maidens at Kempton. *Miss A. M. Newton-Smith* **–**

LITTLE RUFUS 2 b.c. (Mar 27) Lujain (USA) 119 – Compendium (Puissance 110) [2009 5g^4 Jul 26] 20/1, 3¼ lengths fourth to Cian Rooney in maiden at Pontefract. *K. A. Morgan* **56**

LITTLE SARK (IRE) 4 b.g. Singspiel (IRE) 133 – Notenqueen (GER) (Turfkonig (GER) 122) [2009 53: 10.2g 11.5g 10m^6 12.1m^3 16m 12.1v p12m p12g^4 p12f* p12m^2 f14m Nov 11] fair handicapper: won at Kempton in October: stays 1½m: acts on polytrack and good to firm going: tried in cheekpieces: often races prominently. *P. D. Evans* **65**

LITTLE SCOTLAND 2 b.f. (Feb 21) Acclamation 118 – Belladera (IRE) 82 (Alzao (USA) 117) [2009 5g^2 5s^3 5g^5 5m^4 6g 6m Aug 20] 22,000F, £87,000Y: smallish, good-quartered filly: half-sister to 3 winners, including useful Irish 1½m to 2m winner Mrs Gillow (by Danzero) and fairly useful 7f/1m winner Satyricon (by Dr Fong): dam 2-y-o 6f winner: fairly useful maiden: best efforts when in frame in listed races, length third to Misheer at York and 2½ lengths fourth to Strike The Tiger in Windsor Castle Stakes at Royal Ascot: should stay 6f+: acts on soft and good to firm going: has joined R. Fahey. *T. D. Easterby* **85**

LITTLE WEED (IRE) 2 b. or br.g. (Apr 27) Statue of Liberty (USA) 115 – Carna (IRE) 60 (Anita's Prince 126) [2009 p6g^4 Oct 31] 9/1, tailed-off last in maiden at Wolverhampton. *B. Palling* **–**

LIVELY BLADE 3 ch.g. Needwood Blade 117 – Breezy Day 85 (Day Is Done 115) [2009 f6g^5 f7g Feb 6] modest form in maidens at Southwell. *E. S. McMahon* **51**

LIVELY FLING (USA) 3 b.g. Dynaformer (USA) – Creaking Board (Night Shift (USA)) [2009 61p: 11.8m* 11.8f^2 14g 12s 12m^3 11.6g* Oct 5] tall, deep-girthed gelding: fairly useful form: won maiden at Leicester in April and handicap at Windsor (blinkered, beat Souter Point by neck) in October: should stay 1¾m: acts on firm going, well below form on soft: visored penultimate start: sold 25,000 gns, joined Venetia Williams. *J. H. M. Gosden* **94**

LIVING IT LARGE (FR) 2 ch.c. (Feb 23) Bertolini (USA) 125 – Dilag (IRE) (Almutawakel 126) [2009 6m^2 5g* 7g 6g* p5.1g* p5.1g* p6m^4 Nov 26] 10,500F, €21,000Y: **90**

first foal: dam, French 7f winner, half-sister to smart European sprinter Terroir: fairly useful performer: won maiden at Musselburgh in July and nurseries at Ayr and Wolverhampton in October and Wolverhampton (gamely by head from Desert Poppy) in November: winner at 6f, best form at 5f: front runner. *R. F. Fisher*

LIVING THE DREAM 7 b.g. Double Trigger (IRE) 123 – Aquavita 56 (Kalaglow 132) [2009 p12.2g p12g p12g 10m May 22] modest form in bumpers, but little form on Flat: wore cheekpieces first 2 starts. *Karen George* –

LIZARD ISLAND (USA) 4 b.c. Danehill Dancer (IRE) 117 – Add (USA) (Spectacular Bid (USA)) [2009 101: 8g May 14] lengthy colt: smart at 2 yrs: in decline in 2008/9 (for several different trainers): should stay 1m: acts on dirt, soft and good to firm going: sent to Argentina. *P. F. I. Cole* –

LLANDOVERY 2 b.c. (Feb 6) Auction House (USA) 120 – Sweet Coincidence 69 (Mujahid (USA) 125) [2009 7m p7.1g^{3} 7g^{3} 8.3m^{6} p8.6g* p8.6g^{4} 8g Oct 23] workmanlike colt: fair performer: won nursery at Wolverhampton in September: should stay 1¼m: best form on polytrack: sold 17,500 gns. *P. J. McBride* **60 a69**

LOADED 2 b.c. (Apr 27) Tobougg (IRE) 125 – Missed Again 84 (High Top 131) [2009 p7m Aug 20] 25/1, seventh to Lethal Combination in maiden at Lingfield: dead. *P. Winkworth* **57**

LOCAL HERO (GER) 2 b.c. (Mar 22) Lomitas 129 – Lolli Pop (GER) (Cagliostro (GER)) [2009 7m^{5} Jun 16] €46,000Y: lengthy colt: seventh foal: brother to useful German 10.5f to 15f winner Liquido and half-brother to 2 winners in Germany: dam German 9f/1¼m winner: 17/2 and green, 4 lengths fifth to Jehu in maiden at Thirsk, staying on: will be well suited by 1¼m+: should improve. *T. P. Tate* **64 p**

LOCALISER (IRE) 3 b.g. Iron Mask (USA) 117 – Becada (GER) (Cadeaux Genereux 131) [2009 7m^{3} 8m^{3} 6g Oct 16] €10,000 2-y-o: second living foal: half-brother to 5-y-o Wibbadune: dam, German maiden, half-sister to smart German 7f/1m winner Bear King: fair maiden: looked very awkward (hung) final outing: stays 1m. *D. Nicholls* **73**

LOCATION 3 b.f. Dansili 127 – Well Away (IRE) (Sadler's Wells (USA) 132) [2009 51: p6g^{6} p8.6g p7.1g* 7.1m^{4} p8.6g^{4} 10d^{2} 10g^{6} 10m 11.6m^{4} 9.8m^{2} 11.7g^{5} 10g^{4} 8m^{4} 10.9m^{4} 10m p10g^{3} 11.9d^{3} p10g* p9.5g^{4} p10g Nov 5] leggy filly: fair handicapper: won at Wolverhampton in March and, after leaving Ian Williams £6,000 tenth start, Kempton in October: likely to prove best around 1¼m: acts on polytrack, good to firm and good to soft going: held up. *P. D. Evans* **65**

LOCHAN MOR 3 b.g. Kyllachy 129 – Bright Moll 88 (Mind Games 121) [2009 6d^{2} 6g* p6g^{2} 6s^{4} p6g^{2} 6d^{2} p6g^{3} Oct 30] angular gelding: first foal: dam, 5f/6f winner (ran only at 2 yrs), half-sister to smart performer (including in Hong Kong as Helene Brilliant) up to 1m Doctor Brown: fairly useful form: won maiden at Yarmouth in May: in frame in handicaps after: will prove at least as effective at 5f as 6f: acts on polytrack and good to soft going: gelded after final outing. *M. L. W. Bell* **89**

LOCHBROOM SUNSET 2 b.c. (Feb 15) Firebreak 125 – Woore Lass (IRE) 75 (Persian Bold 123) [2009 p6g 6.1g 7d 6d p6g^{2} p7f p7.1g^{4} p6m p7m Oct 7] medium-sized colt: modest maiden: stays 7f: acts on polytrack: tried tongue tied: none too consistent. *S. C. Williams* **56**

LOCHIEL 5 b.g. Mind Games 121 – Summerhill Special (IRE) 80 (Roi Danzig (USA)) [2009 93: p12g^{4} 12m^{5} 12.1m^{3} 12m^{2} 12g f12g 14m* 12m* 12d Oct 24] rather leggy gelding: useful handicapper: better than ever when winning at Haydock in September and Newmarket (beat Resplendent Light 4½ lengths) in October, travelling strongly both times: well below form at Doncaster final outing: stays 1¾m: acts on polytrack, good to firm and good to soft ground: sold 42,000 gns. *G. A. Swinbank* **101**

LOCH JIPP (USA) 4 b.f. Belong To Me (USA) – Miss Keyonna (USA) (Septieme Ciel (USA) 123) [2009 82: 6g 5g 5m Sep 16] strong, workmanlike filly: useful at 2 yrs: very much in decline: tried in headgear: often hangs. *J. S. Wainwright* –

LOCH LINNHE (USA) 3 b.g. Elusive Quality (USA) – Firth of Lorne (IRE) 112 (Danehill (USA) 126) [2009 8m* 7m 8m^{3} 8m Jul 25] well-made gelding: useful form: won maiden at Newmarket (by 8 lengths) in May: improvement when seventh to Ouqba in Jersey Stakes at Royal Ascot and 1¼ lengths third to Spring of Fame in minor event at Newmarket: restless in stall, well held in handicap at Ascot final outing: stayed 1m: dead. *J. H. M. Gosden* **105**

LOCHSTAR 5 b.g. Anabaa (USA) 130 – Lochsong 129 (Song 132) [2009 92p: 5m^{6} p5g* 5d p5g^{4} 5g^{6} 5m p5g^{6} Oct 22] big gelding: useful handicapper on all-weather, fairly useful on turf: won at Lingfield in May: has won at 6f, races mainly at 5f: acts on polytrack: usually races prominently: sold 7,500 gns. *A. M. Balding* **81 a96**

LOCK 'N' LOAD (IRE) 3 b.f. Johannesburg (USA) 127 – Margay (IRE) 98 (Marju (IRE) 127) [2009 61: 8m Sep 27] modest maiden at 2 yrs: stiff task in handicap only outing in 2009: should stay 1m. *B. Smart* **–**

LOCKSLEY HALL (USA) 2 ch.g. (Feb 10) Songandaprayer (USA) 118 – Wonderously (USA) (Awesome Again (CAN) 133) [2009 p6g^2 6m^2 Sep 18] good-topped gelding: second foal: half-brother to winner in USA by Hold That Tiger: dam unraced half-sister to US Grade 2 6f winner Forest Music: shaped well when second in maidens at Kempton (to San Cassiano) and Newbury (split Pastoral Player and Kalypso King, still green): subsequently gelded: sent to USA: likely to improve again. *E. F. Vaughan* **93 p**

LOCUM 4 ch.g. Dr Fong (USA) 128 – Exhibitor (USA) 68 (Royal Academy (USA) 130) [2009 73: 10.1m* 10m^3 p12.2g 10.1g^4 10m^6 10g^2 12.3m^4 12m^4 12m^4 12m Oct 3] angular gelding: fair handicapper: won at Yarmouth in May: stays 1½m: acts on polytrack and good to firm going: held up: has hung/found little, but is consistent. *M. H. Tompkins* **73**

LODEN 2 b.c. (Apr 8) Barathea (IRE) 127 – Tentpole (USA) 85 (Rainbow Quest (USA) 134) [2009 7g 8m^4 p8m Sep 26] well-made colt: fifth foal: brother to 3-y-o Too Much Trouble and half-brother to 5-y-o Bivouac and French 2005 2-y-o 9f winner Playhouse (by Jade Robbery): dam, Irish 1¾m winner, out of half-sister to Oaks winner Snow Bride, herself dam of Lammtarra: not knocked about in maidens, best effort when fourth to Sharaayeen at Ffos Las: should be suited by 1¼m+: capable of better. *L. M. Cumani* **65 p**

LODI (IRE) 4 ch.g. Bertolini (USA) 125 – Lady of Leisure (USA) 76 (Diesis 133) [2009 88: p7g 6g 7m 7m* 7m 7m 7m 8.3m 6g^3 7m^3 7m^4 7d^2 p7m^4 Oct 12] strong, compact gelding: fairly useful handicapper: won at Lingfield in May: free-going sort, best up to 7f: acts on polytrack, soft and good to firm ground: tongue tied. *J. Akehurst* **86**

LOFTHOUSE 2 b.g. (Feb 14) Hunting Lion (IRE) 115 – Noble Destiny 89 (Dancing Brave (USA) 140) [2009 5.2s 5g 6d^3 6m 6g p6g^5 7.1m^6 p7m^6 p7g Nov 13] leggy gelding: modest maiden: barely stays 7f: acts on polytrack and soft going: sold £3,800. *M. R. Channon* **57**

LOGIC WAY (USA) 5 b.g. Freud (USA) 113 – Just A Ginny (USA) (Go For Gin (USA) 123) [2009 12g 11g* 9m^5 10.3m 12s 10m Sep 19] good-topped gelding: smart performer: successful 4 times and good second in Grade 2 in USA in 2008 for R. Dutrow Jnr: won at Doha in March when trained by I. Al Malki in Qatar: little impact in varied company in Britain: stays 1½m: acts on firm and good to soft going: wears headgear, also tongue tied in Britain. *Miss D. Mountain* **?**

LOGOS ASTRA (USA) 2 b.c. (Feb 7) Elusive Quality (USA) – Wild Planet (USA) 106 (Nureyev (USA) 131) [2009 7.1m^4 7.1m^3 p7.1g^2 p8.6g^5 Sep 5] half-brother to several winners abroad, including US Grade 2 8.5f winner Surya (by Unbridled): dam 6f (at 2 yrs) to 1m winner, later successful in USA: similar form in maidens/nursery: stays 8.6f. *D. R. Lanigan* **75**

LOIS DARLIN (IRE) 3 ch.f. Indian Haven 119 – Miriana (IRE) (Bluebird (USA) 125) [2009 52: f6s^4 p7.1g p5g^2 f5g^5 p6g 6f May 12] attractive filly: modest maiden: will be suited by return to 7f+: acts on all-weather: wears headgear. *R. A. Harris* **52**

LOMBOK 3 b.c. Hernando (FR) 127 – Miss Rinjani 83 (Shirley Heights 130) [2009 –: 12m^5 10g^6 11.8g^5 14.1m^4 14.1m* Jul 11] big, strong colt: fair form: improved to win handicap at Nottingham in July: stays 1¾m: acts on good to firm going. *M. L. W. Bell* **77**

LOMICA 3 ch.f. Lomitas 129 – Ecstatic 94 (Nashwan (USA) 135) [2009 55: f8g f11g 9.3g^4 10g^3 12.1m^4 10m Aug 9] modest maiden: stayed at least 1m: acted on soft and good to firm going: in cheekpieces last 4 starts: dead. *Julie Camacho* **50**

LONDON BRIDGE 3 br.g. Beat Hollow 126 – Cantanta 74 (Top Ville 129) [2009 100p: 10.3g^4 10m* 10.1g 12m 10g Aug 12] rather leggy, lengthy gelding: fair performer: won maiden at Newmarket in May: well held in handicaps after: should be suited by 1½m+: unraced on firm going, acts on any other: sold 40,000 gns, joined N. Meade, Ireland, then gelded. *J. H. M. Gosden* **79**

LONDON GIRL (IRE) 2 b.f. (Apr 18) Trans Island 119 – Sweet As A Nut (IRE) 75 (Pips Pride 117) [2009 5g f5g f5g^6 7g^6 p5.1m p6g Sep 11] sixth foal: half-sister to winner in Macau by Imperial Ballet: dam 2-y-o 5f winner: poor maiden plater: tried in cheekpieces. *A. J. McCabe* **38**

LONDON GOLD 2 b.c. (Feb 1) Fraam 114 – Princess Londis 59 (Interrex (CAN)) [2009 6m^4 6d^2 6s* Nov 7] tall colt: second foal: half-brother to fairly useful 5f winner Devine Dancer (by Woodborough): dam maiden: progressive in maidens, second to Carnaby Street at Goodwood then fairly useful form when winning at Doncaster by ½ length from Olney Lass: will prove as effective at 5f as 6f: should continue to improve. *H. Candy* **80 p**

LONDON STRIPE (IRE) 2 ch.c. (Mar 12) Rock of Gibraltar (IRE) 133 – Agenda (IRE) 102 (Sadler's Wells (USA) 132) [2009 8g^5 7d* Oct 27] sturdy colt: first foal: dam, Irish 1¼m winner, out of sister to Breeders' Cup Juvenile/Preakness Stakes winner Timber Country and half-sister to dam of Dubai Millennium: shaped well both starts in maidens, winning at Yarmouth by ½ length from Mass Rally, still green: should be suited by 1¼m: should continue to progress. *Sir Michael Stoute* **87 p**

LONELY STAR (IRE) 3 b.f. Bachelor Duke (USA) 122 – Soviet Belle (IRE) 85 (Soviet Star (USA) 128) [2009 77: 8d^3 10.2g^2 9g^5 Jun 19] rather unfurnished filly: fairly useful maiden: stays 1¼m: raced only on polytrack and good/good to soft ground: sold £4,000. *D. R. Lanigan* **82**

LONE WOLFE 5 b.g. Foxhound (USA) 103 – Fleet Hill (IRE) 99 (Warrshan (USA) 117) [2009 102: p6g^6 Jan 10] heavy-topped gelding: useful performer: finished lame sole outing in 2009: was effective at 6f to 1m: acted on polytrack and good to firm going: front runner/raced prominently: dead. *Jane Chapple-Hyam* **–**

LONGBOAT KEY 3 b.g. Dr Fong (USA) 128 – You Are The One 85 (Unfuwain (USA) 131) [2009 83: p8g^5 p10g^2 f11g 12.5m^3 14.1f^3 12m^5 15m^2 16.2m^2 14g^5 16.1g Aug 8] fairly useful maiden: stays 2m: acts on firm and soft going: blinkered last 4 starts: signs of temperament: sold 11,000 gns. *M. Johnston* **80**

LONG DISTANCE (FR) 4 b. or br.g. Storming Home 128 – Lovers Luck (IRE) (Anabaa (USA) 130) [2009 82: p12.2g^2 12g Oct 10] leggy, useful-looking gelding: fairly useful handicapper, lightly raced: visored, good neck second at Wolverhampton: left J. Fanshawe 5,000 gns, shaped as if amiss at York 9 months later: stays easy 1½m: acts on polytrack and good to soft going. *Miss Lucinda V. Russell* **82**

LONG LASHES (USA) 2 b.f. (Jan 30) Rock Hard Ten (USA) 126 – Border Dispute (USA) (Boundary (USA) 117) [2009 6d* 7g* 7v^4 8m Sep 26] $95,000Y: sturdy filly: second foal: half-sister to 3-y-o Mythical Border: dam unraced out of half-sister to US Grade 2 1m winner Conserve: smart performer: won listed race at the Curragh (by 2½ lengths from Elusive Galaxy, subsequently sold privately from Mrs J. Harrington) in June and skybet.com Sweet Solera Stakes at Newmarket (by length from Blue Maiden) in August: stamina stretched when below form last 2 starts, including in Fillies' Mile at Ascot (tongue tied, threatened penultimate 1f): stays 7f: acts on good to soft ground. *Saeed bin Suroor* **110**

LONGLINER 2 gr.c. (Feb 10) Dalakhani (IRE) 133 – Ive Gota Bad Liver (USA) (Mt Livermore (USA)) [2009 8g^3 8d^2 Oct 27] fifth foal: half-brother to 9f winner Otelcaliforni (by Gulch): dam, US 6f/7f winner, half-sister to 1000 Guineas winner Russian Rhythm: favourite when placed in maidens, better effort when 1¼ lengths second to Commissionaire at Yarmouth, still green: should stay 1¼m: open to further improvement. *Sir Michael Stoute* **84 p**

LONGSPUR 5 br.g. Singspiel (IRE) 133 – Bunting 102 (Shaadi (USA) 126) [2009 81: 12g 10m 10.2v Nov 4] tall, good sort: has been tubed: fairly useful performer at best: ran as if amiss all outings in 2009, including in seller: tried tongue tied: said to have had breathing problems. *M. W. Easterby* **–**

skybet.com Sweet Solera Stakes, Newmarket—Long Lashes (noseband) holds off outsider Blue Maiden (hooped cap) to make a winning debut in Godolphin colours

betfred.com Temple Stakes, Haydock—
tough filly Look Busy (noseband) lowers the colours of Borderlescott in very heavy ground

LONSDALE LAD 3 b.g. Elusive City (USA) 117 – Winchcombe (Danehill (USA) 126) [2009 –: f7s Jan 4] no form: blinkered/in cheekpieces last 4 starts. *R. C. Guest* **–**

LOOBY LOO 3 b.f. Kyllachy 129 – Halland Park Lass (IRE) (Spectrum (IRE) 126) [2009 p5m² p6m⁶ Oct 28] 280,000F, 480,000Y: second foal: half-sister to high-class sprinter/miler Dutch Art (5f/6f winner at 2 yrs, by Medicean): dam, ran 3 times, half-sister to smart Scandinavian sprinter King Quantas: better effort in maidens at Kempton when head second to Edith's Boy, green early but going on strongly at finish: pulled too hard next time. *P. W. Chapple-Hyam* **71**

LOOK BUSY (IRE) 4 b.f. Danetime (IRE) 121 – Unfortunate 55§ (Komaite (USA)) [2009 113: 5.1g* 6.1m³ 5v* 6m³ 5g⁶ 5m 5v 5.2m⁵ 5g² Oct 3] sturdy filly: smart performer: won listed event at Bath in April and betfred.com Temple Stakes at Haydock (beat Borderlescott by neck) in May: good efforts after in handicap at Ayr (sixth to Pavershooz), World Trophy at Newbury (fifth to Strike The Deal) and listed race at Cologne (second to Best Joking): best at 5f: acts on any going: sometimes slowly away: effective held up or ridden prominently: tough and reliable. *A. Berry* **111**

LOOK HERE 4 b.f. Hernando (FR) 127 – Last Look (Rainbow Quest (USA) 134) [2009 123: 12g³ 10d³ 12m⁶ 11m² 10m Oct 17] sparely-made filly: very smart performer in 2008, winning Oaks at Epsom: bit below that form at 4 yrs, best efforts when very close third to Ask in Coronation Cup there on reappearance and when nose second to Doctor Fremantle in Arc Trial at Newbury: third in Pretty Polly Stakes at the Curragh (beaten length by Dar Re Mi, poorly placed), sixth to Conduit in King George VI and Queen Elizabeth Stakes at Ascot (never travelling well) and seventh to Lahaleeb in E. P. Taylor Stakes at Woodbine on other starts: best efforts at 1½m on good going: often warm/edgy in preliminaries: stud. *R. M. Beckett* **119**

LOOK OFFICER (USA) 3 b.f. Officer (USA) 120 – Inn Between (USA) (Quiet American (USA)) [2009 68§: 8f⁶ 10.5m² 9d p10m³ Dec 9] quite good-topped filly: fair maiden handicapper: left David Wachman, Ireland after third start: stays 10.5f: acts on polytrack and good to firm going: sometimes blinkered: ungenuine tail flasher. *Tom Dascombe* **72 §**

LOOKS LIKE SLIM 2 b.c. (Apr 1) Passing Glance 119 – Slims Lady 59 (Theatrical Charmer 114) [2009 6m 6m 5g⁴ p7g 7g² Sep 14] rather unfurnished colt: modest maiden: best effort when runner-up in nursery at Leicester: stays 7f. *P. F. I. Cole* **59**

LOOKS THE BUSINESS (IRE) 8 b.g. Marju (IRE) 127 – Business Centre (IRE) 58 (Digamist (USA) 110) [2009 62, a69: 11.5m 14m⁴ 12.6g* 14.1m 13.1f* p16.5g p13.9g Nov 2] workmanlike gelding: modest handicapper: won at Warwick (apprentices) in July and Bath in August: stays 2m: acts on polytrack and firm going: has worn cheekpieces/tongue strap: often races freely: inconsistent nowadays. *A. B. Haynes* **65**

LOOK TO THIS DAY 4 ch.f. In The Wings 128 – Yanka (USA) (Blushing John **79**
(USA) 120) [2009 81: 11.6g^3 16g 14.1g^3 14.8g^6 Jul 18] rather leggy filly: fair handicapper: stays 1¾m: acts on good to soft ground: wore cheekpieces final start (below form): seemed amiss second outing: sold 4,500 gns in December. *R. Charlton*

LOOK WHOS NEXT 2 ch.c. (Feb 15) Compton Place 125 – Look Here's Carol (IRE) **83**
102 (Safawan 118) [2009 5g^3 5g^3 5m^4 6.1d^3 5.5g^2 p5.1m* Sep 28] close-coupled colt: first foal: dam, 6f/7f winner, half-sister to smart sprinter Now Look Here: fairly useful performer: made all in maiden at Wolverhampton: may prove best at 5f: acts on polytrack, probably on good to soft ground: sold £6,500, sent to Sweden. *E. S. McMahon*

LOOPING THE LOOP (USA) 4 gr. or ro.g. Alphabet Soup (USA) 126 – Citidance **50**
Missy (USA) (Citidancer (USA)) [2009 50: p12g^6 p16g Jun 24] leggy, close-coupled gelding: modest maiden: stays 1½m. *J. G. Portman*

LOOSE CABOOSE (IRE) 4 b.f. Tagula (IRE) 116 – Tama (IRE) 58 (Indian Ridge **80**
123) [2009 82: f6d f5d p6g^2 p6g p5.1g^6 6g^2 6.1f f5g* 5m^5 5f* 5g^5 5m 5m f5g^2 f5g p6g f5m p6m^4 f6g^4 f5m f5g^5 Dec 27] leggy, workmanlike filly: fairly useful handicapper: won at Southwell and Doncaster in May: best at 5f/6f: acts on all-weather, firm and good to soft going: wears headgear: often gets behind. *A. J. McCabe*

LOOTER (FR) 4 b.g. Red Ransom (USA) – Water Echo (USA) 79 (Mr Prospector **–**
(USA)) [2009 57: p8g p13g p12g p8g 10g^6 9m Jun 5] close-coupled, quite attractive gelding: maiden: little form in 2009: wears headgear/tongue tie. *P. Butler*

LOPE DE VEGA (IRE) 2 ch.c. (Feb 19) Shamardal (USA) 129 – Lady Vettori 107 **108**
(Vettori (IRE) 119) [2009 7.5g* 7g* 7g^4 Oct 4] strong, angular colt: powerful galloper: fifth foal: half-brother to several winners in France, including smart 7.5f (at 2 yrs) to 1¼m winner Bal de La Rose (by Cadeaux Genereux): dam, French 2-y-o 5f to 7f winner, out of half-sister to smart middle-distance performers Lowell and Lady Blessington: useful form: won newcomers race at Deauville in August and minor event at Longchamp (readily beat Heaven's Heart 2½ lengths) in September: increasingly edgy but ran well when 2½ lengths fourth to Siyouni in Prix Jean-Luc Lagardere at Longchamp final start: should stay 1¼m. *A. Fabre, France*

LOPINOT (IRE) 6 br.g. Pursuit of Love 124 – La Suquet 72 (Puissance 110) [2009 62, **72**
a73: p8g* p8g^3 p8g* p8g^5 p8g^6 p8g^5 p8g^4 p8g p8g p8m p8m p8m p8m^6 Nov 29] robust gelding: fair handicapper: won at Kempton in January and Lingfield in March: stays 1m: acts on polytrack: wears cheekpieces/visor: none too consistent. *M. R. Bosley*

LORD ADMIRAL (USA) 8 b.h. El Prado (IRE) 119 – Lady Ilsley (USA) (Trempo- **115**
lino (USA) 135) [2009 115: 8g 7m^5 10s^2 8.9m^6 10d^5 p10.7g^5 p7g^2 Nov 27] close-coupled horse: smart performer: won 6 races during career, including Group 2/3 events at Nad Al Sheba in 2008: creditable effort in 2009 only when short-head second to She's Our Mark in Meld Stakes at Leopardstown third start: was effective at 7f to bare 1¼m: ran poorly on heavy going, acted on any other turf: wore blinkers/visor: held up: to stand at Sans Craintes Stud, Coimbatore, Tamil Nadu, India. *Charles O'Brien, Ireland*

LORD AERYN (IRE) 2 b.g. (May 5) Antonius Pius (USA) 123§ – White Paper (IRE) **75 p**
(Marignan (USA) 117) [2009 6m^5 6m* 6m 7m* Oct 3] €6,200F, €12,000Y, £50,000 2-y-o: strong gelding: closely related to Italian 7f/1m winner Golden White (by Mull of Kintyre) and half-brother to 3 winners, including 2001 2-y-o 6f winner Funksoulborough (by Woodborough): dam unraced out of half-sister to high-class 1981 2-y-o 7f/1m performer Paradis Terrestre: fair form: won maiden at Ayr in July and nursery at Epsom in October: subsequently gelded: stays 7f: likely to progress again. *R. A. Fahey*

LORD CHANCELLOR (IRE) 3 b.c. King's Best (USA) 132 – Summer Serenade **91**
75 (Sadler's Wells (USA) 132) [2009 87: p10g* p10g^3 p10g* Mar 4] good-topped colt: fairly useful performer: won maiden at Lingfield in January and handicap there (beat Alexander Gulch 3¼ lengths) in March: likely to stay 1½m: raced only on polytrack and good ground: races prominently: sold £22,000 in December. *M. Johnston*

LORD DEEVERT 4 br.g. Averti (IRE) 117 – Dee-Lady 93 (Deploy 131) [2009 73: **70**
p7.1g^5 p7g^2 6g p6g^5 7s^3 7d^5 p6g p6g^5 p6m^2 Dec 1] strong gelding: fair handicapper: stays 7f: acts on all-weather, soft and good to firm ground: effective with or without headgear: races up with pace. *W. G. M. Turner*

LORD FIDELIO (IRE) 3 b.g. Xaar 132 – Rekindled Affair (IRE) (Rainbow Quest **72**
(USA) 134) [2009 8m p8g 6m^3 6.1m p7g^4 p7g* Dec 2] compact gelding: sixth foal: half-brother to useful French 9.5f/11f winner Porticcio (by Lomitas): dam unraced half-sister to dam of smart performer up to 1½m Sights On Gold: fair form: won maiden at Kempton in December: should stay 1m. *A. M. Balding*

LORD HIGH ADMIRAL (IRE) 2 b.c. (May 17) Galileo (IRE) 134 – Splendid (IRE) (Mujtahid (USA) 118) [2009 7g* 8g 7m 7d^2 Oct 26] €500,000Y: strong colt: half-brother to several winners, including 3-y-o Fanditha: dam, ran 3 times, from excellent family of Cape Cross: useful performer: won maiden at Gowran in May: upped in grade after, good 2 lengths second to Free Judgement in Killavullan Stakes at Leopardstown, making most: lost place 4f out when well held in Dewhurst Stakes at Newmarket third start: likely to be suited by 1¼m/1½m: acts on good to soft going. *A. P. O'Brien, Ireland* **103**

LORD LAING (USA) 6 br.g. Chester House (USA) 123 – Johanna Keene (USA) (Raise A Cup (USA)) [2009 55: p12g Jan 6] workmanlike gelding: modest handicapper at best: well held only outing in 2009: tried visored. *H. J. Collingridge* **–**

LORD OF THE DANCE (IRE) 3 ch.c. Indian Haven 119 – Maine Lobster (USA) 71 (Woodman (USA) 126) [2009 53p: p7.1g^3 p7g^3 10g^6 p8.6g^3 p8m^2 f8f^6 p7g^2 Dec 2] fair maiden: will prove best at 1m+: raced only on all-weather and good ground: blinkered/visored last 3 outings: sold £12,000, joined W. M. Brisbourne. *J. M. P. Eustace* **68**

LORD OF THE FLAME 3 br.g. Largesse 112 – Maylan (IRE) 47 (Lashkari 128) [2009 –: 16f Jun 19] compact gelding: tailed off in minor event at Newbury (at 2 yrs) and Queen's Vase at Royal Ascot: bred to stay 1¼m+. *W. de Best-Turner* **–**

LORD OF THE REINS (IRE) 5 b.g. Imperial Ballet (IRE) 110 – Waroonga (IRE) (Brief Truce (USA) 126) [2009 97: 5m 5g 5v 5g^6 6m 5m 5g^4 5g 5m^3 5.1d 5.1g p5m* p5.1g p5m* p5m Dec 30] good-topped gelding: just fairly useful handicapper nowadays: won at Kempton in November/December: raced at 5f/6f: acts on polytrack, soft and good to firm going: held up. *J. G. Given* **84**

LORD OROKO 5 ch.g. Lord of Men 116 – Wannaplantatree 72 (Niniski (USA) 125) [2009 p12g 18m 11.7m^4 17.2f* 14.1f 17.2m Jul 16] rather leggy, quite attractive gelding: fair handicapper: won at Bath in May: stays 17f: acts on all-weather, firm and soft going: often races freely: held up. *J. G. M. O'Shea* **68**

LORD ORPEN (IRE) 5 b.g. Orpen (USA) 116 – Kenyane (IRE) 82 (Kahyasi 130) [2009 6.1m p12g Oct 8] little form since 2007: often in headgear. *Pat Morris* **–**

LORD RAGLAN (IRE) 2 b.g. (Mar 5) Noverre (USA) 125 – Raglan Rose (USA) (Giant's Causeway (USA) 132) [2009 6g^3 6g^3 6g p7.1g Nov 2] €16,000F, 15,000Y: first foal: dam French maiden (third at 9.5f): fair maiden: trained by K. R. Burke first 2 starts, well below form after (including in seller): should stay 7f. *A. P. Jarvis* **72**

LORDS A LEAPING (IRE) 3 b.c. Bahamian Bounty 116 – Joonayh 81 (Warning 136) [2009 p9.5g^3 p10g^3 12g^2 Jun 5] 36,000Y: fifth foal: half-brother to 3 winners, including 4-y-o Pretty Bonnie and 7-y-o Majehar: dam, 2-y-o 6f winner from 3 starts, half-sister to smart performers Chrysander (up to 1¼m) and Millennium Force (at 7f): fair maiden: may prove best up to 1¼m. *J. A. Osborne* **72**

LORD SHANAKILL (USA) 3 b.c. Speightstown (USA) 124 – Green Room (USA) (Theatrical 128) [2009 117: 8m 8m^3 8g* 8g^5 6.5f Nov 7] **121**

'What's harder—Flat or jumps?' Jockey Jim Crowley presumably didn't take long in nominating that as the 'daftest question' he'd ever been asked by a journalist. 'Let's just say I am minus a collarbone, and that didn't happen on the Flat. As well as the falls, it's harder to get rides over jumps, and you last longer on the Flat and get paid better.' The thirty-one-year-old has certainly had no cause to regret his decision to switch codes in 2006, after achieving just modest success in nine seasons as a jump jockey, the bulk of his career spent on the northern circuit. Crowley's tally of wins for the last three Flat campaigns—92, 116 and 120—comfortably exceed the total accrued during the whole of his National Hunt career, whilst his prize money haul puts his jumps career even more in the shade, even though just over half of his Flat winners over the last three years have come on the all-weather. The next season will see Crowley riding as number-one to Ralph Beckett, the hitherto-freelance Crowley having his sister-in-law Amanda Perrett to thank for the bulk of his wins so far. However, it was one of Crowley's old northern links which put him on the big-race stage with Lord Shanakill, whom he has partnered on his last seven starts (six of them at Group 1 or Grade 1 level).

Crowley first teamed up with Lord Shanakill when springing something of a surprise in the Group 2 Mill Reef Stakes at Newbury as a two-year-old, a performance he followed with a close second in the Dewhurst, which saw him go into the winter as a live outsider for the Two Thousand Guineas. As it was,

Etihad Airways Prix Jean Prat, Chantilly—Jim Crowley drives home Lord Shanakill (far side) to a narrow win over Oiseau de Feu (No.9) and Irian (No.2)

14/1-shot Lord Shanakill failed to live up to expectations at Newmarket, running an uncharacteristically poor race to finish only twelfth of fifteen behind Sea The Stars, after missing his intended preparatory race in the Greenham at Newbury because of a temperature. Lord Shanakill wasted little time bouncing back from his Newmarket flop, establishing himself as one of Europe's leading three-year-old milers on his next two starts. He got much closer to two of the Newmarket principals—Mastercraftsman and Delegator, beaten a neck and a length and a half—when third at 20/1 in the St James's Palace Stakes at Royal Ascot, a performance which was followed by victory in the following month's Etihad Airways Prix Jean Prat at Chantilly. The betting was headed by the Aidan O'Brien-trained Westphalia, who had finished third in both the Poule d'Essai des Poulains (promoted) and the Prix du Jockey Club, but it was the home-trained Oiseau de Feu (promoted fourth in the Poule d'Essai des Poulains) who pushed Lord Shanakill closest. Just a head separated them at the line, with the prominently-ridden Lord Shanakill gamely holding Oiseau de Feu's late challenge, with a further half length back to German-trained Irian in third.

Lord Shanakill's lucrative win in the Prix Jean Prat (£195,350 first prize) was the first at Group 1 level for both Crowley and Lord Shanakill's trainer Karl Burke, though the latter was dealt a major blow when he was banned from racing for twelve months later in July as a long-running investigation into race-fixing, revolving around the activities of racehorse owner Miles Rodgers, was finally concluded (more details of which can be found in the Introduction). Burke's ban came into effect twenty-four hours before Lord Shanakill's next appearance in the Sussex Stakes at Goodwood, by which time the licence at Spigot Lodge had been taken over by Burke's father-in-law Alan Jarvis. Lord Shanakill had an excuse for his below-par fifth behind Rip Van Winkle at Goodwood, finishing lame, but his owners opted for a switch of stables soon afterwards, Lord Shanakill being sent to Richard Mandella in the States to be prepared for what turned out to be an unsuccessful tilt at the Breeders' Cup Turf Sprint at Santa Anita, where he finished a never-dangerous twelfth of fourteen after a three-month absence from the track.

Victory as a six-year-old in the 2004 Breeders' Cup Sprint (held that year at Lone Star Park) was the crowning moment on the track for Lord Shanakill's sire Speightstown, who won ten of his sixteen starts during a stop-start career. Lord Shanakill has been the leading earner from Speightstown's first two crops and, in truth, it was probably the bottom line of his pedigree which prompted connections to pay 110,000 dollars for Lord Shanakill as a yearling. His unraced dam Green Room hails from a very good family, being a half-sister to Spanish Fern, who progressed into a Grade 1 mile and a quarter winner for Bobby Frankel after being exported to the States towards the end of her three-year-old campaign (formerly trained by Roger Charlton). Lord Shanakill's grandam Chain Fern was an unraced sister to the 1985 Irish One Thousand Guineas winner Al Bahathri, a pivotal mare in Hamdan Al Maktoum's bloodstock empire, as recounted in the essay on her grandson Gladiatorus. Another Group 1 winner to emerge from this family in the latest season was Hearts of Fire, a great grandson of Chain Fern. Green Room has some way to go if she is to make a similar impact to Al Bahathri and her other illustrious relatives, but she has produced two more colts since first foal Lord Shanakill, whose exploits hadn't gone unnoticed when that pair passed through the sale-ring. Lord Shanakill's year-younger half-brother Brannagh (by Hennessy) made 105,000 guineas and finished third in two maidens for Jeremy Noseda in the autumn, shaping with promise both times despite not looking entirely straightforward (also tongue tied), whilst Green Room's yearling colt by Dixie Union (as yet unnamed) was bought by Mark Johnston for 140,000 guineas at the Tattersalls October Yearling Sales.

Lord Shanakill (USA) (b.c. 2006)	Speightstown (USA) (ch 1998)	Gone West (br 1984)	Mr Prospector
			Secrettame
		Silken Cat (ch 1993)	Storm Cat
			Silken Doll
	Green Room (USA) (b 2002)	Theatrical (b 1982)	Nureyev
			Tree of Knowledge
		Chain Fern (b 1986)	Blushing Groom
			Chain Store

The notably genuine Lord Shanakill, a good-topped colt with a quick action, seems versatile with regards to both going—he acts on firm and probably on soft—and tactics. He stays a mile well and, although outpaced at Santa Anita, may well still prove effective at sprint distances, given that race-rustiness may have been a factor in that below-par American run. Incidentally, should he be returned to Britain in 2010, it is likely that he will have another new trainer, as his owners removed their other horses from Spigot Lodge in September to join Henry Cecil. *R. E. Mandella, USA*

LORDSHIP (IRE) 5 b.g. King's Best (USA) 132 – Rahika Rose 91 (Unfuwain (USA) **80**
131) [2009 74: 8.1g 7.1m 8.1g^{4} 8.1m^{5} 7.5g 7s^{6} 8.1g 7.2s^{3} 8s* 7.1d* 8.1m 8g 7.2v* 7v^{5} f7m Nov 12] sturdy, close-coupled gelding: fairly useful handicapper: won at Ayr in August, Chepstow in September and Ayr in October: stays 1m: best on going softer than good (acts on heavy): headstrong. *A. W. Carroll*

LORD'S SEAT 2 b.g. (Jan 25) Trade Fair 124 – Clashfern (Smackover 107) [2009 5m^{6} **55**
5g^{4} 5m 5m^{6} 5d^{3} 5.9g 6s 7.2v^{5} 7v^{5} f8m Nov 11] modest maiden: best efforts at 5f on good/good to soft going: inconsistent. *A. Berry*

LORD THEO 5 b.g. Averti (IRE) 117 – Love You Too 88 (Be My Chief (USA) 122) **89**
[2009 88: f8g^{4} p10g^{6} p8g f8g^{3} p8g^{3} 8.3m^{5} p8g 10.9d 8m^{5} 8d^{2} 10g^{5} 9s^{6} 10d* 10m* 12m^{2} 10m* 14v 10.1m 12m^{5} 10.2d Oct 15] tall, close-coupled gelding: fairly useful handicapper: successful 3 times at Newmarket in August: below form after: stays 1½m: acts on all-weather, firm and good to soft going: tried blinkered/visored. *N. P. Littmoden*

LORD VICTOR 2 ch.c. (Mar 20) Needwood Blade 117 – La Victoria (GER) (Rousil- **71**
lon (USA) 133) [2009 p8g^{6} p8.6g 6.1s p7.1g^{3} p7.1g f6m^{2} f7f p6g^{4} f7m* f6g^{3} f7d* Dec 29] 18,000F, 8,000Y: half-brother to several winners abroad: dam, German 1m winner, half-sister to high-class German 1½m performer Lomitas: fair performer: won seller and claimer at Southwell in December: stays 7f: acts on all-weather (once raced on turf): tried blinkered/in cheekpieces: front runner. *A. J. McCabe*

LORD WHEATHILL 2 b.g. (Feb 19) Tobougg (IRE) 125 – Classic Quartet 52 (Clas- **–**
sic Cliche (IRE) 128) [2009 7.1s 7g 8.3g Oct 28] well held in maidens. *Mrs L. Williamson*

LORD ZENITH 2 b.c. (Jan 29) Zamindar (USA) 116 – Lady Donatella 57 (Last **98 p**
Tycoon 131) [2009 6m^{6} 7m* 7m^{5} Jul 10] tall, good-topped colt: sixth foal: half-brother to 4-y-o Maxwil and 6f/7.6f winner Dark Moon (by Observatory): dam, maiden (stayed 1½m), half-sister to very smart 1m/9f performer Right Wing: impressive winner of maiden at Salisbury (by 6 lengths from Cafe Greco) in June: twice hampered when 2½ lengths fifth to Silver Grecian in Superlative Stakes at Newmarket: will stay 1m: already useful, and type to do better still. *A. M. Balding*

LOS NADIS (GER) 5 b.g. Hernando (FR) 127 – La Estrella (GER) (Desert King (IRE) **72**
129) [2009 81: 16m^{4} 14m^{6} 14m 16.1d^{5} May 15] fair handicapper nowadays: stays 2m: acts on heavy and good to firm ground: tried blinkered in France earlier in career: fairly useful hurdler, won later in May. *P. Monteith*

LOSS LEADER (IRE) 2 ch.g. (Jan 29) Captain Rio 122 – Nenagh (IRE) 63 (Barathea (IRE) 127) [2009 5m 5m Sep 17] sturdy gelding: green, well held in maidens 4½ months apart (gelded in between). *T. D. Easterby* –

LOST CAUSE 2 b.c. (Mar 27) Dubawi (IRE) 129 – Crystal (IRE) 93 (Danehill (USA) 126) [2009 7g 7s⁶ 6m⁶ p7g⁴ 8.3d Oct 15] compact colt: modest maiden: should be suited by 1m+: acts on polytrack and good to firm going: sold 11,000 gns, sent to Bahrain. *R. Charlton* 64

LOST HORIZON (IRE) 2 b.f. (Apr 3) Elusive City (USA) 117 – Souvenir Souvenir (Highest Honor (FR) 124) [2009 7s 7m² 7d Oct 12] 17,000F, €70,000Y: good-topped filly: fifth foal: sister to French 6f winner Azagra and half-sister to 2 winners in France, including 1½m winner Sing Faraway (by Galileo): dam, French 1m winner, half-sister to dam of smart French 1m/9f performer Rouvres: easily best effort when ¾-length second to Silver Rock in minor event at Newbury: will stay 1m. *R. Hannon* 83

LOST IN PARIS (IRE) 3 b.g. Elusive City (USA) 117 – Brazilia 63 (Forzando 122) [2009 65: 8.3m⁵ 8m 7.1m³ 7m³ 7g 6v⁵ 7v³ 6g³ 5m² 5m* p5.1g⁴ Nov 14] compact gelding: fair handicapper: won at Ayr in October: best efforts at 5f: acts on polytrack, heavy and good to firm ground: blinkered nowadays: often front runner. *T. D. Easterby* 74

LOST IN THE DESERT (IRE) 3 b.g. Nayef (USA) 129 – Desert Harmony (Green Desert (USA) 127) [2009 10m 8.3g 8.1f⁴ 8g 10m* 9.8m Nov 26] rangy gelding: fair performer: left M. Botti and gelded after fourth start: won maiden seller at Milan in October: stays 1¼m: acts on good to firm ground: blinkered last 2 starts in Britain. *S. Botti, Italy* 67

LOST IN THE FOREST 2 ch.f. (Feb 2) Trade Fair 124 – Fallujah (Dr Fong (USA) 128) [2009 7m 7s⁵ Sep 5] workmanlike filly: second foal: dam, ran once, half-sister to useful 7f winner Tora Bora: poor form in maidens. *A. P. Jarvis* 47

LOST IN THE MOMENT (IRE) 2 b.c. (Apr 29) Danehill Dancer (IRE) 117 – Streetcar (IRE) 69 (In The Wings 128) [2009 7g⁶ Oct 10] €380,000Y: well-made colt: seventh foal: brother to a winner in Japan and closely related to smart Irish 6f (at 2 yrs) to 9.5f winner Luas Line (by Danehill) and Irish 9.5f winner Street Style (by Rock of Gibraltar): dam, lightly raced at 2 yrs in Ireland, half-sister to smart but untrustworthy 6f to 1m winner Intimate Guest: 13/2, very green when sixth to Karaka Jack in maiden at York: should improve. *J. Noseda* – p

LOST SOLDIER THREE (IRE) 8 b.g. Barathea (IRE) 127 – Donya 74 (Mill Reef (USA) 141) [2009 102: 12m p16g 12g⁴ 12m⁴ 15.9m 12m³ 14m⁵ 12g 12g² 12.5d² f12m² f12f² f16m² Dec 15] close-coupled gelding: fairly useful performer nowadays: stays 2m: acts on fibresand, firm and soft going: tried visored: temperament under suspicion. *D. Nicholls* 87

LOU BEAR (IRE) 2 b.c. (May 11) Lujain (USA) 119 – Dream of Dubai (IRE) 61 (Vettori (IRE) 119) [2009 p7m⁴ p7g Dec 31] much better effort in maidens when 4 lengths fourth to Prince of Sorrento at Kempton: likely to stay 1m. *J. Akehurst* 60

LOUGH BEG (IRE) 6 b.g. Close Conflict (USA) 115 – Mia Gigi (Hard Fought 125) [2009 68: p12g⁶ p16.5g p12g Apr 22] modest performer nowadays: stays easy 1½m: acts on polytrack, heavy and good to firm ground: tried blinkered, tongue tied. *Miss Tor Sturgis* 61

LOUIDOR 3 b.g. Lujain (USA) 119 – Simonida (IRE) (Royal Academy (USA) 130) [2009 69: 8.3g 8.1g p6g Jun 5] sturdy gelding: fair maiden at 2 yrs: no form in 2009. *M. R. Bosley* –

LOUIE'S LAD 3 gr.g. Compton Place 125 – Silver Louie (IRE) (Titus Livius (FR) 115) [2009 58§: 5m 5.7f p5g 5m³ 5.3g² 6d² 5.2m⁴ 5.3f² 6m⁵ 5m⁶ 6m 5.3d⁴ 5.3f 6g 5m Sep 12] smallish, leggy gelding: modest maiden handicapper: best at 5f/6f: acts on firm and soft going: wears cheekpieces: ungenuine. *J. J. Bridger* 56 §

LOUISA (GER) 5 b.m. Seattle Dancer (USA) 119 – La Ola (GER) (Dashing Blade 117) [2009 9.2d⁴ 11.5d⁶ 11.5g⁶ 12.1s⁶ 12.1v 13.1d 16.1d Sep 7] €13,000Y: third foal: half-sister to French 1¼m winner Levinas (by Waky Nao): dam, German 6.5f/1m winner, half-sister to smart German performer up to 1½m Lecroix: ran 5 times in Germany for A. Wohler in 2007, winning maiden at Bad Harzburg: modest form at best in handicaps in Britain: stays 1½m: raced mainly on good ground or softer. *P. Monteith* 56

LOUISE BONNE (USA) 3 b. or br.f. Yes It's True (USA) 116 – Blushing Issue (USA) (Blushing John (USA) 120) [2009 –: 8g* 9m Jun 13] good-topped filly: fairly useful form: easily best effort when winning maiden at Goodwood in May by ¾ length from Aqwaas: pulled too hard in handicap at Sandown 2 weeks later: stays 1m: sold 50,000 gns, sent to Saudi Arabia. *C. G. Cox* 82

LOUISE SAUVAGE 3 b.f. Loup Sauvage (USA) 125 – Breezy Louise 60 (Dilum **49**
(USA) 115) [2009 6m 6m^{5} p7m^{5} 7.1m^{6d} 6g Oct 5] rather leggy filly: fourth foal: half-sister to fairly useful but unreliable Irish 7f winner (including at 2 yrs) Rockie (by Bertolini): dam 5f winner, including at 2 yrs: poor maiden. *M. D. I. Usher*

LOUISIADE (IRE) 8 b.g. Tagula (IRE) 116 – Titchwell Lass 57 (Lead On Time (USA) **55**
123) [2009 73d: f8s f8s^{5} f8g f8g^{3} p7.1g^{2} f8g f7g p7.1g 7m f7g^{6} f7g^{5} 6g^{4} 6m p8m^{2} f7f^{5} f8g Dec 27] strong, lengthy gelding: modest performer nowadays: left M. Chapman after thirteenth start: effective at 6f to 8.6f: acts on all-weather and firm ground: usually in headgear: tried tongue tied. *R. C. Guest*

LOUISIANA GIFT (IRE) 2 b.g. (Mar 8) Cadeaux Genereux 131 – Southern Queen **70**
(Anabaa (USA) 130) [2009 p7f^{5} p7.1g^{6} p7g Oct 20] €62,000F, 46,000Y, 10,000 2-y-o: second foal: half-brother to 3-y-o Scottish Affair: dam useful French 2-y-o 5.5f/7f winner: best effort in maidens when fifth to Fallen Idol at Kempton: gelded after final start. *J. W. Hills*

LOULOU (USA) 3 ch.f. El Prado (IRE) 119 – Hatoof (USA) 124 (Irish River (FR) **63**
131) [2009 57: 10.2d* 12.1m^{3} 10s May 27] well-made filly: modest handicapper: won at Nottingham in April: may prove best short of 1½m: acts on good to firm and good to soft going. *S. A. Callaghan*

LOUP BRETON (IRE) 5 b.h. Anabaa (USA) 130 – Louve (USA) 112 (Irish River **118**
(FR) 131) [2009 120: 10s^{4} 10g^{4} 10.5g^{2} 9.3s 10g 9f* 9f^{2} Dec 27] rather leggy, lengthy horse: smart performer: best effort in France in 2009 when ¾-length second to Vision d'Etat in Prix Ganay at Longchamp: well below form next 2 starts, in Prix d'Ispahan on same course and Prix Gontaut-Biron at Deauville: left E. Lellouche, landed odds in allowance race at Hollywood in November, then creditable neck second to Proudinsky in Grade 2 San Gabriel Handicap at Santa Anita: best at 9f/1¼m: acts on any going: in cheekpieces/blinkers nowadays: held up. *J. C. Canani, USA*

LOUPHOLE 7 ch.g. Loup Sauvage (USA) 125 – Goodwood Lass (IRE) 71 (Alzao **72**
(USA) 117) [2009 82: p6g^{2} p6g^{2} p6g 6g 6m^{5} 6m* 6m 7m^{6} 6m^{4} 6m^{3} p6g^{2} p6m^{6} 6m^{2} p6g^{6} Nov 1] close-coupled gelding: fair performer nowadays: won handicap at Brighton in May: best at 6f: acts on polytrack and firm going: tried in cheekpieces/visor: held up, and best in well-run race. *J. R. Jenkins*

LOVE ACTION (IRE) 2 b.f. (Mar 2) Motivator 131 – Speciale (USA) (War Chant **68**
(USA) 126) [2009 7m^{4} 7g p8m^{6} Nov 19] 100,000Y: rather unfurnished filly: first foal: dam, useful French 6f winner (including at 2 yrs), half-sister to smart performer up to 1¼m Common World: fair form in maidens: off 4 months, still green final start: stays 1m. *R. Hannon*

LOVE ALLOWED 3 br.f. Diktat 126 – Love Song 75 (Kris 135) [2009 p6g p7g 7d^{3} **53**
7g^{3} 7m 8.3g 8g 7g p7f p7g p7g Oct 14] 5,000Y: fourth foal: dam, 1¼m winner, half-sister to smart 1¼m winner National Anthem: modest maiden: stays 7f: unraced on extremes of going on turf. *Jamie Poulton*

LOVE AND DEVOTION 2 b.f. (Mar 21) Shamardal (USA) 129 – Romantic Myth **64**
105 (Mind Games 121) [2009 6f^{5} 6m 5.1g^{6} 6g^{5} Sep 30] 42,000Y: sturdy filly: type to carry condition: fifth foal: half-sister to 3-y-o Mythicism, 4-y-o Headache and 5-y-o Stargazy: dam 2-y-o 5f winner, including Queen Mary Stakes: modest form in maidens, finishing weakly last 3 starts: joined H-A. Pantall in France. *Saeed bin Suroor*

LOVE ANGEL (USA) 7 b. or br.g. Woodman (USA) 126 – Omnia (USA) 85 (Green **§§**
Dancer (USA) 132) [2009 56§: p10g Mar 13] good-topped gelding: modest handicapper: became most reluctant/refused to race on Flat and over jumps, and was banned from racing at BHA inquiry in April. *J. J. Bridger*

LOVE CALL (IRE) 3 ch.f. Indian Haven 119 – Cap And Gown (IRE) 81 (Royal **67**
Academy (USA) 130) [2009 8m^{6} p12g^{6} 8.1g* Aug 26] half-sister to 2 winners, including fairly useful 7f winner Arch of Titus (by Titus Livius): dam, 1m winner, half-sister to smart performer up to 1½m Papering: easily best effort in maidens when winning at Warwick in August by short head from Asateer: stays 1m. *W. R. Muir*

LOVE DELTA (USA) 2 b. or br.c. (Feb 3) Seeking The Gold (USA) – Delta Princess **75**
(USA) (A P Indy (USA) 131) [2009 7d^{5} 7.5g^{3} 6d^{6} p8f Dec 16] $260,000Y, 100,000 2-y-o: sturdy colt: first foal: dam, US Grade 3 8.5f/9f winner, sister to smart US Grade 1 9f winner Indy Five Hundred: easily best effort in maidens when fifth to Stags Leap at Goodwood: stays 7f. *M. Johnston*

LOVE GALORE (IRE) 4 b.g. Galileo (IRE) 134 – Lobmille (Mill Reef (USA) 141) **104**
[2009 107: 12g 12m^{3} 10g 12g^{6} p12g^{5} 12g 11.9m 10.4m Jul 11] good-topped gelding:

useful handicapper: 4¾ lengths third to Age of Reason at Nad Al Sheba in January, only creditable effort in 2009: gelded after fifth start: stays 1½m: raced only on good ground or firmer: headstrong sort, has worn net muzzle: tends to wander. *M. Johnston*

LOVE IN THE PARK 4 b.f. Pivotal 124 – Naughty Crown (USA) 84 (Chief's Crown (USA)) [2009 f6g^3 p7g 7.1f 8.1g 7f^2 9m* 10g^3 10g* 10s* 10.9g^6 11.5d^6 Sep 15] 45,000Y: angular filly: fourth foal: half-sister to 7f winner Grand Lucre and winner in USA (both by Grand Slam): dam, 7f and (in USA) 7.5f winner, half-sister to smart performer up to 1¼m Tahreeb: fair handicapper: won at Lingfield in June, July and August: reluctant there final outing: will be suited by 1½m: acts on firm and soft going: held up. *R. Brotherton* **78**

LOVEINTHESAND (IRE) 2 b.c. (Mar 23) Footstepsinthesand 120 – Love Emerald (USA) (Mister Baileys 123) [2009 6m^2 6g^4 6m Sep 9] tall, good-topped colt: fourth foal: half-brother to 4-y-o Sammy The Snake: dam unraced half-sister to useful Irish performer up to 9f Lil's Boy: fair form in maidens/minor event: will probably still do better. *M. Johnston* **70 p**

LOVE IN THE WEST (IRE) 3 b.f. Fruits of Love (USA) 127 – Sandhill (IRE) 96 (Danehill (USA) 126) [2009 8g 10.3m^4 9.8m* 7.5m^2 12.1s^5 12d^3 12.5m Sep 14] €6,200F: angular filly: sister to 9f/10.5f winner in Italy and half-sister to 2 winners in USA: dam, 7f winner, half-sister to smart miler Sand Falcon: fair performer: won seller at Ripon in July: needs to learn to settle to stay 1½m+: acts on soft and good to firm going. *G. A. Swinbank* **67**

LOVELACE 5 b.h. Royal Applause 124 – Loveleaves 93 (Polar Falcon (USA) 126) [2009 117: 7s^4 8.1g^6 8g^4 8.5g^6 8m 8g^5 8m Aug 20] tall horse: smart performer: respectable efforts at best in 2009, including when fourth to Yamal in listed handicap at York and sixth to Mac Love in Diomed Stakes at Epsom third/fourth starts: best at 7f/1m: acts on good to firm and good to soft going: dropped out nowadays. *M. Johnston* **111**

LOVE LOCKDOWN (IRE) 2 gr.g. (May 10) Verglas (IRE) 118 – Out of Thanks (IRE) 89 (Sadler's Wells (USA) 132) [2009 5d^3 6g* 6f* 6m* 6g^6 5m^3 p6g* Sep 5] €14,000Y, resold €35,000Y: sturdy, close-coupled gelding: second foal: dam, Irish 1¼m winner (stayed 1½m): smart performer: won maiden at Leopardstown in May, minor event at Naas (beat Beethoven by head) and listed contest at Cork (by neck from King Ledley) in June, and totepool Sirenia Stakes at Kempton (beat Iver Bridge Lad 1½ lengths) in September: better at 6f than 5f: acts on polytrack and firm ground: races up with pace: sent to Hong Kong. *G. M. Lyons, Ireland* **110**

LOVELY EYES (IRE) 2 b.f. (Mar 29) Red Ransom (USA) – Polygueza (FR) 78 (Be My Guest (USA) 126) [2009 8m^4 10.2m^4 Sep 28] 55,000Y: half-sister to several winners, including very smart 1¼m/1½m winner The Geezer (by Halling) and Irish 2008 2-y-o 7f winner Maziona (by Dansili): dam Irish 7f winner: better effort in maidens when fourth to Exemplary at Bath latter start, still green. *D. M. Simcock* **69**

LOVELY STEPS (USA) 3 b. or br.f. Gone West (USA) – Magicalmysterycat (USA) 111 (Storm Cat (USA)) [2009 46: p8g p6g^2 p6g^6 Feb 25] modest maiden: stays 6f, should be as effective at 5f: raced only on polytrack: blinkered last 2 starts: sold 36,000 gns in July, reportedly in foal to Tiger Hill, and sent to USA. *D. M. Simcock* **56**

LOVELY THOUGHT 3 b.f. Dubai Destination (USA) 127 – Fairy Flight (IRE) 86 (Fairy King (USA)) [2009 74+: 6d* 7d^3 6d 7g 6m 7s 6s* 6s^3 Nov 7] big, rangy filly: fairly useful performer: improved in 2009, winning handicaps at Yarmouth in April and Catterick in October: good third to Fullandby in listed race at Doncaster final outing: effective at 6f/7f: acts on soft going: usually blinkered, tried in cheekpieces: front runner: sold 95,000 gns. *W. J. Haggas* **92**

LOVE MATCH 2 b.f. (Apr 6) Danehill Dancer (IRE) 117 – Name of Love (IRE) 105 (Petardia 113) [2009 6g^5 6s^5 6m^3 p6m 5g^2 p6f^4 Oct 14] useful-looking filly: half-sister to 9.5f winner Almavara (by Fusaichi Pegasus) and winner in USA by Lemon Drop Kid: dam, 7f winner (including Rockfel Stakes), ran only at 2 yrs: fair maiden: second in nursery at Catterick: effective at 5f/6f: acts on polytrack, soft and good to firm ground: blinkered/visored last 2 starts. *R. Charlton* **72**

LOVE PEGASUS (USA) 3 b.c. Fusaichi Pegasus (USA) 130 – Take Charge Lady (USA) 123 (Dehere (USA) 121) [2009 77p: p8g* p8g* 8.3g p10.7g^6 Nov 25] useful performer: won maiden in February and handicap (by 3 lengths from Implication) in June, both at Kempton: below form next 2 starts over 5 months apart, leaving M. Johnston 75,000 gns prior to final outing: stays 1m: best efforts on polytrack: tongue tied final start. *Niall O'Callaghan, Ireland* **96**

LOVERS CAUSEWAY (USA) 2 b.c. (Mar 14) Giant's Causeway (USA) 132 – Heer- **79 p**
emandi (IRE) 105 (Royal Academy (USA) 130) [2009 8m p8.6g^{2} Dec 26] $160,000Y: closely related to useful Irish 1m winner Emerald Cat (by Storm Cat) and half-brother to several winners in USA: dam, 2-y-o 6f winner in Ireland, closely related to dam of US Grade 1 9f/9.5f winner Flawlessly: much better effort in maidens when neck second to Dubai Bounty at Wolverhampton: will stay 1¼m: open to further improvement. *M. Johnston*

LOVE YOU LOUIS 3 b.g. Mark of Esteem (IRE) 137 – Maddie's A Jem 82 (Emperor **79**
Jones (USA) 119) [2009 79: p6g^{6} p6g p5g* f5g^{5} 5g 5m p5g^{3} p5g p5.1g p6f^{5} Dec 13] stocky gelding: fair handicapper: won at Kempton in February: not at best after: likely to prove best at 5f/6f: acts on polytrack and soft ground: usually in headgear: often front runner/races prominently. *J. R. Jenkins*

LOWDOWN (IRE) 2 ch.c. (Mar 4) Shamardal (USA) 129 – Mood Swings (IRE) 77 **99**
(Shirley Heights 130) [2009 6d^{5} 7s^{2} 6g* 6.5m 6m 7m^{4} Oct 3] 77,000F, 100,000Y: sturdy colt: half-brother to several at least useful performers, including 3-y-o Grand Ducal and 5-y-o Al Khaleej: dam 2-y-o 6f winner: useful performer: best effort when winning maiden at Goodwood (by 1¼ lengths from Red Badge, made all) in July: respectable fourth to Oasis Dancer in sales race at Newmarket: should stay 1m: acts on soft going. *M. Johnston*

LOWTHER 4 b.c. Beat All (USA) 120 – Ever So Lonely 63 (Headin' Up) [2009 8g* **104**
7g* 7m^{6} 8.1m 7.6m^{2} 6.5m 6m^{2} 7m^{5} f8g 6g Oct 23] angular colt: eighth living foal: dam 5f winner: well held in bumper: useful performer: won maiden at Yarmouth (100/1) in May and handicap at Chester in June: best effort when neck second to Kaldoun Kingdom in Ayr Silver Cup seventh start: effective at 6f to 1m: acts on good to firm going: blinkered last 4 starts: refused to enter stall intended debut. *A. Bailey*

LOYALISTE (FR) 2 ch.c. (Feb 21) Green Tune (USA) 125 – Whitby (FR) (Gold Away **63**
(IRE) 125) [2009 9m^{3} 10m^{6} Oct 5] modest form in maidens at Goodwood and Pontefract: bred to stay at least 1¼m. *R. Hannon*

LOYAL ROYAL (IRE) 6 b.g. King Charlemagne (USA) 120 – Supportive (IRE) **50**
(Nashamaa 113) [2009 71: p6g^{4} p7.1g^{4} p6g^{3} p7g^{2} p7g^{5} p7.1g^{2} p7g^{6} p7g 7.1m 7.1g p7.1g^{6} **a72**
p7g^{3} 7.6m p6m^{2} p6g p6g^{5} p7.1g^{2} p7m p6g* p6g^{4} p7g p7.1g^{6} p7m^{3} Dec 30] leggy gelding: fair handicapper on all-weather, modest on turf: won at Wolverhampton in October: effective at 6f/7f: acts on polytrack, firm and good to soft going: tried in cheekpieces, wears blinkers: not straightforward (pulls hard and needs strong pace). *J. M. Bradley*

LUBERON 6 b.g. Fantastic Light (USA) 134 – Luxurious (USA) (Lyphard (USA) 132) **–**
[2009 101, a109: p12g^{4} f11m^{5} Dec 5] angular gelding: useful performer at best: well below form both starts in 2009: stays 13.4f: acts on polytrack and firm going: front runner. *M. Johnston*

LUCAYAN DANCER 9 b.g. Zieten (USA) 118 – Tittle Tattle (IRE) 80 (Soviet Lad **72**
(USA)) [2009 80: p9.5g^{6} 9m^{2} 10m 12g^{2} 9m* 7.9g^{2} 9m^{4} 10m* 11.1m^{3} 10m^{2} 9m^{2} 10m^{6} 10g Sep 17] close-coupled gelding: has a markedly round action: fair performer: won seller at Musselburgh in May and claimer at Redcar in June: effective at 1m to 1½m: acts on polytrack and any turf going: tried in cheekpieces/blinkers at 3 yrs: has flashed tail: has run well when sweating: versatile regarding tactics: not straightforward. *D. Nicholls*

LUC JORDAN 3 b.c. Intikhab (USA) 135 – Saphila (IRE) 72 (Sadler's Wells (USA) **93**
132) [2009 8m^{2} 8.1g^{2} 8g^{2} 10.1g^{6} 7s^{3} 7.1m^{2} p8.6g* p10m* 10.3g* Oct 23] close-coupled colt: second foal: half-brother to fairly useful 2007 2-y-o 7f winner Port Quin (by Dr Fong): dam, maiden (stayed 1¾m), sister to smart Irish/German performer up to 1½m Poseidon Adventure: progressed into a fairly useful performer, winning maiden at Wolverhampton in September, and handicaps at Kempton later in month and Doncaster (beat Bruton Street by neck, idling) in October: stays 10.3f: acts on polytrack. *L. M. Cumani*

LUCKETTE 3 b.f. Lucky Story (USA) 128 – Thea (USA) 95 (Marju (IRE) 127) [2009 **–**
–: 7m 9.9m^{6} 12.1m 6m^{6} 6m Jul 1] workmanlike filly: little form: tried visored. *M. Brittain*

LUCKIER (IRE) 3 gr.f. Key of Luck (USA) 126 – Ibiza (GER) (Linamix (FR) 127) **–**
[2009 76p: p8.6g^{2} p8g^{4} 8m 7m f7g p7.1g^{2} p7g Oct 24] fair handicapper on polytrack: **a79**
stays 8.6f: little form on turf: sold 7,000 gns. *S. Kirk*

LUCK OF THE DRAW (IRE) 2 b.g. (Mar 28) Key of Luck (USA) 126 – Sarifa **52 p**
(IRE) (Kahyasi 130) [2009 p7f p6g^{6} p7g Oct 9] €70,000F, €60,000Y: brother to several winners in Ireland, notably 7f (at 2 yrs) to 1¾m winner Right Key, 6.5f (at 2 yrs) to 1m winner Wrong Key and 10.7f winner Starluck (also smart hurdler), all useful: dam unraced half-sister to smart French 7f/1m performer Saratan: modest form in maidens: bred to do better at 1m+. *Sir Mark Prescott*

LUCK WILL COME (IRE) 5 b.m. Desert Style (IRE) 121 – Petite Maxine 70 **82** (Sharpo 132) [2009 75: 8g^4 p8.6g* 8m^2 8m^2 10g p10g^2 9g^2 8.5m p8.6g^3 Oct 3] angular mare: fairly useful handicapper: won at Wolverhampton in May: stays easy 1¼m: acts on polytrack and good to firm ground: consistent. *H. J. Collingridge*

LUCKY ART (USA) 3 b.g. Johannesburg (USA) 127 – Syrian Summer (USA) **82** (Damascus (USA)) [2009 85: 5f 5g^5 5m 5g 5d^2 5g^4 5m^3 5d* 5m^5 5.1m 6.1d^3 6s^3 f5m f6f Nov 24] quite attractive gelding: fairly useful handicapper: left J. Howard Johnson after fifth start: won at Thirsk in August: stays 6f: acts on good to firm and good to soft going: tried in cheekpieces. *Mrs R. A. Carr*

LUCKY BID 3 b.g. Josr Algarhoud (IRE) 118 – Double Fault (IRE) 54 (Zieten (USA) **36** 118) [2009 –: p6g^5 5.7f May 13] sturdy gelding: poor form. *J. M. Bradley*

LUCKY BREEZE (IRE) 2 b.f. (Mar 31) Key of Luck (USA) 126 – Lasting Chance **46 p** (USA) (American Chance (USA) 117) [2009 p8g Dec 7] 25,000Y: fifth foal: half-sister to 3 winners, notably high-class 7f (at 2 yrs)/1¼m (including in Hong Kong) winner Collection (by Peintre Celebre): dam Canadian 6f (at 2 yrs) to 9f (Grade 3) winner: 12/1, very much in need of experience and not knocked about when down the field in maiden at Lingfield: should improve. *W. J. Knight*

LUCKY BUDDHA 3 gr.g. Kyllachy 129 – Heaven-Liegh-Grey 90 (Grey Desire 115) **60** [2009 57: 5.1m^5 6s^3 6f 6g^6 6g 5.9g^3 5g Sep 21] modest maiden handicapper: raced only at 5f/6f: acts on soft and good to firm ground. *Jedd O'Keeffe*

LUCKY CHARACTER 4 b.g. Key of Luck (USA) 126 – Gay Heroine 105 (Caerleon **43** (USA) 132) [2009 47: p7g^4 p7g Feb 18] poor maiden: stays 7f: acts on polytrack and good to firm ground: tongue tied since debut, also tried blinkered/visored: joined Tom Dascombe, sold 800 gns in October. *N. J. Vaughan*

LUCKY DANCE (BRZ) 7 b.h. Mutakddim (USA) 112 – Linda Francesa (ARG) **98** (Equalize (USA)) [2009 99: p8.6g 8m^5 8s 7f^3 8m 8m 8m 7d^6 8m^6 f8g^6 8g^4 p10g p8f^4 Dec 19] tall, good-topped horse: useful performer: best efforts in 2009 in handicaps on second/fourth outings: stays 9f: acts on polytrack/dirt and any turf going: tried blinkered. *A. G. Foster*

LUCKY DANCER 4 ch.g. Selkirk (USA) 129 – Spot Prize (USA) 108 (Seattle Dancer **65** (USA) 119) [2009 60p: p12g^6 p10g^6 16d^5 p16g^2 16m^5 p16g Jun 17] fair maiden handicapper: stays easy 2m: acts on polytrack, probably on good to soft ground: blinkered second/third outings: joined Evan Williams 7,000 gns, won over hurdles in August. *D. R. C. Elsworth*

LUCKY DAN (IRE) 3 b.g. Danetime (IRE) 121 – Katherine Gorge (USA) (Hansel **79** (USA)) [2009 63: p6g^6 p7.1g^6 5m^5 5m 7.6m 6m* 5d 6d 6m 5m^4 6d^2 p6g^2 6g^3 6.1d Oct 15] close-coupled gelding: fair handicapper: won at Hamilton in July: effective at 5f/6f: acts on polytrack, good to firm and good to soft going: signs of temperament. *Paul Green*

Goffs Million Sprint, the Curragh—
the last year of this valuable series of sales races yields another bumper payday for Richard Hannon-trained two-year-olds as Lucky General (third right) wins from stable-companion Full Mandate (second right); King Ledley (rail) and Beethoven (second left, striped cap) finish third and fourth

LUCKY DIVA 2 ch.f. (Apr 20) Lucky Story (USA) 128 – Cosmic Countess (IRE) 74 (Lahib (USA) 129) [2009 5.1g Sep 7] sixth foal: half-sister to 7f/7.6f winner Miss Madame (by Cape Cross) and winner in Greece by Bahhare: dam 2-y-o 6f winner: 18/1, soon outpaced when seventh in maiden at Bath: will be suited by 6f+. *Rae Guest* **41 +**

LUCKY FLYER 2 br.f. (Mar 27) Lucky Story (USA) 128 – Fly Like The Wind 76 (Cyrano de Bergerac 120) [2009 5f Jun 4] sturdy filly: fifth foal: dam 5f winner: 33/1, backward and green, last in maiden at Sandown. *Rae Guest* **–**

LUCKY FORTEEN 6 b.m. Forzando 122 – Grey Blade (Dashing Blade 117) [2009 –: p8g p6g 7.1g May 4] little form. *P. W. Hiatt* **–**

LUCKY FORTUNE (IRE) 3 ch.g. Lucky Story (USA) 128 – Majborah (IRE) (Entrepreneur 123) [2009 64: p7g^3 p7g p8g^3 p8g^6 8.1g May 4] modest maiden: stays easy 1m: raced mainly on polytrack: tried blinkered. *Miss Amy Weaver* **59**

LUCKY GENERAL (IRE) 2 b.c. (Mar 4) Hawk Wing (USA) 136 – Dress Code (IRE) 83 (Barathea (IRE) 127) [2009 6m^5 6m* 7m^4 7g 6m* 7m^4 6.5m^3 6g* Sep 27] €50,000Y: good-topped colt: fourth foal: half-brother to 7f (in Ireland at 2 yrs)/8.5f (in USA) winner Slaney Rock (by Rock of Gibraltar) and 5f winner (including at 2 yrs) Dress To Impress (by Fasliyev): dam, 2-y-o 5f winner, sister to useful performer up to 7f Rag Top: smart performer: won maiden (by 6 lengths) in June and minor event in August, both at Windsor, and Goffs Million Sprint at the Curragh (quickened smartly to beat stable-companion Full Mandate 1¾ lengths) in September: also third to Swilly Ferry in sales race at Doncaster: at least as effective at 6f as 7f: raced only on good/good to firm ground. *R. Hannon* **111**

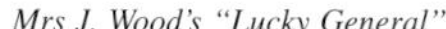

Mrs J. Wood's "Lucky General"

totepool Two-Year-Old Trophy, Redcar—outsiders dominate as Lucky Like pulls clear of Kaptain Kirkup (stars, almost hidden) and Nosedive (right)

LUCKY LEIGH 3 b.f. Piccolo 121 – Solmorin (Fraam 114) [2009 96: 5.1g 5m 6d 5g^{2} 6m 5m p5g 5.2m^{5} p5g* 5g p6m^{6} p5.1g^{5} Dec 4] good-bodied filly: fairly useful handicapper: won at Lingfield in October: best at 5f: acts on polytrack and firm going: tried visored: none too consistent. *M. R. Channon* **82**

LUCKY LIKE (FR) 2 b. or br.c. (Mar 18) Lucky Story (USA) 128 – Land Bound (USA) (Boundary (USA) 117) [2009 5g^{5} 6d^{2} 6g^{4} 5.5g* 7g^{5} 6m* Oct 3] €26,000Y: good-bodied colt: first foal: dam unraced half-sister to Peruvian Grade 2 winner Albret: useful performer: won minor event at Chateaubriant in August and listed totepool Two-Year-Old Trophy at Redcar (beat Kaptain Kirkup by 4 lengths) in October: stays 6f: acts on good to firm going, probably on good to soft: sent to Hong Kong, where renamed Touch Go. *E. J. O'Neill* **109**

LUCKY MELLOR 2 b.c. (Mar 24) Lucky Story (USA) 128 – Lady Natilda 64 (First Trump 118) [2009 5m f5g* 5m^{4} p6g^{5} f5g^{2} 5.3m p5g^{3} p5f^{2} p5.1g^{4} 6g^{3} p5.1g^{3} f5m^{2} f5g* Dec 18] angular colt: third foal: half-brother to Italian 2007 2-y-o 6f winner Velando (by Iron Mask): dam 2-y-o 6f winner: fairly useful performer: won maiden in May and nursery in December, both at Southwell: stays 6f: acts on all-weather: effective with/without blinkers: races prominently. *D. K. Ivory* **83**

LUCKY NUMBERS (IRE) 3 b.c. Key of Luck (USA) 126 – Pure Folly (IRE) 58 (Machiavellian (USA) 123) [2009 87: 6m^{5} 6m^{2} 6.1m^{2} 5.1m 6g^{6} 7m 6m^{6} 6s^{2} 6m 6f^{2} 5m^{6} 6g^{3} 6m^{5} Sep 15] compact colt: fairly useful handicapper: effective at 5f/6f: acts on any going, but has good record on softer than good: tried blinkered. *Paul Green* **90**

LUCKY PUNT 3 ch.g. Auction House (USA) 120 – Sweet Coincidence 69 (Mujahid (USA) 125) [2009 61: 10.2g^{4} f11g* f12g* 12d f12g* f11g^{2} f14g* f11m* Dec 5] workmanlike gelding: much improved on fibresand, winning 5 handicaps at Southwell, in May, June, September, October and December (useful form, beat Dunaskin 5 lengths): just modest form on turf and polytrack: stays 1¾m: races close up. *B. G. Powell* **62 a100**

LUCKY QUAY (IRE) 2 b.g. (Mar 27) Key of Luck (USA) 126 – Lakatoi 82 (Saddlers' Hall (IRE) 126) [2009 p8g Nov 25] 33/1, very backward when behind in maiden at Lingfield: bred to be suited by 1¼m+. *W. R. Swinburn* **–**

LUCKY RAVE 2 b.c. (Feb 14) Lucky Story (USA) 128 – Rave On (ITY) 73 (Barathea (IRE) 127) [2009 6g^{3} 6m^{4} 5.9g^{2} p6g* p7g* a8.5f 8f^{3} Nov 28] £5,500Y: fourth foal: half-brother to 7f winner Hit The Roof (by Auction House): dam, maiden, half-sister to useful Italian performer up to 1¼m Lady Bi: fairly useful performer: won maiden at Wolverhampton in July and nursery at Lingfield (by 5 lengths from Edgewater) in August: left D. Brown after: creditable 2¼ lengths third to Who's Up in Grade 3 Generous Stakes at Hollywood final outing: stays 1m: acts on polytrack and firm going: signs of temperament third start. *P. Eurton, USA* **92**

LUCKY SCORE (IRE) 3 b.f. Lucky Story (USA) 128 – Musical Score 104 (Blushing Flame (USA) 109) [2009 64: 9.9g^{3} 9.9m^{5} p8m^{2} p8.6g^{3} p9.5g^{5} p8f^{5} p7f^{6} Dec 21] good-topped filly: fair maiden handicapper: may prove best up to 1¼m: acts on polytrack, good to firm and good to soft going: in cheekpieces last 2 starts. *Mouse Hamilton-Fairley* **70**

LUCKY TRAVELLER 2 b.g. (Mar 5) Lucky Story (USA) 128 – Bollin Sophie (Efisio 120) [2009 5.9m^{5} 6m^{5} 6m Aug 22] poor form in maidens: gelded after final start. *T. D. Easterby* **44**

LUCKY WINDMILL 2 b.g. (Mar 7) Lucky Story (USA) 128 – Windmill Princess 55 (Gorytus (USA) 132) [2009 6d^{4} 6g Oct 9] tall, unfurnished gelding: modest form in maidens: will be suited by 7f+. *G. A. Swinbank* **57 +**

LUCULLUS 4 b.g. Bertolini (USA) 125 – Calcavella 75 (Pursuit of Love 124) [2009 69: p7g^{4} Apr 8] fair performer, lightly raced: raced at 7f on polytrack and good to soft going. *M. Blanshard* **75**

LUCY BROWN 3 br.f. Compton Place 125 – Harambee (IRE) (Robellino (USA) 127) [2009 –: 7f^{4} 7g^{2} 6g 6m* 6m^{4} 6m^{2} p7m^{6} p7g Nov 11] quite attractive filly: fair handicapper: won at Salisbury in August: stays 7f: acts on good to firm going. *R. Hannon* **79**

LUCY GLITERS 2 ch.f. (May 8) Observatory (USA) 131 – Bombay Sapphire (Be My Chief (USA) 122) [2009 5d^{6} 5d^{6} 6s 5m^{3} Sep 16] £3,000Y: close-coupled filly: seventh foal: half-sister to 3 winners, including 6-y-o Misphire and 8-y-o Mind Alert: dam ran 3 times: poor maiden. *T. P. Tate* **45**

LUCY'S PERFECT 3 ch.f. Systematic 121 – Water Flower 79 (Environment Friend 128) [2009 10.2g 12m^{4} 12.1g 11.7m^{3} 11.7g^{4} 13.1g^{6} 10g* 10g Oct 19] close-coupled filly: third foal: dam 1½m winner: fair performer: won claimer at Windsor in October: stays 1¼m: raced only on good/good to firm ground: blinkered last 2 starts. *B. R. Millman* **65**

LUISANT 6 ch.g. Pivotal 124 – La Legere (USA) (Lit de Justice (USA) 125) [2009 8g^{3} 8m 7.5d^{5} 6v^{3} p6g* p6g* 7g^{6} 6s^{2} p5g^{6} 7s^{3} Nov 5] smart performer: won 2 handicaps at Dundalk in August, beating Miss Gorica 1½ lengths on second occasion: best effort after when neck second to Rayeni in listed race at the Curragh: will prove best at 6f/7f: acts on polytrack and soft going: usually held up. *J. A. Nash, Ireland* **114**

LUISA TETRAZZINI (IRE) 3 b.f. Hawk Wing (USA) 136 – Break of Day (USA) (Favorite Trick (USA) 121) [2009 6d p8.6g^{5} p7g^{5} f7m^{3} p7.1g^{3} p5.1g^{3} f8g^{4} Dec 18] €16,000F: rather leggy filly: second foal: half-sister to useful 6f/7f winner Laddies Poker Two (by Choisir): dam unraced: fair maiden: left K. Ryan £6,000 prior to final start: may prove best at 7f: acts on polytrack: tried in cheekpieces. *John A. Harris* **68**

LUJANO 4 b.g. Lujain (USA) 119 – Latch Key Lady (USA) 48 (Tejano (USA)) [2009 69: f7g 6.9g 8d 8m^{3} 8s p8.6g* 8g* p8.6g p8.6g Nov 9] fair handicapper: won at Wolverhampton and Newcastle in September: stays 8.6f: acts on all-weather and good to firm ground: has raced lazily. *Ollie Pears* **77**

LUJEANIE 3 br.g. Lujain (USA) 119 – Ivory's Joy 109 (Tina's Pet 121) [2009 68: 7m^{5} p6g* p6g^{4} 7g 6m* p6f p6m* Dec 30] good-topped gelding: fairly useful handicapper: won at Kempton in June, Lingfield in August and Kempton in December: best at 6f: acts on all-weather and good to firm going: usually in cheekpieces: held up. *D. K. Ivory* **90**

LUJIANA 4 b.f. Lujain (USA) 119 – Compact Disc (IRE) 48 (Royal Academy (USA) 130) [2009 67: 6d 6m 5m p6g Nov 27] neat filly: handicapper, just poor form in 2009: effective at 5f/6f: acts on all-weather and good to soft going. *M. Brittain* **45**

LUKATARA (USA) 4 b.g. Kayrawan (USA) 91 – Hey Winnie (USA) (Hey Big Spender (USA)) [2009 –: p12g p7g Feb 24] no form: sold £650. *Miss S. West* **–**

LULUTI (IRE) 2 b.f. (Mar 22) Kheleyf (USA) 116 – Amsicora (Cadeaux Genereux 131) [2009 p6m^{6} Jul 15] 4,500F, €45,000Y, 100,000 2-y-o: sixth foal: half-sister to several winners, including 3-y-o Excellerator: dam unraced out of sister to very smart 7f/1m winner Efisio: 6/1 and green, 7¼ lengths sixth to Puff in maiden at Lingfield, soon behind after slow start: likely to do better. *S. A. Callaghan* **55 p**

LUMINOSA 2 ch.f. (Mar 24) Zaha (CAN) 106 – Lightning Blaze 58 (Cosmonaut) [2009 p7.1m Nov 28] fourth foal: sister to 5f (including at 2 yrs) winner Baytown Blaze: dam 2-y-o 5f winner: 66/1, showed little in maiden at Wolverhampton. *D. Donovan* **–**

LUMINOUS GOLD 4 b.f. Fantastic Light (USA) 134 – Nasaieb (IRE) 89 (Fairy King (USA)) [2009 81: 6g 6g* 6m^{4} 6d^{4} 6m^{3} 6g^{3} 5m^{3} 5g Oct 10] rather leggy filly: fair handicapper: won at Yarmouth in May: will prove best at 5f/6f: acts on polytrack and good to firm ground: races prominently. *C. F. Wall* **79**

LUMINOUS STAR (USA) 2 b. or br.g. (Mar 15) Aldebaran (USA) 126 – Best of Memories (USA) (Halo (USA)) [2009 6g^5 6m^6 7m^2 7f* p8.6g^3 p8.6g^5 Oct 3] $125,000Y, resold €45,000Y, 45,000 2-y-o: useful-looking gelding: closely related to 2 winners in USA and half-brother to 3 winners, including fairly useful performer up to 1¼m Jathaab (7f winner at 2 yrs, by Silver Hawk): dam, US 7f/8.5f winner, half-sister to very smart US Grade 1 9f/9.5f winner Memories of Silver: fair performer: won maiden at Brighton in August: stays 8.6f: acts on polytrack and firm going: gelded after final start. *R. M. Beckett* **78**

LUNA LANDING 6 ch.g. Allied Forces (USA) 123 – Macca Luna (IRE) 78 (Kahyasi 130) [2009 83, a–: 16m 14m^4 18m^3 15.8g^6 16.4g^6 15.9m Aug 22] close-coupled gelding: fair handicapper nowadays: effective at 1½m to 2¼m: acts on firm and good to soft going, below form on polytrack: often front runner. *Jedd O'Keeffe* **76**

LUNAR LIMELIGHT 4 b.g. Royal Applause 124 – Moon Magic 62 (Polish Precedent (USA) 131) [2009 –: p10g^4 10d p8.6g^3 p9.5g p10g* p8.6g* Dec 14] smallish, strong gelding: good walker: fair handicapper: improved to win at Lingfield and Wolverhampton in December: stays 1¼m: acts on polytrack. *P. J. Makin* **66**

LUNAR RIVER (FR) 6 b.m. Muhtathir 126 – Moon Gorge 78 (Pursuit of Love 124) [2009 65, a72: p10g^6 p10g* 10d p10g^3 10g^2 9.7m^4 10g^6 p10m^2 p8.6g p9.5m^6 p9.5g^2 p10g^4 p9.5g Nov 14] big mare: fair handicapper, better on all-weather: won at Lingfield in May: effective at 1m to 1½m: acts on polytrack and good to firm going: tried visored: tongue tied: held up/travels well (sometimes finds little). *David Pinder* **67** **a77**

LUNAR ROMANCE 3 b.f. Royal Applause 124 – Witness 71 (Efisio 120) [2009 –: p9.5g f7m Nov 12] close-coupled filly: no solid form. *T. J. Pitt* **–**

LUNAR STORM (IRE) 5 b.g. Machiavellian (USA) 123 – Moonshell (IRE) 117 (Sadler's Wells (USA) 132) [2009 p12.2g f8g^6 9m 10.1g 14.1g 8m Aug 5] modest form in bumpers, little form on Flat: tried in blinkers/cheekpieces. *Mrs R. A. Carr* **–**

LUNAR VICTORY (USA) 2 b.c. (Apr 8) Speightstown (USA) 124 – Lunar Colony (USA) 83 (A P Indy (USA) 131) [2009 8m^3 8g^4 Oct 8] $350,000Y: good sort: third foal: half-brother to winner in USA by Pine Bluff: dam, 1¼m winner, half-sister to smart Irish performer up to 1½m Reform Act: fairly useful form when 1¾ lengths third to Ameer in minor event at Newbury: only fourth to Dancing David in maiden on same course. *J. H. M. Gosden* **87**

LUNATICUS 3 b.f. Lujain (USA) 119 – Steppin Out 63 (First Trump 118) [2009 p6m p7f Dec 21] fifth foal: half-sister to fairly useful 11f to 2m winner Rollin 'N Tumblin (by Zaha): dam 6f winner: last in maidens. *M. J. Attwater* **–**

LUNCES LAD (IRE) 5 gr.g. Xaar 132 – Bridelina (FR) (Linamix (FR) 127) [2009 87§: 6g^6 5f 6m p7m Oct 31] lengthy, good-topped gelding: fair handicapper nowadays: effective at 6f/7f: acts on polytrack, good to firm and good to soft going: sometimes visored: ungenuine, usually hard ride. *G. Brown* **67 §**

LUPITA (IRE) 5 ch.m. Intikhab (USA) 135 – Sarah (IRE) 73 (Hernando (FR) 127) [2009 64: 15.4g 17.2f May 31] modest handicapper at best: little form in 2009: tried in cheekpieces: has joined D. Scott. *B. G. Powell* **–**

LUSCIVIOUS 5 ch.g. Kyllachy 129 – Lloc 79 (Absalom 128) [2009 94: f6s p5.1g p5.1g^3 p6g 5v^2 5g f6g* 5d^2 5d f5g* p6g^6 6v 5m f5g Sep 29] small gelding: fairly useful handicapper, better on all-weather: left A. McCabe, won at Southwell in July and August (made all both times): below form last 3 starts: effective at 5f/6f: acts on all-weather, heavy and good to firm going: usually wears cheekpieces/blinkers. *J. A. Glover* **82** **a94**

LUSH (IRE) 4 b.f. Fasliyev (USA) 120 – Our Hope (Dancing Brave (USA) 140) [2009 78: 12.1g^4 9m 10g 10m^2 p9.5g Sep 18] tall, angular filly: fair maiden handicapper: stays 1½m: acts on polytrack and good to firm ground: tried in cheekpieces: held up: temperament under suspicion. *R. Hannon* **69**

LUSH LASHES 4 b.f. Galileo (IRE) 134 – Dance For Fun 74 (Anabaa (USA) 130) [2009 122: 10.5v^3 8m^6 10d^4 Jun 27] close-coupled, quite good-topped filly: very smart performer in 2008, winning Coronation Stakes at Royal Ascot, Yorkshire Oaks at Newmarket and Matron Stakes at Leopardstown: not same force in 2009, third in Tattersalls Gold Cup and fourth to Dar Re Mi in Pretty Polly Stakes, both at the Curragh, and sixth in Windsor Forest Stakes at Royal Ascot in between: was effective at 1m to 1½m: acted on firm and good to soft going, seemingly not on heavy: often ponied to start/ blanketed for stall entry: sold 1,800,000 gns, to visit Sea The Stars. *J. S. Bolger, Ireland* **110**

LUTHIEN (IRE) 3 b.f. Polish Precedent (USA) 131 – Triplemoon (USA) 77 (Trempolino (USA) 135) [2009 72p: p9.5g^5 9.9f 11.6g 12m^6 14.1g p11m p9.5g^6 8d p9.5g Nov 13] maiden, just modest at 3 yrs: left W. Swinburn after fifth start: should be suited by 1¼m/1½m: best effort on polytrack: in cheekpieces last 4 outings. *A. M. Hales* **63**

LUTINE BELL 2 ch.g. (Apr 14) Starcraft (NZ) 128 – Satin Bell 99 (Midyan (USA) **57 p**
124) [2009 7.1m^5 p7.1g^4 p7g^5 Jul 22] half-brother to several winners, including fairly useful 1m/9f winner Strawberry Leaf (by Unfuwain) and useful 6f (at 2 yrs) to 11f (in Hong Kong) winner Zabaglione (by Zilzal): dam 7f winner: modest form in 3 maidens, still green and best work late final start: type to do better at 1m+. *Sir Mark Prescott*

LUTINE CHARLIE (IRE) 2 b.g. (Apr 11) Kheleyf (USA) 116 – Silvery Halo (USA) **85**
68 (Silver Ghost (USA)) [2009 6s^2 p6g^2 p6g^4 6g 8.3v^5 Nov 4] €10,000F, €23,000Y, £23,000 2-y-o: compact gelding: seventh foal: half-brother to fairly useful 2004 2-y-o 5f winner Percheron (by Perugino) and winner in Italy by Eagle Eyed: dam Irish maiden (stayed 1m): fairly useful maiden: in frame at Doncaster and Kempton (2), below form subsequently: stays 6f: acts on polytrack and soft ground: gelded after final start. *P. Winkworth*

LUTINE LADY 2 b.f. (Apr 3) Exceed And Excel (AUS) 126 – Hillside Girl (IRE) **–**
78 (Tagula (IRE) 116) [2009 5m 5g May 18] £13,500Y: good-topped filly: second foal: half-sister to 3-y-o Arriva La Diva: dam 2-y-o 5f winner: behind in minor event (said to have had breathing problem) and maiden. *P. Winkworth*

LUV U NOO 2 b.f. (Feb 27) Needwood Blade 117 – Lady Suesanne (IRE) 66 (Cape **57**
Cross (IRE) 129) [2009 5m^5 5f^3 5d^5 f6g^5 Oct 27] sturdy filly: first foal: dam 7f/1m winner: modest maiden: trained on debut by K. R. Burke: should stay 6f: acts on firm ground. *A. P. Jarvis*

LYCEANA 4 ch.f. Medicean 128 – Wax Lyrical 94 (Safawan 118) [2009 85: 8m^5 8.3m^5 **83**
12m^2 10.9g 10d Sep 16] rangy filly: fairly useful handicapper: creditable effort in 2009 only when second at Salisbury: stays 1½m: acts on polytrack and good to firm going: sold 14,000 gns, sent to Saudi Arabia. *M. A. Jarvis*

LYDIA'S LEGACY 4 b.f. Bahamian Bounty 116 – Lydia's Look (IRE) 65 (Distant **35**
View (USA) 126) [2009 –: 5m 6m 5.1m Jun 3] close-coupled filly: poor form. *T. J. Etherington*

LYRA'S DAEMON 3 b.f. Singspiel (IRE) 133 – Seven of Nine (IRE) 66 (Alzao (USA) **82**
117) [2009 73: 10.2g* 9g^6 10m p10m^6 p12.2g* p12m^5 p12f Dec 19] lengthy, good-topped filly: fairly useful handicapper: won at Bath in April and Wolverhampton in November: stays 1½m: acts on polytrack, unraced on extremes of going on turf: often forces pace. *W. R. Muir*

LYRICAL INTENT 3 ch.g. Imperial Dancer 123 – Magical Flute 75 (Piccolo 121) **55**
[2009 p7g^5 p8g p8g^4 p7g p8.6m p9.5g p10g p12m p11f^6 p8.6g^4 Dec 19] modest maiden handicapper: stays 11f: raced only on polytrack: often slowly away. *P. Howling*

LYRIC ART (USA) 3 b.f. Red Ransom (USA) – String Quartet (IRE) 109 (Sadler's **65**
Wells (USA) 132) [2009 65: f7g^2 f8g^3 7.1m^4 7m 8m^6 7v* f8g^4 Sep 29] good-topped filly: fair performer: won maiden at Catterick in September: stays 1m: acts on fibresand and heavy ground: tried visored: sold £5,000. *B. Smart*

LYRIC POET (USA) 2 b. or br.c. (Apr 4) Distorted Humor (USA) 117 – Baltic **56**
Nations (USA) (Seattle Slew (USA)) [2009 7g 8.1m^6 Sep 11] strong, deep-girthed colt: very green and only modest form in maidens at Newmarket and Sandown: has left Godolphin. *Saeed bin Suroor*

LYTHAM (IRE) 8 b.g. Spectrum (IRE) 126 – Nousaiyra (IRE) (Be My Guest (USA) **68**
126) [2009 50: p11g* p10g* p11g* p9.5g p12g^3 12g^3 p10g p10g^2 8.3g 10m^3 p12.2g^5 10d p9.5g^4 f11g p9.5g Sep 12] tall gelding: fair handicapper: won at Kempton in January and February (2): effective at 1¼m/1½m: acts on polytrack, firm and soft going: held up. *A. W. Carroll*

LYTTON 4 b.g. Royal Applause 124 – Dora Carrington (IRE) 106 (Sri Pekan (USA) **66**
117) [2009 84d: p5.1m f6g f6g 7m^2 7.5m* p7f 7m Sep 19] well-made gelding: fair performer nowadays: won handicap at Beverley in April: stays 7.5f: acts on polytrack, good to firm and good to soft ground: tried blinkered/in cheekpieces, visored last 5 starts: none too consistent. *R. Ford*

M

MAADRAA (IRE) 4 br.g. Josr Algarhoud (IRE) 118 – Del Deya (IRE) 117 (Caerleon **84**
(USA) 132) [2009 79: 16s 11.6m* 11.6m^6 10.4s^4 Jul 17] angular gelding: fairly useful handicapper: won at Windsor in May: should stay beyond 1½m: acts on polytrack and good to firm ground: tried in cheekpieces. *B. J. Llewellyn*

Investec Diomed Stakes, Epsom—
14/1-shot Mac Love (checked cap) quickens past placed horses Confront (centre) and Deposer (rails)

MAANY (USA) 2 ch.f. (Feb 7) Mr Greeley (USA) 122 – Dixie Card (USA) (Dixieland Band (USA)) [2009 7g Aug 8] $500,000Y: big filly: half-sister to several winners in USA, notably smart Grade 2 9f winner Adonis (by Kris S): dam US 6f (including at 2 yrs) to 8.5f winner, including minor stakes: 10/1 and backward, last in maiden at Newmarket won by Tabassum: type to do better. *M. A. Jarvis* **– p**

MAASHOOQ 2 ch.g. (Feb 13) Observatory (USA) 131 – Chatifa (IRE) 83 (Titus Livius (FR) 115) [2009 p6g 6m^3 Oct 16] smallish, angular gelding: third foal: dam, 1m winner, half-sister to Prix de l'Arc de Triomphe winner Dylan Thomas and Cheveley Park Stakes winner Queen's Logic (dam of 2-y-o Lady of The Desert): much better effort in maidens when 6½ lengths third to Inler at Newmarket, still green: sold 20,000 gns, then gelded and sent to Malaysia. *M. P. Tregoning* **77**

MABAIT 3 b.c. Kyllachy 129 – Czarna Roza (Polish Precedent (USA) 131) [2009 81: 6m* 6m 7g 6g p7.1g* p7.1m* 8.3m* Oct 26] smallish, compact colt: useful handicapper: progressed in 2009, winning at Ripon in June, Wolverhampton (2) in September and Leicester (beat Swift Chap ¾ length) in October: stays 8.3f: acts on polytrack, good to firm and good to soft going. *L. M. Cumani* **99**

MABUYA (UAE) 3 b.g. Halling (USA) 133 – City of Gold (IRE) 91 (Sadler's Wells (USA) 132) [2009 70+: 7g^2 10.2d^2 9.9g^3 9.9f* 10m^2 12g 9g 11m^3 Sep 23] lengthy, useful-looking gelding: fairly useful handicapper: won at Salisbury in June: best around 1¼m: acts on firm and good to soft ground: gelded after final start. *P. J. Makin* **90**

MACADEMY ROYAL (USA) 6 b.g. Royal Academy (USA) 130 – Garden Folly (USA) (Pine Bluff (USA)) [2009 –, a63d: p7g Nov 25] quite good-topped gelding: of little account nowadays: wears tongue tie. *Miss N. A. Lloyd-Beavis* **–**

MACARTHUR 5 b.g. Montjeu (IRE) 137 – Out West (USA) 103 (Gone West (USA)) [2009 125: 9g 12m 12g 12m Sep 27] tall, good-bodied gelding: smart performer nowadays: limited impact at 5 yrs, seventh to Bankable in handicap at Nad Al Sheba on reappearance: ran as if amiss after 6-month absence in Cumberland Lodge Stakes at Ascot final start: better at 1½m/1¾m than shorter, and will probably stay 2m: acts on heavy and good to firm ground: tried tongue tied/blinkered. *M. F. de Kock, South Africa* **114**

MAC DALIA 4 b.f. Namid 128 – Maugwenna 85 (Danehill (USA) 126) [2009 72: f5g a6g 5.5g^6 10.5s a5g a5g^6 Oct 8] fair performer in 2008: little form in 2009, leaving A. McCabe £4,500 after reappearance: usually wore cheekpieces in Britain, tried blinkered in Sweden. *Charlotte Sjogren, Sweden* **–**

MACDILLON 3 b.g. Acclamation 118 – Dilys 84 (Efisio 120) [2009 83: 6m^2 6g 5g^4 6m p6g^6 p5g^5 Nov 1] well-made gelding: useful handicapper: very good efforts in 2009 when in frame: will prove best at 5f/6f: acts on polytrack, good to firm and good to soft going. *W. S. Kittow* **98 a92**

MAC DON (IRE) 5 b.g. Soviet Star (USA) 128 – Sharena (IRE) 78 (Kahyasi 130) [2009 78: f11g Mar 11] maiden: fair at 4 yrs: well held sole start in 2009: effective at 8.5f to 1¼m: acts on heavy and good to firm going: often in cheekpieces/blinkers. *G. J. Smith* **–**

MAC GILLE EOIN 5 b.h. Bertolini (USA) 125 – Peruvian Jade 76 (Petong 126) **105** [2009 105: 6m 6f^6 6m 6g^2 6m^4 6m* 6d^5 6m^2 6m Sep 19] strong horse: useful performer on balance: won handicap at Epsom in July: seemed to run very well when second to Tamagin in listed race at Goodwood penultimate start: blinkered, well below form in Ayr Gold Cup (Handicap) final outing: best at 6f: acts on polytrack and firm going: races prominently. *J. Gallagher*

MACHINATE (USA) 7 b. or br.g. Machiavellian (USA) 123 – Dancing Sea (USA) 80 **56 d** (Storm Cat (USA)) [2009 74: p8.6g^5 p8.6g^4 p8.6g^6 p8.6g p8.6m p7.1g p8.6g^5 p8.6g 7.5m Aug 30] leggy gelding: fair performer in 2008: regressed at 7 yrs: stays 8.6f: acts on polytrack, firm and soft going: tried visored/tongue tied: usually held up. *W. M. Brisbourne*

MACHINE GUN KELLY (IRE) 2 b.g. (Feb 19) Johannesburg (USA) 127 – West **67** Brooklyn (USA) (Gone West (USA)) [2009 6g 6m^3 5m^4 7m 8.3d^6 7d Oct 22] close-coupled gelding: fair maiden: best efforts when in frame: bred to stay 7f+: acts on good to firm going: sold 4,000 gns. *G. L. Moore*

MACHINIST (IRE) 9 br.g. Machiavellian (USA) 123 – Athene (IRE) 83 (Rousillon **98** (USA) 133) [2009 109: 6m 6g 6d* May 16] good-topped gelding: useful handicapper: dropped in weights, won at Thirsk in May: best at 5f/6f: acts on polytrack/dirt, firm and soft going: sometimes slowly away: held up. *D. Nicholls*

MACKINTOSH (IRE) 3 ch.g. Kyllachy 129 – Louhossoa (USA) (Trempolino (USA) **57** 135) [2009 p7g 7v 8g 8g p8g p10.7g p12f^6 p9.5g^3 p9.5g^4 Dec 28] modest maiden handicapper: left G. Lyons in Ireland after sixth start: stays easy 10.7f: acts on polytrack: blinkered last 2 outings. *Pat Morris*

MACKTEN 3 b.g. Makbul 104 – Tender (IRE) 76 (Zieten (USA) 118) [2009 7g^3 7m* **74** p8g May 28] stocky gelding: first foal: dam 5f winner, including at 2 yrs: fair form: won maiden at Lingfield in May: stays 1m: acts on polytrack and good to firm going: gelded after final start. *W. J. Knight*

MAC LOVE 8 b.g. Cape Cross (IRE) 129 – My Lass 91 (Elmaamul (USA) 125) [2009 **120** 110: 8m^4 8.5g* 8m 8m* 8g^4 9.9m* Sep 12] strong, compact gelding: very smart performer: better than ever in 2009, winning Investec Diomed Stakes at Epsom (by ¾ length from Confront) in June, totesport.com Sovereign Stakes at Salisbury (by 1½ lengths from same rival) in August and Select Racing UK On Sky 432 Stakes at Goodwood (by length from Stotsfold) in September: respectable fifth (promoted) behind disqualified Delegator in Celebration Mile at Goodwood on penultimate start: stays easy 1¼m: acts on polytrack and firm going, not on softer than good: edgy, free-going sort (has been early to post): held up. *Stef Liddiard*

totesport.com Sovereign Stakes, Salisbury—
odds-on Confront (left) again has to play second fiddle to Mac Love, who is sent off at 25/1 this time

MACORVILLE (USA) 6 b.g. Diesis 133 – Desert Jewel (USA) (Caerleon (USA) 132) [2009 10.4g 16g 14v Sep 5] leggy, workmanlike gelding: has a markedly round action: useful performer in 2007: unraced at 5 yrs, and no impact in 2009. *G. M. Moore* –

MACROY 2 b.g. (Apr 28) Makbul 104 – Royal Orchid (IRE) 74 (Shalford (IRE) 124§) [2009 5g^6 5.1m 6.1m^4 Sep 30] smallish, sturdy gelding: maiden: fourth at Nottingham: gelded after: likely to be best at 5f/6f. *B. R. Millman* 50

MAC'S POWER (IRE) 3 b.g. Exceed And Excel (AUS) 126 – Easter Girl (Efisio 120) [2009 69p: p5g^4 5.1d p5g^4 p6g^5 p6g* p6g^3 p7g^3 p7g^6 p7g^2 p8m* p8m^4 Sep 24] good-quartered gelding: fairly useful handicapper: progressed to win at Kempton in June and September: stays 1m: acts on polytrack: tongue tied after reappearance: gelded following final outing. *P. J. O'Gorman* 92

MACTRAC 2 b.g. (Feb 4) Marju (IRE) 127 – Zanna (FR) (Soviet Star (USA) 128) [2009 5m p6g^6 6m p10m p7g Dec 31] maiden: form only when eighth in claimer at Kempton fourth start. *R. Hannon* 53

MAC WOLF 3 b.c. Polish Precedent (USA) 131 – Herminoe 83 (Rainbow Quest (USA) 134) [2009 10m 9.7m^4 8m 10g^6 p12m Sep 16] tall, lengthy colt: modest maiden: stays 1¼m: acts on good to firm going: sold 1,200 gns, sent to Hungary. *M. G. Quinlan* 59

MAD ABOUT YOU (IRE) 4 b.f. Indian Ridge 123 – Irresistible Jewel (IRE) 115 (Danehill (USA) 126) [2009 117: 8s^3 7s* 7v^2 8g^4 7s^3 9.5g 8g^3 Oct 18] lengthy filly: smart performer: won Bruce Betting Newbridge Gladness Stakes at the Curragh in April by 2½ lengths from Dohasa: just respectable efforts after, 1¾ lengths second to Emily Blake in Athasi Stakes on same course next time: effective at 7f to 1¼m: acts on soft and good to firm going, probably on heavy: usually blinkered: travels strongly, sometimes finds little. *D. K. Weld, Ireland* 117

MADAME BOOT (FR) 2 b.f. (Feb 1) Diktat 126 – Esprit Libre (Daylami (IRE) 138) [2009 6f 7s Sep 3] €36,000F, 26,000Y: strong, attractive filly: second foal: dam, ran once in France, half-sister to smart French 9f/1¼m performer Di Moi Oui: modest form when down the field in maidens at Windsor (backward and green) and Salisbury (soon poorly placed): bred to stay 1m. *P. J. Makin* 54 +

MADAME EXCELERATE 2 b.f. (Apr 29) Pursuit of Love 124 – Skovshoved (IRE) (Danetime (IRE) 121) [2009 7m^5 7g p7.1g^2 Oct 30] second foal: dam unraced out of sister to Derby third Blues Traveller: easily best effort in maidens when head second to Hudoo at Wolverhampton: should stay 1m. *W. M. Brisbourne* 69

MADAME GUILLOTINE (USA) 3 gr. or ro.f. Proud Citizen (USA) 122 – Paris Gem (USA) (Rubiano (USA)) [2009 8m p8g p7g^5 Oct 8] $35,000Y, 45,000 2-y-o: seventh foal: half-sister to several winners in USA: dam unraced: modest maiden: best effort on debut: sold 1,800 gns. *R. M. Beckett* 62

MADAME JOURDAIN (IRE) 3 b.f. Beckett (IRE) 116 – Cladantom (IRE) 70 (High Estate 127) [2009 66: 5m 5m 5.9d 5s^6 6d^5 5g 8.3v Nov 4] leggy filly: just poor form at 3 yrs, leaving N. Wilson after second start, A. Berry after fifth: effective at 5f/6f: acts on good to firm and good to soft going: sometimes blinkered: not straightforward. *S. A. Harris* 46

MADAME MCMANUS 3 ch.f. Needwood Blade 117 – Madame Jones (IRE) 79 (Lycius (USA) 124) [2009 p8m p7.1g p8.6g Dec 14] fourth foal: half-sister to 6f/7f winner Put It On The Card (by Bertolini): dam 6f to 9.4f winner: well held in maidens/seller: tried visored. *P. D. Evans* –

MADAME RIO (IRE) 4 b.f. Captain Rio 122 – Glenviews Purchase (IRE) 77 (Desert Story (IRE) 115) [2009 –: 6m Jun 25] lengthy filly: little form since 2007. *E. J. Cooper* –

MADAME ROULIN (IRE) 2 b.f. (Jan 24) Xaar 132 – Cradle Rock (IRE) (Desert Sun 120) [2009 p8g^4 8d p8.6g^5 Nov 6] €11,000F, 17,000Y: second foal: dam unraced sister to useful Irish 1m/9.5f winner Fuerta Ventura and half-sister to useful 6f/7f performer Sir Xaar (by Xaar): modest form first 2 starts in maidens (pulled hard in latter). *M. L. W. Bell* 64

MADAME TROP VITE (IRE) 3 b.f. Invincible Spirit (IRE) 121 – Gladstone Street (IRE) (Waajib 121) [2009 102: 6g 5g^6 5m 6d 6m 6m p5g Oct 23] tall, good-topped filly: useful performer: not discredited second/third starts, in listed race at Chantilly (sixth to Delvita) and Sprint Stakes at Sandown (seventh behind Ialysos), but below form after: best at 5f: acts on firm and good to soft going: tried blinkered: sold €190,000. *K. A. Ryan* 102

MADAM ISSHE 2 b.f. (Apr 26) Ishiguru (USA) 114 – Lucky Dip 68 (Tirol 127) [2009 6.1v 5.7g^5 5.7g 5.7g^3 5.1g^4 Sep 7] £6,000Y: half-sister to several winners, including 5-y-o 55

Halsion Chancer and useful 2003 2-y-o 5f winner Fortunately (by Forzando), later successful in USA: dam 5f winner: modest maiden: stays 5.7f. *M. S. Saunders*

MADAMLILY (IRE) 3 b.f. Refuse To Bend (IRE) 128 – Rainbow Dream (Rainbow Quest (USA) 134) [2009 81p: 10.3m 12s 12d⁴ 12m⁴ 12v 12d² p12.2g² 14m⁶ Sep 27] attractive filly: fair handicapper: stays 1½m: acts on polytrack, soft and good to firm going. *J. J. Quinn* **76**

MADAM MACIE (IRE) 2 ch.f. (Mar 3) Bertolini (USA) 125 – Dictatrice (FR) (Anabaa (USA) 130) [2009 7g* 7v⁵ Oct 24] €4,000Y: third foal: half-sister to fairly useful Irish 1m winner Dianella (by Gold Away) and 1m winner in Denmark by Xaar: dam French 1m winner: 66/1, won maiden at Catterick by 3¼ lengths from Huntingfortreasure, making all: only fifth in listed race at Newbury 7 days later: remains open to improvement. *J. Hetherton* **80 p**

MADAM PRESIDENT 4 b.f. Royal Applause 124 – White House 84 (Pursuit of Love 124) [2009 74: p10g* 10m p10m 11.5m⁵ 12s Oct 6] sturdy, useful-looking filly: fair handicapper: won at Kempton in April: should stay 1½m: acts on polytrack and good to firm ground: tried tongue tied. *W. R. Swinburn* **76**

MADAM RUBY (IRE) 2 ch.f. (Mar 8) Observatory (USA) 131 – Azur (IRE) 76 (Brief Truce (USA) 126) [2009 8.1d⁶ 7d 8g⁶ Oct 21] €12,000Y: third foal: dam, 7f (at 2 yrs) to 12.6f winner, half-sister to useful performer up to 1¾m Bryony Brind: modest form in maidens: should stay beyond 1m. *A. King* **60**

MADAM'X 3 b.f. Xaar 132 – Bonne Etoile 94 (Diesis 133) [2009 51: 9.8g⁴ 12.1g⁴ 16.1g⁶ Sep 30] lengthy filly: modest maiden: stays 1½m: raced only on polytrack and good/good to soft ground. *Mrs A. Duffield* **51**

MADDY 4 b.f. Daggers Drawn (USA) 114 – Summer Lightning (IRE) 81 (Tamure (IRE) 125) [2009 62: p8.6g p12g⁶ p10g⁴ 9.8m³ f11g 8.3g³ 10m³ 10m³ 10d⁶ 8f 10.1s⁴ 8g Aug 5] lengthy, angular filly: modest performer: stays easy 1½m: acts on polytrack, soft and good to firm ground: usually wears cheekpieces. *George Baker* **57**

MADE TO RANSOM 4 b.g. Red Ransom (USA) – Maid For The Hills 101 (Indian Ridge 123) [2009 10.2g* 9.9m May 25] well-made gelding: useful performer, very lightly raced: missed 2008: won maiden at Chepstow on belated return in May by 5 lengths: ran as if amiss in listed race at Goodwood later same month: stayed 1¼m: raced on good/good to firm going: retired. *J. H. M. Gosden* **101**

MADHAAQ (IRE) 2 b.f. (May 10) Medicean 128 – Winsa (USA) 80 (Riverman (USA) 131) [2009 7g⁵ Oct 31] useful-looking filly: seventh foal: closely related to fairly useful 1½m winner Majhud (by Machiavellian) and half-sister to 3 winners, including 2003 2-y-o 7f/7.5f winner Mutahayya (by Peintre Celebre) and 1¼m winner Elmaleeha (by Galileo), both useful: dam, 1½m winner, sister to high-class miler Bahri: 16/1 and green, encouraging 4¾ lengths fifth to Field Day in maiden at Newmarket: will be suited by 1m+: sure to do better. *J. L. Dunlop* **70 p**

MADHAL 3 b.g. First Trump 118 – Jane Grey 64 (Tragic Role (USA)) [2009 6f³ 8.1g 8f p7m⁵ p6g⁶ p7g p7.1g Dec 17] modest maiden: may prove best at 6f/7f: acts on polytrack and firm going. *Matthew Salaman* **58**

MADISON BELLE 3 ch.f. Bahamian Bounty 116 – Indian Flag (IRE) 39 (Indian Ridge 123) [2009 66§: p8.6g³ f7s* f6g* f6g² f7d* f6g³ f6g² f6d Dec 29] leggy filly: fair performer: won claimers in January and February (2), all at Southwell: left K. R. Burke prior to final start: stays 7f: best form on fibresand: has looked temperamental. *J. R. Weymes* **74**

MADISON PARK (IRE) 3 b.c. Montjeu (IRE) 137 – Crystal Gaze (IRE) (Rainbow Quest (USA) 134) [2009 10m 10m p12g⁴ p11g Aug 5] good-topped colt: first foal: dam unraced sister to useful 1¼m/1½m winner and smart hurdler Desert Quest: fair maiden: stays 1½m: blinkered/visored and tongue tied after debut: not straightforward: sold 3,500 gns. *H. R. A. Cecil* **71**

MADJ'S BABY 2 b.f. (Feb 8) Footstepsinthesand 120 – Madamoiselle Jones 76 (Emperor Jones (USA) 119) [2009 6m 7g 6m Aug 21] 12,000Y: close-coupled, unfurnished filly: first foal: dam, 1m winner, half-sister to smart performer up to 1¼m Penkenna Princess: signs of ability in maidens: bred to be suited by 1m. *H. S. Howe* **–**

MADMAN (FR) 5 b.g. Kaldou Star 114 – Shirlauges (FR) (Port Lyautey (FR) 115) [2009 p9.5g Oct 10] regressive hurdler: 100/1, no promise in maiden at Wolverhampton. *C. N. Kellett* **–**

MAD MILLIE (IRE) 2 b.f. (Feb 26) Pyrus (USA) 106 – Tipsy Lady 64 (Intikhab (USA) 135) [2009 6g^6 7d^2 6g^2 6m 5v 7.5m f5g Sep 29] sparely-made filly: first foal: dam, maiden (stayed 9f), out of half-sister to high-class performer up to 1½m In The Groove: fair maiden: easily best efforts when runner-up: stays 7f: acts on good to soft going. *J. Hetherton* **68**

MAD RUSH (USA) 5 b.g. Lemon Drop Kid (USA) 131 – Revonda (IRE) (Sadler's Wells (USA) 132) [2009 118: 12m* 14d^5 Jun 27] big, rangy gelding: smart performer: won listed race at Goodwood in June by nose from Halicarnassus, dictating: ran as if amiss when tailed off in Curragh Cup later same month, and not seen after (suffered tendon injury): should stay 2m: acts on soft and good to firm going. *L. M. Cumani* **113**

MAE CIGAN (FR) 6 gr.g. Medaaly 114 – Concert (Polar Falcon (USA) 126) [2009 75: p16g 12g^2 11.9g^5 p13.9g 11.7g Oct 21] angular gelding: fair handicapper: stays 2m: acts on polytrack, heavy and good to firm going: tried visored: held up. *M. Blanshard* **66**

MAFAAZ 3 ch.c. Medicean 128 – Complimentary Pass 80 (Danehill (USA) 126) [2009 101p: p9g* p9f Apr 11] useful form: blinkered, further improvement when winning valuable minor event at Kempton in March by neck from Spring of Fame: stiffish task when eighth to General Quarters in Blue Grass Stakes at Keeneland next time, then joined K. McLaughlin in USA: stays 9f: acts on polytrack and good to firm going. *J. H. M. Gosden* **104**

MAFAHEEM 7 b.g. Mujahid (USA) 125 – Legend of Aragon 67 (Aragon 118) [2009 80: p6g* p6g^6 f6g p6g^4 p6g^4 6s p6g 6s p6m Aug 21] strong, well-made gelding: fair performer: won seller at Great Leighs in January: largely below form after: races mainly at 6f nowadays: acts on polytrack, heavy and good to firm going: sometimes blinkered/in cheekpieces: waited with. *A. B. Haynes* **70 d**

MAFASINA (USA) 4 b.f. Orientate (USA) 127 – Money Madam (USA) (A P Indy (USA) 131) [2009 69d: f8g^3 f7g^3 May 18] fair handicapper: stays 1m: acts on all-weather: sent to France. *B. Smart* **65**

MAFEKING (UAE) 5 b.g. Jade Robbery (USA) 121 – Melisendra (FR) (Highest Honor (FR) 124) [2009 94: p12g^6 10m 10m p11g^2 10d^2 p10g^2 p10m p10m^2 p10m^2 Dec 16] useful-looking gelding: fairly useful handicapper, better on all-weather: probably best at 1¼m: acts on polytrack and good to soft ground: often forces pace: consistent (reportedly bled when pulled up seventh start). *M. R. Hoad* **89 a93**

MAGADAN (IRE) 4 b.c. High Chaparral (IRE) 132 – Molasses (FR) (Machiavellian (USA) 123) [2009 117: 12g* 12g* 12m^3 12m^5 12g Oct 4] well-made colt: smart performer: made successful return from injury in listed race at Longchamp (by 1½ lengths from Fully Funded) in April and followed up in Prix d'Hedouville there (by 2 lengths from Coastal Path, who gave 7 lb) in May: ran at least creditably afterwards when ¾-length third to Scintillo in Grand Prix de Chantilly, 3¼ lengths fifth to Spanish Moon in Grand Prix de Saint-Cloud and keeping-on ninth to Sea The Stars in Prix de l'Arc de Triomphe at Longchamp: suited by 1½m: acts on good to firm ground, won on heavy on debut: held up. *E. Lellouche, France* **118**

MAGALING (IRE) 3 ch.c. Medicean 128 – Fling 89 (Pursuit of Love 124) [2009 91p: 7d* 8g 8m Jun 18] angular, useful-looking colt: good mover: fairly useful handicapper: won at Doncaster in May: should stay 1m: yet to race on extremes of going: sold 13,000 gns. *L. M. Cumani* **94**

MAGENTA STRAIT 2 b.f. (Mar 28) Sampower Star 118 – Vermilion Creek 68 (Makbul 104) [2009 p6g p6g* Dec 14] first foal: dam 1m to 1¼m winner, including 8.5f at 2 yrs: better effort when winning seller at Wolverhampton in December by head from Bubbly Bellini, finishing strongly: should stay 7f. *R. Hollinshead* **61 +**

MAGGIE KATE 4 b.f. Auction House (USA) 120 – Perecapa (IRE) 44 (Archway (IRE) 115) [2009 71: p6g p6g 5.1m 5.1m 5g 7s 6m 5.3g^5 5.3d* 5.1d* Sep 4] good-topped filly: modest handicapper: won at Brighton in August and Chepstow in September: effective at 5f to 7f: acts on polytrack, good to firm and good to soft going: often in cheekpieces/blinkers: races prominently. *R. Ingram* **61**

MAGGIE LOU (IRE) 3 b.f. Red Ransom (USA) – Triomphale (USA) (Nureyev (USA) 131) [2009 83: p5g 6g^4 7.1v^4 7.1m^5 7d 6s Aug 26] good-topped filly: fairly useful handicapper: should stay 1m: acts on heavy going, probably good to firm: tried visored. *K. A. Ryan* **80**

MAGGIE MAGGIE MAY (IRE) 7 b.m. Spectrum (IRE) 126 – Liberty Song (IRE) (Last Tycoon 131) [2009 6m May 26] lightly raced and no form since 2004. *P. C. Haslam* **–**

MAGICAL DESTINY (IRE) 3 b.g. Exceed And Excel (AUS) 126 – Magic Lady (IRE) (Bigstone (IRE) 126) [2009 62: f8g^4 Mar 17] modest maiden: raced only at 7f/1m on fibresand. *B. Smart* **60**

MAGICAL MACEY (USA) 2 ch.g. (Mar 15) Rossini (USA) 118 – Spring's Glory (USA) (Honour And Glory (USA) 122) [2009 5m 5v^2 5m* 5d Oct 28] $6,000F: second foal: dam US 6f winner: best effort when winning maiden at Haydock in September by 1½ lengths from Confessional: well held in nursery: raced only at 5f: acts on good to firm ground: blinkered last 3 starts. *T. D. Barron* **81**

MAGICAL MIMI 8 b.m. Magic Ring (IRE) 115 – Naval Dispatch (Slip Anchor 136) [2009 p6g p6g p9.5g p8.6m Feb 25] no longer of any account. *K. G. Wingrove* **–**

MAGICAL MOLECULE 2 b.g. (Feb 20) Whittingham (IRE) 104 – Fontaine House (Pyramus (USA) 78) [2009 5m^6 Jun 12] 33/1, tailed-off last in maiden at Sandown (reportedly lame). *G. D. Blake* **–**

MAGICALMYSTERYTOUR (IRE) 6 b.g. Sadler's Wells (USA) 132 – Jude 53 (Darshaan 133) [2009 109: 13.3d^5 11.6m^2 14m^3 14m 14v 12g 12d^6 12s Nov 7] strong, good-bodied gelding: useful handicapper: creditable efforts when short-head second to Warringah at Windsor and close third to Hits Only Vic at York: below form after: stays 1¾m: acts on heavy and good to firm going: patiently ridden. *W. J. Musson* **106**

MAGICAL SONG 4 ch.g. Forzando 122 – Classical Song (IRE) 69 (Fayruz 116) [2009 59: f7d f7g^2 f7g^4 f8d^3 f8g^3 f7g f7g^6 7m^4 6m^2 6m^2 Jul 11] rather leggy, lengthy gelding: modest handicapper: left R. Curtis after third start: effective at 6f to 1m: acts on fibresand, good to firm and good to soft going: often blinkered/in cheekpieces: races prominently. *J. Balding* **62**

MAGICAL SPEEDFIT (IRE) 4 ch.g. Bold Fact (USA) 116 – Magical Peace (IRE) 80 (Magical Wonder (USA) 125) [2009 82§: 5.3g* 5.7g 5.3m 5m^4 5g 5m 6g^3 6f 5m^2 5.2g^4 5f^2 5.2m^6 5g^3 5.3d* 5.1g^3 Oct 28] sturdy gelding: fairly useful handicapper: won at Brighton in April and October: effective at 5f/6f: acts on polytrack, firm and soft going: tried blinkered: often gets behind: temperamental. *G. G. Margarson* **82 §**

MAGIC AMIGO 8 ch.g. Zilzal (USA) 137 – Emaline (FR) 105 (Empery (USA) 128) [2009 57: p11g^3 p10g p9.5g^6 10.1g Jul 20] tall, leggy gelding: modest handicapper: stays easy 1½m: acts on all-weather, heavy and good to firm ground: usually wears headgear: sometimes races freely. *J. R. Jenkins* **50**

MAGIC CAT 3 b.g. One Cool Cat (USA) 123 – Magic Music (IRE) 82 (Magic Ring (IRE) 115) [2009 106: 6m 6g 6m 6g Oct 10] tall, good-topped gelding: useful performer at 2 yrs: no form in 2009: best form at 5f: acts on any going: tried in cheekpieces. *A. P. Jarvis* **–**

MAGIC DOLL (USA) 2 ch.f. (Mar 3) Elusive Quality (USA) – Meniatarra (USA) 68 (Zilzal (USA) 137) [2009 7g^3 p7g* Sep 21] tall filly: better effort in maidens when winning at Kempton readily by 1½ lengths from Faithful One: would probably have stayed 1m: dead. *Saeed bin Suroor* **84**

MAGIC ECHO 5 b.m. Wizard King 122 – Sunday News'n'echo (USA) 78 (Trempolino (USA) 135) [2009 96: 10.3m 9.8m 8d^2 10.3d^4 10.4g 10s^6 7.2s^5 8g^5 10g Oct 23] compact mare: fairly useful handicapper: stays 1¼m: acts on fibresand, best on good ground or softer on turf: tactically versatile. *M. Dods* **89**

MAGIC FOOTSTEPS 2 b.c. (Feb 9) Footstepsinthesand 120 – Dayville (USA) 86 (Dayjur (USA) 137) [2009 6g 6m^2 Jun 4] strong, lengthy colt: better effort in maidens when second to Whispered Times at Hamilton: dead. *Jedd O'Keeffe* **69**

MAGIC GLADE 10 b.g. Magic Ring (IRE) 115 – Ash Glade (Nashwan (USA) 135) [2009 86d: p6g^6 p5g^6 p5g p5.1g p5g^6 f5g 5m Jun 27] compact gelding: just modest handicapper nowadays: effective at 5f/6f: acts on all-weather, firm and soft going: tried in cheekpieces/blinkers: has bled. *Peter Grayson* **53**

MAGIC HAZE 3 b.g. Makbul 104 – Turn Back 73 (Pivotal 124) [2009 54: 7m^6 9.9g 8m Sep 23] good-topped gelding: modest maiden: bred to stay 1m: acts on good to firm going. *Miss S. E. Hall* **63**

MAGICIAN'S CAPE (IRE) 2 b.c. (Feb 1) Montjeu (IRE) 137 – Seven Magicians (USA) 106 (Silver Hawk (USA) 123) [2009 7d* p8g^3 Oct 14] first foal: dam, 1¼m winner, closely related to smart performer up to 1½m Ocean Silk, out of sister to Divine Proportions: promising when winning maiden at Lingfield (by ¾ length from Swift Return) in September: creditable last of 3 in minor event at Lingfield won by Fareej, **84 p**

again not knocked about: should be suited by 1¼m: open to further improvement. *Sir Michael Stoute*

MAGIC KAHYASI (IRE) 6 b.g. Kahyasi 130 – Magic Play (IRE) (Deploy 131) **53** [2009 p16g p16g Feb 11] won minor events at Chatillon and Montlucon-Neris in 2007 for T. Fourre/G. Doyen in France (unraced in 2008): just modest form in Britain: probably stays 15f: raced mainly on good ground or softer and polytrack: tried blinkered/in cheek-pieces. *G. L. Moore*

MAGIC LANTERN 2 ch.f. (Mar 7) Halling (USA) 133 – Papabile (USA) 104 **77** (Chief's Crown (USA)) [2009 6m p7g^{2} 7m^{2} 8g 6.5m p6m^{5} Oct 12] 25,000Y: angular filly: third foal: half-sister to 1¼m winner Papality (by Giant's Causeway): dam, 1m winner, sister to high-class performer up to 1¼m Grand Lodge: fair maiden: easily best efforts when runner-up: should stay 1m: sold 25,000 gns, sent to USA. *R. Hannon*

MAGIC MILLIE (IRE) 2 b. or br.f. (Apr 16) Marju (IRE) 127 – Fille de La Terre **53** (IRE) (Namaqualand (USA)) [2009 7g 6m 7m 7.5m Sep 16] €3,800Y: compact filly: third foal: dam ran once in Ireland: regressive form in maidens. *J. Hetherton*

MAGIC PLACE 2 b.c. (Feb 21) Compton Place 125 – Michelle Shift (Night Shift **–** (USA)) [2009 6s Nov 7] 11/1, tailed off in maiden at Doncaster (said to have finished lame). *R. Hannon*

MAGIC QUEEN (IRE) 3 b.f. Aptitude (USA) 128 – Second Wind (USA) (Hennessy **52** (USA) 122) [2009 7m^{5} p7.1g^{6} p7g p9.5g p7m Nov 4] €45,000Y: first foal: dam, US 8.5f winner, out of half-sister to US Grade 1 1½m winner Sligo Bay and smart stayer Wolfe Tone: modest maiden. *A. P. Jarvis*

MAGIC RUSH 7 b.g. Almaty (IRE) 113§ – Magic Legs 54 (Reprimand 122) [2009 79: **76** p8g^{6} p7g^{2} 10m^{2} 8f^{5} p8g^{3} Aug 17] good-topped gelding: fair handicapper, on long losing run: stays 1¼m: acts on polytrack, soft and good to firm going. *Norma Twomey*

MAGIC SPIRIT 2 ch.f. (Feb 21) Kirkwall 118 – Flaming Spirt 78§ (Blushing Flame **60** (USA) 109) [2009 p8m Dec 4] second foal: half-sister to 3-y-o First Spirit: dam unreliable 1m (at 2 yrs)/9f winner: 66/1 and green, eighth in maiden at Lingfield won by Fairy Flight. *J. S. Moore*

MAGIC WARRIOR 9 b.g. Magic Ring (IRE) 115 – Clarista (USA) 67 (Riva Ridge **49** (USA)) [2009 53, a69: p10g^{3} p8g^{5} p9.5g p8g p9.5g^{2} p10g 10.9f 10m^{6} 9m^{5} 8m Aug 21] **a62** strong, compact gelding: modest handicapper on all-weather, poor on turf: stays easy 11f: acts on polytrack and firm ground: held up: tried blinkered: often said to have bled. *J. C. Fox*

MAGISTRATE (IRE) 4 b. or gr.g. Nayef (USA) 129 – Alabastrine 56 (Green Desert **65** (USA) 127) [2009 p9.5g p12g^{5} Nov 13] modest form in bumpers: better effort in maidens on Flat when seventh on debut: will prove best at 1¼m+. *Andrew Turnell*

MAGNERS HILL (IRE) 5 b.g. Desert Sun 120 – Tropicana (IRE) (Imperial Frontier **61** (USA) 112) [2009 70: p8.6g^{3} p12s^{6} p10.7f 10v^{6} 10v 10m p9.5g p12.2g Dec 12] fair **a69** maiden on all-weather, modest on turf: stays 1½m: acts on polytrack and heavy going. *G. Keane, Ireland*

MAGNETIC FORCE (IRE) 2 gr.g. (Feb 19) Verglas (IRE) 118 – Upperville (IRE) **72 p** 79 (Selkirk (USA) 129) [2009 7.1g^{6} 8m^{3} p8g^{2} Oct 8] €160,000Y: good-topped gelding: second foal: half-brother to Irish 3-y-o Blue Ridge Lane: dam, Irish 1½m winner, half-sister to smart Irish performer up to 1¾m Mutakarrim: maiden: placed at Goodwood and Kempton (head second to Art Excellence, strong at finish): subsequently gelded: will be suited by 1¼m+: type to progress further. *Sir Michael Stoute*

MAGNETO (IRE) 2 b.g. (Feb 10) Fasliyev (USA) 120 – Shashana (IRE) 64 (King's **56** Best (USA) 132) [2009 f5g f5g 6m^{6} 5.1m 6g^{4} p6g p7f^{4} p8.6g^{3} p7.1g 8.3g^{6} p8m Nov 4] modest maiden: stays 8.6f: acts on polytrack. *E. J. Creighton*

MAGNIFICENCE 2 b. or gr.f. (Mar 12) Sadler's Wells (USA) 132 – Doctor's Glory **58** (USA) 91 (Elmaamul (USA) 125) [2009 7d^{6} 7s 6m^{5} p7g^{5} 8g^{5} Oct 20] compact filly: half-sister to several winners, including 4-y-o Prescription, 7-y-o Cupid's Glory and useful 7f (at 2 yrs) to 1¼m winner Courting (by Pursuit of Love): dam, 5f (at 2 yrs)/6f winner, half-sister to useful 1½m to 2m winner On Call: modest maiden: will stay 1¼m+: acts on polytrack and soft going: sold 29,000 gns, sent to Norway. *Sir Michael Stoute*

MAGNIFICO (FR) 8 b.g. Solid Illusion (USA) 117 – Born For Run (FR) (Pharly (FR) **–** 130) [2009 p9.5g f16g Apr 21] lightly-raced maiden on Flat: fairly useful hurdler, successful twice in 2009/10, joining P. D. Evans in between. *Mrs K. Waldron*

MAGNITUDE 4 ch.g. Pivotal 124 – Miswaki Belle (USA) 73 (Miswaki (USA) 124) **76**
[2009 85: p8g^5 p8g p8g^4 10.2g 10m 7g^3 8g^5 8d^4 9s 8.3m 7f^4 p12m Dec 9] sturdy gelding: fair performer: claimed from G. L. Moore £6,000 fourth outing: stays 1m: acts on firm and good to soft going: tried in blinkers/cheekpieces. *M. E. Rimmer*

MAGNUS THRAX (USA) 2 b.c. (Feb 21) Roman Ruler (USA) 122 – Wild Catseye **85**
(USA) (Forest Wildcat (USA) 120) [2009 6m 6.1g* 6m 7m^6 p6g^4 Oct 26] $62,000Y, resold 45,000Y: sturdy colt: second foal: half-brother to winner in USA by Came Home: dam US 5f/6f winner, including at 2 yrs: fairly useful performer: won maiden at Chepstow in August: creditable efforts last 2 starts: stays 7f: acts on polytrack and good to firm going. *R. Hannon*

MAGROOM 5 b.g. Compton Place 125 – Fudge (Polar Falcon (USA) 126) [2009 79: **74**
8m 8.1g^6 8f^2 8.3g^6 7f^6 8m^2 9m* 10.2m 8.1d^2 8.1m* 8m^2 8.3g^4 8g^4 p8.6g^4 Oct 30] leggy, lengthy gelding: fair handicapper: won at Newbury (apprentice event) in August and Chepstow in September: stays 9f: acts on polytrack, firm and good to soft going: has worn cheekpieces/visor: held up: consistent. *R. J. Hodges*

MAHADEE (IRE) 4 b. or br.g. Cape Cross (IRE) 129 – Rafiya 89 (Halling (USA) 133) **83**
[2009 96: p8.6g* p8g^4 p7g p8.6g^4 p10g p8g* p8g^3 8m 8g 8m Sep 12] tall, quite attractive **a108**
gelding: useful performer on all-weather, fairly useful on turf: further progress in 2009, winning minor event at Wolverhampton in January and handicap at Kempton (beat Checklow 1¼ lengths) in April: not disgraced when tenth (second home far side) in Hunt Cup (Handicap) at Royal Ascot on eighth start: stays 1¼m: acts on all-weather and good to firm going: blinkered. *C. E. Brittain*

MAHIKI 2 ch.f. (Feb 1) Compton Place 125 – Sound of Sleat (Primo Dominie 121) **66**
[2009 5f^5 5.2m^6 5g^5 f5g* f5g* p5g 5m p5.1g^6 Oct 3] £12,000Y: lengthy, unfurnished filly: fifth foal: half-sister to 9f winner in Italy by Dr Fong: dam unraced half-sister to smart French miler Soft Currency: fair performer: best efforts when winning seller and nursery at Southwell in July: raced only at 5f: acts on fibresand: sold 4,000 gns. *S. A. Callaghan*

MAHJONG GIRL 2 ch.f. (Feb 21) Kirkwall 118 – Gulchina (USA) 72 (Gulch (USA)) **66**
[2009 7g 7.1g 8.1d^4 Aug 31] first foal: dam, maiden (stayed 7f), out of half-sister to smart Irish/US middle-distance performer Phantom Breeze: best effort in maidens when fourth to Leitzu at Chepstow (pulled hard): may prove best short of 1m: sold 2,000 gns. *R. M. Beckett*

MAHLAK (IRE) 2 ch.f. (Mar 5) Pastoral Pursuits 127 – Bint Al Hammour (IRE) **–**
(Grand Lodge (USA) 125) [2009 7g Aug 28] 40,000Y: tall filly: first foal: dam, little form, half-sister to smart Irish 1¼m winner Muakaad: 33/1, very green and well held in maiden at Newmarket. *C. E. Brittain*

MAIDANNI (USA) 7 b. or br.g. Private Terms (USA) – Carley's Birthday (USA) **–**
(Marfa (USA)) [2009 p9.5g p13g f8g Mar 12] rangy gelding: one-time fair performer: very lightly raced, and last all starts in 2009: tried in blinkers/tongue tie. *J. R. Gask*

MAID IN HEAVEN (IRE) 2 b.f. (Mar 14) Clodovil (IRE) 116 – Serious Delight **64 p**
(Lomond (USA) 128) [2009 p7g^5 Nov 11] €39,000Y: seventh foal: half-sister to several winners, including useful 6f (in Ireland at 2 yrs)/7f winner Delphie Queen (by Desert Sun): dam unraced half-sister to dams of high-class sprinter Pipalong and 5-y-o Gris de Gris: 40/1 and green, promising 6¼ lengths fifth to Next Move in maiden at Kempton, finishing strongly: will improve. *W. R. Swinburn*

MAID OF STONE (IRE) 3 ch.f. Rock of Gibraltar (IRE) 133 – Gold Flair 93 (Tap On **53**
Wood 130) [2009 10m^4 p11g 8d 12g 7g Aug 28] €18,000Y: tall filly: half-sister to several winners, including 7f winner Atylan Boy (by Efisio) and fairly useful Irish 2004 2-y-o 1m winner Conquistadores (by Bachir): dam maiden sister to very smart performer up to 1½m Nisnas: modest maiden: sold 800 gns, sent to Italy. *D. R. C. Elsworth*

MAIDTORUN (IRE) 2 ch.f. (Apr 10) Rakti 130 – Bayletta (IRE) 41 (Woodborough **63**
(USA) 112) [2009 5m^5 5m* 6d 5m Jun 10] 11,000Y: unfurnished filly: third foal: half-sister to fairly useful 2008 2-y-o 6f/7f winner Lucky Redback (by Redback) and 4-y-o Rub of The Relic: dam, Irish maiden, half-sister to 2000 Guineas runner-up Lucky Lindy: modest performer: won maiden at Beverley in May: disappointing after: should stay 6f+: acts on good to firm going: sold £2,200. *R. A. Fahey*

MAIGH EO (IRE) 3 b.g. Elusive City (USA) 117 – Princess Magdalena 76 (Penne- **64**
kamp (USA) 130) [2009 –: p5g^4 6g 5f p6g 5f^6 Aug 8] close-coupled gelding: modest maiden: form only on reappearance. *Pat Morris*

Timeform Jury Stakes (John of Gaunt), Haydock—
favourite Main Aim successfully steps up from handicap company; Beacon Lodge takes second

MAIN AIM 4 b.c. Oasis Dream 129 – Orford Ness 107 (Selkirk (USA) 129) [2009 105: 6d* 7.1g* 8m⁴ 6m² 7g 6d 7m⁴ Oct 17] good-topped, attractive colt: very smart performer: much improved in 2009, winning handicap at Newbury (by 7 lengths) and Timeform Jury Stakes (John of Gaunt) at Haydock (beat Beacon Lodge 2 lengths), both in May: ran well after when 2½ lengths fourth to Paco Boy in Queen Anne Stakes at Royal Ascot and 1¼ lengths second to Fleeting Spirit in July Cup at Newmarket (hampered by winner inside final 1f): seemingly amiss next 2 starts (reportedly treated for ulcers after second occasion) then not discredited when fourth to Arabian Gleam in Challenge Stakes at Newmarket final start: effective at 6f to 1m: acts on soft and good to firm ground: edgy type, tends to sweat. *Sir Michael Stoute* **123**

MAIN SPRING 2 b.f. (Mar 16) Pivotal 124 – Fairy Godmother 113 (Fairy King (USA)) [2009 p8g Nov 14] sixth foal: half-sister to 3-y-o Four Winds and 4-y-o Kingdom of Fife: dam, 1¼m winner, half-sister to very smart middle-distance stayer Blueprint: 8/1, worked up in stall when down the field in maiden at Lingfield: should improve. *Sir Michael Stoute* **– p**

MAINSTAY 3 b.f. Elmaamul (USA) 125 – Felucca 94 (Green Desert (USA) 127) [2009 p8m² Nov 19] sister to smart 1m (at 2 yrs) to 10.4f winner Lateen Sails and half-sister to 2 winners abroad by Zafonic: dam, 2-y-o 6f winner, half-sister to very smart French performer up to 1½m Radevore: 11/8 favourite, encouraging 4 lengths second to Penzena in maiden at Kempton: sold 10,000 gns 2 weeks later: bred to stay 1¼m. *J. H. M. Gosden* **76**

MAISON BRILLET (IRE) 2 b.g. (Apr 15) Pyrus (USA) 106 – Stormchaser (IRE) (Titus Livius (FR) 115) [2009 5m³ 6g* 6d³ 6m⁴ 8m 6m⁶ Sep 18] £4,500Y: fourth foal: half-brother to 1m winner in Italy by Mull of Kintyre: dam unraced out of sister to top-class miler Northjet: fair performer: won maiden at Ayr in May, best effort: should stay beyond 6f. *J. Howard Johnson* **72**

MAISON DIEU 6 br. or b.g. King Charlemagne (USA) 120 – Shining Desert (IRE) 82 (Green Desert (USA) 127) [2009 65: f6g 7m² 7.1m³ 5.9m³ 6m³ 6d⁴ 6m* 6m⁴ 7.6m⁴ 7d 7.1m⁵ 6m² 6m⁶ p6g Oct 16] useful-looking gelding: fair handicapper: won at Ayr in June: stays 7f: acts on polytrack and firm going: tried in cheekpieces/blinkers: patiently ridden: sold £4,500. *E. J. Alston* **67**

MAISON D'OR 3 b.g. Auction House (USA) 120 – Figura 87 (Rudimentary (USA) 118) [2009 57: p8g p10g⁶ p8g p8g 8.5g 9m 12.1g Aug 13] rather leggy gelding: modest maiden: stays easy 1¼m: acts on polytrack. *R. Ingram* **54**

MAIWAND 2 b.f. (Apr 1) Reset (AUS) 124 – Iris May 87 (Brief Truce (USA) 126) [2009 p6g 7d 7d 7.5m 7m⁶ 7.5m 6g f6g Oct 27] sturdy filly: seventh foal: half-sister to several winners, including 7-y-o Joseph Henry: dam 5f winner (including at 2 yrs): no form: left Sir Mark Prescott after third outing: tried blinkered. *Mrs R. A. Carr* **–**

MAJAJI 5 b.m. Bal Harbour 113 – Petaz (Petong 126) [2009 7g May 5] fifth foal: dam well beaten: 33/1, very slowly away and never on terms in maiden at Catterick. *P. Salmon* **–**

MAJD ALJAZEERA 3 b.g. King's Best (USA) 132 – Tegwen (USA) 79 (Nijinsky (CAN) 138) [2009 54: p10g^4 11.9f^6 p12g p8g p10g Sep 9] modest maiden: stays 1¼m: acts on polytrack: often tongue tied: sold £1,500. *D. M. Simcock* **54**

MAJEHAR 7 b.g. Marju (IRE) 127 – Joonayh 81 (Warning 136) [2009 –, a69: p10g* p10g f11g* 10.2g 12d^6 p11g^6 p12m^2 f12m* a12g^4 Dec 18] fair performer, better on all-weather: won handicaps at Lingfield in January and Southwell in March and claimer at Southwell (claimed from A. Newcombe £8,000) in November: stays 1½m: acts on all-weather, good to firm and good to soft going: consistent. *E. J. O'Neill* **65 a76**

MAJESTIC CHEER 5 b.g. Royal Applause 124 – Muwasim (USA) (Meadowlake (USA)) [2009 69d: f6s^5 f7g^6 f6g^6 6m^5 7g Jun 27] lengthy, rather leggy gelding: modest performer: effective at 5f to 8.5f: acts on all-weather and firm going, probably on heavy: often wears headgear, formerly tongue tied: ungenuine. *John A. Harris* **50 §**

MAJESTIC CHIEF 5 b.g. Xaar 132 – Grand Splendour 79 (Shirley Heights 130) [2009 12.4s 12.4s May 22] heavy-topped gelding: maiden handicapper: just modest at 5 yrs: stays 1¼m: acts on good to firm going: tried in cheekpieces/tongue tie. *Miss Lucinda V. Russell* **50**

MAJESTIC LADY (IRE) 3 b.f. Royal Applause 124 – Kiris World 107 (Distant Relative 128) [2009 63: 6g^5 6d^5 5m^2 6g^6 p5.1g^4 f6g^3 p5.1g^4 6s Nov 13] lengthy, angular filly: modest maiden: left B. Hills 3,000 gns after seventh start: should prove best at 5f/6f: acts on fibresand, soft and good to firm going. *Mlle C. Comte, France* **63**

Mr K. Abdulla's "Main Aim"

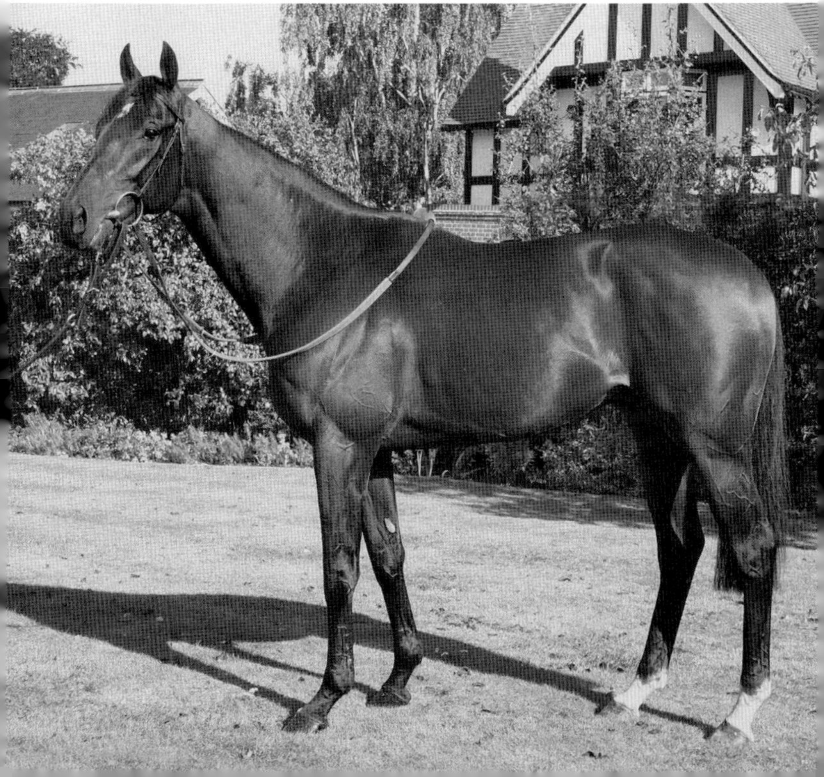

MAJOR CADEAUX 5 ch.h. Cadeaux Genereux 131 – Maine Lobster (USA) 71 (Woodman (USA) 126) [2009 121: 8d^5 6g^3 8d^5 Oct 11] big, strong, angular horse: very smart performer at best, winner of 3 pattern races: best effort in 2009 when fifth to Virtual in Lockinge Stakes at Newbury (final start for R. Hannon): well below form after in minor event at Hamilton and Premio Vittorio di Capua at Milan (behind Gladiatorus): took strong hold, but stayed 1m: acted on soft and good to firm going: to stand at Bearstone Stud, Shropshire, fee £3,500. *R. A. Fahey* **113**

MAJOR EAZY (IRE) 4 b.g. Fasliyev (USA) 120 – Castilian Queen (USA) 82 (Diesis 133) [2009 102: 6m^5 May 30] well-made gelding: useful performer: shaped well only start in 2009 when fifth to High Standing in handicap at Goodwood: was best at 5f/6f: acted on soft and good to firm going: raced prominently: dead. *B. J. Meehan* **101**

MAJOR LAWRENCE (IRE) 3 b.c. Fasliyev (USA) 120 – Ziffany 68 (Taufan (USA) 119) [2009 6g^2 6m^3 p7g^4 p7g p6m^4 p8.6g^3 Dec 28] €310,000F: rather leggy colt: fifth foal: half-brother to smart 5f/6f winner Jessica's Dream (by Desert Style) and very smart 7f/1m winner Majors Cast (by Victory Note): dam 2-y-o 7f seller winner: fair maiden: stays 8.6f: acts on polytrack: tried tongue tied. *J. Noseda* **78 §**

MAJOR MAGPIE (IRE) 7 b.g. Rossini (USA) 118 – Picnic Basket (Pharly (FR) 130) [2009 94: 8.1m 8.5m 8d 7.9m 7.9g 6.9d 8g 8s Aug 26] close-coupled gelding: fairly useful handicapper in 2008: just fair at best at 7 yrs: stays 1¼m: acts on firm and soft going: tried in cheekpieces: held up. *M. Dods* **75**

MAJOR MAXIMUS 2 br.c. (Feb 26) Domedriver (IRE) 128 – Madame Maxine (USA) 89 (Dayjur (USA) 137) [2009 p7.1g^3 p7.1g^4 p6g^4 f6f^5 p8m^3 Dec 30] fourth foal: half-brother to 1m winner Hasty Retreat (by King's Best) and winner in Greece by Cadeaux Genereux: dam, 5f and (including at 2 yrs) 6f winner, half-sister to smart French miler Panis: fair maiden: stays 7f. *George Baker* **70**

MAJOR MONTY (IRE) 2 b.g. (Apr 4) Orpen (USA) 116 – Mari-Ela (IRE) 60 (River Falls 113) [2009 p6g f5m^5 Dec 5] better effort in maidens when fifth to R Woody at Southwell, outpaced. *Tom Dascombe* **61**

MAJOR PHIL (IRE) 3 b.c. Captain Rio 122 – Choral Sundown 81 (Night Shift (USA)) [2009 82p: p6g^5 7.1v 7.1f p7.1g* 8m^5 Jul 16] strong colt: fairly useful handicapper: won at Wolverhampton in June: stays 1m: acts on polytrack and good to firm going. *L. M. Cumani* **77 a82**

MAJOR PROMISE 4 b.g. Lomitas 129 – Distant Diva 86 (Distant Relative 128) [2009 63: p13.9g^5 f14m p12.2g^2 Dec 12] leggy gelding: modest maiden handicapper: stays 1¾m: acts on polytrack and good to soft going: has looked none too genuine. *Jane Chapple-Hyam* **63**

MAJOR VALUE 3 b.c. Tobougg (IRE) 125 – Surrealist (ITY) (Night Shift (USA)) [2009 –: 8.3g^5 8.1m 10s^3 10.2m 10g Oct 19] useful-looking colt: poor maiden: raced only at 1m/1¼m: tried blinkered/in cheekpieces: sold 5,000 gns, sent to Greece. *C. G. Cox* **49**

MAJURO (IRE) 5 b.g. Danetime (IRE) 121 – First Fling (IRE) 63 (Last Tycoon 131) [2009 96: f8s^2 f7g^2 p8g^2 p7g^2 p6g^3 8m^3 8s 8m^4 7m May 9] good-topped gelding: useful handicapper, better on all-weather: placed first 6 starts in 2009, running well when nose second to Capricorn Run at Lingfield and close third to Thebes at Wolverhampton fourth/fifth outings: best of far-side group when third to Manassas in Spring Mile at Doncaster next time: effective at 6f to 1m: acts on all-weather, firm and good to soft going: consistent: gelded after final start. *K. A. Ryan* **101 a106**

MAKAAMEN 3 ch.g. Selkirk (USA) 129 – Bird Key (Cadeaux Genereux 131) [2009 86p: 7m* 7s* 7.1v 7g Oct 10] big, well-made gelding: useful performer: won maiden at Doncaster in March and handicap at Newbury (beat Wannabe King 1¼ lengths) in April: below form after: raced only at 7f: acts on soft and good to firm going. *B. W. Hills* **99**

MAKAAM (USA) 3 ch.c. Giant's Causeway (USA) 132 – Elaflaak (USA) 104 (Gulch (USA)) [2009 p7g^2 p7g^2 6s 7.1g^4 p8g p7m Sep 30] tall colt: third foal: half-brother to winner in USA by Swain: dam, 2-y-o 5f/6f winner, half-sister to US Grade 3 8.5f winner Indescribable: fairly useful maiden: runner-up first 2 starts, well below form after: stays easy 7f: acts on polytrack: sold 9,000 gns, sent to Hungary. *M. P. Tregoning* **84**

MAKARTHY 2 b.c. (Apr 27) Makbul 104 – Royal Shepley (Royal Applause 124) [2009 p6g Dec 14] 66/1, slowly away and never dangerous in seller at Wolverhampton. *H. A. McWilliams* **–**

MAKAYKLA 3 b.f. Makbul 104 – Primum Tempus 49 (Primo Dominie 121) [2009 66p: 6m 5g^5 Jul 20] big filly: maiden: will prove best at 5f/6f. *E. J. Alston* **43**

MAKBULLET 2 gr.g. (Feb 15) Makbul 104 – Gold Belt (IRE) 61 (Bellypha 130) [2009 5f⁶ 5m³ 6g³ 5f⁴ 6d² 6g* 6m Aug 20] £31,000Y: tall, good-topped gelding: brother to useful sprinter Goldeva and half-brother to several winners, including useful 9.4f to 1½m winner Royal Cavalier (by Prince of Birds): dam 1m winner: fairly useful performer: best effort when winning maiden at Ripon in August by 3¾ lengths from Mad Millie: unfavourably drawn final start: better at 6f than 5f: acts on good to soft going: races up with pace. *J. Howard Johnson* **83**

MAKE AMENDS (IRE) 4 b.f. Indian Ridge 123 – Chill Seeking (USA) 102 (Theatrical 128) [2009 72: p12g p9.5g p8.6m³ p12g p10g² 10.2m⁶ 13.1d⁴ 12m⁵ 10.2m² 10.9g⁶ 9.7m* 8m⁵ 8m³ 11m p9.5g p9.5g* Dec 28] fair handicapper: won at Folkestone in July and Wolverhampton in December: may prove best around 1¼m: acts on polytrack, heavy and good to firm going. *R. J. Hodges* **69**

MAKE MY DREAM 6 b.g. My Best Valentine 122 – Sandkatoon (IRE) (Archway (IRE) 115) [2009 82: 5.3g⁴ 5.7g⁴ 5f² 5g 5f 6m³ 6g 6m⁵ 5m* 5m⁶ p5g³ 5.1g² p6g² p5m⁶ p6f Dec 13] close-coupled gelding: fair handicapper: won at Sandown in September: effective at 5f/6f: acts on polytrack, firm and soft going: tried blinkered/visored: tactically versatile: consistent. *J. Gallagher* **79**

MAKHAALEB (IRE) 3 b.g. Haafhd 129 – Summerhill Parkes 105 (Zafonic (USA) 130) [2009 76: p10g⁴ 8d³ 8m⁴ 8.1f³ 10v Aug 4] lengthy gelding: fair maiden: left B. Hills 10,500 gns prior to final start: seems to stay 1¼m: acts on polytrack and good to soft going, probably on firm. *P. Stafford, Ireland* **76**

MAKING MUSIC 6 b.m. Makbul 104 – Crofters Ceilidh 101 (Scottish Reel 123) [2009 61: 5m 5m⁶ 5m Jun 29] lengthy, good-topped mare: just poor handicapper nowadays: best at 5f/6f: acts on firm going: tried in cheekpieces/tongue tie, usually blinkered. *T. D. Easterby* **46**

MAKSHOOF (IRE) 5 b.g. Kyllachy 129 – Tres Sage (Reprimand 122) [2009 91: 6g³ 6f⁵ 6v 6g⁵ f6g 6m 6g 7.5g f7m p6g⁴ p6m³ p6m Dec 16] good-topped gelding: has a fluent action: fair performer: below form after reappearance, leaving K. Ryan after second start: best at 6f: acts on all weather, firm and soft going: often in cheekpieces/blinkers: one to be wary of. *I. W. McInnes* **74 d**

MAL AND DAVE (IRE) 2 b.g. (Apr 24) Redback 116 – Louvolite (IRE) 81 (Fayruz 116) [2009 5m⁴ 6g⁶ 5m⁵ 5m² 5g² 5m* Jun 29] sturdy gelding: fair performer: won maiden at Musselburgh by short head from Mercers Row: may prove best at 5f: raced only on good going or firmer: sold 17,000 gns, sent to Sweden. *D. Nicholls* **69**

MALAPROPISM 9 ch.g. Compton Place 125 – Mrs Malaprop 83 (Night Shift (USA)) [2009 90: 5m 5.3m 5m 5.3m³ 5.2s 5.3f 5m⁴ 5m 5f 5.1m p6g³ p6f² p6g* p6g p6g p5m p6f p5g Dec 31] well-made gelding: just modest handicapper nowadays: won apprentice event at Lingfield in October: stays easy 6f: acts on dirt/polytrack, firm and soft going: tried visored: not straightforward (weak finisher nowadays). *M. R. Channon* **61 §**

MALCHEEK (IRE) 7 br.g. Lend A Hand 124 – Russland (GER) (Surumu (GER)) [2009 88d: 7m* 7f⁴ 6m 7g 6m 7g 6g 7d² p7.1g⁴ 7.1m* 7g 7s p7.1g Nov 27] tall, lengthy gelding: fairly useful handicapper: won at Catterick in April and Musselburgh in September: effective at 6f/7f: acts on polytrack and firm ground: races prominently: unreliable. *T. D. Easterby* **88 §**

MALDON PROM (IRE) 2 br.g. (Apr 28) Kheleyf (USA) 116 – Misty Peak (IRE) 83 (Sri Pekan (USA) 117) [2009 6g⁶ 6g p6g³ p5.1g 6s f5m² p6g* Dec 17] sixth foal: closely related to 3-y-o Grissom and half-brother to 3 winners, including fairly useful 5f/6f winner (including at 2 yrs) Katie Boo (by Namid): dam, Irish maiden (probably stayed 7f), half-sister to useful Irish 1½m winner Golly Gosh: fair performer: won nursery at Wolverhampton in December by 1½ lengths from Sabatini: raced only at 5f/6f: acts on all-weather: tried tongue tied/visored. *C. A. Dwyer* **73**

MALGURU 5 b.g. Ishiguru (USA) 114 – Vento Del Oreno (FR) 67 (Lando (GER) 128) [2009 65: 8g Aug 11] deep-girthed gelding: fair handicapper: well held only start at 5 yrs: stays 1¼m: acts on firm ground: in cheekpieces/blinkers nowadays: races prominently. *J. A. McShane* **–**

MALIBU BAY (USA) 3 b.c. El Prado (IRE) 119 – Favorite Funtime (USA) 118 (Seeking The Gold (USA)) [2009 89p: 10m³ 10.5g 10m 10s 8g Jul 29] tall, deep-girthed colt: useful performer: best efforts in 2009 when 2 lengths third to Above Average in Classic Trial at Sandown and seventh to She's Our Mark in Meld Stakes at Leopardstown on fourth outing: ran in Group 1s otherwise, used as pacemaker on at least one occasion: will stay 1½m: acts on soft and good to firm ground. *A. P. O'Brien, Ireland* **98**

MALINSA BLUE (IRE) 7 b.m. Desert Style (IRE) 121 – Talina's Law (IRE) 83 (Law **61**
Society (USA) 130) [2009 66: 9.9m 7.5m^5 9.3m 8.3m^5 7.9m^6 Jun 15] workmanlike mare: modest handicapper: stays 1¼m: acts on polytrack and firm going: often blinkered/in cheekpieces: races prominently. *B. Ellison*

MALLOREY 3 ch.g. Medicean 128 – In Luck 72 (In The Wings 128) [2009 p7g 8v^4 7d **68**
p10.7f 11d^3 9.5s^4 p11g p12f Dec 21] fair maiden handicapper: left T. Stack in Ireland after sixth start: gelded prior to final outing: should stay 1½m: acts on heavy ground: usually tongue tied. *A. M. Hales*

MALT EMPRESS (IRE) 4 b.f. Second Empire (IRE) 124 – Sunset Malt (IRE) (Red **–**
Sunset 120) [2009 46: p12g Jan 22] maiden: well held sole 4-y-o start: stays 1m: acts on polytrack. *B. W. Duke*

MALT OR MASH (USA) 5 gr.h. Black Minnaloushe (USA) 123 – Southern Tradition **85**
(USA) (Family Doctor (USA)) [2009 114: 11.9m 10g 11m* 10.4d^5 12m^4 14.1s^6 14.6g f12m^6 Nov 11] big, lengthy horse: one-time smart performer, only fairly useful nowadays: won claimer at Newbury in August: stays 1½m: acts on polytrack and good to firm going. *R. Hannon*

MAMBO SPIRIT (IRE) 5 b.g. Invincible Spirit (IRE) 121 – Mambodorga (USA) **77**
(Kingmambo (USA) 125) [2009 90: 5f^5 5m^5 5m^5 5g^4 5.2g^4 5d p6g^4 p5m Dec 9] tall, good-topped gelding: fair handicapper nowadays: left J. Given 17,000 gns after sixth start: best at 5f/6f: acts on polytrack, firm and soft going: tried blinkered: sometimes slowly away. *Stef Liddiard*

MAMBO SUN 6 b.g. Superior Premium 122 – The Manx Touch (IRE) 70 (Petardia **73**
113) [2009 71: f8s* f8g^4 p9.5g^3 f11g^3 Feb 20] leggy gelding: fair handicapper: won at Southwell in January: effective at 1m to easy 11f: acts on all-weather and firm going: tried in blinkers/cheekpieces. *R. Curtis*

MAMLAKATI (IRE) 3 b.f. Invincible Spirit (IRE) 121 – Elba (IRE) (Ela-Mana-Mou **75**
132) [2009 87: 7m^4 6g 7.1m^5 7g 6f 5g^6 5g^4 5.1d* 5m 6m* 6.1d Oct 15] lengthy, useful-looking filly: fair performer: won seller at Chepstow in August and handicap at Brighton in September: should prove best at 5f/6f: acts on good to firm and good to soft going: often races freely/finds little. *R. Hannon*

MAMLOOK (IRE) 5 br.g. Key of Luck (USA) 126 – Cradle Brief (IRE) (Brief Truce **101**
(USA) 126) [2009 97: 18m^2 Oct 17] good-topped gelding: useful handicapper, lightly raced on Flat: placed in Cesarewitch at Newmarket for second year running when 5 lengths second of 32 to Darley Sun: stays 2½m: acts on firm and good to soft going: useful hurdler. *D. E. Pipe*

MANANA MANANA 3 b.g. Tobougg (IRE) 125 – Midnight Allure 85 (Aragon 118) **65**
[2009 65: p8g 6g^3 7.1m f6g^5 Dec 27] fair maiden: left S. Parr prior to final outing: stays 7f: acts on fibresand: tried blinkered. *J. Balding*

MANARAH (USA) 3 ch.f. Giant's Causeway (USA) 132 – Ishtak 90 (Nashwan (USA) **51**
135) [2009 10m 12m May 15] deep-girthed filly: third foal: half-sister to winner in Hungary by Kingmambo: dam, 1½m winner, half-sister to smart Irish performer up to 1½m Mona Lisa (by Giant's Causeway): modest form at best in maidens. *J. H. M. Gosden*

MANASSAS (IRE) 4 b.g. Cape Cross (IRE) 129 – Monnavanna (IRE) 109 (Machia- **106**
vellian (USA) 123) [2009 92: 8m* 8s 8.3m 8m 8m* Sep 12] leggy gelding: useful handicapper, lightly raced: won at Doncaster in March (Spring Mile, beat Extraterrestrial by ½ length) and September (by ½ length from Balcarce Nov): stays 1m: acts on good to firm ground, probably on good to soft. *B. J. Meehan*

MANCHESTERMAVERICK (USA) 4 ch.g. Van Nistelrooy (USA) 108 – Lydia **65**
Louise (USA) (Southern Halo (USA)) [2009 68: p9.5g p7g^3 p7.1g^4 7m^2 6m 7m 7f* 8f p7.1g Dec 28] strong gelding: fair performer: won claimer at Brighton (left H. Morrison £4,000) in August: stays easy 8.6f: acts on polytrack and firm ground: usually visored/tongue tied in 2009: has reportedly bled. *Dr J. R. J. Naylor*

MANDALAY KING (IRE) 4 b.g. King's Best (USA) 132 – Mahamuni (IRE) **79**
(Sadler's Wells (USA) 132) [2009 70: 7m^5 6m* 7.1m 5.9m 6.9g^5 5m^6 5m 6g^2 6g* 6g^2 5d^6 6v Sep 4] smallish, close-coupled gelding: fair handicapper: won at Catterick (apprentices) in April and York in July: best at 5f/6f: acts on firm and soft going: usually held up. *Mrs Marjorie Fife*

MANDARIN EXPRESS 2 ch.g. (Mar 11) Dubai Destination (USA) 127 – Hsi Wang **54**
Mu (IRE) 61 (Dr Fong (USA) 128) [2009 7s 6g 6m^5 p8g 8m Sep 17] small gelding: modest maiden: should be suited by 7f+: acts on soft and good to firm going: sold £900. *B. J. Meehan*

MANDARIN SPIRIT (IRE) 9 b.g. Primo Dominie 121 – Lithe Spirit (IRE) 74 (Dancing Dissident (USA) 119) [2009 80: 8m p8.6g 5g* 7.1m 5m p5.1g^{5} 7.2g 5d^{2} p6g Dec 12] compact gelding: fair handicapper: won at Hamilton in September: best at 5f/6f: acts on all-weather, firm and soft ground: usually wears headgear: front runner. *Miss L. A. Perratt* **78**

MANDELIEU (IRE) 4 b.g. Acclamation 118 – Notley Park 71 (Wolfhound (USA) 126) [2009 73: f5g p5.1g 6m 5.1d 5f^{4} 5m^{6} 5.9g 6f^{4} 6d^{4} 5d Jul 22] good-topped gelding: modest performer nowadays: free-going sort, raced only at 5f/6f: acts on firm and good to soft going: tried blinkered. *Ollie Pears* **54**

MANDHOOMA 3 b.f. Oasis Dream 129 – Shatarah 79 (Gulch (USA)) [2009 48: p6g^{2} 6s 6m* 5.7m p6g f6g Dec 18] modest handicapper: won at Brighton in August: raced only around 6f: acts on polytrack and good to firm ground. *P. W. Hiatt* **60**

MANDRAKE (IRE) 2 b.c. (Mar 31) Bertolini (USA) 125 – Aquaba (USA) (Damascus (USA)) [2009 5m May 25] 3/1 and very green, well beaten in maiden at Carlisle: sold 6,500 gns. *M. Johnston* **–**

MANDURAH (IRE) 5 b.g. Tagula (IRE) 116 – Fearfully Grand (Grand Lodge (USA) 125) [2009 79: p5.1g^{4} 5m 5m* 5g 5.1g 5m* 5m* 5m 5d 5g 5m^{5} 5g 5g^{4} Oct 19] strong, sturdy gelding: fairly useful handicapper: won at Thirsk in May, Haydock in June and Ascot in July: left D. Nicholls after tenth start: has won at 6f, best at 5f: acts on polytrack and good to firm ground: races prominently. *B. P. J. Baugh* **90**

MANERE BAY 4 b.f. Olden Times 121 – Madurai 71 (Chilibang 120) [2009 70: 7d^{5} 7.1m^{3} 8d^{3} 7.1g^{2} 8.3g Oct 19] angular filly: fair maiden: stays 8.3f: acts on soft and good to firm going: sold 9,000 gns, sent to Saudi Arabia. *J. L. Dunlop* **73**

MANGANO 5 b.g. Mujadil (USA) 119 – Secret Dance (Sadler's Wells (USA) 132) [2009 49: 7.1m 7.2g 7.1m^{5} Aug 7] sturdy gelding: poor at 4 yrs: little form in 2009: stays 1m: acts on fibresand and any turf going: held up. *A. Berry* **–**

MANGHAM (IRE) 4 b.g. Montjeu (IRE) 137 – Lovisa (USA) 55 (Gone West (USA)) [2009 103: 8m 8m 8d 8m f8g p8g Sep 21] big, strong gelding: useful handicapper at best: well held after second outing at 4 yrs: best around 1m: acts on soft and good to firm going: tongue tied once: front runner. *D. H. Brown* **93 d**

MANGO MUSIC 6 ch.m. Distant Music (USA) 126 – Eurolink Sundance 85 (Night Shift (USA)) [2009 93, a62: p6g^{3} 5m^{6} 6m^{6} 6m^{2} 6g* 6m 6g 5m 5m 6g^{2} f6g Dec 8] angular mare: fairly useful performer on turf, fair on all-weather: won handicap at Haydock in June: effective at 5f/6f: acts on all-weather and any turf going: races prominently. *M. Quinn* **84** **a68**

MANHATTAN FOX (USA) 2 ch.c. (Mar 23) Elusive Quality (USA) – Safeen (USA) (Storm Cat (USA)) [2009 7m 8d^{2} 8m* 7m 7m Oct 17] deep-girthed colt: fourth foal: dam, unraced half-sister to smart performer up to 11.5f Revere, out of Yorkshire Oaks and Prix Vermeille winner Bint Pasha: fairly useful performer: won maiden at Goodwood in September: stiff tasks in pattern events at Newmarket after, good seventh to Sir Parky in Somerville Tattersall Stakes first occasion: stays 1m: acts on good to firm and good to soft going: sent to USA. *B. J. Meehan* **89**

MANHATTAN SUNRISE (USA) 3 ch.f. Hold That Tiger (USA) 117 – Sellsey (USA) (Pulpit (USA) 117) [2009 57: f7g Jun 2] modest maiden at best: raced only on all-weather. *Paul Mason* **–**

MANIFEST 3 b.c. Rainbow Quest (USA) 134 – Modena (USA) (Roberto (USA) 131) [2009 10g^{2} 12g* 14m^{3} Oct 1] rangy colt: half-brother to numerous winners, notably high-class 7f (at 2 yrs) to 1¼m (Eclipse) winner Elmaamul (by Diesis) and very smart 7f (at 2 yrs, when also won Fillies' Mile) to 1½m (Oaks) winner Reams of Verse (by Nureyev): dam unraced half-sister to smart 7f/1m performer Zaizafon, herself dam of Zafonic: useful form: built on promising debut when winning maiden at Newmarket in August by 19 lengths: again odds on, creditable 2¼ lengths third of 5 to Akmal in listed race there final start: stays 1¾m: remains a smart prospect. *H. R. A. Cecil* **108 p**

MANIGHAR (FR) 3 gr.g. Linamix (FR) 127 – Mintly Fresh (USA) (Rubiano (USA)) [2009 12g* 12g* 12d* 12d* 15m* 15g^{2} 15g* 15.5d^{3} Oct 25] third foal: brother to useful French 1¼m/1½m (Prix de Royaumont) winner Minatlya and half-brother to useful French 6f (at 2 yrs)/6.5f winner Minted (by Clodovil): dam US 6f/6.5f winner: smart performer: progressed really well, winning maiden and minor event at Lyon Parilly in May, minor event at Saint-Cloud and listed race at Nantes in June, listed race at Deauville in August and Qatar Prix Chaudenay at Longchamp (beat Los Cristianos ½ length, despite flashing tail) in October: placed on other starts, length second to Wajir in Prix de **119**

Lutece at Longchamp and good 4½ lengths third to Ask in Prix Royal-Oak at Longchamp, staying on: stays 15.5f: acts on good to firm and good to soft ground: reportedly sold privately, and has joined L. Cumani. *A. de Royer Dupre, France*

MAN IN THE MIRROR (IRE) 2 b.g. (Feb 11) Captain Rio 122 – Shyshiyra (IRE) (Kahyasi 130) [2009 p7g f8g 8.1d 7d⁵ f8f⁶ Dec 12] modest maiden: stays 7f: acts on good to soft going: tried visored. *P. L. Gilligan* **54**

MANNELLO 6 b.m. Mamalik (USA) 115 – Isle of Sodor 63 (Cyrano de Bergerac 120) [2009 61: p6g³ 6d 6m⁶ 7f May 12] leggy mare: modest performer: best at 7f: acts on polytrack, soft and good to firm going: usually in headgear. *S. W. Hall* **55**

MANNLICHEN 3 ch.g. Selkirk (USA) 129 – Robe Chinoise 103 (Robellino (USA) 127) [2009 82: 10.4m 10g⁴ p9.5g⁴ f11g⁴ p12m* p12m² p12m² Dec 4] big, lengthy, good-topped gelding: fairly useful handicapper: won at Kempton in November: good second last 2 starts: stays 1½m: acts on polytrack and good to firm going. *M. Johnston* **88**

MAN OF ACTION (USA) 2 ch.c. (Feb 14) Elusive Quality (USA) – Dixie Melody (USA) (Dixieland Band (USA)) [2009 7g³ Oct 30] $225,000Y: strong, useful-looking colt: half-brother to 3 winners in USA: dam, US 7f/8.5f winner, out of half-sister to top-class 1½m performer Cacoethes: 15/2, promising 2½ lengths third to Quick Wit in maiden at Newmarket, travelling well long way: sure to improve. *J. H. M. Gosden* **79 p**

MAN OF GWENT (UAE) 5 b.g. In The Wings 128 – Welsh Valley (USA) 64 (Irish River (FR) 131) [2009 88§: p12.2g p10g⁵ p10g⁵ p10g³ p12.2g 9.9g⁴ 10.2m² 10m 9.9m 10.3m Jul 11] strong, sturdy gelding: fair handicapper nowadays: stays 11f: acts on polytrack, good to firm and good to soft ground: tried in blinkers/cheekpieces: temperamental. *P. D. Evans* **77 §**

MAN OF IRON (USA) 3 ch.c. Giant's Causeway (USA) 132 – Better Than Honour (USA) 116 (Deputy Minister (CAN)) [2009 –p: 8g 8m* 8g³ 10d 8s⁵ p10.7g* p10.7g⁴ p10.7g* a14f* Nov 6] very smart performer: progressed well, and won maiden at Navan in June, handicap (edged left) and minor event (beat Cochlear 3½ lengths) at Dundalk in September/October and Breeders' Cup Marathon at Santa Anita (upped in trip, beat Cloudy's Knight by a nose with Mastery third, staying on under pressure to lead on line) in November: respectable 7 lengths fourth to Mastercraftsman in Diamond Stakes at Dundalk on seventh start, nearest finish: stays 1¾m: acts on polytrack/pro-ride and good to firm going: has joined L. Cumani. *A. P. O'Brien, Ireland* **123**

Breeders' Cup Marathon Stakes, Santa Anita—Man of Iron (right) provides Ballydoyle with its first Breeders' Cup winner since 2003 as he pips the nine-year-old Cloudy's Knight

MANOLITO MONTOYA (IRE) 3 b.g. High Chaparral (IRE) 132 – Queens Wharf (IRE) 104 (Ela-Mana-Mou 132) [2009 70: p8g^{5} 10m 10g 10m p12g 10g^{5} Jul 4] lengthy gelding: fair maiden: stays 1m: acts on polytrack and good to firm going: usually wears headgear: not straightforward. *J. W. Hills* **66**

MANSHOOR (IRE) 4 gr.g. Linamix (FR) 127 – Lady Wells (IRE) (Sadler's Wells (USA) 132) [2009 p12g* p10g* p13g^{4} 10.1g 10d^{2} Jun 26] sturdy gelding: fairly useful handicapper: trained by F. Head in France at 3 yrs, winning maiden at Le Croise-Laroche: won twice at Lingfield in April: stays 13f: acts on polytrack and good to soft ground. *Mrs L. Wadham* **86**

MANSII 4 b.g. Dr Fong (USA) 128 – Enclave (USA) (Woodman (USA) 126) [2009 69: p6g^{6} p6g^{6} p8g 7f 5.2s^{4} 6g^{3} 6m p7.1g^{2} p7.1g^{3} Oct 10] tall gelding: modest maiden handicapper: stays 7f: acts on polytrack and firm going: tried tongue tied: none too consistent. *P. J. McBride* **59**

MANX MISS (USA) 2 b.f. (Mar 14) El Corredor (USA) 123 – Final Legacy (USA) (Boston Harbor (USA) 122) [2009 p7g^{2} p7g* 6g Oct 30] \$85,000Y: well-made filly: third foal: half-sister to winners in USA by Siphon and Thunder Gulch: dam, US maiden, half-sister to Storm Cat: fair form: won maiden at Dundalk in October: well held in listed race at Newmarket final start: will stay 1m: acts on polytrack. *D. Myerscough, Ireland* **79**

MANY A SLIP 2 gr.g. (Mar 13) Verglas (IRE) 118 – Tri Pac (IRE) (Fairy King (USA)) [2009 6m 6g^{2} 7.1m^{4} 7m* 8g^{5} Aug 28] 2,500Y: quite good-topped gelding: sixth foal: dam unraced half-sister to high-class 7f to 1¼m winner Timarida: fair performer: best effort when winning maiden at Salisbury in August: finished tamely in nursery final start (gelded after): should be well suited by 1m: said to have had breathing problem third start. *J. L. Dunlop* **78**

MANYRIVERSTOCROSS (IRE) 4 b.g. Cape Cross (IRE) 129 – Alexandra S (IRE) (Sadler's Wells (USA) 132) [2009 95: 12m^{3} 12g 12m^{2} 14g* 14m^{6} 14.6m^{2} Sep 11] good sort: useful handicapper: further progress in 2009, winning at Goodwood in July by head from Precision Break: excellent 2¾ lengths second to Nanton in Mallard Stakes at Doncaster final start: will probably stay 2m: acts on soft and good to firm going: useful novice hurdler, won Grade 2 in December. *A. King* **106**

MANY WELCOMES 4 ch.f. Young Ern 120 – Croeso Cynnes 70 (Most Welcome 131) [2009 51: p6g* p6m^{3} 6.1f^{3} 6.1g^{5} 7.6g 7.6m* 7g^{2} 7.6m 7m^{2} 7g^{2} Oct 20] strong, lengthy filly: fair handicapper: won at Wolverhampton in February and Chester (apprentices) in July: stays 7.5f: acts on polytrack and any turf going: held up. *B. P. J. Baugh* **68**

MANZILA (FR) 6 ch.m. Cadeaux Genereux 131 – Mannsara (IRE) (Royal Academy (USA) 130) [2009 109: 5m 5.1g 6m 5g^{6} 6d 5d^{4} 6s^{5} 5s Nov 30] lengthy mare: just fairly useful nowadays: left D. Nicholls after second start: dead-heated for fourth in handicap at Longchamp sixth outing: best at 5f/6f: has form on good to firm ground but best efforts in Britain on going softer than good: in cheekpieces/blinkers last 5 starts. *Mme C. Barande Barbe, France* **93**

MAOI CHINN TIRE (IRE) 2 b.g. (Mar 1) Mull of Kintyre (USA) 114 – Primrose And Rose 72 (Primo Dominie 121) [2009 5d^{6} 5m^{6} 6g^{2} 7d^{3} 6.1d^{4} p7g^{4} p7g^{2} p6m^{6} Dec 4] €2,500Y: sturdy gelding: third foal: dam 5f (at 2 yrs)/6f winner: fair maiden: stays 7f: acts on polytrack: in cheekpieces last 2 starts (gelded in between): has shown signs of temperament. *J. S. Moore* **72**

MAOINEACH (USA) 3 ch.f. Congaree (USA) 127 – Trepidation (USA) (Seeking The Gold (USA)) [2009 98: 7g* 7s 7v 6m^{3} 7g Jul 1] useful-looking filly: has badly scarred near-fore: useful performer: won Leopardstown 1000 Guineas Trial in March by 1¾ lengths from Heart Shaped: best effort after when 1¾ lengths third to Lesson In Humility in Ballyogan Stakes at Leopardstown: well held in Fred Darling Stakes at Newbury second outing: stayed 7f: acted on soft and good to firm going: tried tongue tied: visits Sea The Stars. *J. S. Bolger, Ireland* **106**

MA PATRICE 3 ch.f. Tumbleweed Ridge 117 – Ma Barnicle (IRE) 76 (Al Hareb (USA) 123) [2009 –: p11g 9g 9.7m p8g p10m Sep 26] leggy filly: little form. *T. D. McCarthy* **–**

MAQAAM 3 b.g. Dubai Destination (USA) 127 – Desert Lynx (IRE) 79 (Green Desert (USA) 127) [2009 10m* May 26] odds-on, fair form when winning 5-runner maiden at Redcar by head from Peaceful Rule, getting hang of things late, only outing: dead. *M. Johnston* **77**

MARAASED 4 b.g. Alhaarth (IRE) 126 – Fleeting Rainbow 65 (Rainbow Quest (USA) **74** 134) [2009 95: 12v p12.2g^{2} Dec 17] strong, lengthy gelding: useful maiden early on at 3 yrs: just fair form at best in 2009: stays 1¼m. *S. Gollings*

MARAFONG 2 ch.g. (Feb 23) Dr Fong (USA) 128 – Marakabei 98 (Hernando (FR) **62** 127) [2009 p6g^{5} p7.1g^{5} 7d^{5} 6.1d^{2} p7g Aug 19] close-coupled gelding: modest maiden: near favoured rail and probably flattered when second in minor event at Nottingham: should stay 1m+. *Miss J. Feilden*

MARAGNA (IRE) 2 b.c. (Feb 23) Invincible Spirit (IRE) 121 – Bradwell (IRE) 76 **51** (Taufan (USA) 119) [2009 6s^{6} 6m^{5} 6m^{4} f6m^{5} p6g^{5} Dec 3] close-coupled colt: modest maiden: should stay 7f. *Paul Green*

MARAJAA (IRE) 7 b.g. Green Desert (USA) 127 – Ghyraan (IRE) 106 (Cadeaux **96** Genereux 131) [2009 86: p8g^{6} p8g* p8.6g^{3} 8m^{6} 8m^{2} 8g* 8g^{5} 8g* 8.1g 9m Oct 3] good-topped gelding: useful handicapper: won at Kempton in April, Yarmouth in June and Goodwood in July: well held in Cambridgeshire at Newmarket final start: effective at 7f to easy 8.6f: yet to race on firm going, acts on any other turf and polytrack: patiently ridden. *W. J. Musson*

MARBLED CAT (USA) 3 b.c. Cherokee Run (USA) 122 – Catstar (USA) 105 (Storm **58** Cat (USA)) [2009 69: p6g^{5} p8g p10.7g p8g Nov 25] medium-sized, useful-looking colt: modest maiden: left M. Johnston £10,000 after reappearance: seemingly stays 1m: raced only on all-weather and good/good to firm going. *Niall O'Callaghan, Ireland*

MARCHAND D'OR (FR) 6 gr.g. Marchand de Sable (USA) 117 – Fedora (FR) **106** (Kendor (FR) 122) [2009 127: a6f 5m^{4} 5m May 31] leggy, quite good-topped gelding: high-class performer at best: top sprinter in Europe in 2008, winning 4 times, notably July Cup at Newmarket, Prix Maurice de Gheest at Deauville (for third year running) and Prix de l'Abbaye de Longchamp: ran poorly (as in 2007) in Golden Shaheen at Nad Al Sheba on reappearance and just useful form in Prix de Saint-Georges at Longchamp and Prix du Gros-Chene at Chantilly after: effective at 5f to 7f: acts on heavy and good to firm ground, not on dirt: patiently ridden nowadays: taken early/walked to post. *F. Head, France*

MARCHING TIME 3 b.g. Sadler's Wells (USA) 132 – Marching West (USA) 99 **104** (Gone West (USA)) [2009 86p: 10.4m^{6} 10.1g^{5} 10.4g^{4} 8g* 7g* 7m 8s^{4} Oct 12] sturdy colt: useful handicapper: won at Salisbury and Goodwood (beat Signor Peltro 1¼ lengths) in August: good fourth to Prime Exhibit at Salisbury final start: best at 7f/1m: acts on soft and good to firm ground: sold 270,000 gns. *Sir Michael Stoute*

MARCHIN STAR (IRE) 2 ch.c. (Feb 10) Chineur (FR) 123 – March Star (IRE) 109 **–** (Mac's Imp (USA) 116) [2009 5f^{4} 6d^{6} 5m 6m 7g Sep 3] well-grown colt: little form: has looked awkward. *M. Brittain*

MARCH MATE 5 b.g. Warningford 119 – Daira 72 (Daring March 116) [2009 63: **63** p8.6g* Feb 14] lengthy, unfurnished gelding: modest handicapper: won at Wolverhampton (amateurs) only start at 5 yrs: stays 8.6f: acts on polytrack and firm going: tried in cheekpieces. *B. Ellison*

MARCUS CICERO (IRE) 2 b.g. (Apr 22) Le Vie Dei Colori 126 – Stroke of Six **88** (IRE) 84 (Woodborough (USA) 112) [2009 6.1m^{4} 6m* 6d 6m* 6g^{4} Sep 30] 18,000Y: good-topped gelding: third living foal: half-brother to 3-y-o Sohcahtoa and 2007 2-y-o 7f winner Miss Phoebe (by Catcher In The Rye): dam, 6f (at 2 yrs)/1m winner, half-sister to smart 1¼m performer Revelation: fairly useful performer: won maiden at Windsor in August and nursery at Newbury (best effort, beat Haadeeth by short head) in September: likely to stay 7f: acts on good to firm going: races prominently: sent to Hong Kong. *P. Winkworth*

MARED (USA) 3 ch.c. Speightstown (USA) 124 – Unbridled Lady (USA) (Unbridled **87** (USA) 128) [2009 p8g^{6} 10m^{3} p8g^{2} 9.3g* 10g^{2} 10g^{5} Dec 24] $475,000 2-y-o: strong colt: good sort: fourth foal: half-brother to winner in USA by Forestry: dam US 6f to 8.5f (minor stakes) winner: fairly useful form in maidens first 3 starts, then left J. Noseda: won minor event at Doha in November: stays 1¼m. *J. Smart, UAE*

MAREVA 3 ch.f. Reel Buddy (USA) 118 – Margarets First (Puissance 110) [2009 7g 6m **–** Aug 5] half-sister to 2005 2-y-o 5f winner First Among Equals (by Primo Valentino): dam ran twice: no sign of ability, including in seller. *Ollie Pears*

MARGARETS JOHN (IRE) 2 b.g. (Apr 4) Kalanisi (IRE) 132 – Tarrara (UAE) **– p** (Lammtarra (USA) 134) [2009 7.2v Oct 31] 9,000Y: fourth foal: half-brother to 2008 2-y-o 6f seller winner Anacaona (by Distant Music): dam unraced half-sister to very smart 1¼m performer Torjoun, out of sister to Top Ville: 7/1, very green when last in maiden at Ayr: bred to be suited by 1¼m+: open to improvement. *G. A. Swinbank*

MARGARITA (IRE) 3 b.f. Marju (IRE) 127 – Kalinka (IRE) 88 (Soviet Star (USA) 128) [2009 60p: 7g^5 7m 8.3m^3 p8.6g^6 8.3g 7g Oct 20] neat filly: fair maiden handicapper: stays 8.3f: raced only on polytrack and good/good to firm going: tried tongue tied/visored. *J. R. Fanshawe* **72**

MARIA ANTONIA (IRE) 6 ch.m. King's Best (USA) 132 – Annieirwin (IRE) 94 (Perugino (USA) 84) [2009 66d: f11g^4 f11g^6 Mar 22] modest performer: below form on Flat in 2009: stays 1½m: acts on all-weather and soft ground: takes good hold: usually held up: sold £6,000, joined Mrs A. Thorpe and progressed into fair hurdler. *D. G. Bridgwater* **47 +**

MARIA DI SCOZIA 4 ch.f. Selkirk (USA) 129 – Viva Maria (Hernando (FR) 127) [2009 90: 9.9m 10.3d^6 p10m f11g^4 Dec 22] lengthy filly: fair handicapper nowadays: may prove best around 1¼m: acts on good to firm ground: tongue tied. *P. W. Chapple-Hyam* **75**

MARIA NUNZIATA 3 b.f. Green Desert (USA) 127 – Napoleon's Sister (IRE) 101 (Alzao (USA) 117) [2009 8m^3 10m^3 10m^3 p8.6g* Nov 14] good-topped filly: sixth foal: half-sister to several winners, including useful 9.5f winner Queen of Naples (by Singspiel) who stayed 1½m and fairly useful 2004 2-y-o 6f winner Halle Bop (by Dubai Millennium): dam, 1¼m winner, half-sister to Derby winner Oath and high-class performer up to 10.5f Pelder: fairly useful form in maidens: placed first 3 starts before winning at Wolverhampton in November by 4½ lengths from No Mean Trick: stays 1¼m: sold 50,000 gns. *J. Noseda* **84**

MA RIDGE 5 ch.g. Tumbleweed Ridge 117 – Ma Barnicle (IRE) 76 (Al Hareb (USA) 123) [2009 54: p8g^5 p8g p8g p8g^6 p10g^2 p10g^6 10.9g 9m^6 8.5m Jul 2] workmanlike gelding: modest maiden: stays easy 1¼m: acts on polytrack and firm ground: tried in cheekpieces/blinkers: none too consistent. *T. D. McCarthy* **52**

MARIE CUDDY (IRE) 2 b.f. (Apr 12) Galileo (IRE) 134 – Corrine (IRE) 99 (Spectrum (IRE) 126) [2009 7m^3 Sep 26] €130,000Y: second foal: sister to Irish 3-y-o Liszt: dam, useful 9f to 1½m winner in Norway, half-sister to smart performer up to 1½m Etoile, out of sister to top-class French miler Bellypha: 7/1, 10¼ lengths third to Jacqueline Quest in maiden at Chester, pulling hard in front: bred to be suited by 1¼m+: sold 31,000 gns. *M. R. Channon* **66**

MARIE DE MEDICI (USA) 2 ch.f. (Jan 24) Medicean 128 – Mare Nostrum 117 (Caerleon (USA) 132) [2009 6m^3 7m^3 7m* 8g^2 8g^4 Oct 31] $340,000Y: big filly: fourth foal: half-sister to useful French 2005 2-y-o 1m winner Hurricane Mist (by Spinning World) and 3-y-o Roman Republic: dam, French 9f (including at 2 yrs) winner (stayed 1½m), half-sister to US Grade 1 1¼m winner Aube Indienne: useful performer: won maiden at Leicester in October by 2 lengths from Faithful One, pair well clear: comfortably best effort otherwise when ½-length equal-second to Barouda in Prix des Reservoirs at Deauville: will stay 1¼m: acts on good to firm going. *M. Johnston* **102**

MARIE LOUISE 4 b.f. Helissio (FR) 136 – Self Esteem (Suave Dancer (USA) 136) [2009 65: 12d 12m^6 p16g Jun 17] maiden: tailed off all starts at 4 yrs. *L. A. Dace* **–**

MARIESCHI (USA) 5 b.g. Maria's Mon (USA) 121 – Pennygown 91 (Rainbow Quest (USA) 134) [2009 55: p12.2g f12g^6 Apr 21] tall gelding: modest performer: may prove best around 1½m: acts on all-weather and good to firm going. *R. F. Fisher* **53**

MARIE TEMPEST 4 b.f. Act One 124 – Hakkaniyah 84 (Machiavellian (USA) 123) [2009 56: p8.6g^6 p10g 10m 9m^5 Jun 22] useful-looking filly: poor maiden handicapper: stays 1¼m: acts on polytrack: tried visored. *M. R. Bosley* **49**

MARILLOS PROTERRAS 3 b.f. Fraam 114 – Legend of Aragon 67 (Aragon 118) [2009 68: 10m^6 12.1m 8s 13.8g^2 12g 16.2g^5 Jul 20] sturdy filly: modest maiden: stays 1¾m: tried in visor/cheekpieces. *Mrs A. Duffield* **54**

MARINA'S OCEAN 5 b.m. Beat All (USA) 120 – Ocean Song 61 (Savahra Sound 111) [2009 p8.6g p8.6g 8.3m^6 12s p9.5g f7f Dec 12] tall, close-coupled mare: first foal: dam 9.4f winner: tailed off in bumpers: modest maiden on Flat: tongue tied. *S. R. Bowring* **50**

MARINA WALK 3 ch.f. Compton Place 125 – Raindrop 59 (Primo Dominie 121) [2009 p6g^6 p6g^5 f6g 6f 6m 5.7g Jul 31] fifth foal: sister to 6f/7f winner Glencal and half-sister to 2 winners, including useful 7f/1m winner Kasumi (by Inchinor): dam maiden (best effort at 7f): modest maiden: best effort on debut: tried tongue tied. *H. Morrison* **54 d**

MARINE BOY (IRE) 3 b.g. One Cool Cat (USA) 123 – Bahamamia 92 (Vettori (IRE) 119) [2009 105: 7m^5 6m 6d^4 7m 7m^5 6g^2 Oct 30] tall, angular gelding: useful performer: marginally best effort at 3 yrs when fifth to Esoterica in handicap at Newmarket on penultimate start: barely stays 7f: unraced on extremes of going. *Tom Dascombe* **105**

*William Hill Great St Wilfrid Stakes (Heritage Handicap), Ripon—
hot favourite Markab (No.5) gains a deserved win in a big sprint handicap
as he edges out Tamagin (cheekpieces), Advanced (far side) and Jimmy Styles (No.6)*

MARINE SPIRIT (GER) 2 b.c. (Mar 1) Big Shuffle (USA) 122 – Molly Dancer **85**
(GER) (Shareef Dancer (USA) 135) [2009 6m^{4} 6g^{3} 6m* 6g^{2} 6g^{6} p6m Oct 28] €100,000Y: tall, good-topped colt: has fluent action: fifth foal: brother to 3 winners in Germany, including useful performers up to 1m Molly Art and Molly Max: dam lightly-raced half-sister to useful German performers Mister Big (at 6f/7f) and Molly Mello (at 7f/1m) (both by Big Shuffle): fairly useful performer: won maiden at Folkestone in August: ran creditably in nurseries fourth/fifth starts: likely to stay 7f: blinkered (below form) final outing: has joined M. bin Shafya in UAE. *Saeed bin Suroor*

MARINO PRINCE (FR) 4 b.g. Dr Fong (USA) 128 – Hula Queen (USA) (Irish River **–**
(FR) 131) [2009 61: 10.9g 8.1m^{6} p9.5g Aug 10] modest at 3 yrs: well held in 2009: tried in cheekpieces. *T. Wall*

MARIOL (FR) 6 b.g. Munir 118 – La Bastoche (IRE) (Kaldoun (FR) 122) [2009 115: **118**
6m^{2} 7g^{3} 7g^{6} 6g^{4} 6.5g^{2} 6m* 6m 7g Oct 3] good-bodied gelding: first foal: dam French 1½m winner: smart performer: first past post twice in 2008, including in Prix de Ris-Orangis at Deauville: better than ever at same course fifth/sixth starts in 2009, ½-length second to King's Apostle in Prix Maurice de Gheest before winning Prix de Meautry Lucien Barriere in August by 2½ lengths from Contest, quickening well from rear: had excuses last 2 starts in Diadem Stakes at Ascot (raced alone until halfway) and Prix de la Foret at Longchamp (hampered early stages): best around 6f/7f: acts on soft and good to firm going: held up: tough. *R. Collet, France*

MARISTAR (USA) 2 b.f. (Apr 24) Giant's Causeway (USA) 132 – Jewel Princess **82 p**
(USA) 129 (Key To The Mint (USA)) [2009 7m^{3} p8g^{5} f7f* Oct 21] $200,000Y: tall, unfurnished filly: closely related to 2 winners in USA by Storm Cat: dam US Grade 1 8.5f/9f winner, including Breeders' Cup Distaff: fairly useful form: won maiden at Southwell cosily by 1¼ lengths from Vegas Palace: should stay 1m: acts on fibresand and good to firm going: open to further progress. *G. A. Butler*

MARIUS MAXIMUS (IRE) 2 b.c. (Apr 10) Kheleyf (USA) 116 – Marju Guest (IRE) **59 +**
67 (Marju (IRE) 127) [2009 5.4d 6m^{3} Sep 25] strong colt: better effort in maidens when 8¼ lengths third to Atlaal at Haydock, finishing weakly. *M. Johnston*

MARJOLLY (IRE) 2 b.c. (Mar 2) Marju (IRE) 127 – Lost Icon (IRE) (Intikhab (USA) 135) [2009 6m^6 f6g^3 f6g^5 p7g^5 f6m^3 Dec 15] modest maiden: stays 7f: acts on all-weather: in cheekpieces final outing. *M. Botti* **58**

MARJU KING (IRE) 3 b.c. Marju (IRE) 127 – Blue Reema (IRE) 90 (Bluebird (USA) 125) [2009 –: 10m^3 10.2g 10g^3 Aug 21] workmanlike colt: fair maiden: stays 1¼m: acts on good to firm going. *W. S. Kittow* **70**

MARJURY DAW (IRE) 3 b.f. Marju (IRE) 127 – The Stick 61 (Singspiel (IRE) 133) [2009 61: p10g p10g p9.5g^2 p8g p9.5g Nov 30] compact filly: modest maiden handicapper: stays 9.5f: acts on polytrack. *J. G. Given* **64**

MARKAB 6 b.g. Green Desert (USA) 127 – Hawafiz (Nashwan (USA) 135) [2009 105: 7m^6 6m^4 6d^4 6m* 5.6m 6g^5 Oct 10] sturdy, deep-girthed gelding: smart performer: further improvement in valuable handicaps in 2009, fourth in Wokingham (behind High Standing) and Stewards' Cup (behind Genki) prior to winning William Hill Great St Wilfrid Stakes at Ripon in August by neck from Tamagin: rather isolated and not discredited when equal-fifth to Royal Rock in Bengough Memorial Stakes at Ascot final outing: speedy front runner, best up to 7f: acts on polytrack, heavy and good to firm ground. *H. Candy* **110**

MARKADAM 3 b.g. Mark of Esteem (IRE) 137 – Elucidate 60 (Elmaamul (USA) 125) [2009 62: 8.5g 12.1m 10m^6 14.1m^4 15.8g p12.2g p13.9g Dec 14] modest maiden handicapper: stays 1¾m: acts on heavy and good to firm going: tried in cheekpieces: reportedly bled second start: no easy ride. *Miss S. E. Hall* **56**

MARK ANTHONY (IRE) 2 b.g. (Feb 1) Antonius Pius (USA) 123§ – Zuniga's Date (USA) (Diesis 133) [2009 7g^5 8.1g^3 6m* Aug 15] 7,000Y: tall, good-bodied gelding: first living foal: dam French 7.5f winner: progressive form in maidens, winning at Ripon by 2½ lengths from Royal Record, travelling powerfully in front (gelded after): may prove best at 5f/6f: capable of further improvement. *K. A. Ryan* **84 p**

MARKAZZI 2 b.c. (Apr 5) Dansili 127 – Bandanna 98 (Bandmaster (USA) 97) [2009 7m^2 7m* 7m Oct 3] 200,000F, 300,000Y: rangy colt: fourth foal: half-brother to useful 2007 2-y-o 5f winner Art Sale (by Compton Place) and 3-y-o Rowayton: dam, 5f/6f (latter at 2 yrs) winner, half-sister to July Stakes winner Rich Ground: promising in maidens, second to Pounced at Newbury then won at Leicester in September comfortably by 1¾ lengths from Sand Skier: poorly drawn and well held in sales race at Newmarket: shapes as though will stay 1m: should still go on to better things. *Sir Michael Stoute* **98 p**

MARK CARMERS 2 b.g. (Feb 16) Mark of Esteem (IRE) 137 – Queen Lea (FR) (Alzao (USA) 117) [2009 6g 6d Sep 7] last in maidens at Ayr and Newcastle. *T. D. Barron* **–**

MARKET WATCHER (USA) 8 b.g. Boundary (USA) 117 – Trading (USA) (A P Indy (USA) 131) [2009 58: p16.5g* 16m p16.5g^6 p13.9m Nov 28] strong gelding: modest handicapper: won at Wolverhampton in January: stays 16.5f: acts on polytrack, soft and good to firm going: tried blinkered, formerly tongue tied. *Seamus Fahey, Ireland* **60**

MARKHESA 3 b.f. Sakhee (USA) 136 – Marciala (IRE) (Machiavellian (USA) 123) [2009 52: 8d 8g^3 8g p8f^3 p7.1g^5 7m* 8g Oct 30] big, strong filly: fair performer: won seller at Leicester (sold from C. Wall 5,800 gns) in October: should stay 1¼m: acts on polytrack and good to firm going. *J. R. Boyle* **68**

MARKINGTON 6 b.g. Medicean 128 – Nemesia 111 (Mill Reef (USA) 141) [2009 74: 14.6m* 18m* 16.1m* 21g 18g^2 16g Oct 30] close-coupled gelding: fairly useful handicapper: won at Doncaster, Pontefract and Newcastle, all in June: stays 2¼m: acts on polytrack, firm and soft going: wears blinkers/cheekpieces: lazy. *P. Bowen* **80**

MARK OF MEYDAN 4 ch.g. Mark of Esteem (IRE) 137 – Rose Bounty (Polar Falcon (USA) 126) [2009 81: f6g^3 7s^5 6g 6d* 6d 6g p7.1g^3 p7.1g^2 p7g Oct 9] fairly useful handicapper: won at Newcastle in June: stays 7f: acts on polytrack, soft and good to firm ground: none too consistent. *M. Dods* **83**

MARK TWAIN (IRE) 2 b.g. (Apr 24) Rock of Gibraltar (IRE) 133 – Lady Windermere (IRE) (Lake Coniston (IRE) 131) [2009 7g^6 6m^2 7.2m^5 6s 7s^3 7g^2 8s* 7s^5 Nov 5] 150,000Y: sixth foal: closely related to useful Irish 6f winner Absolutelyfabulous (by Mozart) and half-brother to 3-y-o Russian Jar: dam unraced half-sister to Fillies' Mile winner Listen and Moyglare Stud Stakes winner Sequoyah (dam of Henrythenavigator): fairly useful performer: won maiden at Cork in August: left A. O'Brien in Ireland, creditable fifth in nursery at Leopardstown (gelded after): stays 1m: acts on soft and good to firm going: usually races up with pace. *D. M. Simcock* **86**

MARKYG (USA) 3 b. or br.c. Fusaichi Pegasus (USA) 130 – Spring Pitch (USA) **97**
(Storm Cat (USA)) [2009 91: p7g* p9g p8g^{4} 8.1v^{6} 8m Jun 18] sturdy colt: useful handicapper: won at Kempton in February: good fourth to Pure Poetry in listed race there after: stays 1m: acts on polytrack and good to firm going: tried tongue tied/visored: sent to USA. *K. R. Burke*

MARMOOQ 6 ch.g. Cadeaux Genereux 131 – Portelet 91 (Night Shift (USA)) [2009 **72**
70: p7g^{5} p7g* p7.1g^{4} p7g^{3} p8g^{2} p7g^{2} p8g p8g* p8g^{5} p7g p8g 7g 8m p8m p8m p8g^{5} p8m^{3} p8.6g^{5} p10g* p10m^{3} Dec 10] tall gelding: fair handicapper: won at Kempton in January and March and Lingfield in November: stays 1¼m: acts on polytrack, firm and good to soft going: has worn headgear: held up. *M. J. Attwater*

MARNING STAR 4 b.g. Diktat 126 – Mustique Dream 87 (Don't Forget Me 127) **79**
[2009 85: p8.6g^{5} p8.6g^{3} 10g 8m 8g 8.3v^{3} 8.3d* 8.3m f8g Sep 29] leggy, lengthy gelding: fair handicapper nowadays: won at Nottingham in August: stays 8.6f: acts on polytrack, heavy and good to firm going: tongue tied last 4 starts: sold 6,000 gns, sent to Bahrain. *Ian Williams*

MAROON MACHINE (IRE) 2 ch.c. (Apr 4) Muhtathir 126 – Mediaeval (FR) **99**
(Medaaly 114) [2009 7d* 7.5g^{3} 8g^{2} 8g* 7m 8s^{2} Nov 11] €62,000Y: good-topped colt: third foal: half-brother to useful French 2006 2-y-o 5.5f/6f winner Place Vendome (by Dr Fong) and fairly useful French 7.5f winner Mirleft (by Anabaa): dam unraced half-sister to useful French sprinter Dobby Road: useful performer: won maiden at Dieppe in July and minor event at Saint-Cloud in October: good second in listed races at Deauville (beaten 2½ lengths by Ruler of My Heart in valuable contest) and Toulouse (beaten nose by Bottega) third/final starts: stiff task in Dewhurst Stakes at Newmarket fifth outing: stays 1m: acts on soft ground. *E. J. O'Neill*

MAROSH (FR) 2 b.c. (Feb 7) American Post 121 – Madragoa (FR) (Kaldoun (FR) **69**
122) [2009 5m^{4} 5m^{4} p6g^{4} p6g Jul 13] fair maiden: best effort when fourth in newcomers race at Chantilly: should stay 7f: tried in cheekpieces: has looked awkward. *R. M. H. Cowell*

MARRAYAH 2 b.f. (Jan 23) Fraam 114 – Mania (IRE) (Danehill (USA) 126) [2009 **82 p**
6m* Aug 17] 57,000Y: fourth foal: half-sister to fairly useful 2007 2-y-o 6f winner Fanatical (by Mind Games), later 6f winner in USA, and 3-y-o Gower Valentine: dam unraced half-sister to dam of Youmzain and Creachadoir: 12/1, won maiden at Yarmouth going away by 2½ lengths from Young Simon, clearly green: will stay 7f: will progress. *M. A. Jarvis*

MARSAM (IRE) 6 gr.g. Daylami (IRE) 138 – Dancing Prize (IRE) 99 (Sadler's Wells **–**
(USA) 132) [2009 71: f11m Dec 15] handicapper: very lightly raced since 2007, and well held in seller sole outing on Flat at 6 yrs: tried blinkered: winning hurdler/chaser. *M. G. Quinlan*

MARSHAL PLAT CLUB 2 b.f. (Apr 17) Monsieur Bond (IRE) 120 – Bond May Day **48 p**
79 (Among Men (USA) 124) [2009 f5m^{6} Nov 11] second foal: dam 1¼m/1½m winner: 40/1, better for race when 4¼ lengths sixth to Clear Ice in maiden at Southwell: capable of better. *G. R. Oldroyd*

MARSH WARBLER 2 ch.g. (Jan 31) Barathea (IRE) 127 – Echo River (USA) 101 **85**
(Irish River (FR) 131) [2009 6g* 6m 7g Jul 31] tall gelding: third foal: brother to 5-y-o Ravi River: dam 2-y-o 6f/7f winner: won maiden at Redcar in June by 6 lengths: seemed amiss in Coventry Stakes at Royal Ascot next time, respectable ninth in nursery at Goodwood final start (gelded after): shapes as though will stay 1m. *M. Johnston*

MARSOOL 3 br.g. Key of Luck (USA) 126 – Chatifa (IRE) 83 (Titus Livius (FR) 115) **65**
[2009 –p: 10f^{4} Jun 30] workmanlike gelding: better effort when fourth in maiden at Brighton: sold 17,000 gns, joined D. McCain Jnr and successful in juvenile hurdles in September/October. *M. P. Tregoning*

MARTHA'S GIRL (USA) 3 ch.f. E Dubai (USA) 124 – Blue Stream (USA) (King of **–**
Kings (IRE) 125) [2009 62: 10.3g 12m f12f^{5} f14m f8f Dec 17] rather leggy filly: maiden: left D. Brown and rejoined former trainer after second start: tried tongue tied/visored: weak finisher. *D. Carroll*

MARTINGRANGE BOY (IRE) 4 b.g. Danetime (IRE) 121 – Coloma (JPN) (Forty **68**
Niner (USA)) [2009 –: f5g^{5} p5g 5.1m p6g Apr 28] fair handicapper, lightly raced: stays 6f: acts on all-weather, well held only start on turf: tongue tied since debut: weak finisher. *J. Balding*

MARTINGRANGE LASS (IRE) 4 b.f. Chevalier (IRE) 115 – Jellybeen (IRE) 72 **52**
(Petardia 113) [2009 54: f11s f7g f6g^{4} p5g f6g^{4} Mar 22] lengthy, good-bodied filly: modest maiden: stays 1¼m, effective at much shorter: acts on all-weather and good to firm ground: tried in headgear/tongue tie: signs of temperament. *S. Parr*

MARTIN'S FRIEND (USA) 4 b.g. Grand Slam (USA) 120 – Dans La Ville (CHI) (Winning (USA)) [2009 p10g 10d Jul 17] ex-German-trained gelding: won maiden and handicap at Frankfurt in 2008 for M. Hofer: well held on Flat in Britain: stays 1¼m: acts on good to firm going: tried blinkered/tongue tied: sold £5,000, sent to Switzerland. *Mrs L. Wadham* **–**

MARTYR 4 b.g. Cape Cross (IRE) 129 – Sudeley 65 (Dancing Brave (USA) 140) [2009 87: 10s 10g* 12m* 12g³ 12m³ 12m Jul 10] sturdy gelding: useful handicapper: improved in 2009, winning at Windsor and Newmarket in May: good third at Epsom and Royal Ascot (Duke of Edinburgh Stakes, to Drill Sergeant) after: stays 1½m: acts on polytrack and good to firm going: races prominently. *R. Hannon* **99**

MARVIN GARDENS 6 b.g. Largesse 112 – En Grisaille 53 (Mystiko (USA) 124) [2009 58: p6g p6g p5g⁴ p6g Feb 22] modest handicapper: best form at 6f: acts on polytrack and good to firm ground: blinkered/visored nowadays. *P. S. McEntee* **53**

MARVO 5 b.g. Bahamian Bounty 116 – Mega (IRE) 66 (Petardia 113) [2009 82: 8.3g f7g⁶ 8d* 8m* 8.1m⁴ 8m 9.2v* 10g 10.2d⁵ 8g Oct 31] angular gelding: fairly useful handicapper: won at Pontefract in May, Doncaster in June and Hamilton in August: stays 1¼m: acts on soft and good to firm going: tried blinkered/visored: travels strongly held up. *M. H. Tompkins* **88**

MARY CELEST (IRE) 2 b.f. (Mar 6) Barathea (IRE) 127 – Rack And Ruin (IRE) 59 (King's Best (USA) 132) [2009 6g 6m 7.5m³ p8m 10.2m p9.5g p7.1g Nov 2] €10,000Y: workmanlike filly: first foal: dam, maiden (ran only at 5f/6f at 2 yrs), out of half-sister to Middle Park winner Mister Majestic and Grand Prix de Paris winner Homme de Loi: maiden: third at Beverley, little form otherwise: in cheekpieces last 3 starts. *K. A. Ryan* **50**

MARYGATE (IRE) 3 b.f. Spartacus (IRE) 107 – Thorn Tree (Zafonic (USA) 130) [2009 53: 5m 5m May 12] close-coupled filly: maiden: well held since 2-y-o debut. *M. Brittain* **–**

MARY GOODNIGHT 3 b.f. King's Best (USA) 132 – Disco Volante 105 (Sadler's Wells (USA) 132) [2009 10m* 10m³ p12g Oct 9] 50,000Y: big filly: second foal: half-sister to 1m winner Cinerama (by Machiavellian): dam, 1m winner (stayed 10.5f), closely related to smart but irresolute 7f/1m performer Valentino: fairly useful form: won maiden at Windsor in July: good third in handicap at same track next outing: stays 1¼m. *J. Noseda* **86**

MARY HELEN 2 b.f. (Apr 9) Dandoun 117 – Hotel California (IRE) 58 (Last Tycoon 131) [2009 5m 6d⁴ 6g³ 7s* 7d⁶ 7d² 7.5m⁴ p8g⁴ p9.5g* p10m* p9.5g² Dec 12] 1,000Y: compact filly: half-sister to several winners, including fairly useful 5.7f (at 2 yrs) and 7f winner Goldie (by Celtic Swing) and 5-y-o Dot's Delight: dam 2-y-o 7.5f winner: modest performer: won seller at Yarmouth in June and claimers at Wolverhampton in October and Kempton in November: stays 1¼m: acts on polytrack, soft and good to firm going: signs of temperament. *W. M. Brisbourne* **61**

MARY MASON 3 b.f. Hunting Lion (IRE) 115 – Kalarram (Muhtarram (USA) 125) [2009 73: p6g 6.1g May 25] strong filly: fair performer in 2008: well held at 3 yrs. *M. Hill* **–**

MARYOLINI 4 b.f. Bertolini (USA) 125 – Mary Jane 77 (Tina's Pet 121) [2009 78: p5.1g⁶ p5g p6g³ 6m p5.1g p5g Oct 21] leggy filly: modest handicapper nowadays: left N. Vaughan after third start: effective at 5f/easy 6f: acts on polytrack and firm going: races prominently: sold 2,500 gns. *Tom Dascombe* **60**

MARY WEST (IRE) 3 b.f. Pyrus (USA) 106 – Pivot d'Amour 56 (Pivotal 124) [2009 59: p5.1g 5g Jul 20] leggy filly: maiden: below form since 2-y-o debut. *Pat Morris* **–**

MARZY 3 br.f. Kyllachy 129 – Amarella (FR) (Balleroy (USA) 115) [2009 p5g⁶ p6g p6g Jun 5] poor maiden: should have been suited by 6f: dead. *M. Botti* **46**

MASAFI (IRE) 8 b.g. Desert King (IRE) 129 – Mrs Fisher (IRE) 94 (Salmon Leap (USA) 131) [2009 p12.2g Jun 22] good-bodied gelding: one-time useful performer: has lost way badly, including over hurdles: tried tongue tied. *E. J. Cooper* **–**

MASAI MOON 5 b.g. Lujain (USA) 119 – Easy To Imagine (USA) (Cozzene (USA)) [2009 101: p6g² 6m⁶ 7f 7m⁴ 7g⁶ 7g 7m³ p7.1g⁴ 6m³ f6f⁵ Oct 21] tall, rather leggy gelding: useful handicapper: creditable ½-length second to Mullein at Kempton on return: effective at stiff 6f/7f: acts on all-weather, firm and soft going: tried in cheekpieces. *B. R. Millman* **101**

MASAMAH (IRE) 3 gr.g. Exceed And Excel (AUS) 126 – Bethesda 91 (Distant Relative 128) [2009 100: 6m 5.1m p6g² Oct 9] good-topped gelding: useful performer: gelded, best effort in 2009 when creditable second to Lemon N Sugar in handicap at Lingfield: should prove best at 5f/6f: acts on polytrack and good to firm going: twice blinkered: hangs, and is one to be wary of: sold 30,000 gns. *E. A. L. Dunlop* **98**

MASKAN 2 ch.g. (Mar 8) Starcraft (NZ) 128 – Silence Is Golden 120 (Danehill Dancer (IRE) 117) [2009 8d^5 Oct 15] 5/1 and green, fifth to Avon Lady in maiden at Brighton: should stay 1¼m: sold 5,500 gns. *W. J. Haggas* **55**

MASKATEER (IRE) 3 b.g. Iron Mask (USA) 117 – Indescent Blue 63 (Bluebird (USA) 125) [2009 12.1g 12.1g^6 Jun 22] little form. *Mrs A. M. Thorpe* **–**

MASKED DANCE (IRE) 2 gr.g. (Mar 15) Captain Rio 122 – Brooks Masquerade (Absalom 128) [2009 5m^4 f5g^5 5d^5 6.1v^4 5.2g^3 5s^3 6s^2 6g* 6g^5 7.2v^2 Oct 31] £16,000Y: close-coupled gelding: half-brother to several winners, including useful 6f (at 2 yrs) to 1½m winner Fiveoclock Express (by Woodborough): dam, maiden, half-sister to dam of high-class sprinter Red Clubs: fair performer: won seller at Ripon in August: stays 7f: acts on heavy and good to firm ground: tried visored, in cheekpieces (best form) last 3 starts: usually front runner: formerly temperamental (has hung right). *K. A. Ryan* **79**

MASKING BALDINI (IRE) 5 b.g. Iron Mask (USA) 117 – Royal Baldini (USA) (Green Dancer (USA) 132) [2009 49: 10m 12d^6 12g Aug 3] no longer of any account. *J. Hetherton* **–**

MASLAK (IRE) 5 b.g. In The Wings 128 – Jeed (IRE) 86 (Mujtahid (USA) 118) [2009 90, a95: p12g p12.2m^5 p12g^4 f11g^6 12d^3 14.1g^4 12m 12g^2 11.6f* 12m 11.1v^2 p12f^2 p13.9g^4 12m 12g f12m^6 f12f^2 p12m^2 Dec 16] good-bodied gelding: fairly useful handicapper, better on all-weather: won at Windsor (amateurs) in August: best around 1½m: acts on all-weather and any turf going: none too consistent. *P. W. Hiatt* **82** **a87**

MASON HINDMARSH 2 ch.g. (Mar 17) Dr Fong (USA) 128 – Sierra Virgen (USA) (Stack (USA)) [2009 6d 5m^6 7m 8m^4 8g^2 8d^5 Oct 28] 6,500F, £8,000Y: unfurnished gelding: half-brother to 1m winner Sistos Fascination (by Fasliyev): dam, US Grade 3 8.5f winner, sister to smart US Grade 2 9.5f winner Stay Forever: fair maiden: best efforts last 2 starts, second in nursery at Pontefract: likely to stay 1¼m: acts on good to soft going. *Karen McLintock* **72**

MASSILAH 3 b.f. Namid 128 – Loveleaves 93 (Polar Falcon (USA) 126) [2009 7s^6 7m^4 p7g^3 Oct 26] 18,000F, 90,000Y: sturdy filly: third foal: half-sister to 5-y-o Lovelace: dam 1m winner: fair form in maidens: will be at least as effective at 6f as 7f: sold €5,000. *B. W. Hills* **74**

MASS RALLY (IRE) 2 b.c. (Mar 10) Kheleyf (USA) 116 – Reunion (IRE) 108 (Be My Guest (USA) 126) [2009 7.1m 8m^5 p7g^2 7d^2 p7g* p7.1g* Nov 21] €75,000Y: strong colt: seventh foal: half-brother to 6-y-o Gunfighter and winner in Japan by Giant's Causeway: dam 6f (at 2 yrs) and 7f (Nell Gwyn) winner: useful and progressive form: won maiden at Kempton and nursery at Wolverhampton (beat Quaker Parrot 2 lengths, travelling well and quickening impressively) in November: stays 7f: acts on polytrack, good to firm and good to soft going: tongue tied last 2 starts. *J. H. M. Gosden* **97 +**

MASTA PLASTA (IRE) 6 b.g. Mujadil (USA) 119 – Silver Arrow (USA) 67 (Shadeed (USA) 135) [2009 117: p5g^2 5.8s 5v 5g^3 5g^2 5m^3 5.1m 5g^4 5.1d^4 5m Aug 29] good-topped gelding: smart performer: almost as good as ever in 2009, placed fourth to sixth starts in Scottish Sprint Cup (Handicap) at Musselburgh (length third to Pavershooz), listed race at Chantilly and Sprint Stakes at Sandown (¾-length third to Ialysos): well below form last 2 starts: best at 5f/easy 6f: acts on polytrack, soft and good to firm going: tried visored/blinkered: races up with pace. *D. Nicholls* **115**

MASTER AT ARMS 6 ch.g. Grand Lodge (USA) 125 – L'Ideale (USA) (Alysheba (USA)) [2009 86: 16s 13.1m^3 16g 16m p16g Sep 6] fairly useful handicapper: good third at Ayr on second start: stays 16.5f: acts on polytrack and good to firm ground, possibly not on softer than good. *D. Loughnane, Ireland* **81**

MASTERCRAFTSMAN (IRE) 3 gr.c. Danehill Dancer (IRE) 117 – Starlight Dreams (USA) (Black Tie Affair 128) [2009 120: 8m^5 8v* 8m* 10.4m^2 10d^3 p10.7g* a8f^4 Nov 7] **129**

As usual, a number of the previous season's top two-year-olds failed to add to their reputation, with Crowded House, Naaqoos, Bushranger, Intense Focus, Gallagher, Square Eddie and Proportional running twenty-five times for just one win. There were as many good success stories, though, with seven of the twenty-one colts and fillies rated at least 115 in *Racehorses of 2008* gaining victories, or running very well, in Group 1 events. The septet comprised Mastercraftsman, Rainbow View, Art Connoisseur, Lord Shanakill, Delegator, Rip Van Winkle and Jukebox Jury. Rip Van Winkle's victories in the Sussex Stakes and Queen Elizabeth II Stakes marked him down as the best of that bunch at three, but Mastercraftsman's campaign was nearly as fruitful, yielding victories in the Irish Two Thousand Guineas and St James's Palace Stakes and places in two other Group 1s.

It is a comment on the quality of the Ballydoyle team of three-year-olds that, for much of the year, Mastercraftsman appeared to figure no higher than third in the pecking order behind stable-companions Rip Van Winkle and Fame And Glory. Mastercraftsman's victories in the Phoenix Stakes and the National Stakes at two had marked him down as a colt with classic pretensions, notwithstanding a lacklustre run in the Prix Jean-Luc Lagardere on his final appearance when quite likely feeling the effects of a hard race on heavy in the National. Movements in the betting market for the Two Thousand Guineas in the run-up to the race saw Mastercraftsman drift from 4/1 clear favourite out to 7/1 as support developed for Rip Van Winkle, who himself had drifted to 9/1 from 6/1 in mid-March. Mastercraftsman started 7/1 fourth favourite of fifteen at Newmarket—stable jockey Johnny Murtagh having plumped for Rip Van Winkle—and he finished a respectable fifth, over four lengths behind the winner Sea The Stars and a length and three quarters behind fourth-placed Rip Van Winkle, staying on steadily after losing some ground in the Dip.

Mastercraftsman appeared fit enough on the day, but he left his Newmarket performance well behind on his remaining starts in Europe, beginning with the boylesports.com Irish Two Thousand Guineas at the Curragh three weeks later. The going was heavy and despite the presence of Newmarket second Delegator, Mastercraftsman was sent off 6/4 favourite in a field of nine, his stable saddling three other contenders including Dee Stakes third Drumbeat dropping back in trip; the pick of the other runners were Rayeni, running for the first time since landing the Killavullan Stakes at two, and Soul City, successful in the Prix La Rochette and Goffs Million in his first season and also making his reappearance. Delegator ran way below form in eighth and none of the rest was able to live with Mastercraftsman who chased the Ballydoyle pacemaker early on, took it up three furlongs out and stretched clear in fine style to beat Rayeni by four and a half lengths, with Soul City third. Mastercraftsman gave his trainer a ninth victory in a row in an Irish classic, an astonishing run that had started with Soldier of Fortune in the 2007 Irish Derby. The run couldn't be extended by the trainer's solitary runner in the Irish One Thousand Guineas the next day, Totally Devoted starting at 25/1 and finishing fourteenth of sixteen behind Again, a filly owned by two of the Coolmore principals Michael Tabor and Sue Magnier and ridden by Murtagh. With Rip Van Winkle being trained for the Derby, O'Brien immediately singled out the St James's Palace Stakes at Royal Ascot for Mastercraftsman. On very different going—good to firm—he started at 6/5-on in a field of ten including Delegator again and Soul City,

boylesports.com Irish 2000 Guineas, the Curragh—the grey Mastercraftsman goes four places better than at Newmarket to give Aidan O'Brien his ninth successive Irish classic; Rayeni (left) takes second

St James's Palace Stakes, Royal Ascot—Johnny Murtagh conjures a strong rally from Mastercraftsman to pip Delegator (No.2), with Lord Shanakill (No.5) in third and Evasive in fourth

in addition to the Two Thousand Guineas sixth Evasive and Lord Shanakill, who had come twelfth in that race. Also in the line-up was Intense Focus who had narrowly beaten Lord Shanakill in the 2008 Dewhurst Stakes. Delegator was back to his best and Mastercraftsman had to show all his courage and ability to beat him. There is sometimes a tendency for the pacemakers from Ballydoyle to go blazing off in front, building up a five- or six-length advantage which can lead to the main body of the field almost contesting a separate race, in the process receiving no obvious benefit from the efforts of the pacemakers. This occurs more in races over middle distances and, with Mastercraftsman's natural inclination being to get on with things, his pacemakers were never too far ahead of him at Royal Ascot. Mastercraftsman moved ahead entering the straight, chased by Lord Shanakill on his outside, but Delegator, moving easily immediately behind the leader, proved a much greater danger. Under very strong pressure as Delegator edged ahead inside the last furlong, Mastercraftsman looked beaten but, with Murtagh giving him a great ride, Mastercraftsman took the lead again fifty yards from home and went on to a neck success. Lord Shanakill, who won the Prix Jean Prat next time, finished a length and a half away in third, with Evasive fourth. A memorable race was slightly tarnished for some when Murtagh received a one-day ban for excessive use of the whip; Murtagh found himself in more trouble with the stewards later in the afternoon, picking up a five-day suspension for careless riding on Kayf Aramis in the Ascot Stakes and a further day for not riding out the same horse for sixth place. Suspended for trying too hard, and for not trying hard enough, both on the same day!

The St James's Palace Stakes suggested that Mastercraftsman would be suited by further than a mile and his next three starts were all at a mile and a quarter or more. He ran well in all of them, though two of them were in defeat against Sea The Stars, starting with the International at York. With two pacemakers and a field of only four, Mastercraftsman couldn't have had things more tailormade for him at York and, after taking up the running three furlongs out, he galloped on strongly forcing Sea The Stars to put in plenty of effort to get past him a hundred yards out and win by a length. This was a splendid run by Mastercraftsman, certainly one of the best of his career. He couldn't quite repeat the form in the Irish Champion Stakes at Leopardstown, in which Murtagh chose to ride Fame And Glory instead, though, after leading briefly early in the straight, he was slightly hampered when held over a furlong out, eventually beaten five lengths into third behind Sea The Stars.

Mastercraftsman was declared for the Queen Elizabeth II Stakes at Ascot three weeks later, but only as a precaution in case Rip Van Winkle was unable to take up the engagement. Mastercraftsman ran instead in the Diamond Stakes at Ireland's only all-weather track, Dundalk, which was opened in 2007. Mastercraftsman had had the Breeders' Cup at Santa Anita in November pencilled in for him for some time, whether he ran in the Classic or the Dirt Mile said at the time to depend on how Rip Van Winkle fared in the lead-up to the same event. A year earlier, British-trained Muhannak had won the Diamond Stakes before going on to land the Breeders' Cup Marathon. Given the wet summers that Ireland has had in the last two years, Dundalk has proved a boon, with plenty of runners and competitive racing. Ger Lyons, who has trained more winners at Dundalk than anyone over the last three years, said in 2008: 'If it was not for the polytrack, then I would be out of business as I just would not be able to run my horses.' The top Irish trainers have their share of runners there, with John Oxx among the leaders numerically, and O'Brien sent out eight winners in 2008, including Age of Aquarius who scored on his debut, and nine in 2009, among them Fencing Master, who also won on his debut, and Man of Iron who won twice at Dundalk before he won the Breeders' Cup Marathon. It remains to be seen whether Dundalk proves quite so relevant for the next Breeders' Cup which returns to Churchill Downs, with its traditional dirt surface (the venue for the last two Breeders' Cups, Santa Anita, has a synthetic surface, pro-ride, in place of dirt). The Diamond Stakes was upgraded to Group 3 after being listed in 2008 and, with first prize money of approaching £40,000, is a worthy target in its own right. The field of eleven for the latest edition attracted no runners from Britain and none who boasted anything like the same form as Mastercraftsman, who started at 9/2-on (the second favourite was course specialist Fiery Lad, trained by Lyons and successful five times at Dundalk in 2008). After racing in third behind a helter-skelter gallop set by 33/1-shot Via Galilei and Mastercraftsman's stablemate Augustusthestrong, and still being at least a dozen lengths adrift with three furlongs to go, Mastercraftsman came with an impressive run to lead over a furlong out and surge clear, passing the post eased down five lengths clear of Fiery Lad, with Augustusthestrong third and Man of Iron a staying-on fourth.

Mastercraftsman's win was one of twenty-three for Johnny Murtagh at Dundalk through the year, from an overall total in Ireland of ninety-three which enabled him to finish the year as champion jockey, five ahead of Pat Smullen. It was Murtagh's fourth Irish championship, after landing the title in 1995, 1996 and 1998. Man of Iron provided him with his only winner at the Breeders' Cup where Mastercraftsman eventually went for the Breeders' Cup Dirt Mile, instead of the Classic (in which Rip Van Winkle represented Ballydoyle). The Dirt Mile was upgraded to Grade 1, having had no graded status in its two previous runnings. Mastercraftsman was the clear form pick on his turf form and, having proved himself on a similar surface at Dundalk, started a hot favourite but, in a muddling race, he did himself no favours by starting sluggishly and having to race in the middle of the field. Mastercraftsman did make some ground under pressure in the straight and was beginning to respond just behind the leader when becoming unbalanced and stumbling after colliding with the rail inside the final furlong.

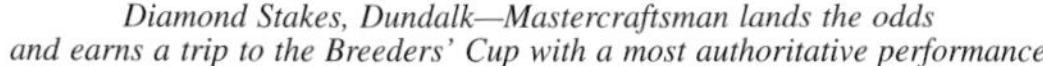

Diamond Stakes, Dundalk—Mastercraftsman lands the odds and earns a trip to the Breeders' Cup with a most authoritative performance

He crossed the line in fourth, just over a length and a half behind the winner Furthest Land, who was gaining his sixth victory of the year. Allowing that the winner was an improving sort, the form shown by Mastercraftsman was almost a stone below his best.

Mastercraftsman (IRE) (gr.c. 2006)	Danehill Dancer (IRE) (b 1993)	Danehill (b 1986)	Danzig Razyana
		Mira Adonde (b or br 1986)	Sharpen Up Lettre d'Amour
	Starlight Dreams (USA) (gr 1995)	Black Tie Affair (gr 1986)	Miswaki Hat Tab Girl
		Reves Celestes (b 1979)	Lyphard Tobira Celeste

Mastercraftsman has been retired to Coolmore at a fee of €20,000 which ranks him fourth among the stud's sires with published fees—behind Duke of Marmalade, Dylan Thomas and Rock of Gibraltar (the fees for Danehill Dancer, Galileo and Montjeu are private). Mastercraftsman should make plenty of appeal. He was precocious and can be expected to sire two-year-old winners himself; he trained on and proved fully effective at a mile to nearly eleven furlongs; and, as a big, strong colt, he certainly looks the part. He was tough, genuine and consistent and, though he did not race on firm going, he acted on any other and on polytrack. Mastercraftsman has what nowadays is sometimes labelled a 'commercial' pedigree, being the best son of Danehill Dancer, who had a remarkable year, topping the sires' table on earnings in Britain and Ireland for the first time. Danehill Dancer's remarkable career has seen his fee rise from just IR4,000 guineas in his first season in 1998 to €115,000 in 2008, after which his fee was made private. Danehill Dancer has now been represented by eight horses who have shown better form than he did, though he himself was no slouch, winning the same major races at two as Mastercraftsman, the Phoenix Stakes and National Stakes. The previous

Mr Derrick Smith's "Mastercraftsman"

leading progeny of Danehill Dancer were sprinter Choisir (126), two-year-old Fast Company (126) and miler Where Or When (124). Besides Mastercraftsman, Danehill Dancer was represented by two other Group 1 winners in the latest season, Again in the Irish One Thousand Guineas and Alfred Nobel, who led home a one, two, three for his sire when winning the Phoenix Stakes from Air Chief Marshal and Walk On Bye. Others to shine were Lillie Langtry (Debutante Stakes), Tamazirte (Prix Daniel Wildenstein, second in the Poule d'Essai des Pouliches and Prix de Diane) and Wajir (Prix Hocquart). The distaff side of Mastercraftsman's pedigree was covered in *Racehorses of 2008* but requires updating. Starlight Dreams's two-year-old Famous, also by Danehill Dancer and purchased for the top price of €1,000,000 at Goffs as a yearling, ran creditably for O'Brien in a fairly busy campaign comprising six races between June and September. She made all to win a maiden at Leopardstown, chased home Termagant in the Moyglare Stud Stakes and finished under a length fourth to Shakespearean in the Goffs Million Mile, looking at least useful and a fair prospect to land a pattern event at three. A yearling filly by Holy Roman Emperor out of Starlight Dreams was knocked down to Demi O'Byrne on behalf of John Magnier for 400,000 guineas at Tattersalls October Sales. *A. P. O'Brien, Ireland*

MASTER FONG (IRE) 3 b.g. Dr Fong (USA) 128 – Last Cry (FR) (Peintre Celebre **84**
(USA) 137) [2009 81: 7.1f p8g 10d^4 10.2g^6 10g* 9.7f^5 11.6g^4 p10m^2 Oct 26] smallish gelding: fairly useful handicapper: won at Sandown in August: stays 11.6f: acts on polytrack, good to firm and good to soft going: has looked irresolute, but is reliable: sold 14,000 gns, joined D. McCain Jnr. *B. W. Hills*

MASTERFUL ACT (USA) 2 ch.g. (Jan 20) Pleasantly Perfect (USA) 130 – Catnip **70**
(USA) (Flying Paster (USA)) [2009 7.6d p7m^6 p8.6g^3 p8m Sep 23] €32,000F: tall, workmanlike gelding: closely related to US Grade 3 8.5f winner Indescribable (by Pleasant Tap) and half-brother to several winners, including useful 1999 2-y-o sprinter Elaflaak (by Gulch): dam, won 8.5f minor stakes in USA, half-sister to Belmont Stakes winner Editor's Note: maiden: easily best effort when third to Sejanus at Wolverhampton (played up beforehand): stays 8.6f: gelded after final start. *J. R. Best*

MASTER LEON 2 b.c. (May 5) Monsieur Bond (IRE) 120 – Bollin Rita 82 (Rambo **71**
Dancer (CAN) 107) [2009 7d 7.5m 8g^3 8d^4 f7m^3 f8m^2 f8f^2 Dec 12] £3,500Y: well-made colt: fourth foal: half-brother to 5f winner Hawaii Prince (by Primo Valentino) and 3-y-o Allformary: dam 6f winner: fair maiden: stays 1m: acts on fibresand and good to soft going: visored last 2 starts. *B. Smart*

MASTER LIGHTFOOT 3 b.c. Kyllachy 129 – Two Step 60 (Mujtahid (USA) 118) **82**
[2009 84: p5g p5g p5g* p5.1g^4 p6f Dec 20] lengthy colt: fairly useful performer: won maiden at Lingfield in November: best kept to 5f/6f: acts on polytrack: front runner/races prominently. *W. R. Swinburn*

MASTER MAHOGANY 8 b.g. Bandmaster (USA) 97 – Impropriety (Law Society **63**
(USA) 130) [2009 72: p8g^6 p9.5g 10.2g^5 10.2m 8d^4 8m 8f^4 8f^4 8.1g 8.1m Aug 20] strong gelding: modest handicapper nowadays: effective at 1m/1¼m: acts on polytrack and any turf going. *R. J. Hodges*

MASTER MYLO (IRE) 2 ch.c. (Feb 5) Bertolini (USA) 125 – Sheboygan (IRE) 95 **72**
(Grand Lodge (USA) 125) [2009 5g^4 5m^5 6m^5 6m 7m 5g^4 Oct 19] €10,000Y: leggy colt: first foal: dam 7f (at 2 yrs)/7.6f winner: maiden: left Mrs L. Jewell and blinkered, easily best effort when fourth at Windsor final start: best form at 5f. *D. K. Ivory*

MASTER NIMBUS 9 b.g. Cloudings (IRE) 112 – Miss Charlie 59 (Pharly (FR) 130) **71**
[2009 71: 14m^2 14.1m^4 14.1m* 14.1f* 12g^3 14g^6 14.1g Sep 3] strong, angular gelding: fair handicapper: won at Redcar in June and July: stays 1¾m: acts on polytrack, firm and soft going: fairly useful chaser, successful in June/August. *J. J. Quinn*

MASTEROFCEREMONIES 6 ch.g. Definite Article 121 – Darakah 78 (Doulab **72**
(USA) 115) [2009 –: p8.6g^5 p12.2g^5 9m* 10g 12m^3 10g^5 11.9m^4 9.2m^6 p12.2g^6 9g* 10m Aug 29] tall, lengthy gelding: fair performer: won sellers at Musselburgh in April and July (sold from James Moffatt £11,000): stays 1½m, effective at shorter: acts on polytrack, soft and good to firm going: often wears headgear: tends to start slowly. *W. M. Brisbourne*

MASTER OF DANCE (IRE) 2 ch.c. (May 4) Noverre (USA) 125 – Shambodia **82**
(IRE) (Petardia 113) [2009 5m^6 6m^4 5m^3 5.7f* 7m^5 7g 6m^4 6m^4 7d^4 p7.1g p7m^2 p7g^2 p8m^6 Dec 9] €16,000F, £30,000Y: leggy colt: fourth foal: half-brother to useful 7f winner

(including at 2 yrs) Bettalatethannever (by Titus Livius): dam unraced: fairly useful performer: won maiden at Bath in June: in frame 5 times after, including in nurseries: stays 1m: acts on polytrack, firm and good to soft ground. *R. Hannon*

MASTER OF DISGUISE 3 b.c. Kyllachy 129 – St James's Antigua (IRE) 79 (Law **102**
Society (USA) 130) [2009 89p: 5g* 6g 5g^4 6m Sep 19] compact colt: useful handicapper: marked improvement when winning at Sandown in April by 2¼ lengths from Noble Storm: good fourth behind same rival at Goodwood easily best subsequent effort: should prove best at 5f/6f: acts on soft going. *C. G. Cox*

MASTER OF SONG 2 ch.g. (Apr 22) Ballet Master (USA) 92 – Ocean Song 61 **–**
(Savahra Sound 111) [2009 8.3d 6m p8.6g f6m Dec 15] unfurnished gelding: little form: tried blinkered. *S. R. Bowring*

MASTEROFTHEHORSE (IRE) 3 b.c. Sadler's Wells (USA) 132 – Shouk 94 **122 d**
(Shirley Heights 130) [2009 108: 12.3m^2 12g^3 12g^4 12g 12m Sep 27] leggy colt: very smart performer: shaped well on reappearance (second to Golden Sword in Chester Vase, plenty to do) before marked improvement when 2 lengths third to Sea The Stars in Derby at Epsom, finishing strongly under exaggerated waiting ride: disappointing after, leaving A. O'Brien after fourth to Fame And Glory in Irish Derby at the Curragh: eighth in Gordon Stakes at Goodwood, then said to have finished lame when ninth in Cumberland Lodge Stakes at Ascot: stays 1½m: acts on good to firm and good to soft going, unraced on extremes: sent to Qatar. *Miss D. Mountain*

MASTER PEGASUS 6 b.g. Lujain (USA) 119 – Seeking Utopia 76 (Wolfhound **–**
(USA) 126) [2009 86d: p10g^5 Jan 5] big, lengthy gelding: handicapper: well held only start in 2009: stays 1¼m: acts on polytrack, soft and good to firm ground. *J. R. Boyle*

MASTER ROONEY (IRE) 3 b. or br.c. Cape Cross (IRE) 129 – Wimple (USA) 101 **98 +**
(Kingmambo (USA) 125) [2009 97p: 6d 5g^3 Oct 19] heavy-bodied colt: useful performer, lightly raced: reportedly suffered from bruised feet during truncated campaign at 3 yrs: needed reappearance, then good third to Hotham in handicap at Pontefract, finishing fast: should prove best at 5f/6f: acts on firm and soft going. *B. Smart*

MASTERSHIP (IRE) 5 ch.g. Best of The Bests (IRE) 122 – Shady Point (IRE) 76 **100**
(Unfuwain (USA) 131) [2009 106: 6m p7g^4 8.9g^6 7m^4 8g^4 7d* 7.6g^6 7g f8g 6m^4 7g Oct 10] good-topped gelding: useful handicapper: won at Newcastle in July: creditable effort after only when fourth in Ayr Silver Cup: has won at 8.6f, better over shorter (effective at 6f): acts on polytrack, firm and soft ground: often wears headgear: tricky ride: sold 21,000 gns. *J. J. Quinn*

MASTERS HOUSE (IRE) 6 b.g. Indian Lodge (IRE) 127 – Aster Aweke (IRE) 87 **–**
(Alzao (USA) 117) [2009 9.3m Jun 15] poor form in bumpers, none over hurdles: well beaten in claimer at Carlisle on Flat debut. *Mrs J. C. McGregor*

MASTERY 3 b.c. Sulamani (IRE) 130 – Moyesii (USA) (Diesis 133) [2009 99p: **122**
p9g^4 11m* 16f^3 12g^3 12m^2 14.6m* a14f^3 Nov 6]

Judged on the number of runners involved, Godolphin was undoubtedly more focused on winning Group 1 races than any other European-based operation, particularly in the second half of the season. Between the start of August and the end of the year, there were forty-four Group 1s and Godolphin had runners in thirty-three of them, winning four through Mastery, Gladiatorus, Schiaparelli and Passion For Gold. Thirty of the races were contested by challengers from the stable of Saeed bin Suroor and three from that of Andre Fabre. Aidan O'Brien and Sir Michael Stoute couldn't even match Godolphin's number of runners between them, though they did win five of the forty-four. The victory that gave Sheikh Mohammed the greatest satisfaction was probably that of Mastery in the St Leger. Not only was the owner on the course to witness the success, with runner-up Kite Wood giving Godolphin a one, two, but it was Godolphin's first British classic success since Rule of Law in the same race five years earlier.

Mastery took a different route to Doncaster to that taken by Rule of Law, who had followed what may be termed a relatively traditional route, finishing second in the Dante Stakes and the Derby, fourth in the Irish Derby and then winning the Great Voltigeur Stakes. In contrast, Mastery ran on the polytrack at Kempton, won the Derby Italiano, finished third in the Queen's Vase and the Grand Prix de Paris and came second in the Great Voltigeur. Mastery readily won a maiden at Nottingham before coming third in a minor event at Newmarket on his two starts as a juvenile, when trained by Mark Johnston. Johnston had won the

Kentucky Derby Challenge Stakes at Kempton with Campanologist in 2008 and Mastery came pretty close, beaten less than a length into fourth behind Mafaaz after being slowly away. Transferred to Saeed bin Suroor not long afterwards (as Campanologist had been after his next race the year before), Mastery took in the Derby Italiano Better at Rome over seven weeks later. The race had been downgraded from Group 1 at a meeting of the European Pattern Committee (EPC) in January because it was not meeting the official standard for a race at that level, in other words not justifying its Group 1 status by the quality of its runners. This, in the words of the Committee, is 'assessed primarily by its Pattern Race Rating (which) is the average of the Annual Ratings achieved by a race over a three-year period. The Annual Rating is the average of the official ratings, as agreed by the World Rankings Supervisory Committee, of the first four horses to finish . . .' Certainly some recent editions of the classic have been well below par, notably those won by De Sica in 2005 and Awelmarduk in 2007, but this was hardly a new situation with nine winners between 1990 and 2004 running to a Timeform rating below 115, the mark Cima de Triomphe ran to in 2008 when the distance was reduced from a mile and a half to eleven furlongs for the first time in a last-ditch attempt to improve the quality of the field. Despite its demotion, the Derby Italiano kept its prize money, the £330,357 on offer for the winner making it very surprising that Mastery was the only foreign challenger in a field of twenty-one. Twelve of the runners had taken part on the same course in either the Premio Parioli (Italian Two Thousand Guineas) or the listed Premio Botticelli, though the short-priced favourite Abaton had won the listed Premio Emanuele Filiberto at Milan by six and a half lengths. Mastery was second choice in the market and won decisively, chasing the leaders before staying on in the final two furlongs to hit the front a hundred yards out, where the weakening leader Jakkalberry hit the rail and faltered. Mastery won by a length and a half from Premio Parioli fourth Turati, with Jakkalberry a head away third.

Derby Italiano Better, Rome—
Frankie Dettori claims just his second win in his home Derby as Mastery (centre) makes a winning start under the Godolphin banner; Jakkalberry (left) hits the rail and is about to lose second to Turati

Mastery was Godolphin's third Derby Italiano winner, following Central Park in 1998 and Mukhalif in 1999. Mastery ran only to 110—none of those behind him landed a pattern or listed event in the rest of the year (although the runner-up showed very smart form himself in the autumn)—but, even so, Mastery was spoken of afterwards as a possible runner in the Derby at Epsom. That race eventually passed by without him, with Kite Wood Godolphin's only representative, and Mastery next appeared at Royal Ascot. The choice was between the Queen's Vase and the King Edward VII Stakes, and the longer race was chosen even though Mastery had to shoulder a 5-lb penalty. After hitting the front under two furlongs out, Mastery wasn't done any favours by one of his rivals, Tactic, who continually bumped him, Mastery had no answer to four-length winner Holberg and lost second to Yankee Doodle by another three quarters of a length. Mastery showed that he stayed two miles but his next two starts were at a mile and a half. He posed no threat to the winner in either the Grand Prix de Paris, for which he was supplemented, or the Great Voltigeur Stakes, though he ran creditably in both, holding every chance at Longchamp until a furlong out when outpaced by the winner Cavalryman, eventually finishing third, and running on strongly at York to finish four and a half lengths second to Monitor Closely.

Everything about Mastery suggested that the Ladbrokes St Leger would be an ideal target but, with Kite Wood definitely heading for Doncaster after winning the Geoffrey Freer Stakes at Newbury, Mastery looked a candidate for a place at best. It is rare for a colt who has already run over two miles to win the classic. There have never been many stakes races for three-year-olds at that distance, though in the last half century Indiana (1964) and Bustino (1974) had both finished second in the Grand Prix de Paris (when it was run over fifteen and a half furlongs) and Son of Love (1979) had run second over fifteen furlongs in both the Grand Prix de Paris and the Prix Kergorlay. Stamina gained the day at Doncaster for Mastery, who started at 14/1. With the defection of the O'Brien-trained favourite Age of Aquarius at the final declaration stage, because connections were not happy with him, the St Leger betting was headed by Kite Wood, the Ebor Handicap runner-up Changingoftheguard from the O'Brien stable and Monitor Closely. The last-named was, however, far from certain to get a strongly-run mile and three quarters, something which also applied to King Edward VII Stakes winner and Great Voltigeur third Father Time. The only other Group 1 form on offer was that shown by Mourayan, though he had been no match for the winner Fame And Glory when third in the Irish Derby; the other two in a line-up of eight were outsiders Above Average and Changingoftheguard's pacemaker Von Jawlensky. The race proved

Ladbrokes St Leger Stakes, Doncaster—Ted Durcan takes over on Mastery (white cap), who overhauls the Dettori-ridden favourite Kite Wood inside the final furlong for a Godolphin 1,2; Monitor Closely (blaze) and Father Time (rail) complete the frame

rather muddling, with fifth-placed Mourayan for one suffering significant trouble in running, but Kite Wood was sent on after Von Jawlensky had made the running for almost a mile and a half, followed by Mastery, still going well, with Monitor Closely also travelling smoothly on the outside and Father Time trying to challenge on the inner. Inside the final furlong, Monitor Closely started to labour, hanging left as he did do, putting a halt to the progress Mourayan was trying to make, and under strong riding by Ted Durcan, Mastery clawed his way past his stable companion. Kite Wood ran on well but Mastery had the edge and gained the day by three quarters of a length, with Monitor Closely, found out by the distance, a length and three quarters back in third. Father Time came fourth, just ahead of Mourayan. Durcan received a one-day ban for excessive use of the whip. It may not have been a vintage St Leger but since Rule of Law's triumph in 2004, Godolphin had had sixteen runners in twenty-four British classics with Dubawi's third in the 2005 Derby the only placing (Godolphin had not had a runner in the four St Legers in that period). The St Leger wasn't the end of Mastery's campaign. He formed part of Godolphin's strong challenge for the Breeders' Cup at Santa Anita, contesting the Breeders' Cup Marathon, a race moved up in distance from a mile and a half, the distance over which Muhannak had won the year before. The field for the Marathon lacked strength in depth, Mastery's form at Doncaster the best on show. He was sent off favourite but failed to justify the confidence, struggling to go the pace and coming home third to the O'Brien-trained Man of Iron, beaten almost two and a half lengths by the winner.

Mastery (b.c. 2006)	Sulamani (IRE) (b 1999)	Hernando (b 1990)	Niniski
			Whakilyric
		Soul Dream (br 1990)	Alleged
			Normia
	Moyesii (USA) (b 1997)	Diesis (ch 1980)	Sharpen Up
			Doubly Sure
		Cherokee Rose (b 1991)	Dancing Brave
			Celtic Assembly

Mastery's campaign provided a shot in the arm for his sire Sulamani, a well travelled and thoroughly admirable middle-distance performer who won six Group or Grade 1 races, five of them—including the Dubai Sheema Classic, Arlington Million and Juddmonte International—after being transferred to Godolphin from the Niarchos Family. In an era when style seems to matter at least as much as substance, Sulamani's pedigree is not strictly commercial and his books of mares at Dalham Hall, then at Haras du Logis, where his fee has been €7,000, have not been huge. Mastery is one of fifty-three from a first crop in which useful middle-distance stayer Quai d'Orsay is the only other notable member. Sulamani, who has also been shuttled to Brazil, did not race over further than a mile and a half but gave the impression he would have managed further, his pedigree containing a number of influences for stamina. This is much less so in the lower half of Mastery's pedigree, the distaff family being one with which Sheikh Mohammed has been involved for many years. Following victories by Eastern Anthem in the Dubai Sheema Classic, Cavalryman in the Grand Prix de Paris and Telling in the Sword Dancer Invitational Stakes, the St Leger was the twenty-first Group or Grade 1 success for a horse bred by Sheikh Mohammed or Darley in the northern hemisphere since 2003. By comparison, Juddmonte have had fifty-seven and the Aga Khan thirty-seven. Moyesii, Mastery's dam, ran respectably without making the frame in listed and Group 3 company after winning a maiden at Cholet in the Provinces for Alex Pantall. She has done much better at stud, her 2004 foal, a colt by Jade Robbery, being Kirklees, successful in the Gran Criterium at two and in good form for Godolphin as a five-year-old, particularly when landing the York Stakes and September Stakes. Since foaling Mastery, Moyesii has produced an unraced sister to that colt named Quiet Queen, a yearling colt by Librettist and a colt foal by Street Cry. Moyesii was one of three winners—the two others included Poule d'Essai des Poulains third Bowman—out of Cherokee Rose, who was bred by Sheikh Mohammed. Cherokee Rose showed form over a mile but was significantly better at shorter, winning the Prix Maurice de Gheest and Haydock Sprint Cup and running second in the Prix de l'Abbaye de Longchamp. This is also the family of Prix du Cadran winner Molesnes, a half-brother to Cherokee Rose's dam

Celtic Assembly. Mastery will stay beyond two miles and his lack of top-class speed suggests strongly that he may well do much better going for glory in the Cup races as a four-year-old than plying his trade over a mile and a half, especially as Godolphin have Cavalryman as their main standard bearer among the older horses in that department. An attractive colt who was still rather on the leg at three, Mastery acts on firm and good to soft going and probably on polytrack and pro-ride. *Saeed bin Suroor*

MASTOORA (IRE) 3 b.f. Acclamation 118 – Sacred Love (IRE) 69 (Barathea (IRE) 127) [2009 7g* 7g 7m^6 7g Jul 8] 110,000Y: rather leggy filly: second foal: dam, maiden (should have stayed at least 1¼m), out of sister to very smart French 1½m performer De Quest: fairly useful form: won maiden at Folkestone in April: best subsequent effort when sixth in handicap at Newmarket: raced only at 7f: sold 11,500 gns. *W. J. Haggas* **85**

MASWERTE (IRE) 3 b.c. Fraam 114 – Rose Chime (IRE) 58 (Tirol 127) [2009 76: 7m* 7.1m^2 8g^4 7.1g 7m^3 p8f Oct 14] good-topped colt: fairly useful handicapper: won at Newbury in June: good efforts when placed after: stays 7f: acts on polytrack and good to firm going: quirky: sold 30,000 gns. *L. M. Cumani* **90**

MATAALEB 2 b.c. (Apr 19) Dalakhani (IRE) 133 – Elfaslah (IRE) 107 (Green Desert (USA) 127) [2009 8.3m Oct 13] rangy, attractive colt: half-brother to numerous winners, several at least useful, notably high-class 7f (at 2 yrs) to 1¼m (Dubai World Cup) winner Almutawakel and smart 1m (including UAE 1000 Guineas) winner Muwakleh (both by Machiavellian): dam, won around 1¼m, half-sister to high-class 1½m performer White Muzzle: 14/1 and green, considerately handled when down the field in maiden at Leicester: sure to improve. *M. A. Jarvis* **50 p**

MATA HARI BLUE 3 ch.f. Monsieur Bond (IRE) 120 – Feeling Blue 60 (Missed Flight 123) [2009 p5.1g^6 6d^2 6m^4 6g^3 Aug 30] 40,000Y: first foal: dam, 5f winner, out of useful sprinter Blues Indigo: fair maiden: should prove best at 5f/6f: acts on good to soft going. *J. R. Holt* **68**

MATA KERANJANG (USA) 2 b. or br.c. (Mar 27) More Than Ready (USA) 120 – Love Sick (USA) (Salt Lake (USA)) [2009 5g^3 7g^2 7m^6 7m^2 7m^3 8d^3 Oct 11] $57,000F, $90,000Y, $260,000 2-y-o: good-topped colt: fifth foal: half-brother to winner in USA by Alphabet Soup: dam, unraced, out of close relative to US Grade 2 9f/11f winner Forty Niner Days: useful maiden: highly tried all starts, best efforts when second in Vintage Stakes (1¼ lengths behind Xtension) and listed race (beaten ½ length by Vale of York) at Goodwood, and third in Gran Criterium at Milan (final start, beaten 5¼ lengths by Hearts of Fire): stays 1m: acts on good to firm and good to soft going. *P. F. I. Cole* **103**

MATARAM (USA) 6 b.g. Matty G (USA) 119 – Kalinka (USA) (Mr Prospector (USA)) [2009 , a91: p8.6g^2 p10g Feb 14] tall, leggy, long-backed gelding: fairly useful performer on all-weather, lightly raced on turf: effective at 1m to 11f: acts on polytrack: patiently ridden. *W. Jarvis* **– a81**

MATER MATER 2 gr.f. (Apr 22) Silver Patriarch (IRE) 125 – Emily-Mou (IRE) 80 (Cadeaux Genereux 131) [2009 p6g p8m p8m Dec 4] good-topped filly: seventh foal: sister to 4-y-o Mr Plod and half-sister to 3 winners, including useful 5f winner Obstructive (by Zilzal) and 1¾m winner Dangerous Deploy (by Deploy): dam 1m/1¼m winner: modest form at best in maidens: left Andrew Reid after debut: should stay 1¼m+. *M. J. Scudamore* **64**

MATHAAQ 3 b.c. Nayef (USA) 129 – Mouwadh (USA) 64 (Nureyev (USA) 131) [2009 10.3s p10g^2 10.9g* Aug 31] sturdy colt: third foal: half-brother to 2006 2-y-o 7f winner Malaath (by Green Desert): dam, ran twice, out of half-sister to 1000 Guineas winner Harayir: fairly useful form: won maiden at Warwick in August: stays 11f: acts on polytrack: sold 20,000 gns, joined Eric McNamara, Ireland. *M. A. Jarvis* **85**

MATILDA POLIPORT 3 b.f. Mind Games 121 – Poppy Carew (IRE) 110 (Danehill (USA) 126) [2009 –: p8g 8d 10d Aug 2] angular filly: modest maiden: best effort on second start: sold 1,500 gns, sent to Spain. *W. R. Swinburn* **64**

MATINEE IDOL 6 ch.m. In The Wings 128 – Bibliotheque (USA) 79 (Woodman (USA) 126) [2009 50: f14s f16g f12g Feb 19] sturdy mare: maiden: well held in 2009: tried in cheekpieces; blinkered. *Mrs S. Lamyman* **–**

MATRAASH (USA) 3 b.c. Elusive Quality (USA) – Min Alhawa (USA) 108 (Riverman (USA) 131) [2009 66p: 8.1m^2 9.2g^2 10.1d* 10m* 12g 10.4m 12m^6 Sep 12] big, deep-girthed colt: useful performer: won maiden at Newcastle and handicap at Leicester, both in June: stays 1¼m: acts on good to firm and good to soft ground: sold 20,000 gns. *M. Johnston* **97**

MATSUNOSUKE 7 b.g. Magic Ring (IRE) 115 – Lon Isa 80 (Grey Desire 115) [2009 107: f5s p6g* p6g^3 p5g* p5g* p6g* p6g p5g 6m 5m p6g 6m^3 5m^4 5m 5g 6m p6m 5g^4 5m 5d p6g^3 Dec 28] workmanlike gelding: smart performer on all-weather, useful on turf: thrived early in 2009, winning handicaps at Great Leighs and Lingfield in January, then handicap (by ½ length from Little Edward) and listed race (beat Duff by short head) at Lingfield in February: best at 5f/6f: acts on all-weather and firm ground: held up. *A. B. Coogan* **101 a116**

MATTAMIA (IRE) 3 b.g. Makbul 104 – Lady Dominatrix (IRE) 112 (Danehill Dancer (IRE) 117) [2009 72: 5.1m* 5s 5d^2 5m* 5d* 5g^2 5g^2 5m^4 5d Sep 5] good-bodied gelding: useful handicapper: much improved in 2009, winning at Nottingham in April, and Leicester (by 4½ lengths) and Newmarket (beat Dark Lane 2 lengths) in June: good head second to Noble Storm at Goodwood 2 outings later: best at 5f: acts on good to firm and good to soft ground: versatile tactically. *B. R. Millman* **101**

MATTEROFACT (IRE) 6 b.m. Bold Fact (USA) 116 – Willow Dale (IRE) 89 (Danehill (USA) 126) [2009 78, a69: 5.3m^4 5.7f^5 5m^2 5m^2 5m* 5m^2 5.1m^2 5.1v 5f^6 5.1d^3 5m^2 5s^6 5.1m^3 Sep 28] strong mare: fair handicapper: won at Lingfield in June: has form at 6f, best at 5f: acts on polytrack, firm and soft going. *M. S. Saunders* **77**

MATUZA (IRE) 6 ch.h. Cadeaux Genereux 131 – Aoife (IRE) 83 (Thatching 131) [2009 6m* 6f 6g^6 Oct 19] big, strong horse: missed 2008: just fair performer in 2009: won seller at Windsor in June: stayed 7f: acted on all-weather and firm going: blinkered once: wasn't straightforward: dead. *P. R. Chamings* **74**

MAUSIN (IRE) 2 b.f. (Apr 22) Monsun (GER) 124 – Cote Quest (USA) 96 (Green Desert (USA) 127) [2009 8.3m^4 Sep 30] unfurnished filly: second foal: half-sister to French 11.5f/13f winner Fitzgerald (by Barathea): dam, French 1m winner, out of half-sister to smart French performers up to 1½m Prospect Wells and Prospect Park: 16/1 and green, encouraging 9 lengths fourth to Bint Almatar in maiden at Nottingham, not knocked about: should be well suited by 1¼m+: should improve. *H. Morrison* **53 p**

MAVALENTA (IRE) 2 b.f. (Jan 9) Montjeu (IRE) 137 – Velouette (Darshaan 133) [2009 7m Sep 18] well-made filly: second foal: dam unraced half-sister to Dubai World Cup winner Moon Ballad, out of half-sister to very smart performer up to 2m Central Park: 66/1 and green, well held in minor event at Newbury (unruly beforehand, carried head awkwardly): bred to be suited by 1¼m+. *J. W. Hills* **–**

MAVERICK'S MAGIC 3 ch.g. Karinga Bay 116 – Magical Day 54§ (Halling (USA) 133) [2009 –: p12g Dec 31] well beaten in sellers: bred for stamina. *W. G. M. Turner* **–**

MAVERIN (IRE) 3 b.c. King's Best (USA) 132 – Minerva (IRE) (Caerleon (USA) 132) [2009 82p: 8d^3 p8g^4 8g^3 6s^2 6d^3 6m* 6g Sep 30] useful-looking colt: fairly useful performer: won maiden at Windsor in June: left J. Noseda 22,000 gns prior to final start: stays 1m: acts on polytrack, soft and good to firm going. *Tom Dascombe* **85**

MAWADDAH (IRE) 2 b.c. (Mar 15) Intikhab (USA) 135 – Handsome Anna (IRE) 67 (Bigstone (IRE) 126) [2009 6m 8.1d^6 8.3s^3 8.3d^3 p7g^3 Nov 11] 28,000F, £70,000Y: rather leggy colt: fifth foal: half-brother to 3 winners, including 5-y-o Hansomis and 6-y-o The History Man: dam Irish maiden: fair maiden: barely stays testing 8.3f: acts on polytrack and soft going. *R. Hannon* **78**

MAWATHEEQ (USA) 4 b.c. Danzig (USA) – Sarayir (USA) 104 (Mr Prospector (USA)) [2009 108p: 8s 10.3m* 12m* 10m^2 Oct 17] **126**

Mawatheeq has quickly made up for time lost through an injury to his off-fore joint, an injury sustained when he was being broken in and serious enough to keep him off the course until August 2008. Successful in a maiden at Newmarket and a handicap at Ascot from four starts in his three-year-old campaign, Mawatheeq had a similar wins-to-runs ratio in the latest season. This time, however, one of the wins was in a Group 3 contest, while he then went on to show high-class form when runner-up in a Group 1. There is a chance that there may be even better to come from Mawatheeq, who looks sure to be winning at the highest level in the next season. He was to have started off in 2010 at the Dubai Carnival meeting, but he injured a fetlock joint during his preparation and is now unlikely to be seen until the summer.

Mawatheeq made an inauspicious return to action, finishing well held in a handicap at Newbury in April. Perhaps he was unsuited by the soft ground there—he had raced only on good to firm at three following a promising run on polytrack on his debut—though there is also the possibility that all wasn't well with him.

Grosvenor Casinos Cumberland Lodge Stakes, Ascot—
Mawatheeq earns a crack at the Champion Stakes with this convincing win over Campanologist

It transpired that many in his stable were under the weather in the spring due to an infection, as a result of which trainer Marcus Tregoning temporarily closed his yard in late-May. Mawatheeq himself was given a five-month break and, back on good to firm ground and stepped up in trip, he resumed his progress. In September he followed up a win in a handicap at Doncaster by justifying favouritism in the twelve-runner Grosvenor Casinos Cumberland Lodge Stakes at Ascot. Patiently ridden, Mawatheeq swept through to lead entering the final furlong at Ascot and looked better the further he went on his first attempt at a mile and a half, winning by two and a quarter lengths from Campanologist. It was Tregoning's fifth Cumberland Lodge victory, having been successful with Nayef in 2001, High Accolade in 2003 and 2004 and Mubtaker in 2005, both Nayef (a near relative of Mawatheeq) and Mubtaker also owned by Hamdan Al Maktoum. Nayef won it as a three-year-old, and three weeks later gave Tregoning his first Group 1 win in the Champion Stakes at Newmarket. Mawatheeq took the same route, though it cost his owner £30,000 to supplement him for the Champion Stakes. The decision to do so was vindicated. Mawatheeq earned just over £81,000 for second to Twice Over, and he wasn't far off claiming the first prize. Making headway under pressure when forced to switch left as the winner hung towards him over a furlong out, Mawatheeq ran on strongly once in the clear and was only half a length down at the line, shaping as though a return to a mile and a half will suit him ideally. Mawatheeq's rider took the relatively rare step nowadays of lodging an objection to the winner, which rather put the cat among the pigeons, Twice Over's trainer, for one, seemingly none too impressed. The stewards left the placings unaltered.

Mawatheeq (USA) (b.c. 2005)	Danzig (USA) (b 1977)	Northern Dancer (b 1961)	Nearctic
			Natalma
		Pas de Nom (b or br 1968)	Admiral's Voyage
			Petitioner
	Sarayir (USA) (b 1994)	Mr Prospector (b 1970)	Raise A Native
			Gold Digger
		Height of Fashion (b 1979)	Bustino
			Highclere

A rangy, good sort who looks the part, Mawatheeq is also choicely bred. He is the sixth foal of the seven-furlong and mile-and-a-quarter winner Sarayir, who is closely related to Nayef and a half-sister to Nashwan and Unfuwain. Full details of the distaff side of the pedigree can be found in the essay on Mawatheeq's half-sister, the One Thousand Guineas and Coronation Stakes winner Ghanaati (by Giant's Causeway). Sarayir's four other winners include Mawatheeq's full sister Itqaan, who was successful in a mile maiden. *M. P. Tregoning*

MAWZOON (IRE) 2 ch.c. (Mar 16) Pivotal 124 – Two Clubs 111 (First Trump 118) [2009 6g^4 Oct 30] 200,000Y: stocky, good-bodied colt: sixth foal: half-brother to 3 winners, notably high-class 5f (at 2 yrs) to 7f winner Red Clubs (by Red Ransom): dam 6f winner, including at 2 yrs: 9/2 and backward, shaped well when 2¼ lengths fourth to Asraab in maiden at Newmarket, smooth headway to be upsides briefly 1f out and not knocked about: should make a useful 3-y-o. *M. A. Jarvis* **79 p**

MAXIJACK (IRE) 2 b.g. (Apr 20) Governor Brown (USA) 104 – Aster Fields (IRE) 50 (Common Grounds 118) [2009 p7m p7g Dec 31] poor form in maidens. *G. Brown* **47**

MAXIMIX 6 gr.g. Linamix (FR) 127 – Time Will Show (FR) (Exit To Nowhere (USA) 122) [2009 –: p12g p16g^5 Apr 29] useful-looking gelding: modest handicapper: probably stays 2m: acts on polytrack and good to soft going: temperamental jumper. *G. L. Moore* **60**

MAXIMUS AURELIUS (IRE) 4 b.g. Night Shift (USA) – Dame's Violet (IRE) (Groom Dancer (USA) 128) [2009 79: 9s p9.5g Oct 9] smallish, strong, close-coupled gelding: handicapper: below form at 4 yrs: stays 10.3f: acts on polytrack, firm and good to soft ground: tried tongue tied: inconsistent: gelded after final start. *J. Jay* **63**

MAX ONE TWO THREE (IRE) 4 b.f. Princely Heir (IRE) 111 – Dakota Sioux (IRE) 90 (College Chapel 122) [2009 –: 6m^6 5.2s 6.1m^4 6v^6 7m^3 Jun 1] useful-looking filly: useful performer, lightly raced: standout effort at 4 yrs when 2¾ lengths fourth to Lesson In Humility in listed event at Nottingham: probably best at 6f: acts on soft and good to firm going: temperament under suspicion. *Tom Dascombe* **102**

MAXWELL HAWKE (IRE) 3 br.g. Rock of Gibraltar (IRE) 133 – Twice The Ease 46 (Green Desert (USA) 127) [2009 68: 7.1m* 7d 7g 6g 6m 7m Sep 19] useful-looking gelding: fairly useful performer: won maiden at Warwick in April: below form in handicaps after (lame third outing, then signs of return to form in tongue tie last 2 starts): stays 7f: acts on good to firm ground. *P. W. Chapple-Hyam* **82**

MAXWIL 4 b.g. Storming Home 128 – Lady Donatella 57 (Last Tycoon 131) [2009 91: p11g 7.1g 10.1m^4 10m p12g Oct 9] tall gelding: fair performer nowadays: left G. L. Moore after reappearance: stays 11f: acts on good to firm and good to soft ground: tried blinkered: held up. *P. M. Phelan* **74**

MAYADEEN (IRE) 7 b.g. King's Best (USA) 132 – Inaaq 109 (Lammtarra (USA) 134) [2009 62: p16g^4 f14g 12g 14.1m^3 16m^6 Jun 29] good-topped gelding: modest handicapper: stays 1¾m: acts on polytrack, firm and soft going: wears headgear: held up: temperamental. *R. A. Fahey* **62 §**

MAYBE I WILL (IRE) 4 b.f. Hawk Wing (USA) 136 – Canterbury Lace (USA) (Danehill (USA) 126) [2009 77: 10m 9g^3 8f^6 May 31] small filly: fair handicapper: stays 1¼m: acts on polytrack, good to firm and good to soft ground: signs of temperament. *S. Dow* **69**

MAYBE I WONT 4 b.g. Kyllachy 129 – Surprise Surprise 91 (Robellino (USA) 127) [2009 74: p6g^4 p6g p8g p8.6g^5 10m^3 10.1m 8.5g 10.2g* 10.9g* p11g 9.9g^3 12g 10.2d^2 10.9g Aug 31] good-topped gelding: fair handicapper: won at Nottingham and Warwick in June: stays 10.9f: acts on polytrack, good to firm and good to soft going: tried in cheek-pieces: held up. *Lucinda Featherstone* **73**

MAYBEME 3 b.f. Lujain (USA) 119 – Malvadilla (IRE) 77 (Doyoun 124) [2009 54: 9d^4 8g^5 9.9m^2 9.9f^4 12.1m^4 10g^5 10.3g^6 Oct 24] sparely-made filly: fair maiden handicapper: stays 1½m: acts on firm going. *N. Bycroft* **74**

MAY CHORUS (IRE) 2 b.f. (Mar 23) Night Shift (USA) – Chorus (USA) (Darshaan 133) [2009 p6f p6g^3 6g p7f Dec 20] smallish filly: sixth foal: half-sister to winning sprinter in USA by Boundary: dam ran once in USA: best effort when length third to Hulcote Rose in maiden at Kempton. *J. R. Boyle* **63**

MAYFAIR'S FUTURE 4 b.c. High Estate 127 – Riva La Belle § (Ron's Victory (USA) 129) [2009 69: p10g p10g 10m^3 10.2m 10m p12g^2 p8.6g^6 10s Aug 7] stocky colt: modest performer: stays easy 1½m: acts on polytrack and good to firm going: visored once. *J. R. Jenkins* **63**

MAY MARTIN 3 b.f. Monsieur Bond (IRE) 120 – Calcavella 75 (Pursuit of Love 124) [2009 f5g* f5g 6d^3 6d p6g Oct 26] 30,000F: sturdy filly: fourth foal: half-sister to 3 winners, including 5-y-o Bertoliver and 6-y-o Skhilling Spirit: dam, maiden who stayed **60**

7f, half-sister to smart Hong Kong 7f/1m performer Dave's Best: modest performer: won 5f maiden at Southwell in February: below form in handicaps after. *Rae Guest*

MAY NEED A SPELL 3 b.g. Needwood Blade 117 – Under My Spell 80 (Wizard King 122) [2009 53: 8.1g 6m p6g Jul 8] maiden: no form at 3 yrs: tried blinkered. *J. G. M. O'Shea* **–**

MAYOLYNN (USA) 3 ch.f. Johannesburg (USA) 127 – Civilynn (USA) (Lost Code (USA)) [2009 8g p11g^3 9m^4 10s^2 9.7m^3 p10g Sep 2] $250,000Y: lengthy filly: fourth foal: sister to winner in USA and half-sister to 2 winners there: dam, US 2-y-o 8.5f winner, half-sister to dam of smart performer up to 1m Flashy Wings: fair maiden: stays 11f: acts on polytrack: tried visored. *H. R. A. Cecil* **64 a74**

MAYOMAN (IRE) 4 b.g. Namid 128 – America Lontana (FR) (King's Theatre (IRE) 128) [2009 70: p5.1g p6g^6 7.6g^4 9.9m^6 7g^4 5d^3 6d* 7m^6 p6g* p6g Oct 29] close-coupled gelding: fair handicapper: left M. Mullineaux after fourth start: won at Newcastle in September and Wolverhampton in October: stays easy 7.5f: acts on polytrack and good to soft going: tried blinkered. *D. Carroll* **67**

MAYORSTONE (IRE) 3 ch.f. Exceed And Excel (AUS) 126 – Coolrain Lady (IRE) 74 (Common Grounds 118) [2009 –: 6g Sep 3] tall filly: well held in maidens 13 months apart. *B. Smart* **–**

MAY PARKIN (IRE) 4 b.f. Acclamation 118 – Pretext (Polish Precedent (USA) 131) [2009 43: p8.6g p7m^5 Nov 4] modest maiden: stays 7f: acts on polytrack: tried blinkered/ tongue tied. *M. Wigham* **52**

MAYS LOUISE 5 ch.m. Sir Harry Lewis (USA) 127 – Maysimp (IRE) (Mac's Imp (USA) 116) [2009 –: f8d p8.6g p8.6g^4 p8.6m 8f 10.4m Jun 11] little form. *B. P. J. Baugh* **–**

MAYTA CAPAC (USA) 3 ch.c. Thunder Gulch (USA) 129 – Yvecrique (FR) 111 (Epervier Bleu 131) [2009 58p: p8.6g^6 p10m^5 Dec 9] well-made colt: maiden: well held late on at 3 yrs. *D. M. Simcock* **–**

MAZAMORRA (USA) 2 b. or br.f. (Mar 19) Orientate (USA) 127 – Mumbo Jumbo (USA) (Kingmambo (USA) 125) [2009 p8g^6 Nov 1] $120,000Y: fourth foal: half-sister to winners in USA by A P Indy and Successful Appeal: dam, minor stakes winner in USA around 1m, sister to 5-y-o King of Dixie: 25/1, mid-field in maiden at Lingfield, slowly away and very green. *M. Botti* **45**

MAZE (IRE) 4 ch.g. Dr Fong (USA) 128 – Aryadne (Rainbow Quest (USA) 134) [2009 95§: 6m^4 7m 6m^4 6m 6d 8s p8.6g Oct 16] leggy, workmanlike gelding: fairly useful handicapper nowadays: best at 6f: acts on good to firm and good to soft going: ungenuine: sold £15,500. *B. Smart* **94 §**

MAZZOLA 3 b.g. Bertolini (USA) 125 – Elegant Dance 71 (Statoblest 120) [2009 83: p6g^4 p5g^4 p5g^3 5.2d^3 6m^2 6g^3 5s 5m 5g 5.1m^5 5m^2 6g^6 5.1g p5g^3 5g^6 5m^{3d} 5m 5m^4 5.3m^5 p5.1g^3 5.1d^3 5g^2 5.1g^3 Oct 28] strong, close-coupled gelding: fairly useful handicapper at best: placed numerous times in 2009, and gradually came down weights: effective at 5f/ 6f: acts on polytrack, firm and good to soft ground: sold 6,500 gns. *M. R. Channon* **82**

MCCARTNEY (GER) 4 b.c. In The Wings 128 – Messina (GER) (Dashing Blade 117) [2009 –: 7m 8m^5 Jun 14] workmanlike colt: smart performer at 2 yrs: lightly raced subsequently and useful form at best, fifth to Beacon Lodge in Prix du Chemin de Fer du Nord at Chantilly final start: should stay 1¼m: winner on good to soft going, best form on good to firm: has left Godolphin. *Saeed bin Suroor* **105**

MCCONNELL (USA) 4 ch.g. Petionville (USA) – Warsaw Girl (IRE) (Polish Precedent (USA) 131) [2009 87: p10g f8g* f8g^4 p8g 10d f8g* p8g^4 f8f^5 f8m^2 f8f* Dec 17] good-topped gelding: useful performer: won handicaps in January and September and claimer (claimed £12,000, joined P. Butler) in December, all at Southwell: best around 1m: acts on all-weather and good to firm going. *G. L. Moore* **95**

MCCORMACK (IRE) 7 b.g. Desert Story (IRE) 115 – La Loba (IRE) 73 (Treasure Kay 114) [2009 10.1g* 8.3m 12.4s 10m^3 12m^4 9.9f 10m 8.5m^6 9.9g Sep 22] close-coupled gelding: modest handicapper: 66/1, won apprentice event at Newcastle in April: stays 1¼m: acts on good to firm ground: tried visored/in cheekpieces. *Miss T. Jackson* **55**

MCELDOWNEY 7 b.g. Zafonic (USA) 130 – Ayodhya (IRE) (Astronef 116) [2009 –: 16m^4 18g 13.8m^5 f12m Nov 11] useful-looking gelding: lightly raced and little form since 2007: tried blinkered/in cheekpieces. *M. C. Chapman* **–**

MCQUEEN (IRE) 9 ch.g. Barathea (IRE) 127 – Bibliotheque (USA) 79 (Woodman (USA) 126) [2009 69: 14g 14.1m Aug 8] lengthy gelding: fair handicapper in 2008: below form in 2009: stays 2m: acts on all-weather, heavy and good to firm ground: tried visored: front runner: fair hurdler. *B. D. Leavy* **53**

MDAWEE (IRE) 2 b.c. (Apr 23) Choisir (AUS) 126 – Its All Eurs (IRE) 67 (Barathea (IRE) 127) [2009 5g* 5m 5.1m² 5g 6m⁵ Oct 5] €4,000Y, £10,000 2-y-o: good-quartered colt: third foal: dam maiden (stayed 7f): won maiden at Warwick in June: creditable efforts 3 of last 4 starts, stamina stretched in nursery final one: best at 5f: hung left throughout second outing. *Tom Dascombe* **83**

MEAN MACHINE (IRE) 7 b.g. Idris (IRE) 118 – Date Mate (USA) (Thorn Dance (USA) 107) [2009 –: f11m⁶ p16.5g Aug 10] maiden: little form since 2007. *J. W. Unett* **–**

MEAN MR MUSTARD (IRE) 3 b.g. Invincible Spirit (IRE) 121 – White Lavender (USA) 69 (Mt Livermore (USA)) [2009 59?: p6g³ p6g³ p6g⁵ a7.5g³ a8g* 7d 8g 7d a4.8g⁵ a7g Aug 9] good-quartered gelding: modest performer: left J. Osborne after third start: won minor event at Mons in March: stays 1m: acts on polytrack/all-weather: blinkered 4 of last 5 starts in Britain. *Peggy Bastiaens-Van Cauwenbergh, Belgium* **55**

MECOX BAY (IRE) 2 b.c. (May 19) Noverre (USA) 125 – Birdsong (IRE) 73 (Dolphin Street (FR) 125) [2009 7.1m 8.1g³ Aug 13] rangy colt: fair form in maidens at Sandown, 8¼ lengths third to Waseet. *A. M. Balding* **69**

MEDIA JURY 2 b.g. (Mar 26) Lucky Owners (NZ) 122 – Landofheartsdesire (IRE) 75 (Up And At 'em 109) [2009 5m 6g Oct 9] close-coupled gelding: well held in maidens. *J. S. Wainwright* **–**

MEDIA STARS 4 gr.g. Green Desert (USA) 127 – Starine (FR) 123 (Mendocino (USA) 108) [2009 73d: p8.6g⁶ p10g p13g* 12.4m⁶ 10.1g 8g 12.4d 12s Oct 27] good-topped gelding: fair performer: won claimer at Lingfield (left J. Osborne £5,000) in February: well below form after: stays 13f: acts on polytrack, little impact on turf: tried in blinkers/cheekpieces: temperament under suspicion. *R. Johnson* **73 d**

MEDICEAN MAN 3 ch.g. Medicean 128 – Kalindi 102 (Efisio 120) [2009 6m 6d⁴ 6m* 6s³ 6d* 6.1g⁴ 6g* 7g⁴ Oct 9] 80,000Y: good-topped gelding: fifth foal: brother to useful Irish 2005 2-y-o 6f/7f winner Abigail Pett and half-brother to 5f/6f winner Mambazo (by Dansili) and 7f (including at 2 yrs) winner Autograph Hunter (by Tobougg), both fairly useful: dam 5f (at 2 yrs) and 7f winner: fairly useful performer: won maiden at Doncaster in June, and handicaps at Haydock in July and Ripon in August: stays 7f: acts on soft and good to firm going. *J. R. Gask* **89**

MEDICEA SIDERA 5 b.m. Medicean 128 – Broughtons Motto 75 (Mtoto 134) [2009 101: p6g⁵ 7m 7m⁶ 7m Sep 26] good-bodied mare: just fairly useful performer in 2009: best form at 6f/7f: acted on polytrack and good to firm ground: raced up with pace: reportedly in foal to Bahamian Bounty. *E. F. Vaughan* **93**

MEDICINAL COMPOUND 2 b.g. (Feb 12) Dr Fong (USA) 128 – Liska's Dance (USA) (Riverman (USA) 131) [2009 8d³ 7m² 8g* Oct 16] £21,000Y: half-brother to numerous winners, including useful French 7f to 9.8f winner Dancing Kris (by Kris): dam useful French 1m/1¼m winner: fair form in maidens, winning at Redcar by short head from Fourth Generation (pair clear): should stay 1¼m. *K. A. Ryan* **79**

MEDICI PEARL 5 b.m. Medicean 128 – In Love Again (IRE) 86 (Prince Rupert (FR) 121) [2009 96: 8m 8s³ 8m 8g 8.9g 10.1m³ 10.4m 10.4g⁶ 8.3s* 8g 7g Oct 10] lengthy, good-topped mare: useful handicapper: won at Hamilton in August: stays easy 1¼m: acts on heavy and good to firm going. *T. D. Easterby* **97**

MEDICI TIME 4 gr.g. Medicean 128 – Pendulum 82 (Pursuit of Love 124) [2009 75§: 6f² 6m⁶ 5.9m 6g 5m³ 5g² 6m* 6m 5g* 5g Oct 9] big, good-topped gelding: has round action: fair handicapper: won at Haydock in August and Ayr in September: effective at 5f/6f: acts on firm ground: in headgear nowadays: ungenuine. *T. D. Easterby* **78 §**

MEDIEVAL MAIDEN 6 gr.m. Zaha (CAN) 106 – Brillante (FR) 118 (Green Dancer (USA) 132) [2009 58, a68: p13g 11.9m² 11.9m² p12g* 12m⁵ p11g⁶ p16f p12m p12f Oct 14] lengthy, quite good-topped mare: modest performer: won seller at Lingfield in June: stays 1¾m: acts on polytrack (all wins) and good to firm going: tried in cheekpieces. *Mrs L. J. Mongan* **60**

MEDITERRANEAN SEA (IRE) 3 b.f. Medecis 119 – High Glider (High Top 131) [2009 8.3g 8g 10m⁴ p11g p12m p11m p12g³ Nov 11] rather leggy filly: half-sister to useful 1m winner Lizop (by Brief Truce) and 2m winner Da Silva (by Double Schwartz), both in Ireland: dam Irish 1½m winner: modest maiden: probably stays 1½m: acts on polytrack and good to firm ground. *J. R. Jenkins* **63**

MEER UND WIND (GER) 2 b.f. (Mar 28) Xaar 132 – Moneypenny (GER) (Neshad (USA) 108) [2009 6g⁶ 7.1m 7.1g p8g Oct 2] €22,000Y: fourth foal: dam German 2-y-o 6f (listed race)/7f winner: modest maiden: stays 1m: acts on polytrack: blinkered (ran well) final start. *P. R. Webber* **58**

MEETHAAQ (USA) 4 b.g. Kingmambo (USA) 125 – New Harmony (USA) (A P Indy (USA) 131) [2009 92p: 10.4m^6 12f^2 16.1d 12m Oct 16] good-topped gelding: useful handicapper: reportedly suffered from colic after final 3-y-o start: best effort when second at Doncaster: stays 1½m: acts on firm going: sold £30,000. *Sir Michael Stoute* **96**

MEETINGS MAN (IRE) 2 br.c. (Apr 13) Footstepsinthesand 120 – Missella (IRE) 63 (Danehill (USA) 126) [2009 6m 6v^6 6d 8m^6 7g Oct 10] leggy colt: modest maiden: form only at 6f. *Micky Hammond* **56**

MEEZAAN (IRE) 2 b.c. (Feb 6) Medicean 128 – Varenka (IRE) 91 (Fasliyev (USA) 120) [2009 7m p7g* Oct 14] 200,000Y: strong, well-made colt: first foal: dam, 7.5f winner (ran only at 2 yrs), half-sister to 2-y-o Steinbeck out of sister to dam of very smart miler Nannina (by Medicean): still green, won maiden at Lingfield readily by 2¼ lengths from Mass Rally, racing freely in front and strong at finish having hung right briefly: stiff task in sales race at Newmarket 11 days earlier: should stay 1m: useful prospect. *J. H. M. Gosden* **87 p**

MEEZNAH (USA) 2 b.f. (Apr 16) Dynaformer (USA) – String Quartet (IRE) 109 (Sadler's Wells (USA) 132) [2009 7g^3 8g^3 Oct 20] $120,000Y, resold $175,000Y: good-bodied filly: sixth foal: closely related to 3-y-o Lyric Art and half-sister to smart but irresolute performer up to 13f Shahin (1m winner at 2 yrs, by Kingmambo): dam, 1¼m/12.5f winner, sister to smart Irish/US performer up to 1¼m Casey Tibbs: fairly useful form when third in maidens at Newmarket (behind Tabassum) and Yarmouth (beaten a length by Principal Role): will stay 1¼m. *D. R. Lanigan* **84**

MEFRAAS (IRE) 3 b.g. King's Best (USA) 132 – Khaizarana 90 (Alhaarth (IRE) 126) [2009 68: 9.7f^2 8.3m^2 9g^3 p10g^3 9.7m^2 10.1m^3 Oct 3] good-topped gelding: fairly useful maiden: placed all 6 starts in 2009: stays 1¼m: acts on polytrack and firm ground: sold 32,000 gns, sent to Qatar. *E. A. L. Dunlop* **84**

MEGA DAME (IRE) 5 b.m. Iron Mask (USA) 117 – Easter Girl (Efisio 120) [2009 p8.6g 10.2g Jun 11] maiden: last both starts since 2007: tried blinkered/tongue tied. *D. Haydn Jones* **–**

MEGALALA (IRE) 8 b.g. Petardia 113 – Avionne 59 (Derrylin 115) [2009 66: 11.9g p10g* 10d^3 11.9s* 9.9m 10g 10g* 11.6g^5 p12m 8d^6 12v p10m^6 Nov 3] lengthy gelding: fair handicapper: won at Kempton and Brighton in May and Brighton in July: stays 1½m: acts on polytrack, soft and good to firm going: tried in cheekpieces: often races freely: front runner. *J. J. Bridger* **73**

MEGALO MANIAC 6 b.g. Efisio 120 – Sharanella (Shareef Dancer (USA) 135) [2009 65: f5g p6g p6g^3 p6g^5 f6g^4 p7.1m p6f Dec 21] modest handicapper: stays 7f: acts on all-weather, soft and good to firm going: often wears cheekpieces/visor. *R. A. Fahey* **61**

MEGASECRET 3 b.c. Falbrav (IRE) 133 – Silver Quest (Rainbow Quest (USA) 134) [2009 79: 5.7g^4 7m^4 7m 7g 7m^6 Aug 13] good-topped colt: fair maiden: stays 7f: acts on polytrack, soft and good to firm going. *R. Hannon* **71**

MEGA STEPS (IRE) 5 b.g. Groom Dancer (USA) 128 – Marmaga (IRE) (Shernazar 131) [2009 –: p13.9g p12.2g Feb 16] neat gelding: maiden handicapper: little form since 2007: tried in cheekpieces. *Jennie Candlish* **–**

MEGAVISTA (USA) 3 gr. or ro.f. Medaglia d'Oro (USA) 129 – Bodhavista (USA) (Pass The Tab (USA)) [2009 10m p12g Jul 22] $62,000Y: half-sister to several winners in USA, notably smart Grade 2 7f/1m winner and Kentucky Derby third Imperialism (by Langfuhr): dam lightly raced in USA: little form: sold 9,000 gns, sent to USA. *Paul Mason* **–**

MEGA WATT (IRE) 4 b.g. Acclamation 118 – Kilshanny 70 (Groom Dancer (USA) 128) [2009 85: 10m^3 10.4m^3 p12g 10m^5 Jul 22] tall, good-topped gelding: fairly useful handicapper: should stay 1½m: acts on firm and good to soft going: tried blinkered/in cheekpieces: joined Venetia Williams. *W. Jarvis* **82**

MEG JICARO 3 b.f. Reel Buddy (USA) 118 – Anita In Wales (IRE) (Anita's Prince 126) [2009 68d: p5.1g p7g p6g^3 p6g^6 5m f6g 9.8m May 8] sturdy, compact filly: poor maiden nowadays: seems to stay 6f: acts on polytrack and good to soft ground: tried in cheekpieces. *Mrs L. Williamson* **47**

MEGLIO ANCORA 2 ch.g. (Feb 11) Best of The Bests (IRE) 122 – May Fox (Zilzal (USA) 137) [2009 6d* 7m 7d Aug 2] useful-looking gelding: first foal: dam unraced: won maiden at Newbury in May by ½ length from Alrasm: down the field in listed Chesham Stakes at Royal Ascot and nursery at Newbury (hampered): should stay 7f. *J. G. Portman* **83**

MEHENDI (IRE) 3 b.g. Indian Danehill (IRE) 124 – Wedding Cake (IRE) 71 (Groom Dancer (USA) 128) [2009 83p: 8.5g 10g 10.2g 8s p12.2m^{3} 12.4d^{5} Oct 13] unfurnished gelding: fair maiden: left B. Meehan 16,000 gns after third start: should stay 1¾m: acts on polytrack and soft going: tried blinkered. *B. Ellison* **69 +**

MEIKLE BARFIL 7 b.g. Compton Place 125 – Oare Sparrow 75 (Night Shift (USA)) [2009 p5g^{5} p5g^{6} p5g^{4} p5g* p5g^{3} f5g p5.1g 5.1m 5.3d^{6} 5m 5.1g^{5} 5.3f^{6} 5g^{6} 5.1d 5.1d 5.1m^{6} p5.1g p5m^{6} Dec 9] strong, good-bodied gelding: missed 2008: modest performer nowadays: won minor event at Kempton in March: best at 5f: acts on polytrack, good to firm and good to soft ground: tried blinkered, wears cheekpieces/tongue strap. *J. M. Bradley* **56**

MEIRIG'S DREAM (IRE) 3 b.g. Golan (IRE) 129 – Women In Love (IRE) (Danehill (USA) 126) [2009 51: 11.6d p10g p12m^{3} p16m^{2} Dec 30] tall gelding: fair maiden handicapper: stays 2m: acts on polytrack. *Miss N. A. Lloyd-Beavis* **69**

MEJALA (IRE) 3 b.f. Red Ransom (USA) – Wissal (USA) (Woodman (USA) 126) [2009 71: 8m 9.9m^{6} 9.9g* 10g 10d^{5} 10.2g^{2} Aug 18] good-topped filly: fair handicapper: won at Goodwood in June: stayed 1¼m: acted on good to firm going: blinkered final outing: temperament under suspicion: visits Cape Cross. *J. L. Dunlop* **74**

MEJD (IRE) 2 b.c. (Apr 25) Desert Style (IRE) 121 – Rainstone 57 (Rainbow Quest (USA) 134) [2009 8m Oct 16] neat, attractive colt: 100/1 and backward, soundly beaten in maiden at Newmarket. *M. R. Channon* **–**

MEKONG MISS 3 ch.f. Mark of Esteem (IRE) 137 – Missouri 86 (Charnwood Forest (IRE) 125) [2009 61?: p12g^{2} p12g f11g^{4} f12g^{2} f12g Dec 22] tall filly: modest maiden handicapper: stays 1½m: acts on all-weather and good to soft going. *J. Jay* **65**

MELANGE (USA) 3 b.g. Alphabet Soup (USA) 126 – Garendare 105 (Vacarme (USA) 121) [2009 –: p7g f11g* 12.6g 12m^{5} 14.1m 11.6d Jun 8] big gelding: fair performer: won maiden at Southwell in April: well below form last 2 starts: probably stays 1½m: best effort on fibresand: sold 5,000 gns, joined G. A. Charlton. *P. F. I. Cole* **69**

MELKATANT 3 b.f. Rock City 120 – Change of Image 65 (Spectrum (IRE) 126) [2009 –: 7.5m 8m^{3} 9.8m 9.8d^{6} 10m^{3} 10m^{4} 12.4d^{3} Oct 13] leggy filly: modest maiden: stays 1½m: acts on good to firm and good to soft ground. *N. Bycroft* **52**

MELLIFERA 2 b.f. (Mar 22) Leporello (IRE) 118 – Christina's Dream 74 (Spectrum (IRE) 126) [2009 p6g^{4} p6m^{4} 7m^{5} p7.1g^{6} p6m Nov 19] second foal: half-sister to 3-y-o Jordaura: dam, maiden (stayed 7f), half-sister to smart sprinter To The Roof: fair maiden: stays 7f: finished weakly (in nurseries) last 2 starts. *W. R. Swinburn* **72**

MELLIFLUOUS (IRE) 4 b.f. Noverre (USA) 125 – Danestar 64 (Danehill (USA) 126) [2009 –: 9m^{6} Aug 27] sturdy filly: poor maiden: stays 9f: acts on good to firm going: tried tongue tied. *W. S. Kittow* **44**

MELLOW MIXTURE 3 b.c. Marju (IRE) 127 – Night Owl 73 (Night Shift (USA)) [2009 78: p10g^{2} p10g^{2} p12g 10.2d^{6} 9.7f^{3} 10m 7g^{6} p11g 10f p12m^{5} p10g* Oct 11] good-topped colt: fair handicapper: left R. Hannon after sixth start: dropped in weights, won apprentice event at Lingfield in October: stays 1¼m: acts on polytrack and firm ground: tried tongue tied. *S. Kirk* **77**

MELODY IN THE MIST (FR) 2 b.f. (May 5) Intikhab (USA) 135 – She's All Class (USA) (Rahy (USA) 115) [2009 5m^{6} 5m^{2} 5g^{3} 5f* 5s* Aug 23] leggy filly: closely related to fairly useful 6f (at 2 yrs) to 8.5f winner Flint River (by Red Ransom) and half-sister to several winners, including 4-y-o Irish Heartbeat: dam, US 6f (at 2 yrs) and 8.3f winner, sister to useful Irish 1996 2-y-o sprinter Raphane: fair performer: won claimer at Ayr and seller at Musselburgh in August: will be suited by 6f: unraced on heavy going, acts on any other turf. *T. D. Barron* **71**

MELTING BOB (USA) 3 gr. or ro.f. Johannesburg (USA) 127 – Dancingonice (USA) (Robyn Dancer (USA)) [2009 p8f Dec 20] $50,000Y: fourth foal: half-sister to useful US 2006 2-y-o 6f winner She's Included (by Include): dam US 1m/9f winner (including at 2 yrs, and minor stakes): signs of ability when 8¼ lengths seventh to Erinjay in maiden at Kempton: will improve. *Dr J. D. Scargill* **54 p**

MELT (IRE) 4 b.f. Intikhab (USA) 135 – Kindle (Selkirk (USA) 129) [2009 63: p8g p7g^{5} p7g^{2} p8g* p7g^{2} p7g^{3} 8g^{4} 7m^{6} May 3] stocky filly: fair handicapper: won at Lingfield in March: stays 1m: acts on polytrack, yet to race on extremes on turf: tried in cheekpieces, blinkered of late. *R. Hannon* **66**

MELUNDY 2 b.f. (Feb 15) Best of The Bests (IRE) 122 – Nova Zembla (Young Ern 120) [2009 6m^{2} 6m^{5} Sep 14] second foal: half-sister to 4-y-o Prince Rhyddarch: dam ran once: easily better effort in maidens at Redcar when 2½ lengths equal-second to Distinctive: bred to be suited by 7f+: slowly away both outings. *Mrs L. Stubbs* **69**

MEML 3 b.f. Mark of Esteem (IRE) 137 – Matisse 65 (Shareef Dancer (USA) 135) **49** [2009 8m^6 8d 9.8m^6 p9.5g^4 p12.2g Nov 9] 8,000Y: seventh foal: half-sister to several winners abroad, including useful German 1m to 11f winner Grantley (by Deploy): dam maiden who stayed 1m: poor maiden. *J. D. Bethell*

MEMORANDUM 2 b.f. (Mar 29) Oasis Dream 129 – Marani 106 (Ashkalani (IRE) **74** 128) [2009 5.7m^5 5.1g^3 p5g* p5m^5 p6m^3 Dec 30] fourth foal: half-sister to useful French 10.5f winner Atlas Silk (by Dansili): dam, 9f/1½m winner, out of close relative to St Leger winner Toulon: fair performer: won maiden at Lingfield in November: creditable third in nursery there final outing: will stay 1m. *R. Charlton*

MEMORY AND MAGIC (USA) 2 b.f. (Apr 26) Sahm (USA) 112 – Aljawza (USA) **66** 86 (Riverman (USA) 131) [2009 5f^2 5g p6f^4 7.1m^4 p7g Nov 13] $85,000F: rather leggy filly: closely related to several winners, including 6-y-o Alsadaa, and half-sister to 3 winners, including useful 2002 2-y-o 7f/1m (Royal Lodge Stakes) winner Al Jadeed (by Coronado's Quest): dam, Irish 2-y-o 6f winner, half-sister to Cheveley Park Stakes winner Gay Gallanta: fair maiden: stays 7f: acts on polytrack and firm ground. *C. G. Cox*

MEMPHIS MAN 6 b.g. Bertolini (USA) 125 – Something Blue (Petong 126) [2009 **80** 93: p6g^5 p6g^5 5g 6g^6 7d^6 6v^5 6m^4 6g* 5g^2 6m^5 5m^3 6d^5 6d^3 6f^5 6m^2 7.2s^3 6.1m 6m 6d 7s Oct 27] leggy, close-coupled gelding: fairly useful handicapper: won at Windsor in June: best at 6f/7f: acts on all-weather and any turf going: tried in cheekpieces: held up: not straightforward, but is consistent. *P. D. Evans*

MEMPHIS MARIE 5 b.m. Desert Sun 120 – Spirito Libro (USA) 89 (Lear Fan (USA) **–** 130) [2009 8s 8m^6 7m Sep 16] workmanlike mare: handicapper: missed 2008: little form at 5 yrs. *P. J. McBride*

MENA RL 2 b.f. (Mar 18) Sulamani (IRE) 130 – Natalie (Dushyantor (USA) 123) [2009 **–** p8m Nov 19] second foal: dam unraced: 66/1, tailed off in maiden at Kempton. *Karen George*

MENDIP (USA) 2 b. or br.c. (Feb 9) Harlan's Holiday (USA) 124 – Well Spring (USA) **96 p** (Coronado's Quest (USA) 130) [2009 p8g* Sep 4] $130,000Y, $375,000 2-y-o: first foal: dam, ran 3 times in US, out of very smart US Grade 1 7f winner Chaposa Springs, herself sister to Grade 1 1m winner You And I: 6/5 on and very green, highly promising when winning maiden at Kempton readily by 2¼ lengths from Musaafer, strong run final 1f: looks sure to go on to better things. *Saeed bin Suroor*

MENEDIVA 2 b.f. (Apr 10) Danbird (AUS) – Princess Ismene 61 (Sri Pekan (USA) **40** 117) [2009 5m 6m 5g^4 5g^4 6m Aug 8] second foal: dam temperamental 7f (at 2 yrs)/1m seller winner: poor maiden plater: form only at 5f. *L. A. Mullaney*

MENELAUS 8 b.g. Machiavellian (USA) 123 – Mezzogiorno 108 (Unfuwain (USA) **47** 131) [2009 16.2v^4 p16.5g Oct 17] temperamental hurdler: lightly-raced maiden on Flat, just poor form in 2009: stays 2¼m: acts on good to firm and good to soft ground: wears cheekpieces. *K. A. Morgan*

MENHIR BAY 3 b.g. Sure Blade (USA) 130 – Turkish Delight 67 (Prince Sabo 123) **51** [2009 60: p5g^6 Jan 16] modest maiden: raced only at 5f/6f on polytrack. *D. K. Ivory*

MENKAURA 6 b.g. Pivotal 124 – Nekhbet 74 (Artaius (USA) 129) [2009 –: f12g **–** Jan 13] no longer of any account. *John R. Upson*

MEOHMY 6 b.m. Marju (IRE) 127 – Meshhed (USA) 102 (Gulch (USA)) [2009 54§: **– §** p12g p10g^3 Feb 10] lengthy mare: maiden: modest at best: last both starts in 2009: tried visored: ungenuine: sold 16,000 gns, reportedly in foal to Zafeen. *M. R. Channon*

MERCERS ROW 2 b.g. (Apr 29) Bahamian Bounty 116 – Invincible 76 (Slip Anchor **68** 136) [2009 5g^4 5m^2 5d 5g^3 5v^6 5m^3 6m^4 Oct 1] leggy gelding: fair maiden: should stay 6f: acts on good to firm going. *A. Dickman*

MERCHANT MAN 3 b.g. Mark of Esteem (IRE) 137 – Birsay (Bustino 136) [2009 **64** 9d^4 8.1f^5 9.3d 9.9g^3 14.1m^5 p13.9g^5 Sep 17] compact gelding: modest maiden: barely stays 1¾m: acts on good to soft going: tried blinkered/in cheekpieces: sold £1,600. *J. D. Bethell*

MERCHANT OF DUBAI 4 b.g. Dubai Destination (USA) 127 – Chameleon 79 **106** (Green Desert (USA) 127) [2009 101+: 10g^3 14.8g* 13g^2 12v 12s^6 p12.2g* Nov 20] good-bodied gelding: useful handicapper: won at Newmarket (dead-heated with Recession Proof) in August and Wolverhampton (beat Dance The Star by neck) in November: stays 14.8f: acts on all-weather, heavy and good to firm going: races prominently. *G. A. Swinbank*

MERCHANT OF MEDICI 2 b.g. (Mar 1) Medicean 128 – Regal Rose 110 (Danehill (USA) 126) [2009 6g^3 6g^2 6.1s p7g^4 p8.6g^3 p8.6g Nov 12] 13,000Y: good-topped gelding: third foal: brother to 6-y-o Regal Royale and half-brother to 2006 2-y-o 7f winner Regal Riband (by Fantastic Light): dam, 2-y-o 6f winner (including Cheveley Park Stakes), out of half-sister to high-class miler Shaadi: fair maiden: stays 8.6f: acts on polytrack: blinkered last 2 starts (pulled too hard final one, gelded after). *W. R. Muir* **72**

MERCOLIANO 2 b.g. (Mar 14) Medicean 128 – Mega (IRE) 66 (Petardia 113) [2009 p8.6g^4 p9.5g^5 Nov 14] 10,500Y, 14,000 2-y-o: third foal: half-brother to 4-y-o Astrodonna and 5-y-o Marvo: dam maiden who should have stayed 1½m: fair form in maidens at Wolverhampton: will stay 1¼m. *M. Botti* **70**

MERDAAM 3 ch.g. Dubai Destination (USA) 127 – Faydah (USA) 72 (Bahri (USA) 125) [2009 –: 8s^3 8m^2 9.8m^3 8g^6 10.2s Oct 7] lengthy, good-topped gelding: fairly useful maiden: best form at 1m: acts on soft and good to firm going: gelded after final start. *J. L. Dunlop* **83**

MERLIN'S DANCER 9 b.g. Magic Ring (IRE) 115 – La Piaf (FR) (Fabulous Dancer (USA) 124) [2009 93: p5g^4 5.3g^3 5g^6 5m^3 5g 6m 6m^4 5m Jul 23] good-bodied gelding: unimpressive mover: fairly useful handicapper: best at 5f: acts on polytrack, firm and good to soft ground: tried blinkered: front runner: has twice bled, including final start: inconsistent. *S. Dow* **89**

MERRION TIGER (IRE) 4 ch.g. Choisir (AUS) 126 – Akita (IRE) (Foxhound (USA) 103) [2009 62: f12g* f16g* p16.5g 14m^2 16.1d 14m^3 13.1g^4 12g 13g 17.5m 16.1d f14m* f14g^2 Dec 22] workmanlike gelding: fair handicapper: won in January, February and December, all at Southwell: stays 2m: acts on all-weather and good to firm ground: tried in headgear. *A. G. Foster* **70**

MERRY DIVA 3 b.f. Bahamian Bounty 116 – Merry Rous 66 (Rousillon (USA) 133) [2009 81p: 6m p6g 6m^2 6g^3 6g^4 6m^2 6d^3 Sep 15] sturdy filly: fair handicapper: in frame last 5 starts: should stay 7f: acts on polytrack, unraced on extremes of going on turf. *C. F. Wall* **76**

MERRYMADCAP (IRE) 7 b.g. Lujain (USA) 119 – Carina Clare (Slip Anchor 136) **78**
[2009 75, a83: 8g^2 9.9m* 10g 8g 9m^5 11.7f* 12m^6 11.5d^4 p9.5g^3 p12g^3 p10g^4 p10m^2 **a82**
Nov 21] leggy gelding: fairly useful handicapper on all-weather, fair on turf: won at Salisbury in June and Bath in August: stays 1½m: acts on polytrack, firm and soft ground: tried blinkered: often forces pace: has found little/idled. *Matthew Salaman*

MERRY MAY 3 b.f. Compton Place 125 – Swift Dame (IRE) 60 (Montjeu (IRE) 137) [2009 –: f6m 6m 6.1d Sep 4] small filly: little form. *S. Kirk* **–**

MERSEYSIDE STAR (IRE) 2 ch.c. (Apr 24) Kheleyf (USA) 116 – The Oldladysays No (IRE) 85 (Perugino (USA) 84) [2009 6v^6 6m^4 5.9m* 6d^4 6m^3 5g^6 7m^4 Aug 20] €28,000Y, £42,000 2-y-o: compact colt: second foal: half-brother to winner up to 1m in Italy by Daggers Drawn: dam Irish maiden (stayed 7f): fair performer: trained first 6 starts by K. R. Burke: won maiden at Carlisle in June: may prove best short of 7f: attitude under suspicion: sold 8,000 gns, sent to Norway. *A. P. Jarvis* **70**

MERTON LAD 3 ch.g. Fantastic Light (USA) 134 – Artistic Blue (USA) 109 (Diesis 133) [2009 67: p12.2g^3 p12g^5 11.6m Apr 20] workmanlike gelding: fair maiden: stays 1½m: acts on polytrack: tried in cheekpieces: reportedly bled final start. *T. G. Mills* **69**

MERTON MATRIARCH 2 ch.f. (Feb 6) Cadeaux Genereux 131 – Tesary 98 (Danehill (USA) 126) [2009 p6g^2 Oct 21] rather leggy filly: first foal: dam, 5f (at 2 yrs) to 7f winner, out of half-sister to dam of top-class sprinter Anabaa: 6/1, length second to Hulcote Rose in maiden at Kempton, leading: should improve. *P. Winkworth* **64 p**

MESBAAH (IRE) 5 b.g. Noverre (USA) 125 – Deyaajeer (USA) 64 (Dayjur (USA) 137) [2009 93: 12m 7.5g 7g 8m 9.9f 12s Oct 27] strong, lengthy gelding: type to carry condition: fairly useful handicapper in 2008: little impact at 5 yrs: stays 9f (not 1½m): acts on good to firm going: effective with/without headgear: successful over hurdles in September/November. *R. A. Fahey* **–**

MESHTRI (IRE) 4 ch.g. Dalakhani (IRE) 133 – Arctic Hunt (IRE) (Bering 136) [2009 103: p16g^3 16.1d Jun 27] leggy gelding: useful handicapper: good third to Desert Sea at Kempton on reappearance: below form in Northumberland Plate at Newcastle only other start: gelded after: stays easy 2m: acts on polytrack, soft and good to firm going. *M. A. Jarvis* **102**

METAL GURU 5 ch.m. Ishiguru (USA) 114 – Gemtastic 70 (Tagula (IRE) 116) [2009 75: p5.1g 5.3m^5 5m p5.1g* p5.1g* p5.1g p5.1g^3 f5g^2 f5g^6 Dec 27] fair handicapper: won at Wolverhampton in September and October: will prove best at 5f/easy 6f: acts on polytrack, firm and good to soft ground: wears cheekpieces. *R. Hollinshead* **68**

METAL MADNESS (IRE) 4 b.g. Acclamation 118 – Dosha 47 (Touching Wood (USA) 127) [2009 80: p10g^6 p10g 10v 8.5s 9g 7s^3 14s Oct 26] fair handicapper: left M. Quinlan after second start: effective at 1m, barely at 1¼m: acts on polytrack and good to soft ground, probably on firm: tried in cheekpieces, blinkered last 2 starts. *P. F. Cashman, Ireland* **70**

METAL SOLDIER (IRE) 2 b.g. (Mar 31) Antonius Pius (USA) 123§ – Shenkara (IRE) 79 (Night Shift (USA)) [2009 5.1m* May 7] compact gelding: 9/1, won maiden at Chester in May readily by length from Reel Credit Crunch: dead. *J. J. Quinn* **73**

METHAALY (IRE) 6 b.g. Red Ransom (USA) – Santorini (USA) (Spinning World (USA) 130) [2009 93: p6g^2 p7.1g^5 p6g^2 p6g^4 p5.1g 7m 6m 6f^6 7m 6d* 5.1g^4 6g^5 7g^6 6f 5d 6g 6m 6m^5 6.1m 6m* f6f p6g p6m^3 p6m^5 Dec 30] compact gelding: fairly useful handicapper: won at Doncaster in May and Warwick in October: effective at 5f to 7f: acts on polytrack, soft and good to firm going: usually blinkered: held up (sometimes slowly away). *M. Mullineaux* **90**

METROLAND 3 b.f. Royal Applause 124 – Chetwynd (IRE) (Exit To Nowhere (USA) 122) [2009 73: 5f 5m^2 6g^2 6m^4 5f^6 5m^5 7g* 7g* 7g^2 7g 10g Dec 24] fairly useful performer: left D. Nicholls 10,000 gns, won handicap and minor event at Doha, both in October: stays 7f: acts on good to firm and good to soft going. *I. Al Malki, Qatar* **81**

METROPOLITAN CHIEF 5 b.g. Compton Place 125 – Miss Up N Go (Gorytus (USA) 132) [2009 63: p7g p6g p6g^6 p6g p5g p6g^6 5.2m p7g 6m^6 p6g 5.3d 6m p7g p7m^3 p6f Dec 16] tall gelding: modest handicapper: best at 6f/7f nowadays: acts on polytrack, firm and good to soft ground: often blinkered/in cheekpieces: finishes weakly, and best avoided. *P. Burgoyne* **52 §**

METROPOLITAN MAN 6 ch.g. Dr Fong (USA) 128 – Preceder (Polish Precedent (USA) 131) [2009 115: p8.6g Sep 17] close-coupled gelding: smart performer at best: well below form in minor event at Wolverhampton only start at 6 yrs: stays 9f: acts on soft and good to firm going. *D. M. Simcock* **–**

MEXICAN BOB 6 b.g. Atraf 116 – Eskimo Nel (IRE) 75 (Shy Groom (USA)) [2009 10g 12.1g* 15g p12.2g^3 Dec 26] strong, good-bodied gelding: type to carry condition: fair handicapper: unraced on Flat (fairly useful hurdler) in 2008: won at Beverley in August: stays 1½m: acts on polytrack, firm and good to soft going. *C. E. Longsdon* **71**

MEXICAN JAY (USA) 3 b.f. Elusive Quality (USA) – Mistle Song 112 (Nashwan (USA) 135) [2009 10.1m^3 May 28] $125,000F, €135,000Y: sixth foal: half-sister to several winners, including useful 1¼m winner Motive (by Machiavellian): dam 1½m/14.6f (Park Hill Stakes) winner: 11/1, some promise when 13 lengths third to Charity Belle in maiden at Newcastle. *B. Smart* **57**

MEXICAN MILLY (IRE) 2 ch.f. (Apr 18) Noverre (USA) 125 – Forest Bride (USA) 51 (Woodman (USA) 126) [2009 5m 6s^3 6m^3 p6m^6 Sep 28] €10,000Y, £7,600 2-y-o: tall filly: has scope: sixth foal: half-sister to 10.5f winner in Italy by Mull of Kintyre: dam, maiden, half-sister to smart Irish performer up to 1¼m Al Mohaajir: modest maiden: below form in nursery: will be suited by 7f+. *B. W. Hills* **60**

MEXICAN PETE 9 b.g. Atraf 116 – Eskimo Nel (IRE) 75 (Shy Groom (USA)) [2009 79: p16.5g^2 p16g^5 Apr 1] close-coupled gelding: fairly useful handicapper, lightly raced on Flat nowadays: barely stays 16.5f: acts on polytrack, firm and good to soft going. *A. King* **80**

MEY BLOSSOM 4 ch.f. Captain Rio 122 – Petra Nova 51 (First Trump 118) [2009 88: 7f^5 7g^5 5.9m^4 7m^5 6m^2 7m 6v^2 5m p6g 6d p6g Oct 31] sturdy, deep-girthed filly: fair handicapper: effective at stiff 5f to 7f: acts on polytrack, heavy and good to firm going: sometimes wears cheekpieces. *R. M. Whitaker* **77**

MEYDAN DUBAI (IRE) 4 b.c. Alzao (USA) 117 – Rorkes Drift (IRE) 55 (Royal Abjar (USA) 121) [2009 92§: p8g p10m Dec 10] smallish, stocky colt: maiden handicapper: once fairly useful, but little impact in 2009: stays 8.3f: acts on good to firm and good to soft going: tried visored: temperamental. *J. R. Best* **– §**

MEYDAN GROOVE 3 b.f. Reset (AUS) 124 – In The Groove 127 (Night Shift (USA)) [2009 70d: p8.6g^6 7.1m^6 6s 6m 6.9m 7.1m 6g^3 5.9g Aug 3] compact filly: poor handicapper: stays 7f: acts on polytrack and good to firm ground. *R. Johnson* **47**

MEYDAN STYLE (USA) 3 b.g. Essence of Dubai (USA) 118 – Polish Ruby (USA) (Polish Pro (USA)) [2009 56: f5g^6 p5.1g^6 f8g 7.1g f6g^5 f7g f8f^6 Oct 21] poor maiden: tried blinkered/in cheekpieces. *J. Balding* **44**

MEYYAL (USA) 3 b.c. War Chant (USA) 126 – Tamgeed (USA) 66 (Woodman (USA) 126) [2009 85p: p10g^3 p10m^3 10.2s^5 Oct 7] good-topped colt: fair maiden: stays 1¼m: acts on polytrack, probably on soft going: sold 16,000 gns. *B. W. Hills* **74**

MEZENAH 3 b.f. Cape Cross (IRE) 129 – Saytarra (USA) 111 (Seeking The Gold (USA)) [2009 83: 8m^2 8.1g* Aug 13] smallish filly: fairly useful performer: placed all starts prior to winning maiden at Sandown in August: stays 1m: unraced on extremes of going: has left Godolphin. *Saeed bin Suroor* **87**

MEZUZAH 9 b.g. Barathea (IRE) 127 – Mezzogiorno 108 (Unfuwain (USA) 131) [2009 71§: f8f Dec 11] lengthy gelding: handicapper: well held (including over hurdles) in 2009: barely stays 1¼m: acts on any going: tried tongue tied/blinkered: unreliable. *Miss J. E. Foster* **– §**

MEZZANISI (IRE) 4 b.g. Kalanisi (IRE) 132 – Mezzanine (Sadler's Wells (USA) 132) [2009 95: 12g^2 p12.2g* 11.9m^3 Jul 4] well-made gelding: useful handicapper: won at Wolverhampton in May: good third in Old Newton Cup at Haydock next time (returned sore): stays 1½m: acts on polytrack and any turf going: held up and usually travels strongly/finds little: lacks resolution, but is consistent. *M. L. W. Bell* **97 §**

MIACARLA 6 b.m. Forzando 122 – Zarzi (IRE) (Suave Dancer (USA) 136) [2009 67: p5.1g 5m 5.1d 5g 5g 5m 5s 5m p5.1g Oct 29] workmanlike mare: just poor handicapper in 2009: best at 5f: acts on heavy and good to firm going: tried in cheekpieces: often tongue tied. *H. A. McWilliams* **41**

MIAMI GATOR (IRE) 2 ch.g. (Apr 23) Titus Livius (FR) 115 – Lovere (St Jovite (USA) 135) [2009 5m 6g* 6d^4 6g^5 6s^6 7.2v p6g^5 p7g* Dec 31] lengthy gelding: modest performer: trained first 4 starts by K. R. Burke, next 2 by A. Jarvis: won claimer at Redcar in June and nursery at Lingfield in December: stays 7f: acts on polytrack and good to soft ground. *J. R. Weymes* **64**

MIAMI MIX 3 gr.c. Fair Mix (IRE) 123 – Granma (Little Wolf 127) [2009 p10g p9.5g^5 p10g 10.2m Apr 18] no solid form. *B. N. Pollock* **–**

MIA'S BOY 5 b.h. Pivotal 124 – Bint Zamayem (IRE) 95 (Rainbow Quest (USA) 134) [2009 110: 8m^4 8s^6 7g^2 8g^3 7m^2 8m^3 8g 8m p8.6g^2 7d* 7s^2 Nov 7] big, deep-girthed horse: smart performer: better than ever in 2009, placed several times (including when third to Forgotten Voice in Hunt Cup at Royal Ascot sixth start) prior to winning minor event at Doncaster in October by 1¼ lengths from Young Pretender: good second to Collateral Damage in handicap at same course final start: best at 7f/1m: acts on polytrack, soft and good to firm ground: held up, and has good turn of foot, but tricky ride. *C. A. Dwyer* **115**

MICCOLO 2 b.c. (Mar 25) Piccolo 121 – Ashkernazy (IRE) 60 (Salt Dome (USA)) [2009 5m^6 5m 5m 5d^5 5d Jul 24] close-coupled colt: modest form at best in maidens. *P. T. Midgley* **59 ?**

MICHAEL COLLINS (IRE) 3 b.g. Oasis Dream 129 – West Virginia (IRE) (Gone West (USA)) [2009 56+: p7.1g^4 f8g^2 8s 7.5v 8m 8.5v f8g f7m Nov 12] medium-sized gelding: fair maiden handicapper: little impact after second start, leaving Ms M. Kelly in Ireland prior to final occasion: best effort at 1m on fibresand: tried in cheekpieces. *G. J. Smith* **68 d**

MICHAEL LASKEY 3 b.g. Lujain (USA) 119 – Enchanted Ocean (USA) 76 (Royal Academy (USA) 130) [2009 p8g^5 10g 10.2g p12m p9.5g Dec 19] poor maiden. *B. R. Millman* **46**

MICHAELMAS DAISY 2 b.f. (Feb 24) Camacho 118 – Desert Daisy (IRE) 67 (Desert Prince (IRE) 130) [2009 p5g^5 5.1g 5.2g^3 6m* 6.1m^2 6.1g^6 p7g p7m f6g^6 p6g^6 Nov 16] first foal: dam 7f winner: modest performer: won nursery at Salisbury in July: left Amy Weaver prior to final start: best efforts at 6f: acts on good to firm ground: tried blinkered. *P. Howling* **64**

MICHAELS DREAM (IRE) 10 b.g. Spectrum (IRE) 126 – Stormswept (USA) 74 (Storm Bird (CAN) 134) [2009 p16.5g Jan 22] smallish gelding: fair handicapper at best: well held both outings on Flat since 2006: wore headgear: was unreliable: dead. *N. Wilson* **– §**

MICHELLE (IRE) 3 b.f. Marju (IRE) 127 – Bel Sole (ITY) (Spectrum (IRE) 126) [2009 p8g^3 p8g^5 p10g p8g Mar 30] €5,000F, €16,500Y: second foal: half-sister to Irish 2007 2-y-o 6.5f winner Rivoletto (by Bahri): dam Italian 5f winner: poor maiden: left J. Osborne £5,000 after debut. *P. Butler* **48**

MICHEVIOUS SPIRIT (IRE) 2 ch.f. (Mar 23) Dalakhani (IRE) 133 – Roseanna (FR) 95 (Anabaa (USA) 130) [2009 7.5f^5 8.3m^2 8d^6 Oct 13] 40,000Y: tall, unfurnished filly: second foal: dam, French 2-y-o 6f winner, stayed 1m: easily best effort in maidens when ½-length second to Bint Almatar at Nottingham: should stay 1¼m. *K. A. Ryan* **74**

MICK IS BACK 5 b.g. Diktat 126 – Classy Cleo (IRE) 102 (Mujadil (USA) 119) [2009 68: 9.7d 10.1m5 8s2 10g2 8d3 8g* 8g 8d 9m5 p9.5g6 p10m 7d 10d 10.2g Oct 28] workmanlike gelding: fair handicapper on turf, modest on all-weather: won at Brighton in July: effective at 1m/1¼m: acts on polytrack, heavy and good to firm going: usually wears headgear/tongue tie: has hung right. *G. G. Margarson* **68 a58**

MICK'S DANCER 4 b.g. Pivotal 124 – La Piaf (FR) (Fabulous Dancer (USA) 124) [2009 62+, a81: 10.2g2 10m6 10g 9.7m* 10.3m* 10g3 10.2m* 9.7f2 10.9m4 Oct 5] good-topped gelding: fairly useful handicapper: won at Folkestone in June, Chester in July and Bath in August: stays 1¼m: acts on polytrack and firm ground: tried blinkered: front runner/races prominently. *W. R. Muir* **89**

MICKY MAC (IRE) 5 b.g. Lend A Hand 124 – Gazette It Tonight 63 (Merdon Melody 98) [2009 72: 7d 6m3 6m2 7g 6.1s3 7g p5.1g2 p6g Nov 27] smallish, lengthy gelding: fair handicapper: stays 9.5f, races mainly at shorter: acts on polytrack, soft and good to firm ground: tried blinkered: usually races prominently. *C. J. Teague* **66**

MICKY P 2 gr.c. (Mar 2) Dr Fong (USA) 128 – Carmela Owen (Owington 123) [2009 6d 7g Oct 30] well-made colt: modest form when never dangerous in maidens at Windsor (backward, green) and Newmarket (not unduly knocked about). *S. C. Williams* **52**

MICKY'S BIRD 2 ch.f. (Mar 9) Needwood Blade 117 – Silver Peak (FR) (Sillery (USA) 122) [2009 5.1f f5g 6g2 7.1s 6.5m f6m f7f f8f Dec 11] £800Y: plain filly: half-sister to several winners abroad: dam, French 9f winner, half-sister to dam of high-class 1¼m performer Alexander Goldrun: form only when second in seller at Yarmouth. *R. C. Guest* **51 d**

MICKY'S KNOCK OFF (IRE) 2 b.g. (Apr 16) Camacho 118 – La Grace 63 (Lahib (USA) 129) [2009 6v 5d 5s2 5g5 5m* 5g6 p5.1g 5d3 p5.1g5 p6g4 f5m Dec 5] £800Y: compact gelding: third foal: dam 2-y-o 1m winner: fair performer: won nursery at Musselburgh in September: stays 6f: acts on polytrack, good to firm and good to soft ground. *R. C. Guest* **73 a69**

MICKYS MATE 4 b.g. Choisir (AUS) 126 – Adept 71 (Efisio 120) [2009 –: p8.6g p7.1g 6m6 7m 6m Apr 30] poor maiden. *A. Crook* **48 ?**

MIDAS TOUCH 2 b.c. (Feb 22) Galileo (IRE) 134 – Approach 105 (Darshaan 133) [2009 8m3 7s* 8s4 Nov 1] second foal: dam, 7.5f (at 2 yrs) to 1¼m winner, half-sister to very smart miler Aussie Rules, out of Nassau and Sun Chariot Stakes winner Last Second: promising efforts in maidens at Gowran (third to stable-companion Jan Vermeer) and the Curragh (landed odds most impressively by 7 lengths): good 5¾ lengths fourth to Jan Vermeer in Criterium International at Saint-Cloud: will be suited by 1¼m/1½m: already useful and will improve further. *A. P. O'Brien, Ireland* **107 p**

MIDAS WAY 9 ch.g. Halling (USA) 133 – Arietta's Way (IRE) 71 (Darshaan 133) [2009 20m Jun 16] leggy, close-coupled gelding: smart performer in 2005: fairly useful hurdler: first run on Flat for 21 months, well-held tenth in Ascot Stakes at Royal Ascot only start at 9 yrs: stays at least 2m: acts on firm and soft going: visored (well beaten) once. *P. R. Chamings* **–**

MIDDAY 3 b.f. Oasis Dream 129 – Midsummer 99 (Kingmambo (USA) 125) [2009 98: 10.1g2 11.5m* 12g2 12v3 9.9d* 10g3 10f* Nov 6] **122**

Understandably, winning a Grade 1 race at the Breeders' Cup tends to be viewed as a career highlight by any European-based trainer, among whom Sir Michael Stoute with five, and Andre Fabre and Aidan O'Brien with four head a table with twenty-one names on it (John Gosden has also trained four, but the first of those was when he was based in America). The latest addition to the list was Henry Cecil, who clearly felt it was a case of better late than never when Midday triumphed in the Emirates Airline Breeders' Cup Filly & Mare Turf. He commented: 'I haven't been a great success at the Breeders' Cup over the years but winning has certainly lived up to my expectations. It's a lovely feeling.' In fact, Cecil was not being fair on himself as from 1984 to 1994, a period when he was champion trainer in Britain six times, he had only three runners at the Breeders' Cup—Indian Skimmer (third in the Turf in 1988), Eltish (runner-up in the Juvenile in 1994) and Distant View (seventh in the Mile in 1994). Cecil then ran Dushyantor in the Turf in 1996 and Royal Anthem in the same race in 1998—both came seventh—after which he had no further runners until 2007 when Passage of Time came third in the Filly & Mare Turf. Midday's success, following her earlier Group 1 success in the Nassau Stakes and another by Breeders' Cup Classic candidate Twice Over in the Champion Stakes, resulted in Cecil's most successful season since 1999 for Group/Grade 1 winners. Ramruma won three Group 1s that year and Oath, Royal Anthem, Shiva and Wince won one each. In between, Cecil's only Group 1s came from Beat Hollow and Love Divine in 2000, Passage of Time in 2006 and Light Shift in 2007. Three of that group—Ramruma, Love Divine and Light Shift—won the Oaks, a race Midday came very close to landing herself. She is altogether an admirable filly, tough, genuine and versatile, except in her going requirements—she acts on firm and good to soft but was well below form on her only outing on heavy. That's hardly a criticism though.

As the season got under way Midday had a record of one win (a narrow one in a maiden at Newmarket) from four starts at two, in the last of which she showed improved form when a staying-on fourth to Enticement in a listed race also at Newmarket. Midday's reappearance in the Blue Riband Trial Stakes at Epsom towards the end of April indicated that she would almost certainly win more races at three. Taking on six colts, and thoroughly at home on the course, she led two furlongs out and kept on after being passed by Debussy to finish a length and a quarter second to him. Midday was stepped up an extra furlong and a half in the totesportcasino.com Oaks Trial at Lingfield just over a fortnight later. This race was downgraded from Group 3 to listed status in 1986 and is nothing like so good a pointer to the Oaks itself as it used to be—between 1969 and 1999, Lingfield Trials winners Sleeping Partner, Ginevra, Juliette Marny, Aliysa, User Friendly, Lady Carla and Ramruma all went on to pass the post first at Epsom while Rafha went on to win the Prix de Diane and Give Thanks the Irish Oaks. Until Midday, none of the winners since Ramruma had run to a rating higher than 104 or gone on to win a Group 1 afterwards, though 2008 Oaks winner Look Here finished an unlucky second at Lingfield. Midday became her trainer's seventh winner of the Trial—he had also trained Lady Carla and Rafha. Starting favourite against eight rivals, Midday was always close up, led three furlongs out and drew clear to beat July Jasmine (in the same ownership) ridden right out by six lengths.

Bookmakers reacted to this win by making Midday a best-priced 10/1 for the Oaks. She needed to improve by around a stone to make her presence felt and, after the Ribblesdale Stakes had been mentioned as a possible alternative, she took her chance, attempting to give her trainer a ninth win in the race. In fifth turning for home, she was just beginning to make some headway when caught flat-footed as Sariska accelerated past, carrying her left and into Wadaat in the process. Midday's momentum was not seriously affected though and she rallied to challenge Sariska under hard riding throughout the final furlong, never quite looking likely to gain the day. She was beaten a head, finishing two and a half lengths in front of third-placed High Heeled. Midday's performance was better than those of her close relative Reams of Verse or of Love Divine when they won the Oaks for Cecil, which boded well for Midday through the rest of the season. Heavy ground at the Curragh for the Irish Oaks in mid-July turned the race into a slog and, despite showing her customary gameness, Midday was left standing in the final furlong, ending up over seven lengths third of ten to Sariska. Midday had been supplemented for the race at a cost of €50,000.

Blue Square Nassau Stakes, Goodwood—conditions are anything but 'glorious' as Midday pulls clear of the favourite Rainbow View and Moneycantbuymelove in a race dominated by three-year-olds

Emirates Airline Breeders' Cup Filly & Mare Turf, Santa Anita—trainer Henry Cecil wins his first Beeeders' Cup race as Tom Queally keeps Midday (right) up to her work to win from Pure Clan (blinkers); the grey Forever Together, the previous year's winner, finishes third

On the face of it, punters appeared to have forgotten the Oaks by the time the Blue Square Nassau Stakes came around at the start of August. Midday started 11/2 third favourite in a field of ten behind champion two-year-old filly Rainbow View, who had yet to win in four outings in Group 1 company at three, and the Irish-trained four-year-old Katiyra. What odds would Sariska have been in such company? Another factor, however, was that it was raining incessantly, the going was officially soft (though in fact it was much nearer good to soft) and the owner's racing manager had warned earlier in the week that Midday probably wouldn't run if conditions were as they had been at the Curragh. Apparently Midday's trainer was in two minds about running her, and afterwards he said: 'I nearly pulled her out but I lost my bottle. She doesn't like it soft but I'd seen her work well on good to soft, and they were going through it . . . so I took a chance, but then thought "God, I've done the wrong thing".' Cecil didn't watch the race. 'I felt quite sick but I heard everyone shouting "Come on Midday, come on Midday" so I knew we weren't tailed off.' Midday was very far from being tailed off and she turned in a superb performance, her best of the year. The other runners included High Heeled again, the improving three-year-old Moneycantbuymelove, successful in the listed Height of Fashion Stakes and the Sandringham Handicap, the five-year-old Lancashire Oaks winner Barshiba and Cheveley Park Stud's smart pair Heaven Sent and Spacious. Never far behind the leading group of Barshiba, Spacious and Katiyra, Midday was ridden to lead on the rail two furlongs out, where Rainbow View was also making some headway. Showing a good turn of foot, Midday drew two lengths clear and, staying on strongly, passed the post two and a quarter lengths ahead of Rainbow View, with Moneycantbuymelove keeping on for third.

Taking on Sariska again in the Yorkshire Oaks was mooted but that race came only three weeks after Goodwood and connections were already looking towards Santa Anita. Midday missed York and went instead for the Prix de l'Opera at Longchamp on Arc day, finishing a below-form third to Shalanaya and Board Meeting. Midday had already gone in her coat but she bounced back to her best in the Breeders' Cup Filly & Mare Turf just over a month later. The seven-strong opposition included just about the pick of the American-trained turf fillies and mares headed by the 2008 winner Forever Together, successful in the Diana Stakes at Saratoga in August but beaten twice since. Also in the line-up were: Magical

Fantasy, who had landed the Grade 1 Gamely Stakes, John C Mabee Stakes and Yellow Ribbon Stakes on her last three starts; ex-British Visit, promoted third in the Filly & Mare Turf a year earlier and twice runner-up to Magical Fantasy; Pure Clan, winner of the Flower Bowl Invitational; and Dynaforce, who had had Pure Clan back in third when winning the Beverly D Stakes. Visit, owned like Midday by Abdulla, made the running at something of a muddling pace. Midday raced in fourth before moving into second entering the straight and then, with Visit weakening, quickening to lead a furlong out as a gap opened up against the rail. Pure Clan and Forever Together, next-to-last and last on the final turn, finished well but never threatened Midday, who won by a length from Pure Clan, with Forever Together a length and a quarter back in third. Midday provided the fifth win for a European-trained runner in the last nine renewals of the Filly & Mare Turf, following Banks Hill, Islington and Ouija Board, the last-named winning it twice. Three of the other winners in that period, Starine, Intercontinental and Lahudood, were ex-European. Sisters Banks Hill and Intercontinental had also been successful for Midday's owner. Midday is being kept in training with the aim of winning a second Breeders' Cup Filly & Mare Turf. If she is in the same form, it will take a good filly to lower her colours at Churchill Downs, while, on the home front, a second successive Nassau Stakes must be on the cards too.

The compact, attractive Midday will eventually be another valuable addition to the Juddmonte broodmare band, a band which has received its share of praise in *Racehorses* before and whose success in North America earned the operation a fifth Eclipse Award as outstanding breeder in 2009. Midday was one of seven Group or Grade 1 winners for her owner during the year, the others being Champs Elysees (Canadian International), Midships (Charles Whittingham Memorial Handicap), Spanish Moon (Grand Prix de Saint-Cloud), Special Duty (Cheveley Park Stakes), Twice Over (Champion Stakes) and Ventura (Santa Mon-

Mr K. Abdulla's "Midday"

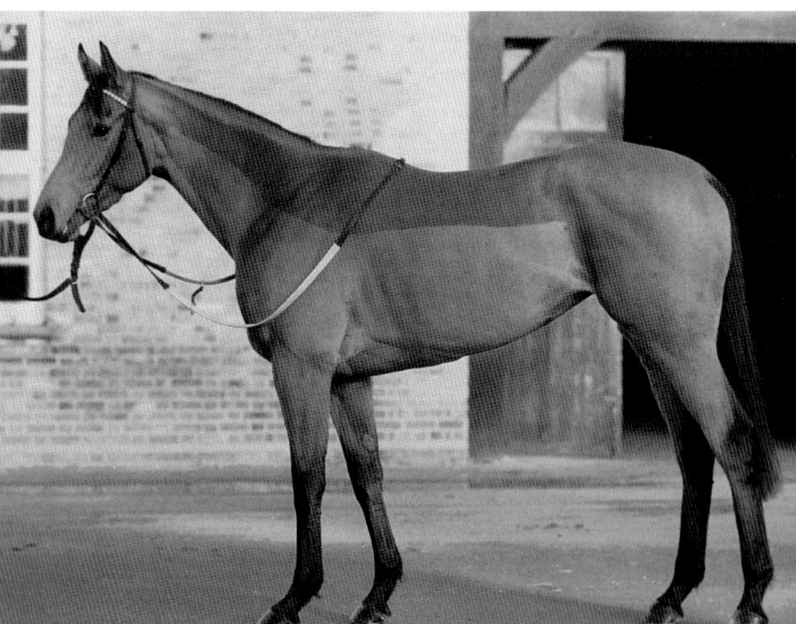

ica Handicap, Woodbine Mile and Matriarch Stakes). Three of those—Champs Elysees, Midships and Ventura—were trained by Bobby Frankel, trainer of the Abdulla horses sent to America in recent years. Frankel died in November at the age of sixty-eight and the majority of the Juddmonte string has been transferred to Bill Mott, one exception being Midships, who is to be trained by Frankel's former assistant Humberto Ascanio. Champion trainer in the States five times, Frankel set the world record for the number of Group/Grade 1 races won in a season with twenty-five in 2003 and saddled a host of top-level performers for Juddmonte including four Grade 1 winners out of Hasili, among them Champs Elysees and the aforementioned Banks Hill and Intercontinental. Midday would have been an ideal type to send to Frankel, but there are now a good number of Group 1s open to fillies aged four and above in Europe and the temptation to send female turf performers to America is not so great as it used to be.

Midday is effective at a mile and a quarter and a mile and a half, though her sire Oasis Dream was a champion two-year-old and a champion sprinter at three. Details of Oasis Dream's burgeoning career as a stallion, and the fact that most of his progeny are suited by distances shorter than a mile, are given in the essay on Arcano. It is worth commenting here, though, on some of his good performers—very much in a minority—who have proved effective at a mile and a quarter or further, such as Monitor Closely, Perfect Stride and Sri Putra, as well as Midday. Oasis Dream may have been a sprinter, but he has a number of horses who stayed a mile and a half close up in his pedigree, particularly on the distaff side, with Dancing Brave, Bahamian, Mill Reef and Sorbus in evidence. Obviously, stamina on the distaff side of his pedigree increases Oasis Dream's chances of getting a horse effective at middle distances.

Midday (b.f. 2006)	Oasis Dream (b 2000)	Green Desert (b 1983)	Danzig
			Foreign Courier
		Hope (b 1991)	Dancing Brave
			Bahamian
	Midsummer (ch 2000)	Kingmambo (b 1990)	Mr Prospector
			Miesque
		Modena (b 1983)	Roberto
			Mofida

Midday is the second foal out of the lightly-raced Midsummer, who also has a yearling colt by Monsun and a filly foal by Oasis Dream. Midsummer's whole racing career was condensed into three runs within a month as a three-year-old. She won a maiden at Kempton, finished runner-up in the Lingfield Oaks Trial and then fourth in the Lupe Stakes. She stayed a mile and a half, as did her half-sister Reams of Verse, winner of the Fillies' Mile and the Oaks and also grandam of the high-class three-year-old Zacinto. Several of Modena's ten other winners stayed even further, including two listed winners over a mile and three quarters, the fillies Novellara and Modesta, while her best son Elmaamul enjoyed his best victories over a mile and a quarter in the Eclipse Stakes and Phoenix Champion Stakes, though he stayed well enough to finish third in the Derby. Modena's final foal, Manifest, figured prominently in the St Leger betting for a while after his wide-margin win in a mile and a half maiden at Newmarket in August. Yet another good winner from this family in the latest season was Confront, a son of Modena's unraced daughter Contiguous. Modena was by Derby winner Roberto but Midday's great grandam Mofida was not a middle-distance filly, her eight wins from forty-one starts coming at up to seven furlongs. She appears in the bottom line of the pedigree of another Group 1 winner during the year, Regal Parade, who landed the Haydock Sprint Cup, and is also the grandam of Two Thousand Guineas winner Zafonic and his good-class brother Zamindar. They were out of Modena's half-sister Zaizafon, a smart miler. *H. R. A. Cecil*

MIDDLE CLUB 2 b.f. (Feb 6) Fantastic Light (USA) 134 – Anna Oleanda (IRE) (Old Vic 136) [2009 7m^3 7g* 7.1m^2 8g* Sep 17] well-made filly: fifth foal: half-sister to useful French 1¼m winner Anna Mona (by Monsun) and German 1m/1¼m winner Anna Royal (by Royal Dragon): dam German 1¼m/10.5f winner: most progressive, winning maiden at Newbury in July and (after ½-length second to Mudaaraah in listed event at Sandown) Prix d'Aumale at Chantilly (by head from Baahama) in September: will be suited by 1¼m+: already useful, and should improve further. *R. Hannon* **103 p**

MIDDLEMARCH (IRE) 9 ch.g. Grand Lodge (USA) 125 – Blanche Dubois (Nashwan (USA) 135) [2009 80: 7m5 7m3 8m 8d4 7.9g 7m 8.3s5 8m 10.4d* 10g 10.3g Oct 24] tall, angular gelding: fairly useful performer: won claimer at York in September: effective at 1m/1¼m: acts on polytrack, firm and soft going: wears headgear: waited with: inconsistent. *J. S. Goldie* **80**

MIDDLE OF NOWHERE (USA) 4 b.c. Carson City (USA) – Ivy Leaf (IRE) 76 (Nureyev (USA) 131) [2009 –: p10g2 p10g2 f12g* Feb 10] tall colt: fair form: won handicap at Southwell in February: not seen after: stays 1½m: acts on all-weather: tongue tied since debut: looked likely to continue improving. *M. A. Magnusson* **74**

MIDFIELDER (USA) 2 ch.c. (Mar 4) Smart Strike (CAN) 121 – Quiet Weekend (USA) (Quiet American (USA)) [2009 p8f Oct 14] $500,000Y: fourth foal: half-brother to fairly useful 7f (including in UAE) winner Step In Line (by Giant's Causeway): dam, French 2-y-o 5f winner, out of close relation to Preakness Stakes winner Summer Squall/ half-sister to A P Indy: 12/1, eighth to Dahaam in maiden at Kempton, forced wide and racing freely. *J. H. M. Gosden* **50**

MIDGET 2 b.f. (Apr 9) Invincible Spirit (IRE) 121 – Sharp Mode (USA) (Diesis 133) [2009 5m* Jun 10] second foal: dam, unraced, out of half-sister to Oaks winner Reams of Verse and Eclipse Stakes winner Elmaamul: 20/1 and green, won claimer at Beverley (claimed £9,000) by ½ length from Mal And Dave: will be suited by 6f+. *M. A. Magnusson* **63 +**

MIDNIGHT BAY 3 br.g. Domedriver (IRE) 128 – Serriera (FR) 51 (Highest Honor (FR) 124) [2009 74: p8.6g4 p12.2g6 p12g 8f 7.1m 8.3m 8d p12.2g3 p11f5 p12g Dec 31] fair maiden: below form after reappearance, leaving M. Channon after seventh start (no impact in juvenile hurdles for Mrs K. Stephens): stays 1½m: acts on polytrack and heavy ground: tried visored: ungenuine. *P. D. Evans* **66 d**

MIDNIGHT CRUISER (IRE) 3 ch.c. Captain Rio 122 – Kriva 69 (Reference Point 139) [2009 94: p8g 8.1m3 8.3g3 10m* 10m 9.9g 10.1m2 a8f Dec 18] good-topped, attractive colt: useful performer: won handicap at Windsor in June: sold from R. Hannon 46,000 gns prior to final start: will stay beyond 1¼m: acts on good to firm and good to soft ground. *M. bin Shafya, UAE* **99**

MIDNIGHT FANTASY 3 b.f. Oasis Dream 129 – Midnight Shift (IRE) 73 (Night Shift (USA)) [2009 70: 6m* 6.1g5 6d5 p6g* 6m 6m* 7d2 6d Oct 13] fairly useful performer: won maiden at Ripon in May, and handicaps at Kempton in June and Newcastle in August: stays 7f: acts on polytrack, soft and good to firm ground: tactically versatile. *Rae Guest* **83**

MIDNIGHT IN MAY (IRE) 3 b.g. Mull of Kintyre (USA) 114 – Birthday (IRE) (Singspiel (IRE) 133) [2009 79p: 8.5g3 Apr 22] sturdy gelding: fair performer: stayed easy 8.5f: acted on soft going: dead. *W. R. Muir* **75**

MIDNIGHT MARTINI 2 b.f. (Feb 21) Night Shift (USA) – Shaken And Stirred (Cadeaux Genereux 131) [2009 5g4 6g4 5m* 5s* 6m* 6m2 Sep 19] £20,000Y: unfurnished filly: second foal: dam unraced half-sister to useful 1¼m performer Sues Surprise: fairly useful performer: won maiden at Carlisle in June, and nursery at Thirsk and DBS £300000 St Leger Yearling Stakes at York (beat Carnaby Street by neck), both in August: creditable second to Distinctive in Firth of Clyde Stakes at Ayr: stays 6f: acts on soft and good to firm going. *T. D. Easterby* **91**

DBS £300000 St Leger Yearling Stakes, Doncaster—
a typically competitive field for this valuable sales race, with Midnight Martini (diamond on cap) just coming out on top from Carnaby Street (third left) and Sole Power (checked cap)

MIDNIGHT STRIDER (IRE) 3 br.c. Golan (IRE) 129 – Danish Gem (Danehill (USA) 126) [2009 p7.1g^2 p8.6g^2 Dec 28] 21,000Y: third foal: half-brother to 5-y-o Ponty Rossa: dam French 9f winner: fair form when runner-up in maidens at Wolverhampton. *Tom Dascombe* **73**

MIDNIGHT UNO 2 b.g. (Feb 1) Desert Style (IRE) 121 – Carati 86 (Selkirk (USA) 129) [2009 f5g^4 5s^3 6m^3 7f p6g Jul 13] modest maiden: went wrong way temperamentally (visored final start). *W. G. M. Turner* **57 §**

MIDNITE BLEWS (IRE) 4 gr.g. Trans Island 119 – Felicita (IRE) 97 (Catrail (USA) 123) [2009 63§: 12d^6 13m Jun 25] workmanlike gelding: modest performer: winner at 5f, seems to stay 1½m: acts on firm and soft going: tried in cheekpieces/blinkers/tongue tie: difficult ride, often very slowly away. *M. A. Barnes* **54 §**

MIDSUMMER MADNESS (IRE) 3 b.f. Alhaarth (IRE) 126 – Robalana (USA) (Wild Again (USA)) [2009 –: 10g Apr 6] lengthy filly: little form. *David Pinder* **–**

MID VALLEY 6 ch.g. Zilzal (USA) 137 – Isabella d'Este (IRE) 65 (Irish River (FR) 131) [2009 64: p12g^4 f12g p13g p10g 11.9m 11.5m^5 14.1s^4 16d p10g p12g Dec 31] stocky gelding: poor handicapper nowadays: stays 1½m: acts on all-weather and firm going: tried visored/in cheekpieces: held up. *J. R. Jenkins* **49**

MIDWESTERN (USA) 2 b. or br.g. (Mar 30) Tiznow (USA) 133 – She's Enough (USA) (Exploit (USA) 117) [2009 6m^6 6.1s 6g^4 Oct 20] $30,000Y, 46,000 2-y-o: good-topped gelding: second foal: dam, US 5.5f/6f winner, closely related to smart US sprinter D'Wildcat: best effort in maidens when 3¾ lengths fourth to Rule of Nature at Yarmouth, finishing well, not knocked about (gelded after): likely to be suited by 7f: will improve further. *M. L. W. Bell* **73 p**

MID WICKET (USA) 3 b.g. Strong Hope (USA) 120 – Sunday Bazaar (USA) (Nureyev (USA) 131) [2009 –p: 10m^6 10f p8.6g Dec 14] big, strong gelding: modest maiden: left B. Hills after reappearance. *Mouse Hamilton-Fairley* **57**

MIESKO (USA) 4 b.g. Quiet American (USA) – Polish Style (USA) (Danzig (USA)) [2009 –: 6.5s 7s p6g a6g p5m^5 Dec 1] modest performer nowadays: left Adrian McGuinness in Ireland after fourth outing: stays 7f: acts on polytrack, good to firm and good to soft going: tried blinkered. *M. G. Quinlan* **58**

MIGHTY APHRODITE 2 b.f. (Feb 12) Observatory (USA) 131 – Sahara Rose (Green Desert (USA) 127) [2009 6.1d Oct 15] 4,000F, 5,000Y: fourth foal: half-sister to 3 winners, including fairly useful 8.5f to 9.8f winner Nelsons Column (by Benny The Dip): dam once-raced close relation to Cheveley Park Stakes winner Regal Rose and half-sister to smart stayer Regal Flush: 12/1, 8¼ lengths seventh to Dormer Street in maiden at Nottingham, not knocked about: should stay 7f/1m. *Rae Guest* **44**

MIGHTY CLARETS (IRE) 2 br.g. (May 7) Whipper (USA) 126 – Collected (IRE) (Taufan (USA) 119) [2009 6d 6m 6g^3 7g^4 8g^3 Oct 19] fair maiden: good fourth in nursery at Leicester: should stay 1m: gelded after final start. *R. A. Fahey* **69**

MIGHTY KITCHENER (USA) 6 br.g. Mighty (USA) 118 – Libeccio (NZ) (Danzatore (CAN) 120) [2009 –: f14g^5 p12g Mar 19] tall gelding: little form since 2007. *P. Howling* **–**

MIGHTY MAMBO 2 b.c. (Jan 18) Fantastic Light (USA) 134 – Mambo's Melody (Kingmambo (USA) 125) [2009 f8f^2 Nov 24] first foal: dam, well held 3 starts, half-sister to 4-y-o Keenes Day: 11/4 and green, 3¾ lengths second to Nazreef in minor event at Southwell, keeping on: will improve. *Jane Chapple-Hyam* **68 p**

MIGHTY MOON 6 gr.g. Daylami (IRE) 138 – Moon Magic 62 (Polish Precedent (USA) 131) [2009 86: p16g 16s* 14m^6 May 16] small, leggy gelding: fairly useful handicapper: won at Newbury in April: stays 2¼m: acts on fibresand and any turf going: has worn tongue tie/blinkers/cheekpieces. *R. A. Fahey* **87**

MIGHTY MOVER (IRE) 7 ch.g. Bahhare (USA) 122 – Ericeira (IRE) (Anita's Prince 126) [2009 67: 8.1d^3 8g^3 p8.6g* p8.6g^6 p9.5g Nov 30] modest handicapper: won at Wolverhampton in October: stays 9.5f: acts on polytrack. *B. Palling* **57 a63**

MIGLIORI 3 b.g. Royal Applause 124 – Millyant 114 (Primo Dominie 121) [2009 f5g^5 6d 6d^4 6m^5 6.1g 5.7g^6 7m Oct 13] close-coupled gelding: modest maiden: stays 6f: yet to race on extremes of going. *Rae Guest* **62**

MIJAS PLAYA 2 b.f. (Mar 10) Avonbridge 123 – Rainbow Spectrum (FR) 57 (Spectrum (IRE) 126) [2009 5m^2 5.1m^5 5.2g^2 5m^2 5m 5g* 5s 5m 5m^5 5g Oct 17] 7,000F: unfurnished filly: third foal: half-sister to 3-y-o Piazza San Pietro: dam maiden (stayed 1m): fair performer: won nursery at Ffos Las in July: below form after: raced only at 5f: acts on good to firm ground: sold 11,000 gns, sent to Sweden. *C. A. Dwyer* **78**

MIK 3 b.g. Baryshnikov (AUS) – Daphne's Doll (IRE) 72 (Polish Patriot (USA) 128) [2009 9.9g Jun 28] 80/1, tailed off in maiden at Salisbury. *Dr J. R. J. Naylor* –

MIKADO 8 b.g. Sadler's Wells (USA) 132 – Free At Last 115 (Shirley Heights 130) [2009 –: f14s^6 Jan 1] smallish, quite attractive gelding: very smart performer for A. O'Brien at 3 yrs: no form on Flat since: tried visored/in cheekpieces. *Jonjo O'Neill* –

MIKHAIL GLINKA (IRE) 2 b.c. (Feb 18) Galileo (IRE) 134 – Lady Karr 76 (Mark of Esteem (IRE) 137) [2009 8.5d* 8.5d^2 8m^6 9s* 10v^2 Nov 14] 250,000F: first foal: dam, 1½m winner, sister to Derby winner Sir Percy: useful performer: successful in maiden at Galway in August and listed race at Leopardstown (beat What A Charm 4 lengths) in November: creditable 6 lengths second to Passion For Gold in Criterium de Saint-Cloud final outing: not best of runs when below form in Royal Lodge Stakes at Ascot third start: will be suited by 1½m: acts on heavy ground: has wandered/carried head high. *A. P. O'Brien, Ireland* **108**

MILDOURA (FR) 4 b.f. Sendawar (IRE) 129 – Miliana (IRE) 108 (Polar Falcon (USA) 126) [2009 p12.2g^5 12d* 10s^2 10g p13g p12m* p12f* Dec 19] sturdy filly: third foal: dam French 1¼m/10.5f winner: useful handicapper: left A. de Royer Dupre in France €22,000 after 3 yrs: won at Folkestone in March, Kempton in November and Lingfield in December: stays 1½m: raced on polytrack and good ground or softer on turf (probably acts on heavy). *Mrs L. J. Mongan* **96**

MILE HIGH LAD (USA) 3 b. or br.g. Sky Mesa (USA) 116 – Thunder Warmth (USA) (Thunder Gulch (USA) 129) [2009 77: p10g^3 p11g^3 10g^4 f11f 10.1d^4 p9.5g^5 p12m p8m Nov 28] fair maiden: below form after second outing: stays 11f: acts on polytrack: tried in cheekpieces/visor/tongue tie: sold 1,500 gns. *George Baker* **69 d**

MILEMILIA (IRE) 3 b.f. Milan 129 – Emilia Romagna (GER) (Acatenango (GER) 127) [2009 p8g p10g p12g^3 12m 14.1f f12g p12g 11.5m^6 16.2g Jul 20] fourth foal: closely related to fairly useful 1½m to 2m winner Rehearsed (by In The Wings) and half-sister to 2 winners abroad: dam, German maiden who stayed 15f, sister to smart German winner up to 10.5f Elacata: modest maiden: should stay beyond 1½m: blinkered last 2 starts: one to treat with caution. *H. Morrison* **54 §**

MILITARIST (USA) 3 b.g. War Chant (USA) 126 – Season's Greetings (IRE) 106 (Ezzoud (IRE) 126) [2009 8m* 8.1m^2 8m^6 8g^5 7.1g^4 p8m Sep 16] tall gelding: third foal: dam, French 2-y-o 5f/6f winner, half-sister to smart 5f to 7f winner Deep Space: fairly useful performer: won newcomers event at Newmarket in April: ran creditably on second, fourth and fifth outings: stays 1m: acts on good to firm going: blinkered final start. *J. H. M. Gosden* **93**

MILITARY CALL 2 b.c. (Feb 21) Royal Applause 124 – Trump Street 77 (First Trump 118) [2009 5.1m^4 5.1d^2 5m^5 6f* 6d^5 6m^6 Aug 7] 33,000F, £42,000Y: leggy colt: fifth foal: half-brother to 3 winning sprinters, including 5-y-o Top Bid: dam 6f winner: fair performer: best effort when winning nursery at Redcar in July: stays 6f: acts on firm and good to soft going: sold £4,500. *E. S. McMahon* **74**

MILITARY POWER 4 b.c. Dubai Destination (USA) 127 – Susun Kelapa (USA) 94 (St Jovite (USA) 135) [2009 100: a8f^2 10g 10g^5 a9f a8f a9g* 10m^4 May 25] rather leggy, quite attractive colt: useful handicapper: won at Jebel Ali (beat Moonquake a head) in March: left M. bin Shafya, creditable fourth to Kingdom of Fife in Zetland Gold Cup at Redcar final start: stays 10.4f: acts on polytrack/dirt and good to firm going. *Saeed bin Suroor* **107**

MILLAGROS (IRE) 9 b.m. Pennekamp (USA) 130 – Grey Galava 64 (Generous (IRE) 139) [2009 p13.9m p9.5g 12.4s 15m^3 Jun 3] lengthy, good-bodied mare: modest handicapper nowadays: stays 15f: acts on polytrack, firm and soft going: tried in visor/cheekpieces: signs of temperament. *I. Semple* **50**

MILL BEATTIE 4 b.f. Beat All (USA) 120 – Step On Degas 69 (Superpower 113) [2009 56: f12g p9.5m^5 f11g Mar 17] rather leggy filly: poor maiden nowadays: stays 9.8f: acts on good to soft going: has hung. *J. Mackie* **40**

MILLDEN 2 b.g. (Feb 10) Compton Place 125 – Pretty Poppy 67 (Song 132) [2009 p6f Dec 13] 16/1 and blinkered, looked hard ride when eighth to Passion Overflow in maiden at Kempton. *H. Candy* **54**

MILLDOWN STORY 3 b.f. Lucky Story (USA) 128 – Barnacla (IRE) 83 (Bluebird (USA) 125) [2009 6m^6 6g^3 6g^3 7.1g^3 f6g^2 5.7g^3 p6m* p6g Oct 29] 10,000F: sixth foal: half-sister to 2005 2-y-o 6f winner Suesam (by Piccolo) and 1m winner Princess Zada (by Best of The Bests): dam 6f winner: fair performer: won maiden at Wolverhampton in September: stays 6f: acts on all-weather and good to firm ground. *B. R. Millman* **69**

MILLERS CROSSING 3 b.g. Tobougg (IRE) 125 – Tweed Mill 88 (Selkirk (USA) 129) [2009 7m^4 6s^5 6g Jun 20] unfurnished gelding: modest maiden: has looked awkward. *W. J. H. Ratcliffe* **61**

MILLFIELD (IRE) 6 br.g. Elnadim (USA) 128 – Eschasse (USA) (Zilzal (USA) 137) [2009 83: p8g^6 p7g^2 p8g^6 p8g p8g^5 p8g 9m 8.3g 8.1g p8g^3 7f^5 p8g* p7m^2 p7m* p7m^4 p7g^3 p8m^5 Nov 28] tall, close-coupled gelding: fairly useful performer: won claimer in September and handicap in October, both at Kempton: was best at 7f/1m: acted on polytrack and firm going: tried blinkered: held up (often missed break): dead. *P. R. Chamings* **81**

MILLFIELDS DREAMS 10 b.g. Dreams End 93 – Millfields Lady 75 (Sayf El Arab (USA) 127) [2009 80: 7.1g^2 6m^4 8.1g^3 7m^5 7.1m^2 10.2g^2 6d^6 8.1m 6.1m^4 6g^6 8g 7.1m Aug 20] tall gelding: fairly useful handicapper: effective from 6f to 1¼m: acts on all-weather, firm and good to soft going: usually wears cheekpieces. *G. C. Bravery* **81**

MILLHARBOUR (IRE) 3 b.g. Nayef (USA) 129 – My Funny Valentine (IRE) 105 (Mukaddamah (USA) 125) [2009 70: 10g^4 12m 12m^4 10m^4 p8.6g^6 10.1m^6 Oct 3] unfurnished gelding: fair maiden: stays 1¼m: unraced on extremes of going: tried blinkered: sold 7,500 gns. *B. W. Hills* **66**

MILLIE'S ROCK (IRE) 4 b.f. Rock of Gibraltar (IRE) 133 – Miletrian (IRE) 113 (Marju (IRE) 127) [2009 76: p10g* p10g^2 p12.2g p8g^4 8m 10g 6g 8g p9.5g Nov 14] workmanlike filly: fair handicapper: won at Lingfield in January: well below form after fourth start: stays 1¼m: acts on polytrack and good to firm ground: sold 15,000 gns. *K. A. Ryan* **78 d**

MILLION DOLLARS (USA) 2 ch.f. (Feb 27) Pleasant Tap (USA) – Six Zeroes (USA) (Hold For Gold (USA)) [2009 7m p8m^4 Sep 16] $35,000Y, 75,000 2-y-o: third foal: half-sister to US Grade 3 7f winner Million Dollar Run (by Tejano Run): dam, US 8.5f winner, half-sister to US Grade 3 9f winner Lager (by Pleasant Tap): better effort in maidens when 4¾ lengths fourth to Wild Rose at Kempton, disputing: very slowly away on debut: has left Godolphin. *Saeed bin Suroor* **67**

MILLOAKS (IRE) 4 b.f. Tamayaz (CAN) 121 – Jaldini (IRE) (Darshaan 133) [2009 –: f6g Jan 27] of no account. *Paul Flynn, Ireland* **–**

MILLVILLE 9 ch.g. Millkom 124 – Miss Top Ville (FR) (Top Ville 129) [2009 91, a115: p12g^3 12g Apr 22] tall, leggy gelding: smart handicapper on all-weather, fairly useful at best on turf: excellent ¾-length third to Evident Pride at Lingfield on reappearance: poorly placed and not knocked about only other start at 9 yrs: stays 1¾m: acts on polytrack, firm and soft going. *M. A. Jarvis* **– a115**

MILLWAY BEACH (IRE) 3 b.g. Diktat 126 – Cape Cod (IRE) 62 (Unfuwain (USA) 131) [2009 73: p7g* p8g^4 p8g^4 7m 9.7f^4 11.6g 10g p10g p12m Sep 30] big, angular gelding: fair handicapper: won at Lingfield in January: stays 1¼m: acts on polytrack and firm going: tried in cheekpieces: sold 3,000 gns. *Pat Eddery* **71**

MILLY ROSE 3 br.f. Diktat 126 – Milly Fleur 67 (Primo Dominie 121) [2009 60: 6d 10f Jun 30] maiden: well held in 2009. *George Baker* **–**

MILNAGAVIE 2 ch.f. (Mar 17) Tobougg (IRE) 125 – Abyaan (IRE) 106 (Ela-Mana-Mou 132) [2009 p8g^3 8.1d^4 p8g^6 Oct 8] 6,000Y: sixth foal: half-sister to 3 winners, including 3-y-o Dhushan and Irish 5-y-o Elyaadi: dam, 1¼m winner who stayed 12.5f, sister to dam of very smart 1m/9f winner Autumn Glory: easily best effort in maidens when 1¼ lengths third to Dyna Waltz at Kempton: will be suited by 1¼m+. *R. Hannon* **78**

MILNE BAY (IRE) 4 b.g. Tagula (IRE) 116 – Fiction 59 (Dominion 123) [2009 80+: p6g* p7.1g^6 p6g^5 p6g^3 6m^2 p7m^2 p6g^6 p6g Oct 9] fair handicapper: won at Great Leighs in January: best at 6f/7f: acts on polytrack and good to firm going: tongue tied. *D. M. Simcock* **77**

MILTON OF CAMPSIE 4 ch.f. Medicean 128 – La Caprice (USA) 84 (Housebuster (USA)) [2009 74: f7g^5 p6g 8m p6g 7m^5 5m^3 5m* 5g* 6m* 6d Oct 13] strong, good-topped filly: fairly useful handicapper: left S. Parr after fifth start: improved when winning at Ffos Las and Hamilton in September and Ayr in October: should stay 7f: acts on good to firm ground: tried tongue tied. *J. Balding* **80**

MILTONS CHOICE 6 b.g. Diktat 126 – Starosta (Soviet Star (USA) 128) [2009 62: 6m 6g p6g^3 Apr 25] workmanlike gelding: modest handicapper: best at 5f/6f: acts on polytrack, soft and good to firm going. *J. M. Bradley* **59**

MIND ALERT 8 b.g. Mind Games 121 – Bombay Sapphire (Be My Chief (USA) 122) [2009 –, a70: p6g^4 p7g f6g p6g^5 Feb 8] good-topped gelding: modest handicapper: races mainly at 6f on all-weather: wears headgear (usually visor): held up. *D. Shaw* **– a56**

MINDER 3 b.g. Mind Games 121 – Exotic Forest 66 (Dominion 123) [2009 62: 8.3m^5 8.1g^6 May 25] tall gelding: modest maiden: stays 8.3f: acts on good to firm and good to soft ground: not straightforward. *J. G. Portman* **62**

MIND OF HER OWN 2 b.f. (Feb 20) Pastoral Pursuits 127 – Mindfulness (Primo Dominie 121) [2009 5m^6 5f^2 6g p7.1g^4 p8g p7g p6g f6f^4 p6g f6m Dec 15] €5,000Y: second foal: dam unraced out of close relative to very smart sprinter Prince Sabo: modest maiden: stays easy 7f: acts on polytrack and firm going: tried visored. *P. D. Evans* **52**

MIND THE MONARCH 2 b.f. (Apr 18) Mind Games 121 – Enford Princess 89 (Pivotal 124) [2009 p5g^4 5g^4 6f p5g^5 f5g^6 p6g^3 p6g^6 p8g p5m^2 p6f^5 p7g^4 Dec 31] neat filly: first foal: dam, 2-y-o 6f winner (stayed 1m), half-sister to smart 2005 2-y-o sprinter Always Hopeful (by Mind Games): modest maiden: stays 7f: acts on polytrack. *R. A. Teal* **57**

MINE BEHIND 9 b.g. Sheikh Albadou 128 – Arapi (IRE) 89 (Arazi (USA) 135) [2009 64§: 6g 6g Apr 21] lengthy gelding: handicapper: has reportedly had breathing problems: well held at 9 yrs: tried in cheekpieces/tongue tie: one to treat with caution. *J. R. Best* **– §**

MING MASTER (FR) 2 b.g. (Mar 3) Tobougg (IRE) 125 – Sakura Queen (IRE) 52 (Woodman (USA) 126) [2009 p6m p7.1g^4 p8f^4 Dec 16] half-brother to several winners, including 1m to 1¼m winner Son of Thunder (by Dr Fong) and 1½m winner Reine Cerise (by Shareef Dancer): dam, maiden who stayed 1¼m, half-sister to dam of Rock of Gibraltar: progressive in maidens, 3½ lengths fourth to Gracious Melange at Kempton final outing: will be well suited by 1¼m+: capable of better still. *W. J. Haggas* **76 p**

MINGUN BELL (USA) 2 b.c. (Jan 26) Mingun (USA) 117 – Miss Tippins (USA) (Squadron Leader (USA)) [2009 6m^3 7m^3 7.1m* f8g* 8.5m^4 10g^6 Oct 31] $25,000F, $55,000Y: third foal: dam unraced half-sister to useful sprinter Access Travel: fairly useful performer: won maiden at Warwick (beat Duplicity ½ length) in July and minor event at Southwell (odds on) in August: seemed amiss last 2 starts (said to have lost a shoe first occasion): stays 1m: acts on fibresand and good to firm going. *H. R. A. Cecil* **83**

MING VASE 7 b.g. Vettori (IRE) 119 – Minstrel's Dance (CAN) (Pleasant Colony (USA)) [2009 57: f8g^4 f8g^6 f11g^3 f11g 8.5m^5 8.3m 9.9g 9.3m^6 10m^2 10m 10g^5 10m^4 10.4g 8d Sep 7] strong gelding: modest performer: stays 11f: acts on all-weather and any turf going: tried in headgear: sometimes hangs: none too consistent. *P. T. Midgley* **58**

MINIBUZZ 3 b.g. Superior Premium 122 – Amy Leigh (IRE) 78 (Imperial Frontier (USA) 112) [2009 –: p6g f6g^4 7m Apr 22] poor maiden: visored in 2009. *Mrs G. S. Rees* **43**

MINI MAX 2 b.f. (Feb 3) Tobougg (IRE) 125 – Maxilla (IRE) 78 (Lahib (USA) 129) [2009 7m p7g^5 7d 7m^4 Oct 26] lengthy, angular filly: first foal: dam, 1¼m winner, stayed 1¾m: modest maiden: should be suited by at least 1¼m. *B. W. Duke* **57**

MINIMUM FUSS (IRE) 5 b.m. Second Empire (IRE) 124 – Jamis (IRE) (Be My Guest (USA) 126) [2009 –: f6g f6g^5 5f^6 6m Jun 1] tall mare: little form since 2007 (flattered third outing). *M. C. Chapman* **–**

MINIMUSIC 2 b.f. (Feb 27) Distant Music (USA) 126 – Minette 55 (Bishop of Cashel 122) [2009 p8.6g Nov 21] fifth foal: dam, sprint maiden, half-sister to useful performer up to 8.5f Coconut Squeak: 100/1, showed nothing in maiden at Wolverhampton. *B. Palling* **–**

MINISTEROFINTERIOR 4 b.g. Nayef (USA) 129 – Maureen's Hope (USA) (Northern Baby (CAN) 127) [2009 65: p12g^4 10d^4 p12g^5 Jun 27] good-bodied, compact gelding: modest performer: stays easy 1½m: acts on polytrack, soft and firm going: tried blinkered/visored: joined B. Leavy. *G. L. Moore* **58**

MINIYAMBA (IRE) 2 b.f. (Mar 8) Sadler's Wells (USA) 132 – Atlantide (USA) (Southern Halo (USA)) [2009 7g 7s^6 8m 8g Oct 23] 78,000F, 230,000Y: useful-looking filly: third foal: half-sister to winner in USA by Grand Slam: dam, French 1¼m winner, half-sister to smart French 1m winners Airline and Art Moderne: easily best effort when 3 lengths sixth to Pipette in maiden at Salisbury: will be well suited by 1¼m+: acts on soft going: type to do better at 3 yrs. *J. L. Dunlop* **77 p**

MINNIE ROCKET 2 ch.f. (Mar 24) Monsieur Bond (IRE) 120 – Real Popcorn (IRE) 52 (Jareer (USA) 115) [2009 5.2m f5g 6g 5s 5m Sep 14] £1,800Y: small filly: half-sister to several winners, including fairly useful 7f (at 2 yrs) to 1½m winner Winners Delight (by First Trump): dam 1½m winner: no form: temperamental. *R. C. Guest* **– §**

MINNOLA 4 b.f. Royal Applause 124 – Miss Anabaa 107 (Anabaa (USA) 130) [2009 58: p5g^5 6v^3 6s p7g 6.1d^4 7v p7m p6g^6 p7.1g^4 p7m Dec 30] leggy filly: modest maiden: stays 7f: acts on polytrack and heavy going: tried blinkered. *Rae Guest* **56**

MINORITY REPORT 9 b.g. Rainbow Quest (USA) 134 – Queen Sceptre (IRE) 97 (Fairy King (USA)) [2009 88: 7m³ 8m 7f⁵ 8.1m 8m 8g⁴ 8m⁶ 8d 8.5m p8g Sep 9] stocky gelding: type to carry condition: fairly useful handicapper: left D. Nicholls after ninth start: effective at 7f/1m: has form on good to soft going, but best on good or firmer: tried visored: held up. *K. A. Ryan* **80**

MINORTRANSGRESSION (USA) 2 ch.c. (Jan 23) Yes It's True (USA) 116 – Casting Pearls (USA) (Fusaichi Pegasus (USA) 130) [2009 p7f⁴ Dec 19] $7,000Y, £24,000 2-y-o: first foal: dam US 8.5f winner: encouraging 5¼ lengths fourth to Kai Mook in minor event at Lingfield: should improve. *G. L. Moore* **61 p**

MINOTAURIOUS (IRE) 3 b.f. Acclamation 118 – Bella Vie (IRE) (Sadler's Wells (USA) 132) [2009 81: p6g² p5g³ p5.1g² 6m Apr 1] leggy filly: just modest form at 3 yrs: free-going sort, probably best at 5f: acts on polytrack, heavy and good to firm going: sold 1,000 gns in July, sent to Greece. *K. R. Burke* **62**

MINSTALAD 5 ch.g. Minster Son 130 – Denby Wood (Lord Bud 121) [2009 12g³ Aug 14] modest form in bumpers: well held over hurdles: 100/1, well-beaten third in maiden at Catterick on Flat debut. *G. R. Oldroyd* **–**

MINTOE 3 b.g. Noverre (USA) 125 – West One 67 (Gone West (USA)) [2009 65: 6d 7g⁶ 8d Jul 24] tall, good-topped gelding: modest maiden: likely to prove best at 5f/6f: in cheekpieces last 2 starts. *K. A. Ryan* **55**

MINTURNO (USA) 3 b.g. Ten Most Wanted (USA) 128 – Panama Jane (USA) (Perrault 130) [2009 56p: 6m⁴ 6f⁴ 7m² 6f 6m* 7.1m² 7m⁴ 6g³ 6g* 6m 7d⁵ 6m⁴ 7.5g Sep 22] sturdy gelding: fair handicapper: won at Redcar in May and Ayr in July: effective at 6f/7f: acts on good to firm ground, below form on good to soft: in cheekpieces last 5 starts: gelded after final outing. *Mrs A. Duffield* **75**

MINT WHIP (IRE) 2 b.f. (Apr 28) Whipper (USA) 126 – Aminata 98 (Glenstal (USA) 118) [2009 6m⁶ p6g⁶ Nov 9] half-sister to several winners, including smart Irish 7f (at 2 yrs) and 1m winner Swift Gulliver (by Gulch), later successful in USA, and useful 1999 2-y-o 6f winner Abderian (by Machiavellian): dam Irish 2-y-o 5f/6f winner (stayed 1m): very green in maidens at Leicester (better effort, flashed tail) and Wolverhampton, slowly away both times: should stay 7f: remains open to improvement. *R. Hannon* **62 p**

MINWIR (IRE) 4 b.g. Green Desert (USA) 127 – Elshamms 107 (Zafonic (USA) 130) [2009 62: p8g p6g⁶ p7.1g p8.6g Oct 15] just poor handicapper in 2009: left M. Quinn £1,000 after second start: probably stays 1m: acts on polytrack and soft ground: tried visored. *W. M. Brisbourne* **48**

MIRABELLA (IRE) 2 b.f. (Feb 23) Motivator 131 – Anayid (A P Indy (USA) 131) [2009 p7g⁴ p8g p7g² p7g* Nov 13] €20,000Y, 38,000 2-y-o: unfurnished filly: second foal: half-sister to fairly useful French 2008 2-y-o 7f winner Sand Tiger (by Indian Ridge): dam unraced daughter of Fillies' Mile winner and 1000 Guineas runner-up Aqaarid: fairly useful performer: improved when winning nursery at Lingfield by 3¼ lengths from Be A Devil (made all, hung markedly right): should stay 1m: open to further progress. *R. Hannon* **86 p**

MIRACLE BABY 7 b.m. Atraf 116 – Musica 82 (Primo Dominie 121) [2009 51: p6g⁶ p7g 7m p7g⁶ Oct 14] strong mare: modest maiden: stays 7.6f: acts on polytrack and firm going. *J. A. Geake* **51**

MIRACLE SEEKER 4 br.f. Rainbow Quest (USA) 134 – Miracle (Ezzoud (IRE) 126) [2009 104: 11.9m Jul 4] tall, leggy, useful-looking filly: useful performer in 2008 (injured after final start): last in Lancashire Oaks at Haydock only start at 4 yrs: stays 1¾m: acts on soft and good to firm going: front runner. *C. G. Cox* **–**

MIRACLE WISH (IRE) 2 b.f. (Feb 19) One Cool Cat (USA) 123 – Bentley's Bush (IRE) 96 (Barathea (IRE) 127) [2009 6m May 30] first foal: dam, 2-y-o 6f winner, out of useful French performer up to 10.5f Veiled Threat: 33/1, behind in maiden at Newbury. *R. M. Beckett* **–**

MIRANDA'S GIRL (IRE) 4 b.f. Titus Livius (FR) 115 – Ela Tina (IRE) (Ela-Mana-Mou 132) [2009 90: 8s 7.2v 8g 7f⁴ 7s² 7s* 8.5s 7d⁶ 7d 7d p7f p7g⁵ p8g⁵ p7g p7g p8g³ p7g³ p7.1g Dec 18] tall, close-coupled filly: useful handicapper: won at Roscommon in July by 6 lengths: respectable efforts at best after: effective at 7f/1m: acts on polytrack and any turf going: wears cheekpieces: races close up. *Thomas Cleary, Ireland* **99**

MIRJAN (IRE) 13 b.g. Tenby 125 – Mirana (IRE) (Ela-Mana-Mou 132) [2009 81: 16.1d May 15] strong, sturdy gelding: regressive handicapper, lightly raced nowadays: stays 2¼m: acts on firm and soft going: blinkered. *L. Lungo* **–**

MIRRORED 3 b.g. Dansili 127 – Reflections (Sadler's Wells (USA) 132) [2009 80: p8g* 8.1g* 8m^3 8.1m^3 9.9g^3 8m 10.3m^4 Sep 26] good-bodied gelding: useful handicapper: won at Kempton in April and Sandown in May: good efforts after when third at Royal Ascot (Britannia Stakes, first home far side) and Goodwood (1¼ lengths behind Roman Republic) third/fifth starts, and when fourth of 5 to Mutamaashi at Chester final outing: effective at 1m to 1¼m: acts on polytrack and good to firm ground: sold 45,000 gns, then gelded. *Sir Michael Stoute* **107**

MIRROR LAKE 2 b.f. (Mar 29) Dubai Destination (USA) 127 – Reflections (Sadler's Wells (USA) 132) [2009 p7g^5 Oct 29] angular filly: third foal: half-sister to 3-y-o Mirrored and 4-y-o My Shadow: dam, ran once, closely related to dam of very smart US 7f/1m performer Ventura: 25/1 and green, promising 3¾ lengths fifth to Padmini in maiden at Lingfield, slowly away and nearest finish under considerate handling: will stay 1m: sure to improve. *Mrs A. J. Perrett* **68 p**

MISARO (GER) 8 b.g. Acambaro (GER) 118 – Misniniski (Niniski (USA) 125) [2009 100: 5g 5g 6m^4 5.7f^3 5.7m^6 5m* 5g^5 5m^5 5m 5f^6 5.1m^4 6v 5.1m^3 5.1m^6 p5.1g* p5g p6m* p5.1g^3 p6m p6f^4 Dec 21] leggy gelding: fairly useful performer: won handicaps at Salisbury in June and Wolverhampton in October, and claimer at Kempton in November: effective at 5f/6f: acts on all-weather, firm and soft going: wears visor/blinkers. *R. A. Harris* **88**

MISBEHAVIOUR 10 b.g. Tragic Role (USA) – Exotic Forest 66 (Dominion 123) [2009 12m Aug 15] leggy gelding: lightly raced and little recent form on Flat: tried in cheekpieces/visor. *P. Butler* **–**

MISCHIEF MAKING (USA) 4 b. or br.f. Lemon Drop Kid (USA) 131 – Fraulein 117 (Acatenango (GER) 127) [2009 101: 16m^2 16g 16.1d 12m^3 16m Oct 17] big, strong filly: useful performer: good efforts in 2009 when 9 lengths second to Patkai in Sagaro Stakes and ½-length third to Spirit of Dubai in listed event, both at Ascot: stays 2m: acts on all-weather, good to firm and good to soft going: usually held up. *E. A. L. Dunlop* **101**

MISDAQEYA 3 br.f. Red Ransom (USA) – Crystal Power (USA) (Pleasant Colony (USA)) [2009 106: 7m 8m 10m^3 10.3s Nov 7] tall, close-coupled filly: useful performer at 2 yrs: respectable effort in 2009 only when third in minor event at Leicester: should have stayed 1¼m: acted on polytrack, easily best effort on turf on soft going: visits Raven's Pass. *B. W. Hills* **90**

MISHEER 2 b.f. (Mar 12) Oasis Dream 129 – All For Laura 99 (Cadeaux Genereux 131) [2009 5.2g* 5s* 5m^2 6g* 5m 6m^2 Oct 2] 70,000Y: smallish filly: first foal: dam, 2-y-o 5f winner, sister to useful 7f/1m winner Kehaar: useful performer: successful in maiden at Yarmouth (by 8 lengths) in April, listed race at York (by head from Aalsmeer) in May and Irish Thoroughbred Marketing Cherry Hinton Stakes at Newmarket (by 3¼ lengths from Habaayib) in July: much better effort after when good 2¾ lengths second to **109**

Irish Thoroughbred Marketing Cherry Hinton Stakes, Newmarket—
Misheer pulls clear of favourite Habaayib; Lady Darshaan (No.6) comes third in a good renewal

Mr Saeed Manana's "Misheer"

Special Duty in Cheveley Park Stakes at Newmarket, again strong at finish: will stay 7f: acts on soft and good to firm ground. *C. E. Brittain*

MISHRIF (USA) 3 b. or br.g. Arch (USA) 127 – Peppy Priscilla (USA) (Latin American (USA) 120) [2009 98: p8g^3 10m^6 7g^5 8m 8.1g^6 p7g f8g p8m 8d 10.3g Oct 23] close-coupled gelding: useful performer at best: good third to Pure Poetry in listed race at Kempton on reappearance: not so good after, leaving P. Chapple-Hyam after fourth start: should stay 1¼m: acts on polytrack and soft ground: tried tongue tied/visored: gelded after final outing. *J. R. Jenkins* **99 d**

MISKIN FLYER 3 b.f. Lend A Hand 124 – Sipsi Fach 100 (Prince Sabo 123) [2009 66: 8.3g 8.1m p9.5g Sep 3] sparely-made filly: maiden: little impact at 3 yrs. *B. Palling* **–**

MISKIN NIGHTS 2 b.f. (May 25) Zafeen (FR) 123 – Risalah (Marju (IRE) 127) [2009 6d 6.1m^3 6g^5 Jul 21] £5,000Y: half-sister to 3 winners, including useful 7f to 9f winner Atlantic Ace (by First Trump) and fairly useful 7f/1m winner Lockstock (by Inchinor): dam ran once: easily best effort in maidens when ¾-length third to Slice at Chepstow: bred to stay at least 7f. *B. Palling* **62 ?**

MISKIN SPIRIT 3 b.f. Bertolini (USA) 125 – Risalah (Marju (IRE) 127) [2009 8.3d p7g p9.5g p7.1g Nov 20] lengthy filly: half-sister to 3 winners, including useful 7f to 9f winner Atlantic Ace (by First Trump) and fairly useful 7f/1m winner Lockstock (by Inchinor): dam ran once: little solid form in maidens: tried in cheekpieces/blinkers. *B. Palling* **–**

MISPHIRE 6 b.m. Mister Baileys 123 – Bombay Sapphire (Be My Chief (USA) 122) [2009 88: 6d 6g 7m^5 7g^5 7.2s 7g 7.2v Oct 31] big, good-topped mare: fair handicapper nowadays: stays 7f: acts on heavy and good to firm going: tried in headgear: sometimes misses break, and generally none too keen. *M. Dods* **78**

MISPLACED FORTUNE 4 b.f. Compton Place 125 – Tide of Fortune (Soviet Star (USA) 128) [2009 67: 7m 6.1f* 5.9m* 6m^2 6d^4 6g^3 6.1g^4 7d^6 6m^2 6d* 7g^5 7s^3 Nov 7] lengthy filly: fairly useful handicapper: won at Nottingham (apprentices) and Carlisle in May and Newcastle in October: stays 7f: acts on firm and soft going: often visored. *N. Tinkler* **88**

MISS ANTONIA (IRE) 2 b.f. (May 1) Antonius Pius (USA) 123§ – Masharik (IRE) 93 (Caerleon (USA) 132) [2009 p7g^3 8.1m^4 8g^4 Oct 20] lengthy filly: has scope: half-sister to 3 fairly useful winners, including 5-y-o Dayia and 1¼m/1½m winner Namat (by Daylami): dam, 1¼m winner, half-sister to high-class middle-distance stayer Ibn Bey and Yorkshire Oaks winner Roseate Tern: fair form when fourth in maidens at Haydock and Yarmouth (to Hymnsheet): will be suited by 1¼m. *H. R. A. Cecil* **73 +**

MISS BEAT (IRE) 3 b.f. Beat Hollow 126 – Bolas 118 (Unfuwain (USA) 131) [2009 77: p9.5g^3 8m 9.9m^5 10m 8d^6 Jul 11] sturdy filly: fair performer on balance: flattered in listed race third start: bred to stay at least 1¼m: acts on polytrack, unraced on extremes of going on turf: tried tongue tied. *B. J. Meehan* **77**

MISS BLUEANDBLACK (IRE) 3 ch.f. Hawkeye (IRE) 122 – Don't Tell Trigger (IRE) 69 (Mujadil (USA) 119) [2009 p12g Oct 21] £2,800Y: smallish, plain filly: first foal: dam 2-y-o 6f/7f seller winner: soon behind in juvenile hurdle on debut: tailed off in claimer at Kempton on Flat debut next time. *Jean-Rene Auvray* **–**

MISS BOOTYLISHES 4 b.f. Mujahid (USA) 125 – Moxby (Efisio 120) [2009 86d: 8d^6 7.1v* 7f 7d 7.2v^2 f6m^6 f7m^4 Dec 15] neat filly: fair handicapper: won at Chepstow in July: stays 1m: acts on fibresand, heavy and good to firm going: temperamental. *A. B. Haynes* **74 §**

MISS CALIFORNIA 2 b.f. (Apr 21) Mtoto 134 – Lightning Princess (Puissance 110) [2009 7m Oct 6] small, leggy filly: fifth foal: half-sister to winner in Holland by Bold Edge: dam unraced half-sister to useful performer up to 1½m Black Monday: 100/1, well held in maiden at Leicester. *Miss Tor Sturgis* **–**

MISS CAMEO (USA) 3 b.f. Mizzen Mast (USA) 121 – Angela Niner (USA) (Forty Niner (USA)) [2009 48+: p9.5g^3 7.5m^3 f8g^2 7.5m May 4] leggy filly: modest maiden: stayed 9.5f: acted on all-weather and good to firm going: dead. *R. M. Whitaker* **57**

MISS CHAMANDA (IRE) 3 ch.f. Choisir (AUS) 126 – Smandar (USA) (Sahm (USA) 112) [2009 73: p6g^3 6m 7m 6g* 6g 6g^3 5f* 5m^5 5.1m^5 Sep 12] lengthy, angular filly: fairly useful handicapper: won at Windsor in June and August: effective at 5f/6f: acts on polytrack and firm ground. *P. D. Evans* **86**

MISS CHAUMIERE 2 b.f. (Feb 20) Selkirk (USA) 129 – Miss Corniche 104 (Hernando (FR) 127) [2009 7d Jul 30] big, strong filly: third foal: sister to 4-y-o Moyenne Corniche and half-sister to 3-y-o Miss Eze: dam, 7f (at 2 yrs) and 1¼m winner, sister to useful 1m winner Miss Riviera Golf: 40/1, very green when tailed off in maiden at Goodwood. *M. L. W. Bell* **–**

MISS CHRISTOPHENE (IRE) 3 b.f. Christophene (USA) 107 – Lotus Flower (IRE) 63 (Grand Lodge (USA) 125) [2009 48: f8g^2 f8g* f8d* 10g 8g^5 12m f8g Aug 25] fair performer: won maiden and handicap, both at Southwell in February: stays 1m: acts on fibresand. *Mrs S. Lamyman* **76**

MISS CLARICE (USA) 4 b. or br.f. Mr Greeley (USA) 122 – Mutton Maniac (USA) (Wolf Power (SAF)) [2009 60: p8.6m^3 p8g Mar 18] big, good-topped filly: maiden handicapper: just poor in 2009: stays 8.6f: acts on polytrack, best turf effort on good to firm ground: has worn cheekpieces: sent to Saudi Arabia. *J. R. Jenkins* **49**

MISS CRACKLINROSIE 3 b.f. Tobougg (IRE) 125 – Anatase (Danehill (USA) 126) [2009 63: p9.5g^5 p12.2m f8g^4 7.5m 9.3g Jun 1] modest maiden: stays 9.5f: acts on polytrack and heavy going: tried in cheekpieces. *J. R. Weymes* **55**

MISS DAAWE 5 b.m. Daawe (USA) 103 – Feiticeira (USA) 79 (Deposit Ticket (USA)) [2009 76: 5m p6g^4 5d^5 5m^3 6g^3 6d^5 5m^5 5d 5g^6 5g^2 5m^5 p6g 5g 5m 5.1d Oct 15] close-coupled, workmanlike mare: fair handicapper: effective at 5f/6f: acts on any turf going: tried tongue tied/blinkered. *B. Ellison* **66**

MISS DEE LADY (IRE) 3 ch.f. Captain Rio 122 – Windomen (IRE) (Forest Wind (USA) 111) [2009 7.1m 7.9g Jul 4] €33,000F, €15,000 2-y-o: fourth foal: half-sister to fairly useful/temperamental 6f (at 2 yrs)/1¼m winner Harvest Joy (by Daggers Drawn) and 7.5f to 1¼m winner Touch of Ivory (by Rossini): dam unraced: always behind in maiden at Musselburgh and seller at Carlisle. *Pat Morris* **–**

MISS DOODLE 3 ch.f. Dubai Destination (USA) 127 – Running Flame (IND) (Steinbeck (USA) 119) [2009 p10g 12m^3 12g^6 14g^6 16g Aug 29] 26,000F: leggy filly: third **64**

foal: sister to French 6f winner Jhansi Rani: dam Indian 1000 Guineas/Oaks winner: modest maiden handicapper: stays 1¾m: acts on good to firm ground. *Eve Johnson Houghton*

MISS DREAMY 2 b.f. (Apr 20) Whipper (USA) 126 – Highest Dream (IRE) (Highest Honor (FR) 124) [2009 5m Apr 30] leggy filly: fifth foal: half-sister to 3 winners, including 6-y-o Smarten Die and 8.5f winner Swainsworld (by Swain): dam, French 2-y-o 1m winner (later successful in USA), half-sister to very smart French/US 1m/9f performer Special Ring: 66/1, tailed off in maiden at Redcar. *P. C. Haslam* **–**

MISSED MONDAYS 3 ch.f. Distant Music (USA) 126 – Lilting Prose (IRE) 55 (Indian Ridge 123) [2009 53: p7.1g[5] p6g p6g f6g[6] 6m[5] p6g Oct 26] poor maiden: stays easy 7f: acts on polytrack and good to firm going: tried visored. *Pat Morris* **45**

MISS EZE 3 b.f. Danehill Dancer (IRE) 117 – Miss Corniche 104 (Hernando (FR) 127) [2009 84p: 7d 7.1v p8g[6] 7s p7.1g[2] p8g[5] Nov 13] tall, unfurnished filly: fairly useful handicapper: likely to prove best at 7f/1m: acts on polytrack and soft going: sold 48,000 gns. *M. L. W. Bell* **82**

MISS FERNEY 5 ch.m. Cayman Kai (IRE) 114 – Jendorcet 57 (Grey Ghost 98) [2009 60: 10.1d 8m 12v[6] 10m* 10.1m* 9.9f[3] 12.4d[6] 10m[2] Sep 23] sturdy mare: modest performer: won seller at Redcar (66/1) and handicap at Newcastle in August: stays 1¼m: acts on good to firm ground: usually travels strongly held up. *A. Kirtley* **64**

MISS FIREFLY 4 b.f. Compton Place 125 – Popocatepetl (FR) 66 (Nashwan (USA) 135) [2009 66§: 5.1m 5g[2] 5m[6] 6.1m[6] 6m p5.1g[2] 5.7m[3] 5.3d[3] 5.7m[6] 6.1d[3] 5.1m p6g[2] p7m p6g[4] p6m Dec 16] leggy filly: fluent mover: modest performer nowadays: best at 5f/6f: acts on polytrack, firm and good to soft going: tried blinkered: ungenuine. *R. J. Hodges* **60 §**

MISS FRANGIPANE (IRE) 3 b.f. Acclamation 118 – Snap Crackle Pop (IRE) 87 (Statoblest 120) [2009 6m[4] 6m[3] 6g[2] 6g[2] 6m* p7g[3] Oct 11] 350,000Y: seventh foal: half-sister to 3 winners, including 8-y-o Handsome Cross and useful 6f (at 2 yrs) to 1m winner Sharp Nephew (by Dr Fong): dam 2-y-o 5f winner: fair performer: won maiden at Yarmouth in September: stays 7f: acts on polytrack, raced only on good/good to firm ground on turf: sold 10,000 gns, then resold 6,500 gns. *J. Noseda* **71**

MISS FRITTON (IRE) 3 b.f. Refuse To Bend (IRE) 128 – Golly Gosh (IRE) 103 (Danehill (USA) 126) [2009 65: f8g* p9.5g a10g Dec 1] neat filly: fair handicapper: won at Southwell in January: left M. Botti after next start: stays 1m: acts on all-weather and good to firm ground. *T. Larriviere, France* **68**

MISS GIBBOA (IRE) 3 ch.f. Spartacus (IRE) 107 – Ludovica (Bustino 136) [2009 53p: 7.5m 12.1m 10g 16.2g Jul 20] modest maiden: barely stayed 1½m: acted on good to firm and good to soft ground: dead. *P. C. Haslam* **53**

MISS GIBBS 2 b.f. (Mar 7) Needwood Blade 117 – Katy-Q (IRE) 58 (Taufan (USA) 119) [2009 5.1g Apr 28] £2,800Y: half-sister to 3 winners, including 10-y-o Mister Benji: dam 2-y-o 5f winner: 20/1, well held in maiden at Bath. *P. D. Evans* **–**

MISS GLITTERS (IRE) 4 b.f. Chevalier (IRE) 115 – Geht Schnell (Fairy King (USA)) [2009 p7g[4] f7g* 7f[2] f7g* 8.1f p8g[6] 6.9g[6] f8g f8g* f8m[2] Dec 15] €60,000Y: lengthy filly: closely related to useful Irish 2005 2-y-o 6f winner Alexander Alliance (by Danetime) and half-sister to several winners, including smart 6f winner (including at 2 yrs) Ruby Rocket (by Indian Rocket) and useful 7f winner (including at 2 yrs) Cool Panic (by Brave Act): dam Irish sprint maiden: fairly useful handicapper: won in April (maiden), May and October, all at Southwell: stays 1m: acts on all-weather and firm going. *H. Morrison* **91**

MISS GORICA (IRE) 5 b.m. Mull of Kintyre (USA) 114 – Allegorica (IRE) (Alzao (USA) 117) [2009 108: 7.5d* 6.5g[3] 6g[5] 6g 6m 5f[2] 7s[4] 5g 7g[4] 6g* p6g[3] p6g[2] 7d[5] 6g p5g Oct 23] sturdy, compact mare: smart performer: won handicap at Nad Al Sheba in January and minor event at Leopardstown (by ½ length from Leandros) in July: placed in handicaps at Dundalk in August, tending to hang on second occasion: effective at 5f to easy 1m: acts on polytrack, firm and good to soft going (seemingly not on soft): tongue tied once as 4-y-o: travels strongly and usually tracks pace. *Ms Joanna Morgan, Ireland* **110**

MISS HOLLYBELL 3 b.f. Umistim 119 – Hollybell 87§ (Beveled (USA)) [2009 75: 6m 6v[6] 6d* 6g[5] 6m 7g p7g p6g Nov 25] good-topped filly: fair handicapper: won at Windsor in June: stays 6f: acts on firm and good to soft going: has finished weakly. *J. Gallagher* **78**

MISSIONAIRE (USA) 2 b. or br.c. (Jan 27) El Corredor (USA) 123 – Fapindy (USA) (A P Indy (USA) 131) [2009 6d[2] 7g* 7m[5] 8g[4] Aug 28] $80,000F, $320,000Y: good-topped colt: third foal: half-brother to winners in USA by Point Given and Saarland: dam US 8.5f winner: fairly useful performer: won maiden at Newmarket (beat Dubawi **85**

Phantom ½ length) in June: better effort after when respectable fourth in nursery at same course: should stay 1m+. *W. J. Knight*

MISSION CONTROL (IRE) 4 ch.g. Dubai Destination (USA) 127 – Stage Manner 104 (In The Wings 128) [2009 82: p12.2g[6] p13g* p16g[2] p16g[3] p16.5g[5] p16g[4] Nov 25] strong, lengthy gelding: fairly useful handicapper: won at Lingfield in January: left J. Boyle and successful 3 times over hurdles prior to final start: stays 2m: acts on polytrack and good to firm going. *Tim Vaughan* **80**

MISSION IMPOSSIBLE 4 b. or gr.g. Kyllachy 129 – Eastern Lyric 93 (Petong 126) [2009 79: p5.1g f6g 7m 5g 6s 6m 7.2g 5.1s* Nov 4] tall gelding: just modest handicapper in 2009: left P. Haslam after fifth start: won at Nottingham in November: stays 6f: acts on all-weather, soft and good to firm going: sometimes slowly away. *Miss Tracy Waggott* **60**

MISSION LODGE 3 b.f. Selkirk (USA) 129 – Hiddendale (IRE) 97 (Indian Ridge 123) [2009 8.3g 10m Jun 11] good-topped filly: second foal: dam 2-y-o 6f winner: tailed-off last in maidens at Windsor (failed to settle) and Newbury: sold 3,500 gns. *B. J. Meehan* **–**

MISS ISLE CONTROL 2 ch.f. (Mar 23) Monsieur Bond (IRE) 120 – Sea Isle 73 (Selkirk (USA) 129) [2009 p6g 7.5g 7m f7g Oct 18] sparely-made filly: fourth foal: half-sister to 6-y-o Cativo Cavallino and 6f winner La Famiglia (by Tobougg): dam maiden (stayed 1m): no form in maidens, said to have been lame when pulled up penultimate start. *A. J. McCabe* **–**

MISSISSIPPIAN (IRE) 5 b.g. Montjeu (IRE) 137 – Swilly (USA) (Irish River (FR) 131) [2009 10f 9f 10g p8g p10m 8.3g Oct 19] good-topped gelding: fairly useful form when winning minor event at Navan on debut at 3 yrs for A. O'Brien: sold 120,000 gns and raced in USA for J. Cassidy in 2008 (best effort when third in optional claimer at Hollywood) and first 2 starts in 2009: just modest efforts back on Flat in Britain: stays 1¼m: acts on firm going: tried tongue tied: sold £1,600. *C. J. Mann* **64**

MISS JABBA (IRE) 3 b.f. Bertolini (USA) 125 – Najaaba (USA) 92 (Bahhare (USA) 122) [2009 –: 7m p7g 8d[3] f8f p8m Dec 6] sturdy filly: poor maiden: stays 1m: acts on good to soft going: tried blinkered. *Miss J. Feilden* **47**

MISS JODARAH (USA) 3 b.f. Action This Day (USA) 121 – Suzie Diamond (USA) (Secreto (USA) 128) [2009 –: p10m p7m p8.6g 9.9m p12g 14m[5] Oct 1] compact filly: little form. *J. R. Best* **–**

MISS KADEE 3 ch.f. Needwood Blade 117 – Deco Lady 65 (Wolfhound (USA) 126) [2009 47: 6.1g 7f p7g[6] Jun 4] poor maiden: tried visored (pulled up). *J. S. Moore* **–**

MISS KECK 5 b.m. Inchinor 119 – En Vacances (IRE) 90 (Old Vic 136) [2009 f11g[3] p12.2g[4] f12g[3] 16m[5] 14m[6] 14.1m 16.1d* 18m[4] 16.2m[3] 16s* 16.2g[4] 15.8v[5] Sep 4] 2,000Y: rather leggy mare: fourth foal: half-sister to 2m/17f winner Sariba (by Persian Bold): dam 2m winner: placed in bumpers: fair handicapper: won at Newcastle in June and Thirsk in August: suited by 2m+: acts on soft and good to firm ground, promise on all-weather. *G. A. Swinbank* **76**

MISS KITTY GREY (IRE) 2 gr.f. (Apr 28) One Cool Cat (USA) 123 – Nortolixa (FR) (Linamix (FR) 127) [2009 5g[6] 5.7g Aug 6] €26,000F, €16,000Y: fourth foal: half-sister to French 2004 2-y-o 1m winner Danse du Desert (by Desert Prince) and French 9f winner Angarika (by Dansili): dam, French 5.5f (at 2 yrs) to 10.5f winner, half-sister to smart French/US performer up to 1½m Northern Quest: better effort in maidens when sixth to Excelling at Lingfield: bred to need further than 5.7f. *J. R. Boyle* **46**

MISS KITTYHAWK (IRE) 3 b.f. Hawk Wing (USA) 136 – Canterbury Lace (USA) (Danehill (USA) 126) [2009 8m[3] 8f[4] 7g 7m[4] 8d Oct 15] leggy filly: second foal: sister to 4-y-o Maybe I Will: dam unraced sister to smart Irish 2002 2-y-o 1m winner Chevalier and half-sister to 1000 Guineas winner Virginia Waters: regressive maiden: stays 1m: acts on good to firm going: sold 9,500 gns. *Rae Guest* **66 d**

MISS LAUZ 2 b.f. (Feb 2) Whipper (USA) 126 – Absolve (USA) (Diesis 133) [2009 5.1g[5] 5.1m 6g[5] Jul 4] 15,000F: fourth foal: half-sister to 5-y-o Windjammer: dam unraced half-sister to smart 1¼m/1½m winner Wunderwood: no form in maidens/seller. *R. Hannon* **–**

MISS LEONA 3 b.f. Kyllachy 129 – Feather Circle (IRE) 64 (Indian Ridge 123) [2009 –: 5.1d Aug 31] little form. *J. M. Bradley* **–**

MISS LESLEY 2 b.f. (Feb 20) Needwood Blade 117 – You Found Me 62 (Robellino (USA) 127) [2009 5g[5] 5g[3] f5g[2] p6g[2] 6m* 6g[5] 6g 6s p7g p6g[4] p6f* p5m[5] Dec 30] sturdy filly: second foal: dam, maiden (stayed 1m), half-sister to smart 1¼m/1½m performer Sri Diamond: fairly useful performer: won maiden at Windsor in July and claimer at **80 §**

Lingfield in December: should stay 7f: acts on all-weather and good to firm ground: blinkered last 3 starts: temperamental. *D. K. Ivory*

MISS MARANI (IRE) 2 b.f. (Mar 22) Statue of Liberty (USA) 115 – Countess Bankes 50 (Son Pardo 107) [2009 f5g 5.1m May 6] third foal: dam, 2-y-o 5f seller winner, half-sister to useful sprinter Simianna: no form in maiden/seller. *W. G. M. Turner* **–**

MISS MEDUSA 4 b.f. Medicean 128 – College Night (IRE) 54 (Night Shift (USA)) [2009 –: p7.1g Feb 20] leggy filly: no form. *Mrs C. A. Dunnett* **–**

MISS MINNIES (IRE) 3 b. or br.f. Fraam 114 – Gold Majesty 50 (Josr Algarhoud (IRE) 118) [2009 73: p8f^4 8s 8g 7.5g 7d^4 9g^2 p8g* p8g* p7.1g^5 p7g^2 p7g Oct 23] fairly useful handicapper: won at Dundalk in August and Kempton in September: effective at 7f, barely at 9f: acts on polytrack and good to soft going: sold 35,000 gns, sent to Saudi Arabia. *D. Myerscough, Ireland* **89**

MISS MIRACLE 2 gr.f. (Feb 21) Motivator 131 – Miracle (Ezzoud (IRE) 126) [2009 7g^4 8m^5 Sep 18] rather leggy filly: fourth foal: half-sister to 4-y-o Miracle Seeker, Irish 5-y-o Prince Erik and fairly useful 1¼m winner/Champion Hurdle winner Katchit (by Kalanisi): dam French/US 1m winner: encouraging efforts in maidens at Newmarket, fourth to Pollenator then fifth to Golden Aria: will be well suited by 1¼m+: capable of further improvement. *C. G. Cox* **72 p**

MISS MITTAGONG (USA) 2 b.f. (Apr 28) Pleasantly Perfect (USA) 130 – Go Go (USA) 120 (Falstaff (USA) 115) [2009 p7g 7g^3 Oct 31] $25,000Y, 32,000 2-y-o: tall, angular filly: fourth foal: half-sister to winners in USA by Distorted Humor and Mr Greeley: dam US Grade 3 6f/Grade 2 7f winner: much better effort in maidens when 1½ lengths third to Revered at Newmarket, alone far side and always prominent. *R. M. Beckett* **77**

MISS MOJITO (IRE) 3 ch.f. Lucky Story (USA) 128 – Lamanka Lass (USA) 79 (Woodman (USA) 126) [2009 47+: p7.1g^2 p7g^6 p8g^2 7.1m 8f^5 8m* p8g^2 8m^4 p8g 8d* 8m Sep 25] rather leggy filly: fair handicapper: won at Salisbury in June and September (apprentices): stays 1m: acts on polytrack, good to firm and good to soft going: tongue tied nowadays: often slowly away: sold 25,000 gns, sent to USA. *J. W. Hills* **76**

MISS MOLONEY (IRE) 3 b.f. Sesaro (USA) 81 – Mickey Towbar (IRE) 41 (Mujadil (USA) 119) [2009 53: f8g 7m Jun 25] workmanlike filly: maiden: well held in 2009. *Mrs S. Lamyman* **–**

MISS MUJANNA 4 b.f. Mujahid (USA) 125 – Robanna 60 (Robellino (USA) 127) [2009 78: p7g^4 p7g 7m* 8m^5 8d^5 8.1g^6 p7f Sep 10] close-coupled filly: fair handicapper: won at Salisbury in June: stays easy 1m: acts on polytrack and good to firm ground: sold 1,700 gns. *J. Akehurst* **77**

MISSOULA (IRE) 6 b.m. Kalanisi (IRE) 132 – Medway (IRE) 60 (Shernazar 131) [2009 95: 16.2g 20m Jun 16] good-topped mare: useful handicapper at best: well held in 2009: stays 2½m: acts on firm and good to soft going: tends to run in snatches. *Miss Suzy Smith* **–**

MISS PELLING (IRE) 4 b.f. Danehill Dancer (IRE) 117 – Morningsurprice (USA) (Future Storm (USA)) [2009 74: 10.2f^2 10m^2 8.1g* 8g Aug 13] angular filly: fair handicapper: won at Warwick in June: left B. Meehan 52,000 gns prior to final start: stays 1¼m: acts on polytrack and firm going. *James G. Burns, Ireland* **75**

MISS PERFECTIONIST 3 b.f. Invincible Spirit (IRE) 121 – To The Woods (IRE) 86 (Woodborough (USA) 112) [2009 69: p6g f8g^6 f7g p10g^6 p9.5g^4 p9.5g p9.5g Dec 19] sturdy filly: modest maiden: stays 1¼m: raced only on all-weather and good to firm ground. *P. Howling* **53**

MISS POLLY PLUM 2 b.f. (Apr 5) Doyen (IRE) 132 – Mrs Plum 72 (Emarati (USA) 74) [2009 p7m Dec 16] third foal: dam, maiden (stayed 6f), form only at 2 yrs: well held in maiden at Lingfield. *C. A. Dwyer* **–**

MISS PORKY 3 b.f. Deportivo 116 – Carati 86 (Selkirk (USA) 129) [2009 6m^5 7m^5 6.1f 8m^5 Jun 14] 7,000Y: leggy filly: sixth foal: half-sister to 6-y-o Sea Salt: dam 2-y-o 6f winner: fair maiden: stays 6f: acts on good to firm going: sold £1,800. *R. Hollinshead* **66**

MISSPRINT 2 b.f. (Feb 2) Ishiguru (USA) 114 – Miss Up N Go (Gorytus (USA) 132) [2009 p6g Nov 27] closely related to several winners, including smart US performer up to 1¼m Al Desima (by Emperor Jones), 7f winner at 2 yrs, and half-sister to several winners, including 7-y-o Scamperdale and useful 1¼m/1½m winner Flight of Esteem (by Mark of Esteem): dam unraced half-sister to dam of Derby winner Oath: 100/1, tailed off in maiden at Wolverhampton. *B. P. J. Baugh* **–**

MISS PUSEY STREET 3 ch.f. Compton Place 125 – Pusey Street Girl 87 (Gildoran 123) [2009 –: 6d^4 6.1f 6m 6d^2 6m^4 5s^3 6d 5.1d p6g p6f^5 f5g Dec 22] modest maiden: left **53**

J. Gallagher £6,000 after fourth start: likely to prove best at 5f/6f: acts on soft and good to firm going: tried visored: often front runner. *P. D. Evans*

MISSREPRESENTATION 3 b.f. Intikhab (USA) 135 – Fairy Story (IRE) 80 (Persian Bold 123) [2009 7d^6 8m 7f^6 7.1v 8d Sep 3] good-topped filly: modest maiden: best effort on debut: dead. *J. C. Fox* **61**

MISS ROMA (IRE) 2 b.f. (Feb 2) Le Vie Dei Colori 126 – Saffa Garden (IRE) 49 (King's Best (USA) 132) [2009 5.3m 5v^6 f5g 5.1g^4 5.7m Sep 28] first foal: dam, maiden, half-sister to very smart sprinter Danetime: poor maiden: tried in cheekpieces. *R. A. Harris* **34**

MISS SAMPOWER (IRE) 3 b.f. Sampower Star 118 – Miss Mimosa (IRE) (Salmon Leap (USA) 131) [2009 p7.1g Jan 22] closely related/half-sister to several winners up to 1m in Italy: dam Italian 9f to 10.5f winner: 40/1, well beaten in maiden at Wolverhampton. *D. Carroll* **–**

MISS SCARLET 3 b.f. Red Ransom (USA) – Give Warning (IRE) (Warning 136) [2009 68?: 8d 7m Jun 25] maiden: well beaten at 3 yrs. *K. A. Ryan* **–**

MISS SERENA 4 gr.f. Singspiel (IRE) 133 – Valnerina (IRE) (Caerleon (USA) 132) [2009 84: p16g^5 p16.5g^4 p16g^4 16g a8f^6 Aug 20] good-topped filly: fair performer: left Mrs P. Sly before final outing (inadequate trip): stays 2¼m: acts on polytrack and soft ground. *L. Delacour, USA* **74**

MISS SMILLA 2 b.f. (Apr 13) Red Ransom (USA) – Snowing 88 (Tate Gallery (USA) 117) [2009 5m^4 6.1m* 6d^5 7m^4 8m^4 p8.6g^3 Oct 23] 50,000Y: smallish filly: half-sister to 3 winners, notably very smart sprinter The Trader (by Selkirk): dam Irish 5f winner: fair performer: won maiden at Nottingham in July: ran well when fourth in nurseries: strong-travelling sort, likely to prove best up to 7f: acts on good to firm going, probably on polytrack: sold 24,000 gns. *K. A. Ryan* **78**

MISS SOPHISTICAT 3 b.f. Alhaarth (IRE) 126 – She's Classy (USA) (Boundary (USA) 117) [2009 78: p12g 11.6g^6 10.3m^5 8d^2 9g^5 8m^2 8.3m p8m^4 8.3g* p10g* 10.2v p9.5g Nov 14] rangy filly: has a round action: fairly useful handicapper: won at Windsor in October and Lingfield in November: stays 1¼m: acts on polytrack, soft and good to firm ground: in visor/cheekpieces nowadays: races prominently. *W. J. Knight* **80**

MISS STARLIGHT 2 b.f. (Mar 17) Trade Fair 124 – Redeem (IRE) (Doyoun 124) [2009 7g^6 p8.6g* p8g Nov 18] 1,500Y: workmanlike filly: seventh foal: half-sister to several winners abroad: dam, French 2-y-o 6f to 9f winner, half-sister to smart stayer Boreas: easily best effort when winning maiden at Wolverhampton (got up late to beat Krymian by length) in September: lacklustre performance in nursery: will stay 1¼m. *P. J. McBride* **82**

MISS TAKEN (IRE) 2 b.f. (Mar 30) Dubai Destination (USA) 127 – Miss Takeortwo (IRE) 95 (Danehill Dancer (IRE) 117) [2009 6v^2 5m^3 6g^5 8m 8m^6 p8.6g f6g^5 f6m^4 f6g^4 f7f^2 p7.1m f7m^3 f7g^3 f7d^5 Dec 29] €5,000Y: small, angular filly: first foal: dam 2-y-o 5f/6f winner: modest maiden: stays 7f: acts on fibresand and heavy ground: usually blinkered. *D. Carroll* **58**

MISS TANGO HOTEL 3 b.f. Green Desert (USA) 127 – Inchyre 102 (Shirley Heights 130) [2009 77: 7m^2 7g^6 May 20] medium-sized filly: fair maiden, lightly raced: stays 7f: acts on good to firm going. *J. H. M. Gosden* **76**

MISS THIPPAWAN (USA) 3 b. or br.f. Street Cry (IRE) 130 – Sheathanna (USA) (Mr Leader (USA)) [2009 47: p5g 5m 5m^6 May 29] leggy filly: poor maiden: form only at 5f: acts on polytrack and good to soft going: tried in cheekpieces. *P. T. Midgley* **–**

MISS TIKITIBOO (IRE) 3 b.f. Elusive City (USA) 117 – Sabindra (Magic Ring (IRE) 115) [2009 62: p8g^6 p7g^3 6m^5 p7g Aug 7] rather leggy filly: modest maiden handicapper: stayed 7f: acted on polytrack and good to firm ground: held up: dead. *E. F. Vaughan* **63**

MISS TOTNES 5 b.m. Bandmaster (USA) 97 – Kingston Black (Shaab 85) [2009 10m Aug 9] sturdy mare: modest form at best in bumpers: 66/1, well beaten on Flat debut in maiden at Windsor. *M. Hill* **–**

MISS UNDERSTANDING 4 br.f. Dansili 127 – Crossed Wire 77 (Lycius (USA) 124) [2009 53: p10g^3 f12g p9.5g^4 p10g^6 f8d 9.8m 9.8m May 8] sturdy filly: modest maiden: should stay 1½m: acts on polytrack and good to firm going: usually in headgear. *J. R. Weymes* **50**

MISS WENDY 2 b.f. (Feb 7) Where Or When (IRE) 124 – Grove Dancer 61 (Reprimand 122) [2009 6s p8g^3 Sep 4] fourth foal: dam, 2-y-o 6f winner, half-sister to smart performer up to 1m Winisk River: easily better effort in maidens when 8¼ lengths third to Mendip at Kempton. *M. H. Tompkins* **61**

MISS WHIPPY 2 b.f. (Mar 25) Whipper (USA) 126 – Glorious (Nashwan (USA) 135) [2009 7d^{4} 8.3m* 8m^{3} Sep 24] 38,000Y: close-coupled filly: half-sister to several winners, including 6-y-o Plush and useful winner around 1¼m Closertobelieving (by Xaar): dam unraced half-sister to smart miler Killer Instinct: modest performer: won seller at Windsor in August: better form when third in nursery at Pontefract: stays 8.3f: acts on good to firm ground: has carried head high/flashed tail. *M. L. W. Bell* **61**

MISS XU XIA 3 b.f. Monsieur Bond (IRE) 120 – Bond Girl (Magic Ring (IRE) 115) [2009 46: f8s^{3} Jan 1] good-bodied filly: poor performer: stays 7f: acts on fibresand: wears cheekpieces: signs of temperament. *G. R. Oldroyd* **–**

MISS ZOOTER (IRE) 2 b.f. (Apr 9) Intikhab (USA) 135 – Laraissa (Machiavellian (USA) 123) [2009 5.7g^{5} 7.1m^{6} 6m* Oct 26] £6,500Y: close-coupled filly: fifth foal: sister to fairly useful 7f (including at 2 yrs)/1m winner Raza Cab and half-sister to winner in Greece by Exceed And Excel: dam unraced: easily best effort in maidens when winning at Leicester by 4 lengths from Adventure Story, going clear final 2f while hanging right: should stay 1m: capable of better still. *R. M. Beckett* **87 p**

MISTA ROSSA 4 br.g. Red Ransom (USA) – Cloud Hill (Danehill (USA) 126) [2009 75: p12g* 12m^{2} 14m^{5} 13.3m p12g p11g^{3} p16g^{5} p12m* 11.8m 12v^{2} Oct 24] good-bodied gelding: fair performer: won handicap in April and claimer in September, both at Kempton: best around 1½m: acts on polytrack, heavy and good to firm going: tried blinkered: sold 24,000 gns, joined Jamie Snowden. *H. Morrison* **78**

MISTER ANGRY (IRE) 2 b.c. (May 4) Cape Cross (IRE) 129 – Yaya (USA) (Rahy (USA) 115) [2009 7.1m^{2} p7.1g* 7d* 8.3s* 8m 8g p8.6g* Dec 11] €22,000Y: lengthy colt: has scope: third living foal: half-brother to winner in Cyprus by Anabaa: dam, French 1¼m/11f winner who stayed 12.5f, sister to 6-y-o Samarinda: fairly useful performer: won maiden at Wolverhampton and minor event at Catterick in July and minor events at Hamilton in August and Wolverhampton (back to form) in December: will stay 1¼m: acts on polytrack, good to firm and good to soft going: races prominently. *M. Johnston* **85**

MISTER ARJAY (USA) 9 b.g. Mister Baileys 123 – Crystal Stepper (USA) (Fred Astaire (USA)) [2009 80, a–: 12.4g^{4} 12m 16.2g May 23] smallish, good-bodied gelding: handicapper: below form in 2009: tried blinkered. *B. Ellison* **–**

MISTER BENEDICTINE 6 b.g. Mister Baileys 123 – Cultural Role 95 (Night Shift (USA)) [2009 p11g Jul 8] sturdy, quite attractive gelding: fairly useful handicapper at best: unraced on Flat in 2008, and below form only start at 6 yrs: tried tongue tied. *B. W. Duke* **–**

MISTER BENJI 10 b.g. Catrail (USA) 123 – Katy-Q (IRE) 58 (Taufan (USA) 119) [2009 –, a56: f7d^{3} f7g f8g^{4} f8g^{3} f7g p8g^{4} p8.6g Apr 4] quite good-topped gelding: modest performer: stays 8.6f: acts on all-weather, little recent form on turf: usually wears headgear. *B. P. J. Baugh* **– a51**

MISTER BISCUIT (USA) 3 b.g. Proud Citizen (USA) 122 – Nouvelle (USA) (Hazaam (USA) 113) [2009 7d 6s 6s 9.2g^{6} 7.2m Oct 1] good-bodied gelding: no form. *Miss L. A. Perratt* **–**

MISTER BOMBASTIC (IRE) 3 ch.c. Monsieur Bond (IRE) 120 – Sheen Falls (IRE) 56 (Prince Rupert (FR) 121) [2009 66p: 10.3g Jun 9] well-made colt: modest maiden: may prove best up to 1m: sold 3,000 gns. *N. J. Vaughan* **62**

MISTER COMPLETELY (IRE) 8 b.g. Princely Heir (IRE) 111 – Blue Goose (Belmez (USA) 131) [2009 63, a72: 16g p16g^{5} Jun 17] sturdy gelding: handicapper, better on all-weather: just modest in 2009: stays 16.5f: acts on all-weather, firm and good to soft going: blinkered once, visored nowadays. *Ms J. S. Doyle* **– a61**

MISTER DEE BEE (IRE) 3 b.g. Orpen (USA) 116 – Acidanthera 81 (Alzao (USA) 117) [2009 87: 8m* 8.1f* 10m* 10m^{4} 8g^{2} Jul 28] lengthy, heavy-topped gelding: useful performer: won maiden at Ripon in April, and handicaps at Warwick in May and Leicester in June: good efforts in frame in handicaps at Newmarket and Goodwood last 2 starts: stays 1¼m: acts on firm and soft ground: sent to Hong Kong, where renamed Great Bauhinia. *B. W. Hills* **98**

MISTER FANTASTIC 3 ch.g. Green Tune (USA) 125 – Lomapamar 76 (Nashwan (USA) 135) [2009 67: 7.1m^{3} 8m 6s 8s Sep 5] smallish, good-bodied gelding: fair maiden: left N. Vaughan and returned to former trainer after second start: should be suited by 1m+: acts on good to firm and good to soft going. *M. Dods* **71**

MISTER FIZZBOMB (IRE) 6 b.g. Lend A Hand 124 – Crocus (IRE) 70 (Mister Baileys 123) [2009 72: 12.5m* 12.1g^{2} 12.3m^{6} 12.1m 10m^{5} Sep 24] smallish, sturdy gelding: fair handicapper: won at Musselburgh in August: stays 12.5f: acts on polytrack, firm and good to soft going: usually wears headgear: races prominently. *T. D. Walford* **74**

MISTER FROSTY (IRE) 3 gr.g. Verglas (IRE) 118 – La Chinampina (FR) 51 (Darshaan 133) [2009 53: p7g 8g 8s 9g p12.2g p10g p11f^3 f11g^2 f11g^5 Dec 27] modest maiden handicapper: stays 11f: acts on all-weather. *G. Prodromou* **61**

MISTER GREEN (FR) 3 b.g. Green Desert (USA) 127 – Summertime Legacy 109 (Darshaan 133) [2009 87: 6.1m p6g p8g^2 Dec 7] good-topped gelding: fairly useful handicapper: left D. Flood after second start: stays 1m: acts on polytrack: tried visored/ blinkered. *K. McAuliffe* **85**

MISTER HARDY 4 b.g. Kyllachy 129 – Balladonia 103 (Primo Dominie 121) [2009 96: 7m* 7m* 7.6m* 7f 7m 7g^6 6m 7m^6 7m^4 7s Nov 7] smallish, close-coupled gelding: useful handicapper: thrived early in 2009, winning at Doncaster (by 6 lengths) in March, Newcastle in April and Chester (beat Opus Maximus 1¼ lengths) in May: best effort after when creditable fourth to Esoterica at Newmarket: will probably stay 1m: acts on all-weather, firm and soft going: gelded after final start. *R. A. Fahey* **104**

MISTER HUGHIE (IRE) 2 b.c. (Feb 10) Elusive City (USA) 117 – Bonne Mere (FR) (Stepneyev (IRE)) [2009 5.7f^6 5m^3 5m^3 5d^5 5.1g* 5m* 5m^2 6m^2 6m* 6m^5 Oct 3] €25,000F, €60,000Y: stocky colt: first foal: dam useful French 9f to 1¾m winner: useful performer: won seller at Bath and nursery at Newmarket in August and nursery at Haydock in September: excellent 5½ lengths fifth to Lucky Like in listed race at Redcar (not favourably drawn and slowly away) final start: stays 6f: acts on good to firm going. *M. R. Channon* **100**

MISTER INCREDIBLE 6 b.g. Wizard King 122 – Judiam 74 (Primo Dominie 121) [2009 58: f6s^6 p6g^4 p6g^5 p6g^3 p5.1g f6g^2 f5g^3 6g f6g May 5] lengthy gelding: modest handicapper: effective at 5f to 7f: acts on all-weather, heavy and good to firm ground: wears headgear. *J. M. Bradley* **58**

MISTERISLAND (IRE) 4 b.c. Spectrum (IRE) 126 – Carranita (IRE) 111 (Anita's Prince 126) [2009 55: p8.6g p7g p5.1g p6g p8.6g Dec 28] angular colt: maiden: well held in 2009: blinkered last 4 starts. *M. Mullineaux* **–**

MISTER JINGLES 6 ch.g. Desert Story (IRE) 115 – Fairy Free (Rousillon (USA) 133) [2009 68: 7.5m^3 7.5m^3 6.9g^6 7.5m^5 8m^5 8m^3 7.5g 8m 7.2m^3 p7.1g* p7m^2 f7m Nov 12] lengthy, workmanlike gelding: modest handicapper: won at Wolverhampton in October: stays 1m: acts on all-weather, firm and soft ground: sometimes in headgear: has hung markedly left. *R. M. Whitaker* **64**

MISTER LAUREL 3 b.g. Diktat 126 – Balladonia 103 (Primo Dominie 121) [2009 80: 6m* 6m 6v 5m^5 5m^6 5.4g^3 6d* 6g Aug 3] strong, good-bodied gelding: fairly useful handicapper: won at Ripon in April and Newcastle in July: will prove best at 5f/6f: acts on good to firm and good to soft going: tried blinkered: gelded after final start. *R. A. Fahey* **86**

MISTER MANANNAN (IRE) 2 b.c. (Apr 5) Desert Style (IRE) 121 – Cover Girl (IRE) 78 (Common Grounds 118) [2009 5m^3 5g* 5m 5g^2 5m^2 5m^3 5m* Sep 18] £30,000Y: sturdy colt: fourth foal: brother to fairly useful 2005 2-y-o 5f winner Shermeen, later 8.5f winner in USA, and half-brother to Irish 7f/1m winner Luxie (by Acclamation): dam 2-y-o 6f/7f winner, later useful winner up to 9f in Scandinavia: smart performer: won maiden at Pontefract (by 7 lengths) in April and listed event at Ayr (impressive show of speed, beat Puff 3½ lengths) in September: placed in between in **110 +**

Mac Asphalt Harry Rosebery Stakes, Ayr—Mister Manannan looks a pattern sprinter in the making as he rounds off his two-year-old campaign with a convincing success in this listed contest

Molecomb Stakes at Goodwood (1¼ lengths second to Monsieur Chevalier), listed race at York (neck second to Star Rover) and Flying Childers Stakes at Doncaster (1¼ lengths third to Sand Vixen): likely to prove best at 5f: raced only on good/good to firm ground: front runner/races prominently. *D. Nicholls*

MISTER MAQ 6 b.g. Namaqualand (USA) – Nordico Princess 71 (Nordico (USA)) [2009 –§: p12.2g^6 8.5m^4 10.1g 8.5g 9.3m^5 Jun 15] leggy gelding: modest performer: stays 1¼m: acts on polytrack and any turf going: wears headgear: unreliable. *A. Crook* **52 §**

MISTER NEW YORK (USA) 4 b.c. Forest Wildcat (USA) 120 – Shebane (USA) 108 (Alysheba (USA)) [2009 –, a94: p8.6g^4 f7g^4 p8g^3 p7.1g^4 8.3d p8g 8d p12f^5 p12m^3 p12g* p10m p12.2g^2 p12f^4 Dec 19] quite attractive colt: useful handicapper: won at Lingfield in October: good second at Wolverhampton penultimate start: stays 1½m: acts on polytrack, little impact on turf: blinkered of late: waited with. *Noel T. Chance* **– a97**

MISTER PETE (IRE) 6 b.g. Piccolo 121 – Whistfilly 49 (First Trump 118) [2009 69: 15.8m^6 16m^6 16.1d^3 16m^5 12d Jun 18] compact gelding: fair handicapper: stays 17f: acts on heavy and good to firm going: reliable. *W. Storey* **66**

MISTER ROSS 4 b.g. Medicean 128 – Aqualina (IRE) 104 (King's Theatre (IRE) 128) [2009 89: 8m 7m May 21] lengthy, angular gelding: fairly useful performer, lightly raced: well held at 4 yrs: should be suited by 1¼m: acts on polytrack and good to soft ground: races prominently. *G. L. Moore* **–**

MISTER STANDFAST 3 b.g. Haafhd 129 – Off The Blocks 55 (Salse (USA) 128) [2009 61: 10.2d Apr 28] leggy gelding: modest maiden: pulled up only start at 3 yrs: bred to stay 1m. *J. M. P. Eustace* **–**

MISTER TINKTASTIC (IRE) 3 ch.g. Noverre (USA) 125 – Psychic (IRE) 72 (Alhaarth (IRE) 126) [2009 69: 6m^2 6s 7g^6 5.9m* 6m* 7g^3 6g* 6f^3 5d Aug 19] fairly useful handicapper: won at Carlisle and Pontefract in June, and Pontefract again (by 6 lengths) in August: stays 6f: acts on good to firm going, probably on soft: in cheekpieces of late. *M. Dods* **89**

MISTER TRICKSTER (IRE) 8 b.g. Woodborough (USA) 112 – Tinos Island (IRE) (Alzao (USA) 117) [2009 62: p7g^2 p8.6g 9.7d^2 p8g^3 10m^6 p11g^3 p8g p8m^6 8.3g Oct 19] sturdy, close-coupled gelding: modest handicapper: stays 11f, effective at shorter: acts on polytrack, firm and good to soft going: usually slowly away/held up. *R. Dickin* **62**

MISTER WILBERFORCE 3 b.g. Paris House 123 – She's A Breeze 35 (Crofthall 110) [2009 –: 6m p12m Sep 16] of no account. *M. Mullineaux* **–**

MISTIC ACADEMY (IRE) 4 ch.f. Royal Academy (USA) 130 – Mistic Sun (Dashing Blade 117) [2009 12g 12g^6 10m 8.3m Sep 30] workmanlike filly: failed to see race out in bumper: well held in maidens on Flat: poor form over hurdles. *Miss J. E. Foster* **–**

MISTIC MAGIC (IRE) 2 b.f. (Apr 12) Orpen (USA) 116 – Mistic Sun (Dashing Blade 117) [2009 5f^4 7m* 7.1m 7m^4 7v Oct 24] 45,000Y: big, good-topped filly: second foal: dam useful 6f (in Germany at 2 yrs) and 1m (in USA) winner: fairly useful performer: won maiden at Newbury (beat subsequent pattern winners) in June: good fourth to Bab At The Bowster in nursery at Newmarket: likely to stay 1m: acts on good to firm ground, ran poorly on heavy final start (in cheekpieces). *P. F. I. Cole* **86**

MISTOFFELEES 3 b.c. Tiger Hill (IRE) 127 – Auenlust (GER) (Surumu (GER)) [2009 10m p12m^6 p10m^5 Sep 26] 10,000Y: half-brother to several winners, including 2002 2-y-o 7f winner Aries (by Big Shuffle) and 7-y-o Irish Ballad: dam German 1m winner: best effort in maidens (fair form) when eye-catching fifth to Mutamayez at Kempton final start, keeping on well and not knocked about: bred to be suited by 1½m: type to do well at 4 yrs. *L. M. Cumani* **73 p**

MISTRESS COOPER 4 b. or br.f. Kyllachy 129 – Litewska (IRE) 86 (Mujadil (USA) 119) [2009 70: p7g p6g^3 Feb 8] good-topped filly: modest handicapper: best at 5f/6f: acts on polytrack and good to firm going. *W. J. Musson* **63**

MISTRESS EVA 4 b.f. Diktat 126 – Foreign Mistress (Darshaan 133) [2009 78: p14g Jan 13] angular filly: fair handicapper: well held only start at 4 yrs: stays 1½m: acts on soft going: joined Mrs S. Leech, let down by jumping over hurdles. *L. Corcoran* **–**

MISTRESS GREELEY (USA) 4 ch.f. Mr Greeley (USA) 122 – My Reem (USA) (Chief's Crown (USA)) [2009 83: p8.6g Feb 26] useful-looking filly: fairly useful performer, lightly raced: well held only start at 4 yrs: should stay 1m. *M. Botti* **–**

MISTY DANCER 10 gr.g. Vettori (IRE) 119 – Light Fantastic 66 (Deploy 131) [2009 87: 12m 14.1s Oct 12] good-topped gelding: has reportedly had sinus problems: useful handicapper at best: well held in 2009. *Miss Venetia Williams* **–**

MISTY KIT 4 b.f. Umistim 119 – River Ensign 63 (River God (USA) 121) [2009 p12.2g p12.2g Dec 7] second foal: half-sister to 5-y-o Ensign's Trick: dam 6f to 1¼m winner: poor form in bumpers: well held in maiden/seller on Flat. *W. M. Brisbourne* **–**

MISYAAR (IRE) 3 b.f. Dubai Destination (USA) 127 – Saafeya (IRE) 111 (Sadler's Wells (USA) 132) [2009 67p: p9.5g^6 p8g^5 p7g^4 Jan 31] modest maiden: best effort at 7f: raced only on polytrack: finds little: sold 4,000 gns. *M. A. Jarvis* **59**

MITH HILL 8 b.g. Daylami (IRE) 138 – Delirious Moment (IRE) 90 (Kris 135) [2009 80: 15.9m* 16m^3 18g^2 Oct 10] smallish gelding: fairly useful handicapper: won at Chester in September: stays 21f: acts on polytrack, soft and good to firm ground: tried in cheekpieces/visor/tongue tie: fairly useful hurdler. *Ian Williams* **87**

MITO 8 b.m. Mtoto 134 – Shibui (Shirley Heights 130) [2009 12.1m 12.1m^6 12.1m Jul 10] ex-French mare: sister to fairly useful stayer Empangeni and half-sister to several winners, including Irish 11-y-o Grisham: dam unraced: placed several times in French Provinces up to 1½m for D. Henderson: missed 2007 and 2008: modest form in Britain: saddle slipped final start. *B. R. Millman* **52**

MITRA JAAN (IRE) 3 b.f. Diktat 126 – Persian Lass (IRE) 103 (Grand Lodge (USA) 125) [2009 72: 8.3g^6 10m^6 8.3g^5 p8f Sep 10] good-bodied filly: fair maiden: stays 1m: often tongue tied: free-going sort: sold 2,000 gns. *W. R. Swinburn* **71**

MIXING 7 gr.g. Linamix (FR) 127 – Tuning 114 (Rainbow Quest (USA) 134) [2009 54, a70: p12g p12g 12d^4 p12g 11.5g^5 p12g* 11m^2 12m^6 12m p11g p12m p13g p13g p12m p11f Dec 16] close-coupled gelding: modest handicapper, better on all-weather: won apprentice race at Kempton in June: stays 13f: acts on polytrack, soft and good to firm ground: tried blinkered. *M. J. Attwater* **58 a63**

MIX N MATCH 5 b.g. Royal Applause 124 – South Wind 62 (Tina's Pet 121) [2009 60: p10m^3 p10g* p10g^3 p11g^5 10g Jul 25] stocky gelding: modest handicapper: won at Lingfield in January: will prove best short of 1½m: acts on polytrack, soft and good to firm ground: held up: sold £2,000, joined J. Frost. *R. M. Stronge* **60**

MIYASAKI (CHI) 7 br.h. Memo (CHI) 118 – Cantame Al Oido (CHI) (Yendaka (USA)) [2009 98: a6g^3 6g 6.8g^4 6.8s^2 a6g^4 5.8g a6g^4 8g Oct 31] useful performer: 5½ lengths second to Chicken Momo in Polar Cup at Ovrevoll before close fourth to Tertio Bloom in listed race at Jagersro fifth start: behind in handicap at Newmarket final outing: effective at 6f, has won up to 9.5f: acts on dirt, soft and good to firm going: usually blinkered/visored: has had tongue tied. *Rune Haugen, Norway* **101**

MIZAIR NOUVAIR (IRE) 2 b.g. (Apr 12) Noverre (USA) 125 – Arzachena (FR) (Grand Lodge (USA) 125) [2009 7d 7m p7.1m Aug 21] well held in claimers/maiden: tried visored. *J. R. Weymes* **–**

M'LADY ROUSSEUR (IRE) 3 ch.f. Selkirk (USA) 129 – Millay (Polish Precedent (USA) 131) [2009 p8g p10g^3 p10g^5 10d p11g^6 p12g^2 p12.2g^4 p16g* Oct 24] €45,000Y: angular filly: second foal: half-sister to Swiss 10.5f winner Redmillson (by Red Ransom): dam, French 1m winner, sister to smart performer up to 1½m Millstreet: fair handicapper: won at Kempton in October: stays 2m: raced only on polytrack and good to soft going: held up: sold 16,000 gns. *D. R. C. Elsworth* **68**

MME DE STAEL 2 ch.f. (Apr 3) Selkirk (USA) 129 – Scandalette (Niniski (USA) 125) [2009 8.3m 8.3m 8g 8.3v^3 Nov 4] big, unfurnished filly: half-sister to several winners, including smart 6f (at 2 yrs) to 9f winner Gateman (by Owington) and 4-y-o Lady Jane Digby: dam unraced half-sister to high-class sprinter Polish Patriot: modest form in maidens, still not finished article when third to Green Lightning at Nottingham: likely to be suited by 1¼m: type to make better 3-y-o. *Sir Mark Prescott* **55 p**

MNARANI (IRE) 2 b.g. (Mar 15) Oasis Dream 129 – Finity (USA) 94 (Diesis 133) [2009 6g 6m 6.1m^4 7g 6s p8m Dec 1] lengthy, rather dipped-backed gelding: modest maiden: stays 6f: acts on good to firm going, probably on polytrack. *J. S. Moore* **60**

MNASIKIA (USA) 2 b.f. (Feb 1) Rahy (USA) 115 – Entendu (USA) (Diesis 133) [2009 p6g p7m^3 p7.1g^2 Dec 28] second foal: half-sister to 3-y-o Dubai Echo: dam, fairly useful French 1m winner, stayed 1¼m: promise in maidens, placed at Lingfield and Wolverhampton (½-length second to Capricornus): will be suited by 1m+: open to further improvement. *L. M. Cumani* **64 p**

MOANDEI 5 b.m. Silver Wizard (USA) 117 – Its All Too Much (Chaddleworth (IRE) 103) [2009 56: p11g Feb 8] angular mare: modest form in maidens. *R. Ingram* **56**

MOAYED 10 b.g. Selkirk (USA) 129 – Song of Years (IRE) 89 (Shareef Dancer (USA) 135) [2009 73: p8.6g^4 p8g^5 p8g^4 p8g p8.6g^2 Apr 6] workmanlike gelding: fair handi- **65**

capper: stays 8.6f: acts on all-weather and any turf going: wears blinkers: formerly tongue tied: held up. *N. P. Littmoden*

MOCHA JAVA 6 b.g. Bertolini (USA) 125 – Coffee Cream 87 (Common Grounds 118) [2009 55: p7g^5 p8.6g^3 p8g^4 f6g* p7g^5 f7g* 7m 6g 7.1m p7.1g* p7g f7g 7.1d p6g^3 p7g^4 f7m^6 p7g^4 f6g^2 p7.1g Dec 26] good-topped gelding: fair performer: won handicaps at Southwell in January and February and claimer at Wolverhampton in June: stays 8.6f, effective at shorter: acts on all-weather, little recent form on turf: tried in cheekpieces, blinkered later in 2009. *Matthew Salaman* – a68

MOCHUA (IRE) 5 ch.g. Moscow Society (USA) 110 – Devilabit (IRE) (Buckskin (FR) 133) [2009 –: f11g Feb 20] maiden hurdler: well held in maidens on Flat: dead. *Adrian Sexton, Ireland* –

MODEYRA 2 br.f. (Apr 3) Shamardal (USA) 129 – Zahrat Dubai 114 (Unfuwain (USA) 131) [2009 8g* Oct 23] tall, useful-looking filly: seventh foal: half-sister to fairly useful 2005 2-y-o 1m winner Shariki (by Spectrum): dam 1¼m (Musidora/Nassau Stakes) winner: well-backed 9/2, promising when winning 21-runner maiden at Doncaster by ½ length from Gertrude Bell, bursting to front 1f out before idling: bred to be suited by 1¼m: useful prospect. *Saeed bin Suroor* **91 p**

MOGGY (IRE) 3 br.f. One Cool Cat (USA) 123 – Termania (IRE) (Shirley Heights 130) [2009 54p: 10.3m 10g^2 10.2v^2 10.1m 13.8m^4 10m^3 12g^6 p12g Nov 11] close-coupled filly: modest maiden: claimed from M. Bell £6,000 third start: stays stiff 1¼m (not 1¾m): acts on heavy and good to firm going. *G. A. Harker* **54**

MOGOK RUBY 5 gr.g. Bertolini (USA) 125 – Days of Grace 79 (Wolfhound (USA) 126) [2009 86: p6g^5 p6g* p6g^3 p6g* p6g^3 p6g^6 6g^3 6m 6g 6m 6m p6m p6g p6m Dec 10] sturdy gelding: fairly useful handicapper on all-weather, fair on turf: won at Kempton in January and February: below form later in year: best at 5f/easy 6f: acts on polytrack and firm ground: tried visored: has bled: waited with. *L. Montague Hall* **76 a87**

MOHANAD (IRE) 3 b.g. Invincible Spirit (IRE) 121 – Irish Design (IRE) (Alhaarth (IRE) 126) [2009 78: p8g^4 p12g^4 12g^6 9.7f 14g^6 Jul 3] quite good-topped gelding: fair maiden: seems to stay 1¾m: acts on polytrack and good to firm going: sold 10,500 gns and joined Miss S. West (gelded), won juvenile hurdle in October. *M. R. Channon* **67**

MOHATHAB (IRE) 4 b.g. Cadeaux Genereux 131 – Zeiting (IRE) 105 (Zieten (USA) 118) [2009 88: p8g* 9m 9s p8g^2 10.1m^6 p10m p8.6g^6 Dec 12] small, round-barrelled gelding: fairly useful performer: won maiden at Lingfield in April: left J. Boyle after fifth start: best efforts at 1m/9f: acts on polytrack, best turf form on good ground: tried blinkered/visored. *Tim Vaughan* **85**

MOHAWK RIDGE 3 b.g. Storming Home 128 – Ipsa Loquitur 69 (Unfuwain (USA) 131) [2009 61d: 9.9m 8d^2 8.3g^3 8g^4 8.3v* 8s^5 8m^3 p9.5g Oct 17] leggy, useful-looking gelding: fair handicapper: won at Hamilton in August: bred to stay 1¼m+: acts on heavy and good to firm ground: tried in cheekpieces. *M. Dods* **73**

MOHAWK STAR (IRE) 8 ch.g. Indian Ridge 123 – Searching Star 63 (Rainbow Quest (USA) 134) [2009 77: p16g p16g^6 16m^2 16g^4 14.1m Aug 13] angular gelding: fair handicapper: stays 16.5f: acts on polytrack and heavy going: blinkered/visored: ridden patiently. *I. A. Wood* **72**

MOHEEBB (IRE) 5 b.g. Machiavellian (USA) 123 – Rockerlong 112 (Deploy 131) [2009 84: 8m^4 8.5m^5 8d^6 8.1v* 9.2m^2 8.9d^3 7.9m^4 8m 9.8v^3 8s* 9.8g* 9.9m 10.4m^3 10m 10g Sep 17] heavy-bodied gelding: useful handicapper: better than ever in 2009, winning at Haydock in May, and Thirsk and Ripon (beat Demolition 3 lengths) 48 hours apart in August: best subsequent effort when creditable third to Royal Destination at York: stays 11f: has form on polytrack and good to firm going, all wins on good or softer (acts on heavy): blinkered: held up. *Mrs R. A. Carr* **100**

MOHTASHEM (IRE) 3 b.c. Haafhd 129 – Showering (Danehill (USA) 126) [2009 p8g^3 8.3g^3 8m* 8m 8s 8m^3 p7g Sep 5] 110,000F: attractive colt: fourth foal: dam once-raced half-sister to smart 7f winner Clearing: fairly useful form: won maiden at Goodwood in June: stays 1m: acts on polytrack and good to firm ground, well below form on soft: visored final start: sold 20,000 gns. *Sir Michael Stoute* **88**

MOI MEL 2 b.f. (Feb 20) Danbird (AUS) – Lady Double U (Sheikh Albadou 128) [2009 7.5m Jul 28] 150/1, tailed off in maiden at Beverley: dead. *L. A. Mullaney* –

MOIQEN (IRE) 4 b.g. Red Ransom (USA) – Za Aamah (USA) (Mr Prospector (USA)) [2009 104: 10v^3 10.5v^4 11.3m^5 12s^4 Jul 6] tall, good-topped gelding: smart performer: improved when 3¼ lengths third to Curtain Call in Mooresbridge Stakes at the Curragh **112**

on reappearance: failed to repeat that form, including when fourth of 5 to Casual Conquest in Tattersalls Gold Cup at the Curragh next time: stays 1¼m, not 1½m: probably acts on any going: sometimes starts slowly: sent to UAE. *Kevin Prendergast, Ireland*

MOJEERR 3 b.g. Royal Applause 124 – Princess Miletrian (IRE) 80 (Danehill (USA) 126) [2009 –: 8.5m 9.9g^{3} p11m^{6} p9.5g^{3} p9.5g^{3} f8f f7g^{3} Dec 18] good sort: modest maiden: stays 11f: acts on all-weather: in cheekpieces last 4 starts. *A. J. McCabe* **58**

MOLLY THE WITCH (IRE) 3 b.f. Rock of Gibraltar (IRE) 133 – Tree Peony 79 (Woodman (USA) 126) [2009 64: 10m 8m* p8.6g p10g Oct 11] quite attractive filly: fair performer: won seller at Yarmouth (left M. Tregoning 9,400 gns) in August: stays 1m: raced only on polytrack/good to firm ground. *W. J. Musson* **63**

MOLLY TWO 4 ch.f. Muhtarram (USA) 125 – Rum Lass 54 (Distant Relative 128) [2009 55: 5.1d* 5d 5f^{6} 5g 5m 5d 5d 5m 5g f5g Oct 18] fair handicapper: won at Nottingham in April: below form after: speedy, raced at 5f: acts on polytrack and good to soft ground: tried visored/in cheekpieces. *L. A. Mullaney* **70 d**

MOLON LABE (IRE) 2 ch.g. (May 4) Footstepsinthesand 120 – Pillars of Society (IRE) 96 (Caerleon (USA) 132) [2009 7g 8d^{6} 8.3v^{2} Nov 4] €35,000Y, 52,000 2-y-o: good-topped gelding: fifth foal: half-brother to fairly useful French 2006 2-y-o 6f winner Good Mood (by Danehill Dancer), later Grade 3 9f winner in USA: dam, Irish 1¼m winner, stayed 1¾m, out of Prix Saint-Alary winner Grise Mine: progressive in maidens, 3¾ lengths second to Burj Nahar at Nottingham: gelded after: will be suited by 1¼m. *T. P. Tate* **79**

MOMENT OF CLARITY 7 b.g. Lujain (USA) 119 – Kicka (Shirley Heights 130) [2009 70: p9.5g^{5} p10g f8g^{2} p8.6g Feb 14] lengthy gelding: handicapper, just modest form at 7 yrs: effective at 1m to 1½m: acts on all-weather and firm ground: wears cheekpieces. *R. C. Guest* **57**

MO MHUIRNIN (IRE) 3 b.f. Danetime (IRE) 121 – Cotton Grace (IRE) 62 (Case Law 113) [2009 78: 5.1d^{3} 6s^{3} 5m^{3} 7g^{2} 6.9m* 7m* 7g^{2} 8m 7s Sep 3] workmanlike filly: fairly useful handicapper: won at Carlisle and Doncaster in June: good equal second at Newmarket next time: should stay 1m: acts on polytrack, soft and good to firm going. *R. A. Fahey* **87**

MOMTAZ 2 b.f. (Feb 26) Motivator 131 – Sahra Alsalam (USA) (Gone West (USA)) [2009 8m^{4} p7g p8g Oct 9] close-coupled filly: first foal: dam unraced out of US Grade 2 9.5f and 1½m winner Fairy Garden: 3½ lengths fourth to Namaskar at Goodwood, only form in maidens: seemed amiss final start: should stay 1¼m+. *C. E. Brittain* **72**

MONAADEMA (IRE) 4 b.f. Elnadim (USA) 128 – Suhaad 111 (Unfuwain (USA) 131) [2009 75p: 7f* Jun 2] fairly useful form: off a year, progressed again to win handicap at Folkestone in June: stayed 7f: acted on firm going: stud. *W. J. Haggas* **88**

MONAADI (IRE) 4 b.g. Singspiel (IRE) 133 – Bint Albaadiya (USA) 108 (Woodman (USA) 126) [2009 71: f12g^{4} p13.9g* p13.9g^{3} p16.5g^{3} p16.5g^{6} 18m^{5} 11.8m^{2} 14g 12.3g 12.6g Jul 3] good-topped gelding: fair handicapper: won at Wolverhampton in February: barely stays 2m: acts on all-weather and good to firm going: in cheekpieces/visor after reappearance: joined F. Sutherland. *R. Hollinshead* **68**

MONACO DREAM (IRE) 3 b.f. Hawk Wing (USA) 136 – Parvenue (FR) 79 (Ezzoud (IRE) 126) [2009 p8g^{3} 8m 10m^{2} 11.8m^{4} Jun 18] €32,000F, €80,000Y: fourth foal: half-sister to 3 winners, including Irish 2007 2-y-o 1m winner Vivaldi (by Montjeu) and fairly useful 2006 2-y-o 6f winner Three Decades (by Invincible Spirit): dam, 2-y-o 6f winner, out of sister to Middle Park Stakes winner/2000 Guineas runner-up Lycius: fair form in maidens: stays 1¼m: raced only on polytrack and good to firm going. *W. Jarvis* **74**

MONACO (GER) 3 b.c. Monsun (GER) 124 – Miss Holsten (USA) (Diesis 133) [2009 p8.6g^{2} Sep 11] 50,000Y: third foal: half-brother to German 7f and (at 2 yrs) 7.5f winner Mona Lisa (by Spinning World): dam, German 8.5f winner, half-sister to smart performer up to 1½m Santillana: 4/1, very green when ½-length second to Awesome Surprise in maiden at Wolverhampton, leading for most of final 1f: bred to be suited by 1¼m+: will improve. *L. M. Cumani* **80 p**

MONACO MISTRESS (IRE) 3 b.f. Acclamation 118 – Bendis (GER) (Danehill (USA) 126) [2009 58: 7.5m 7g 9.1v f12g Nov 17] maiden: little impact in handicaps in 2009, leaving P. Haslam after second start: tried tongue tied. *N. Tinkler* **–**

MONAGASQUE (IRE) 3 ch.f. King Charlemagne (USA) 120 – Amiela (FR) (Mujtahid (USA) 118) [2009 8.1g 8f^{6} p8.6g^{6} 10m f11g Aug 25] sparely-made filly: fourth foal: half-sister to winner in Greece by Second Empire: dam, French maiden, half-sister to smart French/Swedish sprinter Terroir: little form. *S. Kirk* **–**

Sandringham Handicap, Royal Ascot—Jamie Spencer celebrates as Moneycantbuymelove comes from last to first to beat the Queen's Golden Stream (white face); the Channon-trained pair Please Sing (No.6) and the grey Silver Games complete the frame

MONAHULLAN PRINCE 8 b.g. Pyramus (USA) 78 – Classic Artiste (USA) 56 (Arctic Tern (USA) 126) [2009 67: 16s^4 17d 16d^3 16g* 16m^3 14s* 16g^2 p16.5g* 16s Nov 5] fair handicapper: better than ever in 2009, winning at Wexford and Killarney in August and Wolverhampton in October: stays 17f: acts on polytrack, firm and soft ground: used to wear tongue tie (not last 4 starts): in cheekpieces second to fifth outings: tough and consistent. *G. Keane, Ireland* **76**

MONALINI (IRE) 2 b.g. (Mar 4) Bertolini (USA) 125 – Mona Em (IRE) (Catrail (USA) 123) [2009 5m* 5m^5 6m 5m 6m Oct 5] €26,000F, £40,000Y: fourth foal: half-brother to 2 winners in France, including useful 9f/1¼m winner (including at 2 yrs) Nice Applause (by Royal Applause): dam German 2-y-o 5f/6f winner: fair performer: won maiden at Musselburgh in April: soundly beaten last 3 outings, seeming amiss first occasion: should stay at least 6f: gelded after final start. *B. Smart* **73**

MONASHEE ROCK (IRE) 4 b.f. Monashee Mountain (USA) 115 – Polar Rock 66 (Polar Falcon (USA) 126) [2009 78: 8f^2 8f^3 8m^3 8m^6 7m^3 p8m^4 p7g^4 p8m p7.1g* p7g^2 p7g^4 p7.1g^4 Dec 11] useful-looking filly: fair performer: won seller at Wolverhampton in November: effective at 7f/1m: acts on polytrack, firm and good to soft going: held up: reportedly bled fifth start. *Matthew Salaman* **75**

MON BRAV 2 b.c. (Apr 2) Sampower Star 118 – Danehill Princess (IRE) 62 (Danehill (USA) 126) [2009 5g* 6g 5m^4 Jul 11] £5,500Y: rather leggy colt: sixth foal: half-brother to 4-y-o Bahamian Lad: dam maiden (stayed 7f): fair performer: won maiden at Beverley in May: better form when seventh in listed event at Epsom and fourth in nursery at York: should be at least as effective at 6f as 5f. *D. Carroll* **78 +**

MON CADEAUX 2 b.c. (Feb 5) Cadeaux Genereux 131 – Ushindi (IRE) 73 (Montjeu (IRE) 137) [2009 6g^2 6g* 7m 6g* Sep 30] 37,000Y: first foal: dam, 1½m winner, out of half-sister to Fillies' Mile winner and Oaks second Shamshir: quickly made into useful performer: won maiden (beat Dafeef 3 lengths) in August and minor event (beat Chaperno going away by 2¾ lengths) in September, both at Salisbury: should stay 7f. *A. M. Balding* **105**

MONDEGO (GER) 7 b.g. Big Shuffle (USA) 122 – Molto In Forma (GER) (Surumu (GER)) [2009 p9.5g* p12g* Oct 20] fair form: ran 3 times for C. von der Recke in Germany at 2/3 yrs, winning maiden at Neuss on last occasion: well held in 2 races in Ireland for Gerard Cully later in 2005: had several trainers over hurdles (fair winner in **73**

2007, but then lost form): landed gamble on return to Flat in minor event at Wolverhampton, then followed up in handicap at Lingfield 4 days later: stays 1½m: acts on polytrack/sand. *George Baker*

MONDOVI 5 b.m. Kyllachy 129 – Branston Fizz 80 (Efisio 120) [2009 96: p5.1g* 5g p5g f5g Dec 8] neat mare: useful performer: won handicap at Wolverhampton in September by length from Feelin Foxy: may prove best at 5f/6f: acts on polytrack and good to firm ground. *Tom Dascombe* **97**

MONETARY FUND (USA) 3 b.g. Montjeu (IRE) 137 – Maddie G (USA) (Blush Rambler (USA) 119) [2009 83: 10m^6 8m^2 8.1g^5 14s^5 f11g^3 9.8m^2 10.1m* f12g^3 p12g Oct 8] sturdy gelding: fairly useful performer: won maiden at Epsom in September: stays 1½m: acts on all-weather and good to firm going: tongue tied last 5 starts. *G. A. Butler* **87**

MONEYCANTBUYMELOVE (IRE) 3 b.f. Pivotal 124 – Sabreon 85 (Caerleon (USA) 132) [2009 85: 10m^5 10f^3 9.9m* 8m* 9.9d^3 10s^4 Oct 3] angular filly: smart performer: progressed well, winning listed races at Goodwood (by 1½ lengths from Fallen In Love) in May and Royal Ascot (Sandringham Handicap, beat Golden Stream 2 lengths) in June: good 2¾ lengths third to Midday in Nassau Stakes at Goodwood next time: below-form fourth behind Pure Clan in Flower Bowl Invitational at Belmont final outing: effective at 1m/1¼m: acts on good to firm and good to soft going: held up: has joined C. Clement. *M. L. W. Bell* **116**

MONEY LENDER 3 b.c. Lend A Hand 124 – Ellen Mooney 83 (Efisio 120) [2009 10g^5 Apr 29] compact colt: signs of ability in maiden at Pontefract: sold 800 gns in October. *N. J. Vaughan* **55**

MONEY MONEY MONEY 3 b.f. Generous (IRE) 139 – Shi Shi (Alnasr Alwasheek 117) [2009 69: 10.2g^6 12m^6 May 21] rather leggy filly: modest maiden: will stay 1¾m+: acts on polytrack and good to firm ground. *P. Winkworth* **61**

MONEYSUPERMARKET (IRE) 3 b.f. Acclamation 118 – Almaviva (IRE) 93 (Grand Lodge (USA) 125) [2009 p6g^5 7m 5g^4 6g^5 5d^6 5f^4 6s^6 p5.1g p7m Oct 26] 38,000F, £60,000 2-y-o: first foal: dam 2-y-o 7f winner: maiden, modest form only on third start. *Pat Morris* **61 d**

MONFILS MONFILS (USA) 7 b.g. Sahm (USA) 112 – Sorpresa (USA) (Pleasant Tap (USA)) [2009 83, a67: p9.5g^3 p9.5g^3 p8.6g^6 12g* 12.4m 12m^2 12f^5 14.6g 12d 12m^6 12d 10.1d 11.5d 9.9m* 12g^6 10m 12.4d f11g Dec 27] rather leggy gelding: fair handicapper nowadays: won apprentice event at Doncaster in March and, having left A. McCabe after tenth outing, ladies race at Beverley in July: stays 1¾m: acts on polytrack, firm and good to soft going: tried blinkered/in cheekpieces. *R. E. Barr* **77**

MONITOR CLOSELY (IRE) 3 b.c. Oasis Dream 129 – Independence 116 (Selkirk (USA) 129) [2009 99p: 10m^2 8m 10.4g^4 10m^3 10.4g^5 12m* 14.6m^3 Sep 12] tall, good-bodied colt: very smart performer: improved when making all in Ladbrokes Great Voltigeur Stakes at York in August, beating Mastery by 4½ lengths: in frame in good company 4 other occasions in 2009, including when fourth in Dante Stakes at York and when 2½ lengths third to Mastery in St Leger at Doncaster (travelled strongly) final start: will prove best short of 14.6f: acts on heavy and good to firm going: tough and reliable: has joined M. Bell. *P. W. Chapple-Hyam* **122**

Ladbrokes Great Voltigeur Stakes, York—Monitor Closely (white face) leads all the way to spring a 28/1 surprise, chased home by his subsequent St Leger conqueror Mastery (right), Father Time and the grey Jukebox Jury

Weatherbys Super Sprint, Newbury—a seventh win in the race for the Richard Hannon stable as bargain buy Monsieur Chevalier justifies short-priced favouritism from Shamandar

MONKEY GLAS (IRE) 5 b.h. Mull of Kintyre (USA) 114 – Maura's Pet (IRE) 58 (Prince of Birds (USA) 121) [2009 101: p7g p8.6g Feb 7] strong, lengthy horse: useful performer at 4 yrs: well below form both starts in 2009: visored/blinkered. *J. R. Gask* –

MONKTON VALE (IRE) 2 b.g. (Mar 15) Catcher In The Rye (IRE) 115 – Byproxy (IRE) (Mujtahid (USA) 118) [2009 7.2m³ 8g⁶ Oct 23] easily better effort in maidens at Ayr when 8 lengths third to Hanson'd. *N. Wilson* **66**

MON MON (IRE) 2 b.f. (Apr 29) Refuse To Bend (IRE) 128 – Adaja (Cadeaux Genereux 131) [2009 f8m Dec 5] third foal: half-sister to 2006 2-y-o 6f seller winner Merry Moon (by Night Shift): dam unraced half-sister to Racing Post Trophy/Dante Stakes winner Dilshaan: 28/1, shaped as if in need of run in maiden at Southwell: will improve. *G. A. Swinbank* **– p**

MONMOUTHSHIRE 6 b.g. Singspiel (IRE) 133 – Croeso Cariad 107 (Most Welcome 131) [2009 –: 10.2m 10.2g Jul 4] good-topped gelding: no form since 2007: usually visored, tongue tied in 2009. *R. J. Price* –

MONOGRAPH 2 b.g. (Apr 16) Kyllachy 129 – Beading 82 (Polish Precedent (USA) 131) [2009 6m 6.5g p7.1g Dec 28] good-topped gelding: modest form in maidens. *J. W. Hills* **58**

MONOPOLE (IRE) 5 b.g. Montjeu (IRE) 137 – Pretty (IRE) 112 (Darshaan 133) [2009 10g⁵ 10.3m Jun 27] useful-looking gelding: signs of ability in bumper: modest form in maiden on Flat debut: gelded after final start: sold £6,500, joined D. Pipe. *P. R. Webber* **56**

MONO'S ONLY 3 br.f. Red Ransom (USA) – Mono Lady (IRE) 81§ (Polish Patriot (USA) 128) [2009 p10g⁵ 9.7d Apr 9] first foal: dam ungenuine 1m to 1½m winner: well held in maidens. *Paul Mason* –

MONREALE (GER) 5 b.g. Silvano (GER) 126 – Maratea (USA) (Fast Play (USA)) **74**
[2009 94d: 10d 10.2v4 Nov 4] fair handicapper nowadays: left D. Pipe after reappearance: stays 11f: acts on good to soft ground. *G. Brown*

MONROE GOLD 9 ch.g. Pivotal 124 – Golden Daring (IRE) (Night Shift (USA)) **–**
[2009 p12.2g3 12.1m Jun 23] close-coupled gelding: poor hurdler: lightly raced and well held on Flat since 2005: usually wears headgear/tongue tie. *Jennie Candlish*

MONS CALPE (IRE) 3 b.g. Rock of Gibraltar (IRE) 133 – Taking Liberties (IRE) 57 **79**
(Royal Academy (USA) 130) [2009 69: 10.2g 12g4 9.9m* 9.7f* 10g 10.9g5 Jun 25] strong, good sort: fairly useful handicapper: won at Beverley in May and Folkestone in June: stays 1½m: acts on polytrack, raced only on good going or firmer on turf: blinkered last 4 starts. *P. F. I. Cole*

MONSIEUR CHEVALIER (IRE) 2 b.c. (Jan 23) Chevalier (IRE) 115 – Blue Holly **110**
(IRE) 83 (Blues Traveller (IRE) 119) [2009 5g* 5m* 5g* 5m* 5m5 5.2d* 5g* 6m3 p6g3 5g Oct 4] 17,000Y: smallish, well-made colt: third foal: brother to fairly useful 2007 2-y-o 5f winner Mister Fips and half-brother to 2006 2-y-o 5f seller winner Suzieblue (by Redback): dam, 5f (including at 2 yrs)/6f winner, half-sister to smart 7f/1m performer Rockets 'n Rollers: smart performer: won 6 of first 7 starts between April and July (badly hampered other occasion), namely maiden at Folkestone, minor events at Newmarket and Windsor, listed race at Sandown (National Stakes, beat Star Rover 3¼ lengths), Weatherbys Super Sprint at Newbury (by ½ length from Shamandar) and Betfair Molecomb Stakes at Goodwood (beat Mister Manannan 1¼ lengths): at least respectable efforts after, third in Gimcrack Stakes at York and Sirenia Stakes at Kempton and eighth to Total Gallery in Prix de l'Abbaye de Longchamp (plenty to do and not given hard time): effective at 5f/6f: acts on polytrack, good to firm and good to soft going: comes from off pace. *R. Hannon*

Mrs Valerie Hubbard & Mr Ian Higginson's "Monsieur Chevalier"

MONSIEUR FILLIOUX (USA) 3 ch.g. Hennessy (USA) 122 – Eventually (USA) (Affirmed (USA)) [2009 77p: p7g p7f^2 Dec 21] fairly useful handicapper: off further 4 months (said to have finished lame on return), improved when second at Kempton final start: stays 7f: raced only on polytrack. *J. R. Fanshawe* **84**

MONSIEUR HARVEY 3 ch.g. Monsieur Bond (IRE) 120 – Annie Harvey 75 (Fleetwood (IRE) 107) [2009 6m^5 6d 6m May 25] well held in maidens. *B. Smart* **–**

MONSIEUR JOE (IRE) 2 b.c. (Mar 22) Choisir (AUS) 126 – Pascali 61 (Compton Place 125) [2009 5m^2 5m^3 5m* p5.1g* 5g^5 5g Oct 10] 35,000Y: sturdy colt: second foal: half-brother to 3-y-o Cerito: dam, 6f winner, half-sister to useful performer up to 7.5f Obe Brave out of half-sister to Cheveley Park Stakes winner Pass The Peace: fairly useful performer: won maiden at Folkestone in August and nursery at Wolverhampton in September: better effort after when creditable ninth to Our Jonathan in Cornwallis Stakes at Ascot: should stay 6f: acts on polytrack and good to firm ground. *W. R. Swinburn* **88**

MONSIEUR JOURDAIN (IRE) 3 b.g. Royal Applause 124 – Palwina (FR) (Unfuwain (USA) 131) [2009 52: 6v Jul 18] good-topped gelding: modest form at 2 yrs: well held only Flat outing in 2009: won juvenile hurdles in October/November. *T. D. Easterby* **–**

MONSIEUR PONTAVEN 2 b.c. (May 12) Avonbridge 123 – Take Heart 84 (Electric 126) [2009 5g 6g Oct 19] workmanlike colt: well held in maidens. *R. Bastiman* **–**

MONSIEUR REYNARD 4 ch.g. Compton Place 125 – Tell Tale Fox (Tel Quel (FR) 125) [2009 78§: 5f 5.7d p5g^5 5m 5.1m 5.3d 5.1m^2 5g 5.1d^5 5.1m^3 p5.1g^2 p5.1g^2 5g p5g p5.1g^3 p5.1g^2 p5m^5 Dec 6] attractive gelding: fair handicapper: stays easy 6f: acts on polytrack, soft and good to firm ground: tried in cheekpieces/blinkers: temperamental. *J. M. Bradley* **65 §**

MONTAFF 3 b.c. Montjeu (IRE) 137 – Meshhed (USA) 102 (Gulch (USA)) [2009 90p: 11.5m^2 12g 12f 12g^5 10d^2 10m 9.9m^4 Sep 23] rather leggy colt: useful performer: best efforts when second in Derby Trial at Lingfield (beaten neck by Age of Aquarius) and minor event at Newmarket (3¼ lengths behind Prince Siegfried): stays 1½m: acts on heavy and good to firm going: visored last 4 starts: temperamental. *M. R. Channon* **108 §**

MONT AGEL 2 b.c. (Mar 5) Danehill Dancer (IRE) 117 – Miss Riviera Golf 106 (Hernando (FR) 127) [2009 7m^3 8.3g* Oct 5] lengthy, angular colt: sixth foal: half-brother to useful 7f and 1½m winner Hotel du Cap (by Grand Lodge), 3-y-o Gassin and 5-y-o The Carlton Cannes: dam, 1m winner, sister to useful 1¼m performer Miss Corniche: promising in maidens, winning at Windsor easily by 3½ lengths from Fine Sight, quickening impressively: will stay 1¼m: useful prospect. *M. L. W. Bell* **94 p**

MONTBRETIA 4 b.f. Montjeu (IRE) 137 – Bayswater 76 (Caerleon (USA) 132) [2009 105: p10g^4 11.9g^6 May 30] useful-looking filly: useful performer at 3 yrs: below best both starts in 2009 (returned lame after final one): stays 1½m: acts on soft and good to firm going: sold 18,000 gns in December. *H. R. A. Cecil* **93**

MONT CERVIN 4 b.g. Sakhee (USA) 136 – Daylight Dreams 77 (Indian Ridge 123) [2009 80: f8g f8g^4 p8.6g f7g p8.6m 7d Jun 6] regressive handicapper: blinkered last 5 starts: tried tongue tied. *Mrs R. A. Carr* **55 d**

MONTCHARA (IRE) 6 b.g. Montjeu (IRE) 137 – Mochara (Last Fandango 125) [2009 14m^6 12.1g Jun 17] lengthy, angular gelding: little form since 2007, including over hurdles. *M. Todhunter* **–**

MONTE CASSINO (IRE) 4 ch.g. Choisir (AUS) 126 – Saucy Maid (IRE) 69 (Sure Blade (USA) 130) [2009 68: 5m 6m^5 5m^4 p6g^2 p6g 5g^3 5m 5g f5f p5.1g p6f Dec 21] big, workmanlike gelding: fair maiden handicapper: stays 6f: acts on all-weather: tried blinkered. *J. O'Reilly* **67**

MONTEGO BREEZE 3 b.f. Tipsy Creek (USA) 115 – Mofeyda (IRE) 70 (Mtoto 134) [2009 7m^3 8.3g f6g^4 Dec 27] sturdy filly: second foal: dam, maiden, stayed 1¼m: modest form in maidens. *John A. Harris* **54**

MONTELISSIMA (IRE) 2 b.f. (Feb 4) Montjeu (IRE) 137 – Issa (Pursuit of Love 124) [2009 7f 7g^6 Oct 31] first foal: dam, thrice-raced maiden, sister to very smart Yorkshire Oaks winner Catchascatchcan, herself dam of very smart miler Antonius Pius: much better effort in maidens 3 months apart (possibly amiss on debut) when 6½ lengths sixth to Field Day at Newmarket, dropped out and not knocked about: should improve further. *E. A. L. Dunlop* **64 p**

MONTE MAJOR (IRE) 8 b.g. Docksider (USA) 124 – Danalia (IRE) 78 (Danehill (USA) 126) [2009 55, a72: f5d^3 f5g^3 p5.1g^2 p5.1g* p5g p5.1m^5 p5.1g p5.1g^5 p5.1g^3 5.2d p5.1g^6 p6g Nov 21] strong, sturdy gelding: fair handicapper: won at Wolverhampton in February: best at 5f/6f: acts on all-weather, little recent form on turf: visored. *D. Shaw* **– a68**

MONTE MAYOR EAGLE 3 ch.f. Captain Rio 122 – Ink Pot (USA) 73 (Green Dancer (USA) 132) [2009 55: p6g p6g^5 8.3m f6m 7s p6g^2 f6g^2 6.1d p6g f7m Nov 12] rather leggy filly: modest performer: stays 7f: acts on all-weather: sometimes blinkered: none too consistent. *D. Haydn Jones* **– a59**

MONTE MAYOR ONE 2 b.f. (Jan 23) Lujain (USA) 119 – Alvarinho Lady 72 (Royal Applause 124) [2009 5.1f^5 5g^6 5d p6g 5.1v* 5g^6 6g p5.1g Oct 30] well-grown filly: first foal: dam, 2-y-o 5f winner, sister to useful 2002 2-y-o 6f winner All Nines: modest performer: flattered when winning 4-runner maiden at Chepstow in August, coping best with extreme conditions: below form in nurseries after: will prove best at 5f: acts on heavy going, probably on firm. *D. Haydn Jones* **55**

MONTE PATTINO (USA) 5 ch.g. Rahy (USA) 115 – Jood (USA) 87 (Nijinsky (CAN) 138) [2009 –: f11g^5 f11g^4 14m* 14.1m^2 14.1g^3 16m* 16.2m Jul 14] plain gelding: fair handicapper: won at Musselburgh (apprentices) in May and June (amateurs): stays 2m: acts on fibresand and good to firm ground: visored/tongue tied nowadays: front runner. *C. J. Teague* **69**

MONTEREY (IRE) 2 b.c. (Apr 21) Montjeu (IRE) 137 – Magnificient Style (USA) 107 (Silver Hawk (USA) 123) [2009 8.1m p8f^4 Oct 14] 230,000F: closely related to 3 at least useful winners by Sadler's Wells, including 8-y-o Percussionist and Fillies' Mile/ Lancashire Oaks winner Playful Act, and half-brother to 3 winners, including 1m (at 2 yrs)/9f winner Petara Bay (by Peintre Celebre) who stayed 1¾m and 1m (including at 2 yrs)/14.6f (Park Hill Stakes) winner Echoes In Eternity (by Spinning World), both smart: dam 1¼m winner, including Musidora Stakes: much better effort in maidens when 5 lengths fourth to Dahaam at Kempton, still green: bred to be well suited by 1½m: should continue to progress. *T. G. Mills* **67 p**

MONTEROSSO 2 b.c. (Feb 14) Dubawi (IRE) 129 – Porto Roca (AUS) (Barathea (IRE) 127) [2009 p7.1g^5 Nov 13] fifth foal: half-brother to 3 winners in Australia: dam Australian 6f (including at 2 yrs) to 1m winner, including Group 1 7f event: 12/1 and green, 9 lengths fifth to Bronze Prince in maiden at Wolverhampton: will stay 1m: sure to improve. *M. Johnston* **63 p**

MONTIBOLI (IRE) 4 ch.f. Bahamian Bounty 116 – Aunt Sadie 71 (Pursuit of Love 124) [2009 78: f7d p7.1g^6 p7.1g^4 f8d^6 8f f7g^4 8f^4 8d* 8m* 6.9d^4 8.1v^2 Jul 31] leggy, close-coupled filly: fair handicapper: won at Ripon in June and July: stays 1m: acts on all-weather and any turf going: tried blinkered, often wears cheekpieces: usually up with pace. *K. A. Ryan* **78**

MONTIYRA (IRE) 5 b.g. Montjeu (IRE) 137 – Shiyra (Darshaan 133) [2009 f14m p12.2g Nov 21] good-topped gelding: maiden: tailed off in handicaps both starts in 2009. *Miss L. C. Siddall* **–**

MONTMARTRE (USA) 3 b.g. Awesome Again (CAN) 133 – Sacre Coeur (USA) (Saint Ballado (CAN)) [2009 45: 8.3g^5 8m^6 7.1m^4 8f* 7.6m 8d 8m p10g 8d Oct 15] close-coupled gelding: fair performer: won seller at Bath (left B. Meehan 9,000 gns) in June: stays 1m: acts on firm ground. *David Pinder* **65**

MONYATI 2 ch.c. (Mar 7) Kyllachy 129 – Mustique Dream 87 (Don't Forget Me 127) [2009 p8g Dec 7] 70,000F, 130,000Y: fifth foal: half-brother to 3 winners, including useful sprinter Special Day (by Fasliyev), 5f winner at 2 yrs, and fairly useful Italian 7f winner Looking Back (by Stravinsky), herself dam of Rip Van Winkle: dam 1m winner: 12/1 and green, signs of ability when last in maiden at Lingfield: will improve. *D. M. Simcock* **– p**

MOOAKADA (IRE) 3 gr.f. Montjeu (IRE) 137 – Sulaalah (IRE) (Darshaan 133) [2009 83p: 10d^4 12m 12g 10.1m^2 10m 10.3s^2 p12m^2 Nov 29] tall, angular filly: useful performer: best efforts when runner-up in listed events at Yarmouth (¾ length behind Nashmiah), Doncaster (beaten 1¾ lengths by Queen of Pentacles) and Kempton (went down by length to Les Fazzani): stayed easy 1½m: acted on polytrack, soft and good to firm going: had awkward head carriage: said to have had breathing problem third start: visits Dansili. *J. H. M. Gosden* **104**

MOOBEYN 2 ch.g. (Mar 23) Selkirk (USA) 129 – Key Academy 103 (Royal Academy (USA) 130) [2009 p7g 8d p7.1g^3 Nov 6] 155,000Y: sixth foal: half-brother to 3 winners, including 4-y-o Keenes Day: dam, 1¼m (in USA) and 11.7f winner, half-sister to very smart performer up to 1½m Squeak: in cheekpieces, easily best effort in maidens when 1¼ lengths third to Sea of Heartbreak at Wolverhampton: bred to be suited by 1m+: looked awkward last 2 starts: gelded after final one. *M. P. Tregoning* **70**

Prix de Saint-Georges, Longchamp—the strict French interference rules come into action after a late burst by Mood Music (blinkers, light sleeves) to snatch second from Benbaun (second right) leads to his being awarded the race when first-past-the-post Inxile (noseband) is subsequently demoted to third for hampering Benbaun

MOOD MUSIC 5 b.g. Kyllachy 129 – Something Blue (Petong 126) [2009 114: a6g* p5g 5d² 5m* 5m⁵ 6g Jul 12] smallish, quite good-topped gelding: smart performer in 2008, successful in minor event at Dortmund and listed race at Baden-Baden: not quite so good at 5 yrs, but won minor event at Dortmund in March and awarded Prix de Saint-Georges at Longchamp in May after finishing ¾-length second to Inxile: below best in listed races at Lingfield and Milan in between: always behind in Prix de Ris-Orangis at Maisons-Laffitte final start: effective at 5f/6f: acts on sand, soft and good to firm going: usually blinkered: held up. *M. Hofer, Germany* **108**

MOODY TUNES 6 b.g. Merdon Melody 98 – Lady-Love 70 (Pursuit of Love 124) [2009 87: 8.3m² 8m⁴ 7.9m 7d² 7.9d* 7.9g* 8.3s⁴ 8g 8v³ Oct 31] lengthy, good-topped gelding: fairly useful performer: won claimer (final start for K. R. Burke) and ladies handicap at Carlisle in July/August: stays 9.2f: winner on good to firm ground, best efforts on good or softer (acts on heavy): tried blinkered/tongue tied: races prominently. *A. P. Jarvis* **87**

MOOINOOI 2 b.f. (Apr 12) Kyllachy 129 – Amused 78 (Prince Sabo 123) [2009 6m 6s 6m² 6m Sep 25] workmanlike filly: fourth foal: sister to 4-y-o Atlantic Beach: dam, 6f/7f winner, half-sister to smart sprinters Astonished and Bishops Court: easily best effort in maidens when 7 lengths second to Secret Queen at Redcar: not sure to stay beyond 6f: in cheekpieces last 2 starts: sold 800 gns. *T. D. Walford* **63**

MOOJEH (IRE) 3 ch.f. King's Best (USA) 132 – Bahareeya (USA) (Riverman (USA) 131) [2009 p8g p10g⁴ p7g* p7.1g p8m p7f* Dec 21] tall, close-coupled filly: third foal: dam unraced sister to high-class miler Bahri and half-sister to very smart 1996 2-y-o 7f winner (also third in Champion Stakes) Bahhare: fairly useful form: left E. Dunlop 7,000 gns, much improved when winning maiden in September and handicap in December, both at Kempton: should stay 1m+: raced only on polytrack. *M. Botti* **84**

MOONAGE DAYDREAM (IRE) 4 b.g. Captain Rio 122 – Thelma (Blakeney 126) [2009 75: 6m 7s 6f 7.5m⁶ 8m 7.5g* 7d 7.5f⁴ 9.2g⁴ 8m³ 10m Oct 13] lengthy, good-topped gelding: fair handicapper: won at Beverley in July: stays 9.2f: unraced on heavy going, acts on any other turf and fibresand: usually blinkered: tried tongue tied. *T. D. Easterby* **69**

MOONBALEJ 2 ch.g. (Mar 28) Motivator 131 – Glam Rock 102 (Nashwan (USA) 135) [2009 7g 8.3g 8g Oct 21] tall, lengthy gelding: form in maidens only when seventh to Think Its All Over at Hamilton (weakened quickly) second start: bred to be suited by 1¼m+: looked awkward last 2 outings: subsequently gelded. *M. Johnston* **58**

MOONBEAM DANCER (USA) 3 b. or br.f. Singspiel (IRE) 133 – Shepherd's Moon (USA) (Silver Hawk (USA) 123) [2009 71: p12g² p12g⁴ 11.8g³ 10.2m³ p13g* p13.9g p16g* p16m² Dec 10] fairly useful handicapper: won at Lingfield and Kempton in November: stays 2m: acts on polytrack and good to firm going. *D. M. Simcock* **81**

MOON CRYSTAL 4 b.f. Fasliyev (USA) 120 – Sabreon 85 (Caerleon (USA) 132) [2009 77: p8g⁴ f8g³ p8g* p8g² p6g⁴ p8g² p7g³ Mar 24] fair handicapper: won at Kempton in February: stays 1¼m: raced on all-weather: tongue tied: tried blinkered: usually races up with pace: consistent. *E. A. L. Dunlop* **77**

MOONDARRA BLADE 2 b.g. (Feb 18) Needwood Blade 117 – Beechy Bank (IRE) 78 (Shareef Dancer (USA) 135) [2009 7m 7d Jul 22] soundly beaten in sellers: tried visored. *J. R. Weymes* **–**

MOONLIFE (IRE) 3 b.f. Invincible Spirit (IRE) 121 – Marania (IRE) (Marju (IRE) 127) [2009 101: 8s^2 8m 8.3m* p8g* Oct 29] good-topped filly: smart form: tongue tied, improved to win minor event at Leicester and listed race at Lingfield (beat Ahla Wasahl 2¼ lengths, leading on bridle 1f out and soon well in control) both in October: stays 8.3f: acts on polytrack, soft and good to firm going: often front runner. *Saeed bin Suroor* **114**

MOONLIGHT AFFAIR (IRE) 3 b.f. Distant Music (USA) 126 – Petite Maxine 70 (Sharpo 132) [2009 78: 6m^6 6v^2 7m 7d^4 Jul 22] leggy filly: fair handicapper: likely to stay 1m: acts on heavy and good to firm going: sold 2,500 gns in October. *E. S. McMahon* **75**

MOONLIGHT BABE (USA) 2 b.f. (Mar 22) Thunder Gulch (USA) 129 – Autumn Moon (USA) (Mr Prospector (USA)) [2009 5.1m 5m 5m 7.5f Aug 29] $20,000Y, £30,000 2-y-o: sixth foal: half-sister to 3 winners abroad: dam unraced sister to very smart sprinter/miler Lycius: no form in maidens. *I. W. McInnes* **–**

MOONLIGHT BLAZE 2 b.g. (Mar 17) Barathea (IRE) 127 – Moonlight (IRE) 69 (Night Shift (USA)) [2009 6m 7m 7.5g^5 8m 8g Oct 19] workmanlike gelding: form only when fifth to Tominator in maiden at Beverley: stays 7.5f: gelded after final start. *C. W. Fairhurst* **58**

MOONLIGHT MAN 8 ch.g. Night Shift (USA) – Fleeting Rainbow 65 (Rainbow Quest (USA) 134) [2009 88: f8g^2 p10g^4 f8g^6 Dec 27] good-topped gelding: fair performer nowadays: stays easy 1¼m: acts on all-weather, firm and good to soft ground: tried blinkered/in cheekpieces: tongue tied. *C. R. Dore* **76**

MOON LIGHTNING (IRE) 3 b.g. Desert Prince (IRE) 130 – Moon Tango (IRE) 81 (Last Tycoon 131) [2009 74+: 8.1g 7m 9g^5 8g^3 10.3g^4 8m 9.2g 8g^6 8.3v Nov 4] good-bodied gelding: fair handicapper: stays 1m: acts on fibresand, best turf efforts on good ground: tried blinkered/in cheekpieces: gelded after final start. *M. H. Tompkins* **72**

MOONLIGHT SERENADE 2 b.f. (Feb 7) Mind Games 121 – Rasseem (IRE) 76 (Fasliyev (USA) 120) [2009 5g 5.1f^4 6.1g p6g^6 p6g^4 f7d^4 p7g^3 Dec 31] first foal: dam 6f seller winner: modest maiden: stays 7f: acts on polytrack. *W. G. M. Turner* **56**

MOONLINE DANCER (FR) 2 b.f. (Jan 26) Royal Academy (USA) 130 – Tulipe Noire (USA) (Alleged (USA) 138) [2009 7g^3 6m* 7m^5 6g^6 Oct 8] €160,000Y: unfurnished filly: sister to winner in Belgium and half-sister to 3 winners abroad, including French 10.5f/11.5f winner Mogro (by Diesis): dam, ran 3 times in France, sister to Ribblesdale Stakes winner Tulipa and half-sister to smart German 1m/1¼m performer Devil River Peek: fair performer: won maiden at Newbury in August: creditable efforts after, sixth to Freeforaday in nursery at same course: bred to be suited by 7f+. *R. Hannon* **79**

MOON MIX (FR) 6 gr.g. Linamix (FR) 127 – Cherry Moon (USA) (Quiet American (USA)) [2009 69§, a87d: p12g p10g^5 9.7d^6 11.9m 9s 11.5g 16d Jul 27] leggy, workmanlike gelding: just modest handicapper in 2009: stayed 2m: acted on polytrack, good to firm and good to soft going: tried tongue tied/in cheekpieces/visor: headstrong, and wasn't straightforward: dead. *J. R. Jenkins* **53 §**

MOON MONEY (IRE) 3 b.g. King's Theatre (IRE) 128 – Last Drama (IRE) (Last Tycoon 131) [2009 12m^6 9g^2 11.1g^6 7m 9.9g 15.8g^5 p16g^4 f12g Nov 17] smallish gelding: modest maiden: stays 2m: acts on polytrack and good to firm going: sold £2,200. *K. A. Ryan* **61**

MOONQUAKE (USA) 4 b. or br.c. Mr Greeley (USA) 122 – Beaming Meteor (USA) (Pleasant Colony (USA)) [2009 98: a10f* 12g^3 a10f^2 a10f^6 a9g^2 10.4m* 10f^2 10.4m Jul 11] big, good-bodied colt: smart performer: won minor event at Nad Al Sheba in January and, having left M. bin Shafya, handicap at York (by ½ length from Checklow) on return to Britain in May: good neck second to Perfect Stride in listed Wolferton Handicap at Royal Ascot next time: stayed 1½m: acted on dirt and firm going: dead. *Saeed bin Suroor* **110**

MOONRAKER'S CHOICE (IRE) 2 ch.f. (Feb 24) Choisir (AUS) 126 – Staploy 74 (Deploy 131) [2009 7m 5.7g Jul 31] €30,000Y: third foal: half-sister to winner abroad by Tendulkar: dam, maiden (stayed 11.5f), out of half-sister to Prix du Jockey Club winner Sanglamore: poor form in maidens, too free on debut. *R. Hannon* **48**

MOONSHINE BEACH 11 b.g. Lugana Beach 116 – Monongelia 98 (Welsh Pageant 132) [2009 67: 16.2g May 23] leggy, lengthy gelding: handicapper: well held sole start in 2009: stays 2¼m: acts on polytrack, firm and good to soft going: tried visored/in cheekpieces: consistent. *P. W. Hiatt* **–**

MOONSHINE CREEK 7 b.g. Pyramus (USA) 78 – Monongelia 98 (Welsh Pageant 132) [2009 71: p12g 11.9g* 11.7g* 11.7m 13.3m^6 11.6g^2 p12.2g^6 p12.2g^4 p12g* p12m^2 **73**

f12f^2 Dec 17] leggy gelding: fair handicapper: won at Brighton and Bath in April, and Lingfield (amateurs) in November: stays 1½m: acts on all-weather, soft and good to firm going: front runner/races prominently. *P. W. Hiatt*

MOON SISTER (IRE) 4 b.f. Cadeaux Genereux 131 – Tanz (IRE) 79 (Sadler's Wells (USA) 132) [2009 100: 9f^4 8.9g 10.1m 10.4g^4 10g^6 Aug 14] strong, good-bodied filly: type to carry condition: useful performer: respectable effort in 2009 only when 8¼ lengths fourth to High Heeled in listed event at York fourth outing: stays 10.9f: acts on good to firm and good to soft going. *W. Jarvis* **96**

MOONSTREAKER 6 b.g. Foxhound (USA) 103 – Ling Lane (Slip Anchor 136) [2009 75: 9.9m^6 10g 10.1s 7.9g^5 10.1m^4 Jun 25] tall, leggy gelding: fair handicapper: regressive form in 2009: stays 1½m: acts on all-weather, soft and good to firm going: often slowly away. *R. M. Whitaker* **70 d**

MOONWALKING 5 b.g. Danehill Dancer (IRE) 117 – Macca Luna (IRE) 78 (Kahyasi 130) [2009 63: 12g^5 14g 12g^5 Aug 3] angular, quite good-topped gelding: fair handicapper: should stay beyond 1½m: acts on firm and good to soft going: fair winning hurdler. *Jedd O'Keeffe* **65**

MOON WARRIOR 3 b.g. Yoshka 99 – Lunalux 61 (Emarati (USA) 74) [2009 –: 9d May 17] leggy, plain gelding: little form: tried visored. *C. Smith* **–**

MOORHOUSE GIRL 2 b.f. (Jan 30) Makbul 104 – Record Time 69 (Clantime 101) [2009 5m^2 5.4d^3 Sep 6] £46,000Y: fifth foal: half-sister to 3 winning sprinters, notably 6-y-o Moorhouse Lad and Off The Record (smart, by Desert Style): dam 5f winner: placed in maidens, 3¼ lengths third to Coolminx at York: likely to prove best at 5f. *D. H. Brown* **71 +**

MOORHOUSE LAD 6 b.g. Bertolini (USA) 125 – Record Time 69 (Clantime 101) [2009 120: 5m 5g 5m 5m Sep 9] close-coupled gelding: below very smart best in 2009, often finding little, including when ninth in Nunthorpe Stakes at York third outing: best at 5f: acts on all-weather and firm ground, probably on soft: best ridden prominently: has been bandaged behind. *B. Smart* **105**

MOORSIDE DIAMOND 5 b.m. Elmaamul (USA) 125 – Dispol Diamond 72 (Sharpo 132) [2009 58: p8.6g p8g p10g p7g^2 f8d Mar 10] modest maiden: stays 9.5f: acts on polytrack and good to soft ground: tried blinkered/in cheekpieces. *A. D. Brown* **55**

MOOSE MORAN (USA) 2 gr. or ro.c. (Jan 26) Lemon Drop Kid (USA) 131 – After All (IRE) 64 (Desert Story (IRE) 115) [2009 p7g^5 Oct 9] 11/1 and green, 5½ lengths fifth to Sahara Kingdom in maiden at Lingfield, off bridle halfway. *H. R. A. Cecil* **67**

MOOTED (UAE) 4 b.g. Mtoto 134 – Assraar 86 (Cadeaux Genereux 131) [2009 76: 9m 12d^2 12.5m* Jun 29] big, leggy gelding: fair handicapper: won at Musselburgh in June: stays 1½m: acts on polytrack, good to firm and good to soft ground. *Julie Camacho* **72**

MOOTEEAH (IRE) 3 b.f. Sakhee (USA) 136 – Cerulean Sky (IRE) 114 (Darshaan 133) [2009 67: p10g* 12v^3 Jul 17] strong, close-coupled filly: improved when winning maiden at Lingfield in May: favourite, possibly unsuited by heavy ground on handicap debut next time (though ran respectably): should have been suited by 1½m+: visits Muhtathir. *M. A. Jarvis* **77**

MOOTRIBA 3 ch.f. Nayef (USA) 129 – Tarbiyah 89 (Singspiel (IRE) 133) [2009 69: 7.5g^3 8d^3 Jun 26] lengthy, angular filly: fair maiden: stays 1m: acts on polytrack and good to soft going: usually blinkered: quirky: sold 20,000 gns in July. *W. J. Haggas* **69**

MORAL DUTY (USA) 4 ch.c. Silver Deputy (CAN) – Shoogle (USA) 86 (A P Indy (USA) 131) [2009 6m^3 6s 7.1d Aug 31] close-coupled colt: fair performer: winner at 2 yrs for Pat Eddery: well beaten in Austria/Czech Republic for A. Petrlik in 2008: below form after reappearance in 2009: should stay 7f: acts on good to firm and good to soft going. *J. S. Moore* **70**

MORANA (IRE) 2 b.c. (Feb 5) Alhaarth (IRE) 126 – Blushing Barada (USA) 53 (Blushing Groom (FR) 131) [2009 8.1m^2 7m^2 8g* 8d^5 Oct 24] 30,000F, £95,000Y: strong colt: half-brother to several winners, including 9-y-o Blythe Knight and fairly useful 12.5f to 2m winner Bid Me Welcome (by Alzao): dam Irish maiden half-sister to Irish St Leger winner Authaal: quickly made into useful performer: won Jaguar All-New XJ Autumn Stakes at Ascot in October by head from Prompter (pair clear): respectable 7¾ lengths fifth to St Nicholas Abbey in Racing Post Trophy at Doncaster: bred to stay beyond 1m, but needs to learn to settle. *P. W. Chapple-Hyam* **107**

MORAN GRA (USA) 2 ch.g. (Apr 18) Rahy (USA) 115 – Super Supreme (IND) (Zafonic (USA) 130) [2009 5s^6 6m* 6m^4 6g 7s 6g Sep 27] sturdy gelding: fifth foal: half- **93**

brother to useful Irish 2006 2-y-o 7.5f winner Vorteeva (by Bahri), later successful in USA, and 3-y-o Super Academy: dam unraced: fairly useful performer: won maiden at Leopardstown in June: good 8¼ lengths fourth to Canford Cliffs in Coventry Stakes at Royal Ascot: just respectable efforts at best after, blinkered when ninth in sales race at the Curragh final start: gelded after: should be suited by 7f: acts on good to firm ground, possibly not soft: tends to be slowly away: sent to UAE. *Ms Joanna Morgan, Ireland*

MORBICK 5 ch.g. Kyllachy 129 – Direcvil (Top Ville 129) [2009 81: p9.5g p12.2g^3 p12.2g^3 p12.2g^2 p13.9g^4 Mar 2] lengthy, heavy-topped gelding: fair handicapper nowadays: stays 13.8f: acts on polytrack and good to firm ground: reliable: joined J. O'Shea. *W. M. Brisbourne* **75**

MORE FOR LESS 2 b.g. (Apr 29) Danbird (AUS) – Patricia Philomena (IRE) 61 (Prince of Birds (USA) 121) [2009 5m^5 5m^5 6g Jun 9] close-coupled gelding: form only when fifth to Maidtorun in maiden at Beverley second start, possibly flattered. *T. D. Barron* **49 ?**

MORE LASHES (USA) 2 ch.f. (Apr 30) More Than Ready (USA) 120 – Red Piano (USA) (Red Ransom (USA)) [2009 5.2g 5d^5 6m 5g^3 5g^2 5.2m 6m^5 p5.1g Sep 18] $125,000Y: workmanlike filly: first foal: dam, US 1m/8.5f winner, out of close relative to Irish 2000 Guineas winner Prince of Birds: fair maiden: best effort when head second to Excellent Day at Sandown: may prove best at 5f: acts on good to firm going. *M. G. Quinlan* **75**

MORESCO 3 gr.g. Dalakhani (IRE) 133 – Majoune (FR) 105 (Take Risks (FR) 116) [2009 83p: 10g^5 p12g^6 13g^3 14g Aug 12] good-topped gelding: has scope: fair maiden: gelded after second start: should be suited by 2m: signs of temperament. *W. R. Swinburn* **79**

MORESTEAD (IRE) 4 ch.g. Traditionally (USA) 117 – Itsy Bitsy Betsy (USA) (Beau Genius (CAN)) [2009 51§: 18g Aug 13] rangy gelding: modest maiden handicapper: stays 7f: acts on good to soft going: tried visored: temperamental: won over fences in September. *B. G. Powell* **– §**

MORES WELLS 5 b.h. Sadler's Wells (USA) 132 – Endorsement 107 (Warning 136) [2009 122: 10g^4 15.5s^6 10f^5 12.5d^3 12m^2 10.5g 12s^3 12s^2 Nov 21] close-coupled, quite attractive horse: smart performer nowadays: respectable fifth to Perfect Stride in listed handicap at Royal Ascot (hampered before finishing well) third start: placed in 4 listed events subsequently, creditable 2 lengths second to Not Just Swing at La Teste fifth start and demoted to second after beating Eminem short head at Lyon Parilly final outing: effective at 1¼m to 1¾m: acts on firm and soft going: usually tongue tied: blinkered of late (in cheekpieces second start). *R. Gibson, France* **112**

MORE TEA VICAR (IRE) 3 b.f. Bahhare (USA) 122 – Grand Splendour 79 (Shirley Heights 130) [2009 71: p9.5g^6 9.7d 8.3m^6 7.1g^5 8.3v p7f Sep 4] maiden, just poor at 3 yrs: should be suited by 1¼m+: acts on polytrack: visored final start. *Pat Morris* **46**

MORE THAN MANY (USA) 3 b. or br.c. More Than Ready (USA) 120 – Slewnami (AUS) (Seattle Slew (USA)) [2009 66p: 7.5m* Apr 15] useful-looking colt: has scope: fairly useful form: much improved when winning handicap at Beverley in April impressively by 3¾ lengths from Labisa: not seen out again: will stay 1m. *R. A. Fahey* **81**

MORE TIME TIM (IRE) 4 b.g. Namid 128 – Lady Nasrana (FR) (Al Nasr (FR) 126) [2009 73: p8g^3 p8.6g^2 f8g* f8g* f8d* f8g p8g* 8.5g^6 p7.1g* p7.1g^3 f8g Oct 18] useful handicapper: much improved in 2009, winning 3 times (maiden first occasion) at Southwell in January/February, Lingfield in May and Wolverhampton (beat Bond City by length) in July: best at 7f/1m: acts on all-weather, soft and good to firm going: sold 17,000 gns, sent to Qatar. *J. R. Boyle* **96**

MORGANS CHOICE 2 b.g. (Feb 4) Namid 128 – Polar Dawn 72 (Polar Falcon (USA) 126) [2009 6g 5g^2 5.1m^3 5m* p5.1g Oct 16] £8,000Y: first foal: dam 7f (at 2 yrs)/1m winner: fair performer: won maiden at Ffos Las in September (edged left): seemed amiss in nursery at Wolverhampton final start: may prove best at 5f: acts on good to firm going. *J. L. Spearing* **71**

MORMEATMIC 6 b.g. Orpen (USA) 116 – Mimining 83 (Tower Walk 130) [2009 63d: 6g^4 5m 6s Aug 1] good-topped gelding: just poor handicapper in 2009: best at 5f: acts on fibresand, good to firm and good to soft going: tried blinkered: often shapes as if amiss. *M. W. Easterby* **48**

MORNING CALM 3 b.f. Montjeu (IRE) 137 – Tempting Prospect 95 (Shirley Heights 130) [2009 64p: 9.9f 14m^6 14g 12f^5 Jul 23] tall, unfurnished filly: fair maiden: should be suited by 1½m/1¾m: raced only on good going or firmer: visored last 2 outings: sold 5,500 gns. *R. Charlton* **65**

MORNING DRESS (USA) 3 gr. or ro.g. Smart Strike (CAN) 121 – Black Tie Kiss (USA) (Danzig (USA)) [2009 7d p10g 10m a6g^3 Dec 13] workmanlike gelding: well held in maidens first 3 starts: sold from M. Johnston £1,200 and dropped in trip, third in handicap at Taby final outing. *Catharina Vang, Sweden* **?**

MORNING DRIVE 2 ch.f. (Mar 1) Motivator 131 – Bright Hope (IRE) 84 (Danehill (USA) 126) [2009 p7g Sep 21] quite attractive filly: fourth foal: half-sister to 3-y-o Brief Candle, 4-y-o Wintercast and 6-y-o Birkside: dam, 1¼m winner, out of half-sister to Sprint Cup winner Iktamal: 20/1 and green, down the field in maiden at Kempton: bred to be suited by 1m+. *W. R. Swinburn* **–**

MORNING QUEEN (IRE) 3 b.f. Night Shift (USA) – Woodland Glade 72 (Mark of Esteem (IRE) 137) [2009 51: 5.1d^5 6m^2 6f^5 6g^5 Jul 21] fair performer: free-going sort, stays 6f: acts on good to firm ground: tried in cheekpieces. *C. G. Cox* **67**

MORNING SIR ALAN 3 b.c. Diktat 126 – Menhoubah (USA) 107 (Dixieland Band (USA)) [2009 57: p8.6g^4 p8.6g^2 p8.6g^3 9.7g^2 9.9m p10g^2 9.7m* 11.6g^5 Jun 22] useful-looking colt: fairly useful performer: won maiden at Folkestone in June: stays 1¼m: raced only on polytrack and good/good to firm ground: tried in cheekpieces: sold 48,000 gns in July. *S. A. Callaghan* **81**

MORNING SPRING 4 b.f. Montjoy (USA) 122 – Dino's Girl (Sabrehill (USA) 120) [2009 p8.6g Dec 28] third foal: dam no form: soundly beaten in bumper/maiden. *D. Shaw* **–**

MORNING VIEW (USA) 2 b.f. (Mar 5) North Light (IRE) 126 – Vignette (USA) 93 (Diesis 133) [2009 p8m Nov 19] sixth live foal: half-sister to 2 winners, notably very smart 1m to 14.6f (St Leger) winner Lucarno (by Dynaformer): dam, 2-y-o 6f winner (later winning sprinter in USA), out of smart French/US winner up to 9f Be Exclusive: weak 12/1, soundly beaten in maiden at Kempton: bred to be well suited by 1¼m+. *J. H. M. Gosden* **–**

MOROCCHIUS (USA) 4 b.g. Black Minnaloushe (USA) 123 – Shakespearean (USA) (Theatrical 128) [2009 68: 7s 7g 7.1g^3 7.1g* 8d^2 8s* 8m* 8m^3 8.3g^5 Oct 19] compact gelding: fair handicapper: won at Musselburgh (2) and Newcastle in July/August: stays 1m: acts on polytrack, soft and good to firm ground. *Julie Camacho* **73**

MORRISTOWN MUSIC (IRE) 5 b.m. Distant Music (USA) 126 – Tongabezi (IRE) 75 (Shernazar 131) [2009 57: 7s 5d May 15] close-coupled mare: regressive form: tried visored/in cheekpieces. *J. S. Wainwright* **–**

MORSE (IRE) 8 b.g. Shinko Forest (IRE) – Auriga 73 (Belmez (USA) 131) [2009 68: p6g^5 p6g^6 p6g^5 p7.1g^6 Mar 27] close-coupled gelding: modest handicapper nowadays: effective at 6f to 1m: acts on polytrack, heavy and good to firm going: wears cheekpieces. *J. A. Osborne* **55**

MOSA MINE 2 b.f. (May 8) Exceed And Excel (AUS) 126 – Baldemosa (FR) (Lead On Time (USA) 123) [2009 5d^4 p5.1g^4 p5g^5 Nov 13] £9,000Y: half-sister to several winners, including 4-y-o Sirocco Breeze and 11-y-o Caustic Wit: dam, French 1m winner, half-sister to very smart French sprinter Balbonella, herself dam of top-class sprinter Anabaa: modest form in maidens: free-going sort, will prove best at 5f. *D. H. Brown* **61**

MOSCOW ALI (IRE) 9 ch.g. Moscow Society (USA) 110 – Down The Bog (IRE) (Down The Hatch 76) [2009 9.2g May 15] no show in novice hurdles for Lucinda Russell in 2005/6: last in maiden on Flat debut. *J. A. McShane* **–**

MOSCOW EIGHT (IRE) 3 b.c. Elusive City (USA) 117 – Hurricane Lily (IRE) 61 (Ali-Royal (IRE) 127) [2009 90: 6.1m p6g p5.1g p5.1g^5 6.8v^2 6s^2 6s^3 a6.5g^3 a7.5g^2 a6.5g^3 Dec 24] fairly useful performer: left E. O'Neill after reappearance: claimed from Tom Dascombe £12,000 after fourth start and rejoined former stable: placed in varied company in France last 6 outings: stays 7.5f: acts on all-weather, polytrack and heavy ground. *E. J. O'Neill* **85**

MOSCOW OZNICK 4 b. or br.g. Auction House (USA) 120 – Cozette (IRE) 49 (Danehill Dancer (IRE) 117) [2009 71: 10.1s 10.2g 10m^4 10m^5 11.8m^2 f11g p12.2g^3 Dec 17] compact gelding: fair maiden handicapper: left N. Vaughan after second start, Tom Dascombe 6,500 gns after fifth: stays 1½m: acts on polytrack and good to firm ground: tried in headgear. *D. Donovan* **68**

MOSQUERAS ROMANCE 3 gr.f. Rock of Gibraltar (IRE) 133 – Mosquera (GER) 108 (Acatenango (GER) 127) [2009 p7.1g^3 p8g^2 8m p8g* Jul 15] €52,000Y: good-topped filly: fifth foal: closely related to fairly useful Irish 6f winner Bonanza (by Danehill) and half-sister to German/French 7.5f to 8.5f winner Manita (by Peintre Celebre): dam German 6.5f (at 2 yrs) to 9f winner: fairly useful form: improved when winning handicap at Kempton in July: stays 1m: acts on polytrack: likely to improve further. *M. Botti* **85 p**

MOSQUETA 2 b.f. (Mar 8) Doyen (IRE) 132 – Arantxa 77§ (Sharpo 132) [2009 p6g 5g p5.1g^5 Nov 2] sixth foal: half-sister to 3 winners, including 5-y-o Ben Chorley: dam, unreliable 6f winner (including at 2 yrs), half-sister to useful Irish performer up to 1¾m Damancher: easily best effort in maidens when 4¼ lengths fifth to Tartufo Dolce at Wolverhampton: should prove well suited by 6f+. *P. D. Evans* **60**

MOSSMANN GORGE 7 b.g. Lujain (USA) 119 – North Pine (Import 127) [2009 p12.2g 11.5g* 10.9g 12m^5 12.1v^4 13.1f Aug 22] quite good-topped gelding: modest performer: missed 2008: won handicap at Lingfield in May: stays 1½m: acts on all-weather, heavy and good to firm going: wears headgear: tricky ride, often finds little. *A. Middleton* **57 §**

MOST DEFINITELY (IRE) 9 b.g. Definite Article 121 – Unbidden Melody (USA) (Chieftain) [2009 74§: p12g Feb 11] good-bodied gelding: handicapper: well held only start in 2009: tried in blinkers/cheekpieces: temperamental. *R. M. Stronge* **– §**

MOSTOFITLEFT (IRE) 2 ch.f. (Feb 15) Pastoral Pursuits 127 – Gold Majesty 50 (Josr Algarhoud (IRE) 118) [2009 5m 5m^6 5m^6 6m Jun 16] second foal: half-sister to 3-y-o Miss Minnies: dam, sprint maiden (ran only at 2 yrs), half-sister to smart 7f/1m performer Majestic Desert: well beaten in sellers. *A. Berry* **–**

MOTAFARRED (IRE) 7 ch.g. Machiavellian (USA) 123 – Thurayya (Nashwan (USA) 135) [2009 84: 7.9m^2 8g 8g^2 8m 8m 10m^3 10.4g Oct 9] heavy-bodied gelding: fairly useful handicapper: effective at 1m to 1½m: acts on polytrack and firm ground: tried visored: tongue tied at 3 yrs: none too consistent. *Micky Hammond* **86**

MOTARJM (USA) 5 br.g. Elusive Quality (USA) – Agama (USA) 44 (Nureyev (USA) 131) [2009 93: p10g p10m p12m Nov 26] tall gelding: handicapper: well below form in 2009: formerly tongue tied. *J. Pearce* **–**

MOTIVATED CHOICE 4 b.f. Compton Place 125 – Makhsusah (IRE) (Darshaan 133) [2009 74: p7g p7.1g^5 p8g^3 p7g^3 f7g^5 p9.5g^6 Mar 2] rather leggy filly: fair performer: stayed easy 1m: acted on polytrack and good to soft ground: raced prominently: signs of temperament: reportedly in foal to Ishiguru. *Miss Amy Weaver* **69**

MOTIVATIONAL (IRE) 2 ch.c. (Feb 12) Motivator 131 – Park Romance (IRE) 95 (Dr Fong (USA) 128) [2009 6g^3 6.1g p7.1g^3 f7g^3 6g p7.1g Sep 18] 110,000F, 75,000Y: small colt: first foal: dam, 2-y-o 6f winner, half-sister to useful Irish 6f/7f winner Rum Charger, herself dam of US Grade 1 1¼m winner Winchester: fair maiden: stays 7f: acts on all-weather: sold 6,500 gns, sent to Czech Republic. *D. R. Lanigan* **72**

MOTOR HOME 3 b.g. Tobougg (IRE) 125 – Desert Dawn 108 (Belfort (FR) 89) [2009 78: 8.5g 8.1g 7m 7f^2 8g^6 p7g 7f p7g 8m Sep 28] rather leggy, useful-looking gelding: handicapper, just modest at 3 yrs: should stay 1m: acts on firm and good to soft going: tried in cheekpieces/visored: none too consistent. *A. M. Balding* **63**

MOTRICE 2 gr.f. (Mar 20) Motivator 131 – Entente Cordiale (USA) (Affirmed (USA)) [2009 p7g p7g p7.1g 8g Oct 20] close-coupled filly: half-sister to several winners, including smart 7f (at 2 yrs) to 1¾m winner Foreign Affairs (by Hernando) and 3-y-o Quai d'Orsay: dam ran once in France: modest form at best in maidens: type to do better at 1¼m+. *Sir Mark Prescott* **58 p**

MOTTY'S GIFT 2 ch.g. (Jan 28) Lucky Story (USA) 128 – Oatcake 68 (Selkirk (USA) 129) [2009 6g^6 6g p6g p7g Nov 25] compact gelding: well held in maidens/ nursery: subsequently gelded. *W. R. Swinburn* **–**

MOUNTAIN CAT (IRE) 5 b.g. Red Ransom (USA) – Timewee (USA) (Romanov (IRE) 119) [2009 66: 7g^6 6.9g^2 8.3m* 7d* 8m* 8m^5 9.2v^2 p8.6g* 8m^3 8m Oct 3] stocky gelding: fairly useful handicapper: improved in 2009, winning at Hamilton, Brighton and Musselburgh in June and Wolverhampton (4 wins from 6 starts there) in September: stays 9f: acts on polytrack, soft and good to firm going: reliable. *G. A. Swinbank* **94**

MOUNTAIN FAIRY 6 ch.m. Daylami (IRE) 138 – Mountain Spirit (IRE) (Royal Academy (USA) 130) [2009 f14g^6 Mar 3] ex-French-trained mare: no form in Britain: tried blinkered/visored/tongue tied: sold £1,600 in April (reportedly in foal to Act One). *M. W. Easterby* **–**

MOUNTAIN FOREST (GER) 3 b.g. Tiger Hill (IRE) 127 – Moricana (GER) (Konigsstuhl (GER)) [2009 –: f11g 14.1m^6 10f^6 p8f^4 p8g^4 f8f^5 p10g^6 p12f^3 Dec 13] sturdy gelding: modest maiden handicapper: stays 1½m: acts on polytrack: tried tongue tied. *H. Morrison* **53**

MOUNTAIN PASS (USA) 7 b.g. Stravinsky (USA) 133 – Ribbony (USA) (Dayjur (USA) 137) [2009 67: p7m p8.6g^4 p8g^3 p8g p7.1g^2 p8.6g 7.1g^6 8.1g 7g^2 8d^6 8.1m Jul 1] good-topped gelding: fair performer: reportedly has only one eye and paralysed tongue: stays easy 8.6f: acts on polytrack, firm and soft going: tried in headgear/tongue strap, wears cheekpieces nowadays: often slowly away. *B. J. Llewellyn* **65**

Windflower March Stakes, Goodwood—older horses again dominate this one-time Leger trial as Mourilyan (left) proves too strong for Victoria Montoya (white face) and Oasis Knight (blinkers)

MOUNTAIN PRIDE (IRE) 4 b.g. High Chaparral (IRE) 132 – Lioness 74 (Lion Cavern (USA) 117) [2009 92: 8.3m^5 7m 10m* 10m^4 10g^3 9s^2 10g^6 Oct 10] smallish, light-bodied gelding: has a quick, unimpressive action: useful handicapper: won at Sandown in May: good efforts after when placed: stays 1¼m: acts on soft and good to firm going: tried blinkered: awkward ride, and not one to trust: sold 30,000 gns, joined Paul Nolan in Ireland. *J. L. Dunlop* **96 §**

MOUNTAIN QUEST 2 b.c. (Apr 8) Hernando (FR) 127 – Miss Katmandu (IRE) (Rainbow Quest (USA) 134) [2009 8g^5 8.3g Oct 28] first foal: dam, ran once, half-sister to very smart performer up to 13.4f Asian Heights (by Hernando) and smart 1¼m/13f winner St Expedit: green in maidens, much better effort when encouraging 4½ lengths fifth to Medicinal Compound at Redcar: bred to be suited by 1¼m+: type to do better at 3 yrs. *M. L. W. Bell* **68 p**

MOUNT ATHOS (IRE) 2 b.c. (Apr 19) Montjeu (IRE) 137 – Ionian Sea (Slip Anchor 136) [2009 8g 8v Oct 24] useful-looking colt: well held in maidens at Newbury, seemingly modest form on debut: will be suited by 1¼m+. *J. W. Hills* **56**

MOUNT ELLA 3 b.f. Royal Applause 124 – Hiraeth 76 (Petong 126) [2009 –: 7m^4 p7.1g 6d 7.6d 6m^6 7m Aug 20] good-quartered filly: modest maiden: well below form after reappearance, leaving J. Osborne following third start: stays 7f: blinkered final outing. *J. R. Boyle* **60 d**

MOUNT HADLEY (USA) 5 b.g. Elusive Quality (USA) – Fly To The Moon (USA) 90 (Blushing Groom (FR) 131) [2009 97d: 8m^2 p8g^6 7.9g* 8g 8.3m 7.5f* 10.1m^5 8m f8m^4 Nov 6] tall, good-topped gelding: useful handicapper: won at Carlisle in July and Beverley in August: stays 8.3f: acts on polytrack/dirt, firm and good to soft going: tried visored/blinkered: tongue tied once. *G. A. Butler* **95**

MOUNT HERMON (IRE) 5 b.g. Golan (IRE) 129 – Machudi (Bluebird (USA) 125) [2009 89: 8.1g 8.3m^6 10g^2 10d^4 10.2m 10m^2 Oct 3] big, strong, heavy-bodied gelding: fairly useful handicapper: largely below form in 2009: stays 1¼m: acts on all-weather and firm ground: sold 7,000 gns. *H. Morrison* **82**

MOUNT JULIET (IRE) 2 b.f. (Feb 13) Danehill Dancer (IRE) 117 – Stylist (IRE) 76 (Sadler's Wells (USA) 132) [2009 p6g 7s p5.1m^2 Sep 28] good-topped filly: first foal: dam, Irish 8.5f winner, sister to useful Irish performer up to 1¾m French Ballerina and half-sister to Fillies' Mile winner Sunspangled: fair form in maidens last 2 starts, 1½ lengths second to Look Whos Next at Wolverhampton: bred to stay 7f+. *S. A. Callaghan* **73 +**

MOUNTRATH 2 b.g. (Jan 15) Dubai Destination (USA) 127 – Eurolink Sundance 85 (Night Shift (USA)) [2009 p7g 7m^5 6d^5 7d^3 8m^2 8.3d^2 Oct 12] 46,000F: strong, lengthy gelding: fourth foal: half-brother to 6-y-o Mango Music: dam, 6f winner (including at 2 yrs), half-sister to smart 1¼m performers Bonecrusher and Mango Mischief: fairly useful maiden: in cheekpieces, further improvement when short-head second to Agony And Ecstasy in nursery at Windsor (hung badly left) final start: stays 8.3f: acts on good to firm and good to soft going: tongue tied fourth/fifth starts. *B. R. Johnson* **82**

MOUNT USHER 7 br.g. Polar Falcon (USA) 126 – Division Bell (Warning 136) [2009 –§: f7g f8g^5 p8g^5 p10g p8.6g^6 Dec 14] lengthy gelding: modest performer nowadays: left M. Gingell after second start: best at 1m/1¼m: acts on polytrack, firm and good to soft ground: tried blinkered/visored: ungenuine. *Miss Diana Weeden* **59 §**

MOURAYAN (IRE) 3 b.c. Alhaarth (IRE) 126 – Mouramara (IRE) 113 (Kahyasi 130) [2009 108p: 10d³ 10g² 12g³ 12g² 14.6m⁵ Sep 12] lengthy colt: very smart performer: best effort at 3 yrs when 6 lengths third to Fame And Glory in Irish Derby at the Curragh third start, racing prominently and staying on steadily: 1¼ lengths second to Profound Beauty in Ballyroan Stakes at Leopardstown next time, then better than result when 3¼ lengths fifth to Mastery in St Leger at Doncaster, blocked off twice in final 2f after coming from last place: will stay 2m+: acts on soft and good to firm going: blinkered last 3 appearances: sold to race in Australia. *John M. Oxx, Ireland* **121**

MOURILYAN (IRE) 5 b.h. Desert Prince (IRE) 130 – Mouramara (IRE) 113 (Kahyasi 130) [2009 119: 14g³ 16m² 12m 16g² 13.3m⁴ 14g* 16d³ Nov 3] strong, lengthy horse: smart performer: off nearly 5 months and left H. Brown (returned to former trainer G. L. Moore), good length second to Schiaparelli in Goodwood Cup (hung right) fourth start: back to winning ways when beating Victoria Montoya 3 lengths in listed race on same course in August: back with H. Brown, good 2¼ lengths third to Shocking in Melbourne Cup at Flemington final outing, more to do than first 2 and staying on: stays 2m: acts on good to firm and good to soft going, probably on polytrack: below form in visor/cheekpieces: waited with: possibly not straightforward. *H. Brown, South Africa* **119**

MOVES GOODENOUGH 6 ch.g. Woodborough (USA) 112 – Rekindled Flame (IRE) (Kings Lake (USA) 133) [2009 87: 10s³ 10m 10.3d 9.8g 8m 8g Sep 17] compact gelding: fairly useful handicapper: well below form after reappearance: left A. Turnell after second start: stays 1¼m: acts on polytrack, soft and good to firm ground: often blinkered. *A. G. Foster* **87 d**

MOYENNE CORNICHE 4 ch.g. Selkirk (USA) 129 – Miss Corniche 104 (Hernando (FR) 127) [2009 108: 8m⁶ 8d³ 9.9g 8.1v⁴ 10.5d² 8s Nov 1] tall, lengthy gelding: useful performer: creditable efforts when in frame in minor event at Doncaster (¾-length third to Dream Lodge), and listed races at Haydock (3½ lengths fourth to Confront) and Saint-Cloud (1½ lengths second to Capitaine Courage): in rear in Prix Perth on last-named course final outing (gelded after): stays 10.5f: acts on soft and good to firm ground: blinkered (ran poorly) final start in 2008, visored on reappearance: usually races prominently: has got worked up in stall. *M. L. W. Bell* **108**

MOYNAHAN (USA) 4 ch.g. Johannesburg (USA) 127 – Lakab (USA) 74 (Manila (USA)) [2009 104: 8g 7g² 8g² 8g⁴ 9m f8g 8g⁵ p8.6g Nov 13] big, good-bodied gelding: useful performer: best efforts in 2009 when runner-up in minor event at Goodwood (½ length behind Axiom) and handicap at Ascot (beaten 4½ lengths by We'll Come) second/third outings: free-going sort, but stays easy 1¼m: acts on polytrack and good to soft ground: tried blinkered. *P. F. I. Cole* **104**

MOYOKO (IRE) 6 b.m. Mozart (IRE) 131 – Kayoko (IRE) 74 (Shalford (IRE) 124§) [2009 59: p9.5g⁴ p8.6g² p9.5g⁴ p10g f8g⁴ p9.5g⁵ 9.7d³ 11.9m 8f May 12] close-coupled mare: modest handicapper: stays 1¼m: acts on all-weather, firm and good to soft ground: tried in blinkers/cheekpieces. *M. Salaman* **58**

MOZAYADA (USA) 5 ch.m. Street Cry (IRE) 130 – Fatina 98 (Nashwan (USA) 135) [2009 85: f8s⁴ f8g* f7g³ p8.6g⁴ f8g⁵ 8m f8g⁴ 8m 7g⁶ 8d 8s* 8s 7.5g f8g 7.2g f8g⁵ f6f⁴ f8f² f8f³ Dec 17] big mare: fairly useful handicapper on all-weather, fair on turf: won at Southwell in January and Thirsk in August: stays 1m: acts on all-weather and soft going. *M. Brittain* **71 a83**

MR AITCH (IRE) 7 b.g. Soviet Star (USA) 128 – Welsh Mist 102 (Damister (USA) 123) [2009 80: p12.2g⁴ f11g⁴ p16g* p16g² p16.5g³ p16g²ᵈ 16.4m Jun 26] big, good-topped gelding: fairly useful handicapper: won at Lingfield in February: stays easy 2m: acts on all-weather and firm going: tongue tied: joined Eric McNamara in Ireland. *R. T. Phillips* **83**

MR BURTON 5 gr.g. Thethingaboutitis (USA) 106 – Quay Four (IRE) (Barathea (IRE) 127) [2009 62: p12.2g Feb 16] lengthy gelding: regressive maiden: tried in cheekpieces. *M. Mullineaux* **–**

MR CHOCOLATE DROP (IRE) 5 b.g. Danetime (IRE) 121 – Forest Blade (IRE) (Charnwood Forest (IRE) 125) [2009 –, a61: p7g² p8.6g p7g p8.6g⁴ p9.5g⁴ f8d² p7g² f8g⁵ Mar 27] modest handicapper on all-weather, no form on turf: stays 8.6f: acts on all-weather: tried tongue tied: often wears headgear (usually blinkers): held up. *Miss M. E. Rowland* **– a61**

MR CORBY (IRE) 2 b.c. (Mar 20) Camacho 118 – Clochette (IRE) 83 (Namaqualand (USA)) [2009 6d³ 7m⁴ 7m³ p6m² 6g 6g Oct 19] useful-looking colt: third foal: half-brother to 3-y-o Calypso Girl and 6f winner Time Share (by Danetime): dam Irish sprint maiden: fair maiden: second in nursery at Kempton: stays 7f: acts on polytrack, good to firm and good to soft ground: sold 6,000 gns. *M. R. Channon* **70**

MR CRYSTAL (FR) 5 ch.g. Trempolino (USA) 135 – Iyrbila (FR) (Lashkari 128) **87** [2009 84: 21.6m* 17.1g^{2} 18m^{2} 16g 18m^{4} 18g^{3} Oct 10] close-coupled gelding: fairly useful handicapper: won at Pontefract in April: stays 21.5f: acts on soft and good to firm going: won over fences in October. *Micky Hammond*

MR DAVID (USA) 2 b.c. (Apr 18) Sky Mesa (USA) 116 – Dancewiththebride (USA) **104** (Belong To Me (USA)) [2009 6m^{4} 6g* 6m^{4} Aug 19] $50,000Y, $155,000 2-y-o: good-topped colt: has scope: fifth foal: closely related/half-brother to several winners in USA: dam US 5f (at 2 yrs) to 9f winner: quickly made into useful performer: won maiden at Newmarket in July: very good 3¾ lengths fourth to Showcasing in Gimcrack Stakes at York, wide and never on terms: will stay 7f. *B. J. Meehan*

MR DEAL 3 b.g. King's Best (USA) 132 – One of The Family 73 (Alzao (USA) 117) **59** [2009 –: p12g 10.1g^{6} 11.5s p10g^{4} p10g^{5} Dec 7] sturdy gelding: modest maiden: stays 1¼m: tried blinkered: poor form in juvenile hurdles. *Eve Johnson Houghton*

MR EMIRATI (USA) 2 ch.c. (May 17) Mr Greeley (USA) 122 – Kathy K D (USA) **70 p** (Saint Ballado (CAN)) [2009 8g^{3} Oct 23] $140,000Y, 140,000 2-y-o: third foal: half-brother to winner in USA by Stravinsky: dam US 1m (at 2 yrs)/8.5f winner: 12/1, encouraging 3¾ lengths third to Corsica in maiden at Ayr: capable of better. *B. Smart*

MR FANTOZZI (IRE) 4 br.g. Statue of Liberty (USA) 115 – Indian Sand (Indian **70** King (USA) 128) [2009 66: p10g 8f* 7s^{2} 8g 8d 8f 8d p9.5g f8g Dec 27] tall gelding: fair handicapper: won at Brighton in May: stays 1m: acts on all-weather, firm and soft ground: usually in blinkers/cheekpieces: tried tongue tied: often makes running. *D. Donovan*

MR FLANNEGAN 3 ch.g. Forzando 122 – Star of Flanders (Puissance 110) [2009 71: **57** 6g 8.3f^{6} 7f^{2} 7m 8f 7m^{5} 7s 7f Aug 18] compact gelding: maiden: just modest form at best in 2009: stays 7f: tried visored. *H. Candy*

MR FORTHRIGHT 5 b.g. Fraam 114 – Form At Last (Formidable (USA) 125) [2009 **52** 55: 5.1m^{3} 5.7d 5.1g 5.7m^{5} 5.7g^{6} 5.7g^{6} p6g Aug 14] big, lengthy gelding: modest performer: best at 5f/6f: acts on polytrack, firm and soft going: often wears headgear. *J. M. Bradley*

MR FREDDY (IRE) 3 b.g. Intikhab (USA) 135 – Bubble N Squeak (IRE) 91 (Catrail **79 p** (USA) 123) [2009 61p: 8.5g^{6} 8s^{2} 8.5g* 8.1g^{3} 9.8v^{2} 12s^{3} Aug 1] big gelding: has plenty of scope: fair handicapper: won at Beverley (dead-heat) in May: gelded after next start: stays 1½m: raced only on good going or softer: should progress further. *R. A. Fahey*

MR FUNSHINE 4 b.g. Namid 128 – Sunrise Girl 62 (King's Signet (USA) 110) [2009 **59** 61: 7.1g 5f p6g^{6} p5.1g p6g^{6} p6m^{6} f5f^{3} f5g* Dec 22] good-topped gelding: modest handicapper: left R. Hodges, won at Southwell in December: best at 5f: acts on fibresand and good to soft going: none too consistent. *D. Shaw*

MR GARSTON 6 b.g. Mull of Kintyre (USA) 114 – Ninfa of Cisterna (Polish Patriot **–** (USA) 128) [2009 81: p7g Jan 14] good-topped gelding: handicapper: below form sole start in 2009: tried blinkered/tongue tied. *J. R. Boyle*

MR GRINCH (IRE) 2 b.g. (Feb 5) Green Tune (USA) 125 – Flyamore (FR) (Sanglamore (USA) 126) **85 +** [2009 5.9g* 6m* 7m Sep 9] 12,500Y: half-brother to 3 winners in France, including 11f winner Queseraisjesanstoi (by Rainbow Quest) and 1½m/13f winner La Fine Equipe (by Jeune Homme): dam, 1m winner in Denmark, half-sister to smart French winners Daneskaya (miler) and Silverskaya (at 1½m): fairly useful performer: won maiden at Carlisle and minor event at Newcastle (by head from Keyta Bonita) in August: better than result when eighth in well-contested nursery at Doncaster: should stay 7f: sent to Hong Kong, where renamed Win Win Fellowship. *M. Dods*

MR HARMOOSH (IRE) 2 b.g. (Mar 16) Noverre (USA) 125 – Polish Affair (IRE) **61** (Polish Patriot (USA) 128) [2009 7g 8.1m^{6} 7m^{4} 7m Oct 26] neat gelding: modest form at best in maidens: seemed amiss in nursery: gelded after: stays 7f. *E. F. Vaughan*

MR HICHENS 4 b.g. Makbul 104 – Lake Melody (Sizzling Melody 117) [2009 94§: **83 §** p8g^{5} 8.1v^{6} 10m 10s 8.3m 8.3g p8m p8m* p8g Dec 7] big, lengthy, unfurnished gelding: fairly useful handicapper: won at Kempton in November: stays 1¼m: acts on polytrack, soft and good to firm ground: tried in headgear: irresolute. *Karen George*

MR IRONS (USA) 2 ch.c. (Mar 7) Mr Greeley (USA) 122 – Jive Talk (USA) (Kingmambo (USA) 125) **95 p** [2009 7m 7m* Oct 3] $425,000F: well-made colt: second foal: dam unraced close relation to useful 5f (Queen Mary Stakes) to 1m (US Grade 2 event) winner Dance Parade and half-sister to US Grade 3 9f winner Ocean Queen: much better effort in maidens when winning at Redcar by head from Tesslam, still green: likely to be suited by 1m: already useful, and will improve again. *Sir Michael Stoute*

MR KARTOFFEL (IRE) 4 b.g. Night Shift (USA) – Diamant (IRE) (Bigstone (IRE) 126) [2009 8.1g 10g 12.1g Jun 22] workmanlike gelding: well held in maidens. *H. Candy* **–**

MR LAMBROS 8 ch.g. Pivotal 124 – Magical Veil 73 (Majestic Light (USA)) [2009 –, a105: p6g^{6} p6g p7g^{2} Jan 24] good-topped gelding: just fairly useful handicapper in 2009: effective at 6f/7f: acts on polytrack and firm ground: usually visored: tongue tied: often races prominently: has bled. *Miss Gay Kelleway* **– a86**

MR LOIRE 5 b.g. Bertolini (USA) 125 – Miss Sancerre 95 (Last Tycoon 131) [2009 54: p6g p6g p6g^{2} p6g^{5} p6g^{3} p5.1m^{5} p6g 5m 5.7m 6.1g 6m^{5} 5.3g Jul 14] rather leggy gelding: modest performer: left K. Wingrove after seventh outing: best at 5f/6f: acts on polytrack, soft and good to firm ground: tried visored, usually wears blinkers: tried tongue tied: ungenuine. *A. J. Chamberlain* **50**

MR LU 4 b.g. Lujain (USA) 119 – Libretta (Highest Honor (FR) 124) [2009 74: 8m 7.1m 7s 6m^{4} 6m^{6} 7.1g 7d 8s 7g^{6} 7.2m* 7.2g Oct 23] modest handicapper nowadays: left A. G. Foster after seventh start: won at Ayr in October: barely stays 8.6f: acts on polytrack, good to firm and good to soft going: tried in cheekpieces/tongue strap. *J. S. Goldie* **64**

MR MACATTACK 4 b.c. Machiavellian (USA) 123 – Aunty Rose (IRE) 103 (Caerleon (USA) 132) [2009 68: p7.1g^{5} p7.1m* p7.1g* 7m 7f^{4} 7f Jun 19] good-topped, attractive colt: fairly useful handicapper, lightly raced: much improved when winning at Wolverhampton in February and March, impressive both times: raced at 7f on polytrack and going firmer than good: once tongue tied: held up: signs of temperament. *N. J. Vaughan* **90**

MR MAHOGANEIGH 2 b.c. (Mar 14) Mark of Esteem (IRE) 137 – Sweet Cando (IRE) 72§ (Royal Applause 124) [2009 p8f* Sep 4] second foal: half-brother to useful US 6.5f/1m winner Hameildaeme (by Storming Home): dam unreliable 2-y-o 5f winner: 20/1, promising when winning maiden at Lingfield by 2¼ lengths from Rare Malt, travelling strongly and merely shaken up: sent to Hong Kong, where renamed Jacobee: likely to improve. *M. L. W. Bell* **90 p**

MR MAXIMAS 2 ch.g. (Feb 24) Auction House (USA) 120 – Cashiki (IRE) 69 (Case Law 113) [2009 8.1d 7.1m 10.2m^{6} Sep 28] well beaten in maidens: tried in cheekpieces. *B. Palling* **–**

MR MISCHIEF 9 b.g. Millkom 124 – Snow Huntress 80 (Shirley Heights 130) [2009 –: p12g p12g p16g 17.2d May 18] leggy gelding: handicapper: lightly raced since 2007, and just modest form: effective at 1½m to 17f: acts on all-weather, firm and good to soft ground. *C. Gordon* **58**

MR MOHICAN (IRE) 2 b.g. (Feb 14) Barathea (IRE) 127 – Tipi Squaw (King's Best (USA) 132) [2009 7s 8g 7g Oct 17] good-bodied gelding: poor form in maidens: in cheekpieces final start, subsequently gelded. *Mrs A. Duffield* **46**

MR MONEY MAKER 2 ch.c. (Apr 6) Ishiguru (USA) 114 – Ellopassoff 69 (Librate 91) [2009 5g^{5} Oct 19] fourth foal: brother to 3-y-o Crazy Chris: dam 1m/1¼m winner: 3/1 and green, encouraging 2¾ lengths fifth to Hot Pursuits in maiden at Windsor (edged left): has joined B. Palling: capable of better. *Tom Dascombe* **71 p**

MR NAPOLEON (IRE) 7 gr.g. Daylami (IRE) 138 – Dathuil (IRE) 97 (Royal Academy (USA) 130) [2009 79: p11g^{6} p12g^{5} Mar 1] rather leggy gelding: fair handicapper: stays 1½m: acts on polytrack, heavy and good to firm ground: below form in blinkers/cheekpieces: has carried head awkwardly: usually held up. *G. L. Moore* **71**

MR PLOD 4 ch.g. Silver Patriarch (IRE) 125 – Emily-Mou (IRE) 80 (Cadeaux Genereux 131) [2009 –: p12g 10m^{3} p11m^{4} p12f^{4} p12m* p11f Dec 16] strong, plain gelding: fair handicapper: left Andrew Reid after fourth start: successful over hurdles prior to winning at Lingfield in December: stays 1½m: acts on polytrack: tried in cheekpieces/visor. *M. J. Scudamore* **66**

MR PRIZE FIGHTER 2 b.g. (Mar 21) Piccolo 121 – Lv Girl (IRE) 67 (Mukaddamah (USA) 125) [2009 6.1g^{6} 7s 6m^{5} Sep 25] lengthy gelding: little sign of ability in maidens (awkward final start). *I. W. McInnes* **–**

MR PROLIFIC 3 b.g. Haafhd 129 – Rumpipumpy 80 (Shirley Heights 130) [2009 –p: 10.2m^{2} 10.2g 12.1g May 26] lengthy gelding: modest maiden: stays 1¼m: acts on good to firm going: joined N. Twiston-Davies. *B. W. Hills* **57**

MR RAINBOW 3 ch.g. Efisio 120 – Blossom (Warning 136) [2009 p7.1g* 7s^{2} Oct 12] third foal: brother to 2004 2-y-o 6f winner Je Suis Belle and fairly useful 1m winner Champfleurie: dam unraced out of half-sister to very smart 1½m performer Apache: fairly useful form: won maiden at Wolverhampton in October: better effort when second to Victoria Sponge in handicap at Salisbury next time: will stay 1m+: useful prospect. *G. A. Swinbank* **94 p**

MR REV 6 b.g. Foxhound (USA) 103 – Branston Berry (IRE) 86 (Mukaddamah (USA) 125) [2009 70d: p7g p6g^{2} p8g^{3} p7.1g^{6} p8g^{6} f7g p8g^{5} 7d^{4} 6m^{4} 5.7m^{3} 7m^{4} 6m^{3} 6m^{5} 6.1m^{6} 7d^{6} 7f^{5} 7m Aug 23] maiden, just modest at 6 yrs: stays easy 1m: acts on polytrack and good to firm going: tried in cheekpieces, blinkered nowadays: none too genuine. *J. M. Bradley* **54**

MR RIO (IRE) 4 b.g. Captain Rio 122 – Amoras (IRE) 81 (Hamas (IRE) 125§) [2009 59?: f6g^{3} 6g 5.9d 6d p6f^{6} 6g p7m^{4} p7m^{5} p6m^{5} p6f Dec 21] modest maiden: will prove best at 5f/6f: best effort on fibresand: tried visored. *A. P. Jarvis* **64**

MR ROONEY (IRE) 6 b.g. Mujadil (USA) 119 – Desert Bride (USA) (Key To The Kingdom (USA)) [2009 64: f5d^{5} f5g^{4} f5g* p5.1m 5m 5g 5m 5g 5g 5m^{6} 5g 5s 5g 5v Nov 3] strong gelding: modest performer: won handicap at Southwell in February: regressive after: best at 5f nowadays: acts on all-weather, firm and soft going: tried tongue tied. *A. Berry* **60 d**

MRS BEETON (IRE) 3 b.f. Dansili 127 – Eliza Acton 70 (Shirley Heights 130) [2009 70p: 8m* 10g Jul 4] fairly useful form: won maiden at Salisbury in June: should stay 1¼m+: acts on good to firm ground. *W. R. Swinburn* **80**

MRS BOSS 2 b.f. (Jan 30) Makbul 104 – Chorus 80 (Bandmaster (USA) 97) [2009 5m 5m^{3} 5s 6m^{3} p5g^{3} 5m 5.7m^{4} 6.5m Sep 25] £500Y: compact filly: first foal: dam 5f to 7f winner: fair maiden: stays 6.5f: acts on polytrack and good to firm going: tried visored: ungenuine. *B. R. Millman* **71 §**

MRS BUN 4 b.f. Efisio 120 – Card Games 89 (First Trump 118) [2009 64+: f8s* f7g* f8g^{2} f7g^{4} p7.1g Mar 23] strong, lengthy filly: fair handicapper: won twice at Southwell in January: effective at 7f/1m: acts on fibresand and good to soft ground: wears headgear: signs of temperament. *K. A. Ryan* **74**

MRS E 2 b.f. (Mar 15) Doyen (IRE) 132 – Fille de Bucheron (USA) 83 (Woodman (USA) 126) [2009 8.1m 8g^{5} Oct 23] workmanlike filly: fourth foal: dam 6f winner: better effort in maidens when fifth to Corsica at Ayr, still green (wandered). *M. W. Easterby* **59**

MRS JONES AND ME (IRE) 2 b.f. (Jan 13) Namid 128 – Meadow 72 (Green Desert (USA) 127) [2009 5d^{5} 5m 6m^{5} 6d^{6} 5m^{4} 5g f5g^{4} p5.1m f5g Aug 27] €4,000Y: first foal: dam, Irish 7f winner, sister to smart performer up to 1m Green Line: modest maiden: stays 6f: acts on fibresand and good to firm going: tried visored/blinkered: weak finisher. *P. T. Midgley* **51 §**

MR SKIPITON (IRE) 4 b.g. Statue of Liberty (USA) 115 – Salty Air (IRE) (Singspiel (IRE) 133) [2009 59: p7g p6g p6m^{4} p6g* p6g* 5.1m^{5} 6f^{6} 6.1m^{2} 6s* 6d^{4} p6g Sep 2] rather leggy gelding: fair handicapper, better on turf: won at Kempton in March, Lingfield in April and Yarmouth in July: best form at 5f/6f: acts on polytrack, soft and good to firm going: tried visored. *B. J. McMath* **77 a63 +**

MRS MEDLEY 3 b.f. Rambling Bear 115 – Animal Cracker 73 (Primo Dominie 121) [2009 6d p6g p6m p5.1g p5g f5f p7f Dec 21] 1,200Y: second foal: dam 2-y-o 5f winner: no form. *D. Shaw* **–**

MR SMITHSON (IRE) 2 br.g. (Mar 27) Xaar 132 – Amanda Louise (IRE) 60 (Perugino (USA) 84) [2009 5m^{2} 5m 5g^{3} 5m^{2} 5g 5m f5g^{3} f6g^{5} 5m p6m Sep 28] close-coupled gelding: fair maiden: raced mainly at 5f: acts on good to firm going, probably on fibresand: tried visored: ungenuine. *B. Ellison* **68 §**

MRS MOGG 2 b.f. (Apr 13) Green Desert (USA) 127 – Maybe Forever 109 (Zafonic (USA) 130) [2009 5.1g^{6} Jul 4] €20,000Y: fourth foal: dam, French 5f/5.5f winner (including at 2 yrs), sister to useful 7f/1m performer Easy Air and half-sister to high-class 7f/1m performer Court Masterpiece: 11/1 and green, 7¾ lengths sixth to Skylla in maiden at Nottingham, wandering: should improve. *N. J. Vaughan* **48 p**

MR SNOWBALLS 3 gr.g. Monsieur Bond (IRE) 120 – Swissmatic 54 (Petong 126) [2009 58: p6g Apr 17] workmanlike gelding: modest form at 2 yrs: well held in handicap sole outing in 2009: should prove best at 5f/6f. *R. A. Farrant* **–**

MRS PENNY (AUS) 5 br.m. Planchet (AUS) – Respective (AUS) (Noalcoholic (FR) 128) [2009 98: p6g* p6g p6g^{4} p5.1g^{5} p6g Dec 28] fairly useful performer: won handicap at Wolverhampton in January: stays 6.5f: raced on polytrack and good ground or softer: tried in cheekpieces/blinkers. *J. R. Gask* **89**

MRS PUFF (IRE) 2 gr.f. (Mar 27) Trans Island 119 – Canosa (IRE) 53 (Catrail (USA) 123) [2009 5.1g 7.1g 6m 7m 6d 6m^{5} p8m 7d^{4} p7.1g^{5} f8m^{6} Nov 11] €5,000Y: rather leggy filly: third foal: half-sister to winner in Greece by Clodovil: dam sprint maiden: modest maiden: left A. Haynes after debut: stays 7f: acts on good to soft going. *P. D. Evans* **51**

MRS SLOCOMBE (IRE) 3 b.f. Masterful (USA) 119 – Mrs Beatty 62 (Cadeaux Genereux 131) [2009 74?: p7g4 7m3 7.6f 8.1g 10m4 11.7g5 8m Aug 16] leggy filly: fair form at 3 yrs only on second outing: left J. Akehurst £2,000 after fifth start: stays 7f: acts on good to firm and good to soft going: tried in cheekpieces: poor form in juvenile hurdles. *Mrs N. S. Evans* **69 d**

MR TOSHIWONKA 5 b.g. Compton Place 125 – Victoria (Old Vic 136) [2009 73: f7g 7.1m 8.1m4 Jun 11] workmanlike gelding: handicapper: no form in 2009. *D. Nicholls* **–**

MR UDAGAWA 3 b.g. Bahamian Bounty 116 – Untold Riches (USA) 94 (Red Ransom (USA)) [2009 74: 8m3 8.1g 8m2 8d2 p8.6g3 8.3m* 10g Oct 19] useful-looking gelding: fair performer: won maiden at Nottingham in September: stays 8.6f: acts on polytrack, good to firm and good to soft going: in cheekpieces last 2 starts: sold 28,000 gns. *R. M. Beckett* **78**

MR WILLIS 3 b.g. Desert Sun 120 – Santiburi Girl 77 (Casteddu 111) [2009 70p: p7g* p7g* p7g3 p8g* p8m* p9.5g2 Dec 17] sturdy gelding: useful handicapper: won at Lingfield 4 of 6 starts in 2009, in March, April, November and December: further progress when 1½ lengths second to Splinter Cell at Wolverhampton final outing: stays 9.5f: raced only on polytrack and good to firm going. *J. R. Best* **99**

MR WOLF 8 b.g. Wolfhound (USA) 126 – Madam Millie 99 (Milford 119) [2009 84: 5m6 6m 6g6 5g* 5.1m6 6d 5g 6d2 5m 5m3 7g Oct 17] tall, leggy gelding: fairly useful handicapper: won at Pontefract (seventh course win) in June: below form after, leaving D. Barker after sixth start: best at 5f/6f: acts on polytrack, firm and soft going: usually wears cheekpieces: front runner. *J. J. Quinn* **82**

MS SOPHIE ELEANOR (USA) 3 b. or br.f. Grand Slam (USA) 120 – Population (General Assembly (USA)) [2009 6g 7d* 7.1g2 7.1m Sep 14] $140,000Y: half-sister to several winners, notably smart 7f (at 2 yrs, when also won Racing Post Trophy) to 1¼m (Dante Stakes) winner Saratoga Springs (by El Gran Senor): dam, Irish maiden, half-sister to Washington International winner Providential and Prix Marcel Boussac winner Play It Safe: fair performer: won maiden at Thirsk in July: stays 7f: acts on good to soft ground. *T. D. Barron* **70**

MT DESERT 7 b.g. Rainbow Quest (USA) 134 – Chief Bee 89 (Chief's Crown (USA)) [2009 75: f12f Nov 24] strong, lengthy gelding: handicapper: well held sole outing at 7 yrs: stays easy 2m: acts on good to soft going: tried visored/blinkered: not straightforward. *E. W. Tuer* **–**

MT KINTYRE (IRE) 3 b.g. Mull of Kintyre (USA) 114 – Nihonpillow Mirai (IRE) 48 (Zamindar (USA) 116) [2009 74: 10m2 10.2m2 11.1g4 8.3g 9g3 p12g 10.4g 10.1d6 Oct 27] strong gelding: fair maiden: stays 1¼m: acts on soft and good to firm going: ungenuine. *M. H. Tompkins* **73 §**

MTOTO GIRL 5 b.m. Mtoto 134 – Shalati (FR) (High Line 125) [2009 46: p8g Feb 19] medium-sized mare: maiden: well held sole start at 5 yrs. *J. J. Bridger* **–**

MUBROOK (USA) 4 b.g. Alhaarth (IRE) 126 – Zomaradah 118 (Deploy 131) [2009 95p: 10m 12g4 12g4 p12m2 14.6g2 Oct 23] well-made gelding: fairly useful maiden: stays 14.6f: best form on good ground: sold 55,000 gns, joined E. O'Grady, Ireland. *L. M. Cumani* **91**

MUCH ACCLAIMED (IRE) 2 b.g. (Mar 8) Sulamani (IRE) 130 – Much Commended 100 (Most Welcome 131) [2009 7m2 7g6 Oct 23] tall gelding: has scope: brother to Irish 3-y-o Few Are Chosen and half-brother to several winners, including 7-y-o Dabbers Ridge: dam, 2-y-o 6f winner (stayed 1m), sister to smart performer up to 1½m Prize Giving: better effort in maidens when ½-length second to Cash Queen Anna at Redcar: will be suited by 1m+. *T. P. Tate* **77**

MUCHO LOCO (IRE) 6 ch.g. Tagula (IRE) 116 – Mousseux (IRE) (Jareer (USA) 115) [2009 45: p12g6 10m2 May 4] lengthy gelding: poor maiden: stays 1½m: acts on all-weather, firm and soft going: tried in headgear. *R. Curtis* **49**

MUDAARAAH 2 b.f. (Feb 27) Cape Cross (IRE) 129 – Wissal (USA) (Woodman (USA) 126) [2009 6f* 6g 7.1m* 7g2 8m Sep 26] useful-looking filly: fourth foal: closely related to useful 6f/7f winner Ethaara (by Green Desert) and half-sister to useful 7f (at 2 yrs) and 1m winner Sudoor (by Fantastic Light) who stayed 1¼m, and 3-y-o Mejala: dam unraced sister to very smart performer up to 1¼m Bahhare and half-sister to high-class miler Bahri: useful performer: won maiden at Folkestone in June and listed race at Sandown (by ½ length from Middle Club) in July: better effort after when creditable nose second to Sent From Heaven in Prestige Stakes at Goodwood: should stay 1m (laboured when last in Fillies' Mile at Ascot). *J. L. Dunlop* **104**

MUDAWIN (IRE) 8 b.g. Intikhab (USA) 135 – Fida (IRE) (Persian Heights 129) [2009 94d: 16.2g 13.1m^5 14f^3 14s^2 16.4g* Jul 25] big, lengthy gelding: type to carry condition: fairly useful handicapper nowadays: won at York in July: stays 2m: acts on polytrack, firm and soft going. *James Moffatt* **86**

MUDHISH (IRE) 4 b.g. Lujain (USA) 119 – Silver Satire (Dr Fong (USA) 128) [2009 –: f8g* p7.1g^4 p8g^5 f7d p5g p6g^2 p6g^2 7m^2 7g p7.1g^3 7g^4 7g^2 7m^4 Sep 21] good-topped gelding: fair handicapper: won at Southwell in February: effective at 6f to 1m: acts on all-weather and firm going: usually blinkered nowadays. *C. E. Brittain* **73**

MUFARRH (IRE) 2 b.c. (Mar 8) Marju (IRE) 127 – What A Picture (FR) (Peintre Celebre (USA) 137) [2009 7.1g^3 7m^2 7m* Oct 13] 85,000F, 170,000Y: neat, attractive colt: second foal: half-brother to useful French 1m winner Partner Shift (by Night Shift): dam, well held in France, out of half-sister to Irish Derby winner Grey Swallow: progressive form in maidens, winning at Leicester by 4 lengths from Official Style, travelling strongly up with pace and quickening impressively: will stay 1m: a useful prospect. *J. L. Dunlop* **93 p**

MUFFETT'S DREAM 5 b.m. Fraam 114 – Loveless Carla (Pursuit of Love 124) [2009 55: 11.7f 11.9m 11m 11m^4 11.5m^4 Jul 8] sturdy mare: modest performer: stays 11.5f: acts on polytrack and good to firm going: front runner. *J. J. Bridger* **53**

MUFTARRES (IRE) 4 b.c. Green Desert (USA) 127 – Ghazal (USA) 103 (Gone West (USA)) [2009 83: 6g 6d^6 p6g^6 p7m^3 8.1m* 10m^2 p10m^6 Nov 4] rather leggy colt: fairly useful handicapper: won at Warwick in October: stays 1¼m: acts on polytrack, soft and good to firm going: tried in cheekpieces: tongue tied of late. *G. A. Butler* **88**

MUFTI (IRE) 2 b.c. (Jan 30) Noverre (USA) 125 – Dark Indian (IRE) (Indian Ridge 123) [2009 8g^4 7.1g^6 Aug 31] 200,000F: fifth foal: half-brother to 2 winners, including smart 7f (at 2 yrs, also US Grade 3 1m winner) to 9f (US Grade 2) winner Valbenny (by Val Royal): dam Italian 1m/9f winner: better effort in maidens when length fourth to Dashing Doc at Newmarket. *B. J. Meehan* **75**

MUGEBA 8 b.m. Primo Dominie 121 – Ella Lamees 61 (Statoblest 120) [2009 52: 7g p7.1g 6d 5.2d Oct 27] workmanlike mare: poor handicapper nowadays: best at 6f/7f: acts on all-weather and any turf going: tried in headgear: formerly tongue tied. *C. A. Dwyer* **44**

MUHANNAK (IRE) 5 b.g. Chester House (USA) 123 – Opera 84 (Forzando 122) [2009 115: a10m^5 a10f 12g p12m p8.6g 12m^5 a14f^5 Nov 6] sturdy gelding: smart performer: won Breeders' Cup Marathon at Santa Anita in 2008: somewhat disappointing in 2009 and well held in same race (over extra 2f) on final start: best earlier effort when 4 lengths fifth to Mawatheeq in Cumberland Lodge Stakes at Ascot on sixth outing: effective at 1¼m/1½m: acts on polytrack, pro-ride and firm ground: tried in blinkers/cheekpieces: waited with: temperamental (pulled himself up fourth start, reluctant again next time): joined B. Cecil in USA. *R. M. Beckett* **110 §**

MUJAADEL (USA) 4 ch.g. Street Cry (IRE) 130 – Quiet Rumour (USA) (Alleged (USA) 138) [2009 93: 7.1m^5 8d 7m 8.1f^3 10.3m 8s 7m* 7d^6 7.2g 7g* Oct 17] tall gelding: fairly useful handicapper: won at Redcar in August and Catterick in October: stays 1m: acts on polytrack and good to firm going: sometimes in cheekpieces: withdrawn after giving trouble in stall intended reappearance. *D. Nicholls* **83**

MUJADA 4 b.f. Mujahid (USA) 125 – Catriona 75 (Bustino 136) [2009 52: f7g f6g 7m Aug 14] maiden: poor nowadays: best at 6f: acts on fibresand: tried blinkered. *M. Brittain* **41**

MUJAMEAD 5 b.g. Mujahid (USA) 125 – Island Mead 86 (Pharly (FR) 130) [2009 72: p16g Jan 10] fair performer, lightly raced on Flat: well held in 2009, including over hurdles for G. Ham: tried visored, often in cheekpieces. *A. W. Carroll* **–**

MUJDEYA 2 gr.f. (Feb 19) Linamix (FR) 127 – Majhud (IRE) 94 (Machiavellian (USA) 123) [2009 8g^5 Oct 20] second foal: dam, 1½m winner, out of sister to high-class miler Bahri: 15/2, most encouraging when length fifth to Principal Role in maiden at Yarmouth, running on well for hand riding: will be suited by 1¼m/1½m: sure to improve. *J. H. M. Gosden* **83 p**

MUJMA 5 b. or gr.g. Indian Ridge 123 – Farfala (FR) 106 (Linamix (FR) 127) [2009 47§: f8g^6 p8g^6 p5g* f5g^2 p5.1g^3 5.1d 5g May 3] lengthy, good-topped gelding: modest handicapper: won at Lingfield in March: effective at 5f, stays 1¼m: unraced on heavy going, acts on any other turf and all-weather: often in headgear: tongue tied of late: irresolute. *S. Parr* **60 §**

MUJOOD 6 b.g. Mujahid (USA) 125 – Waqood (USA) 75 (Riverman (USA) 131) [2009 100, a80: p8g 7g^5 6m 8m* 8m^2 8.1f^2 8.1m 8f^2 8g^3 8g 7g 7.1g 6g^6 7m* 7m* 7m 6d Oct 11] quite good-topped gelding: useful handicapper on turf, fair on all-weather: won at **97 a73**

Goodwood in May and September (2): effective at 6f to 1m: acts on all-weather, firm and good to soft ground: often in headgear. *Eve Johnson Houghton*

MUKTASB (USA) 8 b.g. Bahri (USA) 125 – Maghaarb 104 (Machiavellian (USA) –
123) [2009 –, a74: p6g^4 f5g^5 p6g* p6g^3 p6g^3 p5.1m^4 p5.1g^3 p5.1g^4 p6g^4 p6g^3 f6g p6g **a66**
Jun 22] good-topped gelding: has a quick action: fair handicapper on all-weather: won amateur event at Wolverhampton in January: best at 5f/6f: acts on all-weather, unraced on turf since 2007: visored: held up (sometimes misses break): consistent. *D. Shaw*

MULAAZEM 6 b.g. King's Best (USA) 132 – Harayir (USA) 119 (Gulch (USA)) **61**
[2009 61: p16g^4 p16g^5 p16g Feb 24] medium-sized, quite attractive gelding: modest performer: stays 2m: acts on polytrack and good to firm going: blinkered/tongue tied. *A. M. Hales*

MULAZEM (USA) 3 gr. or ro.c. El Prado (IRE) 119 – Muwakleh 115 (Machiavellian –
(USA) 123) [2009 8m May 11] very green in maiden at Yarmouth: sold £4,000 in August. *W. J. Haggas*

MULLEIN 4 b.f. Oasis Dream 129 – Gipsy Moth 99 (Efisio 120) [2009 99p: p6g* 6v **110**
6d^3 6g 6m* 6m^3 6m^3 6g Oct 10] strong filly: smart performer: won handicap at Kempton in April and listed race at Pontefract (beat Bouvardia 3½ lengths) in August: further improvement when 2¾ lengths third to Sayif in Diadem Stakes at Ascot seventh start: was best at 6f: acted on polytrack, soft and good to firm going: usually held up: to visit Selkirk. *R. M. Beckett*

MULLGLEN 3 b.g. Mull of Kintyre (USA) 114 – However (IRE) (Hector Protector **83**
(USA) 124) [2009 83: 6m^6 5s 5m 5d* 6d^6 5g 5d^3 6g^6 5g^6 Oct 19] sturdy gelding: fairly useful handicapper: won at Catterick in July: best at 5f: acts on heavy and good to firm going: tried blinkered: tongue tied final outing. *T. D. Easterby*

MULLITOVERMAURICE 3 ch.g. Pursuit of Love 124 – Ellovamul 62 (Elmaamul **66**
(USA) 125) [2009 61: p8.6g^2 p9.5g^2 p8.6g^3 f8d^6 p9.5g Dec 18] fair performer: stays 9.5f: raced only on all-weather. *J. G. Given*

MULL OF DUBAI 6 b.g. Mull of Kintyre (USA) 114 – Enlisted (IRE) 83 (Sadler's **101**
Wells (USA) 132) [2009 101: 10.2d^5 10.3m 12g* 10.3s^4 Aug 1] sturdy gelding: useful handicapper: won Queen Mother's Cup (Lady Amateurs) at York in June by ¾ length from Gifted Leader: stays 13.4f: acts on any going: blinkered once: held up: sold £18,500. *T. P. Tate*

MULL OF KILLOUGH (IRE) 3 b.g. Mull of Kintyre (USA) 114 – Sun Shower **104**
(IRE) (Indian Ridge 123) [2009 7.1m* 8d* 8.3g^2 8.1g^3 9.9f 8.1m* Sep 25] good-bodied gelding: first foal: dam, placed up to 11f in France, out of half-sister to Irish Oaks winner Princess Pati and Great Voltigeur winner Seymour Hicks: useful form, largely progressive: won maiden at Warwick in April and handicaps at Thirsk in May and Haydock (beat Light From Mars ½ length) in September: should be suited by 1¼m: acts on good to firm and good to soft going. *J. L. Spearing*

MULTAHAB 10 b. or br.g. Zafonic (USA) 130 – Alumisiyah (USA) 93 (Danzig (USA)) **70**
[2009 75: p5.1g^3 5.3m 5.3f^3 p5g 5.3m^2 5.3m* 5.3f^4 5m^4 5.3m^4 p5.1g Nov 6] smallish gelding: fair handicapper: won at Brighton (fifth course success) in July: effective at 5f/6f: acts on all-weather and firm ground: tried in blinkers/cheekpieces: tongue tied. *M. Wigham*

MULTAKKA (IRE) 6 b.g. Alhaarth (IRE) 126 – Elfaslah (IRE) 107 (Green Desert **97**
(USA) 127) [2009 92: p8g^2 p8g p8g Oct 9] strong, rangy, attractive gelding: keen walker: useful handicapper: further improvement when 3 lengths second to Forgotten Voice at Kempton on reappearance: better than result both starts after: should stay 1¼m: unraced on heavy going, acts on any other turf and polytrack: tried blinkered: held up: possibly not straightforward. *M. P. Tregoning*

MULTAMES (IRE) 2 b.c. (Feb 13) Cape Cross (IRE) 129 – Elutrah (Darshaan 133) **99 p**
[2009 7m 8v* Oct 24] big, strong colt: third foal: dam unraced sister to Rockfel Stakes winner Sayedah (stayed 1½m): much better effort in maidens 4 months apart when winning at Newbury impressively by 3½ lengths from Total Command, leading 2f out: will stay 1¼m: already useful, and sure to go on improving. *Saeed bin Suroor*

MULTIPLICATION 3 b.f. Marju (IRE) 127 – Lunda (IRE) 60 (Soviet Star (USA) **78**
128) [2009 82: 10.9m* 10m^4 12m 8.3m^6 Oct 13] good-topped filly: just fair performer at 3 yrs: won maiden at Warwick in May: left R. Charlton after next start: stays 10.9f: acts on good to firm and good to soft ground. *W. J. Knight*

MULTI TASKER 3 b.c. Lear Spear (USA) 124 – Lola Lola (IRE) (Piccolo 121) [2009 –
60d: p6g Jan 12] workmanlike colt: regressive maiden: tried blinkered. *Miss J. R. Tooth*

MUMAATHEL (IRE) 6 b.g. Alhaarth (IRE) 126 – Alhufoof (USA) 100 (Dayjur (USA) 137) [2009 –: p6g Jan 8] rather leggy gelding: maiden, lightly raced and regressive since 3 yrs. *W. R. Muir* **–**

MUMTAZ BEGUM 4 ch.f. Kyllachy 129 – Indian Gift 64 (Cadeaux Genereux 131) [2009 7s p7m 7f Sep 8] 2,500Y: second foal: dam maiden (stayed 8.5f): more temperament than ability in maidens. *J. E. Long* **–**

MUNCASTER CASTLE (IRE) 5 b.g. Johannesburg (USA) 127 – Eubee (FR) (Common Grounds 118) [2009 60: f8g* f8g Feb 19] lengthy gelding: modest performer: won handicap at Southwell in February: barely stays 1½m: acts on all-weather, soft and good to firm going: tried blinkered. *R. F. Fisher* **56**

MUNCHING MIKE (IRE) 6 br.g. Orpen (USA) 116 – Stargard (Polish Precedent (USA) 131) [2009 61: f12g p16g p13.9g Jul 13] maiden handicapper: no form in 2009: tried in cheekpieces/visor. *K. M. Prendergast* **–**

MUNDO'S MAGIC 5 b.g. Foxhound (USA) 103 – Amber's Bluff 80 (Mind Games 121) [2009 60: 8m 10m⁴ Aug 9] big, close-coupled gelding: poor performer nowadays: tried in cheekpieces/blinkers/tongue tie. *N. Wilson* **–**

MUNICH (IRE) 5 b.g. Noverre (USA) 125 – Mayara (IRE) 85 (Ashkalani (IRE) 128) [2009 85: p12g p7g p8g^2 p7g^4 p7g^5 p7g 8d^4 Jul 27] good-topped gelding: fair handicapper nowadays: left L. Wells after second outing, Norma Twomey after fourth: probably stays easy 1½m: acts on sand/polytrack and heavy going: tried tongue tied. *Mrs S. Leech* **67**

MUNLOCHY BAY 5 b.m. Karinga Bay 116 – Meghdoot 75 (Celestial Storm (USA) 132) [2009 70p: 12d^2 p16g 17.2d^6 16g^2 14m Jun 13] workmanlike mare: fair handicapper, lightly raced: best at 2m+: acts on heavy ground: tried in cheekpieces: joined M. Sheppard. *W. S. Kittow* **75**

MUNSARIM (IRE) 2 b.c. (Mar 25) Shamardal (USA) 129 – Etizaaz (USA) 117 (Diesis 133) [2009 7d^3 8m^4 8m^3 Oct 16] lengthy, good-topped colt: has plenty of scope: sixth foal: half-brother to smart 5.7f (at 2 yrs) to 7f winner Munaddam (by Aljabr) and 3-y-o Almiqdaad: dam, 7f (at 2 yrs)/1m winner who was second in Prix Vermeille, out of half-sister to Swain: progressive form in maidens, 2¼ lengths third to Invincible Soul at Newmarket (made running) final start: stays 1m: type to progress again at 3 yrs. *J. L. Dunlop* **89 p**

MUNSEF 7 b.g. Zafonic (USA) 130 – Mazaya (IRE) 105 (Sadler's Wells (USA) 132) [2009 111d: 10g 10g 12g 10.3m* 11.9m^2 12m* 13.4m* 12g^2 16d Nov 3] strong, close-coupled gelding: smart performer: left D. Nicholls after third start: rejuvenated after, winning claimer at Chester in June and handicaps at Ascot in July and Chester (listed event, beat Mystery Star ½ length) in August: also good second in Old Newton Cup (Handicap) at Haydock (beaten ½ length by Red Merlin) and Stockholm Cup International at Taby (same distance behind Touch of Hawk): stays 13.4f (reportedly suffered gashed leg when mid-field in 2m Melbourne Cup final start): acts on soft and good to firm going: tried in blinkers. *Ian Williams* **114**

MUNTAMI (IRE) 8 gr.g. Daylami (IRE) 138 – Bashashah (IRE) 83 (Kris 135) [2009 60: f14s 16.5s^6 14.1g 16g^6 f14m^4 Dec 5] sturdy, close-coupled gelding: poor handicapper nowadays: stays 14.8f: acts on fibresand and heavy going: tried in headgear. *John A. Harris* **46**

MURACO 5 b.g. Bertolini (USA) 125 – Miss Honeypenny (IRE) (Old Vic 136) [2009 51: p10g Jan 28] close-coupled gelding: little impact on Flat since 2007. *A. M. Hales* **–**

MURAWEG (IRE) 3 b.c. Kheleyf (USA) 116 – Lady Moranbon (USA) (Trempolino (USA) 135) [2009 73p: p8g* 10m^4 10.4m^5 10.3m^5 11m^5 10.2s Oct 7] well-made, attractive colt: fairly useful performer: won maiden at Lingfield in March: stays 10.4f: acts on polytrack and good to firm going: blinkered last 2 starts: sold 9,000 gns. *J. H. M. Gosden* **90**

MURCAR 4 ch.g. Medicean 128 – In Luck 72 (In The Wings 128) [2009 75: p12g^5 14v^5 13.3m* 14.1g^6 14.1m^4 p13.9g^2 14m^3 18g^4 p16.5g* Oct 23] strong, lengthy gelding: fairly useful handicapper: won at Newbury in May and Wolverhampton in October: probably stays 2¼m: acts on polytrack, heavy and good to firm going: blinkered nowadays: has raced freely: none too straightforward: sold 38,000 gns. *C. G. Cox* **83**

MUREB (USA) 2 b.c. (Apr 10) Elusive Quality (USA) – Sumoto 101 (Mtoto 134) [2009 p7.1g^3 Nov 2] $500,000Y: half-brother to several winners, notably very smart 7f (at 2 yrs) to 1¼m (Eclipse Stakes) winner Compton Admiral (by Suave Dancer) and smart 1m (including at 2 yrs and Queen Elizabeth II Stakes) and 1¼m winner Summoner (by Inchinor): dam 6f (at 2 yrs) and 7f winner: 5/4 favourite, encouraging 3¾ lengths third to Elspeth's Boy in maiden at Wolverhampton, green and getting going only near finish: bred to do lot better. *Saeed bin Suroor* **80 p**

MURFREESBORO 6 b.g. Bahamian Bounty 116 – Merry Rous 66 (Rousillon (USA) 133) [2009 100d: p8g³ p10g³ Jan 15] useful-looking gelding: just fair form in 2009: claimed by A. Jones £8,000 after final outing: probably best around 1m: acts on polytrack and good to firm going: tried visored/blinkered: often looks awkward. *D. Shaw* **79**

MURHEE (USA) 3 b.c. Rahy (USA) 115 – Grand Ogygia (USA) (Ogygian (USA)) [2009 59: p8g⁵ 8.3m⁶ 10m Aug 15] rangy colt: fair maiden: should stay 1¼m: tried blinkered: sold £1,200 in October. *D. R. Lanigan* **68**

MURRAYS MAGIC (IRE) 3 b.f. Bahri (USA) 125 – Fiina 68 (Most Welcome 131) [2009 50: 7.1m f8g Apr 23] leggy filly: maiden: no form at 3 yrs. *D. Nicholls* **–**

MURRIN (IRE) 5 b. or br.g. Trans Island 119 – Flimmering (Dancing Brave (USA) 140) [2009 82: p8g* p8g³ p8g² p8g³ 8m⁴ p8g⁴ 8.5m 8m⁵ 8m⁴ p8g² p8m p8g⁶ Nov 13] close-coupled gelding: fair handicapper: won at Great Leighs in January: stays 1m: acts on polytrack and good to firm going: tried blinkered, in cheekpieces last 3 starts. *T. G. Mills* **79**

MURRUMBIDGEE (IRE) 6 gr.g. Bluebird (USA) 125 – Blanche Neige (USA) (Lit de Justice (USA) 125) [2009 9.7d⁴ 10.1m⁴ 10.2m* Jun 3] good-topped gelding: fair handicapper: won apprentice event at Nottingham in June: effective at stiff 1m/1¼m: acts on polytrack and firm going: tried visored/tongue tied/in cheekpieces: not straightforward. *Mike Murphy* **63**

MUSAAFER (IRE) 2 b.c. (Jan 17) Marju (IRE) 127 – Alexander Icequeen (IRE) 106 (Soviet Star (USA) 128) [2009 p8g² 8m* 8d Oct 24] €105,000F, €300,000Y: good-bodied colt: first foal: dam, Irish 2-y-o 7f winner, half-sister to useful winner up to 1½m Gavroche: progressive form, making running when winning maiden at Pontefract in September easily by 6 lengths from Finest Reserve: stiff task, again raced freely when ninth to St Nicholas Abbey in Racing Post Trophy at Doncaster: raced only at 1m. *M. A. Jarvis* **92 +**

MUSAALEM (USA) 5 gr.g. Aljabr (USA) 125 – Atyab (USA) (Mr Prospector (USA)) [2009 105: 6m⁵ 7f 7g* 7g 6.5m⁴ 7m* Oct 3] tall, lengthy, raw-boned gelding: has reportedly had breathing operation: smart performer, lightly raced: won handicap at Doncaster in July and listed race at Redcar (much improved when beating Able Master by neck) in October: stays 7f: acts on good to firm ground: travels strongly held up: has joined D. Watson in UAE. *W. J. Haggas* **116**

Guisborough Stakes, Redcar—
the grey Musaalem shows improved form stepped up in class to beat Able Master

MUSASHI (IRE) 4 ch.g. Hawk Wing (USA) 136 – Soubrette (USA) (Opening Verse (USA) 126) [2009 75: f11d^5 9.8m^4 f12g^6 p10g p10g 11.6m^5 p12m Nov 27] sturdy gelding: maiden, just modest at 4 yrs: left Jane Chapple-Hyam (gelded) after return, T. Tate £4,500 after third start: stays 1¼m: acts on polytrack and good to firm ground: tried in cheekpieces/blinkers. *Mrs L. J. Mongan* **60**

MUSCA (IRE) 5 b.g. Tendulkar (USA) 114 – Canary Bird (IRE) 59 (Catrail (USA) 123) [2009 80d: 6g 7s May 22] angular gelding: handicapper: no form in 2009. *J. Wade* **–**

MUSHAGAK (IRE) 2 b.f. (Mar 17) Oratorio (IRE) 128 – Tetou (IRE) 70 (Peintre Celebre (USA) 137) [2009 p8m Dec 4] second foal: dam, 1¼m winner, half-sister to smart German miler Sinyar: 16/1 and green, modest form when last in maiden at Lingfield. *E. A. L. Dunlop* **54**

MUSHREQ (USA) 2 b.c. (Apr 1) Distorted Humor (USA) 117 – Casual Look (USA) 114 (Red Ransom (USA)) [2009 7g^4 7m^5 Oct 2] $850,000Y: strong, close-coupled colt: third foal: half-brother to winner in USA by Kingmambo: dam, 1m (at 2 yrs) to 1½m (Oaks) winner, sister to smart French 1¼m winner Shabby Chic: similar form in maidens at Newmarket, most promising fourth to Ameer then not unduly knocked about when fifth to Swiss Cross: should do quite a lot better given looks/pedigree. *Sir Michael Stoute* **72 p**

MUSIARA 2 b.f. (Apr 26) Hunting Lion (IRE) 115 – Search Party 78 (Rainbow Quest (USA) 134) [2009 5g^4 5m^6 5m^3 5m^2 6d 5m^4 7g 8g 8m Sep 23] unfurnished filly: sixth foal: half-sister to 5-y-o Bateleur and 2004 2-y-o 6f winner Evanesce (by Lujain): dam, second at 1m/1¼m from 3 starts, half-sister to US Grade 1 1¼m winner Bequest: poor maiden: form only at 5f: acts on good to firm ground: none too reliable. *M. R. Channon* **46**

MUSICAL BRIDGE 3 b.g. Night Shift (USA) – Carrie Pooter 95 (Tragic Role (USA)) [2009 80: 5.1d^2 5.1m* 6g^5 5d^3 5m^3 5m 5g^3 f5m Nov 12] fair performer: won maiden at Nottingham in June: should stay 6f: acts on good to firm and good to soft going. *Mrs L. Williamson* **74**

MUSICAL DELIGHT 2 b.g. (Apr 9) Oratorio (IRE) 128 – Living Daylights (IRE) 73 (Night Shift (USA)) [2009 p6g 6d 7.2m Sep 18] strong gelding: well held in minor event/maidens: gelded after final start: bred to stay 1m+. *A. P. Jarvis* **–**

MUSICAL MAZE 3 b.f. Distant Music (USA) 126 – Maze Garden (USA) (Riverman (USA) 131) [2009 70: p8.6g 8d 9.3g^3 10.3g^2 9.2g^4 10.3g^5 12.3m^6 10.4s^3 12d 10.3g Aug 2] good-topped filly: fair handicapper: stays 1½m: acts on heavy and good to firm ground. *W. M. Brisbourne* **68**

MUSICAL SCRIPT (USA) 6 b.g. Stravinsky (USA) 133 – Cyrillic (USA) 106 (Irish River (FR) 131) [2009 83: p6g^3 p6g^2 p6g p6g^3 p6g 6d p7m^6 p7m^5 p6g p7m p6g p6m^5 p6g^3 p7g^2 p6g^4 p6f p6f^6 Dec 20] sturdy gelding: fair handicapper: effective up to 7f: acts on all-weather, firm and soft going: tried in cheekpieces, wears blinkers nowadays: often races freely held up. *Mouse Hamilton-Fairley* **79**

MUSIC BOX EXPRESS 5 b.g. Tale of The Cat (USA) 113 – Aly McBe (USA) (Alydeed (CAN) 120) [2009 79: p6g^4 p6g^4 f5g^3 6m 6m 6g 5.7d^3 6f^4 5m^2 5.3m^3 6g 6m f6g p6g Dec 19] sturdy gelding: fair handicapper: best at 5f/6f: acts on all-weather, good to firm and good to soft ground: tried blinkered/in cheekpieces: often tongue tied: front runner. *George Baker* **71**

MUSIC MAESTRO (IRE) 2 b.g. (Apr 20) Oratorio (IRE) 128 – Adjalisa (IRE) 65 (Darshaan 133) [2009 7d^6 7s^2 p8.6g^4 p7.1g^2 Nov 2] €18,000Y: strong gelding: closely related to a winner in Turkey by Danehill and half-brother to several winners, including smart South African/UAE winner up to 1½m Front House (by Sadler's Wells) and smart Irish 1998 2-y-o 5f/6f winner Access All Areas (by Approach The Bench): dam, Irish maiden (stayed 1m), half-sister to Irish 2000 Guineas second Adjareli: progressive form in maidens, 1¼ lengths second to Elspeth's Boy at Wolverhampton: should prove fully effective at 1m. *B. W. Hills* **87**

MUSIC OF THE MOOR (IRE) 2 ch.g. (Mar 12) Rock of Gibraltar (IRE) 133 – A La Longue (GER) (Mtoto 134) [2009 6d^4 7m^4 8.1g^2 8d 8.1m^5 8g 7v^3 Nov 3] €50,000Y: sturdy gelding: fifth foal: half-brother to useful Italian 7f (at 2 yrs) to 1¼m winner Le Giare (by Monashee Mountain): dam German maiden: fair maiden: effective at 7f/1m: acts on heavy going: tried blinkered. *T. P. Tate* **70**

MUSIC SHOW (IRE) 2 b.f. (Apr 18) Noverre (USA) 125 – Dreamboat (USA) 84 (Mr Prospector (USA)) [2009 5.7g* 5.7f* 6m 7m* Oct 17] **111 p**

The list of versatile sportsmen or sportswomen who achieve comparable success in more than one sport is small. John Surtees remains the only person in motor sport to have won world championships on both two and four wheels, the

Lotus Evora Rockfel Stakes, Newmarket—a second successive win in this Guineas pointer for the Channon stable as 25/1-shot Music Show (left) beats Atasari (centre) and Tabassum (right) in a strong renewal

legendary cricketer Denis Compton also won league championship and FA Cup medals for Arsenal, whilst four-times London Marathon winner Ingrid Kristiansen had been the 1974 junior European champion at cross-country skiing! All of which goes to show how well former international footballer Mick Channon has done to make such a success of his second career as a racehorse trainer. A regular in the top twelve of the trainers' championship during the past decade, Channon has had little cause to regret his purchase of West Ilsley from the Queen in 1999, with many of the big-race winners sent out from there carrying the colours of Channon's leading patron Jaber Abdullah. The smart Music Show can be added to that group, having rounded off a largely successful juvenile campaign with victory in the Lotus Evora Rockfel Stakes at Newmarket in October, Channon's third win in the last seven renewals of this Group 2 event.

Music Show is the longest-priced of Channon's three Rockfel winners, sent off at 25/1 in a field of eleven after flopping at Ayr on her previous start. In hindsight, however, her disappointing tenth in the Firth of Clyde Stakes can probably be attributed to a bad draw and she comprehensively reversed placings at Newmarket with the first and third from that race—Distinctive and Astrophysical Jet—who could manage only seventh and fifth respectively. In the event, Music Note's biggest dangers proved to be Irish raider Atasari and odds-on Tabassum, who had won the Group 3 Oh So Sharp Stakes over the same course and distance earlier in the month. Tabassum made most of the running and looked the likely winner for much of the way too, only for Atasari to overhaul her inside the final furlong, the pair of them then collared close home by the more patiently-ridden Music Show, who kept on strongly under pressure to win by a neck and three quarters of a length. The fact that the first three pulled six lengths clear of fourth-placed Gibraltar Blue (who met trouble in running) suggests it was an up-to-scratch renewal of the Rockfel, which has produced a number of One Thousand Guineas contenders in recent years, Speciosa and Finsceal Beo winning both races, whilst 2004 Rockfel winner Maids Causeway was runner-up in the One Thousand Guineas. The value of Music Show's Rockfel win was backed up by a good timefigure, as her performance had been when landing the odds in a five-runner minor event at Bath in late-August, when she quickened smartly under hands and heels to comfortably beat next-time-out winner Ramamara by three and a quarter lengths.

Bath had also been the venue for Music Note's smooth winning debut (in a fourteen-runner fillies' maiden) earlier in August. Bath has no watering system so regular runners there get plenty of experience of racing on ground firmer than good. Music Note's effectiveness under such conditions isn't perhaps surprising given that her sire Noverre has produced only a handful of winners on soft or heavy going from his first four crops. A high-class performer who won the Poule d'Essai des Poulains (subsequently disqualified for failing a drugs test) and the Sussex Stakes in 2001, Noverre enjoyed his finest season as a sire in 2009, thanks largely to the Prix du Jockey Club success of Le Havre. However, it's unlikely that many of Noverre's future progeny will be racing on European soil, as he was offloaded by Darley in 2008 and sold to stand at Sohna Stud in India.

Music Show (IRE) (b.f. Apr 18, 2007)	Noverre (USA) (b 1998)	Rahy (ch 1985)	Blushing Groom Glorious Song
		Danseur Fabuleux (b 1982)	Northern Dancer Fabuleux Jane
	Dreamboat (USA) (b 1992)	Mr Prospector (b 1970)	Raise A Native Gold Digger
		Gorgeous (b or br 1986)	Slew O'Gold Kamar

Music Show is a useful-looking filly but she fetched only €16,000 at the Goresbridge Breeze-Up Sale in May. Her year-older sister Norfolk Broads showed fair form—successful once, at six furlongs, from seven starts—as a two-year-old for Mark Johnston in 2008 but has since also been sold on by Darley, fetching only 9,000 guineas at the 2009 Tattersalls February Sales. That price tag, and the relative lack of interest in Music Show at the sales, is a little surprising given that this is an excellent family, featuring big-race winners on either side of the Atlantic. For example, Music Show's great grandam Kamar won the 1979 Canadian Oaks and her offspring include three top-notch North American performers in Key To The Moon (Canada's champion three-year-old of 1984), Seaside Attraction (1990 Kentucky Oaks winner) and Gorgeous. Gorgeous's eight wins included the 1989 Hollywood Oaks (she was also runner-up in that year's Breeders' Cup Distaff) and she also proved extremely successful at stud, her best winners being the smart sprinter Abundance and the Prix Imprudence winner Stunning, who both plied their trade in France. Seaside Attraction also developed into a top-notch broodmare once her racing days were over, producing the 1998 Florida Derby winner Cape Town and the 1994 Cherry Hinton Stakes winner Red Carnival amongst others, whilst the latter became the dam of the very smart sprinter Desert Lord. There is clearly plenty of speed in the pedigree, though it is worth noting that Kamar was also the grandam of Fantastic Light (by Noverre's sire Rahy), a top-class performer at up to a mile and a half who became the first horse in British racing history to reach £4m in total prize money when winning the 2001 Breeders' Cup Turf on his final start. Music Note's dam Dreamboat—a lightly-raced seven-furlong winner for John Gosden—has produced another winner, in addition to Norfolk Broads and Music Show, in the shape of Irish filly Fantasia Girl (by Caerleon), who showed useful form at up to a mile and a half and has already produced an above-average performer of her own since retiring to stud, the useful 2008 two-year-old Ra Junior (also by Rahy). Music Show should have little trouble staying the One Thousand Guineas trip, particularly as she shaped in the Rockfel as if an extra furlong would suit her. In addition, she gave the impression in the paddock at Newmarket that she needed another winter physically, still looking slightly unfurnished. *M. R. Channon*

MUSIGNY (USA) 3 b. or br.g. Forest Wildcat (USA) 120 – Water Rights (USA) (Kris **62**
S (USA)) [2009 66: 8s p8g 7m 7m^2 8g^2 Oct 20] good-bodied gelding: fair maiden: stays 1m: acts on polytrack and soft ground: none too consistent: joined Miss S. Hall 7,500 gns. *W. Jarvis*

MUSLEH (USA) 3 b.c. Forestry (USA) 121 – Lucifer's Stone (USA) 116 (Horse **99**
Chestnut (SAF) 119) [2009 85p: p8g* p8g* p8g p8m^3 Sep 24] well-made colt: useful handicapper: won twice at Kempton in August, beating Bomber Command 1½ lengths

latter occasion: good third to Stoic there final outing: stays 1m: raced only on polytrack: has left Godolphin. *Saeed bin Suroor*

MUSTAJED 8 b.g. Alhaarth (IRE) 126 – Jasarah (IRE) 70 (Green Desert (USA) 127) **77** [2009 86: p12g^6 p12g* f11g* 10.4v^6 12m^5 10m 12g^3 12d^2 12g^3 11.6f^3 11.6m f11m^4 Dec 15] sturdy gelding: fair handicapper: won at Lingfield (amateurs) in January and Southwell in February: best at 1¼m/1½m: acts on all-weather, soft and firm going: sometimes in headgear. *B. R. Millman*

MUSTAKHLAS (USA) 8 ch.g. Diesis 133 – Katiba (USA) 99 (Gulch (USA)) [2009 **–** f14g Dec 22] rangy gelding: missed 2008: no form over hurdles/on belated Flat return: tried in cheekpieces. *B. P. J. Baugh*

MUSTAKMIL (IRE) 3 b.c. Haafhd 129 – Elfaslah (IRE) 107 (Green Desert (USA) **86** 127) [2009 8m^3 10.3s 8.3g^2 8g^3 10.3m^4 p8m* p8f* Dec 16] good-bodied colt: closely related to Irish 4-y-o Alhabeeb and 6-y-o Multakka and half-brother to several winners, including high-class 7f (at 2 yrs) to 1¼m (Dubai World Cup) winner Almutawakel and smart 1m (including UAE 1000 Guineas) winner Muwakleh (both by Machiavellian): dam, won around 1¼m, half-sister to high-class 1½m performer White Muzzle: fairly useful form: left E. Dunlop 17,000 gns, won maiden at Lingfield in November and handicap at Kempton in December: stays 1¼m: acts on polytrack and good to firm ground. *S. Dow*

MUSTAQER (IRE) 3 b.g. Dalakhani (IRE) 133 – Al Ihtithar (IRE) 106 (Barathea **–** (IRE) 127) [2009 87p: 10.1g 10.4g 8s^5 Dec 27] rangy gelding: fairly useful winner at 2 yrs: well held all starts in 2009, leaving B. Hills 6,000 gns and gelded after second start: should stay at least 1¼m. *A. Onaya, Spain*

MUT'AB (USA) 4 b.g. Alhaarth (IRE) 126 – Mistle Song 112 (Nashwan (USA) 135) **86** [2009 94: p7g 8.1g 6m^2 7m May 28] rangy, good-topped gelding: fairly useful handicapper: seemingly effective from 6f to 1¼m: acts on good to firm going: blinkered: none too consistent: gelded after final start. *C. E. Brittain*

MUTAFAJER 2 b. or br.c. (Feb 4) Oasis Dream 129 – Shahaamah (IRE) (Red Ransom **81 p** (USA)) [2009 6.5g^5 p7m^3 p6m^2 Nov 4] attractive colt: third foal: half-brother to useful 2007 2-y-o 7f winner Zakhaaref (by Daylami) and 2008 2-y-o 5f winner Azwa (by Haafhd): dam unraced out of close relative to July Cup winner Elnadim: fairly useful form when placed in maidens at Kempton, length second to Forest Crown latter occasion (pulled hard): may prove best at 5f/6f: will do better. *Saeed bin Suroor*

MUTAJAASER (USA) 4 b.g. War Chant (USA) 126 – Hazimah (USA) 74 (Gone **67** West (USA)) [2009 7d p8.6g^5 Dec 7] much better effort in maidens over 4 months apart when fifth at Wolverhampton. *K. A. Morgan*

MUTAJARRED 5 ch.g. Alhaarth (IRE) 126 – Bedara 93 (Barathea (IRE) 127) [2009 **–** 112: 10d 8g Aug 1] big, strong gelding: well below smart best both starts in 2009 (said to have bled latter occasion): stays 1¼m: acts on polytrack and heavy going: tried blinkered: has carried head awkwardly. *W. J. Haggas*

MUTAMAASHI 3 b.g. Sakhee (USA) 136 – Almahab (USA) (Danzig (USA)) [2009 **102** p8g* 8m^2 10m^3 8m 10d^3 p10f^2 10.3m* 10g^3 Oct 10] tall, attractive gelding: first foal: dam unraced half-sister to smart 6f/7f performer Munaddam and 3-y-o Almiqdaad: useful performer: won maiden at Lingfield in February and quite valuable handicap at Chester (beat Goliath's Boy by ½ length) in September: good third to Cill Rialaig in handicap at Ascot final outing: stays 10.3f: acts on polytrack, unraced on extremes of going on turf: held up. *W. J. Haggas*

MUTAMARED (USA) 9 ch.g. Nureyev (USA) 131 – Alydariel (USA) (Alydar **92 d** (USA)) [2009 95: p6g* p6g* p7g* p6g* p6g^2 p7.1g^5 p7g^4 p6g^3 6f 6g^5 6d 6f^2 p6g 6d^6 p7.1g^4 6m* p6m^6 p6g p6g p6g p6m Dec 6] lengthy gelding: fairly useful performer at best nowadays: successful in claimer at Kempton, and 2 claimers and handicap at Lingfield in January/February and, having left K. Ryan £7,000, handicap at Goodwood in September: left Andrew Reid prior to penultimate outing: effective at 5f to easy 7f: acts on dirt/polytrack and good to firm going: usually tongue tied nowadays. *M. J. Scudamore*

MUTAMAYEZ 3 b.c. Dalakhani (IRE) 133 – Blue Oasis (IRE) 94 (Sadler's Wells **87 p** (USA) 132) [2009 p10m* Sep 26] 120,000F, 220,000 2-y-o: compact, attractive colt: first foal: dam, 1m winner, sister to useful Irish winners Stage Call (1m) and Humilis (1¼m): 6/5, promising debut when winning maiden at Kempton in September impressively by 3 lengths from Ramora: will improve. *M. A. Jarvis*

MUTAWARATH (IRE) 3 b.c. Marju (IRE) 127 – Castlerahan (IRE) (Thatching 131) **91** [2009 8m 8g^4 8g* 7.2s^4 p8m 8.5m^4 Oct 3] 200,000F: strong colt: brother to smart 7f (including at 2 yrs)/1m winner Brunel: dam unraced: fairly useful performer: won maiden at York in June: good efforts 2 of 3 starts in handicaps after, 2½ lengths fourth to Roar of Applause at Epsom final one: stays 8.5f: acts on soft and good to firm going: sold 32,000 gns. *W. J. Haggas*

MUTAYAM 9 b.g. Compton Place 125 – Final Shot 91 (Dalsaan 125) [2009 48: 5m 5m^6 5m Jun 29] of little account nowadays. *D. A. Nolan* **–**

MUTHEEB (USA) 4 b.c. Danzig (USA) – Magicalmysterykate (USA) (Woodman (USA) 126) [2009 84p: 7g* p6g^3 7f^4 7m^3 Jul 10] lengthy colt: smart performer: won minor event at Yarmouth (beat Mia's Boy by a head) in April: creditable efforts in valuable handicaps last 2 starts, at Royal Ascot (Buckingham Palace Stakes, 3¼ lengths fourth to Giganticus) and Newmarket (Bunbury Cup, again travelled strongly long way when length third to Plum Pudding): will stay 1m, but not short of speed: raced on polytrack and good going or firmer: has joined M. Al Muhairi in UAE. *Saeed bin Suroor* **111**

MUTUALLY MINE (USA) 3 ch.f. Golden Missile (USA) 123 – Gal of Mine (USA) (Mining (USA)) [2009 72: p10g^6 8f^2 8.3f^3 8m^6 7g^3 7m 8.3m^5 8m^6 p9.5g^3 p10g p9.5g Dec 7] sturdy filly: fair maiden handicapper: barely stays 9.5f: acts on polytrack and firm going: tried in cheekpieces. *Mrs P. Sly* **72**

MUWAKABA (USA) 2 ch.f. (Apr 4) Elusive Quality (USA) – Saleela (USA) 85 (Nureyev (USA) 131) [2009 p7g* Sep 21] tall, well-made filly: fifth live foal: half-sister to useful 7f (at 2 yrs) to 1¼m (in UAE) winner Morghim (by Machiavellian) and winner in USA by Miswaki: dam, 12.5f winner, half-sister to 2000 Guineas winner King's Best and Arc winner Urban Sea, herself dam of Sea The Stars and Galileo: 7/2, highly promising when winning maiden at Kempton easily by length from Sing Sweetly, coming from off pace: will stay at least 1m: open to considerable improvement, and should make useful filly at least. *Sir Michael Stoute* **87 P**

MUWALLA 2 b.c. (Apr 21) Bahri (USA) 125 – Easy Sunshine (IRE) 96 (Sadler's Wells (USA) 132) [2009 7.5g^4 7.1g 8m^3 7m^2 Sep 21] 18,000F, 32,000Y: well-made colt: fourth foal: half-brother to 3-y-o Sunshine Always and Irish 4-y-o Second Glance: dam Irish 7f winner: fairly useful maiden: placed at Doncaster and Leicester (minor event): stays 1m. *C. E. Brittain* **83**

MUZMIN (USA) 4 b. or br.g. Seeking The Gold (USA) – In On The Secret (CAN) (Secretariat (USA)) [2009 7g^5 8g 10m^5 Jun 20] tall, leggy gelding: maiden: missed 2008: just modest form in 2009: will be suited by 1½m: raced on good/good to firm going. *E. A. L. Dunlop* **63**

MUZO (USA) 3 b.c. Gone West (USA) – Bowl of Emeralds (USA) (A P Indy (USA) 131) [2009 p9.5g^4 p11g^3 Oct 22] fair form in polytrack maidens: stays 11f. *J. Noseda* **68**

MY ARCH 7 b.g. Silver Patriarch (IRE) 125 – My Desire 88 (Grey Desire 115) [2009 12g Oct 10] big, good-bodied gelding: fairly useful hurdler/chaser, successful in November: off 17 months, signs of retaining similar level of ability on Flat sole outing at 7 yrs: stays 1½m: acts on soft going: tried blinkered/in cheekpieces. *Ollie Pears* **75 +**

MY AUNT FANNY 4 b.f. Nayef (USA) 129 – Putuna 98 (Generous (IRE) 139) [2009 92: 9g^5 9.9g^6 10m Sep 19] tall, quite attractive filly: fairly useful handicapper: below form after reappearance in 2009: stays 1¼m: acts on soft and good to firm ground: suspect temperament: sold £15,000, sent to USA. *A. M. Balding* **92**

MY BEST BET 3 ch.f. Best of The Bests (IRE) 122 – Cibenze 74 (Owington 123) [2009 74: p6g^3 p6g^3 p6g* 7d 7f^6 6.9m 7m^2 7m^2 7g^5 7.1v^3 7m* 7m^4 p7f^2 6d^5 p7.1m^6 p7.1g^5 7g^3 p8g* p8f^3 Dec 16] leggy, lengthy filly: fairly useful handicapper on all-weather, fair on turf: won at Kempton in January, Folkestone in August and, having left M. Channon, Lingfield in November: best at stiff 7f/easy 1m: acts on polytrack and good to firm going: usually held up: tough. *Stef Liddiard* **79 a89**

MY BEST MAN 3 b.g. Forzando 122 – Victoria Sioux 54 (Ron's Victory (USA) 129) [2009 69: p6g^5 f6g^3 f8g^3 f7g^3 8.1g^4 8.1g^3 7m^6 8g^6 5.1v^5 6.1g^6 5.1m Aug 20] good-topped gelding: modest maiden handicapper: best at 7f/1m: acts on all-weather, heavy and good to firm going: tried in blinkers/cheekpieces/tongue tie. *B. R. Millman* **62**

MY BODYGUARD (FR) 3 b.c. Alhaarth (IRE) 126 – Hollow Dynasty (USA) (Deputy Commander (USA) 124) [2009 10g 12d f12g Jun 7] workmanlike colt: showed little in maidens/claimer: tongue tied all starts, also blinkered final one. *H. J. L. Dunlop* **–**

MY BOY NICK 7 b.g. Bold Fort 100 – Suelizelle 54 (Carnival Dancer 117) [2009 p8.6g Apr 25] well beaten over hurdles, and in seller at Wolverhampton on Flat debut. *D. L. Williams* **–**

MYCENEAN PRINCE (USA) 6 b.g. Swain (IRE) 134 – Nijinsky's Beauty (USA) (Nijinsky (CAN) 138) [2009 45: p8.6g 12g 9.9g Sep 22] strong, compact gelding: **–**

maiden: poor on Flat and over jumps nowadays: left R. C. Guest after reappearance. *S. A. Harris*

MY CHESTNUT GIRL (USA) 3 ch.f. Horse Chestnut (SAF) 119 – Mien (USA) **84**
(Nureyev (USA) 131) [2009 61p: 10m 9.9m^4 9.7m^3 10m^4 11.9m^2 12g* Aug 3] good-topped filly: fairly useful performer: improved when winning maiden at Ripon in August: stays 1½m: acts on good to firm ground: sold 115,000 gns. *H. R. A. Cecil*

MY CHOICE 3 b.g. Groom Dancer (USA) 128 – Beleza (IRE) (Revoque (IRE) 122) **–**
[2009 –: f11g Apr 21] strong gelding: no form. *A. P. Jarvis*

MY CONDOR (IRE) 8 b.g. Beneficial 117 – Margellen's Castle (IRE) (Castle Keep **–**
121) [2009 p12.2g Aug 10] maiden hurdler/winning chaser: usually shapes as if amiss/finds little, including in seller at Wolverhampton on Flat debut. *D. McCain Jnr*

MYDY EASY (USA) 3 b. or br.c. Speightstown (USA) 124 – Eze (USA) (Williams- **62**
town (USA) 118) [2009 8.3m^5 7m^5 Oct 6] medium-sized colt: better effort (modest form) in maidens on debut. *P. W. Chapple-Hyam*

MY FLAME 4 b.g. Cool Jazz 116 – Suselja (IRE) 53 (Mon Tresor 113) [2009 59d: 7d^2 **65**
7g^6 7m* 8f^5 7m 7g 7m p7m^4 p7m p8g p7g^5 Dec 2] workmanlike gelding: fair handicapper: won at Brighton in April: stays 7f: acts on polytrack and good to firm going: tried in headgear: front runner/races prominently: gelded after final start. *J. R. Jenkins*

MY FRIEND FRITZ 9 ch.g. Safawan 118 – Little Scarlett 54 (Mazilier (USA) 107) **76**
[2009 76: f14s* f12s^4 f14g f12g^4 f12g* p16g f12g May 18] fair performer: won handicap in January and seller in March, both at Southwell: stays 1¾m: raced mainly on fibresand. *P. W. Hiatt*

MY GACHO (IRE) 7 b.g. Shinko Forest (IRE) – Floralia 81 (Auction Ring (USA) **100**
123) [2009 102: p7g^5 p7g^5 7f 6f 7.2m 6m^6 7m* 8m* 7m* 7m* 6m 7m 6g f7g Dec 22] good-topped gelding: useful handicapper: won at Leicester in July and Brighton, Newcastle and Chester (beat I Confess 1½ lengths) in August: well below form after: stays 1m: acts on all-weather and firm ground: blinkered/visored: none too consistent. *M. Johnston*

MY GIRL JODE 3 ch.f. Haafhd 129 – Brush Strokes (Cadeaux Genereux 131) [2009 **70**
70: 8g 10.2g^5 10.1g* 10.3g^2 11.1g^5 10g p10g^3 p10g Nov 25] angular filly: fair handicapper: won at Yarmouth in July: should stay beyond 1¼m: raced only on polytrack and good ground: pulls hard. *M. H. Tompkins*

MY GRAND DUKE (USA) 2 b.c. (Mar 6) Johannesburg (USA) 127 – Hit It Here **–**
Cafe (USA) (Grand Slam (USA) 120) [2009 p7.1m f8f^6 f8d Dec 29] down the field in maidens. *J. A. Osborne*

MY IMMORTAL 7 b.g. Monsun (GER) 124 – Dame Kiri (FR) 112 (Old Vic 136) **78**
[2009 14m 14g^4 18m^5 15.8g Jul 8] sturdy gelding: handicapper: not seen on Flat between 2005 (for J. Gosden) and 2009 (just fair form), winning hurdler/chaser in that time: stays 2¼m: acts on polytrack, firm and good to soft going. *J. J. Quinn*

MY JEANIE (IRE) 5 ch.m. King Charlemagne (USA) 120 – Home Comforts (Most **48**
Welcome 131) [2009 –: 8.1g p7.1g 8g^5 p10g Dec 7] poor handicapper: stays 1m: acts on polytrack. *J. C. Fox*

MY KAISER CHIEF 4 bl.g. Paris House 123 – So Tempted (So Factual (USA) 120) **–**
[2009 76: p6g p7g Mar 11] leggy, lengthy gelding: handicapper: well below form both starts in 2009: tried tongue tied. *W. J. H. Ratcliffe*

MYKINGDOMFORAHORSE 3 b.c. Fantastic Light (USA) 134 – Charlecote (IRE) **82**
(Caerleon (USA) 132) [2009 77: 8.3m 9.9g^4 9g^2 10.3d^4 10.1g* 10m^3 12m^2 14.1g* 18g Oct 10] compact colt: fairly useful handicapper: won at Yarmouth in August and Salisbury in September: free-going sort, but stays 1¾m: acts on good to firm and good to soft ground: tried visored. *M. R. Channon*

MY KINGDOM (IRE) 3 b.g. King's Best (USA) 132 – Nebraas (Green Desert (USA) **90**
127) [2009 85: 7.1g^4 p8g^4 7m 6d^4 6g^2 6d* 6d^3 6m 6.1m^4 p6m^6 Oct 12] leggy gelding: fairly useful handicapper: won at Brighton in August: effective at 6f to 1m: acts on polytrack, soft and good to firm going: tongue tied. *H. Morrison*

MY LEARNED FRIEND (IRE) 5 b.g. Marju (IRE) 127 – Stately Princess 70 **84**
(Robellino (USA) 127) [2009 84: 7m^4 7m 7m^2 7f* 7m 7.1m^6 7m Oct 3] close-coupled, useful-looking gelding: fairly useful handicapper: won at Brighton in July: stays 7f: acts on good to firm and good to soft going: tried visored. *A. M. Balding*

MY LEGAL EAGLE (IRE) 15 b.g. Law Society (USA) 130 – Majestic Nurse 80 **–**
(On Your Mark 125) [2009 52: 11.9m May 22] smallish gelding: veteran handicapper: well held sole outing in 2009: tried blinkered. *E. G. Bevan*

MY LES 3 b.f. Josr Algarhoud (IRE) 118 – Ashantiana 64 (Ashkalani (IRE) 128) [2009 –: p12g^5 16g 11.9d* p12g^3 Oct 20] sturdy filly: left J. R. Best, vastly improved form when winning seller at Brighton in October: stays 1½m: acts on polytrack and good to soft going. *Jim Best* **76**

MY MANDY (IRE) 2 b.f. (Mar 1) Xaar 132 – Ikan (IRE) 98 (Sri Pekan (USA) 117) [2009 p5g^4 5m^3 5m^2 5.1m^6 5.1m^4 5m^2 5m^3 5d^4 5m^5 f5g^3 p5g^3 p6g^4 Oct 20] £26,000Y: leggy filly: second foal: dam 5f/6f (latter at 2 yrs) winner: modest maiden: flattered (raced alone) third start: stays easy 6f: acts on all-weather and good to firm going: in cheekpieces last 3 starts: sold 7,000 gns. *Ian Williams* **64**

MYMATEERIC 3 b.g. Reset (AUS) 124 – Ewenny 71 (Warrshan (USA) 117) [2009 67: 9.7g 10g p8g 9.8m^5 11.5d^2 11.5m 11.5g^4 p16m^3 p16.5g^4 p16g p16g Oct 24] sturdy, good-topped gelding: modest maiden handicapper: stays 2m: acts on polytrack, soft and good to firm going: wears headgear nowadays: usually held up. *J. Pearce* **60**

MY MATE GRANITE (USA) 5 ch.g. High Yield (USA) 121 – Fellwaati (USA) (Alydar (USA)) [2009 –: f12g^2 f12g^6 p16g Jun 24] poor maiden: trained on return by M. Wigham, second start by M. Rimmer: stayed 1½m: raced only on all-weather: dead. *H. J. Collingridge* **43**

MY MATE MAL 5 b.g. Daawe (USA) 103 – Kandymal (IRE) 52 (Prince of Birds (USA) 121) [2009 66: p8.6g 8.5m^6 p8.6g^2 7m^6 8m* 8d 8d^2 p8g^6 7d 9.1d^3 10g p12.2m^2 p8.6g^5 p9.5g f11m^3 Dec 15] sturdy gelding: fair performer: won seller at Newcastle in May: stays 1½m: acts on all-weather, soft and good to firm going: often forces pace: none too consistent. *B. Ellison* **72**

MY MATE MAX 4 b.g. Fraam 114 – Victory Flip (IRE) 67 (Victory Note (USA) 120) [2009 79: p12g 14m^2 15g^2 15m^6 15.9m 15g^3 15m* 16g^4 Oct 30] sturdy gelding: fair handicapper: won at Warwick in September: stays 2m: acts on polytrack, soft and good to firm ground: wears cheekpieces: not straightforward. *R. Hollinshead* **79**

MY MENTOR (IRE) 5 b.g. Golan (IRE) 129 – Vanille (IRE) 72 (Selkirk (USA) 129) [2009 80§: f8g^4 f11g^2 f11g^4 p10g^6 f7g p11g f12g Jul 27] fair handicapper: effective at 7f to 1½m: raced only on all-weather: often blinkered, once in cheekpieces: temperamental. *Sir Mark Prescott* **74 §**

MY MIRASOL 5 ch.m. Primo Valentino (IRE) 116 – Distinctly Blu (IRE) 70 (Distinctly North (USA) 115) [2009 72: f12s^3 f11g^6 f12g Feb 20] lengthy mare: just modest performer in 2009: barely stays 1¼m: acts on all-weather, heavy and good to firm ground: often wears cheekpieces: has bled: front runner. *D. E. Cantillon* **62**

MYMUMSAYSIMTHEBEST 4 b.g. Reel Buddy (USA) 118 – Night Gypsy 74 (Mind Games 121) [2009 p7g 6m^2 6g^6 Jun 15] lengthy gelding: fairly useful maiden: missed 2008: should prove best up to 7f: acts on good to firm going. *G. L. Moore* **87**

MY ONE WEAKNESS (IRE) 2 ch.g. (Feb 3) Bertolini (USA) 125 – Lucina (Machiavellian (USA) 123) [2009 6d^3 6d^3 5m f7g* 6m^4 8m 6m* Sep 18] £9,000Y: close-coupled gelding: first foal: dam unraced half-sister to 8-y-o Blue Monday out of half-sister to Luso and Warrsan: fair performer: won nurseries at Southwell in July and Ayr in September: stays 7f: acts on fibresand and good to firm going. *B. Ellison* **80**

MY PARIS 8 b.g. Paris House 123 – My Desire 88 (Grey Desire 115) [2009 97d: f8g Apr 23] leggy, lengthy gelding: one-time smart handicapper: well held only start in 2009: tried in headgear. *Ollie Pears* **–**

MYRAID 2 b.g. (May 20) Danbird (AUS) – My Desire 88 (Grey Desire 115) [2009 8g Oct 16] tall gelding: 100/1 and backward, well held in maiden at Redcar: bred to be suited by 1¼m+. *Ollie Pears* **–**

MY RED KITE 2 ch.g. (Apr 4) Avonbridge 123 – Cup of Love (USA) 70 (Behrens (USA) 130) [2009 6m^5 7.1m 7g p8m^6 Nov 4] modest maiden: stays 1m: acts on polytrack and good to firm going: tried in cheekpieces. *G. D. Blake* **54**

MYRIOLA 4 ch.f. Captain Rio 122 – Spaniola (IRE) (Desert King (IRE) 129) [2009 52: p5.1g p5.1g^5 f5g Dec 22] attractive filly: poor maiden: best form at 5f: acts on polytrack, soft and good to firm going: tried blinkered. *D. Shaw* **43**

MY SHADOW 4 b.g. Zamindar (USA) 116 – Reflections (Sadler's Wells (USA) 132) [2009 82: p10g* p10g p8g^2 p10g^2 10.2f^5 8g* 10.1m^3 8.1m p8g Sep 9] good-topped gelding: fair handicapper: won at Kempton in February and Goodwood in June: effective at 1m/1¼m: acts on polytrack and soft ground: held up. *S. Dow* **78**

MYSHKIN 3 b.g. Refuse To Bend (IRE) 128 – Marmaga (IRE) (Shernazar 131) [2009 –: p10g^5 12.5m^4 Apr 12] good-bodied gelding: modest maiden: tried blinkered/visored. *I. Semple* **54**

MY SISTER 2 b.f. (Apr 7) Royal Applause 124 – Mysistra (FR) (Machiavellian (USA) 123) [2009 6m 6m⁴ 6m⁵ 6.5m p6m⁵ 8.3d⁶ Oct 12] smallish filly: half-sister to 3 winners, including fairly useful 9f to 1½m winner Greyfriars Abbey (by Fasliyev): dam, French 11f winner, out of half-sister to Irish St Leger winner Dark Lomond: modest maiden: should stay at least 1m: acts on good to firm going. *M. D. I. Usher* **62**

MYSTERY STAR (IRE) 4 ch.g. Kris Kin (USA) 126 – Mystery Hill (USA) 72 (Danehill (USA) 126) [2009 90: 8.3g³ 10.1d² 9.9g* 10m⁵ 10.1g² 10g⁵ 11.9m 12m² 12g⁶ 13.4m² 14.1m³ 12g Oct 10] smallish, rather leggy gelding: has short, scratchy action: useful handicapper: won at Goodwood in May: good efforts after when placed, including length third to Akmal at Yarmouth penultimate outing: barely stays 1¾m: acts on polytrack, good to firm and good to soft going: tried in cheekpieces: held up. *M. H. Tompkins* **104**

MYSTICAL AYR (IRE) 7 br.m. Namid 128 – Scanno's Choice (IRE) 54 (Pennine Walk 120) [2009 63: 9.2g 8g⁶ 9.2d Jul 17] sturdy mare: no form in 2009: tried in cheekpieces: none too resolute. *Miss L. A. Perratt* **–**

MYSTICAL SPIRIT (IRE) 3 b.f. Xaar 132 – Samsung Spirit 79 (Statoblest 120) [2009 48: 11.4m May 6] poor maiden: out of depth, pulled up only outing at 3 yrs. *J. R. Weymes* **–**

MYSTIC ART (IRE) 4 b.g. Peintre Celebre (USA) 137 – Mystic Lure 70 (Green Desert (USA) 127) [2009 73: p10g* p10g³ p10g² 10.2g 10f⁴ 10.1g p12g Jun 6] angular gelding: fair performer: won seller at Lingfield in February: stays 11f: acts on polytrack, good to firm and good to soft going: tried in cheekpieces/blinkers: signs of temperament. *C. R. Egerton* **65**

MYSTICKHILL (IRE) 4 ch.f. Raise A Grand (IRE) 114 – Lady Eberspacher (IRE) 68 (Royal Abjar (USA) 121) [2009 65: f5g⁵ Jan 15] close-coupled filly: maiden: just modest form sole start at 4 yrs: will prove best at 5f/6f: acts on all-weather and firm going: tried tongue tied. *J. Balding* **53**

MYSTIC MILLIE (IRE) 2 ch.f. (Mar 18) Bertolini (USA) 125 – Present Imperfect 61 (Cadeaux Genereux 131) [2009 6g 6f 7m⁵ Oct 1] €36,000Y: angular filly: seventh foal: half-sister to useful 2002 2-y-o 6f winner who stayed 7f Hector's Girl (by Hector Protector): dam twice-raced half-sister to very smart performer up to 7f College Chapel: well held in maidens: sold 2,500 gns, sent to Germany. *C. G. Cox* **–**

MYSTIC PRINCE 3 b.g. Dubai Destination (USA) 127 – Hazy Heights 56 (Shirley Heights 130) [2009 70: 10d 8m 10.9g Jul 3] rather leggy gelding: maiden: well held in 2009. *Miss Tor Sturgis* **–**

MYSTIC ROLL 6 br.g. Medicean 128 – Pain Perdu (IRE) (Waajib 121) [2009 62: 6g 7g⁶ Jul 16] quite good-topped gelding: maiden: well held both starts in 2009: tried blinkered: none too consistent. *Jane Chapple-Hyam* **–**

MYSTIC TOUCH 3 b.g. Systematic 121 – Lycius Touch 50 (Lycius (USA) 124) [2009 p7g p8g³ p8.6g 9.9g 8m⁴ 8f 7.6d 10m⁶ p9.5g* p10g p7g Nov 25] modest handicapper: left Miss E. Lavelle after seventh start: won at Wolverhampton in October: will prove best up to 1¼m: best efforts on polytrack: tried in cheekpieces. *A. B. Haynes* **63**

MYSTIFIED (IRE) 6 b.g. Raise A Grand (IRE) 114 – Sunrise (IRE) 58 (Sri Pekan (USA) 117) [2009 –: 14.1g* 14.1m² 14.1m² 16m² 13g² 14.1m 16d⁴ 17.1m³ 15.8g Oct 6] useful-looking gelding: modest performer: won apprentice seller at Redcar in June: stays 17f: acts on polytrack, good to firm and good to soft ground: formerly blinkered, in cheekpieces/tongue tie in 2009: front runner/races prominently. *R. F. Fisher* **63**

MY SWEET GEORGIA (IRE) 3 b.f. Royal Applause 124 – Harda Arda (USA) 66 (Nureyev (USA) 131) [2009 79: f6g* p8.6g⁵ p7g² f6g* f7d² f6g⁴ p6m p8m p7g f7m* p6m p7.1g f8g³ Dec 18] sturdy filly: good walker: fair performer: won handicap in January, claimer in February and, having left S. Callaghan after sixth outing, handicap in November, all at Southwell: stays 8.6f: acts on all-weather, soft and good to firm going: best in headgear nowadays. *Stef Liddiard* **74**

MYTHICAL BLUE (IRE) 3 b.g. Acclamation 118 – Proud Myth (IRE) (Mark of Esteem (IRE) 137) [2009 82: 5g³ 5.7f² 5.1g* 5.1f* p5.1g³ 5.1g* 5.1g⁵ 5g* 5m* 5g Oct 9] sturdy gelding: fairly useful performer: won claimers at Chepstow in May and Bath in June, handicap at Bath in July, seller at Warwick in August and handicap at Goodwood in September: best at 5f: acts on firm and good to soft going: tried tongue tied: best when able to dominate: genuine. *J. M. Bradley* **84**

MYTHICAL BORDER (USA) 3 ch.f. Johannesburg (USA) 127 – Border Dispute (USA) (Boundary (USA) 117) [2009 100: 5m Aug 21] sturdy, lengthy filly: useful at 2 yrs: off nearly 11 months, well held in Nunthorpe Stakes at York sole outing in 2009: should prove best at 5f/6f. *J. Noseda* **–**

MYTHICAL CHARM 10 b.m. Charnwood Forest (IRE) 125 – Triple Tricks (IRE) 70 (Royal Academy (USA) 130) [2009 53: p8g Jan 5] good-topped mare: handicapper: well held only start in 2009: tongue tied. *J. J. Bridger* **–**

MYTHICAL FLIGHT (SAF) 6 ch.g. Jet Master (SAF) – Mythical Bird (SAF) (Harry Hotspur (SAF)) [2009 6g^{6} 5m 5m Aug 21] strong, deep-girthed gelding: smart performer at best: won 8 of his first 10 starts in South Africa, including Grade 1s at Kenilworth (Cape Flying Championship) and Turffontein (Computaform Sprint) in 2007: contested same races again first 2 starts in 2008, 1¼ lengths second to O Caesour at Kenilworth before last behind J J The Jet Plane at Turffontein: below form in 2009, including in King's Stand Stakes at Royal Ascot and Nunthorpe Stakes at York: best at 5f: raced mainly on good ground. *Sean Tarry, South Africa* **105**

MYTHICAL THRILL 3 b.g. Alhaarth (IRE) 126 – Mythical Girl (USA) 107 (Gone West (USA)) [2009 –: 8.3v 8.3g Aug 14] no form in maidens. *J. G. Given* **–**

MYTHICISM 3 b.f. Oasis Dream 129 – Romantic Myth 105 (Mind Games 121) [2009 80: 5m 6s May 4] good-topped filly: fairly useful winner at 2 yrs: well below form in handicaps in 2009: tongue tied. *B. Smart* **–**

MYTIVIL (IRE) 3 gr.f. Clodovil (IRE) 116 – Mytilene (IRE) 103 (Soviet Star (USA) 128) [2009 66: p8.6g^{6} 8.3m^{2} 8.1g p8.6g 10.2g Jun 11] rather leggy filly: fair maiden: left Tom Dascombe after reappearance: stays 8.3f: acts on polytrack and good to firm going. *M. Salaman* **72**

MYTTONS MAID 3 b.f. Bertolini (USA) 125 – The In-Laws (IRE) 90 (Be My Guest (USA) 126) [2009 –: 7m 10.1d^{2} Jul 21] close-coupled filly: first form (modest) when second in seller at Yarmouth: stays 1¼m: in cheekpieces in 2009. *A. Bailey* **54**

MY VERSE 3 b.f. Exceed And Excel (AUS) 126 – Reematna 75 (Sabrehill (USA) 120) [2009 80p: 8g* 8.1d* 8m^{4} Oct 5] useful-looking filly: fairly useful form: won maiden at Ripon in August and handicap at Sandown in September: may prove best up to 1m: acts on good to soft ground: signs of temperament: joined D. Selvaratnam in UAE. *M. A. Jarvis* **87**

N

NAAQOOS 3 b.c. Oasis Dream 129 – Straight Lass (IRE) (Machiavellian (USA) 123) [2009 117p: 7g^{2} 8m^{6} 6.5g Aug 9] big, strong colt: had exuberant, powerful action: smart performer: won Prix Jean-Luc Lagardere at Longchamp in 2008: creditable efforts first 2 starts at 3 yrs, beaten head by Le Havre in listed race at Maisons-Laffitte (odds on) then 2¼ lengths third past post (demoted to sixth) behind Silver Frost in Poule d'Essai des Poulains at Longchamp despite pulling hard: off 3 months (missed Prix Jean Prat, reportedly due to coughing/scoping badly) and favourite, well held in Prix Maurice de Gheest at Deauville final outing: stayed 1m: raced mainly on good/good to firm ground (won on good to soft on debut): to stand at Haras du Mezeray, France, fee €6,000. *F. Head, France* **116**

NABEEDA 4 b.g. Namid 128 – Lovellian (Machiavellian (USA) 123) [2009 63: f7d^{4} f6d^{3} f6g^{3} p7.1g^{5} 7m^{5} f6g^{4} f5f^{4} Dec 11] leggy gelding: modest handicapper: stays 7f: acts on all-weather, heavy and good to firm going: races close up: consistent. *M. Brittain* **60**

NABRA 5 b.m. Kyllachy 129 – Muja Farewell 94 (Mujtahid (USA) 118) [2009 52: f7g 6d 5m* 6m 5g 6m Sep 23] modest performer: won maiden at Ripon in August: well held otherwise: best at 5f: acts on polytrack and good to firm going: tried blinkered: none too reliable: sold 6,000 gns. *M. Brittain* **57**

NABRINA (IRE) 2 ch.f. (Feb 24) Namid 128 – My Cadeaux 93 (Cadeaux Genereux 131) [2009 5.1g^{5} 5d^{6} 5g 5d^{6} 5m^{3} 6.1s f6g^{6} f6m^{4} Dec 15] €2,000Y: close-coupled, good-bodied filly: seventh foal: half-sister to 6f winner Milly Fleur (by Primo Dominie): dam, 6f winner, closely related to very smart sprinter Prince Sabo and half-sister to smart sprinter Millyant: modest maiden: stays 6f: acts on fibresand, soft and good to firm going. *M. Brittain* **52**

NACHO LIBRE 4 b.g. Kyllachy 129 – Expectation (IRE) 59 (Night Shift (USA)) [2009 100d: 5m 6g^{6} 6d f7g 6d^{4} 6d 7.2g^{4} p6g* f6g^{3} p6g^{3} Dec 12] strong, good-bodied gelding: fair handicapper nowadays: won at Wolverhampton in November: stays 7f: acts on all-weather, soft and good to firm ground: blinkered last 4 outings. *M. W. Easterby* **70**

NADDWAH 2 ch.f. (Feb 17) Pivotal 124 – My Dubai (IRE) 76 (Dubai Millennium 140) [2009 7d^{6} Oct 12] first foal: dam once-raced half-sister to high-class 6f/7f performer **66 p**

Iffraaj out of half-sister to high-class miler Cape Cross: 7/1 and very green, 3 lengths sixth to Qaraaba in maiden at Salisbury, wandering: likely to do better. *M. A. Jarvis*

NADEEN (IRE) 2 b.c. (May 2) Bahamian Bounty 116 – Janayen (USA) 97 (Zafonic (USA) 130) [2009 5.3m* 5m³ Jun 1] stocky colt: first foal: dam 1m winner out of smart performer up to 1½m Saafeya: shaped well both starts, winning maiden at Brighton in April and close third to Navajo Chief in minor event at Windsor: will be suited by 6f+. *M. R. Channon* **88**

NAFURA 2 b.f. (Mar 28) Dubawi (IRE) 129 – Mysterial (USA) (Alleged (USA) 138) [2009 p7g⁵ 7g 7.5m p8.6g* p8.6g* Nov 12] attractive filly: half-sister to several winners, notably milers Dubai Destination (high class, by Kingmambo) and Librettist (very smart, by Danzig), both also 7f winners at 2 yrs: dam, ran twice, half-sister to very smart Japanese performers Agnes World (sprinter) and Hishi Akebono (sprinter/miler): useful form: in cheekpieces, much improved when winning nurseries at Wolverhampton in October and November, latter easily by 2 lengths from Duty And Destiny: will stay beyond 8.6f: acts on polytrack: should continue to progress. *Saeed bin Suroor* **95 p**

NAHEELL 3 ch.c. Lomitas 129 – Seyooll (IRE) 78 (Danehill (USA) 126) [2009 73: p12.2g⁶ 10m 9.7m² p9.5g* 10.1d p10m p8g Dec 7] rather unfurnished colt: fair handicapper: left M. Jarvis 13,500 gns after reappearance: won at Wolverhampton in October: stays 9.5f: acts on polytrack and good to firm going. *G. Prodromou* **76**

NAIAS (IRE) 4 ch.f. Namid 128 – Sovereign Grace (IRE) 101 (Standaan (FR) 118) [2009 47: p6g Jan 14] poor maiden: should prove best at 5f/6f. *R. A. Fahey* **–**

NAIRANA 3 b.f. Lend A Hand 124 – Flukes (Distant Relative 128) [2009 40: p7.1g⁶ Jan 26] signs of ability on debut only. *J. G. Given* **–**

NAIZAK 3 ch.f. Medicean 128 – Sunny Davis (USA) 71 (Alydar (USA)) [2009 73: 8.3m 7.1g May 4] leggy filly: fair maiden at 2 yrs: well held both starts in 2009 (blinkered final outing): stays 7f: sold 11,000 gns in July. *J. L. Dunlop* **–**

NAJD (USA) 2 ch.c. (Mar 30) Storm Cat (USA) – Miss Halory (USA) (Mr Prospector (USA)) [2009 7m* Aug 14] attractive colt: favourite, won maiden at Newbury by head from Poltergeist: dead. *Saeed bin Suroor* **87**

NAKOMA (IRE) 7 b.m. Bahhare (USA) 122 – Indian Imp (Indian Ridge 123) [2009 55: 9.3d⁴ 12g⁴ 14s 12.4d* p13.9g* p12.2g⁶ p13.9g Dec 17] fair handicapper: won at Newcastle in October and Wolverhampton in November: stays 1¾m: acts on polytrack and good to soft going. *B. Ellison* **70**

NALEDI 5 b.g. Indian Ridge 123 – Red Carnation (IRE) 103 (Polar Falcon (USA) 126) [2009 –§: f7g p9.5g⁵ 10.9f 8.1g Jun 25] temperamental maiden handicapper: one to avoid. *J. R. Norton* **43 §**

NAMASKAR 2 b.f. (Feb 6) Dansili 127 – Namaste 65 (Alzao (USA) 117) [2009 8m* Sep 8] second foal: dam lightly-raced close relative to Irish Oaks winner Wemyss Bight (dam of Beat Hollow) and to dam of high-class sprinter Oasis Dream and Poule d'Essai des Pouliches winner Zenda: 13/2, good impression when winning maiden at Goodwood by head from Silent Secret, weaving through from poor position and not needing to be hard ridden to lead close home: should stay 1¼m: sure to improve. *J. H. M. Gosden* **84 p**

NAMECHECK (GER) 2 ch.c. (Mar 17) Shamardal (USA) 129 – Nadia 116 (Nashwan (USA) 135) [2009 6d³ 7.5g* 8g³ Oct 19] sturdy, compact colt: fourth foal: half-brother to 4-y-o Ace of Spies and French 2008 2-y-o 9f winner Cartel (by Cape Cross): dam French 1¼m (including Prix Saint-Alary) winner: progressive form, winning maiden at Beverley (by 6 lengths) in September before very close third to Gallic Star in listed event at Pontefract: will be suited by 1¼m. *Saeed bin Suroor* **93**

NAMED AT DINNER 8 ch.g. Halling (USA) 133 – Salanka (IRE) 68 (Persian Heights 129) [2009 –: 16m Jun 29] close-coupled gelding: maiden handicapper: retains little ability: tried in headgear. *Miss Lucinda V. Russell* **–**

NAMIBIAN ORATOR (IRE) 3 br.c. Cape Cross (IRE) 129 – Drama Class (IRE) 102 (Caerleon (USA) 132) [2009 10g* 10m⁶ 8m³ 10v⁴ Oct 24] lengthy colt: fifth foal: half-brother to smart 7f (at 2 yrs)/1¼m winner Scottish Stage (by Selkirk) and fairly useful 1¼m winner Voice Coach (by Alhaarth): dam, 1¼m winner, out of sister to high-class performer up to 1¼m Prince of Dance: useful form: won maiden at Windsor in April: off 5 months (amiss second start), in frame in handicaps last 2 starts, at Newmarket (third to Proponent) and Newbury (fourth behind Rainbow Peak): stays 1¼m: acts on heavy and good to firm going: sold 40,000 gns, sent to Bahrain. *Sir Michael Stoute* **96**

Ladbrokes Mallard Stakes (Handicap), Doncaster—
the tough and versatile Nanton is better than ever at the age of seven
and gains a well-deserved big win as he beats Manyriverstocross (hooped cap) and Cosmic Sun (centre)

NAMIR (IRE) 7 b.g. Namid 128 – Danalia (IRE) 78 (Danehill (USA) 126) [2009 86, a74: f5m 6m 5f^2 5g 5m^4 5m^6 5m 5v 5m^6 5g^2 5.1d 5.7g 5m^6 5m^2 5.1g^6 p6g^6 Nov 11] strong, good-topped gelding: fairly useful handicapper on turf, modest on all-weather nowadays: left D. Shaw after tenth start: suited by stiff 5f: acts on polytrack, firm and soft going: tried in cheekpieces/blinkers, wears visor/tongue tie: held up. *H. J. Evans* **85 a60**

NAMPOUR (FR) 4 gr.g. Daylami (IRE) 138 – Nadira (FR) 103 (Green Desert (USA) 127) [2009 12m^4 Sep 13] third foal: half-brother to French 7f winner Nadirana (by Kendor): dam French 10.5f/1½m winner: fairly useful performer: won maiden at Compiegne at 2 yrs and minor event at Nancy in 2008 when trained by A. de Royer Dupre in France: well backed, 2½ lengths fourth to Trachonitis in handicap at Goodwood only outing on Flat in Britain: stays 1½m: acts on soft and good to firm ground: useful hurdler, won in October. *P. J. Hobbs* **89**

NAMU 6 b.m. Mujahid (USA) 125 – Sheraton Heights 52 (Deploy 131) [2009 67: p6g* p7g^6 p6g p7.1g p7g 6.1g 6f^2 6m* 6m^2 5.3f^5 6m^6 p6g 5m 6m^3 p6m^5 5.7g Oct 21] smallish mare: fair handicapper: won at Kempton in January and Brighton in July: stays 7f: acts on polytrack and any turf going: wears cheekpieces: patiently ridden. *Miss T. Spearing* **67**

NANTON (USA) 7 gr. or ro.g. Spinning World (USA) 130 – Grab The Green (USA) (Cozzene (USA)) [2009 101: 8m 10m^2 8m^4 10.4m 7m 10.4m^2 14m^4 14.6m* 10m^4 9m^3 18m p12.2g^4 Dec 11] good-bodied gelding: smart handicapper: won Ladbrokes Mallard Stakes at Doncaster in September by 2¾ lengths from Manyriverstocross: in frame in several other valuable events, doing very well from draw/position when fourth in Hunt Cup at Royal Ascot and Ebor at York, and third to Supaseus in Cambridgeshire at Newmarket third/seventh/tenth starts: top weight, met trouble in running when ninth in Cesarewitch at Newmarket on penultimate outing: stays 14.6f, effective at much shorter: acts on polytrack, firm and good to soft going: held up: tough and versatile, a credit to connections. *J. S. Goldie* **113**

NAOMH GEILEIS (USA) 4 ch.f. Grand Slam (USA) 120 – St Aye (USA) 90 (Nureyev (USA) 131) [2009 p10g p8.6g f8g^5 9.2s 10.2g^4 11.1g 6g^6 f7m* f6f^6 f8f^3 f7m^5 f6d Dec 29] big, lengthy, angular filly: fair performer nowadays: creditable efforts in 2009 on fibresand only, winning at Southwell in November: should stay 1¼m: acts on all-weather, firm and soft going: blinkered nowadays. *M. Johnston* **72**

NAPA STARR (FR) 5 b.g. Marchand de Sable (USA) 117 – Jade d'Eau (IRE) (Lion Cavern (USA) 117) [2009 67§: 7.5v 7m^3 8g* 9g^2 8.5s p8g^2 8g^4 p8g^4 Oct 14] fairly useful handicapper: won at Bellewstown in July: stays 9f: acts on all-weather and good to firm ground: tried blinkered: not one to trust. *Charles Byrnes, Ireland* **81 §**

NAPOLEONS MISTRESS (IRE) 2 ch.f. (Mar 12) Peintre Celebre (USA) 137 – State Crystal (IRE) 114 (High Estate 127) [2009 8.3m^6 Sep 30] compact filly: sister to useful performer up to 11.4f Crystal Curling, 7f winner at 2 yrs, and half-sister to several fairly useful winners, including 1½m winner Time Crystal (by Sadler's Wells): dam, 7f (at 2 yrs) and 1½m (Lancashire Oaks) winner, half-sister to smart performer up to **– p**

1¾m Dubai Success and Fillies' Mile winner Crystal Music: 10/1, sixth to Bint Almatar in maiden at Nottingham, pulling hard: bred to be suited by 1¼m+: capable of better. *P. F. I. Cole*

NAPOLETANO (GER) 8 b.g. Soviet Star (USA) 128 – Noble House (GER) (Siberian Express (USA) 125) [2009 78: p7g^6 p8g p7g 8m^2 7m^4 7g^5 7.6f 7m 7g^2 7m^3 8m^6 p7g^5 Oct 14] strong gelding: fair handicapper: free-going sort, effective at 7f/1m: acts on polytrack, firm and soft ground: wears cheekpieces. *S. Dow* **73**

NAPOLETANO (ITY) 3 b.g. Kyllachy 129 – Nationality (Nashwan (USA) 135) [2009 f7g 12.4g 10.1s 12d Aug 26] little form. *R. Johnson* **–**

NASEBY (USA) 2 ch.c. (Apr 28) Maria's Mon (USA) 121 – Branchbury (USA) (Mt Livermore (USA)) [2009 p7g p7m p6f Oct 14] no impact in maiden/claimers, leaving R. Charlton after second start. *Miss S. L. Davison* **–**

NASEEHAH (USA) 3 ch.c. Rahy (USA) 115 – Helwa (USA) (Silver Hawk (USA) 123) [2009 p9.5g* p9.5g^2 a8f^2 Dec 18] $70,000F, 175,000Y: fourth foal: half-brother to winner in USA by Spinning World: dam unraced sister to dam of smart 1¼m performer Silver Pivotal: landed odds in maiden at Wolverhampton in October: subsequently good second in handicaps, on same course (to Snow Dancer, left Saeed bin Suroor after) and Jebel Ali (behind Blues Ballad): will be suited by 1¼m+. *A. bin Huzaim, UAE* **98**

NASHMIAH (IRE) 3 b.f. Elusive City (USA) 117 – Frond 85 (Alzao (USA) 117) [2009 98: p7g* 8f 8s* 8f 7m^5 9.9d 8.1g^3 9.9g* 10.1m* 8m 10d^4 Oct 25] tall, good-topped filly: smart performer: won listed races at Lingfield in March, York in May, Goodwood (handicap) in August and Yarmouth (readily beat Mooakada ¾ length) in September: good close fourth to Eva's Request in Premio Lydia Tesio at Rome final outing, staying on well: stays 1¼m: acts on polytrack, soft and good to firm going. *C. E. Brittain* **114**

Mr Saeed Manana's "Nashmiah"

NASRI 3 b.c. Kyllachy 129 – Triple Sharp 80 (Selkirk (USA) 129) [2009 106p: 7s^{6} 7m^{2} **105**
7g^{3} 7m Jun 17] well-made colt: useful performer: creditable effort in 2009 only when 1¾ lengths second to Alyarf in listed race at Newmarket: will stay 1m: acts on firm and good to soft going. *B. J. Meehan*

NASSAR (IRE) 6 b.h. Danehill (USA) 126 – Regent Gold (USA) (Seeking The Gold **69**
(USA)) [2009 61: p10g^{5} p9.5g* p10g^{3} 11.9f^{3} 10m^{4} 10d^{5} 11.5g^{4} 10m^{3} 9.7s p9.5g^{4} p10g^{6} Nov 1] compact horse: fair handicapper: won at Wolverhampton in April: stays 1½m: acts on all-weather and firm going: usually in cheekpieces/visor: often starts slowly. *G. Prodromou*

NASSAU BEACH (IRE) 3 b.g. Bahamian Bounty 116 – Oh'cecilia (IRE) 95 (Scenic **46**
128) [2009 –p: 6m^{5} 7m 8m^{5} 5m Jun 19] big, rangy gelding: poor maiden: should be suited by at least 7f: raced only on good/good to firm ground. *T. D. Easterby*

NATALIE N G 2 b.f. (Apr 24) Zamindar (USA) 116 – Tango Teaser (Shareef Dancer **–**
(USA) 135) [2009 6s Nov 7] seventh foal: half-sister to 3 winners, including 8-y-o After The Show: dam, ran twice, out of smart miler Ever Genial: 66/1, down the field in maiden at Doncaster (prominent to 2f out). *J. R. Jenkins*

NATHAN DEE 4 ch.g. Guys And Dolls 113 – Blu Air Flow (ITY) (Entrepreneur 123) **–**
[2009 –: f11g Apr 27] workmanlike gelding: maiden, no form since 2 yrs: tried blinkered/in cheekpieces/tongue tied: sometimes races freely. *M. R. Bosley*

NATIONAL MONUMENT (IRE) 3 b.g. Statue of Liberty (USA) 115 – Panpipes **68**
(USA) 69 (Woodman (USA) 126) [2009 p8g^{3} p8.6g^{3} p9.5g^{4} 11.9f p10m Sep 26] medium-sized gelding: fair maiden: off 5½ months, well held in handicaps last 2 starts: stays 8.6f: acts on polytrack. *J. A. Osborne*

NATIVE DAME (IRE) 3 b.f. Spartacus (IRE) 107 – Wisecrack (IRE) (Lucky Guest **65 d**
109) [2009 50: p8g^{4} p6g^{3} 12.1g p10g 7.1m^{2} 6d^{6} 7f^{5} p6m p6m Dec 10] good-topped ex-Irish filly: fair maiden handicapper: left P. Deegan after second start: stays 1m: acts on polytrack and good to firm going: tried tongue tied: often blinkered. *Edgar Byrne*

NATIVE RULER 3 b.c. Cape Cross (IRE) 129 – Love Divine 120 (Diesis 133) [2009 **106**
10m^{2} 10g* 10.4g 12f 10d^{3} Aug 7] big, well-made colt: type to carry condition: fifth foal: half-brother to 3 winners, notably high-class 1¼m to 1¾m (St Leger) winner Sixties Icon (by Galileo): dam, 1¼m/1½m (Oaks) winner, out of close relation to Champion Stakes winner Legal Case: useful form: won maiden at Pontefract in April: good 4¼ lengths seventh to Black Bear Island in Dante Stakes at York next time: unable to build on that after, including when third to Prince Siegfried in minor event at Newmarket: should stay 1½m: best form on good ground. *H. R. A. Cecil*

NATIVITY 3 ch.f. Kyllachy 129 – Mistral's Dancer (Shareef Dancer (USA) 135) [2009 **67**
61: 5.1f 5m^{6} 7f 6m^{2} 6m p6m^{2} p7m^{5} p7g^{6} p6f^{2} p6f^{5} Dec 21] smallish filly: fair maiden **a61**
on turf, modest on all-weather: stays 7f: acts on polytrack and firm going: none too consistent. *J. L. Spearing*

NATURAL FLAIR (USA) 3 ch.f. Giant's Causeway (USA) 132 – Forest Lady (USA) **90**
(Woodman (USA) 126) [2009 82p: 10s* 10f 11d^{6} 10m^{4} 10g* 10.5s Nov 7] well-made filly: poor mover in slower paces: fairly useful performer: successful at Newbury in maiden in April and handicap (beat Flora Trevelyan by length) in October: well held in listed race at Le Croise-Laroche final outing: will stay 1½m: acts on soft going, well below form both starts on firmer than good. *P. W. Chapple-Hyam*

NATURAL LAW (IRE) 2 b.g. (Feb 20) Lomitas 129 – Flying Squaw 102 (Be My **80**
Chief (USA) 122) [2009 8.1d 8.5m^{3} p8m* 10g^{5} Oct 31] 100,000Y: lengthy gelding: seventh foal: brother to smart 6f (at 2 yrs) to 11f winner Championship Point and half-brother to 2 winners, including fairly useful 7f winner Straight Sets (by Pivotal): dam 2-y-o 5f/6f winner: progressive in maidens, winning at Kempton in September by 1¼ lengths from Inside Track (dictated): below-form fifth (finished weakly) in minor event at Newmarket: gelded after: should stay 1¼m: acts on polytrack and good to firm going: in cheekpieces/visor last 2 starts. *Saeed bin Suroor*

NATURAL RHYTHM (IRE) 4 ch.g. Distant Music (USA) 126 – Nationalartgallery **62 §**
(IRE) (Tate Gallery (USA) 117) [2009 67§: 8.3m 8d 8d 8m 9.2d^{6} 8.5g* 8.1v^{5} 8s 8m p8.6g 9.1v^{4} Oct 31] lengthy, good-topped gelding: modest handicapper: won at Beverley in July: stays 1¼m: acts on all-weather and any turf ground: often in headgear: front runner: untrustworthy. *Mrs R. A. Carr*

NAUGHTY GIRL (IRE) 9 b.m. Dr Devious (IRE) 127 – Mary Magdalene 78 (Night **– §**
Shift (USA)) [2009 52§: f8s f8g Feb 5] smallish, sturdy mare: one-time fair performer: no form in 2009: temperamental. *John A. Harris*

NAUGHTY NORRIS 2 ch.g. (Mar 29) Needwood Blade 117 – Leave It To Lib 66 (Tender King 123) [2009 6s 7m 8.3v Nov 4] close-coupled gelding: well held in maidens. *R. Bastiman* –

NAUTICAL 11 gr.g. Lion Cavern (USA) 117 – Russian Royal (USA) 108 (Nureyev (USA) 131) [2009 63: f6s^2 f7g^4 f6g f8g^2 p8g p9.5g* f8g Mar 12] good-topped gelding: modest handicapper: won at Wolverhampton in February: was effective at 6f to 9.5f: acted on all-weather, firm and good to soft going: tried in headgear/tongue strap: looked awkward under pressure: dead. *J. R. Holt* **52**

NAVAJO CHIEF 2 b.c. (Feb 1) King's Best (USA) 132 – Navajo Rainbow (Rainbow Quest (USA) 134) [2009 5m* 6m^5 7m^3 7v Oct 24] workmanlike colt: third foal: half-brother to Italian winner around 1¼m Flyfong (by Dr Fong): dam unraced half-sister to very smart Irish 1m/1¼m winner Jammaal: fairly useful performer: won minor event at Windsor in June: ran creditably in minor event at Newmarket/listed event at Ascot (9 lengths third to Nideeb) next 2 starts: very stiff task when last in Horris Hill Stakes at Newbury: stays 7f: acts on good to firm ground. *A. P. Jarvis* **80**

NAVAJO JOE (IRE) 4 ch.g. Indian Ridge 123 – Maid of Killeen (IRE) 97 (Darshaan 133) [2009 91: f12g^5 f7g^6 7s 7s^3 7m 6.9g 6d^6 6m 8g Sep 30] useful-looking gelding: fair handicapper: well below form last 5 starts: stays 1¼m: acts on polytrack and soft going: tried blinkered/tongue tied: inconsistent: temperament under suspicion. *R. Johnson* **77**

NAVAJO NATION (IRE) 3 b.g. Indian Haven 119 – Kathy Desert (Green Desert (USA) 127) [2009 73: 7g^3 11d 10.1g^2 p10g 11.5m^4 p9.5g^6 10g^3 Oct 5] good-topped gelding: fair maiden: claimed £8,000 and joined W. G. M. Turner after final outing: may prove best short of 1¼m: best form on good ground: tried blinkered. *B. J. Meehan* **73**

NAVENE (IRE) 5 b.m. Desert Style (IRE) 121 – Majudel (IRE) (Revoque (IRE) 122) [2009 74: 8.3g May 19] good-topped mare: fair handicapper in 2008: last sole outing in 2009 (said to have finished distressed): free-going sort, stays 1m: acts on good to firm and good to soft going: carries head high. *C. F. Wall* –

NAVE (USA) 2 b.c. (Apr 30) Pulpit (USA) 117 – Lakabi (USA) 63 (Nureyev (USA) 131) [2009 6v 6m^3 6v p6g^6 p7.1g^4 p8m* p8g^2 p8m^2 Dec 9] $100,000Y: tall, unfurnished colt: sixth foal: brother to useful 7f/1m winner Throne of Power and half-brother to several winners, including smart French 1m winner (including at 2 yrs) Soneva (by Cherokee Run): dam ran once: fair performer: won nursery at Kempton in November: good second in similar company last 2 starts: shapes as if will stay 1¼m: acts on polytrack and good to firm ground. *M. Johnston* **75**

NAVY LIST (FR) 2 b.c. (Apr 10) Nayef (USA) 129 – Fasliyeva (FR) (Fasliyev (USA) 120) [2009 7g p8m^2 p8g^2 9m* 8g^5 Oct 23] €80,000Y, €165,000 2-y-o: useful-looking colt: first foal: dam, ran 3 times in France, half-sister to useful French sprinter Marchand Volant: useful performer: won maiden at Redcar in September by 11 lengths: good 1¾ lengths fifth to Antoniola in nursery at Doncaster, squeezed out late: stays 9f: acts on polytrack and good to firm going. *Saeed bin Suroor* **99**

NAWAADI (USA) 3 ch.g. El Corredor (USA) 123 – Louise's Time (USA) (Gilded Time (USA)) [2009 84p: p8g^6 10m 9.9m^4 12s 10g^2 10m^5 p12g^6 10g Dec 24] tall, useful-looking gelding: fairly useful handicapper: left J. Gosden 36,000 gns before final start: stays 1½m: acts on polytrack and good to firm going: tried visored. *M. Mubarak, Qatar* **80**

NAWAAFF 4 ch.g. Compton Place 125 – Amazed 58 (Clantime 101) [2009 76d: p6g^4 p5.1g* p6g p5g 7m 5.7m 6d 6d 6m^5 6m^3 p5m^5 p6m Dec 16] leggy, quite good-topped gelding: modest performer nowadays: won handicap at Wolverhampton in February: left M. Channon 4,200 gns after tenth start: effective at 5f to 7f: acts on polytrack, good to firm and good to soft ground: tried visored. *M. Quinn* **55**

NAWAMEES (IRE) 11 b.g. Darshaan 133 – Truly Generous (IRE) 104 (Generous (IRE) 139) [2009 84: p12.2g^4 f12g* f12g* p12.2g^5 f12g^4 p12g^2 11.7m f12g^4 12g* 12m f12g^5 11.8m^3 11.6m^2 12.1v^4 p12.2g^6 11m^2 11.6f^4 12m^4 15.9m^4 12g p13g 12v^6 p13.9g f12m^4 p12m^6 Nov 27] close-coupled gelding: fair performer: won seller/claimer at Southwell in January/February, and seller at Catterick in May: effective at 1¼m to easy 2m: acts on all-weather, soft and firm going: tried blinkered, wears cheekpieces: has hung: usually races up with pace. *P. D. Evans* **74**

NAWOJKA (IRE) 3 gr.f. Daylami (IRE) 138 – Panna 106 (Polish Precedent (USA) 131) [2009 50p: 8.3g 10.2v^6 Jul 17] medium-sized filly: modest maiden: will stay 1½m. *J. G. Given* **53**

NAXOX (FR) 8 ch.g. Cupidon (FR) – Frou Frou Lou (FR) (Groom Dancer (USA) 128) [2009 p13.9m^2 f12f^6 Dec 12] ex-French gelding: won 2 non-thoroughbred events in **74**

2004/2005 for M. Postic: fair hurdler/chaser for Venetia Williams: seemingly fair form when second in claimer at Wolverhampton on British Flat debut: likely to stay 2m. *George Baker*

NAYEF STAR 4 b.g. Nayef (USA) 129 – Satin Bell 99 (Midyan (USA) 124) [2009 10.4v³ May 21] better effort in maidens 18 months apart when sixth to Foolin Myself at Newmarket: travelled well for long way at Haydock: may prove best around 1m. *J. Noseda* **62**

NAYESSENCE 3 ch.g. Nayef (USA) 129 – Fragrant Oasis (USA) 113 (Rahy (USA) 115) [2009 54: 10g⁴ 12s⁶ Oct 27] rangy gelding: modest maiden: stays 1¼m: best efforts on good going: tongue tied. *M. W. Easterby* **59**

NAYWYE 3 b.f. Nayef (USA) 129 – Mount Hillaby (IRE) 80 (Mujadil (USA) 119) [2009 f6g f6g May 1] first foal: dam 7f (including at 2 yrs)/8.6f winner: no form in claimers at Southwell. *M. W. Easterby* **–**

NAZREEF 2 b.c. (May 12) Zafeen (FR) 123 – Roofer (IRE) 80 (Barathea (IRE) 127) [2009 f8f* Nov 24] third foal: half-brother to 3-y-o Assail and 2006 2-y-o 5f winner Relkida (by Bertolini): dam, maiden who stayed 9f, half-sister to smart 7f/1m winner Brunel: 6/1, won minor event at Southwell by 3¾ lengths from Mighty Mambo, making all: unlikely to stay much beyond 1m. *H. Morrison* **79**

NBHAN (USA) 3 b.c. With Approval (CAN) – Crisp And Cool (USA) (Ogygian (USA)) [2009 73p: 10m³ 10m² 10s² p8.6g³ 10m Sep 11] leggy colt: fairly useful maiden: stays 1¼m: acts on polytrack, soft and good to firm ground: sold 17,000 gns, sent to Saudi Arabia. *L. M. Cumani* **83**

NCHIKE 3 b.g. Zaha (CAN) 106 – Tinkerbird 76 (Music Boy 124) [2009 64: f7g 7m 7.1m⁴ 6s² 8f f8g⁵ 6d 7v⁶ 10.1m Sep 16] workmanlike gelding: modest performer: left D. Nicholls after sixth outing: stays 7f: acts on soft and good to firm going: usually in headgear. *R. C. Guest* **64**

NDOLA 10 b.g. Emperor Jones (USA) 119 – Lykoa (Shirley Heights 130) [2009 58: p12g⁴ p13.9g Mar 2] rather leggy gelding: poor performer: stays 1½m: acts on all-weather, best turf effort on good going: usually in headgear. *P. Butler* **44**

NEAR THE FRONT 4 b.g. Compton Place 125 – Once In My Life (IRE) 114 (Lomond (USA) 128) [2009 61: p11g² Feb 14] leggy gelding: modest maiden: likely to prove best short of 11f: acts on polytrack and soft going: visored last 4 starts at 3 yrs. *Miss Gay Kelleway* **59**

NEAT 'N TIDY 5 b.m. Josr Algarhoud (IRE) 118 – Raspberry Sauce 65 (Niniski (USA) 125) [2009 –: 7.1v p6g Nov 20] stocky mare: of little account nowadays, including over hurdles. *A. E. Jones* **–**

NEBOISHA 5 ch.m. Ishiguru (USA) 114 – Mariette 35 (Blushing Scribe (USA) 107) [2009 10m 8.3m 7d Jun 10] modest maiden: stayed 7f: raced on polytrack, good to soft and good to firm ground: tried blinkered: dead. *M. Wigham* **50**

NEBULA STORM (IRE) 2 b.c. (Jan 22) Galileo (IRE) 134 – Epping 81 (Charnwood Forest (IRE) 125) [2009 7s 7s* Nov 5] 470,000F, 460,000Y: fourth foal: brother to smart 1¼m/1½m winner and St Leger runner-up The Last Drop and half-brother to fairly useful French 1m winner Cherry Orchard (by King's Best): dam, 7f winner from 3 starts, closely related to smart performer up to 1¾m Self Defense, out of half-sister to Irish Oaks winner Princess Pati and high-class 1½m performer Seymour Hicks: much better effort in maidens (useful form) when winning at Leopardstown by 1¼ lengths from Is Feidir Linn, staying on strongly: will be suited by 1¼m+: sure to improve further. *John M. Oxx, Ireland* **101 p**

NED LUDD (IRE) 6 b.g. Montjeu (IRE) 137 – Zanella (IRE) 87 (Nordico (USA)) [2009 85: 16s 16g³ 16g⁶ 16d Oct 11] leggy, close-coupled gelding: fair maiden handicapper nowadays: stays 2¾m: acts on soft and good to firm ground. *J. G. Portman* **78**

NEDUARDO 2 ch.c. (Mar 12) Monsieur Bond (IRE) 120 – Bond Shakira 54 (Daggers Drawn (USA) 114) [2009 p6m⁵ Nov 21] 5,000F, €17,000Y: second foal: brother to 3-y-o Fangfoss Girls: dam sprint maiden: 11/2 and green, 8¾ lengths fifth of 11 to Pittodrie Star in maiden at Kempton, late headway not knocked about: capable of better. *P. W. Chapple-Hyam* **43 p**

NEEDSAMAITE 2 b.c. (Jan 23) Needwood Blade 117 – Dekelsmary 61 (Komaite (USA)) [2009 5m⁴ Apr 13] sturdy colt: 12/1 and green, 3 lengths fourth to Transfixed in seller at Warwick: not seen out again. *D. J. S. ffrench Davis* **41**

NEEDS A TREAT 2 b.f. (Mar 19) Needwood Blade 117 – Goes A Treat (IRE) 82 (Common Grounds 118) [2009 5f⁵ 5m Apr 30] 4,000Y: fourth foal: half-sister to 2 winners, including 2004 2-y-o 5f/6f winner Treat Me Wild (by Loup Sauvage), later 7f winner in Jersey: dam 6.8f winner: little show in claimer/seller. *N. Tinkler* –

NEEDWOOD DANCER 2 br.f. (Apr 1) Needwood Blade 117 – Waterline Dancer (IRE) 69 (Danehill Dancer (IRE) 117) [2009 p5g 5m⁶ 5.1m p5.1g⁴ 5.2g⁵ May 29] no form: tried blinkered: dead. *Peter Grayson* –

NEEDY MCCREDIE 3 ch.f. Needwood Blade 117 – Vocation (IRE) 74 (Royal Academy (USA) 130) [2009 7d 7s⁵ 8m 7.1m Sep 14] fourth foal: half-sister to 8-y-o Divine Spirit: dam 2-y-o 7f winner: poor maiden: raced only at 7f/1m. *J. R. Turner* **42**

NEFYN 2 b.f. (Mar 16) Tiger Hill (IRE) 127 – Bread of Heaven 79 (Machiavellian (USA) 123) [2009 8m⁶ 8g p8.6g Oct 29] second foal: dam, 2-y-o 6f winner, half-sister to smart 7f/1m performer Trans Island: modest form first 2 starts in maidens (flashed tail in latter). *W. R. Muir* **61**

NEGOTIATION (IRE) 3 b.g. Refuse To Bend (IRE) 128 – Dona Royale (IRE) 86 (Darshaan 133) [2009 p7g³ 8d* 8.1g² 8m* 9g Aug 30] 150,000Y: half-brother to 3 winners, including 2003 2-y-o 7f winner Old Malt (later successful abroad) and 8.6f/9.5f winner Bazelle (both fairly useful, by Ashkalani): dam, second at 1m/1¼m in Ireland all 3 starts, half-sister to very smart performers Royal Touch (up to 9f) and Foresee (up to 1¾m): fairly useful form: won maiden at Yarmouth in April and handicap at Newmarket (by neck from Russian Jar) in August: should stay 1¼m: unraced on extremes of going: sold 18,000 gns. *J. H. M. Gosden* **93**

NEHAAM 3 b.g. Nayef (USA) 129 – Charm The Stars (Roi Danzig (USA)) [2009 93P: 10m* 10.4g 12f 14m² 16m² Oct 17] lengthy, useful-looking gelding: has fluent action: smart performer: won £400000 Tattersalls Timeform 3-Y-O Trophy at Newmarket (beat Monitor Closely by head) in April: well held in Dante Stakes at York and King Edward VII Stakes at Royal Ascot next 2 starts: off 3½ months and gelded, back to form when second to Akmal at Newmarket last 2 starts, beaten ½ length in Jockey Club Cup final outing: stays 2m: raced only on good going or firmer. *J. H. M. Gosden* **111**

£400000 Tattersalls Timeform 3-Y-O Trophy, Newmarket—the richest three-year-old race of the British season, outside the classics, sees Nehaam (No.9) edge out Monitor Closely (white face); the last-named had come sixth the previous autumn in the Tattersalls Timeform Million, the flagship event in this particularly valuable series of sales races which will have a change of format from 2010

NELSONS PROSPECT (IRE) 4 b.g. Fayruz 116 – Kiva (Indian Ridge 123) [2009 p10g Jun 27] showed nothing in maiden at Lingfield. *R. A. Teal* **–**

NEMO SPIRIT (IRE) 4 gr.g. Daylami (IRE) 138 – La Bayadere 83 (Sadler's Wells (USA) 132) [2009 97: p16g⁴ 16.2g 16.4d* 16.4g 14v² 18m Oct 17] big, workmanlike gelding: useful handicapper: won at York in June by ¾ length from Hawk Mountain: creditable second to Yes Mr President in Old Borough Cup at Haydock after: firmer ground, folded tamely in Cesarewitch final outing: stays 16.4f: acts on polytrack and heavy going: front runner: sold 100,000 gns, then gelded. *W. R. Muir* **99**

NEON BLUE 8 b. or br.g. Atraf 116 – Desert Lynx (IRE) 79 (Green Desert (USA) 127) [2009 66: 10m⁴ 10g 9m 9.3m 9.9m⁴ 10m 10m 12.1m⁶ 10.4d 10g Oct 16] smallish, compact gelding: modest performer at best in 2009: stays 1¼m: acts on firm and soft going (below form all 3 starts on all-weather): effective with or without headgear: often slowly away: slipped up sixth outing. *R. M. Whitaker* **60 d**

NEO'S MATE (IRE) 3 br.f. Modigliani (USA) 106 – Gute (IRE) 77 (Petardia 113) [2009 45§: p6g 5f 6m* 8.1s⁶ 6d* 7g⁵ 5.9d⁵ p8.6g p8.6g p6g p7.1g² Dec 17] close-coupled, good-topped filly: modest handicapper: won twice at Catterick in July (maiden first occasion): stays 7f: acts on polytrack, good to firm and good to soft going: held up. *Paul Green* **59**

NEPOTISM 2 b.c. (Mar 29) Piccolo 121 – Craic Sa Ceili (IRE) 83 (Danehill Dancer (IRE) 117) [2009 5.1f⁵ 5.7f 5g² 5m* p5f⁶ Sep 4] sturdy colt: fair performer: made all in maiden at Lingfield in June: well below form in nursery final start: best at bare 5f: acts on good to firm going. *M. S. Saunders* **69**

NERO WEST (FR) 8 ch.g. Pelder (IRE) 125 – West River (USA) (Gone West (USA)) [2009 79: p13.9g Jan 19] good-topped gelding: fair handicapper in 2008: well held sole outing in 2009: stays 2m: acts on any turf going: wears cheekpieces/blinkers: edgy sort. *I. Semple* **–**

NESAYEM (IRE) 3 b.f. Diktat 126 – Zibet 90 (Kris 135) [2009 68: 8.3g⁴ 7.5g⁴ p10g³ 10m⁵ 10.3m² 11.9d⁴ Oct 15] leggy filly: fair maiden: stays 1¼m: poor efforts both starts on softer than good: sold 6,500 gns. *D. M. Simcock* **68**

NESNO (USA) 6 ch.g. Royal Academy (USA) 130 – Cognac Lady (USA) (Olympio (USA)) [2009 74: 8m p9.5g p8.6g Oct 17] big, lengthy gelding: fair handicapper: below form in 2009: stays 11f: acts on polytrack and firm going: often in headgear: has found little: races up with pace. *J. D. Bethell* **66**

NETTA (IRE) 3 b.f. Barathea (IRE) 127 – Nishan (Nashwan (USA) 135) [2009 63p: 8d⁴ 7m* 8.1d Sep 16] big, lengthy filly: fairly useful form: won maiden at Salisbury in August: possibly amiss on handicap debut at Sandown next time: bred to stay 1¼m+: acts on good to firm going. *P. J. Makin* **86**

NETWORKER 6 ch.g. Danzig Connection (USA) – Trevorsninepoints 71 (Jester 119) [2009 77: p8g p7g³ 7d p8.6g⁴ 8.5g² 7g⁴ p9.5g³ Dec 18] workmanlike gelding: fair handicapper: stays 9.5f: acts on polytrack, firm and good to soft going: has shaped as if amiss, including on reappearance. *P. J. McBride* **74**

NEUCHATEL (GER) 3 b.g. Rahy (USA) 115 – Nalani (IRE) 104 (Sadler's Wells (USA) 132) [2009 83p: p10m⁴ a7.5g a7g a8g⁶ a10.5g* a11.5g* a11.5g* a11g⁶ a10.5g* Dec 5] good-bodied gelding: fairly useful performer at best: sold from M. Johnston £11,000 after reappearance: successful at Mons in claiming handicap, 2 minor events and handicap between September and December: stays 11.5f: won only start on turf, raced on dirt/polytrack otherwise. *Mme L. Braem, Belgium* **75 +**

NEVA A MULL MOMENT (IRE) 3 b.g. Mull of Kintyre (USA) 114 – Serious Contender (IRE) (Tenby 125) [2009 –: 7f³ 7d³ 5m³ 6d² 6g Sep 3] lengthy gelding: fair maiden: stays 7f: acts on good to soft ground: sold £800 and joined R. Barr. *D. Nicholls* **69**

NEVADA DESERT (IRE) 9 b.g. Desert King (IRE) 129 – Kayanga (Green Desert (USA) 127) [2009 87: 8.5m 8.1v 9d 8v⁶ 8.5m⁶ 8s⁶ 8g 8.1m p9.5g p9.5g² p9.5g* 10.3g* p9.5g Oct 31] useful-looking gelding: fairly useful handicapper: won at Wolverhampton and Doncaster in October: stays 11f: acts on all-weather and any turf going: tried in cheekpieces/tongue strap: tends to carry head high. *R. M. Whitaker* **86**

NEVE LIEVE (IRE) 4 b.f. Dubai Destination (USA) 127 – Love of Silver (USA) 110 (Arctic Tern (USA) 126) [2009 89: 15m⁶ 14m⁵ May 16] good-topped filly: fairly useful performer at 3 yrs: below form both starts in 2009: stays 2m: best form on good ground or softer (acts on heavy): effective with or without headgear: makes running/races prominently: sent to Italy. *M. Botti* **80**

NEVER ENDING TALE 4 ch.g. Singspiel (IRE) 133 – Bright Finish (USA) 108 (Zilzal (USA) 137) [2009 88: p8.6g² 10.3m* 8.1g Jun 20] strong, lengthy gelding: fairly useful handicapper: won at Doncaster in June by neck from Shady Gloom: possibly amiss final start: stays 10.3f: acts on polytrack and good to firm going: in cheekpieces last 2 starts: quirky. *E. F. Vaughan* **91**

NEVER LOSE 3 br.f. Diktat 126 – Enchanted Princess 82 (Royal Applause 124) [2009 81: f6d* p6g p7g p6g⁴ 7d* 6v³ 5m⁴ 7g 8d 6g⁵ 6m Oct 16] tall, good-topped filly: useful performer: won maiden at Southwell in March and handicap at Newbury in May: needs good test at 6f, barely stays 1m: acts on all-weather, heavy and good to firm going: quirky (tried blinkered). *C. E. Brittain* **95**

NEVER ON SUNDAY (FR) 4 gr.c. Sunday Break (JPN) 121 – Hexane (FR) 108 (Kendor (FR) 122) [2009 118: 10g⁵ 9.3s* 10m³ 8m 10m Oct 17] **125**

French trainer Jean-Claude Rouget failed to add to his solitary British success, despite saddling some runners with leading chances in the latest season. His Pouliches winner Elusive Wave managed no better than fourth behind Ghanaati in the Coronation Stakes at Royal Ascot and the high-class four-year-old Never On Sunday was beaten on both his trips across the English Channel. However, the stable had an extremely successful year on home turf. Rouget began by training jumpers in the 'eighties before switching his attention to the Flat and he has habitually been the leading trainer in France by number of winners from his base at Pau near the Spanish border, with a record 242 wins in 1994. However, it wasn't until 2009 that he finally became champion trainer by total prize money. His 188 wins (his lowest tally since 2003, ironically) and his 340 places yielded over €6.1m, putting Rouget around €2.3 million clear of runner-up Alain de Royer Dupre. What made the difference for Rouget was winning six Group 1 races, including three classics, Le Havre in the Prix du Jockey Club and Stacelita in the Prix de Diane adding to the success of Elusive Wave. Stacelita also gained two more Group 1 wins, in the Prix Saint Alary and the Prix Vermeille, while Never On Sunday also got in on the act, his victory coming in the Prix d'Ispahan in May.

The d'Ispahan was in the news mostly for the return to action of the Breeders' Cup Mile winner Goldikova. Loup Breton and Never On Sunday seemed her main challengers and both had already been out, finishing fourth and fifth respectively to Trincot in the Group 2 Prix d'Harcourt at Longchamp six weeks before. Loup Breton, better off at the weights, was second choice in the market for the d'Ispahan, ahead of Never On Sunday but neither he nor Goldikova, who appeared unsuited by the soft ground and could finish only seventh, gave their running. Never On Sunday, by contrast, handled the conditions well and stepped up on his previous form, coming through to lead in the final furlong and win by a length from Gris de Gris, who had won the Group 3 Prix Edmond Blanc and been second in the Group 2 Prix du Muguet on his first two starts of the year. Outsiders filled the next two places.

The d'Ispahan was Never On Sunday's seventh win from ten starts, the prize money for his victory greater than that for his six other successes combined. He won both his starts as a two-year-old, in the autumn over a mile at Toulouse and

Prix d'Ispahan, Longchamp—the greys Never On Sunday and Gris de Gris (noseband) battle it out; outsiders Runaway (blaze) and Celebrissime (rail), the latter a pacemaker for disappointing favourite Goldikova (out of shot), complete the 1,2,3,4

Lyon Parilly. He was returned to the latter track for his first start at three, winning a minor event, again over a mile before meeting defeat on his first two starts at the Parisian tracks, though two of the three who finished in front of him at Saint-Cloud on the first occasion also won pattern events subsequently, and he was beaten just a nose at Longchamp the time after. The fitting of blinkers saw Never On Sunday back in the winner's circle on his next two starts, in a minor event at Chantilly and in a listed race at the same track, stepped up to a mile and a quarter for the first time on the second occasion. Rouget himself has described Never On Sunday as 'a slightly complicated individual' and that showed on his next appearance. Again declared to wear blinkers, Never On Sunday wouldn't let them be fitted before the Group 3 Prix du Prince d'Orange at Longchamp. It made not one whit of difference, he won without them and hasn't worn them since.

The d'Ispahan was followed for Never On Sunday by the Prince of Wales's Stakes. If anything, the form he showed in finishing third behind the previous year's Prix du Jockey Club winner Vision d'Etat and Derby runner-up Tartan Bearer was better than his d'Ispahan form. Never On Sunday did well the way the race developed too, having to come from behind in a steadily-run affair, though he might have done even better had he not jinked left under pressure in the last seventy-five yards, probably costing him second. In the light of Never On Sunday's efforts at Longchamp and Royal Ascot, his two subsequent runs were something of a let down. Dropped back to a mile for the first time in listed or pattern company, he was struggling from some way out in the Prix Jacques le Marois at Deauville, managing only seventh of nine to Goldikova. Worse followed when Never On Sunday was returned to Britain for the Champion Stakes at Newmarket, the race in which Rouget had gained his previous British victory, in the 2007 running with Literato. Another win never looked on the cards for second favourite Never On Sunday, who shaped as if possibly amiss, finishing only tenth to Twice Over, who had been behind him in the Prince of Wales's Stakes.

Never On Sunday is a son of Sunday Break, who carries the Japan suffix but raced in the United States. Sunday Break, whose dam ran twice for James Fanshawe in Britain, was a very smart winner at nine furlongs in the Grade 2 Peter Pan Stakes and came a respectable third in the Belmont Stakes. Sunday Break was at stud in the States when Never On Sunday was conceived, though he has since been transferred to Normandy, joining an eclectic team of stallions at the Haras de Grandcamp (headed by the Lingfield Derby Trial winner Linda's Lad, who had been sent to Arnaud Chaille-Chaille for a hurdling career but never started over jumps). Sunday Break struggled to attract mares in the States and his most notable performer is Never On Sunday. The first four dams on the distaff side of Never On Sunday's pedigree were all above average, the fourth dam Tamoure a winner of the Prix d'Astarte. The third dam Texan Girl won handicaps at a mile and a half at Evry and Maisons-Laffitte (two); while both the grandam Texan Beauty and dam Hexane were useful, Texan Beauty winning at up to around ten and a half furlongs, Hexane racing at seven furlongs and a mile. Hexane finished second in the Prix de Sandringham and is a half-sister to another useful miler in Texalina. All told, Texan Beauty has foaled five winners, including Hexane's sister Texalouna, yet another miler. Prior to Never On Sunday, Hexane had three winners, minor ones in the States by Cape Town and Geri and the fairly useful British-trained middle-distance stayer Just Intersky (by Distant View). Her 2007 foal by Gold Away, named Round Midnight, has yet to race. Her latest foal, by Dubawi, was withdrawn from the Tattersalls Foal Sales in December.

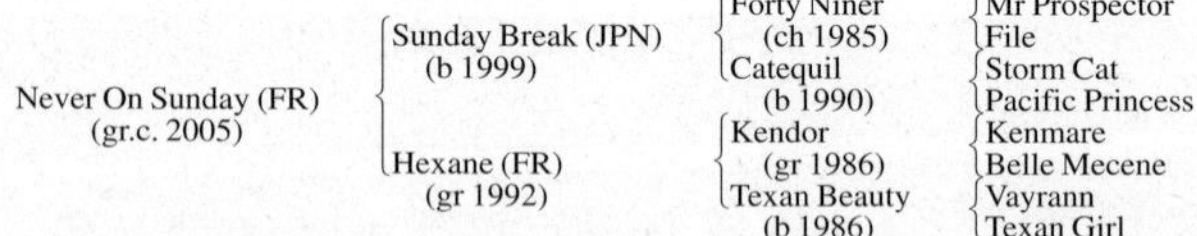

Never On Sunday (FR) (gr.c. 2005)	Sunday Break (JPN) (b 1999)	Forty Niner (ch 1985)	Mr Prospector
			File
		Catequil (b 1990)	Storm Cat
			Pacific Princess
	Hexane (FR) (gr 1992)	Kendor (gr 1986)	Kenmare
			Belle Mecene
		Texan Beauty (b 1986)	Vayrann
			Texan Girl

Never On Sunday has also skipped an appointment in the sale-ring, being withdrawn from the Arc Sale in 2008 after his win in the Prince d'Orange. Never On Sunday is a sturdy colt in appearance and he showed a round action to post at

Ascot. He has raced at up to a mile and a quarter and is not certain to stay further. He acts on soft and good to firm going. It is fair to say Never On Sunday, who has joined Patrick Biancone in the States, hasn't lived up to his name, since three of his seven wins have been achieved on the day of rest. Monday, Wednesday, Thursday and Saturday have produced a single victory each. As things stand, Never On Tuesday or Friday might have been a more appropriate name, though neither of those was the title of an Oscar-winning film starring Melina Mercouri. *J-C. Rouget, France*

NEVER SOLD OUT (IRE) 4 ch.g. Captain Rio 122 – Vicious Rosie (Dancing Spree (USA)) [2009 55: p7g 7m^4 8.1g 8f^3 10.2m 8f 8m Aug 21] modest performer: stays 1¼m: acts on polytrack and firm going: tried blinkered/visored: signs of temperament. *J. G. M. O'Shea* **55**

NEVER THE WAITER 2 b.c. (Feb 7) Kyllachy 129 – Talighta (USA) 62 (Barathea (IRE) 127) [2009 7m^6 p6g* 6g^3 Oct 10] £58,000Y: strong colt: sixth foal: half-brother to several winners, including fairly useful 5f (at 2 yrs)/6f winner Forces Sweetheart (by Allied Forces): dam Irish sprint maiden: useful form: won maiden at Wolverhampton in good style by 3¼ lengths from Hot Spark: excellent 2½ lengths third to Layla's Hero in listed event at York 7 days later: should stay 7f: sent to Hong Kong. *B. J. Meehan* **99 +**

NEW ADVENTURE 3 b.g. Generous (IRE) 139 – Sari 83 (Faustus (USA) 118) [2009 –: 12.1g May 26] small, close-coupled gelding: no form. *P. F. I. Cole* **–**

NEW BEGINNING (FR) 3 b.f. Nayef (USA) 129 – Chrysalu 102 (Distant Relative 128) [2009 67: 10.2g p8.6g 8.3d Jul 22] workmanlike filly: fair maiden at 2 yrs: no form in 2009: blinkered final outing: sold £1,400. *H. J. L. Dunlop* **–**

NEW BEGINNING (IRE) 5 b.g. Keltos (FR) 132 – Goldthroat (IRE) 79 (Zafonic (USA) 130) [2009 85: f8s f8s^5 p9.5g^5 p9.5g^4 10.2m^3 9.9m^2 10g Apr 29] angular gelding: fair handicapper: stays 1½m: acts on polytrack, soft and good to firm going: tried in cheekpieces: has finished distressed (including final outing). *Mrs S. Lamyman* **75**

NEWBURY STREET 2 b.g. (Apr 25) Namid 128 – Cautious Joe 73 (First Trump 118) [2009 5.1d^3 6d^4 5m^3 7m^2 p6m* 6g^3 Oct 23] fourth foal: half-brother to 3-y-o Deadly Encounter and 2005 2-y-o 5f/6f winner Magnolia Blossom (by Superior Premium): dam 5f (at 2 yrs) and 1m winner: fair performer: won nursery at Wolverhampton in September: stays 7f: acts on polytrack, good to firm and good to soft going. *R. A. Fahey* **72**

NEWBY ABBEY (IRE) 8 b.g. Lord of Appeal 109 – Turramurra Girl (IRE) (Magical Wonder (USA) 125) [2009 p8.6g f12g May 18] winning Irish pointer: little impact over hurdles and on Flat: in cheekpieces/tongue tie on debut. *D. Flood* **–**

NEWCASTLE SAM 4 b.g. Atraf 116 – Ballyewry (Prince Tenderfoot (USA) 126) [2009 –§: 10d^6 Sep 15] temperamental and no sign of ability. *J. J. Bridger* **– §**

NEW CHRISTMAS (USA) 2 gr. or ro.c. (Feb 8) Smoke Glacken (USA) 120 – Occhi Verdi (IRE) 77 (Mujtahid (USA) 118) [2009 6g^4 6m 7.1g p7.1g^5 p8m* p8.6g* Dec 18] $54,000F, 48,000Y: fifth foal: half-brother to winners in USA by Royal Academy and Menifee: dam 5f (at 2 yrs) to 1m (in USA) winner: fairly useful performer: improved to win nurseries at Lingfield and Wolverhampton (by neck from Be A Devil, pair well clear) in December: stays 8.6f: acts on polytrack. *B. J. Meehan* **87**

NEW COUTURE (IRE) 3 b.f. Montjeu (IRE) 137 – New Design (IRE) 93 (Bluebird (USA) 125) [2009 p10g p12.2g^4 p10m^6 Dec 30] second foal: dam Irish 2-y-o 5f winner: easily best effort in maidens when fourth at Wolverhampton. *P. W. Chapple-Hyam* **54**

NEW DEN 2 ch.c. (Apr 7) Piccolo 121 – Den's-Joy 85 (Archway (IRE) 115) [2009 p6g 6m p8f^6 f8d Dec 29] modest form in maidens. *J. R. Boyle* **56**

NEW ENGLAND 7 ch.g. Bachir (IRE) 118 – West Escape 95 (Gone West (USA)) [2009 –§: p9.5g^3 f11g^3 p12.2g* p12.2g^2 12d 11.5g 10m^2 12.3g^6 10.3m^5 p12.2g^3 p12.2g* p12.2m p12g^6 p9.5g Oct 23] fair performer: won claimer at Wolverhampton in March and seller at same track in August (left W. M. Brisbourne after next start): effective at 1¼m/1½m: acts on polytrack and good to firm going: often slowly away: free-going sort. *F. Sheridan* **66**

NEWGATE (UAE) 5 b.g. Jade Robbery (USA) 121 – Patruel 93 (Rainbow Quest (USA) 134) [2009 61d: f8g Mar 12] quite good-topped gelding: modest handicapper: won at Wolverhampton in 2008, little form on Flat since (successful over hurdles in May): should stay 1m: acts on polytrack: tried blinkered/in cheekpieces: has shown temperament. *Mrs R. A. Carr* **–**

NEW INNOCENCE 2 ch.c. (Mar 4) Where Or When (IRE) 124 – Scottendale 58 (Zilzal (USA) 137) [2009 7g^{6} 7.5m^{4} p8g^{4} Nov 1] leggy colt: first foal: dam, ran 3 times, half-sister to smart 1½m/13f winner Compton Ace out of Irish St Leger and Cesarewitch winner Mountain Lodge: similar form in maidens, off 3 months before 3½ lengths fourth to Sowaylm at Lingfield (tongue tied) final start: should be suited by 1m+. *G. A. Butler* **78**

NEW LEYF (IRE) 3 b. or br.g. Kheleyf (USA) 116 – Society Fair (FR) (Always Fair (USA) 121) [2009 6d^{6} 6m 6d* 6g 7d^{3} 6m^{5} p6f^{2} Dec 20] €115,000F, £58,000 2-y-o: stocky gelding: sixth foal: closely related to 2 winners by Desert Style, including 6-y-o Bedouin Blue, and half-brother to 7-y-o Society Music: dam, French 2-y-o 5.5f winner, later useful up to 1m: fairly useful performer: won maiden at Ripon in June: gelded prior to final start: stays 7f: acts on polytrack and good to soft ground. *J. R. Gask* **82**

NEWMARKET STORY (IRE) 7 b.m. Desert Story (IRE) 115 – Faramisa (IRE) (Doyoun 124) [2009 11.5m* 10s 12s p12g Aug 29] modest handicapper: off nearly 2 years and 66/1, form in 2009 only when winning at Lingfield in June: stays 11.5f: form only on good to firm going. *W. J. Austin, Ireland* **60**

NEW STAR (UAE) 5 b.g. Green Desert (USA) 127 – Princess Haifa (USA) 69 (Mr Prospector (USA)) [2009 86: p9.5g^{4} p9.5g* p9.5g^{2} p9.5g* p8g^{2} p9.5g^{6} p9.5g^{2} Apr 4] leggy, workmanlike gelding: fairly useful performer: won handicap in February and claimer in March, both at Wolverhampton: stays 1¼m: acts on polytrack, soft and good to firm ground: none too consistent. *W. M. Brisbourne* **82**

NEWTON CIRCUS 2 gr.c. (Mar 11) Verglas (IRE) 118 – Flying Finish (FR) (Priolo (USA) 127) [2009 6m^{3} p7.1g 6s p7g^{5} p7f* p7m^{3} 7g^{2} Oct 16] fair performer: won claimer at Kempton (left R. Hannon £6,000) in September: claimed £8,000 after final start: effective at 6f/7f: acts on polytrack and good to firm going: reportedly finished distressed second start: sent to Switzerland. *Ollie Pears* **67**

NEWTONS CRADLE (IRE) 2 b.g. (Feb 15) Noverre (USA) 125 – Lady of Kildare (IRE) 100 (Mujadil (USA) 119) [2009 7m 6g Aug 3] last in maidens at York and Ripon. *J. Howard Johnson* **–**

NEW TRICKS 3 b.g. Falbrav (IRE) 133 – Numberonedance (USA) (Trempolino (USA) 135) [2009 57: 12.1s^{2} 14.1m 11.1m* 12.3m 12.1s Aug 12] fair handicapper: won at Hamilton in June, making all: stays 1½m (seemed stretched by 1¾m): acts on soft and good to firm going: in cheekpieces/blinkers last 4 starts: races freely: joined P. Monteith. *I. Semple* **74**

NEW WORLD ORDER (IRE) 5 b.g. Night Shift (USA) – Kama Tashoof 72 (Mtoto 134) [2009 p10g p11g 10g^{6} p10m* p8.6g p12g p8.6g^{2} Nov 14] fair handicapper nowadays (missed 2008): left Mrs S. Leech, won at Kempton in September: stays 10.3f: acts on polytrack and soft going: usually tongue tied: often front runner: joined R. Curtis. *Edgar Byrne* **73**

NEW WORLD SYMPHONY (IRE) 2 b.c. (Apr 22) War Chant (USA) 126 – Bold Classic (USA) (Pembroke (USA) 113) [2009 7m^{6} f8g^{6} Aug 25] quite attractive colt: better effort in maidens 10 weeks apart when sixth to Jehu at Thirsk. *J. Howard Johnson* **58**

NEW YORK LIGHTS (IRE) 2 b.f. (Apr 21) Statue of Liberty (USA) 115 – Nautical Light (Slip Anchor 136) [2009 5m 5m 5.1m p7g^{5} p6g^{2} p6g p6g 8m 8.3d p7m p7g Dec 31] lengthy, unfurnished filly: fourth foal: half-sister to French/Spanish 5.5f to (at 2 yrs) 7.5f winner Mariners Doll (by King Charlemagne): dam disappointing maiden: poor maiden: best efforts at 6f/7f on polytrack: finds little and one to treat with caution. *M. D. I. Usher* **49 §**

NEXT MOVE (IRE) 2 b.c. (Apr 25) Tiger Hill (IRE) 127 – Cinnamon Rose (USA) 96 (Trempolino (USA) 135) [2009 p7g* Nov 11] 140,000Y: seventh foal: closely related to very smart Irish 7f (Moyglare Stud Stakes) to 1½m winner Chelsea Rose (by Desert King) and half-brother to several winners, including useful 6f (at 2 yrs in Ireland) to 9f (in US) winner European (by Great Commotion): dam Irish 1¼m winner: 3/1, won maiden at Kempton by ¾ length from Hidden Glory, taking time and pressure to get on top: bred to be suited by 1m+: likely to improve. *Saeed bin Suroor* **83 p**

NEZAMI (IRE) 4 b.g. Elnadim (USA) 128 – Stands To Reason (USA) 80 (Gulch (USA)) [2009 94: p7g^{3} p7g^{4} 7m^{2} p8f Dec 20] workmanlike gelding: useful handicapper: creditable second of 27 to Swift Gift in Victoria Cup at Ascot: races mostly at 7f (effective at 6f): acts on polytrack, firm and soft going. *J. Akehurst* **95**

NIBANI (IRE) 2 ch.c. (Feb 22) Dalakhani (IRE) 133 – Dance of The Sea (IRE) (Sinndar (IRE) 134) [2009 8m^{4} Oct 16] neat colt: first foal: dam unraced half-sister to Irish 2000 Guineas and Champion Stakes winner Spectrum and to dams of Petrushka and Conduit (by Dalakhani): 20/1 and very green, 5¼ lengths fourth to Invincible Soul in maiden at Newmarket, late headway under considerate handling: sure to do better. *Sir Michael Stoute* **81 p**

NICALDANI 2 ch.f. (Feb 28) Compton Place 125 – Thamud (IRE) (Lahib (USA) 129) [2009 7m f6g Aug 10] seventh foal: half-sister to 3 winners, including useful 7f to 8.6f winner Arctic Desert (by Desert Prince) and fairly useful 7f winner Sweet Emily (by Inchinor): dam unraced: well held in maidens. *M. Blanshard* –

NICE TIME (IRE) 3 ch.f. Tagula (IRE) 116 – Nicea (IRE) 90 (Dominion 123) [2009 72: 9.9g[6] 9.9g[6] 10.3m[2] 12m p11g 10m[4] 11.6d[4] Oct 12] sparely-made filly: fair handicapper: stays 1¼m: acts on polytrack and good to firm going. *M. H. Tompkins* 74

NICE TO KNOW (FR) 5 ch.m. Machiavellian (USA) 123 – Entice (FR) 111 (Selkirk (USA) 129) [2009 89: 8g 7g p8g[2] p8g[2] 8g Jul 24] big, leggy mare: fairly useful performer: best efforts when runner-up at Kempton: stays 1m: acts on polytrack and good to firm ground: held up. *G. L. Moore* 88

NICHOLAS POCOCK (IRE) 3 b.g. King's Best (USA) 132 – Sea Picture (IRE) 82 (Royal Academy (USA) 130) [2009 7m[6] Apr 15] tall gelding: fifth foal: half-brother to 7f winner Tableau Vivant (by Pivotal) and 1m winner Sea Nymph (by Spectrum), both fairly useful: dam, maiden who stayed 1¼m, half-sister to Yorkshire Oaks winner/St Leger second Hellenic, herself dam of Greek Dance, Islington and Mountain High: better for experience, 6 lengths sixth to Infiraad in maiden at Newmarket: bred to stay 1m+: sold 6,500 gns in October. *Sir Michael Stoute* 71

NICKEL SILVER 4 ro.g. Choisir (AUS) 126 – Negligee 94 (Night Shift (USA)) [2009 77: p5.1g* p5m* p5g* p5g[3] 5m 5g 5m[3] 5.1m[5] 5m[3] 6m[4] 5m[5] p5.1g[4] 5.1g* p5.1g[2] f5m* Dec 15] quite good-topped gelding: fairly useful handicapper: won at Wolverhampton and Lingfield (2) in January, Nottingham in October and Southwell in December: effective at 5f/6f: acts on polytrack, good to firm and good to soft ground: wears headgear: often forces pace. *B. Smart* 94

NICKY NUTJOB (GER) 3 b.c. Fasliyev (USA) 120 – Natalie Too (USA) (Irish River (FR) 131) [2009 70: p9.5g[5] p10g p12.2m p12g 9.7d[4] 10.2m 10.2d 10g 11.5g Jul 20] close-coupled colt: modest maiden handicapper: stays 1¼m: acts on polytrack and soft ground: tried in headgear: fair juvenile hurdler. *J. Pearce* 62

NICOSIA 2 b.f. (May 7) Imperial Dancer 123 – Stride Home 78 (Absalom 128) [2009 6g 6v[6] Jul 18] small filly: half-sister to several winners, including fairly useful 1¼m/1½m winner Pedro Pete (by Fraam): dam 5f (at 2 yrs) to 1¼m winner: tailed off in sellers. *M. R. Channon* –

NIDAMAR 2 b.f. (Mar 21) Redoubtable (USA) 115 – Marabar 87 (Sri Pekan (USA) 117) [2009 5m 5m 6f p5.1m f5g f5g[5] f6f Dec 11] close-coupled filly: first foal: dam unreliable 6f/7f winner: of little account. *Mrs R. A. Carr* –

NIDEEB 2 ch.c. (Feb 13) Exceed And Excel (AUS) 126 – Mantesera (IRE) (In The Wings 128) [2009 7g[4] 7s* 7m* 8.1v[2] 7m[5] Oct 1] 20,000Y: strong colt: second foal: dam unraced sister to Nell Gwyn Stakes winner Cloud Castle (stayed 1½m) and half-sister to very smart/high-class 1½m performers Luso and Warrsan: useful performer: won maiden at Yarmouth and listed race at Ascot (beat Party Doctor by nose) in July: not discredited last 2 starts, second to Emerald Commander in listed race at Haydock and fifth to Sir Parky in Somerville Tattersall Stakes at Newmarket: stays 1m: unraced on firm going, acts on any other. *C. E. Brittain* 101

NIGHT AFFAIR 3 b.f. Bold Edge 123 – Twilight Mistress 84 (Bin Ajwaad (IRE) 119) [2009 77p: p6g[4] p5g[2] 5g[2] 5g 5m[4] Sep 12] medium-sized filly: fairly useful handicapper: likely to prove best at 5f/6f: acts on polytrack, probably on good to firm ground: prominent runner. *D. W. P. Arbuthnot* 81

NIGHTBOAT TO CAIRO (IRE) 5 b.m. Turtle Island (IRE) 123 – Garryduff Breeze (IRE) (Strong Gale 116) [2009 14.1g[4] Jun 9] no sign of ability in bumpers/seller. *P. A. Kirby* –

NIGHT CRESCENDO (USA) 6 br. or b.g. Diesis 133 – Night Fax (USA) (Known Fact (USA) 135) [2009 103: 12f[5] 14m 12m 12m 12g[6] 12g[2] 10m 12m[3] 12m Sep 27] tall, useful-looking gelding: useful handicapper: stays 1½m: acts on polytrack, firm and soft ground: usually wears cheekpieces: none too reliable. *Mrs A. J. Perrett* 97 §

NIGHTJAR (USA) 4 b.c. Smoke Glacken (USA) 120 – Night Risk (USA) (Wild Again (USA)) [2009 90: f7d* p7.1g[5] f7g* p6g p8.6g f6g* 8m 7m 6m 6m[3] 6d[3] 6m p7.1g 8m f8g[4] f6f[2] f7g[3] Dec 22] good-topped colt: useful handicapper on all-weather, fairly useful on turf: won at Southwell in January (2) and March: good second to Ingleby Arch at same course penultimate outing (left M. Johnston 25,000 gns after): has form at 1¼m, best recent form at 6f/7f: acts on all-weather (best efforts on fibresand), good to firm and good to soft going. *K. A. Ryan* 90 a104

NIGHT KNIGHT (IRE) 3 b.g. Bachelor Duke (USA) 122 – Dark Albatross (USA) 89 (Sheikh Albadou 128) [2009 57?: 9.9m 8f* 8m 8.3g 8g 10.1m* p10g⁴ Oct 2] angular gelding: fair handicapper: won at Redcar in May and Yarmouth (seller) in September: stays 1¼m: acts on firm going: visored last 6 starts: sold 8,000 gns. *M. L. W. Bell* **73**

NIGHT LILY (IRE) 3 b.f. Night Shift (USA) – Kedross (IRE) 63 (King of Kings (IRE) 125) [2009 78: p7g³ 7m 8m⁴ 12m⁵ 7.6g² 10d 10g⁵ p7g² p8m* Sep 24] rather leggy filly: fair performer: all out to win maiden at Kempton: stays 1½m: acts on polytrack, soft and good to firm going: tried in cheekpieces: tongue tied last 3 starts: often held up. *J. Jay* **71**

NIGHT MAGIC (GER) 3 ro.f. Sholokhov (IRE) 121 – Night Woman (GER) (Monsun (GER) 124) [2009 10g³ 10g³ 11g* 11d* 10g 10d² Oct 25] €43,000Y: tall, quite good-topped filly: second foal: half-sister to German 7f/1m winner Night Prince (by Dashing Blade): dam fairly useful German 1¼m/11f winner: smart performer: successful at 2 yrs in maiden at Dresden and valuable auction event at Baden-Baden: improved efforts when making all in Grosser Preis der Jungheinreich Gabelstapler at Hamburg (beat Miss Europa ¾ length) in July and Henkel Preis der Diana at Dusseldorf (beat Soberania 4½ lengths) in August: back to best when beaten head by Eva's Request in Premio Lydia Tesio at Rome final start: stays 11f: acts on soft and good to firm ground. *W. Figge, Germany* **115**

NIGHT ORBIT 5 b.g. Observatory (USA) 131 – Dansara (Dancing Brave (USA) 140) [2009 75: p12m* p12g⁴ p13g⁶ p13.9g⁴ 16g² Oct 28] leggy gelding: fair handicapper: won at Lingfield in January: stays 2m: acts on all-weather and heavy ground: usually visored. *Miss J. Feilden* **72**

NIGHT PREMIERE (IRE) 4 b.f. Night Shift (USA) – Star Studded (Cadeaux Genereux 131) [2009 63: p5m⁴ p5g p5g Feb 27] sturdy filly: modest maiden handicapper: effective at 5f/6f: acts on polytrack, heavy and good to firm going: blinkered: usually races close up. *R. Hannon* **56**

NIGHT PROSPECTOR 9 b.g. Night Shift (USA) – Pride of My Heart 74 (Lion Cavern (USA) 117) [2009 70: p6g Jan 3] close-coupled, good-topped gelding: modest handicapper: well below form sole outing in 2009: best at 5f/6f: acts on all-weather, firm and soft going: wears blinkers/cheekpieces. *R. A. Harris* **–**

NIGHT SKY 2 b.f. (Jan 16) Starcraft (NZ) 128 – War Shanty 66 (Warrshan (USA) 117) [2009 7d Oct 12] seventh foal: half-sister to several winners, including 4-y-o Artsu and 7f/1m winner All Quiet (by Piccolo), both fairly useful: dam lightly-raced half-sister to very smart sprinter Bold Edge: 40/1, always behind in maiden at Salisbury. *P. J. Makin* **–**

NIGHTSTRIKE (IRE) 6 b.m. Night Shift (USA) – Come Together 68 (Mtoto 134) [2009 60: p7g p8g Dec 2] stocky mare: handicapper: just poor form in 2009: stays 7f: acts on polytrack and good to firm ground: tried blinkered. *Luke Comer, Ireland* **47**

NIGHT TRADE (IRE) 2 b.f. (Feb 8) Trade Fair 124 – Compton Girl (Compton Place 125) [2009 6.1g p5.1g³ p5m³ 5g⁴ 5g³ p5.1g⁴ Oct 30] third foal: dam unraced half-sister to smart 5f performer Repertory: fair performer: much improved when making all in nursery at Catterick in October: ran creditably after: should stay 6f. *Mrs D. J. Sanderson* **78**

NIKKI BEA (IRE) 6 ch.m. Titus Livius (FR) 115 – Strong Feeling (USA) (Devil's Bag (USA)) [2009 64: p7m⁴ p8g² p8g² p8g⁶ p8g Feb 27] leggy mare: modest handicapper: effective at 7f to 1¼m: acts on polytrack and firm going: tried blinkered. *Jamie Poulton* **59**

NIMBELLE (IRE) 4 b.f. Namid 128 – Bellissi (IRE) 77 (Bluebird (USA) 125) [2009 58: p6g Jan 30] lengthy filly: modest maiden: likely to prove best at 5f/easy 6f: acts on polytrack: tried in cheekpieces. *J. C. Tuck* **47**

NIMMY'S SPECIAL 3 ch.f. Monsieur Bond (IRE) 120 – Mammas F-C (IRE) 71 (Case Law 113) [2009 66: p9.5g p8.6g⁴ p7.1g⁶ 10g f8g 5.9d² 6d³ Aug 27] small, close-coupled filly: modest maiden handicapper: stays 8.6f: acts on polytrack, soft and good to firm going: temperamental. *M. Mullineaux* **53 §**

NIMUE (USA) 2 b. or br.f. (Feb 1) Speightstown (USA) 124 – Flag Support (USA) (Personal Flag (USA)) [2009 6g² 6m p5m Oct 7] $120,000Y, $310,000 2-y-o: strong filly: seventh foal: half-sister to 2 winners in US, notably Grade 2 9f winner Go Rockin' Robin (by Distorted Humor): dam unraced out of smart French performer up to 1¼m Accommodating: maiden: easily best effort when 1¼ lengths second to Beyond Desire (pair clear) at Goodwood, pulling hard: seemed amiss in Lowther Stakes York, blindfold removed late and hampered start at Kempton: stays 6f. *P. F. I. Cole* **91**

NINA ROSE 2 ro.f. (Mar 31) Pastoral Pursuits 127 – Magnolia 52 (Petong 126) [2009 5.7f² 6d³ 6.1m³ 7g⁴ 7g 8.3d⁴ Oct 15] sparely-made filly: closely related to 8-y-o One Upmanship and half-sister to winner in Italy by Lujain: dam, ran twice, half-sister to **73**

smart 7f winner Naahy: fair maiden: stays 8.3f: acts on good to soft ground, probably on firm. *C. G. Cox*

NINO ZACHETTI (IRE) 3 ch.g. Daggers Drawn (USA) 114 – Paganina (FR) (Galetto (FR) 118) [2009 –: 7g 8.3g^6 6v^4 5.9g 7m 6g 7.2m^6 7s Nov 9] poor maiden: sold from E. Alston £800 after seventh start: free-going sort, likely to prove best at 5f/6f: acts on heavy going: tried in cheekpieces/blinkers. *G. Verheye, Belgium* **46**

NINTH HOUSE (USA) 7 b.h. Chester House (USA) 123 – Ninette (USA) 101 (Alleged (USA) 138) [2009 61, a93d: p8.6g p8.6g p8.6g 8.3m^3 7d 7.5m^3 8m^5 p7.1g* p8.6g^2 p7.1g^4 p7.1g^2 8m* 8s^2 8m^5 8m^2 p7.1g* 8m 8s* 8g p7.1g 8.3g 7.2v p8.6g Dec 4] good-topped horse: fairly useful handicapper: won at Wolverhampton in June, Redcar in July, Wolverhampton in August and Thirsk in September: below form after: effective at 7f to 1¼m: acts on polytrack, firm and soft going: sometimes blinkered, tried in cheekpieces: usually tongue tied: held up. *Mrs R. A. Carr* **80**

NIQAAB 5 ch.m. Alhaarth (IRE) 126 – Shanty 94 (Selkirk (USA) 129) [2009 54: f14s^6 p13.3g Jan 15] useful-looking mare: poor maiden in 2009: stays 1½m: acts on polytrack and soft going. *W. J. Musson* **39**

NIRAN (IRE) 2 b.c. (Mar 11) Captain Rio 122 – Valley Lights (IRE) (Dance of Life (USA)) [2009 6m* 6g* 6m Jul 9] €6,700F, 40,000Y: good-topped colt: has scope: half-brother to several winners, including useful 6f (including at 2 yrs) winner Masha-Il (by Danehill): dam, Irish maiden, half-sister to high-class miler Then Again: fairly useful performer: won minor events at Newmarket (by neck from Shark Man) and Yarmouth (by length from Brisbane) in May: much stiffer task when tailed-off last in July Stakes at Newmarket: raced only at 6f on good/good to firm ground. *C. E. Brittain* **82**

NISAAL (IRE) 4 b.g. Indian Ridge 123 – Kahalah (IRE) 77 (Darshaan 133) [2009 86: 7m^4 8.1g 8.1v 8.1m^2 8.1s^4 8m^6 10m 9.2g^2 p9.5g^5 Oct 9] compact gelding: fair maiden handicapper: stays 9.2f, effective at shorter: acts on soft and good to firm going: in cheekpieces last 3 starts: tried tongue tied: has found little, and one to treat with caution. *J. J. Quinn* **74 §**

NIZAA (USA) 2 b. or br.c. (Feb 16) Dixieland Band (USA) – Star Queen (USA) (Kingmambo (USA) 125) [2009 6g^4 7g^3 p7g^5 Oct 21] $60,000F, £100,000Y: good-bodied colt: fifth foal: half-brother to 2 winners abroad by Cozzene: dam, US 1m/9f winner (including minor stakes), half-sister to US Grade 3 1m winner Patience Game: fair form in maidens: sold £7,000. *B. W. Hills* **69**

NIZHONI DANCER 3 b.f. Bahamian Bounty 116 – Hagwah (USA) 109 (Dancing Brave (USA) 140) [2009 82: 8.1m Jun 12] fairly useful form: respectable seventh in handicap at Sandown only outing in 2009: will be suited by 1¼m: acts on soft going. *C. F. Wall* **76**

NIZHONI (USA) 4 ch.f. Mineshaft (USA) 132 – Carinae (USA) 99 (Nureyev (USA) 131) [2009 65: f6s p5.1m^3 Mar 4] fair maiden at 3 yrs: just poor form in 2009: raced only at 5f/6f: best effort on fibresand. *B. Smart* **46**

NOAFAL (IRE) 2 ch.c. (Apr 18) Bahamian Bounty 116 – Miss Party Line (USA) (Phone Trick (USA)) [2009 6m^3 6.5g* Oct 8] 60,000Y: strong colt: fifth foal: half-brother to smart 6f/7f (at 2 yrs) winner Bentong (by Anabaa), useful French 2004 2-y-o 6f winner Corsario (by Zafonic) and 3-y-o Sister Clement: dam, French 1m winner, sister to US Grade 2 6.5f winner All Chatter: plenty of promise in maidens, considerately-handled third to Dafeef at Newmarket and winning cosily by ½ length from The Rectifier at Newbury: should stay 7f: sure to improve again. *M. A. Jarvis* **86 p**

NOAH JAMEEL 7 ch.g. Mark of Esteem (IRE) 137 – Subtle One (IRE) (Polish Patriot (USA) 128) [2009 61: p10g^2 p11g^2 p9.5g^4 10.9m^2 10.2f^6 10.2m f11g^2 p10m^5 p12m^5 p9.5g^5 Dec 28] modest handicapper: effective at 1m to 11f: acts on all-weather, soft and good to firm ground: usually held up. *A. G. Newcombe* **64**

NOBELIX (IRE) 7 gr.g. Linamix (FR) 127 – Nataliana 103 (Surumu (GER)) [2009 88: p14g* 12m^2 Jun 26] compact gelding: fairly useful handicapper: won at Great Leighs in January: stayed 14.8f: acted on polytrack, firm and good to soft going: dead. *J. R. Gask* **87**

NOBILISSIMA (IRE) 5 b.m. Orpen (USA) 116 – Shadow Smile (IRE) 74 (Slip Anchor 136) [2009 94: p6g Jun 24] lengthy mare: fairly useful handicapper: left J. Spearing and off 9 months, shaped as if in need of race at Kempton: best at 5f/6f: acts on soft and good to firm ground. *Miss Tor Sturgis* **69**

NOBLE ATTITUDE 3 b.f. Best of The Bests (IRE) 122 – Charming Lotte 80 (Nicolotte 118) [2009 6g 10.2v^3 6s^5 Aug 1] fourth foal: half-sister to 2006 2-y-o 5f winner The Italian Job (by Bertolini): dam 6f winner, including at 2 yrs: modest maiden. *N. Tinkler* **60**

NOBLE CITIZEN (USA) 4 b.c. Proud Citizen (USA) 122 – Serene Nobility (USA) (His Majesty (USA)) [2009 98: 8g a7f^{2} a7.5f^{2} 7.6m 7m 6m^{2} 7g 7m^{2} 7m Sep 26] good-topped colt: useful handicapper: best efforts when runner-up behind Snaafy at Nad Al Sheba second/third starts: stays 1m: acts on polytrack/dirt and firm going, probably on soft: tried blinkered: prominent runner. *D. M. Simcock* **98** **a106**

NOBLE DICTATOR 3 b.g. Diktat 126 – Noble Desert (FR) (Green Desert (USA) 127) [2009 66: 8.3m 7m 8.3m 10m p10m^{2} p10g^{3} Oct 14] quite good-topped gelding: fair handicapper: stays 1¼m: acts on polytrack and good to firm going: tried in cheekpieces: temperament under suspicion (carries head awkwardly): sold 12,000 gns. *E. F. Vaughan* **69**

NOBLE GREEK (USA) 2 b. or br.c. (Mar 4) Omega Code (USA) – Regal Beauty (USA) (Explosive Red (CAN) 119) [2009 p6g^{2} 6m 6m^{2} p5g^{3} Oct 2] $10,000Y: sturdy colt: second foal: half-brother to winner in USA by Delaware Township: dam, US maiden, half-sister to US Grade 3 6f winner Don Six: fair maiden: highly tried second start: effective at 5f/6f. *J. R. Best* **78**

NOBLE STORM (USA) 3 b.c. Yankee Gentleman (USA) – Changed Tune (USA) (Tunerup (USA)) [2009 99: 5g^{2} 5.1m^{2} 5g* 5m^{5} 5.1m^{2} 5g* 5m* 5m^{4} 5m^{2} Oct 1] well-made colt: smart performer: won minor event at Beverley in May and handicaps at Goodwood in July and York (by ½ length from Rain Delayed) in August: good neck second to Spin Cycle in listed race at Newmarket final outing, travelling best: exuberant sort, will prove best at sharp 5f: acts on soft and good to firm ground: normally front runner. *E. S. McMahon* **113**

NOCHE DE REYES 4 b.g. Foxhound (USA) 103 – Ashleigh Baker (IRE) 68 (Don't Forget Me 127) [2009 –: 8g^{5} 10g^{6} 10.4g^{6} p9.5g f8f^{4} 9.1v^{5} p9.5g^{3} Nov 30] angular gelding: modest maiden: stays 1¼m: acts on all-weather. *E. J. Alston* **58**

NO COMPLAINING (IRE) 2 b.f. (Feb 21) Alhaarth (IRE) 126 – Rambler 74 (Selkirk (USA) 129) [2009 6m 6m 7d Oct 27] second foal: half-sister to 5-y-o Rambling Light: dam, 7f winner, half-sister to smart sprinter Cassandra Go (dam of Irish 1000 Guineas winner Halfway To Heaven) and Coventry Stakes winner Verglas: well held in maidens (looked awkward final start). *B. J. Curley* **–**

NO EXPLAINING (IRE) 2 b.f. (Apr 22) Azamour (IRE) 130 – Claustra (FR) 91 (Green Desert (USA) 127) [2009 6f 7g 6.1s* Oct 7] smallish, good-bodied filly: fifth foal: half-sister to 3 winners, including 2006 2-y-o 7.5f winner Weld Il Balad (by Alhaarth) and 4-y-o Inspector Clouseau: dam, Irish 9f winner, half-sister to smart French sprinter Wessam Prince: easily best effort in maidens when winning at Nottingham by 2¼ lengths from Skyrider: bred to stay 1m+: acts on soft ground. *B. J. Curley* **80 +**

NO GREATER LOVE (FR) 7 b.g. Take Risks (FR) 116 – Desperate Virgin (BEL) (Chief Singer 131) [2009 f11g^{4} Mar 31] fair performer: respectable fourth in handicap at Southwell on belated Flat return: stays 14.5f: acts on fibresand, has run only on good/good to soft going on turf. *C. E. Longsdon* **70**

NO GROUSE 9 b.g. Pursuit of Love 124 – Lady Joyce (FR) (Galetto (FR) 118) [2009 78, a63: 7m^{4} 7f 6m^{5} 6.9g 6.1g^{2} 6f 7.6m^{6} 7d 7.1m^{2} 7m 6g p7m^{5} Oct 31] strong, round-barrelled gelding: fair handicapper on turf, modest on all-weather: effective at 6f to 7.5f: acts on all-weather, firm and good to soft going: tried in cheekpieces in 2004: inconsistent. *E. J. Alston* **67** **a59**

NO HUBRIS (USA) 2 b.c. (Apr 24) Proud Citizen (USA) 122 – Innateness (USA) (Flying Paster (USA)) [2009 6g* 6m^{6} Jun 16] $160,000F, 85,000Y: tall colt: has scope: half-brother to winners in USA by Wharf and Bon Point: dam, US 6.5f winner, half-sister to very smart 1½m/1¾m performer Yellowstone: useful form: won maiden at York in May impressively by 2¼ lengths from Flying Statesman: similar form when sixth to impressive Canford Cliffs in Coventry Stakes at Royal Ascot (tried to match strides with winner): not seen out again: should stay 7f, though clearly not short of speed. *P. F. I. Cole* **98**

NOLECCE 2 ch.g. (Mar 15) Reset (AUS) 124 – Ghassanah 73 (Pas de Seul 133) [2009 6f 7s 6g Sep 17] close-coupled, workmanlike gelding: well held in maidens. *R. C. Guest* **–**

NOMADIC WARRIOR 4 b.g. Nomadic Way (USA) 104 – Jesmund (Bishop of Cashel 122) [2009 –: p12.2g p12.2g Mar 6] neat gelding: maiden: seemingly modest form final outing. *J. R. Holt* **56 ?**

NOM DE LA ROSA (IRE) 2 b.f. (Apr 26) Oratorio (IRE) 128 – Cheal Rose (IRE) 83 (Dr Devious (IRE) 127) [2009 7d 6f^{4} 7f 7m Sep 27] compact filly: fifth foal: closely related to smart 6f (at 2 yrs) to 8.5f winner in Ireland/UAE Golden Arrow (by Danehill) and half-sister to 2 winners, including fairly useful Irish 1m winner Perpetual Motion (by Spinning World): dam, Irish maiden who stayed 1¼m, half-sister to US Grade 3 8.5f winner Buffalo Berry: fair maiden: best effort when fourth to Emirates Hills at Windsor, hanging badly left: should stay at least 7f: sold 5,000 gns. *G. L. Moore* **67**

NO MEAN TRICK (USA) 3 b.c. Grand Slam (USA) 120 – Ruby's Reception (USA) 110 (Rubiano (USA)) [2009 p8.6g^{2} p8f^{3} Dec 20] $100,000Y: first foal: dam US 5f (at 2 yrs) to 8.5f (Grade 2) winner: fair form when placed in maidens at Wolverhampton (favourite) and Kempton. *C. G. Cox* **75**

NOMOREBLONDES 5 ch.m. Ishiguru (USA) 114 – Statuette 57 (Statoblest 120) [2009 78: p5.1g^{5} 5m^{4} 5f 5m^{3} 5m^{5} 5g^{4} 5m 5m 5g^{5} 5g^{2} 5m* 5m 5m p5m^{6} p5.1g Nov 14] leggy mare: fairly useful handicapper on turf, fair on all-weather: won at Musselburgh in April and Newcastle in August: best at 5f/6f: acts on polytrack and firm going: wears cheekpieces: often forces pace: has finished weakly. *P. T. Midgley* **80 a70**

NOMORETAXES (BRZ) 7 b.g. First American (USA) 115 – Raghida (BRZ) (Roi Normand (USA)) [2009 6g 7g^{6} 6g^{6} 9m p8g Jul 8] good-topped gelding: fairly useful performer in UAE in 2006 for A. Al Raihe, winning minor event at Nad Al Sheba (also successful in Brazil earlier in career): trained in Qatar after, winning handicap at Doha early in 2008: left I. Al Malki and gelded, no sign of retaining ability either start in Britain: stays 8.5f: acts on dirt: often blinkered/tongue tied. *Miss D. Mountain* **–**

NON DOM (IRE) 3 b.g. Hawk Wing (USA) 136 – Kafayef (USA) 46 (Secreto (USA) 128) [2009 77p: 11.6m* 11.8g^{2} 12.5g^{3} 14.1f^{4} 12m^{3} 12m^{2} 14m^{4} 11.6g^{3} Oct 5] strong gelding: fairly useful handicapper: won at Windsor in May: stays 1¾m: acts on good to firm going: consistent, but possibly not straightforward. *H. Morrison* **84**

NO NIGHTMARE (USA) 3 b. or br.f. Lion Heart (USA) 124 – Attasliyah (IRE) (Marju (IRE) 127) [2009 51: p5.1g 6d^{5} 7.2m Oct 1] big, strong filly: poor maiden: left Jane Chapple-Hyam 3,500 gns in July (before reappearance): tongue tied at 2 yrs. *A. P. Jarvis* **43**

NON SUCRE (USA) 4 b. or br.g. Minardi (USA) 119 – Vieille Rose (IRE) (Dancing Spree (USA)) [2009 77: p7g p6g 6m Apr 13] lengthy gelding: fair handicapper: no form in 2009: stays 7f: acts on polytrack, firm and good to soft going: sometimes blinkered: has hung/found little. *J. Gallagher* **–**

NOODLES BLUE BOY 3 b.g. Makbul 104 – Dee Dee Girl (IRE) 60 (Primo Dominie 121) [2009 75: f6g^{4} p7.1g^{6} 6s 5m* 5g^{3} 5d^{2} 5d* 5d^{5} 5m^{2} 5m* 5m 6.1m 6d^{2} 6s^{4} Oct 27] neat gelding: fairly useful performer: won seller at Beverley in May and handicaps at Newcastle in June and August: good neck second penultimate start: effective at 5f/6f: acts on all-weather, good to firm and good to soft going. *Ollie Pears* **82**

NO ONE LIKES US 2 b.g. (May 2) Lucky Owners (NZ) 122 – Habibi 50 (Alhijaz 122) [2009 p8m^{6} 8.3g p8g Nov 21] form only when sixth in claimer at Kempton: has been slowly away/looked awkward. *S. Curran* **52**

NOOR AL BAHAR (IRE) 3 b.f. Bahri (USA) 125 – Barbaresque (IRE) 68 (Green Desert (USA) 127) [2009 10.1d 11.9g^{6} Jun 7] €18,000Y, resold 9,000Y: first foal: dam, Irish 5f winner, half-sister to very smart sprinter Balbonella, herself dam of Anabaa: well held in maidens: sold 3,200 gns. *M. R. Channon* **–**

NOORDHOEK KID 3 b.g. Dansili 127 – Anqood (IRE) 82 (Elmaamul (USA) 125) [2009 75: 10.2d 10.1g^{4} 11.7g^{6} Aug 28] fair maiden: stays 1¼m: acts on polytrack: tried blinkered: tongue tied last 2 starts: sold £1,800. *C. R. Egerton* **68**

NO QUARTER (IRE) 2 b.g. (Mar 8) Refuse To Bend (IRE) 128 – Moonlight Wish (IRE) (Peintre Celebre (USA) 137) [2009 7m 7d 7d^{4} 7.1s 6m Sep 19] workmanlike gelding: modest form at best in maidens. *A. Dickman* **59**

NORA CHRISSIE (IRE) 7 b.m. Bahhare (USA) 122 – Vino Veritas (USA) 72 (Chief's Crown (USA)) [2009 57, a76: p13g 11m Jul 5] fair performer on all-weather, modest on turf: well held both starts in 2009, leaving Niall Moran in between: effective at 10.7f to 13f: acts on polytrack and heavy going, probably on good to firm: usually wears headgear: held up. *D. Loughnane, Ireland* **–**

NORA MAE (IRE) 3 ch.f. Peintre Celebre (USA) 137 – Wurfklinge (GER) (Acatenango (GER) 127) [2009 89p: 7s 7s 8.1d^{6} 10g p7.1g p8g^{2} p8m^{5} p7f Dec 13] attractive filly: fairly useful handicapper: should be suited by 1¼m+: raced only on polytrack and good going or softer. *S. Kirk* **88**

NORCROFT 7 b.g. Fasliyev (USA) 120 – Norcroft Joy 82§ (Rock Hopper 124) [2009 58, a67: f7d* p7g^{5} p7.1g f7g^{6} p7.1g p7g p7g f7g^{3} 7g 7m^{2} 7m^{6} 7m p7.1g 7m^{4} p7.1g p7m f7m Nov 12] leggy, good-topped gelding: fair handicapper on all-weather, modest on turf: won at Southwell in January: effective at 6f/7f: acts on all-weather, firm and good to soft ground: wears headgear. *Mrs C. A. Dunnett* **60 a68**

NORDIC LIGHT (USA) 5 b. or br.g. Belong To Me (USA) – Midriff (USA) (Naevus (USA)) [2009 73d: p7g p7.1g p6g^{4} p6g p5.1g^{3} p5.1g^{2} p5g^{6} p6g f6g p5.1g^{4} 6m 5.7m 5.3d^{5} **53**

5.1g 5g 6.1m p5m Dec 9] small, strong gelding: modest performer: effective at 5f/6f: acts on polytrack and good to firm going: wears blinkers/visor: usually tongue tied: moody. *J. M. Bradley*

NORMAN BECKETT 6 b.g. Beckett (IRE) 116 – Classic Coral (USA) (Seattle Dancer (USA) 119) [2009 f11g Apr 27] rather leggy, close-coupled gelding: fair performer: fit from hurdling, well held on belated return: stays 1½m: acts on any going: in headgear 5 of last 6 starts in 2006: has joined Jim Best. *R. T. Phillips* –

NORMAN THE GREAT 5 b.g. Night Shift (USA) – Encore du Cristal (USA) 82 (Quiet American (USA)) [2009 –: 10m* 13m* 12d* 12m⁶ p12f⁶ Sep 4] close-coupled gelding: fairly useful handicapper: won at Newbury (lady riders) in May, Newmarket in June and Epsom in July: stays 13f: acts on polytrack, good to firm and good to soft going: often hangs left. *A. King* **84**

NORSE WARRIOR (USA) 3 ch.g. Newfoundland (USA) 122 – Spicy Red (USA) (Tactical Advantage (USA)) [2009 7m⁶ 6s² 6.7m 8d 7d 7s p8g p5.1g* p5m Dec 30] $120,000F, $100,000Y: second foal: half-brother to winner in USA by R C Indy Go: dam, US 4f to 1m winner, half-sister to US Grade 3 8.5f winner Sister Swank: fair performer: won maiden at Wolverhampton in December (left D. Myerscough in Ireland £9,000 after): stays 6f: acts on polytrack and soft ground: visored last 2 starts: tried tongue tied. *Peter Grayson* **78**

NORTH CAPE (USA) 3 b.g. Action This Day (USA) 121 – Cape (USA) (Mr Prospector (USA)) [2009 66p: 7.1m⁵ 8.3d³ 9.9m² 10m* 10m⁴ p12g³ Aug 24] good-bodied gelding: fair handicapper: won at Sandown in June: stays 1¼m: acts on polytrack, good to firm and good to soft going. *H. Candy* **79**

NORTH CENTRAL (USA) 2 b. or br.c. (May 4) Forest Camp (USA) 114 – Brittan Lee (USA) (Forty Niner (USA)) [2009 5g⁶ 6m⁶ 6m⁴ Aug 22] good-bodied colt: maiden: best effort when sixth to Capercaillie in minor event at Musselburgh on debut. *J. Howard Johnson* **64**

NORTH EAST CORNER (USA) 3 b.g. Giant's Causeway (USA) 132 – Saree 95 (Barathea (IRE) 127) [2009 87p: 7m May 13] lengthy, good-bodied gelding: fairly useful form: won maiden at Newmarket at 2 yrs: shaped as if amiss next 2 starts 7 months apart: sold 800 gns, sent to Spain. *B. W. Hills* –

NORTHERN ACRES 3 b.g. Mtoto 134 – Bunting 102 (Shaadi (USA) 126) [2009 61p: 8.1m⁴ 10.3m 8m Sep 18] good-bodied gelding: fair maiden: well held last 2 starts over 4 months apart: should be suited by 1¼m+: gelded after final start. *D. Nicholls* **72**

NORTHERN BOLT 4 b.g. Cadeaux Genereux 131 – Shafir (IRE) 68 (Shaadi (USA) 126) [2009 91: p5.1g 5m f6g⁶ 5d⁶ 5m⁶ 5d⁴ 6v³ 6m⁵ 5g 5v* Nov 3] sturdy gelding: fairly useful performer: won claimer at Nottingham in November: effective at 5f/6f: acts on heavy going: visored last 4 starts. *D. Nicholls* **88**

NORTHERN DARE (IRE) 5 b.g. Fath (USA) 116 – Farmers Swing (IRE) (River Falls 113) [2009 101: p5.1g* 5.1m 6g⁴ 5m⁴ 5v* 6g² 5g³ 5d 5.6m 5g 5d Oct 24] lengthy gelding: useful handicapper: won at Wolverhampton in March and Pontefract (beat Haajes 1¾ lengths) in July: good second to Johannes at Goodwood, best subsequent effort: best at 5f/6f: acts on polytrack and has won on firm going, best turf efforts on good or softer (acts on heavy). *D. Nicholls* **103**

NORTHERN DESERT (IRE) 10 b.g. Desert Style (IRE) 121 – Rosie's Guest (IRE) (Be My Guest (USA) 126) [2009 72: p7m* p8g² p7g⁴ p7g* p8g⁶ p7g² 7g p8.6g² 8d² 8.1m⁵ 7.1d p8g³ Oct 11] lengthy gelding: fair performer on all-weather, modest on turf: won sellers at Lingfield in January and February: stays 8.6f: acts on polytrack, firm and good to soft going, probably on soft: wears cheekpieces. *S. Curran* **64** **a79**

NORTHERN DUNE (IRE) 5 b.g. Dilshaan 119 – Zoudie 79 (Ezzoud (IRE) 126) [2009 58: 16m* Apr 13] modest handicapper: won at Redcar sole outing in 2009: stays 2m: raced on all-weather and good to firm ground. *B. J. Curley* **62**

NORTHERN EMPIRE (IRE) 6 ch.g. Namid 128 – Bumble (Rainbow Quest (USA) 134) [2009 99: f5s⁵ p6g³ p5g² p6g p5.1g p5g² p6g* f6g f5g⁴ 5f* 5g⁵ 5m² 5g² p5.1g² 6g⁶ 5.1v 5.1d⁴ 5m³ 5d p5.1g p5m f5g p6g Dec 31] strong, good-topped gelding: fairly useful performer: won claimer at Lingfield in March and seller at Redcar in May: claimed from K. Ryan £6,000 after fourteenth start: lost way after: best at 5f/6f: acts on all-weather and firm going: usually in cheekpieces, tried blinkered/tongue tied: not straightforward. *F. Jordan* **81 d**

NORTHERNER (IRE) 6 b.g. Mark of Esteem (IRE) 137 – Ensorceleuse (FR) (Fabulous Dancer (USA) 124) [2009 –: 12g f12f Nov 24] tall gelding: no form since 2006. *J. O'Reilly* –

NORTHERN FLING 5 b.g. Mujadil (USA) 119 – Donna Anna (Be My Chief (USA) 122) [2009 107: a6g 6.5g^4 6m 5m 5g 7f 5d 6g 5d 5m 5g^6 7.2v^4 Oct 31] tall gelding: useful handicapper at best in 2009: below form after fourth to Balthazaar's Gift at Nad Al Sheba second outing: left D. Nicholls after tenth start: seems to stay 7f: acts on polytrack, good to firm and good to soft going: tried in cheekpieces. *J. S. Goldie* **100 d**

NORTHERN FLYER (GER) 3 b.g. Hawk Wing (USA) 136 – Nachtigall (GER) (Danehill (USA) 126) [2009 55p: f6g^5 f8g^6 8s^3 7.1g^2 7.1m* 7g^2 7.5m^2 6g^3 8s^2 8s^4 8.5g^5 Sep 22] strong gelding: fair handicapper: won at Musselburgh in June: stays 1m: acts on soft and good to firm ground, below form both starts on fibresand: reliable. *J. J. Quinn* **72**

NORTHERN GENES (AUS) 3 b.g. Refuse To Bend (IRE) 128 – Cotswold Dancer (AUS) (Carnegie (IRE) 129) [2009 p10m p10g p10m^4 Nov 27] rather leggy gelding: well held in maidens. *M. R. Bosley* **–**

NORTHERN JEM 5 b.g. Mark of Esteem (IRE) 137 – Top Jem 85 (Damister (USA) 123) [2009 88: 10m^6 8d* 8g 10.4g 10.3g^3 Oct 24] leggy, close-coupled gelding: fairly useful handicapper: won at Newmarket in July: stays 1¼m: acts on good to firm and good to soft ground: has hung left: sold 14,000 gns, joined D. Pipe. *Jane Chapple-Hyam* **86**

NORTHERN SHORE (IRE) 3 br.g. Clodovil (IRE) 116 – Distant Shore (IRE) 71 (Jareer (USA) 115) [2009 –: f7d f8g^4 p7g f7d^5 Feb 26] seemed to show a little ability in 1m seller on second outing: blinkered in 2009: tried tongue tied. *K. A. Ryan* **49 ?**

NORTHERN SPY (USA) 5 b.g. War Chant (USA) 126 – Sunray Superstar 101 (Nashwan (USA) 135) [2009 91d: 11.6m^5 10f p10g 8.5d* 8.3m^4 8.5m^4 8.5m^5 p8g^2 8d p10m p7g Dec 7] well-made gelding: fairly useful handicapper: won at Epsom in July: stays 1¼m: acts on polytrack, good to soft and good to firm going. *S. Dow* **81**

NORTHERN TOUR 3 b.g. Tobougg (IRE) 125 – Swift Spring (FR) 56 (Bluebird (USA) 125) [2009 84: p8g^5 10m p8m p9.5g^4 Dec 19] big gelding: fair performer: well below form after reappearance: stays 1m: acts on polytrack, good to firm and good to soft going: tried tongue tied. *P. F. I. Cole* **76 d**

NORTHGATE LODGE (USA) 4 ch.g. Hold That Tiger (USA) 117 – Sabaah Elfull 75 (Kris 135) [2009 –: 6g p9.5g Dec 11] big, strong gelding: maiden: little form since 2007: tried blinkered. *M. Brittain* **–**

NORTH PARADE 4 b.g. Nayef (USA) 129 – Queen Sceptre (IRE) 97 (Fairy King (USA)) [2009 85: p10g^3 f8g* p9.5g^5 f11g^2 8.1g^5 10m^4 10.4v May 21] strong, lengthy gelding: fairly useful performer: won claimer at Southwell in February: likely to prove best short of 1½m: acts on fibresand (well held both starts on polytrack), good to firm and good to soft ground: tongue tied, tried blinkered: not one to trust. *A. W. Carroll* **84 §**

NORTH SHADOW 2 ch.g. (Feb 28) Motivator 131 – Matoaka (USA) 92 (A P Indy (USA) 131) [2009 7m^6 7s^6 9m 6.1s* f7f^5 p6m^6 p8.6g Nov 30] lengthy, good-topped gelding: has scope: modest performer: best effort when making all in nursery at Nottingham in October: bred to be suited by 1m+: acts on soft ground. *A. D. Brown* **63**

NORTHSIDE PRINCE (IRE) 3 b.g. Desert Prince (IRE) 130 – Spartan Girl (IRE) 91 (Ela-Mana-Mou 132) [2009 58p: 10g^3 12.1g^4 12m^4 10m 10m^2 10s^2 8d^3 Sep 7] lengthy, angular gelding: fair maiden handicapper: stays 1¼m: acts on soft and good to firm ground: brought down fourth outing: consistent. *G. A. Swinbank* **75**

NORTH SOUTH DIVIDE (IRE) 5 b.g. Namid 128 – Bush Rose (Rainbow Quest (USA) 134) [2009 84d: p5g p5g f5g 6s^5 5g^6 p6g^4 p6g p7m Dec 30] good-topped gelding: modest maiden handicapper: claimed from Peter Grayson £5,000 fifth start: best at 5f/6f: acts on polytrack, good to firm and good to soft ground: tried in headgear/tongue tie: ungenuine. *K. A. Ryan* **51 §**

NORTH WALK (IRE) 6 b.g. Monashee Mountain (USA) 115 – Celtic Link (IRE) 66 (Toca Madera 111) [2009 62: p16g Jun 17] good-topped gelding: modest performer: left Tim Vaughan, well held on return to Flat: stays 13.3f: acts on all-weather, firm and soft going: often blinkered/in cheekpieces. *B. N. Pollock* **–**

NO RULES 4 b.g. Fraam 114 – Golden Daring (IRE) (Night Shift (USA)) [2009 60: f12d^5 16d* 16.1d^6 p16g^3 16.5s* 16d^2 17.5m 16d^5 15.8s* Oct 27] workmanlike gelding: fair handicapper: won at Yarmouth in April, Doncaster in July and Catterick in October: stays 2m: acts on polytrack, heavy and good to firm ground: usually races prominently. *M. H. Tompkins* **77**

NORWEGIAN 8 b.g. Halling (USA) 133 – Chicarica (USA) 112 (The Minstrel (CAN) 135) [2009 56: p11g^6 p9.5g^3 f12g^5 Feb 1] good-topped gelding: poor handicapper nowadays: stays 1¼m: acts on all-weather and good to firm going: tried visored/blinkered, usually in cheekpieces nowadays: held up. *Ian Williams* **49**

NORWEGIAN DANCER (UAE) 3 b.c. Halling (USA) 133 – Time Changes (USA) (Danzig (USA)) [2009 66: 10.3m^5 10g 10.3m* 10.3m* 12g 10.3m^4 p10f 10.2m^5 10m 10d 10.3g^5 p12.2g^4 Nov 13] good-bodied colt: fairly useful performer: won maiden in June and handicap in July, both at Chester: stays 10.3f: acts on good to firm going. *E. S. McMahon* **94**

NOSEDIVE 2 ch.g. (Mar 28) Observatory (USA) 131 – Resistance Heroine 75 (Dr Fong (USA) 128) [2009 5m* 5m^4 6m 6g^6 5m^5 5.5g^5 6m^3 Oct 3] smallish gelding: first foal: dam, maiden (stayed 1m), half-sister to useful performer up to 7f Violette (by Observatory) and Nell Gwyn Stakes winner Silca's Gift: fairly useful performer: won maiden at Sandown in June: mainly creditable efforts after, including when last of 5 to Sorciere in Prix d'Arenberg at Chantilly and third to Lucky Like in listed race at Redcar last 2 starts: subsequently gelded: will stay 7f: has started slowly/sweated. *W. J. Haggas* **91**

NOSFERATU (IRE) 6 b.g. In The Wings 128 – Gothic Dream (IRE) 113 (Nashwan (USA) 135) [2009 12m* 18m Jun 21] strong gelding: good mover: fairly useful performer: first run on Flat since 2007 when winning claimer at York in May: stays 1½m: acts on good to firm and good to soft going: blinkered in 2009: joined Jens Erik Lindstol, won over hurdles in Norway in August. *J. Howard Johnson* **89**

NO STING 3 b.f. Exit To Nowhere (USA) 122 – Beacon Silver 75 (Belmez (USA) 131) [2009 –: p11g 12.1g^5 14m 12.1g^3 Jun 22] workmanlike filly: modest maiden: stays 1½m. *W. S. Kittow* **50**

NO SUPPER (IRE) 5 ch.g. Inchinor 119 – Be Thankfull (IRE) 98 (Linamix (FR) 127) [2009 –: 11.8m 10.2m Sep 10] raced only 4 times on Flat, modest form only on debut in 2006: should stay 1¼m: fair winner over hurdles in March. *Tim Vaughan* **–**

NOTA BENE 7 b.g. Zafonic (USA) 130 – Dodo (IRE) 90 (Alzao (USA) 117) [2009 113: 6g 6g^3 6m^3 p6g^4 6m 7m 5d* Jul 17] strong gelding: smart performer: won minor event at Newmarket by length from Icelandic: creditable efforts when in frame earlier at Nad Al Sheba (2) and Lingfield (minor event, fourth to Strike The Deal): effective at 5f/6f: acts on polytrack, soft and good to firm going: tongue tied once. *D. R. C. Elsworth* **111**

NOTA LIBERATA 5 b.g. Spinning World (USA) 130 – Kyda (USA) 78 (Gulch (USA)) [2009 –: p9.5g Feb 16] leggy gelding: fair handicapper in 2007 for G. M. Moore: no recent form, including over hurdles: stays 9f, not 1¼m: acts on fibresand, heavy and good to firm going: tried blinkered/tongue tied. *Ollie Pears* **–**

NOTE PERFECT 4 b.f. Diktat 126 – Better Still (IRE) (Glenstal (USA) 118) [2009 59: 5m f6g May 5] sturdy filly: modest handicapper: well held in 2009: effective at 5f/6f: acts on fibresand and heavy going: blinkered. *M. W. Easterby* **–**

NOTHING IS FOREVER (IRE) 5 b.g. Daylami (IRE) 138 – Bequeath (USA) (Lyphard (USA) 132) [2009 p16g^4 p13.9g Feb 7] sturdy gelding: modest maiden handicapper: stays easy 2m: acts on polytrack, unraced on extremes of going on turf: lost action final outing: fairly useful hurdler. *L. Corcoran* **55**

NOTICE GIVEN 2 b.c. (Mar 3) Oasis Dream 129 – Well Warned 104 (Warning 136) [2009 7s 7g 6m^2 7d^6 Oct 27] best effort in maidens when 5 lengths second to Ongoodform at Yarmouth: stays 6f: acts on good to firm going: not straightforward. *H. R. A. Cecil* **67**

NOT IN THE CLOCK (USA) 2 b.c. (Apr 22) Chapel Royal (USA) 110 – Bavarian Girl (USA) (Unbridled (USA) 128) [2009 p6m p6m^5 p7g Dec 31] easily best effort in maidens when fifth at Lingfield. *J. R. Best* **55**

NOT MY CHOICE (IRE) 4 ch.g. Choisir (AUS) 126 – Northgate Raver (Absalom 128) [2009 88: p5.1g p5.1g 5f 5m 5m^4 p6g p7.1g p6g^4 Nov 27] good-topped, quite attractive gelding: fair handicapper: left S. Parr after third start: stays 6f: acts on polytrack and good to firm going: tried in cheekpieces/tongue tie. *J. Balding* **75 a67**

NOT NOW LEWIS (IRE) 5 b.g. Shinko Forest (IRE) – Pearl Egg (IRE) 55 (Mukaddamah (USA) 125) [2009 66: 6g^5 8m^3 5.9m^6 8m* 8d^6 7.9g 7g^6 8d p8.6g Sep 25] modest handicapper: won at Thirsk in June: barely stays easy 1¼m: acts on polytrack and good to firm going: tried blinkered. *F. P. Murtagh* **64**

NOTORIZE 2 ch.c. (Feb 17) Hernando (FR) 127 – Hypnotize 103 (Machiavellian (USA) 123) [2009 8g* 8g^2 Sep 17] 33,000Y: fifth foal: closely related to 7-y-o Hypnotic and half-brother to 2 winners, including fairly useful 7f winner Macedon (by Dansili): dam, 2-y-o 7f winner, closely related to smart performer up to 1m Dazzle: won maiden at Goodwood in August impressively by ½ length from Baltimore Clipper: better effort when 1¼ lengths second to Simenon in minor event at Ayr: will stay 1¼m: sent to Hong Kong. *R. M. Beckett* **91**

NOTTE DI NOTE (IRE) 2 b.f. (Mar 25) Le Vie Dei Colori 126 – Effetto Ottico (IRE) (Foxhound (USA) 103) [2009 7m^5 p6g^5 p6g^5 Nov 9] first foal: dam, 1m winner in Italy, out of half-sister to very smart 7f/1m performer Tillerman: modest form in maidens: should stay at least 7f. *L. M. Cumani* **59**

NOUAILHAS 3 b.g. Mark of Esteem (IRE) 137 – Barachois Princess (USA) 62 (Barachois (CAN)) [2009 p8.6g 7.1f 10.4g 10m^3 10g^6 13.8m^5 10m 11.9d Oct 15] leggy gelding: poor maiden: stays 1¼m: acts on good to firm going. *R. Hollinshead* **47**

NOUBIAN (USA) 7 ch.g. Diesis 133 – Beraysim 111 (Lion Cavern (USA) 117) [2009 83: p9.5g p12.2g^6 p12.2g p13.9m Feb 25] rangy gelding: just modest handicapper in 2009: effective at 11f, probably at 2m: acts on polytrack, heavy and good to firm going: tongue tied final outing. *C. R. Dore* **61**

NOUNOU 8 b.g. Starborough 126 – Watheeqah (USA) 60 (Topsider (USA)) [2009 66: p13.9g Feb 7] quite good-topped gelding: one-time fairly useful handicapper: well held only outing in 2009: stays 16.5f: acts on all-weather, good to firm and good to soft ground: tried visored/in cheekpieces: tongue tied last 3 starts. *Miss J. E. Foster* **–**

NOURIYA 2 b.f. (Feb 25) Danehill Dancer (IRE) 117 – Majestic Sakeena (IRE) (King's Best (USA) 132) [2009 p8g^4 Oct 9] second foal: dam unraced half-sister to dam of very smart miler Zafeen: 16/1, highly promising 3¼ lengths fourth to Timepiece in maiden at Lingfield, closing strongly when not clear run (would have gone close): sure to do better. *Sir Michael Stoute* **85 p**

NOVASTASIA (IRE) 3 b.f. Noverre (USA) 125 – Pink Sovietstaia (FR) (Soviet Star (USA) 128) [2009 62p: p7g^6 p7g^4 8m 8.3m 8s p8.6m p9.5g Oct 3] smallish filly: modest maiden: should be suited by 1m: in cheekpieces last 3 starts: sold 4,500 gns. *W. R. Swinburn* **64**

NOVAY ESSJAY (IRE) 2 ch.g. (Feb 15) Noverre (USA) 125 – Arabian Hideway (IRE) (Desert Prince (IRE) 130) [2009 5m* 6d^5 6d^3 7g^6 7m^5 f5g^6 Sep 29] strong gelding: fair performer: won maiden at Ripon in May: third in nursery at Ripon: best form at 5f/6f: acts on good to firm and good to soft going: tried in cheekpieces. *P. C. Haslam* **70**

NOVELLEN LAD (IRE) 4 b.g. Noverre (USA) 125 – Lady Ellen 67 (Horage 124) [2009 83: 7m^3 7m^3 6g* 7m* 6d 6m^5 7m^5 6m^2 6m 6m^4 Sep 26] tall gelding: fairly useful handicapper: won at Catterick and Redcar in June: at least as effective over 6f as 7f: acts on firm going (below form on softer than good). *E. J. Alston* **94**

NOVERRE OVER THERE (IRE) 2 b.g. (Mar 10) Noverre (USA) 125 – Shirley Moon (IRE) (Montjeu (IRE) 137) [2009 7d 7g 7g 8m^5 p8.6g^4 p9.5g^5 Oct 29] modest maiden: should be suited by 1¼m+: acts on polytrack: not straightforward. *M. E. Rimmer* **60**

NOVERRE TO GO (IRE) 3 ch.c. Noverre (USA) 125 – Ukraine Venture 96 (Slip Anchor 136) [2009 90p: p6g^4 7s 6m^3 6g* 6m 6m Sep 25] sturdy colt: useful handicapper: best effort when winning at Ascot in August by head from Tropical Paradise: best at 6f: acts on polytrack, soft and good to firm going: tongue tied since debut: signs of temperament. *Tom Dascombe* **97**

NOVERRE TO HIDE (USA) 3 b.g. Noverre (USA) 125 – Zanoubia (USA) 94 (Our Emblem (USA) 114) [2009 66: 6.1g^4 8.3m 6g 6m^5 8g p8g 6m p5m^6 Sep 23] big, strong gelding: regressive maiden: tends to find little: tried visored/blinkered: sold 1,200 gns. *J. R. Best* **52 d**

NOVIKOV 5 ch.g. Danehill Dancer (IRE) 117 – Ardisia (USA) 87 (Affirmed (USA)) [2009 97: 8.1g p8g Oct 9] strong, good-bodied gelding: useful handicapper in 2008 for J. Gosden: well held both starts in 2009: stays 1¼m: acts on polytrack and soft going: tried in cheekpieces/tongue tie/blinkers: sold £2,200, joined P. D. Evans: fairly useful hurdler. *G. L. Moore* **–**

NOVILLERO 2 b.c. (Feb 14) Noverre (USA) 125 – Fairy Story (IRE) 80 (Persian Bold 123) [2009 6m 7m 6.5g p7g^5 Nov 25] rather leggy colt: form only when fifth in nursery at Kempton: will probably stay 1m. *J. C. Fox* **43**

NOW 3 br.f. Where Or When (IRE) 124 – Tup Tim (Emperor Jones (USA) 119) [2009 60: 6.1g 8.1g Jun 22] good-topped filly: little form since debut at 2 yrs. *P. Winkworth* **–**

NOW LOOK WHO'SHERE 2 b.g. (Mar 9) Kyllachy 129 – Where's Carol 67 (Anfield 117) [2009 6d Jul 27] 5/1, slowly away when last in seller at Yarmouth. *E. S. McMahon* **–**

NO WONGA 4 b.g. Where Or When (IRE) 124 – Fizzy Fiona (Efisio 120) [2009 59: 13.1d^3 11.9d* p13.9g 12s^2 13.8v^4 Nov 3] close-coupled gelding: fair handicapper: won amateur event at Haydock in September: stays 13.8f: unraced on firm going, acts on any other: held up. *P. D. Evans* **67**

NOW YOU SEE ME 5 b.m. Anabaa (USA) 130 – Bright Vision (Indian Ridge 123) [2009 68: p5g[2] f5g p5.1g f5g Mar 10] fair handicapper: below form after first start: best form at 5f: acts on all-weather: has hung/flashed tail: has joined R. J. Smith. *D. Flood* **65**

NUFOUDH (IRE) 5 b.g. Key of Luck (USA) 126 – Limpopo 49 (Green Desert (USA) 127) [2009 54: 7m 7.1m[3] 7g[3] 7.1g* 7.1g[4] 6m 7g* 7.1m[2] 7m[2] Sep 19] sturdy, workmanlike gelding: fair handicapper: won at Musselburgh in July and Catterick in August: stays 1m: acts on firm and soft going: prominent runner. *Miss Tracy Waggott* **66**

NUIT SOMBRE (IRE) 9 b.g. Night Shift (USA) – Belair Princess (USA) (Mr Prospector (USA)) [2009 82: 7m 7.5g 7d 7.5f[3] 7.5g 7g[6] p8.6m p8.6g Dec 14] good-topped gelding: fair handicapper: stays 10.5f, though best recent form around 7f: acts on polytrack and any turf going: usually wears headgear: front runner. *G. A. Harker* **73 a–**

NUMBER ONE GUY 2 br.c. (Apr 5) Rock of Gibraltar (IRE) 133 – Dubious (Darshaan 133) [2009 6g[6] 7.1m[5] 7g[6] 9m[6] 8g* Oct 20] 70,000Y: rather leggy colt: fourth foal: half-brother to 4-y-o Linby: dam, ran once in USA, closely related to high-class 1¼m performer Shady Heights: fair performer: improved to win nursery at Yarmouth: should stay beyond 1m: acts on good to firm going. *M. H. Tompkins* **75**

NUMIDE (FR) 6 b.g. Highest Honor (FR) 124 – Numidie (FR) (Baillamont (USA) 124) [2009 106§: p12m[4] Nov 4] strong gelding: useful performer: respectable fourth in listed race at Kempton (raced freely) only outing on Flat in 2009: stays 13.4f: acts on polytrack, heavy and good to firm ground: tried in blinkers/cheekpieces: usually slowly away: quirky and not one to rely on. *G. L. Moore* **99 §**

NUN TODAY (USA) 3 b.f. Chapel Royal (USA) 110 – Oldupai (USA) (Gulch (USA)) [2009 59: p7.1g p7g[4] p7.1g[5] 7.1f p7.1g[3] 8.3m p8g[5] p7g 7g 8.1d p7f p7m Oct 26] workmanlike filly: left J. S. Moore after second start, below form after fifth outing: stays 7f: acts on polytrack (seemingly not on fibresand): wears headgear: has gone in snatches. *Karen George* **57**

NURAI 2 b.f. (Jan 17) Danehill Dancer (IRE) 117 – Lady High Havens (IRE) 102 (Bluebird (USA) 125) [2009 p8g p7.1g Sep 25] third foal: dam, 2-y-o 7f winner (stayed 1¼m), out of half-sister to Irish 2000 Guineas winner Indian Haven: soundly beaten in maidens: tongue tied. *P. W. D'Arcy* **–**

NURTURE (IRE) 2 ch.f. (Feb 3) Bachelor Duke (USA) 122 – Silesian (IRE) (Singspiel (IRE) 133) [2009 p6f[5] p6g[2] 8g[3] 8g[2] Oct 31] €50,000Y, 50,000 2-y-o: good-topped filly: first foal: dam unraced daughter of Prix de Diane winner Sil Sila: highly progressive last 2 starts, very close third to Shakespearean in valuable Goffs Million Mile at the Curragh and nose second to Timepiece, pair clear, in listed event at Newmarket: stays 1m: already useful. *R. Hannon* **104 +**

NUSOOR (IRE) 6 b.g. Fasliyev (USA) 120 – Zulfaa (USA) 97 (Bahri (USA) 125) [2009 76: 5g 5g 5m p5.1g Jun 5] sturdy gelding: fair handicapper in 2008: well held in 2009: usually blinkered/visored: probably not straightforward. *Peter Grayson* **–**

NUT HAND (IRE) 3 b.g. Noverre (USA) 125 – Walnut Lady 91 (Forzando 122) [2009 58?: 7.5m 8f 12.1m[3] 12m[5] f14g[5] 10m[5] Aug 9] tall gelding: modest maiden handicapper: stayed 1½m: acted on good to firm ground: dead. *T. D. Easterby* **55**

NUTS ABOUT YOU (IRE) 2 b.f. (Apr 15) Rakti 130 – La Noisette (Rock Hopper 124) [2009 5m p5.1g 7m 6g Jul 3] half-sister to several winners, including fairly useful 6f winner Minimum Bid (by First Trump): dam unraced half-sister to smart 5f performer Repertory: slowly away when soundly beaten in maidens/sellers. *A. Berry* **–**

NYETIMBER (USA) 3 ch.c. Forest Wildcat (USA) 120 – Once Around (CAN) (You And I (USA) 118) [2009 p9.5g[6] p12m[5] p13.9g[4] f12f[5] Dec 11] modest maiden: stays 1¾m: raced only on all-weather. *J. A. Osborne* **64**

O

OAKBRIDGE (IRE) 7 b.g. Indian Ridge 123 – Chauncy Lane (IRE) 90 (Sadler's Wells (USA) 132) [2009 –: p11g Jan 10] tall, lengthy gelding: one-time fair performer: little form since 2007: tried tongue tied/blinkered. *R. Brotherton* **–**

OAK LEAVES 2 b.f. (Mar 21) Mark of Esteem (IRE) 137 – Exotic Forest 66 (Dominion 123) [2009 6f 6m 8v Oct 24] good-topped filly: half-sister to several winners, including 5f/6f winner (including at 2 yrs) Mesmerize Me (by Mind Games) and 5f (at 2 yrs) to 1m winner Threezedzz (by Emarati), both useful: dam 1m winner: modest maiden: best effort second start: should stay 1m. *J. G. Portman* **51**

Tattersalls Timeform Million, Newmarket—three of the first four start at 50/1 or longer in Britain's most valuable race for juveniles, 66/1-shot Oasis Dancer (left) getting the better of fellow outsider Kona Coast (centre) and Take Ten (right), the last-named touched off for the second time in this series of sales races after his second in the previous month's Tattersalls Timeform Millions Sprint

OASIS DANCER 2 br. or gr.c. (Apr 30) Oasis Dream 129 – Good Enough (FR) 109 (Mukaddamah (USA) 125) [2009 7.1g 7m^2 7m* Oct 3] 52,000Y: rangy colt: has scope: fifth foal: half-brother to 3 winners, notably smart miler Smart Enough (by Cadeaux Genereux): dam, fourth in Prix de Diane and later 9f winner in USA, half-sister to Molecomb Stakes winner Classic Ruler: 66/1, much improved when winning Tattersalls Timeform Million gamely by neck from Kona Coast: likely to stay 1m: acts on good to firm going: useful. *R. M. Beckett* **103**

OASIS JADE 2 b.f. (Apr 16) Oasis Dream 129 – Royal Jade 82 (Last Tycoon 131) [2009 5f^5 5f^3 6m^5 5.3m^6 7f p6m^4 6g Oct 19] quite attractive filly: closely related to fairly useful 6f winner Exmoor (by Cape Cross) and half-sister to several winners, including useful 6f (including at 2 yrs) to 1m winner Million Percent (by Ashkalani) and 3-y-o Finnegan McCool: dam, 7f winner, half-sister to smart sprinter Averti: fair maiden: stays 6f: acts on polytrack and firm going. *G. L. Moore* **65**

OASIS KNIGHT (IRE) 3 b.c. Oasis Dream 129 – Generous Lady 98 (Generous (IRE) 139) [2009 87p: 10m 13.3m* 14g^3 16m^2 16m^5 Oct 17] stocky, compact colt: useful performer: won handicap at Newbury in August by 1¾ lengths from Right Stuff: good efforts after when placed in listed races at Goodwood (to Mourilyan) and Ascot (behind Electrolyser) prior to 1¾ lengths fifth to Akmal in Jockey Club Cup at Newmarket (raced freely and none too keen in finish): stays 2m: acts on good to firm going: visored last 4 starts: quirky. *M. P. Tregoning* **106**

OBARA D'AVRIL (FR) 7 gr.m. April Night (FR) – Baraka de Thaix II (FR) (Olmeto 122) [2009 12g^5 10.4d 10m^3 15.8g^6 12.4d^3 Oct 13] non-thoroughbred mare: modest hurdler: modest maiden on Flat: stays easy 15.8f: unraced on extremes of going: held up. *S. G. West* **58**

OBE BRAVE 6 b.g. Agnes World (USA) 123 – Pass The Rose (IRE) (Thatching 131) [2009 89: 8g 6s 7s 7v 7.1g 7m^5 p7.1g* p6g^3 6m p7.1g p8.6g p8g p7g^3 p6g^6 p7.1g p7.1g Dec 28] strong gelding: has a quick action: fair handicapper nowadays: won at Wolverhampton in September: stays 7.5f: acts on polytrack, soft and good to firm going: usually blinkered/in cheekpieces nowadays. *L. Smyth, Ireland* **69**

OBE GOLD 7 b.g. Namaqualand (USA) – Gagajulu 75 (Al Hareb (USA) 123) [2009 103: f5m^2 p6g* 5m^5 6m^3 6m 6g^6 5m^3 5g* 5d* 5.7g^3 5g^3 6m^5 6d^4 p6g p7g p6m^3 p7.1g^2 p7m^4 p7.1g^3 p6m* Dec 30] tall, useful-looking gelding: fairly useful performer: won handicap at Lingfield in March, claimers at Hamilton and Catterick (left D. Nicholls £15,000) in July and, having left Miss D. Mountain after twelfth start, seller at Lingfield in December: effective at 5f to 7f: acts on all-weather, soft and good to firm going: often wears headgear: tried tongue tied: usually held up: often races lazily. *P. Howling* **91**

OBE ONE 9 b.g. Puissance 110 – Plum Bold 83 (Be My Guest (USA) 126) [2009 61: p6g 6m 6s^6 5m 5.9g 6m 6m 6m^5 6m 6s 5.9d^3 7.2s 7.2m Oct 1] leggy gelding: modest handicapper: effective at 5f to 7f: acts on any turf going: tried in cheekpieces/blinkers: usually held up. *A. Berry* **52**

OBERLIN (USA) 4 ch.g. Gone West (USA) – Balanchine (USA) 131 (Storm Bird (CAN) 134) [2009 52, a73: f14s f16g p16.5g p12g Mar 19] leggy gelding: fair handicapper at 3 yrs: well held in 2009: tried in blinkers/cheekpieces: ungenuine: joined M. Wigham. *T. Keddy* – §

OBE ROYAL 5 b.g. Wizard King 122 – Gagajulu 75 (Al Hareb (USA) 123) [2009 78: p6g[3] p6g[5] p6g[6] p6g[5] f6g[2] f6g[3] p6g[4] f7g* f7g* p7g[2] f7d* p7g[2] p7.1g[2] f7g[2] p7.1g p7g* f7g[4] 7g f7g[5] p7g[4] p8g p8.6g 7.6m p7g[6] p7.1g[3] 7.2s p7.1g p7m p7.1g Sep 17] close-coupled gelding: fairly useful performer on all-weather, fair on turf: won seller and handicap at Southwell in February, seller at same course in March and handicap at Kempton in April: effective at 5f to 7f: acts on all-weather and any turf going: wears headgear: held up: tough. *P. D. Evans* 66 a83

OBEZYANA (USA) 7 ch.g. Rahy (USA) 115 – Polish Treaty (USA) (Danzig (USA)) [2009 87: p7.1m[5] p8.6g[2] p8g[4] 8m[5] p8g[6] 7.9g[6] 8.1g Jun 18] quite good-topped gelding: fairly useful handicapper: below form after second start: stays easy 1¼m: acts on polytrack and firm going: tried tongue tied: often wears headgear nowadays. *A. Bailey* 80

OBSERVATORY STAR (IRE) 6 br.g. Observatory (USA) 131 – Pink Sovietstaia (FR) (Soviet Star (USA) 128) [2009 89: 8.5m[5] 8g[2] 7.9m[4] 8s[3] 8m[2] 8m[6] 7d[3] 8.3g[3] 7s Nov 7] good-topped gelding: fairly useful handicapper: mostly at least respectable efforts in 2009: stays 9f: acts on firm and soft going: wears blinkers/cheekpieces, also usually tongue tied nowadays: held up: often races lazily, but is consistent. *T. D. Easterby* 87

OBVIOUS 3 b.f. Falbrav (IRE) 133 – Bright And Clear 106 (Danehill (USA) 126) [2009 57p: 10.9g 9.9m f7g Dec 18] sturdy filly: maiden: well held in 2009. *Miss J. Feilden* –

OCARITO (GER) 8 b.g. Auenadler (GER) 114 – Okkasion (Konigsstuhl (GER)) [2009 p10g p8.6g Jan 22] winner of 5 races up to 9f in Germany for W. Hickst earlier in career: poor hurdler for M. Keighley: no form on return to Flat. *G. F. Bridgwater* –

OCCASION 4 b.f. Zamindar (USA) 116 – Set Fair (USA) (Alleged (USA) 138) [2009 –: 7d Jul 24] no form in maidens. *G. M. Moore* –

OCEANA BLUE 4 b.f. Reel Buddy (USA) 118 – Silken Dalliance 91 (Rambo Dancer (CAN) 107) [2009 85: p7g[5] p6g[4] 7m* 7g* 7g 7g 7g 7m Oct 3] good-topped filly: fairly useful handicapper: won at Newmarket in May and Doncaster in June: below form after: stays easy 1m: acts on polytrack, heavy and good to firm going: tongue tied: tried visored. *A. M. Balding* 89

OCEAN BLAZE 5 b.m. Polar Prince (IRE) 117 – La Belle Vie 73 (Indian King (USA) 128) [2009 91: 5g[6] 5m[2] 5f[5] 5.1m 5f[5] 5m[3] 5m[5] 5m* 5m* f5g[6] 5g[6] p5g[2] Oct 22] strong, lengthy mare: fairly useful handicapper: won at Goodwood and Newmarket in September: best at easy 5f: acts on firm and soft ground: speedy front runner. *B. R. Millman* 88

OCEAN CLUB 2 ch.g. (Mar 13) Storming Home 128 – Strictly Cool (USA) (Bering 136) [2009 p7g Oct 21] tall gelding: 16/1 and bit backward, last in maiden at Kempton: bred to need 1¼m+. *B. W. Hills* –

OCEAN COUNTESS (IRE) 3 b.f. Storming Home 128 – Pennycairn 84 (Last Tycoon 131) [2009 –: p8g 8d 7m* p8.6g 9g 7f[2] 8g[6] 7m 7m* 8d* 8d* p8g[5] p8f[6] Dec 13] leggy filly: fair performer on turf, modest on all-weather: won minor event at Yarmouth in May and handicaps at Brighton in September and October (2): stays 1m: acts on polytrack, firm and good to soft ground: tried visored. *Miss J. Feilden* 75 a62 +

OCEAN GLORY (IRE) 4 b.g. Redback 116 – Finty (IRE) (Entrepreneur 123) [2009 41: 5m Jun 10] sturdy gelding: fair winner on debut at 2 yrs: regressive since. *Pat Morris* –

OCEANIC DANCER (IRE) 3 b.f. Danetime (IRE) 121 – Almasa 83 (Faustus (USA) 118) [2009 54+: p6g p6g 5.1m 5m 5s Aug 26] smallish filly: maiden: just poor form at 3 yrs: best at 5f: acts on soft going. *Pat Morris* 44

OCEAN LEGEND (IRE) 4 b.g. Night Shift (USA) – Rose of Mooncoin (IRE) 99 (Brief Truce (USA) 126) [2009 86: p8g[2] p8g[5] p8g[3] p8g 8.1g[4] p8g[5] 8.3d p8g[6] p8g 7d[3] f8g p7g f7g p8g* 7m[6] f8g[5] p8.6g[6] Dec 4] workmanlike gelding: fairly useful performer: won seller at Lingfield in October: effective at 1m/1¼m: acts on all-weather and good to soft ground: tried visored/tongue tied. *Miss J. Feilden* 84

OCEAN OF PEACE (FR) 6 b.g. Volochine (IRE) 121 – Sumatra (IRE) (Mukaddamah (USA) 125) [2009 11s[6] 11.9m[4] p11g[3] p12m 10d[6] Oct 22] winner of 3 races in France for C. Boutin in 2008: modest handicapper in Britain: stays 2m: acts on polytrack, heavy and good to firm going: tried blinkered. *M. R. Bosley* 55

OCEAN PRIDE (IRE) 6 b.g. Lend A Hand 124 – Irish Understudy (ITY) (In The Wings 128) [2009 54: p16g Jan 30] strong, neat gelding: modest performer in 2008: well –

held sole start in 2009: stays 1½m: acts on polytrack, heavy and good to firm going: has worn blinkers/cheekpieces: tried tongue tied. *L. Wells*

OCEAN ROSIE (IRE) 2 b.f. (Mar 3) One Cool Cat (USA) 123 – Rose of Mooncoin (IRE) 99 (Brief Truce (USA) 126) [2009 p7g Sep 21] sturdy filly: sixth foal: half-sister to several winners, including smart 7f (including at 2 yrs) to 8.6f winner Russki (by Fasliyev) and 3-y-o The Scorching Wind: dam 2-y-o 6f winner: 100/1 and very green, soundly beaten in maiden at Kempton. *Miss J. Feilden* **–**

OCEAN'S MINSTREL 3 b.c. Pivotal 124 – Minstrel's Dance (CAN) (Pleasant Colony (USA)) [2009 77: p8g* 8m 7g* 7m 7m4 8d Aug 1] leggy, close-coupled colt: useful performer: won listed races at Lingfield (by 2¼ lengths from Deposer) in April and Epsom (beat Ermine And Velvet ¾ length) in June: creditable effort after only when 4 lengths fourth to Regal Parade in similar event at Chester: successful at 1¼m, best efforts at 7f/1m: best form on polytrack and good to firm going: struck into fourth outing: often front runner. *J. Ryan* **102**

OCEAN TRANSIT (IRE) 4 b.f. Trans Island 119 – Wings Awarded 67 (Shareef Dancer (USA) 135) [2009 76: 7.1m2 6m5 8.1f 7.1d* 7.1m2 8d2 9g 8g 10g 7v3 8.3g4 7s Nov 7] strong, compact filly: fairly useful handicapper: won at Warwick in June: stays 8.3f: acts on heavy and good to firm ground: races prominently. *R. J. Price* **89**

OCHILVIEW WARRIOR (IRE) 2 b.c. (Apr 20) Trans Island 119 – Lonely Brook (USA) (El Gran Senor (USA) 136) [2009 5g 7d 7.2s5 7.5m 6.1d 6g2 7.2v Oct 31] strong colt: form only when second in nursery at Ayr: bred to stay 7f: blinkered last 2 starts: has looked very awkward on bends. *R. Bastiman* **54**

ODDSHOES (IRE) 7 b.g. Mujadil (USA) 119 – Another Baileys 60 (Deploy 131) [2009 p9.5g3 Jan 16] tall, good-topped gelding: fair handicapper: respectable effort sole start on Flat in 2009: best at 7f to 9f: acts on polytrack and heavy ground: often in blinkers/cheekpieces/tongue tie prior to 2007: fairly useful hurdler, successful in April and (having joined P. Hobbs) December. *K. M. Prendergast* **61**

ODDSMAKER (IRE) 8 b.g. Barathea (IRE) 127 – Archipova (IRE) (Ela-Mana-Mou 132) [2009 85: 8m 14m 13g 12m 12m 7.9g 12.5s* 12d5 12.5m* 11.1g3 p12.2g 10g5 12.5d* Oct 28] angular gelding: fair performer: won handicaps in August and September and seller in October, all at Musselburgh: stays 1¾m: acts on firm and soft going: tried in headgear: tongue tied: front runner: sometimes hangs. *M. A. Barnes* **75**

OFF CHANCE 3 b.f. Olden Times 121 – La Notte 88 (Factual (USA) 108) [2009 8m3 9.8m* 12s 9.3g* 9.3m4 10.4g6 8m* 8m* 8s3 Sep 5] tall, good-bodied filly: third foal: dam, 2-y-o 6f winner, sister to useful Swedish miler Magic Fact: progressed into a fairly useful performer, winning maiden at Ripon in April, and handicaps at Carlisle in June, then Newcastle and Ripon in August: good third at Thirsk final start: effective at 1m/1¼m: acts on soft and good to firm ground: waited with. *T. D. Easterby* **91**

OFF HAND 3 b.f. Lend A Hand 124 – Off Camera (Efisio 120) [2009 –: 6m 6f 7.5m 6s4 f8g 7.5m3 8m Aug 9] close-coupled filly: modest maiden: stayed 7.5f: acted on soft and good to firm ground: blinkered last 3 starts: dead. *T. D. Easterby* **50**

OFFICER IN COMMAND (USA) 3 b. or br.c. Officer (USA) 120 – Luv To Stay N Chat (USA) (Candi's Gold (USA)) [2009 90+: 8.3g p8g p8g6 10m4 Aug 27] fairly useful performer: stays 1¼m: acts on polytrack and good to firm going: tried tongue tied. *J. S. Moore* **83**

OFFICER MOR (USA) 3 ch.g. Officer (USA) 120 – Hot August Nights (USA) (Summer Squall (USA)) [2009 75d: f6d4 p6g2 6d p6f 5g 6s Oct 27] good-bodied gelding: modest performer: well held after second start, trained by K. R. Burke until after third and by A. Jarvis for fourth: should prove best at 5f/6f: acts on polytrack and good to firm ground: tried blinkered: one to treat with caution. *A. Berry* **62 §**

OFFICIAL STYLE 2 b.c. (Feb 18) Dansili 127 – Reel Style (Rainbow Quest (USA) 134) [2009 7m 7m3 7m2 Oct 13] compact colt: second foal: dam, French 9f winner, out of sister to Queen Mary/Fred Darling Stakes winner Dance Parade: progressive form in maidens, 4 lengths second to Mufarrh at Leicester, best work late: will stay 1m: type to do better in handicaps. *Sir Michael Stoute* **81 p**

OGRE (USA) 4 b. or br.f. Tale of The Cat (USA) 113 – Soverign Lady (USA) (Aloha Prospector (USA)) [2009 84: p8.6g4 8m 10m3 8.5m* 7g* 8.5m 10.1d* 7m2 8d6 Oct 9] sturdy filly: fairly useful performer: won claimers (2) in July and apprentice handicap in September, all at Epsom: probably flattered when sixth in listed race at Saint-Cloud final start: effective at 7f to 1¼m: acts on polytrack, firm and soft going: usually tongue tied nowadays. *P. D. Evans* **84 +**

Mrs June Judd's "Oh Goodness Me"

OH GOODNESS ME 3 b.f. Galileo (IRE) 134 – Coyote 91 (Indian Ridge 123) [2009 96: 8s* 8m 8v³ 12g 12v⁵ 8s² 9v Aug 30] tall filly: useful performer: won Lodge Park Stud EBF Park Express Stakes at the Curragh in March by short head from Firey Red: good efforts after when 3¾ lengths third to Again in Irish 1000 Guineas at the same course and 1¾ lengths second to Latin Love in listed race at Cork: shaped as if amiss final start: may prove best at 1m/1¼m (shaped as if stamina stretched over 1½m in Oaks and Irish Oaks): acts on heavy ground: usually races close up: sold 400,000 gns, reportedly to Australia. *J. S. Bolger, Ireland* **108**

OH LANDINO (GER) 4 b.g. Lando (GER) 128 – Oh La Belle (GER) (Dashing Blade 117) [2009 13g 9.1m⁴ 10g 13.1g 11.1s Aug 1] German-bred gelding: trained by J. Pubben in Holland in 2008, winning minor event at Duindigt: poor form at best in Britain: stays 10.5f. *P. Monteith* **46**

OH SO SAUCY 5 b.m. Imperial Ballet (IRE) 110 – Almasi (IRE) 96 (Petorius 117) [2009 90: 7m 7m⁶ 7d⁶ 7d Sep 6] sturdy mare: fairly useful handicapper: stays 7f: acts on polytrack and good to firm ground, probably on good to soft: said to have had breathing problem final start. *C. F. Wall* **80**

OIL STRIKE 2 b.g. (Apr 19) Lucky Story (USA) 128 – Willisa 67 (Polar Falcon (USA) 126) [2009 5g² p6g* 6s Nov 7] 11,000F, £20,000Y: half-brother to 4-y-o Polar Annie and 5f (at 2 yrs) to 1m winner Waterpark (by Namaqualand): dam, 7f winner, half-sister to useful performers Alzianah (sprinter) and Return of Amin (up to 7f): fairly useful performer: won maiden at Lingfield in October: respectable eighth to Dubai Set in nursery at Doncaster: gelded after: should stay 7f. *P. Winkworth* **82**

OISEAU DE FEU (USA) 3 b.c. Stravinsky (USA) 133 – Slewadora (USA) (Seattle Slew (USA)) [2009 a7.5g* 8g³ 8m⁴ 8g* 8g² 8g⁴ 7g⁶ᵈ Oct 3] $11,000Y, €55,000 2-y-o: second foal: dam US 1m winner: smart performer: successful first 4 starts, including in **118**

minor event at Deauville on reappearance in March, and won Prix Paul de Moussac at Chantilly (by short neck from Handsome Maestro) in June: best efforts next 2 starts, head second to Lord Shanakill in Prix Jean Prat at Chantilly and 4½ lengths fourth to Aqlaam in Prix du Moulin de Longchamp: sixth past post behind Varenar in Prix de la Foret at Longchamp final outing, disqualified for causing interference early on: best at 1m: acts on all-weather, heavy and good to firm ground: often held up. *J-C. Rouget, France*

OISIN'S BOY 3 b.g. Catcher In The Rye (IRE) 115 – Red Storm 61 (Dancing Spree (USA)) [2009 60: 6d⁶ 8.5g Apr 22] good-bodied gelding: modest maiden: well held in 2009: stays 7f: acts on fibresand: tried in cheekpieces. *J. R. Boyle* **–**

OKAFRANCA (IRE) 4 b.g. Okawango (USA) 115 – Villafranca (IRE) (In The Wings 128) [2009 80: 14.1s Oct 12] fairly useful handicapper at 3 yrs: well held only start in 2009: stays 2m: acts on polytrack and heavy going: tried in cheekpieces (pulled hard). *J. A. B. Old* **–**

OKE BAY 3 b.f. Tobougg (IRE) 125 – Barakat 93 (Bustino 136) [2009 –: 10.2g 10.4g³ 14m⁵ f14g² f12g Dec 22] sturdy filly: modest maiden handicapper: stays 1¾m: acts on fibresand and good to firm ground: visored last 4 starts: has looked none too keen. *R. M. Beckett* **62**

OK KATIE 6 b.m. Slip Anchor 136 – Darling Splodge (Elegant Air 119) [2009 p12g p12g Apr 15] half-sister to 2m to 2¼m winner Our Monogram and 1¼m winner Starry Mary (both by Deploy): dam unraced: modest form in bumpers: well beaten in maidens on Flat. *R. M. Beckett* **–**

OLD DEVIL MOON (IRE) 2 br.g. (Jan 21) Johannesburg (USA) 127 – Tencarola (IRE) (Night Shift (USA)) [2009 5m 7m p7g f6g⁴ Oct 27] useful-looking gelding: modest maiden: best effort third start: should stay 1m: tried tongue tied. *T. G. Mills* **56**

OLD FIRM 3 ch.g. Compton Place 125 – Miriam 59 (Forzando 122) [2009 6s 5d p7.1g⁵ Nov 20] seemingly modest form at best in maidens: tongue tied first 2 starts. *D. A. Nolan* **55 ?**

OLDJOESAID 5 b.g. Royal Applause 124 – Border Minstral (IRE) 69 (Sri Pekan (USA) 117) [2009 111: 5.2s⁶ 6f 5g⁴ 6m 5g⁶ 5.6m⁶ 5m Sep 26] rather leggy gelding: smart handicapper in 2008: useful at 5 yrs, best effort when fourth to Indian Trail in 'Dash' at Epsom: effective at 5f/6f: acts on polytrack, soft and good to firm going: sold 40,000 gns. *H. Candy* **103**

OLD MONEY 2 ch.f. (Feb 1) Medicean 128 – Nouveau Riche (IRE) 84 (Entrepreneur 123) [2009 6f 7.1m³ 7d² Oct 6] angular filly: first foal: dam, 1m winner (stayed 1¼m), half-sister to smart performers Guys And Dolls (stayed 1¼m) and Pawn Broker (stayed 1½m): progressive in maidens, ¾-length second to Bint Doyen at Folkestone: will be suited by 1m+: open to further improvement. *H. J. L. Dunlop* **80 p**

OLD ROMNEY 5 br.g. Halling (USA) 133 – Zaeema 93 (Zafonic (USA) 130) [2009 72: p10g* p9.5g² p10g² p10g² p10g² 10g⁴ 10m 10.2m 10m 10d p10g Nov 25] tall, lengthy gelding: fair handicapper: won at Lingfield in January: left M. Wigham after seventh start: below form after: effective at 1¼m/1½m: acts on polytrack and firm going: has worn blinkers: travels strongly. *P. Howling* **77 d**

OLD SARUM (IRE) 3 b.g. Elusive City (USA) 117 – Quintellina 83 (Robellino (USA) 127) [2009 56: p6g Jan 21] good-topped gelding: modest maiden: appeared to stay 6f: raced only on polytrack and good to soft ground: was headstrong: joined P. McEntee in February: reportedly suffered fatal injury while being put through stalls on gallops in early-March. *D. R. C. Elsworth* **–**

OLIVE GREEN (USA) 3 b.f. Diesis 133 – Zaghruta (USA) (Gone West (USA)) [2009 8.3f⁴ 8g⁴ 8m⁵ 8.3v 8.3m² Sep 30] tall, unfurnished filly: sixth live foal: sister to 4-y-o Gifted Leader: dam unraced sister to Zafonic and Zamindar: fair maiden: raced only around 1m: acts on firm going: sold 30,000 gns, sent to France. *Pat Eddery* **77**

OLIVINO (GER) 8 ch.g. Second Set (IRE) 127 – Osdemona (GER) (Solarstern (FR)) [2009 p12g Jan 30] German-bred gelding: modest performer in 2006: tailed off first Flat outing since: fair hurdler, successful 3 times in 2009/10. *B. J. Llewellyn* **–**

OLNEY LASS 2 b.f. (Apr 7) Lucky Story (USA) 128 – Zalebe 52 (Bahamian Bounty 116) [2009 p7g 6.1s³ 6s² Nov 7] compact filly: first foal: dam 7f winner: fair form in maidens last 2 starts, ½-length second to London Gold at Doncaster: may prove best at 5f/6f. *W. J. H. Ratcliffe* **74**

OLYMPIC CEREMONY 2 br.g. (May 7) Kyllachy 129 – Opening Ceremony (USA) 89 (Quest For Fame 127) [2009 5s 5m³ 6m 6d³ 5m⁴ 6m 5m⁵ 6m³ 6s² f5m⁴ Dec 5] close-coupled gelding: fair maiden: effective at 5f/6f: acts on fibresand, soft and good to firm going. *R. A. Fahey* **67**

OLYMPIC DREAM 3 b.g. Kyllachy 129 – Opening Ceremony (USA) 89 (Quest For Fame 127) [2009 81: 7m^5 7.1m^4 8d^6 7m* 8m^6 7m^3 7d Aug 28] good-bodied gelding: fair handicapper: won at Newcastle in June: stays 7f: acts on firm and soft going. *R. A. Fahey* **78**

OLYNARD (IRE) 3 b.g. Exceed And Excel (AUS) 126 – Reddening 82 (Blushing Flame (USA) 109) [2009 90: 6.1m^5 5m^4 5g^3 6m* 6m* 5g Aug 22] strong gelding: useful handicapper: improved to win at Windsor in July and August: has raced freely, and best at 6f: acts on polytrack and good to firm ground. *R. M. Beckett* **98**

OMNIUM DUKE (IRE) 3 ch.c. Indian Haven 119 – Please Be Good (IRE) (Prince of Birds (USA) 121) [2009 69: p8.6g^3 p8.6g* 8g p8g^5 p8g p8.6g^2 p8.6g p8.6g Oct 17] good-bodied colt: fair performer: won maiden at Wolverhampton in July: stays 8.6f: acts on polytrack and soft going: effective visored/blinkered or not: sold 9,000 gns. *J. W. Hills* **78**

OMOKOROA (IRE) 3 b.g. Hawkeye (IRE) 122 – Alycus (USA) (Atticus (USA) 121) [2009 65+: 10m^3 12d^2 12g* 12g^2 14v^2 14.1s^2 Oct 12] sturdy gelding: fairly useful handicapper: won at Catterick in July: good efforts after: stays 1¾m: acts on heavy going, promise on good to firm. *M. H. Tompkins* **90**

ONCEAPONATIME (IRE) 4 b.g. Invincible Spirit (IRE) 121 – Lake Nyasa (IRE) 67 (Lake Coniston (IRE) 131) [2009 86: p6g^6 p6g^4 p7.1g 6d^3 p6g^2 6g^3 6m^3 p6g 5.2m p6m^6 p6g^2 p6g^6 p6m^4 p6g* f5m^3 p6g p6m^5 p6g^3 p6g^4 f6d^2 Dec 29] rangy gelding: fairly useful performer: won handicap at Wolverhampton in October: effective at 6f/7f: acts on all-weather and good to firm going: tried in cheekpieces. *M. D. Squance* **80**

ONCE MORE DUBAI (USA) 4 b.c. E Dubai (USA) 124 – Go Again Girl (USA) (Broad Brush (USA)) [2009 114: 10g^5 10m^3 9.9m^5 10.4g^6 11.8m* p12m* Nov 4] $20,000Y: half-brother to 3 winners in USA, including Grade 3 6f winner Go Again Valid (by Valid Appeal): dam US 8.5f winner: smart performer: successful in 2 listed races in Italy in 2008 for G. Bietolini: largely creditable efforts at 4 yrs, winning minor event at Leicester in October and listed race at Kempton (beat stable-companion Age of Reason 1½ lengths) in November: creditable 8¾ lengths third to Presvis in handicap at Nad Al Sheba earlier: stays 1½m: acts on polytrack, soft and good to firm ground: usually blinkered/tongue tied: held up: shaped as though amiss fourth outing. *Saeed bin Suroor* **111**

ON CUE (IRE) 3 ch.f. Indian Haven 119 – On Time Arrival (USA) (Devil's Bag (USA)) [2009 51: f8g^4 p10g^2 p8.6g 10.1g p12g^2 Jun 27] lengthy, angular filly: modest maiden: stays easy 1½m: acts on all-weather. *J. M. P. Eustace* **56**

ONEBIDKINTYMILL (IRE) 4 b.g. Mull of Kintyre (USA) 114 – More Risk (IRE) 82 (Fayruz 116) [2009 61: 6.1m* 6m^5 Aug 8] fair handicapper, lightly raced: won at Chepstow in July (sole outing for B. Baugh): will stay 7f: acts on good to firm going. *R. Hollinshead* **72**

ONE CAT DIESEL (IRE) 2 b.g. (Jan 14) One Cool Cat (USA) 123 – Awaaser (USA) 63 (Diesis 133) [2009 8g Oct 23] 50/1, last in maiden at Ayr. *N. Wilson* **–**

ONE COOL BUCK (IRE) 2 b.g. (May 14) One Cool Cat (USA) 123 – Simply Katie 93 (Most Welcome 131) [2009 5.2s 6g^5 a8g^4 Nov 13] lengthy gelding: has scope: better effort in maidens (far too green on debut) for R. Hannon when fifth at Goodwood: fourth in similar event at Ovrevoll: stays 1m. *W. Neuroth, Norway* **60**

ONE COOL DEAL (IRE) 2 b.g. (May 2) One Cool Cat (USA) 123 – Acciacatura (USA) 96 (Stravinsky (USA) 133) [2009 5.9m^6 6g p6g^5 7d 6d Aug 27] modest maiden: tried blinkered. *T. D. Easterby* **50**

ONE COOL DREAM 3 b.f. One Cool Cat (USA) 123 – Swift Baba (USA) (Deerhound (USA) 64) [2009 p8g 8.3m^4 7f^4 6m^3 7g Oct 16] 8,000F, €42,000 2-y-o: workmanlike filly: third foal: half-sister to 2007 2-y-o 5f winner Swallow Star (by Oasis Dream): dam ran 3 times: fair maiden: stays 1m: raced only on polytrack and good going or firmer on turf: sold £2,200, joined P. Hiatt. *W. R. Swinburn* **66**

ONE COOL KITTY 3 b.f. One Cool Cat (USA) 123 – Exultate Jubilate (USA) (With Approval (CAN)) [2009 73: p7.1g^4 6m^5 p7g^6 8s p6f^3 p6g p7g Nov 18] angular filly: modest handicapper: stays 7f: acts on polytrack, good to firm and good to soft going: tried tongue tied: usually held up: signs of temperament. *M. G. Quinlan* **62**

ONE COOL MISSION (IRE) 3 b.f. One Cool Cat (USA) 123 – San Luis Rey 75 (Zieten (USA) 118) [2009 55: p6g^3 7.1v^6 p7g Aug 7] modest maiden: should stay 7f: acts on polytrack: tongue tied in 2009: sold £400, sent to Qatar. *Tom Dascombe* **54**

ONE COOL POPPY (IRE) 2 b.f. (Feb 4) One Cool Cat (USA) 123 – Elusive Kitty (USA) 73 (Elusive Quality (USA)) [2009 7m^4 6.5m p8.6g^6 Oct 17] second foal: sister to 3-y-o Elusive Ronnie: dam, maiden (stayed 1¼m), half-sister to US Grade 3 8.5f winner Southern Africa: best effort when fourth to Many A Slip in maiden at Salisbury: may prove best up to 7f. *H. J. L. Dunlop* **58**

ONE COOL SLASH (IRE) 2 b.f. (Mar 27) One Cool Cat (USA) 123 – Sun Slash (IRE) 102 (Entrepreneur 123) [2009 p6g p7f^6 Dec 19] first foal: dam Irish 2-y-o 5f/6f winner: no show in maiden/minor event. *M. J. McGrath* –

ONE FOR JOULES (IRE) 2 b.f. (Mar 11) Choisir (AUS) 126 – Stuttgart 84 (Groom Dancer (USA) 128) [2009 7s^5 p6g 7d 7d^4 p8g Nov 14] first foal: dam, Irish 11f/1½m winner, half-sister to smart Irish performer up to 1¾m Orpington: fair maiden: best effort when fourth in nursery at Leopardstown: weakened quickly in claimer at Lingfield final outing: will stay 1m. *John Joseph Hanlon, Ireland* 67

ONE GOOD EMPEROR (IRE) 2 b.c. (Apr 20) Antonius Pius (USA) 123§ – Break of Day (USA) (Favorite Trick (USA) 121) [2009 6g^5 p6g^3 p7m^3 p6g Oct 16] €24,000Y: unfurnished colt: third foal: half-brother to useful 6f/7f winner Laddies Poker Two (by Choisir): dam unraced: fair maiden: best effort when third to Adele Blanc Sec at Lingfield second start: should be suited by 7f. *J. R. Best* 77

ONE HIT WONDER 2 b.g. (Feb 4) Whipper (USA) 126 – Swiftly 73 (Cadeaux Genereux 131) [2009 p5g^5 p6g^6 Jun 10] compact gelding: better effort in maidens at Kempton when sixth to Iver Bridge Lad (still green, gelded after). *Mouse Hamilton-Fairley* 50

ONEMIX 3 gr.f. Fair Mix (IRE) 123 – One For Philip (Blushing Flame (USA) 109) [2009 79p: p8g^2 p10g^2 10.2g* 10.2g^4 10m^3 11.6g^2 10g^5 p13.9g^3 Oct 10] workmanlike filly: fairly useful performer: won maiden at Bath in April: stays 11.6f: raced only on polytrack and good/good to firm ground: usually makes running/races prominently. *B. W. Hills* 81

ONEMOREANDSTAY 4 ch.f. Dr Fong (USA) 128 – Subito 94 (Darshaan 133) [2009 70: f11d* f11g^5 p10g 12d^3 10.1d^5 f12g* f11m^2 f12f^3 Dec 17] fair performer: won maiden in January (left R. Price after) and handicap in April, both at Southwell: stays 1½m: raced on all-weather and going softer than good: tried in cheekpieces (including for latest win): reliable. *M. D. Squance* 74

ONE MORE ROUND (USA) 11 b.g. Ghazi (USA) – Life of The Party (USA) (Pleasant Colony (USA)) [2009 85: p6g^2 p6g^2 p6g^4 p6g* p6g^4 p6g p6g^4 5.7m^4 6f^2 6g p7g p6g^5 p6g p7g p6m p6g Dec 5] rather leggy gelding: fair performer: won seller at Lingfield in January: largely below form after: form at 8.5f, races mainly at 6f/7f: acts on all-weather, firm and good to soft going: blinkered (tried in cheekpieces): held up. *P. D. Evans* 76 d

ONENIGHTINLISBON (IRE) 5 br.m. Bold Fact (USA) 116 – Mickey Towbar (IRE) 41 (Mujadil (USA) 119) [2009 79: p8g p8g p7g 7.6g 9.7m^3 8g^2 p10m 8.3m p10m^6 8.3g Oct 5] leggy, short-backed mare: modest handicapper nowadays: stays 9.7f: acts on polytrack, good to firm and good to soft going: has found little. *J. R. Boyle* 62

ONEOFAPEAR (IRE) 3 b.g. Pyrus (USA) 106 – Whitegate Way 46 (Greensmith 121) [2009 8.3m^5 f11g^5 8g^2 9.2g* Sep 21] €11,000F, €10,000Y: good-topped gelding: fourth foal: half-brother to 5-y-o Withnail: dam, maiden (raced only at 7f/1m), sister to US Grade 2 1m winner Lord Smith: fairly useful form in maidens: won at Hamilton in September by 5 lengths: stays 9f. *G. A. Swinbank* 87

ONEOFTHESEDAYZ (IRE) 3 b.f. Acclamation 118 – Thornby Park 94 (Unfuwain (USA) 131) [2009 48: 7.5m 8f 7m Jun 25] leggy filly: poor maiden: worth a try at 5f: tried in cheekpieces. *Mrs D. J. Sanderson* –

ONE OI 4 b.g. Bertolini (USA) 125 – Bogus Penny (IRE) 80 (Pennekamp (USA) 130) [2009 67: p8g^2 p8g p8g^4 Aug 5] fair maiden handicapper: will be suited by return to 1¼m: raced only on polytrack. *D. W. P. Arbuthnot* 65

ONE SCOOP OR TWO 3 b.g. Needwood Blade 117 – Rebel County (IRE) 97 (Maelstrom Lake 118) [2009 p8.6g^6 p7.1g^5 p8.6g^3 10.3g 14g p12.2g p9.5g^5 p7m Oct 28] modest maiden: stays 1½m: raced only on polytrack and good going: tongue tied. *F. Sheridan* 59

ONE SLICK CHICK (IRE) 3 b.f. One Cool Cat (USA) 123 – Ms Mary C (IRE) 68 (Dolphin Street (FR) 125) [2009 68p: p8.6g* Feb 14] better effort in maidens (fair form) when winning at Wolverhampton in January, still green: not seen out again: will probably stay 1¼m. *M. Botti* 71

ONE TOU MANY 4 b.f. Tobougg (IRE) 125 – Reine de Thebes (FR) 67 (Darshaan 133) [2009 –: 12.4s^3 16.1d 14.1m f14g 15.8g Aug 4] modest maiden: stays 12.4f: acts on soft ground: tried visored. *C. W. Fairhurst* 51

ONE UPMANSHIP 8 ch.g. Bahamian Bounty 116 – Magnolia 52 (Petong 126) [2009 p8.6g p9.5g Mar 6] modest performer in 2005: off 3½ years, well beaten in 2009: has worn blinkers/cheekpieces: tried tongue tied. *M. Salaman* –

ONE WAY OR ANOTHER (AUS) 6 b.g. Carnegie (IRE) 129 – True Blonde (AUS) (Naturalism (NZ)) [2009 7g 8.1g* 8g^2 8.1m^6 8g 7m^2 7s p8.6g^4 Nov 27] compact gelding: winner of 4 races for D. Hayes in Australia in 2008: useful handicapper in Britain: won at 101

Haydock in June: good head second to Aldermoor at Newmarket sixth start: has form at 1¼m, best form in Britain at 7f/1m: acts on heavy and good to firm ground: tried in cheekpieces: patiently ridden. *J. R. Gask*

ONE WAY TICKET 9 ch.g. Pursuit of Love 124 – Prima Cominna 86 (Unfuwain (USA) 131) [2009 68, a50: p6g p6g p5g³ p5g³ 5.3m 5.1m 5.3d⁴ 5.1g⁴ 5.3m⁶ 5.1d⁶ 5.1d⁶ 5.1m Sep 10] lengthy, workmanlike gelding: modest performer: best at 5f: acts on polytrack, firm and soft going: wears cheekpieces/blinkers: tongue tied of late: carries head high. *J. M. Bradley* **50**

ONE ZERO (USA) 4 ch.f. Theatrical 128 – Binary 109 (Rainbow Quest (USA) 134) [2009 73: p12g⁵ p12.2g⁴ Feb 9] maiden: only modest form in 2009, looking awkward on latter start: worth a try at 1¼m: raced on polytrack and good ground. *M. G. Quinlan* **63**

ONGOODFORM (IRE) 2 b.c. (Mar 15) Invincible Spirit (IRE) 121 – Elfin Queen (IRE) 64 (Fairy King (USA)) [2009 6g p6g³ 6m* 6m² p6g² p7g² Nov 5] 22,000Y: unfurnished colt: half-brother to 1½m winner Edgehill (by Ali-Royal) and winner in Greece by Dolphin Street: dam sprint maiden: useful performer: won maiden at Yarmouth (by 5 lengths) in September: much better form when close second in nursery at Warwick (to Comedy Hall) and minor event at Lingfield (to Chaperno) next 2 starts: stays 6f: acts on polytrack and good to firm ground. *P. W. D'Arcy* **97**

ON HER WAY 2 ch.f. (Feb 9) Medicean 128 – Singed (Zamindar (USA) 116) [2009 7g Oct 31] 65,000Y: big filly: third foal: half-sister to 3-y-o On Our Way: dam, French 1m winner, closely related to useful French 2-y-o 6f/7f winner Inhabitant: 16/1 and very green, soundly beaten in maiden at Newmarket (hung). *H. R. A. Cecil* **–**

ON HOLIDAY 2 b.f. (Mar 25) Dubai Destination (USA) 127 – Mount Hillaby (IRE) 80 (Mujadil (USA) 119) [2009 5d 6s⁵ 7.5f Aug 29] big filly: second foal: dam, 7f (including at 2 yrs)/8.6f winner: well held in maidens: bred to stay 7f+. *M. W. Easterby* **–**

ONIZ TIPTOES (IRE) 8 ch.g. Russian Revival (USA) 125 – Edionda (IRE) (Magical Strike (USA) 114) [2009 –: 14.1m⁶ Aug 8] close-coupled gelding: maiden handicapper, lightly raced on Flat: poor on balance: stays 1½m: acts on good to firm going: wears headgear: fair hurdler/chaser. *J. S. Wainwright* **49**

ON KHEE 2 b.f. (Mar 9) Sakhee (USA) 136 – Star Precision 103 (Shavian 125) [2009 8g p7g p7g⁴ Nov 11] quite attractive filly: fourth foal: half-sister to 3-y-o Benozzo Gozzoli and 5-y-o Sularno: dam 1m to 13f winner: modest form last 2 starts in maidens: will be suited by 1¼m: type to do better. *H. Morrison* **60 p**

ONLY A GAME (IRE) 4 b.g. Foxhound (USA) 103 – Compendium (Puissance 110) [2009 77: p7.1g p7.1g f6g f7d p6g 5.9g⁵ 5m* 5m⁴ 5m 5g 5g 7m 7m³ p7m 7m p6g⁴ f6g² p6m* Dec 16] strong gelding: fair handicapper: left Miss M. Rowland £1,200 after fourth start: won at Beverley in June and Lingfield in December: best at 5f/6f nowadays: acts on all-weather and good to firm going: tried blinkered, in cheekpieces/tongue tied nowadays. *I. W. McInnes* **68**

ONLY A GRAND 5 b.m. Cloudings (IRE) 112 – Magic Orb 81 (Primo Dominie 121) [2009 60: f8s f7g f8g f8g Feb 19] strong mare: modest handicapper at best: well held in 2009: usually blinkered. *R. Bastiman* **–**

ONLY A SPLASH 5 b.g. Primo Valentino (IRE) 116 – Water Well 96 (Sadler's Wells (USA) 132) [2009 45§: 6d⁶ 5m 5m 7.1g² 6v* 7.1g 6g f6g 7.2s⁵ Aug 26] sparely-made gelding: modest handicapper: won at Ripon in July: stays 8.3f, effective at shorter: acts on heavy ground: tried in cheekpieces: ungenuine. *Mrs R. A. Carr* **53 §**

ONLY HOPE 5 b.m. Marju (IRE) 127 – Sellette (IRE) 88 (Selkirk (USA) 129) [2009 54: f6g⁴ p6g f6g⁴ p5g³ f5g Feb 19] big, workmanlike mare: modest maiden: stays 1½m, effective at 6f: acts on all-weather and good to soft ground: often wears headgear. *P. S. McEntee* **52**

ON OFFER (IRE) 3 b.f. Clodovil (IRE) 116 – Camassina (IRE) 62 (Taufan (USA) 119) [2009 84: 8m⁶ 7g 6v³ 6d⁵ 6m⁵ 6d 6s⁵ 6g Sep 3] tall filly: fair handicapper: best form at 6f: acts on heavy and good to firm going: tried in blinkers/cheekpieces. *T. D. Easterby* **75**

ON OUR WAY 3 b.g. Oasis Dream 129 – Singed (Zamindar (USA) 116) [2009 109p: 9m⁴ 10m 7g* 7g² 8g³ Dec 13] big, strong gelding: useful performer: respectable reappearance when 3¾ lengths fourth to Redwood in listed race at Newmarket: well below form in similar event at Ascot next time: left H. Cecil, gelded, off 4½ months and renamed Chater Way, won handicap at Sha Tin in November: races freely, and may prove best up to 1m: acts on good to firm and good to soft ground. *D. E. Ferraris, Hong Kong* **102**

ON TERMS (USA) 3 b.f. Aptitude (USA) 128 – Silver Yen (USA) (Silver Hawk (USA) 123) [2009 p10m⁴ Dec 9] 3,500 3-y-o: second foal: dam, US 9f winner, half-sister **58**

to very smart 1¼m/1½m performer Notable Guest, out of smart half-sister to Derby winner Quest For Fame: promise when fourth in maiden at Lingfield, outpaced: bred to be suited by 1½m. *S. Dow*

ON THE BOUNTY 2 b.c. (Apr 7) Bahamian Bounty 116 – Dark Eyed Lady (IRE) 82 (Exhibitioner 111) [2009 5d* 5m^5 6d^3 6.1d^6 6.5m Sep 10] workmanlike colt: fair performer: won maiden at Doncaster in May: well below form last 2 starts: stays 6f. *R. A. Fahey* **68**

ON THE CUSP (IRE) 2 b.g. (Mar 25) Footstepsinthesand 120 – Roman Love (IRE) (Perugino (USA) 84) [2009 p7g^5 8g 7g Oct 23] modest maiden: gelded after final start: will stay 1m (stiff task when tried). *M. A. Jarvis* **63**

ON THE LOOSE (IRE) 5 gr.g. Great Palm (USA) 119 – Marys Rival (IRE) (Soughaan (USA) 111) [2009 10s^6 12m 10g 14g 12d^4 12s^4 9.1v* p12g Nov 11] fair handicapper: won at Ayr in October: stays 1½m: acts on heavy and good to firm going. *T. G. McCourt, Ireland* **67**

ON THE PISTE (IRE) 2 b.f. (Feb 20) Distant Music (USA) 126 – Lady Piste (IRE) 67 (Ali-Royal (IRE) 127) [2009 5m^3 5.2g* 5m^5 5g* f5g 5m* 5g^5 p5.1g^5 Nov 13] leggy filly: first foal: dam, 5f (at 2 yrs)/7f winner, half-sister to useful 2004 2-y-o 5f/7f winner Silver Wraith: modest performer: won sellers at Yarmouth in May and Catterick (left P. Midgley) in July and nursery at Redcar in September: raced only at 5f: acts on good to firm going: not straightforward. *L. A. Mullaney* **64**

ONYX OF ARABIA (IRE) 2 b.c. (Mar 15) Avonbridge 123 – Fiamma Royale (IRE) 74 (Fumo di Londra (IRE) 108) [2009 6g^5 7m^2 7.1m^4 7g Oct 17] €43,000F, 24,000Y, £34,000 2-y-o: lengthy colt: second foal: half-brother to fairly useful 2008 2-y-o 6f winner Burning Flute (by Piccolo): dam, 5f (including at 2 yrs) to 7f winner, half-sister to useful performer up to 1¼m Another Fantasy: fair maiden: seemed amiss final start: stays 7f. *B. J. Meehan* **75**

OONDIRI (IRE) 2 b.f. (Mar 30) Trans Island 119 – Nullarbor (Green Desert (USA) 127) [2009 5m^6 5m^3 5m* 5m^3 5f^3 5g^5 6m 5m^5 5m^4 5g^5 Oct 6] €4,000Y: smallish filly: half-sister to several winners, including 3-y-o Kuanyao and 9-y-o Desert Opal: dam, French 2-y-o 5.5f winner, out of half-sister to Irish 1000 Guineas winner Al Bahathri, herself dam of Haafhd: fair performer: won maiden at Redcar in May: below form in nurseries after next start: probably best at 5f: acts on good to firm going: tried blinkered: races up with pace (often freely). *T. D. Easterby* **67**

OOPS ANOTHER ACT 4 gr. or ro.f. Act One 124 – Oops Pettie 93 (Machiavellian (USA) 123) [2009 56: p10g 10.1m May 19] good-topped filly: regressive maiden: tried in cheekpieces: has joined A. Hales. *W. R. Swinburn* **–**

OOR WEE MIRACLE (GER) 3 b.f. Tiger Hill (IRE) 127 – Old Tradition (IRE) 76 (Royal Academy (USA) 130) [2009 9.2g Jun 17] €12,000F, 13,500Y: seventh foal: half-sister to 2 winners, including 5f (including at 2 yrs)/6f winner Litewska (by Mujadil): dam, ran twice, out of sister to Cheveley Park and 1000 Guineas winner Ma Biche: 33/1, travelled comfortably for long way before folding in maiden at Hamilton. *M. Dods* **–**

OPEN GLORY (FR) 2 b.f. (Mar 10) Lando (GER) 128 – Lovigna (GER) (Komtur (USA) 118) [2009 7m 7m 6s p7g p8m Sep 16] €35,000Y: rangy filly: fourth foal: half-sister to French 7.5f winner Ciao My Love (by Touch Down): dam, German 2-y-o 7f winner, half-sister to smart German performer up to 1¼m Lord of England: modest maiden: should be suited by 1m+. *Tom Dascombe* **55**

OPENIDE 8 b.g. Key of Luck (USA) 126 – Eyelet (IRE) (Satco (FR) 114) [2009 –§: p16.5g^5 17.2d May 18] sturdy, close-coupled gelding: maiden handicapper: lightly raced and little form on Flat since 2007: tried in cheekpieces/tongue tie: moody: won over hurdles in July, one-time useful chaser but temperamental nowadays. *B. W. Duke* **– §**

OPENING HAND 4 b.g. Observatory (USA) 131 – Belle Ile (USA) 67 (Diesis 133) [2009 –: p8.6g f12g Apr 21] winning hurdler, but little form on Flat: tried in cheekpieces. *G. J. Smith* **–**

OPEN SESAME (IRE) 3 b.g. Key of Luck (USA) 126 – Chiquita Linda (IRE) (Mujadil (USA) 119) [2009 p9.2g* 8m* 10.4v* May 22] €17,000Y: sturdy, dipped-backed gelding: fifth foal: half-brother to 7-y-o Fiefdom and fairly useful 2005 2-y-o 5f winner Puskas (by King's Best): dam, Italian 5.5f (including listed race at 2 yrs)/6f winner, half-sister to very smart 6f/7f performer Mount Abu: fairly useful form: successful all 3 starts, namely maiden at Great Leighs in January (gelded after) and handicaps at Newmarket and Haydock (still green, beat Tropical Blue 3¾ lengths) in May: stays 10.4f: sent to Hong Kong: open to further improvement. *P. W. Chapple-Hyam* **91 p**

OPERA GAL (IRE) 2 b.f. (Mar 8) Galileo (IRE) 134 – Opera Glass 88 (Barathea (IRE) 127) [2009 7m^5 8d^4 7d^2 Oct 12] unfurnished filly: second foal: dam, 8.5f winner, **81**

sister to 6f/7f performer Opera Cape and half-sister to stayer Grey Shot and sprinter Night Shot, all 3 smart: progressive in maidens, 3 lengths second to Thrill at Salisbury: should stay 1m+. *A. M. Balding*

OPERA PRINCE 4 b.g. Kyllachy 129 – Optaria 83 (Song 132) [2009 96: p11g 10.1g 10m 8.1m 8g 8d 10g⁶ Oct 19] smallish gelding: fairly useful handicapper nowadays: stays 1¼m: acts on polytrack and soft ground: has hung left. *S. Kirk* **89**

OPERA WINGS 3 ch.f. Medicean 128 – Wings of Love 61 (Groom Dancer (USA) 128) [2009 65p: 10f⁴ p12g⁵ Aug 17] neat filly: modest maiden: stays 1¼m: sold 5,000 gns. *Sir Michael Stoute* **63**

OPERA WRITER (IRE) 6 b.g. Rossini (USA) 118 – Miss Flite (IRE) (Law Society (USA) 130) [2009 78: f11g Jan 29] strong, compact gelding: fair handicapper: below form sole start in 2009: effective at 1¼m to easy 1¾m: acts on all-weather, heavy and good to firm going: wears cheekpieces. *R. Hollinshead* **–**

OPHISTROLIE (IRE) 7 b.g. Foxhound (USA) 103 – Thoughtful Kate 64 (Rock Hopper 124) [2009 11m Jul 2] tall gelding: poor maiden: well held sole Flat start since 2005: tried blinkered. *H. J. Manners* **–**

OPINION POLL (IRE) 3 b.c. Halling (USA) 133 – Ahead 113 (Shirley Heights 130) [2009 94p: 10f³ 11.9v* 12m 12g* Oct 10] strong, sturdy colt: smart handicapper: won at Haydock (by 1½ lengths from Distant Memories) in May and Ascot (further improvement when beating Kings Destiny 3½ lengths, staying on strongly) in October: below-form seventh in King George V Handicap at Royal Ascot in between: will stay 1¾m: acts on heavy going: capable of better still. *M. A. Jarvis* **111 p**

OPTICAL ILLUSION (USA) 5 b.g. Theatrical 128 – Paradise River (USA) (Irish River (FR) 131) [2009 67§: 7.1m⁴ 7.1m³ 5.9m 6m* 6g 7.1g³ 7.1m⁴ p6g 7g⁵ Oct 20] smallish gelding: modest handicapper: won at Hamilton in June: stays 7f: acts on polytrack, soft and good to firm going: tried in cheekpieces: temperamental. *R. A. Fahey* **64 §**

OPTICAL SECLUSION (IRE) 6 b.g. Second Empire (IRE) 124 – Theda 61 (Mummy's Pet 125) [2009 –: p6g 9m May 19] useful-looking gelding: maiden: lightly raced nowadays, and no form since 2007: left A. Berry after reappearance: blinkered: tried tongue tied. *K. W. Hogg, Isle of Man* **–**

OPTIMISTIC DUKE (IRE) 2 ch.g. (Mar 17) Bachelor Duke (USA) 122 – Gronchi Rosa (IRE) (Nashwan (USA) 135) [2009 p7g 8v p7g Nov 11] sturdy gelding: well held in maidens. *W. R. Muir* **–**

OPTIMUM (IRE) 7 b.g. King's Best (USA) 132 – Colour Dance (Rainbow Quest (USA) 134) [2009 53: f16d f16g⁶ Jan 13] close-coupled gelding: one-time fair handicapper: well held in 2009: tried visored. *J. T. Stimpson* **–**

OPUS DEI 2 b.g. (Apr 1) Oasis Dream 129 – Grail (USA) (Quest For Fame 127) [2009 6d³ 6m⁶ 6s p7.1g² p7.1g Nov 21] 68,000F, 15,000Y: good-bodied gelding: sixth foal: half-brother to 2006 2-y-o 6f winner Divine Right (by Observatory) and Irish 7f winner Aliceinwonderland (by Danehill), both fairly useful: dam, French 1½m winner, half-sister to smart performer up to 1m Three Valleys, out of half-sister to outstanding broodmare Hasili: fair maiden: left A. McCabe after second start: gelded, best effort when second in nursery at Wolverhampton: stays 7f: acts on polytrack: blinkered (hampered) final outing. *J. A. Glover* **75**

OPUS MAXIMUS (IRE) 4 ch.g. Titus Livius (FR) 115 – Law Review (IRE) 63 (Case Law 113) [2009 94: p7g⁵ p8g⁶ p8g⁵ 8m p8g 7.1m* 7.6m² 7m 8.9g 7d⁵ 6d 6d 7.6g⁴ 8.1m³ 7.6m³ 8g 8m² 8m⁵ Oct 3] good-topped gelding: useful handicapper on turf, fairly useful on all-weather: won at Musselburgh in May: several creditable efforts after: suffered condylar fracture of near-fore later in October: effective at 7f/1m: acts on polytrack, firm and good to soft ground: tactically versatile. *M. Johnston* **95 a86**

ORANGELEG 3 b.g. Intikhab (USA) 135 – Red Shareef (Marju (IRE) 127) [2009 –: 7m* 8f³ p7m* Dec 30] fair handicapper, lightly raced: won at Brighton in July and Lingfield in December: stays 1m: acts on polytrack and firm going. *S. C. Williams* **67**

ORANGE PIP 4 ch.f. Bold Edge 123 – Opopmil (IRE) 68 (Pips Pride 117) [2009 85: 6g p6g² 6m⁵ 5f⁵ 6d 5.7g Sep 7] tall, lengthy filly: fairly useful handicapper: best form at 6f: acts on polytrack and good to firm going: usually races prominently: joined P. Makin. *R. Hannon* **82 a89**

ORANGE SQUARE (IRE) 4 br.g. King Charlemagne (USA) 120 – Unaria (Prince Tenderfoot (USA) 126) [2009 67d: f6g⁴ f6g f6g³ p5g⁴ f5g Mar 31] modest performer nowadays: probably best at 5f/6f: acts on all-weather: tried in cheekpieces/tongue tie, visored last 3 starts: temperamental (carries head awkwardly). *D. W. Barker* **– § a50 §**

ladbrokes.com Stakes (Heritage Handicap), Ascot—Opinion Poll (No.19) wins from front-running stable-companion Kings Destiny, with Safari Sunup (checks) and Pevensey (cheekpieces) third and fourth

ORATORY (IRE) 3 b.g. Danehill Dancer (IRE) 117 – Gentle Night (Zafonic (USA) 130) [2009 96: 6d p7g Oct 11] big, strong, good sort: fairly useful performer: strong-traveller, may prove best at 6f/7f: acts on good to firm going: gelded after final start. *R. Hannon* **88**

ORBITOR 3 b.g. Galileo (IRE) 134 – Peacock Alley (IRE) 98 (Salse (USA) 128) [2009 81p: 10.3m^3 11.8f^3 Apr 25] rather leggy gelding: fairly useful winner at 2 yrs: below form in handicaps in spring: reportedly suffered setback after, then gelded: should stay 1½m: acts on polytrack and good to soft going: tongue tied final start. *M. L. W. Bell* **74**

ORCHARD HOUSE (FR) 6 b.g. Medaaly 114 – Louisa May (IRE) (Royal Abjar (USA) 121) [2009 –: p16g^3 21.6m Apr 20] leggy gelding: modest performer: stayed 2m: acted on all-weather: was usually blinkered: modest hurdler/maiden chaser: dead. *Evan Williams* **52**

ORCHARD SUPREME 6 ch.g. Titus Livius (FR) 115 – Bogus Penny (IRE) 80 (Pennekamp (USA) 130) [2009 98, a110: p7.1g* p8g p8g^4 p7g^5 7m 8.3g 8.3m 8m^4 p8g p7g p8m^6 Dec 4] good-topped gelding: useful performer on all-weather, fairly useful on turf: won minor event at Wolverhampton (beat Councellor by head) in January: in-and-out form after: effective at 7f, barely stays easy 1¼m: acts on polytrack, seems best on good ground or firmer on turf (won maiden on soft at 2 yrs): tried in headgear: usually held up. *R. Hannon* **84 a97**

ORCHESTRATION (IRE) 8 ch.g. Stravinsky (USA) 133 – Mora (IRE) 100 (Second Set (IRE) 127) [2009 –, a51: p6g^3 Feb 9] compact gelding: modest performer: best at 5f/6f: acts on all-weather, lightly raced on turf: usually wears headgear. *Garry Moss* **– a51**

ORCHESTRION 4 ch.f. Piccolo 121 – Mindomica 63 (Dominion 123) [2009 67d: 9.9g Jul 20] good-bodied filly: regressive maiden: upset/unseated in paddock before tailed off sole 4-y-o start. *Miss T. Jackson* **–**

ORCHID WING 2 ch.c. (Mar 20) Avonbridge 123 – First Ace (First Trump 118) [2009 6g^5 6m 6s f5g^2 Dec 8] 15,000F, 18,000Y, 68,000 2-y-o: first foal: dam unraced sister to Flying Childers winner Mrs P and closely related to smart sprinter Sarcita: fair maiden: best effort when second in nursery at Southwell: will be as effective at 5f as 6f. *R. A. Fahey* **70**

ORDER ORDER 3 br.f. Diktat 126 – Brocheta 100 (Hector Protector (USA) 124) [2009 61: p7.1g^3 8.3m p8.6g^4 7m p7g p10g^6 p12.2g* p12.2g Nov 16] big, strong filly: fair performer: won maiden at Wolverhampton in November: stays easy 1½m: acts on polytrack: tried visored: joined Tim Vaughan. *H. J. L. Dunlop* **65**

ORDNANCE ROW 6 b.g. Mark of Esteem (IRE) 137 – Language of Love 63 (Rock City 120) [2009 117: 8m^3 7.1g^2 8.3m* 9.9m^6 8.3m^4 8m 7.6m^6 8g^2 7g* 8.1v 8m Oct 2] close-coupled gelding: smart performer: as good as ever in 2009, winning listed race at Windsor (by 2 lengths from Pinpoint) in May and Supreme Stakes at Goodwood (by length, outbattled Asset) in August: good third (promoted to second) behind disqualified Delegator in Celebration Mile at Goodwood 24 hrs before latter race: below form last 2 outings: best at 7f/1m: acts on any going. *R. Hannon* **118**

ORDONEY (IRE) 4 b.c. Intikhab (USA) 135 – Mitawa (IRE) 73 (Alhaarth (IRE) 126) [2009 7d^2 7m* 10g^3 9.7f* p9.5g^2 10g^4 p10m Nov 4] €50,000F, 68,000Y: big, good-bodied colt: type to carry condition: second foal: half-brother to 1¼m selling winner Ful of Grace (by Marju): dam, 2-y-o 7f winner, half-sister to useful 1¼m/1½m performer Balladonia: fairly useful performer: won maiden at Redcar in August and handicap at Folkestone in September: stays 1¼m: acts on polytrack and firm ground: sold £25,000. *L. M. Cumani* **91**

ORIENTAL CAT 2 b.c. (Jan 17) Tiger Hill (IRE) 127 – Sentimental Value (USA) 107 (Diesis 133) [2009 7g^6 Oct 23] 100,000Y: well-made colt: second foal: half-brother to 3-y-o Barwell Bridge: dam 1m/9f winner, including minor US stakes: 9/1, encouraging 10½ lengths sixth to Tamaathul in maiden at Doncaster, closing from rear after slow start: will be suited by 1m+: will improve. *J. H. M. Gosden* **63 p**

ORIENTAL CAVALIER 3 ch.g. Ishiguru (USA) 114 – Gurleigh (IRE) (Pivotal 124) [2009 70: 9.9m^2 10.4v^5 10.3g^3 10.3m^3 10.4m^4 12m p9.5g^2 p9.5g* p9.5g^2 p9.5g^4 p12.2g^4 Dec 26] fairly useful performer: won maiden at Wolverhampton in November: stays 1½m: acts on polytrack, soft and good to firm ground: in cheekpieces later in 2009. *R. Hollinshead* **80**

ORIENTAL GIRL 4 b.f. Dr Fong (USA) 128 – Zacchera 82 (Zamindar (USA) 116) [2009 73: p10g^6 8.1g^4 8m^4 8m 9.9g^2 8.1d 9.9m^2 9.9s Oct 12] tall filly: fair handicapper: stays 1¼m: acts on soft and good to firm ground, probably on polytrack: formerly in cheekpieces (visored last 4 starts): hard ride. *J. A. Geake* **69**

ORIENTALIST ART 4 b.g. Green Desert (USA) 127 – Pink Cristal 113 (Dilum (USA) 115) [2009 99: 7m Aug 15] rangy gelding: useful performer at best, lightly raced: off 16 months (reportedly cracked pelvis in February), not knocked about in handicap at Newbury: stays easy 1m: raced on polytrack and good/good to firm going: slowly away last 2 3-y-o outings: sold 800 gns, later won at 1m in Greece. *P. W. Chapple-Hyam* **89**

ORIENTAL ROSE 3 b.f. Dr Fong (USA) 128 – Sahara Rose (Green Desert (USA) 127) [2009 73: 6d 6.1m^2 6.9m^6 6g^4 6g^2 6m^4 6m^4 5m Sep 24] leggy filly: fair handicapper: stays 6f: acts on good to firm ground. *G. M. Moore* **70**

ORIENTAL SCOT 2 ch.c. (Feb 15) Selkirk (USA) 129 – Robe Chinoise 103 (Robellino (USA) 127) [2009 7g^5 p8.6g^2 f8f^5 Dec 12] 42,000Y: tall, good-topped colt: second foal: brother to 3-y-o Mannlichen: dam, 1¼m to 11.7f winner (stayed 1¾m), half-sister to useful performer up to 2m Kiswahili (by Selkirk): shaped well first 2 starts in maidens, travelling strongly when 2 lengths second to Bowdler's Magic at Wolverhampton: well below form (fibresand) final outing: bred to be suited by 1¼m+, but not short of speed: remains open to improvement. *W. Jarvis* **73 p**

ORIGINAL DANCER (IRE) 2 b.c. (Jan 12) Danehill Dancer (IRE) 117 – Courtier (Saddlers' Hall (IRE) 126) [2009 6g 7.2m Sep 18] lengthy colt: has scope: down the field in maidens at York and Ayr 4 months apart. *M. Johnston* **–**

ORIZABA (IRE) 3 b.c. Orpen (USA) 116 – Jus'chillin' (IRE) 60 (Elbio 125) [2009 111: 8g^3 8m 8g^2 8m^5 Aug 13] useful-looking colt: useful performer: best effort in 2009 when 1¾ lengths second to Khateeb in listed race at Pontefract: stays 1m: acts on good to firm and good to soft going. *Saeed bin Suroor* **109**

ORKNEY (IRE) 4 b.g. Trans Island 119 – Bitty Mary 49 (Be My Chief (USA) 122) [2009 76: f12g 13.1g^6 11.9g Aug 7] good-bodied gelding: fair performer in 2008: well held at 4 yrs: tried in cheekpieces. *Julie Camacho* **–**

ORLANDO'S TALE (USA) 4 ch.g. Tale of The Cat (USA) 113 – Tell Seattle (USA) (A P Indy (USA) 131) [2009 –: 8g 7.1g^2 7m^2 7g 7f* Sep 8] angular gelding: fairly useful performer: won maiden at Lingfield (again raced freely) in September: stays 7f: acts on firm going: sold 5,000 gns. *J. R. Fanshawe* **86**

ORONSAY 4 ch.f. Elmaamul (USA) 125 – Glenfinlass (Lomond (USA) 128) [2009 54: 10m 10.9f^6 12.1g^2 10.2f 11.5m 12.1v^5 10f^5 9.7s^3 10d Oct 22] leggy filly: modest maiden handicapper: barely stays 1½m: acts on soft ground: tongue tied: inconsistent. *B. R. Millman* **60**

ORPEN ALL HOURS (IRE) 2 b.f. (May 10) Orpen (USA) 116 – Devious Miss (IRE) (Dr Devious (IRE) 127) [2009 6d 6g p6g 5v 8m f5g Sep 29] £14,000 2-y-o: fourth foal: half-sister to fairly useful 2007 2-y-o 6f winner Lord Sandicliffe (by Spartacus): dam, of no account in Ireland, half-sister to smart 7f/1m performer Little White Lie (by Orpen): no form: tried in cheekpieces. *P. C. Haslam* **–**

ORPEN ARMS (IRE) 2 b.f. (Feb 18) Orpen (USA) 116 – Lindas Delight 54 (Batshoof 122) [2009 5f^2 5g^3 6d^2 6m^4 5g^5 7g 7.1m^2 7m^6 Oct 26] €5,000Y: lengthy filly: half-sister to several winners, including 11-y-o Fromsong and 6f/7f winner Marshallspark (by Fayruz): dam 2-y-o 6f seller winner: modest maiden on balance: stays 7f: acts on firm and good to soft going. *R. A. Fahey* **58**

ORPEN BID (IRE) 4 b.f. Orpen (USA) 116 – Glorious Bid (IRE) (Horage 124) [2009 51: 12.4s 8.3m Jun 10] maiden: modest at 3 yrs, well held in 2009. *A. M. Crow* **–**

ORPENELLA 4 b.f. Orpen (USA) 116 – M N L Lady 85 (Polar Falcon (USA) 126) [2009 –, a70: f11s^2 p11g^3 f8g^3 Jan 29] modest maiden: probably stayed 11f: acted on fibresand: blinkered: dead. *K. A. Ryan* **61**

ORPEN GREY (IRE) 2 gr.g. (Feb 9) Orpen (USA) 116 – Sky Red 75 (Night Shift (USA)) [2009 6m^{5} 5g* 6g* 6m^{2} 6m^{5} Aug 19] €37,000Y: strong gelding: seventh foal: half-brother to 3 winners, including Irish 2006 2-y-o 5f winner Rose of Battle (by Averti) and Irish 6-y-o Chronomatic: dam 5f winner: smart performer: won maiden at Warwick and minor event at Salisbury (by 8 lengths) in June: excellent ¾-length second of 11 to Arcano in July Stakes at Newmarket: disappointing in Gimcrack Stakes at York final start, then gelded: effective at 5f/6f: raced only on good/good to firm going: front runner: reportedly sold privately, and sent to Hong Kong where renamed Able Grey. *Tom Dascombe* **115**

ORPENINDEED (IRE) 6 b. or br.g. Orpen (USA) 116 – Indian Goddess (IRE) (Indian Ridge 123) [2009 101: p6g^{4} p7.1g^{3} p7g^{2} p7g^{6} 6m^{3} 6g p7.1g^{2} p7.1g^{3} p6g* p5.1g^{4} Nov 16] tall gelding: useful handicapper: won at Wolverhampton in October: won at 1m in Italy earlier in career, races at 6f/7f nowadays: acts on polytrack and good to firm ground: often wore cheekpieces in 2009 (including for win): has been tongue tied: sometimes makes running. *M. Botti* **98**

ORPEN LADY 3 b.f. Orpen (USA) 116 – Gargren (IRE) (Mujtahid (USA) 118) [2009 6g p5.1g Aug 10] 3,600Y: fifth foal: half-sister to 2002 2-y-o 5f winner Miss Twti (by Ali-Royal) and 7f/1m winner in Italy by Sri Pekan: dam unraced: last in maidens. *J. M. Bradley* **–**

ORPEN'S ART (IRE) 4 b.c. Invincible Spirit (IRE) 121 – Bells of Ireland (UAE) (Machiavellian (USA) 123) [2009 77: p7.1g p6g^{6} p5.1g^{3} 5.1m 5.3f* f5g^{3} 5.3m^{5} p5g^{6} 5m 5.3m 5.3f* 5.3m^{2} 8g 5g^{5} 8s 4d^{5} 5f^{2} 5d 5.5s Nov 7] quite good-topped colt: fair performer: claimed from George Baker £6,000 second start: won handicaps at Brighton in May and June: sold from S. Callaghan 8,000 gns after next outing: stays easy 6f: acts on all-weather, firm and good to soft going: tried blinkered. *Ecurie Prince Rose, Belgium* **68**

ORPEN SHADOW (IRE) 2 b.c. (Feb 10) Orpen (USA) 116 – Mujadil Shadow (IRE) (Mujadil (USA) 119) [2009 5m* 6m* 5m* 6m* 5.5g^{4} Jul 26] fourth foal: half-brother to 2 winning sprinters in Italy, including smart performer Titus Shadow (by Titus Livius): dam, Italian 5f (at 2 yrs)/6f winner, half-sister to smart sprinters Evening Time (in Ireland) and Distinctly Dancer (in Italy): smart performer: won newcomers race at Milan, minor events at Rome and Milan, and Premio Primo Passi at Milan (by neck from Marshade, pair clear) in May/June: ran well when 2¼ lengths fourth to Special Duty in Prix Robert Papin at Maisons-Laffitte final start, again making running: effective at 5f/6f: raced only on good/good to firm ground. *B. Grizzetti, Italy* **111**

ORPEN WIDE (IRE) 7 b.g. Orpen (USA) 116 – Melba (IRE) 62 (Namaqualand (USA)) [2009 –: f8g^{3} p7.1m f6g^{5} 7m* 8.3m 8.5m 8.1m^{4} 7m 8d^{3} 7g 7g Oct 9] strong, lengthy gelding: fairly useful handicapper: second start in 48 hrs, won at Leicester in April: largely below form after: best efforts at 7f to 8.3f: acts on all-weather and any turf going: tried tongue tied, usually wears headgear. *M. C. Chapman* **92**

ORPHAN BOY 4 b.g. Tipsy Creek (USA) 115 – Miss Jingles 73 (Muhtarram (USA) 125) [2009 –: p6g Jan 14] no sign of ability. *H. J. Collingridge* **–**

ORPHANED ANNIE 3 b.f. Lend A Hand 124 – Great Exception 84 (Grundy 137) [2009 61: 12m^{4} 12m^{6} Apr 20] rather leggy filly: modest maiden: should stay 1¼m: acts on all-weather, best turf effort on good ground. *B. Ellison* **50**

ORPSIE BOY (IRE) 6 b.g. Orpen (USA) 116 – Nordicolini (IRE) 64 (Nordico (USA)) [2009 101, a108: p6g^{6} p6g^{3} p6g^{2} p6g^{4} 6m^{5} 6f^{4} 6m 7m 7m 6d 5g 5g 5.6m 6.1m 6m^{3} Oct 5] big, useful-looking gelding: useful performer: creditable efforts in early-2009, including third to Matsunosuke in listed race at Lingfield and neck second to Thebes in handicap at Wolverhampton: lost way after sixth start: best at 6f: acts on polytrack and firm ground: has worn headgear/tongue tie. *N. P. Littmoden* **104**

ORSETT LAD (USA) 2 b.g. (Mar 5) Essence of Dubai (USA) 118 – Sofisticada (USA) (Northern Jove (CAN)) [2009 7f^{6} p6g^{4} p7g^{4} 7m^{3} 7m p8m p7g^{6} p7g p7g^{6} Dec 31] modest maiden: should be well suited by 1m+: acts on polytrack and good to firm going. *J. R. Best* **63**

ORSIPPUS (USA) 3 b. or br.g. Sunday Break (JPN) 121 – Mirror Dancing (USA) (Caveat (USA)) [2009 83: p10g^{5} p10g^{6} p10g^{6} 12m^{3} p12g 11.6m^{4} 12.1g 9g 16.1g^{2} 16.1d Oct 13] good-topped gelding: fair handicapper: left M. Channon after eighth start: stays 2m: acts on polytrack and soft ground: tried visored: often races freely: modest form in juvenile hurdles. *Michael Smith* **74**

ORTHOLOGY (IRE) 3 b.g. Kalanisi (IRE) 132 – Al Shakoor (Barathea (IRE) 127) [2009 86p: 12m^{5} 12.4s^{5} 9.7m^{4} p8g^{5} 10g^{5} 11.8m^{5} 10.1d* Oct 27] good-topped gelding: **78**

fair performer nowadays: in cheekpieces, won seller at Yarmouth in October: should stay 1½m: acts on soft ground: tried blinkered: signs of temperament: sold 12,500 gns. *M. H. Tompkins*

OSCAR WILD 7 b.g. Tragic Role (USA) – Minster Lascar (Scallywag 127) [2009 –: 7g⁴ 9.3m 7.2s 9.1v Oct 31] poor form in bumpers/over hurdles: modest maiden on Flat: left James Moffatt after second start: should stay beyond 7f: tried in cheekpieces. *I. Semple* **54**

OSIRIS WAY 7 ch.g. Indian Ridge 123 – Heady (Rousillon (USA) 133) [2009 105: 6m⁴ 6m 6.1m 6d 6m⁵ 6g 6d Oct 11] well-made gelding: useful handicapper: creditable 2 lengths fourth to High Standing at Goodwood on reappearance: below form after: effective at 5f/6f: acts on polytrack, good to firm and good to soft going: often races prominently. *P. R. Chamings* **102**

OSKARI 4 b.g. Lear Spear (USA) 124 – Cedar Jeneva 34 (Muhtarram (USA) 125) [2009 55: f7g² f7g² 8.5g 7m f8m³ 10m⁴ f8g⁵ Aug 25] fair maiden on all-weather, modest on turf: should stay 1¼m: acts on fibresand, probably on good to firm ground. *P. T. Midgley* **60 a69**

OSORIOS TRIAL 2 ch.c. (Feb 18) Osorio (GER) 114 – Skytrial (USA) (Sky Classic (CAN)) [2009 7g 6.8d* 6.8g a8g² Nov 6] good-topped colt: has scope: sold from M. Johnston 11,000 gns after debut (gave impression amiss in maiden at Newmarket): won minor event at Övrevoll in September and second in similar event there final start: stays 1m. *Rune Haugen, Norway* **?**

OSTAADI 3 b.c. Nayef (USA) 129 – Blodwen (USA) 52 (Mister Baileys 123) [2009 10m f11g* p12g² p16g² Jun 25] 280,000Y: good-topped colt: fourth foal: half-brother to useful German 1¼m winner Carolines Secret (by Inchinor): dam, maiden who probably stayed 1½m, out of Cheveley Park Stakes and 1000 Guineas winner Ma Biche: fairly useful performer: won maiden at Southwell in May: improved when runner-up in handicaps at Kempton after: stays 2m: acts on all-weather, promise on good to firm ground only turf start. *M. A. Jarvis* **89**

OSTENTATION 2 ch.g. (Feb 11) Dubawi (IRE) 129 – Oshiponga 72 (Barathea (IRE) 127) [2009 7.5g⁵ 6.1s p8g p7m⁶ Nov 27] well-made gelding: modest maiden: should stay 1m: usually slowly away: signs of temperament third start, gelded after final one. *M. Johnston* **58**

OSTEOPATHIC CARE (IRE) 5 b.g. Montjeu (IRE) 137 – Super Gift (IRE) 96 (Darshaan 133) [2009 –: f7g May 1] workmanlike gelding: little form: tried in cheekpieces. *Miss Tracy Waggott* **–**

OSTEOPATHIC REMEDY (IRE) 5 ch.g. Inchinor 119 – Dolce Vita (IRE) 85 (Ela-Mana-Mou 132) [2009 101: 8m 7m⁶ 7f 8m 6d³ 6m⁶ 7m² 7d² 8m 7d⁵ 8g³ 7.2m² p8g⁵ 8v⁴ Oct 31] sparely-made gelding: fairly useful handicapper nowadays: generally held form well in 2009: effective at 6f to 1m: acts on soft and good to firm going. *M. Dods* **93**

OSTERHASE (IRE) 10 b.g. Flying Spur (AUS) – Ostrusa (AUT) (Rustan (HUN)) [2009 86: 5d³ 5g⁵ 6.3g 5s p6g p5g Sep 6] big, good-topped gelding: formerly very smart, still useful handicapper: ran well at Naas (1½ lengths third to Fol Hollow) and York (fifth to Internationaldebut) first 2 starts in 2009: well below form after: best at 5f/6f: has won on good to soft ground, best on good or firmer: usually blinkered/visored: game front runner. *J. E. Mulhern, Ireland* **100**

Jersey Stakes, Royal Ascot—his stable's second string Ouqba (No.13) comes with a strong late run under Tadhg O'Shea to overhaul long-time leader Deposer (right); Ashram (rail, partly obscured by winner) and Gallagher (No.8) complete the frame

OTHELLO (IRE) 2 b.g. (Apr 5) Azamour (IRE) 130 – Bonheur (IRE) 93 (Royal Academy (USA) 130) [2009 8.3v p7g p7g Nov 18] €25,000F: big, heavy-bodied gelding: fifth foal: half-brother to 3 winners, including smart Irish/US 7f to 8.5f winner Carribean Sunset (by Danehill Dancer) and 1½m winner Ommadawn (by Montjeu): dam, Irish 6f winner, out of US Grade 1 1¼m winner Queen To Conquer: modest form in maidens, still green final start: type to do better at 1m+ at 3 yrs. *E. F. Vaughan* **53 p**

OTTERTON 2 b.f. (Mar 15) Sampower Star 118 – Parkside Prospect 65 (Piccolo 121) [2009 $6g^{6}$ 7d Jul 31] fourth foal: dam 2-y-o 5f/6f winner: better effort when sixth to Bluie in seller at Haydock, finishing well. *R. Hollinshead* **49**

OTTOMAN EMPIRE (FR) 3 ch.g. Pivotal 124 – Chesnut Bird (IRE) 108 (Storm Bird (CAN) 134) [2009 $8m^{5}$ $10g^{2}$ $10m^{5}$ f11g* p12g* $p12g^{2}$ 10.2d Oct 15] €360,000Y: stocky gelding: fourth foal: dam, French 1¼m/10.5f winner, half-sister to smart French 1m/1¼m performer Caesarion: useful performer: won maiden at Southwell in August and handicap at Kempton in September: good length second to Highland Glen in handicap at Kempton penultimate start, again hanging right: stays 1½m: acts on all-weather and good to firm going, well below form on good to soft final start: gelded after. *D. R. Lanigan* **102**

OUQBA 3 b.c. Red Ransom (USA) – Dancing Mirage (IRE) 83 (Machiavellian (USA) 123) [2009 105: 7m* 8m 7m* $7g^{6}$ $7m^{4}$ $7m^{2}$ Oct 17] sturdy colt: good walker, though has quick, unimpressive action in faster paces: very smart performer: won listed Free Handicap at Newmarket (by 2¾ lengths from Awinnersgame) in April and Jersey Stakes at Royal Ascot (beat Deposer ½ length) in June: good efforts in Park Stakes at Doncaster (close fourth to Duff) and Challenge Stakes at Newmarket (better than result when neck second to Arabian Gleam, short of room as winner struck on) last 2 starts: should stay 1m (eleventh in 2000 Guineas when tried): acts on good to firm and good to soft going: finished lame fourth start: has raced lazily/looked reluctant. *B. W. Hills* **122**

Mr Hamdan Al Maktoum's "Ouqba"

OUR ACQUAINTANCE 4 ch.g. Bahamian Bounty 116 – Lady of Limerick (IRE) (Thatching 131) [2009 69: p5.1g f5g 5.1g 5.7m Jun 13] lengthy gelding: fair performer in 2008: just poor form at 4 yrs: usually blinkered. *W. R. Muir* **45**

OUR APOLONIA (IRE) 3 b.f. Intikhab (USA) 135 – Algaira (USA) (Irish River (FR) 131) [2009 51: 6d 7.1m 6v 7.9g⁴ 8.3v 9.8d Sep 1] tall filly: maiden: well held in 2009: tried blinkered. *A. Berry* **–**

OURBELLE 4 b.f. Bertolini (USA) 125 – Guardienne (Hector Protector (USA) 124) [2009 –: 5m Sep 14] small filly: no form. *Miss Tracy Waggott* **–**

OUR BLESSING (IRE) 5 b.g. Lujain (USA) 119 – Berenice (ITY) (Marouble 116) [2009 76: p6g⁴ 6g² 6m May 16] tall, close-coupled gelding: fair handicapper: speedy, all wins at 5f/6f: acts on polytrack, soft and good to firm ground: tried visored: usually races prominently: none too consistent. *A. P. Jarvis* **69**

OUR BOY BARRINGTON (IRE) 2 b.c. (Apr 12) Catcher In The Rye (IRE) 115 – Daily Double (FR) (Unfuwain (USA) 131) [2009 6.1g 7g 7.1g Aug 12] €32,000F, £32,000Y: well-made colt: fifth foal: half-brother to several winners, including 3-y-o Sharpener and 6-y-o Princess Cocoa: dam unraced: best effort in maidens when seventh to Missionaire at Newmarket second start: should be as effective at 6f as 7f: will probably still do better. *R. Hannon* **63 p**

OUR DAY WILL COME 3 b.f. Red Ransom (USA) – Dawnus (IRE) 103 (Night Shift (USA)) [2009 75: 8g⁵ 7.1f 6.1g May 25] smallish, well-made filly: type to carry condition: fair maiden at 2 yrs: well held in 2009, shaping as though amiss. *R. Hannon* **–**

OUR DREAM QUEEN 2 b.f. (Feb 20) Oasis Dream 129 – Our Queen of Kings (Arazi (USA) 135) [2009 5.2s³ 6g⁵ 6g* 6m³ 6g 6s Nov 7] good-bodied filly: sixth foal: half-sister to several winners, including smart 6f (at 2 yrs) to 1m (Sun Chariot Stakes) winner Spinning Queen (by Spinning World) and 3-y-o Changing The Guard: dam, unraced half-sister to Fanmore (high class) and Labeeb (very smart), both best up to 1¼m: fair performer: won maiden at Ffos Las in July: stays 6f: acts on soft and good to firm going: tongue tied final outing (tailed off): sold 55,000 gns. *B. W. Hills* **68**

OUR FUGITIVE (IRE) 7 gr.g. Titus Livius (FR) 115 – Mystical Jumbo (Mystiko (USA) 124) [2009 72d: p6g p5g⁵ f5g⁶ Mar 31] leggy gelding: modest handicapper nowadays: effective at 5f/6f: acts on polytrack, soft and good to firm going: often wears headgear: races prominently: carries head high, and one to treat with plenty of caution. *C. Gordon* **52 §**

OUR GEORGIE GIRL 2 ch.f. (Jan 18) Zafeen (FR) 123 – Rosina May (IRE) 83 (Danehill Dancer (IRE) 117) [2009 5g 5.2g⁶ 6g 7s⁶ 6g Jun 15] workmanlike filly: third foal: dam 2-y-o 5f winner: no form, including in sellers: tried blinkered. *G. G. Margarson* **–**

OUR GIRL ALLY (IRE) 3 b.f. Captain Rio 122 – Glenviews Big Bird (USA) (Danehill (USA) 126) [2009 6s⁶ 5g 6s⁶ 6s⁴ Aug 24] second foal: dam unraced half sister to 5-y-o Athlone: maiden: no form: tried tongue tied. *A. Berry* **–**

OUR GLENARD 10 b.g. Royal Applause 124 – Loucoum (FR) 93 (Iron Duke (FR) 122) [2009 –§: p12g⁶ Mar 14] smallish, sturdy gelding: untrustworthy performer: little form since 2006: tried tongue tied. *J. E. Long* **– §**

OUR JOE MAC (IRE) 2 b.g. (May 3) Celtic Swing 138 – Vade Retro (IRE) 86 (Desert Sun 120) [2009 7g³ 7d* 8m⁵ Sep 19] 9,500F, €25,000Y: good-bodied gelding: second foal: half-brother to 3-y-o Zegna: dam, Irish 2-y-o 7f winner, out of sister to smart Irish 1¼m/1½m winner Dancing Sunset: shaped well in maidens, third to Vale of York at York then winning at Thirsk (odds on, by 4 lengths) in August: respectable fifth to Centigrade in nursery at Ayr: should stay 1m: already useful, and type to do better still at 3 yrs. *R. A. Fahey* **97 p**

OUR JONATHAN 2 b.c. (Apr 19) Invincible Spirit (IRE) 121 – Sheik'n Swing 73 (Celtic Swing 138) [2009 6g³ 5m* p5g* 5m 5g* 6s* Nov 3] 30,000F, 25,000 2-y-o: third foal: dam 7f winner: smart performer: left B. Smart after debut: won maiden at Pontefract and listed race at Dundalk in August, Willmott Dixon Cornwallis Stakes at Ascot (beat Taajub by neck, leading near line from unfavourable draw) in October and Criterium de Maisons-Laffitte (beat Ascot Glory cosily by 1½ lengths) in November: will prove best at 5f/6f: acts on polytrack, soft and good to firm ground: sometimes slowly away, markedly so fourth outing: capable of better still. *K. A. Ryan* **113 p**

OUR KES (IRE) 7 gr.m. Revoque (IRE) 122 – Gracious Gretclo 54 (Common Grounds 118) [2009 68, a75: p10g³ p9.5g p10g p12g 10.2g p8.6g 10g p10g² p9.5g⁴ p12.2g* p12.2g³ p9.5g p12g² p8.6g⁶ p10g⁶ p11f⁵ Dec 16] strong, lengthy mare: fair handicapper, better on all-weather: won at Wolverhampton in September: stays easy 1½m: acts on all-weather/dirt and firm going: tried blinkered: usually held up. *P. Howling* **– a67**

OUR LAST CALL (IRE) 3 gr.f. Hernando (FR) 127 – On Call 103 (Alleged (USA) 138) [2009 p10g p8g p11g p16.5g Oct 30] small filly: seventh foal: half-sister to several winners, including smart 1¼m (including Grade 2 in USA) to 15f winner One Off (by Barathea) and 6-y-o Ahlawy. dam 1½m to 2m winner: little form in maidens/handicap: should stay 2m: blinkered final outing: sold €6,500, sent to Greece. *Sir Mark Prescott* **–**

OUR NATIONS 4 gr.g. Highest Honor (FR) 124 – Lines of Beauty (USA) (Line In The Sand (USA)) [2009 50: f12d² p16.5g Jan 22] close-coupled gelding: fair performer: pulled up amiss at Wolverhampton: stayed 1½m: acted on fibresand: tried visored: dead. *D. Carroll* **74**

OUR PICCADILLY (IRE) 4 b.f. Piccolo 121 – Dilys 84 (Efisio 120) [2009 84: 5g² 5g³ 5m* 5m 5m³ 5d 5.1m⁶ 5m⁴ p5g² p5g Oct 22] leggy filly: fairly useful handicapper: won at Lingfield in May: has won at 6f, best at 5f: acts on polytrack, soft and good to firm ground. *W. S. Kittow* **83**

OUR SERENDIPITY 6 ch.m. Presidium 124 – Berl's Gift 44 (Prince Sabo 123) [2009 –: 10.1m Apr 4] tall mare: maiden: no form since 2005. *R. C. Guest* **–**

OURS (IRE) 6 b.g. Mark of Esteem (IRE) 137 – Ellebanna 69 (Tina's Pet 121) [2009 80: p9.5g³ p8.6g² f8g² 8m f8g f7g³ 8m⁵ 8v² 8g⁴ 8.3s⁴ f8g² 8.3m³ f8g² f11g⁵ 8.3g⁶ f8m³ f8g* Dec 27] strong, close-coupled gelding: fairly useful handicapper: in frame 11 times in 2009 prior to winning at Southwell: stays 9.5f: acts on all-weather and any turf going: tried blinkered, wears cheekpieces: held up: temperament under suspicion. *John A. Harris* **85**

OUR TEDDY (IRE) 9 ch.g. Grand Lodge (USA) 125 – Lady Windley (Baillamont (USA) 124) [2009 p10g Nov 14] sturdy, lengthy gelding: handicapper: missed 2008: well held on belated return: stays 1½m: acts on polytrack and firm ground: tried in headgear. *R. Curtis* **–**

OUR WEE GIRL (IRE) 3 b.f. Choisir (AUS) 126 – Zwadi (IRE) 74 (Docksider (USA) 124) [2009 81d: 5.7g p5.1g p6g Oct 1] strong, medium-sized filly: fairly useful maiden at best: has gone wrong way temperamentally: best at 5f: acts on firm going: tried visored/in cheekpieces. *Miss Tor Sturgis* **55 §**

OUSTE (FR) 7 ch.g. Ragmar (FR) 117 – Elbe (FR) (Royal Charter (FR)) [2009 50+: p11g⁶ Feb 14] fairly useful chaser: poor maiden handicapper on Flat: stays 2m: acts on good to firm going: tried in cheekpieces (ran poorly): has been very slowly away: joined Mrs A. Thorpe. *Mrs S. Leech* **46**

OUSTER (GER) 3 b.c. Lomitas 129 – Odabella's Charm 80 (Cadeaux Genereux 131) [2009 99p: 10.1g⁴ Apr 22] lengthy colt: has plenty of scope: fairly useful performer: respectable fourth in minor event at Epsom sole start in 2009: stays 1¼m: raced only on good/good to soft going. *D. R. C. Elsworth* **84**

Willmott Dixon Cornwallis Stakes, Ascot—the third of four wins in a fine campaign for Our Jonathan (left), who edges out Taajub (centre) and Iver Bridge Lad (right)

OUTDROAD 3 ch.c. Desert Sun 120 – Loch Fyne 70 (Ardkinglass 114) [2009 –: p8g^{6} Feb 7] no sign of ability. *P. M. Phelan* –

OUTER HEBRIDES 8 b.g. Efisio 120 – Reuval 102 (Sharpen Up 127) [2009 61: p7g^{4} p7.1g^{4} p7g p7.1g^{4} p7.1g f6g* 7m f6g^{2} 7.1m^{2} 6m^{2} 6s^{5} 5.7g^{4} 8.1g 7m^{6} 6.1d* 6.1d^{4} 6.1m^{5} 7d 5.7g^{6} p7m^{3} f7m^{3} f6g^{3} p7g p6m^{3} Dec 1] sturdy gelding: has a round action: fair performer: won handicaps at Southwell in May and Chepstow in August: effective at 5.7f to 1m: acts on all-weather and any turf going: wears headgear: formerly tongue tied. *J. M. Bradley* **65**

OUTLAND (IRE) 3 gr.g. Indian Haven 119 – Sensuality (IRE) (Idris (IRE) 118) [2009 –: f11g 11.5s* 12.1m^{2} 11.5g^{5} 14.1g^{2} 16.1d^{2} 16g Oct 28] good-bodied gelding: fair handicapper: won at Yarmouth in June: stays 2m: acts on soft and good to firm ground. *M. H. Tompkins* **68**

OUTLANDISH 6 b.g. Dr Fong (USA) 128 – Velvet Lady 102 (Nashwan (USA) 135) [2009 86: 12m^{2} 12m^{4} 11.9f^{5} 10m Aug 24] good-topped gelding: fairly useful handicapper: effective at 8.6f to 1½m: acts on polytrack and good to firm ground. *Miss E. C. Lavelle* **84**

OUT OF EDEN 2 b.c. (May 23) Monsun (GER) 124 – Eden (USA) (Holy Bull (USA) 134) [2009 8v Oct 24] third foal: half-brother to 3-y-o Warpedsenseofhumor: dam US 8.5f winner: well-backed 9/2, some promise when eighth to Gardening Leave in maiden at Newbury, too free: likely to do better. *H. R. A. Cecil* **60 p**

OUT OF INDIA 7 b.m. Marju (IRE) 127 – Tide of Fortune (Soviet Star (USA) 128) [2009 58: p6g f7g May 1] leggy mare: modest handicapper in 2008: below form at 7 yrs: effective at 5f, stays 8.6f: acts on all-weather, firm and soft going. *P. T. Dalton* –

OUT OF NOTHING 6 br.m. Perryston View 114 – Loves To Dare (IRE) (Desert King (IRE) 129) [2009 72, a58+: 7.1g May 5] angular mare: fair handicapper on turf, modest on all-weather: well held sole 6-y-o start: stays 9f: seems to need soft/heavy ground: sometimes races freely: inconsistent. *K. M. Prendergast* –

OUTOFOIL (IRE) 3 b.g. King's Best (USA) 132 – Simplicity 93 (Polish Precedent (USA) 131) [2009 81: 8m May 25] leggy gelding: fairly useful form at 2 yrs: below form in handicap only outing in 2009: should stay 7f+: possibly not straightforward. *R. M. Beckett* –

OUTRAGEOUS REQUEST 3 ch.g. Rainbow Quest (USA) 134 – La Sorrela (IRE) (Cadeaux Genereux 131) [2009 10.3g^{6} 10m^{6} 10g^{2} 10.3s^{4} 12v^{2} f11f^{2} f14d^{2} Dec 29] leggy, lengthy gelding: half-brother to smart 1m/1¼m winner Colisay (by Entrepreneur) and 1m winner Son of Halling (by Halling): dam unraced half-sister to smart sprinter Central City: fairly useful maiden: stays 1¾m: acts on fibresand, best turf effort on good ground. *Pat Eddery* **88**

OUTSHINE 2 ch.f. (Mar 1) Exceed And Excel (AUS) 126 – Sunny Davis (USA) 71 (Alydar (USA)) [2009 6m^{3} 6m^{3} 6g Aug 30] 32,000Y: lengthy filly: half-sister to several winners, including useful 6f (at 2 yrs) to 1m (in Sweden) winner Warming Trends (by Warning) and fairly useful 1¼m winner Dance In The Sun (by Halling): dam 2-y-o 7f winner: third in maidens at Newmarket and Windsor: tongue tied (well below form) final start: sold 3,500 gns. *J. H. M. Gosden* **69**

OUT THE RING (IRE) 2 b.g. (Mar 8) Acclamation 118 – Residual (IRE) (Trempolino (USA) 135) [2009 p5g^{2} 5m^{3} 5m^{2} p5.1g^{2} 5m^{2} 5m^{4} p6m p6f^{6} f6g p5.1g^{2} p6g p5.1g^{5} Dec 14] maiden: fair form on debut, only modest subsequently (left K. Ryan after fourth outing): best efforts at 5f: acts on polytrack and good to firm going: tried in cheekpieces. *Miss Gay Kelleway* **58 a70**

OVERDOSE 4 b.c. Starborough 126 – Our Poppet (IRE) 58 (Warning 136) [2009 126+: 5g* Apr 19] developed into high-class sprinter in 2008, winning 6 times and also first past post in void running of Prix de l'Abbaye at Longchamp: took unbeaten record to 12 starts when winning minor event at Budapest on reappearance in April (won by 8 lengths conceding 14 lb to runner-up) but reportedly lost shoe on near-fore: missed rest of season with foot problems (stabled with Mrs A. Perrett for much of year in anticipation of British campaign but due to rejoin own trainer, now based in Germany, early in 2010): has won at 7f, but very speedy and best at 5f/6f: acts on soft and good to firm ground, also successful on sand: front runner: tends to sweat. *S. Ribarszki, Hungary* **117**

OVERRULE (USA) 5 b.g. Diesis 133 – Her Own Way (USA) 87 (Danzig (USA)) [2009 81: 13.8m* 14.6g^{4} 12m 10.3m^{3} 11.5m* 12m 16g Aug 8] strong, lengthy gelding: useful handicapper: won at Catterick in April and Carlisle (better than ever when beating Yes Mr President 5 lengths) in June: stays 13.8f: acts on good to firm going, probably on soft: tried tongue tied: ridden patiently: fairly useful form over hurdles. *B. Ellison* **96**

OVERSIGHTED (GER) 8 b.g. Selkirk (USA) 129 – Obvious Appeal (IRE) 82 (Danehill (USA) 126) [2009 60: p8g* p8.6g p8g* p8g^4 Oct 30] fairly useful handicapper: won at Dundalk in September and October: stays 1m: acts on polytrack and any turf going: tried in cheekpieces, seems best in blinkers/tongue tie (wore no equipment when below form at Wolverhampton second start): front runner. *Mrs Yvonne Dunleavy, Ireland* **82 +**

OVER TO YOU BERT 10 b.g. Overbury (IRE) 116 – Silvers Era 72 (Balidar 133) [2009 69: p7g p7.1g* p7g p7g p7.1g p7.1g 7m Apr 26] modest handicapper: won at Wolverhampton in February: effective at 6f to easy 9.5f: acts on all-weather, soft and good to firm going: tried in cheekpieces/visor: usually races up with pace. *R. J. Hodges* **61**

OVERTURN (IRE) 5 b.g. Barathea (IRE) 127 – Kristal Bridge 75 (Kris 135) [2009 93: 8m 10m^3 12g p11g^2 14m^2 14.1s* Oct 12] good-bodied gelding: useful handicapper: won at Salisbury in October by ½ length from Omokoroa: stays 1¾m: acts on polytrack, soft and good to firm ground: tried tongue tied: free-going sort, usually races prominently: has reportedly bled: joined D. McCain Jnr £75,000, fair form over hurdles. *W. R. Swinburn* **100**

OVTHENIGHT (IRE) 4 b.c. Noverre (USA) 125 – Night Beauty 80 (King of Kings (IRE) 125) [2009 74: 12m^6 12m^3 14.1g^2 13m 12m^5 Aug 15] good-topped colt: fair handicapper: stays 1¾m: acts on good to firm and good to soft going: visored last 4 outings: fair hurdler. *Mrs P. Sly* **74**

OWAIN JAMES 4 ch.g. Dancing Spree (USA) – Jane Grey 64 (Tragic Role (USA)) [2009 41: 17.2f 10m^6 Jul 6] leggy, lengthy gelding: poor maiden handicapper: in cheekpieces/blinkers last 4 starts. *M. Salaman* **–**

OWED 7 b.g. Lujain (USA) 119 – Nightingale (Night Shift (USA)) [2009 –, a68: f6g f6g f6g f6g^3 f6g 6g f6g Jul 27] good-topped gelding: modest performer nowadays: stays 7f: best efforts on fibresand, little form on turf: tried visored/blinkered, usually tongue tied/in cheekpieces: said to have had breathing problem on reappearance: has hung/flashed tail. *R. Bastiman* **–** **a51**

OWEN JONES (USA) 3 b.g. Rahy (USA) 115 – Batique (USA) (Storm Cat (USA)) [2009 8.3d^4 Oct 12] \$130,000Y, £4,000 3-y-o: tall gelding: fourth foal: brother to useful US performer up to 1¼m Tejida: dam US Grade 3 9f winner: 28/1 and better for race, encouraging fourth in maiden at Windsor, travelling well before green under pressure: should stay 1¼m: capable of better. *P. W. Hiatt* **64 p**

OWLS FC (IRE) 3 b.f. King's Best (USA) 132 – Sadinga (IRE) 85 (Sadler's Wells (USA) 132) [2009 14m^5 12v f11f Dec 17] 11,000F, 32,000Y, 10,000 3-y-o: workmanlike filly: third foal: half-sister to 4-y-o Cool Judgement: dam, Irish 1½m winner, half-sister to Moyglare Stud Stakes winner Priory Belle and 4-y-o Eva's Request: tailed off in listed race/maidens. *M. C. Chapman* **–**

OXBRIDGE 4 ch.g. Tomba 119 – Royal Passion 78 (Ahonoora 122) [2009 57: 6.1d 6.1d f7m p5g p6m^4 Nov 26] lengthy, heavy-topped gelding: modest maiden handicapper: best up to 1m: acts on polytrack, good to firm and good to soft going: tried in cheekpieces. *J. M. Bradley* **51**

OXFORD CITY (IRE) 5 ch.g. City On A Hill (USA) 114 – Bold Nora (IRE) (Persian Bold 123) [2009 10m 10d^6 10g 10g^3 8d p10f Dec 20] fair handicapper: left D. Marnane in Ireland before final outing: effective at 1¼m/1½m: acts on polytrack, soft and good to firm ground: sometimes tongue tied: tends to wander. *P. M. Phelan* **75**

OXUS (IRE) 4 ch.g. Sinndar (IRE) 134 – River Dancer 118 (Irish River (FR) 131) [2009 49: p10g^3 p11g p9.5g^5 Feb 17] poor maiden. *B. R. Johnson* **48**

OZONE TRUSTEE (NZ) 5 b.g. Montjeu (IRE) 137 – Bold Faith 77 (Warning 136) [2009 86: 11.1m^3 f12g 10m 7d^6 7.9d^6 Jul 26] sturdy gelding: just fair form at best in 2009: stays 11f: acts on good to soft ground. *G. A. Swinbank* **66 d**

P

PAB SPECIAL (IRE) 6 b.g. City On A Hill (USA) 114 – Tinos Island (IRE) (Alzao (USA) 117) [2009 70: p8.6g^2 p8.6g* p8g^2 8m 10g 8d Jun 10] good-topped gelding: fair handicapper, better on all-weather: won at Wolverhampton in February: barely stays easy 1¼m: acts on polytrack, firm and soft going: tried in cheekpieces/visor: free-going sort. *B. R. Johnson* **62** **a71**

PACHAKUTEK (USA) 3 ch.g. Giant's Causeway (USA) 132 – Charlotte Corday 105 (Kris 135) [2009 70p: 8s 10g p9.5g^4 Dec 18] good-topped colt: fair form in maidens/handicap: left E. Vaughan before final start: should stay 1¼m. *L. M. Cumani* **65**

PACHATTACK (USA) 3 ch.f. Pulpit (USA) 117 – El Laoob (USA) 95 (Red Ransom (USA)) [2009 97: 10f^5 10.4m^5 10m^2 10m^2 p10g^2 p12m^4 Nov 29] tall filly: useful performer: good efforts third/fourth starts, runner-up at Newmarket in handicap and listed race (beaten short head by Enticement): stays easy 1½m: acts on polytrack and good to firm going: in blinkers/cheekpieces last 3 outings. *G. A. Butler* **102**

PACIFIC BAY (IRE) 3 b.f. Diktat 126 – Wild Clover (Lomitas 129) [2009 65: 6g^5 7m^3 6s^5 7v 8.5m* 8m^6 p7g^5 Oct 11] compact filly: modest performer: won apprentice minor event at Beverley in September: stays 8.5f: acts on polytrack and good to firm going: sold £2,000 and joined D. McCain Jnr. *R. A. Fahey* **62**

PACIFIC PRIDE 6 b.g. Compton Place 125 – Only Yours 113 (Aragon 118) [2009 83: 6m 5m 5m* 5m 6g 5m^5 5m 7d^6 8m^6 6d 6s 5m^6 5m Oct 3] big, strong gelding: fair handicapper nowadays: won at Beverley in May: best at 6f: acts on good to firm and good to soft going: often wears headgear: one to treat with caution. *J. J. Quinn* **77 §**

PACO BOY (IRE) 4 b.c. Desert Style (IRE) 121 – Tappen Zee (Sandhurst Prince 128) [2009 129: 8.9g 8.1g* 8d^4 8m* 6m^4 8g^2 Jul 29] **129**

The top mile races and the top sprints are considerably different in character and in the demands they make on a horse. But moving backwards and forwards between the two disciplines can be done with the right horse. If any of the latest crop of leading older milers looked worth trying in a top race over six furlongs it was Paco Boy. As was noted in *Racehorses of 2008*, his form at seven furlongs was first rate and he travelled strongly in events contested at an end-to-end gallop before producing a telling turn of foot. After establishing himself at the top of the tree among the leading older milers with an impressive win at Royal Ascot in the Queen Anne Stakes, Paco Boy started second favourite behind the King's Stand winner Scenic Blast in a strong, international field for the July Cup. Unfortunately for Paco Boy, the prevailing good to firm going at Newmarket placed the emphasis firmly on speed—the winner's time was only a fraction off the course record—and Paco Boy didn't help his chances by taking too long to find his stride. Still last at halfway, and with a deal to do, Paco Boy made up ground hand over fist to finish fourth behind the King's Stand runner-up Fleeting Spirit, beaten two and three quarter lengths. There was criticism of Paco Boy's rider Jimmy Fortune for giving him too much to do in a race dominated by those who raced handily (Paco Boy was the only one in the first five who came from the middle of the field or further back). Fortune found a staunch defender in Paco Boy's trainer who used his web site to say that he had 'never heard so much nonsense talked after a race.'

Had Paco Boy been tried at six furlongs again in the Sprint Cup at Haydock (for which the going was on the soft side) there might well have been a different story to tell, but his season was over by then and the July Cup remains the only time he has raced at shorter than seven furlongs since his two-year-old days. Paco Boy won five races at three, including the Prix de la Foret at Longchamp, and he was out early as a four-year-old, tried over nearly nine furlongs in the Dubai Duty Free at Nad Al Sheba in March when he finished eighth of sixteen behind Gladiatorus, beaten nearly ten lengths, after never getting on terms from his wide draw. Paco Boy got off the mark for the year in the bet365 Mile at Sandown a month later, cruising to the front over a furlong out and winning by three quarters of a length and a neck from Dream Eater and Virtual, to both of whom he was giving 6 lb (his Group 1 penalty).

With first prize money totalling £309,397, the Juddmonte Lockinge Stakes and the Queen Anne Stakes provided the older milers with two excellent opportunities in Britain in the first part of the season. Paco Boy had the form to win both but things just didn't go his way when he started a warm favourite at Newbury three weeks after Sandown. He failed to settle in a race run at only a steady pace early on, then got caught behind one of his rivals when the race started to develop in earnest, which left him with ground to make up. Paco Boy did make the ground, getting on terms with Virtual, Alexandros and Twice Over inside the final furlong before being unable to do any more, eased a little and coming home nearly two lengths fourth behind Virtual. Paco Boy was also found to have been suffering from an

Queen Anne Stakes, Royal Ascot—a second Group 1 success for Paco Boy as he beats Royal Ascot regular Cesare (right) and Aqlaam (striped cap), with Main Aim (rail) fourth

infected off-fore hoof. The Queen Anne Stakes was contested on different going to the Lockinge, good to firm, and, with Virtual and Twice Over both having the Prince of Wales's Stakes over a mile and a quarter as their Royal Ascot target, Paco Boy started second favourite to Gladiatorus, who was having his first outing since the Dubai Duty Free. In a high-class renewal, Main Aim, winner of the John of Gaunt Stakes at Haydock, was next in the betting followed by Alexandros, Godolphin's second string. Waited with as usual in mid-division, as Gladiatorus set a strong pace, Paco Boy had no trouble moving up to the leaders when beginning his challenge two furlongs out. He hit the front over a furlong out and, once shaken up, showed a clean pair of heels to the others, despite tending to hang right, and was full value for his winning margin of a length and a half over the veteran Cesare, with Aqlaam and Main Aim coming next, while Gladiatorus weakened dramatically. It was a high-class performance, and marginally better form than Mastercraftsman showed when beating the Two Thousand Guineas runner-up Delegator in the St James's Palace Stakes later in the afternoon.

The nature of the course at Goodwood, and the likelihood in a normal summer of good going or firm, gave Paco Boy the look of a potential winner of the Sussex Stakes, though Hannon had other options to consider before that, including the July Cup and the Prix Maurice de Gheest. Paco Boy's fourth at Newmarket did nothing to jeopardise his chances in the Sussex Stakes, though, in the interim, the Irish-trained three-year-old Rip Van Winkle had run a splendid race to finish second to Sea The Stars in the Coral-Eclipse, and he started favourite with Paco Boy also preceded in the betting by the One Thousand Guineas and Coronation Stakes winner Ghanaati. Paco Boy ran an excellent race at Goodwood, performing up to his best, moving through from sixth to chase Rip Van Winkle resolutely in the last two furlongs. He couldn't get to the leader, going down by two and a half lengths, but he was much too good for the rest in a vintage Sussex, finishing four lengths clear of third-placed Ghanaati, with the others strung out, headed by the smooth Royal Hunt Cup winner Forgotten Voice and the Prix Jean Prat winner (third in the St James's Palace) Lord Shanakill.

After the Sussex Stakes, initial indications were that the Prix Jacques le Marois at Deauville two and a half weeks later might be Paco Boy's next target, but the colt missed that race, his trainer reporting 'There is nothing wrong with Paco Boy, but we've all put in our two penny worth and decided that it's a good time to give him a break. He'll come back for the Prix de la Foret . . . there are plenty of good races for him at the backend, so it makes sense to give him a little holiday as he was on the go early on being prepared for Dubai.' The Breeders' Cup was discounted as a long-term target, but Hong Kong in December was mentioned, though in early-September the following appeared on the trainer's web site: 'Paco Boy has done enough this year . . . you can't keep going with these top horses, so we have decided to give him a long break through the winter and bring him back next year, when he'll be aimed at all the top mile races, with the Lockinge Stakes at

Newbury the logical stepping stone to Royal Ascot.' The presumption had to be that Paco Boy wasn't showing consistent sparkle at home.

Paco Boy (IRE) (b.c. 2005)	Desert Style (IRE) (b 1992)	Green Desert (b 1983)	Danzig
			Foreign Courier
		Organza (b 1985)	High Top
			Canton Silk
	Tappen Zee (ch 1986)	Sandhurst Prince (ch 1979)	Pampapaul
			Blue Shark
		Rossaldene (gr 1975)	Mummy's Pet
			Palestra

Paco Boy's pedigree was covered in some detail in last year's Annual but there are one or two things to add. His sire Desert Style had a fairly quiet year apart from Paco Boy, though Mister Manannan developed into a smart sprinting two-year-old. Paco Boy remains the only top-notch runner from his immediate family on the distaff side and, as an indication of the contrasting fortunes so often seen in breeding and buying bloodstock, his year-younger close relative and stable-companion Tartan Turban, by a more commercial son of Green Desert in Invincible Spirit, went through the sale-ring twice after finishing tailed off in a claimer at Kempton in January. He fetched £1,500 at Doncaster a week later, then €2,000 at Goffs in November, without having run in the meantime. Tartan Turban had cost €80,000 as a yearling. Paco Boy, a compact colt who moves poorly in his slower paces, is thoroughly genuine and a credit to his connections. *R. Hannon*

PADDY BEAR 3 b.c. Piccolo 121 – Lily of The Guild (IRE) 65 (Lycius (USA) 124) **75**
[2009 68: 6f* 6m 6m^6 5d 6d* 6g Jul 20] rather leggy colt: fair performer: won maiden at Thirsk in April and seller at Catterick in July: likely to prove best at 5f/6f: acts on firm and good to soft going. *R. A. Fahey*

PADDY JACK 4 ch.g. Rambling Bear 115 – Bayrami 39 (Emarati (USA) 74) [2009 62: **55**
5.1d^5 5m 5g^6 5m 6m^5 5m^3 5m 5s^6 5s p5.1g Dec 4] close-coupled, workmanlike gelding: modest maiden: best at 5f: acts on firm and good to soft going: usually in headgear: none too consistent. *J. R. Weymes*

PADDY PARTRIDGE 3 b.c. Pivotal 124 – Treble Heights (IRE) 107 (Unfuwain **53**
(USA) 131) [2009 10m 10.3m 10.4v 10.3g Jun 26] stocky colt: second foal: brother to 15f winner Holoko Heights: dam, 1½m winner who stayed 1¾m, half-sister to smart stayer Warm Feeling: modest form in maidens/handicap. *N. J. Vaughan*

PADDY RIELLY (IRE) 4 b.g. Catcher In The Rye (IRE) 115 – The Veil (IRE) **73**
(Barathea (IRE) 127) [2009 70: f12g^2 p12g^5 f12g* f12g^3 12m^2 14.1f^6 12g^6 Jul 21] angular gelding: fair handicapper: won at Southwell in April: stays 1½m: acts on all-weather, good to firm and good to soft going: usually wears cheekpieces. *P. D. Evans*

PADLOCKED (IRE) 5 b.g. Key of Luck (USA) 126 – Accelerating (USA) 76 (Lear **–**
Fan (USA) 130) [2009 p8g Mar 21] deep-girthed, useful-looking gelding: useful performer in 2007: off 18 months and gelded, well below form sole start in 2009: best form at 1m: acts on polytrack and good to firm ground. *D. M. Simcock*

PADMINI 2 b.f. (Apr 1) Tiger Hill (IRE) 127 – Petrushka (IRE) 126 (Unfuwain (USA) **87 p**
131) [2009 p7g* Oct 29] tall, attractive filly: fourth foal: half-sister to 10.5f seller winner Hall of Fame (by Machiavellian): dam 7f (including at 2 yrs) to 1½m (Irish/Yorkshire Oaks) winner: 11/10 favourite, promising when winning maiden at Lingfield going away by 1½ lengths from Mirabella: will be suited by 1¼m+: sure to improve. *Saeed bin Suroor*

PAGAN FLIGHT (IRE) 3 b.g. Hawk Wing (USA) 136 – Regal Darcey (IRE) 67 **51 §**
(Darshaan 133) [2009 –: 8m 14m 11.6m^3 10.1d Jul 21] lengthy gelding: modest maiden: likely to prove best at 1¼m/1½m: acts on good to firm ground: tried tongue tied: one to be wary of: sold £3,800. *Mrs A. J. Perrett*

PAGAN FORCE (IRE) 3 b.c. Green Desert (USA) 127 – Brigitta (IRE) (Sadler's **61**
Wells (USA) 132) [2009 66+: p7g 7d^6 8g p7g Oct 11] sturdy colt: modest maiden: should stay 1m: blinkered last 2 starts: sold £2,500. *Mrs A. J. Perrett*

PAGAN STARPRINCESS 5 b.m. Robertico 111 – Pagan Star (Carlitin 50) [2009 **64**
f16g^4 16.2g^2 17.5m^6 16.1d Oct 13] tall mare: modest handicapper: unraced on Flat in 2008 (fairly useful hurdler): stays 2m: acts on soft and good to firm ground: tried in cheekpieces. *G. M. Moore*

PAGAN SWORD 7 ch.g. Selkirk (USA) 129 – Vanessa Bell (IRE) (Lahib (USA) 129) **–**
[2009 p16.5g Oct 23] tall, well-made gelding: unraced on Flat in 2008 (modest chaser) and well below form only start in 2009: should stay 1½m: acts on polytrack, firm and

good to soft going: often visored/in cheekpieces: sometimes slowly away: tricky ride. *D. G. Bridgwater*

PAINSWICK (USA) 2 ch.c. (Feb 19) Elusive Quality (USA) – Pleine Lune (IRE) (Alzao (USA) 117) [2009 7g 7m 7m Oct 13] well-made colt: modest form at best in maidens, still green final start: seemed amiss second outing: should stay 1m. *J. L. Dunlop* **62**

PAINTBALL (IRE) 2 b.c. (Apr 9) Le Vie Dei Colori 126 – Camassina (IRE) 62 (Taufan (USA) 119) [2009 f6d3 Dec 29] €20,000Y: half-brother to several winners, including 3-y-o On Offer and 9-y-o Bricks And Porter: dam Irish maiden (stayed 9f): 3/1, promising 3¼ lengths third to Exearti in maiden at Southwell: will stay 1m: sure to improve. *W. R. Muir* **67 p**

PAINT BY NUMBERS 2 b.g. (Mar 1) Haafhd 129 – Attention Seeker (USA) 75 (Exbourne (USA) 125) [2009 p6g p8f Dec 20] well held in maidens. *J. A. Glover* **–**

PAINTED SKY 6 ch.g. Rainbow Quest (USA) 134 – Emplane (USA) 101 (Irish River (FR) 131) [2009 –: p10m4 p9.5g6 Dec 19] leggy gelding: fair performer nowadays: stays 1½m: acts on polytrack and soft ground. *R. A. Fahey* **66**

PAINT SPLASH 3 ch.f. Beat Hollow 126 – Questa Nova (Rainbow Quest (USA) 134) [2009 59: f8g6 f7g3 7m3 f6g 8.3g3 8f3 7.9g2 8.3g3 8d4 8m5 8.5m p9.5g Oct 3] modest performer: best up to 1m: acts on all-weather, firm and good to soft going: tried in blinkers: usually held up: has reportedly bled. *T. D. Barron* **56**

PAINT STRIPPER 4 b.g. Prince Sabo 123 – Passing Fancy (Grand Lodge (USA) 125) [2009 –: 8.5m 7s4 8m5 7d 6d 6g5 5.9d 6m Aug 22] smallish, lengthy gelding: poor performer nowadays: barely stays 1m: acts on heavy and good to firm going: tried in cheekpieces. *W. Storey* **41**

PAINT THE TOWN (IRE) 4 b.f. Sadler's Wells (USA) 132 – Minnie Habit (Habitat 134) [2009 10.4v 8m Jun 21] maiden: missed 2008, and little impact in 2009: should stay 1¼m. *J. G. Given* **–**

PAINT THE TOWN RED 4 b.g. Mujahid (USA) 125 – Onefortheditch (USA) 79 (With Approval (CAN)) [2009 80: 10f* 10m 12m5 10m 8g 10.1d p12.2g6 10m p13.9g p13.9g4 Nov 20] good-topped gelding: fairly useful handicapper: won at Leicester in April: below form after: seems to stay easy 1¾m: acts on polytrack and firm going: held up: none too consistent. *H. J. Collingridge* **80 d**

PAIRUMANI PAT (IRE) 4 ch.g. Pairumani Star (IRE) 110 – Golden Skiis (IRE) 73 (Hector Protector (USA) 124) [2009 53: f16g Apr 21] plain gelding: maiden: well held only outing in 2009: should stay beyond 2m: acts on polytrack: lazy. *J. Pearce* **–**

PAISLEY 3 ch.f. Pivotal 124 – Pongee 110 (Barathea (IRE) 127) [2009 7g5 9.9m* 10m4 Sep 13] unfurnished filly: first foal: dam, 1¼m/1½m (Lancashire Oaks) winner, closely related to smart performer up to 1¾m Lion Sands, out of smart middle-distance stayer Puce: fairly useful form: built on debut when highly promising winner of maiden at Salisbury in August by length from Alqaffay, still very green but plenty in hand: odds on, unsuited by steady pace on handicap debut at Ffos Las next time: will prove best at 1¼m+: remains open to further improvement. *L. M. Cumani* **80 p**

PAJADA 5 b.m. Bertolini (USA) 125 – Last Ambition (IRE) 29 (Cadeaux Genereux 131) [2009 52: p10g p8g Feb 10] leggy mare: maiden: below form in 2009: formerly in headgear. *M. D. I. Usher* **–**

PAKTOLOS (FR) 6 b.g. Dansili 127 – Pithara (GR) (Never So Bold 135) [2009 94, a102: p12g6 12g p10g 12g p12.2g f11m4 p12f2 Dec 19] lengthy gelding: fairly useful handicapper nowadays, better on all-weather: left A. King £6,800 after fourth start: stays easy 13f: acts on polytrack, soft and good to firm going: tried in cheekpieces, usually blinkered: moody. *John A. Harris* **– §** **a93 §**

PALACEFIELD (IRE) 3 b.g. Green Desert (USA) 127 – Multaka (USA) 66 (Gone West (USA)) [2009 80p: 8d2 7m2 8.1g* 8g5 8.3m4 8.1m5 p8f5 Oct 14] quite good-topped gelding: fairly useful performer: landed odds in maiden at Chepstow in May: stays 8.3f: acts on soft and good to firm ground: sold 21,000 gns, then gelded and sent to Malaysia. *P. W. Chapple-Hyam* **84**

PALACE MOON 4 b.g. Fantastic Light (USA) 134 – Palace Street (USA) 103 (Secreto (USA) 128) [2009 92p: 6m* 6m2 7m4 6m* 6m 6g Oct 10] tall, lengthy gelding: smart performer: much improved in 2009, winning handicap at Doncaster (impressively by 5 lengths from Advanced) in March and listed event at Newmarket (beat Swiss Diva by neck) in August: respectable efforts in between in listed race at Salisbury (nose second to Judd Street) and Hungerford Stakes at Newbury (unsuitable trip): below form last 2 starts: best around 6f: raced on good/good to firm going: signs of temperament. *H. Morrison* **114**

Sky Bet Strensall Stakes, York—
a first pattern success for Palavicini, who beats outsider Dream Lodge (stars)

PALAIS POLAIRE 7 ch.m. Polar Falcon (USA) 126 – Palace Street (USA) 103 (Secreto (USA) 128) [2009 65§: p7g p7g p7g 7.1v Jul 24] rather leggy mare: handicapper: well below form in 2009: wears cheekpieces: tried tongue tied: ungenuine. *J. A. Geake* – §

PALAVICINI (USA) 3 b.c. Giant's Causeway (USA) 132 – Cara Fantasy (IRE) 84 (Sadler's Wells (USA) 132) [2009 100p: 10s^4 10m^2 10m* 10m 8.9m* 9.9m^4 12m^6 9m^3 Oct 16] big, good-topped colt: smart performer: improved in 2009, winning listed race at Newmarket in May and Sky Bet Strensall Stakes at York (beat Dream Lodge by length) in August: creditable efforts after, 2¾ lengths third to Steele Tango in Darley Stakes at Newmarket final occasion: probably stays 1½m: acts on soft and good to firm going: free-going sort, but is consistent. *J. L. Dunlop* 114

PALAWI (IRE) 2 ch.c. (Mar 15) Dubawi (IRE) 129 – Palwina (FR) (Unfuwain (USA) 131) [2009 8d^3 8d^3 Oct 28] €27,000Y: second foal: dam, ran twice in France, out of sister to Prix du Jockey Club winner Polytain: similar form when third in maidens at Newcastle and Musselburgh (wandered markedly): bred to stay 1¼m: should do better. *J. J. Quinn* 72 p

PALEO (IRE) 2 ch.f. (May 3) Indian Ridge 123 – Crossbreeze (USA) 86 (Red Ransom (USA)) [2009 6s 7d 7g* 6.5m^3 7m 7m Oct 17] €50,000Y: sturdy filly: third foal: half-sister to winner in Italy up to 1m by Refuse To Bend: dam, ran 3 times at 2 yrs (third at 6f), half-sister to St Leger winner Rule of Law: fairly useful performer: won maiden at Newmarket (wandered) in August: good third to In The Slips in nursery at Doncaster, below form after: stays 7f: acts on good to firm going: sold 14,000 gns, sent to USA. *R. Hannon* 86

PALIO SQUARE (USA) 2 b. or br.c. (Mar 14) Harlan's Holiday (USA) 124 – Teewee's Hope (CAN) (Defrere (USA)) [2009 7g 7.1g^4 8.3g^4 Oct 28] close-coupled colt: second foal: half-brother to winner in USA by Golden Missile: dam Canadian 5f (at 2 yrs) to 1m winner: fair maiden: trained by K. R. Burke on debut, by A. Jarvis second start: stays 8.3f. *H. R. A. Cecil* 79

PALISADES PARK 2 b.c. (May 1) Compton Place 125 – Brooklyn's Sky (Septieme Ciel (USA) 123) [2009 5f^6 5f^2 6g* 5.1m^5 5.2d 6d 5g^5 Aug 21] 37,000F, 26,000Y: useful-looking colt: third living foal: half-brother to German 7f winner De Havilland (by Groom Dancer): dam, French 2-y-o 7f winner, out of half-sister to smart French performers up to 1½m Prospect Wells and Prospect Park: fairly useful performer: won maiden at Windsor 80 in June comfortably by 1½ lengths from Many A Slip: below form after (said to have finished lame final start): will prove best at 5f/6f: acts on firm going, probably on good to soft. *R. Hannon*

PALLANTES CROSS 2 b.c. (Mar 1) Cape Cross (IRE) 129 – Palinisa (FR) 106 **99** (Night Shift (USA)) [2009 6v 7.1m* 7g^2 7m^3 p8.6g* 8g^4 Sep 20] big colt: fourth foal: half-brother to 2 winners, including 3-y-o Ethics Girl: dam, 7f (at 2 yrs in France) and 1m (in US) winner, out of sister to Prix du Jockey Club winner Polytain: useful performer: won maiden at Musselburgh in June and 3-runner minor event at Wolverhampton (easily) in September: best effort when 1½ lengths third to Red Badge in nursery at Newmarket: only fourth in listed race at Dusseldorf final outing: stays 8.6f: acts on polytrack and good to firm going. *M. Johnston*

PALLATON 3 ch.g. Bertolini (USA) 125 – Miss Honeypenny (IRE) (Old Vic 136) **61** [2009 10.2g^6 9.9g p12g^6 Jun 13] modest form in maidens only on debut. *R. M. Beckett*

PANADIN (IRE) 7 b.g. Desert King (IRE) 129 – Strident Note 89 (The Minstrel (CAN) **–** 135) [2009 42: 16.4m Jul 9] medium-sized gelding: poor form at best: usually wears cheekpieces: tried tongue tied. *Mrs L. C. Jewell*

PAN AMERICAN 2 b.g. (Mar 1) American Post 121 – Pan Galactic (USA) 105 (Lear **74** Fan (USA) 130) [2009 p6g^4 7.1m^2 p7g^3 p6g^4 p6m* Dec 6] 8,000Y: closely related to useful French 7f winner Battlestar (by Bering) and half-brother to 3 winners: dam French 1m winner: fair performer: won maiden at Lingfield: gelded after: should stay 1m: acts on polytrack and good to firm going. *P. J. Makin*

PANCELTICA 4 b.g. Makbul 104 – Lady Kate (Bay Express 132) [2009 p7.1g p12.2g **–** Jun 22] showed nothing in maiden/seller. *Karen George*

PANPIPER 2 ch.c. (Jan 25) Piccolo 121 – Phi Beta Kappa (USA) 74 (Diesis 133) [2009 **60** 6m 6f^3 Jul 5] better effort in maidens when third of 4 to Velvet Band at Brighton, racing alone. *G. L. Moore*

PANSY POTTER 3 b.f. Auction House (USA) 120 – Ellway Queen (USA) 71 (Bahri **54** (USA) 125) [2009 59: 6.1g 7m 6g p6g Jun 25] good-topped filly: modest maiden handicapper: shapes like a sprinter: sometimes blinkered. *B. J. Meehan*

PANTHERII (USA) 4 ch.f. Forest Wildcat (USA) 120 – Saraa Ree (USA) 102 (Caro **69** 133) [2009 63: 8m^2 Jun 3] strong filly: fair maiden handicapper: stays 1m: raced on polytrack and good going or firmer: sold 10,000 gns. *P. F. I. Cole*

PANTO PRINCESS 3 b.f. Act One 124 – Bob's Princess 69 (Bob's Return (IRE) 123) **76 p** [2009 10g^3 9.9m^2 10.2d^5 10.1d^4 Oct 27] rather leggy filly: sixth foal: half-sister to several winners, including 5-y-o Ingleby Princess and fairly useful 7f/1½m winner The Oil Magnate (by Dr Fong): dam 2-y-o 7f winner (stayed 1½m): fair form: likely to be well suited by 1½m: acts on good to firm and good to soft going: open to improvement. *H. Candy*

PAPAGENO 2 b.c. (Mar 26) Piccolo 121 – Fresh Fruit Daily 92 (Reprimand 122) [2009 **62** 5g 5m^5 5m^4 5m p5g^2 p5g^4 5g p5g Nov 13] workmanlike colt: modest maiden: seemed amiss last 2 starts: should be suited by 6f: acts on polytrack and good to firm ground. *J. R. Jenkins*

PAPA POWER (IRE) 6 b.g. Polish Precedent (USA) 131 – Guignol (IRE) 80 (Anita's **–** Prince 126) [2009 5m Sep 13] maiden handicapper: well held only start since 2007: usually tongue tied: dead. *K. M. Prendergast*

PAPARAAZI (IRE) 7 b.g. Victory Note (USA) 120 – Raazi 46 (My Generation 111) **–** [2009 62: 10m 9.9m Jul 14] lengthy gelding: handicapper: well held in 2009, including over hurdles: usually wears headgear. *I. W. McInnes*

PAPA'S PRINCESS 5 b.m. Mujadil (USA) 119 – Desert Flower (Green Desert (USA) **62** 127) [2009 62: 8.3g^4 9.3m^6 8m^6 10g^6 12.5m^5 10m^4 9g^3 8m^3 8g 8s 8d 9m^5 Sep 14] dipped-backed mare: modest handicapper: stays 1¼m: acts on good to firm and good to soft going: none too consistent. *J. S. Goldie*

PAPILLIO (IRE) 4 b.g. Marju (IRE) 127 – Danish Gem (Danehill (USA) 126) [2009 **78** 71: p7g^6 p7g p7.1g^3 7m 6m^2 6m^3 f6g Jul 7] good-topped gelding: fair maiden: stays 7f: acts on polytrack and good to firm ground: none too genuine: sold 6,000 gns. *J. R. Fanshawe*

PAPPOOSE 4 b.f. Namid 128 – Bryn (Saddlers' Hall (IRE) 126) [2009 54: 6.1g p6g **–** 5.7g Jul 31] compact filly: maiden: well held in 2009. *H. Candy*

PAPRADON 5 b.g. Tobougg (IRE) 125 – Salvezza (IRE) 97 (Superpower 113) [2009 **–** 74: p12g Jan 30] useful-looking gelding: fair handicapper: below form sole Flat start in 2009: stays 1¾m: acts on polytrack: usually visored. *N. A. Twiston-Davies*

PAPYRIAN 3 b.g. Oasis Dream 129 – La Papagena (Habitat 134) [2009 –p: 8m^3 8g^5 7m^2 7.1g^2 8f^4 8.3m^4 p8g^3 Oct 22] well-made gelding: fairly useful maiden: stays 1m: acts on polytrack and good to firm ground: tried blinkered: ungenuine: sold 16,000 gns, sent to Bahrain. *W. Jarvis* **81 §**

PAQUERETTZA (FR) 3 ch.f. Dr Fong (USA) 128 – Cover Look (SAF) (Fort Wood (USA) 117) [2009 70: 8m* 8g* 8m^4 8m^2 8s 8m 10.4g^2 Oct 10] well-made filly: fairly useful handicapper: won at Redcar in April and Newmarket in July: good efforts after when runner-up: stays 10.4f: acts on good to firm ground. *D. H. Brown* **90**

PARADISE DANCER (IRE) 5 b.m. Danehill Dancer (IRE) 117 – Pintada de Fresco (FR) (Marignan (USA) 117) [2009 84: p10g p8g Jan 28] big, strong mare: handicapper, just modest form in 2009: best at 1m/1¼m: acts on polytrack and good to firm going. *J. A. R. Toller* **63**

PARADISE DREAM 2 b.c. (Mar 14) Kyllachy 129 – Wunders Dream (IRE) 107 (Averti (IRE) 117) [2009 p5g^2 5m^3 6.1g 5g^4 Jul 6] well-made colt: modest maiden: best effort on debut: hung left next time: sold 21,000 gns, sent to Qatar. *J. Noseda* **63**

PARADISE SPECTRE 2 b.c. (Apr 20) Firebreak 125 – Amber's Bluff 80 (Mind Games 121) [2009 6m^4 6g^2 6m 6d^2 Jul 25] 45,000F, 42,000Y: fourth foal: half-brother to 5-y-o Mundo's Magic: dam, 6f winner, half-sister to useful 5f/7f winner Golden Nun: fairly useful maiden: second at Hamilton (to Awzaan) and Newcastle (to Flaneur in nursery): raced only at 6f: acts on good to soft going: visored (too free, hung) third start: sold 27,000 gns in October. *K. R. Burke* **80**

PARAGUAY (USA) 6 b.g. Pivotal 124 – Grisonnante (FR) (Kaldoun (FR) 122) [2009 83: f8g^6 7m^2 7.5g* 8m^6 7.9m^6 p8g 8.5m^4 8g Aug 5] small, leggy gelding: fairly useful handicapper: won at Beverley in May: stayed 1¼m, all wins at shorter: acted on all-weather, firm and soft going: tried visored: held up, and had good turn of foot: dead. *Mrs D. J. Sanderson* **84**

PARALLEL (IRE) 3 b.f. Refuse To Bend (IRE) 128 – Iktidar 80 (Green Desert (USA) 127) [2009 8.1g^3 8.3d^6 Oct 12] 95,000Y: lengthy, angular filly: half-sister to several winners, including 5-y-o Follow The Flag and 7-y-o Qadar: dam maiden who stayed 1m: modest form in maidens. *J. H. M. Gosden* **61**

PAR AVION 4 b.f. Efisio 120 – Blow Me A Kiss 72 (Kris 135) [2009 9.2g^5 May 15] fifth foal: sister to 7f winner Goodbye and 2003 2-y-o 5f winner Farewell To Arms, both fairly useful: dam, maiden who stayed 1¼m, out of half-sister to very smart middle-distance performer Apache: bumper winner, but poor hurdler (has had breathing problem): modest form in maiden at Hamilton on Flat debut. *Paul Murphy* **58**

PARBOLD HILL 2 br.f. (Jan 25) Exceed And Excel (AUS) 126 – Let Alone 78 (Warning 136) [2009 5g^5 5d^2 5g 5d^3 5f^6 Jul 2] £41,000Y: tall, unfurnished filly: fifth foal: closely related to 6-y-o Tabulate and half-sister to 2 winners, including 4-y-o Rash Judgement: dam 1m winner: fair maiden: below form last 2 starts, in nursery (blinkered) final one: raced only at 5f: acts on good to soft going: has joined R. Fahey. *T. D. Barron* **70**

PARC DES PRINCES (USA) 3 b. or br.g. Ten Most Wanted (USA) 128 – Miss Orah 91 (Unfuwain (USA) 131) [2009 58: 10.2g^5 11.6m 10g^4 11.6g^3 10.9g* 12m^3 p12g* Jul 22] sturdy gelding: fair handicapper: won at Warwick in June and Lingfield in July: stays 1½m: acts on polytrack, unraced on extremes of going on turf: tried blinkered: held up: not straightforward (tends to edge left): gelded after final start. *A. M. Balding* **79**

PARISIAN ART (IRE) 3 b.g. Clodovil (IRE) 116 – Cafe Creme (IRE) (Catrail (USA) 123) [2009 91: 6m Jun 10] strong gelding: type to carry condition: fairly useful performer at 2 yrs: well below form only outing in 2009: stays 7f: acts on soft and good to firm going: blinkered in 2008: quirky: sold 8,000 gns, sent to Greece. *J. Noseda* **–**

PARISIAN DREAM 5 b.g. Sakhee (USA) 136 – Boojum 101 (Mujtahid (USA) 118) [2009 7g 7g 10g 10m p12.2g p9.5g Oct 23] strong, deep-girthed gelding: fair performer: best up to 1m: acts on good to firm and good to soft ground: tried blinkered. *T. J. Pitt* **70**

PARISIAN GIFT (IRE) 4 b.g. Statue of Liberty (USA) 115 – My Micheline (Lion Cavern (USA) 117) [2009 90?: p6g^3 p7g^3 6m^3 Apr 30] fair performer nowadays: likely to stay 1m: acts on polytrack and good to firm ground: in cheekpieces final start. *J. R. Gask* **70**

PARISIAN PYRAMID (IRE) 3 gr.g. Verglas (IRE) 118 – Sharadja (IRE) (Doyoun 124) [2009 94: 6m^3 6.1m 5.1m 6m^3 7g^4 6g^2 6g^5 6g 7m 5d 6g 5d^5 Oct 24] sturdy gelding: useful handicapper: several creditable efforts in 2009, second to Swiss Diva at York: effective up to 7f: acts on heavy and good to firm going. *D. Nicholls* **98**

PARIS IN MIND 3 b.f. Mind Games 121 – Paris Babe 94 (Teenoso (USA) 135) [2009 6g Jun 18] 3,000Y: half-sister to fairly useful 6f (at 2 yrs)/7f winner Ashtree Belle (by Up And At 'em): dam 6f winner: tailed off in maiden at Warwick. *C. N. Kellett* **–**

PARK LANE 3 b.g. Royal Applause 124 – Kazeem 73 (Darshaan 133) [2009 82p: p8g^{2} p8g^{2} 8.1g^{3} 8d^{2} 8m* 10m^{5} p8m Sep 16] big, lengthy gelding: fairly useful performer: won maiden at Pontefract in August: below form in handicaps after: stays 1m: acts on polytrack, soft and good to firm going: gelded after final start. *B. W. Hills* **83**

PARK MELODY (IRE) 3 b.f. Refuse To Bend (IRE) 128 – Park Charger 105 (Tirol 127) [2009 10m^{4} 12m^{4} 10f p12m p9.5g Oct 17] 250,000Y: rather leggy filly: closely related to fairly useful 1999 2-y-o 6f winner Alpine Park (by Barathea), later successful abroad, and half-sister to several winners, including Irish 6f (at 2 yrs)/7f winner Rum Charger (by Spectrum) and 1m winner Acclaimed (by Hawk Wing), both useful: dam Irish 1m/1¼m winner: modest maiden: best effort at 1¼m: blinkered final outing: sold 31,000 gns. *B. J. Meehan* **64 d**

PARK'S PRODIGY 5 b.g. Desert Prince (IRE) 130 – Up And About 77 (Barathea (IRE) 127) [2009 62: 6m^{4} 16g 10.1m 12.4d^{4} 13.8m^{2} 15.8g^{2} 12s* p16.5g Oct 30] big, workmanlike gelding: fair handicapper: left P. Haslam after second start: stays 16.5f, seems effective at much shorter: acts on all-weather, soft and good to firm going: tried in cheekpieces/tongue tie. *G. A. Harker* **65**

PARK VIEW 2 ch.f. (Feb 25) With Approval (CAN) – Bayswater 76 (Caerleon (USA) 132) [2009 7g Oct 31] tall filly: sixth foal: half-sister to 3 winners, including 4-y-o Montbretia and fairly useful 1m winner Art Work (by Zafonic): dam, 1½m winner, sister to Grand Criterium/Dante Stakes winner Tenby: 20/1 and green, 10 lengths tenth to Field Day in maiden at Newmarket, not knocked about: will stay 1¼m+: open to improvement. *B. W. Hills* **54 p**

PARKVIEW LOVE (USA) 8 b. or br.g. Mister Baileys 123 – Jerre Jo Glanville (USA) (Skywalker (USA)) [2009 62d, a77d: p9.5g^{5} p9.5g p8m f8f Dec 17] leggy, good-topped gelding: regressive handicapper: left J. Given after second start: stays 1½m: acts on all-weather, firm and good to soft going: often wears headgear: temperamental. *A. G. Newcombe* **52 §**

PARNASSIAN 9 ch.g. Sabrehill (USA) 120 – Delphic Way 63 (Warning 136) [2009 66: p12m^{5} 12.1v Jul 24] angular, sparely-made gelding: modest handicapper nowadays: stays 1½m: acts on all-weather and any turf going, goes particularly well on good or softer: visored: temperament under suspicion. *J. A. Geake* **58**

PARSON'S PUNCH 4 b.g. Beat Hollow 126 – Ordained 66 (Mtoto 134) [2009 76: p10g Feb 4] rather leggy gelding: fair maiden: stays 1¼m: raced on polytrack and good to firm going: sold £5,200, joined Mrs L. Normile. *P. D. Cundell* **65**

PARTHENON 3 b.g. Dubai Destination (USA) 127 – Grecian Slipper 102 (Sadler's Wells (USA) 132) [2009 99p: 8.1m* 11.1g* 10.5g Jun 7] well-made gelding: useful performer: improved when winning minor event at Sandown in April and listed race at Hamilton (beat Stately Home 2½ lengths) in May, making all both times: left M. Johnston, well held in Prix du Jockey Club at Chantilly final start (gelded after): will be suited by 1½m+: acts on heavy and good to firm going: has left Godolphin. *Saeed bin Suroor* **107**

PARTNER (IRE) 3 b.g. Indian Ridge 123 – Oregon Trail (USA) (Gone West (USA)) [2009 –: 5.8m^{3} 6s 6d 5s^{6} 5g^{2} 5g* p6g^{3} p6g* Nov 25] sturdy gelding: fair handicapper: won at Cork in October and Lingfield in November: effective at 5f/6f: acts on polytrack, soft and good to firm going: blinkered last 5 starts. *David Marnane, Ireland* **78**

PARTY DOCTOR 2 ch.c. (Mar 4) Dr Fong (USA) 128 – Wedding Party 91 (Groom Dancer (USA) 128) [2009 6m^{2} 6m^{3} 7m^{3} 7m^{2} 7m^{4} Aug 18] 10,000F: tall, unfurnished colt: first foal: dam 2-y-o 6f/7f winner: useful maiden: placed in listed events third/fourth starts, finishing 1½ lengths third to Big Audio in Chesham Stakes at Royal Ascot and nose second to Nideeb at Ascot: further improvement when 2 lengths fourth to Elusive Pimpernel in Acomb Stakes at York: will stay 1m: raced only on good to firm going. *Tom Dascombe* **109**

PARTY IN THE PARK 4 b.g. Royal Applause 124 – Halland Park Girl (IRE) 106 (Primo Dominie 121) [2009 72: p7.1g p8.6g 6.1f 7m 7g^{5} 7.5m^{2} 7g^{5} 7g 7m 7m^{6} p8g^{6} p8m^{2} p8g^{2} p8g p8m^{2} p8.6g^{2} Dec 14] strong, good-topped gelding: modest handicapper: left Miss J. Camacho after ninth start: stays 1m: acts on polytrack and firm ground: tried in headgear. *J. R. Boyle* **63**

PARTY PALACE 5 b.m. Auction House (USA) 120 – Lady-Love 70 (Pursuit of Love 124) [2009 49: 11.7m^3 11.7f^3 12.1g* 11.7f 12m^4 13.3g^4 17.2m^3 Jul 16] small, sparely-made mare: modest handicapper: improved in 2009, winning at Chepstow in May: stays easy 17f: acts on polytrack and firm going: tried in cheekpieces. *H. S. Howe* **64**

PARVAAZ (IRE) 2 ch.c. (Feb 1) Rahy (USA) 115 – Saabga (USA) 83 (Woodman (USA) 126) [2009 8d^3 Oct 27] half-brother to several winners, including 7f (at 2 yrs) and 8.5f winner Jazmeer (by Sabrehill) and 1m to 13f (in France) winner Sabbaag (by Mark of Esteem), both fairly useful: dam, second at 7f at 2 yrs (only outing), half-sister to smart middle-distance performers Close Conflict and Newton's Law: 12/1, encouraging 3½ lengths third to Bullet Train in maiden at Yarmouth, racing freely: bred to stay 1¼m: will do better. *M. A. Jarvis* **75 p**

PASCHENDALE 2 b.c. (Apr 17) Refuse To Bend (IRE) 128 – Fading Light 103 (King's Best (USA) 132) [2009 8.3g^5 8g Oct 16] lengthy colt: first foal: dam, French 2-y-o 1m winner, half-sister to useful performers Putra Kuantan (up to 1¼m) and Faru (up to 13.5f in France): easily better effort in maidens when 5½ lengths fifth to Mont Agel at Windsor (slowly away): bred to stay 1¼m: has left Godolphin. *Saeed bin Suroor* **72**

PASSAGE TO INDIA (IRE) 3 ch.f. Indian Ridge 123 – Kathy College (IRE) 108 (College Chapel 122) [2009 74: f7g^3 p8g Jun 24] fair maiden handicapper: best efforts at 7f on fibresand: sold £7,000 in August. *Miss J. R. Tooth* **71**

PASSIONATE CRY (USA) 2 b. or br.c. (Apr 19) Street Cry (IRE) 130 – Virtus (USA) (Silver Charm (USA) 132) [2009 p7f 8g p7m^5 Oct 26] close-coupled colt: modest form at best in maidens: should stay 1m: form only on polytrack: sold 9,000 gns. *W. J. Knight* **52**

PASSION FOR GOLD (USA) 2 b.c. (Mar 23) Medaglia d'Oro (USA) 129 – C'Est L'Amour (USA) 115 (Thunder Gulch (USA) 129) [2009 8d* 8g^3 10v* Nov 14] **119 p**

The tally of Godolphin's two-year-old winners each year since 2003 provides surprising reading. In 2003, following David Loder's resignation as the trainer of the operation's two-year-olds, Saeed bin Suroor sent out just three winning juveniles. That was followed by forty-eight, thirty-two, five, eleven and sixteen in the next five years, none of which prepared observers for an astonishing campaign in 2009 which yielded sixty-two individual winners, second only to the juvenile total of Richard Hannon among British-based trainers. The total contributed greatly to Godolphin's surpassing its own previous records for the number of horses it ran and, in particular, for its number of wins worldwide. There were two hundred and twenty-seven runners in all who won two hundred and two races; the previous highest figures were two hundred and two for the number of individual runners, in 2005, and one hundred and thirty-three for the number of wins in 2001. The two-year-olds contributed a Group 1 winner in Passion For Gold, a Grade 1 winner in the States in British-trained Vale of York, Group 2 winners in Poet's Voice and Sand Vixen, Group 3 winners in Buzzword, Long Lashes and Zeitoper, not to mention a good number of less highly-tried, promising individuals. Godolphin might have difficulty finding suitable targets for its winning two-year-olds in the first part of their three-year-old season—minor events for which winners are eligible are not so plentiful as maiden races—and it seems likely there will be more Godolphin runners in handicaps in the next season.

Passion For Gold's Group 1 triumph came in the season's final pattern race for juveniles, and the one contested over the longest distance—the Criterium de Saint-Cloud over a mile and a quarter. Any race run in mid-November is likely to be run under testing conditions which can exaggerate the superiority of a winner. Only once since 1990, when Passage of Time won in 2006, has the going been firmer than good to soft for the Criterium de Saint-Cloud. Conditions were certainly testing for the latest renewal, in which Passion For Gold took on eight opponents. All were winners, though none had been successful in pattern company, one of the three contenders trained by Aidan O'Brien, Mikhael Glinka, having gained a four-length success in the listed Eyrefield Stakes. O'Brien's two other runners, Don Carlos, ridden by stable-jockey Johnny Murtagh, and Banyan Tree had landed maidens. British-trained challengers Passion For Gold and Layali Al Andalus had been placed in a pattern race, the Beresford Stakes at the end of September, in which Layali Al Andalus was beaten three quarters of a length by easy winner St Nicholas Abbey, with Passion For Gold a length and a half away third. Passion For

Gold, a five-length winner of an eight-runner maiden at Thirsk a month before his Irish venture, ran well at the Curragh, rallying after being tapped for speed and running distinctly green, at the same time giving the strong impression that he would be suited by further than a mile. The home defence at Saint-Cloud consisted of the Andre Fabre-trained Simon de Montfort, unbeaten in a maiden and a minor event and also representing Godolphin, and the Compiegne winner Kaage. There was a German challenger in Zazou, successful in a valuable sales race at Baden-Baden, while the third British challenger, Gardening Leave, had picked up a maiden at Newbury. This was not the strongest renewal of the Criterium by a long chalk but it produced a very impressive winner, though the horses which raced close to the strong pace, after Layali Al Andalus had made the running from Banyan Tree, Gardening Leave and Simon de Montfort, all dropped out after entering the straight and filled the last four places. Passion For Gold was pushed along to move up on the outside from fifth to take the lead with two and a half furlongs left. Dettori left nothing to chance once in front, riding Passion For Gold firmly until dropping his hands fifty yards out, Passion For Gold winning by six lengths from Mikhael Glinka who came late to take second off Zazou. Although the opposition was not exceptional, and some of them might not have been suited by the heavy going, the trip or by racing too close to an overly strong gallop, there was no denying the quality of Passion For Gold's performance, after which he was given a quote of 10/1 for the Derby. Passion For Gold, who has raced only on good going or softer and clearly acts well in the mud, is a middle-distance performer through and through, so time is unlikely to be wasted in training him for the Two Thousand Guineas. The Dante Stakes would be an obvious race in which to start him off, followed with luck by the Derby. The 2008 Criterium de Saint-Cloud winner, Fame And Glory, enjoyed a good year as a three-year-old and Passion For Gold appeals very much as the sort to do the same.

The increase in the number of two-year-olds racing for Godolphin stemmed from the scale of Sheikh Mohammed's Darley breeding operation and, more particularly, a spending spree at the yearling auctions in 2008 and the various breeze-up sales in the spring. As one of the richest men in the world—he ranks fourth in *Forbes Magazine*'s so-called Royal Rich List with net worth of sixteen billion dollars—Sheikh Mohammed can afford to buy virtually any good or promising horse whose owner is willing to sell. One of the numerous quotes on his web site claims that 'money is like water, block its flow and it will stagnate'. The Sheikh certainly lived up to that dictum in 2008 and early-2009 with one hundred and fifty or so northern hemisphere yearlings and two-year-olds purchased on his behalf at a cost of more than 50,000,000 dollars. The eight who fetched at least a million dollars include dual winner and Racing Post Trophy third Al Zir, and Chimayo, whose win in a maiden race at Aqueduct in November and one place, from four starts, have recouped 35,550 dollars of the 3,100,000 dollars she cost. The six others consist of two who have run but not won so far, and four non-runners. Of Godolphin's big-race contenders among the two-year-olds through the year, Buzzword, Poet's Voice and Zeitoper were all Darley-bred, Long Lashes was a private purchase during the season, Vale of York was bought privately by Godolphin after not reaching his reserve at the Tattersalls Breeze-Up Sale and Passion For Gold

Criterium de Saint-Cloud, Saint-Cloud—Passion For Gold caps a fine season for Godolphin's juveniles with a six-length victory; Mikhail Glinka (centre, dark colours) stays on to pass German challenger Zazou for second, with Mikhail Glinka's Ballydoyle stablemate Don Carlos (second right) taking fourth

cost 260,000 guineas at that same venue. The Flying Childers winner Sand Vixen (130,000 guineas) and the Prix de la Huderie winner Frozen Power (500,000 guineas) have proved the best of the rest so far among the sale purchases. Looking at the whole period between 1991 and 2007, Sheikh Mohammed bought 270 or so yearlings which cost at least 300,000 guineas each (or the equivalent in dollars or euros), his total expenditure on them more than 325,000,000 dollars. Nearly sixty per cent didn't reach the racecourse or failed to win and together they have yielded just over twenty stakes winners, with Moon Ballad and Dubai Destination the only ones successful in Group 1 company. The seven hundred-plus yearlings that cost less than 300,000 guineas or equivalent included only four Group 1 winners to race in the colours of Sheikh Mohammed or Godolphin, led by Kayf Tara. The breeze-up purchases, incidentally, account for fewer than a hundred in the same period but include not only Passion For Gold, Al Zir and, in a manner of speaking, Vale of York but also Rio de La Plata (Prix Jean-Luc Lagardere) and Seventh Street (Apple Blossom Handicap and Go For Wand Handicap).

Passion For Gold (USA) (b.c. Mar 23, 2007)	Medaglia d'Oro (USA) (b or br 1999)	El Prado (gr 1989)	Sadler's Wells
			Lady Capulet
		Cappucino Bay (b 1989)	Bailjumper
			Dubbed In
	C'Est L'Amour (USA) (ch 1997)	Thunder Gulch (ch 1992)	Gulch
			Line of Thunder
		L'Amour Toujours (ro 1986)	Blushing Groom
			Paint The Town

Passion For Gold was the top lot at the Tattersalls Breeze-Up Sale at Newmarket in April. Sheikh Mohammed having already shown interest in his sire Medaglia d'Oro, notably when buying Al Zir. The Sheikh went on to purchase a majority stake in Medaglia d'Oro and moved him from Stonewall to Darley in America at the beginning of June; he then bought ten yearlings by him at auction, headed by a filly who fetched 1,500,000 dollars at Saratoga in August. Medaglia d'Oro's fee for 2010 has risen from 40,000 dollars to 100,000 dollars, after a superb start to his stud career. His first crop included American Horse of The Year Rachel Alexandra, winner of the Preakness Stakes and the Haskell Invitational, and another Grade 1-winning filly Gabby's Golden Gal and three other graded stakes winners. Medaglia d'Oro, by the smart Irish two-year-old El Prado, a son of Sadler's Wells, was a high-class performer at up to a mile and half, winning the Travers Stakes and Whitney Handicap and finishing second in the Belmont Stakes, the Breeders' Cup Classic (twice) and the Dubai World Cup. He is shaping up to be a reasonably strong influence for stamina. Passion For Gold had cost 125,000 dollars as a yearling at Keeneland and comes from a good, though not exceptional, family on the dam's side. C'Est L'Amour won the Grade 2 Nassau County Handicap over seven furlongs and ran second in the Grade 1 Acorn Stakes over a mile. She has foaled one other winner, a colt by Dixieland Band who won in Barbados, and she did not reach her reserve at the Keeneland January Sale in January 2008, when the bidding stopped at 70,000 dollars. C'Est L'Amour is a half-sister to the minor stakes-winning dam of Madeo, who won the Del Mar Derby. The grandam L'Amour Toujours won a listed race over a mile and a quarter at Longchamp but was soundly beaten in pattern events. She was out of Paint The Town, a daughter of Vaguely Noble who showed good form at around a mile and a half, winning the Grand Prix d'Evry and the Prix de Royallieu. *Saeed bin Suroor*

PASSION OVERFLOW (USA) 2 b.f. (Mar 23) Hennessy (USA) 122 – Polar Bird 111 (Thatching 131) [2009 p6m^2 p6f* Dec 13] half-sister to several winners, including 6f (including at 2 yrs)/7f winner Fokine (by Royal Academy) and 1996 Prix Robert Papin winner Ocean Ridge (by Storm Bird), both smart: dam 5f/6f winner, including at 2 yrs: odds on, won maiden at Kempton by 1¼ lengths from Torres del Paine: better form when runner-up in similar event at Lingfield on debut: remains open to improvement. *J. Noseda* **73 p**

PASSKEY 3 b.f. Medicean 128 – Revival 86 (Sadler's Wells (USA) 132) [2009 8.1g^3 p7m^2 9.2g^2 p8m^3 p7.1g Dec 12] good-topped filly: fifth foal: half-sister to 2 winners, including fairly useful Irish 8.7f winner Uva Fragola (by Nashwan): dam, 1¼m winner, half-sister to very smart sprinter Pivotal: fairly useful form in maidens: possibly amiss **83**

third outing: likely to stay 1¼m: raced only on polytrack and good ground: tried blinkered: signs of temperament. *Sir Mark Prescott*

PASS THE PORT 8 ch.g. Docksider (USA) 124 – One of The Family 73 (Alzao (USA) 117) [2009 90: p13.9g² Mar 7] leggy gelding: fairly useful handicapper: stays 1¾m: acts on all-weather, firm and soft going: tried visored/in cheekpieces: held up: consistent. *D. Haydn Jones* **85**

PASTA PRAYER 4 b.g. Bertolini (USA) 125 – Benedicite (Lomond (USA) 128) [2009 61: p6g 7m May 9] strong, stocky gelding: maiden: no form in 2009: tried blinkered/visored. *D. E. Cantillon* **–**

PASTEL BLUE (IRE) 2 b.f. (Mar 11) Shamardal (USA) 129 – Painted Moon (USA) (Gone West (USA)) [2009 6m⁴ p6g⁵ p6m⁵ p7g³ Aug 27] first foal: dam, ran twice, closely related to very smart 1m/1¼m performer Crimplene: fair maiden: good third to Lucky Rave in nursery at Lingfield (made running): will stay 1m. *M. L. W. Bell* **69**

PASTELLO 2 ch.f. (Mar 22) Exceed And Excel (AUS) 126 – Pastel 95 (Lion Cavern (USA) 117) [2009 7d 7f² 8.3m² 8m⁵ 7m⁶ 8.3d p8.6g p7m Nov 27] angular filly: third foal: dam 2-y-o 5f winner: fair maiden: below form in nurseries last 3 starts: stays 8.3f: acts on firm going: signs of temperament. *R. Hannon* **71**

PASTORAL PLAYER 2 b.g. (Mar 21) Pastoral Pursuits 127 – Copy-Cat 60 (Lion Cavern (USA) 117) [2009 6m* 7v 6g Oct 30] 35,000Y: well-made gelding: half-brother to several winners, including useful 2007 2-y-o 7f winner Copywriter (by Efisio) and 3-y-o Laudatory: dam, sprint maiden, half-sister to smart sprinter Averti: fairly useful performer: won maiden at Newbury in September by neck from Locksley Hall: stiff task in Horris Hill Stakes on same course next time: signs of temperament in minor event at Newmarket final start: gelded after: may prove best at 6f/7f: withdrawn after giving trouble at start intended second outing: remains capable of better. *H. Morrison* **92 p**

PATACHOU 2 b.f. (May 5) Domedriver (IRE) 128 – Pat Or Else 72 (Alzao (USA) 117) [2009 6v⁴ 7d³ p8g Oct 26] close-coupled filly: sister to 3-y-o Patronne and half-sister to several winners, including useful Irish 2007 2-y-o 7f winner Triskel (by Hawk Wing) and 7-y-o Trafalgar Square: dam, staying maiden, half-sister to Classic Cliche and My Emma: poor maiden: left Rae Guest £5,000 after second start: should stay 1m. *R. J. Smith* **45**

PATAVIAN (IRE) 5 b.g. Titus Livius (FR) 115 – Five of Wands 71 (Caerleon (USA) 132) [2009 11.1m⁴ 12.1m Jun 23] rather leggy gelding: unraced on Flat in 2008: well held in 2009, including over hurdles: usually in cheekpieces/blinkers. *B. Storey* **–**

PATAVIUM (IRE) 6 b.g. Titus Livius (FR) 115 – Arcevia (IRE) 85 (Archway (IRE) 115) [2009 14m 16g⁴ 12d* 14.1m⁵ 9.9f* 12.5m⁴ 12g³ 12.4d² Oct 13] good-topped gelding: fair handicapper: won apprentice races at Catterick in July and Beverley in August: stays 1¾m: acts on polytrack, firm and good to soft going: has looked temperamental. *E. W. Tuer* **66**

PATAVIUM PRINCE (IRE) 6 ch.g. Titus Livius (FR) 115 – Hoyland Common (IRE) (Common Grounds 118) [2009 82, a56+: p7g³ p6g⁴ p6g² 6g 7g² 7m* 6f² 6d⁴ 7f⁵ 6d Oct 22] compact gelding: fairly useful handicapper on turf, just modest on all-weather: won at Brighton in June: best at 6f/7f: acts on polytrack, firm and good to soft going: tried visored: consistent. *Miss Jo Crowley* **84 a63**

PATCH PATCH 2 b.g. (May 10) Avonbridge 123 – Sandgate Cygnet 75 (Fleetwood (IRE) 107) [2009 5m² 5d* 5g Aug 11] won maiden at Carlisle in July: gave trouble at start/ran as if amiss in nursery: raced only at 5f: acts on good to soft going. *M. Dods* **67**

PATH OF PEACE 2 b.f. (Mar 12) Rock of Gibraltar (IRE) 133 – Persian Song 45 (Persian Bold 123) [2009 6g⁶ 7g Oct 23] unfurnished filly: sister to fairly useful Irish 2006 2-y-o 1m winner Rock Lily and half-sister to several winners, including smart 7f (at 2 yrs) to 1¼m winner Mountain Song (by Tirol) and 3-y-o Please Sing: dam, ran 3 times, sister to high-class performer up to 1¼m Bold Arrangement: better effort in maidens when seventh to Tamaathul at Doncaster: should stay 1m. *J. D. Bethell* **50**

PATH TO GLORY 5 b.g. Makbul 104 – Just Glory (Glory of Dancer 121) [2009 –: 8g Jun 19] sturdy, workmanlike gelding: maiden: refused to race sole Flat outing in 2009: tried in cheekpieces/blinkers: one to treat with caution. *Miss Z. C. Davison* **– §**

PATHWAY TO HEAVEN (IRE) 2 ch.f. (Jan 14) Indian Haven 119 – Beckerson (IRE) 74 (Alzao (USA) 117) [2009 8d Oct 13] first foal: dam, Irish maiden (stayed 1¼m), half-sister to smart performers Mastermind (up to 1¼m) and Housemaster (up to 1½m, including in Hong Kong): 100/1, down the field in maiden at Newcastle, slowly away: bred to stay 1¼m. *J. J. Quinn* **–**

PATIENCE REWARDED 3 ch.f. Dr Fong (USA) 128 – Breathing Space (USA) (Expelled (USA) 116) [2009 p7g p7g Jan 30] first foal: dam French 11f winner: no form in maiden/claimer. *J. S. Moore* –

PATKAI (IRE) 4 ch.c. Indian Ridge 123 – Olympienne (IRE) (Sadler's Wells (USA) 132) [2009 118: 16m* 16.4m^2 20m^2 Jun 18] **124**

A new name will appear on the Gold Cup roll of honour in 2010 following the retirement of four-times winner Yeats. It won't be Reefscape, who was runner-up in 2006 but is now at stud, while time looks to have run out for the enigmatic entire Geordieland, who was second in 2007 and 2008. It might be different, though, for the other horse that finished immediately behind Yeats at Royal Ascot, the relatively lightly-raced Patkai. In pulling fifteen lengths clear of third-placed Geordieland as he chased home Yeats in the latest edition, Patkai showed that he has what it takes to go one better in the 2010 Gold Cup. That he is with a trainer who is second to none when it comes to improving older horses only adds to his credentials.

Patkai, successful in a maiden at Nottingham from two starts as a two-year-old, quickly made up into a smart performer at three and won a handicap at Haydock and the Queen's Vase at Royal Ascot, the latter by seven lengths. At that stage he looked the ideal type for the St Leger, but he missed Doncaster after a disappointing run in the Great Voltigeur (run at Goodwood). In fact, he wasn't seen out for the remainder of 2008, returning from eight months off in the Woodcote Stud Sagaro Stakes at Ascot in April. Patkai made light of a straightforward task, sent to the front three furlongs out and soon asserting as he landed the odds by nine lengths from Mischief Making in a weak renewal. With Yeats flopping on his return, it wasn't long before Patkai was favourite in the Gold Cup betting. He was fully expected to strengthen that position by winning the Henry II Stakes at Sandown, but this time he couldn't get the better of a resurgent Geordieland and was already beaten when hampered in the final furlong. Patkai's reputation had taken a knock and both Yeats and Geordieland were preferred to him in the Gold Cup betting. In the event, Patkai was the only one to pose a threat to Yeats, proving well suited by the longer trip. Held up in a race run at a modest pace, Patkai was hemmed in as the winner made his move over three furlongs out, but quickened well to look a danger two furlongs out before being unable to sustain his effort and going down by three and a half lengths. Patkai reportedly suffered a minor setback shortly afterwards and wasn't seen out again, though there are said to be no concerns about his being able to return at least as good as ever as a five-year-old.

Patkai (IRE) (ch.c. 2005)	Indian Ridge (ch 1985)	Ahonoora (ch 1975)	Lorenzaccio
			Helen Nichols
		Hillbrow (ch 1975)	Swing Easy
			Golden City
	Olympienne (IRE) (b 2000)	Sadler's Wells (b 1981)	Northern Dancer
			Fairy Bridge
		Hellenic (b 1987)	Darshaan
			Grecian Sea

Patkai is the first foal of Olympienne, an unraced mare bred in the purple. She is a sister to four at least smart performers, namely the Brigadier Gerard Stakes winner New Morning and the Gold Cup third Election Day, and Group 1 winners Greek Dance (Grosser Dallmayr-Preis) and Islington, the last-named successful twice in the Yorkshire Oaks and also winner of the Breeders' Cup Filly & Mare Turf. All of those bar New Morning were also trained by Sir Michael Stoute for the Weinstocks and Ballymacoll Stud. Olympienne is also a half-sister to several other winners including another Stoute-trained Group 1 winner in Mountain High, whose most notable triumph came in the Grand Prix de Saint-Cloud. Patkai's grandam Hellenic won three races for Lord Weinstock, including the Ribblesdale Stakes and Yorkshire Oaks, and also finished runner-up in the St Leger. Olympienne's second foal is stablemate Saptapadi, a brother to Patkai who has shown useful form but has had just three runs in two seasons and is still a maiden. Patkai, a strong, useful-looking colt who tends to race freely, acts on firm going and probably on soft. He is genuine, even though he usually hangs right. *Sir Michael Stoute*

PATRICIAN'S GLORY (USA) 3 b.c. Proud Citizen (USA) 122 – Landholder (USA) (Dixieland Band (USA)) [2009 99: 8m² 7m⁶ 7m⁵ 8m Aug 20] compact colt: useful performer: improved first 2 starts in 2009, 2 lengths second to Four Winds in minor event at Newmarket and 5¾ lengths sixth to Ouqba in Jersey Stakes at Royal Ascot: possibly amiss last 2 starts: stays 1m: acts on good to firm going: sold 55,000 gns in October. *T. P. Tate* **103**

PATRICKS LODGE 2 ch.g. (Mar 17) Redoubtable (USA) 115 – Duxford Lodge (Dara Monarch 128) [2009 6m 8.5m Aug 30] well held in maidens. *J. D. Bethell* **–**

PATRONNE 3 b.f. Domedriver (IRE) 128 – Pat Or Else 72 (Alzao (USA) 117) [2009 –: p8.6g⁶ f8g* f8g Feb 20] modest form: won seller at Southwell (left Sir Mark Prescott 3,000 gns) in February: stays 1m: raced only on all-weather. *Miss A. Stokell* **52**

PAT SEAMUR 2 b.g. (Feb 13) Compton Place 125 – Superlove (IRE) (Hector Protector (USA) 124) [2009 6m 6.1g⁶ 6d p7.1g⁴ p7.1g² Oct 16] close-coupled gelding: fair maiden: should be as effective at 6f as 7f: acts on polytrack: sold 15,000 gns. *E. A. L. Dunlop* **67**

PATTERESA GIRL 2 b.f. (Feb 4) Auction House (USA) 120 – Ellway Queen (USA) 71 (Bahri (USA) 125) [2009 p5g 5m* 5g 6f Jun 19] big, lengthy filly: fourth foal: sister to useful 7f (at 2 yrs) to 1¼m (in USA) winner Ghetto and 2007 2-y-o 6f winner Hythe Bay: dam 1m winner: won maiden at Doncaster in April: out of depth after: should be suited by 6f+. *Mrs L. Stubbs* **66**

PATTERN MARK 3 b.g. Mark of Esteem (IRE) 137 – Latch Key Lady (USA) 48 (Tejano (USA)) [2009 52: 8f 10g³ 12m⁶ 14.1g⁶ 14.1m Aug 29] modest maiden handicapper: stays 1¾m: acts on good to firm ground. *Ollie Pears* **56**

PAT WILL (IRE) 5 b.m. Danetime (IRE) 121 – Northern Tara (IRE) 84 (Fayruz 116) [2009 p6g Mar 24] leggy mare: unraced on Flat in 2008 (well held over hurdles for P. Sharp): well beaten sole outing in 2009: often blinkered/visored. *M. R. Hoad* **–**

PAUL'S PET 4 b.g. Tobougg (IRE) 125 – Cape Siren (Warning 136) [2009 p7g 7.1f 8.1g 10.9d 8.3m³ p8g 9.9g p9.5g p7.1g Sep 25] compact gelding: modest maiden: should stay beyond 1m: acts on polytrack and firm going: held up. *Karen George* **57**

PAVEMENT GAMES 2 b.f. (Feb 7) Mind Games 121 – Pavement Gates 81 (Bishop of Cashel 122) [2009 5.9g⁵ 6d 6s⁵ 6.5m 6.1d 5.1s⁵ Nov 4] £3,800Y: angular filly: first foal: dam 6f (at 2 yrs) and 1½m winner: poor maiden: stays 6f: acts on soft going. *R. C. Guest* **48**

PAVERSHOOZ 4 b.g. Bahamian Bounty 116 – Stormswept (USA) 74 (Storm Bird (CAN) 134) [2009 89: 6m² 6s 6m 5g* 5d* 6m² 5g* 5.6m 5g Oct 17] workmanlike gelding: useful handicapper: improvement in 2009, winning at Musselburgh (Scottish Sprint Cup) and Newcastle (Gosforth Park Cup, by neck from Buachaill Dona) in June and Ayr (beat Just For Mary by 1½ lengths) in July: best at 5f/easy 6f: acts on good to firm and good to soft going: tried tongue tied. *N. Wilson* **103**

PAWAN (IRE) 9 ch.g. Cadeaux Genereux 131 – Born To Glamour (Ajdal (USA) 130) [2009 100: f5s* p5.1g⁶ p6g f5m⁴ f5g 5.1m² 5m 6g⁶ 6g f5g⁴ 5.1d⁵ 6g⁵ 5g² f5g⁵ f6g 7d f5g⁵ 8.3v p6m f5g f5m³ f5d⁵ Dec 29] lengthy, angular gelding: useful performer: won handicap at Southwell in January by ½ length from Rebel Duke: best up to 7f nowadays (has won at 9f): acts on all-weather and any turf going: tried in cheekpieces, usually blinkered: held up: trainer ridden: races lazily, but is tough. *Miss A. Stokell* **100**

PAYDAAR 2 ch.c. (Feb 19) Sulamani (IRE) 130 – Eternal Reve (USA) 116 (Diesis 133) [2009 6g 6m 6g⁴ 8.5d² 7s⁵ 8g Oct 21] €40,000Y: good-bodied colt: half-brother to several winners, including useful 6f (at 2 yrs) to 1m (in UAE) winner Infinite Spirit (by Maria's Mon) and 3-y-o Invisible Man: dam, French 6f (at 2 yrs) to 1m winner, half-sister to US Grade 1 9f winner Eternity Star: fair maiden: left D. Marnane in Ireland prior to final start: will prove best at 7f/1m: acts on soft and good to firm going: has looked awkward. *B. J. Meehan* **70**

PAYMASTER IN CHIEF 3 b.g. Minardi (USA) 119 – Allegedly (IRE) 71 (Alhaarth (IRE) 126) [2009 61: f6g⁶ p7g⁶ p8g⁵ 7d³ 10m⁶ f7g⁴ 8f 8.3g 11.6m⁴ 10.2v³ Jul 17] leggy gelding: modest maiden: seems to stay 11.6f: acts on soft and good to firm ground: visored/in cheekpieces last 5 starts. *M. D. I. Usher* **54**

PEACE AND GLORY (IRE) 2 b.f. (Apr 11) Antonius Pius (USA) 123§ – Rosy Lydgate 53 (Last Tycoon 131) [2009 7m Sep 12] half-sister to several winners, including useful 6f and (at 2 yrs) 7f winner Loyal Tycoon (by Royal Abjar) and fairly useful 1m and 9.5f winner Symbol of Peace (by Desert Sun): dam, maiden, half-sister to smart performer up to 11f Supreme Sound and useful stayer Top Cees: 33/1, tailed off in maiden at Chester. *J. W. Unett* **–**

PEACE CONCLUDED 3 b.f. Bertolini (USA) 125 – Effie (Royal Academy (USA) 130) [2009 72: p9.5g 9.7f 7m^4 f8g^5 8m 8d Sep 3] compact filly: fair maiden: regressed after reappearance: seems to stay easy 9.5f: acts on polytrack and good to soft going: tried in cheekpieces/blinkers. *B. R. Millman* **70 d**

PEACE CORPS 3 ch.g. Medicean 128 – Tromond 94 (Lomond (USA) 128) [2009 p8g 8.3g^6 8.1g^4 10m 9.9f^2 Jun 24] angular gelding: brother to smart hurdler Trenchant, closely related to 8-y-o Cesare and half-brother to several winners, including very smart 1m (at 2 yrs) to 1½m winner Nowhere To Exit (by Exit To Nowhere): dam, 9f winner, stayed 1½m: fair form: visored, best effort when second in handicap at Salisbury final start: changed owners privately after: stays 1¼m: acts on firm going: possibly not straightforward. *J. R. Fanshawe* **79**

PEACEFUL RULE (USA) 3 b.g. Peace Rules (USA) 124 – La Cat (USA) (Mr Greeley (USA) 122) [2009 78p: 8.5g 10m^2 12.5g 8.5g^2 7m^2 8d 8g Aug 31] good-bodied gelding: fair maiden: stays 1¼m: acts on good to firm ground: gelded after final start. *D. Nicholls* **77**

PEACEFUL SOUL (USA) 2 b.f. (May 3) Dynaformer (USA) – Serenity Jane (USA) (Affirmed (USA)) [2009 7g Oct 31] $300,000Y: lengthy, useful-looking filly: sixth foal: half-sister to several winners in USA: dam, US maiden, half-sister to US Grade 1 9.5f winner Include: 33/1 and green, 7 lengths eighth to Revered in maiden at Newmarket, never nearer: will stay 1m+: open to improvement. *D. R. Lanigan* **61 p**

PEACE IN PARADISE (IRE) 3 b.f. Dubai Destination (USA) 127 – Paola Maria (Daylami (IRE) 138) [2009 –: p8g p12g^6 12.1m Jun 23] close-coupled filly: little form: tried blinkered. *J. A. R. Toller* **–**

PEACE OFFERING (IRE) 9 b.g. Victory Note (USA) 120 – Amnesty Bay 63 (Thatching 131) [2009 118: p5g^3 5g 5g^5 5d^3 6s^6 5m^2 Sep 1] good-topped gelding: smart performer: respectable efforts in 2009 when 2¼ lengths fifth to Ialysos in listed race at Haydock and 1½ lengths third to Nota Bene in minor event at Newmarket third/fourth outings: best at 5f: acts on polytrack and any turf going: tried in blinkers/cheekpieces: often front runner: genuine. *D. Nicholls* **111**

PEACHEY MOMENT (USA) 4 b. or br.g. Stormin Fever (USA) 116 – Given Moment (USA) (Diesis 133) [2009 f7g Oct 18] fair form in bumpers: well held in maiden on Flat debut. *H. J. Collingridge* **–**

PEAK DISTRICT (IRE) 5 b.g. Danehill (USA) 126 – Coralita (IRE) 98 (Night Shift (USA)) [2009 103: f5g^3 p5g^2 5m^2 p5g* 5g 5m 5.4m 5m 5.6m f5d Dec 29] good-quartered gelding: useful handicapper: claimed from M. Easterby £15,000 after reappearance: won at Lingfield in June: good neck second to Ishetoo at York previous outing: gelded prior to final start: best at 5f: acts on polytrack, firm and good to soft ground: usually travels strongly close up: *K. A. Ryan* **101**

PEAK (IRE) 3 b.c. Exceed And Excel (AUS) 126 – Glympse (IRE) 59 (Spectrum (IRE) 126) [2009 –: p7g 7m^5 8.1g 10d^5 p12g Jun 27] lengthy colt: modest maiden: probably stays 1¼m: unraced on extremes of going: tried blinkered. *H. Morrison* **57**

PEAL PARK 3 b.f. Sulamani (IRE) 130 – Cape Siren (Warning 136) [2009 66: 8f^5 8.1m 9m^5 p8g 11.7g p10g Sep 8] small filly: maiden: little form in 2009. *Karen George* **–**

PEANUT GIRL (IRE) 3 b.f. Tillerman 123 – Phintia (IRE) (Tagula (IRE) 116) [2009 p6g p6g^5 6m^3 p7.1g^2 6.1g^3 6.1g May 25] €1,000Y: second foal: dam unraced half-sister to useful Italian performer up to 9f Sunday's Brunch: modest maiden: stays 7f: acts on polytrack. *B. Palling* **58**

PEARL DEALER (IRE) 4 b.g. Marju (IRE) 127 – Anyaas (IRE) 99 (Green Desert (USA) 127) [2009 70: p9.5g f8g^5 Feb 6] strong, lengthy gelding: fair handicapper at 3 yrs: below form both starts in 2009: stays 8.6f: acts on all-weather: tried tongue tied/in cheekpieces. *N. J. Vaughan* **55**

PEARL OF KENT (IRE) 2 ch.f. (Apr 23) Pearl of Love (IRE) 112 – Kentmere (FR) (Galetto (FR) 118) [2009 6d 8m^4 7d Oct 27] stocky filly: half-sister to several winners, including fairly useful performer up to 1m Danemere (by Danehill), 6f winner at 2 yrs, and 1½m/13f winner Love Bitten (by Darshaan): dam, French 1m (at 2 yrs) and 11f winner, half-sister to Prix de Diane winner Lypharita: poor form in maiden/claimers: bred to be suited by 1m+. *P. D. Evans* **44**

PEARL OF MANACOR (IRE) 3 b.g. Danehill Dancer (IRE) 117 – Mountain Law (USA) (Mountain Cat (USA)) [2009 83p: p6g* p8g^3 p8g^5 8m 8d Oct 11] tall gelding: has scope: fairly useful performer: won maiden at Wolverhampton in January: well below form after next start: stays 1m: acts on polytrack and good to soft ground: tried visored: sold only 3,000 gns. *M. R. Channon* **80**

PEARLY WEY 6 b.g. Lujain (USA) 119 – Dunkellin (USA) (Irish River (FR) 131) **92** [2009 106: 6m 6.1m 6m 6m 6g^{5} 6.5m^{6} 6m^{5} 7m p6g p6m Dec 10] close-coupled gelding: just fairly useful handicapper at 6 yrs: left C. Cox 17,000 gns after eighth start: best at 5f/6f: acts on firm and good to soft going: held up. *I. W. McInnes*

PEAS 'N BEANS (IRE) 6 ch.g. Medicean 128 – No Sugar Baby (FR) (Crystal Glitters **47** (USA) 127) [2009 51: p16g p14g^{6} p12g Feb 4] leggy gelding: poor maiden: seems to stay 2m: acts on polytrack, firm and good to soft going: tried in cheekpieces/blinkers/tongue tie. *T. Keddy*

PEBBLESONTHEBEACH 2 b.g. (Feb 15) Footstepsinthesand 120 – Peep Show (In **69** The Wings 128) [2009 7d^{6} 7.1g^{5} 7m^{4} 8g Sep 7] fair maiden: met trouble in nursery: gelded after: should prove suited by 1m+. *J. W. Hills*

PECKFORTON CASTLE 2 b.g. (Apr 13) Celtic Swing 138 – Fleuve d'Or (IRE) **50 p** (Last Tycoon 131) [2009 p7.1g^{5} Nov 20] 20,000F, 5,000Y: sixth foal: half-brother to 3 winners, including 1¼m winner Gold Card (by First Trump): dam, no form, half-sister to smart sprinter Showbrook: 20/1 and green, 6¼ lengths fifth to Sidney Melbourne in maiden at Wolverhampton, late headway: should improve. *Pat Morris*

PEDASUS (USA) 3 b.c. Fusaichi Pegasus (USA) 130 – Butterfly Cove (USA) (Storm **–** Cat (USA)) [2009 76p: p7g^{d} 7m 9.9m Aug 13] big, workmanlike colt: maiden: little form at 3 yrs: best effort at 7f on polytrack: tried tongue tied. *T. Keddy*

PEDREGAL 3 gr.g. Diktat 126 – Bella Chica (IRE) 95 (Bigstone (IRE) 126) [2009 55: **49** p6g f7g^{3} p7g^{6} p8g 5m^{5} 5m^{3} 5m^{6} 6m^{4} 5m^{3} 6g 5g Jul 20] close-coupled gelding: poor maiden handicapper: left R. Fahey after seventh start: best at 5f/6f: raced only on all-weather and good ground or firmer on turf. *J. S. Goldie*

PEGASUS AGAIN (USA) 4 b.g. Fusaichi Pegasus (USA) 130 – Chit Chatter (USA) **95** (Lost Soldier (USA) 103) [2009 80+: p7g* p7g^{5} p8g^{2} p8g^{2} p8g^{2} 8.3m^{3} 8.3m* 7m^{4} 7g p8m^{2} p8m* Dec 30] leggy, useful-looking gelding: useful handicapper: won at Lingfield in January, Windsor in August and Lingfield in December: stays 8.3f: acts on polytrack and good to firm ground: wears cheekpieces (not final start): usually races prominently: genuine and consistent. *T. G. Mills*

PEGASUS DANCER (FR) 5 b.g. Danehill Dancer (IRE) 117 – Maruru (IRE) (Fairy **56** King (USA)) [2009 70: p5m^{6} p5g 5.1m 5g May 20] quite good-topped gelding: just modest handicapper in 2009: may prove best at 5f: acts on polytrack, firm and good to soft going: wears headgear: usually races prominently. *R. H. York*

PEGASUS GOLD (USA) 4 ch.g. Fusaichi Pegasus (USA) 130 – Little Treasure (FR) **66** 105 (Night Shift (USA)) [2009 p7g^{5} 8.3g^{6} Jun 11] good-quartered gelding: fair form both starts in maidens. *W. R. Swinburn*

PEGASUS LAD (USA) 3 b. or br.g. Fusaichi Pegasus (USA) 130 – Leo Girl (USA) **87 d** 100 (Seattle Slew (USA)) [2009 85: p8g^{2} p8g^{3} 8d 7g 9m 8m^{6} 9.2d 8.1g^{2} 8.1g^{3} 8s^{6} 8.5m^{6} p8g Oct 8] strong, lengthy gelding: fairly useful handicapper: below form after second outing: likely to stay 1¼m: acts on polytrack, firm and good to soft going: none too consistent: sold 6,500 gns. *M. Johnston*

PEGASUS PRINCE (USA) 5 b.g. Fusaichi Pegasus (USA) 130 – Avian Eden (USA) **–** (Storm Bird (CAN) 134) [2009 73: f12f^{6} Nov 24] fair handicapper: well below form only start on Flat in 2009: barely stays 2m: acts on all-weather, good to firm and good to soft going. *J. Wade*

PEINTRE D'ARGENT (IRE) 3 ch.f. Peintre Celebre (USA) 137 – Petite-D-Argent **64** 91 (Noalto 120) [2009 61p: p10g^{3} 12.1g^{5} 12.1m^{5} p12g p9.5g p12m^{5} Dec 9] leggy filly: modest maiden handicapper: trained by N. Vaughan first 3 starts, left Tom Dascombe after fifth: stays 1½m: acts on polytrack. *W. J. Knight*

PEKAN ONE 7 ch.g. Grand Lodge (USA) 125 – Ballet 61 (Sharrood (USA) 124) [2009 **–** 56: p16.5g Sep 12] maiden handicapper: largely below form since early-2008, including over hurdles: usually in tongue tie/blinkers, tried in cheekpieces: joined V. Thompson. *J. G. Carr, Ireland*

PEKAN STAR 2 b.c. (Mar 23) Montjeu (IRE) 137 – Delicieuse Lady (Trempolino **63 P** (USA) 135) [2009 7g^{4} Aug 28] 200,000F, 220,000Y: rangy colt: closely related to French 2007 2-y-o 7.5f winner Ballerina Blue (by High Chaparral) and half-brother to 3 winners, including French 9f (at 2 yrs) to 1½m (Prix du Jockey Club) winner Blue Canari (by Acatenango) and 1m (including at 2 yrs)/1¼m winner Blue Ksar (by Anabaa), both smart: dam, won up to 9f in Scandinavia, out of smart French performer up to 12.5f Savoureuse Lady, herself half-sister to Mtoto: 16/1 and green, highly promising 9 lengths fourth to Treble Jig in maiden at Newmarket, late headway under considerate handling: will be suited by 1¼m+: open to significant improvement. *M. A. Jarvis*

PEKAN THREE (IRE) 2 b.c. (Mar 6) Sadler's Wells (USA) 132 – Frappe (IRE) 93 (Inchinor 119) [2009 8m6 Oct 16] 175,000Y: strong colt: closely related to useful 7f (at 2 yrs) to 1½m (Ribblesdale Stakes) winner Thakafaat (by Unfuwain) and half-brother to 2 winners, including fairly useful 1¼m winner Quantum (by Alhaarth): dam, 2-y-o 6f winner, half-sister to 2000 Guineas winner Footstepsinthesand: 16/1 and green, encouraging 6½ lengths sixth to Invincible Soul in maiden at Newmarket, staying on well: should stay at least 1¼m: will improve. *P. F. I. Cole* **78 p**

PEKING PRINCE 3 b.g. Passing Glance 119 – Brandon Princess (Waajib 121) [2009 78p: p7.1g 7.1m4 8.1g5 8m* 8m3 8m2 7.1g6 Aug 12] lengthy gelding: has scope: fairly useful handicapper: won at Newbury in June: better form when placed next 2 starts, ½-length second to Sri Putra at Ascot: should prove best at 7f/1m: acts on good to firm and good to soft going: visored last 2 outings: quirky: sent to Hong Kong, where renamed Sham Shui Po. *A. M. Balding* **91**

PELHAM CRESCENT (IRE) 6 ch.g. Giant's Causeway (USA) 132 – Sweet Times 60 (Riverman (USA) 131) [2009 69: p9.5g4 p9.5g5 p9.5g2 p12.2g4 p12g2 p9.5g2 10.2g* 11.7m* 10.2f* 10m 10m3 10.2g5 p13.9g5 12m* 9.9s 11.7g Oct 21] close-coupled gelding: fairly useful handicapper: won at Bath (3) in April/May and Goodwood in September: stays easy 1½m: acts on polytrack, good to firm and good to soft ground: tried in blinkers/cheekpieces. *B. Palling* **86**

PELIGROSO (FR) 3 ch.c. Trempolino (USA) 135 – Pitpit (IRE) (Rudimentary (USA) 118) [2009 106p: 10g2 11g6 9m3 10.4g* Oct 9] useful performer: trained by M. Hofer in Germany at 2 yrs: creditable short-head second to Saphir in Bavarian Classic at Munich on reappearance: won minor event at York (by 2¼ lengths from Wasan) in October: stays 10.4f: acts on heavy ground. *Saeed bin Suroor* **108**

PELLINORE (USA) 3 b. or br.f. Giant's Causeway (USA) 132 – Glatisant 104 (Rainbow Quest (USA) 134) [2009 p8g 8.1g6 10.1m4 Sep 9] angular filly: seventh foal: sister to very smart Irish 6f (at 2 yrs) to 1m (2000 Guineas) winner Footstepsinthesand and half-sister to 2 winners, including useful Irish 1½m and 2m winner Theme Song (by Singspiel): dam, 2-y-o 6f and 7f (Prestige Stakes) winner who became unreliable, out of Nassau Stakes winner Dancing Rocks: little impact in maidens: tried visored: sold 35,000 gns. *E. F. Vaughan* **–**

PEMBO 4 b.g. Choisir (AUS) 126 – Focosa (ITY) (In The Wings 128) [2009 57: f8d4 f12g f8g5 p9.5g f8g5 Feb 19] good-bodied gelding: poor performer nowadays: stays 1m: acts on all-weather and heavy going: tried in cheekpieces/blinkers: none too consistent: joined S. Jacobs. *R. A. Harris* **49**

PENA DORADA (IRE) 2 b.c. (Jan 4) Key of Luck (USA) 126 – Uluwatu (IRE) (Unfuwain (USA) 131) [2009 8d5 8.3g2 10m5 Oct 5] €35,000Y: first foal: dam unraced: best effort in maidens when 1¼ lengths second to Think Its All Over at Hamilton: should stay 1¼m (badly hampered when tried): remains likely to do better. *A. P. Jarvis* **75 p**

PENANG CINTA 6 b.g. Halling (USA) 133 – Penang Pearl (FR) 106 (Bering 136) [2009 74: p12g5 p9.5g6 p12g3 p9.5g5 10f4 12m* 11.5g3 12m5 12.3g 11.9m* 11.9f2 10.1d4 11.9g* 11.9d* 12m 10.1d6 Sep 3] smallish gelding: fair handicapper: won at L'Ancresse (Guernsey) in May (by distance) and Brighton in June, July (apprentices) and August: stays 1½m: acts on polytrack and any turf going: sometimes wears headgear: quirky. *P. D. Evans* **79**

PENANGDOUBLE O ONE 2 ch.c. (Mar 28) Starcraft (NZ) 128 – Penang Pearl (FR) 106 (Bering 136) [2009 p8g3 p8g5 Nov 14] rather unfurnished colt: sixth foal: half-brother to 3 winners, notably 3-y-o Harbinger: dam 1m/9f winner: tongue tied, similar form in maidens at Lingfield: will stay 1¼m. *R. M. Beckett* **77**

PENANG PRINCESS 3 br. or gr.f. Act One 124 – Pulau Pinang (IRE) 101 (Dolphin Street (FR) 125) [2009 72p: p8g4 11.6m4 14.1f2 14g* p16g* 14m p16.5g3 Oct 15] medium-sized filly: fairly useful handicapper: improved when winning at Sandown in May and Kempton in June: will stay 2¼m: acts on polytrack and firm ground. *R. M. Beckett* **90**

PENCHESCO (IRE) 4 b.g. Orpen (USA) 116 – Francesca (IRE) (Perugino (USA) 84) [2009 80: f8g4 p8g5 p9.5g 10.2s4 Oct 7] lengthy gelding: fair handicapper: stays 1¼m: acts on all-weather, soft and good to firm going: sold 13,000 gns. *Pat Eddery* **77**

PENDERYN 2 b.f. (Jan 24) Sakhee (USA) 136 – Brecon 89 (Unfuwain (USA) 131) [2009 7d 7d6 p8g6 f8g6 Dec 18] first foal: dam 2-y-o 7f winner who stayed 1¼m: poor maiden: sold out of Mrs A. Perrett's stable £800 prior to final outing. *C. Smith* **48**

PENDRAGON (USA) 6 ch.g. Rahy (USA) 115 – Turning Wheel (USA) 108 (Seeking The Gold (USA)) [2009 63: f8g^3 Dec 27] modest maiden: stays 1¾m: acts on fibresand and good to soft ground. *B. Ellison* **62**

PENEL (IRE) 8 b.g. Orpen (USA) 116 – Jayess Elle 55 (Sabrehill (USA) 120) [2009 64: f8s^5 f7g^5 f7g Jan 20] smallish gelding: poor performer at 8 yrs: stays 1¼m: acts on all-weather, heavy and good to firm going: wears headgear (in cheekpieces nowadays). *P. T. Midgley* **44**

PENINSULA GIRL (IRE) 3 b.f. Cape Cross (IRE) 129 – Rio de Jumeirah 92 (Seeking The Gold (USA)) [2009 76?: p6g^4 6m 6.1g 7m 6d^6 6g^6 6.1m Jul 11] close-coupled filly: maiden: has gone wrong way: should stay 1m: best effort on good to soft going: tried visored. *M. R. Channon* **63 d**

PENINSULAR WAR 3 b.g. Deportivo 116 – Queens Jubilee 71 (Cayman Kai (IRE) 114) [2009 85: p6g^4 5.2d^5 5s^4 5g^6 5m^2 5m 5m^4 p5.1g 5d p7f^5 Dec 21] workmanlike gelding: fairly useful maiden: trained until after fifth outing by K. R. Burke: well worth another try at 6f: acts on firm and soft going. *R. A. Fahey* **82**

PENITENT 3 b.g. Kyllachy 129 – Pious 74 (Bishop of Cashel 122) [2009 6d^2 7g* p7g^2 p8m* f8g^2 Oct 18] sturdy, compact gelding: third foal: closely related to 4-y-o Solemn and 2006 2-y-o 7f winner Blithe (both by Pivotal): dam, 6f (including at 2 yrs) winner, out of half-sister to smart sprinter Ya Malak: useful form: won maiden at Newmarket in July and handicap at Kempton (dead-heated with Stoic) in September: further progress when 2¼ lengths second to Sovereign Remedy at Southwell final start: stays 1m: acts on all-weather and good to soft going. *W. J. Haggas* **107**

PENNINE ROSE 3 b.f. Reel Buddy (USA) 118 – Adorable Cherub (USA) 58 (Halo (USA)) [2009 –: 5m 6m 7.1m May 29] compact filly: little sign of ability. *A. Berry* **–**

PENNYBID (IRE) 7 b.g. Benny The Dip (USA) 127 – Stamatina (Warning 136) [2009 –: 7m 13.8m 10m Jun 19] of little account. *C. R. Wilson* **–**

PENNY'S GIFT 3 b.f. Tobougg (IRE) 125 – Happy Lady (FR) 72 (Cadeaux Genereux 131) [2009 101: 7m^3 8f^6 8g* 8g^5 7g 7m Sep 26] rather leggy, useful-looking filly: useful performer: further improvement in 2009, 3 lengths sixth to Ghanaati in 1000 Guineas at Newmarket prior to winning German 1000 Guineas at Dusseldorf in June by neck from Fabiana, making all: below form after: barely stays 1m, and should prove at least as effective at 7f: acts on firm and soft going. *R. Hannon* **108**

PENOLVA (IRE) 3 b.f. Galileo (IRE) 134 – Jabali (FR) (Shirley Heights 130) [2009 10.9m^5 11.8m^5 12m^2 11.1d^4 14.1m^3 p10.7f^5 p10.7g^6 f14m^4 Nov 11] 55,000Y, 50,000 2-y-o: smallish filly: half-sister to several winners in France, including useful 1¼m to 1½m winner Far From Old (by Vettori): dam twice-raced half-sister to very smart French stayer Floripedes, herself dam of Montjeu: fair maiden: trained by K. R. Burke first 4 starts, by A. Jarvis on fifth: barely stays 1¾m: acts on polytrack and good to firm going: races freely, often up with pace. *P. D. Deegan, Ireland* **65**

PENPERTH 3 b.f. Xaar 132 – Penelewey 97 (Groom Dancer (USA) 128) [2009 72: 8d p7g^5 p8g 10.1g Jul 20] smallish filly: maiden: just modest form at best in 2009: stays 1m: acts on polytrack: tried blinkered. *J. M. P. Eustace* **53**

PENROD BALLANTYNE (IRE) 2 ch.c. (May 3) Indian Ridge 123 – Silvia Diletta (Mark of Esteem (IRE) 137) [2009 7m Oct 13] €50,000F, €55,000Y: lengthy colt: fourth foal: brother to Italian 5f/7.5f winner Sparkling Ridge and half-brother to Italian 5f/6f winner Gioconda (by Fasliyev): dam fairly useful Italian 7f (at 2 yrs)/1m winner: 66/1, shaped well when mid-field behind Mufarrh in maiden at Leicester, travelling well when hampered under 2f out: will stay 1m: sure to do better. *B. J. Meehan* **70 p**

PENSION POLICY (USA) 4 b. or br.f. Danzig (USA) – Domain (USA) (Kris S (USA)) [2009 80: p8g^3 10g p8g 7m^4 May 19] lengthy filly: fair handicapper on all-weather, modest on turf: left R. Charlton after reappearance: stays 1m: acts on polytrack and good to firm ground: tried visored/blinkered. *J. M. P. Eustace* **63 a74**

PENTOMINIUM 2 b.c. (Apr 8) Dubai Destination (USA) 127 – Mouriyana (IRE) (Akarad (FR) 130) [2009 8g^3 Sep 30] 75,000F: sixth foal: half-brother to several winners in France, including 10.5f to 1½m winner Epatha (by Highest Honor) and 1m winner (including at 2 yrs) Skins Game (by Diktat), both useful: dam, French 2-y-o 1m winner, half-sister to smart dam of 3-y-o Mourayan and 5-y-o Mourilyan: 11/2 and green, promising 2¼ lengths third to Arlequin in maiden at Newcastle, late headway: will be suited by 1¼m: sure to improve. *M. Johnston* **74 p**

PENTON HOOK 3 gr.g. Lucky Owners (NZ) 122 – Cosmic Star 58 (Siberian Express (USA) 125) [2009 67: p8g* p10g^{2} Oct 29] tall, angular gelding: fairly useful form: off 14 months, won handicap at Lingfield in October: stays 1¼m: acts on polytrack. *P. Winkworth* **85**

PENZENA 3 ch.f. Tobougg (IRE) 125 – Penmayne 95 (Inchinor 119) [2009 63p: 8.3f^{4} 8g 8m^{2} 8.3m^{4} p8m* p8g^{5} Dec 7] useful-looking filly: fairly useful performer: left W. Knight, much improved when winning maiden at Kempton in November: likely to prove at least as effective at 7f as 1m: acts on polytrack and firm going: races close up. *A. M. Balding* **87**

PEOPLETON BROOK 7 b.h. Compton Place 125 – Merch Rhyd-Y-Grug (Sabrehill (USA) 120) [2009 72: p6g^{2} 6g p6g 6m^{6} 5.3f^{6} 5g* 5f^{4} 5f 5f^{4} 5g^{3} 5f^{4} 5f 6m^{3} 6g^{4} 5m^{5} 5m p6m^{2} p7m^{6} p6g p6m^{4} p5f p6m^{3} Dec 30] leggy horse: fair handicapper: won apprentice event at Goodwood in May: best at 5f: acts on polytrack, firm and soft ground: sometimes wears blinkers/cheekpieces: usually tongue tied: none too consistent. *B. G. Powell* **69**

PEPER HAROW (IRE) 3 b.f. Compton Place 125 – Faraway Moon 61 (Distant Relative 128) [2009 81d: 6.1f 5.1g^{5} 5m 5m 7g* 7d^{6} 6.1g* 6g p7.1g^{2} p7.1g* p7.1g p7.1g Oct 23] workmanlike filly: fair handicapper: won at Newbury in July, Nottingham in August and Wolverhampton in October: stays 7f: acts on polytrack, good to firm and good to soft going: tried visored: sold 13,000 gns. *M. D. I. Usher* **76**

PEPIN (IRE) 3 ch.g. King Charlemagne (USA) 120 – Consignia (IRE) 67 (Definite Article 121) [2009 45: p6g p6g^{6} p7g^{6} 6m^{6} p5.1g^{4} f6g^{3} p5.1g^{4} f6g* 6m f6g^{3} f6m^{6} f6g^{4} p6g Oct 23] small gelding: modest performer on all-weather, no form on turf: won handicap at Southwell in May: stays 6f: acts on all-weather: tried blinkered/in cheekpieces. *D. Haydn Jones* **–** **a59**

PEPI ROYAL (IRE) 2 b.f. (Feb 14) Royal Applause 124 – Alenushka 73 (Soviet Star (USA) 128) [2009 5g^{4} 6m^{6} 6m 6.1d 7g p5.1g^{3} p6f* Oct 14] £8,000Y: unfurnished filly: second foal: dam maiden (stayed 1m): fair performer: won nursery at Kempton, best effort: should stay 7f: acts on polytrack: sold 800 gns. *Pat Eddery* **69**

PEPONI 3 ch.c. Kris Kin (USA) 126 – Polmara (IRE) (Polish Precedent (USA) 131) [2009 p8m^{2} p7f^{2} Dec 21] 20,000Y: fourth foal: half-brother to winner abroad by Compton Place: dam ran once: fairly useful form when runner-up in maidens at Lingfield and Kempton, always prominent: stays 1m. *P. J. Makin* **80**

PEPPER LANE 2 ch.f. (Jan 16) Exceed And Excel (AUS) 126 – Maid To Matter (Pivotal 124) [2009 5m^{2} 5m^{4} 5g 6m^{5} 5d^{4} p6m^{3} 7g^{5} 7g^{5} Oct 16] 20,000F, £15,000Y: smallish, sparely-made filly: first foal: dam unraced sister to useful 6f/7f performer Polar Kingdom: modest maiden: left T. D. Barron after third outing: stays 6f: acts on polytrack and good to firm going. *J. Hetherton* **64**

PEPPERTREE LANE (IRE) 6 ch.g. Peintre Celebre (USA) 137 – Salonrolle (IRE) 103 (Tirol 127) [2009 115: 16m^{6} Sep 27] rather leggy, quite attractive gelding: good walker: well below smart best sole Flat start in 2009 (fair form over hurdles). *A. P. Boxhall* **–**

PERCEPTION (IRE) 3 b.f. Hawk Wing (USA) 136 – Princesse Darsha (GER) (Darshaan 133) [2009 73p: 10.2d 12m^{6} 13g^{6} 15.4m^{4} p16m* Sep 16] rangy filly: fair handicapper: won at Kempton in September: stays 2m: acts on polytrack and good to soft going: visored once: sold 15,000 gns, joined A. King. *R. Charlton* **72**

PERCEPTIVE 2 b.f. (Apr 23) Carnival Dancer 123 – Discerning 96 (Darshaan 133) [2009 7g p8.6g^{4} p8g^{2} Nov 1] fourth foal: half-sister to 3-y-o Phillipina and 5-y-o Star of Pompey: dam, 11.5f winner (would have been suited by 2m+), half-sister to very smart performer up to 1½m Nowhere To Exit and 8-y-o Cesare: progressive in maidens, 2¾ lengths second to Sowaylm at Lingfield (dictated, flashed tail): will be well suited by 1¼m+: capable of better still. *J. R. Fanshawe* **75 p**

PERCOLATOR 3 b.f. Kheleyf (USA) 116 – Coffee Cream 87 (Common Grounds 118) [2009 106: 5g 5m 5g Sep 22] unfurnished filly: useful performer in 2008 (reportedly suffered chip final outing): little impact at 3 yrs in listed races/minor event. *P. F. I. Cole* **86**

PERCUSSIONIST (IRE) 8 b.g. Sadler's Wells (USA) 132 – Magnificient Style (USA) 107 (Silver Hawk (USA) 123) [2009 14s May 15] tall, close-coupled gelding: has a powerful, round action: one-time very smart performer: lightly raced on Flat since 2004 (fairly useful hurdler nowadays), and well held sole start at 8 yrs: stays 2m: raced mostly on good ground or softer nowadays: tried blinkered: hard ride (edgy sort). *J. Howard Johnson* **–**

PERCYS CORISMATIC 3 b.f. Systematic 121 – Corisa (IRE) (Be My Guest (USA) 126) [2009 48: 8f 8g 11.9m Aug 5] maiden: well held in 2009. *J. Gallagher* **–**

PEREZ PRADO (USA) 4 b.g. Kingmambo (USA) 125 – Marisa (USA) (Swain (IRE) 134) [2009 63: 8.1g⁵ 8.3m 7d Aug 7] attractive gelding: modest maiden, lightly raced: tried tongue tied. *W. Jarvis* **59**

PERFECT ACT 4 b.f. Act One 124 – Markova's Dance 64 (Mark of Esteem (IRE) 137) [2009 85: p8.6g⁶ p8g⁴ p7g⁶ 7g p6m³ p6m³ p6g* p6m⁶ p7f p6f* Dec 20] smallish, sturdy filly: fairly useful handicapper: won at Lingfield in October and Kempton in December: effective at 6f to 1m: acts on polytrack, good to firm and good to soft going: usually held up. *C. G. Cox* **86**

PERFECT AFFAIR (USA) 3 b.g. Perfect Soul (IRE) 122 – Caribbean Affair (USA) (Red Ransom (USA)) [2009 76p: p7g p7g 8.3m³ 9.9m May 21] big, strong gelding: fair form: likely to prove best at 1m+: acts on good to firm ground: gelded after final start. *R. M. Beckett* **76**

PERFECT BLOSSOM 2 b.f. (Apr 12) One Cool Cat (USA) 123 – Perfect Peach 100 (Lycius (USA) 124) [2009 6m⁴ 6m⁵ 5s⁵ 5m Aug 13] fourth foal: half-sister to fairly useful 10.3f winner Thumpers Dream (by Cape Cross) and 5-y-o Poppy's Rose: dam 5f (at 2 yrs) and 7f winner: modest form in maidens first 2 starts only: should be as effective at 5f as 6f: acts on good to firm going. *I. W. McInnes* **54**

PERFECT CH'I (IRE) 2 b.f. (Mar 18) Choisir (AUS) 126 – Agouti (Pennekamp (USA) 130) [2009 5g 5.5m⁵ 6g* 6g² 6.1d* 6m³ 6.5m 6.5m p6m⁴ 7g⁵ p7.1g Nov 9] 4,000Y: lengthy filly: second foal: half-sister to French/Spanish 7f (at 2 yrs) to 9f winner Rey Ene (by King Charlemagne): dam, ran twice, half-sister to smart 5f to 1m winner in UAE Conflict, out of close relative to high-class French 6f to 1m performer Polar Falcon and half-sister to dam of 3-y-o Le Havre: fair performer: won maiden at Yarmouth in June and minor event at Nottingham in August: stays 7f: acts on polytrack, good to firm and good to soft going: races prominently. *I. A. Wood* **77**

PERFECT CITIZEN (USA) 3 ch.g. Proud Citizen (USA) 122 – Near Mint (USA) (Dehere (USA) 121) [2009 87: 8.3g p8g 7.1m⁶ f7g³ 9g⁵ p8.6g⁶ Oct 2] angular gelding: fairly useful handicapper: stays 7f: acts on all-weather, good to firm and good to soft going: tried in cheekpieces/tongue tie: not one to trust: sold 9,000 gns. *W. R. Swinburn* **84 §**

PERFECT CLASS 3 b.f. Cape Cross (IRE) 129 – Liberty 71 (Singspiel (IRE) 133) [2009 59: p6g* p6g² p7g⁵ 6g 7.1f³ 7m² 7m³ 7f⁵ p8g² 8g* 8.3f Aug 17] close-coupled filly: fair handicapper: won at Kempton in January and Bath in July: stays 1m: acts on polytrack and firm ground: tried visored/blinkered. *C. G. Cox* **75**

PERFECT FLIGHT 4 b.f. Hawk Wing (USA) 136 – Pretty Girl (IRE) 103 (Polish Precedent (USA) 131) [2009 101: 6d⁴ 7g 7s⁶ 6d Oct 11] neat filly: just fairly useful handicapper at 4 yrs: effective at 5f/6f: has won on good to firm going, best form on softer than good. *M. Blanshard* **92**

PERFECT FRIEND 3 b.f. Reel Buddy (USA) 118 – Four Legs Good (IRE) 58 (Be My Guest (USA) 126) [2009 70: p9.5g p7g² 7.1g* 6.1g² 7m² 7g³ 7m⁴ 7m* 8d² 7m 9g p7f 8g⁵ Oct 8] sturdy filly: fairly useful handicapper: won at Warwick in May and Newbury in July: effective at 6f to 8.6f: acts on polytrack, heavy and good to firm ground: held up. *S. Kirk* **84**

PERFECT HONOUR (IRE) 3 ch.f. Exceed And Excel (AUS) 126 – Porcelana (IRE) (Highest Honor (FR) 124) [2009 –: f6g⁴ p7.1g⁴ p6g⁶ p5g² p5.1g* p5.1g⁵ Apr 25] sturdy filly: modest handicapper: won at Wolverhampton in April: may prove best at 5f/6f: acts on all-weather. *D. Shaw* **56**

PERFECT NOTE 2 b.f. (Apr 19) Shamardal (USA) 129 – Mezzo Soprano (USA) 117 (Darshaan 133) [2009 7g⁴ Oct 31] well-made filly: third foal: half-sister to useful French 11f/1½m winner Claremont (by Sadler's Wells): dam, 1m (at 2 yrs in France) to 1½m (Prix Vermeille) winner, out of sister to Rahy/half-sister to Singspiel: 4/1, promising 3¾ lengths fourth to Field Day in maiden at Newmarket, not knocked about: will be suited by 1¼m: sure to do better. *Saeed bin Suroor* **72 p**

PERFECT PRIDE (USA) 3 b.f. Forest Wildcat (USA) 120 – Kisses To Yall (USA) (Copelan (USA)) [2009 77: 6m* 6m 6g⁴ 7m⁵ Sep 13] good-topped filly: has a quick action: fairly useful handicapper: improved to win at Goodwood in June: should stay 7f: acts on good to firm ground: sold 8,000 gns. *C. G. Cox* **89**

PERFECT SECRET 3 b.f. Spinning World (USA) 130 – Sharp Secret (IRE) 69 (College Chapel 122) [2009 7g⁴ p7f³ Dec 21] first foal: dam 6f (at 2 yrs) to 1m winner: encouraging efforts in frame in maidens at Goodwood and Kempton (better effort): likely to improve again. *A. M. Balding* **70 p**

Wolferton Handicap, Royal Ascot—one of three new course records on the day (though none of the Ascot records is long standing); Perfect Stride wins from Moonquake (No.10) and Salute Him

PERFECT SHOT (IRE) 3 b.g. High Chaparral (IRE) 132 – Zoom Lens (IRE) 65 (Caerleon (USA) 132) [2009 82: 10m 11.6g^{2} 12.1g* 14.1m^{2} 16.1g* 16g^{4} 16m^{6} 18g^{6} 16g Oct 30] sparely-made gelding: fairly useful performer: won maiden at Chepstow in June and handicap at Newmarket in August: stays 2m: acts on soft and good to firm ground: temperament under suspicion: gelded after final start. *J. L. Dunlop* **91**

PERFECT SILENCE 4 b.f. Dansili 127 – Perfect Echo 81 (Lycius (USA) 124) [2009 92p: 6m^{3} 6m^{3} 7.1m* 7g p7f* p7m^{4} p7f 7g^{4} Oct 31] big filly: has scope: has a powerful action: fairly useful handicapper: won at Warwick in July and Kempton in September: stays 7f: acts on polytrack, soft and good to firm ground: blinkered last 4 starts: races prominently. *C. G. Cox* **86 +**

PERFECT STAR 5 b.m. Act One 124 – Granted (FR) 100 (Cadeaux Genereux 131) [2009 107: p8g^{2} 8g^{5} 8v^{6} 8g^{4} 8.3m^{2} 10.3s p8.6g^{5} Nov 27] rather leggy mare: useful performer: in frame 3 times in 2009, including when 2½ lengths second to Born Tobouggie in listed race at Kempton on reappearance: best at 7f/1m: acts on polytrack, good to firm and good to soft ground. *C. G. Cox* **99**

PERFECT STRIDE 4 b.c. Oasis Dream 129 – First (Highest Honor (FR) 124) [2009 111: 8m* 8m^{6} 10f* 8.9m^{3} 9.9m^{3} 9.9m^{2} Sep 23] rangy, good sort: smart performer: improved at 4 yrs, winning listed race at Ascot (awarded race after nose second to General Eliott) in April and Wolferton Handicap (listed) at Royal meeting there (by neck from Moonquake) in June: several other creditable efforts in 2009, including when 2½ lengths second to Twice Over in listed event at Goodwood final start: stays 1¼m: raced only on good ground or firmer. *Sir Michael Stoute* **116**

PERFECT TRUTH (IRE) 3 ch.f. Galileo (IRE) 134 – Charroux (IRE) 75 (Darshaan 133) [2009 91: 10g^{4} p10.7g^{2} 11.4m* 12g 12s^{2} 14.6m Sep 10] big, close-coupled filly: useful performer: won listed Cheshire Oaks at Chester in May by short head from Phillipina: creditable effort after only when 1½ lengths second to Tamarind in Give Thanks Stakes at Cork (tailed-off last in Oaks at Epsom and Park Hill Stakes at Doncaster otherwise): should stay beyond 1½m: acts on polytrack, soft and good to firm going: temperament under suspicion (carries head awkwardly): sold to Australia. *A. P. O'Brien, Ireland* **105**

PERFECT VISION 2 b.f. (Apr 15) Starcraft (NZ) 128 – Auspicious 103 (Shirley Heights 130) [2009 7m 8m p8m* Oct 28] 18,000Y: sixth foal: half-sister to several fairly useful winners, including 4-y-o Istiqdaam and 6-y-o Prince Picasso: dam, 1¼m winner, sister to smart middle-distance stayer Sacrament: easily best effort in maidens when winning at Kempton by ½ length from Anaya: will stay 1¼m+: likely to progress further. *C. G. Cox* **76 p**

PERGAMON (IRE) 3 b.g. Dalakhani (IRE) 133 – Pinaflore (FR) (Formidable (USA) 125) [2009 86+: 10m f11g^{6} May 5] close-coupled gelding: fairly useful maiden at 2 yrs: well below form in blinkers both starts in 2009: should stay 1¼m: sold £5,000, joined Miss C. Dyson. *J. H. M. Gosden* **–**

PERKS (IRE) 4 b.g. Selkirk (USA) 129 – Green Charter 77 (Green Desert (USA) 127) [2009 116: 10v^5 10m 10f 8d^2 8g^3 p10m 10g^5 Oct 31] big, workmanlike gelding: has a round action: smart performer: creditable effort in 2009 only when nose second to Dream Lodge in minor event at Doncaster: should stay 1½m: has form on good to firm ground, acts very well on soft/heavy. *J. L. Dunlop* **113**

PERLACHY 5 b.g. Kyllachy 129 – Perfect Dream 72 (Emperor Jones (USA) 119) [2009 67: p6g^2 p6g* p5.1g* p6g^6 p5.1g p6g p5.1g^2 p6g* p6m^2 p5.1g^3 Dec 4] quite good-topped, close-coupled gelding: fair handicapper: won at Kempton and Wolverhampton in February and, having left D. Shaw after fifth start, Wolverhampton in November: effective at 5f to 7f: acts on all-weather and firm going: wears visor (tried in cheekpieces). *J. R. Holt* **75**

PERLE D'AMOUR (IRE) 2 b.f. (May 8) Pearl of Love (IRE) 112 – Bella Vie (IRE) (Sadler's Wells (USA) 132) [2009 5.7f^4 May 31] 7,500Y: fifth foal: half-sister to 3 winners, including 7f (at 2 yrs) to 8.6f winner Elusive Lady (by Clodovil) and 5-y-o Snow Dancer: dam unraced close relation of useful Irish sprinter Immovable Option: 7/1, well-held fourth in maiden at Bath. *R. Hannon* **–**

PERPETUALLY (IRE) 3 b.c. Singspiel (IRE) 133 – Set In Motion (USA) (Mr Prospector (USA)) [2009 93p: 10m* Apr 16] good-topped colt: has won both his starts, and showed useful form when winning handicap at Newmarket (still green, edged ahead late on under hands and heels when beating Imposing by short head) in April: should stay 1½m: raced only on good to firm going. *M. Johnston* **98**

PERSE 2 br.f. (Feb 5) Rock of Gibraltar (IRE) 133 – La Persiana 112 (Daylami (IRE) 138) [2009 7g Oct 31] first foal: dam, won around 1¼m, half-sister to Dewhurst and St James's Palace Stakes winner Grand Lodge: 50/1, well held in maiden at Newmarket. *W. Jarvis* **–**

PERSIAN BUDDY 3 b.g. Reel Buddy (USA) 118 – Breeze Again (USA) (Favorite Trick (USA) 121) [2009 63: p8g^6 Feb 4] deep-girthed gelding: fair form: improved when sixth in handicap sole start at 3 yrs: stays 1m: acts on polytrack. *Jamie Poulton* **67**

PERSIAN HEROINE (IRE) 2 b.f. (Feb 16) Intikhab (USA) 135 – Persian Fantasy 94 (Persian Bold 123) [2009 6m^5 7m Oct 6] neat filly: closely related to smart 1m to 11.5f winner Persian Lightning (by Sri Pekan) and half-sister to several winners, including useful 1¾m/2m winner Height of Fantasy (by Shirley Heights): dam 1½m winner (stayed 2m): very green and no impact in maidens at Folkestone and Leicester: will be suited by 1m+: sold 3,800 gns. *J. L. Dunlop* **–**

PERSIAN MEMORIES (IRE) 3 br.f. Indian Ridge 123 – Persian Fantasy 94 (Persian Bold 123) [2009 78p: 11.6m p10g 11.8m^3 11.6m^2 12f^2 11.5s^3 13.1d^5 p16m 12m^5 p12m^6 Oct 26] close-coupled filly: fair maiden handicapper: stays 1½m: acts on polytrack, firm and soft going: tried blinkered. *J. L. Dunlop* **71**

PERSIAN PERIL 5 br.g. Erhaab (USA) 127 – Brush Away (Ahonoora 122) [2009 84: f12g f11g* 10g^3 10.2v^3 10s 12s 10.4g^2 f11g^3 p8.6g Nov 13] strong, close-coupled gelding: fairly useful handicapper: won at Southwell in May: very good neck second in apprentice event at York seventh start: stays 1½m: acts on fibresand, heavy and good to firm going. *G. A. Swinbank* **93**

PERSIAN POET 2 b.g. (Mar 6) Dubai Destination (USA) 127 – Salim Toto 107 (Mtoto 134) [2009 8.1m 8.3s 8g Oct 16] good-topped gelding: modest form at best in maidens: bred to be suited by 1¼m+: sold £1,200, joined R. Barr, and gelded. *M. Johnston* **50**

PERSIAN STORM (GER) 5 b.g. Monsun (GER) 124 – Private Life (FR) (Bering 136) [2009 105: p10g^5 8.1g^4 8d^3 Aug 7] smart performer at best: trained in Germany at 3 yrs, winning 2 Group 3s: just useful form in 2 starts for A. Fabre in France in 2008 and well below par all 3 outings in Britain in 2009 (said to have finished lame final one): seemed best around 1¼m: acted on good to firm going: modest form over hurdles: dead. *G. L. Moore* **–**

PERSIAN TOMCAT (IRE) 3 gr.g. One Cool Cat (USA) 123 – Persian Mistress (IRE) (Persian Bold 123) [2009 –: p8g^6 p8g^3 p10g^3 11.5m^2 11.5s p12g^3 12m^4 12f^6 f11g^5 9.9g p10g^3 p10g^5 p9.5g^5 p10g^6 p12f^5 Dec 13] workmanlike gelding: modest maiden handicapper: stays 1½m: acts on polytrack and good to firm going: tried visored/in cheekpieces. *Miss J. Feilden* **58**

PERSISTENT (IRE) 4 b.g. Cape Cross (IRE) 129 – Insistent (USA) (Diesis 133) [2009 60: 11.7g Aug 28] sturdy gelding: modest maiden: well held sole 4-y-o start: stays 1½m: acts on all-weather, well held on turf: tried in cheekpieces/tongue tie. *D. G. Bridgwater* **–**

PERSONA NON GRATA (IRE) 2 b.g. (Mar 16) Azamour (IRE) 130 – Private Life (FR) (Bering 136) [2009 p8g^4 8.3g^6 p8m Oct 12] lengthy, angular gelding: fair maiden: will stay 1¼m: blinkered: has looked reluctant: sold 1,000 gns, joined M. Ramadan in UAE. *R. Charlton* **70**

PERSONIFY 7 ch.g. Zafonic (USA) 130 – Dignify (IRE) 105 (Rainbow Quest (USA) 134) [2009 60: 10.2g^4 12.1m 10g Jul 14] rather leggy gelding: modest performer nowadays: best short of 1½m: acts on polytrack, firm and soft going: usually in headgear: tried tongue tied. *J. L. Flint* **53**

PERTEMPS POWER 5 b.g. Zaha (CAN) 106 – Peristyle 59 (Tolomeo 127) [2009 –: p13.9g^3 p12.2g^2 p13.9g 12m^4 12.6d^5 p12.2g^3 p13.9g^4 p16.5g^5 Oct 30] modest maiden: stays 1¾m: acts on polytrack and good to firm ground: tongue tied last 2 starts. *B. G. Powell* **57**

PETELLA 3 b.f. Tamure (IRE) 125 – Miss Petronella (Petoski 135) [2009 62p: 8.1m^4 10.2g^5 11.1d^5 12d 12.5m 16g^2 16g Oct 28] modest maiden handicapper: worth a try at 1¾m: best efforts on good/good to firm going. *C. W. Thornton* **58**

PETER GRIMES (IRE) 3 ch.g. Alhaarth (IRE) 126 – Aldburgh (Bluebird (USA) 125) [2009 72: 9.7d* 9.7g^4 11d 11.7m^5 10d^3 10d^3 p10g Sep 2] well-made gelding: fair handicapper: won at Folkestone in March: stays 1¼m: acts on good to soft going: joined A. King, won juvenile hurdle in November. *H. J. L. Dunlop* **72**

PETER ISLAND (FR) 6 b.g. Dansili 127 – Catania (USA) (Aloma's Ruler (USA)) [2009 89: p6g^3 6f* 6g^6 6m 6g^4 5m^6 6g 6m^6 6g 6m^3 6d Oct 22] smallish, strong gelding: useful handicapper: better than ever when winning at Leicester (by 4 lengths from Dancing Maite) in April: below that form after: best at 5f/6f: acts on polytrack, firm and good to soft going: visored/blinkered: speedy front runner. *J. Gallagher* **95**

PETER'S FOLLIE 2 gr.f. (Jan 14) Highest Honor (FR) 124 – Fabulous Speed (USA) (Silver Hawk (USA) 123) [2009 5.2d^4 5g^3 5.1g 6.1s Oct 7] small, leggy filly: first foal: dam, French 9f to 1½m winner, half-sister to useful French performer up to 15f High Maintenance (by Highest Honor) out of Prix de Royallieu winner Fabulous Hostess: modest maiden: bred to be well suited by 1¼m+: sold 2,000 gns, sent to Serbia. *Tom Dascombe* **54**

PETER'S GIFT (IRE) 3 b.f. Catcher In The Rye (IRE) 115 – Eastern Blue (IRE) 68 (Be My Guest (USA) 126) [2009 74: 7.1m^2 7g^5 f7g* 8m^5 8.1g^3 p7g^5 8g p7.1m Sep 28] tall, useful-looking filly: fair handicapper: won at Southwell in May: below form after: stays 7f: acts on all-weather, heavy and good to firm ground. *K. A. Ryan* **78**

PETERS PRIDE 7 b.g. Silver Patriarch (IRE) 125 – Manzanilla (Mango Express 106) [2009 f11g May 5] fairly useful bumper winner: modest hurdler: well beaten in maiden only outing on Flat: dead. *M. W. Easterby* **–**

PETER'S STORM (USA) 4 ch.g. Van Nistelrooy (USA) 108 – Fairy Land Flyer (USA) (Lyphard's Wish (FR) 124) [2009 74, a79: p6g^3 p6g^3 f5g p7.1g^6 f6g^6 p6g f6g^4 p6g Mar 23] strong, workmanlike gelding: type to carry condition: fair handicapper: below form after second start: best at 5f/6f: acts on polytrack and good to soft going: tried in cheekpieces: often forces pace. *K. A. Ryan* **75 d**

PETE'S PASSION 3 b.f. Rock of Gibraltar (IRE) 133 – Three Days In May 70 (Cadeaux Genereux 131) [2009 7m Jul 11] 29,000F, 40,000Y: quite attractive filly: first living foal: dam, 6f winner, half-sister to useful 1997 2-y-o 6f winner Crazee Mental: very green in maiden at York. *R. A. Fahey* **–**

PETHERS DANCER (IRE) 3 b.g. Kyllachy 129 – La Piaf (FR) (Fabulous Dancer (USA) 124) [2009 –: p8g 7m Jun 25] rather leggy gelding: no form: tried blinkered. *W. R. Muir* **–**

PETIDIUM 4 b.f. Presidium 124 – Efipetite 54 (Efisio 120) [2009 f7g Oct 18] small filly: well held in maidens. *N. Bycroft* **–**

PETIT BELLE 2 b.f. (Mar 31) Piccolo 121 – Tallulah Belle 92 (Crowning Honors (CAN)) [2009 5g p6g p6g Nov 27] 11,000 2-y-o: fifth foal: sister to 3-y-o Ruby Tallulah: dam 9f to 1½m winner: well held in maidens. *N. P. Littmoden* **–**

PETITE MAMBO 2 b.g. (Feb 24) Miesque's Son (USA) 117 – Chalet 62 (Singspiel (IRE) 133) [2009 6m 7.1m 7d^6 8.3d 8g p8g Nov 14] leggy gelding: modest maiden: should stay beyond 1m: acts on polytrack. *W. de Best-Turner* **59**

PETITE ROCKET (IRE) 3 b.f. Fayruz 116 – Courtisane (Persepolis (FR) 127) [2009 –: 5m May 19] no form in claimer/maiden. *J. A. McShane* **–**

PETOMIC (IRE) 4 ch.g. Dubai Destination (USA) 127 – Petomi 75 (Presidium 124) [2009 –: p7g 8.1m³ 8.3m⁶ 8.1m³ 8.1d* 8.1d⁵ p10m⁴ p8.6g⁵ p8m Nov 4] angular gelding: fair handicapper: left Christian Wroe after reappearance, R. Beckett after second start: improved to win at Chepstow in August: may prove best around 1m: acts on polytrack and good to soft going: tried tongue tied. *M. Hill* **68**

PETOUGG 2 b.g. (Mar 28) Tobougg (IRE) 125 – Piroshka (Soviet Star (USA) 128) [2009 6d* 6.1d⁵ 6m⁶ Sep 25] 7,000F, 11,000Y: sturdy gelding: seventh foal: half-brother to 7-y-o Red Rudy and winner up to 11f in Italy by Case Law: dam unraced: fair performer: won maiden at Haydock in July, best effort: stays 7f. *W. Jarvis* **76**

PETRENKO 3 b.g. Efisio 120 – Lambast 70 (Relkino 131) [2009 p5g f6g⁶ p8.6g Feb 27] well held in maidens: subsequently gelded. *R. A. Fahey* **–**

PETROCELLI 2 b.g. (Mar 24) Piccolo 121 – Sarcita 111 (Primo Dominie 121) [2009 5f⁴ 5m³ 6g⁵ 6f³ p7.1g Aug 10] compact gelding: half-brother to smart 6f/7f winner (including in UAE) Snow Kid (by Indian Ridge) and useful 1998 2-y-o 5f winner Sarson (by Efisio): dam 5f/6f winner, including at 2 yrs: fair performer: best effort when third to Alrasm in maiden at Doncaster fourth start: stays 6f: acts on firm going: blinkered last 2 outings (pulled hard final one, gelded after). *A. J. McCabe* **75**

PETROGLYPH 5 ch.g. Indian Ridge 123 – Madame Dubois 121 (Legend of France (USA) 124) [2009 –: f8g p12f Oct 14] very tall gelding: no form on Flat since 2006: left P. Bowen prior to final outing (wore cheekpieces): fair hurdler, won 3 times in November/ December. *M. G. Quinlan* **–**

PETROVSKY 3 gr.r. Daylami (IRE) 138 – Russian Society 103 (Darshaan 133) [2009 86p: p8.6g* p11g* 12m² 12m* 13g⁵ Sep 20] good-topped colt: useful handicapper: won at Wolverhampton in January, Kempton in February, and having been off 4 months, Ffos Las (by 2 lengths from Sehoy) in September: should stay beyond 1½m: acts on polytrack, heavy and good to firm going: forces pace: has joined A. Al Raihe in UAE. *M. Johnston* **104**

PETSAS PLEASURE 3 b.g. Observatory (USA) 131 – Swynford Pleasure 72 (Reprimand 122) [2009 69: 9.9m f7g 8m⁴ 8.3m² 8.3m* 9.2v 8.3g 8g p8.6g p12.2g Nov 2] leggy gelding: fair handicapper: won at Hamilton in July: below form after: worth another try at 1¼m: acts on good to firm going. *Ollie Pears* **74**

PEVENSEY (IRE) 7 b.g. Danehill (USA) 126 – Champaka (IRE) (Caerleon (USA) 132) [2009 103: p12g⁴ p9.5g 10m⁶ 12f 12g 12m* 12g⁴ 12s Nov 7] compact gelding: useful handicapper on turf, fairly useful on all-weather: won at Catterick in September by 1¼ lengths from Wicked Daze: good fourth to Opinion Poll in quite valuable event at Ascot next time: stays 1½m: acts on polytrack, firm and soft going: tried in blinkers/visor, wears cheekpieces: held up: none too consistent. *J. J. Quinn* **99 a94**

PEZULA 3 b.f. Diktat 126 – Mashmoum 85 (Lycius (USA) 124) [2009 –: 10f⁶ 8.1g p11m p16g Oct 24] good-topped filly: well held in varied company. *R. T. Phillips* **–**

PHA MAI BLUE 4 b.g. Acclamation 118 – Queen of Silk (IRE) 93 (Brief Truce (USA) 126) [2009 80: p8g p8g³ 7g³ p8g* p8g³ p8g 10g⁶ p7g* p8.6g 8.3g⁴ p8g⁴ p8g⁵ p7m p8g p7m Dec 30] lengthy, quite attractive gelding: fair handicapper: won at Lingfield in May and August: best at 7f/1m: acts on polytrack and good to firm going: has worn visor: none too consistent. *J. R. Boyle* **74**

PHANTOM RIDGE (IRE) 3 b.f. Indian Ridge 123 – Phantom Waters 79 (Pharly (FR) 130) [2009 8g p8g⁶ 10m³ 10m⁶ Aug 9] lengthy filly: fifth foal: sister to 1m winner Tina's Ridge and half-sister to 4-y-o Tina's Best and Irish 9f winner Phantom Lad (by Desert Prince): dam, 1½m winner, half-sister to smart dam of Tenby: fair form in maidens: worth another try at 1m. *R. Hannon* **72**

PHANTOM SERENADE (IRE) 4 b.g. Orpen (USA) 116 – Phantom Rain 77 (Rainbow Quest (USA) 134) [2009 56: 8g⁶ 9.2d* 8d 7g 10m⁶ 10m* 12.4d 10g Oct 16] big, rangy gelding: fair performer: won handicap at Hamilton in July and seller at Redcar in September: stays 1¼m: acts on soft and good to firm ground: none too consistent. *M. Dods* **66**

PHANTOM WHISPER 6 b.g. Makbul 104 – La Belle Vie 73 (Indian King (USA) 128) [2009 103: 5.2s 6m 6d⁵ 6m 6g³ 6.1m⁶ 6g 6m 7.1g 6g⁶ 6d⁵ p6g Oct 24] workmanlike gelding: just fairly useful handicapper in 2009: best at 6f/7f: acts on polytrack, soft and good to firm ground: tried in blinkers/cheekpieces. *B. R. Millman* **92**

PHARAOHS JUSTICE (USA) 4 br.g. Kafwain (USA) 118 – Mary Linoa (USA) 113 (L'Emigrant (USA) 129) [2009 –: f7d⁶ p7g p8g p8g p7g 8f 7f Jun 13] just modest handicapper nowadays: should stay 1¼m: raced on all-weather and firm ground: blinkered of late. *N. P. Littmoden* **58**

PHEROUSA 2 b.f. (Mar 25) Dubawi (IRE) 129 – Sea Nymph (IRE) 85 (Spectrum (IRE) 126) [2009 6m² 6m 6g 5g⁴ 5.7g 5.1m⁵ 5.5g⁴ 5.1g* 5m⁶ 6m Oct 1] leggy filly: second foal: dam, 1m winner, out of half-sister to Yorkshire Oaks winner/excellent broodmare Hellenic: modest performer: won maiden at Bath in September, best effort: should stay 7f: inconsistent. *M. Blanshard* **64**

PHILANDER 2 b.c. (Mar 16) Red Ransom (USA) – Fidelio's Miracle (USA) 108 (Mountain Cat (USA)) [2009 8d⁴ 8g⁵ 8.1m³ 8d² 9.5v⁵ Nov 8] 40,000Y: third foal: dam French 7.5f to 1¼m winner: fairly useful maiden: 6½ lengths third to Hot Prospect at Sandown third start, only outing in Britain: ran at least respectably in France otherwise: will stay 1¼m: acts on good to firm and good to soft ground. *E. J. O'Neill* **86**

PHILARIO (IRE) 4 ch.c. Captain Rio 122 – Salva 73 (Grand Lodge (USA) 125) [2009 104: p8g² p7.1g⁵ 8m⁶ 8m 8g² 8v* 8.5g³ 8m Jun 17] close-coupled colt: unimpressive in appearance: smart handicapper: improvement when winning at the Curragh in May by length from Rock And Roll Kid: creditable third to Tartan Gigha at Epsom next time: poorly drawn in Royal Hunt Cup final start: best up to 8.5f: acts on polytrack, heavy and good to firm going: races up with pace: sold £50,000 in October, joined P. Deegan in Ireland. *K. R. Burke* **112**

PHILATELIST (USA) 5 b.h. Rahy (USA) 115 – Polent (Polish Precedent (USA) 131) – [2009 111: p10g⁴ p10g⁴ p11g* 10.4m 10m a10g p10m⁵ 12m p10g³ a9.5g⁶ Dec 10] **a109** tall, lengthy horse: useful performer: won handicap at Kempton in March by 2¾ lengths from King Olav: off 5 months (reportedly suffered injury), below form after: effective at 1¼m/1½m: acts on polytrack, no form on turf in 2009: often wears headgear nowadays. *M. A. Jarvis*

PHILIPPA JANE 2 ch.f. (Apr 9) Muhtathir 126 – Ante Futura (FR) (Suave Dancer (USA) 136) [2009 p8m p8m p7m Dec 10] sixth foal: half-sister to French 8.5f to 1¼m winner Futura Dancer (by Anabaa) and French 9f to 1½m winner Wind of Tea (by Barathea): dam French 1¼m winner: well held in maidens at Kempton: pulled hard first 2 starts. *P. Winkworth* **–**

PHILLIPINA 3 b.f. Medicean 128 – Discerning 96 (Darshaan 133) [2009 87p: 10s⁵ 11.4m² 12g⁶ 10.2v* 12d 12m Sep 25] useful-looking filly: useful performer: landed odds in maiden at Nottingham in July: easily best effort when short-head second to Perfect Truth in listed Cheshire Oaks at Chester second start: should have been suited by 1½m: acted on heavy and good to firm ground: visits Cape Cross. *Sir Michael Stoute* **105**

PHILMACK DOT COM 3 b.g. Traditionally (USA) 117 – Lilli Marlane 82 (Sri Pekan (USA) 117) [2009 53: p8g⁶ p6g p7g p7.1m* p9.5g Dec 11] good-topped gelding: fair handicapper: left Amy Weaver after reappearance: won at Wolverhampton in November: stays 7f: raced only on polytrack: tongue tied last 3 starts. *D. Donovan* **67**

PHINERINE 6 ch.g. Bahamian Bounty 116 – Golden Panda 77 (Music Boy 124) [2009 –, a60: f6s⁴ f6d⁵ f5g⁴ Jan 15] modest handicapper: effective at 5f/6f: acts on all-weather: wears headgear. *A. Berry* **– a54**

PHLUKE 8 b.g. Most Welcome 131 – Phlirty (Pharly (FR) 130) [2009 95, a81: p8g⁶ 8.1g 7.1m³ 7.5g² p8g⁶ 7m 8.5d⁵ 8.1m 8.5m p8m⁴ 7d⁶ p8m p10g Nov 5] good-bodied gelding: regressive handicapper: effective at 7f/1m: acts on all-weather, firm and good to soft going: sometimes visored. *Eve Johnson Houghton* **83 d**

PHOENIX ENFORCER 3 b.f. Bahamian Bounty 116 – Kythia (IRE) 77 (Kahyasi 130) [2009 76: 9.9m 10g⁴ 10.2v* 8.3d* 10.2g⁵ Aug 18] fair performer: won sellers at Nottingham and Leicester 5 days apart in July: stays 1¼m: best form on good going or softer (acts on heavy): in cheekpieces last 4 starts: poor form in juvenile hurdles. *George Baker* **67**

PHOENIX FLIGHT (IRE) 4 b.g. Hawk Wing (USA) 136 – Firecrest (IRE) 107 (Darshaan 133) [2009 89: p10g⁶ p10g f12d² p12g* p16.5g² p12g* 14m² p16g⁴ 13d³ 13.8g³ 11.6f³ p12g² p12.2g⁵ 16g Oct 30] lengthy gelding: fairly useful performer: won claimer at Lingfield and handicap at Kempton in March: claimed from Sir Mark Prescott £21,000 eleventh start: stays 2m: acts on all-weather and good to firm ground: in cheekpieces last 3 starts: quirky. *H. J. Evans* **89**

PHOENIX HILL (IRE) 7 b.g. Montjeu (IRE) 137 – Cielo Vodkamartini (USA) (Conquistador Cielo (USA)) [2009 –: p12g² p12g 12m² 16.4m⁴ Jul 9] quite good-topped gelding: modest maiden: stays 1¾m: acts on polytrack, firm and good to soft going: tried tongue tied. *D. R. Gandolfo* **53**

PHOENIX NIGHTS (IRE) 9 b.g. General Monash (USA) 107 – Beauty Appeal (USA) (Shadeed (USA) 135) [2009 –: 15m⁶ 13.8m Jun 5] smallish, workmanlike gelding: of little account nowadays. *A. Berry* **–**

PHOENIX RISING 3 b.f. Dr Fong (USA) 128 – Dead Certain 123§ (Absalom 128) [2009 p7g 6m 8m Jun 14] sturdy filly: half-sister to numerous winners, including useful Irish 7f/1¼m winner Hamad (by Sadler's Wells): dam, sprinter (wins included Cheveley Park Stakes), became temperamental: well held in maidens. *H. Morrison* **–**

PHOENIX ROSE (IRE) 2 ch.f. (Apr 16) Rakti 130 – Fez 94 (Mujtahid (USA) 118) [2009 p6g⁴ p6g f6g⁵ p5g p7g p7g Nov 25] €3,000Y: smallish filly: fourth foal: dam 2-y-o 5f winner: modest maiden: well held in nurseries: stays 6f: acts on polytrack. *J. R. Best* **62**

PHONIC (IRE) 2 ch.c. (Mar 4) Green Tune (USA) 125 – Superfonic (FR) (Zafonic (USA) 130) [2009 7.1m 8m³ 9d Oct 11] 24,000Y: third foal: half-brother to French 2007 2-y-o 9.5f winner Paradisiac (by Hernando): dam, French 11.5f winner, half-sister to 4-y-o Goldikova and smart French/US 1m/1¼m performer Gold Sound (by Green Tune): easily best effort in maidens when 4¾ lengths third to Wigmore Hall at Newmarket, staying on and not knocked about: bred to be suited by 1¼m+. *J. L. Dunlop* **75**

PHOTOGRAPHIC 3 b.f. Oasis Dream 129 – Prophecy (IRE) 109 (Warning 136) [2009 p8g* 8m* 7m² 8m 7g⁵ 7m⁶ Oct 16] lengthy filly: half-sister to several winners, including smart French 7f (at 2 yrs)/1m winner Modern Look (by Zamindar) and useful 6f winner Arabesque (by Zafonic): dam, 2-y-o 5f/6f (latter including Cheveley Park Stakes) winner who stayed 1m, out of Lancashire Oaks winner Andaleeb: useful performer: won maiden at Kempton in March and handicap at Newmarket in May: good neck equal-second to Brief Encounter in handicap at York next time: stayed 1m: acted on polytrack and good to firm going: visits Zamindar. *B. W. Hills* **99**

PIANOFORTE (USA) 7 b.g. Grand Slam (USA) 120 – Far Too Loud (CAN) (No Louder (CAN)) [2009 72: 8.3m 9.3m⁴ 8d⁴ 7.9m³ 8m 7.9d 9m⁴ 8m⁶ 8d⁵ p9.5g² 8m p8.6g* p8.6g p8.6m p9.5g⁵ Nov 30] strong, close-coupled gelding: modest performer nowadays: won handicap at Wolverhampton in September: stays 8.6f: acts on all-weather, firm and soft ground: wears headgear: not straightforward. *E. J. Alston* **62**

PIAZZA SAN PIETRO 3 ch.g. Compton Place 125 – Rainbow Spectrum (FR) 57 (Spectrum (IRE) 126) [2009 82: p5.1g² p7g 5.7m² 7m² 7.1m* 5.7m* p6g 7f 5.2g³ 5.7g³ 5m 7m² p6m⁶ Nov 26] fair performer: left J. Gask £7,000, won seller at Chepstow and claimer at Bath in July: stays 7f: acts on heavy and good to firm ground: has worn cheek-pieces (including at Bath). *A. B. Haynes* **77**

PICCADILLY FILLY (IRE) 2 ch.f. (Apr 7) Exceed And Excel (AUS) 126 – Tortue (IRE) 89 (Turtle Island (IRE) 123) [2009 p6g² p6g p6m² p5g* 5g* 5m⁶ 5g Oct 10] unfurnished filly: third foal: dam, Irish 1m/9f winner, half-sister to smart French stayer Tiraaz: useful performer: improved to win maiden at Lingfield and listed race at Deauville (by neck from Angel's Pursuit) in August: better effort after when creditable sixth to Sand Vixen in Flying Childers Stakes at Doncaster: will prove best at sharp 5f: acts on polytrack and good to firm going: usually makes running. *E. J. Creighton* **97**

PICCASO'S SKY 3 b.c. Piccolo 121 – Skylark 77 (Polar Falcon (USA) 126) [2009 –: p5g⁵ p5g⁴ 5m 5.7f 5.1f⁵ p5.1g Jul 13] modest maiden, sporadic form: should stay beyond 5f: best efforts on polytrack: tried blinkered/visored: sold £1,000 in August. *A. B. Haynes* **51**

PICCOLA STELLA (IRE) 2 b.f. (Mar 9) Antonius Pius (USA) 123§ – Beeper's Lodge (IRE) (Grand Lodge (USA) 125) [2009 5s Aug 1] €5,500Y: fourth foal: closely related to winner in Russia by Mull of Kintyre and half-sister to 2 winners abroad, including Italian 2008 2-y-o 1m winner Alex Douglas (by Catcher In The Rye): dam of no account: 13/2, last in maiden at Thirsk. *R. M. H. Cowell* **–**

PICCOLINDA 3 b.f. Piccolo 121 – Belinda 64 (Mizoram (USA) 105) [2009 66: p7g p6g⁵ p7g 7d p7g⁴ Aug 24] medium-sized filly: modest performer: stays 7f: acts on polytrack: tried blinkered. *W. R. Muir* **60**

PICCOLO DIAMANTE (USA) 5 b. or br.g. Three Wonders (USA) – Bafooz (USA) 48 (Clever Trick (USA)) [2009 64: f5g⁶ p6g f8g f8g p6m⁶ f7g Mar 3] close-coupled gelding: handicapper, just poor in 2009: usually tongue tied. *S. Parr* **47**

PICCOLO EXPRESS 3 b.g. Piccolo 121 – Ashfield 67 (Zilzal (USA) 137) [2009 –: p8.6g p8.6g⁵ p7.1g⁴ 8f³ 7.6g⁴ 8.1s 8m Aug 9] modest maiden: well worth dropping back to 6f: acts on firm ground. *B. P. J. Baugh* **52**

PICCOLO MONDO 3 b.g. Piccolo 121 – Oriel Girl 65 (Beveled (USA)) [2009 78: p8g³ 8m 7.6f 7g² 8g² p8g⁵ p8m³ Nov 19] leggy gelding: fairly useful maiden: stays 1m: acts on polytrack and good to firm ground: tried tongue tied. *P. Winkworth* **80**

PICCOLO PETE 4 b.g. Piccolo 121 – Goes A Treat (IRE) 82 (Common Grounds 118) [2009 54: 10.1m 16m 6g 7s 6d 6g Jul 16] close-coupled gelding: maiden: little form in 2009: tried in headgear. *R. Johnson* **–**

PICCOLO PRIDE 4 ch.g. Piccolo 121 – Jaycat (IRE) 56 (Catrail (USA) 123) [2009 –
–: 9.2m^6 Jun 25] no sign of ability on Flat (modest maiden hurdler): tried tongue tied.
M. A. Barnes

PICKERING 5 br.g. Prince Sabo 123 – On The Wagon (Then Again 126) [2009 78: **79**
6m* 6m^3 6m^3 7g 5m^6 6m Oct 1] big, strong, lengthy gelding: fair handicapper: won at
Pontefract in April: was effective at 5f to 7f: acted on firm going: tried blinkered, in
cheekpieces at 5 yrs: dead. *E. J. Alston*

PICK OF THE DAY (IRE) 4 ch.g. Choisir (AUS) 126 – Reveuse de Jour (IRE) 79 **50**
(Sadler's Wells (USA) 132) [2009 58: f14s^4 f12g^6 f12d Mar 10] sturdy, compact gelding:
modest maiden: stays 1¾m: acts on fibresand: tried visored. *J. G. Given*

PICKY 5 b.g. Piccolo 121 – Passerella (FR) (Brustolon 117) [2009 11.8m^4 Jun 25] fair –
performer in 2007: well held sole Flat outing since: stays 1¼m: acts on polytrack and
good to firm ground: tried visored/blinkered. *C. C. Bealby*

PICNIC PARTY 2 ch.f. (Jan 27) Indian Ridge 123 – Antediluvian 106 (Air Express **66**
(IRE) 125) [2009 6.1s^6 p6g^2 Nov 18] first foal: dam, 7f (at 2 yrs)/1m winner, half-sister to
useful performer up to 1m Ekhtiaar: similar form in maidens, still green when 4½ lengths
second to Jarrow at Lingfield: will be suited by 7f/1m. *J. Noseda*

PICOT DE SAY 7 b.g. Largesse 112 – Facsimile 67 (Superlative 118) [2009 12.1m^3 **61**
12.1v* 10.2m Sep 10] lightly raced and modest on Flat (fairly useful hurdler): won
handicap at Chepstow in August: stays 1½m: acts on heavy ground. *C. Roberts*

PICTORIAL (USA) 3 b.g. Pivotal 124 – Red Tulle (USA) 66 (A P Indy (USA) 131) **82**
[2009 10d^6 10m* 12m p12g Aug 24] 165,000Y: lengthy gelding: fifth foal: closely
related to 5-y-o Redwater River and half-brother to 2 winners, including 7f/1¼m winner
Danger Zone (by Danzero): dam, third at 1¼m from 3 starts, half-sister to US Grade 3
8.5f winner Namaqualand: fairly useful form: won maiden at Windsor in June: well held
both starts after: raced only at 1¼m/1½m: acts on good to firm ground: sold 14,000 gns in
October. *Sir Michael Stoute*

PICTURE FRAME 5 ch.g. Fraam 114 – Floral Spark 69 (Forzando 122) [2009 p7.1g **59**
7.1m^5 7g 8.1m^4 10m 8d Aug 10] lengthy gelding: modest performer: missed 2008:
possibly best around 1m nowadays: acts on firm and good to soft going: tried in cheekpieces. *J. T. Stimpson*

PICTURES (IRE) 2 b.f. (Feb 27) Le Vie Dei Colori 126 – So Glam So Hip (IRE) 62 **76**
(Spectrum (IRE) 126) [2009 7f^2 p6g^3 p7.1g^2 7d^3 p7g Nov 13] 15,000Y: first foal: dam ran
3 times: fair maiden: third in nursery at Yarmouth fourth start: should stay 1m: acts on
polytrack and good to soft going, probably on firm. *L. M. Cumani*

PICTURETHATMOMENT (USA) 3 b. or br.f. Mr Greeley (USA) 122 – –
I'maknightschoice (USA) (Knights Choice (USA)) [2009 8.3g May 19] $440,000Y:
half-sister to several winners in USA: dam winning US sprinter (including 2-y-o minor
stakes): well held in maiden at Nottingham. *K. R. Burke*

PIC UP STICKS 10 gr.g. Piccolo 121 – Between The Sticks 83 (Pharly (FR) 130) **72**
[2009 71: 5g^6 5m* 5.2m^3 5.3f^5 5.3m 5m 5s^4 5.1m 5m^5 5.1d p7m Oct 31] tall gelding: fair
handicapper: won at Folkestone in June: largely below form after: stays 6.5f: acts on
polytrack, firm and soft going: tried in cheekpieces: none too consistent. *B. G. Powell*

PIE POUDRE 2 ch.g. (Mar 13) Zafeen (FR) 123 – Eglantine (IRE) (Royal Academy **56**
(USA) 130) [2009 6f 6.1m^6 6d p7m p8.6g^2 Dec 17] workmanlike gelding: modest
maiden: stays 8.6f: acts on polytrack: temperament under suspicion. *R. Brotherton*

PIERMARINI 4 b.g. Singspiel (IRE) 133 – Allespagne (USA) (Trempolino (USA) **51**
135) [2009 72: p9.5g p10g p7.1g^4 p9.5g Feb 17] small, sturdy gelding: modest maiden:
likely to stay beyond 1½m: acts on polytrack and good to firm ground: tried visored: none
too consistent. *P. T. Midgley*

PILANNSKI 2 b.f. (May 7) Pilsudski (IRE) 134 – Honey Mill 67 (Milford 119) [2009 –
8m p8g Nov 25] half-sister to several winners, including 1m/1¼m winner Dial Square
and 1¼m winner Bluegrass Boy (both by Bluegrass Prince): dam sprint maiden: well
beaten in maidens. *R. A. Teal*

PILOT LIGHT 3 b.g. Falbrav (IRE) 133 – Bollin Jeannie 74 (Royal Applause 124) **48**
[2009 51: 9.9m 12.1m 8.5g May 27] poor maiden: stays 1½m: best efforts on good to firm
going: in cheekpieces last 2 starts. *T. D. Easterby*

PINBALL (IRE) 3 b.f. Namid 128 – Luceball (IRE) 56 (Bluebird (USA) 125) [2009 **63**
47: p5.1g^2 p5.1g^4 5m^3 5.1m^4 p5.1g^6 5.7f* 5.1g^3 5m 5.7g 5m^6 p6m 6d^5 5.7g 5.1s^4 p6g^6
p5m^4 p6f Dec 21] tall filly: modest handicapper: won at Bath in May: left Pat Morris

after eighth outing: stays 6f: acts on polytrack, firm and soft ground: visored nowadays. *Mrs L. Williamson*

PINCH OF SALT (IRE) 6 b.g. Hussonet (USA) – Granita (CHI) (Roy (USA)) [2009 **88**
102: 10g 10m p11g p12m Oct 12] big, lengthy gelding: has reportedly had wind operation: handicapper, just fairly useful in 2009: stays 1½m: acts on polytrack, soft and good to firm ground: visored final start: tried tongue tied. *A. M. Balding*

PIN CUSHION 2 ch.f. (Mar 20) Pivotal 124 – Frizzante 121 (Efisio 120) [2009 6f 6m^{3} **77**
6d^{4} Oct 12] sturdy, compact filly: second foal: half-sister to 3-y-o Greensward: dam 5f/6f (including July Cup) winner: best effort in maidens when 2½ lengths third to Queen's Grace at Newbury: should stay 7f. *B. J. Meehan*

PINEWOOD LEGEND (IRE) 7 br.g. Idris (IRE) 118 – Blue Infanta (Chief Singer **51**
131) [2009 46: f16g^{3} 16d Aug 10] modest maiden on Flat, lightly raced: stays 2m: acts on fibresand, probably on firm going: tried blinkered/tongue tied. *P. D. Niven*

PINEWOOD LULU 4 bl. or br.f. Lujain (USA) 119 – Lucy Glitters (USA) 60 (Crypto- **–**
clearance (USA)) [2009 55: 8.3g 6m 7m 8.5m p8.6g Sep 17] smallish, workmanlike filly: no form in 2009, leaving R. C. Guest after second outing: blinkered last 2 starts. *S. A. Harris*

PINEWOOD POLLY 2 b.f. (Apr 18) Lujain (USA) 119 – Polmara (IRE) (Polish **–**
Precedent (USA) 131) [2009 p7.1g Nov 14] fifth foal: half-sister to winner abroad by Compton Place: dam ran once: 100/1, badly in need of experience when tailed off in maiden at Wolverhampton. *S. A. Harris*

PINK FLAMES (IRE) 2 ch.f. (Apr 27) Redback 116 – Flames (Blushing Flame **– p**
(USA) 109) [2009 7s^{6} Sep 5] €62,000F, £25,000Y, 210,000 2-y-o: useful-looking filly: fifth foal: sister to 3-y-o Lahaleeb and half-sister to fairly useful 6f (at 2 yrs)/1m winner Precocious Star (by Bold Fact): dam unraced close relative/half-sister to useful performers up to 1¼m Kindlelight Debut and Dance Partner: 5/1, 12 lengths sixth to Layla's Dancer in maiden at Thirsk, weakening: should stay at least 1m: should do better. *T. P. Tate*

PINK PLEASE (IRE) 2 ch.f. (Mar 21) Camacho 118 – Inonder 31 (Belfort (FR) 89) **–**
[2009 6.1s Oct 7] €4,000Y, resold €6,000Y: half-sister to 3 winners by Common Grounds, including 1997 2-y-o 5f to 7.5f winner Chips and 6f (at 2 yrs)/7f winner Aretino, both fairly useful: dam poor maiden: 100/1, tailed off in maiden at Nottingham. *Tom Dascombe*

PINK SYMPHONY 2 b.f. (Feb 17) Montjeu (IRE) 137 – Blue Symphony 73 (Dars- **87**
haan 133) [2009 7d^{5} 7g^{2} 7m^{4} Oct 3] 400,000Y: lengthy, good-topped filly: has scope: third foal: closely related to 3-y-o Fantasia and half-sister to 2007 2-y-o 7f winner Blue Rhapsody (by Cape Cross): dam, 1¼m winner, out of Cheveley Park Stakes winner Blue Duster: progressive form, 5 lengths fourth to Lillie Langtry in sales race at Newmarket, strong at finish: will be suited by 1m+. *P. F. I. Cole*

PINNACLE LAD (IRE) 2 b.g. (Feb 2) Titus Livius (FR) 115 – Alyska (IRE) 80 **65**
(Owington 123) [2009 5.1g^{6} 5m^{3} 5g^{2} 5.1m^{4} p5.1m 6.1d^{4} 5g 5.1s Nov 4] leggy gelding: fair maiden: below form after third start: may prove best at 5f: acts on good to firm going: tried blinkered: usually makes running. *J. L. Spearing*

PINNACLE POINT 4 ch.g. Best of The Bests (IRE) 122 – Alessandra 101 (Generous **56**
(IRE) 139) [2009 61: p12g^{4} 12m^{5} 10m^{5} Jul 6] lengthy, workmanlike gelding: modest maiden handicapper: stays 1½m: acts on good to firm going: blinkered in 2009: sometimes races freely. *G. L. Moore*

PINPOINT (IRE) 7 b.g. Pivotal 124 – Alessia (GER) (Warning 136) [2009 116: 8.3m^{2} **112**
9.9m 10f Jun 19] tall, close-coupled gelding: has a round action: smart performer: creditable 2 lengths second to Ordnance Row in listed race at Windsor on reappearance: well below form after: best at 1m/1¼m: acts on firm and good to soft going: waited with. *W. R. Swinburn*

PINTANO 4 ch.g. Dr Fong (USA) 128 – Heckle 47 (In The Wings 128) [2009 63: p6g **58**
7m 6m 6.1m 6.1g* 6f^{4} 6d 6m^{6} 6.1d 7.1d Sep 4] modest performer: won seller at Nottingham in July: effective at 6f to easy 1m: acts on good to firm ground: tried in blinkers/cheekpieces: tongue tied of late: signs of temperament. *J. M. Bradley*

PINTURA 2 ch.g. (Apr 21) Efisio 120 – Picolette 56 (Piccolo 121) [2009 5m^{3} 5.1d^{6} 6g **77**
6d^{3} 6m* 6m^{5} 7m^{4} 6d^{5} 7m^{5} 7.1m* 7d Oct 11] £30,000Y: neat gelding: fifth foal: half-brother to fairly useful 6f/7f (including at 2 yrs and abroad) winner Pommes Frites (by Bertolini) and 4-y-o Ruby Delta: dam maiden (stayed 7f): fair performer: won nurseries at Redcar in August and Warwick in September: stays 7f: acts on good to firm and good to soft going: sold 21,000 gns. *M. R. Channon*

Qatar Prix Dollar, Longchamp—a bunched finish as Pipedreamer (white face) pips long-time leader Gris de Gris (left) and Famous Name (second right)

PIPEDREAMER 5 b.h. Selkirk (USA) 129 – Follow A Dream (USA) 90 (Gone West (USA)) [2009 123: 10g² 10m⁵ 9.8g* 10m⁴ Oct 17] big, strong, useful-looking horse: has a round action: very smart performer: won Qatar Prix Dollar at Longchamp in October by neck from Gris de Gris: creditable efforts otherwise when in frame, namely in Gordon Richards Stakes at Sandown (short-head second to Tartan Bearer) and Champion Stakes at Newmarket (2 lengths fourth to Twice Over): stays 10.4f: acts on firm going, below form only run on softer than good: genuine. *J. H. M. Gosden* **121**

PIPERS PIPING (IRE) 3 b.c. Noverre (USA) 125 – Monarchy (IRE) (Common Grounds 118) [2009 p7g p6g³ p6g* f6g² 6f 6d³ p6g p6g³ p6m⁵ p7m⁶ Oct 7] fair performer: won claimer at Wolverhampton in April: should be suited by 7f: acts on all-weather and good to soft going: sold £5,500. *J. A. Osborne* **69**

PIPER'S SONG (IRE) 6 gr.g. Distant Music (USA) 126 – Dane's Lane (IRE) (Danehill (USA) 126) [2009 86: p9.5g⁵ p10g⁴ p12.2g⁶ 12.4s² 11.7f² 16g 12.3g 12.5m⁴ 14g² 12g⁵ 14.1g⁴ p11g² 12.5m p12.2g Nov 21] big gelding: just fair handicapper at best in 2009: may prove best short of 1½m: acts on polytrack, firm and soft going: tried visored/in cheekpieces: held up (sometimes slowly away). *Pat Morris* **73 d**

PIPETTE 2 b.f. (Apr 15) Pivotal 124 – Amaryllis (IRE) 71 (Sadler's Wells (USA) 132) [2009 7s* 7v³ Oct 24] half-sister to 3 winners in France, including useful 1m (at 2 yrs) to 1½m winner Day Or Night (by Daylami) and fairly useful 1½m/1¾m winner According (by Dalakhani): dam, 7f (at 2 yrs) to 9f (in France) winner, closely related to smart French/US 1m/9f winner Corrazona: highly promising when winning maiden at Salisbury in September comfortably (despite hanging badly left once in front) by 1½ lengths from Faithful One: still green (missed break), better form when 1¼ lengths third to Electric Feel in listed race at Newbury, finishing strongly: will stay at least 1m: already useful, and likely to go on improving. *A. M. Balding* **98 p**

PIPPBROOK GOLD 4 ch.g. Golden Snake (USA) 127 – Chiaro (Safawan 118) [2009 79: p7g⁶ 7d⁴ 7m⁴ 8.3d 7m⁴ 8.1g 7m⁵ 10m 8d⁵ p10m³ Nov 3] sturdy gelding: fair handicapper: may prove best short of 1¼m: acts on polytrack, unraced on extremes of going on turf. *J. R. Boyle* **77**

PIQUANTE 3 b.f. Selkirk (USA) 129 – China 74 (Royal Academy (USA) 130) [2009 79p: 10s⁴ 8.3g⁶ 10.2g⁴ 12m⁴ 9.8g⁶ p10m⁵ 8d* Oct 22] angular filly: fair handicapper: won at Brighton in October: may prove best around 1m: acts on soft and good to firm going: sold 20,000 gns. *M. L. W. Bell* **78**

PIRATE'S SONG 2 b.c. (Mar 1) Bahamian Bounty 116 – Soviet Terms (Soviet Star (USA) 128) [2009 6m 6m³ p5g⁵ Oct 2] compact colt: fair maiden: needs to learn to settle to stay beyond 6f. *J. A. R. Toller* **66**

PIRES 5 br.g. Generous (IRE) 139 – Kaydee Queen (IRE) (Bob's Return (IRE) 123) [2009 84: 12m⁵ 8.5s 8v p12g² Nov 27] big gelding: useful handicapper: better than ever **101**

when neck second to Avanti Albert at Dundalk: respectable fifth to Drill Sergeant in Duke of Edinburgh Stakes at Royal Ascot earlier: stays 1½m: acts on polytrack and firm going: fairly useful hurdler. *A. J. Martin, Ireland*

PISCEAN (USA) 4 b. or br.g. Stravinsky (USA) 133 – Navasha (USA) (Woodman (USA) 126) [2009 93: 5m* 6g 6m 5d 5m 5d 5.4m 5g^5 5m 6m 5m Sep 26] sturdy, close-coupled gelding: useful handicapper: won at Goodwood in May by 2 lengths from Cake: not at best after: best at 5f/6f: acts on polytrack, good to firm and good to soft going: sometimes blinkered: often slowly away, and not one to trust: gelded after final start. *T. Keddy* **100 §**

PISTE 3 b.f. Falbrav (IRE) 133 – Arctic Char 102 (Polar Falcon (USA) 126) [2009 70: 5.1m^3 5.1g^4 p5g^4 5m^2 5m^4 5m* 5.4g^6 5m 5d 5m^3 5m 6m Oct 1] sturdy filly: fair handicapper: won at Windsor in June: left B. Meehan, below best after: likely to prove best at 5f/6f: acts on polytrack, good to firm and good to soft going: tried blinkered. *Miss T. Jackson* **74**

PITBULL 6 b.g. Makbul 104 – Piccolo Cativo 67 (Komaite (USA)) [2009 69: p9.5g 7.9g 8.1s^3 10g^2 8.1v^6 10.4g 10m Oct 13] smallish, good-bodied gelding: fair handicapper: stays 1¼m: acts on polytrack, firm and soft going: usually wears cheekpieces: usually slowly away: unreliable nowadays. *Mrs G. S. Rees* **65 §**

PITTODRIE STAR (IRE) 2 ch.c. (Mar 3) Choisir (AUS) 126 – Jupiter Inlet (IRE) (Jupiter Island 126) [2009 7g p6m* p7g^5 Dec 2] €12,000F, £12,000Y: half-brother to several winners, including useful 2008 2-y-o 6f winner Kingship Spirit (by Invincible Spirit): dam useful Italian winner up to 1¾m: won maiden at Kempton in November: similar form when last of 5 in nursery at same course, still green and free in front: should be at least as effective at 7f as 6f: open to further improvement. *A. M. Balding* **73 p**

PITTON JUSTICE 7 ch.g. Compton Place 125 – Blind Justice (Mystiko (USA) 124) [2009 5.1g 7m Jul 3] no show in claimers. *Dr J. R. J. Naylor* **–**

PIVERINA (IRE) 4 b.f. Pivotal 124 – Alassio (USA) 90 (Gulch (USA)) [2009 58: 12.4s 12.1g* f14g 12.1m^5 12.1g 12.4d^4 Sep 7] leggy, workmanlike filly: modest handicapper: won apprentice event at Hamilton in June: stays 1¾m: acts on all-weather and soft going. *Julie Camacho* **60**

PIVOTAL EXPRESS (IRE) 3 ch.g. Pivotal 124 – Forest Express (AUS) (Kaaptive Edition (NZ)) [2009 8.3d Oct 12] strong gelding: no show in maiden at Windsor. *J. F. Panvert* **–**

PLACE THE DUCHESS 3 b.f. Compton Place 125 – Barrantes 90 (Distant Relative 128) [2009 51: 6m p6m^6 p5.1g p6m^2 f6g^3 f6d Dec 29] lengthy filly: modest maiden: left Miss S. West after reappearance: raced only at 5f/6f: best form on all-weather: tongue tied after reappearance. *A. J. Lidderdale* **54**

PLACIDITY 3 ch.f. Compton Place 125 – Wittily 69 (Whittingham (IRE) 104) [2009 f6g p6g Mar 27] second foal: dam 2-y-o 5f winner: well held in maidens. *A. J. McCabe* **–**

PLAISTERER 4 b.f. Best of The Bests (IRE) 122 – Lumiere d'Espoir (FR) 81 (Saumarez 132) [2009 79: 11.6g^3 10m^5 10d* 8.3g^2 10.3d* 10g^2 10m^6 10.3s Nov 7] leggy, lengthy filly: useful performer: improved in 2009, winning handicaps at Windsor in June and Doncaster (by 1¾ lengths from Shaloo Diamond) in July: good second to Demolition in similar event at Ayr next time: hampered when sixth at Newmarket, better effort in listed races last 2 starts: should stay 1½m: acts on good to soft going: tail flasher. *C. F. Wall* **100**

PLAKA (FR) 4 gr.f. Verglas (IRE) 118 – Top Speed (IRE) (Wolfhound (USA) 126) [2009 55: p9.5g p8.6g p7.1g^3 8.1g 7.1f 7m Jun 1] lengthy filly: modest maiden: stays easy 9.5f: acts on polytrack: none too consistent. *W. M. Brisbourne* **55**

PLANE PAINTER (IRE) 5 b.g. Orpen (USA) 116 – Flight Sequence 88 (Polar Falcon (USA) 126) [2009 82: 21.7m Jun 20] tall gelding: fairly useful handicapper: well held in Queen Alexandra Stakes at Royal Ascot sole Flat start in 2009: stays 17f: acts on firm and good to soft going: makes running: fair maiden hurdler/chaser. *B. G. Powell* **–**

PLANETARY MOTION (USA) 4 gr. or ro.c. Gone West (USA) – Gaviola (USA) 121 (Cozzene (USA)) [2009 77p: p10g* 10.3g p12g^4 a8f^4 a7f^4 a9f Dec 4] rangy colt: fairly useful handicapper: won at Lingfield in February, dictating: below form subsequently, leaving M. Johnston after third start: stays easy 1¼m: acts on polytrack. *A. bin Huzaim, UAE* **81 d**

PLANET RED (IRE) 2 ch.c. (Feb 25) Bahamian Bounty 116 – Aries (GER) 79 (Big Shuffle (USA) 122) [2009 5.2s^2 6g* 7m Aug 18] 3,500F, 14,000Y: good-topped colt: has scope: third foal: dam 2-y-o 7f winner: promising in maidens, off over 3 months prior to winning at Windsor in July by neck from stable-companion Carnaby Street (pair clear): only seventh in Acomb Stakes at York (hampered): should stay 7f: remains open to improvement. *R. Hannon* **87 p**

PLATINUM BOUNTY 3 ch.f. Bahamian Bounty 116 – Maxizone (FR) (Linamix –
(FR) 127) [2009 8g May 29] 5,000F: lengthy filly: fifth foal: half-sister to 7f (including at 2 yrs)/1m (in Scandinavia) winner Big Player (by Noverre): dam unraced: well held in maiden at Goodwood. *J. A. Geake*

PLATOCHE (IRE) 4 b.c. Galileo (IRE) 134 – Political Parody (USA) (Doonesbury **59**
(USA)) [2009 54: p13g 11.5g p11g p10g^3 p10g Aug 1] leggy colt: modest maiden: stayed 1¼m: acted on polytrack: tried in blinkers/cheekpieces/tongue tie: sold 7,500 gns: dead. *G. A. Butler*

PLATO (JPN) 2 ch.c. (Feb 2) Bago (FR) 130 – Taygete (USA) (Miswaki (USA) 124) **74**
[2009 p8g^5 p8.6g^2 Oct 10] first foal: dam, US 8.5f/9f winner, closely related to smart French 6.5f to 1m winner Byzantium, out of sister to Miesque: much better effort in maidens when 1¼ lengths second to Start Right at Wolverhampton: should stay 1¼m: may do better still. *H. R. A. Cecil*

PLAYBOY BLUES (IRE) 2 b.c. (Mar 19) Bertolini (USA) 125 – Ingeburg 100 **77 p**
(Hector Protector (USA) 124) [2009 p7.1g^4 p7.1g* Dec 18] 4,500F, £15,000Y: fourth foal: half-brother to Irish 13f winner Lios Tulcha (by Barathea): dam, German/French 2-y-o 5f/5.5f winner, out of half-sister to smart 6f/7f performer Inchinor: better effort in maidens when winning at Wolverhampton by 1¼ lengths from Fusaichi Flyer: should improve again. *P. W. Chapple-Hyam*

PLAYFUL ASSET (IRE) 3 ch.f. Johannesburg (USA) 127 – Twickin (USA) (Two **66**
Punch (USA)) [2009 62: 7.1m^4 10d 10d^2 10g* 10.1g^3 12m p12.2g^6 p8m p12f^4 p12g^3 Dec 31] leggy, lengthy filly: fair performer: won claimer at Leicester (left R. Beckett £6,000) in July: stays 1½m: acts on polytrack and good to firm going. *P. Howling*

PLAY IT SAM 3 b.g. Bahamian Bounty 116 – Bombalarina (IRE) (Barathea (IRE) 127) **82**
[2009 62: 7m^5 8.3m^5 8.3m^4 8v* 8g^2 8.1g^2 p8g^5 8m^2 Oct 1] sturdy gelding: fairly useful handicapper: won at Pontefract in July: good efforts after when runner-up: stays 1m: acts on heavy and good to firm going: tongue tied last 5 starts (gelded after final occasion). *W. R. Swinburn*

PLAY MASTER (IRE) 8 b.g. Second Empire (IRE) 124 – Madam Waajib (IRE) **46**
(Waajib 121) [2009 p16g p16g Feb 11] tall, rather leggy, useful-looking gelding: just poor nowadays, including over jumps: tried visored/in cheekpieces. *B. J. Llewellyn*

PLAY TO WIN (IRE) 3 b.c. Singspiel (IRE) 133 – Spot Prize (USA) 108 (Seattle –
Dancer (USA) 119) [2009 68p: 12.6g 11.6m 11.5m Jun 4] big, lengthy, attractive colt: maiden: no form in 2009: tried in cheekpieces. *D. R. C. Elsworth*

PLAY UP POMPEY 7 b.g. Dansili 127 – Search For Love (FR) (Groom Dancer –
(USA) 128) [2009 –, a61: p10g^4 p10g^2 p10g^5 p11g p10g^5 12m p10g^5 p10g 10.1d^3 p10g **a59**
8m^6 9g Aug 30] angular gelding: modest handicapper: effective at 1m to 1½m: acts on polytrack, well held on turf since 2006: usually held up. *J. J. Bridger*

PLEASANT DAY (IRE) 2 b.g. (Mar 7) Noverre (USA) 125 – Sunblush (UAE) 57 **104**
(Timber Country (USA) 124) [2009 7g 7g p7m* 7m^2 7m* 7v^2 Oct 24] €44,000F, €40,000Y: good-topped gelding: first foal: dam twice-raced half-sister to dam of 3-y-o Tamazirte: useful performer: progressed well, winning maiden at Lingfield in August and nursery at Ascot (by 2 lengths from Guest Book) in September: good short-head second to Carnaby Street in Horris Hill Stakes at Newbury after: will stay 1m: acts on polytrack, heavy and good to firm ground: blinkered last 4 outings. *B. J. Meehan*

PLEASANT WAY (IRE) 2 ch.f. (Apr 15) Barathea (IRE) 127 – Eman's Joy 68 (Lion **62**
Cavern (USA) 117) [2009 8g p8g Nov 1] 55,000Y: fifth foal: sister to useful 2005 2-y-o 7f/1m winner Blitzkrieg and 5-y-o Summer Gold, and half-sister to 3-y-o Toledo Gold: dam 6f winner: green in maidens, much better effort when eighth at Yarmouth on debut. *D. R. Lanigan*

PLEASE SING 3 b.f. Royal Applause 124 – Persian Song 45 (Persian Bold 123) [2009 **103**
89: 7s^6 7m^3 8m^3 7g^3 8m^2 8.1g 7m 7m Sep 26] leggy filly: has a quick action: useful performer: several good placed efforts in 2009, namely in Chartwell Fillies' Stakes at Lingfield, listed Sandringham Handicap at Royal Ascot (5 lengths third to Moneycantbuymelove), Oak Tree Stakes at Goodwood (not clear run when 1½ lengths third to Summer Fete) and listed race at Bath (length second to Annabelle's Charm): stays 1m: acts on soft and good to firm going: held up. *M. R. Channon*

PLENILUNE (IRE) 4 b.g. Fantastic Light (USA) 134 – Kathleen's Dream (USA) **63**
(Last Tycoon 131) [2009 69: 12g 8m 9.8m 8.9d 8d^5 10.4g f11g p9.5g^6 f7g^5 p8.6g f8f^4 Dec 17] quite attractive gelding: maiden handicapper, just modest in 2009: stays 1¼m: acts on polytrack and soft ground: blinkered once: temperament under suspicion. *M. Brittain*

Ladbrokes Bunbury Cup (Heritage Handicap), Newmarket— a seventh Newmarket win for Plum Pudding (far side) as he defies top weight to beat favourite Captain Brilliance (No.11), Mutheeb (partly obscured) and Joseph Henry

PLENTY O'TOOLE 2 ch.g. (Jan 28) Monsieur Bond (IRE) 120 – Marie La Rose (FR) (Night Shift (USA)) [2009 f6g p7g4 p7m2 Nov 26] 44,000F, €23,000 2-y-o: half-brother to 3 winners, including French 1m (at 2 yrs)/1¼m winner Contemporary Art (by Blushing Flame): dam French 1¼m winner: progressive in maidens, head second to Too Putra at Kempton: should stay 1m. *Mrs D. J. Sanderson* **71**

PLUMAGE 4 b.f. Royal Applause 124 – Cask 99 (Be My Chief (USA) 122) [2009 62, a67: p6g2 6g2 6.1g5 6.1m 6.1m4 6m* 5.2s5 Jul 17] sturdy filly: fair handicapper: won apprentice event at Leicester in July: effective at 6f/7f: acts on polytrack and good to firm ground. *M. Salaman* **68**

PLUME 2 b.f. (Mar 6) Pastoral Pursuits 127 – Polar Storm (IRE) 76 (Law Society (USA) 130) [2009 7s 6m* Sep 25] 21,000F, €100,000Y: tall filly: half-sister to several winners, including Irish 9f winner Lawnett (by Runnett): dam, 6f (at 2 yrs) to 1m winner, half-sister to smart sprinter Polar Bird: much better effort in maidens when winning at Haydock comfortably by 4½ lengths from Posy Fossil: should stay 7f: sure to improve again. *R. Hannon* **88 p**

PLUM PUDDING (IRE) 6 b.g. Elnadim (USA) 128 – Karayb (IRE) 93 (Last Tycoon 131) [2009 115: 7.1m* 8.5g2 7m2 7m* 7m3 8g5 8.3v2 p10g5 p8m p10f5 Dec 19] strong, good-topped gelding: impresses in appearance: smart performer on turf, just useful on all-weather: as good as ever in 2009, winning minor event at Warwick (by 1¼ lengths from Dream Eater) in April and Ladbrokes Bunbury Cup (Handicap, beat Captain Brilliance by neck) at Newmarket (seventh course success) in July: creditable effort after only when 2¼ lengths second to Alexandros in minor event at Nottingham: best at 7f/1m: acts on polytrack, heavy and good to firm going: tried in cheekpieces: often makes running. *R. Hannon* **116 a103**

PLUSH 6 ch.g. Medicean 128 – Glorious (Nashwan (USA) 135) [2009 79: p8.6g* p8.6g4 p8.6g* p9.5g5 Dec 26] fairly useful handicapper: progressive in 2009, winning at Wolverhampton in January and, having been off over 9 months (reportedly lame after second start), December (fifth course win): stays 9.5f: acts on all-weather (very lightly raced on turf): tried blinkered: held up (often slowly away). *Tom Dascombe* **88**

PLUS ULTRA (IRE) 2 b.g. (May 10) Rock of Gibraltar (IRE) 133 – Tafseer (IRE) (Grand Lodge (USA) 125) [2009 7g Jul 25] 16/1 and blinkered, down the field in maiden at Newmarket, slowly away and hanging (gelded after). *H. R. A. Cecil* **–**

PLUTOCRAFT 2 ch.g. (Feb 7) Starcraft (NZ) 128 – Angry Bark (USA) 62 (Woodman (USA) 126) [2009 6m4 p7g3 Oct 24] 23,000F, 20,000Y: second foal: dam, maiden (stayed 1¼m), out of smart French/US performer up to 1¼m Polemic: much better effort in maidens when 2¾ lengths third to Highland Quaich at Kempton, pulling hard and not unduly knocked about: gelded after: should stay 1¼m: should improve again. *J. R. Fanshawe* **62 p**

PLYMOUTH ROCK (IRE) 3 b.c. Sadler's Wells (USA) 132 – Zarawa (IRE) (Kahyasi 130) [2009 10g* 11.6m3 11m2 Sep 23] 280,000Y, resold 170,000Y: attractive colt: half-brother to fairly useful 1½m winner Dawaarr (by Indian Ridge): dam, ran once **90**

in France, half-sister to smart French 7f/1m winner Zarannda and to grandam of Zarkava: fairly useful form: won maiden at Windsor in June: placed in handicaps after: will stay at least 1½m. *J. Noseda*

POAKA BECK (IRE) 3 b.c. Fath (USA) 116 – Star of The Future (USA) 100 (El Gran Senor (USA) 136) [2009 –: p5.1g^{6} Feb 6] last in maidens. *R. F. Fisher* –

POBS TROPHY 2 b. or br.g. (Mar 26) Umistim 119 – Admonish 57 (Warning 136) [2009 f7g Nov 17] 100/1, tailed off in maiden at Southwell. *R. C. Guest* –

POCA A POCA (IRE) 5 b.m. Namid 128 – Cliveden Gail (IRE) 102 (Law Society (USA) 130) [2009 7g 8.1g^{6} p8g 7s f6g 8.1g^{5} 8v^{6} 6g p10g 8.1m Aug 20] sister to winning sprinter in Italy and half-sister to several winners, including fairly useful 2m winner Precious Persian (by Persian Bold): dam, 1¾m/2m winner, half-sister to very smart 1½m/1¾m winner Rock Hopper: well held in bumper: poor maiden on Flat: wears cheekpieces/blinkers nowadays. *G. C. Bravery* 49

POCKET'S PICK (IRE) 3 ch.g. Exceed And Excel (AUS) 126 – Swizzle (Efisio 120) [2009 81: 5g 6m p5g^{2} 6m p5g^{5} p6m p5m^{4} p6g 6d f6m^{5} p6g^{2} p6m^{4} f5g* p6g Dec 31] strong, lengthy gelding: fair handicapper: won at Southwell in December: stays 6f: acts on all-weather, firm and good to soft going: tried in blinkers/cheekpieces/tongue tie. *G. L. Moore* 73

POCKET TOO 6 b.g. Fleetwood (IRE) 107 – Pocket Venus (IRE) (King's Theatre (IRE) 128) [2009 82: p13.9g Dec 17] close-coupled gelding: fairly useful handicapper: below form only outing at 6 yrs: effective at 1½m to 21f: acts on polytrack and soft going: tried blinkered, wears cheekpieces: modest hurdler nowadays. *Matthew Salaman* –

POET 4 b.c. Pivotal 124 – Hyabella 111 (Shirley Heights 130) [2009 102: 10s^{5} 8d^{4} 8s^{3} 8.5d* 8v* 10d* 8s^{2} Sep 13] tall, lengthy colt: very smart performer: improved to win listed race at Killarney and Irish Cambridgeshire (Handicap, by neck from Raise Your Heart) at the Curragh, both in August, and At The Races Kilternan Stakes at Leopardstown (by 4½ lengths from Allied Powers) in September: effective at 1m/1¼m: acts on heavy ground: races close up: tough and game: joined R. Simpson in UAE. *A. P. O'Brien, Ireland* 121

POET'S PLACE (USA) 4 b.g. Mutakddim (USA) 112 – Legion of Merit (USA) (Danzig (USA)) [2009 f6g* Dec 27] $6,000Y: second foal: dam unraced sister to useful Irish sprinter Remarkable Style: 13/2, good impression when winning maiden at Southwell by 4 lengths from Bandstand, coasting clear: will improve. *T. D. Barron* 80 p

Hackett's Bookmakers European Breeders Fund Irish Cambridgeshire, the Curragh—Poet (white cap) edges out Raise Your Heart (left) in a strong renewal; Worldly Wise (right) finishes third

DFS Champagne Stakes, Doncaster—
Poet's Voice (right) holds on from Viscount Nelson and the grey Silver Grecian

POET'S VOICE 2 b.c. (Mar 7) Dubawi (IRE) 129 – Bright Tiara (USA) (Chief's Crown (USA)) [2009 $7g^3$ 7g* $7m^3$ 7m* $6m^4$ Oct 2] tall, good-topped colt: has scope: half-brother to several winners, including fairly useful French 1¼m winner The World (by Dubai Destination) and Japanese 6f to 9f stakes winner Gold Tiara (by Seeking The Gold): dam, US 2-y-o 6f winner, sister to US Grade 1 11f winner Chief Honcho: smart performer: won minor event at Newmarket (by 10 lengths) in July and DFS Champagne Stakes at Doncaster (by ¾ length from Viscount Nelson) in September: also ran well in **114**

Godolphin's "Poet's Voice"

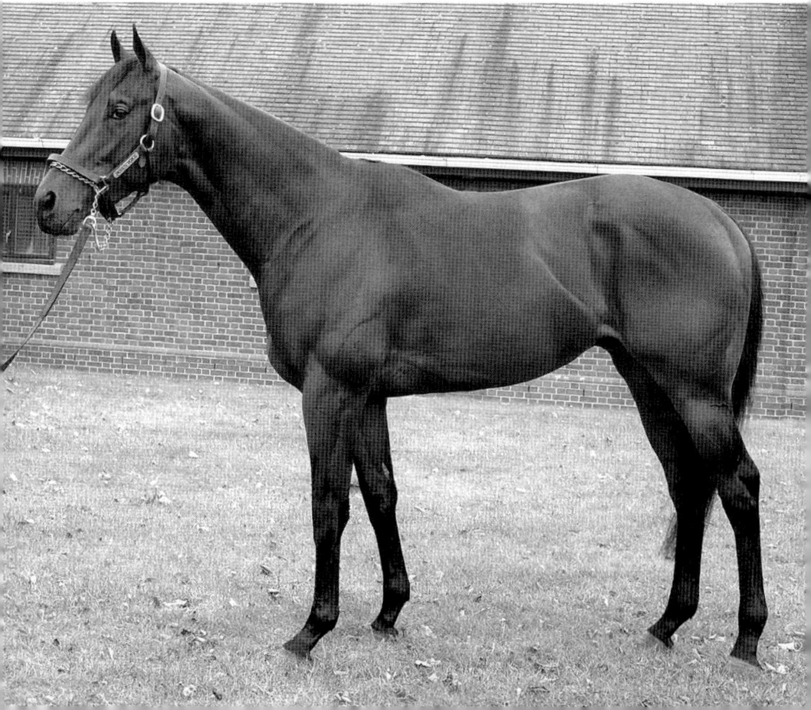

Acomb Stakes at York (¾-length third to Elusive Pimpernel) and Middle Park Stakes at Newmarket (tongue tied, 2 lengths fourth to Awzaan, again pulling hard but keeping on after hampered final 1f): effective at 6f/7f: raced only on good/good to firm ground: has twice hung left. *Saeed bin Suroor*

POINTILLIST (IRE) 3 b.f. Peintre Celebre (USA) 137 – For Example (USA) 66 **62**
(Northern Baby (CAN) 127) [2009 64p: 10m^5 9.9g 9.7m 8f Aug 18] leggy filly: modest maiden: should stay 1¼m: raced only on good going or firmer: tried in cheekpieces. *R. M. Beckett*

POINTING NORTH (SAF) 5 b.g. Joshua Dancer (USA) – Compass Point (SAF) **105**
(Model Man (SAF)) [2009 7.5m 7.5g 7m 6m Aug 29] smart performer at best in South Africa, winning first 4 starts, namely maiden, handicap and Racing Association Secretariat Stakes, all at Turffontein in 2007, and Grade 1 Bloodstock South Africa Cape Guineas at Kenilworth only outing at 4 yrs: left R. Sage, just useful form in handicaps at Nad Al Sheba (for S. Seemar, UAE) and listed races in Britain in 2009: stays 1m: raced mainly on good/good to firm going. *B. Smart*

POINT OF LIGHT 3 b.g. Pivotal 124 – Lighthouse 92 (Warning 136) [2009 54p: 10g* **93**
10.2g* 11.7g* 11.6m* 11.5g* 12.1m* 12m^6 Sep 23] well-made gelding: fairly useful handicapper: most progressive in 2009, winning at Newmarket (apprentices) and Bath in July, Bath (apprentices, best effort when beating Blue Nymph 1½ lengths), Windsor and Yarmouth in August then Beverley in September: not discredited final start: stays 1½m: acts on good to firm ground: front runner/races prominently: sold 100,000 gns, joined Paul Nolan in Ireland. *Sir Mark Prescott*

POINT OUT (USA) 2 ch.c. (Apr 24) Point Given (USA) 134 – Dock Leaf (USA) **70 p**
(Woodman (USA) 126) [2009 p7g^2 Oct 24] fourth foal: half-brother to 3 winners, including 3-y-o Sea of Leaves and 4-y-o Distinctive Image: dam, maiden (third at 9f in USA), half-sister to US Grade 1 1¼m winner and Kentucky Derby/Belmont Stakes runner-up Aptitude: evens favourite, promising nose second to Highland Quaich in maiden at Kempton, headed line: will be suited by 1m+: sure to improve. *J. H. M. Gosden*

POINT TO PROVE 2 b.c. (Feb 28) Refuse To Bend (IRE) 128 – On Point 72 (Kris **67**
135) [2009 5.2g^5 5m^5 5m^2 5m^6 5.3m p6g^2 p6g p6m^6 p5g^4 5.1s f5m^3 p5.1g^4 f5m* Dec 5] fair performer: won nursery at Southwell in December: stays 6f: acts on all-weather and good to firm ground: none too consistent: sold £8,800. *Miss Amy Weaver*

POKFULHAM (IRE) 3 b.g. Mull of Kintyre (USA) 114 – Marjinal (Marju (IRE) 127) **68**
[2009 64: 8.5g 8f^4 7m^4 7f^5 8s^4 6s^3 6d 8m* 8m 7g Oct 23] lengthy, good-topped gelding: fair handicapper: left A. Jarvis after fourth start: back to very best when winning at Ayr in September: stays 1m: acts on heavy and good to firm going: usually visored nowadays. *J. S. Goldie*

POLAR ANNIE 4 b.f. Fraam 114 – Willisa 67 (Polar Falcon (USA) 126) [2009 84: **70**
p6g^6 5.7f 6g 6g 6s 6m^4 7.1d Aug 31] tall filly: just fair handicapper in 2009: may prove best at easy 6f: acts on polytrack, firm and soft going. *M. S. Saunders*

POLAR GOLD 7 b.m. Lujain (USA) 119 – Polar Fair 62 (Polar Falcon (USA) 126) **–**
[2009 7m p8.6g Oct 15] second foal: dam 8.5f winner: maiden in Spain (placed at 5f/6f): off almost 3 years, no form in apprentice handicaps in Britain. *A. J. Chamberlain*

POLEBROOK 2 ch.g. (Apr 14) Lomitas 129 – Fifth Emerald 54 (Formidable (USA) **–**
125) [2009 5g^6 6m 7d 9m 7m Oct 13] workmanlike gelding: no form in maidens: tried visored. *J. R. Jenkins*

POLEMICA (IRE) 3 b.f. Rock of Gibraltar (IRE) 133 – Lady Scarlett (Woodman **68**
(USA) 126) [2009 p8g 8.3g 8m^6 7m 8s^4 7g Jul 30] 90,000Y: quite attractive filly: fourth foal: closely related to 6-y-o Sunrise Safari: dam unraced half-sister to smart Irish/Hong Kong performer up to 1½m Desert Fox: fair maiden: stays 1m: acts on soft ground: sold £5,000 in August, resold 5,500 gns in October. *E. A. L. Dunlop*

POLISH POWER (GER) 9 br.h. Halling (USA) 133 – Polish Queen (Polish Pre- **85 d**
cedent (USA) 131) [2009 97: p10g p10g p12g* 10.3g^5 p10g* f12g 10.1s^5 p10g^2 p11g 11m^6 p12.2g Oct 3] tall horse: useful at 8 yrs: on downgrade in 2009, though won seller in April and claimer in May, both at Lingfield: stays 1¾m: acts on all-weather, heavy and good to firm going: tried in cheekpieces/blinkers. *J. S. Moore*

POLISH PRIDE 3 b.f. Polish Precedent (USA) 131 – Purple Tiger (IRE) (Rainbow **71**
Quest (USA) 134) [2009 94: 6m 7m 7.1v May 23] lengthy filly: just fair form in handicaps in 2009: stayed 6.5f: best efforts on going softer than good (acted on heavy): quirky: dead. *M. Brittain*

POLISH RED 5 b.g. Polish Precedent (USA) 131 – Norcroft Joy 82§ (Rock Hopper 124) [2009 67: 12d 11.6g f14g 11.5g Jul 20] good-topped gelding: handicapper: well held in 2009: tried in cheekpieces. *Jane Chapple-Hyam* –

POLISH STEPS (IRE) 2 b.f. (Mar 26) Footstepsinthesand 120 – Polish Spring (IRE) 104 (Polish Precedent (USA) 131) [2009 5m 5.7g p5m f6g Oct 27] €11,000Y: fifth foal: dam, 6f (at 2 yrs) to 1m (in USA) winner, half-sister to dam of very smart 1m/1¼m performer Ashkal Way: well held in maidens/nursery. *J. A. Osborne* –

POLISH WORLD (USA) 5 b.g. Danzig (USA) – Welcometotheworld (USA) (Woodman (USA) 126) [2009 67: f5g 6f May 11] medium-sized, stocky gelding: just modest form in 2009: effective at 6f/7f: acts on polytrack and good to firm ground: tried blinkered. *T. J. Etherington* **58**

POLLAN BAY (IRE) 2 b.g. (Feb 24) High Chaparral (IRE) 132 – Rossa di Rugiada (IRE) (College Chapel 122) [2009 7m 8.3m 8m^5 p8.6g^6 p8.6g Oct 9] poor maiden: should be suited by 1¼m+. *S. Kirk* **49**

POLLENATOR (IRE) 2 ch.f. (Apr 2) Motivator 131 – Ceanothus (IRE) 61 (Bluebird (USA) 125) [2009 7m^6 7f^2 7g^2 7g* 8m* Sep 11] **111 p**

The 2005 Derby winner Motivator hasn't had things go all his own way since that famous win at Epsom. He couldn't win any of his three subsequents starts (beaten twice by Derby tenth Oratorio), and his first season as a stallion was curtailed by a back injury, leading to a reduced number of foals in his first crop. Partly as a result, Motivator finished fourteenth in the 2009 table of first-season sires—Epsom third Dubawi was runner-up, a place ahead of Oratorio—and he had only seven winners from twenty-nine runners in Britain, though he did register a listed success in Italy with the filly Super Motiva. Motivator's headline performer so far has been another filly, Pollenator, who flew the flag for her sire in more ways than one in 2009, also carrying the same Royal Ascot Racing Club colours worn by Motivator throughout his racing career. Pollenator's win in the DFS May Hill Stakes at Doncaster in September saw her go into the winter vying for favouritism in the ante-post market for the 2010 Oaks. The chances are that we have yet to see the very best of her, a sentiment which applies to Motivator too, particularly as he will have significantly larger numbers in his second and third crops. There won't be any foals from 2010 coverings as he is to miss the breeding season due to a tendon injury in a hind leg, for which he underwent surgery in October.

In truth, Pollenator hardly looked a potential classic winner after her first three starts, particularly as she showed signs of quirkiness, her tendency to hang left arguably costing her victory when beaten a short head by Eolith (who won her only other start) in a seven-furlong fillies' maiden at Newmarket on the third occasion. Pollenator did progress steadily with each run, though, and improved

DFS May Hill Stakes, Doncaster—a first pattern success for Derby winner Motivator as a sire; Pollenator (No.4) beats Hibaayeb (left) and odds-on Seta

The Royal Ascot Racing Club's "Pollenator"

significantly when winning both her subsequent outings. A return to Newmarket's July course later in August yielded a smooth victory in another fillies' maiden when, partnered by stable-jockey Richard Hughes for the first time, Pollenator wasn't extended to beat Boogie Diva by three and a quarter lengths. Then it was on to Doncaster, where Hughes was forced to sit things out having incurred a three-week riding ban under the 'totting-up' rules. Champion jockey Ryan Moore proved a more than able deputy as Pollenator proved well suited by the longer trip and sprung a 14/1 surprise in a field of seven, keeping on strongly to assert herself inside the final furlong, despite again hanging badly left. Pollenator had half a length to spare over 40/1-shot Hibaayeb at the line, with another length back to odds-on Seta in third and a further two and a quarter lengths to fourth-placed Gallic Star. The form didn't look altogether reliable at the time because the race was run at a steady early gallop, but Hibaayeb (Fillies' Mile at Ascot) and Gallic Star (listed event at Pontefract) did the form no harm at all by winning their next starts, whilst Pollenator herself deserved extra credit at Doncaster, having twice been forced to switch round the runner-up in the penultimate furlong. Pollenator shaped as though she will be suited by further than a mile, a view reinforced by some areas of her pedigree.

Pollenator is the fifth foal of Ceanothus, a modest maiden at up to a mile and a half for William Haggas who has done better at stud, producing three other winners, Prince Hector, Wedding Party and Competitor. Haggas also trained the fairly useful but inconsistent winning miler Prince Hector (by Hector Protector), whilst the Amanda Perrett-trained filly Wedding Party (by Groom Dancer) was of a similar standard at up to a mile and is herself the dam of useful two-year-old maiden Party Doctor, placed twice in listed company in 2009. Competitor (by Danzero) might not be so good as those two but, with relevance to Pollenator's Epsom prospects, he stays much further than either of them, having won eight times at up to a mile and a half (mainly on the all-weather). Pollenator's unraced grandam Golden Bloom also did well at stud, her winners including the smart mile and a half performer Golden Wells and a couple of prolific winners over shorter in Golden Pond and Stratton, both above-average performers, the latter successful eight times at seven furlongs in 2001 before being exported to the States, where he failed to add to those wins. Pollenator's great grandam Daffodil Day was a half-sister to several big-race winners owned by Jim Joel—notably the 1968 Derby runner-up Connaught—and produced a classic winner in the 1992 Australian Derby winner Dance The Day Away. Incidentally, Pollenator's Doncaster win came at an opportune time for those selling her year-younger Hurricane Run half-brother named Purification, who was bought to join John Gosden for 180,000 guineas at the Tattersalls October Yearling Sales, at which Pollenator had fetched 50,000 guineas twelve months earlier.

Pollenator (IRE) (ch.f. Apr 2, 2007)	Motivator (b 2002)	Montjeu (b 1996)	Sadler's Wells
			Floripedes
		Out West (br 1994)	Gone West
			Chellingoua
	Ceanothus (IRE) (ch 1994)	Bluebird (b 1984)	Storm Bird
			Ivory Dawn
		Golden Bloom (ch 1985)	Main Reef
			Daffodil Day

Pollenator has raced only on good going or firmer to date, but Ceanothus was second on good to soft and Prince Hector won twice on good to soft, whilst Wedding Party's best effort was put up on heavy ground. It is also worth noting that Motivator's wins in the Racing Post Trophy and Dante Stakes both came on soft. Pollenator seems likely to stay at least a mile and a quarter and, if she develops into an Oaks contender, she will be a rare runner for Richard Hannon, who has saddled only three previously in the Epsom classic during his forty-year training career—Brentwood in 1994 (ninth), Asterita in 1995 (fifth) and The Miniver Rose in 2009 (fifth). *R. Hannon*

POLLISH 3 b.f. Polish Precedent (USA) 131 – Fizzy Fiona (Efisio 120) [2009 –: 6d 5m^5 5m 7.5m^5 Jul 14] leggy filly: little form: tried blinkered. *A. Berry* **–**

POLLY MACHO (IRE) 2 b.g. (Apr 2) Camacho 118 – Polly Mills 89 (Lugana Beach 116) [2009 5f^6 6g 6d 6g^4 6d Jul 27] compact gelding: modest maiden at best: beaten in sellers last 2 starts: tried visored. *P. D. Evans* **61**

POLLY'S MARK (IRE) 3 b.f. Mark of Esteem (IRE) 137 – Kotdiji (Mtoto 134) [2009 76: 9.7d^3 10m^2 10.2g* 12m 10g^3 12d* 12g* 12m^2 Sep 25] leggy filly: useful performer: won handicap at Nottingham in May and listed race at Newbury (much improved to beat Fallen In Love by length) and handicap at Ascot (by 3 lengths from Chiberta King) in August: good short-head second to Spirit of Dubai in listed race at Ascot final start: stays 1½m: acts on soft and good to firm going. *C. G. Cox* **106**

POLMAILY 4 b.g. Hawk Wing (USA) 136 – Hampton Lucy (IRE) 65 (Anabaa (USA) 130) [2009 76: 6g 7f p7g^5 Jun 4] good-topped gelding: maiden, just modest form in 2009: stays 1m: acts on polytrack, good to firm and good to soft going: tried blinkered: said to have bled final start. *J. Akehurst* **55**

POLO SPRINGS 2 b. or gr.f. (Apr 4) Baryshnikov (AUS) – Cristal Springs 55 (Dance of Life (USA)) [2009 8.3m Aug 24] first foal: dam, staying maiden, half-sister to useful 1¼m winner General Sikorski: 20/1, well beaten in seller at Windsor. *W. G. M. Turner* **–**

POLTERGEIST (IRE) 2 b.c. (Mar 28) Invincible Spirit (IRE) 121 – Bayalika (IRE) (Selkirk (USA) 129) [2009 7s 7m^2 Aug 14] tall colt: has scope: half-brother to very smart 2006 2-y-o 6f/7f winner/2000 Guineas runner-up Vital Equine (by Danetime) and fairly useful 1m winner Bramaputra (by Choisir): dam unraced: shaped well in maidens at Newbury, much better effort when head second to Najd, taking while to find stride: likely to improve further. *R. Hannon* **89 p**

POMANDER (IRE) 6 b.m. Bob's Return (IRE) 123 – Pheisty 78 (Faustus (USA) 118) [2009 p11g Jan 10] lightly-raced maiden: well held only Flat start in 2009 (modest hurdler): stays 1½m: acts on soft ground. *C. Gordon* **–**

POMEROY 2 b.c. (Mar 26) Green Desert (USA) 127 – Ela Paparouna 85 (Vettori (IRE) 119) [2009 7m p7.1m^4 p7.1g^6 Dec 18] good-topped colt: modest form in maidens: worth a try at 6f. *Tom Dascombe* **62**

PONG PING 2 ch.f. (Apr 4) Dr Fong (USA) 128 – Hoh Chi Min 103 (Efisio 120) [2009 f5g 5m^5 7m^5 Jun 19] fourth foal: half-sister to 1m winner Khe Sanh (by Mtoto) and 4-y-o Belle Bellino: dam, 2-y-o 5f/6f winner, later stayed 1m and won in USA: well held in maiden/sellers. *T. D. Easterby* **–**

PONTARDAWE 3 ch.f. Noverre (USA) 125 – Blaina 76§ (Compton Place 125) [2009 6m Apr 1] well held in maiden at Catterick: dead. *T. D. Easterby* **–**

PONT D'AVIGNON 2 ch.f. (Apr 16) Avonbridge 123 – Ambonnay 89 (Ashkalani (IRE) 128) [2009 p6f p7m^4 p7m^2 p7.1g Nov 2] third foal: dam, 2-y-o 6f winner, half-sister to useful sprinter Deep Finesse: modest maiden: claimed from P. Winkworth £3,000 after second start: stays 7f. *F. J. Brennan* **57**

PONT DE NUIT 2 b.g. (Mar 23) Avonbridge 123 – Belle de Nuit (IRE) 85 (Statoblest 120) [2009 p6g^5 7m 8g 6.1d^3 f6m Nov 11] useful-looking gelding: fair maiden: should stay 7f: acts on polytrack and good to soft going, never going well on fibresand final start (gelded after). *R. Hannon* **67**

PONTING (IRE) 3 gr.g. Clodovil (IRE) 116 – Polar Lady 69 (Polar Falcon (USA) 126) [2009 65: p7g^5 8.3d 8m 6m^3 f6m^4 6g^2 f6m* p6g f6g* Dec 18] lengthy gelding: fair performer: won maiden in November and, having left R. Beckett £7,000, claimer in December, both at Southwell: best form at 6f: acts on fibresand and good to firm going: tried in cheekpieces. *P. T. Midgley* **73**

PONTY ROSSA (IRE) 5 ch.m. Distant Music (USA) 126 – Danish Gem (Danehill (USA) 126) [2009 –: 6m^6 7m^6 6d* 7g^4 6d Jun 27] sturdy, lengthy mare: fairly useful handicapper: won at Ripon in May: stays 7f: acts on good to firm and good to soft going. *T. D. Easterby* **92**

POOR PRINCE 2 b.g. (Feb 6) Royal Applause 124 – Kahira (IRE) 80 (King's Best (USA) 132) [2009 7.1m^2 7d^3 7m^6 Oct 13] unfurnished gelding: first foal: dam, ran 3 times (second at 7f at 2 yrs), half-sister to high-class sprinter Tamarisk: fair maiden: placed at Sandown and Goodwood: gelded after below form final start: free-going sort, should be as effective at 6f as 7f. *C. G. Cox* **77**

POPCORN ROSIE 6 b.m. Diktat 126 – Real Popcorn (IRE) 52 (Jareer (USA) 115) [2009 p13g Feb 11] half-sister to several winners, including fairly useful 7f (at 2 yrs) to 1½m winner Winners Delight (by First Trump): dam 1½m winner: winning hurdler, modest maiden chaser: similar form in maiden on Flat debut. *C. J. Down* **51**

POPMURPHY 3 b.c. Montjeu (IRE) 137 – Lady Lahar 106 (Fraam 114) [2009 10g* 10.1g^3 11.1g^4 16f^5 13m Jul 9] 160,000Y: strong, useful-looking colt: fourth foal: closely related to 4-y-o Classic Legend and half-brother to 5-y-o Kilburn: dam 6f (at 2 yrs) to 8.3f winner: useful performer: won maiden at Windsor in April: best efforts when 2 lengths third to Debussy in minor event at Epsom and 9 lengths fifth to Holberg in Queen's Vase at Royal Ascot: stays 2m: raced only on good going or firmer (acts on firm): visored last 2 starts. *K. R. Burke* **99**

POPPANAN (USA) 3 b.g. Mr Greeley (USA) 122 – Tiny Decision (USA) (Ogygian (USA)) [2009 6m 5.7g* p6g^2 p5g^5 p6m^3 p7g^5 Dec 31] $100,000Y, 82,000 2-y-o: seventh foal: half-brother to 3 winners, including useful 2002 2-y-o 6f winner Fiddlers Reach (by Kingmambo), later winning sprinter in Hong Kong: dam, US 6f (including at 2 yrs) and 1m winner, out of half-sister to very smart 9f/1¼m performer Running Stag: fair performer: won maiden at Bath in September: at least creditable efforts in handicaps after: likely to prove best at 7f+: acts on polytrack. *S. Dow* **79**

POPPET'S LOVEIN 3 b.f. Lomitas 129 – Our Poppet (IRE) 58 (Warning 136) [2009 8.3g^2 8m 7.1g* 7m* 8m^5 7s Oct 12] angular filly: fifth foal: half-sister to several winners, notably 4-y-o Overdose: dam, ran once, out of very smart 1¼m/1½m winner Upend: fairly useful form: much improved when winning maiden at Chepstow and handicap at Newcastle in August: free-going sort, likely to prove best short of 1m: acts on good to firm going: unruly in stall and withdrawn on intended debut. *A. B. Haynes* **89**

POPPY DEAN (IRE) 4 ch.f. Night Shift (USA) – Miss Devious (IRE) 51 (Dr Devious (IRE) 127) [2009 55: p10g p8g p7g^6 8.3m^5 8.1g Aug 13] compact filly: modest maiden handicapper: should stay 1½m: acts on polytrack and good to firm ground: tried tongue tied. *J. G. Portman* **52**

POPPY MORRIS (IRE) 4 b.f. Namid 128 – Coco Palm 80 (Selkirk (USA) 129) [2009 5.7g 5.1m p6g Oct 2] first foal: dam Irish maiden (stayed 1¼m): well held in seller/claimers. *A. B. Haynes* **–**

POPPY N'PENNY (IRE) 2 b.f. (Apr 7) Redback 116 – Lulu Island (Zafonic (USA) **87**
130) [2009 5.2g^3 5.1g^3 6s^4 p7g^2 p7g^6 6.5m 6g* Oct 19] 5,500Y: strong filly: half-sister to winning 2-y-o sprinter in Sweden by Indian Rocket: dam unraced daughter of Moyglare Stud Stakes winner Twafeaj: fairly useful performer: much improved to win nursery at Windsor by 4½ lengths from Schoolboy Champ: stays 7f: acts on polytrack: hung right penultimate start: sold 12,000 gns. *W. J. Haggas*

POPPY RED 4 ch.f. Lear Spear (USA) 124 – Pooka's Daughter (IRE) 63 (Eagle Eyed **55**
(USA) 111) [2009 55: p12g^2 p12g p12g^4 p12g^4 10.2g May 5] modest maiden: stays 1½m: acts on polytrack and good to firm ground: tried blinkered, in cheekpieces nowadays. *C. J. Gray*

POPPY SEED 2 br.f. (Mar 23) Bold Edge 123 – Opopmil (IRE) 68 (Pips Pride 117) **77 p**
[2009 6s^4 Jul 17] unfurnished filly: sixth foal: sister to 5f (including at 2 yrs) winner Don't Tell Sue and 4-y-o Orange Pip, and half-sister to 6f winner Mission Man (by Revoque), all 3 fairly useful: dam, sprint maiden, sister to very smart sprinter Pipalong: 5/1, good speed when encouraging 5½ lengths fourth to Conniption in maiden at Newbury: likely to be best at 5f/6f: capable of better. *R. Hannon*

POPPY'S ROSE 5 b.m. Diktat 126 – Perfect Peach 100 (Lycius (USA) 124) [2009 75: **69**
7d 7.1m 6g p7.1g^2 p7.1g^3 6v^3 6d^4 p6m^4 Aug 21] lengthy, workmanlike mare: fair handicapper: stays 7f: acts on polytrack, soft and good to firm ground: tried in cheekpieces: has looked quirky. *I. W. McInnes*

POR CHABLIS (IRE) 10 b.g. Key of Luck (USA) 126 – State Princess (IRE) 85 **–**
(Flash of Steel 120) [2009 12.5g 8.3s Aug 12] little form: tried blinkered. *P. J. Lally, Ireland*

PORT HILL 2 ch.g. (Apr 21) Deportivo 116 – Hill Farm Dancer 82 (Gunner B 126) **–**
[2009 p7.1g^6 7.1s 7g Aug 2] well held in maidens. *W. M. Brisbourne*

PORT RONAN (USA) 3 gr. or ro.c. Cozzene (USA) – Amber Token (USA) (Hen- **54**
nessy (USA) 122) [2009 61: p6g 6s 6m 6m 5g 5m^5 5m 5.9g^5 5m^6 5m^3 7m^5 7m^6 Sep 19] small colt: modest maiden: best efforts at 5f/6f: acts on firm going: in cheekpieces/visor nowadays. *J. S. Wainwright*

PORTRUSH STORM 4 ch.f. Observatory (USA) 131 – Overcast (IRE) 72 (Caerleon **71 d**
(USA) 132) [2009 68: 9.3m^3 8.9d 8m^6 7.9m 10.2m 7.9d^5 8d 7.5g Aug 12] workmanlike filly: fair handicapper: below form after reappearance in 2009: should stay 1¼m: acts on good to soft and good to firm ground: tried blinkered. *D. Carroll*

PORTUGESE CADDY 3 b.g. Great Palm (USA) 119 – Paintbrush (IRE) 48 (Groom **73 d**
Dancer (USA) 128) [2009 80: 7.1m p8g 10g p8g^6 7m^4 7m Sep 21] close-coupled gelding: fair performer: well below form after reappearance: best form at 6f: acts on soft and good to firm going: tried blinkered: sold £2,000. *P. Winkworth*

POSE (IRE) 2 b.f. (Apr 11) Acclamation 118 – Lyca Ballerina 76 (Marju (IRE) 127) **85**
[2009 5m 6f^4 5.1m^2 5d^4 6.5m^5 6m^5 Oct 1] £58,000Y: well-made filly: second foal: dam 7.5f winner: fairly useful maiden: easily best effort when fifth to Shamandar in sales race at Ascot penultimate start, comfortably first home stand side: will stay 7f: acts on good to firm going. *R. Hannon*

POSITIVITY 3 ch.f. Monsieur Bond (IRE) 120 – Pretty Pollyanna (General Assembly **57**
(USA)) [2009 68: 5d 5g^5 5g^5 7.1m f6m^3 f6g^3 7.2m f7g^2 f7m f7f^3 f6d Dec 29] close-coupled filly: just modest maiden in 2009: stays 7f: acts on fibresand and good to firm going: in cheekpieces last 2 starts. *B. Smart*

POSSIBLY A TEN (USA) 3 b.f. Seeking The Gold (USA) – Possibly Perfect (USA) **57**
122 (Northern Baby (CAN) 127) [2009 10m 12m^6 May 15] sixth foal: sister to fairly useful 2001 2-y-o 7f winner Dubai Status and closely related to 3 winners, including US 8.5f (at 2 yrs) and 9f (Grade 3 event) winner Promontory Gold (by Gone West) and useful performer up to 1¾m Right To Play (by Kingmambo): dam, champion turf mare in USA, multiple Grade 1 winner at 9f/1¼m: modest form in maidens: sent to USA. *J. H. M. Gosden*

POSTAGE (USA) 6 b. or br.g. Chester House (USA) 123 – Nimble Mind (USA) 103 **62**
(Lyphard (USA) 132) [2009 p10g* p12g p9.5g^2 10.2m p8g May 28] modest performer: won minor event at Lingfield in February: stays 1¼m: raced mainly on polytrack: tried in cheekpieces. *K. A. Morgan*

POSTMAN 3 b.g. Dr Fong (USA) 128 – Mail The Desert (IRE) 110 (Desert Prince **75**
(IRE) 130) [2009 57: f8g* 8.3d* 9f^4 8d^4 8.5g^3 8.1g^5 Aug 7] workmanlike gelding: fair handicapper: successful at Southwell and Nottingham within 6 days in April: stays 8.5f: acts on fibresand and good to soft ground: visored once. *B. Smart*

Breeders' Cup Juvenile Turf, Santa Anita—
Frankie Dettori pounces late on Pounced (white face) to beat Bridgetown (right) and Interactif

POSY FOSSIL (USA) 2 b. or br.f. (May 16) Malibu Moon (USA) – Fire And Shade (USA) 91 (Shadeed (USA) 135) [2009 7m 6m^{2} p5m^{5} p7g Nov 13] $115,000Y: unfurnished filly: half-sister to several winners, including useful 1¼m winner Freedom Flame (by Darshaan): dam, 2-y-o 6f winner, out of Musidora Stakes winner Fatah Flare: fair maiden: second at Haydock: well below form in nursery at Lingfield: should stay 7f+. *S. C. Williams* **67**

POTEMKIN (USA) 4 b. or br.g. Van Nistelrooy (USA) 108 – Bolshoia (USA) (Moscow Ballet (USA)) [2009 58: 10.9g p12g Jun 25] close-coupled gelding: lightly-raced maiden: well held in 2009. *A. King* **–**

POTENTIALE (IRE) 5 ch.g. Singspiel (IRE) 133 – No Frills (IRE) 62 (Darshaan 133) [2009 83: p12g^{2} 12m^{3} 11.9s^{3} 9.9m^{3} 9m^{3} 9g* 10.1m* 10.1m Oct 3] sturdy gelding: fairly useful handicapper: better than ever when winning at Goodwood in August and Epsom in September: effective at 9f to 1½m: acts on polytrack, soft and good to firm ground: usually wears cheekpieces: consistent. *J. W. Hills* **88**

POUNCED (USA) 2 ch.c. (Apr 14) Rahy (USA) 115 – Golden Cat (USA) 102 (Storm Cat (USA)) [2009 7g^{2} 7m* 7g^{2} 8f* Nov 7] big, strong, lengthy colt: has scope: half-brother to several winners, including useful 1¼m winner Pampas Cat (by Seeking The Gold) and 3-y-o Big Bound: dam, Irish 1m winner, out of Irish St Leger winner Eurobird: smart form: won maiden at Newbury (by 3 lengths from Markazzi) in August and Grade 2 Breeders' Cup Juvenile Turf at Santa Anita (beat Bridgetown ¾ length, driven to lead last 50 yds) in November: also ran well in between when 1½ lengths second to Siyouni in Prix Jean-Luc Lagardere at Longchamp: stays 1m: acts on firm going: will improve further. *J. H. M. Gosden* **112 p**

POWERFUL MELODY (USA) 2 br.c. (Feb 15) Dynaformer (USA) – Song Track (USA) (Dixieland Band (USA)) [2009 p9.5g* Nov 14] $550,000Y: second foal: dam, US 8.5f winner, closely related to US Grade 3 8.5f winner High Cotton and half-sister to US Grade 3 1½m winner Symphony Sid: 7/2, promising debut when winning maiden at Wolverhampton comfortably by ½ length from Bowdler's Magic, patiently ridden and leading late: sure to improve. *Saeed bin Suroor* **82 p**

POWERFUL PIERRE 2 ch.g. (Feb 8) Compton Place 125 – Alzianah 102 (Alzao (USA) 117) [2009 6d 6m^{3} 5m 6d 6m^{6} 7g 5m^{2} 5m^{2} 6g^{4} Oct 19] £32,000Y: close-coupled gelding: brother to fairly useful 2005 2-y-o 5f winner Crosby Hall and half-brother to several winners, including fairly useful 5f winner (including at 2 yrs) Leozian (by Lion **71**

Cavern) and 8-y-o Desperate Dan: dam 5f/6f winner, including at 2 yrs: fair maiden: good efforts in nurseries last 2 starts: stays 6f: acts on good to firm going: visored last 3 starts. *Jedd O'Keeffe*

POWER OF DREAMS (IRE) 2 b.c. (Apr 2) Pearl of Love (IRE) 112 – Pussie Willow (IRE) 77 (Catrail (USA) 123) [2009 6m[5] 7g 8.3g 7m[2] 8m Nov 11] €4,000F, €12,000Y: good-topped colt: fifth foal: dam, maiden (second at 5f at 2 yrs), sister to smart 6f winner Lionhearted: fair maiden: easily best effort when second to House Red in nursery at Leicester: should stay 1m: acts on good to firm going. *M. H. Tompkins* 72

POWER OF SPEECH 4 b.g. Advise (FR) – Marsara (Never So Bold 135) [2009 –: p12.2g Mar 20] big, workmanlike gelding: last in maidens: tried tongue tied. *J. Gallagher* –

POWER SERIES (USA) 2 gr. or ro.c. (Feb 27) Mizzen Mast (USA) 121 – Diese (USA) 111 (Diesis 133) [2009 7.6d 7g Aug 14] good-topped colt: half-brother to several winners, including very smart US performer up to 11f Senure (2-y-o 7f winner in Britain, by Nureyev) and smart French performer up to 1m Dexterity (by Kingmambo): dam, French 1¼m winner, half-sister to Xaar: well held in maidens at Lingfield and Newmarket (close up long way): likely to do better. *J. H. M. Gosden* – p

POWER SHARED (IRE) 5 gr.g. Kendor (FR) 122 – Striking Pose (IRE) 77 (Darshaan 133) [2009 64: p16.5g Oct 30] quite good-topped gelding: maiden: well held only Flat start in 2009: stays 1½m: acts on polytrack, raced on going softer than good on turf: modest hurdler, successful in December. *P. G. Murphy* –

POYLE MEG 3 b.f. Dansili 127 – Lost In Lucca 72§ (Inchinor 119) [2009 87: 7m[4] 7f[3] 8.1m[2] 8.3g* 8.1m[2] p10g* p10g[3] p10m* Dec 9] leggy filly: fairly useful performer: won maiden at Nottingham in August and handicaps at Kempton in October and December: stays 1¼m: acts on polytrack and good to firm going: usually in cheekpieces. *R. M. Beckett* 91

PRACTITIONER 2 b.g. (Mar 5) Dr Fong (USA) 128 – Macina (IRE) 102 (Platini (GER) 126) [2009 6m* 6g[3] 7d[2] 7m[2] 7m[3] Sep 11] £5,500Y: leggy gelding: fourth foal: brother to winner in Greece: dam useful German 6.5f/7f winner: useful performer: won maiden at Salisbury in June: progressed next 3 starts, 3½ lengths second to Azmeel in listed event at Newbury: stays 7f: acts on good to firm and good to soft ground: blinkered last 2 outings: sold 80,000 gns, sent to Hong Kong, where renamed Fat Choy Oohlala. *H. J. L. Dunlop* 95

PRAESEPE 2 b.f. (Jan 31) Pivotal 124 – Superstar Leo (IRE) 114 (College Chapel 122) [2009 p5.1g[2] Dec 26] sister to smart 5f performer Enticing and half-sister to fairly useful 5f winner (including at 2 yrs) Speed Song (by Fasliyev): dam 2-y-o 5f winner (including Flying Childers Stakes): 11/10 on, green when 1¼ lengths second to Clifton Bridge in maiden at Wolverhampton: will do better. *W. J. Haggas* 71 p

PRAGMATIST 5 b.m. Piccolo 121 – Shi Shi (Alnasr Alwasheek 117) [2009 71: 7s May 27] smallish mare: fair handicapper: needed outing sole start in 2009: should stay 1m: acts on polytrack and good to soft going. *P. Winkworth* 56

PRAIRIE HAWK (USA) 4 b. or br.g. Hawk Wing (USA) 136 – Lady Carla 122 (Caerleon (USA) 132) [2009 68: p13.9g* p16g* 16.4m[3] Jun 26] good-topped gelding: fair handicapper: progressive in 2009, winning at Wolverhampton and Lingfield in February: will stay beyond 2m: acts on polytrack and good to firm ground: tongue tied. *Tim Vaughan* 73

PRAIRIE SPIRIT (FR) 5 ch.g. Grape Tree Road 122 – Prairie Runner (IRE) 108 (Arazi (USA) 135) [2009 p10g p11g Feb 18] useful form in France for E. Lellouche, successful 5 times: shaped as though amiss in handicaps in 2009: stays 14.5f: acts on soft going: fair hurdler, won twice in spring. *C. E. Longsdon* –

PRAIRIE STORM 4 b.g. Storming Home 128 – Last Dream (IRE) 80 (Alzao (USA) 117) [2009 89+: 10.2d 10g[6] p10g[3] Jun 17] neat gelding: fairly useful handicapper: stays 1¼m: acts on polytrack and heavy going: travels well up with pace: sold 24,000 gns, sent to Qatar. *A. M. Balding* 85

PRAISE OF FOLLY 3 b.f. Selkirk (USA) 129 – Song of Hope 103 (Chief Singer 131) [2009 53: p7.1g[5] p7.1g p10g Apr 8] leggy filly: modest maiden: raced mainly at 7f. *A. G. Newcombe* 56

PRAVDA STREET 4 ch.g. Soviet Star (USA) 128 – Sari 83 (Faustus (USA) 118) [2009 90: 7m[4] p7g 6f[4] 7m* 7.1m 7m[3] 7m 7m Oct 3] tall gelding: useful handicapper: won at Newmarket (dead-heat) in May: good third to Captain Brilliance there following month: best form at 7f: acts on polytrack, soft and firm ground: sometimes blinkered. *P. F. I. Cole* 96

On The House Stakes, Goodwood—one of five wins for Premio Loco (No.3) who gets up in the dying strides to beat Pure Poetry (No.9), with Yamal (right) and the largely obscured Mac Love (checked cap) also involved in the finish

PRAYER BOAT (IRE) 3 b.c. Oasis Dream 129 – Reasonably Devout (CAN) (St Jovite (USA) 135) [2009 83: 7g 7m⁴ 8m² 10d⁵ 8.5s⁵ p10.7g p7g Sep 5] lengthy, good-topped colt: fairly useful maiden: probably stays 1¼m: acts on polytrack, good to firm and good to soft going. *John Joseph Murphy, Ireland* **88 ?**

PRECIOUS CITIZEN (USA) 4 ch.f. Proud Citizen (USA) 122 – Fasateen (USA) (Alysheba (USA)) [2009 57: p8.6g 10g³ 13.1f⁵ 10.2m⁴ Sep 10] modest maiden handicapper: should stay beyond 1¼m: acts on good to firm ground. *J. R. Gask* **57**

PRECIOUS CORAL (IRE) 2 gr.f. (Feb 10) Elusive City (USA) 117 – Somaggia (IRE) (Desert King (IRE) 129) [2009 6m 6g 7g p5g⁶ p6g² 7g³ 7g Oct 16] €60,000Y: big filly: first foal: dam, Italian maiden, half-sister to smart performer up to 1m Speedfit Too: fair maiden: easily best efforts when placed in nurseries: dropped away tamely final outing (claimed £5,000): stays 7f: acts on polytrack: said to have had breathing problem second outing (tongue tied next time). *S. A. Callaghan* **72**

PRECIOUS SECRET (IRE) 3 b.f. Fusaichi Pegasus (USA) 130 – Gharam (USA) 108 (Green Dancer (USA) 132) [2009 63p: 7g⁴ 8.3m 10.1g⁵ Jul 20] neat filly: just poor maiden in 2009: best effort at 7f. *C. F. Wall* **49**

PRECISION BREAK (USA) 4 b.g. Silver Deputy (CAN) – Miss Kitty Cat (USA) (Tabasco Cat (USA) 126) [2009 99: 12f 14g² 14m 12m* Sep 12] big, strong gelding: useful handicapper: improved when winning at Doncaster in September by ½ length from Falcon Rock (gelded after): stays 2m: acts on all-weather, firm and good to soft going. *P. F. I. Cole* **105**

PRECOCIOUS AIR (IRE) 3 b.f. Redback 116 – Wee Merkin (IRE) (Thatching 131) [2009 67: p9.5g² p8g⁶ p8.6g³ p8g⁴ 9g² 9g* Apr 26] modest performer: left J. Osborne after fourth outing: first past post in minor events at Avenches (demoted) and Dielsdorf in April: stayed 9.5f: raced only on polytrack in Britain: dead. *G. J. Raveneau, Switzerland* **61**

PRELUDE 8 b.m. Danzero (AUS) – Dancing Debut 83 (Polar Falcon (USA) 126) [2009 79: 12.3g⁵ 11.9f³ 12.3m 12.3g 13.1d Aug 27] good-topped mare: fair handicapper: stays 13.4f: acts on firm and soft going: races prominently: tends to carry head awkwardly. *W. M. Brisbourne* **71**

PREMIER ANGEL (USA) 3 b.f. Arch (USA) 127 – Angel Song (USA) (Reign Road (USA)) [2009 68p: p8g p10g⁵ 8d Aug 10] regressive maiden: left Jane Chapple-Hyam prior to final start. *Ollie Pears* **–**

PREMIER DEMON (IRE) 3 b.f. Tagula (IRE) 116 – Luisa Demon (IRE) (Barathea (IRE) 127) [2009 –: p6g p7g 8f 7.1m⁵ Jul 1] smallish filly: no solid form: tried tongue tied. *P. D. Evans* **–**

PREMIER KRUG (IRE) 3 gr.f. Xaar 132 – Perugia (IRE) 94 (Perugino (USA) 84) [2009 57§: 7m 9.8m 7.1m^3 8m^4 8m^6 8f^4 Jul 2] leggy filly: poor maiden nowadays: probably stays 8.6f: acts on polytrack and firm going: tried visored: ungenuine. *P. D. Evans* **40 §**

PREMIER LAD 3 b.g. Tobougg (IRE) 125 – Al Joudha (FR) (Green Desert (USA) 127) [2009 69p: f6g* f6g^2 f6g^4 f6m f6f p6f Dec 20] fair performer: won maiden at Southwell in February: stays 6f: acts on fibresand and good to soft going. *T. D. Barron* **76**

PREMIER SUPERSTAR 3 ch.f. Bertolini (USA) 125 – Absolve (USA) (Diesis 133) [2009 55: 10m 11.5m Jun 4] medium-sized filly: no form since debut. *M. H. Tompkins* **–**

PREMIO LOCO (USA) 5 ch.g. Prized (USA) – Crazee Mental 107 (Magic Ring (IRE) 115) [2009 118p: p8g* p8g* p10g^2 8m* 8.3m^2 8g* 8g* Sep 27] lengthy gelding: smart performer: in excellent form again in 2009, winning minor event at Lingfield in January, listed races at Kempton in February and Goodwood (by neck from Pure Poetry) in May and Darley Oettingen-Rennen at Baden-Baden (beat Konig Concorde 2½ lengths) and Grosse Europa Meile at Cologne (by ¾ length from Earl of Fire) in September: effective at 1m/easy 1¼m: raced only on polytrack and good/good to firm ground: often early to post: held up (travels strongly), and has good turn of foot. *C. F. Wall* **118**

PREMIUM CHARGE 2 ch.g. (May 18) Footstepsinthesand 120 – Kallavesi (USA) 64 (Woodman (USA) 126) [2009 7m^4 p9.5g Dec 12] tall, good-bodied gelding: well held in minor event and claimer (raced freely in blinkers/hampered), gelded in between. *C. A. Dwyer* **–**

PRESBYTERIAN NUN (IRE) 4 b.f. Daylami (IRE) 138 – Conspiracy 98 (Rudimentary (USA) 118) [2009 100: 14.1m^3 14g^6 14d 12m^4 10.3m^6 10.4m^2 10g 12g^4 Oct 30] leggy, lengthy filly: useful performer: at least respectable efforts all starts in 2009: stays 1¾m: acts on good to firm and good to soft ground: tried in cheekpieces/blinkers: ungenuine. *J. L. Dunlop* **95 §**

PRESCRIPTION 4 ch.f. Pivotal 124 – Doctor's Glory (USA) 91 (Elmaamul (USA) 125) [2009 92p: 7g^6 p6g* p6g^2 p7g^3 6s^4 p6g^6 Nov 21] tall filly: useful performer: won handicap at Lingfield in August: good efforts when placed in similar events at Wolverhampton (second to Jaconet) and Lingfield (third to Kyllachy Star): below best in listed races last 2 starts, though hampered second occasion: stays 7f: acts on polytrack and heavy ground. *Sir Mark Prescott* **103**

PRESENT 5 ch.m. Generous (IRE) 139 – Miss Picol (Exit To Nowhere (USA) 122) [2009 –: f11g 11.5m 16m^4 16g Oct 28] good-topped mare: little form since 2007, leaving M. Gingell after reappearance: tried in cheekpieces/visor/tongue tie. *Miss Diana Weeden* **–**

PRESENT ALCHEMY 3 ch.c. Cadeaux Genereux 131 – Desert Alchemy (IRE) 103 (Green Desert (USA) 127) [2009 8s^6 8.1v^5 6m^2 6m^2 5m* Aug 29] big, deep-girthed colt: third foal: half-brother to 5-y-o Rosko: dam, 7f winner, closely related to smart 7f/1m winner Madid: vastly improved form (fairly useful) when landing odds in maiden at Beverley in August by 9 lengths from Rainy Night: likely to prove best at 5f: acts on good to firm going. *H. Morrison* **97**

PRESQUE PERDRE 5 ch.g. Desert Prince (IRE) 130 – Kindle (Selkirk (USA) 129) [2009 16.1d^4 May 15] good-topped gelding: fairly useful hurdler: lightly-raced maiden on Flat, first form (modest) in handicap on sole 5-y-o start: stays 2m: acts on good to soft going. *G. M. Moore* **54 +**

PRESSED FOR TIME (IRE) 3 b.f. Traditionally (USA) 117 – Desert Palace (Green Desert (USA) 127) [2009 64: p5.1g 5m^3 5.7f^6 5.1g p5.1g^6 5.3f 5g Aug 3] good-topped filly: modest performer: below form after second outing: tried blinkered/in cheekpieces: usually tongue tied. *E. J. Creighton* **64**

PRESSING (IRE) 6 b.h. Soviet Star (USA) 128 – Rafif (USA) 68 (Riverman (USA) 131) [2009 120: 8d 8m* 10g* 8g* 8v^3 8g Dec 13] **120**

'I am willing to forego the 100,000/1-chance of having the Kentucky Derby or Epsom Derby winner, in favour of buying European horses at the end of their three-year-old season, when owners are looking to sell because they feel there aren't the opportunities for older horses.' Owner Gary Tanaka has had little cause to regret his policy of buying horses with proven form, as the string of big-race wins to his name across the globe will testify. His latest flag-bearer Pressing has finished outside the money only three times in nineteen starts since donning the emerald green, white and yellow colours of Tanaka for the first time early in his four-year-old campaign, amassing more than £1.25m since doing so. Pressing had already

Grosser Dallmayr-Preis - Bayerisches Zuchtrennen, Munich—the much travelled Pressing (right) goes one better than in 2008; strong-finishing Precious Boy (noseband) and Trincot fill the places

shown smart form when trained by Roberto Feligioni in Italy, winning four times there, and he hasn't had to improve significantly (if at all) to claim seven wins since joining Michael Jarvis, who also enjoyed something of a bonanza with another Tanaka-owned Italian import Rakti earlier in the decade.

Newmarket-based Jarvis has clocked up plenty of air miles to find winning opportunities for Pressing, who has raced in six different countries since joining the yard. He isn't in the same class as Rakti, though, and has finished no closer than fourth in his four starts on British soil (three times in Group 1 company), though he possibly needed the run when only eighth of eleven in the Lockinge at Newbury on his reappearance in 2009. The six-year-old didn't look back afterwards, winning his next three starts, including gaining his second successive victory in the Group 2 International Topkapi Trophy at Istanbul's Veliefendi racecourse in early-September, rallying under regular jockey Neil Callan to beat fellow British raider Dream Eater by a head. The race forms the centrepiece of the Turkish track's two-day International Racing Festival, which was dominated by British-based trainers in 2009, with Mick Channon (Eva's Request and Halicarnassus) and Saeed bin Suroor (Balius) taking the three other big prizes (Jarvis, incidentally, wasn't present at Veliefendi as he was recovering from heart surgery at the time). Leading British Flat yards have long been prepared to travel far and wide in search of winning opportunities for performers who fall just below top class, an increasingly rewarding approach given the current weakness of sterling. For example, the Topkapi Trophy, whose first prize was worth £304,878 at prevailing exchange rates, was considerably more valuable than any of the three Group 1s that Pressing has contested in Britain and half as much again as the Group 1 Prix du Moulin at Longchamp three days later.

The most famous international race meeting in the calendar is the Breeders' Cup, which was staged at Santa Anita in 2009, but running there wasn't an option with Pressing because of an ongoing legal tangle involving his owner. The Californian stewards have revoked Tanaka's licence as an owner because of his conviction following a high-profile federal fraud case which took several years to reach the court, Tanaka being kept under virtual house arrest in New York both before and after the trial (his wife, a former employee of Tanaka's firm, runs the family home in London and won't travel to the USA for fear of arrest). Tanaka couldn't appeal against the verdict until he had been sentenced, which eventually took place in February 2010. Tanaka was given five years in prison and ordered to repay millions of dollars to investors. Tanaka has announced his intention to appeal which means the case may still have some way to run. 'When a trainer gets suspended, he just puts an assistant in charge. For owners, it's not quite that easy,' Tanaka remarked in the autumn, explaining that he still maintained a string of about twenty horses outside the States. Pressing presumably provided a welcome distraction for Tanaka and the owner must have followed his exploits, albeit from afar, with much satisfaction in 2009. In addition to that second lucrative pay-day in Turkey, Pressing won the Premio Carlo Vittadini at Milan in late-May (making light work of weaker opposition) and the Grosser Dallmayr-Preis - Bayerisches Zuchtrennen at Munich two months later. The latter was the first time Pressing had run at a mile and a quarter since he had finished runner-up to Linngari in a stronger renewal of the same race twelve months earlier, a slow pace suiting him this time around as he quickened smartly over a furlong and a half out to beat home-trained Precious Boy by three quarters of a length, despite drifting left late on. Pressing ran in the Premio Ribot at Rome in early-November, bidding for a third consecutive win on the card after winning the Ribot the year before and the Group 1 Premio Roma in 2007. He looked like pulling it off when forging a couple of lengths clear a furlong and a half out, only to be caught inside the final furlong by Silver Arrow and Sehrezad. Sent on to Hong Kong the following month, Pressing lost a shoe in the Hong Kong Mile and came back tailed off (he had recorded a rare poor run in the same race the previous year).

Pressing (IRE) (b.h. 2003)	Soviet Star (USA) (b 1984)	Nureyev (b 1977)	Northern Dancer
			Special
		Veruschka (b 1967)	Venture VII
			Marie d'Anjou
	Rafif (USA) (b or br 1990)	Riverman (b 1969)	Never Bend
			River Lady
		Reves Celestes (b 1979)	Lyphard
			Tobira Celeste

Pressing is a tall, leggy, useful-looking horse and hails from a good Flat family, which was covered in detail in *Racehorses of 2007*. Another notable performer has emerged from it since then in the form of top-class three-year-old Mastercraftsman, who shares the same grandam as Pressing. To recap, Reves Celestes was a half-sister to King George VI and Queen Elizabeth Stakes runner-up Celestial Storm and closely related to Ribblesdale Stakes winner Thawakib, the latter the dam of Arc winner Sakhee. As for Pressing's more immediate relatives, there is one more winner to report in his four-year-old half-brother Roughting (by Celtic Swing), who has won in Italy at up to eleven furlongs. Pressing's dam Rafif has since produced another foal to Celtic Swing, the 2008 filly Growling, whilst Pressing's exploits led to a return visit to Soviet Star, which has resulted in a foal full brother to him. Rafif has been represented by several durable performers other than Pressing, notably the one-time useful mile and a half winner Rajam (by Sadler's Wells), who ran forty-seven times on the Flat and has also shown fair winning form at up to twenty-three furlongs over jumps. Pressing doesn't stay anything like so far as that—he is ideally suited by a mile to a mile and a quarter, even though he has won at up to eleven furlongs—but he has proved far more genuine and consistent than Rajam. Pressing also seems versatile with regard to the ground (acts on firm and soft, with a respectable effort in his only race on heavy). He is a credit to his connections. *M. A. Jarvis*

PRESSING MATTERS (IRE) 3 br.c. Oasis Dream 129 – Pasithea (IRE) 101 (Celtic **77**
Swing 138) [2009 80: p8g 7.6f^{4} 7g* p7g 7g 7g^{3} p8g 8g Oct 20] useful-looking colt: fair performer: won handicap at Yarmouth in July: below form after: stays 7f: acts on polytrack and firm ground: in blinkers/cheekpieces last 6 starts. *M. Botti*

PRESS THE BUTTON (GER) 6 b.g. Dansili 127 – Play Around (IRE) 105 (Niniski **99**
(USA) 125) [2009 96: p10g* 10.1g 10.3m^{5} 12g 10m^{2} 12g* 13.4m 10m Sep 19] workmanlike gelding: useful handicapper: won at Kempton in April and Ascot in August: better than result (best of those who forced pace) when seventh in valuable event at Newbury final start: best at 1¼m/1½m: acts on polytrack, firm and soft ground: tried in cheekpieces: often makes running: reliable: fairly useful form over hurdles. *J. R. Boyle*

PRESS TO RESET 2 b.g. (Mar 31) Reset (AUS) 124 – Lady de Londres (Mtoto 134) **43**
[2009 7g 8.3m^{3} 7m p9.5g Oct 29] plain gelding: poor maiden: third in seller, only form. *W. G. M. Turner*

PRESVIS 5 b.g. Sakhee (USA) 136 – Forest Fire (SWE) 88 (Never So Bold 135) **126**
[2009 116p: 10g* 10m* 8.9g^{2} 10d* 10g^{2} p10g^{2} 10g^{3} Dec 13]

'You race in Britain for prestige and abroad for money.' Whilst trainer Luca Cumani's quote in an interview in the latest season might have been a generalisation—as well as a veiled criticism of British prize money levels—it is hard to imagine how Presvis, the best horse in his yard at present, would have earned anything like his 2009 haul of £2m by staying at home. As a five-year-old gelding, Presvis had no future stud career for his connections to consider, so rather than seeking prestige in top ten-furlong contests in Britain, such as the Eclipse, the International and the Champion Stakes (winning all three wouldn't have earned

Audemars Piguet Queen Elizabeth II Cup, Sha Tin—
Ryan Moore produces Presvis (No.3) late to beat 2007 winner Viva Pataca and Thumbs Up (checked cap)

Presvis half the money he picked up on his travels), Presvis was aimed instead at much more valuable targets in Dubai, Hong Kong and Singapore. Cumani has long been alive to the potential rewards to be had from campaigning good horses internationally. He was the first British-based trainer to win the Arlington Million, with Tolomeo in 1983. In the modern era, it is easy to take successes in America for granted, but, in those days, before the advent of the Breeders' Cup, the Arlington Million was the world's richest race and Tolomeo's success was the first by a British-trained horse in top company in North America for well over a decade. A Breeders' Cup win for Cumani's stable came when Barathea took the Mile in 1994, and more recently the stable has exploited other opportunities in the expanding international programme. Alkaased won the 2005 Japan Cup for Cumani and he has come the closest yet of any British-based trainer to landing Australia's richest race the Melbourne Cup, Bauer being beaten a nose in 2008, a year after stable-companion Purple Moon filled the runner-up spot in the same race. Cumani's earnings on foreign soil in 2009 were £2,626,018, according to figures produced by the International Racing Bureau using the 'official' exchange rate; only Saeed bin Suroor (£3,361,108) and Sir Michael Stoute (£3,295,452) won more in a year when British-trained horses picked up £24,574,470 on their travels, smashing the previous record set in 2006 after a significant fall in the value of sterling as a result of the 2008 banking crisis.

Tolomeo had contested the Two Thousand Guineas and the Derby on the way to winning the Arlington Million as a three-year-old, but there were no classics for Presvis who worked his way up, if not from the bottom, then from well down the handicap. In fact, because of injury, he did not see a racecourse at all until he was four, finishing third in a maiden at Haydock in May of that year. Ridden by a 7-lb claimer in his early races, two more runs earned Presvis a BHA mark of 72 on his handicap debut at Sandown, and he made a nonsense of that by winning by nine lengths. After two seconds in similar company, he defied a mark 20 lb higher than the one he had been given at Sandown when running out a seven-length winner of the John Smith's Stakes at Newbury on his final start in 2008. Presvis was clearly destined for better things, though the Dubai International Carnival early in the latest season gave him a couple more opportunities in handicaps, at the same time building up the bank balance. Handicaps are the bread and butter of the Dubai Carnival, but their inflated value is such that almost any would be the main event on a card in Britain. Presvis won his first two starts of the year at Nad Al Sheba, each by more than three lengths, showing a good turn of foot to burst clear on the first occasion and making up ten lengths under a confident ride on the second. That second win came when defying a mark of 112, Presvis putting up a high-class effort to concede 8 lb to the runner-up Yahrab, who had won a listed race at Lingfield the previous autumn.

Although his earnings for the year were staggering, Presvis could have won even more with better luck. After winning his two handicaps in Dubai, Presvis was drawn sixteen of sixteen in the Dubai Duty Free at Nad Al Sheba, a race with a prize exceeded on turf only by the Prix de l'Arc de Triomphe. Presvis needs to be held up and had to take his chance dropped out in rear on the rail. Still behind on the home turn, he was left with an impossible amount of ground to make up on the runaway leader Gladiatorus but he made an eye-catching attempt, weaving his way through the field and finishing strongly to cut into the winner's advantage in the closing stages, beaten just over three lengths into second. The stable had another near-miss later on the Dubai World Cup card when Purple Moon went down by a nose and a short head in the equally valuable Dubai Sheema Classic.

Presvis's successful graduation from handicapper to international Group 1 performer looked merely to have been delayed, and he went one better on his next outing in Hong Kong four weeks later where previous winners Archipenko (sixth in the Duty Free) and Viva Pataca looked the main dangers in a field of ten for the Audemars Piguet Queen Elizabeth II Cup at Sha Tin. The Sha Tin straight is a lot shorter than Nad Al Sheba's, but Presvis quickened through from the back of the field after the home turn to hit the front halfway through the final furlong and run out a length winner from Viva Pataca. The other European runner, French-trained Chinchon, finished fourth, with Archipenko sixth. Presvis had not needed to run to his best form to win in Hong Kong, and the opposition looked no stronger for his next assignment, the International Cup at Kranji. However, it turned out to be almost a carbon copy of the Duty Free, Presvis drawn widest, twelve of twelve, and breaking slowly as he often does before being switched inside to trail the field. Still on the rail turning for home, there was only a furlong and a half left by the time Presvis could be switched wider to begin his challenge. Once in the clear, Presvis came with a storming run in the final furlong and failed by just a head to catch the French-trained Dubai World Cup runner-up Gloria de Campeao, beating his former stable-companion Bankable into third. The Cumani stable had been successful in the race with Endless Hall in 2001.

Although it was still early days in the main European season, Presvis had already had five races in as many months, involving plenty of travelling, and his 2009 campaign effectively ended in Singapore. With a similar campaign planned for him in 2010, it was six months before he was seen again, with his first big target

Mr L. Marinopoulos' "Presvis"

the Hong Kong Cup in December, another prize the stable had won before, with Falbrav in 2003. Before then, though, Presvis had a pipe-opener, making his only appearance of the year in Britain in the listed Churchill Stakes at Lingfield in November. Starting odds on for his all-weather debut, Presvis looked ring-rusty in finishing three lengths second to the smart Tranquil Tiger. He duly improved on that when third behind Vision d'Etat and Collection in the Hong Kong Cup, but was still short of his best form, giving the impression that he would be more fully tuned up for the Dubai Carnival early in 2010. It was planned that he would have one run on turf and one on the synthetic surface, tapeta, at the new track at Meydan, to determine his big-race target on Dubai World Cup night. If proving himself on tapeta, he would be aimed at the Dubai World Cup itself.

Presvis (b.g. 2004)	Sakhee (USA) (b 1997)	Bahri (b 1992)	Riverman
			Wasnah
		Thawakib (b 1990)	Sadler's Wells
			Tobira Celeste
	Forest Fire (SWE) (b 1995)	Never So Bold (b 1980)	Bold Lad
			Never Never Land
		Mango Sampaquita (b or br 1985)	Colombian Friend
			Twins Fire

The lucrative prizes on offer at ten furlongs mean there has been no need to try Presvis over further so far, though a literal interpretation of Presvis's pedigree suggests he would have no problem staying a mile and a half, a distance over which both his sire and dam won. Sakhee, the sire of Presvis, won the Arc and was second in the Derby, but he was just as good at a mile and a quarter, winning the International at York by seven lengths and beaten a nose in the Breeders' Cup Classic. Several of Sakhee's offspring, however, haven't even stayed that far, the high-class sprinter Sakhee's Secret a notable example. Presvis's dam Forest Fire, a fairly useful handicapper who won four times in all (successful at a mile, nine furlongs and ten furlongs, as well as twelve), was by the top-class sprinter Never So Bold, and there are other speedier elements in Presvis's background too. The sturdy Presvis made 15,000 guineas as a foal and twice that sum as a yearling, proving a bargain to those who weren't put off by the fact that his family's exploits had largely been confined to Scandinavia. His great grandam Twins Fire won the Norwegian Oaks and was Norway's champion older mare in 1982, while his grandam Mango Sampaquita won three races in the same country at up to nine furlongs and finished second in a listed race. Apart from Forest Fire, two more of Mango Sampaquita's winners were successful in Britain, both of them over jumps; Pepe Galvez was a fairly useful hurdler at up to two and a half miles and Antonio Mariano a fair two-mile chaser. Presvis is his dam's third foal, and Forest Fire's other winner, Magelan (by Nashwan), won abroad as well, though it was not on the same world stage as his younger brother, both his wins coming in Serbia. Presvis acts on good to firm and good to soft ground (his Hong Kong win was the only time he has encountered ground softer than good), while he shaped at Lingfield as though he will prove effective on an artificial surface, at least on polytrack. Presvis will always need some luck in running, as he is ridden from behind for a turn of foot, his most potent weapon which should see him win another valuable prize or two abroad in 2010. *L. M. Cumani*

PRETTIEST STAR (IRE) 2 ch.f. (Mar 10) Footstepsinthesand 120 – Alyousufeya (IRE) 75 (Kingmambo (USA) 125) [2009 5m^6 5m^4 6m^6 5f^5 7d 7d 6m^5 p5.1m^2 5m 5g^4 7g f6m Nov 12] €15,000Y: rather leggy filly: second foal: dam, ran 3 times (would have proved best at 1m), out of Fred Darling Stakes winner Musicale: modest maiden: best efforts at 5f: acts on good to firm ground, probably on polytrack: in cheekpieces last 5 starts: none too consistent. *K. A. Ryan* **54**

PRETTY BONNIE 4 b.f. Kyllachy 129 – Joonayh 81 (Warning 136) [2009 90: 5.1g p6g* 6d^3 6d^2 6g^5 6s^5 6m^3 7s^5 6m Sep 26] close-coupled filly: fairly useful performer: won handicap at Kempton in May: mostly creditable efforts after: stays 7f: acts on polytrack, soft and good to firm going: tough and genuine. *A. E. Price* **94**

PRETTY OFFICER (USA) 4 b.f. Deputy Commander (USA) 124 – La Samanna (USA) (Trempolino (USA) 135) [2009 57: f11g^6 10.1g^6 10.2m^2 10.1g^3 8.3m^4 10.1g* 8d 9.9g^6 Sep 22] lengthy filly: modest handicapper: won apprentice event at Yarmouth in August: stays 1¼m: acts on good to firm ground. *Rae Guest* **64**

PRETTY ORCHID 4 b.f. Forzando 122 – Dunloe (IRE) 54 (Shaadi (USA) 126) [2009 49: 6m 6v 6d^{3} Aug 26] sturdy filly: modest maiden, lightly raced: may prove best at 7f: acts on good to soft ground: tried in cheekpieces. *P. T. Midgley* **55**

PRIDE OF KINGS 3 b.c. King's Best (USA) 132 – Aunty Mary 82 (Common Grounds 118) [2009 81. 8.5g^{1} 8.3m* 10m^{2} 8.1m^{3} 8.1f* 8m 8m^{6} 8g Aug 31] close-coupled colt: fairly useful handicapper: progressed to win at Nottingham in May and Haydock (by ¾ length from Flipando) in July: stays 1¼m: acts on firm and good to soft going: races prominently: sold 14,000 gns, sent to Bahrain. *M. Johnston* **90**

PRIDE OF NATION (IRE) 7 b.h. Danehill Dancer (IRE) 117 – Anita Via (IRE) (Anita's Prince 126) [2009 113d: p8g p8g 8s f7m p7.1g^{3} p8.6g p8.6m^{2} p8.6g^{4} p8f^{5} p8.6g^{3} Dec 28] tall, quite attractive horse: just fair performer on balance in 2009, leaving J. Hills after third start: tried tongue tied, often in cheekpieces. *A. J. McCabe* **73**

PRIDE OF NORTHCARE (IRE) 5 b. or gr.g. Namid 128 – Pride of Pendle 80 (Grey Desire 115) [2009 79: f5g Mar 3] close-coupled gelding: fair performer: last in handicap sole start in 2009 (collapsed after line): was best at 5f: acted on polytrack and good to firm going: tried visored: raced freely held up: dead. *D. Shaw* **–**

PRIESTLEY (IRE) 2 b.g. (Feb 28) Bahri (USA) 125 – Siskin (IRE) (Royal Academy (USA) 130) [2009 7g 8.3v p7.1g Nov 13] close-coupled gelding: well held in maidens: gelded after. *J. G. Given* **–**

PRIMAEVAL 3 ch.c. Pivotal 124 – Langoustine (AUS) 117 (Danehill (USA) 126) [2009 7g^{2} 7m^{3} 6g* Oct 16] good-topped colt: has scope: fourth foal: half-brother to 4-y-o Cigalas: dam, Australian 2-y-o 5f winner (including Group 2), out of half-sister to Royal Academy and the dam of Storm Cat: fairly useful form in maidens: won at Redcar in October by 2½ lengths from Star Addition: should prove best at 6f/7f: open to further improvement. *J. R. Fanshawe* **82 p**

PRIMA FONTEYN 3 ch.f. Imperial Dancer 123 – Flying Wind 51 (Forzando 122) [2009 –: p10g^{6} p11g p10g Feb 22] lengthy filly: little sign of ability. *Miss S. West* **–**

PRIMARY COLORS 2 ch.c. (Mar 20) Nayef (USA) 129 – Red Yellow Blue (USA) (Sky Classic (CAN)) [2009 7g^{5} 8g^{6} Oct 8] rather leggy colt: similar form in maidens, sixth to Kalypso King at Newbury (prominent over 6f). *C. G. Cox* **61**

PRIME ASPIRATION (USA) 4 b. or br.g. Tale of The Cat (USA) 113 – Bank On Her (USA) 76 (Rahy (USA) 115) [2009 6.9d 7f* 9g^{4} 9.5g* Sep 27] close-coupled gelding: missed 2008 and sold from B. Smart £2,200 after well held on reappearance: gelded, won minor events at Miesau in August and Mannheim in September: stays 9.5f: acts on polytrack, firm and good to soft ground. *C. von der Recke, Germany* **63**

PRIME CIRCLE 3 b.g. Green Desert (USA) 127 – First of Many 83 (Darshaan 133) [2009 6d 7.1g^{3} Jul 3] well-made gelding: third foal: brother to smart Irish/UAE 7f to 9f winner Many Colours and half-brother to fairly useful 1½m winner Forsyte Saga (by Machiavellian): dam, ran 3 times, sister to useful performer up to 15f Without A Trace: much better effort in maidens (fair form) when third at Warwick. *M. Johnston* **73**

PRIME CLASSIQUE (USA) 3 b.f. Elusive Quality (USA) – Via Borghese (USA) 116 (Seattle Dancer (USA) 119) [2009 10d^{6} 8.5g^{5} 9.3g^{3} 12s^{6} Nov 14] €80,000Y: closely related to 2003 2-y-o 6f winner Venetian Pride and 7f winner Pietro Siena (both fairly useful, by Gone West) and half-sister to 3 winners abroad: dam 6f (at 2 yrs in Ireland) to 9f (US Grade 2) winner: well held in maiden at Pontefract on debut (for B. Smart): fair form in maidens/minor event in French Provinces after: seems to stay 1½m. *X. T. Demeaulte, France* **65**

PRIME DEFENDER 5 ch.h. Bertolini (USA) 125 – Arian Da 81 (Superlative 118) [2009 118: 6m* 6g 6m 6d^{2} 7m 7m^{5} 6m^{5} 6g Oct 10] strong, good-bodied horse: impresses in appearance: good walker: has powerful, round action: smart performer: not at very best in 2009, though won listed race at Doncaster (beat Pusey Street Lady ½ length) in March: creditable 1¼ lengths second to High Standing in Hackwood Stakes at Newbury: winner at 7f, very best form at stiff 5f/6f: acts on polytrack, soft and good to firm going: tried blinkered/in cheekpieces. *B. W. Hills* **113**

PRIME EXHIBIT 4 b.g. Selkirk (USA) 129 – First Exhibit (Machiavellian (USA) 123) [2009 86: 8.3v^{4} 7.1g* 7.2m^{3} 8s^{2} Oct 12] rangy gelding: useful handicapper, lightly raced: improved in 2009, winning at Sandown in August: good placed efforts at Ayr and Salisbury after: likely to prove best at 7f/1m: acts on soft and good to firm ground. *R. Charlton* **99**

PRIME MOOD (IRE) 3 ch.c. Choisir (AUS) 126 – There With Me (USA) 63 (Distant View (USA) 126) [2009 90: 6f^6 6g 7m 6g Sep 30] big, dipped-backed colt: fairly useful performer at 2 yrs: below form in 2009, seeming amiss (hung badly left) second start, final one for B. Smart: stays 6.5f: best form on soft/heavy going. *X. T. Demeaulte, France* **80**

PRIMERA ROSSA 3 ch.f. Needwood Blade 117 – Meandering Rose (USA) (Irish River (FR) 131) [2009 p7g p8g 7.1m 8f 11.6m^6 p10g^5 12.1m^5 12.1g* 13.1d^2 16m^5 p12g Oct 2] 2,500Y: leggy filly: fifth foal: half-sister to 7f to 9.5f winner (including 1m winner at 2 yrs) Ella Y Rossa (by Bertolini): dam unraced: modest performer: won seller at Chepstow in August: stays 13f: acts on polytrack, good to firm and good to soft ground. *J. S. Moore* **55**

PRIMERA VISTA 3 b.c. Haafhd 129 – Colorvista (Shirley Heights 130) [2009 8m 8d^6 10.3s^5 p9.5g^4 Sep 3] good-bodied colt: half-brother to several winners, including smart 1997 2-y-o 7f winner Mudeer (by Warning) and 4-y-o Island Vista: dam unraced half-sister to Irish Oaks winner Colorspin, herself dam of Opera House and Kayf Tara: fair maiden: worth a try beyond 1¼m: acts on polytrack and soft ground. *L. M. Cumani* **76**

PRIME SPIRIT (IRE) 3 b.c. Invincible Spirit (IRE) 121 – Turtulla (IRE) 77 (Night Shift (USA)) [2009 94: 7.1s^2 7d 8g^4 8s* 7.8g^4 a7.5g* Dec 9] strong, good-bodied colt: useful performer: off a year, improved when head second of 4 to Welsh Emperor in minor event at Haydock on reappearance: left B. Smart after next outing: won minor events at Saint-Cloud (female jockeys) in October and Deauville (all-weather, by 2½ lengths from Right One) in December: stays 1m: best efforts on all-weather/soft going. *X. T. Demeaulte, France* **100**

PRIMO DE VIDA (IRE) 2 b.g. (Feb 21) Trade Fair 124 – Rampage 88 (Pivotal 124) [2009 5.7g 5.7g^3 f7g^2 Oct 18] 11,000F, £23,000Y: first foal: dam, 6f/7f winner, half-sister to useful performer up to 7f J M W Turner: fair maiden: best effort when 4 lengths second to Tres Amigos at Southwell: gelded after: stays 7f. *R. M. Beckett* **71**

PRIMO DILETTANTE 3 b.g. Primo Valentino (IRE) 116 – Jezadil (IRE) 66 (Mujadil (USA) 119) [2009 59: 10m^3 p10g 10s* p10g 10d^3 p12g^5 10g^4 10d^5 p10g* 10m p10g^5 10d^2 10m 7.5d Dec 5] useful-looking gelding: has scope: fair performer: won handicap at Brighton in May and seller at Lingfield in September: sold from W. Knight 8,500 gns after twelfth start: stays 1¼m: acts on polytrack, soft and good to firm ground: tried in cheekpieces. *F. Turner, Italy* **69**

PRIMO WAY 8 b.g. Primo Dominie 121 – Waypoint 95 (Cadeaux Genereux 131) [2009 68: 8.3g 7s 8g 10g^4 9.1g^3 9.2d^4 9.2s^3 9.2v 10m 9.2g Sep 21] tall gelding: modest handicapper: barely stays 1¼m: acts on polytrack, heavy and good to firm going: tried in headgear/tongue tie: held up. *D. A. Nolan* **62**

PRIMROSE BANKES 2 b.f. (Mar 24) Mark of Esteem (IRE) 137 – Lady Bankes (IRE) 69 (Alzao (USA) 117) [2009 f8g^6 p8f^5 p8m Sep 16] half sister to 3 winners, including 7-y-o Danzili Bay and fairly useful 6f (at 2 yrs) to 1m winner Moten Swing (by Kris): dam, 1¼m winner, half-sister to dam of St Leger winner Rule of Law: best effort in maidens when fifth to Mr Mahoganeigh at Lingfield: should be as effective at 7f as 1m. *W. G. M. Turner* **59**

PRINCABILITY (IRE) 3 b.g. King's Best (USA) 132 – Harmonic Sound (IRE) (Grand Lodge (USA) 125) [2009 79: p8g^3 9.9m^3 9.9m^6 11m 11d 10g^4 12d^6 p12g Oct 22] workmanlike gelding: fair maiden handicapper: below form after third start: stays 1¼m: acts on soft and good to firm ground. *M. R. Channon* **79**

PRINCE ANDJO (USA) 3 b.g. Van Nistelrooy (USA) 108 – Magic Flare (USA) (Danzatore (CAN) 120) [2009 –: p7.1g^2 7.5m p10g Oct 11] modest maiden, sporadic form: stays 7f: acts on polytrack: tried tongue tied. *I. W. McInnes* **58**

PRINCE CHARLEMAGNE (IRE) 6 br.g. King Charlemagne (USA) 120 – Ciubanga (IRE) (Arazi (USA) 135) [2009 57, a82d: p9.5g^5 p12g* p12g* p12g* p10g^4 p12g^3 p13g^2 p16g^3 p10m p12g^5 p12.2g^2 p13.9g* p12m^4 p13.9g Dec 17] quite good-topped gelding: fair handicapper: resurgent in 2009, winning at Lingfield and Kempton (2) in February/March and Wolverhampton (amateurs) in November: effective at 1½m to 2m: acts on polytrack, good to firm and good to soft ground: has worn cheekpieces/blinkers. *G. L. Moore* **77**

PRINCE DE FORTUNE 3 b.g. Lend A Hand 124 – Fortuitious (IRE) 42 (Polish Patriot (USA) 128) [2009 p8.6g 7s 7f p7m p7m Oct 31] medium-sized gelding: modest maiden. *Mrs C. A. Dunnett* **51**

PRINCE EVELITH (GER) 6 b.g. Dashing Blade 117 – Peace Time (GER) (Surumu (GER)) [2009 –: 8.1m^4 9.2s^4 7.9m^3 8.9d* 9.8d Jun 17] workmanlike gelding: fairly useful **92**

handicapper, lightly raced in recent years: better than ever when winning at York by 4½ lengths: broke leg 5 days later: stayed 9f: acted on soft and good to firm going: dead. *J. J. Quinn*

PRINCE FORTUNE 2 b.g. (Apr 6) Namid 128 – Plumeria (Revoque (IRE) 122) [2009 6m^5 5d^6 5.2g* Aug 12] 5,000Y: second foal: dam, ran twice in France, half-sister to useful 7f/1m performers Persiano and Peony (in France): dropped in class, much improved form when winning seller at Yarmouth by ¾ length from Italian Tom (pair clear), still showing signs of greenness: should stay 6f: should continue to progress. *Mrs L. Stubbs* **78 p**

PRINCE GOLAN (IRE) 5 b.g. Golan (IRE) 129 – Mohican Princess (Shirley Heights 130) [2009 76: f12s^5 p9.5g p9.5g^4 f11g 8.3g 10.4g^5 p7.1g f8g^3 p9.5g^5 f8f* p9.5g Dec 7] good-topped gelding: fair handicapper: left J. Unett, won amateur event at Southwell in November: should stay beyond 9.5f: acts on all-weather, heavy and good to firm going: usually wears cheekpieces: none too consistent. *R. J. Price* **70**

PRINCELY HERO (IRE) 5 b.g. Royal Applause 124 – Dalu (IRE) 72 (Dancing Brave (USA) 140) [2009 92: f8g^3 p8g^3 p7g^2 7.1m^6 10m Sep 18] good-topped gelding: fairly useful handicapper: left M. Botti after fourth start: stays 9f: acts on all-weather, heavy and good to firm going: tried blinkered. *C. Gordon* **85**

PRINCELYWALLYWOGAN 7 b.g. Princely Heir (IRE) 111 – Dublivia (Midyan (USA) 124) [2009 75: 10.2m 10f 10m^2 10.2m^2 10d Jul 17] tall gelding: fair handicapper: stayed 11f: acted on polytrack, firm and soft going: dead. *John A. Harris* **70**

PRINCE MAGGIO 3 b.c. Prince Sabo 123 – Pieta (IRE) 52 (Perugino (USA) 84) [2009 7g 7g Jul 25] more temperament than ability in maidens: tried blinkered. *Pat Eddery* **– §**

PRINCE NAMID 7 b.g. Namid 128 – Fen Princess (IRE) 72 (Trojan Fen 118) [2009 82: 6v 6v 5g* 5m 5m 5d Oct 28] quite good-topped gelding: fairly useful handicapper: easily best effort in 2009 when winning at Beverley in July: best at 5f/6f: acts on any turf going: tried in visor/cheekpieces: temperament under suspicion. *D. Nicholls* **80**

PRINCE NOEL 5 b.g. Dr Fong (USA) 128 – Baileys On Line 60 (Shareef Dancer (USA) 135) [2009 72, a84: f7d p8.6g^4 p8.6g^3 p9.5g^2 p8.6g p8.6g^3 8.5m p8.6g^6 Apr 25] short-backed gelding: fair performer: stays 1¼m: acts on polytrack, soft and good to firm going: tried in headgear: temperamental. *N. Wilson* **66 §**

PRINCE OF DANCE 3 b.c. Danehill Dancer (IRE) 117 – Princess Ellen 114 (Tirol 127) [2009 7d* 8s* 8g* Oct 31] good-topped colt: fourth foal: half-brother to 3 winners, including 4-y-o Stravella and 6-y-o La Estrella: dam, 2-y-o 6f/7f winner and runner-up in 1000 Guineas, later 1m winner in USA: smart form: quickly made into a smart performer, unbeaten in maiden at Newbury in May and, having been off 5 months (reportedly suffered hairline fracture of pelvis), handicap at Salisbury and listed race at Newmarket (beat Shaweel by head, racing freely but battling well) in October: stays 1m: acts on soft ground: pattern winner in the making. *Tom Dascombe* **114 p**

PRINCE OF DELPHI 6 b.g. Royal Applause 124 – Princess Athena 119 (Ahonoora 122) [2009 79: p6g p6g^3 p6g^4 p6g^6 5.1m 6m 5.3m Jun 23] strong, good-bodied gelding: fair maiden handicapper: stays easy 7f: acts on polytrack and good to firm going: usually in headgear. *Mrs A. L. M. King* **67**

PRINCE OF DREAMS 2 b.c. (May 2) Sadler's Wells (USA) 132 – Questina (FR) (Rainbow Quest (USA) 134) [2009 8v^2 Oct 24] 140,000Y: eighth foal: closely related to smart French 9f (at 2 yrs) to 10.5f winner Trumbaka (by In The Wings) and half-brother to 2 winners, including 3-y-o Spirit of Dubai: dam French 1¼m winner: 16/1, promising 3½ lengths second to Gardening Leave in maiden at Newbury, going on at finish: will be suited by 1¼m+: will do better. *W. J. Knight* **78 p**

PRINCE OF JOHANNE (IRE) 3 gr.c. Johannesburg (USA) 127 – Paiute Princess (FR) (Darshaan 133) [2009 p7g 8m^4 7d* 8.3f* 10g* 10.3m 10m^5 Sep 19] €105,000F, €275,000Y: good-topped colt: fourth foal: half-brother to winners in USA by Marquetry and Aptitude: dam, ran twice in France, out of smart French performer up to 1½m Papago: fairly useful performer: won maiden at Newbury in May, and handicaps at Windsor and Sandown in August: not discredited last 2 starts: stays 1¼m: acts on firm and good to soft going: sold 40,000 gns. *J. Noseda* **89**

PRINCE OF MEDINA 6 ch.g. Fraam 114 – Medina de Rioseco 70 (Puissance 110) [2009 60: p11g^2 p13.3g^3 p12g p12g^5 p12g^2 p16g^6 p11g^4 p12g p16g^4 Mar 2] rangy gelding: modest handicapper: effective at 11f to 2m: acts on polytrack and good to firm going: usually tongue tied. *J. R. Best* **51**

williamhill.com Doonside Cup Stakes, Ayr—the favourite Prince Siegfried is a class apart; Baila Me (No.9) makes it a 1,2 for Godolphin, followed home by Arch Rebel (noseband), the grey Nanton and Dream Lodge

PRINCE OF SORRENTO 2 ch.c. (Mar 27) Doyen (IRE) 132 – Princess Galadriel 74 (Magic Ring (IRE) 115) [2009 p6g³ p7m* Dec 10] first foal: dam 6f/7f winner: fair form: better effort when winning at Kempton by ½ length from Feeling Fragile (pair clear), soon prominent and leading late: will stay 1m. *J. Akehurst* **72**

PRINCE OF THEBES (IRE) 8 b.g. Desert Prince (IRE) 130 – Persian Walk (FR) (Persian Bold 123) [2009 95: p8g³ p7g⁴ 8.3m 8m 8.1f p8g³ 7m⁶ 8.5d⁶ 7m p8g 8.5m p8g 8m 8g p8g⁴ p8m p8g³ p10f Dec 20] good-topped gelding: fairly useful handicapper, better on all-weather: best around 1m: acts on polytrack, firm and good to soft going: tried visored: races prominently. *M. J. Attwater* **83 a90**

PRINCEOFTHEDESERT 3 b.g. Nayef (USA) 129 – Twilight Sonnet 87 (Exit To Nowhere (USA) 122) [2009 10.3s Aug 1] no show when last in maiden at Doncaster: subsequently gelded. *G. Woodward* **–**

PRINCE OF VASA (IRE) 2 b.c. (Apr 10) Kheleyf (USA) 116 – Suzy Street (IRE) 71 (Dancing Dissident (USA) 119) [2009 f6g³ Aug 25] €9,000F, €5,000Y, 55,000 2-y-o: fifth foal: half-brother to fairly useful Irish 2004 2-y-o 6f winner Jenkins Lane (by Revoque) and winner in Greece by Spartacus: dam Irish 2-y-o 6f/6.5f winner: 5/1, 3¼ lengths third to Circumvent in maiden at Southwell, slowly away and headstrong: has left Godolphin. *Saeed bin Suroor* **71**

PRINCE PICASSO 6 b.g. Lomitas 129 – Auspicious 103 (Shirley Heights 130) [2009 –: 10.1m² 8.1m³ f11m³ p10m⁶ Dec 16] lengthy gelding: fairly useful handicapper: should stay 1½m: acts on fibresand and firm going: tried tongue tied: fairly useful hurdler. *R. A. Fahey* **83**

PRINCE PIPPIN (IRE) 3 b.g. King Charlemagne (USA) 120 – Staploy 74 (Deploy 131) [2009 p12m Sep 16] well held in maiden at Kempton: fairly useful juvenile hurdler, successful twice in November. *S. Curran* **–**

PRINCE RHYDDARCH 4 b.g. Josr Algarhoud (IRE) 118 – Nova Zembla (Young Ern 120) [2009 76: 13d⁵ 12.1s 13.1d 16.1d 17.5m f12m Nov 12] close-coupled gelding: modest handicapper: stays 1½m: acts on heavy ground: tried in cheekpieces: races prominently: joined Mrs S. Bradburne. *I. Semple* **64**

PRINCE ROSSI (IRE) 5 b.g. Royal Applause 124 – Miss Rossi (Artaius (USA) 129) [2009 53: p8g* p8g* 9.7d⁵ 8.1g* 8.1g* 8d 8.1m Jul 10] neat gelding: has a quick action: fair performer: won minor event and handicaps at Kempton and Chepstow (2) between January and May: barely stays 1¼m: acts on polytrack, heavy and good to firm going: tried in cheekpieces, visored nowadays: front runner. *A. E. Price* **69**

PRINCE SAMOS (IRE) 7 b.g. Mujadil (USA) 119 – Sabaniya (FR) (Lashkari 128) [2009 81: 8g⁶ 12m⁶ 12d 10m Jul 29] sturdy gelding: fair handicapper: below form after reappearance in 2009: stays 10.6f: acts on polytrack, soft and good to firm going: tried blinkered/visored. *C. A. Mulhall* **68 d**

PRINCE SIEGFRIED (FR) 3 b.g. Royal Applause 124 – Intrum Morshaan (IRE) 95 **120** (Darshaan 133) [2009 110: p8g^3 10g^3 10d* 10m* 10g^2 Oct 31] angular gelding: progressed into a very smart performer, making all in minor event at Newmarket in August and listed race at Ayr (by 3¼ lengths from stable-companion Baila Me) in September: good length second to Laaheb in listed event at Newmarket final start (gelded after): best form at 1¼m: acts on soft and good to firm going. *Saeed bin Suroor*

PRINCESS ALIUSKA 4 b.f. Domedriver (IRE) 128 – Aliuska (IRE) 70 (Fijar Tango **48** (FR) 127) [2009 9.8m^5 10m^2 12g p12g Aug 17] good-bodied filly: half-sister to several winners, including fairly useful 8.5f to 13f winner Altay (by Erins Isle): dam, Irish 5f winner, ran only at 2 yrs: saddle slipped early in bumper: poor maiden. *Mrs S. Lamyman*

PRINCESS CAGLIARI 3 b.f. Efisio 120 – Queenie 82 (Indian Ridge 123) [2009 64: **75** p6g^2 p6g^2 p6g^2 p6g^2 f6d* p6g^6 Apr 1] fair handicapper: won at Southwell in March: stays 7f: raced only on all-weather: sold 5,000 gns in July. *R. Hannon*

PRINCESS CHARLMANE (IRE) 6 b.m. King Charlemagne (USA) 120 – Bint **60** Alreeys (Polish Precedent (USA) 131) [2009 55: f6g^2 f6g^2 f6g f6g 5m 5m 5g* 5m 5d^4 5g^3 5m* 5.1g 6d 5g 5g Oct 6] quite good-topped mare: modest performer: won seller in July and handicap in August, both at Musselburgh: speedy, best at 5f/6f: acts on fibresand, soft and good to firm ground: formerly tongue tied, in cheekpieces nowadays: front runner: none too reliable. *C. J. Teague*

PRINCESS COCOA (IRE) 6 b.m. Desert Sun 120 – Daily Double (FR) (Unfuwain **72** (USA) 131) [2009 86: p10g p9.5g^6 p9.5g^5 Feb 9] sturdy mare: handicapper, just fair form in 2009: effective at 8.6f to 1½m: acts on polytrack and any turf going. *R. A. Fahey*

PRINCESS EMMA 2 b.f. (Mar 22) Fantastic Light (USA) 134 – Rosablanca (IRE) **64** (Sinndar (IRE) 134) [2009 7.5g^3 p7.1g Oct 9] unfurnished filly: first foal: dam once-raced half-sister to smart performers Rolo Tomasi (sprinter) and Eastern Breeze (up to 1½m): green in maidens, better effort when 8½ lengths third to Namecheck at Beverley: will be suited by 1m+. *R. A. Fahey*

PRINCESS FLAME (GER) 7 br.m. Tannenkonig (IRE) 111 – Pacora (GER) (Lagunas) **72** [2009 81: p13g 12d^5 10s 10g^6 12d^6 10m 12g^2 11.7f^4 11.8m^2 10m^6 12v^5 Oct 24] angular mare: fair handicapper: in-and-out form in 2009: stays 1½m: acts on heavy and good to firm ground. *B. G. Powell*

PRINCESS GEE 4 b.f. Reel Buddy (USA) 118 – Queen G (USA) 57 (Matty G (USA) **–** 119) [2009 66: p8.6g p10g f8g Jun 7] workmanlike filly: maiden handicapper: well held in 2009: tried visored. *B. J. McMath*

PRINCESS JANET 3 ch.f. Deportivo 116 – Idolize 92 (Polish Precedent (USA) 131) **–** [2009 –: p7.1g 8d Apr 14] no form. *A. B. Coogan*

PRINCESS LEXI (IRE) 2 ch.f. (Mar 18) Rock of Gibraltar (IRE) 133 – Etaaq (IRE) **63** (Sadler's Wells (USA) 132) [2009 6m^5 5g Oct 6] £19,000Y: big, lengthy filly: fifth living foal: closely related to Irish 1m winner So So Lucky (by Danehill) and half-sister to winner abroad by Nashwan: dam unraced half-sister to useful performers Hiwaya (up to 1m) and Mutawwaj (up to 1½m): encouraging 6 lengths fifth to Plume in maiden at Haydock, late headway: inadequate trip final start: likely to stay 7f/1m. *K. A. Ryan*

PRINCESS LOMI (IRE) 4 b.f. Lomitas 129 – Athlumney Lady 98 (Lycius (USA) **78** 124) [2009 77: p10.7s^6 10g 12s^5 12m p12g^2 p12g p10m f12f^5 Dec 12] leggy filly: fair handicapper: stays 1½m: acts on all-weather, firm and soft ground: consistent. *A. Heffernan, Ireland*

PRINCESS MANDY (IRE) 2 gr.f. (Jan 31) Desert Style (IRE) 121 – Lady Fabiola **57** (USA) (Open Forum (USA)) [2009 p6g 6s^4 p7.1g^6 p7.1m^3 Nov 28] £25,000Y: first foal: dam, Italian 5f winner (including at 2 yrs), out of smart French performer up to 1¼m Sacre Look: modest maiden: stays 7f: acts on polytrack. *K. A. Ryan*

PRINCESS NEENEE (IRE) 2 b.f. (Jan 15) King's Best (USA) 132 – Precedence **–** (IRE) 88 (Polish Precedent (USA) 131) [2009 7d 8d 6m Sep 25] €20,000Y: lengthy filly: sixth foal: half-sister to fairly useful performer up to 1½m Wingman (by In The Wings), 1m winner at 2 yrs, and 9f winner Charlie Tango (by Desert Prince): dam Irish maiden who stayed 9f: well beaten in maidens: tried tongue tied. *Paul Green*

PRINCESS OF AENEAS (IRE) 6 b.m. Beckett (IRE) 116 – Romangoddess (IRE) **–** (Rhoman Rule (USA)) [2009 –: 10g 12m Jul 1] no form since 2007, including over hurdles: usually wears cheekpieces. *A. G. Foster*

PRINCESS PIVOTAL 4 gr.f. Pivotal 124 – Santa Sophia (IRE) 106 (Linamix (FR) 127) [2009 p7g Oct 26] 80,000Y: small filly: third foal: dam 1¼m/1½m winner: modest form when eighth in maiden at Lingfield, only outing: likely to stay 1m+. *G. A. Butler* **63**

PRINCESS PODGE 2 b.f. (Jan 7) Desert Sun 120 – Medici Princess (Medicean 128) [2009 6g May 20] 1,000F: first foal: dam, unraced, out of half-sister to US Grade 1 9f winner Jovial: 100/1, down the field in maiden at Goodwood, slowly away. *M. D. I. Usher* **–**

PRINCESS RAINBOW (FR) 4 b.f. Raintrap 123 – Chausseneige (FR) (Mad Captain 117) [2009 77: 10g 10.4v* 10.4g³ 11.9f² 14s³ 16.2g⁶ 15.8v² Sep 4] lengthy filly: fairly useful handicapper: won at Haydock in May: good efforts after when placed: stays 2m: acts on any turf going. *Jennie Candlish* **81**

PRINCESS REBECCA 3 ch.f. Compton Place 125 – Sunley Stars (Sallust 134) [2009 47: 7m f6g May 18] maiden: no form in 2009. *H. J. Collingridge* **–**

PRINCESS ROSE ANNE (IRE) 4 ch.f. Danehill Dancer (IRE) 117 – Hawksleys Jill (Mujtahid (USA) 118) [2009 79: p7g⁵ p7g a4s³ a4s* p6g⁴ 5.7g* 5g* 5g 5m 5f³ 5.7f⁵ 5m⁶ a5f* Dec 4] smallish filly: fairly useful performer: won minor event at Saint Moritz in February, handicaps at Bath and Folkestone (made all) in April, and, after sold from J. R. Best 12,000 gns and off over 5 months, Jebel Ali in December: stays 7f, effective at shorter: acts on polytrack/dirt (probably on fibresand) and firm going: tried in cheekpieces. *M. Ramadan, UAE* **84**

PRINCESS SEREN 2 b.f. (Mar 31) King's Best (USA) 132 – Gold Field (IRE) (Unfuwain (USA) 131) [2009 6g Jun 19] 20,000F: fourth foal: dam useful French 10.5f to 12.5f winner: 20/1 and green, tailed-off last in maiden at Goodwood: will need further than 6f. *B. R. Millman* **–**

PRINCESS SHAMAL 2 b.f. (Mar 9) Kheleyf (USA) 116 – Gentle Dame 75 (Kris 135) [2009 5g 6g p5g⁶ 5f⁵ 5.2d⁵ f5g f5g⁵ 6g f6g⁵ p7m⁶ Dec 16] £12,000Y: sixth foal: half-sister to 2 winners, including 1m winner Game Dame (by Nashwan): dam, 1¼m winner, out of half-sister to Oaks winner Diminuendo: modest maiden: stays 6f: acts on fibresand, firm and good to soft going: probably not straightforward. *J. R. Jenkins* **55**

PRINCESS SHIRL 5 b.m. Shahrastani (USA) 135 – Shirl 52 (Shirley Heights 130) [2009 f12f Nov 24] half-sister to 6f winner Waff's Folly (by Handsome Sailor): dam 1½m winner: no form in bumpers/hurdles: tailed off in maiden on Flat debut. *A. D. Brown* **–**

PRINCESS SORAYA 3 ch.f. Compton Place 125 – Eurolink Cafe (Grand Lodge (USA) 125) [2009 –: 8s 6.1f 9.9g May 20] well held in maidens: refused to enter stall intended final outing (later in May). *R. Dickin* **–**

PRINCESS TAYLOR 5 ch.m. Singspiel (IRE) 133 – Tapas En Bal (FR) (Mille Balles (FR) 124) [2009 96: 10.3m⁵ 10g² 10.4g³ 11.9g⁵ 10.9d² 12g² 14d⁴ 12m⁵ 14.6m⁵ 12m⁴ p13g⁴ p12m Nov 29] leggy mare: useful performer: held form well in 2009, best efforts when runner-up in listed events at Warwick (went down by ½ length to Cassique Lady) and Newmarket (beaten 3 lengths by Barshiba) fifth/sixth starts: stays 1¾m: acts on polytrack, soft and good to firm going: tried in cheekpieces: effective with or without tongue tie: reliable: sold 90,000 gns, joined D. Weld in Ireland. *M. Botti* **103**

PRINCESS TEDDY (IRE) 6 b.m. Sayarshan (FR) 117 – Bajan Girl (IRE) (Pips Pride 117) [2009 50: p7g p8g Feb 12] workmanlike mare: maiden handicapper: just poor in 2009: stays 7f: acts on polytrack, good to firm and good to soft going: blinkered nowadays. *Edgar Byrne* **42**

PRINCESS VALERINA 5 ch.m. Beat Hollow 126 – Heart So Blue (Dilum (USA) 115) [2009 83: p6g* p6g⁴ p6g⁵ p6g² p5.1g⁵ p6g* 6.1m 6v 6m p6g 6m 6g⁴ p6g⁶ p6m p6g p6m⁶ Dec 30] tall mare: fairly useful handicapper: won at Wolverhampton in January and April: effective at 6f/7f: acts on polytrack, soft and good to firm ground: often slowly away. *D. Haydn Jones* **91**

PRINCESS ZHUKOVA (IRE) 4 b.f. Terroir (IRE) 110 – Miss Bussell 65 (Sabrehill (USA) 120) [2009 –: p8.6g⁵ p8.6g f6g⁶ p6g f8f Dec 17] maiden: modest form only on third start. *M. Wellings* **50**

PRINCESS ZOHRA 3 b.f. Royal Applause 124 – Desert Royalty (IRE) 96 (Alhaarth (IRE) 126) [2009 61p: p7.1g* p8g⁶ p6g Jun 4] fair form: best effort when winning maiden at Wolverhampton in February: should stay 1m: raced only on polytrack: sold 5,500 gns. *E. A. L. Dunlop* **67**

PRINCE VALENTINE 8 b.g. My Best Valentine 122 – Affaire de Coeur 55 (Imperial Fling (USA) 116) [2009 61, a52: 8m 6m 8f³ 8f⁶ 10d⁴ p8m³ p7m Dec 30] lengthy gelding: modest handicapper: best at 1m: acts on polytrack and any turf going: tried tongue tied/blinkered, wears cheekpieces: held up. *G. L. Moore* **56**

PRINCE YARRAMAN (IRE) 2 b.c. (Apr 28) Chineur (FR) 123 – Church Mice (IRE) 82 (Petardia 113) [2009 p7m^5 f7f^2 p8f^2 f8d^3 Dec 29] modest form in maidens: stays 1m: raced only on all-weather. *J. A. Osborne* **64**

PRINCE ZAFONIC 6 ch.g. Zafonic (USA) 130 – Kite Mark 58 (Mark of Esteem (IRE) 137) [2009 78: 14.1m^5 11.8m^5 Sep 1] big, strong gelding: fair maiden handicapper: modest/ungenuine hurdler for O. Sherwood in first half of 2009: stays 2m: acts on polytrack, firm and soft going: formerly tongue tied. *C. A. Dwyer* **69 §**

PRINCIPAL ROLE (USA) 2 b.f. (Feb 26) Empire Maker (USA) 129 – Interim 117 (Sadler's Wells (USA) 132) [2009 8g* Oct 20] half-sister to several winners, including very smart 6f (at 2 yrs) to 1¾m (in USA) winner Midships (by Mizzen Mast) and 1¼m/1½m winner Staging Post (by Pleasant Colony), later smart up to 1¾m in USA: dam 1m to 1½m (US Grade 2) winner: 5/1, big impression when winning maiden at Yarmouth by head from Tomodachi, missing break (lost around 5 lengths) before cruising into contention and leading final 1f: open to considerable improvement, and is one to follow. *H. R. A. Cecil* **94 P**

PRINT (IRE) 3 b.c. Exceed And Excel (AUS) 126 – Hariya (IRE) 99 (Shernazar 131) [2009 68p: 6m 6.1g May 19] big colt: has scope: fair maiden: should be suited by 7f/1m. *M. R. Channon* **66**

PRITI FABULOUS (IRE) 4 b.f. Invincible Spirit (IRE) 121 – Flying Diva 100 (Chief Singer 131) [2009 92: 8m 8m^4 p7g f5m p5g p5m^6 p5m^6 Dec 30] well-made filly: fairly useful handicapper: below best in 2009, leaving W. Haggas after third start: stays 1m: acts on polytrack and good to firm ground. *A. J. McCabe* **82**

PRIVATE EQUITY (IRE) 3 b.f. Haafhd 129 – Profit Alert (IRE) 97 (Alzao (USA) 117) [2009 –: 8m^6 10m^4 p12g* p13.9g* p12f^5 Dec 13] rangy filly: fair form: upped in trip, much improved when winning handicaps at Kempton and Wolverhampton in November: stays 1¾m: acts on polytrack. *W. Jarvis* **65**

PRIVATE OLLEY 2 ch.c. (Feb 22) Exceed And Excel (AUS) 126 – My Daisychain 79 (Hector Protector (USA) 124) [2009 5f p6g 6d Aug 2] good-topped colt: well held in maidens (said to have finished lame second start). *J. Akehurst* **–**

PRIVATE PASSION (IRE) 3 b.g. Captain Rio 122 – Victoria's Secret (IRE) 70 (Law Society (USA) 130) [2009 61?: p6g* p7g^3 p7g^4 p6g^3 p7.1g 7.1m f7g 6m^2 6m 6m^6 7m Aug 23] good-topped gelding: modest handicapper: won at Kempton in February: effective at 6f/7f: acts on polytrack and good to firm going. *Pat Eddery* **58**

PRIVATE SOLDIER 6 gr.g. Dansili 127 – Etienne Lady (IRE) 67 (Imperial Frontier (USA) 112) [2009 58: 8f^6 8.1g p8.6g^4 Oct 15] modest handicapper: trained until before final start by N. Vaughan: stays easy 9.5f: form only on polytrack. *Tom Dascombe* **–** **a50**

PRIVATE STORY (USA) 2 b.c. (Mar 13) Yes It's True (USA) 116 – Said Privately (USA) (Private Account (USA)) [2009 7.1g* 8m^2 8g 10g^4 Oct 31] $85,000F, €130,000Y: well-made colt: half-brother to several winners in USA: dam US 1m/1¼m winner: fairly useful performer: won maiden at Sandown (by ½ length from Valiant Knight) in August: best effort when ¾-length second to Ameer in minor event at Newbury: should be suited by 1¼m: ran in snatches final start. *R. Hannon* **94**

PRIVY SPEECH (IRE) 2 ch.f. (Apr 10) El Corredor (USA) 123 – Privileged Speech (USA) (General Assembly (USA)) [2009 f8g^3 Dec 18] 21,000F, 27,000Y: half-sister to several winners in North America, notably Canadian 2002 2-y-o 6f to 8.5f (Grade 2) winner Brusque (by Canaveral): dam US 1m/8.5f winner: 8/1, 2½ lengths third to Lily Lily in maiden at Southwell, green early on and caught wide: capable of better. *Rae Guest* **56 p**

PRIX MASQUE (IRE) 5 b.g. Iron Mask (USA) 117 – Prima Marta (Primo Dominie 121) [2009 55: p7g p8g p8g p10g Feb 18] strong, close-coupled gelding: has quick action: poor maiden: stays 1m: acts on polytrack: tried tongue tied: held up: signs of temperament. *Christian Wroe* **46**

PRIZE FIGHTER (IRE) 7 b.g. Desert Sun 120 – Papal (Selkirk (USA) 129) [2009 79d: 7m Apr 18] tall gelding: regressive handicapper: often blinkered: joined Miss L. Siddall. *A. Berry* **–**

PRIZEFIGHTING (USA) 2 ch.c. (Apr 1) Smart Strike (CAN) 121 – Allencat (USA) (Storm Cat (USA)) [2009 p7m* 8s^5 Nov 1] $500,000Y: second foal: dam unraced daughter of smart US Grade 1 9f winner Pharma, herself out of high-class sprinter Committed: 14/1 and green, highly promising when winning maiden at Kempton in October by ¾ length from Silk Street, making up 5 or 6 lengths under hand riding final 1f: much better form when 7¼ lengths fifth to Jan Vermeer in Criterium International at Saint-Cloud 6 days later: stays 1m: will make a smart performer at least. *J. H. M. Gosden* **104 p**

At The Races Curragh Cup, the Curragh—Profound Beauty (noseband) claims the first leg of a summer hat-trick with a hard-fought success over Alandi (right) and the grey Yankee Doodle

PRIZE POINT 3 ch.g. Bahamian Bounty 116 – Golden Symbol 54 (Wolfhound (USA) 126) [2009 79p: 8g^3 6g^4 May 26] good-topped gelding: has scope: fair form: should prove best at 5f/6f: claimed £12,000, joined J. Boyle. *K. A. Ryan* **75**

PROCLAIM 3 b.c. Noverre (USA) 125 – Pescara (IRE) 108 (Common Grounds 118) [2009 82: p7g^6 6m* 6m* 6m^4 6f* 6g 6m 6g 7g^3 6g 6m 6g^3 7m^3 Sep 26] angular colt: useful performer: progressed well early in 2009, winning handicaps at Doncaster and Ripon in April, and minor event Doncaster (beat Akhenaten ¾ length) in May: best effort after when creditable 1¼ lengths equal-third to Advanced in Challenge Cup (Handicap) at Ascot final start: effective at 6f/7f: acts on polytrack and firm going: blinkered/visored last 5 starts: races up with pace: has joined Godolphin. *M. Johnston* **102**

PROFESSOR BOLLINI (IRE) 2 b.c. (Apr 10) Bertolini (USA) 125 – Nofa's Magic (IRE) 92 (Rainbow Quest (USA) 134) [2009 p6g p7g Oct 14] good-topped colt: well held in maidens. *H. J. L. Dunlop* **–**

PROFESSOR JOHN (IRE) 2 b.g. (Apr 10) Haafhd 129 – Dancing Flower (IRE) 96 (Compton Place 125) [2009 6g^6 6g* 7d 7m^3 p7g^6 8m^6 7d 7v Nov 3] €57,000F, €45,000Y, 20,000 2-y-o: sturdy gelding: second foal: half-brother to German/French 7f/1m winner De La Vista (by Big Shuffle): dam German 2-y-o 5f to 7f winner: fair performer: won maiden at Brighton in July: below form in nurseries last 3 starts (gelded after): should be suited by 1m+: acts on polytrack and good to firm ground, seems unsuited by softer than good. *M. L. W. Bell* **79**

PROFESSOR MALONE 4 ch.g. Ishiguru (USA) 114 – Molly Malone 60 (Formidable (USA) 125) [2009 53?: 5.7m p6m p8m Oct 12] modest maiden: stays 6f: in cheekpieces last 2 starts. *M. S. Tuck* **53 ?**

PROFESSOR TWINKLE 5 ch.h. Dr Fong (USA) 128 – Shining High 90 (Shirley Heights 130) [2009 –: p7.1g Jan 25] compact horse: handicapper: very lightly raced and no form since 2007: tried visored/blinkered. *I. W. McInnes* **–**

PROFICIENCY 4 gr.f. El Prado (IRE) 119 – Talent Quest (IRE) (Rainbow Quest (USA) 134) [2009 67: 9.9g 10.2g^6 10.2m^3 10v* 12g Jul 31] workmanlike filly: fair handicapper: won at Pontefract in July: should be suited by 1½m: acts on heavy and good to firm ground: blinkered last 3 starts: sold £5,000, joined Mrs S. C. Bradburne. *T. D. Walford* **68**

PROFIT'S REALITY (IRE) 7 br.g. Key of Luck (USA) 126 – Teacher Preacher (IRE) 37 (Taufan (USA) 119) [2009 98: p12g^3 p12.2g p11g^6 p12g^3 f12d* p16g 12g f11g^4 12f^4 12g^5 14m^5 12g^6 f12f* f11g^2 Dec 22] big gelding: fairly useful handicapper: won at Southwell in February and December: stays 1½m: acts on all-weather, good to firm and good to soft ground: tried blinkered/in cheekpieces/tongue tied. *M. J. Attwater* **88**

PROFLIGATE (IRE) 2 b.f. (Apr 19) Soviet Star (USA) 128 – Profit Alert (IRE) 97 (Alzao (USA) 117) [2009 7g Oct 31] good-topped filly: seventh foal: half-sister to 3-y-o Private Equity and fairly useful 1¼m winner Pound Sign (by Singspiel): dam, Irish 7f and 11f winner, half-sister to dam of Prix de l'Opera winner Kinnaird: 100/1, always behind in maiden at Newmarket: bred to be suited by 1¼m+. *W. Jarvis* –

PROFOUND BEAUTY (IRE) 5 b.m. Danehill (USA) 126 – Diamond Trim (IRE) 111 (Highest Honor (FR) 124) [2009 115: 14d* 14d* 12g* 14s⁴ Sep 12] well-made mare: smart performer: better than ever in 2009, winning At The Races Curragh Cup (by neck from Alandi) in June, listed race at Leopardstown (by ¾ length from Yankee Doodle) in July and Ballyroan Stakes on same course (not hard pressed to beat Mourayan 1¼ lengths) in August: very laboured effort when well-held fourth in Irish St Leger at the Curragh final start: effective at 1½m to 2m: acts on heavy and good to firm ground: game. *D. K. Weld, Ireland* **118**

PROGRESS (IRE) 2 br.f. (Feb 4) Green Desert (USA) 127 – Mille (Dubai Millennium 140) [2009 6m⁵ Oct 16] €50,000Y: small filly: first foal: dam unraced half-sister to US Grade 1 1¾m winner Passinetti out of half-sister to dam of Bosra Sham: 14/1 and very green, 7¾ lengths fifth to Inler in maiden at Newmarket, slowly away and soon ridden: will do better. *J. Noseda* **68 p**

PROHIBIT 4 b.g. Oasis Dream 129 – Well Warned 104 (Warning 136) [2009 114: 6m⁶ 6f 6m⁵ 6d 6m² Sep 26] strong, sturdy gelding: just useful performer in 2009: best effort when short-head second to Hitchens in handicap at Haydock: also shaped well when fifth of 26 to High Standing in Wokingham Stakes (Handicap) at Royal Ascot, second home on stand side: stays 6f: acts on polytrack, firm and good to soft going: tried blinkered: often looks awkward: seems best fresh: sold 85,000 gns, joined R. Cowell. *J. H. M. Gosden* **108**

PROHIBITION (IRE) 3 b.c. Danehill Dancer (IRE) 117 – Crumpetsfortea (IRE) (Henbit (USA) 130) [2009 95p: p9.5g Dec 3] close-coupled colt: fairly useful winner at 2 yrs: odds on, pulled too hard in handicap at Wolverhampton sole outing in 2009: stays 8.3f: acts on heavy ground. *W. J. Haggas* –

PROM 3 b.f. Lujain (USA) 119 – Ball Gown 98 (Jalmood (USA) 126) [2009 49: 9.8m Jul 6] poor form. *M. Brittain* –

PROMISED GOLD 4 ch.g. Bahamian Bounty 116 – Delphic Way 63 (Warning 136) [2009 –: 17.2d May 18] workmanlike gelding: little solid form: tried in cheekpieces. *J. A. Geake* –

PROMISE MAKER (USA) 4 b.g. Empire Maker (USA) 129 – Sunday Bazaar (USA) (Nureyev (USA) 131) [2009 60: 12m* 12.6d 12m² 12d² 12g 15.8d² 15.8v* 17.1m⁵ Sep 17] lengthy, deep-girthed gelding: fair handicapper: won at Ripon (selling event) in June and Catterick in September: stays 2m: acts on heavy and good to firm ground: front runner/races prominently: sold £7,800. *T. D. Walford* **77**

PROMPTER 2 b.c. (Apr 6) Motivator 131 – Penny Cross 99 (Efisio 120) [2009 7g² 7g* 7.1g⁶ 8g² Oct 10] 70,000Y: lengthy, attractive colt: second foal: half-brother to 3-y-o Quinsman: dam, 7f to 8.5f winner, half-sister to smart 7f/1m performer Priors Lodge: quickly made into useful performer: won maiden at Chester in August by 2 lengths from Tominator: excellent head second to Morana in Autumn Stakes at Ascot final start, dictating: likely to stay 1¼m: open to further progress. *M. L. W. Bell* **107 p**

PROPER LITTLEMADAM 2 b.f. (Apr 21) Statue of Liberty (USA) 115 – Aly McBe (USA) (Alydeed (CAN) 120) [2009 6g⁴ 6m⁴ 7g p8g p7f⁶ p8m Oct 12] close-coupled filly: fourth foal: closely related to 5-y-o Music Box Express: dam unraced: fourth in maidens at Doncaster: below form after (seemed amiss third start, unseated early on fourth): may prove best at 5f/6f. *M. Botti* **64**

PROPONENT (IRE) 5 b.g. Peintre Celebre (USA) 137 – Pont Audemer (USA) 108 (Chief's Crown (USA)) [2009 105: 8s 9m 8.1m⁴ 10g³ 10m² 10m 9m⁶ 8m* Oct 1] tall, close-coupled gelding: useful handicapper: tongue tied, back to very best when winning at Newmarket in October by ¾ length from Legislate: effective at 1m, barely stays 1½m: acts on firm and soft ground. *R. Charlton* **107**

PROPORTIONAL 3 b.f. Beat Hollow 126 – Minority 106 (Generous (IRE) 139) [2009 115p: 8g³ 8m⁴ 10g² 10m⁴ 8g² Sep 24] big, strong filly: smart performer: won twice at 2 yrs, notably Prix Marcel Boussac at Longchamp: creditable efforts in 2009 when 2¾ lengths fourth to Elusive Wave in Poule d'Essai des Pouliches at Longchamp second start and short-head second to Board Meeting in Prix de Psyche at Deauville nearly 3 months later: below best in Prix de la Nonette at Deauville and listed race at Saint-Cloud last 2 starts: should have stayed 1½m: acted on good to firm ground: on edge before final 2-y-o start: visits Dansili. *Mme C. Head-Maarek, France* **115**

PUBLIC IMAGE 3 b.f. Bahamian Bounty 116 – Shouting The Odds (IRE) 91 (Victory Note (USA) 120) [2009 7m 6m Aug 8] 5,500Y: angular filly: second foal: dam, 2-y-o 5f winner, half-sister to smart sprinter Lady Dominatrix: well beaten in maidens. *Jamie Poulton* –

PUBLIC SERVICE (IRE) 2 ch.g. (Jan 10) Danehill Dancer (IRE) 117 – Sintra (IRE) (Kris 135) [2009 6f 6m 6s 7f[2] p7.1g p6f[6] Oct 14] 52,000F, €80,000Y: unfurnished gelding: first foal: dam French 8.5f winner: fair maiden: stays 7f: acts on polytrack and firm ground: said to have had breathing problem penultimate start: sold 8,000 gns, sent to Denmark. *B. J. Meehan* **72**

PUFF (IRE) 2 b.f. (Apr 23) Camacho 118 – Kelsey Rose 97 (Most Welcome 131) [2009 p6m* 6m[4] 5m[2] 6m[4] 6g[2] Oct 30] 95,000 2-y-o: attractive filly: fourth foal: closely related to 3-y-o Golden Rosie: dam 2-y-o 5f winner (stayed 1m): useful performer: won maiden at Lingfield in July by length from Piccadilly Filly: in frame after, best effort when 3¾ lengths fourth to Special Duty in Cheveley Park Stakes at Newmarket fourth outing: length second to Queen's Grace in listed race on same course final start: likely to stay 7f: acts on polytrack and good to firm ground. *R. M. Beckett* **106**

PUITIN 4 b.g. Red Ransom (USA) – Pagoda (FR) (Sadler's Wells (USA) 132) [2009 p8f Dec 20] well held in bumper/maiden. *M. Madgwick* –

PULLYOURFINGEROUT (IRE) 2 b.c. (Mar 27) Indian Haven 119 – Sandomierz (IRE) 76 (Nordico (USA)) [2009 5m 5.2s 5m[4] 6m[2] 6g[4] 6m[5] 7g[6] 7g 7g* 8.3d[2] Oct 15] €2,700F, £14,000Y: good-topped colt: fifth foal: dam Irish 5f winner: fair performer: won nursery at Leicester in September: stays 8.3f: acts on good to firm and good to soft ground. *B. G. Powell* **79**

PUMPKIN 3 ch.f. Pivotal 124 – Gallivant 93 (Danehill (USA) 126) [2009 60p: 7m[2] 6s* p6g* 6g[2] 6g Jul 31] unfurnished filly: fairly useful form: won maiden at Yarmouth in June and handicap at Kempton in July: good second in handicap at Newmarket next time: raced only at 6f/7f: acts on polytrack, soft and good to firm ground. *Sir Michael Stoute* **90**

PUNCH DRUNK 3 b.f. Beat Hollow 126 – Bebe de Cham 75 (Tragic Role (USA)) [2009 77: 9.9m p8.6g[3] p8.6g 10.3m[4] 10.3d[2] 10.4v[2] 10.2g[2] 12v[6] 10.3m[5] 12m 10.3g[5] Oct 24] angular filly: fair handicapper: stays 10.4f: acts on polytrack, heavy and good to firm going: in cheekpieces 5 of last 6 starts: quirky (usually hangs left). *J. G. Given* **77**

PUNCHING 5 b.g. Kyllachy 129 – Candescent (Machiavellian (USA) 123) [2009 78: p5.1g p5m[4] p6g[5] f6g* f5g[4] f6g[3] f5m[3] 7m f7g* 7.1g[3] 7s[5] 6.1g 6m 5m p6g p6g p5.1g[5] p5m f6g* p6g[3] Nov 21] good-topped, quite attractive gelding: fair handicapper, better on all-weather: won at Southwell in January, April and November: effective at 5f to 7f: acts on all-weather and firm ground: tried blinkered/visored/tongue tied. *C. R. Dore* **67 a79**

PUNTA GALERA (IRE) 6 br.g. Zafonic (USA) 130 – Kobalt Sea (FR) (Akarad (FR) 130) [2009 71: p12g p8.6g 12g 12d 5.9d Aug 19] big, strong, close-coupled gelding: handicapper: well held in 2009: tried in headgear. *Paul Green* –

PURE CRYSTAL 3 ch.f. Dubai Destination (USA) 127 – Crystal Flute (Lycius (USA) 124) [2009 55: p10g 12.1m[2] 14.1m[5] 14.1s[5] 16v p12m[3] p13.9g[5] Nov 27] workmanlike filly: modest maiden handicapper: should stay beyond 1¾m: acts on polytrack, soft and good to firm going: tried blinkered: modest form over hurdles. *M. G. Quinlan* **58**

PURE HEIR (USA) 3 b.f. Perfect Soul (IRE) 122 – Regal Baby (USA) (Northern Baby (CAN) 127) [2009 7d[4] 7s 7m[6] 7m Sep 15] $22,000Y: tall filly: half-sister to numerous winners, including useful 2000 2-y-o 6f winner Dim Sums (by Repriced) and 8-y-o Imperial Echo: dam US maiden: modest maiden: best effort on debut. *T. D. Barron* **59 d**

PURELY BY CHANCE 4 b.f. Galileo (IRE) 134 – Sioux Chef 78 (Be My Chief (USA) 122) [2009 65: p16g* p16.5g[6] p13.9g Dec 14] rather leggy filly: modest handicapper: won at Kempton in November: stays 2m: acts on polytrack, soft and good to firm going: usually visored/blinkered. *J. Pearce* **59**

PURE NOSTALGIA (IRE) 2 ch.f. (May 7) Choisir (AUS) 126 – Montmartre (IRE) 98 (Grand Lodge (USA) 125) [2009 6m[4] 6g[2] 6m 6v* 6s[4] 7g[4] Oct 6] workmanlike filly: second foal: dam, 7f (at 2 yrs) to 1½m winner, half-sister to smart miler Rebel Rebel: modest performer: dead-heated in seller at Ripon in July: stays 7f: acts on heavy and good to firm going. *J. Howard Johnson* **61**

PURE POETRY (IRE) 3 b.g. Tagula (IRE) 116 – Express Logic (Air Express (IRE) 125) [2009 102: p8g* 8m[3] 8m 8m[2] 8m[6] 8d[3] 10m 10m[5] Aug 29] good-topped gelding: has a quick action: smart performer: won listed race at Kempton in April by head from Shampagne: good placed efforts after, in Craven Stakes at Newmarket (3½ lengths third **110**

to Delegator) and listed races at Goodwood (beaten neck by Premio Loco on first occasion and ¾ length when third to Zacinto on second one): also ran well when seventh to Sea The Stars in 2000 Guineas at Newmarket on third outing: barely stays easy 1¼m: acts on polytrack, good to firm and good to soft going: reliable: gelded, then sent to Hong Kong, where renamed Cheerful Delights. *R. Hannon*

PURE RHYTHM 3 b.f. Oasis Dream 129 – Degree 81 (Warning 136) [2009 53p: 6.1m³ 6m* Jun 13] sturdy filly: modest form: won handicap at Leicester in June: stays 6f: raced only on polytrack and good to firm going: tongue tied in 2009. *S. C. Williams* **62 +**

PURISSIMA (USA) 3 b.f. Fusaichi Pegasus (USA) 130 – Willstar (USA) (Nureyev (USA) 131) [2009 88p: 7g Jul 29] lengthy filly: fairly useful form: favourite, repeatedly blocked in run in minor event at Goodwood sole start in 2009: should have stayed 7f: visits Dansili. *Sir Michael Stoute* **88**

PURPLE GALLERY (IRE) 2 b.c. (Mar 6) Whipper (USA) 126 – Daftara (IRE) (Caerleon (USA) 132) [2009 p6m p7m Dec 16] 42,000F, 5,000Y, 24,000 2-y-o: sixth foal: half-brother to Irish 4-y-o Dahindar and Irish 7-y-o Dafarabad: dam unraced daughter of very smart sprinter Dafayna, herself half-sister to 2000 Guineas winner Doyoun: much better effort in maidens at Lingfield when seventh latter start: will continue to progress. *J. S. Moore* **57 p**

PURPLE HEART (IRE) 2 b.c. (Apr 4) Sadler's Wells (USA) 132 – Brigid (USA) (Irish River (FR) 131) [2009 7s³ 7g³ 7.5v⁴ 7m² p8g 8d* Oct 21] brother to 3 winners, including Fillies' Mile winner Listen and Moyglare Stud Stakes winner Sequoyah (stayed 1½m, dam of top-class Henrythenavigator), and half-brother to useful Irish 6f winner Oyster Catcher (by Bluebird): dam, French 1m winner, sister to dam of Irish 2000 Guineas winner Saffron Walden (by Sadler's Wells) and high-class sprinter/miler Dolphin Street: fairly useful performer: blinkered, best effort when winning nursery at Navan by ¾ length from Captains Dilemma: may prove best at 1m/1¼m: acts on good to soft going: carries head high. *A. P. O'Brien, Ireland* **94**

PURPLE MOON (IRE) 6 ch.g. Galileo (IRE) 134 – Vanishing Prairie (USA) 93 (Alysheba (USA)) [2009 118: 12m⁴ 12g³ Mar 28] tall, quite good-topped gelding: good walker and a fluent mover: very smart performer: better effort at Nad Al Sheba in 2009 when excellent close third to Eastern Anthem and Spanish Moon in Dubai Sheema Classic, handily placed throughout and rallying: ideally needs good test at 1½m and stays 2m: acts on firm and soft ground: has worn ear plugs in preliminaries. *L. M. Cumani* **123**

PURSESTRINGS 2 b.f. (Mar 15) Red Ransom (USA) – New Assembly (IRE) 99 (Machiavellian (USA) 123) [2009 p8m p8m⁴ Dec 4] fifth foal: half-sister to several winners, including 3-y-o Instalment and fairly useful 1¼m winner Regent's Park (by Green Desert): dam, 9f (in USA) to 1½m winner, sister to very smart 1m/1¼m performer Right Approach: better effort in maidens when 8 lengths fourth to Gifted Apakay at Lingfield: will stay 1¼m+: should improve again. *R. Charlton* **55 p**

PURSUIT OF GLORY (IRE) 3 b.f. Fusaichi Pegasus (USA) 130 – Sophisticat (USA) 117 (Storm Cat (USA)) [2009 108: 8f 6m 6.5f⁵ a8.5f⁶ Nov 28] leggy filly: useful at 2 yrs: below that form in 2009, in 1000 Guineas at Newmarket (10 lengths eighth to Ghanaati) and Ballyogan Stakes at Leopardstown first 2 starts (left D. Wachman in Ireland and off 4½ months after): should stay 1m: acts on polytrack and good to firm going. *E. Harty, USA* **93**

PURSUIT OF GOLD 2 b.f. (Mar 7) Pastoral Pursuits 127 – Sheer Gold (USA) (Cutlass (USA)) [2009 5f 5.1f⁶ 5g⁵ p6g⁶ p6f 6g⁶ p7g Nov 25] rather leggy filly: half-sister to several winners, including smart 5f/6f winner (including in UAE) San Salvador (by Dayjur): dam US 4.5f (at 2 yrs) to 9f winner: modest maiden: stays 6f: best efforts on good ground. *J. R. Best* **61**

PURSUIT OF PURPOSE 3 b.f. Dansili 127 – Sinead (USA) (Irish River (FR) 131) [2009 –: p8g 9.7d p10g 10f⁴ p12g⁵ Oct 2] poor maiden: probably stays 1½m: tried blinkered. *G. L. Moore* **45**

PURUS (IRE) 7 b.g. Night Shift (USA) – Pariana (USA) (Bering 136) [2009 91: p7g² p7g⁴ 7m² 7f³ 7.1d 7m 8m 7m⁶ 7m 7d p7m p8m Nov 29] close-coupled gelding: fairly useful handicapper: below form after fourth outing: best at 7f: acts on polytrack, firm and soft going: tried in tongue tie/cheekpieces/blinkers. *R. A. Teal* **87 d**

PUSEY STREET LADY 5 b.m. Averti (IRE) 117 – Pusey Street Girl 87 (Gildoran 123) [2009 102: 6m² 5.1g⁶ 6v² 6d³ 6m⁵ 6g 6m⁵ 6m 6m Oct 16] rather leggy mare: useful performer: best efforts in 2009 when placed in listed races at Doncaster and Haydock and Chipchase Stakes at Newcastle (1¾ lengths third to Knot In Wood): raced mainly at 6f: acts on polytrack, heavy and good to firm going. *J. Gallagher* **103**

PUSH ME (IRE) 2 gr.f. (Jan 17) Verglas (IRE) 118 – Gilda Lilly (USA) 80 (War Chant **65**
(USA) 126) [2009 p7.1g* 7m^6 p7.1g^2 f8f^5 f7g^4 Dec 18] €16,000F, €8,500Y: first foal: dam Irish 2-y-o 7f winner: fair performer: won seller at Wolverhampton (for M. Tuck) in September: left John Quinn in Ireland, good fourth in nursery at Southwell final outing: stays 7f: acts on all-weather. *A. J. McCabe*

PUTERI (IRE) 2 b.f. (May 4) One Cool Cat (USA) 123 – London Pride (USA) 106 **65 +**
(Lear Fan (USA) 130) [2009 7d 7.6d^3 p8g^5 f8g^4 Dec 18] neat filly: half-sister to 3 winners, including 11f winner Bukit Fraser and 1999 2-y-o 7f winner Pekan's Pride (both by Sri Pekan): dam 1m winner: fair form in maidens: likely to stay 1¼m. *M. A. Jarvis*

PUTRA LAJU (IRE) 5 b.h. Trans Island 119 – El Corazon (IRE) (Mujadil (USA) 119) **–**
[2009 52, a73: p8g^3 p8.6g^6 Jan 19] compact horse: modest performer, better on all- **a56**
weather: stays 8.6f: acts on polytrack: has worn cheekpieces/visor: waited with: sold 2,000 gns in February. *J. W. Hills*

PUTRA ONE (IRE) 3 b.g. Danehill Dancer (IRE) 117 – Veronica Cooper (IRE) 86 **86**
(Kahyasi 130) [2009 70p: 8d^2 10g^3 12m* p12f^4 p10m^3 Oct 7] good-topped gelding: fairly useful performer: won maiden at Newbury in July: good efforts in frame in handicaps after: stays 1½m: acts on polytrack, good to firm and good to soft going. *M. A. Jarvis*

PUY D'ARNAC (FR) 6 b.g. Acteur Francais (USA) 118 – Chaumeil (FR) (Mad **83**
Captain 117) [2009 86: f12g^4 f14g 13g^4 14v^4 17.1g^4 15.8g^4 14s^5 14g^6 14s* 12v* 16.1d^3 14.6g^6 15v^3 Oct 31] close-coupled gelding: unimpressive mover: fairly useful handicapper: won at Musselburgh in August and Catterick in September: stays 2m: raced mostly on ground softer than good on turf (acts on heavy): strong traveller, sometimes finds little. *G. A. Swinbank*

PUZZLEMASTER 3 ch.g. Lomitas 129 – Norcroft Joy 82§ (Rock Hopper 124) [2009 **92**
70p: p8.6g* 10.4m 10m^6 10.2v* p12g^6 12g^5 10.3g Oct 23] neat gelding: fairly useful performer: won maiden at Wolverhampton in April and handicap at Nottingham in July: left M. Botti after fifth start: appears to stay 1½m: acts on polytrack, heavy and good to firm going: sold 40,000 gns, joined H. Morrison, then gelded. *Jane Chapple-Hyam*

PYCIAN 2 b.g. (Mar 4) Mark of Esteem (IRE) 137 – Beejay 77 (Piccolo 121) [2009 6g* **78**
7m^3 7d Jul 18] 7,000Y: first foal: dam 5f (at 2 yrs)/6f winner: similar form first 2 starts, winning maiden at Haydock (by ½ length from Atacama Crossing, almost detached at one point) in May: seemed amiss final start: stays 7f: acts on good to firm going. *Mrs L. Stubbs*

PYRRHA 3 b.f. Pyrus (USA) 106 – Demeter (USA) 79 (Diesis 133) [2009 91: 6m^3 7g^4 **107**
7g* 7g* Aug 14] good-topped filly: useful handicapper: much improved when winning at Newmarket in July and August (beat Iasia 3 lengths): stays 7f: acts on good to firm ground: races prominently. *C. F. Wall*

PYRUS TIME (IRE) 3 b.g. Pyrus (USA) 106 – Spot In Time (Mtoto 134) [2009 60: **77**
p8g^5 p8g^3 p8g^3 p8g^2 p10g^2 p12g^2 p10g^2 11.9m^3 p10m^3 p12g^4 10m^6 10.4m^2 8m^5 p10m* Dec 9] leggy gelding: fair performer: won maiden at Lingfield in December: effective from 1m to 1½m: acts on polytrack and good to firm going: tried in cheekpieces: usually held up: reliable. *J. S. Moore*

PYTHEAS (USA) 2 b.g. (Apr 21) Seeking The Gold (USA) – Neptune's Bride (USA) **81**
110 (Bering 136) [2009 7m^2 7.1m 7.5m^3 p8.6g^2 8d^2 8.3g^3 Oct 28] rather leggy, quite attractive gelding: sixth foal: brother to useful French 6f/7.5f winner Poseidon's Bride and closely related to 1¼m winner Evening Affair (by Kingmambo): dam French 1m to 10.5f winner: fairly useful maiden: stays 8.6f: acts on polytrack and good to firm going: front runner: gelded after final start. *M. Johnston*

Q

QADAR (IRE) 7 b.g. Xaar 132 – Iktidar 80 (Green Desert (USA) 127) [2009 92: p6g^5 **85**
p6g^2 p5g^2 p6g^5 p6g^4 p5.1g^4 7m^3 7m 7d a6g* p8f^3 6g^4 p8g^5 p6g^6 p8g^3 p7g^4 Nov 27] strong, good sort: fairly useful handicapper: trained first 6 starts by N. Littmoden: won at Laytown in September: effective at 5f to 1m: acts on all-weather/sand and firm going: often wears headgear: sometimes tongue tied. *David Marnane, Ireland*

QALAHARI (IRE) 3 b.f. Bahri (USA) 125 – Daqtora 70 (Dr Devious (IRE) 127) **82**
[2009 92: p7g 7m^2 8m 9g Jul 29] tall filly: fairly useful performer: will prove best around 6f: acts on polytrack, firm and good to soft going: reportedly lost action final outing. *D. J. Coakley*

QARAABA 2 b.f. (Jan 27) Shamardal (USA) 129 – Mokaraba 86 (Unfuwain (USA) 131) [2009 7d^2 7g^3 7d* Oct 12] tall filly: has scope: first foal: dam, 1½m winner (stayed 1¾m), granddaughter of Salsabil: won maiden at Salisbury by short head from Cojo, hanging left: better form when second to Champagnelifestyle at Newmarket: will be suited by 1m+. *J. L. Dunlop* **82**

QARAQUM (USA) 2 b. or br.f. (Feb 14) Vindication (USA) 122 – Code of Ethics (USA) (Honour And Glory (USA) 122) [2009 p8m^5 p8m^5 Dec 4] $42,000Y: first foal: dam, US 1m/8.5f winner, sister to 2002 Canadian Grade 3 2-y-o 1m winner One And Twenty: green, similar form in maidens at Kempton and Lingfield. *D. J. Coakley* **51**

QEDAAM (IRE) 3 b.f. Daylami (IRE) 138 – Zafzala (IRE) 115 (Kahyasi 130) [2009 p12g Apr 15] €17,000Y: closely related to fairly useful Irish 1m winner (stayed 1½m) Zafaraniya (by Doyoun) and half-sister to 2 winners in Ireland, including 5-y-o Gwens Spirit: dam Irish 6f (at 2 yrs) and 1½m winner: well held in maiden at Kempton: sent to Saudi Arabia. *Pat Morris* **–**

QELAAN (USA) 3 b.f. Dynaformer (USA) – Irtahal (USA) 94 (Swain (IRE) 134) [2009 71: 9.7d^4 10f^2 p11g^6 12f* 11.5d* 12m^2 12g^5 Oct 30] tall filly: fairly useful handicapper: won at Folkestone (by 12 lengths) and Lingfield in September: stayed 1½m: acted on firm and good to soft going: front runner: visits Dubawi. *M. P. Tregoning* **93**

QUADRIFOLIO 3 b.g. Key of Luck (USA) 126 – Berkeley Note (IRE) 69 (Victory Note (USA) 120) [2009 –: 8.3g Oct 28] leggy gelding: no form: tried visored. *Paul Green* **–**

QUADRILLE 2 b.c. (Feb 7) Danehill Dancer (IRE) 117 – Fictitious 100 (Machiavellian (USA) 123) [2009 6d* p7g* 7g^2 Oct 10] well-made colt: third foal: half-brother to 5-y-o Hunting Tower: dam, 1¼m winner (later Grade 3 8.5f winner in USA), sister to smart performer up to 13f Phantom Gold: most progressive, winning maiden at Newbury (7/4 favourite, readily by 4 lengths from Chips O'Toole) in August and minor event at Kempton (beat Circumvent by head) in September: very good head second to Corporal Maddox in minor event at Ascot: will stay 1m: smart prospect. *R. Hannon* **102 p**

QUAESTOR (IRE) 2 b.c. (Feb 14) Antonius Pius (USA) 123§ – Lucky Oakwood (USA) 75 (Elmaamul (USA) 125) [2009 p6g^6 6m^5 p6g^2 6s^6 6s 6f^2 6m Sep 19] €15,000F, €15,000Y: good-topped colt: sixth foal: half-brother to winner in Japan by Grand Lodge: dam, 2-y-o 7f winner, closely related to useful 1¼m winner Gisarne: fair maiden: stays 6f: acts on polytrack and firm ground. *Tom Dascombe* **78**

QUAI D'ORSAY 3 ch.c. Sulamani (IRE) 130 – Entente Cordiale (USA) (Affirmed (USA)) [2009 88p: 12.3m^2 11.9v 12.5g* 12m 11.9m* 14m^5 14g 12g^5 12m^5 13.1m* 12g Oct 10] good-topped colt: useful handicapper: won at Musselburgh in June, Haydock in July and Ayr (beat Hunting Tower ½ length) in October: stays 13f: unraced on firm going, acts on any other: races up with pace: has joined Godolphin. *M. Johnston* **105**

QUAKER PARROT 2 ch.f. (Mar 14) Compton Place 125 – Little Greenbird 39 (Ardkinglass 114) [2009 5.1g 5.5f* 5g 5m^6 5d^3 5.1m* 6g 5.7m^2 6m^2 p5.1g^4 p7.1g^2 p7.1g Dec 26] 20,000F, £20,000Y: smallish filly: fourth foal: half-sister to 3 winners, including 5f (at 2 yrs) to 8.5f (in Austria) winner Green Pride (by Piccolo) and 2008 2-y-o 7f winner Brazilian Art (by Captain Rio), both fairly useful: dam maiden: fairly useful performer: won maiden at Warwick in May and nursery at Bath in July: good efforts when runner-up in nurseries after: stays 7f: acts on polytrack, firm and good to soft ground: races prominently. *Tom Dascombe* **83**

QUALITAS 3 b.g. Orpen (USA) 116 – Kiss Me Kate 73 (Aragon 118) [2009 6d^5 6d f5m 6s p9.5g^5 Oct 16] modest maiden: should stay beyond 6f. *M. W. Easterby* **62**

QUALITY MOVER (USA) 2 b. or br.f. (Feb 2) Elusive Quality (USA) – Katherine Seymour 107 (Green Desert (USA) 127) [2009 7g^6 p8g Aug 19] $140,000Y: third foal: closely related to fairly useful 7f winner Liberation Spirit (by Gone West): dam 7f (in Ireland at 2 yrs) to 8.5f (in USA) winner: green in maidens, better effort when sixth to Seta at Newmarket. *D. M. Simcock* **63**

QUALITY STREET 7 ch.m. Fraam 114 – Pusey Street Girl 87 (Gildoran 123) [2009 72d: p8g p7g Feb 13] rather leggy, lengthy mare: one-time fairly useful handicapper, on downgrade: wears cheekpieces, tried visored. *P. Butler* **–**

QUAM CELERRIME 4 b.g. Xaar 132 – Divine Secret (Hernando (FR) 127) [2009 81: p12.2g Jan 29] useful-looking gelding: fairly useful performer at 2 yrs: lightly raced and regressive since. *R. Curtis* **–**

QUANAH PARKER (IRE) 3 b.c. Namid 128 – Uncertain Affair (IRE) 79 (Darshaan 133) [2009 89: 7.1v^3 7m^2 6g^5 6m Jul 4] big, workmanlike colt: useful handicapper: **96**

best efforts when placed first 2 starts, beaten nose by Kyllachy Star at York on second occasion: will probably stay 1m: acts on heavy and good to firm going: usually races prominently. *R. M. Whitaker*

QUAROMA 4 ch.f. Pivotal 124 – Quiz Time 90 (Efisio 120) [2009 103: 6f^{4} 6.1m May 9] neat filly: useful performer at 3 yrs: well held both starts in 2009, eased and seemingly amiss final outing: raced only at 5f/6f: acts on good to firm and good to soft going, probably on polytrack. *Jane Chapple-Hyam* –

QUARREL (USA) 2 gr. or ro.c. (Jan 14) Maria's Mon (USA) 121 – Gender Dance (USA) (Miesque's Son (USA) 117) [2009 6m* 6.1m* 6m^{3} Sep 19] $32,000Y, £80,000 2-y-o: sturdy colt: second foal: dam US 7f to 8.3f winner: most progressive, winning maiden at Ascot (by ¾ length from Atlaal) in July and 3-runner minor event at Chester (beat Atlantis Star by length) in August: good 2¼ lengths third to Awzaan in Mill Reef Stakes at Newbury, dictating: should stay 7f: already useful. *W. J. Haggas* **102**

QUASI CONGAREE (GER) 3 ch.g. Congaree (USA) 127 – Queens Wild (USA) (Spectacular Bid (USA)) [2009 7m^{6} 6g^{2} 6d^{2} p6m^{4} p5.1g p6g^{3} p6g p5m^{5} p5g^{6} Nov 5] 14,000F: workmanlike gelding: half-brother to several winners in USA: dam, US 6f to 1m winner, half-sister to several US graded stakes winners, including 1990 Grade 1 2-y-o 7f winner Eastern Echo: fair maiden: will prove best at 5f/6f: acts on polytrack and good to soft going: usually tongue tied: front runner: weak finisher: gelded after final start. *I. A. Wood* **77**

QUE BEAUTY (IRE) 4 b.f. Val Royal (FR) 127 – Ardbess (Balla Cove 119) [2009 –: f16d^{3} p16.5g^{6} f14g f16g^{5} Feb 5] smallish, workmanlike filly: poor maiden: stays 16.5f: acts on all-weather: tried blinkered, in cheekpieces at 4 yrs. *R. C. Guest* **49**

QUE BELLE (IRE) 2 b.f. (Apr 14) Hawk Wing (USA) 136 – Enaya 99 (Caerleon (USA) 132) [2009 f8g Dec 18] 40,000F, €2,000Y: half-sister to several winners, including useful 6f to 1m winner (including in UAE) Jila (by Kris): dam, 2-y-o 6f winner (later stayed 1¼m), half-sister to very smart performer around 1m Gabr: 12/1, very green when well held in maiden at Southwell. *Tom Dascombe* –

QUE CALOR LA VIDA (FR) 5 b.m. Lavirco (GER) 125 – Hasta Manana (FR) (Useful (FR)) [2009 12.5m 12m May 2] lengthy non-thoroughbred mare: soundly beaten in mares bumpers for G. Harker: no form in maidens on Flat. *N. Wilson* –

QUEEN ELEANOR 3 b.f. Cape Cross (IRE) 129 – Rainbow Queen 92 (Rainbow Quest (USA) 134) [2009 82p: p8g^{3} 9g^{2} 10m^{3} p10g* 10.2g Aug 14] good-topped filly: fairly useful performer: won handicap at Lingfield in July: hung badly left and probably amiss final outing: stays 1¼m: acts on polytrack: sold 13,000 gns. *J. H. M. Gosden* **85**

QUEEN EXCALIBUR 10 ch.m. Sabrehill (USA) 120 – Blue Room 70 (Gorytus (USA) 132) [2009 64?: 12.1v Jul 24] rather leggy mare: modest performer at best in 2008: well held only outing in 2009: stays 1½m: acts on soft going: tried blinkered, often in cheekpieces. *B. J. Llewellyn* –

QUEEN MARTHA (USA) 3 b.f. Rahy (USA) 115 – Cryptoqueen (USA) (Cryptoclearance (USA)) [2009 p7g^{6} 8.3m 8.3f* 8m* 10.1m^{6} Jun 25] $100,000Y: rangy filly: half-sister to several winners in US, notably Grade 3 8.5f/9f winner Clearly A Queen (by Lucky North): dam lightly raced in USA: fairly useful form: won maiden at Nottingham in May and handicap at Doncaster in June: far from discredited in listed race at Newcastle final outing: stays 1¼m: acts on firm going: front runner: sent to USA. *M. A. Magnusson* **85**

QUEEN OF PENTACLES (IRE) 3 b.f. Selkirk (USA) 129 – Maid To Perfection 102 (Sadler's Wells (USA) 132) [2009 10d^{4} p10g* 12d^{4} 10.1m^{4} 10m^{4} 10.3s* Nov 7] good-bodied filly: third foal: half-sister to Irish 5-y-o Perfect Reward: dam, 7f (at 2 yrs) to 1¼m winner, closely related to useful performer up to 1½m Maid To Believe: useful form, progressive: won maiden at Kempton in June and 19-runner listed race at Doncaster (beat Mooakada 1¾ lengths) in November: appears to stay 1½m, though failed to settle when tried: acts on polytrack, soft and good to firm going: held up. *J. Noseda* **105**

QUEEN OF THEBES (IRE) 3 b.f. Bahri (USA) 125 – Sopran Marida (IRE) (Darshaan 133) [2009 79: 8.1g 5f 7m^{5} 8.1m^{6} p7g^{6} p7f p10g Oct 2] useful-looking filly: fair performer: not quite so good in 2009: stays 7f: tongue tied last 5 starts. *G. L. Moore* **68**

QUEEN OF TROY (IRE) 2 b.f. (Feb 17) Storm Cat (USA) – Warrior Queen (USA) 113 (Quiet American (USA)) [2009 6s p7g^{2} p5g* 6s^{6} 7g^{4} p7g Oct 9] fourth foal: half-sister to smart US Grade 2 8.5f winner A P Warrior (by A P Indy): dam, Irish 2-y-o 6f winner, out of half-sister to dam of high-class French 1m/1¼m winner Green Tune and Cheveley Park winner Pas de Reponse: useful performer: won maiden at Dundalk in August: 2¾ lengths fourth to Lady Springbank in C. L. Weld Park Stakes at the Curragh, **95**

best effort: not sure to stay much beyond 7f: acts on polytrack, best turf effort on good going: usually races close up: sometimes carries head high/flicks tail. *A. P. O'Brien, Ireland*

QUEEN OF WANDS 2 b.f. (Feb 18) Sakhee (USA) 136 – Maid To Treasure (IRE) 77 (Rainbow Quest (USA) 134) [2009 7g 8.1d Aug 31] second foal: half-sister to 3-y-o King of Wands: dam, maiden (should have stayed 1½m+), half-sister to useful performer up to 1½m Maid To Believe: green when mid-field in maidens at Newmarket (better effort) and Chepstow: bred for 1¼m+: type to do better in handicaps. *J. L. Dunlop* **53 p**

QUEEN SALLY (IRE) 3 b.f. Key of Luck (USA) 126 – Crystal Blue (IRE) (Bluebird (USA) 125) [2009 70: 7.1v[3] 6.1g[6] p7m 5.1d Oct 15] modest maiden nowadays: best at 6f: raced only on polytrack and good ground or softer on turf. *Tom Dascombe* **63**

QUEEN'S ENVOY 2 b.f. (Feb 5) King's Best (USA) 132 – Allied Cause 73 (Giant's Causeway (USA) 132) [2009 7m[6] p7g[3] Oct 29] tall, lengthy filly: has scope: first foal: dam, 2-y-o 7f winner, half-sister to very smart 1m/1¼m winner Kissogram: much better effort in maidens when 2½ lengths third to Padmini at Lingfield: bred to stay 1m. *L. M. Cumani* **72**

QUEENS FLIGHT 3 b.f. King's Best (USA) 132 – Birdie 99 (Alhaarth (IRE) 126) [2009 56: 8d[5] p7g 6m Sep 28] close-coupled filly: poor maiden: stays 1m: sold 8,000 gns. *Tom Dascombe* **47**

QUEENS FORESTER 3 b.f. Needwood Blade 117 – Bonsai (IRE) 66 (Woodman (USA) 126) [2009 –: 8f Jun 5] close-coupled filly: no form. *P. F. I. Cole* **–**

QUEEN'S GRACE 2 ch.f. (Feb 23) Bahamian Bounty 116 – Palace Affair 113 (Pursuit of Love 124) [2009 6d 6m* 6s[3] 6g* Oct 30] smallish, strong filly: third foal: half-sister to 5-y-o April Fool: dam, 5f to 7f winner (including 6f at 2 yrs), half-sister to high-class sprinter Sakhee's Secret: useful and progressive: won maiden at Newbury (by neck from Jacqueline Quest) in August and listed race at Newmarket (beat Puff by length, making all gamely) in October: acts on soft and good to firm going. *H. Morrison* **107**

QUEEN'S HAWK 2 ch.c. (Mar 29) Hawk Wing (USA) 136 – Queen of Africa (USA) (Peintre Celebre (USA) 137) [2009 5.1g 6m* 7m 7g[5] 6d 7d 8g[6] 7.1m[6] 7d[6] Oct 22] smallish, rather leggy colt: fair performer: won maiden at Goodwood in May: below form in nurseries last 5 starts, visored final one: stays 7f: acts on good to firm ground: quirky, and one to treat with caution: sold 7,500 gns, sent to Denmark. *D. J. Coakley* **72 §**

QUELLA 3 ch.f. Falbrav (IRE) 133 – Qirmazi (USA) 113 (Riverman (USA) 131) [2009 p8g 10.2g Apr 3] half-sister to several winners, including very smart 6f to 1m winner Quito (by Machiavellian) and useful French 7f (at 2 yrs) to 1m winner Quarter Note (by Danehill): dam French 6f (at 2 yrs) and 9f winner: well held in maidens (green). *J. H. M. Gosden* **–**

QUERIDO (GER) 5 b.g. Acatenango (GER) 127 – Quest of Fire (FR) (Rainbow Quest (USA) 134) [2009 59: 7m 9.1v Oct 31] modest form at best in Britain: well held in 2009: stays 10.5f: acts on heavy ground: tried tongue tied. *M. Bradstock* **–**

QUEST FOR SUCCESS (IRE) 4 b.g. Noverre (USA) 125 – Divine Pursuit 69 (Kris 135) [2009 92: 7m[5] 7f* 7m 6m 7.1m[2] 6d* 6m[6] 6g[6] f6f[4] 5d* Oct 24] rather leggy, close-coupled gelding: useful handicapper on turf, fairly useful on all-weather: progressive in 2009, winning at Thirsk in April, Hamilton in July and Doncaster (beat Excusez Moi ½ length) in October: has form at 7f, will prove best at 5f/6f: acts on any going: blinkered once. *R. A. Fahey* **108** **a89 +**

QUICK GOURMET 3 b.f. Lend A Hand 124 – Rhiann (Anshan 119) [2009 44p: 9.2g[6] 7.1g[5] 7.1m[6] 6s[3] 6s[3] 6s[4] 12.4d Oct 13] fair maiden: left J. McShane before final outing: likely to prove best up to 7f: acts on soft ground: difficult ride. *G. A. Swinbank* **65**

QUICK OFF THE MARK 4 b.f. Dr Fong (USA) 128 – Equity Princess 106 (Warning 136) [2009 71: f8g[2] p8.6g[2] f11d[4] p9.5g[6] 10.1s 10.2g p8.6g[3] 8.3m[4] 8g p9.5g[3] p9.5g Aug 17] good-topped filly: fair handicapper on all-weather, modest on turf: stays 11f: acts on all-weather, probably on soft going: tongue tied 4 of last 5 starts: races prominently. *J. G. Given* **53** **a71**

QUICK REACTION 2 b.g. (Feb 22) Elusive Quality (USA) – Arutua (USA) (Riverman (USA) 131) [2009 7m 8m[5] 8g Sep 30] good-topped gelding: half-brother to several winners, including 7f (at 2 yrs) and 1½m winner Juliette (by Sadler's Wells) and 6f (at 2 yrs) and 1m winner Plato (by Lure), both useful in Ireland: dam unraced out of top-class middle-distance mare All Along: best effort in maidens when fifth to Coordinated Cut at Doncaster, staying on under considerate ride: stays 1m: gelded after final start. *R. Hannon* **80**

QUICK RELEASE (IRE) 4 b.c. Red Ransom (USA) – Set The Mood (USA) (Dixie Brass (USA)) [2009 75: p8g^5 p8g p8g^4 p8g^6 p9.5g^2 p10g^5 p8g^4 p8m^4 p8.6g* Dec 19] close-coupled colt: fairly useful handicapper: won at Wolverhampton in December: stays 1¼m: acts on polytrack and good to firm going: consistent. *D. M. Simcock* **85**

QUICK SINGLE (USA) 3 b. or br.g. Doneralle Court (USA) – Summer Strike (USA) (Smart Strike (CAN) 121) [2009 73: p6g^5 p6g^3 p5g^4 p6g^3 p6g* p6g* p6g^6 6g^5 7m 8m^6 7m 6m^4 p6g^4 8m p6m 5d 6f^4 p7g p7g p10g p10g^4 p8m Nov 29] sturdy gelding: fair performer: left D. Elsworth 3,000 gns after third start: won maiden and handicap at Lingfield in February: below form after: best at 6f: acts on polytrack: usually blinkered/visored: tried tongue tied. *P. S. McEntee* **73 d**

QUICKS THE WORD 9 b.g. Sri Pekan (USA) 117 – Fast Tempo (IRE) 74 (Statoblest 120) [2009 66: 5m 5.9g 6m 6m Aug 29] rather leggy gelding: modest handicapper: best around 6f: acts on any turf going: tried blinkered. *T. A. K. Cuthbert* **50**

QUICK WIT 2 b.c. (Apr 16) Oasis Dream 129 – Roo 97 (Rudimentary (USA) 118) [2009 p7g^5 7g^2 7g* Oct 30] 98,000F, 190,000Y: fifth foal: half-brother to several winners, including 3-y-o Gallagher and 4-y-o Averoo: dam, 2-y-o 5f/6f winner, half-sister to Gimcrack Stakes winner Bannister: fairly useful form last 2 starts in maidens, making all when landing odds at Newmarket by 1½ lengths from Youm Jamil: raced only at 7f. *Saeed bin Suroor* **90**

QUIET 2 ch.f. (Mar 7) Observatory (USA) 131 – Quandary (USA) 104 (Blushing Groom (FR) 131) [2009 8.3m* 8m Sep 11] small, compact filly: half-sister to several winners, including useful 1¼m/11.5f winner Double Crossed (by Caerleon), dam of 4-y-o Twice Over (by Observatory), and 1½m winner Clepsydra (by Sadler's Wells), dam of smart performers up to 1½m Passage of Time and Father Time: dam 9f/1¼m winner: won maiden at Leicester in September by 2½ lengths from Pastello: creditable last of 7 to Pollenator in May Hill Stakes at Doncaster, dictating: bred to be suited by 1¼m. *R. Charlton* **91**

QUIET ELEGANCE 4 b.f. Fantastic Light (USA) 134 – Imperial Bailiwick (IRE) 104 (Imperial Frontier (USA) 112) [2009 96: 6m 6.1m 8.1v 6m 6g^3 6g 6m Sep 18] strong, sturdy filly: fairly useful handicapper nowadays: best at 5f/6f: acts on soft and good to firm going. *E. J. Alston* **82**

QUIET MOUNTAIN (IRE) 4 ch.g. Monashee Mountain (USA) 115 – Shalstayholy (IRE) 84 (Shalford (IRE) 124§) [2009 f7g p7.1g^6 p8.6g^5 Dec 14] modest form in maidens: raced at 7f/8.6f on all-weather. *Ollie Pears* **59**

QUIJANO (GER) 7 ch.g. Acatenango (GER) 127 – Quila (IRE) (Unfuwain (USA) 131) [2009 120: 12m^2 12g^6 12m* 11f^3 12f^6 12f^2 12m Oct 17] very smart performer: won Gran Premio di Milano Trofeo SNAI at Milan (beat Age of Reason a length) in June for second year running: good efforts when placed in Dubai City of Gold at Nad Al Sheba (½-length second to Front House), Man o' War Stakes at Belmont (2¼ lengths third to Gio Ponti) and Northern Dancer Turf Stakes at Woodbine (beaten ¾ length, promoted second on demotion of Marsh Side): ran as though amiss when tailed off in Canadian International at Woodbine final start: best at 11f/1½m: acts on firm ground, won on soft earlier in career: races in mid-division: reliable. *P. Schiergen, Germany* **120**

QUINCE (IRE) 6 b.g. Fruits of Love (USA) 127 – Where's Charlotte 53 (Sure Blade (USA) 130) [2009 91: p12.2g^2 p13g^2 p11g^4 p12g^2 p12.2g* 12m^6 10g^3 10g 10m 10.1m^3 10.4d 10g^2 10m p12g^2 p13.9g^2 p13.9m^5 p12m Dec 16] strong, close-coupled gelding: fairly useful performer: won claimer at Wolverhampton in February: placed 5 times after: effective at 1¼m to easy 1¾m: acts on polytrack, good to firm and good to soft going: tried in cheekpieces, usually visored: held up: quirky. *J. Pearce* **81**

QUINMASTER (USA) 7 gr.g. Linamix (FR) 127 – Sherkiya (IRE) (Goldneyev (USA) 114) [2009 109: 8v 8m^2 8m 7m 8s^4 Aug 16] useful performer: creditable effort in 2009 only when 3 lengths second to Shreyas in listed race at Leopardstown: well held in Hunt Cup at Royal Ascot next time: effective at 1m to 10.5f: acts on polytrack, good to firm and good to soft ground: often in tongue tie and/or cheekpieces. *M. Halford, Ireland* **106**

QUINNER (IRE) 2 ch.c. (Apr 28) Arakan (USA) 123 – Quintellina 83 (Robellino (USA) 127) [2009 6.1v^6 6d^3 6m 6d p6m Sep 28] sturdy colt: form only when third in maiden at Newbury: bred to stay 7f: tried tongue tied. *P. D. Evans* **57**

QUINSMAN 3 b.c. Singspiel (IRE) 133 – Penny Cross 99 (Efisio 120) [2009 8s 6m^4 7m^5 8.3m^6 8d^6 8d^5 10.4m^3 p10g* p12g^3 p12f* Dec 21] good-bodied colt: first foal: dam, 7f to 8.5f winner, half-sister to smart 7f/1m performer Priors Lodge: fair handicapper: **79**

won at Lingfield in October and Kempton in December: stays 1½m: acts on polytrack, good to firm and good to soft going. *J. S. Moore*

QUIQUILLO (USA) 3 ch.f. Cape Canaveral (USA) 115 – Only Seventeen (USA) (Exploit (USA) 117) [2009 61p: 8g^4 10m^4 10.3d^5 6.1g* p7.1g 6.1d^5 Oct 15] tall, rather unfurnished filly: fair handicapper: left H. Cecil, won at Chepstow in August: ran well final outing: will prove best short of 1m: acts on good to soft ground. *P. D. Evans* **73**

QUIRINA 4 b.f. Red Ransom (USA) – Qirmazi (USA) 113 (Riverman (USA) 131) [2009 94: p10g^3 10m^5 p8g Jul 1] good-topped, quite attractive filly: fairly useful handicapper: below form after reappearance: will prove best short of 1½m: acts on polytrack, soft and good to firm going: sent to Australia. *R. M. Beckett* **92**

QUITE A FELLA (USA) 4 b.g. Swain (IRE) 134 – Magnificent Star (USA) 122 (Silver Hawk (USA) 123) [2009 p12g* p12g Mar 1] 800 3-y-o: half-brother to 3 winners, including 1¾m winner Patrixprial (by Linamix) and 1½m winner Profiler (by Capote), both fairly useful: dam 1¼m/1½m (Yorkshire Oaks) winner: some promise in 3-y-o bumper: won maiden at Lingfield in January by 1½ lengths from Regal Angel, running on strongly: pulled up (said to have been lame) in handicap there next time: will stay 1¾m+. *Andrew Turnell* **73 +**

QUITE SOMETHING 2 b.f. (Feb 1) Footstepsinthesand 120 – Quite Elusive (USA) (Elusive Quality (USA)) [2009 6.5g^4 Oct 8] rangy filly: first foal: dam unraced half-sister to useful French 7f/9f winner Quittance: 50/1, encouraging 4 lengths fourth to Noafal in maiden at Newbury, green (and free) before finishing strongly: sure to improve. *A. M. Balding* **69 p**

QUITE SPARKY 2 b.g. (Feb 24) Lucky Story (USA) 128 – Imperialistic (IRE) 99 (Imperial Ballet (IRE) 110) [2009 7d^6 7s^2 Sep 5] £6,000 2-y-o: leggy gelding: first foal: dam 6f (at 2 yrs) to 1m winner: much better effort in maidens at Thirsk when neck second to Cracking Lass, making most. *T. P. Tate* **77**

QUITIT (IRE) 4 b.g. Kalanisi (IRE) 132 – Wattrey 62 (Royal Academy (USA) 130) [2009 77: 16.2m^5 Jul 4] compact gelding: fair handicapper: fit from hurdling and in cheekpieces, well held only outing on Flat in 2009: stays 15.8f: acts on soft ground: blinkered last 6 starts in 2008. *Mrs S. A. Watt* **–**

R

RAAEIDD (IRE) 3 b.c. King's Best (USA) 132 – Bahr 119 (Generous (IRE) 139) [2009 86p: 10.4m^3 10m^5 9.8v^4 8g^4 8.5m Aug 31] good-topped colt: fairly useful handicapper: stays 10.4f: acts on good to firm going: in cheekpieces final outing (well held). *M. A. Jarvis* **87**

RABBIT FIGHTER (IRE) 5 ch.g. Observatory (USA) 131 – Furnish 87 (Green Desert (USA) 127) [2009 81: f7d p6g^5 p6g* 7s p7.1g p7.1g 6d p6g^5 Oct 16] strong, close-coupled gelding: fair handicapper: won amateur event at Wolverhampton in April: below form after: effective at 5f to 8.6f: acts on polytrack, soft and good to firm going: usually visored. *D. Shaw* **72**

RABEERA 4 b.f. Beat Hollow 126 – Gai Bulga 110 (Kris 135) [2009 58: 10.2g Apr 21] angular filly: modest maiden: well held sole 4-y-o start: stays 1¼m: tried visored: looks irresolute: sold 8,000 gns. *A. M. Balding* **–**

RACCOON (IRE) 9 b.g. Raphane (USA) 102 – Kunucu (IRE) 94 (Bluebird (USA) 125) [2009 73: 5.1m* 5g^3 5m^3 5g* 5m^3 5m^3 5m^2 5g^4 5g^2 5d^2 5m* 5g* 5s 5m Sep 9] strong, good-quartered gelding: has been tubed: fairly useful performer: won handicaps at Nottingham in April and Catterick in June and handicap/seller at Musselburgh in August: best at sharp 5f: acts on firm and soft going: effective visored or not: tried tongue tied: usually forces pace. *Mrs R. A. Carr* **84**

RACER FOREVER (USA) 6 b.g. Rahy (USA) 115 – Ras Shaikh (USA) 105 (Sheikh Albadou 128) [2009 115: 7f^5 7f^5 7m^5 7m 7.6m Aug 22] well-made gelding: smart performer at best: just useful in handicaps in 2009, fifth in valuable events at Royal Ascot (Buckingham Palace Stakes, beaten 3½ lengths by Giganticus) and Newmarket (Bunbury Cup): stays 7.5f: acts on polytrack and firm going: blinkered: suspect temperament. *J. H. M. Gosden* **109**

RACHEL ALEXANDRA (USA) 3 b.f. Medaglia d'Oro (USA) 129 – Lotta Kim (USA) (Roar (USA) 116) [2009 115: a8f* a8.5s* a8.5f* a9f* a9.5f* a9f* a9s* a9f* Sep 5] first foal: dam US 6f (at 2 yrs) and 1m (minor stakes) winner: improved into a top-class **130**

performer (voted Horse of The Year at Eclipse awards), winning all 8 of her races at 3 yrs, including 3 against males: successful in non-graded event at Oaklawn in February, Grade 2 Fair Ground Oaks in March, Grade 2 Fantasy Stakes at Oaklawn in April, Kentucky Oaks at Churchill Downs (by 20¼ lengths, sold privately and left H. Wiggins after) and Preakness Stakes at Pimlico (first filly to win the race since 1924 when beating Mine That Bird by a length, despite tiring in closing stages), both in May, Mother Goose Stakes at Belmont (by 19¼ lengths from Malibu Prayer in 3-runner race) in June, Haskell Invitational at Monmouth (beat top 3-y-o colt Summer Bird by 6 lengths) in August and Woodward Stakes at Saratoga (first filly to win race, gamely by a head from Macho Again) in September: will stay 1¼m: raced only on dirt (effective on sloppy going) except when successful in allowance race on polytrack at 2 yrs: effective from front or just off pace: missed Breeders' Cup (connections reportedly didn't want to race her on the pro-ride surface): stays in training. *S. M. Asmussen, USA*

RACINGER (FR) 6 b.h. Spectrum (IRE) 126 – Dibenoise (FR) (Kendor (FR) 122) **119**
[2009 119: 8d^3 8d^4 8m* 8g 8s^3 Nov 1] good-topped horse: smart performer: off 4 months, change of tactics and back to best when winning Prix Quincey Lucien Barriere at Deauville in August by ¾ length from Sahpresa, improving from rear to lead inside final 1f: better subsequent start when respectable third to Zafisio in Prix Perth at Saint-Cloud: best at 1m/9f: acted on heavy ground, probably on good to firm: blinkered second start: used to race prominently, but held up last 3 outings: to stand at French National Stud, Le Lion d'Angers, fee €1,400. *F. Head, France*

RACING HERO (IRE) 3 b.g. Montjeu (IRE) 137 – Aim For The Top (USA) 111 **92**
(Irish River (FR) 131) [2009 10g^3 12m* 10m^5 p10m 10.3d* 10.1d^2 Oct 27] 160,000Y: good-topped gelding: closely related to several winners, including useful 1993 2-y-o 7f winner/Fillies' Mile second Dance To The Top (by Sadler's Wells), dam of 5-y-o Bankable, and half-brother to 2 winners, notably smart 7f to 9f winner Polar Bear (by Polar Falcon): dam 6f (at 2 yrs) to 8.5f winner: fairly useful form: won maiden at Doncaster in June and handicap there in October: good second in handicap at Yarmouth 3 days after latter success: stays 1½m: acts on good to firm and good to soft going: sent to Hong Kong, where renamed Industrial Hero. *J. Noseda*

RACKETEER (IRE) 3 b.c. Cape Cross (IRE) 129 – Flirtation (Pursuit of Love 124) **107**
[2009 87p: 8.1m* 8.1m^5 May 28] lengthy, good-topped colt: much improved when winning handicap at Sandown in April by 6 lengths from Thief of Time, travelling strongly to lead 2f out: disappointing fifth to Border Patrol in listed race on same course next time: should have stayed 1¼m: raced only on all-weather and good to firm going: dead. *J. H. M. Gosden*

RACY 2 b.c. (Jan 29) Medicean 128 – Soar 110 (Danzero (AUS)) [2009 5m^2 6m* p6g^3 **89 p**
Oct 26] sturdy colt: first foal: dam, 2-y-o 5f/6f (Lowther Stakes) winner, half-sister to smart 6f/7f winner Feet So Fast: landed odds in maiden at Pontefract in September by 5 lengths from Antarctic Desert, making all: similar form when third to Chaperno in minor event at Lingfield: useful sprinting prospect. *Sir Michael Stoute*

RADDY 'ELL PAULINE (IRE) 2 ch.f. (Apr 25) Dubawi (IRE) 129 – Run For Me **84**
(IRE) (Danehill (USA) 126) [2009 6g p6g* 6g 5m^2 6m 6d Sep 5] €40,000Y: well-made filly: sixth foal: half-sister to several winners abroad, including smart Italian 6f to 1m winner Remarque (by Marju): dam unraced half-sister to Rockfel Stakes winner Negligent: fairly useful performer: won maiden at Kempton in June by 1¼ lengths from Piccadilly Filly: ran creditably next 2 starts, including seventh to Misheer in Cherry Hinton Stakes at Newmarket: stays 6f when conditions not testing: acts on polytrack and good to firm going: races prominently. *K. A. Ryan*

RADIATOR ROONEY (IRE) 6 br.g. Elnadim (USA) 128 – Queen of The May **63**
(IRE) 80 (Nicolotte 118) [2009 61, a74: p6g^6 5m 5g 6m^4 p6g^5 6m^3 6f p6g p5m p6g p5.1g^3 p5m^3 p6m^3 p6f p5g^5 Dec 31] good-topped gelding: modest handicapper nowadays: best at 5f/6f: acts on all-weather and firm going: usually wears headgear: held up: sometimes carries head awkwardly: has reportedly bled. *Pat Morris*

RADIO CITY 2 b.g. (Jan 31) Intikhab (USA) 135 – Red Shareef (Marju (IRE) 127) **82**
[2009 p5g^4 5m^3 6d^6 5m^3 5.3m* 5m^6 6m* p5.1g^6 6m^3 Oct 5] 22,000Y: lengthy gelding: fifth foal: brother to 3-y-o Orangeleg and half-brother to 3 winners, notably smart 6f (at 2 yrs) and 7.5f (in UAE) winner Caesar Beware (by Daggers Drawn), later winning sprinter in USA: dam Italian 1m (at 2 yrs) to 11f winner: fairly useful performer: won nurseries at Brighton in August and Epsom (best effort) in September: stays 6f: acts on polytrack and good to firm going: has raced freely: sold 13,000 gns. *R. M. Beckett*

Norfolk Stakes, Royal Ascot—Jamie Spencer produces Radiohead (star on cap) to win impressively in the end from outsider Reignier (breastgirth) and Tawaabb (left) in an incident-packed race

RADIOHEAD 2 ch.c. (Apr 26) Johannesburg (USA) 127 – Security Interest (USA) (Belong To Me (USA)) [2009 5f² 5.1d* 5m* 5m³ 6m⁴ 6m² a8.5f Nov 7] €130,000F, 78,000Y: lengthy, useful-looking colt: has scope: third foal: half-brother to winner in USA by Smoke Glacken: dam unraced: smart form: won minor event at Bath in May and Norfolk Stakes at Royal Ascot (by 2 lengths from Reignier, showing fine turn of foot) in June: further improvement when placed in Nunthorpe Stakes at York (1½ lengths third to Borderlescott) and Middle Park Stakes at Newmarket (¾-length second to Awzaan, possibly shade flattered to get so close): fair seventh to Vale of York in Breeders' Cup Juvenile at Santa Anita final outing: may prove best short of 1m: acts on good to firm and good to soft going: tongue tied after second outing, also ponied to start on 3 occasions: has twice hung right: has joined R. Dutrow Jnr, USA. *B. J. Meehan* **115**

RADIO WAVE 2 ch.f. (Mar 22) Dalakhani (IRE) 133 – Tuning 114 (Rainbow Quest (USA) 134) [2009 8g³ Oct 20] seventh foal: half-sister to 3 winners, including 7-y-o Mixing and 9-y-o Tuning Fork: dam 1¾m (including Ebor) winner: 11/1, most encouraging 2¼ lengths third to Hymnsheet in maiden at Yarmouth, finishing well from rear under considerate handling: will be suited by 1¼m+: sure to progress. *J. H. M. Gosden* **78 p**

RADSKY 2 ch.c. (Feb 23) Where Or When (IRE) 124 – Radiant Sky (IRE) 62 (Spectrum (IRE) 126) [2009 7m 8.3m 10.2m Sep 28] unfurnished colt: no form in maidens/seller. *J. G. Portman* **–**

RAFAAN (USA) 3 b. or br.g. Gulch (USA) – Reem Al Barari (USA) 69 (Storm Cat (USA)) [2009 79: 10.1m* 10m 10.4g Jun 13] unfurnished gelding: fairly useful form: won maiden at Newcastle in April: shaped as if amiss in handicaps after (gelded in between): stays 1¼m: sold 15,000 gns in July. *M. Johnston* **85**

RAFFANETTI (IRE) 3 b.g. Raphane (USA) 102 – Proud Boast 104 (Komaite (USA)) [2009 6m⁶ 5m Jun 16] well held in maidens. *T. D. Barron* **–**

RAFIKI (IRE) 2 b.g. (Feb 24) Kheleyf (USA) 116 – Jemalina (USA) 52 (Trempolino (USA) 135) [2009 p6g Oct 15] 28/1 and very green, well held in maiden at Wolverhampton (gelded after). *W. R. Swinburn* **–**

RAFIQA (IRE) 3 b.f. Mujahid (USA) 125 – Shamara (IRE) 99 (Spectrum (IRE) 126) [2009 89p: 7m³ 8d² 8m⁵ 10m⁴ Sep 25] angular filly: useful performer: best effort when second to Elliptical in handicap at Salisbury: probably stays 1¼m: acts on good to firm and good to soft going. *C. F. Wall* **99**

RAFTA (IRE) 3 b.f. Atraf 116 – First Kiss (GER) 65 (Night Shift (USA)) [2009 –: 7m 6f* 6.1v* 7d* 6d* 7s² p7g 6g Aug 30] fairly useful handicapper: much improved to win at Salisbury in June and Nottingham, Leicester and Thirsk in July: refused to race last 2 outings: effective at 6f/7f: acts on any turf going. *T. T. Clement* **83 §**

RAGAMUFFIN MAN (IRE) 4 gr.g. Dalakhani (IRE) 133 – Chamela Bay (IRE) 106 (Sadler's Wells (USA) 132) [2009 85: 16.1g⁴ 16d² 18m⁵ 18g* Oct 19] good-topped gelding: fairly useful handicapper: in cheekpieces, won at Pontefract in October: stays 2¼m: acts on polytrack and good to soft going: visored prior to win: front runner: joined P. Hobbs. *W. J. Knight* **88**

RAGDOLLIANNA 5 b.m. Kayf Tara 130 – Jupiters Princess 54 (Jupiter Island 126) [2009 87: 14m 14f⁵ p13g⁴ Nov 1] leggy mare: fairly useful in 2008: well below form in 2009. *Norma Twomey* **–**

PROSPECT COURT 7 ch.g. Pivotal 124 – Scierpan (USA) 86 (Sharpen Up 127) [2009 71: 6m 7.2g 5s 6.9d 5s 6d Sep 7] close-coupled gelding: no form in 2009: tried blinkered. *A. C. Whillans* –

PROTARAS (USA) 2 b. or br.c. (Mar 10) Lemon Drop Kid (USA) 131 – Seven Moons (JPN) (Sunday Silence (USA)) [2009 8m 8.3m² Oct 13] sturdy colt: second foal: dam, US 1m/8.5f winner, out of close relative to Kingmambo and half-sister to East of The Moon: still green, much better effort in maidens when 2¾ lengths second to Botanist at Leicester: will stay 1¼m: should improve again. *H. R. A. Cecil* **78 p**

PROTECTOR (SAF) 8 b.g. Kilconnel (USA) 99 – Mufski (SAF) (Al Mufti (USA) 112) [2009 103: 6d 7d 6m 7d 6s Nov 7] big gelding: just fairly useful in 2009: barely stays 7f: acts on dirt and any turf going: tried in headgear: tongue tied: edgy type, and sometimes early to post. *A. G. Foster* **93**

PROTIVA 3 ch.f. Deportivo 116 – Prowse (USA) 55 (King of Kings (IRE) 125) [2009 64: p7g⁵ p8g³ p10g 9g 7d⁵ 8m Aug 16] sturdy filly: modest maiden: left A. Jarvis after fourth outing: stays 1m: acts on polytrack and good to soft going: sometimes visored. *Karen George* **– a62**

PROUD JUNIOR (USA) 3 b.c. Proud Citizen (USA) 122 – Endless Reward (USA) (End Sweep (USA)) [2009 8d 7m 6f⁶ 8f⁴ 10m Jul 15] rangy colt: poor maiden. *S. A. Callaghan* **45**

PROUD KILLER 6 b.g. Killer Instinct 111 – Thewaari (USA) 68 (Eskimo (USA)) [2009 72: 6s Jul 21] big, leggy, useful-looking gelding: fair handicapper: well held only start in 2009: stays 7f: acts on fibresand and heavy going: has been visored/blinkered. *J. R. Jenkins* –

PROUD LINUS (USA) 4 b.g. Proud Citizen (USA) 122 – Radcliffe Yard (USA) (Boston Harbor (USA) 122) [2009 61: p7.1g p5.1g Nov 30] rather leggy, useful-looking gelding: maiden: once fairly useful, has regressed (shaped as though amiss both starts in 2009): edgy sort. *J. Ryan* –

PROUD TIMES (USA) 3 b.g. Proud Citizen (USA) 122 – Laura's Pistolette (USA) (Big Pistol (USA)) [2009 80p: 7g² 8.1v² 8g⁶ 11.1g² 12d⁵ Jul 24] rangy gelding: has scope: fairly useful maiden: seems to stay 1½m: raced only on good ground or softer (acts on heavy). *G. A. Swinbank* **80**

PROVISO 4 b.f. Dansili 127 – Binche (USA) 51 (Woodman (USA) 126) [2009 113: 8d* 9.3s⁵ 8m 8d³ 7g* p9f² a9f⁴ Nov 6] strong, deep-girthed filly: smart performer: first past post in minor event at Longchamp in April, Prix du Pin on same course (by neck from Varenar, final start for A. Fabre) in September and Juddmonte Spinster Stakes at Keeneland (beat Mushka 1¼ lengths but demoted to second after veering right inside final 1f) in October: creditable 4½ lengths third to Goldikova in Prix Rothschild at Deauville on fourth start: below-form fourth to Life Is Sweet in Breeders' Cup Ladies Classic at Santa Anita final start: effective at 7f to 10.5f: acts on polytrack, soft and good to firm ground: has made running, but often held up: races freely (ruined chance by refusing to settle in Windsor Forest Stakes at Royal Ascot third outing). *R. J. Frankel, USA* **118**

PROVOST 5 ch.g. Danehill Dancer (IRE) 117 – Dixielake (IRE) 84 (Lake Coniston (IRE) 131) [2009 68: f8g* f11g³ f8g p8.6g f7g f8g⁵ Dec 27] strong gelding: fair handicapper: won at Southwell in March: should stay beyond 1m: acts on all-weather, heavy and good to firm ground: none too consistent. *M. W. Easterby* **71**

PROWL 3 b.f. One Cool Cat (USA) 123 – Go Supersonic 66 (Zafonic (USA) 130) [2009 80: 6g⁵ 5.7g⁶ Sep 7] maiden: little impact in 2009. *E. A. L. Dunlop* **55**

PSEUDONYM (IRE) 7 ch.g. Daylami (IRE) 138 – Stage Struck (IRE) 83 (Sadler's Wells (USA) 132) [2009 74: p16g² p16.5g³ 16.4m⁶ 15g* 16.2m* 16.1g⁶ 16.2g⁵ 15.9m⁶ 15g⁴ 15g² 17.2m Sep 13] big, lengthy gelding: fair handicapper (including over hurdles): won at Warwick and Beverley in July: stayed 17f: acted on polytrack, good to firm and good to soft going: tried visored: tongue tied: dead. *M. F. Harris* **76**

PSYCHIC ABILITY (USA) 2 b.c. (Feb 4) Kingmambo (USA) 125 – Speed of Thought (USA) (Broad Brush (USA)) [2009 p8.6g⁶ 8.3g* Oct 28] 200,000 2-y-o: fourth foal: dam, French/US 1m/11f winner, half-sister to US Grade 3 1¼m winner Intensive Command: easily better effort in maidens when winning at Nottingham by 4 lengths from Dandino (wore cheekpieces): should stay 1¼m: open to further improvement. *Saeed bin Suroor* **87 p**

PSYCHOPATHICSANDRA (IRE) 2 ch.f. (Mar 21) Reel Buddy (USA) 118 – Waltzing Star (IRE) (Danehill (USA) 126) [2009 5.1m 7g⁵ 5.1m 5m⁴ 6s Oct 27] big, strong filly: fifth foal: half-sister to 6-y-o Isphahan and French 9.5f winner J'Attends Vincent (by Inchinor): dam unraced: no form. *A. Berry* –

RAGETTI (IRE) 2 b.f. (Feb 1) Hawk Wing (USA) 136 – Renada 67 (Sinndar (IRE) 134) [2009 7s⁴ Sep 5] close-coupled filly: 16/1 and green, fourth to Layla's Dancer in maiden at Thirsk, hanging left: dead. *J. Howard Johnson* **62**

RAGGLE TAGGLE (IRE) 3 b.f. Tagula (IRE) 116 – Jesting (Muhtarram (USA) 125) [2009 95: 5.1g 6d* 6g 5.7m f6f Oct 21] small, deep-girthed filly: fairly useful performer: won minor event at Newmarket in June: below form in handicaps after: stays 6f: acts on polytrack, soft and good to firm going. *R. M. Beckett* **92**

RAGSTA (IRE) 2 b.f. (Feb 25) Key of Luck (USA) 126 – Rag Top (IRE) 101 (Barathea (IRE) 127) [2009 5.1d² 6m⁴ 6g* p7g 7m² 7g p7m⁶ p8.6g p7g 8g⁴ 7d Oct 27] close-coupled filly: second foal: dam 2-y-o 5f to 7f winner: fair performer: won seller at Windsor in June: left R. Hannon £6,000 after fifth start, below form subsequently: stays 7f: acts on good to firm and good to soft going: claimed £7,000 after final start. *C. A. Dwyer* **68**

RAHAALA (IRE) 2 b.f. (Apr 5) Indian Ridge 123 – Mythie (FR) (Octagonal (NZ) 126) [2009 p7g⁵ Sep 8] 170,000F: well-made filly: third foal: half-sister to 3-y-o Versaki: dam French 10.5f winner: 4/1 and bit backward, encouraging 4¾ lengths fifth to Dawnbreak in maiden at Lingfield, not unduly knocked about: sure to improve. *Sir Michael Stoute* **57 p**

RAIMOND RIDGE (IRE) 3 b. or br.g. Namid 128 – Jinsiyah (USA) 98 (Housebuster (USA)) [2009 70: p6g⁴ p6g* p6g² p6g* p6g² p6g* p6g³ 6m² 6m⁶ 6m⁶ 5.9m⁴ 6m⁴ 6m³ p6m⁴ 6f² 6m³ 5.7f³ 5.1d² 6m 5m³ 6d⁶ 5.1m⁶ 5.3d⁶ p6g⁴ p5f⁶ Dec 19] compact gelding: fair performer: won seller at Lingfield in January, and handicaps at Kempton in February and Lingfield in March: placed 8 times after, leaving M. Channon 6,000 gns prior to final start: stays 6f: acts on polytrack, firm and soft ground: usually held up: tough. *J. Jay* **77**

RAIN AND SHADE 5 ch.g. Rainbow Quest (USA) 134 – Coretta (IRE) 118 (Caerleon (USA) 132) [2009 –: 9.9m 12m 12d May 16] tall, good-topped gelding: maiden: little form since 2007 (said to have had breathing problem last 2 outings): tried tongue tied. *E. W. Tuer* **–**

RAINBOW BAY 6 b.g. Komaite (USA) – Bollin Victoria 51 (Jalmood (USA) 126) [2009 64: f5g 6g 6f 6m 6d⁵ 6d⁵ 5g 6m⁴ 5g⁶ Sep 30] smallish, close-coupled gelding: modest performer: effective at 5f/6f: acts on polytrack, firm and soft going: wears headgear: inconsistent. *Miss Tracy Waggott* **54**

RAINBOW DESERT (USA) 3 b. or br.f. Dynaformer (USA) – Tuscoga (USA) (Theatrical 128) [2009 8.3d* 10.3s Nov 7] $650,000Y: closely related to smart US Grade 1 9f winner Dublino (by Lear Fan) and half-sister to several winners in USA: dam twice-raced sister to US Grade 1 1¼m winner Duda: highly promising when winning maiden at Windsor in October by 5 lengths from Etruscan, making most: similar form when eighth of 19 to Queen of Pentacles in listed race at Doncaster next time, still green: stays 1¼m: useful prospect. *Saeed bin Suroor* **86 p**

RAINBOW MIRAGE (IRE) 5 b.g. Spectrum (IRE) 126 – Embers of Fame (IRE) (Sadler's Wells (USA) 132) [2009 96: p8.6g² 8.1g⁴ f8g³ Aug 27] strong gelding: useful handicapper: in frame all 3 starts at 5 yrs: effective at 6f to 8.6f: acts on all-weather, heavy and good to firm going: tried blinkered. *E. S. McMahon* **94**

RAINBOW PEAK (IRE) 3 b.g. Hernando (FR) 127 – Celtic Fling 77 (Lion Cavern (USA) 117) [2009 p8g* 10m* 10v* Oct 24] useful-looking gelding: fifth foal: brother to smart 7f (at 2 yrs)/1m winner Celtic Heroine and half-brother to 2 winners, including fairly useful 7f winner Jacaranda Ridge (by Indian Ridge): dam, 1m winner, closely related to Celtic Swing: smart form: unbeaten in maiden at Kempton in May (suffered hairline fracture of pelvis after), minor event at Ascot in September and handicap at Newbury (comfortably beat Dr Livingstone ¾ length) in October: stays 1¼m: acts on polytrack, heavy and good to firm going: pattern performer in the making. *M. A. Jarvis* **112 p**

RAINBOW SIX 2 b.g. (Mar 13) Tiger Hill (IRE) 127 – Birthday Suit (IRE) 94 (Daylami (IRE) 138) [2009 p8.6g p8.6g⁴ Nov 21] 26,000Y: second foal: half-brother to fairly useful 3-y-o Excelsior Academy: dam, 2-y-o 5f winner, half-sister to Irish 1000 Guineas winner Classic Park, herself dam of Derby runner-up Walk In The Park: better effort in maidens at Wolverhampton when fourth to Bowdler's Magic, weakening quickly (gelded after): should be suited by 1¼m+: open to further improvement. *M. Botti* **57 p**

RAINBOW VIEW (USA) 3 b.f. Dynaformer (USA) – No Matter What (USA) 110 (Nureyev (USA) 131) [2009 119p: 8f⁵ 12g⁴ 8f³ 8g⁴ 9.9d² 8d* 10m² a9f⁵ Nov 6] **120**

'. . . Unbeaten Rainbow View reinforced her position as the top two-year-old filly with victory over the very promising Fantasia in the Fillies' Mile. If the top French filly Proportional, winner of the Prix Marcel Boussac, also makes the trip to

Coolmore Fusaichi Pegasus Matron Stakes, Leopardstown—
Rainbow View returns to winning ways in first-time cheekpieces; she shows an impressive turn of foot to beat Heaven Sent, Again (second left), Totally Devoted (second right) and San Sicharia (left)

Newmarket, the One Thousand Guineas will be a race to savour.' As the Introduction to *Racehorses of 2008* pointed out, there was much to anticipate in a meeting between three potentially top-class fillies, who had clearly been better than the usual run of leading juvenile fillies and had good prospects of improving again at three. Sadly, though, the savouring was all that there was. Rainbow View was the only one of the trio to make the line-up at Newmarket and she didn't even make the frame in the race itself. Subsequent events suggest the absence of Fantasia and Proportional was no great loss to the race. Fantasia had been bought in the winter by Rainbow View's owner and she won the principal Guineas trial, the Nell Gwyn at the Craven meeting, by seven lengths before being sent instead for the Poule d'Essai des Pouliches in which she finished third (the decision to avoid a clash with Rainbow View causing quite a commotion in the media at the time). A place behind Fantasia at Longchamp was Proportional, who had also been rerouted from Newmarket after a defeat in her trial race. Proportional failed to win a race all season, Fantasia was found wanting twice more at Group 1 level before gaining a consolation of sorts in a victory in the listed Sceptre Stakes at Doncaster in September. Despite being physically less imposing than the other pair and despite her reverse in the Guineas, Rainbow View went on to achieve the most success of the trio. All the same, she wasn't able to progress enough to maintain her position as the best of her generation and, in a series of races at between a mile and a mile and a half, she was generally beaten on merit, even if she did occasionally meet trouble in running and shape better than the result. A full campaign took in eight Group or Grade 1 races, of which she was able to win only the weakest, the Matron Stakes at Leopardstown.

Rainbow View won all four starts at two, including the Sweet Solera and May Hill Stakes as well as the Fillies' Mile, and she didn't reappear until the One Thousand Guineas. It was never intended that she should have a trial run, her trainer John Gosden happy to give her a much publicised piece of work on the course during the Craven meeting. Rainbow View's form was still boosted by the May Hill third Lahaleeb's win in the Fred Darling, as well as by Fantasia's success in the Nell Gwyn, and Rainbow View was sent off at 11/8-on, the first odds-on shot in the One Thousand Guineas since Bosra Sham in 1996. Although her form fully entitled Rainbow View to short-priced favouritism, she managed no better than fifth, not travelling with anything like the fluency expected and failing to produce the trademark turn of foot which had characterised her performances at two. She was beaten just under three lengths by Ghanaati, her trainer inclined to blame the prevailing firm ground; even if that was not the reason for her defeat it seemed wise at the time to give her the benefit of the doubt. At two, Rainbow View tended to sweat and be excitable, as she was before her gallop at the Craven meeting, but she was a fair bit calmer in the Guineas preliminaries.

It may be that a little of the spark had gone, for Rainbow View also stayed relatively calm (brought late into the paddock and trainer fined £140) before her next start, in the Oaks, and again before the Coronation Stakes. Although better than the result in both of those races, neither performance suggested she was about to show a return to the form of the previous autumn. There was sufficient expectation of a revival at the time for Rainbow View to start second favourite at Epsom, despite doubts about her ability to stay a mile and a half; she finished fourth behind the favourite Sariska, seemingly beaten on merit rather than by lack of stamina, spared an unnecessarily hard race after suffering interference two furlongs out. Rainbow View reopposed Ghanaati at Royal Ascot and might well have finished second, instead of third, had she not found herself very short of room, getting out with only a furlong left, as she tried to come from well off the pace in a truly-run race. The Coronation Stakes performance offered hope of a return to something like her best and the Falmouth Stakes at Newmarket's July meeting looked a good stepping stone. However, a steadily-run race did Rainbow View no favours and she was the first of the principals off the bridle, finishing only fourth behind Goldikova. The Falmouth confirmed that Rainbow View needed a true test at a mile and was probably ready for a return to further.

Rainbow View started favourite, ahead of the Oaks runner-up Midday on her next start in the Nassau Stakes over a mile and a quarter at Goodwood but Midday confirmed the Epsom form with authority, Rainbow View beaten on merit by two and a quarter lengths and producing her best effort of the season up to that point, matching the pick of her two-year-old form. Rainbow View thoroughly deserved her victory back at a mile in the Coolmore Fusaichi Pegasus Matron

Augustin Stables' "Rainbow View"

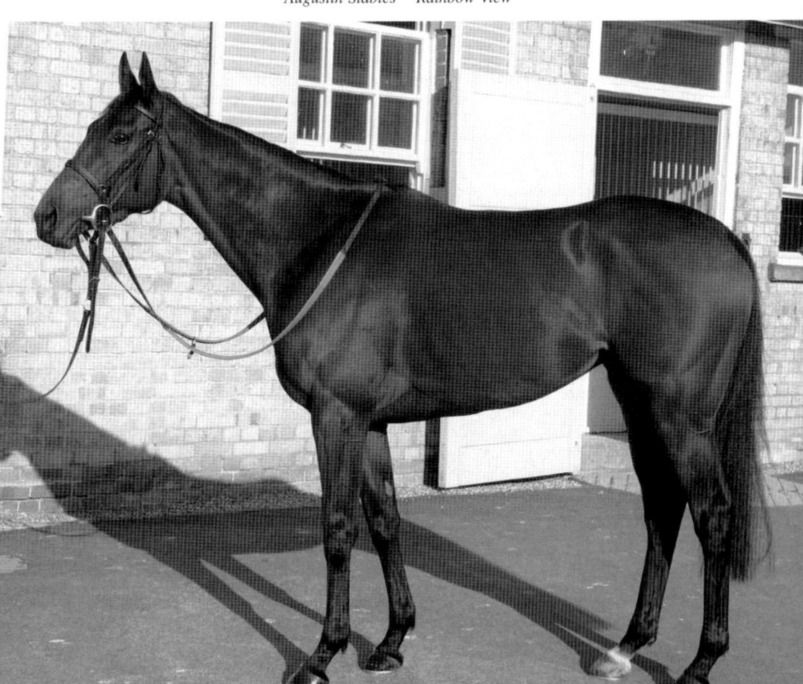

Stakes at Leopardstown in early-September, justifying favouritism to beat the six-year-old Heaven Sent, who had finished runner-up in the Falmouth, by two lengths. The only other contender with serious claims was the Irish One Thousand Guineas winner Again, though she had flopped in the Coronation Stakes and was having her first outing since. Tried in cheekpieces for the first time (she also wore them on both subsequent starts), Rainbow View produced her old turn of foot and quickened away in good style after travelling strongly from the start; Again finished a further four and a half lengths behind Heaven Sent in third.

Rainbow View (USA) (b.f. 2006)	Dynaformer (USA) (b or br 1985)	Roberto (b 1969)	Hail To Reason
			Bramalea
		Andover Way (b or br 1978)	His Majesty
			On The Trail
	No Matter What (USA) (ch 1997)	Nureyev (b 1977)	Northern Dancer
			Special
		Words of War (b 1989)	Lord At War
			Right Word

Rainbow View's last two runs were in North America. She wasn't discredited when second to Lahaleeb in the E. P. Taylor Stakes at Woodbine but her campaign ended on a low note when she managed only fifth of eight in the Breeders' Cup Ladies Classic at Santa Anita on her first start on an artificial surface. She remained in the States after that run and has joined Jonathan Sheppard. Sheppard already had charge of Rainbow View's half-brother Just As Well (by A P Indy), whose form improved markedly at the age of six in 2009 when he was awarded the Grade 1 Northern Dancer Stakes at Woodbine and finished second in the Arlington Million. If Rainbow View goes on to make an impact in the States, she won't be the first in her family to do well after being transferred there. Her year-older half-sister Winter View (by Thunder Gulch) won a couple of Grade 3 events in the States in 2009 (including the Bewitch Stakes over a mile and a half at Keeneland) after being moved from France, while their dam No Matter What won the Grade 1 Del Mar Oaks after winning in listed company in France. Rainbow View's erstwhile stable-companion Raven's Pass, out of a sister to No Matter What, won the Breeders' Cup Classic as a three-year-old after a full campaign in Europe in which he showed himself a top-class miler. The smallish Rainbow View has shown her best form at a mile to a mile and a quarter, though she probably stays a mile and a half, unlikely as it is that she will run again at that distance. She acts on soft and good to firm going, and probably on firm too, conditions which prevailed in the Coronation Stakes as well as the Guineas. She is usually waited with. Her tendency to get on edge in the preliminaries, very noticeable in her two-year-old days, was much less marked at three, though she had to be mounted on the walkway out to the course before the Nassau. *J. H. M. Gosden*

RAINBOW ZEST 6 b.g. Rainbow Quest (USA) 134 – Original (Caerleon (USA) 132) – [2009 70: 12.4m 8f 10g 7.9g 8m 10g Oct 16] good-topped gelding: fair performer at best: well below form in 2009 (said to have had breathing problem fourth start). *W. Storey*

RAIN DELAYED (IRE) 3 b.g. Oasis Dream 129 – Forever Phoenix 106 (Shareef 112 Dancer (USA) 135) [2009 92p: 6g^{5} 5g* 5m^{3} 5g* 5m^{2} p5g^{2} Oct 23] smart performer: much improved, and won minor events at Down Royal (beat Sioduil 2 lengths) in May and Tipperary (odds on) in June: second in handicap at York (beaten ½ length by Noble Storm) and listed race at Dundalk (length behind Arganil) after: best at 5f: acts on polytrack and good to firm going: tried tongue tied. *G. M. Lyons, Ireland*

RAINE'S CROSS 2 b.c. (Feb 22) Cape Cross (IRE) 129 – Branston Jewel (IRE) 95 97 (Prince Sabo 123) [2009 5.1g* 5m^{3} 6m 6g^{4} 7g^{3} 8m^{4} 8d* 8.5m^{2} Oct 3] 5,000F, £12,500Y: rather leggy colt: half-brother to useful 5f/6f (including at 2 yrs) winner Falcon Hill (by Polar Falcon): dam, 2-y-o 5f winner, half-sister to Branston Abby (smart at 6f/7f) and Desert Deer (very smart at 1m/1¼m): useful performer: won maiden at Bath in April and minor event at Salisbury (beat Dancing David ½ length) in September: stays 8.5f: acts on good to firm and good to soft going: consistent. *P. Winkworth*

RAINE SUPREME 2 b.f. (Jan 17) Mind Games 121 – Supreme Angel 85 (Beveled 53 (USA)) [2009 5.1m^{6} 5m 7g^{3} 7m^{6} p6g Dec 14] £1,200Y: small, leggy filly: third foal: half-sister to winner in North America by Vettori: dam 5f (including at 2 yrs)/6f winner: maiden plater: barely stays 7f. *E. S. McMahon*

RAIN FOREST 2 b.c. (Apr 14) Sadler's Wells (USA) 132 – Gryada 93 (Shirley Heights 130) [2009 8d Oct 21] 200,000Y: closely related to 3 winners, notably 3-y-o Fame And Glory, and half-brother to several winners, including smart 7f (at 2 yrs) to 1½m winner Grampian (by Selkirk): dam, 2-y-o 7f/1m winner, closely related to useful stayer Gondolier: 20/1 and very green, eighth to stable-companion Flying Cross in maiden at Navan, soon off bridle and best work late on: will be suited by 1¼m+: will improve. *A. P. O'Brien, Ireland* **67 p**

RAINIERS GIRL 3 b.f. Tobougg (IRE) 125 – Premier Night 102 (Old Vic 136) [2009 p10m p12g p8m^5 p8m^5 Dec 6] big filly: seventh foal: half-sister to fairly useful 11.5f winner Sir Brastias (by Shaamit) and 1¾m winner Flamenco Bride (by Hernando): dam 1½m to 2m winner: modest maiden: bred to stay 1¼m+. *R. A. Teal* **50**

RAIN IN THE COURSE 2 b.f. (Feb 10) Royal Applause 124 – Numanthia (IRE) 56 (Barathea (IRE) 127) [2009 8.1d 7.5m Sep 16] £11,000Y: neat filly: first foal: dam, maiden (stayed 9.5f), half-sister to 2-y-o Layali Al Andalus: very green and well held in maidens. *M. R. Channon* **–**

RAIN ON THE WIND (IRE) 2 b.g. (Apr 8) Bahamian Bounty 116 – Mix Me Up (FR) (Linamix (FR) 127) [2009 p6g p6g p5m^4 Sep 23] rather unfurnished gelding: modest form in maidens, bit awkward final start (gelded after): free-going sort, may prove best at 5f/6f. *S. C. Williams* **63**

RAINSBOROUGH 2 b.g. (Apr 30) Trans Island 119 – Greeba 63 (Fairy King (USA)) [2009 6m^5 7m 6g* 7g 8m p7f^2 7m^3 p7m p8m 7m f8m^2 p8g^2 f8f^5 p7f Dec 20] tall, angular gelding: modest performer: won seller at Leicester in July: claimed from M. Channon £7,000 sixth start: stays 1m: acts on all-weather and good to firm going: tried tongue tied/blinkered/in cheekpieces. *S. Curran* **64**

RAIN STOPS PLAY (IRE) 7 b.g. Desert Prince (IRE) 130 – Pinta (IRE) (Ahonoora 122) [2009 64§: p9.5g^5 9.1g^2 8g^4 7.9g^4 10m^4 9.9g 10g Oct 16] leggy gelding: modest handicapper: stays 1¼m: acts on soft and good to firm going: tried visored/in cheekpieces: sometimes hangs/carries head awkwardly: one to be wary of. *N. G. Richards* **59 §**

RAINY NIGHT 3 b.g. Kyllachy 129 – Rainy Day Song 61 (Persian Bold 123) [2009 65+: 6.1f^6 6.1g^2 6.1m^4 6m^5 6.1g 5m^2 5.7g^4 p5.1g* p6g^4 Oct 16] fair handicapper: won at Wolverhampton in September: raced only at 5f/6f: acts on polytrack and firm going: races prominently. *R. Hollinshead* **72**

RAISE ALL IN (IRE) 3 b.f. Exceed And Excel (AUS) 126 – Inforapenny 111 (Deploy 131) [2009 67d: 6m 7m May 26] compact filly: regressive maiden. *N. Wilson* **–**

RAISE YOUR HEART (IRE) 6 b.g. Raise A Grand (IRE) 114 – Gobolino (Don 128) [2009 10d* 10s^2 8v^2 10s* 10d* Oct 26] good-topped gelding: useful hurdler, successful in August: improved into a smart performer on Flat (having missed 2008), winning handicaps at Leopardstown (apprentices, by 8 lengths) in July and the Curragh (by 1¾ lengths from Precious Gem) in September, and listed race at Leopardstown (beat Distant Memories 2 lengths) in October: stays 1¼m: acts on heavy going: usually travels strongly held up: game. *Ms Joanna Morgan, Ireland* **113**

RAJAMAND (FR) 3 gr.g. Linamix (FR) 127 – Ridafa (IRE) (Darshaan 133) [2009 12g 13d^4 p10g^5 p12g^4 Dec 2] second foal: half-brother to French 9f winner Rijaiyma (by Desert Prince): dam French 1½m winner: fairly useful performer: trained by A. de Royer Dupre in France first 2 starts: 7¼ lengths fourth of 5 to Tripitaka in handicap at Kempton final outing, unsuited by emphasis on speed. *Miss E. C. Lavelle* **81 +**

RAJEH (IRE) 6 b.g. Key of Luck (USA) 126 – Saramacca (IRE) 54 (Kahyasi 130) [2009 99: 12g^3 14.1m^3 20m 12m^5 14g^6 Jul 28] sturdy gelding: useful handicapper: at least respectable efforts most starts in 2009: stays 14.8f (didn't stay 2½m): acts on good to firm and good to soft ground: reliable: fairly useful hurdler, won in August/September. *J. L. Spearing* **97**

RA JUNIOR (USA) 3 b.g. Rahy (USA) 115 – Fantasia Girl (IRE) 101 (Caerleon (USA) 132) [2009 100: a9f 10.4m 9.9g 10.4m 10.2d Oct 15] good-topped gelding: fairly useful performer: creditable effort at 3 yrs only when seventh in quite valuable handicap at Goodwood third outing: stays 1¼m: acts on good to firm going: tried blinkered/tongue tied/in cheekpieces: sometimes slowly away: sold only 4,500 gns, then gelded. *B. J. Meehan* **94**

RAKAAN (IRE) 2 ch.g. (Jan 23) Bahamian Bounty 116 – Petite Spectre 74 (Spectrum (IRE) 126) [2009 6g^2 6m^2 6m^3 6g 6m^2 p6g^2 6.5m 5.7m* Sep 28] 45,000F, 140,000Y: compact colt: first foal: dam, 2-y-o 6f winner, half-sister to useful 2002 2-y-o 5f to 7f winner Rag Top: fairly useful performer: landed odds in maiden at Bath in September: **90 §**

runner-up in similar company earlier, and also good third to Canford Cliffs in Coventry Stakes at Royal Ascot (flattered coming off strong pace): stays 6f: acts on good to firm going: tried blinkered: not one to trust: sold 26,000 gns. *B. J. Meehan*

RAKHAPURA (IRE) 2 b.c. (Mar 10) Arakan (USA) 123 – Indistinto (Groom Dancer (USA) 128) [2009 6g p8f⁵ p8g⁶ Oct 26] modest form last 2 starts in maidens: stays 1m: sold 5,500 gns, sent to Serbia. *P. R. Webber* **62**

RAKHINE (IRE) 2 b.g. (Feb 4) Arakan (USA) 123 – Amorous Pursuits (Pursuit of Love 124) [2009 6d⁵ 5.7f⁴ 6d 6g⁶ 8m* p8m Oct 12] good-topped gelding: modest performer: won selling nursery at Yarmouth in September: stays 1m: acts on firm going: blinkered once: sold 3,000 gns. *P. F. I. Cole* **59**

RALEIGH QUAY (IRE) 2 b.c. (Mar 27) Bachelor Duke (USA) 122 – Speedbird (USA) 76 (Sky Classic (CAN)) [2009 6m⁶ 5.9g⁶ 6g² 7.1s* 8g Oct 19] €7,000F, £2,400Y, £12,000 2-y-o: strong colt: first living foal: dam, maiden (stayed 7f), out of half-sister to Poule d'Essai des Pouliches winner Rose Gypsy: fair performer: won maiden at Musselburgh in August: stays 7f: acts on soft ground. *Micky Hammond* **70**

RAMAMARA (IRE) 2 ch.f. (Mar 7) Trans Island 119 – Kaskazi (Dancing Brave (USA) 140) [2009 5.1m⁶ p6g* 5.7f² 6m* p7g³ 6.5m 5.1m³ 5g p6g⁶ p6g³ p7g³ p7m⁴ p6m³ p6g² p6f⁴ p7f Dec 20] small, close-coupled filly: eighth foal: half-sister to fairly useful 5f/6f winner Trinity (by College Chapel): dam Irish 9f/1¼m winner: fairly useful performer: won seller at Lingfield and minor event at Windsor in August: stays 7f: acts on polytrack and firm going: none too consistent. *P. D. Evans* **81**

RAMAYANA (IRE) 2 b.f. (May 19) Arakan (USA) 123 – Dance Land (IRE) (Nordance (USA)) [2009 7m 6m p5m p8g Nov 14] €1,800Y, €5,500 2-y-o: lengthy, angular filly: half-sister to several winners, including 4-y-o Barraland and Irish 1½m/1¾m winner Dariole (by Priolo): dam unraced: little form, including in claimer. *M. R. Channon* **–**

RAMBLIN BOB 4 b.g. Piccolo 121 – Bijan (IRE) 75 (Mukaddamah (USA) 125) [2009 54§: p7g p5g* p6g p6g 5g p8g⁶ 7g Jun 27] quite attractive gelding: modest handicapper: form in 2009 only when winning at Lingfield in March: best at 5f/6f: acts on polytrack: sometimes blinkered/tongue tied (including for win): unreliable: withdrawn after rearing over in stall intended fifth outing. *W. J. Musson* **54 §**

RAMBLING LIGHT 5 b.g. Fantastic Light (USA) 134 – Rambler 74 (Selkirk (USA) 129) [2009 81, a87: 8m⁴ 7m Jun 12] smallish, well-made, attractive gelding: fairly useful handicapper: stayed 8.6f: raced only on polytrack and good ground or firmer: wore cheekpieces/visor: tongue tied final outing: dead. *A. M. Balding* **81**

RAMBLING ROSIE (IRE) 3 b.f. Rambling Bear 115 – La Noisette (Rock Hopper 124) [2009 7s p8g p6g 6.1g⁴ Jul 4] poor form in maidens/sellers: dead. *C. Drew* **42**

RAMONA CHASE 4 b.g. High Chaparral (IRE) 132 – Audacieuse 113 (Rainbow Quest (USA) 134) [2009 103: p10g⁴ 10.1g 9m 10.1g⁶ 10m⁵ 10m 10.1m³ 9.9m Sep 13] leggy gelding: fairly useful handicapper nowadays: stays 1¼m: acts on polytrack, soft and good to firm ground: held up: headstrong, attitude under suspicion. *M. J. Attwater* **94**

RAMORA (USA) 3 br.f. Monsun (GER) 124 – Madame Cerito (USA) 100 (Diesis 133) [2009 12m³ 12m² 11.7m³ p10m² p13.9g² p12g Oct 22] $475,000F: rather leggy filly: second foal: dam, Irish 1m winner (later successful in USA), half-sister to smart German performer up to 1½m Ransom O'War: fair maiden: placed first 5 starts: possibly amiss when tailed off final outing: stays easy 1¾m: raced only on polytrack and good to firm ground. *H. R. A. Cecil* **77**

RAMPANT RONNIE (USA) 4 b.g. Honor Glide (USA) 119 – Jalfrezi 103 (Jalmood (USA) 126) [2009 62: p10g p9.5g f8g⁴ 8.1m Aug 20] compact gelding: modest performer: sold out of P. D'Arcy's stable £900 after third outing: stays 10.9f: acts on all-weather and firm ground: fair hurdler. *Mrs A. M. Thorpe* **51**

RAMVASWANI (IRE) 6 b.g. Spectrum (IRE) 126 – Caesarea (GER) (Generous (IRE) 139) [2009 –: f11g² p12.2g p16.5g⁴ Feb 20] modest maiden handicapper: probably stays 2m: acts on all-weather: tried in cheekpieces (below form): none too consistent. *N. B. King* **58**

RANDAMA BAY (IRE) 4 b. or br.g. Frenchmans Bay (FR) 118 – Randama 77 (Akarad (FR) 130) [2009 85: p8.6g² p8.6g⁴ p7g³ p8g⁶ p8g 8m 10d⁶ 10.4g⁴ 11.9d² p10m⁶ Sep 26] leggy gelding: fair handicapper: stayed 1½m: acted on polytrack, good to firm and good to soft going: dead. *I. A. Wood* **78**

RANGEFINDER 5 gr.h. Linamix (FR) 127 – Risen Raven (USA) 111 (Risen Star (USA)) [2009 9.8m³ 12m 10.3d³ 10s² 12s* 12g 12s Nov 7] sturdy horse: half-brother to **95**

several winners in Germany, including 9f to 11f winner Rinconada (by Lavirco): dam German 1m (at 2 yrs) to 11f (Preis der Diana) winner: useful handicapper: winner of 5 races in Italy, including at Livorno and Varese in 2008 for M. Gasparini: won at Thirsk in September: below form after, leaving L. Cumani 28,000 gns prior to final outing: stays 1½m: acts on soft and good to firm ground. *Jane Chapple-Hyam*

RANK BAJIN 2 b.f. (Feb 1) Red Ransom (USA) – Sharp As A Tack (IRE) 86 (Zafonic –
(USA) 130) [2009 6m Jun 10] first foal: dam, 2-y-o 7f winner, half-sister to smart 6f/7f performer Twilight Blues: 18/1 and very green, last in maiden at Haydock. *E. J. Alston*

RANN NA CILLE (IRE) 5 b.m. Agnes World (USA) 123 – Omanah (USA) (Kayra- 46
wan (USA) 91) [2009 62: p5g^{4} p5.1g Mar 30] good-bodied mare: just poor form in 2009, reportedly lame final outing: best at 5f: acts on all-weather, good to firm and good to soft going (below form on soft): tried blinkered/in cheekpieces: races prominently. *P. T. Midgley*

RANNOCH ROSE (IRE) 3 b.f. Court Cave (IRE) – Lady Semillon (IRE) 84 52
(Semillon 116) [2009 p9.5g p11g^{2} p12.2g 9.8m^{5} 11.5m Jun 4] third foal: dam Irish 7f winner: modest maiden: stays 11f: raced only on polytrack and good to firm going: tried in cheekpieces: looked awkward last 2 outings. *J. L. Spearing*

RANSOM NOTE 2 b.c. (Feb 20) Red Ransom (USA) – Zacheta (Polish Precedent 81 +
(USA) 131) [2009 7g 7m* 7m 7d* Oct 11] 30,000Y: sturdy, compact colt: fourth foal: half-brother to fairly useful 11.5f winner Dawn Sky (by Fantastic Light): dam unraced half-sister to Prix de l'Arc de Triomphe winner Marienbard: progressive form, winning maiden at Chester in August and nursery at Goodwood (beat Brick Red by nose) in October: will be suited by 1m: acts on good to firm and good to soft going. *B. W. Hills*

RAPANUI BELLE 3 b.f. Compton Place 125 – Belle Ile (USA) 67 (Diesis 133) [2009 50
44: p7g^{5} p5g p5.1g^{2} p5.1g 5.7f 5.3g^{4} 5.3m 6d^{3} 5.3f 6.1d p5.1g^{3} p5m^{4} p5m Oct 7] lengthy filly: had a quick action: modest maiden handicapper: lost action and pulled up final outing: was effective at 5f to 7f: acted on polytrack and good to soft going: blinkered last 3 starts: inconsistent: dead. *G. L. Moore*

RAPID CITY 6 b.g. Dansili 127 – West Dakota (USA) (Gone West (USA)) [2009 93d: 77
p10g^{6} p12g* f12g^{6} p10g^{3} p10g^{3} p12.2g^{4} p10g* p9.5g^{2} 10m* 10.2m p10m^{5} Dec 16] lengthy gelding: fair performer nowadays: won seller in January and claimer in March, both at Lingfield, and, having left A. McCabe £8,000 eighth outing, handicap at Brighton in April: left Jim Best before final start (claimed to join P. D. Evans £10,000): stays easy 1½m: acts on polytrack and good to firm going: usually in cheekpieces: held up. *G. L. Moore*

RAPID DESIRE (IRE) 3 b.f. Statue of Liberty (USA) 115 – Whistfilly 49 (First 57 §
Trump 118) [2009 10.1d^{3} 10.3s f11g 16d^{5} 16.1d 15.8s Oct 27] €6,500Y: third foal: half-sister to 2007 2-y-o 6f winner Hansinger (by Namid), later smart 6f/7f winner in Scandinavia, and 6-y-o Mister Pete: dam, maiden, sister to Flying Childers Stakes winner Mrs P: modest maiden: stays 2m: tried in cheekpieces: ungenuine. *J. R. Weymes*

RAPID FLOW 7 b.g. Fasliyev (USA) 120 – Fleet River (USA) 93 (Riverman (USA) 44
131) [2009 36: f6s p5.1g^{5} 5m Jun 25] lengthy, workmanlike gelding: poor maiden: probably stays 8.6f: acts on polytrack: inconsistent. *J. W. Unett*

RAPID LIGHT 3 ch.f. Tobougg (IRE) 125 – La Coqueta (GER) (Kris 135) [2009 66p: –
p8g Jun 6] third in maiden at Great Leighs sole outing at 2 yrs: tailed off in similar event at Lingfield 6 months later: bred to stay 1¼m: sold 2,000 gns. *E. A. L. Dunlop*

RAPID WATER 3 b.g. Anabaa (USA) 130 – Lochsong 129 (Song 132) [2009 65p: 6m* 88
6g^{5} 6g^{5} 6m* 6m^{4} Aug 14] good-quartered gelding: fairly useful form: won maiden at Salisbury in May and handicap at Ascot in July: reportedly pulled a muscle final outing (gelded after): will prove best at 5f/6f: raced only on good/good to firm going. *A. M. Balding*

RAPTOR (GER) 6 b.g. Auenadler (GER) 114 – Royal Cat (Royal Academy (USA) 92
130) [2009 106: p8.6g 8m 8.1v^{3} 8m^{3} 8m 7.2s Aug 27] big, good-topped gelding: fairly useful handicapper nowadays: trained by K. R. Burke prior to final outing: effective at testing 6f to 1m: acts on polytrack and heavy going: tried blinkered, visored last 3 starts: has worn tongue tie: sold 4,000 gns, joined M. Rimmer. *A. P. Jarvis*

RAQEEB (USA) 2 b.c. (May 2) Seeking The Gold (USA) – Sayedah (IRE) 105 –
(Darshaan 133) [2009 p8g Nov 14] fifth foal: dam, won Rockfel Stakes, out of half-sister to US Grade 2 7f winner Kayrawan: 12/1 and very green, down the field in maiden at Lingfield. *Sir Michael Stoute*

RAQUEL WHITE 5 b.m. Robellino (USA) 127 – Spinella (Teenoso (USA) 135) [2009 71: f12s* f12g^{6} Feb 1] workmanlike mare: modest handicapper: won at Southwell in January: free-going sort: stays 1½m: acts on all-weather and soft ground: tried in blinkers. *J. L. Flint* **63**

RARE ART 3 b.c. Kyllachy 129 – Succumb (Pursuit of Love 124) [2009 74: 6g^{3} f6g^{5} p6g Jul 8] sturdy colt: fair handicapper: should prove best at 5f/6f: raced only on all-weather and good going or softer (acts on heavy): sold 6,000 gns, sent to Bahrain. *S. A. Callaghan* **74**

RARE BET 3 b.f. Bertolini (USA) 125 – Rare Old Times (IRE) 72 (Inzar (USA) 112) [2009 6f 7.1m^{5} 5.7g Sep 7] third foal: dam 2-y-o 5f winner: no form. *W. G. M. Turner* **–**

RARE COINCIDENCE 8 ch.g. Atraf 116 – Green Seed (IRE) 78 (Lead On Time (USA) 123) [2009 71: p16.5g* 16m^{3} f16g 13m^{6} p16.5g 16.1d p12.2g^{5} p13.9g p13.9g Dec 14] quite good-topped gelding: fair handicapper: won at Wolverhampton in April: stays easy 16.5f: acts on all-weather, firm and soft ground: wears cheekpieces: tried tongue tied (including last 4 starts): makes running. *R. F. Fisher* **69**

RARE MALT (IRE) 2 b.f. (Feb 26) Intikhab (USA) 135 – A'Bunadh (USA) (Diesis 133) [2009 7g^{4} p8g^{2} p8f^{2} Sep 4] €6,500Y, €9,000 2-y-o: third foal: dam unraced: best effort in maidens when length second to Dyna Waltz at Kempton second start, shaping as though will stay beyond 1m. *Miss Amy Weaver* **79**

RARE RUBY (IRE) 5 b.m. Dilshaan 119 – Ruby Setting 91 (Gorytus (USA) 132) [2009 70: 16g^{2} 14.1g* 15m* 17.1m^{5} 15g^{6} 14d^{3} 15.8s Oct 27] lengthy mare: fair handicapper: won at Nottingham in June and Warwick in July: seemingly stays 17f: acts on good to firm and good to soft going: tried blinkered/in cheekpieces. *Jennie Candlish* **73**

RARE VIRTUE (USA) 3 b.f. Empire Maker (USA) 129 – Heat Haze 120 (Green Desert (USA) 127) [2009 10s Apr 17] rangy filly: first living foal: dam, French/US 6.5f to 9.5f winner, out of outstanding broodmare Hasili: 14/1 and green (fell over entering paddock and walked to post), soundly beaten in maiden at Newbury: stud. *H. R. A. Cecil* **–**

RASAMAN (IRE) 5 b.g. Namid 128 – Rasana 74 (Royal Academy (USA) 130) [2009 91: 5f^{2} 5d* 5m^{6} 6m^{4} 6m 5.1m^{4} 6m 5d^{3} 6g* 5.1m 5m^{2} 6m^{6} 6m 6.1m* 5g Oct 9] sturdy gelding: type to carry condition: fairly useful performer: won handicap at Thirsk in May, claimer at Catterick (left K. Ryan £15,000) in August and handicap at Chester in September: poorly drawn at York final outing: best at 5f/6f: acts on all-weather, firm and soft ground: often wears cheekpieces/visor: sometimes tongue tied. *J. S. Goldie* **93**

RASCAL IN THE MIX (USA) 3 gr. or ro.f. Tapit (USA) 118 – Ready Cat (USA) (Storm Cat (USA)) [2009 56p: 6m^{3} 6g^{6} 8g 8.5m p9.5g^{2} p8g Nov 1] modest maiden: seems to stay 9.5f: acts on all-weather and good to firm going. *R. M. Whitaker* **56**

RASCASSE 4 b.g. Where Or When (IRE) 124 – Sure Flyer (IRE) (Sure Blade (USA) 130) [2009 52: 7m 11.1g 7.9g 14.1m Jun 15] workmanlike gelding: maiden: little form in 2009: tried blinkered. *Bruce Hellier* **–**

RASHAAD (USA) 2 b.c. (Mar 28) Smart Strike (CAN) 121 – Martinique (USA) (Pleasant Colony (USA)) [2009 7g* Oct 23] $650,000Y: rangy colt: third foal: brother to 2 winners in US, including smart Grade 3 9.5f/1½m winner Communique: dam, US 9f winner, half-sister to high-class 1¼m performer Muhtarram: 3/1, highly promising when winning maiden at Doncaster by ½ length from Robinson Cruso, travelling strongly and showing excellent attitude: should stay at least 1¼m: useful prospect. *B. W. Hills* **90 p**

RASH JUDGEMENT 4 b.g. Mark of Esteem (IRE) 137 – Let Alone 78 (Warning 136) [2009 92: 6d* 6g^{2} 6m^{3} 6g 6m 6d Oct 11] deep-girthed gelding: useful handicapper: won at Folkestone in April: below form last 3 starts: may prove best at stiff 5f/6f: acts on firm and good to soft going: nervy sort, often rears as stall opens. *W. S. Kittow* **95**

RASLAN 6 b.g. Lomitas 129 – Rosia (IRE) (Mr Prospector (USA)) [2009 17.2m^{3} 18m Oct 17] lengthy gelding: has a round action: fairly useful handicapper: fit from hurdling (useful form), better effort in 2009 when third at Bath: stays 2½m: acts on polytrack and good to firm ground: often visored, also tongue tied in 2009. *D. E. Pipe* **91**

RASMY 2 b.c. (May 31) Red Ransom (USA) – Shadow Dancing 110 (Unfuwain (USA) 131) [2009 7m^{5} 8g* Oct 21] 68,000Y: sturdy colt: third foal: half-brother to 3-y-o Hazy Dancer: dam, 1m (at 2 yrs) and 11.4f winner, out of smart performer up to 1¾m Salchow: plenty of promise in maidens, winning at Bath by 5 lengths from Breakheart: will stay 1¼m: already useful, and should continue to progress. *M. P. Tregoning* **97 p**

RASSELAS (IRE) 2 b.g. (Apr 28) Danehill Dancer (IRE) 117 – Regal Darcey (IRE) 67 (Darshaan 133) [2009 7g^{5} 7g^{4} 7m 8m Oct 16] 120,000Y: compact gelding: has a fluent action: fourth foal: dam, lightly-raced sister to smart 1½m winner Talaash, out of sister to **77**

King George VI and Queen Elizabeth Stakes winner King's Theatre: fair maiden: should stay 1m (pulled hard when tried at trip): has carried head awkwardly: gelded after final start. *B. W. Hills*

RATHBAWN GIRL (IRE) 2 b.f. (Apr 1) Alamshar (IRE) 133 – Rathbawn Realm (Doulab (USA) 115) [2009 6d p6f^4 f6d^5 Dec 29] half-sister to several winners, including 4-y-o Spirit of Sharjah: dam Irish 7f winner: best effort in maidens (trained by M. Squance on debut) when fourth at Kempton: likely to stay 7f. *Miss J. Feilden* **57**

RATHLIN LIGHT (USA) 3 b. or br.f. Grand Slam (USA) 120 – Baltic Sea (CAN) (Danzig (USA)) [2009 60p: p5g^2 5m^2 5m* 5m Jun 20] fair form: won handicap at Lingfield in May: stiff task in listed race at Ayr final outing: raced only at 5f: acts on polytrack and good to firm going: tongue tied last 2 starts: tail swisher. *W. R. Swinburn* **70**

RATHMOLYON 4 ch.f. Bahamian Bounty 116 – Feather Circle (IRE) 64 (Indian Ridge 123) [2009 61: 5.1m 5.3m 5g 5.1d 5.1m Sep 28] workmanlike filly: poor maiden nowadays: best at bare 5f: acts on firm and good to soft going, probably on polytrack: tried visored, blinkered last 2 starts. *D. Haydn Jones* **46**

RATTAN (USA) 4 ch.c. Royal Anthem (USA) 135 – Rouwaki (USA) (Miswaki (USA) 124) [2009 96: 8m 8.1v^2 p10g^2 8g Aug 31] big, close-coupled colt: fairly useful handicapper: creditable efforts when runner-up at Haydock and Kempton: stays 1¼m: acts on polytrack and heavy going. *Rae Guest* **93**

RAUCOUS (GER) 6 b.g. Zinaad 114 – Roseola (GER) (Acatenango (GER) 127) [2009 f12g^4 12.5m* 14m 12.4g* 12g^4 May 5] tall, leggy gelding: fair performer nowadays (missed 2008): won seller at Musselburgh and handicap at Newcastle in April: said to have finished lame final outing: stays 2m: raced mostly on good going or firmer: blinkered (found little) third outing: races prominently. *Mrs R. A. Carr* **77**

RAVENFIELD (IRE) 2 b.c. (Mar 8) Xaar 132 – Rubyanne (IRE) 83 (Fasliyev (USA) 120) [2009 5m^6 Sep 16] €6,000Y: neat colt: first foal: dam 2-y-o 5f winner: 33/1, 3½ lengths sixth to Elusive Trader in maiden at Beverley, finishing well from rear: will stay 6f: should improve. *D. H. Brown* **59 p**

RAVENS ROSE 2 b.f. (Mar 13) Bold Edge 123 – Marjeune 70 (Marju (IRE) 127) [2009 6m p8g* Oct 2] leggy filly: first foal: dam, 2-y-o 1¼m winner, stayed 2m: still green, much better effort in maidens over 3 months apart when winning at Lingfield by nose from Folletta, rallying: open to further improvement. *J. G. Portman* **71 p**

RAVI RIVER (IRE) 5 ch.g. Barathea (IRE) 127 – Echo River (USA) 101 (Irish River (FR) 131) [2009 84: p7.1g^2 p7.1g* p7g* p8.6g p7g^2 p6g^5 p7.1g^6 p7g* p7g^5 p7g p7.1g^3 p7.1g^6 p8m^4 Dec 30] strong, good-bodied gelding: fairly useful performer: won handicap at Wolverhampton and claimer at Kempton in February and, having left Tom Dascombe after fifth start, handicap at Lingfield in October: left J. Boyle, respectable efforts last 2 starts: best at 7f: acts on polytrack and good to firm going. *P. D. Evans* **87**

RAWAABET (IRE) 7 b.g. Bahhare (USA) 122 – Haddeyah (USA) 68 (Dayjur (USA) 137) [2009 53: 12.1m^4 12d 11.8m Jul 16] good-topped gelding: modest performer: stays 1½m: acts on all-weather, good to firm and good to soft going: often tongue tied nowadays: sometimes slowly away. *R. Hollinshead* **55**

RAWAAJ 3 gr.g. Linamix (FR) 127 – Inaaq 109 (Lammtarra (USA) 134) [2009 62p: p12g Oct 22] close-coupled gelding: modest maiden at 2 yrs: well held in handicap only outing in 2009: should be suited by 1¼m/1½m: sold 10,000 gns, joined D. McCain Jnr. *Sir Michael Stoute* **–**

RAWDON (IRE) 8 b.g. Singspiel (IRE) 133 – Rebecca Sharp 122 (Machiavellian (USA) 123) [2009 80: p10g f12g^2 f12g* f12g^2 p12.2g f12d^2 p13g^2 12m f12g^2 11.6m f12g^3 11.9s^4 p12g^5 11.9m^5 Jun 23] tall, good-topped gelding: fair performer: claimed from M. Bell £5,500, easily won seller at Southwell in February: runner-up 4 times after: stays 1½m: acts on all-weather, soft and good to firm going: usually visored/blinkered: often tongue tied: finds little (reportedly has breathing problem). *Miss Gay Kelleway* **78 §**

RAWNAQ (IRE) 2 b.c. (Mar 9) Azamour (IRE) 130 – Sharemata (IRE) (Doyoun 124) [2009 7m^4 Sep 10] 28,000F: seventh foal: half-brother to 2 winners in Ireland, including fairly useful 1¼m winner Sharesha (by Ashkalani): dam, French 10.5f winner, out of half-sister to Derby winner Shahrastani: 7/1 and green, 6 lengths fourth to Five Cents in maiden at Epsom, slowly away and soon pushed along: will be suited by 1¼m+: should improve. *M. Johnston* **63 p**

RAY DIAMOND 4 ch.g. Medicean 128 – Musical Twist (USA) 97 (Woodman (USA) 126) [2009 52: p10g^4 Jan 10] close-coupled gelding: poor maiden: stays 1m: acts on polytrack, little form on turf: often sweats: tried in cheekpieces: fair hurdler. *M. Madgwick* **–**

RAYENI (IRE) 3 ch.c. Indian Ridge 123 – Rayyana (IRE) 102 (Rainbow Quest (USA) 134) [2009 109p: 8v^2 8s^4 6s* 7s^2 Nov 5] lengthy, good-topped colt: smart performer: reportedly had setback in March: won listed race at the Curragh in October by neck from Luisant: in frame other starts, in Irish 2000 Guineas (best effort, 4½ lengths second to Mastercraftsman despite twice being hampered) and Solonaway Stakes (fourth to Border Patrol), both on same course, and listed race at Leopardstown (2 lengths second to Libano): effective at 6f (given test) to 1m: acts on heavy going (unraced on good or firmer). *John M. Oxx, Ireland* **118**

RAYHANI (USA) 6 b.g. Theatrical 128 – Bahr Alsalaam (USA) (Riverman (USA) 131) [2009 100: 10m 12s 12s 13.1m 12g* Oct 6] big, strong, attractive gelding: type to carry condition: fairly useful handicapper: easily best effort in 2009 when making all at Catterick: stays 1½m: acts on polytrack and good to firm going: tried blinkered: joined J. Nash in Ireland. *D. Nicholls* **88**

RAY OF JOY 3 b.f. Tobougg (IRE) 125 – Once Removed 65 (Distant Relative 128) [2009 77: p6g* 6m p6g^3 6m^6 p6g p6g^2 p7g^3 p6m^4 p6m p6m Dec 30] sturdy filly: fairly useful handicapper: won at Kempton in April: good efforts in frame there 4 times after: best at 6f: acts on polytrack, good to firm and good to soft going. *J. R. Jenkins* **92**

REACH FOR THE SKY (IRE) 2 b.f. (Apr 11) Elusive City (USA) 117 – Zara Whetei (IRE) (Lomond (USA) 128) [2009 6m* 5.2d 6g 6m^4 p6g^6 p6m 6g^4 Oct 19] 2,000Y: small, sturdy filly: sixth foal: half-sister to winner in Spain by Lake Coniston: dam Italian 7f (at 2 yrs) to 1¼m winner: fair performer: won maiden at Goodwood in May: will stay 7f: acts on good to firm going: sold 3,500 gns, joined A. Bailey. *R. Hannon* **68**

REACTION 3 ch.g. Alhaarth (IRE) 126 – Hawas 93 (Mujtahid (USA) 118) [2009 82: 8g^4 p8g Oct 22] good-topped gelding: fairly useful performer at 2 yrs: off 12 months, ran as if in need of race on belated return: shaped as if amiss next time: stays 1m: acts on polytrack, good to firm and good to soft going: hard ride: sold 15,500 gns. *M. R. Channon* **76**

READILY 3 ch.f. Captain Rio 122 – Presently 48 (Cadeaux Genereux 131) [2009 59: f5d^4 p6g p6g^4 p5g Mar 25] compact filly: just poor performer in 2009: likely to stay 7f: acts on all-weather and firm going (unraced on softer than good): races prominently: sent to Switzerland. *J. G. Portman* **49**

READ THE SCRIPT (IRE) 4 b.g. King's Best (USA) 132 – Grizel 93 (Lion Cavern (USA) 117) [2009 50: p7.1g^3 p7.1g Oct 10] modest maiden, lightly raced: amiss (said to have bled) final start: needs to settle to stay beyond 7f. *Tom Dascombe* **59**

READY FOR BATTLE (IRE) 3 b.g. Namid 128 – Enamoured 76 (Groom Dancer (USA) 128) [2009 58p: 8m 6v 9.3d 12d 7v Sep 4] well-made gelding: maiden: no form in 2009: in cheekpieces last 3 starts. *D. W. Thompson* **–**

READYMADE (IRE) 2 b.g. (Feb 23) Dubai Destination (USA) 127 – Onda Nova (USA) 115 (Keos (USA) 120) [2009 7m^6 8.3d^2 9s^5 a7.5s^6 Dec 31] rather leggy, lengthy gelding: second foal: dam, French 7f and (including at 2 yrs) 1m winner, half-sister to dam of high-class 1¼m performer Shiva and Oaks winner Light Shift out of top-class middle-distance filly Northern Trick: fair form: best effort when 7 lengths second to Saboteur in maiden at Nottingham: sold from Sir Michael Stoute 16,000 gns after: stays 1m. *C. von der Recke, Germany* **76**

READY TO CROWN (USA) 5 b.m. More Than Ready (USA) 120 – Dili (USA) 73 (Chief's Crown (USA)) [2009 61: p12.2g p10m^2 p10g^4 p13.9g 11.5g p10g^3 Aug 15] modest maiden handicapper: left Andrew Turnell £5,000 after third start: should stay 1½m: acts on polytrack, good to firm and good to soft going: tried blinkered, in cheekpieces final outing: fairly useful hurdler. *J. Mackie* **58**

READY TO PRIME 3 ch.f. Primo Valentino (IRE) 116 – Blue Topaz (IRE) (Bluebird (USA) 125) [2009 43: p7m p10g Nov 18] lengthy filly: poor maiden. *Mike Murphy* **–**

REAL DESIRE 3 ch.g. Haafhd 129 – Stop Press (USA) 93 (Sharpen Up 127) [2009 10.1d 12m 9.2m^2 11.1d 9.8g 11.1g 12.4g Sep 30] modest maiden at best: should stay 1½m: acts on good to firm going: tried blinkered/in cheekpieces. *I. Semple* **62 d**

REAL DIAMOND 3 b.f. Bertolini (USA) 125 – Miss Fit (IRE) 87 (Hamas (IRE) 125§) [2009 62: 6m 6g* 5d^5 6g 7m 6d 6s^2 Oct 27] fair handicapper: won at Catterick in July: in cheekpieces, back to form there final outing: best efforts at 6f: acts on soft ground. *A. Dickman* **74**

REALISATION (USA) 2 b.g. (May 7) Alhaarth (IRE) 126 – Live Your Dreams (USA) (Mt Livermore (USA)) [2009 7.1s^3 7g^3 8.5m* 10m^2 Oct 6] fourth foal: half-brother to fairly useful 2007 2-y-o 5.5f winner Enactment (by Pivotal): dam, US 1m (at 2 yrs)/8.5f winner (second in Grade 2 8.5f event), out of half-sister to champion US **91**

sprinter Housebuster: fairly useful performer: won 4-runner maiden at Epsom in September by 1¾ lengths from Ebony Boom: stays 1¼m: acts on good to firm going, probably on soft: gelded after final start. *M. Johnston*

REALISM (FR) 9 b.g. Machiavellian (USA) 123 – Kissing Cousin (IRE) 116 (Danehill (USA) 126) [2009 –: f12g^2 12m f12g* 12d 12g^6 10.4d^6 12.4d t11g^6 p10m Dec 16] strong, good-bodied gelding: fairly useful performer: won claimer at Southwell in June: well below form after: stays 1½m: acts on fibresand, good to firm and good to soft going: tried tongue tied/in cheekpieces/visored: held up. *M. W. Easterby* **83 d**

REALLYMISSGREELEY (USA) 2 b. or br.f. (Apr 1) Mr Greeley (USA) 122 – Holiday Gold (USA) (Touch Gold (USA) 127) [2009 6m^4 5.9m 6m p5.1g p8.6g^2 Oct 29] $100,000Y: second foal: dam lightly raced in USA: fair maiden: easily best effort when second to Addahab (pair clear) at Wolverhampton: stays 8.6f: blinkered fourth start: sold £20,000. *K. A. Ryan* **75**

REALT NA MARA (IRE) 6 b. or br.g. Tagula (IRE) 116 – Dwingeloo (IRE) 83 (Dancing Dissident (USA) 119) [2009 83: f6d* f6g^4 p7.1g 6m f6g^3 6.1f 5m 6g^2 6d^5 f6g* 5.9d* 6d 5.7g 6d 7m* 7s Nov 7] strong gelding: fairly useful handicapper: won at Southwell in January and August, and amateur events at Carlisle in August and Leicester in October: stays 7f: acts on all-weather (goes particularly well on fibresand), good to soft and good to firm going: usually in cheekpieces, blinkered once. *H. Morrison* **82**

RE BAROLO (IRE) 6 b.h. Cape Cross (IRE) 129 – Dalaiya (USA) (Irish River (FR) 131) [2009 106, a112: p10g* p10g^6 p10g^4 10m^3 10f^4 10.4m 10.4m^6 p10.7g^3 p8m^2 Nov 29] sturdy horse: smart performer: won listed race at Lingfield (beat Suits Me by neck) in February: mostly respectable efforts after, good third to Kingdom of Fife in Zetland Gold Cup (Handicap) at Redcar fourth start: effective at 1¼m/easy 1½m: acts on all-weather, firm and soft going: effective with/without tongue tie: waited with. *M. Botti* **111**

REBECCA DE WINTER 3 b.f. Kyllachy 129 – Miss Adelaide (IRE) 85 (Alzao (USA) 117) [2009 83: p5g^6 p5g^6 5m p5.1g^5 p5g^2 p6g p5g^6 Oct 24] smallish, robust filly: fair performer nowadays: will prove best at 5f/6f: acts on polytrack and firm going: said to have finished lame final outing. *David Pinder* **74**

REBECCA ROMERO 2 b.f. (Apr 17) Exceed And Excel (AUS) 126 – Cloud Dancer 94 (Bishop of Cashel 122) [2009 6m 6m p6g^6 p7g 7d Sep 3] has scope: second foal: dam 6f (including at 2 yrs) to 1m winner: poor maiden: form only at 6f: has flashed tail/looked awkward. *D. J. Coakley* **46**

REBEL CHIEFTAIN (IRE) 2 b.c. (Mar 1) Dansili 127 – Desert Royalty (IRE) 96 (Alhaarth (IRE) 126) [2009 7m Oct 3] strong colt: 5/1, tailed off in maiden at Redcar, very slowly away and driven throughout: has left Godolphin. *Saeed bin Suroor* **–**

REBEL CITY 3 b.c. Elusive City (USA) 117 – Seguro (IRE) (Indian Ridge 123) [2009 73: p7m^2 p7g^2 7m 7m^5 f6g Jul 7] fair maiden: well held last 3 starts (said to have had breathing problem final outing): likely to stay 1m: form only on polytrack: sold 15,000 gns. *S. A. Callaghan* **73**

REBEL DUKE (IRE) 5 ch.g. Namid 128 – Edwina (IRE) 63 (Caerleon (USA) 132) [2009 92: f5s^2 f5s* f5m^3 f5g^2 5g^4 f5g^3 p5.1g f5g^5 f5d^2 Dec 29] angular gelding: useful handicapper: won at Southwell in January: left D. Barker after fifth outing: best at 5f: acts on all-weather (best on fibresand), firm and soft going (unraced on heavy): tried blinkered/tongue tied/in cheekpieces: travels strongly close up: consistent. *Ollie Pears* **96**

REBELLIOUS SPIRIT 6 b.g. Mark of Esteem (IRE) 137 – Robellino Miss (USA) (Robellino (USA) 127) [2009 88: p9.5g Jan 7] tall, quite good-topped gelding: fairly useful handicapper: well held sole outing in 2009: stays easy 1¼m: acts on all-weather, soft and good to firm going: often makes running. *S. Curran* **–**

REBEL PRINCE (IRE) 3 b.g. Barathea (IRE) 127 – Rebel Clan (IRE) (Tagula (IRE) 116) [2009 –: p10g p9.5g 10.2d^2 12.1m^6 12.1g f12g^4 14v^5 f11g 11.5g Oct 20] close-coupled gelding: modest maiden: stays 1½m: acts on fibresand, good to firm and good to soft ground: tried blinkered: possibly not straightforward. *M. G. Quinlan* **56**

REBEL RAIDER (IRE) 10 b.g. Mujadil (USA) 119 – Emily's Pride (Shirley Heights 130) [2009 53: p13.9g^5 Feb 7] modest performer: well held sole outing in 2009: stays 16.5f: acts on polytrack and soft going, possibly not on fibresand: tried visored. *B. N. Pollock* **–**

REBEL SWING 3 b.g. Robellino (USA) 127 – Ninia (USA) 102 (Affirmed (USA)) [2009 73: 11.6g^5 12.1g^6 May 26] angular gelding: maiden: just modest form in 2009: should be suited by 1¼m+: acts on heavy going. *W. R. Muir* **59**

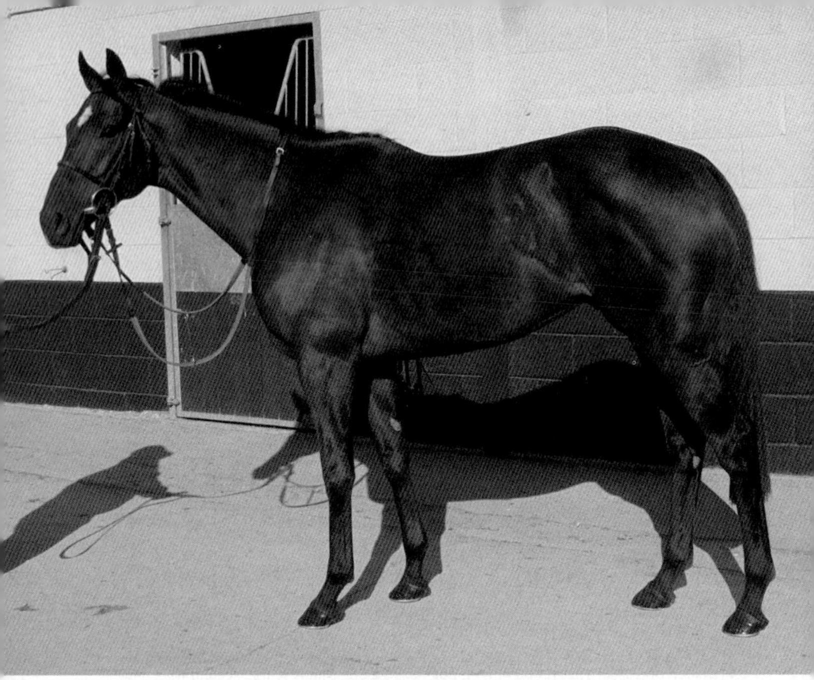

Triplin Racing's "Record Breaker"

REBELWITHOUTACAUSE (IRE) 3 b.g. Redback 116 – Christmas Kiss 82 (Taufan (USA) 119) [2009 –: p9.5g Jan 12] poor maiden: tried in cheekpieces. *George Baker* **40**

REBEL WOMAN 3 b.f. Royal Applause 124 – Wild Woman (Polar Falcon (USA) 126) [2009 p7g 6g 7.1m⁶ p8f² p8m⁶ p9.5g⁵ p7g⁶ Nov 25] 42,000Y: fifth foal: half-sister to 3 winners abroad, including useful German 7f/1m winner Wild Advice (by Desert Prince): dam, German 2-y-o 6f winner, sister to smart 6f/7f performer Resplendent Cee: modest maiden: stays 9.5f: acts on polytrack. *J. A. Osborne* **59**

RECALCITRANT 6 b.g. Josr Algarhoud (IRE) 118 – Lady Isabell 62 (Rambo Dancer (CAN) 107) [2009 64: 10m³ 12g⁶ 8f* 10f² 10m* 10.2m* 9.7s² Oct 6] workmanlike gelding: fair handicapper: won at Brighton and Lingfield in August and Chepstow in September: best at 1m/1¼m: acts on polytrack, firm and soft going: races prominently. *S. Dow* **68**

RECESSION PROOF (FR) 3 ch.g. Rock of Gibraltar (IRE) 133 – Elevate 98 (Ela-Mana-Mou 132) [2009 86: 11.6g⁵ 8m 8.3m⁴ 10g² 10d* 10g* 10g² 14.8g* 14m⁵ Sep 12] strong gelding: useful handicapper: won at Newbury, Pontefract (both amateur events) and Newmarket (dead-heated with Merchant of Dubai) in August: stays 14.8f: acts on polytrack and good to soft going: sold 95,000 gns. *S. A. Callaghan* **98**

RECETTE 2 b.f. (Feb 18) Reset (AUS) 124 – Sunny Times (IRE) 59 (Raise A Grand (IRE) 114) [2009 5m 5m⁴ 6m⁶ p7g Nov 14] angular filly: first foal: dam 7f winner: poor maiden. *R. Ingram* **47**

RECHARGE (IRE) 3 b.c. Cape Cross (IRE) 129 – Rebelline (IRE) 122 (Robellino (USA) 127) [2009 107p: 8g* 8v⁴ 12g⁵ Jun 28] tall, good sort; smart performer: won Leopardstown 2000 Guineas Trial in March by length from Intense Focus: respectable 7¾ lengths fourth to Mastercraftsman in Irish 2000 Guineas at the Curragh: failed to stay in Irish Derby at same track final outing: may prove best up to 1¼m: acts on good to soft going. *Kevin Prendergast, Ireland* **113**

RECOIL (IRE) 4 b.g. Red Ransom (USA) – Dazilyn Lady (USA) 105 (Zilzal (USA) 137) [2009 –: 10.1d 10.1m 7.9d 6m 7m^5 Aug 14] big, strong gelding: poor maiden: stays 7f: acts on good to firm going: tried blinkered/tongue tied/in cheekpieces. *R. Johnson* **49**

RECORD BREAKER (IRE) 5 b.g. In The Wings 128 – Overruled (IRE) 91 (Last Tycoon 131) [2009 101: 12g 12f 14m^2 16.2g^4 12.1m* 12m^2 16.1d 12m^5 14m 14.6m^4 12m* 12g^5 Oct 10] tall gelding: smart handicapper: won at Hamilton in June and Ascot (career best when beating Australia Day 3¾ lengths, running on strongly) in September: also ran well when runner-up to stablemate Drill Sergeant in Duke of Edinburgh Stakes at Royal Ascot sixth outing: suited by 1½m nowadays: acts on good to firm and good to soft going: usually blinkered: tactically versatile. *M. Johnston* **110**

RECURRING DREAM 3 b.f. Beat All (USA) 120 – Rewbell (Andy Rew 103) [2009 11.7g Jul 31] half-sister to smart staying chaser Dream Alliance (by Bien Bien): dam of little account: well held in maiden at Bath. *P. J. Hobbs* **–**

RED 5 ch.m. Fraam 114 – Great Tern 59 (Simply Great (FR) 122) [2009 –: f12g Jun 2] leggy mare: little form in 2 races on Flat since 2007. *Mrs S. J. Humphrey* **–**

RED AMARYLLIS 4 ch.f. Piccolo 121 – Passiflora 75 (Night Shift (USA)) [2009 61: 6m p6g 6m 6.1m Jun 12] sturdy filly: modest maiden at 3 yrs: little form in 2009: blinkered (looked reluctant) second outing: sold 4,000 gns. *H. J. L. Dunlop* **–**

RED AMY 2 b.f. (Mar 24) Hawk Wing (USA) 136 – Ballet Ballon (USA) 81 (Rahy (USA) 115) [2009 7d 7m^5 p7m^5 Aug 20] 48,000Y: neat filly: first foal: dam, 1¼m winner, half-sister to useful 1¼m winner Design Perfection, out of sister to high-class 1¼m performer Stagecraft: modest form in maidens, not knocked about final start: will be suited by 1m+: should do better. *M. L. W. Bell* **51 p**

RED ARMY COMMANDER (IRE) 4 b.g. Soviet Star (USA) 128 – Penny Fan 58 (Nomination 125) [2009 p12g^4 9.9m^6 10m^5 16m 11.9d Oct 22] good-topped gelding: modest form in maidens/handicaps. *J. A. Geake* **54**

REDARSENE 4 ch.c. Sakhee (USA) 136 – Triple Zee (USA) (Zilzal (USA) 137) [2009 73: p8.6g^6 Jan 19] tall colt: just modest form in seller sole outing in 2009: stays 8.6f: acts on polytrack and good to soft ground. *S. Wynne* **55**

RED AVALANCHE (IRE) 2 gr.c. (Mar 9) Verglas (IRE) 118 – Maura's Guest (IRE) (Be My Guest (USA) 126) [2009 p5g 5.1m^2 5.1d* 5m^2 6g^3 5m 5.1m^4 5.2d^4 5g^3 p6g^5 5g Oct 10] €26,000F, €45,000Y: strong colt: half-brother to several winners, including useful 2002 2-y-o 7f winner Rainbows For All and 7f (at 2 yrs) to 9f winner Always Rainbows (both in Ireland, by Rainbows For Life): dam unraced: useful performer: won maiden at Nottingham in April: good efforts eighth to tenth starts, including 3 lengths fifth to Love Lockdown in Sirenia Stakes at Kempton: effective at stiff 5f/6f: acts on polytrack, good to firm and good to soft going: has run well tongue tied: usually races prominently. *P. F. I. Cole* **97**

RED BADGE (IRE) 2 ch.c. (Mar 1) Captain Rio 122 – Red Fuschia (Polish Precedent (USA) 131) [2009 6.1m^2 6m^3 6g^2 6m^6 7m* 7v Oct 24] €8,000F, £46,000Y: workmanlike colt: second foal: dam unraced half-sister to useful performer up to 1½m Red Peony: useful performer: best effort when winning nursery at Newmarket in August by ½ length from Azizi: stays 7f: acts on good to firm ground, well below form on heavy (in Horris Hill Stakes at Newbury). *R. Hannon* **102**

RED BARCELONA (IRE) 2 ch.c. (Feb 19) Indian Haven 119 – Purepleasureseeker (IRE) (Grand Lodge (USA) 125) [2009 6s 8g 8m Sep 24] easily best effort in maidens when 5¼ lengths eighth to Notorize at Goodwood second start: stays 1m. *M. H. Tompkins* **64**

RED BIRR (IRE) 8 b.g. Bahhare (USA) 122 – Cappella (IRE) 75 (College Chapel 122) [2009 86: 8.3d 10.2g^3 10.2g Jul 4] leggy, quite good-topped gelding: fairly useful handicapper: may prove best at 1¼m/1½m nowadays: acts on polytrack, firm and good to soft going: tongue tied: has shaped as if amiss more than once, including final outing. *P. R. Webber* **80**

RED CADEAUX 3 ch.g. Cadeaux Genereux 131 – Artisia (IRE) (Peintre Celebre (USA) 137) [2009 8d^6 p8g 9d^3 p12.2g* p12.2g^2 12s* 14v^5 Sep 5] lengthy gelding: useful handicapper: won at Wolverhampton in June and Doncaster (beat Advisor ½ length) in August: stays 1¾m: raced only on polytrack and going softer than good (acts on heavy): gelded after final outing. *E. A. L. Dunlop* **95**

RED CAPE (FR) 6 b.g. Cape Cross (IRE) 129 – Muirfield (FR) (Crystal Glitters (USA) 127) [2009 85d: f6s^4 p7.1g^2 p7.1g^3 p6m^3 7m 6m p6g^4 7.1m^3 6d* 6g 6m* 6d^4 6m* 6d^2 7m^3 6g 6d^2 6g* 6m^2 6m^2 6m 6m 6m^3 6g Oct 23] big, rangy gelding: useful handicapper: won at Catterick and Thirsk in June, Catterick in July and Ripon in August: placed **96**

10 other occasions in 2009, including when good third at Haydock penultimate start: has form at 1m, best at 6f: acts on all-weather, good to firm and good to soft going: used to wear cheekpieces/blinkers (not when successful): races prominently: tough. *Mrs R. A. Carr*

RED CELL (IRE) 3 b.g. Kheleyf (USA) 116 – Montana Lady (IRE) 83 (Be My Guest (USA) 126) [2009 64: p5g* p5.1g^6 5m^5 5m 5g 5g^2 5m 5v^3 p5.1g 5.3m 5g Oct 6] small gelding: modest performer: won seller at Lingfield in January: best at 5f: acts on all-weather, heavy and good to firm going: wears blinkers/cheekpieces: none too consistent. *I. W. McInnes* **62**

RED CENTURY 4 ch.f. Captain Rio 122 – Red Millennium (IRE) 102 (Tagula (IRE) 116) [2009 –: p8.6g Apr 4] no form in maiden/seller (blinkered/tongue tied) 10 months apart. *Paul Mason* **–**

RED CHIEFTAIN (FR) 4 b.g. Red Ransom (USA) – Delimara (IRE) (In The Wings 128) [2009 p7g 8.1v May 22] well held in maidens: dead. *Mrs H. S. Main* **–**

RED CHINA BLUES (USA) 3 ch.g. Royal Academy (USA) 130 – Viewy (USA) (Majestic Light (USA)) [2009 –p: 10g 10.1d^4 7.1m^3 7m 7.9d^2 9.8m^5 8s Sep 5] leggy gelding: modest maiden: claimed from J. Howard Johnson £6,000 after fifth start: seems to stay 1¼m: acts on good to firm and good to soft going. *R. E. Barr* **64**

RED COURTIER 2 b.c. (Apr 9) Red Ransom (USA) – Lady In Waiting 113 (Kylian (USA)) [2009 7g^6 p8.6g^3 p10m* Dec 9] 25,000Y: fifth foal: half-brother to 3 winners, including 3-y-o Dream In Waiting and 5-y-o Wait For The Light: dam, 5f (at 2 yrs) to 1¼m (Sun Chariot Stakes) winner, closely related to smart stayer Savannah Bay: fair form: further improvement when winning maiden at Kempton by 6 lengths from Cast of Stars, dominating throughout: stays 1¼m. *P. F. I. Cole* **78**

RED CURRENT 5 b.m. Soviet Star (USA) 128 – Fleet Amour (USA) (Afleet (CAN)) [2009 69, a57: p8g^2 p8g^4 p8.6g^3 p8g^5 p7.1g p8g p8g^2 10.9m 8g^6 10.2g^6 10.2g^5 8f^6 10m^6 9m 10.2m 8.1m* p8.6g^4 f8g 8.1g^5 8.1m^4 p8g^6 p8g^3 p8g^6 p10g p7.1g Dec 17] leggy, close-coupled mare: modest performer: won claimer at Chepstow in July: stays 11f: acts on polytrack, heavy and good to firm going: tried blinkered/in cheekpieces: often finds little: none too consistent. *R. A. Harris* **58**

RED DAGGER (IRE) 3 b.g. Daggers Drawn (USA) 114 – Dash of Red (Red Sunset 120) [2009 –: p8g 8.5g p10g 10m^5 11.5m 9m 6.1d^3 7m Sep 16] compact gelding: poor maiden: left T. McCarthy after sixth start: stays 1¼m, effective at much shorter: acts on good to soft going. *R. J. Price* **47**

REDDEN 2 b.g. (Feb 11) Pivotal 124 – Coy (IRE) 112 (Danehill (USA) 126) [2009 6m^6 7g 6s^4 Nov 7] strong gelding: second foal: dam, 6f (at 2 yrs) to 1m winner, half-sister to smart 7f/1m winner Il Warrd (by Pivotal): fair form in maidens, fourth to London Gold at Doncaster: gelded after: type to do better at 3 yrs. *W. J. Haggas* **67 p**

RED DUNE (IRE) 4 b.f. Red Ransom (USA) – Desert Beauty (IRE) 103 (Green Desert (USA) 127) [2009 102: 8.5g 7m^6 7g^4 6m 7m^4 7m^2 8d^3 a7.5g^6 Dec 3] good-topped filly: useful performer: creditable efforts in Oak Tree Stakes at Goodwood (1¾ lengths fourth to Summer Fete) and listed races at Doncaster and Ascot (strong-finishing length second to Golden Stream) third/fifth/sixth outings: has won at 1m, better at 7f: acts on soft and good to firm going: reportedly bled first/fourth starts: free-going sort: used to make running, patiently ridden of late. *M. A. Jarvis* **101**

REDDY RONNIE (IRE) 5 b.g. Redback 116 – Daffodil Dale (IRE) 78 (Cyrano de Bergerac 120) [2009 58: 8m 9.3m 8m 7g 7.1m^4 8m 8.5m Sep 16] workmanlike gelding: just poor form in 2009: stays 1m: acts on good to firm going: tried in cheekpieces/visor. *D. W. Thompson* **40**

REDDY TO STAR (IRE) 2 b.g. (Mar 27) Redback 116 – Grade A Star (IRE) (Alzao (USA) 117) [2009 5g 5.5m^2 5m^2 5.1g^2 5g^2 5.2d p5g 5.7m^4 7d p7g^3 Oct 20] 12,000Y: good-bodied gelding: half-brother to several winners, including useful 6f winner March Star (by Mac's Imp) and fairly useful 1¼m winner Jimmy Swift (by Petardia): dam Irish 2-y-o 1m winner: fair maiden: stays 7f: acts on polytrack and good to firm going: tried blinkered: signs of temperament: sold 10,000 gns, and gelded. *C. G. Cox* **71**

RED EDDIE 2 b.c. (Apr 7) Red Ransom (USA) – Sister Bluebird 94 (Bluebird (USA) 125) [2009 7d 7.1g 7.1m^6 7.1m 8g Oct 19] sturdy colt: modest maiden: should stay 1m: blinkered (dropped away tamely) final start. *B. J. Meehan* **51**

REDEEMED 4 b.f. Red Ransom (USA) – Pastel 95 (Lion Cavern (USA) 117) [2009 –: f8d p8.6g Jan 19] close-coupled filly: maiden: little form since 2007: tried tongue tied. *M. Brittain* **–**

RED ERIC 3 ch.g. Reset (AUS) 124 – Lady Soleas (Be My Guest (USA) 126) [2009 –: p9.5g Jan 12] no sign of ability. *W. M. Brisbourne* –

REDESIGNATION (IRE) 4 b.g. Key of Luck (USA) 126 – Disregard That (IRE) (Don't Forget Me 127) [2009 102: 10.3m* 12f^{2} 12s a12g^{4} 12g^{3} 12.5g^{2} a12g^{5} Oct 20] tall gelding: useful performer: won handicap at Doncaster in April by ¾ length from Granston: ran at least respectably when placed afterwards, leaving R. Hannon after third outing: stays 1½m: acts on any turf going, below form both starts on all-weather at Deauville. *Rupert Pritchard-Gordon, France* **106**

RED EXPRESSO (IRE) 4 ch.g. Intikhab (USA) 135 – Cafe Creme (IRE) (Catrail (USA) 123) [2009 71: p12.2m* f11g^{6} p12.2g^{6} Dec 5] strong, compact gelding: fair performer: won apprentice handicap at Wolverhampton in September: stays 1½m: acts on all-weather and firm ground: tried visored (raced lazily): held up. *Ollie Pears* **70**

RED FAMA 5 ch.g. Fraam 114 – Carol Again 48 (Kind of Hush 118) [2009 85: f12g^{6} 10.3d 16.4g Jul 25] good-topped gelding: fairly useful handicapper in 2008: well held in 2009: should stay 2m: acts on fibresand, soft and good to firm going. *N. Bycroft* –

RED FANTASY (IRE) 2 b.f. (May 2) High Chaparral (IRE) 132 – Petite Fantasy 110 (Mansooj 118) [2009 7m^{4} 7.1m^{5} Sep 29] €52,000F: sturdy filly: sixth foal: closely related to Irish 7f winner Aidin And Abetting (by Entrepreneur) and half-sister to 2 winners, notably smart Irish 6f/7f winner Desert Fantasy (by Desert King): dam Irish 5f (including at 2 yrs)/6f winner: better effort when 3¾ lengths fourth to Silver Rock in minor event at Newbury: drawn wide in maiden at Warwick (again slowly away): edgy sort. *B. W. Hills* **74**

RED FARASI (IRE) 2 ch.g. (Apr 28) Redback 116 – Boristova (IRE) 79 (Royal Academy (USA) 130) [2009 7m p6g f8m Nov 11] well held in maiden/sellers: tried in cheekpieces. *B. W. Duke* –

REDFORD (IRE) 4 b.g. Bahri (USA) 125 – Ida Lupino (IRE) (Statoblest 120) [2009 108p: 6g^{4} 7f^{3} 7m^{6} 7m^{3} 6m 7m Sep 26] tall, good-topped gelding: impresses in appearance: useful handicapper: ran well in valuable events second to fourth starts, especially when third in Buckingham Palace Stakes at Royal Ascot (to Giganticus) and International Stakes at same course (beaten 2 lengths by Al Muheer): poorly drawn last 2 outings: best at 7f/1m: acts on firm and good to soft going: visored final outing: held up, travels strongly: sold 130,000 gns. *M. L. W. Bell* **108**

RED GULCH 2 b.c. (Mar 31) Kyllachy 129 – Enrapture (USA) 85 (Lear Fan (USA) 130) [2009 p7m^{3} Nov 26] 16,000Y, 32,000 2-y-o: second foal: dam 7f winner: 8/1, encouraging 2¾ lengths third to Bramshaw in steadily-run maiden at Kempton, racing wide and challenging early in straight: likely to improve. *E. A. L. Dunlop* **67 p**

RED HORSE (IRE) 3 ch.g. Bachelor Duke (USA) 122 – Miss Childrey (IRE) 97 (Dr Fong (USA) 128) [2009 –: 8f p7f 10m^{5} p10g Oct 24] unfurnished gelding: modest maiden: stays 1¼m: acts on firm going. *M. L. W. Bell* **50**

RED HOT DESERT 3 b.g. Green Desert (USA) 127 – Red Carnation (IRE) 103 (Polar Falcon (USA) 126) [2009 p9.5g p11g p12g* p12g^{6} p10f Dec 20] 70,000Y: third foal: dam, 1m to 1½m winner, half-sister to smart 1¼m/1½m performer Red Fort (by Green Desert): fair form: won maiden at Lingfield in November: stays 1½m: raced only on polytrack. *W. R. Swinburn* **79**

RED INTRIGUE (IRE) 2 b.f. (Mar 12) Selkirk (USA) 129 – Red Affair (IRE) 95 (Generous (IRE) 139) [2009 7s 7.1m p8f^{3} Oct 14] good-topped filly: seventh foal: sister to useful 6f (at 2 yrs)/7f winner Red Liason and half-sister to 2 winners, including smart Irish 7f/1m (at 2 yrs) winner Redstone Dancer (by Namid): dam, Irish 1¼m winner, out of sister to Rainbow Quest: fair form in maidens, 1½ lengths third to Dahaam at Kempton: stays 1m: appeared to lose action second start (bit said to have slipped through mouth). *Mrs A. J. Perrett* **71**

RED JADE 4 ch.g. Dubai Destination (USA) 127 – Red Slippers (USA) 111 (Nureyev (USA) 131) [2009 89p: 10.2d^{2} 10v 8.9g 10d^{4} 10.3s^{6} 10s^{3} 10.1m^{3} 10.1m^{6} 10.4g^{3} Oct 9] angular gelding: fairly useful handicapper: trained by K. R. Burke until after fourth start, left A. Jarvis after next: will stay 1½m: acts on soft and good to firm going: gelded after final outing. *R. A. Fahey* **93**

RED JAZZ (USA) 2 b.c. (Feb 3) Johannesburg (USA) 127 – Now That's Jazz (USA) (Sword Dance) [2009 5g* 5m* 6m 6m^{3} Jul 9] $37,000F, €95,000Y: useful-looking colt: half-brother to winner in USA by Halo's Image: dam US 9f winner: useful performer: won maiden at Windsor (by 5 lengths from Iver Bridge Lad) and minor event at Ascot (by ½ length from Archers Road) in April: good 3¾ lengths third to Arcano in July Stakes at Newmarket (warm/edgy): will probably stay 7f: raced only on good/good to firm going. *B. W. Hills* **105**

RED KESTREL (USA) 4 ch.g. Swain (IRE) 134 – The Caretaker 113 (Caerleon (USA) 132) [2009 99: 10.4m 12g 12m^6 14.1d^4 14m^6 Sep 26] sturdy gelding: fairly useful handicapper: stays 1½m: acts on polytrack and good to firm going: weak finisher. *K. A. Ryan* **92**

RED KYTE 3 br.f. Hawk Wing (USA) 136 – Ruby Affair (IRE) 68 (Night Shift (USA)) [2009 91: p7g 6m p6g 6g^3 7f^5 6g 5d* 5s^4 6g^5 6d^6 6g Sep 14] workmanlike filly: fair handicapper: won at Pontefract in July: below form after: stays 7f: acts on firm and soft going: in cheekpieces last 5 outings: sometimes finds little. *K. A. Ryan* **76**

REDLYNCH 4 b.g. Sinndar (IRE) 134 – Red Azalea 95 (Shirley Heights 130) [2009 –: f11d f12g f8d 6m Jun 29] no sign of ability: tried in cheekpieces/visor. *S. Parr* **–**

RED MARGARITA (IRE) 3 ch.f. Dalakhani (IRE) 133 – Red Bartsia 99 (Barathea (IRE) 127) [2009 –: p10g 8d 11.6g^6 10.1g p12g 16.2g Jul 20] sturdy filly: modest maiden: should stay 1½m: signs of temperament. *D. R. C. Elsworth* **51**

RED MAX (IRE) 3 b.g. Kheleyf (USA) 116 – Set Trail (IRE) 76 (Second Set (IRE) 127) [2009 59: 6s 5.1g May 19] lengthy, good-topped gelding: just poor maiden handicapper in 2009: barely stays 7f: tried blinkered/in cheekpieces. *T. D. Easterby* **44**

RED MERLIN (IRE) 4 ch.g. Soviet Star (USA) 128 – Truly Bewitched (USA) 81 (Affirmed (USA)) [2009 84: p12g^3 11.6g^2 12.3m* 12m* 11.9m* 14m Aug 19] rather leggy, attractive gelding: smart handicapper: much improved in 2009, winning at Chester (dead-heated) and Goodwood in May and Haydock (Old Newton Cup, beat Munsef ½ length) in July: pulled too hard in Ebor at York final outing: stays 1½m: acts on polytrack, heavy and good to firm ground: blinkered/visored: waited with: quirky, but reliable. *C. G. Cox* **110**

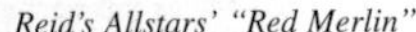

Reid's Allstars' "Red Merlin"

RED ORIENTAL 3 ch.f. Zamindar (USA) 116 – Pan Galactic (USA) 105 (Lear Fan (USA) 130) [2009 6m^4 7.5g^4 10.5g^3 10g^3 10.5g^3 9g Jul 20] closely related to French/ Spanish 9f winner Chinese Cookie (by Zafonic) and half-sister to 3 winners, including useful French 7f winner Battlestar (by Bering): dam French 1m winner: fairly useful maiden: below form last 2 starts, leaving A. Fabre in France 32,000 gns in between: better around 1¼m than shorter. *N. P. Littmoden* **90**

REDOUBTABLE GRACE 2 b.g. (May 3) Redoubtable (USA) 115 – Full of Grace (Lucky Wednesday 124) [2009 5v 5m p5.1m f5g^6 Dec 8] leggy gelding: well held in maidens/nursery. *Mrs R. A. Carr* **–**

RED RED RASCAL 3 b.f. Red Ransom (USA) – Normandy (CHI) (Great Regent (CAN)) [2009 10m p8g Jun 25] fifth foal: half-sister to 2 winners, including fairly useful 2005 2-y-o 7f and (in Canada) 1m winner Santiago Star (by Hussonet): dam unraced: no form in maidens. *A. M. Balding* **–**

RED REEF 3 ch.f. King's Best (USA) 132 – Rafiya 89 (Halling (USA) 133) [2009 65: 9.9f 11.7m^4 10.2g^6 10s^2 10f 10m p11g p12m p9.5g Oct 15] tall, unfurnished filly: fair handicapper: below form after fourth start: should stay 1½m: acts on soft and good to firm going: tried visored. *D. J. Coakley* **70 d**

RED RIVER BOY 4 ch.g. Bahamian Bounty 116 – Riviere Rouge (Forzando 122) [2009 57: 6m^5 5m^5 5m^6 5m 5.9g^5 5g^5 Jul 16] angular gelding: modest handicapper: raced at 5f/6f: acts on good to firm ground. *C. W. Fairhurst* **57**

RED RIVER REBEL 11 b.g. Inchinor 119 – Bidweaya (USA) 45 (Lear Fan (USA) 130) [2009 58: f12g p12.2g May 11] tall, leggy gelding: regressive handicapper: effective at 11.8f to 2m: acts on all-weather and any turf going: tried visored: races up with pace. *J. R. Norton* **–**

RED ROCK CANYON (IRE) 5 b.h. Rock of Gibraltar (IRE) 133 – Imagine (IRE) 119 (Sadler's Wells (USA) 132) [2009 111: 10.5g 8g^6 7.5v^3 10s* 9s^3 14d^2 10s^5 10s^3 12v^5 Aug 31] well-made horse: useful performer: landed odds in maiden at Roscommon in July: best effort after when 5½ lengths third to Famous Name in International Stakes at the Curragh next time: best at 9f to 1½m: acts on soft and good to firm going: sometimes in cheekpieces/blinkers: often front runner (sometimes as pacemaker): sometimes finds little: slipped final outing: has joined M. de Kock. *A. P. O'Brien, Ireland* **109**

RED ROCKS (IRE) 6 b. or br.h. Galileo (IRE) 134 – Pharmacist (IRE) 108 (Machiavellian (USA) 123) [2009 124: 9f 12g 12m^4 12f^5 Nov 7] rather leggy, attractive horse: had a quick, fluent action: very smart performer at best: won 6 races, notably Breeders' Cup Turf at Churchill Downs in 2006 and Man o'War Stakes at Belmont in 2008: well below form for M. Hennig first 2 starts at 6 yrs, then rejoined former trainer: smart form last 2 outings, 4¼ lengths fifth to Conduit in Breeders' Cup Turf at Santa Anita final one: was best at 1¼m/1½m: acted on firm and soft going: blinkered/visored 4 starts prior to last 2: edgy sort, often sweated: reported to have scoped dirty after second outing: versatile tactically: to stand at Allevamento Il Grifone, near Turin, Italy. *B. J. Meehan* **116**

RED ROSANNA 3 b.f. Bertolini (USA) 125 – Lamarita 92§ (Emarati (USA) 74) [2009 69: 5m^4 5m 5f^4 5m^2 5m* 5g 5g* 5.1m^5 5s^5 Jul 17] tall filly: fairly useful handicapper: won at Newmarket in June and Haydock in July: best at 5f: acts on firm and good to soft going: races prominently. *R. Hollinshead* **82**

RED ROSSINI (IRE) 3 b.g. Rossini (USA) 118 – La Scala (USA) 80 (Theatrical 128) [2009 78: 6g^6 6f^3 6.1g^6 6.1m^5 6g 6f^5 6m 5g^5 5.7g^5 Sep 7] rather leggy, useful-looking gelding: fair performer: below form after third outing: stays 6f: acts on polytrack and any turf going: tried visored/blinkered: withdrawn after unruly in stall intended fifth outing: sold £800. *R. Hannon* **73 d**

RED RUDY 7 ch.g. Pivotal 124 – Piroshka (Soviet Star (USA) 128) [2009 78: p6g p6g^4 p6g p7g* p10g^3 p8.6g^2 p8g^3 p8.6g 6g May 4] tall, close-coupled gelding: fair handicapper: won at Kempton in February: best up to 1m: acts on polytrack, firm and good to soft going. *A. W. Carroll* **70**

RED SCINTILLA 2 b.f. (Apr 15) Doyen (IRE) 132 – Red To Violet 85 (Spectrum (IRE) 126) [2009 6s Nov 7] third foal: dam 6f (at 2 yrs) to 1m winner: 66/1, 6¼ lengths tenth to Adventure Story in maiden at Doncaster, slowly away and hanging. *N. Tinkler* **55**

RED SKIPPER (IRE) 4 ch.g. Captain Rio 122 – Speed To Lead (IRE) 90 (Darshaan 133) [2009 69: 7.1m 9m^5 10m^2 9.1g^5 9g^2 10.4g^4 8s 8s^4 10g^4 8m 9.1v^4 Oct 31] strong, compact gelding: fair performer: stays 1¼m: acts on heavy and good to firm going: tried in cheekpieces/visor. *N. Wilson* **65**

RED SOMERSET (USA) 6 b.g. Red Ransom (USA) – Bielska (USA) (Deposit Ticket (USA)) [2009 98: p8g^{2} p8g* p8.6g^{2} p8g^{5} p8g^{6} p7g^{2} 8g^{3} p7g^{6} p8g^{4} 7m p8g p7g p8.6g p8.6g^{2} p8m p9.5g p7.1g* Dec 26] strong, good-bodied gelding: useful performer: won handicap at Lingfield in January: best effort when ½-length second to Abbondanza in similar event there on sixth outing: below form later in year, though won claimer at Wolverhampton in December: best at 7f/1m: acts on polytrack, soft and good to firm going. *R. J. Hodges* **102 d**

RED STILETTO 3 b.f. Red Ransom (USA) – The Blade (GER) 101 (Sure Blade (USA) 130) [2009 –: 7g Apr 21] no form: sent to Saudi Arabia. *Rae Guest* **–**

RED SUEDE SHOES 3 ch.g. Storming Home 128 – Dipple 80 (Komaite (USA)) [2009 p8g p10g^{2} p12g^{2} 9.9m^{6} 8.3m^{4} 8.1m^{4} 8.1g^{4} p8g^{3} 10g^{4} p8m^{5} p8m* p8g^{2} p8.6g^{3} p8m* p8m^{3} p8f^{4} Dec 16] close-coupled gelding: second foal: dam 6f (at 2 yrs) to 9f (in Scandinavia) winner: fairly useful handicapper: won at Kempton in October and November: stays 8.6f: acts on polytrack and good to firm going: in cheekpieces last 6 outings. *B. R. Millman* **84**

RED TARN 4 gr.g. Fraam 114 – Cumbrian Melody 83 (Petong 126) [2009 73: f11s* f12g Jan 13] big gelding: fair performer: won apprentice maiden at Southwell in January: stays 1½m: acts on all-weather and good to firm going: tried tongue tied/visored: not straightforward (races lazily/has hung). *B. Smart* **66**

RED TWIST 4 b.g. Red Ransom (USA) – Spinning The Yarn 70 (Barathea (IRE) 127) [2009 64: p11g^{4} f14g 13.3m 10.2g Jun 11] big, good-topped gelding: modest maiden handicapper: well beaten after reappearance: stays 11f: acts on polytrack and good to soft going: inconsistent. *M. Hill* **64**

RED VALERIAN TWO (IRE) 2 ch.c. (Mar 25) Hawk Wing (USA) 136 – La Turque (IRE) (Diesis 133) [2009 f7g f8m Nov 6] well beaten in maidens at Southwell. *P. T. Midgley* **–**

REDWATER RIVER 5 b.g. Kyllachy 129 – Red Tulle (USA) 66 (A P Indy (USA) 131) [2009 70: f8d^{5} f8g^{6} p9.5g p7.1g 7s 5.9m f6g^{6} 6v^{6} 6d^{3} 6m^{3} 6d^{5} 6g* 5.9d 6m^{5} 7g Sep 3] modest handicapper: won at Catterick in August: stays 9f, effective at much shorter: acts on fibresand, heavy and good to firm going: blinkered nowadays. *Mrs R. A. Carr* **64**

RED WILLOW 3 ch.f. Noverre (USA) 125 – Chelsea Blue (ITY) 71 (Barathea (IRE) 127) [2009 6m 7.1g^{5} 7f Sep 8] 5,000F: lengthy filly: first foal: dam sprint maiden: little form. *J. E. Long* **–**

RED WINE 10 b.g. Hamas (IRE) 125§ – Red Bouquet (Reference Point 139) [2009 **82 §**
86§: f14s p12g p13g^{5} p13g 12g^{2} 12m^{4} 14.6g^{2} 12d* 14m 12s^{4} 11.9g^{6} 16d^{3} 15.8v^{6} 16.1d^{5} **a62 §**
15.8s^{3} 13.8v^{5} f12f^{4} f14m Dec 5] smallish, leggy gelding: fairly useful handicapper on turf, modest on all-weather: won apprentice event at Doncaster (fifth course success) in May: left A. McCabe after next outing: below form after: effective at 1½m to 2m: acts on all-weather and any turf going: tried blinkered/in cheekpieces: held up (often slowly away): ungenuine. *J. A. Glover*

REDWOOD 3 b.c. High Chaparral (IRE) 132 – Arum Lily (USA) (Woodman (USA) 126) [2009 96p: 9m* 10.4g May 14] sturdy colt: smart form, lightly raced: much improved to win listed race at Newmarket in April by 2 lengths from Drumbeat: beat only one home in Dante Stakes at York next time: should stay 1¼m: acts on good to firm going. *B. W. Hills* **111**

RED YARN 2 b.f. (Mar 14) Lucky Story (USA) 128 – Aunt Ruby (USA) 67 (Rubiano (USA)) [2009 p7m^{6} p7g^{3} Dec 31] fifth foal: half-sister to several winners, including useful 7f winner (including at 2 yrs) Relative Order (by Diktat) and 6-y-o South Cape: dam 7f seller winner: better effort in maidens when 2½ lengths third to Cuthbert at Lingfield. *G. L. Moore* **60**

RED ZOE (USA) 3 b.f. Danehill Dancer (IRE) 117 – Starbourne (IRE) 105 (Sadler's Wells (USA) 132) [2009 8.3g 8.1g May 29] $180,000F, 80,000Y: has scope: third foal: dam Irish 1m/1¼m winner: modest form in maidens: sold 3,500 gns in December. *M. L. W. Bell* **59**

REEDS BAY (IRE) 2 br.c. (Feb 28) Monsieur Bond (IRE) 120 – Paradise Blue (IRE) 63 (Bluebird (USA) 125) [2009 6g^{3} 6s^{5} 6m* 7m^{4} 7.1g 7d^{4} 6g^{3} 6m^{3} Oct 5] €23,000F, £31,000Y: close-coupled colt: third foal: dam, maiden (raced at 6f/7f), half-sister to smart winner up to 1m Speedfit Too: fairly useful performer: won maiden at Haydock in June: good efforts when third in nurseries: stays 7f: acts on good to firm and good to soft going: blinkered last 4 outings: sold 13,000 gns. *E. S. McMahon* **81**

REEL BLUFF 3 b.g. Reel Buddy (USA) 118 – Amber's Bluff 80 (Mind Games 121) [2009 51: 12m 7.1m 8f 10m Oct 3] good-bodied gelding: poor maiden: left D. Barker prior to final start: should prove best at 5f/6f. *N. Wilson* **48**

REEL BUDDY STAR 4 ch.g. Reel Buddy (USA) 118 – So Discreet (Tragic Role (USA)) [2009 80: 10.1d 8.1m^{5} 9d^{6} 8m^{2} 8m^{6} 8m* 8.1g 8g^{3} 8.1m^{4} 8m Oct 3] big, good-bodied gelding: fairly useful handicapper: won at Newcastle in August: stays 1m: acts on good to firm and good to soft going: in cheekpieces once. *G. M. Moore* **90**

REEL CREDIT CRUNCH 2 ch.f. (Jan 28) Reel Buddy (USA) 118 – Four Legs Good (IRE) 58 (Be My Guest (USA) 126) [2009 p5.1g^{3} 5m^{5} 5.1m^{2} 5m^{2} 5.1m^{4} 5m^{6} p5.1m^{5} 5m 5m p7m Oct 7] £600Y, resold £5,000Y: workmanlike filly: fourth foal: sister to 3-y-o Perfect Friend and half-sister to 5-y-o Benllech: dam maiden (best at 7f): maiden: regressive after third start (claimed from P. D. Evans £10,000 after fourth): raced mainly at 5f: tried blinkered. *I. W. McInnes* **65 d**

REEL EASY 2 b.c. (Feb 7) Reel Buddy (USA) 118 – Easy Feeling (IRE) 84 (Night Shift (USA)) [2009 5m 5m f5g Jul 7] sturdy colt: no form in minor event/sellers. *J. R. Holt* **–**

REEL HOPE 3 b.f. Reel Buddy (USA) 118 – Compton Amber 78 (Puissance 110) [2009 47: p7f p12g Sep 21] workmanlike filly: poor maiden. *J. R. Best* **–**

REEL LOVE 2 b.c. (Mar 13) Reel Buddy (USA) 118 – Love Affair (IRE) 78 (Tagula (IRE) 116) [2009 6d p7.1g Jun 29] well held in maidens. *J. R. Holt* **–**

REEL MAN 4 ch.g. Reel Buddy (USA) 118 – Yanomami (USA) 71 (Slew O' Gold (USA)) [2009 –: p11g p12m p12g Oct 21] big, strong gelding: maiden: little form since 2007. *D. K. Ivory* **–**

REFLECTIVE GLORY (IRE) 5 ch.m. City On A Hill (USA) 114 – Sheznice (IRE) 58 (Try My Best (USA) 130) [2009 –: 9m Aug 8] good-topped mare: maiden: well held both Flat starts since 2007: tried in visor, usually in cheekpieces. *J. S. Wainwright* **–**

REFUSE TO DECLINE 3 ch.f. Refuse To Bend (IRE) 128 – Oulianovsk (IRE) (Peintre Celebre (USA) 137) [2009 –: p8.6g Jan 16] lengthy filly: more signs of temperament than ability: sold €4,500, reportedly in foal to Tiger Hill. *D. M. Simcock* **–**

REFUSE TO TELL 2 b.g. (May 3) Refuse To Bend (IRE) 128 – Zibet 90 (Kris 135) [2009 6g p7g 8.5d^{6} 9m Sep 18] well held in maidens/nursery: sold 2,000 gns. *C. E. Brittain* **–**

REFUSE TOULOUSE (IRE) 3 b.c. Refuse To Bend (IRE) 128 – Continuous (IRE) 89 (Darshaan 133) [2009 10.3g 8s 10g^{6} p11g p10m 11.8m Oct 13] lengthy colt: modest maiden: tried blinkered/tongue tied: sold £800, sent to Greece. *C. G. Cox* **52**

REFUSE TO WAIT (IRE) 2 b.f. (Feb 27) Refuse To Bend (IRE) 128 – I'll Be Waiting (Vettori (IRE) 119) [2009 5m^{4} 6v^{3} 6d* 6g 7m 6d^{4} Sep 1] €13,000Y: good-topped filly: second foal: dam unraced half-sister to smart stayer Witness Box: fair performer: won maiden at Newcastle in June: should be suited by 7f+: acts on heavy ground: blinkered (ran creditably) final start. *T. D. Easterby* **65**

REGAL ANGEL 6 ch.m. Roi de Rome (USA) 112 – Dominion's Dream 68 (Dominion 123) [2009 p12m^{3} p12g^{2} p13g^{3} 12g^{4} 14.1m 13.1g^{4} Sep 7] fifth foal: dam 7f and hurdles winner: dual bumper winner: fair maiden: should stay 1¾m. *Jean-Rene Auvray* **65**

REGAL BLUSH 3 b.f. Bachelor Duke (USA) 122 – Royale Rose (FR) 75 (Bering 136) [2009 7d 8m 10g 10d^{2} 9.9g 13.1g^{3} p16m 11.9d^{3} 10m 7.5d 11g Dec 13] 42,000F, 48,000Y: tall, angular filly: seventh foal: half-sister to 3 winners, including useful French 9f to 1½m winner Antioquia (by Singspiel) and fairly useful 1½m and 2m winner Vin du Pays (by Alzao): dam, 1m winner, sister to useful French miler Rouen: fair maiden: sold from A. Balding 6,200 gns after eighth start: stays 13f: unraced on extremes of going. *G. Miliani, Italy* **67**

REGAL DREAM (IRE) 7 b.g. Namid 128 – Lovely Me (IRE) 70 (Vision (USA)) [2009 43: 5.9m Jun 15] close-coupled gelding: poor performer nowadays: should stay 1m: acts on polytrack and firm going, probably on good to soft: tried tongue tied/visored. *J. W. Unett* **–**

REGAL GUEST 2 b.c. (Mar 30) King's Best (USA) 132 – Zuleika Dobson 106 (Cadeaux Genereux 131) [2009 8.1d 9m^{2} 9d^{2} Oct 11] 26,000F, 30,000Y: fourth foal: half-brother to fairly useful French 9f/9.8f winner Midnight Dreamer (by Fantastic Light): dam 9f winner: easily best effort in maidens when 1½ lengths second to Ted Spread at Goodwood final start: should be suited by 1¼m+. *M. R. Channon* **80 +**

REGAL LYRIC (IRE) 3 b.g. Royal Applause 124 – Alignment (IRE) 98 (Alzao (USA) 117) [2009 74: 7g4 7f 8m 8m 12g2 12.1m4 11.1g2 12m3 Oct 5] close-coupled gelding: fair handicapper: stays 1½m: acts on good to firm ground: sold £11,500. *T. P. Tate* **71**

REGAL PARADE 5 ch.g. Pivotal 124 – Model Queen (USA) 76 (Kingmambo (USA) 125) [2009 115: p6g6 7f2 7m* 6m 7m* 7g3 7m2 6d* Sep 5] **123**

Regal Parade followed in the footsteps of two other stalwarts for his Yorkshire stable, Continent and Bahamian Pirate, in winning a Group 1 sprint after landing the Ayr Gold Cup. All three were thoroughly tried and tested by the time of their most important victory, though Regal Parade himself seemed to improve by a fair margin when defeating Fleeting Spirit in the Sprint Cup at Haydock. That was the twenty-ninth start of Regal Parade's career; Continent won the 2002 July Cup on his twenty-first outing; and Bahamian Pirate took until his sixty-eighth start to gain a Group 1 triumph, in the 2004 Nunthorpe Stakes (Ya Malak, the other Nicholls-trained Group 1 winner, who dead-heated in the 1997 Nunthorpe, was making his forty-second appearance on that occasion). Continent went on to gain a second Group 1 victory in the Prix de l'Abbaye, while Bahamian Pirate had already finished runner-up in an Abbaye and a July Cup before his York win. Both Continent and Bahamian Pirate proved notably durable too, Continent still capable of fairly useful form and winning twice at ten, going on to make seventy starts in total in his career; Bahamian Pirate was still capable of useful form as a twelve-year-old, when placed in handicaps, and he ran in one hundred and four races in all. Continent, Bahamian Pirate and Regal Parade were all 'hand-me-downs', joining David Nicholls after being with other stables. Bahamian Pirate ran his first two races for Con Collins, while both Continent and Regal Parade had a full season or more for another yard before being bought to join Nicholls (Ya Malak joined Nicholls as a six-year-old). Continent was acquired for 40,000 guineas after showing fairly useful form at three for Pascal Bary in France, Regal Parade was even more of a bargain, bought for just 16,000 guineas out of Mark Johnston's stable at the Newmarket Autumn Sales towards the end of his three-year-old days.

That Regal Parade made so little, after showing himself a useful performer, was presumably a result of the fact that his form seemed to have peaked. Regal Parade, a 430,000-guinea yearling, had been gelded as a two-year-old, when with Godolphin. He didn't race for Godolphin at two and was sent to Johnston, for whom he made a winning debut in a maiden at Wolverhampton at the end of January as a three-year-old. He followed up a month later in a handicap at Southwell before completing a hat-trick at Newmarket at the Guineas meeting. Regal Parade seemed to have earned a try in listed company but his eight further appearances at three were all in handicaps, the Silver Bowl, Britannia and the International among them, and he failed to reach so much as a place, looking increasingly temperamental as the season progressed (he ended the year with a Timeform 'squiggle'). Regal Parade's three wins came at seven furlongs and all his later races at three were at

Betfred Sprint Cup, Haydock—Regal Parade shows improved form in the tacky ground as he overhauls Fleeting Spirit (left) late on; High Standing (hooped cap) is third

that trip or further, including when tried over a mile and a quarter at Chester (where he ran badly) on his final one.

After joining Nicholls, Regal Parade was at first campaigned at a mile, finishing runner-up on three occasions, before a drop to seven furlongs brought some improvement. Regal Parade's first success for Nicholls came in the Buckingham Palace Handicap at Royal Ascot and he followed that with a third in the Bunbury Cup at Newmarket. When he arrived at Ayr for the Gold Cup it was his first start at six furlongs and his success that day seemed to owe plenty to the very testing conditions, which made for a thorough test at the trip. Five of Regal Parade's first seven runs in the latest season were at seven furlongs and he showed smart form on each occasion, winning a well-run conditions event at York in May and the listed totepool City Plate at Chester. Regal Parade got first run on the favourite Balthazaar's Gift at Chester and the tables were turned on Regal Parade's next two starts, the pair second and third to Finjaan in the Betfair Cup (Lennox) at Goodwood and Balthazaar's Gift beating Regal Parade by three lengths in the Hungerford Stakes at Newbury. Regal Parade had two runs at six furlongs, the first on the polytrack at Kempton on his reappearance and the second on his first outing in Group 1 company in the Golden Jubilee at Royal Ascot, in which he ran as if a little out of his depth.

All in all, Regal Parade looked to have plenty against him, stepping back up to Group 1 company in the Betfred-sponsored Sprint Cup over six furlongs on good to soft ground, conditions not nearly so testing as at Ayr the previous September. Truth to tell, most of the thirteen others in the field looked to have much better credentials on their best form, headed by the first three in the July Cup, Fleeting Spirit, Main Aim and J J The Jet Plane, the first two in the Wokingham Handicap, High Standing and Asset, the Betfair Cup winner Finjaan, and the Golden Jubilee winner Art Connoisseur. However, Main Aim and J J The Jet Plane had both run poorly in the Betfair Cup, while Art Connoisseur had lost his way since Ascot and was sent off at 33/1. That trio ran well below their best again, filling the last three places. And the form of the race was further weakened by below-par efforts on the day from Finjaan, who appeared to find the ground against him, and the unreliable Asset, who put in one of his forgettable efforts. The run of the race suited Regal Parade, the 2008 King's Stand winner Equiano taking the field along at a good pace from the Maurice de Gheest fifth Sayif, with Fleeting Spirit tucked in behind the leaders. Regal Parade, who had made the running in his time with Mark Johnston, was, as usual nowadays for his current stable, held up in rear. Fleeting Spirit cruised to the front over a furlong out with Regal Parade coming through to chase her, his pursuit looking forlorn at first, until Fleeting Spirit began to falter in the ground. Regal Parade stayed on strongly to lead in the last half furlong and eventually beat Fleeting Spirit by half a length, with High Standing, unable to land a blow, two lengths further back in third, and Sayif clear of the rest in fourth. Fleeting Spirit was below her July Cup form on the softish going but, even so, Regal Parade still showed form only just behind the best by a British-trained sprinter in 2009. Fleeting Spirit ran to a similar level when second in the Abbaye next time, while Sayif went on to win the Diadem at Ascot. Regal Parade himself wasn't seen out again but he is set to return in 2010 for a campaign in the top six- and seven-furlong events.

Regal Parade (ch.g. 2004)	Pivotal (ch 1993)	Polar Falcon (b or br 1987)	Nureyev
			Marie d'Argonne
		Fearless Revival (ch 1987)	Cozzene
			Stufida
	Model Queen (USA) (ch 1998)	Kingmambo (b 1990)	Mr Prospector
			Miesque
		Model Bride (ch 1985)	Blushing Groom
			Mofida

Regal Parade isn't the only one of his dam Model Queen's progeny to fetch a good price at the yearling sales for breeders the Highclere Stud. His year-younger half-brother Mount Helicon (by Montjeu) made 600,000 guineas before showing useful form at up to fifteen furlongs in France. Model Queen's 2006 foal by Danehill Dancer, the ill-fated Canyon Ranch who was placed at a mile, made 350,000 guineas, while the 2009 two-year-old Hot Prospect (by Motivator), a 230,000-guinea yearling, won a mile maiden in September on the second of his three starts, showing useful form already. Model Queen's 2008 filly foal by Encosta de Lago made 280,000 guineas at Newmarket in the autumn. The dam's first foal Sister Sylvia (by Fantastic Light) won over just short of ten furlongs in France. Model Queen herself made 92,000 guineas when sent up to the 2001 Newmarket December Sales after winning a maiden over seven and a half furlongs at Beverley for Barry Hills, and also showing her form at a mile and a quarter. Model Queen is a half-sister to five winners, the useful milers Arabride and Mediterraneo, the fairly useful performers Tableau, another miler, and Naked Ambition, successful at six and seven furlongs, and the fair mile and a half winner Theatre Groom. A twice-raced half-sister, Veiled Beauty, is the dam of the useful but fragile The Cheka, a seven-furlong winner at two and on his only start at three in 2009. Further back, this is a tremendous family, the third dam Mofida, a smart sprinter, featuring in the extended pedigrees of numerous pattern winners, including as grandam of Zafonic. Also among them is the Oaks runner-up Midday in whose essay further details of the family appear. The strong, lengthy Regal Parade has won on both fibresand and polytrack, as well as on going from firm to heavy on turf. He is a credit to his trainer and, as a tough, genuine and very smart performer, a credit to himself as well. *D. Nicholls*

REGAL PARK (IRE) 2 b.c. (Jan 13) Montjeu (IRE) 137 – Classic Park 115 (Robellino (USA) 127) [2009 8g^5 Oct 8] 180,000Y: lengthy colt: seventh foal: brother to Derby runner-up Walk In The Park, French 1m winner at 2 yrs, and half-brother to 2 winners, including smart 1m winner Secret World (by Spinning World): dam Irish 5f (at 2 yrs) to 1m (Irish 1000 Guineas) winner: 9/1, 16 lengths fifth to Kalypso King in maiden at Newbury, late headway: will stay 1¼m+: type to do better at 3 yrs. *J. Noseda* **61 p**

REGAL RANSOM (USA) 3 b. or br.c. Distorted Humor (USA) 117 – Kelli's Ransom (USA) (Red Ransom (USA)) [2009 a7g^2 a8f^2 a9f* a10s a9f* a10f Nov 7] $675,000 2-y-o: third foal: half-brother to useful 6f/7f (latter at 2 yrs) winner Speedy Dollar (by Dixie Union): dam, US maiden (stayed 8.5f), half-sister to Breeders' Cup Juvenile runner-up Minister Eric: very smart form: won maiden at Saratoga when trained by K. McLaughlin in 2008: improved in 2009, second to Desert Party at Nad Al Sheba in minor event and UAE 2000 Guineas before beating same rival ½ length (pair well clear) in UAE Derby there in March, holding on determinedly: off 3½ months (reported in June to have suffered a tendon injury on off-hind hock), won Grade 2 Super Derby at Louisiana Downs in September by 1¼ lengths from Blame, eased: stays 9f (possibly didn't stay 1¼m when eighth to Mine That Bird in Kentucky Derby at Churchill Downs and when eighth to Zenyatta in Breeders' Cup Classic at Santa Anita): raced only on dirt/pro-ride: tongue tied: races up with pace. *Saeed bin Suroor* **122**

REGAL RAVE (USA) 2 b.c. (Jan 28) Wild Event (USA) 120 – Golden Crown (USA) (Defensive Play (USA) 118) [2009 6m 6m 6.1g^6 7m Oct 26] strong colt: modest maiden: well held in nursery: should stay 1m. *J. R. Best* **55**

REGAL ROYALE 6 b.g. Medicean 128 – Regal Rose 110 (Danehill (USA) 126) [2009 80§: f6g^3 6d f5g^3 f5m^3 5d 5f 6g p6g^4 6d* p6g^3 Aug 11] well-made gelding: fair handicapper: won at Lingfield in August: races at 5f/6f: acts on all-weather, soft and good to firm going: has worn blinkers, visored nowadays: said to have bled: ungenuine. *Peter Grayson* **72 §**

REGAL TRADITION (IRE) 4 b.g. Traditionally (USA) 117 – Dathuil (IRE) 97 (Royal Academy (USA) 130) [2009 p9.5g 12m^4 9.8m f12g May 18] leggy, dipped-backed gelding: fair maiden at 2 yrs: missed 2008 and no form in 2009: tried blinkered. *G. J. Smith* **–**

REGARDLESS 2 ch.f. (May 8) Reset (AUS) 124 – Princess of Garda 79 (Komaite (USA)) [2009 5g 5m^3 f5g^3 6.1m^4 6d^2 6m^2 6d Sep 5] fourth foal: half-sister to 6f (including at 2 yrs) winner Tipsy Prince (by Tipsy Creek): dam, 2-y-o 5f winner, sister to useful sprinter Castelletto: fair maiden: effective at 5f/6f: acts on good to firm and good to soft going: visored last 3 outings: races prominently: sold £3,200. *Mrs G. S. Rees* **67**

REGENCY ART (IRE) 2 b.c. (Apr 18) Titus Livius (FR) 115 – Honey Storm (IRE) 73 (Mujadil (USA) 119) [2009 5.1d 6m* Oct 5] 40,000Y: attractive colt: fourth foal: brother to 7f (at 2 yrs)/1m winner Coalpark and half-brother to 3-y-o Rumble of Thunder: dam, 1m winner, half-sister to smart performer up to 13.4f Compton Bolter: much better effort in maidens over 5 months apart when winning at Warwick by ½ length from Libertino: sure to be suited by 7f+: sold 50,000 gns: will go on improving. *D. R. C. Elsworth* **71 p**

REGENERATION (IRE) 3 b.g. Chevalier (IRE) 115 – Cappuchino (IRE) 59 (Roi Danzig (USA)) [2009 67p: 6s^4 p6g* f7g^2 p7m* 7m^2 p7.1g* 8m^6 7g Oct 31] sturdy gelding: fairly useful performer on all-weather, fair on turf: won maiden at Lingfield in July and handicaps there in August and Wolverhampton in September: left S. Callaghan after next start: stays 7f: acts on all-weather and good to firm going. *M. L. W. Bell* **78 a84**

REGENT'S SECRET (USA) 9 br.g. Cryptoclearance (USA) – Misty Regent (CAN) (Vice Regent (CAN)) [2009 70: 12.1g^6 9.2m^4 11.1m^4 9.2d^3 12.5g^2 12.1v^4 12.5m Sep 14] leggy, useful-looking gelding: modest performer nowadays: stays 1½m: acts on polytrack, firm and good to soft going: tried visored, usually in cheekpieces: held up. *J. S. Goldie* **62**

REGGANE 3 b.f. Red Ransom (USA) – Reine Zao (FR) 107 (Alzao (USA) 117) [2009 8g* 8m^2 8f^2 8d^6 8g^6 Oct 3] sturdy, deep-girthed filly: third foal: half-sister to French 6.5f winner Ramita (by Fasliyev): dam, French 1¼m winner, out of Prix de Diane third Raintree Renegade: won newcomers race at Chantilly in May: smart form next 2 starts when ½-length second to Homebound in Prix de Sandringham at same course and 2 lengths second to Ghanaati in Coronation Stakes at Royal Ascot, on both occasions running on strongly: just fair efforts after, sixth to Goldikova in Prix Rothschild at Deauville and to Tamazirte in Prix Daniel Wildenstein at Longchamp: likely to stay 1¼m: acts on firm ground: has had tongue tied. *A. de Royer Dupre, France* **116**

REGIONAL COUNSEL 5 b.g. Medicean 128 – Regency Rose (Danehill (USA) 126) [2009 92: 10m^6 10d 8.3m p8g^6 Sep 9] lengthy gelding: fair handicapper nowadays: stays easy 1½m: acts on polytrack and good to firm ground: tried in blinkers. *A. M. Hales* **72**

REGISTRAR 7 ch.g. Machiavellian (USA) 123 – Confidante (USA) 95 (Dayjur (USA) 137) [2009 68: 7d 7g^6 8.3g 7g^2 6s 7g* 7m 7m^3 7g Oct 20] lengthy, good-topped gelding: modest handicapper: won at Yarmouth in August: best up to 7f: acts on polytrack, soft and good to firm ground: wears cheekpieces: held up: inconsistent: sold 1,000 gns. *Mrs C. A. Dunnett* **60**

REHABILITATION 4 ch.g. Dr Fong (USA) 128 – Lamees (USA) (Lomond (USA) 128) [2009 77: 10d 10m 10s^4 10m^4 10.9m p12.2g Nov 2] sturdy gelding: modest handicapper nowadays: stays 1¼m: acts on polytrack, soft and good to firm going: tried visored, wears cheekpieces/tongue tie nowadays: gelded after final start. *W. R. Swinburn* **62**

REIGNIER 2 b.c. (Apr 8) Kheleyf (USA) 116 – Komena 84 (Komaite (USA)) [2009 5.1d^5 5m* 5g^2 5m^2 6m^4 5g^6 Jul 28] £25,000Y: good-bodied colt: first foal: dam 2-y-o 6f winner: useful performer: won maiden at Musselburgh in May: best efforts in Norfolk Stakes at Royal Ascot (2 lengths behind Radiohead) and Molecomb Stakes at Goodwood (sixth to Monsieur Chevalier, never really comfortable with pace) fourth/final starts: should stay 6f: acts on good to firm going. *K. R. Burke* **95**

REIGNING IN RIO (IRE) 3 br.f. Captain Rio 122 – Saibhreas (IRE) 83 (Last Tycoon 131) [2009 –: f8g* f8g f8g^3 Apr 23] quite attractive filly: modest handicapper: won at Southwell in February: stays 1m: acts on fibresand. *P. C. Haslam* **53**

REIGNING MONARCH (USA) 6 b.g. Fusaichi Pegasus (USA) 130 – Torros Straits (USA) 82 (Boundary (USA) 117) [2009 66: p6g p6g^3 6f 7m 5.2s^3 6d 5g^5 p6m^3 p6m^4 p6m^4 Dec 10] leggy gelding: modest handicapper: effective at 5f/6f: acts on all-weather, firm and soft going: often in cheekpieces/blinkers. *Miss Z. C. Davison* **58**

REJECT 3 b.g. Green Desert (USA) 127 – Wardat Allayl (IRE) 87 (Mtoto 134) [2009 6m^6 6m^2 6m* 7m^4 6m 7m^6 6d^2 6m^4 6.1d Oct 15] 78,000Y: good-bodied gelding: fourth foal: brother to 8.5f winner Shot Gun and 2007 2-y-o 6f winner Ramatni, both fairly useful: dam, 2-y-o 7f winner, half-sister to smart performers Bint Allayl (leading 2-y-o filly in 1998) and Kheleyf (6f/7f performer), both by Green Desert: fairly useful performer: won maiden at Hamilton in May: not in same form in handicaps after: should stay 7f: unraced on extremes of going: sold 10,500 gns, sent to Greece. *W. J. Haggas* **85**

RELATIVE STRENGTH (IRE) 4 ch.g. Kris Kin (USA) 126 – Monalee Lass (IRE) 72 (Mujtahid (USA) 118) [2009 82: 11.6g 12m^3 14g^3 12g^2 21g p16g^6 15.9m^3 16m^5 Sep 26] workmanlike gelding: fairly useful handicapper: placed 4 times in 2009: stays 2m: acts on polytrack and good to firm going: visored nowadays. *A. M. Balding* **84**

REMARK (IRE) 5 b.g. Machiavellian (USA) 123 – Remuria (USA) 93 (Theatrical 128) [2009 11.8m p8.6g^6 f8f Nov 24] unfurnished gelding: little form since 2006: tongue tied: said to have had breathing problem. *M. W. Easterby* **–**

REMEMBER DOUGIE (IRE) 2 b.f. (Feb 5) Namid 128 – Proud Myth (IRE) (Mark of Esteem (IRE) 137) [2009 5m 5s 5m Sep 16] €3,000Y: close-coupled filly: second foal: half-sister to 3-y-o Mythical Blue: dam unraced: well held in maidens/seller. *A. Berry* **–**

REMEMBER RAMON (USA) 6 ch.g. Diesis 133 – Future Act (USA) 94 (Known Fact (USA) 135) [2009 84: p12g^4 p13.9g* p12g^4 12g* 12g p13.9g Sep 25] good-topped gelding: fairly useful handicapper: won at Wolverhampton in February and Newmarket (by ¾ length from Snoqualmie Boy) in July: well below form last 2 starts: barely stays 2m: acts on polytrack and good to soft going: races prominently. *J. R. Gask* **90**

REMEMBER WHEN (IRE) 2 ch.f. (Apr 7) Danehill Dancer (IRE) 117 – Lagrion (USA) 68 (Diesis 133) [2009 7s^2 Nov 5] closely related to top-class Irish 7f (at 2 yrs) to 1½m (Irish Derby and Prix de l'Arc de Triomphe) winner Dylan Thomas (by Danehill) and half-sister to several winners, notably high-class 5f (at 2 yrs, won Cheveley Park Stakes) to 7f winner Queen's Logic (by Grand Lodge): dam Irish maiden (stayed 13f): 8/1 and green, encouraging neck second to Karasiyra in maiden at Leopardstown (head bit high): will stay 1m+: will progress. *A. P. O'Brien, Ireland* **84 p**

REMINISCENT (IRE) 10 b.g. Kahyasi 130 – Eliza Orzeszkowa (IRE) 69 (Polish Patriot (USA) 128) [2009 –, a53: f16d f14g^5 f11g^4 p13.9g^5 Mar 2] rather leggy gelding: poor handicapper nowadays: stays 2m: acts on all-weather and firm going: wears head-gear: inconsistent. *B. P. J. Baugh* **43**

RENDEZVOUS (IRE) 3 b.c. Sadler's Wells (USA) 132 – Gwynn (IRE) (Darshaan 133) [2009 10m^4 10g 12m Oct 16] useful form in France at 2 yrs when trained by A. Fabre, winning maiden at Chantilly: little impact in 2009, visored in handicap final start: should stay 1¼m/1½m: sold 12,000 gns, sent to Hungary. *Sir Michael Stoute* **–**

RENEGE THE JOKER 6 b.g. Alflora (IRE) 120 – Bunty 57 (Presidium 124) [2009 –: 16d 14.1g Aug 30] no sign of ability: tried tongue tied. *Sean Regan* **–**

REPEALED 3 b.c. Reset (AUS) 124 – Great Verdict (AUS) (Christmas Tree (AUS)) [2009 64p: f11g^2 Apr 21] fair form in 2 maidens: stays 11f. *H. Morrison* **69**

REPETISCHA (IRE) 3 ch.f. Peintre Celebre (USA) 137 – Brief Escapade (IRE) 95 (Brief Truce (USA) 126) [2009 8m^6 9.9m^3 p8g^3 8g 11m Oct 11] lengthy filly: has scope: closely related to fairly useful 9.5f to 2m winner Newnham (by Theatrical) and half-sister to useful 7f and (in USA) 1m winner Illuminise (by Grand Lodge): dam, 1m winner, half-sister to high-class 7f to 9f performer Indian Lodge: fair maiden: left E. Dunlop before final outing: stays 1¼m, but travels strongly and may prove best at shorter. *E. J. O'Neill* **75**

REPLICATOR 4 b.g. Mujahid (USA) 125 – Valldemosa 81 (Music Boy 124) [2009 74: f6d^4 p6g f5g f5m 6.1f^5 p7.1g Jun 5] compact gelding: fair handicapper at best in 2009: should prove best at 5f/6f: acts on all-weather, good to firm and good to soft going: often blinkered/visored: finds little: fell final outing. *Pat Eddery* **69 d**

REPORTAGE (USA) 3 b.g. Elusive Quality (USA) – Journalist (IRE) 102 (Night Shift (USA)) [2009 8s^6 8.1g^3 10g 8g^2 8.5v Aug 31] sturdy gelding: fourth foal: closely related to useful 2006 2-y-o 6f winner La Presse (by Gone West) and half-brother to 7f/1m winner Paper Talk and French 1m winner Emirates Girl (both by Unbridled's Song), all useful: dam, 2-y-o 6f winner, half-sister to useful sprinter Sheer Viking: fair maiden: left J. Gosden prior to final outing: gelded after: should stay 1¼m. *R. A. Hennessy, Ireland* **78**

REPRIEVED 4 ch.g. Bertolini (USA) 125 – Crystal Seas 47 (Zamindar (USA) 116) [2009 54: f11g^5 p13.9g Mar 26] leggy gelding: poor maiden: likely to prove best short of 11f: acts on fibresand and good to firm ground. *Julie Camacho* **48**

REQUISITE 4 ch.f. Pivotal 124 – Chicarica (USA) 112 (The Minstrel (CAN) 135) [2009 89, a80: p6g^5 p5g 6s^3 5d* 5.2m 5m^5 5g^3 5s^2 5g 5d^4 5m 5.3d p6g p6g f6m Nov 11] attractive filly: fair handicapper, better on turf: won at Ripon in June: effective at 5f/6f: acts on polytrack, soft and good to firm ground: usually visored. *I. A. Wood* **79 a70**

RESCENT 2 ch.f. (Mar 7) Reset (AUS) 124 – Bukhoor (IRE) (Danehill (USA) 126) [2009 6d^2 p6g^4 7m* 8g^6 7.2v f8m f7g Dec 18] sturdy filly: second foal: dam unraced: poor performer: won claimer at Newcastle (left Rae Guest £6,000) in August: stays 7f: acts on polytrack, good to firm and good to soft going. *Mrs R. A. Carr* **49**

RESENTFUL ANGEL 4 b.f. Danehill Dancer (IRE) 117 – Leaping Flame (USA) (Trempolino (USA) 135) [2009 71: 8f 7.1g^2 8.3g^4 p7g^3 7.6d^3 p10m^5 12d p10g* p10g^3 p9.5g* p10m^2 Dec 10] tall, close-coupled filly: fair handicapper: won apprentice events at Lingfield in November and Wolverhampton in December: may prove best up to 1¼m: acts on polytrack and good to soft ground: blinkered twice. *Pat Eddery* **75**

RESET CITY 3 ch.f. Reset (AUS) 124 – City of Angels (Woodman (USA) 126) [2009 10m^6 11.7g^2 11.7g^5 12d Oct 11] half-sister to several winners, including useful 7f (at 2 yrs) to 11f winner I'm So Lucky (by Zilzal) and fairly useful 1½m winner Star of Angels (by Diktat): dam unraced: fair maiden: stays 11.7f: best efforts on good going. *A. B. Haynes* **70**

RESIDENCY (IRE) 3 b.g. Danetime (IRE) 121 – Muckross Park 41 (Nomination 125) [2009 –: 5m^6 f5m^2 5m 5s^2 5d f6m^5 p6g^4 Dec 19] useful-looking gelding: fair maiden: raced only at 5f/6f: acts on fibresand and soft going: visored/in cheekpieces last 2 starts. *B. Smart* **70**

RESOLUTE DEFENDER (IRE) 4 b.g. Namid 128 – Snowspin 75 (Carwhite 127) [2009 53: 7d 8m Aug 5] maiden: no form in 2009: tried blinkered. *R. Johnson* **–**

RESORT 3 b.f. Oasis Dream 129 – Gay Gallanta (USA) 112 (Woodman (USA) 126) [2009 79P: 7m* 7.6m 7g 8g^3 8.3f* 9m^2 8m Sep 26] close-coupled filly: useful performer: won maiden at Newmarket in April and handicap at Windsor in August: good neck second to Tartan Gunna in handicap at Goodwood next time: stayed 9f: raced only on good going or firmer (acted on firm): visits Pivotal. *Sir Michael Stoute* **97**

RESOUNDING GLORY (USA) 4 b.g. Honour And Glory (USA) 122 – Resounding Grace (USA) (Thunder Gulch (USA) 129) [2009 82: 9.2s Aug 1] rangy gelding: fairly useful handicapper at best: said to have finished distressed only outing on Flat in 2009: stays 1¼m: acts on heavy going. *R. A. Fahey* **–**

RESPITE 3 b.f. Pivotal 124 – Truce (Nashwan (USA) 135) [2009 74p: p7g* 7d^5 8.3m p7g^2 p8g^6 p7.1g a6.5g a6.5g Dec 24] strong, lengthy filly: fairly useful performer: won maiden at Kempton in April: second in handicap there, best effort after: sold from W. Haggas 12,000 gns after sixth outing: should stay 1m: acts on polytrack. *H-A. Pantall, France* **83**

RESPLENDENT ACE (IRE) 5 b.g. Trans Island 119 – Persian Polly 99 (Persian Bold 123) [2009 69, a84: p12g p12g p12.2g^4 p10g^6 p12.2g* p9.5g^2 p10m p12m^2 p9.5g^6 p10m^3 f12m* p13g^3 p10m^5 p9.5g^2 f16m^3 f11g^6 Dec 27] sturdy gelding: fairly useful handicapper on all-weather, fair at best on turf: won at Wolverhampton (claimer) in July and Southwell in November: stays 1½m: acts on all-weather, soft and good to firm going: has looked none too keen: held up. *P. Howling* **–** **a83**

RESPLENDENT ALPHA 5 ch.g. Best of The Bests (IRE) 122 – Sunley Scent 85 (Wolfhound (USA) 126) [2009 88: p6g^6 p6g* p6g^4 p6g^4 p6g p6g^2 6d^6 6g 6m^5 6m 6m 6f^4 p7g 6m p6g^6 f6m p6f^2 p6f^4 Dec 20] lengthy gelding: fairly useful handicapper: won at Lingfield in February: best at 6f/7f: acts on all-weather, firm and good to soft ground: tried tongue tied/blinkered: sometimes slowly away: held up. *P. Howling* **86**

RESPLENDENT LIGHT 4 b.g. Fantastic Light (USA) 134 – Bright Halo (IRE) (Bigstone (IRE) 126) [2009 100: 12f^6 10m^5 12g 11.6m^4 12m^3 12g^2 12m 12m^3 12m^2 Oct 3] leggy gelding: useful handicapper: runner-up at Pontefract and Newmarket: stays 1½m: acts on soft and good to firm ground: has found little. *W. R. Muir* **96**

RESPLENDENT NOVA 7 b.g. Pivotal 124 – Santiburi Girl 77 (Casteddu 111) [2009 76, a93: f7d^3 p7g* p8g^5 7g 7s 7m p7.1g p8g p7g p7g p7g^3 p7f^4 p7m^4 Dec 30] sturdy gelding: fairly useful handicapper on all-weather, fair when last showed form on turf in 2008: won at Kempton in January: below best after: best at 7f: acts on all-weather, soft and good to firm going: tried visored: held up. *P. Howling* **–** **a87 d**

RESTART (IRE) 8 b.g. Revoque (IRE) 122 – Stargard (Polish Precedent (USA) 131) [2009 55: f16d^6 p16g Jan 16] sturdy gelding: modest handicapper in 2008: well held in 2009: sometimes in cheekpieces. *Lucinda Featherstone* **–**

REST BY THE RIVER 3 ch.f. Reset (AUS) 124 – Palace Green (IRE) 71 (Rudimentary (USA) 118) [2009 54: 6m 6f Jun 24] close-coupled filly: maiden: little form in 2009. *A. G. Newcombe* **–**

RESTLESS GENIUS (IRE) 4 b.g. Captain Rio 122 – Mainmise (USA) (Septieme Ciel (USA) 123) [2009 80: p6g^2 5m^6 5g^6 p6g* 6m^4 5g^4 5m^5 f7g^4 p7f f5m^2 p6g^5 p6g f6d^6 Dec 29] good-topped gelding: fair handicapper: won at Wolverhampton in May: stays 1m: acts on all-weather, good to firm and good to soft going: tongue tied at 3 yrs. *B. Ellison* **73**

RESTLESS SWALLOW 4 gr.g. Bandmaster (USA) 97 – Pink Petal (Northern Game) [2009 10g 12.1g 13.1g Sep 7] big, workmanlike gelding: no form. *R. A. Harris* **–**

RESTYLE 2 b.f. (Mar 13) Reset (AUS) 124 – Surrealist (ITY) (Night Shift (USA)) [2009 5g 6m 7g 6f p7f Sep 10] £16,000Y: strong filly: half-sister to 3 winners, including fairly useful but unreliable 5f/6f winner (including at 2 yrs) Mitsuki (by Puissance) and 6f/7f winner Crafty Fox (by Foxhound): dam unraced: temperamental maiden: no form: tried in cheekpieces: sold £600. *D. K. Ivory* **– §**

RESURGE (IRE) 4 b.g. Danehill Dancer (IRE) 117 – Resurgence (Polar Falcon (USA) 126) [2009 102: 8.1g 8m 8m^5 8.3m^4 10m* 10g^2 10g^5 8.1g 9m 9.9s^5 p12g^6 Oct 26] stocky gelding: type to carry condition: useful handicapper: won at Windsor by 7 lengths in June: generally struggled after: stays 1¼m: acts on polytrack and firm ground. *W. S. Kittow* **97**

RESUSCITATOR (USA) 2 b.c. (May 6) Bernstein (USA) 115 – Lac du Printemps (USA) (Meadowlake (USA)) [2009 p7m² p7f⁴ Sep 10] fifth foal: half-brother to 3 winners in USA: dam, US maiden, sister to US 1999 Grade 1 2-y-o 1m winner Greenwood Lake and closely related to Breeders' Cup Juvenile winner Success Express: similar form in maidens at Lingfield (66/1, runner-up to Lethal Combination) and Kempton (fourth to Fallen Idol). *Mrs H. S. Main* **74**

RETRATO (USA) 2 b. or br.f. (Apr 24) Fusaichi Pegasus (USA) 130 – Painted Lady (USA) (Broad Brush (USA)) [2009 8.3s³ Oct 7] $70,000Y: tall, unfurnished filly: third living foal: half-sister to 2 winners in US, notably Grade 2 8.5f winner Skylighter (by Sky Mesa): dam, US 1m winner, sister to smart Japanese performer up to 1¼m Nobo True: 22/1, encouraging 6¼ lengths third to Ceilidh House in maiden at Nottingham, shuffled back 3f out: capable of better. *Rae Guest* **67 p**

RETRO (IRE) 3 b.c. Tagula (IRE) 116 – Cabcharge Princess (IRE) 64 (Rambo Dancer (CAN) 107) [2009 77: 9g 7m p6m p7m 6g Oct 19] close-coupled colt: fair performer at 2 yrs: well held in 2009. *R. Hannon* **–**

RETTORICAL LAD 4 gr. or ro.g. Vettori (IRE) 119 – Reciprocal (IRE) 88 (Night Shift (USA)) [2009 –: p13g⁵ p16g p12g Mar 12] big, strong gelding: seemingly modest form at best: has reportedly suffered breathing problems. *Jamie Poulton* **59 ?**

REVE DE MARDI 2 b.g. (Feb 14) Cyrano de Bergerac 120 – Dreams Forgotten (IRE) 63 (Victory Note (USA) 120) [2009 p8.6g 8d Oct 12] well held in maidens. *George Baker* **–**

REVELATOR (IRE) 2 b.c. (Mar 21) One Cool Cat (USA) 123 – Capades Band (FR) (Chimes Band (USA) 117) [2009 6m⁴ 6s* Oct 27] €30,000F: second foal: dam, US 1m winner, half-sister to smart French/US performers up to 1½m Vangelis and Marichal: much better effort in maidens nearly 3 months apart when winning at Catterick by 2½ lengths from Olympic Ceremony, making all: should stay 7f/1m: will improve again. *A. P. Jarvis* **74 p**

REVERED 2 b.f. (Mar 29) Oasis Dream 129 – Arrive 109 (Kahyasi 130) [2009 7d³ 7g* Oct 31] lengthy filly: fourth foal: sister to smart 6f (at 2 yrs)/7f winner Visit (stays 1¼m) and half-sister to very smart 7f to 1¼m (Pretty Polly Stakes) winner Promising Lead (by Danehill): dam, 1¼m to 15f winner, sister to outstanding broodmare Hasili: promising in maidens, winning at Newmarket by ½ length from Call To Reason, in control final 1f: will stay 1¼m: looks sure to go on to much better things. *Sir Michael Stoute* **81 P**

REVERENCE 8 ch.g. Mark of Esteem (IRE) 137 – Imperial Bailiwick (IRE) 104 (Imperial Frontier (USA) 112) [2009 111: 5d² 5v 5g⁴ 5g⁴ 5g 5v* 5g Oct 4] heavy-bodied gelding: has reportedly fractured pelvis twice: one-time high-class performer, still smart nowadays: won Grenzen Flying Five Stakes at the Curragh in August by length from Judge 'N Jury: below form in Prix de l'Abbaye de Longchamp final outing: effective at 5f/6f: has form on good to firm going, all wins on good or softer (acts on heavy). *E. J. Alston* **113**

REVE VERT (FR) 4 b.c. Oasis Dream 129 – Comme d'Habitude (USA) 72 (Caro 133) [2009 60: 8.1g 8.3m f8g Jun 7] strong colt: modest maiden: worth a try at 1¼m: acts on polytrack, good to firm and good to soft ground. *Tim Vaughan* **51**

REVOLTINTHEDESERT 2 b.f. (Mar 5) Dubai Destination (USA) 127 – Cloud Hill (Danehill (USA) 126) [2009 6m⁶ 7d⁴ Jul 22] 17,000F, £18,000Y: fourth foal: half-sister to 2 winners, including 4-y-o Mista Rossa: dam unraced half-sister to St Leger runner-up High And Low and dam of very smart French miler American Post: better effort in maidens when fourth to Giulietta da Vinci at Leicester, still green: will stay 1¼m+: sold 4,000 gns in October. *E. S. McMahon* **49**

REVOLVING WORLD (IRE) 6 b.g. Spinning World (USA) 130 – Mannakea (USA) (Fairy King (USA)) [2009 48: 16m 10g Oct 16] handicapper: no form in 2009: tried in blinkers/cheekpieces: tongue tied. *L. R. James* **–**

REVUE PRINCESS (IRE) 4 b.f. Mull of Kintyre (USA) 114 – Blues Queen 85 (Lahib (USA) 129) [2009 72§: 5m 5d* 5f 5d 5g⁶ 5g 5g³ 5g* 6d⁵ p5.1g⁵ 5s f5m Nov 6] strong, sturdy filly: fair handicapper: won at Newcastle in May and September: best at 5f: acts on polytrack, heavy and good to firm ground: blinkered: inconsistent, and one to treat with caution. *T. D. Easterby* **75 §**

REZWAAN 2 b.g. (Mar 22) Alhaarth (IRE) 126 – Nasij (USA) 101 (Elusive Quality (USA)) [2009 p7g 7s⁵ 7m⁶ 8g² 9m³ 8.3d* p7m Dec 6] good-bodied gelding: second foal: dam, 6f (at 2 yrs) and 1m winner, stayed 1¼m: fair performer: won nursery at Nottingham in October, then left E. Dunlop 55,000 gns: stays 8.3f: acts on good to firm and good to soft going. *M. J. McGrath* **78**

RHAPSILIAN 5 b.m. Dansili 127 – Rivers Rhapsody 104 (Dominion 123) [2009 68: 6m^5 6f^2 6f^4 6m 6m^5 5.1g^4 5.2g 6m p5m^4 Oct 7] tall mare: modest handicapper nowadays: left J. Geake after fourth start: free-going sort, best at 5f/6f: acts on polytrack and firm ground: often in headgear: one to treat with caution. *J. R. Jenkins* **62 §**

RHYTHMIC STAR 2 ch.c. (Mar 10) Starcraft (NZ) 128 – Markova's Dance 64 (Mark of Esteem (IRE) 137) [2009 7g Aug 14] 62,000F, 52,000Y: fifth foal: half-brother to 4-y-o Perfect Act: dam, sprint maiden, half-sister to smart middle-distance stayers Azzilfi and Khamaseen: 25/1, down the field in maiden at Newmarket, pulling hard after slow start, not knocked about: capable of better. *W. J. Haggas* **– p**

RICCI DE MARE 4 b.f. Cadeaux Genereux 131 – Procession 72 (Zafonic (USA) 130) [2009 60: f12s^5 p9.5g Jan 22] lengthy filly: modest performer in 2008: poor efforts all 4 starts for current connections: tried blinkered/in cheekpieces. *G. J. Smith* **–**

RICCOCHE (IRE) 2 b.f. (Jan 21) Oasis Dream 129 – Ammo (IRE) (Sadler's Wells (USA) 132) [2009 p8.6g Nov 21] first foal: dam, French 1½m winner, sister to useful 1½m (Prix de Royaumont) winner Sadler's Flag, out of smart French 1½m performer Animatrice: 16/1 and very green, slowly away and tailed off in maiden at Wolverhampton. *J. H. M. Gosden* **–**

RICHARDLIONHEART (USA) 3 ch.g. Lion Heart (USA) 124 – Cleito (USA) (Unbridled's Song (USA) 125) [2009 –: 7m 6m^6 p8f 10d Oct 22] workmanlike gelding: little form: left B. Gubby after second start. *M. Madgwick* **–**

RICHARDTHESECOND (IRE) 4 b.g. Acclamation 118 – Tahlil 46 (Cadeaux Genereux 131) [2009 61: p5.1g p5.1g 5.1m Apr 18] robust gelding: poor maiden handicapper: effective at 5f/6f: acts on polytrack and good to firm going: tried blinkered: quirky. *W. M. Brisbourne* **48**

RICH BOY 2 ch.g. (Mar 10) Bahamian Bounty 116 – West Humble 93 (Pharly (FR) 130) [2009 6m^6 p6g^4 p7m^4 Nov 26] compact gelding: similar form when fourth in maidens at Lingfield and Kempton (to Too Putra, dictating): gelded after: seems to stay 7f. *Mrs L. J. Mongan* **66**

RICHELIEU 7 b.g. Machiavellian (USA) 123 – Darling Flame (USA) 101 (Capote (USA)) [2009 80: 6s^5 5.8s p8f^3 6s^2 5g^5 5g^2 6.3g a7g* p7.1g p8f p6g^3 p7g p8g Nov 25] fairly useful handicapper: won at Laytown in September: best at 6f/7f: acts on polytrack/sand, firm and soft going: none too consistent. *J. J. Lambe, Ireland* **87**

RICHO 3 ch.g. Bertolini (USA) 125 – Noble Water (FR) 46 (Noblequest (FR) 124) [2009 83: 7g^2 7f 7.1m^3 7m 7.6m 7d 7m^4 7m 8m^4 8g^6 8.3v Nov 4] big, workmanlike gelding: fairly useful performer: left D. Brown after seventh start: stays 1m: acts on polytrack, good to firm and good to soft going: tried blinkered/in cheekpieces. *S. A. Harris* **80**

RICH RED (IRE) 3 ch.g. Redback 116 – Pink N Prosperous (IRE) (Grand Lodge (USA) 125) [2009 62: p6g Jan 14] sturdy gelding: modest maiden at 2 yrs: well held sole outing in 2009: stays 6f. *R. Hannon* **–**

RIDE A WHITE SWAN 4 gr.g. Baryshnikov (AUS) – The Manx Touch (IRE) 70 (Petardia 113) [2009 71: p7.1g p7g p8g 6m 8m^6 6m^5 6.1m^5 p6g^4 p6m^3 f7f Dec 12] modest maiden handicapper nowadays: stays 1m: acts on polytrack and good to firm ground: tried in cheekpieces. *D. Shaw* **51**

RIDGEWAY JAZZ 4 b.f. Kalanisi (IRE) 132 – Billie Holiday (Fairy King (USA)) [2009 49: p8.6g^4 p8.6g^5 p9.5g* p9.5g^3 p12g^4 p9.5g* p9.5g^2 p9.5g* p9.5g Mar 27] fair handicapper: won at Wolverhampton in January, February (apprentices) and March: will prove best short of 1½m: raced on all-weather. *M. D. I. Usher* **73**

RIDGEWAY SAPPHIRE 2 b.f. (Mar 5) Zafeen (FR) 123 – Barefooted Flyer (USA) 67 (Fly So Free (USA) 122) [2009 6s 6.1g^5 p7f f5g Sep 29] tall filly: third foal: half-sister to 3-y-o Ridgeway Silver and 5f/6f (latter including at 2 yrs) winner Totally Free (by Woodborough): dam 7f winner: form only in maidens first 2 starts: should stay 7f. *M. D. I. Usher* **54**

RIDGEWAY SILVER 3 b.f. Lujain (USA) 119 – Barefooted Flyer (USA) 67 (Fly So Free (USA) 122) [2009 66: f6s^5 p6g^4 p7.1g^4 6.1g p7.1g^4 p6g 6f p7g p6g^4 p7f^5 p7g Oct 2] tall filly: modest performer at 3 yrs: stays 7f: acts on polytrack and good to firm ground: tried in cheekpieces: has looked tricky ride. *M. D. I. Usher* **60**

RIDLEY DIDLEY (IRE) 4 b.g. Tagula (IRE) 116 – Dioscorea (IRE) (Pharly (FR) 130) [2009 63: p5m^2 f5g^2 f5g 5m^5 5m^2 5g 5m^6 Jun 19] modest maiden handicapper: will prove best at 5f: acts on all-weather and good to firm ground: tried blinkered (pulled too hard): tongue tied last 3 starts. *N. Wilson* **62**

RIEVAULX WORLD 3 b.g. Compton Place 125 – Adhaaba (USA) 76 (Dayjur (USA) 137) [2009 106: 5.1m^6 5m^5 5g^2 5m 5.1m^6 5g Jul 30] strong, compact gelding: useful performer: creditable efforts in 2009 in Palace House Stakes at Newmarket (3¾ lengths fifth behind Amour Propre), minor event at York (length second to Anglezarke) and listed race at Chester (sixth to Borderlescott): last in King George Stakes at Goodwood final outing (gelded after): speedy front runner, best kept to 5f: acts on firm going: none too consistent. *K. A. Ryan* **105**

RIFFELALP (IRE) 2 ch.f. (Mar 19) Bachelor Duke (USA) 122 – Alpenrot (IRE) (Barathea (IRE) 127) [2009 5g^6 5g p7g^5 7m^6 7m Sep 1] workmanlike filly: first foal: dam German 2-y-o 6.8f winner: maiden: best effort on debut: should stay 6f. *Eve Johnson Houghton* **55**

RIFLESSIONE 3 ch.c. Captain Rio 122 – Hilites (IRE) 85 (Desert King (IRE) 129) [2009 75: p6g^4 p5.1g^3 f6d^3 p6g^2 6g 5.1g* 6f^4 6m^3 6m^3 7m p6m^3 5.1g^4 5.1d^4 6d p7.1g Dec 28] angular, good-topped colt: fair handicapper: dead-heated at Bath in April: best at 5f/6f: acts on all-weather, firm and soft going: wears cheekpieces/blinkers: looks hard work, but often finishes strongly. *R. A. Harris* **78**

RIGAT 6 b.g. Dansili 127 – Fudge (Polar Falcon (USA) 126) [2009 61: p9.5g p8.6g^3 Mar 20] tall, good-topped gelding: modest handicapper: stays easy 1½m: acts on polytrack, firm and good to soft going: held up. *J. S. Goldie* **57**

RIGGED 3 b.g. Desert Sun 120 – Emma Peel 113 (Emarati (USA) 74) [2009 47: p8.6g^3 p8.6g^6 f8g^4 a7.5g^2 a8g^4 7g 6.8g Aug 15] compact gelding: modest maiden: left J. Osborne after third start: stays 8.6f: acts on polytrack: tried blinkered. *Jozef Oost, Belgium* **51**

RIGGINS (IRE) 5 b.g. Cape Cross (IRE) 129 – Rentless (Zafonic (USA) 130) [2009 101p: 8m 8m* 10.4m Jul 11] useful handicapper: has won 3 of 5 career starts, best effort when beating Mujood ¾ length at Goodwood in May: well held in John Smith's Cup at York subsequent outing (on edge beforehand): should stay 1¼m: raced on polytrack and good to firm ground: sold 18,000 gns, then gelded. *L. M. Cumani* **104**

RIGGS (IRE) 3 b.c. Daggers Drawn (USA) 114 – Jay And-A (IRE) 98 (Elbio 125) [2009 p5f p5g Nov 5] tailed off in maidens at Lingfield, blinkered latter outing. *Peter Grayson* **–**

RIGHTCAR 2 b.c. (Feb 14) Bertolini (USA) 125 – Loblolly Bay 99 (Halling (USA) 133) [2009 5m^6 5m^6 7.1m^6 p5g^4 f5g^4 p5g f5g p6m p5g^6 p5.1g^5 5.1s p5.1g^6 p6g^4 f6m f6g^5 p7g^2 Dec 31] lengthy colt: modest maiden: effective at 5f/6f: acts on all-weather: tried blinkered: unreliable. *Peter Grayson* **51 §**

RIGHTCAR DOMINIC 4 b.c. Kyllachy 129 – Vallauris 94 (Faustus (USA) 118) [2009 59: p6g p5.1g p5g p7m p5.1g^6 f6d Dec 29] maiden: little form at 4 yrs: tried blinkered. *Peter Grayson* **–**

RIGHTCAR LEWIS 4 ch.f. Noverre (USA) 125 – Abeyr 106 (Unfuwain (USA) 131) [2009 48: p5g^3 f5g p5g^5 p5g 5m^5 6d 6m^6 5m 5m 5m^4 5m 5s^3 5m^4 5.1d^4 Sep 4] modest maiden: may prove best at 5f: acts on polytrack and soft ground: blinkered. *Peter Grayson* **54**

RIGHTCAR MARIAN 2 b.f. (Apr 17) Oasis Dream 129 – Top Flight Queen 82 (Mark of Esteem (IRE) 137) [2009 p5.1g p5m p5m f5f p5.1g Dec 26] 3,000Y: fifth foal: sister to 4-y-o Anne of Kiev and half-sister to 3 winners, including 5-y-o Big Robert: dam, 1¼m winner, half-sister to smart performer up to 1¾m Sacrament: no form. *Peter Grayson* **–**

RIGHTFUL RULER 7 b.g. Montjoy (USA) 122 – Lady of The Realm (Prince Daniel (USA)) [2009 57: p12.2g May 11] strong gelding: lightly raced and modest on Flat in 2008: well held only outing in 2009: should stay 2m: acts on polytrack, soft and firm going: tried in cheekpieces: sold £2,700. *N. Wilson* **–**

RIGHT GRAND 2 b.c. (Mar 10) Exceed And Excel (AUS) 126 – Baileys Dancer 90 (Groom Dancer (USA) 128) [2009 p7.1m f7f* Dec 11] 58,000F, 40,000Y: second foal: dam 1m (at 2 yrs) to 1½m winner, half-sister to useful 1¼m performer Deal Fair: much better effort in maidens when winning at Southwell by 6 lengths from Prince Yarraman, clear final 1f: will stay beyond 7f: will improve further. *W. J. Haggas* **77 p**

RIGHT OPTION (IRE) 5 b.g. Daylami (IRE) 138 – Option (IRE) 52 (Red Ransom (USA)) [2009 78: p16g* p16g^4 16s 17.2m^5 Sep 13] smallish, close-coupled gelding: fairly useful handicapper: won at Kempton (by 9 lengths) in February: stays 2m: acts on polytrack, firm and good to soft ground (below form on fibresand and soft/heavy ground): tried in cheekpieces/blinkers: fairly useful hurdler, won twice in 2009. *J. L. Flint* **83**

RIGHT RAVE (IRE) 2 b.f. (Mar 24) Soviet Star (USA) 128 – Genuinely (IRE) 43 (Entrepreneur 123) [2009 6m 5.2d* 6m[6] 7m[5] p8m[2] 8m[3] Sep 23] 5,500Y: good-topped filly: second foal: sister to Italian 1¼m winner Henry Gondorff: dam maiden (stayed 1½m), out of half-sister to very smart sprinter Pivotal: fair performer: won maiden at Yarmouth in July: good efforts in nurseries last 2 starts: will stay 1¼m: acts on polytrack, good to soft and good to firm going. *P. J. McBride* **73**

RIGHT STEP 2 b.c. (Jan 20) Xaar 132 – Maid To Dance 62 (Pyramus (USA) 78) [2009 6m[3] 7m* 8g[5] Sep 17] big, lengthy colt: has scope: fourth foal: half-brother to 5-y-o Everyman: dam, ran 3 times, half-sister to very smart performer up to 1½m Filia Ardross, herself dam of Fillies' Mile winner Sunspangled: best effort when winning maiden at Newcastle in August by 2½ lengths from Elmfield Giant: should stay 1m (raced freely when tried). *A. P. Jarvis* **84**

RIGHT STUFF (FR) 6 b.g. Dansili 127 – Specificity (USA) 103 (Alleged (USA) 138) [2009 82: p12g[2] p12g* 13.3m[2] Aug 14] rangy gelding: fairly useful handicapper: won at Kempton in April: off 4 months, good second at Newbury final outing, meeting interference: stays 13.3f: acts on all-weather, soft and good to firm going: held up. *G. L. Moore* **93**

RIGHT YOU ARE (IRE) 9 ch.g. Right Win (IRE) 119 – Ancadia (Henbit (USA) 130) [2009 57: 10m Jun 29] modest maiden in 2008: well held only outing on Flat in 2009: should stay beyond 1½m: acts on polytrack and good to soft ground: tried visored. *Paul Green* **–**

RIGID 2 ch.g. (Apr 10) Refuse To Bend (IRE) 128 – Supersonic 80 (Shirley Heights 130) [2009 6f[4] 7m 7d[4] p7.1g Oct 16] 2,000Y: rather leggy gelding: sixth foal: half-brother to 1½m seller winner Whirling (by Groom Dancer): dam, maiden (stayed 10.5f), sister to useful stayer Upper Strata: maiden: easily best effort on debut: should stay at least 1¼m: sold 8,000 gns, then gelded. *J. G. Given* **70**

RIGIDITY 2 b.c. (Mar 6) Indian Ridge 123 – Alakananda 92 (Hernando (FR) 127) [2009 8g[2] 8m* Sep 17] 95,000Y: fourth foal: half-brother to 3 winners, including 1½m performer (Derby runner-up) Dragon Dancer (by Sadler's Wells) and 5-y-o Ajaan: dam, won around 1½m, half-sister to dual Champion Stakes winner Alborada and smart 1½m performer Albanova: promising in maidens, winning at Yarmouth by 2 lengths from Bab Al Shams, not fully extended: will be well suited by 1¼m+: useful prospect. *H. R. A. Cecil* **90 p**

RIGUEZ DANCER 5 b.g. Dansili 127 – Tricoteuse (Kris 135) [2009 80: p13.9g* p16.5g* f11g* 12g Jun 13] workmanlike gelding: fairly useful handicapper: much improved to complete hat-trick at Wolverhampton/Southwell in January/February: off over 4 months, weakened quickly in ladies event at York final outing: effective at 11f to 2m: acts on all-weather, soft and good to firm ground: tongue tied: races prominently: sold £32,000, joined Ferdy Murphy. *P. C. Haslam* **89**

RILEY BOYS (IRE) 8 ch.g. Most Welcome 131 – Scarlett Holly 81 (Red Sunset 120) [2009 83: 8.5m 9.9g 12d[5] Jun 17] close-coupled gelding: fairly useful handicapper at best: well held in 2009: tried in cheekpieces/visor. *J. G. Given* **–**

RILEY QUEEN BEE (USA) 3 b.f. Mr Greeley (USA) 122 – Quarrel Over Halo (USA) (Halo (USA)) [2009 7m 7.2g 7d Jun 26] €80,000Y: tall filly: closely related to winner in USA by Elusive Quality and half-sister to several winners abroad, including useful French 7f/9f winner Quittance (by Riverman): dam, US 6f/7f winner, half-sister to US Grade 2 9f winner Suivi: maiden: modest form only on debut: saddle slipped second start, said to have finished distressed final outing. *K. R. Burke* **60**

RIMSKY KORSAKOV (IRE) 5 b.g. Sadler's Wells (USA) 132 – Tedarshana (Darshaan 133) [2009 –: 21.6m[3] Apr 20] well-made gelding: modest maiden: stayed 21.5f: acted on good to firm going: visored final start: dead. *Micky Hammond* **60**

RINDLESS 4 b.f. Bertolini (USA) 125 – Streaky (IRE) 63 (Danetime (IRE) 121) [2009 –: p6g 7f 10d Sep 15] no solid form. *J. F. Panvert* **–**

RING OF FIRE 2 b.c. (May 6) Firebreak 125 – Sweet Patoopie 72 (Indian Ridge 123) [2009 p7m p8f Dec 16] little impact in maidens at Kempton. *J. L. Spearing* **–**

RINGO ZAAR 3 b.g. Xaar 132 – Tomanivi (Caerleon (USA) 132) [2009 56: p10g f8g Feb 12] maiden: no form in 2009: blinkered last 3 starts. *A. B. Haynes* **–**

RINKY DINK LADY (IRE) 3 b.f. Tiger Hill (IRE) 127 – Glady Starlet (GER) (Big Shuffle (USA) 122) [2009 8.3g[5] Jul 27] €25,000Y, resold €13,000Y: third foal: half-sister to winner in Italy by Tertullian: dam German 7f winner: poor form when fifth in maiden at Windsor: sold 1,000 gns. *W. R. Swinburn* **45**

RIO CARIBE (IRE) 2 b.g. (Apr 28) Captain Rio 122 – Kadja Chenee (Spectrum (IRE) 126) [2009 5m^5 5d^2 5g^5 6s Aug 1] best effort in maidens when ½-length second to On The Bounty at Doncaster: should be suited by 6f+. *T. D. Walford* **66**

RIO CARNIVAL (USA) 3 b.f. Storm Cat (USA) – Zenda 115 (Zamindar (USA) 116) [2009 –p: 8m Apr 4] sturdy filly: well held in maidens 7 months apart: stud. *J. H. M. Gosden* **–**

RIO COBOLO (IRE) 3 b.c. Captain Rio 122 – Sofistication (IRE) 68 (Dayjur (USA) 137) [2009 68: f6g^5 5m 6.1g 5g^2 6m^3 5m^3 7.6g* 6.9g^3 7.6m^2 7s 6m^2 7d^3 6v* 5.1m 6m^4 7.5g* p6g 6.1d p8.6g^5 f6m^2 f6f Nov 24] good-bodied colt: fairly useful handicapper: won at Chester in June, and Catterick and Beverley in September: effective at 5f to 7.6f: acts on fibresand, heavy and good to firm going: visored (below form when blinkered once). *Paul Green* **80**

RIO COMMAND (IRE) 2 b.g. (Feb 8) Captain Rio 122 – Happy To Chat (IRE) 80 (Alzao (USA) 117) [2009 7s 7s^4 7g^2 8.1d^3 8s^5 Sep 15] €7,500F, €44,000Y: first foal: dam Irish 1m winner: fair maiden: placed at Leopardstown and Chepstow: likely to prove better at 7f than 1m: needs to learn to settle: sent to Hong Kong. *D. Loughnane, Ireland* **78**

RIO DE LA PLATA (USA) 4 ch.c. Rahy (USA) 115 – Express Way (ARG) (Ahmad (ARG)) [2009 118: 8.1v 8m^2 9m^5 Oct 16] rangy, good-topped colt: usually impresses in appearance: has fluent action: smart performer: reportedly suffered setback in spring and not seen out until September: creditable effort in 2009 only when ½-length second to Confront in Joel Stakes at Newmarket: only fifth in Darley Stakes there final outing, not moving well at finish: stays 1m: acts on good to firm ground, below form both starts on softer than good. *Saeed bin Suroor* **118**

RIO GURU (IRE) 4 b.f. Spartacus (IRE) 107 – Montessori (Akarad (FR) 130) [2009 90: 10.3m^4 10g 10.4g^5 9.9m^4 8g^5 10m^2 10g 10.4g^4 10.4v^5 10m^3 10.4m^5 10.2v^2 p10m Dec 9] good-bodied filly: fairly useful performer: stays 1½m: acts on polytrack, heavy and good to firm going: held up. *M. R. Channon* **81**

RIOJA RUBY (IRE) 3 b.f. Redback 116 – Bacchanalia (IRE) 69 (Blues Traveller (IRE) 119) [2009 45: 8f 10g Jun 9] smallish filly: poor maiden: best efforts at 5f: acts on soft ground: tried in headgear. *S. G. West* **–**

RIOLIINA (IRE) 3 b.f. Captain Rio 122 – Anneliina 80 (Cadeaux Genereux 131) [2009 84: p6g^6 7d 7m 7m* p7g^3 p7g Dec 7] angular filly: fair performer: won claimer at Leicester in October: stays 7f: acts on good to firm and good to soft going. *J. G. Portman* **77**

RIO L'OREN (IRE) 4 ch.f. Captain Rio 122 – Princess Sofie 84 (Efisio 120) [2009 66: p7g p7g p7g^2 p7g p7.1g 5.9g p7.1g 5m^6 Jun 30] modest performer: below form last 5 starts: stays 7f: acts on polytrack: tried in cheekpieces, often blinkered. *N. J. Vaughan* **63**

RIO MIST 2 b.f. (Apr 26) Captain Rio 122 – Welsh Mist 102 (Damister (USA) 123) [2009 5f^6 p6g Jun 24] €26,000Y, 18,000 2-y-o: half-sister to several winners, including 3-y-o Anglezarke and useful 7f/8.5f winner Brighter Future (by Night Shift): dam 5f (including at 2 yrs)/6f winner: similar form in maidens at Lingfield and Kempton. *R. Hannon* **56**

RIO POMBA (IRE) 3 b.f. Captain Rio 122 – Lyrebird (USA) (Storm Bird (CAN) 134) [2009 52: 5.1g 5m 5m Jun 23] leggy filly: maiden: little form at 3 yrs: tried blinkered. *D. Carroll* **–**

RIO ROYALE (IRE) 3 b.g. Captain Rio 122 – Lady Nasrana (FR) (Al Nasr (FR) 126) [2009 80: p8g^3 p7g p8g^5 6f* 6v 6m^2 6m^4 6m 6f^4 7g^5 6d p5g p6g Nov 11] deep-girthed gelding: fairly useful handicapper: won at Salisbury in May: below form last 4 starts: free-going sort, effective at 6f/7f: acts on polytrack, firm and good to soft ground: tried in cheekpieces: prominent runner: gelded after final start. *Mrs A. J. Perrett* **82**

RIO SANDS 4 b.g. Captain Rio 122 – Sally Traffic 57 (River Falls 113) [2009 79: 6m 5m^6 5g 5m^3 5m 6m^5 f6g 5g^5 6m^3 5m 5g* p6g 6d Oct 13] quite good-topped gelding: fair handicapper: won at Newcastle in September: best at 5f/6f: unraced on heavy going, acts on any other: none too consistent. *R. M. Whitaker* **66**

RIO'S GIRL 2 b.f. (Apr 6) Captain Rio 122 – African Breeze 79 (Atraf 116) [2009 5d Jun 17] £800Y: first foal: dam, 5f (at 2 yrs)/6f winner, half-sister to useful sprinter Tabaret: 25/1, soundly beaten in maiden at Ripon. *R. M. Whitaker* **–**

RIPTIDE 3 b.g. Val Royal (FR) 127 – Glittering Image (IRE) (Sadler's Wells (USA) 132) [2009 –: 10.4v 12m^4 11.5d Jul 21] good-bodied gelding: fair maiden: stays 1½m: joined D. McCain Jnr, won juvenile hurdles in October and November. *C. F. Wall* **65**

RIP VAN WINKLE (IRE) 3 b.c. Galileo (IRE) 134 – Looking Back (IRE) (Stravinsky (USA) 133) [2009 115p: 8m^4 12g^4 10m^2 8g* 8m* a10f Nov 7] **134**

Racing in the United States has taken one particularly notable step towards weaning itself off drugs by banning steroids (at least in most of its thirty-eight separate jurisdictions). That move came after public outrage over the extent of steroid use that became apparent after revelations about the training regime of America's leading three-year-old of 2008 Big Brown. His trainer Rick Dutrow had a long history of medication violations and his admission that he regularly (and legally, it should be said) administered steroids to his horses widened discussion, which led to a congressional sub-committee examining safety and medication issues in American racing. Its main recommendation was that a national horse-racing commission should be set up to regulate the sport. American racing was, however, first given the chance to make reforms without federal intervention, the banning of the use of steroids one of the most significant first steps.

An article by respected commentator Andy Beyer, published in the *Washington Post* and then *Daily Racing Form* on successive days in January 2009, certainly fanned the flames. 'Thoroughbred racing has become less a test of horses than it is a competition among trainers,' wrote Beyer. 'The most successful have been dubbed "supertrainers" because they achieve results almost without precedent. They compile winning percentages that dwarf the records of horsemen enshrined in the Hall of Fame. They acquire horses and transform them in ways that history's greatest trainers never dreamed of. Accordingly, bettors disregard the normal logic of handicapping when they evaluate horses saddled by Rick Dutrow in New York, Bruce Levine or Jason Servis in New Jersey, Marty Wolfson in Florida, Kirk Ziadie and Jamie Ness at Tampa Bay Downs, Jeff Mullins in California and countless other miracle workers.' Beyer went on to say that 'in an era when certain trainers repeatedly perform feats that defy the laws of nature and the logic of handicapping, bettors invariably suspect they are using illegal substances . . . such distrust has corroded the very foundation of the sport . . . the public at large is alienated when it suspects that drugs are tainting the sport's greatest events.'

Some of the trainers named by Beyer responded angrily to any suggestion that the improved performances of horses in their care might be put down to anything other than their own skill, horsemanship and experience (Marty Wolfson and Jason Servis, for example, both pointed out that they had never been suspended for any drug offence). A committee of trainers condemned Beyer, saying that 'Writing that type of stuff is a discredit to the game.' Beyer was unrepentent. 'Some of these very trainers on the committee have records of drugs violations that should make them hesitant to accuse anyone of discrediting the game,' he declared. Interestingly, of the top ten American-based trainers by earnings in 2009, only one, Christophe Clement, had never been cited for a medication violation. The chairman of the International Federation of Horseracing Authorities, Jean Romanet, given a platform at America's influential annual Round Table conference in August, called for American racing to bring its medication rules into line with the rest of the major racing countries. He particularly criticised the raceday use of the diuretic drug furosemide (lasix) and the continued liberal use of non-steroidal anti-inflammatory drugs such as phenylbutazone (bute). 'You can do it if you want to do it,' said

BGC Sussex Stakes, Goodwood—Rip Van Winkle, kicked clear early in the straight, gallops on too strongly for Paco Boy and Ghanaati, recording the best performance in the race in thirty years

Romanet as he asked American racing to start by banning the use of lasix in all 'black-type' races by 2012. No other major racing country permits the use of lasix on raceday but it is legal throughout North America and virtually every runner races on it. The *Journal of the American Veterinary Medical Association* published the results in July of a practical study of 167 racehorses conducted in South Africa in November 2007. Each horse raced twice, once on lasix and once lasix-free. The study, financed mainly by North American racing interests, purported to show that lasix is effective in reducing the severity of internal bleeding in horses who break blood vessels when racing. By doing that, lasix is therefore effective in enhancing performance, as well as having beneficial welfare effects for the horses affected. The argument over lasix seems set to run and run.

Not all North American jurisdictions, however, allow the use of painkillers such as bute close to a race, and the Jockey Club's Thoroughbred Safety Committee is attempting to bring about a standard approach which will prohibit their use within forty-eight hours of a race. The creation of an umbrella organisation among supportive racing states will, it is hoped, allow state jurisdictions to adopt rule changes together, rather than individually. North America still has a long way to go, though, before it is ready to participate in the international effort being made to standardise drug rules worldwide. American horses have to comply with strict rules on doping when they race overseas, on the Dubai World Cup day programme for example, at which they have a good record. Yet, despite that record, the mistrust of American performances has continued to grow over the years. American racing must continue to address its drug problem if it is to play a full part in the new era that beckons for racing as a truly competitive international sport.

Europe's principal trainers mostly adopt a 'when in Rome . . .' approach to the use of permitted drugs on challengers sent for America's top races. One notable exception at the latest Breeders' Cup was the Ballydoyle contingent saddled by Aidan O'Brien, only one of whom, Man of Iron (who won the Marathon), ran on lasix. Many of the stable's runners in previous years had been given the medication but Aidan O'Brien explained the change of policy. 'Some of our horses won on lasix and we went along with it, but, just because we won on it, it doesn't mean it was necessarily a good policy . . . it might have been better not to have run on lasix in previous Breeders' Cups. We scope our horses a lot and, this year, none of them has ever shown anything, except Man of Iron who had little colds through the season while the others didn't. We have decided to be natural and do what we've been doing all year at home with them.' Interestingly, the connections of Goldikova and Conduit, both of whom were lasix-free European-trained Breeders' Cup winners in 2008, decided to race them on lasix this time; by contrast, British sprinter Fleeting Spirit, who raced on lasix in 2008, was the only runner not on it in the latest edition of the Sprint.

Andre Fabre—who did not have a runner in 2009—has conspicuously stood out against the use of lasix at the Breeders' Cup and it would be laudable if more European trainers followed the example set on this vexing issue by Ballydoyle in the latest season. It would make Europe's strict drugs policy more tenable and would focus more attention on the permissive approach of the Breeders' Cup organisers towards medication which continues to detract from the meeting's considerable value to international racing. The Californian racing jurisdiction is among those that also permits the use of the pain-masking drug bute and 139 of the 147 runners in the fourteen races at the latest Breeders' Cup at Santa Anita ran on it, including all seven Ballydoyle challengers and all the other European challengers with the exception of Goldikova and Only Green (both trained by Freddie Head) and German-trained Junia Tepzia (the only one of the 147 runners to run on neither bute nor lasix).

The introduction of more resilient artificial surfaces on some American tracks was seen as an important step towards 'cleaning up' American racing. A shortage of horses able to stand repeated racing on the unforgiving traditional dirt surfaces in the 'seventies was at the root of American racing's increasing acceptance of the use of drugs. The Breeders' Cup was staged in 2009 for the second year running at Santa Anita, which replaced its traditional dirt track with a synthetic surface in 2007, resulting in the fatality rate falling significantly at the track (as has happened at the other Californian tracks with artificial surfaces). There

Queen Elizabeth II Stakes (Sponsored By Sony), Ascot—in a gruelling encounter, Rip Van Winkle is up with the very strong pace all the way and wins from the most patiently ridden of the quartet Zacinto (right); Delegator and front-running Aqlaam both pay for the early pace

is, however, some talk of a return to dirt being on the cards at Santa Anita. Whatever happens, European challengers have enjoyed two good years on the pro-ride, a surface said to ride the same as good to firm going on turf. After Raven's Pass and Henrythenavigator filled the first two places for Europe in the 2008 Breeders' Cup Classic, there were hopes of another success in North America's richest race in the latest season. Ballydoyle has targeted the Classic with some of its very best horses over the years but has yet to win it (the John Gosden-trained Raven's Pass was only the second European-trained winner of the Classic, following the Andre Fabre-trained rank outsider Arcangues in 1993).

Since Giant's Causeway, 'The Iron Horse', finished second to Tiznow at Churchill Downs in 2000, Ballydoyle has had ten further runners in the mile and a quarter Classic, Galileo (sixth) and Black Minnaloushe (tenth) in 2001, Hawk Wing (seventh) in 2002, Hold That Tiger (fifth) in 2003, Oratorio (eleventh) in 2005, George Washington (sixth) in 2006, George Washington (suffered severe injuries and had to be put down) in 2007, Henrythenavigator (second) and Duke of Marmalade (ninth) in 2008, and Rip Van Winkle in the latest season. Aidan O'Brien assessed Rip Van Winkle as the stable's best chance so far of winning the Classic. 'He's the most natural athlete we've ever had, his main asset is class,' said O'Brien. 'Some who are like that can be a bit soft but he's as hard as concrete mentally. He's very special and there is no doubt he is good enough.' Rip Van Winkle went into the Classic rated behind only Hawk Wing (he achieved 136 the year after he ran in the Classic) among the O'Brien-trained stars who have tackled the race that the Ballydoyle/Coolmore partners evidently regard as providing a very important opportunity to show off their best to American breeders. Rip Van Winkle is rated the equal of his sire Galileo, while George Washington (133), Giant's Causeway (132), Duke of Marmalade (132) and Henrythenavigator (131) are also among the pick of the horses O'Brien has trained. Raven's Pass and Henrythenavigator both had a full campaign before the Breeders' Cup Classic, actually meeting four times in the process—in the Two Thousand Guineas, the St James's Palace Stakes, the Sussex Stakes and the Queen Elizabeth II Stakes. Neither ran beyond a mile before the Breeders' Cup Classic. Rip Van Winkle had a more varied campaign, starting off in the Two Thousand Guineas, then running in the Derby and the Eclipse before reverting to a mile in the Sussex and the Queen Elizabeth II Stakes. He finished behind Sea The Stars in his first three races, getting closer to him each time, but hopes of a fourth meeting in the Classic came to nothing when Sea The Stars was retired after winning the Prix de l'Arc de Triomphe, the world's richest turf race. Sea The Stars had been favourite in ante-post betting on the Classic and his absence, coupled with that of the outstanding American three-year-old filly, Rachel Alexandra, was an anticlimax at the time (Rachel Alexandra's connections didn't want to run her on pro-ride, after blaming the surface for the defeat of their champion Curlin in the previous year's Classic).

Rip Van Winkle was beset by hoof problems throughout his three-year-old campaign—there was even a late scare with his off-hind hoof before the Classic—and his trainer encountered plenty of worrying moments. 'Nine out of ten horses wouldn't have still been racing this season,' O'Brien said after Rip Van Winkle finally lived up to the highest expectations held for him when winning the BGC Sussex Stakes at Goodwood on his fourth start. 'He has had problems all the way and hasn't had a clean run before any race this season,' said O'Brien, explaining that Rip Van Winkle was 'ten out of ten' lame on the eve of the Sussex, having sustained a crack in his near-hind foot. O'Brien explained that Rip Van Winkle had infections in all four of his heels in the spring which spread to his feet. 'They kept going down so the bottom layer of his foot was coming away all the time, the setback before the Sussex was probably from all this still coming through.'

Rip Van Winkle had first been held up in his Two Thousand Guineas preparation after suffering an over-reach in the winter (a setback only revealed two months after it had happened) but stable-jockey Johnny Murtagh chose to ride him instead of Mastercraftsman, the highest-rated of the stable's juveniles the previous season after the highly-regarded Rip Van Winkle had been beaten when favourite for the Dewhurst (though he still retained his position afterwards at the head of the Guineas market). Rip Van Winkle was held up again in his preparation for Newmarket by a stone bruise in the immediate run-up to the meeting, but he missed out only narrowly on third in the Two Thousand Guineas behind Sea The Stars and the favourite Delegator, and Murtagh chose him again—this time ahead of five stablemates (including the favourite Fame And Glory)—in the Derby. He was a picture of well-being beforehand but managed only fourth behind Sea The Stars, beaten also by Fame And Glory and another Ballydoyle runner Masterofthehorse. Rip Van Winkle's performance in running Sea The Stars to a length in the Eclipse at Sandown next time (ridden by Jimmy Fortune as Murtagh was suspended), almost drawing alongside at one stage as he put in a strong challenge in the home straight, was worthy of winning most Group 1s (he finished four and a half lengths ahead of third-placed Conduit who went on to win the King George next time).

Rip Van Winkle started hot favourite for a vintage Sussex and beat the Queen Anne winner Paco Boy by two and a half lengths, the pair clear of the One Thousand Guineas winner Ghanaati in third in a race that further endorsed the quality of the season's leading three-year-olds in Europe. Rip Van Winkle couldn't have been more impressive or more convincing, sent for home in earnest soon after halfway and galloping on really well to record the best performance in the Sussex for thirty years, since Kris won a memorable renewal by five lengths in a season when he dominated racing at around a mile in a way that no other horse had done since Brigadier Gerard.

Unfortunately, Rip Van Winkle aggravated his near-hind foot injury in the Sussex and wasn't seen out again until the Queen Elizabeth II Stakes (Sponsored by Sony) over eight weeks later. Only three took him on at Ascot—stablemate Mastercraftsman a late withdrawal after being left in as a precaution—but Rip Van Winkle had to win the race the hard way, matching the breakneck gallop set by the Prix du Moulin winner Aqlaam from the start before being sent for home fully three furlongs out. The patiently-ridden Zacinto came from a detached last to finish second, beaten a length and a quarter, while Aqlaam and Delegator, who looked Rip Van Winkle's most dangerous opponents beforehand, both paid for the overly strong gallop. Rip Van Winkle took longer to run the last three furlongs of the Queen Elizabeth II Stakes than the winners of the three other races on the round mile that day, the falsely-run Rosemary Handicap, the Royal Lodge and the Fillies' Mile. His timefigure, equivalent to a timerating of only 103 (below those recorded by Joshua Tree in the Royal Lodge and Hibaayeb in the Fillies' Mile), was 26 lb below the Timeform rating given to the performance, another indication that Rip Van Winkle would probably have done better ridden a shade more conservatively. Rip Van Winkle won the race but it took a lot out of him and it may be significant that Delegator and Zacinto also disappointed at the Breeders' Cup, both of them finishing unplaced on turf behind Goldikova in the Mile.

As for Rip Van Winkle, who started second favourite to Zenyatta in the Classic, he weakened after rounding the home turn and managed only tenth of twelve (British-trained Twice Over did best of the overseas challengers to fill third behind the historic winner Zenyatta, the Belmont winner Summer Bird being the first of the three-year-olds in fourth). If Rip Van Winkle gets a second chance in the Breeders' Cup Classic, he will have to show he can handle traditional American dirt because the Breeders' Cup returns to Churchill Downs, home of the Kentucky Derby, in 2010. All being well, he should enhance his reputation even further in Europe in the meantime, his versatility so far as distance goes affording his connections plenty of choice when it comes to targeting the big races.

Rip Van Winkle (IRE) (b.c. 2006)	Galileo (IRE) (b 1998)	Sadler's Wells (b 1981)	Northern Dancer
			Fairy Bridge
		Urban Sea (ch 1989)	Miswaki
			Allegretta
	Looking Back (IRE) (b 2001)	Stravinsky (b 1996)	Nureyev
			Fire The Groom
		Mustique Dream (b 1995)	Don't Forget Me
			Jamaican Punch

The sturdy Rip Van Winkle was bought as a yearling in Italy for €170,000. He wasn't in the top thirty by sale price among sixty-eight Galileo yearlings offered for auction that autumn, his not particularly striking physique and the relatively modest achievements of the first three dams on the bottom line of his pedigree probably weighing against him. Full details of Rip Van Winkle's pedigree were given in *Racehorses of 2008* but, to summarise, he is the first foal of his fairly useful dam the Stravinsky mare Looking Back, placed in listed company at seven and a half furlongs in Italy and closely related to the useful British sprinter Special Day (by another Nureyev sprint stallion, Fasliyev) who is the only relative of any note close up in the pedigree (though brothers Ace, Danish and Hawkeye crop up further back). Looking Back's second foal Le Vie Infinite (by Le Vie dei Colori) was a two-year-old in the latest season and finished fourteenth of eighteen in a six-furlong maiden at Rome in October on his only start; her third, a yearling filly by Ad Valorem, passed through the sale-ring at Tattersalls in October, bought back for 70,000 guineas; there was no return for Looking Back in the 2009 *Return of Mares*. Rip Van Winkle has good form at a mile and a half, but his form at a mile and at a mile and a quarter is better. He is unraced on extremes of going on turf and was a long way below his best on his only start on an artificial surface. *A. P. O'Brien, Ireland*

RIQAAB (IRE) 4 b.g. Peintre Celebre (USA) 137 – Jeed (IRE) 86 (Mujtahid (USA) 118) [2009 78: 10g^{2} 11.7g^{6} Apr 28] rather leggy gelding: fair handicapper: stays 11.6f: acts on polytrack and good to firm ground: held up: gelded and sold 11,000 gns in October, resold £2,200 in December. *E. A. L. Dunlop* **78**

RISING FORCE (IRE) 6 b.g. Selkirk (USA) 129 – Singing Diva (IRE) (Royal Academy (USA) 130) [2009 74: 11.5g^{6} p11g p12.2g Dec 7] angular gelding: modest handicapper nowadays: barely stays 1½m: acts on polytrack, firm and good to soft going: blinkered: held up. *J. L. Spearing* **58**

RISING KHELEYF (IRE) 3 ch.g. Kheleyf (USA) 116 – Rising Spirits 77 (Cure The Blues (USA)) [2009 62p: 7m* 8m^{2} 7d^{4} 7.1m^{5} 6.9g* 7.5g^{4} 6.9g^{5} 7.2g Sep 17] good-topped gelding: fair handicapper: won at Catterick in April and Carlisle in July: stays easy 1m: acts on good to firm and good to soft going. *G. A. Swinbank* **78**

RISING PROSPECT 3 ch.c. Traditionally (USA) 117 – La Sylphide 94 (Rudimentary (USA) 118) [2009 86: p8.6g p8.6g Oct 29] sturdy colt: fairly useful performer at 2 yrs: left G. M. Moore and off nearly a year prior to reappearance: broke down fatally at Wolverhampton: would have stayed beyond 1m: went well on testing ground (both wins on heavy): twice hung badly at 3 yrs. *L. M. Cumani* **79**

Investec Sir Clement Freud Memorial Stakes (Heritage Handicap), Epsom—River Captain is a clear-cut winner of a race commemorating the veteran Racing Post columnist and bon viveur who died in April; Tepmokea, Lasso The Moon (light-coloured cap) and History Lesson come next

RISING SHADOW (IRE) 8 b.g. Efisio 120 – Jouet 71 (Reprimand 122) [2009 103: **80**
6s 6g 6m 8.5m 7.2g^3 6d^5 7g 7s Nov 7] close-coupled gelding: fairly useful handicapper nowadays: left C. Thornton after fourth start: best at 6f: acts on heavy and good to firm going: tried blinkered: held up: none too consistent. *A. D. Brown*

RISK RUNNER (IRE) 6 b.g. Mull of Kintyre (USA) 114 – Fizzygig 71 (Efisio 120) **–**
[2009 75: 16.1d Jun 6] rather leggy gelding: fairly useful handicapper at best: lightly raced on Flat nowadays (fairly useful hurdler): stays 11.6f: acts on heavy and good to firm going: visored/blinkered: none too consistent. *James Moffatt*

RISKY LADY (IRE) 3 b.f. Tamarisk (IRE) 127 – My Croft 64 (Crofter (USA) 124) **–**
[2009 –: p7.1g 7m f6g 8.3m 10m Jun 4] sparely-made filly: little form. *J. Ryan*

RISQUE BELLE 3 b.f. Fantastic Light (USA) 134 – Risque Lady 109 (Kenmare (FR) **–**
125) [2009 –: p10g Jan 23] last in maidens: sold £380. *E. J. Creighton*

RISQUE HEIGHTS 5 b.g. Mark of Esteem (IRE) 137 – Risque Lady 109 (Kenmare **77**
(FR) 125) [2009 85: p10g^6 p10g p10g 12g^4 12m 10m Aug 15] medium-sized gelding: just fair handicapper in 2009: barely stays 1½m: acts on polytrack, soft and good to firm going: tried in cheekpieces/blinkers/tongue tie: held up: formerly tricky ride. *J. R. Boyle*

RIVER ARDECHE 4 b.g. Elnadim (USA) 128 – Overcome (Belmez (USA) 131) **87**
[2009 –: p12.2g^3 f12g* 13.8m^2 p12g^3 12m^3 f11m^6 Dec 5] fairly useful handicapper: won at Southwell in January: stays 13.8f: acts on all-weather, soft and good to firm going: front runner. *P. C. Haslam*

RIVER CAPTAIN (IRE) 3 ch.c. Captain Rio 122 – Pardoned (IRE) 74 (Mujadil **103**
(USA) 119) [2009 75: p9.5g^3 8.5g* 10d^6 10.1g* 8m^5 9.9g^4 Jul 30] useful-looking colt: useful handicapper: won at Epsom in April and June (by 5 lengths from Tepmokea): good efforts in valuable events after, at Royal Ascot (fifth to Fareer in Britannia Stakes) and Goodwood (warm beforehand, fourth to Roman Republic): effective at 1m/1¼m: acts on polytrack, heavy and good to firm going: sent to Hong Kong. *S. Kirk*

RIVER DANUBE 6 b.g. Dansili 127 – Campaspe 79 (Dominion 123) [2009 70: f16g **49**
16.1d 16s 15.8v 15.8s^5 13.8v^6 f14m^6 Dec 5] good-topped gelding: just poor maiden in 2009: stays 2m: acts on fibresand and heavy going: tried tongue tied. *T. J. Fitzgerald*

RIVER DEE (IRE) 3 b.g. Almutawakel 126 – Fiaba 66 (Precocious 126) [2009 75: 8m **63**
6s^3 6m^5 8.1g^4 7.5m^3 6s f6g Aug 25] smallish gelding: modest performer: should stay 1m: acts on good to firm and good to soft going: blinkered second start: held up. *D. Donovan*

RIVER FALCON 9 b.g. Pivotal 124 – Pearly River 72 (Elegant Air 119) [2009 104: **103**
6m 5m^5 6s^5 5m^3 5g^2 5d 5g^3 6g 5.4m 5.6m 6m 5m 6g 5d Oct 24] useful-looking gelding: useful handicapper: placed 3 times in competitive events in 2009, at York, Musselburgh and Ayr (to Pavershooz): effective at 5f/6f: acts on polytrack, probably on any turf going: tried in cheekpieces: comes from behind. *J. S. Goldie*

RIVER KIROV (IRE) 6 b.g. Soviet Star (USA) 128 – Night Shifter (IRE) 74 (Night **88**
Shift (USA)) [2009 80: p6g* p6g* p6g 6g 6m* 6g^3 6d^2 6g^5 p6g 6g p6g* p6g^2 p6m p6m p6m p7g Dec 7] strong gelding: fairly useful handicapper: won at Kempton and Wolverhampton in January, Newmarket in June and Wolverhampton (claimer) in October: good second at Lingfield next time: below form after: raced mainly at 6f, stays 7f: acts on polytrack, good to firm and good to soft going: usually held up. *M. Wigham*

RIVER LANDING 2 b.c. (Apr 29) Lucky Story (USA) 128 – Beechnut (IRE) (Mujadil **–**
(USA) 119) [2009 7m 8d a5.5g Nov 27] little sign of ability: sold from R. Beckett 1,500 gns after second start (tongue tied). *Pal Jorgen Nordbye, Norway*

RIVER RYE (IRE) 3 b.f. Acclamation 118 – Rye (IRE) 75 (Charnwood Forest (IRE) 125) [2009 72: p6g^{6} p7g^{4} p6g^{4} p7g^{2} 7d^{2} p7.1g 6.1g May 25] small filly: modest performer nowadays: stays 7f: acts on polytrack and firm going: often in cheekpieces: sold 3,000 gns. *J. S. Moore* **60**

RIVERSIDE 4 b.f. Kyllachy 129 – My Cadeaux 93 (Cadeaux Genereux 131) [2009 –: 8.5m f7g Dec 8] leggy filly: little form. *M. Brittain* **–**

RIVER THAMES 6 b.g. Efisio 120 – Dashing Water 87 (Dashing Blade 117) [2009 86, a75: f6d Jan 2] sturdy, useful-looking gelding: fair handicapper at best, better on turf: below form sole outing in 2009: best at 5f/6f: acts on polytrack, firm and soft going: tried in blinkers/cheekpieces: held up: has joined J. Goldie. *K. A. Ryan* **61**

RIVER TILL (IRE) 3 b.f. Bachelor Duke (USA) 122 – The Poachers Lady (IRE) (Salmon Leap (USA) 131) [2009 6s^{3} 6m Jun 26] €10,500Y, resold €15,000Y, 15,000 2-y-o: half-sister to several winners, including useful 1999 2-y-o 7f winner Sir Ninja (by Turtle Island): dam Irish 1¼m/1½m winner: much better effort in maidens when 2½ lengths third to Pumpkin at Yarmouth: likely to be suited by 7f+. *W. Jarvis* **67**

RIVIERA CHIC (USA) 2 b.f. (Mar 21) Medaglia d'Oro (USA) 129 – Hurricane Warning (USA) (Thunder Gulch (USA) 129) [2009 p7.1m^{3} p8.6g^{3} Dec 19] $40,000F, $60,000Y: fifth foal: half-sister to winners in USA by Honour And Glory and Victory Gallop: dam unraced half-sister to US Grade 2 9f winner Recoup The Cash: modest form when third in maidens at Wolverhampton, awkward under pressure both times: will stay 1¼m: remains open to improvement. *R. M. Beckett* **62 p**

RIVIERA RED (IRE) 9 b.g. Rainbow Quest (USA) 134 – Banquise (IRE) (Last Tycoon 131) [2009 48: p8g p8g^{4} p8g* p8g Nov 1] modest performer: won minor event at Lingfield in February: should stay beyond 1m: acts on polytrack: often blinkered/visored. *L. Montague Hall* **56**

RIVITIVO 2 b.f. (Apr 4) Deportivo 116 – River Ensign 63 (River God (USA) 121) [2009 5m p6g 7d Jul 22] third foal: half-sister to 5-y-o Ensign's Trick: dam 6f to 1¼m winner: well held, including in seller. *W. M. Brisbourne* **–**

RJEEF (IRE) 2 b.c. (Feb 14) Red Ransom (USA) – Sun Chaser (IRE) (King's Best (USA) 132) [2009 6v^{2} 6m^{2} 7m^{5} Sep 1] 8,000Y: deep-girthed colt: first foal: dam unraced half-sister to smart performers Mastermind (at 1m/1¼m) and Housemaster (up to 1½m): fair form in maidens at Ripon (second to Audacity of Hope) and Leicester (fifth to Markazzi) 3 months apart last 2 starts: will be suited by 1m. *C. E. Brittain* **73**

ROAD TO LOVE (IRE) 6 ch.g. Fruits of Love (USA) 127 – Alpine Flair (IRE) (Tirol 127) [2009 94: 9m 10.4m 12m 10m 10m 10d^{4} Aug 6] strong, close-coupled gelding: one-time smart performer: little impact in handicaps in 2009: usually front runner. *M. Johnston* **–**

ROARING FORTE (IRE) 4 b.c. Cape Cross (IRE) 129 – Descant (USA) (Nureyev (USA) 131) [2009 109: 7m* 7m 8m* Aug 20] strong, rangy colt: smart handicapper: won at Newmarket (by 2½ lengths from Tryst) in May and York (beat Alazeyab 2 lengths) in August: folded tamely in International Stakes at Ascot in between: best form at 7f/1m: acts on polytrack, soft and good to firm going: front runner: second favourite, unruly in stall and withdrawn from Royal Hunt Cup intended second outing. *W. J. Haggas* **114**

Addleshaw Goddard Stakes (Heritage Handicap), York—
front runners dominate as Roaring Forte beats Alazeyab (striped cap) and Acrostic (stars)

ROAR OF APPLAUSE 3 b.g. Royal Applause 124 – Les Hurlants (IRE) (Barathea (IRE) 127) [2009 69p: 8.1g* 8.3m^5 8.3m* 8.1g^3 8.1m^4 8d 8m^6 p8g^2 8.5m^3 p8g 8m^3 8m^3 8.5m* 8m^2 Oct 5] big, strong gelding: useful handicapper: won at Chepstow and Windsor in May, and Epsom (beat Sovereign Remedy 1¾ lengths) in October: stays 8.5f: acts on polytrack and good to firm ground: usually blinkered: waited with: sold 48,000 gns, sent to USA. *B. J. Meehan* **95**

ROAR OF THE KING (USA) 3 b.c. Lion Heart (USA) 124 – V V S Flawless (USA) (Deputy Minister (CAN)) [2009 p7g 8m^6 May 23] modest form both starts in maidens: dead. *J. Noseda* **59**

ROAR TALENT (USA) 2 ch.c. (Feb 15) Roar of The Tiger (USA) 98 – Laurie's Folly (USA) (Kris S (USA)) [2009 p8m p6g Oct 20] good-topped colt: no sign of ability in maidens, pulled up latter start. *J. R. Best* **–**

ROBBMAA (FR) 4 br. or bl.g. Cape Cross (IRE) 129 – Native Twine 114 (Be My Native (USA) 122) [2009 42: 11.9f^4 10.2m 10.2f^5 Jun 24] rather leggy gelding: poor maiden: stays 1½m: acts on firm ground: signs of temperament. *A. W. Carroll* **46**

ROBBY BOBBY 4 ch.g. Selkirk (USA) 129 – Dancing Mirage (IRE) 83 (Machiavellian (USA) 123) [2009 93: p12g* f11g^2 p11g p11g^4 p11g 12g 10.3m^3 12s 10m 12.9m^6 12g^5 12m 12.3g^6 f12g^4 Aug 10] tall gelding: useful handicapper on all-weather, fairly useful on turf: won at Lingfield in January: needs good test at 1¼m, and stays easy 13f: acts on all-weather, good to firm and good to soft going: gelded after final outing. *M. Johnston* **90** **a99**

ROBENS ROCK (IRE) 2 b.g. (Jan 27) Rock of Gibraltar (IRE) 133 – Qhazeenah 101 (Marju (IRE) 127) [2009 7.5g 6m^6 p5g^2 5.1g^5 Oct 21] well-made gelding: modest maiden: should stay beyond 6f, but needs to learn to settle: gelded after final start. *A. B. Haynes* **63**

ROBERT BURNS (IRE) 4 b.g. Invincible Spirit (IRE) 121 – Double Red (IRE) 70 (Thatching 131) [2009 72d: p8g Apr 29] good-topped gelding: fair maiden at best in 2008: tongue tied, no form for new trainer last 4 starts. *Miss D. Mountain* **–**

ROBERT THE BRAVE 5 b.g. Primo Valentino (IRE) 116 – Sandicliffe (USA) 66 (Imp Society (USA)) [2009 71: 11s^4 Jul 17] rangy gelding: just fair handicapper in 2008, and well held sole outing in 2009: effective at 8.6f to 1½m: acts on polytrack: races freely: fairly useful chaser, won in August. *P. R. Webber* **–**

ROBINSON CRUSO 2 b.c. (Jan 23) Footstepsinthesand 120 – Miss Hawai (FR) (Peintre Celebre (USA) 137) [2009 6m^2 6m^6 7g^2 Oct 23] 100,000Y: attractive colt: third foal: half-brother to smart Irish 4-y-o Beach Bunny: dam unraced half-sister to smart French performer up to 12.5f Mer de Corail, out of Prix Marcel Boussac winner Miss Tahiti: fairly useful maiden: second at Windsor and Doncaster (to Rashaad, going freely): also sixth to Society Rock in sales race at Newmarket: should stay at least 1m. *M. A. Jarvis* **89**

ROBIN THE TILL 3 ch.g. Bold Edge 123 – My Dancer (IRE) 79 (Alhaarth (IRE) 126) [2009 59: p6g^3 p6g^2 6m 6.1m^4 5.2d 5g^5 6.1g 5m 5.1d^5 Aug 31] big, strong gelding: fair maiden handicapper: best at 5f: acts on polytrack, firm and good to soft going: hangs left: none too consistent. *R. Hannon* **67**

ROBUST WISH (USA) 2 b.g. (Apr 7) Strong Hope (USA) 120 – Copper Rose (USA) (Unbridled (USA) 128) [2009 p7f p7.1g^2 p8f^2 p7.1m* Nov 28] $140,000Y, resold $70,000Y, 34,000 2-y-o: fourth foal: half-brother to winner in USA by Lemon Drop Kid: dam unraced half-sister to Grade 3 8.5f winner Namaqualand: fairly useful performer: blinkered, won maiden at Wolverhampton by 5 lengths from Seamster: stays 1m. *B. J. Meehan* **85**

ROCKABILLY REBEL 2 b.c. (Apr 28) Kyllachy 129 – Its All Relative 90 (Distant Relative 128) [2009 6g 6m^5 5m^3 5m^5 5.5g^6 Aug 31] €17,000F, £32,000Y: compact colt: eighth foal: half-brother to 2005 2-y-o 7f/7.5f winner King Alfie (by Foxhound): dam 2-y-o 5f winner: fair maiden: should prove better at 6f than 5f. *B. W. Hills* **71**

ROCKABOUT (IRE) 3 b.f. Rock of Gibraltar (IRE) 133 – Capades Dancer (USA) (Gate Dancer (USA)) [2009 8.3f^6 8g 8.3g^4 8.1m p8g 8d 10.2m p10g^4 p9.5g Oct 29] angular filly: half-sister to several winners, notably 8.5f/1¼m winner Vangelis and 5f (at 2 yrs) to 1½m winner Marichal, both smart in France by Highest Honor: dam US 2-y-o 6.5f winner: fair maiden: stays 8.3f: acts on polytrack and firm ground: blinkered last 2 starts. *B. J. Meehan* **65**

ROCK A DOODLE DOO (IRE) 2 b.c. (Apr 27) Oratorio (IRE) 128 – Nousaiyra (IRE) (Be My Guest (USA) 126) [2009 6m 6m 6d Oct 12] €42,000Y: good-bodied colt: **– p**

half-brother to 8-y-o Lytham: dam, ran twice in France (second at 1¼m), half-sister to very smart 1½m performer Narwala: signs of ability in maidens (hung badly right second start): will be suited by 1m+: type to do better at 3 yrs. *W. Jarvis*

ROCK AND ROLL KID (IRE) 4 b.g. Danehill Dancer (IRE) 117 – Milly's Song 110 (Millfontaine 114) [2009 97: 8s^4 8v^2 8g^2 8.5s* 8.1v^5 7s^5 Nov 5] tall, lengthy gelding: smart performer: further improvement when winning valuable Tote Galway Mile EBF Handicap at Galway in July by 2 lengths from Maundy Money: not at best in listed races after, including when fifth to Confront at Haydock next time: stays 8.5f: acts on heavy going: travels well. *Anthony Mullins, Ireland*

ROCK ANTHEM (IRE) 5 ch.g. Rock of Gibraltar (IRE) 133 – Regal Portrait (IRE) 83 57 (Royal Academy (USA) 130) [2009 83: f8s^2 p8g^2 f8g^6 f8d^5 8d^2 10m^4 p8g 8.5d^3 8m^4 8d^5 7.6m* 8m* p8g 8.1m* 8.3m^3 p8m^5 Nov 3] leggy, close-coupled gelding: fairly useful handicapper: won at Lingfield and Salisbury (ladies event) in August and Sandown (length second to Desert Kiss but awarded race) in September: best at 1m/1¼m: acts on all-weather, good to firm and good to soft going: often held up. *Mike Murphy*

ROCK ART (IRE) 3 ch.f. Rock of Gibraltar (IRE) 133 – Lindesberg 71 (Doyoun 124) 59 [2009 58p: 8m 7g^2 8s^6 9.7m 9m 7.1d p8m f11g Dec 8] tall filly: modest maiden: left B. Meehan after sixth start: seems to stay 9.7f: blinkered/in cheekpieces last 4 starts: sold £1,000. *Karen George*

ROCK ASCOT (URU) 5 gr.h. Mantle Rock (USA) – Maria Fumadora (URU) 102 (Sportin' Gold (USA)) [2009 a8.5g 10d 14g p10m p8g* p10m^6 Nov 3] tall horse: useful performer: successful 5 times in Uruguay (all at Maronas), including only start in 2008 in Grade 1 Gran Premio Jose Pedro Ramirez: left H. Gonzales at end of 2008 and H. Brown after reappearance: easily best effort in 2009 when winning handicap at Lingfield in October: shaped as if amiss next time: stays 1½m, but best effort in Britain at 1m: acts on polytrack and dirt: tried tongue tied, blinkered last 2 starts. *G. L. Moore*

ROCKER 5 b.g. Rock of Gibraltar (IRE) 133 – Jessica's Dream (IRE) 114 (Desert Style 83 (IRE) 121) [2009 88: 5g^3 5v^3 5f 5m^2 5g^4 5m* 5d 5f^4 6d^4 5g 6d^5 Oct 22] smallish gelding: fairly useful handicapper: won at Epsom in July: effective at 5f/6f: acts on polytrack and any going on turf: effective with or without visor/blinkers: held up. *G. L. Moore*

ROCKETBALL (IRE) 4 b.g. Namid 128 – Luceball (IRE) 56 (Bluebird (USA) 125) 71 [2009 64: p5g f5g^4 f5g^6 5.1d^2 5g* 5d 5m^4 5m* 5m* 5g^4 5g^4 5d 5m^6 5m^6 5m^4 Sep 27] lengthy gelding: fair handicapper: won at Hamilton in May and, having left Pat Morris after sixth start, Musselburgh (2, apprentices first occasion) in June: best at 5f/easy 6f: acts on fibresand, good to firm and good to soft ground: tried visored/tongue tied: prominent runner. *Mrs L. Williamson*

ROCKET (IRE) 8 ch.g. Cadeaux Genereux 131 – Prends Ca (IRE) 98 (Reprimand – 122) [2009 12m Aug 15] of no account nowadays. *H. J. Manners*

ROCKET ROB (IRE) 3 b.g. Danetime (IRE) 121 – Queen of Fibres (IRE) 65 (Scenic 88 128) [2009 75: p6g^5 5m^5 6g 6g* 7f^3 5m* 6g^4 5g* 5f^2 5g* 5m^4 5m Sep 12] good-quartered gelding: fairly useful handicapper: won at Yarmouth in June, Epsom in July and Sandown (2) in August: has won at 7f, best at 5f/6f: acts on polytrack and firm going: held up: not entirely straightforward. *S. A. Callaghan*

ROCKET RUBY 3 br.f. Piccolo 121 – Kitty Kitty Cancan 73 (Warrshan (USA) 117) 64 [2009 51: p5.1g^5 p6g^2 p6g^4 p6g^{4d} 5.1g^2 f5g 5g^2 5g^2 p5.1g p5.1g^2 p5.1g^3 p5g Dec 31] small, sturdy filly: modest maiden: effective at 5f/6f: acts on all-weather, raced only on good ground on turf: tried visored. *D. Shaw*

ROCK EXHIBITION 4 ch.f. Rock of Gibraltar (IRE) 133 – Finity (USA) 94 (Diesis – 133) [2009 86: 8.3m f8g^6 p10m Nov 3] smallish, good-topped filly: fairly useful performer at 3 yrs for J. Bolger: well held in 2009: sold 8,000 gns. *B. W. Duke*

ROCKFELLA 3 ch.g. Rock of Gibraltar (IRE) 133 – Afreeta (USA) (Afleet (CAN)) 85 [2009 73: 10.2d^3 10m^5 10f^5 10m* 12m* 11m^5 11.7g* p12.2g^6 Nov 13] compact gelding: fairly useful handicapper: won at Windsor in July, Goodwood in September and Bath in October: may prove best up to 1½m: acts on good to firm and good to soft going: not straightforward. *D. J. Coakley*

ROCKFIELD LODGE (IRE) 4 b.g. Stravinsky (USA) 133 – La Belle Simone (IRE) 67 (Grand Lodge (USA) 125) [2009 84: p6g^6 5.7m^6 5.1g^6 6m^6 5.1v^4 5.7g^3 p7m^6 f7m^3 f7f^5 Dec 12] leggy gelding: fair performer at best in 2009: left R. Harris after sixth start: effective at 5f to 7f: acts on all-weather and good to firm ground, probably on heavy: often in headgear: probably not straightforward. *Ian Williams*

ROCKHAMPTON (IRE) 3 b.c. Galileo (IRE) 134 – Green Rosy (USA) (Green Dancer (USA) 132) [2009 81p: 10g* 10m³ p12f* 8m 12g 9s⁴ 12m 10d Sep 5] useful-looking colt: useful performer: won maiden at Leopardstown in March and minor event at Dundalk (4 ran) in May: 7¼ lengths fourth to Famous Name in International Stakes at the Curragh, only creditable effort after: acted as pacemaker in Group 1 races on fifth and last 2 outings: stays 1½m: acts on polytrack, soft and good to firm going, probably on heavy: tends to get worked up beforehand. *A. P. O'Brien, Ireland* **101**

ROCKINIT (IRE) 3 b.f. Rock of Gibraltar (IRE) 133 – Tidal Reach (USA) 68 (Kris S (USA)) [2009 68: f8g p8.6g Mar 2] angular filly: fair maiden at 2 yrs: well held both starts in 2009. *R. A. Harris* **–**

ROCKJUMPER 4 br.g. Cape Cross (IRE) 129 – Bronzewing 103 (Beldale Flutter (USA) 130) [2009 59: p11g⁴ f12g Apr 21] close-coupled gelding: modest maiden: seems to stay easy 11f: acts on polytrack, best effort on turf on good going: tried blinkered. *Mrs Lawney Hill* **51**

ROCK ME (IRE) 4 ch.g. Rock of Gibraltar (IRE) 133 – Final Farewell (USA) (Proud Truth (USA)) [2009 43: p10m⁵ Dec 30] strong gelding: maiden: last sole 4-y-o start: stays 1¼m: tried in blinkers/cheekpieces: fair hurdler. *Mrs Lawney Hill* **–**

ROCK MY WORLD (IRE) 2 b.f. (May 2) Rock of Gibraltar (IRE) 133 – Arctic Hunt (IRE) (Bering 136) [2009 p8g² Nov 25] 35,000Y: fifth foal: half-sister to 3 winners, including 4-y-o Meshtri and 5-y-o Arctic Wings: dam, useful French 1m to 1¼m winner (including 9f at 2 yrs), half-sister to smart French 1¼m/1½m performer Trumbaka: 9/1 and green, promising 2½ lengths second to Whistleinthewind in maiden at Lingfield, taking while to settle: likely to stay 1¼m: should improve. *M. A. Jarvis* **74 p**

ROCKNEST ISLAND (IRE) 6 b.m. Bahhare (USA) 122 – Margin Call (IRE) 75 (Tirol 127) [2009 61: 14.1m 14.1m⁶ 16m 16d Aug 10] small, close-coupled mare: poor handicapper nowadays: stays 2¼m: acts on polytrack and any turf going: usually wears cheekpieces/visor. *P. D. Niven* **46**

ROCK 'N' ROYAL 2 b.c. (Apr 8) Royal Applause 124 – Grande Terre (IRE) 71 (Grand Lodge (USA) 125) [2009 6g* Oct 19] £2,500Y: angular colt: first foal: dam, 7.5f/1m winner, half-sister to smart performers up to 1m Sentinelese and Soul City: 8/1, won maiden at Pontefract by 1¾ lengths from Filwa, showing good attitude and leading final 1f: will stay 7f: sure to progress. *R. A. Fahey* **81 p**

ROCK OF BEHISTUN (IRE) 2 b.g. (Apr 24) Antonius Pius (USA) 123§ – Persian Flower (Persian Heights 129) [2009 p7g p7.1m p7f 8.3g Oct 28] no sign of ability. *P. L. Gilligan* **–**

ROCK OF EIRE 2 b.g. (Apr 12) Rock of Gibraltar (IRE) 133 – Graceful Lass 96 (Sadler's Wells (USA) 132) [2009 6m³ p8g 7m⁶ f8f⁵ Nov 24] compact gelding: modest maiden: should stay 1¼m+. *E. J. Creighton* **53**

ROCK OF LOVE (IRE) 2 b.c. (Feb 8) Rock of Gibraltar (IRE) 133 – Ridotto (Salse (USA) 128) [2009 5g⁴ 5s⁴ 6m² 6m³ 7.5m* 7m⁴ 7g Jul 31] strong, lengthy colt: sixth foal: half-brother to 3 winners, including useful 2004 2-y-o 5f winner Salsa Brava (by Almutawakel): dam French maiden (stayed 7.5f): fairly useful performer: improved to win maiden at Beverley in June by 9 lengths: similar form in nursery next time: will stay 1m+: acts on good to firm going. *M. Johnston* **90**

ROCK OF ROCHELLE (USA) 4 br.c. Rock of Gibraltar (IRE) 133 – Recoleta (USA) (Wild Again (USA)) [2009 114: 6m⁵ 7m 6m³ 7s⁶ 8g⁶ 7s³ Oct 25] tall, close-coupled colt: smart performer: creditable efforts in 2009 when 2¼ lengths fifth to Utmost Respect in Duke of York Stakes at York and 3¼ lengths third to High Standing in Wokingham Stakes (Handicap) at Royal Ascot: effective at 6f to 7f: acts on soft and good to firm going: used to wear tongue tie. *Andrew Kinsella, Ireland* **113**

ROCK PEAK (IRE) 4 b.g. Dalakhani (IRE) 133 – Convenience (IRE) (Ela-Mana-Mou 132) [2009 78: p12m⁶ p12g p16g⁴ Feb 11] rather leggy gelding: fair maiden handicapper: not at best in 2009: stays 1¾m: acts on polytrack and good to firm ground: effective in cheekpieces or not: used to make running: not straightforward. *B. J. Llewellyn* **65**

ROCK RELIEF (IRE) 3 gr.g. Daylami (IRE) 138 – Sheer Bliss (IRE) 86 (Sadler's Wells (USA) 132) [2009 70p: p12g⁵ p11g Aug 5] maiden: just modest form in 2009: probably stays 1½m: best effort on soft going. *Sir Mark Prescott* **61**

ROCKSON (IRE) 3 b. or br.f. Rock of Gibraltar (IRE) 133 – Opera Star (IRE) 56 (Sadler's Wells (USA) 132) [2009 –: p10g p9.5g p8g⁶ f8g 8.3d² p7g 7m p8m f7m f8f p9.5g⁶ Dec 19] angular filly: modest maiden: claimed from B. Hills £6,000 after fifth start: free-going sort, should prove best short of 1¼m: acts on polytrack and good to soft going: tried tongue tied/visored. *Ian Williams* **54**

ROCKSY 3 b.f. Kyllachy 129 – Sea Music (Inchinor 119) [2009 62: 7.1m Apr 13] tall filly: modest maiden: well held only outing in 2009: stays 7f. *D. J. Coakley* –

ROCK TECH 4 b.c. High Estate 127 – Mrs Fire Cracker (Rock City 120) [2009 p7g 7.1g^6 6m 8g p8g p11f^4 Dec 16] close-coupled colt: form (modest) only when fourth in handicap at Kempton final start: stays 11f: acts on polytrack. *J. R. Jenkins* 52

ROCK THE STARS (IRE) 2 ch.g. (Apr 18) Rock of Gibraltar (IRE) 133 – Crimphill (IRE) 106 (Sadler's Wells (USA) 132) [2009 8.3v p7m Dec 16] lengthy gelding: similar form when down the field in maidens at Nottingham and Lingfield (not knocked about): bred to be suited by 1m+. *M. G. Quinlan* 53

ROCKWEILLER 2 b.c. (Apr 13) Rock of Gibraltar (IRE) 133 – Ballerina Suprema (IRE) 87 (Sadler's Wells (USA) 132) [2009 6m 6m^3 p5.1g p7.1g Oct 16] form only when third to Katehari in maiden at Windsor: bred to be suited by 7f+: blinkered (none too keen) final start. *C. R. Egerton* 62

ROCKY HEIGHTS (IRE) 3 b.f. Rock of Gibraltar (IRE) 133 – Height of Fantasy (IRE) 101 (Shirley Heights 130) [2009 –: 10m 9.9f 11.5m^3 12m^2 Jun 29] close-coupled filly: modest maiden: will be well suited by 1¾m: sold 7,000 gns. *J. L. Dunlop* 59

ROCKY'S PRIDE (IRE) 3 b.g. Rock of Gibraltar (IRE) 133 – L'Animee (Green Tune (USA) 125) [2009 8m^2 8.3g^2 10f* 10g p12g^3 p10m* Dec 30] 135,000Y: fifth foal: half-brother to fairly useful French 1m winner Miguel do Brazil (by Spectrum) and 4-y-o Bosamcliff: dam, French 9f winner, half-sister to smart French 1¼m performer Bailador: fairly useful form: won maiden at Brighton in June (left J. Noseda 67,000 gns after) and claimer at Lingfield in December: stays 1½m: acts on polytrack and firm going. *G. L. Moore* 86

ROCOPPELIA (USA) 3 ch.c. Hennessy (USA) 122 – Eternally (USA) (Timeless Moment (USA)) [2009 63: p8g^6 p6g* p6g^3 a6g a6g Oct 22] medium-sized, good-bodied colt: modest performer: won handicap at Lingfield in January: sold from Mrs A. Perrett £7,000 after next start: stays 7f: acts on polytrack and good to firm ground: has been blinkered, including for win. *Carlos Figueroa, Sweden* 63

RODRIGO DE FREITAS (IRE) 2 b.g. (Feb 11) Captain Rio 122 – Brazilian Sun (IRE) 78 (Barathea (IRE) 127) [2009 p6g 7g 7.6d^6 p8g^2 p8m^5 8.3d^4 8.3d Oct 15] good-topped gelding: fair maiden: in frame in nurseries: seemed amiss final start: stays 8.3f: acts on polytrack and good to soft going. *J. R. Boyle* 66

RODRIGO DE TORRES 2 ch.c. (Feb 17) Bahamian Bounty 116 – Leonica 92 (Lion Cavern (USA) 117) [2009 6g* 6m 6m 8m^4 Oct 16] £48,000Y: lengthy, good-topped colt: has scope: first living foal: dam, 1m winner, half-sister to useful performers South Rock (up to 1m) and Greek Envoy (up to 1½m): fairly useful form: won maiden at York (trained by K. R. Burke) in July in good style: trained by A. Jarvis second start: creditable fourth to Champagne Style in minor event at Newmarket (too free): should be as effective at 7f as 1m: remains open to improvement. *H. R. A. Cecil* 86 p

ROGALT (IRE) 3 b.c. Rock of Gibraltar (IRE) 133 – Rills (USA) (Clever Trick (USA)) [2009 –: 10.1s 6d^3 6m^2 5d^5 6m^5 Jul 11] tall colt: fair maiden: likely to prove best at 6f/7f: sent to France. *B. Smart* 68

ROI DE VITESSE (IRE) 2 ch.c. (Apr 28) Chineur (FR) 123 – Face The Storm (IRE) 72 (Barathea (IRE) 127) [2009 5d 5.1m* 6d* 6m^3 7m^2 7g^5 7g^4 7m^4 7g Oct 4] 8,000Y: small colt: fourth foal: half-brother to 6f (at 2 yrs) and 8.6f winner Cavort (by Vettori), later successful in Saudi Arabia: dam 2-y-o 1m winner: useful performer: won maiden at Nottingham in April and minor event at Pontefract in May: mostly creditable efforts in higher grade after, including in Superlative Stakes at Newmarket (length second to Silver Grecian) and Champagne Stakes at Doncaster (5 lengths fourth to Poet's Voice) fifth/eighth starts: stiff task final outing: will stay 1m: sold 39,000 gns. *B. R. Millman* 98

ROISIN'S PRINCE (IRE) 7 br.g. Bold Fact (USA) 116 – Rosie Jaques 47 (Doyoun 124) [2009 –: f16g^2 17.2f 17.2g Jul 4] modest maiden handicapper: stays 2m: acts on fibresand, heavy and good to firm ground: tongue tied: tried blinkered: fair hurdler. *M. Sheppard* 56

ROKER PARK (IRE) 4 b.g. Choisir (AUS) 126 – Joyful (IRE) 71 (Green Desert (USA) 127) [2009 98: 6s 5g 6m* 6d* 6d^3 6g 5m^3 6m 7m Sep 26] strong, good-bodied gelding: useful performer: won handicaps at Doncaster and Newcastle (beat Barney McGrew 1½ lengths) in June: good efforts after when third at Hamilton (Scottish Stewards' Cup) and Beverley (listed race, ½ length behind Exceptional Art): best at 5f/6f: acts on heavy and good to firm going: tried blinkered, in cheekpieces nowadays. *K. A. Ryan* 106

ROLEPLAY (IRE) 4 b.f. Singspiel (IRE) 133 – In Your Dreams (IRE) (Suave Dancer **66**
(USA) 136) [2009 70: 7g p6g^{2} p7g 8m p12.2g^{3} p12.2g p9.5g^{6} Nov 13] medium-sized filly: fair maiden: stays easy 1½m: acts on polytrack: blinkered. *J. M. P. Eustace*

ROLLING HILLS (IRE) 2 b.g. (Apr 9) Celtic Swing 138 – Silk Suivante (IRE) **74**
(Danehill (USA) 126) [2009 6d 6m^{2} Oct 26] €16,500F, 16,000Y: first foal: dam unraced: much better effort in maidens when 1¼ lengths second to Deacon Blues at Leicester, making running (gelded after): should stay 7f. *H. Candy*

ROLY BOY 3 b.g. Dansili 127 – Night At Sea 107 (Night Shift (USA)) [2009 96: p8g^{4} **85 d**
8.3g 8.1f^{6} 9.9g 10m^{6} 8.5m^{4} 7g^{4} 7g Aug 28] strong gelding: type to carry condition: fairly useful performer at best at 3 yrs: stays 1m: acts on polytrack, good to firm and good to soft going: tried blinkered: usually held up. *R. Hannon*

ROMANCEA (USA) 2 ch.f. (Feb 17) Mr Greeley (USA) 122 – Two Halos (USA) **49 p**
(Saint Ballado (CAN)) [2009 7d Jul 17] $400,000Y: tall filly: first foal: dam unraced out of US Grade 2 1m (at 2 yrs)/8.5f winner Top Secret: 10/1 and very green, tenth to Champagnelifestyle in maiden at Newmarket, always towards rear: should do better. *E. F. Vaughan*

ROMAN EMPRESS (IRE) 3 b.f. Sadler's Wells (USA) 132 – Ionian Sea (Slip **114**
Anchor 136) [2009 77p: 10g 11.3m* 10d^{6} 12v^{6} 12s^{5} 9.5g^{2} 12m^{3} 10s^{2} 9.5m 12s 8g^{4} Oct 18] rangy filly: smart performer: won maiden at Limerick in June: good efforts when placed after, 2¼ lengths third to Dar Re Mi in Yorkshire Oaks at York and second to Chinese White in listed race at Gowran (beaten 1½ lengths) and Blandford Stakes at the Curragh (went down by 2 lengths) either side: stayed 1½m: acted on soft and good to firm going: sometimes found little and was one to treat with some caution: visits Fastnet Rock. *A. P. O'Brien, Ireland*

ROMAN GLORY (IRE) 3 b.g. Soviet Star (USA) 128 – Putout 69 (Dowsing (USA) **69**
124) [2009 95: 7.1f^{4} 8.1v 7g Jun 5] attractive gelding: useful maiden at 2 yrs: well below that form in 2009: stays 1m: acts on good to soft going. *B. J. Meehan*

ROMAN HISTORY (IRE) 6 b.g. Titus Livius (FR) 115 – Tetradonna (IRE) 102 **55**
(Teenoso (USA) 135) [2009 64: 10.1m^{6} 9m^{3} 10.1m Aug 13] sturdy gelding: modest performer: stays 1½m: acts on polytrack and firm going: tried visored, wears cheekpieces: has shown temperament. *Miss Tracy Waggott*

ROMAN MAZE 9 ch.g. Lycius (USA) 124 – Maze Garden (USA) (Riverman (USA) **–**
131) [2009 71: p7.1g p7.1g p8.6g p7m p6g Nov 20] good-bodied gelding: regressive handicapper: usually held up. *W. M. Brisbourne*

ROMAN REPUBLIC (FR) 3 b.c. Cape Cross (IRE) 129 – Mare Nostrum 117 (Caer- **107**
leon (USA) 132) [2009 86p: 8g* 8m 8.1m^{6} 10m^{2} 9.9g* Jul 30] tall, good-topped colt: useful handicapper: won at Doncaster in June and Goodwood (beat Sopranist ¾ length in quite valuable event) in July: will stay 1½m: acts on good to firm ground: has joined Godolphin. *M. Johnston*

ROMAN SIOUX (IRE) 2 b.c. (Feb 15) Antonius Pius (USA) 123§ – Blue Sioux 69 **–**
(Indian Ridge 123) [2009 7g Oct 10] leggy colt: 50/1, last in maiden at York. *R. Bastiman*

ROMAN THE EMPEROR (IRE) 3 ch.g. Spartacus (IRE) 107 – Honey Bee (Alnasr **–**
Alwasheek 117) [2009 10.1d 9.7m^{5} 11.5g May 20] well held in maidens. *S. W. Hall*

ROMANTIC BOND 3 ch.f. Monsieur Bond (IRE) 120 – Romantic Drama (IRE) 65 **–**
(Primo Dominie 121) [2009 7d 5m Aug 29] 10,000Y: workmanlike filly: first foal: dam maiden (stayed 1m): well held in maidens at Thirsk and Beverley (blinkered). *T. D. Easterby*

ROMANTIC INTERLUDE (IRE) 3 b.f. Hawk Wing (USA) 136 – Kissin A Lot **51**
(USA) (Kissin Kris (USA) 122) [2009 60: p12g 10.2m f11g 10.1g p10g 7m Aug 14] good-topped filly: modest maiden: seems to stay 1m: best effort on polytrack: visored last 3 starts. *A. P. Jarvis*

ROMANTICIZE 3 b.f. Kyllachy 129 – Romancing 79 (Dr Devious (IRE) 127) [2009 **85**
6m* 6m^{2} 7m Jun 20] 4,200 2-y-o: workmanlike filly: third foal: sister to 4-y-o Romantic Verse: dam, maiden (stayed 1¼m), half-sister to useful dam of smart 7f/1m performer Infallible: fairly useful form: won maiden at Salisbury in May: best effort when length second to White Shift in handicap at Newmarket (best work late) next time: should be suited by 7f: raced only on good to firm going. *Dr J. D. Scargill*

ROMANTIC QUEEN 3 b.f. Medicean 128 – Bandit Queen 90 (Desert Prince (IRE) **68**
130) [2009 68: p6g* p6g^{4} p6g^{4} p7g^{3} p6g^{6} 5f p6g* 6m p7g p6g^{3} p6g p6g^{6} p6g^{5} p6m Dec 1] small, angular filly: fair performer: won maiden in January and, after leaving E. Dunlop fifth start, seller in September, both at Wolverhampton: should prove best at 5f/6f: acts on polytrack: tongue tied of late. *George Baker*

ROMANTIC RETREAT 4 ch.f. Rainbow Quest (USA) 134 – Magical Retreat (USA) 115 (Sir Ivor (USA) 135) [2009 63: p12m^{5} p13g^{6} p13.9g Mar 26] sturdy filly: modest maiden: likely to prove best at 1¾m+: raced on polytrack and good/good to firm going. *G. L. Moore* **60**

ROMANTIC VERSE 4 b.f. Kyllachy 129 – Romancing 79 (Dr Devious (IRE) 127) [2009 74: p7.1g p7.1g^{2} p7.1g p6g* f6g p7.1g 8.3m p7f p8m p7.1m^{5} p6m p6g Dec 19] tall, angular filly: fair handicapper: won seller at Wolverhampton (left E. McMahon 5,000 gns) in March: below form after: stays 7f: acts on polytrack and good to soft going: tried tongue tied, often blinkered: has joined R. Harris. *S. Curran* **69 d**

ROMANY PRINCESS (IRE) 4 b.f. Viking Ruler (AUS) – Fag End (IRE) 88 (Treasure Kay 114) [2009 92: p6g^{3} 7m p7g^{5} p8g 8.3m* 8.1m* 9g^{6} 8.1g^{5} 7s^{4} 8m^{6} Sep 27] good-topped filly: useful handicapper: won at Windsor and Sandown in July: mostly creditable efforts after: stays 9f: acts on polytrack, soft and good to firm going: held up. *R. Hannon* **97**

ROMEOS GIRL 2 b.f. (Mar 6) Statue of Liberty (USA) 115 – Fadaki Hawaki (USA) 60 (Vice Regent (CAN)) [2009 6s^{4} 8.3m 6g^{5} Sep 14] £4,800Y: workmanlike filly: half-sister to several winners, including fairly useful Irish 2004 2-y-o 6f winner King of Love (by King's Best): dam, maiden who stayed 1m, closely related to smart 1990 2-y-o sprinter Mujadil and half-sister to high-class 1½m performer Fruits of Love: modest form at best in maidens: should stay beyond 6f. *Jennie Candlish* **53**

RONDEAU (GR) 4 ch.g. Harmonic Way 121 – Areti (GR) (Wadood (USA) 97) [2009 78: 6.1g^{5} 6g^{5} p6g* 5f p6g^{6} 5.7g p6m 7d* p7g^{4} p7m^{2} p7f Dec 21] rather leggy gelding: fairly useful handicapper: won at Lingfield in July and Brighton in October: effective at 6f/7f: acts on polytrack, firm and good to soft going: tactically versatile: none too consistent. *P. R. Chamings* **82**

RONNIE HOWE 5 b.g. Hunting Lion (IRE) 115 – Arasong 76 (Aragon 118) [2009 72: f7d f5g^{4} f6g^{3} f5g p6g^{5} f6g 5.1m^{3} 5.1d^{4} 5.1m 5m 5m 5d 5g 6m f5g Dec 22] sturdy gelding: fair handicapper: effective at 5f/6f: acts on all-weather, firm and good to soft going (well held on soft/heavy): usually in headgear/tongue tie: none too consistent. *S. R. Bowring* **66**

RONNIES GIRL 5 b.m. Tobougg (IRE) 125 – Tryptonic (FR) (Baryshnikov (AUS)) [2009 –: f7d f7g Mar 26] of no account: tried visored. *C. J. Teague* **–**

RON THE DON 2 ch.g. (May 20) Paris House 123 – Hillside Heather (IRE) 65 (Tagula (IRE) 116) [2009 5s 5g 5m 6v 7g 7g f7g Nov 17] small gelding: of no account. *A. Berry* **–**

RONY DONY (IRE) 5 b.g. Revoque (IRE) 122 – Farrans Guest (IRE) (Tagula (IRE) 116) [2009 p7g 8g p8g 15.4m 8g 7f Aug 18] little sign of ability: tried blinkered/tongue tied. *M. E. Rimmer* **–**

ROODEE KING 3 b.g. Auction House (USA) 120 – Antithesis (IRE) 75 (Fairy King (USA)) [2009 5g^{6} 6m^{2} p5f^{4} p5m^{5} p7m Oct 26] regressive maiden: best effort at 5f: raced only on polytrack and good/good to firm going. *Pat Morris* **65 d**

ROODLE 2 b.f. (Mar 10) Xaar 132 – Roodeye 100 (Inchinor 119) [2009 5f^{2} 5.1m* 6m^{6} 5.2m^{5} 6m^{2} 6m 6g^{6} Oct 30] lengthy, unfurnished filly: first foal: dam, 5f (at 2 yrs)/7f winner, half-sister to 3-y-o Gallagher: fairly useful performer: won minor event at Chepstow in July: mostly creditable efforts after, sixth in listed event at Newmarket final start: effective at 5f/6f: raced only on good ground or firmer. *Eve Johnson Houghton* **90**

ROOKWITH (IRE) 9 b.g. Revoque (IRE) 122 – Resume (IRE) 69 (Lahib (USA) 129) [2009 74: 7g p8g 8d 10m 8m 8m 9g^{4} 8m* 8v Aug 26] tall gelding: modest handicapper: won at Musselburgh in August: stayed 1¼m: acted on all-weather/sand and any turf going: usually in headgear: sometimes slowly away/found little: dead. *T. G. McCourt, Ireland* **64**

ROSABEE (IRE) 3 ch.f. No Excuse Needed 123 – Tilbrook (IRE) 78 (Don't Forget Me 127) [2009 96: 6m 7g 8g Jul 26] lengthy filly: just fairly useful performer at 3 yrs: should stay 7f: acts on good to firm and good to soft ground: has wandered: sold £18,000 in December. *Mrs D. J. Sanderson* **88**

ROSA GURNEY (IRE) 2 b.f. (Jan 25) Antonius Pius (USA) 123§ – Nonsense (IRE) (Soviet Star (USA) 128) [2009 6f 7d 6d^{5} Oct 6] £19,000Y: rather leggy, attractive filly: first foal: dam unraced half-sister to smart 1m winner Prince Arthur: modest maiden: should stay 7f/1m. *J. R. Best* **55**

ROSALEEN (IRE) 4 b.f. Cadeaux Genereux 131 – Dark Rosaleen (IRE) (Darshaan 133) [2009 101: 8g* 8m 8g^{5} 12d^{3} 8.1g p8g^{5} Oct 29] angular, useful-looking filly: useful performer: won listed race at Pontefract (beat Just Lille 2 lengths) in June: largely creditable efforts after: stays 1½m: acts on polytrack, firm and soft going: sold 120,000 gns. *B. J. Meehan* **99**

ROSANARA (FR) 2 gr.f. (Feb 8) Sinndar (IRE) 134 – Rosawa (FR) 111 (Linamix (FR) 127) [2009 8g* 8g* 8s³ Nov 1] **110**

Britain had its share of news stories about jockeys during the year, including the return in September of six-times champion Kieren Fallon at the end of an eighteen-month suspension. None of the stories in Britain, though, made the same impact as the most significant one in France, the sacking by the Aga Khan of his retained jockey Christophe Soumillon towards the end of August. A statement by the owner read: 'Christophe Soumillon will not be retained to ride the Aga Khan-owned horses in France after the 2009 Flat racing season. After eight years under contract as the first rider in France, it has been decided as human relations have become difficult and after mutual agreement, that his contract will not be renewed for 2010.' Reportedly the action was precipitated by derogatory remarks by the jockey about trainer Andre Fabre made in a speech at a charity dinner the previous weekend; a few days afterwards Fabre crisply summed up his view of the rider by saying 'He is not a friend of mine, he never has been and he never will be.' The position of retained rider to the Aga Khan is one of the best in French racing, Soumillon having been fortunate enough to partner such as Dalakhani, Darjina, Mandesha, Shawanda and Zarkava. Within a week of the original announcement came another about a replacement: 'The Aga Khan Studs have announced that Christophe Lemaire will be retained as their first jockey in France next season. He recently signed a one-year contract with the Niarchos family and they will have priority on his services in 2010. When the jockey is not riding for them, he will ride the Aga Khan Studs' French-trained horses.' Lemaire had been enjoying an excellent season thanks largely to runners trained by Jean-Claude Rouget for whom he partnered classic winners Elusive Wave, Le Havre and Stacelita. Matters did not improve in the short term for Soumillon when he broke his elbow at Nancy in early-September.

As Arc weekend approached, Lemaire had accumulated a tremendous book of rides over the two-day meeting headed by Stacelita in the Arc and several big-race candidates for the Aga Khan including Siyouni in the Prix Jean-Luc Lagardere and Rosanara in the Total Prix Marcel Boussac. In a great stroke of irony, Lemaire himself broke his collarbone in a race for Arab horses at Saint-Cloud on the Friday and had to give up his mounts at Longchamp, which included, as it turned out, no fewer than eight winners, four of them in Group 2s and three in Group 1s with Rosanara, Siyouni and Shalanaya, the last-named also owned by the Aga Khan and successful in the Prix de l'Opera. In a further twist, Soumillon made an unexpectedly early return to the saddle and partnered several of Lemaire's intended rides, notably Tamazirte, who won the Prix Daniel Wildenstein, Stacelita, who ran equal seventh in the Arc, and Rosanara. To complete what might almost be termed a round of musical chairs, it was announced at the end of October that Soumillon would be riding for Rouget in 2010. All being well, of course, Lemaire will be the man on board the three missed Longchamp Group 1 winners in 2010, along with plenty of other quality horses. With Rosanara and Siyouni he has the

Total Prix Marcel Boussac - Criterium des Pouliches, Longchamp—
Rosanara makes it two wins from two races; it's close for the minor honours as On Verra (No.10) snatches second off Joanna and Wedding March (rail), with Green Dandy fifth

H.H. Aga Khan's "Rosanara"

chance of making an impact in the classics, though Rosanara, on what she has shown so far, is no Zarkava. Like Zarkava, she made her debut at Longchamp early in September, in her case in a ten-runner maiden in which all her rivals had the benefit of at least one race already (Zarkava started in a newcomers event). Rosanara won in some style, leading nearly two furlongs out and leaving the others for dead and winning by four lengths from Aruna, who went on to win on her next start. After Rosanara's initial success, Alain de Royer Dupre gave the impression that the filly had not been showing so much at home as another in his stable, Darma, a daughter of Danehill Dancer who finished lame after being successful in a newcomers race at Chantilly three days after Rosanara's win at Longchamp. Darma could be one to watch out for if making a full recovery as a three-year-old but, be that as it may, what the trainer called 'an interesting gallop' towards the end of September indicated to Royer Dupre that Rosanara was well up to contesting the Prix Marcel Boussac.

With only one 'British' runner among the ten others, in the shape of Green Dandy trained by Eoghan O'Neill (who established a base in France in the latest season), and no runner that had shown form at Group 1 level, the latest Marcel Boussac was not a high-ranking renewal. The only pattern successes by any of the runners had been in Group 3 company, by Italian-trained Joanna in the Prix du Calvados and by the Aidan O'Brien-trained Cabaret in the Silver Flash Stakes. Several had profiles similar to Rosanara's, notably Wedding March, trained by

Andre Fabre and an easy winner of a newcomers event over the course and distance. Rosanara started a shade of odds on ahead of Wedding March and Cabaret. Rosanara stumbled leaving the stalls but immediately recovered and was always reasonably close up in the tightly-bunched field. Once shaken up and switched outside in the home straight she made impressive headway and took it up seventy-five yards out, going on to a two-length win from the strong-finishing rank outsider On Verra, with Joanna and Wedding March close behind in third and fourth, Cabaret finishing tailed-off last after her saddle slipped.

The Poule d'Essai des Pouliches is likely to be Rosanara's first classic target, though bookmakers in Britain priced her up at only 7/1 for the One Thousand Guineas and 10/1 favourite for the Oaks. By the end of the season she was a top-priced 20/1 for both classics, though it would still be a surprise if she ran in either. Rosanara ran once more after the Prix Marcel Boussac, and lost her unbeaten record against the colts in the Criterium International at Saint-Cloud. Her performance in that race, in which she again started odds on, suggested that a mile and quarter or more might suit her best at three. She was never really dangerous, running on without being subjected to too hard a race and snatching third on the line, nearly six lengths behind impressive winner Jan Vermeer. The mile of the Poule d'Essai des Pouliches isn't likely to show Rosanara to best advantage, though it will be no surprise to see her lining up. The Prix de Diane looks altogether more suitable for her, though she will almost certainly have to improve on her Boussac form to win.

Rosanara (FR) (gr.f. Feb 8, 2007)	Sinndar (IRE) (b 1997)	Grand Lodge (ch 1991)	Chief's Crown
			La Papagena
		Sinntara (b 1989)	Lashkari
			Sidama
	Rosawa (FR) (gr 2002)	Linamix (gr 1987)	Mendez
			Lunadix
		Rose Quartz (b 1997)	Lammtarra
			Graphite

Rosanara's pedigree has plenty of stamina in it. Her sire Sinndar has also had Group 1 winners in Youmzain and Shawanda (who won the Irish Oaks and Prix Vermeille for the Aga Khan) but the fact that he now stands at Haras de Bonneval (having started out at Gilltown) at just €10,000 tells its own story. Sinndar is a strong influence for stamina, and the dam Rosawa—Rosanara is her first foal—was effective at a mile and a quarter, the furthest she tried. Rosawa was a smart performer, winning her first four races including two listed events, the Prix de la Calonne and Prix de Liancourt, before coming last in the Prix de l'Opera on her final appearance. Rosawa, who has subsequently produced a colt by Selkirk and a filly by Red Ransom, was originally owned by Jean-Luc Lagardere, whose bloodstock interests the Aga Khan purchased on his death in 2005. Rosanara's grandam Rose Quartz, who won a thirteen-furlong maiden at Wexford for Sheikh Mohammed and John Oxx, cost Lagardere 42,000 guineas as a three-year-old; her latest progeny Rajsaman, a two-year-old brother to Rosawa trained by de Royer Dupre, won the listed Criterium de Lyon at Lyon Parilly in September. Rosanara's great grandam Graphite is also the third dam of the high-class Australian four-year-old Whobegotyou, successful in the Group 1 Yalumba Stakes in October. Graphite was a winning sister to Cuddles, successful in the Hollywood Starlet Stakes, out of Stellarette, who won at Grade 3 level and was a half-sister to the 1990 broodmare of the year Kamar and to Grade 1 scorer Love Smitten, the dam of Swain. This is an excellent family and, whatever else the leggy, quite attractive Rosanara achieves on the racecourse, she should prove a valuable addition to her owner's fine collection of broodmares. Rosanara has raced only on good going or softer. *A. de Royer Dupre, France*

ROSBAY (IRE) 5 b.g. Desert Prince (IRE) 130 – Dark Rosaleen (IRE) (Darshaan 133) **89**
[2009 93: 12.4g^2 12m 9.9g^3 10.3g^4 9.8d^2 12m 10.2v^5 9.8g^5 9.9m^4 10s 12s 10.4g^4 Oct 9] strong gelding: fairly useful handicapper: best efforts in 2009 when second at Newcastle and Ripon: effective at 1¼m to 13f: acts on any going: usually waited with: tried blinkered. *T. D. Easterby*

ROSCO FLYER (IRE) 3 b.g. Val Royal (FR) 127 – Palace Soy (IRE) (Tagula (IRE) **69**
116) [2009 66: p8g^6 p8m^2 p10g^6 12d^5 Oct 11] rangy gelding: fair maiden: stays 1m: raced only on polytrack and good going or softer on turf. *J. R. Boyle*

ROS CUIRE (IRE) 4 br.c. Expelled (USA) 116 – Haven Island (IRE) (Revoque (IRE) 122) [2009 64: f7g 8m 7.2m^3 p7.1g 7.2g Oct 23] quite good-topped colt: modest maiden: stays 1m: acts on polytrack and good to firm ground. *W. A. Murphy, Ireland* **54**

ROSE ALBA (IRE) 2 ch. or gr.f. (May 11) Verglas (IRE) 118 – Green Rosy (USA) (Green Dancer (USA) 132) [2009 7g 7.6d 8.1d^2 9m Sep 18] lengthy, rather unfurnished filly: half-sister to numerous winners, including French/US 7f (at 2 yrs) to 1½m winner Majorien (by Machiavellian) and French 9f (at 2 yrs) to 1½m winner America (by Arazi), both smart: dam French 1½m winner: easily best effort in maidens when second to Leitzu at Chepstow: seemed amiss in nursery: should be suited by 1¼m. *J. L. Dunlop* **68**

ROSE AURORA 2 gr.f. (Feb 18) Pastoral Pursuits 127 – Khaladja (IRE) (Akarad (FR) 130) [2009 6f^5 p6m Nov 4] sturdy filly: seventh foal: half-sister to French 1m winner Khalafa (by College Chapel) and winner in Greece by Vettori: dam, French maiden, half-sister to dam of high-class 1½m performer Predappio: well held in maidens. *M. P. Tregoning* **–**

ROSE AVELINA 3 b.f. Xaar 132 – B'Elanna Torres 66 (Entrepreneur 123) [2009 7.5m^5 8m 8g 8m 9.9m 13.8m Sep 19] 1,500Y: third foal: dam maiden: no form: tried blinkered. *I. W. McInnes* **–**

ROSE BED (IRE) 2 ch.f. (Mar 13) Namid 128 – Daqtora 70 (Dr Devious (IRE) 127) [2009 5m p7m Sep 24] £15,000Y: fourth foal: half-sister to 3 winners, including 3-y-o Qalahari and Irish 4-y-o Almolahek: dam Irish 11f winner: poor form in maiden and claimer almost 5 months apart. *M. G. Quinlan* **45**

ROSE BIEN 7 b. or br.m. Bien Bien (USA) 125 – Madame Bovary 82 (Ile de Bourbon (USA) 133) [2009 72: p16g^3 16d^6 p16g 18g^2 14.6m^5 16d^3 17.1m* Aug 16] sparely-made mare: fair handicapper on turf, modest on all-weather: won at Pontefract in August: stays 2¼m: acts on polytrack, firm and good to soft going: wears cheekpieces. *P. J. McBride* **66 a58**

ROSE BLOSSOM 2 b.f. (Apr 6) Pastoral Pursuits 127 – Lamarita 92§ (Emarati (USA) 74) [2009 5m* 5m 6f* 6m 5m^4 Sep 11] 2,000F, £21,000 2-y-o: tall, unfurnished filly: fifth foal: half-sister to 3 winners, including 6f/7f winner St Ivian (by Inchinor) and 3-y-o Red Rosanna: dam untrustworthy 5f winner: useful performer: won maiden at Hamilton (impressive) in May and minor event at Haydock in July: creditable 2½ lengths fourth to Sand Vixen in Flying Childers Stakes at Doncaster: effective at 5f/6f. *R. A. Fahey* **98**

ROSE CHEVAL (USA) 3 ro.f. Johannesburg (USA) 127 – La Samanna (USA) (Trempolino (USA) 135) [2009 74: p8.6g^3 p9.5g 8.1g 8.1s 8m^3 9m^3 8m^2 10m Sep 23] angular filly: modest maiden: stays 8.6f: acts on polytrack, good to firm and good to soft going: has looked temperamental. *M. R. Channon* **62**

ROSEDALE 2 b.f. (Apr 23) Pastoral Pursuits 127 – Wyoming 62 (Inchinor 119) [2009 5g 5m^5 p6g^4 6d* 6.1d p6g^6 6m^3 7d^4 Oct 27] 1,000Y: angular filly: first foal: dam 1½m winner: modest performer: won nursery at Leicester in July: stays 7f: acts on polytrack, good to firm and good to soft going. *J. A. R. Toller* **57**

ROSE DE RITA 4 br.f. Superior Premium 122 – Rita's Rock Ape 87 (Mon Tresor 113) [2009 38: 5.1g Jun 22] sturdy filly: poor maiden. *L. P. Grassick* **–**

ROSE DIAMOND (IRE) 3 gr.f. Daylami (IRE) 138 – Tante Rose (IRE) 126 (Barathea (IRE) 127) [2009 100: 7m^4 8m^3 8m 6.5f* 6f^4 a7f^4 Dec 26] neat filly: useful performer: best effort in Britain in 2009 when 4½ lengths fourth to Ouqba in listed Free Handicap at Newmarket on reappearance: left R. Charlton, won allowance race at Santa Anita in October: good 2¾ lengths fourth to Evita Argentina in La Brea Stakes on same course final outing: stays 1m: acts on pro-ride, firm and soft going: patiently ridden. *P. L. Biancone, USA* **103**

ROSEMARKIE 5 br.m. Diktat 126 – Sparkling Isle 66 (Inchinor 119) [2009 –: p8.6g 10.2g 7f Aug 18] no sign of ability: tried in cheekpieces. *J. M. Bradley* **–**

ROSE OF COMA (IRE) 3 b.f. Kheleyf (USA) 116 – Rosalia (USA) 66 (Red Ransom (USA)) [2009 60: 8d 7m 9.8m^3 10m* p10g^5 10d^3 9g^4 10.1m^2 10f^2 10d 11.9f^5 9.9m^6 11.5g^4 10.1d^6 Oct 27] leggy filly: modest performer: won seller at Leicester in May: left Gay Kelleway after twelfth start: barely stays 11.5f: acts on soft and good to firm going, below form on polytrack: tried in cheekpieces/visor: held up: not straightforward. *A. G. Juckes* **57**

ROSE ROW 5 gr.m. Act One 124 – D'Azy 91 (Persian Bold 123) [2009 77: p12g^4 11.6m^4 10g 12g p12.2m* p16f* p13.9g^2 p13.9g^4 Oct 9] sparely-made mare: fairly useful handicapper: won at Wolverhampton in August and Kempton in September: good efforts in frame at Wolverhampton last 2 starts: stays easy 2m: acts on polytrack, soft and good to firm ground. *Mrs Mary Hambro* **86**

ROSES 4 b.f. Muhtarram (USA) 125 – Sublime (Conquering Hero (USA) 116) [2009 13.8g^5 Jul 8] fifth foal: half-sister to 7f winner Submissive (by Young Ern): dam unraced half-sister to smart 1m/1¼m performer Penny Drops: useful bumper performer, successful all 4 starts: favourite, only modest form in maiden at Catterick on Flat debut: should be capable of better. *G. A. Swinbank* **51 p**

ROSES FOR THE LADY (IRE) 3 b.f. Sadler's Wells (USA) 132 – Head In The Clouds (IRE) 114 (Rainbow Quest (USA) 134) [2009 74p: 10g* 11.4m^3 12m^5 12v^2 Jul 12] tall, lengthy filly: smart performer: won maiden at Leopardstown in March: easily best effort when 3 lengths second to Sariska in Irish Oaks at the Curragh, setting good pace: given a break after, then prevented from running in autumn by firm ground: stays 1½m: acts on heavy ground, probably on good to firm: tends to carry head high under pressure: stays in training. *John M. Oxx, Ireland* **117**

ROSE STREET (IRE) 5 b.m. Noverre (USA) 125 – Archipova (IRE) (Ela-Mana-Mou 132) [2009 102p: 10.4m^5 May 13] big, lengthy mare: useful handicapper, lightly raced: raced freely and considerately handled when fifth to Moonquake at York only start in 2009: should stay 1½m: acts on polytrack and good to soft ground, probably on good to firm: joined Miss P. Robson, second on hurdling debut in December. *M. A. Jarvis* **93 +**

ROSETTA HILL 2 ch.f. (Feb 17) Compton Place 125 – Fruit of Glory 106 (Glory of Dancer 121) [2009 5m 6m 5g Oct 19] first foal: dam 5f to 1m winner (including 7f at 2 yrs): well held in maidens (looked awkward final start). *J. R. Jenkins* **–**

ROSEWIN (IRE) 3 b.f. Hawkeye (IRE) 122 – African Scene (IRE) 31 (Scenic 128) [2009 –: 8.5m 10g 10.9m^3 12.1m* 12.1m^5 12d^3 14.1m 12d* 12.4d* 12.1m^2 12g^6 Oct 6] sparely-made filly: fair handicapper: won at Beverley in June and, having left O. Brennan after sixth start, Catterick in August and Newcastle in September: should be suited by 1¾m: acts on good to firm and good to soft ground. *A. Dickman* **74**

ROSIE CROSS (IRE) 5 b.m. Cape Cross (IRE) 129 – Professional Mom (USA) (Spinning World (USA) 130) [2009 67d: p7g p6g^5 p7g^4 p8g Mar 11] modest performer nowadays: effective at 5f to 7f: acts on polytrack and firm going: tried blinkered, in cheekpieces nowadays. *Eve Johnson Houghton* **51**

ROSIE SAYS NO 4 b.f. Catcher In The Rye (IRE) 115 – Curlew Calling (IRE) 51 (Pennine Walk 120) [2009 69: p6g^4 f6g 6d^3 p6g^2 p6m^4 5.1d 5.2d* p5.1g^5 p7.1g p6g^4 f5g^3 f5g Dec 27] stocky filly: fair handicapper: won at Yarmouth in October (left R. Cowell after): effective at 5f to 7f: acts on all-weather and soft going: wears cheekpieces. *A. J. McCabe* **71**

ROSIE'S MAGIC 2 b.f. (Apr 26) Auction House (USA) 120 – Sachiko 54 (Celtic Swing 138) [2009 7m 7m^5 Oct 13] compact filly: second foal: dam maiden: well held in minor events. *W. de Best-Turner* **–**

ROSIE TWO 3 b.f. Acclamation 118 – Just A Glimmer 93 (Bishop of Cashel 122) [2009 6m 6g 6m^5 5.1g^6 6.1g p7g^6 7m Sep 21] 50,000Y: smallish, angular filly: first foal: dam 7f (including at 2 yrs) winner: modest maiden. *W. S. Kittow* **55**

ROSIKA 3 b.f. Sakhee (USA) 136 – Blush Rambler (IRE) (Blushing Groom (FR) 131) [2009 71p: 10.2g* 9.9f* 11.9m 10.2m^2 12m* p13g^2 Oct 29] good-bodied filly: progressive form: won maiden at Bath in April and handicaps at Salisbury in May and Goodwood in October: good 4 lengths second to Baila Me in listed race at Lingfield final outing, poorly placed and finishing well: stays 13f: acts on polytrack and firm ground: smart prospect. *Sir Michael Stoute* **104 p**

ROSILIANT (IRE) 2 ch.f. (Mar 15) Refuse To Bend (IRE) 128 – Rosy Dudley (IRE) 72 (Grand Lodge (USA) 125) [2009 6f p6g 6g 7.1m p7.1g 7m^5 Oct 26] £25,000Y: rather unfurnished filly: second foal: half-sister to 3-y-o Grand Honour: dam, Irish 8.5f winner, half-sister to smart 1996 2-y-o sprinter Deadly Dudley: modest maiden: stays 7f: acts on good to firm going: blinkered last 2 starts. *C. G. Cox* **53**

ROSKO 5 b.g. Selkirk (USA) 129 – Desert Alchemy (IRE) 103 (Green Desert (USA) 127) [2009 p12.2g p9.5g^3 p9.5g^3 9m^6 10m^5 8.3g^2 9m^6 8m^4 8d* 8s^3 8m^4 9.2v Aug 19] 110,000Y, 13,000 2-y-o: tall gelding: first foal: dam, 7f winner, closely related to smart 7f/1m winner Madid: fair form in bumpers: fair handicapper: won at Newcastle in June: free-going sort, may prove best at 1m: acts on polytrack, soft and good to firm ground. *B. Ellison* **76**

ROSSATRON 3 b.c. Primo Valentino (IRE) 116 – Sunday Night (GER) 51 (Bakharoff (USA) 130) [2009 p11g^4 p12.2g^6 10.2m^4 8m May 14] modest maiden: free-going sort, may prove best short of 1¼m. *T. T. Clement* **62 ?**

ROSSETT ROSE (IRE) 3 ch.f. Rossini (USA) 118 – Sabaah Elfull 75 (Kris 135) **53** [2009 62: 5d^4 5g^6 6g 6v 8d 6m^5 Aug 22] workmanlike filly: modest maiden: best form at 6f: acts on any turf ground: races prominently. *M. Brittain*

ROSSINI'S DANCER 4 b.g. Rossini (USA) 118 – Bint Alhabib (Nashwan (USA) **77** 135) [2009 63: p8.6g* 7.5m^4 8.5m^6 8.5g 8d 9.2d^2 9.9m 8g^6 9.8d* 10g^5 12.4d* Oct 13] rather leggy gelding: fair performer: won amateur handicap at Wolverhampton in April, seller at Ripon in September and amateur handicap at Newcastle in October: stays 12.4f: acts on polytrack, soft and good to firm ground: effective in cheekpieces or not: sold £20,000, joined Mrs S. C. Bradburne. *R. A. Fahey*

ROSS MOOR 7 b.g. Dansili 127 – Snipe Hall 93 (Crofthall 110) [2009 74: p13g^5 10.2m **69** p10g 10g^2 10.4g^3 12g 10m* 10g^3 10.9g p12m p10m Dec 16] big, strong, close-coupled gelding: fair handicapper: won at Sandown (apprentices) in July: was effective at 1¼m to 1¾m: acted on polytrack, good to firm and good to soft ground: tried blinkered/in cheekpieces: often slowly away: suspect temperament: dead. *Mike Murphy*

ROSY ALEXANDER 4 ch.f. Spartacus (IRE) 107 – Sweet Angeline 74 (Deploy 131) **–** [2009 73: 10m May 15] sturdy filly: fair handicapper at 3 yrs: shaped as if amiss only outing in 2009: should stay 1¼m: acts on firm and good to soft going. *G. G. Margarson*

ROSY DAWN 4 ch.f. Bertolini (USA) 125 – Blushing Sunrise (USA) (Cox's Ridge **58** (USA)) [2009 52: p12g p10g p10g 10f^2 11.9m p12g^2 p10g^4 10.9g 11m^5 9.7m^2 12m 10g^4 9.7m* 10f 10m p11g 9.7s^6 p12f p10g Nov 5] workmanlike filly: modest handicapper: won at Folkestone in August: stays easy 1½m: acts on polytrack and firm ground: used to wear visor/blinkers: front runner. *J. J. Bridger*

ROTATIVE 4 ch.f. Spinning World (USA) 130 – Kristal Bridge 75 (Kris 135) [2009 **97** 79p: p12.2g* p12g 11.8d^2 14.1d* 16m* Sep 13] workmanlike filly: useful handicapper: won at Wolverhampton in June, Nottingham in August and Goodwood (further improvement when beating Wicked Daze ½ length) in September: stays 2m: raced on polytrack, good to soft and good to firm going: tends to race in snatches. *W. R. Swinburn*

ROTHESAY DANCER 6 b.m. Lujain (USA) 119 – Rhinefield Beauty (IRE) 52 **87** (Shalford (IRE) 124§) [2009 80: p5.1g^2 5m^4 5m^2 5d^3 5v^6 5m* 5g 5m^3 5m* 5m 5g 5s^6 5m 5d* 5s 5m 5m 6g^5 5g Oct 19] leggy mare: has a quick action: fairly useful handicapper: better than ever in 2009, winning at Ayr and Hamilton in June and Carlisle in August: effective at 5f/6f: acts on polytrack, firm and soft going: tried blinkered/in cheekpieces: travels strongly held up: tough and consistent. *J. S. Goldie*

ROUGHAM 3 b.g. Red Ransom (USA) – Louella (USA) (El Gran Senor (USA) 136) **78** [2009 12g^4 11.7m^2 p12m^4 Sep 24] sixth foal: half-brother to very smart 7f (at 2 yrs) to 1½m winner Leadership (by Selkirk) and 2 winners abroad: dam, French maiden, sister to useful 1¼m performer Himself: fair maiden: raced only around 1½m: joined P. Hobbs, won juvenile hurdle in December. *A. M. Balding*

ROUGH ROCK (IRE) 4 ch.g. Rock of Gibraltar (IRE) 133 – Amitie Fatale (IRE) **60** (Night Shift (USA)) [2009 70, a–: p7g 6g^4 6g 6s^4 7.1g^5 7g 5.2s* 5.1v 6g^5 5.1g 7m^4 6d^4 **a–** 5.2d^2 Oct 27] close-coupled gelding: modest handicapper nowadays: won at Yarmouth in July: best up to 7f: acts on firm and soft going, well below form on all-weather: tried blinkered/tongue tied. *C. A. Dwyer*

ROUGH SKETCH (USA) 4 b.g. Peintre Celebre (USA) 137 – Drama Club (IRE) **65** (Sadler's Wells (USA) 132) [2009 p10g^5 p10g p13.9m* p13g^4 f16g^4 16.1d 12m 11.9f* 14.1g^5 11.5m 12s Oct 6] useful-looking gelding: fair handicapper: missed 2008: won at Wolverhampton in February and Brighton in June: stays 1¾m: acts on polytrack (below form on fibresand) and firm ground: tried blinkered (including for last success)/visored: sold 4,000 gns. *Sir Mark Prescott*

ROUNDTHETWIST (IRE) 4 b.g. Okawango (USA) 115 – Delta Town (USA) **47** (Sanglamore (USA) 126) [2009 69d: p12g^5 p10g^5 Mar 18] maiden: just poor at 4 yrs: barely stays easy 1½m: acts on polytrack and firm ground: tried visored/in cheekpieces. *K. R. Burke*

ROUND WON (USA) 2 ch.c. (Mar 3) Two Punch (USA) – Indy Go Go (USA) (A P **73** Indy (USA) 131) [2009 7g 8m p7g^3 Oct 9] $150,000 2-y-o: brother to winner in USA and half-brother to several winners there: dam, US 6f (including at 2 yrs)/1m winner, half-sister to 5-y-o King of Dixie: easily best effort in maidens when 3½ lengths third to Sahara Kingdom at Lingfield: may prove best at 6f/7f. *W. J. Knight*

ROWAAD 4 ch.g. Compton Place 125 – Level Pegging (IRE) 48 (Common Grounds **55** 118) [2009 74d: 7m 7.1m 6.1g 8f^3 8.3m^3 8m 9.8d Sep 1] sturdy, useful-looking gelding: modest maiden nowadays: stays 1m: acts on polytrack and firm going: visored last 5 outings. *A. E. Price*

ROWAN LIGHT 3 b.f. Fantastic Light (USA) 134 – Filippa (GER) (Dashing Blade 117) [2009 8d Apr 14] fourth foal: dam, German 6f/7f winner, sister to smart German miler Faberger: eighth to Wadaat in maiden at Yarmouth, green and late headway. *J. R. Boyle* **54**

ROWAN LODGE (IRE) 7 ch.g. Indian Lodge (IRE) 127 – Tirol Hope (IRE) 100 (Tirol 127) [2009 69: p8g^3 p9.5g 8.5m* 9m^2 7.9g* 9.3m* 10m^5 7.9d^3 p9.5g 8m^3 p8.6g^4 9.1g p9.5g p8.6g Dec 14] sturdy gelding: fair performer: won seller at Beverley in April and claimers at Carlisle (2) in June: stays 1¼m, effective at shorter: acts on polytrack and any turf ground: tried visored, wears blinkers nowadays: held up. *Ollie Pears* **69**

ROWAN RIO 4 ch.g. Lomitas 129 – Lemon Tree (USA) (Zilzal (USA) 137) [2009 93: 12m 14m p12g 10.2g 10m 10g 12g Aug 1] leggy gelding: fairly useful handicapper: below form in 2009: stayed 1½m: acted on polytrack and heavy going: dead. *W. J. Haggas* **81**

ROWAN RIVER 5 b.m. Invincible Spirit (IRE) 121 – Lemon Tree (USA) (Zilzal (USA) 137) [2009 78: 10d Jun 10] workmanlike mare: fair handicapper at best: ran poorly in seller at Brighton only outing in 2009: stays 1¼m: acts on polytrack and firm going: tried in cheekpieces/tongue tied: quirky: sold £4,800 in July and joined Mrs A. Thorpe. *A. Middleton* **–**

ROWAN TIGER 3 b.g. Tiger Hill (IRE) 127 – Lemon Tree (USA) (Zilzal (USA) 137) [2009 65p: 8.5g p10g^5 11.5s^6 p12m* p12m* p12g* Oct 9] rangy gelding: fairly useful handicapper: won at Kempton (2) in September and Lingfield (beat Wind Flow 1¼ lengths, travelling smoothly) in October: stays 1½m: acts on polytrack. *J. R. Boyle* **85**

ROWAYTON 3 br. or gr.f. Lujain (USA) 119 – Bandanna 98 (Bandmaster (USA) 97) [2009 90: 6m 6g^4 5m^5 6g^4 5g^6 Aug 3] rangy filly: fairly useful handicapper: free-going sort, best kept to 5f/6f: acts on polytrack and good to firm going. *J. D. Bethell* **86**

ROWE PARK 6 b.g. Dancing Spree (USA) – Magic Legs 54 (Reprimand 122) [2009 109: p5g^6 p5g* 5m^6 5m^6 5g^6 6m 6g f5g* p6g Nov 21] lengthy gelding: smart performer: won minor events at Lingfield (by ¾ length from Masta Plasta) in April and Southwell (beat Excellerator by nose) in October: best at 5f: acts on all-weather and good to firm going: tried in cheekpieces: held up: tends to sweat. *Mrs L. C. Jewell* **110**

ROXY FLYER (IRE) 2 b.f. (Mar 16) Rock of Gibraltar (IRE) 133 – Dyna Flyer (USA) (Marquetry (USA) 121) [2009 7d^4 p7g^6 Oct 29] 35,000Y: workmanlike filly: second foal: dam, US 1m (at 2 yrs) to 9f winner, out of Yorkshire Oaks winner Condessa: better effort in maidens when 5½ lengths fourth to Thrill at Salisbury: will stay 1m. *Mrs A. J. Perrett* **74**

ROYAATY (IRE) 3 b.c. Singspiel (IRE) 133 – Whisper To Dream (USA) (Gone West (USA)) [2009 p10g* Nov 18] first foal: dam, French 1½m/12.5f winner, out of very smart 1m to 1½m performer Hatoof: 5/2, won maiden at Lingfield by short head from Trooping-thecolour (pair well clear), green but finding extra: will stay 1½m: has joined M. Al Subouse, UAE. *Saeed bin Suroor* **93**

ROYAL ACCLAMATION (IRE) 4 b.g. Acclamation 118 – Lady Abigail (IRE) (Royal Academy (USA) 130) [2009 75: p6g 6m 6g 6d^2 5.9m^4 6m^4 Jun 25] good-topped gelding: modest handicapper nowadays: stays 6f: acts on good to firm and good to soft ground: visored last 3 starts. *G. A. Harker* **61**

ROYAL ADELAIDE (IRE) 3 ch.f. Redback 116 – Ball Cat (FR) (Cricket Ball (USA) 124) [2009 7.1m f6g 7m 7m^5 8d p7m Oct 28] €8,000F, 30,000Y: leggy filly: half-sister to 3 winners, including useful 2007 2-y-o 5f/6f winner Drawnfromthepast (by Tagula): dam Belgian 7.5f winner: poor maiden. *J. A. Osborne* **44**

ROYAL AMNESTY 6 b.g. Desert Prince (IRE) 130 – Regal Peace 94 (Known Fact (USA) 135) [2009 87: p9.5g p9.5g^5 p10g* 9m^2 10.4m 12.1m 10.3m^3 9.9m^4 Sep 13] close-coupled gelding: fairly useful handicapper: won at Lingfield in March: stays easy 1¼m: acts on polytrack and good to firm going: blinkered: held up. *I. Semple* **92**

ROYAL AND REGAL (IRE) 5 b.g. Sadler's Wells (USA) 132 – Smart 'n Noble (USA) (Smarten (USA)) [2009 120: 12s^4 14s 16.4m^3 Aug 19] tall, good-topped, attractive gelding: very smart performer at best: not so good or reliable in 2009, off 3 months prior to 5 lengths third of 5 to Askar Tau in Lonsdale Cup at York final outing, looking sure to win before curling up under pressure: effective at testing 1½m to 2m: acts on heavy and good to firm ground: bled in Yorkshire Cup second start: races up with pace: one to treat with caution: sold 31,000 gns, joined Luke Comer, Ireland: fair form on hurdling debut. *M. A. Jarvis* **106 §**

ROYAL APPLORD 4 b.g. Royal Applause 124 – Known Class (USA) (Known Fact (USA) 135) [2009 73: 8g 8.5m 8m 7g^{6} Jun 20] strong gelding: has a quick action: fair performer at best: well held in 2009: often wears cheekpieces: not entirely straightforward. *P. T. Midgley* –

ROYAL ARTHUR 3 ch.g. Imperial Dancer 123 – Scenic Lady (IRE) 68 (Scenic 128) [2009 –: p8g 9.9g 10s 11.6g^{6} 12f 11.9m 16g 16m Sep 2] sturdy, lengthy gelding: little form: tried in headgear. *L. A. Dace* –

ROYAL BET (IRE) 3 b.g. Montjeu (IRE) 137 – Queen of Norway (USA) (Woodman (USA) 126) [2009 –p: 10f 9d 11.5g^{2} 14.1m^{4} p11m^{5} Sep 30] tall, good-topped gelding: modest and ungenuine maiden: stays 11.5f: acts on polytrack. *M. L. W. Bell* 59 §

ROYAL BLADE (IRE) 2 ch.g. (Feb 8) Needwood Blade 117 – Royal Dream 81 (Ardkinglass 114) [2009 6v 5f^{6} 5g* 5m p5f Sep 4] strong gelding: form only when making all in maiden at Windsor in July: seemed amiss last 2 starts (gelded after). *A. P. Jarvis* 68

ROYAL BLOOM (IRE) 4 b.f. Royal Applause 124 – Bethesda 91 (Distant Relative 128) [2009 –: 8.3g 8.3g 9m 6.1g^{2} 6f^{6} Jul 23] sparely-made filly: modest maiden: seemingly stays 1m: tried in cheekpieces. *J. R. Fanshawe* 52

ROYAL BOX 2 b.c. (Feb 15) Royal Applause 124 – Diamond Lodge 98 (Grand Lodge (USA) 125) [2009 6g 6s* p6g^{4} 7m^{6} p7g^{5} p8.6g Dec 7] smallish colt: first foal: dam, 1m/9f winner, out of Prix des Reservoirs winner Movieland: fair performer: won maiden at Leicester in July, best effort: left R. Hannon after fifth start: should stay 1m: acts on soft going: tried blinkered. *A. J. McCabe* 78 d

ROYAL CHALLENGE 8 b.g. Royal Applause 124 – Anotheranniversary 95 (Emarati (USA) 74) [2009 82: f6g p7.1g^{2} f7g^{6} p6g^{6} f7g 7.1m 6g 6v p7.1g 7.5m p7.1g* p7.1g 7m^{2} p7g p7.1g Nov 6] well-made gelding: fair performer nowadays: won claimer at Wolverhampton in September: best at 6f/7f nowadays: acts on polytrack (well held on fibresand), firm and good to soft going: tried blinkered: temperament under suspicion. *I. W. McInnes* 71

ROYAL CHEER 2 b.f. (Mar 15) Royal Applause 124 – Rise 'n Shine 67 (Night Shift (USA)) [2009 6m 5m^{6} Sep 15] 33,000F, £36,000Y: half-sister to 3 winners, including 6-y-o Total Impact: dam, 5f winner, half-sister to useful French sprinter Touch And Love: well held in maidens. *Mrs A. Duffield* –

ROYAL CHOIR 5 ch.m. King's Best (USA) 132 – Harmonic Sound (IRE) (Grand Lodge (USA) 125) [2009 61: p10m p9.5g 10.9m p10g Apr 28] little form in 2009. *H. E. Haynes* –

ROYAL COLLECTION (IRE) 3 b.c. Val Royal (FR) 127 – Rachel Green (IRE) 46 (Case Law 113) [2009 72p: p7g* p8g* Jan 28] sturdy colt: progressive form: won both starts in 2009, namely maiden at Lingfield and 3-runner handicap at Kempton (beat Bushveld by length): stays easy 1m: sent to USA. *J. Pearce* 85

ROYAL COMPOSER (IRE) 6 b.g. Mozart (IRE) 131 – Susun Kelapa (USA) 94 (St Jovite (USA) 135) [2009 65: 6f^{4} 5m 5.9g 7g^{4} 7.5g 7g^{3} 6m 8.3m Sep 21] lengthy, good-topped gelding: has a quick action: modest handicapper: effective at 5f to 8.5f: acts on firm and soft going: has worn headgear. *T. D. Easterby* 64

ROYAL CONFIDENCE 4 b.f. Royal Applause 124 – Never A Doubt 107 (Night Shift (USA)) [2009 107: 7m^{4} 7.1g^{6} 8m 7g 7m^{3} 7m^{5} 7m^{6} 7m^{4} Oct 3] rangy, good sort: useful performer: patchy form in 2009, good ¾-length third to dead-heaters Confront and Dream Eater in listed race at York: below form after: barely stays 1m: acts on soft and good to firm going: in cheekpieces final outing. *B. W. Hills* 108

ROYAL CREST 3 b.g. Royal Applause 124 – Noble Lady 77 (Primo Dominie 121) [2009 f7g^{3} f6g* 7m 7m 7g p8.6g^{5} p9.5g Oct 15] sturdy gelding: modest performer: won maiden at Southwell in March: stays 7f: raced only on all-weather and good/good to firm ground: sold £1,000. *J. A. Osborne* 63

ROYAL DEFENCE (IRE) 3 b.g. Refuse To Bend (IRE) 128 – Alessia (GER) (Warning 136) [2009 76p: 7m^{4} 8.3g^{4} 9.8m 8d* 9.8m* 8s^{4} Sep 5] quite attractive gelding: fairly useful performer: won maiden at Thirsk in July and handicap at Ripon in August: stays 1¼m: acts on soft and good to firm going: said to have had breathing problem third outing. *D. Nicholls* 87

ROYAL DESERT 2 b.c. (Apr 27) Pastoral Pursuits 127 – Overcome (Belmez (USA) 131) [2009 5.1m^{6} 5f^{3} 5.1m* 6g 6g^{2} 6s^{5} Jul 17] £17,000Y: close-coupled colt: sixth foal: closely related to 7.5f/1m winner Brace of Doves (by Bahamian Bounty) and half-brother to 2 winners, including 4-y-o River Ardeche: dam, German 1¼m winner, out of half-sister to Deutsches Derby winners Orofino and Ordos: fair performer: won maiden at Bath in May, best effort: will stay 7f: sold 8,000 gns in October. *M. R. Channon* 78

ROYAL DESTINATION (IRE) 4 b.g. Dubai Destination (USA) 127 – Royale (IRE) **102**
102 (Royal Academy (USA) 130) [2009 81p: 8.1g* 8g* 9.9g^3 10.4m* 10m 9m Oct 3] rangy gelding: useful handicapper: won at Haydock (maiden) in June, Ayr in July and York (overcame plenty of trouble when beating Stevie Thunder by head) in August: disappointing at Newbury and Newmarket (Cambridgeshire) last 2 starts: effective at 1m/1¼m: raced on good/good to firm ground. *J. Noseda*

ROYAL DIAMOND (IRE) 3 b.g. King's Best (USA) 132 – Irresistible Jewel (IRE) **103 p**
115 (Danehill (USA) 126) [2009 65p: 12.1s 14s^2 14g* 14.1g* 14m* p13.9g* Oct 10] strong gelding: useful handicapper: most progressive in 2009, winning at Sandown in July, Yarmouth in August, Ffos Las in September and Wolverhampton (by 10 lengths from Ramora) in October: stays 1¾m: acts on polytrack and good to firm going, probably on soft: sold 400,000 gns, joined M. Dods: likely to improve again. *Sir Mark Prescott*

ROYAL DIGNITARY (USA) 9 br.g. Saint Ballado (CAN) – Star Actress (USA) **90**
(Star de Naskra (USA)) [2009 88: f7g* p8g f8g* 7g^2 8g^5 7.5m* p8g^4 8m Sep 23] useful-looking gelding: fairly useful performer: won handicap in March and claimer in May, both at Southwell, and claimer at Beverley in August: best at 7f/1m: acts on all-weather and firm going, unsuited by softer than good: tried blinkered/visored: front runner. *D. Nicholls*

ROYAL ENCORE 5 b.m. Royal Applause 124 – Footlight Fantasy (USA) 68 (Nure- **59**
yev (USA) 131) [2009 69: p9.5g^3 Jan 19] leggy, quite attractive mare: fair maiden at best: below form sole start at 5 yrs: stays 9.5f: raced on polytrack and good/good to firm going: held up: sold 3,500 gns, reportedly in foal to Dutch Art. *J. R. Fanshawe*

ROYAL ENTOURAGE 4 b.g. Royal Applause 124 – Trempkate (USA) (Trempolino **85**
(USA) 135) [2009 69: p8g^2 p7g^2 p10.7g* p8g^2 p8g 9g a7g* p16g* 12m^6 18g Oct 10] **a93**
fairly useful performer, better on all-weather: won handicap at Dundalk in April, and claimer at Laytown and handicap at Dundalk in September: left G. M. Lyons in Ireland after eighth start: effective at 7f to 2m: acts on sand/polytrack and good to firm going: held up, and no easy ride. *C. A. Mulhall*

ROYAL ENVOY (IRE) 6 b.g. Royal Applause 124 – Seven Notes (Zafonic (USA) **73**
130) [2009 83: p7g p6g* f8g^4 p8g^3 6g^4 6v p8g^5 p6g^6 p7.1g^6 p6g^2 p7.1g p7g^6 p6m p7.1g f6f Nov 24] strong, lengthy gelding: fair handicapper nowadays: won at Kempton in February: effective at 5f to easy 1m: acts on polytrack, firm and good to soft going (well below form on soft/heavy): usually held up. *P. Howling*

ROYAL ETIQUETTE (IRE) 2 b.g. (Mar 9) Royal Applause 124 – Alpine Gold **75 +**
(IRE) 86 (Montjeu (IRE) 137) [2009 7d^3 6s^5 8m^2 p9.5g^3 Nov 14] first foal: dam, 2-y-o 1m winner, half-sister to 4-y-o Downhiller: fair maiden: stays 9.5f: acts on polytrack, good to firm and good to soft going: gelded after final start. *H. J. L. Dunlop*

ROYAL EXECUTIONER (USA) 3 b.c. Royal Academy (USA) 130 – Guillotine **91**
(USA) (Proud Truth (USA)) [2009 80: p8g* p8g^2 p8g^3 8.1g* 7g Dec 19] quite attractive colt: fairly useful performer: won maiden at Lingfield in February and handicap at Haydock (by 2½ lengths from Captainrisk) in June: left D. Simcock, renamed Royal Knight and off 6 months before final outing (tongue tied): stays 1m: acts on polytrack and good to firm ground. *S. Woods, Hong Kong*

ROYAL FANTASY (IRE) 6 b. or br.m. King's Best (USA) 132 – Dreams 88 (Rain- **69**
bow Quest (USA) 134) [2009 87: 8.9d 10.4g^6 10f 10g^4 9m^5 10m 10m^6 9.9g Sep 22] leggy mare: just fair handicapper at best in 2009: stays 11.5f: acts on polytrack, good to firm and good to soft ground: tried in cheekpieces/visor: held up: tricky ride. *N. Tinkler*

ROYAL FLYNN 7 b.g. Royal Applause 124 – Shamriyna (IRE) (Darshaan 133) [2009 **65**
86: 10.3g 10.3g 12d^5 12g^4 12g^4 13v 12.4d 14.1g Oct 16] rather leggy, close-coupled gelding: just fair handicapper at best in 2009: stays 1½m: has form on good to firm ground, possibly best under more testing conditions (acts on heavy): wears cheekpieces/blinkers: held up. *Mrs K. Walton*

ROYAL GOD (USA) 4 b.g. Royal Academy (USA) 130 – Gold Splash (USA) 116 **–**
(Blushing Groom (FR) 131) [2009 108: 8.3m^6 Jun 3] half-brother to French 7.8f winner Ziggy Gold (by Danzig) and winner in USA by Storm Cat: dam, won Prix Marcel Boussac and Coronation Stakes, sister to dam of Goldikova: useful performer at 3 yrs, winning listed race at Toulouse and second in similar event at Deauville: left F. Head in France, well held in minor event at Nottingham only outing in 2009 (said to have finished lame): gelded after: stays 1m: raced mainly on good ground or softer (probably acts on heavy): held up. *Saeed bin Suroor*

ROYAL HOLIDAY (IRE) 2 ch.g. (Apr 28) Captain Rio 122 – Sunny Slope 77 (Muj- **66**
tahid (USA) 118) [2009 6g f6g* p7.1g Oct 16] won maiden at Southwell in August: laboured effort on polytrack final start: should stay 7f: acts on fibresand. *B. Ellison*

ROYAL INTRUDER 4 b.g. Royal Applause 124 – Surprise Visitor (IRE) (Be My Guest (USA) 126) [2009 99, a93: 5d 5.8s 5v 6v 7g 6m^4 5m* 7s 5g* 6g^5 5m^3 6g* p5g* Oct 22] sturdy gelding: fairly useful handicapper: won at Sandown in June and August, Salisbury in September and Kempton (beat Ocean Blaze 1½ lengths) in October: has form at 7f, best at 5f/6f: acts on polytrack, good to firm and good to soft ground: tried in cheekpieces: somewhat quirky. *S. Donohoe, Ireland* **94**

ROYAL ISLAND (IRE) 7 b.g. Trans Island 119 – Royal House (FR) 104 (Royal Academy (USA) 130) [2009 89: p7g p10g f7g p9.5g 10g 7.6g p8g 6m p8.6g^2 Sep 25] sturdy gelding: has a round action: just modest handicapper nowadays: best at 7f to easy 1¼m: acts on polytrack (below form on fibresand), heavy and good to firm ground: tried blinkered. *M. G. Quinlan* **62**

ROYAL JASRA 5 b.g. Royal Applause 124 – Lake Pleasant (IRE) 90 (Elegant Air 119) [2009 84: p12g Feb 11] strong gelding: fairly useful performer at best: well held sole start in 2009: stays 10.6f: acts on good to firm going: tried blinkered. *Mrs S. Leech* **–**

ROYAL JET 7 b.g. Royal Applause 124 – Red Bouquet (Reference Point 139) [2009 99: p12g^3 16m p12g Jun 27] leggy gelding: useful performer at best: well below form in 2009, claimed from M. Channon £6,000 after reappearance: stays 1½m: acts on polytrack, firm and good to soft going: tried visored: sold £1,200. *Mrs S. Leech* **60**

ROYAL KEVA (IRE) 3 b.g. Medecis 119 – Karmafair (IRE) (Always Fair (USA) 121) [2009 69: 8s 10.1d^5 8.3g 7.1m^6 9.3d 13.8m^6 p12.2g p12.2g p9.5g^4 p9.5g^4 f8f^3 f7f^2 Dec 12] just modest maiden at 3 yrs: should stay 1¼m: acts on all-weather: blinkered last 3 starts. *A. D. Brown* **51** **a63**

ROYAL MANOR 4 b.f. King's Best (USA) 132 – She's Classy (USA) (Boundary (USA) 117) [2009 73: p5.1g^6 6m^6 p7.1g^6 p8m^2 p8.6g^6 Dec 5] compact filly: fair handicapper: trained until after reappearance by N. Vaughan: may prove best at 6f/7f: raced on polytrack, good to firm and good to soft going. *Tom Dascombe* **68**

ROYAL MAX (IRE) 3 b.g. Hawkeye (IRE) 122 – Baccara (IRE) (Sri Pekan (USA) 117) [2009 53: 9.9g^5 p12g^3 Jul 1] sturdy gelding: modest maiden handicapper: stays 1½m: acts on all-weather and heavy going: tried visored, blinkered final outing: fair hurdler. *C. G. Cox* **56**

ROYAL MISCHIEF (IRE) 3 b.f. Val Royal (FR) 127 – Anearlybird (USA) 53 (Sheikh Albadou 128) [2009 –: p6g^5 p6g p8.6g f7g Feb 5] little sign of ability. *P. D. Evans* **–**

ROYAL ORISSA 7 b.g. Royal Applause 124 – Ling Lane (Slip Anchor 136) [2009 37: f6g p7g p8g Feb 19] leggy gelding: no form in 2009. *D. Haydn Jones* **–**

ROYAL PATRIOT (IRE) 2 b.c. (Feb 7) King's Best (USA) 132 – Lady Ragazza (IRE) (Bering 136) [2009 7g Aug 28] rather leggy, attractive colt: 80/1, last in maiden at Newmarket: sold 4,500 gns. *W. J. Haggas* **–**

ROYAL POWER (IRE) 6 b.g. Xaar 132 – Magic Touch (Fairy King (USA)) [2009 108: 8g 8g a7f^4 a7.5f 8m 8.5g^4 8m 8.5s 8g 8m^6 9m^3 Sep 27] tall, good sort: useful handicapper: creditable efforts in 2009 only when fourth at Nad Al Sheba and Epsom (to Tartan Gigha): stays 8.5f: acts on polytrack, dirt, firm and good to soft going: waited with: none too consistent. *D. Nicholls* **102**

ROYAL PREMIER (IRE) 6 b.g. King's Theatre (IRE) 128 – Mystic Shadow (IRE) 80 (Mtoto 134) [2009 77, a68: 12m^6 14g^6 14.1g^4 16.5s^4 16d 14.1g^2 14.1g 11.5m^6 f12m p11f Dec 16] quite good-topped gelding: modest handicapper nowadays: stays 1¾m: acts on polytrack and good to firm going: wears visor (tried in cheekpieces/tongue tie): unreliable. *H. J. Collingridge* **56 §**

ROYAL PREMIUM 3 b.c. Superior Premium 122 – Royal Shepley (Royal Applause 124) [2009 51: f6g^6 8f^2 8.3g^2 7.6g^3 6.9g^5 8.1v* 8m^4 8s^5 7m 8m Oct 1] small, leggy colt: modest handicapper: won at Haydock in July: stays 1m: acts on any going: usually in cheekpieces in 2008, visored of late: has joined James Moffatt. *Mrs G. S. Rees* **63**

ROYAL PRODIGY (USA) 10 ch.g. Royal Academy (USA) 130 – Prospector's Queen (USA) (Mr Prospector (USA)) [2009 17m* 17.2f^6 May 31] close-coupled gelding: modest performer: lightly raced on Flat nowadays (poor hurdler), though won 4-runner handicap at L'Ancresse (Guernsey) in May: stays 17f: acts on all-weather and good to soft going: visored (well held) once. *R. J. Hodges* **51**

ROYAL RAINBOW 5 ch.g. Rainbow Quest (USA) 134 – Royal Future (IRE) (Royal Academy (USA) 130) [2009 –: 10m 11.8g^6 p13.9g f12m^6 p13.9g^3 Dec 14] tall gelding: modest maiden: stays 1¾m: acts on polytrack. *P. W. Hiatt* **56**

Willmott Dixon Bengough Memorial Stakes, Ascot—a career-best effort from Royal Rock (blaze), who has just a head to spare over Triple Aspect (seams); Brave Prospector (left) and Bonnie Charlie (light-coloured cap, behind Triple Aspect) are third and fourth

ROYAL RATIONALE (IRE) 5 b.g. Desert Prince (IRE) 130 – Logic 94 (Slip Anchor 136) [2009 20m³ 18m Oct 17] strong, good-bodied gelding: fairly useful handicapper (useful hurdler, but ungenuine): good third to Judgethemoment in Ascot Stakes at Royal Ascot: disappointing in Cesarewitch at Newmarket other Flat outing at 5 yrs: stays 2½m: acts on polytrack, good to firm and good to soft going: blinkered: usually dropped out. *D. E. Pipe* **92**

ROYAL RECORD 2 b.f. (Mar 7) Royal Applause 124 – First Musical 107 (First Trump 118) [2009 6m⁶ 7g⁶ 6s⁴ 6m² 6s³ 6.5m 6g Oct 16] 7,500Y: rather leggy filly: sixth foal: half-sister to 5-y-o Avertuoso and 5.7f winner Casterossa (by Rossini): dam 5f/6f winner at 2 yrs: fair maiden: should be as effective at 5f as 6f: acts on soft and good to firm going. *M. Brittain* **65**

ROYAL ROCK 5 b.g. Sakhee (USA) 136 – Vanishing Point (USA) (Caller I D (USA)) [2009 107+: 6g* 5g⁶ 6s⁴ 6g* 6s Nov 3] strong, well-made gelding: smart performer: won minor event at Haydock (by 4 lengths from Abraham Lincoln) in May and Willmott Dixon Bengough Memorial Stakes at Ascot (better than ever when beating Triple Aspect by head, edging ahead late) in October: below form back on soft ground in Prix de Seine-et-Oise at Maisons-Laffitte final outing: has won at 7f, best at 6f: acts on polytrack, good to firm and good to soft ground: usually waited with/travels strongly. *C. F. Wall* **114**

ROYAL SALSA (IRE) 3 b.f. Royal Applause 124 – Lady Salsa (IRE) (Gone West (USA)) [2009 51: p8.6g³ p8.6g f8g Feb 3] close-coupled filly: poor maiden: stays 8.6f: acts on polytrack: in cheekpieces final outing. *R. A. Fahey* **49**

ROYAL SOCIETY 3 b.g. King's Best (USA) 132 – Nawaiet (USA) (Zilzal (USA) 137) [2009 –: p8.6g³ p12g² 14.1m 8.3g 10s 9.1g p9.5g* p12m p9.5g Dec 28] big gelding: fair handicapper: left M. Johnston £14,500 after second start, A. G. Foster after fifth and Miss L. Perratt after sixth: won at Wolverhampton in November: stays 1½m: acts on polytrack, little form on turf: tried tongue tied. *R. A. Farrant* **– a65**

ROYAL STRAIGHT 4 ch.g. Halling (USA) 133 – High Straits 74 (Bering 136) [2009 79: p10g⁴ p8g⁶ p10g Feb 11] rangy gelding: fair performer: stays 1¼m: acts on polytrack and good to soft going: visored/blinkered last 2 starts: none too consistent. *B. N. Pollock* **70**

ROYAL SUPERLATIVE 3 b.f. King's Best (USA) 132 – Supereva (IRE) (Sadler's Wells (USA) 132) [2009 –p: 8.1g⁴ 8.1g* 8.1m² 10d 8.5m⁴ p9.5m Sep 28] good-topped filly: fair performer: won maiden at Chepstow in June: should stay 1¼m: acts on good to firm ground, below form on good to soft. *R. M. Beckett* **78**

ROYAL TORBO (ISR) 2 b.c. (Mar 3) Tabari (GER) – Royal Dutch (GER) (Monsun (GER) 124) [2009 p7.1g Dec 18] 100/1, well held in maiden at Wolverhampton. *George Baker* **–**

ROYAL TREASURE (IRE) 2 b.c. (Feb 8) Arakan (USA) 123 – Isticanna (USA) 96 (Far North (CAN) 120) [2009 p8.6g p8g Nov 14] well held in maiden/claimer. *J. A. Osborne* –

ROYAL TROOPER (IRE) 3 b.g. Hawk Wing (USA) 136 – Strawberry Roan (IRE) 113 (Sadler's Wells (USA) 132) [2009 62: 9.9m³ 12m³ 12d⁴ 12m³ 12d* 11.9g⁵ 14m 14.8g p12.2g⁴ f12g⁴ 14.6g⁵ 13.8v* Nov 3] good-topped gelding: fair handicapper: won at Thirsk in July and Catterick in November (gelded after): stays 14.6f: acts on all-weather, heavy and good to firm ground. *J. G. Given* **79**

ROYAL WEDDING 7 b.g. King's Best (USA) 132 – Liaison (USA) (Blushing Groom (FR) 131) [2009 p10g p13g⁵ p13g Feb 21] good-topped gelding: fair performer in 2005: just modest form on return to Flat in 2009: stays 1¼m: acts on all-weather and good to firm ground: fair hurdler/fairly useful chaser. *N. J. Gifford* **61**

ROYAL WILLY (IRE) 3 b.g. Val Royal (FR) 127 – Neat Dish (CAN) 90 (Stalwart (USA)) [2009 75: 8m p8.6g³ 9g⁴ 12d 14.1g p10g⁶ p8.6g Nov 2] lengthy gelding: fair maiden handicapper: stays 9f: acts on polytrack and good to soft going. *W. Jarvis* **73**

ROYBUOY 2 b.c. (May 15) Royal Applause 124 – Wavy Up (IRE) (Brustolon 117) [2009 7m 8d p7m p8m⁶ p7m⁶ p7g Dec 31] modest maiden: should stay 1m: acts on polytrack: blinkered last 3 starts. *H. J. L. Dunlop* **58**

RUBBINGHOUSEDOTCOM (IRE) 3 b.g. Desert Style (IRE) 121 – Marain (IRE) (Marju (IRE) 127) [2009 49: p7g 8g⁴ 10m p10g May 12] poor maiden: stays 1m: raced only on polytrack and good/good to firm ground: blinkered final outing. *P. M. Phelan* **49**

RUBENSTAR (IRE) 6 b.g. Soviet Star (USA) 128 – Ansariya (USA) 83 (Shahrastani (USA) 135) [2009 74: p7.1g p7.1g³ 7d³ p7g* p7g p7.1g² Dec 28] strong gelding: fair handicapper: won at Lingfield in April: stays 1m: acts on polytrack, soft and good to firm going: strong traveller: held up. *Pat Morris* **74**

RUBICON BAY (IRE) 2 b.f. (Apr 24) One Cool Cat (USA) 123 – Mrs Moonlight (Ajdal (USA) 130) [2009 6g 7.1d⁶ Oct 28] £14,000 2-y-o: compact filly: half-sister to 3 winners, notably smart 7f (at 2 yrs)/1m winner Soviet Flash (by Warning): dam unraced half-sister to Japan Cup winner Jupiter Island: trouble at start before soundly beaten in maidens over 4 months apart. *C. J. Teague* –

RUBLEVKA STAR (USA) 3 b.f. Elusive Quality (USA) – Al Desima 93 (Emperor Jones (USA) 119) [2009 77p: 5m p5g⁵ 5s Aug 2] good-bodied filly: fair performer: left J. Noseda after second start: should be suited by 7f/1m. *James M. Ryan, Ireland* **66**

RUB OF THE RELIC (IRE) 4 b.g. Chevalier (IRE) 115 – Bayletta (IRE) 41 (Woodborough (USA) 112) [2009 59, a66: f8s⁴ f8g f8g³ f12g p9.5g f8d² f8g Mar 27] lengthy gelding: modest handicapper: should stay 1¼m: acts on all-weather and heavy going: wears headgear (usually visor): moody: gelded after final start. *P. T. Midgley* **62**

RUBY BEST 3 b.f. Best of The Bests (IRE) 122 – Ice Bird (Polar Falcon (USA) 126) [2009 –: p7g Jan 14] workmanlike filly: little form. *D. K. Ivory* –

RUBY DELTA 4 b.g. Delta Dancer – Picolette 56 (Piccolo 121) [2009 59: p13.9g Feb 7] tall, short-backed gelding: modest performer: well held only outing in 2009: stays 1½m: acts on polytrack, firm and soft ground: blinkered/visored last 4 starts. *A. G. Juckes* –

RUBY TALLULAH 3 b.f. Piccolo 121 – Tallulah Belle 92 (Crowning Honors (CAN)) [2009 78: p5g⁴ p5.1g⁴ p5g⁵ p5.1g⁵ p6g⁵ p6g⁶ p5g⁶ p5g Mar 25] small, sturdy filly: fair performer at best at 3 yrs: effective at 5f/6f: acts on polytrack and firm going. *C. R. Dore* **69 d**

RUDOLPH SCHMIDT (IRE) 3 br.f. Catcher In The Rye (IRE) 115 – Enaya 99 (Caerleon (USA) 132) [2009 82: 8v 7s 8s³ 8.5d 7m p7g* Oct 2] fairly useful performer: won seller at Lingfield (sold 8,600 gns and joined D. ffrench Davis) in October: effective at 7f/1m: acts on polytrack and soft ground: tongue tied last 5 starts, also in cheekpieces/blinkers last 3: sent to Greece. *D. Myerscough, Ireland* **81**

RUDRY WORLD (IRE) 6 ch.g. Spinning World (USA) 130 – Fancy Boots (IRE) 62 (Salt Dome (USA)) [2009 74: 12d² 12.1v 13v⁴ 12.4d² 12v p12g Nov 18] workmanlike gelding: fair handicapper: will be suited by further than 1¾m: acts on all-weather, heavy and good to firm going: held up. *M. Mullineaux* **65**

RUE SOLEIL 5 ch.m. Zaha (CAN) 106 – Maria Cappuccini 70 (Siberian Express (USA) 125) [2009 59: 5s 5s Aug 24] tall mare: modest at best: well held in 2009. *J. R. Weymes* –

RUFF DIAMOND (USA) 4 b. or br.g. Stormin Fever (USA) 116 – Whalah (USA) 76 (Dixieland Band (USA)) [2009 83§: p10g³ p10g³ p12g⁴ 14.1g⁴ p13g 21.7m Jun 20] big, close-coupled, good-topped gelding: fair handicapper: stays 1½m: acts on polytrack, soft and good to firm going: below form in headgear: ungenuine: joined M. Harris. *J. S. Moore* **77 §**

RUFUS ROUGHCUT 2 b.c. (Feb 26) Auction House (USA) 120 – Shining Oasis (IRE) 73 (Mujtahid (USA) 118) [2009 5g 7m 7s 6g 7d Oct 27] well held in maidens/ claimer: tried tongue tied. *S. C. Williams* **–**

RUGELL (ARG) 4 b. or br.c. Interprete (ARG) – Realize (ARG) (Confidential Talk (USA)) [2009 10.1d4 10g5 14.8g3 14.1m6 Sep 17] Argentinian-bred colt: raced at San Isidro in native country in 2008, winning maiden and Grade 2 Clasico Provincia de Buenos Aires: well held in Gran Premio Carlos Pellegrini final start before leaving J. Udaondo: best effort in Britain (fairly useful form) when third in handicap at Newmarket: stays 14.8f: acts on firm going. *H. R. A. Cecil* **91**

RULE OF NATURE 2 b.f. (Jan 26) Oasis Dream 129 – Jolie Etoile (USA) (Diesis 133) [2009 7.1m2 6g* Oct 20] strong, lengthy filly: first foal: dam lightly-raced half-sister to smart French/US 7f/1m performer Etoile Montante: promising in maidens, landing odds at Yarmouth by length from Dherghaam despite finding drop in trip against her: will prove best at 7f+: sure to improve again. *Sir Michael Stoute* **82 p**

RULER OF ALL (IRE) 3 b.g. Sadler's Wells (USA) 132 – Shabby Chic (USA) 114 (Red Ransom (USA)) [2009 60p: 10.1m2 11s 14.1s 11.7g Oct 21] tall, leggy gelding: fairly useful maiden: left B. Hills and off 6 months after second start: should be suited by 1½m+: acts on good to firm ground. *H. Candy* **80**

RULER OF MY HEART (IRE) 2 br.f. (Mar 25) Green Tune (USA) 125 – Dirigeante (FR) (Lead On Time (USA) 123) [2009 7g5 8g* 8g 9g5 Nov 14] €80,000Y: tall, unfurnished filly: half-sister to several winners abroad, including smart French 5.5f (at 2 yrs) to 10.5f winner Al Namix (by Linamix): dam French 7f winner: useful form: vastly improved from debut (green in maiden at Newmarket) when winning valuable listed race at Deauville in August by 2½ lengths from Maroon Machine: below best in Prix d'Aumale at Chantilly (sold from T. Dascombe €128,000 after) and listed race at Marseille Borely last 2 starts: stays 1m. *F. Rossi, France* **102**

RULER'S HONOUR (IRE) 2 b.g. (Apr 24) Antonius Pius (USA) 123§ – Naughty Reputation (IRE) 31 (Shalford (IRE) 124§) [2009 p5g6 Nov 21] 33/1 and green, well held in maiden at Lingfield. *T. J. Etherington* **–**

RULESN'REGULATIONS 3 b.c. Forzando 122 – Al Awaalah 52 (Mukaddamah (USA) 125) [2009 97p: 6m* 5d p6m Nov 3] useful-looking colt: useful handicapper: improved to win at Ascot in September by neck from Enact: below form after: speedy, effective at 5f/6f: acts on polytrack and good to firm ground. *Matthew Salaman* **100**

RULING REEF 7 b.m. Diktat 126 – Horseshoe Reef 88 (Mill Reef (USA) 141) [2009 54: p12.2g Feb 16] close-coupled mare: modest performer at best: well held only outing on Flat in 2009: stays 1¾m: acts on fibresand, firm and soft going (well held on polytrack). *M. R. Bosley* **–**

RUMBLE OF THUNDER (IRE) 3 b.g. Fath (USA) 116 – Honey Storm (IRE) 73 (Mujadil (USA) 119) [2009 82: p11g3 12.3m 10.2d* 9.9g 10.2g2 10g2 10m2 Oct 2] leggy, close-coupled gelding: fairly useful handicapper: won at Bath in May: good second last 3 starts: stays 12.3f: acts on polytrack, good to firm and good to soft going: front runner. *D. W. P. Arbuthnot* **88**

RUM JUNGLE 5 b.g. Robellino (USA) 127 – Anna Karietta 82 (Precocious 126) [2009 90+: 7g 7m 7g6 Jul 31] big, strong gelding: just fair handicapper in 2009: best at 7f: acts on soft and good to firm ground. *H. Candy* **76**

RUM KING (USA) 2 b. or br.c. (Mar 7) Montbrook (USA) – Cut Class Leanne (USA) (Cutlass (USA)) [2009 7d 6f3 6m* 6g* Oct 30] $57,000 2-y-o: sturdy, close-coupled colt: brother to 2 winners in USA, notably smart 2003 2-y-o Grade 2 6f winner Chapel Royal, also third in Breeders' Cup Juvenile, and half-brother to winner in USA by Notebook: dam, US 5.5f (at 2 yrs) to 8.5f winner, out of half-sister to Night Shift: most progressive: won maiden and minor event (beat Marine Boy by head) at Newmarket in October: stays 6f: acts on good to firm ground: already useful. *R. Hannon* **100**

RUMOOL 2 b.c. (Apr 4) Exceed And Excel (AUS) 126 – Silent Heir (AUS) 82 (Sunday Silence (USA)) [2009 6m5 p6g* Jun 3] useful-looking colt: third foal: half-brother to 4-y-o Young Pretender: dam, 1¼m winner, out of close relative to Derby winner New Approach: easily better effort when winning minor event at Kempton by 1½ lengths from Janeiro, hanging badly left: seems likely to improve further. *C. E. Brittain* **92 p**

RUMOUSH (USA) 2 b.f. (Apr 13) Rahy (USA) 115 – Sarayir (USA) 104 (Mr Prospector (USA)) [2009 p8g* Nov 14] sister to fairly useful 1½m winner Atayeb and half-sister to several winners, notably 3-y-o Ghanaati and 4-y-o Mawatheeq: dam, 7f (at 2 yrs) and 1¼m winner, closely related to Nayef and half-sister to Nashwan and Unfuwain: 11/2 and **81 P**

green, most promising when winning maiden at Lingfield comfortably by ½ length from Street Entertainer: likely to improve considerably. *M. P. Tregoning*

RUM RAISIN 3 b.f. Invincible Spirit (IRE) 121 – Femme Femme (USA) (Lyphard (USA) 132) [2009 71: 7v 8.5g⁶ 6m p8g 8.5d 6.3s⁶ 8g⁵ 9d 7g² Oct 17] good-topped filly: fair maiden handicapper: stays 8.5f: acts on polytrack and heavy going: tried blinkered (ran poorly): tends to carry head high. *John Joseph Murphy, Ireland* **71**

RUMRAMAH (USA) 3 b.f. Mr Greeley (USA) 122 – She's Vested (USA) (Boundary (USA) 117) [2009 57: p7m 7.1m⁵ p9.5g Oct 3] maiden: little form at 3 yrs. *D. M. Simcock* **–**

RUNAWAY PEGASUS (USA) 4 b.f. Fusaichi Pegasus (USA) 130 – Runaway Venus (USA) (Runaway Groom (CAN)) [2009 12g⁵ Apr 21] fourth foal: half-sister to winners in North America by Honour And Glory (2) and El Prado: dam US 6f to 8.5f winner: well beaten in 2 maidens at Milan for V. Valiani in Italy in 2008, and in similar event at Folkestone on British debut: sold 800 gns. *H. R. A. Cecil* **–**

RUN FOR EDE'S 5 b.m. Peintre Celebre (USA) 137 – Raincloud (Rainbow Quest (USA) 134) [2009 76: 11.6g* 10g⁴ 10.1d³ 12g* 12g* 12m⁴ 12g² 11.7g Oct 21] leggy, close-coupled mare: fairly useful handicapper: won at Windsor in April and Ascot (apprentices) and Epsom in July: effective at 1m to 1½m: acts on polytrack and good to soft going: tried in cheekpieces: races freely held up: has awkward head carriage. *P. M. Phelan* **83**

RUN FOR THE HILLS 3 b.c. Oasis Dream 129 – Maid For The Hills 101 (Indian Ridge 123) [2009 103p: 6d 6g 6g⁶ 5m³ Oct 1] tall, quite attractive colt: useful performer: career-best effort when 1¾ lengths third to Spin Cycle in listed race at Newmarket final outing, coming from off strong pace: raced only at 5f/6f, likely to stay further: unraced on extremes of going. *J. H. M. Gosden* **107**

RUN FREE 5 b.g. Agnes World (USA) 123 – Ellie Ardensky 100 (Slip Anchor 136) [2009 67: f8s⁶ f7g f7g³ f7g f8g 10.1m 9.9m f7g⁶ 12.5g³ 12.5s 10m Sep 14] good-bodied gelding: modest performer: effective at 7f to 12.5f: acts on all-weather, soft and good to firm going: tried in visor/cheekpieces: races prominently: inconsistent. *N. Wilson* **61**

RUNNING BUCK (USA) 4 b.c. Running Stag (USA) 124 – Dinghy (USA) (Fortunate Prospect (USA)) [2009 46: p6g p7g⁴ p9.5g Mar 6] sturdy colt: poor maiden: stays 7f: acts on polytrack, probably on good to soft ground: tried in blinkers, visored in 2009. *A. Bailey* **49**

RUNNING FLUSH (USA) 3 ch.g. Grand Slam (USA) 120 – Holiday Gold (USA) (Touch Gold (USA) 127) [2009 6m 6g p5.1g³ 6.1d⁶ p6g⁶ p6g⁶ p7m p7g³ f7g Dec 18] modest maiden: stays 7f: acts on polytrack, unraced on extremes of going on turf: blinkered last 2 starts. *J. R. Gask* **63**

RUNNING MATE (IRE) 2 b.c. (Feb 22) Acclamation 118 – It Takes Two (IRE) (Alzao (USA) 117) [2009 6g⁴ 6m⁴ 5m 6.1v* 6d Aug 1] €68,000F, £180,000Y: lengthy colt: has scope: half-brother to several winners, including smart Irish sprinter Final Exam (by College Chapel): dam ran 3 times at 2 yrs in Ireland: fair performer: won at Nottingham in July: ran poorly in nursery at Goodwood: may prove best at 5f/6f: unraced on firm going, acts on any other: tried visored: sold 10,000 gns. *J. H. M. Gosden* **71**

RUNSWICK BAY 4 b.g. Intikhab (USA) 135 – Upend 120 (Main Reef 126) [2009 –: 8d 12d 10d 12d Jul 15] big, useful-looking gelding: fairly useful performer at 2 yrs: lightly raced and no form since. *G. M. Moore* **–**

RUPESTRIAN 3 b.g. Fantastic Light (USA) 134 – Upper Strata 109 (Shirley Heights 130) [2009 81: p12g* 10.3m⁶ Mar 29] good-topped gelding: fairly useful form at 2 yrs: didn't need to be at best to win maiden at Lingfield in March: will prove best at 1½m+: acts on polytrack and heavy ground: joined Tim Vaughan £4,000, fairly useful juvenile hurdler, successful first 4 starts. *M. Johnston* **62 +**

RUSSIAN ANGEL 5 gr.m. Baryshnikov (AUS) – Eventuality 77 (Petoski 135) [2009 56: p11g⁴ 10.9g 8.1m³ 8m³ 9m⁴ 8.1m⁵ p7m⁵ p8g³ p9.5g² p8.6g Dec 18] modest maiden handicapper: stays 11f: acts on polytrack and good to firm ground: races prominently: signs of temperament. *Jean-Rene Auvray* **56**

RUSSIAN BRIGADIER 2 b.g. (Feb 20) Xaar 132 – Brigadiers Bird (IRE) (Mujadil (USA) 119) [2009 7g Oct 23] leggy gelding: 100/1 and very green, well held in maiden at Doncaster (gelded after). *M. Brittain* **–**

RUSSIAN DAVIS (IRE) 2 b.c. (Apr 14) Mull of Kintyre (USA) 114 – Sunny Isles Beauty (USA) (Tale of The Cat (USA) 113) [2009 5d 5.1g⁴ f5g⁶ p7g* p7.1g³ p7.1g⁶ 6g⁵ Oct 23] €35,000Y: sturdy colt: first foal: dam US 2-y-o 1m winner: fair performer: won nursery at Kempton in August: should be as effective at 6f as 7f: acts on polytrack: sold 21,000 gns. *R. M. H. Cowell* **73**

RUSSIAN EMPRESS (IRE) 5 b.m. Trans Island 119 – Russian Countess (USA) 104 (Nureyev (USA) 131) [2009 101: 8s^4 7v 8v 8.5d 7d 6g 6s^5 p8g^6 p8g^3 p6g^2 p6g Nov 27] angular mare: useful performer: best efforts in 2009 when fourth to Oh Goodness Me in Park Express Stakes at the Curragh, seventh in handicap at Leopardstown on fifth outing and 2½ lengths third to Fourpenny Lane in listed race at Dundalk: effective at 6f to 1m: acts on polytrack and soft ground: often slowly away: sold 77,000 gns. *D. Myerscough, Ireland* **101**

RUSSIAN EPIC 5 b.g. Diktat 126 – Russian Rhapsody 100 (Cosmonaut) [2009 85: 11.6g^5 May 4] lengthy, good-topped gelding: fairly useful handicapper at best: well below form only start in 2009: barely stays 1¼m: acts on any going: has had breathing problems, tried tongue tied. *Andrew Turnell* **70**

RUSSIAN GEORGE (IRE) 3 ch.g. Sendawar (IRE) 129 – Mannsara (IRE) (Royal Academy (USA) 130) [2009 79: 8m* 8m^2 7.9m 8.5m^4 9.8m^2 10m 10.4g Oct 10] stocky gelding: fairly useful performer: won maiden at Thirsk in May: left T. Tate after fourth start: well held last 2 outings: stays 1¼m: acts on good to firm going. *S. Gollings* **83**

RUSSIAN INVADER (IRE) 5 ch.g. Acatenango (GER) 127 – Ukraine Venture 96 (Slip Anchor 136) [2009 –: f12g^4 f12g^2 p16.5g 16d^3 f16g^5 16g f14m f12g^5 Dec 22] good-bodied gelding: fair handicapper: stays easy 16.5f: acts on all-weather and good to firm ground: blinkered last 3 starts. *R. C. Guest* **70**

RUSSIAN JAR (IRE) 3 b.g. Xaar 132 – Lady Windermere (IRE) (Lake Coniston (IRE) 131) [2009 8.3m* 8m^2 7m^2 7m^5 8s Oct 12] useful-looking gelding: fifth foal: half-brother to useful Irish 6f winner Absolutelyfabulous (by Mozart): dam unraced half-sister to Fillies' Mile winner Listen and Moyglare Stud Stakes winner Sequoyah (dam of Henrythenavigator): fairly useful form: won maiden at Leicester in May: good second in handicaps at Newmarket next 2 starts: below par after: at least as good at 7f as 1m: acts on good to firm going: sold 26,000 gns. *M. A. Jarvis* **94**

RUSSIAN MUSIC (USA) 4 b.g. Stravinsky (USA) 133 – Private Seductress (USA) (Private Account (USA)) [2009 6m 6m 5.1d f8g^2 7.2s 8.5m^5 p12m^2 p13.9g* Dec 14] stocky, deep-girthed gelding: modest form when third in bumper: modest handicapper on Flat: left C. Mulhall after fifth start, M. Easterby after sixth: won at Wolverhampton in December: stays 1¾m: acts on all-weather: tried blinkered. *Ian Williams* **62 +**

RUSSIAN RAVE 3 ch.f. Danehill Dancer (IRE) 117 – Russian Ruby (FR) 85 (Vettori (IRE) 119) [2009 71: p7g^3 7.1f^5 7m^6 p7g* p8g^4 p7g^5 8.3m p7g Oct 11] tall filly: fair handicapper: won at Kempton in June: worth a try back at 6f, stamina stretched at 1m: acts on polytrack and firm ground. *J. G. Portman* **74**

RUSSIAN ROCKET (IRE) 7 b.g. Indian Rocket 115 – Soviet Girl (IRE) (Soviet Star (USA) 128) [2009 77: f5m^4 6d^6 f5m^4 p5.1g^5 5.1m* p5g^3 5.1d^6 f5g 5.2m 5.1d 5.2d^3 Oct 27] small, leggy gelding: fair handicapper: won at Nottingham in July: stays 6f: acts on all-weather, firm and soft going. *Mrs C. A. Dunnett* **68** **a72**

RUSSIAN ROCK (IRE) 2 b.c. (Apr 14) Rock of Gibraltar (IRE) 133 – Mala Mala (IRE) 104 (Brief Truce (USA) 126) [2009 5g^5 5f* 5m Jun 16] 21,000F, £20,000Y, £26,000 2-y-o: close-coupled colt: fifth foal: closely related to 3 winners, including 4-y-o Silvanus and 5-y-o Contest: dam, Irish 5f winner, half-sister to very smart 1¼m performer Mister Monet and Irish 1000 Guineas winner Tarascon: still green, won maiden at Salisbury in May: only twelfth in listed Windsor Castle Stakes at Royal Ascot, wide: will stay at least 6f. *R. A. Teal* **76**

RUSSIAN SAGE (SAF) 5 b.h. Jallad (USA) 89 – Sage Blue (SAF) (Badger Land (USA)) [2009 8g^2 9m^2 12g 8.9m 9m p10g^4 Nov 11] angular horse: very smart performer: won Cape Derby at Kenilworth and Daily News 2000 at Greyville (both Grade 1) in 2008: twice runner-up at Nad Al Sheba early in 2009, ½ length behind Kachgai in handicap, then beaten 1¼ lengths by Balius in Jebel Hatta: reportedly bled in Dubai Sheema Classic there next time and well below form in Group 3s/minor event in Britain after: effective at 7f to 11f: acts on good to firm ground. *M. F. de Kock, South Africa* **122**

RUSSIAN SAINT 3 b.f. Red Ransom (USA) – Tessara (GER) (Big Shuffle (USA) 122) [2009 –: p8g Apr 29] last in maidens. *D. Shaw* **–**

RUSSIAN SPIRIT 3 b.f. Falbrav (IRE) 133 – Russian Rhapsody 100 (Cosmonaut) [2009 70p: 6m^2 6d* 6g^2 6m^3 5g* 6g Oct 23] attractive filly: fairly useful performer: won maiden at Doncaster in July and handicap at York in October: raced too freely final outing: stays 6f: unraced on extremes of going: prominent runner. *M. A. Jarvis* **94**

RUSSIAN SYMPHONY (USA) 8 ch.g. Stravinsky (USA) 133 – Backwoods Teacher (USA) (Woodman (USA) 126) [2009 –, a79: p5.1g^4 p6m^6 p6g^2 Mar 20] lengthy gelding: fair performer: effective at 5f to 7f: acts on polytrack and firm going: usually in blinkers (tried in cheekpieces). *C. R. Egerton* **–** **a75**

RUSTY PELICAN 2 ch.g. (Mar 9) Tobougg (IRE) 125 – Opalite 57 (Opening Verse (USA) 126) [2009 p7g Oct 24] 33/1 and green, tailed off in maiden at Kempton: sold £800. *P. J. Makin* –

RUTBA 4 b.f. Act One 124 – Elhilmeya (IRE) 94 (Unfuwain (USA) 131) [2009 74: 15.4g p16g⁶ May 4] strong, close-coupled filly: fair handicapper at 3 yrs: folded tamely both starts in 2009: visored last 6 starts. *M. P. Tregoning* –

RUTHIE BABE 2 b.f. (Feb 17) Exceed And Excel (AUS) 126 – Lady Oriande 59 (Makbul 104) [2009 5g⁶ 6m⁵ p5.1g⁴ 5m* 5m³ p5.1g⁴ Oct 16] €90,000F, £90,000Y: smallish, strong filly: first foal: dam, sprint maiden, sister to very smart sprinter Striking Ambition: fair performer: won nursery at Ffos Las in September: likely to be best at 5f/6f: acts on polytrack and good to firm going: sold 11,000 gns. *W. J. Haggas* **69**

RUUD REVENGE (USA) 3 b.g. Van Nistelrooy (USA) 108 – Savannah's Revenge (USA) (West By West (USA) 116) [2009 –: 12m³ 12d² 12f⁴ 12g Jun 13] sturdy gelding: fair maiden: likely to stay beyond 1½m: acts on good to firm and good to soft going. *Mrs D. J. Sanderson* **79**

RUWAIN 5 b.g. Lujain (USA) 119 – Ruwaya (USA) 80 (Red Ransom (USA)) [2009 58: p10g* p12g p9.5g p10g⁴ p9.5g⁶ 10.2m⁴ p8g⁶ 9m p9.5g Nov 20] close-coupled gelding: modest handicapper: won at Great Leighs in January: stays 1¼m (not 1½m): acts on polytrack, good to firm and good to soft going: tried blinkered: front runner. *P. J. McBride* **56**

R WOODY 2 ch.g. (Feb 9) Ishiguru (USA) 114 – Yarrita 77 (Tragic Role (USA)) [2009 6m p6g p6g f5m* p5m⁴ Dec 30] €4,500Y, €8,800 2-y-o: rather unfurnished gelding: third foal: half-brother to winner in Greece by Fraam: dam 2-y-o 5f winner: fair performer: gelded prior to showing much improved form (100/1) to win maiden at Southwell in December by 3 lengths: fourth in nursery at Kempton: likely to be best at 5f/6f: acts on all-weather. *Mrs L. C. Jewell* **77**

RYAN'S ROCK 4 b.g. Lujain (USA) 119 – Diamond Jayne (IRE) (Royal Abjar (USA) 121) [2009 53: 8.1g May 4] tall gelding: modest maiden at best: stays 1m: acts on polytrack. *R. J. Price* –

RYDAL (USA) 8 ch.g. Gilded Time (USA) – Tennis Partner (USA) (Northern Dancer) [2009 68: p7g⁵ p7g⁶ p7g⁵ 7f p6g Sep 25] good-topped gelding: modest performer: effective at stiff 5f to 8.5f: acts on all-weather, firm and good to soft going: tried tongue tied: effective with or without headgear. *Miss Jo Crowley* **56**

RYEDALE OVATION (IRE) 6 b.g. Royal Applause 124 – Passe Passe (USA) 78 (Lear Fan (USA) 130) [2009 76: p11g p12g⁴ p12g f6g p7g* p8g² 8m⁵ 7m⁶ May 9] big, useful-looking gelding: fair performer: won claimer at Kempton (claimed from M. Hill £5,000) in April: effective at 7f, barely stays 1½m: acts on polytrack, soft and good to firm ground: tried in blinkers/cheekpieces: held up: quirky. *G. L. Moore* **76**

RYEDANE (IRE) 7 b.g. Danetime (IRE) 121 – Miss Valediction (IRE) (Petardia 113) [2009 72: p5.1g⁵ 5.1d 5.1m⁶ 5m* 5m³ 5m³ 6m 6g⁵ 6m³ 5d⁵ p6g 5m 6m Sep 23] tall, leggy gelding: fair handicapper: won at Carlisle in May: largely respectable efforts after: stays 6f: acts on polytrack, firm and good to soft going: blinkered: held up. *T. D. Easterby* **67**

RYEDON BYE 3 ch.g. Distant Music (USA) 126 – Payphone (Anabaa (USA) 130) [2009 50: 6f 7m 8f May 11] sturdy, lengthy gelding: poor maiden. *T. D. Easterby* **45**

RYKER (IRE) 3 ch.g. Halling (USA) 133 – Charlock (IRE) 108 (Nureyev (USA) 131) [2009 7d 7m p8g p8m p9.5g⁴ p11f³ Dec 16] close-coupled gelding: fair maiden: stays easy 11f: acts on polytrack, unraced on extremes of going on turf. *J. W. Hills* **65**

S

SAACHI'S VISION (IRE) 2 ch.f. (Jan 19) Compton Place 125 – Ash Moon (IRE) 92 (General Monash (USA) 107) [2009 5g p5g⁶ p5.1g 6g⁶ 6g f5g 5m p6g Oct 8] 3,000F, 3,000Y: plain, sturdy filly: fourth foal: dam 2-y-o 5f/6f winner (stayed 1½m): poor maiden: pulled up (said to have been lame) penultimate outing: blinkered last 5 starts, also tried in tongue tie: sold £650. *D. K. Ivory* **40**

SAAFIA (USA) 2 b. or br.f. (Apr 22) Swain (IRE) 134 – Reem Al Barari (USA) 69 (Storm Cat (USA)) [2009 7g⁵ 7d⁶ 7.5f* Aug 29] unfurnished filly: third foal: half-sister to 3-y-o Rafaan and a winner in Qatar by Nayef: dam once-raced half-sister to Derby winner Erhaab: best effort in maidens when winning at Beverley comfortably by 5 **77**

lengths from Whirly Dancer, making all: will stay 1m+: sold 13,000 gns, sent to Bahrain. *M. Johnston*

SAA'IDA (IRE) 3 ch.f. Diesis 133 – Westernize (USA) (Gone West (USA)) [2009 9.7d 10m 9.9m* 10.1g 10s 8.3d 8.3g^{4} 11m^{6} Oct 1] $70,000F, 40,000Y: lengthy filly: first foal: dam, US maiden, out of smart French 1¼m/1½m performer Palme d'Or, herself half-sister to top-class French 1½m performer Pistolet Bleu: fair performer: won maiden at Goodwood in May: stays 1¼m: acts on good to firm going: blinkered last 2 starts. *C. E. Brittain* **78**

SAAMEQ (IRE) 8 b.g. Bahhare (USA) 122 – Tajawuz 82 (Kris 135) [2009 –, a62: p12.2g Jun 22] strong gelding: modest performer: very lightly raced nowadays, and well held sole start in 2009: stays 1½m: acts on polytrack and good to firm going: tried in cheekpieces. *D. W. Thompson* **–**

SABANCAYA 4 b.f. Nayef (USA) 129 – Serra Negra 83 (Kris 135) [2009 66: f14s* f16g^{4} f14g* f16g^{3} f14g^{6} p13.9g^{3} Mar 2] neat filly: fair handicapper: won twice at Southwell in January, latter amateur event: stays 2m: acts on all-weather, firm and good to soft going: reliable. *Mrs P. Sly* **70**

SABANDER BLEUE (IRE) 2 b.c. (Mar 5) Peintre Celebre (USA) 137 – Sabander Bay (USA) 51 (Lear Fan (USA) 130) [2009 7d^{6} 7m^{5} 8.5m^{2} 8.5m^{3} 8.3g^{3} 8g^{6} Sep 30] 48,000F, 40,000Y: close-coupled colt: second foal: half-brother to 3-y-o Aim To Achieve: dam twice-raced granddaughter of Lowther Stakes winner Kingscote: fair maiden: should stay 1¼m: acts on good to firm going: sold 22,000 gns, sent to Switzerland. *M. R. Channon* **75**

SABATINI (IRE) 2 b.f. (Feb 12) One Cool Cat (USA) 123 – Two Sets To Love (IRE) (Cadeaux Genereux 131) [2009 6m 8d^{4} 6g^{4} p6g* p6m* p6g^{2} Dec 17] €26,000Y: workmanlike filly: first foal: dam unraced half-sister to very smart miler Swallow Flight: fairly useful performer: much improved when winning claimer at Wolverhampton (left R. Hannon £10,000) in November and nursery at Lingfield in December: should be suited by 7f+: acts on polytrack. *J. Pearce* **84**

SABII SANDS (IRE) 2 b.c. (Feb 25) Invincible Spirit (IRE) 121 – Miriana (IRE) (Bluebird (USA) 125) [2009 6m* 6m^{3} 7d^{4} Jul 18] €120,000Y: strong colt: third foal: dam lightly-raced sister to smart French miler Fine Fellow: fairly useful performer: won maiden at Goodwood in June: better effort in minor events when creditable third at Newmarket: should be suited by 7f: sent to Hong Kong, where renamed Dreams Maker. *R. Hannon* **82**

SABI STAR 3 b.c. Green Desert (USA) 127 – Balisada 115 (Kris 135) [2009 64p: 8g^{5} 8.3g^{3} 8d^{3} 8.3g^{6} Jul 27] attractive colt: fair maiden: should stay 1¼m: unraced on extremes of going: races prominently: signs of temperament: sold 12,000 gns, sent to Germany. *J. H. M. Gosden* **79**

SABORIDO (USA) 3 gr.g. Dixie Union (USA) 121 – Alexine (ARG) (Runaway Groom (CAN)) [2009 67: 10.2g^{3} 12.6g^{2} 11.8g^{4} 14m 10v^{3} 12f^{4} 14.1m* 15g* 16m^{2} 17.2g* Oct 21] big, useful-looking gelding: fair handicapper: won at Salisbury and Warwick in August, and Bath in October: gelded after: stays 17f: acts on heavy and good to firm going: tried in cheekpieces (seemed amiss)/blinkered. *Mrs A. J. Perrett* **75**

SABOTAGE (UAE) 3 b.g. Halling (USA) 133 – Cunas (USA) 86 (Irish River (FR) 131) [2009 9.9g^{2} 11.8m* 16f 14m^{2} 12m^{3} 12g 12g^{3} 13.4m^{3} Aug 22] lengthy, good-topped gelding: third foal: half-brother to French 9f winner Portobela (by Silver Hawk) and 1¼m winner Try Me (by Singspiel): dam, 1m winner from 2 starts, out of 1000 Guineas winner Sayyedati: useful form: won maiden at Leicester in June: good efforts when placed in handicaps after, last 2 at Ascot (3½ lengths third to Polly's Mark) and Chester (length third to Munsef, looking ill at ease on track): raced only on good going or firmer: has joined Godolphin: remains capable of better, particularly returned to 1¾m+. *M. Johnston* **104 p**

SABOTEUR 2 b.c. (Mar 7) Shamardal (USA) 129 – Croeso Cariad 107 (Most Welcome 131) [2009 6m^{4} p7f^{3} 6m^{4} 7m 8.3d* 8g Oct 23] 130,000Y: small, attractive colt: fourth foal: half-brother to 6-y-o Monmouthshire and a winner in Switzerland by Fantastic Light: dam, 5f (at 2 yrs) and 7.5f winner, half-sister to smart Irish 1½m winner Mona Lisa out of half-sister to Irish Oaks winner Colorspin, herself dam of Kayf Tara and Opera House: fairly useful performer: won maiden at Nottingham in October by 7 lengths: should stay 1¼m: acts on good to firm and good to soft going, probably on polytrack: found little final start: has joined A. bin Huzaim in UAE. *Saeed bin Suroor* **92**

SABRE LIGHT 4 b.g. Fantastic Light (USA) 134 – Good Grounds (USA) (Alleged (USA) 138) [2009 84: p10g* p10g* p9.5g^{3} p10g^{2} 9.8m^{3} a12g a10g a10g* a12g* a10g^{3} Dec 13] compact gelding: fairly useful performer: won claimers at Lingfield and Kempton in January and (after being claimed from J. Pearce £12,000 fourth start) 2 handicaps **90**

at Taby in November: effective at 1m to 1½m: acts on polytrack/dirt and good to firm going: in headgear nowadays. *C. Bjorling, Sweden*

SACCO D'ORO 3 b.f. Rainbow High 121 – Speedy Native (IRE) (Be My Native (USA) 122) [2009 p10m Dec 30] second foal: dam placed in bumper/points: well held in bumpers and in maiden at Lingfield (blinkered). *M. Mullineaux* –

SACRED KINGDOM (AUS) 6 b.g. Encosta de Lago (AUS) – Courtroom Sweetie (AUS) (Zeditave (AUS)) [2009 126: 5g^4 6g^3 7g^6 6m* 6g* 6m^5 6g^2 6g* Dec 13] sturdy, dipped-backed gelding: top-class performer: reported in September 2008 to have suffered hairline fracture of sesamoid bone: took while to find form in 2009, but won Group 2 Sprint Cup at Sha Tin and KrisFlyer International Sprint at Kranji (beat Rocket Man by neck), both in May, and repeated 2007 success when winning Cathay Pacific Hong Kong Sprint at Sha Tin in December by ½ length from One World, coming off strong pace to lead in final 1f: sweated badly prior to below-par 4½ lengths fifth to Art Connoisseur in Golden Jubilee Stakes at Royal Ascot sixth start, leading briefly over 1f out: seems best at 6f: raced only on good/good to firm ground: tongue tied. *P. F. Yiu, Hong Kong* **130**

SACRED STAR (IRE) 2 b.f. (Apr 15) Xaar 132 – Mono Star (IRE) (Soviet Star (USA) 128) [2009 5m^5 5d 5d 5g^6 Jul 8] €6,500Y: good-bodied filly: second foal: dam unraced half-sister to useful sprinters Morinqua and Topkamp: poor maiden: tried blinkered. *M. Brittain* **42**

SADASKA 3 ch.f. Fantastic Light (USA) 134 – Sadaka (USA) 77 (Kingmambo (USA) 125) [2009 p7.1g^3 p7g 10m^6 12m 14.1s^3 16g p12m Sep 30] 9,000Y: fifth foal: sister to fairly useful 1½m to 17f winner Strobe and half-sister to 4-y-o Benhego and 7-y-o Hawridge King: dam 1m winner: modest maiden: stays 1¾m: acts on polytrack and soft going: sold 800 gns. *S. C. Williams* **54**

SADDLERS LODGE 2 b.g. (Feb 10) Motivator 131 – Grandalea 85 (Grand Lodge (USA) 125) [2009 5g^2 6.1g^2 Aug 14] 29,000Y: second foal: dam, 7f winner, half-sister to useful performer up to 1½m Red Peony: better effort in maidens when ½-length second to Society Rock at Nottingham (finished strongly, pair clear) latter outing: will be suited by 1m+: capable of further progress. *G. A. Swinbank* **80 p**

SADEEK 5 ch.g. Kyllachy 129 – Miss Mercy (IRE) 62 (Law Society (USA) 130) [2009 87: 7m 7d 7d 7g p7.1g^4 p7f Dec 21] strong, lengthy gelding: easy walker: has a quick action: just fair handicapper in 2009: stays 7f: acts on polytrack, soft and good to firm ground. *B. Smart* **70**

SADLER'S KINGDOM (IRE) 5 b.g. Sadler's Wells (USA) 132 – Artful Pleasure (USA) (Nasty And Bold (USA)) [2009 82: 12d May 22] good-topped gelding: one-time useful handicapper: poor effort sole 5-y-o start: should stay 2m: winner on good to firm ground, best form on soft. *R. A. Fahey* –

SADLER'S MARK 2 b.c. (Mar 1) Sadler's Wells (USA) 132 – Waldmark (GER) 106 (Mark of Esteem (IRE) 137) [2009 8.3d 8.3v^5 Nov 4] 160,000Y: strong colt: third foal: dam, 2-y-o 7f winner, half-sister to 5-y-o Waldvogel out of smart Deutsches St Leger winner Wurftaube: better effort in maidens at Nottingham when fifth to Green Lightning: bred to be suited by 1¼m+: should improve again. *T. P. Tate* **57 p**

SADLER'S STAR (GER) 6 b.g. Alwuhush (USA) 121 – Sadlerella (IRE) (King's Theatre (IRE) 128) [2009 –: 10s^5 Aug 9] fairly useful in Germany earlier in career: well held in Britain: tried tongue tied: fair maiden hurdler. *A. King* –

SAFARI 6 b.m. Namaqualand (USA) – Breakfast Creek 63 (Hallgate 127) [2009 8.1g 10m^5 11.6m^6 Jul 20] lengthy mare: maiden: little form since 2006: tried blinkered. *S. Curran* –

SAFARI CAMP (IRE) 2 b.c. (Mar 10) Camacho 118 – Consensus (IRE) 91 (Common Grounds 118) [2009 5g^5 5.3m^6 5.1m^6 5m^3 5.1g^3 5.3m 5v 5m 5g^3 5d p5.1g f5m^6 Dec 5] modest maiden: left P. Winkworth £400 after sixth start: raced only at 5f: acts on good to firm ground: tried tongue tied: tends to travel strongly/find little. *A. Berry* **60**

SAFARI GUIDE 3 b.g. Primo Valentino (IRE) 116 – Sabalara (IRE) 61 (Mujadil (USA) 119) [2009 63: 7g^2 7m^2 6s^6 p6g 7g^3 7m^4 p7g^6 8.3v Nov 4] smallish gelding: fair maiden: should be as effective at 6f as 7f (has raced freely): acts on good to firm ground. *P. Winkworth* **76**

SAFARI JOURNEY (USA) 5 ch.h. Johannesburg (USA) 127 – Alvernia (USA) (Alydar (USA)) [2009 10.3g^5 11m^4 Jun 23] tall horse: fair handicapper: successful 3 times in France for T. Clout in 2008: creditable efforts in 2009: stays 1½m: acts on heavy and good to firm ground: fairly useful hurdler/useful chaser. *P. J. Hobbs* **76**

SAFARI MISCHIEF 6 b.g. Primo Valentino (IRE) 116 – Night Gypsy 74 (Mind Games 121) [2009 100: 5m^{4} 5g 5m 5m Jul 26] sturdy gelding: useful handicapper at 5 yrs: just fairly useful in 2009: effective at 5f/6f: acts on polytrack and any turf going: versatile regarding tactics. *P. Winkworth* **91**

SAFARI SONG (IRE) 3 b.c. War Chant (USA) 126 – Leopard Hunt (USA) 89 (Diesis 133) [2009 –: 7d^{2} 8d 7m^{6} Sep 14] good-bodied colt: fair maiden: raced only at 7f/1m: acts on good to soft ground: sold £2,500. *B. Smart* **74**

SAFARI SPECIAL 2 ch.g. (Feb 16) Pastoral Pursuits 127 – Quiz Time 90 (Efisio 120) [2009 5m^{3} 5.1g^{5} p6g^{5} p6f* Oct 14] fair performer: off 3 months and gelded, won claimer at Kempton: will prove best at 5f/6f: acts on polytrack and good to firm ground. *P. Winkworth* **66**

SAFARI SUNUP (IRE) 4 b.g. Catcher In The Rye (IRE) 115 – Nuit Des Temps (Sadler's Wells (USA) 132) [2009 98: 10.1g p10g^{2} 10d^{3} 10.3s^{3} p11g^{2} 12g^{3} 12s Nov 7] compact gelding: useful handicapper: several good efforts in 2009, notably when ½-length second to Charm School at Kempton and 4¾ lengths third to Opinion Poll at Ascot fifth/sixth starts: stays 1½m: acts on polytrack, heavy and good to firm going: reliable. *P. Winkworth* **103**

SAFASEEF (IRE) 4 b.f. Cadeaux Genereux 131 – Asaafeer (USA) (Dayjur (USA) 137) [2009 60: 6m p8g f7f p6f Dec 16] workmanlike filly: maiden: well held in 2009: stays easy 1m: visored last 2 starts. *K. A. Morgan* **–**

SAFEBREAKER 4 b.g. Key of Luck (USA) 126 – Insijaam (USA) 112 (Secretariat (USA)) [2009 77: p8g* f8g* p8g^{2} f8g^{3} 10m* f11g^{2} 12d^{2} 10.1s^{3} 10g^{3} 12m^{2} 12.3m* 12m^{2} 10g^{3} Oct 19] good-topped gelding: fair handicapper: won at Great Leighs in January, Southwell in February, Pontefract (apprentices) in April and Chester (amateurs) in August: stays 1½m: acts on all-weather, soft and good to firm going: usually wears cheek-pieces nowadays: not straightforward, but very consistent. *K. A. Ryan* **78**

SAFE INVESTMENT (USA) 5 b.g. Gone West (USA) – Fully Invested (USA) 99 (Irish River (FR) 131) [2009 60: p8g Mar 4] small gelding: modest performer at 4 yrs: just poor form sole start in 2009: likely to stay 1¼m: raced only on polytrack and good to firm going: tried visored/tongue tied: has been early to post. *B. N. Pollock* **44**

SAFFRON'S SON (IRE) 3 b.g. Saffron Walden (FR) 123 – Try My Rosie 93 (Try My Best (USA) 130) [2009 52: p12.2m 12.1m 12.4g^{6} 12.1m 14.1m^{3} 14.1m^{3} 16.2g^{4} 12.1m^{3} 12.1m^{4} 12d^{4} 13.8m* 10.5s Nov 7] plain gelding: fair performer: won seller at Catterick in September: sold from P. Midgley £800 following month: very stiff task final outing: stays 2m: acts on polytrack and good to firm going: visored/blinkered of late. *R. Ducasteele, Belgium* **65**

SAFINA 2 ch.f. (Jan 29) Pivotal 124 – Russian Rhythm (USA) 123 (Kingmambo (USA) 125) [2009 7g^{3} Oct 31] strong, attractive filly: second foal: dam 6f (at 2 yrs) to 1¼m winner, including 1000 Guineas and Nassau Stakes: 11/4 favourite, promising 3 lengths third to Field Day in maiden at Newmarket, challenging briefly and not unduly knocked about: sure to progress. *Sir Michael Stoute* **75 p**

SAFIN (GER) 9 b.g. Pennekamp (USA) 130 – Sankt Johanna (GER) (High Game) [2009 p12.2g* p12g^{2} p16.5g f14g^{2} p16g f12g* p13.9m f12d^{3} p13.9g^{4} f11g Apr 27] fair handicapper: won at Wolverhampton in January and Southwell in February: stays 1¾m: acts on sand/all-weather and heavy ground: often races freely: joined Mrs S. Bradburne. *R. Curtis* **65**

SAFRANINE (IRE) 12 b.m. Dolphin Street (FR) 125 – Webbiana (African Sky 124) [2009 53: f5g Feb 1] rather leggy mare: modest performer: tailed off sole start at 12 yrs: effective at 5f to 7f: acts on all-weather, firm and soft ground: tried tongue tied/in head-gear. *Miss A. Stokell* **–**

SAGACIOUS (IRE) 2 b.f. (Feb 12) Dalakhani (IRE) 133 – Sadima (IRE) 103 (Sadler's Wells (USA) 132) [2009 8v* Jul 26] fourth foal: sister to 4-y-o Shreyas and half-sister to 5-y-o Creachadoir and 6-y-o Youmzain: dam, Irish 1¼m winner, out of half-sister to Pilsudski: 11/4 and ponied to start, won maiden at the Curragh in July by ½ length from Alsalwa (pair clear), good attitude: will stay at least 1¼m: sure to prove at least useful. *J. S. Bolger, Ireland* **92 P**

SAGA DE TERCEY (FR) 4 b.g. Sagacity (FR) 125 – Fanciulla Del West (USA) (Manila (USA)) [2009 12.5m* 11.5d^{2} 13.8g* 16.4m^{2} 16d* 18m Sep 19] €17,000Y, €47,000 2-y-o: seventh foal: half-brother to 2 winners abroad, including French 1¼m winner Pasar de La Raya (by Trempolino): dam, unraced, out of sister to dam of Dancing Brave: bumper winner: useful handicapper: won at Musselburgh (maiden) in April and **96**

Catterick and Thirsk in August: also ran well when second to Swingkeel at York fourth start: stays 2m: acts on good to firm and good to soft going. *G. A. Swinbank*

SAGARA (USA) 5 b.g. Sadler's Wells (USA) 132 – Rangoon Ruby (USA) 105 (Kingmambo (USA) 125) [2009 118: 12m^5 20m^4 Jun 18] leggy, useful-looking gelding: smart performer at 4 yrs: below form in listed race at Goodwood and Gold Cup at Royal Ascot (distant fourth to Yeats, typically looking awkward) in 2009: stays 2½m: acts on firm and good to soft ground: wore cheekpieces third start at 3 yrs, visored last 4 outings: has raced lazily: has left Godolphin. *Saeed bin Suroor* **104**

SAGARICH (FR) 5 gr.m. Sagamix (FR) 129 – Baranciaga (USA) (Bering 136) [2009 73: 10.1d 10g^3 12.1g 12m Sep 25] rather leggy mare: just poor handicapper nowadays: effective at 1¼m to 2m: acts on heavy and good to firm going: has been slowly away. *M. G. Quinlan* **49**

SAGGIATORE 2 b.f. (Apr 24) Galileo (IRE) 134 – Madame Dubois 121 (Legend of France (USA) 124) [2009 8m Sep 18] closely related to useful 1½m winner and excellent broodmare Place de l'Opera (by Sadler's Wells) and half-sister to several winners, including smart 6f (at 2 yrs) to 1m (Irish 2000 Guineas) winner Indian Haven (by Indian Ridge): dam 9f to 14.6f (Park Hill Stakes) winner: 40/1, down the field in maiden at Newmarket: bred to be well suited by 1¼m+. *E. A. L. Dunlop* **53**

SAGREDO (USA) 5 b.g. Diesis 133 – Eternity 77 (Suave Dancer (USA) 136) [2009 16m 14.1s f14g^5 p12.2g^4 Nov 16] tall, useful-looking gelding: useful handicapper in 2007: unraced on Flat in 2008: fair nowadays: probably stays 1¾m: acts on polytrack, soft and good to firm going: patiently ridden: fair form over hurdles. *Jonjo O'Neill* **78**

SAGUNT (GER) 6 ch.g. Tertullian (USA) 115 – Suva (GER) (Arazi (USA) 135) [2009 63: p12.2g 10.9m* 12m* 11.9g^2 12.1v* 12s^5 Oct 6] workmanlike gelding: fair handicapper: won at Warwick in April, Folkestone in June and Chepstow (amateurs) in July: stays 1½m: acts on polytrack, heavy and good to firm going: not the easiest of rides. *S. Curran* **77**

SAHAAL (USA) 3 b.c. Rahy (USA) 115 – Thaminah (USA) 91 (Danzig (USA)) [2009 8.3g 8m^3 9.9g 7g^6 7g^3 8f* 8.5m^5 p10g Oct 22] good-topped colt: first foal: dam, 2-y-o 6f winner, out of sister to dam of 1000 Guineas winner Ghanaati and close relative to Nayef/half-sister to Nashwan and Unfuwain: fairly useful performer: won maiden at Bath in August: may prove best at 1m: acts on firm ground: tried in cheekpieces, tongue tied last 4 starts: sold 14,000 gns. *M. P. Tregoning* **82**

SAHARA KINGDOM (IRE) 2 gr.c. (Apr 5) Cozzene (USA) – Rose Indien (FR) 108 (Crystal Glitters (USA) 127) [2009 p7g* p7g* Nov 5] 50,000F, €200,000Y: closely related to US 8.5f minor stakes winner Salty Sea (by Siberian Express) and half-brother to several winners there: dam, 6f/7f winner (including at 2 yrs and in US), half-sister to smart French/US performer up to 1½m Majorien: created most favourable impression when winning maiden (by 3¼ lengths from Essexbridge) and 4-runner minor event (beat Ongoodform 5 lengths, again slowly away but able to coast final 1f) within a month at Lingfield: should stay 1m: smart prospect, open to considerable improvement. *Saeed bin Suroor* **98 P**

SAHARAN ROYAL 3 b.f. Val Royal (FR) 127 – Saharan Song (IRE) 64 (Singspiel (IRE) 133) [2009 70: 8m p10g p10m Dec 16] maiden: fair at 2 yrs: no form in 2009, said to have finished lame on reappearance: should stay 1m+. *Matthew Salaman* **–**

SAHARA PRINCE (IRE) 9 b.g. Desert King (IRE) 129 – Chehana 78 (Posse (USA) 130) [2009 –: p8g Jan 11] tall gelding: modest performer in 2007: little form since: usually wears headgear. *K. A. Morgan* **–**

SAHARA SUNSHINE 4 b.f. Hernando (FR) 127 – Sahara Sunrise (USA) (Houston (USA)) [2009 p16g 11.6g 11.5m^3 10m 11.5s Aug 7] ex-French-trained filly: sixth foal: sister to useful French 1m (at 2 yrs)/1¼m winner Shifting Sands and fairly useful French 9f winner Sand Dune: dam unraced close relation of Ribblesdale Stakes winner Sahara Slew: fair maiden: sold from Y. de Nicolay €26,000 after final 3-y-o start: stays 12.5f: acts on firm and soft ground. *Mrs L. J. Mongan* **69**

SAHARIA (IRE) 2 b.c. (May 1) Oratorio (IRE) 128 – Inchiri 108 (Sadler's Wells (USA) 132) [2009 p6m p7.1g* Dec 5] 37,000Y: fifth foal: half-brother to useful 11.6f to 13f winner Inchwood (by Dubai Destination), 3-y-o Hawk's Eye and 5-y-o Celtic Step: dam, 1¼m/1½m winner, out of half-sister to smart performer up to 1m Inchinor: easily better effort in maidens when winning at Wolverhampton readily by ½ length from Barreq, still green (wanted to hang): will stay 1¼m+: open to further improvement. *J. Noseda* **83 p**

SAHPRESA (USA) 4 b.f. Sahm (USA) 112 – Sorpresa (USA) (Pleasant Tap (USA)) [2009 112: 8g* 8m2 8d4 8m2 8m* 8f3 Nov 22] **118**

Some unpredictable results in the last fillies' Group 1 mile of the European season, the Sun Chariot Stakes at Newmarket, have meant that the list of fillies beaten in the race includes names that are more illustrious than those of some recent winners. Ghanaati, 6/5 favourite for the latest renewal, was the latest One Thousand Guineas winner to meet with defeat, hot on the heels of Speciosa, beaten as a four-year-old in 2007, and Virginia Waters, who finished last in 2005. Spinning Queen was the outsider of five when beating a field that included Soviet Song, Alexander Goldrun and Red Evie in 2006, and Majestic Roi was another long-shot, winning at 16/1 in 2007. Irish One Thousand Guineas winner Halfway To Heaven was a classic winner who fared better, though her victory in 2008 came at the chief expense of another short-priced favourite, Darjina.

Darjina's trainer, Alain de Royer Dupre, was represented in the latest Sun Chariot by Alnadana but it was the other French-trained four-year-old, 16/1-shot Sahpresa, who became the latest filly to upset the form-book in the Kingdom of Bahrain-sponsored contest. As well as a wintry-looking Ghanaati, Sahpresa's three-year-old rivals included Strawberrydaiquiri, who had completed a hat-trick in listed races, and the Nell Gwyn winner Fantasia, while the older brigade included the Cheveley Park Stud pair Spacious and Heaven Sent who had come first and second in the Windsor Forest Stakes at Royal Ascot. Spacious made the running and Ghanaati made hard work of getting past her from over a furlong out, only for Sahpresa, travelling strongly, to emerge from the pack to beat them both, winning by a length and a half from Ghanaati with the same distance back to Spacious in third. Those held up, notably Strawberrydaiquiri and Fantasia, who finished fourth and sixth respectively, failed to land any sort of blow.

The Sun Chariot was Sahpresa's second visit to Newmarket, where she had finished fourth in the Darley Stakes the previous autumn. That was only the fourth start of Sahpresa's career which did not begin until the summer of her three-year-old season. She made an eye-catching start, winning a newcomers race at Maisons-Laffitte by eight lengths, and made virtually all for a six-length win in a listed race at Saint-Cloud on her third outing. It seemed only a matter of time before she made her mark in better company, an impression reinforced by another clear-cut success (by three lengths) in a listed race at Longchamp on her reappearance in May. Sahpresa ran at least respectably in defeat in pattern company before the Sun Chariot, though it was still a surprise when her first pattern success came in a Group 1. She finished second to Beacon Lodge in the Prix du Chemin de Fer du Nord at Chantilly and was beaten three quarters of a length by Racinger in the Prix Quincey at Deauville, either side of a fourth place behind Goldikova in the Prix Rothschild, also at Deauville. Sahpresa had one more run after the Sun Chariot.

Kingdom of Bahrain Sun Chariot Stakes, Newmarket—French-trained four-year-old Sahpresa upsets favourite Ghanaati (left); Spacious (partially hidden) and Strawberrydaiquiri are next

Already proven on firm ground, she was sent to Japan for the Mile Championship at Kyoto and, without quite repeating her Newmarket form, she earned the equivalent of around £170,000 when beaten a length and a half into third behind the improved eight-year-old Japanese horse Company. Eva's Request, the other European-trained runner, finished tenth.

Sahpresa comes from an unexceptional American family but her sire is the very well-bred Sahm, who is by Mr Prospector out of Salsabil. Sahm looked like living up to his breeding initially, winning his first two starts at York, but was a disappointing favourite for the National Stakes on his final outing at two for John Dunlop. His career resumed in the States after a wind operation, and after he recovered from fracturing a pastern. He gained his biggest success there as a four-year-old in the Grade 2 Knickerbocker Handicap. Sahm died early in 2007, his best runner at that time the very smart Irish horse at up to a mile and a quarter Mustameet. Sahpresa's seven-year-old brother Monfils Monfils won in France earlier in his career and has shown himself a fairly useful handicapper at best in Britain in the last couple of seasons, winning at up to a mile and a half. In between, the dam Sorpresa produced Miofilio Miofilio (by Dayjur), a winner at around a mile and a half in France and successful over hurdles there in 2009. Sorpresa won three times at around a mile in the States and is a half-sister to numerous winners, including some fair performers in Britain. Sahpresa's grandam Dubiously won as a two-year-old in the States, including in a minor stakes event, and was a half-sister to Bill E. Shears, a winner of three Grade 3 events at around a mile who was twice placed in Grade 1 company.

Sahpresa (USA) (b.f. 2005)	Sahm (USA) (b 1994)	Mr Prospector (b 1970)	Raise A Native Gold Digger
		Salsabil (b 1987)	Sadler's Wells Flame of Tara
	Sorpresa (USA) (b or br 1996)	Pleasant Tap (b 1987)	Pleasant Colony Never Knock
		Dubiously (b 1987)	Jolie Jo Skeptic Lady

The good-topped Sahpresa has raced only at a mile and nine furlongs so far, though she would prove effective at a mile and a quarter given the chance, something which would increase the options of her connections. She has run respectably on good to soft ground, but all her wins have come on good ground or firmer and her best chance of further top-level success might still come outside France, perhaps across the Atlantic. She has already given her trainer Rodolphe Collet, son of Robert Collet, his biggest success to date, and, with just ten races behind her, making the frame each time, there may be more victories to come. *Rodolphe Collet, France*

SAHRATI 5 ch.g. In The Wings 128 – Shimna 62 (Mr Prospector (USA)) [2009 98, **96**
a77+: p12g^2 12s^2 p12g^6 12m^5 10.3s^5 12m Aug 19] leggy gelding: useful handicapper on **a80**
turf, fairly useful on all-weather: creditable efforts when runner-up first 2 starts: below form after: barely stays 1¾m: acts on polytrack, firm and soft ground: wears headgear: none too genuine: joined A. King, fair form over hurdles. *D. R. C. Elsworth*

SAIF AL FAHAD (IRE) 3 ch.c. Shinko Forest (IRE) – Golden Ciel (USA) (Septieme Ciel (USA) 123) [2009 76: 5.1m^4 6g May 19] fair performer: should stay 7f: acts on all-weather, good to firm and good to soft going. *E. J. O'Neill* **76**

SAINGLEND 4 b.g. Galileo (IRE) 134 – Verbal Intrigue (USA) (Dahar (USA) 125) [2009 81: 11.6m^5 Jun 1] tall gelding: fairly useful handicapper (similar standard over hurdles): respectable effort sole 4-y-o start: may prove best short of 11.6f: acts on firm and good to soft going. *S. Curran* **76**

SAINT ARCH (CAN) 3 b.g. Arch (USA) 127 – Halo Silver (USA) (Silver Buck (USA)) [2009 98p: p8g* p8g^6 10.1g^5 Apr 22] tall, attractive gelding: useful performer: further progress when winning handicap at Kempton in March by 2½ lengths from Royal Executioner: subsequently below form (gelded after final start): should stay 1¼m: acts on polytrack and soft ground (unraced on firmer than good). *M. Johnston* **100**

SAINT CHAPELLE (IRE) 3 b.f. Noverre (USA) 125 – Chartres (IRE) 105 (Danehill (USA) 126) [2009 56p: p12m 10.2m^6 Sep 28] modest form sole 2-y-o start: no form at 3 yrs. *Mrs A. J. Perrett* **–**

SAINTS BAY (IRE) 3 b.f. Redback 116 – Alexander Eliott (IRE) 73 (Night Shift (USA)) [2009 p7g³ p6g² p6g³ p7g 6m Apr 26] 28,000Y: fourth foal: half-sister to 4-y-o Artistic License and 6-y-o Brandywell Boy: dam Irish maiden (stayed 1¼m): modest maiden: finished lame final outing. *R. Hannon* **56**

SAINT SEBASTIAN (IRE) 2 ch.c. (Mar 27) Captain Rio 122 – Paris Song (IRE) 69 (Peintre Celebre (USA) 137) [2009 6d⁴ 6m² 5m⁶ 5.9g⁴ 6s³ p7.1g 5m⁵ 6.1s² Oct 7] close-coupled colt: modest maiden: stays 6f: acts on soft and good to firm going: tried in cheekpieces: races prominently: sold £5,200, sent to Sweden. *E. S. McMahon* **57**

SAINT THOMAS (IRE) 2 b.c. (Apr 8) Alhaarth (IRE) 126 – Aguilas Perla (IRE) (Indian Ridge 123) [2009 7f³ 7.1m p8.6g⁴ 8.3d p8g² p10m² Nov 21] €40,000Y: fourth foal: half-brother to 3 winners, including fairly useful Irish 2006 2-y-o 5f/6.5f winner Spirit of Pearl (by Invincible Spirit): dam unraced sister to useful Irish 7f winner Cool Clarity: fair maiden: stays 1¼m: acts on polytrack and firm going: blinkered fourth start: ridden prominently: claimed £8,000 after final start then gelded. *J. A. Osborne* **70**

SAIRAAM (IRE) 3 b. or br.f. Marju (IRE) 127 – Sayedati Eljamilah (USA) 64 (Mr Prospector (USA)) [2009 61: 8.5g 10g⁵ 8m 16.2g 8m 10.1m 7m* 7m³ 7g⁴ 7m³ 8.3v f7m⁴ p9.5g⁴ f7f p9.5g Dec 28] close-coupled filly: modest performer: sold from J. Dunlop 3,000 gns after third start: won seller at Yarmouth in September: effective at 7f to 1¼m: acts on all-weather and good to firm going: has found little: none too consistent. *C. Smith* **61**

SAKHEE'S PEARL 3 gr.f. Sakhee (USA) 136 – Grey Pearl 97 (Ali-Royal (IRE) 127) [2009 73p: 7g* 7g⁴ 6g⁶ p7.1g⁴ 7v Oct 24] close-coupled filly: fairly useful performer: won maiden at Doncaster in July: stays 7f: acts on polytrack, best turf efforts on good ground. *Miss Gay Kelleway* **89**

SAKILE 2 ch.f. (Apr 20) Johannesburg (USA) 127 – Crooked Wood (USA) 93 (Woodman (USA) 126) [2009 6m⁵ 5f⁶ p5g³ p5g* Nov 21] second foal: dam, 2-y-o 7f/1m winner (later won in USA), out of US Grade 2 1½m winner Crockadore: fair performer: made all in maiden at Lingfield: likely to prove best at 5f: acts on polytrack. *P. W. Chapple-Hyam* **78**

SALADIN'S VOW (USA) 2 ch.c. (Apr 17) Broken Vow (USA) 117 – Morena Park 105 (Pivotal 124) [2009 6m p7m Sep 30] down the field in maidens at Newmarket and Kempton (blinkered, still green). *G. A. Butler* **–**

SALAMON 3 gr.f. Montjeu (IRE) 137 – Farfala (FR) 106 (Linamix (FR) 127) [2009 –p: 8.3g 10.2v⁴ 7d⁵ 9.9m⁵ Aug 30] close-coupled filly: modest maiden: should stay beyond 1¼m: best effort on heavy ground: tongue tied once: sold 115,000 gns. *P. F. I. Cole* **57**

SALDEN LICHT 5 b.g. Fantastic Light (USA) 134 – Salde (GER) (Alkalde (GER)) [2009 p8.6g 8s 10v³ 12s⁵ Nov 7] ex-French gelding: half-brother to several winners in Germany, including 1¼m/1½m performers Saldentigerin (smart, by Tiger Hill) and Saldenschwinge (useful, by In The Wings): dam German 1m/9f winner: useful performer: has won 3 times, including listed race at Chantilly in 2007 and minor event at Vichy in 2008: left A. Fabre and off 12 months prior to reappearance: best effort in 2009 when 2¼ lengths third to Rainbow Peak in handicap at Newbury: respectable fifth to Charm School in November Handicap at Doncaster final start: stays 1½m: acts on heavy ground: joined A. King, successful on hurdling debut in December. *J. M. P. Eustace* **102**

SALEROSA (IRE) 4 b.f. Monashee Mountain (USA) 115 – Sainte Gig (FR) (Saint Cyrien (FR) 128) [2009 68: 9.9m⁶ 7.5m² 8.5g* 8f⁴ 8m* 9.2g³ 8v 7g³ 8.5m 7.5g³ f7g* 7g⁵ f8g² f8m* f8f* Dec 11] sturdy filly: fairly useful handicapper: won at Beverley in May, Ayr in June and Southwell (5 wins from 6 starts there) in September, November and December: effective at 7f to 8.5f: acts on all-weather and good to firm ground: sometimes pulls hard. *Mrs A. Duffield* **86**

SALIENT 5 b.g. Fasliyev (USA) 120 – Savannah Belle 84 (Green Desert (USA) 127) [2009 96: 8.3m⁴ 7.1m⁴ 7m p8g³ 7.1d p8g 8.1m⁶ 8g⁴ p7g⁴ 8.1g⁶ 7g⁴ 7m³ 8m 8d p7g f8m Nov 6] sturdy, compact gelding: fairly useful handicapper: stays 1m: acts on polytrack, soft and good to firm ground: races prominently. *M. J. Attwater* **88**

SALLY FORTH 3 b.f. Dubai Destination (USA) 127 – Daralbayda (IRE) 102 (Doyoun 124) [2009 12m⁶ 12.6m³ 12g³ f16g* 16m⁵ Sep 30] tall filly: half-sister to several winners in France, including smart 1¼m to 15f winner Darkara (by Halling) and useful 1½m winner Darinska (by Zilzal), now dam of high-class miler Darjina: dam, French 1½m winner, half-sister to dam of Prix du Jockey Club winner Darsi: fairly useful performer on all-weather, fair on turf: easily best effort when wide-margin winner of handicap at Southwell in August: stays 2m: acts on fibresand. *R. Charlton* **71** **a89**

SALLY O'RILEY 3 ch.f. Vettori (IRE) 119 – Swallow Breeze 62 (Salse (USA) 128) [2009 10m 9.3d Jul 26] 800Y: fourth foal: dam 2-y-o 1¼m winner: tailed off in maidens, in cheekpieces on second start. *F. Watson* –

SALLY'S DILEMMA 3 b.f. Primo Valentino (IRE) 116 – Lake Mistassiu 86 (Tina's Pet 121) [2009 83d: f6d^5 f7s^4 Jan 6] sturdy filly: won minor event at Doncaster on 2-y-o debut: has regressed since: wore cheekpieces final outing, tongue tied 6 starts prior to that. *W. G. M. Turner* –

SALLY'S SWANSONG 3 b.f. Mind Games 121 – Sister Sal 74 (Bairn (USA) 126) [2009 –: 6m p7.1g f7g 6d 6.1g^5 6d Jul 24] poor maiden: in cheekpieces last 4 starts. *M. Wellings* **41**

SALONTIGER (GER) 7 b.g. Tiger Hill (IRE) 127 – She's His Guest (IRE) (Be My Guest (USA) 126) [2009 10.2g May 26] fairly useful performer in Germany earlier in career for A. Kleinkorres: well held in handicap at Chepstow sole start in Britain: stays 1m: acts on soft ground. *P. J. Hobbs* –

SALOON (USA) 5 b.g. Sadler's Wells (USA) 132 – Fire The Groom (USA) 115 (Blushing Groom (FR) 131) [2009 64: p12g* p13.9g^2 12m* 11.9m^2 12m^3 14.6m^2 14.8g^4 12m 12g^2 14.6g p12m^4 f14g^2 Dec 8] leggy gelding: fairly useful handicapper: improved in 2009, winning at Kempton in April and Goodwood in May: in frame 7 times after: stays 14.6f: acts on all-weather, soft and good to firm going: tried tongue tied, wore cheekpieces in 2009: often looks uncooperative, and probably best coming off strong pace: one to treat with caution. *Jane Chapple-Hyam* **84 §**

SALTAGIOO (ITY) 5 b.g. Dr Devious (IRE) 127 – Sces (Kris 135) [2009 94: p8.6g^4 p8g^2 p8g* p8g 8m^3 10.3m 8g 8.1g* 9.7f Sep 7] sturdy gelding: fairly useful performer: won handicap at Kempton in March and claimer at Sandown (claimed from M. Botti £15,000) in July: effective at 1m/1¼m: acts on polytrack, heavy and good to firm ground: sometimes tongue tied: joined A. King, modest form over hurdles. *I. A. Wood* **94**

SALT OF THE EARTH (IRE) 4 b.g. Invincible Spirit (IRE) 121 – Get The Accountant (Vettori (IRE) 119) [2009 77: p8g^5 p7.1g^3 p8g p7g^4 p8g^3 7f 8m p7g Jun 3] fair handicapper: possibly amiss last 3 starts: free-going sort, but stays easy 1m: acts on polytrack: tried in cheekpieces. *T. G. Mills* – **a69**

SALUSCRAGGIE 7 b.m. Most Welcome 131 – Upper Caen (High Top 131) [2009 67: 12m^2 13g May 3] workmanlike mare: modest handicapper: broke leg at Hamilton: was effective at 1¼m to 1¾m: acted on firm and soft going: tried in cheekpieces: had flashed tail, and wasn't easiest of rides: dead. *R. E. Barr* **64**

SALUTE HIM (IRE) 6 b.g. Mull of Kintyre (USA) 114 – Living Legend (ITY) (Archway (IRE) 115) [2009 99: 10g 10m* 10f^3 9m Oct 3] big gelding: useful handicapper: won at Navan in June: more progress when ¾-length third to Perfect Stride in listed Wolferton Handicap at Royal Ascot, closing strongly from poor position: off 4 months, eased once held in Cambridgeshire at Newmarket final start: effective at 1¼m to 13f: acts on any going: usually slowly away/held up. *A. J. Martin, Ireland* **107**

SALUTE (IRE) 10 b.g. Muhtarram (USA) 125 – Alasib 93 (Siberian Express (USA) 125) [2009 81, a86: p16g^2 p16g^6 p13.9g* p16g^3 p16g f12g p16g^5 p16g^6 p13.9g Sep 11] lengthy, quite attractive gelding: fairly useful handicapper: won at Wolverhampton in March: stays 16.5f: acts on polytrack, firm and soft going: tried in headgear: often races up with pace: edgy sort. *P. G. Murphy* **83**

SALUT SAINT CLOUD 8 b.g. Primo Dominie 121 – Tiriana (Common Grounds 118) [2009 62: p13g p16g 16g May 29] close-coupled gelding: modest handicapper in 2008: well held at 8 yrs (said to have finished lame final start): has worn headgear, often in cheekpieces. *G. L. Moore* –

SALVATION 2 b.f. (Mar 20) Montjeu (IRE) 137 – Birdie 99 (Alhaarth (IRE) 126) [2009 8.3v Nov 4] 70,000Y: unfurnished filly: third foal: dam 1m to 11.5f winner: 10/1 and green, well held in maiden at Nottingham, hampered early: should do better. *M. L. W. Bell* **– p**

SALYBIA BAY 3 b.f. Fraam 114 – Down The Valley 73 (Kampala 120) [2009 70: 8.3m 10.2g 10.2g^2 11.6m^2 12m^2 12m^3 11.6g p12g^4 10d 12m^2 p12m^4 p12m^2 9.9g^3 10g^3 p10g^3 Nov 14] sturdy filly: fair maiden handicapper: stays 1½m: acts on polytrack and good to firm going. *R. Hannon* **68**

SAMAAHA 3 b.f. Singspiel (IRE) 133 – Genovefa (USA) 107 (Woodman (USA) 126) [2009 10.2v^2 10m^3 11.5m^2 p12g* p16m^2 p16.5g^5 Nov 14] lengthy filly: closely related to 2 winners by In The Wings, notably very smart middle-distance stayer Mamool (1m winner at 2 yrs), and half-sister to 2 winners, including useful French 1999 2-y-o 1m **83**

winner Ejlaal (by Caerleon): dam French 1¼m/1½m winner: fairly useful performer: won maiden at Kempton (made all) in September: creditable efforts in handicaps after: stays 2m: acts on polytrack and good to firm going: has left Godolphin: sent to UAE. *Saeed bin Suroor*

SAMARINDA (USA) 6 ch.g. Rahy (USA) 115 – Munnaya (USA) 101 (Nijinsky (CAN) 138) [2009 –, a103: p8g^3 p8g^6 p8.6g p8g^4 p8g^6 8m 8m p8m Dec 4] good-topped gelding: useful handicapper on all-weather: best efforts in 2009 at Kempton on fourth/fifth starts, including when fourth to Mahadee: just fair form on turf in 2009: best at 1m/1¼m: acts on polytrack. *Mrs P. Sly* **76 a100**

SAMBA MIRANDER 3 b.f. Zaha (CAN) 106 – Silent Scream (IRE) (Lahib (USA) 129) [2009 –: p10g^3 p11g Jul 1] medium-sized filly: modest maiden: stays 1¼m: tried in cheekpieces. *C. Drew* **59**

SAMBULANDO (FR) 6 gr.g. Kouroun (FR) 112 – Somnambula (IRE) (Petoski 135) [2009 f11g^2 Feb 20] fairly useful maiden for J-M. Beguigne in France in 2006: plenty of encouragement when runner-up in maiden at Southwell on British debut: stays 1¾m: fairly useful hurdler, successful twice in 2009/10. *T. R. George* **70 +**

SAMIZDAT (FR) 6 b.g. Soviet Star (USA) 128 – Secret Account (FR) (Bering 136) [2009 12m^5 12.4s^5 10.1m^5 12.4d Oct 13] fair performer for E. Libaud in France in 2006, winning maiden at Saumur: modest in Britain (including over hurdles): left James Moffatt after third start: stays 15f: acts on good to soft ground: wears headgear, also tongue tied final start. *Mrs Dianne Sayer* **62**

SAM JICARO 2 b.g. (Feb 17) Mind Games 121 – Claradotnet 82 (Sri Pekan (USA) 117) [2009 6d 7g Aug 2] showed little in maidens at Ripon and Chester: subsequently gelded. *Mrs L. Williamson* **–**

SAM LORD 5 ch.g. Observatory (USA) 131 – My Mariam 79 (Salse (USA) 128) [2009 89: p12g 12m^5 14m 14.1g* 14.8g^5 Jul 18] stocky, close-coupled gelding: fairly useful handicapper (including over hurdles): won at Salisbury in June: stays 1¾m: acts on polytrack, good to firm and good to soft ground: sold £25,000, joined James Moffatt. *A. King* **91**

SAMMY THE SNAKE (IRE) 4 b.g. Diktat 126 – Love Emerald (USA) (Mister Baileys 123) [2009 p6g^5 7.1g 6m p8g p7.1g 8.3g Oct 19] workmanlike gelding: fairly useful form when winning maiden at 2 yrs: missed 2008: seemingly similar standard when last of 5 in minor event at Kempton on return, but well below form after: bred to stay 7f/1m: tried blinkered/in cheekpieces: reportedly had breathing problem fifth outing. *B. W. Duke* **91 d**

SAMPI 3 ch.f. Beat Hollow 126 – Delta (Zafonic (USA) 130) [2009 86p: 9.9m 9g Aug 30] big, rangy filly: fairly useful 2-y-o winner: well held in handicaps both outings in 2009, tongue tied final one: should stay 1¼m/1½m: sold 10,000 gns, sent to Bahrain. *Mrs A. J. Perrett* **–**

SAMPOWER QUIN (IRE) 3 b.g. Sampower Star 118 – Quinolina (Shareef Dancer (USA) 135) [2009 68: 12.1g 10.3g 10f p12.2g 11.5g Oct 20] unfurnished gelding: maiden: fair form on final 2-y-o start: well held in 2009: stays 1m: acts on soft ground: tried blinkered. *D. Carroll* **–**

SAMPOWER ROSE (IRE) 3 b.f. Sampower Star 118 – Rosebank (USA) (El Prado (IRE) 119) [2009 68: 8d 8.5g 8.1g^2 10s 8s^2 8.5g p7.1g 8g Oct 20] angular filly: fair handicapper: stays 1m: acts on firm and soft going: tried blinkered. *D. Carroll* **71**

SAMPOWER SARGE (IRE) 3 b.f. Sampower Star 118 – Desert Skimmer (USA) 44 (Shadeed (USA) 135) [2009 p7.1g Jan 22] seventh foal: half-sister to 2 winners abroad: dam, sprint maiden, half-sister to smart 7f/1m performer Vanderlin: 50/1, well held in maiden at Wolverhampton. *D. Carroll* **–**

SAMPOWER SHAMROCK (IRE) 3 b.f. Sampower Star 118 – Sans Escale (USA) (Diesis 133) [2009 p7.1g f6g^6 Feb 1] €20,000F: half-sister to several winners, notably smart 5f/6.5f (including at 2 yrs and in UAE) winner Cartography (by Zafonic) and useful 1m winner West Escape (by Gone West): dam, useful French 11f winner, out of Prix de Diane winner Escaline: well held in maidens. *D. Carroll* **44**

SAM'S CROSS (IRE) 4 b.g. Cape Cross (IRE) 129 – Fancy Lady 99 (Cadeaux Genereux 131) [2009 85: p8g p7g^4 6m^4 6m^3 6g^4 6m 6m* 7m 6d 6m^5 7g 6g^6 p7f 7m p6m* p6g p6m p6m^6 Dec 30] rather leggy gelding: fair performer: left K. R. Burke after second start: won seller at Brighton (left Pat Eddery 3,500 gns) in July and handicap at Kempton in September: effective at 6f to easy 1m: acts on polytrack, firm and good to soft going: tried in headgear/tongue tie: none too consistent. *J. J. Bridger* **73**

SAM SHARP (USA) 3 b. or br.g. Johannesburg (USA) 127 – Caffe (USA) (Mr Prospector (USA)) [2009 64p: p8g^{2} 10d* 10.1g 10d^{6} p8g 10.3m^{6} 12m^{5} 11m^{2} 10.4g^{4} Oct 10] rather leggy gelding: fairly useful performer: won maiden at Newbury in May: stays 11f: acts on polytrack, good to firm and good to soft going: tried tongue tied. *H. R. A. Cecil* **85**

SAMS LASS 3 b.f. Refuse To Bend (IRE) 128 – Dina Line (USA) 60 (Diesis 133) [2009 60p: 6g 7g 6g* Jul 21] strong filly: easily best effort in maidens when winning at Ffos Las in July, soon dominating: bred to stay 1m: open to further improvement. *D. Nicholls* **76 p**

SAMSON QUEST 7 b.g. Cyrano de Bergerac 120 – Zenita (IRE) (Zieten (USA) 118) [2009 51: p8g* p8g^{4} Jan 11] sturdy gelding: modest performer: won minor event at Lingfield in January: stays easy 1¼m: acts on polytrack and good to firm going: formerly in headgear. *B. Smart* **52**

SAM'S SECRET 7 b.m. Josr Algarhoud (IRE) 118 – Twilight Time (Aragon 118) [2009 97: 7m 7f^{3} 7m 8m^{4} 7g^{5} Jun 20] quite good-topped mare: fairly useful performer: not at best in 2009: free-going sort, best up to 1m: acts on polytrack and firm going: tried in visor/cheekpieces, not since 2006: held up: tough. *G. A. Swinbank* **86**

SAMS SPIRIT 3 br.g. Diktat 126 – Winning Girl (Green Desert (USA) 127) [2009 61?: p8g^{6} 7d 7.5m Apr 15] maiden: little form at 3 yrs. *P. J. McBride* **–**

SAMURAI WARRIOR 4 br.g. Beat All (USA) 120 – Ma Vie 69 (Salse (USA) 128) [2009 70: p10g* p10g^{2} p9.5g^{3} p8.6g^{2} p8.6g^{6} 8.1g 10g* 10.2f* p10g 11.6g 8f^{3} 10.3m^{3} 10.2m 10.1s^{2} 10.2g^{2} 14.1m Aug 13] compact gelding: fair performer: won handicaps at Great Leighs (apprentices) in January and Lingfield and Bath in May: left P. D. Evans £6,000 after penultimate start: effective at 7f to 1¼m: acts on polytrack and firm ground, probably on soft: tried in blinkers/cheekpieces. *Jamie Snowden* **76**

SANA ABEL (IRE) 3 b.f. Alhaarth (IRE) 126 – Midway Lady (USA) 126 (Alleged (USA) 138) [2009 8d^{4} 10.1d^{6} 10m^{5} 11.7g^{4} p12g^{2} 11.7g 14m* Oct 1] rather leggy filly: closely related to smart 1¼m/1½m (Oaks) winner Eswarah (by Unfuwain) and half-sister to numerous winners, including smart 9f to 1½m winner Itnab (by Green Desert): dam won 1000 Guineas and Oaks: fair performer: won maiden at Goodwood in October: stayed 1¾m: acted on polytrack, unraced on extremes of going on turf: in cheekpieces last 3 outings: visits Teofilo. *M. A. Jarvis* **78**

SAN ANTONIO 9 b.g. Efisio 120 – Winnebago 63 (Kris 135) [2009 82: 8.1g^{2} Jun 18] strong, well-made gelding: has a round action: fairly useful handicapper: stays 1m: acts on polytrack and any turf going: tried in cheekpieces: blinkered: usually front runner. *Mrs P. Sly* **83**

SA NAU 6 b.g. Generous (IRE) 139 – Trellis Bay 100 (Sadler's Wells (USA) 132) [2009 p16.5g p16g Oct 14] rather leggy, quite good-topped gelding: modest handicapper in 2007: off almost 2 years, well held on return. *T. Keddy* **–**

SAN CASSIANO (IRE) 2 b.g. (May 4) Bertolini (USA) 125 – Celtic Silhouette (FR) (Celtic Swing 138) [2009 p6g* 6g^{3} Sep 30] third foal: closely related to useful 2007 2-y-o 7f/1m winner Celtic Slipper (by Anabaa) and half-brother to 3-y-o Dreamwalk: dam, French maiden (stayed 11.5f), sister to smart performer up to 2m Celtic Silence and 5-y-o Royal And Regal: won maiden at Kempton in September by length from Locksley Hall: good 3 lengths third to Mon Cadeaux in minor event at Salisbury (still green, strong at finish): will stay 7f: open to further progress. *R. M. Beckett* **92 p**

SANCHO PANZA 2 b.g. (Feb 21) Zafeen (FR) 123 – Malvadilla (IRE) 77 (Doyoun 124) [2009 p6g 7g f6g Aug 10] close-coupled gelding: little form. *Miss J. Feilden* **–**

SANCTUARY 3 ch.g. Dr Fong (USA) 128 – Wondrous Maid (GER) (Mondrian (GER) 125) [2009 10.1d^{3} 10.4g^{2} 10.4m* 9.9m^{4} 12s^{2} 13g Sep 20] 10,000Y: rather leggy gelding: fourth foal: dam, German 1¼m winner, half-sister to dam of Nassau Stakes winner Zahrat Dubai: fairly useful performer: won maiden at Haydock in June: good second in handicap at Thirsk penultimate start: stays 1½m: acts on soft and good to firm ground. *B. Smart* **87**

SANCTUM 3 b.f. Medicean 128 – Auspicious 103 (Shirley Heights 130) [2009 p10g p10g 10m^{5} Aug 9] 1,100 2-y-o: leggy filly: fifth foal: half-sister to several fairly useful winners, including 4-y-o Istiqdaam and 6-y-o Prince Picasso: dam, 1¼m winner, sister to smart middle-distance stayer Sacrament: best effort in maidens (modest form) when fifth at Windsor. *Dr J. D. Scargill* **60**

SAN DENG 7 gr.g. Averti (IRE) 117 – Miss Mirror 77 (Magic Mirror 105) [2009 62: 15.8m^{5} 16m^{4} Apr 13] tall gelding: modest handicapper: stays 2m: acts on polytrack, good to firm and good to soft going: possibly none too resolute. *Micky Hammond* **55**

SANDFAIRYANN 2 b.f. (Mar 12) Dubai Destination (USA) 127 – Alhufoof (USA) 100 (Dayjur (USA) 137) [2009 p7g p6g p8m Oct 28] leggy filly: sixth foal: half-sister to 2 winners, notably 3-y-o Finjaan: dam, 2-y-o 6f winner, half-sister to useful dam of 1000 Guineas winner Lahan: well held in maidens at Kempton. *B. R. Johnson* **–**

SANDOR 3 ch.g. Fantastic Light (USA) 134 – Crystal Star 100 (Mark of Esteem (IRE) 137) [2009 82: p8g* 9g^{2} p10g^{3} 10m* 9.9g^{5} 10.3m Aug 21] good-topped gelding: useful performer: won maiden at Lingfield (idled) in April and handicap at Sandown in July: good fifth to Roman Republic in valuable handicap at Goodwood, better effort after: worth a try at 1½m: raced only on polytrack and good/good to firm going: hung both ways second outing. *P. J. Makin* **96**

SAND REPEAL (IRE) 7 b.g. Revoque (IRE) 122 – Columbian Sand (IRE) (Salmon Leap (USA) 131) [2009 70: f11g^{5} p13g p13.9g 12d^{3} 17.2d^{4} 12.6d^{3} 12m* 16.4m^{2} 12.3m 11.6m^{3} 11m^{2} 15.4m^{6} 12m^{6} 11.9d Oct 22] leggy gelding: fair handicapper: won at Folkestone in June: effective at 11f to 2m: acts on all-weather and any turf going: effective with or without headgear: usually races prominently. *Miss J. Feilden* **69**

SANDS CROONER (IRE) 6 b.g. Imperial Ballet (IRE) 110 – Kurfuffle (Bluebird (USA) 125) [2009 69, a87: f5s 5f* 5g 5m^{2} 5f* 5m^{4} 5m 5g^{6} 5.1m 5m^{6} 5g 5g 5.1g^{5} p5.1g Nov 14] workmanlike gelding: fairly useful handicapper: won at Warwick in May and Lingfield in June: largely below form after: effective at 5f/easy 6f: acts on all-weather, firm and soft going: visored: tried tongue tied: refused to race third outing: usually held up. *J. G. Given* **86**

SAND SKIER 2 b.c. (Mar 4) Shamardal (USA) 129 – Dubai Surprise (IRE) 115 (King's Best (USA) 132) [2009 6.1g^{4} 7m^{2} 6g* 7g^{3} Oct 24] 150,000Y: sturdy, useful-looking colt: first foal: dam 7f (at 2 yrs) to 1¼m (Premio Lydia Tesio) winner: fairly useful performer: second to Markazzi at Leicester prior to making all in weaker maiden at Hamilton in September: creditable third in nursery at Doncaster: will be suited by 1m: remains open to improvement. *M. Johnston* **93 p**

SANDS OF BARRA (IRE) 6 gr.g. Marju (IRE) 127 – Purple Risks (FR) 80 (Take Risks (FR) 116) [2009 76: p7g^{6} p7g 7d 7.5m 7.1m^{5} 7.1g^{4} 7.6m 7.1g^{5} 6s 8d^{3} Aug 10] quite good-topped gelding: just modest handicapper at 6 yrs: stayed easy 1m: acted on polytrack, firm and soft going: tried in blinkers/cheekpieces: was unreliable: dead. *I. W. McInnes* **57**

Polypipe Flying Childers Stakes, Doncaster—Sand Vixen lowers the two-year-old course record set by Sing Sing in 1959; Bould Mover (rail) and Mister Manannan chase her home

Godolphin's "Sand Vixen"

SANDS OF DEE (USA) 2 b.g. (Apr 13) Dixieland Band (USA) – Diamond Bracelet (USA) (Metfield (USA)) [2009 5m 6m^4 6g 5f^2 6s* p7.1g Sep 18] smallish, compact gelding: fair performer: won claimer at Hamilton (claimed from R. Fahey £7,000) in August: well held in nursery (said to have finished lame) final start: best effort at 6f: acts on soft and good to firm going: tried visored. *J. A. Glover* **65**

SAND VIXEN 2 b.f. (Feb 28) Dubawi (IRE) 129 – Fur Will Fly 66 (Petong 126) [2009 6m^5 p6g* 6m^3 5.2m* 5m* 6m Oct 2] 30,000Y, 130,000 2-y-o: strong, close-coupled filly: half-sister to 3 winning sprinters, notably smart 6f (including at 2 yrs)/6.5f (in UAE) winner So Will I (by Inchinor): dam sprint maiden: useful performer: won maiden at Kempton in July, listed race at Newbury (beat Shamandar by nose) in August and Polypipe Flying Childers Stakes at Doncaster (further progress, beat Bould Mover a length) in September: well below form in Cheveley Park Stakes at Newmarket final start: likely to prove best at 5f/6f: raced only on polytrack and good to firm ground. *Saeed bin Suroor* **107**

SANDWITH 6 ch.g. Perryston View 114 – Bodfari Times 72 (Clantime 101) [2009 85: p5.1g 5m^2 5m^2 5m 5d^2 5g 5g^2 5d 5g 5m 6d 5d^5 Oct 28] lengthy, good-topped gelding: fairly useful handicapper on turf, fair on all-weather: best at 5f: acts on polytrack, firm and good to soft ground: effective with/without cheekpieces: travels strongly but has wandered. *A. G. Foster* **83** **a66**

SANDY PAR 4 ch.g. No Excuse Needed 123 – Nesting 47 (Thatching 131) [2009 47: p5.1g p5g 5m^4 5.1d^6 5.1m^4 5m 5.3g 5.1g 5g^3 6.1d 5.1d 5.1m 5g^4 p6m p6g p5g^5 p5.1g^4 Dec 11] tall gelding: modest maiden at best: raced mainly at 5f: acts on polytrack, good to firm and good to soft going: wears cheekpieces/blinkers. *J. M. Bradley* **60 d**

SANDY SHAW 2 ch.f. (Mar 9) Footstepsinthesand 120 – Susi Wong (IRE) (Selkirk (USA) 129) [2009 p7g 8g 8m^3 Sep 13] rather unfurnished filly: sixth foal: half-sister to several winners, including 5-y-o Buccellati: dam German 1m winner: best effort in maidens when third to Chain of Office at Ffos Las, staying on strongly under hands and heels: will stay 1¼m. *J. W. Hills* **71 +**

*Ladbrokes Portland (Heritage Handicap), Doncaster—
Santo Padre improves again, beating Everymanforhimself (hidden, left), Captain Dunne (far right), Green Manalishi (cheekpieces, centre) and Ishetoo (cheekpieces, right)*

SANDY TOES 2 b.g. (Apr 23) Footstepsinthesand 120 – Scrooby Baby 66 (Mind Games 121) [2009 5g 6f 6m^5 Aug 7] leggy, close-coupled gelding: well held in maidens (first 2 starts for A. McCabe). *J. A. Glover* **–**

SANJAY'S CHOICE (IRE) 3 br.g. Trans Island 119 – Livy Park (IRE) (Titus Livius (FR) 115) [2009 72: 10g 8g p7g 6s p7.1g^3 p5g p6g^3 p6g^3 p8g Nov 25] fair maiden handicapper: stays easy 7f: form only on polytrack: tried in cheekpieces: wandered first 2 starts. *T. G. McCourt, Ireland* **– a78**

SAN JEMENIANO (IRE) 2 b.c. (Apr 30) Bertolini (USA) 125 – Kafayef (USA) 46 (Secreto (USA) 128) [2009 6m^3 6g^3 p6g^3 6m^4 a6g^4 Nov 29] 47,000Y: useful-looking colt: half-brother to several winners, including French 2004 2-y-o 5.5f to 7f winner Ascot Dream (by Pennekamp) and 1½m/13.4f winner Blimey O'Riley (by Kalanisi), both useful: dam, ran 3 times, half-sister to smart stayer Melrose Avenue: fair maiden: in frame all starts, sold from P. Chapple-Hyam 12,000 gns before final outing: raced only at 6f: acts on polytrack, dirt and good to firm ground. *Ms K. Stenefeldt, Sweden* **75**

SAN MARCO (GER) 7 br.g. Military (USA) 118 – Stormin' Sun (USA) (Buddy (USA) 76) [2009 10v p10g Nov 25] 3-time winner in Germany in 2006 for A. Wohler: well held in 2009, leaving Gerald Cully in Ireland prior to final start (said to have finished lame). *P. Butler* **–**

SANS FRONTIERES (IRE) 3 ch.c. Galileo (IRE) 134 – Llia 94 (Shirley Heights 130) [2009 80P: 8m^2 10.4g^3 May 14] good-topped colt: smart form: won maiden at Lingfield sole 2-y-o start: plenty of improvement in 2009, 2¾ lengths second to Delegator in Craven Stakes at Newmarket (pulled hard early, hung right) and length third to Black Bear Island in Dante Stakes at York (off bridle and shuffled back to last but finished best of all): reported in early-June to have suffered a setback: will be well suited by 1½m+: raced only on good/good to firm ground: stays in training. *J. Noseda* **112**

SAN SICHARIA (IRE) 4 ch.f. Daggers Drawn (USA) 114 – Spinamix 67 (Spinning World (USA) 130) [2009 100: 7m* 6m^2 7m^6 8g^6 7g^6 8d^5 p8g^2 Nov 13] strong filly: useful performer: won totesportbingo.com Chartwell Fillies' Stakes at Lingfield in May by nose from Baileys Cacao: good efforts after when runner-up in Ballyogan Stakes at Leopardstown (beaten 1¾ lengths by Lesson In Humility) and listed race at Dundalk (went down by ½ length to Fourpenny Lane): stays easy 1m: acts on polytrack, heavy and good to firm ground: tried in cheekpieces: sold 370,000 gns. *Ms Joanna Morgan, Ireland* **108**

SANSILI 2 gr.c. (Feb 3) Dansili 127 – Salinova (FR) (Linamix (FR) 127) [2009 8.3g p8g^6 Nov 14] much better effort in maidens (fair form) when sixth to Rumoush at Lingfield, prominent when hampered 2f out: bred to be suited by 1¼m+. *Pat Eddery* **64**

SAN SILVESTRO (IRE) 4 b.g. Fayruz 116 – Skehana (IRE) 69 (Mukaddamah (USA) 125) [2009 74: 8.3m 8d 8m^2 9m* 10g 8m* 8.5g^4 8.3s^2 8g^4 Aug 11] compact gelding: fair performer: won seller and handicap at Musselburgh in June: stays 1¼m: acts on soft and good to firm going: usually wears cheekpieces. *Mrs A. Duffield* **70**

SANTA MARGHERITA 2 b.f. (Mar 21) Titus Livius (FR) 115 – A Simple Path (IRE) (Imperial Ballet (IRE) 110) [2009 7d^4 7m^4 8d^4 Oct 15] first foal: dam unraced: modest form in maidens: stays 1m. *H. J. L. Dunlop* **63**

SANTAS PAL 2 b.f. (Apr 9) Chineur (FR) 123 – Khafayif (USA) 62 (Swain (IRE) 134) [2009 5m 5d f5g f5g Jul 7] little form: dead. *C. J. Teague* **–**

SANTEFISIO 3 b.g. Efisio 120 – Impulsive Decision (IRE) 71 (Nomination 125) [2009 6m 6m* 7m² 7.1m³ 7m³ p7g* 7m* Sep 19] 36,000Y: good-topped gelding: sixth foal: brother to useful 2004 2-y-o 6f winner Cammies Future (later 1m winner in US) and half-brother to 3 winners, including 4-y-o Fabreze: dam 6f (at 2 yrs) and 1m winner: fairly useful performer: won maiden at Newbury (100/1) in May and handicaps at Lingfield and Newbury (idled, beat Wilfred Pickles by a nose) in September: stays 7f: raced only on polytrack and good to firm going. *P. J. Makin* **88**

SANTIAGO ATITLAN 7 b.g. Stravinsky (USA) 133 – Sylvette (USA) (Silver Hawk (USA) 123) [2009 106: 6.5g 6g 6d 7d 8m 8s 14m 7.2v Oct 31] one-time useful performer: lightly raced and well below form since early-2008, leaving A. Wohler in Germany and gelded after second start in 2009: stays 7f: acts on dirt, soft and good to firm going: tried visored/blinkered: well held over hurdles. *P. Monteith* **88 d**

SANTO PADRE (IRE) 5 b.g. Elnadim (USA) 128 – Tshusick 81 (Dancing Brave (USA) 140) [2009 87: 5g⁴ 5d⁶ 5v⁵ 5s* 5s* 5.6m* p5g⁴ Oct 23] workmanlike gelding: smart performer: much improved when winning handicaps at Tipperary and Down Royal in August and Doncaster (beat Everymanforhimself by 1¼ lengths in Ladbrokes Portland) in September: respectable length fourth to Arganil in listed race at Dundalk final start, bit slowly away and never nearer: will prove best at 5f/6f: acts on polytrack, heavy and good to firm going: held up. *David Marnane, Ireland* **110**

SANVEAN (IRE) 3 b.f. Danehill Dancer (IRE) 117 – Russian Muse (FR) (Machiavellian (USA) 123) [2009 87: p8g* 8m 11.5m 11.9v 8.5m⁶ 8d 7d⁵ 7m² 7m³ Aug 31] lengthy, good-topped filly: fair performer: landed odds in maiden at Kempton in March: effective at 7f/1m: acts on polytrack, soft and good to firm going: usually held up: sold 4,500 gns, sent to Greece. *M. R. Channon* **75**

SAPHIRA'S FIRE (IRE) 4 b.f. Cape Cross (IRE) 129 – All Our Hope (USA) 96 (Gulch (USA)) [2009 111: 11.9m⁵ 9.9d 12m⁶ 12m³ 10g³ p12m³ p10f⁴ Dec 19] tall, useful-looking filly: smart performer: creditable efforts when third in Pride Stakes (for second year running, beaten 1½ lengths by Ashalanda) and listed race (1¾ lengths behind Laaheb) fourth/fifth starts, both at Newmarket: stays 1½m: acts on polytrack and good to firm ground. *W. R. Muir* **111**

SAPPHIRE PRINCE (USA) 3 b.c. Read The Footnotes (USA) 114 – Anna Jackson (USA) (Houston (USA)) [2009 79: 8m p8g 8m⁵ 8d 7s p7m 8.3g* 8.3g p10m⁴ p12m⁶ p8m p8f Dec 13] big colt: fair handicapper: won at Windsor in October: seems to stay easy 1¼m: acts on polytrack and good to firm going: none too consistent (has looked awkward). *J. R. Best* **77**

SAPPHIRE ROSE 3 b.f. Tobougg (IRE) 125 – Pearly River 72 (Elegant Air 119) [2009 58+: 10.2d 8f* 8m³ 8m 10.2g p8m Sep 30] modest handicapper: won at Bath in May, despite idling: stays 1m: acts on firm going. *J. G. Portman* **63**

SAPPHIRE SPIRIT (USA) 2 gr. or ro.g. (Feb 11) Unbridled Time (USA) – Mimi's Tizzy (USA) (Cee's Tizzy (USA)) [2009 p5g 6d 5g Oct 19] well held in maidens (gelded after). *J. R. Best* **–**

SAPTAPADI (IRE) 3 ch.g. Indian Ridge 123 – Olympienne (IRE) (Sadler's Wells (USA) 132) [2009 77p: 10m⁴ 12.3m⁵ May 7] well-made gelding: useful maiden, raced only 3 times: 4¼ lengths fourth to Above Average in Classic Trial at Sandown prior to 5¼ lengths fifth to Golden Sword in Chester Vase (took time to gather full stride before barged slightly, going on again at finish): gelded after: will be suited by 1¾m+: type to keep on improving. *Sir Michael Stoute* **104 p**

SARAH PARK (IRE) 4 ch.f. Redback 116 – Brillano (FR) 75 (Desert King (IRE) 129) [2009 78: p8g 8.3d* p8g³ 8g³ 8g⁶ 8.5m* 8m* 8m⁴ p8g² p8g p8m⁵ Nov 29] small, close-coupled filly: useful handicapper: improved through year, winning at Windsor in June, Epsom in August and Goodwood in September: good neck second to Rock Ascot at Lingfield after: effective at 7f to 8.5f: acts on polytrack, unraced on extremes of going on turf: races prominently. *B. J. Meehan* **100**

SARAH'S ART (IRE) 6 gr.g. City On A Hill (USA) 114 – Treasure Bleue (IRE) (Treasure Kay 114) [2009 65: p7g³ p6g* p6g* p6g⁴ p5.1g⁴ p6g⁶ p6g⁵ 6g² 6m* 6f 6m* 6g p6g* Dec 12] lengthy gelding: fairly useful handicapper: won at Wolverhampton (2) in January, Warwick in April, Newmarket in August and Wolverhampton in December: effective at 6f/7f: acts on polytrack and firm going: formerly blinkered, tongue tied last 5 starts: held up: has looked wayward. *Stef Liddiard* **83**

SARANDO 4 b.g. Hernando (FR) 127 – Dansara (Dancing Brave (USA) 140) [2009 61: p13.3g⁶ Jan 11] robust gelding: fair maiden: will stay 2m: acts on all-weather and good to firm ground: joined P. Webber. *R. Charlton* **66**

SARASOTA SUNSHINE 3 b.f. Oasis Dream 129 – Never Explain (IRE) 80 (Fairy King (USA)) [2009 54+: p7g* p7g³ 6d² 6d* p6g* 6.1v³ 6m* p7g* 7m Aug 29] fairly useful handicapper: progressive form, winning at Lingfield in February, Warwick and Wolverhampton in June, and Haydock and Kempton in August: effective at 6f/7f: acts on polytrack, good to firm and good to soft going: blinkered last 6 starts. *N. P. Littmoden* **84**

SARD 2 b.f. (Mar 14) Bahamian Bounty 116 – Clincher Club 77 (Polish Patriot (USA) 128) [2009 6m 6d Oct 6] 80,000Y: eighth foal: half-sister to 3 winners, including smart 2004 2-y-o 6f winner Henrik (by Primo Dominie) and fairly useful 6f (at 2 yrs) and 1m winner Spritzeria (by Bigstone): dam, 5f (at 2 yrs) and 7.5f winner, half-sister to smart sprinter Paradise Isle (by Bahamian Bounty): much better effort in maidens when eighth to Dafeef at Newmarket on debut, considerately handled and going on well finish. *M. A. Jarvis* **62**

SARDAN DANSAR (IRE) 3 b.f. Alhaarth (IRE) 126 – Peruvian Witch (IRE) (Perugino (USA) 84) [2009 50: 7.5m⁵ p8.6g 7.1m 6g⁵ 6d⁶ 6d³ 6m 7v Sep 4] close-coupled filly: modest maiden: stays 7.5f: acts on good to soft ground. *Mrs A. Duffield* **55**

SARISKA 3 b.f. Pivotal 124 – Maycocks Bay 100 (Muhtarram (USA) 125) [2009 93P: 7s⁴ 10.4m* 12g* 12v* 12m² 10m³ Oct 17] **123**

Small-scale British owner-breeders enjoyed a good run in the Oaks in the first decade of the new millennium. Following the success of Love Divine (Lordship Stud), Ouija Board (19th Earl of Derby) and Look Here (Julian Richmond-Watson), Sariska made it four in ten years, carrying the colours of Lady Bamford who bred her at Daylesford Stud in the Cotswolds, though Sariska's family on the distaff side came from Yorkshire. Sariska's dam Maycocks Bay, who was bought as a yearling for 32,000 guineas on behalf of Lady Bamford, was from a family developed at Lord Halifax's Garrowby Stud in the 'sixties, 'seventies and 'eighties, its Yorkshire roots originally put down at nearby Burton Agnes Stud by Sariska's fifth dam the Lancashire Oaks winner Eyewash who came from a family developed by another peer of the realm, the 17th Earl of Derby, Eyewash being a granddaughter of the celebrated Stanley House broodmare Selene (the dam of Hyperion). Marcus Wickham-Boynton, owner of Burton Agnes Stud, gave Eyewash away to the Earl and Countess of Halifax when she was in her dotage and she produced Sariska's fourth dam Fiddlededee, her last foal, at Garrowby.

Sariska will do very well to get anywhere near the astonishing career achievements of Ouija Board, the other recent home-bred Oaks winner with Stanley House studs connections, but she has already emulated Ouija Board by completing the Oaks/Irish Oaks double. Sariska became only the twelfth to do so, following Masaka, Altesse Royale, Juliette Marny, Fair Salinia, Blue Wind, Unite, Diminuendo (dead heated in the Irish Oaks), User Friendly, Ramruma, Ouija Board and Alexandrova. Sariska ran only once at two but she couldn't have made a much better impression, strongly supported when winning a maiden in good style at Newmarket's final meeting of the year and possessing the physical attributes—big and strong with a good action—which made her look just the type to improve considerably and develop into a pattern performer at three. With good reports of her

Investec Oaks, Epsom—for the second successive year, a triumph for a small British owner-breeder as Sariska holds off Midday (right); High Heeled and Rainbow View are next

Darley Irish Oaks, the Curragh—much easier this time, as Sariska cruises to the front; Roses For The Lady is an excellent second, while Midday is only third

home work emanating from the Newmarket gallops in March, Sariska's ante-post odds for the One Thousand Guineas halved from 20/1 to 10/1, but she didn't quite run up to expectations in her trial, the Fred Darling at Newbury, starting slowly and then being stopped in her run entering the final furlong, eventually finishing fourth behind Lahaleeb. A change of plan meant that Sariska's next appearance came in the Tattersalls Musidora Stakes at York in the middle of May. The race featured three of the first five in the Oaks betting and looked a good rehearsal for Epsom. Sariska's clear-cut win, by three and three quarter lengths and three and a half lengths from Star Ruby (who didn't hold an Oaks entry) and the Stoute-trained favourite Enticement in the royal colours, saw her promoted to clear Oaks favouritism.

The Musidora fourth High Heeled was the only one who took on Sariska again in the Investec Oaks for which the first three in the betting in a field of ten were Sariska (9/4), the beaten One Thousand Guineas favourite Rainbow View (3/1) and the winner of the Oaks Trial at Lingfield, Midday (5/1). The representative field also included the first two in the Cheshire Oaks, Perfect Truth and Phillipina, and the Irish One Thousand Guineas third Oh Goodness Me. Sariska looked set to take charge of the race three furlongs out, but she veered off a true line as she made her run and caused interference to both Phillipina and Midday, with Wadaat and Perfect Truth also caught up in the trouble. Sariska, Midday, High Heeled and Rainbow View were clear of the rest two furlongs out but Rainbow View was hampered soon afterwards by Sariska and High Heeled, though Rainbow View was under strong pressure and seemed destined for fourth anyway. Sariska was pushed all the way to the line by Midday but always just looked like holding on. The winning margin was only a head, however, with 33/1-shot High Heeled two and a half lengths further back and then another four and a half to Rainbow View. Nothing else finished within sixteen lengths of the winner. The lengthy stewards inquiry which followed the Oaks resulted in the placings remaining unaltered, but Sariska's jockey Jamie Spencer received a five-day suspension for careless riding after being held responsible for causing the interference—allowing Sariska to drift right—at the three-furlong marker. It was a second British classic winner for both Sariska's rider (Spencer won the 2003 St Leger on Brian Boru) and for her trainer. Michael Bell saddled the 2005 Derby winner Motivator and joins Sir Michael Stoute, Henry Cecil, Saeed bin Suroor, Aidan O'Brien, John Dunlop and Jim Bolger, among trainers currently holding a licence, in having saddled winners of both Epsom classics.

Despite turning into a rough race, Sariska's Oaks was a slightly above-average renewal, an excellent timefigure providing confirmation of the value of the form. The first two met again in the Darley Irish Oaks at the Curragh the following month when they were the only British-trained challengers in a ten-runner line-up in which there was surprisingly strong support in the market for the Oxx-trained

Beauty O'Gwaun, who hadn't been seen since winning the Group 3 Blue Wind Stakes at Naas in May. Sariska was sent off the even-money favourite, with Beauty O'Gwaun at 4/1, Midday at 9/2 and the Oaks seventh Oh Goodness Me at 10/1. There wasn't a lot of strength in depth (three of the runners started at 50/1 or longer) but Sariska produced a most impressive performance, held up some way off the leaders and cruising to the front on the bridle inside the final furlong after the very confident Spencer had spent the home straight playing cat and mouse with his rivals. 'She was never out of second gear, I was going to win by a neck but I thought I'd better not!' Nonetheless, Spencer barely had to move to ease Sariska to a three-length win from the front-running 25/1-shot Roses For The Lady, ostensibly in the race as a pacemaker for Beauty O'Gwaun, with Midday, below her best on the very soft going and off the bridle some way out, a further four and a half lengths away in third. The rest were strung out, with Oh Goodness Me fifth, a place in front of Roman Empress (trying to give the Coolmore partners a twelfth successive Irish classic success) and Beauty O'Gwaun last.

Of the fillies who have completed the Oaks/Irish Oaks double, Fair Salinia, Diminuendo, User Friendly, Ramruma and Alexandrova went on to add the Yorkshire Oaks as well, the three last-named in the period since the Yorkshire Oaks has been open to older fillies and mares. Sariska started at 11/4-on at York, where two three-year-olds—the O'Brien-trained pair Tamarind and Roman Empress—and three of the older brigade took her on. The four-year-old Dar Re Mi, runner-up in the race the year before when it had been relocated to Newmarket, produced what was a turn-up at the time to beat Sariska by three quarters of a length, with Roman

Lady Bamford's "Sariska"

Empress third. It emerged that Sariska was in season, though Dar Re Mi's subsequent very good efforts when passing the post first in the Prix Vermeille and when just run out of the frame in the Prix de l'Arc de Triomphe showed Sariska's task at York in a different light. Sariska looked set to take on the colts for the first time herself in the Prix de l'Arc, for which she would have had to be supplemented at a cost of €100,000. Connections decided not to run her because of the prospect of firmish going, though, ironically, it came up good to firm when she took her chance in the Champion Stakes at Newmarket a fortnight afterwards. She was far from discredited in third, beaten half a length and a length by Twice Over and Mawatheeq, but gave the impression that a mile and a quarter was possibly on the short side for her in top company when conditions are not testing. With Kieren Fallon standing in for suspended Jamie Spencer, Sariska was never travelling within herself at any stage after a slow start, though she kept on gamely to eventually edge into a place, never nearer than at the line.

Sariska is by the sprinter Pivotal, and the Oaks runner-up Midday is by another winner of the Nunthorpe, Oasis Dream. Sadler's Wells has the joint-best record (with the late-nineteenth and early-twentieth century sire St Simon) of any stallion in the history of the Oaks, siring five winners of the race, one more than Hyperion. Sadler's Wells, who had the first three in 2001, proved a strong influence for stamina, and his sons Montjeu, Galileo and High Chaparral are following him in that regard, the two last-named each represented by two runners in the latest Oaks. There have been Oaks winners before by stallions who were not themselves middle-distance performers. In the last thirty years, those stallions include the brothers Diesis and Kris, neither of whom ran at beyond a mile yet respectively sired three winners of the Oaks (Diminuendo, Ramruma and Love Divine) and two winners (Oh So Sharp and Unite). The 1982 winner Time Charter was by the July Cup winner Saritamer. The average distance of the races won by the offspring of Sariska's sire Pivotal at three and upwards is around a mile and, until Sariska won the Oaks, he had not had a major winner at a mile and a half or more (though one of his daughters Silvester Lady had won the Preis der Diana, the German Oaks, which is run over a mile and three furlongs).

Sariska (b.f. 2006)	Pivotal (ch 1993)	Polar Falcon (b or br 1987)	Nureyev
			Marie d'Argonne
		Fearless Revival (ch 1987)	Cozzene
			Stufida
	Maycocks Bay (b 1998)	Muhtarram (b 1989)	Alleged
			Ballet de France
		Beacon (b 1987)	High Top
			Mountain Lodge

There is plenty of stamina on the distaff side of Sariska's pedigree, so much in fact that it is easy to see why her dam was sent to an influence for speed like Pivotal. Maycocks Bay, a useful racemare at her best, was by the Alleged stallion Muhtarram and the better of her two wins on the racecourse came on the last of her seventeen starts, when she was already in foal, in a listed rated stakes (from 13 lb out of the weights) over a mile and three quarters at York as a four-year-old. That first foal (a filly by Vettori named Cassava) never made the racecourse in Britain, and was exported to Greece after making only 1,000 guineas at the July Sales as a two-year-old. The now six-year-old Cassava resurfaced at the latest Tattersalls December Sale, this time fetching 22,000 guineas. Maycocks Bay's second foal Gull Wing (by the Sadler's Wells stallion In The Wings) was useful, winning a listed race at Nottingham over a mile and three quarters and running another good race at the trip when runner-up to the smart Yellowstone in the same listed rated stakes at York that her dam had won. After being barren to Rock of Gibraltar, Maycocks Bay produced her third foal Sariska, her fourth being the unraced two-year-old Zigato (by Azamour), with a yearling colt by Cape Cross following on, after which she was barren to Singspiel. Sariska's grandam Beacon was unraced and was bought privately from Lord Halifax, reportedly for £1,000, by John Johnson, then the stud groom at Garrowby who, along with his wife Trisha, has also been breeding horses at Bishop Wilton Stud, near Garrowby, since the 'sixties. Although Beacon didn't see a racecourse, it is a fair bet she would have stayed very well, being a half-sister to the smart performer at up to two and a half miles (third in the Gold Cup) Compton Ace out of Mountain Lodge who won the Cesarewitch as a three-year-old and the Irish St Leger at four in the Halifax colours (making history at the Curragh by becoming the first horse above the age of three to win a 'classic' in Britain or Ireland). Mountain Lodge was the best winner bred by Sariska's fourth dam Fiddlededee, who was placed in the Park Hill Stakes. Another of Fiddlededee's winning daughters, Fiddle-Faddle, who stayed well, produced the out-and-out stayer El Conquistador (runner-up in the Goodwood Cup) and his sister Piffle, dam of Prix Vermeille winner Pearly Shells and the Hollywood Turf Cup winner Frenchpark. As well as being chock-full of stamina, Sariska's family on the distaff side contains plenty who trained on from three to four, perhaps a good omen for Sariska herself who stays in training. She needs a good test at a mile and a quarter and stays a mile and a half very well. She acts on heavy and good to firm going. *M. L. W. Bell*

SARMAD (USA) 2 b. or br.f. (Mar 16) Dynaformer (USA) – Performing Arts 104 (The Minstrel (CAN) 135) [2009 6m 7.5m 8.3m Sep 1] $60,000F, $180,000Y: sturdy, deep-girthed filly: closely related to useful 2002 2-y-o 1m winner Choir Master (by Red Ransom), later successful in USA, and half-sister to several winners, including smart 1995 2-y-o 6f winner Woodborough (by Woodman) and useful 1997 2-y-o 6f winner Dance Trick (by Diesis): dam, 2-y-o 5f/6f winner, third in Irish 1000 Guineas: green/not knocked about in maidens (modest form on debut): bred to do better. *C. E. Brittain* **56 p**

SARRAAF (IRE) 13 ch.g. Perugino (USA) 84 – Blue Vista (IRE) (Pennine Walk 120) [2009 61: p8.6g 10.1g^6 9.2m^4 May 29] smallish, strong gelding: modest handicapper: stays 9.5f: acts on all-weather and any turf going: tried blinkered/visored: held up, and suited by well-run race. *I. Semple* **56**

SARRSAR 2 b.g. (Jan 29) Shamardal (USA) 129 – Bahr 119 (Generous (IRE) 139) [2009 8d^3 Oct 27] half-brother to several winners, including smart 7f to 8.6f winner Baharah (by Elusive Quality) and useful 7f (in UAE)/7.5f (at 2 yrs) winner Naaddey (by Seeking The Gold): dam 7f (at 2 yrs) to 1½m (Ribblesdale Stakes) winner and second in Oaks: 4/1 and sweating, encouraging 2¾ lengths third to Commissionaire in maiden at Yarmouth, soon prominent (gelded after): bred to stay 1¼m: capable of better. *M. A. Jarvis* **80 p**

SARWIN (USA) 6 gr. or ro.g. Holy Bull (USA) 134 – Olive The Twist (USA) 94 (Theatrical 128) [2009 –: f7g p7.1g p8.6g* 8.5m* 9m^3 9.2m* 7.9g^6 8m 8s^6 8m^5 10g Oct 19] strong gelding: fair handicapper: won at Wolverhampton in April and Beverley and Hamilton in May: stays 1½m, effective at much shorter: acts on polytrack and good to firm ground: sometimes looks no easy ride (has carried head awkwardly). *G. A. Swinbank* **76**

SASHEEN 2 b.f. (Feb 27) Zafeen (FR) 123 – Sashay 72 (Bishop of Cashel 122) [2009 p8g p8m^3 p8f^5 Dec 16] strong filly: second foal: dam 1½m to 2m winner: fair form last 2 starts in maidens (didn't find much final one): bred to stay beyond 1m: has twice refused at stall. *J. R. Boyle* **74**

SASSANIAN (IRE) 2 b.g. (Apr 27) Clodovil (IRE) 116 – Persian Sally (IRE) (Persian Bold 123) [2009 6g 7d^4 7m^5 6m f8m^4 p9.5g^4 Dec 12] close-coupled gelding: modest maiden: claimed from J. Howard Johnson £6,000 second start: stays 9.5f: acts on all-weather, probably on good to firm going. *Jane Chapple-Hyam* **56**

SATINDRA (IRE) 5 b.g. Lil's Boy (USA) 109 – Voronova (IRE) 71 (Sadler's Wells (USA) 132) [2009 71d: p11g^4 f12g p12g^4 Feb 4] modest performer nowadays: stays 1½m: acts on all-weather and good to soft going: tongue tied/in cheekpieces. *C. R. Dore* **53**

SATIN PRINCESS (IRE) 2 b.f. (Mar 21) Royal Applause 124 – College of Arms (Lujain (USA) 119) [2009 5d 5g 5m 5g^4 p5.1g p6m Nov 19] €15,500Y: second foal: dam unraced half-sister to smart performers up to 1m Mister Cosmi and Auditorium (both by Royal Applause): poor maiden: left Paul Mason after second start. *A. M. Hales* **44**

SATISFACTION LIFE (IRE) 3 b.f. Acclamation 118 – Etica (IRE) (Barathea (IRE) 127) [2009 7.5g^6 8d^4 9m^4 9m 10.5m^2 11m p11g p9.5g^6 Sep 3] €26,000Y, £14,000 2-y-o: first foal: dam Italian 2-y-o 7f/7.5f winner: fair performer: won maiden at Naples on debut late in 2008: stiff task in Oaks d'Italia at Milan sixth start (final outing for G. Chianese): mid-field in handicaps in Britain: stays 10.5f: acts on good to firm and good to soft ground, probably on polytrack. *M. Botti* **76**

SATURN GIRL (IRE) 3 ch.f. Danehill Dancer (IRE) 117 – Lilissa (IRE) (Doyoun 124) [2009 8.3m^4 8.3g* 8s 8.3m Sep 21] 210,000Y: lengthy filly: half-sister to several **78**

winners, including smart Irish 1m to 1¼m winner Livadiya (by Shernazar), 4-y-o Cape Express and dam of very smart performer up to 1¼m Linngari: dam French 9f/10.5f winner: fair performer: won maiden at Windsor in June: raced only around 1m: best effort on good ground. *S. A. Callaghan*

SATURN WAY (GR) 3 b.g. Bachelor Duke (USA) 122 – Senseansensibility (USA) 75 (Capote (USA)) [2009 79: 7m^6 8g^2 8.3m 8.5g 8.1g^4 Aug 13] rather leggy gelding: fair handicapper: stays 1m: acts on soft ground: gelded after final start. *P. R. Chamings* **75**

SATWA CROWN 2 b.c. (May 24) Dubai Destination (USA) 127 – Crown of Spring (USA) (Chief's Crown (USA)) [2009 p6g 6g p7g Jul 22] close-coupled colt: well beaten in maidens. *E. A. L. Dunlop* **–**

SATWA EXCEL 2 b.f. (Mar 14) Exceed And Excel (AUS) 126 – Pericardia 60 (Petong 126) [2009 7g Aug 1] €92,000F, €65,000Y: closely related to fairly useful 7f (at 2 yrs)/1m winner Dansa Queen (by Dansili) and half-sister to several winners, including useful 7f (at 2 yrs)/1¼m winner Halicardia (by Halling): dam lightly-raced half-sister to smart 6f/7f performer Prince Ferdinand: 20/1, very green and well held in maiden at Newmarket: should do better. *E. A. L. Dunlop* **– p**

SATWA GOLD (USA) 3 ch.c. Rahy (USA) 115 – No More Ironing (USA) (Slew O' Gold (USA)) [2009 –: p8.6g* p8g^2 p8g p10f 10.2s p10g* p10g^3 p12m* p12g^5 Dec 2] good-topped colt: fairly useful performer: won maiden at Wolverhampton in March, and claimers at Kempton in October and November: stays 1½m: acts on polytrack (lightly raced on turf). *E. A. L. Dunlop* **85**

SATWA LAIRD 3 b.c. Johannesburg (USA) 127 – Policy Setter (USA) (Deputy Minister (CAN)) [2009 98: 7m^4 7g 8m 7m 7m^4 7m^2 8m^2 p7g Oct 11] attractive colt: fairly useful handicapper: creditable efforts when runner-up: stays 1m: acts on soft and good to firm ground: held up. *E. A. L. Dunlop* **94**

SATWA MOON (USA) 3 ch.c. Horse Chestnut (SAF) 119 – Double Schott (USA) (Demons Begone (USA)) [2009 p10m^6 p8.6m^3 p8.6g^6 Sep 3] $50,000Y, 95,000 2-y-o: half-brother to 3 winners in USA: dam, US 8.5f winner, half-sister to very smart US Grade 1 11f winner Down The Aisle and half-sister to dam of high-class US performer up to 1½m Kitten's Joy: best effort in maidens when third at Wolverhampton: not knocked about at same course final start: will be suited by return to 1¼m+. *E. A. L. Dunlop* **79**

SATWA RUBY (FR) 3 gr.f. Verglas (IRE) 118 – Vezina (FR) (Bering 136) [2009 a9.5g^4 10.5d* 10d* 11.5d^5 10m 10d a12g^2 Dec 10] €110,000Y: rather leggy, attractive filly: second foal: half-sister to fairly useful French 1¼m winner Zina Blue (by Anabaa Blue): dam French maiden (stayed 1½m): useful performer: won maiden at Le Croise-Laroche in April and minor event at Le Lion-d'Angers in May: creditable efforts in listed races at Le Lion-d'Angers and Vichy (seventh to Danehill's Pearl) fourth/sixth starts, but well held in similar event at Royal Ascot in between: stays 11.5f: acts on good to soft ground, below form both starts on all-weather at Deauville. *Jean de Roualle, France* **96**

SATWA SON (IRE) 2 gr.c. (Mar 11) Oasis Dream 129 – Cozy Maria (USA) 105 (Cozzene (USA)) [2009 6g p7m Aug 20] in need of experience in maidens, showing a little ability on polytrack at Lingfield. *E. A. L. Dunlop* **54**

SATWA STAR (IRE) 3 b.g. King's Best (USA) 132 – Sheppard's Watch 108 (Night Shift (USA)) [2009 p7g^5 8.3g^5 6d p7m^5 p7.1g^4 p7m p7g 8v a6.5g^6 Dec 24] well-made gelding: second foal: dam 6f (at 2 yrs) to 8.5f winner: fair maiden: sold from E. Dunlop 8,000 gns after seventh start: stays 7f: acts on polytrack. *F. Alloncle, France* **74**

SATWA STREET (IRE) 3 br.c. Elusive City (USA) 117 – Black Tribal (IRE) (Mukaddamah (USA) 125) [2009 88: p6g^4 p6g^3 p6g^2 p6g^3 5.1m 5g^5 5.7f^5 p6g^5 6m* 6g^2 6m^3 6m Aug 15] lengthy colt: fairly useful handicapper: won at Brighton in July: speedy, raced only at 5f/6f: acts on polytrack and good to firm going: front runner: joined E. Charpy in UAE. *D. M. Simcock* **88**

SAUCY 8 b.m. Muhtarram (USA) 125 – So Saucy 59 (Teenoso (USA) 135) [2009 75: p10g^3 p8g^5 Feb 22] sturdy mare: fair handicapper: best around 1¼m: acts on polytrack and good to firm ground: tried blinkered earlier in career. *Tom Dascombe* **68**

SAUCY BROWN (IRE) 3 b.g. Fasliyev (USA) 120 – Danseuse du Bois (USA) (Woodman (USA) 126) [2009 89: 6m^3 7s 7g* 6f^3 7m 7g^5 7g 7m^5 Aug 15] lengthy gelding: useful performer: won minor event at Doncaster in May: creditable third to Proclaim in similar race next time, best effort after: effective at 6f/7f: acts on firm and good to soft going: usually races prominently: sold 30,000 gns, then gelded. *R. Hannon* **97**

John Guest Diadem Stakes, Ascot—Sayif (far side) puts up a very smart performance and is clear of the opposition, including Tamagin (nearest camera), who raced alone

SAUCY GIRL (IRE) 2 b.f. (Jan 28) Footstepsinthesand 120 – Leenane (IRE) (Grand Lodge (USA) 125) [2009 5m^2 5m^3 6d 6m 5v p6m Sep 28] €32,000Y: quite good-topped filly: first foal: dam unraced half-sister to smart 5f winner Watching: maiden: seemingly easily best effort on debut: should stay 6f: acts on good to firm going. *T. D. Easterby* **68 ?**

SAUNTON SANDS 3 ch.g. Best of The Bests (IRE) 122 – Victoriet 54 (Hamas (IRE) 125§) [2009 45: 8m Jun 14] big, workmanlike gelding: poor maiden. *A. G. Newcombe* **–**

SAUTE 3 b.g. Hawk Wing (USA) 136 – Lifting (IRE) (Nordance (USA)) [2009 –p: 8m p8g f8m p12.2g^3 p12g p12m* f14m^2 f14m* Dec 5] useful-looking gelding: fair handicapper: won at Kempton in October and Southwell in December: should stay 2m: acts on all-weather: signs of temperament. *W. R. Swinburn* **73**

SAVARONOLA (USA) 4 ch.g. Pulpit (USA) 117 – Running Debate (USA) (Open Forum (USA)) [2009 81: f12s^5 f11g Apr 27] lengthy gelding: just modest maiden in 2009: should stay 1½m: acts on polytrack and firm ground. *B. J. Curley* **60**

SAVEIRO (FR) 5 b.g. Raintrap 123 – Branceilles (FR) (Satin Wood 117) [2009 12m May 2] useful bumper performer: 7/2, shaped as though amiss on Flat debut in maiden at Thirsk: fair form over hurdles. *G. A. Swinbank* **–**

SAVILE'S DELIGHT (IRE) 10 b.g. Cadeaux Genereux 131 – Across The Ice (USA) (General Holme (USA) 128) [2009 87: f5d p5g^5 f6g f6g p6g Mar 2] lengthy gelding: just fair performer in 2009: best at 5f/6f: acts on all-weather, heavy and good to firm going: formerly in headgear/tongue tie: tends to hang left: versatile regarding tactics. *Tom Dascombe* **70**

SAVING GRACE 3 br.f. Lend A Hand 124 – Damalis (IRE) 106 (Mukaddamah (USA) 125) [2009 –: f7g p8.6g Dec 14] leggy filly: modest maiden handicapper: best effort final start. *E. J. Alston* **51**

SAVIOUR SAND (IRE) 5 b.g. Desert Sun 120 – Teacher Preacher (IRE) 37 (Taufan (USA) 119) [2009 82: p8g^5 p9.5g^4 p8g May 8] good-topped gelding: fair performer: left M. Rimmer after second start: stays 1¼m: acts on polytrack and good to firm going: front runner/races prominently: signs of temperament. *T. Keddy* **70**

SAWAB 3 b.f. Tobougg (IRE) 125 – Skew (Niniski (USA) 125) [2009 p8.6g^2 p8g^3 8g 10g 8m^4 10.1g^5 Jul 2] 26,000F, 32,000Y: half-sister to 3 winners, including 2003 2-y-o 7f winner Sketch (by Perugino), later successful in USA, and 2m winner Skit (by In The Wings): dam unraced half-sister to smart performer up to 13.5f Spout: fair maiden: stays 1¼m: acts on polytrack and good to firm ground: blinkered last 2 starts: sold 12,000 gns. *C. E. Brittain* **71**

SAWPIT SUNSHINE (IRE) 4 b.f. Mujadil (USA) 119 – Curie Express (IRE) 65 (Fayruz 116) [2009 60: 7.1g p7g 7.1m 6.1s Oct 7] close-coupled filly: modest handicapper in 2008: well below form at 4 yrs: blinkered last 2 starts. *J. L. Spearing* –

SAXBY (IRE) 2 ch.c. (Mar 3) Pastoral Pursuits 127 – Madam Waajib (IRE) (Waajib 121) [2009 5.1g^6 6m^6 6m* 6f^3 6m^6 6d^6 p7.1g^5 7m^2 p7.1g^2 p6m* 7g Oct 6] €17,000Y, £15,000 2-y-o: workmanlike colt: fifth foal: half-brother to fairly useful 2006 2-y-o 5f winner (later 1m winner in USA) Deadshot Keen (by Invincible Spirit) and 8-y-o Play Master: dam lightly raced: fair performer: won seller at Thirsk in June and claimer at Kempton (claimed from M. Channon £13,000) in September: stays 7f: acts on polytrack and good to firm going, probably on firm: usually races prominently: signs of temperament. *G. A. Harker* 71

SAXFORD 3 b.g. Reset (AUS) 124 – Bint Makbul 65 (Makbul 104) [2009 103: 7m 6d May 15] leggy gelding: useful performer at 2 yrs: last in listed races in 2009: effective at 5f/6f: acts on soft and good to firm going. *Mrs L. Stubbs* –

SAXONA (IRE) 5 b.m. Jade Robbery (USA) 121 – Saxon Maid 108 (Sadler's Wells (USA) 132) [2009 10.4g 12.1m 12.1g^2 17.2g* 15.4m^5 17.1m Aug 16] plain mare: half-sister to several winners, including 6f (in UAE) to 11.6f winner Saxe-Coburg (by Warning) and French 11.5f/12.5f winner Marion (by Doyoun): dam 1½m/1¾m winner: fair bumper winner: modest performer on Flat: won handicap at Carlisle in July: stays 17.2f: raced on good/good to firm ground. *Ian Williams* 63

SAYIF (IRE) 3 b.c. Kheleyf (USA) 116 – Sewards Folly 70 (Rudimentary (USA) 118) [2009 115: 6m* 6g^4 6.5g^5 6d^4 6m* Sep 27] good sort: very smart performer: won minor event at Leicester in April (reportedly scoped dirty after) and John Guest Diadem Stakes at Ascot (best effort, beat Tamagin 2½ lengths, showing good turn of foot before edging left) in September: not discredited in Prix Maurice de Gheest at Deauville (fifth to King's Apostle) and Sprint Cup at Haydock (fourth to Regal Parade) third/fourth starts: best around 6f: acts on good to firm and good to soft going (unraced on extremes): usually races prominently. *P. W. Chapple-Hyam* 122

SAY NO NOW (IRE) 3 b.f. Refuse To Bend (IRE) 128 – Star Studded (Cadeaux Genereux 131) [2009 86p: 8.3f* 9.9m^3 8m 8.1m^2 8.1g^5 7m^3 7g^4 Oct 4] good-topped, attractive filly: useful performer: won maiden at Nottingham in May: best efforts when placed in listed races at Sandown (2 lengths second to Strawberrydaiquiri) and Doncaster (2½ lengths third to Fantasia) fourth/sixth starts: stays 1m: raced only on polytrack and good going or firmer: front runner/races prominently. *D. R. Lanigan* 103

SAY YOU SAY ME 3 b.f. Acclamation 118 – Mindfulness (Primo Dominie 121) [2009 65p: 6d 6m^2 Jun 10] fair form in maidens: would have proved best kept to 5f/6f: dead. *N. J. Vaughan* 65

SCAMPERDALE 7 br.g. Compton Place 125 – Miss Up N Go (Gorytus (USA) 132) [2009 –, a97: p9.5g^5 p10g p9.5g^2 p8.6g^5 p9.5g^3 10g 10.3m p11g* p12.2g p10m p9.5g* Dec 26] good-topped gelding: fairly useful handicapper on all-weather, lightly raced on turf: won at Kempton in July and Wolverhampton in December: stays 11f: acts on polytrack: effective with/without cheekpieces: usually waited with: has looked awkward under pressure. *B. P. J. Baugh* – a94

SCANDAL 4 b.g. Reel Buddy (USA) 118 – Milliscent 49 (Primo Dominie 121) [2009 p13g^4 p12g^3 Feb 27] won bumper at Lingfield: fair form in maidens there on Flat: worth a try at 1¼m: modest form over hurdles. *Andrew Turnell* 70

SCARAB (IRE) 4 b. or br.g. Machiavellian (USA) 123 – Russian Society 103 (Darshaan 133) [2009 88: p12g* p12g^5 14d 12g Oct 10] deep-girthed gelding: fairly useful handicapper: won at Kempton in January: left M. Johnston £20,000 and off 7 months (gelded), well held last 2 starts: stays 1½m: raced on polytrack and going softer than good (acts on heavy). *T. D. Walford* 86

SCARBORO WARNING (IRE) 2 ch.g. (Mar 31) Footstepsinthesand 120 – Spring Easy (IRE) (Alzao (USA) 117) [2009 7s^3 p7.1g 7g Oct 30] €40,000F, £12,000 2-y-o: tall gelding: has scope: half-brother to several winners, including fairly useful Irish 11f winner Spring Opera (by Sadler's Wells): dam, well held only start, half-sister to smart dam of 1000 Guineas winner Virginia Waters: form in maidens only when ¾-length third to Layla's Dancer at Thirsk: should stay 1m+: gelded after final start. *J. G. Given* 71

SCARCITY (IRE) 2 b.f. (Mar 16) Invincible Spirit (IRE) 121 – Sanpa Fan (ITY) (Sikeston (USA) 124) [2009 6m 7d Oct 12] €46,000F, 62,000Y: fourth foal: half-sister to winners in Italy by Wixim and Dane Friendly: dam Italian 7.5f to 9f winner, including at 2 yrs: down the field in maidens at Yarmouth and Salisbury (better effort). *E. A. L. Dunlop* 61

SCARLET OAK 5 b.m. Zamindar (USA) 116 – Flamenco Red 93 (Warning 136) **57**
[2009 77, a67: p5m^5 p6g^5 p5g^2 p5g p5.1g^2 Apr 4] angular mare: modest performer nowadays: best at 5f/6f: acts on polytrack and good to soft going: often wears cheekpieces: held up: not straightforward. *A. M. Hales*

SCARLET RIDGE 2 ch.f. (Mar 21) Tumbleweed Ridge 117 – Kayartis 57 (Kaytu **–**
112) [2009 p8m p8g Dec 7] seventh foal: sister to 4-y-o Kaystar Ridge and half-sister to 2 winners, including 1m/1¼m winner Glendale (by Opening Verse): dam 1½m to 2m winner: very green, down the field in maidens. *D. K. Ivory*

SCARLETT ANGEL (IRE) 3 b.f. Xaar 132 – Mildred (IRE) (Peintre Celebre (USA) **–**
137) [2009 8.3g 9.9g p12g May 30] 20,000Y: second foal: dam unraced: no form. *W. J. Knight*

SCARTH HILL (IRE) 3 ch.g. Selkirk (USA) 129 – Louve Sereine (FR) 70 (Sadler's **–**
Wells (USA) 132) [2009 55: 8m 8f May 11] workmanlike gelding: modest form on 2-y-o debut: little form since. *G. M. Moore*

SCAR TISSUE 5 ch.m. Medicean 128 – Possessive Lady 62 (Dara Monarch 128) [2009 **–**
–: 10m^6 17.2f May 31] close-coupled mare: maiden, no form since 2007: tried blinkered. *E. J. Creighton*

SCARTOZZ 7 b.g. Barathea (IRE) 127 – Amazing Bay 100 (Mazilier (USA) 107) **87**
[2009 105: p8.6g p8g* p8.6g Sep 17] strong, lengthy gelding: fairly useful performer nowadays: won claimer at Kempton in April: stays 8.5f: acts on all-weather, soft and good to firm ground: usually wears headgear (not at Kempton): has been tongue tied. *M. Botti*

SCEILIN (IRE) 5 b.m. Lil's Boy (USA) 109 – Sharifa (IRE) (Cryptoclearance (USA)) **69**
[2009 65, a56: p12.2g 10m^5 10.2f* 10g^2 10f* 10.9m* 10m^6 Oct 13] sturdy mare: fair handicapper: won at Bath in June, Brighton in August and Warwick (amateurs) in September: stays 10.9f: acts on polytrack and firm going: tongue tied. *J. Mackie*

SCENE TWO 3 gr.g. Act One 124 – Gleaming Water 81 (Kalaglow 132) [2009 83P: **83**
p12g^5 12g^6 p11g 12d* Oct 11] big, rangy gelding: fairly useful handicapper: won at Goodwood (hung badly left) in October: stays 1½m: acts on polytrack and good to soft going: visored third start: temperament under suspicion: sold 45,000 gns. *L. M. Cumani*

SCENIC BLAST (AUS) 5 b. or br.g. Scenic 128 – Daughter's Charm (AUS) **128**
(Delgado (USA)) [2009 5.5g^2 5g* 5.5g^5 6g* 5m* 6m 6f 6g Dec 13]

Choisir, Takeover Target, Miss Andretti and now Scenic Blast. In the space of just seven years, the success of top Australian sprinters at Royal Ascot has gone from the remarkable to the commonplace, from the shock of Choisir's 25/1 win in the King's Stand in 2003 to Miss Andretti and Scenic Blast justifying favouritism in the same race in two of the last three years. Royal Ascot's big sprints, the King's Stand and the Golden Jubilee, both now Group 1 contests and the first two British legs of the Global Sprint Challenge series, received a further increase in prize money for 2009. The Golden Jubilee is now the most valuable prize at the Royal meeting (ahead of the Prince of Wales's Stakes), with the King's Stand the third richest race. Scenic Blast was the only antipodean challenger for the big sprints (Miss Andretti had been among a raiding party of four from Australia two years earlier). However, even in the absence of the most eagerly-awaited runner from abroad, the unbeaten Hungarian sprinter Overdose, who was ruled out with a foot problem, the King's Stand and Golden Jubilee succeeded between them in attracting Cannonball from North America, Mythical Flight and J J The Jet Plane from South Africa and Hong Kong's best sprinter Sacred Kingdom.

Scenic Blast's King's Stand win might not have been so newsworthy as Choisir's ground-breaking victory, but there was nothing mundane about the style of his win. Drawn fifteen of fifteen, Scenic Blast was covered up on the outside of the field, which raced in one pack down the centre of the course, but from two out he began making ground with ease. Hitting the front over a furlong out, Scenic Blast was soon a couple of lengths clear and well on top. Second favourite Fleeting Spirit was the only one to raise a serious challenge, and she was somewhat flattered to get within three quarters of a length, with a gap of almost three lengths back to the third, the three-year-old filly Anglezarke. Neither of the other foreign raiders, Cannonball and Mythical Flight, made any impression and there was a disappointing performance from the Palace House Stakes winner Amour Propre, who reportedly tore off a shoe. The previous year's winner Equiano and regular challenger Dandy Man, who had made the frame in the last three years, were others to perform well below their best. That said, Scenic Blast's performance still looked on a par, at the very least, with those put up by the other high-class Australian winners of the King's Stand, though, unlike his predecessors, Scenic Blast wasn't turned out again for the Golden Jubilee four days later.

The rest of Scenic Blast's season was focussed on consolidating his lead in the Global Sprint Challenge. However, in contrast to Fleeting Spirit, who went on to win the July Cup, and the King's Stand fifth Borderlescott, successful in the Nunthorpe, Scenic Blast himself suffered a catalogue of problems. He was sent off the 11/8 favourite for the July Cup on his next outing, but managed only tenth behind Fleeting Spirit, afterwards reported to have swallowed his tongue. Even worse followed when Scenic Blast finished last in both Japan in October and Hong Kong in December. In the Sprinters Stakes at Nakayama, a bad stumble just before the home turn didn't help matters, but he was found to be suffering afterwards from the condition known as the thumps (contractions of the diaphragm) which necessitated his being put on an intravenous drip. Scenic Blast then bled in the Hong Kong Sprint, the final leg of the Global Sprint Challenge, having missed an intended preparatory run at Sha Tin in the Sprint Trial with a foot problem. Victory for Scenic Blast in either Japan or Hong Kong would have earned connections an extra 1,000,000 dollars for winning legs of the Challenge in three different countries. Though the bonus eluded him, Scenic Blast had already done enough to win the Global Sprint Challenge and his exploits also earned him the title of Australian Horse of the Year for the 2008/9 season, as well as champion sprinter and champion international performer.

Scenic Blast had taken a well-trodden route to Royal Ascot early in the year. Like all the other Australian sprinters successful in the King's Stand before him, he won the Coolmore Lightning Stakes (the first leg of the Global Sprint Challenge) over five furlongs at Flemington in January, where he had short-priced favourite Weekend Hussler, Australia's 2007/8 Horse of the Year, back in fourth. After meeting trouble when finishing fifth in the Oakleigh Plate at Caulfield next time, Scenic Blast made a successful return to Flemington to win another Group 1, the twenty-two-runner Crown Newmarket Handicap over six furlongs, by a head from the Oakleigh Plate winner Swiss Ace. Both Takeover Target and Miss Andretti had also completed the Lightning/Newmarket double before winning at Royal Ascot. Prior to the latest season, Scenic Blast had shown no better than smart form in Australia, earning ratings of 116 and then 117 in the last two editions of *Racehorses*. He hadn't won above Group 3 level until the Lightning Stakes, though he had twice been placed behind Weekend Hussler in Group 1 company as a three-year-old, including when second in the Caulfield Guineas. That was over a mile, and sprinting clearly wasn't uppermost in connections' minds in 2008 when he was reportedly backed to win the Cox Plate, Australia's top weight-for-age contest, over an extended ten furlongs, before he was forced to miss the race with a setback and then required a throat operation.

Reflecting on the experience of taking Scenic Blast to Britain, his trainer Dan Morton told *The Aushorse Magazine* 'One thing that made it special for me

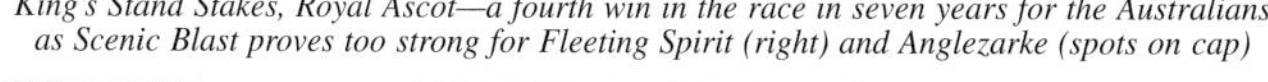

King's Stand Stakes, Royal Ascot—a fourth win in the race in seven years for the Australians as Scenic Blast proves too strong for Fleeting Spirit (right) and Anglezarke (spots on cap)

was the people you meet over there. I got to meet some really good people and some of the bigger trainers invited me to trackwork.' But not all of the British training fraternity were quite so accommodating. 'I still can't help but wonder,' wrote Mark Johnston on his web site, 'how it is possible to get a son of a moderate National Hunt sire, which in turn is a son of Saddler's [sic] Wells, to look like a cross between Alan [sic] Wells and a Quarter Horse and to win a Group 1 race over five furlongs. I suppose we can only conclude that they must be better trainers.' Whilst he claimed to be 'not one of the "smoking syringe theorists"', Johnston's remarks could have been taken to imply that the good-topped Scenic Blast's physique was not entirely natural, and that perhaps he owed his speed to something more than his pedigree. Not surprisingly, the Australian Press in particular responded to what was interpreted as a slur on the integrity of their nation's racing as a whole, some of them reminding readers that Johnston was the trainer of the 1995 Melbourne Cup favourite Double Trigger who was beaten more than fifty lengths into seventeenth. Morton played down the story, saying 'I have never actually heard of the bloke'. On a general point, for all the benefits of the internet, the uncensored nature of web sites, blogs and forums means that individuals are able to (or even feel the need to) express themselves in a cavalier way they would never do in mainstream print, where there is, on the whole, much more accountability and quality control. Johnston himself is fully aware of this, alerting anyone who might be tempted to take views like those about Scenic Blast too seriously by expressing them under the title of 'Bletherings'.

Scenic Blast may not have the pedigree of a one-dimensional sprinter, but there's no lack of speed in it either and, given the stud records of both his sire and dam, nobody should be surprised, or suspicious for that matter, that he has become a Group 1 winner. Scenic Blast's sire Scenic, who stayed a mile and a quarter (well beaten in Breeders' Cup Turf only try at further), had more speed than many by Sadler's Wells, enough to dead heat in the Dewhurst Stakes. Initially retired to Coolmore (at no stage in his stud career, incidentally, did he stand as a National Hunt sire), Scenic was shuttled to the southern hemisphere for several seasons before settling in Australia permanently. Scenic has had more than a dozen Group 1 winners there and, as is often the way, has never been more successful than in the years since his death in 2005. Scenic's best horses have won at a range of distances, and Scenic Blast is by no means the only sprinter among them. He has also been represented by the 2008 Melbourne Cup winner Viewed, also winner of the Caulfield Cup in the latest season and third in the Mackinnon Stakes to Scenic Shot, another by the same sire, who races for the same connections as Scenic Blast.

Scenic Blast (AUS) (b. or br.g. 2004)	Scenic (b 1986)	Sadler's Wells (b 1981)	Northern Dancer
			Fairy Bridge
		Idyllic (b or br 1982)	Foolish Pleasure
			Where You Lead
	Daughter's Charm (AUS) (b 1987)	Delgado (b 1980)	Hoist The Flag
			Princess Pout
		Romantic's Daughter (br or bl 1971)	Romantic
			Lorraine Lee

Scenic Blast's grandam Romantic's Daughter was a sprinter purely and simply, with all six of her wins in Australia coming at five or six furlongs. She was by Romantic, who was exported to Australia at the end of his two-year-old season when his wins included the July Stakes and Richmond Stakes. Scenic Blast apparently inherited his size from his dam, 'a giant' according to her breeders. Daughter's Charm also won six races and, while she too had the speed to win over five and a half furlongs, she was by Delgado, a brother to Alleged, and won over as far as a mile and a quarter, also having the stamina and ability to be beaten a head in the Group 1 West Australian Oaks over a mile and a half. Daughter's Charm bred four winners in all at a variety of distances at up to a mile and a half, though each of them was successful at least once over sprint trips. Scenic Blast is Daughter's Charm's second Group 1 winner in Australia after Gilded Venom (by Golden Snake), winner of Perth's richest race, the Railway Stakes, over a mile in 2008 when earning a Timeform rating of 119. Gilded Venom had to be put down early in 2009 after suffering a serious bacterial infection in his knee. *D. Morton, Australia*

SCHIAPARELLI (GER) 6 ch.h. Monsun (GER) 124 – Sacarina (Old Vic 136) **120**
[2009 120: 12m^3 16g* 15m* 14s^3 12m* 15.5d^2 Oct 25]

Schiaparelli more than made up for lost time in his second season with Godolphin, having been restricted to a couple of unsuccessful appearances for them in his first. He put his name into the Godolphin record books in the process, the six-year-old's victory in the Prix Kergorlay being the five hundredth at listed or pattern level in a tally stretching back to Balanchine's Oaks win in 1994.

Schiaparelli spent two seasons with Peter Schiergen in Germany before he was purchased by Godolphin towards the end of 2007, during which time he won nine of his thirteen races. They included the Deutsches Derby and Deutsches St Leger at three and the Deutschlandpreis, Preis von Europa and Gran Premio del Jockey Club at four. His new connections were reported to be aiming Schiaparelli at the Dubai Sheema Classic as a five-year-old, but a minor foot problem meant that he was on the sidelines until the September of 2008. Although he made a pleasing return in finishing second to Zambezi Sun in the Prix Foy, Schiaparelli cut no ice in the Arc three weeks later and it was nine months before he was seen again. Reappearing in the Princess of Wales's Stakes at Newmarket, he looked very much Godolphin's second string, behind Campanologist, and started at 25/1. He belied those odds, finishing runner-up to Doctor Fremantle, though he hampered Alwaary when hanging right and was subsequently demoted a placing.

Clearly as good as ever at a mile and a half, Schiaparelli was stepped up to two miles on his next start and showed himself to be just as effective at that trip, winning the Coutts Goodwood Cup in July by a length from Mourilyan, the pair finishing a long way clear of the rest. In a strongly-run race, 6/4 favourite

Coutts Goodwood Cup, Goodwood—Schiaparelli and Mourilyan have left the opposition well behind

Gran Premio del Jockey Club e Coppa d'Oro, Milan—a ninth pattern-race victory for Schiaparelli as he repeats his 2007 success in the race; third-placed Voila Ici is the other horse in the photo

Schiaparelli was sent on half a mile out and Dettori didn't get serious with him until the final furlong when Mourilyan, hanging right, threatened briefly. Schiaparelli had made the running several times previously, and the tactics were used in his four subsequent races. He won two of them, starting at odds on both times. Not at all troubled to account for a couple of no-more-than-useful rivals in the Darley Prix Kergorlay at Deauville in August, Schiaparelli gave a relentless display of galloping when beating Sant'Antonio a length and three quarters in the Gran Premio del Jockey Club e Coppa d'Oro at Milan in October. Schiaparelli is one of only three dual winners—and the first for fifty-five years—of the Gran Premio del Jockey Club, a race which was one of the casualties of the month-long strike which brought racing in Italy to a halt in 2008. In between those wins, Schiaparelli was a respectable third behind Alandi in the Irish St Leger at the Curragh, easing clear early in the straight, but then finding the testing ground and the strong pace he had set taking their toll and he had no answer to the winner in the final furlong. Schiaparelli signed off in the latest season with a good effort in the Prix Royal-Oak at Longchamp, collared only well inside the final furlong by Ask, who beat him by a length and a half.

Schiaparelli (GER) (ch.h. 2003)	Monsun (GER) (br 1990)	Konigsstuhl (br 1976)	Dschingis Khan
			Konigskronung
		Mosella (b 1985)	Surumu
			Monasia
	Sacarina (ch 1992)	Old Vic (b 1986)	Sadler's Wells
			Cockade
		Brave Lass (ch 1974)	Ridan
			Bravour II

The visits of the unraced Sacarina to Monsun have resulted in three German classic winners all told. The high-class Samum won the Deutsches Derby six years before Schiaparelli did, while the smart Salve Regina, who was runner-up in the Deutsches Derby, won the 2002 Preis der Diana (German Oaks). A sister to the trio, Sortita, was a useful winner at a mile and a quarter in Britain in 2008. Sacarina has also produced minor winners in Germany by Platini and Dashing Blade. The next dam Brave Lass was a smart two-year-old sprinter and is herself a daughter of another German classic winner, Bravour II, successful in the German equivalent of

Godolphin's "Schiaparelli"

the One Thousand Guineas. Schiaparelli, a big, strong sort, acts on heavy and good to firm ground. He is thoroughly game and genuine. *Saeed bin Suroor*

SCHINKEN OTTO (IRE) 8 ch.g. Shinko Forest (IRE) – Athassel Rose (IRE) (Reasonable (FR) 119) [2009 –, a62: p12g p12.2g⁴ p13.9g⁵ Mar 2] strong gelding: modest handicapper: barely stays 1¾m: acts on all-weather, little solid form on turf. *J. M. Jefferson* **– a55**

SCHOLARS LASS (IRE) 4 b.f. Spartacus (IRE) 107 – Blanche Neige (USA) (Lit de Justice (USA) 125) [2009 49: p7g f6g⁴ p6g f6g Apr 27] modest maiden: should stay 1m: acts on fibresand. *J. Balding* **50**

SCHOOLBOY CHAMP 2 ch.g. (Mar 7) Trade Fair 124 – Aswhatilldois (IRE) 84 (Blues Traveller (IRE) 119) [2009 5g* p5g⁵ 6m 6m 6g² 6g Oct 23] €50,000F, £4,000Y: close-coupled gelding: fifth foal: half-brother to 4-y-o Wiseman's Diamond: dam 7f (at 2 yrs) to 8.5f (US minor stakes) winner: fair performer: won maiden at Haydock in June: should stay 7f: best efforts on good ground: tried tongue tied. *Pat Morris* **75**

SCILLY BREEZE 2 gr.g. (Jan 22) Linamix (FR) 127 – Mitraillette (USA) 87 (Miswaki (USA) 124) [2009 6g⁴ 7s² 7.5m⁴ 7s² Jul 14] modest maiden: claimed from Rae Guest £5,000 second outing: should stay 1m+: acts on soft going. *A. M. Hales* **56**

SCINTILLATING (IRE) 2 b.f. (Apr 29) Cape Cross (IRE) 129 – Announcing Peace (Danehill (USA) 126) [2009 6m 6m p7.1g p7.1g 8g 8.3g p7.1g f7g⁴ f8f⁶ Dec 11] €140,000F: seventh foal: sister to smart 6f (at 2 yrs) to 1½m winner Crosspeace and **41**

useful 2006 2-y-o 7f winner So Sweet, closely related to 1m winner Tatbeeq (by Invincible Spirit) and half-sister to 2 winners: dam maiden: poor maiden: stays 7f: acts on all-weather: pulled up second and third starts: tried in cheekpieces. *R. Hollinshead*

SCINTILLO 4 ch.c. Fantastic Light (USA) 134 – Danseuse du Soir (IRE) 121 (Thatching 131) [2009 112: p10g³ p12g* p10g* 12s 13.4m² 12m* 12m 12m 12d⁶ 12f Nov 29] sturdy colt: good walker: smart performer: better than ever in first half of 2009, winning listed race at Kempton and sportingbet.com Winter Derby at Lingfield (beat Premio Loco by nose) in March, and Grand Prix de Chantilly (beat Chinchon a head) in May: well held next 3 starts, in Grand Prix de Saint-Cloud, King George VI and Queen Elizabeth Stakes at Ascot and Prix du Conseil de Paris at Longchamp: changed ownership privately, not discredited when eleventh to Vodka in Japan Cup at Tokyo final outing: effective at 1¼m, seemingly at easy 13.4f: acts on polytrack, heavy and good to firm going: blinkered last 4 starts at 3 yrs: to continue career in USA. *R. Hannon* **117**

SCOOBY DEE 2 b.f. (Mar 7) Captain Rio 122 – Scooby Dooby Do 62 (Atraf 116) [2009 6g 5m⁵ 6m 8g Oct 19] smallish, deep-girthed filly: second foal: sister to 3-y-o Captain Scooby: dam sprint maiden: form only when fifth in maiden at Beverley: bred to prove best at 5f/6f. *R. M. Whitaker* **50**

SCORN (USA) 2 b.f. (Apr 28) Seeking The Gold (USA) – Sulk (IRE) 111 (Selkirk (USA) 129) [2009 7d⁴ 7g² Oct 31] fourth foal: sister to smart UAE 7f winner Ibn Battuta and closely related to winner abroad by Kingmambo: dam, 2-y-o 7f/1m (Prix Marcel Boussac) winner (stayed 15.5f), half-sister to very smart performer up to 1½m Eagle Mountain: promise in maidens, better effort when 1½ lengths second to Field Day at Newmarket: will be suited by 1m+: open to further improvement. *J. H. M. Gosden* **78 p**

SCOTCH AND SODA (IRE) 3 b.f. Mull of Kintyre (USA) 114 – Buddy And Soda (IRE) 75 (Imperial Frontier (USA) 112) [2009 6m⁵ 7m⁶ 6f⁵ 8v 5.9g 7v f7g Oct 18] 4,500Y: sturdy, compact gelding: sixth foal: half-sister to 5f (including at 2 yrs)/6f winners Sahara Silk (fairly useful, by Desert Style) and Dunn Deal (by Revoque): dam Irish 7f winner: modest form in maidens first 2 starts: regressed after. *Jedd O'Keeffe* **57 d**

SCOTTISH AFFAIR 3 b.g. Selkirk (USA) 129 – Southern Queen (Anabaa (USA) 130) [2009 57p: p8g⁵ p9.5g* 10.2g 11.8g⁶ p12g Jul 1] rather unfurnished gelding: fair handicapper: won at Wolverhampton in March, easily best effort: stays 9.5f: acts on polytrack: sold 8,000 gns. *E. A. L. Dunlop* **67**

SCOTTISH BOOGIE (IRE) 2 b.c. (Mar 22) Tobougg (IRE) 125 – Scottish Spice 92 (Selkirk (USA) 129) [2009 6m 7m 6.5g³ 7d* Oct 27] rather unfurnished colt: fourth foal: dam 7f (at 2 yrs)/1m winner: improved to win nursery at Yarmouth by 2¾ lengths from Landowner: should be suited by 1m: acts on good to soft going. *S. Kirk* **81**

SCOTTISH GLEN 3 ch.g. Kyllachy 129 – Dance For Fun 74 (Anabaa (USA) 130) [2009 7.1g⁵ Jun 25] sturdy gelding: 8/1, well held in maiden at Warwick. *P. R. Chamings* **–**

SCOTTY'S FUTURE (IRE) 11 b.g. Namaqualand (USA) – Persian Empress (IRE) 51 (Persian Bold 123) [2009 54§: 9.9g 9.9m 7.9g 10g Oct 16] close-coupled gelding: modest performer at 10 yrs: no form in 2009: visored once: temperamental/unreliable. *A. Berry* **– §**

sportingbet.com Winter Derby, Lingfield—a second win in four days for Scintillo (right), who edges out Premio Loco in the winter showpiece; behind them are Bronze Cannon (left) and Halicarnassus (dark colours, centre)

SCRAPPER SMITH (IRE) 3 b.g. Choisir (AUS) 126 – Lady Ounavarra (IRE) (Simply Great (FR) 122) [2009 59: 5g^{3} 6g^{6} 6g^{4} 5d* 6s^{6} 5s* 5g^{6} 7.2v^{3} Oct 31] smallish, compact gelding: fair handicapper: won at Carlisle in July and Ayr in August: stays 7f: acts on heavy ground: visored once (went too fast). *A. C. Whillans* **69**

SCREAMING BRAVE 3 b.g. Hunting Lion (IRE) 115 – Hana Dee 72 (Cadeaux Genereux 131) [2009 60: p8g p8.6g^{4} p12.2m p12g^{5} p12g^{4} 12.1m^{3} 14.1m^{2} 10.1g* 11.5m* 12m^{3} 12d^{5} 11.5d^{6} 11.5m^{4} 11.9f^{6} 9.9m^{2} p12.2g^{6} 10m^{2} Sep 12] angular gelding: fair handicapper: won at Yarmouth in May and Lingfield in June: stays 1¾m: acts on polytrack, good to firm and good to soft ground: tried visored: usually held up: joined Miss S. West, fairly useful form over hurdles. *M. R. Channon* **68 a60**

SCRUFFY SKIP (IRE) 4 b.g. Diktat 126 – Capoeira (USA) (Nureyev (USA) 131) [2009 62§: f6g^{6} p6g 6m^{5} 7g 6f 7g 6f^{5} 6m^{2} 6g 6s^{6} 6d 6f* 6m 6m p6g p6f 6g Oct 20] workmanlike gelding: modest performer: won seller at Brighton in September: stays 7f: acts on all-weather and firm going: often in headgear: temperamental, and not one to rely on. *Mrs C. A. Dunnett* **58 §**

SCRUPULOUS 3 gr.f. Dansili 127 – Mrs Gray 61 (Red Sunset 120) [2009 62: 8s 10g 8m 10.7g^{3} 9d* 8.5d p9.5g^{6} Dec 3] lengthy, rather leggy filly: fair performer: won claimer at Ballinrobe in August: left David Wachman in Ireland, pulled too hard in handicap at Wolverhampton final outing: stays 10.7f: acts on good to soft going: none too consistent. *Tom Dascombe* **70**

SCUFFLE 4 gr.f. Daylami (IRE) 138 – Tantina (USA) 115 (Distant View (USA) 126) [2009 106: p8g^{3} 8g^{6} 10g^{4} 8m^{5} 8m^{5} Sep 19] leggy filly: useful performer, lightly raced: best effort in 2009 when 5 lengths fourth to Whispering Gallery in handicap at Newmarket: respectable efforts in similar events after: stayed 1¼m: acted on polytrack, good to firm and good to soft going: visits Oasis Dream. *R. Charlton* **103**

SCUTCH MILL (IRE) 7 ch.g. Alhaarth (IRE) 126 – Bumble (Rainbow Quest (USA) 134) [2009 64: p9.5g^{2} p10g^{4} Jan 13] small, close-coupled gelding: modest handicapper: stays 1¼m: acts on polytrack and firm going: tongue tied: often slowly away: fair hurdler: has joined W. B. Stone. *P. C. Haslam* **57**

SEA CLIFF (IRE) 5 b.g. Golan (IRE) 129 – Prosaic Star (IRE) 81 (Common Grounds 118) [2009 47+: f16g* p16g^{5} f14g^{2} p13.9g^{3} f14g^{3} p16g^{4} Apr 29] fair handicapper: won at Southwell in January: may prove best at 2m+: acts on all-weather: effective in cheekpieces or not: often slowly away earlier in career: fair hurdler/chaser. *Jonjo O'Neill* **65**

SEA COVE 9 b.m. Terimon 124 – Regal Pursuit (IRE) 61 (Roi Danzig (USA)) [2009 17.2g^{5} 13g 16d Aug 10] workmanlike mare: poor maiden: stays easy 1½m: acts on fibresand and good to firm ground. *Mrs Dianne Sayer* **45**

SEA CREST 3 b.f. Xaar 132 – Talah 87 (Danehill (USA) 126) [2009 69: 5m 5s^{2} 6m^{3} 5m^{2} f6g^{6} 5m 5g Oct 23] rather leggy filly: modest maiden: best at 5f: acts on soft and good to firm ground. *M. Brittain* **65**

SEADER (USA) 4 b. or br.g. Mr Greeley (USA) 122 – Evangel (USA) (Danzig (USA)) [2009 58: p8g^{5} 8d 8g 12.1v p9.5g^{5} Aug 17] useful-looking gelding: fair maiden: left M. Halford in Ireland after third start: worth another try at 1½m: acts on polytrack, best turf effort on firm going: tried in cheekpieces. *Tim Vaughan* **68**

SEA DUBAI 2 b.c. (Mar 23) Mark of Esteem (IRE) 137 – Royal Flame (IRE) 72 (Royal Academy (USA) 130) [2009 7m^{6} p7g^{2} 7.1g Aug 31] 23,000Y: fifth foal: half-brother to 3 winners, including 4-y-o Arabian Spirit: dam 1¼m winner: easily best effort in maidens when second to Astonishment at Kempton: seemed amiss final outing: will stay 1m. *R. Hannon* **78**

SEAFIELD TOWERS 9 ch.g. Compton Place 125 – Midnight Spell 79 (Night Shift (USA)) [2009 48: 5m 5m 6f 6g^{6} 5m 6m Jun 20] good-bodied gelding: poor performer: often in blinkers/cheekpieces. *D. A. Nolan* **–**

SEA LAND (FR) 5 ch.g. King's Best (USA) 132 – Green Bonnet (IRE) (Green Desert (USA) 127) [2009 –: p6g* p7g 6s^{4} 5.9d p7.1g^{5} p7.1g p7.1g^{2} p7.1g p8.6g Oct 17] well-made gelding: fair performer on all-weather, poor on turf nowadays: won handicap at Wolverhampton in July: should stay 1m: acts on polytrack: tried visored: has been slowly away. *B. Ellison* **46 a69**

SEA LAVENDER 3 b.f. Diktat 126 – Satin Bell 99 (Midyan (USA) 124) [2009 7s p8g 10f^{5} 10m^{2} 11.6d p12g a8g^{3} a11.5g^{2} Dec 5] unfurnished filly: eighth foal: half-sister to several winners, including fairly useful 1m/9f winner Strawberry Leaf (by Unfuwain) and useful 6f (at 2 yrs) to 11f (in Hong Kong) winner Zabaglione (by Zilzal): dam 7f winner: fair maiden: sold from R. Charlton 4,000 gns after sixth start: stays 11.5f: acts on all-weather and good to firm going: tried blinkered. *N. Minner, Belgium* **77**

SEA LORD (IRE) 2 b.c. (Feb 18) Cape Cross (IRE) 129 – First Fleet (USA) 106 (Woodman (USA) 126) [2009 7g² 7g* 7m 6d 7m² 7g Oct 24] sturdy colt: fifth foal: half-brother to winner in Canada by Storm Cat: dam, French 1m/1¼m winner (including at 2 yrs), out of close relative to high-class middle-distance performer Assatis: fairly useful performer: won maiden at Ascot (by neck from Pounced) in July: only form after when good head second to Audacity of Hope in nursery at Newmarket: should be suited by 1m+: acts on good to firm going: races prominently. *M. Johnston* **93**

SEAMSTER 2 ch.g. (May 2) Pivotal 124 – Needles And Pins (IRE) 104 (Fasliyev (USA) 120) [2009 6g 7s p7.1m² Nov 28] maiden: left Saeed bin Suroor/off over 4 months after second start: easily best effort when second to Robust Wish at Wolverhampton: gelded after: stays 7f. *M. Johnston* **71**

SEAMUS SHINDIG 7 b.g. Aragon 118 – Sheesha (USA) (Shadeed (USA) 135) [2009 96: 6m⁵ 6m 6m 6g⁴ 6g* 6m 6d⁴ 6g Oct 23] small, sturdy gelding: useful handicapper: won at Newmarket in August: only creditable effort after when fourth at Goodwood: best at 6f: acts on polytrack, firm and good to soft going: tried in cheekpieces at 4 yrs. *H. Candy* **95**

SEA OF HEARTBREAK (IRE) 2 b.f. (Mar 20) Rock of Gibraltar (IRE) 133 – Top Forty (Rainbow Quest (USA) 134) [2009 8v p7.1g* Nov 6] second foal: dam unraced half-sister to smart winner up to 13.5f Self Defense, out of half-sister to Irish Oaks winner Princess Pati and high-class middle-distance performer Seymour Hicks: much better effort in maidens when winning at Wolverhampton by ¾ length from Akamon, quickening impressively: will stay 1¼m: should go on improving. *R. Charlton* **68 p**

SEA OF LEAVES (USA) 3 b.f. Stormy Atlantic (USA) – Dock Leaf (USA) (Woodman (USA) 126) [2009 79: 7g 5g⁵ 6m² 6d 6m 6m* 6m⁴ Oct 16] neat filly: useful performer: won handicap at Newmarket in October by neck from Bounty Box: respectable 2½ lengths fourth to Damaniyat Girl in listed race at same course final start: effective at 5f/6f: acts on good to firm going: tongue tied last 3 outings at 2 yrs. *J. S. Goldie* **103**

SEAQUEL 3 b.f. Kyllachy 129 – Broughton Singer (IRE) 61 (Common Grounds 118) [2009 61: 8d⁴ 9.1v⁶ p10g p12f² Dec 13] close-coupled filly: modest maiden handicapper: stays easy 1½m: acts on polytrack, raced only on ground softer than good on turf. *A. B. Haynes* **57**

SEARCH FOR THE KEY (USA) 2 b. or br.c. (Feb 26) El Corredor (USA) 123 – Lo Cal Bread (USA) (Native Prospector (USA) 90) [2009 6d³ p6g⁶ Sep 9] $135,000Y, resold 26,000Y: fifth foal: closely related to fairly useful Italian 5f (at 2 yrs) to 1m winner Fresh Bread (by Mr Greeley) and half-brother to 2 winners in USA: dam once-raced half-sister to smart US sprinter/miler Richter Scale: better effort in maidens when sixth to San Cassiano at Kempton: should stay 7f. *P. F. I. Cole* **75**

SEA ROVER (IRE) 5 b.h. Jade Robbery (USA) 121 – Talah 87 (Danehill (USA) 126) [2009 –: 6m² 5.9m⁵ 5f 5g 7m 6f* 5m 6m 6g 6m 6m 6d p6g² p5.1g Nov 30] tall, useful-looking horse: fairly useful handicapper on his day: won at Haydock in July: mostly below form after: stays 7f: acts on firm going: has twice finished lame. *M. Brittain* **80**

SEA SALT 6 b.g. Titus Livius (FR) 115 – Carati 86 (Selkirk (USA) 129) [2009 76: 6f 6d³ 7d⁵ 7d⁴ 6m* 7g² 6d 6m 6s* 6g⁴ 7.1m² 6d 7s⁶ Oct 27] good-topped gelding: has one eye (usually wears eyecover): fairly useful performer: left A. McCabe after reappearance: won seller at Newcastle in August and handicap at Thirsk in September: stays 7f: acts on firm and soft ground: has hung. *R. E. Barr* **82**

SEASIDER 4 b.g. Zamindar (USA) 116 – Esplanade 77 (Danehill (USA) 126) [2009 78+: 7f Jun 19] well-made gelding: easy mover: very lightly raced: useful at 2 yrs: well held both starts since: sold 13,000 gns, joined D. Simcock. *Sir Michael Stoute* **–**

SEASIDE SIZZLER 2 ch.g. (Feb 23) Rahy (USA) 115 – Via Borghese (USA) 116 (Seattle Dancer (USA) 119) [2009 7g 7.1m⁵ 8g⁴ Sep 30] 55,000F, 62,000Y: lengthy gelding: half-brother to several winners, including 2003 2-y-o 6f winner Venetian Pride and 7f winner Pietro Siena (both fairly useful, by Gone West): dam 6f (at 2 yrs in Ireland) to 9f (US Grade 2) winner: best effort in maidens when 1½ lengths fourth to Spoken at Salisbury (still green, gelded after): should stay 1¼m. *R. M. Beckett* **73**

SEASONAL CROSS 4 b.f. Cape Cross (IRE) 129 – Seasonal Blossom (IRE) (Fairy King (USA)) [2009 57, a65: p7g 8.1g³ 8m² 8.3g⁴ 8m³ 9g³ 8g² 7g 8m* 8g* 7d⁵ Oct 15] sturdy filly: fair handicapper: won at Bath and Salisbury in September: should stay 1¼m: acts on polytrack and good to firm ground: usually held up. *S. Dow* **73**

SEASONS ESTATES 7 b.m. Mark of Esteem (IRE) 137 – La Fazenda (Warning 136) [2009 8.1g Jun 25] smallish mare: fairly useful handicapper in 2005: has since been to stud (had foal by Tobougg in 2007): tailed off only outing since. *F. J. Brennan* –

SEA STORM (IRE) 11 b.g. Dolphin Street (FR) 125 – Prime Interest (IRE) (Kings Lake (USA) 133) [2009 –: 12.4d^6 Oct 13] big, strong gelding: fair hurdler: very lightly raced on Flat nowadays, modest form sole start at 11 yrs: stays 1m: acts on polytrack, soft and firm ground: has worn cheekpieces, blinkered once. *James Moffatt* 58

SEA THE STARS (IRE) 3 b.c. Cape Cross (IRE) 129 – Urban Sea (USA) 126 (Miswaki (USA) 124) [2009 109p: 8m* 12g* 10m* 10.4m* 10d* 12g* Oct 4] 140

'I was always reading about racing and great horses of the past. So when you grow up with the history of racing and the history of breeding, the landmark horses that came along over a century—to train one that's in that league gives you the greatest satisfaction.' John Oxx was careful not to get too closely involved in the academic debate about the place of his 'landmark horse' Sea The Stars in the pantheon of the Flat-racing greats, but he showed a keen appreciation of racing history. 'Sea-Bird was the flashiest Arc winner in my time. Mill Reef was such a generous sort, he could stretch clear and win by wide margins. Brigadier Gerard ran a lot of races over a variety of distances and was outstanding. Nijinsky was a triple crown winner. They are the ones . . . it's marvellous just that Sea The Stars is up there with them.' Thomas Carlyle's famous essay *On History* begins by describing history as 'the first distinct product of man's spiritual nature; his earliest expression of what can be called thought . . . of all mankind, there is no tribe so rude that it has not attempted history, though several have not arithmetic enough to count five.' Carlyle described all knowledge as recorded experience, and a product of history. 'History has become a schoolmistress . . . all learners, all inquiring minds of every order, are gathered round her footstool, and reverently pondering her lessons, as the true basis of wisdom.' Carlyle pointed out that the 'conflict of testimonies' that occur when history is recorded is usually 'settled by majority of votes'. 'Suppose, however, that the majority of votes was all wrong; that the real cardinal points lay far deeper; and had been passed over unnoticed, because no seer, but only mere onlookers, chanced to be there!' Carlyle acknowledged that the most gifted man can observe, still more can record, only the series of his own impressions. 'Vigilance and reverent humility' should be the bywords for those inquiring into history, said Carlyle who bemoaned the fact that 'a well-written life is almost as rare as a well-spent one, and there are certainly many more men whose history deserves to be recorded than persons able and willing to furnish the record.'

stanjames.com 2000 Guineas, Newmarket—Sea The Stars opens his campaign with a classic success; favourite Delegator (blaze) hangs left but still takes second ahead of Gan Amhras (breastgirth), Rip Van Winkle (left) and Mastercraftsman (striped sleeves)

The seventeen handicappers from fourteen countries around the world who compile horseracing's World Thoroughbred Rankings now meet in Hong Kong in December to provide 'official recognition' of the achievements of the world's top horses. The rankings, though, according to the World Rankings Supervisory Committee, apparently have their limitations. In its 'statement of handicapping practice' issued with the latest rankings, it republished the foreword written by the then International Classification Committee chairman in 1996. 'There is some confusion as to what a rating now represents and as to the purpose of the Classifications. Many people believe a rating to represent the absolute inherent ability of a particular thoroughbred and therefore, the Classifications to represent the qualitative assessment of the breed in any one year or as between one year and another. This view is no longer sustainable, as a rating is now primarily a measurement of relative performance and only in particular circumstances will it demonstrate the ultimate inherent ability of a particular thoroughbred. This being the case, Classifications are now a retrospective measure of performances, not necessarily the inherent abilities of those thoroughbreds included.' This witless admission of its own shortcomings was presumably an attempt by the World Rankings Supervisory Committee to diffuse criticism of its assessment of Sea The Stars when the World Thoroughbred Rankings for 2009 were published in January 2010.

Sea The Stars had been labelled 'the best we have ever seen' by many, among them BBC TV's leading racing presenter Clare Balding ('the best horse I think we'll ever see') and long-serving Channel 4 commentator John Francome ('the best in my lifetime') who delivered their verdicts after—and in Francome's case before—Sea The Stars made it six Group 1 wins from six starts as a three-year-old when winning the world's most valuable race on turf, the Prix de l'Arc de Triomphe at Longchamp in October. Ian Balding (father of Clare), who trained Mill Reef, was quoted as saying that, among the great horses of his experience, he thought Sea The Stars was 'probably the best'. In the print media, Alan Lee of *The Times* wrote 'I always believed no Flat horse could ever supplant Dancing Brave in my estimation . . . but he has not achieved as much as Sea The Stars'; the bloodstock correspondent of the *Racing Post* Tony Morris, whose experience stretches beyond that of Lee, wrote 'I can't quite persuade myself that he would have beaten Sea-Bird . . . but I can believe that the superstar we have been

Investec Derby, Epsom—rounding Tattenham Corner, Sea The Stars is on the rail disputing third with Kite Wood; two of the Ballydoyle contingent, Golden Sword and Age of Aquarius, have opened up a clear lead after a relatively steady first three furlongs

privileged to watch this year would have defeated every other great horse of my era, so I rank him above such favourites as Vaguely Noble, Nijinsky, Mill Reef, Brigadier Gerard, Shergar and Dancing Brave.' The debate about whether Sea The Stars had eclipsed all other past champions even prompted *TIME* magazine to publish an article posing the question 'Is Sea The Stars the best racehorse of all time?' The author's answer: 'He might just be the greatest of them all.'

The World Thoroughbred Rankings put Sea The Stars on 136, only the eighth highest figure awarded since its forerunner the International Classifications were established in 1977 (North American horses have been included since 1995). Dancing Brave (141) heads the list, with Alleged, Shergar, El Gran Senor, Generous, Three Troikas and Peintre Celebre also higher than Sea The Stars. According to an article in the *Daily Telegraph* in early-December, the senior BHA handicapper Phil Smith was going to Hong Kong armed with files of statistics to ensure that Sea The Stars 'should gain proper official recognition.' 'Dominic Gardiner-Hill [another BHA handicapper] has put together our draft,' said Smith. 'He has spent three weeks on its preparation, and we are satisfied we have arrived at the correct ratings.' Smith stressed the 'vigorous debate' that goes on at the Hong Kong conference. 'It gets tetchy at times, sometimes people feel very strongly that they're right, and you have to remember that all the representatives are bosses in their own respective jurisdictions, and they are used to getting their own way.' While Smith claimed that, with the rating of Sea The Stars, there was 'no need for a vote, no doubts about what he had achieved at his best', the decision-making process that arrives at the World Thoroughbred Rankings—handicapping by committee—makes expediency inevitable.

The lack of leadership and of a cohesive, long-term strategy was bound to bring the World Rankings/International Classifications into disrepute over time. In its 'statement of handicapping practice' the supervisory committee finally admitted to inconsistencies in the level of the 'official' ratings in the thirty years or so that the Rankings/Classifications have been in existence. 'In the circumstances,' the committee wrote, 'one would have to seriously question whether the likes of Dancing Brave, Alleged, Shergar and El Gran Senor would have achieved their ratings were they racing today.' The committee didn't go into details about the reasons for the variations in the level of ratings—the level has slipped by around 4 lb since the early-'nineties alone, for example—but its statement exposed the Rankings/Classifications as virtually worthless as a comparative historical record. The International Classifications were introduced to provide a way of monitoring the quality of the official pattern races, to see whether they were living up to their designation. Its originators did not have to start from scratch—they had the *Timeform* model which had already been established for thirty years—but mistakes were made right from the start (an initial 0-100 scale was soon dropped in favour of mirroring the *Timeform* scale). Even for the purpose of monitoring the quality of pattern races, it should have been self-evident that the Classifications needed to be maintained at roughly the same level, year-on-year. That they weren't was a gross dereliction of duty on the part of those responsible—Carlyle's 'mere onlookers'—and led to the embarrassing position in which the World Rankings Supervisory Committee found itself in the latest season.

The first 'Timeform Annual'—a pocket-sized supplement to the late-out 1947 edition of Phil Bull's *Best Horses*—became the forerunner of the *Racehorses* series. *Racehorses* has built up a worldwide readership and become established, in the words of eminent turf historian John Randall, as the 'definitive record of the racing year and the most authoritative source of reference for future historians.' The highest-rated horse in that slim, concise first edition was the brilliant miler Tudor Minstrel, rated 144. The Timeform handicap was expressed in pounds, on a level which corresponded to 'an average official Free Handicap', the maximum weight in those days being 9-7 (133 lb); at 144, therefore, Tudor Minstrel, runaway winner of the Two Thousand Guineas, was rated 11 lb superior to the top horse in an average year. Only one horse has been rated more highly by Timeform—the peerless Sea-Bird whose rating of 145 is still the highest achieved in more than sixty years of the *Racehorses* annuals. The trio of Sea-Bird, Tudor Minstrel and Brigadier Gerard (144) remain secure at the top of the 'all-time' Timeform list, but, among the champion three-year-olds and upwards, only the sprinter Abernant

(142), the unbeaten Ribot (142) and Mill Reef (141) have been rated more highly than Sea The Stars who stands on a par with Vaguely Noble, Shergar, Dancing Brave and Dubai Millennium, each rated 140.

Comparisons between past and present champions are always difficult to make but, when an exceptional horse like Sea The Stars comes along, the desire to make them becomes well-nigh irresistible. Absolute comparisons between top horses of different generations are notoriously unfair, more so when the horses are separated by decades. The present learns from the past and no sport stands still, each succeeding generation of performers shaped by an ever-changing environment with, for example, advances made in nutrition and training methods. The story in most sports is of modern-day, professional competitors generally bettering the achievements and skills of their predecessors, sometimes with the help of technological advances in equipment and kit (and, it has to be said, sometimes with the help of performance-enhancing drugs). It should almost go without saying that the average thoroughbred racehorse is superior to its ancestors from half a century ago. But by how much? How can any intrinsic improvement—if there has been any—be quantified accurately, given the unevenness of the landscape of the sport over the years? A general improvement in the racing surfaces, and the use of artificial watering, is a stumbling block to using the stop-watch to measure improvement. Worthwhile comparisons can be made only by accurate assessment of what the sport's great horses achieve against their own generations and by putting them in historical context. The level of the ratings in the Timeform Annuals has been carefully monitored, and maintained or amended as required, to allow valid comparisons to be made between crops.

Naturally, in a publication that has been going as long as *Racehorses*, the methods used to arrive at Timeform ratings have evolved over time. There was probably a little more reliance at Timeform on 'time' than on 'form' in the early days when linking lines of form between horses was the most widely-used method of handicapping. Time analysis is still a very important aid, mostly through analysis of overall times. But the Timeform handicappers have had a variety of other tools at their disposal for much of Timeform's history, including extensive, historical race standards, based on Timeform's assessments of previous runnings of a race (or of similar races), adjusted for such things as the time taken, the size of the field, the weights carried and the distance between the horses at the finish. Handicapping will, though, always be an art, not a science, and an inevitable degree of subjectivity—influenced by lessons learned from experience—goes into determining the definitive Annual ratings. Enough good horses usually remain in training for their performances from one year to another also to be used to tie in the ratings from one Annual to the next. For example, Vaguely Noble, Nijinsky (rated 138 by Timeform) Mill Reef and Brigadier Gerard all ran in a golden five-year period between 1968 and 1972. The 1968 Derby winner Sir Ivor, triple crown winner Nijinsky and Mill Reef, who won the Derby after coming second to Brigadier Gerard in the Two Thousand Guineas, all made their mark on the Prix de l'Arc de Triomphe as three-year-olds after being tested in a full series of top races beforehand. All three had been leading two-year-olds (as had Brigadier Gerard) in an era when success by a horse as a juvenile was regarded as much more important than it is nowadays.

It became clear, however, in the 'eighties, that some of the leading two-year-olds were no longer living up to their ratings. They weren't training on, or more likely, they were being overtaken by those whose development was, by then, being planned more with a three-year-old campaign in mind (Shergar and Dancing Brave were both relatively lightly raced at two). The globalisation of racing, and the fact that most of the new, big international races were being created for three-year-olds and older horses, was an incentive to keep more good horses in training after their three-year-old career. The change in emphasis among owners and trainers has led to an enormous shift in the number of older horses kept in training: from being the smallest group in 1968 (when there were 821 four-year-olds and upwards with a rating in *Racehorses*), four-year-olds and upwards are now much the largest (numbering 3,723 in *Racehorses of 2008*). The corresponding figures for the two-year-olds with a rating were 1,527 in *Racehorses of 1968* and 2,689 in *Racehorses of 2008*; and for the three-year-olds, the figures were 1,059 and 3,047 respectively.

Investec Derby, Epsom—Sea The Stars comes home ahead of four Ballydoyle challengers, Fame And Glory, Masterofthehorse (striped cap), Rip Van Winkle (left) and Golden Sword (blaze); Crowded House (white armlets) does best of the British-trained colts in sixth

With Timeform ratings, it is always a question of being flexible and putting them in context. If a horse is rated too highly, for example, it becomes apparent in the light of subsequent results. One consequence of having to lower the general level of the ratings of the two-year-olds over time has been an inevitable effect on the level for the three-year-olds, particularly in the first part of the season when the classics take place (the Timeform weight-for-age scale was amended in favour of the older horses in 1990 which also had the effect of depressing the three-year-old level). The performance required to win an average edition of the Two Thousand Guineas has fallen from around 130 in the 'sixties and 'seventies to around 124 in the last decade or so. Sir Ivor ran to 133, Nijinsky to 135+ and Brigadier Gerard to 141, while the only winners of the race to run to a rating above 130 since 1980 are El Gran Senor (136 in 1984) and Dancing Brave (134 in 1986). Sea The Stars ran to 128 in winning the latest edition (125 would have been good enough to come out on top). He had shown progressive form in three races as a juvenile, winning the Beresford Stakes at the Curragh on the last of them and being promoted towards the head of the ante-post Derby lists. His stable's main hope for the Two Thousand Guineas seemed to be another choicely-bred prospect the Futurity Stakes winner Arazan, who had taken the place of Sea The Stars in the National Stakes and started odds on, finishing third to Mastercraftsman. Sea The Stars began fast work in March but he missed a fortnight after running a high temperature in the middle of that month and his participation in the Two Thousand Guineas was still in the balance two weeks before Newmarket when he worked upsides with Arazan—who was as short as 10/1 for the Guineas at the time—in a gallop at Leopardstown. With Newmarket having to water, Arazan's connections eventually decided the going would be too firm (he missed the whole season), while the trainer reported at the start of Guineas week that Sea The Stars had 'failed to sparkle' in a gallop at home. 'It's very soft and he hasn't worked as well as he has been working on good ground, or as well as he worked at Leopardstown eight days ago.' Oxx spoke more encouragingly, however, as the race approached and Sea The Stars was sent off at 8/1, half the odds he had been after his gallop with Arazan at Leopardstown (25/1 had been generally available at the start of April). Sea The Stars was still only sixth choice in the betting on the day, behind the impressive Craven Stakes winner Delegator (a stablemate of the previous year's top two-year-old Crowded House, who was headed for the Derby via the Dante Stakes at York). Rip Van Winkle, Evasive, Mastercraftsman and Gan Amhras also started at shorter odds than Sea The Stars. The race was truly run, the field keeping together up the centre of the course after the stalls were positioned in the middle. Sea The Stars took a while to settle but produced a strong run on the stand-side flank coming out of the Dip and won, without his rider having to go for everything, by a length and a half and three quarters of a length from Delegator and Gan Amhras. Rip Van Winkle, Mastercraftsman and Evasive came next in an above-average Guineas. Sea The Stars really took the eye beforehand, towering over most of his rivals in the paddock, and he was made Derby favourite immediately after the Guineas.

'The Derby is the Derby' was John Oxx's reply when asked at the end of the season to nominate his personal highlight of the magnificent campaign enjoyed by Sea The Stars. The Derby has the most distinguished roll of honour of any event in the sport and is still the biggest draw in Britain's Flat calendar (watched on the BBC by 2.8m in the latest season). However, until the banking group Investec stepped in to sign a five-year deal in early-May, Jockey Club Racecourses seemed resigned to the latest Derby being run without a sponsor, just as a major grandstand redevelopment costing £38m was being completed at Epsom. The Derby is still the richest prize in British racing—Sea The Stars earned £709,625 for winning the latest edition—but the weakness of the pound saw the race fall from thirteenth to forty-second in the list of the world's most valuable races compiled by the International Racing Bureau. The Tokyo Yushun (Japanese Derby), the Kentucky Derby, the Prix du Jockey Club, the Irish Derby, the Hong Kong Derby and the UAE Derby were all worth more than the Derby at Epsom. Crowded House's Derby aspirations took a knock when he ran disappointingly in the Dante and the market was monopolised by Irish-trained runners, with Fame And Glory, one of six representing Ballydoyle, advancing his claims with an impressive win in the Derrinstown Stud Derby Trial at Leopardstown and supplanting Sea The Stars as Derby favourite. Ballydoyle's number-one Johnny Murtagh stuck with Rip Van Winkle at Epsom and he started third favourite, ahead of the Dante winner Black Bear Island (another representing Ballydoyle) and the Two Thousand Guineas third Gan Amhras, half of the field of twelve—only four of whom were trained in Britain—starting at odds ranging from 20/1 to 40/1. It was a smaller field than usual, no Derby having had fewer runners since Nijinsky's year, when there were eleven, the race having had twelve runners in 1989 (Nashwan), 2001 (Galileo) and 2002 (High Chaparral) in the period since.

The Derby got under way eight minutes late, Aidan O'Brien fined a total of £840 for his runners being late into the parade ring. Sea The Stars became the first since Nashwan, and only the second since Nijinsky, to win both the Two Thousand Guineas and the Derby. His trainer's stated misgivings about whether Sea The Stars

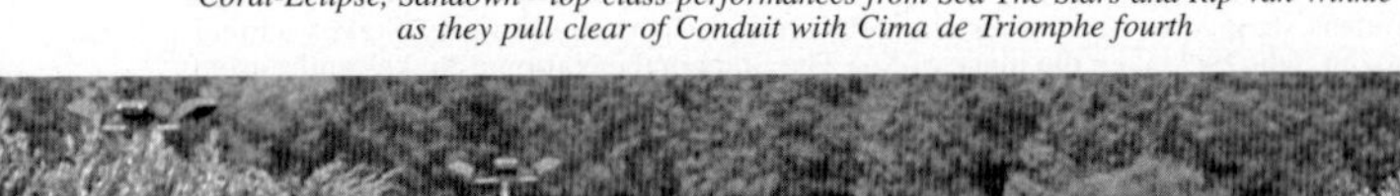

Coral-Eclipse, Sandown—top-class performances from Sea The Stars and Rip Van Winkle as they pull clear of Conduit with Cima de Triomphe fourth

would stay a strongly-run mile and a half must have been relieved somewhat by the steady pace over the first three furlongs, though the strong-travelling Sea The Stars did himself no favours by pulling his way to the front of the main pack as two of the Ballydoyle contingent, Golden Sword and Age of Aquarius, eventually quickened and opened up a clear lead. The result was never in much doubt after Sea The Stars responded really well when ridden halfway up the straight, catching and overtaking the leaders approaching the final furlong. Nothing ever looked like coming from behind, Fame And Glory (after tracking Sea The Stars throughout) outpaced in the penultimate furlong when Sea The Stars began to quicken, but still emerging best of the Ballydoyle challengers. Sea The Stars won with something in hand by a length and three quarters from Fame And Glory who was all out to hold on to second by a neck in a very close finish with three of his stablemates, Masterofthehorse, Rip Van Winkle and Golden Sword, the last-named collared by his compatriots only in the dying strides. The first British-trained finisher was Crowded House, six lengths behind Golden Sword in sixth; Black Bear Island and Gan Amhras came tenth and eleventh, neither making any impression, the latter's performance blamed by his jockey on his inability to handle Epsom's gradients.

Sea The Stars was a second Derby winner for his trainer, following Sinndar, and a third for Michael Kinane, his forty-nine-year-old rider (the oldest winning jockey since Willie Carson, successful at fifty-one on Nashwan). Kinane also won the Derby on Commander In Chief and on Galileo, a half-brother to Sea The Stars. Galileo's win came during Kinane's five years as number one at Ballydoyle when he also rode High Chaparral in most of his races, though he partnered runner-up Hawk Wing instead at Epsom, and when he also rode French-trained Montjeu, another of the stars associated with the Coolmore partners at that time. Kinane, who retired at the end of the latest season, won the Irish jockeys' title thirteen times and he was very much a jockey for the big occasion, as his outstanding record in the major races showed. The performance of Sea The Stars at Epsom, judged strictly on the form-book, didn't match those of Galileo and High Chaparral and was also not up with the Derby-winning efforts of Motivator, Authorized or the previous year's winner New Approach. Kinane, though, privately already had no doubts that Sea The Stars was the best he had ever ridden; John Oxx revealed later in the year that Kinane whispered to him, as he dismounted at Epsom, 'This is one of the greats.'

The performances of recent Derby winners Sir Percy and New Approach, among others, has gone some way to showing that the all-round classic performer, one possessing the range of qualities needed for the Rowley Mile, Epsom's switchback mile and a half and possibly Doncaster's galloping mile and three quarters, may not yet be extinct. Neither Sir Percy nor New Approach, both of whom came second in the Two Thousand Guineas, went on to run in the St Leger and, in fact, no Derby winner has done so since Reference Point won both races in 1987. Connections of Sea The Stars were quick to pour cold water on the idea that he might be aimed at the triple crown. The passing in Derby week of Nijinsky's trainer Vincent O'Brien, one of the legends of the turf, was another poignant reminder of an era when the Derby was still almost universally regarded as the greatest race in the world (O'Brien saddled the winner six times between 1962 and 1982) and when the highest status attainable by a thoroughbred on the British turf was that of triple crown winner. Since Nijinsky, the filly Oh So Sharp is the only horse to win three English classics (One Thousand Guineas, Oaks and St Leger). The decision four years after Oh So Sharp's achievement of Nashwan's owner to bypass the St Leger in favour of an Arc preparatory race in France caused a stir among traditionalists, whose criticism—some of it vitriolic—ranged from 'unadventurous' to 'defying any sporting explanation'. But there was no wholesale criticism of the connections of Sea The Stars. The St Leger, the oldest classic, faces much stiffer competition on the international stage nowadays for the best of the classic horses than it did, for example, in Nijinsky's day. It is fair to question whether Nijinsky himself would have contested the St Leger had the richly-endowed Irish Champion Stakes been in existence in 1970. John Oxx is among those who think the triple crown will be won again. He points to the make-up of Coolmore's current stallion band, which includes the influential Sadler's Wells stallions Montjeu, Galileo and High Chaparral, and is resulting in more stayingbreds coming through to Ballydoyle. Sea The Stars would have been a red-hot favourite had he turned up at Doncaster but, in the opinion of his trainer, he was not another genuine all-rounder like Nijinsky. 'I am a believer in the triple crown, it's a nice dream, but it might be a bridge too far for this fellow,' he said straight after the Derby. The position became even clearer when Oxx gave a further interview shortly after Sea The Stars returned home from Epsom. 'The St Leger is a great race, but it's a gruelling race and a big test of stamina, and I don't think this is the horse to do it,' he said. 'Cape Cross [sire of Sea The Stars] is Cape Cross and our fellow is just not bred for the St Leger—you can't ignore it. In any case, we want Sea The Stars to run in the Irish Champion Stakes [a week before the St Leger], ground permitting . . . if he doesn't run there he could run in the Arc if the ground is suitable.'

A tilt at the triple crown, then, was not on the agenda for Sea The Stars but he was still expected to emulate one of Nijinsky's notable achievements by completing a classic treble in the Irish Derby ('the obvious race for him,' according to his trainer). Sea The Stars would almost certainly have won at Epsom however the race had been run, but, with Ballydoyle likely to do more to ensure a strong gallop throughout at the Curragh, the Irish Derby rematch between Sea The Stars and Fame And Glory was still eagerly anticipated. Unfortunately, amid accusations that the course had been overwatered in the week leading up to the race, Sea The Stars was pulled out following heavy rain two days before (Fame And Glory went on to win by five lengths from Golden Sword). Instead, Sea The Stars took the path taken by Nashwan after his Two Thousand Guineas and Derby successes, dropping back to a mile and a quarter after Epsom.

Conditions at Sandown for the Coral-Eclipse, a week after the Curragh, were on the firm side and odds-on Sea The Stars, again looking in excellent shape beforehand, faced nine opponents, headed by the previous year's St Leger and Breeders' Cup Turf winner Conduit and by Rip Van Winkle, whom he was meeting for the third time in three outings as a three-year-old. No Derby winner had been successful in the Eclipse since Nashwan—Reference Point, Erhaab, Benny The Dip, Motivator and Authorized those beaten in the interim—but Sea The Stars put up a top-class performance, his effort, on form, better than those in winning the Two Thousand Guineas and the Derby and matched by his timefigure of 1.28 fast (equivalent to a timerating of 132) which was the fastest recorded by any horse over any distance in Britain in the latest season. With pacemakers for Rip Van Winkle and Conduit ensuring an unrelenting gallop, Kinane again had Sea The Stars at the head of the main pack and the response in the home straight was as impressive as it had been at Epsom. Sea The Stars quickened really well and was two lengths clear entering the penultimate furlong before idling a little in front and briefly allowing Rip Van Winkle almost alongside, before reasserting himself to win by a length, the shortest distance between the pair in their three meetings. Sea The Stars and Rip Van Winkle pulled clear of the rest, Conduit finishing four and a half lengths away in third after challenging briefly in the home straight, with the rest stretched right out (the only other runners to start at odds shorter than 50/1, Cima de Triomphe and Twice Over, were well beaten in fourth and seventh respectively).

Both Nijinsky and Nashwan contested the King George VI and Queen Elizabeth II Stakes in their signature seasons but there had been another indication of the changed fashions in racing when, of all the possible future targets mentioned for Sea The Stars in the aftermath of the Derby, there had been no mention of the Ascot race. The inauguration of the King George in 1951 was one of the first major developments which undermined the traditional classic races (and, as a consequence, the concept of the triple crown). Races like the King George and the Arc, which had its prize money raised substantially in 1949, challenged the supremacy of the classics, bringing the leaders of the classic generation into regular competition with the best of the older horses who remained in training. The Eclipse, first run in 1886 when it was the most valuable race in England, sometimes brought the generations together, most famously in 1903 when the previous year's Derby winner Ard Patrick beat another four-year-old the great filly Sceptre (who had won all the classics except the Derby) and the three-year-old Rock Sand, who had won the Two Thousand Guineas and the Derby (and went on to complete the triple crown). Until the second half of the twentieth century, though, the classic races reigned supreme. Bahram, the last horse to complete the triple crown before

Juddmonte International Stakes, York—
only four runners, two of them pacemakers for Mastercraftsman, in an all-Irish affair;
Sea The Stars continues his faultless season, breaking the course record to beat Mastercraftsman

Nijinsky, retired undefeated but never competed outside his own age group, though the previous year's Derby and St Leger winner Windsor Lad was still in training in 1935 and Bahram could have taken him on in the Eclipse (which Windsor Lad won). It was not necessary, however, for him to do so to attain exalted status.

Nowadays, the classics are seldom the most rigorous tests that a three-year-old faces in the course of a full season and an outstanding classic performer has to go on to prove himself in the top open-aged championship events. In later conversations, John Oxx did say that Sea The Stars would probably have been aimed at the King George if he had been able to run in the Irish Derby. 'Missing the Curragh and going to Sandown instead did change the situation, in terms of the time we have between upcoming races.' Whereas Oxx's previous Derby winner Sinndar (who didn't contest the King George either) was given a break after completing the Derby/Irish Derby double, Sea The Stars was regarded by his trainer as a summer horse ('the ground is very important for him') and was kept on the go. He didn't do any fast work for three weeks after the Eclipse, once the decision had been taken to miss the King George, but, other than that, his training regime wasn't relaxed. 'He actually needs to work, because he gets fresh if he doesn't, so it was not as big a drawback as it would be with some other horses.'

Sea The Stars went on thriving through the summer and made his next appearance in mid-August in the Juddmonte International, which carried the biggest first prize ever at York (£340,620), just over six weeks after the Eclipse and two and a half weeks before his 'definite' target the Irish Champion at Leopardstown. The International's inaugural running, as the Benson and Hedges Gold Cup, in 1972 saw Brigadier Gerard sensationally beaten at 3/1-on by the Derby winner Roberto, a defeat which prevented his equalling the Italian-trained Ribot's unbeaten sequence of sixteen victories (including successive Arcs—the second by six lengths—and a King George) achieved in the 'fifties. Brigadier Gerard ended his career with seventeen wins from eighteen starts (though he never ran on foreign soil), excelling at the top level over three seasons and winning championship events at a mile, a mile and a quarter (including the Eclipse) and a mile and a half (the King George VI and Queen Elizabeth Stakes). The task of assessing Brigadier Gerard was easier because in most of his races he was made to show the full measure of his superiority over those he ran against. His performances were there in black and white. It wasn't so straightforward with Sea The Stars, his racing style and general demeanour often contributing to his winning with something in reserve, while he wasn't usually made to race right through to the end and demonstrate his superiority to the full ('He only does enough but, sure, enough is enough if he wins,' was how his trainer put it). Nobody can be certain how much Sea The Stars had in hand at the end of some of his races. It was a matter of opinion, not of fact, and therefore will always be open to challenge.

By the time Sea The Stars lined up against Mastercraftsman and two Ballydoyle pacemakers in a rather disappointing four-runner, all Irish line-up at

Tattersalls Millions Irish Champion Stakes, Leopardstown—the race lives up to its title as Sea The Stars puts up a performance of tip-top merit, beating Fame And Glory and Mastercraftsman

York, his Timeform rating had gone up a further 3 lb to 136p after Rip Van Winkle and Conduit went on to boost the Eclipse form with winning performances in the Sussex Stakes (the best in the race for thirty years) and the King George VI and Queen Elizabeth Stakes respectively. Mastercraftsman had won the Irish Two Thousand Guineas and the St James's Palace Stakes since finishing fifth to Sea The Stars at Newmarket. Sea The Stars landed odds of 4/1-on at York but not before his supporters had endured an anxious moment when he briefly looked short of room while following Mastercraftsman through a gap between the two pacemakers early in the straight. Steadied again once through the gap, before Kinane asked him for his final effort, Sea The Stars took a while to hit top gear but swept through in the closing stages to beat Mastercraftsman (the pair a distance clear) with something in hand by a length, first and second both inside the previous time record for the course and distance (the time value of the performance was excellent, only a fraction behind the effort of Sea The Stars in the Eclipse).

'I'll see you at Leopardstown' was Johnny Murtagh's parting shot as Sea The Stars and Mastercraftsman were being pulled up at York. The Tattersalls Millions Irish Champion Stakes, with a first prize of £518,646 (over £200,000 more than the St Leger), certainly lived up to its billing, with Ballydoyle launching its biggest challenge yet to Sea The Stars. The management and staff at Leopardstown produced the track in very good shape, taking the precaution of preparing an inner and an outer course (the less-used latter circuit kept for the two Group 1s). Fortunately, the racecourse missed much of the heavy rain that led to several meetings elsewhere in Ireland being lost to the weather during the week, though the appearance of Sea The Stars wasn't finally confirmed until two hours before the race, which may have contributed to the fact that just 9,000 Irish racegoers took their only chance to get a view of Sea The Stars in the flesh as a three-year-old. The race provided a fascinating prospect, with Ballydoyle saddling both Mastercraftsman (pulled out of the Prix du Moulin to take part) and Fame And Glory (ridden by Murtagh), in addition to three others. Sea The Stars started at 6/4-on, Fame And Glory at 9/4 and Mastercraftsman at 6/1, with the Tattersalls Gold Cup winner Casual Conquest at 16/1 the only other runner in the nine-strong line-up at shorter than 100/1.

What established Sea The Stars as a great horse was not just the fact of his winning six Group 1 races in a row, but rather his performances in some of those races. His Eclipse performance was that of a true champion, but his performance at Leopardstown was even better, probably the best on turf in Europe since Dancing Brave in the 1986 Prix de l'Arc de Triomphe. That performance had been matched by Dubai Millennium when he put on a display of the same sheer brilliance to spreadeagle his field in the Dubai World Cup on dirt in 2000. Any fears that Sea

The Stars might be inconvenienced by the prevailing good to soft ground proved absolutely ill-founded. He completed his Group 1 five-timer in spectacular fashion, settled in mid-field and not beginning his unanswerable finishing run until after Fame And Glory had been sent clear early in the straight. Sea The Stars forged ahead over a furlong out and won by two and a half lengths, merely kept up to his work after taking the lead, drifting slightly left but giving the distinct impression he could have found more if needed. Mastercraftsman finished third, a further two and a half lengths behind Fame And Glory, with another nine back to Ballydoyle's third string Grand Ducal in fourth, Casual Conquest managing only seventh. Sea The Stars returned to the type of reception usually reserved for an Irish-trained winner of one of the championship events at Cheltenham's National Hunt Festival. It was thoroughly deserved—seeing that he had just proved himself the best Flat horse trained in Ireland in the now-extensive period since the Second World War, surpassing Nijinsky and dual Arc winner Alleged, the last-named also trained by Vincent O'Brien. John Oxx and his team at Currabeg deserved great credit for their handling of Sea The Stars, who was turned out once again in the pink of condition, while the unflappable Michael Kinane kept his nerve admirably when Fame And Glory suddenly surged past Sea The Stars early in the home straight. 'I wasn't worried. I was happy to let Fame And Glory go past me because my fellow was still running away. This is a hell of a racehorse,' he said afterwards.

Next step was the Qatar Prix de l'Arc de Triomphe, the world's richest race on turf (£2,096,881 to the winner). The race was, at one time, said to be an unlikely port of call but, with the Irish Champion showing that softish ground did not inconvenience Sea The Stars (he had won on soft at two), and the horse himself still thriving, he was sent to Longchamp with an outstanding chance. Three-year-olds generally have a very good record in the Arc but the great post-war trainer Noel Murless always maintained that the race was 'just three weeks too late for a horse who has undergone a proper classic preparation, working up to the Guineas in the spring, followed by Epsom and Ascot [the King George].' Murless was champion trainer in Britain nine times and saddled the winners of nineteen English classics, two of his best horses Crepello and Royal Palace arguably denied triple crown glory by injury after winning the Two Thousand Guineas and Derby (the St Leger being won by the respective Derby runners-up in their years, Ballymoss and Ribocco). The triple crown winner Nijinsky, whose three-year-old campaign was interrupted by an attack of ringworm in the summer, lost his unbeaten record when going down narrowly in the Arc and was beaten again in the Champion Stakes, his seventh and eighth outings at three. Sir Ivor and Mill Reef, however, defied the Murless adage, Sir Ivor's campaign continuing beyond Longchamp—where he was a fine second to Vaguely Noble—with wins in the Champion Stakes and the Washington International (the last-named run on November 11th). Mill Reef made six appearances as a three-year-old, having a preparatory run before the Guineas (as did Nijinsky and Sir Ivor) and winning the Derby, the Eclipse (by four lengths), the King George (by six) and the Arc (by three) after his defeat by Brigadier Gerard in the Two Thousand Guineas. Dancing Brave was the outstanding example between Mill Reef and Sea The Stars of a top three-year-old winning the Arc after following a full programme of top races beforehand. Dancing Brave suffered an unlucky defeat in the Derby, eating up the ground to finish second, after winning the Two Thousand Guineas (before which he was warmed up in the Craven) but he swept the board otherwise until managing only fourth in the Breeders' Cup Turf on his eighth outing as a three-year-old (the Breeders' Cup didn't exist in the days of Sir Ivor, Nijinsky and Mill Reef). Dancing Brave had a similar record to Sea The Stars, winning the Eclipse (the first Derby winner to run in it since Mill Reef), turning the tables decisively on Derby winner Shahrastani in the King George and, after a warm-up in the Select Stakes at Goodwood, taking the Arc in breathtaking fashion from one of the best fields ever assembled for the race. The comparisons with Mill Reef and Dancing Brave became irresistible after Sea The Stars duly extended his one-a-month sequence of Group 1 victories to six.

The prestige of the Arc and the attention focussed on Sea The Stars—who was cheered when he came into the paddock—led to the victory being lauded as the finest of his career though, judged solely on the quality of performance, it wasn't on a par with his Eclipse and Irish Champion efforts. The going at Longchamp was

Qatar Prix de l'Arc de Triomphe, Longchamp—
a worthy winner of the world's richest turf race as Sea The Stars and Michael Kinane complete a unique sequence, making light of a less than clear run in the straight; Youmzain finishes runner-up for the third year in a row as Cavalryman, Conduit (No.2) and Dar Re Mi take the rest of the prize money

good, if anything on the firm side, and with his main rival on form Fame And Glory proving difficult to settle and then never really threatening, Sea The Stars effectively had 10 lb in hand of the rest of the Arc field. Although there was an anxious moment when Sea The Stars looked like being crowded on the inside in the home straight, the incident was never going to cost him the race. Kinane had eventually anchored the hard-pulling Sea The Stars about halfway down the main field, the two Ballydoyle pacemakers essentially ignored as they raced a long way clear, and, once extricated in the straight, Sea The Stars quickened between the leaders Stacelita and Dar Re Mi to take command a furlong out. He was well on top at the finish, winning by two lengths from the running-on Youmzain, who filled the runner-up spot for the third time. The impression that Sea The Stars had plenty left was confirmed when Sea The Stars took off again as Stacelita came alongside after the leaders had crossed the line; it took Kinane some time to pull him up. The Grand Prix de Paris winner Cavalryman was the first home-trained runner to finish, a head behind Youmzain and the same in front of Conduit, with Dar Re Mi (whose dam Darara finished sixth in Dancing Brave's Arc) a further length away in fifth. Fame And Glory came sixth and Stacelita dead-heated for seventh. Sea The Stars, who received the expected rousing reception, was the first Derby winner to go on to success in the Arc since Sinndar in 2000; he was the third Arc winner ridden by Michael Kinane ('I was never worried, when I got the gap the race was over, I was on the fastest horse in the race'), following Carroll House and Montjeu. Sea The Stars carried very similar colours to those worn by his dam Urban Sea when she won the race for the Hong Kong-based Tsui (pronounced Choy) family in 1993 (Christopher Tsui, registered owner of Sea The Stars, was in the Longchamp winner's circle as an eight-year-old to greet Urban Sea with his father David). Urban Sea is the second Arc winner in the post-war era to produce a winner of the race, following Detroit who became the dam of 1994 winner Carnegie.

Sea The Stars's claim to greatness does not hinge on his performance in the Arc, though some of the post-race hype might have suggested otherwise. An article in the *Racing Post* by John Randall, which put a well-reasoned historical perspective on Sea The Stars's Arc performance, came in for adverse comment in some quarters. Randall was accused by one critic of viewing history through 'spectacles tinted to such a rosy hue that he can no longer see clearly', his appreciation—and indeed *Timeform*'s—of the performance of 1965 Arc winner Sea-Bird coming in for the strongest criticism. The fact that the Arc field in Sea-Bird's year was 'strung out like washing' is regarded by some modern-day form students as a clear indication that there must have been little strength in depth. Racing, they say, was nowhere near so competitive in 1965 as it is nowadays. The latest Arc had nineteen runners, one fewer than in Sea-Bird's year, and a big field for the race by modern standards. There were eight other Group 1 winners, apart from Sea The Stars, though a good third of the field was made up of makeweights or pacemakers (the last six finishers started at 172/1, 100/1, 163/1, 151/1, 153/1 and 198/1). Sea-Bird's Arc victory came against a field which included the best middle-distance performers from Britain, Ireland, Italy, the United States and Russia, as well as the unbeaten Prix du Jockey Club winner Reliance. Five of the runners were Derby winners, including Sea-Bird who had won at Epsom without coming off the bridle. Sea-Bird pulverised the field by a distance given as six lengths (*Timeform* used four and a half) and there is no question of his merit being exaggerated by his rating of 145. The classic crop headed by Sea-Bird and the Arc runner-up Reliance was undoubtedly one of superlative merit; Sea-Bird was the only horse to beat Reliance, while, that year, only Sea-Bird and Reliance beat third-placed Diatome (officially eleven lengths behind Sea-Bird). Diatome went on to beat a representative field on his next start in the Washington International (with Arc eighth Carvin in second), the focus of European ambition in North America before the advent of the Breeders' Cup in 1984. The Arc fifth Anilin (beaten nearly twelve lengths) and seventh Demi Deuil (beaten over twenty lengths) also franked the form when going on to win the Preis von Europa (by four) and Premio Roma (by seven) respectively. Form analysis is more sophisticated than simply applying collateral form—how horses have run against each other—but Youmzain's effort in second invited direct comparisons between Sea The Stars and the two previous winners Dylan Thomas and Zarkava. Youmzain has won only once in the last three seasons and, unless the proposition that he improved markedly at six is accepted, his performance alone suggests that the 2009 Arc was no better a race overall than those in 2007 and 2008. Comparing some of the links between the 1965 Arc and the editions each side of it is also interesting. Timmy Lad finished fourth in the 1964 Arc, beaten about two lengths, but couldn't reach the first ten in Sea-Bird's year when he was beaten around thirty lengths; Carvin, beaten nearly twenty-five lengths in Sea-Bird's year, came sixth the following year, finishing about four and a half lengths behind the winner, while Sigebert, not in the first ten in Sea-Bird's year, finished second. Too simplistic a view, of course, but, perhaps, if nothing else, the overall performances of horses like Carvin, Sigebert and Timmy Lad refute the suggestion that the 1965 Arc field 'lacked strength in depth'. Unlike the latest Arc, there were virtually no makeweights.

The achievements of Raven's Pass, Henrythenavigator and New Approach in 2008 provided a timely reminder that top three-year-olds can have a full campaign and still be at their best for autumn's big championship races. Raven's Pass and Henrythenavigator finished first and second in the Breeders' Cup Classic, North America's richest race, and, with that race being staged on Santa Anita's synthetic surface for the second year running, the connections of Sea The Stars faced an awkward decision about whether or not to take up the challenge. Victory for Sea The Stars would have been a real feather in his cap, adding further to his reputation by succeeding where Dancing Brave had failed and, in the process, successfully completing just about the toughest programme that could be set for a European classic three-year-old. Sea The Stars's Arc performance clearly indicated that he was still in peak form. Kinane reported that the horse had been 'scintillating' in his homework leading up to the race, though the fact that he was starting to go in his coat at Longchamp and sweated up at the start seemed to put his rider off the idea of going on to the Breeders' Cup. 'Does he need to achieve anything more? It's questionable,' said Kinane who partnered the two-year-old Johannesburg and High Chaparral (twice) to victory at the Breeders' Cup in his spell at Ballydoyle, though he also came in for criticism when narrowly beaten on Giant's Causeway(losing his reins in the closing stages) in the Classic in 2000, and when a strong-finishing second on Rock of Gibraltar in the Mile two years later. Both Giant's Causeway and Rock of Gibraltar gained five straight Group 1 victories as three-year-olds, the only European horses to achieve that particular feat before Sea The Stars, who went one better (Nijinsky won five championship races in a row the year before the official pattern system was introduced). The announcement that Sea The Stars was being retired came nine days after the Arc, his trainer saying that the horse had come out of the race 'in his usual good form' but connections felt it was 'unfair to keep him going any further given his unprecedented record of achievement in the last six months.' Although some writers sought to set Sea The Stars apart as the only winner of the Two Thousand Guineas, Derby and Arc, which they dubbed 'the modern triple crown', it was Sea The Stars's unparalleled, sustained excellence, in remaining unbeaten in six genuine championship events as a three-year-old, that underpinned his claims to greatness.

Hardly any regrets were expressed in the mainstream media that Sea The Stars would not be in training at four. He was very mature physically as a three-year-old and it is unlikely he would have made more than the regulation progress from three to four and, in any event, what could he have achieved at four that would have added significantly to his record as a racehorse—or to his value? Sea-Bird, Tudor Minstrel, Nijinsky, Vaguely Noble, Sir Ivor, Shergar and Dancing Brave are among those who laid claims to immortality without running beyond the age of three. One last hurrah in the Breeders' Cup Classic—and a clash with the unbeaten American mare Zenyatta—would have brought Sea The Stars to an even wider audience, as well as giving him a chance to conquer North America, in addition to Britain, Ireland and France (not to mention one last opportunity to show whether he might indeed have proved capable of an even higher Timeform rating than the one he has been given). As it was, Sea The Stars left the stage just as the general public was getting an inkling of his greatness.

Zenyatta's spectacular victory in the Breeders' Cup Classic transcended the confines of the sport in North America, the news in January that she is to remain in training a tremendous boost to racing there. The greatest American horse of the

Mr Christopher Tsui's "Sea The Stars"

modern era, by the way, Triple Crown winner Secretariat, was also retired at the end of his three-year-old campaign. Secretariat, who made the front cover of *TIME* in June 1973, was mentioned in an interesting American insight provided by Steven Crist in *Daily Racing Form.* Maintaining that different standards are used in American and European racing to define greatness, Crist wrote: 'We don't say that Secretariat had a lovely way of going and a magnificent turn of foot—we note that he set track records in all three legs of the Triple Crown and won the Belmont by thirty-one lengths . . . we cite Rachel Alexandra's 2009 campaign as perhaps the best ever by a three-year-old filly, with nineteen- and twenty-length victory margins and three triumphs against colts in Grade 1 races . . . Sea The Stars set one course record, when he won the International . . . what am I missing?' Crist pertinently pointed out the record of Arc winners in Breeders' Cup races. All ten have been beaten, one in the Classic (Sakhee, beaten a nose in 2001) and nine in the Turf. 'Maybe Sea The Stars really is better than those Arc winners, but neither running him in the Classic—if he's the greatest turf horse ever shouldn't he run in the Turf? —nor retiring him as a three-year-old is going to prove it.' Dancing Brave, Trempolino and Saumarez are the only three-year-olds to have run at the Breeders' Cup meeting immediately after their Arc victories, and all three of them ran in the period up to 1990 (since then, four others have run the year after). Success at the Breeders' Cup would certainly have given Sea The Stars the wider public recognition that a horse of his ability deserved, both in America and back home in Europe, where full recognition of what he achieved in a glittering season came a little too late to help racing in its battle to regain recognition as a mainstream sport.

Sea The Stars (IRE) (b.c. 2006)	Cape Cross (IRE) (b 1994)	Green Desert (b 1983)	Danzig
			Foreign Courier
		Park Appeal (br 1982)	Ahonoora
			Balidaress
	Urban Sea (USA) (ch 1989)	Miswaki (ch 1978)	Mr Prospector
			Hopespringseternal
		Allegretta (ch 1978)	Lombard
			Anatevka

Sea The Stars is a big, lengthy, good sort who developed into a real powerhouse through his three-year-old season, very much taking the eye with his appearance and displaying a most relaxed disposition in the preliminaries. He has the pedigree to go with his good looks, being by the high-class miler Cape Cross, who stands under the Darley banner at Kildangan Stud in County Kildare, out of Urban Sea, who won the Arc at 37/1 as a four-year-old. Urban Sea ran for an unfashionable stable and her four-year-old campaign was unorthodox. She won the Prix Exbury at Saint-Cloud in March in preparation for a tilt at the Hong Kong International Cup (in which she came sixth) at Sha Tin four weeks later, running again at Saint-Cloud before looking a shade unlucky when beaten in the Prince of Wales's Stakes at Royal Ascot and then kept busy in the summer, winning at Le Lion d'Angers in the Provinces in July and in the Prix Gontaut-Biron at Deauville in August, before lining up for the Arc against fifteen Group 1 winners (she herself had never won a Group 1).

The winning trophy for the latest Derby was a bronze of Arthur Budgett with his Derby winners Blakeney and Morston, both sons of his Oaks runner-up Windmill Girl. Urban Sea joined Windmill Girl as a producer of two Derby winners, becoming only the twelfth mare to achieve the feat in the long history of the race, the last one before Windmill Girl being at the turn of the last century when Morganette produced Galtee More and then Ard Patrick. As well as producing Galileo (by Sadler's Wells) and Sea The Stars, Urban Sea has also built up a notable record in the Oaks, being the dam of Melikah (by Lammtarra), third in the 2000 Oaks, All Too Beautiful (by Sadler's Wells), second to Cape Cross's daughter Ouija Board in 2004, and Cherry Hinton (by Cape Cross's sire Green Desert), fifth in 2007. Cherry Hinton is the only non-winner among Urban Sea's eight foals to reach the racecourse so far. Of those not mentioned yet, Black Sam Bellamy, a brother to Galileo and All Too Beautiful, and the Giant's Causeway filly My Typhoon were both Group/Grade 1 winners, Black Sam Bellamy winning the Tattersalls Gold Cup and the Gran Premio del Jockey Club and Urban Sea's 2002 foal My Typhoon (who fetched a record-breaking 1,800,000 guineas as a foal at the December Sales)

including the Diana Stakes among her nine wins. Urban Sea's first foal Urban Ocean (by Bering, who was runner-up in Dancing Brave's Arc) won the Group 3 Gallinule Stakes. Urban Sea was barren to Shamardal and slipped her foal to Pivotal in the two years following Sea The Stars and she died suddenly with complications after foaling a colt by another Green Desert stallion Invincible Spirit in March at the Irish National Stud where Urban Sea was based.

Urban Sea's final foal will go into training with John Oxx, who described Sea The Stars as 'the most beautiful yearling' when he saw him at the Irish National Stud—'He would have topped any sale, but luckily for me Mrs Tsui decided not to sell him. I thought they were taking a chance, but thank goodness they did.' Sea The Stars was the first of his dam's progeny to carry the Tsui colours since Urban Ocean, some of the others being sold at auction while Urban Sea's offspring by Sadler's Wells—of which there were four in total—were bred in conjunction with Coolmore under foal share agreements, the Tsui family selling its interest privately in Galileo and Black Sam Bellamy (both of whom ran for a Coolmore partnership) but opting to send Urban Sea's 2001 Sadler's Wells filly (All Too Beautiful) to the December Sales, where she was bought as a foal on behalf of the Coolmore partners for a then-record 1,100,000 guineas. Since Urban Sea's Arc win, her half-brother King's Best has won the Two Thousand Guineas and become a successful sire, her half-sister Allez Les Trois, a Group 3 winner, has bred a Prix du Jockey Club winner Anabaa Blue, and a daughter of Allez Les Trois, Al Ishq, bred Tamayuz, winner of the Prix Jacques le Marois, while yet another half-sister to Urban Sea, Anzille, bred the German Group 1 winner Anzillero. Urban Sea's dam Allegretta, who finished tailed off in the Oaks after coming second in the Lingfield Oaks Trial, was from a leading German family and was herself a half-sister to the German Group 2 winners in the 'eighties Anno and Anatas.

Galileo has followed his own sire Sadler's Wells in becoming a star of the Coolmore stallion band, but his half-brother Sea The Stars won't be standing under the Coolmore banner, or that of its great rival Darley. He will stand at the Aga Khan's 'neutral' Gilltown Stud in Ireland where he is expected to cover between one hundred and twenty and one hundred and thirty mares at a fee of €85,000. Among the first mares to visit him will be the Aga Khan's 2008 Arc winner Zarkava. The outstanding Sea The Stars was effective at a mile to a mile and a half and he showed tip-top form on going ranging from good to firm to good to soft (also won on soft). Patiently ridden to make the most effective use of his fine turn of foot, Sea The Stars is the embodiment of that hardy Timeform epithet, tough, genuine and consistent, and he thoroughly deserves his place among the select group of horses who have fulfilled the time-honoured Timeform definition of greatness, being 'a horse of such superlative merit as to make him, or her, far superior to the general run of classic winners.' *John M. Oxx, Ireland*

SEATTLE SPEIGHT (USA) 2 b.f. (Apr 6) Speightstown (USA) 124 – Gal From Seattle (USA) (A P Indy (USA) 131) [2009 7s p7g Sep 8] rather unfurnished filly: fourth foal: closely related/half-sister to winners in Japan by Grand Slam and Tale of The Cat: dam unraced half-sister to top-class Japanese performer up to 1½m El Condor Pasa: soundly beaten in maidens. *W. J. Knight* –

SEAWAY 3 b.c. Dr Fong (USA) 128 – Atlantic Destiny (IRE) 99 (Royal Academy (USA) 130) [2009 95: 8m² 8g³ 10m* Jul 16] tall, angular colt: useful form at 2 yrs (lame and off 11 months after final start): just fair form on return, winning maiden at Leicester in July: winner at 1¼m, but may prove best at shorter: raced only on good/good to firm ground: tongue tied last 2 starts: tends to sweat. *Saeed bin Suroor* **76 +**

SEBASTIAN FLYTE 2 ch.c. (Mar 24) Observatory (USA) 131 – Aravonian 82 (Night Shift (USA)) [2009 5s 7g* 6v³ 7m² Oct 1] £38,000Y: compact colt: fourth foal: half-brother to smart Irish 5f (at 2 yrs)/6f (Ballyogan Stakes) winner Age of Chivalry (by Invincible Spirit) and 3-y-o The Cuckoo: dam 1m winner: useful performer: won maiden at Gowran in August: good efforts when placed in Round Tower Stakes at the Curragh (5½ lengths third to Arctic) and Somerville Tattersall Stakes at Newmarket (½-length second to Sir Parky): will stay 1m: acts on heavy and good to firm ground. *Francis Ennis, Ireland* **102**

SECOND BROOK (IRE) 2 b.g. (May 15) Celtic Swing 138 – Mur Taasha (USA) 108 (Riverman (USA) 131) [2009 7m⁴ 7g p6g p8.6g f8f⁴ Dec 12] modest maiden: stays 1m. *R. Hollinshead* **57**

SECOND REEF 7 b.g. Second Empire (IRE) 124 – Vax Lady 98 (Millfontaine 114) [2009 –: 6m 7.9g^6 5.9d 8m 10g Oct 16] good-topped gelding: poor performer: best short of 1½m: acts on all-weather, firm and good to soft going: has worn headgear/tongue tie: one to avoid. *T. A. K. Cuthbert* **41 §**

SECOND TO NUN (IRE) 3 b.f. Bishop of Cashel 122 – One For Me 62 (Tragic Role (USA)) [2009 65: 8g* 8f^3 8m 8.1m^5 10d 8d 8m^5 p8m Nov 29] lengthy, good-topped filly: modest performer: won minor event at Bath in April: stays 1m: acts on firm and good to soft ground. *Jean-Rene Auvray* **61**

SECRECY 3 b.g. King's Best (USA) 132 – Wink (Salse (USA) 128) [2009 111p: 8m^3 8s^3 8g* Oct 31] tall, leggy gelding: smart performer, lightly raced: improved again when winning handicap at Newmarket by 5 lengths from Benandonner, short of room before quickening clear 1f out: stays 1m: acts on soft and good to firm going: headstrong/hung badly at 2 yrs. *Saeed bin Suroor* **119**

SECRET CITY (IRE) 3 b.g. City On A Hill (USA) 114 – Secret Combe (IRE) 81 (Mujadil (USA) 119) [2009 61: 7m 7g^5 6g* 6d 7m^5 6g Oct 20] good-bodied gelding: modest handicapper: won at Ayr in July: effective at 5f to 7f: acts on soft and good to firm ground: usually blinkered. *R. Bastiman* **61**

SECRET DESERT 3 b.g. Dubai Destination (USA) 127 – Lady Bankes (IRE) 69 (Alzao (USA) 117) [2009 8.3g p10g^6 11.5m^4 10g 11.9d^4 11.5g^2 Oct 20] leggy gelding: fair maiden: stays 1½m: unraced on extremes of going: not straightforward: sold 8,000 gns, then gelded. *D. M. Simcock* **65**

SECRET DUBAI (IRE) 4 b.c. Dubai Destination (USA) 127 – Secret Pride 89 (Green Desert (USA) 127) [2009 82: p7.1g^6 p7g^5 f7g^4 6d^2 6g^5 6m 5.9m 6m^4 p6g^6 6s 6m 6m Aug 29] fair performer: claimed from M. Botti £6,000 fourth start: lost way after next outing: effective at 6f to 1m: acts on polytrack, heavy and good to firm ground: sometimes tongue tied, tried blinkered. *Mrs L. Stubbs* **71 d**

SECRET HERO 3 b.c. Cadeaux Genereux 131 – Valiantly 103 (Anabaa (USA) 130) [2009 p7g 8s 7d^6 7m* 7.1m^5 7.1v^2 7d* 7m 8.3g^6 p8.6g Dec 7] sturdy, lengthy colt: second foal: dam, 6f winner, out of half-sister to dam of very smart sprinter Continent: fair handicapper: won at Salisbury in June and Lingfield in August: left R. Hannon prior to final start: stays 8.3f: acts on heavy and good to firm ground: blinkered seventh to ninth outings: sold 5,000 gns. *L. Smyth, Ireland* **74**

SECRETIVE 2 b.c. (Mar 9) Shamardal (USA) 129 – Samsung Spirit 79 (Statoblest 120) [2009 f7g* Dec 22] 60,000Y: half-brother to 3 winners, including useful 5f (including at 2 yrs) winner Mystical Land (by Xaar): dam, 6f winner (including at 2 yrs), half-sister to dam of smart sprinter Indian Rocket: 11/8 on, ran green (hung left) when winning maiden at Southwell by 3 lengths from Golden Tiger: sure to improve. *M. Johnston* **78 p**

SECRET LIFE 3 b.c. Montjeu (IRE) 137 – Bright Halo (IRE) (Bigstone (IRE) 126) [2009 8m p10g^4 10m^3 p10g^4 p12.2g^2 10v a12g Dec 29] 200,000Y: well-made colt: fifth foal: half-brother to 3 winners, including 6f (at 2 yrs)/1m winner Nantyglo (by Mark of Esteem) and 4-y-o Resplendent Light, both useful: dam, French 1¼m winner, half-sister to smart/very smart fillies up to 1½m Cerulean Sky, L'Ancresse and Moonstone: fairly useful maiden: sold from J. Noseda 12,500 gns after fifth start: stays 1½m: acts on polytrack: signs of temperament. *H-A. Pantall, France* **84**

SECRET MILLIONAIRE (IRE) 2 b.g. (Apr 18) Kyllachy 129 – Mithl Al Hawa 99 (Salse (USA) 128) [2009 5.1m^2 5d^3 5.1m* 5m^4 p5f* 5m^2 6m Oct 3] €21,000F, £40,000Y, £56,000 2-y-o: quite attractive gelding: half-brother to several winners, including 7f/1m winner Cornflower Fields (by Cadeaux Genereux), later successful in USA, and 1m/9f winner Eastern Spice (by Polish Precedent), both fairly useful: dam, 2-y-o 6f winner, half-sister to 5-y-o Abraham Lincoln: fairly useful performer: won maiden at Chepstow in August and nursery at Lingfield in September: creditable efforts after, eighth in listed race at Redcar: may prove best at 5f: acts on polytrack and good to firm going. *Pat Morris* **92**

SECRET NIGHT 6 gr.m. Dansili 127 – Night Haven 99 (Night Shift (USA)) [2009 91: p7g* 7m^3 8m^2 7g^3 7m^5 Jul 25] tall, useful-looking mare: fairly useful handicapper: won at Lingfield in April: stays 1m, all wins at shorter: acts on polytrack and good to firm going: wears headgear: quirky, but reliable: has reportedly been covered by Manduro. *C. G. Cox* **90**

SECRET PLOY 9 b.g. Deploy 131 – By Line 64 (High Line 125) [2009 15m 16s^5 17.1m 17.1m^6 Sep 17] leggy, attractive gelding: missed 2008: just fair nowadays: stays 21f: acts on firm and soft going: in cheekpieces once: difficult ride and needs treating with caution. *H. Morrison* **75 §**

SECRET QUEEN 2 b.f. (Jan 18) Zafeen (FR) 123 – Gold Queen 83 (Grand Lodge (USA) 125) [2009 5.7f³ 7m² 7g² p8g⁴ 6m* 6m⁶ Oct 3] tall filly: first foal: dam, 2-y-o 7.5f winner, half-sister to smart 1m/1¼m winner Silver Pivotal: fairly useful performer: won maiden at Redcar in September by 7 lengths: not ideally drawn when creditable sixth to Lucky Like in listed race at Redcar: likely to prove best at 6f/7f: acts on good to firm going. *B. J. Meehan* **90**

SECRET ROSE 2 b.f. (May 6) Deportivo 116 – Kingston Rose (GER) (Robellino (USA) 127) [2009 p5g 5m Apr 13] £600Y: close-coupled, workmanlike filly: second foal: sister to 3-y-o Dispol Diva: dam, maiden, stayed 1½m in Germany: last in maiden and seller (tongue tied). *W. G. M. Turner* **–**

SECRET SOCIETY 3 b.c. Exceed And Excel (AUS) 126 – Shady Point (IRE) 76 (Unfuwain (USA) 131) [2009 87p: p7g* 8m⁴ 7f* 8m² 7m* 7m² 7m⁴ 7g⁶ Sep 6] strong colt: smart performer: won maiden at Lingfield in April and handicaps at Thirsk in June and Ascot (beat Suruor by head) in July: also ran well when runner-up in valuable handicaps in large fields at Ascot fourth/sixth starts, in Britannia Stakes (beaten a head by Fareer) and International Stakes (½ length behind Al Muheer) and when ¾-length fourth to dead-heaters Confront and Dream Eater in listed race at York: blinkered, below form in Prix du Pin at Longchamp final start: stays 1m, all wins at 7f: acts on polytrack and firm going: held up, and travels strongly. *M. L. W. Bell* **114**

SECRET VENUE 3 ch.g. Where Or When (IRE) 124 – Sheila's Secret (IRE) 97 (Bluebird (USA) 125) [2009 75: 5m 5m* 5m* 5g* 5.4g² 5g 5m 5.1m 5.1m* Sep 30] strong, workmanlike gelding: fair handicapper: won at Musselburgh in May, June and July, and Nottingham in September: raced only at 5f/6f: acts on good to firm going: speedy, usually races prominently: game. *Jedd O'Keeffe* **79**

SECRET WITNESS 3 ch.g. Pivotal 124 – It's A Secret 95 (Polish Precedent (USA) 131) [2009 p7g* 7.1v 7g p7g² p7m p7f p7g⁶ f6g⁵ Dec 18] big, strong, lengthy gelding: fourth foal: dam, 1m/9f winner, half-sister to useful dam of high-class miler Excellent Art (by Pivotal): fairly useful performer: won maiden at Lingfield in May: left J. Noseda 10,000 gns after sixth start: raced only at 6f/7f: form only on polytrack: tried visored/blinkered. *R. A. Harris* **–** **a84**

SECURITISATION (IRE) 2 ch.c. (Feb 22) Rock of Gibraltar (IRE) 133 – Maria Delfina (IRE) 72 (Giant's Causeway (USA) 132) [2009 6g 5m 8.3s 7g Oct 23] good-topped colt: no form in maidens: slowly away. *B. J. Curley* **–**

SEDGE (USA) 9 b.g. Lure (USA) 131 – First Flyer (USA) (Riverman (USA) 131) [2009 66: p8.6g Apr 6] good-topped gelding: modest handicapper: well held sole start at 9 yrs: had form up to 9f, but probably best at 7f: acted on all-weather, firm and good to soft ground: usually wore cheekpieces/blinkers: none too consistent: dead. *P. T. Midgley* **–**

SEDUCTIVE WITCH 4 ch.f. Zamindar (USA) 116 – Thicket 87 (Wolfhound (USA) 126) [2009 61: p6g⁵ p5g Apr 8] lengthy filly: modest handicapper: best at 5f/6f: acts on polytrack: has reportedly bled. *J. Balding* **54**

SEEDLESS 4 br.f. Mtoto 134 – Unseeded 93 (Unfuwain (USA) 131) [2009 61: 13.1d⁵ 13.3m May 30] well-made filly: maiden: below form at 4 yrs: should be suited by 1¾m+: has looked temperamental: joined D. McCain Jnr, fair form over hurdles. *A. M. Balding* **–**

SEE ELSIE PLAY 3 b.f. King O' The Mana (IRE) 112 – Liebside Lass (IRE) (Be My Guest (USA) 126) [2009 6s 6f Jun 20] half-sister to several winners, including fairly useful Irish 1996 2-y-o 1m winner Mo Chos Chle (by Indian Ridge): dam unraced daughter of Oaks second Val's Girl: easily better effort in maidens on debut: bred to stay further than 6f. *Miss Z. C. Davison* **51**

SEEKER RAINBOW 2 ch.f. (Mar 6) Mark of Esteem (IRE) 137 – Seeker 75 (Rainbow Quest (USA) 134) [2009 7f p7g Jul 22] 800F, 9,000 2-y-o: sixth foal: half-sister to 5-y-o Caoba: dam, 1½m winner, out of half-sister to Kris and Diesis: too free when well held in maidens. *Mrs L. C. Jewell* **–**

SEEKING DUBAI 2 b.f. (Feb 5) Dubawi (IRE) 129 – Placement (Kris 135) [2009 6m³ 6g² 6f* p6g* 6.5m⁴ 6g Oct 30] £5,000Y: rather leggy filly: seventh foal: half-sister to useful 5f (at 2 yrs) and 7f winner Presto Vento (by Air Express) and 4-y-o Amanjena: dam unraced close relative of smart French sprinter Pole Position: fairly useful performer: won maiden at Windsor and nursery at Kempton in August: very good fourth to Wonderfilly at Maisons-Laffitte, much better effort in listed events after: will be suited by 7f. *E. F. Vaughan* **93**

SEEKING FAITH (USA) 3 b. or br.f. Chapel Royal (USA) 110 – Padrao Global 52
(USA) (Storm Bird (CAN) 134) [2009 –p: 8.3g 10m Jul 20] lengthy, angular filly: modest
maiden: sold 3,500 gns. *C. G. Cox*

SEEKING RIO 2 b.f. (Feb 22) Captain Rio 122 – True Seeker (Lujain (USA) 119) –
[2009 p7.1g p6g p7.1g Dec 28] £4,500Y: first foal: dam unraced half-sister to very smart
sprinter Pivotal Point: no impact in maidens/seller at Wolverhampton. *R. J. Hodges*

SEEKING ROSE 2 b.f. (Mar 14) Where Or When (IRE) 124 – Selkirk Rose (IRE) 74 –
(Pips Pride 117) [2009 8.3m p8m 8d Oct 12] 4,500Y: good-topped filly: fifth foal:
half-sister to fairly useful 5f (at 2 yrs)/7f winner Miss Meggy (by Pivotal) and a winner in
Greece by Kyllachy: dam 5f (at 2 yrs)/6f winner: behind in maidens: sold 2,500 gns.
E. A. L. Dunlop

SEEKING STARDOM 2 ch.g. (Mar 27) Starcraft (NZ) 128 – Lunar Goddess (Royal 53
Applause 124) [2009 6m 6f 6m Sep 18] strong gelding: form in maidens only when ninth
at Newbury final start (gelded after): should stay 7f/1m. *P. M. Phelan*

SEEKING THE BUCK (USA) 5 b.g. Seeking The Gold (USA) – Cuanto Es (USA) 98
(Exbourne (USA) 125) [2009 10m* 10.1g* 10m^2 10.4m^4 12m^5 Aug 19] close-coupled
gelding: useful handicapper: ran only once over hurdles in 2008/9 for Carl Llewellyn:
better than ever back on Flat in 2009, winning at Newmarket in May and Epsom (beat
Lake Poet ¾ length) in June: at least respectable efforts after: stays 1½m: raced on good
ground or firmer: used to be tongue tied, also tried blinkered. *R. M. Beckett*

SEEK N' DESTROY (IRE) 3 b.c. Exceed And Excel (AUS) 126 – Very Nice (Day- 100
lami (IRE) 138) [2009 75p: p7g* p7g^2 7m* 7m^4 7m^3 7m* 7m Sep 26] rangy colt: useful
performer: won maiden at Kempton in March, and handicaps at Lingfield in May and
Newmarket (best effort, beat Russian Jar 3 lengths) in August: stays 7f: acts on polytrack
and good to firm going: tactically versatile: sent to Hong Kong. *B. W. Hills*

SEEK THE CASH (USA) 2 ch.c. (Apr 28) Mr Greeley (USA) 122 – Cash Deal 51
(USA) (Danzig (USA)) [2009 p7m Dec 16] 20/1, eighth to Licence To Till in maiden at
Lingfield. *M. Quinn*

SEEK THE FAIR LAND 3 b.g. Noverre (USA) 125 – Duchcov 101 (Caerleon (USA) 96
132) [2009 65p: p7.1g* p7g* 7m^5 p6g^4 p6g p7f^4 7g p7.1g^4 p8m^4 p7m* p7f* p7f^2 Dec 21]
workmanlike gelding: useful performer: largely progressive in 2009, winning maiden
at Wolverhampton in April, and handicaps at Kempton later in month, and Lingfield and
Kempton in December: effective at 6f/7f: acts on polytrack and good to firm going: has
sweated up. *J. R. Boyle*

SEE THAT GIRL 3 b.f. Hawk Wing (USA) 136 – Hampton Lucy (IRE) 65 (Anabaa 47
(USA) 130) [2009 –: 7d 7m^4 p6m Oct 31] workmanlike filly: poor maiden: raced only at
6f/7f. *B. Smart*

SEFTON PARK 2 b.g. (Apr 22) Dansili 127 – Optimistic 90 (Reprimand 122) [2009 47
7.1g 7d p8f Oct 14] poor maiden: should stay 1m+: gelded after final start. *C. R. Egerton*

SEGAL (IRE) 4 b.g. Cadeaux Genereux 131 – Camcorder (Nashwan (USA) 135) [2009 –
83: 12f^6 Jun 2] sturdy gelding: fairly useful performer in 2008: fair form over hurdles:
well held on Flat return: likely to prove best around 1¼m: acts on polytrack. *A. M. Hales*

SEHOY (USA) 3 b. or br.c. Menifee (USA) 124 – Another Storm (USA) (Gone West 93
(USA)) [2009 52p: p12g* p12g^2 10d 10d^4 12m^4 12m^2 p12m Oct 12] good-topped colt:
fairly useful performer: won maiden at Lingfield (despite failing to handle bend) in
March: much better form when runner-up in handicaps after: stays 1½m: acts on polytrack and good to firm ground: sold 40,000 gns. *J. H. M. Gosden*

SEJANUS 2 b.g. (Feb 19) Dubai Destination (USA) 127 – Agrippina 99 (Timeless 82
Times (USA) 99) [2009 6v^6 6m^5 6v^4 f7g^2 7.5m p8.6g* p8.6g^2 p8.6g Oct 15] £23,000Y:
third foal: half-brother to smart 6f winner Cartimandua (by Medicean) and useful
5f winner (including at 2 yrs) Terentia (by Diktat): dam 2-y-o 7f winner: fairly useful
performer: won maiden at Wolverhampton in September: good head second in nursery
there next time: stays easy 8.6f: acts on all-weather: races prominently: sold £22,000.
K. A. Ryan

SELDOM (IRE) 3 b.g. Sesaro (USA) 81 – Daisy Dancer (IRE) 57 (Distinctly North 71
(USA) 115) [2009 6f^2 7m* 5s 6m^3 7f 7g 7m 7g 7g p7.1g^2 Dec 11] good-bodied gelding:
third foal: dam Irish 6.5f winner: fair performer: won maiden at Redcar in April: stays 7f:
acts on polytrack and good to firm going. *M. Brittain*

SELDOM SEEN KID (IRE) 2 ch.c. (Mar 16) Captain Rio 122 – North Cider Rose (IRE) (Goldmark (USA) 113) [2009 6d p7.1g 6v 7d 6m Aug 8] smallish, deep-girthed colt: poor maiden: tried blinkered: dead. *T. D. Easterby* **44**

SELECT COMMITTEE 4 b.g. Fayruz 116 – Demolition Jo 89 (Petong 126) [2009 68: 5d^5 5d^4 5m^3 5d^2 5g^2 5g 5m* 5.1d 5d^5 5m* 5m 5g^2 5m 5m* Oct 3] sturdy gelding: fair handicapper: won at Beverley in July and August and Redcar in October: speedy, raced mainly at 5f: acts on heavy and good to firm going: wears visor/cheekpieces. *J. J. Quinn* **77**

SELECT (IRE) 3 ch.f. Choisir (AUS) 126 – Intercession 90 (Bluebird (USA) 125) [2009 89: 6m* 7m 7.1g^3 7g^4 7g^2 Jul 31] sturdy, attractive filly: useful performer: won maiden at Pontefract in April: better form after, including when in frame in listed races at Warwick and Deauville (length fourth to Emergency) and Oak Tree Stakes at Goodwood (1¼ lengths second to Summer Fete): stays 7f: acts on good to firm going: sold 50,000 gns. *P. W. Chapple-Hyam* **102**

SELINA RIO 2 ch.f. (Apr 22) Captain Rio 122 – Encanto (IRE) 80 (Bahhare (USA) 122) [2009 5m 5m^6 5g 5g^6 6v f6m^6 f7f Nov 24] £1,000Y: close-coupled filly: first foal: dam 2-y-o 6f winner: little form: tried in cheekpieces. *L. A. Mullaney* **–**

SELMIS 5 ch.h. Selkirk (USA) 129 – Nokomis (Caerleon (USA) 132) [2009 109: 10m* 10s* 10m* May 17] half-brother to several winners in Italy: dam, Italian 7.5f (including at 2 yrs)/1m winner, half-sister to smart Italian sprinter Beat of Drums: smart performer: improved to win all 3 starts in 2009, minor event and Premio Ambrosiano (forged clear final 1f to beat Papetti 6 lengths), both at Milan in April, and Premio Presidente della Repubblica at Rome (by ¾ length from Trincot) in May: stays 1¼m: acts on soft and good to firm ground: has worn blinkers/cheekpieces. *V. Caruso, Italy* **116**

SEMAH HAROLD 4 b.g. Beat All (USA) 120 – Semah's Dream 39 (Gunner B 126) [2009 67: p9.5g^5 p7.1g^6 Jan 23] good-bodied gelding: just poor form in 2009: probably best around 1m: acts on all-weather, good to firm and good to soft going: blinkered/visored of late: joined J. Holt. *E. S. McMahon* **46**

SEMI DETACHED (IRE) 6 b.g. Distant Music (USA) 126 – Relankina (IRE) (Broken Hearted 124) [2009 65: p12.2g^6 Jan 9] tall, quite good-topped gelding: modest maiden handicapper: below form sole start in 2009: stays easy 1½m: acts on polytrack and soft ground: tried tongue tied: has found little. *J. W. Unett* **–**

SEMINAL MOMENT 3 b.f. Sakhee (USA) 136 – Thracian 92 (Green Desert (USA) 127) [2009 –: 8.3g 13.8g^4 f14m* 16v^5 14.1g p16g^6 f12m f14m Dec 5] leggy filly: modest handicapper: won at Southwell in July: stays 1¾m: acts on all-weather. *J. G. Given* **60**

SENATE 2 ch.c. (Mar 11) Pivotal 124 – Sauterne 98 (Rainbow Quest (USA) 134) [2009 p8.6g Nov 21] 160,000Y: fourth foal: half-brother to fairly useful 2007 2-y-o 7f winner Determind Stand (by Elusive Quality): dam, 7.5f/1¼m winner, closely related to Cherry Hinton Stakes winner Applaud: well-backed 7/2, very green and always behind in maiden at Wolverhampton: should do better. *J. H. M. Gosden* **– p**

SENATE MAJORITY 2 ch.g. (Mar 21) Avonbridge 123 – Benjarong 50 (Sharpo 132) [2009 5m^6 5g^4 5d^4 5s^5 6.1d p5.1g Sep 18] well-made gelding: modest maiden: should be suited by 6f: acts on soft going: tried blinkered: gelded after final start. *T. D. Easterby* **62**

SENDALI (FR) 5 b.g. Daliapour (IRE) 122 – Lady Senk (FR) (Pink (FR) 123) [2009 59: 16.1d* Sep 7] rather leggy gelding: modest handicapper: won at Newcastle: stays 2m: acts on soft and good to firm going: tried in cheekpieces: often held up. *J. D. Bethell* **58**

SENDRENI (FR) 5 b.g. Night Shift (USA) – Sendana (FR) (Darshaan 133) [2009 78: p7g p6g^3 7d* 7s p7g p7m p7.1g p7.1g p7.1g Nov 30] sturdy gelding: fair performer: won handicap at Folkestone in March: little impact after: effective at 7f to 9f: raced on all-weather and going softer than good on turf: tongue tied third to eighth starts: free-going sort. *M. Wigham* **80 d**

SENESCHAL 8 b.g. Polar Falcon (USA) 126 – Broughton Singer (IRE) 61 (Common Grounds 118) [2009 77: p8g^6 p7g^2 7d* 8m 7f* 7f* 7g^4 7m^6 7f^3 7g 7s^2 7f^6 7.1m 6f^6 Sep 2] big, leggy gelding: fairly useful performer: won handicap at Yarmouth in April and seller at Brighton and handicap at Salisbury (apprentices) in May: stays 1m: acts on polytrack, soft and firm going: tried in cheekpieces: usually races prominently. *A. B. Haynes* **83**

SENORA VERDE 3 ch.f. Bahamian Bounty 116 – Spain 62 (Polar Falcon (USA) 126) [2009 43: f6s f5g 6m Apr 2] temperamental maiden: little form at 3 yrs: tried in cheekpieces. *P. T. Midgley* **– §**

SENOR BERTI 3 b.g. Bertolini (USA) 125 – Pewter Lass 56 (Dowsing (USA) 124) [2009 76: 7m^6 Jun 13] close-coupled gelding: fair performer at best: would have stayed 1m: acted on good to soft going: dead. *B. Smart* **–**

SENSACION SENSUAL 3 b.f. Josr Algarhoud (IRE) 118 – Charlie Girl 70 (Puissance 110) [2009 53: 6m Apr 7] workmanlike filly: maiden: well held only outing in 2009. *J. G. Given* –

SENSES (USA) 3 ch.c. Rahy (USA) 115 – Sweet And Steady (USA) (Steady Growth (CAN)) [2009 p8g^6 10m^2 10f* 10m^4 12m^5 10m* 12m^3 Oct 3] $120,000Y, resold 75,000Y: lengthy colt: sixth foal: half-brother to several winners in USA, including Grade 2 8.5f winner Sweet And Ready (by El Prado): dam US 1m/8.5f winner: fairly useful performer: won maiden in June and handicap in September, both at Sandown: stays 1½m: raced only on polytrack and ground firmer than good: tried visored: suspect temperament (looks ungainly). *J. Noseda* **85**

SENT FROM HEAVEN (IRE) 2 b.f. (Apr 7) Footstepsinthesand 120 – Crystal Valkyrie (IRE) 81 (Danehill (USA) 126) [2009 p7g* 7g^3 7g* 8m^4 Sep 26] well-made filly: fourth foal: half-sister to 3-y-o Above Average and 2006 2-y-o 6f winner Spinning Crystal (by Spinning World), later successful in Hungary: dam 2-y-o 6f winner (stayed 11f): useful performer: won maiden at Kempton in July and Berry Brothers And Rudd Prestige Stakes at Goodwood (beat Mudaaraah by nose, dictated/idled/flashed tail) in August: good 2¾ lengths fourth to Hibaayeb in Fillies' Mile at Ascot, headed and hampered in final 1f: stays 1m: edgy sort. *B. W. Hills* **103**

SEPTEMBERINTHERAIN 2 gr.c. (Mar 9) Verglas (IRE) 118 – Gwyneth 62 (Zafonic (USA) 130) [2009 7.1m p8g^4 Nov 14] 60,000Y: first foal: dam, maiden (stayed 1m), out of smart performer up to 9f Llyn Gwynant: much better effort in maidens 5 months apart when 3½ lengths fourth to Con Artist at Lingfield, still green and going on at finish: may improve further. *T. G. Mills* **76**

SEQUILLO 3 b.g. Lucky Story (USA) 128 – Tranquillity 70 (Night Shift (USA)) [2009 78: p8g 9.9g^4 10g* 9.7f* 10d^2 10g^2 p8g^3 10m^4 10.9m^3 10.3g Oct 23] big, strong gelding: fairly useful handicapper: won at Windsor in June and Folkestone in July: stays 1¼m: acts on polytrack, firm and good to soft going: gelded after final start. *R. Hannon* **84**

SERADIM 3 ch.f. Elnadim (USA) 128 – Seren Devious (Dr Devious (IRE) 127) [2009 93: 8f 8s^3 8d^5 7.1g^4 8.1m^6 8m^4 Aug 19] good-topped filly: useful performer: creditable efforts in listed races second to fourth starts, third to Nashmiah at York: reportedly finished lame final outing: stays 1m: acts on polytrack, heavy and good to firm ground: ran poorly in blinkers fifth start: sometimes races freely. *P. F. I. Cole* **95**

SERAFINA'S FLIGHT 2 b.f. (Apr 19) Fantastic Light (USA) 134 – Seven of Nine (IRE) 66 (Alzao (USA) 117) [2009 7s^4 p8m^3 p7.1g^2 Oct 9] fifth foal: half-sister to 3-y-o Lyra's Daemon and winner in Greece by Hernando: dam, ran 3 times (should have stayed 1¼m), sister to smart performer up to 1¼m Rabi: similar form when placed in maidens, second to Chardonnay at Wolverhampton (again flashed tail): will stay 1¼m+. *W. R. Muir* **73**

SEREN ARIAN 3 ro.f. Dreams End 93 – Westfield Mist (Scallywag 127) [2009 10.2g p9.5g p7.1g Nov 30] fourth foal: half-sister to 11.6f winner Cirrious (by Cloudings): dam poor bumper winner: no form in maidens/seller. *B. Palling* –

SERETH (IRE) 6 b.g. Monsun (GER) 124 – Saderlina (IRE) (Sadler's Wells (USA) 132) [2009 109: 12s 12f 14m 12m 12g^5 18m^3 Oct 17] tall gelding: brother to 2 winners, notably smart 1m (in Germany at 2 yrs)/9.8f (in France) winner Salutino, and half-brother to 3 winners abroad: dam, useful French 10.5f winner, half-sister to Prix de Diane winner Caerlina: useful handicapper: trained by J. Hirschberger in Germany in 2008, winning 2 listed races: gambled on, best effort in Britain when 5½ lengths third to Darley Sun in Cesarewitch at Newmarket: stays 2¼m: acts on good to firm and good to soft ground: fairly useful form over hurdles. *B. J. Curley* **98**

SERGEANT PINK (IRE) 3 b.c. Fasliyev (USA) 120 – Ring Pink (USA) 111 (Bering 136) [2009 73: 10.4v^3 12g^4 15.8s^6 Oct 27] tall, lengthy colt: fair performer: probably stays 1½m: acts on heavy ground. *S. Gollings* **68**

SERGEANT SHARPE 4 ch.g. Cadeaux Genereux 131 – Halcyon Daze 82 (Halling (USA) 133) [2009 66: f12g^5 f11g Mar 22] well-made gelding: maiden: fair at 3 yrs: below form in 2009. *H. J. Evans* –

SERHAAL (IRE) 2 b.c. (Feb 3) Green Desert (USA) 127 – Lucky For Me (USA) (King of Kings (IRE) 125) [2009 6m^2 p7g Oct 14] 240,000F: second foal: half-brother to Spanish 5f (at 2 yrs)/6.5f winner Our Chairman (by Okawango): dam unraced daughter of high-class performer up to 1m Vilikaia: easily better effort in maidens when 4 lengths second of 4 to Excellent Guest at Yarmouth: still green/bit awkward at Lingfield 2 months later: should stay 7f. *Sir Michael Stoute* **72**

Cuisine de France Summer Stakes, York—
Serious Attitude's return to sprinting is a successful one as she edges out Lesson In Humility (far side)

SERIOUS ATTITUDE (IRE) 3 b.f. Mtoto 134 – Zameyla (IRE) 86 (Cape Cross (IRE) 129) [2009 112: 8f 6m* 6 5g Aug 9] workmanlike filly: smart performer: won all 3 starts at 2 yrs, notably Cheveley Park Stakes at Newmarket: easily best effort in 2009 when winning Cuisine de France Summer Stakes at York in July by head from Lesson in Humility: raced in unfavoured group when behind in Prix Maurice de Gheest at Deauville final start (reportedly returned with muscle problems): will prove best at 5f/6f (raced freely and failed to stay when seventh in 1000 Guineas at Newmarket on reappearance): acts on good to firm and good to soft going: stays in training. *Rae Guest* **112**

SERIOUS CHOICE (IRE) 4 b.g. Choisir (AUS) 126 – Printaniere (USA) (Sovereign Dancer (USA)) [2009 78: 10.1d* 10m 14m p11g Jul 8] fairly useful handicapper: won at Yarmouth in April, easily best effort at 4 yrs: stays 1¼m: acts on good to firm and good to soft ground: joined P. Hobbs. *J. R. Boyle* **82**

SERIOUS DRINKING (USA) 3 b.f. Successful Appeal (USA) 118 – Cup Match (USA) (Kingmambo (USA) 125) [2009 p7.1g^4 8.3d^3 Oct 12] $50,000Y: angular filly: second foal: half-sister to winner in USA by Forest Wildcat: dam US 6f winner: better effort in maidens when third at Windsor: stays 1m. *W. R. Swinburn* **69**

SERIOUS IMPACT (USA) 4 b.g. Empire Maker (USA) 129 – Diese (USA) 111 (Diesis 133) [2009 –: 10f* 12m^3 10m^6 a12g* Dec 24] well-made gelding: fairly useful performer: won maiden at Leicester in April and, having been sold from J. Gosden 15,500 gns, minor event at Deauville (all-weather, by 3 lengths from Kibaar) in December: stays 1½m: raced on ground firmer than good on turf: hung right third start (off 4 months afterwards). *F. Vermeulen, France* **92**

SERIOUS SPIRIT 2 b.f. (Jan 27) Pastoral Pursuits 127 – Motto (FR) 95 (Mtoto 134) [2009 8g Oct 8] 2,200F, €4,000Y: angular filly: fourth foal: half-sister to winners abroad by Vettori and Dr Fong: dam, 1½m winner, out of Park Hill Stakes winner Coigach: 100/1, soundly beaten in maiden at Newbury. *Rae Guest* **–**

SERMONS MOUNT (USA) 3 b. or br.g. Vicar (USA) 120 – Ginny Auxier (USA) (Racing Star (USA)) [2009 48: p8g^4 10.2g 7m p8.6g 7m^2 6g^5 7f^2 7d 7g^5 p7f^2 p7m^2 p7g^2 p7m^2 Oct 26] fair maiden: stays 7f: acts on polytrack and firm going: in cheekpieces last 3 outings. *Mouse Hamilton-Fairley* **67**

SERVA JUGUM (USA) 3 b. or br.c. Fusaichi Pegasus (USA) 130 – Shake The Yoke 122 (Caerleon (USA) 132) [2009 100p: 10m^4 10.3g^2 12g Sep 22] well-made colt: smart performer: good efforts in Winter Hill Stakes at Windsor (1½ lengths fourth to Campanologist) and minor event at Doncaster (1¾ lengths second to Twice Over): last in listed race at Chantilly final start: stays 1¼m: acts on good to firm ground. *P. F. I. Cole* **110**

SERVETIUS (USA) 2 b.c. (Apr 21) Eurosilver (USA) 118 – Golden Envoy (USA) 68 (Dayjur (USA) 137) [2009 p6g^4 p6g Oct 3] better effort in maidens at Wolverhampton when fourth to Armour. *G. A. Butler* **47**

SERVOCA (CAN) 3 gr.c. El Prado (IRE) 119 – Cinderellaslipper (USA) (Touch Gold (USA) 127) [2009 91: p6g* 6m^3 6.1m^2 5g 6m^2 7d 6g 6m^5 6m^6 5g^2 6g* p6m^2 Nov 3] big, strong colt: has scope: reportedly had wind operation after final 2-y-o start: improved into a useful performer in 2009, winning maiden at Wolverhampton in March and handicap at Doncaster (beat We Have A Dream 1¾ lengths, left B. Hills 60,000 gns after) in October: creditable 1¼ lengths second to Fullandby at Kempton final start: effective at 5f/6f: acts on polytrack, firm and good to soft going: tried tongue tied: has got worked up in preliminaries: has high head carriage. *Mike Murphy* **102**

SESENTA (IRE) 5 b.m. King's Theatre (IRE) 128 – Cincuenta (IRE) 87 (Bob Back (USA) 124) [2009 95: 12v* 20m^2 12s 14m* 14.6m^6 Sep 10] small mare: useful performer (similar standard over hurdles): better than ever in 2009, winning handicaps at the Curragh in May and York (totesport Ebor, by head from Changingoftheguard) in August: also ran well when ½-length second to Judgethemoment in Ascot Stakes (Handicap) at Royal Ascot: never dangerous in Park Hill Stakes at Doncaster final start: needs good test at 1½m, and stays 2½m: unraced on firm going, acts on any other. *W. P. Mullins, Ireland* **105**

SESTET 4 b.f. Golden Snake (USA) 127 – Sestina (FR) 86 (Bering 136) [2009 60: p11g^5 p10g p10g^3 p10m^5 p10g^4 Dec 7] lengthy filly: modest maiden: should stay 1½m: raced on polytrack since debut. *S. Dow* **59**

totesport Ebor (Heritage Handicap)—a 1,2 for the Irish as Sesenta just gets the better of favourite Changingoftheguard (No.15) in a rough race; Hits Only Vic (hidden, far side), the grey Nanton, Warringah (right), Manyriverstocross (hooped cap) and The Betchworth Kid (hidden, second right) are close behind

SETA 2 ch.f. (May 1) Pivotal 124 – Bombazine (IRE) 97 (Generous (IRE) 139) **104 p**
[2009 7g* 8m^3 Sep 11]

'Quality not quantity' was very much the maxim of late owner-breeder Gerald Leigh, who enjoyed remarkable success from a small string of well-bred broodmares. Leigh died aged seventy-one in 2002 and, although most of his bloodstock was subsequently acquired by Sheikh Mohammed's Darley Stud, Leigh's son and daughter, Robin and Sarah, continued to run a reduced breeding operation at Eydon Hall Farm Stud in Northamptonshire until prominent sales consignor Ted Voute took over the lease there in March. The family's involvement in racing isn't quite at an end, however, as the famous brown and beige colours seem set to be carried with distinction in 2010 by the exciting filly Seta, who hails from Leigh's most successful bloodline. Seta's third dam Canton Silk was one of Leigh's foundation mares in the 'seventies, her offspring including the very smart seven-furlong/mile winner Brocade, who became one of the best broodmares of the past twenty-five years. Brocade's most notable performer was the high-class miler Barathea (whom Leigh owned in partnership with Sheikh Mohammed), but she also produced the smart fillies Gossamer (a sister to Barathea) and Free At Last, as well as several other above-average winners. The last group included Seta's dam Bombazine, a useful performer at up to a mile and a half for Luca Cumani, a trainer who has had a long association with the family, having also trained Barathea and Gossamer.

Miss Sarah J. Leigh's "Seta"

Seta's background largely explains why she was so prominent in the betting on her debut in a seven-furlong fillies' maiden at Newmarket in early-August, though it was also clear she must have been showing plenty at home to start so heavily backed, sent off 11/8 favourte in a field of fourteen. The support wasn't misplaced as Seta ran out a most impressive winner, cruising clear under Dane O'Neill to beat main market rival Dyna Waltz by eight lengths. The runner-up went on to frank the form by winning her next start, as did the third (Moonline Dancer) and fifth (Tipperary Boutique), by which time Seta was already heading the ante-post market for the 2010 One Thousand Guineas. She lost that position when failing to land the odds on her only subsequent outing, in the May Hill Stakes at Doncaster, where she faded into third of seven behind Pollenator (14/1) and Hibaayeb (40/1), beaten a length and a half, after looking the likely winner when breezing through to lead over two furlongs out (after racing freely early on). Inexperience may have been a factor, an explanation shared by Kieren Fallon, who took over from O'Neill at Doncaster: 'She just felt a little leggy and ran green. I know she is a good filly.' Fallon, incidentally, had only recently returned to the saddle after an absence from British racing that dated back over three years, due to his involvement in a 'race-fixing' case brought by City of London police and an eighteen-month drugs ban. Cumani has been especially keen to support Fallon—'He's one hell of a jockey who I'll use whenever possible'—and supplied the jockey with a third of his 2009 wins, the new association seeming set to continue into 2010, when Seta is likely to be one of Fallon's best mounts during the first half of the campaign. She remains prominent (16/1) in the ante-post betting for Newmarket, at considerably shorter odds than either Pollenator (25/1) or Hibaayeb (40/1), despite the fact that the latter went on to win the Fillies' Mile at Ascot.

Seta (ch.f. May 1, 2007)	Pivotal (ch 1993)	Polar Falcon (b or br 1987)	Nureyev
			Marie d'Argonne
		Fearless Revival (ch 1987)	Cozzene
			Stufida
	Bombazine (IRE) (ch 1994)	Generous (ch 1988)	Caerleon
			Doff The Derby
		Brocade (b 1981)	Habitat
			Canton Silk

Seta's dam Bombazine was restricted to just five starts (winning once) as a three-year-old, though the decision to switch her to stud so quickly has proved a successful one, with Seta the sixth winner out of the seven runners she has produced to date. Most of the sextet have been useful or better, including the French stayers Affirmative Action (by Rainbow Quest) and Armure (by Dalakhani), the latter successful in the Prix de Pomone at Deauville in 2009 having begun her career in Britain, whilst Gravitas (by Mark of Esteem) has proved a smart mile and a half performer in the UAE since being exported from France. Dubai Venture (by Rainbow Quest) has also shown winning form at a mile and a half in the Middle East (Saudi Arabia), though he became temperamental when trained in Britain by Sir Michael Stoute. As her offspring attest, Bombazine has proved a bigger influence for stamina than the better-known members in her family tree, this being largely on account of her sire Generous. However, her 1999 foal Camelot proved best at around a mile and, like Seta, he was by a speedier influence in Machiavellian. Seta's sire Pivotal is an even greater influence for speed than Machiavellian, so it is by no means certain that Seta will stay so well as some of her immediate siblings. She will stay at least a mile and a quarter, though, and, despite her defeat in the May Hill, she looks just the type to improve from two to three and is no forlorn hope to provide the distaff side of her family with its first British classic success. Free At Last finished a good fourth to Salsabil in the 1990 One Thousand Guineas, but Gossamer managed only eighth when hot favourite for the same race twelve years later, though she gained consolation in the Irish version, becoming her owner's final winner before he lost his battle with cancer that summer. Barathea won the 1993 Irish Two Thousand Guineas after finishing runner-up to Zafonic at Newmarket.

A tall chestnut with plenty of scope, Seta has got quite a high action so it is possible her Doncaster defeat might have been related in part to the prevailing going, with good or softer likely to suit her ideally. Incidentally, her name is Italian for 'silk', the vast majority of Canton Silk's best descendents having been named with a silk and/or fabric reference—including Brocade, Barathea, Gossamer and Bombazine. *L. M. Cumani*

SET BACK 2 b.g. (Mar 31) Reset (AUS) 124 – No Comebacks 70 (Last Tycoon 131) [2009 5g^4 6g 6s Nov 7] rather leggy gelding: modest form in maidens (seemed amiss second start): bred to stay 7f+: gelded after final start. *D. Nicholls* **59**

SET EM UP MO 3 b.f. Reset (AUS) 124 – Mo Stopher 47 (Sharpo 132) [2009 55: p7g p7g p7g p8m p12g p10g^5 p10m Dec 30] leggy filly: modest maiden: tried in cheekpieces/visor. *M. J. Attwater* **54 ?**

SET IN ICE 2 b.g. (Apr 7) Reset (AUS) 124 – Masrora (USA) 71 (Woodman (USA) 126) [2009 5.7g 8.1g^6 8.3m 8g p8g p7.1g Dec 5] rather leggy gelding: well beaten, including in seller. *Mark Gillard* **–**

SET SAIL (IRE) 3 ch.c. Danehill Dancer (IRE) 117 – Ahdaab (USA) 73 (Rahy (USA) 115) [2009 103: 8g^4 10.5g 8m 10m 10s^2 10.4m^3 10d 12g 10m Oct 17] big, lengthy colt: useful performer: acted as pacemaker most outings in 2009, seeming to run well when 2¼ lengths fourth to Silver Frost in Prix de Fontainebleau at Longchamp on reappearance: below best when 3 lengths second to Nafaath in minor race at Fairyhouse in July: stays 1m: best efforts on good going. *A. P. O'Brien, Ireland* **104**

SET THE TREND 3 b. or br.c. Reset (AUS) 124 – Masrora (USA) 71 (Woodman (USA) 126) [2009 p7g* p7g^3 p8g* 8.1v^2 p8g^2 9.9g p8g Sep 5] 7,000F: good-topped colt: third foal: half-brother to 2004 2-y-o 7f winner Daisy Bucket (by Lujain), later successful in Germany up to 9f: dam, maiden, stayed 1½m: reportedly suffered stress fracture to pelvis in 2008: useful performer: won maiden at Lingfield in February and handicap at Kempton in April: creditable efforts after: stays 1¼m: acts on polytrack and heavy ground (unraced on firmer than good). *A. M. Balding* **99**

SETTIGANO (IRE) 6 b.g. Sadler's Wells (USA) 132 – Bonita Francita (CAN) (Devil's Bag (USA)) [2009 110: 8.5s p8g* p10f^3 Dec 19] lengthy, quite good-topped gelding: useful performer: off 9 months before reappearance: won minor event at Dundalk in November: best effort in 2009 when 2¾ lengths third to Tranquil Tiger in listed race at Lingfield: stays easy 1¼m: acts on polytrack, heavy and good to firm going: tongue tied once: usually in cheekpieces: tends to take time to warm to task. *Michael Joseph Fitzgerald, Ireland* **107**

SET TO GO 2 b.g. (Feb 26) Reset (AUS) 124 – Golubitsa (IRE) (Bluebird (USA) 125) [2009 p8m 8d p7g p8m Nov 4] angular gelding: form only when mid-field in maiden at Kempton third start. *H. J. L. Dunlop* **51**

SET TO ROCK 2 ch.g. (Feb 3) Reset (AUS) 124 – Crocolat 77 (Croco Rouge (IRE) 126) [2009 f8g 8.3d 8.3g Oct 28] close-coupled gelding: well beaten in maidens/seller. *J. G. Portman* **–**

SEVENNA (FR) 4 b.f. Galileo (IRE) 134 – Silvassa (IRE) (Darshaan 133) [2009 98: p16g^5 12f^6 14g^2 14d* 15.5d Oct 25] well-made filly: useful performer: much improved when winning Moet Hennessy Fillies' Stakes (Lillie Langtry) at Goodwood in July by 1½ lengths from Cassique Lady: off 3 months and sweating, stiff task when last in Prix Royal-Oak at Longchamp subsequent start: should stay 2m: acts on polytrack, good to firm and good to soft ground. *H. R. A. Cecil* **107**

SEVEN OF DIAMONDS (IRE) 2 gr.f. (Apr 9) Clodovil (IRE) 116 – Tres Sage (Reprimand 122) [2009 6m^4 6m^4 7d^4 6g^4 Oct 16] 48,000Y: unfurnished filly: seventh foal: half-sister to 3 winners, including 5-y-o Makshoof: dam, French 1m winner, closely related to smart performer up to 1m Aragon: fair maiden: stays 6f: acts on good to firm going: tongue tied second/third outings: found little final start. *T. D. Easterby* **65**

SEVEN ROYALS (IRE) 4 b.g. Val Royal (FR) 127 – Seven Notes (Zafonic (USA) 130) [2009 61: p7m Oct 28] lengthy, workmanlike gelding: modest maiden: well held sole 4-y-o start: bred to stay 1m: acts on soft and good to firm going. *Miss A. M. Newton-Smith* **–**

SEVEN SKY (FR) 6 b.g. Septieme Ciel (USA) 123 – Nuit de Crystal (FR) (Crystal Glitters (USA) 127) [2009 f12g p10g Mar 18] 10.5f winner in France earlier in career: modest form at best over hurdles for Carl Llewellyn: no form on Flat in Britain: tried blinkered. *P. F. I. Cole* **–**

SEVENTH CAVALRY (IRE) 4 gr.g. No Excuse Needed 123 – Mixwayda (FR) (Linamix (FR) 127) [2009 83§: 10d^6 10m 9.9m^2 12d^3 10d^2 10g^4 12m^2 Sep 10] sturdy gelding: fair maiden handicapper: stays 1½m: unraced on firm/heavy going, acts on **75 §**

polytrack and any other turf: often visored/blinkered at 3 yrs: finds little, and one to treat with caution: successful on hurdling debut. *A. King*

SEVENTH HILL 4 ch.g. Compton Place 125 – Dream Baby (Master Willie 129) [2009 73: p10g³ 11.7g³ 10d 13.3m⁵ 10.2m³ 9.9m⁶ 10.2m p12.2g² p12.2g p12m p10m² p10g⁴ Nov 25] workmanlike gelding: fair maiden handicapper: stays 1½m: acts on polytrack, soft and good to firm going. *M. Blanshard* **70**

SEVERIO (IRE) 3 b.f. Captain Rio 122 – Good Forecast (Unfuwain (USA) 131) [2009 7d 7m⁵ 8d⁵ f8f 9.1v Oct 31] tall filly: third foal: dam unraced half-sister to useful performers Cloudy Start (at 7f/1m) and Valentine Girl (up to 1½m): trained by K. R. Burke on debut: easily best effort when fifth in maiden at Newcastle third start: well held otherwise: stays 1m: acts on good to soft going: sold 1,000 gns. *A. P. Jarvis* **66**

SEW'N'SO CHARACTER (IRE) 8 b.g. Imperial Ballet (IRE) 110 – Hope And Glory (USA) 87 (Well Decorated (USA)) [2009 p8.6g⁶ p8g p7g² p7g³ p7.1g⁵ p8g⁵ p8g⁶ p7g p8g f11g p11g⁵ p10m Sep 23] good-topped gelding: fair handicapper: below form after fourth start: effective at 7.5f to 10.5f: acts on polytrack, soft and good to firm going: often waited with. *M. Blanshard* **78 d**

SGT ROBERTS (IRE) 3 b.g. Diktat 126 – Ann's Annie (IRE) 78 (Alzao (USA) 117) [2009 74: p10g⁴ p12g⁶ p10g⁵ 11.6m 10.2d May 18] workmanlike gelding: fair maiden: likely to prove best short of 1½m: acts on polytrack and good to soft ground. *J. S. Moore* **73**

SGT SCHULTZ (IRE) 6 b.g. In The Wings 128 – Ann's Annie (IRE) 78 (Alzao (USA) 117) [2009 84+, a104: p10g³ a10f a8f p12g* p12g 11.6g 11.5m² 12m⁴ 12f⁵ 12g p10m⁵ p12.2g Dec 11] big, good-topped gelding: useful handicapper on all-weather, fairly useful on turf: won at Lingfield (beat Distinctive Image by nose) in March: effective at 1¼m to easy 1¾m: acts on polytrack and firm going. *J. S. Moore* **84 a100**

SHAARIDH (USA) 3 b. or br.f. Dixieland Band (USA) – Boston Lady (USA) (Boston Harbor (USA) 122) [2009 –p: 10m³ 8.1g⁴ Aug 13] rangy filly, has scope: progressive form in maidens: fourth at Sandown final start, best work at finish: likely to prove best at 1¼m+: sold 3,000 gns. *M. Johnston* **78**

SHAAYEQ (IRE) 2 b. or br.c. (Feb 10) Dubawi (IRE) 129 – Shohrah (IRE) 103 (Giant's Causeway (USA) 132) [2009 p7m³ 8.5d* 8m⁴ 10m³ Oct 6] sturdy colt: first foal: dam, 2-y-o 6f winner, half-sister to 1¼m winner Haadef and 7f winner (stayed 1¼m) Ma-Arif, both useful, out of half-sister to Ibn Bey and Roseate Tern: fairly useful performer: won maiden at Epsom in September: good 2¾ lengths fourth to Ameer in minor event at Newbury: bred to stay 1¼m: visored last 2 starts, tailed off final one: sold 15,000 gns. *M. P. Tregoning* **89**

SHABAK HOM (IRE) 2 b.c. (Jan 26) Exceed And Excel (AUS) 126 – Shbakni (USA) (Mr Prospector (USA)) [2009 p7m 8.5d² p8.6g⁵ Sep 19] eighth foal: half-brother to 2 winners abroad by Green Desert, including UAE 1¼m winner Pentland Firth: dam, placed in France/UAE up to 9f, out of Kentucky Derby winner Winning Colors: easily best effort in maidens when 2½ lengths second to Shaayeq at Epsom: seemed amiss final start. *D. M. Simcock* **70**

SHABIB (USA) 3 b.c. Intidab (USA) 115 – Muklah (IRE) 101 (Singspiel (IRE) 133) [2009 81p: p7g² 7g* 7d* 7.1g Aug 13] sturdy colt: useful performer: won maiden at Folkestone in April and handicap at Newmarket (further marked improvement, beat Invincible Isle 2¼ lengths) in July: reportedly finished lame final start: will be suited by 1m: acts on polytrack, soft and good to firm going: joined M. Al Muhairi in UAE. *B. W. Hills* **97**

SHADED EDGE 5 b.g. Bold Edge 123 – Twilight Mistress 84 (Bin Ajwaad (IRE) 119) [2009 68: p7g p7g² p7g³ p7g* p7g⁴ 7m* 7m* 7m⁵ 7m p7g² 7.1g p7g p7m² p7g⁶ p8g² p7m p7g² Dec 31] rather leggy gelding: fair handicapper: won at Lingfield in March and Salisbury and Lingfield (both ladies) in May: effective at 6f to 1m: acts on polytrack and good to firm going: tried visored, effective with/without cheekpieces: sometimes races lazily. *D. W. P. Arbuthnot* **78**

SHADOW BAY (IRE) 3 b.g. Deportivo 116 – Champion Tipster (Pursuit of Love 124) [2009 78: 6g 5g* 7m⁵ 5f⁶ p6g p6m⁵ p7g p6m Oct 26] small, sturdy gelding: fair performer: won seller at Folkestone in April: effective at well-run 5f to 1m: acts on polytrack, soft and good to firm ground: inconsistent. *Miss Z. C. Davison* **70**

SHADOW JUMPER (IRE) 8 b.g. Dayjur (USA) 137 – Specifically (USA) (Sky Classic (CAN)) [2009 –: f8d p8.6g f7g f12g⁵ f11g Mar 3] one-time fair performer: little form since 2007: usually wears headgear. *J. T. Stimpson* **–**

SHADOWS LENGTHEN 3 b.g. Dansili 127 – Bay Shade (USA) 90 (Sharpen Up 127) [2009 57: f11g^5 f11g 10.1m^3 10s^6 p12.2g 12.4d f12g* p12.2g* f11m* f11g* f12f* Dec 11] workmanlike gelding: fairly useful performer: much improved to complete 5-timer at Southwell (4) and Wolverhampton in November/December: stays 1½m: acts on all-weather and good to firm ground: often blinkered, including for all wins: best making running. *M. W. Easterby* **92**

SHADOWTIME 4 b.g. Singspiel (IRE) 133 – Massomah (USA) 90 (Seeking The Gold (USA)) [2009 75: 7m 8f^4 8g 8.5m^2 8.5g^3 7.9m^2 7.9m 8.3m^2 7g^6 8.5m^3 9.2v 8m^5 8m^4 9.2g 8g^4 Sep 30] smallish gelding: fair handicapper: stays 8.5f: acts on polytrack, firm and good to soft going. *Miss Tracy Waggott* **75**

SHADY GLOOM (IRE) 4 b.g. Traditionally (USA) 117 – Last Drama (IRE) (Last Tycoon 131) [2009 88: 10.3g p12g 10.3m^2 12g^4 9.9m^5 10.4g^5 10s 11.1v^3 11.9d p12.2g^2 Oct 16] big, lengthy gelding: fairly useful handicapper: stays 1½m: acts on polytrack, firm and good to soft going: tried visored: races up with pace: sold £8,000. *K. A. Ryan* **84**

SHADY LADY (IRE) 3 b.f. Celtic Swing 138 – Viola Royale (IRE) 90 (Royal Academy (USA) 130) [2009 84: p12g Oct 26] good-topped filly: fairly useful winner at 2 yrs: well held only outing in 2009: dead. *M. Johnston* **–**

SHAFRONS CANYON (IRE) 6 b.m. Lend A Hand 124 – Carroll's Canyon (IRE) (Hatim (USA) 121) [2009 57: p9.5g Apr 24] maiden: lightly raced: well held sole start in 2009: tried tongue tied. *P. J. Lally, Ireland* **–**

SHAKALAKA (IRE) 3 b.g. Montjeu (IRE) 137 – Sweet Times 60 (Riverman (USA) 131) [2009 74: 10m^2 9m^2 p8m^4 p10m^4 p10m^3 p12f^2 p10m* Dec 30] tall gelding: fairly useful performer: won maiden at Lingfield in December: effective at 1m to 1½m: acts on polytrack, soft and good to firm going: tried in blinkers/cheekpieces: ungenuine. *G. L. Moore* **83 §**

SHAKE ON IT 5 b.g. Lomitas 129 – Decision Maid (USA) 105 (Diesis 133) [2009 90d: p8g^3 p8g^2 p8g p8g^4 p8g p8g p7g 10g 8m 8f p8g^4 7.6g p8g^6 p7m^3 p7m p8g^3 p8m^4 p8g p7m p8m^4 p8.6g* Dec 18] sparely-made gelding: fair handicapper: left M. Gingell after seventh start: won at Wolverhampton in December: stays 1¼m: acts on polytrack and good to firm ground: tried visored/in cheekpieces: formerly tongue tied: used to finish tamely. *M. R. Hoad* **71**

SHAKER STYLE (USA) 3 ch.g. Gulch (USA) – Carr Shaker (USA) (Carr de Naskra (USA)) [2009 66: p9.5g^4 p9.5g* p12.2g^4 12m^5 Apr 1] lengthy gelding: fair handicapper: won at Wolverhampton in February: stays 1½m: acts on polytrack: blinkered/visored: sold £4,000, joined M. Todhunter. *J. D. Bethell* **65**

SHAKESPEAREAN (IRE) 2 b.c. (Mar 21) Shamardal (USA) 129 – Paimpolaise (IRE) (Priolo (USA) 127) [2009 6g* 7m^5 7m^3 7.1g* 8g* 8d^6 Oct 24] €80,000Y: big, strong colt: fourth foal: dam, French maiden, half-sister to smart French sprinter (also second in Poule d'Essai des Pouliches) Pont-Aven, herself dam of smart French 5f **106**

Goffs Million Mile, the Curragh—the last running of this very richly endowed sales race goes to Shakespearean, who gets a narrow verdict over Marfach (No.7) and Nurture (in between first two) with Famous (No.17), Is Feidir Linn and Cadley Road next

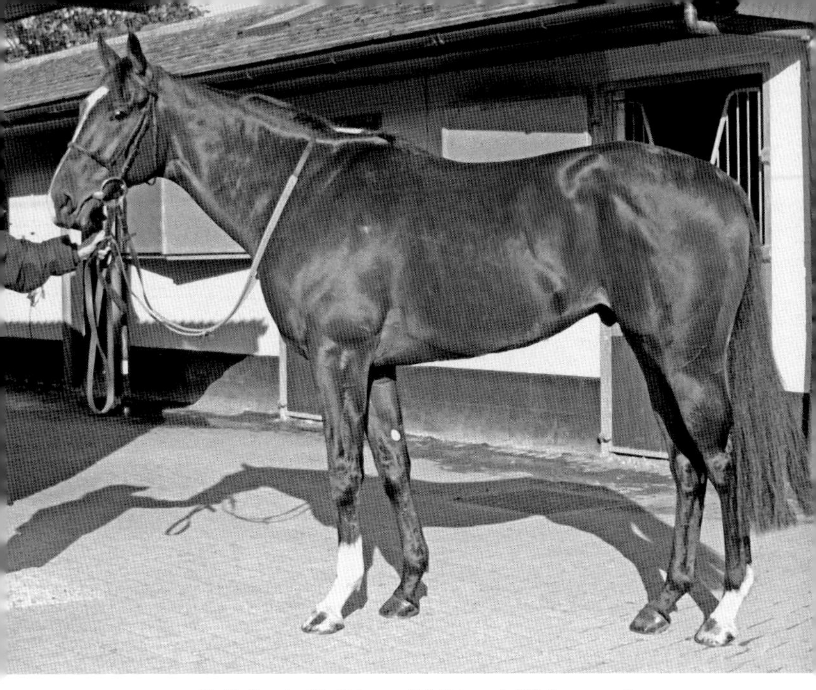

Sheikh Hamdan bin Mohammed Al Maktoum's "Shakespearean"

performer Sainte-Marine and smart 7f/1m performer Josr Algarhoud: useful performer: won maiden at Haydock in May, Solario Stakes at Sandown (beat Buzzword 1¼ lengths) in August and Goffs Million Mile at the Curragh (by short head from Marfach) in September: respectable sixth to St Nicholas Abbey in Racing Post Trophy at Doncaster: stays 1m: made running last 3 starts: has joined Godolphin. *M. Johnston*

SHAKESPEARE'S SON 4 b.g. Mind Games 121 – Eastern Blue (IRE) 68 (Be My Guest (USA) 126) [2009 78: p7g 5g 7.1m 6m^5 6g^3 6m^2 6s f5g 5.1m^4 6m^5 p6g^2 p7.1g p6g f5f p5.1g^6 p6f^3 p5g^3 Dec 31] angular gelding: fair handicapper: best at 5f/6f: acts on all-weather, good to firm and good to soft going: often visored/blinkered. *H. J. Evans* **68**

SHAKIN JOHN 3 b.g. Refuse To Bend (IRE) 128 – Qudrah (IRE) 88 (Darshaan 133) [2009 53: f11g 10.2d Apr 28] strong, close-coupled gelding: maiden: modest at 2 yrs: well held in handicaps in 2009: bred to stay 1¼m/1½m: tried blinkered (looked awkward). *E. J. O'Neill* **–**

SHALANAYA (IRE) 3 ch.f. Lomitas 129 – Shalamantika (IRE) 102 (Nashwan (USA) 135) [2009 10.5d^3 10g* 10g^5 10.5g* 10g* 11f^4 Nov 15] **120**

One of the chief beneficiaries of Christophe Lemaire's absence through injury during Arc weekend was the rising star among French jockeys, Maxime Guyon. He came in for the ride on Shalanaya in the Qatar Petroleum Prix de l'Opera at Longchamp in October, and the filly provided him with his ninth pattern-race victory, all gained in the space of just over five months, It was also his second at Group 1 level, the first having come on Cavalryman in the Grand Prix de Paris. Guyon, who now rides the majority of the Andre Fabre-trained horses not owned by either Khalid Abdulla or the Wertheimer brothers, both of whom have retained riders, ended the year with one hundred and thirteen wins, which took him into third place in the jockeys' championship in France.

Qatar Petroleum Prix de l'Opera, Longchamp—three-year-olds occupy the first three places as Shalanaya leads late on from Board Meeting (No.8) and Midday; Alpine Rose (checks) does best of the four-year-olds

Guyon probably wouldn't have been expecting too much from Shalanaya, whose only previous appearance in pattern company had seen her finish fifth to Board Meeting in the Prix de Psyche at Deauville two starts earlier. While Shalanaya had gone on to justify favouritism in good style in a twelve-runner listed event at Longchamp in September and was clearly improving, her form was still short of that shown by the majority of her eight rivals in the Prix de l'Opera, Board Meeting among them. Five were Group 1 winners, namely Again (Irish One Thousand Guineas), Alpine Rose (Prix Jean Romanet), Lady Marian (2008 Prix de l'Opera), Midday (Nassau Stakes) and Night Magic (Preis der Diana), so it was no surprise that Shalanaya was one of the outsiders. She proved more than ready for the task, though. Ridden in contrasting fashion to previously, Shalanaya was last into the straight, delivered her challenge out wide and led well inside the final furlong to win by a length and a half from Board Meeting and Midday, who were separated by a short head. It was the second successive year that three-year-olds had filled the first three places. Shalanaya ran some way below this very smart form on her only subsequent appearance. Racing on ground firmer than good for the first time, she was a never-nearer fourth to Queen Spumante in the Queen Elizabeth II Commemorative Cup at Kyoto in Japan, an extraordinary race in which the first two pinched a long lead.

Shalanaya (IRE) (ch.f. 2006)	Lomitas (ch 1988)	Niniski (b 1976)	Nijinsky
			Virginia Hills
		La Colorada (ch 1981)	Surumu
			La Dorada
	Shalamantika (IRE) (b 1999)	Nashwan (ch 1986)	Blushing Groom
			Height of Fashion
		Sharamana (b 1991)	Darshaan
			Sharmeen

Shalanaya, a small, sturdy filly who did not race at two, opened her account at the second attempt, in a minor event at Longchamp in June. Raced only at around a mile and a quarter, she is bred to stay a mile and a half, being by Lomitas out of Shalamantika, who finished a good third in a listed race at that trip on her final start. Shalamantika, who was trained by Sir Michael Stoute, gained her only win in a maiden over a mile and a quarter at Epsom in her three-year-old season. Shalamantika is from one of the Aga Khan's most notable families, being a daughter of the Prix Minerve winner Sharamana, a half-sister to Shergar and Shernazar. *M. Delzangles, France*

SHALLAL 4 b.c. Cape Cross (IRE) 129 – First Waltz (FR) 117 (Green Dancer (USA) 132) [2009 94: 7.1g^5 6d^4 6d 7m Oct 16] strong, sturdy colt: useful performer: ran well when 3¼ lengths fourth to Knot In Wood in Chipchase Stakes at Newcastle: below form after: stays 7f: acts on soft going. *P. W. Chapple-Hyam* **101**

SHALOO DIAMOND 4 b.g. Captain Rio 122 – Alacrity 62 (Alzao (USA) 117) [2009 **94**
90: 9.8m 8.1v 10.4m^4 11.5m^4 12s* 10.3d^2 10.3s^2 12g^5 10s^2 12s 12g Oct 10] well-made
gelding: fairly useful handicapper: won at Doncaster in July: good efforts after when
runner-up: stays 1½m: acts on soft ground. *R. M. Whitaker*

SHALUCA 2 b. or br.f. (Jan 23) Shamardal (USA) 129 – Noushkey 118 (Polish **73**
Precedent (USA) 131) [2009 8.3m^3 p8.6g^4 Oct 29] 31,000Y: lengthy filly: has scope:
seventh foal: half-sister to several winners, including 6-y-o January and 10.5f winner
Anaamil (by Darshaan): dam, 7f (at 2 yrs) and 1½m (Lancashire Oaks) winner, half-
sister to very smart stayer San Sebastian and to dam of high-class 1½m performer
Alkaased: easily better effort in maidens when length third to Bint Almatar at Nottingham
(made running): raced freely/dropped away tamely final start: bred to stay 1¼m+.
E. S. McMahon

SHAMALI 4 ch.c. Selkirk (USA) 129 – Shamaiel (IRE) 113 (Lycius (USA) 124) [2009 **110 p**
97p: 8.1m 10m^3 10m* 10m* Jul 26] strong, heavy-topped colt: smart performer: much
improved when winning handicap (by 2¾ lengths from Mabuya) and minor event (2/1
on, easily beat Proponent 3¾ lengths) in July, both at Ascot: suffered minor injury to a
leg after: should stay 1½m: acts on polytrack and good to firm going: open to further
improvement. *W. J. Haggas*

SHAMANDAR (FR) 2 ch.f. (Apr 11) Exceed And Excel (AUS) 126 – Sensational **106**
Mover (USA) 68 (Theatrical 128) [2009 6m* 5.2d^2 5.2m^2 6s* 6.5m* 6m^5 Oct 2] strong
filly: third foal: dam, placed at 1½m, out of US Grade 2 8.5f winner Blushing Heiress:
useful performer: won maiden at Ripon in July, and listed race at Salisbury (by ¾ length
from Sweet Sonnet) and Watership Down Stud Sales Race at Ascot (by ½ length from
Dubawi Heights) in September: also ran well when second in Super Sprint and listed race
(beaten nose by Sand Vixen) second/third starts, both at Newbury: laboured when only
fifth in Cheveley Park Stakes at Newmarket: stays 6.5f: acts on soft and good to firm
ground. *W. J. Haggas*

SHAME THE DEVIL (IRE) 4 b.g. Danehill Dancer (IRE) 117 – Iles Piece (Shirley **–**
Heights 130) [2009 8.1v May 22] in need of experience both starts in bumpers: 50/1,
slowly away when well held in maiden at Haydock. *Jonjo O'Neill*

SHAMIR 2 b.c. (Apr 12) Dubai Destination (USA) 127 – Lake Nyasa (IRE) 67 (Lake **84**
Coniston (IRE) 131) [2009 7m p7g^2 p7g^2 p8g^3 Nov 14] £7,000Y, £11,000 2-y-o: rather
leggy colt: sixth foal: half-brother to 3 winners, including useful Irish 2005 2-y-o 6f
winner Mrs Snaffles (by Indian Danehill) and 4-y-o Onceaponatime: dam, Irish maiden
who stayed 1¼m, half-sister to Gold Cup winner Mr Dinos: fairly useful maiden: similar
form when placed: stays 1m. *Miss Jo Crowley*

SHAMPAGNE 3 b.c. Orpen (USA) 116 – Arndilly 75 (Robellino (USA) 127) [2009 **109**
102: p9g^6 p8g^2 8m^2 8m^3 8m 8m^5 8d^2 8g^3 p8m^4 Nov 29] tall, good-topped colt: impresses
in appearance: useful performer: best efforts when placed in listed race at Kempton
(beaten head by Pure Poetry) and handicap (½-length second to Photographic) and minor
event (4¼ lengths third to Four Winds) at Newmarket second/third/fourth outings: below
form after: stays easy 9f: acts on all-weather, best turf form on ground firmer than good.
P. F. I. Cole

SHAMROCK LADY (IRE) 4 b.f. Orpen (USA) 116 – Shashi (IRE) 79 (Shaadi **78**
(USA) 126) [2009 88: 7g^6 6d 8.3f^6 7m p7g Oct 9] deep-girthed filly: fair handicapper:
barely stays 1m: acts on polytrack, soft and good to firm ground: has found little.
J. Gallagher

SHAM SHEER 3 b.g. Cape Cross (IRE) 129 – Viola Da Braccio (IRE) 58 (Vettori **87**
(IRE) 119) [2009 64p: p7.1g^4 8m 12m^6 10.3g^6 7f* p8.6g* 8.1m^2 p8g* Oct 22] well-made
gelding: fairly useful handicapper: gelded, improved to win at Folkestone and Wolverhampton in September then Kempton in October: stays 8.6f: acts on polytrack and good
to firm ground: visored once: sold 44,000 gns, sent to Bahrain. *L. M. Cumani*

SHAMWARI LODGE (IRE) 3 b.f. Hawk Wing (USA) 136 – Ripalong (IRE) 68 **109**
(Revoque (IRE) 122) [2009 94p: 6m* 7g^2 6g 7d^2 8m* 7m^2 8m^5 8g Oct 3] well-made filly:
useful performer: won handicaps at Newmarket in May and York (beat Paquerettza 1¾
lengths) in August: generally creditable efforts otherwise, particularly in face of stiffer
task when 3 lengths seventh to Tamazirte in Prix Daniel Wildenstein at Longchamp final
start: stays 1m: acts on good to firm and good to soft going. *R. Hannon*

SHANAFARAHAN (IRE) 4 b.g. Marju (IRE) 127 – Sedna (FR) (Bering 136) [2009 **69**
61: p13.3g p13g* p12g* p12g* 12d p12g p13.9g p12.2g^5 Dec 12] compact gelding: fair
handicapper: completed hat-trick at Lingfield and Kempton (2) in March/April: barely
stays easy 13f: acts on polytrack and firm going: versatile regards tactics. *K. A. Morgan*

SHANAVAZ 3 gr.f. Golden Snake (USA) 127 – Safinaz 50 (Environment Friend 128) [2009 64: 8.3d 10.4v 10.3g5 10.9g4 p12.2g4 12g5 10.4g 9.9m 12.4d 13.8m5 16.1g4 15.8g4 15.8s f12g p13.9g6 Nov 27] workmanlike filly: modest maiden handicapper: left Mrs G. Rees after seventh start: stays 2m: acts on polytrack: in cheekpieces last 6 starts: often slowly away: held up. *C. J. Teague* **60**

SHANDELIGHT (IRE) 5 b.m. Dilshaan 119 – By Candlelight (IRE) 84 (Roi Danzig (USA)) [2009 60: p12.2g2 Dec 7] deep-girthed mare: modest performer: stays 1½m: acts on all-weather, soft and good to firm going: often wears cheekpieces. *Julie Camacho* **60**

SHANGANI 3 b.f. Ishiguru (USA) 114 – Sheesha (USA) (Shadeed (USA) 135) [2009 64p: 7m* 7m5 6g* 6.1g6 6m3 7s4 7v5 Oct 24] angular filly: fairly useful performer: won maiden at Salisbury in June and handicap at Windsor in July: effective at 6f/7f: acts on heavy and good to firm ground, promise on polytrack: sold 15,000 gns, sent to Bahrain. *H. Candy* **86**

SHANGHAI STAR (IRE) 5 b.g. Soviet Star (USA) 128 – Sweet Surrender (IRE) 84 (Pennekamp (USA) 130) [2009 78: 16s 10m 10g* 10.7g 10m5 p12.2g 12v Oct 25] sturdy, lengthy gelding: fair performer at best: won claimer at Sligo in June: below form after, leaving W. Mullins after first occasion, Irene Monaghan after second: effective at 1¼m/1½m: acts on good to firm and good to soft going: sometimes slowly away: blinkered (raced freely) final outing. *Patrick Allen, Ireland* **78**

SHANNERSBURG (IRE) 4 b. or br.g. Johannesburg (USA) 127 – Shahoune (USA) (Blushing Groom (FR) 131) [2009 –: 9.7f6 p8g 8g p10m p12g* Dec 31] leggy gelding: fair performer: left A. Haynes after third start: won seller at Lingfield in December: stays 1½m: acts on polytrack and soft going: often blinkered/tongue tied. *D. E. Pipe* **74**

SHANNON GOLDEN 3 b.g. Tumbleweed Ridge 117 – Cledeschamps 46 (Doc Marten 104) [2009 f7g4 6d f5m5 5.1g f6g p6g* 5.1s p8.6g5 Dec 3] fair performer on all-weather, poor on turf: best effort when winning minor event at Wolverhampton in October: stays 6f: acts on all-weather: tongue tied last 4 starts. *S. R. Bowring* **47 a66**

SHANNON WEIR (IRE) 7 br.g. Norwich 118 – Go Meekly (IRE) (Bulldozer 93) [2009 11.9g Jun 7] no form in bumper/over hurdles/on Flat debut. *E. J. Creighton* **–**

SHANZU 4 b.f. Kyllachy 129 – Limuru (Salse (USA) 128) [2009 79: 8.3g 8.1g 9.9m p8g 8g Jul 24] close-coupled filly: fair handicapper in 2008: below form at 4 yrs (blinkered last 3 starts). *G. L. Moore* **–**

SHAPE SHIFTER (USA) 3 ch.g. Performing Magic (USA) 98 – Shot Gun Frances (USA) (Commemorate (USA)) [2009 –: 10f 14.1g 15.4m 11.8m Oct 13] workmanlike gelding: no form. *J. R. Best* **–**

SHARAAYEEN 2 br.c. (Mar 24) Singspiel (IRE) 133 – Corinium (IRE) 116 (Turtle Island (IRE) 123) [2009 p8g5 8m* 8g Oct 23] 85,000Y: good sort: third foal: half-brother to useful 2004 2-y-o 6f winner Dramaticus (by Indian Ridge) and 3-y-o Decision: dam, 1m winner, half-sister to smart 7f/1m winner Fa-Eq: won maiden at Ffos Las in September by length from Royal Etiquette: caught wide/hampered in nursery at Doncaster: should stay 1¼m: remains open to improvement. *B. W. Hills* **80 p**

SHARAKTI (IRE) 2 b.g. (Mar 28) Rakti 130 – Easter Parade 78 (Entrepreneur 123) [2009 p8.6g Sep 19] 40/1 and green, tailed off in maiden at Wolverhampton. *A. J. McCabe* **–**

SHARED MOMENT (IRE) 3 ch.f. Tagula (IRE) 116 – Good Thought (IRE) (Mukaddamah (USA) 125) [2009 8d3 9g2 8.3m* 8d5 8m3 10f6 8.1d4 8.3g2 8.3m 8g Sep 30] compact filly: second foal: sister to 4-y-o Sir Boss: dam unraced: modest performer: claimed from S. Hall £10,000 after debut, from D. Cantillon £4,500 after second start: won seller at Nottingham in July: left Ollie Pears £10,000 after next outing: stays 1m: acts on good to firm and good to soft going: in cheekpieces after debut. *J. Gallagher* **64**

SHARE OPTION 7 b.g. Polish Precedent (USA) 131 – Quota 102 (Rainbow Quest (USA) 134) [2009 p16g Apr 29] fairly useful winner in France in 2005: lightly raced on Flat in Ireland next 2 seasons (just modest in 2007): fair hurdler for new connections (successful in May), but well held in handicap on return to Flat: stays 2m: acts on soft and good to firm ground. *A. W. Carroll* **–**

SHARK MAN (IRE) 2 b.g. (Apr 3) Arakan (USA) 123 – Sharkiyah (IRE) 75 (Polish Precedent (USA) 131) [2009 5m5 p5g2 p5.1g* 6m2 6d 6g p7g5 7.1g 8m p7m* p6f2 p7.1g* Nov 9] €16,500F: small, leggy gelding: sixth foal: half-brother to 2 winners abroad, including useful winner in Europe up to 7.5f Swing The Ring (by Rossini): dam maiden (best at 1m): fair performer: won maiden at Wolverhampton in April and claimers at **70**

Kempton (only run in cheekpieces) in October and Wolverhampton (subsequently joined Miss J. Tooth £8,000, then gelded) in November: stays 7f: acts on polytrack and good to firm ground. *P. J. McBride*

SHARP AND CHIC 2 b.f. (May 4) Needwood Blade 117 – Morcover (IRE) 69 (Caerleon (USA) 132) [2009 p8g 8d Oct 12] 8,000F, 6,000Y: third live foal: dam, staying maiden, sister to smart performer up to 1½m Overbury: green, down the field in maidens at Lingfield and Salisbury: sold 1,200 gns. *M. L. W. Bell* **–**

SHARPAZMAX (IRE) 5 b.g. Daggers Drawn (USA) 114 – Amour Toujours (IRE) (Law Society (USA) 130) [2009 p10g⁵ 10m⁶ 12m⁴ p11g³ 12m⁶ p10m² p10m Dec 16] tall gelding: fairly useful handicapper: missed 2008: twice said to have finished distressed in 2009: stays 11f: acts on polytrack and good to firm ground. *P. J. Makin* **84**

SHARP BULLET (IRE) 3 b.g. Royal Applause 124 – Anna Frid (GER) 99 (Big Shuffle (USA) 122) [2009 86p: 5g⁴ 5f p5g⁵ p6g Oct 1] compact gelding: fair handicapper: raced only at 5f/6f: acts on polytrack and soft ground: reportedly bled on reappearance: sold £2,000, then gelded. *W. R. Swinburn* **78**

SHARP DISCOVERY 3 b.f. Needwood Blade 117 – You Found Me 62 (Robellino (USA) 127) [2009 –: 6.1g 8.3f f7g Jun 7] workmanlike filly: no form: in cheekpieces/blinkers last 3 starts. *J. M. Bradley* **–**

SHARP ECLIPSE 2 ch.g. (Apr 1) Exceed And Excel (AUS) 126 – Helen Sharp (Pivotal 124) [2009 5m⁵ 5s³ 6d May 17] good-bodied gelding: best effort in maidens when 1¼ lengths third to Tres Coronas at Newcastle: should stay 6f: gelded after final start. *K. A. Ryan* **69**

SHARPENED EDGE 3 b.f. Exceed And Excel (AUS) 126 – Beveled Edge 60 (Beveled (USA)) [2009 66p: 7s 6m³ 5m* 5m³ 5m⁶ 5m³ 5g⁴ 5m³ 5g Oct 10] leggy filly: fairly useful handicapper: won at Sandown in June: best at 5f: acts on good to firm ground. *B. Palling* **88**

SHARPENER (IRE) 3 b.f. Invincible Spirit (IRE) 121 – Daily Double (FR) (Unfuwain (USA) 131) [2009 73: p6g⁵ Jan 17] big, good-topped, close-coupled filly: fair performer at 2 yrs: below form sole start in 2009: effective at 5f/6f: acts on polytrack and soft going: usually front runner/races prominently. *R. Hannon* **58**

SHARPS GOLD 4 ch.f. Twice As Sharp 99 – Toking N' Joken (IRE) (Mukaddamah (USA) 125) [2009 57: p7g f8g p7g* p8g⁶ p7g p8g Jun 13] big, workmanlike filly: modest performer: won minor event at Kempton in February: stays 1m: acts on polytrack, raced only on good/good to soft ground on turf: often tongue tied (has reportedly had breathing problem): tried blinkered/visored. *D. Morris* **56**

SHARP SHOES 2 br.g. (Apr 29) Needwood Blade 117 – Mary Jane 77 (Tina's Pet 121) [2009 5s 5m⁵ 6m² 6m³ Oct 5] lengthy, good-topped gelding: modest form when placed in maidens: stays 6f. *Mrs A. Duffield* **58**

SHARP SOVEREIGN (USA) 3 b.g. Cactus Ridge (USA) 109 – Queen of Humor (USA) (Distorted Humor (USA) 117) [2009 71: 8.1m⁶ 12.1s⁴ 12.1g 12d⁵ 12.1m 9.3d 11.1s 10.1m⁵ 12.5s 12.4d 11.1g⁴ 9.1g Oct 23] good-bodied gelding: fair handicapper: largely on downgrade in 2009, leaving T. D. Barron after third start, I. Semple after eleventh: stays 1½m: acts on soft and good to firm ground: tried blinkered/in cheekpieces. *Miss L. A. Perratt* **69 d**

SHAVA 9 b.g. Atraf 116 – Anita Marie (IRE) (Anita's Prince 126) [2009 57: f7d p7g⁶ p7g⁶ Feb 24] poor performer nowadays: effective at 6f to 8.6f: acts on all-weather and good to firm going: tried in cheekpieces/blinkers/tongue strap: often carries head awkwardly. *H. J. Evans* **47**

SHAVANSKY 5 ch.g. Rock of Gibraltar (IRE) 133 – Limelighting (USA) 107 (Alleged (USA) 138) [2009 88: 10f* 10m* 10m⁴ 9s 10m⁵ 9m⁵ p9.5g Oct 31] tall, attractive gelding: fairly useful handicapper: won at Sandown (dead-heat) and Lingfield in June: creditable fifth in Cambridgeshire at Newmarket sixth start: stays 1¼m: acts on polytrack and firm ground. *B. R. Millman* **92**

SHAVOULIN (USA) 5 b. or br.g. Johannesburg (USA) 127 – Hello Josephine (USA) (Take Me Out (USA)) [2009 –: 10m² 9m³ p11g 10m⁴ 10v⁵ 8f 8g Aug 12] leggy gelding: modest maiden handicapper: stays 1¼m: acts on dirt, soft and good to firm going: tried in headgear. *P. W. Hiatt* **59**

SHAWEEL 3 b.c. Dansili 127 – Cooden Beach (IRE) 56 (Peintre Celebre (USA) 137) [2009 115: 7s⁵ 8m 8g² Oct 31] strong colt: has scope: smart performer: lightly raced at 3 yrs, below form in Greenham Stakes at Newbury and Poule d'Essai des Poulains at **113**

Longchamp, but ran creditably (after 5-month absence) when head second to Prince of Dance in listed race at Newmarket: stays 1m: acts on heavy and good to firm going: races prominently. *Saeed bin Suroor*

SHAWS DIAMOND (USA) 3 ch.f. Ecton Park (USA) 124 – Dear Abigail (USA) (Dehere (USA) 121) [2009 80: p7.1g^2 p8.6g^2 p7.1g^2 6m^6 7g 6d^4 7m* 7g 7g^4 Aug 14] good-topped filly: fairly useful performer: won maiden at York in July: probably best at 7f: acts on polytrack, good to firm and good to soft ground. *D. Shaw* **81**

SHAYERA 4 b.f. Hawk Wing (USA) 136 – Trick (IRE) 76 (Shirley Heights 130) [2009 71: p12m^4 p16g Jan 30] tall, angular filly: modest maiden: stays 1½m: acts on polytrack and good to soft ground: tried in cheekpieces, tongue tied in 2009. *B. R. Johnson* **61**

SHAYLA 2 ch.f. (Apr 25) Pastoral Pursuits 127 – Honours Even (Highest Honor (FR) 124) [2009 6g^5 8d Oct 13] £3,000Y: third foal: half-sister to winner in Greece by Diktat: dam unraced half-sister to smart performers Millennium Force (at 7f) and Chrysander (up to 1¼m): similar form in maidens at Hamilton and Newcastle. *G. A. Swinbank* **61**

SHAYLEE 4 b.f. Muhtarram (USA) 125 – Fairywings 85 (Kris 135) [2009 60: 10.1s^6 7.9g^3 9.9m^4 12.1m* Jul 3] neat filly: modest handicapper: won at Beverley in July: stays 1½m: acts on soft and good to firm going: possibly quirky. *T. D. Walford* **62**

SHEER FANTASTIC 4 b.g. Fantastic Light (USA) 134 – Sheer Bliss (USA) (Relaunch (USA)) [2009 71: p10g^4 p13.9g^5 p12.2g* Feb 6] good-topped gelding: fair handicapper: won at Wolverhampton in February: stays 1¾m: acts on polytrack: wears headgear: quirky. *P. C. Haslam* **73**

SHEER FORCE (IRE) 2 b.g. (May 9) Invincible Spirit (IRE) 121 – Imperial Graf (USA) (Blushing John (USA) 120) [2009 6m 6g^3 6g p7m^4 7m^3 p7g^3 Oct 9] €68,000F, 68,000Y: compact gelding: seventh foal: half-brother to several winners, including 3-y-o Ginobili and useful Irish 7f/7.5f (including at 2 yrs) winner Dynamo Dancer (by Danehill Dancer): dam, Italian maiden, out of US Grade 3 8.5f winner Sharp Ascent: fairly useful maiden: good placed efforts at Goodwood (nursery) and Lingfield last 2 starts (gelded after): stays 7f: sometimes slowly away. *W. J. Knight* **82**

SHEGARRDI 2 b.c. (Apr 7) Efisio 120 – Elleray (IRE) (Docksider (USA) 124) [2009 5d 6d Aug 27] lengthy colt: well beaten in maidens at Thirsk and Ayr. *K. A. Ryan* **–**

SHE GOES NOWHERE (IRE) 3 br.f. Pyrus (USA) 106 – Peking Dancer (USA) (King of Kings (IRE) 125) [2009 p7g p6m^6 Sep 28] €8,500Y: compact filly: second foal: dam unraced: seemingly better effort in maidens when equal-sixth at Wolverhampton. *M. S. Tuck* **54**

SHEIK'N'KNOTSTERD 4 ch.g. Zaha (CAN) 106 – Royal Ivy 71 (Mujtahid (USA) 118) [2009 48: 8.5m f6g^4 6f^6 6m f6g 6d^4 6g^3 7f^4 6m^6 6m 6m Aug 22] lengthy gelding: modest maiden: stays 7f: acts on firm and good to soft going: tried blinkered. *J. F. Coupland* **63**

SHEILA'S CASTLE 5 b.m. Karinga Bay 116 – Candarela 41 (Damister (USA) 123) [2009 p12g* 11.8m^3 p13g^6 p13.9g p13.9g Dec 17] 5,000 3-y-o: half-sister to 7-y-o Byron Bay: dam, maiden, half-sister to useful 1¼m performer Game Ploy: modest form in bumpers: fair performer on Flat: won maiden at Lingfield in August: should stay 1¾m: raced on polytrack and good to firm ground. *Sean Regan* **73**

SHEILA TOSS (IRE) 2 b.f. (Apr 16) Galileo (IRE) 134 – Palacoona (FR) 105 (Last Tycoon 131) [2009 p7g^5 Sep 21] 155,000Y: good-topped filly: seventh foal: half-sister to smart 1m winner/US Grade 3 9f winner Diamond Tycoon (by Johannesburg) and 4-y-o Cassique Lady: dam, French/US 1m/9f winner, out of sister to Prix du Jockey Club winner Polytain: 25/1, promising 3¼ lengths fifth to Magic Doll in maiden at Kempton, best work at finish, not unduly knocked about: will stay 1¼m+: will improve. *R. Hannon* **74 p**

SHEKA 2 b.f. (Jan 5) Ishiguru (USA) 114 – Maid For Running 80 (Namaqualand (USA)) [2009 5m^4 5m* 5g^6 5m^4 Jul 3] £15,000Y: compact filly: second foal: half-sister to winner in Hong Kong by Fraam: dam 2-y-o 5f winner: fair performer: won maiden at Ripon in April by short head from Forbidden Paradise: creditable efforts after in listed race and minor event, both at Beverley: raced only at 5f. *I. W. McInnes* **68**

SHEKAN STAR 7 b.m. Sri Pekan (USA) 117 – Celestial Welcome 96 (Most Welcome 131) [2009 47: 9.9m* 10d^3 13m^4 10m 12.1m^2 12.1m^5 9.9m^4 11.5g^2 12.1g^3 12.1m^6 12.4d^2 12.5m^5 Sep 27] smallish, close-coupled mare: modest handicapper: won at Beverley in April: stays 13f: acts on polytrack, firm and soft going. *K. G. Reveley* **62**

SHE KNOWS IT ALL (IRE) 2 gr.f. (Mar 4) Verglas (IRE) 118 – Tatamagouche (IRE) 70 (Sadler's Wells (USA) 132) [2009 5m 7.5m* 5.8g a8g^4 a6g^2 a10g^2 a6.8g^2 **57**

Dec 13] €5,000Y: first foal: dam, Irish maiden (stayed 1½m), out of sister to smart miler Darnay: modest performer: won claimer at Beverley (claimed from G. A. Swinbank £8,000) in July: second in minor events at Taby last 3 starts: stays 7.5f: acts on dirt and good to firm ground. *C. Bjorling, Sweden*

SHELFAH (IRE) 2 b.f. (Apr 10) Selkirk (USA) 129 – Pass The Peace 116 (Alzao (USA) 117) [2009 7s 6m⁴ 8.3d⁵ Oct 15] well-made filly: sister to fairly useful 1¼m winner Bayhirr and half-sister to several winners, including smart 7f (at 2 yrs) to 1¼m winner Tarfshi (by Mtoto) and 1997 Cheveley Park Stakes winner Embassy (by Cadeaux Genereux): dam won Cheveley Park Stakes and second in Poule d'Essai des Pouliches: best effort in maidens when fourth to Plume at Haydock: bred to stay 1m. *M. A. Jarvis* **63**

SHEMIMA 4 gr.f. Dalakhani (IRE) 133 – Shemaka (IRE) 116 (Nishapour (FR) 125) [2009 107: 10d* 10.5g⁴ 14g³ 12.5g² 14.6m⁴ Sep 10] tall, rather leggy filly: closely related to useful French 9f/1¼m winner Shemaya (by Darshaan) and half-sister to useful French 1¼m/10.5f winner Shemala (by Danehill) and French 10.5f to 1½m winner Shemdani (by Unfuwain): dam French 1m (at 2 yrs) to 10.5f (Prix de Diane) winner: smart performer: awarded Prix de Lutece at Longchamp in 2008 and won Prix Allez France at Chantilly in April by short neck from Tres Rapide: in frame all subsequent starts, including Prix Maurice de Nieuil at Longchamp (close third to Voila Ici), Prix de Pomone at Deauville (¾-length second to Armure) and Park Hill Stakes at Doncaster (didn't convince with attitude, hanging left/carrying head high, when fourth to The Miniver Rose): stays 15f: acts on good to firm and good to soft going. *A. de Royer Dupre, France* **114**

SHEMOLI 3 ch.g. Singspiel (IRE) 133 – Felawnah (USA) 111 (Mr Prospector (USA)) [2009 61p: 11.8m² 12m² 12d³ 12m* 14.1m⁴ 12m Aug 21] big gelding: has a round action: fairly useful performer: won maiden at Pontefract in June: stays 1½m: raced mainly on good to firm going. *M. A. Jarvis* **82**

SHENANDOAH GIRL 6 b.m. Almushtarak (IRE) 122 – Thundering Papoose (Be My Chief (USA) 122) [2009 62: f11g p12g* p12g⁵ Feb 19] lengthy mare: modest handicapper: won at Lingfield in February: stays 1½m: acts on polytrack, soft and good to firm going: wears headgear: sometimes slowly away: has reportedly bled: sold £3,000, joined Miss A. Newton-Smith. *Miss Gay Kelleway* **54**

SHERCON (IRE) 2 ch.g. (Jan 22) Redback 116 – Snow Eagle (IRE) 57 (Polar Falcon (USA) 126) [2009 7m 6s 7g Oct 16] lengthy gelding: well held in maidens/claimer. *N. Tinkler* **–**

SHERIFF'S SILK 5 b.g. Forzando 122 – Sylhall (Sharpo 132) [2009 –, a73: f8g 6g⁶ 8g Aug 30] tall gelding: fair handicapper at 4 yrs: well held in 2009, leaving Paul Mason prior to final start: tried visored: blinkered. *B. N. Pollock* **–**

SHERJAWY (IRE) 5 b.g. Diktat 126 – Arruhan (IRE) 87 (Mujtahid (USA) 118) [2009 59: p6g⁶ p6g* p6g⁴ p6g³ p5g p6g* f5g f5g² p5g⁵ 6g⁴ 5f⁵ 6m 6m* 6s 5f 6m 5g 6g 5m f5f³ f5f² p6f* Dec 21] stocky gelding: modest handicapper: won at Kempton in January (minor event), March and December, and Goodwood in June: best at 5f/6f: acts on all-weather, good to firm and good to soft going: wears blinkers/cheekpieces: withdrawn after unruly in stall intended twentieth start. *Miss Z. C. Davison* **63**

SHERMAN MCCOY 3 ch.g. Reset (AUS) 124 – Naomi Wildman (USA) (Kingmambo (USA) 125) [2009 69: 10.2g² 11.6m³ 11m* 11.6g² 13g* 14g⁴ 14v³ 16m⁴ Sep 30] lengthy gelding: fairly useful handicapper: won at Goodwood in May and Newmarket in July: creditable efforts in frame next 2 starts: stays 1¾m: unraced on firm going, acts on any other turf. *B. R. Millman* **88**

SHERNANDO 2 b.c. (Feb 11) Hernando (FR) 127 – Shimmering Sea 89 (Slip Anchor 136) [2009 8.3s⁵ Oct 7] 22,000Y: lengthy, good-topped colt: half-brother to several winners, including sprinter Sea Dane (by Danehill), later successful in Scandinavia, and 1m winner South Atlantic (by Sadler's Wells), both useful: dam, 2-y-o 5f and 7f winner, half-sister to Petoski: 20/1, 5½ lengths fifth to Anhar in maiden at Nottingham, soon close up and not knocked about: likely to improve. *M. Johnston* **70 p**

SHE'S A CHARACTER 2 b.f. (Jan 30) Invincible Spirit (IRE) 121 – Cavernista 75 (Lion Cavern (USA) 117) [2009 6g* 6f⁴ 7g⁶ 6s 6m Sep 19] 26,000F, 28,000Y: close-coupled filly: fifth foal: half-sister to 3 winners, including 6-y-o Celtic Spirit and 6f winner Capetown Girl (by Danzero): dam lightly-raced half-sister to smart stayer Give Notice: fairly useful performer: won maiden at Doncaster in June: creditable efforts after when fourth to Habaayib in Albany Stakes at Royal Ascot and sixth to Xtension in **91**

Vintage Stakes at Goodwood: stays 7f: acts on firm going: bit said to have slipped through mouth fourth outing. *R. A. Fahey*

SHE'S A MODEL 3 b.f. Erhaab (USA) 127 – Bedtime Model (Double Bed (FR) 121) [2009 10m p12g Jun 27] fifth foal: dam unraced: well beaten in maiden/seller. *R. Ingram* –

SHESHA BEAR 4 b.f. Tobougg (IRE) 125 – Sunny Davis (USA) 71 (Alydar (USA)) [2009 79: 9.7m^5 10g 10.1d^2 10m^3 11.5s* Aug 7] rather leggy filly: fair handicapper: won at Lingfield: stays 11.5f: acts on soft and good to firm ground: blinkered last 3 starts: reportedly in foal to Haafhd. *W. R. Muir* 72

SHESHALI (IRE) 5 b.g. Kalanisi (IRE) 132 – Sheshara (IRE) 107 (Kahyasi 130) [2009 11.7g* Jul 31] twice raced at 2 yrs for J. Oxx: fit from hurdling (fairly useful, stays very well), won maiden at Bath in July on return to Flat: will be suited by 1¾m+: capable of better still. *Evan Williams* 77 p

SHE'S IN THE MONEY 3 b.f. High Chaparral (IRE) 132 – Luminda (IRE) (Danehill (USA) 126) [2009 6m^2 7m 5g^2 6m^6 8g^5 7m* 7d^2 7m^5 7.2g* 8m^2 Sep 27] 30,000Y: smallish, compact filly: second foal: half-sister to fairly useful French 2007 2-y-o 7.5f winner Lazy Afternoon (by Hawk Wing): dam French 9.5f winner: fairly useful handicapper: left J. Given after fourth start: progressive after, winning at Newcastle in August and Ayr in September: good second at Musselburgh final start: may prove best short of 1m: acts on good to firm and good to soft ground. *R. A. Fahey* 90

SHE'S MY ROCK (IRE) 2 b.f. (Jan 30) Rock of Gibraltar (IRE) 133 – Love And Affection (USA) (Exclusive Era (USA)) [2009 p7g p6m p6g^6 p8.6g^3 f8f p7g^4 Dec 31] 35,000Y: small, angular filly: sister to 5-y-o Yellowstone, closely related to 2005 2-y-o 8.6f winner Danamour (by Dansili) and half-sister to several winners, including useful 7f (including at 2 yrs)/1m winner Londoner (by Sky Classic): dam, US 5f (at 2 yrs) to 1m winner, closely related to very smart 1¼m performer Zoman: modest maiden: stays 8.6f: raced only on all-weather. *S. Kirk* 55

SHE'S OK (IRE) 2 b.f. (Feb 11) Xaar 132 – Silvertine (IRE) 84 (Alzao (USA) 117) [2009 5g^6 6g^2 5.1m^2 7d^2 6g* 6m 6d 6.5m^4 Sep 25] €16,000F, 10,000Y: workmanlike filly: second foal: dam, Irish maiden (stayed 7f), half-sister to smart performer up to 1¼m Kinnaird: fairly useful performer: improved to win nursery at Newmarket in August: creditable fourth to Shamandar in sales race at Ascot final outing: stays 7f: acts on good to firm and good to soft going. *C. E. Brittain* 81

SHE'S OUR BEAUTY (IRE) 6 b.m. Imperial Ballet (IRE) 110 – Eleonora d'Arborea 78 (Prince Sabo 123) [2009 58: f5d^6 f5g^4 p5g f5m^5 Mar 22] modest performer: best at 5f: acts on fibresand and heavy going: usually wears headgear: none too consistent. *S. T. Mason* 57

SHE'S OUR DREAM 4 b.f. Statue of Liberty (USA) 115 – Mainly Sunset (Red Sunset 120) [2009 –: f5g p7g 7m 6m 6g May 3] sturdy filly: maiden: modest at 2 yrs, no form since: tried visored: often tongue tied. *R. C. Guest* –

SHE'S OUR MARK 5 ch.m. Ishiguru (USA) 114 – Markskeepingfaith (IRE) 86 (Ajraas (USA) 88) [2009 113: 10s 9.5v* 10s^2 8m^5 9s* 10s* 9.5g^3 10s^3 9.5m 8g^2 10d^4 Oct 26] good-topped mare: smart performer: won listed races at Gowran (by ½ length from Chinese White) in May and the Curragh (beat Latin Love 2 lengths) in July, and Meld Stakes at Leopardstown (by short head from Lord Admiral) later in July: creditable 2 lengths second to Aspectoflove in listed event at Naas penultimate start: effective at 1m/1¼m: promise on polytrack, best form on good ground or softer (acts on heavy): usually held up: tough and genuine. *Patrick J. Flynn, Ireland* 113

SHE'S PIVOTAL (IRE) 3 ch.f. Pivotal 124 – Born Beautiful (USA) (Silver Deputy (CAN)) [2009 8.3g p7.1g 7m^6 p9.5g Nov 13] small filly: sixth foal: half-sister to fairly useful 7f (at 2 yrs)/1m winner Denver (by Danehill) and French 1m winner We Will Rock You (by Rock of Gibraltar), later successful in USA: dam unraced half-sister to dam of Cheveley Park winner Pas de Reponse and Poule d'Essai des Poulains winner Green Tune: well held in maidens/minor event. *J. A. Osborne* –

SHE'S SO PRETTY (IRE) 5 ch.m. Grand Lodge (USA) 125 – Plymsole (USA) 84 (Diesis 133) [2009 76: p12g^5 Jan 30] angular, useful-looking mare: fair handicapper: stays 1½m: acts on polytrack, firm and soft going: usually in headgear (blinkered of late). *G. L. Moore* 65

SHE WHO DARES WINS 9 b.m. Atraf 116 – Mirani (IRE) 55 (Danehill (USA) 126) [2009 45: f5g^4 Mar 31] smallish, workmanlike mare: poor maiden: had a foal in 2007 by Sugarfoot: best at 5f: acts on firm going and fibresand, probably on polytrack. *L. R. James* 40

SHIANDA 2 b.f. (May 1) Kyllachy 129 – Limuru (Salse (USA) 128) [2009 7g Oct 31] unfurnished filly: fifth foal: sister to 4-y-o Shanzu and half-sister to 5-y-o Shimoni: dam unraced sister to very smart Italian/US performer up to 1½m Timboroa out of half-sister to Efisio: 100/1 and green, signs of ability when down the field in maiden at Newmarket: likely to do better. *G. L. Moore* **– p**

SHIBHAN 2 ch.f. (Mar 13) Compton Place 125 – Untold Riches (USA) 94 (Red Ransom (USA)) [2009 5.2m³ 6g³ 6m⁵ 7m 5.2d 5m³ 7m* 7f⁴ 6m² Oct 5] 6,000Y: rather unfurnished filly: fourth foal: half-sister to 1¼m seller winner Ciccone (by Singspiel) and 3-y-o Mr Udagawa: dam 1m/9f winner: fair performer: won nursery at Chester in August: good short-head second in similar event at Pontefract final outing: stays 7f: acts on good to firm going: tried in cheekpieces. *C. E. Brittain* **78**

SHIFTING GOLD (IRE) 3 b.g. Night Shift (USA) – Gold Bust (Nashwan (USA) 135) [2009 61: f8g* f8d 12m 11.8g³ f12g 11.1s* 12.1s⁴ 12.1v² 12.4d* Sep 7] sturdy, close-coupled gelding: fair handicapper: won at Southwell in January, Hamilton in August and Newcastle in September: stays 1½m: acts on fibresand and heavy ground: tried in cheekpieces, blinkered nowadays: races prominently: game: fair form on hurdling debut, amiss next time. *K. A. Ryan* **77**

SHIFTING STAR (IRE) 4 ch.g. Night Shift (USA) – Ahshado 70 (Bin Ajwaad (IRE) 119) [2009 106: 6f 6m 7f 7m p6m³ Nov 19] strong, sturdy gelding: useful handicapper: best effort in 2009 when 2½ lengths third to Earlsmedic at Kempton: raced mainly at 6f: acts on polytrack, good to firm and good to soft going: tongue tied last 3 starts. *W. R. Swinburn* **100**

SHIMAH (USA) 3 ch.f. Storm Cat (USA) – Sayedat Alhadh (USA) (Mr Prospector (USA)) [2009 107: 8f May 3] small filly: useful performer at 2 yrs: well below form when eleventh to Ghanaati in 1000 Guineas at Newmarket sole outing in 2009 (reportedly jarred up): stayed 7f: acted on firm and soft ground: visits Oasis Dream. *Kevin Prendergast, Ireland* **–**

SHIMMERING MOMENT (USA) 2 ch.f. (May 7) Afleet Alex (USA) 128 – Vassar (USA) (Royal Academy (USA) 130) [2009 p6g³ 7d Oct 12] $280,000Y: fourth foal: half-sister to 3 winners in USA, including smart Coast Guard (by Stormy Atlantic), third in Grade 1 9f event: dam French 7.5f winner: better effort in maidens 2 months apart (trained by A. Jarvis on debut) when 6½ lengths seventh to Thrill at Salisbury. *H. R. A. Cecil* **72**

SHIMMERING SURF (IRE) 2 b.f. (Apr 10) Danehill Dancer (IRE) 117 – Sun On The Sea (IRE) 109 (Bering 136) [2009 p7g⁴ p8g² Oct 9] 54,000Y: useful-looking filly: second foal: half-sister to 3-y-o Brother Cha: dam 1¼m winner: easily better effort in maidens at Lingfield when 1¾ lengths second to Timepiece, showing good attitude: bred to stay 1¼m. *P. Winkworth* **80**

SHIMONI 5 b.m. Mark of Esteem (IRE) 137 – Limuru (Salse (USA) 128) [2009 90: 11.6g* May 4] big, good-topped mare: fairly useful handicapper: won at Windsor: should stay 1¾m: acts on polytrack, soft and good to firm going: sometimes visored: has been slowly away: lazy sort. *G. L. Moore* **89**

SHINING TIMES (IRE) 3 br.f. Danetime (IRE) 121 – Shining Desert (IRE) 82 (Green Desert (USA) 127) [2009 47: 5.9d 5d 5m 5m f6m⁶ Nov 6] poor maiden: tried blinkered. *P. T. Midgley* **37**

SHINTOH (USA) 2 br.c. (Feb 27) Giant's Causeway (USA) 132 – Hollywood Wildcat (USA) 125 (Kris S (USA)) [2009 7s⁴ 7g* Oct 17] closely related to winner in USA by Storm Cat and half-brother to several winners, including Breeders' Cup Mile winner War Chant (by Danzig) and smart 6f (at 2 yrs)/1m winner Ivan Denisovich (by Danehill): dam won Breeders' Cup Distaff: confirmed highly promising debut at the Curragh (6¾ lengths fourth to Kingsfort, leading or disputing until over 1f out) when winning 18-runner event at Cork 4 months later by 1½ lengths from Timeless Whisper, still green, going away finish: should be suited by 1m: useful prospect. *J. S. Bolger, Ireland* **90 p**

SHIP'S BISCUIT 2 b.f. (Jan 25) Tiger Hill (IRE) 127 – Threefold (USA) 99 (Gulch (USA)) [2009 p8m⁵ Nov 19] fourth foal: half-sister to 3 winners, notably smart 7f (at 2 yrs) to 14.6f (Park Hill Stakes) winner Hi Calypso (by In The Wings) and 4-y-o Warringah: dam, 1m winner, would have stayed 1½m: 7/1, promising 2¾ lengths fifth to Aviate in maiden at Kempton, staying on from poor position and not knocked about: bred to be well suited by 1¼m+: open to significant improvement. *Sir Michael Stoute* **71 P**

SHIRLEY HIGH 3 b.f. Forzando 122 – Ripple Effect 88 (Elmaamul (USA) 125) [2009 53: p6g 6g p5.1g⁵ p5.1g² p6g p5g⁴ p5.1g⁵ p5.1g Dec 11] modest maiden: raced only at 5f/6f: acts on polytrack (very lightly raced on turf): tried tongue tied. *P. Howling* **53**

Irish Thoroughbred Marketing Gimcrack Stakes, York—Showcasing puts up the best performance in the race in nearly twenty years; Taajub (right) and Monsieur Chevalier (second left) are second and third; the grey Orpen Grey is fifth

SHI SHAN 2 b.c. (Feb 5) Sampower Star 118 – Nanna (IRE) 74 (Danetime (IRE) 121) [2009 5d^6 6m^4 Aug 29] sturdy colt: similar form in maidens at Thirsk and Redcar: dead. *T. D. Barron* **64**

SHOOTING PARTY (IRE) 3 b.g. Noverre (USA) 125 – L-Way First (IRE) 59 (Vision (USA)) [2009 77: 8.1m^6 p8g 10d 9.9s Oct 12] unfurnished gelding: fair performer: well below form last 2 starts: gelded after: should stay 1¼m: acts on polytrack and good to firm ground. *R. Hannon* **79**

SHOOT THE POT (IRE) 2 b.g. (Apr 26) Intikhab (USA) 135 – Kerasana (IRE) (Kahyasi 130) [2009 8d p8f* Dec 20] €5,000Y: third foal: half-brother to Irish 6f winner Karasay (by Royal Applause): dam unraced half-sister to useful French 7f/1m performer Keramani: better effort in maidens when winning at Kempton by ½ length from Prince Yarraman, still green and getting up close home: should improve again. *R. M. Beckett* **65 p**

SHORE THING (IRE) 6 b.g. Docksider (USA) 124 – Spicebird (IRE) 67 (Ela-Mana-Mou 132) [2009 21g 15g^4 Aug 31] big, strong gelding: fair handicapper: will stay 2m: acts on firm going: tried tongue tied: sometimes finds little: fairly useful hurdler, successful in November. *C. R. Egerton* **75**

SHORT AFFAIR 4 b.f. Singspiel (IRE) 133 – L'Affaire Monique 101 (Machiavellian (USA) 123) [2009 10.3g* 10.4g^5 9.9g 10.3s Nov 7] neat filly: second foal: sister to 5-y-o Bon Spiel: dam, 1¼m winner, sister to smart performer up to 1¾m Whitewater Affair and half-sister to very smart 1½m performer Little Rock: useful performer: trained by M. Gasparini in Italy prior to 2009, winning maiden at Merano at 2 yrs: improved when winning handicap at Doncaster in June: below form after: effective at 1m to 10.3f: acts on soft and good to firm ground. *L. M. Cumani* **99**

SHORT CUT 3 b.g. Compton Place 125 – Rush Hour (IRE) (Night Shift (USA)) [2009 –: 6m 6m^3 7d^2 6.1g^4 p7f^4 6m^3 p7.1g^4 Dec 17] stocky gelding: modest maiden handicapper: left S. Kirk prior to final start: stays 7f: acts on polytrack and good to soft ground: tongue tied after reappearance. *Ian Williams* **56**

SHORT SHARP SHOCK 3 b.c. Mujahid (USA) 125 – Possibility 59 (Robellino (USA) 127) [2009 59: 10.4v f8g 8d Aug 10] unfurnished colt: maiden: well held at 3 yrs. *J. Mackie* **–**

SHORT SUPPLY (USA) 3 b.f. Point Given (USA) 134 – Introducing (USA) 87 (Deputy Minister (CAN)) [2009 8g^6 8d f7m Nov 12] 2,500 3-y-o: deep-girthed filly: second foal: dam, 9f winner who stayed 1½m, half-sister to very smart US Grade 1 1¼m winner Midships (also winner up to 1¾m): best effort in maidens when seventh at Newcastle second outing: should be suited by 1¼m+: type to do better in handicaps. *T. D. Walford* **55 p**

SHORTWALL LADY (IRE) 4 b.f. Court Cave (IRE) – Vanished (IRE) 77 (Fayruz 116) [2009 –: f8d^5 p8g Jan 18] little form: blinkered in 2009: dead. *J. L. Spearing* **–**

SHOSOLOSA (IRE) 7 br.m. Dansili 127 – Hajat 64 (Mujtahid (USA) 118) [2009 65: 8.5m 10d 8.3m 9.8m 10m 10m Sep 12] close-coupled mare: modest handicapper at 6 yrs: out of sorts in 2009, leaving R. C. Guest after third start: tried in cheekpieces. *S. A. Harris* **–**

SHOTLEY MAC 5 ch.g. Abou Zouz (USA) 109 – Julie's Gift (Presidium 124) [2009 87: 7m 6g 7m* 7m^4 7d Jul 25] workmanlike gelding: fairly useful handicapper: better than ever when winning at Doncaster in June: creditable fourth at York next time: stays 1m: acts on heavy and good to firm ground: usually blinkered: front runner/races prominently. *N. Bycroft* **92**

SHOULDNTBETHERE (IRE) 5 ch.g. Soviet Star (USA) 128 – Octomone (USA) 74 (Hennessy (USA) 122) [2009 –, a69: p12g^6 p12g^6 Feb 13] good-topped gelding: modest performer: barely stays 1½m: races mostly on all-weather. *Mrs P. N. Dutfield* **–** **a50**

SHOWCASING 2 b.c. (Mar 31) Oasis Dream 129 – Arabesque 100 (Zafonic (USA) 130) [2009 6m^2 6g* 6m* 6m^3 Oct 2] strong, stocky colt: type to carry condition: sixth foal: brother to 3-y-o Bouvardia and half-brother to smart 6f (including at 2 yrs) winner Camacho (by Danehill): dam, 6f winner, out of Cheveley Park Stakes winner Prophecy: smart form: head second to Arcano at Newbury on debut, then won maiden at Yarmouth in July and Irish Thoroughbred Marketing Gimcrack Stakes at York (beat Taajub 2 lengths) in August: raced freely when respectable length third to Awzaan in Middle Park Stakes at Newmarket final outing: likely to prove best at 5f/6f: should hold his own in top sprints. *J. H. M. Gosden* **117**

SHOW WILLING (IRE) 2 b.f. (Mar 20) Elusive City (USA) 117 – Showboat (USA) (Theatrical 128) [2009 6g p6m 5g p7g^5 p7m^5 Oct 31] 2,000Y: leggy filly: half-sister to several winners, including 4-y-o Flashy Photon: dam, French maiden, daughter of US Grade 1 9f winner Fitzwilliam Place: modest maiden: stays 7f. *A. P. Jarvis* **54**

Mr K. Abdulla's "Showcasing"

SHREYAS (IRE) 4 gr.f. Dalakhani (IRE) 133 – Sadima (IRE) 103 (Sadler's Wells (USA) 132) [2009 109: 10v[4] 8m* 9g* 12g[3] 10d[3] 9.5m[5] Sep 26] smart performer: successful in 2 listed events at Leopardstown in June, beating Quinmaster 3 lengths then holding Fiery Lad by short head: below form after, finding little and hanging right in Denny Cordell Lavarack Stakes at Gowran (in cheekpieces) final start: best at 1m/1¼m: acts on heavy and good to firm ground: tongue tied on reappearance. *J. S. Bolger, Ireland* **115**

SHUBBAAN (USA) 4 b. or br.c. Kingmambo (USA) 125 – Sayedah (IRE) 105 (Darshaan 133) [2009 p11g[2] Oct 22] third foal: dam, won Rockfel Stakes, out of half-sister to US Grade 2 7f winner Kayrawan: 4/1, 2¾ lengths second to King's Salute in maiden at Kempton, running on having been hampered 1f out: will improve. *M. P. Tregoning* **73 p**

SHUNKAWAKHAN (IRE) 6 b.g. Indian Danehill (IRE) 124 – Special Park (USA) (Trempolino (USA) 135) [2009 72: 8m 8m 7.2g 7.1g 7.1g[6] 8s 7.1m[3] 7.2m[2] p7.1g Oct 9] quite good-topped gelding: modest handicapper: free-going sort, though stays 8.6f: acts on all-weather, firm and good to soft going: has worn blinkers, usually in cheekpieces. *Miss L. A. Perratt* **64**

SHY 4 ch.f. Erhaab (USA) 127 – Shi Shi (Alnasr Alwasheek 117) [2009 82: 13.1d[2] 14.1g 16g Jul 25] sturdy filly: fair maiden handicapper: stays 13f: unraced on firm going, acts on any other turf and polytrack: usually front runner. *P. Winkworth* **78**

SHYBUTWILLING (IRE) 4 ch.f. Best of The Bests (IRE) 122 – Reticent Bride (IRE) 71 (Shy Groom (USA)) [2009 –: 6m 6m 5.1m[5] 7m[6] 5.7m Jul 16] strong filly: little form: ungenuine. *Mrs P. N. Dutfield* **– §**

SHY GLANCE (USA) 7 b.g. Red Ransom (USA) – Royal Shyness 104 (Royal Academy (USA) 130) [2009 77: 8.3g[5] 10.1d[3] 10g[3] 10m* 9.2s 9.2v 10s 9.2g* 10.4g Oct 9] good-topped gelding: fairly useful handicapper: won at Ayr in June and Hamilton in September: stays 1¼m: acts on polytrack, firm and good to soft going: tried tongue tied: usually held up. *P. Monteith* **80**

SI BELLE (IRE) 4 gr.f. Dalakhani (IRE) 133 – Stunning (USA) 103 (Nureyev (USA) 131) [2009 93: 14m[6] 16g 12d 13.4m Aug 22] close-coupled filly: useful performer: stiff task, seemed to run well when seventh to Munsef in listed handicap at Chester final start: stays 2m: acts on all-weather, good to firm and good to soft ground. *Rae Guest* **95**

SIBERIAN TIGER (IRE) 4 b.g. Xaar 132 – Flying Millie (IRE) 99 (Flying Spur (AUS)) [2009 110: 12m 14m 12g[6] 12s Nov 7] tall, angular gelding: useful handicapper: fit from hurdling (fairly useful), limited impact in valuable events in 2009, best effort when 7½ lengths sixth to Opinion Poll at Ascot: stays 1½m: acts on soft and good to firm going: in cheekpieces/blinkers last 3 starts: temperament under suspicion. *A. J. Martin, Ireland* **99**

SICILIAN WARRIOR (USA) 3 b.c. War Chant (USA) 126 – Gravina (CAN) (Sir Ivor (USA) 135) [2009 56: p8.6g[4] p9.5g* Jan 12] fair handicapper: won at Wolverhampton in January: stays 9.5f: acts on polytrack: tongue tied last 3 starts: sold 10,000 gns in February, sent to Kazakhstan. *P. F. I. Cole* **66**

SIDE GLANCE 2 br.g. (Mar 15) Passing Glance 119 – Averami 68 (Averti (IRE) 117) [2009 6m* 7g[2] Sep 30] second foal: brother to 3-y-o Advertise: dam 7f winner: won maiden at Newmarket (by ½ length from Sophie's Beau) in September: marginally better form when 2½ lengths second to Fremont in minor event at Salisbury: stays 7f: should continue to progess. *A. M. Balding* **87 p**

SIDNEY MELBOURNE (USA) 2 ch.c. (May 7) Lemon Drop Kid (USA) 131 – Tolltally Light (USA) (Majestic Light (USA)) [2009 6g[4] 7.1m p7.1g* Nov 20] $7,500Y, resold $27,000Y: tall, lengthy colt: half-brother to several winners, including untrustworthy 1½m winner Crimson Monarch (by Red Ransom): dam, US maiden, half-sister to dam of smart US 9f/1¼m performer Riskaverse: best effort in maidens when winning at Wolverhampton by length from Wishformore: will stay 1m. *J. R. Best* **69 +**

SIEGFRIEDS NIGHT (IRE) 8 ch.g. Night Shift (USA) – Shelbiana (USA) (Chieftain) [2009 –: f12s[6] f16g p16.5g Jan 22] quite good-topped gelding: no form since early-2007: tried tongue tied. *M. C. Chapman* **–**

SIENA 4 b.f. Lomitas 129 – Sea Lane (Zafonic (USA) 130) [2009 47: f8g p7g f7g[6] p10g Mar 12] leggy filly: poor maiden: visored nowadays. *Mrs C. A. Dunnett* **46**

SIENA STAR (IRE) 11 b.g. Brief Truce (USA) 126 – Gooseberry Pie 63 (Green Desert (USA) 127) [2009 64, a70: p10g[6] p10g 9.7d* 10.2m[2] 10.2f[3] 10.2f[6] p10g p10m[6] Dec 10] close-coupled gelding: has a quick action: fair handicapper: won at Folkestone in April: stays easy 1½m: acts on polytrack, firm and soft going: tried blinkered earlier in career. *Stef Liddiard* **70**

SIENNA LAKE (IRE) 3 b.f. Fasliyev (USA) 120 – Lolita's Gold (USA) 66 (Royal Academy (USA) 130) [2009 65: p7g Oct 11] leggy filly: fair performer: off 12 months, tailed off sole 3-y-o start: should stay 1m: acts on polytrack and good to soft going: not straightforward. *T. D. McCarthy* **–**

SIERRA ALPHA 2 b.c. (Apr 19) Dansili 127 – Sound Asleep (USA) (Woodman (USA) 126) [2009 7.1g* Aug 31] fourth foal: half-brother to 1½m winner Warming Up (by Kalanisi) and winner in Sweden by Selkirk: dam unraced out of US Grade 1 9f winner Sleep Easy, herself closely related to US Grade 1 1¼m winner Aptitude: 28/1, won maiden at Warwick cosily by ½ length from Dahaam: will stay 1m+: likely to improve. *Mrs A. J. Perrett* **80 p**

SIGHT UNSEEN 3 b.c. Sadler's Wells (USA) 132 – High Praise (USA) 111 (Quest For Fame 127) [2009 11s* 12.3m[4] 11g[3] May 20] useful-looking colt: second foal: half-brother to fairly useful 1½m winner Critical Acclaim (by Peintre Celebre): dam, 7f (at 2 yrs) to 1½m (Prix de Malleret) winner, half-sister to top-class miler Observatory: useful form: won maiden at Newbury in April by 4 lengths: improved after when in frame in Chester Vase (5¼ lengths fourth to Golden Sword) and listed race at Goodwood (favourite, 3¾ lengths third to Alwaary, travelling smoothly most of way before hanging down camber and finding little, reportedly had breathing problem): stays 1½m: acts on soft and good to firm going: tongue tied: sold 20,000 gns in October, joined F. Vermeulen in France. *H. R. A. Cecil* **104**

SIGNALLER (USA) 3 ch.g. Rahy (USA) 115 – Tango Charlie (USA) (Cure The Blues (USA)) [2009 8m[3] 9.8m[2] 10m[6] May 9] $90,000F, €280,000Y: strong gelding: seventh foal: half-brother to several winners abroad, notably Canadian Grade 3 1¼m winner Ballroom Deputy (by Silver Deputy): dam US 6f (including at 2 yrs) to 9.5f (Grade 3) winner: maiden: shaped well when third at Ripon on debut: went wrong way after (gelded): sold 6,000 gns, sent to USA. *M. Johnston* **78**

SIGNALMAN 5 gr.g. Silver Patriarch (IRE) 125 – Kairine (IRE) (Kahyasi 130) [2009 66: 13g May 3] leggy gelding: fair handicapper: below form sole 5-y-o start: stays 15f, effective at shorter: acts on heavy and good to firm ground: fair hurdler. *P. Monteith* **–**

SIGNELLA 3 ch.f. Selkirk (USA) 129 – Sarah Georgina 79 (Persian Bold 123) [2009 –: p10g* 9.7d[6] Mar 31] leggy filly: fair performer: won maiden at Lingfield in January: likely to be suited by 1½m: raced only on polytrack and good to soft ground. *P. W. Chapple-Hyam* **66**

SIGN OF APPROVAL 3 b.c. Refuse To Bend (IRE) 128 – Scarlet Plume 103 (Warning 136) [2009 81: p7g[3] p11g[5] p9.5g* 10m 9.8m[2] p10g[2] 10f[2] Jul 2] well-made colt: fairly useful performer: won maiden at Wolverhampton in February: good second in handicaps last 3 starts: stays 1¼m: acts on polytrack and firm going: tried visored, wore cheekpieces last 2 outings: often slowly away: sold 20,000 gns. *K. R. Burke* **82**

SIGN OF LIFE 2 b.f. (May 6) Haafhd 129 – Three Piece (Jaazeiro (USA) 127) [2009 p7g 7m[4] Oct 6] good-topped filly: half-sister to several winners, including very smart 6f (at 2 yrs) to 1m (Poule d'Essai des Poulains) winner Victory Note (by Fairy King), useful 1¼m/1½m winner Dance So Suite (by Shareef Dancer) and 3-y-o Sweet Hollow: dam Irish maiden: similar form in maidens at Lingfield and Leicester (still green): should be suited by 1m+: capable of better. *W. R. Swinburn* **59 p**

SIGN OF THE CROSS 5 b.g. Mark of Esteem (IRE) 137 – Thea (USA) 95 (Marju (IRE) 127) [2009 86: p10g[6] p10g p8.6g* 8.3g* 8.3d 7.6g p8g 8.5g[5] p8g f8g p7.1g p8.6m p8m p7g[3] p7m Nov 4] good-topped gelding: fair performer: won sellers at Wolverhampton in April and Leicester (left G. L. Moore 7,200 gns) in May: below that level after: stays 1¼m: acts on polytrack and good to soft ground: temperamental, and one to treat with plenty of caution. *C. R. Dore* **77 d**

SIGNORA FRASI (IRE) 4 b.f. Indian Ridge 123 – Sheba (IRE) (Lycius (USA) 124) [2009 74d: p6g[3] 6.1g 8g[3] p8g* Oct 21] useful-looking filly: modest handicapper nowadays: won at Kempton: stays easy 1m: acts on polytrack and good to firm going: tends to race freely. *A. G. Newcombe* **64**

SIGNOR PELTRO 6 b.g. Bertolini (USA) 125 – Pewter Lass 56 (Dowsing (USA) 124) [2009 101: 7m[4] 7f* 7m 7m[5] 7g[2] 7g[2] 6m 7m 8s[6] Oct 12] strong, rangy gelding: useful handicapper: won at Doncaster in May by length from Celtic Sultan: better form still when second at Newmarket (unlucky, beaten ½ length by Jeninsky) and Goodwood (went down by 1¼ lengths to Marching Time) after: best at 7f (stretched by 1m final start): acts on polytrack, firm and soft ground: tried blinkered/visored: reliable. *H. Candy* **109**

SIGNOR VERDI 2 b.c. (Feb 17) Green Tune (USA) 125 – Calling Card (Bering 136) [2009 7g Oct 23] good-topped colt: 40/1 and green, down the field in maiden at Doncaster. *B. J. Meehan* **–**

SILAAH 5 b.g. Mind Games 121 – Ocean Grove (IRE) 84 (Fairy King (USA)) [2009 **98**
90p: p7g^{3} 6g^{5} 7m^{6} p6g^{2} p7g* 6g^{2} 6m^{2} 6m^{6} Sep 18] good-topped gelding: useful performer: won handicap at Kempton in June (left E. Dunlop 22,000 gns after): good second in minor event at Haydock penultimate start: free-going sort, likely to prove best at 6f/7f: raced only on polytrack and good going or firmer: looked none too keen under pressure third/fourth outings: joined D. Watson in UAE. *D. Nicholls*

SILCA MEYDAN 3 b.g. Diktat 126 – Golden Silca 115 (Inchinor 119) [2009 p8g^{6} **62**
p7g^{4} p6g^{4} p5.1m^{2} 6m p5.1g^{5} 8.1m p7.1m p8.6g Dec 14] third foal: half-brother to 7f/1m winner Silca Destination (by Dubai Destination): dam 5f (at 2 yrs) to 9f winner: modest maiden: off 5 months, below form last 5 starts, leaving M. Channon £1,300 after seventh outing: should stay 1m: acts on polytrack. *R. J. Price*

SILENCEOFTHEWIND (USA) 2 b.c. (Feb 13) Eddington (USA) 120 – Betty's **93**
Solutions (USA) (Eltish (USA) 120) [2009 6d^{6} 6m* 7m Jul 10] $310,000Y: good-topped colt: third foal: half-brother to useful 2007 2-y-o 6f winner Francesca d'Gorgio (by Proud Citizen) and a winner in USA by Lion Heart: dam, US 6f and 8.3f winner, out of US Grade 3 8.5f/9f winner Betty Lobelia: won maiden at Newcastle in June comfortably by 3 lengths from Antoniola: better than result when last in Superlative Stakes at Newmarket (failed to settle, hampered final 1f) final start (subsequently joined H. Cecil): should stay 7f. *K. R. Burke*

SILENT ACT (USA) 3 b.f. Theatrical 128 – Vinista (USA) (Jade Hunter (USA)) **77**
[2009 54p: 10m^{5} 10.9m^{2} 11.5g 9.9g^{4} p12m^{3} 12m^{2} p12m* p12m^{2} Nov 4] big, lengthy filly: fair handicapper: won at Kempton in October: stays 1½m: acts on polytrack and good to firm going: tried tongue tied. *Mrs A. J. Perrett*

SILENT APPLAUSE 6 b.g. Royal Applause 124 – Billie Blue 63 (Ballad Rock 122) **73**
[2009 73: 12m* Jun 19] lengthy gelding: fair handicapper: won at Newmarket in June: stays 1½m: acts on firm and good to soft going: tried visored: looks hard ride (has wandered). *Dr J. D. Scargill*

SILENT DANCER (IRE) 2 b.g. (Apr 29) Danehill Dancer (IRE) 117 – Silent Crystal **75 ?**
(USA) 94 (Diesis 133) [2009 5g 7s 7s 5v 7d^{3} 8d p7m Oct 26] 52,000 2-y-o: third foal: half-brother to 4-y-o Greylami: dam, 1m and (at 2 yrs) 9f winner, out of half-sister to top-class performer up to 1m Moorestyle: maiden: third at Listowel: little form otherwise, including at Kempton final outing: stays 7f. *S. Donohoe, Ireland*

SILENT HERO 3 b.g. Oasis Dream 129 – Royal Passion 78 (Ahonoora 122) [2009 82: **89**
p7g^{5} 7m f7g* 8.3g^{5} f6g 7d^{3} p7.1m^{3} f8f^{6} Oct 21] stocky gelding: fairly useful handicapper: won at Southwell in June: should stay 1m: acts on all-weather, very best turf effort on good ground: in cheekpieces last 2 starts: probably not straightforward: sold 19,000 gns. *M. A. Jarvis*

SILENT LUCIDITY (IRE) 5 ch.g. Ashkalani (IRE) 128 – Mimansa (USA) (El Gran **55**
Senor (USA) 136) [2009 12g p13.9g 13.8g p12.2g^{6} Dec 12] modest performer nowadays: off over 2 years prior to reappearance: stays 11f: acts on firm going. *P. D. Niven*

SILENT MAJORITY (IRE) 2 b.c. (Mar 14) Refuse To Bend (IRE) 128 – Queen Shy **65 p**
(Marju (IRE) 127) [2009 7g^{5} p7.1g Nov 13] €52,000Y, 72,000 2-y-o: tall colt, has scope: second foal: half-brother to Italian 8.5f winner Valore Assoluto (by One Cool Cat): dam, Italian 1m (at 2 yrs)/10.5f winner, sister to smart Italian performer up to 1½m Toto Le Moko: better effort in maidens when fifth to Tamaathul at Doncaster: seemed amiss subsequent start: should stay 1m+: should still do better. *E. A. L. Dunlop*

SILENT OASIS 3 b.f. Oasis Dream 129 – Silence Is Golden 120 (Danehill Dancer **80**
(IRE) 117) [2009 8.3g^{4} 8m^{2} 9g^{3} 8.1g^{4} 8g Oct 8] 10,000 2-y-o: smallish filly: second foal: dam 7f (at 2 yrs) to 1¼m winner (runner-up in Nassau Stakes): fairly useful maiden: will stay 1¼m: raced only on good/good to firm going. *B. J. Meehan*

SILENT SECRET (IRE) 2 ch.f. (Mar 30) Dubai Destination (USA) 127 – Charita **81**
(IRE) 103 (Lycius (USA) 124) [2009 6m 6m^{4} 6m^{3} 8m^{2} 7.5m* 7v Oct 24] €47,000F, 30,000 2-y-o: useful-looking filly: sixth foal: half-sister to 3 winners, including smart Irish 6f to 1m (including at 2 yrs) winner Cheyenne Star (by Mujahid) and 3-y-o Vivachi: dam Irish 7f (at 2 yrs)/1m winner: fairly useful performer: won maiden at Beverley in September: stays 1m: acts on good to firm going. *R. Hannon*

SILENT TREATMENT (IRE) 3 ch.f. Captain Rio 122 – Without Words 71 (Lion **63**
Cavern (USA) 117) [2009 64: 7g p8g^{4} f8g 8d Jul 24] close-coupled filly: modest handicapper: stays 1m: acts on all-weather, soft and good to firm going: tried in cheekpieces, often tongue tied. *Miss Gay Kelleway*

SILIDAN 6 b.g. Dansili 127 – In Love Again (IRE) 86 (Prince Rupert (FR) 121) [2009 69?: p7m p7g* p7g p7g5 f7m Nov 12] compact gelding: modest handicapper: won at Lingfield in February: left G. L. Moore after fourth start: stays 7f: acts on polytrack, sand and good to firm ground: none too consistent and signs of temperament. *Miss M. E. Rowland* 59

SILK AFFAIR (IRE) 4 b.f. Barathea (IRE) 127 – Uncertain Affair (IRE) 79 (Darshaan 133) [2009 95: 18m Oct 17] sturdy filly: useful performer at best, including over hurdles: never competitive in Cesarewitch (Handicap) sole start on Flat in 2009: should stay 1¾m+: acts on heavy ground. *M. G. Quinlan* –

SILK AND SATIN (USA) 3 b. or br.f. Storm Cat (USA) – Rafina (USA) (Mr Prospector (USA)) [2009 10m 10.3m4 11.7g 9.7m3 Sep 22] good-topped filly: sixth foal: sister to useful Irish 2007 2-y-o 7f winner Lucifer Sam and half-sister to 3 winners, notably smart Royal Lodge and Dee Stakes winner Admiralofthefleet (by Danehill): dam, placed up to around 1m in France, sister to very smart performer up to 1m Machiavellian and half-sister to very smart 1m/1¼m performer Exit To Nowhere: modest maiden: stays 10.3f: raced only on good/good to firm going: tongue tied last 3 starts: sold 210,000 gns. *H. R. A. Cecil* 55

SILK COTTON (USA) 3 b.f. Giant's Causeway (USA) 132 – Calico Moon (USA) (Seeking The Gold (USA)) [2009 71p: 10m p8.6g Jun 5] well-made filly: fair maiden at 2 yrs: well held in handicaps in 2009: should be suited by 1¼m/1½m: blinkered final start: sold 8,000 gns in July, sent to Kuwait. *E. A. L. Dunlop* –

SILKEN AUNT 2 b.f. (Feb 4) Barathea (IRE) 127 – Aunt Susan (Distant Relative 128) [2009 p7.1g4 p7.1g4 Dec 4] 40,000Y: fifth foal: half-sister to useful 2005 2-y-o 5f/6f winner BA Foxtrot and 5f winner Belvedere Vixen (both by Foxhound): dam no form: fourth in maidens at Wolverhampton, better effort on debut. *J. A. R. Toller* 60

SILKEN PROMISE (USA) 3 b. or br.f. Pulpit (USA) 117 – Banksia (Marju (IRE) 127) [2009 69p: 10m4 9.9f5 11.6m6 p12m5 p12m p10g p12m2 p11f2 Dec 16] fair maiden handicapper: stays 1½m: raced only on polytrack and good going or firmer: in cheekpieces last 2 starts. *W. R. Swinburn* 68

SILKEN SANDS (IRE) 3 b.f. Green Desert (USA) 127 – Arctic Silk 80 (Selkirk (USA) 129) [2009 8.3d5 p8f5 Dec 20] 30,000Y: long-backed, sparely-made filly: first foal: dam, maiden (stayed 1m), out of 1000 Guineas winner Cape Verdi: modest form in maidens. *C. G. Cox* 57

SILKENVEIL (IRE) 2 b.f. (Feb 5) Indian Ridge 123 – Line Ahead (IRE) (Sadler's Wells (USA) 132) [2009 p8.6g Dec 19] €95,000F: second foal: half-sister to winner in Italy by Hawk Wing: dam, ran once, out of half-sister to smart performer up to 14.6f Bonny Scot and to dam of Golan and Tartan Bearer: 7/1, always behind in maiden at Wolverhampton. *R. A. Fahey* –

SILK GALLERY (USA) 4 b.f. Kingmambo (USA) 125 – Moon Flower (IRE) 95 (Sadler's Wells (USA) 132) [2009 57: f6s2 f6g2 p6g4 p6g3 f6g5 5m 8.1s5 7s2 6s2 7v4 p6g 5s* 5.1s3 f5m f5f Nov 24] strong, good-topped filly: fair handicapper: won at Catterick in October: stays 7f, effective at shorter: acts on all-weather and heavy ground: tongue tied. *E. J. Alston* 66

SILK HALL (UAE) 4 b.g. Halling (USA) 133 – Velour 94 (Mtoto 134) [2009 91: 14.1m2 14m6 May 23] rather leggy gelding: fairly useful handicapper: developed into useful novice hurdler in early-2009: good nose second at Nottingham, better effort on Flat at 4 yrs: stays 2m: acts on polytrack, unraced on extremes of going on turf. *A. King* 92

SILK RUNNER (IRE) 2 ch.f. (May 9) Barathea (IRE) 127 – Sao Gabriel (IRE) (Persian Bold 123) [2009 7g p8m Sep 16] €120,000F: fifth foal: half-sister to fairly useful Irish 7f winner Spring Snowdrop (by Danehill Dancer): dam unraced half-sister to Champion Stakes winner Legal Case and to dam of Oaks winner Love Divine, herself dam of St Leger winner Sixties Icon: well held in maidens at Newmarket (backward) and Kempton. *J. W. Hills* –

SILK SLIPPERS 2 b.f. (Apr 19) Oasis Dream 129 – Interpose (Indian Ridge 123) [2009 p6g4 6g Sep 27] €32,000Y: closely related to 2007 2-y-o 6f winner Rinterval and 7f/1¼m winner Go Figure (both fairly useful, by Desert Prince) and half-sister to 2 winners, including 3-y-o Interdiamonds: dam unraced half-sister to smart French winner up to 12.5f Short Pause: fourth to Ferris Wheel in maiden at Kempton: tailed off in sales race at the Curragh (hung right) later in month. *John Joseph Murphy, Ireland* 57

SILK STAR (IRE) 3 b.f. Pyrus (USA) 106 – Silk Feather (USA) (Silver Hawk (USA) 123) [2009 –: 8g p8.6g f8f6 Nov 24] poor maiden. *Pat Morris* 43

SILK STREET (USA) 2 b.c. (Jan 28) Street Cry (IRE) 130 – High Potential (USA) (Pleasant Colony (USA)) [2009 6.1d^2 p7m^2 Oct 26] $60,000Y: sturdy colt: second foal: half-brother to winner in USA by Langfuhr: dam, US 1m/8.5f winner, half-sister to US Grade 3 9f winner Personal Legend: shaped well when runner-up in maidens at Nottingham (green) and Kempton (beaten ¾ length by Prizefighting): will stay 1m: sent to USA: should improve again. *R. A. Fahey* **85 p**

SILK TRAIL 3 b.f. Dubai Destination (USA) 127 – Satin Flower (USA) 115 (Shadeed (USA) 135) [2009 76p: 8.3g^3 8m^3 7d^2 7f* 8d^3 8s^2 7v Nov 24] rather leggy filly: fairly useful performer: won maiden at Folkestone in July on final start for Saeed bin Suroor: good 1½ lengths second to Sokar in minor event at Nantes before stiff task (not discredited) in listed race at Saint-Cloud final outing: stays 1m: probably acts on polytrack and any ground on turf. *H-A. Pantall, France* **81**

SILKY WAY (GR) 3 b.f. Harmonic Way 121 – Flourishing Way 78 (Sadler's Wells (USA) 132) [2009 67: 5m* p5.1g^6 5.1g^5 5m Sep 12] fair performer: won handicap at Goodwood in May: should prove best at 5f/6f: raced only on polytrack and good ground or firmer on turf: returned to Greece. *P. R. Chamings* **68**

SILLS VINCERO 3 b.f. Piccolo 121 – Aegean Magic 76 (Wolfhound (USA) 126) [2009 71d: p5g^5 f5d^5 p6g^4 p6g^3 p5.1g* p5.1g^2 p5.1g^3 p5g p5.1g^3 5.1m p5.1g^6 p5.1g Apr 25] tall filly: modest handicapper: won at Wolverhampton in February: best at 5f: acts on all-weather and good to firm ground. *D. Shaw* **62**

SILLY GILLY (IRE) 5 b.m. Mull of Kintyre (USA) 114 – Richly Deserved (IRE) (Kings Lake (USA) 133) [2009 64: 8f 7m* 8f^3 8m^3 7g^2 7.5g 7.9g^3 8.5m 8s^4 8m^3 7g^3 9.9g f8f Nov 24] lengthy mare: fair handicapper: won at Thirsk in May: stays 1m: acts on fibresand, heavy and good to firm going: tried in cheekpieces: usually races prominently: consistent. *R. E. Barr* **67**

SILVADOR 3 gr.g. Selkirk (USA) 129 – Dali's Grey (Linamix (FR) 127) [2009 73p: 11.5g^2 May 20] rangy, unfurnished gelding: fairly useful form in maidens: shaped well when second to Akmal at Lingfield only start in 2009 (gelded after): will stay 1½m. *W. R. Muir* **85**

SILVANUS (IRE) 4 b.g. Danehill Dancer (IRE) 117 – Mala Mala (IRE) 104 (Brief Truce (USA) 126) [2009 81: p5g^2 p6g^3 p5.1g 5m^6 5m^5 6g^4 5d 5m^6 5g^3 5m* 5m^4 5m^3 5d^5 5g* 5m p6g^4 5m^5 f5g Oct 18] angular, useful-looking gelding: fairly useful performer at best: won seller at Musselburgh in June and claimer at Catterick (left I. Semple £5,000) in August: best at 5f/6f: acts on polytrack and good to firm going: effective with or without blinkers/cheekpieces: usually pulls hard. *P. T. Midgley* **81 d**

SILVEE 2 gr.f. (Mar 15) Avonbridge 123 – Silver Louie (IRE) (Titus Livius (FR) 115) [2009 5g 5m 6m^6 5f 5m 6m 5.3m 8m p6g 6d^5 Sep 15] workmanlike filly: second foal: dam very temperamental maiden: poor maiden: stays 6f: acts on good to firm and good to soft going. *J. J. Bridger* **43**

SILVER BLUE (IRE) 6 ch.g. Indian Lodge (IRE) 127 – Silver Echo (Caerleon (USA) 132) [2009 75: 11.9s^5 8.1m^6 10f 11.6m^6 Aug 29] good-topped gelding: fair handicapper at 5 yrs: well below form in 2009: probably stays 1½m: acts on polytrack and firm going: tried blinkered/visored. *W. K. Goldsworthy* **–**

SILVER DEAL 4 b.f. Lujain (USA) 119 – Deal In Facts 61 (So Factual (USA) 120) [2009 46: p5.1g Jan 29] leggy, angular filly: poor maiden at best. *J. A. Pickering* **–**

SILVER FROST (IRE) 3 gr.c. Verglas (IRE) 118 – Hidden Silver (Anabaa (USA) 130) [2009 109: 8g* 8g* 8m* 10.5g^6 8m^6 Aug 16] **122**

Reports of Silver Frost's retirement would appear to have been premature. An injury sustained in the Prix Jacques le Marois at Deauville in August looked to have ended his racing career, but, following an operation on his near-fore knee in October, there is said to be a good chance that the Poule d'Essai des Poulains winner will be back in action in 2010. With offers for Silver Frost to go to stud already received before the news that he is to stay in training, his future still looks assured even if he does not make the expected full recovery.

Silver Frost is owned by John Cotton, whose yellow and purple hooped colours are quite familiar to British racegoers, though probably more so over jumps through the likes of smart chaser Dear Villez, who actually gained his biggest win in Ireland in the 2008 Munster National. It didn't take long for Silver Frost to demonstrate that he was comfortably the best of his owner's horses on the Flat to date, his three wins in his first season including those in the Prix de Cabourg and

Poule d'Essai des Poulains, Longchamp—
high point of the season for Silver Frost as he beats Le Havre (No.2), Naaqoos (second left) and Westphalia (right); Naaqoos was demoted to sixth for causing interference

Prix Thomas Bryon, while he also finished a good third in the Criterium International. Further victories in a listed race at Saint-Cloud in March and the Prix de Fontainebleau at Longchamp in April showed that Silver Frost had trained on well, and he started second favourite on his return to Longchamp in May for the Poule d'Essai des Poulains. The favourite was Prix Jean-Luc Lagardere winner Naaqoos, who had been narrowly beaten by another Poulains runner Le Havre on his return; third choice in the betting was Westphalia, a half-length second to Silver Frost in the Fontainebleau and one of five in the eleven-runner field trained outside France. The named quartet dominated the finish. Silver Frost, held up in rear as Handsome Maestro set a strong pace, still had only a couple behind him turning for home, but he then made good headway down the outer and took control inside the final furlong. He finished two lengths clear of close-finishers Le Havre and Naaqoos, with unlucky in running Westphalia taking fourth. Naaqoos was subsequently demoted to sixth for hampering the weakening Handsome Maestro and Westphalia promoted to third. The first three met again in the Prix du Jockey Club, the extra two and a half furlongs at Chantilly bringing out improvement in Le Havre and Westphalia, who came first and third. The trip proved too far for Silver Frost, however, and he managed only sixth to Le Havre. His only other outing came when he was well held behind Goldikova in the Jacques le Marois.

Silver Frost (IRE) (gr.c. 2006)	Verglas (IRE) (gr 1994)	Highest Honor (gr 1983)	Kenmare
			High River
		Rahaam (gr 1987)	Secreto
			Fager's Glory
	Hidden Silver (b 2000)	Anabaa (b 1992)	Danzig
			Balbonella
		Hint of Silver (ch 1991)	Alysheba
			Hot Silver

Silver Frost, a €95,000 yearling, is by the Coventry Stakes winner and Irish Two Thousand Guineas runner-up Verglas, now based at the Irish National Stud after beginning his stud career in France. Verglas had already produced a very smart miler in Stormy River, winner of the Prix de Fontainebleau three years before Silver Frost who went on to Group 1 success in the Prix Jean Prat after finishing placed in the Poule d'Essai des Poulains and St James's Palace Stakes. Silver Frost is the first foal of Hidden Silver, a winner at nine and a half furlongs on her debut in a maiden at Lisieux, who was placed up to eleven furlongs in her three remaining starts. Hidden Silver is a half-sister to several winners, including the smart French performers Homeland (by Highest Honor, the sire of Verglas) and High Rock. Homeland won at up to eleven furlongs, while High Rock started favourite for the 2008 Prix du Jockey Club after winning the Prix La Force, finishing a creditable fourth to Vision d'Etat on what proved his final start. Their dam Hint of Silver, successful at seven and a half furlongs in France as a two-year-old, is a sister to the smart French miler Hill Silver. Silver Frost has done the majority of racing on good ground or softer and acts on soft, though his best performance was put up on good to firm in the Poulains. *Y. de Nicolay, France*

Meydan Superlative Stakes, Newmarket—Silver Grecian (second right) quickens best in a bunched finish with Roi de Vitesse (centre), Shakespearean (left), Lucky General (second left), Lord Zenith (noseband), Emperor Claudius (right), Big Audio (black cap, hidden) and Silenceofthewind (No.8)

SILVER GAMES (IRE) 3 gr.f. Verglas (IRE) 118 – Mise (IRE) (Indian Ridge 123) **95**
[2009 94: p7g 7s 8m⁴ 9g³ 8m* 8m⁴ 8.3m² 8m³ 8d⁵ 8m³ 7s³ 8m Sep 26] strong filly: useful handicapper: won at Newcastle in May: in frame most starts after: stays 9f, effective at shorter: acts on soft and good to firm going: waited with: reliable: sent to USA. *M. R. Channon*

SILVERGLAS (IRE) 3 gr.g. Verglas (IRE) 118 – Yellow Trumpet 75 (Petong 126) **84**
[2009 63p: p7g³ p8g⁵ 9g² 9.7m* 10d Oct 12] tall gelding: fairly useful handicapper: generally progressive, and won at Folkestone in September: stays 9.7f: acts on polytrack and good to firm going. *M. P. Tregoning*

SILVER GRECIAN 2 gr.c. (Jan 27) Haafhd 129 – Regrette Rien (USA) (Unbridled's **111**
Song (USA) 125) [2009 7m* 7.1g* 7m* 7m³ 7m Oct 17] 16,000 2-y-o: compact colt: second foal: brother to Irish 3-y-o Chebona Bula: dam, ran once in France, out of useful 6f/7f performer Rose Indien: smart performer: won maiden at Newmarket in June, and minor event at Warwick and Meydan Superlative Stakes at Newmarket (beat Roi de Vitesse comfortably by length) in July: further marked improvement when ¾-length third to Poet's Voice in Champagne Stakes at Doncaster: slowly away and stuck wide when only seventh in Dewhurst Stakes at Newmarket: will stay 1m: held up and has turn of foot. *J. Ryan*

SILVER GREY (IRE) 2 gr.f. (Jan 19) Chineur (FR) 123 – Operissimo (Singspiel **95**
(IRE) 133) [2009 5.1g² 6d* 6g 6m² 7.1g³ 7m⁵ 8d² Oct 9] 5,000Y: lengthy filly: first foal: dam unraced sister to smart performer up to 2m Songlark and half-sister to smart miler Blatant: useful performer: won maiden at Epsom in July: further improvement last 2 starts, fifth to Vale of York in listed race at Goodwood and staying-on 1½ lengths second of 4 to Circumvent in Prix Thomas Bryon at Saint-Cloud: stays 1m: acts on good to firm and good to soft ground. *R. Ingram*

SILVER GUEST 4 br.g. Lujain (USA) 119 – Ajig Dancer 86 (Niniski (USA) 125) **85**
[2009 90§: 5m 7f 6m 7m 6g 6m⁴ 6m p7.1g* p6g* p7.1g⁴ p8m³ p7m³ Dec 4] tall, good-topped gelding: has a quick action: fairly useful handicapper: won twice at Wolverhampton (latter apprentice event) in October: stays 1m: acts on polytrack and good to firm going: not straightforward. *M. R. Channon*

SILVER HOTSPUR 5 b.g. Royal Applause 124 – Noble View (USA) 68 (Distant **65**
View (USA) 126) [2009 –, a98: p9.5g p8.6g⁵ p8.6g⁵ f8g² f8g⁶ p10g⁶ p7.1g 7g 8s 8.3d **a88 d**
8g⁵ 8f p7m p7m p8m p7.1g f8f⁶ f8g Dec 27] neat gelding: fairly useful handicapper on all-weather, fair on turf: became disappointing in 2009: stays 1¼m: has form on polytrack, good to firm and good to soft ground, best on fibresand: tried blinkered/in cheekpieces: reportedly resents whip. *C. R. Dore*

SILVER IN THE SAND 2 b.f. (Jan 25) Fasliyev (USA) 120 – Dances With Dreams **60**
109 (Be My Chief (USA) 122) [2009 5d⁶ 5g³ 5d⁴ 6g 6d 8m Sep 23] tall filly: seventh foal: dam, 2-y-o 6f winner who stayed 1¼m, half-sister to very smart performer up to 1½m Dark Moondancer: modest maiden: no impact in nurseries: should stay 7f. *J. D. Bethell*

SILVER LINNET (IRE) 2 gr.f. (May 12) Acclamation 118 – Nadeema (FR) (Linamix **70**
(FR) 127) [2009 5d 5m³ 5m⁵ 5d² 6.5m 5m³ 5g* f6g⁶ Dec 27] tall, unfurnished filly: third

foal: dam, French 11f winner, half-sister to useful French performer up to 12.5f Nadira: fair performer: blinkered, best effort when winning nursery at Catterick in October: left T. Easterby after: raced mainly at 5f. *M. G. Quinlan*

SILVERMINE BAY (IRE) 2 br.f. (Apr 2) Act One 124 – Quittance (USA) (Riverman (USA) 131) [2009 6s 6g p8g Oct 2] 2,500Y: leggy filly: sixth foal: half-sister to useful 2005 2-y-o 7f winner Daggernought (by Diesis) and French 1½m/13f winner Trendy Queen (by Traditionally): dam useful French 7f/9f winner: behind in maidens: should stay 1¼m. *A. P. Jarvis* **–**

SILVER PRELUDE 8 gr.g. Prince Sabo 123 – Silver Blessings (Statoblest 120) [2009 69, a94: p5g⁶ p6g p6g⁵ 6g⁵ 5.1m p5g² 5.2s* 5.2s p5g* 5.2g² 5m p5.1g³ p5m⁴ p5m p5m⁴ Dec 9] good-bodied gelding: fair handicapper, better on all-weather: won at Yarmouth in July and Kempton in August: best at bare 5f: unraced on heavy going, acts on polytrack and any other turf: tongue tied last 9 starts: speedy front runner. *S. C. Williams* **68 a75**

SILVER PRINT (USA) 3 gr. or ro.g. Maria's Mon (USA) 121 – Shutterbug (USA) (Deputy Minister (CAN)) [2009 80: p8g⁵ 8g 10g⁶ p9.5g³ p12m⁵ Sep 30] well-made gelding: fair maiden: stays 1½m: acts on polytrack, soft and good to firm ground: sold £12,000. *W. R. Swinburn* **76**

SILVER RIME (FR) 4 gr.c. Verglas (IRE) 118 – Severina (Darshaan 133) [2009 94: 8.1m 7.2s 8g³ 7g 8v⁶ Oct 31] leggy colt: fairly useful handicapper: creditable effort in 2009 only when third at Ayr: stays 1m: acts on soft and good to firm going: tends to get warm in preliminaries. *Miss L. A. Perratt* **92**

SILVER ROCK (IRE) 2 ch.f. (May 23) Rock of Gibraltar (IRE) 133 – Ribblesdale 80 (Northern Park (USA) 107) [2009 7m* 7m Oct 17] €52,000Y: sturdy filly: fifth foal: half-sister to 3 winners, including smart performer up to 9f in Italy/USA Silver Cup and useful 1½m winner Silver Mitzva (both by Almutawakel): dam far from reliable 1¼m winner who stayed 11.6f: fairly useful form when winning minor event at Newbury in September by ¾ length from Lost Horizon: well held in Rockfel Stakes at Newmarket (raced freely/not clear run): should stay 1m+. *M. A. Magnusson* **85**

SILVER SALSA 3 b.f. Lujain (USA) 119 – Tango Teaser (Shareef Dancer (USA) 135) [2009 54: p6g⁵ 6d 8g 6d⁶ 6m Jun 29] lengthy filly: maiden: modest at 2 yrs: no form in 2009: tried visored. *J. R. Jenkins* **–**

SILVER SCEPTRE (IRE) 3 b.g. Intikhab (USA) 135 – Silver Pursuit (Rainbow Quest (USA) 134) [2009 –: f11g⁴ Aug 25] rather leggy gelding: poor maiden, lightly raced: bred to stay 1m+. *W. J. Musson* **46 +**

SILVER SOCKS 2 br.c. (Apr 15) Captain Rio 122 – Silver Blessings (Statoblest 120) [2009 6d⁵ 7.2m⁵ 6m 6g Oct 23] modest maiden: trained by I. Semple prior to final outing: may prove best at 5f/6f. *Miss L. A. Perratt* **60**

SILVER SPRUCE 4 gr.g. First Trump 118 – Red Typhoon 75 (Belfort (FR) 89) [2009 67d: p10m p10g p10g⁵ p8g Jan 22] good-topped gelding: just modest performer nowadays: stays 1¼m: tried blinkered/in cheekpieces. *D. Flood* **50**

SILVER SURPRISE 5 gr.m. Orpen (USA) 116 – Dim Ofan 80 (Petong 126) [2009 59§: 11.6m 16.4m³ 16g⁶ 11.9d 12m 14.1m 16m Sep 2] lengthy mare: modest maiden: stays 2m: acts on polytrack and firm ground, probably on good to soft: blinkered last 3 starts: unreliable. *J. J. Bridger* **51 §**

SILVER SYMPHONY (IRE) 2 b. or br.f. (Feb 6) Pastoral Pursuits 127 – Streak of Silver (USA) 66 (Dynaformer (USA)) [2009 5m 6m⁴ 6m² p7g* p7.1g³ 6.5m Sep 10] 11,000F, 12,000Y: lengthy filly: fifth foal: half-sister to 3-y-o Brilliana and French 2005 2-y-o 1m winner Star Dancing (by Danehill Dancer): dam, Irish maiden (stayed 1½m), closely related to US Grade 2 11f winner Mio Robertino and half-sister to US Grade 2 1½m winner Star of Manila: fairly useful performer: won maiden at Kempton in June: good third in nursery at Wolverhampton: likely to stay 1m: acts on polytrack and good to firm going: front runner/races prominently. *P. F. I. Cole* **81**

SILVERTOWN BOY 3 gr.g. Cape Town (IRE) 119 – Optimistic Dreamer (IRE) (Topanoora 118) [2009 10m⁵ p8.6m 8d p9.5g p7.1g Nov 20] little form in maidens: in cheekpieces last 2 starts. *H. A. McWilliams* **–**

SILVER WATERS 4 gr.g. Fantastic Light (USA) 134 – Silent Waters (Polish Precedent (USA) 131) [2009 79: 11.6g 11.8m⁵ Jun 25] strong gelding: fair handicapper at best: well held in 2009. *Tim Vaughan* **–**

SILVER WIND 4 b.g. Ishiguru (USA) 114 – My Bonus 79 (Cyrano de Bergerac 120) [2009 92: p7.1g⁴ p7.1g* p7.1g⁵ 6m⁶ 6g² 6m 6m⁵ 7g 6g² 6d* 6m 6g⁴ 6d⁵ 6m* 6m 6m 6g **93**

Oct 23] small, strong, compact gelding: fairly useful performer: won claimer at Wolverhampton in January and handicaps at Newmarket in August and Doncaster in September: best at 6f: acts on polytrack, soft and good to firm going: visored/blinkered: has hung right: often races lazily. *P. D. Evans*

SILVESTER 3 gr.g. Silver Patriarch (IRE) 125 – Raintree Venture (Good Times (ITY)) [2009 p8g p8g 10.2d p12.2g p10m Dec 9] big gelding: well held in maidens: tried in cheekpieces. *R. M. H. Cowell* **–**

SIMENON (IRE) 2 b.c. (Feb 25) Marju (IRE) 127 – Epistoliere (IRE) (Alzao (USA) 117) [2009 7g^3 7g* 7.1g^5 8g* 8g^3 Oct 10] 60,000Y: unfurnished colt: fourth foal: half-brother to Irish 3-y-o Vivacious Vivienne and 11f winner in Italy by Indian Danehill: dam, French maiden (stayed 1¼m), sister to smart French performer up to 13f Epistolaire and half-sister to smart French stayer Epitre: useful performer: won maiden at Newmarket (by neck from Timely Jazz) in July and minor event at Ayr (comfortably by 1¼ lengths from Notorize) in September: good 4¾ lengths third to Morana in Autumn Stakes at Ascot final outing, staying on again after badly squeezed 2f out: will stay 1¼m: type to do better still at 3 yrs. *A. M. Balding* **101 p**

SIMLA SUNSET (IRE) 3 b.f. One Cool Cat (USA) 123 – Simla Bibi 69 (Indian Ridge 123) [2009 76p: 8g^3 7d^4 6s^3 7m p7.1g^2 p7.1g* p7f Dec 21] fair performer: left D. Myerscough in Ireland after third start: won maiden at Wolverhampton in November: barely stays 1m: acts on polytrack and good to soft going: tongue tied last 3 starts. *J. R. Gask* **78**

SIMOLA 3 ch.f. Bold Edge 123 – Amused 78 (Prince Sabo 123) [2009 5m^6 7d^5 Jul 24] lengthy filly: third foal: half-sister to 4-y-o Atlantic Beach: dam, 6f/7f winner, half-sister to smart sprinters Astonished and Bishops Court: poor form in maidens at Thirsk. *R. A. Fahey* **45**

SIMON GRAY 3 b.c. Act One 124 – Shardette (IRE) (Darshaan 133) [2009 79: 8.1m* 11d* p10g* Jun 17] unfurnished colt: fairly useful performer: much improved in 2009, winning handicaps at Haydock in April, Newbury in May and Kempton in June: stays 11f: acts on polytrack, good to firm and good to soft ground (shaped well on heavy): joined D. Hughes in Ireland. *R. Hannon* **92**

SIMONSIDE 6 b.g. Shahrastani (USA) 135 – Only So Far (Teenoso (USA) 135) [2009 p9.5g p12.2g* p13.9g^4 12m^3 16m 11.5m 12d^3 16.1m^3 11.5d* 12m^6 16.4d^3 17.5m^3 16.1d^4 Oct 13] leggy, angular gelding: fairly useful bumper winner (modest form over hurdles): fair handicapper on Flat: won at Wolverhampton (maiden) in March and Carlisle (ladies event) in July: stays 17.5f: acts on polytrack, good to firm and good to soft going. *B. Ellison* **79**

SIMPLE JIM (FR) 5 b.g. Jimble (FR) – Stop The Wedding (USA) (Stop The Music (USA)) [2009 66: 13m 16g^5 12.1m^4 16d^6 14.1g* 13.8m* 15.8g^4 13.8g* 12s^4 Oct 27] modest handicapper: won at Redcar and Catterick (2) in September/October: stays 1¾m: acts on all-weather, soft and good to firm ground: tried in cheekpieces. *J. Hetherton* **63**

SIMPLE RHYTHM 3 b.f. Piccolo 121 – Easy Beat (IRE) (Orpen (USA) 116) [2009 72: p6g^3 p6g p6g^2 5m 5m^2 5.1g^4 f5g* 5m^4 p5g^4 5g^3 6m^2 5f^4 6d* p6m 5.3m* 6.1s* 5.3d^4 f5g Oct 18] leggy, close-coupled filly: fairly useful handicapper: left N. Tinkler after fourth start: won at Southwell in June and, having left J. Given after eleventh start, Lingfield and Brighton in September and Nottingham (apprentices) in October: best at 5f/6f: acts on all-weather, soft and good to firm ground: often front runner. *J. Ryan* **87**

SIMPLE SOLUTION (USA) 3 b.f. Dynaformer (USA) – Super Staff (USA) 91 (Secretariat (USA)) [2009 91p: 11.4m^5 11.9v 12f^5 p12g^5 Sep 21] attractive filly: fairly useful performer: fifth in Cheshire Oaks at Chester on reappearance, disappointing after: seemingly stays 11.4f: acts on polytrack: sold 48,000 gns. *B. W. Hills* **83**

SIMPLIFICATION 3 gr.f. Daylami (IRE) 138 – Bella Cantata (Singspiel (IRE) 133) [2009 77p: p7g^2 p8g^3 10.3g^3 10g^6 10g^5 Jul 8] lengthy filly: fair maiden: stays 10.3f: acts on polytrack and good to firm ground: sold 25,000 gns, sent to Kuwait. *R. Hannon* **78**

SIMPLIFIED 6 b.m. Lend A Hand 124 – Houston Heiress (USA) (Houston (USA)) [2009 –: p8g^6 Jan 11] sparely-made mare: modest performer in 2007: tongue tied, little form on Flat since. *M. C. Chapman* **–**

SIMPLY SENSATIONAL (IRE) 3 ch.g. Tendulkar (USA) 114 – Grange Clare (IRE) 72 (Bijou d'Inde 127) [2009 7f 7.5m^6 Jul 14] well held in maiden/claimer, looking reluctant in latter. *Pat Morris* **–**

SIMPSONS GAMBLE (IRE) 6 b.g. Tagula (IRE) 116 – Kiva (Indian Ridge 123) **65**
[2009 –, a68: p6g^4 p6g^3 p6g p6g^3 p6g 8f^4 p8g p8g^4 p7g p8g 9m* 10d^4 p8m Oct 28] strong gelding: fair performer: won seller at Lingfield in August: effective at 6f to 9f: acts on polytrack and good to firm going: tried blinkered: wears cheekpieces: has found little: none too consistent. *R. A. Teal*

SIMULATE 3 b.c. Dansili 127 – Orford Ness 107 (Selkirk (USA) 129) [2009 10.2d **–**
Oct 15] big, strong colt: 12/1, well held in maiden at Nottingham: sold 5,000 gns. *Sir Michael Stoute*

SINBAD THE SAILOR 4 b.g. Cape Cross (IRE) 129 – Sinead (USA) (Irish River **70**
(FR) 131) [2009 79: 10.3g^6 10d 10m 10g* 11m^5 12m^4 14.1m^4 14.1m^6 11m^3 p10m^4 p12m^3 11.9d^2 Oct 22] strong, compact gelding: fair handicapper: won at Brighton in June: stays 1½m: acts on polytrack, firm and good to soft going: visored nowadays: sold 18,000 gns. *J. W. Hills*

SINCHIROKA (FR) 3 b.c. Della Francesca (USA) 118 – Great Care (USA) (El Gran **–**
Senor (USA) 136) [2009 66: p10m Dec 9] workmanlike colt: encouraging effort sole 2-y-o start: tailed off only outing in 2009. *R. J. Smith*

SINGAPORE GIRL 3 b.f. Danehill Dancer (IRE) 117 – Musical Refrain (IRE) **52 d**
(Dancing Dissident (USA) 119) [2009 f6s^4 p7.1g^5 f6g 5m 5d^6 7.6g^6 5m f5m f5f Dec 11] fifth foal: half-sister to fairly useful Irish 5f/6f winner Ms Victoria (by Fasliyev): dam unraced half-sister to very smart 6f/7f performer Monsieur Bond (by Danehill Dancer): regressive maiden: tried visored. *G. R. Oldroyd*

SINGBELLA 3 b.f. Singspiel (IRE) 133 – B Beautiful (IRE) 57 (Be My Guest (USA) **–**
126) [2009 8.3m 8.3g 8m Jun 14] 32,000Y: rather sparely-made filly: third foal: half-sister to fairly useful 1m winner Eastern Emperor (by Halling) and a winner in Italy by Lomitas: dam, 1m winner, half-sister to Phoenix Stakes winner Lavery: signs of ability in maidens. *C. G. Cox*

SINGEUR (IRE) 2 b.c. (Mar 10) Chineur (FR) 123 – Singitta (Singspiel (IRE) 133) **105**
[2009 f5g^2 f5g* 5f* 5g* 5m* 5m^4 6m 6g^4 6d^2 Oct 24] 15,000Y: lengthy colt: has scope: second foal: half-brother to winner abroad by Needwood Blade: dam, maiden, half-sister to useful 6f/7f winner Injaaz: useful performer: won maiden at Southwell in June, nurseries at Redcar and York in July and minor event at Musselburgh (by 1½ lengths from Raddy 'ell Pauline) in August: in frame in listed events after, particularly good effort when head second to Layla's Hero at Doncaster: stays 6f: acts on fibresand, firm and good to soft ground. *R. Bastiman*

SINGINGINTHERAIN (IRE) 2 ch.f. (Mar 6) Kyllachy 129 – Comeraincomeshine **60**
(IRE) 67 (Night Shift (USA)) [2009 p6m p7m^4 Dec 16] second foal: half-sister to 3-y-o Danehill Destiny: dam, 6f winner, half-sister to very smart miler Where Or When and smart middle-distance stayer All The Way: similar form in maidens at Kempton and Lingfield: may prove best at 5f/6f. *T. G. Mills*

SINGING SCOTT (IRE) 2 b.g. (Mar 18) Royal Applause 124 – Ciel Bleu (Septieme **–**
Ciel (USA) 123) [2009 6g 6s Nov 7] lengthy, unfurnished gelding: well held in maidens (looked awkward). *R. Bastiman*

SINGIN' THE BLUES 2 b.g. (Apr 15) Superior Premium 122 – Not So Generous **63**
(IRE) 68 (Fayruz 116) [2009 p6g 6.1d^5 6s Nov 7] modest form in maidens: raced only at 6f, unlikely to stay much further. *J. M. P. Eustace*

SINGLEB (IRE) 5 b.g. Intikhab (USA) 135 – Bubble N Squeak (IRE) 91 (Catrail **77**
(USA) 123) [2009 78: p8g* p8.6g* p7.1g* p7g^4 f7g^6 8.3d^6 p7g 8g^3 p8g Jul 15] workmanlike gelding: fair performer: won sellers at Great Leighs and Wolverhampton in January, and handicap on latter course in February: stays 8.6f: acts on all-weather, soft and good to firm going: wears cheekpieces nowadays: tried in tongue tie. *Miss Gay Kelleway*

SING OF RUN 2 bl.c. (Apr 22) Singspiel (IRE) 133 – Crimson Rosella 54 (Polar Fal- **–**
con (USA) 126) [2009 8.1d Aug 31] 100/1, tailed off in maiden at Chepstow. *J. F. Panvert*

SINGORA LADY (IRE) 4 ch.f. Intikhab (USA) 135 – Unicamp 84 (Royal Academy **67**
(USA) 130) [2009 67: f8g f8g^5 f8g^4 p9.5g 8d^4 8.3m^2 8.3m^3 8m* 8m^3 10m* 9m^3 10m Aug 15] fair handicapper: won at Pontefract in June and Redcar in July: stays 1¼m: acts on fibresand, good to firm and good to soft going: tried in cheekpieces: held up: reportedly in foal to Bertolini. *P. T. Midgley*

SING SWEETLY 2 b.f. (Apr 17) Singspiel (IRE) 133 – Sweetness Herself 106 (Unfu- **80 p**
wain (USA) 131) [2009 p7g^2 7m Oct 3] 70,000Y: lengthy, useful-looking filly: has scope: seventh foal: closely related to Irish 5-y-o Miss Fancy Pants and half-sister to 3 winners,

including 4-y-o Sweet Lightning and 9-y-o Jagger: dam 1½m to 16.5f winner: much bettter effort when promising length second to Muwakaba in maiden at Kempton: met trouble in sales race at Newmarket: will be suited by 1¼m+: remains capable of better. *G. A. Butler*

SION HILL (IRE) 8 b.g. Desert Prince (IRE) 130 – Mobilia 67 (Last Tycoon 131) **66** [2009 73: f7s^{6} p8.6g^{2} p8.6g 6.1f 8f 8m^{3} p8g^{2} 8m^{2} 8.3m^{2} 8d^{3} 8g^{6} 8g 7m^{6} p8.6g^{5} p8.6g Dec 14] well-made gelding: fair handicapper: stays 8.6f: acts on all-weather, good to firm and good to soft going: wears cheekpieces (also tried blinkered/visored): usually makes running. *John A. Harris*

SIOUX CITY SUE 3 b.f. Noverre (USA) 125 – Sartigila 67 (Efisio 120) [2009 10m **–** Aug 24] eighth foal: half-sister to 3 winners, including 1m to 1½m winner Alfano (by Priolo) and 1½m to 2m winner Montosari (by Persian Bold): dam 6f/1m winner: 50/1, slowly away in maiden at Windsor. *J. R. Boyle*

SIOUX RISING (IRE) 3 b.f. Danetime (IRE) 121 – Arvika (FR) (Baillamont (USA) **87** 124) [2009 72p: 6d* 6m* 7m^{6} 6m Aug 15] leggy filly: fairly useful performer: won maiden in May and handicap in June, both at Pontefract: disappointing after: should stay 7f+: unraced on extremes of ground. *R. A. Fahey*

SIRAJ 10 b.g. Piccolo 121 – Masuri Kabisa (USA) 48 (Ascot Knight (CAN) 130) [2009 **–** p7g p6g p6g Mar 16] good-bodied gelding: modest handicapper in 2007: off 15 months, well beaten at 10 yrs: usually wears headgear: tried tongue tied. *J. Ryan*

SIR BILLY NICK 4 b.c. Bertolini (USA) 125 – Follow Flanders 92 (Pursuit of Love **–** 124) [2009 74: f8s p12.2m p8.6g Oct 23] lengthy colt: fair performer at best: well held in 2009: tried in headgear. *S. Wynne*

SIR BOSS (IRE) 4 b.g. Tagula (IRE) 116 – Good Thought (IRE) (Mukaddamah (USA) **88** 125) [2009 75: 10m^{3} 10m^{6} 10m^{2} 12.1m* 12g* 12g^{6} 12m p11g 10m 12m^{6} Oct 3] rather leggy gelding: fairly useful handicapper: improved to win at Chepstow (apprentices) and Ffos Las in July: well below form last 4 outings: stays 1½m: acts on fibresand, good to firm and good to soft ground. *D. E. Cantillon*

SIR BRUNO (FR) 2 ch.g. (Feb 4) Hernando (FR) 127 – Moon Tree (FR) (Groom **76** Dancer (USA) 128) [2009 7m 7.1m^{2} 7f^{3} 8.1d^{4} 7.1m^{3} Sep 29] €27,000Y: close-coupled gelding: first foal: dam French 1m winner: fair maiden: should stay 1m+: acts on firm going: races up with pace. *B. Palling*

SIR CHRISTIE 2 b.g. (Feb 25) Auction House (USA) 120 – Dazzling Quintet 73 **54** (Superlative 118) [2009 5m 5g^{6} 6g 5m^{4} 5m^{6} Jun 29] modest maiden: best form at 5f: dead. *N. Tinkler*

SIRCOZY (IRE) 3 b.g. Celtic Swing 138 – Furnish 87 (Green Desert (USA) 127) **78** [2009 59: 5m 8.3g 12g p10g^{2} p11m^{2} p12m p9.5g* p12g* p12m* p12f^{2} Dec 21] strong gelding: fair performer: improved when winning minor event at Wolverhampton in November and 2 handicaps at Lingfield in December: stays 1½m: acts on polytrack: held up. *S. C. Williams*

SIR DON (IRE) 10 b.g. Lake Coniston (IRE) 131 – New Sensitive (Wattlefield 117) **44** [2009 63: p5m 5m p5.1g Sep 3] sparely-made gelding: handicapper: lightly raced since 2006, and just poor at 10 yrs: often wears headgear. *E. S. McMahon*

SIR EDWIN LANDSEER (USA) 9 gr.g. Lit de Justice (USA) 125 – Wildcat Blue **94 §** (USA) (Cure The Blues (USA)) [2009 86, a99: p5g^{2} 6m p6f p5g^{5} p5m^{3} p6m^{5} Dec 30] good-quartered gelding: fairly useful performer at best nowadays: below form after reappearance: effective at 5f to 7f: acts on polytrack, dirt, firm and soft going: tried blinkered/visored, usually wore cheekpieces prior to 2009: tends to get behind (often starts slowly): temperamental and often refuses to enter stall. *G. L. Moore*

SIREN'S GIFT 5 ch.m. Cadeaux Genereux 131 – Blue Siren 113 (Bluebird (USA) 125) **101** [2009 104: 5.1g^{3} 5m 5g^{6} 5m^{4} 5g 5m* 5m 5m Oct 1] lengthy mare: useful performer: won handicap at Epsom in August: had earlier run creditably when narrow third to Look Busy in listed race at Bath: below form otherwise: was probably best at 5f: acted on polytrack, firm and soft going: blinkered: travelled strongly, but often didn't battle: stud. *A. M. Balding*

SIRENUSE (IRE) 3 b.f. Exceed And Excel (AUS) 126 – Cefira (USA) 66 (Distant **89** View (USA) 126) [2009 80p: 5d^{2} 5d^{2} p5.1g Sep 25] tall filly: fairly useful handicapper, lightly raced: improved when second at Thirsk and Carlisle: said to have finished distressed final start: all speed, best at 5f: acts on good to soft ground (promise on good to firm): probably suited by forcing pace. *B. Smart*

SIR FRANK WAPPAT 2 b.c. (May 18) Oasis Dream 129 – Trevillari (USA) (Riverman (USA) 131) [2009 6m^4 6.1m^5 Sep 30] rather leggy colt: very green in maidens at Yarmouth (better effort) and Nottingham (hung badly): bred to stay 7f. *M. Johnston* **55**

SIR FREDDIE 3 b.g. Fraam 114 – Height of Folly 81 (Shirley Heights 130) [2009 53: 10.2g^4 10.2d 14g^4 Jul 29] fair maiden: stays 1¾m: best efforts on good ground. *Lady Herries* **73**

SIR GEOFFREY (IRE) 3 b.g. Captain Rio 122 – Disarm (IRE) (Bahamian Bounty 116) [2009 87: p6g^6 p6g p6g^5 p5g 5f^3 5s^6 5g^3 p6g 5.1m p5.1g 6d Oct 13] sturdy gelding: fair performer: left A. McCabe after eighth start: best at 5f: acts on polytrack, firm and good to soft going: tried blinkered: tongue tied of late (has reportedly had breathing problem): headstrong, and sometimes makes running. *J. A. Glover* **79**

SIR GEORGE (IRE) 4 b.g. Mujadil (USA) 119 – Torrmana (IRE) (Ela-Mana-Mou 132) [2009 81: 7m^6 p7.1g^5 p7.1g* p7.1g^4 p7.1g^2 Dec 28] quite good-topped gelding: fair performer: won seller at Wolverhampton in November: likely to stay 1m: acts on polytrack and soft ground. *P. D. Evans* **74**

SIR GERRY (USA) 4 ch.c. Carson City (USA) – Incredulous (FR) 95 (Indian Ridge 123) [2009 118: 6m 6s p6g p7f Dec 16] good-topped colt: smart at 2/3 yrs: useful at best in 2009: left J. Fanshawe and off 6 months (reportedly had pelvic injury) after reappearance: said to have been struck into second outing: best at 6f: acts on soft and good to firm ground: held up. *J. R. Best* **99**

SIR HAYDN 9 ch.g. Definite Article 121 – Snowscape (Niniski (USA) 125) [2009 62: p12g p12g^3 p11g^3 p10g^3 p12g^2 12d^6 f11g* 10.1g p11g f11g^5 p11g p10g^4 f12m^5 p12m p11f^4 Dec 16] big, leggy gelding: modest handicapper: won apprentice event at Southwell in May: stays 1½m: acts on all-weather, firm and soft ground: usually wears headgear: often held up. *J. R. Jenkins* **52 a58**

SIR IKE (IRE) 4 b.g. Xaar 132 – Iktidar 80 (Green Desert (USA) 127) [2009 67: p7g^6 p8g^2 p8g^5 p8g^3 8.1m* 8m^4 7m* p7.1g 7m Oct 13] well-made gelding: fair performer: won handicap at Chepstow in July and seller at Folkestone in August: stays 9f: acts on polytrack and firm going: mainly in cheekpieces in 2009, once in visor: tongue tied: sold £1,600. *W. S. Kittow* **72**

SIR ISAAC 3 b.g. Key of Luck (USA) 126 – Rainbow Queen (FR) 88 (Spectrum (IRE) 126) [2009 –: 7g* 7.1f^4 8.1m^2 8m^2 7g^3 7.1g* Aug 12] sturdy gelding: fairly useful performer: won maiden at Goodwood in May and handicap at Sandown in August: stays 1m: raced only on good going or firmer: not straightforward. *W. J. Haggas* **89**

SIR JAKE 5 b.h. Killer Instinct 111 – Waikiki Dancer (IRE) 48 (General Monash (USA) 107) [2009 54: 14.1g^6 p16g f14m Nov 11] angular horse: maiden: modest at 4 yrs: no form in 2009. *T. T. Clement* **–**

SIR JOEY 4 ch.g. Forzando 122 – Estabella (IRE) 67 (Mujtahid (USA) 118) [2009 46§: p13.3g f12g Jan 27] strong, workmanlike gelding: temperamental maiden: tried in headgear. *B. D. Leavy* **– §**

SIRJOSH 3 b.g. Josr Algarhoud (IRE) 118 – Special Gesture (IRE) (Brief Truce (USA) 126) [2009 8m^5 p10g 12m p8.6g^6 p7g 7s^3 p7g^5 8g 9.8d Sep 1] good-topped gelding: fair maiden: stays 1m: acts on polytrack, soft and good to firm ground: tongue tied/visored last 5 outings. *D. Donovan* **60**

SIR KYFFIN'S FOLLY 4 b.f. Dansili 127 – Persia (IRE) (Persian Bold 123) [2009 73: 8.1d f12f f12g Dec 22] workmanlike filly: maiden: well held in 2009. *J. A. Geake* **–**

SIR LIAM (USA) 5 b.g. Monarchos (USA) 129 – Tears (USA) (Red Ransom (USA)) [2009 75: p12.2g p12g^3 p16g* p16g^2 p13g^3 p12g^5 Mar 18] neat gelding: modest handicapper: won selling event at Lingfield in January: effective at 1¼m to 2m: acts on polytrack and firm going: tried in cheekpieces/blinkers: joined Tim Vaughan. *Tom Dascombe* **63**

SIR LOIN 8 ch.g. Compton Place 125 – Charnwood Queen 61 (Cadeaux Genereux 131) [2009 61: p5g p5g p5g^5 5m p5.1g^6 p6g^5 Nov 20] leggy gelding: poor handicapper nowadays: best at 5f: acts on polytrack, good to firm and good to soft going, well beaten on soft: wears headgear: front runner: has bled. *P. Burgoyne* **45**

SIR LOUIS 2 b.g. (Mar 3) Compton Place 125 – Heuston Station (IRE) 72 (Fairy King (USA)) [2009 6v^5 6m 6g Oct 9] big gelding: fifth to Tamanaco in maiden at Pontefract, best effort: bred to be best at 5f/6f: gelded after final start. *R. A. Fahey* **55**

SIR NOD 7 b.g. Tagula (IRE) 116 – Nordan Raider 81 (Domynsky 110) [2009 78: p6g* p6g^6 6d 6g 5m* 5m^4 5g^4 5g^6 5m^4 5m Sep 9] lengthy gelding: fairly useful handicapper: won at Wolverhampton in January and Carlisle in June: effective at 5f/6f: acts on polytrack, firm and good to soft ground: tried visored: often races prominently. *Julie Camacho* **80**

SIROCCO BREEZE 4 b.c. Green Desert (USA) 127 – Baldemosa (FR) (Lead On Time (USA) 123) [2009 97p: p7g* Oct 29] good-topped colt: smart form: off 12 months, much improved when winning handicap at Lingfield by 4 lengths from Beckermet, quickening away: not certain to stay beyond 7f. *Saeed bin Suroor* **112**

SIR ORPEN (IRE) 6 gr.g. Orpen (USA) 116 – Yalciyna 92 (Nishapour (FR) 125) [2009 8m 7m^6 p8g Nov 1] lengthy, good-topped gelding: one-time fairly useful handicapper: off 23 months, modest form at best in 2009: was effective at stiff 6f to 1m: acted on firm and soft going: tried blinkered/in cheekpieces: dead. *J. F. Panvert* **50**

SIR PARKY (IRE) 2 b.c. (Feb 14) Choisir (AUS) 126 – Jorghinia (FR) (Seattle Slew (USA)) [2009 6g 5m* 6.1m* 7m^3 7d* 6m 7m^6 7m* Oct 1] £50,000Y: good-topped colt: fourth foal: half-brother to winner in USA by Charismatic: dam, placed in France up to 10.5f, half-sister to useful Irish performer up 1¾m Jade Quest: useful performer: won maiden at Salisbury in May, minor events at Chepstow in June and Newbury in July and Somerville Tattersall Stakes at Newmarket (allowed easy lead, beat Sebastian Flyte ½ length for best effort) in October: stays 7f: acts on good to firm and good to soft going. *R. Hannon* **104**

SIR PITT 2 b.c. (Feb 15) Tiger Hill (IRE) 127 – Rebecca Sharp 122 (Machiavellian (USA) 123) [2009 8d^5 8v Oct 24] sixth foal: closely related to useful 6f (at 2 yrs)/1m winner Miss Pinkerton (by Danehill) and half-brother to 3 winners, notably smart Irish 7f (at 2 yrs)/1¼m winner Grand Central (by Sadler's Wells): dam 7f/1m (Coronation Stakes) winner: better effort in maidens when fifth to Burnett at Newcastle, going on under considerate handling: possibly unsuited by heavy ground next time. *J. H. M. Gosden* **76**

SIRRI 2 b.f. (Mar 26) Ishiguru (USA) 114 – Sumitra 56 (Tragic Role (USA)) [2009 p6g 7s Sep 3] 7,000Y: third foal: sister to 3-y-o Itshim: dam maiden (stayed 2m): down the field in maidens at Lingfield and Salisbury over 3 months apart. *C. E. Brittain* **–**

SIR ROYAL (USA) 4 b.c. Diesis 133 – Only Royale (IRE) 121 (Caerleon (USA) 132) [2009 83: 12.1m^5 12m^6 8g^2 8g^2 7.9m Jun 24] good-topped colt: fairly useful maiden handicapper: may prove best up to 1¼m: acts on heavy going. *G. A. Swinbank* **84**

SIR SANDICLIFFE (IRE) 5 b.g. Distant Music (USA) 126 – Desert Rose (Green Desert (USA) 127) [2009 72: 15m^2 14v^3 14.6m^6 15g 16m^3 15.9m^5 16s p16.5g^2 15.8d^4 15.8v^4 13.8m^3 p16.5g p16.5g p16.5g p13.9g Dec 14] workmanlike gelding: fair handicapper: stays 16.5f: acts on polytrack, heavy and good to firm ground: tried in headgear: held up: often races lazily: temperamental. *W. M. Brisbourne* **71 §**

SIR TOM 4 b.g. Medicean 128 – Shasta 81 (Shareef Dancer (USA) 135) [2009 p7g p8f Dec 20] seemingly modest form in maidens. *J. J. Bridger* **52 ?**

SIRVINO 4 b.g. Vettori (IRE) 119 – Zenita (IRE) (Zieten (USA) 118) [2009 74: 9.9m* 9m* 9.8d* 10g* 10.4m* 9m Oct 3] tall, lengthy gelding: useful handicapper: most progressive in 2009, winning at Beverley in April, Musselburgh, Ripon and Ayr in May, and York (John Smith's Cup, beat Kingdom of Fife 2¾ lengths) in June: off 3 months, unfavourably drawn in Cambridgeshire at Newmarket final start: likely to stay 1½m: acts on good to firm and good to soft going. *T. D. Barron* **109**

SIR WALTER RALEIGH 2 b.g. (Mar 10) Galileo (IRE) 134 – Elizabethan Age (FR) 78 (King's Best (USA) 132) [2009 8.3v Nov 4] 120,000Y: well-made gelding: first foal: dam, 7f winner, half-sister to 4-y-o Drill Sergeant: 7/2 favourite, very green when seventh to Green Lightning in maiden at Nottingham (gelded after): should stay 1¼m+: likely to improve. *Sir Michael Stoute* **55 p**

SIR WILLIAM ORPEN 2 b.g. (Apr 9) Orpen (USA) 116 – Ashover Amber 81 (Green Desert (USA) 127) [2009 p6g 7m^3 p7m^6 Sep 30] workmanlike gelding: modest form in maidens: may prove best short of 7f. *P. M. Phelan* **60**

SIR XAAR (IRE) 6 b. or br.g. Xaar 132 – Cradle Brief (IRE) (Brief Truce (USA) 126) [2009 98§: 7m^4 7.1m 7d 8m 7d Sep 6] good-topped gelding: has a quick action: fairly useful handicapper: respectable fourth at Newcastle on reappearance: well below form after: effective at 6f/7f: acts on good to firm and good to soft going: tried tongue tied: blinkered/visored: ungenuine: sold £1,800. *B. Smart* **92 §**

SIRYENA 4 b.f. Oasis Dream 129 – Ard Na Sighe (IRE) (Kenmare (FR) 125) [2009 64: p8g^6 p10g p9.5g^6 10m Apr 26] good-topped filly: modest performer: stays 1¼m: acts on polytrack, heavy and good to firm ground: tried visored, wears cheekpieces/tongue tie. *B. I. Case* **53**

SISTER CLEMENT (IRE) 3 b.f. Oasis Dream 129 – Miss Party Line (USA) (Phone Trick (USA)) [2009 59: 7g 6m^2 5.2s* 6g^2 5f^5 6.1g p6g^2 p6g* Nov 1] close-coupled filly: **85**

fairly useful handicapper: left C. Egerton after reappearance: won at Newbury in July and Lingfield (in cheekpieces, further improvement) in November: should prove best at 5f/6f: acts on polytrack, soft and good to firm going. *R. Hannon*

SISTER EARTH (IRE) 2 ch.f. (Apr 8) Galileo (IRE) 134 – Time Ahead 112 (Spectrum (IRE) 126) [2009 p8.6g³ Oct 29] third foal: half-sister to 4-y-o World Time: dam, 1¼m winner (second in Prix de Diane), half-sister to Musidora Stakes winner Time Away: 9/1 and very green, encouraging 7 lengths third to Addahab in maiden at Wolverhampton, very slowly away and rousted along early: will be suited by 1¼m+: will improve. *J. H. M. Gosden* **60 p**

SISTER MOONSHINE 4 b.f. Averti (IRE) 117 – Cal Norma's Lady (IRE) 87 (Lyphard's Special (USA) 122) [2009 65: p6g³ 6m May 9] leggy, attractive filly: maiden: just poor form in 2009: will stay 7f: probably not straightforward. *W. R. Muir* **49**

SISTERS WARNING 2 b.f. (Mar 11) Bishop of Cashel 122 – Slite 55 (Mind Games 121) [2009 f5g 6d p8m p7.1g p10m Dec 9] first foal: dam maiden (probably stayed 1m): no form in maidens. *J. Ryan* **–**

SITWELL 3 b.g. Dr Fong (USA) 128 – First Fantasy 97 (Be My Chief (USA) 122) [2009 52p: 9.9g 10m 10d⁶ 9m 12m* 11.8m⁶ p13.9g⁵ 11.8m* Oct 13] leggy gelding: fair performer: won handicap at Folkestone in August and claimer at Leicester in October: stays 13.9f: acts on polytrack, good to firm and good to soft going: visored last 2 starts: sold 17,000 gns, joined A. King. *J. R. Fanshawe* **72**

SIXBOX 2 br.f. (Feb 19) Kyllachy 129 – Lady's Walk (IRE) (Charnwood Forest (IRE) 125) [2009 6m p6g p5.1g Sep 3] third foal: half-sister to 3-y-o Johnmanderville: dam unraced: tailed off in maidens. *D. Shaw* **–**

SIX DIAMONDS 2 b.f. (Feb 17) Exceed And Excel (AUS) 126 – Daltak (Night Shift (USA)) [2009 5g 5.7f² 5.1m* 6g 5m² p5m* p5f³ 5m⁴ Sep 14] 7,000F: good-topped filly: seventh foal: half-sister to 2003 2-y-o 6f winner Scarlet Empress (by Second Empire): dam unraced close relative to smart sprinter Ya Malak out of half-sister to Cadeaux Genereux: fairly useful performer: won maiden at Bath in June and nursery at Lingfield in August: best at 5f: acts on polytrack and good to firm going: races up with pace. *H. Morrison* **80**

SIX OF CLUBS 3 ch.g. Bertolini (USA) 125 – Windmill Princess 55 (Gorytus (USA) 132) [2009 –: p12m Sep 16] workmanlike gelding: tailed off in maidens: wore cheekpieces only outing in 2009. *W. G. M. Turner* **–**

John Smith's Cup (Heritage Handicap), York—the progressive Sirvino stays ahead of the handicapper again to record a fifth straight win; Kingdom of Fife is second

SIX OF HEARTS 5 b.g. Pivotal 124 – Additive (USA) 81 (Devil's Bag (USA)) [2009 92: 7.2v 5.8s 7d* 7f* 7f 8.5s 8g 5s^4 5s^3 6m 7g^3 6s^6 8.5g^3 7s p6g^6 p8g^2 p7g* Nov 27] good-topped gelding: useful performer: won handicaps at Gowran in May and Naas (under 10-0, beat Funatfuntasia by a neck) in June, and minor event at Dundalk in November: ran well otherwise when in frame, including in listed event, but well held in competitive handicaps in Britain fifth/tenth starts: effective at testing 5f to easy 8.5f: acts on polytrack, firm and soft going: wears cheekpieces/blinkers: effective held up or racing close up: game. *Cecil Ross, Ireland* **102**

SIXPENNY MOON (USA) 2 b.f. (Feb 9) Johannesburg (USA) 127 – Shirazi (USA) (Stephen Got Even (USA) 125) [2009 5g 6m 7m p7g^3 8m^6 p8g 10.2m p7m^5 p8m Oct 12] $105,000F, £25,000Y, £19,000 2-y-o: compact filly: first foal: dam, ran once in US, half-sister to US Grade 3 6.5f (at 2 yrs)/1m winner Tasha's Miracle: modest maiden: should stay 1m: blinkered last 2 outings: sold 3,500 gns, sent to Bahrain. *R. Hannon* **60**

SIXTH ZAK 4 br.g. Fantastic Light (USA) 134 – Zakuska 96 (Zafonic (USA) 130) [2009 65: f7g^5 p8.6g p16.5g p12.2g^5 12d Jun 18] modest maiden handicapper: left S. R. Bowring after reappearance: likely to prove best at 1½m+: acts on all-weather: blinkered last 2 outings. *M. W. Easterby* **58**

SIXTIES GIFT (UAE) 3 b. or br.f. Singspiel (IRE) 133 – Sicily (USA) 74§ (Kris S (USA)) [2009 62p: p7.1g 10m 11.9d^5 Oct 15] disappointing maiden. *Rae Guest* **–**

SIXTIES ROCK 2 ch.g. (Feb 19) Rock of Gibraltar (IRE) 133 – Scene (IRE) 87 (Scenic 128) [2009 7.2m 6g^2 7m p6g f7g^6 Dec 18] small gelding: modest maiden: stays 7f. *J. A. Glover* **55**

SIXTIES SWINGER (USA) 3 b.g. Refuse To Bend (IRE) 128 – Kardashina (FR) (Darshaan 133) [2009 78p: p12g 11d 11.9g^2 11.9m^5 9.9g 10.1g^2 9.9g^2 p10g Oct 21] good-topped gelding: fair performer: stays 1¼m: acts on soft ground: tried in tongue tie/blinkers/cheekpieces: often finds little, and one to treat with caution: sold 12,000 gns. *M. A. Jarvis* **74 §**

SIX WIVES 2 b.f. (Feb 16) Kingsalsa (USA) 118 – Regina 97 (Green Desert (USA) 127) [2009 5m^6 5g^3 p5.1g* 5g p6g^3 p5g^3 5m^6 5g p5g* p5m^2 5m^6 p5f^5 p6f^3 p5.1g^2 p5.1g^3 p6m f5m^3 f5g^2 p5m Dec 30] sturdy filly: first foal: dam, 2-y-o 5f winner, out of smart performer up to 1m Dazzle: fair performer, better on all-weather: won claimer at Wolverhampton in May (left W. Haggas £14,000, trained next 2 starts by A. McCabe) and nursery at Lingfield in August: effective at 5f/6f: acts on all-weather and good to firm going: races up with pace. *J. A. Glover* **65 a75**

SIYAADAH 2 b.f. (Jan 29) Shamardal (USA) 129 – River Belle 113 (Lahib (USA) 129) [2009 7m* 7g 7m^6 Oct 3] 110,000Y: useful-looking filly, unfurnished at present: first foal: dam, 6f (Princess Margaret Stakes) to 8.5f (US Grade 2) winner, half-sister to smart miler Rio Riva: won maiden at Redcar in August by 1¾ lengths from Cash Queen Anna: similar form when sixth to Lillie Langtry in sales race at Newmarket: should stay 1m: hung right second start. *Saeed bin Suroor* **84**

SIYOUNI (FR) 2 b.c. (Feb 14) Pivotal 124 – Sichilla (IRE) 108 (Danehill (USA) 126) [2009 5g* 5d* 5g* 5.5g^2 7g^2 7g* Oct 4] **117**

Of the forty or so active sires whose progeny earned at least £1,000,000 in Europe during 2009 only five—Elusive City, Green Tune, King's Best, Sinndar and Slickly—are based in France. The dominance of British- and Irish-based sires partly accounts for a drop in the number of good, precocious youngsters coming through in France which, coupled with the greater readiness of trainers in Britain and Ireland, particularly Aidan O'Brien, to challenge for the best French juvenile races, has made it much tougher for French owners and trainers to keep their Group 1 two-year-old races at home. Between 1970 and 1989, only seven of the winners of the four Group 1 events open to colts—the Prix Morny, Prix de la Salamandre, Grand Criterium and Criterium de Saint-Cloud—were trained outside France. Since 1990, this group of races, with the Criterium International replacing the Prix de la Salamandre and the distance of the Grand Criterium (Prix Jean-Luc Lagardere) dropping from a mile to seven furlongs, has produced thirty-eight foreign-trained winners. In the last five years, only five French two-year-old colts (Thewayyouare, Hello Morning, Naaqoos, Milanais and Siyouni) have run to a Timeform rating of 115 or higher, as against sixty trained in Britain or Ireland who have achieved the same mark.

Siyouni was the best two-year-old colt trained in France in the latest season but he isn't the champion French two-year-old, the filly Special Duty having the edge on him. Even so, Siyouni's emphatic victory in the Prix Jean-Luc Lagardere put him in a class of his own among the colts and he looks to have a fairly good chance in the Poule d'Essai des Poulains. Possessing much more speed than stamina, he is closer in racing character and style to some of the big two-year-old winners owned by the present Aga Khan's father Prince Aly Khan—Venture VII (Middle Park Stakes in 1959) being a notable example—and by the Aga Khan himself with Silver Shark (Prix de l'Abbaye in 1965) and Zeddaan (Prix Robert Papin in 1967) in the early days after taking over the bloodstock empire founded by his grandfather. There have been Group 1 successes for Aga Khan-owned two-year-old colts in recent times with Manntari and Sinndar in the National Stakes and Carlotamix and Dalakhani in the Criterium International, but none of those had won three races over five furlongs by the middle of June, as Siyouni did.

Siyouni started off in a newcomers race at Longchamp at the beginning of May, making all to beat Dolled Up by a length and a half, after which mention was made of a trip to Royal Ascot for the Norfolk Stakes. Next, though, was a minor event at Maisons-Laffitte, which Siyouni won by the same margin from the filly Quintalina after leading entering the final furlong. Royal Ascot was eventually ruled out because connections seemed to believe it might harm Siyouni's long-term prospects, trainer Alain de Royer Dupre saying 'I have spoken with several people about the Ascot race and have been told that it is a very hard race for a two-year-old and they often leave their career behind when they run in it.' Instead, Siyouni had his first start in pattern and listed company in the listed Prix La Fleche at Maisons-Laffitte. The race has been won in the last thirty years by several horses who went on to make their mark in Group 1 company—Ma Biche, Hector Protector, Arazi, Zieten, Noverre and Natagora—and the style in which Siyouni landed the odds against nine rivals suggested he might well follow suit. Held up and making smooth progress to lead a furlong and a half out, Siyouni went on to beat Ladoga comfortably by three lengths.

The Prix Robert Papin, also at Maisons-Laffitte nearly six weeks later, presented Siyouni with an excellent chance of getting off the mark in pattern company. Unfortunately, sent off at 2/1-on, he caught a tartar in once-raced Special Duty, trying to challenge on the rail inside the last furlong after being waited with but failing to get past under strong riding, eventually going down by a length and a half. Given what Special Duty went on to achieve in the Prix Morny and Cheveley Park Stakes, the result could be seen in a different light at the end of the season but, at the time, Siyouni's bubble seemed to have been burst. His next appearance came at seven furlongs—for the first time—in the Prix La Rochette at Longchamp in early-September. Favourite again, Siyouni was held up, perhaps because of concerns about his staying the trip, and he was given more to do than the winner before going down by a length and a half to Buzzword, who had been close up from the outset. Siyouni started only third favourite in a field of seven for the Qatar Prix Jean-Luc Lagardere at Longchamp a month later. The field didn't have much strength in depth, containing only two pattern winners in the shape of Buzzword

Qatar Prix Jean-Luc Lagardere (Grand Criterium), Longchamp—
a tactical affair is won by Siyouni from Pounced, Buzzword, Lope de Vega, Dick Turpin and Beethoven

and the market leader Dick Turpin, who had been successful in the Richmond Stakes. National Stakes third Beethoven represented Aidan O'Brien, while the other runners trained outside France were Newbury maiden winner Pounced and Superlative Stakes runner-up Roi de Vitesse. The second favourite was Lope de Vega from the Andre Fabre stable and unbeaten in a newcomers event at Deauville and a minor event at Longchamp. Dick Turpin had a poor run and Beethoven wasn't in the form he showed next time, when visored in the Dewhurst Stakes, but Siyouni's performance was still a revelation. Waited with, and evidently going well in fourth as Pounced made the running, Siyouni took closer order halfway up the straight, was pushed into the lead over a furlong out and quickened well to finish a length and a half clear of Pounced. Buzzword kept on well for third, half a length further back, with Lope de Vega fourth. Siyouni's performance was not quite the best by a winner of the race since the distance was shortened—that was by Holy Roman Emperor in 2006—but it wasn't far off it, and Pounced franked the form when winning the Breeders' Cup Juvenile Turf next time. Siyouni could do well at around a mile as a three-year-old, perhaps tackling the Prix Jean Prat as well as the Poule d'Essai des Poulains in the first part of the year. He is a strong, good-bodied colt who carries condition and looks sure to train on, and is in the hands of a very good trainer. Siyouni has so far raced only on good or good to soft going.

Siyouni (FR) (b.c. Feb 14, 2007)	Pivotal (ch 1993)	Polar Falcon (b or br 1987)	Nureyev
			Marie d'Argonne
		Fearless Revival (ch 1987)	Cozzene
			Stufida
	Sichilla (IRE) (b 2002)	Danehill (b 1986)	Danzig
			Razyana
		Slipstream Queen (b 1990)	Conquistador Cielo
			Country Queen

H.H. Aga Khan's "Siyouni"

Siyouni's prospects of staying beyond a mile may not be strong, but his relaxed demeanour and calm temperament will help—he looked lethargic before the Prix Jean-Luc Lagardere and is certainly no tearaway, although he has won three times at around five furlongs. He is another good horse produced by the Jean-Luc Lagardere broodmare band, which was bought by the Aga Khan in 2005 (victory in the race named after Lagardere was particularly appropriate). Siyouni is not by a French-based stallion. His sire, the British-based Pivotal, enjoyed another good year thanks also to Regal Parade, Sariska and Virtual, as well as Buzzword and Emerald Commander among the juveniles. Siyouni came from just two foals bred by the Aga Khan from Pivotal's 2007 crop; Buzzword came from twenty bred by Darley. Pivotal sires a good number of horses who are effective at a mile or further and the distaff side of Siyouni's pedigree has some stamina elements in it. The dam Sichilla—Siyouni is her first foal—won twice at seven furlongs from three starts, showing smart form when winning the listed Prix Amandine. Since Siyouni, Sichilla has produced a filly by Medicean and a colt by Dalakhani. Sichilla's dam Slipstream Queen was bought on behalf of Jean-Luc Lagardere for 110,000 dollars at Keeneland in 1995. For him she produced the high-class Slickly, who was effective at up to eleven furlongs, as he showed when landing the Prix Noailles and Grand Prix de Paris as a three-year-old, but was better at a mile, over which distance he won the Prix du Moulin and the Premio Vittorio di Capua (twice) for Godolphin. Slipstream Queen, a stakes-placed winner of three races, is the dam of several other winners notably No Slip, successful in the Grade 2 Oak Tree Derby. Siyouni's great grandam Country Queen ran forty-two times, her twelve victories highlighted by the Grade 1 Yellow Ribbon Stakes over a mile and a quarter. She was a half-sister to the dam of Procida, a good three-year-old in 1984 when he won the Prix de la Foret and Hollywood Derby. This is a successful family and Siyouni has every chance of adding further to its reputation. *A. de Royer Dupre, France*

SKHILLING SPIRIT 6 b.g. Most Welcome 131 – Calcavella 75 (Pursuit of Love 124) [2009 106§: 6s^6 May 15] strong, close-coupled gelding: has a short, unimpressive action: useful handicapper: poorly drawn sole start in 2009 (sixth at York): best at 6f/7f, seemingly on good ground or softer: tried blinkered/visored: virtually refused to race final outing at 5 yrs: often hangs: held up: temperamental. *T. D. Barron* **102 §**

SKYBOB 3 b.g. Tobougg (IRE) 125 – Heavens Above (FR) (Pistolet Bleu (IRE) 133) [2009 7g 8g 12g 16d 13.8m Sep 19] no form: visored when pulled up final start: dead. *D. W. Thompson* **–**

SKY CRUSADER 7 b.g. Mujahid (USA) 125 – Red Cloud (IRE) 61 (Taufan (USA) 119) [2009 a7.5g^4 a10g* a10g^6 a9.5g* a12g^3 a9.5g* a9.5g* p12m^4 a9.5g* p10f^6 Dec 19] tall, leggy gelding: fairly useful handicapper in Britain for R. Ingram in 2006: useful and prolific winner in Europe since: better than ever in 2009, successful at Cagnes-sur-Mer in handicap in January and at Deauville in minor events in March, July (ladies) and August, and listed race (by 2 lengths from Eire) in December: creditable 5½ lengths fourth to Kirklees in September Stakes at Kempton eighth start, but well held in listed race at Lingfield final outing: effective at 7.5f to 1½m: raced only on all-weather nowadays (winner of 7 of his 9 starts at Deauville): visored (well held) once at 4 yrs. *M. Nigge, France* **107**

SKYFLIGHT 2 ch.f. (Apr 12) Observatory (USA) 131 – Flight Soundly (IRE) 78 (Caerleon (USA) 132) [2009 6g p7g 6.1m* Sep 30] unfurnished filly: half-sister to several winners, including useful German 5f (at 2 yrs)/6f winner Elli (by Polar Falcon): dam, 2-y-o 6f winner, out of Queen Mary Stakes winner Night of Wind: modest form: sweating, won maiden at Nottingham (hung left): stays 7f. *Eve Johnson Houghton* **64**

SKY GATE (USA) 3 b.c. Arch (USA) 127 – Mista Mayberry (USA) (Touch Gold (USA) 127) [2009 87p: 10g^6 12m a8f^3 a8.3f^6 a8f^4 Dec 20] workmanlike colt: fairly useful performer at best: changed owners 47,000 gns in February: well held in handicaps first 2 starts in 2009 (refused to settle at Royal Ascot on second one): left B. Meehan and off 5 months, in frame in claimers at Calder late in year: stays 1m: acts on dirt/fibresand: blinkered. *Martin D. Wolfson, USA* **?**

SKY HIGH KID (IRE) 3 b.g. One Cool Cat (USA) 123 – Market Hill (IRE) 67 (Danehill (USA) 126) [2009 66p: 8d 5.1g 5.7g 6m^2 5m 5.7g p6f p7g Oct 2] modest performer: may prove best short of 1m: acts on polytrack and good to firm going: visored once. *M. R. Channon* **59**

SKYLARKER (USA) 11 b.g. Sky Classic (CAN) – O My Darling (USA) 76 (Mr Prospector (USA)) [2009 –: 10.4g 12.4d Oct 13] tall, rather leggy gelding: no form since 2005. *T. A. K. Cuthbert* **–**

SKYLLA 2 b.f. (Mar 5) Kyllachy 129 – Day Star 77 (Dayjur (USA) 137) [2009 5.1g* 6g^2 5m* 6g^2 5m^6 6g Oct 30] £14,000Y: leggy, close-coupled filly: sixth foal: half-sister to several winning sprinters, including 2004 2-y-o 6f winner Tractor Boy (by Mind Games) and 2008 2-y-o 5f winner Sunset Crest (by Reel Buddy), both later successful abroad: dam, 6f winner, closely related to Poule d'Essai des Pouliches winner Rose Gypsy: fairly useful performer: won maiden at Nottingham in July and nursery at Haydock in August: ran in listed races after, creditable effort only when length second to Hold Your Colour at Ripon: speedy front runner, may prove best at 5f: raced only on good/good to firm ground: has given trouble in preliminaries. *J. R. Holt* **92**

SKY QUEST (IRE) 11 b.g. Spectrum (IRE) 126 – Rose Vibert (Caerleon (USA) 132) [2009 73: p11g* p10g p10g p12g 11s* 10g^4 12m^5 11.6m* 11m^4 12m^5 Sep 25] smallish gelding: fair handicapper: won at Kempton in January, Newbury (apprentices) in July and Windsor (amateurs) in August: effective at 1¼m/1½m: acts on polytrack, firm and soft going: tried in cheekpieces/tongue tie: has carried head awkwardly/found little: held up: inconsistent. *J. R. Boyle* **74**

SKYRIDER (IRE) 2 gr.f. (Mar 16) Dalakhani (IRE) 133 – Future Flight 85 (Polar Falcon (USA) 126) [2009 6.1s^2 Oct 7] 42,000Y, €85,000 2-y-o: unfurnished filly: fourth foal: half-sister to 3-y-o Flying Silks: dam, 7f winner, half-sister to high-class sprinter Tante Rose: 16/1, promising 2¼ lengths second to No Explaining in maiden at Nottingham, very green off bridle: will be suited by 7f+: sure to improve. *R. Charlton* **73 p**

SKYSURFERS 3 b.c. E Dubai (USA) 124 – Fortune (IRE) 80 (Night Shift (USA)) [2009 f7g* Oct 18] third foal: half-brother to smart UAE 5f/7f winner Change Alley and 5-y-o Celtic Gold (both by Elusive Quality): dam, Irish 6f winner, sister to smart French sprinter Dyhim Diamond and US Grade 1 2-y-o 8.5f winner Creaking Board: 13/8 on, won maiden at Southwell in October by 10 lengths from Positivity, barely off bridle: useful prospect. *Saeed bin Suroor* **88 P**

SLAM 4 b.g. Beat Hollow 126 – House Hunting (Zafonic (USA) 130) [2009 100: 9.8m^2 10.4m May 13] big, strong, well-made gelding: usually impresses in appearance: useful performer: good neck second to Halicarnassus in minor event at Ripon, easily better effort in 2009 (pulled hard other occasion): stays 1¼m: acts on polytrack and good to firm ground: sold 20,000 gns early in July, and gelded. *B. W. Hills* **100**

SLANT (IRE) 3 b.f. Spinning World (USA) 130 – Sweet Honesty (IRE) (Charnwood Forest (IRE) 125) [2009 85: p7g 8m May 14] leggy, close-coupled filly: fairly useful maiden at 2 yrs: well below form at Kempton on return, then pulled up amiss next time: should stay 7f: best form on soft/heavy ground. *Eve Johnson Houghton* **–**

SLASL 2 b.f. (Feb 16) Dubawi (IRE) 129 – Mazuna (IRE) 110 (Cape Cross (IRE) 129) [2009 p6g p6m p8g^4 6.1s Oct 7] 15,000Y: first foal: dam, 11.5f/1½m (Princess Royal Stakes) winner, out of half-sister to dam of 3-y-o Mastercraftsman: modest form at best: should stay beyond 1m. *C. E. Brittain* **56**

SLEEPY BLUE OCEAN 3 b.c. Oasis Dream 129 – Esteemed Lady (IRE) 96 (Mark of Esteem (IRE) 137) [2009 8d 6m* 6g 7g f6g Nov 17] 40,000Y: first foal: dam, in frame both starts around 6f at 2 yrs, half-sister to useful performers Revenue (up to 7f) and La Mottie (up to 9f): fair form when winning maiden at Haydock in June (left J. Noseda £10,000 after): no form otherwise (said to have had breathing problem third start): likely to stay 7f: acts on good to firm ground. *J. Balding* **72**

SLEEPY DOVE 4 b.f. Muhtarram (USA) 125 – Robins Meg (Skyliner 117) [2009 8m^5 p9.5g Nov 12] first foal: dam third in bumper, only form: well held in bumper/maidens. *M. E. Sowersby* **–**

SLEEPY HOLLOW 4 b.g. Beat Hollow 126 – Crackling 57 (Electric 126) [2009 92: 12m^2 p12g 14.1s^3 Oct 12] good-topped, attractive gelding: fairly useful handicapper: creditable placed efforts 2 of 3 starts in 2009: stays 14.6f: unraced on heavy ground, acts on any other turf going: none too resolute: fairly useful form over hurdles. *H. Morrison* **92**

SLEEPY MOUNTAIN 5 ch.g. Beat Hollow 126 – La Sorrela (IRE) (Cadeaux Genereux 131) [2009 68: f12g p12m Nov 27] fair maiden at best: off 11 months, well held in 2009: stays 1¾m: acts on polytrack: often races prominently. *A. Middleton* **–**

SLEEPY SILVER 4 gr.f. Silver Patriarch (IRE) 125 – Hustle An Bustle (USA) 59 (Lomond (USA) 128) [2009 10.4g May 29] workmanlike filly: second foal: dam maiden (stayed 7f): well beaten in bumper/maiden. *J. Mackie* **–**

SLEEPY VALLEY (IRE) 3 b.f. Clodovil (IRE) 116 – Kilkee Bay (IRE) 61 (Case Law 113) [2009 60: 6m 6g 6g^2 5d 5v 5m 6g Oct 16] modest maiden: should prove best at 5f/6f: acts on good to firm going: in cheekpieces of late. *A. Dickman* **59**

SLEW CHARM (FR) 7 b.g. Marathon (USA) 116 – Slew Bay (FR) (Beaudelaire (USA) 125) [2009 p12.2g^2 f12g^4 Feb 10] modest maiden: stays 1½m: acts on polytrack and heavy going: tried tongue tied. *Noel T. Chance* **62**

SLEY (FR) 3 ch.f. Lomitas 129 – Samara (IRE) 108 (Polish Patriot (USA) 128) [2009 66: p8.6g 8f 7m Jun 27] small, attractive filly: fair form on debut at 2 yrs, but little impact since: blinkered last 2 starts: sold 5,000 gns. *B. J. Meehan* **50**

SLICE (IRE) 2 b.c. (Mar 19) Daggers Drawn (USA) 114 – Windomen (IRE) (Forest Wind (USA) 111) [2009 5.1g^5 6.1m* 6d 6s 6m p8m Sep 23] €12,500Y: sturdy colt: fifth foal: brother to fairly useful/temperamental 6f (at 2 yrs)/1¼m winner Harvest Joy and half-brother to 7.5f to 1¼m winner Touch of Ivory (by Rossini): dam unraced: fair performer: won maiden at Chepstow in July: should stay 7f/1m: acts on good to firm going: tried blinkered: sold 6,500 gns. *Eve Johnson Houghton* **70**

SLICK MOVER (IRE) 4 gr.f. Slickly (FR) 128 – Agnessa (FR) (Niniski (USA) 125) [2009 p12g^6 14m^4 8.3d p12m^5 Oct 28] €17,500Y, €24,000 3-y-o: big filly: fourth foal: dam French 10.5f to 1½m winner: modest form in bumpers/over hurdles: modest maiden on Flat: will stay beyond 1½m: acts on polytrack. *B. G. Powell* **62**

SLIGO 4 b.c. Sadler's Wells (USA) 132 – Arabesque 100 (Zafonic (USA) 130) [2009 93?: 12v 12s Nov 7] tall, attractive colt: seemingly fairly useful at 3 yrs: left A. P. O'Brien and off 18 months, well held in 2009: best effort at 1¼m on soft ground: blinkered/tongue tied final start. *A. J. McCabe* **–**

SLIP 4 b.g. Fraam 114 – Niggle 65 (Night Shift (USA)) [2009 94: p10g* p10g^5 10m* 10.1g^4 p12m^5 Dec 4] compact gelding: fair performer nowadays: won claimer in January and seller in July, both at Lingfield: left J. Boyle and successful over hurdles prior to final outing: stays 1½m: acts on polytrack, good to firm and good to soft ground: tried in blinkers/cheekpieces: not straightforward. *Tim Vaughan* **79**

SLIP SILVER 5 gr.m. Slip Anchor 136 – New Wind (GER) (Windwurf (GER)) [2009 16m f12g p12.2g Apr 25] big mare: poor maiden in 2007: unraced in 2008: no form at 5 yrs: often in cheekpieces in 2007. *R. C. Guest* **–**

SLIP SLIDING AWAY (IRE) 2 b.c. (Apr 5) Whipper (USA) 126 – Sandy Lady (IRE) 91 (Desert King (IRE) 129) [2009 p7g^3 p7g p5g^4 p6g^3 p6m^4 p7.1g^4 Dec 26] fair maiden: stays 7f: raced only on polytrack. *J. R. Best* **66**

SLIP STAR 6 b.m. Slip Anchor 136 – Shiny Kay 65 (Star Appeal 133) [2009 60: 7m 8m^6 8f 9.2g^5 7m 6d 7g 7.1m^6 10m Sep 23] quite good-topped mare: modest handicapper: may prove best up to 7f: acts on good to firm ground. *T. J. Etherington* **53**

SLOOP JOHNB 3 b.g. Bahamian Bounty 116 – Soundwave (Prince Sabo 123) [2009 78: 5m^2 5m* 5s* 6g 6g 5d^4 5g Jul 31] workmanlike gelding: fairly useful handicapper: won at Beverley and York in May: in-and-out form after: best at 5f: acts on firm and soft going. *R. A. Fahey* **87**

SLUGGER O'TOOLE 4 br.g. Intikhab (USA) 135 – Haddeyah (USA) 68 (Dayjur (USA) 137) [2009 102: 8m 8s 7m 7f 7s Nov 7] tall, rather leggy gelding: has a short, scratchy action: useful handicapper at best: well held in 2009. *S. C. Williams* **–**

SLUMDOG (IRE) 4 b.c. Alzao (USA) 117 – Chardania (IRE) 34 (Rainbows For Life (CAN)) [2009 8g 7s Aug 9] tailed off in maiden/seller. *Garry Moss* **–**

SMALLJOHN 3 ch.g. Needwood Blade 117 – My Bonus 79 (Cyrano de Bergerac 120) [2009 79: f7s^3 7m 7d 7g p7.1g p7.1g^4 p7m^2 Dec 9] sparely-made, close-coupled gelding: fair performer: stays 7f: acts on all-weather, good to firm and good to soft ground: wears visor: races prominently: has looked difficult ride. *B. Smart* **68**

SMART ENDEAVOUR (USA) 3 ch.g. Smart Strike (CAN) 121 – Luminance (USA) (Deputy Minister (CAN)) [2009 55p: p7.1g* 7m^6 8.3g^4 10d Aug 6] lengthy gelding: fairly useful performer: won maiden at Wolverhampton in April: gelded after final start: likely to prove best up to 1m: acts on polytrack, best turf effort on good ground: tried tongue tied. *W. R. Swinburn* **88**

SMARTEN DIE (IRE) 6 ch.h. Diesis 133 – Highest Dream (IRE) (Highest Honor (FR) 124) [2009 101: a6g* a6g* p6g^6 6g* 6m 6g 6g^2 6g a5.5s^2 Nov 29] useful performer: won handicaps at Dortmund in January and February and Hoppegarten in May: also creditable 4½ lengths sixth of 7 to Matsunosuke in listed race at Lingfield third start: brought down sixth outing: best up to 6f: acts on polytrack/sand and good to soft ground. *Frau E. Mader, Germany* **101**

SMARTERTHANUTHINK (USA) 4 b.g. Smart Strike (CAN) 121 – Dance Gaily (USA) (Nureyev (USA) 131) [2009 76: 12m 9.9m^6 Jun 23] good-topped gelding: fair handicapper: well below form in 2009: tried in cheekpieces/visor: signs of temperament. *R. A. Fahey* **–**

SMARTIES PARTY 6 b.m. Tamure (IRE) 125 – Maries Party (The Parson 119) [2009 10.1m^4 12v^6 p13.9g^3 Nov 27] modest winning 2½m hurdler: modest form in maidens on Flat. *C. W. Thornton* **64**

SMART JOHN 9 b.g. Bin Ajwaad (IRE) 119 – Katy-Q (IRE) 58 (Taufan (USA) 119) [2009 15g Aug 31] good-topped gelding: modest handicapper in 2007: fit from hurdling, tailed off only Flat start since: stays 12.6f: acts on good to firm going: has shown signs of temperament. *S. T. Lewis* **–**

SMART PICK 6 ch.m. Piccolo 121 – Nevita (Never So Bold 135) [2009 47: 9g 9.9g Sep 22] close-coupled mare: maiden: poor at 5 yrs: well held in 2009: tried in headgear. *Mrs L. Williamson* **–**

SMART TAZZ 4 b.g. Mujahid (USA) 125 – Katy-Q (IRE) 58 (Taufan (USA) 119) [2009 –: 10.2g 10m p12.2g p8.6g^4 p8.6g Sep 3] big gelding: well held in maidens/handicaps: left H. Evans after third start: tried blinkered: dead. *S. T. Lewis* **–**

SMARTY SOCKS (IRE) 5 ch.g. Elnadim (USA) 128 – Unicamp 84 (Royal Academy (USA) 130) [2009 80: f7g* f7g^4 7m 7m* 7m^6 8m^5 7m 7m* 7d^4 6.9g^3 f8g Aug 27] rather leggy gelding: useful handicapper: won at Southwell in February, Doncaster (ladies) in April and York in July: best at 7f/1m: acts on all-weather, soft and good to firm going: tried in cheekpieces/tongue tie: usually held up (often slowly away). *P. T. Midgley* **95**

SMAYAL (USA) 2 b.f. (Mar 20) Kingmambo (USA) 125 – Cloud Castle 119 (In The Wings 128) [2009 7m^6 Oct 3] unfurnished filly: closely related to several winners, notably smart 6f (at 2 yrs) to 1½m winner Queen's Best (by King's Best), and half-sister to smart French 1½m winner Reverie Solitaire (by Nashwan): dam, won Nell Gwyn Stakes and second in Prix Vermeille, half-sister to Luso, Warrsan and Needle Gun: 28/1 and green, always behind in maiden at Redcar, hanging: should do better. *C. E. Brittain* **– p**

SMELLY CAT 3 b.f. One Cool Cat (USA) 123 – Grecian Halo (USA) 59 (Southern Halo (USA)) [2009 –: 6m^5 5m^5 6m^6 7.9g 6m Jul 11] unfurnished filly: modest form first 2 starts in 2009: left T. Easterby £800, well beaten after: may prove best at 5f: acts on good to firm ground: has shaped as if amiss more than once. *D. W. Thompson* **50**

SMETANA 4 b.g. Kylian (USA) – Shimmer 55 (Bustino 136) [2009 59: p16g^6 f11g^6 f12g Jun 2] good-topped gelding: modest maiden at 3 yrs: no form in 2009: tried visored. *E. J. Creighton* **–**

SMICKER SMACKER 2 gr.f. (Jan 27) Verglas (IRE) 118 – Vallee Blanche (IRE) 78 (Zafonic (USA) 130) [2009 6m 6g p7g^6 8.1d Aug 31] close-coupled filly: first foal: dam, Irish maiden (stayed 1¼m), out of half-sister to smart performer up to 1m Three Valleys: modest form at best in maidens: should stay 1m: slowly away last 2 outings: sold 1,500 gns. *George Baker* **50**

SMIRFYS COPPER (IRE) 2 ch.f. (May 14) Choisir (AUS) 126 – Fer de Lance (IRE) (Diesis 133) [2009 6d Jul 22] 7,000Y: seventh foal: half-sister to 3 winners, including useful 7f (at 2 yrs) to 10.4f winner Ferzao (by Alzao): dam unraced: 8/1, very slowly away and tailed off in maiden at Catterick. *D. Nicholls* **–**

SMIRFY'S SILVER 5 b.g. Desert Prince (IRE) 130 – Goodwood Blizzard 97 (Inchinor 119) [2009 73: 10m Aug 29] short-backed gelding: fair handicapper: off 13 months, tailed off sole outing in 2009: stays 1¼m: acts on good to firm and good to soft going: races prominently. *E. S. McMahon* **–**

SMIRFYS SYSTEMS 10 b.g. Safawan 118 – Saint Systems 68 (Uncle Pokey 116) [2009 67: p6g^2 p6g* p6m^5 p7g^5 p6g^4 p7.1g Dec 28] close-coupled, workmanlike gelding: fair performer: won claimer at Wolverhampton in February: stays 7f: acts on polytrack, firm and good to soft going: tried in blinkers/cheekpieces. *E. S. McMahon* **69**

SMITAIN 3 b.g. Lujain (USA) 119 – Mitsuki 91§ (Puissance 110) [2009 –: 7m 8.5m^6 Jun 23] no form in maidens. *Mrs S. Lamyman* **–**

SMOG (IRE) 2 gr.c. (Feb 26) Verglas (IRE) 118 – Dollysister (FR) (Alydar (USA)) [2009 6g 6.1v^4 8.1g p7.1g Sep 3] poor maiden: should stay 7f+: tried blinkered. *B. J. Meehan* **49**

SMOKEY OAKEY (IRE) 5 b.g. Tendulkar (USA) 114 – Veronica (Persian Bold 123) [2009 115: 10m 8.1m 10d^5 10.4g 8g^6 8.1v 9m 8.3v^5 Nov 4] smallish, leggy gelding: **105**

just useful in 2009, best effort when 3¼ lengths fifth to Crime Scene in listed race at Newbury on third start: stays 1¼m: goes well on ground softer than good (acts on heavy). *M. H. Tompkins*

SMOKEY RYDER 3 ch.f. Bertolini (USA) 125 – Another Secret 87 (Efisio 120) [2009 80: p6g* p6g^4 f5g* p6g* p7g^3 p6g 7m 6m^6 6.1m^4 6d 6g p6g Dec 28] strong filly: fairly useful handicapper: won at Wolverhampton in January, and Southwell and Lingfield in February: creditable efforts when in frame after, including when third to Nashmiah in listed race at Lingfield: stays 7f: acts on all-weather, good to firm and good to soft ground: races up with pace. *R. A. Harris* **94**

SMOKEY RYE 4 b.f. Bertolini (USA) 125 – Another Secret 87 (Efisio 120) [2009 82: p8g^4 p8g* p8g p7g* p8g^3 p8.6g* p8g 8d^3 Apr 13] good-topped filly: fair performer: won seller and handicap at Lingfield and apprentice claimer at Wolverhampton (simple task) in February/March: stays 8.6f: acts on polytrack, good to firm and good to soft ground: tried blinkered/in cheekpieces: usually held up: flashes tail: reportedly sent to Libya. *George Baker* **76**

SMOKIN BEAU 12 b.g. Cigar 68 – Beaù Dada (IRE) 66 (Pine Circle (USA)) [2009 72: p5g Mar 25] smallish, robust gelding: one-time smart performer: well held sole start at 12 yrs: tried in headgear: has bled. *N. P. Littmoden* **–**

SMOKIN JOE 8 b.g. Cigar 68 – Beau Dada (IRE) 66 (Pine Circle (USA)) [2009 –, a82d: p7g p10g Apr 28] small, quite attractive gelding: fairly useful handicapper at best on all-weather: on downgrade: wears blinkers, tried visored. *J. R. Best* **–**

SMOOTH AS SILK (IRE) 4 b.f. Danehill Dancer (IRE) 117 – Doula (USA) (Gone West (USA)) [2009 72: p12g^3 11m p13.9g^4 f12g p12.2m^4 p12.2g^4 p12m^3 p12g Nov 18] tall, useful-looking filly: fair maiden handicapper: barely stays 13.8f: acts on polytrack and good to firm ground: tried blinkered/in cheekpieces: signs of temperament. *C. R. Egerton* **73**

SMOOTHLY DOES IT 8 b.g. Efisio 120 – Exotic Forest 66 (Dominion 123) [2009 61, a52: p12g Apr 22] leggy gelding: has been fired: modest handicapper: well held sole 8-y-o start on Flat: stays 1½m: has form on polytrack/good to firm ground, ideally suited by softer than good (acts on heavy). *Jim Best* **–**

SMOOTH SOVEREIGN (IRE) 4 ch.g. King's Best (USA) 132 – Mellow Park (IRE) 114 (In The Wings 128) [2009 75: p9.5g^5 p8.6g f8g 12.4m^2 Apr 4] fair maiden: stays 12.4f: acts on polytrack and good to firm ground: sold £2,000, joined W. Clay. *M. Johnston* **68**

SMUGGLERS BAY (IRE) 5 b.g. Celtic Swing 138 – Princess Mood (GER) (Muhtarram (USA) 125) [2009 78: 9.9m^5 16.1d 11.5m May 25] useful-looking gelding: shows plenty of knee action: fair handicapper: stays 1¾m: acts on heavy and good to firm going: tried blinkered: has found little: fairly useful hurdler. *T. D. Easterby* **69**

SNAEFELL (IRE) 5 gr.g. Danehill Dancer (IRE) 117 – Sovereign Grace (IRE) 101 (Standaan (FR) 118) [2009 114: 5d^6 6v^5 6m* 5g^2 7s 6s^2 5s^2 6s^6 5v^4 6s* 6s Oct 11] strong gelding: smart performer: won minor event at Cork in June and Irish Daily Mail Renaissance Stakes at the Curragh (beat Girouette 2½ lengths) in September: creditable efforts otherwise in 2009 only when runner-up in Sapphire Stakes at the Curragh (beaten 2½ lengths by Benbaun) and in listed races at Fairyhouse (to Aine) and Tipperary (to Perfect Polly), beaten a neck both times: should prove effective at stiff 5f to 7f: acts on heavy and good to firm ground: wears cheekpieces/blinkers nowadays: tongue tied earlier in career. *M. Halford, Ireland* **114**

SNAKE SKIN 6 ch.m. Golden Snake (USA) 127 – Silken Dalliance 91 (Rambo Dancer (CAN) 107) [2009 68: p10g f12g Feb 20] leggy mare: handicapper: well held both starts in 2009: tried blinkered/in cheekpieces. *J. Gallagher* **–**

SNEAK PREVIEW 3 ch.f. Monsieur Bond (IRE) 120 – Harryana 79 (Efisio 120) [2009 100+: 6m^2 Apr 2] sturdy, useful-looking filly: useful form: further progress when head second to Sayif in minor event at Leicester only outing at 3 yrs: speedy, well worth a try at 5f: acts on heavy and good to firm going: sent to USA. *E. S. McMahon* **104**

SNEEM'S ROCK 8 br.g. Daylami (IRE) 138 – Urchin (IRE) (Fairy King (USA)) [2009 p10g Aug 15] off over 4 years, no encouragement on return (including over hurdles): tried in cheekpieces/blinkers. *P. R. Hedger* **–**

SNOOZING 3 b.f. Where Or When (IRE) 124 – Tenpence 60 (Bob Back (USA) 124) [2009 f7d^5 p8g f8g 7d Mar 31] second foal: dam ran twice: no form: sold from M. Tompkins 800 gns prior to final start: tried in cheekpieces. *Mrs L. C. Jewell* **–**

SNOQUALMIE BOY 6 b.g. Montjeu (IRE) 137 – Seattle Ribbon (USA) 70 (Seattle Dancer (USA) 119) [2009 105: 9.8m^4 10m 10m^6 12g^2 16.4m 12m^4 12g^2 f11g 12d Oct 24] rangy, good-bodied, attractive gelding: handicapper, just fairly useful in 2009: stays 1½m: acts on polytrack, firm and good to soft going: temperament under suspicion: sold 16,000 gns. *T. P. Tate* **94**

SNOQUALMIE GIRL (IRE) 3 b.f. Montjeu (IRE) 137 – Seattle Ribbon (USA) 70 (Seattle Dancer (USA) 119) [2009 101: 7m^6 10f 10m^5 12m^4 12.3m* 12m^6 12m p13g Oct 29] angular filly: useful performer: best effort in 2009 when winning listed race at Chester in September by head from Traffic Guard: will stay 1¾m: acts on soft and good to firm going. *D. R. C. Elsworth* **103**

SNOQUALMIE STAR 2 ch.f. (Feb 22) Galileo (IRE) 134 – Seattle Ribbon (USA) 70 (Seattle Dancer (USA) 119) [2009 7d^5 7g^5 8d Oct 27] rather leggy filly: closely related to 3-y-o Snoqualmie Girl and 6-y-o Snoqualmie Boy and half-sister to several winners: dam, maiden (stayed 1¼m), sister to Racing Post Trophy winner Seattle Rhyme: similar form when fifth in maidens at Newmarket: found little final start: bred to be suited by at least 1¼m. *D. R. C. Elsworth* **66**

SNOW BAY 3 ch.c. Bahamian Bounty 116 – Goodwood Blizzard 97 (Inchinor 119) [2009 74: 7f^4 7g* 8g 7d^6 p7.1m^5 p7m^3 p7g f8m* f7g Dec 22] neat colt: fairly useful handicapper: won at Catterick in July and Southwell in December: stays 1m: acts on all-weather, firm and good to soft going: visored final outing. *B. Smart* **89**

SNOWBERRY HILL (USA) 6 b.g. Woodman (USA) 126 – Class Skipper (USA) (Skip Trial (USA)) [2009 65: p16g^2 f14g p13.9g^6 18m^2 16.2g 17.1g 16.5s p16.5g^6 15.8d^6 16m^3 p16.5g* p13.9g^4 Sep 17] workmanlike gelding: fair handicapper: won at Wolverhampton in September: stays 2¼m: acts on all-weather and firm going: tried in blinkers/cheekpieces. *Lucinda Featherstone* **65**

SNOW DANCER (IRE) 5 b.m. Desert Style (IRE) 121 – Bella Vie (IRE) (Sadler's Wells (USA) 132) [2009 64: p12.2g^6 p9.5g* p9.5g^2 p9.5g^2 9.9m 9.9m^3 10.1d 9m 10.4m^2 9m^2 9.3m^2 10.4g^2 9.9m 8m^3 8.1m p9.5g^2 p9.5g^3 p9.5g* p9.5m^5 p9.5g^6 Dec 26] leggy mare: fairly useful handicapper: won at Wolverhampton in January and November: stays easy 1½m: acts on polytrack and any turf going: often wears cheekpieces/blinkers (not last 5 starts): tactically versatile. *H. A. McWilliams* **84**

SNOWED UNDER 8 gr.g. Most Welcome 131 – Snowy Mantle 54 (Siberian Express (USA) 125) [2009 86: 9.9m* 10g 9.9m^3 10s Jul 29] good-topped gelding: fairly useful handicapper: won at Beverley in May: stays 1½m: acts on polytrack, firm and good to soft going: none too consistent. *J. D. Bethell* **86**

SNOW FAIRY (IRE) 2 b.f. (Feb 12) Intikhab (USA) 135 – Woodland Dream (IRE) 93 (Charnwood Forest (IRE) 125) [2009 6m^3 p6g* 6g^2 7g^4 7g^3 7v Oct 24] €1,800Y: smallish, workmanlike filly: first foal: dam, Irish 7f winner, half-sister to smart 1¼m performer Big Bad Bob: useful performer: won maiden at Lingfield in July comfortably: good efforts next 3 starts, particularly when very close third to Sent From Heaven in Prestige Stakes at Goodwood: will stay 1m: acts on polytrack, best turf efforts on good ground (well below form on heavy final start). *E. A. L. Dunlop* **99**

SNOWY INDIAN 4 b.f. Indian Ridge 123 – Snow Princess (IRE) 111 (Ela-Mana-Mou 132) [2009 73: p8.6g p8g^6 Feb 12] lightly-made filly: regressive maiden: should stay 1½m: acts on soft going: tried in cheekpieces. *M. Botti* **–**

SOAP WARS 4 b.g. Acclamation 118 – Gooseberry Pie 63 (Green Desert (USA) 127) [2009 101: p6g* 6m p6g^2 p6g 6g p6g^4 p6g p6g^5 Nov 27] strong, lengthy gelding: useful handicapper: won at Dundalk in April: in frame there in August (2 lengths second to Luisant) and October (1½ lengths fourth to Copper Dock): likely to prove best at 5f/6f: acts on polytrack, soft and good to firm going: in cheekpieces of late. *M. Halford, Ireland* **101**

SOBA JONES 12 b.g. Emperor Jones (USA) 119 – Soba 127 (Most Secret 119) [2009 63: f6s^6 f6g f6g f6g^6 f6g Mar 3] tall gelding: modest performer: regressive since early-2008: effective at 5f/6f: acts on fibresand and any turf going: tried in blinkers/cheekpieces. *J. Balding* **50**

SO BAZAAR (IRE) 2 b.g. (Feb 28) Xaar 132 – Nature Girl (USA) (Green Dancer (USA) 132) [2009 6m^3 7d^5 5d^5 6m^5 Sep 19] modest maiden: stays 7f. *G. A. Swinbank* **62**

SO BLISSFUL (IRE) 3 b.f. Cape Cross (IRE) 129 – Royal Devotion (IRE) 101 (Sadler's Wells (USA) 132) [2009 p8g^6 7g* 7.1g 8g 8g^6 10m^4 Oct 13] €220,000Y: good-topped filly: first foal: dam, Irish 1¼m/1½m winner, out of half-sister to Oaks/Irish Derby winner Balanchine: fair performer: won maiden at Goodwood in May: left T. Mills **77**

prior to final start: stays 1¼m: raced only on polytrack and good/good to firm going. *Mrs L. Wadham*

SOCCERJACKPOT (USA) 5 b.g. Mizzen Mast (USA) 121 – Rahbaby (USA) (Rahy **101** (USA) 115) [2009 –: p8g* p8.6g* 8m 7g^{4} p8g^{3} p7g^{5} Nov 18] quite good-topped gelding: useful handicapper: improved to win at Kempton and Wolverhampton (beat Tartan Gigha ¾ length) in March: creditable effort after only when third at Kempton: stays 8.6f: acts on polytrack and firm going. *C. G. Cox*

SOCCER (USA) 2 ch.c. (Feb 21) Van Nistelrooy (USA) 108 – Bonita Gail (USA) **93** (Geiger Counter (USA)) [2009 p5g* 5m^{2} 5m^{4} p5g^{2} 5g 5.7f^{3} 5g Oct 5] lengthy, good-topped colt: fifth foal: half-brother to winner in USA by Lure: dam ran twice in USA: fairly useful form: won maiden at Lingfield in April: good efforts in frame next 3 starts, including fourth to Monsieur Chevalier in listed race at Sandown: finished tamely last 2 outings: should be suited by 6f: acts on polytrack and good to firm ground: tongue tied: sold 33,000 gns, sent to Bahrain. *Tom Dascombe*

SOCIAL GRACE 2 gr.f. (Feb 28) Pastoral Pursuits 127 – Zilkha 50 (Petong 126) **65** [2009 5m^{2} 5m^{4} 5.1g^{2} 5.1m* 5.2d 5s 6g 5m 5m 5g^{6} 7g Oct 16] £5,000Y: tall filly: has scope: fourth foal: half-sister to 2007 2-y-o 5f seller winner Llab Nala (by Tobougg) and winner in Switzerland by Bertolini: dam, maiden (stayed 7f), out of sister to very smart French/US performer up to 1½m Millkom: fair performer: won maiden at Chester in July: largely below form after: raced mainly at 5f: acts on good to firm ground: tried in cheekpieces: sold £3,800. *D. H. Brown*

SOCIAL RHYTHM 5 b.m. Beat All (USA) 120 – Highly Sociable 56 (Puissance 110) **69** [2009 72: 8g* 8s^{6} 9.2g^{5} 8m* 9.1v^{3} Oct 31] sturdy mare: fair handicapper: won at Musselburgh in August and Ayr in October: stays 9.2f: acts on polytrack, heavy and good to firm going: tried in cheekpieces: usually held up. *A. C. Whillans*

SOCIETY MUSIC (IRE) 7 b.m. Almutawakel 126 – Society Fair (FR) (Always Fair **74** (USA) 121) [2009 77: 8f^{2} 8m 8.5g 8m^{3} 8d 8g Sep 30] leggy mare: fair handicapper: best around 1m: acts on any going: tried blinkered, usually wears cheekpieces: often races freely: sold 1,000 gns. *M. Dods*

SOCIETY ROCK (IRE) 2 b.c. (Feb 8) Rock of Gibraltar (IRE) 133 – High Society **105** (IRE) 97 (Key of Luck (USA) 126) [2009 7g^{5} 6.1g* 6m* 7m Oct 3] 75,000Y: good-bodied colt: second foal: half-brother to German 2006 2-y-o 6f winner Johannesburg Cat (by Johannesburg): dam 5f (in Ireland at 2 yrs) to 6.5f (in USA) winner: quickly made into useful performer: won maiden at Nottingham in August and Tattersalls Timeform Millions Sprint at Newmarket (beat Take Ten a head, again pulling hard in rear, then quickening impressively) in September: poorly drawn when only seventh in similar event at Newmarket final outing: will probably prove best short of 7f. *J. R. Fanshawe*

SOCIETY VENUE 4 b.g. Where Or When (IRE) 124 – Society Rose 88 (Saddlers' **80** Hall (IRE) 126) [2009 75: 8m^{3} 9.9m^{3} 10.1s^{2} 9.3m* 10.1d^{2} 12g^{6} 9.8g^{6} 9.8d 9.2g^{3} 10m^{3} Oct 13] tall, angular gelding: fairly useful handicapper: won at Carlisle in May: stays 1¼m: acts on firm and soft going: front runner/races prominently: reliable: sold £14,000, joined M. Scudamore. *Jedd O'Keeffe*

SOFIA'S STAR 4 b.g. Lend A Hand 124 – Charolles 82 (Ajdal (USA) 130) [2009 83: **80** p7g^{3} p8g^{5} p8g 8.3m^{5} 8m 8d^{2} Jun 10] short-backed gelding: fairly useful performer: stays 8.3f: acts on all-weather, good to firm and good to soft going: tried blinkered/in cheekpieces: held up (often slowly away). *S. Dow*

SOFINELLA (IRE) 6 gr.m. Titus Livius (FR) 115 – Mystical Jumbo (Mystiko (USA) **55** 124) [2009 64: p5g^{2} p5g^{4} 5.1m^{6} 5g 5v 5.1g^{5} 5g 5.1d^{5} 5.1d 5.1d 5.2d^{5} Oct 27] leggy mare: modest handicapper: best around 5f: acts on polytrack, good to firm and good to soft going: tried tongue tied/in cheekpieces: races prominently. *A. W. Carroll*

SOFONISBA 3 b.f. Rock of Gibraltar (IRE) 133 – Lothlorien (USA) 80 (Woodman **–** (USA) 126) [2009 57+: f8g p8.6g May 18] unfurnished filly: modest maiden at 2 yrs: well held in 2009: should be suited by 1m+. *M. L. W. Bell*

SOFTLY KILLING ME 4 b.f. Umistim 119 – Slims Lady 59 (Theatrical Charmer **–** 114) [2009 p8g p7g Mar 18] workmanlike filly: maiden: missed 2008: little form in 2009: tried visored. *B. Forsey*

SOFTLY SPOKEN 2 b.f. (Mar 22) Forzando 122 – Star of Flanders (Puissance 110) **46** [2009 6m^{5} 5m^{6} 5g 5d Sep 16] close-coupled filly: seventh foal: half-sister to 2004 2-y-o 5f winner Komac (by Komaite) and 9-y-o Davids Mark: dam unraced: sixth in maiden at Windsor, only form. *A. W. Carroll*

SO GLAMOROUS 4 b.f. Diktat 126 – Gena Ivor (USA) (Sir Ivor (USA) 135) [2009 7s 6m[6] 7m 6g Oct 20] poor maiden, lightly raced. *C. F. Wall* **49**

SOHCAHTOA (IRE) 3 b.g. Val Royal (FR) 127 – Stroke of Six (IRE) 84 (Woodborough (USA) 112) [2009 97: p9g[3] p8g 8.1m[5] 8m[5] 7.1m[4] 8g[5] 8s 10v p10m[5] Nov 3] good-topped gelding: useful performer: improved when close third to Mafaaz in minor event at Kempton on reappearance: below form after: stays 9f: acts on polytrack and good to firm ground. *R. Hannon* **103**

SOHO SECRETS 3 b.f. Lucky Owners (NZ) 122 – Meritxell (IRE) (Thatching 131) [2009 p7g 8.3f[5] 8m[5] Jun 18] tall, lengthy filly: fourth foal: closely related to winner in USA by Danehill and half-sister to winner in Sweden by King's Best: dam, French 1½m winner, half-sister to very smart 1m/1¼m performer Almushtarak: form in maidens (fair) only on second outing: likely to be suited by 1¼m: sold £800. *M. Johnston* **66**

SOHO THEATRE 2 b.c. (Jan 20) Indian Ridge 123 – Costa Brava (IRE) (Sadler's Wells (USA) 132) [2009 7g 7.1m[5] p7g[3] 8d Oct 27] good-topped colt: fair maiden: should be suited by 1m+: acts on polytrack and good to firm going. *D. R. C. Elsworth* **68**

SOHRAAB 5 b.g. Erhaab (USA) 127 – Riverine (Risk Me (FR) 127) [2009 105: 5.2s[2] 5.1m* 6m[4] 6m 5.1m[4] 6.1g[2] 5m[2] 5.2m 5g Oct 4] compact gelding: useful performer: won handicap at Chester in May by 1¼ lengths from Strike Up The Band: good efforts when in frame in listed races fifth to seventh starts, beaten head by Exceptional Art at Beverley on final occasion: best at 5f/6f: acts on all-weather, soft and good to firm going. *H. Morrison* **107**

SOKOKE 8 ch.g. Compton Place 125 – Sally Green (IRE) 79 (Common Grounds 118) [2009 –: 5m 5m Jul 11] workmanlike gelding: no longer of any account. *D. A. Nolan* **–**

SOLAR GRAPHITE (IRE) 3 b.g. Rock of Gibraltar (IRE) 133 – Solar Crystal (IRE) 110 (Alzao (USA) 117) [2009 64: 9.7g* 11m[3] 12d[2] 12m[4] 12m[5] 11.7g[6] Oct 21] close-coupled gelding: fairly useful handicapper: won at Folkestone in April: good placed efforts next 2 starts: stays 1½m: unraced on extremes of going: sold 16,000 gns and joined R. Hennessy in Ireland. *J. L. Dunlop* **80**

SOLAR SPIRIT (IRE) 4 b.g. Invincible Spirit (IRE) 121 – Misaayef (USA) 82 (Swain (IRE) 134) [2009 87: 6g[2] 6m[3] 6m[3] 5d 6d[5] 5v[3] 6d[5] 6m 6.1m[6] p7f[5] Oct 14] tall, good-topped gelding: fairly useful handicapper: in-and-out form in 2009: seems best at 5f/6f: acts on any going: tried in cheekpieces/visor. *J. J. Quinn* **92**

SOLAS ALAINN (IRE) 4 b.g. Fantastic Light (USA) 134 – Littlepacepaddocks (IRE) 110 (Accordion) [2009 68: 12f[3] 14m[3] 12d 16.2g[4] 12.1m[6] 12.5m[3] 13.8g[3] 14.8g[3] 14g Aug 7] rangy gelding: fair maiden handicapper: stays 2m: acts on firm ground: blinkered/visored 5 of last 6 starts: ungenuine. *M. Johnston* **79 §**

SOLDIER SOLDIER 3 ch.g. Tobougg (IRE) 125 – Bijan (IRE) 75 (Mukaddamah (USA) 125) [2009 –: 7g 8m 7f[5] 7m Sep 15] good-bodied gelding: no form: tried visored/tongue tied. *J. R. Jenkins* **–**

SOLEMN 4 b.g. Pivotal 124 – Pious 74 (Bishop of Cashel 122) [2009 64d: 5g 5.1g* 5m* 5m[2] 5.1v* 5f* 5g[3] 5.7g[4] 6m[5] 6d[2] 5.1d* f5m[2] Nov 6] workmanlike gelding: fairly useful handicapper: much improved in 2009, winning at Chepstow (claimer) in June, Beverley and Chepstow in July, Windsor in August and Nottingham in October: best at 5f/6f: acts on all-weather and any turf going: usually in cheekpieces/blinkers. *J. M. Bradley* **82**

SOLENT RIDGE (IRE) 4 b.g. Namid 128 – Carrozzina 70 (Vettori (IRE) 119) [2009 95d: p8g[4] p8.6g[3] p8g[4] p8g* 8g p8g 8m 10f[6] 8m p8m Sep 30] good-topped gelding: fairly useful handicapper: won at Lingfield in March: well below form after: stays 1m: acts on polytrack and good to firm going: tried blinkered/in cheekpieces. *J. S. Moore* **81 d**

SOLE POWER 2 b.g. (Mar 18) Kyllachy 129 – Demerger (USA) (Distant View (USA) 126) [2009 6d[3] 5v[2] 6m[3] 5g p5g* p6g[4] Nov 18] £32,000Y: third foal: half-brother to 7-y-o Cornus: dam unraced: useful performer: landed odds easily in maiden at Dundalk in November: also ran well previous 3 outings, including ½-length third to Midnight Martini in sales race at York (met trouble briefly): likely to prove best at 5f/6f (very free final start): acts on polytrack, heavy and good to firm ground: gelded after final outing. *Edward Lynam, Ireland* **99**

SOLICITOR 2 ch.c. (Mar 24) Halling (USA) 133 – Tolzey (USA) 94 (Rahy (USA) 115) [2009 8d[4] f7g* Nov 17] second foal: dam, 2-y-o 6f winner, granddaughter of high-class sprinter/miler Golden Opinion: promising in maidens, better effort when winning at Southwell by 9 lengths from Dandarrell: will stay 1m: sure to improve again. *M. Johnston* **85 p**

SOLICITUDE 6 ch.m. Bertolini (USA) 125 – Sibilant (Selkirk (USA) 129) [2009 –, a67: f7d^6 p7m^3 p7g Jan 14] workmanlike mare: just modest performer at 6 yrs: best at 7f: acts on all-weather (no form on turf): wears cheekpieces (tried blinkered): usually held up. *D. Haydn Jones* – a63

SOLIS 3 b.g. Josr Algarhoud (IRE) 118 – Passiflora 75 (Night Shift (USA)) [2009 54: f6d^6 7.1m* 6s^2 7.1m^3 May 19] strong gelding: fair performer: won handicap at Warwick in April: stays 7f: acts on soft and good to firm going. *J. J. Quinn* 67

SOLIS (GER) 6 b.g. In The Wings 128 – Seringa (GER) 102 (Acatenango (GER) 127) [2009 74: 12.4d 10g 11.1g Sep 21] fair at 5 yrs: well held in 2009: tried visored. *P. Monteith* –

SOLITARY 3 b.f. Lahib (USA) 129 – Bond Solitaire 66 (Atraf 116) [2009 83: 7d^6 6.1g p6g Sep 19] angular filly: fair maiden: well below form last 2 starts: will prove best at 5f/6f: sold 3,200 gns. *H. Candy* 75

SOLO ATTEMPT 3 b.f. Anabaa (USA) 130 – Sonja's Faith (IRE) 116 (Sharp Victor (USA) 114) [2009 85: p8g^3 Jul 1] good-bodied filly: has scope: fairly useful performer: should stay 9f: acts on polytrack and good to firm going: sold 30,000 gns. *M. Botti* 89

SOLO CHOICE 3 b.g. Needwood Blade 117 – Top of The Class (IRE) 69 (Rudimentary (USA) 118) [2009 63: p9.2g^2 f8g^2 p11g^2 p10g 11.6g^4 12.3m f12g^6 10g p10g 10g p9.5g f12g Nov 17] rangy gelding: fair maiden: below form later in 2009, leaving D. Flood after eighth start: stays 1½m: acts on all-weather: usually blinkered of late. *I. W. McInnes* 68 d

SOLO RIVER 4 b.f. Averti (IRE) 117 – Surakarta 67 (Bin Ajwaad (IRE) 119) [2009 72: p10g^4 p10g^2 10m p10g^4 10m^2 10m* 10.2f^4 10.1m^4 8f^3 8g^2 p10g^6 Nov 25] sturdy filly: fair performer: won claimer at Leicester in June: stays 1¼m: acts on polytrack and firm ground. *P. J. Makin* 72

SOME SUNNY DAY 3 ch.f. Where Or When (IRE) 124 – Palace Street (USA) 103 (Secreto (USA) 128) [2009 p8g^5 p8g^6 8.3m^2 8m^2 8.1m^4 p10m^2 p10m* 10m* 10.4g^5 p10g^3 Oct 29] smallish, angular filly: half-sister to several winners, notably high-class sprinter Sakhee's Secret (by Sakhee): dam 6f/7f winner: fairly useful handicapper: won at Lingfield in August and Ffos Las in September: stays 1¼m: acts on polytrack and good to firm going: signs of temperament. *H. Morrison* 82

SOMETHING (IRE) 7 b.g. Trans Island 119 – Persian Polly 99 (Persian Bold 123) [2009 100: p7g* 6g^3 7f 6.3g^5 6g 7g^5 p6g 7.2m 7m^3 7m^5 7g^6 Oct 10] big, strong, lengthy gelding: useful handicapper: won at Kempton in April: creditable efforts after at Epsom (1½ lengths third to Baldemar, hampered), the Curragh (fifth to Mountain Coral) and Ascot (third to Advanced) second/fourth/ninth starts: effective at 6f/7f: acts on polytrack, good to firm and good to soft going: tried tongue tied: in cheekpieces last 3 starts: not entirely straightforward. *D. Nicholls* 103

SOMETHING PERFECT (USA) 3 b.f. Perfect Soul (IRE) 122 – Lady Angharad (IRE) 95 (Tenby 125) [2009 82: p8g^3 8m^3 8m^3 10m^2 8.1d p8f Oct 14] tall filly: fairly useful handicapper: stays 1¼m: acts on polytrack and good to firm going: tried visored: signs of temperament (flashes tail): sold 23,000 gns, sent to Qatar. *H. R. A. Cecil* 87

SOME TIME GOOD (IRE) 3 br. or gr.g. Clodovil (IRE) 116 – El Alma (IRE) (Goldmark (USA) 113) [2009 73: p12g^4 11.6m 12.1s^6 10s May 27] leggy gelding: just modest maiden at 3 yrs: barely stays 1½m: acts on polytrack and good to firm ground: sold £2,300 and joined Miss J. Davis. *M. R. Channon* 59

SOMETSUKE 3 br.g. Efisio 120 – Peyto Princess 85 (Bold Arrangement 127) [2009 p7g 5.7g^2 p7.1g^3 6.1d Oct 15] 16,000Y: lengthy gelding: second foal: half-brother to 5f winner Hurricane Hen (by Compton Place): dam, 6f winner, half-sister to useful sprinters Abbajabba and Blue Iris: fair maiden: best effort at 5.7f on good ground: tongue tied. *P. J. Makin* 76

SOMEWHERE ELSE 2 b.f. (Apr 26) Firebreak 125 – Royal Future (IRE) (Royal Academy (USA) 130) [2009 5m 7d 5f^5 f5g Sep 29] half-sister to several winners, including 3-y-o Dubai Legend and 6-y-o They All Laughed: dam unraced half-sister to very smart miler Where Or When: no form. *A. Berry* –

SOMMERSTURM (GER) 5 b.g. Tiger Hill (IRE) 127 – Sommernacht (GER) (Monsun (GER) 124) [2009 –: f12g p12.2g p12g^5 f12g f12g Jul 27] one-time useful performer in Germany: just modest form in 2009, trained by A. Stringer on reappearance: stays 11f: raced on all-weather and good ground or softer. *B. J. Curley* 64

John Smith's Northumberland Plate (Heritage Handicap), Newcastle— the outcome turns on jockeyship, as Som Tala is allowed to dictate a sedate pace; he holds off Wells Lyrical and top weight Friston Forest who are also prominent throughout

SOM TALA 6 ch.g. Fantastic Light (USA) 134 – One of The Family 73 (Alzao (USA) 117) [2009 104: 18.7m 20m^{5} 16.1d* 21g 14m 14v 18m 16d^{6} Oct 28] workmanlike gelding: useful handicapper: won John Smith's Northumberland Plate at Newcastle (dictated) in June by ¾ length from Wells Lyrical: below form after: stays 21f: acts on polytrack, firm and good to soft going: usually up with pace. *M. R. Channon* **102**

SONARA (IRE) 5 b.g. Peintre Celebre (USA) 137 – Fay (IRE) 64 (Polish Precedent (USA) 131) [2009 15.8m^{2} 14m^{5} 16.1m^{2} Jun 25] strong, good-bodied gelding: fair handicapper: stays 2m: acts on firm ground. *J. Howard Johnson* **79**

SONATE DE LA TOUR (FR) 4 b.f. Timboroa 121 – Damanka (IRE) (Slip Anchor 136) [2009 12.1v Jul 24] €3,500Y: sixth foal: half-sister to 7f winner Durandana (by Selkirk) and French 1½m winner Danaw (by Lomitas): dam, maiden, half-sister to useful stayer Bondstone: raced only in claimers in France (had several trainers), winning at Bordeaux and Saint-Cloud in 2007: little impact in juvenile hurdles for D. Brace in 2008: well held in amateur handicap on British debut: stays 1m: acts on soft ground. *J. L. Flint* **–**

SONGFUL (IRE) 3 b. or br.f. Captain Rio 122 – Trillie 86 (Never So Bold 135) [2009 p8g^{5} p8g^{6} p7g 8g^{6} 6d 7s 6m p8g Sep 2] 8,000Y: second living foal: dam 2-y-o 6f/7f winner: poor maiden on balance: stays 1m: acts on polytrack. *Pat Eddery* **43**

SONG OF MY HEART (IRE) 2 ch.f. (Mar 12) Footstepsinthesand 120 – Catch The Moon (IRE) (Peintre Celebre (USA) 137) [2009 6g^{6} 6v* 6s* 6m^{6} Oct 2] €47,000F, €55,000Y: tall filly: has scope: second foal: half-sister to useful 2008 2-y-o 6f winner Catskill Mountain (by One Cool Cat): dam French 9f winner out of useful French performer up to 1¼m Sensitivity: useful form: won maiden at the Curragh in August and listed contest there (by 1½ lengths from Wrong Answer) in September: well below form in Cheveley Park Stakes at Newmarket (firmer ground/hung right from before halfway): will stay 7f+: acts on heavy ground: type to do better still at 3 yrs. *David Wachman, Ireland* **107 p**

SONG OF PARKES 2 b.f. (Mar 21) Fantastic Light (USA) 134 – My Melody Parkes 102 (Teenoso (USA) 135) [2009 7.2v^{4} Oct 31] sister to fairly useful 2006 2-y-o 6f winner Fantasy Parkes and half-sister to 6-y-o Bajan Parkes: dam, 5f winner (including at 2 yrs), half-sister to useful sprinters Summerhill Parkes and Lucky Parkes: 14/1, signs of ability when well-held fourth in maiden at Ayr: capable of better. *E. J. Alston* **– p**

SONG OF PRAISE 3 b.f. Compton Place 125 – Greensand 96 (Green Desert (USA) 127) [2009 66: p7g^{4} p6g* p6g* p6g^{2} 6f p6g^{2} 5m 6g p6m^{6} p7f p6m^{5} p6g Oct 20] workmanlike filly: fairly useful handicapper on all-weather, fair on turf: won at Kempton in February and Wolverhampton in March: best at 5f/6f: acts on polytrack, firm and good to soft going. *M. Blanshard* **67 a80**

SONG TO THE MOON (IRE) 2 b.f. (Feb 10) Oratorio (IRE) 128 – Jojeema (Barathea (IRE) 127) [2009 7m 8g Oct 23] 46,000F, 26,000Y: well-made filly: second foal: **66 p**

half-sister to 2008 2-y-o 1m winner Hum Cat (by One Cool Cat): dam unraced half-sister to very smart performer up to 1½m Riyadian out of Irish Oaks winner Knight's Baroness: reportedly fractured a tibia early in year: much better effort (stiff task in sales race on debut) when seventh to Modeyra in maiden at Doncaster: should improve again. *A. M. Balding*

SONHADOR 3 b.g. Compton Place 125 – Fayre Holly (IRE) 57 (Fayruz 116) [2009 73: 5.3m^{6} 6g p6g p5.1g 6m p5m^{2} p6m* p6g p6f^{6} p5g^{6} Dec 31] useful-looking gelding: modest performer nowadays: won handicap at Kempton in October (gelded after): effective at 5f/6f: acts on polytrack and firm ground: tried blinkered. *G. Prodromou* **63**

SONIC ANTHEM (USA) 7 b.g. Royal Anthem (USA) 135 – Whisperifyoudare (USA) (Red Ransom (USA)) [2009 12.1g f12m Nov 12] tall, good-topped gelding: lightly raced and just poor on Flat nowadays (modest hurdler): stays 11f: acts on fibresand and firm ground. *B. D. Leavy* **47**

SONNENGOLD (GER) 8 b.m. Java Gold (USA) – Standing Ovation (ITY) (Law Society (USA) 130) [2009 61§: 16.2v^{5} Jul 24] modest performer: below form sole outing on Flat in 2009: stays 2m: acts on soft and good to firm ground: has been blinkered: ungenuine: poor hurdler nowadays. *B. J. Llewellyn* **– §**

SONNING GATE 3 b.g. Desert Sun 120 – Sunley Scent 85 (Wolfhound (USA) 126) [2009 94p: 8.1m^{3} 8.3g^{4} 8.1v May 23] fairly useful performer: stays 1m: acts on polytrack and good to firm going: held up. *D. R. C. Elsworth* **93**

SONNY G (IRE) 2 ch.c. (Apr 22) Desert Sun 120 – Broughton Zest 71§ (Colonel Collins (USA) 122) [2009 7m 6m^{6} p7g p7g^{5} Dec 31] heavy-bodied colt: poor form in maidens: bred to be suited by 1¼m+. *J. R. Best* **49 +**

SONNY PARKIN 7 b.g. Spinning World (USA) 130 – No Miss Kris (USA) (Capote (USA)) [2009 82: 8m^{6} 8m* 8d 8g^{6} 10d 8g 8m^{6} p8g p10g Nov 25] tall, leggy gelding: fair handicapper: won apprentice event at Newmarket in June: largely below form after: stays 1¼m: acts on polytrack, soft and good to firm ground: usually wears headgear: held up: ungenuine. *J. Pearce* **76 §**

SONNY RED (IRE) 5 b.g. Redback 116 – Magic Melody 62 (Petong 126) [2009 112: 5.2s^{4} 5g 5m* 6d 5.4m^{6} 5d 6m^{5} 7m Sep 26] well-made gelding: good walker: useful handicapper: won at Ascot in July by head from Group Therapy: best effort after when 2 lengths fifth to Jimmy Styles in Ayr Gold Cup: has form at 1m, best at 5f/6f: acts on soft and good to firm going: tried in cheekpieces. *D. Nicholls* **109**

SONNY SAM (IRE) 4 b.g. Black Sam Bellamy (IRE) 121 – Purple Risks (FR) 80 (Take Risks (FR) 116) [2009 62: 16m^{2} 14m^{3} 18g May 14] smallish, strong gelding: modest maiden handicapper: stays 2m: raced on polytrack and good to firm going. *R. A. Fahey* **61**

SONOFDON 2 ch.g. (Apr 27) Stage Pass 108 – Moore Appeal (Homo Sapien 121) [2009 6m Aug 22] leggy gelding: 100/1 and on edge, soundly beaten in maiden at Ripon. *C. W. Moore* **–**

SON OF MONSIEUR 3 ch.g. Monsieur Bond (IRE) 120 – Triple Tricks (IRE) 70 (Royal Academy (USA) 130) [2009 8m^{6} 7f^{4} 10m 12d 10m p7.1g p8.6g^{4} p9.5g Dec 19] leggy gelding: modest maiden: stays 8.6f: acts on polytrack and good to firm ground. *G. R. Oldroyd* **54**

SON OF MY HEART (USA) 4 b. or br.g. Dynaformer (USA) – Sophie My Love (USA) (Danzig (USA)) [2009 69p: 10m f11g 10m^{3} p10g^{3} Jun 20] well-made gelding: fair maiden: stays 11f: acts on all-weather and good to firm going: tried blinkered: gelded after final start, then sold £6,500 in October. *P. F. I. Cole* **69**

SON OF THE CAT (USA) 3 b.g. Tale of The Cat (USA) 113 – Dixieland Gal (USA) (Dixieland Band (USA)) [2009 93: p7g 6m^{5} p6g^{6} p6g^{4} 6m* p7g^{5} 6m^{3} 6d^{2} p6g^{2} p6g^{4} Nov 21] neat gelding: useful performer: won 4-runner handicap at Lingfield in August by 5 lengths from Kingswinford: creditable efforts last 4 starts, beaten a neck by Global City in minor event then 3¾ lengths when fourth to Jaconet in listed race, both at Lingfield, on last 2: best at 6f: acts on polytrack, good to firm and good to soft going: tongue tied. *B. Gubby* **103**

SOOPACAL (IRE) 4 b.g. Captain Rio 122 – Fiddes (IRE) 52 (Alzao (USA) 117) [2009 97: p6g^{3} p6g p6g^{6} p5.1g f5g^{4} Mar 26] sturdy, deep-girthed gelding: just fairly useful performer at 4 yrs: said to have bled final start: best at 5f/6f: acts on all-weather and heavy going: tried blinkered/visored. *B. Smart* **85**

SOPHIE'S BEAU (USA) 2 b.g. (Mar 21) Stormy Atlantic (USA) – Lady Buttercup (USA) (Meadowlake (USA)) [2009 7g^{5} 6m^{2} p6g^{4} Oct 23] $77,000Y, 46,000 2-y-o: fourth **79**

foal: half-brother to winners in US by Omega Code and Forest Camp: dam, US maiden, half-sister to Beresford Stakes winner Victory Piper: easily best effort in maidens when ½-length second to Side Glance at Newmarket: free-going sort: gelded after final start. *B. J. Meehan*

SOPHIST (IRE) 6 b.g. Montjeu (IRE) 137 – Cordon Bleu (USA) (D'Accord (USA)) [2009 53: f12g³ Feb 19] modest maiden handicapper: stays 9.5f: acts on polytrack: usually in cheekpieces/blinkers. *Evan Williams* **52**

SOPRANIST 3 b.c. Singspiel (IRE) 133 – Trefoil 111 (Kris 135) [2009 10m* 10m 10d² 9.9g² Jul 30] lengthy, good-topped colt: half-brother to several winners, including smart 7f/1m winner Three Graces (by Peintre Celebre) and useful French 1¼m/1½m winner Trefula (by Rainbow Quest): dam French 10.5f/11f winner: smart form: won maiden at Newmarket in April: much improved when ¾-length second in handicaps there (to Laaheb) and Goodwood (quite valuable event, behind Roman Republic): raced only around 1¼m: unraced on extremes of going: has joined Godolphin. *J. H. M. Gosden* **110**

SORREL POINT 6 b.h. Bertolini (USA) 125 – Lightning Princess (Puissance 110) [2009 –: 8.1g 7g 6s 6m⁶ 6m⁵ p5.1g³ 5.2d p6g³ Nov 13] modest maiden handicapper: stays 8.2f: acts on polytrack and good to soft going: visored last 3 starts: usually tongue tied: none too consistent. *H. J. Collingridge* **61**

SORREL RIDGE (IRE) 3 ch.g. Namid 128 – She Legged It (IRE) 66 (Cape Cross (IRE) 129) [2009 57: p6g⁵ p6g² p5.1g² p5g p6g 6m⁴ 5g⁵ 7f May 12] leggy gelding: modest maiden: best at 5f/6f: acts on polytrack and good to soft ground: usually wears cheekpieces/blinkers: tried tongue tied. *M. G. Quinlan* **57**

SORRENTO MOON (IRE) 5 b.m. Tagula (IRE) 116 – Honey For Money (IRE) 72 (Alzao (USA) 117) [2009 53: 12.4s 12m 14.1m Jun 20] close-coupled mare: poor performer nowadays: stays 9.8f: acts on soft going. *G. A. Harker* **46**

SORY 2 b.g. (Jan 27) Sakhee (USA) 136 – Rule Britannia 89 (Night Shift (USA)) [2009 8d Oct 27] 16/1 and very green, tailed-off last in maiden at Yarmouth: sold 7,500 gns. *L. M. Cumani* **–**

SOSTENUTO 2 ch.f. (Jan 15) Compton Place 125 – Hufflepuff (IRE) 102 (Desert King (IRE) 129) [2009 6m Oct 26] 11,000Y, €8,000 2-y-o: first foal: dam 5f and (at 2 yrs) 6f winner: 66/1, always behind in maiden at Leicester. *T. H. Caldwell* **–**

SO SUBLIME 4 b.g. Bertolini (USA) 125 – Petalite 63 (Petong 126) [2009 67d: p7.1g f7g f7g p5.1g⁴ p5.1g² f6g p6g p9.5g f7g 9.8m 6g May 29] regressive form: stays 7f: acts on all-weather: often blinkered/visored: sometimes tongue tied. *M. C. Chapman* **51 d**

SO SURREAL (IRE) 2 b.f. (Feb 22) Avonbridge 123 – Secret Circle (Magic Ring (IRE) 115) [2009 5m⁶ p6m³ 6g 6m 6.5m p6g* p6m p7m⁵ Nov 27] 9,500F, £24,000Y: compact filly: closely related to 1m winner Ambrosiano (by Averti) and half-sister to several winners, including 6-y-o Ektimaal and useful 5f (in UAE)/7f winner Secret Place (by Compton Place): dam unraced half-sister to high-class 1m/1¼m performer Bijou d'Inde: fair performer: won maiden at Wolverhampton in October: stays 7f: acts on polytrack and good to firm ground: blinkered last 4 starts. *G. L. Moore* **74**

SOTELO 7 ch.h. Monsun (GER) 124 – Seringa (GER) 102 (Acatenango (GER) 127) [2009 11.8d⁵ p9.5g Oct 10] first foal: dam German 9f/11f winner: fairly useful performer for A. Wohler in Germany in 2006, winning handicap at Cologne: just fair form in Britain in 2009: stays 11f: acts on soft ground: has been blinkered. *S. Gollings* **69**

SOTIK STAR (IRE) 6 b.g. Elnadim (USA) 128 – Crystal Springs (IRE) 79 (Kahyasi 130) [2009 83: p8g² p8g p8g p8.6g⁴ 8g² p8.6m* Aug 21] strong gelding: fair performer: won handicap at Wolverhampton in August: stays 8.6f: acts on polytrack and good to firm going: tried in tongue strap/cheekpieces: tends to hang. *K. A. Morgan* **74**

SOTO 6 b.g. Averti (IRE) 117 – Belle of The Blues (IRE) (Blues Traveller (IRE) 119) [2009 74: f6g 6f⁶ 6f³ 6g² 5m² 6d² 5.9g⁴ 6m⁴ 6m³ 5.9d⁵ 7m⁴ 7.2m² 7g Oct 17] small, leggy gelding: fair performer: stays easy 7f: acts on fibresand, firm and soft going: tried visored, often blinkered. *M. W. Easterby* **67**

SOUL CITY (IRE) 3 b.c. Elusive City (USA) 117 – Savage (IRE) 98 (Polish Patriot (USA) 128) [2009 109: 8v³ 8m Jun 16] strong colt: has round action: smart performer: ran well when 6¼ lengths third to Mastercraftsman in Irish 2000 Guineas at the Curragh on reappearance, keeping on: eased off when beaten in St James's Palace Stakes at Royal Ascot only subsequent start: stays 1m: acts on heavy going: races close up. *R. Hannon* **114**

SOUL HEAVEN 2 b.g. (Jan 16) Oratorio (IRE) 128 – Pilgrim Spirit (USA) 66 (Saint Ballado (CAN)) [2009 5.5m⁴ p6g* 6m* Jul 11] well-made gelding: third foal: dam, **85 p**

maiden who stayed 1¾m, out of sister to dams of high-class miler Aragorn and very smart sprinter One Cool Cat: progressive form, winning maiden at Lingfield in May and nursery at Ascot (beat Step In Time by neck, gelded after) in July: will stay 7f+: likely to improve further. *M. L. W. Bell*

SOUL MURMUR (IRE) 4 br.g. Indian Ridge 123 – My Potters (USA) (Irish River (FR) 131) [2009 78: p7.1g 7m Oct 13] tall gelding: fair maiden at 3 yrs: well held in 2009: tried blinkered: tongue tied at 4 yrs: sent to Italy. *F. Sheridan* **–**

SOUL SINGER 3 br.f. Where Or When (IRE) 124 – Tancholo (So Factual (USA) 120) [2009 p11g^{6} p11g* p12g p12g 11.5m 11.6m^{3} 12.1g^{3} 11.7g^{3} p16m^{4} p13.9g p12g Nov 11] 6,000Y: tall, angular filly: third foal: dam once-raced half-sister to dam of Sussex Stakes winner Reel Buddy: modest performer: won maiden at Kempton in February: barely stays 2m: acts on polytrack and good to firm ground. *J. G. Portman* **56**

SOUL SISTA (IRE) 3 b.f. City On A Hill (USA) 114 – Fraamtastic 54 (Fraam 114) [2009 80: 6m 6v^{5} 6s 6d 7g^{4} 8.3v^{6} p8m Nov 29] lengthy filly: just modest handicapper at 3 yrs: stays 1m, effective at shorter: acts on heavy ground (not on good to firm): tried blinkered. *J. L. Spearing* **62**

SOUL STATION (FR) 2 b.g. (Apr 20) Starcraft (NZ) 128 – Allumette (Rainbow Quest (USA) 134) [2009 p7m^{5} 8d* Oct 12] 12,000Y: fourth foal: half-brother to 3-y-o Granny McPhee: dam unraced out of smart 1¼m winner Flame Valley: much better effort in maidens when winning at Salisbury by 2 lengths from Flouncing, making all: will stay 1¼m. *R. Charlton* **79**

SOUNDBYTE 4 b.g. Beat All (USA) 120 – Gloaming 74 (Celtic Swing 138) [2009 83: p12g^{3} 14m^{3} 14.1g^{3} 18g 14.1g^{5} 12g^{5} 11.9f 11m* 11.9d^{5} p12g^{6} 14.6g^{4} 13.8v^{2} Nov 3] angular gelding: fair handicapper nowadays: won amateur event at Goodwood in September: should stay 2m: acts on polytrack, heavy and good to firm going: tried visored. *J. Gallagher* **78**

SOUNDS OF JUPITER (IRE) 3 ch.g. Galileo (IRE) 134 – Sena Desert 89 (Green Desert (USA) 127) [2009 60p: p11g* p12.2g^{2} 12m^{4} 14.1f 12.1g 11.7g^{3} 11.9f* 12m* p11g Sep 4] well-made gelding: fairly useful performer: won maiden at Kempton in January (left E. Vaughan 36,000 gns after) and handicaps at Brighton and Folkestone 6 days apart in August: should stay 1¾m: acts on polytrack, yet to race on ground softer than good on turf: sold 58,000 gns, joined Charles Byrne in Ireland. *D. M. Simcock* **89**

SOUNDS OF THUNDER 2 b.f. (Feb 6) Tobougg (IRE) 125 – Distant Music (Darshaan 133) [2009 7m^{6} 7f^{5} 7.1g^{4} 7g^{5} 8.3d p8.6g^{4} p8.6g* Nov 30] 8,000F, 11,000Y: compact filly: seventh foal: half-sister to several winners, including fairly useful 10.5f to 2m winner Desert Island Disc (by Turtle Island) and 1m (at 2 yrs)/1¼m winner Rock Lobster (by Desert Sun): dam unraced: fair performer: won nursery at Wolverhampton: stays 8.6f: acts on polytrack, best turf efforts on good going. *H. J. L. Dunlop* **72**

SOUR MASH (IRE) 2 b.c. (Mar 24) Danehill Dancer (IRE) 117 – Landmark (USA) (Arch (USA) 127) [2009 8m Oct 16] 140,000Y: good-bodied colt: first foal: dam, US 2-y-o 1m winner, sister to Canadian/US Grade 1 9f/1¼m winner Arravale: 18/1 and very green, always behind in maiden at Newmarket: capable of better. *L. M. Cumani* **– p**

SOUTER POINT (USA) 3 b. or br.g. Giant's Causeway (USA) 132 – Wires Crossed (USA) (Caller I D (USA)) [2009 86p: 10g^{2} 10m^{4} 9.9g^{3} 12.6m^{2} p12g* 10.2m^{3} 10.9g^{2} 10.2m^{3} 11.6g^{2} 11.8m^{2} Oct 6] tall gelding: fairly useful performer: won maiden at Lingfield in July: good efforts in handicaps after: stays easy 1½m: raced only on polytrack and good/good to firm ground: travels strongly but finds little: sold 55,000 gns. *R. Charlton* **91**

SOUTH AFRICAN GOLD (USA) 2 ch.c. (Feb 17) Johannesburg (USA) 127 – Coesse Gold (USA) (Seeking The Gold (USA)) [2009 6m p6m p7.1g^{4} Dec 28] quite attractive colt: fair maiden: easily best effort when 1½ lengths fourth to Capricornus at Wolverhampton: will stay 1m. *J. M. P. Eustace* **66**

SOUTH AFRICAN (USA) 3 gr. or ro.f. Johannesburg (USA) 127 – River Cache (USA) (Unbridled (USA) 128) [2009 p5.1g^{2} p6g^{2} Sep 12] $150,000Y: third foal: half-sister to 2 winners in USA, including 6f minor stakes winner Sentimental Charm (by Silver Charm): dam unraced: fair form when runner-up in maidens at Wolverhampton, showing plenty of speed: capable of further improvement. *M. A. Magnusson* **71 p**

SOUTHANDWEST (IRE) 5 ch.g. Titus Livius (FR) 115 – Cheviot Indian (IRE) 71 (Indian Ridge 123) [2009 93: p7.1g* p7g^{3} p7g p7.1g^{2} p7g^{3} p8g p7g p7g p8g p7g 7g 8.1g 8.3m^{6} p7g^{2} p7.1g^{3} p8.6g^{5} p8m^{3} Dec 30] strong, lengthy gelding: fairly useful **94 §**

handicapper: won at Wolverhampton in January: best at 7f: acts on polytrack, firm and good to soft going: tried in cheekpieces: ungenuine. *J. S. Moore*

SOUTH CAPE 6 b.g. Cape Cross (IRE) 129 – Aunt Ruby (USA) 67 (Rubiano (USA)) [2009 97: 8.5g 7f 7m^6 8g 7.1g 7m^3 8m 7g 8.3g* Oct 28] small, leggy gelding: just fairly useful handicapper in 2009: won at Nottingham in October: stays 8.3f: acts on polytrack and any turf going: effective with/without cheekpieces. *G. L. Moore* **89**

SOUTH EASTER (IRE) 3 ch.c. Galileo (IRE) 134 – Dance Treat (USA) 115 (Nureyev (USA) 131) [2009 8s^2 10.3m* 12f^6 Jun 19] 210,000Y: useful-looking colt: has scope: brother to Italian 1m to 1½m winner Jupiters Moon and half-brother to several winners, including useful 1m to 10.5f winner First Buddy (by Rock of Gibraltar): dam, won La Coupe (1¼m) and Prix de Flore (10.5f), out of half-sister to Derby winner Golden Fleece: useful form: best effort when winning Addleshaw Goddard Dee Stakes at Chester in May by head from Gitano Hernando: missed Derby reportedly due to coughing: found little in King Edward VII Stakes at Royal Ascot final start: should stay 1½m: acts on soft and good to firm going. *W. J. Haggas* **107**

SOUTHERN BREEZE 2 b.c. (Mar 19) Dansili 127 – Michelle Ma Belle (IRE) 90 (Shareef Dancer (USA) 135) [2009 p7m Nov 26] 20/1, tailed-off last in maiden at Kempton. *S. Kirk* **–**

SOUTHERN GODDESS (IRE) 2 b.f. (Mar 15) Avonbridge 123 – Northern Secret 70 (Sinndar (IRE) 134) [2009 5.1m 6.1g May 25] first foal: dam, maiden (stayed 7f), half-sister to smart French/US performer up to 1½m Northern Quest: little impact in seller/claimer. *P. D. Evans* **–**

SOUTHERN MISTRAL 4 b.g. Desert Prince (IRE) 130 – Hyperspectra 91 (Rainbow Quest (USA) 134) [2009 66: 9.7d 9.8m* p10g^5 10.2m May 9] compact gelding: fair performer: won seller at Ripon in April: stays 11f: acts on polytrack, good to firm and good to soft going: tried in cheekpieces (including for win): none too consistent: sold 5,000 gns in July. *Miss Gay Kelleway* **66**

Addleshaw Goddard Dee Stakes, Chester—South Easter (No.8), unlucky-in-running Gitano Hernando (right), Drumbeat (left) and Deposer (second left) fight out a tight finish

SOUTHERN WATERS (FR) 5 b.g. Sinndar (IRE) 134 – Due South 104 (Darshaan 133) [2009 12.5m Apr 3] modest form in bumper: last in seller at Musselburgh on Flat debut: sold £1,300, resold £1,200. *G. A. Swinbank* –

SOUTHOFFRANCE (IRE) 3 b.f. Dr Fong (USA) 128 – Mystery Solved (USA) 57 (Royal Academy (USA) 130) [2009 38: 11.9d p9.5g Nov 13] poor maiden: tried in cheekpieces/blinkers. *W. G. M. Turner* –

SOUTHWARK NEWSHAWK 2 ch.f. (Apr 13) Piccolo 121 – Be Bop Aloha 50 (Most Welcome 131) [2009 5.2g 5.2m f5g³ p6g 5.2g f5g³ f6m⁴ 5.2d³ 5.2g f5g⁵ 5m f5m⁴ Nov 11] 1,800F, 1,000Y: plain filly: first foal: dam, maiden, sister to smart 1m/1¼m winner Welcome Stranger: modest maiden: best form at 5f: acts on fibresand, good to firm and good to soft going: races up with pace. *Mrs C. A. Dunnett* **53**

SOUTH WING (IRE) 5 ch.g. In The Wings 128 – Desert Grouse (USA) (Gulch (USA)) [2009 85: 10g³ 12g² 16g 12s⁵ 12m 10s 16s Nov 5] lengthy gelding: fairly useful handicapper: left E. Griffin after fifth start: stays 1½m: acts on polytrack, soft and good to firm ground: tried blinkered. *Ms Caroline Hutchinson, Ireland* **89**

SOVENTO (GER) 5 ch.g. Kornado 120 – Second Game (GER) (Second Set (IRE) 127) [2009 12v 12g 12s⁶ 13.8g⁵ p12m² Dec 9] won twice in Germany at 4 yrs for W. Hickst: modest form in 2009: stays 1½m: acts on polytrack and soft going. *Shaun Harley, Ireland* **63**

SOVEREIGN REMEDY (USA) 3 ch.c. Elusive Quality (USA) – Lailani 122 (Unfuwain (USA) 131) [2009 p8g² 8.3g* 10.4g⁶ 8m³ 8g² 8.5m² f8g* 8.3m⁶ Oct 26] strong colt: third foal: half-brother to 2 winners in USA by A P Indy: dam, 1m to 1½m (Irish Oaks) winner, out of half-sister to very smart performer up to 1½m Faithful Son: useful performer: progressed well to win maiden at Nottingham in May and handicap at Southwell (beat Penitent 2¼ lengths) in October: stays 8.5f: acts on all-weather and good to firm ground. *Saeed bin Suroor* **101 a108**

SOVEREIGN SECURE (IRE) 2 ch.f. (Jan 26) Kyllachy 129 – Affaire Royale (IRE) 95 (Royal Academy (USA) 130) [2009 7g p6g 6m³ 6m 6g p5.1g⁶ p5g⁵ p5.1g⁴ Nov 13] €45,000F: rather leggy filly: third foal: half-sister to 5-y-o Dancing Duo: dam, 7f winner, out of close relation to US Grade 1 1m winner Quiet American: standout effort when third to Hold Your Colour in sales race at Ripon: stays 6f: acts on polytrack and good to firm going: in cheekpieces last 3 starts: usually races prominently. *L. Smyth, Ireland* **71**

SOVEREIGN SPIRIT (IRE) 7 b.g. Desert Prince (IRE) 130 – Sheer Spirit (IRE) 86 (Caerleon (USA) 132) [2009 66: 15.5g a11.5g² a11.5g a11.5g p16m Dec 1] leggy gelding: fair handicapper at best: trained by Mme L. Braem in Belgium first 4 starts in 2009 before rejoining former stable: stays 2m: acts on all-weather and good to soft going: often tongue tied: tried in cheekpieces. *C. Gordon* **?**

SOVEREIGNTY (JPN) 7 b.g. King's Best (USA) 132 – Calando (USA) 110 (Storm Cat (USA)) [2009 75: 6m 7m p5.1g⁵ f6g p8g* p8g* p8g⁵ f8g p7f⁵ p8m³ p8m 6g p8m⁶ p7m⁴ p7m p6f⁶ Dec 21] lengthy gelding: fair handicapper: won at Kempton in June and July: effective at 7f/1m: acts on all-weather and good to firm going: tried visored/in cheekpieces: tends to wander. *D. K. Ivory* **70**

SOVIET RHYTHM 3 b.f. Soviet Star (USA) 128 – Aldevonie 75 (Green Desert (USA) 127) [2009 62: 8m 7g 5m 5.9d⁴ Aug 19] compact filly: modest maiden: left G. M. Moore after second start: best form at 5f/6f on good ground or softer. *M. Dods* **50**

SOVIET SCEPTRE (IRE) 8 ch.g. Soviet Star (USA) 128 – Princess Sceptre (Cadeaux Genereux 131) [2009 66: 11.8m⁶ May 25] lengthy gelding: fair handicapper: below form only outing in 2009: effective at 1¼m to 1¾m: acts on polytrack, soft and good to firm going: wears cheekpieces/tongue tie: fair hurdler. *Tim Vaughan* –

SOVIETTA (IRE) 8 b.m. Soviet Star (USA) 128 – La Riveraine (USA) 90 (Riverman (USA) 131) [2009 58: f16d p12g p13.9g p12g Jun 3] modest at 7 yrs: well held in 2009: tried in cheekpieces: tongue tied. *Ian Williams* –

SOWAYLM 2 b.c. (Jan 21) Tobougg (IRE) 125 – Ameerat 116 (Mark of Esteem (IRE) 137) [2009 p8g* Nov 1] second foal: half-brother to fairly useful 7f winner Own Boss (by Seeking The Gold): dam 7f (at 2 yrs) and 1m (1000 Guineas) winner: 9/4, promising when winning maiden at Lingfield easily by 2¾ lengths from Perceptive, travelling strongly close up after slow start and not hard ridden: useful prospect. *Saeed bin Suroor* **90 p**

SPACE PIRATE 4 b.g. Bahamian Bounty 116 – Science Fiction (Starborough 126) [2009 58: p10m p10g 10m p10g 10g 8g Aug 5] leggy, close-coupled gelding: has round action: handicapper: well held in 2009 (gelded after second start): tried in headgear. *J. Pearce* –

Windsor Forest Stakes, Royal Ascot—a good battle between the Cheveley Park Stud pair, Spacious (right) and Heaven Sent; Eva's Request (left) gets the better of Chantilly Tiffany for third

SPACE STATION 3 b.g. Anabaa (USA) 130 – Spacecraft (USA) (Distant View (USA) 126) [2009 8g4 8g6 p7g 7d2 7m4 p6g5 p7g4 p6f2 p7m5 Dec 30] stocky gelding: first foal: dam, second at 5.5f/6.5f in France, closely related to smart French/US performer up to 1m Etoile Montante: fairly useful maiden: left P. Bary in France 15,000 gns after second start: stays 1m: acts on polytrack. *S. Dow* **80**

SPACIOUS 4 b.f. Nayef (USA) 129 – Palatial 101 (Green Desert (USA) 127) [2009 113: 8.5g3 8m* 8g3 9.9d 8m3 Oct 3] big, rangy filly: good sort: smart performer: better than ever when winning Windsor Forest Stakes at Royal Ascot by length from Heaven Sent: creditable effort otherwise in 2009 only when length third behind Goldikova in Falmouth Stakes at Newmarket next time: not disgraced at same track (Sun Chariot Stakes, third to Sahpresa) final start: should stay 1¼m: acts on firm and good to soft going: races prominently nowadays: stays in training. *J. R. Fanshawe* **115**

SPANISH ACCLAIM 2 b.g. (Apr 7) Acclamation 118 – Spanish Gold 82 (Vettori (IRE) 119) [2009 5.2s 5f2 5.7f 6m Aug 24] £90,000Y: good-bodied gelding: second foal: half-brother to 4-y-o Spanish Bounty: dam 8.5f winner: easily best effort when second to Russian Rock in maiden at Salisbury: very temperamental after: needs treating with caution. *J. G. Portman* **74 §**

SPANISH ACE 8 b.g. First Trump 118 – Spanish Heart 86 (King of Spain 121) [2009 55: p7.1g6 p6g p5.1g4 p5g4 p6g5 p5.1m6 p5g3 p5.1g6 5.7m 5.1g Jun 22] rather leggy, close-coupled gelding: poor performer nowadays: effective at 5f/6f: acts on polytrack, firm and good to soft going: usually wears headgear. *J. M. Bradley* **49**

SPANISH BOUNTY 4 b.g. Bahamian Bounty 116 – Spanish Gold 82 (Vettori (IRE) 119) [2009 97: p6g6 6f 6d6 6m3 7m 7g4 7g 6.5m 7m Oct 3] good-topped gelding: useful performer: best efforts in 2009 when in frame in listed race at Salisbury (2 lengths third to Judd Street) and minor event at Goodwood (1¾ lengths fourth to Axiom): effective at 6f/7f: acts on good to firm and good to soft going: tried in cheekpieces: races prominently. *J. G. Portman* **101**

SPANISH CONQUEST 5 b.g. Hernando (FR) 127 – Sirena (GER) (Tejano (USA)) [2009 77: 15m2 Sep 29] tall, leggy, useful-looking gelding: fair handicapper: stayed easy 16.5f: acted on all-weather and good to firm going: fair hurdler, won 3 times in spring: dead. *P. J. Hobbs* **77**

SPANISH CROSS (IRE) 4 gr.f. Cape Cross (IRE) 129 – Espana 69 (Hernando (FR) 127) [2009 67: p12.2g 8g 10d5 10.1d3 p9.5g4 Nov 20] just modest maiden at 4 yrs: stays 1¼m: acts on heavy and good to firm going: blinkered once. *G. Prodromou* **59**

SPANISH CYGNET (USA) 3 b.f. El Corredor (USA) 123 – Dixie Dos (USA) (Dixieland Band (USA)) [2009 87: 7g 7g Aug 14] good-topped filly: fairly useful winner at 2 yrs: well held in handicaps both starts in 2009: stays 7f: acts on polytrack and good to firm going: sold 3,000 gns, joined M. Ramadan in UAE. *Mrs A. J. Perrett* **–**

SPANISH DUKE (IRE) 2 b.g. (Feb 12) Big Bad Bob (IRE) 118 – Spanish Lady (IRE) 61 (Bering 136) [2009 7m 7g5 7m4 8g2 7m* p8.6g* Oct 15] sixth foal: half-brother to 5-y-o Spanish Hidalgo and fairly useful/ungenuine 1½m winner Spanish Ridge (by Indian Ridge): dam, lightly-raced maiden, out of half-sister to Mtoto: fairly useful performer: won maiden at Brighton in September and nursery at Wolverhampton (improved again, beat Diam Queen ¾ length) in October: should be suited by 1¼m+: acts on polytrack and good to firm ground: will continue to progress. *J. L. Dunlop* **89 p**

SPANISH HIDALGO (IRE) 5 b.g. Night Shift (USA) – Spanish Lady (IRE) 61 (Bering 136) [2009 111: 12m³ 13.3d May 16] sturdy gelding: smart at 4 yrs: tongue tied, shaped as if amiss both starts in 2009: stays 15f: has form on good to firm going, races mainly on good or softer (acts on heavy). *J. L. Dunlop* –

SPANISH MOON (USA) 5 b.h. El Prado (IRE) 119 – Shining Bright 98 (Rainbow Quest (USA) 134) [2009 121: 12g² 12m* 12g* 12f⁴ 12g² Dec 13] **123**

'Horses are like people. I knew that with the proper treatment, you could make a horse do whatever you wanted him to do.' Clay Puett, the inventor of the electronic starting stalls, was responding to the considerable resistance he faced whilst developing his revolutionary product during the 'thirties, the general perception being that thoroughbreds were too temperamental to be confined in the moments before the start. The doubters were silenced after a trouble-free debut for the stalls in a twelve-runner race over five furlongs at Lansdowne Park in Vancouver during the summer of 1939. Every major track in the States switched to the electronic stalls over the next eighteen months, with Whirlaway lowering the course record when winning the Kentucky Derby in 1941, the first time the Churchill Downs showpiece was started from electronic stalls. Unfortunately, the British racing authorities adopted an ostrich-like approach, ploughing on with manual tape and flag starts for another quarter of a century. Timeform's founder Phil Bull was one of the fiercest critics—'Only those who have seen the starts effected in America can appreciate how bad our starting is by comparison,' he said in a wide-ranging speech at the 1957 Gimcrack dinner (after the success in the race of Pheidippides whom he bred and owned). As it was, British racing had to wait until Thursday July 8th 1965 for starting stalls to be used in Britain for the first time in the Chesterfield Stakes at Newmarket, coincidentally, another twelve-runner event over five furlongs (for two-year-olds). Track Spare went into the record books as the first winner of a race in Britain started from stalls, though it was another two years before the Derby at Epsom was started by the same method.

It could be argued that British racing still lags behind its foreign cousins with regard to starting stalls. Some British trainers have long maintained that starting stalls in this country are too confining, whilst modifications in the decade since the introduction of new stalls (manufactured by Australian firm Steriline) have prompted concerns from trainers, jockeys and stalls' handlers about safety. It still seems that British-trained runners tend to lose ground at the start against their rivals when they compete on foreign soil and their behaviour before entering the stalls sometimes leaves plenty to be desired.

The latest edition of the Grand Prix de Saint-Cloud in late-June got under way some six minutes late because of the antics at the start of two awkward British raiders—Scintillo and Spanish Moon. The latter, who finally went into the stalls after a slap with the long tom (not allowed in Britain), was having his first outing since being hit with a six-month ban (which applied in Britain only) by the British Horseracing Authority after being reported by the starter three times in twelve

Grand Prix de Saint-Cloud, Saint-Cloud—Spanish Moon, banned from racing in Britain, eventually consents to be loaded into his stall before beating Alpine Rose (right), Youmzain (striped sleeves), Curtain Call (rail), Magadan (left) and Ideal World

months for his behaviour at the stalls, the final one coming when Spanish Moon was well fancied for the Jockey Club Stakes at Newmarket in early-May. 'We'll just have to take him to countries where they want him,' was the reaction of a spokesman for owner Khalid Abdulla, connections reportedly unhappy that Spanish Moon hadn't been given more chances by the Newmarket starter. In France, the only restriction placed on him was that he had to start from the outside stall. Whatever the merits of this individual case, the BHA's strict stance on such matters is to be applauded and it is perhaps time that some British trainers took a leaf out of the book of their American peers in the way they prepare young racehorses for the starting experience. For example, American trainer Wesley Ward revealed after saddling two Royal Ascot winners in the latest season that his juveniles are put into stalls 'forty or fifty' times before making their debut—'so that they are used to the rattling around and used to having other horses in there with them.' Further details can be found in the essay on Jealous Again.

Although his aversion to starting stalls makes him something of a problem horse, Spanish Moon has proved a model of consistency over the past season and a half, when he has consented to be loaded, winning four of his eight races during this period and making the frame in good company on the four other occasions. That haul included the aforementioned Grand Prix de Saint-Cloud, Spanish Moon's first victory in a Group 1, in which the 2008 winner Youmzain started odds on in a field of ten. Spanish Moon had beaten Youmzain when a close second to Eastern Anthem in the Dubai Sheema Classic at Nad Al Sheba on his reappearance and he repeated the form at Saint-Cloud, finding plenty under pressure to get on top inside the final half-furlong, winning by a length and a half from Alpine Rose, with Youmzain the same distance away in third. Spanish Moon was returned to France for his next outing, eleven weeks later in the Qatar Prix Foy at Longchamp which attracted just four runners. Ryan Moore was seen to particularly good effect, dictating matters throughout to beat Vision d'Etat by three quarters of a length. The Arc was a possibility at one stage for Spanish Moon, but connections ventured instead to the States (where the stalls are wider) and to Hong Kong for his last two starts, when he made the frame in both the Breeders' Cup Turf (fourth to stablemate Conduit) at Santa Anita and the Hong Kong Vase. Spanish Moon was sent off favourite at Sha Tin and, as at Nad Al Sheba, was deprived of a big first prize in the dying strides, collared by the unbeaten French filly Daryakana and beaten a short head in a bunched finish (second favourite Youmzain came a below-par tenth). Incidentally, Spanish Moon had to pass a stalls test in Hong Kong before that final start and will need to come through a similar test successfully before he is allowed to race again on British soil. At present, a horse cannot take a stalls test for six months after it has been banned, but there are plans to be more flexible if good behaviour can be shown (supported by written submission and DVD) in at least two races overseas where comparable loading procedures are used. In the meantime, another tilt at big prizes in Dubai is reportedly on the cards for Spanish Moon in the spring of 2010.

Spanish Moon's versatility on different surfaces—he acts on good to firm and good to soft going on turf and won a listed event on the polytrack at Kempton on his final four-year-old outing—is typical of the progeny of his successful sire El Prado, who died of a heart attack in September at the age of twenty. The Vincent O'Brien-trained El Prado was a leading two-year-old in 1991 but proved a disappointment at three and his prospects seemed anything but bright when he was sent to stand in the States, where breeders at the time viewed Sadler's Wells (El Prado's sire) as an unlikely source of dirt track winners. El Prado, however, sired major winners on dirt and turf in the States and his stud fee rose from an initial 7,500 dollars to a high of 125,000 dollars in 2006; he has sired over five hundred winners and was champion sire in North America in 2002. His biggest money spinner was Medaglia d'Oro, who performed exclusively on dirt, winning the Travers Stakes, the Whitney Stakes and the Donn Handicap, as well as being runner-up in the Belmont, the Breeders' Cup Classic (twice) and the Dubai World Cup. Medaglia d'Oro is the sire of the top three-year-old filly and Horse of The Year in the States in the latest season, Rachel Alexandra, and now stands as a Darley stallion. Among El Prado's progeny who did well on the turf were Breeders' Cup Mile winner Artie Schiller and Secretariat Stakes and Turf Classic winner Kitten's Joy, also runner-up in the Breeders' Cup Turf.

Mr K. Abdulla's "Spanish Moon"

Spanish Moon (USA) (b.h. 2004)	El Prado (IRE) (gr 1989)	Sadler's Wells (b 1981)	Northern Dancer
			Fairy Bridge
		Lady Capulet (gr 1974)	Sir Ivor
			Cap And Bells
	Shining Bright (b or br 1989)	Rainbow Quest (b 1981)	Blushing Groom
			I Will Follow
		Bourbon Girl (b 1984)	Ile de Bourbon
			Fleet Girl

Although El Prado was a product of Coolmore Stud, the bottom line of this pedigree has been a very productive family for Juddmonte Farms, which acquired the third dam Fleet Girl and Spanish Moon's fourth dam Fleet Noble when it bought Ferrans Stud in Ireland. Fleet Girl had won twice at up to a mile and a half in Ireland (by wide margins both times). Fleet Girl was the dam of eight winners, the best of them being the smart filly Bourbon Girl, who was runner-up to Unite in both the Oaks and Irish Oaks in 1987. Bourbon Girl did even better for Juddmonte at stud, her progeny including a couple of smart pattern-winning French fillies at a mile and a half, Apogee and Daring Miss (second in the Grand Prix de Saint-Cloud in 2000), who have since produced above-average performers in their own right. Apogee is the dam of smart French performers Apsis (at a mile/mile and a quarter) and Dance Routine (Prix de Diane runner-up), whilst Daring Miss is the dam of Musidora runner-up Quickfire. The last-named was trained by Sir Michael Stoute, who has also handled several other notable performers in the family's recent history. Spanish Moon's dam Shining Bright was actually trained by Andre Fabre before being transferred to Ron McAnally in the States—she won at a mile and a quarter at Longchamp before finishing a remote fifth of seven in the 1992 Oaks—but Stoute has also trained Shining Bright's two other offspring by El Prado. Both of them won twice during light careers, Certain Promise showing fairly useful form at around a mile, whilst Spanish Sun won the Ribblesdale Stakes. Shining Bright, also the dam of three other minor winners, produced fillies by Royal Anthem in 2007 (named Phrase but as yet unraced) and by Dansili in 2008, and had a colt by Montjeu in 2009.

Several of Spanish Moon's siblings have been lightly raced and Spanish Moon had his share of training troubles in his younger days too, having just two starts almost a year apart before his career finally got under way at four—he reportedly suffered a cracked pelvis early on at three when prominent in the Derby betting. Spanish Moon has stood up well to fairly busy schedules in both 2008 and 2009 (when raced exclusively at a mile and a half), and should continue in a similar vein in 2010, particularly as he is with a trainer who has no peers when it comes to handling older horses. *Sir Michael Stoute*

SPARES AND REPAIRS 6 b.g. Robellino (USA) 127 – Lady Blackfoot 108 (Prince Tenderfoot (USA) 126) [2009 63: p9.5g^6 f11g^2 f12g^5 10m 10.2m 10.1m 8g f8g Jun 7] good-bodied gelding: modest maiden: should be suited by 1¾m+: raced on all-weather and good/good to firm going. *Mrs S. Lamyman* **60**

SPARKAWAY 3 ch.g. Gold Away (IRE) 125 – West River (USA) (Gone West (USA)) [2009 44: p12g^5 12m* 14.1s* p13.9g^6 11.6d^2 p13.9g Nov 2] close-coupled gelding: has pronounced knee action: fair handicapper: won at Pontefract in June and Yarmouth in July: likely to stay 2m: acts on soft and good to firm going. *W. J. Musson* **69**

SPARKBRIDGE (IRE) 6 b.g. Mull of Kintyre (USA) 114 – Persian Velvet (IRE) (Distinctly North (USA) 115) [2009 42: p16g^6 Jun 24] good-topped gelding: poor maiden: seems to stay 2m: acts on polytrack, heavy and good to firm going: tried blinkered/in cheekpieces/tongue tied. *S. C. Burrough* **39**

SPARKING 2 ch.f. (Apr 29) Exceed And Excel (AUS) 126 – Twilight Time (Aragon 118) [2009 5g p6g^3 Dec 3] half-sister to several winners, including 7-y-o Sam's Secret: dam unraced half-sister to smart 1¼m/1½m performer Punishment: better effort in maidens when third to Wellmarked at Wolverhampton, nearest finish: should stay 7f. *Mrs G. S. Rees* **59**

SPARKLE PARK 2 b.f. (Apr 13) Kyllachy 129 – Petonellajill 73 (Petong 126) [2009 p7g Dec 31] closely related to useful 7f to 9f (Dahlia Stakes) winner Violet Park (by Pivotal) and half-sister to 3 winners, including 5-y-o Golden Prospect: dam 7f winner: 25/1, tailed-off last in maiden at Lingfield. *B. J. Meehan* **–**

SPARKLING CROWN 2 br.f. (May 13) Xaar 132 – Crown Water (USA) (Chief's Crown (USA)) [2009 7d 7g p8m p10m Dec 9] sister to winner in Italy and half-sister to several winners abroad: dam US 2-y-o 1m winner: well held in maidens (reportedly lame final start). *J. Ryan* **–**

SPARKLING CRYSTAL (IRE) 3 ch.f. Danehill Dancer (IRE) 117 – Crystal Curling (IRE) 100 (Peintre Celebre (USA) 137) [2009 72: 7m^3 8m^2 8.3g* 8d^5 8g^5 9.8m^3 10m p12g Oct 22] sparely-made filly: fairly useful handicapper: won at Windsor in June: stays 1m: acts on polytrack, good to firm and good to soft going: front runner/races prominently. *B. W. Hills* **80**

SPARKLING SMILE (IRE) 2 b. or br.f. (Feb 21) Cape Cross (IRE) 129 – Starlight Smile (USA) (Green Dancer (USA) 132) [2009 6m 7m^4 p8g Oct 9] 80,000Y: sixth foal: half-sister to 3 winners, including useful 1½m winner Portrait of A Lady (by Peintre Celebre) and Irish 3-y-o Bay Swallow: dam unraced half-sister to dam of Irish Derby winner Grey Swallow: green and steadily progressive in maidens, 7½ lengths ninth to Timepiece at Lingfield, again not knocked about: should be suited by 1¼m+: open to further improvement. *D. R. Lanigan* **65 p**

SPARKLING SUZIE 3 b.f. Deportivo 116 – Sparkling Jewel 77 (Bijou d'Inde 127) [2009 57: 6m 7f^5 p7g p7f p12g Oct 2] little impact in 2009: tried blinkered. *J. S. Moore* **–**

SPARKY VIXEN 5 b.m. Mujahid (USA) 125 – Lucy Glitters (USA) 60 (Cryptoclearance (USA)) [2009 61: f8d^4 9m^5 f8g 9m f8f Nov 24] quite good-topped mare: modest performer: stays 11f: acts on all-weather and good to firm ground. *C. J. Teague* **53**

SPARTAN DANCE 5 ch.g. Groom Dancer (USA) 128 – Delphic Way 63 (Warning 136) [2009 –: 11.5m 11.9d^6 10f^5 Aug 18] useful-looking gelding: maiden: little form since 2006: tried visored. *J. A. Geake* **–**

SPARTAN PRINCESS (IRE) 3 ch.f. Spartacus (IRE) 107 – Stormchaser (IRE) (Titus Livius (FR) 115) [2009 7s Aug 1] €3,000Y: third foal: half-sister to 1m winner in Italy by Mull of Kintyre: dam unraced out of sister to top-class miler Northjet: last in maiden at Thirsk. *M. Brittain* –

SPARTAN PRINCE (USA) 3 b.c. Mr Greeley (USA) 122 – Yalta (USA) (Private Terms (USA)) [2009 46: p9.5g^4 p9.5g* 9.9m 10m^2 12m 10m^4 Jul 29] fair performer: won maiden at Wolverhampton in February: stays 1¼m: acts on polytrack and good to firm ground: tried tongue tied: sold 3,500 gns in October. *T. D. Barron* 72

SPARTAN STORM (IRE) 3 b.c. Spartacus (IRE) 107 – Sylvan Princess 73 (Sylvan Express 117) [2009 6d 7m Aug 8] well beaten in maidens. *M. Brittain* –

SPARTON DUKE (IRE) 4 b.g. Xaar 132 – Blueberry Walk (Green Desert (USA) 127) [2009 87: 6f^5 6d 7m^6 p8g^4 p8g 7.9g Jul 4] good-topped gelding: handicapper, just fair at 4 yrs: effective at 6f to 1m: acts on polytrack, soft and good to firm going: wears cheekpieces: tends to start slowly/get behind: sold 16,500 gns. *K. A. Ryan* 76

SPA'S DANCER (IRE) 2 b.c. (Apr 14) Danehill Dancer (IRE) 117 – Spa (Sadler's Wells (USA) 132) [2009 7.1m^4 7m 7.1d^2 8g^3 Oct 21] good-bodied colt: closely related to 1¼m/11f winner in Italy by Rock of Gibraltar and half-brother to several winners, notably smart performer up to 1½m Persian Majesty (by Grand Lodge): dam unraced half-sister to very smart 1½m performer Sandmason out of smart close relation to Slip Anchor: fair maiden on balance (probably flattered when second in minor event at Sandown): should be well suited by 1m+. *J. W. Hills* 76

SPATE RIVER 4 b.g. Zaha (CAN) 106 – Rion River (IRE) (Taufan (USA) 119) [2009 89: 7.1g^5 p8g p8.6g* Oct 2] sturdy gelding: fairly useful handicapper: improved to win at Wolverhampton in October: stays 8.6f: acts on polytrack, good to firm and good to soft going: joined Jonjo O'Neill. *C. F. Wall* 94

SPEAGLE (IRE) 7 ch.g. Desert Sun 120 – Pohutakawa (FR) (Affirmed (USA)) [2009 68: f12g f12g p8.6m f11g 11.7m 11.7f^4 11.5g^4 f12g 12m^6 11.9m^6 12.6g 17.2m Jul 16] strong gelding: just poor handicapper nowadays: left D. Shaw after third start: stays 1½m: acts on all-weather/sand and good to firm going: tried visored/tongue tied. *A. J. Chamberlain* 45

SPEAK FREELY 3 b.f. Domedriver (IRE) 128 – Miss Tolerance (USA) 74 (Mt Livermore (USA)) [2009 –: f6g 10.2m Apr 18] last in 3 maidens. *C. Smith* –

SPEAK THE TRUTH (IRE) 3 br.g. Statue of Liberty (USA) 115 – Brave Truth (IRE) (Brief Truce (USA) 126) [2009 57: p5g^2 p5.1g* p5.1g^2 p5.1g p5g* p6g* p5.1g^3 5.1g* 5m^5 p5g^6 5.1g* 5m^2 p5g p6g^4 6.1d^6 p6g p6g* p6m p6f^5 Dec 13] close-coupled gelding: fair performer: won maiden at Wolverhampton in February, sellers at Lingfield in March/April and handicaps at Bath in April/July and Kempton in November: effective at 5f/6f: acts on polytrack, good to firm and good to soft ground: in cheekpieces nowadays. *J. R. Boyle* 78

SPEAR THISTLE 7 ch.g. Selkirk (USA) 129 – Ardisia (USA) 87 (Affirmed (USA)) [2009 –: 10.2v^3 Nov 4] tall, close-coupled gelding: handicapper: fair form sole Flat outing in 2009: effective at 1½m to 2m: acts on polytrack, heavy and good to firm going: fairly useful hurdler, successful in November. *C. J. Mann* 71

SPECIAL ADVISER 3 b.g. Dr Fong (USA) 128 – Dimakya (USA) 83 (Dayjur (USA) 137) [2009 52: 7f^6 10m Jun 19] maiden: well held at 3 yrs. *T. J. Etherington* –

SPECIAL BETTY 2 b.f. (May 25) Tamayaz (CAN) 121 – Natural Key 74 (Safawan 118) [2009 p6g p6g p6g^4 p6g p5m Dec 30] sixth foal: dam 5f/6f winner, including at 2 yrs: maiden: seemingly best effort when fourth to Wellmarked at Wolverhampton. *D. Haydn Jones* 54

SPECIAL BOND 3 b.f. Monsieur Bond (IRE) 120 – Fizzy Treat 79 (Efisio 120) [2009 68: p10g^3 p8g f8g^3 p8g^5 Feb 7] well-made filly: modest maiden: well below form after reappearance in 2009: stays 1¼m: acts on polytrack: tried blinkered. *J. A. Osborne* 63

SPECIAL CHAPTER (IRE) 4 b.f. Acclamation 118 – Literary 79 (Woodman (USA) 126) [2009 –: p8g^6 p12.2g^4 p12g^5 10m 11.8m^5 11.9m^3 11.7g f14m f11m Dec 15] poor maiden: stays 11.8f: acts on good to firm going. *A. B. Haynes* 49

SPECIAL CUVEE 3 b.g. Diktat 126 – Iris May 87 (Brief Truce (USA) 126) [2009 75: f5g f6g^5 f7g^4 7d* 8d* 8.3d 7.1m^6 8d 8m^6 9.1v f7f^4 f8f^3 p9.5g Dec 19] fair performer: won sellers at Folkestone in March and Yarmouth in April: mostly below form after: stays 1m: acts on all-weather and good to soft going: tried visored: held up: not straightforward. *A. B. Haynes* 70

SPECIAL DUTY 2 ch.f. (Feb 12) Hennessy (USA) 122 – Quest To Peak (USA) **118**
(Distant View (USA) 126) [2009 5g² 5.5g* 6m² 6m* Oct 2]

There is no such thing as a certainty in horse racing, but Special Duty's credentials for the One Thousand Guineas are impeccable. She has shown herself the best of her generation with pretensions to staying a mile, no European-based juvenile filly in that category having faced tougher competition through the year or having comparable form—American-trained Jealous Again, a sprinter purely and simply, showed only marginally better form when recording her brilliant victory in the Queen Mary Stakes. Special Duty's appeal as a One Thousand Guineas candidate is also supported by the fact that she is a useful-looking filly who impresses with her physical well-being and looks sure to train on. Her pedigree suggests that the Guineas trip should be within her capabilities, and she is in the very capable hands of Criquette Head-Maarek, who has already saddled three winners of the One Thousand Guineas, putting her joint-second with John Dunlop among active trainers in a roll of honour headed by Henry Cecil on six.

In many respects, Special Duty resembles the best French two-year-old filly of 2007, Natagora. Like her, she won the Prix Robert Papin and the Cheveley Park Stakes and was runner-up in the Prix Morny and, like her, she is blessed with the speed to enable her to have most of her rivals in trouble some way before the end of any race. Special Duty obviously hadn't been hiding her light under a bushel before her debut in the listed Prix Yacowlef at Deauville in early-July, a race her trainer has won a record nine times. Special Duty started 5/4 favourite but she didn't have the run of the race and went down by a length and a half to another filly, Sorciere. The experience looked sure to do Special Duty good but, even so, she looked to have a tough task against odds-on Siyouni in the Prix Robert Papin just over three weeks later. The four other runners included Italian-trained Premio Primi Passi winner Orpen Shadow, and a pattern-winning filly in Dolled Up, successful in the Prix du Bois. Though still looking green, carrying her head on one side and looking a little ungainly at times, Special Duty showed speed all the way on the outside and asserted herself under the whip inside the final furlong, having a length and a half to spare over Siyouni at the line. There was more talk afterwards about Siyouni's defeat than there was about Special Duty's victory, but that wouldn't have bothered Special Duty's trainer who was gaining a sixth win in the race, following those of Ma Biche (1982), Baiser Vole (1985), Balawaki (1987), Didyme (1992) and Psychobabble (1993). The race record is held by Marcel Boussac's trainer Charles Semblat who sent out nine winners between 1943 and 1955. Despite her excellent record in the Prix Robert Papin, Head-Maarek has never trained the winner of the

Prix Robert Papin, Maisons-Laffitte—Special Duty floors the odds on Siyouni (noseband) with Dolled Up (left) and Orpen Shadow (rail) next, second and fourth losing their unbeaten records

Electrolux Cheveley Park Stakes, Newmarket—Special Duty puts herself firmly at the head of the One Thousand Guineas market as she sees off Misheer (No.3) and Lady of The Desert (striped sleeves)

Prix Morny at Deauville. It isn't for want of trying. Psychobabble and the Robert Papin-placed Divine Danse and Magic America came second in the Morny, while Ma Biche, Baiser Vole, Balawaki and Prix Yacowlef winner Pas de Reponse finished third, and Didyme only fifth. Special Duty faced a small but select field at Deauville, including the impressive Coventry Stakes winner Canford Cliffs and the July Stakes winner Arcano. Special Duty very nearly won, making the running, having Canford Cliffs in trouble a furlong out and only just failing to hold the late challenge of Arcano, who prevailed by a short neck. Special Duty came closer to success than Natagora who was beaten two lengths by Myboycharlie in 2007. Once again, Special Duty displayed a somewhat odd head carriage but the trait is clearly nothing to worry about as there is absolutely no mistaking her enthusiasm for racing.

The Electrolux Cheveley Park Stakes at Newmarket almost six weeks after the Prix Morny was an obvious next step for a filly like Special Duty. Of the Head-trained fillies in the Prix Morny already referred to, Balawaki did not run again at two, and Baiser Vole won the Prix de la Salamandre, while Ma Biche, Divine Danse, Pas de Reponse and Magic America all contested the Cheveley Park. Divine Danse and Pas de Reponse won the Prix d'Arenberg in between, a race another Head-trained filly Ravinella won before going for the Cheveley Park. Ma Biche, Ravinella and Pas de Reponse all went on to win at Newmarket, Divine Danse came third and Magic America sixth. The day before the Cheveley Park, bookmaker Stan James was offering 33/1 about Special Duty's completing a double in the Cheveley Park and One Thousand Guineas (the latter a race which they have sponsored). Anyone who took those odds must have been patting themselves on the back after Special Duty's stunning display in the Cheveley Park, one which led to her being cut from 10/1 joint-favourite to 8/1 clear favourite for the classic on the day, and backed down further to a best-priced 5/1 by the end of the season.

Jealous Again apart, just about all the best fillies at five and six furlongs were in the field of eight, the market headed by Lady of The Desert, an authoritative winner of the Princess Margaret Stakes and the Lowther Stakes. Special Duty looked in tremendous shape, well muscled up and bursting with well-being. She started second favourite, then came Sand Vixen, winner of the Flying Childers, Misheer, successful in the Cherry Hinton, Shamandar, whose tally included the Watership Down Stud Sales Race, the Irish challenger Song of My Heart, the Cherry Hinton runner-up Habaayib and 50/1-shot Puff. Soon in front, racing with plenty of gusto, from Misheer and Lady of The Desert, Special Duty quickened again in the closing stages and surged clear up the hill. Lady of The Desert had no answer to Special Duty from the Dip and was a spent force inside the final furlong. Special Duty won by two and three quarter lengths from Misheer, who rallied to catch Lady of The Desert on the line. The victory enabled Head-Maarek to equal Alec Taylor's record of four successes in the race, his gained between 1908 and 1924. It came as no surprise to learn that the proposed route for Special Duty at three will be to go for the One Thousand Guineas after a preparatory race in the Prix

Mr K. Abdulla's "Special Duty"

Imprudence, a race Head-Maarek has won ten times including with Ma Biche and Ravinella before they won the One Thousand Guineas; her other winner of the classic, Hatoof, finished second in the Imprudence (Natagora, trained by Pascal Bary, also took the Prix Imprudence before winning the Guineas).

Special Duty (ch.f. Feb 12, 2007)	Hennessy (USA) (ch 1993)	Storm Cat (b or br 1983)	Storm Bird Terlingua
		Island Kitty (ch 1976)	Hawaii T C Kitten
	Quest To Peak (USA) (b 2002)	Distant View (ch 1991)	Mr Prospector Seven Springs
		Viviana (b 1990)	Nureyev Nijinsky Star

Special Duty isn't the first good juvenile sired by Hennessy, who died the year she was foaled, nor is she the first top-level winner from her immediate family on the distaff side. Hennessy was precocious and raced only at two, winning four of his nine starts including the Grade 1 Hopeful Stakes at Saratoga over seven furlongs and two Grade 2s both over six furlongs. Hennessy was beaten only a neck by Unbridled's Song in the Breeders' Cup Juvenile over eight and a half furlongs. One of the Coolmore band of stallions, Hennessy had spells at stud in Kentucky,

Australia, Japan and Argentina and proved principally an influence for speed. His best performers have been the champion juvenile of 2001 Johannesburg, successful in three Group 1s and the Breeders' Cup Juvenile, and the high-class Henny Hughes, runner-up in the Breeders' Cup Juvenile and winner of Grade 1s at six and seven furlongs as a three-year-old. Hennessy's best Australian son Grand Armee did, however, win four Group 1s over a mile and a quarter headed by the Mackinnon Stakes, while Half Hennessy landed the Queensland Derby at a mile and a half. The bottom half of Special Duty's pedigree is first-rate. She is the first foal out of Quest To Peak, who ran once unplaced at three in America. Quest To Peak has since produced a yearling filly by Dansili and a filly foal by Galileo. Her high-class sister Sightseek won seven Grade 1s at seven furlongs to nine furlongs on dirt in the States, while her half-sister Tates Creek (by Rahy) won the Grade 1 Gamely Handicap over nine furlongs and the Yellow Ribbon Stakes over a mile and a quarter on turf. Special Duty's grandam Viviana was twice successful in listed races over a mile and a quarter in France before finishing runner-up in the Group 3 Prix de Psyche over the same trip. There is another top-flight winner at this point in the pedigree, since Viviana's sister Willstar foaled Etoile Montante, successful in the Prix de la Foret. The next dam, Nijinsky Star, did not run but was a half-sister, out of champion three-year-old Chris Evert, to Six Crowns, the dam of champion two-year-old Chief's Crown. This is also the family of Kentucky Derby winner Winning Colors, and Special Duty looks like boosting its reputation even further. *Mme C. Head-Maarek, France*

SPECIALISING 2 ch.f. (Feb 6) Nayef (USA) 129 – Spry 84 (Suave Dancer (USA) 136) [2009 6g^6 8g Oct 21] 75,000Y: leggy filly: half-sister to 3 winners, including 5-y-o Bajan Pride and 1¼m winner Stow (by Selkirk): dam 1½m winner out of smart half-sister to Derby winner Slip Anchor: modest form in maidens at Goodwood (green, better effort) and Bath (again free) 3 months apart: bred to be suited by 1¼m+: remains open to improvement. *M. R. Channon* **63 p**

SPECIAL RESERVE (IRE) 4 b.c. Sadler's Wells (USA) 132 – Ionian Sea (Slip Anchor 136) [2009 87: 9.7m^2 10m* 10m^3 12m^6 10g^6 10g^4 10m* 10.2s 10g^3 Oct 19] big, good-bodied colt: fairly useful handicapper: won at Windsor in May and August: stays 1½m: acts on soft and good to firm going: tried in cheekpieces: consistent, but often finds little. *R. Hannon* **91**

SPECTAIT 7 b.g. Spectrum (IRE) 126 – Shanghai Girl 102 (Distant Relative 128) [2009 85+: p9.5g* p8.6g* p9.5g* 8m 8s^4 7g 8g^2 Jul 31] big, lengthy gelding: useful handicapper: completed hat-trick at Wolverhampton between January/March: good efforts at Newbury (Spring Cup, fourth to Extraterrestrial) and Goodwood (second to Laa Rayb in totesport Mile) after: stays 9.5f: acts on all-weather, firm and soft going. *Jonjo O'Neill* **99**

SPEED DATING 3 ch.g. Pivotal 124 – Courting 108 (Pursuit of Love 124) [2009 –p: 8s^3 8.1s^2 9.3d* 10f^4 9.8g^2 Aug 31] big, strong gelding: fair performer: won handicap at Carlisle in July: will stay 1½m: acts on soft going: gelded after final start. *Sir Mark Prescott* **72**

SPEED SONG 4 b.f. Fasliyev (USA) 120 – Superstar Leo (IRE) 114 (College Chapel 122) [2009 92+: 5.1g 6d 5.7f^3 Jun 5] rather leggy, lengthy filly: fairly useful performer: will prove best kept to 5f/6f: acts on firm and good to soft going: tried blinkered: sold 270,000 gns, reportedly in foal to Pivotal. *W. J. Haggas* **89**

SPEEDYFIX 2 b.g. (Apr 16) Chineur (FR) 123 – Zonnebeke 64 (Orpen (USA) 116) [2009 5.2g p6g^6 6s p5g 5m p6m^4 p6g^2 f6g f6m p6m Nov 19] leggy gelding: poor maiden: stays 6f: acts on polytrack and good to firm going: usually tongue tied/in cheekpieces. *Mrs C. A. Dunnett* **47**

SPEEDY GURU 3 b.f. Ishiguru (USA) 114 – Gowon (Aragon 118) [2009 75p: 7m 6.1v^5 6m* 7g p6g p6f Dec 13] useful-looking filly: fair handicapper: won at Leicester in October: below form after: stays 6f: acts on soft and good to firm ground: tongue tied twice at 2 yrs, including for win. *H. Candy* **79**

SPEEDY SENORITA (IRE) 4 b.f. Fayruz 116 – Sinora Wood (IRE) 70 (Shinko Forest (IRE)) [2009 79: 5m^4 5d^3 5f^3 5m 5m^2 5g^5 5m^5 5m* 5m 5m 5m 5.1g Oct 28] sturdy filly: fair handicapper: won at Beverley in August: best at 5f: acts on polytrack and firm going: tried in cheekpieces: often races prominently: tough. *J. J. Quinn* **77**

SPELL CASTER 4 ch.f. Bertolini (USA) 125 – Princess Claudia (IRE) 58 (Kahyasi 130) [2009 92: 10m^4 9.9m^2 10m^5 10v Oct 24] close-coupled filly: fairly useful handicapper: stays 1¼m, not 1½m: acts on polytrack and firm going: sold 16,000 gns, sent to USA. *R. M. Beckett* **93**

SPENSLEY (IRE) 3 ch.g. Dr Fong (USA) 128 – Genoa 96 (Zafonic (USA) 130) [2009 p8g 10m 10m^5 12s 10d^6 10m* Oct 13] 35,000Y: good-bodied gelding: seventh foal: brother to useful 1m winner Brindisi and half-brother to several fairly useful winners, including 1½m winner Wild Fell Hall (by Grand Lodge): dam temperamental 11.5f winner: fair form: gelded, improved when winning handicap at Leicester in October, still looking rather ungainly: stays 1¼m: acts on good to firm ground. *J. R. Fanshawe* **79**

SPENT 4 b.g. Averti (IRE) 117 – Top 74 (Shirley Heights 130) [2009 67: p7g p8g^6 8d Jun 10] tall gelding: handicapper: just poor form in 2009: tried blinkered: sold £2,400, joined Mrs A. Thorpe. *Mouse Hamilton-Fairley* **47**

SPHERE (IRE) 4 b.f. Daylami (IRE) 138 – Apple Town 91 (Warning 136) [2009 77: 12d^4 14.1m^4 16.4m^6 15g^6 12g^4 p10g p12.2g^4 12.5m^3 12.1g* 13.8g p13.9g^6 Nov 12] small, angular filly: fair performer: claimed from J. Fanshawe £6,000 seventh start: won seller at Beverley (left P. Midgley 8,000 gns) in September: stays 15f: acts on soft and good to firm ground: tried in cheekpieces/tongue strap. *J. Mackie* **69**

SPHINX (FR) 11 b.g. Snurge 130 – Egyptale (Crystal Glitters (USA) 127) [2009 95: 16d 17.5m 18g 15v* Oct 31] smallish, workmanlike gelding: fairly useful handicapper: best effort in 2009 when winning at Ayr in October: stays 17.5f: has form on polytrack and good to firm ground, seems best on soft/heavy nowadays: usually in headgear: held up. *E. W. Tuer* **81**

SPICE FAIR 2 ch.g. (Jan 10) Trade Fair 124 – Focosa (ITY) (In The Wings 128) [2009 p8g^2 p7g^6 Dec 31] fourth foal: half-brother to 4-y-o Pembo: dam, Italian 11f winner, half-sister to US Grade 3 1¼m winner I'm Indy Mood: much better effort in maidens at Lingfield when 3 lengths second to Hidden Glory: subsequently gelded, hampered start final outing. *M. D. I. Usher* **68**

SPICE RUN 6 b.g. Zafonic (USA) 130 – Palatial 101 (Green Desert (USA) 127) [2009 68: p7g^6 p6g* Nov 16] good-topped gelding: fairly useful form, lightly raced: improved when winning maiden at Wolverhampton in November: best effort at 6f, will prove at least as effective at 7f: form only on polytrack: capable of better still. *Stef Liddiard* **83 p**

SPIC 'N SPAN 4 b.g. Piccolo 121 – Sally Slade 80 (Dowsing (USA) 124) [2009 70: f5g* p5g^6 f5g f5g^5 f5g^5 f5g* f5g^2 f5g^2 f5m^2 5g 5.1g p5.1g^4 p5.1g* 5.1m^3 f5g^4 5.1d^3 5.1m p5.1g Oct 10] good-topped gelding: fair performer on all-weather, modest on turf: won handicaps in January/March, both at Southwell, and seller at Wolverhampton in July: best at 5f/6f: acts on all-weather, good to firm and good to soft ground: wears blinkers/cheekpieces: tried tongue tied: front runner. *R. A. Harris* **64** **a72**

SPIDERS STAR 6 br.m. Cayman Kai (IRE) 114 – Kiss In The Dark 55 (Starry Night (USA)) [2009 49: 16m^4 16g* 16.2m* 16.2g^3 17.1m^2 15.8d* 16.4d Sep 6] angular mare: fair handicapper, lightly raced: much improved in 2009, winning at Thirsk in June, Beverley in July and Catterick in August: stays 17.1f: acts on good to firm and good to soft ground: held up. *S. G. West* **74**

SPIDERS TERN 4 b.g. Sooty Tern 79 – Miss Money Spider (IRE) 65 (Statoblest 120) [2009 10m p9.5g p7.1g Nov 30] no form. *J. M. Bradley* **–**

SPIEKEROOG 3 ch.c. Lomitas 129 – Special 91 (Polar Falcon (USA) 126) [2009 10g^2 12m^2 13.8g* 14m^4 p16.5g^4 Oct 15] 20,000Y: leggy colt: second foal: dam, 1¾m winner, closely related to very smart 7f/1m performer Soviet Line: fairly useful form: won maiden at Catterick in July: should stay 2m: raced only on polytrack and good/good to firm ground: tried blinkered: said to have finished lame final start. *H. R. A. Cecil* **87**

SPIN AGAIN (IRE) 4 b.g. Intikhab (USA) 135 – Queen of The May (IRE) 80 (Nicolotte 118) [2009 80: f7g^6 7m 8m^5 8m 8.5m 7g 6d 7.5m^2 p7.1g^5 8d^5 Aug 10] fair performer nowadays: should stay 1m: acts on polytrack, soft and good to firm going: tried visored: races prominently. *D. Nicholls* **72**

SPIN CYCLE (IRE) 3 b.c. Exceed And Excel (AUS) 126 – Spinamix 67 (Spinning World (USA) 130) [2009 103: 5m* 5m 5g 5m^5 5m^2 5.2m^6 5m* Oct 1] sturdy, good-bodied colt: type to carry condition: smart performer: improved in 2009, winning minor event at Musselburgh in May and listed race at Newmarket (by neck from Noble Storm) in October: only good effort in between when length second to Strike The Deal in listed race at Doncaster: raced mainly at 5f: acts on firm going: visored penultimate start. *B. Smart* **114**

SPINIGHT (IRE) 3 b.c. Spinning World (USA) 130 – Adjtiya (IRE) (Green Desert **65**
(USA) 127) [2009 64: p7g^3 f7g^5 p7g^2 p7g^4 7m^3 6.1g Jul 4] sturdy colt: fair maiden: stays 7f: acts on polytrack, good to firm and good to soft ground: in cheekpieces/blinkers in 2009. *M. Botti*

SPINNERS END (IRE) 3 b.c. Royal Applause 124 – Needwood Epic 61 (Midyan **92**
(USA) 124) [2009 72: 8.3m^3 8d* 8m^3 8m* 8m 8m 7m* 6.9g^4 Aug 3] sturdy colt: fairly useful handicapper: won at Pontefract in May, Musselburgh in June and Salisbury in July when trained by K. R. Burke: effective at 7f, likely to stay 1¼m: acts on good to firm and good to soft going: races prominently: sold 50,000 gns in October. *A. P. Jarvis*

SPINNING 6 ch.g. Pivotal 124 – Starring (FR) 74 (Ashkalani (IRE) 128) [2009 92: f8s^6 **103**
p8.6g* 7m^5 8m 8v^5 8s 8m 8m p8.6g p8.6g^2 p8.6g^4 p9.5g^4 p8.6g* p8.6g* p8f^3 Dec 20] leggy gelding: useful handicapper: won at Wolverhampton in February and twice there in November: much improved for last 2 successes, beating Chapter And Verse by length in latter: effective at 7f to 9.5f: acts on polytrack and any turf going: blinkered: held up (tends to miss break/race lazily). *T. D. Barron*

SPINNING BAILIWICK 3 b.f. Spinning World (USA) 130 – Zietunzeen (IRE) 99 **81**
(Zieten (USA) 118) [2009 7g 6m^4 5.5g^6 5f^5 p5g^4 p5g* p6m* p5m* p6f^3 Dec 20] third foal: half-sister to 4-y-o The Magic Blanket: dam 2-y-o 6f winner: poor form in 4 starts in Channel Islands for Ms V. Lucas: much improved (fairly useful form) to win 3 handicaps at Kempton and Lingfield in November/December: effective at 5f/6f: best form on polytrack: blinkered once. *G. L. Moore*

SPINNING JOY 3 b.f. Josr Algarhoud (IRE) 118 – Den's-Joy 85 (Archway (IRE) 115) **–**
[2009 –: p8g p10g 8g May 29] small filly: little form. *J. R. Boyle*

SPINNING RIDGE (IRE) 4 ch.g. Spinning World (USA) 130 – Summer Style (IRE) **68**
70 (Indian Ridge 123) [2009 68: p8g p9.5g p8m p8.6g p8g* p8g^2 p7.1m^2 p7.1g^3 f8f p9.5g^5 Dec 28] fair handicapper: 50/1, won at Lingfield in November: barely stays 1¼m: acts on polytrack and good to soft ground: tried in cheekpieces. *R. A. Harris*

SPINNING SPIRIT (IRE) 2 b.g. (Apr 20) Invincible Spirit (IRE) 121 – Vencera (FR) **67**
(Green Tune (USA) 125) [2009 6.1g 7.1g^3 7m^5 8.3d f6g^3 p7g Nov 25] well-made gelding: fair maiden: barely stays 7f: acts on fibresand: again found little final start (gelded after). *J. G. Given*

SPINNING WATERS 3 b.g. Vettori (IRE) 119 – Secret Waters 100 (Pharly (FR) 130) **68**
[2009 62: 12m* 12.6g^6 11m 11.7m^2 11.9f^3 12m^5 p16m^6 17.2m^4 Sep 28] useful-looking gelding: fair handicapper: won at Pontefract in April: stays 12.6f: acts on firm going: tried in cheekpieces. *Eve Johnson Houghton*

Newsells Park Stud 'Golden Bonus' Rous Stakes, Newmarket—three-year-olds fill the first three places, Spin Cycle (nearest camera) just getting the better of Noble Storm as Run For The Hills (far left) finishes well to pip Dandy Man for third

SPINNING WELL (IRE) 3 ch.f. Pivotal 124 – Kiltubber (IRE) 104 (Sadler's Wells (USA) 132) [2009 p7g³ 8g 8s² 9.5m⁴ p10g⁴ Nov 18] second foal: dam, 1½m winner in Ireland/Italy, out of Moyglare Stud Stakes winner Priory Belle: fairly useful maiden: standout effort when second at the Curragh (testing conditions): left D. Weld/off 5 months, well beaten at Lingfield final start: should stay 1¼m: acts on soft ground: tongue tied last 3 outings. *R. M. Beckett* **83**

SPIN SISTER 3 b.f. Umistim 119 – Gloaming 74 (Celtic Swing 138) [2009 –: p10g 7.1d p8.6g 11.9d Oct 15] little form. *J. Gallagher* **–**

SPIOSRA (USA) 3 ch.f. Mr Greeley (USA) 122 – Laptop (USA) (Phone Trick (USA)) [2009 8d 7m 6g Oct 16] $100,000Y, resold €100,000Y, 1,500 3-y-o: fifth foal: half-sister to winners in USA by Anees and Buddha: dam US maiden: well held in maidens: tongue tied last 2 starts. *C. J. Teague* **–**

SPIRIT CHILD (USA) 3 b. or br.f. Hennessy (USA) 122 – Babeinthewoods (USA) (Woodman (USA) 126) [2009 p7.1g 7m Oct 6] $32,000Y: rather leggy filly: sixth foal: closely related/half-sister to winners in USA by Forest Wildcat and Southern Halo: dam, US 6f (at 2 yrs)/6.5f winner, out of US Grade 1 2-y-o 7f winner Delicate Vine: last in maidens. *J. A. Osborne* **–**

SPIRIT IS NEEDED (IRE) 3 b.g. No Excuse Needed 123 – The Spirit of Pace (IRE) (In The Wings 128) [2009 11.8m 11.8g* 14m² Sep 27] first foal: dam unraced close relative to very smart performer up to 2m Yavana's Pace: said to have been lame on debut: off 3½ months and gelded, fairly useful form when winning maiden at Leicester in September: further progress when second to Ascendant in handicap at Musselburgh 13 days later: likely to stay beyond 1¾m: may well prove useful. *M. Johnston* **90 p**

SPIRIT LAND (IRE) 2 ch.c. (Apr 8) Indian Haven 119 – Reborn (IRE) 48 (Idris (IRE) 118) [2009 7m 8m⁵ 7.1m f8m⁴ p8g⁶ Nov 21] smallish colt: poor maiden: stays 1m. *M. H. Tompkins* **48**

SPIRIT OF ADJISA (IRE) 5 b.g. Invincible Spirit (IRE) 121 – Adjisa (IRE) (Doyoun 124) [2009 88: p12g² p12.2g⁴ 14v 11.6m² 12d⁴ 12g⁶ 12g⁴ 12d* 13.4m* 16g⁶ Oct 30] leggy gelding: fairly useful handicapper: won at Epsom and Chester in September: effective at 1¼m to 13.4f: acts on polytrack, heavy and good to firm going: often wears blinkers/visor: edgy sort, but reliable: joined A. King, fair form over hurdles. *Pat Eddery* **93**

SPIRIT OF A NATION (IRE) 4 b.c. Invincible Spirit (IRE) 121 – Fabulous Pet (Somethingfabulous (USA)) [2009 94+: p8g³ 8g² Sep 17] lengthy, good-topped, quite attractive colt: fairly useful handicapper, lightly raced: creditable placed efforts both starts in 2009: will stay 1¼m: acts on polytrack, soft and good to firm ground. *D. H. Brown* **94**

SPIRIT OF CONISTON 6 b.g. Lake Coniston (IRE) 131 – Kigema (IRE) 58 (Case Law 113) [2009 69: p6g³ p5.1g f5g³ f5g³ 5m³ p6g 5m 5m⁴ 5m³ 5m⁵ 5g 5d* 5.1d⁵ 5m⁶ 5s* p5.1g Nov 14] stocky gelding: fair handicapper: won at Catterick in August and October (seemingly better than ever): best at 5f: acts on all-weather, firm and soft going: has worn headgear. *P. T. Midgley* **78 ?**

SPIRIT OF DUBAI (IRE) 3 b.f. Cape Cross (IRE) 129 – Questina (FR) (Rainbow Quest (USA) 134) [2009 65: 11.5m⁴ 11m 10.3m² 10m⁴ 11.5m* 12m* Sep 25] tall filly: useful performer: won maiden at Lingfield and listed race at Ascot (much improved when beating Polly's Mark by short head), both in September: stays 1½m: acts on good to firm going. *D. M. Simcock* **103**

SPIRIT OF FRANCE (IRE) 7 b.g. Anabaa (USA) 130 – Les Planches (Tropular) [2009 78: 6m 7m 8d 9m² 9.8m³ 7.5m⁴ 8.9d⁵ 10m⁵ Jun 19] tall, rather leggy gelding: fair handicapper: should stay 1¼m: acts on firm and good to soft going. *D. Carroll* **74**

SPIRIT OF LOVE (IRE) 2 b.g. (Apr 5) Pearl of Love (IRE) 112 – Sesleria (IRE) (Mark of Esteem (IRE) 137) [2009 p6g⁴ Nov 27] €8,000Y, 14,000 2-y-o: second foal: dam unraced half-sister to very smart US Grade 1 11f winner Lunar Sovereign: 28/1, encouraging 3 lengths fourth to Kingsgate Choice in maiden at Wolverhampton, staying on under considerate handling: will be well suited by 7f+: should improve. *M. Wigham* **69 p**

SPIRIT OF NORMANDY 2 ch.f. (Apr 20) Auction House (USA) 120 – Charlottevalentina (IRE) 80 (Perugino (USA) 84) [2009 p7g Nov 18] fifth foal: sister to 2006 2-y-o 5f winner Loves Bidding and half-sister to 6-y-o Double Valentine: dam 2-y-o 6f winner: 66/1, tailed off in maiden at Kempton. *R. Ingram* **–**

SPIRIT OF SHARJAH (IRE) 4 b.g. Invincible Spirit (IRE) 121 – Rathbawn Realm (Doulab (USA) 115) [2009 99: 6m 5g⁶ 5g⁶ 6m⁶ 6m⁴ 6m³ 7m⁶ 7m* 6g 7.1g³ 8.1g 8m⁴ 7m⁶ p7g² p7g⁴ Oct 29] big, good-topped gelding: useful handicapper: won at Epsom in July: **96**

stays 1m, effective at shorter: acts on polytrack and good to firm going: tried visored: held up: signs of temperament. *Miss J. Feilden*

SPIRIT OF THE GLEN 3 b.f. Catcher In The Rye (IRE) 115 – Sentiment (Dancing Brave (USA) 140) [2009 p10g⁵ p12g⁴ 10m 10d Aug 2] 7,500Y: sparely-made filly: seventh foal: closely related to winner in Japan by Danehill and half-sister to 2 winners, including useful Irish 1997 2-y-o 7f winner Brief Sentiment (by Brief Truce): dam unraced half-sister to Chester Vase winner Nomrood and to dam of Racing Post Trophy winner Dilshaan: modest form only on second start. *Jamie Poulton* **53**

SPIRITOFTHEWEST (IRE) 3 b.g. Invincible Spirit (IRE) 121 – Rosie's Guest (IRE) (Be My Guest (USA) 126) [2009 81: 6m⁶ 5g⁴ 6m³ 5m 5m 6g 5m 5m⁵ p6g⁵ 6.1d p8m⁴ f8m Dec 15] sturdy gelding: fairly useful handicapper at best: left S. Parr after reappearance: stays 6f: acts on good to firm and good to soft going, probably on polytrack: tried tongue tied/visored. *D. H. Brown* **82**

SPIRITONTHEMOUNT (USA) 4 b. or br.g. Pulpit (USA) 117 – Stirling Bridge (USA) (Prized (USA)) [2009 74§: f16d p13.3g p13g f14g⁵ f14g⁴ f16g⁶ f16g² 15.8g f14m p16m³ Dec 30] tall, leggy gelding: modest maiden handicapper nowadays: stays easy 2m: acts on all-weather, soft and good to firm going: often blinkered: one to treat with plenty of caution. *P. W. Hiatt* **59 §**

SPIRITUAL ART 3 b.f. Invincible Spirit (IRE) 121 – Oatey 68 (Master Willie 129) [2009 76p: 6m⁶ p7g 6g⁵ 7m p7g⁶ p7g² p8g² p8g* p8g⁴ p8m⁶ Dec 30] good-bodied filly: fairly useful handicapper: left S. Callaghan 2,500 gns after reappearance: improved when winning at Lingfield in November: stays easy 1m: acts on all-weather and good to soft ground: in cheekpieces nowadays. *L. A. Dace* **85**

SPIRITUAL BOND 3 b.f. Monsieur Bond (IRE) 120 – Country Spirit (Sayf El Arab (USA) 127) [2009 48: p7g Jan 23] poor maiden, sporadic form: best effort at 7f on polytrack. *R. A. Harris* **–**

SPIRITUAL HEALING (IRE) 3 b.f. Invincible Spirit (IRE) 121 – Tarbela (IRE) 68 (Grand Lodge (USA) 125) [2009 p6g⁵ f6g* Feb 3] €55,000F, 68,000Y: first foal: dam, Irish maiden (best at 7f), half-sister to dam of 2-y-o Arcano: modest form in maidens, winning at Southwell in February: will stay 7f: sold 6,000 gns in May, resold 30,000 gns in November. *J. A. Osborne* **64**

SPIRITUAL TREASURE (USA) 3 b. or br.g. Perfect Soul (IRE) 122 – Storm Runner (USA) (Miswaki (USA) 124) [2009 80p: p10g p12.2g⁵ 10.2g p12.2g Oct 16] useful-looking gelding: has scope: no form in 2009: tongue tied third outing (gelded after). *M. A. Magnusson* **–**

SPIT AND POLISH 3 b.g. Polish Precedent (USA) 131 – Brooklyn's Sky (Septieme Ciel (USA) 123) [2009 66: p7g⁶ p7g² 7f² 6g p5g⁶ p6g 6m p6g⁶ Jun 22] fair maiden: below form after second start (claimed from J. Dunlop £5,000 after next one): stays 7f: acts on polytrack: tried visored, often blinkered: weak finisher: sold 4,000 gns in July. *C. A. Dwyer* **66**

SPITFIRE 4 b.g. Mujahid (USA) 125 – Fresh Fruit Daily 92 (Reprimand 122) [2009 100: p7g⁴ 7m 7f 6g³ 6g⁶ 7m⁶ p8g³ p7g⁴ p10g⁴ p8m Dec 4] tall, good-topped gelding: fairly useful handicapper: effective at 6f to 1m: acts on polytrack, good to firm and good to soft going: free-going sort: visored final outing. *J. R. Jenkins* **94**

SPLASHDOWN 3 ch.f. Falbrav (IRE) 133 – Space Time (FR) (Bering 136) [2009 99p: 9.9m⁴ 10m* 12g⁵ 9.9g² 10.1m³ 10m³ Oct 16] good-bodied filly: useful performer: improved when winning listed race at Newbury (by short head from Apple Charlotte) in June: creditable efforts when placed in similar events last 3 starts, at Salisbury (1¼ lengths second to Ave), Yarmouth (2¼ lengths third to Nashmiah) and Newmarket (1½ lengths third behind Enticement): should be suited by 1½m: raced only on polytrack and good/good to firm going. *L. M. Cumani* **105**

SPLASH THE CASH 4 b.g. Lomitas 129 – Bandit Queen 90 (Desert Prince (IRE) 130) [2009 74: p6g p7g⁵ p6g⁵ p7.1g 7m* 6g 7.1m 7g* 6g⁴ 7m Jun 16] fairly useful performer on turf, modest on all-weather: won seller at Catterick in April and handicap there in May: stayed 7f: acted on polytrack, soft and good to firm ground: tried in cheekpieces/tongue tie: sometimes found little: dead. *K. A. Ryan* **82 a57**

SPLENDORINTHEGRASS (IRE) 3 ch.c. Selkirk (USA) 129 – Portelet 91 (Night Shift (USA)) [2009 93p: 7f² 8d* 7g³ 7g Oct 10] tall, close-coupled colt: useful form: changed hands 160,000 gns in May: improved when winning maiden at Newmarket in July by 9 lengths from Park Lane: creditable length third to Jeninsky in handicap on same course next time: said to have finished sore behind at York final start: stays 1m: best form on going softer than good (acts on heavy): sold 75,000 gns. *R. Charlton* **102**

SPLINTER CELL (USA) 3 b. or br.c. Johannesburg (USA) 127 – Rock Salt (Selkirk (USA) 129) [2009 88p: p8.6g² 10m 11.9v⁵ 10g³ 8.5g* 8s⁵ 10d* 10.3g⁴ p10m p9.5g* Dec 17] attractive colt: useful handicapper: generally progressive, and won at Beverley in July, Windsor in October and Wolverhampton (beat Mr Willis 1½ lengths) in December: stays 1¼m: acts on polytrack and good to soft going. *M. Botti* **102**

SPLIT THE POT (IRE) 2 b.g. (Feb 24) Chevalier (IRE) 115 – Autumn Fall (USA) (Sanglamore (USA) 126) [2009 6m⁶ 5g⁵ 6f⁴ p8g p6g Oct 8] neat gelding: poor maiden. *P. R. Chamings* **49**

SPOKEN 2 ch.c. (May 18) Medicean 128 – Spout 115 (Salse (USA) 128) [2009 8.1m⁴ 8g* Sep 30] sixth foal: half-brother to 3 at least fairly useful winners, including useful 1½m winner Sea Wall (by Giant's Causeway): dam 7f (at 2 yrs) to 1½m (including Lancashire Oaks) winner who stayed 13.5f: promising in maidens at Sandown (fourth to Hot Prospect) and Salisbury (beat Youm Jamil cosily by ¾ length): will be suited by 1¼m+: should make an even better 3-y-o. *R. Charlton* **84 p**

SPONGE 4 b.g. Zaha (CAN) 106 – Glensara (Petoski 135) [2009 –: p10g 11.6m 12.1v Jul 24] tall, angular gelding: poor maiden. *P. R. Chamings* **43**

SPOOF MASTER (IRE) 5 b.g. Invincible Spirit (IRE) 121 – Talbiya (IRE) (Mujtahid (USA) 118) [2009 83: p5m⁵ f5g³ p6g⁶ f6g⁴ f6g⁵ p8g⁵ p8g⁶ p5g* p5m⁶ f5g Dec 22] sturdy gelding: handicapper, just modest form in 2009: won at Kempton in October: has form at 1m, best at 5f: acts on all-weather, firm and soft going: often wears cheekpieces: often forces pace. *C. R. Dore* **63**

SPORTING GESTURE 12 ch.g. Safawan 118 – Polly Packer 81 (Reform 132) [2009 79: 12f⁶ f12g 12d 12m 12g⁵ 12g* 12.5m⁵ 12d 11.9d⁴ Sep 15] rather leggy, close-coupled gelding: has a round action: fair handicapper: won at Pontefract in July: stays 13.8f: acts on firm and good to soft going: blinkered once. *M. W. Easterby* **67**

SPOTTY MULDOON (IRE) 4 b.g. Mull of Kintyre (USA) 114 – Fashion Guide (IRE) 87 (Bluebird (USA) 125) [2009 84: 8.1g p8g 8.3g Jun 15] sturdy, compact gelding: well held in handicaps in 2009: tried visored. *R. M. Beckett* **–**

SPOUK 4 b.f. Pivotal 124 – Souk (IRE) 98 (Ahonoora 122) [2009 81p: 10.4g² Jul 25] smallish filly: fairly useful form: second to Summer Gold on handicap debut at York sole outing in 2009: would have stayed 1½m: acted on polytrack, best effort on turf on good ground: dead. *L. M. Cumani* **89**

SPRING ADVENTURE 3 b.f. Dr Fong (USA) 128 – Yavari (IRE) 79 (Alzao (USA) 117) [2009 80p: 7m³ p8g* p8g 8g⁴ 8.3m³ 8.1g³ 8m p8g Oct 22] lengthy filly: fairly useful performer: won maiden at Lingfield in May: stays 1m: acts on polytrack, unraced on extremes of going on turf: has run well in a visor: often forces pace: sold 13,500 gns. *E. A. L. Dunlop* **80**

SPRING BREEZE 8 ch.g. Dr Fong (USA) 128 – Trading Aces 71 (Be My Chief (USA) 122) [2009 66: 16.5s³ Jul 9] workmanlike gelding: handicapper, lightly raced on Flat since 2005: just modest form only start in 2009: stays 16.5f: acts on all-weather, firm and soft going: usually wears headgear: fairly useful hurdler, successful in October/November. *J. J. Quinn* **57**

SPRING BRIDGE (IRE) 3 b.g. Tagula (IRE) 116 – Miss Lainey (IRE) 62 (Woodborough (USA) 112) [2009 7f⁴ 7g 6m 7m p5f³ p5.1g p5m Sep 23] modest maiden: best effort at 5f: tried in cheekpieces/tongue tie: gelded after final start. *Mrs L. C. Jewell* **53**

SPRING FASHION (IRE) 3 b.f. Galileo (IRE) 134 – Darina (IRE) 103 (Danehill (USA) 126) [2009 10.2g⁶ p9.5g⁴ p13.9g p12m Dec 9] 3,500 3-y-o: seventh foal: sister to fairly useful Irish 1¼m winner Galilean and closely related to Irish 13f winner Massuci (by Montjeu): dam Irish 7f to 1¼m winner: modest maiden: should stay 1½m. *M. Botti* **54**

SPRING GODDESS (IRE) 8 b.m. Daggers Drawn (USA) 114 – Easter Girl (Efisio 120) [2009 87: 8m* 10.3m 8g⁶ 8g⁶ 12s 10g⁶ 8g* p10m Nov 21] good-topped mare: fairly useful performer: won handicap at Doncaster in March and claimer at Yarmouth in October: stays 1¼m: acts on polytrack, soft and good to firm going: held up. *A. P. Jarvis* **89**

SPRING GREEN 3 b.f. Bahamian Bounty 116 – Star Tulip 99 (Night Shift (USA)) [2009 –: 6m 5.1d* p6g³ p5g* 6g 6g⁶ p6g⁴ 5m⁴ 5g Oct 9] sturdy filly: fairly useful performer: won maiden at Bath in May and handicap at Kempton in July: may prove best at 5f: acts on polytrack, good to firm and good to soft going. *H. Morrison* **86**

SPRING HEATHER (IRE) 2 b.f. (Mar 12) Montjeu (IRE) 137 – Spotlight 110 (Dr Fong (USA) 128) [2009 7d 7.1m Sep 29] unfurnished filly: first foal: dam, 7f (at 2 yrs) to 9f (US Grade 2) winner, out of smart 1¼m Prix de la Nonette winner Dust Dancer: clear signs of ability when down the field in maidens at Lingfield and Warwick (tongue tied, not knocked about): will be suited by 1¼m+: should do better. *J. L. Dunlop* **– p**

SPRING JIM 8 b.g. First Trump 118 – Spring Sixpence 60 (Dowsing (USA) 124) [2009 10.3g* 10.3m6 12m* 11.9m4 12m 14v6 14.1m2 12d Oct 24] close-coupled gelding: useful handicapper: off 3½ years, won at Doncaster in March and York in May: good fourth to Red Merlin in Old Newton Cup at Haydock fourth start: stays 1¾m: acts on heavy and good to firm ground: held up: successful on hurdling debut in November. *J. R. Fanshawe* **95**

SPRING OF FAME (USA) 3 b.c. Grand Slam (USA) 120 – Bloomy (USA) (Polish Numbers (USA)) [2009 91p: p8.6g* p9g2 10m3 8.1m3 10m 8m* 8g* 8.9m4 8g Oct 3] lengthy, attractive colt: fluent mover: smart performer: won handicap at Wolverhampton in March (left M. Magnusson after next start), minor event at Newmarket in July and listed race at Deauville (easily by 3 lengths from Mantoro) in August: below form after in Strensall Stakes at York and Prix Daniel Wildenstein at Longchamp: best at 1m: acts on polytrack and good to firm ground. *Saeed bin Suroor* **112**

SPRING QUARTET 3 b.g. Captain Rio 122 – Alice Blackthorn 70 (Forzando 122) [2009 58: p8.6g p10g5 p12.2m3 p12g3 p12g f11g3 12.1g 11.9m f11g2 Aug 25] lengthy gelding: modest maiden handicapper: stays 1½m: acts on all-weather: tried blinkered, usually visored in 2009: signs of temperament. *Pat Eddery* **59**

SPRING SECRET 3 b.g. Reset (AUS) 124 – Miss Brooks 81 (Bishop of Cashel 122) [2009 58: 8.1g 12.1g 10m 7.1m4 8g3 7s4 8f5 8d* 8.1d2 8.1d* 8.1m2 10.2v Nov 4] workmanlike gelding: fair handicapper: won at Bath in August and Chepstow in September: will prove best around 1m: acts on firm and soft ground. *B. Palling* **73**

SPRINGWELL GIANT (IRE) 2 ch.g. (Mar 21) Choisir (AUS) 126 – Glasnas Giant 60 (Giant's Causeway (USA) 132) [2009 7m3 p7.1g3 p8.6g4 p8.6g Oct 23] small gelding: modest maiden: stays 8.6f. *A. J. McCabe* **62**

SPRINKLER 6 b.m. Emperor Fountain 112 – Ryewater Dream 72 (Touching Wood (USA) 127) [2009 14.1g5 Jun 9] winning hurdler: well held in seller on Flat debut. *C. W. Thornton* **–**

SPRUZZO 3 b.g. Emperor Fountain 112 – Ryewater Dream 72 (Touching Wood (USA) 127) [2009 –: p9.5g f11g 10.2m p13.9g Dec 14] rather leggy gelding: little sign of ability. *C. W. Thornton* **–**

SPUME (IRE) 5 b.g. Alhaarth (IRE) 126 – Sea Spray (IRE) 101 (Royal Academy (USA) 130) [2009 71§: p13.3g p12.2g3 f14g4 p16g5 p13.9g p13g6 p8.6g f12d Mar 10] strong, lengthy gelding: modest handicapper: stays 2m: acts on all-weather, soft and good to firm going: tried blinkered/in cheekpieces: tongue tied: unreliable. *S. Parr* **58 §**

SPUTNIK ONE (IRE) 2 b.c. (Apr 21) Soviet Star (USA) 128 – Walnut Lady 91 (Forzando 122) [2009 5.7g 7g 7m Sep 1] big colt: no form: tried blinkered/in cheekpieces: ungenuine. *J. S. Moore* **– §**

SPY GUN (USA) 9 ch.g. Mt Livermore (USA) – Takeover Target (USA) (Nodouble (USA)) [2009 52§: f7g f7g p9.5g2 p9.5g p9.5g p9.5g Feb 17] angular, useful-looking gelding: modest performer: stays 9.5f: acts on all-weather, soft and good to firm going: usually wears headgear: unreliable. *T. Wall* **50 §**

SPYING 2 ch.g. (Mar 16) Observatory (USA) 131 – Mint Royale (IRE) 44 (Cadeaux Genereux 131) [2009 7.5m* 7m* 6.5m Sep 10] rangy gelding: fifth foal: half-brother to useful 5f (at 2 yrs) to 9f (in USA) winner La Neige (by Royal Applause) and fairly useful 5f to 8.6f winner Ten Shun (by Pivotal): dam, sprint maiden, sister to Prix Morny/Middle Park Stakes winner Bahamian Bounty: fairly useful performer: won maiden at Beverley in July and minor event at Newcastle (beat Bow Beaver 3½ lengths) in August: well below form in sales race at Doncaster (gelded after): will stay 1m. *Mrs A. Duffield* **94**

SQUAD 3 ch.g. Choisir (AUS) 126 – Widescreen (USA) (Distant View (USA) 126) [2009 60: p8g p10g4 p10g4 10.2g3 12m 10d6 8.3m3 9m5 8.5g3 10d* 10m2 11.5d2 10m* 12s3 p10m Dec 10] angular gelding: fair handicapper: won at Brighton in August and September: stays 11.5f: acts on polytrack, good to firm and good to soft going: tried visored. *S. Dow* **76**

SQUADRON 5 b.g. Sakhee (USA) 136 – Machaera (Machiavellian (USA) 123) [2009 16s5 Apr 18] well-made gelding: unraced on Flat in 2008 (useful hurdler): fair form only outing in 2009: stays 2m: raced only on polytrack and good ground or softer on turf. *A. King* **72**

SQUANDER 3 b.f. Dr Fong (USA) 128 – Ghariba 112 (Final Straw 127) [2009 7s Jul 21] half-sister to several winners, including Italian sprinter Reinaldo (by Green Desert) and French 10.5f winner Lord Darnley (by Darshaan), both useful: dam, won Nell Gwyn Stakes, half-sister to smart performer up to 2m Braashee: badly in need of experience in maiden at Yarmouth: sold 22,000 gns. *Sir Michael Stoute* **–**

SQUARE OF GOLD (FR) 3 ch.g. Gold Away (IRE) 125 – All Square (FR) (Holst (USA) 119) [2009 8.1g^{6} 7.1g 6d 6.1d Sep 4] signs of a little ability. *A. W. Carroll* –

SQUARE PANTS (IRE) 2 b.g. (Apr 10) Kheleyf (USA) 116 – Bron Hilda (IRE) 50 (Namaqualand (USA)) [2009 p8.6g Oct 1] 33/1, soundly beaten in claimer at Wolverhampton. *J. A. Osborne* –

SQUIRTLE (IRE) 6 ch.m. In The Wings 128 – Manilia (FR) (Kris 135) [2009 73§: p16g^{5} p16.5g^{5} 15g* 16d 16s^{6} 16d p16.5g^{4} p16.5g^{4} p16.5g^{3} p13.9g^{3} p16.5g^{3} p16.5g^{4} p13.9g* Dec 14] workmanlike mare: modest handicapper nowadays: won at Warwick in June and Wolverhampton in December: stays 16.5f: acts on polytrack, firm and soft going: has been visored: held up (often races lazily): not one to rely on. *W. M. Brisbourne* **63 §**

SRI KANDI 3 ch.f. Pivotal 124 – Aunt Pearl (USA) (Seattle Slew (USA)) [2009 79: 9.9f p10g^{6} May 27] lengthy, unfurnished filly: fair handicapper: may prove best short of 1¼m: acts on polytrack, firm and good to soft going. *P. F. I. Cole* **75**

SRI KUANTAN (IRE) 5 ch.g. Spinning World (USA) 130 – Miss Asia Quest 70 (Rainbow Quest (USA) 134) [2009 85: f8d f11g^{4} p10g^{2} 10.1d^{2} 10.1d^{4} 14.1g* 14.1m^{6} 11.5m^{3} 9.9g^{2} 10g 12m 12m 10.1m 10.4g Oct 9] sturdy gelding: fairly useful handicapper: won at Yarmouth in April: left R. C. Guest prior to final start: free-going sort, but seems to stay 1¾m: acts on polytrack, unraced on extremes of going on turf: tried blinkered: usually tongue tied nowadays: not straightforward. *R. A. Harris* **82**

SRI PUTRA 3 b.c. Oasis Dream 129 – Wendylina (IRE) (In The Wings 128) [2009 101: 7s^{4} 8d^{5} 8m* 10m* 10g^{5} 10v Nov 8] well-made colt: smart performer: improved to win handicap at Ascot (beat Peking Prince ½ length) in July and followed up in Prix Guillaume d'Ornano at Deauville (readily by ¾ length from Three Bodies) in August: stays 1¼m: best efforts on good to firm going, ran poorly on heavy in Premio Roma at Rome final start. *M. A. Jarvis* **115**

H.R.H. Sultan Ahmad Shah's "Sri Putra"

STACELITA (FR) 3 b.f. Monsun (GER) 124 – Soignee (GER) 104 (Dashing Blade 117) [2009 10v* 10.5s* 10s* 10.5m* 12g* 12g Oct 4] **123**

Jean-Claude Rouget's success in the French trainers' championship was the first by a trainer based in the French Provinces, his stable being at Pau in the far south-west. Chantilly's traditional dominance as a training centre is coming under pressure nowadays from Rouget, Alex Pantall and Eric Libaud. Pantall trains in the Loire Valley east of Nantes and has regularly finished in the top six in the table since 2000, while Eric Libaud, trainer of Vision d'Etat, trains around one hundred and fifty miles south-west of Paris beyond Le Mans. For all the merits of Pau as a warm location for training, there are some inconveniences. Early in the season Rouget revealed: 'I have to take over one hundred and fifty flights a year and cover about one hundred thousand kilometres in my car. We have five horseboxes in the yard and they each clock up around eighty thousand kilometres.' He doubtless feels it is all worthwhile.

As may be deduced from the €6,110,140 prize money his runners earned, Rouget enjoyed success both in terms of quality as well as quantity—his ratio of winners to runners is remarkably high, twenty-seven per cent in the latest season, and never below twenty-six per cent since 2000—though his ground-breaking success caused little more than a ripple outside racing circles. References to Rouget on the internet are few and far between, for example. The free encyclopaedia *Wikipedia* has entries for Fabre, de Royer Dupre and Criquette Head-Maarek, among others, but there's no entry for Rouget. His achievement was recognised tangibly when Hamdan Al Maktoum decided to send him ten horses late in the year, the most notable of them the Prix Marcel Boussac third Joanna. Rouget won six French Group 1 events in 2009, the Poule d'Essai des Pouliches with Elusive Wave, the Prix Saint-Alary, Prix de Diane and Prix Vermeille with Stacelita, the Prix d'Ispahan with Never On Sunday and the Prix du Jockey Club with Le Havre. Le Havre was not one of the best winners of the Prix du Jockey Club (unfortunately he was unable to run again) and Stacelita was no Zarkava. Stacelita is a fine filly all the same and she remained unbeaten (admittedly by virtue of Dar Re Mi's controversial disqualification in the Vermeille) until the Prix de l'Arc de Triomphe. Typically for a Rouget runner, she had her first race as a two-year-old far from the metropolitan tracks, at Salon-de-Provence, landing the odds in a newcomers event in October. She was out early as a three-year-old, starting long odds on and making all—she invariably races prominently—in a minor event at Toulouse in February. Stepped up in grade just over a month later in the Prix Rose de Mai, a listed race at Saint-Cloud, Stacelita made short work of four opponents at odds on again, defeating Divine Comedy by four lengths, after which a bout of coughing reportedly prevented her contesting the Prix Cleopatre.

Stacelita's next appearance came in the Montjeu Coolmore Prix Saint-Alary at Longchamp in mid-May, a race that Rouget had won three times, with Ask For The Moon, Germance and Coquerelle between 2004 and 2007, but a race that struggles to justify its Group 1 status and is effectively viewed as a trial for the Prix de Diane. In twenty runnings of the Prix Saint-Alary between 1989 and 2008, only four winners, Behera in 1989, Rosefinch in 1992, Zainta in 1998 and Vadawina in 2005, achieved a rating of 117 or higher in the race, and a number of modest fillies by Group 1 standards have run into a place. There was only one pattern winner

Montjeu Coolmore Prix Saint-Alary, Longchamp—Stacelita is stepped up in class and takes her unbeaten record to four; the grey Article Rare is her nearest pursuer

among Stacelita's six opponents, Article Rare, who achieved a Timeform rating of 103 when landing the Prix des Reservoirs at two and had finished last in the Prix de la Grotte on her reappearance. Stacelita started favourite and justified the confidence in great style, soon leading going smoothly and drawing clear after the field turned into the straight, eventually being allowed to coast home over the last seventy-five yards as she beat Article Rare by six lengths.

The Prix de Diane at Chantilly a month later lacked a sponsor but its first prize of £400,982 still dwarfed the £198,695 earned by Sariska for her success in the Oaks at Epsom. Rouget had saddled Le Havre to win the Prix du Jockey Club the previous week so he was attempting to emulate Charlie Elliott, who completed the double in 1956 with Philius and Apollonia. Since then, some outstanding trainers had won the two classics, Alain de Royer Dupre, for instance, training five winners of each race, though none had managed to win both classics in the same year. Stacelita was a short-priced favourite to beat eleven rivals headed by Celimene (Prix Penelope), Board Meeting (promoted to second in the Prix Cleopatre), Fantasia (the only runner trained outside France, who had come third in the Poule d'Essai des Pouliches), Rouget's other contender Tamazirte (second in the Poule d'Essai des Pouliches) and the Aga Khan's lightly-raced Shediyama. The others included Prix Vanteaux winner Denomination and Plumania, who had come fifth in the Prix Saint-Alary. None of them could hold a candle to Stacelita, who moved easily behind Board Meeting's pacemaker Onega Lake for much of the race, took up the running entering the home straight and quickened in eye-catching fashion a furlong and a half out. Christophe Lemaire had an armchair ride and Stacelita won comfortably by four lengths from Tamazirte, with Plumania half a length away third. Stacelita ran in different colours at Chantilly, her original owners having sold a half share to Martin Schwartz, who was completing a memorable classic double, as he also owns Elusive Wave.

Stacelita was the tenth Prix Saint-Alary winner to land the Prix de Diane, following La Sega, Belle Sicambre, Pistol Packer, Madelia, Reine de Saba, Harbour, Lacovia, Indian Skimmer and Zainta. The standard policy with a Prix de Diane winner who can be expected to stay a mile and a half is to have the best part of three months off before being brought back for the Prix Vermeille at Longchamp, to be followed, if successful, by a tilt at the Prix de l'Arc de Triomphe. That was what connections did with Stacelita, though only Pistol Packer, among the fillies listed above, had been successful in the Vermeille. The form of Stacelita's Prix de Diane victory was well up to standard for the race, and was almost on a par with the form shown by the best winners over the previous decade—Egyptband, Divine Proportions and Zarkava—but it was hardly fair to regard her, as some observers did, as another Zarkava. The controversy surrounding Stacelita's victory in the Qatar Prix Vermeille is dealt with in the essay on Dar Re Mi, but one thing was not disputed: Stacelita was not the best filly in the race on the day, and she did not reproduce her Chantilly form. Stacelita started at a shade of odds on in a field of twelve including five four-year-olds headed by second favourite Dar Re Mi, fresh from her victory over Sariska in the Yorkshire Oaks, and the Prix de Pomone winner Armure. Among the three-year-olds, Board Meeting and Plumania, first and third in the Prix de Psyche, lined up again. Plumania's trainer Andre Fabre also ran

Prix de Diane, Chantilly—a third classic winner in France in 2009 for trainer Jean-Claude Rouget and jockey Christophe Lemaire; Stacelita is again impressive as she quickens clear of stable-companion Tamazirte, Plumania (right), Celimene, Board Meeting (rail) and Shediyama (noseband)

Qatar Prix Vermeille, Longchamp—
Stacelita is caught close home by Dar Re Mi but is awarded the race following the latter's disqualification; Plumania, Board Meeting (right) and Soberania (rail) are also promoted

Kalla, successful in the Prix Minerve, and there were two German-trained runners, notably Preis der Diana runner-up Soberania, though it was not a vintage renewal. Stacelita had the run of the race, tracking her pacemaker Volver until being allowed to slip through on the rail to lead a furlong and a half out. However, on this occasion, she did not accelerate anything like so strikingly as she had in some of her earlier races and she looked vulnerable with a furlong to go as Dar Re Mi tried to make ground. Stacelita battled on gamely but had no answer to Dar Re Mi, who caught her in the final strides to win by a short neck. Plumania was a length and a half away third, with Board Meeting and the hampered Soberania breathing down her neck in fourth and fifth. The third and fourth past the post were much closer to Stacelita than at Chantilly. Stacelita's final appearance came in the Prix de l'Arc de Triomphe back at Longchamp three weeks later, for which she had to be supplemented at a cost of €100,000. Starting 10/1 joint-second favourite with Fame And Glory, behind odds-on Sea The Stars, with Dar Re Mi at 23/1, Stacelita got worked up going out on to the course and broke away early from the parade. She was ridden by Christophe Soumillon in place of the injured Lemaire, who rode all Rouget's runners in the top races and had partnered Stacelita to her last four successes. Lemaire replaces the sacked Soumillon on the Aga Khan's horses in 2010, when Soumillon will take over as Rouget's metropolitan jockey. Stacelita led the main body of the Arc field and was the first to gather in the Ballydoyle pacemakers with less than two furlongs left. However, like all the others, Stacelita had no answer to Sea The Stars as he burst to the front a furlong out. Stacelita kept on, but was unable to hold off other challengers either and, at the line, she was only equal seventh with La Boum, almost five lengths behind the winner, with Dar Re Mi two places ahead of her. Stacelita's form was of a similar order to that in the Prix Vermeille, around 7 lb below her best.

Stacelita (FR) (b.f. 2006)	Monsun (GER) (br 1990)	Konigsstuhl (br 1976)	Dschingis Khan
			Konigskronung
		Mosella (b 1985)	Surumu
			Monasia
	Soignee (GER) (b 2002)	Dashing Blade (b 1987)	Elegant Air
			Sharp Castan
		Suivez (b 1990)	Fioravanti
			Sea Symphony

Scarcely a year goes by without Stacelita's sire Monsun being represented by a top-flight runner and, in addition to Stacelita, the now blind stallion was also represented in the latest season by Getaway, successful in two Group 1 races in Germany, and by Schiaparelli, who won a similar event in Italy. That took to twenty-seven the number of Group 1s won by the progeny of Monsun, a remarkable figure considering he has spent his career based in Germany, where he stood at a private fee at Gestut Schlenderhan in the latest season, after being advertised at €150,000 in 2008. Monsun is the most successful German-based sire in the history of the European pattern scheme with most of his runners suited by a mile and a quarter or further. Stacelita is his best filly to date, just ahead of the miler Anna

M. Schwartz/Ecurie Monastic's "Stacelita" (C. Lemaire)

Monda, rated 122 after winning the Premio Vittorio di Capua in 2005. Stacelita is the first foal out of her dam Soignee, whose 2007 foal, a filly by Footstepsinthesand named Sandy Girl, was led out unsold as a yearling at Deauville after the bidding reached €130,000 and finished second in a maiden at Bordeaux for the Rouget stable on her only start so far. Next came a filly by Shamardal foaled in 2008. Soignee, sold for €150,000 as a yearling at Baden-Baden, won two races as a juvenile, notably the listed Kronimus Rennen over seven and a half furlongs which she won by five lengths; she also finished second in the Group 3 Prix des Reservoirs over a mile. Soignee was one of four listed or pattern winners out of Suivez, a listed-placed winner out of a half-sister to the top-class miler Steinlen from the family of Irish Derby winner Zagreb. Two of the other stakes winners out of Suivez were by Monsun, the better of them the smart middle-distance colt Simoun, successful in the Group 2 Grosser Mercedes-Benz-Preis and Idee Hansa-Preis over eleven furlongs as a four-year-old. In a varied career, Simoun later contested the Supreme Novices' Hurdle in a spell with Martin Pipe and even ended up winning in the pointing field. Further back on the distaff side is the outstanding German racemare Schwarzgold, whose name is found in the pedigrees of exceptional middle-distance performers Slip Anchor and Sagace, among others. Stacelita, a tall, leggy, close-coupled filly with a rather unimpressive action, stays a mile and a half and acts on heavy and good to firm going. She remains in training. *J-C. Rouget, France*

STADIUM OF LIGHT (IRE) 2 b.g. (Jan 26) Fantastic Light (USA) 134 – Treble Seven (USA) 58 (Fusaichi Pegasus (USA) 130) [2009 7f 8g 8d Oct 22] useful-looking gelding: well held in maidens (gelded after): bred to stay 1m+. *H. Morrison* –

STAFFORD CHARLIE 3 ch.g. Silver Patriarch (IRE) 125 – Miss Roberto (IRE) 63 (Don Roberto (USA)) [2009 –: p9.5g^6 10.2g Apr 28] no form. *J. G. M. O'Shea* –

STAFF SERGEANT 2 b.c. (Jan 26) Dubawi (IRE) 129 – Miss Particular (IRE) 86 (Sadler's Wells (USA) 132) [2009 p7g Nov 18] first foal: dam, 1¼m/1½m winner, sister to Oaks third Relish The Thought: 7/4, seventh to Khanivorous in maiden at Kempton, **52 p**

slowly away and not unduly knocked about: likely to be suited by 1m+: sure to improve. *M. Johnston*

STAGE ACCLAIM (IRE) 4 b.g. Acclamation 118 – Open Stage (IRE) (Sadler's Wells (USA) 132) [2009 75: p12.2g^6 Nov 2] lengthy gelding: fair performer: well below form only outing on Flat in 2009: stays 1¼m: acts on firm and good to soft going, probably on polytrack: tried blinkered/in cheekpieces. *C. J. Down* **–**

STAGECOACH EMERALD 7 ch.g. Spectrum (IRE) 126 – Musician 104 (Shirley Heights 130) [2009 –: p13.9g 11.5g f14g p16g f14m* f14m^4 Dec 5] close-coupled gelding: modest handicapper: won at Southwell in November: stays 2m: acts on all-weather and good to soft ground: often wears headgear: tried tongue tied. *R. W. Price* **59**

STAGECOACH JADE (IRE) 3 ch.f. Peintre Celebre (USA) 137 – Starring Role (IRE) (Glenstal (USA) 118) [2009 p9.5g* p9.5g* 10m^2 10.1d^4 Jun 27] half-sister to several winners, including useful French 1m to 11f winner Blasket Island (by Kenmare) and Irish 8-y-o Baggio: dam unraced: fair performer: won maiden in March and handicap in April, both at Wolverhampton: stayed 1¼m: acted on polytrack and good to firm going: stud. *M. Johnston* **78**

STAGE PERFORMANCE (IRE) 3 ch.f. Danehill Dancer (IRE) 117 – Stage Presence (IRE) 95 (Selkirk (USA) 129) [2009 10m 10.2g Oct 21] 375,000Y: big, rangy filly: fourth foal: sister to useful 2006 2-y-o 6f and 7f (Sweet Solera Stakes) winner English Ballet and half-sister to 2005 2-y-o 5f winner Spectacular Show (by Spectrum): dam, 7f/1m winner, half-sister to dam of smart Irish/US performer up to 1½m Winchester: well held in maidens. *J. H. M. Gosden* **–**

STAGS LEAP (IRE) 2 b.c. (Mar 26) Refuse To Bend (IRE) 128 – Swingsky (IRE) (Indian Ridge 123) [2009 7.1m^5 7d* 7.1g* 8g Oct 10] €110,000Y: first foal: dam, French 7.5f winner, sister to useful French winner up to 13f Indianski: fairly useful performer: won maiden at Goodwood and minor event at Warwick (by ½ length from Avonrose) in August: stiff task, not disgraced in Autumn Stakes at Ascot final start: should stay beyond 1m. *R. Hannon* **84**

STALKING SHADOW (USA) 4 b.c. Storm Cat (USA) – Strategic Maneuver (USA) (Cryptoclearance (USA)) [2009 96: a8f a5f^5 a8g* 6.5m* 8m^4 7m Jun 19] neat colt: useful handicapper: improved when winning at Jebel Ali in February and Abu Dhabi (beat Taqseem 1¼ lengths) in March for M. bin Shafya: rejoined former trainer, better effort back in Britain when creditable fourth to Cadre at Yarmouth: effective at 6.5f to 1m: acts on dirt, soft and good to firm going: returned to UAE, joining S. Seemar. *Saeed bin Suroor* **101**

STAMFORD BLUE 8 b.g. Bluegrass Prince (IRE) 110 – Fayre Holly (IRE) 57 (Fayruz 116) [2009 87, a–: 6m^6 5.3m^6 6m 6.1g 7f 6.1m^3 6d^4 6g* 5.1v^3 6d^6 5.1m 7.1d 5.7g Sep 7] workmanlike gelding: just fair handicapper at 8 yrs: won at Lingfield in July: has won at 1m, best at 6f: acts on any turf going: tried in cheekpieces, blinkered nowadays. *R. A. Harris* **69**

STAND AND FIGHT (IRE) 2 b.g. (Mar 29) Invincible Spirit (IRE) 121 – Up On Points 97 (Royal Academy (USA) 130) [2009 5s 5d^4 p5g^2 p5f^3 5g* 5m Jun 16] €20,000Y: good-topped gelding: fourth foal: half-brother to fairly useful 6f (including at 2 yrs)/7f winner Buckie Massa (by Best of The Bests) and 2005 2-y-o 7f winner Zafantage (by Zafonic): dam 2-y-o 7f winner: fairly useful performer: made all in maiden at Down Royal in May, winning readily by 5½ lengths from Money Trader: down the field in listed Windsor Castle Stakes at Royal Ascot next time: gelded after: will prove best at 5f/6f: acts on polytrack and good to soft ground: sent to Hong Kong, where renamed Young Supreme. *Kevin Prendergast, Ireland* **93**

STAND GUARD 5 b.g. Danehill (USA) 126 – Protectress 110 (Hector Protector (USA) 124) [2009 88: p9.5g^2 p10g^4 p9.5g^4 p9.5g* p10g* p11g 10.1g 12m p11g^4 p8g^2 p9.5g p9.5g^3 p8.6g* p10m p8f Dec 20] lengthy gelding: useful handicapper on all-weather, little form on turf: won at Wolverhampton in February, Kempton in March and Wolverhampton in November: effective at 8.6f to 1½m: acts on polytrack: consistent. *P. Howling* **– a98**

STAND IN FLAMES 4 b.f. Celtic Swing 138 – Maid of Arc (USA) 58 (Patton (USA) 110) [2009 86: 6m 7m 7.1m 8.3v 7s* 7.1d 7.1d^3 7m^3 10d 7m^6 f7m p8.6g Nov 16] angular filly: just fair performer at 4 yrs: won seller at Leicester (left Pat Eddery 5,200 gns) in August: effective at 6f to 8.3f: acts on heavy and good to firm going: races prominently: none too consistent. *George Baker* **65**

STANDPOINT 3 b.g. Oasis Dream 129 – Waki Music (USA) 97 (Miswaki (USA) 124) [2009 76: 6m^2 7.1f* 8g^6 7.1m Jul 4] well-made gelding: has markedly round action: fairly useful performer: won maiden at Warwick in May: effective at 6f/7f: acts on polytrack and firm ground, unraced on softer than good: sold 10,000 gns in October. *Sir Michael Stoute* **80**

STANLEY BRIDGE 2 b.g. (Feb 22) Avonbridge 123 – Antonia's Folly 64 (Music Boy 124) [2009 5m 5g 5m 6d⁶ 8g 7.2v Oct 31] no form. *A. Berry* –

STANLEY GOODSPEED 6 ch.g. Inchinor 119 – Flying Carpet 76 (Barathea (IRE) 127) [2009 90: p6g⁴ p7g 6d⁶ 6v⁶ 7.1m p7.1g⁶ 7g⁴ 7m⁵ 8.3s⁵ 7.1d² p7f³ p7.1g² p7.1g⁶ p7.1g p7m³ p7.1g f6d Dec 29] big, good-topped gelding: fair handicapper nowadays: effective at 6f to 8.6f: acts on polytrack, soft and good to firm going: usually in headgear/ tongue tie: held up: not one to trust. *J. W. Hills* **77 §**

STANLEY RIGBY 3 b.g. Dr Fong (USA) 128 – Crystal (IRE) 93 (Danehill (USA) 126) [2009 –: 10.4v 10m⁶ Aug 24] sturdy gelding: well held in maidens. *C. F. Wall* –

STAN'S COOL CAT (IRE) 3 b.f. One Cool Cat (USA) 123 – Beautiful France (IRE) (Sadler's Wells (USA) 132) [2009 83: 7f 8g³ 10s* 10.2g³ p10f 10.4m⁴ p10g⁴ p8m⁶ Nov 26] leggy, attractive filly: fairly useful handicapper, better on turf: improved when winning at Newbury in July: worth a try at 1½m: acts on soft and good to firm going: tried blinkered. *P. F. I. Cole* **90 a84**

STANSTILL (IRE) 3 b.g. Statue of Liberty (USA) 115 – Fervent Wish (Rainbow Quest (USA) 134) [2009 60: 11.1g² 10.1d² 10g² 12.3m* 12m* 14m* 13.1m⁶ Sep 19] good-topped gelding: useful handicapper: progressed in 2009, winning at Chester in June, Ascot in July and Haydock (beat Interdiamonds by length in 4-runner event) in August: often races freely, but stays 1¾m: acts on good to firm and good to soft ground. *G. A. Swinbank* **97**

STAR ACCLAIM 4 b.f. Acclamation 118 – Tropical Lass (IRE) 67 (Ballad Rock 122) [2009 70?: 6.1g f6g f8m f8g p7.1g⁵ Sep 12] lengthy filly: modest maiden: stays 1m: acts on all-weather and soft ground: often tongue tied. *E. V. Stanford* **52**

STAR ADDITION 3 ch.g. Medicean 128 – Star Cast (IRE) 82 (In The Wings 128) [2009 6m⁶ 5m 6s 5m 5g³ 5m 6g² 5g⁵ Oct 23] maiden: seemed to show fair form when second at Redcar: bred to stay 7f: best efforts on good going. *E. J. Alston* **65 ?**

STARBOUGG 5 b.m. Tobougg (IRE) 125 – Celestial Welcome 96 (Most Welcome 131) [2009 –: 15.8s Oct 27] good-topped mare: maiden: little form on Flat since 2006. *K. G. Reveley* –

STARBURST 4 b.f. Fantastic Light (USA) 134 – Rasmalai 71 (Sadler's Wells (USA) 132) [2009 61: p12g 10m⁵ p12g² p12m² p12.2g* Dec 17] lengthy filly: fair performer: won maiden at Wolverhampton in December: stays 1½m: acts on polytrack. *A. M. Balding* **78**

STARBURST EXCEL 2 b.f. (Feb 26) Exceed And Excel (AUS) 126 – Homeward (IRE) 49 (Kris 135) [2009 5m⁴ 5m⁵ 5f p5.1g p5g Oct 22] unfurnished filly: second foal: dam lightly-raced half-sister to very smart 6f/7f winner Susu: easily best effort when fourth to Its Alright in maiden at Newmarket: seemed amiss next 2 starts: raced only at 5f. *M. G. Quinlan* **70 d**

STAR CHOICE 4 ch.g. Choisir (AUS) 126 – Bay Queen 85 (Damister (USA) 123) [2009 71: p12m² p13g⁴ p12.2g² p16g⁵ p12.2g* p12g⁴ 11.9g² p12g⁵ 11.9f² 12m 10.9d⁴ 11.9g 12g⁵ p12m Dec 9] tall, lengthy gelding: fair handicapper: won at Wolverhampton in March: said to have had breathing problem penultimate start: stays 13f: acts on polytrack, firm and good to soft ground: tried in cheekpieces, often visored. *J. Pearce* **75**

STARCLASS 2 b.f. (Mar 8) Starcraft (NZ) 128 – Classic Millennium 72 (Midyan (USA) 124) [2009 7d Oct 12] 3,000Y: second foal: dam 1½m/1¾m winner: 66/1, 3¼ lengths seventh to Qaraaba in maiden at Salisbury, staying on under considerate handling: will be suited by 1¼m+: should do better. *W. R. Swinburn* **66 p**

STARCROSS MAID 7 ch.m. Zaha (CAN) 106 – Maculatus (USA) (Sharpen Up 127) [2009 51§, a62§: f12d⁶ f11g³ f11g² May 1] poor performer: stays 1½m: acts on all-weather and firm going: tried blinkered: travels strongly held up, but often finds little: one to treat with caution. *A. G. Juckes* **47 §**

STAR CRUISER (USA) 2 b.g. (Feb 13) Golden Missile (USA) 123 – Beautiful Star (USA) (War Chant (USA) 126) [2009 7m 6m Jul 29] well-made gelding: better effort in maidens when mid-field at Redcar (still backward, not knocked about) latter start. *T. D. Easterby* **52**

STARDUST MEMORIES (UAE) 3 b.f. Halling (USA) 133 – Clarinda (IRE) 91 (Lomond (USA) 128) [2009 p8g 10.2d p12g Nov 13] 1,200Y: smallish, sturdy filly: third foal: dam, 2-y-o 5f winner, half-sister to dam of smart 1¼m performer Parasol (by Halling): always behind in maidens. *John Berry* –

STARFALA 4 gr.f. Galileo (IRE) 134 – Farfala (FR) 106 (Linamix (FR) 127) [2009 98p: 12m^2 11.9g^4 11.9m^3 14d 12m 14.6m^2 16m^6 Oct 17] leggy filly: useful performer: improved in 2009, best effort when short-head second to The Miniver Rose in Park Hill Stakes at Doncaster sixth start: made frame earlier in listed races at Ascot and Haydock, and Lancashire Oaks at Haydock (third to Barshiba): sweated up prior to below-form sixth in Jockey Club Cup at Newmarket final outing: should stay 2m: acts on all-weather and good to firm going. *P. F. I. Cole* **108**

STARGAZE (IRE) 2 b.c. (Jan 26) Oasis Dream 129 – Dafariyna (IRE) 71 (Nashwan (USA) 135) [2009 5.2s 5.1g^4 5m* 5.1g* 6g^3 6m^5 p7f^2 Dec 19] 70,000F: sturdy colt: fourth foal: half-brother to 2006 2-y-o 7f winner Bayonyx (by Montjeu): dam Irish maiden (second at 1m/9f), out of Cork And Orrery winner Dafayna, herself half-sister to 2000 Guineas winner Doyoun: useful performer: won maiden at Lingfield in May and minor event at Bath (by head from Angel's Pursuit) in July: best effort when 3¼ lengths third to Dick Turpin in Richmond Stakes at Goodwood: left A. Balding and off 3 months, well below form in minor event at Lingfield final start: effective at 5f/6f: acts on good to firm ground. *A. Bailey* **101**

STARGAZING (IRE) 3 b.f. Galileo (IRE) 134 – Autumnal (IRE) 104 (Indian Ridge 123) [2009 8.3m Sep 30] useful-looking filly: has scope: third foal: dam 5f (at 2 yrs)/6f winner: signs of ability in maiden at Nottingham: likely to do better. *B. J. Meehan* **– p**

STARGAZY 5 b.g. Observatory (USA) 131 – Romantic Myth 105 (Mind Games 121) [2009 56: p7g p7.1g* p7.1g^6 p7.1g^3 p7.1g p8g p7f Dec 16] sturdy, well-made gelding: modest performer: won minor event at Wolverhampton in January: left W. Turner after fifth start: stays easy 7f: acts on polytrack and firm going: tried blinkered/in cheekpieces/tongue tied: none too consistent. *A. J. Lidderdale* **56**

STARKAT 3 b.f. Diktat 126 – Star of Normandie (USA) 93 (Gulch (USA)) [2009 p8g 9g^2 10.2d^4 Oct 15] unfurnished filly: first foal: dam 1m/1¼m winner: left J. Toller, best effort in maidens (fair form) when fourth at Nottingham final start: should prove best around 1¼m. *Jane Chapple-Hyam* **78**

STARK CONTRAST (USA) 5 ch.g. Gulch (USA) – A Stark Is Born (USA) (Graustark) [2009 71: p10g p8.6g^6 p8.6g^5 p8.6g p8.6g^4 p9.5g p9.5g p8.6g^6 7f 10.2f^3 10d 8f^6 p8m^3 p8m^6 p9.5g Dec 28] tall, lengthy gelding: modest handicapper nowadays: stays 1¼m: acts on polytrack and firm ground: tried in blinkers/cheekpieces/tongue tie. *M. D. I. Usher* **60**

STARLA DANCER (GER) 3 b.f. Danehill Dancer (IRE) 117 – Starla (GER) (Lando (GER) 128) [2009 52: 8m^3 7.5g^2 8.5m^4 9.3d^2 8m^2 9.8m^4 p9.5g^4 10.4g* 10.3g^2 Oct 24] leggy filly: fairly useful handicapper: improved when winning at York in October: good second to Nevada Desert at Doncaster next time: will prove best up to 10.4f: acts on polytrack, good to firm and good to soft going. *R. A. Fahey* **88**

STARLIGHT BOY 2 b.c. (Apr 19) Firebreak 125 – Dispol Verity 60 (Averti (IRE) 117) [2009 6m Sep 15] 66/1 and very green, tailed off in maiden at Haydock. *S. Wynne* **–**

STARLIGHT GAZER 6 b.g. Observatory (USA) 131 – Dancing Fire (USA) (Dayjur (USA) 137) [2009 80: p7.1g f8f^5 Dec 12] small, close-coupled gelding: fair handicapper at 5 yrs: off 12 months, just modest form in 2009: stays 1m: raced mainly on good ground or softer on turf: tongue tied/visored nowadays. *J. A. Geake* **55**

STAR LINKS (USA) 3 b.c. Bernstein (USA) 115 – Startarette (USA) (Dixieland Band (USA)) [2009 88: 9g^4 8m^2 p7g^3 8d^3 7.1m^2 7g^6 8.5m^4 8.1m 8m 8m^6 Oct 5] leggy colt: fairly useful handicapper: stays 9f: acts on polytrack, good to firm and good to soft going: sold 8,000 gns. *R. Hannon* **88**

STARLISH (IRE) 4 b. or br.c. Rock of Gibraltar (IRE) 133 – Stylish (Anshan 119) [2009 109: a9.5g^4 9m^2 9.3d* 10g^2 10s^6 10g 9.8g^5 10d* 10g^6 Dec 13] fourth foal: closely related to 6-y-o Count Trevisio and fairly useful 7f (including at 2 yrs)/1m winner Due Respect (both by Danehill) and half-brother to smart 7f (at 2 yrs) to 2m winner Solent (by Montjeu): dam unraced half-sister to very smart sprinter Eveningperformance: smart performer: won minor event at Longchamp in May and Prix Andre Baboin at Lyon Parilly (asserted close home to beat Capitaine Courage a neck) in October: also ran creditably at Longchamp in between when short-neck second to Stotsfold in La Coupe and 1¼ lengths fifth to Pipedreamer in Prix Dollar, and at Sha Tin when 4¼ lengths sixth to Vision d'Etat in Hong Kong Cup final start: stays 11f: acts on heavy ground: has hung left. *E. Lellouche, France* **117**

STARLIT SANDS 4 b.f. Oasis Dream 129 – Shimmering Sea 89 (Slip Anchor 136) [2009 104: 5.1g 5m Aug 31] good-topped filly: well below useful best both starts in 2009: **–**

will prove best at 5f/easy 6f: raced only on polytrack and good/good to firm going: tried blinkered: usually front runner. *Sir Mark Prescott*

STARMAAMUL 2 b.g. (Mar 31) Elmaamul (USA) 125 – Catwalk Girl 53 (Skyliner 117) [2009 8d Aug 28] 33/1 and very green, tailed off in maiden at Thirsk. *K. A. Ryan* –

STAR OF KALANI (IRE) 2 b.g. (Mar 7) Ashkalani (IRE) 128 – La Bekkah (FR) (Nononito (FR) 121) [2009 8.5m 8.3d 8.3g Oct 28] workmanlike gelding: well held in maidens/seller, then gelded. *G. M. Moore* –

STAR OF MEMORY (FR) 5 b.g. Starborough 126 – Desert Memory (FR) (Desert King (IRE) 129) [2009 11.7m 10.2m Sep 30] strong ex-French gelding: placed both starts in France in 2007 for D. de Watrigant: well beaten both starts in Britain: stays 1¼m. *D. G. Bridgwater* –

STAR OF POMPEY 5 b.m. Hernando (FR) 127 – Discerning 96 (Darshaan 133) [2009 64?: p12g p16g* 17.2m^2 16g^5 14g 16g^6 p16g Oct 14] good-topped mare: fair handicapper: won at Kempton in June: stays 17f: acts on polytrack and good to firm ground. *A. B. Haynes* 68

STAR OF SOHO (IRE) 2 b.f. (Mar 8) Starcraft (NZ) 128 – Trois Graces (USA) (Alysheba (USA)) [2009 7g Oct 31] €28,000Y: half-sister to several winners, including smart 7f (at 2 yrs)/1m winner Flat Spin (by Spinning World) and useful French 2008 2-y-o 5f winner Abbeyside (by Danehill Dancer): dam, French 1m winner, half-sister to smart French sprinter/miler Crack Regiment and to Prix de l'Abbaye second La Grande Epoque: 125/1, well held in maiden at Newmarket. *E. J. Creighton* –

STAR OF SOPHIA (IRE) 3 b.f. Hawk Wing (USA) 136 – Sofia Aurora (USA) (Chief Honcho (USA)) [2009 35: p10g Apr 8] sturdy filly: poor maiden: tried visored: signs of temperament. *Mrs A. Duffield* –

STAR PROMISE 2 b.f. (Jan 26) Mujahid (USA) 125 – Diamond Promise (IRE) 72 (Fayruz 116) [2009 5d f5g* 5g^2 p5.1g f5g^2 Dec 27] rather leggy filly: fourth foal: dam 5f/6f winner, including at 2 yrs: fair performer: won maiden at Southwell in July: good second in nursery at Musselburgh (hung right) next time: raced only at 5f: acts on fibresand. *T. D. Barron* 74

STAR ROVER (IRE) 2 ch.c. (Mar 19) Camacho 118 – Charlene Lacy (IRE) 77 (Pips Pride 117) [2009 p5g* 5.1m* 5f* 5.1m* 5m^3 5m^2 5m^6 5m 5.2d^6 5g^4 5m* 5m 6m 5g Oct 10] €17,000Y: small colt: seventh foal: half-brother to 8.6f winner Tetcott (by Definite Article) and winner in Italy by Bad As I Wanna Be: dam 2-y-o 5f winner: useful performer: won maiden at Kempton in March, minor events at Nottingham and Thirsk in April and at Chester in May, and listed race at York (by neck from Mister Manannan) in 103

Julia Graves Roses Stakes, York—the tough and genuine Star Rover (left) gains a well-deserved listed win at the chief expense of Mister Manannan, the pair clear of Love Lockdown

August: respectable seventh to Our Jonathan in Cornwallis Stakes at Ascot final start: speedy, likely to prove best at 5f: acts on polytrack and firm going, probably on good to soft: front runner/races prominently: tough and genuine. *P. D. Evans*

STAR RUBY (IRE) 3 b.f. Rock of Gibraltar (IRE) 133 – Purple Spirit (IRE) 81 (Sadler's Wells (USA) 132) [2009 10m* 10.4m² May 13] 105,000Y: well-made filly: first foal: dam, Irish maiden (placed up to 1½m), half-sister to Irish 1000 Guineas winner Matiya: useful form: 9/4 favourite, won maiden at Sandown in April by 2¼ lengths from Hidden Brief: better form when 3¾ lengths second to Sariska in Musidora Stakes at York next time: not seen out again: likely to stay 1½m. *P. W. Chapple-Hyam* **109**

STARRY MOUNT 2 ch.c. (Feb 3) Observatory (USA) 131 – Lady Lindsay (IRE) 105 (Danehill Dancer (IRE) 117) [2009 6.1g 7m⁴ 8.3g⁵ 7.2v* Oct 31] third foal: half-brother to fairly useful French 6.5f to 1m (including 7f at 2 yrs) winner Mount Hollow (by Beat Hollow): dam 2-y-o 6f winner who stayed 1m: progressive form, winning nursery at Ayr by 2¼ lengths from Masked Dance: should be at least as effective at 1m as 7f: acts on heavy ground. *A. B. Haynes* **77 +**

STARSTREAMER (IRE) 2 ch.f. (Jan 22) Captain Rio 122 – Petra Nova 51 (First Trump 118) [2009 6m Aug 15] £32,000Y: sturdy filly: fifth foal: sister to 3-y-o Ingleby Lady and 4-y-o Mey Blossom and half-sister to 2 winners: dam sprint maiden: 9/1, last in maiden at Newbury. *M. P. Tregoning* **–**

STAR STRIDER 5 gr.g. Royal Applause 124 – Onefortheditch (USA) 79 (With Approval (CAN)) [2009 70, a82: p8.6g² p8g⁴ p8g⁵ 10g⁶ 8m 8m 7m⁴ 7g⁵ 7.6g 6d³ 6m 6g p8m⁵ p7.1g⁶ p7m* p9.5g p7.1g Dec 28] leggy gelding: fair handicapper, better on all-weather: left Gay Kelleway after eleventh start: won at Kempton in November: stays 1m: acts on polytrack, firm and good to soft going: tried in headgear: held up: no easy ride. *T. Keddy* **65 a77**

STARSTRUCK PETER (IRE) 5 b.g. Iron Mask (USA) 117 – Daraliya (IRE) (Kahyasi 130) [2009 63: p16g p12g 12.1m* 16.4m* p13.9g Jul 13] fair handicapper: left S. Curran and off 5 months, won at Chepstow and Folkestone in July: stays 2m: acts on polytrack and any turf going: blinkered nowadays: tongue tied at 3/4 yrs: races prominently: formerly weak finisher. *Jim Best* **72**

START RIGHT 2 b.c. (Apr 23) Footstepsinthesand 120 – Time Crystal (IRE) 83 (Sadler's Wells (USA) 132) [2009 6g 7g⁶ 7.1g² 8m³ 8.1m² p8.6g* Oct 10] 58,000F, €38,000Y: attractive colt: third foal: dam, 1½m winner, out of Lancashire Oaks winner State Crystal: fairly useful performer: won maiden at Wolverhampton: best effort when third to Azizi in nursery at Doncaster: stays 8.6f. *L. M. Cumani* **91**

STAR TWILIGHT 2 b.f. (Mar 8) King's Best (USA) 132 – Star Express 80 (Sadler's Wells (USA) 132) [2009 6m 7f⁴ p7g p6g Dec 3] tall, good-topped filly: third foal: sister to 2007 2-y-o 6f winner Haedi: dam, French 11.5f winner, sister to smart 7f/1m performer Yalaietanee: modest form in maidens first 2 starts: has found little, including in tongue tie final outing. *D. R. Lanigan* **55**

STARWATCH 2 b.g. (Apr 17) Observatory (USA) 131 – Trinity Reef 80 (Bustino 136) [2009 6m 6m² 7.1d⁶ 8m⁶ 6d p8m⁴ p7g⁴ p7f⁴ Dec 20] rather unfurnished gelding: modest maiden: bred to stay 1¼m: acts on polytrack, good to firm and good to soft going. *J. J. Bridger* **60**

STASH 3 b.g. Bold Edge 123 – Gemtastic 70 (Tagula (IRE) 116) [2009 81: p6g³ f5g³ p5.1g⁶ 5.3d 5.1g p5.1g⁵ p6g Dec 7] fair performer: likely to prove best kept to 5f/6f: best efforts on polytrack, no form on turf. *R. Hollinshead* **– a75**

STATE BANQUET (USA) 3 br.g. Fusaichi Pegasus (USA) 130 – Gracie Lady (IRE) (Generous (IRE) 139) [2009 83p: 10g² 10g³ 12g² p12g⁵ 11m⁶ Sep 23] deep-girthed gelding: fairly useful handicapper: improved when placed at Windsor and Goodwood second/third starts: let down by attitude in cheekpieces last 2 outings: effective at 1¼m/1½m: best efforts on good ground: sold 42,000 gns, then gelded: sent to USA. *H. Morrison* **92**

STATE FAIR 2 b.g. (Feb 20) Marju (IRE) 127 – Baralinka (IRE) 93 (Barathea (IRE) 127) [2009 5.2s⁵ 5g² 6m³ 7m³ 8v p7.1g Nov 2] lengthy gelding: has scope: second foal: dam, 5f (at 2 yrs)/6f winner, half-sister to high-class miler Soviet Song (by Marju): fairly useful form in maidens second/third starts (off over 4 months after): weakened tamely last 2 outings (gelded after): probably stays 7f: acts on good to firm ground. *P. F. I. Cole* **85**

STATE FUNCTION (IRE) 4 b.g. Grand Slam (USA) 120 – Well Designed (IRE) 70 (Sadler's Wells (USA) 132) [2009 61: 6f⁶ p8.6g Sep 25] maiden, very lightly raced: well held in 2009: tried tongue tied. *G. Prodromou* **–**

STATE GATHERING 2 b.c. (May 4) Royal Applause 124 – Flag (Selkirk (USA) 129) **58 +** [2009 6.5g 6g Oct 30] good-topped colt: modest form when down the field in maidens at Newbury and Newmarket (not unduly knocked about). *H. Candy*

STATE GENERAL (IRE) 3 b.g. Statue of Liberty (USA) 115 – Nisibis (In The Wings **–** 128) [2009 79: p10m* 10m p12g 11.6f 10.4g Oct 10] big, useful-looking gelding: fair **a77** performer: won handicap at Lingfield in January: well below form after: should stay 1½m: acts on polytrack, little form on turf. *Miss J. Feilden*

STATELY HOME (IRE) 3 b.c. Montjeu (IRE) 137 – Pescia (IRE) 98 (Darshaan 133) **106 §** [2009 10d* 11.1g^{2} 16f^{6} 12g^{6} Aug 13] well-made colt: fourth foal: dam, French 1¼m/ 1½m winner, out of half-sister to Dewhurst winner Tobougg: useful form: won maiden at Leopardstown in April easily by 2½ lengths from Yankee Doodle: failed to impress with attitude when showing similar form next 2 starts, 2½ lengths second to Parthenon in listed race at Hamilton and 9¼ lengths sixth to Holberg in Queen's Vase at Royal Ascot: broke down badly around 1f out in Ballyroan Stakes at Leopardstown final outing: stayed 2m: carried head most awkwardly, and was one to be wary of: dead. *A. P. O'Brien, Ireland*

STATESIDE (CAN) 4 b.f. El Corredor (USA) 123 – Double Trick (USA) (Phone Trick **70** (USA)) [2009 –: 10.9f^{2} 9.1g* 9.2m* 10f^{2} 12v^{5} 9.2v^{3} 12d Sep 6] workmanlike filly: fair handicapper: marked improvement in 2009, winning at Ayr in May and Hamilton in June: should stay 1½m: acts on any turf going. *R. A. Fahey*

STATE VISIT 2 b.c. (Mar 31) Dr Fong (USA) 128 – Saint Ann (USA) 66 (Geiger **57** Counter (USA)) [2009 8m 8.1m p7g^{5} Oct 24] strong colt: similar form in maidens, in blinkers final start: stays 1m. *W. R. Muir*

STATION PLACE 4 b.f. Bahamian Bounty 116 – Twin Time 77 (Syrtos 106) [2009 **–** 60: 7m 7.6g 7m^{5} p6g Oct 26] medium-sized filly: little impact in 2009. *A. B. Haynes*

STATUTE BOOK (IRE) 3 b.c. Statue of Liberty (USA) 115 – Velvet Slipper 50 **81** (Muhtafal (USA)) [2009 60+: f8g* p8g* p8g* f8g^{3} p8g 8d^{4} 10m p8g^{3} 8m^{3} p8g^{3} p8g p7.1g^{6} p8m Sep 30] fairly useful performer: won handicaps at Southwell, Lingfield and Kempton in February/March: in-and-out form after: stays 1m: acts on all-weather and good to soft going: sold 4,000 gns. *S. Kirk*

STAYING ON (IRE) 4 b.g. Invincible Spirit (IRE) 121 – Lakatoi 82 (Saddlers' Hall **113** (IRE) 126) [2009 110: 8m* 10.3m^{2} 10m^{6} 9s^{2} 10.4m^{5} 10m^{6} Aug 29] sturdy gelding: type to carry condition: smart performer: won listed race at Doncaster in April by ¾ length from Unnefer: held form well after in pattern company, best effort when 2 lengths second to Famous Name in International Stakes at the Curragh fourth outing: effective at 1m to 10.3f: acts on polytrack, firm and soft ground: visored (sweated up and raced freely) final start: tongue tied in 2009: front runner: game: sent to USA. *W. R. Swinburn*

STAY ON TRACK (IRE) 2 b.c. (Feb 19) Refuse To Bend (IRE) 128 – Blue Lightning **–** (Machiavellian (USA) 123) [2009 6d Jun 8] 11/1, down the field in maiden at Windsor, in touch until halfway. *E. F. Vaughan*

STEADY GAZE 4 b.g. Zamindar (USA) 116 – Krisia (Kris 135) [2009 –: p12g p9.5g **39** p12g Apr 2] poor maiden: tongue tied. *M. A. Allen*

STEAMER (IRE) 3 b.g. Xaar 132 – Antigone (IRE) 75 (Cape Cross (IRE) 129) [2009 **–** 7f 6g 8.1m Jul 1] little sign of ability in claimers. *P. Winkworth*

STEEL BLUE 9 b.g. Atraf 116 – Something Blue (Petong 126) [2009 79, a62: 6m 6v **68** 6d 6d 6m^{6} 6g 5m 6m^{6} 5s* 6d^{2} 6s^{4} 7m^{5} 6m p6g f6g Nov 17] leggy gelding: fair performer **a–** nowadays: won seller at Hamilton in August: best at 5f/6f: acts on dirt, firm and soft going, probably on polytrack: tried visored, usually in cheekpieces. *R. M. Whitaker*

STEEL CITY BOY (IRE) 6 b.g. Bold Fact (USA) 116 – Balgren (IRE) (Ballad Rock **74** 122) [2009 81: p5g^{4} p5g^{4} f5g^{5} p5g* p5.1g^{5} p6g p5.1g f5g 5.1g p6g p5.1g p5f Dec 19] lengthy, good-bodied gelding: fair handicapper: won at Kempton in February: stays 6f: acts on all-weather, soft and good to firm ground: tried in cheekpieces. *D. Shaw*

STEELCUT 5 b.g. Iron Mask (USA) 117 – Apple Sauce 70 (Prince Sabo 123) [2009 85: **87** 5m^{3} 5f* 5g^{5} 5d^{3} 5g 5d^{5} 5m^{4} 5m 5s^{4} 5d 5s^{4} 5.9d^{2} 5m 5m^{3} p6m* 6g^{3} p5g f5m Dec 15] good-topped gelding: fairly useful performer: won handicap at Thirsk in April and claimer at Kempton (left R. Fahey £7,000) in September: left Andrew Reid prior to final outing: stays 6f: acts on polytrack, firm and good to soft going: below form in headgear: none too consistent. *M. J. Scudamore*

STEELE TANGO (USA) 4 ch.c. Okawango (USA) 115 – Waltzing Around (IRE) **114** (Ela-Mana-Mou 132) [2009 107: 9m^{2} 10g^{4} 12m^{3} 10m 12m 10m^{5} 12g 9m* Oct 16] good-bodied colt: smart performer: better than ever when winning Thurlow Nunn Standen

Thurlow Nunn Standen Darley Stakes, Newmarket—25/1-shot Steele Tango (near side) edges out Glass Harmonium as Palavicini hangs on to third from the previous year's winner Charlie Farnsbarns

Darley Stakes at Newmarket in October by head from Glass Harmonium: ran creditably earlier when 3½ lengths second to Tazeez in Earl of Sefton Stakes at Newmarket, fourth to Tartan Bearer in Gordon Richards Stakes at Sandown and seventh to Cima de Triomphe in Brigadier Gerard Stakes at same course on fourth start: effective at 9f, seems to stay 1½m: acts on polytrack, soft and good to firm going. *R. A. Teal*

STEELEY FLYER 2 b.f. (Mar 3) Needwood Blade 117 – Gymcrak Flyer 73 (Aragon 118) [2009 5m 6m 6g^2 7s^5 p6g Aug 7] £2,000Y: leggy filly: fifth foal: half-sister to 2004 2-y-o 5f seller winner Bob's Flyer (by Lujain): dam 6f to 1m winner: poor maiden: stays 6f. *P. D. Evans* **48**

STEEL FREE (IRE) 3 b.f. Danehill Dancer (IRE) 117 – Candelabra 94 (Grand Lodge (USA) 125) [2009 7s^2 6g^3 7.1g* 7g p7g^6 7d^6 7.2g^4 7g^5 Oct 23] €150,000Y: strong, lengthy filly: second foal: half-sister to German 1m winner Eneyda (by Cape Cross): dam 7f winner: fairly useful performer: won maiden at Warwick in July: will stay 1m: acts on soft going: usually races prominently. *M. L. W. Bell* **81**

STEEL MASK (IRE) 4 b.c. Iron Mask (USA) 117 – Thorn Tree (Zafonic (USA) 130) [2009 47: f5f Dec 11] poor maiden: raced at 5f/6f: tongue tied sole 4-y-o start: looks hard ride. *M. Brittain* **42**

STEEL MY HEART (IRE) 2 b.f. (Apr 20) Clodovil (IRE) 116 – Antigonel (IRE) 59 (Fairy King (USA)) [2009 6g 6d^4 7d^6 7g^5 p6g Sep 2] 1,000Y: plain filly: fifth foal: half-sister to fairly useful 7f winner Lavenham (by Kalanisi): dam maiden (stayed 1m): poor form in sellers: tried visored: signs of temperament. *Miss D. Mountain* **44**

STEEL STOCKHOLDER 3 b.c. Mark of Esteem (IRE) 137 – Pompey Blue 71 (Abou Zouz (USA) 109) [2009 64: 6f^3 7g^6 6s^6 8d^4 8m 6m^5 7g^4 8g^4 8s 8d^4 8m^2 7v^2 7m^2 7g* p7.1g Dec 12] close-coupled colt: fair performer: won apprentice handicap at Doncaster in October: stays 1m: acts on any turf going. *M. Brittain* **73**

STEEL TRADE 3 b.g. Sakhee (USA) 136 – Hammiya (IRE) 103 (Darshaan 133) [2009 8m^6 7m^5 7.5m^2 8g 8.5m^3 8m^4 10.3g 8m^3 9.9g^6 9.8m^3 8.5g^4 Sep 22] €3,500Y: tall gelding: second foal: half-brother to smart 7f winner Masaalek (by Green Desert): dam 8.5f to 11.4f (Cheshire Oaks) winner: fair maiden: stays 1¼m: raced only on good/good to firm going: held up (sometimes slowly away). *M. Brittain* **76**

STEELY BIRD 2 gr.g. (Mar 15) Needwood Blade 117 – La Cygne Blanche (IRE) 46 (Saddlers' Hall (IRE) 126) [2009 8g 8g Oct 21] down the field in maidens. *Miss Jo Crowley* **–**

STEEPLE CASTER 3 ch.g. Compton Place 125 – Antonia's Double 84 (Primo Dominie 121) [2009 5.7g 5.1d May 18] well held in maidens. *J. M. Bradley* **–**

STEF AND STELIO 2 ch.g. (Feb 11) Bertolini (USA) 125 – Cashmere 86 (Barathea (IRE) 127) [2009 6m 5.9g f6g^3 6m p7.1g* f7f^2 p7.1g Nov 9] £17,000Y: tall gelding: fourth foal: dam, won around 7f, half-sister to Irish 1000 Guineas winner Classic Park, herself dam of Derby runner-up Walk In The Park: fair performer: won claimer at Wolverhampton in September: seemed amiss final start (gelded after): stays 7f: form only on all-weather: blinkered last 3 starts: temperament under suspicion. *G. A. Butler* **–** **a76**

STEFANKI (IRE) 2 b.g. (May 4) Danehill Dancer (IRE) 117 – Ghana (IRE) (Lahib (USA) 129) [2009 6m^2 7g p7.1m Nov 28] 23,000Y: fifth foal: half-brother to Irish 6f/1m winner Akua'ba (by Sadler's Wells) and Irish 2005 2-y-o 7f winner Ice Princess (by Grand Lodge) who stayed 11.3f, both useful: dam, French 9f winner, half-sister to National Stakes winner Heart of Darkness: best effort in maidens when ½-length second to Glen Shiel at Ffos Las: should stay at least 7f: gelded after final start. *R. Curtis* **77**

STEIG (IRE) 6 b.g. Xaar 132 – Ring of Kerry (IRE) 67 (Kenmare (FR) 125) [2009 75: p8.6g[2] 8.3g[6] 8m[3] 8s[3] 8d* 10m[2] 8.5d[2] 9g* 8.5s* 8.5s[3] 8v 8s p10.7g Oct 2] good-topped gelding: fairly useful performer: won claimer at Brighton in June (left George Baker after next start) and handicaps at Ballinrobe and Galway in July: best at 1m/9f: acts on polytrack, firm and soft going: tends to race freely close to pace. *C. Moore, Ireland* **92**

STEINBECK (IRE) 2 b.c. (Feb 9) Footstepsinthesand 120 – Castara Beach (IRE) 74 (Danehill (USA) 126) [2009 6g* 7m[4] Oct 17] **115 p**

'We have a very nice Footstepsinthesand colt called Steinbeck and the birds in the trees around here are singing about him!' Aidan O'Brien is not renowned nowadays for a surfeit of overt bullishness when discussing his horses, so this statement about the then-unraced Steinbeck in a *Racing Post* 'stable tour' back in April made a refreshing change. Unfortunately, the physically-imposing Steinbeck didn't really get the chance to show what he could do in a two-year-old campaign restricted by injury which kept him off the course all summer. However, he still goes into 2010 as one of Ballydoyle's main hopes for classic glory and figures, at the time of writing, at shorter odds (9/1 in some places) in the ante-post betting for the Two Thousand Guineas than stable-companions Beethoven and Fencing Master, behind whom he finished fourth, thrown in at the deep end, in the Dewhurst Stakes on his belated comeback in October. Steinbeck was still ostensibly the Ballydoyle first string at Newmarket that day, when he was ridden by stable number-one Johnny Murtagh and started 4/1 second favourite in a field of fifteen, with Beethoven and Fencing Master at 33/1 and 20/1 respectively. Although he managed only minor honours in the end, Steinbeck arguably shaped like the best prospect in the field (it was later reported that he hadn't been back in training very long), showing up well against largely more experienced rivals and having most of them in trouble when briefly clear over two furlongs out, only for his exertions to tell when collared late on, beaten a neck, a nose and a neck into fourth by three rivals racing much wider than him. Steinbeck fared much better than the two Jim Bolger-trained runners (including favourite Chabal) who had kept up with him for a long way against the inside rail. On his Dewhurst performance, Steinbeck is well worth another chance to build on his huge home reputation and appeals as one to follow as a three-year-old.

Despite the reports of his prowess on the Ballydoyle gallops, Steinbeck wasn't sent off favourite on his debut in a six-runner minor event over six furlongs at Naas in mid-May, though this might have had something to do with the fact that Ballydoyle's four previous two-year-old newcomers that spring had all been beaten. Steinbeck, a 9/4-shot, ended the run in no uncertain manner, travelling smoothly throughout and quickening well to win by two and a half lengths from the Bolger-trained favourite Gold Bubbles, who met trouble in running. The Coventry Stakes at Royal Ascot and the Railway Stakes at the Curragh were mooted as possible summer targets, but Steinbeck was forced to sit things out until his comeback in the Dewhurst after reportedly striking into himself. That five-month absence probably prevented his sire Footstepsinthesand finishing higher than fourth in the first-season sires' table—a place behind fellow first-season Coolmore sire Oratorio (sire of Beethoven and Fencing Master)—which presumably caused extra frustration given that the first-season sire standings were headed by the Darley-based pair Shamardal and Dubawi. It is to be hoped, incidentally, that Steinbeck proves more durable than his unbeaten sire, who also had just two outings as a two-year-old and was then retired because of a heel problem after only one appearance at three, on which he won the 2005 Two Thousand Guineas (Oratorio and Dubawi finished fourth and fifth respectively).

Steinbeck (IRE) (b.c. Feb 9, 2007)	Footstepsinthesand (b 2002)	Giant's Causeway (ch 1977)	Storm Cat
			Mariah's Storm
		Glatisant (b 1991)	Rainbow Quest
			Dancing Rocks
	Castara Beach (IRE) (b 1996)	Danehill (b 1986)	Danzig
			Razyana
		Sea Harrier (ch 1979)	Grundy
			Anchor

Footstepsinthesand himself seemed bred more for speed than stamina, but that doesn't necessarily mean he'll prove a strong influence for speed as a stallion (he stood initially in Australia), particularly as his own requirements so far as distance was concerned were never fully tested in an all too brief career; his Group 1 entries after the Two Thousand Guineas ranged from the Derby to the July Cup! Steinbeck's dam Castara Beach, who raced in the same Michael Tabor colours as Steinbeck, was also not tried beyond a mile during her five-race career (fair form at best) and is a sister to the useful six-furlong/seven-furlong performer Hill Hopper, herself the dam of the very smart miler Nannina. However, there is stamina to be found elsewhere in Castara Beach's pedigree, as her other winning siblings include the above-average stayers Prairie Falcon and Water Boatman, the latter successful in the two-mile Adelaide Cup in 1990 (then a Group 1 event) after being transferred to Australia from Barry Hills. Steinbeck's grandam Sea Harrier was a half-sister to Sea Anchor, a high-class stayer in the mid-'seventies, whilst his great grandam Anchor is the grandam of the very smart performer Indigenous, a prolific winner at up to a mile and a half in Hong Kong during the late-'nineties. Steinbeck attracted plenty of interest when coming under the hammer twice before seeing a racecourse, fetching 100,000 guineas as a foal before current connections paid 250,000 guineas for him as a yearling. Steinbeck's year-younger half-brother Corsicanrun (by Nannina's sire Medicean) fetched 175,000 guineas at the latest yearling sales to join Richard Fahey. Castara Beach has had three other foals to reach the racecourse so far, her only winner before Steinbeck being the fairly useful filly Varenka, who raced only as a two-year-old for Sir Mark Prescott, winning a seven-furlong maiden at Beverley and finishing runner-up in listed company at Rome before being retired to stud, her first foal being Meezaan (also by Medicean), who looked a useful prospect when winning a seven-furlong maiden at Lingfield for John Gosden in the autumn. An attractive good-bodied colt, Steinbeck is bred to stay a fair bit further than seven furlongs—he holds Derby entries at Epsom and the Curragh—but it will not be a big surprise if he proves ideally suited by distances around a mile, particularly as he looks the type who prefers to get on with things, racing prominently on both his starts at two. *A. P. O'Brien, Ireland*

STELLAR CAUSE (USA) 3 ch.g. Giant's Causeway (USA) 132 – Stellar (USA) (Grand Slam (USA) 120) [2009 10d^5 10g 8.1g^4 8.3g 10.4m^6 Sep 25] $130,000Y: big, rangy, attractive gelding: third foal: brother to winner in USA: dam, useful US 6f/7f winner, half-sister to very smart US Grade 1 7f winner Gygistar: fair maiden: easily best effort when fifth at Newbury on debut: stays 1¼m: sold 8,500 gns, joined R. Curtis. *P. F. I. Cole* **72 d**

STELLARINA (IRE) 3 b.f. Night Shift (USA) – Accelerating (USA) 76 (Lear Fan (USA) 130) [2009 71: 6m 7.1g^3 6g Jun 8] strong filly: fair maiden: should stay 1m: acts on polytrack, unraced on extremes of ground on turf. *G. A. Swinbank* **69**

STELLINO (GER) 6 b.g. Monashee Mountain (USA) 115 – Sweet Tern (GER) (Arctic Tern (USA) 126) [2009 –: 12m Sep 19] useful-looking gelding: little form on Flat in Britain: fairly useful hurdler at best: dead. *James Moffatt* **–**

STELLITE 9 ch.g. Pivotal 124 – Donation (Generous (IRE) 139) [2009 76: 7s^6 7.1m* 7.1m 7.2g* 8g^6 6g^2 6f^4 7.1g^2 8s^2 7.2g 7.1m^4 7.2g^2 7.2v^3 Oct 31] workmanlike gelding: fair handicapper: won at Musselburgh in May and Ayr in June: stays 8.6f, all wins around 7f: acts on all-weather, heavy and good to firm going: has played up in stall. *J. S. Goldie* **79**

STEP AT A TIME (IRE) 3 ch.f. Danehill Dancer (IRE) 117 – Zing Ping (IRE) 80 (Thatching 131) [2009 10d Jul 7] 72,000Y: half-sister to several winners, including 2-y-o 6f winners Fear And Greed (in 1998, later stayed 1m) and Serious Play (in 2001), both by Brief Truce, and 1¼m winner Superius (by High Chaparral), all 3 useful in Ireland: dam Irish maiden (stayed 7f): well held in maiden at Pontefract: sold 4,000 gns later in month, sent to Greece. *M. Johnston* **–**

STEP FAST (USA) 3 ch.f. Giant's Causeway (USA) 132 – Nannerl (USA) (Valid Appeal (USA)) [2009 –: 12.1m 11.1m^4 12.1m Jun 30] sturdy filly: little form: tried blinkered. *M. Johnston* **–**

STEP IN TIME (IRE) 2 b.c. (Apr 24) Giant's Causeway (USA) 132 – Cash Run (USA) 119 (Seeking The Gold (USA)) [2009 6g^2 6m* 7m 6m^2 6m 6.5m 6g Sep 27] €50,000Y: leggy colt: fifth foal: closely related to 3 winners by Storm Cat, including smart Irish 2007 2-y-o 7f winner Great War Eagle: dam, won Breeders' Cup Juvenile Fillies, half-sister to very smart US Grade 1 7f winner Forestry: fairly useful performer: **84**

won maiden at Newmarket in May: easily best effort after when good second in nursery at Ascot: bred to stay at least 7f (has raced freely). *M. Johnston*

STEP INTO SUNSHINE (USA) 3 b.f. The Cliff's Edge (USA) 123 – Iridescence (USA) (Mt Livermore (USA)) [2009 8d 8m 8.1g^6 Aug 26] $80,000F: tall filly: fifth foal: half-sister to 3 winners in US, including smart 7f to 9f (Grade 1) winner Flashy Bull (by Holy Bull): dam US 6f/6.5f winner: fractured off-hind pedal bone at 2 yrs: well held in maidens: sold 12,000 gns in December. *M. Johnston* **–**

STEP IT UP (IRE) 5 ch.g. Daggers Drawn (USA) 114 – Leitrim Lodge (IRE) 64 (Classic Music (USA)) [2009 74: p6g^4 p6g^2 p5g^2 p5g^2 p5g^3 5g^3 6m^6 5f^3 5.1m^6 5f 5g^2 5m* 5g* 6g 5m^2 5g^4 p5g* p5g^3 Oct 22] close-coupled gelding: fairly useful handicapper: won at Folkestone and Sandown 3 days apart in August and Lingfield (career-best effort) in October: best at 5f: acts on polytrack and firm going, below form on softer than good. *J. R. Boyle* **84**

STEP THIS WAY (USA) 4 ch.f. Giant's Causeway (USA) 132 – Lady In Waiting (USA) (Woodman (USA) 126) [2009 93: 13.8m^4 14m^4 12.1m^3 14.1m^5 14m^2 14m^2 16.4d 11.9f^3 12m 16.4m Aug 21] tall, close-coupled filly: fairly useful handicapper: stays 1¾m: acts on polytrack and firm going: races prominently. *M. Johnston* **87**

STEP TO IT (IRE) 2 b.g. (Apr 15) Footstepsinthesand 120 – Lilly Gee (IRE) 56 (Ashkalani (IRE) 128) [2009 6d 6g 7.1m Sep 14] unfurnished gelding: well held in sellers. *K. A. Ryan* **–**

STERLING MOLL 6 gr.m. Lord of Men 116 – Princess Maud (USA) (Irish River (FR) 131) [2009 21.7m Jun 20] little form on Flat. *W. de Best-Turner* **–**

STERLING SOUND (USA) 3 b.f. Street Cry (IRE) 130 – Lady In Silver (USA) 127 (Silver Hawk (USA) 123) [2009 78: 8m^3 8.3m^3 8m* 9.9g^3 9.9g Aug 30] close-coupled filly: fairly useful performer: won maiden at Ascot in July: possibly flattered when 4¼ lengths third to Ave in listed race at Salisbury penultimate start: stays 1¼m: acts on polytrack and good to firm going. *M. P. Tregoning* **95**

STERNIAN 2 ch.f. (Mar 24) Where Or When (IRE) 124 – Fly In Style (Hernando (FR) 127) [2009 f8d^6 Dec 29] fourth foal: half-sister to 2006 2-y-o 6f seller winner Distant Flash (by Mujahid): dam unraced: 150/1, slowly away and well held in maiden at Southwell. *M. E. Rimmer* **–**

STERNLIGHT (IRE) 2 b.c. (Apr 29) Kheleyf (USA) 116 – Sail By Night (USA) (Nureyev (USA) 131) [2009 6m 7m^4 7.1m^3 Sep 29] €14,500F, £30,000Y: well-made colt: fifth foal: half-brother to 2 winners in Italy by Alhaarth, including 1m winner Sail By Roos: dam unraced out of half-sister to US Grade 1 7f winner Mining: best effort in maidens when fourth to Business As Usual at Yarmouth: plenty to do final start. *E. S. McMahon* **72**

STEVIE GEE (IRE) 5 b.g. Invincible Spirit (IRE) 121 – Margaree Mary (CAN) (Seeking The Gold (USA)) [2009 98: p7g 6m 7g 7g^2 6m 7.9m* 7.9g^5 7d 9.8g 8s 8.3m p7g Nov 5] leggy gelding: fairly useful handicapper: won at Carlisle in June: below form after, leaving G. A. Swinbank after ninth outing: stays 1m: acts on fibresand, firm and soft going: tried blinkered. *Ian Williams* **90**

STEVIE THUNDER 4 ch.g. Storming Home 128 – Social Storm (USA) (Future Storm (USA)) [2009 96: 8.1g^3 8d^4 8g^4 7.6g 10.4m^2 10g^5 9m^6 10g Oct 10] rangy gelding: useful handicapper: best effort in 2009 when head second to Royal Destination at York: stays 10.4f: acts on polytrack, soft and good to firm ground: tried tongue tied, visored last 2 starts. *Ian Williams* **96**

ST IGNATIUS 2 b.g. (Feb 17) Ishiguru (USA) 114 – Branston Berry (IRE) 86 (Mukaddamah (USA) 125) [2009 p7m p7g^4 p7m^5 Dec 10] similar form in maidens at Kempton: should be as effective at 6f as 7f. *R. M. Beckett* **60**

STILL DREAMING 5 ch.m. Singspiel (IRE) 133 – Three Green Leaves (IRE) 97 (Environment Friend 128) [2009 66: p12.2g 11.6f^6 11.6m^5 11.9d Sep 15] workmanlike mare: handicapper, just poor at 5 yrs: stays 14.6f: acts on polytrack, good to firm and good to soft ground: wears blinkers. *R. J. Price* **44**

STIMULATION (IRE) 4 b.c. Choisir (AUS) 126 – Damiana (IRE) (Thatching 131) [2009 121: 7m^5 7m^4 Sep 18] big, good-bodied colt: usually impresses in appearance: very smart performer at 3 yrs: respectable 2½ lengths fifth to Duff in Park Stakes at Doncaster (shaped as though needing run), but well below form in listed race at Newbury later in month: should prove as effective at 1m as 7f: acts on firm and good to soft going. *H. Morrison* **114**

ST JEAN CAP FERRAT 4 b. or br.g. Domedriver (IRE) 128 – Miss Cap Ferrat 53 (Darshaan 133) [2009 96: 10.2d 10.3f 9.9m* 12m⁶ 9g⁴ 9s* Oct 24] smallish gelding: useful performer: won handicaps at Salisbury (beat Cill Rialaig a nose) in July and (after sold from P. Hobbs 21,000 gns later in month) Klampenborg in October: ran well when 3¾ lengths sixth to Peas And Carrots in Scandinavian Open Championship at Klampenborg fourth start: stays 1½m: acts on polytrack, soft and good to firm ground: visored/blinkered nowadays: has looked none too straightforward. *S. Jensen, Denmark* **102**

ST MORITZ (IRE) 3 b.g. Medicean 128 – Statua (IRE) 98 (Statoblest 120) [2009 p7m* p7.1g* 8.5d⁵ Apr 19] €110,000Y: half-brother to 3 winners, including 6f to 1m winner Annemasse (by Anabaa) and 5f (at 2 yrs) to 1¼m (in Saudi Arabia) winner Dance Anthem (by Royal Academy), both useful: dam, US 6f to 1m winner, half-sister to smart 7f to 9f performer Bluegrass Prince: fairly useful form: won maiden at Lingfield in January and 4-runner handicap at Wolverhampton (still very green, beat Changing The Guard 3¼ lengths) in February: only fifth in Dr Busch-Memorial at Krefeld final start (gelded after): should stay 1m: stays in training. *M. Johnston* **94**

ST NICHOLAS ABBEY (IRE) 2 b.c. (Apr 13) Montjeu (IRE) 137 – Leaping Water (Sure Blade (USA) 130) [2009 8s* 8g* 8d* Oct 24] **126 p**

It is a reasonable precept that the emergence of a truly exceptional performer in any sphere is not an everyday or even an every year occurrence. The belief sometimes prompts repetition of the old saw 'After the Lord Mayor's Show comes the dust cart'. Sea The Stars was indeed the equine equivalent of the Lord Mayor's Show, but is there anything in logic or history to suggest that the arrival of one majestic thoroughbred automatically excludes the possibility of another appearing straight afterwards? Is there anything to suggest that providence, or some other supposed supernatural force, controls which racehorses we have at any one time and how good they are? St Nicholas Abbey has a long way to go before he can be spoken of in the same tones as Sea The Stars, but he showed as much potential in winning the Racing Post Trophy as any two-year-old in any race during the last decade. He has 'outstanding classic candidate'—not 'dust cart'—written all over him, and being foaled the year after Sea The Stars won't stop his emulating that colt if he is good enough. As it happens, there has been no shortage of outstanding horses foaled in successive years. Not all triple crown winners are brilliant, but they tend to be the best of their age, and there are three instances of such colts achieving the feat in successive seasons—Gladiateur in 1865 and Lord Lyon in 1866, Flying Fox in 1899 and Diamond Jubilee in 1900, and Gay Crusader in 1917 and Gainsborough in 1918 (Pommern won the triple crown in 1915). More recently, 1970 triple crown winner Nijinsky (rated 138) was followed immediately by two of the best horses ever to race in Britain, Brigadier Gerard and Mill Reef (both rated 141 as three-year-olds, Brigadier Gerard rated 144 at four), while 1987 Derby winner Reference Point (139) was foaled a year after another exceptional colt, Dancing Brave (140). In France, Helissio (136) and Peintre Celebre (137) came from successive crops in the 'nineties, with Montjeu (137) following two years after Peintre Celebre. Among the fillies, 1971 Prix de l'Arc de Triomphe runner-up Pistol Packer (133) preceded Arc winner San San (133), who was followed straight away by Allez France and Dahlia (both 132 at three but higher later). In America, Seattle Slew and Affirmed respectively won the triple crown in 1977 and 1978, while Buckpasser, a champion at two, three (when also Horse of the Year) and four, was foaled in 1963, the year before Damascus, who was also a champion and Horse of the Year at three. For good measure Dr Fager, champion sprinter in 1967 and a multiple champion and Horse of the Year in 1968, was another from the 1964 crop. So it can happen, has happened and will doubtless happen again.

St Nicholas Abbey followed a well-trodden path for a highly-regarded two-year-old colt trained by Aidan O'Brien, starting by making short work, at short odds, of ten opponents in a maiden at the Curragh in mid-August, beating Saajidah by four lengths. O'Brien had already won the Juddmonte Beresford Stakes, over the same course towards the end of September, nine times, though never with the best youngster in his stable. Just two of the nine, Saratoga Springs in 1997 and Septimus in 2005, went on win a Group 1 for O'Brien. St Nicholas Abbey started at 5/2-on against eight rivals in the Beresford including two from Britain, Layali Al Andalus and Passion for Gold, successful between them in two maiden races

Juddmonte Beresford Stakes, the Curragh—
St Nicholas Abbey has the measure of Layali Al Andalus and gives his trainer a tenth win in the race

and a nursery. There was no outstanding performer among the rest of the Irish-trained contingent and it was the British pair who chased home St Nicholas Abbey. The winner was always going well, a few lengths off a rather muddling pace set by his stable-companion Lastofthemohicans, and soon went on when asked to quicken over a furlong out, eventually beating Layali Al Andalus by three quarters of a length, value for more, with the rallying Passion For Gold a length and a half further back in third. The form was slightly better than that Sea The Stars had shown when winning the same race by half a length in 2008 and St Nicholas Abbey was made favourite for the Derby by all bookmakers, as short as 8/1 in a couple of places. By contrast, he was available at the same time at 20/1 for the Two Thousand Guineas.

Just over a month later, St Nicholas Abbey was as short as 2/1 for the Derby and 3/1 for the Guineas. Most of O'Brien's earlier Beresford Stakes winners had gone on to contest the Racing Post Trophy, with Saratoga Springs winning the race, Lermontov, Castle Gandolfo and Albert Hall finishing second, Septimus third and Eagle Mountain fourth. In his customary fashion, the trainer had a sizeable initial entry for the Doncaster race, responsible for forty-one of the one hundred and fifty-eight nominated. By the time of the race, the forty-one had come down to just one, St Nicholas Abbey, who this time didn't have a pacemaker. Every Racing Post Trophy runner had won his latest start, not a common occurrence in an eleven-strong field, though all ten in a minor event won by Awzaan at Newmarket in July had managed the same feat. There were some proven colts in the Racing Post line-up, as well as several distinctly promising ones. St Nicholas Abbey started 13/8 favourite ahead of Acomb Stakes winner Elusive Pimpernel and Godolphin's highly-regarded Al Zir. Next in the betting came Coordinated Cut, who had been joint-favourite for the Derby before even appearing on the racecourse and justifying favouritism in a maiden event at Doncaster. He was followed by decisive Newbury maiden winner Dancing David, Solario Stakes and Goffs Million Mile winner Shakespearean and Autumn Stakes winner Morana. The other runners were all at 25/1 or longer. It is rare to see a jockey ride such a confident race in a championship event as Johnny Murtagh did on St Nicholas Abbey. Dropped out last, around six lengths off the pace set by Shakespearean and Al Ghazal, St Nicholas Abbey was still cantering two and a half furlongs out, with Murtagh sitting motionless while his rivals were all pushing and shoving. Once asked to quicken a furlong and a half out, St Nicholas Abbey produced an electrifying turn of speed and swept from sixth to first in the space of half a furlong. Nor was that the end of it, St Nicholas Abbey maintaining his run under hand riding to draw three and three quarter lengths clear of Elusive Pimpernel, who kept on gamely but was made to look one paced compared to the winner. Al Zir was a further two and a half lengths away third, with Dancing David, Morana and Shakespearean next and Coordinated Cut only tenth. St Nicholas Abbey, still full of running at the end, made a good field look second rate and there was no room to doubt that this was the outstanding performance during the year by a two-year-old, not just in Europe but anywhere in the northern hemisphere. It was the best in the Racing Post Trophy since Celtic Swing's runaway success in 1994.

The Racing Post Trophy has been by far the best recent guide to the colts' classics. O'Brien's other winners this century (Aristotle won for him in 1999) were High Chaparral in 2001 and Brian Boru the year after; they went on to land the Anglo/Irish Derby double and win the St Leger respectively. American Post (2003) was successful in the Poule d'Essai des Poulains, and Motivator (2004) and Authorized (2006) won the Derby. Among the beaten horses in the Racing Post Trophy in the same period, Septimus, Dylan Thomas and Frozen Fire—all trained at Ballydoyle—went on to win classics, though Septimus was five when successful in the Irish St Leger. Straight after his victory, St Nicholas Abbey was being quoted at 6/1 to win both the Guineas and Derby, and at 14/1 for the triple crown. He looks sure to make further progress and is the clear form choice for the Two Thousand Guineas, certainly possessing the ability and the speed needed for that race. There are some strong opponents who will be trained especially for Newmarket because they have no pretensions to getting the Derby trip, the most dangerous of them probably Arcano, Awzaan and Canford Cliffs, the last-named's form in landing the Coventry Stakes only marginally behind that of St Nicholas Abbey in the Racing Post Trophy. There are also others in the Ballydoyle team to consider, chiefly Steinbeck and Fencing Master. Both look likely to improve on their efforts in the Dewhurst Stakes, and their best chance of classic success looks like being at Newmarket rather than Epsom. Given the usual glut of Derby prospects at Ballydoyle, including Jan Vermeer, winner of the Criterium International, O'Brien could find it tricky shuffling his pack. It is to be hoped, however, that St Nicholas Abbey does run in the Two Thousand Guineas. However he fares at Newmarket, though, nothing else in the Derby market makes anything like so much appeal and, at this stage, St Nicholas Abbey looks like taking a tremendous amount of beating at Epsom.

St Nicholas Abbey, a sturdy, attractive colt who has not raced on going firmer than good and acts on soft, cost 200,000 guineas as a yearling at the Newmarket October Sales. Since 1995, the year before Aidan O'Brien took over at Ballydoyle, the operation has spent a small fortune on yearlings, and to a lesser extent on foals and two-year-olds, all of whom run in the colours of one or more of the Coolmore partners Sue Magnier, Derrick Smith and Michael Tabor. Getting on for 300,000,000 dollars has been spent on more than five hundred horses in that time and, while there have inevitably been expensive failures, there have

Racing Post Trophy, Doncaster—a most impressive performance from the season's top juvenile; St Nicholas Abbey is clear of Elusive Pimpernel, Al Zir (right) and Dancing David (rail)

Mr D. Smith, Mrs J. Magnier, Mr M. Tabor's "St Nicholas Abbey" (J. Murtagh)

been twenty-five Group or Grade 1 winners, mostly trained by O'Brien. These include champion sprinters Stravinsky (625,000 dollars, rated 133) and Mozart (340,000 guineas, 131), Rip Van Winkle (€170,000, 134), and classic winners Beckett (1,700,000 guineas, 116), Fame And Glory (190,000 guineas, 133), Footstepsinthesand (170,000 guineas, 120), George Washington (1,150,000 guineas, 133), Halfway To Heaven (€450,000, 118), High Chaparral (270,000 guineas, 132), Landseer (260,000 guineas, 125), Milan (650,000 guineas, 129), Moonstone (700,000 guineas, 119), Rose Gypsy (115,000 guineas, 114) and Septimus (€220,000, 129). The Coolmore sires include many of the best in Europe, and buying youngsters by them makes sense, in more ways than one, as part of the purchasing strategy. As some indication of the focus on 'home-grown' horses, in the last three years eighty-five per cent of the horses John Magnier and Demi O'Byrne have bought have been by sires based at Coolmore or its American wing Ashford. They include St Nicholas Abbey, whose sire Montjeu is building a fine record, much as Rip Van Winkle's sire Galileo is doing. St Nicholas Abbey is Montjeu's third winner of the Racing Post Trophy following Motivator and Authorized, whose subsequent careers have been taken by many to be a good omen for St Nicholas Abbey. Montjeu, whose progeny tend to improve with age, is now the sire of sixteen Group 1 winners, seven of them in the latest season also including Fame And Glory, Jan Vermeer and Jukebox Jury. Three of the winners were in Australia and New Zealand, led by a second successive winner of the AJC Australian Derby in Roman Emperor (Montjeu was shuttled to Windsor Park Stud in New Zealand from 2001 to 2004). Add such as the Royal Lodge winner Joshua Tree, and Montjeu looks to be in for another good year in 2010. He is a strong influence for stamina, Tavistock, successful in the Mudgway Stakes over seven furlongs at Hastings in New Zealand in August, being his only winner aged three and upwards to have won a Group 1 over shorter than a mile and a quarter. Most of Montjeu's top horses have been suited by a mile and a half. What has gone before with Montjeu's runners is, of course, relevant, but not so relevant as the racing characteristics that St Nicholas Abbey has already shown on the track. He clearly possesses the speed to win a Group 1 race over a mile as a three-year-old.

St Nicholas Abbey (IRE) (b.c. Apr 13, 2007)	Montjeu (IRE) (b 1996)	Sadler's Wells (b 1981)	Northern Dancer
			Fairy Bridge
		Floripedes (b 1985)	Top Ville
			Toute Cy
	Leaping Water (ch 1990)	Sure Blade (b 1983)	Kris
			Double Lock
		Flamenco Wave (ch 1986)	Desert Wine
			Armada Way

Given the rivalry between Coolmore and Sheikh Mohammed's Darley operation, there is an element of irony in St Nicholas Abbey's background on the distaff side. Not only is he out of Leaping Water, a mare sold by her owner-breeder Sheikh Mohammed for 3,200 guineas as an unraced three-year-old, but St Nicholas Abbey's grandam Flamenco Wave was also sold by the Sheikh, to John Magnier, for 45,000 guineas as a nine-year-old in 1995, and went on to foal two Group 1 winners for her new connections. Leaping Water had done quite well without setting the world alight before St Nicholas Abbey, breeding three winners from eight living foals, four of whom did not reach the racecourse. The three winners included Grammarian (by Definite Article), successful in the Grade 2 San Gabriel Handicap over nine furlongs and the Sunset Handicap over a mile and a half, and St Nicholas Abbey's three-year-old sister Cascata, who won a mile maiden at Great Leighs in November 2008 and showed she stayed a mile and a half when fourth in a handicap at Newmarket. Leaping Water has not produced a reported live foal since St Nicholas Abbey. Going back one generation, Flamenco Wave ran only four times, winning both her starts at two over six furlongs, including the Moyglare Stud Stakes, but then finishing last in two races as a three-year-old which included the Irish One Thousand Guineas. Before she was sold by Sheikh Mohammed, her first two foals had both won, though neither had made a real mark. Culling is essential in any large stud, but it must, nonetheless, have frustrated Sheikh Mohammed, or his advisers, to see what happened to Flamenco Wave after her sale. Most of the runners she had from 1995 onwards won in pattern company, including two who raced for Sheikh Mohammed in Spanish Falls (Prix de Royaumont) and Starborough (Prix Jean Prat, St James's Palace Stakes), and two trained by O'Brien in Aristotle (Racing Post Trophy) and Ballingarry (Criterium de Saint-Cloud, Canadian International). Starborough stayed nine furlongs and ran respectably at a mile and a quarter, while the three others all stayed further. Two of Flamenco Wave's minor winners were successful at a mile and a half. Flamenco Wave was easily the best of four winners produced by her dam Armada Way, who was successful in two minor stakes events including the Searching Stakes over eight and a half furlongs at Aqueduct, in which coincidentally Six Crowns, dam of champion Chief's Crown, finished third. This is also the family of such top-notch performers as Lacovia, Manila, Miswaki and Targowice. Let's hope St Nicholas Abbey can add further to the family's distinguished record and, who knows, even give Irish racing its second brilliant three-year-old in a row. *A. P. O'Brien, Ireland*

STOCKMAN 5 b.g. Kylian (USA) – Fabriana 82 (Northern State (USA) 91) [2009 –: f12d f11g^5 f11g p12g Apr 28] lightly-raced maiden: form (modest) only when fifth in seller at Southwell (probably flattered). *H. Morrison* **52 ?**

STOIC (IRE) 3 b.g. Green Desert (USA) 127 – Silver Bracelet 92 (Machiavellian (USA) 123) [2009 69p: 8.3f^2 8m* 8.1m* p8m* Sep 24] attractive gelding: useful form: most progressive in 2009, winning maiden at Newmarket in August, and handicaps at Sandown and Kempton (dead-heated with Penitent) in September: gelded after: stays 1m: raced only on polytrack and ground firmer than good. *J. Noseda* **111**

STOIC LEADER (IRE) 9 b.g. Danehill Dancer (IRE) 117 – Starlust 79 (Sallust 134) [2009 80: p9.5g^4 p7g p8.6m^2 p8.6g 8m^4 8m 8m 7.9m^4 8m^6 7.2g^4 p9.5g^6 p9.5g p9.5g p8.6g Dec 14] sturdy gelding: fair handicapper on turf, modest on all-weather: best up to 8.6f: acts on all-weather, firm and soft going: tried in cheekpieces: sometimes races freely: tends to edge left. *R. F. Fisher* **72 a63**

STOLEN AFFECTION 2 b.g. (Feb 26) Pursuit of Love 124 – Thieves Welcome 61 (Most Welcome 131) [2009 7.1m Sep 14] 40/1 and green, tailed off in seller at Musselburgh. *J. R. Weymes* –

STOLT (IRE) 5 b.g. Tagula (IRE) 116 – Cabcharge Princess (IRE) 64 (Rambo Dancer (CAN) 107) [2009 96: 5g 5m 5g 5m^5 5g 5s^6 5m^6 5.1m* 5m 5g p5g^6 p5.1g f5m^4 Dec 15] close-coupled gelding: useful handicapper: won at Chester in September by 3½ lengths from Bel Cantor: largely below form otherwise: best at 5f: acts on polytrack, firm and soft going: races prominently: in cheekpieces final outing. *N. Wilson* 96

STONEACRE BABY (USA) 4 ch.f. Stravinsky (USA) 133 – Katiba (USA) 99 (Gulch (USA)) [2009 –: p5g p5.1m f5g 5m 5m Jun 4] poor maiden. *Peter Grayson* 42

STONEACRE DONNY (IRE) 5 br.h. Lend A Hand 124 – Election Special 78 (Chief Singer 131) [2009 59d: p6g^5 p6g 5d 8f May 30] no form in 2009: tried blinkered: dead. *Peter Grayson* –

STONEACRE JOE (IRE) 2 b.c. (Mar 2) Iron Mask (USA) 117 – Jarmar Moon (Unfuwain (USA) 131) [2009 p5g p5g f5g^4 Dec 27] last in maidens/seller. *Peter Grayson* –

STONEACRE LAD (IRE) 6 b.h. Bluebird (USA) 125 – Jay And-A (IRE) 98 (Elbio 125) [2009 103§: p5g p5g f5g^6 p5g^5 5g 5d^4 5m 5d^4 p5g 5g f5g^6 5s^5 Aug 23] good-topped horse: useful handicapper: regressive form in 2009: best at 5f: acts on all-weather, firm and soft ground: blinkered: quirky and unreliable. *Peter Grayson* 97 d

STONEACRE PAT (IRE) 4 b.c. Iron Mask (USA) 117 – Sans Ceriph (IRE) 75 (Thatching 131) [2009 60: p6g p5g p5.1m p5g p5.1g^6 p5m p5m Dec 6] workmanlike colt: poor handicapper: raced at 5f/6f: acts on polytrack and soft ground: sometimes blinkered: often slowly away. *Peter Grayson* 41

STONECRABSTOMORROW (IRE) 6 b.g. Fasliyev (USA) 120 – Tordasia (IRE) (Dr Devious (IRE) 127) [2009 p6g^3 p6g^2 p6g* p6m* p6g^2 p6g^2 7.1m^3 6g* 6f* 7m May 28] leggy gelding: fairly useful performer: missed 2008: won seller in February and handicap in March, both at Wolverhampton, and claimers at Hamilton and Redcar in May: effective at 6f/7f: acts on all-weather and any turf going: often in cheekpieces/blinkers nowadays: reliable. *R. A. Fahey* 80

STONEHAUGH (IRE) 6 b.g. King Charlemagne (USA) 120 – Canary Bird (IRE) 59 (Catrail (USA) 123) [2009 84d: 7m 7.5m^5 6.9g* 6g Aug 4] good-bodied gelding: fair performer: easily best effort in 2009 when winning handicap at Carlisle in June: best form short of 1m: acts on firm ground: usually tongue tied. *J. Howard Johnson* 77

STONE OF SCONE 4 b.g. Pivotal 124 – Independence 116 (Selkirk (USA) 129) [2009 93: 10.2d* 10.4m^3 10f Jun 19] very big, rangy gelding: useful form, lightly raced: off nearly 12 months, won handicap at Nottingham (beat Red Jade by neck) in April: creditable third to Moonquake in similar event at York: favourite, reportedly slipped and returned with serious tendon injury in listed handicap at Royal Ascot final start (gelded after): stays 10.4f: acts on polytrack, good to firm and good to soft ground. *E. A. L. Dunlop* 102

STOOP TO CONQUER 9 b.g. Polar Falcon (USA) 126 – Princess Genista 108 (Ile de Bourbon (USA) 133) [2009 80: p13g^6 15g^4 16g Oct 28] big, leggy, lengthy gelding: fair handicapper nowadays: stays 2¼m: acts on all-weather and any turf going: sometimes races freely. *A. W. Carroll* 68

STOREY HILL (USA) 4 b. or br.g. Richter Scale (USA) 119 – Crafty Nan (USA) (Crafty Prospector (USA)) [2009 79: p5g p6g^4 p5g p6m Mar 4] fair handicapper: below best in 2009: effective at 5f/6f: acts on polytrack. *D. Shaw* 70

STORMBEAM (USA) 4 b.g. Tale of The Cat (USA) 113 – Broad Smile (USA) (Broad Brush (USA)) [2009 69: p12g Jun 3] lengthy gelding: fair maiden: below form sole outing in 2009: likely to prove best short of 1½m: acts on polytrack, good to firm and good to soft ground: tongue tied last 2 starts: carries head awkwardly. *G. A. Butler* 60

STORMBURST (IRE) 5 b.m. Mujadil (USA) 119 – Isca 66 (Caerleon (USA) 132) [2009 57: p7.1g p6g p6g^6 p7g f6g 6m^4 p6g p6g p6m^3 f6d^6 Dec 29] quite good-topped mare: modest performer: barely stays 7f: acts on polytrack, firm and good to soft ground: tried visored/blinkered. *A. J. Chamberlain* 55

STORM COMMAND (IRE) 2 ch.g. (Apr 30) Halling (USA) 133 – Clarinda (IRE) 91 (Lomond (USA) 128) [2009 7.5m 8.1g^5 8.5m^4 9m^2 10.2m Sep 30] smallish, stocky gelding: modest maiden: bred to stay 1¼m: gelded after final start. *B. Smart* 58

STORMGLASS 2 ch.c. (Feb 7) Galileo (IRE) 134 – Aberdovey 82 (Mister Baileys 123) [2009 9m^6 7m Oct 3] leggy colt: always behind in maiden at Goodwood and sales race at Newmarket: dead. *W. R. Muir* –

STORM HAWK (IRE) 2 b.g. (Mar 30) Hawk Wing (USA) 136 – Stormy Larissa (IRE) 79 (Royal Applause 124) [2009 5f^5 6d^5 6m^3 7d^2 7.5m 7g 8.3d 8g^4 Oct 19] compact gelding: fair maiden: stays 1m: acts on good to soft going: tried visored: gelded after final start: temperamental and one to treat with caution. *Pat Eddery* **68 §**

STORMING SIOUX 3 b.f. Storming Home 128 – Sueboog (IRE) 109 (Darshaan 133) [2009 79: 8.1g^2 8m^2 8m p12m^3 p12g^4 Oct 21] tall filly: fair maiden: below form after reappearance in 2009: should stay beyond 1m. *W. J. Haggas* **76**

STORMY MORNING 3 ch.g. Nayef (USA) 129 – Sokoa (USA) (Peintre Celebre (USA) 137) [2009 10m 10g 10m^4 12g 13.1d* p16m p13.9g Oct 2] sturdy gelding: fair handicapper: best effort when winning at Bath in August: stays 13f: acts on polytrack and good to soft ground: sold £11,000. *W. R. Swinburn* **68**

STORMY'S PRELUDE 3 ch.f. Alhaarth (IRE) 126 – Far Reaching (USA) 76 (Distant View (USA) 126) [2009 p10g^3 9.7d^5 12m May 15] 4,000Y: tall filly: third foal: dam, maiden (stayed 1m), half-sister to very smart performer up to 1¼m Eltish and smart sprinter Forest Gazelle: fair form first 2 starts in maidens: pulled up amiss final outing: bred to stay 1½m+. *P. Winkworth* **66**

STORMY SUMMER 4 b.g. Observatory (USA) 131 – Khambani (IRE) 80 (Royal Academy (USA) 130) [2009 –: 10.1d 10m p10g f14g^6 10g f12m^2 f12f f12f^2 f14g Dec 22] workmanlike gelding: fair maiden handicapper: improved when runner-up 2 of last 4 starts at 4 yrs: tried in cheekpieces, in blinkers last 4 starts: often tongue tied. *R. W. Price* **73**

STORMY WEATHER (FR) 3 gr.g. Highest Honor (FR) 124 – Stormy Moud (USA) (Storm Bird (CAN) 134) [2009 98: 11.9v^3 12s Nov 7] €55,000Y: fifth foal: half-brother to French 2006 2-y-o 7f winner Palm Academy (by Royal Academy) and 2 winners in USA by Quiet American: dam, won at around 1m in USA, half-sister to very smart US Grade 2 11f winner Irish Warrior: useful performer: won newcomers race at Longchamp at 2 yrs, when also second in listed event at Saint-Cloud: left J-L. Pelletan in France, improved when 4 lengths third to Opinion Poll in handicap at Haydock on reappearance in May: well held in November Handicap at Doncaster when next seen on Flat: barely stays testing 1½m: acts on heavy ground. *J. Howard Johnson* **106**

STORYLAND (USA) 4 b.f. Menifee (USA) 124 – Auspice (USA) (Robellino (USA) 127) [2009 103: 12f 12g^4 14g^5 12m^6 12m 12m^2 12m^5 p13g^3 Oct 29] useful-looking filly: has a quick action: useful performer: several creditable efforts in 2009, including 6¾ lengths third to Baila Me in listed race at Lingfield final outing: stays 13f: acts on polytrack, soft and good to firm going: held up. *W. J. Haggas* **99**

STOTSFOLD 6 b.g. Barathea (IRE) 127 – Eliza Acton 70 (Shirley Heights 130) [2009 118: 8.1g^4 10m^3 10g* 10g^3 9.9m^2 9.8g^4 9m^6 Oct 16] strong, good-bodied gelding: smart performer: won La Coupe at Longchamp in June by short neck from Starlish: good efforts after in Arlington Million (1½ lengths third to Gio Ponti), Select Stakes at Goodwood (length second to Mac Love) and Prix Dollar at Longchamp (length fourth to Pipedreamer): rare poor effort in Darley Stakes at Newmarket final start: stays 1½m: acts on polytrack and firm going: held up: reliable. *W. R. Swinburn* **118**

STRABINIOS KING 5 b.g. King's Best (USA) 132 – Strawberry Morn (CAN) (Travelling Victor (CAN)) [2009 76: p7g^3 p7.1g* p7.1g^2 p7g^3 7.1m 7d 6g 6g p7.1g 6g^6 5.9d Aug 19] workmanlike gelding: fairly useful handicapper: better than ever when winning at Wolverhampton (final start for M. Wigham) in January: left K. J. Burke after fourth outing: regressive after: stays 7f: acts on all-weather, soft and good to firm going: tried blinkered. *A. Berry* **83 d**

STRABOE (USA) 3 b.g. Green Desert (USA) 127 – Staff Nurse (USA) (Arch (USA) 127) [2009 –: 7d 7g 8.3g 6m* p6f^5 Dec 21] modest handicapper: gambled on, improved when making all at Yarmouth in August: best efforts at 6f: acts on polytrack and good to firm ground. *S. C. Williams* **63 +**

STRAIGHT AND LEVEL (CAN) 4 gr. or ro.g. Buddha (USA) 122 – Azusa (USA) (Flying Paster (USA)) [2009 78: p8g p10g p8g p8m Nov 29] leggy gelding: fair handicapper: below best in 2009, gelded after second start: stays 1m: acts on polytrack, firm and good to soft going: tried in cheekpieces/visor. *Miss Jo Crowley* **68**

STRAIGHT FACE (IRE) 5 b.g. Princely Heir (IRE) 111 – Dakota Sioux (IRE) 90 (College Chapel 122) [2009 62: p7g f6g^5 f6g^3 p6g^2 f7g* f8d^6 6g^6 7s* 7m 7f p8.6g^6 7g 7d^3 7g^3 8d^5 8d p7m* p7m p7g* f7m f7f^4 Dec 12] sturdy gelding: fair performer: won **72**

handicap at Southwell in March, apprentice claimer at Newcastle in May, handicap at Kempton in September and claimer at Lingfield in October: best at 7f nowadays: acts on all-weather, soft and good to firm going: wears headgear: none too consistent. *Miss Gay Kelleway*

STRAIGHT LACED 3 b.f. Refuse To Bend (IRE) 128 – Gaelic Swan (IRE) 80 (Nashwan (USA) 135) [2009 10.9m⁶ 11.5g⁶ 12.1m Jun 12] third foal: dam, maiden (placed at 1½m), sister to smart 1¼m/1½m winner Mary Stuart and half-sister to smart middle-distance stayer Bonny Scot and to dam of Golan and Tartan Bearer: modest form in maidens only on second start. *W. J. Knight* **62**

STRAITJACKET 3 b.f. Refuse To Bend (IRE) 128 – Thara'a (IRE) 69 (Desert Prince (IRE) 130) [2009 73§: p6g³ 6.1g p7g* p6g⁶ p8g 7g p7g Jul 22] smallish, good-topped filly: modest performer: won seller at Lingfield in June: went wrong way after: stays 7f: acts on polytrack: often in blinkers/cheekpieces (wore latter for win): temperamental: sold £1,600, joined A. Hales. *Miss J. R. Tooth* **61 §**

STRAITS OF HORMUZ (USA) 3 gr. or ro.f. War Chant (USA) 126 – Tjinouska (USA) 86 (Cozzene (USA)) [2009 –: 10m* 10s³ 12g³ 12m⁶ p13.9g⁵ Oct 10] lengthy filly: fairly useful performer: won maiden at Pontefract in June: stays 1½m: acts on soft and good to firm going: races prominently. *M. Johnston* **87**

STRAIT STREET (IRE) 2 gr.f. (Feb 21) Verglas (IRE) 118 – Savoy Street (Vettori (IRE) 119) [2009 p7g Oct 29] rather leggy filly: first foal: dam unraced half-sister to useful performers Widyan (up to 1½m) and Street General (up to 1¾m): 100/1, last in maiden at Lingfield. *P. Winkworth* **–**

STRANGE FICTION 2 ch.c. (Mar 18) Avonbridge 123 – Science Fiction (Starborough 126) [2009 5m 5m Apr 30] last in maiden/seller (blinkered): dead. *R. A. Fahey* **–**

STRATEGIC KNIGHT (USA) 4 b.g. Johannesburg (USA) 127 – Western Friend (USA) (Gone West (USA)) [2009 p8g f8g p9.5g p7.1g 7d 8m⁴ 10m 8.3g 10m 10.1g 8m p8.6g Jul 7] sturdy gelding: missed 2008: modest handicapper at best at 4 yrs: stays 1m: acts on all-weather and good to firm going: sometimes tongue tied. *R. C. Guest* **62 d**

STRATEGIC MOUNT 6 b.g. Montjeu (IRE) 137 – Danlu (USA) (Danzig (USA)) [2009 106: 12m 12m 12m Aug 19] big, strong gelding: useful performer: below best in 2009, respectable effort only when seventh in handicap at York (tongue tied) final start: effective at 1½m/1¾m: acts on firm and good to soft going: tried blinkered. *P. F. I. Cole* **99**

STRATEGIC MOVER (USA) 4 ch.g. Grand Slam (USA) 120 – Efficient Frontier (USA) (Mt Livermore (USA)) [2009 77: p7g⁵ p5.1g⁶ 7m³ p10g p12g p8m p9.5g p6f⁴ Dec 21] strong, useful-looking gelding: fair maiden: claimed from P. Cole £6,000 after third start: stays 1m: acts on good to firm and good to soft going: tried blinkered/visored: sometimes tongue tied. *P. Butler* **66**

STRATEGIC PRINCESS (IRE) 3 b.f. Hawk Wing (USA) 136 – Puteri Wentworth 88 (Sadler's Wells (USA) 132) [2009 12.1m 12m⁵ f12g⁴ 18g⁵ 16g⁴ p16m Sep 16] lengthy, angular filly: sixth foal: half-sister to 3 winners, including 1¾m and 16.4f winner Bukit Tinggi (by Peintre Celebre) and 1m (at 2 yrs)/8.6f winner Putra Sas (by Sri Pekan), both useful: dam 1½m to 2½m winner: modest maiden handicapper: stays 2¼m: acts on fibresand and good to firm going. *P. F. I. Cole* **63**

Coral Distaff, Sandown—the second of Strawberrydaiquiri's four wins; she readily draws clear of Say No Now (rail) and Wadaat

STRATFORD BRIDGE 6 b.g. Fraam 114 – Moorland Stroll (IRE) (Inzar (USA) 112) [2009 6g Oct 5] workmanlike gelding: soundly beaten in bumper for R. Tudor: 40/1, tailed off in maiden at Windsor on Flat debut. *J. L. Spearing* **–**

STRATHCAL 3 b.g. Beat Hollow 126 – Shall We Run 59 (Hotfoot 126) [2009 66p: 12.6g^4 12m* 12m* 14m^2 14g^3 13.3m^6 p16m^3 p12m^3 Nov 21] tall, useful-looking gelding: fairly useful handicapper: improved to win at Salisbury in May and Newbury in June: stays 1¾m: acts on polytrack and good to firm ground. *H. Morrison* **83**

STRATHMORE (IRE) 5 gr.g. Fath (USA) 116 – In The Highlands (Petong 126) [2009 75: p6g^3 f5g^3 p6g p6g^2 5m^2 5m 5d^6 5.9m 6m^2 6m^4 5m 5m^4 5g 6s^4 5s^4 5m^4 6d 5m Sep 23] good-topped gelding: fair handicapper: below form after fifth start: best at 5f/6f: acts on all-weather, good to firm and good to soft going: tried in cheekpieces/blinkers: races lazily. *R. A. Fahey* **71 d**

STRATTON BANKER (IRE) 2 b.g. (Feb 5) One Cool Cat (USA) 123 – Birthday (IRE) (Singspiel (IRE) 133) [2009 7m 7f Sep 7] €28,000F, £20,000Y, £20,000 2-y-o: fourth foal: closely related to 4-y-o Liberty Island and half-brother to 3-y-o Midnight In May: dam unraced: better effort in maidens at Folkestone (gelded in between) when seventh to Diam Queen latter start, again showing speed: likely to improve further. *S. C. Williams* **57 p**

STRAVELLA (IRE) 4 b.f. Stravinsky (USA) 133 – Princess Ellen 114 (Tirol 127) [2009 8m^5 8.1g* 8.3d^5 10g^3 9s Aug 1] third foal: closely related to 6-y-o La Estrella and half-sister to French 2006 2-y-o 5.5f winner Candelabro (by Elusive Quality): dam, 2-y-o 6f/7f winner and runner-up in 1000 Guineas, later 1m winner in USA: fairly useful performer: won maiden at Chepstow in May: stays 1¼m: best efforts on good ground: races prominently. *R. M. Beckett* **84**

STRAVERSJOY 2 b.f. (Mar 30) Kayf Tara 130 – Stravsea 65 (Handsome Sailor 125) [2009 8g 8.3v f8m Dec 5] tall, workmanlike filly: third foal: sister to 2005 2-y-o 1m winner Stravara and half-sister 5-y-o Stravita: dam 7f/1m winner: best effort in maidens when mid-field at Nottingham second start: should stay 1¼m+. *R. Hollinshead* **50**

STRAVITA 5 b.m. Weet-A-Minute (IRE) 106 – Stravsea 65 (Handsome Sailor 125) [2009 66: f16d^5 f14g^3 f12g f14m^5 p13.9g^6 f12g^6 Dec 22] compact mare: fair performer: stays 1¾m: acts on all-weather and soft ground: usually wears cheekpieces. *R. Hollinshead* **65**

STRAVONIAN 9 b.g. Luso 124 – In The Evening (IRE) 73 (Distinctly North (USA) 115) [2009 52§: 16m Apr 3] maiden: well held only outing in 2009: stays 1¾m: acts on soft and good to firm ground: tried in cheekpieces: ungenuine. *D. A. Nolan* **– §**

STRAWBERRYDAIQUIRI 3 gr.f. Dansili 127 – Strawberry Morn (CAN) (Travelling Victor (CAN)) [2009 8.3m^2 8.3g* 8.1m* 8g* 8.1g* 8m^4 Oct 3] 105,000Y: rather leggy filly: fifth foal: half-sister to fairly useful 8.6f to 1¼m winner Strawberry Lolly (by Lomitas) and 5-y-o Strabinios King: dam North American 6.5f to 8.5f minor stakes winner: smart form: successful 4 times in a row, namely maiden at Windsor in May, and listed races at Sandown and Ascot in July, and Sandown again (best effort, beat Ada River 4½ lengths) in August: fair 4¼ lengths fourth to Sahpresa in Sun Chariot Stakes at Newmarket final start, hold-up tactics counting against her: will stay 1¼m: raced only on good/good to firm going: type to improve further. *Sir Michael Stoute* **117 p**

STRAWBERRY MOON (IRE) 4 b.f. Alhaarth (IRE) 126 – Dancing Drop 103 (Green Desert (USA) 127) [2009 78: 7f* 7.9m^4 May 25] close-coupled filly: fairly useful handicapper: won at Redcar (all 3 wins there) in May: effective from 6f to 1m: acts on any going: often slowly away, but is consistent. *B. Smart* **80**

STREET CRIME 4 b.g. Tagula (IRE) 116 – Brandon Princess (Waajib 121) [2009 73: p12.2g Jun 22] big gelding: fair maiden at 3 yrs: well held only start in 2009: stays 9.5f: raced only on polytrack and good/good to soft ground: attitude under suspicion: sold £2,500 in July, resold £2,000 in October. *R. Lee* **–**

STREET DEVIL (USA) 4 gr.g. Street Cry (IRE) 130 – Math (USA) (Devil's Bag (USA)) [2009 75: f8g* 10.2g^4 f8g^3 9.9g^6 May 23] lengthy gelding: fairly useful performer: won maiden at Southwell in March: seems to stay 1¼m: acts on fibresand and soft ground: none too reliable. *R. Curtis* **80**

STREET DIVA (USA) 4 ch.f. Street Cry (IRE) 130 – Arctic Valley (USA) (Arctic Tern (USA) 126) [2009 65: 8g 8f 5.1m 6.1d^5 6.1d Sep 4] compact filly: maiden handicapper: just poor form in 2009, leaving R. Curtis after second start: should stay 1m: acts on polytrack. *A. B. Haynes* **45**

STREET ENTERTAINER (IRE) 2 br.c. (Feb 20) Danehill Dancer (IRE) 117 – Opera Ridge (FR) (Indian Ridge 123) [2009 8g p8g^2 p8g^4 Nov 25] lengthy colt: first foal: dam, placed at 1¼m in France, half-sister to smart French winners up to 15f Stretarez and Street Shaana: easily best effort in maidens when ½-length second to Rumoush at Lingfield: will be suited by 1¼m. *Mrs A. J. Perrett* **85**

STREET POWER (USA) 4 b. or br.g. Street Cry (IRE) 130 – Javana (USA) (Sandpit (BRZ) 129) [2009 –: p7g* p7g* p7g p6g* p6m^2 6m^3 6v^4 p7g* 6g* p6g* p6f^2 p7.1g Nov 27] useful handicapper: progressive in 2009, winning at Kempton (2) in January, Lingfield in February, Kempton in June, Ascot in July and Kempton (best effort, beat We Have A Dream 3¼ lengths) in August: free-going sort, will probably prove best at 6f/7f: acts on polytrack and good to firm going, promise on heavy: held up. *J. R. Gask* **96**

STREETS APART (USA) 4 b.f. Street Cry (IRE) 130 – Saintly Speaking (USA) (Dahar (USA) 125) [2009 72: 10.1m^4 12m^3 12d 10d^2 9.9g^3 p9.5g^4 Sep 18] big, good-topped filly: fair maiden handicapper: stays 1½m: acts on polytrack, good to firm and good to soft ground: visored/in cheekpieces after reappearance in 2009: front runner/races prominently: sold 13,000 gns. *W. R. Swinburn* **72**

STREETS OF WAR (USA) 2 b. or br.c. (Apr 29) Street Cry (IRE) 130 – Saint Boom (USA) (Saint Ballado (CAN)) [2009 8v^6 Oct 24] $45,000F, 55,000Y: fourth foal: dam ran twice in US: 8/1 and backward, encouraging sixth to Gardening Leave in maiden at Newbury, smooth headway before tiring: sure to do better. *P. W. Chapple-Hyam* **62 p**

STREET SPIRIT (USA) 3 b. or br.f. Street Cry (IRE) 130 – Be Good Or Be Gone (USA) (Gulch (USA)) [2009 6m^2 6m 5.1d f7g^3 8.3g 7.1m Jun 29] $10,000F: workmanlike filly: first foal: dam unraced out of close relation to smart 1¼m/1½m performer Mamaluna (grandam of Papal Bull): modest maiden, sporadic form: stays 7f: acts on fibresand: tongue tied last 4 starts: sold 5,000 gns. *T. D. Easterby* **57**

STREET WARRIOR (IRE) 6 b.g. Royal Applause 124 – Anne Bonny 105 (Ajdal (USA) 130) [2009 10.3m Mar 29] rather leggy gelding: missed 2008: below form sole outing on Flat in 2009 (fair hurdler, successful in April): stays 1¼m: acts on polytrack and firm ground. *H. J. Evans* **–**

STRENSALL 12 b.g. Beveled (USA) – Payvashooz 78 (Ballacashtal (CAN)) [2009 53: 5f 5m^3 5g 5g^6 5m^4 5g^2 5m^6 5g^2 5s Oct 27] sturdy gelding: modest performer: best at 5f: acts on fibresand, firm and soft ground. *R. E. Barr* **58**

STREVELYN 3 br.g. Namid 128 – Kali 83 (Linamix (FR) 127) [2009 –: 8s 11.1m f8g Jul 7] angular gelding: little form on Flat. *Mrs A. Duffield* **–**

STRICTLY 3 b.f. Falbrav (IRE) 133 – Dance On 93 (Caerleon (USA) 132) [2009 76p: 5.1d^2 6d* 5m^3 5m^2 5g 5g^2 5.7m^3 p6g Sep 21] rather leggy, attractive filly: fairly useful performer: landed odds in maiden at Doncaster in May: good efforts when runner-up in handicaps after: raced only at 5f/6f: unraced on extremes of going: sold 17,000 gns, sent to Saudi Arabia. *Sir Michael Stoute* **87**

STRICTLY DANCING (IRE) 2 b.f. (Mar 28) Danehill Dancer (IRE) 117 – Lochangel 119 (Night Shift (USA)) [2009 6m^5 6.5g^2 Oct 8] useful-looking filly: sixth foal: half-sister to 3 winners, including fairly useful 7f winner Star Pupil (by Selkirk) and 3-y-o Celestial Dream: dam, won Nunthorpe Stakes (also 6f winner at 2 yrs), half-sister to high-class sprinter Lochsong: better effort in maidens when 3½ lengths second to Exceedingly Bold at Newbury, finishing well: should improve again. *A. M. Balding* **71 p**

STRICTLY LAMBADA 2 b.f. (Feb 23) Red Ransom (USA) – Bella Lambada 87 (Lammtarra (USA) 134) [2009 8g^5 Oct 20] fifth foal: half-sister to several winners, including 3-y-o Yankee Doodle and useful 6f (including at 2 yrs) winner Fontana Amorosa (by Cadeaux Genereux): dam, 10.4f winner from 2 starts, half-sister to high-class 1¼m performer Stagecraft: 12/1, 3¾ lengths fifth to Hymnsheet in maiden at Yarmouth, prominent long way and not knocked about: will stay 1¼m: should do better. *J. H. M. Gosden* **72 p**

STRICTLY ROYAL 3 ch.g. Imperial Dancer 123 – Royal Logic (Royal Applause 124) [2009 –: p12g 8d Apr 14] deep-girthed gelding: no form: tried visored. *M. R. Channon* **–**

STRIDENT (USA) 8 ch.g. Deputy Commander (USA) 124 – Regrets Only (USA) (Black Tie Affair 128) [2009 61: p13.3g Jan 15] modest performer at 7 yrs: well held sole Flat outing in 2009 (poor hurdler/chaser): tried in visor/cheekpieces. *N. P. Moore* **–**

STRIDING EDGE (IRE) 3 b. or br.g. Rock of Gibraltar (IRE) 133 – For Criquette (IRE) (Barathea (IRE) 127) [2009 72: p7g 8m 8.3g^2 8.3m^3 8.3f^5 p8g* p8g^2 p8m^6 p8.6g^4 Oct 3] good-topped gelding: fairly useful handicapper: won apprentice event at Kempton in August: should stay beyond 1m: acts on polytrack and firm ground. *W. R. Muir* **81**

STRIKE A DEAL (IRE) 2 b.f. (Feb 15) Chineur (FR) 123 – Bishop's Lake 87 (Lake Coniston (IRE) 131) [2009 6s 8d^6 8d^5 Oct 27] 17,000Y: second foal: half-sister to 3-y-o Lakeman: dam 2-y-o 6f winner: progressive form in maidens, fifth to Commissionaire at Yarmouth: may prove best up to 7f: capable of better still. *C. F. Wall* **68 p**

STRIKE FORCE 5 b.g. Dansili 127 – Miswaki Belle (USA) 73 (Miswaki (USA) 124) [2009 74: p12g p9.5g^6 p9.5g 10.2m^6 12m^2 10m 11.9m^2 10m^3 11.9g^5 10f^3 12g^5 p9.5g^3 p12.2g^5 10.9m p12.2g^4 p9.5g^3 p9.5g p12.2g Nov 21] well-made gelding: fair handicapper: stays 1½m: acts on polytrack, soft and good to firm going: has worn cheekpieces/blinkers: held up. *Miss J. Feilden* **70**

STRIKEMASTER (IRE) 3 b.g. Xaar 132 – Mas A Fuera (IRE) (Alzao (USA) 117) [2009 55: p9.5g^3 p12.2m^2 p12g 14.1f^4 12.1g^3 16.2g* 16v^2 Jul 30] leggy gelding: fair handicapper: left J. Hills, improved when winning at Beverley in July: stays 2m: acts on polytrack and any turf going: won juvenile hurdle in August (subsequently gelded). *B. Ellison* **75**

STRIKER TORRES (IRE) 3 ch.g. Danehill Dancer (IRE) 117 – Silver Skates (IRE) 89 (Slip Anchor 136) [2009 83: 7.1m^5 7d^6 8m 8m^5 10.4g 7g p7.1g^2 p7.1g* Dec 19] compact gelding: fairly useful handicapper: won at Wolverhampton in December: needs to settle to stay 1m: acts on polytrack, best turf efforts on good going: visored last 2 starts (looked awkward first occasion). *B. Smart* **76**

STRIKE SHOT 2 b.g. (Mar 20) Avonbridge 123 – Final Shot 91 (Dalsaan 125) [2009 5m^6 5g* 6.1m^5 5.2d 6d^5 p5m^6 Aug 20] £30,000Y: compact gelding: half-brother to several winners, including smart sprinters Double Action and Sir Nicholas (both by Cadeaux Genereux), latter also successful up to 1¼m in Hong Kong: dam won Ayr Gold Cup: fair performer: won maiden at Haydock in May, best effort: will probably prove best at 5f: tried in cheekpieces. *W. R. Muir* **75**

STRIKE THE DEAL (USA) 4 ch.c. Van Nistelrooy (USA) 108 – Countess Gold (USA) (Mt Livermore (USA)) [2009 116: 5m^4 6m^4 p6g* 6m 6g^5 6m^6 5m* 5.2m* 6.5f Nov 7] quite attractive colt: smart performer: better than ever in 2009, winning minor event at Lingfield in May, and listed race at Doncaster (by length from Spin Cycle) and Dubai Duty Free World Trophy at Newbury (beat Total Gallery by neck) in September: reportedly suffered from foot trouble in week before finishing last in Breeders' Cup Turf Sprint at Santa Anita (blinkered) final outing: effective at 5f to 7f: acts on polytrack, firm and good to soft ground: usually visored: tactically versatile: normally reliable. *J. Noseda* **118**

Dubai Duty Free World Trophy, Newbury—Strike The Deal (visor) finishes strongly to collar Total Gallery; J J The Jet Plane (rail) is third

Windsor Castle Stakes, Royal Ascot—Strike The Tiger is the first-ever US-trained winner on the Flat in Britain; he is strongly pressed by Fratellino (noseband) and Di Stefano

STRIKE THE TIGER (USA) 2 b.g. (Feb 9) Tiger Ridge (USA) – R Lucky Strike (USA) (In Excess 116) [2009 a4.5s* 5m* 5.5f* a8.5g Sep 7] compact gelding: first foal: dam US 2-y-o 5.5f winner: useful form: won first 3 starts, namely 5-runner maiden claimer at Churchill Downs in April, 22-runner listed Windsor Castle Stakes at Royal Ascot (33/1, beat Fratellino by neck, getting across from wide draw) in June and non-graded stakes at Colonial Downs (by 3¼ lengths from Red Rally, again making all) in July: favourite, only seventh of 9 behind Gleam of Hope in non-graded event at River Downs final outing: stays 5.5f: acts on firm ground and on sloppy going on dirt: blinkered first 3 outings: has worn tongue tie. *Wesley A. Ward, USA* **98**

STRIKE UP THE BAND 6 b.g. Cyrano de Bergerac 120 – Green Supreme (Primo Dominie 121) [2009 114: a6g a5f a5.5f p5g^4 5.1m^4 5.1m^2 5g^6 5g^3 5.1m 5d^3 5g f5g^4 Oct 27] strong, good-topped gelding: just useful performer nowadays: mostly creditable efforts on turf in 2009, placed in handicaps at Chester, Epsom (third to Indian Trail in 'Dash') and Haydock: stiff task when tenth to Total Gallery in Prix de l'Abbaye de Longchamp penultimate outing: best at 5f: acts on polytrack (well held on fibresand and dirt), firm and soft going: tried visored: usually front runner. *D. Nicholls* **108**

STRIKING SPIRIT 4 b.g. Oasis Dream 129 – Aspiring Diva (USA) (Distant View (USA) 126) [2009 92: 6m* 6m 6g 6m 6m* 6g 6d 6m 5.6m 6m Sep 19] good-topped gelding: useful handicapper: improved when winning at Ascot in May and York (beat Pavershooz 1¾ lengths) in July: respectable efforts at best after: best at 5f/6f: unraced on extremes of going. *D. Nicholls* **104**

STRINGSOFMYHEART 5 b.m. Halling (USA) 133 – Heart's Harmony (Blushing Groom (FR) 131) [2009 84: f12g 12.1g^3 May 25] big, rangy mare: just fair handicapper in 2009: stays 1¾m: acts on all-weather, soft and good to firm going: has worn cheekpieces/ blinkers. *J. J. Quinn* **74**

STRONGARM 3 b.g. Refuse To Bend (IRE) 128 – Surf The Net 91 (Cape Cross (IRE) 129) [2009 –: 11.6g 10.9g^6 p12.2g Jul 13] workmanlike gelding: little form: tried blinkered. *A. Bailey* **–**

STRONG STORM (USA) 3 ch.g. Giant's Causeway (USA) 132 – Sweeping Story (USA) (End Sweep (USA)) [2009 –p: p8g* 11.6m^5 10m 10m^3 10f^3 10.1g* p10g Nov 18] **76**

good sort: fair performer: won maiden at Lingfield in January and, having been gelded after third start, claimer at Yarmouth (left J. Noseda £7,000, originally demoted for causing interference, but later reinstated on appeal) in August: should stay 1½m: raced only on polytrack and good going or firmer: in cheekpieces final outing. *H. J. Collingridge*

STRONG VIGILANCE (IRE) 2 ch.c. (Jan 20) Mr Greeley (USA) 122 – Zabadani 52 (Zafonic (USA) 130) [2009 7g⁴ Oct 23] 87,000F, 135,000Y: heavy-topped colt: first foal: dam, ran twice, half-sister to very smart French/US winner up to 1½m Radevore, out of half-sister to Irish 1000 Guineas winner Al Bahathri, herself dam of 2000 Guineas/ Champion Stakes winner Haafhd: 13/2, promising 6½ lengths fourth to Rashaad in maiden at Doncaster: bred to stay 1m: sure to improve. *P. W. Chapple-Hyam* **70 p**

STROPPI POPPI 5 b.m. Mtoto 134 – Capricious Lass (Corvaro (USA) 124) [2009 –: p12g p10g Feb 22] no form since 3 yrs. *Norma Twomey* **–**

ST SAVARIN (FR) 8 ch.g. Highest Honor (FR) 124 – Sacara (GER) (Monsagem (USA) 117) [2009 94: f12s² f12g p12g f11g Dec 8] sturdy gelding: just fair performer at best in 2009, leaving B. Johnson and off almost 10 months before final outing: seems to stay easy 2m: acts on all-weather, firm and soft ground: tried in cheekpieces. *M. S. Tuck* **72**

STUBBS ART (IRE) 4 ch.c. Hawk Wing (USA) 136 – Rich Dancer 70 (Halling (USA) 133) [2009 113: 7.5g³ a8f 7m 8g⁶ Aug 1] rather leggy colt: easily best effort in 2009 when 2¼ lengths third to Valedictum in handicap at Nad Al Sheba on reappearance: best form around 1m: acts on good to firm going: tried blinkered/tongue tied: races freely. *M. F. de Kock, South Africa* **109**

STYLE AWARD 4 b.f. Acclamation 118 – Elegant (IRE) (Marju (IRE) 127) [2009 88: p5g⁵ p6g⁵ p5g 5m 6g* 6m 5.2g 8d⁶ 6d 5.3m³ 6d p5.1g³ Nov 6] leggy, lengthy filly: fair handicapper: won at Windsor (apprentices) in May: best at 5f/6f: acts on polytrack, heavy and good to firm going: usually in cheekpieces nowadays. *W. J. H. Ratcliffe* **71**

STYLE ICON 4 ch.g. Mark of Esteem (IRE) 137 – Break Point (Reference Point 139) [2009 70: 7d⁶ 5.1m 6s⁵ 5.7f⁶ Jun 24] strong, good-bodied gelding: maiden, just modest at 4 yrs: should stay 1m+: acts on polytrack. *Rae Guest* **63**

STYLISH MOVER 4 b.g. Auction House (USA) 120 – Dam Certain (IRE) 61 (Damister (USA) 123) [2009 p6g⁶ p7g 7g 6m⁴ p7.1g Sep 25] poor maiden: should stay 7f: acts on polytrack and good to firm going: tongue tied last 2 starts. *R. Ingram* **45**

SUAILCE (IRE) 4 gr.f. Singspiel (IRE) 133 – Katch Me Katie 77 (Danehill (USA) 126) [2009 103: 14v³ 14g⁴ 14d⁴ 14d⁶ p10.7g Oct 2] useful-looking filly: useful performer: creditable fourth in listed race at Leopardstown and Curragh Cup (beaten 5 lengths by Profound Beauty): effective at 1½m to 2m: unraced on firm going, acts on any other turf/ polytrack: often blinkered: held up at 4 yrs. *D. K. Weld, Ireland* **103**

SUAKIN DANCER (IRE) 3 ch.f. Danehill Dancer (IRE) 117 – Wedding Morn (IRE) 62 (Sadler's Wells (USA) 132) [2009 61: 10.2g 8m 6m 7f⁶ Jul 23] small filly: modest maiden at 2 yrs: little form in 2009: should stay 1m+. *H. Morrison* **–**

SUBASTA 4 b.f. Auction House (USA) 120 – Travel Mystery 99 (Godswalk (USA) 130) [2009 12.4d Oct 13] 2,000Y: half-sister to 9f winner Pugilist (by Fraam): dam won Sagaro Stakes/useful 2m hurdler: well held in bumpers and in maiden at Newcastle. *M. Brittain* **–**

SUBA (USA) 3 b.f. Seeking The Gold (USA) – Zomaradah 118 (Deploy 131) [2009 81: 8.3m* 8m⁵ 9g⁴ p9.5m⁴ Sep 28] close-coupled filly: fairly useful handicapper: won at Nottingham (dead-heated with Charlotte Point) in June: stays 9.5f: acts on polytrack and good to firm going. *L. M. Cumani* **85**

SUBTEFUGE 2 b.f. (Apr 19) Observatory (USA) 131 – Artifice 80 (Green Desert (USA) 127) [2009 6m² 6g⁵ 7.1m* 7g Oct 24] sturdy filly: fifth foal: half-sister to fairly useful 7.5f winner Ramaad (by Dr Fong), later 1¼m winner in Qatar: dam, 6f winner, sister to smart 7f/1m performer Ardkinglass: fair performer: made all in maiden at Warwick in September by 3 lengths from Rule of Nature: creditable seventh in nursery at Doncaster: stays 7f. *H. R. A. Cecil* **76**

SUBURBIA (USA) 3 b.g. Street Cry (IRE) 130 – Green Lady (IRE) 104 (Green Desert (USA) 127) [2009 7f 8.3m Sep 30] sturdy gelding: better effort in maidens on second start: sold £9,500. *M. A. Jarvis* **53**

SUCH OPTIMISM 3 b.f. Sakhee (USA) 136 – Optimistic 90 (Reprimand 122) [2009 88: 8d 9g 10.2g⁶ f11g³ Dec 22] sturdy filly: has round action: fairly useful performer: should be suited by 1¼m+: acts on good to soft going: tends to hang right. *R. M. Beckett* **88**

SUDDEN IMPACT (IRE) 4 b. or br.f. Modigliani (USA) 106 – Suddenly 86 (Puissance 110) [2009 97§: f8g³ 7m 5g³ 5m² 5s* 6d* 6m⁴ 7.1g⁶ 5d 6m Sep 19] lengthy filly: useful handicapper: won at Haydock and Thirsk in July: poor and temperamental efforts last 3 starts: best at 5f/6f: acts on soft and good to firm going: moody. *Paul Green* **99 §**

SUDDEN IMPULSE 8 b.m. Silver Patriarch (IRE) 125 – Sanshang (FR) (Astronef 116) [2009 79: 10g² 12d⁵ 10.1s⁵ 10.1d 10.9d⁵ Jun 15] strong mare: fair handicapper: stays 1½m: acts on all-weather, firm and soft ground: tried in cheekpieces. *A. D. Brown* **66**

SUE AND SUE 2 b.f. (Mar 13) Needwood Blade 117 – Bahamian Belle 62 (Bahamian Bounty 116) [2009 6g Sep 14] first foal: dam, unreliable sprint maiden, half-sister to Princess Margaret Stakes winner Mixed Blessing: 100/1, last in maiden at Leicester. *G. Woodward* **–**

SUFAD 4 b.g. Alhaarth (IRE) 126 – Alshakr 108 (Bahri (USA) 125) [2009 82: p10g 21g p16g 12m⁵ 14.1g⁶ 12s Oct 6] useful-looking gelding: just modest handicapper in 2009, leaving G. L. Moore £6,800 after reappearance: stays 1¾m: acts on firm and good to soft going: blinkered last 2 starts. *T. D. McCarthy* **63**

SUFFICIENT WARNING 5 b.g. Warningford 119 – Efficacious (IRE) 49 (Efisio 120) [2009 9g a8.8g³ a10.5g³ p8g p8m p8g p8g Nov 18] won 2 handicaps at Mijas in 2008: third twice there early in year and modest form at best in similar events in Britain last 4 starts: stays 11f: acts on sand, well held on turf: tried blinkered. *R. J. Smith* **51**

SUFFOLK PUNCH (IRE) 2 ch.c. (May 4) Barathea (IRE) 127 – Lamanka Lass (USA) 79 (Woodman (USA) 126) [2009 6.1m³ p6g⁴ 7m* 7g 7.1g⁵ Aug 26] €25,000Y: good-topped colt: fifth foal: half-brother to several winners, notably smart 7f (including at 2 yrs) to 9f (in USA) winner Dark Islander (by Singspiel) and 3-y-o Miss Mojito: dam, 1m winner, half-sister to very smart 1¼m performer Far Lane: fairly useful performer: much improved when winning maiden at Epsom in July by 2½ lengths from Interakt: creditable eighth in nursery at Goodwood: stays 7f. *A. M. Balding* **84**

SUGARBABY PRINCESS (IRE) 3 gr.f. Verglas (IRE) 118 – Alkifaf (USA) (Mtoto 134) [2009 –: 12.1g Jun 22] well beaten in maidens. *S. W. James* **–**

SUGAR FREE (IRE) 3 b.f. Oasis Dream 129 – Much Faster (IRE) 113 (Fasliyev (USA) 120) [2009 98: 5.8v² 6m⁴ 5m* 5g 5v³ 5m Oct 1] strong, useful-looking filly: useful performer: improved when winning listed race at Ayr in June by ¾ length from City Dancer: below best after, twice in Britain: best at 5f: acts on soft and good to firm going: sold 540,000 gns in December. *T. Stack, Ireland* **104**

SUGAR RAY (IRE) 5 b.g. Danehill (USA) 126 – Akuna Bay (USA) 88 (Mr Prospector (USA)) [2009 110: 12d⁵ 12g³ 12m⁴ 14m⁴ 14g Jul 28] good-topped gelding: useful performer: creditable efforts first 4 starts in 2009, including when fifth to Crime Scene in handicap at Nad Al Sheba and 3¼ lengths fourth to Furmigadelagiusta in listed race at Pontefract first/third outings: stays 1½m: acts on firm and good to soft going: effective with/without visor: tongue tied: races prominently: reliable. *Saeed bin Suroor* **108**

SUGAR STATE 4 gr.g. M'Bebe 50 – Sweet Patoopie 72 (Indian Ridge 123) [2009 p9.5g p12.2g p9.5g 16d Jul 27] no form. *J. L. Spearing* **–**

SUHAILAH 3 ch.f. Sulamani (IRE) 130 – Vrennan 74 (Suave Dancer (USA) 136) [2009 p10g p12g⁵ p12g⁶ p12g⁵ p12g⁵ 11.5m 10.1m⁶ p12m p10g p12g p12g p12m⁶ Nov 29] fifth foal: half-sister to 7-y-o Baba Ghanoush and winner around 1¼m Blu Manruna (both by Zaha): dam 1½m winner: modest maiden: stays 1½m: acts on polytrack: in cheekpieces/visor last 5 starts. *M. J. Attwater* **53**

SUHAYL STAR (IRE) 5 b.g. Trans Island 119 – Miss Odlum (IRE) 81 (Mtoto 134) [2009 54§: p6g² p6g p8g² p7g* p7g⁴ p7g* p7g⁶ p6g* 6m² p6g² 6m p6g⁵ p7m Dec 4] strong, close-coupled gelding: fair handicapper: won at Lingfield in March and April (2): effective at 6f to 8.6f: acts on polytrack and good to firm going: tried in visor/cheekpieces: weak finisher, needs treating with caution. *P. Burgoyne* **71 §**

SUITABLY ACCOUTRED (IRE) 3 b.f. Acclamation 118 – Cliveden Gail (IRE) 102 (Law Society (USA) 130) [2009 –: 8m f11g 12.1m 14.1m⁵ 12.1m* 12.1m Jul 3] modest handicapper: won at Hamilton in June: stays 1½m: acts on good to firm ground: reluctant to enter stall last 3 outings. *Mrs A. Duffield* **57**

SUITED AND BOOTED (IRE) 2 ch.c. (Feb 24) Tagula (IRE) 116 – Carpet Lady (IRE) 70 (Night Shift (USA)) [2009 7g 7g⁴ 7g² 6m⁴ Sep 18] 48,000Y: compact colt: fifth foal: brother to 3-y-o Tagula Night and half-brother to 3 winning sprinters, including 4-y-o Cake: dam, maiden (should have stayed at least 7f), out of sister to smart middle- **85**

distance stayer Shambo: best effort in maidens when 1¾ lengths second to Treble Jig at Newmarket, dictating: stays 7f. *R. Hannon*

SUITS ME 6 ch.g. Bertolini (USA) 125 – Fancier Bit (Lion Cavern (USA) 117) [2009 113: p10g* p10g² p10g 8m 9m⁶ 9.8g 10g⁶ p10g³ p10f² Dec 19] tall, close-coupled gelding: smart performer on all-weather, useful on turf: won 3-runner listed race at Lingfield in February by ½ length from Dansant: creditable efforts after when runner-up in listed races at same course on second (neck behind Re Barolo) and final (beaten short head by Tranquil Tiger) outings: stays 10.5f: acts on polytrack and any turf going: usually front runner. *T. P. Tate* **105 a114**

SULA DREAM 3 ch.g. Sulamani (IRE) 130 – Bonella (IRE) 56 (Eagle Eyed (USA) 111) [2009 9g 10f 11.8g p12g Oct 2] angular gelding: little impact in maidens/handicap. *J. Pearce* **–**

SULARNO 5 ch.g. Medicean 128 – Star Precision 103 (Shavian 125) [2009 –, a76: f8g f11g f12g 8.3g² f8g³ p8g 8g p8.6g Oct 17] strong, good-bodied gelding: fair performer: claimed from H. Morrison £7,000 fourth start: stays 1m: acts on all-weather: tried in headgear. *J. Pearce* **67**

SULLENBERGER (IRE) 3 ch.g. Namid 128 – Bint Alhaarth (IRE) 78 (Alhaarth (IRE) 126) [2009 p8.6g² p8.6g* 8.3m 9.9g p12g p9.5g⁴ p9.5g³ p8.6g² p8g Oct 26] €70,000Y, 14,000 2-y-o: rather leggy gelding: first foal: dam, 1m winner, half-sister to smart 1½m performer Come On Jonny: fair performer: won maiden at Wolverhampton in March: stays 9.5f: acts on polytrack: often looks awkward, including in cheekpieces final start: sold 7,000 gns in October. *J. A. Osborne* **72**

SULTANA (GER) 7 b.m. Law Society (USA) 130 – Sweet Second (IRE) (Second Set (IRE) 127) [2009 p7g 11.3d 13m Jun 25] ex-German mare: first foal: dam, useful German 2-y-o 7.5f winner, stayed 1¼m: won maiden at Hassloch for C. von der Recke in 2005 (since been to stud): well held in handicaps in 2009, leaving L. Smyth in Ireland after second start: stays 1¼m: acts on good to soft ground: joined J. Lambe in Ireland. *Mrs L. C. Jewell* **–**

SULTAN'S CHOICE 2 b.f. (Feb 10) Sulamani (IRE) 130 – Royal Wish 45 (Royal Applause 124) [2009 7s⁴ 7d* p7.1g⁴ p8g⁵ Sep 2] rather unfurnished filly: first foal: dam ran twice: modest performer: claimed from J. Eustace £5,000 after debut: won seller at Catterick in July: should be suited by 1m+: acts on polytrack and good to soft going. *P. D. Evans* **58**

SULTANS WAY (IRE) 3 b.g. Indian Ridge 123 – Roses From Ridey (IRE) 78 (Petorius 117) [2009 73: 8m 8.5g p7g⁴ 7m⁶ p7g⁴ 7m Sep 28] good-topped gelding: fair performer: worth a try at 6f: acts on polytrack and good to soft going: tried blinkered: often finishes weakly. *P. F. I. Cole* **62**

SULUTION 3 b.c. Sulamani (IRE) 130 – Streccia (Old Vic 136) [2009 p8g² 8.5f⁶ 8f Jul 11] second foal: dam, maiden, half-sister to useful stayer Saltrio: best effort in maidens when second at Lingfield (only outing for M. Botti): stays 1m. *J. C. Canani, USA* **75**

SULWAAN (IRE) 2 b.g. (Apr 19) King's Best (USA) 132 – Iktidar 80 (Green Desert (USA) 127) [2009 7m⁴ 8.5m* 8m* Sep 15] £52,000Y: half-brother to several winners, including 5-y-o Follow The Flag and 7-y-o Qadar: dam maiden who stayed 1m: most progressive, winning maiden at Beverley in August and nursery at Yarmouth (slowly away, made most to beat Togiak ½ length, pair well clear) in September: stays 1m: open to further progress. *M. Johnston* **91 p**

SUMANI (FR) 3 b.g. Della Francesca (USA) 118 – Sumatra (IRE) (Mukaddamah (USA) 125) [2009 55: p7g⁴ p8g⁵ 9.9g p10g* 9.9g³ 12m² p12g² 10g 12f² p12m⁴ Sep 30] good-bodied gelding: fair handicapper: won at Lingfield in May: stays 1½m: acts on polytrack and firm going: front runner. *S. Dow* **75**

SUMAY BUOY (IRE) 2 b.c. (May 12) Fasliyev (USA) 120 – Mourir d'Aimer (USA) (Trempolino (USA) 135) [2009 6d 6g 6m Oct 1] down the field in maidens. *Mrs J. C. McGregor* **–**

SUMBE (USA) 3 b. or br.g. Giant's Causeway (USA) 132 – Sumoto 101 (Mtoto 134) [2009 78p: 10m 11.5m⁵ May 9] compact, attractive gelding: fair form sole outing at 2 yrs: in excellent shape, lost all chance when badly hampered in sales race at Newmarket on reappearance: tailed off in Derby Trial at Lingfield next time (gelded after): should stay 1¼m. *M. P. Tregoning* **–**

SUMMA CUM LAUDE 2 gr.f. (Apr 19) With Approval (CAN) – Sulitelma (USA) 63 (The Minstrel (CAN) 135) [2009 5m 5v⁵ p6g 6m 5m p6m Sep 28] small, leggy filly: half-sister to several winners, including Irish 5f winner Neeze (by Cadeaux Gene- **44 §**

reux) and 1¼m/1½m winner Tromp (by Zilzal), both fairly useful: dam, 2-y-o 5f winner, out of half-sister to Petoski: poor maiden: visored (looked reluctant) last 2 starts. *Mrs A. Duffield*

SUMMER AFFAIR (IRE) 4 b.g. Alhaarth (IRE) 126 – Late Summer (USA) 71 (Gone West (USA)) [2009 p12m^{4} p11g p9.5g^{3} p12.2g^{4} Nov 21] achieved little in 3-y-o bumpers: modest maiden on Flat: stays 1½m: raced on polytrack. *B. I. Case* **61**

SUMMER BOUNTY 13 b.g. Lugana Beach 116 – Tender Moment (IRE) 78 (Caerleon (USA) 132) [2009 58: p13.3g p9.5g^{4} p9.5g^{4} 12d^{5} 17.2d 12m p12g Oct 20] leggy, close-coupled gelding: modest performer: stays 12.6f: acts on all-weather and any turf going: tried blinkered/tongue tied: held up. *F. Jordan* **52**

SUMMER CAPERS (USA) 4 b.f. Mt Livermore (USA) – Crown Capers (USA) 83 (Chief's Crown (USA)) [2009 66: 7.1g p6g^{6} May 20] maiden handicapper: just poor form in 2009: effective at 5f to easy 1m: acts on polytrack, soft and good to firm going. *J. Gallagher* **48**

SUMMER DANCER (IRE) 5 br.g. Fasliyev (USA) 120 – Summer Style (IRE) 70 (Indian Ridge 123) [2009 86: 8f 8g^{6} 7.1m^{6} 7d^{5} 7.1m* 7.5m* 7m^{4} 7g^{4} 7m^{5} 7.1g* 7m^{2} 7.1g^{3} 6m 7m Sep 26] tall gelding: fairly useful handicapper: won at Musselburgh and Beverley in June and Musselburgh in August: best at 7f/1m: acts on polytrack, soft and good to firm going: headstrong: usually held up. *P. T. Midgley* **89**

SUMMER FETE (IRE) 3 gr.f. Pivotal 124 – Tamarillo 105 (Daylami (IRE) 138) [2009 99p: 7m 7s^{3} 7g* 8g Sep 6] good-topped filly: useful performer: improved in 2009, winning Oak Tree Stakes at Goodwood in July by 1¼ lengths from Select, staying on well: stiff task in Prix du Moulin de Longchamp only subsequent outing: free-going sort, though should stay 1m: acts on heavy ground, once raced on firmer than good. *B. Smart* **104**

SUMMER GOLD (IRE) 5 b.m. Barathea (IRE) 127 – Eman's Joy 68 (Lion Cavern (USA) 117) [2009 91: 10g^{4} 8g 8.1m^{3} 8.1f^{4} 8d^{2} 10.4g* 10.4m 10.3m 10.4m^{3} 8m Oct 3] lengthy mare: fairly useful handicapper: won at York in July: below form after: stays 10.4f: acts on good to firm and good to soft going: sold 25,000 gns. *E. J. Alston* **91**

SUMMERINTHECITY (IRE) 2 ch.c. (Apr 17) Indian Ridge 123 – Miss Assertive 88 (Zafonic (USA) 130) [2009 6g^{2} 6g* Jul 16] 67,000F, €80,000Y: sturdy colt: second foal: half-brother to useful 6f (at 2 yrs) to 8.5f (in USA) winner Meydan Princess (by Choisir): dam, 2-y-o 6f winner, half-sister to useful performer up to 1¼m Ascertain: better effort when winning minor event at Doncaster by neck from Skylla: should stay 7f: verging on useful. *J. Noseda* **94 +**

SUMMER LODGE 6 b.g. Indian Lodge (IRE) 127 – Summer Siren (FR) (Saint Cyrien (FR) 128) [2009 70: p12.2g p13.9g^{2} p16.5g^{4} 12m^{2} p11g^{2} 12d* 13.3g^{2} 12.1m* 12.3m^{5} 12v^{4} 12.4g^{2} p12m^{5} p13.9g^{3} Nov 12] small, sturdy gelding: fairly useful handicapper: won at Ripon (final start for A. McCabe) in June and Beverley in July: effective at 1½m, barely stays 2m: acts on all-weather, firm and soft going: often wears headgear: consistent. *J. A. Glover* **80**

SUMMER ROSE 4 gr.f. Kyllachy 129 – Roses of Spring 93 (Shareef Dancer (USA) 135) [2009 59: p5g^{5} 5.2d p5g p6m Dec 10] neat filly: modest handicapper: raced at 5f/6f: acts on all-weather: wears headgear. *R. M. H. Cowell* **55**

SUMMERS LEASE 4 b.f. Pivotal 124 – Finlaggan 83 (Be My Chief (USA) 122) [2009 92p: 10g 8m May 9] tall, angular filly: fairly useful at 3 yrs: well held in handicaps in 2009: stays 1¼m: acts on soft ground. *M. L. W. Bell* **–**

SUMMER SOUL (IRE) 7 b.g. Danehill (USA) 126 – Blend of Pace (IRE) 104 (Sadler's Wells (USA) 132) [2009 69: 16.1d* 13.1g^{3} 14s^{3} 17.5m^{4} 16.1d^{6} 15v^{6} Oct 31] fair handicapper: fit from hurdling, won at Newcastle in May: stays 17.5f: acts on firm and soft going: wears headgear: often front runner nowadays. *Miss Lucinda V. Russell* **77**

SUMMERS TARGET (USA) 3 ch.g. Mr Greeley (USA) 122 – She's Enough (USA) (Exploit (USA) 117) [2009 89: 7m^{5} 6f^{3} 6m^{3} 6m 7m^{5} 7g 7d Sep 3] leggy gelding: maiden, just fair at 3 yrs: free-going type, will prove best up to 7f: acts on firm ground: tried in cheekpieces. *R. M. H. Cowell* **70**

SUMMER WINDS 4 ch.g. Where Or When (IRE) 124 – Jetbeeah (IRE) 95 (Lomond (USA) 128) [2009 85: p10g^{2} p10g^{4} 10m* 10f 10d* 10m^{3} 9g^{4} 9.7f Sep 7] lengthy gelding: fairly useful handicapper: won at Newmarket in May and June: stays 1¼m: acts on polytrack, good to firm and good to soft ground: usually blinkered in 2009: consistent. *T. G. Mills* **91**

Amethyst Stakes, Leopardstown—Summit Surge returns to form; Three Rocks, Beach Bunny (hoops) and Mad About You (No.3) are next

SUMMIT SURGE (IRE) 5 b.g. Noverre (USA) 125 – Lady Peculiar (CAN) (Sunshine Forever (USA)) [2009 115: 7.5g* 8g^5 8m 7s^5 8g* May 10] sturdy gelding: smart performer: better than ever in 2009, winning handicap at Nad Al Sheba (by 1¼ lengths from Calming Influence) in February and Amethyst Stakes at Leopardstown (beat Three Rocks 1½ lengths) in May: effective at 7f/1m: acts on polytrack and good to firm going, not on softer than good: tongue tied: has joined L. Cumani. *G. M. Lyons, Ireland* **119**

SUMMON UP THEBLOOD (IRE) 4 b.g. Red Ransom (USA) – Diddymu (IRE) 66 (Revoque (IRE) 122) [2009 101: 8m May 2] tall, quite attractive gelding: handicapper, well below useful best sole outing in 2009: stays 8.3f: acts on firm and good to soft going. *M. R. Channon* **–**

SUNARISE (IRE) 2 b.f. (Mar 17) Galileo (IRE) 134 – Sun Silk (USA) 64 (Gone West (USA)) [2009 7m p7g* 8g Oct 31] 22,000Y: sturdy filly: fourth foal: half-sister to useful 1m (in USA)/9f winner Victory Design (by Danehill) and fairly useful Irish 2005 2-y-o 7.5f winner Sakkara Star (by Mozart): dam lightly-raced daughter of Fillies' Mile winner Silk Slippers: won maiden at Lingfield in October in good style: seemed amiss in listed event final start: should stay 1m. *R. Hannon* **81 +**

SUN CATCHER (IRE) 6 b.g. Cape Cross (IRE) 129 – Taalluf (USA) 82 (Hansel (USA)) [2009 82: 7m^5 6g 7f p7.1g^2 p7g Jul 15] good-topped gelding: just fair performer nowadays: effective at 6f to 1m: acts on all-weather, good to firm and good to soft going: wears headgear: none too consistent. *P. G. Murphy* **66**

SUNCELEB (IRE) 3 ch.f. Peintre Celebre (USA) 137 – Suntory (IRE) 89 (Royal Applause 124) [2009 8.3m^5 8.3f^3 8m^4 8f* 8g 10f^6 11.6d^6 Oct 12] angular filly: second foal: dam, Irish 6f/7f winner, half-sister to smart Irish 1¼m/1½m performer Fracas: fair performer: awarded race on appeal after nose second to Altimatum in maiden at Brighton in July: stays 1m: acts on firm going: sold 800 gns. *H. Morrison* **77**

SUNDAE 5 b.g. Bahamian Bounty 116 – Merry Rous 66 (Rousillon (USA) 133) [2009 99: 6d 6m^6 6d* 6g p6m Nov 19] useful-looking gelding: fairly useful handicapper: easily best effort in 2009 when winning at Yarmouth in July: effective at 5f/6f: acts on good to firm and good to soft ground: tried blinkered: often shapes as if amiss. *C. F. Wall* **94**

SUN DREAM 2 b.f. (Feb 24) Desert Sun 120 – I Have A Dream (SWE) (Mango Express 106) [2009 7m 7.1g^5 8d Oct 12] seventh foal: dam unraced: best effort in maidens when fifth to Sierra Alpha at Warwick. *Tom Dascombe* **63**

SUNLEY SMILES 4 ch.f. Arkadian Hero (USA) 123 – Sunley Scent 85 (Wolfhound (USA) 126) [2009 52: 7m May 11] modest maiden, lightly raced: shaped as though amiss only run in 2009: stays 7f: raced only on polytrack and good to firm ground. *P. Howling* **–**

SUNLEY SOVEREIGN 5 b.g. Josr Algarhoud (IRE) 118 – Pharsical 80 (Pharly (FR) 130) [2009 55: 5g^5 5m* 5m 6m 6m^4 7g 6g^6 6g^4 6m 7m 5s^2 5.9d^4 5s^2 5m^2 5g^6 5g^2 Sep 21] big, angular gelding: fair handicapper: won at Hamilton in May: was effective at 5f to 7f: acted on all-weather and any turf going: wore blinkers/cheekpieces: had looked reluctant: dead. *Mrs R. A. Carr* **65**

SUNLEY SPINALONGA 2 ch.f. (Mar 19) With Approval (CAN) – Sunley Scent 85 (Wolfhound (USA) 126) [2009 p7m Dec 16] fourth foal: half-sister to 3-y-o Sonning Gate and 5-y-o Resplendent Alpha: dam 6f/7f winner: 20/1 and very green, well held in maiden at Lingfield, not knocked about: capable of better. *D. R. C. Elsworth* **– p**

SUNNANDAEG 2 ch.c. (Jan 26) Haafhd 129 – Come Away With Me (IRE) 75 (Machiavellian (USA) 123) [2009 7d^3 6f* 6g^5 7g^4 Oct 24] £31,000Y: sturdy colt: first foal: dam, 5f/7f winner, half-sister to Norfolk Stakes winner Russian Valour: fairly useful performer: won maiden at Ayr in August by 4½ lengths from Happy Dubai: creditable efforts in listed race/nursery after: stays 7f: acts on firm going. *I. Semple* **86**

SUNNY FUTURE (IRE) 3 b.g. Masterful (USA) 119 – Be Magic 57 (Persian Bold 123) [2009 80: 7m 8.1g^2 8m 7.1v^4 8d^4 8d^3 p8g Oct 26] big, rangy gelding: fair maiden handicapper: stays 1m: acts on polytrack, good to firm and good to soft going (below form on soft/heavy). *M. S. Saunders* **73**

SUNNYSIDE TOM (IRE) 5 b.g. Danetime (IRE) 121 – So Kind 90 (Kind of Hush 118) [2009 82: 7s^6 7.9m* 8g^3 7.9m* 7.9g^2 8g 9.2v* 9.2g^2 9m^2 f8f^4 Oct 21] big, strong gelding: fairly useful performer: better than ever in 2009, winning handicaps at Carlisle in May and June and claimer at Hamilton in August: races freely, but stays 9.2f: acts on fibresand and any turf going: tried visored/in cheekpieces: often makes running. *R. A. Fahey* **92**

SUNNY SPELLS 4 b.g. Zamindar (USA) 116 – Bright Spells 93 (Salse (USA) 128) [2009 70p: p8m p10m p12.2g^5 f12g* f14d^3 Dec 29] big, good-topped gelding: fair handicapper: won at Southwell in December: stays 1¾m: acts on all-weather. *S. C. Williams* **73**

SUNNY SPRITE 4 b.g. Lujain (USA) 119 – Dragon Star 54 (Rudimentary (USA) 118) [2009 75: p7g^5 Feb 11] good-topped gelding: maiden: fair at 3 yrs: well held sole start in 2009. *J. M. P. Eustace* **–**

SUNRAIDER (IRE) 2 b.c. (Mar 6) Namid 128 – Doctrine 97 (Barathea (IRE) 127) [2009 6m^3 6m* 6.5m Sep 10] 25,000Y: well-made colt: second foal: half-brother to Irish 3-y-o Always Be True: dam, 2-y-o 7f/1m winner, out of sister to smart middle-distance stayer Sacrament: won maiden at Windsor in August by ½ length from Robinson Cruso, best effort: not clear run in sales race at Doncaster final start: remains useful prospect. *B. W. Hills* **89 p**

SUNRISE LYRIC (IRE) 2 b.f. (Mar 7) Rock of Gibraltar (IRE) 133 – Dawn Air (USA) 53 (Diesis 133) [2009 p7g^6 Sep 8] 68,000F, 50,000Y: good-topped filly: second foal: dam, maiden, half-sister to smart winner up to 1½m Midnight Line, out of May Hill Stakes winner Midnight Air: 16/1, 5½ lengths sixth to Dawnbreak in maiden at Lingfield: will stay 1m+: likely to improve. *P. F. I. Cole* **55 p**

SUNRISE SAFARI (IRE) 6 b.g. Mozart (IRE) 131 – Lady Scarlett (Woodman (USA) 126) [2009 95: 5m 6g^2 6m^4 7g^6 6g 6d^3 7m^5 6g* 6g 6m^5 6m^4 6m 6g^6 p6g Nov 14] lengthy gelding: useful handicapper: won at Pontefract (by 1¼ lengths from Harrison George) in July: best at 5f/6f: acts on soft and good to firm going: usually visored, tried in cheekpieces: moody, and hard ride (tends to get behind). *R. A. Fahey* **96 §**

SUNRISE SHUFFLE 2 b.f. (Mar 9) Danehill Dancer (IRE) 117 – Silky Dawn (IRE) 100 (Night Shift (USA)) [2009 7g Oct 31] 25,000Y: fourth foal: half-sister to fairly useful 2008 2-y-o 5f winner Sun Ship (by Xaar) and 7f winner Catbang (by Zafonic): dam 1m winner: 40/1, mid-field in maiden at Newmarket, slowly away and brief trouble. *B. W. Hills* **62 +**

SUNSET BOULEVARD (IRE) 6 b.g. Montjeu (IRE) 137 – Lucy In The Sky (IRE) 59 (Lycius (USA) 124) [2009 71: p12m^6 p12g* p12g p12g^2 p12g* p12g^2 p12g^2 10m p12g^2 p12.2g Jul 13] leggy, useful-looking gelding: fair performer: won handicap in January and seller in March, both at Lingfield: likely to stay beyond 1½m: acts on polytrack, unraced on extremes of going on turf: tried visored. *Miss Tor Sturgis* **69**

SUNSHINE ALWAYS (IRE) 3 gr.g. Verglas (IRE) 118 – Easy Sunshine (IRE) 96 (Sadler's Wells (USA) 132) [2009 p7.1g* 7.1m^4 8d^2 8g^2 7s^4 p8g* p8m^3 p7m^2 p8f^6 p7m^4 p8m^4 p7f^6 p7g^4 Dec 31] €110,000Y, resold 80,000Y: third foal: half-brother to Irish 4-y-o Second Glance: dam, Irish 7f winner, closely related to 3-y-o Fortuni: fairly useful performer: won maiden at Wolverhampton in May and claimer at Kempton (left W. Haggas £20,000) in September: stays 1m: acts on polytrack, good to firm and good to soft going: held up (often races freely). *T. D. McCarthy* **89**

SUNSHINE BUDDY 2 b.f. (Feb 1) Reel Buddy (USA) 118 – Bullion 85 (Sabrehill (USA) 120) [2009 p7g Jul 15] workmanlike filly: seventh foal: half-sister to several winners, including 5-y-o Hart of Gold: dam 2-y-o 1m winner: 40/1, well beaten in maiden at Kempton. *J. R. Holt* **–**

totesport.com Cambridgeshire (Heritage Handicap), Newmarket— Supaseus (rail) just holds the strong challenge of Tartan Gigha; they are followed, from right to left, by Nanton, Applause, Shavansky and Stevie Thunder; Nanton also ran in the second leg of the autumn double two weeks later

SUNSHINE ELLIE 3 ch.f. Desert Sun 120 – Lindoras Glory (USA) (Gone West (USA)) [2009 48: f6s^6 p7g p5.1g p5.1g^6 Dec 11] smallish filly: poor maiden: may prove best at 5f/6f: acts on all-weather. *D. Shaw* **44**

SUNTRAP 2 ch.g. (Feb 17) Desert Sun 120 – Regal Gallery (IRE) 76 (Royal Academy (USA) 130) [2009 7g^5 7m^6 Sep 23] small gelding: modest form in maidens at Newmarket and Goodwood: should stay at least 1m. *W. J. Knight* **64**

SUPASEUS 6 b.g. Spinning World (USA) 130 – Supamova (USA) 88 (Seattle Slew (USA)) [2009 114: a9f 8g 10.4m^6 10m^5 9m* 9m Oct 16] big, good-bodied gelding: smart performer: lightly raced in 2009 (cracked pelvis after reappearance), but gradually back to best, winning 32-runner totesport.com Cambridgeshire Handicap at Newmarket (beat Tartan Gigha by nose) in October, soon in front against far rail and finding plenty: well held in Darley Stakes there final outing: stays 10.4f: acts on firm and good to soft going: makes running. *H. Morrison* **113**

SUPAVERDI (USA) 4 br. or b.f. Green Desert (USA) 127 – Supamova (USA) 88 (Seattle Slew (USA)) [2009 75p: 8g* 8m^6 8m p10g^6 10.4v* 10.2g* Aug 18] tall filly: useful handicapper: won at Bath in April, Haydock in July and Nottingham (further improvement when beating Mejala by 4½ lengths, again making all) in August: likely to stay 1½m: acts on polytrack and heavy going. *H. Morrison* **95**

SUPER ACADEMY (USA) 3 ch.f. Royal Academy (USA) 130 – Super Supreme (IND) (Zafonic (USA) 130) [2009 p7.1g^2 p7g^2 7f* p7g 5.7m Sep 13] 90,000Y: fourth foal: half-sister to useful Irish 2006 2-y-o 7.5f winner Vorteeva (by Bahri), later successful in USA: dam unraced: fair form: won maiden at Salisbury in June: not sure to stay much beyond 7f: acts on polytrack and firm ground: sold 26,000 gns, sent to USA. *J. A. Osborne* **78**

SUPERA (IRE) 3 ch.f. Spartacus (IRE) 107 – Lauretta Blue (IRE) (Bluebird (USA) 125) [2009 –: 8m 7.5m^4 10.1d Jul 21] close-coupled filly: poor form: best effort at 7.5f on good to firm going. *M. H. Tompkins* **47**

SUPERCAST (IRE) 6 b.g. Alhaarth (IRE) 126 – Al Euro (FR) 57 (Mujtahid (USA) 118) [2009 83: p9.5g p9.5g^2 p10g^3 p9.5g^5 10.3g^4 10.4v^4 9.9m* 10.2g 9.9m p9.5g^4 10m p10m^5 p9.5g^4 Dec 26] lengthy gelding: fairly useful handicapper: won at Goodwood in June: trained by F. Sheridan on ninth start only: stays 1¼m: acts on polytrack and any turf going: tried in cheekpieces/blinkers/tongue strap: races prominently: tough. *N. J. Vaughan* **83**

SUPER COLLIDER 2 b.g. (Feb 5) Montjeu (IRE) 137 – Astorg (USA) 106 (Lear Fan (USA) 130) [2009 7g^6 8d^2 8.1m^3 Sep 26] 230,000Y: tall, good-topped gelding: seventh foal: closely related to French/US 8.5f to 10.5f winner Asti (by Sadler's Wells) and half-brother to French 5.5f to 1m winner (latter at 2 yrs) Amazon Beauty (by Wolfhound), both useful: dam, French 1m winner, half-sister to smart French 1m/1¼m performer Android: similar form when placed in maidens at Thirsk and Haydock (third to Graymalkin, gelded after): will be suited by 1¼m. *M. A. Jarvis* **79**

SUPERDUPER 4 b.f. Erhaab (USA) 127 – I'm Magic 75 (First Trump 118) [2009 89: 6g^2 6m^6 6m 5g p6g^3 Aug 14] good-topped filly: fairly useful handicapper: well below form after reappearance in 2009: effective at 6f/7f: acts on firm and soft ground. *R. Hannon* **84**

SUPER DUPLEX 2 b.c. (Apr 6) Footstepsinthesand 120 – Penelope Tree (IRE) (Desert Prince (IRE) 130) [2009 p5g^4 6m^3 6d^3 6g^6 p5f 6d 6g Oct 19] fair form in maidens first 3 starts: went wrong way in nurseries, often let down by attitude: stays 6f. *P. M. Phelan* **65**

SUPER FOURTEEN 3 b.c. Lucky Story (USA) 128 – Beechnut (IRE) (Mujadil (USA) 119) [2009 67: 8.3m p8g^3 8.3g^3 8.1m p7g p8m^3 Sep 30] useful-looking colt: fair performer: stays 1m: acts on polytrack and good to soft going, seemingly not on firmer than good: usually races prominently: claimed £5,000 final start, joined Ray Fielder. *R. Hannon* **65**

SUPER FRANK (IRE) 6 b.g. Cape Cross (IRE) 129 – Lady Joshua (IRE) 88 (Royal Academy (USA) 130) [2009 –, a89: p7g^5 p7g^3 p7g* p6g* p6g 6g* 6m* 7f^6 6g 6m 6g 7d Oct 6] rather leggy gelding: fairly useful handicapper on all-weather, fair on turf: won at Lingfield in February and March and Folkestone (2, apprentices on first occasion) in April: below form after: effective at 6f to 1m: acts on polytrack and good to firm ground: tried blinkered/tongue tied, usually in cheekpieces. *J. Akehurst* **75 a86**

SUPERHOOPS 2 b.g. (Feb 5) Hunting Lion (IRE) 115 – Colonial Lady (Dansili 127) [2009 p8m 8.3m 8m Sep 12] no form, including in seller. *H. S. Howe* **–**

SUPERIOR DUCHESS 4 b.f. Superior Premium 122 – Downclose Duchess 49 (King's Signet (USA) 110) [2009 59: 8g^6 7g^6 8g^4 p12m p8m Dec 6] close-coupled filly: modest maiden: stays 8.3f: acts on fibresand and soft ground. *Jane Chapple-Hyam* **53**

SUPERIOR EDGE 2 b.f. (Apr 30) Exceed And Excel (AUS) 126 – Beveled Edge 60 (Beveled (USA)) [2009 6m 5.1g^5 Aug 28] tall filly: has scope: sister to 3-y-o Sharpened Edge, closely related to 6f (including at 2 yrs) winner Bright Edge (by Danehill Dancer) and 6f (at 2 yrs) to 1m winner Elidore (by Danetime), both useful, and half-sister to 2 winners: dam 6f winner: faded in maidens at Newbury and Bath (better effort, took good hold). *B. Palling* **55**

SUPERIOR SERVICE 2 b.f. (May 3) Superior Premium 122 – Dolly Bevan 53 (Another Realm 118) [2009 5v Jul 18] half-sister to several winners, including useful 6f winner (including at 2 yrs) Oggi and fairly useful 6f (at 2 yrs) to 1m winner Pengamon (both by Efisio): dam, 2-y-o 6f seller winner who stayed 1m, half-sister to smart sprinter Pips Pride: 12/1, tailed off in maiden at Ripon. *C. C. Bealby* **–**

SUPER KING 8 b.g. Kingsinger (IRE) 94 – Super Sisters (AUS) (Call Report (USA)) [2009 –: f8g f11g p10g^5 f12g 10m 9.9f Aug 29] leggy gelding: maiden: little form since 2005: tried visored/blinkered. *A. D. Brown* **–**

SUPERMASSIVE MUSE (IRE) 4 br.g. Captain Rio 122 – Cautionary (IRE) 78 (Warning 136) [2009 98: 5m^6 5g 5g 5.1g 6m 5.1m^5 5.1m^4 p5.1g Oct 2] strong gelding: handicapper: well below useful best after 4-y-o reappearance: best at 5f: acts on polytrack, soft and good to firm going: tried blinkered/tongue tied, wears cheekpieces. *E. S. McMahon* **91 d**

SUPERNOVERRE (IRE) 3 b.g. Noverre (USA) 125 – Caviare (Cadeaux Genereux 131) [2009 75: p10g^4 p10g^5 p11g^4 p10g* p8.6g^3 p12g* 12m* 12d^6 10.1g^5 14g p10g^5 p12.2g p12m^6 p12.2g^3 p16g^5 p13.9g^6 Nov 2] good-bodied gelding: fair performer: won claimer at Lingfield (left Mrs A. Perrett £8,000) in February and handicaps at Kempton in March and Catterick in April: stays 1½m: acts on polytrack and good to firm going: tried blinkered/in cheekpieces. *P. Howling* **78**

SUPER SENSATION (GER) 8 b.g. Platini (GER) 126 – Studford Girl 43 (Midyan (USA) 124) [2009 p12.2g^4 p16g^3 Mar 2] modest performer: missed 2008: stays easy 1½m: acts on all-weather and soft going: blinkered nowadays. *G. L. Moore* **53**

SUPER SLEUTH (IRE) 3 ch.f. Selkirk (USA) 129 – Enemy Action (USA) 105 (Forty Niner (USA)) [2009 101p: 7s^2 8f^3 8v May 24] big, strong filly: smart maiden: further improvement when placed first 2 starts in 2009, head second to Lahaleeb in Fred Darling Stakes at Newbury and 2¾ lengths third to Ghanaati in 1000 Guineas at Newmarket, finishing fast: heavy ground, ran poorly in Irish 1000 Guineas at the Curragh final start: suffered setback after: not sure to stay beyond 1m: acts on soft and good to firm going. *B. J. Meehan* **113**

SUPERSTITIOUS ME (IRE) 3 b.f. Desert Prince (IRE) 130 – Royal Rival (IRE) (Marju (IRE) 127) [2009 52: 10.2d p8.6g^2 7m^4 8m 8d p8.6g p8.6g Nov 16] modest maiden handicapper: stays 8.6f: acts on polytrack and firm going: races freely. *B. Palling* **60**

SUPER YELLOW 2 b.g. (Jan 25) Exceed And Excel (AUS) 126 – Almost Amber (USA) 88 (Mt Livermore (USA)) [2009 p6g^5 p7.1g Nov 13] better effort in maidens at Wolverhampton when fifth to Little Garcon: likely to prove best at 5f/6f: gelded after final start. *J. A. Osborne* **59**

SUPPLEMENTARY (IRE) 7 b.m. Rudimentary (USA) 118 – Will She What (IRE) (Lafontaine (USA) 117) [2009 p9.5g p11g p12g p10g Dec 7] has shown more temperament than ability, including in bumpers/over hurdles. *M. J. Coombe* –

SUPPORT FUND (IRE) 5 ch.m. Intikhab (USA) 135 – Almost A Lady (IRE) 70 (Entitled 126) [2009 83: 7m 7m³ 8.3d⁴ 7m⁴ 7.1m² 7g* 7g⁶ 8m p7m³ p7m⁵ 8g² p8m³ p8g⁶ p8g⁶ Dec 7] deep-girthed mare: fairly useful handicapper on turf, fair on all-weather: won at Epsom in July: best at 7f/1m: acts on polytrack, soft and good to firm going: has run well when sweating: held up. *Eve Johnson Houghton* **83 a76**

SUPREME GLIMPSE 3 b.f. Piccolo 121 – Running Glimpse (IRE) 84 (Runnett 125) [2009 5.7g 7m May 8] compact filly: sister to 5f winners Intriguing Glimpse (useful, also won at 2 yrs) and Espy (fairly useful) and half-sister to 2 winners, including fairly useful 6f/7f winner Another Glimpse (by Rudimentary): dam, 5f (at 2 yrs)/6f winner, half-sister to smart 1¼m/1½m performer Captain Horatius: last in maidens. *Mrs N. Smith* –

SUPREME SPEEDSTER 5 br.g. Superior Premium 122 – Effervescent 89 (Efisio 120) [2009 68: f5g f6g⁵ 6g 7m 6m² 6f 5.7g 5.1m 6.1d⁶ 6.1m Sep 10] rather leggy, close-coupled gelding: modest performer nowadays: raced mostly at 5f/6f: acts on fibresand and good to firm ground. *A. G. Newcombe* **52**

SUPSONIC 6 br.g. Marju (IRE) 127 – Nicely (IRE) 94 (Bustino 136) [2009 f12g² f14g* f12g³ f16g* 16.4d 14m a12g a12g 12g* 15g² 15d² 15.5s Nov 1] lengthy, good-topped gelding: fair performer: won claimer at Deauville in 2006 when trained by U. Suter, France: unraced again on Flat until 2009, winning claimer and handicap at Southwell in March and (having left R. Price after sixth outing) women jockeys claimer at Chantilly in September: stays 2m: acts on fibresand and good to soft ground: tried in cheekpieces. *R. Le Gal, France* **73 a77**

SURANAM 2 ch.g. (Mar 27) Tobougg (IRE) 125 – Miss Grimm (USA) 69 (Irish River (FR) 131) [2009 5m⁶ p6g² p7.1g p5.1m³ Nov 28] small, sturdy gelding: fourth foal: brother to fairly useful 2006 2-y-o 6f winner Ela Aleka Mou: dam, maiden, out of useful performer up to 1m Gretel: best effort in maidens when neck second to So Surreal at Wolverhampton: likely to be best at 5f/6f. *W. J. Haggas* **76**

SURE FIRE (GER) 4 b.g. Monsun (GER) 124 – Suivez (FR) (Fioravanti (USA) 115) [2009 p12g⁶ f12f³ Dec 12] brother to 2 winners in Germany, including smart 9f to 11f winner Simoun and half-brother to 3 winners, including useful dam of 3-y-o Stacelita (by Monsun): dam German 6f (at 2 yrs) and 1m winner: fair form when fifth in bumper: better effort in maidens on Flat (fair form) when third to Lava Steps at Southwell: will stay 1¾m. *B. J. Curley* **68**

SURPRISE PARTY 3 b.f. Red Ransom (USA) – Surprise Visitor (IRE) (Be My Guest (USA) 126) [2009 68: 8.3f⁵ 8m⁵ 8s² 8s* 8m* 8.1g* 8f* Dec 17] rather leggy filly: useful performer: progressed well, winning handicaps at Yarmouth (2) and Sandown in July/August, and, having left C. Wall, allowance race at Hollywood in December: stays 1m: acts on firm and soft going: held up in Britain. *Kathy Walsh, USA* **96**

SURPRISE PENSION (IRE) 5 b.g. Fruits of Love (USA) 127 – Sheryl Lynn (Miller's Mate 116) [2009 69: p9.5g⁶ 12g 10.9m 10m* 9.9m³ Jun 28] stocky gelding: fair handicapper: best effort in 2009 when winning at Leicester in May: stays 1½m: acts on heavy and good to firm going. *J. J. Quinn* **65**

SURUOR (IRE) 3 b.g. Intikhab (USA) 135 – Kismah 111 (Machiavellian (USA) 123) [2009 73: p7.1g² 7.1g* 8m* 8m 7m² 7d* 7m Sep 12] workmanlike gelding: useful handicapper, generally progressive in 2009: won at Warwick and Newmarket in May, and Goodwood (beat Shamwari Lodge ¾ length, idled) in July: effective at 7f/1m: acts on polytrack, good to firm and good to soft going: held up (sometimes gets behind). *D. M. Simcock* **104**

SURWAKI (USA) 7 b.g. Miswaki (USA) 124 – Quinella (Generous (IRE) 139) [2009 74: p8g* p7g³ Feb 9] close-coupled gelding: just modest form both starts in 2009, though won seller at Lingfield in January: stays 1m: acts on polytrack, firm and soft ground: tried in cheekpieces: races prominently. *R. M. H. Cowell* **63**

SUSHITAN (GER) 4 ch.g. Lomitas 129 – Subia (GER) (Konigsstuhl (GER)) [2009 9.9g⁶ p12g³ 13.1g⁵ p13.9g⁵ Sep 25] brother to 3 winners abroad, notably very smart German/US performer up to 1½m Sumitas, and half-brother to German 1m winner Sargentos (by Linamix): dam, German 8.3f to 10.5f winner, sister to smart German middle-distance performer Surako: ran twice in maidens for P. Schiergen in Germany in 2008: fair form all 4 starts in Britain (gelded after final occasion): seems to stay 1¾m: raced on polytrack and good ground. *G. L. Moore* **72**

SUSSEX DANCER (IRE) 3 ch.f. Danehill Dancer (IRE) 117 – Wadud 59 (Nashwan (USA) 135) [2009 71: p8.6g p7g 10f^5 Jul 5] rather unfurnished filly: maiden: well held at 3 yrs: sold 57,000 gns. *J. A. Osborne* –

SUSURRAYSHAAN 3 b.g. Dilshaan 119 – Magic Mistral (Thowra (FR)) [2009 –: 10.2m^4 9.9m^5 14.1m 10.4m^4 12m 10.4g 10.1m p8.6g^5 p16.5g Sep 12] good-bodied gelding: modest maiden, sporadic form: stays 1¼m: acts on soft and good to firm ground: wears cheekpieces/visor. *Mrs G. S. Rees* 53

SUTTON VENY (IRE) 3 b.f. Acclamation 118 – Carabine (USA) (Dehere (USA) 121) [2009 6m 6g^4 6m* 5g 6g p6g^2 p6g p6f* Dec 13] €14,500Y, resold 52,000Y: workmanlike filly: fourth foal: half-sister to Irish/US 6f to 7.5f winner Glorificamus (by Shinko Forest) and 5f (at 2 yrs) to 9.5f winner Fiore di Bosco (by Charnwood Forest): dam maiden half-sister to 2000 Guineas winner Mystiko: fair performer: won maiden at Lingfield in August and handicap at Kempton in December: stays 6f: acts on polytrack and good to firm ground. *J. R. Gask* 79

SUZHOU 2 b.f. (Mar 10) Tiger Hill (IRE) 127 – Tora Bora 101 (Grand Lodge (USA) 125) [2009 6s Nov 7] second foal: dam 7f winner: 16/1, green when eleventh in maiden at Doncaster: likely to improve. *Tom Dascombe* 53 p

SUZIE QUW 3 ch.f. Bahamian Bounty 116 – Bonkers 63 (Efisio 120) [2009 77: 6g 6v* 6d 7g 6g f6g Oct 18] close-coupled filly: fairly useful handicapper: won at Haydock in May: well held after, trained by K. R. Burke until after fourth outing: stays 6f: acts on heavy going, yet to race on firmer than good. *A. P. Jarvis* 83

SUZI'S A SMARTLADY (IRE) 2 b.f. (Apr 19) Rakti 130 – Shesasmartlady (IRE) (Dolphin Street (FR) 125) [2009 p6m 6m^3 6m^4 7g 7g Oct 17] €20,000Y: fifth foal: half-sister to several winners, including smart 5f (at 2 yrs) to 7f winner Captain Marvelous (by Invincible Spirit) and useful 1¼m/1½m winner Hero Worship (by Kalanisi): dam Irish maiden half-sister to useful Irish performer up to 1m Dashing Colours: best effort when third to Bond Fastrac in maiden at Redcar: well held in nurseries: should be suited by 7f+. *M. Johnston* 68

SUZI'S CHALLENGER 2 b.f. (Apr 23) Tobougg (IRE) 125 – La Tiziana 83 (Rudimentary (USA) 118) [2009 8.3m 8.3m 6m Oct 26] tall filly: seventh foal: dam, 1¼m winner, half-sister to useful stayer Taffrail: behind in maidens: probably capable of better over further. *H. J. Collingridge* – p

SUZI'S DANCER 3 b.f. Groom Dancer (USA) 128 – La Tiziana 83 (Rudimentary (USA) 118) [2009 p7g p8.6g^5 p7g^4 p6m^3 Dec 9] leggy filly: sixth foal: dam, 1¼m winner, half-sister to useful stayer Taffrail: modest form in maidens: should stay 1m+: raced only on polytrack. *H. J. Collingridge* 60

SUZI'S DECISION 4 gr.f. Act One 124 – Funny Girl (IRE) 78 (Darshaan 133) [2009 104: 11.9g* May 30] big filly: smart performer: off 10 months, further progress when winning listed event at Haydock by 2½ lengths from Les Fazzani, travelling strongly and asserting final 1f: will stay 1¾m: acts on firm ground. *P. W. D'Arcy* 110

SUZI SPENDS (IRE) 4 b.f. Royal Applause 124 – Clever Clogs 96 (Nashwan (USA) 135) [2009 94: 8m^5 10.3g^3 10.4g 10s^4 p9.5m^5 p8g^3 p10m p10m^5 Dec 16] workmanlike filly: fairly useful handicapper: stays 1¼m: acts on polytrack, soft and good to firm going: held up. *H. J. Collingridge* 87

SUZY ALEXANDER 2 b.f. (Apr 21) Red Ransom (USA) – Fiveofive (IRE) 61 (Fairy King (USA)) [2009 6g Aug 30] closely related to fairly useful 1m/9.7f winner Lilli Marlane (by Sri Pekan) and half-sister to several winners, notably smart 1m/US Grade 2 9f winner Medici Code (by Medicean): dam 5f (at 2 yrs) and 1m winner: 66/1, last in maiden at Yarmouth. *G. G. Margarson* –

SUZYBEE 2 b.f. (May 6) Bahamian Bounty 116 – Greenfly (Green Desert (USA) 127) [2009 p8m p8f Dec 20] fourth foal: half-sister to 3-y-o Desert Bump and winner in Greece by Vettori: dam, French 1m winner, out of sister to smart 1m/1¼m performer Darnay: well held in maidens at Kempton. *M. R. Hoad* –

SUZYS DREAM (IRE) 2 gr.f. (Apr 16) Arakan (USA) 123 – Blue Velvet 100 (Formidable (USA) 125) [2009 6d f5g 5m Jun 10] £10,000Y: second foal: half-sister to 4-y-o Lieutenant Pigeon: dam 5f (including at 2 yrs)/6f winner: well held in maidens/claimer. *P. T. Midgley* –

SVINDAL (IRE) 3 ch.g. Tomba 119 – Princess Sadie 86 (Shavian 125) [2009 68: p10g^2 p9.5g* 8s p8g Jun 24] strong, lengthy gelding: fair handicapper: won at Wolverhampton in January: stays 1¼m: acts on all-weather: wears blinkers/cheekpieces: races prominently: sold £7,600 in August, sent to Kuwait. *K. A. Ryan* 68

SWAIN'S QUEST (USA) 2 b.f. (May 5) Swain (IRE) 134 – Questonia 107 (Rainbow Quest (USA) 134) [2009 p8.6g Dec 19] half-sister to several winners, including 3-y-o Bea Menace and fairly useful 11.6f winner Sharp Reply (by Diesis): dam, 1m winner, out of half-sister to champion 1997 2-y-o Xaar: 25/1, showed nothing in maiden at Wolverhampton. *Eve Johnson Houghton* **–**

SWALLOW SENORA (IRE) 7 b.m. Entrepreneur 123 – Sangra (USA) 69 (El Gran Senor (USA) 136) [2009 32: f7s p9.5g Mar 27] lightly-made mare: poor maiden: tried blinkered/tongue tied. *M. C. Chapman* **40**

SWANS A SWIMMING (IRE) 3 b.c. Mujadil (USA) 119 – Danestar 64 (Danehill (USA) 126) [2009 p6g² p6g⁴ 7f³ 7g⁵ a7g* a8g⁴ 7g⁵ 7d Oct 29] modest performer: left J. Osborne after third start: won at Mons in August: should stay 1m: acts on all-weather and firm ground: has had tongue tied. *Mme L. Braem, Belgium* **58**

SWANSEA JACK 2 ch.g. (Feb 2) Singspiel (IRE) 133 – Welsh Diva 112 (Selkirk (USA) 129) [2009 6d 6g Oct 20] good-topped gelding: third foal: half-brother to 4-y-o Welsh Opera: dam, 1m winner, sister to smart 7f/1m performer Trans Island: down the field in maidens at Windsor (very backward) and Yarmouth (not knocked about) 9 days apart (gelded after): should do better. *S. C. Williams* **– p**

SWAN WINGS 2 b.f. (Mar 24) Bahamian Bounty 116 – Star Tulip 99 (Night Shift (USA)) [2009 5m² 5f* 6g 6m 5.2m⁴ 5m Sep 11] sturdy filly: sister to 3-y-o Spring Green and 2007 2-y-o 7f winner Kamal, closely related to smart sprinter Texas Gold (by Cadeaux Genereux) and half-sister to several winners: dam 6f winner, including at 2 yrs: fairly useful performer: won maiden at Salisbury (made all to beat Roodle 2 lengths) in June: highly tried after, good fourth to Sand Vixen in listed race at Newbury: seemed amiss final start: likely to be best at 5f/6f. *A. M. Balding* **89**

SWEET APPLAUSE (IRE) 3 b.f. Acclamation 118 – Nice Spice (IRE) (Common Grounds 118) [2009 84: p5g⁵ p5g³ 5s 6g⁵ 5.1f² 5g p5.1g⁴ p6g⁴ Nov 16] leggy filly: fair maiden at 3 yrs: best at 5f: acts on polytrack and firm ground. *A. P. Jarvis* **78**

SWEET AVON 2 gr.f. (Apr 2) Avonbridge 123 – Sweet Whisper 63 (Petong 126) [2009 p6m Nov 29] half-sister to several winners, including useful 5f (including at 2 yrs)/6f winner Blue Velvet (by Formidable): dam 2-y-o 5f/6f winner: 50/1 and green, 6¼ lengths eighth to Key Light in maiden at Kempton. *Matthew Salaman* **54**

SWEET BABY JANE (IRE) 2 b.f. (Feb 22) Royal Applause 124 – Nebulae (IRE) 82 (Unfuwain (USA) 131) [2009 5.5m⁶ 5m 6g 8g Oct 20] €17,000F: third foal: dam, Irish 1¼m winner, sister to Irish Oaks winner Bolas: well held in maidens/nursery: sold 800 gns. *R. A. Fahey* **–**

SWEET CAROLINE (IRE) 2 b.f. (Feb 15) Motivator 131 – Figlette (Darshaan 133) [2009 p7.1g Nov 14] third foal: closely related to 3-y-o Eightdaysaweek and half-sister to fairly useful 8.6f (at 2 yrs)/11f winner Moment's Notice (by Beat Hollow): dam unraced half-sister to smart 1m/1¼m performers Marbush and Sublimity, latter also Champion Hurdle winner: 20/1, well held in maiden at Wolverhampton: bred to be well suited by 1¼m+. *B. W. Hills* **–**

SWEET CHILD O'MINE 2 b.f. (Feb 15) Singspiel (IRE) 133 – Vendors Mistake (IRE) 61 (Danehill (USA) 126) [2009 f8f* p8.6g³ Dec 26] 11,000F, £2,200 2-y-o: first foal: dam, maiden (effective at 6f/7f), out of Fillies' Mile winner Sunspangled: 100/1 and green, won maiden at Southwell by 1¼ lengths from Master Leon: similar form when third in minor event at Wolverhampton 2 weeks later: will probably stay beyond 8.6f. *R. C. Guest* **69**

SWEET CLEMENTINE (IRE) 2 b.f. (Mar 24) Shamardal (USA) 129 – Heavenly Whisper (IRE) 105 (Halling (USA) 133) [2009 7d p7g Oct 29] good-topped filly: fifth foal: half-sister to 3 winners, including 2008 2-y-o 1m/8.6f winner Premier Banker (by Cape Cross) and Irish/UAE miler River Tiber (by Danehill), both useful: dam 1m winner (including at 2 yrs): backward, modest form when down the field in maidens: will stay 1m: probably capable of better. *W. J. Knight* **53 p**

SWEET GALE (IRE) 5 b.m. Soviet Star (USA) 128 – Lady Moranbon (USA) (Trempolino (USA) 135) [2009 76: f7g³ p7g f7g p7.1g² p7g* 6m* p7g² 6m⁴ 7m⁵ 6f³ 6g⁶ 6g² p7f⁵ 6m⁴ p7m⁵ p7m Oct 12] fairly useful handicapper: won at Kempton and Leicester in June: effective at 6f to easy 1m: acts on all-weather and firm going: tried tongue tied: held up: reliable. *Mike Murphy* **81**

Range Rover Best of British Goodwood Stakes (Handicap), Goodwood—useful staying hurdler Sweetheart proves well suited by this thorough test of stamina; Tyrrells Wood (rail) and Swingkeel are the next two home

SWEETHEART 5 b.m. Sinndar (IRE) 134 – Love And Adventure (USA) (Halling (USA) 133) [2009 –: 16g* 16.4m* 16.4m^4 16g^2 21g* 16m^4 18m Oct 17] lengthy mare: fairly useful handicapper (also useful hurdler): improvement in 2009, winning at Goodwood in May, Folkestone in June and Goodwood in July: stays 21f: acts on polytrack, good to firm and good to soft ground. *Jamie Poulton* **84**

SWEET HEARTH (USA) 3 ch.f. Touch Gold (USA) 127 – Sweet Gold (USA) (Gilded Time (USA)) [2009 100: 7g* 8g^3 8d 8g* 7g^2 8g Dec 13] fifth foal: half-sister to several winners abroad, notably US Grade 1 8.5f winner Santa Teresita (by Lemon Drop Kid): dam US maiden: smart performer: trained by R. Betti in Italy in 2008, winning maiden and listed race at Rome: would also have gone close in Premio Primi Passi at Milan but for swerving out through rail and unseating rider in final 1f: successful at Chantilly in 2009 in minor event in July and listed race in September (beat Rosey de Megeve a short neck): excellent short-head second to Varenar in Prix de la Foret at Longchamp next time, up with strong pace throughout: never on terms in Hong Kong Mile at Sha Tin final start: effective at 7f/1m: won on good to soft ground on debut, best efforts since on good/good to firm. *A. de Royer Dupre, France* **119**

SWEET HOLLOW 3 b.f. Beat Hollow 126 – Three Piece (Jaazeiro (USA) 127) [2009 76p: 12m^2 12.1m^2 12g 11.9g p11g* p11g^5 12m* 12m^6 11.7g^3 Oct 21] useful-looking filly: fairly useful handicapper: won at Kempton in August and Newbury in September: will be suited by 1¾m+: acts on polytrack and good to firm going: blinkered last 5 starts: sold 62,000 gns. *C. G. Cox* **86**

SWEET KISS (USA) 4 gr.f. Yes It's True (USA) 116 – Always Freezing (USA) (Robyn Dancer (USA)) [2009 69: p7g 8m 6m p6m^3 6g f6m^4 p6g p6m p6f Dec 16] rather leggy filly: handicapper, just modest and patchy form in 2009: may prove best at 5f/6f: raced on polytrack and good going or firmer: tried in headgear. *M. J. Attwater* **53**

SWEET LIGHTNING 4 b.g. Fantastic Light (USA) 134 – Sweetness Herself 106 (Unfuwain (USA) 131) [2009 94: p11g^2 10.1g^6 10.4m^6 9.9g^2 10.4m 10m^3 Sep 19] tall gelding: useful handicapper: placed in several competitive events in 2009, best effort when 1¾ lengths third to Almiqdaad in John Smith's Stakes at Newbury: stays 1½m: acts on polytrack, good to firm and good to soft ground: held up: sold 110,000 gns. *W. R. Muir* **100**

SWEET LILLY 5 b.m. Tobougg (IRE) 125 – Maristax 74 (Reprimand 122) [2009 107§: 10.4g^3 9.9g^6 10.3g^5 10.1m Sep 16] big, rangy mare: useful performer: respectable efforts at best in 2009, including when 6 lengths third to High Heeled in listed race at York: stays 10.4f: acts on polytrack, firm and soft going: free-going sort: difficult ride, and one to treat with plenty of caution. *M. R. Channon* **101 §**

SWEET MIRASOL (IRE) 2 b.f. (Apr 15) Celtic Swing 138 – Sallwa (IRE) (Entrepreneur 123) [2009 6v^6 6m^3 6d^5 f6g^6 6m 5g 8g Oct 19] €27,000F, €28,000Y: rather leggy filly: fourth foal: half-sister to 3 winners, including fairly useful 2007 2-y-o 6f winner Italian Art (by Captain Rio) and 6f (at 2 yrs) to 1m winner Smash N'Grab (by Jade Robbery): dam French 9.5f/11.5f winner: form only when third in maiden at Hamilton: tried in cheekpieces: sold £800, joined Miss M. Rowland. *K. A. Ryan* **63 d**

SWEET PILGRIM 2 b.f. (Mar 15) Talkin Man (CAN) 120 – Faraway Moon 61 (Distant Relative 128) [2009 6.5g p5g Nov 13] sixth foal: half-sister to 3 winners, includ- **47**

ing 3-y-o Peper Harow and 5-y-o Kelamon: dam maiden (stayed 1m): poor form in maidens at Newbury and Lingfield. *M. D. I. Usher*

SWEET POSSESSION (USA) 3 b.f. Belong To Me (USA) – Bingo Meeting (USA) (General Meeting (USA)) [2009 71: p7g⁴ 8.1m 6g³ 7g³ 6m⁶ 7m⁴ Aug 13] tall filly: fair maiden: stays 7f: acts on polytrack and good to firm going. *A. P. Jarvis* **65**

SWEET REQUEST 5 ch.m. Best of The Bests (IRE) 122 – Sweet Revival 41 (Claude Monet (USA) 121) [2009 –: p12g⁶ p12.2g 12.1m Jul 10] tall mare: modest maiden handicapper: should stay 1¾m: acts on polytrack, firm and soft ground: tried in cheekpieces/blinkers: often held up. *Dr J. R. J. Naylor* **54**

SWEET SECRET 2 ch.f. (Mar 16) Singspiel (IRE) 133 – Ballymore Celebre (IRE) (Peintre Celebre (USA) 137) [2009 6.5g 8v⁵ Oct 24] rather leggy filly: third foal: dam, French 11f/13.5f winner, half-sister to smart 1¼m performer Nysaean: much better effort in maidens at Newbury when fifth to Multames, still green and finishing well: will be suited by 1¼m/1½m: open to further improvement. *R. Hannon* **70 p**

SWEET SIXTEEN (IRE) 4 b.f. Sadler's Wells (USA) 132 – User Friendly 128 (Slip Anchor 136) [2009 91?: p10g⁵ Mar 19] maiden: just fair form only start at 4 yrs: best effort at 1½m on good to soft ground: sent to Saudi Arabia. *J. R. Jenkins* **65**

SWEET SONNET (USA) 2 ch.f. (Mar 23) Seeking The Gold (USA) – Minister's Melody (USA) 115 (Deputy Minister (CAN)) [2009 6m* 6f 6s² Sep 3] leggy filly: fifth live foal: sister to smart US Grade 1 9f winner Bob And John and half-sister to winner in USA by Storm Cat: dam US 7f (at 2 yrs) to 9f (Grade 3) winner: progressive form: won maiden at York in May by neck from Falling Angel: off 2½ months, ¾-length second to Shamandar in listed race at Salisbury: will stay 7f: already useful. *Saeed bin Suroor* **95**

SWEET VIRGINIA (USA) 3 b. or br.f. Arch (USA) 127 – Hey Hey Sunny (USA) (Known Fact (USA) 135) [2009 38: p8.6g p8g³ p10g⁶ p8.6g⁵ Apr 3] leggy filly: poor maiden: stays 1¼m: acts on polytrack: tried blinkered. *K. R. Burke* **45**

SWEET WORLD 5 b.g. Agnes World (USA) 123 – Douce Maison (IRE) 67 (Fools Holme (USA)) [2009 67: p10g Feb 11] lengthy gelding: fair performer: well held only start in 2009: stays 11f: acts on all-weather, firm and soft going: tried visored/in cheekpieces: fair hurdler, successful in August. *B. J. Llewellyn* **–**

SWIFT CHAP 3 b.g. Diktat 126 – Regent's Folly (IRE) 101 (Touching Wood (USA) 127) [2009 88: p8g 8d 8.1g⁵ 10g³ 10m 10m 8m* 8g* 8.3m² 7g Oct 31] sturdy gelding: fairly useful handicapper: won at Goodwood and Newbury, both in October: stays 1¼m: acts on good to firm going: usually races prominently. *B. R. Millman* **93**

SWIFT GIFT 4 b.g. Cadeaux Genereux 131 – Got To Go 99 (Shareef Dancer (USA) 135) [2009 94: 7m* 7f 7m* 7m Sep 26] compact gelding: useful handicapper: gelded, much improved when winning at Ascot (27-runner totesport Victoria Cup, beat Nezami 1¾ lengths) in May and Newbury (by ¾ length from Golden Desert) in August: will stay 1m: acts on polytrack and good to firm ground: held up. *B. J. Meehan* **108**

SWIFT RETURN 2 b.g. (Feb 13) Fantastic Light (USA) 134 – Swift Dispersal 87 (Shareef Dancer (USA) 135) [2009 6m⁵ 7d² p8m³ 7d Oct 27] smallish gelding: third foal: half-brother to 2006 2-y-o 7f winner Swift Image (by Act One): dam 6f/7f winner: fair maiden: placed at Lingfield and Kempton: stays 1m: found little last 2 starts (gelded after). *S. C. Williams* **73**

totesport Victoria Cup (Heritage Handicap), Ascot—Swift Gift wins readily from Nezami; Dhaular Dhar (left) takes third, ahead of Signor Peltro and Trafalgar Bay

Weatherbys Insurance £300,000 2-Y-O Stakes, Doncaster—Swilly Ferry sweeps through to win this valuable sales event from Taajub; stable-companions Lucky General and Fremont also make the frame

SWILLY FERRY (USA) 2 b.c. (Feb 23) Wiseman's Ferry (USA) 102 – Keepers Hill (IRE) 99 (Danehill (USA) 126) [2009 5m^3 5.1m^3 p6g* 6m 6g^3 6m^3 6m^4 6.5m* 7m 6g Oct 10] $14,000Y, resold £58,000Y: stocky colt: second foal: dam, Irish/US 5f/5.5f winner, half-sister to 4-y-o Forgotten Voice: useful performer: won maiden at Lingfield in June and Weatherbys Insurance £300,000 2-Y-O Stakes at Doncaster (beat Taajub by length) in September: well below form last 2 outings: stays 6.5f: acts on polytrack, raced only on good/good to firm ground on turf. *B. W. Hills* **96**

SWINBROOK (USA) 8 ch.g. Stravinsky (USA) 133 – Dance Diane (USA) (Affirmed (USA)) [2009 82: f6s f6g* f6g* 6m f6g^2 5f^3 p6g* 6g^3 6g* 6d^6 f6g* 5.7g* 5.7m^3 5m 5.1m^5 p6g^2 p5.1g f6m p6g f6g Dec 8] workmanlike gelding: fairly useful performer: won seller and handicap at Southwell in March, seller at Lingfield in May, handicap at Pontefract in June and claimers at Southwell (left R. Fahey £6,000) in July and Bath in August: below form after next start: best at 6f/7f: acts on all-weather, firm and soft ground: often wears headgear: tried tongue tied. *R. A. Harris* **81**

SWINDLER (IRE) 3 b.g. Sinndar (IRE) 134 – Imitation (Darshaan 133) [2009 80p: 12g Jul 28] tall, quite attractive gelding: reportedly split a pastern after sole 2-y-o start: having only second outing (fit and ready, but decidedly nervy in preliminaries), fairly useful form when 13 lengths last of 9 to Harbinger in Gordon Stakes at Goodwood only outing in 2009 (gelded after): should be suited by 1½m: nervy sort. *A. M. Balding* **90**

SWING IT RUBY (IRE) 3 br.f. Celtic Swing 138 – Golconda (IRE) 92 (Lahib (USA) 129) [2009 49: 12.1m f12g 10m Jun 29] modest maiden, sporadic form: stays 1½m. *Mrs D. J. Sanderson* **50**

SWINGKEEL (IRE) 4 ch.g. Singspiel (IRE) 133 – Anniversary 101 (Salse (USA) 128) [2009 88: 16s^2 16m^2 p16g* 21g^3 16.4m* 16m^3 18m Oct 17] good-bodied gelding: useful performer: progressive in 2009, winning handicaps at Kempton in July and York (by 2 lengths from Saga de Tercey) in August: respectable third to Electrolyser in listed race at Ascot: well held in Cesarewitch (Handicap) at Newmarket final start: suited by 2m+: acts on polytrack, soft and good to firm ground: held up. *J. L. Dunlop* **106**

SWIRL TANGO 3 b.f. Lujain (USA) 119 – Tangolania (FR) (Ashkalani (IRE) 128) [2009 p8m 10.2d Oct 15] close-coupled filly: second foal: dam French maiden (best at 1¼m): tailed off in maidens. *F. Jordan* **–**

SWISH DISH (CAN) 2 b. or br.f. (Mar 2) El Corredor (USA) 123 – Amelia Saratoga (JPN) (Dehere (USA) 121) [2009 6.5g 7g Oct 31] €140,000Y: lengthy, angular filly: first foal: dam, US 6.5f winner, half-sister to dam of 2000 Guineas winner Cockney Rebel: better effort in maidens when 9 lengths ninth to Field Day at Newmarket. *R. Hannon* **57**

SWISS ACT 5 ch.g. Act One 124 – Dancing Mirage (IRE) 83 (Machiavellian (USA) 123) [2009 p8g^5 p8g a4s^6 a10s p12.2m^2 f12g* p11g^6 11.5g^6 Apr 26] lengthy, good-topped gelding: fairly useful performer: missed 2008: won handicap at Southwell in March: will be suited by 1¾m: acts on all-weather, good to firm and good to soft going. *M. Johnston* **93**

SWISS ART (IRE) 3 b.g. One Cool Cat (USA) 123 – Alpine Park (IRE) 87 (Barathea (IRE) 127) [2009 63: f6d^3 p7g^5 f7d^3 f8g* f8g* p7.1g^6 10m 7f^5 f7g* p6g^5 f8g* f6g^2 f8m* 8g f7g^4 8s^3 f8g^4 f8f f8m f8g* p8.6g f8f^5 p8.6g^5 Dec 28] good-topped gelding: fair performer, better on all-weather than turf: won sellers in March (2) and June (left R. Harris 4,000 gns), claimer and handicap in July and seller in November, all at Southwell: left Mrs R. Carr after next start: stays 1m: best on fibresand, also has form on polytrack and soft going: sometimes in blinkers/cheekpieces/tongue tie: tough. *R. Hollinshead* **66 a78**

SWISS CROSS 2 b.c. (Jan 30) Cape Cross (IRE) 129 – Swiss Lake (USA) 115 (Indian Ridge 123) [2009 6.1g^5 5m^3 7m* 7g^6 Oct 24] 100,000Y: useful-looking colt: has scope: third foal: half-brother to 3-y-o Swiss Diva and 4-y-o Swiss Franc: dam 5f winner, including at 2 yrs: progressive in maidens, fairly useful form when winning at Newmarket in October by ½ length from Esaar: laboured in nursery at Doncaster next time: stays 7f: acts on good to firm going. *G. A. Butler* **91**

SWISS DIVA 3 br.f. Pivotal 124 – Swiss Lake (USA) 115 (Indian Ridge 123) [2009 90: 6m^3 p6g* 6m^3 6g* 6m^4 6m^2 Aug 29] rangy filly: useful performer: won handicaps at Lingfield in May and York (Reg Griffin Memorial Trophy, beat Parisian Pyramid 1¼ lengths) in June: very good neck second to Palace Moon in listed race at Newmarket final start: raced only at 6f: acts on polytrack, soft and good to firm going: travels strongly. *D. R. C. Elsworth* **108**

SWISS FRANC 4 br.g. Mr Greeley (USA) 122 – Swiss Lake (USA) 115 (Indian Ridge 123) [2009 106: p5g^2 p6g^4 Feb 21] leggy, useful-looking gelding: useful performer: creditable efforts in frame both starts in 2009, in cheekpieces when 2¾ lengths fourth behind Matsunosuke in listed race at Lingfield latter occasion: suffered minor injury after, then gelded: free-going sort, best at 5f/6f: acts on polytrack, good to firm and good to soft going: quirky. *D. R. C. Elsworth* **104**

SWISS LAKE SWEETIE (USA) 3 ch.f. Action This Day (USA) 121 – Almost Blue (USA) (Mr Greeley (USA) 122) [2009 58: p6g Jan 2] maiden: has seemingly gone wrong way: sold 800 gns. *George Baker* **–**

SWOP (IRE) 6 b.g. Shinko Forest (IRE) – Changing Partners 58 (Rainbow Quest (USA) 134) [2009 106: 8g 8g^4 7.5g* 8m 7g^6 8m 9m Oct 3] strong, attractive gelding: smart handicapper: best effort in 2009 when winning at Nad Al Sheba in February by ½ length from dead-heaters Ragheed and Yamal: seventh in Cambridgeshire at Newmarket final outing: best up to 9f: raced on polytrack and good/good to firm ground. *L. M. Cumani* **111**

SWORDS 7 b.g. Vettori (IRE) 119 – Pomorie (IRE) 67§ (Be My Guest (USA) 126) [2009 74: f14s^4 p13.9g 12.6d f14g^3 p13.9g^5 f12g p16.5g^5 p12.2g^4 p13.9g f12m* f12g^2 f14m^5 Dec 5] sturdy gelding: fair handicapper: won at Southwell in November: effective at 1½m to 16.5f: raced mainly on all-weather nowadays: usually held up. *R. E. Peacock* **– a68**

SWORDSMAN (GER) 7 b.g. Acatenango (GER) 127 – Saiga (Windwurf (GER)) [2009 16.4m^5 16.4m^2 16m* 16d^3 21g 16.1g 16d Oct 11] good-topped gelding: fair handicapper: won at Lingfield in July: stays 2m: acts on firm and good to soft going: tried blinkered/tongue tied. *C. Gordon* **79**

Reg Griffin Memorial Trophy (Heritage Handicap), York—
Swiss Diva leads them home in this valuable 3-y-o handicap with Parisian Pyramid (left), Favourite Girl (partially obscured by winner) and Rowayton (noseband) the next three to finish; for the first time in nearly four decades, Timeform's name was not associated with York's annual charity day which was rebranded as the Macmillan Charity Day and raised £242,012

SYBIL'S SURPRISE 4 b.f. Puissance 110 – Fervent Fan (IRE) 65 (Soviet Lad (USA)) [2009 8.3m 9.8d Sep 1] tall filly: fifth foal: half-sister to 1¼m winner Pigeon Flight (by Compton Admiral): dam 2-y-o 6f winner: showed little in bumper and sellers. *J. Mackie* **–**

SYDNEY BRIDGE 2 b.g. (Mar 9) Danbird (AUS) – Miss Prim (Case Law 113) [2009 5m^6 6g^5 6g 7g 6g Oct 23] neat gelding: modest maiden: best effort on third start: tried in cheekpieces. *I. Semple* **60**

SYDNEY COVE (IRE) 3 b.g. Cape Cross (IRE) 129 – First Fleet (USA) 106 (Woodman (USA) 126) [2009 –: 9.2g 8s 11.1m^3 12.1m^6 11.1d^6 9.3d 10.1m 10s Aug 26] good-bodied gelding: little form on Flat. *R. Allan* **–**

SYDNEYSIDER 4 b.g. Averti (IRE) 117 – Cajole (IRE) 72 (Barathea (IRE) 127) [2009 70: 6g p8m^5 p7m^5 p7g Dec 2] tall, angular gelding: fair maiden: stays 7f, should prove effective at 5f: acts on polytrack and good to firm ground. *Eve Johnson Houghton* **67**

SYNONYMY 6 b.g. Sinndar (IRE) 134 – Peony 108 (Lion Cavern (USA) 117) [2009 66d: 16.4m Jun 8] good-bodied gelding: handicapper: well held sole outing on Flat in 2009: stays 17f: acts on polytrack, good to firm and good to soft going: blinkered: unreliable. *M. Blanshard* **– §**

SYRIAN 2 b.g. (Jan 20) Hawk Wing (USA) 136 – Lady Lahar 106 (Fraam 114) [2009 7d* 8.1v^5 8g^3 Sep 17] 30,000Y: rangy gelding: has plenty of scope: fifth foal: half-brother to 3-y-o Popmurphy, 4-y-o Classic Legend and 5-y-o Kilburn: dam 6f (at 2 yrs) to 1m winner: won maiden at Yarmouth (well-backed favourite, beat Astonishment readily by 1½ lengths) in July: similar form in listed race at Haydock and minor event at Ayr (still green, third to Simenon, gelded after): stays 1m. *M. L. W. Bell* **90**

SYRINX (IRE) 3 b.f. One Cool Cat (USA) 123 – Latest Chapter (IRE) (Ahonoora 122) [2009 69: p7g* Jan 14] good-topped filly: fair performer: improved when winning maiden at Kempton in January: may prove best up to 7f: raced only on polytrack and good going. *J. Noseda* **76**

SYVILLA 4 b.f. Nayef (USA) 129 – Dance Steppe (Rambo Dancer (CAN) 107) [2009 93: 10g^4 11.9g 10.9d 10.1m^2 12g^6 9.9g^4 9.9g 10.3s^5 Nov 7] sparely-made filly: useful performer: best efforts in 2009 when fourth in handicap at Pontefract and runner-up in listed race at Newcastle (beaten 5 lengths by Lady Jane Digby) first/fourth starts: seems to stay 12.5f: acts on heavy and good to firm going. *Rae Guest* **97**

SZABA 4 ch.f. Tipsy Creek (USA) 115 – Compton Alice 58 (Compton Place 125) [2009 51: p6g p8g p6g p8g^6 Feb 19] good-topped filly: poor maiden: bred to prove best at 5f/6f: form only on polytrack: tried blinkered/in cheekpieces. *J. Akehurst* **39**

T

TAAJUB (IRE) 2 b.c. (Mar 11) Exceed And Excel (AUS) 126 – Purple Tiger (IRE) (Rainbow Quest (USA) 134) [2009 6g^2 6g* 6m^2 6.5m^2 5g^2 Oct 10] 80,000Y: good-bodied colt: has scope: second foal: half-brother to 3-y-o Polish Pride: dam unraced out of Park Hill Stakes winner Noble Rose: smart performer: comfortably landed odds in maiden at Newmarket in July: excellent efforts when runner-up in Gimcrack Stakes at York (beaten 2 lengths by Showcasing) and Cornwallis Stakes at Ascot (beaten neck by Our Jonathan) third/final starts: below-form second to Swilly Ferry in sales race at Doncaster in between: effective at 5f/6f: raced only on good/good to firm ground. *W. J. Haggas* **110**

TA ALEEM 3 ch.f. Galileo (IRE) 134 – Tadris (USA) 106 (Red Ransom (USA)) [2009 9.7m^5 Aug 19] second foal: dam, 1m winner, half-sister to smart US performer up to 1½m Mustanfar, out of close relative to Unfuwain and half-sister to Nashwan and Nayef: 4/1, eased as if amiss in maiden at Folkestone: sold 3,000 gns. *M. P. Tregoning* **–**

TAAMEER 3 b.c. Beat Hollow 126 – Vayavaig 78 (Damister (USA) 123) [2009 110p: 10m^5 Apr 24] well-made colt: smart form at 2 yrs: laboured when disappointing fifth in Classic Trial at Sandown only outing in 2009: not sure to stay 1¼m. *M. P. Tregoning* **89**

TAARAB 3 ch.g. Refuse To Bend (IRE) 128 – Tanzania (USA) (Darshaan 133) [2009 87p: 10.1s^2 12d^5 May 16] rather leggy gelding: just fair maiden at 3 yrs: should stay 1¼m: raced only on soft/good to soft going: gelded after final start. *Saeed bin Suroor* **71**

TAARESH (IRE) 4 b.c. Sakhee (USA) 136 – Tanaghum 104 (Darshaan 133) [2009 82: p13g^6 p10f Dec 20] rather leggy colt: fairly useful form at 3 yrs: last both starts in 2009: should stay 1¼m. *K. A. Morgan* **–**

Sakhee Oh So Sharp Stakes, Newmarket—Tabassum has her rivals well strung out; Electric Feel is a clear second

TABARAN (FR) 6 ch.g. Polish Precedent (USA) 131 – Tabariya (IRE) (Doyoun 124) [2009 p12g^5 p16g 16g May 29] ex-French maiden: no solid form on Flat: tried blinkered: sold £5,500 and joined Mrs A. Thorpe, modest hurdler. *L. A. Dace* **–**

TABARET 6 ch.g. Bertolini (USA) 125 – Luanshya 78 (First Trump 118) [2009 102: 6m 5d^6 5m^2 6m^3 6g 5.4m 5d^4 f5g 5g^4 p5g p5.1g Nov 16] small, good-bodied gelding: fluent mover: fairly useful handicapper: raced at 5f/6f: acts on polytrack, firm and good to soft going: sometimes wears cheekpieces: tactically versatile. *R. M. Whitaker* **94**

TABASSUM (IRE) 2 b.f. (Apr 8) Nayef (USA) 129 – Tomoohat (USA) 96 (Danzig (USA)) [2009 7g* 7m* 7m^3 Oct 17] smallish, attractive filly: first foal: dam, 2-y-o 6f winner, sister to useful US miler Prussian out of half-sister to Prix de l'Arc de Triomphe runner-up Mubtaker: smart performer: created big impression when winning maiden in August and Sakhee Oh So Sharp Stakes in October (beat Electric Feel readily by 4 lengths), both at Newmarket: creditable length third to Music Show in Rockfel Stakes there, looking in command for long way and well clear of remainder: bred to stay 1m. *Sir Michael Stoute* **111**

TABOOR (IRE) 11 b.g. Mujadil (USA) 119 – Christoph's Girl 50 (Efisio 120) [2009 63: p5g^2 p6g^4 p5.1g^3 p5g^6 5.2s^3 5.2s 5.2d Oct 27] heavy-topped gelding: modest handicapper: best at 5f/easy 6f: acts on all-weather, firm and soft ground: tried blinkered/tongue tied/in cheekpieces: held up. *R. M. H. Cowell* **53**

TABORCILLO 2 b.g. (May 7) Lucky Story (USA) 128 – Trust In Paula (USA) 54 (Arazi (USA) 135) [2009 5s^2 5.4d 5m Sep 16] compact gelding: easily best effort in maidens when 4 lengths second to Ignatieff at Thirsk: finished weakly both subsequent starts: bred to stay beyond 5f. *T. D. Barron* **68**

TABULATE 6 b.m. Dansili 127 – Let Alone 78 (Warning 136) [2009 67: p10m^6 p10g^5 p10g^4 p11g^5 p8.6m^4 11.6m^4 8g Aug 5] close-coupled mare: modest handicapper: best up to 1¼m: acts on all-weather, lightly raced on turf: travels strongly: held up. *P. Howling* **46 a54**

TACTFUL (IRE) 4 b.f. Intikhab (USA) 135 – Crozon 68 (Peintre Celebre (USA) 137) [2009 96: p8g^4 10.3g^4 9s f8g Oct 18] rangy filly: fairly useful performer: stays 1¼m: acts on polytrack, possibly not on soft ground: sold 18,000 gns, sent to Saudi Arabia. *R. M. Beckett* **91**

TACTIC 3 b.c. Sadler's Wells (USA) 132 – Tanaghum 104 (Darshaan 133) [2009 83p: 11s^2 12m* 11.9v^4 16f^4 13m^2 12g^4 14.1s^5 11.8m^4 Oct 26] neat colt: useful performer: won maiden at Goodwood in May: held form well after, including when 2½ lengths second to Kite Wood in Bahrain Trophy at Newmarket and when 4 lengths fourth to Harbinger in Gordon Stakes at Goodwood fifth/sixth starts: stays 1¾m: acts on any going. *J. L. Dunlop* **107**

TACTICIAN 2 b.c. (Feb 26) Motivator 131 – Tempting Prospect 95 (Shirley Heights 130) [2009 8m^2 8g^4 Oct 8] useful-looking colt: fifth foal: half-brother to smart 1¼m winner Promotion (by Sadler's Wells), fairly useful 1m (at 2 yrs)/1¼m winner Border Castle (by Grand Lodge) and 5-y-o Garden Party: dam, 2-y-o 1m winner (stayed 1½m), half-sister to smart performer up to 13.3f Phantom Gold: much better effort in maidens when 1¼ lengths second to Coordinated Cut at Doncaster: will be well suited by 1¼m+. *M. L. W. Bell* **86**

TADALAVIL 4 gr.g. Clodovil (IRE) 116 – Blandish (USA) (Wild Again (USA)) [2009 84: 5m 5m 5m 6g 5d^3 Jul 25] small, strong, close-coupled gelding: just fair form at best in 2009: effective at stiff 5f/6f: acts on soft and good to firm going. *Miss L. A. Perratt* **68**

TADHKEER 2 ch.g. (Apr 25) Refuse To Bend (IRE) 128 – Shuruk 73 (Cadeaux Genereux 131) [2009 6m^5 7g Oct 17] well-made gelding: behind in maidens at Warwick (odds on, poor form) and Catterick: sold 5,000 gns. *W. J. Haggas* **42**

TADLIL 7 b.g. Pivotal 124 – Pretty Poppy 67 (Song 132) [2009 61: f6s p6g^2 p6g^3 p6g^5 p7.1g^5 5.7f^3 6.1m 5.1m 6s 6.1d^4 p6m p6m f6g^2 f6d^3 Dec 29] well-made gelding: modest handicapper: best at 5f/6f: acts on all-weather and good to firm going: often visored, tried blinkered: inconsistent and signs of temperament. *J. M. Bradley* **58**

TAE KWON DO (USA) 3 b.g. Thunder Gulch (USA) 129 – Judy's Magic (USA) (Wavering Monarch (USA)) [2009 63: f8g^5 p9.5m^3 p9.5g^3 f11g^3 12.1m^2 14.1m^4 12.1m 14.1m 12d^6 14.1m Sep 14] modest maiden handicapper: stays 1¾m: acts on all-weather and good to firm ground: tried in cheekpieces. *Julie Camacho* **60**

TAEPING (IRE) 2 b.c. (May 17) Invincible Spirit (IRE) 121 – Simil (USA) 91 (Apalachee (USA) 137) [2009 6m 6m^4 6m f6g^3 p7.1m^6 p6g f5f f5g^6 Dec 18] rather leggy colt: modest maiden: should be at least as effective at 5f as 6f: acts on all-weather and good to firm going: tried in cheekpieces. *R. Hollinshead* **54**

TAFAOOL (IRE) 3 b.f. Green Desert (USA) 127 – Sundus (USA) 80 (Sadler's Wells (USA) 132) [2009 66p: 8m^3 8.3g^3 Oct 28] compact filly: easily best effort in maidens when third to Stoic at Newmarket on reappearance, shaping as if needing run: hung badly left next time: stays 1m: sold 82,000 gns. *M. P. Tregoning* **78 +**

TAFAWUT 2 b.f. (Apr 30) Nayef (USA) 129 – Rohita (IRE) 94 (Waajib 121) [2009 7g Aug 28] 85,000Y: quite attractive filly: half-sister to several winners, including 5f (at 2 yrs) to 7f winner Kalindi (by Efisio) and French 5.5f/6.5f winner Tayseer (by Medicean), both useful: dam 2-y-o 5f/6f winner: 4/1 and backward, prominent long way when down the field in maiden at Newmarket: sold €18,000, joined C. Cox: should improve. *B. W. Hills* **– p**

TAGALURA (IRE) 3 b.g. Tagula (IRE) 116 – Allurah (IRE) (Goldmark (USA) 113) [2009 –: f11g Feb 20] strong gelding: no form in maidens 9 months apart. *P. T. Midgley* **–**

TAGSEED (IRE) 3 b.c. Elusive City (USA) 117 – Allegorica (IRE) (Alzao (USA) 117) [2009 6.1f^3 May 8] €120,000F, 100,000Y: strong, useful-looking colt: fourth foal: half-brother to 5-y-o Miss Gorica and fairly useful 5f (at 2 yrs) to 1m winner Celtic Spa (by Celtic Swing): dam Italian 5f (at 2 yrs) to 7.5f winner: 4/1, promising 1¾ lengths third to Devil You Know in maiden at Nottingham, travelling strongly and not unduly knocked about: sure to improve. *W. J. Haggas* **81 p**

TAG TEAM (IRE) 8 ch.g. Tagula (IRE) 116 – Okay Baby (IRE) 67 (Treasure Kay 114) [2009 46+, a73: f6d f5g^5 f6g^6 f6g p6g^3 f6g f6g^4 6m p5.1g p6g^2 f6g^6 f6g^4 f6d^2 Dec 29] tall gelding: modest handicapper: probably best at 6f nowadays: acts on all-weather, firm and good to soft going: often wears headgear: inconsistent. *John A. Harris* **55**

TAGULA BREEZE (IRE) 3 b.g. Tagula (IRE) 116 – Pearl Egg (IRE) 55 (Mukaddamah (USA) 125) [2009 80: 6m^5 6m^4 6m^3 5m^4 6m 6g^6 5g 5g 5d* 5m Aug 29] strong gelding: fairly useful handicapper: won at Thirsk in August: stays 6f: acts on good to firm and good to soft going: sometimes tongue tied at 2 yrs: tried in cheekpieces/blinkers. *I. W. McInnes* **83**

TAGULA MINX (IRE) 3 b.f. Tagula (IRE) 116 – Persian Fantasia (Alzao (USA) 117) [2009 –: p9.5g p7g p9.5g Dec 19] little form. *J. Pearce* **–**

TAGULA NIGHT (IRE) 3 ch.g. Tagula (IRE) 116 – Carpet Lady (IRE) 70 (Night Shift (USA)) [2009 75: 6f* p6g* 6m p6g^5 Oct 9] fairly useful handicapper: won at Windsor and Lingfield in August: raced only at 6f, should be as effective at 5f: acts on polytrack and firm going: tongue tied/visored. *W. R. Swinburn* **90**

TAGULA PEARL (IRE) 2 b.f. (Mar 17) Tagula (IRE) 116 – Pearl Egg (IRE) 55 (Mukaddamah (USA) 125) [2009 5m 5m^4 6g 5m 6m p7.1g p6g Dec 11] £11,000Y: unfurnished filly: third foal: sister to 3-y-o Tagula Breeze and half-sister to 5-y-o Not Now Lewis: dam Irish sprint maiden: poor maiden: tried blinkered/in cheekpieces. *I. W. McInnes* **46**

TAGULA SANDS (IRE) 5 b.g. Tagula (IRE) 116 – Pomme Pomme (USA) (Dayjur (USA) 137) [2009 –: p8g p6g p6g Jan 22] little form: in cheekpieces last 2 starts. *J. C. Fox* **–**

TAGUNA (IRE) 3 ch.f. Tagula (IRE) 116 – Tahlil 46 (Cadeaux Genereux 131) [2009 6m 7v Sep 4] well held in seller/claimer. *M. Brittain* **–**

TAHAYAB (ITY) 3 b.f. Nayef (USA) 129 – Zaffrani (IRE) 98 (Danehill (USA) 126) [2009 7.5g^6 7.2g a8g^5 a8g^6 a8g^2 a8g^2 a8.8g^6 a8g^3 a8g^4 a8g* a8g Dec 13] modest performer: sold from M. Johnston 800 gns after second start: won minor event at Ovrevoll in November: stays 1m: acts on dirt. *Cathrine Witso Slettemark, Norway* **59**

TAHFEEZ (IRE) 3 b.f. Alhaarth (IRE) 126 – Ghazal (USA) 103 (Gone West (USA)) [2009 61: 8.1m 8.3g^5 Jul 16] modest maiden: left Sir Michael Stoute 5,500 gns in February before reappearance: may prove best short of 1m: tried in cheekpieces. *I. Semple* **53**

TAHKEEM 3 b.f. Green Desert (USA) 127 – Katayeb (IRE) (Machiavellian (USA) 123) [2009 –: 9.9m* 11m Oct 1] fair form: won maiden at Goodwood in September: in cheekpieces in 2009: sold 15,000 gns. *M. P. Tregoning* **75**

TAHSEEN 2 b.c. (Mar 25) Haafhd 129 – Merayaat (IRE) 80 (Darshaan 133) [2009 8m^5 7d^4 Oct 22] lengthy colt: first foal: dam 1¾m winner: still very green, better effort when 3¾ lengths fourth to Essexbridge in maiden at Brighton: should be suited by 1m+: capable of better still. *M. P. Tregoning* **65 p**

TAI HANG (IRE) 2 br.f. (Mar 31) Celtic Swing 138 – Victoria Peek (IRE) 66 (Cape Cross (IRE) 129) [2009 6g 6m Sep 19] first foal: dam 6f winner: tailed off in maidens at Ascot and Catterick. *A. P. Jarvis* **–**

TAIKOO 4 b.g. Dr Fong (USA) 128 – So True 116 (So Blessed 130) [2009 90: p14g^4 f11g^2 12d^2 12g Jun 13] big, strong gelding: fairly useful handicapper: stays 1¾m: acts on all-weather and soft going: tried in cheekpieces: usually races up with pace. *H. Morrison* **90**

TAINE (IRE) 4 b.c. Invincible Spirit (IRE) 121 – Farjah (IRE) (Charnwood Forest (IRE) 125) [2009 5.7g Sep 7] fair form when third in maiden on debut in 2007: well held in similar event only outing since: should stay 6f. *J. R. Gask* **–**

TAJAAWEED (USA) 4 br.c. Dynaformer (USA) – Uforia (USA) (Zilzal (USA) 137) [2009 112: 10.5g 12m Jun 20] big, strong, close-coupled colt: smart performer at 3 yrs: last both starts in 2009, in Prix Ganay at Longchamp (not discredited) and Hardwicke Stakes at Royal Ascot: stays 10.4f: acts on firm and good to soft going: sent to USA. *Sir Michael Stoute* **107**

TAJNEED (IRE) 6 b.g. Alhaarth (IRE) 126 – Indian Express 61 (Indian Ridge 123) [2009 105: f5g^5 6d 6d 6g^5 7d 6d 6m 6m Sep 26] tall, lengthy gelding: useful handicapper: has won at 8.5f, best form at 5f/6f: acts on heavy going, probably on fibresand: sometimes blinkered: tongue tied in 2007: usually tracks leaders. *D. Nicholls* **100**

TAKAAMUL 6 ch.g. Almutawakel 126 – Mafaatin (IRE) (Royal Academy (USA) 130) [2009 63: p8g^4 p7g p6g^2 p7g^5 8.1g^2 p8g 7g* 7g^6 7g* Aug 5] modest handicapper: won at Yarmouth in June and August (apprentices): stays easy 1m: acts on polytrack, best efforts on turf on good going: tried in tongue tie/cheekpieces: held up. *K. A. Morgan* **64**

TAKAATUF (IRE) 3 b.g. Dubai Destination (USA) 127 – Karlaka (IRE) (Barathea (IRE) 127) [2009 88p: 10m^3 10f* 10m^4 12m 10m 9.9g 10.3m 12m Sep 19] big, lengthy, angular gelding: fairly useful handicapper: won at Newmarket in May: largely below form after: stays 1¼m: acts on firm going: often makes running: sold 21,000 gns, then gelded. *M. Johnston* **94**

TAKAFU (USA) 7 b.g. Lemon Drop Kid (USA) 131 – Proper Protocol (USA) (Deputy Minister (CAN)) [2009 16g^4 14m 13.3m Aug 14] tall, leggy, useful-looking gelding: fairly useful handicapper: missed 2008: showed he retains ability when fourth at Goodwood: below form after: barely stays 17f: acts on good to firm and good to soft going. *W. S. Kittow* **83**

TAKE IT EASEE (IRE) 4 b.f. Noverre (USA) 125 – Fairy Lore (IRE) 89 (Fairy King (USA)) [2009 65: 10g^5 p10.7g 9.5v^2 9s 8g 7.5v^5 7g 8d^3 10.2v* Nov 4] fairly useful handicapper: improved when winning at Nottingham in November by 5 lengths from Jennie Jerome: stays 1¼m: acts on heavy and good to firm going. *Mrs Prunella Dobbs, Ireland* **85**

TAKE IT THERE 7 ch.m. Cadeaux Genereux 131 – Feel Free (IRE) 86 (Generous (IRE) 139) [2009 57: p10m Sep 23] lengthy mare: modest handicapper, lightly raced on Flat nowadays: barely stays easy 9.5f: acts on all-weather and firm ground: tried tongue tied: held up. *A. J. Lidderdale* **–**

TAKE IT TO THE MAX 2 b.c. (Mar 29) Bahamian Bounty 116 – Up And About 77 (Barathea (IRE) 127) [2009 5m 5m 6v^3 6m^2 6d* 7m 8.1v^4 10g* Oct 31] 11,000Y: good-topped colt: half-brother to several winners, including useful 1m (at 2 yrs)/9f (in UAE) winner Tamarillo (by Daylami) and 3-y-o Wake Up Call: dam, 15f winner, half-sister to dam of 4-y-o Overdose: fairly useful performer: won nursery at Pontefract in July and minor event at Newmarket (by short head from Anhar) in October: stays 1¼m: unraced on firm going, acts on any other. *G. M. Moore* **93**

TAKE ME THERE 6 b.g. Cape Cross (IRE) 129 – Mill Path (Mill Reef (USA) 141) [2009 76p: f12g^2 f14g^3 Jan 29] fairly useful in bumpers/over hurdles: similar standard on Flat: should stay 1¾m. *John Berry* **80**

TAKE MY HAND 2 ch.f. (Feb 18) Imperial Dancer 123 – Royal Logic (Royal Applause 124) [2009 5f 7m^6 7m p6m^3 6.1s^6 Oct 7] 1,400F: sturdy filly: second foal: dam little form: modest maiden: stays 7f: acts on polytrack and good to firm ground. *M. R. Channon* **55**

Sydney City Lexus T. J. Smith Stakes, Randwick—Takeover Target makes a successful reappearance in his final season, showing himself better than ever at the age of ten

TAKEOVER BID (USA) 3 b.g. Empire Maker (USA) 129 – Seba 95 (Alzao (USA) 117) [2009 72: f6s* p6g^6 f6g* p7g^2 8.5s 8.5d p7g p10.7g^6 Nov 25] sturdy gelding: fairly useful handicapper: won at Southwell in January and March: left M. Johnston after fourth outing: well held after: stays 7f: acts on all-weather: blinkered and/or tongue tied last 4 starts. *Niall M. O'Callaghan, Ireland* **85**

TAKEOVER TARGET (AUS) 10 b.g. Celtic Swing 138 – Shady Stream (AUS) (Archregent (CAN)) [2009 126: 6d* 6s* 6g 6m Jul 10] sturdy, good-bodied gelding: high-class performer: better than ever first 2 starts in 2009, winning Sydney City Lexus T. J. Smith Stakes at Randwick (by 2¾ lengths from Northern Meteor) in April and Distinctive Homes Goodwood Handicap at Morphettville (beat I Am Invincible by a length for his eighth Group 1 success) in May: below form after in KrisFlyer International Sprint at Kranji and July Cup at Newmarket (his eighth outing in Britain): was effective at 5f to 7f: acted on firm and soft going, bit below form on heavy: raced prominently: tough, game and genuine: reportedly fractured a cannon bone in July Cup, and underwent surgery (had 5 screws inserted): retired. *Joe Janiak, Australia* **128**

TAKE TEN 2 b.c. (Apr 9) Bahamian Bounty 116 – See You Later 98 (Emarati (USA) 74) [2009 5g^5 5.1m^2 5d* 6g* 6.5m^5 6m^2 7m^3 Oct 3] 210,000Y: useful-looking colt: has scope: closely related to 4-y-o Thebes and half-brother to 2 winners, notably smart 5f (at 2 yrs)/6f winner Aahayson (by Noverre): dam 5f winner (including at 2 yrs): useful performer: won maiden at Thirsk and nursery at Warwick (by 5 lengths) in August: much improved when placed in sales races at Newmarket last 2 starts, head second to Society Rock and ½-length third to Oasis Dancer: stays 7f: winner on good to soft ground, best efforts on good to firm: races up with pace: game. *M. Johnston* **102**

TAKE THAT 4 b.g. Kasakov – Baby Be (Bold Arrangement 127) [2009 –: 6m 5s 5g 5v Nov 3] no form: tried in cheekpieces. *S. P. Griffiths* **–**

TAKE THE HINT 3 b.f. Montjeu (IRE) 137 – Insinuate (USA) 99 (Mr Prospector (USA)) [2009 91p: 10f* 12m^6 11.9m^6 10.5s^5 10.5s^4 Nov 11] rather leggy filly: useful performer: won listed race at Newmarket in May by 1¼ lengths from Three Moons: below form in Ribblesdale Stakes at Royal Ascot and Lancashire Oaks at Haydock next 2 starts: off nearly 4 months, back to best last 2 starts when fourth past post in Prix de **107**

Flore at Saint-Cloud (demoted to fifth behind Celimene, final start for J. Gosden) and Prix Fille de l'Air at Toulouse (to Synergy): stayed 10.5f: acted on firm and soft ground: was quirky: visits Dansili. *Mme C. Head-Maarek, France*

TAKE THE MICKY 3 b.g. Beat Hollow 126 – Ailincala (IRE) 94 (Pursuit of Love 124) [2009 77p: p8g 8m p8g p8f Dec 16] neat gelding: fair performer: disappointing at 3 yrs, leaving W. Knight after third outing: should stay 1m: raced only on polytrack and good/good to firm going: often slowly away: has bled. *C. F. Wall* **69**

TAKITWO 6 b.g. Delta Dancer – Tiama (IRE) 50 (Last Tycoon 131) [2009 63: p7g* p7g⁶ p7g⁵ p8g² p8g⁵ p8g⁵ p7g⁶ 7m³ p8g p8g p7m p8m Oct 12] sturdy gelding: fair handicapper: won at Kempton in January: effective at 7f/1m: acts on polytrack, firm and soft going: effective blinkered/visored or not: held up. *P. D. Cundell* **66**

TAKIZADA (IRE) 4 b.f. Sendawar (IRE) 129 – Takarouna (USA) 114 (Green Dancer (USA) 132) [2009 p8.6g 10.4v⁴ p12.2m Aug 21] half-sister to several winners, including Irish 1¼m/1½m winner Takali (by Kris) and Irish 1m (at 2 yrs) to 1¼m winner Takarian (later successful in US Grade 2 9f event, by Doyoun), both smart: dam, Irish 1¼m winner, sister to Dante Stakes winner Torjoun: fairly useful maiden at best in France for A. de Royer Dupre (sold €40,000 after final start in 2008): easily best effort in Britain (fair form) when fourth in handicap at Haydock: stays 10.5f: showed promise on soft going on debut: sold 30,000 gns. *J. R. Gask* **71**

TALAMAHANA 4 b.f. Kyllachy 129 – Bahawir Pour (USA) (Green Dancer (USA) 132) [2009 59§: 5.7m⁴ 6g 7m 5.1g⁶ 5.7m 5.1g³ 5.5d 5.7g⁵ 5f³ 5.7g³ 5.1m p6g p7g p7m² Nov 29] close-coupled filly: modest performer: effective at 5f to 7f: acts on polytrack and firm going: usually wears headgear: temperamental. *A. B. Haynes* **54 §**

TALAYEB 4 b. or br.g. Nayef (USA) 129 – Paper Chase (FR) 78 (Machiavellian (USA) 123) [2009 82§: 8m³ 10m Aug 9] big, rangy gelding: fair maiden: best form at 7f/1m: acts on good to firm going: tried in blinkers/cheekpieces: has reportedly had breathing problem: one to be wary of. *M. P. Tregoning* **75 §**

TALENTI (IRE) 6 b.g. Sadler's Wells (USA) 132 – Sumoto 101 (Mtoto 134) [2009 98: p16g Mar 28] strong gelding: useful performer, very lightly raced on Flat: well beaten sole start in 2009: stays 1¾m: acts on good to soft going, probably good to firm. *Miss E. C. Lavelle* **–**

TALIESIN 2 br.g. (Apr 14) Passing Glance 119 – Silver Bird (IRE) (Vision (USA)) [2009 5.1m 8m 10.2m Sep 28] tailed off in maidens. *Mrs A. M. Thorpe* **–**

TALIMOS (IRE) 3 b.g. Lomitas 129 – Silvertone (FR) (Highest Honor (FR) 124) [2009 12m² 11.5g⁴ 11.9g* 16f 14m⁶ Jul 10] €25,000Y: tall gelding: first foal: dam, French 11.5f winner, out of half-sister to dam of high-class 1¼m performer Alexander Goldrun: fairly useful form: won maiden at Brighton in June: should be well suited by 1¾m+: tried blinkered: signs of temperament: joined D. Pipe, won juvenile hurdle in September. *R. M. Beckett* **84**

TALKING HANDS 3 b.g. Mujahid (USA) 125 – With Distinction 59 (Zafonic (USA) 130) [2009 95: p9g 7g 10m Sep 19] sturdy gelding: useful performer at 2 yrs: well held in 2009: sold 16,000 gns, sent to Saudi Arabia. *S. Kirk* **–**

TALK OF SAAFEND (IRE) 4 b.f. Barathea (IRE) 127 – Sopran Marida (IRE) (Darshaan 133) [2009 89: 8m 7.1m 8.1m 9.2s⁶ 8g⁶ 9.2g⁶ 9.3m⁵ 9.2m² 10m 9.2s⁶ 8.3s³ Aug 12] rather leggy filly: fair handicapper nowadays: stays 9f: acts on polytrack, heavy and good to firm going: none too consistent nowadays. *P. Monteith* **77**

TALLAWALLA (IRE) 2 b.f. (May 3) Oratorio (IRE) 128 – Edetana (USA) 70 (Diesis 133) [2009 7g 7m⁶ 8m Sep 8] 62,000Y: leggy filly: second foal: dam, Irish maiden (stayed 1¼m), out of Moyglare Stud Stakes winner Edabiya, herself half-sister to Gold Cup winner Enzeli and Irish Oaks winner Ebadiyla: best effort in maidens when sixth to Creese at Folkestone: likely to stay 1¼m: sold £1,500. *M. R. Channon* **66**

TALLEST PEAK (USA) 4 b. or br.g. Giant's Causeway (USA) 132 – Hum Along (USA) (Fappiano (USA)) [2009 58: p8g p9.5g p7.1g* p8.6g⁶ Dec 18] workmanlike gelding: fair handicapper: won at Wolverhampton in December: may prove best around 1m: raced only on all-weather: blinkered last 2 starts. *M. G. Quinlan* **66**

TALLULAH MAI 2 b.f. (Apr 10) Kayf Tara 130 – Al Awaalah 52 (Mukaddamah (USA) 125) [2009 p8m Dec 4] third foal: half-sister to 3-y-o Rulesn'regulations and 5-y-o Venir Rouge: dam maiden (stayed 9.4f): 50/1 and green, down the field in maiden at Lingfield. *Matthew Salaman* **56**

TALLULAH'S SECRET 3 b.f. Bertolini (USA) 125 – Ascend (IRE) (Glint of Gold 128) [2009 –: 7d^{6} Mar 31] little form. *J. Gallagher* –

TALLULAH SUNRISE 4 b.f. Auction House (USA) 120 – Tallulah Belle 92 (Crowning Honors (CAN)) [2009 68: p6g p7g p10g^{6} p10g p8g p8g 10g 7.6d 8m Aug 16] good-topped filly: regressive maiden: stays 1¼m: acts on polytrack. *M. D. I. Usher* 59 d

TALON (IRE) 4 ch.g. Indian Ridge 123 – Brief Lullaby (IRE) (Brief Truce (USA) 126) [2009 60: 6g May 28] lengthy, sturdy gelding: modest performer: well held sole start in 2009: stays 1m: acts on good to firm and good to soft ground: tried in blinkers/ cheekpieces: has worn tongue tie, including for win: inconsistent. *G. A. Swinbank* –

TALSARNAU (IRE) 3 b.g. Kheleyf (USA) 116 – Ezilana (IRE) (Shardari 134) [2009 –: p8.6g^{5} p9.5g p8.6g Jan 16] leggy gelding: signs of a little ability. *W. M. Brisbourne* –

TALULAH BELLS 3 br.f. Superior Premium 122 – Hullo Mary Doll § (Lidhame 109) [2009 –: f8s^{5} Jan 1] quite good-topped filly: little form: tried blinkered. *A. W. Carroll* –

TAMAATHUL 2 gr.c. (Feb 8) Tiger Hill (IRE) 127 – Tahrir (IRE) 100 (Linamix (FR) 127) [2009 8g^{2} 7g* Oct 23] lengthy colt: first foal: dam, 7f winner, sister to useful French performer up to 1m Mister Charm and half-sister to smart French 1m/9f performer Mister Sacha: most promising in maidens at Newbury (second to Dancing David) and Doncaster (made all to beat Quick Wit by 1½ lengths, pair clear): should be suited by at least 1m: smart prospect. *B. W. Hills* 97 p

TAMAGIN (USA) 6 b.g. Stravinsky (USA) 133 – Luia (USA) (Forty Niner (USA)) [2009 109: p6g^{5} p7g^{2} p6g^{3} 6m 6g* 6g^{5} p6g^{2} 6m 6m* 6d^{2} 6d 6m^{2} 6m^{4} 6m* 6m^{2} 6g Oct 10] tall, close-coupled gelding: smart performer: won handicaps at Newcastle in April and Windsor (beat Genki 1½ lengths, left K. Ryan 70,000 gns after) in June and listed race at Goodwood (by head from Mac Gille Eoin) in September: good 2½ lengths second to Sayif in Diadem Stakes at Ascot penultimate start, isolated towards far side: has won at easy 1m, best at 5f/6f: acts on polytrack, firm and good to soft going: often wears cheekpieces: early to post: free-going front runner. *J. Pearce* 116

TAMANACO (IRE) 2 b.g. (Apr 6) Catcher In The Rye (IRE) 115 – Right After Moyne (IRE) (Imperial Ballet (IRE) 110) [2009 6g^{3} 6m 6v* Jul 17] £8,500Y: lengthy, good-bodied gelding: first foal: dam, unraced, out of half-sister to St Leger runner-up Air Marshall: won maiden at Pontefract in July: better form when third to Shakespearean in similar event at Haydock: will stay at least 1m. *T. D. Walford* 74

TAMARAH 3 b.f. Beat Hollow 126 – Valagalore 91 (Generous (IRE) 139) [2009 80?: 9g 8m 8g* 9.3g^{4} 8g 8g^{2} 10g^{3} Dec 24] tall filly: fairly useful performer: well held first 2 starts in 2009, then left Miss D. Mountain: won maiden at Doha in November: good third to Brief Encounter in valuable Qatar International Derby there final outing: stays 1¼m: tried tongue tied. *I. Al Malki, Qatar* 85

TAMARIND HILL (IRE) 2 b.g. (Feb 23) Shamardal (USA) 129 – Amandian (IRE) 84 (Indian Ridge 123) [2009 6m p7g^{6} p7g^{6} p7.1g p7g^{4} p6g^{2} p6g^{3} p6f f5g^{3} Dec 27] compact gelding: fair maiden: left C. Egerton after eighth start: stays 7f: acts on all-weather: tried in cheekpieces, usually blinkered: not one to trust. *A. J. McCabe* 66 §

TAMARIND (IRE) 3 b.f. Sadler's Wells (USA) 132 – Sharata (IRE) (Darshaan 133) [2009 9.5v^{4} 10g^{5} 12d* 12s* 12m^{5} Aug 20] leggy filly: sister to smart 7f (at 2 yrs) to 1½m winner Crimson Tide and useful Irish/US 9.5f and 1½m winner Arosa, closely related to smart French 1m (including at 2 yrs)/9f winner Pharatta (by Fairy King), and half-sister to 2 useful winners: dam unraced half-sister to Derby winner Shahrastani: useful performer: won maiden at Tipperary in July and Ladbrokes Give Thanks Stakes at Cork (much improved to beat Perfect Truth 1½ lengths) in August: much firmer ground and stiff task when 10¼ lengths fifth to Dar Re Mi in Yorkshire Oaks at York final outing: stayed 1½m: acted on soft going: stud. *A. P. O'Brien, Ireland* 107

TAMASOU (IRE) 4 b.g. Tamarisk (IRE) 127 – Soubresaut (IRE) (Danehill (USA) 126) [2009 73: 8d^{2} 8g^{4} 10m^{3} 8.1v p7f* p7m^{2} p8.6g^{2} p7g 7v* 7s p8.6g^{2} f8m^{5} Dec 15] strong, lengthy gelding: fairly useful handicapper: left Garry Moss after fourth start: won at Kempton in September and Catterick in November: stays 8.6f: acts on all-weather and heavy going. *A. J. McCabe* 85

TAMAZIRTE (IRE) 3 b.f. Danehill Dancer (IRE) 117 – Tanami Desert (Lycius (USA) 124) [2009 a8g* a7.5g* 8g* 8m^{2} 10.5m^{2} 10m^{6} 8g* Oct 3] €40,000 2-y-o: second foal: dam French maiden half-sister to Rockfel Stakes winner Cairns: smart performer: won maiden at Cagnes-sur-Mer in January, minor event at Deauville in February, Prix de la Grotte at Longchamp (beat Soneva a neck) in April and Qatar Prix Daniel Wildenstein at 117

Longchamp (beat Danse Grecque a length) in October: also ran well when runner-up to stable companions in Poule d'Essai des Pouliches at Longchamp (beaten ½ length by Elusive Wave) and Prix de Diane at Chantilly (ran on but no chance with 4-length winner Stacelita) fourth/fifth starts: stays 10.5f: acts on all-weather and good to firm ground: held up. *J-C. Rouget, France*

TAMIMI'S HISTORY 5 b.g. Kalanisi (IRE) 132 – Polish Pink (IRE) (Polish Precedent (USA) 131) [2009 –: p9.5g p11g 16m^4 Apr 25] strong gelding: fairly useful handicapper: lightly raced on Flat since 2007, best effort in 2009 when fourth to Downhiller at Ripon: stays 2m, effective at much shorter: acts on heavy and good to firm going. *P. D. Evans* **92**

TAMINAS DESERT 4 b.f. Green Desert (USA) 127 – Tamise (USA) 113 (Time For A Change (USA)) [2009 65: p9.5m Feb 25] lengthy filly: modest form sole start at 3 yrs: off 8 months, pulled up amiss at Wolverhampton: dead. *M. Botti* **–**

TAMINO (IRE) 6 b.g. Mozart (IRE) 131 – Stop Out 89 (Rudimentary (USA) 118) [2009 71, a66: p6g p6g^3 p7g^6 p6m 7m 7f p7.1g p8g^3 p6m* p8.6g^6 p7m^2 Dec 30] big gelding: modest handicapper: won at Lingfield in December: stays 7f: acts on polytrack, good to firm and good to soft ground: often tongue tied: races up with pace. *P. Howling* **61**

TAMMELA 2 b.f. (Mar 2) Beat Hollow 126 – On The Wing 78 (Pivotal 124) [2009 p8m p8g Oct 8] sturdy filly: first foal: dam 2-y-o 7f winner: modest form at best in maidens at Kempton. *A. P. Jarvis* **53**

TAMPA BOY (IRE) 7 b.g. Montjeu (IRE) 137 – Tirolean Dance (IRE) (Tirol 127) [2009 60: f12d^4 p16.5g^4 p16.5g^6 Jan 29] fair maiden: stays 16.5f: raced on all-weather: tried blinkered: fair hurdler, won in April. *M. F. Harris* **70**

TAMTARA 2 b.f. (Feb 20) Red Ransom (USA) – Tamalain (USA) 80 (Royal Academy (USA) 130) [2009 7g 8m^6 p7g^6 Oct 14] close-coupled filly: first foal: dam, ungenuine maiden (stayed 1¼m), sister to Coventry Stakes winner Cd Europe: easily best effort in maidens when sixth to Namaskar at Goodwood second start: stays 1m. *Mrs A. J. Perrett* **66**

TAN BONITA (USA) 4 b. or br.f. More Than Ready (USA) 120 – Time For Hennessy (USA) (Hennessy (USA) 122) [2009 5g^3 a6g 5.3f 5m p6f p5m Dec 9] neat filly: fair at 2 yrs: won minor event at Mijas on reappearance in 2008: just poor form back in Britain after second start in 2009: stays 6.5f: acts on sand and good to firm going: tried tongue tied. *R. J. Smith* **44**

TANFIDH 3 b.f. Marju (IRE) 127 – Wijdan (USA) 101 (Mr Prospector (USA)) [2009 8g 11.8g^2 10.2m* 10m* 10.3g^6 Oct 23] good-topped filly: seventh foal: sister to smart 1m winner Oriental Fashion and half-sister to 3 winners, including smart 7f/1m (later US Grade 2 1¼m) winner Makderah (by Danehill) and useful 1m (at 2 yrs)/1¼m winner Ezdiyaad (by Galileo): dam, 1m and 10.4f winner, sister to dam of 3-y-o Ghanaati, closely related to Nayef and half-sister to Nashwan and Unfuwain: useful form: won maiden at Bath in September and handicap at Leicester (by 6 lengths) in October: bit too free in front when below form final outing: stayed 1¼m: acted on good to firm going: visits Dansili. *M. P. Tregoning* **93**

TANFORAN 7 b.g. Mujahid (USA) 125 – Florentynna Bay 61 (Aragon 118) [2009 72: p9.5g 8g 8.3g 8.1g^2 8.3m^6 8d 8.1g* 8.3g* 8.3m^5 8.1s^2 8.1v^4 8.3m^2 9.2v^5 8m^6 8m^6 Sep 23] quite attractive gelding: fair handicapper: won at Warwick (amateurs) in June and Nottingham in July: stays 1m: acts on polytrack and any turf going: formerly in blinkers/cheekpieces. *B. P. J. Baugh* **75**

TANGERINE TREES 4 b.g. Mind Games 121 – Easy To Imagine (USA) (Cozzene (USA)) [2009 75: 5m^3 5.9m^2 6m* 6m* 6g* 6g 5m 7g^3 p7.1g^3 f6f Nov 24] big, strong gelding: fair handicapper: won at Hamilton in June (2) and July: stays 7f: acts on polytrack and firm going: tried in headgear: races prominently. *B. Smart* **79**

TANGO STEP (IRE) 9 b.g. Sesaro (USA) 81 – Leitrim Lodge (IRE) 64 (Classic Music (USA)) [2009 50: p5g 5.8s 7m p7g 5s p5.1g f8f^5 Dec 12] poor performer nowadays: left Bernard Lawlor in Ireland after third start: best at 5f/6f: acts on polytrack, firm and soft going: often in cheekpieces/blinkers: sometimes looks none too keen. *D. Carroll* **45**

TANLEY 4 gr.g. Compton Admiral 121 – Schatzi 54§ (Chilibang 120) [2009 62: 5g^2 f5g 5s 5.1s p5g^3 p6g f5f p6g^6 Dec 19] close-coupled gelding: modest handicapper: effective at 5f/6f: acts on all-weather, heavy and good to firm going: usually wears cheekpieces, tried in blinkers: temperament under suspicion. *J. F. Coupland* **60**

H.H. Aga Khan's "Tanoura"

TANOURA (IRE) 3 b.f. Dalakhani (IRE) 133 – Takarouna (USA) 114 (Green Dancer (USA) 132) [2009 93p: 9.5v⁶ 12m² 12m* 14.6m³ 12.5g³ Oct 3] well-made filly: useful performer: unlucky short-head second to Grace O'Malley in Noblesse Stakes at Cork prior to winning listed race at York in August by ½ length from Leocorno: third after in Park Hill Stakes at Doncaster (bit below best behind The Miniver Rose, said to have finished lame) and Prix de Royallieu at Longchamp (ran creditably, stayed on to dead-heat 3¼ lengths behind Daryakana): should have proven fully effective at 1¾m: acted on good to firm going, winner on soft: stud. *John M. Oxx, Ireland* **109**

TANTO FAZ (IRE) 4 b.g. Rock of Gibraltar (IRE) 133 – Sharakawa (IRE) (Darshaan 133) [2009 92: 8d*dis 8.1m³ 8.1m p8.6g 12m³ p12m Oct 12] sturdy gelding: fairly useful handicapper: first past post at Ripon in May, but disqualified after failing dope test: below form after next start: stays 1¼m: acts on polytrack and good to soft ground: suspect temperament: sold 15,000 gns, joined J. J. Quinn, runner-up on hurdling debut. *W. J. Haggas* **90**

TANTO QUANTO (IRE) 2 b.c. (Apr 25) Le Vie Dei Colori 126 – Fear Not (IRE) 64 (Alzao (USA) 117) [2009 6g⁶ 7g² f8g* 8m p8.6g⁶ Oct 3] €30,000F: fourth foal: dam 7f winner: fair performer: won maiden at Southwell in August: stays 8.6f: acts on all-weather: blinkered after debut: sold 15,000 gns. *W. R. Muir* **70**

TANTRIS (IRE) 4 b.g. High Chaparral (IRE) 132 – Emerald Cut (Rainbow Quest (USA) 134) [2009 67: p12g⁵ p9.5g Apr 16] rangy, useful-looking gelding: modest maiden handicapper: stays 1½m: acts on polytrack, yet to race on extremes of going on turf: joined Peter McCreery in Ireland. *J. A. Osborne* **62**

TANTSOR (FR) 2 ch.g. (Apr 9) Brier Creek (USA) 111 – Norova (FR) (Hawker's News (IRE) 105) [2009 8.5m 8d f8m Nov 6] well held in maidens (gelded after). *P. T. Midgley* **–**

TAPAS LAD (IRE) 4 b.c. Modigliani (USA) 106 – Missish (Mummy's Pet 125) [2009 61§: p9.5g p9.5g f8d p9.5g 10m May 25] compact colt: modest performer at best: out of form in 2009: visored/blinkered: tried tongue tied: irresolute. *G. J. Smith* **– §**

TAP DANCE WAY (IRE) 2 b.f. (Apr 7) Azamour (IRE) 130 – Dance Lively (USA) (Kingmambo (USA) 125) [2009 p7g Sep 21] €25,000Y: lengthy filly: third foal: half-sister to 2 winners abroad, including smart Japanese miler Live Concert (by Singspiel): dam unraced half-sister to US Grade 3 6f winner Reunited: 100/1 and very green, down the field in maiden at Kempton: likely to do better. *P. R. Chamings* **52 p**

TAPER JEAN GIRL (IRE) 2 b.f. (May 5) Elusive City (USA) 117 – Ruacana Falls (USA) 86 (Storm Bird (CAN) 134) [2009 p7g[4] p8f p7m p7.1g[4] f7g* f7f f8f[4] f7m[6] Dec 15] €25,000F, £28,000Y: compact filly: fifth foal: half-sister to 3 winners, including fairly useful 2007 2-y-o 7f winner Casa Catalina (by King's Best): dam, 2-y-o 1m winner, stayed 11.4f: modest performer: won seller at Southwell (left M. Botti 3,000 gns) in November: stays 7f: raced only on all-weather. *Mrs R. A. Carr* **58**

TAPIS WIZARD 3 b.g. Alhaarth (IRE) 126 – Just Call Me (NZ) (Blues Traveller (IRE) 119) [2009 75: 8.3d 8s[5] 12s[3] 12d 10.3d[3] 12d[2] Jul 24] workmanlike gelding: fair maiden handicapper: stayed 1½m: acted on heavy going: dead. *M. W. Easterby* **74**

TAPPANAPPA (IRE) 2 b.c. (Feb 24) High Chaparral (IRE) 132 – Itsibitsi (IRE) (Brief Truce (USA) 126) [2009 8v Oct 24] 30,000F, 105,000Y: fourth foal: half-brother to 3 winners, including 5-y-o Baltimore Jack: dam unraced out of half-sister to Yorkshire Oaks winner/excellent broodmare Hellenic: 9/1, well held in maiden at Newbury, not knocked about: should do better. *A. M. Balding* **– p**

TAQDEYR 4 ch.g. Dubai Destination (USA) 127 – Pastorale 91 (Nureyev (USA) 131) [2009 89p: p7g* p7g* 7m[5] 6m[2] 7m[6] 7g 7.1g* 7m[3] Oct 3] good sort: useful performer: gelded and had wind operation prior to reappearance: much improved, winning handicaps at Kempton (2) in April and minor event at Warwick (dictated, beat Khor Dubai 1¼ lengths) in August: respectable third to Musaalem in listed race at Redcar final outing, pulling hard and veering left until halfway: all wins at 7f, at least as effective at 6f: acts on all-weather, good to firm and good to soft going: sold 75,000 gns, joined A. bin Huzaim in UAE. *M. A. Jarvis* **107**

TAQLEED (IRE) 2 b. or br.c. (Feb 2) Shamardal (USA) 129 – Thakafaat (IRE) 107 (Unfuwain (USA) 131) [2009 8g Oct 8] good sort: first foal: dam, 7f (at 2 yrs) to 1½m (Ribblesdale Stakes) winner, out of half-sister to 2000 Guineas winner Footstepsinthesand: 14/1, well beaten in maiden at Newbury (coltish and unruly beforehand). *J. H. M. Gosden* **–**

TARAN TREGARTH 5 b.m. Tobougg (IRE) 125 – Little Change 70 (Grundy 137) [2009 p12.2g[6] Jan 21] workmanlike mare: maiden: well held sole start on Flat since 2007: tried in blinkers/cheekpieces. *W. M. Brisbourne* **–**

TARA'S GARDEN 4 b.f. Dr Fong (USA) 128 – Tremiere (FR) (Anabaa (USA) 130) [2009 65: 8.1g 10.2g 12.1m 8.3m f8g Jul 27] sturdy filly: maiden: well held in 2009: blinkered last 2 starts. *M. Blanshard* **–**

TARAWA ATOLL 3 b.f. Imperial Dancer 123 – Musical Capers (Piccolo 121) [2009 54: p8.6g[3] p7g[5] p8g 8f May 31] angular filly: modest maiden: should be suited by 1¼m: acts on polytrack: has joined Miss S. West. *M. R. Channon* **56**

TARGS (IRE) 3 b.c. Elusive City (USA) 117 – Cannikin (IRE) 82 (Lahib (USA) 129) [2009 7g 7s Jul 29] well held in maiden and seller: dead. *Peter Grayson* **–**

TARIQ 5 ch.h. Kyllachy 129 – Tatora (Selkirk (USA) 129) [2009 122: 8d[6] 7.1g 7m[6] 7m Oct 17] small, leggy horse: good walker: just smart performer at 5 yrs, best efforts when sixth to Virtual in Lockinge Stakes at Newbury and seventh to Main Aim in John of Gaunt Stakes at Haydock first 2 starts: well below form after: stays 1m, all wins at shorter: acts on soft and good to firm ground: has moved poorly to post: held up. *P. W. Chapple-Hyam* **112**

TAR (IRE) 5 b.g. Danzig (USA) – Royal Show (IRE) 63 (Sadler's Wells (USA) 132) [2009 10v f11g[3] f8g p9.5g f12m f8f Nov 24] neat gelding: modest maiden nowadays: stays 11f: acts on fibresand, soft and good to firm going: tried blinkered, visored last 5 starts: sold £800, joined Tim Vaughan. *John A. Harris* **61**

TARITA (IRE) 2 ch.f. (Jan 25) Bahamian Bounty 116 – Zonic 59 (Zafonic (USA) 130) [2009 6m[4] 5m[4] 5m* 6.5m Sep 10] €65,000F, 32,000Y: sturdy filly: first foal: dam, maiden (probably stayed 7f), half-sister to useful 6f/7f winner Injaaz: fair performer: easily best effort when winning maiden at Beverley in August: should stay 6f. *R. Hannon* **73**

TARKAMARA (IRE) 5 ch.m. Medicean 128 – Tarakana (USA) 101 (Shahrastani (USA) 135) [2009 56: p9.5g[3] p8g[2] p8g[4] Jan 18] big, useful-looking mare: has a round **57**

action: modest performer: stays 1¼m: acts on polytrack and good to firm ground: tried tongue tied/blinkered: quirky (has flashed tail) but reliable. *P. F. I. Cole*

TARQUA (IRE) 3 b.f. King Charlemagne (USA) 120 – Shining Creek (CAN) (Bering 136) [2009 6m 7m 8m 9m 5.1g Jul 23] €36,000Y: leggy filly: seventh foal: half-sister to useful 2005 2-y-o 5f/6f (Mill Reef Stakes) winner Cool Creek (by Desert Style): dam Italian 7f (at 2 yrs)/7.5f winner: well held all starts. *R. Hannon* **–**

TARRAAD 3 b.g. Selkirk (USA) 129 – Mingora (USA) 89 (Mtoto 134) [2009 10.3g p12g Apr 15] unfurnished gelding: tailed off in maidens. *M. Botti* **–**

TARRANTS WAY 2 b.c. (Feb 8) Auction House (USA) 120 – Thicket 87 (Wolfhound (USA) 126) [2009 6v f5g^4 5m^3 5s 5d 5.5g 7g Sep 14] sturdy, lengthy colt: modest maiden: no form after third start: best efforts at 5f: acts on fibresand and good to firm ground: tried in cheekpieces: sold £800 in October, sent to Sweden. *Jennie Candlish* **51**

TARRUJI (IRE) 3 gr.g. Verglas (IRE) 118 – Polish Affair (IRE) (Polish Patriot (USA) 128) [2009 59: p5.1g 6s^5 p6g a7.5g^5 a9.5g^3 a9.5g^3 9g a9.5g^5 a9g^4 a9g^4 a7.5g^5 a9.5g Dec 23] close-coupled gelding: fair maiden: sold from S. Callaghan 4,000 gns after third start, trained next outing only by Mme G. Rarick: in frame in claimers/handicaps subsequently: stays 9.5f: raced mainly on all-weather: tried blinkered. *P. Monfort, France* **74**

TARTAN BEARER (IRE) 4 ch.c. Spectrum (IRE) 126 – Highland Gift (IRE) 95 (Generous (IRE) 139) [2009 127: 10g* 10m^2 12m^2 Jul 25] **126**

Tartan Bearer will have to race on if he is to clinch that elusive Group 1 victory, one which will be thoroughly deserved if and when it does come. The 2008 Derby runner-up gave his all but again had to settle for second on both starts in Group 1 company in another foreshortened campaign. Around three weeks after making a bold bid to emulate his brother Golan by winning the King George VI and Queen Elizabeth Stakes at Ascot, Tartan Bearer was reported to be lame and was ruled out for the remainder of the season.

Tartan Bearer's three-year-old season had ended even earlier, when he wasn't seen out again after a below-par performance in the Irish Derby for which he started favourite on the strength of his excellent second to New Approach at Epsom. Tartan Bearer reportedly picked up an infection after he returned from Ireland, one of the consequences being that his tail fell out. Tartan Bearer made a full recovery, although his tail was slow to grow back, and he was able to return to action in April in the bet365 Gordon Richards Stakes at Sandown. Both Tartan Bearer's previous wins had come at a mile and a quarter, in a maiden at Leicester and in the Dante Stakes at York, and he made it three from three at the trip at Sandown. Tartan Bearer started even-money favourite, dominating the betting with Pipedreamer in an eight-runner field. The pair also dominated the race itself, Tartan Bearer winning by a short head, doing well to peg back Pipedreamer who poached a three-length advantage when quickening clear over two furlongs out. Tartan Bearer had prevailed in a steadily-run race at a mile and a quarter, but wasn't quite able to do the same when stepped back up in class in the Prince of Wales's Stakes at Royal Ascot, where he went down by half a length to French-trained Vision d'Etat. It was a high-class performance from Tartan Bearer, nonetheless, one which he managed to improve only marginally when returned to a mile and a half in the King George VI and Queen Elizabeth Stakes. After leading briefly in the penultimate furlong, Tartan Bearer found the favourite Conduit, in the same ownership, just too strong, held when hampered in the closing stages and beaten a length and three quarters. Tartan Bearer and third-placed Ask (the first three were all trained by Sir Michael Stoute) were both tightened up by Conduit as he edged right after taking the lead but a stewards' inquiry left the placings unaltered. Tartan Bearer's rider Michael Kinane was cautioned for using his whip improperly down the shoulder after being left short of room.

Tartan Bearer (IRE) (ch.c. 2005)	Spectrum (IRE) (b 1992)	Rainbow Quest (b 1981)	Blushing Groom
			I Will Follow
		River Dancer (b 1983)	Irish River
			Dancing Shadow
	Highland Gift (IRE) (b 1993)	Generous (ch 1988)	Caerleon
			Doff The Derby
		Scots Lass (b 1982)	Shirley Heights
			Edinburgh

Tartan Bearer is the seventh foal of the mile and a quarter winner Highland Gift. Golan, winner of the Two Thousand Guineas as well as the King George, was her first. All of Highland Gift's five other foals to reach the racecourse have been successful too. The pick of the quintet are the useful fillies Gift Range, a sister to Golan and Tartan Bearer, and Leocorno (by Pivotal), the latter the winner of a handicap at Sandown and in the frame in both the Ribblesdale and Galtres Stakes in the latest season. Leocorno has a year-younger brother named Highland Park, also with Sir Michael Stoute, but unraced. Highland Gift is a half-sister to Great Voltigeur and Gordon Stakes winner and St Leger third Bonny Scot, and is out of a half-sister to the Prix du Cadran winner Sought Out, the dam of 2004 Derby winner North Light. The good-bodied Tartan Bearer had sweated up before the Irish Derby, but he gave no cause for concern on that score in the latest season and looked in excellent shape on his final appearance. A poor mover in his slower paces, Tartan Bearer acts on good to firm going. The Irish Derby, which was run on good to soft, is the only race in which he has raced on softer than good. *Sir Michael Stoute*

TARTAN GIGHA (IRE) 4 b.g. Green Desert (USA) 127 – High Standard 83 (Kris 135) [2009 88: p7g* p8.6g² 7m⁶ p8g² 8.1g 8.5m* 8m² 8d 8.5g* 7f 8m 8g 8g⁴ 7.6m p8g² 8m 9m² Oct 3] good-topped gelding: useful handicapper: won at Kempton in March, Beverley in May and Epsom (beat Plum Pudding 2¼ lengths) in June: good nose second to Supaseus in Cambridgeshire at Newmarket final outing, favourably drawn and positioned: stays 9f: acts on polytrack and firm going: can look ungainly when pressured. *M. Johnston* **103**

TARTAN GUNNA 3 b.g. Anabaa (USA) 130 – Embraced 103 (Pursuit of Love 124) [2009 78: p7.1g* p8g* p7.1g³ 7.5m* 7.6m² 7m⁵ 7g⁵ 8m f8g⁵ 9m* 8m⁵ 10g⁴ Oct 10] lengthy gelding: useful performer: won maiden at Wolverhampton in January and handicaps at Lingfield in February, Beverley in April and Goodwood (beat Resort by neck, well placed in steadily-run race) in September: stays 1¼m: acts on all-weather and good to firm ground. *M. Johnston* **98**

TARTAN TRIP 2 b.g. (Feb 27) Selkirk (USA) 129 – Marajuana 82 (Robellino (USA) 127) [2009 6g⁴ 7m⁴ p7g³ Oct 21] good-topped gelding: first foal: dam, 2-y-o 5f winner (stayed 7f), half-sister to smart performer up to 7f Border Music (by Selkirk): best effort in maidens when 2½ lengths fourth to Swiss Cross at Newmarket (drifted left) second start: likely to stay 1m: gelded after final outing. *A. M. Balding* **83**

TARTAN TURBAN (IRE) 3 b.c. Invincible Spirit (IRE) 121 – Tappen Zee (Sandhurst Prince 128) [2009 70d: p6g p8g Jan 21] good-topped colt: won maiden at 2 yrs: well below form since: sold £1,500, resold €2,000. *R. Hannon* **–**

TARTATARTUFATA 7 b.m. Tagula (IRE) 116 – It's So Easy 63 (Shaadi (USA) 126) [2009 80, a94: f5s 5v³ 5f² 5g² 5.1m⁵ 5.1v f5g⁵ 6s² 5.1d 5s³ f5m f5m p6m f5g³ Dec 27] strong mare: fair performer nowadays: best at 5f: acts on all-weather and any turf going: usually wears visor, blinkered once: sometimes hangs: usually races prominently. *J. G. Given* **75**

TARTUFO DOLCE (IRE) 2 b.f. (Feb 27) Key of Luck (USA) 126 – Corn Futures 78 (Nomination 125) [2009 5.1f⁴ p6g⁴ p6g⁵ p5.1g* f5m⁵ Dec 5] £26,000Y: sturdy filly: sister to useful 2004 2-y-o 5f winner Siena Gold and half-sister to several winners, including useful 1997 2-y-o 6f winner Crazee Mental (by Magic Ring): dam 2-y-o 6f winner: fair performer: won maiden at Wolverhampton in November: will prove best at 5f/6f: acts on polytrack. *J. G. Given* **73**

TARUS (IRE) 5 ch.m. Tagula (IRE) 116 – Wasaif (IRE) 79 (Lomond (USA) 128) [2009 58: 6m 5m 6m 5m 6f⁵ 5m⁴ 6d⁶ 5m 5d 5m Oct 1] poor maiden: stays 7.5f: acts on firm and soft ground: tried tongue tied. *A. Berry* **49**

TARZAN (IRE) 3 ch.g. Spinning World (USA) 130 – Run To Jane (IRE) (Doyoun 124) [2009 66p: 9.9m⁴ 8m² 9f* 8m² 10.1g 8m 8.5d⁴ 8.5m⁵ 8m⁴ 8m⁶ 10.4g Oct 10] sturdy gelding: fairly useful handicapper: won at Redcar in May: generally below form after next start: best at 1m/9f: acts on firm going: blinkered last 2 starts: sold 14,000 gns, sent to Bahrain. *M. Johnston* **89**

TASHEBA 4 ch.g. Dubai Destination (USA) 127 – Tatanka (IRE) (Lear Fan (USA) 130) [2009 93: 21.7m⁴ Jun 20] strong, well-made gelding: useful performer on Flat (smart hurdler): good fourth to Caracciola in Queen Alexandra Stakes at Royal Ascot sole outing on Flat in 2009: effective at 1¾m to 21.7f: acts on polytrack, good to firm and good to soft going. *N. J. Henderson* **96**

TASHKANDI (IRE) 9 gr.g. Polish Precedent (USA) 131 – Tashiriya (IRE) 106 (Kenmare (FR) 125) [2009 –: f12g p12g Feb 13] sturdy, lengthy gelding: lightly **–**

raced on Flat in recent years (poor hurdler): blinkered, well beaten both starts in 2009. *Mrs S. J. Humphrey*

TASHZARA (IRE) 2 ch.f. (Apr 6) Intikhab (USA) 135 – Sun Shower (IRE) (Indian Ridge 123) [2009 7.5m^3 8g^2 8g^6 Oct 31] rather leggy filly: second foal: half-sister to 3-y-o Mull of Killough: dam, placed up to 11f in France, out of half-sister to Irish Oaks winner Princess Pati and Great Voltigeur winner Seymour Hicks: progressive form, 8 lengths sixth to Timepiece in listed event at Newmarket: will stay 1¼m. *Christopher Phillips, Ireland* **83**

TASMEEM (IRE) 2 b. or gr.c. (Apr 1) Acclamation 118 – Park Approach (IRE) 77 (Indian Ridge 123) [2009 6.1v^5 6d^2 6m* 6d Sep 5] 135,000Y: lengthy colt: has scope: first foal: dam, sprint maiden, half-sister to useful Irish 1m winner Poetical, out of half-sister to Middle Park Stakes winner Hayil and smart winner up to 1¼m Tamhid: best effort when winning maiden at Ripon (hung right) in August: raced only at 6f: acts on good to firm going: sold 20,000 gns. *B. W. Hills* **93**

TASTAHIL (IRE) 5 ch.g. Singspiel (IRE) 133 – Luana 101 (Shaadi (USA) 126) [2009 105: 12m* 12s^3 13.3d* 16.4m^3 12v^2 12s Nov 7] strong, good sort: smart performer: won minor event at Doncaster (by 1½ lengths from Drill Sergeant) in March and listed race at Newbury (beat All The Aces ½ length, making all) in May: best effort after when respectable 6 lengths second to High Heeled in St Simon Stakes at Newbury: stays 2m: acts on polytrack, heavy and good to firm ground. *B. W. Hills* **115**

TASTE OF HONEY (IRE) 3 b.f. Deportivo 116 – Long Tall Sally (IRE) 71 (Danehill Dancer (IRE) 117) [2009 –: p7g^5 p7g* 7f 6g p7g p8g 9m Jul 8] small filly: modest performer: won claimer at Lingfield in April: well below form after: stays 7f: acts on polytrack: sold £900. *D. W. P. Arbuthnot* **63**

TASTE THE VICTORY (USA) 2 b.g. (Jan 28) Victory Gallop (CAN) 130 – Tastetheteardrops (USA) (What Luck (USA)) [2009 7g^2 8d^2 Oct 28] $45,000F, €40,000Y: tall gelding: half-brother to several winners in USA, including Grade 1 6f winner Taste of Paradise (by Conquistador Cielo): dam US 6f winner: similar form when runner-up in maidens at York and Musselburgh (still green). *G. A. Swinbank* **77**

TASTE THE WINE (IRE) 3 gr.g. Verglas (IRE) 118 – Azia (IRE) 71 (Desert Story (IRE) 115) [2009 61: 8.3m 10.2d^4 f11g 12.1g* 14.1m* 14.1s 14.1m^5 12g 14g^5 13.1d^6 12m 15m^4 p12g^2 p12m^4 p12f^2 Dec 21] rather leggy gelding: fair handicapper: won at Chepstow in May and Nottingham in June: should stay 2m: acts on polytrack and good to firm ground (poor efforts on soft/fibresand): said to have had breathing problem sixth start. *J. S. Moore* **74**

TATAWOR (IRE) 2 b.g. (Mar 26) Kheleyf (USA) 116 – Romea (Muhtarram (USA) 125) [2009 6g p5g^3 Aug 1] 37,000F, 65,000Y: medium-sized gelding: first foal: dam, Italian 1m/8.5f winner, half-sister to US Grade 3 9f winner Where We Left Off: much better effort in maidens when third to Piccadilly Filly at Lingfield (still green): should stay 6f: sold 11,000 gns, joined J. Boyle and gelded. *M. P. Tregoning* **71**

TATIANA ROMANOVA (USA) 2 ch.f. (May 2) Mr Greeley (USA) 122 – Bank On Her (USA) 76 (Rahy (USA) 115) [2009 6g^2 p6m^4 7.1d* Oct 28] $150,000F, 38,000 2-y-o: seventh foal: closely related to useful 7f to 8.5f (in USA) winner I'm In Love (by Zafonic) and half-sister to winner in Hong Kong by Marju: dam, 7f winner from 3 starts, half-sister to smart 7f performer Weldnaas: best effort in maidens when winning comfortably by 6 lengths from Brink at Musselburgh, making all: stays 7f: should progress again. *R. A. Fahey* **81 p**

TATTERCOATS (FR) 3 b.f. Whywhywhy (USA) 115 – Driscilla (USA) (Stately Don (USA) 122) [2009 –: 8m Sep 13] little form. *M. Botti* **–**

TAURUS TWINS 3 b.g. Deportivo 116 – Intellibet One 74 (Compton Place 125) [2009 55: f5g^6 p6g f5g^2 f5g* f5g 5.1m^6 5m* 6f^2 6.1g* 5d^5 5d^2 6g 5g^2 5g^5 5g^2 5.1g* p6g Nov 14] workmanlike gelding: fairly useful handicapper: won at Southwell in March, Musselburgh and Nottingham in May and Nottingham (beat Frisbee by length) in October: best at 5f/6f: acts on fibresand, firm and good to soft ground: blinkered nowadays: races prominently. *R. J. Price* **86**

TAWAABB 2 ch.c. (Jan 21) Kyllachy 129 – Penmayne 95 (Inchinor 119) [2009 5g^2 5g* 5m^3 6m 5d^5 5g^5 Oct 10] 25,000F, 82,000Y: compact colt: sixth foal: brother to useful 2007 2-y-o 5f/6f winner Kylayne (stayed 1m) and half-brother to 3-y-o Penzena and winner in Sweden by Dr Fong: dam 2-y-o 7f winner: useful performer: won maiden at Leicester in May: very good 2¾ lengths fifth to Our Jonathan in Cornwallis Stakes at Ascot final start: should stay 6f: acts on good to firm going. *M. R. Channon* **100**

*Connaught Access Flooring Abernant Stakes, Newmarket—
Tax Free (left) and Equiano dominate throughout*

TAX FREE (IRE) 7 b.g. Tagula (IRE) 116 – Grandel (Owington 123) [2009 117: 6m* 6m³ 5m* 5m 5m⁴ 5g Oct 4] strong gelding: smart performer: won listed race at Newmarket (by ½ length from Equiano) in April and Prix du Gros-Chene at Chantilly (by neck from Black Mambazo, rallying) in May: good 1¾ lengths fourth to Borderlescott in Nunthorpe Stakes at York: respectable seventh to Total Gallery in Prix de l'Abbaye de Longchamp final outing: effective at 5f/6f: yet to race on heavy ground, acts on any other turf: races up with pace: consistent. *D. Nicholls* **117**

TAXMAN (IRE) 7 ch.g. Singspiel (IRE) 133 – Love of Silver (USA) 110 (Arctic Tern (USA) 126) [2009 56: p16.5g² p13.9g⁴ Feb 7] close-coupled gelding: modest handicapper: stays 16.5f: acts on all-weather, firm and soft going: often wears cheekpieces (not last 3 outings). *A. G. Newcombe* **60**

TAYACOBA (CAN) 2 b. or br.g. (Feb 24) Smart Strike (CAN) 121 – Bienandanza (USA) (Bien Bien (USA) 125) [2009 8g⁶ Oct 21] $240,000Y: fourth foal: dam US 9f/1¼m winner: 12/1 and green, 12½ lengths sixth to Rasmy in maiden at Bath, slowly away and off bridle throughout: sold 6,000 gns. *J. H. M. Gosden* **60**

TAYMAN (IRE) 7 b. or br.g. Sinndar (IRE) 134 – Sweet Emotion (IRE) 97 (Bering 136) [2009 66: p16.5g Oct 23] quite good-topped gelding: handicapper: lightly raced on Flat nowadays, and well held sole start in 2009: may prove best up to 15.4f: acts on all-weather, good to firm and good to soft going: tried blinkered/in cheekpieces: fair hurdler, won in September. *N. A. Twiston-Davies* **–**

TAZBAR (IRE) 7 b.g. Tiraaz (USA) 115 – Candy Bar (IRE) (Montelimar (USA) 122) [2009 80: 12v Nov 3] sturdy gelding: useful bumper performer/smart hurdler/novice chaser: seemingly fairly useful form on Flat debut: well held both outings since. *K. G. Reveley* **–**

TAZEEZ (USA) 5 b. or br.g. Silver Hawk (USA) 123 – Soiree Russe (USA) (Nureyev (USA) 131) [2009 116: 9m* 9.3s 10m⁵ 10.4g⁶ Jul 25] good-topped gelding: smart performer: won Weatherbys Earl of Sefton Stakes at Newmarket in April by 3½ lengths from Steele Tango: creditable effort in pattern company after only when 4 lengths fifth to Vision d'Etat in Prince of Wales's Stakes at Royal Ascot: stays 1¼m: acts on soft and good to firm going: usually races prominently. *J. H. M. Gosden* **117**

TEALING 2 ch.g. (Feb 9) Ishiguru (USA) 114 – Renaissance Lady (IRE) 65 (Imp Society (USA)) [2009 6g f7m^4 f7f* f8f^2 f7g* Dec 18] smallish, sturdy gelding: fair performer: won claimer (left T. D. Barron £6,000) in November and nursery in December, both at Southwell: should be as effective at 1m as 7f. *R. C. Guest* **67**

TEASING 5 b.m. Lujain (USA) 119 – Movieland (USA) 109 (Nureyev (USA) 131) [2009 88: p10g^2 p10g^4 p8.6g^3 p8.6g* p8.6g* p8g^4 p9.5g p8g^4 8m^3 10g^4 10.3m^5 11.6m^3 p12.2g^3 12m May 30] close-coupled mare: fairly useful performer: won claimer and handicap at Wolverhampton in January: hampered and fell in claimer at York final outing: stays 1½m: acts on polytrack and good to firm going: wears cheekpieces/visor: held up. *J. Pearce* **80**

TECKTAL (FR) 6 ch.m. Pivotal 124 – Wenge (USA) (Housebuster (USA)) [2009 –: p12g^5 p11g* p11g^4 p12g^4 p12g^6 10.1d^5 12m^2 12g^3 Jul 30] leggy mare: modest handicapper: had a foal in 2008: won at Kempton in February: stays 1½m: acts on polytrack, good to firm and good to soft going. *P. M. Phelan* **58**

TEDDY WEST (IRE) 3 b.g. Trans Island 119 – Duckmore Bay (IRE) (Titus Livius (FR) 115) [2009 58: f11g p9.5g^5 9m^6 8.3g^6 May 3] poor maiden: probably stays 9f: visored/blinkered last 2 starts: looks reluctant, and one to treat with caution. *Pat Morris* **45 §**

TED SPREAD 2 b.c. (Mar 6) Beat Hollow 126 – Highbrook (USA) 88 (Alphabatim (USA) 126) [2009 7g 9d* 10g^3 Oct 31] good-topped colt: half-brother to 3 winners, including 2003 2-y-o 6f winner Pink Sapphire (by Bluebird) and 6f (at 2 yrs) to 1½m winner Niagara (by Rainbows For Life): dam, 1¼m to 13f winner, also useful hurdler: progressive form, winning maiden at Goodwood (by 1½ lengths from Regal Guest) in October and length third to Take It To The Max in minor event at Newmarket (plenty to do): will stay 1½m. *M. H. Tompkins* **91 +**

TEEKY 3 b.f. Daylami (IRE) 138 – Las Flores (IRE) 102 (Sadler's Wells (USA) 132) [2009 73p: 10.2g^2 10.2g 12g* p11g^2 p16g^5 12g* 12.5s Nov 27] big, deep-girthed filly: fairly useful handicapper: won at Newmarket in July and October (beat Featherweight 3 lengths): well held in listed race at Fontainebleau final start: should be suited by 1¾m+: acts on polytrack, best turf efforts on good ground. *J. H. M. Gosden* **89**

TEEN AGER (FR) 5 b.g. Invincible Spirit (IRE) 121 – Tarwiya (IRE) 103 (Dominion 123) [2009 73: p6g p5g^4 p5.1g p5g* p5.1g p5g^5 p5g^6 p6g p6g^3 6m^5 p7g^4 p8g* p8g^2 8g^6 Jun 19] strong, compact gelding: fair handicapper on all-weather, modest on turf: won at Lingfield in February and May: stays 1m: acts on polytrack, probably on good to firm going: none too consistent. *P. Burgoyne* **51 a73**

TEERAHA (IRE) 2 b.f. (Apr 12) Arakan (USA) 123 – Lovely Me (IRE) 70 (Vision (USA)) [2009 6m 5d p7.1g p6g^6 6m 6.1s Oct 7] €15,000F, £3,000Y: eighth foal: half-sister to useful 5f winner (including at 2 yrs) Red Millennium (by Tagula) and 7-y-o Regal Dream: dam maiden (stayed 7f): little form: joined Miss M. Rowland. *D. Shaw* **42**

TEIA TEPHI 3 ch.f. Elnadim (USA) 128 – Tatora (Selkirk (USA) 129) [2009 6g f6g Aug 27] 50,000F, 65,000 2-y-o: fourth foal: half-sister to 5-y-o Tariq: dam unraced: last in maidens. *P. W. Chapple-Hyam* **–**

TEJIME 3 b.g. Royal Applause 124 – Pizzicato 64 (Statoblest 120) [2009 p7.1g^2 p7.1g^3 f6g Dec 27] 42,000Y: half-brother to several winners, including smart Irish 5f to 1m (Ridgewood Pearl Stakes) winner Grecian Dancer (by Dansili) and useful 2002 2-y-o 5f (including Flying Childers) winner Wunders Dream (by Averti): dam 5f winner: best effort in maidens when head second at Wolverhampton on debut: should prove effective at 6f. *J. H. M. Gosden* **79**

TELL HALAF 2 b.c. (Mar 9) Oasis Dream 129 – Topkamp 104 (Pennekamp (USA) 130) [2009 6g 6s^6 Nov 7] unfurnished colt: second foal: half-brother to fairly useful 7f/1m winner Topazes (by Cadeaux Genereux): dam 5f (at 2 yrs)/6f winner: better effort in maidens when 5 lengths sixth to Adventure Story at Doncaster: should stay 7f: type to make a better 3-y-o. *M. L. W. Bell* **63 p**

TELLING STORIES (IRE) 3 b.f. Lucky Story (USA) 128 – Yes Virginia (USA) (Roanoke (USA)) [2009 56: p12.2g^4 f11g^6 Apr 21] modest maiden: stays 1½m: acts on all-weather. *B. D. Leavy* **53**

TELL ME A STORY 2 ch.f. (Apr 10) Lucky Story (USA) 128 – Cantina 103 (Tina's Pet 121) [2009 5v^2 5m* 6g Oct 23] £3,200Y: workmanlike filly: third foal: half-sister to 2 winners, including 2005 2-y-o 5f winner Miss Lovat (by Wizard King): dam won around 7f: won maiden at Beverley in July: off 3 months, well beaten in nursery at Ayr: should stay 6f. *M. Brittain* **68**

TEMPERENCE HALL (USA) 3 ch.g. Graeme Hall (USA) 119 – Sue's Temper (USA) (Temperence Hill (USA)) [2009 69: 7m 9.7f 7g 8.3m p6g^3 p6m^2 6g a7.5g^2 p7g^3 Sep 2] tall, useful-looking gelding: fair maiden: stays 7.5f: acts on all-weather and good to firm going: visored last 6 outings: inconsistent: sold 7,500 gns. *J. R. Best* **65**

TEMPLAR KNIGHT 3 b.g. Montjeu (IRE) 137 – Vas Y Carla (USA) 80 (Gone West (USA)) [2009 9.9g 10m^4 9d p10.7g Nov 25] compact gelding: first foal: dam, maiden (raced only at 7f/1m), out of Oaks winner Lady Carla: fair maiden: easily best effort when fourth at Windsor on final start for Sir Michael Stoute (then sold £18,500): slowly away first 2 outings. *Gordon Elliott, Ireland* **71**

TEMPLE FAIR (USA) 2 b.g. (Jan 31) Tiger Hill (IRE) 127 – Forty Marchanta (ARG) (Roar (USA) 116) [2009 p7.1g 8m^4 8g Oct 21] best effort in maidens when 1¼ lengths fourth to Rigidity at Yarmouth: bred to stay 1¼m+: gelded after final start. *M. Johnston* **57**

TEMPLE QUEEN 2 ch.f. (Apr 9) Sulamani (IRE) 130 – Indiana Blues 90 (Indian Ridge 123) [2009 p8m^5 p8m^4 p7.1g^6 6g Oct 19] leggy filly: first foal: dam, 6f winner, half-sister to useful 5f winners Siren's Gift and Speed Cop, out of smart sprinter Blue Siren: fair maiden: seems to stay 1m: sold 800 gns. *S. Kirk* **66**

TEMPLETUOHY MAX (IRE) 4 b.g. Orpen (USA) 116 – Eladawn (IRE) 57 (Ela-Mana-Mou 132) [2009 72: p9.5g* p9.5g^2 p9.5g 10.2f^4 9m* 8m^4 10m 10.3m 9.8g^4 8m^4 10m^4 Oct 3] leggy, lengthy gelding: fair handicapper: won at Wolverhampton in January and Redcar in May: best form at 1m/9f: acts on polytrack and firm going: visored. *J. D. Bethell* **82**

TEMPLET (USA) 9 b.g. Souvenir Copy (USA) 113 – Two Step Trudy (USA) (Capote (USA)) [2009 –§: p12g 10.1g 11.5g Jul 2] stocky gelding: little form since 2007: usually wears headgear: ungenuine. *T. T. Clement* **– §**

TENACESTREAM (CAN) 2 b.c. (Feb 17) Grand Slam (USA) 120 – Heart Lake (CAN) (Unbridled (USA) 128) [2009 p6m* p6m^4 Dec 30] $115,000Y: third foal: half-brother to winner in USA by Lion Heart: dam unraced half-sister to dam of 2-y-o Free Judgement: fairly useful form when winning maiden at Lingfield in November by ¾ length from Passion Overflow: looked awkward when last of 4 in nursery at same course: will stay 7f: should still improve. *J. R. Best* **81 p**

TENACIOUS 5 b.m. Pivotal 124 – Invincible 76 (Slip Anchor 136) [2009 f5g Mar 27] 8,000 2-y-o: ex-Italian mare: second foal: dam, 11f winner, half-sister to useful dam of 7-y-o Icelandic: maiden: left R. Oliviero in Italy, last in handicap at Southwell only outing in 2009 (tongue tied): stays 7.5f: acts on good to firm ground. *F. Sheridan* **–**

TENANCY (IRE) 5 b.g. Rock of Gibraltar (IRE) 133 – Brush Strokes (Cadeaux Genereux 131) [2009 59: p6g 5g f5g 5v^2 5.1g 5g^5 5s f6g f5f^4 f6d^5 Dec 29] close-coupled gelding: has round action: modest handicapper: left R. C. Guest after fourth start: best at 5f/6f: acts on all-weather and heavy ground: tried in cheekpieces/blinkers: none too consistent. *S. A. Harris* **57**

TEN DAY WONDER 4 gr.f. Daylami (IRE) 138 – Tenable (Polish Precedent (USA) 131) [2009 10m Jul 20] 12,000Y, 1,100 3-y-o: sturdy filly: third foal: half-sister to 1m/9.5f winner Milla's Rocket (by Galileo): dam unraced half-sister to very smart performer up to 13.4f Day Flight and to dam of high-class 1m/1¼m performer Phoenix Tower: second in bumper on debut before shaping as if amiss in similar event next time: 100/1 and backward, eighth in maiden at Windsor: will be suited by 1½m. *R. W. Price* **54**

TENDER CHARM (USA) 3 b. or br.g. Malibu Moon (USA) – Tender Years (CAN) (Regal Classic (CAN)) [2009 p6g^3 6m^6 6m p8g 8m Jul 25] rather leggy gelding: fair maiden: best effort on second start: tried visored. *R. M. Beckett* **66**

TENDER MOMENTS 5 br.m. Tomba 119 – Cherish Me 88 (Polar Falcon (USA) 126) [2009 64: 10.1s f8g 9.2d^3 12.1m^2 12.1g^6 13.1d 13.8g Oct 17] workmanlike mare: modest handicapper: stays 1½m: acts on soft and good to firm ground: inconsistent. *B. Smart* **57**

TENDER PROCESS (IRE) 6 b.g. Monashee Mountain (USA) 115 – Appledorn 99 (Doulab (USA) 115) [2009 72: f7s^4 p6g^3 p7.1g* f6g* f6g f7g Apr 21] big, strong gelding: fair performer: won handicap at Wolverhampton (hung left) in January and claimer at Southwell (claimed from R. Fahey £5,000) in February: stays 7f: acts on all-weather and heavy going: usually blinkered/visored: has found little. *J. R. Boyle* **74**

TEN DOWN 4 b.g. Royal Applause 124 – Upstream 79 (Prince Sabo 123) [2009 83: p5.1g p5m* p5g p5g^5 p5g^2 p5g* 5g^4 5f 5g p5g 5m 5f^3 5m p5g p5m p5f^6 Dec 19] close-coupled gelding: fair handicapper at best: won at Lingfield in January and March: below **78 d**

form after next start: best at 5f: acts on polytrack and firm going: tried blinkered: races prominently: none too consistent. *M. Quinn*

TENEMENT (IRE) 5 b.g. Mull of Kintyre (USA) 114 – Afifah 66 (Nashwan (USA) **60** 135) [2009 60: p10g^{5} p10g^{5} p10g Jan 16] strong gelding: modest maiden: stays 1¼m: acts on polytrack: tried in cheekpieces: none too consistent. *Jamie Poulton*

TENESSEE 2 b.c. (Jan 29) Nayef (USA) 129 – Shukran 99 (Hamas (IRE) 125§) [2009 **82 p** 8g^{3} Oct 8] tall, rather unfurnished, attractive colt: second foal: half-brother to 5-y-o Hazytoo: dam 2-y-o 5f/6f winner: 12/1, promising 4 lengths third to Dancing David in maiden at Newbury, keeping on well: should stay 1¼m: sure to improve. *C. G. Cox*

TENGA VENGA 2 ch.g. (Jan 23) Beat Hollow 126 – Fanny's Fancy 99 (Groom **51** Dancer (USA) 128) [2009 6m f8g p6m f7f^{4} f7f^{4} f8d Dec 29] modest maiden: stays 7f: acts on fibresand: tried in cheekpieces. *P. S. McEntee*

TENJACK KING 4 b.g. Kyllachy 129 – Rash (Pursuit of Love 124) [2009 81: 8.9d **–** 8.5m f14d Dec 29] good-topped gelding: fairly useful performer at best: well held in 2009. *Joss Saville*

TEN POLE TUDOR 4 b.g. Royal Applause 124 – Amaniy (USA) 96 (Dayjur (USA) **68 §** 137) [2009 81d: p9.5g^{6} p7.1g^{2} p7g p8.6g^{4} p8.6g^{6} p7g f8g^{2} 10g^{4} p9.5g^{2} p8.6g 7m f8g^{4} 7.1m^{6} p7.1g^{6} p8.6g f8f p8.6m* p9.5g p9.5g f8f* f8f^{4} p9.5g^{2} p8.6g^{2} Dec 28] lengthy gelding: fair performer: won sellers at Wolverhampton in November and Southwell in December: stays easy 8.6f: acts on all-weather, good to firm and good to soft going: tried blinkered, usually in cheekpieces: held up: not one to trust. *R. A. Harris*

TEN SPOT (IRE) 4 b.f. Intikhab (USA) 135 – Allergy 99 (Alzao (USA) 117) [2009 **56** 64: p9.5g^{3} p9.5g^{6} p16g f12g^{3} Feb 12] sturdy filly: modest performer: stays 9.5f: acts on all-weather: usually wears headgear: tongue tied: suspect temperament. *Stef Liddiard*

TENTEARS 3 b.f. Cadeaux Genereux 131 – Garmoucheh (USA) 99 (Silver Hawk **80** (USA) 123) [2009 8m 8m p7m^{3} Aug 20] lengthy, quite attractive filly: sister to fairly useful 6f/1m winner Dubai Power: dam 7f (at 2 yrs) to 1¼m winner: easily best effort in maidens when third at Lingfield, again looking awkward: best effort at 7f on polytrack: virtually refused to race second outing. *H. R. A. Cecil*

TEN TO THE DOZEN 6 b. or ch.g. Royal Applause 124 – Almost Amber (USA) 88 **54** (Mt Livermore (USA)) [2009 66, a57: p8g^{3} Jan 18] strong, close-coupled gelding: just modest form sole outing in 2009: stays easy 1m: acts on all-weather, firm and good to soft going: tried blinkered. *S. T. Mason*

TEPMOKEA (IRE) 3 ch.c. Noverre (USA) 125 – Eroica (GER) (Highest Honor (FR) **84** 124) [2009 77: 10.3m^{2} 12s^{2} 10.1g^{2} 10.4g 9.9f^{5} Aug 29] strong, workmanlike colt: fairly useful handicapper: runner-up first 3 starts in 2009: left K. R. Burke before final outing: stays 1½m: acts on polytrack, firm and soft going: often front runner: genuine. *R. A. Fahey*

TERENZIUM (IRE) 7 b.g. Cape Cross (IRE) 129 – Tatanka (ITY) (Luge 113) [2009 **62** –: 14.1m^{6} 16m^{3} 16g^{6} 16.5s^{2} 14.1m 13v* 18g Oct 19] leggy gelding: modest handicapper: won at Hamilton (amateurs) in August: stays 2m: acts on polytrack, heavy and good to firm ground: tried visored, wears cheekpieces nowadays. *Micky Hammond*

TERMAGANT (IRE) 2 b.f. (Jan 28) Powerscourt 126 – Rock Salt (Selkirk (USA) **111 p** 129) [2009 7m* 7v* Aug 30]

Irish racing has been hit particularly hard by the consequences of the global banking crisis, with the prospect of even worse to come going into 2010. Horse Racing Ireland announced severe cuts in the funding for the sport in late-December, with chief executive Brian Kavanagh warning that the country's equine industry could 'unravel' over the coming years due, in part, to a series of reductions in Government support. 'HRI estimates that up to 1,500 jobs have been lost in the racing and breeding industry in the last eighteen months and, regrettably, the measures being announced will lead to further job losses,' explained Kavanagh, revealing at the same time that there was also evidence of stallions being moved from Ireland as a result of the crisis. In amongst all the gloom, veteran trainer Kevin Prendergast bucked the trend by continuing the revival of fortunes he has enjoyed in recent years, topping the £1m prize money mark for the third time in the last four seasons, his leading earners in the latest campaign being the unbeaten two-year-olds Kingsfort and Termagant, both bargain buys who won Group 1s. 'My policy at the sales is to buy what you can afford—you get lucky sometimes,' Prendergast

Moyglare Stud Stakes, the Curragh—a surprise result as 16/1-shot Termagant (noseband) gets the better of 66/1-shot Famous; odds-on Lillie Langtry (partially hidden by winner) finishes third

told the audience attending the Irish Racing Awards in December, when he picked up the Outstanding Achievement award. The seventy-seven-year-old has already made a healthy return on Kingsfort and Termagant, who cost just €36,000 and €34,000 respectively at the 2008 Goffs Sportsman Yearling Sale. Kingsfort was purchased privately by Godolphin after winning the Vincent O'Brien National Stakes at the Curragh in September, and Termagant, who will remain in Prendergast's care for 2010, also changed hands, being bought by Swiss owner Jorg Vasicek before her win in the Moyglare Stud Stakes.

The Vasicek maroon and blue colours are probably best known for their association with successful Francois Doumen-trained jumpers such as Bilboa and Millenium Royal, but the owner has had horses with Prendergast before. The latest Moyglare win for Kevin Prendergast was his stable's fourth in the race, following Milly Whiteway in 1973, Arctique Royale in 1980 and Miss Beatrix in 2006. Prendergast has a good record with fillies and has also saddled four winners of the Pretty Polly Stakes and won the Irish One Thousand Guineas twice, with Arctique Royale in 1981 and Pidget in 1972. The Irish Guineas is reportedly Termagant's first target in 2010, though she would be an interesting runner if she was turned out for the Newmarket version, for which her ante-post odds of 20/1 would look good value if she was a confirmed runner. The Aidan O'Brien-trained Lillie Langtry started odds on in the seven-runner Moyglare, but she could manage only third (beaten four and a quarter lengths) behind 16/1-shot Termagant, who made smooth headway under a patient ride before staying on strongly to beat the Ballydoyle second string Famous (66/1) by two and a half lengths. Although Lillie Langtry was possibly unsuited by the heavy ground, the Moyglare still looked an up-to-scratch renewal despite the fact that Belle Genius in 1995 was the last winner to start at longer odds (20/1) than Termagant.

According to her jockey Declan McDonogh, Termagant 'doesn't do a whole lot at home but she certainly saves it for the track.' This presumably explains why

Mr J. Vasicek's "Termagant"

she had also been largely unconsidered in the betting on her debut in a seven-furlong fillies' maiden at Leopardstown two and a half months earlier, when starting 14/1 fourth choice in a field of five in which the betting was dominated by the once-raced Anaverna. Fellow debutante Cabaret chased Termagant home without, in truth, ever really posing a serious threat to the easy two-length winner, who acted well under the firmish conditions despite displaying quite a high knee action. Cabaret went on to frank the form by winning her next two starts, including the Group 3 Silver Flash Stakes back at Leopardstown in July. Prendergast is reportedly reluctant to risk Termagant again on firm ground, which partly explains why he is planning to miss the Newmarket classic. His 2008 Moyglare runner-up Shimah was retired after returning jarred up when down the field behind Ghanaati in the latest One Thousand Guineas and didn't run again.

Termagant is the only winner from just four runners in Britain and Ireland so far by Coolmore stallion Powerscourt, who is now based in Ireland after having begun his stud career in the States. He also had a couple of winners on American soil in 2009 from a sizeable first crop, though the chances are that his progeny won't really come into their own until given the chance to tackle longer trips. Powerscourt's biggest success came on his final start, when he won the Arlington Million, twelve months after he had been controversially demoted to fourth in the same race after causing interference. Powerscourt wasn't always an entirely straightforward ride and he was often equipped with headgear in the later part of his career, but he did show largely consistent form at a variety of distances (effective at up to a mile and three quarters) in four seasons with Aidan O'Brien, when he raced in seven different countries, his other big-race wins including the 2003 Great Voltigeur Stakes and the 2004 Tattersalls Gold Cup. The distaff side of Termagant's pedigree, also suggests that she will stay a good deal further than seven furlongs. Her dam Rock Salt was placed twice at up to eleven furlongs from four starts as a three-year-old for Criquette Head-Maarek and has already produced an above-average performer in Termagant's year-older half-brother Splinter Cell (by Johannesburg), who showed useful form at up to a mile and a quarter in the latest season, winning three times. The exploits of Splinter Cell and Termagant resulted in Rock Salt's next foal, a colt named Planet Waves (by Red Ransom), fetching 100,000 guineas as a yearling at the December Sales. Rock Salt raced in the Khalid Abdulla colours and her family has been productive for Juddmonte Farms, who were also the breeders of Powerscourt. Rock Salt is a sister to the Prix Eugene Adam winner Kirkwall, who also won in Grade 2 company at a mile in the States later in his career. Third dam Populi is the grandam of Distant Music, the leading two-year-old of 1999 and third in the following year's Champion Stakes. Populi, incidentally, was a half-sister to the 1980 Belmont Stakes winner Temperence Hill and proved an extremely successful broodmare, her ten winners (from thirteen runners) including the prolific Vanlandingham, whose win in the 1985 Washington DC International Stakes helped him to the award that year as America's Champion Older Horse.

Termagant (IRE) (b.f. Jan 28, 2007)	Powerscourt (b 2000)	Sadler's Wells (b 1981)	Northern Dancer
			Fairy Bridge
		Rainbow Lake (b 1990)	Rainbow Quest
			Rockfest
	Rock Salt (ch 2001)	Selkirk (ch 1988)	Sharpen Up
			Annie Edge
		Kamkova (b 1984)	Northern Dancer
			Populi

Backing up the evidence provided by her breeding, Termagant shaped on both her starts as if she will prove well suited by a step-up in trip at three. Her optimum distance is likely to be further than a mile and she might well make up into an Irish Oaks contender. She seems versatile with regards to ground and looks a very smart prospect. *Kevin Prendergast, Ireland*

TERMINATE (GER) 7 ch.g. Acatenango (GER) 127 – Taghareed (USA) 93 (Shadeed (USA) 135) [2009 68: p12g^{2} p13.9g^{2} p13g 11.7m^{2} 11.7f* 12g^{3} 13.8m^{2} p12g* 10.2g^{5} p12.2g^{2} 11.1v^{3} 14m^{4} 13.8m 10g^{6} 9d Oct 28] leggy gelding: fair performer: won handicap at Bath in May and seller at Lingfield in June: claimed from Ian Williams £6,000 after tenth start: well below form after: stays 13.8f: acts on polytrack, firm and good to soft going: tried in cheekpieces/blinkers: often tongue tied: held up (sometimes slowly away): often takes good hold. *A. Berry* **66 d**

TERRACOTTA WARRIOR 3 ch.g. Dubai Destination (USA) 127 – Tamesis (IRE) 55 (Fasliyev (USA) 120) [2009 46: f11g f8g 9g^{6} 8.3d Jul 22] small gelding: poor maiden: stays 9f: tried blinkered. *J. Jay* **49**

TERRASINI (FR) 4 gr.g. Linamix (FR) 127 – Trazando (Forzando 122) [2009 61: 21.6m^{4} Apr 20] sturdy gelding: modest maiden: stays 21.5f: acts on firm ground. *J. Howard Johnson* **63**

TERRYMENE PRINCE 3 b.g. Bollin Terry 88 – Princess Ismene 61 (Sri Pekan (USA) 117) [2009 12m 9d^{6} 10.1d 12.1m 9.8m f8g Jul 7] leggy gelding: little form: visored last 3 outings. *L. A. Mullaney* **–**

TERTIARY (USA) 2 b.c. (Mar 12) Singspiel (IRE) 133 – Allez Les Trois (USA) 114 (Riverman (USA) 131) [2009 8d* f8m^{5} Nov 6] half-brother to several winners, including very smart French 1¼m/1½m winner (including Prix du Jockey Club) Anabaa Blue (by Anabaa) and smart 1m (at 2 yrs)/1¼m winner Reunite (by Kingmambo): dam, French 10.5f winner, half-sister to Arc winner Urban Sea, herself dam of Sea The Stars and Galileo: better effort when winning maiden at Brighton in October by head from **82 p**

Activate, rallying: well held in nursery at Southwell (probably amiss and/or unsuited by surface): bred to be suited by 1¼m+: remains open to improvement. *Saeed bin Suroor*

TESSERAE 3 b.f. Reset (AUS) 124 – Moxby (Efisio 120) [2009 11.5g[5] 10.4g[6] 11.9g[3] 11.7f[3] 12.1g[2] 12.5m[4] 11.9d p12g[5] p12.2g[4] Dec 7] fair maiden: regressed after debut: stays 1½m. *A. B. Haynes* **65 d**

TESSIE BEAR 4 b.f. Red Ransom (USA) – Macaerleon (IRE) (Caerleon (USA) 132) [2009 f12g Apr 21] little form. *E. J. Creighton* **–**

TESSLAM 2 ch.g. (Mar 21) Singspiel (IRE) 133 – Rowaasi 103 (Green Desert (USA) 127) [2009 7d 7m[2] p7.1g[4] Nov 2] well-made gelding: fifth foal: half-brother to 3 winners abroad, including Swedish 7f winner Mesyaal (by Alhaarth): dam 2-y-o 5f winner: easily best effort in maidens when head second to Mr Irons at Redcar: raced only at 7f, should prove as effective at 6f: gelded after final start. *M. A. Jarvis* **91 +**

TEVEZ 4 b.g. Sakhee (USA) 136 – Sosumi 101 (Be My Chief (USA) 122) [2009 78: f8g[6] 10g[3] 10.9d p12g[4] 9.9m 7g[2] 8g 10m[3] f8g[6] Aug 25] strong gelding: fair performer: left Amy Weaver after reappearance: stays 1¼m: acts on all-weather and good to firm ground: tried in headgear/tongue tie. *D. Donovan* **66**

TEWIN WOOD 2 ch.g. (Mar 10) Zaha (CAN) 106 – Green Run (USA) (Green Dancer (USA) 132) [2009 7g 7g[4] 6g[3] p7.1g* p7.1g[6] p7m Dec 6] fourth foal: half-brother to German 6f/6.5f winner Avertigo (by Averti): dam French 7f/1m winner: fair performer: trained by M. Squance on debut: won nursery at Wolverhampton in November: raced too freely last 2 starts: stays 7f: acts on polytrack. *A. Bailey* **77**

TEXAN STAR (IRE) 2 b.c. (Mar 5) Galileo (IRE) 134 – Guignol (IRE) 80 (Anita's Prince 126) [2009 7s[2] 7d Aug 1] 85,000Y: close-coupled colt: fourth foal: dam, Irish 5f winner, half-sister to dam of smart miler Bachir: much better effort in maidens when promising 2½ lengths second to Emerald Commander at Newbury: seemed amiss at Goodwood (strong favourite): should stay 1m. *J. H. M. Gosden* **84**

TEXAS QUEEN 2 b.f. (Apr 21) Shamardal (USA) 129 – Min Asl Wafi (IRE) 75 (Octagonal (NZ) 126) [2009 6m[6] 7g[4] p7g[2] 6m[3] 7m p6g[3] p5.1g[3] Dec 26] neat filly: second foal: dam, ran once (third at 7f), half-sister to very smart miler Zafeen: fair maiden: likely to prove best up to 7f: acts on polytrack and good to firm ground. *M. R. Channon* **69**

THAAHIRA (USA) 2 b.f. (Feb 23) Dynaformer (USA) – Mehthaaf (USA) 121 (Nureyev (USA) 131) [2009 7d[5] Oct 12] half-sister to several winners, including smart 1¼m winner Najah (by Nashwan) and useful 7f (including at 2 yrs)/1m winner Tasdeer (by Rahy): dam, 6f (at 2 yrs) to 1m (Irish 1000 Guineas) winner, closely related to July Cup winner Elnadim: 14/1 and green, encouraging 5¾ lengths fifth to Thrill in maiden at Salisbury, considerately handled: will do better. *M. A. Jarvis* **77 p**

THABAAT 5 ch.g. Pivotal 124 – Maraatib (IRE) 93 (Green Desert (USA) 127) [2009 64: p7g[4] p7g[6] p7g[5] p7g f7d Mar 10] rather leggy, useful-looking gelding: modest handicapper: should stay 1m: acts on polytrack, best turf effort on good ground: blinkered: tongue tied final outing. *J. M. Bradley* **59**

THABIT (USA) 3 ch.c. Mr Greeley (USA) 122 – Matsue (USA) (Lure (USA) 131) [2009 p8g[5] May 4] $800,000Y: good-topped, attractive colt: first foal: dam, French 9f winner, out of high-class 1m/1¼m performer Kooyonga: 4/1 from 7/1, shaped well when 7¾ lengths fifth to Uniquely Poised in maiden at Kempton, not unduly knocked about and getting hang of things late: will improve. *M. A. Jarvis* **75 p**

THALIWARRU 2 b.g. (Jan 24) Barathea (IRE) 127 – Autumn Pearl 102 (Orpen (USA) 116) [2009 5g 6g[6] 7d 7g[2] p7g Oct 8] workmanlike gelding: modest maiden: left G. Margarson after fourth start: stays 7f: has looked difficult ride. *J. R. Gask* **59**

THAT BOY RONALDO 3 b.f. Pyrus (USA) 106 – Red Millennium (IRE) 102 (Tagula (IRE) 116) [2009 52§: f7d[4] f8g Feb 1] workmanlike filly: poor maiden: stayed 7f: acted on fibresand and good to soft going: ungenuine: dead. *A. Berry* **37 §**

THATLITTLECOLT 2 ch.g. (Feb 4) Ishiguru (USA) 114 – Bhima (Polar Falcon (USA) 126) [2009 f5m p6m f7d[6] Dec 29] well held in maidens: tried in cheekpieces. *D. H. Brown* **–**

THAT'LL DO NICELY (IRE) 6 b.g. Bahhare (USA) 122 – Return Again (IRE) 81 (Top Ville 129) [2009 68: p8.6g p9.5g[3] f11g* 12.4m[3] 14m* 14m[3] 14m[4] 14g[4] 13.8g 12.5s 12.4g Sep 30] fair handicapper: won at Southwell in March and Musselburgh in May: stays 1¾m: acts on polytrack and good to firm going: has found little: held up. *N. G. Richards* **71**

THAT'LLDONOWTHEN (IRE) 2 ch.c. (Apr 17) Chineur (FR) 123 – Credit Crunch (IRE) 51 (Caerleon (USA) 132) [2009 6d 6g 5m^5 6d^6 5.1g^6 5.2g^5 p7.1g^6 Sep 3] poor maiden: stays 6f: tried in cheekpieces: sold £2,500. *J. S. Moore* **48**

THAT'S MY STYLE 2 gr.f. (Mar 20) Dalakhani (IRE) 133 – Pearl Dance (USA) 102 (Nureyev (USA) 131) [2009 8g Oct 23] third foal: half-sister to useful 2007 2-y-o 7f winner Ridge Dance (by Selkirk): dam, 2-y-o 6f winner (stayed 1m), half-sister to dam of Melbourne Cup winner Delta Blues: 33/1 and very green, signs of ability when down the field in maiden at Doncaster. *J. H. M. Gosden* **–**

THAT'S SHOWBIZ 2 pt.g. (Apr 7) I Was Framed (USA) – Angelic Dancer 49 (Komaite (USA)) [2009 p8g Dec 7] sixth foal: dam 6f winner: 20/1 and green, seventh to Hidden Glory in maiden at Lingfield, hanging right. *W. J. Knight* **56**

THAUMATOLOGY (USA) 3 ch.f. Distorted Humor (USA) 117 – Crystal Ballet (USA) (Royal Academy (USA) 130) [2009 62: f5g^6 f7d^4 p6g f8g Mar 11] regressive maiden: barely stays 1m: raced only on all-weather: tried in cheekpieces/tongue tie: sold 5,000 gns, reportedly in foal to Pastoral Pursuits. *S. Parr* **38**

THEATRE STREET (IRE) 3 b.f. Invincible Spirit (IRE) 121 – Markova (IRE) 78 (Marju (IRE) 127) [2009 73: p5g^2 p5g* p6g^3 5.2d 6m* 6m^6 Sep 10] good-topped filly: fairly useful performer: won maiden at Lingfield in January and, having left J. Noseda 13,000 gns, handicap at Epsom in August, making all: will prove best kept to 5f/6f: acts on polytrack and good to firm going: temperament under suspicion. *S. Dow* **84**

THE BEAR 6 ch.g. Rambling Bear 115 – Precious Girl 76 (Precious Metal 106) [2009 80: f5m 5m 6g 6g 5d^3 5g^6 5s* 5s* 5g 5g^4 6m 7.2v Oct 31] angular gelding: fair handicapper nowadays: left A. G. Foster after second start, D. Nolan after fourth: successful twice at Hamilton in August: below form after: best at 5f/6f: acts on any going: tried visored: front runner. *Miss L. A. Perratt* **72**

THE BEAT IS ON 3 b.f. Beat All (USA) 120 – Lady Ezzabella (Ezzoud (IRE) 126) [2009 –: p12m p12g Oct 20] leggy filly: no form. *A. W. Carroll* **–**

THEBES 4 ch.g. Cadeaux Genereux 131 – See You Later 98 (Emarati (USA) 74) [2009 98: p6g* p7g^4 6m p7g 6m^2 6g^3 6f^2 6m^4 6d^5 6.1m* 6d 7m 6d 6m 6d 6m 7m^4 7m p6m^6 Nov 3] strong, lengthy gelding: useful handicapper: won at Wolverhampton in March and Chepstow (beat Barons Spy 6 lengths) in July: has won at 7f, best at 6f: acts on all-weather, firm and good to soft going: races prominently: gelded after final start. *M. Johnston* **100 a95**

THE BETCHWORTH KID 4 b.g. Tobougg (IRE) 125 – Runelia (Runnett 125) [2009 111: 14.1m^2 13s^3 13.3d^3 14g^5 16.1d 16g^3 14m 14.1s* 16m^5 Sep 27] rather leggy gelding: useful performer: won minor event at Salisbury in September by nose from Basaltico: mostly creditable efforts otherwise, including third to Alandi in listed race at Navan and seventh to Sesenta in Ebor (Handicap) at York second/seventh outings: barely stays 2m: has form on polytrack and good to firm going, all wins on good or softer: no easy ride (held up), but consistent: joined A. King, fairly useful form over hurdles. *M. L. W. Bell* **108**

THE BLUE DOG (IRE) 2 b.f. (Apr 15) High Chaparral (IRE) 132 – Jules (IRE) 76 (Danehill (USA) 126) [2009 8.3m f7f^4 p7.1g p7.1g^6 p8.6g^6 Dec 19] 30,000Y: sturdy, good-bodied filly: fourth foal: half-sister to 5-y-o Golden Desert and winner in Hungary by Fasliyev: dam, 7f winner, out of US Grade 1 2-y-o 6f/7f winner Before Dawn: modest maiden: not at all knocked about third/fourth starts: should stay 1m. *George Baker* **53**

THE BOAT SHED (IRE) 3 b.g. Barathea (IRE) 127 – Silver Hut (USA) 80 (Silver Hawk (USA) 123) [2009 11s f11g^5 10d May 16] sturdy gelding: well held in maidens: gelded after final start. *B. W. Duke* **–**

THE BULL HAYES (IRE) 3 b.c. Sadler's Wells (USA) 132 – No Review (USA) (Nodouble (USA)) [2009 92: 10g^4 10s* 10v^3 12g 12g^5 12v^2 12d Sep 16] sturdy colt: smart performer: won maiden at Navan in April: good placed efforts in Gallinule Stakes at the Curragh (1½ lengths third to Grand Ducal) and listed race at Galway (½-length second to Aliyfa) after: ran poorly in minor event at Listowel final start: stays 1½m: acts on heavy going: in cheekpieces/blinkers last 4 starts: not one to rely on. *Mrs J. Harrington, Ireland* **111 §**

THE BULLY WEE 3 b.c. Bishop of Cashel 122 – Red Barons Lady (IRE) (Electric 126) [2009 –p: f8g^3 10m f11g 8m 9.7f 9m Jul 8] close-coupled colt: regressive maiden: should stay 11f: acts on fibresand. *J. Jay* **66 d**

THE CANNY DOVE (USA) 3 b.g. Monashee Mountain (USA) 115 – Who's Sorry Now (USA) (Ogygian (USA)) [2009 –: f8g f8g f8g^6 p6g^6 6d Jun 17] leggy gelding: poor form: tried blinkered. *T. D. Barron* **38**

THE CAPED CRUSADER (IRE) 2 b.g. (Mar 31) Cape Cross (IRE) 129 – Pharisee (IRE) 99 (Rainbow Quest (USA) 134) [2009 6f 7m^6 7m^5 7.5m Jul 28] good-topped gelding: modest maiden: stays 7f: gelded after final start. *T. P. Tate* **55**

THE CARDINAL'S HAT (FR) 2 b.c. (Jan 12) High Yield (USA) 121 – Rince Deas (IRE) 53 (Alzao (USA) 117) [2009 5.1f^3 6.1g p8f p8m Sep 23] modest maiden: best effort on debut: tongue tied: sold 4,000 gns. *P. Winkworth* **58**

THE CARLTON CANNES 5 b.h. Grand Lodge (USA) 125 – Miss Riviera Golf 106 (Hernando (FR) 127) [2009 97: p12g^5 Apr 4] compact horse: fairly useful handicapper, lightly raced: stayed 2m: acted on polytrack: dead. *M. L. W. Bell* **93**

THE CAYTERERS 7 b.g. Cayman Kai (IRE) 114 – Silky Smooth (IRE) (Thatching 131) [2009 82: p7g^4 p7g^6 8.3m^3 8m^5 8.3g* 8.3m* 10g* 10m^4 8.1m^6 9m p10m^2 Nov 28] angular gelding: useful handicapper: much improved in 2009, completing hat-trick at Windsor in June/July, beating Resurge by neck final occasion: creditable effort after when length second to Bound By Honour at Lingfield: best at 1m/1¼m nowadays: acts on polytrack, firm and good to soft going: tried in cheekpieces/blinkers: patiently ridden. *A. W. Carroll* **100**

THE CHEKA (IRE) 3 b.c. Xaar 132 – Veiled Beauty (USA) (Royal Academy (USA) 130) [2009 105p: 7s* Jul 17] rangy, good-topped colt: useful performer: has had just 3 races: won minor event at Newbury in July by neck from Ashram, staying on strongly from rear: looked smart prospect, but suffered hairline fracture of near-fore cannon bone after: will stay 1m: raced only on good going or softer (acts on soft). *Eve Johnson Houghton* **107**

THE CHIP CHOPMAN (IRE) 7 b.g. Sri Pekan (USA) 117 – Firstrusseofsummer (USA) (Summer Squall (USA)) [2009 58: 12g^3 14d 14d p13.9m Nov 28] modest handicapper: left Seamus O'Donnell in Ireland prior to final start: stays 2m: acts on heavy and good to firm ground: usually tongue tied for previous stable: wore cheekpieces third start. *R. A. Harris* **52**

THE CITY KID (IRE) 6 b.m. Danetime (IRE) 121 – Unfortunate 55§ (Komaite (USA)) [2009 68: f7d^5 p6m^6 7.1d p7.1g f7m^5 p7.1m^3 f7g^6 p7m^6 Dec 30] leggy mare: modest handicapper: left Gay Kelleway after reappearance: best short of 1¼m: acts on all-weather and heavy going: has worn headgear: held up. *G. D. Blake* **58**

THE COACH 3 ch.g. Central Park (IRE) 123 – E Minor (IRE) 86 (Blushing Flame (USA) 109) [2009 p8.6g p8.6m p8.6g p13.9g Nov 27] no form in maidens at Wolverhampton. *T. Wall* **–**

THE COMPOSER 7 b.g. Royal Applause 124 – Superspring (Superlative 118) [2009 64: p16g 11.5g 16g^4 14.1m^4 16m 17.2m^3 16d Oct 11] good-bodied gelding: poor handicapper nowadays: stays 17f: acts on polytrack, soft and good to firm ground. *M. Blanshard* **46**

THE CONFESSOR 2 b.c. (Mar 12) Piccolo 121 – Twilight Mistress 84 (Bin Ajwaad (IRE) 119) [2009 6.1m 6d^3 6g^3 Oct 19] £14,000Y: strong colt: third foal: half-brother to 3-y-o Night Affair and 5-y-o Shaded Edge: dam 5f to 7f winner: similar form when third in maidens at Goodwood (to Carnaby Street) and Pontefract (to Rock 'N' Royal): not certain to stay beyond 6f. *H. Candy* **71**

THE CUCKOO 3 b.g. Invincible Spirit (IRE) 121 – Aravonian 82 (Night Shift (USA)) **–**
[2009 72: p5g^5 f5g^4 p5g^2 5.1m p6g 5m 5.1s Nov 4] fair performer at best: well below **a66**
form after third outing in 2009: should prove best at 5f: acts on all-weather. *M. Quinn*

THE DESERT SAINT 3 b.g. Dubai Destination (USA) 127 – Maria Theresa (Primo Dominie 121) [2009 74: 6m^4 7.1v 7m p7g Jul 15] angular, useful-looking gelding: fair maiden: reportedly fractured hock after final outing at 2 yrs: well held after return: should stay 7f: tried visored: sold 1,800 gns, sent to Holland. *A. M. Balding* **74**

THE DIAL HOUSE 3 b.g. Tagula (IRE) 116 – Marliana (IRE) (Mtoto 134) [2009 82: p9.5g^5 8.1m 10f p10m^3 p10g^5 p12m^3 p10m p10m^4 Dec 16] strong gelding: fair performer: in-and-out form in 2009: stays 1¼m: acts on polytrack and good to firm going: tried tongue tied. *J. A. Osborne* **79**

THE DUCKING STOOL 2 ch.f. (Jan 27) Where Or When (IRE) 124 – Dance Sequel 54 (Selkirk (USA) 129) [2009 7m 6g f7g Oct 18] big filly: first foal: dam, ran 3 times, out of Lowther Stakes winner Dance Sequence: no form in maidens. *H. J. Collingridge* **–**

THE FIFTH MEMBER (IRE) 5 b.g. Bishop of Cashel 122 – Palace Soy (IRE) (Tagula (IRE) 116) [2009 98: 8m⁴ p8g⁴ 8.1m 8.9g 8d³ 10g² 10v p8.6g² p8.6g Nov 27] tall, close-coupled gelding: useful handicapper: ran well when fourth to Manassas in Spring Mile at Doncaster on reappearance: creditable efforts after only when placed: stays easy 1¼m: acts on polytrack and any turf going: often races prominently. *J. R. Boyle* **98**

THEFILLYFROMEPSOM 3 b.f. Royal Academy (USA) 130 – For Love (USA) (Sultry Song (USA)) [2009 58: p7g p10g 7m 7g 6m Aug 5] modest maiden at best: well held in handicaps: best up to 1m: visored once. *P. M. Phelan* **55**

THEFLYINGSCOTTIE 7 gr.g. Paris House 123 – Miss Flossa (FR) (Big John (FR) 125) [2009 –: 12m May 24] modest handicapper at best: well held both starts on Flat since 2007: visored. *D. Shaw* **–**

THE FONZ 3 b.g. Oasis Dream 129 – Crystal Cavern (USA) 89 (Be My Guest (USA) 126) [2009 75: 8.5m* 10g³ 10m⁴ 12m² Jul 25] useful-looking gelding: fairly useful performer: won maiden at Beverley in April: good second in handicap at Ascot final outing, racing freely (gelded after): stays 1½m: raced only on polytrack and good/good to firm ground. *Sir Michael Stoute* **87**

THE FRYING PAN (IRE) 2 ch.f. (Apr 18) Barathea (IRE) 127 – Hello Mary (IRE) (Dolphin Street (FR) 125) [2009 p7g⁶ 7d 7g 8.3d f7f f8f Dec 11] £11,000 2-y-o: smallish filly: fifth foal: half-sister to Irish 2005 2-y-o 1m winner Crosshaven (by Cape Cross), later successful up to 9.5f in Switzerland: dam, Italian 5f winner (including at 2 yrs), half-sister to dam of very smart sprinter Moss Vale: no form: usually blinkered. *Dr J. D. Scargill* **–**

THE GALLOPING SHOE 4 b.g. Observatory (USA) 131 – My Way (IRE) (Marju (IRE) 127) [2009 85: 8.3g² p8g⁴ 8.1v 6g 7m⁴ 6g 6m³ 7m⁶ 6d³ 6d⁴ 7s⁴ Nov 7] rather leggy gelding: fairly useful handicapper: left J. Noseda 12,000 gns after tenth start: stays 1m: acts on polytrack, soft and good to firm going: consistent. *A. C. Whillans* **89**

THE GAME 4 b.g. Compton Place 125 – Emanant (Emarati (USA) 74) [2009 106: p6g⁴ Jan 17] strong gelding: useful handicapper at best: respectable fourth at Lingfield sole start in 2009: free-going sort, was best at 5f/6f: acted on polytrack, good to firm and good to soft ground: dead. *Tom Dascombe* **92**

THE GEESTER 5 b.g. Rambling Bear 115 – Cledeschamps 46 (Doc Marten 104) [2009 53, a66: f5g² f5g* p5.1g² f5g⁶ p5f Dec 19] strong gelding: fair handicapper on all-weather, modest at best on turf: won at Southwell in January: left S. R. Bowring prior to final start: best at 5f/6f: acts on all-weather (all wins on fibresand): blinkered, tried in cheekpieces/tongue tie: races prominently. *Stef Liddiard* **–** **a65**

THE GILLIE 2 b.g. (Apr 30) Pivotal 124 – Red Tiara (USA) 60 (Mr Prospector (USA)) [2009 6s⁶ Nov 7] 7,000 2-y-o: seventh foal: brother to US 5f (minor stakes) to 8.5f winner Red Diadem, closely related to 3-y-o Adorn and half-brother to 2 winners, including 1m winner Argent (by Barathea): dam, disappointing maiden, closely related to very smart Japanese sprinter Meiner Love out of 1000 Guineas runner-up Heart of Joy: 7/1 and green, 7¼ lengths sixth to London Gold in maiden at Doncaster: should improve. *R. A. Fahey* **59 p**

THEGIRLSGONEWILD (USA) 3 b. or br.f. Gone West (USA) – Coconut Girl (USA) (Cryptoclearance (USA)) [2009 60p: p8g 10.4v⁶ p10g Jun 6] sparely-made filly: regressive maiden. *H. J. L. Dunlop* **50**

THE GRAIG 5 b.g. Josr Algarhoud (IRE) 118 – Souadah (USA) (General Holme (USA) 128) [2009 56: p8.6g² p8g* p10g p8.6g³ f8d⁵ p9.5g* 10.9m⁶ 10f p8.6g p8g p8.6g Dec 14] leggy gelding: modest handicapper: won at Kempton in January and Wolverhampton in March: seems to stay 11f: acts on all-weather and firm ground: tried blinkered/tongue tied. *J. R. Holt* **61**

THE GREAT HUSK (IRE) 2 b.g. (Mar 17) Alamshar (IRE) 133 – Stardance (USA) (Rahy (USA) 115) [2009 7f 7d 7m⁴ p10m⁶ Dec 9] sturdy gelding: poor maiden: should stay at least 1m. *J. S. Moore* **45**

THE GREY ONE (IRE) 6 gr.g. Dansili 127 – Marie Dora (FR) 86 (Kendor (FR) 122) [2009 73: p10g 8m⁶ 7m 8.3g 8m 10.2g 8.1g p8.6g⁶ p8.6g² p8g 8.1g p9.5g² p8.6m⁴ p8.6g³ p8.6g⁵ p9.5g⁵ p8m³ p8m⁵ p9.5g* p8m³ f8g⁵ p10g³ p9.5g² p10m⁴ p10f⁵ Dec 20] tall, close-coupled gelding: fair handicapper, better on all-weather: won at Wolverhampton in October: effective at 1m to 11.5f: acts on all-weather and any turf going: tried blinkered, wears cheekpieces: has hung/looked none too keen. *J. M. Bradley* **65** **a74**

THE HAGUE 3 b.c. Xaar 132 – Cox Orange (USA) 108 (Trempolino (USA) 135) **69** [2009 58: p6g^3 f8g^4 8.1g^5 9.9g^2 Jun 19] close-coupled colt: fair maiden: stays easy 1¼m: acts on all-weather: signs of temperament: sold £20,000. *J. H. M. Gosden*

THE HAPPY HAMMER (IRE) 3 b.g. Acclamation 118 – Emma's Star (ITY) **68** (Darshaan 133) [2009 61: p7.1g^6 p8g^4 7d 8.1g* 8m p8g p8.6g^5 p7.1g^3 p7m^3 p7m Nov 21] workmanlike gelding: fair handicapper: trained on reappearance only by M. Squance: won at Sandown in July: stays 1m: acts on polytrack, unraced on extremes of going on turf. *E. V. Stanford*

THE HERMITAGE (IRE) 2 b.f. (Mar 30) Kheleyf (USA) 116 – Russian Countess **81** (USA) 104 (Nureyev (USA) 131) [2009 5m^2 5m* 5g^2 5m 6m Oct 3] 85,000Y: unfurnished filly: sister to 3-y-o Crimea and half-sister to several winners, including smart 7f (at 2 yrs) and 11.5f winner Crown of Light (by Mtoto) and useful 7f and 8.5f winner Romanzof (by Kris): dam French 2-y-o 1m winner: fairly useful performer: won maiden at Newmarket in May easily: form after only when good second to Don't Tell Mary in listed race at Beverley: seemed amiss after lay-off final start: may prove best at 5f. *M. Johnston*

THE HISTORY MAN (IRE) 6 b.g. Titus Livius (FR) 115 – Handsome Anna (IRE) **64** 67 (Bigstone (IRE) 126) [2009 76: p6g^2 5.1m^3 5m^3 6m 5m 5g 5.1g^3 f5g 6.1d^2 p5.1g^3 p6g^5 6.1s^4 5.7g* 5s^4 Oct 27] workmanlike gelding: fair handicapper: left M. Mullineaux after sixth start: won at Bath in October: stays 6f: acts on polytrack and any turf going (poor efforts on fibresand): usually in headgear (cheekpieces last 2 starts): races prominently: quirky. *B. D. Leavy*

THE HUMAN LEAGUE 2 b.g. (Feb 7) Tobougg (IRE) 125 – Noble Desert (FR) **90** (Green Desert (USA) 127) [2009 6m^3 6d* 6m^6 7g Jul 31] £72,000Y: sturdy gelding: second foal: half-brother to 3-y-o Noble Dictator: dam, little form, out of smart French performer up to 10.5f Sporades, herself half-sister to Arlington Million winner Mill Native and high-class French 1m/9f performer French Stress: fairly useful performer: won maiden at Newcastle in June by 2 lengths from Chaperno: creditable effort in nursery at Goodwood (slowly away/wide/hung right) final start: will be better at 7f+ than shorter: sold 16,000 gns in October, and gelded. *M. R. Channon*

THE JAILER 6 b.m. Mujahid (USA) 125 – Once Removed 65 (Distant Relative 128) **38** [2009 67: p7g p6g 7m 7.1m 7g^6 Jul 14] leggy mare: poor performer nowadays: stays 1m: acts on all-weather, firm and soft going: tried visored/in cheekpieces. *J. G. M. O'Shea*

THE JOBBER (IRE) 8 b.g. Foxhound (USA) 103 – Clairification (IRE) 57 (Sherna- **90** zar 131) [2009 95: p5.1g 5g 5v^5 p5g^4 5m* 5m^2 5m^3 5m 5.2d^4 5f 5m^2 5m p5.1g^5 5g p5g Oct 22] big, strong gelding: fairly useful handicapper: won at Salisbury in June: effective at 6f, races mainly at 5f: acts on polytrack, firm and good to soft going: travels strongly *M. Blanshard*

THE JOSTLER 4 b.f. Dansili 127 – The Jotter 99 (Night Shift (USA)) [2009 92: p8g **76** 7g 7m Jul 2] robust, good-bodied filly: type to carry condition: handicapper: just fair form in 2009, leaving B. Hills after reappearance: stays 7f: acts on polytrack and good to firm going: sold 12,000 gns, reportedly in foal to Sir Percy. *Mrs L. Wadham*

THE KYLLACHY KID 3 b.g. Kyllachy 129 – All Business 92 (Entrepreneur 123) **96** [2009 88: 6.1m^3 6g 6d^2 6m^6 f6f 7s p7.1g* p7.1g^5 Nov 27] close-coupled gelding: useful handicapper: left T. Tate after fourth start: won at Wolverhampton in November by ¾ length from Labisa: needs good test at 6f, and stays 7.5f: acts on polytrack, heavy and good to firm going: once refused at stall: versatile regards tactics. *S. Gollings*

THELADYINQUESTION 2 b.f. (Apr 6) Dubawi (IRE) 129 – Whazzat 105 **84 +** (Daylami (IRE) 138) [2009 6m^5 6m* 6.5m Sep 25] 22,000Y: close-coupled filly: first foal: dam, 2-y-o 6f/7f winner, out of half-sister to Prix de Diane winner Rafha, herself dam of very smart sprinter Invincible Spirit: best effort when winning maiden at Salisbury in August by 1½ lengths from King of Windsor: still green in sales race at Ascot: will be suited by 7f. *A. M. Balding*

THELADYISATRAMP 2 b.f. (Jan 24) Bahamian Bounty 116 – Affair of State (IRE) **50** 99 (Tate Gallery (USA) 117) [2009 6f p7m p6f Oct 14] rather leggy filly: half-sister to numerous winners, including 2004 2-y-o 5f to 7f winner Bibury Flyer and 1¼m/1½m winner Mojalid (both useful, by Zafonic): dam 2-y-o 5f/6f winner: modest form at best in maiden/claimers: signs of temperament. *M. L. W. Bell*

THE LAST ALZAO (IRE) 3 b.f. Alzao (USA) 117 – Balakera (FR) (Lashkari 128) **75** [2009 p5.1m f6g^6 6m 8s 10g* p12.2g* 9.9m* 10.2g Aug 14] neat filly: half-sister to 9.4f winner Sheer Guts (by Hamas): dam unraced half-sister to Prix de l'Arc de Triomphe runner-up Behera: fairly useful handicapper: won at Redcar in June and Wolverhampton and Beverley (ladies) in July: below form final outing: stays 1½m: acts on polytrack and good to firm ground. *R. A. Fahey*

THE LAST BOTTLE (IRE) 4 ch.g. Hawk Wing (USA) 136 – Mesmerist (USA) 65 (Green Desert (USA) 127) [2009 68: p12.2g Dec 5] good-topped gelding: maiden: well held sole outing at 4 yrs: stays 1¾m: acts on polytrack: has looked awkward. *W. M. Brisbourne* **–**

THE LAST DON (IRE) 3 b.c. Redback 116 – Banco Solo (Distant Relative 128) [2009 8d^6 p8g p8g p12g* f14m^2 12g* p16g* p13.9g* Sep 19] 21,000Y: good-topped colt: fifth foal: half-brother to several winners, including Italian 5f to 7f performer Golden Danetime (by Danetime) and 1m/1¼m winner Internationalguest (by Petardia), both useful: dam unraced sister to dam of Sprint Cup winner Tante Rose and half-sister to smart middle-distance stayer/high-class hurdler Celestial Halo: useful handicapper, progressive: won at Kempton in July, Newmarket in August, and Kempton and Wolverhampton (by 7 lengths from Fin Vin de Leu in 4-runner event) in September: stays 2m: acts on all-weather: sometimes races lazily: sold 100,000 gns. *D. R. Lanigan* **104**

THE LITTLE MASTER (IRE) 5 b. or br.g. Tendulkar (USA) 114 – Minatina (IRE) 78 (Ela-Mana-Mou 132) [2009 57: p10g Jan 16] sturdy gelding: maiden: well held sole outing in 2009: should stay 1½m: acts on polytrack: tried tongue tied. *D. R. C. Elsworth* **–**

THE LONDON GANG 6 b.g. Mind Games 121 – Nom Francais 39§ (First Trump 118) [2009 53§: p8.6g p8.6g p9.5g^6 f7g p7.1g* p8.6g p7.1g p7.1g Jun 29] leggy, angular gelding: modest performer: won claimer at Wolverhampton in March: probably stays easy 1¼m: acts on all-weather, heavy and good to firm going: usually wears headgear: unreliable. *S. Wynne* **63 §**

THE LORD 9 b.g. Averti (IRE) 117 – Lady Longmead (Crimson Beau 124) [2009 78: f5g^6 p5g^3 5g^6 p6g f5g May 18] close-coupled, quite good-topped gelding: has a quick action: fair handicapper on turf, modest on all-weather: best at 5f: acts on all-weather, firm and soft going: tried in cheekpieces/visor/tongue tie: inconsistent. *W. G. M. Turner* **72 a63**

THE LOVE GURU 2 b.g. (Jan 29) Ishiguru (USA) 114 – Beauty (IRE) 74 (Alzao (USA) 117) [2009 p8g 8.3d f7g p7m^5 f6m* f6g^2 Dec 27] stocky gelding: fair performer: won nursery at Southwell in December: good second in similar event there next time: best form at 6f on fibresand: usually blinkered. *J. R. Boyle* **65**

THE MAGIC BLANKET (IRE) 4 b.g. Bahamian Bounty 116 – Zietunzeen (IRE) 99 (Zieten (USA) 118) [2009 60: p5g* p5g* 5f p5g 5.2m p5m^5 Dec 9] lengthy gelding: fair handicapper: won at Lingfield in January/March: well below form after: best at 5f: acts on polytrack, firm and good to soft going: tried tongue tied: prominent runner. *Stef Liddiard* **72**

THE MAGIC OF RIO 3 b.f. Captain Rio 122 – Good Health 78 (Magic Ring (IRE) 115) [2009 87: p5g 6f^5 p5m^5 p5g p6g p5.1g p5.1g Oct 29] strong, close-coupled filly: just fair performer at best at 3 yrs: effective at 5f/6f: acts on all-weather, good to firm and good to soft going: blinkered last 2 starts. *Peter Grayson* **65**

THEMANFORACRISIS (IRE) 2 b.c. (Apr 25) Oratorio (IRE) 128 – Sister Golden Hair (IRE) (Glint of Gold 128) [2009 7d^5 7m 7.1g 10.2m^6 Sep 30] big, good-topped colt: modest maiden: best effort on debut: bred to stay 1m+: sold 6,200 gns. *R. M. Beckett* **58**

THEME CATCHER (IRE) 4 b.g. Red Ransom (USA) – Canouan (IRE) 94 (Sadler's Wells (USA) 132) [2009 65: 12m^6 p8.6g Sep 5] maiden: little form in 2009: probably stays 1¼m: acts on soft going: tried visored. *G. Brown* **–**

THE MIDSHIPMAID 2 b.f. (Jan 27) Zafeen (FR) 123 – Ebba 88 (Elmaamul (USA) 125) [2009 6g 5.1m^5 6m^6 p5g 5.5g Aug 31] £3,000Y: strong filly: fifth living foal: dam 2-y-o 5f/6f winner: modest maiden: well beaten in nurseries: stays 6f. *Lucinda Featherstone* **53**

THE MIGHTY ATOM (USA) 2 ch.f. (Apr 3) Sky Mesa (USA) 116 – Nurse Cleo (USA) (Rahy (USA) 115) [2009 p5g 5m^5 7s Oct 12] $15,000 2-y-o: first foal: dam US maiden out of half-sister to Breeders' Cup Distaff winner Hollywood Wildcat: maiden (ran at Ffos Las second start): best effort when eighth in listed race at Dundalk on debut: should stay 7f: blinkered final outing. *P. J. Prendergast, Ireland* **76 ?**

THE MIGHTY MOD (USA) 2 b.g. (Mar 3) Gone West (USA) – Michelle's Monarch (USA) (Wavering Monarch (USA)) [2009 7m 8m 8g 8g Oct 19] tall, rather leggy gelding: modest maiden: well held in nursery (gelded after). *M. Johnston* **50**

DFS Park Hill Stakes, Doncaster—two outsiders fight out the finish, The Miniver Rose (right) just edging out Starfala; it's also close between Tanoura and Shemima (noseband) for third

THE MINIVER ROSE (IRE) 3 b.f. High Chaparral (IRE) 132 – Bloemfontain (IRE) 71 (Cape Cross (IRE) 129) [2009 94p: 10m^4 10f^4 10d^2 12g^5 14.6m* 15.5d Oct 25] rangy filly: useful performer: off 3 months, improved when winning DFS Park Hill Stakes at Doncaster in September by short head from Starfala: tailed off in Prix Royal-Oak at Longchamp final outing: stays 14.6f: acts on firm and good to soft going: often held up: sold 340,000 gns, reportedly to continue career in Australia. *R. Hannon* **108**

THE MOUSE CARROLL (IRE) 5 b.g. Barathea (IRE) 127 – Grecian Glory (IRE) 88 (Zafonic (USA) 130) [2009 10v 7s^3 10.7g 7s a7g^2 7m p8g 6g^5 p6g p7f Dec 21] fair maiden: left D. Leigh in Ireland prior to final start: should stay at least 1m: acts on sand and soft going: tried blinkered. *B. R. Johnson* **76**

THE MUMBO 3 b.f. Bahamian Bounty 116 – Mandolin (IRE) 69 (Sabrehill (USA) 120) [2009 –p: p8g* 8.3m p7g^5 p8m^4 p8m^6 Nov 19] useful-looking filly: fair performer: won maiden at Lingfield in January: stays 1m: acts on polytrack. *W. Jarvis* **66**

THE NAME IS FRANK 4 b.g. Lujain (USA) 119 – Zaragossa 80 (Paris House 123) [2009 64: 5.1g 6.1m 5.7m^2 5.1g 5.1g^2 5m^3 6m 6d^3 5m^2 6m^2 5g* 5.7g^2 p6g^3 f6g^6 p5m^6 p6m^2 p6f Dec 21] tall gelding: modest handicapper: won amateur event at Catterick in October: best at 5f/6f: acts on polytrack, soft and good to firm going: tongue tied nowadays: races prominently: reliable. *Mark Gillard* **64**

THE NIFTY FOX 5 b.g. Foxhound (USA) 103 – Nifty Alice 80 (First Trump 118) [2009 90: 5d 5m^6 5m^3 5d* 5m^4 5d^5 5s* 6v^2 5m^5 f5g^4 5g* 5d Oct 24] big, lengthy gelding: has a rather round action: useful handicapper: won at Catterick in July, Musselburgh in August and Catterick (better than ever when beating Cape Vale 1¼ lengths) in October: effective at 5f/6f: acts on fibresand, heavy and good to firm going: tried blinkered/visored: tactically versatile: reliable. *T. D. Easterby* **98**

THEOCRITUS (USA) 4 b.g. Theatrical 128 – Candace In Aspen (USA) (Woodman (USA) 126) [2009 98: 10.1g 11.6g^6 10m* 10d* 8.5m^2 10.3m^4 10g 10f* 10.1m* 9g^2 10d^3 Sep 15] tall gelding: fairly useful performer nowadays: won sellers in May and June and ladies handicap in August, all at Brighton, and claimer at Yarmouth later in August: stays easy 11f: acts on polytrack, firm and good to soft going: tried in blinkers: said to have bled on 3 occasions in 2009: held up: looked reluctant final start. *D. M. Simcock* **85**

THEOLA (IRE) 3 b.f. Kalanisi (IRE) 132 – Third Dimension (FR) (Suave Dancer (USA) 136) [2009 55: 12.1m^6 12m^3 14v^3 14.1m^2 16g^2 17.1m* 18g* Oct 10] lengthy filly: fairly useful handicapper: improved to win at Pontefract in September and York (landed **93**

gamble when beating Mith Hill 1¼ lengths, well on top) in October: out-and-out stayer: acts on heavy and good to firm ground. *M. H. Tompkins*

THEOLOGIST (IRE) 3 b.g. Galileo (IRE) 134 – Medina (IRE) 97 (Pennekamp (USA) 130) [2009 58: 7m³ 9.9m⁴ 11m⁶ 12g⁵ 14.1m² 16g³ 14.1g² 15m³ 17.2g³ Oct 21] good-topped gelding: fair maiden handicapper: stays 2m: raced only on good/good to firm going: tried visored: consistent: sold 25,000 gns, then gelded. *Mrs A. J. Perrett* **77**

THEOLOGY 2 b.c. (Apr 24) Galileo (IRE) 134 – Biographie (Mtoto 134) [2009 8m³ 8m Oct 16] 70,000Y: good-bodied colt: second foal: dam, useful Italian 1¼m winner, half-sister to smart French 1¼m performer Di Moi Oui: promising 3½ lengths third to Fareej, much better effort in maidens at Newmarket: seemed amiss second occasion: will stay 1¼m+. *J. Noseda* **80**

THEONEBOX (USA) 4 ch.g. Johannesburg (USA) 127 – Khalifa of Kushog (USA) (Air Forbes Won (USA)) [2009 87: p8.6g⁶ p9.5g⁶ 7.9m 8.1g³ 9.2m p10m f8m Dec 15] big gelding: fairly useful handicapper: left N. Vaughan after fifth outing: stays 9.5f: acts on polytrack and good to soft going: none too consistent. *N. P. Moore* **81**

THE ONLY BOSS (IRE) 2 ch.c. (Feb 14) Exceed And Excel (AUS) 126 – Aljafliyah (Halling (USA) 133) [2009 7m⁵ 6g* 5g* Oct 17] €34,000F, 42,000Y: strong, lengthy colt: second foal: dam well beaten: most progressive, winning maiden at Newcastle in September and minor event at Catterick (beat Chips O'Toole cosily by ½ length, pair clear) in October: likely to prove best at 5f/6f: already useful, and open to further progress. *W. J. Haggas* **97 p**

Mrs J. Wood's "The Miniver Rose"

THE OSTEOPATH (IRE) 6 ch.g. Danehill Dancer (IRE) 117 – Miss Margate (IRE) 60 (Don't Forget Me 127) [2009 95: 8m 8m 7d* 8m* 8.1m 8m 7g 7s Nov 7] leggy gelding: useful handicapper: won at Newcastle in May and June (beat Flipando readily by length): below form after: best at 7f/1m: acts on soft and good to firm going: used to wear cheekpieces/blinkers: held up: sometimes looks tricky ride (carries head awkwardly/has hung). *M. Dods* **100**

THE POWER OF PHIL 5 b.g. Komaite (USA) – Starboard Tack (FR) 76 (Saddlers' Hall (IRE) 126) [2009 56: p8g^{5} p8g^{5} f8g^{4} Jan 29] modest maiden: stays 9.5f: acts on all-weather: tried visored. *Tom Dascombe* **52**

THE QUIET GENIUS 3 b.g. Daylami (IRE) 138 – Shallat (IRE) 59 (Pennekamp (USA) 130) [2009 6f 9.8m^{6} 10.1d^{5} 12m 10.3g^{5} 14.1g 12.4d^{3} p16.5g Oct 1] sturdy gelding: modest maiden: stayed 12.4f: acted on good to soft going: dead. *Jedd O'Keeffe* **63**

THEREAFTER (USA) 2 ch.f. (Feb 16) Lion Heart (USA) 124 – Alvernia (USA) (Alydar (USA)) [2009 p6g^{3} p7g Sep 21] compact filly: half-sister to several winners, including 1m to 10.5f winner Acrobatic (by Storm Boot) and 1m winner Verbose (by Storm Bird), both useful, latter dam of smart 7f/1m performer Thousand Words: dam US 8.5f/9f winner: better effort in maidens at Kempton when third to Ferris Wheel: should be well suited by 7f+. *R. Charlton* **67**

THE RECTIFIER (USA) 2 b. or br.c. (Jan 15) Langfuhr (CAN) 124 – Western Vision (USA) (Gone West (USA)) [2009 7m 7m^{4} 6.5g^{2} Oct 8] 30,000F, €38,000Y, £42,000 2-y-o: compact colt: first foal: dam unraced half-sister to US Grade 2 1m winner Rahys' Appeal: progressive in maidens, ½-length second to Noafal at Newbury (dictated): will probably stay 1m. *Stef Liddiard* **85**

THERE WE GO (IRE) 3 b.g. Pyrus (USA) 106 – Ghayaat (USA) (Lyphard (USA) 132) [2009 7g^{6} 9.3d 6s^{4} Aug 1] €14,500Y: half-brother to several winners abroad, including French winners around 1¼m Ghayakal (by Akarad) and Ghayouna (by Doyoun): dam ran 3 times: signs of ability in maidens, keeping on not knocked about when well-held fourth at Hamilton: type to do better in handicaps. *G. A. Swinbank* **– p**

THE SALWICK FLYER (IRE) 6 b.g. Tagula (IRE) 116 – Shimla (IRE) 55 (Rudimentary (USA) 118) [2009 67: 6g Jun 17] small, leggy gelding: handicapper: said to have bled sole start in 2009: stays easy 8.6f: acts on all-weather, firm and soft going: tried in cheekpieces. *I. Semple* **–**

THE SAUCY SNIPE 3 b.f. Josr Algarhoud (IRE) 118 – The Dark Eider (Superlative 118) [2009 65: 9.7g 10g 11.5m^{5} 11.6m* 11.6f^{5} p16f^{4} p16m^{5} p12g Oct 2] angular filly: modest performer: won seller at Windsor in July: stays easy 2m: acts on polytrack and good to firm going: sold £400. *P. Winkworth* **61**

THE SCORCHING WIND (IRE) 3 b.c. Fasliyev (USA) 120 – Rose of Mooncoin (IRE) 99 (Brief Truce (USA) 126) [2009 64p: 7g 6.1g 6g^{2} 6m* 7d^{6} 7g^{2} p8g* p7g* p8g^{2} 8m p8f Dec 20] big, good-topped colt: fairly useful handicapper on all weather, fair on turf: won at Doncaster in June and Kempton (twice, 4 days apart) in September: stays 1m: acts on polytrack and good to firm ground: tongue tied of late. *S. C. Williams* **74 a93**

THESCOTTISHSOLDIER 2 ch.g. (Jan 19) Observatory (USA) 131 – Twenty Seven (IRE) 75 (Efisio 120) [2009 7d 6m 8d Oct 28] well held in maidens, then gelded. *A. G. Foster* **–**

THE SHUFFLER 2 b.g. (Mar 23) Reset (AUS) 124 – Lucky Dice (Perugino (USA) 84) [2009 5m 5m^{4} p6g^{5} 6m^{6} 5m^{5} 6d^{4} p5g 6.1s Oct 7] compact gelding: modest maiden: stays 6f: acts on polytrack, good to firm and good to soft going. *G. L. Moore* **59**

THE SLIDER 5 b.m. Erhaab (USA) 127 – Cottage Maid (Inchinor 119) [2009 49: p10g p12g Jun 6] quite good-topped mare: little form since early-2008. *Mrs L. C. Jewell* **–**

THE SNATCHER (IRE) 6 b.h. Indian Danehill (IRE) 124 – Saninka (IRE) 82 (Doyoun 124) [2009 100: p8g p8g^{3} 8g 7.1g p8g p7m^{6} p8m Oct 26] rather leggy, attractive horse: fairly useful handicapper at best in 2009: best at 7f/1m: acts on polytrack, heavy and good to firm going: tried visored. *R. Hannon* **90 d**

THE SPICER 4 b.g. Lujain (USA) 119 – Spicey (Mizoram (USA) 105) [2009 p7g p8.6g 6g p8g 6.1g Jul 4] good-topped gelding: little form: tried blinkered: tongue tied. *F. Sheridan* **–**

THE STAFFY (IRE) 4 b.g. Redback 116 – Lady Charlotte 75 (Night Shift (USA)) [2009 55: p9.5g^{2} p9.5g^{6} 8.1g 10.9d p7.1g p9.5g Oct 16] regressive maiden: left N. Vaughan after fourth start: visored, broke down final outing: should have been suited by 1¼m+: dead. *Tom Dascombe* **67**

THE STARBOARD BOW 2 b.c. (Feb 22) Observatory (USA) 131 – Overboard (IRE) 73 (Rainbow Quest (USA) 134) [2009 7g* 8m p8.6g^{2} 7m p8.6g Oct 15] close-coupled colt: fourth foal: half-brother to 3-y-o Bin End and 1½m winners Sea Admiral (by Sinndar) and Summer of Love (by Fasliyev): dam, maiden (placed at 1½m), half-sister to smart performer up to 1½m Red Sea: fairly useful performer: won maiden at Yarmouth in August: best effort when seventh in listed race at Salisbury next time: will stay 1¼m+. *S. Kirk* **85**

THE STRIG 2 b.g. (Feb 21) Mujahid (USA) 125 – Pretty Kool 68 (Inchinor 119) [2009 5m p5g^{5} p6m^{3} Nov 28] has scope: first foal: dam 5f/6f winner: progressive in maidens, third to Tenacestream at Lingfield: likely to prove best at 5f/6f: should improve further. *S. C. Williams* **70 p**

THE TATLING (IRE) 12 b.g. Perugino (USA) 84 – Aunty Eileen (Ahonoora 122) [2009 93: f5s^{4} f5g* p6g f5m^{5} f5g^{3} 5f^{6} 5.7g^{3} 6m^{2} 6m^{4} 6m^{3} 5.7f^{2} 5.7f^{4} 5.1g^{2} 5g^{4} 5.7m^{3} 5.1g* 5.2d* 5.1m^{5} 5m^{2} 5m^{3} 5.7m^{3} 5m 5g^{5} p6g p5g^{5} p5m^{3} f5m p5m^{2} Dec 30] strong, lengthy gelding: one-time very smart performer, fairly useful nowadays: won handicap at Southwell in February, claimer at Bath in July and handicap at Newbury (by neck from Kingswinford) in August: generally held form after: best at 5f/6f: acts on all-weather, firm and soft going: tried tongue tied: held up: tough and reliable. *J. M. Bradley* **89**

THETA WAVE (USA) 3 ch.g. Buckhar (USA) 120 – Let's Dance (USA) (Thorn Dance (USA) 107) [2009 51: p6g^{4} p5g^{3} p6g 6.1m 5g* 6m 5.7g p6g Sep 25] fair performer: won selling handicap at Ripon in August: stays 6f: acts on polytrack, best turf effort on good ground: in cheekpieces last 2 starts. *J. R. Gask* **66**

THETEARSTHATICRY (IRE) 5 b.g. King Charlemagne (USA) 120 – Zeddaana (FR) (Arctic Tern (USA) 126) [2009 48: p8.6g 10.2m^{6} Jun 13] poor maiden: stays 1½m. *A. E. Jones* **48**

THE THRIFTY BEAR 6 ch.g. Rambling Bear 115 – Prudent Pet 65 (Distant Relative 128) [2009 –: p5.1g Feb 13] big, workmanlike gelding: of little account nowadays. *C. W. Fairhurst* **–**

THE TWO G'S 2 b.f. (Apr 27) Mark of Esteem (IRE) 137 – Intellibet One 74 (Compton Place 125) [2009 5.5f 6m p5m^{5} p6g f5m^{5} p5.1g f6f^{5} f6m^{6} Dec 15] third foal: half-sister to 3-y-o Taurus Twins: dam 5f (including at 2 yrs)/6f winner: modest maiden: likely to be best at 5f/6f: form only on all-weather: tried in cheekpieces. *P. D. Evans* **51**

THEWAYTOSANJOSE (IRE) 3 b.f. Fasliyev (USA) 120 – Soltura (IRE) (Sadler's Wells (USA) 132) [2009 57: p8.6g* p9.5g^{5} p8.6g^{5} p8g 10v 8.5g Oct 17] tall filly: modest handicapper: won at Wolverhampton in January: regressive after (left S. Kirk after fourth start): stays 8.6f: acts on all-weather. *Patrick J. Flynn, Ireland* **58 d**

THEWAYYOUARE (USA) 4 b.c. Kingmambo (USA) 125 – Maryinsky (IRE) 107 (Sadler's Wells (USA) 132) [2009 109: 10.5g^{4} 10.5v^{5} May 24] good-topped colt: smart performer: won Criterium International at Saint-Cloud at 2 yrs: left A. Fabre in France, as good as ever when 1¾ lengths fourth to Vision d'Etat in Prix Ganay at Longchamp on reappearance: tailed-off last of 5 in Tattersalls Gold Cup at the Curragh next time: stayed 10.5f: acted on soft ground, probably on good to firm: to stand at Ashford Stud, Kentucky, fee $10,000. *A. P. O'Brien, Ireland* **117**

THE WEE CHIEF (IRE) 3 ch.g. King Charlemagne (USA) 120 – La Belle Clare (IRE) 61 (Paris House 123) [2009 6m^{4} p6m* p6f Dec 13] €1,300Y: third foal: dam, 5f winner, half-sister to smart 6f/7f performer Nice One Clare: fair form: won maiden at Kempton in November: pulled too hard in handicap there next time: raced only at 6f. *J. C. Fox* **75**

THE WHICH DOCTOR 4 b.g. Medicean 128 – Oomph 83 (Shareef Dancer (USA) 135) [2009 96: 8.3m p8m^{4} 8g^{3} 10.4m^{5} 10m 10.1m^{6} 10m* 9m 10v^{5} Oct 24] strong, close-coupled gelding: fairly useful handicapper: won at Newbury in September: effective at 1m/1¼m: acts on polytrack and good to firm going, probably on heavy: held up. *J. Noseda* **94**

THE WILY WOODCOCK 5 b.g. Mark of Esteem (IRE) 137 – Lonely Shore (Blakeney 126) [2009 72§: p8g^{6} 8.3m p7.1g p9.5g p7.1g f8f Nov 24] useful-looking gelding: regressive and temperamental maiden handicapper: left G. L. Moore after reappearance: should stay at least 1¼m: acts on polytrack: tried in blinkers/cheekpieces. *T. Wall* **55 §**

THE WINGED ASSASIN (USA) 3 b.g. Fusaichi Pegasus (USA) 130 – Gran Dama (USA) (Rahy (USA) 115) [2009 60: p6g^{2} p8g^{5} 6g* 8.5g^{5} 8.1g 8.3m 7m^{6} 9.7m 8.3g Oct 5] tall, useful-looking ex-Irish-trained gelding: fair performer: won handicap at Folkestone in April: well below form after next outing, refusing to race final one (gelded after): stays easy 8.5f, effective at 6f: acts on polytrack, best turf efforts on good going: one to treat with caution. *J. Akehurst* **74 §**

THEWINNATAKESITALL 2 ch.f. (Feb 15) King's Best (USA) 132 – Powder Puff (IRE) (Sadler's Wells (USA) 132) [2009 p6g 6.1m 7s4 p8m 6.1s 7m f5m2 p5.1g f5f5 Dec 17] first foal: dam unraced half-sister to useful performer up to 1¼m Little Good Bay: modest maiden: effective at 5f to 7f: acts on all-weather and soft ground: in cheek-pieces last 3 outings. *H. J. Evans* **54**

THEY ALL LAUGHED 6 ch.g. Zafonic (USA) 130 – Royal Future (IRE) (Royal Academy (USA) 130) [2009 80: f14s p13.9g2 p12g4 p13g3 p16g3 f14g2 f14g3 f12d* 13.8m3 f12g5 14.1g5 14v 12.3g3 12.1m* 11.1v5 12d 13.8m5 15.8g3 f14m3 f12g5 f14g4 Dec 22] tall, useful-looking gelding: fair performer: won handicap at Southwell in March and claimer at Beverley (left P. Hiatt £8,000) in June: below form after: effective at 1½m to 2m: acts on all-weather, firm and good to soft ground: effective with/without blinkers/cheekpieces: usually waited with. *Mrs Marjorie Fife* **78 d**

THEYMISTIM 2 b.g. (May 4) Kyllachy 129 – Dance Sequence (USA) 105 (Mr Prospector (USA)) [2009 5g* Aug 12] sturdy gelding: half-brother to several winners, including 5f and (at 2 yrs) 6f winner Hornpipe (by Danehill) and 1¼m/1½m winner Sequential (by Rainbow Quest), both useful: dam 2-y-o 6f (Lowther Stakes) winner (stayed 1m): 12/1 and green, won maiden at Beverley readily by 3¾ lengths from Lieu Day Louie, drifting right: will stay 6f: sent to Hong Kong, where renamed Fun And Fast: should improve. *Mrs L. Stubbs* **79 p**

THIEF 3 b.c. Falbrav (IRE) 133 – Eurolink Raindance (IRE) 109 (Alzao (USA) 117) [2009 60p: 8.3m5 May 25] big, close-coupled colt: fair form in 3 maidens at 1m: still green when fifth at Leicester, only outing in 2009. *L. M. Cumani* **66**

THIEF OF TIME (IRE) 3 b.g. Clodovil (IRE) 116 – Cape Flattery (IRE) 66 (Cape Cross (IRE) 129) [2009 p7g2 p8g* 10m2 8.1m2 8.1v 9m5 7.1g4 8m p7g2 Oct 21] €45,000F, 32,000Y: good-topped gelding: first foal: dam Irish 11f winner: useful performer: won maiden at Lingfield in January: good second in handicaps after, including to Captain Macarry at Kempton final outing, finishing strongly: should prove best at 1m/1¼m: acts on polytrack and good to firm going, below form on heavy: held up. *P. W. Chapple-Hyam* **98**

THINKING 2 b.g. (Mar 15) Makbul 104 – Concentration (IRE) (Mind Games 121) [2009 6f 6s 5m5 f5g 6g 5.1s3 Nov 4] strong, lengthy gelding: modest maiden: best efforts at 5f: acts on soft and good to firm going: blinkered (ran creditably) final start. *T. D. Easterby* **62**

THINK ITS ALL OVER (USA) 2 b.c. (Feb 22) Tiznow (USA) 133 – A P Petal (USA) (A P Indy (USA) 131) [2009 7m4 8.3g* Sep 20] $25,000F, €55,000Y: third foal: dam unraced close relative of very smart US performer up to 1¼m Golden Larch: better effort when winning maiden at Hamilton by 1¼ lengths from Pena Dorada (still green): will be suited by 1¼m: should improve again. *T. P. Tate* **78 p**

THIN RED LINE (IRE) 3 b.c. Red Ransom (USA) – Albaiyda (IRE) (Brief Truce (USA) 126) [2009 87p: p9.5g4 8.1g 10g* 11.9m2 11d 10.3m p12m* Oct 12] sturdy colt: useful handicapper: won at Pontefract in June and Kempton (beat Howdigo 1½ lengths) in October: stays 1½m: acts on polytrack and good to firm going: sold 80,000 gns. *E. A. L. Dunlop* **96**

THIRTYFOURTHSTREET (IRE) 4 gr.f. Beat Hollow 126 – Peacock Alley (IRE) 98 (Salse (USA) 128) [2009 –: p9.5m6 p12.2g3 f12g 12d p12g6 Apr 21] workmanlike filly: modest maiden at best: seems to stay 1½m: acts on polytrack: tried blinkered: sold 7,000 gns, reportedly in foal to Dr Fong. *W. R. Muir* **55**

THIS ONES FOR EDDY 4 b.g. Kyllachy 129 – Skirt Around 69 (Deploy 131) [2009 81: f5g2 f6g4 f6g3 p6g6 f7g* 12g 8.3m3 8m* 8g2 8.3g3 7g4 7.9m 8.3m2 7.1m 8.3m 8.1g 9.2d 7.5f6 p7.1g 8m4 7g3 6g2 p7.1g Oct 31] neat gelding: fair handicapper: won at Southwell in March and Pontefract in April: left S. Parr after seventeenth start: stays 8.3f: acts on all-weather and good to firm ground (below form on soft): tried in blinkers/cheekpieces/tongue strap. *J. Balding* **76**

THIS ONES FOR PAT (USA) 4 b. or br.g. Proud Citizen (USA) 122 – Lace Curtain Irish (USA) (Cryptoclearance (USA)) [2009 68: f5g2 6m f7g 5.1d Apr 28] fair handicapper: well held after reappearance: best at 5f/6f: acts on all-weather: tried in cheekpieces (including when successful)/blinkers/tongue tie. *S. Parr* **– a70**

THISTLE 8 ch.g. Selkirk (USA) 129 – Ardisia (USA) 87 (Affirmed (USA)) [2009 f8g6 f11g Aug 27] good-topped gelding: modest handicapper nowadays: stays 11f: acts on good to firm ground: tried in cheekpieces/tongue tie. *George Baker* **53**

THISTLESTAR (USA) 2 b. or br.f. (Feb 19) Lion Heart (USA) 124 – Katiba (USA) 99 (Gulch (USA)) [2009 7.2m^3 p6m^5 p7.1g^5 Dec 18] €28,000Y, resold €66,000Y: half-sister to several winners, including 1999 2-y-o 7f winner Meadaaar (by Diesis) and 1m/1¼m winner Badaayer (by Silver Hawk), both useful: dam, 6f (at 2 yrs)/7f winner (stayed 1¼m), out of half-sister to Breeders' Cup Sprint winner Very Subtle: modest form in maidens: should stay 1m. *R. A. Fahey* **64**

THOMAS BAINES (USA) 2 b.g. (Feb 2) Johannesburg (USA) 127 – Foofaraw (USA) (Cherokee Run (USA) 122) [2009 5g^3 5m 5.2g^3 5m^5 7g^6 p7.1g* p7.1g^3 a8.5f^4 8f^3 Dec 28] 55,000Y: useful-looking gelding: first foal: dam, Canadian 7f winner (including at 2 yrs), granddaughter of champion US turf mare Laugh And Be Merry: useful performer: won nursery at Wolverhampton in September: sold from M. Bell 19,000 gns after next start: returned to turf, improved effort when third to Macias in non-graded event at Santa Anita final outing: stays 1m: acts on polytrack and firm going: looked ungenuine earlier in year (gelded after third start). *D. F. O'Neill, USA* **95**

THOMPSONS WALLS (IRE) 4 b.g. Trans Island 119 – Nordic Living (IRE) 53 (Nordico (USA)) [2009 77: p9.5g 8.5m 6m^6 8.5m May 12] strong gelding: fairly useful performer at best: well held in 2009, leaving S. Mason after third start: tried tongue tied/ blinkered. *D. Nicholls* **–**

THOOSA 3 ch.f. Best of The Bests (IRE) 122 – Natural Grace (Zamindar (USA) 116) [2009 p5.1g p5g^4 p6g^3 f5g^6 6d 6g 6s Jun 11] second foal: dam ran once: poor maiden: will stay 7f: tried in visor. *P. S. McEntee* **44**

THORNABY GREEN 8 ch.g. Whittingham (IRE) 104 – Dona Filipa 51 (Precocious 126) [2009 64: f8s^3 p8.6g f11g f12g Feb 1] tall, quite good-topped gelding: modest handicapper: stays 1¼m: acts on all-weather and any turf going: tried in headgear. *T. D. Barron* **58**

THORNTON GEORGE 4 b.g. Piccolo 121 – Princess Emily (IRE) 68 (Dolphin Street (FR) 125) [2009 12.4s 10m Jun 19] always behind in bumpers: well beaten in maidens on Flat: tried blinkered. *T. J. Fitzgerald* **–**

THORNY MANDATE 7 b.g. Diktat 126 – Rosa Canina 91 (Bustino 136) [2009 68: p12.2g^4 p12g^6 p13.9g* p16.5g^6 14m^4 p13.9g^4 13.3m^3 12.3g 13m^5 12.5m^2 12.3m^6 12.3m 15g p12.2g p13.9g 13.4m Sep 26] strong, close-coupled gelding: fair handicapper: won at Wolverhampton in March: stays 1¾m: acts on polytrack, firm and good to soft going (below best on soft): usually travels strongly held up. *W. M. Brisbourne* **65**

THOUGHTFUL (IRE) 2 b.f. (Mar 26) Acclamation 118 – Truly Generous (IRE) 104 (Generous (IRE) 139) [2009 p6g^5 6.5m Sep 25] neat filly: half-sister to 3 winners, including useful French 7f/1m winner Antique (by Dubai Millennium) and 11-y-o Nawamees: dam, French 1¼m winner who stayed 12.5f, half-sister to very smart French middle-distance performer Modhish: fifth to Ferris Wheel in maiden at Kempton: very stiff task in sales race at Ascot: will probably do better. *J. W. Hills* **52 p**

THOUGHTSOFSTARDOM 6 b.g. Mind Games 121 – Alustar 71 (Emarati (USA) 74) [2009 85: p5g^5 p5g^6 f6g^6 p6g^5 p6g^4 p5g p5.1g 5.7g^6 5.3g^6 5.1m 5.3f^5 5m^6 6g 5m 5.3d^3 5m^5 5m^3 5m^5 5.3m 5d 5.1g p5.1g^3 p5.1g^4 5m* 5.3m p6m^5 p5m^2 f5f* p6m^6 p5f* f5g^4 Dec 22] lengthy gelding: fair handicapper: won at Folkestone in September, and Southwell and Lingfield in December: best at 5f: acts on all-weather, firm and soft going: effective with or without headgear: tough. *P. S. McEntee* **79**

THOUSANDKISSESDEEP (IRE) 2 b.f. (Feb 10) Night Shift (USA) – Interim Payment (USA) 88 (Red Ransom (USA)) [2009 8.1d 8g^2 Oct 20] 36,000F, 140,000Y: first foal: dam, 1¼m winner, half-sister to smart US performer up to 1¾m Midships, out of US Grade 2 1½m winner Interim: much better effort in maidens when length second to Hymnsheet at Yarmouth: should improve again. *J. H. M. Gosden* **79 p**

THOUSAND MILES (IRE) 3 br.c. Danehill Dancer (IRE) 117 – Mille Miglia (IRE) 96 (Caerleon (USA) 132) [2009 73: 8d* 8d^5 8m^5 7.1m^3 7.1g^5 8g 7s Oct 12] sturdy colt: fairly useful performer: won maiden at Yarmouth in April: stays 1m: acts on good to firm and good to soft going, below form on soft final outing: usually races prominently. *P. W. Chapple-Hyam* **90**

THREE BOARS 7 ch.g. Most Welcome 131 – Precious Poppy 70 (Polish Precedent (USA) 131) [2009 79: p14g f16g^2 16g f16m^6 Dec 15] quite good-topped gelding: fair handicapper on all-weather, lightly raced and well held on turf since 2007: effective at 1¼m to 16.5f: acts on all-weather (probably best on fibresand): blinkered: held up: none too consistent. *S. Gollings* **– a65**

THREE DUCKS 3 b.f. Diktat 126 – Three Terns (USA) (Arctic Tern (USA) 126) [2009 78p: 8.3m 9.9g 9g^2 Jul 2] tall filly: fair performer: stays 9f: acts on polytrack. *L. M. Cumani* **77**

THREE GOLD LEAVES 4 ch.g. Zaha (CAN) 106 – Tab's Gift (Bijou d'Inde 127) [2009 –: 10.1m^5 10.1s 7.9g Jun 1] big gelding: little form: tongue tied in 2009. *D. W. Thompson* **–**

THREE GOOD FRIENDS (IRE) 2 b.f. (Apr 7) Orpen (USA) 116 – Eastern Blue (IRE) 68 (Be My Guest (USA) 126) [2009 5d f5g* Jun 7] £5,000Y: third foal: half-sister to 3-y-o Peter's Gift and 4-y-o Shakespeare's Son: dam 6f winner, including at 2 yrs: well backed and better effort in maidens over 2 months apart when winning at Southwell cosily by 1½ lengths from Diamond Affair: will stay 6f. *P. T. Midgley* **58**

THREE MOONS (IRE) 3 b.f. Montjeu (IRE) 137 – Three Owls (IRE) 79 (Warning 136) [2009 93: 9.7d* 10f^2 May 3] good-topped filly: useful performer: landed odds in maiden at Folkestone in April: improved when 1¼ lengths second to Take The Hint in listed race at Newmarket next time: missed Oaks at Epsom in June after reportedly suffering minor injury in final work: likely to stay 1½m: acts on firm and good to soft going, promise on polytrack. *H. J. L. Dunlop* **104**

THREE ROCKS (IRE) 4 b.c. Rock of Gibraltar (IRE) 133 – Top Crystal (IRE) (Sadler's Wells (USA) 132) [2009 94: 6s* 7g* 7.5v* 8d^2 8g^2 6v^6 7f^2 7m^4 5g^5 7s* 6s^6 8s^2 7.5m^3 Oct 4] tall, good-topped colt: smart performer: much improved in 2009, winning handicaps at the Curragh and Leopardstown in March, minor event at Tipperary in April and Keeneland Minstrel Stakes at the Curragh (by 1¼ lengths from Georgebernardshaw) in July: good 1½ lengths third to Duff in Concorde Stakes at Tipperary final outing: effective at 6f, barely at testing 1m: acts on polytrack and any turf ground: usually blanketed for stall entry: often slowly away. *J. S. Bolger, Ireland* **116**

THREE'S A CROWD 2 b.f. (Apr 18) Royal Applause 124 – Thracian 92 (Green Desert (USA) 127) [2009 6m^6 p5g^4 7g p6f Oct 14] lengthy filly: half-sister to several winners, including 2001 2-y-o 7f winner Thrasher (by Hector Protector) and 2m winner Trilemma (by Slip Anchor), both fairly useful: dam, 2-y-o 6f/7f winner, half-sister to very smart performers up to 1½m Richard of York, Maysoon and Three Tails: modest maiden: should stay 7f. *D. R. C. Elsworth* **53**

THREE SONS 2 b.g. (Mar 19) Reset (AUS) 124 – Zuloago (USA) 62 (Stravinsky (USA) 133) [2009 5m p6g 6v 5g Jul 20] no form in claimers/seller: blinkered. *I. W. McInnes* **–**

THREESTEPSTOHEAVEN 3 b.g. Haafhd 129 – Bella Bianca (IRE) 78 (Barathea (IRE) 127) [2009 74: 10g^5 10.2d 10g 7g 10f^2 9f* 9s* Oct 25] rather leggy gelding: fair performer: sold from B. Hills 2,500 gns after third start: won minor event and handicap at Duindigt in October: stays 1¼m: acts on firm and soft ground. *K. Davies, Netherlands* **70**

THREE STRINGS (USA) 6 b.g. Stravinsky (USA) 133 – Just Cause (Law Society (USA) 130) [2009 67: f12s^6 f11g* f12g^3 Jul 27] fair handicapper: won at Southwell in April: stays 1½m: acts on fibresand, firm and soft going: wears cheekpieces. *P. D. Niven* **71**

THREE THIEVES (UAE) 6 ch.g. Jade Robbery (USA) 121 – Melisendra (FR) (Highest Honor (FR) 124) [2009 52: p12m^6 p12m^6 Dec 9] tall gelding: modest handicapper nowadays: stays 1¾m: acts on all-weather, best turf efforts on good going: tried visored. *Jim Best* **51**

THREE TIMES 2 ch.f. (Mar 22) Bahamian Bounty 116 – Triple Joy 104 (Most Welcome 131) [2009 f7f^6 7g Oct 31] 85,000Y: well-made filly: half-sister to several winners, including smart 6f (at 2 yrs) and 1m winner Triple Dash (by Nashwan) who stayed 1¼m, and useful French 1m (at 2 yrs) and 10.5f winner Trinity Joy (by Vettori): dam, 6f/7f winner, half-sister to smart middle-distance performer Talented: green, well beaten in maidens. *D. R. Lanigan* **–**

THRILL 2 ch.f. (Feb 28) Pivotal 124 – Irresistible 98 (Cadeaux Genereux 131) [2009 p7g^3 7d* 8g Oct 31] useful-looking filly: third foal: sister to smart 7f (at 2 yrs and Nell Gwyn Stakes) winner Infallible who stayed 1m: dam 5f/6f winner, including at 2 yrs: made all when winning maiden at Salisbury in October comfortably by 3 lengths from Opera Gal: only eighth in listed event at Newmarket: should stay 1m: already verging on useful. *J. H. M. Gosden* **92 +**

THROUGH THE FOREST (USA) 3 b. or br.f. Forestry (USA) 121 – Lakefront (USA) (Deputy Minister (CAN)) [2009 8.3g 8.1m 10m p10g^4 p11m^3 f11g* Dec 18] $160,000Y: angular filly: second foal: half-sister to winner in USA by Thunder Gulch: dam unraced daughter of US Grade 1 1m/9f winner Lakeway: modest performer: won handicap at Southwell in December: stays 11f: acts on all-weather: tried in cheekpieces. *W. R. Swinburn* **62**

THROW THE DICE 7 b.g. Lujain (USA) 119 – Euridice (IRE) 66 (Woodman (USA) 126) [2009 –: 5m 5g Jul 5] strong, lengthy gelding: modest handicapper in 2007: no form since: has worn cheekpieces, usually visored: has bled. *A. Berry* –

THRUST CONTROL (IRE) 2 ch.g. (Mar 13) Fath (USA) 116 – Anazah (USA) (Diesis 133) [2009 7.1m* Oct 5] sturdy gelding: first foal: dam, Irish maiden, out of useful miler Tadwiga: 10/1, made all when winning maiden at Warwick by head from Pan American: not sure to stay beyond 7f. *M. R. Channon* 75

THUMBERLINA 3 b.f. Choisir (AUS) 126 – Capstick (JPN) (Machiavellian (USA) 123) [2009 –: p6g p6g p5g p5g 5.1m^4 5.1m 5m^5 5.1g 5.3f^5 5.2s 6d 5.3d p5.1g 5.2g 5.2m 6m Sep 28] poor maiden handicapper: raced only at 5f/6f: acts on polytrack and good to firm ground: often in visor/cheekpieces, blinkered last 2 starts. *Mrs C. A. Dunnett* 49

THUNDERBALL 3 ch.g. Haafhd 129 – Trustthunder 87 (Selkirk (USA) 129) [2009 92: 10.3m 7.5m^3 7.1g^2 7d 7f^3 7m^2 8m p8f^2 p10g^4 p9.5g^4 Nov 12] close-coupled gelding: fairly useful handicapper: left A. McCabe after sixth start: stays 1¼m: acts on polytrack, firm and soft going: tried in headgear: usually races prominently. *J. A. Glover* 89

THUNDER BAY 4 b.g. Hunting Lion (IRE) 115 – Floral Spark 69 (Forzando 122) [2009 78: 5m 6g 5m* 5g 5m 5m^3 5m 5g 6f^5 5m 6m 5m^3 5g p6m^2 p6g^2 p5.1g^5 f5f p6g Dec 5] good-quartered gelding: fair handicapper: won at Musselburgh in May: stays 6f: acts on polytrack, firm and good to soft going: tried in headgear. *R. A. Fahey* 68

THUNDER GORGE (USA) 4 b.g. Thunder Gulch (USA) 129 – Renaissance Fair (USA) (Theatrical 128) [2009 80: p8g^5 8m 8m* 8.9d 8.1m^3 9s^6 8f 8m 7m Oct 6] good-topped gelding: fairly useful handicapper: won at Newmarket in May: stays 1m: acts on polytrack, soft and good to firm going: not one to rely on: sold 2,500 gns. *Mouse Hamilton-Fairley* 81 §

THUNDERING HOME 2 gr.c. (Jan 25) Storming Home 128 – Citrine Spirit (IRE) 76 (Soviet Star (USA) 128) [2009 p8g p8g^3 f8d* Dec 29] second foal: dam, 1m winner, half-sister to useful performer up to 9.4f New Century: progressive form in maidens in 2009, winning at Southwell (by length from Gold Party) in December: raced only at 1m on all-weather. *E. A. L. Dunlop* 69

THUNDERONTHEMOUNT 4 ch.g. Zaha (CAN) 106 – Vrennan 74 (Suave Dancer (USA) 136) [2009 12.6m Jul 9] well beaten in bumper: 100/1, no encouragement in maiden at Warwick on Flat debut. *M. J. Attwater* –

THUNDEROUS MOOD (USA) 3 b. or br.c. Storm Cat (USA) – Warm Mood (USA) (Alydar (USA)) [2009 103: 5g 7m 6g 5.7m^4 6m 7m p6g^5 p6g^4 Dec 2] sturdy colt: has moderate, quick action: just fairly useful handicapper at 3 yrs: stays 6f: acts on polytrack, good to firm and good to soft going: sometimes blinkered/tongue tied. *P. F. I. Cole* 85

THUNDER ROCK (IRE) 7 b.g. King's Best (USA) 132 – Park Express 123 (Ahonoora 122) [2009 16.1g^5 Aug 8] tall, useful-looking gelding: useful handicapper in 2006: well below form sole Flat start since (fairly useful hurdler/chaser): stayed 1½m: acted on good to firm and good to soft going: tried in cheekpieces: dead. *Jonjo O'Neill* –

THUNDERSTRUCK 4 b.g. Bertolini (USA) 125 – Trustthunder 87 (Selkirk (USA) 129) [2009 81: 10g 8.5g 9.8m 11.9d 9.9g^4 10g^2 p9.5g^2 p10m* p8.6g* p10g^2 p9.5g^4 p10f^3 Dec 20] big, workmanlike gelding: fairly useful handicapper: left A. McCabe after third outing: won at Kempton and Wolverhampton in November: stays 1¼m: acts on polytrack, firm and good to soft going: tried blinkered, in cheekpieces later in 2009. *J. A. Glover* 83

THUNDERWING (IRE) 7 b. or br.g. Indian Danehill (IRE) 124 – Scandisk (IRE) 88 (Kenmare (FR) 125) [2009 68§: p13.9g 15.8g^3 16.1d May 15] good-topped gelding: modest handicapper: stays easy 15.8f: acts on fibresand, heavy and good to firm going: tried in visor/cheekpieces: ungenuine. *James Moffatt* 58 §

THURSTON (IRE) 3 ch.g. Barathea (IRE) 127 – Campiglia (IRE) (Fairy King (USA)) [2009 64: f7g^6 f7g f7g p7.1g p7g Oct 2] modest maiden at 2 yrs: well held in 2009: tried blinkered/tongue tied. *D. J. S. ffrench Davis* –

TIA JUANA (IRE) 2 b.f. (Apr 6) Shamardal (USA) 129 – Tiavanita (USA) (J O Tobin (USA) 130) [2009 p6g^4 5.1g^4 6m^4 Sep 15] €50,000Y: half-sister to several winners, including very smart 6f (at 2 yrs) to 1m (2000 Guineas) winner Island Sands (by Turtle Island) and 7-y-o King's Majesty: dam French maiden: similar form when fourth in maidens: bred to be suited by 7f+: sold 10,500 gns. *Saeed bin Suroor* 61

TICKET TO FREEDOM (NZ) 7 bl.g. Cape Cross (IRE) 129 – Macrowave (NZ) (Crested Wave (USA)) [2009 14.6m^3 Jun 14] won 1¼m maiden at Wanganui in 2006 65 from 5 starts in New Zealand for W. Thurlow: fit from hurdling (modest form), fair form when third in handicap at Doncaster on British Flat debut (tongue tied): stays 14.6f. *J. J. Quinn*

TICKET TO PARADISE 2 b.c. (Mar 16) Singspiel (IRE) 133 – Dream Ticket (USA) 73 (Danzig (USA)) [2009 8.3v Nov 4] strong colt: half-brother to several winners, including smart French/US 1m/1¼m performer Magic Mission (by Machiavellian) and 3-y-o Box Office: dam, 7f winner, out of smart performer up to 11f Capo di Monte: 50/1 and very green, down the field in maiden at Nottingham: looks sort to do better. *D. R. Lanigan* **– p**

TIDAL FORCE (USA) 3 ch.g. High Yield (USA) 121 – Shady Waters (CAN) (Rahy (USA) 115) [2009 75: p8g 7m^3 7m 8d^5 7m 7s p7m Dec 4] tall, close-coupled gelding: fair performer: in-and-out form in 2009, leaving P. Cole prior to final start: stays 1m: acts on good to firm and good to soft going: often blinkered. *A. J. McCabe* **71**

TIDDLIWINKS 3 b.g. Piccolo 121 – Card Games 89 (First Trump 118) [2009 p8.6m^4 7m^4 p7.1g* 7g 7.2v p8m^2 p7m* Dec 9] third foal: half-brother to 4-y-o Mrs Bun: dam, 5f (at 2 yrs) and 6f winner, half-sister to useful 1¼m performer Halicardia: fairly useful form: won maiden at Wolverhampton in September and handicap at Lingfield in December: stays 1m, will prove effective at 6f: best form on polytrack: has further improvement in him. *K. A. Ryan* **86 p**

TIEGS (IRE) 7 ch.m. Desert Prince (IRE) 130 – Helianthus (Groom Dancer (USA) 128) [2009 54§: p11g f14g Jan 27] angular mare: handicapper: well held in 2009: tried in cheekpieces: untrustworthy. *P. W. Hiatt* **– §**

TIFERNATI 5 b.g. Dansili 127 – Pain Perdu (IRE) (Waajib 121) [2009 95: 12g Apr 22] good-topped gelding: useful handicapper at 4 yrs: well below form sole Flat outing in 2009 (seemed unsuited by track at Epsom): stays 1¾m: acts on polytrack, firm and soft going: tried in blinkers/cheekpieces. *G. L. Moore* **–**

TIFFANY LADY 3 ch.f. Generous (IRE) 139 – Art Deco Lady 51 (Master Willie 129) [2009 –: p9.5g p7.1g^5 f8g p9.5g^6 p12g p12g p10g Dec 7] poor maiden: stays 1¼m: raced only on all-weather. *M. D. I. Usher* **47**

TIGER BREEZE (USA) 3 b.g. Roar of The Tiger (USA) 98 – M S Gripsholm (USA) (Goldwater (USA)) [2009 7m 7g^6 Jul 25] lengthy gelding: better effort in maidens on debut: looked awkward under pressure both starts. *Miss Jo Crowley* **58**

TIGERBYTHETALE (IRE) 4 b.g. Tiger Hill (IRE) 127 – Goldkatze (GER) (Czaravich (USA)) [2009 p10g^5 Jan 15] modest form in bumpers: tongue tied, similar form in seller on Flat debut. *D. R. C. Elsworth* **61**

TIGER COURT 2 b.f. (May 6) Tiger Hill (IRE) 127 – Cruinn A Bhord 107 (Inchinor 119) [2009 7g Oct 31] leggy filly: seventh foal: half-sister to 5-y-o Viva Vettori and 1½m winner Chess Board (by Vettori): dam, 7f winner, half-sister to Ouija Board: 66/1 and very green, well held in maiden at Newmarket. *E. A. L. Dunlop* **–**

TIGER DREAM 4 b.g. Oasis Dream 129 – Grey Way (USA) 109 (Cozzene (USA)) [2009 90: 7m 8m f7g^2 7s^2 8.1v^2 10.1d^5 8m^2 7m 7m 8.5m 8s 8.3s^3 8m^2 7.5g^5 8.1m* p9.5g^5 10g p8g^2 Nov 25] tall, angular gelding: has round action: fairly useful handicapper: won apprentice event at Haydock in September: effective at 7f/1m: acts on all-weather and any turf going: tried blinkered, often in cheekpieces nowadays: sold £10,500. *K. A. Ryan* **81**

TIGER FLASH 3 b.c. Dansili 127 – Miss Penton 66 (Primo Dominie 121) [2009 65p: 8d^3 10f^3 10m 10.1g^2 10.1g^3 p12.2g^3 10g^2 11.8m^4 Oct 13] well-made colt: fair maiden: stays 1½m: acts on polytrack, firm and good to soft going: tried blinkered: reliable: sold 18,000 gns, sent to Kazakhstan. *W. J. Haggas* **74**

TIGER GIRL 2 b.f. (Mar 7) Tiger Hill (IRE) 127 – Girl of My Dreams (IRE) 51 (Marju (IRE) 127) [2009 7g Aug 8] compact filly: half-sister to smart 2002 2-y-o 6f/7f (Rockfel Stakes) winner Luvah Girl (by Alzao), later 6.5f winner in USA, and 5-y-o Farley Star: dam 7f winner: 18/1 and very green, soundly beaten in maiden at Newmarket. *R. Charlton* **–**

TIGER HAWK (USA) 2 b.c. (Feb 2) Tale of The Cat (USA) 113 – Aura of Glory (CAN) (Halo (USA)) [2009 7g 7g^6 7g^3 7.1m p7.1g f8m* p10m p8.6g p8.6g^4 f8f* f7g Dec 18] smallish, compact colt: fair performer: claimed from S. Callaghan after third start, left K. M. Prendergast after fourth: won sellers at Southwell in November and December: stays 1m: acts on fibresand: usually blinkered. *P. D. Evans* **67**

TIGER REIGNS 3 b.g. Tiger Hill (IRE) 127 – Showery 76 (Rainbow Quest (USA) 134) [2009 68: 6m* 8s* 10m^4 8m^2 8d* 8.1g* 8s* 8m^4 Sep 19] workmanlike gelding: **99**

useful performer: won maiden at Catterick in April, then handicaps at Newcastle in May and June, Haydock in August and Thirsk (beat Canwinn by nose) in September: not best of runs final outing: should stay beyond 1m: unraced on firm going, has form on any other turf: game. *M. Dods*

TIGER'S ROCKET (IRE) 4 b.c. Monashee Mountain (USA) 115 – Brown Foam (Horage 124) [2009 69: f8d³ f8g f12g f8g Feb 12] big, strong colt: modest performer: stays 1¼m: acts on all-weather and soft ground: blinkered/visored in 2009: sold £1,200. *S. Gollings* **60**

TIGER STAR 2 b.g. (Feb 25) Tiger Hill (IRE) 127 – Rosy Outlook (USA) 79 (Trempolino (USA) 135) [2009 p7m p8f² Dec 16] half-brother to useful 2001 2-y-o 6f/7f winner Rapscallion (by Robellino) and smart 6f (at 2 yrs) to 1½m winner Orcadian (by Kirkwall), both temperamental: dam 6f winner: much better effort in maidens when 2 lengths second to Gracious Melange at Kempton, slowly away and running on strongly: will stay 1¼m: blinkered on debut: possibly not entirely straightforward, but should progress again. *J. M. P. Eustace* **80 p**

TIGER TEE (IRE) 4 b.g. Spectrum (IRE) 126 – Frill (Henbit (USA) 130) [2009 –: p16.5g* Aug 10] good-topped gelding: modest handicapper: won at Wolverhampton on sole 4-y-o outing: stays 16.5f: acts on polytrack. *John A. Quinn, Ireland* **59**

TIGER TRAIL (GER) 5 b.g. Tagula (IRE) 116 – Tweed Mill 88 (Selkirk (USA) 129) [2009 67: 5.7g 6m 6m⁴ 5.2m 5m² 5m⁴ Oct 1] big, strong gelding: modest maiden: best form at 6f: acts on polytrack, good to firm and good to soft going: tried in cheekpieces. *Mrs N. Smith* **63**

TIGHTROPE (IRE) 3 b.g. Refuse To Bend (IRE) 128 – Sisal (IRE) 84 (Danehill (USA) 126) [2009 –: p8g⁵ p7g p6g⁴ p6g⁶ 6m³ 5m 6f⁵ 5.1g 6f 6f 5f⁵ 6f⁵ 6m⁵ p5g⁵ p6m Dec 16] sturdy gelding: poor maiden: stays 6f: blinkered nowadays. *T. D. McCarthy* **48**

TIGNELLO (IRE) 4 b.g. Kendor (FR) 122 – La Genereuse (Generous (IRE) 139) [2009 67: 10m 8d³ 8m³ p8g³ 8.3m⁵ 8.1m⁶ 7.6d 8m Sep 13] modest maiden handicapper: stays 1m: acts on polytrack, good to firm and good to soft ground: often pulls hard. *G. L. Moore* **64**

TIKKA MASALA (IRE) 3 b.f. One Cool Cat (USA) 123 – Raysiza (IRE) (Alzao (USA) 117) [2009 60p: p7g² p7g 7m* 8m⁶ 8.3m 7m p6g Oct 24] tall, close-coupled filly: fair performer: easily best effort when winning handicap at Leicester in June: free-going sort, but stays 7f: acts on good to firm ground: visored final start: tongue tied in 2009: one to treat with caution: sold 4,000 gns. *Tom Dascombe* **77 §**

TILAPIA (IRE) 5 ch.g. Daggers Drawn (USA) 114 – Mrs Fisher (IRE) 94 (Salmon Leap (USA) 131) [2009 96d: p12.2g Jul 7] useful handicapper at best, regressive nowadays: said to have finished lame sole start at 5 yrs: tried blinkered. *Miss Gay Kelleway* **–**

TILERIUM'S DREAM (IRE) 3 b.g. Tillerman 123 – Thai Princess (IRE) 79 (Hamas (IRE) 125§) [2009 –: 8m 7m⁵ 8f⁴ 6s 8m 7m Sep 15] smallish gelding: modest maiden: stays 1m: acts on firm going: tried in cheekpieces. *K. A. Ryan* **55**

TILLERS SATISFIED (IRE) 3 b.f. Tillerman 123 – Lady of Pleasure (IRE) (Marju (IRE) 127) [2009 62: p7.1g⁴ p6g² 6.1g p6g 6d p6g³ Jun 22] rather leggy filly: modest performer: may prove best at 7f: acts on polytrack and firm ground. *R. Hollinshead* **62**

TILLIETUDLEM (FR) 3 gr.g. Kutub (IRE) 123 – Queenhood (FR) (Linamix (FR) 127) [2009 –: p9.5g 11.1m⁶ 12.1m³ 11.1d³ 11.1s⁶ 14.1m³ Aug 29] modest maiden: stays 1¾m: acts on good to firm going: won 2 juvenile hurdles in September. *J. S. Goldie* **50**

TILLY SHILLING (IRE) 5 b.m. Montjeu (IRE) 137 – Antiguan Jane 71 (Shirley Heights 130) [2009 p12g⁴ p12.2g 17.2d May 18] well-made mare: modest maiden: stays 17f: sold £1,200, no form over hurdles for Tim Vaughan. *Norma Twomey* **53**

TILLYS TALE 2 ch.f. (Mar 24) Lucky Story (USA) 128 – Otylia 57 (Wolfhound (USA) 126) [2009 5m⁵ 5g⁴ 5d* 5g 5m² 5.1m³ 5m 5s² 5g⁵ 5d² Sep 1] small, sparely-made filly: first foal: dam, maiden (stayed 6f), out of high-class sprinter Soba: fairly useful performer: won maiden at Thirsk in May: seemed to improve when length second to Absolute Music in minor event at Ripon final start: raced only at 5f: acts on soft and good to firm ground: usually races prominently. *P. T. Midgley* **81**

TILOS GEM (IRE) 3 ch.c. Trans Island 119 – Alpine Flair (IRE) (Tirol 127) [2009 77p: p8.6g² 8f* 8g 8.5g³ 9g 12m³ 12m³ p12g² p12.2g Nov 13] tall colt: has scope: fairly useful handicapper: won maiden at Bath in June: stays 1½m: acts on polytrack and firm going: races prominently. *M. Johnston* **86**

TILSWORTH GLENBOY 2 b.c. (Feb 20) Doyen (IRE) 132 – Chara 72 (Deploy 131) [2009 p7g p7m^5 Nov 26] easily better effort in maidens at Kempton when fifth to Too Putra: bred to be suited by 1¼m+. *J. R. Jenkins* **62**

TILT 7 b.g. Daylami (IRE) 138 – Tromond 94 (Lomond (USA) 128) [2009 97: 12g 18.7m 12s^3 16.2g^3 16.1d^6 18m f14g 12s p12.2g^5 Nov 20] useful-looking gelding: useful handicapper, on long losing run: effective at 1½m to 2¼m: acts on polytrack, heavy and good to firm going: tried blinkered, often wears cheekpieces: held up: temperamental (twice refused to race in 2009): won novice hurdle in December. *B. Ellison* **98 §**

TIMBAA (USA) 3 b.g. Anabaa (USA) 130 – Timber Ice (USA) 76 (Woodman (USA) 126) [2009 –: p12g^4 p12g 10f^3 10m^6 Jul 8] maiden, modest and sporadic form: barely stays 1½m. *Rae Guest* **56**

TIMBER TREASURE (USA) 5 b. or br.g. Forest Wildcat (USA) 120 – Lady Ilsley (USA) (Trempolino (USA) 135) [2009 89: 7m 5m 6f 6m 6f^6 6.9d* 6.9g^4 6d^3 7d 8s^3 10m 8.1m p6g^6 p7.1g^5 Nov 6] sturdy, close-coupled gelding: fair handicapper: won at Carlisle in July: stays 7f: acts on polytrack, good to firm and good to soft going: tried visored, often blinkered. *Paul Green* **78**

TIME BOOK (IRE) 3 b.c. Galileo (IRE) 134 – Pocket Book (IRE) 60 (Reference Point 139) [2009 11s 10.2d^3 12v^5 f12f* Nov 24] 260,000F: good-topped colt: third foal: half-brother to useful 2001 2-y-o 5f winner Berk The Jerk (by Bahamian Bounty), later successful in Australia, and 6-y-o Grand Palace: dam, Irish maiden who stayed 1¼m, half-sister to high-class 7f to 9f winner Indian Lodge: fairly useful form: won maiden at Southwell in November: stays 1½m: raced only on fibresand and going softer than good: sold £28,000. *J. H. M. Gosden* **83**

TIME FOR OLD TIME 3 b.f. Olden Times 121 – Pink Supreme 70 (Night Shift (USA)) [2009 61: 6m 5.1d 6m p7m p7m Nov 29] close-coupled filly: modest winner at 2 yrs: no form in 2009: tried in cheekpieces: tail flasher. *I. A. Wood* **–**

TIMELESS DREAM 3 b.f. Oasis Dream 129 – Simply Times (USA) 64 (Dodge (USA)) [2009 79: p7g 6m^2 p6g* p6g 6m^6 7g^6 Oct 16] sturdy filly: fair performer: won handicap at Lingfield in September: may prove best at 5f/6f: acts on polytrack and good to firm going. *P. W. Chapple-Hyam* **76**

TIMELESS ELEGANCE (IRE) 2 b.f. (Mar 4) Invincible Spirit (IRE) 121 – Tidy Wager (IRE) 62 (Catrail (USA) 123) [2009 7d 5v^4 6g^3 Sep 30] €34,000F, €65,000Y: compact filly: third foal: half-sister to Irish 6-y-o Holly Hill: dam Irish 7f winner: modest form in frame in maidens, not knocked about final start: should stay 7f: probably capable of better. *J. Howard Johnson* **54 p**

TIMELORD (IRE) 2 ch.g. (Jan 12) Chineur (FR) 123 – My Gray (FR) (Danehill (USA) 126) [2009 5.1g 6m^3 6m^4 6g 6m^3 6m 7d^2 8g p7m p7m 7d^5 Oct 22] workmanlike gelding: fair maiden: stays 7f: acts on good to firm and good to soft going: sold 800 gns, sent to France. *S. Kirk* **66**

TIME LOUP 3 b.g. Loup Sauvage (USA) 125 – Bird of Time (IRE) 75 (Persian Bold 123) [2009 57d: f6g^5 6m^5 5m^6 f5g Jun 2] small gelding: modest winner at 2 yrs: well held in 2009: tried tongue tied/blinkered. *S. R. Bowring* **–**

TIMELY JAZZ (IRE) 2 b.c. (Mar 8) Noverre (USA) 125 – Ricadonna (Kris 135) [2009 7g 7g^2 7g^2 p7.1g* 7m^4 8m 7m Oct 17] 58,000Y: strong colt: fourth foal: half-brother to 3 winners, including useful 2006 2-y-o 7f/7.5f winner Iron Fist (by Desert Style) and 3-y-o Valid Point: dam unraced out of sister to 1000 Guineas/Oaks winner Midway Lady, herself dam of Oaks winner Eswarah: useful performer: won maiden at Wolverhampton (by 5 lengths) in August: best effort when 1½ lengths fourth to Vale of York in listed race at Goodwood: stiff tasks last 2 starts: should stay 1m: acts on polytrack and good to firm going: usually makes running. *B. J. Meehan* **100**

TIME MACHINE (UAE) 3 ch.g. Halling (USA) 133 – Tempting Fate (IRE) 113 (Persian Bold 123) [2009 10.1d^2 12m^4 9.7m^2 10m* p10.7g^6 9.5m^6 Sep 26] rather leggy gelding: second foal: half-brother to Irish 4-y-o Enigma Code: dam 6f (at 2 yrs)/7f winner: fairly useful performer: won maiden at Newmarket in June (left J. Gosden 95,000 gns after): stays 1¼m: acts on good to firm ground. *R. A. Hennessy, Ireland* **88**

TIME MEDICEAN 3 gr. or ro.g. Medicean 128 – Ribbons And Bows (IRE) 91 (Dr Devious (IRE) 127) [2009 65p: p7g^6 6m* 6g^2 7g^3 6d^4 7m 6g^5 Aug 31] lightly-made gelding: fairly useful performer: won maiden at Pontefract in April: likely to prove best around 7f: acts on soft and good to firm going: sold 30,000 gns, then gelded. *M. R. Channon* **88**

TIME 'N' TALENT 3 b.c. Act One 124 – Turn of A Century 85 (Halling (USA) 133) [2009 56: 8.5g* 7d[4] 9m 9.5m p10.7g[3] Nov 13] tall, leggy colt: fairly useful handicapper: won maiden at Killarney in May: stays 10.7f: acts on polytrack and good to soft going: usually tongue tied in 2009. *James Leavy, Ireland* **92**

TIMEPIECE 2 b.f. (Feb 3) Zamindar (USA) 116 – Clepsydra 78 (Sadler's Wells (USA) 132) [2009 8m[2] p8g* 8g* Oct 31] useful-looking filly: sixth foal: closely related to useful 1¼m winner Sandglass (by Zafonic) and half-sister to 3 winners, including 3-y-o Father Time and smart 7f to 1¼m (including at 2 yrs) winner Passage of Time (by Dansili): dam, 1½m winner, out of half-sister to very smart 1m to 1½m filly All At Sea: most progressive: won maiden at Lingfield (made all) and listed event at Newmarket (beat Nurture by nose, pair clear, taking time to wind up fully), both in October: will be well suited by 1¼m+: smart prospect. *H. R. A. Cecil* **104 p**

TIMES AHEAD (USA) 2 b.c. (Feb 26) Proud Citizen (USA) 122 – Nanas Cozy Account (USA) (Langfuhr (CAN) 124) [2009 7d Aug 7] $57,000Y: third foal: half-brother to winners in USA by Parents' Reward and Van Nistelrooy: dam US 2-y-o 5f winner: 80/1 and backward, encouraging ninth to Al Zir in maiden at Newmarket: capable of better. *P. W. Chapple-Hyam* **65 p**

TIMES UP 3 b.g. Olden Times 121 – Princess Genista 108 (Ile de Bourbon (USA) 133) [2009 81p: 10m[2] 11.8m[3] 10m[3] 12d* 12s[5] 12m* 14m[3] 14.1s Oct 12] leggy gelding: useful performer: won maiden at Pontefract in July and handicap at Newmarket in August: good 1¾ lengths third to Royal Diamond at Ffos Las next time: stays 1¾m: acts on good to firm and good to soft going. *J. L. Dunlop* **98**

TIMETEAM (IRE) 3 b.g. Danetime (IRE) 121 – Ceannanas (IRE) 77 (Magical Wonder (USA) 125) [2009 89: 7s 6m[2] 6m 7g 6g 6g p7m[4] Dec 9] smallish, close-coupled gelding: fairly useful handicapper: left S. Kirk 2,500 gns prior to final start: stays 6f: acts on polytrack, soft and good to firm ground: tried tongue tied. *A. Bailey* **89**

TIME TO PLAY 4 b.g. Best of The Bests (IRE) 122 – Primavera 65 (Anshan 119) [2009 71: f8g 7g p12m[6] Dec 9] sturdy gelding: maiden, just modest form at 4 yrs: stays 1¼m: acts on polytrack and good to soft going. *T. T. Clement* **56**

TIME TO REGRET 9 b.g. Presidium 124 – Scoffera 63 (Scottish Reel 123) [2009 66: p8.6g p8.6g[5] 8.3m p9.5g[3] 8.3m[4] 8g[2] p8.6g[4] p8g[4] 8d Jul 25] tall gelding: modest handicapper: stays 9.5f: acts on all-weather and any turf going: wears cheekpieces: tends to hang: often races up with pace. *I. W. McInnes* **62**

TIMETOWYNAGAIN 2 ch.g. (May 5) Reset (AUS) 124 – Ideal Figure (Zafonic (USA) 130) [2009 6m 8d Oct 13] well beaten in maidens. *C. W. Fairhurst* **–**

TIMOCRACY 4 br.g. Cape Cross (IRE) 129 – Tithcar 67 (Cadeaux Genereux 131) [2009 85: 10g* 12m[3] 12s 10s[3] 10s Aug 26] medium-sized gelding: fairly useful handicapper: landed gamble at Pontefract in April: probably best around 1¼m: acts on soft and good to firm going. *T. D. Walford* **83**

TINAAR (USA) 3 b.f. Giant's Causeway (USA) 132 – Seattle Tac (USA) (Seattle Slew (USA)) [2009 10g[6] 8m[4] 10m* p11g* p12g[3] p12g[2] Oct 26] $400,000Y: big filly: first foal: dam, US 5.5f (at 2 yrs) and 9f winner, half-sister to very smart 6f/7f winner One Cool Cat: useful performer: won maiden at Windsor in August and handicap at Kempton in September: good efforts in handicaps last 2 starts, second to Mister New York at Lingfield: stays 1½m: raced only on polytrack and good/good to firm ground. *G. A. Butler* **99**

TINA'S BEST (IRE) 4 b.f. King's Best (USA) 132 – Phantom Waters 79 (Pharly (FR) 130) [2009 82: 7m 8m[3] 7m 7m Oct 13] close-coupled filly: modest performer nowadays: stays 8.3f: acts on polytrack, firm and good to soft going. *E. J. Alston* **60**

TIN CHA WOODY (USA) 4 b. or br.g. Johannesburg (USA) 127 – I'm Beguiled Again (USA) (Wild Again (USA)) [2009 86: p7g p8g p6g p7.1g[3] p9.5g Dec 14] just fair performer in 2009: may prove best at 1m: acts on polytrack, well held only outing on turf (heavy going): tried tongue tied. *D. Loughnane, Ireland* **76**

TING TING (USA) 2 b.f. (Mar 13) Empire Maker (USA) 129 – My Sweet Heart (USA) (You And I (USA) 118) [2009 8.5m[3] 9m[3] p8.6g Oct 10] $180,000Y: sturdy filly: second foal: dam, US 1m winner, half-sister to Kentucky Derby/Preakness Stakes winner War Emblem: modest form when third in maidens at Beverley and Redcar: tailed off final start: bred to stay 1¼m. *T. P. Tate* **52**

TINKERBELLE (IRE) 3 br.f. Marju (IRE) 127 – Pershaan (IRE) 92 (Darshaan 133) [2009 –: p10g[4] 12.1g[2] 14.1s[3] p12g[3] 12m p12.2g[4] p12g* p12.2g[5] Oct 15] leggy filly: fair handicapper: won handicap at Lingfield in October: stays 1¾m: acts on polytrack and soft ground: in cheekpieces last 2 starts. *J. L. Dunlop* **71**

TINSHU (IRE) 3 ch.f. Fantastic Light (USA) 134 – Ring of Esteem (Mark of Esteem (IRE) 137) [2009 52p: p9.5g* p10g² p10g⁵ 10.3m⁴ p12g 10m* 10g² 9.9m 8.3m² 8.3f² 8.1d⁵ 10d⁵ p10m* p10g* p10g⁶ Nov 21] good-topped filly: fairly useful performer: won maiden at Wolverhampton in January, then handicaps at Windsor in May, and Kempton and Lingfield in November: stays 1¼m: acts on polytrack and firm going: probably not straightforward. *D. Haydn Jones* **94**

TIPPERARY BOUTIQUE (IRE) 2 b.f. (Apr 1) Danehill Dancer (IRE) 117 – Moselle 108 (Mtoto 134) [2009 7g⁵ 7.2v* Oct 31] €90,000Y: fifth foal: half-sister to 2 winners in France by Sadler's Wells, including useful 9f (at 2 yrs)/1¼m winner Leitmotiv (stays 1½m): dam 1m to 10.4f winner: promising in maidens 3 months apart, winning at Ayr by 2¾ lengths from Xilerator, travelling strongly up with pace: bred to be well suited by 1m+: will improve further. *B. W. Hills* **83 p**

TIP TOP STYLE 6 b.g. Tipsy Creek (USA) 115 – Eliza Jane (Mistertopogigo (IRE) 118) [2009 12g May 23] maiden: tailed off in seller sole Flat start since 2007: often tongue tied/in cheekpieces. *A. Crook* **–**

TIRADITO (USA) 2 b. or br.c. (Apr 30) Tale of The Cat (USA) 113 – Saratoga Sugar (USA) (Gone West (USA)) [2009 5.2g² 5f⁵ 6m³ p7f Dec 20] $50,000Y: third foal: closely related to winner in USA by Forestry: dam, US maiden, sister to US Grade 1 9f winner Link River: fair maiden: off 7 months, well held in nursery: should be suited by 7f. *M. Botti* **72**

TISIFONE 3 b.f. American Post 121 – Mary Rose (ITY) (Royal Academy (USA) 130) [2009 8.1g⁴ 10m 9g p9.5g Aug 17] fourth foal: half-sister to useful Italian 7.5f (including at 2 yrs) to 9f winner Mary Pekan (by Sri Pekan): dam, Italian 9f/1¼m winner, half-sister to dam of very smart sprinter Amadeus Wolf: fair form in maiden on debut: below form after: should stay beyond 1m. *C. G. Cox* **66**

TISLAAM (IRE) 2 gr.c. (Feb 25) With Approval (CAN) – Lady Angola (USA) 83 (Lord At War (ARG)) [2009 6g 6g³ 6m⁵ 6m² 6m⁵ 6g Sep 17] €12,000F, €35,000Y: tall colt: third foal: half-brother to fairly useful 2007 2-y-o 6f winner Raiding Party (by Orpen), later successful in USA: dam, 1½m winner, half-sister to dam of US Grade 1 9f winner Honor In War: fair maiden: well below form last 2 starts, including in visor: will be suited by 7f+: sold 20,000 gns. *M. R. Channon* **74**

TISLIMEEN 2 b.f. (Mar 6) Alhaarth (IRE) 126 – Torgau (IRE) 109 (Zieten (USA) 118) [2009 7s⁵ 7v Oct 24] 34,000Y: fifth foal: half-sister to fairly useful 7f winner Knapton Hill (by Zamindar) and German 11f winner Timur Danon (by Lando): dam 2-y-o 5f/6f (Cherry Hinton Stakes) winner: 16/1, encouraging 2¾ lengths fifth to Kithonia in maiden at Salisbury, isolated on outer: well held in listed event at Newbury. *M. R. Channon* **74**

TITAN TRIUMPH 5 b.g. Zamindar (USA) 116 – Triple Green 69 (Green Desert (USA) 127) [2009 96: p8g² p8g* 8m p8g p7g⁶ May 1] well-made gelding: useful handicapper: improved again when winning at Lingfield in February by 1¼ lengths from Majuro: well held after, then gelded: effective at 7f/1m: acts on polytrack and good to firm ground: tongue tied: held up, and has good turn of foot. *W. J. Knight* **100**

TITFER (IRE) 4 ch.g. Fath (USA) 116 – Fur Hat (Habitat 134) [2009 58d: p11g Jan 10] compact gelding: lost way at 3 yrs, and well held only start in 2009. *A. W. Carroll* **–**

TITINIUS (IRE) 9 ch.g. Titus Livius (FR) 115 – Maiyria (IRE) 68 (Shernazar 131) [2009 72: 12.5m⁴ 9.9m 12m³ 12g⁴ 9.8m⁴ 10m Jun 29] good-bodied gelding: modest performer: stays 1½m: acts on any turf going: usually wears cheekpieces/visor nowadays: none too resolute. *Micky Hammond* **64**

TITO (IRE) 4 b.g. Diktat 126 – T G'S Girl 57 (Selkirk (USA) 129) [2009 73: p6g 7.5m Aug 30] tall, good-topped gelding: maiden: well held in 2009, leaving Paul Mason after reappearance: stayed 6f: acted on good to firm and good to soft ground: dead. *B. N. Pollock* **–**

TITOLI DI CODA (IRE) 2 ch.f. (Apr 23) Bertolini (USA) 125 – Mystic Tempo (USA) 76 (El Gran Senor (USA) 136) [2009 5f 5g 6m p5g Oct 21] neat filly: half-sister to several winners, notably high-class 7f/1m performer Le Vie dei Colori (by Efisio): dam 6f winner, including at 2 yrs: well held in maidens/nursery: sold 10,000 gns. *L. M. Cumani* **–**

TITUS ANDRONICUS (IRE) 3 b.g. Danetime (IRE) 121 – Scarlet Empress 79 (Second Empire (IRE) 124) [2009 81: 5m* 5s⁵ 5g² 5.1g² 5m³ 5.1m 5d² 5g 5m Aug 20] sturdy gelding: fairly useful handicapper: won at Musselburgh in April: best at bare 5f: acts on any going: usually front runner. *K. A. Ryan* **94**

TITUS GENT 4 ch.g. Tumbleweed Ridge 117 – Genteel (IRE) 58 (Titus Livius (FR) 115) [2009 59: p8g p7.1g^{5} f8g p7g^{4} p5g^{5} p6g 6d 7f p6g^{2} 6s* 6m^{5} 6m^{6} p6g^{3} p6g* p6g^{3} p6g^{2} p6g p6g^{2} p6g^{6} Dec 7] fair performer: won ladies handicap at Thirsk in August and seller at Wolverhampton (left J. Ryan 7,000 gns) in October: best at 6f: acts on polytrack and soft ground: tried in cheekpieces. *R. A. Harris* **74**

TIVERS SONG (USA) 5 gr.g. Buddha (USA) 122 – Rousing (USA) (Alydar (USA)) [2009 f12d f12g 10.2m^{3} 9.9m^{2} 10.1m^{2} 9.9f^{5} 9.9g^{2} 10.9m^{3} p12f^{3} p13.9g^{4} p13.9g Nov 30] close-coupled, workmanlike gelding: modest maiden handicapper: may prove best beyond 1½m: acts on polytrack and good to firm ground: usually wears headgear nowadays: tried tongue tied. *John A. Harris* **60**

TIZA (SAF) 7 b.g. Goldkeeper (USA) – Mamushka (SAF) (Elliodor (FR) 114) [2009 117: 5.5d* 6m^{6} 6g* 6.5g 6s^{4} 6s^{5} Nov 19] smart performer: as good as ever when winning listed race at Fontainebleau (by ¾ length from Contest) in March and Prix de Ris-Orangis at Maisons-Laffitte (for second time, led near line to beat Delvita a neck) in July: just respectable efforts next 2 starts, seventh in Prix Maurice de Gheest at Deauville and fourth in Prix de Seine-et-Oise at Maisons-Laffitte: below form in listed race at Fontainebleau final outing: effective at 5.5f to 7f: acts on soft going, below form on dirt and good to firm: tried blinkered, usually in cheekpieces nowadays: has had tongue tied: held up, and ideally suited by well-run race. *A. de Royer Dupre, France* **117**

TOBAGO BAY 4 b.g. Tobougg (IRE) 125 – Perfect Dream 72 (Emperor Jones (USA) 119) [2009 68: 15.4g^{2} 17.2f^{5} 15.4m^{3} Aug 6] neat gelding: fair maiden: stays 2m: acts on firm and good to soft ground: tried visored, blinkered nowadays: front runner. *Miss S. West* **65**

TOBAGO REEF 5 b.g. Tobougg (IRE) 125 – Silly Mid-On (Midyan (USA) 124) [2009 –: p8.6m^{6} 7.6g 7.6m 10.4g Aug 6] good-topped gelding: just poor form in handicaps in 2009: stays 7f: acts on polytrack, raced on good/good to firm going on turf: wears headgear. *C. W. Moore* **48**

TOBALLA 4 b.f. Tobougg (IRE) 125 – Ball Gown 98 (Jalmood (USA) 126) [2009 57: 10f^{6} 8g 10.1g^{6} 10m 8m p8g^{5} p7g f7f Dec 12] leggy filly: modest maiden: stays 11.5f: acts on polytrack and good to soft going: tried in cheekpieces: tongue tied last 3 starts. *P. Leech* **55**

TOBAR SUIL LADY (IRE) 4 b.f. Statue of Liberty (USA) 115 – Stellarette (IRE) 73 (Lycius (USA) 124) [2009 74: p8g 7g 7s 8s p8g 7s 7s^{6} 5d p7g^{2} Nov 26] tall, good-topped filly: fair handicapper: left J. Spearing after reappearance: stays 1m: acts on polytrack, firm and good to soft going: tried blinkered/in cheekpieces: irresolute. *David Christie, Ireland* **66 §**

TO BE OR NOT TO BE 4 b.f. Tobougg (IRE) 125 – Lady Mayor (Kris 135) [2009 80: f7g^{2} p7.1g^{4} 7m* 7m 6.1g 7d^{4} p7f 8m^{4} 7v^{6} Oct 24] fairly useful handicapper: won at Yarmouth in May: effective at 7f to 8.6f: acts on all-weather, heavy and good to firm ground: sold 20,000 gns, sent to Qatar. *John Berry* **84**

TOBOGGAN LADY 5 b.m. Tobougg (IRE) 125 – Northbend (Shirley Heights 130) [2009 75: 16m^{6} 16.2g^{6} May 23] tall, close-coupled mare: modest handicapper: stays 2¼m: acts on soft and good to firm ground: tried in cheekpieces: often races lazily. *Mrs A. Duffield* **60**

TOBOND (IRE) 3 b.g. Tobougg (IRE) 125 – Rajmata (IRE) 66 (Prince Sabo 123) [2009 96+: p7g^{6} 6m^{6} 7m 8.3g^{6} Jun 11] compact gelding: fairly useful handicapper: has form at 1m, best efforts at 7f: acts on polytrack and good to firm ground: sold 22,000 gns in July. *M. Botti* **92**

TOBOUGGIE ON DOWN 2 ch.f. (Mar 12) Tobougg (IRE) 125 – Park Ave Princess (IRE) 63 (Titus Livius (FR) 115) [2009 6m^{6} Sep 14] leggy filly: first foal: dam, 2-y-o 7f winner, sister to useful sprinter Dusty Dazzler: 100/1, looked awkward when sixth to Secret Queen in maiden at Redcar (also caused trouble at start). *J. A. Glover* **53**

TOBRATA 3 ch.g. Tobougg (IRE) 125 – Sabrata (IRE) (Zino 127) [2009 7d^{5} 8g^{5} f8f^{2} f7m^{2} p8.6g^{3} p8.6g^{3} Dec 14] workmanlike gelding: fair form in maidens: stays 8.6f: acts on all-weather. *M. Brittain* **69**

TO BUBBLES 4 b.f. Tobougg (IRE) 125 – Effervescent 89 (Efisio 120) [2009 63: f7d f7g^{6} f8g^{3} p8.6g f8g Mar 27] compact filly: modest handicapper: stays 1m: acts on fibresand. *A. G. Newcombe* **53**

TOBY TYLER 3 b.g. Best of The Bests (IRE) 122 – Pain Perdu (IRE) (Waajib 121) [2009 72: f7g* 8.1m f7g^{5} 7m^{4} 7m 8g^{6} Aug 5] big, close-coupled gelding: fair handicapper: won at Southwell in March: should stay 1m: acts on fibresand, heavy and good to firm ground. *P. T. Midgley* **76**

TODAY'S THE DAY 3 b.f. Alhaarth (IRE) 126 – Dayville (USA) 86 (Dayjur (USA) 137) [2009 72: 6m4 5.1m5 6m2 Apr 30] workmanlike filly: fair maiden: stays 7f: acts on polytrack, good to firm and good to soft ground: wears cheekpieces/blinkers. *M. A. Jarvis* **69**

TODBER 4 b.f. Cape Cross (IRE) 129 – Dominica 115 (Alhaarth (IRE) 126) [2009 72: 5.1m4 p5g5 p6g* p6g4 p6g Nov 25] good-topped filly: fairly useful handicapper: won apprentice event at Kempton in October: stays 6f: acts on polytrack, unraced on extremes of going on turf: visored. *M. P. Tregoning* **80**

TOGA TIGER (IRE) 2 b.g. (Mar 29) Antonius Pius (USA) 123§ – Minerwa (GER) (Protektor (GER) 120) [2009 5.1g3 5.1f2 6m2 6d5 7f* 7.1g3 p7g* 8m 8m5 7d 8g6 Oct 23] €40,000F, 13,000Y: rather leggy gelding: second foal: dam useful German 5.5f to 7f winner: fairly useful performer: won maiden at Lingfield in June and nursery at Kempton in July: stays 1m: acts on polytrack and firm going: sold 24,000 gns, then gelded. *M. R. Channon* **90**

TOGIAK (IRE) 2 b.c. (Feb 18) Azamour (IRE) 130 – Hawksbill Special (IRE) (Taufan (USA) 119) [2009 7d4 p8g* 8m2 8g5 Oct 10] €100,000F, 45,000 2-y-o: smallish, strong colt: half-brother to several winners, including useful 2000 2-y-o 6f winner Zietunzeen (by Zieten) and 5-y-o Cape Hawk: dam, unraced, out of half-sister to high-class sprinter Sayf El Arab: won maiden at Kempton (by neck from Navy List, pair clear) in August: good efforts after, including 4¾ lengths fifth to Morana in Autumn Stakes at Ascot: stays 1m: acts on polytrack and good to firm ground: useful. *E. A. L. Dunlop* **99 +**

TOLEDO GOLD (IRE) 3 ch.g. Needwood Blade 117 – Eman's Joy 68 (Lion Cavern (USA) 117) [2009 69: 7m2 7.6m3 6g 8.1g 8m 8m Oct 3] fairly useful performer: clear best efforts on first 2 starts: gelded prior to final outing: stays 7.6f: acts on good to firm going: has joined Mrs S. Smith. *E. J. Alston* **81**

TOLL ROAD 3 b.f. Dubai Destination (USA) 127 – Endorsement 107 (Warning 136) [2009 51: p8g6 Jan 10] modest form in 2 polytrack maidens: will be suited by 1¼m+: sold 11,000 gns in February, sent to Kazakhstan. *E. A. L. Dunlop* **49**

TOMATIN 2 b.c. (Mar 9) Kyllachy 129 – Lowrianna (IRE) 50 (Cyrano de Bergerac 120) [2009 p6g4 6d Oct 24] 40,000F, 65,000Y: lengthy colt: half-brother to 3 winners, including useful 5f (at 2 yrs)/6f winner Simianna (by Bluegrass Prince) and 6f (including at 2 yrs) to 7.5f winner Bodfari Anna (by Casteddu): dam 2-y-o 5f winner: much better effort when 7½ lengths eighth to Layla's Hero in listed event at Doncaster: sold 6,500 gns. *P. W. Chapple-Hyam* **82**

TOMBI (USA) 5 b.g. Johannesburg (USA) 127 – Tune In To The Cat (USA) (Tunerup (USA)) [2009 113: 7m4 6m6 6d6 7m 6m6 7m Oct 3] rangy gelding: just useful performer in 2009, best efforts when fourth to Regal Parade in minor event at York and sixth to Jimmy Styles in Ayr Gold Cup fifth outing, first home on stand side: effective at 5f to 7f: acts on firm and good to soft going: tried tongue tied: has shaped as if amiss (including on final start). *J. Howard Johnson* **109**

TOMBOV (FR) 3 b. or br.g. Laveron 111 – Zamsara (FR) (Zino 127) [2009 74p: 10.2g 11.7g6 Aug 6] fair winner at 2 yrs: no form in 2009, including in juvenile hurdles: bred to stay 1½m+. *A. King* **–**

TOM FOLAN 2 b.f. (Feb 18) Namid 128 – My Golly (Mozart (IRE) 131) [2009 5d2 5m3 5.1m3 5m5 5s* 6g p5g6 Aug 11] 3,500Y: angular filly: first foal: dam unraced out of sister to smart 1¼m/1½m performer Bustan: fair performer: dead-heated in nursery at Haydock in July: will prove best at 5f: acts on soft and good to firm going: in cheekpieces last 3 starts, slowly away last 2. *H. J. Collingridge* **70**

TOMINATOR 2 gr.g. (Mar 20) Generous (IRE) 139 – Jucinda 58 (Midyan (USA) 124) [2009 7.1s5 7g2 7.5g* 7d6 7m* 8g2 Oct 19] 7,500Y: tall, good-bodied gelding: seventh foal: brother to Italian 1m (including at 2 yrs)/10.5f winner Gina Parrini and half-brother to fairly useful 5.7f (at 2 yrs) to 1m winner Gems Bond (by Magic Ring): dam, 15.4f winner, sister to Goodwood Cup winner Tioman Island: fairly useful performer: won maiden at Beverley in August and nursery at Catterick in September: good short-head second to Gallic Star in listed event at Pontefract final start, dictating: should be suited by 1¼m+: acts on good to firm going. *R. Hollinshead* **93**

TOMINTOUL SINGER (IRE) 2 ch.f. (Mar 2) Johannesburg (USA) 127 – Shivaree 88 (Rahy (USA) 115) [2009 5g2 6g2 5f* 6g3 Oct 30] 25,000Y: first foal: dam, 2-y-o 6f winner, out of half-sister to smart French miler Firth of Lorne: most progressive: won maiden at Folkestone in July: off 3 months, excellent 1¼ lengths third to Queen's Grace in listed race at Newmarket, travelling best most of way: acts on firm ground: smart sprinting prospect. *H. R. A. Cecil* **98 p**

TOMINTOUL STAR 3 gr.f. Dansili 127 – Lixian (Linamix (FR) 127) [2009 68p: 10m 12g^6 12m^6 Aug 23] tall, leggy filly: modest maiden: stays 1½m: unraced on ground softer than good: sold 3,000 gns in October. *H. R. A. Cecil* **62**

TOMMY TOBOUGG 5 ch.g. Tobougg (IRE) 125 – Celebrate (IRE) 77 (Generous (IRE) 139) [2009 10.1g^3 9.1g 11.1m^5 7.1m Jun 19] sturdy gelding: modest performer: missed 2008: stays 1½m: yet to race on extremes of going. *Miss Lucinda V. Russell* **54**

TOMODACHI (IRE) 2 b.f. (Feb 21) Arakan (USA) 123 – Ivory Bride 86 (Domynsky 110) [2009 8g^2 Oct 20] €26,000F, £32,000Y: half-sister to several winners, including smart 5f to (at 2 yrs) 7f winner Funfair Wane (by Unfuwain) and fairly useful 6f to 1m winner Pure Imagination (by Royal Academy): dam 2-y-o 6f winner: 66/1, head second to Principal Role in maiden at Yarmouth, slightly awkward under pressure. *M. Botti* **86**

TOMS LAUGHTER 5 ch.g. Mamalik (USA) 115 – Time Clash 67 (Timeless Times (USA) 99) [2009 110: 5m 5m^6 5.2m 5g^5 p5g^3 p6m p5.1g f5g p6g Dec 28] lengthy gelding: just useful handicapper in 2009: effective at 5f/6f: acts on all-weather, soft and good to firm going: wears cheekpieces/blinkers. *R. A. Harris* **95**

TOM TOWER (IRE) 5 b.g. Cape Cross (IRE) 129 – La Belle Katherine (USA) (Lyphard (USA) 132) [2009 –: 8g* 7.2g^3 8.1s* 8.1v 8s^3 8s^2 Sep 5] tall, good-topped gelding: fair handicapper: won at Ayr in June and Haydock in July: was effective at 7f/1m: acted on soft and good to firm ground: tried tongue tied: often front runner: dead. *A. C. Whillans* **78**

TOM WADE (IRE) 2 b.g. (Feb 2) Rakti 130 – Plutonia (Sadler's Wells (USA) 132) [2009 p8g^5 p8g p8g Nov 1] close-coupled gelding: best effort in maidens when fifth to Get A Grip at Kempton: mulish behind stall/soon off bridle final outing (gelded after): likely to be suited by 1¼m. *M. A. Jarvis* **64**

TONGALOOMA 3 ch.f. Shinko Forest (IRE) – Schatzi 54§ (Chilibang 120) [2009 7m p6g^4 p5.1g* p5.1g Nov 30] third foal: half-sister to 4-y-o Tanley: dam unreliable sprint maiden: modest form: won maiden at Wolverhampton in October: bred to prove best at 5f/6f: raced only on polytrack and good to firm going. *James Moffatt* **58**

TONY THE TAP 8 b.g. Most Welcome 131 – Laleston 73 (Junius (USA) 124) [2009 98: 5m^6 5m^5 5m 5.1m* 5g^2 5.6m Sep 12] smallish gelding: useful handicapper: won at Chepstow in August: better than ever when length second to Blue Jack at Sandown next time: best at 5f/6f: acts on polytrack, firm and good to soft going: effective visored/blinkered or not: held up (sometimes gets behind). *W. R. Muir* **100**

TOO GRAND 4 ch.f. Zaha (CAN) 106 – Gold Linnet 69 (Nashwan (USA) 135) [2009 62: p7g* p8g^5 p8g p7g p8g^4 p7g^4 Mar 24] modest handicapper: won at Kempton in January: stays 1¼m: acts on polytrack and good to firm going: often visored in 2009: held up. *J. J. Bridger* **60**

TOOLENTIDHAAR (USA) 5 b.m. Swain (IRE) 134 – Rababah (USA) (Woodman (USA) 126) [2009 8m^3 p8g^2 10.1m^3 8.3f 8.3m p8g Sep 9] 5,000 3-y-o: workmanlike mare: first foal: dam unraced half-sister to useful performer up to 1½m Nakheel out of Irish 1000 Guineas winner Matiya: well held in bumpers: fair maiden on Flat: stays 1¼m: raced on polytrack and ground firmer than good. *Andrew Turnell* **78**

TOO MUCH TROUBLE 3 b.g. Barathea (IRE) 127 – Tentpole (USA) 85 (Rainbow Quest (USA) 134) [2009 92p: 12m* 12.3m^6 10m^4 13m^5 12g^6 14m 10m^4 Sep 19] close-coupled gelding: useful performer: won 3-runner minor event at Catterick in April: creditable fourth after, to Glass Harmonium in listed race at Royal Ascot and to Honimiere in handicap at Newmarket: gelded after: stays 1½m: acts on good to firm and good to soft going: suspect attitude. *M. R. Channon* **99**

TOO PUTRA (IRE) 2 b.c. (Apr 7) Oratorio (IRE) 128 – Urgent Liaison (IRE) (High Estate 127) [2009 p7m* Nov 26] 100,000Y: seventh foal: closely related to useful 1¼m winner Imoya (by Desert King) and half-brother to 2 winners, including Irish 8-y-o Qudraat: dam unraced half-sister to very smart performer up to 1¼m Great Dane: 5/2 favourite, promising when winning maiden at Kempton by head from Plenty O'Toole, taking time to find stride/strong at finish: will be suited by 1m+: will do better still. *R. Charlton* **76 p**

TOO TALL 3 b.c. Medicean 128 – Embark (Soviet Star (USA) 128) [2009 69p: 8m 7m^5 6d^5 7f^2 p9.5g^3 p12.2g^3 10.1d^3 p10g^2 Nov 18] big, good-topped colt: fair maiden handicapper: left L. Cumani prior to final start: stays 1½m: acts on polytrack, firm and good to soft ground: tried blinkered: joined Tim Vaughan. *J. R. Boyle* **78**

TOP BID 5 b.g. Auction House (USA) 120 – Trump Street 77 (First Trump 118) [2009 65: 5.1m6 5m2 5g 5g* 5m4 6g2 5.1v4 5m 6s 6m 6d6 6g 5.1g4 Oct 28] smallish, lengthy gelding: has a quick action: fair handicapper: won apprentice event at Haydock in July: best at 5f/6f: acts on polytrack, heavy and good to firm ground: blinkered. *T. D. Easterby* **70**

TOPCROFT 3 b.g. Mujahid (USA) 125 – Starminda 50 (Zamindar (USA) 116) [2009 –: p8g 8g5 p8.6g5 7g p8g5 p8g* p6m* f8f* Dec 17] fairly useful handicapper: left Mrs C. Dunnett, vastly improved when winning at Kempton (2 apprentice races) and Southwell, all in December: effective at 6f to 1m: acts on all-weather: visored last 3 starts. *D. Shaw* **82 +**

TOPFLIGHTREBELLION 4 b.f. Mark of Esteem (IRE) 137 – Jamarj 113 (Tyrnavos 129) [2009 57d: p8.6g4 f11g Apr 27] modest maiden: stays 8.6f: acts on all-weather: tried in cheekpieces. *Mrs G. S. Rees* **55**

TOP FLIGHT SPLASH 3 b.f. Bertolini (USA) 125 – Making Waves (IRE) 70 (Danehill (USA) 126) [2009 56: 7m4 f6g2 f7g2 6d 7g p7m3 f7m6 p6g f7f Dec 12] lengthy filly: modest performer on all-weather, poor on turf: stays 7f: acts on all-weather: wears cheekpieces/visor. *Mrs G. S. Rees* **48 a56**

TOP JARO (FR) 6 b.g. Marathon (USA) 116 – Shahmy (USA) (Lear Fan (USA) 130) [2009 76: f8g6 p8.6g6 f14g f11g p12.2g Feb 16] sturdy gelding: just modest performer in 2009 (blinkered): stays 1¼m: acts on all-weather, heavy and good to firm going. *Mrs R. A. Carr* **50**

TOP MAN DAN (IRE) 4 b.g. Danetime (IRE) 121 – Aphra Benn (IRE) 67 (In The Wings 128) [2009 60: 12.4s6 10.9d Jun 15] lengthy, workmanlike gelding: modest maiden handicapper: stays 1½m: acts on firm ground, possibly unsuited by softer than good: tried tongue tied/visored. *T. D. Walford* **54**

TOPOLSKI (IRE) 3 b.g. Peintre Celebre (USA) 137 – Witching Hour (IRE) 88 (Alzao (USA) 117) [2009 65p: 9.9m* 10m* 10.4m 12f2 12m5 12g 12m Aug 19] leggy gelding: fairly useful handicapper: won at Beverley and Redcar in April: best effort after when second to Akmal at Thirsk: stays 1½m: acts on firm going. *M. Johnston* **94**

TOP ROCKER 5 b.g. Rock City 120 – Top Hand 77 (First Trump 118) [2009 16d Aug 10] modest maiden in 2007: well held only Flat start since: stays 1½m: acts on soft and good to firm ground: modest maiden hurdler. *E. W. Tuer* **–**

TOP SEED (IRE) 8 b.g. Cadeaux Genereux 131 – Midnight Heights 104 (Persian Heights 129) [2009 74: p9.5g6 p12.2g 10.3m2 10s 8.1d p12.2g p9.5g6 Oct 15] quite good-topped gelding: fair handicapper: left Ian Williams after third start: well below form after: stays 1¾m: acts on polytrack, firm and soft going: tried visored/tongue tied: patiently ridden. *M. S. Tuck* **72 d**

TOP SPIN (IRE) 2 b. or br.c. (May 14) Cape Cross (IRE) 129 – Beguine (USA) 77 (Green Dancer (USA) 132) [2009 7s 7m3 8g 8g Oct 19] narrow, leggy colt: seventh foal: half-brother to several winners, including useful Irish 1¼m winner Liss Ard (by In The Wings) and fairly useful Irish 2001 2-y-o 5f/7f winner Master Papa (by Key of Luck): dam, lightly-raced maiden (form on only 2-y-o outing), half-sister to Grand Lodge: maiden (third at Leicester): best effort when seventh to St Nicholas Abbey in Beresford Stakes at the Curragh penultimate start: seemed amiss final start: stays 1m. *John Joseph Murphy, Ireland* **90**

TOP TICKET (IRE) 4 ch.g. Alhaarth (IRE) 126 – Tathkara (USA) (Alydar (USA)) [2009 84: 10d 14.1m5 Aug 21] compact gelding: fairly useful handicapper in 2008: well below form both Flat outings in 2009: should stay beyond 11f: acts on heavy ground: tried in cheekpieces. *D. E. Pipe* **–**

TOP TIGER 5 b.g. Mtoto 134 – Topatori (IRE) 89 (Topanoora 118) [2009 70: p12g f12g2 f12g6 f14g6 15.8m Apr 1] small, angular gelding: modest handicapper: left M. Tompkins after reappearance: barely stays 1¾m: acts on all-weather and soft going. *D. W. Barker* **63**

TOP TIGRESS 2 b.f. (Mar 17) Tiger Hill (IRE) 127 – Top Romance (IRE) 105 (Entrepreneur 123) [2009 p7.1g4 Nov 6] second foal: half-sister to 3-y-o Worth A King's: dam, 2-y-o 7f winner (should have stayed 1¼m), half-sister to smart performer up to 1½m National Anthem: 10/1 and green, promising when 2½ lengths fourth to Sea of Heartbreak in maiden at Wolverhampton, impeded 1f out (would have gone close): will be suited by 1m+: sure to do very much better. *Sir Michael Stoute* **62 P**

TOP TINKER 3 b.g. Vettori (IRE) 119 – Topatori (IRE) 89 (Topanoora 118) [2009 –: p10g 14.1m f12g6 p12g a10g* a12g3 a8g3 a10g a10g Dec 6] sold from M. Tompkins 1,500 gns after fourth start: first form when winning maiden at Taby in September: third in handicaps there next 2 starts: stays 1½m: tried blinkered. *Annika Kallse, Sweden* **?**

TOP TOWN GIRL 3 b.f. Efisio 120 – Halland Park Girl (IRE) 106 (Primo Dominie 121) [2009 90: p6g 6g 5d^4 p6g^4 6g^4 6m^4 p6m 6d^4 Oct 12] good-topped filly: fair handicapper: in-and-out form in 2009: should prove best at 5f/6f: acts on polytrack and soft ground: in cheekpieces last 2 starts: sold 5,000 gns, sent to Saudi Arabia. *R. M. Beckett* **75**

TOP TRIBUTE 4 b.g. Acclamation 118 – Mary Hinge 100 (Dowsing (USA) 124) [2009 71: 7m f7g 8m^2 8m^5 Sep 23] good-topped gelding: maiden, just modest form at 4 yrs: stays 1m: acts on good to firm and good to soft going: sold £4,000. *T. P. Tate* **62**

TORA PETCHA (IRE) 6 b.g. Bahhare (USA) 122 – Magdalene (FR) (College Chapel 122) [2009 –: 14g Aug 7] quite attractive gelding: one-time fairly useful winner: well held both Flat starts since 2006: modest but unreliable hurdler. *B. D. Leavy* **–**

TORCH OF FREEDOM (IRE) 4 b.g. Statue of Liberty (USA) 115 – Danse Royale (IRE) 112 (Caerleon (USA) 132) [2009 81: p8g^4 f8g p8.6g^6 p10g p10g* p9.5g^5 10g 10.1m^5 Aug 17] big gelding: fair performer: won 3-runner claimer at Kempton in March: stays 1¼m: acts on polytrack and good to firm going: held up: sold 4,200 gns. *Sir Mark Prescott* **78**

TORNADODANCER (IRE) 6 b.g. Princely Heir (IRE) 111 – Purty Dancer (IRE) 71 (Foxhound (USA) 103) [2009 94: 6s p5g 5.8s 5g^3 6.3g^4 5v 5s^6 5s^2 p5g^5 6g^2 p6g p6g p6g* p6g Nov 27] good-topped gelding: poor walker: useful performer: won minor event at Dundalk in November: best at 5f/6f: acts on polytrack and any turf going: blinkered/visored later in 2009: usually up with pace: often finishes weakly. *T. G. McCourt, Ireland* **98**

TORQUEMADA (IRE) 8 ch.g. Desert Sun 120 – Gaelic's Fantasy (IRE) (Statoblest 120) [2009 63§: p7g^5 p7g^3 p7g^3 p7g p6g 7m 7m p7g^5 p7g Nov 25] compact gelding: modest handicapper: stays 1m: acts on polytrack, good to firm and good to soft going: often in cheekpieces: tongue tied: often finds little and one to treat with caution. *M. J. Attwater* **58 §**

TORRAN SOUND 2 b.g. (Feb 10) Tobougg (IRE) 125 – Velvet Waters 80 (Unfuwain (USA) 131) [2009 p6m p6m Nov 28] down the field in maidens: bred to be suited by 1¼m+. *J. M. P. Eustace* **–**

TORRENS (IRE) 7 b.g. Royal Anthem (USA) 135 – Azure Lake (USA) (Lac Ouimet (USA)) [2009 70: 10.2g^3 10.2g p13.9g May 11] good-bodied gelding: modest performer: stays 1½m: acts on polytrack, firm and soft ground: tongue tied: held up. *P. D. Evans* **61**

TORRES DEL PAINE 2 b.c. (Apr 4) Compton Place 125 – Noble Story 61 (Last Tycoon 131) [2009 p6g p6m^4 p6f^2 Dec 13] improved gradually in maidens, second to Passion Overflow at Kempton, dictating: likely to be best at 5f/6f: slowly away first 2 outings. *J. C. Fox* **65**

TOSHI (USA) 7 b.g. Kingmambo (USA) 125 – Majestic Role (FR) 107 (Theatrical 128) [2009 –: 12g 9.2m^5 12.3g* 13g^3 Jul 30] close-coupled gelding: modest handicapper nowadays: won ladies event at Chester in June: stays 13f: acts on polytrack, firm and good to soft going: tried in cheekpieces/visor: has hinted at temperament: useful hurdler. *J. S. Goldie* **63**

TOTAL COMMAND 2 b.c. (Apr 11) Sadler's Wells (USA) 132 – Wince 117 (Selkirk (USA) 129) [2009 7m^6 8v^2 Oct 24] strong, well-made colt: fourth foal: brother to very smart 1¼m/1½m (Yorkshire Oaks, also second in St Leger) winner Quiff and smart 1¼m winner/Chester Vase runner-up Arabian Gulf: dam, won 1000 Guineas, half-sister to very smart performer up to 1½m Ulundi: still green, much better effort in maidens when 3½ lengths second to Multames at Newbury, best work late: will be suited by 1½m: looks a useful prospect at least. *Sir Michael Stoute* **88 p**

TOTAL GALLERY (IRE) 3 br.c. Namid 128 – Diary (IRE) (Green Desert (USA) 127) [2009 106: 6m* 5v^5 7m 5m 6g* 5g^2 5.2m^2 5g* 6g^6 Dec 13] **123**

The gulf between being a useful two-year-old and developing into a leading sprinter at three is generally too wide for most to bridge. However, Total Gallery managed it in style, his progress in the second half of the latest season taking him to victory in the Prix de l'Abbaye de Longchamp. He was the first three-year-old to win the Abbaye since Carmine Lake in 1997 and only the eighth three-year-old winner in thirty years. The ill-fated Carmine Lake and two other winning fillies at three Kistena (1996) and Polonia (1987), met with setbacks subsequently. The four others are among the very best sprinters of the last half century. Marwell (1981) won the Abbaye on her final start to set the seal on a brilliant career, and Moorestyle (1980), Habibti (1983) and Dayjur (1990) had enjoyed outstanding campaigns on their way to Paris. Habibti was kept in training at four but couldn't match the achievements of her three-year-old campaign, though she won the King's Stand Stakes. Total Gallery's record is more in the mould of that of Cadeaux Genereux who progressed very well through the ranks at three and passed the post first in the 1988 Abbaye only to be disqualified for interference. Cadeaux Genereux went on to establish himself as a top-class sprinter at four. Total Gallery was near the top of the tree in a year that lacked a top European-trained sprinter, and he should continue to play a major part in the next season.

Total Gallery had six starts at two, winning twice, including the valuable Two-Year-Old Trophy at Redcar by a nose on his final outing. He made a winning return, too, in the listed Cleanevent Pavilion Stakes over six furlongs at Ascot in April, giving a performance which suggested that further progress at sprint distances, especially dropped back to five furlongs, might well be in the offing. However, Total Gallery seemed to find very heavy ground against him in the Temple Stakes at Haydock. He then probably found seven furlongs too far in the Jersey Stakes at Royal Ascot, though the fact that he hung right suggested he might not have been right that day. He then met interference when unplaced behind Ialysos in the Sprint Stakes at Sandown at the start of July, though he faced a stiffish task anyway on the day.

Total Gallery was beginning to look as if he was not quite up to pattern class and he was switched to handicap company on his next start, recording his best performance to that point when winning the six-furlong totesport.com Stakes (Heritage Handicap) at Newmarket in July by a neck from Desert Icon, to whom he was conceding 23 lb. Back in pattern company, he finished clear of the rest when runner-up to a revitalised Kingsgate Native in the King George Stakes at Goodwood and was beaten a neck by Strike The Deal in the World Trophy at Newbury in September, collared late on after seeing off the others that forced the pace in a race in which he made the running (he had been held up in rear at Goodwood).

It was still a big step up for Total Gallery from being beaten in two Group 3s to contesting a Group 1, facing a line-up which included runners from Italy, Slovakia, Sweden and the Czech Republic. Remarkably there was only one French-trained runner in the Qatar Prix de l'Abbaye, Stern Opinion. The remaining ten runners were all trained in Britain and included the 2007 winner Benbaun and two dual Group 1 winners who had been placed in the Abbaye previously,

totesport.com Stakes (Heritage Handicap), Newmarket—Total Gallery (centre) holds off Desert Icon (diamonds on sleeves) in a typically competitive renewal of this 3-y-o handicap

Qatar Prix de l'Abbaye de Longchamp, Longchamp—
British-trained sprinters dominate and Total Gallery, the only 3-y-o in the field, comes out on top;
Fleeting Spirit, War Artist (No.12) and Benbaun also make the frame

Borderlescott and Reverence. Reverence was some way past his prime, but Borderlescott and Benbaun had fought out the finish of the Nunthorpe at York and looked leading candidates on recent form. War Artist, another with plenty of form at the highest level, had won his two most recent races and started second favourite behind the July Cup winner Fleeting Spirit. It might not have been the strongest renewal of the Abbaye but it was a representative one and winning it called for further improvement from Total Gallery, the only three-year-old (there was also one two-year-old, the smart Monsieur Chevalier). Several of the outsiders took the field along, with Total Gallery moving smoothly alongside some of the more strongly-fancied runners tracking the pace before taking over with a little more than a furlong to go and holding off all challengers in game fashion. The slow-starting Fleeting Spirit finished a neck away in second, with around two and a half lengths covering the first eight home. Only the smart Italian sprinter Black Mambazo in fifth prevented total British dominance. Fleeting Spirit didn't run up to her best, nor did Borderlescott, who met interference before reaching sixth, but War Artist and Benbaun in third and fourth gave the form some solidity and confirmed that Total Gallery had recorded a performance about 6 lb better than anything he had achieved before.

Total Gallery had one more run, in the six-furlong Hong Kong Sprint at Sha Tin in December. He proved no match for the strong local team headed by the top-class Sacred Kingdom and finished sixth, below the form he showed in the Abbaye but still well there until over a furlong out and again in front of Borderlescott and War Artist. A campaign in the top European sprints in 2010—with the King's Stand his first main target—seems on the cards for Total Gallery, though, at the time of writing, a run in the International Sprint at Kranji in Singapore before that was said to be under consideration.

Total Gallery (IRE) (br.c. 2006)	Namid (b 1996)	Indian Ridge (ch 1985)	Ahonoora
			Hillbrow
		Dawnsio (b 1990)	Tate Gallery
			Welsh Dancer
	Diary (IRE) (b or br 1999)	Green Desert (b 1983)	Danzig
			Foreign Courier
		Darrery (b 1990)	Darshaan
			Flamenco

The angular, good-topped Total Gallery is a son of an Abbaye winner in Namid, who was successful in 2000. Namid is very much an influence for speed at stud and his best-known runners, apart from Total Gallery, include the Dash and Portland Handicap winner Hogmaneigh, the Gosforth Park Cup winner Buachaill Dona and the smart sprinter Resplendent Glory. Total Gallery's family isn't exactly short on stamina. His grandam Darrery was a useful middle-distance three-year-old, who was placed at listed level and in the Bessborough Handicap at Royal Ascot. Three of her five winning offspring are, or were, effective over at least a mile and half, including the smart mile and three quarter Mallard Handicap winner Sunday Symphony and the fairly useful Made In Japan, who has since shown himself a useful hurdler/chaser. Made In Japan won the Triumph Hurdle at Cheltenham and is fully effective at three miles over jumps nowadays. Total Gallery's dam Diary was in training with Michael Jarvis but didn't run for him, sent to Greece where she achieved three wins at seven furlongs. Diary had one foal in Greece, the winning filly Chrisalice (by Lujain), before being sold for 11,000 guineas at the Tattersalls February Sales in 2005. Total Gallery was the first result of that purchase, followed by Lady Darshaan (by High Chaparral), who managed a win over five furlongs but showed much better form over further subsequently, finishing third in the Cherry Hinton and second in the Fillies' Mile in 2009. Like Total Gallery, Lady Darshaan is trained by Stan Moore, joining him after he bought her at the Doncaster Breeze-Up Sale for £24,000. Total Gallery made three visits to the sale-ring before he ran and failed to find a buyer on each occasion, bought back for 45,000 guineas as a foal and unsold as a yearling and at a breeze-up. There was, not surprisingly, no such difficulty finding a buyer for Diary's latest foal, a filly by High Chaparral who made 300,000 guineas at the Newmarket December Sales. The mare also had a colt by the same sire in 2008. Total Gallery will prove best at five and six furlongs. He showed form on heavy ground as a two-year-old but may prove better under less testing conditions. *J. S. Moore*

TOTAL IMPACT 6 ch.g. Pivotal 124 – Rise 'n Shine 67 (Night Shift (USA)) [2009 95: 5m* 5g 5d^4 5v 5d 5.1m 5m* 5.2m^3 5m^2 5.1m^4 p6m^2 f6g^3 f5g* Dec 27] close-coupled gelding: has a short, scratchy action: fairly useful performer, better on turf: won handicaps at Redcar in May and Doncaster in September, and claimer at Southwell in December: has won at 6f, best at 5f: acts on all-weather, firm and good to soft ground (probably not soft/heavy): tried blinkered: has joined C. Dore. *R. A. Fahey* **93 a81**

TOTALITARIAN 3 ch.g. Pivotal 124 – Shalimar (IRE) 95 (Indian Ridge 123) [2009 p7g^3 7m^3 p7.1g^5 Oct 1] 25,000Y, £20,000 2-y-o: sturdy gelding: fifth foal: dam 7f/1m winner: fair form in maidens when third: likely to stay 1m: raced only on polytrack and good to firm going. *S. A. Callaghan* **73**

TOTALLY DEVOTED (USA) 3 b. or br.f. Seeking The Gold (USA) – Crystal Crossing (IRE) 99 (Royal Academy (USA) 130) [2009 8d^3 8g 8v 12m 8d^2 8g^4 8.5d* 8d^4 7.5v^3 7m 7.5m^5 8g^5 Oct 18] $1,600,000Y: close-coupled filly: seventh foal: closely related to 2 winners, notably high-class 7f (at 2 yrs) to 14.6f (St Leger) winner Rule of Law (by Kingmambo), and half-sister to fairly useful 2006 2-y-o 7f winner Cast In Gold (by Elusive Quality): dam, 2-y-o 6f winner, sister to smart performer up to 8.5f Circle of Gold: useful performer: won maiden at Killarney in August: best efforts in Matron Stakes at Leopardstown (7¾ lengths fourth to Rainbow View) and Concorde Stakes at Tipperary (5¼ lengths fifth to Duff) eighth/eleventh starts: stayed 8.5f: acted on good to firm and good to soft going: visits Giant's Causeway. *A. P. O'Brien, Ireland* **104**

TOTALLY FOCUSSED (IRE) 4 gr. or ro.g. Trans Island 119 – Premier Place (USA) (Out of Place (USA)) [2009 87: p7g^2 p8g^4 p7g^6 p8g^5 p7m^3 p8m Dec 30] rangy gelding: fairly useful handicapper: effective at 7f to 1¼m: acts on polytrack and good to firm going: held up. *S. Dow* **84**

TOTALLY INVINCIBLE (IRE) 2 b.f. (Feb 5) Invincible Spirit (IRE) 121 – Sebastene (IRE) 70 (Machiavellian (USA) 123) [2009 5g 5d^4 5m* 5.1m* 5g Jul 28] 31,000F, £32,000Y: compact filly: first foal: dam, Irish maiden, stayed 7f: fairly useful performer: successful in July in maiden at Catterick (made all) and minor event at Chester (beat Mdawee by short head): stiff task and trouble to post, last in Molecomb Stakes at Goodwood final outing: may prove best at 5f: sold 12,000 gns in October. *E. S. McMahon* **87**

TOTALLY OURS 2 b. or br.f. (Apr 20) Singspiel (IRE) 133 – Totally Yours (IRE) 90 (Desert Sun 120) [2009 p6m p7m* Oct 31] first foal: dam, 2-y-o 6f winner, half-sister to Dewhurst Stakes winner Tout Seul: much better effort in maidens at Kempton when winning by length from Flouncing: will stay 1m: will progress further. *W. R. Muir* **77 p**

TOT HILL 6 b.m. Syrtos 106 – Galava (CAN) (Graustark) [2009 –§: 10.2g Jul 4] has more temperament than ability. *C. N. Kellett* **– §**

TOTO SKYLLACHY 4 b.g. Kyllachy 129 – Little Tramp (Trempolino (USA) 135) [2009 89: 8.5m 8d* 8.9g 8.3v^5 p7f^3 7s^4 7s p7.1g^5 Dec 3] strong, deep-girthed gelding: fairly useful handicapper: awarded race at Ripon in May after ½-length second to Tanto Faz: left T. Tate after fourth start: stays 1m: acts on polytrack, soft and good to firm going. *S. Gollings* **86**

TOTTIE 3 b.f. Fantastic Light (USA) 134 – Katy Nowaitee 112 (Komaite (USA)) [2009 96: 11.5m³ 12g 10.1m⁵ 10.4g⁵ 9g⁴ 10d⁶ Aug 6] leggy filly: useful performer: best efforts at 3 yrs in listed race at Lingfield (6¾ lengths third to Midday) and handicap at Goodwood (fourth to Alsace Lorraine): barely stays 11.5f: acts on good to firm and good to soft ground: in cheekpieces/blinkers last 3 starts: sent to USA. *Mrs A. J. Perrett* **95**

TOUCHING (IRE) 3 b.f. Kheleyf (USA) 116 – Feminine Touch (IRE) (Sadler's Wells (USA) 132) [2009 89: 7s p8g 8.1g p7m⁶ Oct 31] tall filly: fairly useful at 2 yrs: well held in 2009: tried tongue tied: sold 12,000 gns. *R. Hannon* **–**

TOUCH OF STYLE (IRE) 5 b.g. Desert Style (IRE) 121 – No Hard Feelings (IRE) 86 (Alzao (USA) 117) [2009 77: p10g⁵ p12g⁶ p11g p10g³ p10g⁵ 10.2m 10.9m p12f Oct 14] good-bodied gelding: modest handicapper: left J. Boyle after third outing: stays easy 1½m: acts on all-weather and good to firm going: usually wears headgear. *T. D. McCarthy* **58**

TOUCH TONE 2 b.f. (Mar 1) Selkirk (USA) 129 – Payphone (Anabaa (USA) 130) [2009 7g⁶ 7g⁵ Aug 28] tall filly: has plenty of scope: second foal: dam, useful French 5.5f winner, sister to Prix Marcel Boussac runner-up Conference Call: better effort in maidens when encouraging 7¾ lengths fifth to Pollenator at Newmarket, not knocked about: sure to do better still. *B. W. Hills* **68 p**

TOUFAN EXPRESS 7 ch.g. Fraam 114 – Clan Scotia 47 (Clantime 101) [2009 79: p8g² p8g 9.5d 8m³ 8g² 8m³ 9.5s³ 8s³ 7s⁴ 9.5s³ 8g³ 9d 8s 7d* 6g* 6g Oct 10] lengthy gelding: useful handicapper: won at Listowel and the Curragh (beat Tornadodancer by neck), both in September: effective at 6f to 9.5f: acts on polytrack, soft and good to firm going: blinkered seventh outing. *Adrian McGuinness, Ireland* **95**

TOUGH REGIME (IRE) 2 ch.f. (Mar 13) Trans Island 119 – Lady Naryana (IRE) (Val Royal (FR) 127) [2009 6s 7s 7s p7g⁴ p9.5g p8.6g⁴ Dec 19] €2,000Y: first foal: dam unraced: modest maiden: stays 8.6f: form only on polytrack: tongue tied last 4 starts. *Niall Moran, Ireland* **59**

TOUJOURS SOURIANTE 3 b.f. Lucky Story (USA) 128 – Tous Les Jours (USA) 70 (Dayjur (USA) 137) [2009 7.1m 8.1m 8.1g³ 10g³ 12.5g 13d* 13.3m Aug 14] sixth foal: half-sister to 1¾m to 17.5f winner Rule For Ever (by Diktat) and 2 winners abroad: dam 7f winner, including at 2 yrs: fair handicapper: best effort when winning at Hamilton in July: will stay 2m: acts on good to soft ground: sold £4,200, and joined Miss T. Waggott. *M. Johnston* **78**

TOUR D'AMOUR (IRE) 6 b.m. Fruits of Love (USA) 127 – Touraneena (Robellino (USA) 127) [2009 59: f8g⁴ 10.1s⁴ 9m 10f* Jul 2] sparely-made mare: modest handicapper: won at Redcar (cheekpieces) in July: stays 1¼m: acts on all-weather and any turf going: sometimes blinkered. *R. Craggs* **59**

TOURIST 4 b.g. Oasis Dream 129 – West Devon (USA) (Gone West (USA)) [2009 82: p8.6g⁴ p8.6g³ p9.5g² p9.5g³ p8.6g⁵ 10.3g p8g² p8g⁶ p8.6g³ p7.1g 7.5f⁵ p8g 8.3m⁵ p9.5g p8.6g² p7.1g* p7g p6m* p7.1g³ p7.1g³ f5d⁴ Dec 29] big, well-made, attractive gelding: fairly useful handicapper: won at Wolverhampton in October and November: stays 9.5f, best at 6f/7f: acts on all-weather and good to firm going. *D. Shaw* **91**

TOURNEDOS (IRE) 7 b.g. Rossini (USA) 118 – Don't Care (IRE) 93 (Nordico (USA)) [2009 104: f5g 5.1m⁴ 5g 5g 5d 5.1m 5m 6.1g 5g⁴ p6g Oct 10] sturdy gelding: good walker: has a quick action: useful performer on turf: seemingly best effort in 2009 when seventh to Borderlescott in listed race at Chester sixth start: best at 5f: acts on any going: tried in cheekpieces: none too consistent: sold £6,000, joined Mrs R. Carr. *D. Nicholls* **102 d**

TOUS LES DEUX 6 b.g. Efisio 120 – Caerosa 70 (Caerleon (USA) 132) [2009 –, a84: p7g p8g* p8g* p7.1g² p8.6g³ p8g² p8g⁶ Apr 15] strong gelding: fairly useful performer: won handicaps at Lingfield and Kempton in February: effective at 7f to easy 1¼m: acts on polytrack, firm and good to soft going: often held up: reliable. *G. L. Moore* **87**

TOWANDA (USA) 3 b.f. Dynaformer (USA) – Desert Gold (USA) (Seeking The Gold (USA)) [2009 9.7d⁶ p12g⁴ Apr 21] second foal: half-sister to winner in USA by Cozzene: dam, US 5.5f to 9f winner, out of sister to Breeders' Cup Sprint winner Desert Stormer: better effort in maidens on debut: will prove best short of 1½m. *J. H. M. Gosden* **65**

TOWBAAT 2 b.f. (Mar 7) Halling (USA) 133 – Nasmatt 96 (Danehill (USA) 126) [2009 8g Oct 20] fifth foal: half-sister to 4-y-o Emmrooz: dam, 2-y-o 6f winner, closely related to smart 1998 2-y-o sprinter Bint Allayl and smart performer up to 7f Kheleyf and half-sister to 5-y-o Laa Rayb: 12/1, encouraging 4¾ lengths seventh to Hymnsheet in maiden at Yarmouth, switched across from wide draw: will do better. *M. A. Jarvis* **70 p**

TOWN AND GOWN 4 br.f. Oasis Dream 129 – Degree 81 (Warning 136) [2009 63d: 5m 5g 5g 5f 6g 5d^2 5m^5 5g^4 5g^4 Sep 21] useful-looking filly: modest maiden: best at 5f/6f: best form on all-weather: tried tongue tied/in cheekpieces: not one to trust. *J. S. Goldie* **57 §**

TOWNELEY ARMS (IRE) 2 b.c. (May 5) Pyrus (USA) 106 – Grangeclare Lily (UAE) (Green Desert (USA) 127) [2009 7.5m Jul 28] leggy colt: 80/1, signs of ability when mid-field in maiden at Beverley. *G. A. Harker* **–**

TOWN HOUSE 7 gr.m. Paris House 123 – Avondale Girl (IRE) 73 (Case Law 113) [2009 60: p5.1g p5.1m 5v 5m 5g^5 5g^6 5.2s^3 5.1d 5m 5g^5 5.2d Oct 27] close-coupled mare: modest handicapper: best at 5f: acts on all-weather, good to firm and good to soft going: none too consistent. *B. P. J. Baugh* **50**

TOWTHORPE 3 ch.g. Tobougg (IRE) 125 – Snow Shoes 84 (Sri Pekan (USA) 117) [2009 7m^3 8m^4 9.8m 8s 7m Sep 14] compact gelding: modest maiden on balance: stays 1m: raced only on soft and good to firm going: gelded after final start. *M. Brittain* **50**

TOWY BOY (IRE) 4 b.g. King Charlemagne (USA) 120 – Solar Flare (IRE) (Danehill (USA) 126) [2009 76: p6g p6g 6g p6g^6 5.7d 6g 6.1m^4 7f^2 p6g^4 6s p6g^2 5m^3 5.1m^5 p6g^4 5g^6 f7g^3 Oct 18] lengthy gelding: modest maiden handicapper: stays 7f: acts on all-weather, firm and good to soft going: often tongue tied: visored nowadays (tried blinkered). *I. A. Wood* **62**

TOWY VALLEY 4 b.f. Bertolini (USA) 125 – Ulysses Daughter (IRE) 88 (College Chapel 122) [2009 67p: p6g^4 p5g* p5g^3 p5.1m^2 5.7g^4 p5.1g^5 Apr 20] sturdy filly: fair performer: won maiden at Kempton in January: will prove best at 5f: acts on polytrack. *C. G. Cox* **73**

TOY RAZOR (IRE) 2 b.c. (Jan 24) Refuse To Bend (IRE) 128 – Child Prodigy (IRE) 87 (Ballad Rock 122) [2009 7m Oct 2] angular colt: 20/1, well held in maiden at Newmarket: will stay 1m+. *H. Candy* **–**

TOY TOP (USA) 6 gr. or ro.m. Tactical Cat (USA) 116 – I'll Flutter By (USA) (Concorde's Tune (USA)) [2009 70: 5m 5d 5f* 5m^2 5g^2 5d^6 5f 5d^4 5m 5m Sep 23] leggy, angular mare: fair handicapper: won at Thirsk in June: best at 5f/easy 6f: acts on firm and good to soft going: blinkered: races up with pace. *M. Dods* **68**

TRACHONITIS (IRE) 5 b.g. Dansili 127 – Hasina (IRE) 81 (King's Theatre (IRE) 128) [2009 90: 11.6g 13m^3 13.3g 12m^6 14.1g^5 12m* 12m^4 p13g^5 p12.2g f11g* Dec 27] quite good-topped gelding: fairly useful handicapper: won at Goodwood in September and Southwell in December: effective at 11f to 2m: acts on all-weather, firm and soft going: held up: travels strongly (often finds little). *J. R. Jenkins* **83**

TRADE CENTRE 4 b.g. Dubai Destination (USA) 127 – Khubza 86 (Green Desert (USA) 127) [2009 p6g^2 p6g* p6g^4 6g^3 7m 7.1d p7.1g p7g p7m* p7g^3 p8m p7g^3 p7m* p7.1g^4 Dec 26] 375,000Y, £10,000 3-y-o: workmanlike gelding: half-brother to several winners, including 6f (at 2 yrs) to 8.5f winner Trans Island and 1m winner Welsh Diva (both smart, by Selkirk): dam, 7f winner, half-sister to smart performers Barrow Creek (at 6f to 1m in Germany) and Last Resort (7f): fairly useful performer: won maiden at Lingfield in March, handicap at Kempton in September and seller at Lingfield (left W. Muir 9,200 gns) in December: stays 7f: acts on polytrack, best turf effort on good going. *George Baker* **83**

TRADE FAIRLE 2 ch.c. (Feb 11) Trade Fair 124 – Lady Le Quesne (IRE) 78 (Alhaarth (IRE) 126) [2009 5m^6 p6g 5.7g Jul 23] last in maidens: tried visored. *P. R. Webber* **–**

TRADE NAME (IRE) 2 b.f. (Apr 27) Trade Fair 124 – Red Rabbit 86 (Suave Dancer (USA) 136) [2009 p7g 6d^4 6m^5 Oct 26] £10,000Y, £12,000 2-y-o: rather unfurnished filly: seventh foal: half-sister to several winners, including 6f (including at 2 yrs) winner Kabreet (by Night Shift) and 6f (at 2 yrs) and 7.6f winner Spinning Ruby (by Pivotal), both fairly useful: dam maiden (stayed 1¼m): improved gradually in maidens, fifth to Miss Zooter at Leicester (blinkered): stays 6f: sold 2,700 gns, sent to Spain. *H. Candy* **66**

TRADE PRICE (GR) 3 b.g. Kyllachy 129 – Snowdrift (Desert Prince (IRE) 130) [2009 p5g^5 5m 6m^4 5m 7.1m^3 6s 5f^5 8s 9.2g^5 7.2m Oct 1] modest maiden, sporadic form: left J. Osborne prior to third start, gelded after fifth: likely to prove best at 6f: often in headgear. *I. Semple* **54**

TRADE SECRET 2 b.c. (Apr 7) Trade Fair 124 – Kastaway 91 (Distant Relative 128) [2009 5m^4 5m^2 6g^4 5d^2 5m^5 6g^6 Oct 9] £2,500Y: tall colt: half-brother to fairly useful 2003 2-y-o 5f winner Oro Verde (by Compton Place) and 4-y-o Big Boom: dam 2-y-o 5f winner: fair maiden: likely to prove best at 5f. *M. Brittain* **74**

*totequadpot August Stakes, Windsor—
Traffic Guard steps up in trip and easily outpaces his four rivals in a steadily-run contest*

TRADING NATION (USA) 3 b.g. Tiznow (USA) 133 – Nidd (USA) 112 (Known **82**
Fact (USA) 135) [2009 –: 6.1f^2 6m 7m p7m Dec 4] fairly useful maiden: easily best effort when second at Nottingham on reappearance: well held after, off 6 months and left R. Charlton 3,500 gns prior to final outing: bred to stay 7f+. *P. W. Hiatt*

TRAFALGAR BAY (IRE) 6 b.g. Fruits of Love (USA) 127 – Chatsworth Bay (IRE) **98**
(Fairy King (USA)) [2009 –: 7m^5 8m* 7m^5 7.1m Jun 13] compact gelding: useful handicapper: back to best in 2009, winning at Ascot in April by 1¼ lengths from Mount Hadlee: creditable fifth to Swift Gift in Victoria Cup there following month: broke down final start: stayed 1m: acted on firm and good to soft going: dead. *K. R. Burke*

TRAFALGAR SQUARE 7 b.g. King's Best (USA) 132 – Pat Or Else 72 (Alzao **69**
(USA) 117) [2009 84: p7g* p7g* p7g^3 8m 7g p7g p8g 8g 9g p8g p7m p7g^2 8.3g p7g p7g^6 **a89**
p8m^5 Dec 1] strong, compact gelding: fairly useful handicapper on all-weather, just fair on turf in 2009: successful twice at Lingfield in January: best at 7f/1m: acts on polytrack, heavy and good to firm going: tried in cheekpieces: usually held up: often starts slowly. *M. J. Attwater*

TRAFFIC GUARD (USA) 5 b.h. More Than Ready (USA) 120 – Street Scene (IRE) **115**
(Zafonic (USA) 130) [2009 123: 9m^6 8g^6 a9f^6 10d^3 10.4m^4 11.6m* 12.3m^2 12d Oct 18] big, strong, lengthy horse: trained by H. Brown first 3 starts at Nad Al Sheba: smart form back in Britain after, winning listed race at Windsor in August by 8 lengths from Warringah: creditable efforts either side in Rose of Lancaster Stakes at Haydock (fourth to Jukebox Jury) and listed race at Chester (head second to Snoqualmie Girl): stays 12.3f: acts on dirt, good to firm and good to soft going: has worn cheekpieces. *P. F. I. Cole*

TRAILBLAZING 2 b.c. (Feb 14) Green Desert (USA) 127 – Pioneer Bride (USA) **88**
(Gone West (USA)) [2009 6m^6 5.9m^2 6g* 6.5m 7m^3 Oct 3] heavy-topped colt: fourth foal: brother to 4-y-o Yamal: dam, ran once in USA, half-sister to very smart pair Faithful Son (stayed 1½m) and Always Fair (winner up to 1m): fairly useful performer: won maiden at Ascot (beat Taajub 1½ lengths) in July: good third in nursery at Epsom: will stay 1m. *M. Johnston*

TRANOS (USA) 6 b.g. Bahri (USA) 125 – Balancoire (USA) (Diesis 133) [2009 12d^6 **–**
Jun 17] good-topped gelding: maiden handicapper: well held sole start on Flat since 2007: tried visored. *Micky Hammond*

TRANQUIL TIGER 5 ch.h. Selkirk (USA) 129 – Serene View (USA) 105 (Distant **119**
View (USA) 126) [2009 119: 9.9m* 10m^3 10.4m 10.1m^3 p10g* p10f* Dec 19] big, strong, lengthy horse: smart performer: won listed races at Goodwood (by neck from Halicarnassus) in May and Lingfield in November (by 3 lengths from Presvis) and December (landed odds by short head from Suits Me): also ran creditably when third to Kirklees in listed race at Sandown: effective at 1¼m to 1¾m: acts on polytrack and good to firm going: blinkered: sometimes front runner: quirky. *H. R. A. Cecil*

TRANSCEND 5 ch.g. Beat Hollow 126 – Pleasuring 68 (Good Times (ITY)) [2009 **–**
104: 7m Jun 19] sturdy gelding: useful handicapper: well held sole start in 2009: effective at 6f to 1m: acts on polytrack, good to firm and good to soft ground: tried blinkered/in cheekpieces. *J. H. M. Gosden*

TRANSCENTRAL 3 ch.f. Kheleyf (USA) 116 – Khafayif (USA) 62 (Swain (IRE) **51**
134) [2009 68: p5.1g 6f f5g^4 p6g^4 p6g p5.1g f6g Aug 25] smallish filly: just modest performer nowadays: left W. M. Brisbourne £1,600 prior to final start: effective at 5f/6f: acts on polytrack, soft and good to firm going. *T. Wall*

TRANSFER 4 br.g. Trans Island 119 – Sankaty Light (USA) 55 (Summer Squall **77**
(USA)) [2009 85: p7g^4 p7m 8.3g^5 Oct 5] good-topped gelding: fair handicapper: should
stay 1m: acts on polytrack: sold £4,400. *A. M. Balding*

TRANSFERED (IRE) 3 b.f. Trans Island 119 – Second Omen (Rainbow Quest (USA) **61**
134) [2009 48: 14.1g^2 15g 16.1d p12g^6 p13.9g p13.9g Nov 27] modest maiden: stays
1¾m: best effort on good ground. *Lucinda Featherstone*

TRANSFIXED (IRE) 2 b.f. (Mar 7) Trans Island 119 – Rectify (IRE) (Mujadil (USA) **80**
119) [2009 5m* 5m^2 5.1m^3 6d* 6.1g^3 6f^2 6.1m* 6m^3 6g^2 5g^3 6.1g^3 6m 7m* 7m^2 7m 7m^2
6m 5.1m^5 6g 7g* 7d^2 7v^4 p7.1g^5 p7m* p6m^5 p6g^3 p7.1g^6 p6m^2 Dec 30] £5,000Y: plain
filly: first foal: dam unraced out of half-sister to Cheveley Park Stakes winners Desirable
and Park Appeal and Irish Oaks winner Alydaress: fairly useful performer: won sellers at
Warwick in April and Ripon in May, nurseries at Chester in July, Epsom in August and
Catterick in October and minor event at Lingfield in November: stays 7f: acts on polytrack, firm and good to soft going: front runner/races prominently: tough and consistent.
P. D. Evans

TRANSFORMER (IRE) 3 b.g. Trans Island 119 – Lady At War (Warning 136) [2009 **69**
59: p8g^4 8.3m 10d^4 9g^6 10g^3 p10g^2 p11g^4 p12m p10g* p10g^2 Oct 11] good-topped
gelding: fair handicapper: won at Lingfield in October: stays 11f: acts on polytrack,
unraced on extremes of going on turf: tried visored, in cheekpieces last 2 starts: sold
11,000 gns, joined M. Banks. *W. J. Knight*

TRANSMISSION (IRE) 4 b.g. Galileo (IRE) 134 – Individual (USA) 83 (Gulch **72**
(USA)) [2009 74: f8d* f8s^2 f8d^2 f8g 10.2m 10m 8.5m^2 9.2g p8.6g p8.6g f8f^2 f8g^4 Dec 27]
workmanlike gelding: fair performer: won claimer at Southwell in January: possibly best
around 1m: acts on all-weather, heavy and good to firm going: tried visored. *B. Smart*

TRANSMIT (IRE) 2 ch.g. (Mar 9) Trans Island 119 – Apple Brandy (USA) (Cox's **–**
Ridge (USA)) [2009 6g^6 8d Aug 28] well held in maidens (gelded after). *T. D. Easterby*

TRANSPORTER (IRE) 3 b.g. Trans Island 119 – Ascoli (Skyliner 117) [2009 –: 12d^4 **–**
16.2g Jul 20] no form on Flat: modest form in juvenile hurdles. *T. D. Easterby*

TRANS SIBERIAN 5 b.g. Soviet Star (USA) 128 – Dina Line (USA) 60 (Diesis 133) **92**
[2009 95: 8.3g^5 10s^5 10g^2 p10g 10m^4 10.2d Oct 15] tall, good-topped gelding: fairly
useful handicapper: below form after third start: stays 1¼m: acts on polytrack, good to
firm and good to soft going: tried in cheekpieces: often pulls hard: versatile tactically.
P. F. I. Cole

TRANS SONIC 6 ch.g. Trans Island 119 – Sankaty Light (USA) 55 (Summer Squall **69**
(USA)) [2009 69, a78: f12s^2 f11g^3 f12g^5 f11g^5 7.5m f8g f8g^2 Dec 27] big, workmanlike
gelding: fair handicapper: left A. Lockwood prior to final outing: effective at 7f to 1½m:
acts on all-weather and soft going: often wears headgear: races up with pace. *J. Hetherton*

TRANSVAAL SKY 2 b. or br.f. (Feb 1) Avonbridge 123 – Glider (IRE) 65 (Silver Kite **90 +**
(USA) 111) [2009 6s^6 p6g* 6m^4 7m^5 Oct 3] 6,500F, £50,000Y: sturdy filly: fourth foal:
dam, 1m winner, half-sister to Prix Morny winner Bad As I Wanna Be: fairly useful
performer: made all easily in maiden at Lingfield in August: good efforts after, fifth to
Bab At The Bowster in nursery at Newmarket: stays 7f: sold 40,000 gns. *Tom Dascombe*

TRANSVESTITE (IRE) 7 b.g. Trans Island 119 – Christoph's Girl 50 (Efisio 120) **78**
[2009 80: p12.2g* Jan 29] quite good-topped gelding: fair handicapper: won at Wolverhampton sole Flat start at 7 yrs: stays 1½m: acts on polytrack, firm and soft going:
effective with/without visor. *Miss Tor Sturgis*

TRAPHALGAR (IRE) 4 br.g. Cape Cross (IRE) 129 – Conquestadora 98 (Hernando **90**
(FR) 127) [2009 91, a97: 8.5m 8m^6 10d^2 9.9m* 10g 10.4d 10g^3 10m* 10m* p12.2g^2
p10m^2 p10m^3 p9.5g Dec 26] good-topped gelding: fairly useful performer: won handicap
at Beverley in June, claimer at Leicester (left P. Cole £8,000) in September and seller at
Redcar in October: left Ollie Pears after eleventh start: stays easy 1½m: acts on polytrack,
unraced on extremes of going on turf: often held up. *P. D. Evans*

TRAVELLERS KINGDOM (IRE) 2 b.f. (Apr 18) Xaar 132 – Mermaid Melody **43**
(Machiavellian (USA) 123) [2009 5m Apr 20] €6,200F, €8,000Y: rather unfurnished
filly: third foal: half-sister to unreliable 2007 2-y-o 1m seller winner Adam Eterno (by
Spartacus): dam unraced daughter of Oaks winner Jet Ski Lady: 50/1, mid-field in maiden
at Windsor: will need further than 5f. *P. D. Evans*

TREADINGTHEBOARDS 2 b.f. (May 3) Haafhd 129 – Rada's Daughter 107 (Rob- **–**
ellino (USA) 127) [2009 p7m Sep 30] fifth foal: half-sister to 1¼m winner Theatre Royal
(by Royal Applause): dam 1¼m/1½m winner (stayed 2m): 66/1, slowly away and tailed
off in maiden at Kempton. *Mouse Hamilton-Fairley*

TREADWELL (IRE) 2 b.c. (Mar 23) Footstepsinthesand 120 – Lady Wells (IRE) (Sadler's Wells (USA) 132) [2009 5f* 6m5 7m2 7.1d5 p6m* p6g5 Oct 26] 40,000Y: sturdy colt: third foal: half-brother to 4-y-o Manshoor and winner in Greece by Rock of Gibraltar: dam, French 11.5f winner, closely related to useful French winner up to 13f Okabango: fairly useful performer: won maiden at Sandown in June and minor event at Kempton (by ¾ length from Bagamoyo) in October: also good fifth to Canford Cliffs in Coventry Stakes at Royal Ascot second start: bred to stay 1m: acts on polytrack and firm going: has hung right. *J. A. Osborne* **94**

TREASURE ISLANDS (IRE) 4 b.f. Trans Island 119 – Gold Prospector (IRE) 78 (Spectrum (IRE) 126) [2009 58: p11g Feb 25] good-bodied filly: modest maiden at best: stays 1m. *S. W. Hall* **–**

TREASURE TOWN 2 b.c. (Feb 17) King's Best (USA) 132 – Shinko Hermes (IRE) (Sadler's Wells (USA) 132) [2009 8.3m3 p8g* Oct 26] strong colt: half-brother to several winners, including smart 1¼m/11f winner Lake Toya (by Darshaan) and useful 1m winner Glen Innes (by Selkirk): dam, ran once in Japan, sister to Oaks winner Imagine and half-sister to Generous: promising debut then landed odds in maiden at Lingfield easily by 3 lengths from Life And Soul: will be suited by 1¼m+: sure to improve further. *Saeed bin Suroor* **89 p**

TREASURE WAY 2 ch.f. (Apr 9) Galileo (IRE) 134 – Gold Mark (Mark of Esteem (IRE) 137) [2009 8m Sep 8] 87,000Y: second foal: half-sister to winner in Sweden by Singspiel: dam, French maiden, half-sister to smart Irish 2000 2-y-o 6f/7f winner Honours List: 66/1, mid-field in maiden at Goodwood, close up long way: sure to improve. *P. R. Chamings* **62 p**

TREASURY BOND 2 ch.g. (Apr 17) Monsieur Bond (IRE) 120 – Rainbow Treasure (IRE) 57 (Rainbow Quest (USA) 134) [2009 6g 6s 7m4 7s4 Jul 14] lengthy gelding: poor maiden plater: stays 7f. *P. T. Midgley* **36**

TREBLE JIG (USA) 2 b.c. (Mar 17) Gone West (USA) – Light Jig 121 (Danehill (USA) 126) [2009 7d 7g* Aug 28] useful-looking colt: second foal: dam French/US 1m to 1¼m (including Grade 1) winner: most promising in maidens at Newmarket, still green when beating Suited And Booted comfortably by 1¾ lengths (pair clear): will stay 1m+: smart prospect and will make mark at much higher level. *Sir Michael Stoute* **93 P**

TREEKO (IRE) 4 b.g. Alhaarth (IRE) 126 – Allegheny River (USA) (Lear Fan (USA) 130) [2009 –: 10m Aug 29] maiden: well held both starts on Flat since 2007: tried in cheekpieces. *P. A. Kirby* **–**

TREES OF GREEN (USA) 5 b.g. Elusive Quality (USA) – Grazia 111 (Sharpo 132) [2009 –: p8.6m Mar 4] tall, attractive gelding: regressive maiden: stays 1m: acts on soft and good to firm ground: tried visored/blinkered. *M. Wigham* **–**

TREETOPS HOTEL (IRE) 10 ch.g. Grand Lodge (USA) 125 – Rousinette (Rousillon (USA) 133) [2009 64d: p13.3g 12g 12m 10.1g 10.2m 14.1m 15.8d 10m 10g p12.2g Dec 12] quite attractive gelding: little form in 2009: tried in headgear/tongue tie. *L. R. James* **–**

TREGONY BRIDGE 2 b.g. (Mar 29) Avonbridge 123 – Serotina (IRE) 73 (Mtoto 134) [2009 8.1d p7g p7m Oct 31] down the field in maidens. *M. Blanshard* **–**

TRELAWNY WELLS 2 b.g. (Mar 2) Pastoral Pursuits 127 – Kythia (IRE) 77 (Kahyasi 130) [2009 5.1d3 6m 6.1m Jul 1] well beaten in minor event/maidens (gelded after). *M. R. Channon* **–**

TREMPARI 6 ch.g. Trempolino (USA) 135 – Ariadne (GER) (Kings Lake (USA) 133) [2009 p12g 12g4 11.8m 17.2g6 16g 18g4 16m* 17.1m 16d p16m Dec 1] plain gelding: fair form in bumpers: modest handicapper on Flat: won at Lingfield in September: stays 2¼m: acts on good to firm ground: often blinkered. *Mike Murphy* **58**

TRES AMIGOS 2 ch.g. (Apr 9) Exceed And Excel (AUS) 126 – Canterloupe (IRE) 98 (Wolfhound (USA) 126) [2009 7.2m6 7m5 f7g* Oct 18] 56,000F, 65,000Y: tall gelding: second foal: dam, 5f/6f winner, half-sister to useful Norwegian performer up to 1½m Miss The Boat: progressive in maidens, making all at Southwell to win by 4 lengths from Primo de Vida: raced only at 7f, should prove as effective at 6f. *D. Nicholls* **82 +**

TRES CHIC (FR) 3 gr.f. Kaldounevees (FR) 118 – Chic Emilie (FR) (Policeman (FR) 124) [2009 –: 10s 8.3g May 4] modest form in maidens. *S. Curran* **58**

TRES CORONAS (IRE) 2 b.g. (Mar 15) Key of Luck (USA) 126 – Almansa (IRE) (Dr Devious (IRE) 127) [2009 5m3 5s* 6d2 7m2 7g 8m4 8m 8g3 f8m* Nov 6] €7,000Y: leggy gelding: second foal: dam, French 1½m winner, half-sister to smart performer up to **85**

1¼m Alasha: fairly useful performer: won maiden at Newcastle in May and nursery at Southwell (blinkered, improved to beat Cornish Beau 4½ lengths) in November: should stay 1¼m: acts on fibresand, soft and good to firm ground: front runner/races prominently. *T. D. Barron*

TRES FROIDE (FR) 4 ch.f. Bering 136 – Charmgoer (USA) (Nureyev (USA) 131) **70**
[2009 12m 10.1d 8m^{6} 8.1v f8g 12d 10g* 10.2g Oct 28] good-bodied filly: third foal: sister to useful French 7f (at 2 yrs) to 13f winner Beringoer and half-sister to French 11.5f winner Specialiste (by Poliglote): dam, French 13f winner, half-sister to high-class US Grade 1 1¼m winner Dare And Go: fair handicapper: left F. Head in France €42,000 after final start in 2008: won ladies race at Redcar in October: effective at 9f to 11.5f: acts on all-weather and heavy going. *N. Tinkler*

TREVIAN 8 ch.g. Atraf 116 – Ascend (IRE) (Glint of Gold 128) [2009 57: 13.1f Aug **–**
22] big gelding: modest handicapper at 7 yrs: visored/tongue tied, bumped and lost action sole outing on Flat in 2009: stayed 1¼m: acted on polytrack and firm going: fair hurdler: dead. *Tim Vaughan*

TREWARTHENICK 2 br.g. (Mar 9) Cape Cross (IRE) 129 – Play With Fire (FR) **62 p**
(Priolo (USA) 127) [2009 6d^{6} p8g^{6} Aug 24] 50,000F, 48,000Y: good-topped gelding: sixth foal: brother to useful 5f/6f (including at 2 yrs) winner Millbag and half-brother to 2 winners, including useful 2002 2-y-o 5f/6f winner Coconut Penang (by Night Shift): dam French 1½m winner: better effort in maidens when 9¾ lengths sixth to Togiak at Kempton (gelded after): likely to progress again. *A. M. Balding*

TRIBAL MYTH (IRE) 2 b.g. (Apr 5) Johannesburg (USA) 127 – Shadow Play **53**
(USA) (Theatrical 128) [2009 6m 7d^{6} 7g^{6} 7g Sep 3] good-topped gelding: modest maiden: no impact in nursery: should stay 1m. *K. A. Ryan*

TRIBAL RULE 3 gr.c. Daylami (IRE) 138 – Native Justice (USA) 115 (Alleged (USA) **61**
138) [2009 10m^{6} 9.7m^{6} p10m Sep 26] useful-looking colt: easily best effort in maidens (modest form) when sixth on debut: bred to stay 1½m: raced only on polytrack and good to firm going: tried tongue tied: sold 5,500 gns. *Mrs A. J. Perrett*

TRIBE 7 b.g. Danehill (USA) 126 – Leo Girl (USA) 100 (Seattle Slew (USA)) [2009 74: **73**
16.4m^{2} 16.1m^{6} 16m^{3} Jul 15] very big gelding: fair handicapper nowadays: stays 2¼m: acts on good to firm and good to soft ground: tried tongue tied. *P. R. Webber*

TRI CHARA (IRE) 5 ch.g. Grand Slam (USA) 120 – Lamzena (IRE) 92 (Fairy King **–**
(USA)) [2009 70: f7d* f7g^{4} f7g^{5} p7.1g^{6} f7g^{4} f6g^{4} 7g p7.1g^{5} 6g f6g^{6} p6g^{2} p7.1g f7m^{4} **a72**
f6g Dec 8] tall gelding: fair handicapper on all-weather, little form on turf since 3 yrs: won at Southwell in January: effective at 7f to 9.5f: acts on all-weather: usually wears cheekpieces/visor: races prominently. *R. Hollinshead*

TRICK OR TWO 3 gr.g. Desert Style (IRE) 121 – Vax Star 96 (Petong 126) [2009 66: **61**
p5g^{4} f6g^{4} p5.1g^{5} 5m Apr 12] just modest performer at 3 yrs: bred to prove best at 5f/6f: raced only on all-weather and good to firm going: tried blinkered. *Mrs R. A. Carr*

TRICKY SITUATION 3 b.f. Mark of Esteem (IRE) 137 – Trick of Ace (USA) **70**
(Clever Trick (USA)) [2009 78p: 8.1g^{3} 10.4m^{3} Jun 11] regressive form in 3 maidens: should be well suited by 1¼m+. *J. G. Given*

TRICKY TREV (USA) 3 ch.g. Toccet (USA) 118 – Lady Houston (USA) (Houston **56**
(USA)) [2009 66: p7.1g^{6} 8f 5m 6f^{3} 5.3g^{3} 6m p6m Nov 28] modest maiden handicapper: stays 7f: acts on polytrack and firm ground: tried blinkered: tongue tied last 5 starts. *S. Curran*

TRIED AND TRUE (FR) 4 b.f. Marju (IRE) 127 – Test The Rest (USA) (Take Me **72**
Out (USA)) [2009 10f^{4} p10g 10m^{5} Jun 1] small, rather leggy filly: first foal: dam, fairly useful maiden in UAE (stayed 1m), half-sister to US Grade 2 8.5f winner Notation: lightly raced in Italy: left V. Valiani, best effort in Britain (fair form) when fourth in maiden at Leicester: worth a try around 1m: tried blinkered: sold 1,500 gns. *H. R. A. Cecil*

TRIFTI 8 b.g. Vettori (IRE) 119 – Time For Tea (IRE) 73 (Imperial Frontier (USA) 112) **–**
[2009 –, a80: p10g^{3} p10g* p10g^{5} 10m p10g^{5} p10f^{6} Dec 20] medium-sized gelding: fairly **a80**
useful handicapper on all-weather, very lightly raced on turf nowadays: won at Lingfield in March: best at 1m/1¼m: acts on polytrack and good to firm going: tried blinkered: often held up: has bled, including fourth start. *Miss Jo Crowley*

TRIMLESTOWN (IRE) 6 b.g. Orpen (USA) 116 – Courtier (Saddlers' Hall (IRE) **66**
126) [2009 81: p6g^{6} p5.1g p7.1g^{6} p7.1g p6g^{3} p7m^{5} f7m Dec 15] strong, good-topped gelding: fair performer nowadays: effective at 6f/7f: acts on polytrack, heavy and good to firm going: often in headgear: tried tongue tied. *P. D. Evans*

TRINCOT (FR) 4 b.c. Peintre Celebre (USA) 137 – Royal Lights (FR) (Royal Academy (USA) 130) [2009 117: 10s 10g* 10m^2 10m 10g^3 Jul 26] attractive colt: smart performer: won Prix d'Harcourt at Longchamp in April in good style by 3 lengths from The Bogberry: left P. Demercastel in France, just respectable efforts when placed after in Premio Presidente della Repubblica at Rome (¾-length second to Selmis) and Grosser Dallmayr-Preis at Munich (2¼ lengths third to Pressing): only seventh in Prince of Wales's Stakes at Royal Ascot in between: stays 1¼m: acts on soft and good to firm going: in cheekpieces last 4 starts: usually held up. *Saeed bin Suroor* **118**

TRINCULO (IRE) 12 b.g. Anita's Prince 126 – Fandangerina (USA) (Grey Dawn II 132) [2009 74§: p6g f6g p5.1m^6 p6g^4 p6g^4 f5g f6g May 18] good-bodied gelding: has a long, round action: modest performer nowadays: stays 7f: acts on all-weather and any turf going: wears headgear: races up with pace: has hung/found little: unreliable. *R. A. Harris* **58 §**

TRINDER 2 b.c. (Apr 24) Pastoral Pursuits 127 – Quiz Show 82 (Primo Dominie 121) [2009 5g^2 6g^6 5m^2 6g^4 6m 5g Oct 6] £20,000Y: sturdy colt: reportedly has no near eye: half-brother to several winners, including 3-y-o Excellent Show and useful 2004 2-y-o 5f winner Right Answer (by Lujain): dam, 7f winner, half-sister to very smart sprinter Mind Games: fair maiden: best effort at 5f on good to firm going: sold £4,500. *R. A. Fahey* **77**

TRIPBIYAH (USA) 3 b.g. Trippi (USA) 121 – Jathibiyah (USA) 89 (Nureyev (USA) 131) [2009 8g^5 8m^3 5d^4 p7.1g^5 Oct 9] fair maiden: stays 1m: acts on polytrack, unraced on extremes of going on turf. *G. A. Swinbank* **65**

TRIPITAKA 3 b.g. Sulamani (IRE) 130 – Memo (Groom Dancer (USA) 128) [2009 p11g* p12g p12g* Dec 2] third foal: dam unraced out of useful 1994 2-y-o 5f/6.5f winner The Jotter: fairly useful form: won maiden in April and handicap (easily beat Brett Vale 1½ lengths) in November, both at Kempton: shaped as though amiss in between: stays 1½m: should improve further. *M. A. Jarvis* **94 p**

TRIPLE ASPECT (IRE) 3 b.c. Danetime (IRE) 121 – Wicken Wonder (IRE) 71 (Distant Relative 128) [2009 108p: 6d^2 5m* 5m^2 5.2m^4 6g^2 Oct 10] angular colt: smart performer: improved in 2009, and won listed race at Sandown in June by 2¼ lengths from Jargelle: second on 3 other occasions, in similar event at Newbury (to Border Patrol), Sprint Stakes at Sandown (behind Ialysos) and Bengough Memorial Stakes at Ascot (beaten head by Royal Rock): effective at 5f/6f: unraced on extremes of going: tends to wander. *W. J. Haggas* **116**

TRIPLE AXEL (IRE) 5 b.m. Danehill Dancer (IRE) 117 – Across The Ice (USA) (General Holme (USA) 128) [2009 72: f7g^3 p7.1g^3 Jan 26] lengthy mare: fair performer: effective at 6f/7f: acts on all-weather and heavy going: tried in cheekpieces: sold 3,500 gns. *J. Noseda* **66**

TRIPLE CEE (IRE) 3 b.f. Cape Cross (IRE) 129 – Karri Valley (USA) (Storm Bird (CAN) 134) [2009 73: p10g^4 10.2g^6 8.1g 9.9m^6 10.2g^3 10d^6 13.1d 10.3m^3 10m^2 p10g^4 p10g^5 p10g^6 p9.5g Dec 28] small filly: fair maiden handicapper: worth a try at 1½m: acts on polytrack and good to firm going: consistent. *M. R. Channon* **66**

TRIPLE DREAM 4 ch.g. Vision of Night 115 – Triple Joy 104 (Most Welcome 131) [2009 73: 7d^6 p7g 7m^5 5.1m^2 6m 5m^5 5.2m^2 5.2s^5 5f^4 5.7m* 6g^2 5s* 5m* 6g^2 5m^3 5g Oct 10] well-made gelding: fairly useful handicapper: improved at 4 yrs, winning at Bath (apprentices) in August and Salisbury and Redcar in September: best at 5f/easy 6f: acts on polytrack, firm and soft going: wears cheekpieces. *J. M. Bradley* **86**

TRIP SWITCH 3 b.g. Reset (AUS) 124 – Caribbean Star 81 (Soviet Star (USA) 128) [2009 p6g^2 p6g* p6g^4 7.1g^6 p6g 7.1m p6m p6g p6g Dec 31] lengthy gelding: fair performer: won maiden at Lingfield in March: below form after next start, leaving W. Muir prior to final outing: bred to stay 7f: acts on polytrack: tried blinkered. *G. Prodromou* **68**

TRIP THE LIGHT 4 b.g. Fantastic Light (USA) 134 – Jumaireyah 91 (Fairy King (USA)) [2009 71: 12g 12m* 14.6g^6 12m^5 12m* 14f^2 11.9g* 12g^2 14.8g^4 p13.9g^3 14d^5 12g* f14g^2 p12.2g^4 Nov 20] neat gelding: fairly useful handicapper: won at Catterick in April, Thirsk in June, Haydock (apprentices) in August and York in October: should stay 2m: acts on all-weather, firm and good to soft going: usually visored: tough and genuine. *R. A. Fahey* **94**

TRIREME (IRE) 5 b.g. Fantastic Light (USA) 134 – Dreamboat (USA) 84 (Mr Prospector (USA)) [2009 56: p10g 10.2g Jul 23] big gelding: in frame once in bumpers: maiden on Flat: well held both starts at 5 yrs, said to have bled again former occasion: tried tongue tied. *K. A. Morgan* **–**

TRISKAIDEKAPHOBIA 6 b.g. Bertolini (USA) 125 – Seren Teg 80 (Timeless Times (USA) 99) [2009 –, a70: p5.1g p5g p5.1m^{4d} p5g p5.1g 5g 5.1m p5.1g p5m* Dec 6] **49 a57**

small, sturdy gelding: modest handicapper on all-weather nowadays, poor on turf: won at Lingfield in December: speedy front runner, best at 5f: acts on all-weather and good to firm going: often visored/blinkered: tongue tied. *Miss J. R. Tooth*

TRIUMPHANT WELCOME 4 b.g. Piccolo 121 – Shoof (USA) 72 (Dayjur (USA) 137) [2009 71d: p6g 5.1g f6g³ p6g 5.7g p6m f6d Dec 29] compact gelding: just modest handicapper at 4 yrs: stays 6f: acts on fibresand and good to soft going: tried blinkered. *H. J. Evans* **62**

TRIVIA (IRE) 5 br.m. Marju (IRE) 127 – Lehua (IRE) (Linamix (FR) 127) [2009 67: p7g⁶ p6g⁶ 6m 7f 8m 7m⁶ 5.2m⁵ 5.2s Jul 17] leggy mare: modest handicapper: left Ms J. Doyle after third start: stays easy 8.6f: acts on polytrack and good to firm going. *J. J. Bridger* **59**

TROOPINGTHECOLOUR 3 b.c. Nayef (USA) 129 – Hyperspectra 91 (Rainbow Quest (USA) 134) [2009 10m² 10.3s² 10.2d² p10g² p10m* Nov 27] 230,000Y: good-topped colt: sixth foal: closely related to 1½m winner Spectral Star (by Unfuwain) and half-brother to 3 winners, including smart Irish 7f winner (including at 2 yrs) France (by Desert Prince) and Irish 6-y-o Green Tobasco: dam 1¼m winner: fairly useful form: won maiden at Lingfield in November: likely to be suited by 1½m: acts on polytrack and soft going: sold £41,000. *J. H. M. Gosden* **92**

TROPICAL BACHELOR (IRE) 3 b.g. Bachelor Duke (USA) 122 – Tropical Coral (IRE) 82 (Pennekamp (USA) 130) [2009 55p: 10.2m⁵ 7m³ 12s⁵ 12.1g³ 12.5g 14m² 14g⁵ 17.1m 13.8m² 12.1g² 13.8g Oct 17] smallish gelding: fair maiden handicapper: left D. Arbuthnot £2,200 in April before reappearance: stays 1¾m: acts on soft and good to firm ground: races up with pace: in blinkers/cheekpieces last 4 starts. *T. J. Pitt* **73**

TROPICAL BLUE 3 b.g. Fath (USA) 116 – Tropical Zone (Machiavellian (USA) 123) [2009 73: 10.4v² 10.3m³ 14.1m⁶ 10s⁴ 10m p13.9g³ Dec 17] rather leggy gelding: fairly useful maiden handicapper: gelded prior to final start: stays 1¾m: acts on polytrack, heavy and good to firm ground: tried visored. *Jennie Candlish* **83**

TROPICAL DUKE (IRE) 3 ch.g. Bachelor Duke (USA) 122 – Tropical Dance (USA) 93 (Thorn Dance (USA) 107) [2009 –: p10g⁴ p10g 11.6m 14.1f 9.3d 8m* 8.5m³ 9.9g* 10g³ Oct 16] rather leggy gelding: fair performer: left D. Arbuthnot £5,000 and gelded after fourth start: won handicaps at Redcar in August and Beverley (amateurs) in September: should stay 1½m: acts on polytrack and good to firm ground: waited with. *R. E. Barr* **66**

TROPICAL PARADISE (IRE) 3 gr.f. Verglas (IRE) 118 – Ladylishandra (IRE) 82 (Mujadil (USA) 119) [2009 97: 7s⁴ 6g² 7s* 7m Sep 26] workmanlike filly: useful performer: improved when winning handicap at Salisbury in September by neck from Enact: below form in listed race at Ascot final start: stays 7f: acts on polytrack and soft going. *P. Winkworth* **108**

TROPICAL STRAIT (IRE) 6 b.g. Intikhab (USA) 135 – Tropical Dance (USA) 93 (Thorn Dance (USA) 107) [2009 109: 13.3d⁴ May 16] sturdy gelding: useful performer: set to finish third (behind Tastahil) in listed race at Newbury before breaking down close home: stayed 1¾m: acted on polytrack, soft and good to firm ground: dead. *D. W. P. Arbuthnot* **106**

TROPICAL TRADITION (IRE) 4 ch.g. Traditionally (USA) 117 – Tropical Coral (IRE) 82 (Pennekamp (USA) 130) [2009 67: p11g³ p12g 12g⁵ Apr 19] close-coupled gelding: fair performer: sold from D. Arbuthnot 2,500 gns after second start, well held on turf debut: stays 1½m: raced only on polytrack in Britain. *C. von der Recke, Germany* **65**

TROPICAL TREAT 2 b.f. (Feb 27) Bahamian Bounty 116 – Notjustaprettyface (USA) 98 (Red Ransom (USA)) [2009 5m* 6d Oct 24] 28,000F: angular filly: first foal: dam, 2-y-o 5f winner, out of half-sister to smart 1994 2-y-o performer up to 7f Sri Pekan: won maiden at Windsor in July by 1½ lengths from Bush Tucker: 4 lengths seventh to Layla's Hero in listed event at Doncaster: likely to be best at 5f/6f: already fairly useful, and probably capable of better still. *R. M. Beckett* **88 p**

TROUBLE MOUNTAIN (USA) 12 br.g. Mt Livermore (USA) – Trouble Free (USA) (Nodouble (USA)) [2009 72: 9.9m 10.1s 10.1d⁶ 10m* 10.1d⁴ 10.2m 10m⁶ 10.4g² 10g⁶ f11g Oct 27] small, sparely-made gelding: fair handicapper: won at Redcar in June: best around 1¼m: acts on fibresand and any turf going: tried blinkered: tongue tied: none too reliable. *M. W. Easterby* **66**

TROUBLETIMESTWO (FR) 3 gr.g. Linamix (FR) 127 – Time of Trouble (FR) 82 (Warning 136) [2009 60p: p9.5g⁴ 12.1m⁵ 10m May 7] modest maiden: should prove best beyond 9.5f: joined A. Carroll, fair form over hurdles. *H. J. L. Dunlop* **60**

TROVARE (USA) 2 b.c. (May 18) Smart Strike (CAN) 121 – Abita (USA) (Dynaformer (USA)) [2009 7m 8g 7g Oct 30] tall, angular colt: best effort in maidens when mid-field at Newmarket final start: should stay 1m. *Mrs A. J. Perrett* **66**

TRUCKERS DELIGHT (IRE) 8 b.g. Darazari (IRE) 123 – Windmill Star (IRE) (Orchestra 118) [2009 79: 16m² 16g* 16s 18m Oct 17] angular gelding: fairly useful hurdler/chaser: lightly raced on Flat but similar standard in handicaps: best effort when winning at the Curragh in June: well held in Cesarewitch at Newmarket final outing: stays 2m: acts on polytrack and good to firm going. *John Joseph Hanlon, Ireland* **91**

TRUEBLUE WIZARD (IRE) 3 ch.g. Bachelor Duke (USA) 122 – Truly Bewitched (USA) 81 (Affirmed (USA)) [2009 71p: p7.1g⁴ f8d⁴ p10m⁶ p8g⁶ p8g Oct 22] fair handicapper: stays 1¼m: raced only on all-weather: blinkered last 3 starts (gelded after final one): races prominently. *W. R. Muir* **72**

TRUE BRITANNIA 3 b.f. Lujain (USA) 119 – Surf Bird (Shareef Dancer (USA) 135) [2009 58: p10g* p10g⁶ p10g* p10g³ p10g 10g⁶ 7f³ 8m³ May 19] rather leggy filly: fair performer on all-weather, modest on turf: won handicaps at Lingfield in January and February: stays 1¼m: acts on polytrack and firm ground: usually visored nowadays: sold £6,000, fair juvenile hurdler for N. King. *A. M. Hales* **58 a65**

TRUE DECISION 3 b.g. Reset (AUS) 124 – True Precision 84 (Presidium 124) [2009 –: p6g² f7g* p6g 5.1g 6f⁵ p8g p7g p8.6m⁵ p6g⁵ p7m⁴ p10m⁵ f8g p10g³ Nov 18] modest performer: won maiden at Southwell in March: stays 1¼m: acts on all-weather and firm ground. *S. Kirk* **64**

TRUE LOVES KISS 2 ch.f. (Feb 24) Tobougg (IRE) 125 – Bob's Princess 69 (Bob's Return (IRE) 123) [2009 5d⁶ 6m⁴ᵈ 7s Sep 5] £6,500Y: neat filly: seventh foal: half-sister to several winners, including 5-y-o Ingleby Princess and fairly useful 7f/1½m winner The Oil Magnate (by Dr Fong): dam 2-y-o 7f winner (stayed 1½m): best effort in maidens when fourth (disqualified after rider failed to weigh in) to Avonrose at Redcar (left A. McCabe after): should be suited by 7f+: sold £800. *J. A. Glover* **62**

TRUE RED (IRE) 2 ch.f. (Apr 14) Redback 116 – Red Trance (IRE) 79 (Soviet Star (USA) 128) [2009 p5g 5.1g² 5.3m⁵ 5.1m⁵ 6.1g⁴ 5.1g² f5g² 5g⁵ 5.1g² 5g³ 5m p6m⁵ p5g² p5.1g p5.1g f5f⁶ Dec 17] small filly: second foal: dam, 2-y-o 5f winner, sister to 4-y-o Red Merlin: modest maiden: left B. R. Millman after tenth start: likely to prove best at 5f: acts on all-weather and good to firm ground: usually makes running. *Mrs N. S. Evans* **61**

TRUE TO FORM (IRE) 2 b.g. (May 13) Rock of Gibraltar (IRE) 133 – Truly Yours (IRE) (Barathea (IRE) 127) [2009 f6g p6g p6g p7m Oct 31] €9,000Y: fourth foal: brother to Irish 9f and 10.8f winner Truly Mine and half-brother to 7f to 9f (in Hong Kong) winner Days of My Life (by Daylami), both useful: dam, French 2-y-o 1m winner, half-sister to Poule d'Essai des Poulains runner-up Catcher In The Rye: behind in maidens (gelded after): will stay 1m: should do better. *Sir Mark Prescott* **– p**

TRUISM 3 b.g. Daylami (IRE) 138 – Real Trust (USA) (Danzig (USA)) [2009 86p: 7s⁵ 8.3m² 8m² 8m² Oct 5] rangy, attractive gelding: useful handicapper: good second last 3 starts, beaten 1½ lengths by Good Again at Pontefract final occasion: will stay 1¼m: acts on soft and good to firm ground. *Mrs A. J. Perrett* **96**

TRULY ASIA (IRE) 3 b.g. Acclamation 118 – Tasha's Dream (USA) 74 (Woodman (USA) 126) [2009 7d⁴ 8.3g³ 7g² 8d² 9.7m² 8.1m³ 8g* Oct 21] €48,000F, 160,000Y: strong, lengthy gelding: second foal: half-brother to fairly useful 7f (at 2 yrs in Ireland) to 9.5f (in France) winner Unquenchable Fire (by Invincible Spirit): dam, Irish maiden (stayed 8.5f), sister to smart Irish 7f/1m performer Major Force and half-sister to smart Irish performer up to 1¾m Quality Team: fairly useful performer: improved last 2 starts, tongue tied when winning apprentice handicap at Bath in October (gelded after): likely to prove best at 1m: unraced on extremes of going. *R. Charlton* **86**

TRULY DIVINE 4 b.g. Invincible Spirit (IRE) 121 – Shabarana (FR) (Nishapour (FR) 125) [2009 68: p6g⁴ 7d p6g f8g p6m p7m Dec 30] sturdy, lengthy gelding: modest maiden handicapper: should stay at least 7f: acts on polytrack, soft and good to firm ground: tried in cheekpieces/visor: often slowly away: signs of temperament. *C. A. Dwyer* **61**

TRULY MAGIC 2 ch.f. (Mar 19) Traditionally (USA) 117 – Truly Bewitched (USA) 81 (Affirmed (USA)) [2009 p6g 7.1m 5.7g 5.7g⁶ 7g* 7.1m⁴ 8g Oct 19] 5,000Y: angular filly: sixth foal: half-sister to several winners, including useful 1m winner Arabian Spell (by Desert Prince) and 4-y-o Red Merlin: dam, 2-y-o 6f winner, half-sister to smart US miler Chinese Dragon: fair performer: won nursery at Leicester in September: unlucky in similar event at Warwick next time: should stay 1m. *H. J. L. Dunlop* **65**

TRUMPET LILY 4 b.f. Acclamation 118 – Periwinkle (FR) (Perrault 130) [2009 88: 8.3m* 8m³ 8.1m 8g⁶ 8g⁵ 9g 8.3f³ 10g⁴ p8g Oct 29] rangy filly: useful handicapper: won at Windsor in April: often better than result after: should stay 1¼m: acts on firm and soft ground: travels strongly held up. *J. G. Portman* **95**

TRUMPSTOO (USA) 3 b.g. Perfect Soul (IRE) 122 – Cozzy Love (USA) (Cozzene (USA)) [2009 76p: 8m 10.4m 8.5g⁵ 8g³ 8s 10.3m⁶ 16.1g⁵ Sep 30] useful-looking gelding: fair handicapper: gelded prior to third start: stays 1m: acts on heavy ground: won juvenile hurdle in October. *R. A. Fahey* **67**

TRUSTED VENTURE (USA) 3 b.g. Trust N Luck (USA) 118 – Afleet Canadian (CAN) (Bucksplasher (USA)) [2009 63: p7g⁶ p7g⁴ p8g p8m p9.5g Oct 23] neat gelding: modest performer: below form after second start (gelded after next outing): stays 1m: acts on polytrack. *J. R. Best* **57**

TRYST 4 gr.g. Highest Honor (FR) 124 – Courting 108 (Pursuit of Love 124) [2009 86p: p7g* 7m² 10m³ 9m Oct 3] lengthy, good sort: useful performer, very lightly raced: won maiden at Lingfield in May: shaped well in handicap at Newmarket (2½ lengths second to Roaring Forte) and, after 4-month absence, minor event at Ascot (third to Rainbow Peak): possibly found Cambridgeshire (Handicap) at Newmarket coming too soon 8 days later: stays 1¼m: raced on polytrack and good/good to firm ground: sold 24,000 gns. *Sir Michael Stoute* **101**

TSAR BOMBA (USA) 2 b. or br.g. (Feb 28) Red Bullet (USA) 126 – Larry's Blackhoney (USA) (Hennessy (USA) 122) [2009 5m⁵ May 25] $12,000F: good-bodied gelding: second foal: dam US 6f winner: 16/1, 3¾ lengths fifth to Oondiri in maiden at Redcar, green before late headway: should improve. *T. D. Barron* **63 p**

TUBBY LITTLEJOHNS (IRE) 5 ch.h. Desert Sun 120 – Brookhouse Lady (IRE) 61 (Polish Patriot (USA) 128) [2009 15.8g² 11.7m⁵ Aug 16] well beaten in bumper: modest form in seller/maiden on Flat. *B. J. Llewellyn* **61**

TUCKER'S LAW 2 b.g. (Apr 7) Country Reel (USA) 113 – Silvereine (FR) (Bering 136) [2009 5.1g 5m² 6m⁵ 5g⁶ 6.1v⁵ p6g⁴ p6g⁶ p5g⁶ p5.1g⁵ p6f² p7.1g* Nov 2] angular gelding: fair performer: won seller at Wolverhampton: stays 7f: acts on polytrack and good to firm going. *B. R. Millman* **66**

TUDOR KEY (IRE) 3 br.g. Key of Luck (USA) 126 – Anne Boleyn (Rainbow Quest (USA) 134) [2009 91: 10m⁵ 10m⁵ 8m p8m* 8m p8g 8.1g 8m⁶ 8.5m³ Oct 3] good-bodied gelding: useful performer on all-weather, fairly useful on turf: won minor event at Lingfield in July by short head from Film Set: largely held form in handicaps after: effective at 1m/1¼m: acts on polytrack and good to firm going. *Mrs A. J. Perrett* **92 a97**

TUDOR PRINCE (IRE) 5 b. or br.g. Cape Cross (IRE) 129 – Savona (IRE) 70 (Cyrano de Bergerac 120) [2009 84: p6g* 6v 6m³ 6m⁴ p6g⁴ 6d 6g p6g² 6d p7m* p6g Nov 21] well-made gelding: fairly useful handicapper: won at Kempton in April and October: effective at 6f/7f: acts on polytrack, soft and good to firm going: tried blinkered/visored. *A. W. Carroll* **80**

TUDOR PRINCESS 2 b.f. (Feb 15) King's Best (USA) 132 – Santorini (USA) (Spinning World (USA) 130) [2009 6m 6d Oct 6] fourth foal: half-sister to 3 winners, including 6-y-o Methaaly: dam unraced half-sister to St Leger winner Mutafaweq and smart performer up to 1¼m Dimitrova: modest form when seventh in maidens. *W. R. Muir* **53**

TUFTON 6 b.g. King's Best (USA) 132 – Mythical Magic (Green Desert (USA) 127) [2009 86: 10.3g² 10.1d⁵ 10m³ 11.1m* 10m* 9.9m 10g 12.5d⁴ Oct 28] fairly useful performer: won claimers at Hamilton and Redcar in July: below form after: stays 11f: acts on polytrack and firm going: formerly tongue tied. *R. A. Fahey* **82**

TUKITINYASOK (IRE) 2 b.g. (Feb 15) Fath (USA) 116 – Mevlana (IRE) (Red Sunset 120) [2009 7m³ 7.2g* 7d³ 6.1g⁴ 7m p8.6g³ Dec 11] €9,000Y, resold €5,500Y: workmanlike gelding: half-brother to several winners, including 2000 2-y-o 6f winner Ladylishandra (by Mujadil) and 2003 2-y-o 7f winner Vade Retro (by Desert Sun), both fairly useful in Ireland: dam French 11f/1½m winner: fair performer: won maiden at Ayr in July: ran creditably next 3 starts: should stay 1m: acts on good to firm and good to soft ground. *R. F. Fisher* **78**

TULIP EXPLOSION 2 b.f. (Feb 4) Exceed And Excel (AUS) 126 – Comme Ca (Cyrano de Bergerac 120) [2009 5.1g f5g 5g p5.1m³ p5g Sep 9] £11,000Y: sixth foal: half-sister to 2003 2-y-o 6f winner Even Easier (by Petong) and 2004 2-y-o 5f winner Grand Place (by Compton Place): dam unraced: poor maiden. *D. Shaw* **48**

TUMBLED AGAIN 2 br.g. (Mar 17) Tumbleweed Ridge 117 – Amber Brown 67 (Thowra (FR)) [2009 6g p8g Nov 1] slowly away and well held in maidens over 3 months apart (gelded in between). *M. E. Rimmer* –

TUMBLEWEED DI 5 ro.m. Tumbleweed Ridge 117 – Peggotty 50 (Capricorn Line 111) [2009 54: 8.5m Sep 16] modest maiden: well held sole start in 2009: raced mostly at 5f/6f on polytrack and good ground or firmer: tried in cheekpieces. *John A. Harris* –

TUMP MAC 5 ch.g. Compton Admiral 121 – Petite Elite 47 (Anfield 117) [2009 62d: 6m 7g 10v 7.5m 7m 10m Oct 3] strong, close-coupled gelding: maiden: little form in 2009: tried tongue tied. *N. Bycroft* –

TUNDER BOOL (IRE) 4 b.g. Intikhab (USA) 135 – Tirolean Dance (IRE) (Tirol 127) [2009 11s p9.5g Feb 13] ex-Italian handicapper: won at Florence in 2008, placed several times subsequently: left P. Giannotti, well held in minor event on British debut (wore blinkers/tongue tie): stays 11.3f: acts on heavy ground (unraced on firmer than good). *F. Sheridan* –

TUNE UP THE BAND 5 b.g. Bandmaster (USA) 97 – Name That Tune 40 (Fayruz 116) [2009 60: p6g Feb 9] maiden: has only made the track twice since 2 yrs, well held in seller sole outing in 2009. *R. J. Hodges* –

TUNGSTEN STRIKE (USA) 8 ch.g. Smart Strike (CAN) 121 – Bathilde (IRE) 102 (Generous (IRE) 139) [2009 113: 16m[5] 16.4m[4] 16g 16g 14.8g[6] 16m Sep 26] good-bodied gelding: still smart in 2008, very much on downgrade in 2009: stays 2m (seemingly not 2½m): acts on firm and soft going: usually wears cheekpieces/visor: usually forces pace. *Mrs A. J. Perrett* –

TUNING FORK 9 b.g. Alzao (USA) 117 – Tuning 114 (Rainbow Quest (USA) 134) [2009 54: p7g p11g p8g Jun 24] strong, lengthy, attractive gelding: no form in 2009: tried in headgear: has had tongue tied. *M. J. Attwater* –

TUPPENNY PIECE 3 ch.f. Sakhee (USA) 136 – Tuppenny 57 (Salse (USA) 128) [2009 –: p11g[4] 11.5m p11g[4] p12m[4] p13.9g Nov 2] medium-sized filly: fair maiden handicapper: best efforts third/fourth outings: should be suited by 1¾m+: raced only on polytrack and good to firm ground: tried in cheekpieces/tongue tie. *W. R. Swinburn* **65**

TURATI 3 b.c. Lomitas 129 – Torrigiana 110 (Celtic Swing 138) [2009 8d* 8d[4] 11m[2] 10m* 10v[2] Nov 8] €95,000Y: second foal: half-brother to Italian 10.5f winner Tanzio (by Peintre Celebre): dam Italian 7.5f (including at 2 yrs) to 10.5f winner: very smart performer: successful at 2 yrs in maiden at Naples and minor event and listed race at Rome: progressed well at Rome in 2009, winning minor event in March and listed race in October: also runner-up there in Derby Italiano (beaten 1½ lengths by Mastery) and Premio Roma (beaten ½ length by Voila Ici, keeping on): stays 11f: acts on heavy and good to firm ground: tongue tied. *G. Pucciatti, Italy* **120**

TURBO SHANDY 6 b.g. Piccolo 121 – Carn Maire 83 (Northern Prospect (USA)) [2009 6m 5.1d[6] 8f[6] p12.2g Nov 21] modest hurdler/chaser: well held on Flat. *D. Burchell* **46**

TURF TIME 2 b.g. (Feb 1) Zafeen (FR) 123 – Next Time (IRE) 54 (Danetime (IRE) 121) [2009 f5g[5] 5d p5.1g 5m 5g f5f[2] Dec 17] compact gelding: modest maiden: left A. McCabe after second outing: raced only at 5f: acts on fibresand: tried in cheekpieces. *J. A. Glover* **50**

TURF TRIVIA 2 gr.g. (Mar 21) Alhaarth (IRE) 126 – Exclusive Approval (USA) (With Approval (CAN)) [2009 6v[4] 7m[5] 7d[3] 8.3d Oct 15] unfurnished gelding: fair maiden: off nearly 3 months, well held in nursery at Nottingham (gelded after): should be suited by 1m+. *G. M. Moore* **65**

TURFWOLKE (GER) 4 b.f. Medicean 128 – Turfaue (GER) (Big Shuffle (USA) 122) [2009 71: 7.1g[4] f7g 8m 7.6d[6] p10m p7g Dec 2] workmanlike filly: fair maiden: well below form after reappearance: should stay 1¼m: unraced on extremes of ground. *Mrs H. S. Main* **69 d**

TURJUMAN (USA) 4 ch.g. Swain (IRE) 134 – Hachiyah (IRE) 91 (Generous (IRE) 139) [2009 91d: 10d[4] 11.6g* 11.6g* 12m[3] 12m[5] 12m[5] Oct 3] lengthy gelding: fair handicapper nowadays: won at Windsor in June and July: stays 1½m: acts on heavy and good to firm ground: tried blinkered. *W. J. Musson* **75**

TURKISH LOKUM 3 b.f. Bertolini (USA) 125 – Malabarista (FR) (Assert 134) [2009 65: p7g 6g 7.1g[3] 8s[5] p6m[3] p7.1g[3] p7m Oct 26] good-topped filly: fair maiden handicapper: stays 7f: acts on polytrack and good to soft ground: signs of temperament: sold 6,000 gns, sent to Greece. *J. M. P. Eustace* **66**

TURKISH SULTAN (IRE) 6 b.g. Anabaa (USA) 130 – Odalisque (IRE) (Machia- **56**
vellian (USA) 123) [2009 59: p9.5g p10m p8g^{6} p10g^{5} p9.5g^{3} p11g p8g^{4} p8.6g^{3} 10.2g p8.6g f8g p9.5g^{5} p8m^{3} p9.5g Dec 11] good-topped gelding: modest performer: stays 1¼m: acts on polytrack and any turf going: wears headgear, usually cheekpieces: held up. *J. M. Bradley*

TURNER'S TOUCH 7 ch.g. Compton Place 125 – Chairmans Daughter 68 (Unfu- **62 §**
wain (USA) 131) [2009 75§, a80§: p12g^{3} p12g^{3} p12g^{4} p12g^{2} p12g p12g p12.2g^{6} 11.9g^{4} 11.9m^{5} 11.9d p12m p12m^{5} Dec 6] deep-girthed gelding: modest performer: stays 1½m: acts on polytrack and good to firm ground: wears headgear (blinkered nowadays): held up: ungenuine. *G. L. Moore*

TURNING CIRCLE 3 b.c. Spinning World (USA) 130 – Willow Dale (IRE) 89 **53**
(Danehill (USA) 126) [2009 p8.6g Dec 7] modest form when ninth to Heathyards Junior in maiden at Wolverhampton, looking in need of experience. *M. Brittain*

TURNING TOP (IRE) 3 b.f. Pivotal 124 – Pietra Dura 96 (Cadeaux Genereux 131) **87**
[2009 64p: 8g^{3} p8g^{6} 7.1g* 8g 7g^{2} 6f^{3} 8.3m* 7s Sep 3] quite attractive filly: fairly useful performer: won maiden at Warwick in June and handicap at Windsor (improved, beat West With The Wind 2¾ lengths) in August: stays 8.3f: acts on firm going: sent to USA. *S. A. Callaghan*

TURNKEY 7 br.g. Pivotal 124 – Persian Air (Persian Bold 123) [2009 100: 6m 6m^{6} 6d* **90**
5v^{5} 6g^{3} 6f* 5.9d* 6m Sep 18] strong, close-coupled gelding: has a quick action: fairly useful performer nowadays: won claimers at Ripon in June, and Ayr and Carlisle in August: effective at 6f/7f: acts on any turf going (best recent efforts largely on softer than good): effective blinkered or not: held up. *D. Nicholls*

TURN ME ON (IRE) 6 b.g. Tagula (IRE) 116 – Jacobina 71 (Magic Ring (IRE) 115) **88**
[2009 82: 7f* 7g* 7g 7m^{2} 7m 7d^{5} 7d 8m^{2} p9.5g^{6} 7g 7s Oct 27] tall gelding: fairly useful handicapper: better than ever in 2009, winning at Thirsk in April and Catterick in May: effective at 6f to 9.5f: acts on polytrack, firm and good to soft going: tried blinkered/ tongue tied: reliable. *T. D. Walford*

TURN ON THE STYLE 7 ch.g. Pivotal 124 – Elegant Rose 72 (Noalto 120) [2009 **106**
114: p6g^{2} p5g^{4} f5g^{6} p6g Nov 21] good-topped gelding: useful performer nowadays: best effort in 2009 when 1¼ lengths fourth to Matsunosuke in handicap at Lingfield: best at 5f/6f: acts on all-weather, soft and good to firm going: blinkered: usually front runner/ races prominently. *J. Balding*

TURN TO DREAMS 3 b.f. Auction House (USA) 120 – Seren Teg 80 (Timeless **59**
Times (USA) 99) [2009 53: p8.6g^{2} p8.6g^{4} p8.6g^{5} p8g^{4} p8.6g^{2} p8.6g^{3} p9.5g^{4} p8.6g^{6} p9.5g^{2} p8g^{5} p9.5g^{2} p9.5m^{5} p8.6g f8g^{6} 10.2g p8g p9.5g^{5} Dec 19] lengthy filly: modest maiden: stays 9.5f: acts on polytrack, soft and good to firm ground: often visored: usually races up with pace. *P. D. Evans*

TUSCAN GOLD 2 ch.c. (Apr 2) Medicean 128 – Louella (USA) (El Gran Senor (USA) **55 p**
136) [2009 6m p7m p7g^{6} Oct 20] 16,000Y: half-brother to very smart 7f (at 2 yrs) to 1½m winner Leadership (by Selkirk) and 2 winners abroad: dam, French maiden, sister to useful 1¼m performer Himself: never dangerous in maidens, showing modest form: likely to do better in handicaps at 1m+. *Sir Mark Prescott*

TUSCAN KING 2 ch.g. (Mar 23) Medicean 128 – Castaway Queen (IRE) 76 (Selkirk **67**
(USA) 129) [2009 7d^{5} p7g^{6} p8g^{3} p8.6g* p9.5g^{3} p8.6g^{3} Dec 17] chunky gelding: fair performer: won claimer at Wolverhampton (left W. Muir £10,000) in November: stays 8.6f: blinkered last 4 starts: joined P. D. Evans. *P. Howling*

TUSCULUM (IRE) 6 b.g. Sadler's Wells (USA) 132 – Turbaine (USA) (Trempolino **64**
(USA) 135) [2009 –: p12g* 15.8g May 5] leggy, close-coupled gelding: one-time smart performer: modest form when landing gamble in minor event at Kempton in February: should stay 2m: acts on polytrack, soft and good to firm going: tried in visor/cheekpieces: signs of temperament. *B. J. Curley*

TUT (IRE) 2 b.f. (Mar 14) Intikhab (USA) 135 – Radiant Energy (IRE) 78 (Spectrum **71**
(IRE) 126) [2009 5m^{3} 7.2s* 8m Sep 19] €17,000F, 11,000Y: third foal: dam 1m winner: much better effort in maidens (trained by K. R. Burke on debut) when winning at Ayr in August by 1½ lengths from Golden Shaheen: well held in nursery: stays 7f. *A. P. Jarvis*

TUTOR (IRE) 5 ch.g. Dr Fong (USA) 128 – Glandore (IRE) 95 (Persian Bold 123) **71**
[2009 p16g^{3} p13g Feb 21] fair handicapper: likely to prove best short of 13f: acts on polytrack: tried in blinkers/cheekpieces/tongue strap: signs of temperament. *Mrs A. M. Thorpe*

TUXEDO 4 ch.g. Cadeaux Genereux 131 – Serengeti Bride (USA) 91 (Lion Cavern **80**
(USA) 117) [2009 72: p8g p7g* p7.1g^{3} p7g^{5} 7m 7f^{6} 7.1g^{2} 8.1m^{4} 7s* 7d^{3} 7m p7m^{4} p7g^{4} p7g^{2} Nov 11] rangy gelding: fairly useful handicapper: won at Kempton in February and Yarmouth in July: stays 7f: acts on polytrack and soft going: usually held up: bled fifth outing. *P. W. Hiatt*

TUXSUMDOIN 5 ch.m. Zaha (CAN) 106 – Roisin Clover 73 (Faustus (USA) 118) **–**
[2009 f11s^{6} Jan 1] 2,000Y: third foal: dam 1½m winner: modest form in bumpers: always outpaced in maiden on Flat debut. *J. R. Weymes*

TWENTY SCORE 3 ch.f. Lear Spear (USA) 124 – Milladella (FR) (Nureyev (USA) **49**
131) [2009 67: p7.1g p6g^{5} 5.7f 7g p9.5g^{6} Jun 5] regressive maiden: best effort at 6f on polytrack: tried in cheekpieces. *Miss J. R. Tooth*

TWICE OVER 4 b.c. Observatory (USA) 131 – Double Crossed 102 (Caerleon **127**
(USA) 132) [2009 119: 9m^{3} 8d^{3} 10m^{4} 10m 10.3g* 9.9m* 10m* a10f^{3} Nov 7]

One of the ideas that is gathering momentum as a way to reinvigorate Flat racing in Britain is the staging of a single major championship meeting in September that would circulate annually around some of the country's top tracks. Combining the best of Champions Day and Ascot's Queen Elizabeth II Stakes fixture, for example, would give the British Flat a fitting finale to the season's 'narrative', to use modern marketing terminology. This latest idea follows hard on the heels of the apparently lapsed proposal for the £10m Sovereign Series, which was supposed to link ten existing Group 1 events through the season, boosting their prize money and staging them all on Saturdays, as a way of increasing general public interest in racing. A similar initiative in the States in 2002, the Thoroughbred Championship Tour, linking Grade 1 races leading up to the Breeders' Cup and involving bonuses totalling 25,000,000 dollars was heralded with similar fanfare but never launched.

For all its traditions and somewhat old-fashioned public image, racing actually never stands still for long, and the sport has undergone some revolutionary changes, none more significant than its globalisation, with prestigious international races and meetings throughout the year. The international programme has, amongst other things, largely provided the impetus for keeping more top horses in training as four-year-olds, which is a change to the racing landscape that has yielded considerable benefits, domestically as well as internationally. Taking up foreign challenges is now almost part and parcel of a top European middle-distance horse's campaign, with the Breeders' Cup dominating European ambition in North America, an important market in the increasingly-globalised thoroughbred breeding business.

However, the growth in the number of big and very lucrative international races has undoubtedly diminished the status of the British domestic programme, particularly in the second half of the year. Champions Day, inaugurated in 1997 when Newmarket concentrated the big races at its Houghton meeting into a single day, has provided its share of mouth-watering international clashes, but its proximity to Longchamp's similarly revamped and much more valuable Prix de l'Arc de Triomphe meeting means it has lost some of its lustre. Ascot's Festival of British Racing, built around the Queen Elizabeth II Stakes, predated Champions Day by a decade but it too could not live up to the admirable aim of providing an international showcase for British racing. The idea of combining the best of these two fine meetings into a September extravaganza—with significantly increased prize money—certainly has the merit of avoiding a head-on clash with some of the more spectacular, firmly established events in the international programme. It is probably also time to consider the future of the St Leger, a race that has the potential to enhance a new Flat finale, especially if it is opened up to four-year-olds and upwards to provide a European championship for the true mile and three quarter horses, many of whom are campaigned at distances short of their best as four-year-olds because of the absence of a richly endowed event for horses of their type. No horse has ever won both the St Leger and the Prix de l'Arc de Triomphe—and there have been some spectacular failures among those who have attempted the double—but a new-look Leger carrying substantial stakes could potentially prove an attractive alternative to the Arc for the best middle-distance stayers.

Sixty years ago, the St Leger was the most valuable race in the British calendar, the year 1949 coincidentally, like 2009, featuring a colt (Nimbus) who completed the Two Thousand Guineas/Derby double but missed the Leger. Nimbus had not been 'nominated' for the St Leger and was due to contest the Arc before jarring himself at exercise. The St Leger, it might be argued, has largely outlived its usefulness as a classic and would be much more informative and interesting if it provided a clash of the generations (*Timeform* is opposed to the shortening of its distance on the grounds that top performers over all distances should have really big stakes to compete for). A day in September featuring the St Leger, the Queen Elizabeth II Stakes, the Champion Stakes and the (Haydock) Sprint Cup might be a pipe dream but it would provide a varied top-class programme that would be a splendid advertisement for British racing.

The latest Emirates Airline Champion Stakes at Newmarket in mid-October had a distinct end-of-season feel to it, highlighted by the poor run of hot favourite Fame And Glory who was the clear form choice. It was 14/1-shot Twice Over—sixth choice in the betting—who took advantage of the below-par performances of Fame And Glory and others, including French-trained second favourite Never On Sunday. Twice Over's victory did produce a rousing reception in the winner's enclosure for his ever-popular trainer Henry Cecil, whose career has undergone something of a resurgence after a period in which his fortunes had declined markedly. His perseverance paid off with one-time Derby favourite Twice Over, whose Champion Stakes success finally gave the horse a Group 1 win at the sixth attempt, following placed efforts in the St James's Palace Stakes and the Champion Stakes at three, and two good performances in the first part of the latest season when in the frame in the Lockinge Stakes and the Prince of Wales's Stakes. Twice Over had a rare off-day when only seventh in the Eclipse at Sandown in July and he was given a two-month break. Dropped in class on his return, Twice Over won a five-runner minor event at Doncaster (easily from Serva Jugum) and a four-runner listed race at Goodwood (comfortably from Perfect Stride), both in September. The successes put him in good heart for the rest of his autumn campaign, in which he recorded the two best performances of his career, his Champion Stakes victory followed by an even better performance when third in the Breeders' Cup Classic at Santa Anita in November on his first outing on an artificial surface. Twice Over's appearance in the Champion Stakes as a three-year-old coincided with the start of his partnership with jockey Tom Queally, who has ridden him in all his races since. The pair had nothing of New Approach's calibre to contend with in the latest Champion, at least with Irish Derby winner Fame And Glory running way below his best, but Twice Over still showed high-class form, travelling strongly in touch before being sent for home in earnest two furlongs out. He was always holding the runner-up Mawatheeq, who was half a length behind at the line, with the Oaks winner Sariska a further length away third. Twice Over sometimes hangs right under pressure and he did so at Newmarket, prompting an objection—something of a rarity nowadays—from the rider of the runner-up Richard Hills. There seemed little chance of the Newmarket stewards deciding to reverse the placings, and Cecil

Emirates Airline Champion Stakes, Newmarket—
Twice Over gives jockey Tom Queally his fourth Group 1 win of the year;
Mawatheeq (striped cap) and Sariska (left) do their best work late on as Pipedreamer (blaze) fades

himself seemed to take a dim view of Hills's actions. 'You wouldn't object to that, would you? I wouldn't, I'm a sportsman,' he told a Channel 4 interviewer after watching a replay.

Becoming champion apprentice is no guarantee of future success. The 2003 title winner Ryan Moore has gone on to win the jockeys' championship, but there are plenty of star apprentices who have failed to make the grade once they have ridden out their claim. Two champion apprentices from the 'nineties Stephen Davies and Carl Lowther are no longer riding in Britain, while the 2000 winner Lee Newman—whose eighty-seven wins remains a post-Second World War record—was forced to retire less than two years later with weight problems. Saleem Golam has found life tough since sharing the apprentice title with Hayley Turner in 2005, registering just nineteen wins in the latest campaign. Tom Queally, Moore's successor as champion apprentice, also failed initially to make quite the expected impact as a fully-fledged professional, but he has made up for lost time, topping the century in each of the last two seasons and making his breakthrough on the big-race stage in 2009. Although his Group 1 wins on sprinters Art Connoisseur and Fleeting Spirit were supplied by Michael Bell and Jeremy Noseda respectively, it was Queally's burgeoning association with trainer Henry Cecil that provided him with forty-one of his wins in the latest season. The benefits of the link-up are clearly felt to be reciprocal as connections gave Queally a vote of confidence by allowing him to keep the ride on stable stars Midday—on whom Queally won the Group 1 Nassau Stakes—and Twice Over (both owned by Khalid Abdulla) when they contested the Breeders' Cup.

Queally gave Midday a textbook ride to win the Filly & Mare Turf after getting first run on the two placed horses, but it could be argued that he rather blotted his copybook with his display on Twice Over, who finished third in the Classic, two and a quarter lengths behind the impressive winner Zenyatta. The twenty or so backhanders that Queally administered in the straight in that race would undoubtedly have earned him a hefty ban in Britain, particularly as several came in 'rat-a-tat-tat' fashion without Twice Over being given time to respond. In mitigation, Queally certainly isn't the first European jockey—and he won't be the last—to take advantage of the permissive whip rules in the States, Piggott and Dettori among the big names who have also been involved in similar incidents down the years, like Queally escaping censure from the local stewards. 'When in Rome, do as the Romans do' has long appeared to be the policy favoured by the connections of most European raiders when tackling the Breeders' Cup, both in terms of whip use and drug use (Midday and Twice Over both ran on bute and lasix at Santa Anita). The use of a new low-impact whip has recently been made mandatory by some state jurisdictions in North America in the interests of horse welfare and public opinion may continue to play a role in the whip issue, judging by the comments after the Woodward Stakes at Saratoga in September, which was won in hard-fought fashion by the outstanding three-year-old filly Rachel Alexandra. Her jockey Calvin Borel was using one of the new whips, but that didn't prevent an outcry in letters' pages and on internet sites afterwards with complaints that Borel (who struck his mount around twenty times) had abused Rachel Alexandra, who wasn't seen out again in 2009.

Ironically, the one time Queally fell foul of the stewards on Twice Over in 2009 came in a race which highlighted the advantages of a whip in a tight finish. Twice Over's close third to Virtual in the Lockinge Stakes at Newbury on his second start earned the jockey a three-day ban for excessive whip use, though the fact that Queally accidentally knocked Frankie Dettori's whip out of his hand a furlong from home arguably cost Dettori's mount Alexandros victory (he was beaten just a nose). A close fourth to Vision d'Etat in the Prince of Wales's Stakes at Royal Ascot came next, which was the tenth time in eleven career starts that Twice Over had finished in the frame. As that record would suggest, Twice Over can boast largely consistent form. The Eclipse and a below-form third when odds-on, but in need of the run, in the Earl of Sefton Stakes at Newmarket on his reappearance were his only below-par performances in the latest season.

Twice Over's dam Double Crossed was also the subject of a stewards' inquiry when claiming the biggest win of her racing career, when she was trained by Twice Over's trainer, in the 2001 Lingfield Oaks Trial. She was initially demoted to second behind Silver Grey Lady, after hanging left into that rival, but was reinstated after an appeal. Third foal Twice Over is her only runner to date, with Double Crossed's latest foal being a brother to Twice Over. This pedigree was covered in detail by *Racehorses of 2007*, but it bears repeating that Twice Over comes from a family which has served both Khalid Abdulla and trainer Cecil very well down the years. In addition to Double Crossed, Twice Over's grandam Quandary was a useful listed mile and a quarter winner for the same connections and has been a successful broodmare, her most recent winner being the twice-raced 2009 two-year-old Quiet (by Twice Over's sire Observatory). Quandary is also the grandam of another two-year-old, the promising Timepiece, as well as a couple of smart middle-distance performers in Passage of Time (won 2006 Criterium de Saint-Cloud and following year's Musidora Stakes) and Father Time (won 2009 King Edward VII Stakes), the latter a temperamental sort who was another member of Cecil's raiding party at the latest Breeders' Cup. Third dam Lost Virtue also became a prolific source of winners at stud, her most notable performer being the high-class filly All At Sea, who won the Musidora Stakes and Prix du Moulin for the Abdulla-Cecil combination in 1992, when she also finished an excellent second in both the Oaks and International Stakes.

Twice Over (b.c. 2005)	Observatory (USA) (ch 1997)	Distant View (ch 1991)	Mr Prospector
			Seven Springs
		Stellaria (ch 1986)	Roberto
			Victoria Star
	Double Crossed (b 1998)	Caerleon (b 1980)	Nijinsky
			Foreseer
		Quandary (b 1991)	Blushing Groom
			Lost Virtue

Mr K. Abdulla's "Twice Over"

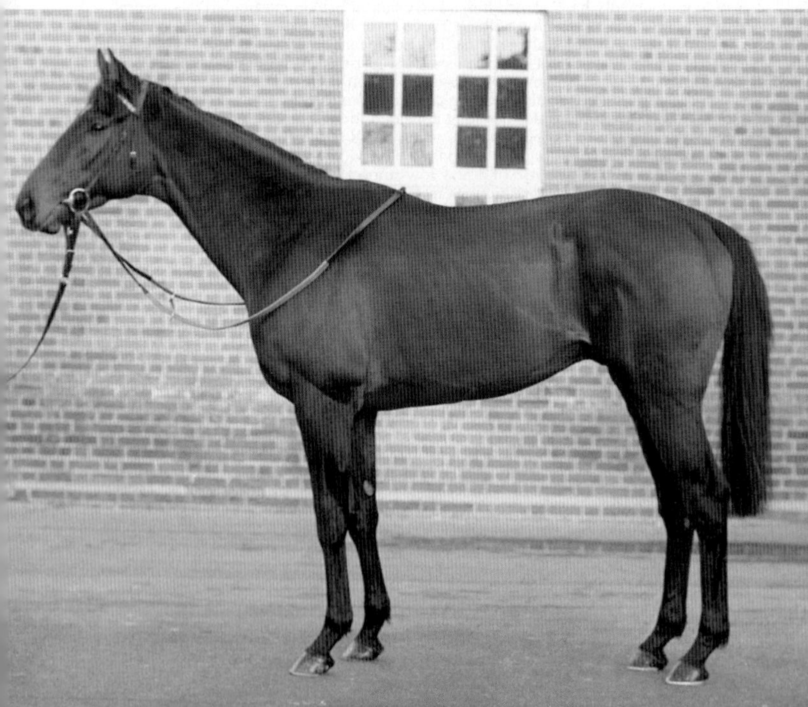

Twice Over, like All At Sea, seems best at around a mile and a mile and a quarter—he has never been tried over a mile and a half, failing to make the Derby line-up after losing his unbeaten record when third in the Dante. Twice Over has raced mainly on good ground or firmer, though he coped well with good to soft in the Lockinge. In addition, his good effort on the synthetic pro-ride surface at Santa Anita bodes well for a tilt at the Dubai World Cup, his reported early-season target in 2010. *H. R. A. Cecil*

TWILIGHT DAWN 5 ch.m. Muhtarram (USA) 125 – Indigo Dawn 78 (Rainbow Quest (USA) 134) [2009 75: 9.9m^4 14g^3 May 29] strong, useful-looking mare: fair handicapper, lightly raced: stays 1¾m: acts on soft and good to firm ground: very slowly away final start. *L. Lungo* **71**

TWILIGHT MEMORY (USA) 2 ch.f. (Feb 2) Smart Strike (CAN) 121 – Southern Swing (USA) (Dixieland Band (USA)) [2009 7s 8.3m^5 Sep 30] $300,000F, $300,000Y: attractive filly: has scope: sixth foal: half-sister to several winners in USA: dam, US 5f winner, closely related to US Grade 3 1½m winner Jaded Dancer: better effort in maidens when fifth to Bint Almatar at Nottingham. *B. J. Meehan* **49**

TWILIGHT STAR (IRE) 5 b.g. Green Desert (USA) 127 – Heavenly Whisper (IRE) 105 (Halling (USA) 133) [2009 86: 8.1g* 8m^6 p7g 8.5d^2 7m^3 8m^6 8.5m 7m^3 Sep 28] lengthy gelding: fairly useful handicapper: won Flat v Jump jockeys event at Sandown in April: creditable effort after only when third at Epsom fifth start: said to have had breathing problem final outing: stays 1m: acts on polytrack and good to soft going: tried blinkered: formerly tongue tied: none too consistent. *R. A. Teal* **82**

TWILIGHT TEAR 2 ch.f. (Jan 26) Rock of Gibraltar (IRE) 133 – Clara Bow (IRE) 84 (Sadler's Wells (USA) 132) [2009 8g Oct 20] first foal: dam, 7f winner, sister to Fillies' Mile winner Listen and Moyglare Stud Stakes winner Sequoyah (dam of Henrythenavigator): 16/1, well held in maiden at Yarmouth. *M. L. W. Bell* **–**

TWILL (IRE) 6 ch.g. Barathea (IRE) 127 – Khafaya 68 (Unfuwain (USA) 131) [2009 –: p12.2g^4 p12.2g Jul 7] big, good-bodied gelding: fair handicapper, lightly raced since 2006: stays 2m: acts on fibresand, good to firm and good to soft ground: tried blinkered/visored: none too resolute. *D. Burchell* **70**

TWINNED (IRE) 6 ch.g. Soviet Star (USA) 128 – Identical (IRE) (Machiavellian (USA) 123) [2009 60: f5g Jan 15] leggy, well-grown gelding: modest handicapper at 5 yrs: well held only outing in 2009: best at 5f: acts on all-weather, firm and good to soft going: tried blinkered/in cheekpieces: races prominently. *Mike Murphy* **–**

TWIST AGAIN (IRE) 3 b.f. Sakhee (USA) 136 – Dance Clear (IRE) 99 (Marju (IRE) 127) [2009 p8g 10m^5 10f p12g 11.5d^3 11.5m^3 14.1g* 14.1m* 14.1m^6 16.1g* Sep 30] 50,000Y: small filly: fifth foal: half-sister to fairly useful 1½m winner Rosecliff (by Montjeu) and 8.6f winner Dyanita (by Singspiel): dam 6f (in Ireland at 2 yrs) to 9f (in USA) winner: fairly useful handicapper: improved to win at Nottingham and Redcar in August and Newcastle in September: stays 2m: acts on good to firm and good to soft ground: usually slowly away in first half of season. *P. Howling* **80**

TWIST BOOKIE (IRE) 9 b. or br.g. Perugino (USA) 84 – Twist Scarlett (GER) (Lagunas) [2009 67: p8.6g Apr 6] tall gelding: fair handicapper at best, lightly raced on Flat in recent years: below form sole start at 9 yrs: stays 1¾m: acts on polytrack, soft and good to firm going: tried blinkered: fair hurdler/chaser. *S. Lycett* **53**

TWISTED 3 ch.c. Selkirk (USA) 129 – Winding (USA) (Irish River (FR) 131) [2009 68p: 10d^3 10f^4 12m Jun 14] rangy colt: has scope: fair maiden: easily best effort when third at Newbury: stays 1¼m: sold 8,500 gns in October. *J. H. M. Gosden* **77**

TWOELLIES 2 ch.f. (Apr 5) Trade Fair 124 – Fancier Bit (Lion Cavern (USA) 117) [2009 5m 6m p8.6g Dec 17] close-coupled filly: sixth foal: half-sister to several winners, including 3-y-o Fantasy Gladiator and 6-y-o Suits Me: dam unraced: well held in maidens/claimer. *Ollie Pears* **–**

TWO KISSES (IRE) 2 b.f. (Feb 12) Spartacus (IRE) 107 – Flight Sequence 88 (Polar Falcon (USA) 126) [2009 5g^5 6m^6 6f^5 5.7f^3 7d 5.7g^5 p8m p7m^6 p6g* Dec 18] 1,200Y: medium-sized filly: fourth foal: half-sister to 3 winners, including 5-y-o Plane Painter: dam 1¼m winner: fair performer: won maiden at Wolverhampton: best efforts around 6f: acts on polytrack and firm ground. *B. G. Powell* **65**

TWOS AND EIGHTS (IRE) 3 gr.g. Kyllachy 129 – Docklands Grace (USA) 62 (Honour And Glory (USA) 122) [2009 59: p6g Mar 13] sturdy gelding: modest maiden at best at 2 yrs, well held only outing in 2009: best effort at 5f: tried blinkered. *Paul Mason* **–**

TWOSHEETSTOTHEWIND 5 ch.m. Bahamian Bounty 116 – Flag (Selkirk (USA) 129) [2009 73d: 5m^4 5d^2 5m 5m* 5m^6 5g^4 5m* 5g^2 Jul 20] lengthy mare: fair handicapper: won at Thirsk in June and Ayr in July: raced at 5f/6f: acts on polytrack, good to soft and good to firm going: has worn cheekpieces, including last 2 outings: ungenuine. *M. Dods* **77 §**

TWO TOGETHER (USA) 3 b.c. Theatrical 128 – Miasma (USA) 92 (Lear Fan (USA) 130) [2009 10.2d p11g Oct 22] lengthy, good-topped colt: modest form in maidens: bred to stay 1¼m: tried tongue tied: sold £2,500. *D. R. Lanigan* **–**

TWO TONE 3 b. or br.g. Diktat 126 – Fireburst (Spectrum (IRE) 126) [2009 8m 8.1f^6 8g Jul 26] tall gelding: no form in maidens. *G. Woodward* **–**

TWO TURTLE DOVES (IRE) 3 b.f. Night Shift (USA) – Purple Rain (IRE) 46 (Celtic Swing 138) [2009 7m 6d 8g^6 p6g^6 7.5m^6 5.9g^2 6.1g 6s^2 6g^4 7g^5 6s^5 Oct 27] 18,000Y: leggy filly: first foal: dam, maiden (raced only at 1m), out of sister to smart 1¼m performer Leporello: modest maiden: largely held form in handicaps: stays 1m: acts on soft going. *M. Mullineaux* **64**

TYCOON'S BUDDY 4 ch.g. Reel Buddy (USA) 118 – Tycoon's Last 64 (Nalchik (USA)) [2009 –: f7g p8.6g Jan 22] no form. *S. Wynne* **–**

TYFOS 4 b.g. Bertolini (USA) 125 – Warminghamsharpish (Nalchik (USA)) [2009 78: 6g^4 6s* 6m^6 6d* 6g^3 6d^4 5.1m^3 Aug 22] lengthy gelding: fairly useful handicapper: won at Yarmouth in June and Epsom in July: best at 5f/6f: acts on polytrack, firm and soft going: reliable. *W. M. Brisbourne* **84**

TYPICAL FEMALE 2 b.f. (Apr 4) Pursuit of Love 124 – Angel Maid (Forzando 122) [2009 p7g 7.1m p9.5g p8.6g Dec 7] second foal: dam well beaten: no form in maidens/ claimers. *A. B. Haynes* **–**

TYRANA (GER) 6 ch.m. Acatenango (GER) 127 – Tascalina (GER) 105 (Big Shuffle (USA) 122) [2009 60: f12g^4 10.2m 10.9g^5 p8g p11f* Dec 16] fair handicapper: left J. Spearing after reappearance, G. Bridgwater after third start: landed gamble at Kempton in December: stays 1½m: raced mainly on all-weather and good ground or firmer. *Ian Williams* **66**

TYRANNOSAURUS REX (IRE) 5 b.g. Bold Fact (USA) 116 – Dungeon Princess (IRE) 62 (Danehill (USA) 126) [2009 70: p6g p5.1g* p5.1g^6 p5.1g^6 p5.1g* p5.1g^2 5.1m* 5.1g* 5g^2 5g 5g 5.1m Aug 22] good-topped gelding: fairly useful handicapper: won at Wolverhampton in February and March, Nottingham in May and Chester in June: seems best at 5f nowadays: acts on polytrack and good to firm ground: sometimes visored. *D. Shaw* **86**

TYRRELLS WOOD (IRE) 4 b.g. Sinndar (IRE) 134 – Diner de Lune (IRE) (Be My Guest (USA) 126) [2009 79: p13g^2 17.1g* 21.7m^2 21g^2 Jul 29] sturdy gelding: useful performer: won handicap at Pontefract in June: better form when runner-up after in Queen Alexandra Stakes at Royal Ascot (beaten 2½ lengths by Caracciola) and handicap at Goodwood (went down by 3¾ lengths to Sweetheart): best at 2m+ (stays 21.7f): acts on polytrack, good to firm and good to soft going. *T. G. Mills* **103**

TYZACK (IRE) 8 b.g. Fasliyev (USA) 120 – Rabea (USA) 61 (Devil's Bag (USA)) [2009 60: f7g^2 f8g^6 Feb 20] good-topped gelding: fair handicapper: stays 1m: acts on fibresand and firm going: usually held up. *Stef Liddiard* **74**

U

UACE MAC 5 b.m. Compton Place 125 – Umbrian Gold (IRE) 83 (Perugino (USA) 84) [2009 76: 6d 7m 6d 6d^3 6m 5.9d Aug 19] tall, rather leggy mare: modest handicapper nowadays: stays 7f: acts on heavy and good to firm ground. *N. Bycroft* **60**

UBENKOR (IRE) 4 b.g. Diktat 126 – Lucky Dancer (FR) (Groom Dancer (USA) 128) [2009 78: 7s 7.5g^4 May 23] good-topped gelding: fair handicapper: stays 7.5f: acts on soft and good to firm going: sold £3,000, then gelded. *B. Smart* **73**

UBIQUITOUS 4 b.f. Erhaab (USA) 127 – Lady Isabell 62 (Rambo Dancer (CAN) 107) [2009 48: 10f 10g^5 11.5m^2 11.6g^2 12m^2 Aug 19] rather leggy filly: modest maiden handicapper: stays 1½m: acts on good to firm going: often held up. *S. Dow* **59**

UDABAA (IRE) 2 b. or br.c. (Feb 21) Alhaarth (IRE) 126 – Addaya (IRE) (Persian Bold 123) [2009 p8g^3 Aug 24] €160,000F, 190,000Y: attractive colt: half-brother to several winners, including smart 7f (including at 2 yrs)/1m winner Priors Lodge (by Grand Lodge) and fairly useful 1½m/2m winner Night Cruise (by Docksider): dam ran once: 12/1, promising 4¼ lengths third to Togiak in maiden at Kempton: sure to improve. *M. P. Tregoning* **77 p**

UDDY MAC 2 ch.f. (Apr 1) Reel Buddy (USA) 118 – Befriend (USA) 76 (Allied Forces (USA) 123) [2009 5d^5 6m 7g 6m^4 6m 7d^5 7.5m^4 Sep 16] £1,800Y: small filly: first foal: dam 2-y-o 6f winner: modest maiden: stays 7.5f: acts on good to firm ground: blinkered (best effort) final start. *N. Bycroft* **64**

UGENIUS 5 b.g. Killer Instinct 111 – I'm Sophie (IRE) 64 (Shalford (IRE) 124§) [2009 69: f7g p8g^4 p7g f8g 7d^4 p8g 8g 7g p8g^3 p8g^3 p8g^2 f7g* p7.1g^6 f8g^4 p7f^2 p7.1g* f7g p8g* Oct 26] fair handicapper on all-weather, modest on turf: better than ever in 2009, winning at Southwell in July, Wolverhampton in September and Lingfield in October: effective at 7f/1m: acts on all-weather, raced on good/good to soft ground on turf: consistent. *Mrs C. A. Dunnett* **60 a78**

UGLY BETTY 4 b.f. Where Or When (IRE) 124 – Dancing Steps (Zafonic (USA) 130) [2009 –: p9.5g 10.3m 12.4d Oct 13] strong, long-backed filly: of no account. *Bruce Hellier* **–**

UHURU PEAK 8 ch.g. Bal Harbour 113 – Catherines Well 99 (Junius (USA) 124) [2009 62: 8m 8.3m 7.9g 8.5m Aug 13] lengthy gelding: handicapper: well held in 2009: was usually blinkered/tongue tied: dead. *M. W. Easterby* **–**

UIG 8 ch.m. Bien Bien (USA) 125 – Madam Zando 51 (Forzando 122) [2009 77, a71: 10.2f^4 9g^5 10.2g^5 9.9m 10.2m^5 10.2g^5 11.6m^3 12g 11.5s 10.2m^3 p12f Oct 14] compact mare: just modest handicapper in 2009: stays 11.7f: acts on polytrack, soft and good to firm going. *H. S. Howe* **62**

ULLALUJAH 7 b.m. Josr Algarhoud (IRE) 118 – Ulla Laing 107 (Mummy's Pet 125) [2009 12g^6 Apr 21] well held in mares bumper/over hurdles, and in maiden at Folkestone on Flat debut. *L. Wells* **–**

ULTIMATE 3 b.c. Anabaa (USA) 130 – Nirvana 82 (Marju (IRE) 127) [2009 79p: f8g* 9.9m^5 11d^4 10.4g f8f* Oct 21] useful-looking colt: fairly useful performer: won maiden at Southwell in January and handicap there in October: effective at 1m, barely at 11f: acts on fibresand, good to firm and good to soft ground: free-going sort: sold 52,000 gns, joined B. Ellison, and won over hurdles in November. *H. Morrison* **92**

ULTIMATE RESPECT (USA) 3 b.c. Elusive Quality (USA) – Zelanda (IRE) 108 (Night Shift (USA)) [2009 8.1m p8g^6 6s^4 6m^6 p8.6g^3 7.5g p8.6g Oct 2] sturdy colt: sixth foal: brother to 2007 2-y-o 6f winner Chatham Islands, closely related to 2 winners by Gone West, including useful 2003 2-y-o 5f/6f winner Pearl Grey and half-brother to fairly useful 6f (at 2 yrs) to 2m winner Silver Seeker (by Seeking The Gold): dam, 5f/6f (including at 2 yrs) winner, out of smart Irish St Leger third Zafadola: fair maiden on all-weather, modest on turf: stays 8.6f: acts on polytrack: tried blinkered: sold £7,000. *M. Johnston* **61 a75**

ULTRAVOX (USA) 2 b.c. (Mar 3) Lemon Drop Kid (USA) 131 – Lynnwood Chase (USA) (Horse Chestnut (SAF) 119) [2009 7s^5 7.1g^3 Aug 12] 65,000Y: good-topped colt: first foal: dam, ran twice in France, half-sister to 8-y-o Lord Admiral: better effort in maidens when 1½ lengths third to Al Ghazal at Sandown: should be suited by 1m+. *B. J. Meehan* **83**

ULYSEES (IRE) 10 b.g. Turtle Island (IRE) 123 – Tamasriya (IRE) (Doyoun 124) [2009 58: 11.1s^5 8s^2 8d 11.1g^2 9d 9.1v Oct 31] quite good-topped gelding: modest handicapper: stays 11f: acts on heavy and good to firm going: tried in visor/cheekpieces. *I. Semple* **58**

ULZANA (IRE) 3 b.g. High Chaparral (IRE) 132 – Maritsa (IRE) 59 (Danehill (USA) 126) [2009 p8.6g^3 Sep 11] 65,000Y: third foal: half-brother to 4-y-o Eton Rifles and Irish 9f winner Camolin (by Fantastic Light): dam, third at 6f on only start, half-sister to high-class miler Marling and very smart 6f to 1m performer Caerwent out of top-class sprinter Marwell: 10/1 and green, encouraging 3½ lengths third to Awesome Surprise in maiden at Wolverhampton, quickening into contention before effort petered out: capable of better. *Sir Mark Prescott* **73 p**

UMPA LOOMPA (IRE) 5 ch.g. Indian Lodge (IRE) 127 – Bold Fashion (FR) (Nashwan (USA) 135) [2009 56d: p6g^6 Aug 14] close-coupled gelding: regressive performer: will prove best at 5f/6f: acts on good to soft going: tried blinkered, usually visored. *B. J. McMath* **–**

UMVERTI 4 b.f. Averti (IRE) 117 – Umbrian Gold (IRE) 83 (Perugino (USA) 84) [2009 62: 9.9m^5 8.5m^3 10d* 9.9m^6 9.9m^2 9.9m* 12v* 10g 12s Sep 5] leggy filly: fair handicapper: improved in 2009, winning at Pontefract in May and Beverley and Pontefract in July: stays 1½m: acts on heavy and good to firm going: tried in cheekpieces. *N. Bycroft* **78**

UNA PELOTA (IRE) 3 b.c. Refuse To Bend (IRE) 128 – Sombreffe 71 (Polish Precedent (USA) 131) [2009 8.1m^5 10.3m^3 8.1v^4 May 22] good-bodied colt: half-brother to several winners, including smart 1m (at 2 yrs)/1¼m (in Germany) winner Ransom O'War (by Red Ransom) and useful Irish 1m winner Madame Cerito (by Diesis): dam, 7f winner, closely related to smart performers up to 7f Russian Bond and Snaadee: fair form in maidens: may prove best at 1¼m. *N. J. Vaughan* **76**

UNAWATUNA 4 b.f. Golden Snake (USA) 127 – Laylee (Deploy 131) [2009 65: 16m^2 17.2g^4 16s 17.1m 16d* 16.1d* Oct 13] angular filly: fair handicapper: won at Ripon in September and Newcastle in October: stays 2¼m well: acts on heavy and good to firm ground. *Mrs K. Walton* **68**

UNBELIEVABLE JEFF 3 b.g. Oasis Dream 129 – Sunshine N'Showers 72 (Spectrum (IRE) 126) [2009 f6g f8g p6g 5g^2 5m^2 6m^4 6g^5 Sep 20] modest maiden handicapper: left S. Parr before final outing: may prove ideally suited by 6f: acts on good to firm going. *J. Balding* **52**

UNBREAK MY HEART (IRE) 4 ch.g. Bahamian Bounty 116 – Golden Heart 77 (Salse (USA) 128) [2009 100: 8m* 10.1g^5 10m^6 10.4m 9.9g 10g 10m Sep 19] useful-looking gelding: useful performer: won handicap at Pontefract in April by head from Bencoolen: creditable effort after only when sixth to Kingdom of Fife in quite valuable similar event at Redcar: stays 1¼m: acts on soft and good to firm going: usually held up. *R. A. Fahey* **100**

UNCLE BERTIE 4 b.g. Bertolini (USA) 125 – Resourceful (IRE) (Entrepreneur 123) [2009 p9.5g p9.5g* 10g 10.4v 9m^4 p9.5g Oct 2] 16,000Y: first foal: dam once-raced half-sister to smart 6f/7f performer Hot Tin Roof: fair performer: won maiden at Wolverhampton in March: left N. Vaughan prior to final outing: stays 1¼m: acts on polytrack and good to firm ground: joined Tim Vaughan. *Tom Dascombe* **75**

UNCLE BRIT 3 b.c. Efisio 120 – Tarneem (USA) 87 (Zilzal (USA) 137) [2009 p6g p6g f6g p7.1g f7g^4 f8g* f8m^4 10.3g p8g^4 p8f Sep 10] fair handicapper: won at Southwell in July: should be suited by 1¼m: best efforts on fibresand: signs of temperament: sold 11,000 gns. *Sir Mark Prescott* **68**

UNCLE FRED 4 b.g. Royal Applause 124 – Karla June (Unfuwain (USA) 131) [2009 81: p8g^2 8m* p8g^2 8m p10m* p10m Nov 4] useful-looking gelding: fairly useful handicapper, lightly raced: won at Newbury in May and Kempton in October: stays 1¼m: acts on polytrack and good to firm ground: held up. *P. R. Chamings* **92**

UNCLE KEEF (IRE) 3 b.g. Sadler's Wells (USA) 132 – Love For Ever (IRE) (Darshaan 133) [2009 10.1m 10.2d p11g Oct 22] 100,000Y: big, strong gelding: brother to several winners, including smart 7f (at 2 yrs) and 10.3f winner Gypsy King and useful 1½m and (in France) 2m winner Albanov: dam, French 1m and 9.5f winner: signs of ability despite greenness in maidens (gelded after final start): type to do better in handicaps. *M. P. Tregoning* **56 p**

UNCONSOLED 3 b.f. Ishiguru (USA) 114 – Chantilly (FR) (Sanglamore (USA) 126) [2009 66: 7g^4 7m 7s^6 6m 5m^6 8.5m f7m^4 f7g Dec 8] lengthy filly: just modest maiden in 2009: tried blinkered/tongue tied. *J. Hetherton* **52**

UNDAUNTED AFFAIR (IRE) 3 ch.f. Spartacus (IRE) 107 – Party Bag (Cadeaux Genereux 131) [2009 89+: 7g^5 8m 6s 6m 7v p7g Nov 7] well-made filly: fairly useful performer: good 4 lengths fifth to Maoineach in Leopardstown 1000 Guineas Trial in March: respectable efforts at best in varied company after: stays 7f: probably acts on polytrack and any turf going: sold £33,000. *K. A. Ryan* **94**

UNDER FIRE (IRE) 6 b.g. Lear Spear (USA) 124 – Kahyasi Moll (IRE) 35 (Brief Truce (USA) 126) [2009 72: p8m p8m 8d p7m p11f^2 Dec 16] sturdy gelding: handicapper, just modest at 6 yrs: effective at 1m to 1½m: acts on all-weather and any turf going. *A. W. Carroll* **61**

UNDER REVIEW (IRE) 3 b.g. Danetime (IRE) 121 – Coloma (JPN) (Forty Niner (USA)) [2009 p5g^2 f5g* p6g^5 5m 5m^5 5m 5m^4 5g^4 f5m^6 Nov 12] €9,000F, €110,000Y, 60,000 2-y-o: good-bodied gelding: second foal: brother to 4-y-o Martingrange Boy: dam ran once in France: fair performer: won maiden at Southwell in February: left S. Callaghan after fourth start: should stay 6f: acts on all-weather and good to firm going: tried blinkered. *T. D. Barron* **73**

UNDER WARRANTY (ITY) 5 ch.g. Della Scala (IRE) 99 – Serengate (GER) **68**
(Highest Honor (FR) 124) [2009 p6g^2 p6g^4 p6g* Jan 30] fair handicapper: won 3 times in 2008 for S. Santella in Italy: best effort in Britain when winning at Wolverhampton in January: stays 6f: acts on all-weather and soft ground: tried in cheekpieces: tongue tied: sold 6,500 gns. *F. Sheridan*

UNDERWORLD DANDY 2 gr.g. (Apr 17) Fraam 114 – Eastern Lyric 93 (Petong **69**
126) [2009 5g^5 6.1g* 6.1m^6 7d 7g p7.1g^4 p8m* p8.6g^5 p8.6g^5 7d p9.5g^3 p8m^5 p10m^4 p8.6g^5 Dec 7] fair performer: won claimer at Chepstow (left Tom Dascombe £6,000) in May and nursery at Kempton in September: stays 1m: acts on polytrack: tried in cheekpieces/visor: has hung/looked lazy. *P. D. Evans*

UNION ISLAND (IRE) 3 b.g. Rock of Gibraltar (IRE) 133 – Daftiyna (IRE) 74 **91**
(Darshaan 133) [2009 84: 9m* 10.4m^2 10.1g 10.4g^2 10m 9.9m^5 10.3m p10m Sep 23] strong gelding: fairly useful performer: won maiden at Musselburgh in April: good second in handicaps at York after: stays 10.4f: acts on good to firm and good to soft going: tried visored: gelded after final start. *K. A. Ryan*

UNION JACK JACKSON (IRE) 7 b.g. Daggers Drawn (USA) 114 – Beechwood **59**
Quest (IRE) 65 (River Falls 113) [2009 47: 6d 5m 6m 8g^5 7.5g* 8m p7.1g Oct 10] good-topped gelding: modest performer: form in 2009 only when winning claimer at Beverley in August: stays 8.6f: acts on all-weather and good to soft ground: wears headgear. *John A. Harris*

UNIQUELY POISED (USA) 3 b. or br.g. More Than Ready (USA) 120 – No Other **95**
Like You (USA) (Cozzene (USA)) [2009 10m p8g* 8g 8m p8g Oct 9] $40,000Y: good-bodied gelding: first foal: dam US 9f winner: useful performer: won maiden at Kempton (by 5 lengths) in May: below form in handicaps after: stays 1m: acts on polytrack: tried in cheekpieces: gelded after final start: has joined D. Watson in UAE. *J. H. M. Gosden*

UNITED NATIONS 8 ch.g. Halling (USA) 133 – Congress (IRE) 86 (Dancing Brave **86**
(USA) 140) [2009 74: f8s* f8d* p8.6g^3 f8g^3 p12.2g^6 f8g^2 f8f^6 Dec 12] sturdy, lengthy gelding: fairly useful performer: won 2 handicaps at Southwell in January: not at best after: effective at 1m to 10.5f: acts on all-weather, good to firm and good to soft going: tried in visor/cheekpieces, usually blinkered nowadays. *N. Wilson*

UNIVERSAL CIRCUS 2 b.f. (Jan 19) Imperial Dancer 123 – Wansdyke Lass 59 (Josr **81**
Algarhoud (IRE) 118) [2009 7m 7g^4 7d^3 7g* 8.1v^6 7m^3 7m^4 p8.6g^6 Oct 15] smallish, angular filly: first foal: dam 1¼m winner: fairly useful performer: won maiden at Epsom in July: should be suited by 1m+: acts on polytrack and good to firm going. *M. R. Channon*

UNIVERSAL PRIDE 2 b.f. (Mar 24) Danbird (AUS) – Frisson (Slip Anchor 136) **–**
[2009 6m 7.1m Oct 5] plain filly: closely related to fairly useful 5f (including at 2 yrs)/6f winner Wanchai Lad (by Danzero) and half-sister to 1m/9f winner Princes Theatre (by Prince Sabo): dam unraced out of useful 7f to 9f winner Comic Talent: well held in maidens. *J. Gallagher*

UNLEASHED (IRE) 4 br.g. Storming Home 128 – Uriah (GER) 109 (Acatenango **108**
(GER) 127) [2009 106: 12s 13.3d 12m^4 12m^3 12g^5 13.4m 12m^3 12g Oct 10] tall, close-coupled gelding: useful performer: good efforts in 2009 when third in listed race at Pontefract (3¼ lengths behind Furmigadelagiusta) and handicap at Ascot (beaten 4¼ lengths by Record Breaker): stays 13f: acts on polytrack and firm going: blinkered last 2 starts: sold 55,000 gns, then gelded. *H. R. A. Cecil*

UNNEFER (FR) 4 b.c. Danehill Dancer (IRE) 117 – Mimalia (USA) (Silver Hawk **114**
(USA) 123) [2009 112: 8m^2 10m* 8m 10g 10d^2 Oct 30] good-topped colt: smart performer: won minor event at Lingfield in May by 1½ lengths from Halicarnassus: below form last 3 starts, in listed race at Goodwood (short of room), Prix Gontaut-Biron at Deauville (final start for H. Cecil) and minor event at Maisons-Laffitte (short-head second to Blue Rockies): stays 10.3f: acts on firm and soft ground: races in touch. *P. Bary, France*

UNSHAKABLE (IRE) 10 b.g. Eagle Eyed (USA) 111 – Pepper And Salt (IRE) **–**
(Double Schwartz 128) [2009 101: 8.1m 7.1m 10m 10.2s Oct 7] good-bodied gelding: handicapper: well below useful best in 2009: stays 1¼m: acts on polytrack, soft and good to firm ground. *Bob Jones*

UNSHAKABLE WILL (IRE) 2 b.g. (Apr 2) Refuse To Bend (IRE) 128 – Miss **87**
Devious (IRE) 51 (Dr Devious (IRE) 127) [2009 6m^5 7m^2 7.2m* 7g^2 7g Oct 24] €34,000F, £30,000Y: third foal: half-brother to 3-y-o Inheritor: dam, Irish 1½m to 2m winner, out of sister to smart 1¼m/1½m performer Monsajem: fairly useful performer: won maiden at Ayr (by ¾ length from Huntingfortreasure) in September: good second to Bahraj in nursery at Catterick next time: seemed amiss final start (gelded after): will stay 1m. *B. Smart*

Phil Bull Trophy Conditions Stakes, Pontefract—
Urban Poet, the most expensive horse ever to run at Pontefract, has little difficulty in justifying favouritism

UNTIL THE MAN (IRE) 2 b.c. (Mar 15) Tillerman 123 – Canoe Cove (IRE) 55 (Grand Lodge (USA) 125) [2009 6m 7m 7m 6.1s^5 8g^2 p8m^3 p7g^2 Dec 31] sturdy colt: fair maiden: good second in nursery at Lingfield final start: stays 1m: in cheekpieces last 4 starts. *R. Ingram* **68**

UNTIL WHEN (USA) 5 b.g. Grand Slam (USA) 120 – Chez Cherie 108 (Wolfhound (USA) 126) [2009 75: 5m^3 Apr 3] good-topped gelding: fair maiden handicapper: effective at 5f, should stay 1m: acts on firm going: visored nowadays. *B. Smart* **66**

UP AT LAST 2 b.f. (Mar 13) Cape Cross (IRE) 129 – Upend 120 (Main Reef 126) [2009 8g Oct 20] sister to smart 1m winner Musicanna and half-sister to several winners, including useful 1m (at 2 yrs) to 1½m winner Al Azhar (by Alzao) and dam of 4-y-o Overdose: dam, 1¼m/1½m (St Simon Stakes) winner, half-sister to dam of high-class stayer/Champion Hurdle winner Royal Gait: 25/1 and green, down the field in maiden at Yarmouth: should do better. *W. J. Haggas* **51 p**

UPHOLD 2 b.c. (May 8) Oasis Dream 129 – Allegro Viva (USA) (Distant View (USA) 126) [2009 7g Oct 30] second foal: dam unraced sister to Dewhurst Stakes winner Distant Music: 14/1 and backward, down the field in maiden at Newmarket (said to have been struck into): should do better. *B. W. Hills* **62 p**

UP IN ARMS (IRE) 5 b.g. Daggers Drawn (USA) 114 – Queenliness (Exit To Nowhere (USA) 122) [2009 69: p12m f16g^4 p16g^6 12d 15.4g^4 11.7f^6 May 13] strong gelding: modest handicapper nowadays: stays 16.5f: acts on polytrack, firm and good to soft going: tried blinkered. *P. Winkworth* **60**

UPPER KEY 3 b.g. Exceed And Excel (AUS) 126 – Ard Na Sighe (IRE) (Kenmare (FR) 125) [2009 8m 6s May 22] quite good-topped gelding: well held in maiden/claimer. *K. A. Ryan* **–**

UPSTAIRS 5 ch.g. Sugarfoot 118 – Laena 72 (Roman Warrior 132) [2009 70: p8g^5 p6g^4 p8g^6 7f 6m 9.9m Jun 28] rangy gelding: just modest handicapper in 2009: left D. Elsworth £4,200 after second start: probably best at 6f/7f: acts on polytrack. *Paul Henderson* **59**

UPTON SEAS 3 b.f. Josr Algarhoud (IRE) 118 – Crystal Seas 47 (Zamindar (USA) 116) [2009 55: 9.9m* 12d* 9.9g^5 9.8g* 12m^5 10.4g f11f^6 10.3d^4 Oct 24] workmanlike filly: fairly useful handicapper: much improved, winning at Beverley and Thirsk in July then Ripon in August: below form after: stays 1½m: acts on good to firm and good to soft going. *M. W. Easterby* **83**

UPTOWN LAD (IRE) 10 b.g. Definite Article 121 – Shoka (FR) 86 (Kaldoun (FR) 122) [2009 16.1d 16.1m 17.2g^3 16.1d 16.1d 18g^6 Oct 19] good-bodied gelding: modest maiden: stays 17.2f: acts on fibresand and any turf going: tried visored. *R. Johnson* **50**

URBAN BOUNTY 4 ch.f. Bahamian Bounty 116 – Bathe In Light (USA) 72 (Sunshine Forever (USA)) [2009 10m Jun 4] 5,500F, £600 3-y-o: half-sister to 9.5f (at 2 yrs) to 1½m winner Liberty Run (by Grand Lodge): dam 1½m/1¾m winner: 66/1, tailed off in maiden at Lingfield. *M. J. McGrath* **–**

URBAN CLUBBER 2 b.g. (Feb 22) Dubai Destination (USA) 127 – Surprise Visitor (IRE) (Be My Guest (USA) 126) [2009 6g^6 6d^5 5.9m^4 7d^6 Jul 22] close-coupled gelding: fair maiden: best effort at 6f on good to soft going. *J. Howard Johnson* **67**

URBAN POET (USA) 3 b. or br.c. Dynaformer (USA) – Preach (USA) (Mr Prospector (USA)) [2009 11.1g* 12g^3 14g^6 12.3m^6 18m* 16m Oct 17] $2,900,000Y: big colt: has scope: half-brother to several winners in USA, notably smart US Grade 2 8.5f/9f winner Pulpit (by A P Indy): dam US Grade 1 2-y-o 1m winner: useful performer: created very good impression first 2 starts, winning maiden at Hamilton (by 9 lengths) in July and 2 lengths third to Harbinger in Gordon Stakes at Goodwood: left M. Johnston, easily best subsequent effort when winning 4-runner minor event at Pontefract in October: stays 2¼m: raced only on good/good to firm ground: races prominently. *Saeed bin Suroor* **109**

URBAN SPACE 3 ch.g. Sulamani (IRE) 130 – Rasmalai 71 (Sadler's Wells (USA) 132) [2009 –: p12g^6 f11g^6 10.2m* 12g^3 11.6m^5 11.8m 11.6d^2 11.6g* 12m^4 13g 11.6f^2 12m^5 Sep 19] small gelding: fair handicapper: won at Nottingham in April and Windsor in June: in-and-out form otherwise, leaving B. Powell £7,000 prior to final start: stays 1½m: acts on firm ground. *D. Burchell* **75**

URBAN TIGER (GER) 6 b.g. Marju (IRE) 127 – Ukraine Venture 96 (Slip Anchor 136) [2009 p12m Oct 12] tall, useful-looking gelding: fluent mover: one-time fairly useful performer: well held both outings on Flat since 2006: ungenuine hurdler/chaser. *Tim Vaughan* **–**

URBAN WARRIOR 5 b.g. Zilzal (USA) 137 – Perfect Poppy 73 (Shareef Dancer (USA) 135) [2009 77: p9.5g p12.2g^6 Mar 13] leggy gelding: has a markedly round action: fair handicapper: below form both starts in 2009: stays 1¾m: acts on all-weather and heavy going: tried visored. *Ian Williams* **62**

URSIS (FR) 8 b.g. Trempolino (USA) 135 – Bold Virgin (USA) (Sadler's Wells (USA) 132) [2009 80: 14v^2 14g^2 p16g Jul 1] sturdy gelding: fair handicapper: should stay 2m: acts on heavy and good to firm going, well held on polytrack: tried blinkered. *S. Gollings* **78**

URSULA (IRE) 3 b.f. Namid 128 – Fritta Mista (IRE) (Linamix (FR) 127) [2009 79p: 7.1v^3 7g^5 6g* 6d^4 p7.1g^3 p7m^5 p6m Nov 21] fairly useful handicapper: won at Doncaster in July (left K. R. Burke after next outing): likely to stay 1m: raced only on polytrack and good going or softer: sold 18,000 gns. *R. M. Beckett* **87**

URSUS 4 ch.g. Rambling Bear 115 – Adar Jane (Ardar 87) [2009 63: 5d^3 5m^6 5d^4 6m 5m^6 6d 5g^2 5s f5f f5f Dec 11] modest handicapper: effective at 5f/6f: acts on heavy and good to firm ground: in cheekpieces/blinkers last 6 starts. *C. R. Wilson* **61**

USETHEFORCE (IRE) 4 ch.g. Black Minnaloushe (USA) 123 – Polynesian Goddess (IRE) (Salmon Leap (USA) 131) [2009 56: p7m p12g^6 10.1g May 28] poor maiden: likely to prove best at 7f+: form only on polytrack: tried visored. *M. Quinn* **47**

USQUAEBACH 2 b.f. (Feb 22) Trade Fair 124 – Mashmoum 85 (Lycius (USA) 124) [2009 5m 5m f5g^3 6m^6 6g f5g^3 f6g p5g Oct 22] 1,000Y: close-coupled filly: half-sister to several winners, including useful 7f/1m winner Indian's Feather (by Indian Ridge): dam 7f winner: modest maiden: left H. Collingridge after fifth start: should stay 6f: form only on fibresand: tried visored/blinkered: one to treat with caution. *S. Curran* **– § a53 §**

USUAL SUSPECTS 3 b.f. Royal Applause 124 – Soft Breeze 99 (Zafonic (USA) 130) [2009 –: p5.1g Jan 23] lengthy filly: no solid form. *Peter Grayson* **–**

UTMOST RESPECT 5 b.g. Danetime (IRE) 121 – Utmost (IRE) 30 (Most Welcome 131) [2009 120: 6m* 6v* May 23] **123**

Richard Fahey's stable at Musley Bank, Malton, enjoyed a remarkable season, sending out one hundred and sixty-five winners in Britain (a total bettered only by the stables of Mark Johnston and Richard Hannon) and earning over £1.5m in prize money to finish ninth in the trainers' table. The campaign was the best by some way that the burgeoning stable has enjoyed so far, but the demise of star turn Utmost Respect, the apple of his trainer's eye, was a big blow. He met a sad end in July after contracting peritonitis following surgery on a foot. Gelded after winning a maiden and a nursery on his only starts at two, Utmost Respect began to fulfil his obvious potential when developing into a smart handicapper at three, winning the Ayr Silver Cup on the third of his four starts that season. He established himself as a pattern performer at four, winning the Chipchase Stakes at Newcastle and the Prix de Seine-et-Oise at Maisons-Laffitte, and also making the frame in Group 1 company in the Prix Maurice de Gheest and the Sprint Cup.

Duke of York Blue Square Stakes, York—
Utmost Respect (right) shows that he doesn't need the mud as he runs on strongly ahead of King's Apostle (second left), Tax Free (blaze), and Strike The Deal (visor)

Utmost Respect proved himself even better as a five-year-old, winning his two starts, both of them in pattern races in May. The first was in an up-to-standard renewal of the Duke of York Blue Square Stakes at York where Utmost Respect won by three quarters of a length and a neck from King's Apostle and Tax Free after being close up all the way, the win being his first under firmish conditions and belying the seemingly widely-held view that Utmost Respect needed some give in the ground to produce his best. In contrast to York, the going at the Curragh ten days later for the Weatherbys Ireland Greenlands Stakes could hardly have been more testing. Starting a hot favourite, Utmost Respect was again close up throughout and stayed on strongly (despite flashing his tail) to win by two and a half lengths from Jumbajukiba who pushed him all the way. The really big sprints sadly went by

Weatherbys Ireland Greenlands Stakes, the Curragh—a very smart performance from Utmost Respect on his final appearance; Jumbajukiba (blinkers) and Icelandic battle it out for the minor placings

without Utmost Respect, who would almost certainly have made his mark in them. The way the race turned out, he might even have fulfilled his trainer's prediction after York that 'Maybe the Sprint Cup at Haydock will be his race.'

Richard Fahey put down his stable's fine season to the fact that 'the horses were very healthy all the way through . . . you can train them if they're healthy.' Fahey doesn't believe, however, in galloping his horses too much at home. 'We have one work morning a week, we put a good level of fitness on our horses but we don't over-gallop them . . . there's no prize money to be won on the gallops and if the horses are sound and well, and we're happy with them, we race them; that's what they're here for.' Among the biggest beneficiaries of the Fahey philosophy—the stable sent out over eleven hundred runners in the latest season—are the jockeys who ride for the stable. The stable's number-one Paul Hanagan, who rode Utmost Respect in most of his races (picking up a two-day ban for excessive whip use in the Duke of York), finished eighth in the jockeys' table with 119 winners (his first century). Hanagan was champion apprentice in 2002 and the latest champion apprentice also emerged from the Fahey stable. Frederik Tylicki won the Jockeys' Association's title, decided over the turf season, by one—68 to 67—from the previous year's joint winner David Probert, though Probert beat Tylicki by ten—81 to 71—over the calendar year. German-born Tylicki spent time with Dermot Weld and Jim Bolger before moving to Malton. He is set to be stable jockey to Nottinghamshire trainer Jeremy Glover in 2010 after spending the winter acquiring further experience in the States.

Utmost Respect (b.g. 2004)	Danetime (IRE) (b 1994)	Danehill (b 1986)	Danzig Razyana
		Allegheny River (b 1987)	Lear Fan Allesheny
	Utmost (IRE) (ch 1998)	Most Welcome (ch 1984)	Be My Guest Topsy
		Bint Alhabib (ch 1991)	Nashwan El Fabulous

The good-bodied Utmost Respect owed his speed to his also now-deceased sire Danetime, who made his name as a sire of sprinters. Utmost Respect's dam Utmost, who has had no other winners, was a poor maiden whose 'best' efforts came when finishing a rather remote third in claiming and selling company on the all-weather. Utmost stayed eleven furlongs and was a half-sister to French mile and a half winner Chocolate Cake and fair handicapper Rossini's Dancer, who also stays a mile and a half. Utmost Respect showed his best form at six furlongs and acted on heavy and good to firm going. He had a tendency to wander and sometimes idled once in front. *R. A. Fahey*

UVINZA 3 ch.f. Bertolini (USA) 125 – Baddi Heights (FR) (Shirley Heights 130) [2009 94: 8m4 10d3 12m3 12g3 12m 12m5 p13g Oct 29] tall, angular filly: useful performer: best efforts when third in listed races at Newbury and Newmarket, and Ribblesdale Stakes at Royal Ascot in between (5¼ lengths behind Flying Cloud) and fifth in listed race at Ascot (beaten 1¼ lengths by Spirit of Dubai): stays 1½m: acts on polytrack, soft and good to firm going. *W. J. Knight* **100**

V

VADITION (IRE) 2 b.f. (Apr 19) Halling (USA) 133 – Retail Therapy (IRE) 50 (Bahhare (USA) 122) [2009 5f p5g 7m 8m 9m 8.3d p8g Nov 14] €16,000F: workmanlike filly: second foal: dam, maiden (stayed 1½m), winning hurdler: little form. *J. J. Bridger* **–**

VADUZ 2 b.f. (Mar 9) Imperial Dancer 123 – Summer Shades 79 (Green Desert (USA) 127) [2009 5.1g 5m3 5f4 6g p6g Jul 7] sparely-made filly: first foal: dam 7f/1m winner: poor maiden. *M. R. Channon* **48**

VAIN BOTELI (GER) 3 b.g. Bertolini (USA) 125 – Vanity Fair (Nashwan (USA) 135) [2009 8g* 8.5s2 8g2 8g* 8.3g f12m Nov 6] second foal: dam unraced daughter of Prix Cleopatre winner Allurement: won minor events at Bremen in April and Hamburg (final start for P. Schiergen in Germany) in June: well held in handicaps both British starts: stays 1m. *R. Ford* **?**

VAINGLORY (USA) 5 ch.h. Swain (IRE) 134 – Infinite Spirit (USA) 108 (Maria's Mon (USA) 121) [2009 97: p8g[4] 10.3m[6] 8m[3] 8.3m* 8.3m[2] 10g[3] 10g[5] p8g[6] 8m[4] f8g[5] Oct 18] smallish horse: useful handicapper: won at Leicester in June: best at 1m/1¼m: acts on dirt/all-weather, soft and good to firm ground: often forces pace. *D. M. Simcock* **95**

VALANTINO OYSTER (IRE) 2 b. or br.g. (Apr 15) Pearl of Love (IRE) 112 – Mishor 83 (Slip Anchor 136) [2009 5s[5] 6s 6m Jun 14] €12,000Y: second living foal: dam 15f winner: signs of ability given inadequate trip in maidens: bred to need 1m+: should do better. *J. Howard Johnson* **– p**

VALATRIX (IRE) 4 b.f. Acclamation 118 – Dramatic Entry (IRE) 68 (Persian Bold 123) [2009 89: p6g[2] p6g[5] 6g[5] 7.1m[4] 6g 7.1g p7g Oct 9] leggy, angular filly: fairly useful handicapper: stays 7f: acts on polytrack and good to firm going: sold 6,500 gns, sent to Greece. *C. F. Wall* **87**

VAL C 2 b.f. (Feb 19) Dubawi (IRE) 129 – Valjarv (IRE) 97§ (Bluebird (USA) 125) [2009 5.1m 5d[3] 5m[3] 5m[4] p5g[5] 5m[3] 6d 5m[5] Sep 14] 30,000Y: close-coupled filly: first foal: dam, 2-y-o 6f winner, half-sister to 7-y-o Qadar: fair maiden: should stay 6f: acts on good to firm and good to soft going. *N. P. Littmoden* **65**

VALDAN (IRE) 5 b.g. Val Royal (FR) 127 – Danedrop (IRE) (Danehill (USA) 126) [2009 77: 12m* 11.5m[6] 12.1m[4] 12m[5] 12.3m[2] 21g 11.9f p12.2g[6] Oct 17] leggy, close-coupled gelding: fairly useful handicapper: won at Thirsk in May: left P. D. Evans prior to final start: stays 1½m: acts on polytrack, firm and good to soft going: has been tongue tied: travels strongly held up. *M. A. Barnes* **83**

VALDEMAR 3 ch.g. Tobougg (IRE) 125 – Stealthy Times 80 (Timeless Times (USA) 99) [2009 50: f5d p5g[2] p6g[6] f5g p6g* p6g 7m[4] 7m[5] f7g[5] 5.9m[3] Jun 15] big gelding: modest performer: won apprentice handicap at Kempton in February: stays 6f: acts on all-weather and good to firm ground: usually in headgear. *A. D. Brown* **55**

VALENTINE BAY 3 b.f. Reel Buddy (USA) 118 – Bullion 85 (Sabrehill (USA) 120) [2009 –: 6m p6m f8f f6m Nov 6] workmanlike filly: little form: tried in cheekpieces/blinkers. *M. Mullineaux* **–**

VALENTINE BLUE 4 ch.g. Tobougg (IRE) 125 – Blue Topaz (IRE) (Bluebird (USA) 125) [2009 55: p12.2g[2] f12d[4] f11g[5] Mar 22] workmanlike gelding: modest maiden: stays 1½m: acts on all-weather and soft ground: in cheekpieces nowadays: formerly tongue tied: signs of temperament. *A. B. Haynes* **55**

VALENTINO ROSSI (BRZ) 7 b.g. New Colony (USA) – Great Sola (BRZ) (Duke of Marmalade (USA)) [2009 ?: 14m 20m 16.1d Jun 27] tall gelding: no worthwhile form in Britain: gelded after final start. *A. G. Foster* **–**

VALENTINO SWING (IRE) 6 ch.g. Titus Livius (FR) 115 – Farmers Swing (IRE) (River Falls 113) [2009 72: p7g[4] p6g[4] p7.1g p7.1g[5] 6d p7m p6m[3] p7.1g p6f* p6g[2] Dec 31] sturdy gelding: fair handicapper: won at Kempton in December: stays 1m: acts on polytrack, firm and good to soft going: tried in headgear: held up. *Miss T. Spearing* **70**

VALE OF YORK (IRE) 2 b.c. (Apr 4) Invincible Spirit (IRE) 121 – Red Vale (IRE) (Halling (USA) 133) [2009 7g* 7m[5] 7m* 8m[3] 8d[2] a8.5f* Nov 7] **117**

In a remarkably busy international season for Godolphin, a fair number of the hundred plus North American Grade 1 events came under scrutiny and then under assault. By the time that the two-day Breeders' Cup meeting came around, Saeed bin Suroor had already trained the winners of seven Grade 1 races since August, and it was no surprise to see the stable field its largest number of starters at any Breeders' Cup. Since Godolphin was started in the early-'nineties, it had had twenty-nine runners at the fixture, winning the Breeders' Cup Turf with Daylami in 1999 and with Fantastic Light in 2001. The latest Breeders' Cup attracted fifteen Godolphin runners in nine races (fourteen trained by Suroor, one by Kiaran McLoughlin), including five of the earlier Grade 1 scorers in America—Flashing, Gayego, Music Note, Pyro and Seventh Street—who were joined from Europe by Gladiatorus and Mastery, winners respectively of the Premio Vittorio di Capua and the St Leger. In truth, the Godolphin challengers did not excel themselves, six making the frame and only one winning. That winner wasn't one of their Group 1 winners from earlier in the year either, the closest the two-year-old Vale of York had come to winning a Group 1 in Europe before his shock success in the Grey Goose Breeders' Cup Juvenile being a close second in the Gran Criterium at Milan on his latest outing.

Grey Goose Breeders' Cup Juvenile, Santa Anita—Vale of York (noseband) overcomes brief trouble and finds extra to edge ahead of Lookin At Lucky, Noble's Promise (No.4) and Piscitelli (No.2)

The American two-year-olds did not impress as a vintage collection in the run-up to the Breeders' Cup, and not all of their Grade 1 winners lined up in a field of thirteen for the Juvenile at Santa Anita. The absentees were Dublin, winner of the Hopeful Stakes at Saratoga, and Homeboykris, who had had Dublin back in fifth when landing the Champagne Stakes at Belmont Park. One of those who had finished behind Homeboykris, third-placed Aspire, who had also come second in the Hopeful Stakes, started at almost 23/1 in a market on the Juvenile headed by the only dual Grade 1 scorer in the race, Lookin At Lucky, unbeaten in four outings including in the Del Mar Futurity and, over the course and distance of the Juvenile, the Norfolk Stakes. Second favourite was Noble's Promise, successful in the Grade 1 Breeders' Futurity on polytrack at Keeneland, then came the second in the Breeders' Futurity, Aikenite, and Homeboykris's stable-companion D'Funnybone, a wide-margin winner of the Grade 2 Saratoga Special Stakes and Futurity Stakes on dirt. The four European challengers, attempting to follow in the footsteps of Breeders' Cup Juvenile winners Arazi in 1991, Johannesburg in 2001 and Wilko in 2004, all started at 14.2/1 or longer. Two had won Group 1 events, Beethoven in a blanket finish to the Dewhurst Stakes when visored for the first time—he wore the same headgear at Santa Anita—and Alfred Nobel who had won the Phoenix Stakes before losing his next two starts. Radiohead, successful in the Norfolk Stakes at Royal Ascot and runner-up in the Middle Park Stakes, was running over a new trip that was far from certain to suit him. In contrast, Vale of York, the outsider of the European quartet at 30.6/1—only two of his rivals started at longer odds—had already shown twice that a mile suited him really well. He kept on gamely after being bumped by the winner Joshua Tree as they both made headway in the straight in the Royal Lodge Stakes at Ascot, eventually coming a length and half third to that colt. Then he was beaten a neck by Hearts of Fire, the pair clear, in the Gran Criterium, leading soon after halfway and running on once headed in the final furlong. Both runs represented improvement on Vale of York's three earlier starts over seven furlongs, though he had won two of them, a median auction maiden at York in July and a listed event at Goodwood in September, the latter by half a length from Mata Keranjang after finishing very strongly. In between, Vale of York finished a never-dangerous fifth of ten to Elusive Pimpernel in a strong renewal of the Acomb Stakes at York.

Ridden by his usual partner Ahmed Ajtebi at Santa Anita, Vale of York was ridden along as soon as the stalls opened, racing in fifth behind Piscitelli and D'Funnybone and then moving up to third on the rail after three furlongs. He looked briefly outpaced when Noble's Promise accelerated to take the lead a furlong and a half out, with Piscitelli keeping on and Lookin At Lucky, forced to race wide all the way from his outside draw, beginning a run. Switched outside, Vale of York challenged with Lookin At Lucky and just got the better of him by a head. Noble's Promise was half a length back in third, with Piscitelli a close fourth. In some respects, Lookin At Lucky, who won the Grade 1 CashCall Futurity in workmanlike style from Noble's Promise on his only subsequent start, was unlucky, having to work much harder from his draw to get into a challenging position, but it wouldn't be fair to underestimate Vale of York who is a likely runner in the Kentucky Derby. Lookin At Lucky won the Eclipse Award for the Two-Year-Old Male of the Year, but Vale of York's narrow victory over him at Santa Anita helped to clinch the Outstanding Owner award for Godolphin, the first it has won in North America. The year's leading owner in North America was Michael Gill who topped the tables for number of winners (370) and most prize money (6,670,490 dollars); Godolphin received 61 of the 232 possible votes, Gill received only six.

Collectively, the twenty-five winners of the Breeders' Cup Juvenile up to 2008 have had an ordinary record as three-year-olds, providing only two classic winners, Timber Country in the 1995 Preakness Stakes and Street Sense in the 2007 Kentucky Derby. Street Sense also won the Travers Stakes, while the only other Grade 1 winners at three were Unbridled's Song (Florida Derby and Wood Memorial), Brocco (Santa Anita Derby), Fly So Free (Florida Derby), Rhythm (Travers Stakes) and Chief's Crown (Travers Stakes and Marlboro Cup). Ten Grade 1 victories from twenty-five colts, twenty of whom were named as champion in the annual Eclipse Awards, is hardly spectacular but that, in itself, won't stop Vale of York winning. Godolphin's challenge for the Kentucky Derby in the latest season was no more successful than several previous challenges with Regal Ransom and Desert Party only eighth and fourteenth. Two other big hopes at the start of the season, Midshipman and Vineyard Haven, and two other potential Kentucky Derby runners, Coronet of A Baron and Jose Adan, were out of action for one reason or another in May. Vale of York's form is not good enough to win a normal renewal of the classic; he is at the bottom end of the top ten colts in Europe on Timeform ratings. Nor is there any guarantee that he will act on a dirt course—making the transition from turf to polytrack or pro-ride seems more straightforward than from turf to dirt. If the usual policy of running Godolphin's Kentucky Derby candidates in Dubai rather than the United States is followed, he will be less acquainted with a dirt track than previous hopefuls because the Meydan track, built to replace Nad Al Sheba, has a synthetic surface (tapeta). Nad Al Sheba's track consisted of fine dune sand, silt and clay, which was much closer to an American dirt track. Finally, there is the question of whether Vale of York has the stamina for a mile and a quarter given his style of racing—he takes a pretty keen hold—and also given his pedigree.

Vale of York's sire Invincible Spirit stayed seven furlongs but was better over shorter distances, putting up his best performances when winning the Duke of York Stakes and Haydock Sprint Cup as a five-year-old. He has been at the Irish National Stud since 2003, when his fee was €10,000, rising to €75,000 in 2008 before dropping back to €50,000 then €45,000 for 2010. As this pattern suggests, Invincible Spirit has done pretty well, and he has two other top-flight winners to his name in Fleeting Spirit (July Cup) and Lawman (Prix du Jockey Club, Prix Jean Prat). He had another smart juvenile in the latest season in Our Jonathan, successful in the Cornwallis Stakes and Criterium de Maisons-Laffitte. Lawman, who stayed ten and a half furlongs, was an exception for Invincible Spirit, the vast majority of whose progeny are best at up to a mile. Those who get further, including Allied Powers and Staying On, tend to be out of mares with plenty of stamina in their pedigree. The maternal grandsires of the two horses just mentioned are High Line and Saddlers' Hall, while Lawman was a half-brother to Latice, a classic winner who was by the miler Inchinor but stayed a mile and a half.

Vale of York (IRE) (b.c. Apr 4, 2007)	Invincible Spirit (IRE) (b 1997)	Green Desert (b 1983)	Danzig
			Foreign Courier
		Rafha (b 1987)	Kris
			Eljazzi
	Red Vale (IRE) (b 1998)	Halling (ch 1991)	Diesis
			Dance Machine
		Hamsaat (b 1992)	Sadler's Wells
			Steel Habit

How much encouragement is there on the dam's side of the pedigree for thinking Vale of York will stay a mile and a quarter? Vale of York's dam Red Vale did not run, nor did her first foal, while the second, the Kalanisi filly Violet Flame, showed just modest form on her only start at Dundalk in October. The next offspring after Vale of York was a colt by Elusive City who fetched 60,000 guineas at Tattersalls October Sales; Red Vale was then barren to Elusive City before visiting Iffraaj in the latest season. Vale of York was withdrawn from the 2008 October Sales, then sold for 23,000 guineas at the Newmarket December Sales. Contrary to some reports, this was not the only time he appeared in the sale-ring. Vale of York was offered at the Tattersalls Breeze-Up Sale in April and, with the bidding stopping at 65,000 guineas, failed to reach his reserve. He was purchased privately for Godolphin afterwards. Further to the question of stamina, Red Vale is by Halling, who stayed a mile and a quarter and has sired such well above average horses as Cavalryman, Coastal Path, Franklins Gardens, Hala Bek and The Geezer who have proved effective over further. Vale of York's grandam Hamsaat ran only once, winning a maiden over a mile at Haydock as a three-year-old, but she was by Sadler's Wells, whose influence for stamina is well established. Hamsaat has foaled seven winners, just one of them in stakes company—the filly Uraib, successful in the Buena Vista Handicap over a mile at Santa Anita. Her three-year-old Carrig Girl won a maiden over a mile and a half at Tipperary in June. Hamsaat is a sister to Batshoof, a very smart performer at around a mile and a quarter who won the Tattersalls Gold Cup and Prince of Wales's Stakes in 1990. Speed is the dominant element in the next two generations on the distaff side of Vale of York's pedigree, his third dam Steel Habit being a sister to Ancestral, a winner from six furlongs to eight and a half furlongs, and to Zummerudd, dam of Two Thousand Guineas winner King of Kings and Prix Robert Papin winner General Monash, out of Ampulla, who won the Cherry Hinton Stakes. Ampulla was a half-sister to two horses who also showed their best form at two, Group 1 winners Steel Heart and Smokey Lady. On pedigree, Vale of York, an unfurnished colt who acts on pro-ride and on good to firm and good to soft going, should find a mile and a quarter within his compass. To some extent, though, much will depend upon Vale of York's conserving his energy more than he tended to do in his first season. *Saeed bin Suroor*

VALERY BORZOV (IRE) 5 b.g. Iron Mask (USA) 117 – Fay's Song (IRE) 84 (Fayruz 116) [2009 111: 6.5g 6g $6g^4$ 6s* $p6g^5$ 6g $6d^6$ 6m 6m Sep 19] lengthy gelding: smart handicapper: best effort in 2009 when winning at York in May by 2¾ lengths from Harrison George, making all: respectable effort after only when sixth to Genki in Stewards' Cup at Goodwood: stays 6f: acts on polytrack, best turf form on ground softer than good (acts on heavy): often visored/blinkered: tried tongue tied: not straightforward. *D. Nicholls* **111**

VALFURVA (IRE) 3 b.f. Celtic Swing 138 – Kiriyaki (USA) (Secretariat (USA)) [2009 $p8g^5$ 9g $p7g^6$ p8m $p7.1g^5$ Oct 1] €12,000Y: lengthy, useful-looking filly: half-sister to several winners, including useful 1998 2-y-o 5f winner Thunder Dragon (by Zieten), later successful in USA: dam, second at 1m in France, sister to smart French 9f to 1½m winner Athyka: fair form: should prove suited by 1m: acts on polytrack: sold 4,500 gns. *L. M. Cumani* **66**

VALIANT KNIGHT (FR) 2 ch.c. (Feb 12) Night Shift (USA) – Pilgrim of Grace **81**
(FR) (Bering 136) [2009 7g 8.1g^3 7.1g^2 7m 7m Sep 23] €40,000F, €115,000Y: well-made colt: first foal: dam useful French 10.5f to 12.5f winner: fairly useful maiden: well below form last 2 outings: stays 1m. *R. Hannon*

VALIANT ROMEO 9 b.g. Primo Dominie 121 – Desert Lynx (IRE) 79 (Green Desert **53**
(USA) 127) [2009 53: 7m 5f^5 5m^4 5m 5m Jun 29] sturdy gelding: modest performer: raced mainly at 5f: acts on firm and soft ground: usually wears headgear. *R. Bastiman*

VALID POINT (IRE) 3 b.g. Val Royal (FR) 127 – Ricadonna (Kris 135) [2009 –p: **87**
p6g^6 p7g^6 8f^4 10s* 9.9m* p9.5g* 11.1g* 10m* f12g^5 Sep 29] lengthy, good-topped gelding: fairly useful handicapper: completed 5-timer at Ayr, Beverley, Wolverhampton, Hamilton and Pontefract in August/September: should stay 1½m: acts on polytrack, soft and good to firm going: races prominently: sold 82,000 gns. *Sir Mark Prescott*

VALID REASON 2 b.c. (Jan 18) Observatory (USA) 131 – Real Trust (USA) (Danzig **80 p**
(USA)) [2009 p8g^3 p8f* Dec 16] third foal: half-brother to 3-y-o Truism: dam, French maiden (best around 7f), half-sister to US Grade 1 7f winner Latent Heat and French/US 7f/1m performer Art Master, both smart: promising in maidens at Lingfield and Kempton (beat Balducci ¾ length, making most and strong at finish): capable of better still. *Mrs A. J. Perrett*

VALKOV 2 b.f. (Mar 10) Val Royal (FR) 127 – Petrikov (IRE) (In The Wings 128) **68**
[2009 p6g 7m^6 7.1g^4 7g p7g^3 Nov 25] eighth foal: half-sister to 3 winners, including 8.6f seller winner Glasson Lodge (by Primo Dominie): dam unraced out of sister to 1000 Guineas/Oaks winner Midway Lady: fair maiden: bred to stay 1m. *Tom Dascombe*

VALKYRIE (IRE) 3 b.f. Danehill Dancer (IRE) 117 – Ridotto (Salse (USA) 128) **58**
[2009 61?: p7g^6 p10g f8g^5 f11g^6 10.1g^3 p12g 10.1g^4 f11g^3 p12g^3 p16g^3 p12g^4 Nov 11] big, lengthy, angular filly: modest maiden handicapper: stays 2m: raced mostly on all-weather: tried in cheekpieces/blinkers. *N. P. Littmoden*

VALMARI (IRE) 6 b.m. Kalanisi (IRE) 132 – Penza 79 (Soviet Star (USA) 128) [2009 **91**
12m p16g 11.5m^4 12m* 16.4m 14.1m^4 12m^5 Sep 19] half-sister to 2 winners by Bahri, including fairly useful 11f winner Trullitti: dam, second in Ireland at 1¼m, half-sister to high-class 1½m performer White Muzzle and to dam of Dubai World Cup winner Almutawakel: trained in Greece prior to 2009, winning 4 times: fairly useful handicapper in Britain: won at Doncaster in June: stays 1¾m: acts on good to firm ground: usually blinkered: joined G. Prodromou. *C. E. Brittain*

VALMINA 2 b.c. (Feb 21) Val Royal (FR) 127 – Minnina (IRE) (In The Wings 128) **76**
[2009 7m 6d p6g^2 p5.1g* p6m^2 f6f^2 Dec 11] workmanlike colt: third foal: half-brother to 4-y-o Willridge: dam, ran once, out of useful 6f/7f performer Cheyenne Spirit: fair performer: won nursery at Wolverhampton in November: stays 6f: acts on all-weather: usually tongue tied: hung right final start. *Tom Dascombe*

VAL'S PRINCESS 2 b.f. (Mar 22) Trade Fair 124 – Eleonora d'Arborea 78 (Prince **–**
Sabo 123) [2009 f5g 6g May 28] 800F: half-sister to 5f to 1¼m winner Leonora Truce (by Brief Truce) and 6-y-o She's Our Beauty: dam, 6f winner, ran only at 2 yrs: last in maiden/seller. *J. R. Jenkins*

VALVIGNERES (IRE) 4 gr.g. Dalakhani (IRE) 133 – Albacora (IRE) 98 (Fairy King **77**
(USA)) [2009 69: p12g^3 p13g^3 14.1g^3 Aug 5] tall, narrow gelding: fair maiden handicapper, lightly raced: stays 13f: acts on polytrack and good to soft going. *E. A. L. Dunlop*

VAMOS (IRE) 3 b.g. Royal Applause 124 – Feather Boa (IRE) 81 (Sri Pekan (USA) **71**
117) [2009 61p: p5g^3 p6g^2 5.1g^3 6f p6g^5 6m^4 6.1v^2 p7g^3 p7g^5 p7g^5 p8.6g* p8.6g^4 p8.6g^2 Nov 16] fair handicapper: won at Wolverhampton in October: stays 8.6f: acts on polytrack and good to firm going: tried blinkered/tongue tied. *J. R. Gask*

VANADIUM 7 b.g. Dansili 127 – Musianica 92 (Music Boy 124) [2009 74: p7.1g^2 8g^5 **68**
7f^4 p7.1g^6 6g^6 7.6g^2 6d 7.6m p7.1g^5 p8.6g^3 p7m^2 5.7g p7m^4 6s p8g^5 p7m Nov 29] tall, good-topped gelding: fair handicapper: left G. L. Moore after eleventh start: effective at 6f to 8.6f: acts on polytrack, soft and good to firm going: tried in cheekpieces: tongue tied later in 2009. *A. J. Lidderdale*

VANATINA (IRE) 5 b.m. Tagula (IRE) 116 – Final Trick (Primo Dominie 121) [2009 **49**
50: f6s^5 p7.1g^5 f7g* f6g p7.1g f7g f6g May 5] workmanlike mare: poor performer: won minor event at Southwell in January: effective at 6f to 1m: acts on all-weather and soft ground. *W. M. Brisbourne*

VAN BOSSED (CAN) 4 ch.g. Van Nistelrooy (USA) 108 – Embossed (CAN) (Silver **84**
Deputy (CAN)) [2009 103: 5g 6m 6g 6m 6d 5m 6g 5g 7d Sep 6] good-bodied gelding: just fairly useful handicapper in 2009: best at 5f/6f: acts on polytrack, soft and good to firm ground: once tongue tied at 2 yrs (won). *D. Nicholls*

VANILLA BALLY (ISR) 4 ch.f. Supreme Commander (FR) 112 – Rozalyn Bally (ISR) (Verardi) [2009 p8.6g 10.1g 8.1g Aug 13] Israeli-bred filly: winner of 7 of her 9 races in Israel for O. Sada: well held in handicaps in Britain in 2009: stays 7f: acts on dirt. *George Baker* **–**

VANILLA LOAN (IRE) 2 b.f. (May 2) Invincible Spirit (IRE) 121 – Alexander Anapolis (IRE) 94 (Spectrum (IRE) 126) [2009 p7g p7.1g f7f³ Oct 21] third foal: half-sister to useful 6f winner Film Maker (by Danetime) and 3-y-o Cut The Cackle: dam, 1½m winner, out of half-sister to very smart sprinter Ballad Rock: modest form in maidens: should be as effective at 6f as 7f. *M. Botti* **61**

VANILLA RUM 2 b.g. (Apr 12) Reset (AUS) 124 – Snoozy (Cadeaux Genereux 131) [2009 6.1d⁶ 6m⁴ Oct 26] 4,000F, £14,000Y: leggy gelding: seventh foal: half-brother to 2 winners, including fairly useful 6f (including at 2 yrs in Ireland) to 1m (in France) winner Bermeco (by Dr Fong): dam unraced out of half-sister to Moyglare Stud Stakes winner Lemon Souffle: easily better effort in maidens when 1¾ lengths fourth to Deacon Blues at Leicester (gelded after): should stay 7f. *H. Candy* **73**

VANISHING GREY (IRE) 2 gr.f. (Jan 31) Verglas (IRE) 118 – Native Force (IRE) 82 (Indian Ridge 123) [2009 5g⁴ 6g⁶ 6.1g³ 5.1g* 5m 6m 5g Oct 10] €220,000Y: well-made filly: third foal: half-sister to 4-y-o Kingsgate Native and 7f winner Assumption (by Beckett): dam, 1m winner, out of close relation to 1000 Guineas winner Las Meninas: fairly useful performer: won maiden at Bath in August: should prove best at 5f/6f: blinkered (stiff task) final start. *B. J. Meehan* **84**

VANQUISHER (IRE) 5 b.g. Xaar 132 – Naziriya (FR) (Darshaan 133) [2009 72: p11g² p16.5g² p16g² p13.9g Feb 7] leggy, useful-looking gelding: modest handicapper nowadays: stays 2m: acts on all-weather, soft and good to firm going: sometimes wears headgear: tongue tied in 2009. *Ian Williams* **55**

VARACHI 2 b.g. (Mar 13) Kyllachy 129 – Miss Rimex (IRE) 84 (Ezzoud (IRE) 126) [2009 8m 8.3s⁶ 7d⁵ Oct 22] well-made gelding: just gradual improvement in maidens: may prove best up to 7f: *E. A. L. Dunlop* **64**

VARAH 3 b.g. Tobougg (IRE) 125 – Relativity (IRE) (Distant Relative 128) [2009 p9.5g Oct 10] showed nothing in maiden at Wolverhampton: subsequently gelded. *R. A. Harris* **–**

VARENAR (FR) 3 ch.c. Rock of Gibraltar (IRE) 133 – Visor (USA) (Mr Prospector (USA)) [2009 8g 7.5g* 8g* 7g² 6.5g⁴ 7g² 7g* Oct 3] **122**

Of the Aga Khan's seven pattern-race winners (five of them Group 1) at Longchamp over a magnificent Arc weekend, Varenar's success in the Total Prix de la Foret on the Saturday was perhaps the least expected. The horse was scheduled to come under the hammer later that day at the Arc sale, his career-best performance leading to an about-turn over the decision to sell! Only one of the Aga Khan's seven winners on Arc weekend, the Marcel Boussac winner Rosanara, started favourite and Varenar was a near-20/1 chance, odds which reflected not only the fact that Varenar was facing the toughest challenge of his career in the Foret, but also that Goldikova was a long odds-on favourite. Goldikova's defeat was the main talking point afterwards, though Varenar certainly did not win simply by default.

Neither Goldikova nor Varenar was favoured by the draw over Longchamp's seven-furlong course, which starts on a spur to the main track running slightly downhill into an early bend to join the straight. A low draw near the inside rail is considered an advantage, a smart break there reducing the chances of interference on the bend. With a field of fourteen rushing into the turn in the Foret, scrimmaging was inevitable and second favourite Oiseau de Feu, who caused it, was afterwards disqualified and placed last after passing the post in sixth. Varenar, drawn thirteen with only Goldikova outside him, missed the trouble and settled down on the outside of the field in mid-division. Goldikova got a clear run too and was rushed into a handy position with Varenar's stable-companion Sweet Hearth and the rank outsiders Welsh Emperor and Opera Comica. These four opened up a gap over the remainder and when Brazilian-trained Opera Comica ran wide and veteran Welsh Emperor (second twice in the race before) began to struggle to hold his place, Goldikova got across to the inside rail and continued in front at a cracking pace tracked by Sweet Hearth. The pacesetters paid for their exertions in the last two furlongs of the Foret and Varenar joined them passing the first winning post before edging ahead close home for a short head verdict over 60/1-shot Sweet Hearth, with Goldikova half a length away in third and a three-length break to the

Total Prix de la Foret, Longchamp—stable-companions Varenar (right) and Sweet Hearth (noseband) fight out the finish with odds-on Goldikova

best of the British-trained runners, Cat Junior and Balthazaar's Gift, who came fourth and fifth.

Varenar had made the running himself when narrowly beaten on two occasions in Group 3 company over the same course and distance earlier in the season, caught close home both times, firstly by the German-trained Smooth Operator in the Prix de la Porte Maillot in June and then by the filly Proviso in the Prix du Pin four weeks before the Foret, Varenar's jockey losing his whip in the final furlong on the second occasion and having to improvise with slaps of his hand in the closing stages. Between those two races, Varenar emerged with plenty of credit from his first run in Group 1 company in the Prix Maurice de Gheest at Deauville in August, when he was the only one in the stand-side group involved in the finish, keeping on to finish a close fourth to King's Apostle. Varenar's sights had been set fairly low before he contested the Porte Maillot. He had shown useful form at best from six starts in minor company, winning at Compiegne on the last of three outings as a two-year-old and then successful twice in the first part of his three-year-old season, at Saint-Cloud and Compiegne again in May.

Varenar (FR) (ch.c. 2006)	Rock of Gibraltar (IRE) (b 1999)	Danehill (b 1986)	Danzig Razyana
		Offshore Boom (ch 1985)	Be My Guest Push A Button
	Visor (USA) (b 1989)	Mr Prospector (b 1970)	Raise A Native Gold Digger
		Look (b 1984)	Spectacular Bid Tuerta

Varenar's dam Visor had already established an excellent record as a broodmare for her late owner Jean-Luc Lagardere before she was integrated into the Aga Khan's Studs, along with the rest of the Lagardere bloodstock in the spring of 2005. Among several winners Visor produced to race in the grey and pink Lagardere colours, no fewer than four proved smart. Visionary and Visionnaire (both by Linamix) were placed in French classics, third in the Poule d'Essai des Poulains and Prix de Diane respectively, while Visorama (also by Linamix) won the Prix de Flore and Visorhill (by Danehill) was runner-up in La Coupe de Maisons-Laffitte. Visor has kept up the good work for the Aga Khan, her first winner in his colours being the 2006 Derby favourite Visindar (by Sinndar). Visindar earned that position after impressive wins on his first three starts, including the Prix Greffulhe, but he returned from Epsom badly jarred and ran only once more, suffering a recurrence of his tendon injury in a minor event at Longchamp the following year. Varenar is his dam's best offspring yet, and the most like her too in terms of distance requirements. Visor's only win came in a six-furlong maiden at Turfway Park, and while a mile has been a minimum for her other foals it looks a maximum for Varenar. The

H.H. Aga Khan's "Varenar"

fact that Visor was by Mr Prospector was clearly a factor when Jean-Luc Lagardere bought her for 65,000 dollars at the end of her racing days. Much of the Lagardere stock had North American origins and Mr Prospector also figures in the pedigrees of the dams of Siyouni, Rosanara and Manighar, the three other pattern winners among the Aga Khan's successes at the Arc meeting which owed their origins to the Lagardere breeding operation (two-year-olds Siyouni and Rosanara are among the first crop from the Lagardere mares to be bred by the Aga Khan). Visor was well related, being out of a half-sister to the 1984 Kentucky Derby and Belmont Stakes winner Swale. Varenar's grandam Look was another minor winner in the States, out of Grade 3 winner Tuerta, a half-sister to the dam of the champion North American two-year-old and Kentucky Derby runner-up Forty Niner (also by Mr Prospector) and a full sister to the grandam of Two Thousand Guineas winner Shadeed. Varenar's career so far has offered few clues about his going requirements; his two-year-old win came on soft ground but he has raced only on good going otherwise. *A. de Royer Dupre, France*

VAULTAGE (USA) 2 ch.f. (Mar 8) El Corredor (USA) 123 – Ten Carats (USA) (Capote (USA)) [2009 7g p7g^2 Nov 18] €65,000F, 130,000Y: tall, unfurnished filly: third foal: half-sister to winners in USA by Siphon and Medaglia d'Oro: dam, US 6f (including at 2 yrs)/7f winner, half-sister to useful performer up to 1¼m Coqueteria: much better effort in maidens when 2½ lengths second to Hypnotized at Kempton: will improve again. *E. A. L. Dunlop* **74 p**

VEGAS BABY (IRE) 3 ch.f. Kheleyf (USA) 116 – Gift of Spring (USA) (Gilded Time (USA)) [2009 83: p6g^3 p6g^5 p7g^5 5.7f^4 6g* 6g 6m^6 Jun 8] lengthy, good-topped filly: fairly useful performer: below form after reappearance, though won claimer at Windsor in May: should stay 7f: acts on polytrack and firm going: blinkered last 4 starts. *J. A. Osborne* **81**

VEGAS PALACE (IRE) 2 ch.f. (Mar 30) Captain Rio 122 – Verify (IRE) (Polish Precedent (USA) 131) [2009 7d^3 f7f^2 f7m* Nov 12] €6,500Y: sister to Italian 2008 2-y-o 5.5f winner Artilliana and half-sister to several winners, including 1¼m/1½m winner La Via Ferrata (by Mark of Esteem): dam Italian maiden: progressive in maidens, beating Brigadoon 5 lengths in 4-runner event at Southwell (made all): raced only at 7f. *Tom Dascombe* **79 +**

VEILED 3 b.f. Sadler's Wells (USA) 132 – Evasive Quality (FR) (Highest Honor (FR) 124) [2009 59p: f14m^3 14.1m* f16g^3 14.1m* 16m* p13.9g^4 Sep 25] compact filly: fairly useful handicapper, better on turf: won at Yarmouth in August then Redcar and Yarmouth (by 9 lengths) within 4 days in September: stays 2m: acts on polytrack and good to firm going: sold 48,000 gns, joined J. Pearce. *Sir Mark Prescott* **93 a86**

VEILED APPLAUSE 6 b.g. Royal Applause 124 – Scarlet Veil 75 (Tyrnavos 129) [2009 94: f8g p13.9g^6 10.3g^4 8m^6 10.3g^3 9.8m^6 9.8d^5 8g^6 8m 8g^5 10.4g* 10m^3 10.3g^4 Oct 24] good-topped gelding: fairly useful handicapper: won apprentice event at York in October: stays 10.4f: acts on polytrack, firm and soft going: tricky ride (tends to hang). *J. J. Quinn* **86**

VELLA 3 b.f. Mtoto 134 – Villella (Sadler's Wells (USA) 132) [2009 –: 10.2g^6 9.9f 12.1g p12g Jun 25] modest form only when sixth in maiden at Bath: bred to stay 1½m: tried blinkered. *H. J. L. Dunlop* **54**

VELLE EST VALERE 2 b.f. (Feb 19) Reset (AUS) 124 – Bond Solitaire 66 (Atraf 116) [2009 6s Nov 7] €1,600F: second foal: dam, maiden, half-sister to useful sprinter Cape Merino, herself dam of very smart sprinter Cape of Good Hope: 100/1 and very green, tailed off in maiden at Doncaster. *C. J. Teague* **–**

VELVET BAND 2 gr.f. (Feb 12) Verglas (IRE) 118 – Applaud (USA) 105 (Rahy (USA) 115) [2009 6g^3 5.1m^2 5d^6 6f* 6g 5.5g 7m p6f^4 Oct 14] sturdy filly: seventh foal: half-sister to several winners, including useful 1m (including at 2 yrs) to 1½m (in USA) winner Jazz Jam (by Pivotal): dam 2-y-o 5f/6f (Cherry Hinton Stakes) winner: fair performer: won maiden at Brighton in July: effective at 5f/6f: acts on polytrack and firm going: races up with pace: sold 8,000 gns, joined D. Carroll. *P. F. I. Cole* **73**

VELVET NAYEF 3 b.f. Nayef (USA) 129 – Laughing Girl (USA) 85 (Woodman (USA) 126) [2009 12g Jul 24] 800 2-y-o: third foal: half-sister to 2 winners abroad, including fairly useful French 1¼m to 1½m winner Vraona (by Fantastic Light): dam 1¼m winner: showed nothing in maiden at Newmarket. *J. Pearce* **–**

VENETIAN LADY 3 b.f. Tobougg (IRE) 125 – Perfect Partner (Be My Chief (USA) 122) [2009 60: 7.5m p7.1g^5 6m 6v 6d p7.1g Sep 25] sturdy filly: maiden: well held in 2009: tried blinkered/in cheekpieces. *Mrs A. Duffield* **–**

VENIR ROUGE 5 ch.g. Dancing Spree (USA) – Al Awaalah 52 (Mukaddamah (USA) 125) [2009 78: 10m^5 11m* 13.3g^6 p12g^5 f11g^4 p12.2g^6 Dec 26] big, lengthy gelding: fair handicapper: won at Newbury (apprentices) in June: stays 1½m: acts on polytrack, firm and good to soft going: tried blinkered: held up. *Matthew Salaman* **77**

VENI VEDI VECI (IRE) 2 b.f. (May 4) Antonius Pius (USA) 123§ – Consultant Stylist (IRE) (Desert Style (IRE) 121) [2009 p8g 8g Oct 8] €42,000Y, £20,000 2-y-o: good-topped filly: second foal: dam unraced: much better effort in maidens when mid-field at Newbury latter start. *A. M. Balding* **60**

VENTURA COVE (IRE) 2 ch.g. (Feb 11) Bahamian Bounty 116 – Baby Bunting 63 (Wolfhound (USA) 126) [2009 5m^2 5m^2 5g^5 May 23] €30,000F, £80,000Y: lengthy, well-made gelding: fifth foal: brother to 3-y-o Bahamian Babe and 4-y-o Victorian Bounty: dam, sprint maiden, half-sister to smart sprinter Atraf: similar form in maiden/minor events (gelded after): likely to be best at 5f/6f. *R. A. Fahey* **76**

VENTURE CAPITALIST 3 b.c. Diktat 126 – Ventura Highway (Machiavellian (USA) 123) [2009 66p: 8.3d 10g^2 11.5s 10m^2 11.5d 11.9f^3 p12.2g p8.6g Dec 28] well-made colt: fair maiden: only marginal improvement in handicaps in 2009 before leaving L. Cumani 11,000 gns after sixth start: probably stays 1½m: acts on polytrack and firm going, possibly not on softer than good. *B. Ellison* **69**

VENTURE GIRL (IRE) 2 ch.f. (Feb 16) Footstepsinthesand 120 – Bold Assumption (Observatory (USA) 131) [2009 6d^6 6m^6 6s^5 f5g^4 6m Sep 21] €33,000Y: first foal: dam **55**

unraced out of half-sister to Zafonic: modest maiden: stays 6f: best efforts on fibresand and soft ground. *T. D. Easterby*

VENUTIUS 2 b.g. (May 13) Doyen (IRE) 132 – Boadicea's Chariot (Commanche Run 133) [2009 7d^3 8.1d^3 p8.6g^2 p8.6g* p8.6g^4 Oct 23] half-brother to useful 1999 2-y-o 7f winner Agrippina (by Timeless Times), dam of smart sprinter Cartimandua: dam Irish 1½m and hurdles winner: fair performer: won maiden at Wolverhampton in October: stays 8.6f. *E. S. McMahon* **79**

VERACITY 5 ch.h. Lomitas 129 – Vituisa (Bering 136) [2009 115: 14g^2 16m* 14s^3 20m Jun 18] lengthy, good-quartered horse: smart performer: won minor event at Nad Al Sheba in February by ½ length from Mourilyan: had earlier run well at same course when nose second to Friston Forest in handicap: respectable third to Ask in Yorkshire Cup at York: pulled up in Gold Cup at Royal Ascot (broke cannon bone and subsequently put down): stayed 2¼m: acted on polytrack, soft and good to firm going: raced prominently. *Saeed bin Suroor* **119**

VERDANT 2 b.c. (Mar 24) Singspiel (IRE) 133 – Orford Ness 107 (Selkirk (USA) 129) [2009 7m^2 p7g* Oct 9] closely related to very smart winner around 1¼m Weightless (by In The Wings) and half-brother to 3 winners, including 4-y-o Main Aim and smart 7f (at 2 yrs)/1m winner Home Affairs (by Dansili): dam French 1m winner, including at 2 yrs: easily better effort in maidens when winning at Lingfield readily by 1¼ lengths from Shamir, still green: should be suited by 1m+: useful prospect. *Sir Michael Stoute* **89 p**

VERINCO 3 b.g. Bahamian Bounty 116 – Dark Eyed Lady (IRE) 82 (Exhibitioner 111) [2009 74: 6d^3 6d^4 6m^3 6d^4 5g f6m^3 f7m Dec 15] compact gelding: fair maiden: stays 7f: acts on polytrack, heavy and good to firm going: tried blinkered, in cheekpieces nowadays: temperamental. *B. Smart* **71 §**

VERITY LANE (USA) 2 b.f. (Feb 13) Yes It's True (USA) 116 – Easy Pass (USA) (Easy Goer (USA)) [2009 p8.6g^3 p8g p8.6g^4 Nov 6] $65,000F, $60,000Y: fourth foal: half-sister to 3 winners in USA: dam, ran 3 times in USA, half-sister to very smart 6f/7f performer Gold Seam: fair maiden: stays 8.6f. *R. M. H. Cowell* **70**

VERONA LAD 2 gr.c. (Mar 23) Needwood Blade 117 – Silver Spell 54 (Aragon 118) [2009 7.1s^6 6s 7d 7g Sep 14] maiden: form only when sixth at Haydock: sold £2,200. *Jennie Candlish* **56**

VERONICAS BOY 3 br.c. Diktat 126 – Thamud (IRE) (Lahib (USA) 129) [2009 72: 10m^4 9.9m^4 8m^4 8v^4 9.3d^4 12g^4 14.1g Aug 14] leggy colt: handicapper, just modest at 3 yrs: best form up to 1m: acts on heavy and good to firm going: tried in cheekpieces: modest form in juvenile hurdles. *G. M. Moore* **61**

VERONICAS WAY 4 b.f. High Estate 127 – Mimining 83 (Tower Walk 130) [2009 46: p8g f8g p8.6g^5 Feb 13] good-bodied filly: poor performer: stays 8.6f: acts on polytrack and good to firm going: tried in cheekpieces/visor. *G. J. Smith* **–**

VEROON (IRE) 3 b.g. Noverre (USA) 125 – Waroonga (IRE) (Brief Truce (USA) 126) [2009 71: 8.3m^2 8m* 8.1g^4 10.2g^6 12g^6 10.3g^2 9.9g* 9.8m^4 p9.5g^2 10.3m* p10m^2 10.4g p10m^5 Nov 4] sturdy gelding: type to carry condition: fairly useful performer: won maiden at Ripon in June then handicaps at Beverley in August and Chester in September: stays 10.3f: acts on polytrack and good to firm going, probably on soft: tried blinkered, in cheekpieces later in 2009: often races prominently. *J. G. Given* **88**

VERSAKI (IRE) 3 gr.g. Verglas (IRE) 118 – Mythie (FR) (Octagonal (NZ) 126) [2009 99: a7g 6.5g p6g 7.1g 7.1g p7.1g 7m^3 7m^3 f8g^6 p7m^6 a9.5g a6.5g^2 Dec 24] leggy gelding: just fair at best in 2009: left D. Nicholls after fourth start and sold from Ian Williams 4,000 gns after tenth outing: possibly best up to 7f: acts on all-weather at Deauville and good to soft going: tried tongue tied/blinkered: inconsistent. *Mme G. Rarick, France* **67**

VERT CHAPEAU 2 ch.f. (Jan 20) Sakhee (USA) 136 – Green Bonnet (IRE) (Green Desert (USA) 127) [2009 p7g p6m Oct 12] 20,000Y: rather leggy filly: seventh foal: half-sister to several winners, including fairly useful 7f winners Edaara (by Pivotal) and Scientist (by Dr Fong): dam, French maiden, sister to useful 7f/1m performer Mauri Moon: better effort in maidens at Kempton when seventh to Muwakaba on debut. *E. F. Vaughan* **60**

VERTIGINEUX (FR) 5 b.h. Nombre Premier 114 – Very Gold (FR) (Goldneyev (USA) 114) [2009 114: 8g^3 8m^2 9m 8d* May 1] first foal: dam French maiden (stayed 1½m): very smart performer: successful in 2008 in Prix de la Porte Maillot at Longchamp, Prix Perth at Saint-Cloud and listed race at Deauville: improved again in 2009, placed at Nad Al Sheba in handicap (¾-length third behind Kachgai) and Zabeel Mile (¾-length second to Archipenko) and won Prix du Muguet at Saint-Cloud in May by ¾ length from Gris de Gris: stays 9f: acts on all-weather, soft and good to firm ground: has had tongue tied. *Mme C. Dufreche, France* **121**

VERTIGO ON COURSE (IRE) 4 b.f. Anabaa (USA) 130 – Due South 104 (Darshaan 133) [2009 63: 7m* p8.6m^3 9d^3 Oct 28] lengthy filly: fair handicapper: improved when winning at Yarmouth in September: probably best at 7f/1m: acts on polytrack, heavy and good to firm ground. *R. A. Fahey* **69**

VERTUEUX (FR) 4 gr.g. Verglas (IRE) 118 – Shahrazad (FR) (Bering 136) [2009 15g p16.5g 16g Oct 28] ex-French gelding: trained by N. Clement in 2008, winning maiden at Lisieux (also second in claimer at Longchamp final start): well beaten in handicaps in Britain in 2009: stays 15f: tried tongue tied/in cheekpieces. *A. W. Carroll* **–**

VERY DISTINGUISHED 3 b.f. Diktat 126 – Dignify (IRE) 105 (Rainbow Quest (USA) 134) [2009 70: 8.3m 9.7g 11.5m 9.9g 11.5d p8m^6 p9.5g p8m^3 p12g^2 p12f p9.5g Dec 28] good-topped filly: modest maiden: left M. Quinlan after fifth start: stays 1½m: acts on polytrack, good to firm and good to soft going. *S. Kirk* **61**

VERY GOOD DAY (FR) 2 b.c. (Apr 18) Sinndar (IRE) 134 – Picture Princess (Sadler's Wells (USA) 132) [2009 8.1g^2 Aug 13] 13,000Y: strong colt: fifth foal: half-brother to 1m winner Perfect Blend and winner in Italy (both by Linamix): dam, ran once in France, half-sister to Oaks third Pictavia (by Sinndar) out of smart half-sister to very smart mare up to 1½m Hatoof: 14/1 and backward, promising 4½ lengths second to Waseet in maiden at Sandown, getting hang of things late: will stay 1½m: sure to improve. *M. R. Channon* **80 p**

VERY WELL RED 6 b.m. First Trump 118 – Little Scarlett 54 (Mazilier (USA) 107) [2009 78, a63: f8s p8g^3 p8g^5 f8g^2 f8g f8d* p8g* f8g^4 8g 8.5g 8m* 8.3m^4 8m^6 8.3s^2 8m^3 8.3m 8s 8.3m^6 8.1m p8m f8f Dec 17] compact mare: fair performer on turf, modest on all-weather: won claimer at Southwell and apprentice handicap at Lingfield in March, and handicap at Bath in June: stays 8.5f: acts on all-weather, firm and soft going: tried blinkered: front runner/races prominently. *P. W. Hiatt* **78 a63**

VESTED INTEREST 2 ch.g. (Apr 28) Footstepsinthesand 120 – Ingozi 91 (Warning 136) [2009 f5g 6g* Jul 2] 5,000Y: half-brother to several winners, including smart 6f (at 2 yrs) to 1½m winner Tissifer (by Polish Precedent) and Irish 3-y-o Miss Keller: dam, 7f/1m winner, half-sister to smart 7f/1m performer Inchinor: gelded and well backed, won seller at Yarmouth (sold 17,500 gns) by 10 lengths from Steeley Flyer, still green yet able to make all: likely to stay beyond 6f: open to further improvement. *George Baker* **84 p**

VHUJON (IRE) 4 b.g. Mujadil (USA) 119 – Livius Lady (IRE) (Titus Livius (FR) 115) [2009 94: p6g^4 6d^4 6m^4 6f 6m* 6g^5 6m^2 6m^2 6m 5d 6g^4 6m^4 6m 6g 6m 6m 7m^5 6g p6m p6f^2 p6m^2 Dec 30] neat gelding: useful handicapper: won at Salisbury in May: effective at 5f/6f: acts on polytrack, firm and good to soft going: tried visored: has worn tongue tie: held up: not straightforward. *P. D. Evans* **96**

VIA AURELIA (IRE) 2 b.f. (Mar 18) Antonius Pius (USA) 123§ – Goldthroat (IRE) 79 (Zafonic (USA) 130) [2009 6m^4 6m^4 6m Oct 26] €55,000Y: fourth foal: half-sister to 3-y-o Zafisio, 4-y-o Harald Bluetooth and 5-y-o New Beginning: dam, Irish 2-y-o 7f winner, out of half-sister to smart miler Killer Instinct: best effort in maidens when fourth to Marrayah at Yarmouth on debut: bred to stay 7f+. *J. R. Fanshawe* **52**

VIABLE 7 b.g. Vettori (IRE) 119 – Danseuse Davis (FR) (Glow (USA)) [2009 52§: 10.1g May 28] one-time fair handicapper: lightly raced on Flat in recent years (fairly useful hurdler), and well held sole start in 2009: barely stays 11.8f: acts on polytrack, good to firm and good to soft going: ungenuine. *Mrs P. Sly* **– §**

VIA GALILEI (IRE) 4 b.c. Galileo (IRE) 134 – Manger Square (IRE) (Danehill (USA) 126) [2009 106: 10g 10g 10g 14d^5 12g* 12s^3 10s^5 12d^5 p10.7g 8.5g Oct 17] good-topped colt: smart performer: easily best effort when winning handicap at the Curragh in June by 4½ lengths from Drunken Sailor: stays 1½m: acts on soft going, probably on good to firm: tongue tied last 2 outings: not to be trusted: sold 60,000 gns, joined G. L. Moore. *J. S. Bolger, Ireland* **114 §**

VIA MIA 3 b.f. Namid 128 – Coming Home (Vettori (IRE) 119) [2009 74: 5m p6g^6 p7g^3 p8.6g^2 p10g^3 p8.6g^6 Dec 3] fair performer: left P. Cole 8,000 gns and off 6 months after third start: barely stays 1¼m: acts on polytrack and good to soft going. *George Baker* **74**

VICIOUS WARRIOR 10 b.g. Elmaamul (USA) 125 – Ling Lane (Slip Anchor 136) [2009 81: 10.4v 12m 9.8d^3 Jun 17] big, strong gelding: handicapper, just fair nowadays: seems to stay 1½m: acts on polytrack, heavy and good to firm going: usually front runner. *R. M. Whitaker* **72**

VICTOIRE DE LYPHAR (IRE) 2 b.g. (Apr 27) Bertolini (USA) 125 – Victory Peak (Shirley Heights 130) [2009 6g^6 6m* 7m^2 7m 7d^2 7m^6 Sep 17] €62,000F: compact gelding: sixth foal: closely related to winner in Spain by Perugino and half-brother to 3 winners, including 3-y-o Global City: dam lightly-raced daughter of Prix de Diane **87 §**

winner Lypharita: fairly useful performer: won maiden at Doncaster in June: visored, good ½-length second to William Morgan in nursery at York penultimate start: blinkered, tailed off final outing: stays 7f: acts on good to firm and good to soft going: unreliable. *P. C. Haslam*

VICTORIA MONTOYA 4 br.f. High Chaparral (IRE) 132 – Spurned (USA) 91 (Robellino (USA) 127) [2009 91: 14m* 14m^2 16.4m^2 14d^3 14g^2 14.6m Sep 10] rangy filly: useful performer: improved in 2009, winning handicap at Newmarket in May by 4½ lengths from Record Breaker: better form after when placed in listed/pattern events, including 1½ lengths third to Sevenna in Lillie Langtry Stakes and 3 lengths second to Mourilyan in listed race, both at Goodwood, fourth/fifth outings: stays 16.4f: acts on polytrack, good to firm and good to soft going: tried in cheekpieces: reliable. *A. M. Balding* **104**

VICTORIAN ART (IRE) 2 b.f. (Jan 16) Chineur (FR) 123 – Alexander Nitelady (IRE) (Night Shift (USA)) [2009 p5g^3 p5.1g^5 6m 5.1m^2 5.2g^5 a5g^2 6s^3 a5g^2 5.8g^3 4.5g^2 Oct 9] €10,000Y: first foal: dam unraced half-sister to Dewhurst Stakes runner-up Fast Company: fair maiden: sold from M. Magnusson 10,500 gns after fifth start: placed at Jagersro/Ovrevoll all 5 starts for new stable: best at around 5f: acts on good to firm ground, probably on dirt: visored/blinkered last 7 starts. *Pia Hoiom, Sweden* **70**

VICTORIAN BOUNTY 4 b.g. Bahamian Bounty 116 – Baby Bunting 63 (Wolfhound (USA) 126) [2009 95: p6g 6g 5f^6 5m Jun 14] strong gelding: just fair handicapper nowadays: will prove best at 5f/6f: acts on polytrack, firm and soft going: tried blinkered/visored: speedy front runner. *Stef Liddiard* **78**

VICTORIAN TYCOON (IRE) 3 b.c. Choisir (AUS) 126 – New Tycoon (IRE) (Last Tycoon 131) [2009 69: 8.3m^2 9.9m^4 8d p8.6g^4 a7.5g a12g^2 12f^6 13.8d^2 15d^3 12s Oct 24] close-coupled colt: fair maiden: second in handicap at Nottingham on reappearance and placed in 3 claimers in France later in year: stays 15f: acts on all-weather, good to firm and good to soft ground: tried in cheekpieces (below form), blinkered last 2 starts. *E. J. O'Neill* **69**

VICTORIA SPONGE (IRE) 3 b.f. Marju (IRE) 127 – Trill 78 (Highest Honor (FR) 124) [2009 76p: p8g^3 7.1g 8m^2 7g* 7m* 6m^4 7g^6 p6g^3 6g^5 7s* Oct 12] tall, attractive filly: has scope: useful handicapper: won at Goodwood in June, Epsom in July and Salisbury (beat Mr Rainbow 1¼ lengths) in October: best form at 7f: acts on polytrack, soft and good to firm going: sold £30,000. *R. Hannon* **96**

VICTORY IDE SAY (IRE) 2 ch.g. (Apr 11) Fath (USA) 116 – Ide Say (IRE) (Grand Lodge (USA) 125) [2009 p6f^3 Dec 13] €20,000Y: fifth foal: dam unraced half-sister to smart 1m/1¼m performer Spindrift: 40/1, eye-catching 1½ lengths third to Passion Overflow in maiden at Kempton, finishing strongly and not at all knocked about: will stay 7f: sure to do better. *P. W. Chapple-Hyam* **64 p**

VICTORY QUEST (IRE) 9 b.g. Victory Note (USA) 120 – Marade (USA) (Dahar (USA) 125) [2009 77: f14s^3 f14g f14g* f14g^3 f14g^5 21.6m^5 f14g^5 f16m^5 f14d Dec 29] big, strong gelding: fair handicapper: won at Southwell (eleventh course win) in February: appears to stay 21.6f: acts on all-weather and firm going: visored. *Mrs S. Lamyman* **77**

VICTORY SPIRIT 5 b.g. Invincible Spirit (IRE) 121 – Tanouma (USA) 114 (Miswaki (USA) 124) [2009 59: p9.5g p8.6g p7.1g 6g^4 9m 7.1m 5g Jul 5] poor handicapper nowawdays: left I. Semple after third start: stays easy 8.6f: acts on polytrack and good to firm going: tried blinkered/in cheekpieces: temperamental. *D. A. Nolan* **46**

VIEN (IRE) 3 b.c. Captain Rio 122 – Fairy Free (Rousillon (USA) 133) [2009 56: p8.6g p9.5g^6 p8.6g Jan 26] close-coupled colt: modest maiden: stays 1m: acts on polytrack and soft ground. *R. Hannon* **52**

VIEWFORTH 11 b.g. Emarati (USA) 74 – Miriam 59 (Forzando 122) [2009 –: p6g^5 6d Apr 13] good-bodied gelding: poor performer nowadays: left M. Wigham after reappearance: best at 5f/6f: acts on all-weather and any turf going: tried in cheekpieces/visor, usually blinkered. *S. T. Mason* **42**

VIGOROSA (IRE) 3 b.f. Red Ransom (USA) – Hejraan Two (IRE) (Green Desert (USA) 127) [2009 p8g 7m 7m p12g p9.5g p9.5g^5 p10g^6 p10g Dec 7] €4,000Y, £20,000 2-y-o: third foal: half-sister to winner in Greece by Dr Fong: dam unraced: modest maiden: stays 1¼m: raced only on polytrack and good to firm ground: in cheekpieces last 2 starts. *P. Howling* **50**

VIKING AWAKE (IRE) 3 b.g. Almutawakel 126 – Norwegian Queen (IRE) (Affirmed (USA)) [2009 72: 7.1g 8.3m^6 5.9m^6 6m^4 7.1d 7m Sep 21] good-bodied gelding: maiden, just modest at 3 yrs: likely to prove best at 5f/6f: acts on good to soft ground: tongue tied last 5 starts, then gelded. *J. W. Unett* **53**

VIKING DANCER 2 b.c. (Apr 12) Danehill Dancer (IRE) 117 – Blue Siren 113 **83**
(Bluebird (USA) 125) [2009 6g 7.1g^{5} 7.1m^{2} 7.1m^{4} Sep 29] good-topped colt: half-brother to several winners, including 5-y-o Siren's Gift and useful 5f winner (including at 2 yrs) Speed Cop (by Cadeaux Genereux): dam, 5f (at 2 yrs) to 7f winner, first past post in Nunthorpe Stakes: easily best effort in maidens when ½-length second to Guest Book at Chepstow: shapes as if will stay 1m. *A. M. Balding*

VIKING SPIRIT 7 b.g. Mind Games 121 – Dane Dancing (IRE) 68 (Danehill (USA) **98**
126) [2009 109: 6m^{6} 6.1m^{3} 6g 6g^{2} 6m p6f^{4} 6d^{6} p6m Nov 3] tall, quite attractive gelding: useful handicapper: in-and-out form in 2009, best effort when runner-up at Ripon: effective at 6f/7f: acts on polytrack, soft and good to firm going: tried in cheekpieces/ visor: usually tongue tied in 2009: has shaped as if amiss. *W. R. Swinburn*

VILLARUZ (IRE) 3 b.g. Fayruz 116 – Villaminta (IRE) (Grand Lodge (USA) 125) **64**
[2009 47: p6g^{3} p6g p6g^{2} p7.1g^{2} p7g 5m^{4} p5.1g* p6g p6g Dec 19] modest handicapper: left Karen George after reappearance: won at Wolverhampton in April: stays easy 7f: acts on polytrack and good to firm ground, promise on soft: blinkered twice, including for win. *J. W. Unett*

VILNIUS 2 b.f. (Apr 19) Imperial Dancer 123 – Aces Dancing (GER) 75 (Big Shuffle **61**
(USA) 122) [2009 5.1g^{4} 5m* 5f^{2} 5g^{2} 5m^{3} 5s^{5} 5g^{6} 5.3m^{2} p5m^{4} 5g^{4} 5m p5g^{5} 5m 5g^{3} p5.1g^{2} 5.1s* p5.1g* p5m p7g Dec 31] leggy filly: second foal: dam, 2-y-o 5f winner, sister to smart sprinter Auenklang: modest performer: won seller at Catterick in April and nurseries at Nottingham and Wolverhampton in November: raced mainly at 5f, should stay further: acts on polytrack, firm and soft going. *M. R. Channon*

VIMIERO (USA) 2 b. or br.c. (Feb 26) Dynaformer (USA) – Merrymaker (ARG) **84 p**
(Rainbow Corner 124) [2009 7m^{4} 7g^{3} Oct 10] $155,000Y: good sort: half-brother to several winners, including very smart US Grade 2 9f winner Magnum and Argentinian Grade 1 5f winner Medal of Honor (both by El Compinche): dam unraced: promising in maiden at Newbury (fourth to Critical Moment) and minor event at Ascot (still green, third to Corporal Maddox): will stay at least 1m: will do better. *W. R. Swinburn*

VINCES 5 b.g. Lomitas 129 – Vadinaxa (FR) (Linamix (FR) 127) [2009 74: p13g^{6} p13g **74**
p10g* p10g^{6} p10g* 9.9m^{5} 9.7m^{3} 10g^{4} 10g^{5} 10s 10m^{5} 12s^{2} p10g^{2} p10g p12m Dec 16] leggy gelding: fair handicapper: won at Lingfield in March and April: stays 13.3f: acts on polytrack, soft and good to firm going. *T. D. McCarthy*

VIN DE ROSE 3 b.g. Tipsy Creek (USA) 115 – Rosewings 66 (In The Wings 128) **–**
[2009 –: 8g p8.6g 10.1g 11.5m 10.1g p8.6g 7m Sep 21] little form. *John A. Harris*

VINTAGE (IRE) 5 b.g. Danetime (IRE) 121 – Katherine Gorge (USA) (Hansel (USA)) **86**
[2009 87: p6g^{4} p6f Dec 21] lengthy gelding: fairly useful handicapper: probably best at 6f: acts on polytrack, lightly raced on turf: tried tongue tied. *J. Akehurst*

VIOLA ROSA (IRE) 4 b.f. Fraam 114 – Bleu Cerise (Sadler's Wells (USA) 132) **–**
[2009 –: 10.1d 10.3m 7s Aug 1] maiden, little form since 2 yrs. *J. G. Given*

VIOLENT VELOCITY (IRE) 6 b.g. Namid 128 – Lear's Crown (USA) 82 (Lear **83**
Fan (USA) 130) [2009 88: 7m 8f 8m 7g* 7g^{5} 7.6m^{3} 7.5g^{3} 7d^{2} 7m* 7m* 7d 7d^{2} 7.1m 7v Nov 3] neat gelding: fairly useful handicapper: won at Newmarket (apprentices) in June and Newcastle and Epsom in August: best at 7f/1m: acts on polytrack and any turf going: tried visored: held up. *J. J. Quinn*

VIPER 7 b.g. Polar Prince (IRE) 117 – Maradata (IRE) 68 (Shardari 134) [2009 98: **94**
16.4m 18m p16g^{2} p16m^{5} Dec 10] big gelding: fairly useful performer: creditable effort in 2009 only when second in handicap at Kempton: stays 2m: acts on polytrack: bled in Cesarewitch second outing. *R. Hollinshead*

VIRGINIA HALL 2 b.f. (Mar 6) Medicean 128 – Odette 72 (Pursuit of Love 124) **103**
[2009 5d p5g^{2} 5m* 5.1m^{2} f6m* 6d^{2} 7g^{2} 8m^{6} Sep 11] good-topped filly: seventh foal: half-sister to several winners, including 5f (at 2 yrs) to 7f (Nell Gwyn Stakes) winner Silca's Gift (by Cadeaux Genereux) and 2005 2-y-o 6f winner Violette (by Observatory): dam, 5f/5.7f winner, half-sister to useful 6f/7f performer Caballero: useful performer: won maiden at Windsor in June and minor event at Southwell in July: plenty of improvement when ¾-length second to Chantilly Creme in listed race at La Teste and ½-length second to Joanna in Prix du Calvados at Deauville: stays 7f (only sixth of 7 in 1m May Hill Stakes at Doncaster): has won on fibresand, best efforts on turf (acts on good to firm and good to soft going). *Sir Mark Prescott*

VIRTUAL 4 b.c. Pivotal 124 – Virtuous 92 (Exit To Nowhere (USA) 122) [2009 118: 8.1g^3 8d* 10m^6 8m^3 8g^3 10m Oct 17] **122**

While one leading stud sponsored the race for twenty-five years, another became noted in that same period for harvesting some of the substantial prize money on offer. At Newbury in May, Virtual became the seventh winner of the Juddmonte Lockinge Stakes to carry the colours of either the Cheveley Park Stud or its owners David and Patricia Thompson, Scottish Reel having set the ball rolling in 1986, two years after Juddmonte began its sponsorship, a sponsorship which came to an end after the latest edition. Scottish Reel was followed by Safawan (1990), Polar Falcon (1991), Medicean (2001), Russian Rhythm (2004) and Peeress (2006).

Sir Michael Stoute has been the trainer most often associated with Cheveley Park's Lockinge winners, but the latest winner Virtual was trained by John Gosden, who won the race in 1994 with another four-year-old colt, the Sheikh Mohammed-owned Emperor Jones. Virtual, brought along steadily by Gosden, opened his account in a three-year-old maiden at Newmarket and won three more races that year, including listed events at Maisons-Laffitte and Newmarket. Virtual looked a pattern winner in the making, and an encouraging reappearance at four, when third to Paco Boy in the Sandown Mile, only served to reinforce that impression. Virtual and Paco Boy met again in the Lockinge, the latter 11/8 favourite in an eleven-runner field with Virtual next in the betting at 6/1. Paco Boy wasn't at his best on the day and the latest Lockinge turned out to be an ordinary renewal. That said, it still took a very smart and game performance from Virtual to come out on top on his first start in a Group 1. Never far away in a steadily-run contest, Virtual found plenty under pressure and got up on the line to beat Alexandros a nose with Twice Over half a length back in third. The runner-up seemed an unlucky loser, his rider having his whip accidentally knocked out of his hand a furlong from home by Twice Over's jockey. Virtual didn't repeat his Lockinge form in four subsequent starts, though he twice finished third in Group 1s, to Goldikova in the Prix Jacques le Marois at Deauville and to Aqlaam in the Prix du Moulin de Longchamp. His two other runs came at a mile and a quarter, a distance Virtual, whose win at Maisons-Laffitte had come at nine furlongs, should have stayed. As in the Jacques le Marois, however, the ground was on the firm side when Virtual tackled the longer trip in the Prince of Wales's Stakes at Royal Ascot and the Champion Stakes at Newmarket. Virtual put up his best performances on good and good to soft going.

Juddmonte Lockinge Stakes, Newbury—Virtual (star on forehead) gets up to snatch the prize from Alexandros (second right) in the last renewal after twenty-five years of sponsorship by Juddmonte; Twice Over (right) is close up, while Paco Boy fades into fourth

Cheveley Park Stud's "Virtual"

Virtual (b.c. 2005)	Pivotal (ch 1993)	Polar Falcon (b or br 1987)	Nureyev
			Marie d'Argonne
		Fearless Revival (ch 1987)	Cozzene
			Stufida
	Virtuous (b 1995)	Exit To Nowhere (b 1988)	Irish River
			Coup de Folie
		Exclusive Virtue (b 1988)	Shadeed
			Exclusive Order

Virtual is the sixth foal of Virtuous. All five to have reached the racecourse are winners and include Virtual's full sister Virtuosity, a fairly useful mile and a quarter winner, and Virtual's close relative the ill-fated Coventry Stakes winner Iceman (by Polar Falcon). Virtuous' eighth foal, also by Pivotal and named Judicious, is in training with Stoute. Virtuous, a winner at a mile at two, stayed eleven and a half furlongs, finishing third in the Lingfield Oaks Trial on her final start; Virtual's grandam Exclusive Virtue was a seven-furlong winner at two who stayed a mile and a half. Exclusive Virtue is a half-sister to the Two Thousand Guineas winner Entrepreneur, to the Coronation Stakes winner Exclusive (dam of dual Celebration Mile winner Chic and Celebration Mile and Matron Stakes winner Echelon) and to the smart middle-distance performers Dance A Dream (the grandam of Pipedreamer) and Sadler's Image. Virtual's great grandam Exclusive Order won the Prix Maurice de Gheest. As well as Pipedreamer, another good winner from this family in the latest season, though not one in Cheveley Park ownership, is the E.P. Taylor Stakes winner Lahaleeb. Virtual, a big, good-topped colt, had a quick, unimpressive action. He has been retired and will join his sire Pivotal, Dutch Art, Kyllachy and Medicean at the Cheveley Park Stud, his fee for 2010 set at £5,000, 1st October free return. *J. H. M. Gosden*

VERTIGO ON COURSE (IRE) 4 b.f. Anabaa (USA) 130 – Due South 104 (Darshaan 133) [2009 63: 7m* p8.6m³ 9d³ Oct 28] lengthy filly: fair handicapper: improved when winning at Yarmouth in September: probably best at 7f/1m: acts on polytrack, heavy and good to firm ground. *R. A. Fahey* **69**

VERTUEUX (FR) 4 gr.g. Verglas (IRE) 118 – Shahrazad (FR) (Bering 136) [2009 15g p16.5g 16g Oct 28] ex-French gelding: trained by N. Clement in 2008, winning maiden at Lisieux (also second in claimer at Longchamp final start): well beaten in handicaps in Britain in 2009: stays 15f: tried tongue tied/in cheekpieces. *A. W. Carroll* **–**

VERY DISTINGUISHED 3 b.f. Diktat 126 – Dignify (IRE) 105 (Rainbow Quest (USA) 134) [2009 70: 8.3m 9.7g 11.5m 9.9g 11.5d p8m⁶ p9.5g p8m³ p12g² p12f p9.5g Dec 28] good-topped filly: modest maiden: left M. Quinlan after fifth start: stays 1½m: acts on polytrack, good to firm and good to soft going. *S. Kirk* **61**

VERY GOOD DAY (FR) 2 b.c. (Apr 18) Sinndar (IRE) 134 – Picture Princess (Sadler's Wells (USA) 132) [2009 8.1g² Aug 13] 13,000Y: strong colt: fifth foal: half-brother to 1m winner Perfect Blend and winner in Italy (both by Linamix): dam, ran once in France, half-sister to Oaks third Pictavia (by Sinndar) out of smart half-sister to very smart mare up to 1½m Hatoof: 14/1 and backward, promising 4½ lengths second to Waseet in maiden at Sandown, getting hang of things late: will stay 1½m: sure to improve. *M. R. Channon* **80 p**

VERY WELL RED 6 b.m. First Trump 118 – Little Scarlett 54 (Mazilier (USA) 107) [2009 78, a63: f8s p8g³ p8g⁵ f8g² f8g f8d* p8g* f8g⁴ 8g 8.5g 8m* 8.3m⁴ 8m⁶ 8.3s² 8m³ 8.3m 8s 8.3m⁶ 8.1m p8m f8f Dec 17] compact mare: fair performer on turf, modest on all-weather: won claimer at Southwell and apprentice handicap at Lingfield in March, and handicap at Bath in June: stays 8.5f: acts on all-weather, firm and soft going: tried blinkered: front runner/races prominently. *P. W. Hiatt* **78 a63**

VESTED INTEREST 2 ch.g. (Apr 28) Footstepsinthesand 120 – Ingozi 91 (Warning 136) [2009 f5g 6g* Jul 2] 5,000Y: half-brother to several winners, including smart 6f (at 2 yrs) to 1½m winner Tissifer (by Polish Precedent) and Irish 3-y-o Miss Keller: dam, 7f/1m winner, half-sister to smart 7f/1m performer Inchinor: gelded and well backed, won seller at Yarmouth (sold 17,500 gns) by 10 lengths from Steeley Flyer, still green yet able to make all: likely to stay beyond 6f: open to further improvement. *George Baker* **84 p**

VHUJON (IRE) 4 b.g. Mujadil (USA) 119 – Livius Lady (IRE) (Titus Livius (FR) 115) [2009 94: p6g⁴ 6d⁴ 6m⁴ 6f 6m* 6g⁵ 6m² 6m² 6m 5d 6g⁴ 6m⁴ 6m 6g 6m 6m 7m⁵ 6g p6m p6f² p6m² Dec 30] neat gelding: useful handicapper: won at Salisbury in May: effective at 5f/6f: acts on polytrack, firm and good to soft going: tried visored: has worn tongue tie: held up: not straightforward. *P. D. Evans* **96**

VIA AURELIA (IRE) 2 b.f. (Mar 18) Antonius Pius (USA) 123§ – Goldthroat (IRE) 79 (Zafonic (USA) 130) [2009 6m⁴ 6m⁴ 6m Oct 26] €55,000Y: fourth foal: half-sister to 3-y-o Zafisio, 4-y-o Harald Bluetooth and 5-y-o New Beginning: dam, Irish 2-y-o 7f winner, out of half-sister to smart miler Killer Instinct: best effort in maidens when fourth to Marrayah at Yarmouth on debut: bred to stay 7f+. *J. R. Fanshawe* **52**

VIABLE 7 b.g. Vettori (IRE) 119 – Danseuse Davis (FR) (Glow (USA)) [2009 52§: 10.1g May 28] one-time fair handicapper: lightly raced on Flat in recent years (fairly useful hurdler), and well held sole start in 2009: barely stays 11.8f: acts on polytrack, good to firm and good to soft going: ungenuine. *Mrs P. Sly* **– §**

VIA GALILEI (IRE) 4 b.c. Galileo (IRE) 134 – Manger Square (IRE) (Danehill (USA) 126) [2009 106: 10g 10g 10g 14d⁵ 12g* 12s³ 10s⁵ 12d⁵ p10.7g 8.5g Oct 17] good-topped colt: smart performer: easily best effort when winning handicap at the Curragh in June by 4½ lengths from Drunken Sailor: stays 1½m: acts on soft going, probably on good to firm: tongue tied last 2 outings: not to be trusted: sold 60,000 gns, joined G. L. Moore. *J. S. Bolger, Ireland* **114 §**

VIA MIA 3 b.f. Namid 128 – Coming Home (Vettori (IRE) 119) [2009 74: 5m p6g⁶ p7g³ p8.6g² p10g³ p8.6g⁶ Dec 3] fair performer: left P. Cole 8,000 gns and off 6 months after third start: barely stays 1¼m: acts on polytrack and good to soft going. *George Baker* **74**

VICIOUS WARRIOR 10 b.g. Elmaamul (USA) 125 – Ling Lane (Slip Anchor 136) [2009 81: 10.4v 12m 9.8d³ Jun 17] big, strong gelding: handicapper, just fair nowadays: seems to stay 1½m: acts on polytrack, heavy and good to firm going: usually front runner. *R. M. Whitaker* **72**

VICTOIRE DE LYPHAR (IRE) 2 b.g. (Apr 27) Bertolini (USA) 125 – Victory Peak (Shirley Heights 130) [2009 6g⁶ 6m* 7m² 7m 7d² 7m⁶ Sep 17] €62,000F: compact gelding: sixth foal: closely related to winner in Spain by Perugino and half-brother to 3 winners, including 3-y-o Global City: dam lightly-raced daughter of Prix de Diane **87 §**

unraced out of half-sister to Zafonic: modest maiden: stays 6f: best efforts on fibresand and soft ground. *T. D. Easterby*

VENUTIUS 2 b.g. (May 13) Doyen (IRE) 132 – Boadicea's Chariot (Commanche Run 133) [2009 7d^3 8.1d^3 p8.6g^2 p8.6g* p8.6g^4 Oct 23] half-brother to useful 1999 2-y-o 7f winner Agrippina (by Timeless Times), dam of smart sprinter Cartimandua: dam Irish 1½m and hurdles winner: fair performer: won maiden at Wolverhampton in October: stays 8.6f. *E. S. McMahon* **79**

VERACITY 5 ch.h. Lomitas 129 – Vituisa (Bering 136) [2009 115: 14g^2 16m* 14s^3 20m Jun 18] lengthy, good-quartered horse: smart performer: won minor event at Nad Al Sheba in February by ½ length from Mourilyan: had earlier run well at same course when nose second to Friston Forest in handicap: respectable third to Ask in Yorkshire Cup at York: pulled up in Gold Cup at Royal Ascot (broke cannon bone and subsequently put down): stayed 2¼m: acted on polytrack, soft and good to firm going: raced prominently. *Saeed bin Suroor* **119**

VERDANT 2 b.c. (Mar 24) Singspiel (IRE) 133 – Orford Ness 107 (Selkirk (USA) 129) [2009 7m^2 p7g* Oct 9] closely related to very smart winner around 1¼m Weightless (by In The Wings) and half-brother to 3 winners, including 4-y-o Main Aim and smart 7f (at 2 yrs)/1m winner Home Affairs (by Dansili): dam French 1m winner, including at 2 yrs: easily better effort in maidens when winning at Lingfield readily by 1¼ lengths from Shamir, still green: should be suited by 1m+: useful prospect. *Sir Michael Stoute* **89 p**

VERINCO 3 b.g. Bahamian Bounty 116 – Dark Eyed Lady (IRE) 82 (Exhibitioner 111) [2009 74: 6d^3 6d^4 6m^3 6d^4 5g f6m^3 f7m Dec 15] compact gelding: fair maiden: stays 7f: acts on polytrack, heavy and good to firm going: tried blinkered, in cheekpieces nowadays: temperamental. *B. Smart* **71 §**

VERITY LANE (USA) 2 b.f. (Feb 13) Yes It's True (USA) 116 – Easy Pass (USA) (Easy Goer (USA)) [2009 p8.6g^3 p8g p8.6g^4 Nov 6] $65,000F, $60,000Y: fourth foal: half-sister to 3 winners in USA: dam, ran 3 times in USA, half-sister to very smart 6f/7f performer Gold Seam: fair maiden: stays 8.6f. *R. M. H. Cowell* **70**

VERONA LAD 2 gr.c. (Mar 23) Needwood Blade 117 – Silver Spell 54 (Aragon 118) [2009 7.1s^6 6s 7d 7g Sep 14] maiden: form only when sixth at Haydock: sold £2,200. *Jennie Candlish* **56**

VERONICAS BOY 3 br.c. Diktat 126 – Thamud (IRE) (Lahib (USA) 129) [2009 72: 10m^4 9.9m^4 8m^4 8v^4 9.3d^4 12g^4 14.1g Aug 14] leggy colt: handicapper, just modest at 3 yrs: best form up to 1m: acts on heavy and good to firm going: tried in cheekpieces: modest form in juvenile hurdles. *G. M. Moore* **61**

VERONICAS WAY 4 b.f. High Estate 127 – Mimining 83 (Tower Walk 130) [2009 46: p8g f8g p8.6g^5 Feb 13] good-bodied filly: poor performer: stays 8.6f: acts on polytrack and good to firm going: tried in cheekpieces/visor. *G. J. Smith* **–**

VEROON (IRE) 3 b.g. Noverre (USA) 125 – Waroonga (IRE) (Brief Truce (USA) 126) [2009 71: 8.3m^2 8m* 8.1g^4 10.2g^6 12g^6 10.3g^2 9.9g* 9.8m^4 p9.5g^2 10.3m* p10m^2 10.4g p10m^5 Nov 4] sturdy gelding: type to carry condition: fairly useful performer: won maiden at Ripon in June then handicaps at Beverley in August and Chester in September: stays 10.3f: acts on polytrack and good to firm going, probably on soft: tried blinkered, in cheekpieces later in 2009: often races prominently. *J. G. Given* **88**

VERSAKI (IRE) 3 gr.g. Verglas (IRE) 118 – Mythie (FR) (Octagonal (NZ) 126) [2009 99: a7g 6.5g p6g 7.1g 7.1g p7.1g 7m^3 7m^3 f8g^6 p7m^6 a9.5g a6.5g^2 Dec 24] leggy gelding: just fair at best in 2009: left D. Nicholls after fourth start and sold from Ian Williams 4,000 gns after tenth outing: possibly best up to 7f: acts on all-weather at Deauville and good to soft going: tried tongue tied/blinkered: inconsistent. *Mme G. Rarick, France* **67**

VERT CHAPEAU 2 ch.f. (Jan 20) Sakhee (USA) 136 – Green Bonnet (IRE) (Green Desert (USA) 127) [2009 p7g p6m Oct 12] 20,000Y: rather leggy filly: seventh foal: half-sister to several winners, including fairly useful 7f winners Edaara (by Pivotal) and Scientist (by Dr Fong): dam, French maiden, sister to useful 7f/1m performer Mauri Moon: better effort in maidens at Kempton when seventh to Muwakaba on debut. *E. F. Vaughan* **60**

VERTIGINEUX (FR) 5 b.h. Nombre Premier 114 – Very Gold (FR) (Goldneyev (USA) 114) [2009 114: 8g^3 8m^2 9m 8d* May 1] first foal: dam French maiden (stayed 1½m): very smart performer: successful in 2008 in Prix de la Porte Maillot at Longchamp, Prix Perth at Saint-Cloud and listed race at Deauville: improved again in 2009, placed at Nad Al Sheba in handicap (¾-length third behind Kachgai) and Zabeel Mile (¾-length second to Archipenko) and won Prix du Muguet at Saint-Cloud in May by ¾ length from Gris de Gris: stays 9f: acts on all-weather, soft and good to firm ground: has had tongue tied. *Mme C. Dufreche, France* **121**

VEGAS BABY (IRE) 3 ch.f. Kheleyf (USA) 116 – Gift of Spring (USA) (Gilded Time (USA)) [2009 83: p6g³ p6g⁵ p7g⁵ 5.7f⁴ 6g* 6g 6m⁶ Jun 8] lengthy, good-topped filly: fairly useful performer: below form after reappearance, though won claimer at Windsor in May: should stay 7f: acts on polytrack and firm going: blinkered last 4 starts. *J. A. Osborne* **81**

VEGAS PALACE (IRE) 2 ch.f. (Mar 30) Captain Rio 122 – Verify (IRE) (Polish Precedent (USA) 131) [2009 7d³ f7f² f7m* Nov 12] €6,500Y: sister to Italian 2008 2-y-o 5.5f winner Artilliana and half-sister to several winners, including 1¼m/1½m winner La Via Ferrata (by Mark of Esteem): dam Italian maiden: progressive in maidens, beating Brigadoon 5 lengths in 4-runner event at Southwell (made all): raced only at 7f. *Tom Dascombe* **79 +**

VEILED 3 b.f. Sadler's Wells (USA) 132 – Evasive Quality (FR) (Highest Honor (FR) 124) [2009 59p: f14m³ 14.1m* f16g³ 14.1m* 16m* p13.9g⁴ Sep 25] compact filly: fairly useful handicapper, better on turf: won at Yarmouth in August then Redcar and Yarmouth (by 9 lengths) within 4 days in September: stays 2m: acts on polytrack and good to firm going: sold 48,000 gns, joined J. Pearce. *Sir Mark Prescott* **93 a86**

VEILED APPLAUSE 6 b.g. Royal Applause 124 – Scarlet Veil 75 (Tyrnavos 129) [2009 94: f8g p13.9g⁶ 10.3g⁴ 8m⁶ 10.3g³ 9.8m⁶ 9.8d⁵ 8g⁶ 8m 8g⁵ 10.4g* 10m³ 10.3g⁴ Oct 24] good-topped gelding: fairly useful handicapper: won apprentice event at York in October: stays 10.4f: acts on polytrack, firm and soft going: tricky ride (tends to hang). *J. J. Quinn* **86**

VELLA 3 b.f. Mtoto 134 – Villella (Sadler's Wells (USA) 132) [2009 –: 10.2g⁶ 9.9f 12.1g p12g Jun 25] modest form only when sixth in maiden at Bath: bred to stay 1½m: tried blinkered. *H. J. L. Dunlop* **54**

VELLE EST VALERE 2 b.f. (Feb 19) Reset (AUS) 124 – Bond Solitaire 66 (Atraf 116) [2009 6s Nov 7] €1,600F: second foal: dam, maiden, half-sister to useful sprinter Cape Merino, herself dam of very smart sprinter Cape of Good Hope: 100/1 and very green, tailed off in maiden at Doncaster. *C. J. Teague* **–**

VELVET BAND 2 gr.f. (Feb 12) Verglas (IRE) 118 – Applaud (USA) 105 (Rahy (USA) 115) [2009 6g³ 5.1m² 5d⁶ 6f* 6g 5.5g 7m p6f⁴ Oct 14] sturdy filly: seventh foal: half-sister to several winners, including useful 1m (including at 2 yrs) to 1½m (in USA) winner Jazz Jam (by Pivotal): dam 2-y-o 5f/6f (Cherry Hinton Stakes) winner: fair performer: won maiden at Brighton in July: effective at 5f/6f: acts on polytrack and firm going: races up with pace: sold 8,000 gns, joined D. Carroll. *P. F. I. Cole* **73**

VELVET NAYEF 3 b.f. Nayef (USA) 129 – Laughing Girl (USA) 85 (Woodman (USA) 126) [2009 12g Jul 24] 800 2-y-o: third foal: half-sister to 2 winners abroad, including fairly useful French 1¼m to 1½m winner Vraona (by Fantastic Light): dam 1¼m winner: showed nothing in maiden at Newmarket. *J. Pearce* **–**

VENETIAN LADY 3 b.f. Tobougg (IRE) 125 – Perfect Partner (Be My Chief (USA) 122) [2009 60: 7.5m p7.1g⁵ 6m 6v 6d p7.1g Sep 25] sturdy filly: maiden: well held in 2009: tried blinkered/in cheekpieces. *Mrs A. Duffield* **–**

VENIR ROUGE 5 ch.g. Dancing Spree (USA) – Al Awaalah 52 (Mukaddamah (USA) 125) [2009 78: 10m⁵ 11m* 13.3g⁶ p12g⁵ f11g⁴ p12.2g⁶ Dec 26] big, lengthy gelding: fair handicapper: won at Newbury (apprentices) in June: stays 1½m: acts on polytrack, firm and good to soft going: tried blinkered: held up. *Matthew Salaman* **77**

VENI VEDI VECI (IRE) 2 b.f. (May 4) Antonius Pius (USA) 123§ – Consultant Stylist (IRE) (Desert Style (IRE) 121) [2009 p8g 8g Oct 8] €42,000Y, £20,000 2-y-o: good-topped filly: second foal: dam unraced: much better effort in maidens when mid-field at Newbury latter start. *A. M. Balding* **60**

VENTURA COVE (IRE) 2 ch.g. (Feb 11) Bahamian Bounty 116 – Baby Bunting 63 (Wolfhound (USA) 126) [2009 5m² 5m² 5g⁵ May 23] €30,000F, £80,000Y: lengthy, well-made gelding: fifth foal: brother to 3-y-o Bahamian Babe and 4-y-o Victorian Bounty: dam, sprint maiden, half-sister to smart sprinter Atraf: similar form in maiden/minor events (gelded after): likely to be best at 5f/6f. *R. A. Fahey* **76**

VENTURE CAPITALIST 3 b.c. Diktat 126 – Ventura Highway (Machiavellian (USA) 123) [2009 66p: 8.3d 10g² 11.5s 10m² 11.5d 11.9f³ p12.2g p8.6g Dec 28] well-made colt: fair maiden: only marginal improvement in handicaps in 2009 before leaving L. Cumani 11,000 gns after sixth start: probably stays 1½m: acts on polytrack and firm going, possibly not on softer than good. *B. Ellison* **69**

VENTURE GIRL (IRE) 2 ch.f. (Feb 16) Footstepsinthesand 120 – Bold Assumption (Observatory (USA) 131) [2009 6d⁶ 6m⁶ 6s⁵ f5g⁴ 6m Sep 21] €33,000Y: first foal: dam **55**

H.H. Aga Khan's "Varenar"

fact that Visor was by Mr Prospector was clearly a factor when Jean-Luc Lagardere bought her for 65,000 dollars at the end of her racing days. Much of the Lagardere stock had North American origins and Mr Prospector also figures in the pedigrees of the dams of Siyouni, Rosanara and Manighar, the three other pattern winners among the Aga Khan's successes at the Arc meeting which owed their origins to the Lagardere breeding operation (two-year-olds Siyouni and Rosanara are among the first crop from the Lagardere mares to be bred by the Aga Khan). Visor was well related, being out of a half-sister to the 1984 Kentucky Derby and Belmont Stakes winner Swale. Varenar's grandam Look was another minor winner in the States, out of Grade 3 winner Tuerta, a half-sister to the dam of the champion North American two-year-old and Kentucky Derby runner-up Forty Niner (also by Mr Prospector) and a full sister to the grandam of Two Thousand Guineas winner Shadeed. Varenar's career so far has offered few clues about his going requirements; his two-year-old win came on soft ground but he has raced only on good going otherwise. *A. de Royer Dupre, France*

VAULTAGE (USA) 2 ch.f. (Mar 8) El Corredor (USA) 123 – Ten Carats (USA) (Capote (USA)) [2009 7g p7g^2 Nov 18] €65,000F, 130,000Y: tall, unfurnished filly: third foal: half-sister to winners in USA by Siphon and Medaglia d'Oro: dam, US 6f (including at 2 yrs)/7f winner, half-sister to useful performer up to 1¼m Coqueteria: much better effort in maidens when 2½ lengths second to Hypnotized at Kempton: will improve again. *E. A. L. Dunlop* **74 p**

VIRTUALITY (USA) 4 b. or br.f. Elusive Quality (USA) – Hold To Ransom (USA) 111 (Red Ransom (USA)) [2009 60: 6m5 6g f6g 7m Jul 29] lengthy filly: modest maiden: stays 6f: acts on good to firm and good to soft going. *B. Smart* **60**

VISCAYA (IRE) 4 b.f. Xaar 132 – Fearfully Grand (Grand Lodge (USA) 125) [2009 55: p8.6g Jan 19] rather leggy filly: maiden: well held sole start in 2009: stays 1m: tried in cheekpieces. *N. J. Vaughan* **–**

VISCOUNT NELSON (USA) 2 b.c. (Feb 6) Giant's Causeway (USA) 132 – Imagine (IRE) 119 (Sadler's Wells (USA) 132) [2009 7s3 8d* 7.5s* 7m2 8f Nov 7] good-bodied colt: fourth foal: half-brother to very smart 2005 2-y-o 7f (including Prix Jean-Luc Lagardere) winner Horatio Nelson (by Danehill), 2007 2-y-o 6f/7f (Rockfel Stakes) winner Kitty Matcham (useful, by Rock of Gibraltar) and 5-y-o Red Rock Canyon: dam, won Irish 1000 Guineas and Oaks, half-sister to Generous: smart performer: won maiden at Leopardstown in July and listed event at Tipperary (beat Bobbyscot ½ length, pair well clear) in August: further marked improvement when ¾-length second to Poet's Voice in Champagne Stakes at Doncaster: slowly away and never threatened in Breeders' Cup Juvenile Turf at Santa Anita: likely to prove best at 1m+: acts on soft and good to firm going. *A. P. O'Brien, Ireland* **111**

VISCOUNT ROSSINI 7 b. or br.g. Rossini (USA) 118 – Spain 62 (Polar Falcon (USA) 126) [2009 55: p13.3g5 Jan 15] modest maiden: below form sole outing in 2009: stays 1¾m: acts on all-weather, good to soft and good to firm ground: tried in headgear: fair hurdler. *S. Gollings* **45**

VISION D'ETAT (FR) 4 b.c. Chichicastenango (FR) 119 – Uberaba (FR) (Garde Royale 120) [2009 126: 10g3 10.5g* 10m* 12g2 12g 10g* Dec 13] **127**

Flat racing produces only a small number of rags to riches stories nowadays, at least outside the sprinting or two-year-old divisions, but Vision d'Etat, reportedly seen more as a prospective jumper when bought for €39,000 as a yearling, took his career earnings to over £2.2m in the latest season. He added three more Group 1s to the Prix du Jockey Club he won as a three-year-old and remains in training as a five-year-old, with the Dubai World Cup reportedly first on the agenda. Vision d'Etat's successes were great reward for his co-owners Jacques Detre (whose colours had previously been seen far more frequently at Auteuil) and trainer Eric Libaud, who must have found offers for the horse hard to resist. To their credit, they also resisted the obvious temptation to send Vision d'Etat to stud at the end of his three-year-old campaign. In addition to his three victories at four, Vision d'Etat also suffered three defeats, having been beaten just once in the two previous seasons. Vision d'Etat can race lazily at times but he finds plenty under pressure and his record overall of nine wins from thirteen starts is very hard to fault, the only performance that might be described as disappointing being his run in the latest Arc.

Prix Ganay Grand Prix Air Mauritius, Longchamp—Vision d'Etat pricks his ears as he approaches the line ahead of Loup Breton (No.3), Adlerflug (blaze) and Thewayyouare (rail)

Nearly half of the prize money won by Vision d'Etat came from the victory in the Cathay Pacific Hong Kong Cup at Sha Tin in December on his final start. He was only allowed to take his chance after passing the vet on the morning of the race, having picked up what could have proved a very costly knock on a hind leg in his box the day before. Vision d'Etat was faced in the Cup by a pair who had won Group 1 races at the track in the spring, Collection, winner of the Hong Kong Derby, and the British-trained Presvis, successful in the Queen Elizabeth II Cup. Like Presvis, locally-trained Collection had once been trained at Newmarket, winning the listed Hampton Court Stakes at Royal Ascot in 2008 when with William Haggas. Collection was sent off at odds on, with Presvis second best and Vision d'Etat, who hadn't raced in Hong Kong previously, only third choice. There was, in truth, little between the trio on form but Vision d'Etat produced the most telling turn of foot on the day to win by three quarters of a length from Collection, with Presvis two and a half lengths away in third. Presvis was probably a bit below his best but Vision d'Etat, up against a high-class rival on his home patch, probably ran as well as he had in any other race in his career, his performance auguring well for 2010.

Much earlier in the year, Vision d'Etat had landed two of Europe's most significant mile and a quarter prizes for older horses, the Prix Ganay at Longchamp in April and the Prince of Wales's Stakes at Royal Ascot. The Prix Ganay Grand Prix Air Mauritius, the first European Group 1 of the year, provided a fairly straightforward opportunity, the Prince of Wales's Stakes a rather more demanding one. Vision d'Etat's main opponents in the Ganay were The Bogberry and Loup Breton, the trio having been involved in a bunched finish for the placings behind Trincot in the Prix d'Harcourt at Longchamp earlier in the month. Vision d'Etat finished third in the Harcourt on his reappearance after racing rather too freely and he was better off at the weights with the other pair in the Ganay. Vision d'Etat settled better, despite a steady pace, and he didn't need to be at his best to get home by three quarters of a length in the Ganay from Loup Breton.

Between the Ganay and Royal Ascot, Vision d'Etat had a change of jockey. Ioritz Mendizabal, who had ridden him at Longchamp and in all his races at three, lost his job with trainer Libaud after the inappropriately named Feels All Right virtually bolted with him in the Prix du Jockey Club, eventually finishing last. Olivier Peslier was engaged for Vision d'Etat at Royal Ascot and kept the ride for the rest of the season. The Prince of Wales's Stakes attracted nothing of the calibre of Manduro and Duke of Marmalade, the winners in the two previous years. The 2008 Derby runner-up Tartan Bearer started favourite after winning the Gordon Richards Stakes on his reappearance, with another French raider Never On Sunday, winner of the Prix d'Ispahan since finishing fifth in the Harcourt, narrowly preferred to Vision d'Etat as second favourite. The Champion Stakes runner-up

Prince of Wales's Stakes, Royal Ascot—in a bunched finish, Vision d'Etat holds on gamely from Tartan Bearer (blaze), Never On Sunday (grey) and Twice Over

Cathay Pacific Hong Kong Cup, Sha Tin—the three high-class performers come to the fore, as Vision d'Etat is followed home by Collection and Presvis (stars); Ashalanda (rail) finishes fourth

Twice Over and the Lockinge winner Virtual were others with claims, the field completed by the Harcourt winner Trincot (now with Godolphin), the Earl of Sefton winner Tazeez, and the German-trained Premio Roma winner Estejo. Rather like the Ganay, the Prince of Wales's was not truly run and less than a length covered the first four home, neither Vision d'Etat nor Tartan Bearer well served by the run of the race but still taking the first two placings, Peslier seen at his strongest in getting the game Vision d'Etat home by half a length, with Never On Sunday and Twice Over close behind the first two.

As in 2008, Vision d'Etat was given a break after June and wasn't seen out again until the Arc trials meeting at Longchamp in early-September. As a three-year-old Vision d'Etat won the Prix Niel but, in the latest Prix Foy, he had to settle for second of four behind front-running Spanish Moon. Vision d'Etat still shaped fairly well, so it was disappointing that he couldn't at least match his Arc fifth of the previous year, tenth being all he could manage behind Sea The Stars on his second appearance in the race. Vision d'Etat had been reported to be a little stiff after the Prix Foy and perhaps, in hindsight, he hadn't enjoyed the ideal preparation for the Arc.

Vision d'Etat (FR) (b.c. 2005)	Chichicastenango (FR) (gr 1998)	Smadoun (gr 1990)	Kaldoun
			Mossma
		Smala (ch 1993)	Antheus
			Small Partie
	Uberaba (FR) (b 1986)	Garde Royale (br 1980)	Mill Reef
			Royal Way
		Ile d'Amour (b 1974)	Montevideo
			Old England

The good-topped Vision d'Etat has a jumping background which was fully detailed in *Racehorses of 2008*. He is by some way the best horse sired so far by the Prix du Jockey Club runner-up Chichicastenango, who is now based in Japan. His second best runner is the Group 3 winner Chichi Creasy, who, like Vision d'Etat, is out of a mare by Garde Royale. Chichi Creasy now stands at the Haras du Grandcamp, from where Vision d'Etat was consigned as a yearling. Vision d'Etat's veteran dam Uberaba has had two foals subsequently by Chichicastenango. The filly Nataba, a year younger than Vision d'Etat, has yet to race; the colt Affaire d'Etat will be a two-year-old in 2010. Vision d'Etat wasn't the only winner from his family in Britain in 2009, though the Wincanton hurdling success of Painter Man, out of a half-sister to Vision d'Etat, hardly has much bearing on Vision d'Etat's prospects, either on the track or, eventually, at stud. Vision d'Etat is effective at a mile and a quarter and a mile and a half. He acts on soft and good to firm going. He has worn a tongue strap since the beginning of his career, though connections forgot to declare one for the Prince of Wales's Stakes. *E. Libaud, France*

VISIONS OF JOHANNA (USA) 4 b.g. Johannesburg (USA) 127 – Belle Turquoise (FR) (Tel Quel (FR) 125) [2009 88: $8.1v^5$ $11.1m^2$ $10.4s^2$ 9s 8m 7d Aug 28] attractive gelding: fairly useful performer: stays 11f: acts on polytrack, heavy and good to firm going: tried in cheekpieces: suspect temperament. *R. A. Fahey* **82**

VISITE ROYALE (USA) 3 b.f. Danehill Dancer (IRE) 117 – Fantasy Royale (USA) 96 (Pleasant Colony (USA)) [2009 73p: $7g^2$ $8m^4$ $10g^2$ 9.3d* Jul 26] angular filly: fairly useful form: landed odds in maiden at Carlisle in July: stays 1¼m: acts on good to soft going: sold 30,000 gns in November. *Sir Michael Stoute* **81**

VISTERRE (IRE) 3 ch.f. Noverre (USA) 125 – Twiggy's Sister (IRE) 100 (Flying Spur (AUS)) [2009 84: 5g 6g Jun 19] lengthy filly: fairly useful performer at 2 yrs: well below form both starts in 2009: best at 5f: acts on soft and good to firm going: placed over hurdles for N. Bertran de Balanda in France in autumn. *B. Smart* –

VITA MIA 3 b.f. Central Park (IRE) 123 – Ma Vie 69 (Salse (USA) 128) [2009 –: 9.7d 9m^4 f11g 8.1g 8.5g^4 10.1g^5 11.8m* 14.1s^6 10f^2 12m* 10.3g* 11.6m^6 13.1d^4 10.3m 13.4m^3 10m^3 p10g^5 Oct 14] good-bodied filly: fair handicapper: won at Leicester in June, Folkestone in July and Chester in August: best at 1¼m/1½m: acts on firm and soft ground. *P. D. Evans* **70**

VITORIA (IRE) 3 b.f. Exceed And Excel (AUS) 126 – Karayb (IRE) 93 (Last Tycoon 131) [2009 99: 10m 8m 7g^2 8m^6 7m^2 6g* 6m^3 6m^2 Oct 16] strong, deep-girthed filly: useful performer: won handicap at Hamilton in September: improved again when head second to Damaniyat Girl in listed race at Newmarket final start: has won at 7f, best form at 6f: raced only on polytrack and good/good to firm going. *B. Smart* **108**

VITO VOLTERRA (IRE) 2 b.c. (Mar 20) Antonius Pius (USA) 123§ – River Abouali (Bluebird (USA) 125) [2009 6m p7g^6 7g* 7d* p7.1g^3 p6g* Dec 7] 23,000F, €35,000Y: angular colt: closely related to 3 winners, including fairly useful 2002 2-y-o 5f winner Maugwenna (by Danehill) and 6f winner Trouble Maker (by Green Desert), and half-brother to winner in Greece by Diktat: dam unraced half-sister to dam of 2-y-o Beethoven: fair performer: won claimers at Redcar (claimed from J. R. Best £8,000) and Yarmouth in October and seller at Lingfield in December: effective at 6f/7f: acts on polytrack and good to soft going: makes running. *A. B. Haynes* **72**

VITTACHI 2 b.g. (Feb 10) Bertolini (USA) 125 – Miss Lorilaw (FR) 104 (Homme de Loi (IRE) 120) [2009 7d 7m^5 7.5m^6 8g^5 f8f p8.6g^4 Dec 17] plain gelding: poor maiden: likely to stay 1¼m: acts on polytrack: tried in cheekpieces/blinkers. *J. D. Bethell* **49**

VITZNAU (IRE) 5 b.h. Val Royal (FR) 127 – Neat Dish (CAN) 90 (Stalwart (USA)) [2009 109: p7.1g^2 6m^4 7.1g 8.5g^5 7g 7m^6 8g p8g^5 7m^4 7m 8s^5 Oct 12] tall, useful-looking horse: useful performer: creditable efforts in 2009 only when second in listed race at Wolverhampton (beaten head by Ceremonial Jade) and fifth in Diomed Stakes at Epsom (3 lengths behind Mac Love) first/fourth starts: has form at easy 8.5f, ideally suited by 7f: unraced on heavy ground, acts on any other turf and polytrack: consistent, but no easy ride (best produced late). *R. Hannon* **109**

VIVA AVERTI 4 b.g. Averti (IRE) 117 – Julia Domna (Dominion 123) [2009 6m 6m Jun 29] lengthy gelding: well held in maiden on debut (for Christian Wroe): broke down fatally in similar event following month. *R. M. Beckett* –

VIVACHI (IRE) 3 b.f. Red Ransom (USA) – Charita (IRE) 103 (Lycius (USA) 124) [2009 p10g 9.9g^4 10m^2 10s* p11g^6 10d^6 Oct 12] €125,000F: useful-looking filly: fifth foal: half-sister to smart Irish 6f to 1m winner Cheyenne Star (by Mujahid) and 11f/2m winner Herne Bay (by Hernando): dam Irish 7f (at 2 yrs)/1m winner: fair handicapper: won 4-runner event at Leicester in August: stays 1¼m: acts on polytrack, soft and good to firm going: sold 22,000 gns. *R. M. Beckett* **78**

VIVA LA VIDA 3 ch.f. Medicean 128 – Moonlight (IRE) 69 (Night Shift (USA)) [2009 p7g 7m^6 7m^5 9.9g 8m 8s p8f Sep 10] 26,000 2-y-o: sturdy filly: sixth foal: half-sister to winners abroad by Xaar and Golan: dam, maiden who stayed 1¼m, half-sister to useful performer around 1m Lady Miletrian: fair maiden: regressive form, leaving Jane Chapple-Hyam 7,500 gns after fourth start: worth a try at 6f: acts on good to firm ground: tried visored. *J. Ryan* **70**

VIVA RONALDO (IRE) 3 b.g. Xaar 132 – Papaha (FR) 103 (Green Desert (USA) 127) [2009 97: p8g^5 7.6m^4 8.1v 8m 7s^6 7m Aug 29] lengthy, good-topped gelding: useful performer: best effort at 3 yrs when 3 lengths fourth to Fareer in handicap at Chester: stays 1m: acts on polytrack, soft and good to firm going: not straightforward. *R. A. Fahey* **97**

VIVA VETTORI 5 ch.h. Vettori (IRE) 119 – Cruinn A Bhord 107 (Inchinor 119) [2009 97: p8g^2 p10g^5 9m^2 8m 8f^3 Jun 24] big, leggy, lengthy horse: useful handicapper: best efforts in 2009 when runner-up: winner at 1¼m, but free-going front runner and may prove best around 7f/1m: acts on polytrack and firm going. *D. R. C. Elsworth* **95**

VIVA VOLTA 6 b.g. Superior Premium 122 – La Volta 86 (Komaite (USA)) [2009 69: 7.1m^2 7g^2 6d* Oct 13] strong, lengthy gelding: fairly useful handicapper: visored, won at Newcastle in October: best at 6f/7f: acts on polytrack, good to firm and good to soft going: often blinkered: often races prominently. *A. C. Whillans* **80**

VIVIANI (IRE) 2 ch.g. (Apr 24) Galileo (IRE) 134 – Bintalreef (USA) 99 (Diesis 133) [2009 7m 8g^6 9d 8d^5 Oct 22] fair maiden: form only at 1m: blinkered final start (gelded after). *Mrs A. J. Perrett* **68**

VOCABULARY 2 br.f. (Apr 25) Observatory (USA) 131 – Zathonia 68 (Zafonic (USA) 130) [2009 p7g Nov 11] second foal: dam, placed all 3 starts at 1m, sister to useful 1m/1¼m winner Zante and half-sister to smart French/US performer up to 11f Requete: 22/1, slowly away when behind in maiden at Kempton: likely to do better. *B. W. Hills* **– p**

VOCALISED (USA) 3 b.c. Vindication (USA) 122 – Serena's Tune (USA) (Mr Prospector (USA)) [2009 92p: 7s* 7s* 7v* 8m $6s^5$ $6s^5$ Sep 13] tall colt: smart performer: won listed race at the Curragh and Bathwick Tyres Greenham Stakes (by length from Cityscape) at Newbury, both in April, and Dylan Thomas EBF Tetrarch Stakes at the Curragh (landed odds readily by 1¾ lengths from Chief Lone Eagle) in May: below best after (off 3 months following fourth outing): stays 7f: acts on heavy going, possibly not on good to firm: usually tongue tied: sometimes carries head awkwardly. *J. S. Bolger, Ireland* **114**

VODKA (JPN) 5 b.m. Tanino Gimlet (JPN) 118 – Tanino Sister (JPN) (Rousillon (USA) 133) [2009 121: $9m^5$ 8.9g 8f* 8f* $9f^2$ $10f^3$ 12f* Nov 29] high-class performer: became first filly since 1943 to win Tokyo Yushun (Japanese Derby) at Tokyo in 2007: successful 5 times on same course since, including Victoria Mile (beat Bravo Daisy by 7 lengths) in May, Yasuda Kinen (for second year in a row, by ¾ length from Deep Sky) in June and Japan Cup (seventh Group 1 win, held on by a nose from Oken Bruce Lee after going 2½ lengths clear inside final 1f, suffering nosebleed in process) in November (subsequently named Horse of The Year in Japan for second successive year): ran twice at Nad Al Sheba in March, meeting trouble when fifth to Balius in Jebel Hatta but only seventh to Gladiatorus in Duty Free: placed behind Company at Tokyo in Group 2 Mainichi Okan (length second) and Tenno Sho (Autumn) (2 lengths third, not enjoying clearest of runs): effective at 1m to 1½m: acts on firm going (yet to race on softer than good). *K. Sumii, Japan* **125**

VODKA SHOT (USA) 3 b. or br.f. Holy Bull (USA) 134 – Absoluta (IRE) 90 (Royal Academy (USA) 130) [2009 53: p8.6g p8.6g Jan 26] maiden: little form at 3 yrs: weak finisher. *M. L. W. Bell* **–**

VOGARTH 5 ch.g. Arkadian Hero (USA) 123 – Skara Brae 49 (Inchinor 119) [2009 68: f7s* $p8g^4$ $f8g^2$ $7g^6$ p7.1g Dec 19] medium-sized gelding: fair performer: won seller at Southwell (left B. R. Millman 3,000 gns) in January: stays 1m: acts on all-weather and heavy ground: visored/blinkered at 5 yrs. *M. C. Chapman* **68**

VOILA ICI (IRE) 4 gr.c. Daylami (IRE) 138 – Far Hope 95 (Barathea (IRE) 127) [2009 114: 12m* 12m* $12m^3$ 14g* 11g* $12m^3$ 10v* Nov 8] €60,000Y: second foal: dam, Italian 5f (at 2 yrs) to 7f winner, also runner-up at 1m: smart performer: successful 3 times at Milan in 2008, including in Premio Federico Tesio: in excellent form in 2009, winning minor event at Milan in April, Premio Carlo d'Alessio at Rome (beat Gimmy ¾ length) in May, Prix Maurice de Nieuil at Longchamp (stuck to task well, beat Winkle short head) in July, Premio Federico Tesio again at Milan (more easily than head margin suggests over Ashalanda) in September and Premio Roma At The Races (gamely beat Turati ½ length) in November: good third at Milan other 2 starts, behind Quijano in Gran Premio di Milano (beaten 1¼ lengths) and to Schiaparelli in Gran Premio del Jockey Club (beaten 2¼ lengths): effective at testing 1¼m, stays 1¾m: acts on heavy and good to firm ground: usually races in touch: reliable. *V. Caruso, Italy* **118**

VOLATILIS (IRE) 2 b.c. (Mar 22) Antonius Pius (USA) 123§ – Fire Flower (Sri Pekan (USA) 117) [2009 6d $6g^6$ $6m^5$ $6g^3$ $p7g^5$ 7d Sep 3] leggy colt: modest maiden: stays 7f: acts on polytrack and good to firm going. *J. W. Hills* **58**

VOLITO 3 ch.c. Bertolini (USA) 125 – Vax Rapide 80 (Sharpo 132) [2009 $p7g^3$ $p6g^4$ $p6g^5$ 5.1g $6f^4$ 6.1m* 6.1g 6m 6m Aug 8] half-brother to 3 winners, including 5-y-o Equuleus Pictor: dam 2-y-o 5f winner: fair handicapper: won at Nottingham in June: stays easy 7f: raced only on polytrack and good ground or firmer (acts on firm). *Jonjo O'Neill* **73**

VOLOCHKOVA (USA) 3 b.f. War Chant (USA) 126 – Ballerina Princess (USA) (Mr Prospector (USA)) [2009 73p: $8d^6$ p7g* 7d $7m^5$ p7.1g* $7g^4$ 8g Aug 8] fairly useful handicapper: improved to win at Lingfield in April and Wolverhampton in July: stays 7f: acts on polytrack: tongue tied last 3 starts: held up. *J. R. Fanshawe* **84**

VON JAWLENSKY (IRE) 3 b.c. Montjeu (IRE) 137 – Zivania (IRE) 101 (Shernazar 131) [2009 74p: 10s* $12s^2$ $14d^6$ 14.6m 12d* 12s Oct 11] good-topped colt: smart performer: won maiden at the Curragh in June and minor event at Listowel (by 3½ lengths from Eytarna) in September: not discredited in listed races at Roscommon (3½ lengths second to Alaivan) and Leopardstown (5 lengths last of 6 behind Profound Beauty) in between: probably stays 1¾m (acted as pacemaker when last in St Leger at 14.6f): acts on soft going: sold 125,000 gns, sent to Qatar. *A. P. O'Brien, Ireland* **111**

VOORTREKKER 3 b.g. Imperial Dancer 123 – Sweet Wilhelmina 87 (Indian Ridge 123) [2009 $8.3g^3$ $8f^2$ p8.6g* 10.2g 9.9m 8.3g Oct 19] fifth foal: half-brother to 2 winners, **74**

including fairly useful 6f (including at 2 yrs)/7f winner Sweet Pickle (by Piccolo): dam 7f (at 2 yrs)/1m winner: fair form: won maiden at Wolverhampton in June: below form after: stays 8.6f: acts on polytrack. *D. J. Coakley*

VUMBURA (IRE) 2 b.g. (May 24) Alhaarth (IRE) 126 – Mathaayl (USA) 79 (Shadeed (USA) 135) [2009 7g 7g Oct 30] down the field in maidens at Doncaster and Newmarket (gelded after): will stay 1m+. *W. J. Knight* –

W

WAABEL 2 b. or br.c. (Mar 9) Green Desert (USA) 127 – Najah (IRE) 110 (Nashwan (USA) 135) [2009 6g^{6} Jul 18] useful-looking colt: fourth foal: dam, 1¼m winner (including Premio Lydia Tesio), out of Irish 1000 Guineas winner Mehthaaf: 9/1, backward and green, 8½ lengths sixth to Mr David in maiden at Newmarket, hanging left: should stay at least 7f: sure to improve. *M. A. Jarvis* **61 p**

WAAHEJ 3 b.g. Haafhd 129 – Madam Ninette (Mark of Esteem (IRE) 137) [2009 73: 8m 8d^{5} 8m 8.3g^{3} p8f^{6} p9.5g* p10g^{2} f11f^{3} f8g p9.5g^{3} p9.5g^{6} Dec 14] angular gelding: fair handicapper: left J. Dunlop 2,000 gns after second start: won at Wolverhampton in September: stays 11f: acts on all-weather and good to soft ground. *P. W. Hiatt* **73**

WAARID 4 b.g. Alhaarth (IRE) 126 – Nibbs Point (IRE) 107 (Sure Blade (USA) 130) [2009 65§: f14g^{6} Jan 27] good-topped gelding: maiden: fit from hurdling (modest) and in cheekpieces, just modest form sole outing in 2009: stays 1½m: tried blinkered: temperamental. *G. L. Moore* **54 §**

WABBRAAN (USA) 4 b.g. Aldebaran (USA) 126 – Madame Modjeska (USA) (Danzig (USA)) [2009 65: f12g* p16g^{6} f12g* p16g^{2} 16s 12d 14.1g f12m^{5} p16.5g^{4} p13.9g^{6} Dec 17] rather leggy gelding: fair performer on all-weather, no form on turf in 2009: improved to win seller in February and handicap in March, both at Southwell: below form after: stays easy 16.5f: acts on all-weather: tried blinkered/visored. *M. Hill* **–** **a78 d**

WABI SABI (IRE) 3 b.f. Xaar 132 – Taroudannt (IRE) (Danehill (USA) 126) [2009 62: 7m 8d^{5} 8d 7m^{5} 10m^{5} Jun 18] leggy filly: modest maiden: stays 1m: acts on polytrack and soft going: tried in cheekpieces. *N. Tinkler* **52**

WACATO KING (IRE) 3 br.g. King Charlemagne (USA) 120 – Daralaka (IRE) (The Minstrel (CAN) 135) [2009 –: p7g p7.1g p8.6g Dec 14] angular gelding: little form: tried tongue tied. *R. A. Farrant* **–**

WADAAT 3 b.f. Diktat 126 – Shining Vale (USA) (Twilight Agenda (USA) 126) [2009 p8g^{3} p10g^{2} 8d* 11.5m 11m^{2} 12g 8.1m^{3} 12g Jul 18] 42,000Y: lengthy filly: fifth foal: half-sister to 3 winners abroad, including useful German performer up to 1m Mrs Snow (by Singspiel), 7.5f winner at 2 yrs, and French 1m winner Agent Almeida (by Dubai Destination): dam unraced half-sister to smart German 1m/1¼m performer Walzerkoenigin (dam of 3-y-o Wiener Walzer): useful performer: won maiden at Yarmouth in April: much better form after when nose second to Night of Magic in Oaks d'Italia at Milan and 2¼ lengths third to Strawberrydaiquiri in listed race at Sandown: stays 11f (well held at 1½m, in Oaks at Epsom on first occasion): unraced on extremes of going on turf. *C. E. Brittain* **102**

WADNAAN 2 ch.c. (Feb 16) Shamardal (USA) 129 – Australian Dreams (Magic Ring (IRE) 115) [2009 f8g^{3} Aug 27] 60,000F, 160,000Y: third foal: dam, German 8.5f to 1¼m winner, half-sister to smart 6f/7f winner Needwood Blade: 7/1 and green, 2¾ lengths third to Tanto Quanto in maiden at Southwell, running on under considerate handling: will stay 1¼m: sure to improve. *M. Johnston* **72 p**

WAFFLE (IRE) 3 ch.g. Kheleyf (USA) 116 – Saphire 93 (College Chapel 122) [2009 110: 5g^{5} 5g^{2} 6g 5d^{3} Oct 24] strong, attractive gelding: smart performer: easily best effort in 2009 when close third to Quest For Success in handicap at Doncaster: gelded after: best at 5f: acts on good to soft ground. *J. Noseda* **112**

WAHAN (USA) 3 b.g. Theatrical 128 – Abrade (USA) (Mr Prospector (USA)) [2009 –: f7g f8g p12g^{6} p12g^{2} f11g 10.1g p10g^{4} 9g 10m^{5} Jul 15] leggy gelding: modest maiden handicapper: stays 1½m: acts on polytrack: sometimes tongue tied: sold £2,000, joined Tim Vaughan, then gelded. *C. E. Brittain* **59**

WAHOO SAM (USA) 9 ch.g. Sandpit (BRZ) 129 – Good Reputation (USA) (Gran Zar (MEX)) [2009 72: p10g^{2} p8.6g p9.5g 8m* 8.3m May 9] lengthy, good-topped gelding: modest performer nowadays: won handicap at L'Ancresse (Guernsey) in May: stays 1¼m: acts on all-weather, firm and soft going: tried blinkered/in cheekpieces: usually front runner: none too consistent. *P. D. Evans* **63**

WAIT FOR THE LIGHT 5 b.g. Fantastic Light (USA) 134 – Lady In Waiting 113 (Kylian (USA)) [2009 79: p12g² p12g⁶ p16g⁵ 13.3m Aug 14] rangy gelding: fair handicapper: stays 2m: acts on polytrack and firm ground: tried in cheekpieces/blinkers. *Mrs S. Leech* **78**

WAJAHA (IRE) 3 ch.f. Haafhd 129 – Amanah (USA) 100 (Mr Prospector (USA)) [2009 88p: p8g* 7m 8m p8m Sep 24] useful-looking filly: fairly useful performer: won handicap at Kempton in April: well below form after: stayed 1m: acted on polytrack: visits Singspiel. *J. H. M. Gosden* **94**

WAJANAAT 2 b. or br.f. (May 8) Sakhee (USA) 136 – Tadris (USA) 106 (Red Ransom (USA)) [2009 p8f⁴ Sep 4] third foal: dam, 1m winner, half-sister to smart US performer up to 1½m Mustanfar, out of close relative to Unfuwain and half-sister to Nashwan and Nayef: 13/8 and green, encouraging 3¾ lengths fourth to Mr Mahoganeigh in maiden at Lingfield, closing late: will stay 1¼m+: will improve. *M. P. Tregoning* **66 p**

WAJIR (FR) 3 b.c. Danehill Dancer (IRE) 117 – War Game (FR) 107 (Caerleon (USA) 132) [2009 10.5s* 10.5g³ 11g* 10.5g 12g⁵ 15g* Sep 6] fourth foal: half-brother to French 1¼m winner Warden (by Halling) and 5-y-o War Party: dam, French 9f to 12.5f (Prix Maurice de Nieuil) winner, half-sister to top-class performer up to 2½m Westerner: very smart performer: progressed in 2009, winning listed race at Saint-Cloud in March, Prix Hocquart (by ½ length from Telluride) in May and Prix de Lutece at Longchamp (gave plenty of weight away all round, led 1½f out to beat Manighar a length) in September: fifth to Cavalryman in Grand Prix de Paris at Longchamp on penultimate start: stays 15f: acts on heavy ground: held up. *E. Lellouche, France* **120**

WAKE ME NOW (IRE) 3 b.f. Almutawakel 126 – Shiyra (Darshaan 133) [2009 71: 10.2d⁵ 10.2g* 8f 8.5f⁵ a8.5f a8.5f⁵ 8f⁶ Dec 31] fairly useful performer: won handicap at Nottingham in June: left R. Beckett, ran in allowance races/claimers after: stays 10.2f: blinkered final outing. *Gary L. Stevens, USA* **81**

WAKE UP CALL 3 b.f. Noverre (USA) 125 – Up And About 77 (Barathea (IRE) 127) [2009 8m² 7f² p6m* p6g³ Nov 25] 30,000Y: close-coupled filly: sixth foal: half-sister to 3 winners, including useful 1m (at 2 yrs)/9f (in UAE) winner Tamarillo (by Daylami) and 2007 2-y-o 9.5f winner Tiger Spice (by Royal Applause): dam, 15f winner, half-sister to dam of 4-y-o Overdose: fairly useful form: won maiden at Kempton in October: good third to Billberry in handicap at Lingfield next time: bred to stay beyond 1m, but not short of speed: raced only on polytrack and ground firmer than good: open to further improvement. *C. F. Wall* **81 p**

WALCOT SQUARE (IRE) 2 b.g. (Feb 7) Marju (IRE) 127 – Lyrical Dance (USA) (Lear Fan (USA) 130) [2009 7s⁶ 7m⁶ 7f² Sep 2] 70,000Y: sturdy gelding: half-brother to several winners, including 5-y-o Furnace: dam, US 8.5f winner, half-sister to 2000 Guineas winner Pennekamp and Irish 2000 Guineas winner Black Minnaloushe: best effort in maidens when ¾-length second to Kona Coast at Brighton, making running (gelded after): will stay 1m. *R. Charlton* **76**

WALDORF (IRE) 4 b.c. Sadler's Wells (USA) 132 – Durrah Green 79 (Green Desert (USA) 127) [2009 56: p8.6g⁴ p12.2g⁶ p8.6m* p8.6g² p10g p12.2g 8.1g⁵ p7.1g 12d⁴ Jul 9] modest handicapper: won apprentice event at Wolverhampton in February: stays 8.6f: acts on polytrack. *W. R. Muir* **63**

WALDVOGEL (IRE) 5 ch.g. Polish Precedent (USA) 131 – Wurftaube (GER) 119 (Acatenango (GER) 127) [2009 109: 12g⁶ 14g 14m 14.6m 12m⁶ p10m² p9.5g³ Dec 17] rather leggy, lengthy gelding: fifth foal: half-brother to 3 winners, including useful performer up to 1¼m Waldmark (by Mark of Esteem), 7f winner at 2 yrs, and 11f/1½m winner in Italy Waldbrand (by Tiger Hill): dam German 10.5f to 1¾m winner: useful performer: second in listed/pattern company in Germany at 4 yrs for A. Wohler: creditable efforts in handicaps in 2009 when 3¾ lengths sixth to Young Mick at Nad Al Sheba, 3¼ lengths second to Bab Al Salam at Lingfield and 1½ lengths third to Splinter Cell at Wolverhampton first/sixth/seventh outings: stays 2m: acts on polytrack, heavy and good to firm ground. *L. M. Cumani* **104**

WALKINGONTHEMOON 2 ch.c. (Apr 15) Footstepsinthesand 120 – Bendis (GER) (Danehill (USA) 126) [2009 5.2s* 5m⁵ 6d² 6g² 6s⁴ 7m³ 6m 6d Oct 24] £26,000Y: rather leggy colt: fourth foal: half-brother to useful 6f (including at 2 yrs)/6.5f (in France) winner Rubirosa (by Acclamation): dam, German 7f winner, half-sister to useful German performer up to 11f Basilea Gold: useful performer: won maiden at Newbury in April: ran creditably in listed events at Epsom (neck second to Corporal Maddox) and Deauville (6½ lengths third to Hearts of Fire) fourth/sixth starts: stays 7f: acts on soft and good to firm going: sent to Hong Kong. *Tom Dascombe* **98**

WALKING TALKING 5 b.g. Rainbow Quest (USA) 134 – Wooden Doll (USA) 98 **100**
(Woodman (USA) 126) [2009 105p: 12s^5 12s May 15] big, well-made gelding: useful performer, lightly raced: better effort in 2009 when 7 lengths fifth to Enroller in John Porter Stakes at Newbury: stays 1½m: acts on polytrack and soft ground: sold 6,500 gns in October, sent to Greece where successful at 7f. *H. R. A. Cecil*

WALK ON BYE (IRE) 2 b.f. (Apr 22) Danehill Dancer (IRE) 117 – Pipalong (IRE) **105**
121 (Pips Pride 117) [2009 6d* 6.3s* 6v^3 6g^6 Sep 27] €68,000Y: fifth foal: sister to winner abroad: dam 5f/6f winner (including at 2 yrs and Sprint Cup): useful performer: won maiden at the Curragh in June and Jebel Ali Stables & Racecourse Anglesey Stakes there (by 1¾ lengths from King Ledley, swishing tail under pressure) in July: below form in Phoenix Stakes (3 lengths third to Alfred Nobel) and valuable sales race at same course, though went best long way in latter: likely to prove as effective at 5f as 6f. *T. Stack, Ireland*

WALK ON WATER 2 ch.f. (Jan 28) Exceed And Excel (AUS) 126 – The Cat's **99 p**
Whiskers (NZ) 91 (Tale of The Cat (USA) 113) [2009 6g* 6.1m* 6s^6 Sep 3] first foal: dam, winner in New Zealand (raced mainly at 7f/1m), half-sister to Australian Group 3 5.5f winner Tully Dane, out of champion New Zealand 2-y-o filly Good Faith: won maiden at Ascot in July and minor event at Chester (readily by 4 lengths from Fly Silca Fly) in August: below form in listed race at Salisbury (possibly unsuited by soft ground): will prove best at 5f/6f: already useful, and remains open to improvement. *H. R. A. Cecil*

WALLGATE 2 b.f. (Jan 19) Namid 128 – Lay A Whisper 72 (Night Shift (USA)) [2009 **–**
5s^6 6m 6m Aug 8] well beaten in maidens/seller: dead. *Julie Camacho*

WALLS WAY 5 ch.g. Karinga Bay 116 – Wilming 35 (Komaite (USA)) [2009 10m **–**
p12m Sep 24] little form in bumpers/maidens. *A. W. Carroll*

WALNUT RISE 2 b.f. (Mar 15) Mujahid (USA) 125 – Seasonal Blossom (IRE) (Fairy **– §**
King (USA)) [2009 6m 7d 7d 7g 7d Oct 27] sturdy filly: fifth foal: half-sister to 3 winners, including 4-y-o Seasonal Cross and 6-y-o Wee Charlie Castle: dam, Irish maiden, half-sister to dam of high-class US performer up to 1½m Relaxed Gesture: temperamental maiden: sold 800 gns. *M. H. Tompkins*

WALRAGNEK 5 gr.g. Mind Games 121 – Eastern Lyric 93 (Petong 126) [2009 62: **–**
5.1g 5m 6.1m 5.3g 5g Aug 26] maiden: well held in 2009: tried visored/blinkered. *J. G. M. O'Shea*

WALTZALONG (IRE) 3 b.f. Carnival Dancer 123 – Flawless 107 (Warning 136) **–**
[2009 9d 10.1m 12g^4 10f 16.2g 8m Aug 9] 6,500Y: half-sister to useful 2006 2-y-o 7f/1m winner Duke of Tuscany (by Medicean) and 4-y-o Jelly Mo: dam 2-y-o 7f winner: well held in maidens/handicaps. *T. D. Easterby*

WALTZ AROUND (IRE) 2 b.f. (Jan 24) Bertolini (USA) 125 – Mellow Jazz 86 **65**
(Lycius (USA) 124) [2009 6s* 6.1d^3 7m 5d^5 Sep 16] fair performer: won maiden at Leicester in July: stayed 6f: acted on soft ground: dead. *C. E. Brittain*

WALTZING BUDDY 3 ch.f. Reel Buddy (USA) 118 – Waltzing Star (IRE) (Danehill **53**
(USA) 126) [2009 –: 7m 6m f6g 5m 6m^5 Jun 4] big, workmanlike filly: modest maiden: very headstrong: may prove best at 5f. *P. T. Midgley*

WALVIS BAY (IRE) 2 gr.g. (Apr 8) Footstepsinthesand 120 – Limpopo 49 (Green **85 p**
Desert (USA) 127) [2009 5.4d^2 6g^5 6g* 6s^6 Nov 7] €45,000Y: half-brother to several winners, including very smart sprinter Pipalong (by Pips Pride) and useful 2003 2-y-o 5f winner China Eyes (by Fasliyev): dam maiden half-sister to smart French performer up to 1½m Alost: fairly useful performer: won maiden at York (by 3 lengths from George Benjamin) in October: good sixth to Dubai Set in nursery at Doncaster (gelded after): likely to prove best at 5f/6f: should improve further. *T. P. Tate*

WANCHAI WHISPER 2 b.f. (Mar 13) Bahamian Bounty 116 – Tiger Waltz (Pivotal **71**
124) [2009 6s^5 7g^6 p5.1m* 5.7m p5.1g p5.1g p5g* p5.1g p6m^3 p5.1g p5m^2 p5m* p5m* Dec 30] first foal: dam unraced out of half-sister to very smart sprinter Bolshoi: fair performer: won seller at Wolverhampton (sold from W. Haggas 11,500 gns) in August, claimer at Kempton in October and claimer and nursery (best effort) at Kempton in December: best at 5f: acts on polytrack: signs of temperament. *P. D. Evans*

WANDERING MINSTRAL 6 br.g. Accordion – Vagrancy 64 (Dancing Brave **44**
(USA) 140) [2009 10.4m^6 8.1f Jul 2] fair form in bumpers/poor form over hurdles: sixth at Haydock, better effort in maidens on Flat. *H. J. L. Dunlop*

WANNABEE (IRE) 2 ch.f. (Feb 15) Bahamian Bounty 116 – Lyric Dances (FR) 49 **–**
(Sendawar (IRE) 129) [2009 p6f 6d p6m Nov 29] first foal: dam, maiden, half-sister to US Grade 2 1m winner Reine de Romance: last in maidens. *J. J. Bridger*

WANNABE KING 3 b.c. King's Best (USA) 132 – Wannabe Grand (IRE) 116 (Danehill (USA) 126) [2009 87p: 7s^2 8.3g^6 7.1v^4 7d^4 8m^2 8.3m* 8.5m* 8g* 9m Oct 3] compact, well-made colt: useful handicapper: improved to win at Windsor, Epsom and Ripon (best effort when beating Billy Dane 2¾ lengths) in August: joint favourite, only mid-field in Cambridgeshire at Newmarket final start: stays 8.5f: acts on soft and good to firm going: best in cheekpieces. *D. R. Lanigan* **108**

WANNAROCK (IRE) 4 b. or br.g. Rock of Gibraltar (IRE) 133 – Propensity 93 (Habitat 134) [2009 –: 11.8m^6 10m 12.1m^6 18g^6 11.5g^5 12d^4 16.2m^3 9.9m 16d^5 16d 16m^3 Sep 17] compact gelding: modest maiden handicapper: seems to stay 2¼m: acts on good to firm and good to soft ground. *M. C. Chapman* **58**

WAR AND PEACE (IRE) 5 b.g. Danehill (USA) 126 – Pipalong (IRE) 121 (Pips Pride 117) [2009 80: p6g^2 p5g^2 p6g^2 6m^3 6m^5 6g p7.1g p6g^5 f6g^6 Dec 8] neat gelding: fair maiden handicapper: effective at 5f/6f: acts on polytrack, soft and good to firm going. *Jane Chapple-Hyam* **78**

WAR ARTIST (AUS) 6 b.g. Orpen (USA) 116 – Royal Solitaire (AUS) (Brocco (USA) 124) [2009 122: 6d^4 6s^4 6m* 5g* 5g^3 6g Dec 13] rangy gelding: very smart performer: off 12 months prior to reappearance (reportedly underwent colic surgery early in year): won bestwetten.de Goldene Peitsche at Baden-Baden (by 1¼ lengths from Smooth Operator) in August and Qatar Prix du Petit Couvert at Longchamp (led close home when beating Stern Opinion short neck) in September: good ¾-length third to Total Gallery in Prix de l'Abbaye de Longchamp next time: well held in Hong Kong Sprint at Sha Tin final start: stays 6f: acts on good to firm going. *J. M. P. Eustace* **120**

WARLING (IRE) 2 br.f. (Feb 7) Montjeu (IRE) 137 – Walkamia (FR) 114 (Linamix (FR) 127) [2009 7g Oct 31] tall, unfurnished filly: second foal: half-sister to 3-y-o War Native: dam, French 1m to 10.5f winner (stayed 1½m), sister to smart French performers up to 1½m Walk On Mix and Walking Around: 16/1, 8½ lengths eighth to Field Day in maiden at Newmarket, in touch long way: will be suited by 1¼m+: likely to improve. *J. Noseda* **58 p**

WAR NATIVE (IRE) 3 b.c. Cape Cross (IRE) 129 – Walkamia (FR) 114 (Linamix (FR) 127) [2009 95: 7s 7g^3 8f^4 8f Oct 10] rather leggy colt: useful performer: creditable third to Saucy Brown in minor event at Doncaster second start: left J. Noseda and off 4 months after: probably stays 1m: acts on polytrack and firm going: blinkered last 2 starts: not straightforward (pulls hard). *N. D. Drysdale, USA* **98**

WARNERS BAY (IRE) 4 b.g. Iron Mask (USA) 117 – Romangoddess (IRE) (Rhoman Rule (USA)) [2009 –: 6m 6m 7.1g 6s 6m 7m Sep 16] good-topped gelding: modest maiden: should stay beyond 6f: acts on good to firm ground. *R. Bastiman* **50**

WARNE'S WAY (IRE) 6 ch.g. Spinning World (USA) 130 – Kafayef (USA) 46 (Secreto (USA) 128) [2009 12v* Oct 24] sturdy gelding: useful hurdler at best (missed 2008/9): fair chaser nowadays: similar level on first start on Flat since 2006 when winning ladies handicap at Newbury: stays 1½m: acts on heavy ground. *B. G. Powell* **76**

Qatar Prix du Petit Couvert, Longchamp—
War Artist collars Stern Opinion (grey) close home; Bluster is in third

WARNING SONG (USA) 2 b. or br.c. (Feb 14) Successful Appeal (USA) 118 – Tia Lea (USA) (Songandaprayer (USA) 118) [2009 5f^4 6m^3 5f^3 6d^5 p7g^2 p7g^3 Nov 11] $75,000Y: quite attractive colt: first foal: dam ran twice in USA: fair maiden: stays 7f: acts on polytrack and firm ground. *Mrs A. J. Perrett* **79**

WAR OF THE ROSES (IRE) 6 b.g. Singspiel (IRE) 133 – Calvia Rose (Sharpo 132) [2009 –, a94: p12g p12g* p12g^6 p16g Apr 11] lengthy, angular gelding: fairly useful handicapper: won at Lingfield in February: effective at 1½m to easy 2m: acts on polytrack, no form on turf since 2007: travels strongly held up. *R. Brotherton* **– a88**

WAR PARTY 5 b.g. Fantastic Light (USA) 134 – War Game (FR) 107 (Caerleon (USA) 132) [2009 12m^6 12g^5 12g 14m Jul 3] neat gelding: fairly useful handicapper: won at Longchamp in 2008 when trained by E. Lellouche (sold €42,000): similar form in Britain first 2 starts in 2009: stays 1½m: acts on good to firm and good to soft ground: fair hurdler. *Dr R. D. P. Newland* **87**

WARPEDSENSEOFHUMOR (FR) 3 ch.c. Distorted Humor (USA) 117 – Eden (USA) (Holy Bull (USA) 134) [2009 9m* 10m^5 Aug 9] useful-looking colt: second foal: dam, US 8.5f winner, half-sister to useful French performer up to 1¼m Mais Oui: fairly useful form: mid-division in newcomers race at Milan at 2 yrs for V. Valiani: won maiden at Redcar in April: not sure to stay beyond 1¼m: raced only on good to firm ground. *H. R. A. Cecil* **81**

WARRANTS ATTENTION (IRE) 3 b.g. Fruits of Love (USA) 127 – Irish Lover (USA) (Irish River (FR) 131) [2009 10m 12.1g^5 12.6m^6 14g 12.1g^6 p10g Sep 9] modest maiden: stays 1¾m: raced only on polytrack and good/good to firm ground. *A. M. Balding* **53**

WARREN BANK 4 b.g. Nayef (USA) 129 – Neptunalia 70 (Slip Anchor 136) [2009 p9.5g^2 f12f p11f Dec 16] lengthy gelding: maiden: modest form only on reappearance. *Mrs Mary Hambro* **60**

WARRINGAH 4 ch.g. Galileo (IRE) 134 – Threefold (USA) 99 (Gulch (USA)) [2009 103p: 12s 11.6m* 14m^2 12g^2 14m^5 11.6m^2 16d Nov 3] big, strong gelding: smart performer: won handicap at Windsor in June by 6 lengths from Magicalmysterytour: good efforts next 3 starts, second in listed handicap at York (beaten short head by Hits Only Vic) and Glorious Stakes at Goodwood (beaten neck by Illustrious Blue), and length fifth to Sesenta in Ebor Handicap at York: sold privately and left Sir Michael Stoute, last in Melbourne Cup (Handicap) at Flemington final outing: effective at 1½m/1¾m: acts on good to firm going (below form on softer than good): usually front runner. *C. Waller, Australia* **114**

WARRIOR CONQUEST 4 b.g. Alhaarth (IRE) 126 – Eilean Shona 102 (Suave Dancer (USA) 136) [2009 51: 12m 11.5g^3 12m^6 p16g^2 16g p16g^3 p16g 14.1g^4 Sep 30] good-topped gelding: fair maiden handicapper: stays 2m: acts on polytrack and good to firm ground: tried visored. *W. J. Knight* **76**

WARRIOR NATION (FR) 3 br.g. Statue of Liberty (USA) 115 – Tadawul (USA) 73 (Diesis 133) [2009 72: p10.7g^2 p10.7g 10d 11.5d p8g p8g p12.2g Dec 12] good-topped gelding: fair maiden: no form after second start, leaving G. Lyons in Ireland after next outing: stays 10.7f: acts on polytrack, firm and good to soft going: tried blinkered/in cheekpieces. *A. J. Chamberlain* **77 d**

WARRIOR ONE 3 ch. or gr.g. Act One 124 – River Cara (USA) 86 (Irish River (FR) 131) [2009 90p: 10.4m 10g^5 Jun 8] useful-looking gelding: just fair form at 3 yrs: will stay 1½m: acts on soft going. *J. Howard Johnson* **72**

WARSAW PACT (IRE) 6 b.g. Polish Precedent (USA) 131 – Always Friendly 111 (High Line 125) [2009 18.7m May 6] lengthy gelding: useful handicapper in 2006: fit from hurdling (fairly useful), well held sole Flat start since: stays 1¾m: acts on polytrack, good to firm and good to soft going: sold £5,500. *P. J. Hobbs* **–**

WAR WOLF 2 br.g. (Feb 10) Lucky Story (USA) 128 – Bollin Janet 83 (Sheikh Albadou 128) [2009 6d 6g^4 5d 6m 8g Oct 16] leggy gelding: no form: sold £1,000. *T. D. Easterby* **–**

WASAN 4 ch.c. Pivotal 124 – Solaia (USA) 110 (Miswaki (USA) 124) [2009 114: 8g p10g* 12g^2 p10m^2 10.4g^2 Oct 9] well-made colt: useful performer: won minor event at Lingfield in May by 4½ lengths from Fairmile: at least respectable efforts when runner-up all 3 starts after, including when beaten neck by Heliodor in similar event at Kempton: stays 10.3f: acts on polytrack and soft going: tried blinkered. *E. A. L. Dunlop* **109**

WASEET 2 ch.c. (Feb 22) Selkirk (USA) 129 – Najayeb (USA) (Silver Hawk (USA) 123) [2009 7g^3 8.1g* 8m^2 Sep 26] well-made colt: fourth foal: half-brother to Irish 5-y-o Mutadarrej: dam unraced half-sister to top-class 1¼m/1½m performer Sakhee: landed **114 p**

odds in maiden at Sandown in August: much improved when 1¼ lengths second to Joshua Tree in Royal Lodge Stakes at Ascot, still on bridle when short of room 2f out then running on well once in clear: will stay 1¼m: already smart, and should continue on upgrade. *J. L. Dunlop*

WASHINGTON IRVING (IRE) 4 b.g. Montjeu (IRE) 137 – Shouk 94 (Shirley Heights 130) [2009 115: 14s^4 20m Jun 18] useful-looking gelding: smart at 3 yrs: respectable 12 lengths fourth to Ask in Yorkshire Cup: pulled up in Gold Cup at Royal Ascot month later: should stay 2m+: acts on soft going: created good impression when winning on hurdling debut in November. *J. Howard Johnson* **106**

WASMI (IRE) 2 b.f. (Feb 7) Exceed And Excel (AUS) 126 – Trim (IRE) (Ela-Mana-Mou 132) [2009 6m 5.2g^4 p7.1g* 6g^4 p7g^4 p6g* p6m* 6g Oct 9] €32,000F, 6,000Y: third foal: dam unraced: fairly useful performer: won maiden at Wolverhampton in July and nurseries (2) at Kempton in September: best form at 6f: acts on polytrack, well below form on turf: races up with pace. *C. E. Brittain* **54 a81**

WASP (AUS) 7 b. or br.g. Octagonal (NZ) 126 – Establishment (AUS) (Star Watch (AUS)) [2009 93: p8.6g* p8g^5 p8g^4 8m 10m^5 7.1m^5 8.5m 9.3g* 9.3g*^{dis} 10.3g^{2d} Aug 2] compact gelding: fairly useful performer: won handicap at Wolverhampton in January: sold from W. Jarvis 7,500 gns, first past post in 2 minor events in 4 days at Bad Harzburg in July but disqualified (failed dope test) second occasion and again on final outing: stays 10.3f: acts on polytrack, soft and good to firm ground: has bled. *C. von der Recke, Germany* **82 a92**

WATCH AMIGO (IRE) 3 b.g. Royal Applause 124 – Miss Red Ink (USA) (Red Ransom (USA)) [2009 p7.1g^2 p7.1g* Dec 12] 11,000F, 19,000Y, 30,000 2-y-o: second foal: half-brother to winner in Canada by Valid Expectations: dam, US maiden, half-sister to dam of smart miler Passing Glance: fair form in maidens at Wolverhampton: won in December by length from Midnight Strider, held up off overly-strong pace but headway readily and just pushed out to assert, still green under pressure: should stay 1m: likely to improve. *W. R. Swinburn* **79 p**

WATCH CHAIN (IRE) 2 b.c. (Mar 12) Traditionally (USA) 117 – Dangle (IRE) 102 (Desert Style (IRE) 121) [2009 5m^5 6d^6 6g^6 5.3m^4 f5g* 6f^3 5m^6 6m f5m^6 Nov 6] good-topped colt: modest performer: won nursery at Southwell in August: likely to stay 7f: acts on fibresand and firm ground. *M. H. Tompkins* **64**

WATCHMAKER 6 b.g. Bering 136 – Watchkeeper (IRE) 86 (Rudimentary (USA) 118) [2009 76: p9.5g^2 p9.5g* p10g^4 10d May 15] fair performer: won claimer at Wolverhampton in April: stays 1½m: acts on polytrack (lightly raced on turf): often races prominently. *Miss Tor Sturgis* **– a76**

WATCH OUT 5 b.g. Observatory (USA) 131 – Ballet Fame (USA) 79 (Quest For Fame 127) [2009 56: p16.5g^6 Oct 30] neat gelding: modest maiden: stays 16.5f: acts on polytrack, soft and good to firm ground: tried blinkered/tongue tied. *D. Burchell* **50**

WATCHOVERME 3 ch.f. Haafhd 129 – Bryony Brind (IRE) 105 (Kris 135) [2009 10g 12d^5 p12g 10.1m^6 14.1g^6 Aug 30] lengthy filly: fifth foal: half-sister to 4-y-o Bugaku: dam 1m to 12.5f winner: little form: visored last 2 starts. *J. R. Fanshawe* **–**

WATCH THE MASTER 3 b.g. Passing Glance 119 – Fine Arts 86 (Cadeaux Genereux 131) [2009 60: 12g p10g f11g Aug 25] maiden: no form in 2009: tried visored/tongue tied. *B. I. Case* **–**

WATER BISCUIT 2 b.f. (Jan 26) Bertolini (USA) 125 – Waterfall One 62 (Nashwan (USA) 135) [2009 6d^2 6m^2 7d* 7g^6 6.5m 7g Oct 17] compact filly: third foal: half-sister to winner in Russia by Intikhab: dam, maiden, out of Lancashire Oaks winner Spout: fairly useful performer: won maiden at Goodwood in July: below form in nurseries last 2 starts: will stay beyond 7f: acts on good to firm and good to soft going. *B. J. Meehan* **82**

WATERGATE (IRE) 3 gr.g. Verglas (IRE) 118 – Moy Water (IRE) 87 (Tirol 127) [2009 90: 8g^4 10.3m 9.9f 9.7f^3 p8m 10.2s^2 Oct 7] tall gelding: fairly useful handicapper: stays 1¼m: acts on soft and good to firm going: front runner/races prominently: sold 85,000 gns, joined P. Nicholls. *Sir Mark Prescott* **91**

WATER GIPSY 2 b. or br.f. (Feb 20) Piccolo 121 – Creek Dancer 58 (Josr Algarhoud (IRE) 118) [2009 6m Sep 18] first foal: dam maiden (stayed 1¼m): 66/1, 6¾ lengths ninth to Side Glance in maiden at Newmarket. *G. L. Moore* **55**

WATER HEN (IRE) 3 b.f. Diktat 126 – Waterfall One 62 (Nashwan (USA) 135) [2009 65: 11.8m^5 9.9f Jun 24] rather leggy filly: fair maiden: likely to prove best short of 1½m: sold 3,000 gns. *R. Charlton* **65**

WATERLOO CORNER 7 b.g. Cayman Kai (IRE) 114 – Rasin Luck (Primitive Rising (USA) 113) [2009 66: 10.2g^5 14.1m^4 16g^3 10m 10.1m Aug 13] smallish, close- **59**

coupled gelding: modest handicapper nowadays: stays easy 1¾m: acts on all-weather and firm going: tried in headgear. *R. Craggs*

WATERLOO DOCK 4 b.g. Hunting Lion (IRE) 115 – Scenic Air (Hadeer 118) [2009 58: p8g^4 p6g* p6g^2 p6m p7m Dec 9] leggy gelding: fair performer: won maiden at Lingfield in February: effective at 6f, seemingly stays 1m: acts on polytrack and good to firm ground: often races prominently. *M. Quinn* **66**

WATERSIDE (IRE) 10 b.g. Lake Coniston (IRE) 131 – Classic Ring (IRE) 50 (Auction Ring (USA) 123) [2009 94: p8g p10g f11g^5 p8.6g* p9.5g p8.6g^5 10m p12.2g^5 10m^2 p9.5g^5 8.1m^2 Aug 20] strong, heavy-topped gelding: has a round action: just fair performer nowadays: won seller at Wolverhampton in April: best short of 1¼m: acts on all-weather and any turf going: tongue tied later in 2009. *S. Curran* **70**

WATSON'S BAY 4 b.c. Royal Applause 124 – Multaka (USA) 66 (Gone West (USA)) [2009 75: p8.6g* p8.6g^5 p9.5g^4 p9.5g^3 p10g p10g^3 10m^4 11.6m^3 p12.2g^3 11.6g^3 13m^4 12m^2 12d^3 12g^3 12m^3 12g^4 11.9f^6 10m p12.2m^2 11.5m^3 12m Sep 25] good-topped colt: fair performer: won maiden at Wolverhampton in January: claimed from Tor Sturgis £7,000 seventh outing: stays 13f: acts on polytrack and good to firm going: patiently ridden. *P. Howling* **75**

WAVEBAND 2 ch.f. (Apr 29) Exceed And Excel (AUS) 126 – Licence To Thrill 83 (Wolfhound (USA) 126) [2009 5m^4 5.1m^3 6m^2 5g^3 6m^3 p5.1g* 6m 7m^3 Oct 3] 75,000Y: rather leggy, lengthy filly: fifth foal: half-sister to several winners, including 3-y-o Cheap Thrills and 4-y-o Group Therapy: dam 5f winner: fairly useful performer: won maiden at Wolverhampton in September: much improved when 4 lengths third to Lillie Langtry in sales race at Newmarket: stays 7f: acts on polytrack and good to firm ground: front runner. *M. Johnston* **91**

WAVERTREE BOUNTY 2 b.f. (Apr 2) Pastoral Pursuits 127 – Grecian Halo (USA) 59 (Southern Halo (USA)) [2009 7.1m 8d^6 8d Oct 27] 6,500Y: fourth foal: dam 1m winner: improved only gradually in maidens, still green and again never dangererous final start: seems to stay 1m. *C. F. Wall* **52 +**

WAVERTREE PRINCESS (IRE) 4 gr.f. Invincible Spirit (IRE) 121 – Blushing Queen (IRE) 75 (Desert King (IRE) 129) [2009 68: 5.1d 5.1m 5.2d 5.1s Nov 4] good-topped filly: handicapper: well held in 2009. *C. F. Wall* **–**

WAVERTREE WARRIOR (IRE) 7 br.g. Indian Lodge (IRE) 127 – Karamana (Habitat 134) [2009 –, a84: p8g^4 p8g^2 p8g^3 p8g^4 p10g p8g 8.1g^4 8d 8.1g^6 7.6d 8.1m Sep 10] leggy gelding: fair handicapper on all-weather, modest on turf nowadays: best at 7f/1m: acts on polytrack, soft and good to firm going: wears headgear. *N. P. Littmoden* **56 a78**

WAZIRI (IRE) 8 b.g. Mtoto 134 – Euphorie (GER) (Feenpark (GER) 115) [2009 12.1m^5 9m Aug 14] close-coupled gelding: handicapper: first Flat outings since 2005, well held at 8 yrs. *M. Hill* **–**

WEALD PARK (USA) 3 ch.g. Cozzene (USA) – Promptly (IRE) 88 (Lead On Time (USA) 123) [2009 98: p9g^5 10m 10d 8m 10g 8d p10g^6 Nov 14] good-topped gelding: useful performer: regressed after creditable 2¼ lengths fifth to Mafaaz in valuable minor event at Kempton: best up to 9f: acts on polytrack and firm going: tried visored. *R. Hannon* **99 d**

WEBBOW (IRE) 7 b.g. Dr Devious (IRE) 127 – Ower (IRE) 71 (Lomond (USA) 128) [2009 99: 8m^2 8d^3 7f 8m^2 8g^4 8m^4 8m 7g^3 7s^5 Nov 7] strong gelding: useful handicapper: best effort in 2009 when nose second to City of The Kings at York fourth start: largely respectable efforts otherwise: effective at 7f/1m: acts on all-weather, heavy and good to firm going: usually held up. *N. Tinkler* **101**

WEDDING DREAM 2 b.f. (Feb 17) Oasis Dream 129 – Gretna 77 (Groom Dancer (USA) 128) [2009 5m f5g 6m f7g^5 f7g^5 f8f* Dec 12] 16,000Y, 26,000 2-y-o: close-coupled filly: first foal: dam, 9.7f winner, half-sister to useful miler Kootenay and 3-y-o Sans Frontieres: modest performer: much improved when winning nursery at Southwell by 6 lengths, flashing tail and wandering: stays 1m: acts on fibresand: tried blinkered/in cheekpieces. *K. A. Ryan* **58**

WEDDING LIST 3 ch.f. Pivotal 124 – Confetti (Groom Dancer (USA) 128) [2009 88p: 6m Jun 10] first foal: dam, ran twice, out of half-sister to very smart US performer up to 1¼m Golden Apples (by Pivotal): fairly useful form in 2008: well held in handicap sole outing at 3 yrs: has plenty of speed, raced only at 6f: acts on polytrack. *W. J. Haggas* **–**

WEDDING MARCH (IRE) 2 gr.f. (Feb 9) Dalakhani (IRE) 133 – Elopa (GER) 119 (Tiger Hill (IRE) 127) [2009 8g* 8g^4 Oct 4] 300,000Y: big, useful-looking filly: has plenty of scope: first foal: dam, German 1¼m/11f winner, half-sister to very smart **104 p**

German 1¼m/11f performer Epalo: won newcomers race at Longchamp in September by 4 lengths from Sahitas: 2¼ lengths fourth to Rosanara in Prix Marcel Boussac there, not clearest of runs: will be suited by 1¼m/1½m: has joined Saeed bin Suroor: very much type to progress further. *A. Fabre, France*

WEDNESDAYS BOY (IRE) 6 b.g. Alhaarth (IRE) 126 – Sheen Falls (IRE) 56 (Prince Rupert (FR) 121) [2009 66: 8d 8d 8.5g 7.9g p9.5g⁴ 9.1v⁵ Oct 31] modest handicapper nowadays: best at 1m/1¼m: acts on polytrack and heavy ground: wears cheekpieces (tried blinkered): held up. *P. D. Niven* **59**

WEE BIZZOM 3 b.f. Makbul 104 – Lone Pine (Sesaro (USA) 81) [2009 48: f6s⁵ f5d² p5.1g⁴ p5.1g 5m⁶ 5m 7.1m⁶ 7.1m 6g Jul 5] poor maiden handicapper: best efforts at 5f: acts on all-weather: tried in blinkers: has reportedly bled. *A. Berry* **48**

WEE BOBBIE 2 b.f. (Apr 7) Acclamation 118 – Bobbie Dee 93 (Blakeney 126) [2009 5.1g p7g Oct 20] seventh foal: half-sister to 5-y-o Colonel Flay and 1¾m winner In Deep (by Deploy): dam maiden who should have stayed 1½m: well held in maidens. *Mrs P. N. Dutfield* **–**

WEE BUNS 4 b.g. Piccolo 121 – Gigetta (IRE) (Brief Truce (USA) 126) [2009 68: p6g p7g p6g 6g Apr 6] rather leggy gelding: little form in 2009: tried blinkered. *P. Burgoyne* **–**

WEE CHARLIE CASTLE (IRE) 6 b.g. Sinndar (IRE) 134 – Seasonal Blossom (IRE) (Fairy King (USA)) [2009 80: 11.1m² 10m³ 14g* 14s⁴ 12.1m* 12m 14m⁵ 10g³ Oct 23] rangy gelding: fairly useful handicapper: won at Musselburgh in July and Beverley in August: stays 1¾m: acts on all-weather, firm and good to soft going: tried visored/blinkered. *I. Semple* **85**

WEE GIANT (USA) 3 ch.g. Giant's Causeway (USA) 132 – Christmas In Aiken (USA) (Affirmed (USA)) [2009 81p: 10m 10.4g 10.3g p8.6g⁶ Oct 29] good-bodied gelding: fairly useful winner at 2 yrs: well held in handicaps in 2009: should stay 1¼m: acts on polytrack. *K. A. Ryan* **–**

WEEKEND AWAY (IRE) 3 b.g. Invincible Spirit (IRE) 121 – March Star (IRE) 109 (Mac's Imp (USA) 116) [2009 8.1g 6g⁵ p8g 8.1d p6g p6g p7.1g Nov 6] fair maiden: best effort on third outing. *S. Kirk* **65**

WEEKEND MILLIONAIR (IRE) 2 b.g. (Apr 10) Arakan (USA) 123 – Almi Ad (USA) 78 (Silver Hawk (USA) 123) [2009 6.1v³ 7.2s³ 7m⁴ Sep 23] fair maiden: bred to be suited by 1m+: hung left final start. *P. D. Evans* **69**

WEEPING WILLOW (IRE) 2 b.f. (Apr 29) Kheleyf (USA) 116 – Bezant (IRE) 51 (Zamindar (USA) 116) [2009 6f Aug 3] €26,000Y, resold £65,000Y: tall filly: has scope: second foal: sister to 3-y-o Deposer: dam maiden (stayed 1m): 9/2, badly hampered at start when well held in maiden at Windsor: will do better. *J. H. M. Gosden* **– p**

WEE SONNY (IRE) 3 b.g. Refuse To Bend (IRE) 128 – Coup de Coeur (IRE) (Kahyasi 130) [2009 78p: 11s 10m³ 9.9f⁴ 11.6g⁴ 10.3g³ Aug 2] fair maiden handicapper: gelded prior to final start: stays 1¼m: acts on firm ground: tends to hang: sold £1,600, joined N. Chance. *Tom Dascombe* **77**

WEET A SURPRISE 4 b.f. Bertolini (USA) 125 – Ticcatoo (IRE) 60 (Dolphin Street (FR) 125) [2009 76: f5m⁶ f6g⁵ 5v⁴ p5.1g* 5m⁵ 5.5g³ 5d³ 5.1v³ 5.1d² p6g* p6g⁵ 6m⁴ p5.1g⁶ p7.1g³ p6g* Nov 6] sparely-made filly: fairly useful handicapper on all-weather, fair on turf: left R. Hollinshead after second start: won at Wolverhampton in June, September and November (apprentices): best at 5f/6f: acts on all-weather and soft going: visored nowadays. *J. W. Unett* **70 a84**

WEETENTHERTY 2 b.c. (Mar 28) Bertolini (USA) 125 – Binaa (IRE) 69 (Marju (IRE) 127) [2009 5m 5m 6g 6d⁵ Jul 17] poor maiden: tried visored. *J. S. Goldie* **48**

WEETFROMTHECHAFF 4 gr.g. Weet-A-Minute (IRE) 106 – Weet Ees Girl (IRE) 75 (Common Grounds 118) [2009 59: p6g p7.1g⁵ p9.5g p5.1g⁴ p6g⁴ 12.4g Apr 27] leggy, close-coupled gelding: modest maiden: left R. Hollinshead prior to final start: free-going sort, best up to 7f: acts on all-weather and good to firm going: usually in cheekpieces/visor. *M. A. Barnes* **59**

WEET IN NERJA 3 b.g. Captain Rio 122 – Persian Fortune 53 (Forzando 122) [2009 58: p6g² p6g⁵ p5.1g⁵ p6g³ p6g p7.1g⁵ p6g⁴ p7.1g 8d p8g Dec 2] good-bodied gelding: modest maiden: left R. Hollinshead prior to final start: effective at 5f/6f: acts on all-weather: tried visored, usually in cheekpieces nowadays. *J. W. Unett* **55**

WEE ZIGGY 6 b.g. Ziggy's Dancer (USA) 97 – Midnight Arrow 81 (Robellino (USA) 127) [2009 p16m⁶ Dec 1] compact gelding: little form on Flat. *M. Mullineaux* **–**

WE HAVE A DREAM 4 b. or br.g. Oasis Dream 129 – Final Shot 91 (Dalsaan 125) [2009 82: 6d 6m 6m² 6m⁵ 6m 6d³ 6g* p6g² 6d² 6m* 6d* 6d 6g² Oct 23] good-bodied **95**

gelding: useful handicapper: won at Ayr in July, Goodwood in September and Folkestone (beat Idle Power 3¼ lengths) in October: raced only at 6f (should prove as effective at 5f): acts on polytrack, heavy and good to firm ground: blinkered once: front runner/races prominently. *W. R. Muir*

WEIMARLAND (IRE) 2 b.c. (Apr 21) Elusive City (USA) 117 – Night Spirit (IRE) 78 (Night Shift (USA)) [2009 f6g^{6} p6m^{6} p5.1m^{5} p5m Dec 10] poor maiden. *J. A. Osborne* **45**

WELCOME APPLAUSE (IRE) 3 b.f. Acclamation 118 – Waseyla (IRE) 71 (Sri Pekan (USA) 117) [2009 58: 10.1g 10m^{4} 8.3m Jul 11] unfurnished filly: maiden, just poor form at 3 yrs: best form at 6f/7f. *M. G. Quinlan* **47**

WELCOME APPROACH 6 b.g. Most Welcome 131 – Lucky Thing (Green Desert (USA) 127) [2009 69: p6g^{5} p6g 5.9g 5m 5g^{6} 7.1m^{3} p5.1g^{6} p6g^{2} p6g^{6} p6g* p6g* Dec 19] sturdy, angular gelding: fair handicapper: won at Wolverhampton in November/December: best at 5f/6f: acts on polytrack, firm and good to soft ground: tried blinkered: held up. *J. R. Weymes* **46 a67**

WELCOME BOUNTY 2 ch.c. (Apr 30) Bahamian Bounty 116 – Welcome Home 55 (Most Welcome 131) [2009 8.3v Nov 4] big, well-made colt: 25/1 and green, tailed off in maiden at Nottingham. *D. R. Lanigan* **–**

WELCOME CAT (USA) 5 b.g. Tale of The Cat (USA) 113 – Mangano (USA) (Quiet American (USA)) [2009 56: f14g f11g Mar 11] little form in 2009: has worn blinkers/tongue strap/cheekpieces. *A. D. Brown* **–**

WELCOME RELEAF 6 ch.g. Most Welcome 131 – Mint Leaf (IRE) 78 (Sri Pekan (USA) 117) [2009 64d: f7g f11g^{6} p12g Feb 19] close-coupled gelding: poor performer nowadays: stays 8.6f: acts on all-weather: tried in headgear. *P. Leech* **42**

WELIKETOBOUGGIE 2 b.c. (Mar 29) Tobougg (IRE) 125 – Country Spirit (Sayf El Arab (USA) 127) [2009 6g p7g^{6} Jul 22] better effort in maidens when sixth to Azizi at Lingfield. *J. S. Moore* **53**

WELL ARMED (USA) 6 b.g. Tiznow (USA) 133 – Well Dressed (USA) (Notebook (USA)) [2009 123: a8.5f^{4} a9f^{2} a10f* p8.5f Aug 2] **129**

Considering that the Dubai World Cup is the most valuable race in the world, a status which ought to make it a prime target for enough high-class horses to ensure a highly competitive contest, there have been a remarkable number of decisive, even wide-margin, winners in the first fourteen renewals. This century alone, Curlin won by seven and three quarter lengths, Dubai Millennium by six, Moon Ballad by five, Street Cry by four and a quarter, and Captain Steve and Roses In May by three. None of these, however, comes near to the victory margin achieved by Well Armed, who stormed home by an official fourteen lengths at Nad Al Sheba in March (the margin looked a shade exaggerated when assessed on time, just over twelve lengths probably closer to the mark.) Dominance of this order is exceptionally rare in a high profile event open to different age groups—Turtle Island's fifteen-length victory in the 1994 Irish Two Thousand Guineas and those of Rachel Alexandra in the Kentucky Oaks (twenty and a quarter lengths) and Mother Goose Stakes (nineteen and a quarter) in the first part of the latest northern hemisphere season came in races restricted to three-year-olds, while there was a fourteen-length success for Folklore in the 2005 Matron Stakes for juvenile fillies. The closest any winner has come to matching Well Armed's feat in an 'open' Group 1 event in recent years was when Septimus landed the Irish St Leger by thirteen lengths in 2008, though not even the greatest supporters of the Curragh race would claim it has the prestige of the Dubai World Cup. Perhaps even more remarkable than Well Armed's winning margin was that this was the same horse who had run to a rating of 99 when fourth in the Autumn Stakes at Salisbury in October 2005, then to 84 in landing a maiden at Lingfield the following month on the last of eight starts as a two-year-old for Clive Brittain.

Well Armed's career has been interrupted by a succession of injuries and the Dubai World Cup Sponsored by Emirates Airline was only his twelfth start in three years since being transferred to North America, seven of his appearances coming in a relatively trouble-free campaign as a five-year-old in 2008. As a three-year-old, still trained by Brittain, Well Armed showed some improvement to win a minor event at Nad Al Sheba in January but, after finishing well held in the UAE 2000 Guineas (in which he started favourite) and UAE Derby, he was found to have chipped his near-fore knee leaving the stalls in the latter event and subsequently underwent arthroscopic surgery to remove a large fragment from the inner carpal joint. Three days after he left the clinic following that operation, Well Armed was found in his box with a fractured hip joint and a heart rate of 100 beats per minute (the normal rate is between 30 and 40 beats.) Reportedly he was unable to get up at first; then, once up, was unable to support any weight on the leg. His connections considered putting him down but, luckily, decided to persevere with treatment of the fracture. Well Armed made a slow recovery, his recuperation including a ten-month stay at his owner's ranch where a steady programme of swimming, walking and jogging enabled Well Armed to make a gradual return to full fitness. Well Armed was gelded in this period, and he resumed his career in October 2007, towards the end of his four-year-old days, winning an allowance race at Hollywood Park on his second appearance. He then did well for new trainer Eoin Harty at the winter meeting at Santa Anita, finishing second in the San Pasqual Handicap and winning the Grade 2 San Antonio Handicap. This was followed by third behind Curlin in the Dubai World Cup, beaten eight lengths. Well Armed continued in good form back in the States, racing entirely on pro-ride and polytrack, with victories in the Grade 2 San Diego Handicap at Del Mar and the Grade 1 Goodwood Stakes at Santa Anita, with a second in between in the Pacific Classic at Del Mar again. He didn't run anywhere near his best in the Breeders' Cup Dirt Mile won by Albertus Maximus at Santa Anita, and was below par when fourth in the San Pasqual Handicap on his reappearance at six, but, on his final start before the Dubai World Cup, he returned to top form when second in the San Antonio Handicap, caught near the finish and going down by a length after making the running as usual.

The quality of the field for the latest renewal of the Dubai World Cup was the lowest in its history. Not one of the fourteen starters had run to a Timeform rating of 125 or higher and there were only two challengers from Europe, the Breeders' Cup Marathon winner Muhannak from Britain and ex-Brazilian Group 2 winner Gloria de Campeao from France. The line-up included only three other Group or Grade 1 winners apart from Well Armed. They were the second favourite Albertus Maximus, who had followed up victory in the Breeders' Cup Dirt with success in the Donn Handicap in January, and Joe Louis and Muller, winners respectively of Group 1 events in Argentina and Peru before their successes in the last two runnings of Saudi Arabia's most important race, the Custodian of The Two Holy Mosques Cup, also known as The King's Cup. The Dubai World Cup favourite was Asiatic Boy, successful in the UAE Derby and runner-up in the World Cup in 2008 and in good form after winning Round 3 of the Maktoum Challenge earlier in March. The American challenge was completed by Grade 2 winners Anak Nakal and Arson Squad, while the others included Godolphin's ex-Argentinian colt My Indy, who had won Rounds 1 and 2 of the Maktoum Challenge, Japan's Casino Drive, runner-up in the Group 1 February Stakes a month before the World Cup, and ex-South African Paris Perfect, second to Muller in the big Saudi Arabian race. Well Armed, who started 10/1 joint-fourth favourite, slaughtered his field, settling in front and moving so strongly that he was able to draw five lengths clear soon after turning for home without being asked a serious question. Everything else was under pressure and, with his rider Aaron Gryder rousting him along two furlongs out, Well Armed drew further and further clear; Gryder eased off in the last hundred

Dubai World Cup Sponsored by Emirates Airline, Nad Al Sheba—
the previous year's third Well Armed wins in stunning style from Gloria de Campeao (noseband);
after 14 years, the world's richest race switches to a new home at state-of-the-art Meydan in 2010

and twenty-five yards, patting his mount down the neck. Gloria de Campeao came second, four and a half lengths ahead of Paris Perfect, with Muller next. Asiatic Boy ran no sort of race after starting tardily and being hampered after two furlongs. The runners were well strung out at the end, though the time was only the ninth fastest in the history of the event.

Performances that seem too good to be true often turn out to be just that, which is another way of saying that wide-margin victories cannot always be taken at face value. Well Armed almost certainly benefited from being allowed an uncontested lead on a track favouring speed, though, if he really was twelve to fourteen lengths superior to the runner-up Gloria de Campeao, who ran to a Timeform rating of 123 next time in the Singapore International Cup on turf, it would make Well Armed one of the best horses in the history of the sport. Any such idea takes a lot of swallowing, particularly as Well Armed was able to run only once after his triumph, finishing last of eight in the Grade 2 San Diego Handicap at Del Mar at the start of August. He was being aimed at the Breeders' Cup Classic which would have given him the opportunity to show whether or not he was flattered by his Dubai World Cup performance. However, he sustained a chip in an ankle at Del Mar that required yet another operation. If Well Armed makes it back for a third appearance in the Dubai World Cup, it is unlikely that the first renewal on the new track of Meydan will be so relatively poorly contested as the last edition at Nad Al Sheba. Gloria de Campeao was the only subsequent winner from the race and several of the field, including Albertus Maximus and Casino Drive, weren't seen out again. Be that as it may, Well Armed's victory was still one of the most striking of the year and, given the training troubles he has had during his career, he is a real credit to his connections.

Well Armed (USA) (b.g. 2003)	Tiznow (USA) (b 1997)	Cee's Tizzy (gr or ro 1987)	Relaunch
			Tizly
		Cee's Song (b or br 1986)	Seattle Song
			Lonely Dancer
	Well Dressed (USA) (b or br 1997)	Notebook (b 1985)	Well Decorated
			Mobcap
		Trithenia (b 1992)	Gold Meridian
			Tri Argo

Well Armed is another top winner by the unfashionably-bred Tiznow who defied his pedigree on the track, winning two Breeders' Cup Classics, and has gone on to make a significant mark at stud, his fee in the latest covering season 75,000 dollars. Tiznow is nearly seventeen hands and Well Armed, a big, strong gelding, takes after him in having an imposing physique. Tiznow's other major winners include the champion two-year-old filly Folklore, mentioned above, the good 2008 three-year-olds Colonel John (Santa Anita Derby and Travers Stakes) and Da' Tara (Belmont Stakes), and Bullsbay, winner of the Whitney Handicap in August. Well Armed's dam, Well Dressed, had eight starts, all at Delaware Park, winning three of them including a maiden over a mile at two and a minor stakes event, the American Holly Stakes, over six furlongs as a three-year-old. She has bred three other winners, including Helsinki, third in the 2007 Travers Stakes, and the unbeaten three-year-old filly Witty, winner of the Grade 3 Railbird Stakes at Hollywood in May, both of them by Distorted Humor. Well Armed's grandam Trithenia failed to win in nine starts but produced six other winners besides Well Dressed. She was a sister to Tee Kay, who landed the Grade 3 Martha Washington Stakes and became the dam of Symboli Kris S, Horse of The Year in Japan in 2002 and 2003. *E. Harty, USA*

WE'LL COME 5 b.g. Elnadim (USA) 128 – Off The Blocks 55 (Salse (USA) 128) **116 §**
[2009 102: 7m 8f* 8.1m 8g* 8m 8m Oct 2] big, heavy-bodied gelding: has a quick action: smart performer: won handicaps at Salisbury in June and Ascot (career-best effort, beat Moynahan 4½ lengths) in August: well below form in Joel Stakes at Newmarket final start: effective at 7f/1m: acts on any turf going: wears blinkers/cheekpieces: ungenuine: sold 75,000 gns, joined A. bin Huzaim in UAE. *M. A. Jarvis*

WE'LL DEAL AGAIN 2 b.c. (Apr 14) Gentleman's Deal (IRE) 114 – Emma Amour **70 +**
67 (Emarati (USA) 74) [2009 6d^2 7m 6g^3 6m 7d^3 8g^5 f6g^2 7.2v^3 Oct 31] workmanlike colt: sixth foal: half-brother to 2007 2-y-o 7f seller winner Indecision (by Muhtarram): dam, sprint maiden, half-sister to smart 7f/1m performer Pulau Tioman: fair maiden: stays 7f: acts on fibresand and heavy going. *M. W. Easterby*

Les Ambassadeurs Club Shergar Cup Mile (Handicap), Ascot—We'll Come is the second of three winners for Richard Hughes, who leads Ireland to victory in the Shergar Cup, with Great Britain second, Europe third and the Rest of the World fourth; the fixture attracted a crowd of 27,772 (down from 33,115 in 2008)

WELLESLEY 3 b.g. Bertolini (USA) 125 – Markova's Dance 64 (Mark of Esteem (IRE) 137) [2009 68: 7.1m 8.3m^4 8s^4 10m^6 p9.5g 9.9g Sep 22] stocky gelding: modest maiden handicapper: will prove best short of 1m: acts on polytrack: tried in cheekpieces: sold £4,200, then gelded. *W. R. Swinburn* **60**

WELLINGTON FAIR 2 br.g. (Feb 17) Trade Fair 124 – Milly's Lass 79 (Mind Games 121) [2009 6m^5 5g 5.1m^5 5m* 5g^3 Oct 5] angular gelding: third foal: dam 2-y-o 5f winner: fairly useful performer: visored, much improved when winning maiden at Sandown (by 1¼ lengths from Racy) in September: best form at 5f: acts on good to firm ground: blinkered third/final starts: sold 20,000 gns. *C. G. Cox* **87**

WELLINGTON SQUARE 4 b.g. Millkom 124 – Tempestosa 41 (Northern Tempest (USA) 120) [2009 91: 12m 7m* 7m^3 8g 7.1g 8d^5 p8.6g^3 Oct 16] leggy gelding: fairly useful handicapper: won at Goodwood in June: effective at 7f to 1¼m: acts on polytrack and good to firm ground: sold 21,000 gns. *H. Morrison* **92**

WELLMARKED (IRE) 2 b.g. (May 25) Choisir (AUS) 126 – Radiance (IRE) 54 (Thatching 131) [2009 p6g^2 p6g* p7.1g* Dec 26] half-brother to 3 winners, including 5-y-o Chjimes: dam, sprint maiden, half-sister to smart 1m to 1½m performer Bustan: fairly useful performer: won maiden and nursery (beat Itsthursdayalready 2½ lengths) at Wolverhampton in December: stays 7f: raced only on polytrack: tongue tied on debut: should progress again. *John A. Quinn, Ireland* **87 p**

WELL OF ECHOES 3 b.f. Diktat 126 – Seeker 75 (Rainbow Quest (USA) 134) [2009 59: 8m^3 10.3m p8.6m p7f^4 8.5m p6g 7m^4 p5g f7m^5 f8g p7.1g^3 p7m Dec 30] good-topped filly: modest maiden handicapper: left A. McCabe after second outing, sold from J. Glover £1,200 and rejoined former trainer after eighth: stays 1m: acts on polytrack: unraced on extremes of going on turf: tried blinkered, in cheekpieces last 2 starts: tongue tied later in year: races prominently. *A. J. McCabe* **61**

WELLS LYRICAL (IRE) 4 b.c. Sadler's Wells (USA) 132 – Lyrical 65 (Shirley Heights 130) [2009 98: 16m^2 16.1d^2 16.4m^3 13.1m^6 18m Oct 17] good-topped colt: useful performer: good efforts when placed first 3 starts, including at Newcastle (Northumberland Plate, ¾-length second to Som Tala) and listed race at Sandown (2 lengths third to Desert Sea): stays 2m: acts on firm and good to soft going. *B. Smart* **103**

WELSH ANTHEM 3 b.f. Singspiel (IRE) 133 – Khubza 86 (Green Desert (USA) 127) [2009 77p: 8.3m^3 8g^6 8m p8g^5 10.2g^2 12g Jul 31] sturdy filly: fair maiden: stays 10.2f: acts on good to firm and good to soft ground: blinkered 3 of last 4 outings: often races prominently. *W. R. Muir* **76**

WELSH ARTIST 2 b.g. (Mar 20) Sakhee (USA) 136 – Gwen John (USA) 70 (Peintre Celebre (USA) 137) [2009 p6m p7g^6 p7m^3 Nov 26] second foal: dam, maiden (stayed 9f), half-sister to useful 5f (Queen Mary Stakes) to 1m (US Grade 2 event) winner Dance Parade and US Grade 3 9f winner Ocean Queen: progressive form in maidens at Kempton, length third to Too Putra: should stay 1m. *Mrs A. J. Perrett* **68**

WELSH EMPEROR (IRE) 10 b.g. Emperor Jones (USA) 119 – Simply Times (USA) 64 (Dodge (USA)) [2009 113: 7.1g^6 7.1g 7.1s* 7g 7d Oct 24] tall gelding: smart performer: creditable effort in 2009 only when winning minor event at Haydock (for second successive year) in July, beating Prime Spirit a head: clipped heels final outing: effective at 6f/7f: raced on good ground or softer nowadays (acts on heavy): sometimes blinkered: front runner. *T. P. Tate* **110**

WELSH LEGACY (IRE) 2 b.g. (Feb 28) Saffron Walden (FR) 123 – Silver Harbour (USA) 53 (Silver Hawk (USA) 123) [2009 6g 6m 6g f7g^5 7m Oct 26] good-topped gelding: poor maiden. *B. W. Duke* **47**

WELSH OPERA 4 b.f. Noverre (USA) 125 – Welsh Diva 112 (Selkirk (USA) 129) [2009 66: p6g^3 p6g^6 p6g^2 p5g* p5g p5.1g^4 p5.1g* 5.2s 6g 5.1g^5 6m* 5m^3 6m^3 p5.1g^3 6g Oct 20] compact filly: fair handicapper, better on all-weather: won at Kempton in February, Wolverhampton in March and Yarmouth in September: effective from 5f to 7f: acts on polytrack and good to firm going: often visored/tongue tied. *S. C. Williams* **67 a73**

WELSH PASSION 3 b.f. Marju (IRE) 127 – Focosa (ITY) (In The Wings 128) [2009 –: 8.3m 7.1m Sep 10] angular filly: no form: tried blinkered. *D. Haydn Jones* **–**

WE'RE DELIGHTED 4 b.g. Tobougg (IRE) 125 – Samadilla (IRE) 83 (Mujadil (USA) 119) [2009 79: 8m^3 7s^5 7g 10m^6 9.9m^4 10g 8m^5 Aug 13] close-coupled gelding: fair handicapper: stays 1m: acts on firm and soft going: sold £1,500. *T. D. Walford* **77**

WESSEX (USA) 9 ch.g. Gone West (USA) – Satin Velvet (USA) 103 (El Gran Senor (USA) 136) [2009 95: p8.6g f6g^6 f7g Jun 2] big, rather leggy gelding: handicapper, well below form in 2009: tried visored/tongue tied. *R. Curtis* **–**

WEST END LAD 6 b.g. Tomba 119 – Cliburnel News (IRE) 76 (Horage 124) [2009 73: f8g* f8g f8g^4 f8g f8g 8.3g* 8.3g^6 8.3m* 8.3v^6 8.3g^6 7.5f 7.5g^6 8.1m^6 7m f8f^4 Dec 17] fairly useful handicapper: won at Southwell in January, and Nottingham in May and July: below form after: effective at 7f/1m: acts on all-weather, heavy and good to firm going: tried in cheekpieces, wears blinkers nowadays. *S. R. Bowring* **83**

WESTER LODGE (IRE) 7 ch.g. Fraam 114 – Reamzafonic 46 (Grand Lodge (USA) 125) [2009 64: p12g^3 p8.6g^5 p13.9g^2 10.3m^6 p8.6g^6 p13.9g^5 10m 12.6d 11m^6 p16.5g^3 p16.5g^3 p16.5g^2 Oct 30] big, close-coupled gelding: modest handicapper: stays 2m: acts on polytrack and firm going: tried in headgear. *J. M. P. Eustace* **64**

WESTERN ART (USA) 4 b. or br.g. Hennessy (USA) 122 – Madam West (USA) (Gone West (USA)) [2009 –: p7.1g f6g f7g f7g 6d 8.5m^3 7v p8.6g Dec 18] good-bodied gelding: form since 2 yrs (modest) only on sixth start in 2009 (left M. Easterby after): stays 8.5f: acts on good to firm and good to soft ground. *Miss Gay Kelleway* **53**

WESTERN PEARL 2 b.f. (Mar 6) High Chaparral (IRE) 132 – Pulau Pinang (IRE) 101 (Dolphin Street (FR) 125) [2009 p8m^5 Nov 19] third foal: half-sister to 3-y-o Penang Princess: dam 1¼m to 13f winner: 25/1, encouraging 6¼ lengths fifth to Eleanora Duse in maiden at Kempton, slowly away and not knocked about: will be suited by 1¼m/1½m: capable of better. *W. J. Knight* **66 p**

WESTERN ROOTS 8 ch.g. Dr Fong (USA) 128 – Chrysalis 66 (Soviet Star (USA) 128) [2009 75: p10g^2 10g* 10.2g^3 10m 9m 10f 8m p9.5g p10m Dec 16] lengthy gelding: fair performer: won claimer at Brighton in April: below form after, leaving A. Balding following next start: stays 1¼m: acts on polytrack and good to firm ground: tried visored/in cheekpieces: forces pace. *P. Butler* **70 d**

WESTER ROSS (IRE) 5 b.g. Fruits of Love (USA) 127 – Diabaig 76 (Precocious 126) [2009 74: 10f^4 14.1g^5 16g^4 Oct 8] compact gelding: modest handicapper nowadays: stays 2m: acts on soft and good to firm going: blinkered once: fair hurdler. *J. M. P. Eustace* **61**

WEST KIRK 3 b.g. Alhaarth (IRE) 126 – Naughty Crown (USA) 84 (Chief's Crown (USA)) [2009 p7g^5 8g^5 p8m^4 p9.5g Dec 18] 13,000Y, resold 67,000Y: fifth foal: half-brother to 3 winners, including 4-y-o Love In The Park: dam, 7f/7.5f (in USA) winner, half-sister to smart performer up to 1¼m Tahreeb: gelded, best effort when fifth in claimer second start: best effort at 1m: raced only on polytrack and good ground. *W. Jarvis* **75**

WEST LEAKE (IRE) 3 b.g. Acclamation 118 – Kilshanny 70 (Groom Dancer (USA) 128) [2009 65: 8.3m⁶ f6g* 6.1g³ 6.1g 6.1m 6.1v Jul 17] compact, attractive gelding: fair handicapper: won at Southwell in April: likely to prove best at testing 6f/7f: acts on all-weather, soft and good to firm going: blinkered final outing: sold £800 in October. *B. W. Hills* **67**

WEST LEAKE STAR (IRE) 2 b.c. (Feb 20) Antonius Pius (USA) 123§ – Red Beach (IRE) (Turtle Island (IRE) 123) [2009 6.1g 5.7g 6s² p6g⁴ f6g 6d⁵ Oct 12] €22,000F, £44,000Y: first foal: dam unraced out of half-sister to smart performer up to 1½m Lord Helpus: fair maiden: should stay 7f: acts on soft going: sold £7,500. *B. W. Hills* **77**

WESTLIN' WINDS (IRE) 3 b.c. Montjeu (IRE) 137 – Uliana (USA) 95 (Darshaan 133) [2009 p8g⁶ 10m⁵ 11.7m⁴ p13.9g⁴ Sep 17] €60,000Y: good-topped, attractive colt: fourth foal: closely related to fairly useful Irish 2006 2-y-o 1m winner So Amazing (by Galileo), later successful in USA, and Irish 4-y-o Festival Princess: dam, Irish 1¼m winner, half-sister to smart German 1¼m/1½m winner Ransom o'War: fair maiden: progressive form, fourth in handicap final start: stays 1¾m: raced only on polytrack and good to firm going. *C. R. Egerton* **75**

WESTPHALIA (IRE) 3 b.c. Danehill Dancer (IRE) 117 – Pharapache (USA) (Lyphard (USA) 132) [2009 110: 8g² 8m³ 10.5g³ 8g⁵ 7g Dec 19] tall, useful-looking colt: smart performer: improved when third at Longchamp (Poule d'Essai des Poulains, promoted from fourth when beaten 3 lengths by Silver Frost) and Chantilly (Prix du Jockey Club, 3 lengths behind Le Havre): below form after, in Prix Jean Prat at Longchamp (blinkered, pulled too hard, left A. O'Brien in Ireland and off over 5 months after) and handicap at Sha Tin (under new name of Super Pistachio, tongue tied): stays 10.5f: acts on firm and soft going: held up: has high head carriage. *A. S. Cruz, Hong Kong* **117**

WESTPORT 6 b.g. Xaar 132 – Connemara (IRE) 100 (Mujadil (USA) 119) [2009 86: 5m 5g 5.9d⁴ 7m⁶ 9d f8f Nov 24] strong gelding: fair handicapper nowadays: best at 6f: acts on all-weather, soft and good to firm going: tried in cheekpieces. *R. Bastiman* **65**

WESTSTERN (GER) 6 b.g. Dashing Blade 117 – Westafrika (GER) (Aspros (GER)) [2009 p12g 12m Sep 23] successful 4 times up to around 1¼m in Germany for C. von der Recke, including in handicaps at Cologne (2) and Bad Harzburg in 2007: modest hurdler: fair form (but little impact) in handicaps on Flat in Britain: tried tongue tied. *G. L. Moore* **73**

WEST WITH THE WIND 4 b.g. Fasliyev (USA) 120 – Midnight Angel (GER) 108 (Acatenango (GER) 127) [2009 91: 11.5m 12s⁶ 10m 10m Sep 23] big, lengthy gelding: has long stride: well held in handicaps on Flat in 2009: sold £10,000, joined Evan Williams. *T. P. Tate* **–**

WEST WITH THE WIND (USA) 3 b.f. Gone West (USA) – Opera Aida (IRE) (Sadler's Wells (USA) 132) [2009 79: p7g⁵ 8.1g² 7g⁴ 8m* 8.3m² p9.5g Sep 25] leggy filly: fair performer: won maiden at Newcastle in August: likely to stay 1¼m: acts on polytrack, good to firm and good to soft ground. *P. W. Chapple-Hyam* **77**

WESTWOOD 4 ch.g. Captain Rio 122 – Consignia (IRE) 67 (Definite Article 121) [2009 78: 6g* 6v 5m 6m p6g p6f Dec 20] rather leggy gelding: fair handicapper: won at Windsor in April: barely stays 7f: acts on fibresand and soft ground: none too consistent. *D. Haydn Jones* **73**

WESTWOOD DAWN 4 gr.g. Clodovil (IRE) 116 – Ivory Dawn 85 (Batshoof 122) [2009 –, a65: p6g⁵ p6g² p5.1g² p6g² p7m⁴ p6g⁵ p5g² Nov 25] leggy gelding: fair maiden handicapper: best at 5f/6f: acts on all-weather, well held on turf: tried in cheekpieces, visored nowadays: tongue tied last 2 starts: sold £3,500. *D. Shaw* **–** **a65**

WET FEET 2 br.g. (Jan 31) Footstepsinthesand 120 – Swoon (Night Shift (USA)) [2009 6g Aug 12] 50/1, eighth to Mon Cadeaux in maiden at Salisbury (gelded after). *P. R. Chamings* **58**

WEYBRIDGE LIGHT 4 b.g. Fantastic Light (USA) 134 – Nuryana 107 (Nureyev (USA) 131) [2009 78: 16g 14d p16g⁶ p13.9g³ p16m Dec 10] fair handicapper: stays 1¾m: acts on polytrack and soft going: blinkered/visored nowadays. *E. Griffin, Ireland* **75**

WHASTON (IRE) 4 b.g. Hawk Wing (USA) 136 – Sharafanya (IRE) (Zafonic (USA) 130) [2009 65: p8.6g 8f 9.8m² 9.8m⁶ 9.3m⁵ 8m⁶ 10m* 10m⁵ 8m Aug 31] deep-girthed gelding: modest performer: won handicap at Ayr in July: stays 1¼m: acts on polytrack and good to firm going: usually visored: none too consistent: sold £6,000 in October. *J. D. Bethell* **63**

WHAT A DAY 3 b.g. Daylami (IRE) 138 – Sensation 114 (Soviet Star (USA) 128) [2009 71: 8f⁵ 8.3m 8.5g 12m 10.3d 9.9g² 9.9m Aug 30] smallish gelding: just modest handicapper at 3 yrs: stays 1¼m: acts on good to soft going: tried in cheekpieces. *J. J. Quinn* **63**

WHAT A FELLA 3 b.g. Lujain (USA) 119 – Fred's Dream 67 (Cadeaux Genereux 131) [2009 65d: 6m⁴ 7.1m⁵ 6m³ 5m³ 5m 5m* 5g³ 5g 5f² p5.1g 5m⁴ 5g Sep 21] compact gelding: modest performer: won maiden seller at Hamilton in July: effective at 5f/6f: acts on firm ground: tried blinkered, often wears cheekpieces: one to be wary of. *Mrs A. Duffield* **54 §**

WHATAGOODCATCH (IRE) 3 b.f. Bachelor Duke (USA) 122 – Truly Generous (IRE) 104 (Generous (IRE) 139) [2009 8g 10g³ 10.5m⁴ p8g Aug 5] 82,000Y: half-sister to 3 winners, including useful French 7f/1m winner Antique (by Dubai Millennium) and 11-y-o Nawamees: dam, French 1¼m winner who stayed 12.5f, half-sister to very smart French middle-distance performer Modhish: fair form when in frame in maidens, leaving John Oxx in Ireland after third outing: should prove better at 1¼m than 1m: sold 6,500 gns in October. *R. Hannon* **70**

WHATAMI 3 br. or gr.f. Daylami (IRE) 138 – Wosaita 70 (Generous (IRE) 139) [2009 57p: p10g⁶ p12g³ Jun 13] angular filly: fair form in maidens: stays 1½m: acts on polytrack. *E. A. L. Dunlop* **69**

WHAT DO YOU KNOW 6 b.g. Compton Place 125 – How Do I Know 91 (Petong 126) [2009 88: 5g⁵ p8g 6m² May 22] sturdy gelding: handicapper, just fair form at 6 yrs: has form at 7f, best at 5f/6f: acts on polytrack and firm going: usually wears headgear: once tongue tied. *A. M. Hales* **73**

WHAT KATIE DID (IRE) 4 b.g. Invincible Spirit (IRE) 121 – Chatterberry 67 (Aragon 118) [2009 76: p6g* p5g³ p6g p6g* p6g* 6g* 5g⁴ 5f 5.7m Jun 13] rather leggy gelding: fair handicapper: won at Kempton in January and March (2) and Windsor in April: well below form after: effective at 6f/7f: acts on polytrack, promise on good to firm: tried blinkered, in cheekpieces nowadays. *J. M. Bradley* **74 a78**

WHAT'S UP DOC (IRE) 8 b.g. Dr Massini (IRE) 117 – Surprise Treat (IRE) 75 (Shalford (IRE) 124§) [2009 83: p10g f8g³ p8g⁴ p9.5g* 10m* 10.1g* Jul 30] fairly useful performer: won seller at Wolverhampton in April and claimers at Brighton in June and Epsom (claimed £11,000) in July: effective at 1m/1¼m: acts on all-weather, heavy and good to firm going: tried in cheekpieces: tongue tied once: sold £2,600. *Mrs Trelawney Hill* **82**

WHATYOUWOODWISHFOR (USA) 3 ch.g. Forestry (USA) 121 – Wishful Splendor (USA) (Smart Strike (CAN) 121) [2009 81: 6m⁴ 7d 6m⁵ 6g 6g p7.1g Dec 19] smallish, workmanlike gelding: fair handicapper: well below form after 3-y-o reappearance: should be suited by 7f: acts on polytrack, soft and good to firm ground. *R. A. Fahey* **76**

WHAXAAR (IRE) 5 b.g. Xaar 132 – Sheriyna (FR) (Darshaan 133) [2009 71: p16g² p16m Dec 30] rather leggy gelding: modest handicapper: stays 2m: acts on polytrack and good to soft going: held up. *R. Ingram* **63**

WHELKEEN ROCK (IRE) 2 b.c. (Jan 10) Xaar 132 – Mizillablack (IRE) 95 (Eagle Eyed (USA) 111) [2009 6v 5m May 29] well-grown colt: behind in maiden at Haydock: broke down after 1f next time: dead. *K. A. Ryan* **–**

WHEN DOVES CRY 3 b.f. Grandera (IRE) 129 – Deeply (IRE) 105 (Darshaan 133) [2009 58p: 11.6g 8.3m³ 8.1g 8.3g⁶ Jul 6] rather leggy filly: fair maiden handicapper: should stay beyond 1m: acts on firm going, probably on polytrack: sold 4,000 gns, sent to Bahrain. *B. W. Hills* **66**

WHENEVER 5 ch.g. Medicean 128 – Alessandra 101 (Generous (IRE) 139) [2009 90: 14m 16g⁶ 16.4d 14.1g³ Sep 30] strong gelding: just fair form in handicaps at 5 yrs: stays 2m: acts on soft ground: tried blinkered: suspect temperament: successful over hurdles in October. *R. T. Phillips* **70**

WHERE'S CHARLIE 3 br.g. Where Or When (IRE) 124 – Kennedys Prima 65 (Primo Dominie 121) [2009 8m⁶ Aug 29] workmanlike gelding: 40/1, always behind in maiden at Newmarket. *P. Leech* **–**

WHERE'S DIDS 4 b.f. Piccolo 121 – Who Goes There 63 (Wolfhound (USA) 126) [2009 49: p6g p7.1g Jan 9] rather leggy filly: maiden: well held in 2009: tried in cheekpieces. *P. D. Evans* **–**

WHERE'S KILLORAN 4 b.f. Iron Mask (USA) 117 – Calypso Lady (IRE) 88 (Priolo (USA) 127) [2009 45: f7g⁴ p8.6g⁴ 7m f7g⁵ Apr 23] poor maiden: will prove best short of 1m: acts on all-weather. *E. J. Alston* **49**

WHERE'S REILEY (USA) 3 b. or br.g. Doneraile Court (USA) – Plateau (USA) (Seeking The Gold (USA)) [2009 70: p5.1g³ f5g³ 5m⁵ 6s* 6g⁵ 6m² 7.1g⁴ 6g³ 6.1v⁴ 6m p6g Dec 19] fair handicapper: won at Newcastle in May: likely to prove best at 5f/6f: acts on all-weather, heavy and good to firm going: tried blinkered. *T. D. Barron* **67**

WHERE'S SUSIE 4 ch.f. Where Or When (IRE) 124 – Linda's Schoolgirl (IRE) **72**
(Grand Lodge (USA) 125) [2009 69: 13.1d* 11.7f^{4} 14m^{2} 11.5m* 12m^{3} p16g^{3} p12m^{6}
Dec 9] workmanlike filly: fair handicapper: won at Bath in May and Lingfield in July:
stays 1¾m: acts on polytrack, firm and good to soft going: tried in cheekpieces: consistent: fair hurdler. *M. Madgwick*

WHERE'S THE SOAP (FR) 2 bl. or br.f. (Apr 15) Country Reel (USA) 113 – Sister **89**
Celestine 78 (Bishop of Cashel 122) [2009 5m^{5} 6m^{4} a6.5g* a6.5g^{4} 7g^{5} 6.5m 8d^{3} 7d^{5} 6s
a7.5g Dec 3] €27,000Y: workmanlike filly: third foal: half-sister to French 6f (at 2 yrs)/
9.5f winner Sister Arwen (by Pennekamp): dam 2-y-o 7.5f winner (later winner up to
1½m in Sweden): fairly useful performer: won minor event on all-weather at Deauville in
August: better form in similar/listed contests next 5 outings, sold from Tom Dascombe
€26,000 after sixth start: stays 1m: acts on good to firm and good to soft ground: in
cheekpieces (ran poorly) penultimate outing. *Cedric Boutin, France*

WHERE TO NOW 4 b.f. Where Or When (IRE) 124 – Starminda 50 (Zamindar **–**
(USA) 116) [2009 –: p8g p8.6g Mar 5] no form: tried visored. *Mrs C. A. Dunnett*

WHERE YOU WILL 3 ch.f. Where Or When (IRE) 124 – Red Duchess 64 (Halling **45**
(USA) 133) [2009 59: p8.6g f8g^{5} Feb 12] poor form in 2009. *S. W. Hall*

WHIEPA SNAPPA (IRE) 2 b.g. (Mar 7) Whipper (USA) 126 – Boudica (IRE) (Alha- **70**
arth (IRE) 126) [2009 7f^{5} 7g^{6} 7g^{5} 8m^{3} p8g^{3} 10.2m^{3} 8.3d^{3} Oct 12] 7,500Y: good-topped
gelding: fourth foal: half-brother to fairly useful 6f (including at 2 yrs) winner Sandrey
(by Noverre) and 5f winner Chivola (by Invincible Spirit): dam, no form, half-sister to 3
useful sprinters: fair maiden: stays 1¼m: acts on polytrack, good to firm and good to soft
ground: signs of temperament fifth start, gelded after final one. *P. M. Phelan*

WHINHILL HOUSE 9 ch.g. Paris House 123 – Darussalam 78 (Tina's Pet 121) [2009 **–**
77: p5.1g^{6} 5.1m p6g f5g 6g 7g^{6} 7f Jun 24] strong gelding: well below form in 2009: wears
headgear. *T. T. Clement*

WHIPMA WHOPMA GATE (IRE) 4 b.f. Rossini (USA) 118 – The Gibson Girl **65**
(IRE) (Norwich 118) [2009 49: 8g 8m^{2} 10m 10v^{2} 9.9m 10.1m^{6} 12.5s^{4} 9.8d 8d* 10m
p8.6g^{3} Oct 23] rather leggy filly: fair performer: won seller at Newcastle in September:
stays 1¼m: acts on polytrack, heavy and good to firm going: blinkered last 4 starts: none
too consistent. *D. Carroll*

WHIPPER'S DELIGHT (IRE) 2 b.f. (May 14) Whipper (USA) 126 – Darling **52**
Smile (IRE) (Darshaan 133) [2009 6g p6g p7g Oct 29] €21,000Y, resold 13,000Y, 7,000
2-y-o: workmanlike filly: sixth foal: half-sister to winner in Belgium by Tagula: dam
unraced daughter of smart French miler Once In My Life: down the field in maidens,
modest form at Wolverhampton second start. *D. Donovan*

WHIPPERS LOVE (IRE) 2 b.c. (Feb 27) Whipper (USA) 126 – Danadoo (FR) **85**
(Septieme Ciel (USA) 123) [2009 5m 5m 6g 6m^{4} p7g^{2} 7d^{3} 7.5m* 8g* 8m^{4} 8g Oct 23]
€70,000F: sturdy colt: first foal: dam, French 5.5f winner, half-sister to useful French
sprinter Dobby Road: fairly useful performer: won nurseries at Beverley and Newmarket
in August: stays 1m: acts on polytrack and good to firm going: races prominently.
M. Johnston

WHIPPERWAY (IRE) 2 b.f. (Apr 15) Whipper (USA) 126 – Prince's Passion 80 **64**
(Brief Truce (USA) 126) [2009 6m 7d^{3} 7f 7m^{4} 8.3d 7d^{2} p7.1g^{5} p7.1g^{6} p8g* Nov 21]
€20,000: rather leggy filly: third foal: dam 2-y-o 5.7f winner (stayed 1¼m): modest performer: visored, won seller at Lingfield in November: stays easy 1m: acts on polytrack,
good to firm and good to soft going. *M. R. Channon*

WHIP UP (IRE) 2 b.g. (Apr 15) Whipper (USA) 126 – Fizz Up 77 (Alzao (USA) 117) **–**
[2009 5.1g 5.1m 6.1g May 25] no form and signs of temperament: tried blinkered.
J. G. Portman

WHIRLIJIG (IRE) 4 ch.f. Spinning World (USA) 130 – Dariyba (IRE) (Kahyasi 130) **76**
[2009 9.2g^{3} 10.3m^{2} 10d^{3} 12g 9.8d^{3} Sep 1] €6,000F, €9,000Y: rather leggy filly: sixth
foal: closely related to winner in Greece by Fasliyev and half-sister to useful Irish 1m/9f
winner Major Title (by Brief Truce): dam, French 1¼m winner, half-sister to smart stayer
Far Cry: placed in bumper: fair maiden on Flat: stays 1¼m: unraced on extremes of going.
G. A. Swinbank

WHIRLY DANCER 2 b.f. (May 1) Danehill Dancer (IRE) 117 – Whirly Bird 101 **76**
(Nashwan (USA) 135) [2009 6.1m 7.5f^{2} 7.5m^{2} p7.1g^{3} 7g^{2} Oct 17] smallish filly: first
foal: dam, 9.5f to 11f winner, out of useful half-sister to smart performer up to 1m
Inchinor: fair maiden: stays 7f: acts on polytrack and good to firm ground. *H. R. A. Cecil*

WHISKEY CREEK 4 ch.g. Tipsy Creek (USA) 115 – Judiam 74 (Primo Dominie 121) [2009 67: p6g⁵ p6g* f5g* p5g* f5g* f5g² p5.1g² p5g² f5g⁴ 5m 5g 5m 5m⁴ p5g⁵ 6g Jun 13] stocky gelding: fairly useful handicapper, better on all-weather: won twice at both Lingfield and Southwell in January/February: effective at 5f/6f: acts on all-weather and good to firm going: blinkered/visored. *C. A. Dwyer* **84 a87**

WHISKEY JUNCTION 5 b.g. Bold Edge 123 – Victoria Mill 59 (Free State 125) [2009 98: p6g 5.3g⁵ 5.7g⁵ 6m⁶ p6g⁶ p5g 5.7m* p6g* p6g⁵ 5.2m² 5g Oct 10] quite good-topped gelding: fairly useful performer: won handicap at Bath in July and claimer at Kempton in August: best kept to 5f/6f: acts on polytrack and good to firm going: tried in cheekpieces: races prominently. *M. Quinn* **86**

WHISKY GALORE 3 ch.c. Kyllachy 129 – Owdbetts (IRE) 69 (High Estate 127) [2009 76: 8m 10g⁵ 10m 11.5s² 16g 11.6d⁵ Oct 12] sturdy colt: fair maiden handicapper: stays 2m: acts on soft going: visored last 2 starts: one to treat with caution: sold 11,000 gns. *C. G. Cox* **76 §**

WHISKY JACK 3 b.g. Bahamian Bounty 116 – Dress Design (IRE) 84 (Brief Truce (USA) 126) [2009 70: p6g p8.6g⁴ 7g p7g* p7.1g p7.1g Oct 23] lengthy gelding: fair handicapper: won at Lingfield in September: well held after: stays 7f: acts on polytrack, soft and good to firm going: often blinkered: signs of temperament. *W. R. Muir* **73**

WHISPERED DREAMS (GER) 4 ch.f. Platini (GER) 126 – Waconda (GER) (Pursuit of Love 124) [2009 6d* 7d* 7g* 8d⁴ 8g² 8g² 8m⁵ 7g³ Aug 23] useful performer: missed 2008, leaving Saeed bin Suroor €15,000 towards end of year: successful in 2009 in minor events at Krefeld, Cologne and Baden-Baden in April/May: good efforts last 4 starts, in Preis der Spielbank Hamburg (neck second to Caro Jino) and listed races at Munich (¾-length second to Magic Eye), Bath (fifth to Annabelle's Charm) and Dusseldorf (length third to Sarabia): stayed 1m: acted on polytrack, good to firm and good to soft ground: consistent: stud. *M. Hofer, Germany* **99**

WHISPERED LANDS (IRE) 3 b.f. Elusive City (USA) 117 – Happy Talk (IRE) 74 (Hamas (IRE) 125§) [2009 p7g 10g 10m p8g p10m Sep 26] compact filly: third foal: half-sister to fairly useful 2006 2-y-o 5f winner Frisky Talk (by Fasliyev) and 4-y-o Foreign Rhythm: dam Irish 1¼m winner: little form. *J. R. Boyle* **–**

WHISPERED TIMES (USA) 2 b. or br.g. (Mar 26) More Than Ready (USA) 120 – Lightning Show (USA) (Storm Cat (USA)) [2009 5d⁴ 6m* 6f 6s⁵ 7m 5.1s f7g Nov 17] $50,000Y, 29,000 2-y-o: close-coupled gelding: first foal: dam, US maiden, sister to smart US 1998 Grade 1 2-y-o 8.5f winner Tactical Cat: fair performer: won maiden at Hamilton in June: below form after: stays 6f: acts on good to firm going: tried blinkered/in cheekpieces. *P. C. Haslam* **75 d**

WHISPERED WISH 3 b.f. Rainbow Quest (USA) 134 – Cyclone Connie 98 (Dr Devious (IRE) 127) [2009 8d Apr 14] third foal: half-sister to 5-y-o Judge 'N Jury and fairly useful 2007 2-y-o 7f winner Flight Plan (by Best of The Bests): dam, 6f winner, half-sister to smart sprinter Colonel Cotton: 33/1, well held in maiden at Yarmouth: refused to enter stall intended debut: sold £800. *W. J. Haggas* **–**

WHISPERING GALLERY 3 b.g. Daylami (IRE) 138 – Echoes In Eternity (IRE) 111 (Spinning World (USA) 130) [2009 9.2g* 12m⁴ 10g* 12m* Aug 19] tall, lengthy, good-topped gelding: has scope: first foal: dam, won Sun Chariot and Park Hill Stakes, **117 p**

RSA and Motability Stakes (Handicap), York—Whispering Gallery makes all and shows smart form in beating Class Is Class (left) and Yes Mr President (star on cap)

closely related to smart performer up to 1¾m Petara Bay and half-sister to very smart performer up to 2m Percussionist and smart performer up to 1½m Playful Act: made impressive start to career, winning 3 of 4 starts, namely maiden at Hamilton (by 10 lengths) in June and handicaps at Newmarket and York (beat Class Is Class 3¾ lengths, again making all), both in August: stays 1½m: raced only on good/good to firm ground: has joined Godolphin: smart already, and will improve further. *M. Johnston*

WHISPERING SPIRIT (IRE) 3 b.f. Catcher In The Rye (IRE) 115 – Celtic Guest **61**
(IRE) (Be My Guest (USA) 126) [2009 60: 8s^4 7g* f7g 8d 7v* Sep 4] compact filly: modest performer: won maiden in June and claimer in September (visored), both at Catterick: may prove best up to 7f: acts on polytrack and heavy ground. *Mrs A. Duffield*

WHISPER SOFTLY (IRE) 3 b.f. Tagula (IRE) 116 – Whisper Dawn (IRE) (Fasliyev **47**
(USA) 120) [2009 6d 5g 6m 5m^5 5m Jul 14] €2,800Y: second foal: half-sister to 4-y-o Al Gillani: dam unraced: poor maiden: raced only at 5f/6f. *T. D. Walford*

WHISTLE BLOWER 2 b.c. (Feb 17) Exceed And Excel (AUS) 126 – Song of Hope **70**
103 (Chief Singer 131) [2009 7d 8.5d^4 8m 7d* p7g^3 Nov 13] £32,000Y: compact colt: half-brother to several winners, including 2001 2-y-o 6f winner Xtrasensory (by Royal Applause) and 5f (at 2 yrs)/7f winner Song of Skye (by Warning), both fairly useful: dam 2-y-o 5f winner: fair performer: won nursery at Brighton in October: should prove at least as effective at 6f as 7f: acts on polytrack and good to soft going: tried blinkered. *J. H. M. Gosden*

WHISTLEDOWNWIND 4 b.g. Danehill Dancer (IRE) 117 – Mountain Ash 107 **96**
(Dominion 123) [2009 106: p8g^4 p8g^2 8m 8s Apr 18] big, good-bodied gelding: useful performer: not at best in 2009, including when respectable second to Al Muheer in minor event at Lingfield: stays 1¼m: acts on polytrack and good to soft ground: visored last 2 starts: gelded after final outing, then sold 6,500 gns. *J. Noseda*

WHISTLEINTHEWIND (IRE) 2 b.g. (Mar 11) Oratorio (IRE) 128 – Lady Scarlett **86 p**
(Woodman (USA) 126) [2009 8g^2 p8g^3 p8g* Nov 25] 40,000Y, 55,000 2-y-o: fifth foal: closely related to 6-y-o Sunrise Safari: dam unraced half-sister to smart Irish/Hong Kong performer up to 1½m Desert Fox: won maiden at Lingfield in November by 2½ lengths from Rock My World: should stay 1¼m: already fairly useful, and likely to do better still. *G. L. Moore*

WHISTLEUPTHEWIND 6 b.m. Piccolo 121 – The Frog Queen 64 (Bin Ajwaad **54**
(IRE) 119) [2009 –: p6g^6 Jan 8] neat mare: modest performer: effective at 6f to 1m: acts on polytrack, firm and soft ground: often blinkered/in cheekpieces. *J. M. P. Eustace*

WHISTLING WIND 2 b.g. (Feb 23) Needwood Blade 117 – Empire of The Sun 53 **–**
(Second Empire (IRE) 124) [2009 5.1m 6g Jul 3] leggy gelding: well held in maiden/seller. *Paul Green*

WHISTON PAT 4 ch.g. Lomitas 129 – Fille de Bucheron (USA) 83 (Woodman (USA) **54**
126) [2009 –: f12d^6 f12g^5 Jan 15] modest maiden: stays 1½m: raced on fibresand. *S. R. Bowring*

WHITBARROW (IRE) 10 b.g. Royal Abjar (USA) 121 – Danccini (IRE) 78 (Dancing **76**
Dissident (USA) 119) [2009 81: f6d^3 f7d^3 p7.1g^5 f6g^2 f7g^3 f7g^5 p7g^2 p7.1g p7.1g^4 p6g^3 f7m* Dec 15] strong, good sort: fair handicapper: won at Southwell in December: effective at 6f/7f: acts on all-weather, firm and soft going: usually wears headgear: front runner: reliable. *B. R. Millman*

WHITBY (IRE) 2 br.f. (Mar 20) Dubawi (IRE) 129 – Hymenee (USA) (Chief's Crown **55 p**
(USA)) [2009 f8f^4 f8m^5 f7f^3 Dec 11] 38,000Y: half-sister to useful French 1¼m/10.5f winner Harlem Dancer (by Dr Devious) and fairly useful French 11f/11.5f winner Harambee (by Robellino): dam French 1¼m winner out of high-class French 2-y-o Hippodamia: modest form in maidens at Southwell, not knocked about last 2 starts: should stay 1¼m: likely to do better. *M. W. Easterby*

WHITCOMBE MINISTER (USA) 4 b.c. Deputy Minister (CAN) – Pronghorn **97**
(USA) (Jaipur) [2009 103: p8.6g^3 p11g p10g p10.7g 9d 8m Sep 26] tall, leggy colt: useful handicapper: third in quite valuable race at Wolverhampton in March, best effort in 2009: left M. Botti after third start: stays 1¼m: acts on polytrack, best turf form on good/good to soft going: blinkered last 3 starts: has run well when sweating. *M. Halford, Ireland*

WHITCOMBE SPIRIT 4 b.g. Diktat 126 – L'Evangile 105 (Danehill (USA) 126) **67**
[2009 65: 15.4g^6 16g^4 16.1d^3 16m^4 16.1d^2 16g^3 16d^6 Oct 11] lengthy gelding: fair maiden handicapper: stays 2m: acts on all-weather, unraced on extremes of going on turf. *Jamie Poulton*

WHITECHAPEL 2 b.g. (Mar 10) Oasis Dream 129 – Barathiki 81 (Barathea (IRE) 127) [2009 6m Jul 25] fourth foal: half-brother to 3-y-o Albertine Rose and winner in Greece by Docksider: dam, 2-y-o 6f winner, half-sister to useful 7f winner Peacock Alley: 7/1 and very green, last in maiden at Salisbury. *W. R. Muir* **–**

WHITE DAFFODIL (IRE) 2 b.f. (Apr 29) Footstepsinthesand 120 – Sparky's Song 63 (Electric 126) [2009 5m^4 5g^2 5.1m* 5m 5m^4 6g^4 6m Sep 21] €35,000Y: quite attractive filly: half-sister to several winners, including 6f (including at 2 yrs) winner Lady Links (by Bahamian Bounty) and 2004 2-y-o 6f winner Umniya (by Bluebird), both useful: dam, 1¼m/1½m winner, half-sister to very smart sprinter Bold Edge: fair performer: won maiden at Nottingham in June: should stay 6f. *R. Hannon* **69**

WHITE DART 2 b.c. (Mar 25) Rakti 130 – Feather Boa (IRE) 81 (Sri Pekan (USA) 117) [2009 7d 7g 7g^6 7g^2 p8m^2 p8m* Sep 30] 60,000Y: third foal: half-brother to fairly useful 2007 2-y-o 5f winner Mazzanti (by Piccolo) and 3-y-o Vamos: dam, 2-y-o 6f winner, half-sister to useful miler Wagtail: fairly useful performer: won nursery at Kempton readily by 2 lengths from Jairzihno: stays 1m. *M. R. Channon* **81**

WHITE DEER (USA) 5 b.g. Stravinsky (USA) 133 – Brookshield Baby (IRE) (Sadler's Wells (USA) 132) [2009 88: f7g^6 7f^2 f8g^4 10.3g 7m* 8g^3 7m 7m 7m 8m* 8m 7g p8.6g Nov 21] lengthy, good-topped gelding: fairly useful performer: left D. Nicholls after fourth outing: won handicap at Thirsk in June and claimer at Redcar in September: said to have had breathing problem final start: stays 9f, effective at shorter: acts on polytrack, firm and good to soft going: wears headgear: tried tongue tied: ungenuine. *G. A. Harker* **90 §**

WHITE DEVIL 2 ch.g. (Mar 13) Zafeen (FR) 123 – Costa Balena (CHI) (Great Regent (CAN)) [2009 7.1m 7.1g^3 7.1g^4 7m^2 Sep 10] tall gelding: has scope: sixth foal: half-brother to winner in Chile by Rich Man's Gold: dam winner in Chile: fairly useful maiden: free-going sort, should be as effective at 6f as 7f: carried head high second start, gelded after final one. *A. M. Balding* **80**

WHITE LEDGER (IRE) 10 ch.g. Ali-Royal (IRE) 127 – Boranwood (IRE) (Exhibitioner 111) [2009 54: 7.6g 8.3m 5.1d^2 f6g p6g Dec 19] useful-looking gelding: modest handicapper: best at 5f/6f: acts on all-weather, firm and soft going: sometimes wears headgear: none too consistent. *R. E. Peacock* **54**

WHITE MOSS (IRE) 5 b.m. Peintre Celebre (USA) 137 – Saint Ann (USA) 66 (Geiger Counter (USA)) [2009 72: p12g 11.9g^5 p10g Apr 17] lengthy mare: just modest handicapper in 2009: may prove best up to 1¼m: acts on soft and good to firm going. *Jim Best* **50**

WHITEOAK LADY (IRE) 4 ch.f. Medecis 119 – French Toast (IRE) (Last Tycoon 131) [2009 76: 6g 6m f6g 6s 6d* 6.1s Oct 7] good-bodied filly: fair performer: won seller at Thirsk in August: effective at 6f/7f: acts on soft ground: blinkered last 2 starts. *J. L. Spearing* **76**

WHITEROCKS 3 ch.g. Imperial Dancer 123 – Thailand (Lycius (USA) 124) [2009 8f^5 10m 11.7g 12.1g^5 16g p10g Sep 9] leggy gelding: modest maiden: stays 1½m: unraced on ground softer than good: joined Miss S. West. *M. R. Channon* **55**

WHITE SHIFT (IRE) 3 b.f. Night Shift (USA) – Ivy Queen (IRE) (Green Desert (USA) 127) [2009 87: p5.1g^4 p5.1g^4 6g 5f^5 5m^5 5.7f* 6m* 6m^2 6m^2 6d* 5m 6d^6 6m 6m^4 5.7f^2 5.7m^5 6d^6 p6g p6m p6g p6f Dec 13] compact filly: fairly useful performer: won claimer at Bath (left P. D. Evans £12,000) in May and handicaps at Newmarket later in month and Ripon in June: below form after: effective at 5f/6f: acts on polytrack, firm and good to soft going. *P. Howling* **86**

WHITLEY BAY (USA) 2 b.c. (Apr 2) Lion Heart (USA) 124 – Sea Witch (USA) (Sea Hero (USA) 124) [2009 p7.1g Nov 13] 66/1, tailed off in maiden at Wolverhampton. *J. R. Best* **–**

WHO ART THOU (USA) 3 b. or br.g. More Than Ready (USA) 120 – Silk Sails (USA) (Ocean Crest (USA)) [2009 56: 10m Sep 12] lengthy gelding: maiden: well held on Flat and over hurdles (for L. Corcoran) in 2009. *D. R. Gandolfo* **–**

WHODUNIT (UAE) 5 b.g. Mark of Esteem (IRE) 137 – Mystery Play (IRE) 104 (Sadler's Wells (USA) 132) [2009 57: p9.5g p8g* p8.6m p7m Dec 30] good-topped gelding: modest handicapper: form in 2009 only when winning at Kempton in February: effective at 1m to 1½m: acts on polytrack, form on turf only on good going: blinkered nowadays: often makes running. *P. W. Hiatt* **64**

WHOOSHKA (USA) 3 b.f. Smart Strike (CAN) 121 – Bushra (USA) (Danzig (USA)) [2009 10m* 10g^4 11.9g 10.3g Oct 23] $70,000Y: third live foal: dam, US 1m winner, **81**

sister to US Grade 3 8.5f/9f winner Lech: fairly useful form: won maiden at Newbury in June: below form last 2 starts (reported breathing problem first occasion): stays 1¼m: acts on good to firm ground. *P. W. Chapple-Hyam*

WHO'S SHIRL 3 b.f. Shinko Forest (IRE) – Shirl 52 (Shirley Heights 130) [2009 –: 6f^{2} 6m^{2} 5.9m^{3} 7m 6m^{2} 6m^{2} 6m* 6m^{5} 7.1m Sep 27] workmanlike filly: fairly useful handicapper: much improved when winning apprentice event at Newcastle in August: will prove as effective at 7f as 6f: acts on firm going. *C. W. Fairhurst* **81**

WHO'S WINNING (IRE) 8 ch.g. Docksider (USA) 124 – Quintellina 83 (Robellino (USA) 127) [2009 66: 6g^{6} 5.1m^{5} 5.7d^{6} 6f^{3} 6.1g^{4} 6f^{6} 6m^{5} 7f^{4} 6f^{3} 6.1m* p6m^{2} 6m^{2} p7m^{3} Oct 7] sturdy gelding: fair performer: won claimer at Chepstow in September: best around 6f: acts on polytrack, firm and good to soft going: tried in headgear: usually tongue tied: has bled. *B. G. Powell* **66**

WHOTSIT (IRE) 3 ch.g. Choisir (AUS) 126 – Charming Victoria (IRE) (Mujadil (USA) 119) [2009 p7g p8.6g p8g* p8g^{2} p8.6g^{5} p8g^{5} 8.1g 8m^{6} 8m^{6} 8g^{2} 8d^{2} 7.6d* 7.6m^{2} 9g 8m^{6} Sep 18] fair performer: won claimer in February and apprentice handicap in August, both at Lingfield: stays 1m: acts on polytrack, good to firm and good to soft ground: blinkered nowadays: often makes running. *Miss Amy Weaver* **67**

WHOZART (IRE) 6 b.g. Mozart (IRE) 131 – Hertford Castle (Reference Point 139) [2009 63: f5g^{2} f6g^{6} f5g^{6} f6g^{5} f5g^{5} 5g^{4} 5m 6m^{5} 5m Jun 16] good-topped gelding: modest handicapper: effective at stiff 5f/6f: acts on fibresand and any turf going: tried in cheek-pieces/blinkers. *A. Dickman* **62**

WHOZTHECAT (IRE) 2 b.c. (Mar 22) One Cool Cat (USA) 123 – Intaglia (GER) (Lomitas 129) [2009 5g^{5} 5f* 6m^{6} Aug 15] €33,000F, £15,000 2-y-o: leggy colt: first foal: dam unraced half-sister to useful German/French performer up to 1½m Irulan: easily best effort when winning maiden at Redcar in May comfortably by 3 lengths from Orpen Arms: off 3 months, seemed amiss final start. *D. Carroll* **84**

WHY NEE AMY 3 ch.f. Tipsy Creek (USA) 115 – Ashleen (Chilibang 120) [2009 62: p7g^{4} p8g^{3} f7g^{5} p8g^{2} p10g^{3} 8d^{2} 8m* 10.1g 8s 9g 8d 8.5m* p9.5g^{5} 8g^{3} p8.6g^{2} p10g* Nov 18] fair performer: won seller at Yarmouth in May and, after leaving Gay Kelleway tenth start, apprentice race at Beverley in September and claimer at Kempton in November: stays easy 1¼m: acts on polytrack, good to firm and good to soft going: tried visored/in cheekpieces. *T. Keddy* **66**

WIBBADUNE (IRE) 5 ch.m. Daggers Drawn (USA) 114 – Becada (GER) (Cadeaux Genereux 131) [2009 86: p5g^{5} p5g p5.1g^{6} 5m 5m^{5} 5m 5g 5.1m 5s 5.1d^{2} 5.1d Aug 11] angular mare: fair handicapper: raced mainly at 5f: acts on all-weather, firm and good to soft going (probably not on soft/heavy): tried in headgear. *D. Shaw* **71**

WICKED DAZE (IRE) 6 ch.g. Generous (IRE) 139 – Thrilling Day 112 (Groom Dancer (USA) 128) [2009 101: p16g^{6} 16m 14.6m^{4} 15.9m^{5} 16m^{2} 12m^{2} 16g p16.5g^{2} p13m^{4} p16m^{3} Dec 10] tall gelding: fairly useful handicapper, better on all-weather nowadays: left Ian Williams after third start: first past post at Wolverhampton (edged right into runner-up and demoted) in November: effective at 1½m to 2m: acts on all-weather and good to firm ground: tried tongue tied/visored/in cheekpieces. *K. A. Ryan* **88** **a94**

WICKEDLY FAST (USA) 3 b.f. Gulch (USA) – Need More Business (IRE) (Alzao (USA) 117) [2009 49: p7g p7g Feb 18] poor form only on debut: raced only at 7f on polytrack: tongue tied. *George Baker* **–**

WICKED WILMA (IRE) 5 b.m. Tagula (IRE) 116 – Wicked 40 (Common Grounds 118) [2009 64: 5m^{2} 5m^{2} 5m^{3} 5m^{5} 5d^{5} 5g^{6} 5m^{5} 5d^{6} 5d^{3} 5m* 5g 5m^{2} 5d Oct 28] fair handicapper: won at Musselburgh in September: raced only at 5f: acts on heavy and good to firm going. *A. Berry* **69**

WICKLEWOOD 3 b.g. Mujahid (USA) 125 – Pinini 63 (Pivotal 124) [2009 –: p6g^{5} p6g 7m 7m^{6} 6m f8g^{4} f6g^{5} 6d 6m 7m^{4} f6g 7m^{6} 11.5g p8m p7g^{4} p7.1g Dec 17] angular gelding: modest maiden: stays 1m: acts on all-weather: usually in headgear. *Mrs C. A. Dunnett* **58**

WICKSY CREEK 4 b.g. Tipsy Creek (USA) 115 – Bridal White 66 (Robellino (USA) 127) [2009 –: p5g^{2} f5g 5m p5.1g 5g 7f p6g^{5} 5g 10g^{5} 11.6f 6m 12m Aug 31] rather leggy gelding: modest maiden: best short of 1½m: tried blinkered/in cheekpieces: often tongue tied. *G. C. Bravery* **50**

WIDE RANGING 2 gr.c. (Mar 25) With Approval (CAN) – Widescreen (USA) (Distant View (USA) 126) [2009 p8g Oct 8] 14/1 and green, well held in maiden at Kempton. *R. Charlton* **52**

WIDEZAIN (IRE) 2 b.c. (Apr 3) Chineur (FR) 123 – Silk Fan (IRE) 100 (Unfuwain (USA) 131) [2009 8m6 Sep 18] 8,000Y, 55,000 2-y-o: first foal: dam Irish 7f winner, including at 2 yrs: 50/1, encouraging 8½ lengths sixth to Wigmore Hall in maiden at Newmarket, slowly away, not knocked about and never nearer: should improve. *M. R. Channon* **65 p**

WI DUD 5 b.g. Elnadim (USA) 128 – Hopesay 84 (Warning 136) [2009 111: 6f3 5.8s4 5d3 5v3 5g 5m 5.1d2 5.4m 6m 6g5 5d Oct 24] small, sturdy gelding: carries condition: smart performer: creditable effort in 2009 only when ½-length third to Look Busy in Temple Stakes at Haydock fourth start: respectable third to Biniou in handicap at Thirsk previous outing: best effort later in year when fifth in similar event at York: effective at 5f/6f: acts on heavy and good to firm going: has worn blinkers, in cheekpieces final start (gelded after): often races prominently: not straightforward. *K. A. Ryan* **111**

WIENER WALZER (GER) 3 b.c. Dynaformer (USA) – Walzerkoenigin (USA) 116 (Kingmambo (USA) 125) [2009 10.5g* 11g* 12g* 12g* 12d4 Sep 6] **124**

For once, the rains stayed away from Hamburg in early-July to give Germany only its second Derby on good going since 1999. The soft or even heavy ground that has so often prevailed for the race in the last decade would doubtless have produced a very different outcome to the one which resulted in victory in the latest edition for Germany's top three-year-old colt Wiener Walzer. He is unbeaten in four starts on good ground but has met with defeat on the two occasions he has encountered softer conditions. So convinced are connections that Wiener Walzer is unsuited by soft that his trainer declared, after a disappointing fourth in the Grosser Preis von Baden on his final start, that Wiener Walzer wouldn't be raced again on anything softer than good. Wiener Walzer's only outing at two—on soft ground—in a maiden at Cologne saw his being beaten more than ten lengths into fifth and, while there are any number of reasons to excuse a horse for defeat on its debut, the fact that Wiener Walzer left that effort way behind suggests that underfoot conditions were almost certainly against him.

Wiener Walzer reappeared at three with a seven-length win in a minor event at Bremen in April. He returned with a bone chip but it was minor enough not to require an operation, though it was still two months before Wiener Walzer was seen out next, in the main trial for the Deutsches Derby, the Oppenheim-Union-Rennen at Cologne. Godolphin's ex-German Peligroso started a short-priced favourite but finished a well-beaten sixth of the seven runners behind Wiener Walzer, who led entering the last two furlongs of a steadily-run affair and won by a length and a quarter. Wiener Walzer clearly didn't impress everyone, though. When the Deutsches Derby came round, stable number-one jockey Adrie de Vries opted to ride the yard's other runner, the unbeaten listed winner Suestado, who started favourite ahead of Wiener Walzer. There were seventeen runners, all of them trained in Germany, for the Idee-sponsored Deutsches Derby. Wiener Walzer was never far off the pace and saw out the longer trip well, leading under two furlongs

Idee Deutsches Derby, Hamburg—
Wiener Walzer (left) gives his connections their second win in the race in three years; Sordino (right), Toughness Danon (cheekpieces) and Eliot (between those two) also make the frame

Rheinland-Pokal, Cologne—
stable-companions Wiener Walzer (left) and Getaway are clear of Eastern Anthem (noseband)

out and winning by a length and a quarter from Sordino, with a neck and the same back to Toughness Danon and Eliot in third and fourth. There have been more impressive winners of the race in recent seasons and the form looked nothing special, with the third and fourth maidens, though both went on to confirm themselves smart performers later in the season (the runner-up wasn't seen out again). Suestado ran poorly and among the others who failed to make the first ten was the filly Bolivia, who started third favourite, in addition to the pair placed behind Wiener Walzer at Cologne, Oriental Lion and Panyu.

Wiener Walzer was the second Deutsches Derby winner in three years for trainer Jens Hirschberger, Swedish jockey Fredrik Johansson and owners Gestut Schlenderhan, following Adlerflug's success in 2007. Trainer and owner were also completing a classic double after winning the German Two Thousand Guineas, the Mehl-Mulhens-Rennen, at Cologne in May with Irian. Most significantly, though, Wiener Walzer's success at Hamburg came little more than a month after the death, at the age of eighty-seven, of Gestut Schlenderhan's owner Baroness Karin von Ullmann, a leading figure in the German breeding industry who inherited Germany's oldest private stud in 1988. Wiener Walzer was the stud's eighteenth winner of the Deutsches Derby since the black, blue and red colours were carried to victory in the classic for the first time in 1908.

Whatever the reservations at the time about the Hamburg form, Wiener Walzer was clearly going the right way and he was given the opportunity to show just how progressive he was when pitched in against older horses for the first time in the Rheinland-Pokal at Cologne in August. His six rivals included his own stable companion, the high-class six-year-old Getaway, carrying the colours of the late Baroness's son Baron Georg von Ullmann. The line-up also included Godolphin representative Eastern Anthem, who had won the Dubai Sheema Classic earlier in the year. The race was, however, dominated throughout by the stable companions, Getaway fractionally shading Wiener Walzer for favouritism. Wiener Walzer led in the race, with Getaway close up, and for a while in the straight it looked as though Getaway might prove the stronger, but, keeping on tenaciously against the rail, Wiener Walzer came out on top by a short head, with Eastern Anthem staying on two and a half lengths away in third. By our reckoning, Wiener Walzer had improved another 10 lb on his Hamburg form. Getaway started favourite again to beat him when they next met in the Grosser Preis von Baden. Wiener Walzer had been far from a certain starter because of the prospect of soft ground at Baden-Baden, but, with conditions drying out (though still good to soft), he was allowed to take his chance. Making the running again, he was unable to find any extra this time when tackled over a furlong out and managed only fourth behind Getaway, beaten five lengths by the winner. Eastern Anthem also turned the form round from Cologne to finish second, with Youmzain keeping Wiener Walzer out of the places.

Lack of stamina, rather than soft ground, had been the primary concern—with good cause as it turned out—when Wiener Walzer's year-older half-brother Walzertraum (by Rahy) was sent off third favourite for the 2008 Deutsches Derby, in which he ended up beating only one home. There was more confidence in Wiener Walzer staying the Derby trip, as he is by Dynaformer, also sire of the 2007 St Leger winner Lucarno. Dynaformer has now sired classic winners in three different countries, most notably at home in the States with the ill-fated 2006 Kentucky Derby winner Barbaro. Walzertraum has gone on to prove a smart performer over a mile and a quarter, winning a Group 3 contest over that trip at Munich prior to his Deutsches Derby bid and running his best race in the latest season when second in a similar event at Baden-Baden. Walzertraum and Wiener Walzer are the first two foals out of Walzerkoenigin, a smart filly at a mile and ten furlongs. She won on soft ground on her debut but finished tailed-off last under similar conditions when favourite for the German One Thousand Guineas, all her wins in better company coming on good ground or firmer. They included the Prix Chloe at Chantilly and the Euro-Cup at Frankfurt at three and the Premio Emilio Turati when progressing further as a four-year-old. Raced exclusively outside Germany that season, she also finished third in the Falmouth Stakes on her one start in Britain and ran one of her best races, on firm ground, when second in the Flower Bowl Invitational at Belmont before ending her racing career with an unlucky fifth in the E. P. Taylor Stakes in Canada.

Wiener Walzer (GER) (b.c. 2006)	Dynaformer (USA) (b or br 1985)	Roberto (b 1969)	Hail To Reason
			Bramalea
		Andover Way (b or br 1978)	His Majesty
			On The Trail
	Walzerkoenigin (USA) (b 1999)	Kingmambo (b 1990)	Mr Prospector
			Miesque
		Great Revival (ch 1992)	Keen
			Prudent Girl

Walzerkoenigin, a daughter of Kingmambo, was a 275,000-dollar yearling purchase at Keeneland's July Sale, and started out with visits to North American-based stallions in her first couple of years at stud. Wiener Walzer's origins are therefore a far cry from those of the traditional Deutsches Derby winner, usually a product of generation upon generation of German breeding. Walzerkoenigin was repatriated and visited Gestut Schlenderhan's own outstanding stallion Monsun in 2006 (resulting in an unraced two-year-old colt named Waltzing Wonder who holds a Deutsches Derby entry for 2010) before producing a colt foal to Montjeu in 2009. Walzerkoenigin's unraced half-sister Shining Vale went close to coming up with a Continental classic winner of her own in the latest season when Wadaat, trained by Clive Brittain, was just touched off in the Oaks d'Italia. Walzerkoenigin and Shining Vale are out of Great Revival who showed precious little in three starts in Ireland (blinkered once) as a four-year-old which made her something of the poor relation among her dam Prudent Girl's numerous other offspring who included Providential, whose wins included the Washington International, and the Prix Marcel Boussac winner Play It Safe. Other daughters of Prudent Girl included the dam of the Racing Post Trophy and Dante Stakes winner Saratoga Springs and the grandam of the Goodwood Cup winner Tioman Island. Prudent Girl was no better than a fairly useful mile and a quarter winner herself, but the 1962 St Leger winner Hethersett was among some notable half-brothers. *J. Hirschberger, Germany*

WIGAN LANE 2 b.f. (Apr 21) Kheleyf (USA) 116 – Nesting 47 (Thatching 131) [2009 **66** 6m^6 5.1g^3 6m* 6m 6m p5.1m^4 p6g^3 p6m p6g^5 p7g Nov 14] £45,000Y, resold 28,000Y: close-coupled filly: fifth foal: half-sister to 7-y-o Hoh Hoh Hoh and 2006 2-y-o 5f winner Miss Otis (by Danetime): dam, ran 3 times, half-sister to dam of 5-y-o Wi Dud: fair performer: won maiden at Doncaster in June: claimed from R. Fahey £6,000 after sixth outing: below form last 3 starts: may prove best at 6f: acts on polytrack and good to firm ground: signs of temperament. *P. Howling*

WIGGY SMITH 10 ch.g. Master Willie 129 – Monsoon 66 (Royal Palace 131) [2009 **88** 89: 10.2d^3 10m 10d^3 10m^4 12m^3 Aug 15] angular gelding: fairly useful handicapper: stays 1½m: acts on polytrack, soft and good to firm going: held up nowadays: reliable. *H. Candy*

WIGHTGOLD 3 ch.f. Golden Snake (USA) 127 – Main Brand 63 (Main Reef 126) **56** [2009 –: 6d^6 8g p10g^4 p10g 12f^3 15.4m^4 17.2g^2 Oct 21] modest maiden: stays 17f: unraced on heavy going, acts on any other turf and polytrack: usually held up. *H. J. L. Dunlop*

WIGMORE HALL (IRE) 2 b.g. (Feb 15) High Chaparral (IRE) 132 – Love And Laughter (IRE) 74 (Theatrical 128) [2009 7g 8m* 7g5 Oct 10] €38,000F, 60,000Y: first foal: dam, 2-y-o 7f winner, half-sister to useful performer up to 1m Kissing The Camera: again heavily backed, easily better effort in maidens when winning at Newmarket in September impressively by 4½ lengths from Mountrath, quickening clear under 2f out before hanging left: seemed amiss (reportedly lost 2 shoes) in minor event at Ascot final start (gelded after): should stay 1¼m: remains useful prospect. *M. L. W. Bell* **93 p**

WIGRAM'S TURN (USA) 4 ch.g. Hussonet (USA) – Stacey's Relic (USA) (Houston (USA)) [2009 90: p7g2 p7g5 7f p7g3 p7m* p7g Nov 18] leggy gelding: useful handicapper: easily best effort in 2009 when winning at Kempton in September: should prove at least as effective at 1m as 7f: acts on polytrack, good to firm and good to soft ground: sometimes visored. *A. M. Balding* **96**

WIGWAM WILLIE (IRE) 7 b.g. Indian Rocket 115 – Sweet Nature (IRE) 71 (Classic Secret (USA) 91) [2009 91: 8.1m 8.5m6 9.8d2 9.8d* 8.5s4 8v 8m Sep 19] quite good-topped gelding: useful handicapper: won at Ripon in June: good fourth in Galway Mile next time: stays 9.8f: acts on heavy and good to firm ground: tried blinkered, wears cheekpieces nowadays: usually tongue tied in 2009: not straightforward. *K. A. Ryan* **97**

WIJIKURA (IRE) 2 ch.c. (Apr 28) Zafeen (FR) 123 – Azolia (IRE) (Alzao (USA) 117) [2009 5m5 5g5 6m6 5g4 6g6 8m Sep 23] close-coupled colt: modest maiden: should stay beyond 5f: tried visored. *J. J. Quinn* **56**

WIKAALA (USA) 4 ch.g. Diesis 133 – Roseate Tern 123 (Blakeney 126) [2009 85: 12s a7g6 9d6 p9.5g6 p12.2g3 p12g* Nov 26] strong gelding: fairly useful handicapper: won at Dundalk in November: stays 1½m: acts on polytrack, soft and good to firm ground: tried visored, blinkered last 4 starts: fairly useful but untrustworthy hurdler. *Gordon Elliott, Ireland* **84**

WILBURY STAR (IRE) 3 b.g. Trans Island 119 – Gold Blended (IRE) 59 (Goldmark (USA) 113) [2009 83: p10g 10m6 8.5g2 8.1g5 p8g3 9.7m2 p8g6 8.3m 9.9g* 10m3 10.3m2 8m3 Oct 1] good-topped gelding: fairly useful handicapper: won at Salisbury in August: creditable placed efforts after: stays 1¼m: acts on polytrack, unraced on extremes of going on turf: blinkered last 4 outings: joined N. Henderson, then gelded. *R. Hannon* **81**

WILD BY NATURE 4 b.f. Tipsy Creek (USA) 115 – Kinraddie (Wuzo (USA) 99) [2009 –: p11g 8m 8g 8m Jun 23] lengthy filly: well held in maidens/handicap. *P. Leech* **–**

WILD CAT CARD (USA) 3 b. or br.f. Mr Greeley (USA) 122 – Wildcat Victory (USA) (Forest Wildcat (USA) 120) [2009 p6g4 Mar 2] $100,000Y, 55,000 2-y-o: third foal: closely related to winner in North America by Grand Slam and half-sister to winner there by Orientate: dam, winning US sprinter, half-sister to US Grade 3 6.5f winner Secret Liaison: needed experience when 2¼ lengths last of 4 behind Trade Centre in maiden at Lingfield: should do better. *D. M. Simcock* **57 p**

WILDCAT WIZARD (USA) 3 b.g. Forest Wildcat (USA) 120 – Tip The Scale (USA) (Valiant Nature (USA) 118) [2009 96: 7m 7m3 7m6 7m Oct 3] sturdy gelding: type to carry condition: useful handicapper: creditable third at Newmarket: gelded after final start: should prove best up to 7f: raced only on good/good to firm going. *P. F. I. Cole* **96**

WILD DESERT (FR) 4 br.g. Desert Prince (IRE) 130 – Sallivera (IRE) (Sillery (USA) 122) [2009 83: p12.2g5 p12g3 Feb 14] strong, angular gelding: fairly useful performer, lightly raced: stays 1½m: acts on polytrack. *Ian Williams* **85**

WILD FELL HALL (IRE) 6 ch.g. Grand Lodge (USA) 125 – Genoa 96 (Zafonic (USA) 130) [2009 83: 12g 12g 12g Aug 14] smallish, workmanlike gelding: handicapper: little form in 2009: often wears cheekpieces/blinkers. *J. Hetherton* **–**

WILD HEATHER 2 b.f. (Mar 2) Bertolini (USA) 125 – Heather Mix 84 (Linamix (FR) 127) [2009 p6g p5g5 p5m p6g6 p5.1g Dec 26] £1,800Y: fifth foal: half-sister to German 7f to 1¼m winner Spy Glass (by Observatory), 7.6f winner in Britain at 2 yrs: dam, 10.5f winner, half-sister to smart miler Castleton: poor maiden. *J. R. Holt* **44**

WILD LYPH 3 b.g. Loup Sauvage (USA) 125 – A Lyph (USA) 78 (Lypheor 118) [2009 p12g 8g Apr 8] last in maidens. *N. P. Mulholland* **–**

WILD RHUBARB 4 ch.f. Hernando (FR) 127 – Diamant Noir (Sir Harry Lewis (USA) 127) [2009 81: 12g2 15m* 16.2g6 14m3 14.6m3 Jun 27] rather sparely-made filly: fairly useful handicapper, lightly raced: won at Warwick in May: creditable third last 2 starts: should stay 2m: acts on good to soft and good to firm ground: joined Jonjo O'Neill. *C. G. Cox* **88**

WILD ROCKETTE 2 b.f. (Mar 4) Rock of Gibraltar (IRE) 133 – Wild Floridian (IRE) 98 (Indian Ridge 123) [2009 6m 7s^4 p7g 8.3d^2 p8g^4 Nov 18] workmanlike filly: second foal: dam Irish 1m (including at 2 yrs) winner: fair maiden: stays 8.3f: acts on polytrack and soft going. *B. J. Meehan* **79**

WILD ROSE 2 gr.f. (Mar 19) Doyen (IRE) 132 – Makhsusah (IRE) (Darshaan 133) [2009 8.1d^5 p8m* p8.6g* 8g Oct 31] 20,000Y: fourth foal: half-sister to useful 2006 2-y-o 6f/7f winner Market Day (by Tobougg), later 1m winner in USA, and 4-y-o Motivated Choice: dam unraced out of half-sister to very smart 1¼m/1½m performer Mutamam: fairly useful performer: won maiden at Kempton in September and nursery at Wolverhampton (slowly away/met trouble, beat Sejanus a head) in October: seemed amiss final start: will stay 1¼m: acts on polytrack. *M. L. W. Bell* **88 +**

WILFRED PICKLES (IRE) 3 ch.g. Cadeaux Genereux 131 – Living Daylights (IRE) 73 (Night Shift (USA)) [2009 77: 8.5m^2 10g^6 8g^2 8f^3 8m^4 7m^2 6g^4 Oct 16] strong, rangy gelding: fairly useful maiden: stays 1m: acts on good to firm ground: tried in tongue tie/cheekpieces: sold 26,000 gns, then gelded. *Mrs A. J. Perrett* **82**

WILLENT 3 b.g. Lend A Hand 124 – Lapu-Lapu 62 (Prince Sabo 123) [2009 9d 8.1g 6d 5.9d Aug 19] sturdy gelding: little form: signs of temperament. *Julie Camacho* **–**

WILL EXELL (IRE) 6 b.m. Exit To Nowhere (USA) 122 – Woodhouse Bay (IRE) (Zaffaran (USA) 117) [2009 p9.5m Feb 25] fourth in bumper on debut, but no form over hurdles: well held in maiden at Wolverhampton sole Flat outing. *M. J. Scudamore* **–**

WILL HE WISH 13 b.g. Winning Gallery 94 – More To Life (Northern Tempest (USA) 120) [2009 94: p11g^2 p9.5g^2 8g^2 10m^5 8.1g 8.5g^6 8g^2 8g^5 Aug 14] good-bodied gelding: fairly useful handicapper nowadays: stays easy 11f: acts on polytrack, firm and good to soft going: usually blinkered/visored. *S. Gollings* **81**

WILLIAM ARNOLD 2 ch.g. (Apr 22) Rambling Bear 115 – Dancing Shirl 54 (Dancing Spree (USA)) [2009 5m 5d 7m^5 7g^2 7.5m^3 7g 7m 7g Oct 6] smallish gelding: modest maiden: probably flattered fourth start: stays 7f: acts on good to firm going. *C. W. Fairhurst* **50**

WILLIAM BLAKE 4 b.g. Rainbow Quest (USA) 134 – Land of Dreams 115 (Cadeaux Genereux 131) [2009 94: 10.1g^4 10m^3 12m^6 10g^2 9.9g^4 12g^4 10.4m 10m^3 p11g^3 10m^2 12m^6 10v Oct 24] sturdy gelding: fairly useful handicapper: held form well in 2009: stays 1½m: acts on all-weather, soft and good to firm ground: has found little: sold 40,000 gns and sent to Bahrain, where reportedly won at 9f. *M. Johnston* **94**

WILLIAM HOGARTH 4 b.g. High Chaparral (IRE) 132 – Mountain Holly 69 (Shirley Heights 130) [2009 96: 12m Sep 13] good-topped gelding: well held sole Flat outing in 2009: stays 1½m: acts on polytrack and good to soft going: suspect temperament: fairly useful form over hurdles. *W. K. Goldsworthy* **–**

WILLIAM MORGAN (IRE) 2 ch.g. (Mar 31) Arakan (USA) 123 – Dry Lightning 63 (Shareef Dancer (USA) 135) [2009 5.9m^4 5.9g^3 6m^6 7m^2 7g* 7d* 6.5m Sep 10] €10,000Y: close-coupled gelding: closely related to winner in Italy by Russian Revival and half-brother to several winners, including 4-y-o Harrison George and fairly useful Irish 1m (at 2 yrs)/10.7f winner Harper Valley (by Val Royal): dam 1¼m winner: fairly useful performer: won nurseries at Redcar and York within 4 days in September: well held in sales race at Doncaster 4 days later (gelded after): likely to stay 1m: acts on good to firm and good to soft going. *R. A. Fahey* **85 +**

WILLIAM'S WAY 7 b.g. Fraam 114 – Silk Daisy 74 (Barathea (IRE) 127) [2009 82, a74: p12m p10g^5 p12g* p13g^4 p13.9g* f14g^2 10.3m^5 11.6g^5 p13g May 12] quite good-topped gelding: just fair handicapper nowadays: won amateur events at Lingfield in January and Wolverhampton in March: stays 13.8f: acts on all-weather, firm and good to soft going: held up. *I. A. Wood* **73**

WILLIAMTOWN LAD (IRE) 8 b.g. Anshan 119 – Hazy River (Over The River (FR)) [2009 p12g Jul 22] poor maiden hurdler: never a threat in maiden on Flat debut. *J. R. Boyle* **–**

WILLIAM VAN GOGH 2 b.c. (Feb 7) Dansili 127 – Flower Girl 108 (Pharly (FR) 130) [2009 8m^2 8m^5 Oct 16] tall, useful-looking colt: has scope: brother to fairly useful 2007 2-y-o 7f winner Honky Tonk Sally and half-brother to several winners, including smart performer up to 14.6f Eco Friendly (1m winner at 2 yrs by Sabrehill) and fairly useful 1m winner Roaring Twenties (by Halling): dam 6f winner, including at 2 yrs: slightly better effort in maidens at Newmarket when 2¼ lengths second to Fareej, travelling strongly in front: finished tamely next time: may progress at 3 yrs. *J. H. M. Gosden* **83 +**

WILLIE EVER 5 b.g. Agnes World (USA) 123 – Miss Meltemi (IRE) 100 (Miswaki **– §**
Tern (USA) 120) [2009 78: p7.1g p8.6g p8.6g p7g Mar 18] lengthy gelding: handicapper: well held in 2009, refusing to race final outing: tried blinkered/visored: one to treat with caution. *I. W. McInnes*

WILLING FOE (USA) 2 b.c. (Apr 9) Dynaformer (USA) – Thunder Kitten (USA) **65 p**
(Storm Cat (USA)) [2009 p9.5g^{6} Nov 14] sixth foal: brother to smart 1m (at 2 yrs) to 1½m winner Michita and half-brother to several winners in USA: dam, US 6.5f to 8.5f (including Grade 3) winner, half-sister to Japanese Grade 1 1m winner Nobo True out of US Grade 1 winner up to 1¼m Nastique: evens favourite, 5¾ lengths sixth to Powerful Melody in maiden at Wolverhampton, not knocked about: bred to stay 1¼m+: should improve. *Saeed bin Suroor*

WILLKANDOO (USA) 4 b.g. Unbridled's Song (USA) 125 – Shannkara (IRE) **84**
(Akarad (FR) 130) [2009 94: p7.1g^{6} p7g p8g^{2} p8g^{3} Mar 2] big gelding: fairly useful performer: stays 1¼m: acts on polytrack and good to firm going: tried in cheekpieces: not straightforward: sold 14,000 gns in July. *D. M. Simcock*

WILLOW DANCER (IRE) 5 ch.g. Danehill Dancer (IRE) 117 – Willowbridge **90**
(IRE) (Entrepreneur 123) [2009 96: 8.1f 8.1m 8g p8g^{6} Oct 9] leggy, lengthy gelding: fairly useful handicapper: respectable efforts at best in 2009: best at 1m: acts on polytrack, good to firm and good to soft going: wears cheekpieces. *W. R. Swinburn*

WILLOW MIST 2 b.f. (Apr 26) Gentleman's Deal (IRE) 114 – Baymist 68 (Mind **–**
Games 121) [2009 6d Jun 12] 66/1, showed nothing in seller at York: dead. *M. W. Easterby*

WILLRIDGE 4 ch.g. Tumbleweed Ridge 117 – Minnina (IRE) (In The Wings 128) **–**
[2009 78: 6m 7.1m p7.1g 7.6m Aug 15] sturdy gelding: no form in handicaps at 4 yrs: tried in cheekpieces/tongue tie. *J. M. Bradley*

WILLYN (IRE) 4 b.f. Lujain (USA) 119 – Lamasat (USA) (Silver Hawk (USA) 123) **60**
[2009 56: 9.1g^{3} 8m^{4} 10g^{3} 9.1g 10m^{2} 8m 10m 9m Sep 14] compact filly: modest handicapper: stays 1¼m: acts on soft and good to firm going: tried visored/in cheekpieces: usually held up. *J. S. Goldie*

WILMINGTON 5 ch.g. Compton Place 125 – Bahawir Pour (USA) (Green Dancer **55**
(USA) 132) [2009 64: f8g 9m^{6} 9.1g 7.9m 8g^{3} 8m 9.1g 12.5m Sep 14] strong, useful-looking gelding: modest maiden: stays 1m: acts on polytrack and good to firm ground: tried blinkered/in cheekpieces. *Mrs J. C. McGregor*

WILTSHIRE (IRE) 7 br.g. Spectrum (IRE) 126 – Mary Magdalene 78 (Night Shift **64**
(USA)) [2009 67: p6g p6g^{2} p6g^{3} p6g p6g f6g^{3} f6g^{4} f6g^{2} 7m^{5} 6f^{4} f6g^{2} 6m^{6} 5.9m^{2} f6g^{2} 7g* 6.8g^{2} a5.5s* Nov 29] leggy gelding: modest performer: sold from P. Midgley £3,800 after fourteenth start: won minor event at Mannheim in September and handicap at Neuss in November: effective at 5.5f to easy 8.6f: acts on all-weather, sand and firm ground: often in headgear: held up. *Christian Peterschmitt, Germany*

WIND FLOW 5 b.g. Dr Fong (USA) 128 – Spring 112 (Sadler's Wells (USA) 132) **81**
[2009 80: p16g* p13g^{2} p13g^{3} p13g p12.2g* p13.9g^{4} p12g^{5} p12g^{2} p12.2g^{2} f12g^{4} p12g p11g p11g p12.2m p12.2g^{3} p12.2g^{2} p12g^{2} p12.2g p12g Oct 26] leggy gelding: fairly useful performer: won claimer at Lingfield in January and handicap at Wolverhampton in February: effective at 1½m to 2m: acts on polytrack: wears headgear: makes running: has looked moody: sold 11,500 gns. *C. A. Dwyer*

WINDJAMMER 5 b.g. Kyllachy 129 – Absolve (USA) (Diesis 133) [2009 73: 5g 5g **49**
5d^{2} 5m 5.1s Nov 4] strong gelding: just poor handicapper nowadays: best at 5f: acts on polytrack, firm and good to soft going: tried visored, often blinkered. *L. A. Mullaney*

WINDPFEIL (IRE) 3 b.g. Indian Ridge 123 – Flying Kiss (IRE) (Sadler's Wells **69**
(USA) 132) [2009 56: 11.5s^{3} p12g 11.5d^{5} 14.1g p16m 11.6d* Oct 12] angular gelding: fair handicapper: won at Windsor in October: should stay 1¾m: raced only on polytrack and good ground or softer: tried in cheekpieces, blinkered last 3 starts: sold 15,000 gns. *J. H. M. Gosden*

WIND SHUFFLE (GER) 6 b.g. Big Shuffle (USA) 122 – Wiesensturmerin (GER) **88**
(Lagunas) [2009 86: 8m^{3} 9m^{3} 9.2s^{2} 7.9m 9.8v Jul 18] big, leggy gelding: fairly useful handicapper: good placed efforts first 3 starts in 2009: stays 1¼m: acts on heavy and good to firm going: often makes running: game. *J. S. Goldie*

WIND STAR 6 ch.g. Piccolo 121 – Starfleet 66 (Inchinor 119) [2009 89: 9m^{4} 10.1d* **92**
9.9g* 10.3f^{6} 10.3m^{4} Jun 27] leggy, lengthy gelding: fairly useful handicapper: won at Newcastle and Beverley in May: may prove best up to 1¼m nowadays: acts on firm and good to soft going: tried blinkered: travels strongly, and often finds little. *G. A. Swinbank*

WINE 'N DINE 4 b.g. Rainbow Quest (USA) 134 – Seasonal Splendour (IRE) 95 (Prince Rupert (FR) 121) [2009 91p: p16g* p12g³ p12.2g² p16g p16g² 14m 12m May 30] deep-girthed gelding: useful handicapper on all-weather, little form on turf since 2007: won at Kempton in January: good placed efforts 3 of next 4 starts: stays 2m: acts on polytrack: quirky: joined B. Llewellyn. *G. L. Moore* – a95

WING COLLAR 8 b.g. In The Wings 128 – Riyoom (USA) 83 (Vaguely Noble 140) [2009 96: 16m Apr 25] tall gelding: useful handicapper: lightly raced in recent years, and well held sole outing in 2009 (returned lame): stayed 2m: acted on any going: often wore cheekpieces: sometimes raced freely: held up: reportedly retired through injury. *T. D. Easterby* –

WING DIVA (IRE) 4 b.f. Hawk Wing (USA) 136 – Sasimoto (USA) (Saratoga Six (USA)) [2009 65: f11d⁴ 10v⁶ f11g² f12m³ f8f² Dec 12] fair maiden handicapper, lightly raced: stays 11f: raced only on fibresand (best efforts) and soft/heavy going. *B. Smart* 65

WINGED ARROW (IRE) 7 b.g. In The Wings 128 – Lightstorm (IRE) 58 (Darshaan 133) [2009 71: p16.5g³ p16g Feb 8] quite good-topped gelding: fair handicapper: stays 16.5f: acts on polytrack and heavy going: none too consistent. *Jonjo O'Neill* 68

WINGED D'ARGENT (IRE) 8 b.g. In The Wings 128 – Petite-D-Argent 91 (Noalto 120) [2009 90§: 16s⁴ 18g 16d Jul 18] sturdy gelding: handicapper, just fair form at best at 8 yrs: stays 2½m: acts on heavy and good to firm going: wears headgear: ungenuine (races in snatches). *B. J. Llewellyn* 79 §

WINGED FARASI 5 b.h. Desert Style (IRE) 121 – Clara Vale (IRE) (In The Wings 128) [2009 59: p8.6g⁴ p8.6g f8d 8.5m Apr 15] angular horse: modest performer: stays 9.5f: acts on all-weather, good to firm and good to soft going: wears cheekpieces/blinkers nowadays: none too consistent. *Miss J. E. Foster* 57

WINGED HARRIET (IRE) 3 b. or br.f. Hawk Wing (USA) 136 – Hawala (IRE) 97 (Warning 136) [2009 85p: 7m⁴ 6g* May 23] angular filly: fairly useful form: below best in 2009, though won maiden at Catterick in May: should stay 1m: temperament under suspicion: sold 62,000 gns in November. *W. J. Haggas* 72 +

WINGED (IRE) 2 b.f. (Jan 25) Hawk Wing (USA) 136 – Aurelia 80 (Rainbow Quest (USA) 134) [2009 7d p7g⁴ Aug 5] 38,000Y: strong filly: second foal: half-sister to 3-y-o Aurorian: dam, 2-y-o 1¼m winner, out of half-sister to Fillies' Mile winner/Oaks runner-up Shamshir: much better effort in maidens when 4 lengths fourth to Astonishment at Kempton: will be suited by 1m+: sent to Canada: should progress further. *B. W. Hills* 65 p

WING FORWARD (IRE) 2 b.f. (Apr 8) Hawk Wing (USA) 136 – Stroppy (IRE) (Xaar 132) [2009 5s⁶ 6f⁶ 7m Aug 31] first foal: dam, ran twice, half-sister to useful Irish 1m/1½m winner Khalafiya, herself dam of high-class 1¼m/1½m performer Predappio: soundly beaten in maidens. *A. Berry* –

WING N PRAYER (IRE) 2 b.f. (Jan 23) Xaar 132 – Jazmeer 88 (Sabrehill (USA) 120) [2009 7.1m⁴ 7.1s 6m Oct 1] €2,000F, €4,000Y: fourth foal: half-sister to winners abroad by Diktat and Cape Cross: dam 7f (at 2 yrs) and 8.5f winner: no form in maidens (said to have lost a shoe second start). *A. Berry* –

WING OF FAITH 2 ch.c. (Feb 11) Kirkwall 118 – Angel Wing (Barathea (IRE) 127) [2009 6m 5g⁶ 7.1m⁶ 6d⁴ 8m p6g² 6d p6g⁴ p5g⁵ Oct 22] rather leggy colt: modest maiden: stays 7f: acts on polytrack, good to firm and good to soft going: sold 3,000 gns. *S. Kirk* 60

WING PLAY (IRE) 4 b.g. Hawk Wing (USA) 136 – Toy Show (IRE) 86 (Danehill (USA) 126) [2009 79: p7.1g⁶ 7m 8f p10g* 10.3m² 10g² 10d* 9.8d 10m³ 10.2s⁵ p9.5g* p10m³ Nov 28] strong gelding: useful handicapper on all-weather, fairly useful on turf: won at Lingfield in June, Sandown in August and Wolverhampton in October: stays 11f: acts on polytrack, soft and good to firm ground: tried tongue tied, usually in cheekpieces/blinkers: held up. *H. Morrison* 90 a96

WINGS OF KINTYRE (IRE) 5 b.m. Mull of Kintyre (USA) 114 – Tiger Wings (IRE) (Thatching 131) [2009 8d Sep 7] €12,000Y, resold 27,000Y: fourth foal: half-sister to useful 2004 2-y-o 5f winner Dance Night (by Danehill Dancer): dam well beaten in Ireland: well held in maiden at Newcastle. *A. Berry* –

WING STEALTH (IRE) 4 br.f. Hawk Wing (USA) 136 – Starlight Smile (USA) (Green Dancer (USA) 132) [2009 76: f12d Jan 2] lengthy, good-topped filly: maiden: well held sole outing in 2009: stays 1½m: best effort on good going: blinkered nowadays. *M. G. Quinlan* –

WINIFRED JO 2 ch.f. (Feb 11) Bahamian Bounty 116 – Coming Home (Vettori (IRE) 119) [2009 p5m⁶ p6m Oct 12] 18,000Y: second foal: half-sister to 3-y-o Via Mia: dam French 11f/1½m winner: better effort in maidens at Kempton when sixth to Felsham. *J. R. Gask* 46

WINKER WATSON 4 ch.c. Piccolo 121 – Bonica 56 (Rousillon (USA) 133) [2009 **101**
118: 7.1m^{4} 8d 7g Jun 27] useful-looking colt: smart performer at best: won all 3 starts at 2 yrs, including July Stakes at Newmarket: just useful form in 2009 when fourth to Plum Pudding in minor event at Warwick and seventh in Criterion Stakes at Newmarket (blinkered) on third start: joined B. Meehan after, but did not race again: barely stayed 1m: raced mainly on good/good to firm ground: to stand at Norman Court Stud, nr Salisbury, Wiltshire, fee £3,500. *P. W. Chapple-Hyam*

WINNING SHOW 5 b.g. Muhtarram (USA) 125 – Rose Show (Belmez (USA) 131) **60**
[2009 71d: p12g^{3} p12g p11f* Dec 16] stocky gelding: modest handicapper: tongue tied and fit from hurdling (successful in November), first win on Flat at Kempton in December: stays 1½m: acts on polytrack, good to firm and good to soft going. *C. Gordon*

WINROB 3 b.g. Exceed And Excel (AUS) 126 – High Standard 83 (Kris 135) [2009 **62**
7m 7.1m^{6} p7.1g 10.3g 10f^{4} 8.3g^{2} 8d* 7.9g Aug 3] leggy, close-coupled gelding: modest handicapper: won selling event at Thirsk in July: best effort at 1m on good to soft going. *Pat Morris*

WINSTON'S LAD 2 gr.g. (Apr 1) Act One 124 – Hernani (FR) (Ezzoud (IRE) 126) **–**
[2009 6g 6g p8.6g Sep 11] soundly beaten in maidens. *P. Howling*

WINTERBOURNE 3 ch. or gr.f. Cadeaux Genereux 131 – Snowing 88 (Tate Gallery **48**
(USA) 117) [2009 49: p5.1g^{4} 6g p5.1g p5m Dec 6] workmanlike filly: poor maiden: raced only at 5f/6f: acts on polytrack. *M. Blanshard*

WINTERBROOK KING 3 b.g. Gleaming (IRE) – Alice Holt (Free State 125) [2009 **65**
63: 9.9m p10g 11.7m p12g^{6} 12.1m^{2} 16v* 15.4m* Aug 6] compact gelding: fair handicaper: won at Nottingham in July and Folkestone in August: stays 2m: acts on polytrack, heavy and good to firm going: held up. *J. R. Best*

WINTERCAST 4 ch.g. Spinning World (USA) 130 – Bright Hope (IRE) 84 (Danehill **100**
(USA) 126) [2009 p8g^{3} 8.1m^{5} 10m^{2} 10g^{2} 10g 10v p8.6g^{5} Nov 13] sturdy, attractive gelding: useful handicapper: missed 2008: best efforts in 2009 when runner-up at Sandown and Newmarket (beaten length by Alazeyab): likely to stay 1½m: acts on polytrack and good to firm going. *W. R. Swinburn*

WINTERFELL 3 b.f. Haafhd 129 – It Girl 83 (Robellino (USA) 127) [2009 –p: 8.3m **56**
9d 6g^{4} 8d^{6} p7f^{3} p8f^{3} Oct 14] good-bodied filly: modest maiden: stays 1m: acts on polytrack: sold 2,000 gns, sent to Holland. *C. F. Wall*

WINTER FEVER (SAF) 5 ch.g. Western Winter (USA) 116 – Fashion Fever (SAF) **92**
(Model Man (SAF)) [2009 a8f^{4} 7m a8g p8f Dec 20] won 2 of his 7 races in South Africa for H. Brown, including listed race at Clairwood (narrowly beat Art of War) final start in 2008: fairly useful form in handicaps for A. Manuel in UAE early in 2009: well held in similar event on British debut final start: stays 9.5f: acts on dirt and soft ground. *J. M. P. Eustace*

WISDOM'S KISS 5 b.g. Ocean of Wisdom (USA) 106 – April Magic (Magic Ring **75**
(IRE) 115) [2009 73, a85: p8.6g^{5} Jan 2] leggy gelding: just fair form only start in 2009: stays 8.6f: acts on polytrack, firm and good to soft ground: wears blinkers/cheekpieces: held up. *J. D. Bethell*

WISECRAIC 2 ch.c. (Mar 21) Kheleyf (USA) 116 – Belle Genius (USA) 111 (Beau **82**
Genius (CAN)) [2009 5.7g* 6s^{4} 6m Sep 19] €14,000Y: good-quartered colt: brother to 2008 2-y-o 7f winner Zelloof, closely related to 3 winners, including useful 6f/7f winner Birjand (by Green Desert) and fairly useful Irish 1m/8.7f winner Fereeji (by Cape Cross), and half-brother to 2 winners: dam won Moyglare Stud Stakes: won maiden at Bath in July in good style: similar form after, fourth to Dick Turpin in sales race at Fairyhouse and last in Mill Reef Stakes at Newbury: should stay 7f. *Tom Dascombe*

WISE DENNIS 7 b.g. Polar Falcon (USA) 126 – Bowden Rose 100 (Dashing Blade **108 d**
117) [2009 114: 8m^{5} 8g^{5} 10g^{4} 8m 10g 8m 10g f8g Oct 18] big, lengthy gelding: useful performer: ran at Nad Al Sheba first 4 starts, best effort there when 2½ lengths fourth to Charlie Cool in handicap: off 5 months, no show back in Britain after: stays 1¼m: acts on all-weather, soft and good to firm going: tried visored: held up. *A. P. Jarvis*

WISEMAN'S DIAMOND (USA) 4 b.f. Wiseman's Ferry (USA) 102 – Aswhat- **80**
illdois (IRE) 84 (Blues Traveller (IRE) 119) [2009 68: f7g 7.5m 7.1m 7m 7m^{3} 7g^{3} 8f^{2} 8.3m^{2} 8m^{2} 8m* 8.5m* 8m 8m* Sep 17] sturdy filly: fairly useful performer: improved in 2009, winning handicaps at Newcastle (apprentices) and Beverley (amateurs) in August and Pontefract in September: stays 8.6f: acts on polytrack, firm and good to soft going: has won in cheekpieces. *P. T. Midgley*

WISE MELODY 4 b.f. Zamindar (USA) 116 – Swellegant 84 (Midyan (USA) 124) [2009 97: 6f^5 6d^2 May 17] sturdy filly: useful handicapper: creditable second at Ripon: likely to prove at least as effective at 5f as 6f: acts on polytrack, firm and good to soft going: races prominently. *W. J. Haggas* **96**

WISE PRINCESS 3 ch.f. Riverwise (USA) – Princess Penny 46§ (King's Signet (USA) 110) [2009 p10g 10d Jun 10] fourth foal: sister to River Prince and half-sister to Champagner Queen (in Germany, by Tomba), both 6f winners: dam, disqualified 2-y-o 6f seller winner, temperamental: last in maiden/seller on Flat. *W. G. M. Turner* **–**

WISHBONE (IRE) 2 b.f. (May 11) Danehill Dancer (IRE) 117 – Intricate Design (Zafonic (USA) 130) [2009 6m^6 6g^3 6g* Sep 30] good-topped filly: has scope: first foal: dam unraced half-sister to useful 1m/1¼m winners Fashionable and Artistic Style: promising in maidens all starts, winning at Newcastle impressively by 1½ lengths from Brinscall, leading on bridle final 1f: bred to stay 7f: already fairly useful, and capable of better still. *M. G. Quinlan* **85 p**

WISHFORMORE (IRE) 2 b.f. (Feb 14) Chevalier (IRE) 115 – Terra Nova 71 (Polar Falcon (USA) 126) [2009 p7.1g^2 Nov 20] €9,000Y: first foal: dam maiden (stayed 7f): 16/1, length second to Sidney Melbourne in maiden at Wolverhampton, keeping on: should improve. *J. S. Moore* **59 p**

WITCH OF THE WAVE (IRE) 3 ch.f. Dr Fong (USA) 128 – Clipper 95 (Salse (USA) 128) [2009 46: p8g^5 p12.2m^4 12.6g May 4] modest maiden: stays 1½m: form only on polytrack: tried visored: poor form in juvenile hurdles. *Miss J. S. Davis* **61**

WITCHRY 7 gr.g. Green Desert (USA) 127 – Indian Skimmer (USA) 133 (Storm Bird (CAN) 134) [2009 74: 6s^2 6m 7m^3 p6g p7.1g Nov 6] smallish, strong gelding: fair handicapper: stays 6f well: acts on polytrack and any turf going: held up. *A. G. Newcombe* **69**

WITHOUT A PRAYER (IRE) 4 ch.c. Intikhab (USA) 135 – Prayer (IRE) 83 (Rainbow Quest (USA) 134) [2009 114: a8.5g 10g^3 10g^2 p10g^5 8.5g^4 8.3m* 8m^6 8m^6 p8m* Nov 29] strong, well-made colt: smart performer: best efforts in 2009 when winning listed events at Windsor (by length from Premio Loco) in June and Kempton (beat Re Barolo 3 lengths) in November: stays 1¼m: acts on all-weather and firm going: usually held up. *R. M. Beckett* **116**

WITHOUT PREJUDICE (USA) 4 ch.g. Johannesburg (USA) 127 – Awesome Strike (USA) 84 (Theatrical 128) [2009 90: 7m 7g 7m^3 7m 7g* 7m^4 7d* 7m p7g 7m^6 Oct 16] angular gelding: useful handicapper: won at Newmarket in July and York (impressive when beating Violent Velocity 3¾ lengths) in September: effective at 6f/7f: acts on polytrack, good to firm and good to soft going: visored nowadays. *J. Noseda* **97**

WIVNY (USA) 4 b.f. Yonaguska (USA) 112 – Mostly Sassy (USA) (Green Dancer (USA) 132) [2009 –: 8.1g p8g 7.1g 5.2s 5.7g Sep 7] lengthy filly: little sign of ability: tried blinkered. *H. J. Evans* **–**

WIZARD LOOKING 8 b.g. Wizard King 122 – High Stepping (IRE) (Taufan (USA) 119) [2009 71: p12g f12g^6 p12.2g^2 11.5g^6 12.4s^4 p12.2g Jun 22] tall, close-coupled gelding: modest handicapper nowadays, better on all-weather: barely stays 1¾m: acts on all-weather, firm and good to soft going (possibly not soft): tried blinkered/tongue tied/in cheekpieces: held up. *P. T. Midgley* **51 a61**

WIZARD OF US 9 b.g. Wizard King 122 – Sian's Girl (Mystiko (USA) 124) [2009 54: 7.9g 13.1d^6 12.4d Sep 7] smallish, workmanlike gelding: one-time fairly useful hurdler: modest handicapper on Flat: stays 1½m: acts on polytrack and heavy going: often makes running. *M. Mullineaux* **50**

WIZZY IZZY (IRE) 4 gr.f. Shinko Forest (IRE) – Strelitzia (IRE) (Bluebird (USA) 125) [2009 p8.6g f6g Jan 20] workmanlike filly: no form: tried blinkered. *N. Wilson* **–**

WOGAN'S SISTER 4 b.f. Lahib (USA) 129 – Dublivia (Midyan (USA) 124) [2009 77: 10m^5 10d May 22] just modest form in 2009: stays 1¼m: acts on polytrack and good to soft going: often forces pace. *D. R. C. Elsworth* **60**

WOLDGATE 2 b.g. (Mar 10) Monsieur Bond (IRE) 120 – Chicago Bond (USA) 64 (Real Quiet (USA) 131) [2009 5m p6g 7g Oct 10] rather leggy gelding: modest form in maidens first 2 starts: rider lost iron final outing: not bred to need 7f. *G. R. Oldroyd* **57**

WOLVERTON (IRE) 3 ch.g. Alhaarth (IRE) 126 – Debbie's Next (USA) 82 (Arctic Tern (USA) 126) [2009 –: p10g 10m f14m^6 Jul 21] leggy gelding: well beaten in maidens/ handicap. *N. P. Littmoden* **–**

WOMANISER (IRE) 5 b.g. Rock of Gibraltar (IRE) 133 – Top Table 65 (Shirley Heights 130) [2009 –: 8.1g^{5} p8.6m^{4} p9.5g p9.5g p7g^{6} p8g p7g Dec 7] modest maiden: should stay 1¼m: raced mainly on polytrack: tried in cheekpieces, blinkered last 3 starts. *T. Keddy* **55**

WOODCOTE (IRE) 7 b.g. Monashee Mountain (USA) 115 – Tootle (Main Reef 126) [2009 90: p5g f5g^{2} p5g^{4} p5g^{3} p5.1m^{2} p5.1m^{6} p5.1g^{4} 5d 5.2g p5g p5g p5.1g p5g p5g f5f Dec 11] strong, lengthy gelding: fair performer at best in 2009: won seller at Lingfield in February: claimed from P. Chamings £6,000 fifth start: lost form after: effective at 5f/6f: acts on polytrack, firm and soft going: usually wears headgear: often tongue tied: usually very slowly away for current stable. *Peter Grayson* **77 d**

WOODCOTE PLACE 6 b.g. Lujain (USA) 119 – Giant Nipper (Nashwan (USA) 135) [2009 90: p7g p7g^{2} 7m* p7g^{2} 7g^{2} 8g Jul 28] small, well-made, attractive gelding: useful handicapper: won at Goodwood in May: good second next 2 starts: stays 8.3f: acts on polytrack, firm and good to soft going: normally held up: reliable. *P. R. Chamings* **95**

WOODENITBENICE 2 gr.f. (Feb 1) Needwood Blade 117 – Nightingale (Night Shift (USA)) [2009 p6g p7.1g p6g p7.1m f8f Dec 12] 4,500F: fifth foal: half-sister to 6-y-o John Keats and 7-y-o Owed: dam little form: no form. *D. Shaw* **–**

WOODEN KING (IRE) 4 b.g. Danetime (IRE) 121 – Olympic Rock (IRE) (Ballad Rock 122) [2009 60: p8g p7g 6.1g^{2} 8g 6d 7g^{6} 5.7m Aug 16] lengthy gelding: modest handicapper: left P. D. Evans after fourth outing: best efforts at 6f/7f: acts on polytrack and good to soft going: tried visored/in cheekpieces: front runner. *M. S. Saunders* **54**

WOODFACE 2 ch.c. (Feb 8) Avonbridge 123 – Amazed 58 (Clantime 101) [2009 6m 6m 6g 7g Aug 12] close-coupled colt: no form: tried blinkered: temperamental. *B. J. Meehan* **– §**

WOOD FAIR 2 b.f. (Mar 11) Trade Fair 124 – To The Woods (IRE) 86 (Woodborough (USA) 112) [2009 6m 6g^{6} 6m 8m Sep 23] 11,500F, £26,000Y: tall filly: fourth foal: half-sister to winner in Hungary by Intikhab: dam 5f (at 2 yrs) and 7f winner who became unreliable: modest maiden: trained by K. R. Burke first 3 starts: off 3 months, better than result in nursery final outing: likely to stay 7f. *A. P. Jarvis* **54 +**

WOOD FAIRY 3 b.f. Haafhd 129 – Woodbeck 90 (Terimon 124) [2009 7d* 8.3s 8m 10m^{5} 8g p10g^{4} p12g^{4} Dec 7] seventh foal: half-sister to 7f (at 2 yrs) to 1¾m (Yorkshire Cup) winner Franklins Gardens (by Halling), 7f (at 2 yrs) and 1m winner Polar Ben (by Polar Falcon), both smart, and useful 9.8f winner Wood Chorus (by Singspiel): dam, 7f winner, out of half-sister to Prix de Diane winner Madam Gay: fair performer: won maiden at Thirsk in July: likely to prove best short of 1½m: acts on polytrack, good to firm and good to soft going. *R. A. Fahey* **71**

WOODFORD BELLE (USA) 2 b. or br.f. (Mar 5) Arch (USA) 127 – Tis Me (USA) (Notebook (USA)) [2009 8m^{4} 8d^{4} Oct 13] second foal: half-sister to winner in Canada by Peace Rules: dam US winner around 1m, including at 2 yrs, sister to dam of Dubai World Cup winner Well Armed: fourth in maidens at Newmarket (to Golden Aria, better effort) and Newcastle (still green): remains open to improvement. *B. J. Meehan* **75 p**

WOODHOUSE MILL (IRE) 2 b.f. (Jan 21) Oratorio (IRE) 128 – Wurfklinge (GER) (Acatenango (GER) 127) [2009 6g 6m 6s 6m 7g 7.5m Sep 16] £20,000Y: compact filly: second foal: half-sister to 3-y-o Nora Mae: dam, German 2-y-o 1m winner (later useful up to 1¾m), sister to smart German 1½m/1¾m performer Wurftaube: no form: tried visored. *N. Tinkler* **–**

WOODLAND VIOLET 3 b.f. Reset (AUS) 124 – Be My Tinker 75 (Be My Chief (USA) 122) [2009 39: p8m p8m^{5} p8m p10g^{6} Dec 7] modest maiden: will prove best short of 1¼m: raced only on polytrack. *I. A. Wood* **50**

WOODLARK ISLAND (IRE) 3 b.g. Tagula (IRE) 116 – Be My Lover (Pursuit of Love 124) [2009 65p: p7g^{2} p8.6g^{4} 10m^{2} p8g* 8m^{5} p10m^{5} Oct 7] lengthy gelding: fairly useful performer: won maiden at Lingfield in September: stays 1¼m: acts on polytrack and good to firm going: tried in cheekpieces/visored: sold 29,000 gns, joined D. Pipe. *M. P. Tregoning* **84**

WOODSLEY HOUSE (IRE) 7 b.g. Orpen (USA) 116 – Flame And Shadow (IRE) (Turtle Island (IRE) 123) [2009 79: 6f 6g^{6} 6s 7.1m* 7.2g^{3} 7m 6g 7d^{5} 7m^{6} 8s^{5} 8s^{4} 9.2g 8m^{6} 7.2g^{5} 9d Oct 28] tall gelding: fair handicapper: won at Musselburgh in May: possibly best at 7f nowadays: acts on soft and good to firm going: in cheekpieces last 5 starts. *A. G. Foster* **78**

WOODY VALENTINE (USA) 8 ch.g. Woodman (USA) 126 – Mudslinger (USA) (El Gran Senor (USA) 136) [2009 51: 15.8m Apr 1] rather leggy gelding: has a round action: one-time fairly useful performer on Flat: well held sole start at 8 yrs: tried in cheekpieces: fair hurdler/chaser. *Mrs Dianne Sayer* **–**

WOODY WALLER 4 ch.g. Lomitas 129 – Reamzafonic 46 (Grand Lodge (USA) 125) [2009 77: 12m^5 17.5m Sep 18] lengthy gelding: fair handicapper, lightly raced: stays 13.8f: unraced on extremes of going. *J. Howard Johnson* **71**

WOOLFALL SOVEREIGN (IRE) 3 b.c. Noverre (USA) 125 – Mandragore (USA) (Slew O' Gold (USA)) [2009 p8.6g* Dec 14] 60,000F: seventh foal: half-brother to useful French 7f (at 2 yrs) to 1½m winner Marie de Bayeux (by Turgeon): dam lightly-raced daughter of Prix Royal-Oak winner Mersey: 7/2, won maiden at Wolverhampton in December by ½ length from Barbarian: likely to stay at least 1¼m. *G. G. Margarson* **70**

WOOLFALL TREASURE 4 gr.g. Daylami (IRE) 138 – Treasure Trove (USA) 62 (The Minstrel (CAN) 135) [2009 97: 14.1m* 20m^6 21g^4 17.2m^2 16m^2 18m Oct 17] close-coupled gelding: useful handicapper: won at Salisbury in May: good second at Bath and Ascot: stays 2½m: acts on good to firm and good to soft going: tried in cheekpieces/blinkers: suspect attitude (often lazy): sold 35,000 gns. *G. L. Moore* **98**

WOOLSTON FERRY (IRE) 3 b.g. Fath (USA) 116 – Cathy Garcia (IRE) (Be My Guest (USA) 126) [2009 87: p6g^4 p7g* p7g* p8g^6 p8g 7.6f p7g^6 p8g^5 p7m p7.1g^5 p7g Nov 18] good-topped gelding: fairly useful performer: won claimers at Lingfield in January and March, leaving M. Channon £14,000 after latter: below form after next start: stays easy 1m: acts on polytrack: held up. *David Pinder* **81 d**

WOQOODD 5 b.g. Royal Applause 124 – Intervene (Zafonic (USA) 130) [2009 66: p5.1g 6d^6 5m p5.1g Jun 29] well-made gelding: poor performer nowadays: stays 6f: acts on polytrack and firm ground: often blinkered/visored. *D. Shaw* **48**

WORKFORCE 2 b.c. (Mar 14) King's Best (USA) 132 – Soviet Moon (IRE) (Sadler's Wells (USA) 132) [2009 7m* Sep 23] **106 P**

It is all too easy to get carried away when a well-bred two-year-old colt from a leading stable makes an impressive winning debut in one of the many maidens which take place in the autumn. That the opposition might have amounted to very little is usually overlooked in the face of the visual impression created by the winner, who so often ends up being introduced into the Two Thousand Guineas/Derby betting at odds which rarely represent value. Numerous are the examples of those who have failed to live up to the hype and didn't even make it to Newmarket and/or Epsom, leaving ante-post punters counting the cost. Not only punters can be misled. Back in 1968, a story circulated that four-times champion jockey Scobie Breasley had considered postponing his retirement from the saddle to continue his partnership with Hymn, who had looked a colt of great potential on his only start as a two-year-old. Such was Hymn's home reputation that he was sent off 6/4 favourite in a forty-five-runner maiden at Newmarket's Cambridgeshire meeting. On that occasion, those who followed the money, going along with the old adage 'the bigger the field, the bigger the certainty', had little cause for concern at any stage. Hymn was always in a good position, moving easily, took the lead a furlong out and drew five lengths clear. Unfortunately, Hymn damaged his pelvis early the following year and made only two more appearances, winning a minor event at Salisbury before finishing a well-held third in the Irish St Leger, for which he started favourite.

Which brings us to Workforce. He created such a favourable impression when making a successful first appearance, starting 3/1 favourite in a twelve-runner maiden at Goodwood at the end of September, that he was quoted at odds as short as 20/1 for both the Guineas and Derby immediately afterwards. It has to be said that Workforce's performance took the breath away. Held up in rear following a rather slow start from the widest stall, Workforce quickened into a challenging position as soon as he was asked, led a furlong out and stormed clear. He was still going strongly passing the post, by which time he had extended his lead to six lengths. At the time the race looked ordinary overall, the subsequent performances of the majority of those behind doing nothing to suggest otherwise. However, there were a couple who went on to give the form a boost, a major boost in the case of runner-up Oasis Dancer, who was having his second outing. Next time out, Oasis

Electrolux Professional EBF Maiden Stakes, Goodwood—
an impressive debut from Workforce, who storms clear of Oasis Dancer

Dancer won the Tattersalls Timeform Million. There is no doubt that Workforce ran to a useful level of form at Goodwood, a level backed up by the timefigure, and he clearly has the potential to improve considerably. Unfortunately, there was no opportunity to take a further look at Workforce as a two-year-old. He did hold an entry at the five-day stage for the Autumn Stakes at Ascot, but connections decided to give that race a miss and put him away until 2010. His return will be eagerly awaited. He is a most exciting prospect.

Workforce (b.c. Mar 14, 2007)	King's Best (USA) (b 1997)	Kingmambo (b 1990)	Mr Prospector
			Miesque
		Allegretta (ch 1978)	Lombard
			Anatevka
	Soviet Moon (IRE) (b 2001)	Sadler's Wells (b 1981)	Northern Dancer
			Fairy Bridge
		Eva Luna (b 1992)	Alleged
			Media Luna

Workforce's sire King's Best won the Two Thousand Guineas and the pick of those to represent him on the racecourse so far, Proclamation and Creachadoir, both proved best at up to a mile. However, King's Best is responsible for plenty who are effective beyond a mile and a few who have won at a mile and a half and further, and, given that there is plenty of stamina on his dam's side, it is more than likely that Workforce will stay at least a mile and a quarter and may well get a mile and a half. Workforce is the third foal of the unraced Soviet Moon, a sister to the 2003 St Leger winner Brian Boru and a half-sister to the Prix de Royallieu winner Moon Search, who promised to stay beyond a mile and a half. Soviet Moon's first foal Rocket Launch (by Oasis Dream) has won in Greece, while her three-year-old Extreme Impact (by Rock of Gibraltar) made the frame in his two starts in maidens (up to a mile and three quarters) in Ireland for Dermot Weld. Soviet Moon's dam Eva Luna didn't race until she was four, when she won the Park Hill Stakes. Eva Luna is a daughter of Media Luna, who was beaten only a neck in the Oaks, while Media Luna herself was a half-sister to another Oaks-placed filly, Suni. *Sir Michael Stoute*

WORLD OF CHOICE (USA) 4 b.g. Distorted Humor (USA) 117 – Palace Weekend **59**
(USA) (Seattle Dancer (USA) 119) [2009 61: f7g^5 f11g* f12g* f12g^5 p12.2g 11.5g 12.4d^5 **a64**
Sep 7] lengthy, angular gelding: modest handicapper: won at Southwell in February (amateurs) and May: stays 1½m: best efforts on fibresand: blinkered nowadays: sold 1,500 gns. *M. W. Easterby*

WORLD TIME 4 ch.g. Dalakhani (IRE) 133 – Time Ahead 112 (Spectrum (IRE) 126) [2009 80: 10g^5 Sep 14] rather leggy, useful-looking gelding: little form in 2009, including over hurdles: stays 11.5f: acts on good to firm ground: tried blinkered/visored: misses break. *Tim Vaughan* **–**

WORTH A KING'S 3 b.g. Red Ransom (USA) – Top Romance (IRE) 105 (Entrepreneur 123) [2009 80+: 10m^4 12m 12s^4 12m^3 p11g^4 p13.9g* 12m* p13.9g^2 Oct 9] strong, compact gelding: fairly useful handicapper: much improved to win at Wolverhampton in September and Epsom (apprentices) in October: good second on former course final start: stays 1¾m: acts on polytrack and good to firm going: visored last 4 outings: sold 18,000 gns, joined D. McCain Jnr. *Sir Michael Stoute* **94**

WOTASHIRTFULL (IRE) 4 ch.g. Namid 128 – Madrina 70 (Waajib 121) [2009 86: p5g* f5g^3 f6g^2 p6g* f6g^3 f6g^2 5.3g^2 5g^2 5g 5.2d p5m* 6d^6 Sep 3] strong, lengthy gelding: fairly useful handicapper: won at Great Leighs (left K. Ryan after) in January, and Lingfield in February and August: best at 5f/easy 6f: acts on all-weather, heavy and good to firm ground: usually wears cheekpieces, has been visored: front runner. *J. R. Boyle* **92**

WOTASPARKLER 3 b.f. Pyrus (USA) 106 – Colourflash (IRE) (College Chapel 122) [2009 7s 6m^6 6g^2 6d 6g* 6g^3 6g^5 6m 8m^5 p7g Sep 2] big, workmanlike filly: fair performer: won maiden at Warwick in June: best efforts at 6f on good going: tried visored: dead. *W. S. Kittow* **67**

WOTATOMBOY 3 ch.f. Captain Rio 122 – Keen Melody (USA) 60 (Sharpen Up 127) [2009 65: 7m 5m^4 6g^6 p6g 8.5g 7g p7m p8.6g^6 Nov 16] just modest handicapper at 3 yrs: best effort at 6f on fibresand. *R. M. Whitaker* **56**

WOTAVADUN (IRE) 6 ch.g. King of Kings (IRE) 125 – Blush With Love (USA) (Mt Livermore (USA)) [2009 –: p6g p7.1g Jan 25] strong, workmanlike gelding: little form since 2006: often blinkered. *D. Flood* **–**

WOTCHALIKE (IRE) 7 ch.g. Spectrum (IRE) 126 – Juno Madonna (IRE) (Sadler's Wells (USA) 132) [2009 62, a68: 16.1d^5 16m^5 16d Aug 10] strong, good-topped gelding: modest performer: stays 2m: acts on polytrack, soft and good to firm ground: wears visor/cheekpieces nowadays. *Miss S. Johnstone* **55**

WOTEVA 3 b.f. Kyllachy 129 – Happy Omen (Warning 136) [2009 76: 12.1m p8.6g 8d 8s 7g 8.3v^5 p10g p8.6g Dec 5] leggy filly: modest handicapper: left B. Ellison after fourth start: stays 8.6f: acts on polytrack and heavy going: used to wear cheekpieces (not last 4 starts): quirky. *T. P. Tate* **63**

WOULD I LIE TO YOU 5 b.g. Bahamian Bounty 116 – Pallas Athene (Jupiter Island 126) [2009 p8g p7g 8m May 11] no sign of ability. *J. R. Jenkins* **–**

WOVOKA (IRE) 6 b.g. Mujadil (USA) 119 – Common Cause 87 (Polish Patriot (USA) 128) [2009 84§: 8m* 8m* 8.1m 8d* 8m^6 8g^5 8m^4 8m 7d 9m^6 8s 8m* 9m^5 10m^6 8g Oct 20] workmanlike gelding: fairly useful performer: won handicaps at Newcastle and Redcar in April, and Doncaster in May and, having left D. Barker after eighth start, claimer at Newcastle in August: stays 1¼m: acts on dirt, heavy and good to firm going: tried visored: has run well when sweating: held up: tricky ride. *K. A. Ryan* **85**

WRAY CASTLE (IRE) 4 b.g. Desert Prince (IRE) 130 – Blushing Gleam 111 (Caerleon (USA) 132) [2009 p12.2g^2 p12g^5 Feb 27] half-brother to several winners, including French 1¼m to 13f winner Blushing Name (by Danehill): dam, French 6f/7f winner (including at 2 yrs), half-sister to high-class French performer up to 9f Gold Away: modest form in bumper: better effort in maidens on Flat when second at Wolverhampton on debut: sold £8,000, joined C. Heard. *Ian Williams* **74**

WRECKER'S MOON (IRE) 4 b.f. Shinko Forest (IRE) – Coast Is Clear (IRE) 60 (Rainbow Quest (USA) 134) [2009 –: 8g Jun 9] lengthy filly: no form. *T. J. Etherington* **–**

WRENINGHAM 4 br.g. Diktat 126 – Slave To The Rythm (IRE) 63 (Hamas (IRE) 125§) [2009 72: 5.1m 5.2s^5 5.1m p6m^6 p5.1g^5 p5g p5.1g^6 Nov 14] angular gelding: fair performer on all-weather, modest on turf: left M. Squance after fourth start: best at 5f/6f: acts on polytrack and soft going: tried blinkered: races prominently. *P. Leech* **60 a66**

WRENS HOPE 3 ch.f. Shinko Forest (IRE) – Star Dancer (Groom Dancer (USA) 128) [2009 –: 5m^6 6d 6m^4 5g Aug 3] smallish filly: poor maiden. *N. Bycroft* **42**

WRIGGLE (IRE) 2 b.g. (Mar 16) Refuse To Bend (IRE) 128 – Isana (JPN) (Sunday Silence (USA)) [2009 7.1m^3 p7g^6 p6g^6 a6g* a6.8g^4 Dec 13] 54,000F, €55,000Y: second foal: half-brother to 4-y-o Guertino: dam, third at 6.5f at 2 yrs in France, out of half-sister to smart miler King of Happiness: fair form: best effort in maidens in Britain when third at Warwick: sold from W. Haggas 5,000 gns prior to winning similar event at Taby in **78**

November: raced only at 6f/7f: acts on dirt and good to firm ground: in cheekpieces third start. *V. Sandrup, Sweden*

WRIGHTY ALMIGHTY (IRE) 7 b.g. Danehill Dancer (IRE) 117 – Persian **67** Empress (IRE) 51 (Persian Bold 123) [2009 78: p8g^4 p10g p8g 8f^3 7m^{3d} 7s^4 8d^5 Jun 10] tall, useful-looking gelding: fair handicapper: stays 1m: acts on polytrack, firm and soft going: tried in tongue tie/cheekpieces/blinkers: held up: sometimes races freely. *P. R. Chamings*

WRIT (IRE) 7 ch.g. Indian Lodge (IRE) 127 – Carnelly (IRE) 101 (Priolo (USA) 127) **–** [2009 –: p7.1g Jan 25] quite good-topped gelding: handicapper: lightly raced and little form since 2007. *I. Semple*

WULFRIDA (IRE) 2 b.f. (Mar 31) King's Best (USA) 132 – Panna 106 (Polish **83** Precedent (USA) 131) [2009 8m 8g^4 Oct 20] fifth foal: half-sister to 5-y-o Hot Diamond and 9.5f winner Red Lily (by Red Ransom): dam, 1¼m winner (stayed 1½m), half-sister to top-class 1¼m/1½m performer Pentire: much better effort in maidens when length fourth to Principal Role at Yarmouth: will be suited by 1¼m+. *J. R. Fanshawe*

WULIMASTER (USA) 6 b. or br.g. Silver Hawk (USA) 123 – Kamaina (USA) (Mr **53** Prospector (USA)) [2009 61: 15.8g 14m^4 13m^5 13.8m^4 13m^4 12d^6 Jul 15] close-coupled gelding: modest performer: stays 2m: acts on all-weather, soft and good to firm ground: tried in cheekpieces/visor: held up: quirky: joined Paula Hearn. *D. W. Barker*

WUNDER STRIKE (USA) 3 b.g. Smart Strike (CAN) 121 – Bishop's Mate (USA) **70** (Lyphard (USA) 132) [2009 –: p8g* p8g^4 8g^2 8.3f* 8.3d^2 8.3m^6 8.3m 8.3m 8.1g 6m 8d p8g^3 p8g* p8m* p8f* Dec 13] good-topped gelding: fair performer: won minor event at Kempton in March and handicaps at Leicester in April, then Lingfield (2) and Kempton in November/December: stays 8.3f: acts on polytrack and firm going: usually in cheekpieces. *J. R. Boyle*

WUSUUL 4 br.f. Kyllachy 129 – Cartuccia (IRE) (Doyoun 124) [2009 70d: p9.5g **61** p9.5m^3 p8.6g^5 p8g^4 p7g 7m Apr 26] good-topped filly: modest maiden nowadays: stays 9.5f: acts on polytrack and good to firm ground: blinkered nowadays. *R. A. Harris*

WYATT EARP (IRE) 8 b.g. Piccolo 121 – Tribal Lady 80 (Absalom 128) [2009 101: **91** 6g^3 6d^6 6g^2 6g^5 6m^5 6m 6g 6m^6 6m^5 Aug 31] smallish, sturdy gelding: fairly useful handicapper nowadays: best at 5f/6f: has form on polytrack and soft ground, seems best on good or firmer nowadays: sometimes blinkered. *P. Salmon*

WYETH 5 ch.g. Grand Lodge (USA) 125 – Bordighera (USA) 104 (Alysheba (USA)) **73** [2009 75: p16g* Feb 24] good-topped gelding: fair handicapper: won apprentice event at Lingfield sole Flat outing in 2009: stays 2m: unraced on firm going, acts on any other turf and polytrack: in blinkers/cheekpieces nowadays: has looked temperamental. *G. L. Moore*

WYMERING FILE (IRE) 4 b.f. Medecis 119 – Ensenada (IRE) 74 (Sri Pekan (USA) **95** 117) [2009 a5g* a12g* a9g* 9.9g p8.6g p10.7g^6 p10.7g p10.7g^4 p10.7g Nov 13] second foal: dam second from 2 starts at 5f in Ireland at 2 yrs: useful performer: won 8 of 12 starts in Cyprus (all at Nicosia), including 1000 Guineas and Oaks in 2008 and St Leger in March on second start in 2009: also won at Markopoulou (Greece) in June: left Petros Petroutsios (Cyprus) after fourth start: good 1¾ lengths fourth to Indiana Gal in listed race at Dundalk penultimate start: stays 1½m: raced only on dirt/polytrack and good going. *M. J. Grassick, Ireland*

WYNBERG (IRE) 4 b.g. Danetime (IRE) 121 – Jayzdoll (IRE) (Stravinsky (USA) **55** 133) [2009 74d: p5g^6 p6g p7g Feb 24] good-quartered gelding: modest handicapper: best at 5f/6f: acts on polytrack and good to soft going: tried blinkered/in cheekpieces/tongue tied. *Stef Liddiard*

WYN DIXIE (IRE) 10 b.g. Great Commotion (USA) 123 – Duchess Affair (IRE) 57 **–** (Digamist (USA) 110) [2009 12.5g^6 Aug 11] modest hurdler/chaser at best: tailed off in claimer on Flat debut. *B. Storey*

X

XAARA STAR (IRE) 2 b.f. (Feb 6) Xaar 132 – Bint Kaldoun (IRE) 82 (Kaldoun (FR) **52** 122) [2009 5m 6f^6 6m 6m^4 5g^3 6d 5.1g Aug 6] €4,500Y: lengthy filly: seventh foal: half-sister to several winners, including 4-y-o Kaldoun Kingdom and 6-y-o Zabeel Tower: dam, maiden (effective at 1m to 1½m), sister to dam of very smart miler Zafeen:

modest maiden: may prove best around 5f: acts on firm going: blinkered (below form) last 2 starts. *Eve Johnson Houghton*

XANDRA (IRE) 4 b.f. Xaar 132 – Talah 87 (Danehill (USA) 126) [2009 55: p9.5g p7.1g 8.1g May 4] sturdy filly: maiden: little form in 2009. *W. M. Brisbourne* **–**

XILERATOR (IRE) 2 b.g. (Apr 20) Arakan (USA) 123 – Grandel (Owington 123) [2009 7.2v^{2} Oct 31] €70,000F, £90,000Y: fifth foal: half-brother to 3-y-o Green Beret, 4-y-o Inxile and 7-y-o Tax Free: dam unraced: promising 2¾ lengths second to Tipperary Boutique (pair clear) in maiden at Ayr, travelling strongly long way: sprint bred: will improve. *D. Nicholls* **83 p**

XPRES MAITE 6 b.g. Komaite (USA) – Antonias Melody 86 (Rambo Dancer (CAN) 107) [2009 85, a96: f7d^{5} f6s* f6g^{2} f6g* p6g p7.1g^{4} f6g^{2} 7m 8g 7m 7g* 8g^{5} 7m p7.1g^{5} 6s^{6} f5g^{3} p6g^{5} f8g^{2} p7.1g^{6} f8f p8.6g^{2} f8m Dec 15] sturdy, compact gelding: fairly useful handicapper on all-weather, just fair on turf in 2009: won at Southwell in January and February, and Yarmouth in May: effective at 6f to 1m: acts on all-weather and firm ground, not on softer than good: wears headgear: consistent. *S. R. Bowring* **78 a92**

XTENSION (IRE) 2 br.c. (Feb 2) Xaar 132 – Great Joy (IRE) (Grand Lodge (USA) 125) [2009 6g* 6m^{2} 7g* 7m^{3} Oct 17] €15,000Y: useful-looking colt: has scope: third living foal: dam, fairly useful German 7f winner, half-sister to useful 1m winner A La Carte: smart and progressive: won maiden in May (favourite) and Veuve Clicquot Vintage Stakes in July (beat Mata Keranjang 1¼ lengths, again edged right), both at Goodwood: placed other 2 starts, in Coventry Stakes at Royal Ascot (6 lengths second to Canford Cliffs) and Dewhurst Stakes at Newmarket (raced wide), further improvement when close third to Beethoven in latter: will stay 1m: raced only on good/good to firm going. *C. G. Cox* **116**

XTRA SPECIAL 3 b.f. Xaar 132 – Misleading Lady (Warning 136) [2009 10m^{4} p12m^{5} Sep 16] sixth foal: half-sister to useful 7f (at 2 yrs) and 1¼m winner Lord Mayor (by Machiavellian) and 7-y-o Dinner Date: dam, ran twice, sister to smart 1½m performer Little Rock and closely related to smart 1¼m/1½m performer Short Skirt: easily better effort (fair form) in maidens 4 months apart when fourth at Newmarket on debut: sold 16,000 gns. *Sir Michael Stoute* **69**

XTRA TORRENTIAL (USA) 7 b.g. Torrential (USA) 117 – Offering (USA) (Majestic Light (USA)) [2009 –: p8.6g^{6} p7.1g^{6} p8.6g^{6} Apr 16] tall, leggy gelding: one-time useful performer: lightly raced in recent years, and just fair form in 2009: stays 8.6f: acts on polytrack and good to soft going: races freely. *D. M. Simcock* **70**

XTRAVAGANZA (IRE) 4 b.f. Xaar 132 – Royal Jubilee (IRE) 81 (King's Theatre (IRE) 128) [2009 73: 8.1d Sep 4] rather leggy filly: has a round action: fair handicapper at 3 yrs: well held only outing in 2009: stays 1½m: acts on polytrack and soft ground. *Jamie Snowden* **–**

Veuve Clicquot Vintage Stakes, Goodwood—Xtension overcomes trouble in running to win from Mata Keranjang (quartered cap) and Corporal Maddox (No.3)

Brighthelm Racing's "Xtension"

XTREME (IRE) 2 b.g. (Jan 13) Xaar 132 – Emerald Storm (USA) 74 (Diesis 133) [2009 p8.6g 8.3g Oct 28] modest form at best in maiden/seller: tried blinkered: sold 2,500 gns. *A. Bailey* **52**

Y

YAA WAYL (IRE) 2 b.g. (Apr 8) Whipper (USA) 126 – Lidanna 113 (Nicholas (USA) 111) [2009 6m^4 5d* 6d^2 6m^4 7g^2 Oct 24] 38,000Y: good-topped gelding: sixth foal: half-brother to several winners, including useful Irish 6.7f winner Lidanski (by Soviet Star) and Irish 4-y-o Capall An Ibre: dam Irish 5f (including at 2 yrs)/6f winner: fairly useful performer: won maiden at Thirsk in July: good efforts when second in nurseries, blinkered when beaten ½ length by Leviathan at Doncaster final outing (gelded after): free-going sort, but stays 7f: acts on good to soft going: tongue tied third/fourth starts. *M. A. Jarvis* **93**

YAB ADEE 5 b.g. Mark of Esteem (IRE) 137 – Kotdiji (Mtoto 134) [2009 75: p12.2m Sep 28] good-topped gelding: fair performer at 4 yrs: well held sole start in 2009: stays 1½m: acts on polytrack and good to firm ground: usually claimer ridden. *M. P. Tregoning* **–**

YA BOY SIR (IRE) 2 ch.c. (Mar 30) Alhaarth (IRE) 126 – Champs Elysees (USA) (Distant Relative 128) [2009 6m^4 5.9m^6 7.1s^5 7.1m^3 6g^6 p5.1g f6m^2 Dec 15] modest maiden: trained by I. Semple first 6 starts: best effort at 6f on fibresand: possibly quirky. *N. Wilson* **54**

YABTREE (IRE) 2 b.c. (Mar 29) Clodovil (IRE) 116 – Lorientaise (IRE) (Xaar 132) [2009 7.1m^3 8g^5 p7g Nov 11] best effort in maidens when fifth to Rasmy at Bath: bred to be best up to 1m. *R. Charlton* **67**

YAHRAB (IRE) 4 gr.g. Dalakhani (IRE) 133 – Loire Valley (IRE) (Sadler's Wells (USA) 132) [2009 115: 10g 9g 10m² 12m 11m² 10.3m 9.9m May 25] close-coupled gelding: smart performer: trained by M. bin Shafya in UAE first 5 starts in 2009, best efforts when 3¼ lengths second to Presvis in handicap at Nad Al Sheba and ½-length second to Mr Brock in listed race at Abu Dhabi: well below form in Britain after: stays 1¼m, not 1½m: unraced on heavy going, acts on polytrack and any other turf: often makes running: returned to C. Brittain, and gelded. *Saeed bin Suroor* **114**

YAHWUDHEE (FR) 4 b.g. Zamindar (USA) 116 – Lady Marshall (FR) (Octagonal (NZ) 126) [2009 81: f5g⁶ f6g 6g 5d p7.1g Sep 12] quite attractive gelding: little form in 2009, leaving M. Easterby after reappearance, N. Wilson after fourth outing: dead. *M. W. Easterby* **–**

YAKAMA (IRE) 4 b.g. Indian Danehill (IRE) 124 – Working Progress (IRE) (Marju (IRE) 127) [2009 66: p8g 10.1d 7.5m 8g⁶ 8f² 8.3g⁵ p7.1g Dec 11] angular gelding: modest maiden: stays 1¼m: acts on polytrack, firm and soft going: often in headgear: tried tongue tied. *Mrs C. A. Dunnett* **62**

YALDAS GIRL (USA) 3 gr. or ro.f. Unbridled's Song (USA) 125 – Marina de Chavon (USA) (Exploit (USA) 117) [2009 49: p8g p7f p9.5g⁶ p16g p12g Nov 11] rather leggy, lengthy filly: maiden: little form in 2009. *J. R. Best* **–**

YAMAL (IRE) 4 b.g. Green Desert (USA) 127 – Pioneer Bride (USA) (Gone West (USA)) [2009 104: 7.5m² a8f* 7.5g² 8g* 8m³ May 30] good-bodied gelding: smart performer: continued progress in 2009, winning handicaps at Nad Al Sheba in February and York (listed event, by ½ length from Philario) in May: also ran creditably when equal-second to Swop in handicap at Nad Al Sheba and close third to Premio Loco in listed race at Goodwood third/final starts: best up to 1m: acts on polytrack/dirt, good to firm and good to soft going: strong traveller. *Saeed bin Suroor* **115**

YANBU (USA) 4 b.f. Swain (IRE) 134 – Dufoof (USA) (Kingmambo (USA) 125) [2009 8g f12g Jul 14] 1,500 3-y-o: first foal: dam unraced half-sister to smart performer up to 9f Iqte Saab: soundly beaten in maidens. *R. W. Price* **–**

YANKEE BRIGHT (USA) 2 b.f. (Mar 26) Elusive Quality (USA) – Sharp Minister (CAN) (Deputy Minister (CAN)) [2009 8.1m⁵ 8d³ 8g Oct 31] leggy, close-coupled filly: seventh foal: half-sister to several winners, including 5-y-o Dijeerr and useful UAE 1m winner Plavius (by Danzig): dam, ran twice in USA, sister to very smart French/US performer up to 1½m Flag Down: fair form in maidens first 2 starts: very stiff task final outing: should stay 1¼m. *J. G. Given* **69 +**

YANKEE DOODLE 3 gr.c. Dalakhani (IRE) 133 – Bella Lambada 87 (Lammtarra (USA) 134) [2009 76p: 10d² 10g² 11.7s* 16f² 14d³ 14d² Jul 16] good sort: smart performer: won maiden at Wexford in May: placed after in Queen's Vase at Royal Ascot (4 lengths second to Holberg), Curragh Cup (close third to Profound Beauty) and listed race at Leopardstown (¾-length second to Profound Beauty): should stay beyond 2m: unraced on heavy going, acts on any other: held up. *A. P. O'Brien, Ireland* **116**

YANKEE STORM 4 b.g. Yankee Gentleman (USA) – Yes Virginia (USA) (Roanoke (USA)) [2009 80: p7g f6g⁵ f6g³ f6g² f5g³ p6g⁶ p7f² p7g p6g³ p6f Dec 13] quite attractive gelding: fair handicapper: left M. Quinn after sixth start: effective at truly-run 5f, and has form at 1¼m: raced only on all-weather and going firmer than good on turf: tried in cheekpieces. *H. J. Collingridge* **77**

YANZA 3 b.f. Bahamian Bounty 116 – Locharia 91 (Wolfhound (USA) 126) [2009 77: p5g* 5m 6.1g p6g p6g p6g⁴ p6g² p6g² p6g³ p5.1g p6g f5g Dec 27] fair performer: won maiden at Kempton in April: in-and-out form after: may prove best at 5f: acts on polytrack and heavy ground: blinkered last 6 outings. *J. R. Gask* **71**

YARRA RIVER 2 b. or br.g. (Apr 2) Dr Fong (USA) 128 – River Cara (USA) 86 (Irish River (FR) 131) [2009 6m² 7g³ 7d² 7m² 7m Oct 3] 20,000Y: smallish, compact gelding: half-brother to several winners, including 3-y-o Warrior One and 4-y-o Basque Beauty: dam French 2-y-o 1m winner: similar form when placed in maidens first 4 starts: stiff task final outing (gelded after): will stay 1m. *A. M. Balding* **78**

YASHKUR 3 ch.f. Needwood Blade 117 – Silent Tribute (IRE) 104 (Lion Cavern (USA) 117) [2009 10.1m⁶ 6g⁶ 9g 8m p8g p8m Sep 24] 18,000F, 27,000Y: angular filly: sixth foal: closely related to winner in Russia by Pivotal: dam 2-y-o 6f/1m winner: modest form. *C. E. Brittain* **52**

YAWARY 2 b.f. (Feb 19) Medicean 128 – Sociable 77 (Danehill (USA) 126) [2009 6m 6g⁴ 6m² 6m 7g⁵ p5g⁴ p8g⁶ 6g⁶ Sep 14] 6,500Y: angular filly: fourth foal: dam, 9f winner, out of half-sister to Cheveley Park Stakes winner Regal Rose: modest maiden: stays 7f: has finished weakly. *C. E. Brittain* **62**

YEADON 2 b.c. (Feb 18) Fraam 114 – Harryana 79 (Efisio 120) [2009 6d³ 5g² f5g² 6f⁴ p6g⁴ 6m⁴ p5.1g⁴ f5m⁴ f6m² p6f⁶ Dec 19] fair maiden: reportedly had wind operation after second start: should stay 7f: acts on all-weather and good to soft going: tried blinkered: signs of temperament. *R. A. Fahey* **68**

YEAH 2 b.g. (May 26) Gentleman's Deal (IRE) 114 – Snugfit Dubarry 69 (Ali-Royal (IRE) 127) [2009 5g⁴ 6g⁶ 6g⁴ f5g p6g Oct 8] poor maiden: should be at least as effective at 5f as 6f. *Pat Morris* **49**

YEATS (IRE) 8 b.h. Sadler's Wells (USA) 132 – Lyndonville (IRE) (Top Ville 129) [2009 128: 13s⁶ 20m* 14s 20g³ Oct 4] **126**

With the natural flow of retirement and recruitment among horses and humans, plus changes in so many other things, no two seasons can ever be the same. There will be one notable difference, though, in 2010, not just from the latest season but from the seven previous ones. Yeats will be on duty at Coolmore, not on the racecourse. He has captured the hearts of racegoers in remarkable style in a career spanning twenty-six starts and producing fifteen wins, seven of them at Group 1, for earnings in excess of £1.3m. Yeats wasn't the best stayer in the history of the sport but, when he was on top form, none of his rivals could hold a candle to him over long distances. His record of four successive victories in the Gold Cup is one which it is hard to imagine being equalled, let alone surpassed. It is testimony to his ability and his longevity, as well as to the skill of his trainer Aidan O'Brien, that he also holds records for having won Group 1 races in five successive years, and for being the subject of an essay in seven editions of *Racehorses*, something no other runner on the Flat, and precious few over jumps, has earned before. Yeats was, in short, a giant who will be virtually impossible to replace on the track and will be sorely missed when Royal Ascot comes round again.

As the year got under way, making history by winning that fourth Gold Cup was the sum total of Aidan O'Brien's ambition for Yeats. Nothing else entered the equation. For the third year running, Yeats reappeared in the Vintage Crop Stakes at Navan in April, which he had won in 2007 and 2008. He had also won on his debut as a two-year-old and on his reappearance in 2004 (the Ballysax Stakes) and also 2006 (the Gold Cup) and, conceding a minimum of 7 lb to his five rivals on soft going, he started at 5/4-on. Yeats ran the worst race of his career, having every chance turning for home but finding nothing when asked and being beaten over thirty lengths into sixth behind Alandi. Coral immediately pushed out Yeats to 7-2 (from 6-4) for the Gold Cup and various commentators started questioning his prospects of making history at the Royal meeting, propounding the theory that age might finally have caught up with him. Yeats blew fairly hard after the Vintage Crop Stakes—a number of Ballydoyle runners did seem to need an outing in the spring—and the explanation offered by his trainer was illuminating. 'Obviously he's a year older and a year wiser than he was last year and than every year that he was before . . . To have him in top gear would have made it hard to get him to peak again at Ascot. I wouldn't read too much into it and hopefully he will leave that well behind him.' Yeats worked over a mile and a half after racing at the Curragh at the end of May with three-year-old Von Jawlensky. Seemingly, he responded well to a couple of cracks of the whip from Johnny Murtagh to overtake his stable companion and go clear towards the end of gallop, O'Brien saying 'He's very lazy, but that will have done him good.'

Which was the best Gold Cup in the long history of the race? A leading candidate would have to be the edition of 1874, won by Boiard (1873 Prix du Jockey Club, Grand Prix de Paris and Prix Royal-Oak, 1874 Prix du Cadran) from dead-heaters Doncaster (1873 Derby, runner-up in the St Leger) and Flageolet (1872 Prix Morny, 1873 Goodwood Cup, runner-up that year in the Prix du Jockey Club, Grand Prix de Paris and Gold Cup). Following them home came Marie Stuart (1873 Oaks, Coronation Stakes, Yorkshire Oaks and St Leger), Gang Forward (1873 Two Thousand Guineas and St James's Palace Stakes, equal second in the Derby) and Kaiser (runner-up in the Two Thousand Guineas and equal second in the Derby in 1873). The nine runners who took on Yeats were hardly in the same league judged on their credentials. They were headed by the first two in the Henry II Stakes, Geordieland (who had chased home Yeats in the 2007 and 2008 Gold Cups) and Patkai (who had landed the Sagaro Stakes on his reappearance). Saeed

Gold Cup, Royal Ascot—the 203rd year of this great race and Yeats becomes the first to win it four times; Patkai is the only one to finish anywhere near him

bin Suroor fielded three for Godolphin: Veracity, successful in the Jockey Club Cup and third to Yeats in the Prix Royal-Oak in 2008; Sagara, who hadn't won for more than two years; and Dubai Sheema Classic winner Eastern Anthem, who was unproven at the trip. Great Voltigeur Stakes winner Centennial was also unproven at the distance and the two others were Hindu Kush, successful in the Saval Beg Stakes after finishing second in the Vintage Crop Stakes, and Washington Irving, fourth in the Yorkshire Cup last time, both of them former stable-companions of Yeats. The good to firm going was much more suitable for Yeats than the going had been at Navan, and the betting suggested he was back to his best. After starting the day as 9/4 favourite, he was finally sent off at 6/4 (he started 7/1 in 2006, 13/8-on in 2007 and 11/8 in 2008). The tactics employed on Yeats in the Gold Cup varied little from year to year—he was ridden for stamina, racing quite close up before challenging for the lead over two furlongs out and making the best of his way home from there. Murtagh rode a cracking race on him in the latest edition, waiting in fourth as Hindu Kush led from Veracity at a relatively moderate gallop. Veracity took over with half a mile to go, but Yeats was soon challenging him. With three furlongs left, both Patkai and Geordieland were somewhat hemmed in on the rail. When Veracity went wrong—he had to be put down after fracturing a cannon bone—Murtagh used Yeats's useful turn of foot to send him all of four lengths clear with two furlongs to go. It was a winning lead. Patkai had got clear soon after entering the straight and stayed on gamely but he never looked like getting to Yeats, while Geordieland made some headway to chase the first two but found nothing more from a furlong out. At the line, to the delight of the Royal Ascot crowd (though not the bookmakers, who claimed to have lost a scarcely believable £10m on the race nationwide), Yeats was the winner by three and a half lengths, with Geordieland fifteen lengths further back. After the winner had received his deserved rapturous reception, O'Brien was quite revealing in expressing how he felt about the record. 'I've never felt such pressure for any race before, this horse was the only time. I was so sick this morning as I really believed this couldn't happen. History is very hard to change, we knew we had a wonderful horse but usually fairytales don't come true. You dream and dream and dream, we were in this position and we never would be again.' To put the achievement into perspective, Yeats had broken Sagaro's record of three Gold Cup victories from

1975 to 1977 and, among out-and-out stayers, he had equalled Marsyas's record of four Prix du Cadrans from 1944 to 1947; Vinnie Roe won four successive Irish St Legers between 2001 and 2004 and, in America, Kelso notched five successive Jockey Club Gold Cups over two miles from 1960 to 1964 (the Cheltenham Gold Cup winner of the 'thirties Golden Miller is the only horse to win the same championship race in Britain five times). Yeats matched Triptych in notching at least one Group 1 race five years in a row, though John Henry (1980 to 1984) and Sunline (1998 to 2002) had also achieved the feat in the States and Australia and New Zealand respectively. Yeats was also only the second eight-year-old to win the Gold Cup. The 1900 winner Merman was the first, though the pair are not the oldest winners, Beeswing being nine when she triumphed in 1842.

Four wins in a row at the Royal meeting is not a record either, Brown Jack having landed the Ascot Stakes in 1928 before winning the Queen Alexandra Stakes six years running from 1929 to 1934. Trelawny won four races in a row at the meeting in just two years, landing the Ascot Stakes/Queen Alexandra Stakes double in both 1962 and 1963. Coincidentally, the day after Boiard won the Gold Cup he contested the Alexandra Plate, forerunner of the Queen Alexandra Stakes, but he managed only second, supposedly due to over-confidence on the part of his jockey.

The King George VI and Queen Elizabeth Stakes was mentioned as a possible target for Yeats, as was the Goodwood Cup, which he had won in 2006 and 2008, but, in the end, he wasn't seen out until the Irish Field St Leger at the Curragh in mid-September, which he had won in 2007. Murtagh preferred to ride Changingoftheguard (who came sixth) in the St Leger at Doncaster on the same day, and on soft going Yeats again ran way below his best, starting only fourth favourite and virtually friendless in the market. Struggling well over half a mile out, he was allowed to come home in his own time, eventually finishing around sixty lengths behind the much improved winner Alandi. A much better effort followed in the Prix du Cadran at Longchamp three weeks later, though Yeats still ran below the form he had shown at Royal Ascot. He had contested the Cadran twice before, running below his best when third in 2007 and fifth in 2008 and, although starting favourite this time and taking over from his pacemaker Windsor Palace half a mile out he could do no more in the final furlong and went down by a short head and a length and a half to Alandi and Kasbah Bliss. Not long afterwards the decision was taken to retire him to Coolmore, his fee for 2010 set at €10,000. On the face of it, in the modern era, Yeats has the profile of a jumps sire rather than a Flat one, but there must be a chance that John Magnier will ensure his old favourite covers at least some mares with the potential to produce above-average Flat runners. Ballydoyle's other top stayer Septimus, who recorded the top staying performances of both 2007 (Doncaster Cup) and 2008 (Irish St Leger), was still in training in the latest season but didn't reach the racecourse. He too has now been retired to stud but, unlike Yeats, is being marketed specifically as a jumps stallion.

Yeats (IRE) (b.h. 2001)	Sadler's Wells (USA) (b 1981)	Northern Dancer (b 1961)	Nearctic
			Natalma
		Fairy Bridge (b 1975)	Bold Reason
			Special
	Lyndonville (IRE) (b 1988)	Top Ville (b 1976)	High Top
			Sega Ville
		Diamond Land (br 1978)	Sparkler
			Canaan

At the seventh time of asking, there is little fresh to write about Yeats's pedigree. His sire Sadler's Wells holds the record for the number of Gold Cup wins, his progeny now having won six (Kayf Tara won twice), putting him two clear of Son-In-Law who had three individual scorers, Foxlaw in 1927, Bosworth in 1930 and Trimdon in 1931 and 1932. 2009 was another good year for the retired Sadler's Wells, with Ask winning twice in Group 1 company (the offspring of Sadler's Wells won twelve European pattern races in all). His very successful stallion sons Galileo, High Chaparral and Montjeu also kept his name to the fore. The Gold Cup field showed just how influential Sadler's Wells has become in staying races— apart from Yeats (whose victory took him clear at the top of the list of Group 1 winners numerically by Sadler's Wells), he sired both Sagara and Hindu

Kush, is in the second generation of Patkai's, Geordieland's and Washington Irving's pedigrees, and in the third generation of Eastern Anthem's (Sadler's Wells is also the sire of Septimus). Yeats's dam Lyndonville won a maiden at Galway over a mile and three quarters by six lengths from only three starts. Like the dam of St Nicholas Abbey, she initially belonged to Sheikh Mohammed, who sold her for 76,000 guineas as a four-year-old at the December Sales. Lyndonville went through the sale-ring there twice more, fetching 96,000 guineas in 1994 and 220,000 guineas in 1999, when she was bought by Yeats's breeders and part-owners the Nagles of Barronstown Stud (not long after his Gold Cup victory Yeats was paraded at the Curragh after the Barronstown Stud Two-Year-Old Maiden). Lyndonville is the dam of two other stakes winners, notably Solskjaer (by Danehill), who landed the Royal Whip Stakes, and comes from a family with plenty of stamina. One half-sister Ivanka won the Fillies' Mile and another Sahara Breeze foaled Lady of Chad (Prix Marcel Boussac) and Alcazar (Prix Royal-Oak). Others from the family include Cantelo (St Leger), Bracey Bridge (Park Hill Stakes), Tug of War (Goodwood Cup) and Biskrah (Doncaster Cup). As already mentioned, Yeats had a useful turn of speed and was no dyed-in-the-wool plodder. One-time ante-post Derby favourite, he won twice over a mile and a quarter at three and won the Coronation Cup over a mile and a half at four before going on to excel over long distances. He acted on any going but was probably at his very best on firmer than good. A tall, good-topped horse and a good walker who impressed in appearance and had a powerful, round action, he was a credit to his connections. *A. P. O'Brien, Ireland*

YELLOW PRINTER 3 b.g. Royal Applause 124 – Robsart (IRE) 91 (Robellino (USA) 127) [2009 80: p8g 8.1g^3 8.1f^3 8m^4 7m^2 8.3m^3 8g p8g^6 p8g p8m^3 Nov 19] sturdy gelding: fairly useful handicapper: left Tom Dascombe after fifth start: stays 1m: acts on polytrack and firm ground: tried visored. *F. J. Brennan* **80**

YELLOW RIDGE (IRE) 6 ch.g. On The Ridge (IRE) 115 – Jonathan's Rose (IRE) (Law Society (USA) 130) [2009 51: p16.5g p12g Oct 20] compact gelding: one-time fair performer: well held in 2009: tried blinkered/tongue tied. *Luke Comer, Ireland* **–**

YELLOW RIVER (USA) 3 ch.f. Johannesburg (USA) 127 – Ascension (IRE) 110 (Night Shift (USA)) [2009 45: f7d^2 p6g p7g f8g^5 7g 7s 5g 6.1g 6m Sep 28] poor form in Britain, leaving S. Callaghan after reappearance: below form after: stays 7f: tried in headgear. *E. J. Creighton* **43 d**

YELLOWSTONE (IRE) 5 b.h. Rock of Gibraltar (IRE) 133 – Love And Affection (USA) (Exclusive Era (USA)) [2009 119: 13.3d^6 14m^4 12m 12g^4 12g 14.5s^2 Oct 24] big, good-bodied horse: well below smart best in 2009, best effort (useful form) when fourth in listed race won by All The Aces at Newmarket fourth outing: stays 1¾m: acts on any going: often in cheekpieces, tried blinkered. *P. F. I. Cole* **96**

YEOMAN OF ENGLAND (IRE) 3 b.g. Pyrus (USA) 106 – Regal Lustre 50 (Averti (IRE) 117) [2009 66: 7m 7.1g 6s 8m 10.1m^4 10m 11.5g^5 Oct 20] sturdy gelding: modest maiden at 3 yrs, patchy form: stays 1¼m: acts on polytrack, soft and good to firm ground: blinkered once: sold 5,000 gns. *C. F. Wall* **58**

YER WOMAN (IRE) 2 b.f. (Apr 30) Kyllachy 129 – Genny Lim (IRE) 91 (Barathea (IRE) 127) [2009 5.1m^2 5g* 6g 5m* 6.5m 6m^4 p6m* Nov 26] 7,500Y: compact filly: second foal: half-sister to Irish 3-y-o Palazzone: dam Irish 1m winner: useful performer: won maiden at Windsor in May and nurseries at Sandown in July and Kempton (in good style, showing improved form) in November: stays easy 6f: acts on polytrack, raced only on good/good to firm going on turf. *R. Hannon* **95**

YES CHEF 2 ch.c. (Feb 1) Best of The Bests (IRE) 122 – Lady Chef 75 (Double Trigger (IRE) 123) [2009 8.3m 7g^4 Oct 23] plain, lengthy colt: first foal: dam 2-y-o 7f winner: much better effort in maidens when 8 lengths fourth to Tamaathul at Doncaster: should stay 1m. *J. Gallagher* **70**

YES MAGGIE (IRE) 2 b.f. (Jan 29) Vindication (USA) 122 – Westerly Gale (USA) (Gone West (USA)) [2009 7m Sep 19] first foal: dam, US 8.5f winner, half-sister to smart US Grade 1 9f winner Scorpion: 18/1, soundly beaten in maiden at Newbury. *M. R. Channon* **–**

YES MR PRESIDENT (IRE) 4 b.g. Montjeu (IRE) 137 – Royals Special (IRE) 72 (Caerleon (USA) 132) [2009 86: 12g^4 14g* 11.5m^2 11.9m 14g^4 16g^2 12m^3 14v* 18m Oct 17] strong, rangy gelding: useful handicapper: largely progressive in 2009, winning **107**

betfred.com Old Borough Cup Stakes (Heritage Handicap), Haydock—Yes Mr President revels in the mud; Alanbrooke (blinkers) and Kings Destiny finish third and fourth respectively

at Goodwood in June and Haydock (Old Borough Cup, beat Nemo Spirit by 6 lengths) in September: finished lame in Cesarewitch final start: stays 2m: acts on polytrack, heavy and good to firm ground: tried blinkered: races prominently. *M. Johnston*

YESNABAY (USA) 2 b. or br.g. (Jan 31) Grand Slam (USA) 120 – Speedy Sonata (USA) (Stravinsky (USA) 133) [2009 5m^3 6g* 8f Sep 19] 36,000Y: first foal: dam, US 5f/5.5f winner (including at 2 yrs), out of sister to Prix de Diane winner Lady In Silver: much improved when winning maiden at Ayr in July by 7 lengths from Benrish, taking strong hold yet quickening impressively: left G. A. Swinbank, below form in Grade 3 Summer Stakes at Woodbine: best effort at 6f. *L. Rivelli, USA* **97**

YES ONE (IRE) 5 ch.g. Peintre Celebre (USA) 137 – Copious (IRE) (Generous (IRE) 139) [2009 89: f7d p8.6g^6 p7g^5 p8g^5 p9.5g^4 Apr 20] small, sturdy gelding: handicapper, just fair at 5 yrs: effective at 7f to 1¼m: acts on all-weather, firm and soft ground: tried tongue tied. *K. A. Ryan* **72**

YES PLEASE 4 b.g. Efisio 120 – Shall We Dance 83 (Rambo Dancer (CAN) 107) [2009 f6g 7.2g 6s^3 7v p7.1g Sep 11] form (modest) only when placed in maiden third start: stays 6f: raced on all-weather and going softer than good: tried visored. *K. A. Ryan* **57**

YES SHE CAN CAN 3 ch.f. Monsieur Bond (IRE) 120 – Antonia's Folly 64 (Music Boy 124) [2009 –: p6g p5g^4 f5g p5g 5m Apr 1] little form: tried blinkered. *Peter Grayson* **–**

YIRGA 3 b.c. Cape Cross (IRE) 129 – Auratum (USA) 93 (Carson City (USA)) [2009 75: 8.1v^3 8.1m* 8g* 9.7f^2 10g Aug 8] leggy, attractive colt: fairly useful handicapper: won at Sandown and Thirsk, both in June: stays easy 9.7f: acts on firm going: tongue tied in 2009: joined A. Al Raihe in UAE. *Saeed bin Suroor* **91**

YKIKAMOOCOW 3 b.f. Cape Town (IRE) 119 – Pigeon 84 (Casteddu 111) [2009 68: 7d* 7g 8d^5 7g 7.2g^3 Oct 23] fair handicapper: won at Catterick in June: stays 7.2f: raced only on good/good to soft ground. *G. A. Harker* **72**

YMIR 3 b.c. Zaha (CAN) 106 – Anastasia Venture 70 (Lion Cavern (USA) 117) [2009 69: p8g 8.5g 7g 8g^3 7.1m^3 8g p8g p7f^2 p8m p7m p8g^2 p8m^4 p8m^6 Dec 9] fair maiden handicapper: stays 1m: acts on polytrack and good to firm ground: often in cheekpieces: not straightforward. *M. J. Attwater* **66**

YOGAROO (USA) 2 b.g. (Apr 14) Bring The Heat (USA) – Harper N Abbey (USA) (Outflanker (USA) 83) [2009 a2.5f^2 p4.5f* 5m p6f Sep 7] good-topped gelding: first foal: dam unraced daughter of Breeders' Cup Sprint runner-up Meafara: won maiden at Keeneland in April by 5½ lengths: well held after in Norfolk Stakes at Royal Ascot (veered badly left when weakening) and non-graded stakes at Del Mar (last of 10): acts on polytrack: blinkered all starts: has worn tongue tie. *Wesley A. Ward, USA* **?**

YONDER 5 br.m. And Beyond (IRE) 113 – Dominance (Dominion 123) [2009 65: p12.2g^4 18m^3 21.6m 12m* 14m* 16.2m 12m 12m Sep 10] workmanlike mare: fair handicapper on Flat: improved when winning at Salisbury and Lingfield in June: stays 2¼m, effective at shorter: acts on good to firm ground: tried blinkered. *H. Morrison* **71**

YORGUNNABELUCKY (USA) 3 b.c. Giant's Causeway (USA) 132 – Helsinki (Machiavellian (USA) 123) [2009 75p: 10m* 10d 10.4m 9.9f 8.1m[5] 8.1m[5] 8m[5] Oct 5] tall colt: fairly useful performer: won maiden at Redcar in June by 16 lengths: stays 1¼m: acts on good to firm ground: tried blinkered. *M. Johnston* **87**

YORK CLIFF 11 b.g. Marju (IRE) 127 – Azm (Unfuwain (USA) 131) [2009 66: f16d p12g[4] f11g p12.2g[6] 16.2v[3] 12.1m 12.3m p12.2g Dec 7] good-bodied gelding: modest performer nowadays: stays 2m: acts on all-weather and any turf going: tried in headgear: none too consistent. *W. M. Brisbourne* **53**

YORKE'S FOLLY (USA) 8 b.m. Stravinsky (USA) 133 – Tommelise (USA) (Dayjur (USA) 137) [2009 54: 5m[2] 5m[6] Aug 15] big, lengthy mare: modest maiden: effective at 5f/6f: acts on fibresand and firm going: usually visored/blinkered: none too consistent. *C. W. Fairhurst* **53**

YORK KEY BAR 3 b.g. Presidium 124 – Onemoretime (Timeless Times (USA) 99) [2009 72: 7m p6g[3] 5m[4] 6s[6] p6g[5] 5d[3] 5g Jul 16] close-coupled gelding: just modest maiden in 2009: stayed 6f: acted on heavy ground: tried tongue tied: bolted to post third outing: dead. *B. Ellison* **61**

YORKSHIRE BLUE 10 b.g. Atraf 116 – Something Blue (Petong 126) [2009 76§: 6f 6m[6] 7g[5] 6m* 6m[6] 6m[2] 6g[6] Oct 23] close-coupled gelding: fair handicapper: won apprentice event at Redcar in September: effective at 6f/7f: acts on all-weather and any turf going: tried blinkered, in cheekpieces of late: often gets behind: unreliable. *J. S. Goldie* **68 §**

YORKSTERS GIRL (IRE) 3 ch.f. Bachelor Duke (USA) 122 – Isadora Duncan (IRE) (Sadler's Wells (USA) 132) [2009 93: 7s 8.1m Jul 4] leggy, lengthy filly: fairly useful performer: below best both starts in 2009, stiff task in Fred Darling Stakes on reappearance: not sure to stay beyond 7f: acts on heavy and good to firm going: sold 40,000 gns in July, resold 18,000 gns in December. *M. G. Quinlan* **81**

YORKSTERS PRINCE (IRE) 2 b.g. (Apr 1) Beat Hollow 126 – Odalisque (IRE) (Machiavellian (USA) 123) [2009 8m p8.6g[4] Dec 26] lengthy gelding: better effort in maidens when 7¼ lengths last of 4 at Wolverhampton: should stay 1¼m. *M. G. Quinlan* **54**

YOSSI (IRE) 5 b.g. Montjeu (IRE) 137 – Raindancing (IRE) 94 (Tirol 127) [2009 85: 12d[2] 12g 12m Sep 10] good-bodied gelding: fairly useful handicapper: below form after reappearance: effective at 1¼m to 1¾m: acts on soft ground: tried blinkered/visored: quirky and not one to trust. *Jim Best* **85 §**

YOU AVIN A LAUGH 3 ch.g. Bertolini (USA) 125 – High Stepping (IRE) (Taufan (USA) 119) [2009 –: p6g[6] p5.1g p5g[3] f5g[4] p6g[5] p5.1g[2] 5m p6g[3] 5m p6g[4] p6g Jun 29] useful-looking gelding: modest maiden: effective at 5f/6f: acts on polytrack, no form on turf: tried blinkered: sold 5,000 gns in July. *C. A. Dwyer* **– a64**

YOUCANALWAYSDREAM (IRE) 2 b.f. (Mar 28) Exceed And Excel (AUS) 126 – Al Shadeedah (USA) 86 (Nureyev (USA) 131) [2009 5.1g p5.1g p5g[2] p5g[2] p5.1m* Nov 28] 32,000F, £27,000Y: eighth foal: half-sister to 3 winners, including fairly useful 9f/1¼m winner Shirazi (by Mtoto): dam, 1m winner, out of Australian Group 1 1m winner Copperama: fairly useful performer: won maiden at Wolverhampton in November easily by 5 lengths: speedy, and may prove best at 5f: raced only on polytrack after debut: open to further improvement. *K. A. Ryan* **80 p**

YOU'LL BE MINE (USA) 2 b.f. (Mar 7) Kingmambo (USA) 125 – Quarter Moon (IRE) 120 (Sadler's Wells (USA) 132) [2009 7g[4] 7d* 8m[3] Sep 26] **105 P**

Ballydoyle is well represented as usual in the ante-post markets for the Two Thousand Guineas and Derby, but has less of a strong hand in the fillies' classics. This situation reflects the success that Ballydoyle has enjoyed with its three-year-olds in the Aidan O'Brien era, winning twenty-three of those classics in Britain and Ireland with its colts compared to eleven with its fillies. The filly who looks best placed to add to the latter tally in the next season is You'll Be Mine, who is available at 33/1 for the One Thousand Guineas at the time of writing, but generally favourite for the Oaks (best odds 16/1). You'll Be Mine progressed with each of her three starts as a two-year-old, on the final occasion rather unfortunate when two and a quarter lengths third of nine to Hibaayeb in the Fillies' Mile at Ascot. The Fillies' Mile was by no means a vintage edition but You'll Be Mine deserves particular credit for her effort, as she was the only one of those held up who proved able to get into things. She certainly looks the one from the race with most potential, especially since her career was little more than six weeks old when she ran at Ascot.

You'll Be Mine was promoted to Group 1 company after having her first two starts in maidens. After finishing fourth under a considerate ride to Miss Laa Di

Da in a fillies' event at Leopardstown on her debut in August, she confirmed that promise in a similar contest at the same track twenty-three days later. Both races were over seven furlongs and on the second occasion she took a while to really find her stride before staying on strongly to beat Hedaaya by two lengths.

You'll Be Mine (USA) (b.f. Mar 7, 2007)	Kingmambo (USA) (b 1990)	Mr Prospector (b 1970)	Raise A Native
			Gold Digger
		Miesque (b 1984)	Nureyev
			Pasadoble
	Quarter Moon (IRE) (b 1999)	Sadler's Wells (b 1981)	Northern Dancer
			Fairy Bridge
		Jude (b 1994)	Darshaan
			Alruccaba

You'll Be Mine's pedigree suggests that she will certainly stay at least a mile and a quarter and may well get the Oaks trip. You'll Be Mine's grandam Jude achieved little in four outings but, a sister to the useful Irish mile and a quarter winner Alouette and Irish Oaks third Arrikala, as well as a half-sister to the Nassau and Sun Chariot Stakes winner Last Second, she has enjoyed notable success as a broodmare. Her first foal was You'll Be Mine's dam Quarter Moon, who was runner-up in three classics. Jude has produced a classic winner in Yesterday, who won the Irish One Thousand Guineas at the Curragh in 2003 before going on to finish runner-up in the Oaks at Epsom. Jude's sixth foal All My Loving finished third in both the English and Irish Oaks. The winner of the Moyglare Stud Stakes as a two-year-old, Quarter Moon came fifth in the One Thousand Guineas on her three-year-old reappearance before finishing second in the Irish version and then repeating the feat in both the Oaks at Epsom and the Curragh. Quarter Moon's first foal never ran, but both You'll Be Mine's brother King of Westphalia and her half-brother Born To Be King (by Storm Cat) were useful at up to a mile and a quarter and a mile respectively, though neither ever looked like figuring among the brighter lights at Ballydoyle for whom they each acted as pacemaker on occasions. The good-topped, attractive You'll Be Mine has the potential to bring more credit to the family name as a three-year-old. *A. P. O'Brien, Ireland*

YOUM JAMIL (USA) 2 gr. or ro.c. (Feb 2) Mizzen Mast (USA) 121 – Millie's Choice (IRE) 110 (Taufan (USA) 119) [2009 $8g^{2}$ $7g^{2}$ Oct 30] 140,000Y: half-brother to several winners in USA, including Grade 3 8.5f winner Millie's Quest (by Quest For Fame): dam, Irish 7f/1m winner, half-sister to dam of 7-y-o Doctor Dino: runner-up in maidens at Salisbury and Newmarket (still green, beaten 1½ lengths by Quick Wit): stays 1m: capable of better still. *B. J. Meehan* **82 p**

YOUMZAIN (IRE) 6 b.h. Sinndar (IRE) 134 – Sadima (IRE) 103 (Sadler's Wells (USA) 132) [2009 131: $12g^{4}$ $12g^{2}$ $12m^{3}$ $12d^{3}$ $12g^{2}$ 12g Dec 13] **130**

Who says you get nothing for finishing second? Youmzain has earned a total of £1,884,333 (at prevailing exchange rates) for his three splendid second places in the Prix de l'Arc de Triomphe. The last two editions, sponsored by Qatar, have seen the Arc assume the mantle of the richest race in the world on turf. Youmzain earned £838,899 in the latest Arc, £129,274 more than Arc winner Sea The Stars earned for *winning* Britain's most valuable race the Derby and £271,199 more than the *first* prize won by Arc fourth Conduit in 'Britain's Arc' the King George VI and Queen Elizabeth Stakes. It is said that nobody ever remembers who finishes second, but at least Youmzain's connections should be able to draw comfort from the entries made on their bank balances as a result of the horse's efforts on his three visits to Longchamp. Deep down, though, their feelings were probably similar to those of top American golfer Tom Weiskopf, who was runner-up in four editions of the US Masters between 1969 and 1975, twice to Jack Nicklaus. 'I'm absolutely delighted to have come second,' he said. 'Who cares about winning when you can be second? Oh yeah, how I love being runner-up to Jack Nicklaus.'

Weiskopf's only victory in a major championship came in the Open at Troon in 1973, a year when he also won seven other tournaments around the world. Nicknamed the 'Towering Inferno', partly because he was one of the taller players but also because of a short temper, Weiskopf did not achieve the greatness as a golfer once expected of him. It could also be said of Youmzain that he hasn't made the most of his ability. His last eighteen outings have been in Group 1 company—spread around six different countries—and, on his Arc form, he is a top-class performer who should certainly have won more of them. His two Group 1 victories have come in the Preis von Europa (odds on) at Cologne, on his final start as a three-year-old, and in the Grand Prix de Saint-Cloud as a five-year-old. Unfortunately, Youmzain rarely runs two consecutive races alike, though his form figures might suggest otherwise to those who do not know him well. Youmzain has finished in the frame in fifteen of the Group 1s he has contested, his disappointing tenth behind Daryakana in the Hong Kong Vase after his latest Arc second the only aberration in that regard in the latest season. For the third year running, Youmzain's campaign opened in the Dubai Sheema Classic. He was thereabouts again at the line, a strong-finishing fourth to Eastern Anthem after being caught in early scrimmaging and still behind on the home turn. Next came the Coronation Cup, Youmzain's only race on British soil as a six-year-old and the one in which he went closest to victory. Second to Soldier of Fortune twelve months earlier, Youmzain finished second again, hanging and not looking altogether keen when going down by a nose to fellow six-year-old Ask in a three-way photo also involving the previous year's Oaks winner Look Here.

Youmzain's performances at Nad Al Sheba and Epsom were some way below the form of his very best efforts, but he started favourite for the third time in the latest season, at odds on this time, to pull off a second successive victory in the Grand Prix de Saint-Cloud at the end of June. Once more, he failed to run up to his best, managing only third behind Spanish Moon and Alpine Rose, showing form nearly a stone below that of his win and also falling short of his latest effort in the Coronation Cup. Youmzain was provided with a pacemaker at Saint-Cloud and also had a change of jockey, Christophe Soumillon replacing Richard Hills. Kieren Fallon partnered Youmzain on his last three outings, starting in the Grosser Preis von Baden, Germany's most important all-aged event, its 'King George' (Youmzain has been placed twice in the King George at Ascot but missed the latest edition with a swollen joint in his near-fore). Considering he had had a setback and was returning from a ten-week absence, Youmzain performed respectably at Baden-Baden, finishing third behind Getaway and Eastern Anthem and giving the impression he was just in need of the run (though his connections blamed the fairly slow early pace, the experiment with a pacemaker having been short-lived).

Youmzain sported a visor for the first time in the Prix de l'Arc de Triomphe and ran his best race of the season, staying on strongly in the home straight after keeping tabs on Sea The Stars round the inner for most of the way. Youmzain was two lengths behind Sea The Stars at the line, though he had only a head and the same to spare over the Grand Prix de Paris winner Cavalryman and Conduit. Youmzain started at 21/1 at Longchamp, having been sent off at 80/1 and 14/1 on his first two Arc appearances. Youmzain's campaigns at four and five had ended at Longchamp and it was initially announced that he wouldn't appear again after his latest run. Hong Kong came on to the agenda when Youmzain was reported by his trainer to have come out of the Arc 'really well'. He was the clear pick on his best form in the Hong Kong Vase (though Spanish Moon started favourite) but, visored again, he ran a long way below his Longchamp form, even allowing for the fact that he was squeezed up on the rail behind a weakening front runner early in the straight and had no chance afterwards. Youmzain is to remain in training at seven, with the aim of following a similar programme to those in the last two seasons, which will probably mean a fourth appearance in the Sheema Classic, a fourth in the Grand Prix de Saint-Cloud and, all being well, a fourth in the Arc.

Discussion about Sea The Stars's place among the best horses in history touched on the subject of the weight-for-age concession that three-year-olds receive from older horses. Brough Scott claimed in the *Racing Post* that the weight-for-age scale is to blame for the retirement of so many of racing's champions after only a short reign. Scott and others have advocated the abolition of weight-for-age allowances in championship races. It was, in many ways, a shame to see the retirement of Sea The Stars just as he had been widely identified as a genuine champion, a superstar whose exploits could have brought racing to a wider audience had he been kept in training. However, the argument that it is unfair that older horses such as Youmzain (beaten by a three-year-old in the last two Arcs) and Conduit should have to concede weight to three-year-olds like Sea The Stars and Cavalryman simply doesn't hold water. The weight-for age scale is bound to have imperfections, some necessarily arising from the fact that all racehorses are treated for weight-for-age purposes, within their own age group, as if they were exactly the same age. Some horses also mature faster than others, very few tip-top three-year-olds like Sea The Stars, for example, being capable of showing real improvement from three to four greater than, or even in line with, the weight-for-age table. There are too many variables for the weight-for-age scale to be proved categorically either right or wrong, but it is indisputable that three-year-olds as a group, because of their immaturity, would not be able to hold their own against older horses at level weights, certainly not at a mile and upwards. It would mean a return to the days before races like the King George and the Arc, when the leading three-year-olds rarely raced against horses from outside their own age group.

As for the weight-for-age scale itself: if it was a long way out, three-year-olds racing against older horses would record consistently higher (or lower) ratings than those they recorded in races against horses of their own age. As it is, the ratings are generally compatible. The weight-for-age scale was purely empirical in the first instance when devised by Admiral Rous in the middle of the nineteenth century. The Jockey Club/BHA scale remained more or less intact for over a century until it was revised in the 'seventies. It has been amended several times since, the last occasion being in 1995. Although critics point out that no other sport gives immature performers an allowance against the best, there are clear benefits for racing in having a weight-for-age scale. It intensifies competition in the top open-aged races, providing top-level clashes which attract public interest, and it also enables direct comparisons to be made between successive classic crops, something that would only be possible otherwise if the best horses routinely remained in training until they were five. Not many top horses are like Youmzain, capable of remaining at their best for four seasons, and, from a commercial point of view anyway, it would make no sense to keep a champion three-year-old like Sea The Stars in training at four and five, risking two seasons' stud fees, not to mention the horse's reputation. Perhaps one way to reward connections who keep their best horses in training is through the programme of racing, by creating restricted races for the offspring of sires who won pattern races at four and upwards, or by giving such offspring an extra allowance in maiden races, for example. The idea would at least be worth investigating more closely.

Youmzain (IRE) (b.h. 2003)	Sinndar (IRE) (b 1997)	Grand Lodge (ch 1991)	Chief's Crown
			La Papagena
		Sinntara (b 1989)	Lashkari
			Sidama
	Sadima (IRE) (b 1998)	Sadler's Wells (b 1981)	Northern Dancer
			Fairy Bridge
		Anima (b 1989)	Ajdal
			Cocotte

The pedigree of Youmzain has been fully documented in earlier Annuals but a couple of updates are necessary. Youmzain's year-younger half-brother the Lockinge winner Creachadoir (by King's Best) was seen out only once in the latest season, beating only one home in the Dubai Duty Free in March, and has now been retired to stud in France. Sadima's smart four-year-old filly Shreyas (by Dalakhani) added listed events at a mile and nine furlongs at Leopardstown to her record in the latest season, while her fifth foal, the two-year-old Sagacious (also by Dalakhani) looked a useful prospect when winning a maiden over a mile at the Curragh on her only outing. The Sadler's Wells mare Sadima, a useful performer who won at a mile and a quarter, is out of a half-sister to Pilsudski who, coincidentally, twice finished second in the Arc (his record included more big wins than Youmzain's, though, headed by the Breeders' Cup Turf, the Japan Cup, the Champion Stakes and the Irish Champion). Youmzain is suited by a good test at a mile and a half and would stay further if required. He acts on good to firm and good to soft going, and has run well when sweating. He is held up. *M. R. Channon*

YOUNG AMERICANS (IRE) 3 b.f. Nayef (USA) 129 – Life At Night (IRE) (Night 92
Shift (USA)) [2009 7.5g* 8.1m 10.4g p11g 8g 10d^{4} 11g Dec 13] good-topped filly: second foal: dam, Italian 7.5f to 9f winner, half-sister to very smart sprinter/miler Missed Flight: fairly useful performer: won maiden at Milan (for A. & G. Botti) in March: well below form in 2 listed races and handicap in Britain (for M. Botti), then returned to former

trainers for next race: creditable efforts last 2 starts: stays 11f: acts on good to soft going: has been tongue tied. *S. Botti, Italy*

YOUNG BERTIE 6 ch.g. Bertolini (USA) 125 – Urania 66 (Most Welcome 131) [2009 81: p8g p8g Feb 11] strong gelding: fairly useful handicapper at best: just modest form in 2009: stayed 1m: acted on polytrack, firm and good to soft going: usually visored, tried in cheekpieces: dead. *H. Morrison* **63**

YOUNG DOTTIE 3 b.f. Desert Sun 120 – Auntie Dot Com 70 (Tagula (IRE) 116) [2009 77: 8.5g 7m^4 7m^3 7m^6 8.3f^5 p10g 8m 10g^4 p8g* Dec 7] angular filly: fairly useful handicapper on all-weather, fair on turf: improved when winning handicap at Lingfield in December: stays 1¼m: acts on polytrack and good to firm going: often races freely. *P. M. Phelan* **74 a84**

YOUNG FIRTH 2 b.g. (Feb 28) Lucky Story (USA) 128 – Le Petit Diable (IRE) (Trans Island 119) [2009 p7.1g 7d^6 8.1g^6 p8.6g Oct 9] modest form at best in maidens: tailed off in nursery final start: stays 7f. *J. R. Norton* **55**

YOUNG GEORGE 2 b.g. (May 9) Danroad (AUS) 112 – Bo' Babbity 75 (Strong Gale 116) [2009 5g p6g Nov 27] well held in maidens (bit said to have slipped through mouth on debut). *C. W. Fairhurst* **–**

YOUNG GLADIATOR (IRE) 4 b.g. Spartacus (IRE) 107 – Savona (IRE) 70 (Cyrano de Bergerac 120) [2009 68: f7g 7d* p7.1g 5.9g^6 7d* 7g 7.2g^6 f7m^2 Nov 12] big, strong gelding: fair performer: won handicap in June and claimer in July, both at Newcastle: stays 7f: acts on all-weather, good to firm and good to soft ground: wears headgear: front runner/races prominently. *Julie Camacho* **70**

YOUNG IVANHOE 4 b.g. Oasis Dream 129 – Cybinka 107 (Selkirk (USA) 129) [2009 72d: p6g^4 p5g f6g^4 p6g^6 f6g 7f^4 6m^6 6g May 29] sturdy gelding: modest performer nowadays: should stay 7f: acts on all-weather: usually wears visor/blinkers: has been tongue tied. *C. A. Dwyer* **54**

YOUNG MICK 7 br.g. King's Theatre (IRE) 128 – Just Warning (Warning 136) [2009 113: p12g 12m^2 14g^6 12g* 12m 12m 16m^4 14m^3 12m^4 12g p12m^5 Nov 4] sturdy, lengthy gelding: useful performer nowadays: won handicap at Nad Al Sheba in February by ½ length from Classic Punch: creditable efforts otherwise when placed in similar events at same course (4¾ lengths second to Age of Reason) and Newmarket (7¾ lengths third to Victoria Montoya): barely stays 1¾m: acts on soft and good to firm going, little recent form on all-weather: usually visored: tried tongue tied: patiently ridden: signs of temperament. *G. G. Margarson* **107 a–**

YOUNG OLLIE 4 ch.f. Piccolo 121 – Miss Michelle 38 (Jalmood (USA) 126) [2009 –: 8g Apr 21] no form. *E. A. Wheeler* **–**

YOUNG PRETENDER (FR) 4 b.c. Oasis Dream 129 – Silent Heir (AUS) 82 (Sunday Silence (USA)) [2009 111: 8m^5 7d^2 8.3v^4 Nov 4] sturdy colt: has a round action: smart performer, lightly raced: off 16 months, good 2 lengths fifth to Confront in Joel Stakes at Newmarket: bit below that form in minor events after, including when 1¼ lengths second to Mia's Boy at Doncaster: stays 8.5f: acts on good to firm ground. *Saeed bin Suroor* **114**

YOUNG SIMON 2 ch.c. (Apr 21) Piccolo 121 – Fragrant Cloud 37 (Zilzal (USA) 137) [2009 6m 6m^2 5g p6m^5 Nov 4] sturdy colt: easily best effort in maidens when 2½ lengths second to Marrayah at Yarmouth, making running: stays 6f. *G. G. Margarson* **70 ?**

YOUNG STAR GAZER 3 ch.g. Observatory (USA) 131 – Ash Glade (Nashwan (USA) 135) [2009 8.3g 8.3m^3 10m^6 9s^3 Jul 14] 2,500F, 24,000Y: brother to winner in Greece and half-brother to 2 winners, including 10-y-o Magic Glade: dam unraced half-sister to 1000 Guineas winner Wince: fair maiden: stays 9f: acts on soft and good to firm going: gelded, joined D. Pipe. *H. R. A. Cecil* **73**

YOU'RELIKEMEFRANK 3 ch.g. Bahamian Bounty 116 – Proudfoot (IRE) (Shareef Dancer (USA) 135) [2009 –: f5d^6 p5.1g^3 p5g^3 p5.1g^4 5s^6 p5.1g^2 p5.1g^6 p5m^3 Sep 23] poor maiden handicapper: raced only at 5f: acts on polytrack: in cheekpieces/ blinkers in 2009. *J. Balding* **49**

YOUR GOLF TRAVEL 4 b.f. Bertolini (USA) 125 – Scottish Spice 92 (Selkirk (USA) 129) [2009 45: p8g^2 8f 10.1g 10.1g Jun 16] lengthy filly: maiden: modest form when second in minor event on return: no form after: stays 1m: acts on polytrack: tried blinkered. *M. Wigham* **56**

YOURGOLFTRAVEL COM 4 b.g. Fasliyev (USA) 120 – Hiddnah (USA) 105 (Affirmed (USA)) [2009 6s Jun 11] last in maiden at Yarmouth: subsequently gelded. *M. Wigham* **–**

YOUR LAD 2 b.c. (Mar 19) Dubawi (IRE) 129 – Krisalya 98 (Kris 135) [2009 p8f Dec 16] 20/1, slowly away and always behind in maiden at Kempton. *C. F. Wall* **–**

YOUR OLD PAL 3 ch.c. Rock of Gibraltar (IRE) 133 – Questabelle (Rainbow Quest (USA) 134) [2009 104P: 10s^5 10m* 10m^4 12f^2 Jun 19] rather leggy colt: useful performer: won listed event at Newmarket in May by head from Palavicini: good 4 lengths second to Father Time in King Edward VII Stakes at Royal Ascot final start: stays 1½m: acts on any going: sent to Hong Kong. *J. Noseda* **109**

YOUR TRUE LOVE (IRE) 3 b.f. Pyrus (USA) 106 – Columbine (IRE) 82 (Pivotal 124) [2009 6m 6s^6 5m May 19] second foal: dam, 5f (including at 2 yrs)/6f winner, half-sister to useful sprinter Fast Heart: well held in maidens. *A. Berry* **–**

YOU SAY I SAY (USA) 3 b. or br.f. Unbridled's Song (USA) 125 – Insight (FR) 115 (Sadler's Wells (USA) 132) [2009 60P: 9.9f^6 May 14] big, strong filly: fair form in maidens 6½ months apart: worth a try at 1m: sold 27,000 gns in November. *Sir Michael Stoute* **66**

YOU'VE BEEN MOWED 3 ch.f. Ishiguru (USA) 114 – Sandblaster 55 (Most Welcome 131) [2009 68: p6g^3 p5.1g 5.1g^6 5.7f 6g^3 f7g* 8m^2 8.1g* 8.3g^5 8g^6 f7g 7g^6 p7.1g 8m* p8g Oct 14] angular filly: fair handicapper: won at Southwell and Chepstow in June, and Brighton in September: effective at 7f/1m: acts on all-weather, firm and good to soft going. *R. J. Price* **68**

YTARTFAWN (IRE) 2 ch.c. (Apr 18) Chineur (FR) 123 – Lady Montekin (Montekin 125) [2009 5m^6 5f^5 5g 6g^5 6g^6 Jul 4] poor maiden: tried blinkered. *P. T. Midgley* **36**

YUGHANNI 3 b.f. Oasis Dream 129 – Bedazzling (IRE) 105 (Darshaan 133) [2009 56p: p7g p6g 7m 7m^3 5g 7f^6 Jun 30] modest maiden: stays 7f: acts on good to firm going: one to treat with caution. *C. E. Brittain* **56 §**

YUNGABURRA (IRE) 5 b.g. Fath (USA) 116 – Nordic Living (IRE) 53 (Nordico (USA)) [2009 73, a93: p6g^3 p5.1m^4 p5.1g^6 5m^5 5m^6 5g Jul 26] quite good-topped gelding: fairly useful performer on all-weather, fair on turf: below form after reappearance, leaving S. Parr £6,000 after next start: effective at 5f/6f: acts on all-weather and good to firm ground: often in blinkers/cheekpieces: usually tongue tied. *J. Balding* **67 a87 d**

YURITUNI 2 b.f. (Mar 9) Bahamian Bounty 116 – Vax Star 96 (Petong 126) [2009 5m^4 5f^4 6f 6m* 6.5m^2 5.7m* 5.1m^2 5g Oct 10] 32,000Y: sturdy filly: half-sister to several winners, including fairly useful 2001 2-y-o 6f winner Negligee (by Night Shift) and 7f winner Vandal (by Entrepreneur): dam, 2-y-o 5f winner, became one to treat with caution: fairly useful performer: won nurseries at York in August and Bath in September: stiff task, well held in Cornwallis Stakes at Ascot final outing: stays 6.5f: acts on good to firm going: races prominently: genuine. *Eve Johnson Houghton* **85**

YVONNE EVELYN (USA) 4 gr. or ro.f. Cozzene (USA) – One Great Lady (USA) (Fappiano (USA)) [2009 72: 10g^6 12d p10m^3 11.5d^5 p12m Oct 7] tall filly: fair maiden handicapper, lightly raced: stays 1¼m: raced on polytrack and good/good to soft going. *J. R. Gask* **69**

Z

ZAAHID (IRE) 5 ch.h. Sakhee (USA) 136 – Murjana (IRE) 80 (Pleasant Colony (USA)) [2009 109: 8m^2 8s 7m May 9] strong, deep-girthed horse: type to carry condition: useful handicapper: creditable 2½ lengths second to Expresso Star in Lincoln at Doncaster on reappearance: well beaten in valuable events after: effective at 7f/1m: acts on soft and good to firm going: versatile tactically: usually travels strongly. *B. W. Hills* **105**

ZAAHY (USA) 2 ch.c. (May 18) More Than Ready (USA) 120 – Sangam (USA) (Majestic Light (USA)) [2009 7g^4 p7g* Sep 2] $105,000Y: fourth live foal: half-brother to winners in USA by Woodman and Dixie Union: dam 7f (at 2 yrs) to 1¼m winner in USA/Canada: much improved from debut when winning minor event at Lingfield easily by 2½ lengths from Champagne Style, travelling strongly and quickening well to lead final 1f: should stay 1m: already useful, and will improve again. *P. W. Chapple-Hyam* **101 p**

ZAAQYA 3 b.f. Nayef (USA) 129 – Classical Dancer 98 (Dr Fong (USA) 128) [2009 82: 10m 9.9f^6 9.9m^3 12m* 12v^3 13.3m^3 12m 12g^3 12g^6 Oct 30] close-coupled filly: fairly useful handicapper: won at Newbury in July: very good efforts after when placed: stayed 13f: acted on heavy and good to firm going: probably not straightforward: visits Aqlaam. *J. L. Dunlop* **94**

ZABEEL HOUSE 6 b.g. Anabaa (USA) 130 – Divine Quest 81 (Kris 135) [2009 68: p9.5g f8g^6 p8g^2 p10g p8g^4 8.5m Apr 15] strong, well-made gelding: modest performer: stays 8.6f: acts on all-weather and firm ground: tried visored, wears cheekpieces. *John A. Harris* **54**

ZABEEL TOWER 6 b.g. Anabaa (USA) 130 – Bint Kaldoun (IRE) 82 (Kaldoun (FR) 122) [2009 82: 7.9m 7.2m^3 7.2g^5 7.6g^6 8.3m^4 6.9d^5 7.1g^2 8m^6 7.1g^4 9.2v 7.1m^5 7g p8.6g Nov 14] leggy, useful-looking gelding: fair handicapper on turf, well held sole start on all-weather since 2007: effective at 7f to 1¼m: acts on soft and good to firm going (had form on polytrack at 4 yrs): tried visored/tongue tied, often wears cheekpieces. *R. Allan* **74 a–**

ZABELLAH 4 ch.f. Zaha (CAN) 106 – Polar Refrain 59 (Polar Falcon (USA) 126) [2009 f8g^5 Jan 29] third foal: dam 1m winner: last in maiden at Southwell, only outing. *J. Balding* **–**

ZABOUGG 4 b.g. Tobougg (IRE) 125 – Double Fault (IRE) 54 (Zieten (USA) 118) [2009 52§: 15.8m 16m 10.1g Apr 27] useful-looking gelding: type to carry condition: poor maiden handicapper: free-going sort, barely stays 1m: acts on good to firm and good to soft ground: tried visored/in cheekpieces: awkward ride, and one to treat with plenty of caution. *D. W. Barker* **49 §**

ZACHARY BOY (IRE) 2 b.c. (Apr 11) Orpen (USA) 116 – Shun (Selkirk (USA) 129) [2009 6m 6m 7d p7.1g^2 Nov 9] modest maiden: stayed 7f: best effort on polytrack: dead. *B. G. Powell* **59**

ZACH'S HARMONEY (USA) 5 ch.g. Diesis 133 – Cool Ashlee (USA) (Mister Baileys 123) [2009 73: p9.5g Jan 9] rather leggy, quite attractive gelding: fair maiden handicapper at 4 yrs: well beaten in seller sole start in 2009: tried in cheekpieces/tongue tie. *Miss M. E. Rowland* **–**

ZACINTO 3 b.c. Dansili 127 – Ithaca (USA) 100 (Distant View (USA) 126) [2009 109p: 8d* 8g* 8m^2 8f Nov 7] **126**

Sir Michael Stoute and Saeed bin Suroor continued their dominance of Goodwood's Celebration Mile in the latest season. Ten of the last fourteen runnings have now gone to a representative of one or other of their stables, and Saeed bin Suroor looked to have won it for a fourth time when Delegator got the better of the Stoute-trained Zacinto. However, when Delegator was disqualified some time later for failing a dope test, Zacinto was promoted to make it win number eight for Stoute, who first won it with Milligram in 1987 when it was known as the Waterford Crystal Mile. It was the second time a Stoute-trained runner had been promoted to first in the Celebration Mile. Back in 1997, the Stoute-trained Among Men finished runner-up to Cape Cross, owned by Sheikh Mohammed and trained by John Gosden at the time, but Cape Cross was disqualified for causing inter-

Blue Square Premier Stakes (Thoroughbred), Goodwood— hard to pick them out in the sea mist as Zacinto (second left) narrowly justifies favouritism from Hartley on his belated return, the pair just ahead of Pure Poetry (rail) and Four Winds (left)

totesport.com Celebration Mile, Goodwood—
Zacinto is awarded the prize and Ordnance Row promoted to second following the disqualification at a hearing over three months later of Delegator (No.6), who failed a dope test after the race

ference. Cape Cross, carrying the Godolphin colours, went on to provide Saeed bin Suroor with the second of his victories in the Celebration Mile two years later.

It says much for his trainer's skill that Zacinto should have run so well as he did at Goodwood and then gone on to show high-class form afterwards, given that minor injuries had restricted him to just three appearances before the Celebration Mile. Installed as favourite for the following year's Two Thousand Guineas following an impressive debut in a Sandown maiden, Zacinto finished a close second to Westphalia in the Champagne Stakes at Doncaster on his only other start at two but was then off the course in his three-year-old season until August after suffering a training setback in early-March. Goodwood had also been the scene of his return, in a nine-runner listed event for which he started favourite despite his lengthy absence. Confidently ridden, Zacinto came from off the pace to lead inside the final furlong and win by a head from Hartley, having a little more in hand than the bare margin.

Zacinto was supplemented for the totesport.com Celebration Mile four weeks later at a cost of £10,000. The race attracted seven runners but the betting suggested that it concerned only the Two Thousand Guineas runner-up Delegator, who started at 6/4-on, and Zacinto, who was sent off at 5/2. In a steadily-run affair, Zacinto was kept closer to the pace than on his reappearance, but he pulled far too hard out wide. He managed to collar the leader Ordnance Row inside the final furlong only to forfeit the lead almost immediately as Delegator produced an impressive turn of speed which took him a length and a half clear. On his next start, in the Queen Elizabeth II Stakes at Ascot, Zacinto faced not only Delegator but an even more formidable opponent in Rip Van Winkle. Zacinto was the outsider of four in a race which also attracted the Prix du Moulin winner Aqlaam. Helped by the overly-strong pace set by Aqlaam, Zacinto settled much better and showed further significant improvement in finishing a length and a quarter second to Rip Van Winkle in a race which was run at a breakneck pace and took its toll on the runners. Zacinto reportedly suffered a minor setback after Ascot and ran as though amiss when he finished tailed-off last of eleven, eased early in the straight, in the Breeders' Cup Mile at Santa Anita, a meeting at which Rip Van Winkle and Delegator also ran below their best.

Mr K. Abdullah's "Zacinto"

Zacinto (b.c. 2006)	Dansili (b 1996)	Danehill (b 1986)	Danzig
			Razyana
		Hasili (b 1991)	Kahyasi
			Kerali
	Ithaca (USA) (ch 2001)	Distant View (ch 1991)	Mr Prospector
			Seven Springs
		Reams of Verse (ch 1994)	Nureyev
			Modena

Zacinto, a sturdy, attractive colt who acts on good to firm and good to soft going, has raced only at seven furlongs and a mile so far. His trainer, though, reportedly has no doubts that he will stay a mile and a quarter (Zacinto was favourite for the Champion Stakes until the decision was made to go for the Breeders' Cup Mile instead). A cursory glance at Zacinto's pedigree might suggest that he would not have the necessary stamina. By the miler Dansili, as is Delegator, Zacinto is the first foal of Ithaca, a two-year-old seven-furlong winner who stayed a mile and seemingly no further. Delve deeper, though, and there are some more positive pointers. Ithaca is closely related to the very smart mile and a quarter performer Many Volumes, and is a daughter of the Oaks winner Reams of Verse, who is herself a half-sister to the Eclipse winner Elmaamul. Further details on Zacinto's pedigree can be found in the essay on his relative Midday, who completed a family double when winning the Nassau Stakes on the same card at Goodwood where Zacinto made his reappearance. Zacinto and Ithaca, incidentally, are named after Greek islands, Zacinto being Italian for Zakynthos, which is better known to British holidaymakers as Zante. *Sir Michael Stoute*

ZAFFAAN 3 ch.g. Efisio 120 – Danceabout 110 (Shareef Dancer (USA) 135) [2009 95: 8.1m 7.1v May 23] strong, deep-girthed gelding: useful performer at 2 yrs: well held in handicaps in 2009: should stay 7f: acts on polytrack, best turf effort on good ground: tried tongue tied. *E. A. L. Dunlop* –

ZAFFATURE 2 b.f. (Mar 8) Zafeen (FR) 123 – Alice Blackthorn 70 (Forzando 122) [2009 p7.1g⁴ p7g⁵ 7g⁴ p7.1m² p7.1g² 8.3g² a8g⁴ Nov 28] £8,000Y: lengthy filly: second foal: dam, 6f (at 2 yrs)/7f winner, half-sister to smart sprinter Ratio: modest maiden: left M. Botti before final start: stays 8.3f: blinkered (ran creditably) fifth start: quirky. *Mme L. Braem, Belgium* **58**

ZAFFEU 8 ch.g. Zafonic (USA) 130 – Leaping Flame (USA) (Trempolino (USA) 135) [2009 72: f16d² f14g⁴ f14g² f16g p13.9g May 11] leggy, useful-looking gelding: has only one eye: fair performer: stays 16.5f: raced mainly on all-weather: tried blinkered. *A. G. Juckes* **68**

ZAFISIO (IRE) 3 b.c. Efisio 120 – Goldthroat (IRE) 79 (Zafonic (USA) 130) [2009 111: 8d² 10.5g 8s³ 8s* 10v* Nov 14] well-made colt: very smart performer: creditable placed efforts in German 2000 Guineas at Cologne (1½ lengths second to Irian, hanging left) and Solonaway Stakes at the Curragh (3¾ lengths third to Border Patrol) prior to improved efforts when winning Prix Perth at Saint-Cloud (by 1½ lengths from Border Patrol) and Hessen Pokal at Frankfurt (by 2 lengths from Liang Kay) in November: stays 1¼m: goes well on soft/heavy going (yet to race on firmer than good): usually races close up. *R. Curtis* **120**

ZAFRANAGAR (IRE) 4 b.g. Cape Cross (IRE) 129 – Zafaraniya (IRE) 106 (Doyoun 124) [2009 12v Nov 3] fairly useful maiden in France for A. Fabre (2 yrs) and A. de Royer Dupre: well held in maiden only Flat start in Britain: stays 9.8f: fair hurdler, successful in November. *A. W. Carroll* **–**

ZAFTIL (IRE) 3 b.f. Tillerman 123 – Zafine 67 (Zafonic (USA) 130) [2009 –: p8g 6.1g⁵ 5.7f 7m 8.1g Jun 22] lengthy filly: poor form. *H. S. Howe* **37**

ZAGAROCK 2 b.f. (Apr 11) Rock of Gibraltar (IRE) 133 – Zagaleta 81 (Sri Pekan (USA) 117) [2009 8.3m 8g 8g⁵ Oct 21] 26,000F: tall, plain, close-coupled filly: fourth foal: half-sister to fairly useful Irish 9f winner Sweet Petite (by Mark of Esteem): dam 1¼m winner: modest maiden: may stay 1¼m. *B. Palling* **56**

ZAHAM (USA) 5 ch.g. Silver Hawk (USA) 123 – Guerre Et Paix (USA) (Soviet Star (USA) 128) [2009 117: 12m⁶ p10g⁴ 12m⁶ Jun 21] lengthy, good-topped gelding: smart performer at best: lightly raced nowadays, and just useful in 2009, seemingly best effort when last of 6 behind Furmigadelagiusta in listed race at Pontefract final start: stays 1½m: acts on polytrack, soft and good to firm going: tried blinkered: often makes running. *M. Johnston* **103**

ZAHOO (IRE) 2 b.f. (May 12) Nayef (USA) 129 – Tanaghum 104 (Darshaan 133) [2009 7g⁵ 8m³ 8.1m* Sep 26] attractive filly: third foal: half-sister to 3-y-o Tactic and 4-y-o Taaresh: dam, 1¼m winner who stayed 1½m, out of Irish 1000 Guineas winner Mehthaaf: similar form in maidens, winning at Haydock by length from Dancing Queen: will be suited by 1¼m/1½m. *J. L. Dunlop* **77**

Prix Perth, Saint-Cloud—Zafisio gains his first win since taking the Criterium International on the same card twelve months earlier; another British-trained 3-y-o, Border Patrol (No.4), finishes second ahead of Racinger (rail) and Schutzenjunker

ZAIF (IRE) 6 b.g. Almutawakel 126 – Colourful (FR) 97 (Gay Mecene (USA) 128) [2009 87: 10g 10g p11g^5 12m 12m p10m p12m 11.9d* p12.2g Nov 21] close-coupled gelding: fair handicapper nowadays: won at Brighton (apprentices) in October: stays 1½m: acts on polytrack, soft and good to firm going: tried blinkered, in cheekpieces last 2 starts: reportedly bled on reappearance. *D. J. S. ffrench Davis* **68 §**

ZAIN (IRE) 5 b.g. Alhaarth (IRE) 126 – Karenaragon (Aragon 118) [2009 53: 10.1g 8.1g 8d p8.6m Nov 28] good-topped gelding: handicapper: well held in 2009: usually tongue tied. *J. G. Given* **–**

ZALKANI (IRE) 9 ch.g. Cadeaux Genereux 131 – Zallaka (IRE) (Shardari 134) [2009 –, a68: p12g^5 p10g^4 p13g^5 p13g^4 p13g^2 p12g^4 p13g p12.2g* p12g^5 p13.9g^3 p12.2g^6 p12m^5 p12.2m p13g p12g^6 Oct 20] fair handicapper: won at Wolverhampton in April: stays 1¾m: acts on polytrack, unraced on turf since 2005: usually held up. *J. Pearce* **– a68**

ZAMBUKA (FR) 2 gr.f. (Feb 28) Zieten (USA) 118 – Mercalle (FR) 108 (Kaldoun (FR) 122) [2009 5m 6g May 9] 60,000F: quite good-topped filly: half-sister to several winners, including 4-y-o Lady Deauville and Japan Cup runner-up Fabulous La Fouine (by Fabulous Dancer): dam French 1m (at 2 yrs) to 2½m (Prix du Cadran) winner: green when down the field in maidens at Newmarket and Haydock. *R. Curtis* **–**

ZANDO'S PEARL 2 b.f. (Apr 25) Forzando 122 – Siouxtabul (Makbul 104) [2009 p6g Nov 27] £1,200Y: second foal: dam unraced: 100/1, tailed off in maiden at Wolverhampton. *C. J. Price* **–**

ZANZIBARI (USA) 2 b.c. (Mar 21) Smart Strike (CAN) 121 – Zinziberine (USA) 108 (Zieten (USA) 118) [2009 5d* 6g^2 6d* 6m^5 Aug 23] third foal: dam, French 2-y-o 4.5f/6f (Criterium de Maisons-Laffitte) winner, out of sister to high-class French stayer Amilynx: smart form: won newcomers race at Maisons-Laffitte in May and Prix de Cabourg Jockey-Club de Turquie at Deauville (by 1½ lengths from Sorciere) in August: not at all discredited when very close last of 5 to Arcano in Prix Morny at Deauville final start, off bridle before halfway: will be well suited by 7f/1m: acts on good to firm and good to soft ground. *A. Fabre, France* **112**

ZAPLAMATION (IRE) 4 b.g. Acclamation 118 – Zapatista (Rainbow Quest (USA) 134) [2009 49: 10m^4 10m 8d* 8m^2 8s^2 8.5m^2 10g* Oct 16] workmanlike gelding: fair performer: left D. Barker after second start: won handicaps at Newcastle (apprentices) in July and Redcar (ladies) in October: stays 11f: acts on firm and soft going: sometimes races freely. *J. J. Quinn* **69**

ZARILAN (IRE) 4 b.g. Namid 128 – Zarlana (IRE) (Darshaan 133) [2009 67?: f8g^3 Feb 10] lengthy gelding: lightly-raced maiden: just modest form sole start on Flat in 2009: should stay 1¼m. *Evan Williams* **57**

ZARINSKI (IRE) 3 b.g. Dalakhani (IRE) 133 – Zarafsha (IRE) 98 (Alzao (USA) 117) [2009 79: p12g* 12m^4 11d Aug 1] tall, useful-looking gelding: has scope: fairly useful form: won maiden at Dundalk in April: favourite, improved when fourth to Cosmic Sun in King George V Handicap at Royal Ascot next time: left John Oxx in Ireland, ran as though amiss only subsequent start on Flat: stays 1½m: acts on polytrack and good to firm ground: tried in cheekpieces: joined N. Henderson, and gelded. *Jim Best* **91**

ZARS GOLD (IRE) 4 b.f. Xaar 132 – Affirmed Crown (USA) 55 (Affirmed (USA)) [2009 72: p6g^5 p7g 7g^4 6m p7g May 20] sturdy filly: just modest maiden nowadays: stays 7f: acts on polytrack and heavy going: tried in blinkers/cheekpieces: ungenuine: sold 2,500 gns, sent to Greece. *J. Gallagher* **63 §**

ZASKIA (IRE) 2 ch.f. (Apr 15) Tomba 119 – Flamenco Dancer (Mark of Esteem (IRE) 137) [2009 p5.1g^5 5m 6f^4 6g f5g^5 p6m 5g^3 f6g Oct 27] second foal: dam unraced: poor maiden: tried blinkered. *K. A. Ryan* **47**

ZA ZA 3 br.f. Barathea (IRE) 127 – Madiyla 73 (Darshaan 133) [2009 –: 10.3m^3 12g a9.5g Dec 18] leggy filly: form (modest) only when third in maiden at Doncaster on reappearance: left H. Cecil after next outing: stays 1¼m. *Mlle H. van Zuylen, France* **64**

ZA ZA ZOOM (IRE) 2 b.f. (Jan 30) Le Vie Dei Colori 126 – Emma's Star (ITY) (Darshaan 133) [2009 6m^5 6d* 7v^2 Oct 24] £28,000Y: lengthy filly: has scope: sixth foal: half-sister to 3 winners, including 4-y-o Hazelrigg and 5-y-o Genki: dam Italian 8.5f winner: won maiden at Windsor in October: significant improvement when 1¼ lengths second to Electric Feel in listed race at Newbury, again strong at finish: will stay 1m: already useful, and capable of further improvement. *B. W. Hills* **96 p**

ZAZOUS 8 b.g. Zafonic (USA) 130 – Confidentiality (USA) (Lyphard (USA) 132) [2009 65: 7m May 3] well-made gelding: fair handicapper at 7 yrs: well held only outing in 2009. *J. J. Bridger* **–**

ZAZY'S GIFT 2 b.f. (Apr 7) Pastoral Pursuits 127 – Tintac 53 (Intikhab (USA) 135) **–**
[2009 7.1m 8d Oct 22] unfurnished filly: first foal: dam, maiden (stayed 9.5f), half-sister to useful performer up to 1½m Balladonia, out of half-sister to dam of Silver Patriarch: last in maidens. *George Baker*

ZEBRANO 3 b.g. Storming Home 128 – Ambience Lady (Batshoof 122) [2009 80: 10m **86**
p8g^{5} 7m 7f^{2} 7.1v* 7m 6d^{3} p6g Nov 14] workmanlike gelding: fairly useful handicapper: won at Chepstow in July: worthwhile form otherwise in 2009 only when placed: stays 7f: acts on polytrack and any turf going: none too consistent. *Miss E. C. Lavelle*

ZEFFIRELLI 4 ch.g. Tomba 119 – Risky Valentine 68 (Risk Me (FR) 127) [2009 64: **64**
p7g^{4} 7d^{5} 8g 7f^{6} 7s^{5} f7g^{2} f7g^{6} Dec 18] angular gelding: modest handicapper: likely to prove best short of 1m: acts on all-weather and soft going: often makes running. *M. Quinn*

ZE FINALE 2 b.f. (Jan 20) Zafeen (FR) 123 – Dominelle 74 (Domynsky 110) [2009 5m **–**
5m Apr 30] sturdy filly: fifth foal: half-sister to 2004 2-y-o 7f seller winner Caloosa (by Fraam), later winner up to 9f in Spain: dam 5f and (including at 2 yrs) 6f winner: well held in maiden and seller. *T. D. Easterby*

ZEFOOHA (FR) 5 ch.m. Lomitas 129 – Bezzaaf 97 (Machiavellian (USA) 123) [2009 **72**
12g 16m 14m^{5} 14.1m* 14.1m* 14.1f^{2} 14g^{2} 14.1g^{4} 11.9d 12.4g^{5} Sep 30] fair handicapper: missed 2008: won at Redcar in May and Carlisle in June: stays 1¾m: acts on polytrack and firm going: tried in cheekpieces: usually races prominently. *T. D. Walford*

ZEGNA (IRE) 3 b. or gr.g. Clodovil (IRE) 116 – Vade Retro (IRE) 86 (Desert Sun 120) **80**
[2009 80: p6g^{2} p6m* p6m Dec 30] good-topped gelding: fairly useful performer: won maiden at Kempton in December: will be at least as effective at 5f as 6f: raced only on polytrack and soft/heavy ground. *B. Smart*

ZEITOPER 2 b.c. (Feb 14) Singspiel (IRE) 133 – Kazzia (GER) 121 (Zinaad 114) **105 p**
[2009 8.1d* 8.5m* 9d* Oct 18] second foal: brother to 5-y-o Eastern Anthem: dam won 1000 Guineas and Oaks: unbeaten in maiden at Sandown in September, and minor event at Epsom (still green, beat Raine's Cross 1½ lengths) and Prix de Conde at Longchamp (gamely by short neck from Circumvent) in October: bred to be well suited by 1¼m/1½m: acts on good to firm and good to soft going: already useful, and capable of even better. *Saeed bin Suroor*

ZELOCA (IRE) 2 ch.f. (Mar 7) Refuse To Bend (IRE) 128 – Lily's Girl (IRE) (Hamas **–**
(IRE) 125§) [2009 6m p8f p7.1g Sep 19] €2,000 2-y-o: rather unfurnished filly: first foal: dam, ran once in Irish bumper, half-sister to smart performer around 1¼m Flying Clarets: last in maidens/seller: tried tongue tied. *Mrs L. C. Jewell*

ZELOS DIKTATOR 3 br.g. Diktat 126 – Chanterelle (IRE) 88 (Indian Ridge 123) **62**
[2009 50: p8.6g^{6} 10.3g 8d^{6} 10.3s 12m^{6} 12.4d* Oct 13] workmanlike gelding: modest performer: left J. Given after fourth start: best effort when winning maiden at Newcastle in October: stays 1½m: best effort on good to soft ground: tried visored, in cheekpieces last 2 outings. *Rae Guest*

ZELOS DREAM (IRE) 2 ch.f. (Apr 6) Redback 116 – Endless Peace (IRE) 62 **63**
(Russian Revival (USA) 125) [2009 f5g^{4} 6m^{5} 5.2d^{2} 5.7g^{2} 5.1m^{4} 5m* p6f p5g^{3} f6m^{3} p6g^{3} p6g^{6} Dec 11] 2,000Y: sturdy filly: first foal: dam, maiden (stayed 9.5f), half-sister to smart sprinters Hoh Mike and Hogmaneigh: modest performer: won selling nursery at Beverley in September: left Rae Guest after eighth start: stays easy 6f: acts on polytrack and good to firm going. *R. A. Harris*

ZELOS GIRL (IRE) 3 ch.f. Exceed And Excel (AUS) 126 – Sedna (FR) (Bering 136) **57**
[2009 72p: 5m 5.3g^{6} 5m^{4} 5g^{6} 6m 5v^{4} p5.1g 5m^{3} Sep 27] workmanlike filly: just modest form in handicaps at 3 yrs, leaving Rae Guest after fifth outing: will probably prove best kept to 5f: not straightforward. *J. G. Given*

ZELOS SPIRIT 2 b.f. (Apr 24) Tiger Hill (IRE) 127 – Good Mood (USA) (Devil's Bag **–**
(USA)) [2009 6.1d Oct 15] 7,000Y: half-sister to several winners, including useful US/UAE 8.5f to 1¼m winner Dubai World (by Deputy Minister): dam US Grade 3 2-y-o 9f winner: 33/1 and backward, well held in maiden at Nottingham: bred to be well suited by 1m+. *Rae Guest*

ZEMARIO (IRE) 3 b.g. Dalakhani (IRE) 133 – Noushkey 118 (Polish Precedent **81 p**
(USA) 131) [2009 10m* Aug 24] sixth foal: closely related to 6-y-o January and fairly useful 10.5f winner Anaamil (by Darshaan) and half-brother to winner in Greece by Fantastic Light: dam, 7f (at 2 yrs) and 1½m (Lancashire Oaks) winner and second in Oaks, half-sister to very smart stayer San Sebastian and to dam of high-class 1½m performer Alkaased: 5/1, won maiden at Windsor in August by head from Cherish The Moment: will be suited by 1½m: likely to improve. *M. A. Jarvis*

ZENARINDA 2 b.f. (Mar 31) Zamindar (USA) 116 – Tenpence 60 (Bob Back (USA) 124) [2009 6g^4 8d^4 Oct 27] third foal: dam, ran twice, out of half-sister to smart sprinter Grey Desire: much better effort in maidens 3 months apart when 3¾ lengths fourth to Bullet Train at Yarmouth latter start (raced freely but stayed on): stays 1m. *M. H. Tompkins* **70**

ZENNERMAN (IRE) 6 b.g. Observatory (USA) 131 – Precocious Miss (USA) 88 (Diesis 133) [2009 71: 7.6m 9g 8d 8.3g* p8.6m^6 p8.6g p7.1g Sep 17] smallish, strong gelding: fair handicapper on turf, modest on all-weather: easily best effort in 2009 when winning at Nottingham (apprentices) in August: stays 1m: acts on polytrack, firm and soft going: usually wears headgear: sold £450, sent to Qatar. *W. M. Brisbourne* **72 a56**

ZENYATTA (USA) 5 b. or br.m. Street Cry (IRE) 130 – Vertigineux (Kris S (USA)) [2009 128: a8.5f* a9f* p8.5f* a8.5f* a10f* Nov 7] top-class performer: unbeaten in 14 races, including Breeders' Cup Ladies Classic at Santa Anita in 2008: gained repeat wins on first 4 starts in 2009, in Grade 2 Milady Handicap at Hollywood (easily) in May, Vanity Handicap (gave 13 lb and more away all round) on same course in June, Clement L. Hirsch Stakes at Del Mar (got home by only a head from Anabaa's Creation after being set a lot to do in steadily-run race) in August and Lady's Secret Stakes at Santa Anita (beat Lethal Heat 1¼ lengths, coasting home unchallenged) in October: surpassed Personal Ensign's sequence of wins when winning Breeders' Cup Classic at Santa Anita in November by a length from Gio Ponti, coming from last and quickening to lead final 50 yards in her first race against males: stays 1¼m: acts on dirt and synthetic surfaces: held up (usually comes wide into straight): stays in training. *J. A. Shirreffs, USA* **131**

ZEPNOVE (IRE) 3 b.f. Noverre (USA) 125 – Royal Zephyr (USA) 62 (Royal Academy (USA) 130) [2009 61: 8.3g 9.9m 8m p12g^4 May 30] lengthy filly: just poor form on Flat at 3 yrs: should stay 1m: tried blinkered: sold £1,500 in July, successful twice in juvenile hurdles for N. King. *M. Wigham* **37**

ZERO COOL (USA) 5 b. or br.g. Forestry (USA) 121 – Fabulous (USA) (Seeking The Gold (USA)) [2009 87: p10g^4 p10g^2 p8g^4 p10g^3 p10g^6 Apr 29] big, close-coupled gelding: just fair performer nowadays: stays 1¼m: acts on polytrack, raced only on good ground or softer on turf: in cheekpieces last 3 outings. *G. L. Moore* **65**

ZERO MONEY (IRE) 3 ch.g. Bachelor Duke (USA) 122 – Dawn Chorus (IRE) (Mukaddamah (USA) 125) [2009 84p: 6g* 7m^3 7d^5 p7g^5 Oct 22] good sort: fairly useful form: won maiden at Leicester in May: stays 7f: acts on good to firm ground: gelded after final start. *R. Charlton* **80**

ZERO SEVEN 2 b.c. (Feb 28) Halling (USA) 133 – Tempting Fate (IRE) 113 (Persian Bold 123) [2009 5m 6g May 26] last in minor event at Newmarket and maiden at Leicester (still green, too free). *C. E. Brittain* **–**

ZERZURA 3 b.g. Oasis Dream 129 – River Fantasy (USA) (Irish River (FR) 131) [2009 p10m^5 Dec 30] sixth living foal: half-brother to smart 7f winner Frenchmans Bay (by Polar Falcon): dam, no worthwhile form, half-sister to Norfolk Stakes winner Romeo Romani: 11/8, fifth to Shakalaka in maiden at Lingfield: open to improvement. *H. R. A. Cecil* **52 p**

ZEYADAH (IRE) 3 b.f. Red Ransom (USA) – Beraysim 111 (Lion Cavern (USA) 117) [2009 –p: p8g^5 p10g^2 p10g Jul 18] rangy filly: has scope: fair form: best effort when second in maiden at Kempton: ran poorly in handicap final outing: stays 1¼m: sold €8,000. *M. A. Jarvis* **74**

ZEYDNAA (IRE) 9 b.g. Bahhare (USA) 122 – Hadawah (USA) 68 (Riverman (USA) 131) [2009 14.1m May 25] close-coupled gelding: handicapper: lightly raced and little form since 2006. *C. R. Wilson* **–**

ZHUKHOV (IRE) 6 ch.g. Allied Forces (USA) 123 – Karameg (IRE) 90 (Danehill (USA) 126) [2009 89: 6s 5d 5.8s^4 7d 6v 7m 8g^2 6s^2 8v 5s 6.3s* 6g p8f 5d 7.2v^5 p7g^3 p8g Nov 25] close-coupled gelding: fairly useful handicapper: won at Listowel in September: effective at 5f to easy 1m: acts on polytrack and any turf going: sometimes slowly away: often takes strong hold. *T. G. McCourt, Ireland* **87**

ZIDANE 7 b.g. Danzero (AUS) – Juliet Bravo 61 (Glow (USA)) [2009 113: 6m 6g^3 6m 6s* 6m^5 6m 6g 7s Nov 7] lengthy, dipped-backed gelding: just useful performer at 7 yrs: won minor event at Doncaster in August by ¾ length from Eisteddfod: better form when 1¾ lengths fifth to Palace Moon in listed event at Newmarket next time: well below form otherwise: best at 6f: acts on polytrack, soft and good to firm going: tongue tied once: held up. *J. R. Fanshawe* **109**

ZIGGY LEE 3 b.g. Lujain (USA) 119 – Mary O'Grady (USA) (Swain (IRE) 134) [2009 59: p7g^6 f7g p5.1g* 5m^2 5.3m* May 22] fairly useful form: first past post in handicaps at Wolverhampton in April, and Newmarket (demoted to second) and Brighton in May: should stay 6f: acts on polytrack and good to firm going: tried tongue tied. *S. C. Williams* **83**

ZIM HO 3 b.c. Zilzal (USA) 137 – Robanna 60 (Robellino (USA) 127) [2009 70: 7m p7g 7g p7g p7f p6f Oct 14] rather sparely-made colt: just poor form in handicaps in 2009, visored final occasion: should prove best up to 7f: form only on polytrack. *J. Akehurst* **46**

ZINJBAR (USA) 2 b.f. (Jan 21) Dynaformer (USA) – Renowned Cat (USA) (Storm Cat (USA)) [2009 5m 6m^3 6m^3 p7g^4 p6g^5 7m^4 Sep 18] $350,000Y: strong filly: first foal: dam unraced half-sister to Breeders' Cup Distaff winner Escena: fair maiden: best efforts at 6f on good to firm going. *C. E. Brittain* **70 a60**

ZIP LOCK (IRE) 3 b.g. Invincible Spirit (IRE) 121 – Buckle (IRE) 77 (Common Grounds 118) [2009 6m May 3] compact gelding: favourite when well held in maiden at Salisbury on debut: subsequently gelded. *J. Noseda* **–**

ZIZOU (IRE) 6 b.g. Fantastic Light (USA) 134 – Search Committee (USA) (Roberto (USA) 131) [2009 p11f Dec 16] neat gelding: maiden: of little account nowadays. *S. Curran* **–**

ZOMERLUST 7 b.g. Josr Algarhoud (IRE) 118 – Passiflora 75 (Night Shift (USA)) [2009 98: 7m 7m 7g^4 7g^5 7g* 7m^5 7.2s* 7.2m^6 7m 8.3m Oct 26] good-topped gelding: fairly useful handicapper nowadays: won at York in July and Ayr in August: best at 6f/7f: acts on heavy and good to firm going: tried in headgear, including last 6 starts. *J. J. Quinn* **93**

ZONIC BOOM (FR) 9 ch.g. Zafonic (USA) 130 – Rosi Zambotti (IRE) 104 (Law Society (USA) 130) [2009 14.1g Aug 30] modest handicapper in 2007: well held sole start on Flat since: tried blinkered/in cheekpieces/tongue tied. *Heather Dalton* **–**

ZOUK 3 ch.g. Zilzal (USA) 137 – Annette Vallon (IRE) 92 (Efisio 120) [2009 8m^4 8.3g^5 8m 8d^5 8.1d^3 Aug 31] lengthy gelding: fair performer: not bred to stay beyond 1m: refused to enter stall intended third outing: sold £2,500. *W. R. Swinburn* **69**

ZOWINGTON 7 gr.g. Zafonic (USA) 130 – Carmela Owen (Owington 123) [2009 91§: 5g 6g 5m^3 6m^2 6m* 6m* 5m 6g^6 6d^2 6m^2 7m 7m 5g 7g Oct 31] quite good-topped gelding: fairly useful handicapper: won at Leicester and Folkestone in June: effective at 5f/6f: acts on polytrack, firm and good to soft ground: often blinkered/visored: ungenuine. *S. C. Williams* **93 §**

ZUBOVA 2 b.f. (Apr 15) Dubawi (IRE) 129 – Jalousie (IRE) 108 (Barathea (IRE) 127) [2009 6s^2 6g^4 6f^3 p5g^3 p6m^2 p7m^2 p6f^2 f6d^2 Dec 29] 30,000 2-y-o: compact filly: fourth foal: half-sister to 3-y-o Kings Destiny: dam 1¼m/1½m winner (stayed 1¾m): fair maiden: claimed from R. Hannon £7,000 prior to final outing (tongue tied): should stay 1m+: acts on polytrack, firm and soft going: wayward and one to treat with caution. *M. J. Attwater* **73 §**

ZULU CHIEF (USA) 4 b.g. Fusaichi Pegasus (USA) 130 – La Lorgnette (CAN) (Val de L'Orne (FR) 133) [2009 106: 8.1d^5 Sep 16] useful performer: well below form in listed race sole outing in 2009: stays 1¼m: acts on soft going. *M. F. de Kock, South Africa* **–**

ZULU MOON 3 b.g. Passing Glance 119 – Mory Kante (USA) (Icecapade (USA)) [2009 71p: p8g^4 May 12] quite attractive gelding: fair form in maidens: will stay 1¼m: sold £800 in October. *A. M. Balding* **74**

ZUWAAR 4 b.g. Nayef (USA) 129 – Raheefa (USA) 75 (Riverman (USA) 131) [2009 78: p16g* p16g^5 p16.5g 14m* 14.1m^3 14v 15g^2 15.9m^2 16.4g^5 15.9m^3 15g^5 17.1m^2 13.4m^4 p13.9m^3 p16.5g^3 f16m^4 Dec 15] good-bodied gelding: fair handicapper: won at Kempton in January and Haydock in April: stays 17f: acts on all-weather and firm going (below form on soft/heavy): tried visored, usually in cheekpieces: tongue tied: reliable. *Ian Williams* **79**

ZUZU (IRE) 3 b.f. Acclamation 118 – Green Life 63 (Green Desert (USA) 127) [2009 94: 6v^4 6m 5d 5d Sep 5] smallish, well-made filly: fairly useful performer: respectable effort at 3 yrs only when fourth to Festoso in listed race at Haydock: will prove best at 5f/6f: acts on heavy going: tried in cheekpieces: front runner/races prominently: sold 8,000 gns. *M. A. Jarvis* **85**

PROMISING HORSES

Selected British-trained horses (plus those trained by Aidan O'Brien) with either a p or P in *Racehorses of 2009* are listed under their trainers for 2010.

A. M. BALDING
Balducci 2 b.c 80p
Brick Red 2 ch.g 88p
Lord Zenith 2 b.c 98p
Pipette 2 b.f 98p
Side Glance 2 br.g 87p
Simenon (Ire) 2 b.g 101p

R. M. BECKETT
Ceilidh House 2 ch.f 84p
Miss Zooter (Ire) 2 b.f 87p
San Cassiano (Ire) 2 b.g 92p
Tropical Treat 2 b.f 88p

M. L. W. BELL
Activate 2 b.g 82p
Coordinated Cut (Ire) 2 b.c 94p
Hypnotized (USA) 2 b.c 86p
Mont Agel 2 b.c 94p
Prompter 2 b.c 107p
Soul Heaven 2 b.g 85p
Wigmore Hall (Ire) 2 b.g 93p

J. R. BEST
Christopher Wren (USA) 2 ch.c 80p
Elspeth's Boy (USA) 2 b.c 90p
Inler (Ire) 2 br.c 98P
Kingsgate Choice (Ire) 2 b.c 80p

M. BOTTI
Gracious Melange 2 b.f 83p
Little Garcon (USA) 2 b.g 80p
Mosqueras Romance 3 gr.f 85p

C. E. BRITTAIN
Bint Doyen 2 br.f 82p
Rumool 2 b.c 92p

G. A. BUTLER
Maristar (USA) 2 b.f 82p
Sing Sweetly 2 b.f 80p

H. CANDY
Beauchamp Yorker 2 ch.c 94p
London Gold 2 b.c 80p

H. R. A. CECIL
Aviate 2 b.f 86p
Bullet Train 2 b.c 86p
Creese 2 b.f 88p
Jacqueline Quest (Ire) 2 b.f 93p
Kithonia (Fr) 2 b.f 90p
Principal Role (USA) 2 b.f 94P
Rigidity 2 b.c 90p
Rodrigo de Torres 2 ch.c 86p
Timepiece 2 b.f 104p
Tomintoul Singer (Ire) 2 ch.f 98p
Walk On Water 2 ch.f 99p
Doggerbank (Ire) 3 b.f 95p
Manifest 3 b.c 108p

M. R. CHANNON
Jibrrya 2 b.c 82p
Music Show (Ire) 2 b.f 111p
Very Good Day (Fr) 2 b.c 80p

JANE CHAPPLE-HYAM
Abayaan 3 gr.c 89p

P. W. CHAPPLE-HYAM
Zaahy (USA) 2 ch.c 101p

R. CHARLTON
Centurio 2 b.c 84p
Spoken 2 ch.c 84p
Too Putra (Ire) 2 b.c 76p
First Service (Ire) 3 ch.c 80p

D. J. COAKLEY
Huygens 2 b.c 86p

C. G. COX
Miss Miracle 2 gr.f 72p
Tenessee 2 b.c 82p

L. M. CUMANI
Blue Lyric 2 b.f 81p
Cheetah 2 b.f 82p
Diam Queen (Ger) 2 b.f 93p
Gold Rules 2 ch.c 82p
Loden 2 b.c 65p
Seta 2 ch.f 104p
Cygnet 3 b.g 92p
Mistoffelees 3 b.c 73p
Monaco (Ger) 3 b.g 80p
Paisley 3 ch.f 80p

TOM DASCOMBE
Adele Blanc Sec (Fr) 2 b.f 93p
Classic Colori (Ire) 2 b.c 96p
Jonny Mudball 3 b.c 104p
Prince of Dance 3 b.c 114p
King Red 5 ch.h 84p

H. J. L. DUNLOP
Green Moon (Ire) 2 b.c 81p
Old Money 2 ch.f 80p

J. L. DUNLOP
Elusive Pimpernel (USA) 2 b.c 116p
Haatheq (USA) 2 b.c 72p
Hajjaan (USA) 2 b.c 83p
Harlestone Times (Ire) 2 b.c 73p
Mufarrh (Ire) 2 b.c 93p
Munsarim (Ire) 2 b.c 89p
Spanish Duke (Ire) 2 b.g 89p
Waseet 2 ch.c 114p
King of Wands 3 b.c 105p

T. D. EASTERBY
Escape Artist 2 gr.g —p

R. A. FAHEY
Bubber (Ire) 2 b.f 59p
Coolminx (Ire) 2 b.f 95p
Layla's Dancer 2 b.c 89p

Our Joe Mac (Ire) 2 b.g 97p
Rock 'n' Royal 2 b.c 81p
Tatiana Romanova (USA) 2 ch.f 81p
Mr Freddy (Ire) 3 b.g 79p

J. R. FANSHAWE
Deacon Blues 2 b.c 83p
Deportment 3 b.f 90p
Primaeval 3 ch.c 82p

J. H. M. GOSDEN
Commissionaire 2 b.c 90p
Deirdre 2 b.f 79p
Dyna Waltz 2 b.f 101p
Fallen Idol 2 b.c 94p
Hunting Tartan 2 b.c 93p
Meezaan (Ire) 2 b.c 87p
Mujdeya 2 gr.f 83p
Namaskar 2 b.f 84p
Pounced (USA) 2 ch.c 112p
Prizefighting (USA) 2 ch.c 104p

W. J. HAGGAS
Centigrade (Ire) 2 gr.g 99p
Cloud's End 2 b.f 83p
Redden 2 b.g 67p
The Only Boss (Ire) 2 ch.c 97p
Tagseed (Ire) 3 b.c 81p
Shamali 4 ch.c 110p

R. HANNON
Gene Autry (USA) 2 b.c 81p
Higgy's Ragazzo (Fr) 2 b.c 86p
Kalypso King (USA) 2 ch.c 105p
Middle Club 2 b.f 103p
Mirabella (Ire) 2 b.f 86p
Planet Red (Ire) 2 ch.c 87p
Plume 2 b.f 88p
Pollenator (Ire) 2 ch.f 111p
Poltergeist (Ire) 2 b.c 89p
Quadrille 2 b.c 102p

B. W. HILLS
Champagnelifestyle 2 b.f 93p
Critical Moment (USA) 2 b.c 98p
Esaar (USA) 2 b.c 96p
Khattaab (USA) 2 b.c 96p
Rashaad (USA) 2 b.c 90p
Sharaayeen 2 br.c 80p
Sunraider (Ire) 2 b.c 89p
Tamaathul 2 gr.c 97p
Tipperary Boutique (Ire) 2 b.f 83p
Za Za Zoom (Ire) 2 b.f 96p
Do The Strand (Ire) 3 b.c 93p

M. A. JARVIS
Atlaal (USA) 2 ch.c 81p
Beyond Desire 2 b.f 105p
Business As Usual 2 b.c 87p
Decorative (Ire) 2 b.f 96P
Hot Prospect 2 b.c 102p
Marrayah 2 b.f 82p
Noafal (Ire) 2 ch.c 86p
Pekan Star 2 b.c 63P
Sarrsar 2 b.g 80p
Alainmaar (Fr) 3 b.g 108p
Laaheb 3 b.g 118p
Libel Law 3 ch.c 112p
Mutamayez 3 b.c 87p

Opinion Poll (Ire) 3 b.c 111p
Rainbow Peak (Ire) 3 b.g 112p
Tripitaka 3 b.g 94p
Zemario (Ire) 3 b.g 81p

M. JOHNSTON
Awzaan 2 br.c 119p
Babylonian 2 b.f 66p
Below Zero (Ire) 2 b.c 94p
Bowmaker 2 b.g 84p
Doctor Zhivago 2 b.c 75P
Exemplary 2 b.c 85p
Green Lightning (Ire) 2 b.c 84p
Guest Book (Ire) 2 b.c 88p
Hafawa (Ire) 2 b.f 99p
Jarrow (Ire) 2 ch.c 92p
Karaka Jack 2 ch.c 96p
Sand Skier 2 b.c 93p
Solicitor 2 ch.c 85p
Sulwaan (Ire) 2 b.g 91p
King's Salute (USA) 3 b.c 97p
Spirit Is Needed (Ire) 3 b.g 90p

W. J. KNIGHT
Eolith 2 ch.f 99p
Fairy Flight (USA) 2 b.f 80p

D. R. LANIGAN
Cape Marien (Ire) 3 b.f 92p

P. J. MCBRIDE
Audacity of Hope 2 b.c 103p

B. J. MEEHAN
Arcano (Ire) 2 b.c 122p
Cockney Class (USA) 2 gr.c 82p
Dancing David (Ire) 2 b.c 105p
Field Day (Ire) 2 br.f 85p
Harvest Dancer (Ire) 2 ch.c 83p
Youm Jamil (USA) 2 gr.c 82p
Dangerous Midge (USA) 3 b.c 99p

G. L. MOORE
Whistleinthewind (Ire) 2 b.g 86p

H. MORRISON
Pastoral Player 2 b.g 92p

D. NICHOLLS
Xilerator (Ire) 2 b.g 83p

J. NOSEDA
Brannagh (USA) 2 gr.c 82p
Call To Reason (Ire) 2 ch.f 80p
Illustrious Prince (Ire) 2 b.c 86p
Leahurst (Ire) 3 gr.g 109p

A. P. O'BRIEN, IRELAND
Amber Grey (Ire) 2 ch.c 86p
Ancient Kingdom (USA) 2 ch.c 87p
At First Sight (Ire) 2 ch.c 83p
Await The Dawn (USA) 2 b.c 99p
Black Quartz (Fr) 2 b.c 107p
Cape Blanco (Ire) 2 ch.c 110p
Dance On By (Ire) 2 b.f 63P
Don Carlos (Ger) 2 b.c 102p
Dynasty 2 b.c 97p
Encompassing (Ire) 2 b.c 92p
Falcon Flight (Ire) 2 b.c 80p
Fencing Master 2 b.c 116p

Fighting Brave (USA) 2 br.c 97p
Flying Cross (Ire) 2 b.c 98P
Jan Vermeer (Ire) 2 b.c 119p
Joshua Tree (Ire) 2 b.c 115p
Lady Lupus (Ire) 2 b.f 100p
Midas Touch 2 b.c 107p
Remember When (Ire) 2 ch.f 84p
Steinbeck (Ire) 2 b.c 115p
St Nicholas Abbey (Ire) 2 b.c 126p
You'll Be Mine (USA) 2 b.f 105P
Age of Aquarius (Ire) 3 b.c 118p
Crimson Sky (Ire) 3 b.c 91P

MRS A. J. PERRETT
Bramshaw (USA) 2 gr.c 80p
Sierra Alpha 2 b.c 80p
Valid Reason 2 b.c 80p

SIR MARK PRESCOTT
Allannah Abu 2 b.f —p
Fortuni (Ire) 3 b.g 99p
Royal Diamond (Ire) 3 b.g 103p

M. G. QUINLAN
Wishbone (Ire) 2 b.f 85p
Celtic Sovereign (Ire) 3 b.g 84p

K. A. RYAN
Mark Anthony (Ire) 2 b.g 84p
Our Jonathan 2 b.c 113p
Youcanalwaysdream (Ire) 2 b.f 80p
Tiddliwinks 3 b.g 86p

SIR MICHAEL STOUTE
Botanist 2 b.c 88p
Eleanora Duse (Ire) 2 b.f 82p
Giants Play (USA) 2 b.f 80p
Hymnsheet 2 b.f 84p
London Stripe (Ire) 2 ch.c 87p
Longliner 2 gr.c 84p
Magician's Cape (Ire) 2 b.c 84p
Markazzi 2 b.c 98p
Mr Irons (USA) 2 ch.c 95p
Muwakaba (USA) 2 ch.f 87P
Nibani (Ire) 2 ch.c 81p
Nouriya 2 b.f 85p
Official Style 2 b.c 81p
Racy 2 b.c 89p
Revered 2 b.f 81P
Rule of Nature 2 b.f 82p
Ship's Biscuit 2 b.f 71P
Top Tigress 2 b.f 62P
Total Command 2 b.c 88p
Treble Jig (USA) 2 b.c 93P
Verdant 2 b.c 89p
Workforce 2 b.c 106P
Jedi 3 ch.g 89p
Rosika 3 b.f 104p
Saptapadi (Ire) 3 ch.g 104p
Strawberrydaiquiri 3 gr.f 117p

SAEED BIN SUROOR
Al Zir (USA) 2 b.c 111p
Ameer (Ire) 2 b.c 98p
Anhar (USA) 2 b.c 96p
Asraab (Ire) 2 b.c 90p
Bab Al Shams (Ire) 2 b.c 85p
Bronze Prince 2 b.c 91p
Burj Nahar 2 b.c 97P
Chabal (Ire) 2 b.c 114p
Dafeef 2 b.c 97p
Destination Aim 2 b.c 89p
Fareej (USA) 2 b.c 93p
Huroof (Ire) 2 ch.f 87p
Judiciary (Ire) 2 b.c 85p
Kingsfort (USA) 2 b.c 115p
Lion Mountain 2 b.c 85p
Mendip (USA) 2 b.c 96p
Modeyra 2 br.f 91p
Multames (Ire) 2 b.c 99p
Mureb (USA) 2 b.c 80p
Mutafajer 2 b.c 81p
Nafura 2 b.f 95p
Next Move (Ire) 2 b.c 83p
Padmini 2 b.f 87p
Passion For Gold (USA) 2 b.c 119p
Powerful Melody (USA) 2 br.c 82p
Psychic Ability (USA) 2 b.c 87p
Sahara Kingdom (Ire) 2 gr.c 98P
Sowaylm 2 b.c 90p
Tertiary (USA) 2 b.c 82p
Treasure Town 2 b.c 89p
Zeitoper 2 b.c 105p
Anmar (USA) 3 ch.c 117p
Darley Sun (Ire) 3 b.c 114p
Emirates Champion 3 b.c 106p
La de Two (Ire) 3 ch.c 103p
Rainbow Desert (USA) 3 b.f 86p
Skysurfers 3 b.c 88P
Whispering Gallery 3 b.g 117p

G. A. SWINBANK
Fortunes of Fire 2 ch.g 94p
Saddlers Lodge 2 b.g 80p
Mr Rainbow 3 ch.g 94p

W. R. SWINBURN
Vimiero (USA) 2 b.c 84p

T. P. TATE
Walvis Bay (Ire) 2 gr.g 85p

J. A. R. TOLLER
At Wits End 3 b.g 88p

M. P. TREGONING
Haadeeth 2 b.g 93p
Latansaa 2 b.c 83p
Rasmy 2 b.c 97p
Rumoush (USA) 2 b.f 81P
Uncle Keef (Ire) 3 b.g 56p

C. F. WALL
Azaday (Ire) 2 b.f 54p
Wake Up Call 3 b.f 81p

SELECTED BIG RACES 2009

Prize money for racing abroad has been converted to £ sterling at the exchange rate current at the time of the race. The figures are correct to the nearest £. The Timeform ratings (TR) recorded by the principals in each race appear on the last line.

NAD AL SHEBA Saturday, Mar 28 Turf course: GOOD, Dirt course: FAST

1 **Dubai Duty Free Sponsored By Dubai Duty Free (Gr 1) (3yo+)** 1m195y (Turf) £2,075,471

GLADIATORUS (USA) *MbinShafya,UAE* 4-9-0 AhmedAjtebi (2)............. 12/1 1
PRESVIS *LMCumani,GB* 5-9-0 RyanMoore (16).. 10/1 3¼ 2
ALEXANDROS *SaeedbinSuroor,UAE* 4-9-0 MJKinane (9)......................... 40/1 2 3
Niconero (AUS) *DAHayes,Australia* 8-9-0 CraigAWilliams (4) 25/1 3 4
Bankable (IRE) *MFdeKock,SouthAfrica* 5-9-0 (t) JMurtagh (1).................... 14/1 ½ 5
Archipenko (USA) *MFdeKock,SouthAfrica* 5-9-0 (b+t) KShea (10)............. 7/2f sh 6
Vodka (JPN) *KSumii,Japan* 5-8-10 YTake (3).. 6/1 hd 7
Paco Boy (IRE) *RHannon,GB* 4-9-0 RichardHughes (13).............................. 9/2 ¾ 8
Tuesday Joy (NZ) *GaiWaterhouse,Australia* 6-8-10 DBeadman (11)........... 16/1 1¾ 9
Kip Deville (USA) *REDutrow,jnr,USA* 6-9-0 (b+t) CVelasquez (7) 16/1 1¾ 10
Jay Peg (SAF) *HBrown,SouthAfrica* 6-9-0 (v) WCMarwing (15) 16/1 3¾ 11
Charlie Farnsbarns (IRE) *BJMeehan,GB* 5-9-0 JamieSpencer (14).............. 50/1 ¼ 12
Balius (IRE) *AbinHuzaim,UAE* 6-9-0 (b) WilliamSupple (8) .... 18/1 ¾ 13
Hyperbaric (USA) *JCCanani,USA* 6-9-0 (b+t) TBaze (5) .... 50/1 ¾ 14
Creachadoir (IRE) *SaeedbinSuroor,UAE* 5-9-0 TedDurcan (6)...................... 25/1 1½ 15
Lady Marian (GER) *SaeedbinSuroor,UAE* 4-8-10 LDettori (12).................. 16/1 4 16

Sheikh Mansoor bin Mohammed Al Maktoum 16ran 1m46.92
TR: 128/118+/114/106/105/105

2 **Dubai Sheema Classic Sponsored By Nakheel (Gr 1) (3yo+)** £2,075,471 1½m (Turf)

EASTERN ANTHEM (IRE) *MbinShafya,UAE* 5-9-0 (t) AhmedAjtebi (2).. 14/1 1
SPANISH MOON (USA) *SirMichaelStoute,GB* 5-9-0 RyanMoore (4)......... 14/1 ns 2
PURPLE MOON (IRE) *LMCumani,GB* 6-9-0 JamieSpencer (7) .... 15/2 sh 3
Youmzain (IRE) *MRChannon,GB* 6-9-0 RHills (6).. 7/2f 2¼ 4
Marsh Side (USA) *NDDrysdale,USA* 6-9-0 (t) EPrado (8)............................ 25/1 3¼ 5
Quijano (GER) *PSchiergen,Germany* 7-9-0 AStarke (10) .... 9/1 hd 6
Deem (IRE) *JBarton,SaudiArabia* 4-8-8 MJKinane (9).................................. 50/1 ½ 7
Doctor Dino (FR) *RGibson,France* 7-9-0 OPeslier (13).................................. 6/1 1¼ 8
Front House (IRE) *MFdeKock,SouthAfrica* 4-8-8 KShea (1) 8/1 4 9
Kirklees (IRE) *SaeedbinSuroor,UAE* 5-9-0 LDettori (14)............................. 12/1 hd 10
Russian Sage (SAF) *MFdeKock,SouthAfrica* 5-9-0 BFayd'herbe (3)............ 16/1 2¼ 11
Red Rocks (IRE) *MAHennig,USA* 6-9-0 (b) JCastellano (12) 25/1 6¼ 12
King of Rome (IRE) *MFdeKock,SouthAfrica* 4-8-13 (t) JMurtagh (5)............ 9/1 hd 13
Macarthur *MFdeKock,SouthAfrica* 5-9-0 (t) DBeadman (15)........................ 25/1 ½ 14
Kings Gambit (SAF) *HBrown,SouthAfrica* 5-9-0 (t) JohnEgan (11) 33/1 4½ 15

Sheikh Hamdan Bin Mohammed Al Maktoum 15ran 2m31.84
TR: 123/123/123/119+/114/113

3 **Dubai World Cup Sponsored By Emirates Airline (Gr 1) (3yo+)** 1¼m (Dirt) £2,490,566

WELL ARMED (USA) *EHarty,USA* 6-9-0 (t) AGryder (7)......................... 10/1 1
GLORIA DE CAMPEAO (BRZ) *PBary,France* 6-9-0 JLeme (6) 25/1 14 2
PARIS PERFECT (SAF) *NBruss,SaudiArabia* 5-9-0 (t) BFayd'herbe (13).. 66/1 4½ 3
Muller (ARG) *NBruss,SaudiArabia* 6-9-0 (t) WCMarwing (11) .... 50/1 ½ 4
My Indy (ARG) *SaeedbinSuroor,UAE* 5-9-0 LDettori (14) 10/1 3½ 5
Albertus Maximus (USA) *KPMcLaughlin,USA* 5-9-0 AGarcia (10)............... 7/2 1¾ 6
Snaafy (USA) *MAlMuhairi,UAE* 5-9-0 (v) RHills (3) .... 12/1 ½ 7
Casino Drive (USA) *KFujisawa,Japan* 4-9-0 KAndo (8)................................ 4/1 2¼ 8
Happy Boy (BRZ) *MbinShafya,UAE* 6-9-0 AhmedAjtebi (5) .... 25/1 ½ 9
Muhannak (IRE) *RMBeckett,GB* 5-9-0 (b) RyanMoore (1) 50/1 1¼ 10
Arson Squad (USA) *REDutrow,jnr,USA* 6-9-0 (t) EPrado (2)........................ 33/1 1¼ 11
Asiatic Boy (ARG) *MFdeKock,SouthAfrica* 6-9-0 JMurtagh (4).................... 2/1f 3¼ 12
Joe Louis (ARG) *JBarton,SaudiArabia* 6-9-0 (t) WRamos (9)...................... 66/1 ¾ 13
Anak Nakal (USA) *NPZito,USA* 4-9-0 (t) JBravo (12)............................... 100/1 7½ 14

WinStar Farm LLC 14ran 2m01.01 TR: 129/108/102/101/97/94

SANDOWN Saturday, Apr 25 GOOD

4 **bet365 Mile (Gr 2) (4yo+)** £56,770 1m14y

1 PACO BOY (IRE) *RHannon* 4-9-6 RichardHughes (1)................................ 15/8f 1
DREAM EATER (IRE) *AMBalding* 4-9-0 (t) FrancisNorton (6)..................... 7/1 ¾ 2

VIRTUAL *JHMGosden* 4-9-0 JimmyFortune (4) 11/4 nk 3
Stotsfold *WRSwinburn* 6-9-0 AdamKirby (3) 5/1 2¾ 4
Forthe Millionkiss (GER) *UweOstmann,Germany* 5-9-0 WMongil (2) 40/1 1¼ 5
Lovelace *MJohnston* 5-9-4 RoystonFfrench (7) 7/1 1½ 6
Kandidate *CEBrittain* 7-9-0 SebSanders (8) 14/1 6 7
The Calvera Partnership No 2 7ran 1m43.04 TR: 125+/117/116/110/107/107

LONGCHAMP Sunday, Apr 26 GOOD

5 **Prix Ganay - "Grand Prix Air Mauritius" (Gr 1) (4yo+)** £151,700 1¼m110y

VISION D'ETAT (FR) *ELibaud,France* 4-9-2 IMendizabal 14/10f 1
LOUP BRETON (IRE) *ELellouche,France* 5-9-2 (s) ACrastus 3/1 ¾ 2
ADLERFLUG (GER) *JHirschberger,Germany* 5-9-2 AdeVries 10/1 sh 3
Thewayyouare (USA) *APO'Brien,Ireland* 4-9-2 JMurtagh 11/1 1 4
The Bogberry (USA) *AdeRoyerDupre,France* 4-9-2 GMosse 17/4 1½ 5
Cima de Triomphe (IRE) *LMCumani,GB* 4-9-2 CPLemaire 24/1 nk 6
Red Rock Canyon (IRE) *APO'Brien,Ireland* 5-9-2 DavidMcCabe 58/1 1 7
Tajaaweed (USA) *SirMichaelStoute,GB* 4-9-2 RHills 13/1 1½ 8
Mr J. Detre 8ran 2m09.43 TR: 120+/117/117/117/113/112

SHA TIN Sunday, Apr 26 GOOD to SOFT

6 **Audemars Piguet Queen Elizabeth II Cup (Gr 1) (3yo+)** £701,755 1¼m

1 PRESVIS *LMCumani,GB* 5-9-0 RyanMoore 29/10 1
VIVA PATACA *JMoore,HongKong* 7-9-0 (h) DBeadman 15/10f 1 2
THUMBS UP (NZ) *CSShum,HongKong* 5-9-0 CSoumillon 62/10 nk 3
Chinchon (IRE) *CLaffon-Parias,France* 4-9-0 (s) ODoleuze 12/1 ½ 4
Packing Winner (NZ) *LHo,HongKong* 6-9-0 ESaint-Martin 25/1 nk 5
1 Archipenko (USA) *MFdeKock,SouthAfrica* 5-9-0 (b+t) KShea 41/10 nk 6
Viva Macau (FR) *JMoore,HongKong* 6-8-9 (s+t) KTYeung[5] 47/1 4½ 7
1 Niconero (AUS) *DAHayes,Australia* 8-9-0 CraigWilliams 29/1 sh 8
Danesis (IRE) *ASCruz,HongKong* 5-9-0 (t) FCoetzee 26/1 3¼ 9
Bullish Cash (NZ) *ASCruz,HongKong* 6-9-0 (t) BPrebble 35/1 1¾ 10
Mr L. Marinopoulos 10ran 2m02.97 TR: 121+/119+/118/118/116/115

NEWMARKET Saturday, May 2 GOOD to FIRM (Rowley Mile Course)

7 **stanjames.com 2000 Guineas Stks (Gr 1) (3yo c+f)** £241,840 1m

SEA THE STARS (IRE) *JohnMOxx,Ireland* 3-9-0 MJKinane (1) 8/1 1
DELEGATOR *BJMeehan* 3-9-0 JamieSpencer (15) 3/1f 1½ 2
GAN AMHRAS (IRE) *JSBolger,Ireland* 3-9-0 KJManning (14) 15/2 ¾ 3
Rip Van Winkle (IRE) *APO'Brien,Ireland* 3-9-0 JMurtagh (5) 9/2 nk 4
Mastercraftsman (IRE) *APO'Brien,Ireland* 3-9-0 PJSmullen (12) 7/1 1¾ 5
Evasive *SirMichaelStoute* 3-9-0 RyanMoore (13) 13/2 hd 6
Pure Poetry (IRE) *RHannon* 3-9-0 RichardHughes (16) 66/1 1¾ 7
Monitor Closely (IRE) *PWChapple-Hyam* 3-9-0 AlanMunro (11) 28/1 ½ 8
Finjaan *MPTregoning* 3-9-0 TPO'Shea (8) 25/1 2 9
Ocean's Minstrel *JRyan* 3-9-0 JerryO'Dwyer (6) 100/1 1¼ 10
Ouqba *BWHills* 3-9-0 RHills (17) 25/1 1 11
Lord Shanakill (USA) *KRBurke* 3-9-0 JimCrowley (10) 14/1 6 12
Ashram (IRE) *SaeedbinSuroor* 3-9-0 LDettori (2) 16/1 1¼ 13
Cityscape *RCharlton* 3-9-0 SteveDrowne (9) 16/1 5 14
Imperial Guest *GGMargarson* 3-9-0 JohnEgan (3) 150/1 dist 15
Mr Christopher Tsui 15ran 1m35.88 TR: 128+/124/122/121+/116+/115+

NEWMARKET Sunday, May 3 FIRM (Rowley mile course)

8 **stanjames.com 1000 Guineas Stks (Gr 1) (3yo f)** £227,080 1m

GHANAATI (USA) *BWHills* 3-9-0 RHills (8) 20/1 1
CUIS GHAIRE (IRE) *JSBolger,Ireland* 3-9-0 KJManning (14) 12/1 1½ 2
SUPER SLEUTH (IRE) *BJMeehan* 3-9-0 MartinDwyer (3) 33/1 1¼ 3
Heart Shaped (USA) *APO'Brien,Ireland* 3-9-0 JMurtagh (10) 14/1 ns 4
Rainbow View (USA) *JHMGosden* 3-9-0 JimmyFortune (6) 8/11f hd 5
Penny's Gift *RHannon* 3-9-0 RichardHughes (15) 66/1 hd 6
Serious Attitude (IRE) *RaeGuest* 3-9-0 PJSmullen (12) 8/1 2½ 7
Pursuit of Glory (IRE) *DavidWachman,Ireland* 3-9-0 WMLordan (9) 33/1 4½ 8
Nashmiah (IRE) *CEBrittain* 3-9-0 JamieSpencer (13) 20/1 4 9
Lahaleeb (IRE) *MRChannon* 3-9-0 DarryllHolland (4) 14/1 1 10
Shimah (USA) *KevinPrendergast,Ireland* 3-9-0 DPMcDonogh (5) 16/1 2½ 11
Seradim *PFICole* 3-9-0 SPasquier (1) 100/1 4½ 12
Devotee (USA) *SaeedbinSuroor* 3-9-0 (t) LDettori (7) 50/1 2¼ 13
Aspen Darlin (IRE) *ABailey* 3-9-0 (s) JimmyQuinn (11) 40/1 pu
Mr Hamdan Al Maktoum 14ran 1m34.22 TR: 117/113/109+/109/108/108

LONGCHAMP Sunday, May 10 GOOD to FIRM

9 **Poule d'Essai des Poulains (Gr 1) (3yo c)** £204,071 1m

Order as they passed the post: Naaqoos was demoted to sixth for hampering Handsome Maestro

SILVER FROST (IRE) *YdeNicolay,France* 3-9-2 CSoumillon (7) ... 43/10 1
LE HAVRE (IRE) *J-CRouget,France* 3-9-2 CPLemaire (2) ... 11/1 2 2
NAAQOOS *FHead,France* 3-9-2 DBonilla (1) ... 3/1f sn 3
Westphalia (IRE) *APO'Brien,Ireland* 3-9-2 JMurtagh (3) ... 21/4 ¾ 4
Oiseau de Feu (USA) *J-CRouget,France* 3-9-2 IMendizabal (5) ... 9/1 1½ 5
Handsome Maestro (IRE) *DSmaga,France* 3-9-2 OPeslier (8) ... 29/4 hd 6
Shaweel *SaeedbinSuroor,GB* 3-9-2 LDettori (9) ... 14/1 1½ 7
Diableside (FR) *YDurepaire,Spain* 3-9-2 (s) J-BEyquem (10) ... 64/1 ns 8
Roi Des Sables (FR) *BdeMontzey,France* 3-9-2 (b) TJarnet (4) ... 69/1 2 9
Vocalised (USA) *JSBolger,Ireland* 3-9-2 KJManning (6) ... 23/4 15 10
Born To Be King (USA) *APO'Brien,Ireland* 3-9-2 (b) JamieSpencer (11)... 52/1 6 11

Mr J. D. Cotton 11ran 1m35.43 TR: 122/116/116/113+/110/109+

10 **Poule d'Essai des Pouliches (Gr 1) (3yo f)** £204,071 1m

ELUSIVE WAVE (IRE) *J-CRouget,France* 3-9-0 CPLemaire (5) ... 54/10 1
TAMAZIRTE (IRE) *J-CRouget,France* 3-9-0 IMendizabal (1) ... 7/1 ½ 2
FANTASIA *LMCumani,GB* 3-9-0 LDettori (2) ... 5/4f 1½ 3
Proportional *MmeCHead-Maarek,France* 3-9-0 SPasquier (10) ... 7/2 ¾ 4
Soneva (USA) *YdeNicolay,France* 3-9-0 CSoumillon (9) ... 11/1 nk 5
Entre Deux Eaux (FR) *RCollet,France* 3-9-0 JMurtagh (3) ... 29/1 1½ 6
Providanza (FR) *MDelzangles,France* 3-9-0 GMosse (4) ... 56/1 1½ 7
Doriana (FR) *AdeRoyerDupre,France* 3-9-0 TThulliez (7) ... 50/1 2½ 8
Oh Goodness Me *JSBolger,Ireland* 3-9-0 KJManning (11) ... 30/1 2 9
Queen America (FR) *RCollet,France* 3-9-0 DBoeuf (8) ... 83/1 ¾ 10
Undaunted Affair (IRE) *KARyan,GB* 3-9-0 OPeslier (6) ... 86/1 1 11

Mr Martin S. Schwartz 11ran 1m39.87 TR: 118/117/114/112/111/107

NEWBURY Saturday, May 16 GOOD to SOFT

11 **Juddmonte Lockinge Stks (Gr 1) (4yo+)** £141,925 1m

4 VIRTUAL *JHMGosden* 4-9-0 JimmyFortune (10) ... 6/1 1
1 ALEXANDROS *SaeedbinSuroor* 4-9-0 LDettori (6) ... 16/1 ns 2
TWICE OVER *HRACecil* 4-9-0 TPQueally (2) ... 15/2 ½ 3
4 Paco Boy (IRE) *RHannon* 4-9-0 RichardHughes (7) ... 11/8f 1¼ 4
Major Cadeaux *RHannon* 5-9-0 RyanMoore (12) ... 12/1 1½ 5
Tariq *PWChapple-Hyam* 5-9-0 JamieSpencer (1) ... 33/1 nk 6
Atlantic Sport (USA) *MRChannon* 4-9-0 DarryllHolland (5) ... 40/1 2¾ 7
Pressing (IRE) *MAJarvis* 6-9-0 NCallan (8) ... 8/1 3½ 8
4 Dream Eater (IRE) *AMBalding* 4-9-0 (t) FrancisNorton (11) ... 20/1 1¾ 9
Aqlaam *WJHaggas* 4-9-0 RHills (3) ... 15/2 3¼ 10
Winker Watson *PWChapple-Hyam* 4-9-0 AlanMunro (4) ... 33/1 15 11

Cheveley Park Stud 11ran 1m40.32 TR: 122/122/120/117+/113/112

KRANJI Sunday, May 17 GOOD

12 **Krisflyer International Sprint (3yo+)** £253,235 6f

SACRED KINGDOM (AUS) *PFYiu,HongKong* 6-9-0 (t) BPrebble (1)..... 46/10 1
ROCKET MAN (AUS) *PShaw,Malaysia* 4-8-10 RFradd (9) ... 1/1f nk 2
DIABOLICAL (USA) *SaeedbinSuroor,GB* 6-9-0 LDettori (7) ... 158/10 3½ 3
Waikato (NZ) *LLaxon,Singapore* 6-9-0 (b) JSaimee (13) ... 45/1 ¾ 4
Capablanca (AUS) *DBaertschiger,Singapore* 7-9-0 JPowell (5) ... 113/1 2½ 5
Mythical Flight (SAF) *SeanTarry,SouthAfrica* 6-9-0 KShea (11) ... 196/10 nk 6
Fantastic Owners (AUS) *BDean,Singapore* 5-9-0 MGallagher (4) ... 123/1 nk 7
Takeover Target (AUS) *JoeJaniak,Australia* 10-9-0 JFord (3) ... 46/10 hd 8
Inspiration (AUS) *JMoore,HongKong* 6-9-0 (t) DBeadman (12) ... 174/10 1¾ 9
Beau Brummell (NZ) *DHill,HongKong* 4-9-0 MCahill (10) ... 51/1 ¾ 10
Madame Trop Vite (IRE) *KARyan,GB* 3-8-2 JimmyQuinn (2) ... 27/1 1¼ 11
Lim's Fighter (AUS) *JMeagher,Singapore* 6-9-0 (b) DinAzis (6) ... 80/1 nk 12
Prime Defender *BWHills,GB* 5-9-0 MichaelHills (14) ... 70/1 3½ 13

Sin Kang Yuk 13ran 1m07.80 TR: 130/125/117/114/106/105

LONGCHAMP Sunday, May 17 SOFT

13 **Prix d'Ispahan (Gr 1) (4yo+)** £127,545 1m1f55y

NEVER ON SUNDAY (FR) *J-CRouget,France* 4-9-2 CPLemaire ... 88/10 1
GRIS DE GRIS (IRE) *AdeRoyerDupre,France* 5-9-2 GMosse ... 10/1 1 2
RUNAWAY *RupertPritchard-Gordon,France* 7-9-2 TJarnet ... 56/1 2½ 3
Celebrissime (IRE) *FHead,France* 4-9-2 DBonilla ... 39/1 ½ 4
Proviso *AFabre,France* 4-8-13 SPasquier ... 12/1 2 5

Curtain Call (FR) *LMCumani,GB* 4-9-2 FMBerry 11/1 2½ 6
Goldikova (IRE) *FHead,France* 4-8-13 OPeslier.......... 1/1f 2 7
5 Loup Breton (IRE) *ELellouche,France* 5-9-2 (s) ACrastus 4/1 5 8
Tazeez (USA) *JHMGosden,GB* 5-9-2 RHills 11/1 8 9
Mr D-Y. Treves 9ran 1m57.20 TR: 119+/117+/111/110/102/99

CURRAGH Saturday, May 23 HEAVY

14 boylesports.com Irish 2000 Guineas (Gr 1) (3yo c+f) £204,018 1m

7 MASTERCRAFTSMAN (IRE) *APO'Brien* 3-9-0 JMurtagh (6) 6/4f 1
RAYENI (IRE) *JohnMOxx* 3-9-0 MJKinane (4) 5/1 4½ 2
SOUL CITY (IRE) *RHannon,GB* 3-9-0 RichardHughes (5).......... 9/1 1¾ 3
Recharge (IRE) *KevinPrendergast* 3-9-0 CDHayes (7).......... 10/1 1½ 4
Fergus McIver (IRE) *JSBolger* 3-9-0 (b) KJManning (2).......... 20/1 3½ 5
Drumbeat (IRE) *APO'Brien* 3-9-0 JAHeffernan (9).......... 10/1 1½ 6
Hail Caesar (IRE) *APO'Brien* 3-9-0 CO'Donoghue (8).......... 40/1 1¾ 7
7 Delegator *BJMeehan,GB* 3-9-0 JamieSpencer (1) 3/1 3 8
Viceroy of India (USA) *APO'Brien* 3-9-0 SMLevey (3) 100/1 30 9
Mr Derrick Smith 9ran 1m48.16 TR: 129/118/114/110/102+/98

CURRAGH Sunday, May 24 HEAVY

15 Tattersalls Gold Cup (Gr 1) (4yo+) £154,688 1¼m110y

CASUAL CONQUEST (IRE) *DKWeld* 4-9-0 (t) PJSmullen (3) 11/4 1
FAMOUS NAME *DKWeld* 4-9-0 MJKinane (4) 9/4f 5½ 2
LUSH LASHES *JSBolger* 4-8-11 KJManning (5) 4/1 1¾ 3
Moiqen (IRE) *KevinPrendergast* 4-9-0 DPMcDonogh (1).......... 14/1 1¼ 4
5 Thewayyouare (USA) *APO'Brien* 4-9-0 JMurtagh (2) 5/2 13 5
Moyglare Stud Farm 5ran 2m26.45 TR: 123/112+/106/107/82+

16 boylesports.com Irish 1000 Guineas (Gr 1) (3yo f) £200,446 1m

AGAIN (IRE) *DavidWachman* 3-9-0 JMurtagh (3).......... 5/2f 1
8 LAHALEEB (IRE) *MRChannon,GB* 3-9-0 DPMcDonogh (13).......... 11/2 nk 2
10 OH GOODNESS ME *JSBolger* 3-9-0 DJMoran (14) 16/1 3½ 3
Rare Ransom *DKWeld* 3-9-0 PShanahan (16) 25/1 4 4
Chintz (IRE) *DavidWachman* 3-9-0 WMLordan (9) 12/1 4 5
Hallie's Comet (IRE) *AndrewKinsella* 3-9-0 SFoley (6).......... 66/1 ½ 6
Love Bird (IRE) *DavidWachman* 3-9-0 JAHeffernan (2).......... 10/1 2 7
Always Be True (IRE) *DavidWachman* 3-9-0 FMBerry (12) 33/1 5 8
Luminous Eyes (IRE) *DKWeld* 3-9-0 MJKinane (1).......... 14/1 1¼ 9
Monivea (IRE) *BrianNolan* 3-9-0 (s) CDHayes (7).......... 66/1 4½ 10
Dance Pass (IRE) *DKWeld* 3-9-0 PJSmullen (10) 10/1 4 11
Beauthea (IRE) *HarryRogers* 3-9-0 (t) DMGrant (5).......... 150/1 7 12
8 Super Sleuth (IRE) *BJMeehan,GB* 3-9-0 LDettori (11) 3/1 5½ 13
Totally Devoted (USA) *APO'Brien* 3-9-0 CO'Donoghue (4).......... 25/1 ½ 14
8 Cuis Ghaire (IRE) *JSBolger* 3-9-0 KJManning (8) 13/2 10 15
Duaisbhanna (IRE) *JSBolger* 3-9-0 DEMullins (15).......... 66/1 2½ 16
Mr Michael Tabor 16ran 1m46.34 TR: 115/114/105/95/85/84

EPSOM DOWNS Friday, Jun 5 GOOD

17 Investec Coronation Cup (Gr 1) (4yo+) £137,809 1½m10y

ASK *SirMichaelStoute* 6-9-0 RyanMoore (8).......... 5/1 1
2 YOUMZAIN (IRE) *MRChannon* 6-9-0 RHills (5) .... 2/1f ns 2
LOOK HERE *RMBeckett* 4-8-11 SebSanders (1).......... 9/2 ns 3
Duncan *JHMGosden* 4-9-0 JimmyFortune (3) .... 9/2 ¾ 4
Frozen Fire (GER) *APO'Brien,Ireland* 4-9-0 JMurtagh (7).......... 17/2 3¼ 5
2 Eastern Anthem (IRE) *SaeedbinSuroor* 5-9-0 (t) LDettori (6).......... 12/1 7 6
Expresso Star (USA) *JHMGosden* 4-9-0 RichardMullen (4).......... 25/1 3½ 7
Buccellati *AMBalding* 5-9-0 (v) WilliamBuick (2) .... 9/1 nk 8
Mr Patrick J. Fahey 8ran 2m37.00 TR: 121/121/119/120/115/101

18 Investec Oaks (Gr 1) (3yo f) £198,695 1½m10y

SARISKA *MLWBell* 3-9-0 JamieSpencer (5).......... 9/4f 1
MIDDAY *HRACecil* 3-9-0 TPQueally (2).......... 5/1 hd 2
HIGH HEELED (IRE) *BWHills* 3-9-0 MichaelHills (9).......... 33/1 2½ 3
8 Rainbow View (USA) *JHMGosden* 3-9-0 JimmyFortune (10).......... 3/1 4½ 4
The Miniver Rose (IRE) *RHannon* 3-9-0 RichardHughes (4) 33/1 9 5
Phillipina *SirMichaelStoute* 3-9-0 RyanMoore (3) 13/2 5 6
16 Oh Goodness Me *JSBolger,Ireland* 3-9-0 KJManning (6) .... 8/1 ¾ 7
Tottie *MrsAJPerrett* 3-9-0 JimCrowley (8).......... 66/1 2¼ 8
Wadaat *CEBrittain* 3-9-0 NCallan (7).......... 33/1 29 9
Perfect Truth (IRE) *APO'Brien,Ireland* 3-9-0 JMurtagh (1).......... 10/1 dist 10
Lady Bamford 10ran 2m35.28 TR: 112+/122/117/109+/92/83

EPSOM DOWNS Saturday, Jun 6 GOOD

19 **Investec Derby (Gr 1) (3yo c+f)** £709,625 1½m10y

7 SEA THE STARS (IRE) *JohnMOxx,Ireland* 3-9-0 MJKinane (4) ... 11/4 1
FAME AND GLORY *APO'Brien,Ireland* 3-9-0 JAHeffernan (10) ... 9/4f 1¾ 2
MASTEROFTHEHORSE (IRE) *APO'Brien,Ireland* 3-9-0 nk 3
RichardHughes (2) ... 16/1
7 Rip Van Winkle (IRE) *APO'Brien,Ireland* 3-9-0 JMurtagh (9) ... 6/1 ns 4
Golden Sword *APO'Brien,Ireland* 3-9-0 CO'Donoghue (7) ... 25/1 sh 5
Crowded House *BJMeehan* 3-9-0 JamieSpencer (12) ... 20/1 6 6
Age of Aquarius (IRE) *APO'Brien,Ireland* 3-9-0 PJSmullen (1) ... 25/1 ½ 7
Debussy (IRE) *JHMGosden* 3-9-0 JimmyFortune (5) ... 33/1 nk 8
Kite Wood (IRE) *SaeedbinSuroor* 3-9-0 LDettori (8) ... 28/1 4½ 9
Black Bear Island (IRE) *APO'Brien,Ireland* 3-9-0 RyanMoore (3) ... 7/1 hd 10
7 Gan Amhras (IRE) *JSBolger,Ireland* 3-9-0 KJManning (6) ... 8/1 5 11
Montaff *MRChannon* 3-9-0 RHills (11) ... 40/1 11 12

Mr Christopher Tsui 12ran 2m36.74 TR: 126+/123/122/122/122/111+

CHANTILLY Sunday, Jun 7 GOOD

20 **Prix du Jockey Club (Gr 1) (3yo c+f)** £751,842 1¼m110y

9 LE HAVRE (IRE) *J-CRouget,France* 3-9-2 CPLemaire (4) ... 119/10 1
FUISSE (FR) *MmeCHead-Maarek,France* 3-9-2 DBoeuf (3) ... 84/10 1½ 2
9 WESTPHALIA (IRE) *APO'Brien,Ireland* 3-9-2 JMurtagh (13) ... 68/10 1½ 3
Beheshtam (FR) *AdeRoyerDupre,France* 3-9-2 CSoumillon (15) ... 9/2 1½ 4
Calvados Blues (FR) *PHDemercastel,France* 3-9-2 GMosse (5) ... 33/1 ½ 5
9 Silver Frost (IRE) *YdeNicolay,France* 3-9-2 OPeslier (2) ... 27/10f 1½ 6
Vesuve (IRE) *ELellouche,France* 3-9-2 TThulliez (9) ... 8/1 hd 7
14 Drumbeat (IRE) *APO'Brien,Ireland* 3-9-2 JimmyFortune (1) ... 68/10 1½ 8
Topclas (FR) *PHDemercastel,France* 3-9-2 SPasquier (8) ... 31/1 ½ 9
Glamstar (FR) *J-CRouget,France* 3-9-2 FranckBlondel (12) ... 76/1 hd 10
Guest Ville (FR) *MlleS-VTarrou,France* 3-9-2 TJarnet (7) ... 24/1 1½ 11
Wajir (FR) *ELellouche,France* 3-9-2 ACrastus (10) ... 8/1 sn 12
Zafisio (IRE) *RCurtis,GB* 3-9-2 WMLordan (14) ... 40/1 3 13
Parthenon *SaeedbinSuroor,GB* 3-9-2 LDettori (11) ... 13/1 15 14
Set Sail (IRE) *APO'Brien,Ireland* 3-9-2 JAHeffernan (17) ... 68/10 ns 15
Malibu Bay (USA) *APO'Brien,Ireland* 3-9-2 DBonilla (6) ... 68/10 2½ 16
Feels All Right (IRE) *ELibaud,France* 3-9-2 IMendizabal (16) ... 12/1 20 17

Mr G. Augustin-Normand 17ran 2m06.80 TR: 124/120/117/114/113/109

CHANTILLY Sunday, Jun 14 GOOD to FIRM

21 **Prix de Diane (Gr 1) (3yo f)** £400,982 1¼m110y

STACELITA (FR) *J-CRouget,France* 3-9-0 CPLemaire (4) ... 13/10f 1
10 TAMAZIRTE (IRE) *J-CRouget,France* 3-9-0 IMendizabal (10) ... 9/1 4 2
PLUMANIA *AFabre,France* 3-9-0 OPeslier (12) ... 44/1 ½ 3
Celimene (IRE) *CLerner,France* 3-9-0 YLerner (11) ... 6/1 1 4
Board Meeting (IRE) *ELellouche,France* 3-9-0 ACrastus (8) ... 17/2 ½ 5
Shediyama (FR) *AdeRoyerDupre,France* 3-9-0 CSoumillon (2) ... 10/1 ½ 6
10 Fantasia *LMCumani,GB* 3-9-0 SPasquier (7) ... 17/2 2½ 7
Eclair de Lune (GER) *YdeNicolay,France* 3-9-0 TThulliez (3) ... 14/1 1 8
Denomination (USA) *MmeCHead-Maarek,France* 3-9-0 DBoeuf (9) ... 19/1 ½ 9
Ana Americana (FR) *PHDemercastel,France* 3-9-0 GMosse (6) ... 37/1 ½ 10
Celebra (FR) *CLaffon-Parias,France* 3-9-0 DBonilla (5) ... 92/1 10 11
Onega Lake (IRE) *ELellouche,France* 3-9-0 SFargeat (1) ... 101/1 20 12

M. Schwartz/Ecurie Monastic 12ran 2m06.23 TR: 123/113+/112+/110/108/107

ASCOT Tuesday, Jun 16 GOOD to FIRM

22 **Queen Anne Stks (Gr 1) (4yo+)** £167,472 1m (Str.)

11 PACO BOY (IRE) *RHannon* 4-9-0 RichardHughes (3) ... 10/3 1
CESARE *JRFanshawe* 8-9-0 JMurtagh (1) ... 11/1 1½ 2
11 AQLAAM *WJHaggas* 4-9-0 RHills (2) ... 10/1 ½ 3
Main Aim *SirMichaelStoute* 4-9-0 RyanMoore (4) ... 5/1 ½ 4
11 Dream Eater (IRE) *AMBalding* 4-9-0 (t) FrancisNorton (7) ... 20/1 4 5
1 Gladiatorus (USA) *SaeedbinSuroor* 4-9-0 AhmedAjtebi (9) ... 9/4f 13 6
Arabian Gleam *JNoseda* 5-9-0 (s) SebSanders (6) ... 25/1 3¼ 7
11 Alexandros *SaeedbinSuroor* 4-9-0 LDettori (8) ... 13/2 19 8
Mac Love *StefLiddiard* 8-9-0 MickyFenton (5) ... 33/1 3¾ 9

The Calvera Partnership No 2 9ran 1m39.31 TR: 127/123/122/120/110/75+

23 **King's Stand Stks (Gr 1) (3yo+)** £170,310 5f

SCENIC BLAST (AUS) *DMorton,Australia* 5-9-4 StevenArnold (15) ... 11/4f 1
FLEETING SPIRIT (IRE) *JNoseda* 4-9-1 RyanMoore (1) ... 7/2 ¾ 2
ANGLEZARKE (IRE) *TDEasterby* 3-8-9 DavidAllan (2) ... 33/1 2¾ 3

	Captain Gerrard (IRE) *BSmart* 4-9-4 TomEaves (7)	66/1	½ 4
	Borderlescott *RBastiman* 7-9-4 PatCosgrave (8)	10/1	nk 5
	Cannonball (USA) *WesleyAWard,USA* 4-9-4 (t) JVelazquez (4)	33/1	1¼ 6
	Dandy Man (IRE) *SaeedbinSuroor* 6-9-4 (t) LDettori (13)	20/1	½ 7
	Equiano (FR) *BWHills* 4-9-4 (b) MichaelHills (9)	14/1	½ 8
	Wi Dud *KARyan* 5-9-4 (b) AlanMunro (11)	66/1	1½ 9
	Amour Propre *HCandy* 3-8-12 DaneO'Neill (6)	4/1	hd 10
12	Mythical Flight (SAF) *SeanTarry,SouthAfrica* 6-9-4 KShea (3)	20/1	½ 11
	Spin Cycle (IRE) *BSmart* 3-8-12 RichardMullen (14)	33/1	nk 12
	Hoh Hoh Hoh *RJPrice* 7-9-4 RobertWinston (5)	33/1	1½ 13
	Tax Free (IRE) *DNicholls* 7-9-4 AdrianTNicholls (10)	12/1	4 14
	Rievaulx World *KARyan* 3-8-12 NCallan (12)	66/1	8 15

Elio Anthony Galante & Partners 15ran 59.54secs TR: 126+/120/109/112/111+/106

24 St James's Palace Stks (Gr 1) (3yo c) £141,925 1m (Rnd)

14	MASTERCRAFTSMAN (IRE) *APO'Brien,Ireland* 3-9-0 JMurtagh (8)	5/6f	1
14	DELEGATOR *BJMeehan* 3-9-0 JimmyFortune (10)	4/1	nk 2
7	LORD SHANAKILL (USA) *KRBurke* 3-9-0 JimCrowley (9)	20/1	1½ 3
7	Evasive *SirMichaelStoute* 3-9-0 RyanMoore (3)	11/2	1¾ 4
	Intense Focus (USA) *JSBolger,Ireland* 3-9-0 (v+t) KJManning (4)	12/1	1½ 5
7	Pure Poetry (IRE) *RHannon* 3-9-0 DaneO'Neill (1)	40/1	1¼ 6
	Orizaba (IRE) *SaeedbinSuroor* 3-9-0 LDettori (7)	33/1	7 7
14	Soul City (IRE) *RHannon* 3-9-0 RichardHughes (5)	16/1	10 8
9	Born To Be King (USA) *APO'Brien,Ireland* 3-9-0 CO'Donoghue (6)	200/1	12 9
20	Set Sail (IRE) *APO'Brien,Ireland* 3-9-0 JAHeffernan (2)	100/1	6 10

Mr D. Smith, Mrs J. Magnier, Mr M. Tabor 10ran 1m39.21
TR: 126/125/121/116/112/109

25 Coventry Stks (Gr 2) (2yo) £56,770 6f

	CANFORD CLIFFS (IRE) *RHannon* 2-9-1 RichardHughes (9)	7/4f	1
	XTENSION (IRE) *CGCox* 2-9-1 AdamKirby (11)	20/1	6 2
	RAKAAN (IRE) *BJMeehan* 2-9-1 JamieSpencer (8)	28/1	¾ 3
	Moran Gra (USA) *MsJoannaMorgan,Ireland* 2-9-1 KJManning (5)	20/1	1½ 4
	Treadwell (IRE) *JAOsborne* 2-9-1 ShaneKelly (12)	33/1	ns 5
	No Hubris (USA) *PFICole* 2-9-1 MartinDwyer (2)	11/2	½ 6
	Red Jazz (USA) *BWHills* 2-9-1 MichaelHills (3)	11/2	¾ 7
	Fremont (IRE) *RHannon* 2-9-1 RyanMoore (6)	20/1	1½ 8
	Alrasm (IRE) *MAJarvis* 2-9-1 RHills (4)	12/1	1¾ 9
	Flying Statesman (USA) *RAFahey* 2-9-1 PaulHanagan (10)	16/1	2¾ 10
	Air Chief Marshal (IRE) *APO'Brien,Ireland* 2-9-1 JMurtagh (1)	11/1	½ 11
	Raine's Cross *PWinkworth* 2-9-1 JimCrowley (14)	16/1	3¾ 12
	Marsh Warbler *MJohnston* 2-9-1 LDettori (13)	16/1	9 13

The Heffer Syndicate 13ran 1m13.64 TR: 119+/100/98?/93/93+/91+

ASCOT Wednesday, Jun 17 GOOD to FIRM

26 Prince of Wales's Stks (Gr 1) (4yo+) £255,465 1¼m

5	VISION D'ETAT (FR) *ELibaud,France* 4-9-0 OPeslier (7)	4/1	1
	TARTAN BEARER (IRE) *SirMichaelStoute* 4-9-0 RyanMoore (2)	6/4f	½ 2
13	NEVER ON SUNDAY (FR) *J-CRouget,France* 4-9-0 CPLemaire (5)	7/2	hd 3
11	Twice Over *HRACecil* 4-9-0 TPQueally (1)	9/1	nk 4
13	Tazeez (USA) *JHMGosden* 5-9-0 RHills (8)	16/1	3¼ 5
11	Virtual *JHMGosden* 4-9-0 JimmyFortune (3)	14/1	¾ 6
	Trincot (FR) *SaeedbinSuroor* 4-9-0 (s) LDettori (4)	16/1	4 7
	Estejo (GER) *RalfRohne,Germany* 5-9-0 DanielePorcu (6)	66/1	16 8

Mr J. Detre 8ran 2m06.90 TR: 126+/125/125/124/117/115

27 Queen Mary Stks (Gr 2) (2yo f) £51,093 5f

	JEALOUS AGAIN (USA) *WesleyAWard,USA* 2-8-12 (b+t) JVelazquez (1)	13/2	1
	MISHEER *CEBrittain* 2-8-12 NCallan (4)	9/1	5 2
	CEEDWELL *BSmart* 2-8-12 TomEaves (3)	12/1	2 3
	Capercaillie (USA) *MJohnston* 2-8-12 LDettori (11)	4/1f	ns 4
	Chantilly Creme (USA) *RGibson,France* 2-8-12 SPasquier (7)	16/1	ns 5
	Lady of The Desert (USA) *BJMeehan* 2-8-12 MartinDwyer (5)	11/2	3½ 6
	Rose Blossom *RAFahey* 2-8-12 PaulHanagan (10)	5/1	2 7
	Crown (IRE) *RHannon* 2-8-12 RichardHughes (9)	20/1	¾ 8
	High Spice (USA) *RMHCowell* 2-8-12 EddieAhern (6)	25/1	nk 9
	Don't Tell Mary (IRE) *TomDascombe* 2-8-12 RichardKingscote (12)	11/2	3¼ 10
	Grand Zafeen *MRChannon* 2-8-12 TonyCulhane (8)	33/1	1¼ 11
	Itwasonlyakiss (IRE) *JWHills* 2-8-12 MichaelHills (2)	40/1	8 12
	Lady Royal Oak (IRE) *MBotti* 2-8-12 RyanMoore (13)	33/1	11 13

R Abrams,R Brewer,M Dutko,W Ward 13ran 1m00.53 TR: 119/102/95/95/94/82+

ASCOT Thursday, Jun 18 GOOD to FIRM

28 Gold Cup (Gr 1) (4yo+) £141,925 2½m

YEATS (IRE) *APO'Brien,Ireland* 8-9-2 JMurtagh (6) 6/4f 1
PATKAI (IRE) *SirMichaelStoute* 4-9-0 RyanMoore (8) 9/2 3½ 2
GEORDIELAND (FR) *JAOsborne* 8-9-2 ShaneKelly (3) 11/4 15 3
Sagara (USA) *SaeedbinSuroor* 5-9-2 (v) TedDurcan (5) 50/1 3¼ 4
17 Eastern Anthem (IRE) *SaeedbinSuroor* 5-9-2 (t) AhmedAjtebi (1) 25/1 1¾ 5
Hindu Kush (IRE) *DNicholls* 4-9-0 JimCrowley (7) 40/1 4 6
Centennial (IRE) *JHMGosden* 4-9-0 (v) JimmyFortune (9) 33/1 12 7
Veracity *SaeedbinSuroor* 5-9-2 LDettori (4) .... 13/2 pu
Washington Irving (IRE) *JHowardJohnson* 4-9-0 PaulMulrennan (2) .... 50/1 pu
Mrs John Magnier & Mrs David Nagle 9ran 4m20.73 TR: 126/124/107+/104/102/100

ASCOT Friday, Jun 19 FIRM

29 Coronation Stks (Gr 1) (3yo f) £154,698 1m (Rnd)

8 GHANAATI (USA) *BWHills* 3-9-0 RHills (6) 2/1f 1
REGGANE *AdeRoyerDupre,France* 3-9-0 (t) GMosse (7) 9/1 2 2
18 RAINBOW VIEW (USA) *JHMGosden* 3-9-0 JimmyFortune (3) 13/2 2¼ 3
10 Elusive Wave (IRE) *J-CRouget,France* 3-9-0 CPLemaire (1) 4/1 2 4
16 Lahaleeb (IRE) *MRChannon* 3-9-0 DarryllHolland (5) .... 16/1 ns 5
8 Heart Shaped (USA) *APO'Brien,Ireland* 3-9-0 RichardHughes (9) 12/1 2½ 6
16 Again (IRE) *DavidWachman,Ireland* 3-9-0 RyanMoore (10) 8/1 11 7
8 Nashmiah (IRE) *CEBrittain* 3-9-0 NCallan (4) 50/1 3¼ 8
16 Chintz (IRE) *DavidWachman,Ireland* 3-9-0 JAHeffernan (8) 40/1 10 9
Baliyana (IRE) *JohnMOxx,Ireland* 3-9-0 MJKinane (2) 15/2 13 10
Mr Hamdan Al Maktoum 10ran 1m38.32 TR: 121+/116/109+/104/104/97

ASCOT Saturday, Jun 20 GOOD to FIRM

30 Hardwicke Stks (Gr 2) (4yo+) £70,963 1½m

BRONZE CANNON (USA) *JHMGosden* 4-9-3 JimmyFortune (3) 8/1 1
CAMPANOLOGIST (USA) *SaeedbinSuroor* 4-9-0 LDettori (9) .... 2/1f ½ 2
DANSANT *GAButler* 5-9-0 EddieAhern (1) 8/1 3 3
Enroller (IRE) *WRMuir* 4-9-0 MartinDwyer (7) 14/1 3 4
Barshiba (IRE) *DRCElsworth* 5-8-11 RichardHughes (5) .... 25/1 ½ 5
Illustrious Blue *WJKnight* 6-9-0 JimCrowley (4) .... 20/1 hd 6
Doctor Fremantle *SirMichaelStoute* 4-9-0 RyanMoore (2) 5/2 2½ 7
Steele Tango (USA) *RATeal* 4-9-0 LukeMorris (8) 11/1 2¼ 8
5 Tajaaweed (USA) *SirMichaelStoute* 4-9-0 RHills (6) 11/1 1¼ 9
Mr A. E. Oppenheimer 9ran 2m27.59 TR: 123/119/112/107/102/104

31 Golden Jubilee Stks (Gr 1) (3yo+) £278,457 6f

ART CONNOISSEUR (IRE) *MLWBell* 3-8-11 TPQueally (4) 20/1 1
23 CANNONBALL (USA) *WesleyAWard,USA* 4-9-4 (t) OPeslier (2) .... 11/1 nk 2
LESSON IN HUMILITY (IRE) *KRBurke* 4-9-1 AndrewElliott (10) 33/1 2½ 3
J J The Jet Plane (SAF) *MFdeKock,SouthAfrica* 5-9-4 KShea (9) 5/2f 1½ 4
12 Sacred Kingdom (AUS) *PFYiu,HongKong* 6-9-4 (t) BPrebble (8) .... 4/1 hd 5
12 Diabolical (USA) *SaeedbinSuroor* 6-9-4 LDettori (6) .... 12/1 sh 6
Strike The Deal (USA) *JNoseda* 4-9-4 (v) PhilipRobinson (11) .... 22/1 nk 7
Duff (IRE) *EdwardLynam,Ireland* 6-9-4 KJManning (1) .... 25/1 ¾ 8
Regal Parade *DNicholls* 5-9-4 AdrianTNicholls (13) .... 66/1 sh 9
King's Apostle (IRE) *WJHaggas* 5-9-4 (v) LiamJones (12) 12/1 1 10
Bushranger (IRE) *DavidWachman,Ireland* 3-8-11 (v) PJSmullen (3) .... 12/1 ½ 11
Ialysos (GR) *LMCumani* 5-9-4 WilliamBuick (5) 7/1 18 12
Kingsgate Native (IRE) *SirMichaelStoute* 4-9-4 RyanMoore (14) 9/1 3¾ 13
Intrepid Jack *HMorrison* 7-9-4 GeorgeBaker (15) 50/1 7 14
Mr R. A. Green 14ran 1m14.90 TR: 121/122/112/110/110/109+

CURRAGH Sunday, Jun 28 GOOD

32 Dubai Duty Free Irish Derby (Gr 1) (3yo c+f) £714,407 1½m

19 FAME AND GLORY *APO'Brien* 3-9-0 JMurtagh (12) 8/11f 1
19 GOLDEN SWORD *APO'Brien* 3-9-0 CO'Donoghue (7) 11/1 5 2
MOURAYAN (IRE) *JohnMOxx* 3-9-0 (b) MJKinane (10) 8/1 1 3
19 Masterofthehorse (IRE) *APO'Brien* 3-9-0 JAHeffernan (3) 9/2 10 4
14 Recharge (IRE) *KevinPrendergast* 3-9-0 CDHayes (2) 20/1 8 5
19 Gan Amhras (IRE) *JSBolger* 3-9-0 KJManning (8) 10/1 2½ 6
The Bull Hayes (IRE) *MrsJHarrington* 3-9-0 (s) FMBerry (6) .... 40/1 ½ 7
Loch Long (IRE) *MissTAMCollins* 3-9-0 PShanahan (5) .... 100/1 sh 8
Rockhampton (IRE) *APO'Brien* 3-9-0 SMLevey (13) 200/1 3 9
Byzantine *APO'Brien* 3-9-0 JPO'Brien (9) 200/1 25 10
20 Drumbeat (IRE) *APO'Brien* 3-9-0 PJSmullen (1) 50/1 13 11
Mr Derrick Smith 11ran 2m30.87 TR: 130+/122/121/106/93+/89

SAINT-CLOUD Sunday, Jun 28 GOOD to FIRM

	Grand Prix de Saint-Cloud (Gr 1) (4yo+) £193,695		1½m
33			
2	SPANISH MOON (USA) *SirMichaelStoute,GB* 5-9-2 RyanMoore	8/1	1
	ALPINE ROSE (FR) *AdeRoyerDupre,France* 4-8-13 GMosse	35/4	1½ 2
17	YOUMZAIN (IRE) *MRChannon,GB* 6-9-2 CSoumillon	8/10f	1½ 3
13	Curtain Call (FR) *LMCumani,GB* 4-9-2 CPLemaire	39/1	sn 4
	Magadan (IRE) *ELellouche,France* 4-9-2 ACrastus	21/4	hd 5
	Ideal World (USA) *AFabre,France* 4-9-2 SPasquier	17/1	¾ 6
	Scintillo *RHannon,GB* 4-9-2 RichardHughes	13/1	15 7
	Full of Gold (FR) *MmeCHead-Maarek,France* 4-9-2 DBoeuf	13/1	1½ 8
	Dream Desert (IRE) *MRChannon,GB* 4-9-2 SamHitchcott	80/1	1½ 9
	Petrograd (IRE) *ELellouche,France* 8-9-2 (s) DBonilla	63/1	dist 10

Mr K. Abdulla 10ran 2m27.40 TR: 123/118+/117/118/118/116

SANDOWN Saturday, Jul 4 GOOD to FIRM

	Coral-Eclipse (Gr 1) (3yo+) £283,850		1¼m7y
34			
19	SEA THE STARS (IRE) *JohnMOxx,Ireland* 3-8-10 MJKinane (5)	4/7f	1
19	RIP VAN WINKLE (IRE) *APO'Brien,Ireland* 3-8-10 JimmyFortune (6)	11/2	1 2
	CONDUIT (IRE) *SirMichaelStoute* 4-9-7 RyanMoore (9)	9/2	4½ 3
5	Cima de Triomphe (IRE) *LMCumani* 4-9-7 CPLemaire (2)	11/1	5 4
30	Steele Tango (USA) *RATeal* 4-9-7 DarryllHolland (1)	100/1	3¾ 5
	Jukebox Jury (IRE) *MJohnston* 3-8-10 RoystonFfrench (3)	50/1	½ 6
26	Twice Over *HRACecil* 4-9-7 TPQueally (8)	14/1	2½ 7
20	Malibu Bay (USA) *APO'Brien,Ireland* 3-8-10 CO'Donoghue (4)	100/1	11 8
	Lang Shining (IRE) *SirMichaelStoute* 5-9-7 RichardHughes (10)	150/1	6 9
24	Set Sail (IRE) *APO'Brien,Ireland* 3-8-10 JAHeffernan (7)	200/1	1½ 10

Mr Christopher Tsui 10ran 2m03.40 TR: 136+/134/125/113/105/101

NEWMARKET Friday, Jul 10 GOOD to FIRM (July Course)

	Darley July Cup (Gr 1) (3yo+) £227,080		6f
35			
23	FLEETING SPIRIT (IRE) *JNoseda* 4-9-2 TPQueally (9)	12/1	1
22	MAIN AIM *SirMichaelStoute* 4-9-5 RyanMoore (10)	14/1	1¼ 2
31	J J THE JET PLANE (SAF) *MFdeKock,SouthAfrica* 5-9-5 KShea (5)	13/2	½ 3
22	Paco Boy (IRE) *RHannon* 4-9-5 JimmyFortune (1)	9/2	1 4
31	King's Apostle (IRE) *WJHaggas* 5-9-5 JMurtagh (13)	20/1	nk 5
	African Rose *MmeCHead-Maarek,France* 4-9-2 SPasquier (11)	25/1	hd 6
12	Takeover Target (AUS) *JoeJaniak,Australia* 10-9-5 JFord (8)	16/1	1¼ 7
23	Equiano (FR) *BWHills* 4-9-5 (b) MichaelHills (7)	66/1	1¼ 8
12	Prime Defender *BWHills* 5-9-5 RHills (3)	66/1	sh 9
23	Scenic Blast (AUS) *DMorton,Australia* 5-9-5 StevenArnold (2)	11/8f	1 10
31	Intrepid Jack *HMorrison* 7-9-5 JimCrowley (6)	125/1	1 11
31	Art Connoisseur (IRE) *MLWBell* 3-8-13 JamieSpencer (4)	12/1	12 12
	Ancien Regime (IRE) *SaeedbinSuroor* 4-9-5 LDettori (12)	25/1	6 13

The Searchers 13ran 1m09.58 TR: 124/123/121/117+/116+/113

CURRAGH Sunday, Jul 12 HEAVY

	Darley Irish Oaks (Gr 1) (3yo f) £239,744		1½m
36			
18	SARISKA *MLWBell,GB* 3-9-0 JamieSpencer (3)	1/1f	1
	ROSES FOR THE LADY (IRE) *JohnMOxx* 3-9-0 FMBerry (9)	25/1	3 2
18	MIDDAY *HRACecil,GB* 3-9-0 TPQueally (1)	9/2	4½ 3
	Grace O'Malley (IRE) *DKWeld* 3-9-0 PJSmullen (6)	12/1	4 4
18	Oh Goodness Me *JSBolger* 3-9-0 KJManning (4)	10/1	4½ 5
	Roman Empress (IRE) *APO'Brien* 3-9-0 JMurtagh (2)	16/1	3½ 6
	Rory Anna (IRE) *JohnJWalsh* 3-9-0 RPCleary (11)	150/1	15 7
	Chirkova (USA) *APO'Brien* 3-9-0 JAHeffernan (10)	50/1	10 8
	Belle Chose (IRE) *JohnJosephMurphy* 3-9-0 DMGrant (8)	66/1	25 9
	Beauty O' Gwaun (IRE) *JohnMOxx* 3-9-0 (b) MJKinane (7)	4/1	22 10

Lady Bamford 10ran 2m45.84 TR: 122+/117/110/104+/97+/91

LONGCHAMP Tuesday, Jul 14 GOOD

	Juddmonte Grand Prix de Paris (Gr 1) (3yo) £295,552		1½m
37			
	CAVALRYMAN *AFabre,France* 3-9-2 MGuyon	34/10	1
19	AGE OF AQUARIUS (IRE) *APO'Brien,Ireland* 3-9-2 JMurtagh	12/1	1½ 2
	MASTERY *SaeedbinSuroor,GB* 3-9-2 LDettori	13/2	2 3
	Freemantle *APO'Brien,Ireland* 3-9-2 JAHeffernan	47/1	sn 4
20	Wajir (FR) *ELellouche,France* 3-9-2 ACrastus	10/1	nk 5
20	Beheshtam (FR) *AdeRoyerDupre,France* 3-9-2 CSoumillon	8/10f	1½ 6
19	Black Bear Island (IRE) *APO'Brien,Ireland* 3-9-2 CO'Donoghue	28/1	3 7
14	Hail Caesar (IRE) *APO'Brien,Ireland* 3-9-2 (b) SMLevey	37/1	dist 8

Sheikh Mohammed 8ran 2m27.60 TR: 121/118/114/114/113/110+

ASCOT Saturday, Jul 25 GOOD to FIRM

38 King George VI and Queen Elizabeth Stks (Sponsored By Betfair) (Gr 1) (3yo+) £567,700 1½m

34	CONDUIT (IRE) *SirMichaelStoute* 4-9-7 RyanMoore (2)	13/8f		1
26	TARTAN BEARER (IRE) *SirMichaelStoute* 4-9-7 MJKinane (4)	7/2	1¾	2
17	ASK *SirMichaelStoute* 6-9-7 OPeslier (7)	9/1	hd	3
	Alwaary (USA) *JHMGosden* 3-8-9 RHills (3)	12/1	2¼	4
32	Golden Sword *APO'Brien,Ireland* 3-8-9 JMurtagh (1)	9/2	4	5
17	Look Here *RMBeckett* 4-9-4 SebSanders (8)	7/1	2½	6
17	Frozen Fire (GER) *APO'Brien,Ireland* 4-9-7 JAHeffernan (6)	20/1	2	7
32	Rockhampton (IRE) *APO'Brien,Ireland* 3-8-9 CO'Donoghue (5)	125/1	8	8
33	Scintillo *RHannon* 4-9-7 RichardHughes (9)	66/1	dist	9

Ballymacoll Stud 9ran 2m28.73 TR: 130/126/126/122/114/106

GOODWOOD Wednesday, Jul 29 GOOD

39 BGC Sussex Stks (Gr 1) (3yo+) £170,310 1m

34	RIP VAN WINKLE (IRE) *APO'Brien,Ireland* 3-8-13 JMurtagh (2)	6/4f		1
35	PACO BOY (IRE) *RHannon* 4-9-7 RichardHughes (7)	7/2	2½	2
29	GHANAATI (USA) *BWHills* 3-8-10 RHills (5)	2/1	4	3
	Forgotten Voice (IRE) *JNoseda* 4-9-7 LDettori (8)	16/1	1¼	4
24	Lord Shanakill (USA) *APJarvis* 3-8-13 JimCrowley (6)	12/1	1¼	5
	Beacon Lodge (IRE) *CGCox* 4-9-7 AdamKirby (3)	33/1	2¾	6
	Mia's Boy *CADwyer* 5-9-7 RyanMoore (1)	50/1	7	7
34	Malibu Bay (USA) *APO'Brien,Ireland* 3-8-13 SeanLevey (4)	100/1	dist	8

Mrs John Magnier,Mr M.Tabor & Mr D.Smith 8ran 1m37.16
TR: 134/129/113/114/109/103

GOODWOOD Thursday, Jul 30 GOOD

40 Audi Stks (King George) (Gr 3) (3yo+) £39,739 5f

31	KINGSGATE NATIVE (IRE) *SirMichaelStoute* 4-9-0 RyanMoore (2)	7/1		1
	TOTAL GALLERY (IRE) *JSMoore* 3-8-10 RichardHughes (1)	16/1	2¾	2
	INXILE (IRE) *DNicholls* 4-9-0 AdrianTNicholls (3)	8/1	1½	3
23	Borderlescott *RBastiman* 7-9-0 PatCosgrave (16)	9/4f	sh	4
23	Dandy Man (IRE) *SaeedbinSuroor* 6-9-0 (t) LDettori (6)	16/1	sh	5
	Rowe Park *MrsLCJewell* 6-9-0 SteveDrowne (11)	28/1	1	6
23	Spin Cycle (IRE) *BSmart* 3-8-10 RichardMullen (8)	33/1	nk	7
35	Equiano (FR) *BWHills* 4-9-0 MichaelHills (10)	14/1	ns	8
	Reverence *EJAlston* 8-9-0 EddieAhern (5)	40/1	hd	9
	Sugar Free (IRE) *TStack,Ireland* 3-8-7 WMLordan (13)	16/1	1	10
	Moorhouse Lad *BSmart* 6-9-0 TomEaves (12)	12/1	2¼	11
	Fat Boy (IRE) *PWChapple-Hyam* 4-9-0 JimmyFortune (15)	20/1	nk	12
31	Ialysos (GR) *LMCumani* 5-9-5 GMosse (14)	6/1	½	13
	Matsunosuke *ABCoogan* 7-9-0 LukeMorris (9)	66/1	½	14
	Siren's Gift *AMBalding* 5-8-11 (b) WilliamBuick (18)	33/1	3½	15
	Jargelle (IRE) *KARyan* 3-8-7 AlanMunro (7)	66/1	11	16
23	Rievaulx World *KARyan* 3-8-10 NCallan (4)	66/1	4½	17

Cheveley Park Stud 17ran 57.96secs TR: 124/113+/111/111+/110/107+

GOODWOOD Saturday, Aug 1 GOOD to SOFT

41 Blue Square Nassau Stks (Gr 1) (3yo+ f+m) £113,540 1m1f192y

36	MIDDAY *HRACecil* 3-8-10 TPQueally (1)	11/2		1
29	RAINBOW VIEW (USA) *JHMGosden* 3-8-10 JimmyFortune (9)	5/2f	2¼	2
	MONEYCANTBUYMELOVE (IRE) *MLWBell* 3-8-10 JamieSpencer (4)	17/2	½	3
30	Barshiba (IRE) *DRCElsworth* 5-9-5 PaulHanagan (5)	14/1	2¼	4
18	High Heeled (IRE) *BWHills* 3-8-10 MichaelHills (8)	8/1	nk	5
	Katiyra (IRE) *JohnMOxx,Ireland* 4-9-5 MJKinane (10)	7/2	2½	6
	Heaven Sent *SirMichaelStoute* 6-9-5 RyanMoore (3)	8/1	5	7
	Saphira's Fire (IRE) *WRMuir* 4-9-5 MartinDwyer (2)	50/1	3½	8
	Spacious *JRFanshawe* 4-9-5 LDettori (6)	11/1	3¼	9
29	Nashmiah (IRE) *CEBrittain* 3-8-10 NCallan (7)	50/1	7	10

Mr K. Abdulla 10ran 2m09.42 TR: 122/117/116/112/111/107

DEAUVILLE Sunday, Aug 2 GOOD to SOFT

42 Prix Rothschild (Ex Prix d'Astarte) (Gr 1) (3yo+ f+m) £123,147 1m

13	GOLDIKOVA (IRE) *FHead,France* 4-9-0 OPeslier	9/10f		1
29	ELUSIVE WAVE (IRE) *J-CRouget,France* 3-8-7 CPLemaire	7/1	1½	2
13	PROVISO *AFabre,France* 4-9-0 SPasquier	38/1	3	3
	Sahpresa (USA) *RodolpheCollet,France* 4-9-0 CSoumillon	11/1	½	4
	Eva's Request (IRE) *MRChannon,GB* 4-9-0 TThulliez	88/1	¾	5
29	Reggane *AdeRoyerDupre,France* 3-8-7 GMosse	5/1	¾	6

1 Lady Marian (GER) *SaeedbinSuroor,GB* 4-9-0 LDettori .... 9/1 sn 7
29 Lahaleeb (IRE) *MRChannon,GB* 3-8-7 DarryllHolland 34/1 2 8
Danse Grecque (USA) *ELellouche,France* 4-9-0 ACrastus 26/1 2½ 9
Testama (FR) *JeandeRoualle,France* 5-9-0 JAuge 76/1 5 10
Only Green (IRE) *FHead,France* 3-8-7 (b) DBonilla .... 53/1 ns 11
Homebound (USA) *J-CRouget,France* 3-8-7 IMendizabal .... 20/1 ½ 12
Wertheimer et Frere 12ran 1m35.70 TR: 125+/120/112/111/109/106

ARLINGTON Saturday, Aug 8 GOOD

43 Arlington Million Stks (Gr 1) (3yo+) £354,217 1¼m

GIO PONTI (USA) *CClement,USA* 4-9-0 RADominguez 15/10f 1
JUST AS WELL (USA) *JESheppard,USA* 6-9-0 EBaird 191/10 1¼ 2
4 STOTSFOLD *WRSwinburn,GB* 6-9-0 AdamKirby .... 287/10 hd 3
34 Cima de Triomphe (IRE) *LMCumani,GB* 4-9-0 CPLemaire 84/10 6 4
Einstein (BRZ) *HelenPitts,USA* 7-9-0 JLeparoux 3/1 1¼ 5
Mr Sidney (USA) *WIMott,USA* 5-9-0 (b) KDesormeaux .... 67/10 ns 6
3 Gloria de Campeao (BRZ) *PBary,France* 6-9-0 TPereira .... 113/10 ½ 7
Presious Passion (USA) *MaryHartmann,USA* 6-9-0 (b) ETrujillo 49/10 3 8
Castleton Lyons Inc 8ran 2m04.19 TR: 121/118/118/104/101/101

DEAUVILLE Sunday, Aug 9 GOOD

44 Prix Maurice de Gheest (Gr 1) (3yo+) £122,094 6f110y

35 KING'S APOSTLE (IRE) *WJHaggas,GB* 5-9-2 RyanMoore (7) 14/1 1
MARIOL (FR) *RCollet,France* 6-9-2 CPLemaire (10) .... 45/1 ½ 2
31 LESSON IN HUMILITY (IRE) *APJarvis,GB* 4-8-13 AndrewElliott (9) .... 13/1 hd 3
Varenar (FR) *AdeRoyerDupre,France* 3-8-11 CSoumillon (4) .... 10/1 nk 4
Sayif (IRE) *PWChapple-Hyam,GB* 3-8-11 JamieSpencer (8) .... 71/1 hd 5
Dunkerque (FR) *MmeCHead-Maarek,France* 4-9-2 (s) DBoeuf (11) 16/1 1½ 6
Tiza (SAF) *AdeRoyerDupre,France* 7-9-2 GMosse (12) .... 22/1 nk 7
8 Serious Attitude (IRE) *RaeGuest,GB* 3-8-8 EddieAhern (1) 58/10 2½ 8
Asset (IRE) *SaeedbinSuroor,GB* 6-9-2 (b) LDettori (5) .... 10/1 hd 9
9 Naaqoos *FHead,France* 3-8-11 DBonilla (3) 2/1f 1½ 10
35 African Rose *MmeCHead-Maarek,France* 4-8-13 SPasquier (6) 55/10 1½ 11
Delvita (FR) *J-VToux,France* 5-8-13 OPeslier (2) 17/1 1½ 12
Mr Bernard Kantor 12ran 1m15.70 TR: 120/118/115/116/115/112

COLOGNE Sunday, Aug 16 GOOD

45 Rheinland-Pokal (Gr 1) (3yo+) £85,740 1½m

WIENER WALZER (GER) *JHirschberger,Germany* 3-8-10 FJohansson ... 18/10 1
GETAWAY (GER) *JHirschberger,Germany* 6-9-6 AdeVries .... 15/10f sh 2
28 EASTERN ANTHEM (IRE) *SaeedbinSuroor,GB* 5-9-6 AhmedAjtebi 48/10 2½ 3
Schiller Danon (GER) *WHickst,Germany* 3-8-10 EPedroza 159/10 2 4
Saphir (GER) *PSchiergen,Germany* 3-8-10 FMinarik 197/10 2½ 5
Poseidon Adventure (IRE) *WFigge,Germany* 6-9-6 (b) KKerekes 140/10 3 6
Flamingo Fantasy (GER) *WHickst,Germany* 4-9-6 ASuborics 37/10 6 7
Gestut Schlenderhan 7ran 2m29.89 TR: 124/123/118/114/110/103

DEAUVILLE Sunday, Aug 16 GOOD to FIRM

46 Prix du Haras de Fresnay-Le-Buffard - Jacques le Marois (Gr 1) (3yo+) £293,026 1m

42 GOLDIKOVA (IRE) *FHead,France* 4-9-0 OPeslier 8/10f 1
22 AQLAAM *WJHaggas,GB* 4-9-3 RHills 17/1 6 2
26 VIRTUAL *JHMGosden,GB* 4-9-3 JimmyFortune 27/1 5 3
Irian (GER) *JHirschberger,Germany* 3-8-11 SPasquier 13/1 1 4
13 Runaway *RupertPritchard-Gordon,France* 7-9-3 TJarnet .... 55/1 nk 5
20 Silver Frost (IRE) *YdeNicolay,France* 3-8-11 CSoumillon 58/10 2 6
26 Never On Sunday (FR) *J-CRouget,France* 4-9-3 CPLemaire .... 9/1 sn 7
22 Gladiatorus (USA) *SaeedbinSuroor,GB* 4-9-3 LDettori 55/10 6 8
42 Only Green (IRE) *FHead,France* 3-8-8 (b) DBonilla 45/1 20 9
Wertheimer et Frere 9ran 1m33.50 TR: 133/122/109/106/105/101

YORK Tuesday, Aug 18 GOOD to FIRM

47 Ladbrokes Great Voltigeur Stks (Gr 2) (3yo c+g) £82,964 1½m

7 MONITOR CLOSELY (IRE) *PWChapple-Hyam* 3-8-12 JimmyFortune (5) 28/1 1
37 MASTERY *SaeedbinSuroor* 3-9-1 LDettori (1) 12/1 4½ 2
FATHER TIME *HRACecil* 3-9-1 EddieAhern (4) 7/2 1¼ 3
34 Jukebox Jury (IRE) *MJohnston* 3-8-12 RoystonFfrench (6) 5/1 2¾ 4
Above Average (IRE) *BWHills* 3-8-12 MichaelHills (7) 66/1 3½ 5
38 Alwaary (USA) *JHMGosden* 3-8-12 RHills (2) 7/2 3¼ 6
Harbinger *SirMichaelStoute* 3-8-12 RyanMoore (3) 13/8f 12 7
Mr Lawrie Inman 7ran 2m29.50 TR: 122/116/114/105/98/92

48 Juddmonte International Stks (Gr 1) (3yo+) £340,620 — 1¼m88y

	Horse / Trainer / Age-Wt / Jockey (draw)	SP	Dist	Pos
34	SEA THE STARS (IRE) *JohnMOxx,Ireland* 3-8-11 MJKinane (3)	1/4f		1
24	MASTERCRAFTSMAN (IRE) *APO'Brien,Ireland* 3-8-11 JMurtagh (2)	3/1	1	2
34	SET SAIL (IRE) *APO'Brien,Ireland* 3-8-11 JAHeffernan (5)	125/1	dist	3
	Georgebernardshaw (IRE) *APO'Brien,Ireland* 4-9-5 CO'Donoghue (1)	100/1	3½	4

Mr Christopher Tsui 4ran 2m05.29 — TR: 131+/129

YORK Thursday, Aug 20 GOOD to FIRM

49 Darley Yorkshire Oaks (Gr 1) (3yo+ f+m) £175,987 — 1½m

	Horse / Trainer / Age-Wt / Jockey (draw)	SP	Dist	Pos
	DAR RE MI *JHMGosden* 4-9-7 JimmyFortune (4)	11/2		1
36	SARISKA *MLWBell* 3-8-11 JamieSpencer (6)	4/11f	¾	2
36	ROMAN EMPRESS (IRE) *APO'Brien,Ireland* 3-8-11 JAHeffernan (5)	40/1	1½	3
41	Barshiba (IRE) *DRCElsworth* 5-9-7 RyanMoore (3)	12/1	1	4
	Tamarind (IRE) *APO'Brien,Ireland* 3-8-11 JMurtagh (2)	11/1	7	5
41	Saphira's Fire (IRE) *WRMuir* 4-9-7 MartinDwyer (1)	50/1	6	6

Lord Lloyd-Webber 6ran 2m30.98 — TR: 118/117/114/112/98/86

YORK Friday, Aug 21 GOOD to FIRM

50 Coolmore Nunthorpe Stks (Gr 1) (2yo+) £136,248 — 5f

	Horse / Trainer / Age-Wt / Jockey (draw)	SP	Dist	Pos
40	BORDERLESCOTT *RBastiman* 7-9-11 NCallan (2)	9/1		1
	BENBAUN (IRE) *KARyan* 8-9-11 (v) JoeFanning (11)	25/1	nk	2
	RADIOHEAD *BJMeehan* 2-8-1 (t) MartinDwyer (9)	9/2	1¼	3
23	Tax Free (IRE) *DNicholls* 7-9-11 AdrianTNicholls (1)	12/1	hd	4
23	Amour Propre *HCandy* 3-9-9 DaneO'Neill (3)	6/1	sh	5
40	Kingsgate Native (IRE) *SirMichaelStoute* 4-9-11 RyanMoore (7)	5/2f	1	6
40	Dandy Man (IRE) *SaeedbinSuroor* 6-9-11 (t) LDettori (10)	14/1	1¼	7
40	Equiano (FR) *BWHills* 4-9-11 MichaelHills (12)	18/1	ns	8
40	Moorhouse Lad *BSmart* 6-9-11 JimCrowley (8)	25/1	¾	9
40	Ialysos (GR) *LMCumani* 5-9-11 JimmyFortune (4)	16/1	hd	10
	Look Busy (IRE) *ABerry* 4-9-8 SladeO'Hara (17)	20/1	2	11
23	Mythical Flight (SAF) *SeanTarry,SouthAfrica* 6-9-11 KShea (5)	28/1	½	12
23	Captain Gerrard (IRE) *BSmart* 4-9-11 TomEaves (14)	33/1	1½	13
	Excellerator (IRE) *GeorgeBaker* 3-9-6 (v+t) DO'Donohoe (15)	80/1	1½	14
35	Art Connoisseur (IRE) *MLWBell* 3-9-9 HayleyTurner (6)	18/1	7	15
	Mythical Border (USA) *JNoseda* 3-9-6 WilliamBuick (16)	80/1	17	16

James Edgar & William Donaldson 16ran 57.50secs — TR: 123/122/110+/117/116/113

DEAUVILLE Sunday, Aug 23 GOOD to FIRM

51 Darley Prix Morny (Gr 1) (2yo) £172,405 — 6f

	Horse / Trainer / Age-Wt / Jockey	SP	Dist	Pos
	ARCANO (IRE) *BJMeehan,GB* 2-9-0 RHills	45/10		1
	SPECIAL DUTY *MmeCHead-Maarek,France* 2-8-11 SPasquier	43/10	sn	2
25	CANFORD CLIFFS (IRE) *RHannon,GB* 2-9-0 RichardHughes	8/10f	nk	3
	Dolled Up (IRE) *RCollet,France* 2-8-11 OPeslier	15/1	nk	4
	Zanzibari (USA) *AFabre,France* 2-9-0 LDettori	48/10	hd	5

Mr Hamdan Al Maktoum 5ran 1m07.90 — TR: 115+/111+/113+/109/112

GOODWOOD Saturday, Aug 29 GOOD

52 totesport.com Celebration Mile (Gr 2) (3yo+) £67,443 — 1m

Delegator was disqualified after failing a dope test

	Horse / Trainer / Age-Wt / Jockey (draw)	SP	Dist	Pos
24	DELEGATOR *SaeedbinSuroor* 3-8-9 LDettori (5)	4/6f		1
	ZACINTO *SirMichaelStoute* 3-8-9 RyanMoore (2)	5/2	1½	2
	ORDNANCE ROW *RHannon* 6-9-1 DaneO'Neill (4)	33/1	hd	3
39	Beacon Lodge (IRE) *CGCox* 4-9-1 AdamKirby (6)	16/1	½	4
22	Mac Love *StefLiddiard* 8-9-1 MickyFenton (1)	14/1	½	5
22	Cesare *JRFanshawe* 8-9-1 EddieAhern (3)	16/1	1	6
	Smokey Oakey (IRE) *MHTompkins* 5-9-1 RobertWinston (7)	66/1	4½	7

Mr K. Abdulla 7ran 1m41.54 — TR: 121+/117+/118/117+/115/113

CURRAGH Sunday, Aug 30 HEAVY

53 Moyglare Stud Stks (Gr 1) (2yo f) £128,348 — 7f

	Horse / Trainer / Age-Wt / Jockey (draw)	SP	Dist	Pos
	TERMAGANT (IRE) *KevinPrendergast* 2-8-12 DPMcDonogh (1)	16/1		1
	FAMOUS (IRE) *APO'Brien* 2-8-12 JAHeffernan (3)	66/1	2½	2
	LILLIE LANGTRY (IRE) *APO'Brien* 2-8-12 JMurtagh (7)	8/11f	1¾	3
	Long Lashes (USA) *SaeedbinSuroor,GB* 2-8-12 LDettori (2)	5/2	8	4
	Gile Na Greine (IRE) *JSBolger* 2-8-12 KJManning (5)	13/2	2	5
	Gold Bubbles (USA) *JSBolger* 2-8-12 (b) DJMoran (6)	66/1	5	6
	Wrong Answer *KevinPrendergast* 2-8-12 CDHayes (4)	16/1	1¼	7

Mr J. Vasicek 7ran 1m35.18 — TR: 111/104/100/79+/74

HAYDOCK Saturday, Sep 5 GOOD to SOFT

54 Betfred Sprint Cup (Gr 1) (3yo+) £163,810 6f

31	REGAL PARADE *DNicholls* 5-9-3 AdrianTNicholls (13)	14/1	1
35	FLEETING SPIRIT (IRE) *JNoseda* 4-9-0 TPQueally (12)	10/3f	½ 2
	HIGH STANDING (USA) *WJHaggas* 4-9-3 KFallon (8)	4/1	2 3
44	Sayif (IRE) *PWChapple-Hyam* 3-9-1 NCallan (10)	28/1	½ 4
50	Equiano (FR) *BWHills* 4-9-3 OPeslier (5)	33/1	2¼ 5
44	Asset (IRE) *SaeedbinSuroor* 6-9-3 (b) TedDurcan (4)	20/1	½ 6
	Corrybrough *HCandy* 4-9-3 DaneO'Neill (7)	20/1	½ 7
7	Finjaan *MPTregoning* 3-9-1 RHills (11)	7/1	1¾ 8
31	Bushranger (IRE) *DavidWachman,Ireland* 3-9-1 WMLordan (1)	28/1	nk 9
	Judd Street *EveJohnsonHoughton* 7-9-3 (v) ShaneKelly (9)	100/1	½ 10
	Al Qasi (IRE) *PWChapple-Hyam* 6-9-3 GMosse (14)	33/1	2 11
50	Art Connoisseur (IRE) *MLWBell* 3-9-1 HayleyTurner (6)	33/1	7 12
35	Main Aim *SirMichaelStoute* 4-9-3 SPasquier (3)	9/2	9 13
35	J J The Jet Plane (SAF) *RHannon* 5-9-3 JimCrowley (2)	6/1	7 14

Dab Hand Racing 14ran 1m13.74 TR: 123/118+/115/114/107/105

LEOPARDSTOWN Saturday, Sep 5 GOOD to SOFT

55 Tattersalls Millions Irish Champion Stks (Gr 1) (3yo+) £518,646 1¼m

48	SEA THE STARS (IRE) *JohnMOxx* 3-9-0 MJKinane (2)	4/6f	1
32	FAME AND GLORY *APO'Brien* 3-9-0 JMurtagh (5)	9/4	2½ 2
48	MASTERCRAFTSMAN (IRE) *APO'Brien* 3-9-0 JAHeffernan (7)	6/1	2½ 3
	Grand Ducal (IRE) *APO'Brien* 3-9-0 CO'Donoghue (1)	100/1	9 4
	Lord Admiral (USA) *CharlesO'Brien* 8-9-7 (b) DPMcDonogh (9)	150/1	4½ 5
32	Loch Long (IRE) *MissTAMCollins* 3-9-0 PShanahan (8)	150/1	5 6
15	Casual Conquest (IRE) *DKWeld* 4-9-7 (b+t) PJSmullen (3)	16/1	½ 7
38	Rockhampton (IRE) *APO'Brien* 3-9-0 SMLevey (6)	150/1	19 8
48	Set Sail (IRE) *APO'Brien* 3-9-0 JPO'Brien (4)	150/1	4 9

Mr Christopher Tsui 9ran 2m03.90 TR: 138+/133/128/112/104/94

BADEN-BADEN Sunday, Sep 6 GOOD to SOFT

56 Grosser Mercedes-Benz Preis von Baden (Gr 1) (3yo+) £132,743 1½m

45	GETAWAY (GER) *JHirschberger,Germany* 6-9-6 AdeVries	2/1f	1
45	EASTERN ANTHEM (IRE) *SaeedbinSuroor,GB* 5-9-6 LDettori	9/2	3 2
33	YOUMZAIN (IRE) *MRChannon,GB* 6-9-6 KFallon	13/5	½ 3
45	Wiener Walzer (GER) *JHirschberger,Germany* 3-8-11 FMinarik	12/5	1½ 4
	Kamsin (GER) *PSchiergen,Germany* 4-9-6 AStarke	63/10	3 5
	Adelar (GER) *WernerBaltromei,Germany* 4-9-6 DBoeuf	115/10	1¾ 6

Baron G. von Ullmann 6ran 2m36.06 TR: 127/122/121/118/113/109

LONGCHAMP Sunday, Sep 6 GOOD

57 Prix du Moulin de Longchamp (Gr 1) (3yo+) £202,265 1m

46	AQLAAM *WJHaggas,GB* 4-9-2 RHills	38/10	1
15	FAMOUS NAME *DKWeld,Ireland* 4-9-2 PJSmullen	3/1	1½ 2
46	VIRTUAL *JHMGosden,GB* 4-9-2 JimmyFortune	10/1	2½ 3
9	Oiseau de Feu (USA) *J-CRouget,France* 3-8-12 IMendizabal	10/1	½ 4
46	Gladiatorus (USA) *SaeedbinSuroor,GB* 4-9-2 AhmedAjtebi	27/1	sh 5
20	Calvados Blues (FR) *AFabre,France* 3-8-12 MGuyon	21/1	½ 6
	Balthazaar's Gift (IRE) *CGCox,GB* 6-9-2 PhilipRobinson	21/1	8 7
	Summer Fete (IRE) *BSmart,GB* 3-8-8 RichardMullen	58/1	nk 8
42	Elusive Wave (IRE) *J-CRouget,France* 3-8-8 CPLemaire	3/2f	rtr

Mr Hamdan Al Maktoum 9ran 1m38.87 TR: 125/121/115/115/114/113

DONCASTER Saturday, Sep 12 GOOD to FIRM

58 Ladbrokes St Leger Stks (Gr 1) (3yo c+f) £306,586 1¾m132y

47	MASTERY *SaeedbinSuroor* 3-9-0 TedDurcan (7)	14/1	1
19	KITE WOOD (IRE) *SaeedbinSuroor* 3-9-0 LDettori (4)	9/4f	¾ 2
47	MONITOR CLOSELY (IRE) *PWChapple-Hyam* 3-9-0 JimmyFortune (2)	7/2	1¾ 3
47	Father Time *HRACecil* 3-9-0 JamieSpencer (5)	7/1	1 4
32	Mourayan (IRE) *JohnMOxx,Ireland* 3-9-0 (b) FMBerry (8)	6/1	sh 5
	Changingoftheguard (IRE) *APO'Brien,Ireland* 3-9-0 JMurtagh (3)	3/1	2¼ 6
47	Above Average (IRE) *BWHills* 3-9-0 MichaelHills (6)	50/1	4½ 7
	Von Jawlensky (IRE) *APO'Brien,Ireland* 3-9-0 CO'Donoghue (1)	80/1	dist 8

Godolphin 8ran 3m04.81 TR: 122/121/118+/117/116+/113

59 DFS Park Stks (Gr 2) (3yo+) £90,832 7f

31	DUFF (IRE) *EdwardLynam,Ireland* 6-9-4 FMBerry (6)	7/1	1
	CAT JUNIOR (USA) *BJMeehan* 4-9-4 (t) JamieSpencer (3)	5/1	nk 2
22	ARABIAN GLEAM *JNoseda* 5-9-4 (s) JMurtagh (1)	11/2	hd 3

7 Ouqba *BWHills* 3-9-0 RHills (4) .... 4/1 nk 4
Stimulation (IRE) *HMorrison* 4-9-4 DarryllHolland (5) 7/4f 1¾ 5
Himalya (IRE) *JNoseda* 3-9-0 LDettori (2) .... 10/1 dist 6
Kilboy Estate 6ran 1m24.38 TR: 122/121/121/119/114

CURRAGH Saturday, Sep 12 SOFT

60 Irish Field St Leger (Gr 1) (3yo+) £139,174 1¾m

ALANDI (IRE) *JohnMOxx* 4-9-11 MJKinane (8) 3/1 1
CLOWANCE *RCharlton,GB* 4-9-8 KJManning (1) .... 25/1 ½ 2
SCHIAPARELLI (GER) *SaeedbinSuroor,GB* 6-9-11 OPeslier (6) 2/1f 5 3
Profound Beauty (IRE) *DKWeld* 5-9-8 PJSmullen (4) 7/2 18 4
All The Aces (IRE) *MAJarvis,GB* 4-9-11 PhilipRobinson (2) 8/1 2½ 5
Moon Indigo *APO'Brien* 3-9-0 JPO'Brien (5) 33/1 19 6
Bashkirov *LukeComer* 4-9-11 RPWalsh (7) 100/1 12 7
28 Yeats (IRE) *APO'Brien* 8-9-11 JAHeffernan (3) 4/1 3 8
H. H. Aga Khan 8ran 3m14.82 TR: 121/117/114+/88/88

61 ladbrokes.com Vincent O'Brien National Stks (Gr 1) (2yo c+f) £130,435 7f

KINGSFORT (USA) *KevinPrendergast* 2-9-1 DPMcDonogh (4) 9/4 1
CHABAL (IRE) *JSBolger* 2-9-1 KJManning (1) .... 9/2 nk 2
BEETHOVEN (IRE) *APO'Brien* 2-9-1 MJKinane (3) 25/1 1¾ 3
25 Air Chief Marshal (IRE) *APO'Brien* 2-9-1 JPO'Brien (2) .... 20/1 ¾ 4
Senior *EdwardLynam* 2-9-1 PJSmullen (6) .... 28/1 ¾ 5
Alfred Nobel (IRE) *APO'Brien* 2-9-1 JAHeffernan (5) .... 1/1f hd 6
Mr Norman Ormiston 6ran 1m33.63 TR: 109+/108+/104/102/100/99

LONGCHAMP Sunday, Sep 13 GOOD

62 Qatar Prix Vermeille (Gr 1) (3yo+ f+m) £130,435 1½m

Order as they passed the post: Dar Re Mi was demoted to fifth for causing interference to Soberania

49 DAR RE MI *JHMGosden,GB* 4-9-3 JimmyFortune (3) 2/1 1
21 STACELITA (FR) *J-CRouget,France* 3-8-8 CPLemaire (9) .... 9/10cpf sn 2
21 PLUMANIA *AFabre,France* 3-8-8 OPeslier (5) 27/1 1½ 3
21 Board Meeting (IRE) *ELellouche,France* 3-8-8 ACrastus (11) .... 19/1 sh 4
Soberania (GER) *AWohler,Germany* 3-8-8 JVictoire (2) .... 83/1 sn 5
Becqu Adoree (FR) *MmeGLecomte,France* 3-8-8 FranckBlondel (4) .... 93/1 ½ 6
Armure *AdeRoyerDupre,France* 4-9-3 GMosse (7) 81/10 1½ 7
Tres Rapide (IRE) *H-APantall,France* 4-9-3 DBoeuf (6) 40/1 1 8
Tangaspeed (FR) *RLaplanche,France* 4-9-3 LDettori (13) .... 62/1 hd 9
Volver (IRE) *J-CRouget,France* 3-8-8 IMendizabal (1) 9/10cpf 6 10
Kalla *AFabre,France* 3-8-8 MGuyon (8) 21/1 2 11
Umirage *HBlume,Germany* 4-9-3 TThulliez (10) 81/1 3 12
M. Schwartz/Ecurie Monastic 12ran 2m29.10 TR: 118+/117+/114+/114+/114/113

63 Qatar Prix Foy (Gr 2) (4yo+ c+f) £64,435 1½m

33 SPANISH MOON (USA) *SirMichaelStoute,GB* 5-9-2 RyanMoore (6) 9/10cp 1
26 VISION D'ETAT (FR) *ELibaud,France* 4-9-2 OPeslier (5) .... 4/5f ¾ 2
CROSSHARBOUR *AFabre,France* 5-9-2 SPasquier (2) .... 9/10cp ½ 3
17 Buccellati *AMBalding,GB* 5-9-2 (b) WilliamBuick (4) 10/1 2½ 4
Mr K. Abdulla 4ran 2m28.70 TR: 123/121+/120/115

ASCOT Saturday, Sep 26 GOOD to FIRM

64 Juddmonte Royal Lodge Stks (Gr 2) (2yo c+g) £86,188 1m (Rnd)

JOSHUA TREE (IRE) *APO'Brien,Ireland* 2-8-12 CO'Donoghue (5) 12/1 1
WASEET *JLDunlop* 2-8-12 RHills (2) 6/1 1¼ 2
VALE OF YORK (IRE) *SaeedbinSuroor* 2-8-12 AhmedAjtebi (4) .... 5/1 hd 3
High Twelve (IRE) *JHMGosden* 2-8-12 JimmyFortune (7) 7/2jf 2¾ 4
Dreamspeed (IRE) *AMBalding* 2-8-12 WilliamBuick (3) 25/1 4 5
Mikhail Glinka (IRE) *APO'Brien,Ireland* 2-8-12 JMurtagh (8) .... 9/1 ns 6
Frozen Power (IRE) *SaeedbinSuroor* 2-8-12 LDettori (1) 7/2jf 4 7
Timely Jazz (IRE) *BJMeehan* 2-8-12 MartinDwyer (10) 16/1 6 8
Black Spirit (USA) *CGCox* 2-8-12 (t) AdamKirby (9) .... 7/1 sh 9
Dubai Miracle (USA) *DMSimcock* 2-8-12 JamieSpencer (11) 20/1 1½ 10
Mr D. Smith, Mrs J. Magnier, Mr M. Tabor 10ran 1m39.55
TR: 115/112+/111+/104/93/93+

65 Meon Valley Stud Fillies' Mile (Gr 1) (2yo f) £123,759 1m (Rnd)

HIBAAYEB *CEBrittain* 2-8-12 NCallan (6) 8/1 1
LADY DARSHAAN (IRE) *JSMoore* 2-8-12 RichardHughes (3) .... 9/1 ¾ 2
YOU'LL BE MINE (USA) *APO'Brien,Ireland* 2-8-12 JMurtagh (4) 7/2 1½ 3
Sent From Heaven (IRE) *BWHills* 2-8-12 MichaelHills (8) .... 8/1 ½ 4

Dyna Waltz *JHMGosden* 2-8-12 JimmyFortune (1) .... 20/1 ½ 5
Blue Angel (IRE) *RHannon* 2-8-12 RyanMoore (5) 14/1 1 6
27 Chantilly Creme (USA) *RGibson,France* 2-8-12 SPasquier (9) .... 18/1 hd 7
53 Long Lashes (USA) *SaeedbinSuroor* 2-8-12 (t) LDettori (7) 5/2f 1 8
Mudaaraah *JLDunlop* 2-8-12 RHills (2) 11/2 2¾ 9
Mr Mohammed Al Nabouda 9ran 1m39.78 TR: 110/108+/104+/103/101/99

66 Queen Elizabeth II Stks (Sponsored By Sony) (Gr 1) (3yo+) £141,925 1m (Rnd)

39 RIP VAN WINKLE (IRE) *APO'Brien,Ireland* 3-8-13 JMurtagh (1) 8/13f 1
52 ZACINTO *SirMichaelStoute* 3-8-13 RyanMoore (5) 18/1 1¼ 2
52 DELEGATOR *SaeedbinSuroor* 3-8-13 LDettori (2) 5/2 3¼ 3
57 Aqlaam *WJHaggas* 4-9-3 RHills (3) 15/2 10 4
Mrs John Magnier,Mr M.Tabor & Mr D.Smith 4ran 1m38.82 TR 129+/126/117+/90

COLOGNE Sunday, Sep 27 GOOD

67 Preis von Europa (Gr 1) (3yo+) £90,090 1½m

47 JUKEBOX JURY (IRE) *MJohnston,GB* 3-8-12 RoystonFfrench 32/10 1
56 EASTERN ANTHEM (IRE) *SaeedbinSuroor,GB* 5-9-6 LDettori .... 13/10f ns 2
ELIOT (GER) *TMundry,Germany* 3-8-12 THellier 67/10 2½ 3
45 Poseidon Adventure (IRE) *WFigge,Germany* 6-9-6 (b) KKerekes .... 233/10 nk 4
45 Schiller Danon (GER) *WHickst,Germany* 3-8-12 ASuborics 198/10 2 5
30 Enroller (IRE) *WRMuir,GB* 4-9-6 DarryllHolland .... 251/10 hd 6
30 Bronze Cannon (USA) *JHMGosden,GB* 4-9-6 RichardMullen 51/10 1½ 7
Ambassador (GER) *TMundry,Germany* 5-9-6 AStarke 232/10 2½ 8
Guantana (GER) *JHirschberger,Germany* 4-9-3 SPasquier .... 109/10 hd 9
Toughness Danon *AWohler,Germany* 3-8-12 (b) JBojko 11/1 18 10
Mr A. D. Spence 10ran 2m29.56 TR: 123/122/118/116/113/112

NEWMARKET Friday, Oct 2 GOOD to FIRM (Rowley Mile Course)

68 Electrolux Cheveley Park Stks (Gr 1) (2yo f) £96,509 6f

51 SPECIAL DUTY *MmeCHead-Maarek,France* 2-8-12 SPasquier (7) 3/1 1
27 MISHEER *CEBrittain* 2-8-12 NCallan (6) 9/1 2¾ 2
27 LADY OF THE DESERT (USA) *BJMeehan* 2-8-12 MartinDwyer (3) .... 11/8f hd 3
Puff (IRE) *RMBeckett* 2-8-12 JimCrowley (4) .... 50/1 ¾ 4
Shamandar (FR) *WJHaggas* 2-8-12 MichaelHills (1) 12/1 3½ 5
Song of My Heart (IRE) *DavidWachman,Ireland* 2-8-12 JMurtagh (5) 14/1 9 6
Sand Vixen *SaeedbinSuroor* 2-8-12 LDettori (2) 6/1 5 7
Habaayib *EALDunlop* 2-8-12 RHills (8) 14/1 9 8
Mr K. Abdulla 8ran 1m10.38 TR: 118/109/108+/106/94/63

69 Shadwell Middle Park Stks (Gr 1) (2yo c) £104,116 6f

AWZAAN *MJohnston* 2-8-12 RHills (5) 4/1 1
50 RADIOHEAD *BJMeehan* 2-8-12 (t) MartinDwyer (1) .... 14/1 ¾ 2
SHOWCASING *JHMGosden* 2-8-12 JimmyFortune (2) .... 2/1 nk 3
Poet's Voice *SaeedbinSuroor* 2-8-12 (t) LDettori (3) 15/8f 1 4
Arctic (IRE) *MissTAMCollins,Ireland* 2-8-12 PJSmullen (4) 6/1 2¾ 5
Mr Hamdan Al Maktoum 5ran 1m10.11 TR: 118+/115/114+/111+/102

LONGCHAMP Saturday, Oct 3 GOOD

70 Total Prix de la Foret (Gr 1) (3yo+) £131,055 7f

Order as they passed the post: Oiseau de Feu was disqualified for causing interference on the first bend

44 VARENAR (FR) *AdeRoyerDupre,France* 3-9-0 SPasquier (13) 196/10 1
SWEET HEARTH (USA) *AdeRoyerDupre,France* 3-8-11 GMosse (1) .... 60/1 sh 2
46 GOLDIKOVA (IRE) *FHead,France* 4-8-13 OPeslier (14) .... 4/10f ½ 3
59 Cat Junior (USA) *BJMeehan,GB* 4-9-2 LDettori (10) 21/1 3 4
57 Balthazaar's Gift (IRE) *CGCox,GB* 6-9-2 AdamKirby (2) .... 32/1 ¾ 5
57 Oiseau de Feu (USA) *J-CRouget,France* 3-9-0 CSoumillon (7) .... 78/10 hd 6
44 Dunkerque (FR) *MmeCHead-Maarek,France* 4-9-2 (s) DBoeuf (4) 43/1 1½ 7
Smooth Operator (GER) *MHofer,Germany* 3-9-0 MGuyon (12) .... 33/1 nk 8
Calrissian (GER) *FReuterskiold,Sweden* 5-9-2 JVictoire (8) .... 78/1 nk 9
Border Patrol *RCharlton,GB* 3-9-0 KJManning (3) 10/1 2½ 10
44 Mariol (FR) *RCollet,France* 6-9-2 FranckBlondel (11) .... 78/1 ¾ 11
10 Soneva (USA) *YdeNicolay,France* 3-8-11 IMendizabal (9) 41/1 8 12
Welsh Emperor (IRE) *TPTate,GB* 10-9-2 (b) MickyFenton (5) 106/1 3 13
Opera Comica (BRZ) *GDuarte,Brazil* 3-8-7 TPereira (6) 100/1 6 14
H.H. Aga Khan 14ran 1m19.20 TR: 122/119/116/110/107/108

LONGCHAMP Sunday, Oct 4 GOOD

71 Qatar Prix de l'Abbaye de Longchamp (Gr 1) (2yo+) £131,055 5f

40 TOTAL GALLERY (IRE) *JSMoore,GB* 3-9-11 JMurtagh (3) 13/1 1

54	FLEETING SPIRIT (IRE) *JNoseda,GB* 4-9-8 TPQueally (8)	15/10f	nk 2
	WAR ARTIST (AUS) *JMPEustace,GB* 6-9-11 OPeslier (9)	48/10	½ 3
50	Benbaun (IRE) *KARyan,GB* 8-9-11 (v) PJSmullen (12)	23/1	hd 4
	Black Mambazo (IRE) *LRiccardi,Italy* 4-9-11 LDettori (2)	15/1	¾ 5
50	Borderlescott *RBastiman,GB* 7-9-11 NCallan (7)	68/10	½ 6
50	Tax Free (IRE) *DNicholls,GB* 7-9-11 AdrianTNicholls (1)	12/1	nk 7
	Monsieur Chevalier (IRE) *RHannon,GB* 2-8-7 RichardHughes (5)	16/1	hd 8
	Stern Opinion (USA) *PBary,France* 4-9-11 SPasquier (14)	10/1	1 9
	Strike Up The Band *DNicholls,GB* 6-9-11 DO'Donohoe (4)	77/1	hd 10
54	Equiano (FR) *BWHills,GB* 4-9-11 KFallon (15)	51/1	2½ 11
	Exhibition (IRE) *FCastro,Sweden* 4-9-11 MMartinez (11)	121/1	¾ 12
40	Reverence *EJAlston,GB* 8-9-11 MJKinane (13)	96/1	1½ 13
	Sohraab *HMorrison,GB* 5-9-11 DarryllHolland (16)	128/1	3 14
	Atlantic Wave (USA) *RTugusev,Slovakia* 4-9-11 MKappushev (6)	79/1	2½ 15
	Another True Story *ZKoplik,CzechRepublic* 5-9-11 VJanacek (10)	164/1	¾ 16

Coleman Bloodstock Limited 16ran 55.10secs TR: 123/118/119/119/116/114+

72 Total Prix Marcel Boussac - Criterium des Pouliches (Gr 1) (2yo f) £157,266 1m

	ROSANARA (FR) *AdeRoyerDupre,France* 2-8-11 CSoumillon (3)	9/10f	1
	ON VERRA (IRE) *FDoumen,France* 2-8-11 TThulliez (6)	61/1	2 2
	JOANNA (IRE) *BGrizzetti,Italy* 2-8-11 DVargiu (5)	18/1	ns 3
	Wedding March (IRE) *AFabre,France* 2-8-11 LDettori (1)	35/10	hd 4
	Green Dandy (IRE) *EJO'Neill,GB* 2-8-11 KFallon (9)	59/1	1½ 5
	American Nizzy (FR) *YdeNicolay,France* 2-8-11 IMendizabal (8)	82/1	1½ 6
	Olvia (IRE) *CLaffon-Parias,France* 2-8-11 GMosse (4)	24/1	¾ 7
	Baahama (IRE) *AFabre,France* 2-8-11 OPeslier (2)	9/1	¾ 8
	Kilo Alpha (FR) *MmeCHead-Maarek,France* 2-8-11 SPasquier (11)	24/1	1½ 9
	Hard Life (IRE) *ACandi,Italy* 2-8-11 MJKinane (7)	50/1	1½ 10
	Cabaret (IRE) *APO'Brien,Ireland* 2-8-11 JMurtagh (10)	65/10	dist 11

H.H. Aga Khan 11ran 1m37.20 TR: 110/105/105/104/99/95

73 Qatar Prix Jean-Luc Lagardere (Grand Criterium) (Gr 1) (2yo c+f) 7f
£183,477

	SIYOUNI (FR) *AdeRoyerDupre,France* 2-9-0 GMosse (6)	6/1	1
	POUNCED (USA) *JHMGosden,GB* 2-9-0 JimmyFortune (2)	15/1	1½ 2
	BUZZWORD *SaeedbinSuroor,GB* 2-9-0 AhmedAjtebi (3)	68/10	½ 3
	Lope de Vega (IRE) *AFabre,France* 2-9-0 MGuyon (4)	2/1	½ 4
	Dick Turpin (IRE) *RHannon,GB* 2-9-0 RichardHughes (5)	15/10f	1 5
61	Beethoven (IRE) *APO'Brien,Ireland* 2-9-0 JMurtagh (7)	16/1	ns 6
	Roi de Vitesse (IRE) *BRMillman,GB* 2-9-0 JamesMillman (1)	64/1	6 7

H.H. Aga Khan 7ran 1m19.50 TR: 116+/111/109/108/105+/105

74 Qatar Petroleum Prix de l'Opera (Gr 1) (3yo+ f+m) £131,055 1¼m

	SHALANAYA (IRE) *MDelzangles,France* 3-8-12 MGuyon (4)	19/1	1
62	BOARD MEETING (IRE) *ELellouche,France* 3-8-12 ACrastus (8)	11/1	1½ 2
41	MIDDAY *HRACecil,GB* 3-8-12 TPQueally (7)	38/10	sh 3
33	Alpine Rose (FR) *AdeRoyerDupre,France* 4-9-2 GMosse (3)	2/1f	¾ 4
	Crystal Capella *SirMichaelStoute,GB* 4-9-2 RyanMoore (5)	45/10	1½ 5
42	Lady Marian (GER) *SaeedbinSuroor,GB* 4-9-2 LDettori (10)	11/1	½ 6
29	Again (IRE) *DavidWachman,Ireland* 3-8-12 (s) JMurtagh (9)	29/1	1½ 7
	Article Rare (USA) *ELellouche,France* 3-8-12 (s) OPeslier (2)	25/1	1½ 8
	Night Magic (GER) *WFigge,Germany* 3-8-12 KKerekes (6)	5/1	½ 9

H.H. Aga Khan 9ran 2m01.80 TR: 120/116/116/112/108/107

75 Qatar Prix de l'Arc de Triomphe (Gr 1) (3yo+ c+f) £2,096,881 1½m

55	SEA THE STARS (IRE) *JohnMOxx,Ireland* 3-8-11 MJKinane (6)	8/10f	1
56	YOUMZAIN (IRE) *MRChannon,GB* 6-9-5 (v) KFallon (1)	21/1	2 2
37	CAVALRYMAN *AFabre,France* 3-8-11 LDettori (19)	17/1	hd 3
38	Conduit (IRE) *SirMichaelStoute,GB* 4-9-5 RyanMoore (12)	14/1	hd 4
62	Dar Re Mi *JHMGosden,GB* 4-9-2 JimmyFortune (2)	23/1	1 5
55	Fame And Glory *APO'Brien,Ireland* 3-8-11 JMurtagh (10)	10/1	1 6
	La Boum (GER) *RCollet,France* 6-9-2 TJarnet (8)	136/1	½ 7
62	Stacelita (FR) *J-CRouget,France* 3-8-8 CSoumillon (16)	10/1	dh 7
33	Magadan (IRE) *ELellouche,France* 4-9-5 ACrastus (17)	76/1	¾ 9
63	Vision d'Etat (FR) *ELibaud,France* 4-9-5 OPeslier (9)	16/1	½ 10
62	Tangaspeed (FR) *RLaplanche,France* 4-9-2 IMendizabal (11)	129/1	¾ 11
37	Beheshtam (FR) *AdeRoyerDupre,France* 3-8-11 GMosse (15)	23/1	sh 12
56	Getaway (GER) *JHirschberger,Germany* 6-9-5 SPasquier (3)	24/1	3 13
5	The Bogberry (USA) *AdeRoyerDupre,France* 4-9-5 MKappushev (18)	172/1	sn 14
	Hot Six (BRZ) *GDuarte,Brazil* 4-9-4 TPereira (4)	100/1	8 15
	Tullamore (USA) *ZKoplik,CzechRepublic* 4-9-5 VJanacek (13)	163/1	2 16
55	Grand Ducal (IRE) *APO'Brien,Ireland* 3-8-11 PJSmullen (5)	151/1	4 17
55	Set Sail (IRE) *APO'Brien,Ireland* 3-8-11 SMLevey (14)	153/1	2 18

34 Steele Tango (USA) *RATeal,GB* 4-9-5 DarryllHolland (7) 198/1 15 19
Mr Christopher Tsui 19ran 2m26.30 TR: 129+/125+/125+/124+/119+/120+

76 Qatar Prix du Cadran (Gr 1) (4yo+) £131,055 2½m

60 ALANDI (IRE) *JohnMOxx,Ireland* 4-9-2 MJKinane (3) 49/10 1
KASBAH BLISS (FR) *FDoumen,France* 7-9-2 TThulliez (5) .... 4/1 sh 2
60 YEATS (IRE) *APO'Brien,Ireland* 8-9-2 JMurtagh (4) 3/1f 1½ 3
Pouvoir Absolu *ELellouche,France* 4-9-2 (b) ACrastus (8) 20/1 2½ 4
Askar Tau (FR) *MPTregoning,GB* 4-9-2 (v) RyanMoore (11) 78/10 3 5
Orion Star (FR) *H-APantall,France* 7-9-2 DBoeuf (12) .... 39/1 ½ 6
62 Armure *AdeRoyerDupre,France* 4-8-13 GMosse (2) 12/1 1 7
Incanto Dream *CLerner,France* 5-9-2 (s) YLerner (1) 55/10 2½ 8
Bluefields (FR) *ELeray,France* 8-9-2 DBonilla (7) 78/1 3 9
Pointilliste (USA) *ELellouche,France* 6-9-2 OPeslier (10) .... 15/1 sn 10
Windsor Palace (IRE) *APO'Brien,Ireland* 4-9-2 SMLevey (9) .... 97/1 pu
Bassel (FR) *H-APantall,France* 4-9-2 MGuyon (6) .... 79/1 pu
H. H. Aga Khan 12ran 4m12.70 TR: 121/120+/118/116/113/111

SANTA ANITA Saturday, Oct 10 FAST

77 Goodwood Stks (Gr 1) (3yo+) £103,774 1m1f (Pro-Ride)

GITANO HERNANDO *MBotti,GB* 3-8-9 KFallon 18/1 1
COLONEL JOHN (USA) *EHarty,USA* 4-8-12 GGomez .... 25/10f nk 2
RICHARD'S KID (USA) *RBaffert,USA* 4-8-12 (b) ASolis .... 68/10 ¾ 3
Parading (USA) *CRMcGaugheyIII,USA* 6-8-12 (b) RBejarano .... 44/10 ¾ 4
Chocolate Candy (USA) *JHollendorfer,USA* 3-8-9 VEspinoza 117/10 1¾ 5
Mine That Bird (USA) *BLWoolley,Jnr,USA* 3-8-9 CBorel .... 34/10 nk 6
Monzante (USA) *MikeRMitchell,USA* 5-8-12 JRosario .... 164/10 ¾ 7
Informed (USA) *DFO'Neill,USA* 5-8-12 (b) MBaze .... 335/10 hd 8
Tres Borrachos (USA) *CBGreely,USA* 4-8-12 JTalamo 248/10 7¼ 9
Tiago (USA) *JAShirreffs,USA* 5-8-12 MikeESmith 79/10 3 10
Team Valor 10ran 1m48.39 TR: 124/121/119/117/115/114

MILAN Sunday, Oct 11 GOOD to SOFT

78 Gran Criterium (Gr 1) (2yo c+f) £168,317 1m

HEARTS OF FIRE *PatEddery,GB* 2-8-11 OPeslier 24/10 1
64 VALE OF YORK (IRE) *SaeedbinSuroor,GB* 2-8-11 AhmedAjtebi .... 35/10 nk 2
MATA KERANJANG (USA) *PFICole,GB* 2-8-11 MDemuro 64/10 5 3
Ladiesandgentlemen (ITY) *RFeligioni,Italy* 2-8-11 SLandi 29/10 3 4
Marshade (ITY) *SBotti,Italy* 2-8-11 UmbertoRispoli 23/10f 4½ 5
Blow Up (IRE) *RMenichetti,Italy* 2-8-11 GMarcelli 89/10 2¼ 6
Air Crew (USA) *RMenichetti,Italy* 2-8-11 LManiezzi .... 89/10 nk 7
Dancer Cat (IRE) *BGrizzetti,Italy* 2-8-11 SUrru 57/10 2¼ 8
Fantastic Shift *BGrizzetti,Italy* 2-8-11 DVargiu 57/10 1¾ 9
Collesano (IRE) *RBiondi,Italy* 2-8-11 MarcoMonteriso .... 98/10 nk 10
Davie's Story *BGrizzetti,Italy* 2-8-11 SPasquier 57/10 3¼ 11
Pat Eddery Racing (Detroit) 11ran 1m38.90 TR: 117+/116+/103/95/83/77

79 Premio Vittorio di Capua (Gr 1) (3yo+) £149,399 1m

57 GLADIATORUS (USA) *SaeedbinSuroor,GB* 4-9-0 AhmedAjtebi 18/10f 1
WIN FOR SURE (GER) *AWohler,Germany* 4-9-0 EPedroza 48/10 4½ 2
ROCKHORSE (IRE) *BGrizzetti,Italy* 4-9-0 DVargiu .... 36/10 hd 3
King of Sydney (USA) *MHofer,Germany* 3-8-10 MGuyon .... 116/10 ¾ 4
11 Major Cadeaux *RAFahey,GB* 5-9-0 OPeslier 53/10 1½ 5
Blue Coral (IRE) *TSatra,CzechRepublic* 5-9-0 MTellini .... 309/10 sh 6
Freemusic (IRE) *LRiccardi,Italy* 5-9-0 GMarcelli .... 267/10 ½ 7
Precious Boy (GER) *WHickst,Germany* 4-9-0 AndreasSuborics .... 39/10 hd 8
Aspectus (IRE) *HBlume,Germany* 6-9-0 MDemuro .... 146/10 ¾ 9
Miles Gloriosus (USA) *RMenichetti,Italy* 6-9-0 LManiezzi .... 33/1 sn 10
Wilside (IRE) *MDelzangles,France* 3-8-7 SPasquier .... 45/10 dist 11
Godolphin 11ran 1m38.00 TR: 124/113/113/111/107/107

NEWMARKET Saturday, Oct 17 GOOD to FIRM (Rowley Mile Course)

80 Victor Chandler Challenge Stks (Gr 2) (3yo+) £60,829 7f

59 ARABIAN GLEAM *JNoseda* 5-9-3 (s) JMurtagh (8) 7/1 1
59 OUQBA *BWHills* 3-9-1 RHills (4) .... 5/1 nk 2
DONATIVUM *SaeedbinSuroor* 3-9-1 TedDurcan (10) .... 9/1 ¾ 3
54 Main Aim *SirMichaelStoute* 4-9-3 RyanMoore (7) .... 5/1 ½ 4
7 Ashram (IRE) *SaeedbinSuroor* 3-9-1 (v) LDettori (6) 7/2f 1½ 5
54 Asset (IRE) *SaeedbinSuroor* 6-9-3 (b) RichardHughes (3) .... 8/1 ½ 6
16 Cuis Ghaire (IRE) *JSBolger,Ireland* 3-8-12 KJManning (1) 9/2 4½ 7
11 Tariq *PWChapple-Hyam* 5-9-3 KFallon (2) .... 20/1 ¾ 8

54 Al Qasi (IRE) *PWChapple-Hyam* 6-9-3 JimmyFortune (9) 28/1 9 9
Mr Saeed Suhail 9ran 1m23.81 TR: 121/120+/118/116/112/110

81 Jumeirah Dewhurst Stks (Gr 1) (2yo c+f) £180,160 7f

73 BEETHOVEN (IRE) *APO'Brien,Ireland* 2-9-1 (v) RyanMoore (3) 33/1 1
FENCING MASTER *APO'Brien,Ireland* 2-9-1 CO'Donoghue (13) 20/1 nk 2
25 XTENSION (IRE) *CGCox* 2-9-1 AdamKirby (11) 6/1 ns 3
Steinbeck (IRE) *APO'Brien,Ireland* 2-9-1 JMurtagh (1) 4/1 nk 4
73 Buzzword *SaeedbinSuroor* 2-9-1 AhmedAjtebi (7) 14/1 1¾ 5
73 Dick Turpin (IRE) *RHannon* 2-9-1 RichardHughes (5) 8/1 2 6
Silver Grecian *JRyan* 2-9-1 MichaelHills (15) 13/2 1 7
Free Judgement (USA) *JSBolger,Ireland* 2-9-1 DJMoran (14) 66/1 nk 8
Awesome Act (USA) *JNoseda* 2-9-1 DarryllHolland (10) 14/1 1½ 9
61 Chabal (IRE) *JSBolger,Ireland* 2-9-1 KJManning (4) 7/2f ½ 10
Maroon Machine (IRE) *EJO'Neill* 2-9-1 CSoumillon (2) 33/1 hd 11
64 High Twelve (IRE) *JHMGosden* 2-9-1 KFallon (6) 9/1 3 12
64 Timely Jazz (IRE) *BJMeehan* 2-9-1 EddieAhern (9) 66/1 nk 13
Lord High Admiral (IRE) *APO'Brien,Ireland* 2-9-1 SeanLevey (8) 66/1 7 14
Manhattan Fox (USA) *BJMeehan* 2-9-1 LDettori (12) 66/1 1¼ 15
Mr M. Tabor, D. Smith & Mrs John Magnier 15ran 1m23.49
TR: 117/116/116/115/109/103

82 Emirates Airline Champion Stks (Gr 1) (3yo+) £213,739 1¼m

34 TWICE OVER *HRACecil* 4-9-3 TPQueally (8) 14/1 1
MAWATHEEQ (USA) *MPTregoning* 4-9-3 RHills (13) 7/1 ½ 2
49 SARISKA *MLWBell* 3-8-9 KFallon (2) 8/1 1 3
Pipedreamer *JHMGosden* 5-9-3 SebSanders (4) 25/1 ½ 4
City Leader (IRE) *BJMeehan* 4-9-3 (b) TedDurcan (11) 100/1 ¾ 5
75 Fame And Glory *APO'Brien,Ireland* 3-8-12 JMurtagh (5) 6/4f 1½ 6
49 Barshiba (IRE) *DRCElsworth* 5-9-0 PaulHanagan (12) 33/1 ¾ 7
57 Virtual *JHMGosden* 4-9-3 JimmyFortune (6) 33/1 1¼ 8
30 Campanologist (USA) *SaeedbinSuroor* 4-9-3 LDettori (7) 25/1 11 9
46 Never On Sunday (FR) *J-CRouget,France* 4-9-3 CPLemaire (14) 5/1 1¾ 10
30 Doctor Fremantle *SirMichaelStoute* 4-9-3 RyanMoore (3) 8/1 5 11
39 Forgotten Voice (IRE) *JNoseda* 4-9-3 RichardHughes (1) 66/1 5 12
74 Alpine Rose (FR) *AdeRoyerDupre,France* 4-9-0 CSoumillon (9) 16/1 9 13
75 Set Sail (IRE) *APO'Brien,Ireland* 3-8-12 CO'Donoghue (10) 200/1 1¼ 14
Mr K. Abdulla 14ran 2m01.31 TR125/124+/118/120/118/115

WOODBINE Saturday, Oct 17 GOOD to FIRM

83 E. P. Taylor Stks Presented By Emirates Airline (Gr 1) (3yo+ f+m) £361,446 1¼m

42 LAHALEEB (IRE) *MRChannon,GB* 3-8-6 WilliamBuick 444/10 1
41 RAINBOW VIEW (USA) *JHMGosden,GB* 3-8-6 (s) JLeparoux 9/4f 1¾ 2
PRINCESS HAYA (USA) *MRMatz,USA* 4-8-12 RBejarano 76/10 2¼ 3
Eastern Aria (UAE) *MJohnston,GB* 3-8-6 RoystonFfrench 183/10 2¼ 4
Salve Germania (IRE) *TAPletcher,USA* 4-8-12 JCastellano 63/10 1¾ 5
Treat Gently *RJFrankel,USA* 4-8-12 GGomez 245/100 ns 6
38 Look Here *RMBeckett,GB* 4-8-12 JimCrowley 315/100 ¾ 7
Roses 'n' Wine (CAN) *DRBell,USA* 4-8-12 (b) ChantalSutherland 217/10 2¼ 8
Mr M. Al-Qatami & Mr K. M. Al-Mudhaf 8ran 2m02.89
TR: 120+/116/112/105/102/102

84 Pattison Canadian International Stks (Gr 1) (3yo+) £722,891 1½m

CHAMPS ELYSEES *RJFrankel,USA* 6-9-0 GGomez 26/10f 1
67 JUKEBOX JURY (IRE) *MJohnston,GB* 3-8-7 RoystonFfrench 345/100 ½ 2
63 BUCCELLATI *AMBalding,GB* 5-9-0 (b) WilliamBuick 94/10 2 3
2 Marsh Side (USA) *NDDrysdale,USA* 6-9-0 JCastellano 495/100 hd 4
43 Just As Well (USA) *JESheppard,USA* 6-9-0 JLeparoux 325/100 6¾ 5
Spice Route *RLAttfield,Canada* 5-9-0 (b) JMcAleney 158/10 ns 6
Allied Powers (IRE) *MLWBell,GB* 4-9-0 JimCrowley 27/1 1¾ 7
2 Quijano (GER) *PSchiergen,Germany* 7-9-0 AndraschStarke 785/100 20 8
Mr K. Abdulla 8ran 2m28.36 TR: 124/123/119/119/106/105

DONCASTER Saturday, Oct 24 GOOD to SOFT

85 Racing Post Trophy (Gr 1) (2yo c+f) £113,540 1m (Str.)

ST NICHOLAS ABBEY (IRE) *APO'Brien,Ireland* 2-9-0 JMurtagh (9) 13/8f 1
ELUSIVE PIMPERNEL (USA) *JLDunlop* 2-9-0 EddieAhern (8) 4/1 3¾ 2
AL ZIR (USA) *SaeedbinSuroor* 2-9-0 LDettori (2) 9/2 2½ 3
Dancing David (IRE) *BJMeehan* 2-9-0 MartinDwyer (5) 12/1 nk 4
Morana (IRE) *PWChapple-Hyam* 2-9-0 AlanMunro (10) 18/1 1¼ 5
Shakespearean (IRE) *MJohnston* 2-9-0 JoeFanning (7) 14/1 nk 6
Hanson'd (IRE) *KARyan* 2-9-0 NCallan (11) 50/1 2 7

Al Ghazal (USA) *SaeedbinSuroor* 2-9-0 AhmedAjtebi (4)........................... 40/1 ¾ 8
Musaafer (IRE) *MAJarvis* 2-9-0 RHills (6)... 25/1 ½ 9
Coordinated Cut (IRE) *PWChapple-Hyam* 2-9-0 KFallon (3)........................ 11/1 2½ 10
Elusive Award (USA) *AndrewOliver,Ireland* 2-9-0 KJManning (12)........... 50/1 10 11

Mr D. Smith, Mrs J. Magnier, Mr M. Tabor 11ran 1m39.62
TR: 122+/112+/105/105/101/101

LONGCHAMP Sunday, Oct 25 GOOD to SOFT

86 Prix Royal-Oak (Gr 1) (3yo+) £129,864 1m7f110y

38 ASK *SirMichaelStoute,GB* 6-9-4 RyanMoore.. 24/10f 1
60 SCHIAPARELLI (GER) *SaeedbinSuroor,GB* 6-9-4 LDettori......................... 3/1 1½ 2
MANIGHAR (FR) *AdeRoyerDupre,France* 3-8-9 CPLemaire........................ 3/1 3 3
60 Clowance *RCharlton,GB* 4-9-1 KFallon.. 45/10 1½ 4
76 Pouvoir Absolu *ELellouche,France* 4-9-4 (b) ACrastus.............................. 12/1 6 5
76 Askar Tau (FR) *MPTregoning,GB* 4-9-4 (v) RichardHughes........................ 31/1 2½ 6
Sassoaloro (GER) *HBlume,Germany* 5-9-4 DBoeuf....................................... 46/1 nk 7
18 The Miniver Rose (IRE) *RHannon,GB* 3-8-6 SPasquier.............................. 53/1 20 8
Sevenna (FR) *HRACecil,GB* 4-9-1 CSoumillon.. 16/1 2 9

Mr Patrick J. Fahey 9ran 3m32.17 TR: 122+/120/119/112/108/106

SAINT-CLOUD Sunday, Nov 1 SOFT

87 Criterium International (Gr 1) (2yo) £131,055 1m

JAN VERMEER (IRE) *APO'Brien,Ireland* 2-9-0 CO'Donoghue............... 4/1cp 1
EMERALD COMMANDER (IRE) *SaeedbinSuroor,GB* 2-9-0 LDettori..... 47/10 4 2
72 ROSANARA (FR) *AdeRoyerDupre,France* 2-8-11 CPLemaire.................. 7/10f 1½ 3
Midas Touch *APO'Brien,Ireland* 2-9-0 JMurtagh.. 4/1cp hd 4
Prizefighting (USA) *JHMGosden,GB* 2-9-0 JimmyFortune............................ 9/1 1½ 5
Royal Bench (IRE) *RCollet,France* 2-9-0 IMendizabal.................................. 23/1 1½ 6
Arasin (IRE) *PBary,France* 2-9-0 OPeslier.. 78/10 ¾ 7

Mr Michael Tabor 7ran 1m45.60 TR: 119/110/104/107/104/102

FLEMINGTON Tuesday, Nov 3 GOOD to SOFT

88 Emirates Melbourne Cup (Hcap) (Gr 1) (3yo+) £1,895,604 2m

SHOCKING (AUS) *MKavanagh,Australia* 4-8-0 (b) CoreyBrown................ 9/1 1
CRIME SCENE (IRE) *SaeedbinSuroor,GB* 6-8-5 (b) KerrinMcEvoy........... 40/1 ¾ 2
MOURILYAN (IRE) *HBrown,SouthAfrica* 5-8-8 GSchofield........................ 20/1 1½ 3
Master O'Reilly (NZ) *DO'Brien,Australia* 7-8-9 VDuric.............................. 11/1 1½ 4
Harris Tweed (NZ) *M&BBaker,NewZealand* 4-8-4 (b) CNewitt................. 100/1 nk 5
Alcopop (AUS) *JakeStephens,Australia* 5-8-4 DominicTourneur................. 15/4f hd 6
Viewed (AUS) *JBCummings,Australia* 6-9-2 (b) BRawiller........................... 11/2 sh 7
C'Est La Guerre (NZ) *JDSadler,Australia* 5-8-10 NicholasHall.................... 25/1 ½ 8
Kibbutz (NZ) *JMcLean,Australia* 5-8-4 (s) ChrisSymons............................ 70/1 ½ 9
Newport (AUS) *PaulPerry,Australia* 7-8-4 PeterWells................................. 40/1 hd 10
Daffodil (NZ) *KGray,NewZealand* 4-8-2 CMunce... 14/1 ¾ 11
Munsef *IanWilliams,GB* 7-8-5 ZPurton.. 50/1 hd 12
Gallions Reach (NZ) *RYuill,NewZealand* 7-8-3 (b) DDunn......................... 200/1 ½ 13
Leica Ding (AUS) *DWeir,Australia* 5-7-13 CraigAWilliams.......................... 25/1 hd 14
Ista Kareem (NZ) *CLittle,Australia* 9-8-6 LNolen.. 90/1 hd 15
Allez Wonder (AUS) *JBCummings,Australia* 4-7-13 (b) MichellePayne...... 25/1 ½ 16
Capecover (NZ) *AFieldes,NewZealand* 7-8-2 NoelHarris............................. 100/1 nk 17
Basaltico (IRE) *LMCumani,GB* 5-8-2 DNikolic... 25/1 3½ 18
Zavite (NZ) *ACummings,Australia* 7-8-5 (b) MZahra................................... 60/1 1¼ 19
Spin Around (AUS) *StevenCooper,Australia* 9-8-3 MduPlessis................. 200/1 nk 20
Roman Emperor (NZ) *JBCummings,Australia* 4-8-7 (b) HBowman............. 10/1 3½ 21
Fiumicino (NZ) *M,W&JHawkes,Australia* 6-8-10 SKing............................... 70/1 3½ 22
Warringah *CWaller,Australia* 4-8-5 DMOliver.. 30/1 30 23

Eales Racing Pty Ltd 23ran 3m23.87 TR: 117+/118/119/118/115/112

SANTA ANITA Friday, Nov 6 Turf course: FIRM, Pro-Ride course: FAST

89 Breeders' Cup Marathon Stks (3yo+) £163,636 1¾m (Pro-Ride)

MAN OF IRON (USA) *APO'Brien,Ireland* 3-8-10 JMurtagh (9)............... 64/10 1
CLOUDY'S KNIGHT (USA) *JESheppard,USA* 9-9-0 ns 2
RosemaryBHomeister (4)... 78/10
58 MASTERY *SaeedbinSuroor,GB* 3-8-10 LDettori (6)................................. 14/10f 2¼ 3
Gangbuster (USA) *JKDesormeaux,USA* 4-9-0 KDesormeaux (10)........... 304/10 12 4
3 Muhannak (IRE) *RMBeckett,GB* 5-9-0 (s) RMoore (2)............................. 239/10 1 5
58 Father Time *HRACecil,GB* 3-8-10 EddieAhern (5)..................................... 34/10 8 6
Eldaafer (USA) *DianeAlvarado,USA* 4-9-0 RBejarano (8)........................ 294/10 1½ 7
Nite Light (USA) *TAPletcher,USA* 5-9-0 JVelazquez (3)............................ 62/10 1 8
Black Astor (USA) *LisaLLewis,USA* 5-9-0 ASolis (1)................................. 222/10 10 9

Sir Dave (USA) *JCarava,USA* 4-9-0 (b) JRosario (7) .... 426/10 pu
Mr Derrick Smith 10ran 2m54.11 TR: 123/118/119/94/92/83

90 Emirates Airline Breeders' Cup Filly & Mare Turf (Gr 1) (3yo+ f+m) 1¼m (Turf)
£654,545

74 MIDDAY *HRACecil,GB* 3-8-8 TPQueally (6) 23/10 1
PURE CLAN (USA) *REHolthus,USA* 4-8-12 (b) GGomez (5) 76/10 1 2
FOREVER TOGETHER (USA) *JESheppard,USA* 5-8-12 JLeparoux (2) . 22/10f 1¼ 3
Visit *RJFrankel,USA* 4-8-12 JVelazquez (1) .... 113/10 nk 4
Magical Fantasy (USA) *PGallagher,USA* 4-8-12 ASolis (4) .... 45/10 ns 5
Maram (USA) *ChadCBrown,USA* 3-8-8 JLezcano (8) 161/10 1 6
Rutherienne (USA) *CClement,USA* 5-8-12 AGarcia (3) .... 13/1 ½ 7
Dynaforce (USA) *WIMott,USA* 6-8-12 KDesormeaux (7) 135/10 4¼ 8
Mr K. Abdulla 8ran 1m59.14 TR: 122/119+/115+/114/114/113

SANTA ANITA Saturday, Nov 7 Turf course: FIRM, Pro-Ride course: FAST

91 Grey Goose Breeders' Cup Juvenile (Gr 1) (2yo c+g) £654,545 1m110y (Pro-Ride)

78 VALE OF YORK (IRE) *SaeedbinSuroor,GB* 2-8-10 AhmedAjtebi (7)..... 306/10 1
LOOKIN AT LUCKY (USA) *RBaffert,USA* 2-8-10 GGomez (13)............ 22/10f hd 2
NOBLE'S PROMISE (USA) *KGMcPeek,USA* 2-8-10 WMartinez (4) .... 6/1 ½ 3
Piscitelli (USA) *GDSacco,USA* 2-8-10 KDesormeaux (2)........................ 506/10 hd 4
Aikenite (USA) *TAPletcher,USA* 2-8-10 AGarcia (9) 61/10 1¾ 5
81 Beethoven (IRE) *APO'Brien,Ireland* 2-8-10 (v) RyanMoore (3)............... 142/10 ns 6
69 Radiohead *BJMeehan,GB* 2-8-10 MartinDwyer (11) 101/10 1½ 7
William's Kitten (USA) *MJMaker,USA* 2-8-10 (b) RADominguez (12)... 783/10 ¾ 8
Eskendereya (USA) *TAPletcher,USA* 2-8-10 JCastellano (8) 124/10 1¾ 9
61 Alfred Nobel (IRE) *APO'Brien,Ireland* 2-8-10 JMurtagh (1).................... 143/10 1½ 10
Pulsion (USA) *PLBiancone,USA* 2-8-10 (b) MikeESmith (6) 144/10 2½ 11
Aspire (USA) *EKenneally,USA* 2-8-10 JLeparoux (10) 229/10 9 12
D'Funnybone (USA) *REDutrow,jnr,USA* 2-8-10 EPrado (5) 67/10 8 13
Godolphin 13ran 1m43.48 TR: 117/116+/115/115/110/110+

92 TVG Breeders' Cup Mile (Gr 1) (3yo+) £654,545 1m (Turf)

70 GOLDIKOVA (IRE) *FHead,France* 4-8-11 OPeslier (11).......................... 14/10f 1
COURAGEOUS CAT (USA) *WIMott,USA* 3-8-11 GGomez (6).............. 229/10 ½ 2
JUSTENUFFHUMOR (USA) *KPMcLaughlin,USA* 4-9-0 AGarcia (10) .. 164/10 1 3
Court Vision (USA) *REDutrow,jnr,USA* 4-9-0 (b) RAlbarado (1) .... 17/1 hd 4
66 Delegator *SaeedbinSuroor,GB* 3-8-11 LDettori (4)....................................... 63/10 1¾ 5
Karelian (USA) *GRArnoldII,USA* 7-9-0 RMaragh (5) .... 406/10 ½ 6
Ferneley (IRE) *BDACecil,USA* 5-9-0 RBejarano (7) 144/10 3¾ 7
Whatsthescript (IRE) *JWSadler,USA* 5-9-0 KDesormeaux (2).................. 192/10 1½ 8
79 Gladiatorus (USA) *SaeedbinSuroor,GB* 4-9-0 AhmedAjtebi (9)................ 132/10 ¾ 9
Cowboy Cal (USA) *TAPletcher,USA* 4-9-0 JVelazquez (3) .... 94/10 ½ 10
66 Zacinto *SirMichaelStoute,GB* 3-8-11 RyanMoore (8) 44/10 28 11
Wertheimer et Frere 11ran 1m32.26 TR: 122+/124/121/120/115/114

93 Emirates Airline Breeders' Cup Turf (Gr 1) (3yo+) £981,818 1½m (Turf)

75 CONDUIT (IRE) *SirMichaelStoute,GB* 4-9-0 RyanMoore (2) 9/10f 1
43 PRESIOUS PASSION (USA) *MaryHartmann,USA* 6-9-0 (b) ETrujillo (6) 59/10 ½ 2
75 DAR RE MI *JHMGosden,GB* 4-8-11 LDettori (5) 57/10 1¼ 3
63 Spanish Moon (USA) *SirMichaelStoute,GB* 5-9-0 KFallon (7)................... 32/10 1¼ 4
2 Red Rocks (IRE) *BJMeehan,GB* 6-9-0 JLeparoux (3) 191/10 1¼ 5
77 Monzante (USA) *MikeRMitchell,USA* 5-9-0 RBejarano (8) .... 182/10 hd 6
Telling (USA) *SteveHobby,USA* 5-9-0 JCastellano (1)................................ 175/10 6 7
Ballymacoll Stud 7ran 2m23.75 TR: 125/124/118/118/116/115

94 Breeders' Cup Classic (Gr 1) (3yo+) £1,636,364 1¼m (Pro-Ride)

ZENYATTA (USA) *JAShirreffs,USA* 5-8-11 MikeESmith (4).................... 28/10f 1
43 GIO PONTI (USA) *CClement,USA* 4-9-0 RADominguez (7)........................ 12/1 1 2
82 TWICE OVER *HRACecil,GB* 4-9-0 TPQueally (5).................................... 92/10 1¼ 3
Summer Bird (USA) *TAIce,USA* 3-8-10 (b) KDesormeaux (3) .... 68/10 ¾ 4
77 Colonel John (USA) *EHarty,USA* 4-9-0 GGomez (2)................................. 119/10 1½ 5
77 Richard's Kid (USA) *RBaffert,USA* 4-9-0 (b) ASolis (6) 114/10 1 6
Awesome Gem (USA) *CDollase,USA* 6-9-0 (b) DFlores (13).................. 521/10 1 7
Regal Ransom (USA) *SaeedbinSuroor,GB* 3-8-10 RMigliore (11)............ 391/10 3½ 8
77 Mine That Bird (USA) *BLWoolley,Jnr,USA* 3-8-10 CBorel (1) .... 144/10 ¾ 9
66 Rip Van Winkle (IRE) *APO'Brien,Ireland* 3-8-10 JMurtagh (10) 34/10 6¼ 10
43 Einstein (BRZ) *HelenPitts,USA* 7-9-0 JLeparoux (8)................................. 104/10 2 11
Girolamo (USA) *SaeedbinSuroor,GB* 3-8-10 AGarcia (9) 252/10 9¾ 12
Mr & Mrs Jerome S. Moss 12ran 2m00.62 TR: 129+/130/127/126/121/119

SAINT-CLOUD Saturday, Nov 14 HEAVY

95 Criterium de Saint-Cloud (Gr 1) (2yo c+f) £127,545 1¼m

PASSION FOR GOLD (USA) *SaeedbinSuroor,GB* 2-9-0 LDettori ... 6/4cpf 1
64 MIKHAIL GLINKA (IRE) *APO'Brien,Ireland* 2-9-0 JAHeffernan ... 26/10cp 6 2
ZAZOU (GER) *MHofer,Germany* 2-9-0 MGuyon ... 63/10 ¾ 3
Don Carlos (GER) *APO'Brien,Ireland* 2-9-0 JMurtagh ... 26/10cp 2½ 4
Kaage (IRE) *FHead,France* 2-9-0 OPeslier ... 9/1 2½ 5
Gardening Leave *AMBalding,GB* 2-9-0 WilliamBuick ... 29/1 2½ 6
Banyan Tree (IRE) *APO'Brien,Ireland* 2-9-0 CO'Donoghue ... 26/10cp 2½ 7
Simon de Montfort (IRE) *AFabre,France* 2-9-0 MickaelBarzalona ... 6/4cpf 1½ 8
Layali Al Andalus *MJohnston,GB* 2-9-0 JoeFanning ... 35/10 5 9
Godolphin 9ran 2m19.10 TR: 117+/107/106/101+/97/93

TOKYO Sunday, Nov 29 FIRM

96 Japan Cup (Gr 1) (3yo+) £1,728,024 1½m

1 VODKA (JPN) *KSumii,Japan* 5-8-10 CPLemaire ... 26/10f 1
OKEN BRUCE LEE (JPN) *HOtonashi,Japan* 4-9-0 HiroyukiUchida ... 37/10 ns 2
RED DESIRE (JPN) *MMatsunaga,Japan* 3-8-5 HShii ... 86/10 1½ 3
93 Conduit (IRE) *SirMichaelStoute,GB* 4-9-0 RyanMoore ... 39/10 1¼ 4
Air Shady (JPN) *MIto,Japan* 8-9-0 HGoto ... 44/1 1¼ 5
Eishin Deputy (JPN) *ANomoto,Japan* 7-9-0 (h) KTosaki ... 38/1 ½ 6
84 Just As Well (USA) *JESheppard,USA* 6-9-0 JLeparoux ... 46/1 ½ 7
Meiner Kitz (JPN) *SKunieda,Japan* 6-9-0 (b) MMatsuoka ... 31/1 ns 8
Reach The Crown (JPN) *KHashiguchi,Japan* 3-8-10 YTake ... 76/10 1½ 9
Never Bouchon (JPN) *MIto,Japan* 6-9-0 HKitamura ... 144/1 2 10
38 Scintillo *RHannon,GB* 4-9-0 GMosse ... 114/1 nk 11
Cosmo Bulk (JPN) *KTabe,Japan* 8-9-0 FIgarashi ... 123/1 3½ 12
Screen Hero (JPN) *YShikato,Japan* 5-9-0 MDemuro ... 75/10 ½ 13
Inti Raimi (JPN) *SSasaki,Japan* 7-9-0 CSoumillon ... 123/1 ½ 14
Interpatation (USA) *RBarbara,USA* 7-9-0 DCohen ... 89/1 dh 14
Asakusa Kings (JPN) *ROkubo,Japan* 5-9-0 YIwata ... 43/1 5 16
84 Marsh Side (USA) *NDDrysdale,USA* 6-9-0 JCastellano ... 32/1 ½ 17
Yamanin Kingly (JPN) *HKawachi,Japan* 4-9-0 (h) YShibayama ... 70/1 6 18
Y. Tanimizu 18ran 2m22.40 TR: 123/127/121/121/118/117

SHA TIN Sunday, Dec 13 GOOD

97 Cathay Pacific Hong Kong Vase (Gr 1) (3yo+) £622,951 1½m

DARYAKANA (FR) *AdeRoyerDupre,France* 3-8-6 GMosse ... 57/10 1
93 SPANISH MOON (USA) *SirMichaelStoute,GB* 5-9-0 RyanMoore ... 17/10f sh 2
76 KASBAH BLISS (FR) *FDoumen,France* 7-9-0 TThulliez ... 44/1 nk 3
Jaguar Mail (JPN) *NHori,Japan* 5-9-0 (b) CSoumillon ... 10/1 sh 4
Cirrus Des Aigles (FR) *MmeCBarandeBarbe,France* 3-8-9 FBlondel ... 17/2 ½ 5
6 Viva Pataca *JMoore,HongKong* 7-9-0 DBeadman ... 89/10 1¼ 6
6 Thumbs Up (NZ) *CSShum,HongKong* 5-9-0 (b) BPrebble ... 84/10 ½ 7
Jamesina (AUS) *DEFerraris,HongKong* 6-9-0 (t) JLloyd ... 61/1 ½ 8
84 Buccellati *AMBalding,GB* 5-9-0 (v) WilliamBuick ... 40/1 1 9
75 Youmzain (IRE) *MRChannon,GB* 6-9-0 (v) KFallon ... 22/5 1 10
6 Packing Winner (NZ) *LHo,HongKong* 6-9-0 BrettDoyle ... 29/1 4½ 11
Jackpot Delight (NZ) *CFownes,HongKong* 6-9-0 (t) JWinks ... 100/1 1½ 12
Black Mamba (NZ) *JWSadler,USA* 6-8-10 (t) ODoleuze ... 66/1 dist 13
H.H. Aga Khan 13ran 2m27.51 TR: 118+/121/120+/120/119/116

98 Cathay Pacific Hong Kong Sprint (Gr 1) (3yo+) £533,958 6f

31 SACRED KINGDOM (AUS) *PFYiu,HongKong* 6-9-0 (t) BPrebble ... 31/20f 1
ONE WORLD (AUS) *JMoore,HongKong* 5-9-0 (t) DBeadman ... 9/1 ½ 2
JOY AND FUN (NZ) *DCruz,HongKong* 6-9-0 BrettDoyle ... 20/1 nk 3
Green Birdie (NZ) *CFownes,HongKong* 6-9-0 ODoleuze ... 13/1 ¾ 4
California Flag (USA) *BJKoriner,USA* 5-9-0 (b+t) JTalamo ... 10/1 sh 5
71 Total Gallery (IRE) *JSMoore,GB* 3-9-0 JMurtagh ... 28/1 1¼ 6
Apache Cat (AUS) *GEurell,Australia* 7-9-0 (b) DMOliver ... 12/1 ½ 7
All Silent (AUS) *GBegg,Australia* 6-9-0 (b+t) NicholasHall ... 4/1 hd 8
12 Inspiration (AUS) *JMoore,HongKong* 6-9-0 (t) JWinks ... 34/1 ns 9
31 Cannonball (USA) *WesleyAWard,USA* 4-9-0 (t) RADominguez ... 34/1 hd 10
71 Borderlescott *RBastiman,GB* 7-9-0 NCallan ... 83/1 1¾ 11
71 War Artist (AUS) *JMPEustace,GB* 6-9-0 OPeslier ... 42/1 2¼ 12
Laurel Guerreiro (JPN) *MKon,Japan* 5-9-0 SFujita ... 40/1 ½ 13
35 Scenic Blast (AUS) *DMorton,Australia* 5-9-0 (t) StevenArnold ... 83/10 6¼ 14
Sin Kang Yuk 14ran 1m09.16 TR: 123/121/120/118/117+/114+

99 Cathay Pacific Hong Kong Mile (Gr 1) (3yo+) £711,943 1m

GOOD BA BA (USA) *DCruz,HongKong* 7-9-0 (t) ODoleuze ... 53/20 1

HAPPY ZERO (AUS) *JMoore,HongKong* 5-9-0 DBeadman .... 9/10f ½ 2
FELLOWSHIP (NZ) *PO'Sullivan,HongKong* 7-9-0 (t) ZPurton .... 12/1 hd 3
Egyptian Ra (NZ) *ASCruz,HongKong* 7-9-0 (t) FCoetzee .... 18/1 nk 4
92 Ferneley (IRE) *BDACecil,USA* 5-9-0 (t) KFallon .... 70/1 ¾ 5
Confront *SirMichaelStoute,GB* 4-9-0 RyanMoore .... 33/1 sh 6
22 Alexandros *SaeedbinSuroor,GB* 4-9-0 LDettori 21/1 1¼ 7
Able One (NZ) *JMoore,HongKong* 7-9-0 BPrebble .... 16/1 nk 8
70 Sweet Hearth (USA) *AdeRoyerDupre,France* 3-8-9 GMosse .... 25/1 ns 9
13 Gris de Gris (IRE) *AdeRoyerDupre,France* 5-9-0 TThulliez .... 75/1 sh 10
Sight Winner (NZ) *JSize,HongKong* 6-9-0 DJWhyte .... 21/1 nk 11
59 Duff (IRE) *EdwardLynam,Ireland* 6-9-0 FMBerry .... 100/1 sh 12
Racing To Win (AUS) *JohnO'Shea,Australia* 7-9-0 (b) JHBowman 30/1 2¼ 13
11 Pressing (IRE) *MAJarvis,GB* 6-9-0 NCallan .... 65/1 dist 14
Mr John Yuen Se Kit 14ran 1m34.06 TR: 124+/123/122/121/119/119

100 Cathay Pacific Hong Kong Cup (Gr 1) (3yo+) £889,929 1¼m

75 VISION D'ETAT (FR) *ELibaud,France* 4-9-0 OPeslier 61/10 1
COLLECTION (IRE) *JMoore,HongKong* 4-9-0 (t) DBeadman .... 9/10f ¾ 2
6 PRESVIS *LMCumani,GB* 5-9-0 KFallon 5/2 2½ 3
Ashalanda (FR) *AdeRoyerDupre,France* 3-8-7 GMosse .... 12/1 nk 4
Eagle Mountain *MFdeKock,SouthAfrica* 5-9-0 KShea .... 18/1 ¾ 5
Starlish (IRE) *ELellouche,France* 4-9-0 ACrastus .... 90/1 sh 6
Special Days (NZ) *JSize,HongKong* 5-9-0 CraigWilliams .... 83/1 ¾ 7
Mr Medici (IRE) *LHo,HongKong* 4-9-0 LDettori 12/1 1¼ 8
Eyshal (IRE) *JMoore,HongKong* 5-9-0 (b+t) WCMarwing .... 62/1 nk 9
Queen Spumante (JPN) *SKojima,Japan* 5-8-10 HTanaka 34/1 2¾ 10
Mr J. Detre 10ran 2m01.86 TR: 127/125/119+/115/117/116

INDEX TO SELECTED BIG RACES

Timeform Horse of the Year

Timeform's 'Racehorses' series stretches back to 1948 when the first prototype Annual—the 'Timeform Supplement'—was produced covering the 1947 season. The selecting of a 'horse of the year' began in the 'sixties. The title has usually been awarded to the highest rated horse, except in 1969 (when Habitat was rated higher at 134), 1984 (El Gran Senor 136), 1985 (Slip Anchor 136) and 2003 (Hawk Wing 136). Raven's Pass was also rated 133 in 2008.

1960	Charlottesville	**135**	1984	Provideo	**112**
	Floribunda	**135**	1985	Pebbles	**135**
1961	Molvedo	**137**	1986	Dancing Brave	**140**
1962	Match	**135**	1987	Reference Point	**139**
1963	Exbury	**138**	1988	Warning	**136**
1964	Relko	**136**	1989	Zilzal	**137**
1965	Sea-Bird	**145**	1990	Dayjur	**137**
1966	Danseur	**134**	1991	Generous	**139**
1967	Petingo	**135**	1992	St Jovite	**135**
1968	Vaguely Noble	**140**	1993	Opera House	**131**
1969	Levmoss	**133**	1994	Celtic Swing	**138**
1970	Nijinsky	**138**	1995	Lammtarra	**134**
1971	Brigadier Gerard	**141**	1996	Mark of Esteem	**137**
	Mill Reef	**141**	1997	Peintre Celebre	**137**
1972	Brigadier Gerard	**144**	1998	Intikhab	**135**
1973	Apalachee	**137**	1999	Daylami	**138**
	Rheingold	**137**	2000	Dubai Millennium	**140**
1974	Allez France	**136**	2001	Sakhee	**136**
1975	Grundy	**137**	2002	Rock of Gibraltar	**133**
1976	Youth	**135**	2003	Falbrav	**133**
1977	Alleged	**137**	2004	Doyen	**132**
1978	Alleged	**138**	2005	Hurricane Run	**134**
1979	Troy	**137**	2006	George Washington	**133**
1980	Moorestyle	**137**	2007	Manduro	**135**
1981	Shergar	**140**	2008	Zarkava	**133**
1982	Ardross	**134**	2009	Sea The Stars	**140**
1983	Habibti	**136**			

Highest Annual Ratings

(3-y-os+ in Europe)

145	Sea-Bird
144	Brigadier Gerard, Tudor Minstrel
142	Abernant, Ribot
141	Mill Reef
140	Dancing Brave, Dubai Millennium, Sea The Stars, Shergar, Vaguely Noble
139	Generous, Pappa Fourway, Reference Point
138	Alleged, Alycidon, Daylami, Exbury, Nijinsky

THE TIMEFORM 'TOP HORSES ABROAD'

Horses not rated highly enough in this review of 2009 for inclusion in the main lists, but which were placed in a European pattern race or (Japan and North America) won a Grade 1, are included below the cut-off line.

IRELAND Commenting on Irish horseracing in 2009 brings to mind the opening words of Charles Dickens' *A Tale of Two Cities*, for it was both the best of times and the worst of times. Horse Racing Ireland's chief executive Brian Kavanagh struggled to put a favourable gloss on proceedings when looking back at the year's end. From an industry point of view, most of the year-on-year measures made grim reading: attendances were down 12%; prize money was down 12%; total betting was down 21%; and bloodstock sales were down a whopping 32%. HRI also estimated that between 1,500 and 2,000 jobs had been lost in racing during the current economic crisis, around 10% of the industry's workforce, while Weatherbys predicted a drop in Irish foals in 2010 of about 30% compared with just three years earlier.

An *Irish Times* editorial, commenting on the wider economic picture, declared in January: 'We have gone from the Celtic Tiger to an era of financial fear with the suddenness of a Titanic-style shipwreck, thrown from comfort, even luxury, into a cold sea of uncertainty'. As an industry that had, for many years, been riding the wave of the boom and benefiting greatly from remarkable levels of government support and subsidy, Irish racing was bound to suffer badly. The Irish Government, and as a result HRI, has been forced into swingeing cuts, with the former's contribution to the Horse and Greyhound Fund due to be reduced by 13% and the latter announcing that prize money will have to return to something like 2002 levels.

When the sun is shining it is all too easy to forget about mending that hole in the roof. The parties concerned must regret not having secured a better funding mechanism for the future of Irish racing long before it became such a pressing need. In the event, a proposal made by Ireland's Labour Party early in 2010 to end direct funding by increasing betting levy and applying it to bets across all platforms (something which may prove difficult to enforce in any case), if not necessarily too little, would clearly come too late to avoid the worst consequences of the economic downturn.

Irish racing should also regret not having taken bolder steps to make the most of the assets that already existed. For instance, it is very difficult to understand why the country's only all-weather track at Dundalk should continue to lie idle through the winter months. That there would be significant interest in an all-weather programme—one that is planned well in advance rather than wheeled out only if the weather turns bad—can be inferred from the number of Irish-trained horses that are sent to Britain during this period. If it was not already abundantly clear how well received an Irish all-weather winter racing programme could be, it probably is now, following severe disruption to the jumps fixture lists on both sides of the Irish Sea in 2009/10.

Against all these, and other, tales of doom and gloom, Irish racing enjoyed spectacular success on the track, notably through the magnificent **Sea The Stars**. The three-year-old's unbeaten season—which took in the Two Thousand Guineas at Newmarket, the Derby at Epsom, the Eclipse at Sandown, the International at York, the Irish Champion at Leopardstown and the Prix de l'Arc de Triomphe at Longchamp—marked him down as one of the best horses in Timeform's history and as the most highly-rated Flat performer ever trained in Ireland. The previous best was 138, posted by Nijinsky in 1970 and Alleged in 1978, both horses trained by the legendary Vincent O'Brien, who died, aged 92, a few days before Sea The Stars won the Derby.

For once, this was an Irish champion that was not trained by an O'Brien—Vincent or more latterly Aidan—but by John Oxx, whose handling of the colt, and of himself in the glare of the media, was exemplary. Sea The Stars also struck up a tremendous partnership with jockey Michael Kinane, who was on board for all of his races. Kinane went out on a high, announcing his retirement at the age of 50 after the end of the season. He will be replaced as Oxx's number-one by Fran Berry, who finished behind only Johnny Murtagh (winning the title for the first time in over a decade) and Pat Smullen in the 2009 Irish jockeys' championship.

It is a matter of dispute, not to mention of personal preference, as to which of Sea The Stars's wins represented his finest hour. The Eclipse and the Irish Champion were his best in terms of bare form, but his Arc win may well live longest in the memory after he overcame difficulties under a remarkably composed ride to beat eighteen rivals.

After only a little public deliberation, Sea The Stars was retired at season's end and will stand at Gilltown Stud, County Kildare, at a fee of €85,000. While this must have provided a fillip to the Irish breeding industry in such trying times, it does raise questions as to how marketable Flat racing can be when its superstars are hurried off to stud at such a young age with 'nothing left to prove'. It should also be noted that only one of Sea The Stars's six races in his classic season took place on home soil. Despite the affluence of Irish racing, at least until recently, and the fact that many of the best horses in the world are trained there, there are only a few events in the calendar that have much chance of attracting horses of Sea The Stars's calibre. This situation will not have been improved by particularly harsh cuts to prize money at the highest level.

It was not just a one-horse show, however. The Aidan O'Brien-trained **Fame And Glory** chased home Sea The Stars in both The Derby and the Irish Champion, between which he was a five-length winner of the Irish Derby at the Curragh, and the former's stablemates, **Mastercraftsman** and **Rip Van Winkle**, managed to run the champion to a length in the International and the Eclipse respectively. Rip Van Winkle went on to win the Sussex Stakes at Goodwood and the Queen Elizabeth II Stakes at Ascot (he did not run in Ireland at all in 2009) and emerges just ahead of Fame And Glory on the ratings, while Mastercraftsman was an easy winner of the Irish Two Thousand Guineas at the Curragh and the Diamond Stakes at Dundalk but had to fight much harder to land the St James's Palace Stakes at Royal Ascot.

While Mastercraftsman joined Sea The Stars in being retired to stud, the good news is that Rip Van Winkle and Fame And Glory remain in training. All eleven runners in the latter's Irish Derby were home-trained, with Aidan O'Brien landing a one, two courtesy of **Golden Sword**, and perhaps even more remarkably all four of the runners in York's International Stakes came from Ireland. Add to that the fact that eight of the twelve runners in the Derby at Epsom were trained in Ireland, including the first six in the betting and the first five to finish, and it can be seen that the male middle-distance division was in a particularly healthy state. The older horse **Casual Conquest** also chipped in with wins in the Tattersalls Gold Cup and Royal Whip at the Curragh.

Things were tougher for the females at all distances, with British-trained raiders winning three of the five Group 1s confined to that sex (Dar Re Mi in the Pretty Polly Stakes at the Curragh, Sariska in the Irish Oaks on the same course and Rainbow View in the Matron Stakes at Leopardstown). The David Wachman-trained **Again** was one of the exceptions, but her win in the Irish One Thousand Guineas came in a fairly weak renewal, run on particularly testing ground, and she failed to win again.

Yeats is another to have been retired, joining his former stablemate Mastercraftsman at Coolmore. He managed just four runs and one win in 2009, but what a win it was! His defeat of Patkai in the Gold Cup at Royal Ascot showed he was very nearly as good as ever as an eight-year-old and meant that he was the first horse to win the race in four successive years. Yeats was clearly never easy to train, managing no more than five runs in any of his seven seasons in action, and his record paid yet another compliment to the consummate skills of Aidan O'Brien, who picked up the Irish trainers' title once more.

Yeats's swansong was at Longchamp in the Prix du Cadran, in which he came third to the John Oxx-trained **Alandi**, who himself had previously won the Irish St Leger at the Curragh. With Alandi, along with another Cup type in the Irish Derby third **Mourayan**, sold to race in Australia at the end of the year, the staying division threatens to be weak in 2010.

That has been the situation with the sprinters for quite some time now, a consequence, at least in part, of there being no five-furlong or six-furlong races for three-year-olds and older at higher than Group 3 level in Ireland. Several of the better races went to British-trained horses, and no single sprinter stamped its mark among the home team. Better efforts were put up at seven furlongs by **Duff** (winner of the Ballycorus Stakes at Leopardstown and Concorde Stakes at Tipperary, as well as in Britain, for trainer Edward Lynam) and **Libano**. The latter was transferred to Dermot Weld after success in the Premio

Parioli at Rome in April and put up a very smart effort when penalised and beating the Irish Two Thousand Guineas runner-up **Rayeni** by two lengths in a listed contest at Leopardstown in November. It will be a surprise if Libano does not score back at a higher level in 2010 if all remains well.

Mastercraftsman and Sea The Stars (in winning at Newmarket) achieved more at a mile than did any of the older contingent, but **Famous Name**, the winner of the International Stakes and the Desmond Stakes at the Curragh, and **Poet**, who took the valuable Irish Cambridgeshire on the same course, posted notable victories. The latter's success under 10-0 and an Irish Turf Club mark of 107 represented the best handicap performance of the year in Ireland, and he ran every bit as well when landing the ten-furlong Kilternan Stakes at Leopardstown soon after. Among the fillies, **Chinese White** was not far behind that pair judged on three victories at between nine and ten furlongs, culminating in the Blandford Stakes over the latter trip at the Curragh. There was also a notable handicap success abroad in the Ebor Handicap at York for **Sesenta**, partnered by Irish champion apprentice Gary Carroll.

The Irish-trained two-year-olds made their presence felt once more, with pride of place going to **St Nicholas Abbey**, unbeaten in three races, including the Beresford Stakes at the Curragh, and top-rated juvenile in Europe courtesy of his easy win in the Racing Post Trophy at Doncaster. The colt's trainer, Aidan O'Brien, had three of the first four in the Dewhurst Stakes at Newmarket, but in the opposite order to that suggested by the betting. **Beethoven**, who won only one other race from a total of eleven starts, emerged victorious in a blanket finish at 33/1, but the runner-up **Fencing Master** and the fourth **Steinbeck** (each with one run and one win to their name beforehand) look better prospects for 2010.

The Jim Bolger-trained **Chabal** edged favouritism over Steinbeck in the Dewhurst but could finish only tenth. He is better judged on his running-on neck second to the Kevin Prendergast-trained **Kingsfort** (unbeaten in two runs) in a muddling contest for the National Stakes at the Curragh. Both Chabal and Kingsfort (whose essay deals with the remarkably wet summer in Ireland and the testing ground that went with it) were acquired by Godolphin after their final starts.

Alfred Nobel gained big wins at the Curragh in the Phoenix Stakes and Railway Stakes (to add to a maiden success), but both were in substandard affairs, and the colt was unplaced on three subsequent starts. Aidan O'Brien looks to have better prospects for 2010 with **Jan Vermeer**, winner of the Criterium International at Saint-Cloud, and the unbeaten **Cape Blanco**, though the latter was not seen after a workmanlike victory at long odds on in the Futurity Stakes at Fairyhouse in August.

Termagant sealed a memorable season for veteran trainer Kevin Prendergast by winning the only domestic Group 1 for two-year-old fillies, the Moyglare Stud Stakes at the Curragh, and went into winter quarters unbeaten in two starts. The highly-touted Aidan O'Brien-trained **Lillie Langtry** managed only third in that race—another to be run in very testing conditions—but picked up big prizes at Naas, Leopardstown (Debutante Stakes) and Newmarket before sustaining a knee fracture at the Breeders' Cup.

The two hugely valuable sales races at the Curragh in September, the Goffs Million Sprint and the Goffs Million Mile, went to British raiders Lucky General (trained by Richard Hannon) and Shakespearean (trained by Mark Johnston) respectively. It is likely that Hannon, who has compiled a tremendous record in such events, in particular will rue the fact that Goffs announced earlier in the year that the 2009 Million races would be the last. In another sign of the times, the sales company announced a fall in turnover from 2008 to 2009 of €21.5m.

Two-Year-Olds

126p	St Nicholas Abbey	111p	Termagant (f)	107p	Black Quartz
119p	Jan Vermeer	111	Free Judgement	107p	Midas Touch
117	Beethoven	111	Viscount Nelson	107p	Song of My Heart (f)
116p	Fencing Master	110p	Cape Blanco	106	Lillie Langtry (f)
116+	Arctic	110	Alfred Nobel	106	Mister Tee
115p	Joshua Tree	110	Atasari (f)	106	Montecchio
115p	Kingsfort	110	Love Lockdown	105P	You'll Be Mine (f)
115p	Steinbeck	110	*Long Lashes (f)	105	Cabaret (f)
114p	Chabal	108	Air Chief Marshal	105	Walk On Bye (f)
		108	Mikhail Glinka	104	Famous (f)

103p Keredari
103p Thunder Bridge
103 *King Ledley
103 Lord High Admiral
102p Don Carlos
102 Emperor Claudius
102 Lady Springbank (f)
102 Rock Jock
102 Sebastian Flyte
102 Stunning View
102 Wrong Answer (f)
101p Nebula Storm
101 Elusive Award
100p Lady Lupus (f)
100 Famous Warrior
100 In Some Respect
100 Marfach
100 *Roan Inish (f)
100? Senior
99p Await The Dawn
99 Beat Surrender
99 Devoted To You (f)
99 Dream Deer
99 Miracle Match
99 Perfect Symmetry
99 Sole Power
98P Flying Cross
98p Gibraltar Blue (f)
98 Bobbyscot
98 *Elusive Galaxy (f)
98 En Un Clin d'Oeil
98 Is Feidir Linn
97p Dynasty
97p Fighting Brave
97 Corcovada (f)
97 Gold Bubbles (f)
97 Moonreach
97 Utrillo
97 What A Charm (f)
96 Sense of Purpose (f)
95p Foolish Ambition (f)
95 Akdarena (f)
95 Legendary Lad
95 Picture Perfect (f)
95 Queen of Troy (f)
95 Rahya Cass (f)

---

93 Kitty Kiernan (f)
91 A Mind of Her Own (f)
89 Alshahbaa (f)

Three-Year-Olds

140 Sea The Stars
134 Rip Van Winkle
133 Fame And Glory
129 Mastercraftsman
123 Man of Iron
122 Gan Amhras
122 Golden Sword
122d *Masterofthehorse
121 *Libano
121 Mourayan
118p Age of Aquarius
118 Rayeni
118 Changingoftheguard
117 Roses For The Lady (f)
117 Westphalia
116 Alaivan
116 Grand Ducal
116 Yankee Doodle
115 Again (f)
114 *Black Bear Island
114 Fergus McIver
114 *Freemantle
114 Intense Focus
114 Roman Empress (f)
114 Vocalised
113 Aspectoflove (f)
113 Cuis Ghaire (f)
113 Recharge
112 Aliyfa (f)
112 Rain Delayed
111 Johann Zoffany
111 Von Jawlensky
111§ The Bull Hayes
109 *Ard Na Greine
109 Choose Me (f)
109 Heart Shaped (f)
109 Tanoura (f)
108p Tarankali
108 Baliyana (f)
108 Chief Lone Eagle
108 Hallie's Comet (f)
108 Luminous Eyes (f)
108 Oh Goodness Me (f)
108 Trojan War
107 *Beauty O'Gwaun (f)
107 Grace O'Malley (f)
107 Latin Love (f)
107 Tamarind (f)
106 Adjaliya (f)
106 Drumbeat
106 Galileo's Choice
106 Maoineach (f)
106 Palazzone
106§ Peter Tchaikovsky
106§ Stately Home
105 Across The Rhine
105 Born To Be King
105 Bushranger
105 Count John
105 Enchanted Evening (f)
105 Liszt
105 Nafaath
105 Perfect Truth (f)
105 Seachantach
105 Slieve Mish (f)
104 Augustusthestrong
104 Barack
104 Croisultan
104 Dance Pass (f)
104 Dixie Music
104 Eytarna (f)
104 French Irish
104 Hail Caesar
104 *Miss Keller (f)
104 Moon Indigo
104 Set Sail
104 Sioduil (f)
104 Sugar Free (f)
104 Totally Devoted (f)
103 Big Game Hunter
103 *Cambiaso
103 Dandy Boy
103 Jakarta Jazz (f)
103 Timabiyra (f)
103 Toraidhe
102 Alaiyma (f)
102 Aristocrat
102 Casual (f)
102 *Ebashan
101 *Aaroness (f)
101 Douze Points
101 Rockhampton
101 Sunwise
100 Chintz (f)
100 The Tooth Fairy
100 Vitruvian Man
99 Coolcullen Times
99 Firey Red (f)
99 Forest Storm (f)
99 Gluteus Maximus
99 Noble Galileo (f)
99 Pittoni
99 Sirgarfieldsobers
99d *Lastkingofscotland
98 Alexander Youth (f)
98 Bangalore Gold
98 Crowfoot
98 Malibu Bay
98 Ohiyesa (f)
98 Smart Coco (f)
98 Tarrsille
98 The Pier
97 Beidh Tine Anseo
97 Chirkova (f)
97 Few Are Chosen (f)
97 Handsome Batchelor
97 Like Magic
97 Monivea (f)
97 Mr Topaz
97 Precious Gem (f)
96 Always Be True (f)
96 Carefree Smile (f)
96 Chorus of Angels (f)
96 Curling Bird
96 Izagonawin (f)
96 *Liebermann
96 Mean Lae (f)
96 Penthesilea Eile (f)
96 Space Telescope
96 What's Up Pussycat (f)
95p Zaralanta (f)
95 L'Impresario
95 Kinetic Quest
95 Loch Long
95 Rare Ransom (f)
95 Wanna (f)

Older Horses

126 Yeats
123 Casual Conquest
123 Famous Name
122 Duff
121 Alandi
121 Poet
119 Summit Surge
118 Profound Beauty (f)
117 Chinese White (f)
117 Fiery Lad
117 Mad About You (f)

117	Thewayyouare	106	Cochlear	99	Green Tobasco
116	Jumbajukiba	106	Indiana Gal (f)	99	Kitty Hawk Miss (f)
116	Three Rocks	106	Pollen (f)	99	Magen's Star (f)
115	Dohasa	106	Quinmaster	99	Miranda's Girl (f)
115	Emily Blake (f)	106	Rose Hip (f)	99	Siberian Tiger
115	Lord Admiral	105	Aine (f)	98	Andre Mon Ami
115	Shreyas (f)	105	Bashkirov	98	Angels Story (f)
115§	Frozen Fire	105	Le Cadre Noir	98	Designated Decoy
114	Beach Bunny (f)	105	Maundy Money	98	Fit The Cove
114	Luisant	105	Mojito Royale	98	Kingsdale Ocean
114	Snaefell	105	Senor Benny	98	Romeo's On Fire
114§	Via Galilei	105	Sesenta (f)	98	Tornadodancer
113	Kargali	105	Sublimity	98§	Mooretown Lady (f)
113	Raise Your Heart	105	Varsity (f)	98§	Shela House
113	Rock of Rochelle	105	Windsor Palace	98d	Crooked Throw
113	She's Our Mark (f)	104	Invincible Ash (f)	98d	Tis Mighty (f)
113§	Georgebernardshaw	104	Kalidaha (f)	97	Arc Bleu
112	*Leandros	104	Mid Mon Lady (f)	97	Greatwallofchina
112	Moiqen	104	Mountain Coral	97	Gwens Spirit
111	Worldly Wise	104	Zaralabad	97	Irish Heartbeat
111d	Estrela Brage	103	Award Ceremony	97	Kaitlins Joy (f)
110	Deauville Vision (f)	103	Belle's Ridge	97	Laurel Creek
110	Fourpenny Lane (f)	103	Drive Time	97	Merveilles
110	Ghimaar	103	Eagle's Pass	97	Ransomed Bride (f)
110	Impossible Dream	103	Excelerate	97	Toirneach (f)
110	*King Jock	103	Festival Princess (f)	97	Valentine Hill (f)
110	Lush Lashes (f)	103	Fingers	96	Astonish (f)
110	Miss Gorica (f)	103	Funatfuntasia	96	Ballivor
110	Rock And Roll Kid	103	Love Intrigue (f)	96	Dahindar
110	Santo Padre	103	Suailce (f)	96	Good Time Sue (f)
110	Silverhand	102	Ask Jack	96	Grand Opera
109	Dirar	102	Bobs Pride	96	Harrington
109	Red Rock Canyon	102	Emmpat	96	Marias Dream (f)
109§	Arch Rebel	102	Headford View (f)	96	Mourinho
109d	Monteriggioni	102	Six of Hearts	96	Red Eye Express
108	Baron De'l	102	Speed Ticket	96	Royal Intruder
108	Deutschland	101	Castle Bar Sling	96	Show Blessed
108	Empirical Power	101	Dedo	96d	Glitter Baby (f)
108	Girouette (f)	101	Donegal	95	Avanti Albert
108	*Glowing (f)	101	Hard Rock City	95	Daasij
108	*High Court Drama	101	Northgate	95	Donnas Palm
108	Katiyra (f)	101	Orpailleur	95	Evening Rushour (f)
108	Nanotech	101	Pires	95	First In Line
108	San Sicharia (f)	101	Russian Empress (f)	95	Gunga Din
107	Copper Dock	101	Soap Wars	95	Just For Mary
107	Drunken Sailor	100	Al Eile	95	Lime Tree Valley
107	Finicius	100	Bahrain Storm	95	Master Marvel
107	Majestic Concorde	100	Osterhase	95	Mourad
107	Perfect Polly (f)	100	Rajik	95	Prince Erik
107	Salute Him	100	Zorija Rose (f)	95	Scarlet O'Hara (f)
107	Settigano	100§	An Tadh	95	Separate Ways
106p	Rite of Passage	99	Alhabeeb	95	Toufan Express
106	Bravely Fought	99	Ashka (f)	95	Valain
106	Celtic Dane	99	Ebadiyan	95	Wymering File (f)
		99	End of The Affair (f)		
		99	Fictional Account (f)		

FRANCE Successful as it was, **Goldikova**'s three-year-old season was put in the shade by the exploits of her top-class contemporary Zarkava who beat her in both of the French fillies' classics. But with Zarkava retiring unbeaten after her Arc victory at the end of 2008, Goldikova had the stage to herself as a four-year-old, improving into a top-class filly herself with four more wins at the highest level. The last of those, her second success in the Breeders' Cup Mile, gave substance to comparisons between her and Miesque, France's outstanding miling filly of the late-'eighties and the regular partner of Goldikova's trainer Freddie Head. The fact that Goldikova stays in training for another season gives her the opportunity to rival Miesque's record total of ten Group/Grade 1 wins. Unlike the year before, Goldikova did not need to show her best form of the season to win at Santa Anita; her top-class performance came instead at Deauville where she lowered the race record with a six-length win in the Prix Jacques le Marois a fortnight after winning her second Prix Rothschild at the same course. Goldikova also made her first appearance in Britain a winning one when taking the Falmouth Stakes at Newmarket, while there were plausible excuses for her two defeats of the season which both came at Longchamp, in the Prix d'Ispahan and Prix de la Foret.

Goldikova stood out in a French season where it was human rather than equine achievements that tended to steal the headlines. Trainer Jean-Claude Rouget hadn't saddled a classic winner before the latest season but won three in 2009 in a tremendous run of success in the first part of the year, while the Aga Khan dominated the Arc meeting to an extraordinary degree in the autumn. Rouget broke his duck in the classics when **Elusive Wave** won the Poule d'Essai des Pouliches. She proved no match for Goldikova in the Rothschild, though that was much her best effort subsequently, coming between a below-form fourth in the Coronation Stakes and a refusal to race in the Prix du Moulin. The stable had an even better filly in **Stacelita** who completed the rare double of the Prix Saint-Alary and Prix de Diane, winning both races impressively to remain unbeaten. That record remained intact after the Prix Vermeille as well, but only after the year's most controversial stewards' decision which left her as the fortunate recipient of the prize on the demotion of Dar Re Mi. The disqualification of the British-trained winner under the very strict French rules was widely condemned on both sides of the Channel, sections of the Longchamp crowd making its feelings known at the prize-giving and *Paris Turf* describing the decision as 'unjust and incomprehensible'. Sent off joint second favourite, Stacelita finished two places behind Dar Re Mi when dead-heating for seventh in the Arc, for which she was supplemented, three weeks later. Underlining the Rouget stable's strength in the three-year-old fillies' department, **Tamazirte** finished runner-up to her stable companions in both the Pouliches and the Diane, though gained pattern-race wins at Longchamp in the Prix de la Grotte in the spring and the Prix Daniel Wildenstein in the autumn.

Rouget became the first trainer since Charlie Elliott in 1956 to win the two Chantilly classics, with Stacelita's Prix de Diane win coming a week after the Poule d'Essai des Poulains runner-up **Le Havre** had gone one better in the Prix du Jockey Club. Tendon problems meant that Le Havre had to be retired after the Jockey Club (runner-up **Fuisse** was not seen out again either) in which he had the Poulains winner **Silver Frost** back in sixth. Silver Frost had completed an early-season hat-trick in the Poulains to prevent a clean sweep of the first four classics by the Rouget stable, and while retirement beckoned after another below-form effort in the Jacques le Marois, Silver Frost may return to action in 2010. The top French two-year-old colt of the previous season **Naaqoos** was third past the post in the Poulains (demoted to sixth for causing interference) but that was to prove his best run in a disappointing three-race campaign which had begun with an odds-on defeat to Le Havre in the Prix Djebel. **Oiseau de Feu** proved another smart performer at Group 1 level among the three-year-olds for the Rouget stable, making the frame in the Poulains (promoted to fourth), Prix Jean Prat and Prix du Moulin and winning the Group 3 Prix Paul de Moussac.

Jockey Christophe Lemaire partnered all three of the Rouget stable's classic winners but his luck ran out when breaking a collarbone in a fall on the eve of Arc weekend. As a result, he missed out on eight winning rides at the two-day meeting which was monopolised by the Aga Khan, for whom Lemaire becomes first jockey in 2010 in place of Christophe Soumillon. The Aga Khan won seven of the weekend's eleven pattern races, five of them Group 1 contests, with runners from three different stables, just about the best of them being the three-year-old colt **Varenar** who had Goldikova back in third in the Prix de la Foret. The Aga Khan remarked afterwards that he wouldn't have swapped those successes for an Arc win (his representative in the big race, the Prix Niel runner-up **Beheshtam**, finished twelfth), though even the Arc result ultimately had a more positive outcome for the Aga Khan when his Gilltown Stud was chosen for Sea The Stars to begin his stallion career.

It was Beheshtam's Prix Niel conqueror **Cavalryman** who fared best of the home-trained horses when third behind Sea The Stars and Youmzain in the Arc, the only French horse to finish in the first six. Cavalryman had also had the odds-on Beheshtam behind him (in sixth) in the Grand Prix de Paris and was the most successful representative of the newly-strengthened partnership between Andre Fabre and Sheikh Mohammed. From Deauville's August meeting onwards, the higher-profile members of Sheikh Mohammed's Fabre-trained string began appearing in Godolphin's beige French colours which were last seen when the Godolphin two-year-olds were trained for a couple of seasons by David Loder at Evry around the turn of the millennium. Another interesting Sheikh Mohammed colt is **Cutlass Bay** who is unbeaten in three starts and missed the rest of the season after beating stable-companion Cavalryman in the Prix Greffulhe in May.

The latest crop of French three-year-olds included a couple of above-average stayers in **Wajir** and **Manighar**. Wajir won the Prix Hocquart before finding the Jockey Club an inadequate test, but he put up his best effort when stepped up in trip to give Manighar 9 lb and a length beating in the Prix de Lutece at Longchamp in the autumn. Wajir did not run again but the gelding Manighar, unbeaten in five previous outings, went on to further success, winning the Prix Chaudenay at the Arc meeting before running a good third against older horses in the Prix Royal-Oak. Another gelding to blossom at pattern level at Longchamp in the autumn was **Cirrus des Aigles**, winner of the Prix du Prince d'Orange and Prix du Conseil de Paris. He proved remarkably tough and consistent, winning six times all told and never finishing worse than third in his sixteen starts in France before finishing a close fifth in the Hong Kong Vase.

The Prix de Diane came a bit too early for them, but by the autumn the Aga Khan had three smart three-year-old fillies over middle-distances. **Shalanaya** showed plenty of improvement to beat a good field in the Prix de l'Opera, the unbeaten **Daryakana** was another of the owner's Arc meeting winners when successful in the Prix de Royallieu before taking some notable scalps against older rivals in the Hong Kong Vase, while **Ashalanda** showed her Prix de Malleret win (when acting as pacemaker) was no fluke when sent over to land the Pride Stakes at Newmarket. The last-named pair are trained by Alain de Royer Dupre, along with **Sweet Hearth** who completed a one, two for the stable in the Foret a short head behind Varenar. The same yard's **Reggane** was an excellent second in the Coronation Stakes on just her third start but was below that form in a couple of starts back in France afterwards. The previous season's Prix Marcel Boussac winner **Proportional** failed to win at three, coming closest when beaten a short head by subsequent Opera runner-up **Board Meeting** in the Prix de Psyche at Deauville. **Plumania**'s third place in the Psyche was one of several placings in pattern company which included being third past the post in the Diane and Vermeille.

Among the older horses, **Vision d'Etat** was much the best French three-year-old colt of the previous season to stay in training and while he failed to run as well in the Arc as he had the year before, he proved every bit as good otherwise, winning the Prix Ganay and the Prince of Wales's Stakes at Royal Ascot, (the latter race also seeing a career-best effort in third from the Prix d'Ispahan winner **Never On Sunday**) and ending the year with victory in the Hong Kong Cup. **Trincot** beat a field that included both Vision d'Etat and Never On Sunday in the Prix d'Harcourt in the spring on what proved his final start before joining Godolphin. Another to show his best form outside France—he did all his racing outside Europe in 2009—was **Gloria de Campeao** who was a remote second in the Dubai World Cup (after winning a handicap at Nad Al Sheba) before beating an unlucky Presvis in the Singapore International Cup. **Vertigineux** was another to run well at the Dubai International Carnival (placed twice) before winning the Prix du Muguet at Saint-Cloud on his only appearance of the year in France from the previous year's winner **Gris de Gris**. The reliable Gris de Gris also had to settle for second in the Prix d'Ispahan and Prix Dollar but he did make up for a narrow defeat the year before when making a winning reappearance in the Prix Edmond Blanc. Smart miler **Racinger** was successful in pattern company for the third year running when beating the subsequent Sun Chariot Stakes winner **Sahpresa** in the Prix Quincey.

Other smart performances at pattern level came from **Crossharbour**, who returned from injury to win the Prix Gontaut-Biron, and La Coupe de Maisons-Laffitte winner **Chinchon** who was rewarded for some good efforts in defeat earlier in the season, including when finishing second in the Grand Prix de Chantilly, one place in front of the Prix d'Hedouville winner **Magadan**. The best older filly over middle-distances was **Alpine Rose**, a cast-off from the Aga Khan at the end of the previous season. She showed plenty of improvement at four, winning the Prix Corrida and the first running of the Prix Jean Romanet at Deauville as a Group 1 race, and fared much the best of the home contingent when second to Spanish Moon in the Grand Prix de Saint-Cloud. Seven-year-old gelding **Kasbah Bliss** had to miss the Gold Cup after finishing distressed on his return to the Flat in the spring but was in top form again later in the year, winning a second successive Prix Gladiateur before being beaten a short head by Irish-trained Alandi in an above-average Prix du Cadran and finishing a close third in the Hong Kong Vase. Such has been the improvement shown by Kasbah Bliss on the level in the last couple of seasons that he is now reportedly to concentrate solely on the Flat. Injury restricted the previous season's top stayer **Coastal Path** to just two appearances, though he ran well conceding weight to Magadan over an inadequate trip on his return. At the other end of the distance scale, France's top sprinter of 2008 **Marchand d'Or** proved badly out of sorts, while another sprinter who had been successful in Group 1 company in Britain the previous season, **African Rose**, sixth in the July Cup, likewise struggled to find her best form. That left the seemingly fully-exposed **Mariol** as the best of an ordinary group of French sprinters, the six-year-old gelding peaking at Deauville in August when runner-up in the Prix Maurice de Gheest before winning the Prix de Meautry.

Few would have guessed at the time, given that it is just the second pattern race of the year for two-year-olds in France, but the top juvenile filly and colt crossed swords in the Prix Robert Papin at Maisons-Laffitte at the end of July. **Special Duty**'s defeat of the odds on **Siyouni** looked a surprise result, though subsequent events proved otherwise, the winner going on to be beaten narrowly by Arcano in course-record time in the Prix Morny and then becoming trainer Criquette Head-Maarek's fourth winner of the Cheveley Park Stakes in the manner of a filly who looks the one to beat in the One Thousand Guineas. Siyouni had won his first three starts over five furlongs but after the Robert Papin proved himself more than just a precocious sprinter when landing the Prix Jean-Luc Lagardere over seven furlongs in the autumn after losing out to Buzzword (third in the Lagardere) in the Prix La Rochette when the Godolphin colt had had the better of things tactically. The other Group 1 contest for two-year-olds on Arc day, the Prix Marcel Boussac, was another that fell to the Aga Khan, and while **Rosanara** made it two wins from two starts, she lost her unbeaten record when finishing third against colts in the Criterium International. In both that race and the Criterium de Saint-Cloud (each won impressively by Jan Vermeer and Passion For Gold, for Ballydoyle and Godolphin respectively) French-trained youngsters made little impression, but there were others who showed plenty of promise in winning lesser pattern races. Beheshtam's half-brother **Behkabad** was unbeaten in three starts after winning the Prix des Chenes at Longchamp, while **Eightfold Path** (the first foal of high-class filly Divine Proportions) ended the season with a win in the six-furlong Prix Eclipse and should go on to better things over longer trips at three. The Prix de Cabourg winner **Zanzibari**, along with Longchamp listed winner **Colonial** (both Sheikh Mohammed/Godolphin) and the Lagardere fourth **Lope de Vega**, were all Andre Fabre-trained colts who figured not far behind the leading French two-year-olds, while stable-companion **Wedding March**, fourth in the Marcel Boussac, has the size and pedigree to make a much better three-year-old. Among other fillies to make their mark at pattern level, the Prix du Bois winner **Dolled Up** was kept busy in sprints and ran some good races to reach the frame behind the top two-year-olds in the Robert Papin and Morny, while **Sorciere** prevented Special Duty from making a winning debut in the Prix Yacowlef and gave another speedy display when beating Dolled Up in receipt of weight in the Prix d'Arenberg.

Two-Year-Olds

118 Special Duty (f)
117 Siyouni
112 Zanzibari
110 Rosanara (f)
109 Dolled Up (f)
108p Behkabad
108 Colonial
108 Lope de Vega
107 Sorciere (f)
106 Arasin
105p Planteur
105 On Verra (f)
104p Eightfold Path
104p Wedding March (f)
103p Barouda (f)
103 Baahama (f)
102 Ayun Tara (f)
102 Lixirova (f)
102 Royal Bench
101 Boltcity
101 Melodyman
101? Irish Cat (f)
100 Barbegal
100 Marceti
100 Saying (f)
100 Wonderfilly (f)

---

99 Ascot Glory (f)
99 Chantilly Creme (f)
97 American Nizzy (f)
97 Kelty In Love (f)

Three-Year-Olds

130 Cavalryman
124 Le Havre

123 Stacelita (f)
122 Silver Frost
122 Varenar
120p Daryakana (f)
120 Elusive Wave (f)
120 Fuisse
120 Shalanaya (f)
120 Wajir
119 Cirrus des Aigles
119 Manighar
119 Sweet Hearth (f)
118 Ashalanda (f)
118 Cashelgar
118 Oiseau de Feu
117 Tamazirte (f)
116 Board Meeting (f)
116 Naaqoos
116 Reggane (f)
115 Beheshtam
115 Handsome Maestro
115 Los Cristianos
115 Plumania (f)
115 Proportional (f)
114 Aizavoski
114 Celimene (f)
113+ Cutlass Bay
113 Calvados Blues
113 Claremont
113 World Heritage
112 Broken In Light
112 Golden Century
112 Homebound (f)
112 On Est Bien
112 Soneva (f)
111 Allybar
111 Byword
111 Emergency (f)
111 Three Bodies
110p Dalghar
110 *Denomination (f)
110 Feels All Right
110 Kalla (f)
110 Peinture Rare (f)
110 Shemiyla (f)
109 Bluster
109 Entre Deux Eaux (f)
109 *Flying Cloud (f)
109 Rosey de Megeve (f)
109 Telluride
109 Vesuve
109 Wilside (f)
109? Terre du Vent (f)
108 Berouni
108 Dovil Boy
108 Gallilei
108 Grandcamp
108 Guest Ville
108 Mary Boleyn (f)
108 One Clever Cat (f)
108 *Providanza (f)
108 Quetsche (f)
108 Shamakiya (f)
107 Aiboa (f)
107 Coubiza
107 Dreamt (f)
107 Prankster
107 Shediyama (f)
107 Topclas
106 Acteur Celebre
106 Almail
106 Ana Americana (f)
106 Article Rare (f)
106 Ashaaq
106 Eclair de Lune (f)
106 *Little Dreams
106 Milanais
106 Mojave Moon
106 Only Green (f)
106 Rex Regina (f)
106 Skins Game
106 Usbeke
105 Celebra (f)
105 Desertar
105 Kissing The Camera (f)
105 Makt
105 Pearlescence (f)
105 Validor
105 Villa Molitor (f)

104+ Shahwardi
104 Alpine Snow (f)
104 Cavaliere (f)
103 Investissement
103 Tassara (f)
100§ Excellent Girl (f)

Older Horses

133 Goldikova (f)
127 Vision d'Etat
125 Never On Sunday
123 Gloria de Campeao
122 Kasbah Bliss
121 Vertigineux
120 Crossharbour
120 Gris de Gris
119 Alpine Rose (f)
119 Coastal Path
119 Racinger
118 Chinchon
118 *Loup Breton
118 Magadan
118 Mariol
118 *Proviso (f)
118 Sahpresa (f)
118 *Trincot
117 Starlish
117 Tiza
116 Ideal World
116 Murcielago
116 Not Just Swing
116 Pouvoir Absolu
115 Alnadana (f)
115 *Americain
115 Pointilliste
115 Putney Bridge
114 Armure (f)
114 Dunkerque
114 Mundybash
114 Prospect Wells
114 Shemima (f)
113 African Rose (f)
113 Capitaine Courage
113 Court Canibal
113 Full of Gold
113 Kachgai
113 Stern Opinion
113 The Bogberry
113 Trois Rois
113 Young Tiger
112 Blek
112 Bon Grain
112 *Contest
112 Danse Grecque (f)
112 Incanto Dream
112 Mores Wells
111 La Boum (f)
111 Orion Star
111 Runaway
110 Albisola (f)
110 Blue Bresil
110 Chopastair
110 Doctor Dino
110 Goose Bay (f)
110 *Mr Brock
110 Salut L'Africain
110 Sans Chichi (f)
110 Tempelstern
110 Tres Rapide (f)
110 Willywell
109 Arcadia's Angle
109 Barongo
109 Darabani
109 Timos
108 Blue Cayenne (f)
108 Candy Gift
108 Delvita (f)
108 Fully Funded
108 Light Green (f)
108 Rainbow Dancing (f)
108 Salsalavie
108 Tangaspeed (f)
108 Tayseer
108 Winkle (f)
107 Celebrissime
107 Inestimable
107 Sceptre Rouge
107 Sky Crusader
106 Burn The Breeze (f)
106 Celtic Wolf
106 Daly Daly (f)
106 Diyakalanie (f)
106 Eye of The Tiger
106 Far From Old
106 Marchand d'Or
106 Parfum des Dieux
106 Rento
106 Testama (f)
106 Ticoz
106 Violon Sacre
105 Cadeau For Maggi
105 Cinq Cinq
105 Green Tango
105 Krataios
105 Libertador
105 Quartz Jem
105 Representing
105 Stikine
105 Verba (f)
105 Wing Express

GERMANY Although several good horses from the previous year remained in training, a couple of new names came to the fore to dominate Germany's top middle-distance races, both of them in the same stable. **Wiener Walzer** emerged as much the best among the classic generation, while the older horses had a new leader in the six-year-old **Getaway**. The Baron Georg von Ullmann-owned Getaway was already established as a high-class performer in France with Andre Fabre but a Group 1 success had eluded him until he joined Jens Hirschberger, private trainer to the von Ullmann family's horses, in the latest season. Wiener Walzer ran in the colours of the von Ullmann family's stud, Gestut Schlenderhan, which had been run by Baron von Ullmann's mother Karin prior to her death in June. It was Wiener Walzer who came out on top in a first meeting with Getaway in the Rheinland-Pokal at Cologne in August, but only by a short head after a protracted duel. Softer ground for Germany's top race, the Grosser Preis von Baden the following month, was more in Getaway's favour however, and he put up the best performance of the year in Germany to win by three lengths, with Wiener Walzer only fourth. Getaway's season ended with his third appearance in the Arc, finishing down the field after not having the best of runs. He had progressed with each run, though, earlier in the season, finishing second to the improved four-year-old **Flamingo Fantasy** (who was following up a win in the two-mile Betty Barclay-Rennen) on his German debut in the Hansa-Preis at Hamburg before turning the tables on that rival for his first Group 1 success in the Deutschland-Preis at Dusseldorf in July.

The two former Deutsches Derby winners who'd fought out the previous season's Grosser Preis von Baden, **Kamsin** and **Adlerflug**, both remained in training. Adlerflug, another Schlenderhan representative, made a promising reappearance to finish third in the Prix Ganay but broke a leg in training a month later and was retired to stud. Kamsin enjoyed a full season, starting with a winning reappearance in the Gerling-Preis at Cologne, though never encountered his favoured soft ground all year, finishing only fourth in the Hansa-Preis and Deutschland-Preis and fifth when attempting a repeat win at Baden-Baden. Kamsin's stable-companion **Quijano**, another former Grosser Preis von Baden winner, on the other hand, goes well under firmer conditions and at the age of seven enjoyed another good season campaigned outside Germany. He won the Gran Premio di Milano for the second year running after beginning the year in Dubai again, and went on to be placed in Grade 1 events in North America in the Man o'War Stakes at Belmont and the Northern Dancer Turf Stakes at Woodbine. **Poseidon Adventure** got his head in front for the first time in three years in a listed race at Munich in May and saved one of his best runs once again for the Preis von Europa, finishing fourth to make the frame for the third time.

Several smart older horses had claims to being the best at around a mile and a quarter. **Zaungast**'s win in the Grosser Preis der Wirtschaft at Dortmund stood out as his best effort all year, while **Precious Boy** stepped up from some good efforts in France at a mile to finish second to Pressing in the Grosser Dallmayr-Preis at Munich. **Liang Kay** was another to start off the season well at a mile, and while he ran poorly at Munich, he came back to form at the end of the year, winning the Baden-Wurttemberg-Trophy at Baden-Baden and running a good second in another Group 3 event at Frankfurt. **Adelar** ran his best race when second in the Prix Gontaut-Biron at Deauville (one place ahead of Precious Boy), while **Wiesenpfad** was retired to stud after winning a second Preis der Sparkassen-Finanzgruppe at Baden-Baden, his sixth pattern win all told.

There was no clear hierarchy among the older milers either, with a short head separating **Earl of Fire** and **Sehrezad** in the Hamburger Meile in June, arguably Germany's most competitive contest of the year at that trip, with Liang Kay third. Earl of Fire was placed behind the British-trained Premio Loco in two similar contests later in the year, while Sehrezad went on to a Group 3 win of his own at Frankfurt next time (by nine lengths) and was a good second in the Premio Ribot at Rome. Other leading older milers **Aspectus** and **Konig Turf** finished down the field at Hamburg, but they had fought out a short-head finish of their own in another Group 3 contest at Baden-Baden's May meeting ahead of Liang Kay and Earl of Fire.

The German sprint division was all the weaker for the absence of Hungary's high-class sprinter Overdose with foot problems in the latest season, though if he recovers well enough to return to action in 2010 (his trainer Sandor Ribarszki moved his stable to Berlin at the end of the year), he shouldn't have much to fear from Germany's older sprinters at least. Six-year-old **Contat** ran as many poor races as good ones, though he did win twice at pattern level, the Benazet-Rennen at Baden-Baden and the Silberne Peitsche at Cologne. Similar form was shown by **Le Big**, a dual listed winner at Munich and third in Germany's top sprint, the Goldene Peitsche, who ended the season with a win in the Premio Chiusura at Milan. **Best Joking** had Le Big back in third place (the pair split by smart British-trained filly Look Busy) in a five furlong listed race at Cologne in October, and though getting weight from the placed horses, she ran out a clear cut winner to show a level of form which would see her go close at pattern level.

Wiener Walzer's defeat of Getaway in the Rheinland-Pokal was his first race against older horses and required him to improve a good deal upon his win against just useful rivals for the most part in the Deutsches Derby on his previous start. Derby runner-up **Sordino** was not seen out again, and the next two home were still maidens at the time, though third-placed **Toughness Danon** went on to win the Furstenberg-Rennen at Baden-Baden and fourth-placed **Eliot** ran very well to finish third behind the British-trained pair Jukebox Jury and Eastern Anthem (also placed in the Rheinland-Pokal and Grosser Preis von Baden) in the Preis von Europa at Cologne. Wiener Walzer completed a hat-trick in the Deutsches Derby after winning the main trial, the Oppenheim-Union-Rennen at Cologne, though was his stable's apparent second string at Hamburg behind the unbeaten listed winner **Suestado** who proved disappointing. The Deutsches Derby was the second German classic success of the year for Jens Hirschberger and Gestut Schlenderhan after **Irian** won the Mehl-Mulhens-Rennen (German 2000 Guineas). He was beaten for the first time when a good third in the Prix Jean Prat on his next outing and was sold to Hong Kong later in the year. **Querari** was placed twice in pattern company at a mile against older horses but ran his best race when making all on a first try at a mile and a quarter in the Euro-Cup at Frankfurt on his final start. Two more of the better German three-year-olds performed at distances short of a mile. **Smooth Operator** landed the third French pattern race of his career when winning the Prix de la Porte Maillot and was a good second in the Goldene Peitsche to the British-trained War Artist, though when starting favourite for the Badener Sprint Cup on his final outing he was a below-form fourth to **Walero** who had graduated from handicap company.

There were few fillies of note in the latest crop of three-year-olds. **Night Magic** was a clear-cut winner of the Preis der Diana (German Oaks), seemingly improving for forcing tactics after winning a Group 3 at Hamburg from the front as well on her previous start. She found the Prix de l'Opera tougher but ran well when beaten a head in the Premio Lydia Tesio at Rome on her final outing. The German Oaks winner was not be confused with **Night of Magic** who won the Italian equivalent and ran her best race at home when runner-up in the Deutsches St Leger. **Soberania** was second in the German Oaks, and while it was Dar Re Mi and Stacelita who were the centre of attention after a controversial Prix Vermeille, it was the slight interference suffered by Soberania, running her best race when a close fifth past the post (promoted fourth), which prompted the stewards to amend the result. **Antara** had raced only at a mile and in listed company at best until her final start when stepped up another two furlongs to win the Preis der Deutschen Einheit at Hoppegarten by eight lengths from Liang Kay, making her an interesting prospect at four.

Glad Tiger enhanced trainer Uwe Ostmann's excellent record in the Preis des Winterfavoriten, traditionally Germany's top two-year-old contest, beating the Zukunfts-Rennen runner-up **Noble Alpha**, though that form was bettered by **Neatico** who had the

Henkel Preis der Diana, Dusseldorf—Night Magic (left) makes all for a clear-cut victory in the German Oaks; Soberania (five from the left) comes out best of some just useful opposition

Winterfavoriten third **Kite Hunter** behind him in fourth when winning the most recent addition to Germany's two-year-old pattern races, the Herzog von Ratibor-Rennen from **Cabimas**. **Zazou** was only fourth in the Zukunfts-Rennen between winning a couple of auction events, but he improved a good deal when stepped up in trip to finish third in the Criterium de Saint-Cloud. Among the two-year-old fillies, **Neon Light** showed the best form, the only rival to finish within seven lengths of her in her two starts being **Elle Shadow** (a daughter of smart mare Elle Danzig) who went down by three quarters of a length when odds on for the Preis der Winterkonigin at Baden-Baden. After two wins in Italy, including a listed race at Milan, **Junia Tepzia** became Germany's first two-year-old runner at the Breeders' Cup, though clearly wasn't herself when finishing last in the Juvenile Fillies Turf.

Two-Year-Olds
107p Neatico
106 Zazou
105p Neon Light (f)
103 Cabimas
103 Elle Shadow (f)
103 Junia Tepzia (f)
102p Glad Tiger
101 Noble Alpha
99 Kite Hunter
98p Lamool
97 Keep Cool
96 Eternal Power
95 Good Hope (f)
95 Nightdance Paolo
95 Paradise Rain (f)
95 Nianga (f)

Three-Year-Olds
124 Wiener Walzer
118 Eliot
116+ Antara (f)
116 Irian
116 Smooth Operator
115 Night Magic (f)
115 Walero
114 Querari
114 Schiller Danon
114 Soberania (f)
112 King of Sydney
111 Sordino
111 Toughness Danon
110 Saphir
109 Ravenel (f)
108 Daring Tiger
108 Falun
108 Miss Europa (f)
108 Palermo
107 Bolivia (f)
107 Fabiana (f)
107 Rock My Soul (f)
107 Suestado
107 Sworn Pro (f)
106 Lady Alida (f)
106 Night of Magic (f)
106 Ordenstreuer
106 Quo Dubai
105 Egon
105 Hansom
105 Mambo Light (f)
105 Norderney (f)
105 Oriental Lion
105 Panyu

---

104 Lukrecia (f)
104 Addicted (f)
104 Glad Panther
103 *Andrea (f)
103 Glad Sky
103 Globus
103 Muriel (f)
101+ Steuben
100 Caro Jina (f)
100 Novita (f)

Older Horses
127 Getaway
120 Quijano
118 Flamingo Fantasy
117 Adlerflug
117 Kamsin
116 Adelar
116 Earl of Fire
116 Poseidon Adventure
116 Precious Boy
116 Zaungast
115 Best Joking (f)
115 Le Big
115 Liang Kay
114 Aspectus
114 Konig Turf
114 *Pont des Arts
114 Sassoaloro
114 Sehrezad
114 Wiesenpfad
113 Ambassador
113 Contat
113 Estejo
113 Prince Flori
113 *Salve Germania (f)
111 Ostland
113 Win For Sure
111 Schutzenjunker
110 Etoile Nocturne (f)
110 Guantana (f)
110 Lauro
110 Ruten
110 Shinko's Best
110 Walzertraum
109 Abbashiva
109 Caudillo
109 Northern Glory
108 Eminem
108 Key To Pleasure
108 Mood Music
108 Peace Royale (f)
108 Shawnee Saga
107 Adolfina (f)
107 Black Out
107 Daveron (f)
107 Dwilano
107 Il Divo
107 Lips Arrow (f)
107 Lord Hill
107 Sacho
107 Setareh
107§ Forthe Millionkiss
106 Bella Platina (f)
106 Integral
106 Konig Concorde
106 La Bamba (f)
106 Le Miracle
106 Tarkheena Prince
106 Valdino
105 Abbadjinn
105 Akiem
105 Duellant
105 Iolith
105 Umirage (f)
105 Zaya (f)

---

102 Themelie Island (f)
99 Whispered Dreams (f)

ITALY Recent years have seen plenty of success for horses that began their career in Italy before enjoying a higher profile abroad and the latest season was no exception. Gladiatorus (Premio Vittorio di Capua) and Pressing (Premio Carlo Vittadini) both won back in Italy for Saeed bin Suroor and Michael Jarvis respectively, while 2008 Derby Italiano winner Cima de Triomphe has been returned to his former trainer Bruno Grizzetti after a season with Luca Cumani. The latest successful Italian export was **Libano**, winner of the Premio Parioli (2000 Guineas) in April, who showed very smart form when winning

Premio Presidente della Repubblica At The Races, Rome—
Selmis (noseband) stays on well to keep this Group 1 prize at home;
Godolphin's challenger Trincot (right) catches Freemusic (white cap, fourth left) for second

a listed race at Leopardstown in the autumn for his new stable, that of Dermot Weld. Libano was one of few horses of note among the three-year-old generation. **Turati** was fourth in the Parioli but proved much better over longer trips, finishing runner-up in the Derby Italiano, which in 2009 became the last of Italy's classics to succumb to the inevitable fate of losing its Group 1 status. Ironically, as it turned out, as both the first two in the Derby developed into very smart colts, winner Mastery going on to success in the St Leger and Turati finishing an excellent second against older rivals (in receipt of only 2 lb, rather than the 5 lb on Timeform's scale) in the Premio Roma. The three-year-old fillies were only useful at best, making minimal impact in pattern races, though the Premio Regina Elena (1000 Guineas) winner **My Sweet Baby** was at least of note for being a half-sister to Gladiatorus.

After an autumn ravaged by industrial action in 2008 it was back to a full programme of pattern races in Italy in the latest season. Two of the country's Group 1 contests were kept at home thanks to **Selmis** and **Voila Ici**. Selmis was unbeaten for the year in three starts but wasn't seen out again after winning the Premio Presidente della Repubblica at Rome in May in which **Freemusic** finished third for the second year running. Voila Ici rounded off an excellent campaign when winning the Premio Roma over the same course and distance in November, the heavy ground offsetting the shorter trip. That was his fourth pattern win of the year after the Premio Carlo d'Alessio at Rome, the Prix Maurice de Nieuil over a mile and three quarters at Longchamp and, for the second year, the Premio Federico Tesio at Milan. Voila Ici was also a good third behind foreign-trained winners in the two Group 1 mile and a half contests at Milan, the Gran Premio di Milano and the Gran Premio del Jockey Club. The latter race saw a career-best effort from **Sant'Antonio** to finish second and he confirmed himself a smart colt with third place in the Premio Roma. Another improved performer in the autumn was **Silver Arrow** who had the previous year's winner Pressing back in third when winning the Premio Ribot at Rome over a mile on what was his twenty-third outing of the year, while similar comments apply to **Rockhorse** who ended the year with good placed efforts in the Premio Vittorio di Capua and Premio Chiusura.

Black Mambazo was Italy's top sprinter for the second year running, gaining a repeat win in a listed race at Naples in July and putting up two good performances in France to finish second in the Prix du Gros-Chene and fifth in the Prix de l'Abbaye. He didn't have things all his own way at home though, going down to **Remarque** in the Premio Tudini at Rome and finding **Titus Shadow** too good in a listed race at Milan in September. That was one of three listed wins at the track for Titus Shadow who also won the Premio Omenoni there. **Morgan Drive**, placed in the Tudini and Omenoni, didn't always enjoy the best of luck but came good when dead-heating with **Thinking Robins** in the Premio Carlo & Francesco Aloisi at Rome in November ahead of both Titus Shadow and Remarque.

Italy's two-year-olds failed to make much impact in the country's top juvenile contest, the Gran Criterium. Favourite **Marshade** disappointed after two listed wins at Milan and a good second prior to that in the Premio Primi Passi behind Titus Shadow's half-brother **Orpen Shadow** who went on to run a good fourth behind some of the top French two-year-olds in the Prix Robert Papin. **Joanna** was another Italian youngster to do well in France, winning the Prix du Calvados and finishing third in the Prix Marcel Boussac; she was bought by Hamdan Al Maktoum after the Calvados and is to continue her career in France with Jean-Claude Rouget. The Premio Dormello won by **Blessed Luck** was a modest race by Group 3 standards but Stefano Botti recorded a training feat of note by saddling the first three home.

Two-Year-Olds

111	Orpen Shadow
107	Marshade
105	Joanna (f)
102	Air Crew
101	Grenso
101	Charming Woman (f)
100	Tauman
99p	Super Motiva (f)
99	Blessed Luck (f)
99	Collesano
98	Pontallmagne (f)
98	Cronsa (f)
98	Nantha (f)
97	Paloma Varga (f)
97	Dagda Mor
97	Blow Up
96	Cool Contest (f)
96	Ladiesandgentlemen
96	Martilzo
96	Kidnapping
96	Occhio della Mente

Three-Year-Olds

121	*Libano
120	Turati
111	Sottone
109	Abaton
108	Suchita Devious (f)
107	Jakkalberry
106	Louise Aron (f)
105	Apprimus
105	Johannes Mozart
105	My Sweet Baby (f)
105	Quiza Quiza Quiza (f)
105	Tuliangreen

103	Aria di Festa (f)
100	Osservatorio
98	Catch Wind (f)
97	Oh Mambo Girl (f)

Older Horses

118	Voila Ici
116	Black Mambazo
116	Sant'Antonio
116	Selmis
116	Silver Arrow
114	Freemusic
113	Gimmy
113	Rockhorse
112	Gesture
112	Remarque
112	Titus Shadow
111	Farrel
111	Miles Gloriosus
111	Permesso
110	Morgan Drive
110	Thinking Robins
110	Vol de Nuit
109	Cottonmouth (f)
109	Eldest
109	Rastignano
108	Papetti
107	Storm Mountain
106	Docksil (f)
106	Montalegre
106	Zenone
105	Awelmarduk
105	L'Indiscreta (f)
105	Pedra Pompas
105	Polar Wind

104	Allegoria (f)
101	Ekta (f)
94	Ruby Dancer (f)

SCANDINAVIA **Appel Au Maitre** enjoyed his third consecutive season as Scandinavia's leading performer in 2009, but with a strong-looking crop of three-year-olds emerging, his position at the top could be under threat from now on. He began the year with three wins, which included a defeat of his long-standing rival **Peas And Carrots** and **Luca Brasi** in the Stockholms Stora Preis, and belatedly showed his best form outside Scandinavia for the first time when beaten less than a length into third behind Getaway in the Deutschland-Preis at Dusseldorf. But on his final start, when starting odds on to win a third consecutive Stockholm Cup International, he was beaten into third place behind his three-year-old stable-companion **Touch of Hawk** who looks a serious challenger to Appel Au Maitre from now on. Touch of Hawk had previously finished third to another stable-companion, **Handsome Hawk** (both gelded sons of Hawk Wing), in the Swedish Derby on dirt before turning the tables back on turf in the Norwegian version and ended the year with a ten-length win in the Norwegian St Leger. Handsome Hawk went on to run a good race of his own against older rivals when splitting Luca Brasi and Peas And Carrots in a mile and a half listed race at Jagersro in September. Peas And Carrots profited from Appel Au Maitre's absence to win the Scandinavian Open Championship at Klampenborg from the previous year's winner **Chinese Mandarin**, with Luca Brasi third again, and beat the latter horse into second, this time on dirt, when winning his second listed race of the year, at Taby in October.

There was little doubt which race drew the strongest line-up all year in Scandinavia; the intermediate distance (nine furlongs) of the Marit Sveaas Minnelop at Ovrevoll in August brought together a number of good horses at a range of distances. Appel Au Maitre started odds on and ran up to his best although beaten into second by the four-year-old filly **Theatrical Award**, winner of the Norwegian 1000 Guineas and Derby the year before. Neither Peas And Carrots nor Luca Brasi gave their running this time, the first two instead finishing clear of the formerly British-trained **Smart Enough** in third, who showed he was still capable of smart form when winning a mile listed race at Taby in July.

The Marit Sveaas was also contested by the three-year-old **Chicken Momo**, who was far from discredited in finishing fourth; although he'd won the Norwegian 2000 Guineas (from Touch of Hawk) over a slightly shorter trip, it was as a sprinter that he proved best, improving out of all recognition on his two-year-old form in Britain when beaten in sellers. As well as the Guineas at Ovrevoll, Chicken Momo won his four other races at the track over shorter distances, notably the Polar Cup in July by five and a half lengths. The Polar Cup is now Scandinavia's only Group 3 sprint after the demotion of the Taby Open Sprint, though even in listed guise (and without Chicken Momo) the latter still drew a good field of older sprinters. The Polar Cup third **Calrissian** won it for the second year running (one of four course-and-distance wins during the year) from the formerly British-trained pair **Exhibition** and **Hansinger**, though the first two were unable to make any impact subsequently at the Arc meeting in the Prix de la Foret and Prix de l'Abbaye respectively. Two further members of the three-year-old generation worth highlighting are the fillies **Una Hora** and **Entangle**. Una Hora won a mile and a half listed event for fillies and mares by six lengths at Jagersro in November, while Entangle's five wins included both fillies' classics in Norway as well as listed races against older fillies and mares in the autumn at Ovrevoll and Taby.

Three-Year-Olds		110	Calrissian	107	Steve's Champ
115	Touch of Hawk	110	Smart Enough	107	Volo Cat
112	Chicken Momo	108	Exhibition	106	Alpacco
110	Una Hora (f)	108	Hansinger	106	Highway (Ire)
109	Handsome Hawk	108	Luca Brasi	106	Novasky (f)
108	Entangle (f)	108	Prince Fasliyev	106	Sydney (f)
		108	Quilboquet	106	Woy Woy
Older Horses		108	Tertio Bloom	105	Alnitak
116	Appel Au Maitre	108	Tertullus	105	Eldfote
113	*Echoes Rock	107	Alcohuaz		
111	Peas And Carrots	107	Chinese Mandarin		
111	Theatrical Award (f)	107	Dollar Hill	101	Miyasaki

SPAIN Madrid's La Zarzuela racecourse was reopened in the autumn of 2005 after racing had been absent from the Spanish capital for the best part of ten years. While Spain is no longer part of the European pattern (two of its races had Group 3 status until 1996), a number of Spanish-trained horses have proven themselves well up to pattern-race standard in France and Britain since Madrid's return to the fixture list for the first time since 1996 gave Spanish owners more confidence to invest in better-quality bloodstock. That was particularly evident in 2008 when the then stable-companions Equiano and **Bannaby** gained Group 1 wins in the King's Stand Stakes and Prix du Cadran respectively. Bannaby was less successful in the latest season, though still needed to run right up to his best to finish third, giving weight all round, in the Prix Vicomtesse Vigier. Stable-companion **Faramir** filled the same position in the Prix de Barbeville, also at Longchamp, while his wins included the Gran Premio de Madrid, a race Bannaby had won the year before. The four-year-old **Synergy** became the first Spanish-trained filly to win a pattern race when successful in the Prix Fille de l'Air at Toulouse in November, adding to a listed win at Maisons-Laffitte in the summer. **Aranel** met trouble when finishing in mid-division in the Jersey Stakes at Royal Ascot and showed he was better than that on his other start in pattern company when fifth in the Prix de Seine-et-Oise on his final outing. **As de Trebol**, runner-up in the Spanish 2000 Guineas, was another three-year-old to run well in pattern company in France, though was demoted to second after passing the post first in the Prix du Palais-Royal. The two-year-old filly **Ercolini** also picked up place money from a Group 3 event when third in the Prix Miesque at Maisons-Laffitte.

The following Spanish-trained horses achieved significant ratings in major races

Two-Year-Olds		Three-Year-Olds		Older Horses	
100p	Ivory Land	110	As de Trebol	115	Bannaby
99	Bottega	106	Aranel	108	Synergy (f)
96	Ercolini (f)	105	Diableside	107	Faramir
				106	Lorgan
				105	Shumookh

The following European-trained horses also achieved significant ratings

Two-Year-Olds		Older Horses			
100	Shamalgan (Slovakia)	117	Overdose (Hungary)	108	Sabirli (Turkey)
		112	Pan River (Turkey)	107	Ryan (Slovakia)
		108	Blue Coral (Czech Republic)	106	Ailton (Switzerland)
				106	Kurtiniadis (Turkey)

UNITED ARAB EMIRATES Originally no more than a training track, a refurbished Nad Al Sheba opened as a racecourse proper in 1992 and has since been the setting for the major developments in what are still the early years of Dubai's rapidly-developing racing programme. Later that same year, the first season of professional racing in the UAE got under way, while the introduction of the Dubai World Cup in 1996, the strengthening of the supporting card around it, and the start of the Dubai International Racing Carnival in 2004 have quickly followed, attracting ever-greater interest from around the world. The pace of change has been such, though, that even a track whose newest stands were then barely more than five years old became obsolete when, on the eve of the 2007 Dubai World Cup, Sheikh Mohammed announced ambitious plans for the creation of Nad Al Sheba's successor, Meydan, as detailed in this piece in *Racehorses* of that year.

Scheduled at the outset to be ready for the start of the new UAE season in November, in the event, Meydan was to become operational instead in January 2010 to coincide with the start of the Carnival meeting, ahead of an official opening on Dubai World Cup night. Meydan's inauguration followed soon after the opening of the Burj Khalifa, the world's tallest building, in Dubai's business district. Estimated costs of these two projects alone—US$2.7 billion for Meydan and US$1.5 billion for the Burj Khalifa—show the importance of real estate and construction to Dubai, a sector which accounts for almost a quarter of the economy (compared with oil and gas which contribute only 6%). Following a boom which lasted for several years, Dubai's property bubble burst just as spectacularly in 2009 with consequences which, it was feared, could have repercussions for racing in Britain. Sheikh Mohammed is the major stakeholder in Dubai World, an investment company which, in November, asked for a six-month delay in repaying its debts (reportedly $59 billion). As Sheikh Mohammed's business interests and his bloodstock operation are entirely separate entities, his investments at the sales (without which the recession would have been felt even more keenly by breeders and vendors in Britain in the last eighteen months or so) in theory should not be affected—though whether he feels he can still be seen to be spending as freely, given Dubai's current financial situation, is another matter.

On the track, Sheikh Mohammed, through his Godolphin operation, enjoyed a second successive highly successful Carnival early in the year, another twenty-one wins (after twenty-four in 2008) taking Saeed bin Suroor past Mike de Kock as the most successful trainer since the Carnival was inaugurated. In contrast to the year before, that success was sustained through to Dubai World Cup night itself, when Godolphin representatives **Two Step Salsa** and Gayego (Godolphin Mile) and **Regal Ransom** and **Desert Party** (UAE Derby) finished first and second in their respective races. Better at six furlongs, Gayego also won the Group 3 Mahab Al Shimaal earlier at the Carnival at that trip, while the latter pair of three-year-olds had also been the first two, though in reverse order, in the UAE 2000 Guineas. Godolphin's other classic winner was Devotee (rated 103), successful in the UAE Oaks. After winning the first two rounds of the Maktoum Challenge, **My Indy** was Godolphin's representative in the Dubai World Cup itself, where he finished a non-staying fifth, but the winners of the two turf big races on the card, the Dubai Duty Free and Dubai Sheema Classic, although not representing Godolphin on the night (both later joined the stable for European campaigns), could be counted as 'home' wins. **Gladiatorus** and **Eastern Anthem** each carried the colours of sons of Sheikh Mohammed

*UAE Derby sponsored by Saeed & Mohammed Al Naboodah, Nad Al Sheba—
a 1,2 for Godolphin as Regal Ransom (right) overturns UAE 2000 Guineas form with Desert Party;
the pair finish fifteen lengths clear*

and both were ridden by Ahmed Ajtebi, Dubai's champion apprentice and very much a protege of the Sheikh. Both horses, trained by Mubarak bin Shafya, had won their two previous starts at the Carnival, Gladiatorus taking the Group 2 Al Fahidi Fort beforehand. Other notable Carnival winners for Godolphin included **Alexandros**, winner of two handicaps before finishing third in the Duty Free, **Kirklees**, who put up one of the best performances in handicaps with an impressive defeat of **Hattan**, and **Veracity**, winner of the DRC Gold Cup, the first two-mile contest to be run at the Carnival.

As well as Gladiatorus and Eastern Anthem, other Carnival winners who earned promotion to Godolphin from other Dubai stables included subsequent Melbourne Cup runner-up **Crime Scene**, winner of a mile and a half handicap and runner-up to Eastern Anthem in another, and the ex-French horse **Balius** who accounted for one of the strongest fields outside the World Cup card in the Group 2 Jebel Hatta. Among the best performances from other UAE-trained horses at the Carnival, **Kalahari Gold** was third in the Zabeel Mile, **Snaafy** won three races on dirt, notably the Group 3 Burj Nahaar over a mile, and **Happy Boy** was a good second in the last two rounds of the Maktoum Challenge.

South African Mike de Kock assembled what looked his strongest team yet for Dubai but after an otherwise successful Carnival, none of his ten runners on World Cup night so much as managed to reach the frame. That was particularly disappointing given that some had won major prep races. **Asiatic Boy** was the biggest flop, starting favourite for the World Cup after beating Kirklees, among others, in Round 3 of the Maktoum Challenge. The filly **Front House** (Dubai City of Gold) and **Archipenko** (Zabeel Mile) also landed big prizes before failing to make an impact in the Sheema Classic and Duty Free respectively. Other pattern-race wins during the Carnival for the de Kock stable came courtesy of **Silver Mist** in the Al Rashidiya and the much-vaunted sprinter **J J The Jet Plane**, winner of the Al Quoz Sprint on turf (a race that has been transferred to the World Cup card for 2010), while the mare **Diana's Choice** and **Hunting Tower** landed three sprint handicaps between them on turf. Fellow South African Herman Brown also made his mark in pattern company with the ex-Italian mare **My Central** who beat Front House in the Balanchine, though much better form was shown by **Strategic News** and **Bankable** in winning handicaps. **Jay Peg** was unable to repeat his 2008 win in the Dubai Duty Free, but had looked back to near his best when dead-heating for second (with de Kock's **Russian Sage**) in the prep race for that event, the Jebel Hatta.

The last race ever to be run at Nad Al Sheba, the fourteenth edition of the Dubai World Cup, failed to draw a field worthy of the occasion, the weakest in the race's history in fact, but it did see a record winning margin—officially fourteen lengths—from Well Armed who had finished a well-held third to Curlin (the previous record holder) the year before. It is unlikely that future World Cups at Meydan, with its synthetic rather than dirt surface, will yield such wide-margin winners; a more important consequence of the tapeta surface should be that the World Cup attracts more horses with a turf background, thereby giving more strength in depth to the field—as befits the world's richest race, which will be worth 10,000,000 dollars in 2010.

The Dubai Golden Shaheen, the big sprint on the World Cup card, has been an even more successful race for American-trained horses in recent years, but the Saudi-trained **Big City Man**, ended that run, even though he too had begun his career in the USA. The Golden Shaheen was his third win from four starts at Nad Al Sheba in 2009, having won the Al Shindagha Sprint and finished second to Gayego in the Mahab Al Shimaal, but he died from a stomach ailment back in the USA later in the year. Another big-race success for Saudi Arabia came from **Deem** who beat Front House in the Cape Verdi for fillies and mares.

British-trained horses claimed a total of seven wins at the Carnival, mainly in handicaps, the most notable of those being dual winner Presvis who went on to finish second in the Duty Free. Luca Cumani also went close in the Sheema Classic with Purple Moon who came off worst in a three-way finish behind Eastern Anthem, Spanish Moon pipping him for second. Ballydoyle remain conspicuous by their absence from Dubai, but one Irish trainer to do well was Ger Lyons who won a handicap with Summit Surge and whose three other Carnival runners all earned place money.

The performances reviewed here are those that took place in the calendar year 2009. Horses which were trained and raced in the UAE but showed significantly better form elsewhere are not included in the list below.

Three-Year-Olds
122 *Regal Ransom
115 *Desert Party
111 City Style
106 *Redding Colliery

Older Horses
128 *Gladiatorus
127 *Big City Man
126 *Archipenko
123 *Eastern Anthem
123 *Gayego
123 *Kirklees
122 *Alexandros
122 *Asiatic Boy
122 *Jay Peg
122 *Russian Sage
122 Silver Mist
121 *Asset
121 *Balthazaar's Gift
121 *J J The Jet Plane
121 *Two Step Salsa
120 *Balius
120 Kalahari Gold
119 *Imbongi
119 *Mourilyan
119 My Indy
119 Snaafy
119 Strategic News
119 Third Set
119 *Veracity
118 *Bankable
118 *Crime Scene
118 Happy Boy
118 Hattan
118 Hunting Tower
117 *Diabolical
117 Engrupido
117 Mashaahed
117 Munaddam
116 *Age of Reason
116 Fathayer
116 *King of Rome
116 Yaddree
115 Deem (f)
115 *Diana's Choice (f)
115 Instant Recall
115 Ragheed
115 Star Crowned
115 Warsaw
115 *Yamal
115d League Champion
114 Art of War
114 Force Freeze
114 Front House (f)
114 *Hatta Fort
114 Ibn Battuta
114 *Kings Gambit
114 *Macarthur
114 *Yahrab
113 *Basaltico
113 *Brave Tin Soldier
113 Calming Influence
113 *Dijeerr
113 Don Renato
113 Jet Express
113 Sanbuch
113 Summer Doldrums
113 With Interest
112 Al Shemali
112 Biarritz
112 Dynamic Saint
112 *Honour Devil
112 Jaasoos
112 Prince Shaun
112 Tiz Now Tiz Then
112d Fateh Field
111 Gravitas
111 Green Coast
111 *Jonquil
111 Meeriss
111 *Once More Dubai
111 Seihali
111 So Will I
111 Yaddree
110 Alo Pura (f)
110 Blue Ksar
110 Change Alley
110 Eddie Jock
110 *Furnace
110 Glen Nevis
110 *King Jock
110 *Mr Brock
110 Oracle West
110 Pompeyano
110 Salaam Dubai
110 Soy Libriano
109 Blue Sky Basin
109 *Emmrooz
109 Familiar Territory
109 Golden Arrow
109 Happy Spirit (f)
109 Lion Sands
109 *Stubbs Art
108 Alsadeek
108 Amarna
108 Book of Music
108 Frosty Secret
108 Grantley Adams
108 Hammadi
108 Lucky Ray
108 My Central (f)
108 *Sugar Ray
108 Tasteyville
107 Barbaricus
107 *Halkin
107 Lipocco
107 Little White Lie
107 *Military Power
107 Montpellier
107 *Nights Cross
107 Weald
107 Yasoodd
106 Arqaam
106 *Lucky Find
106 Mulaqat
106 Roman's Run
106d *Charlie Cool
105 Ans Bach
105 Emirates Gold
105 Emirates Skyline
105 Escape Route
105 Fleeting Shadow
105 Grand Hombre
105 Kal Barg

105	Monte Alto	105	Prince Tamino
105	*Pointing North	105	Tawaassol

NORTH AMERICA In Europe there is nothing unusual about the best fillies and mares taking on and beating male rivals. In fact, it would be surprising for a European filly campaigned at the highest level not to compete against male rivals at least once in her career, at least if her credentials as a champion were to be taken seriously. Even with the expansion of pattern race opportunities in recent seasons, particularly for older fillies and mares, competition between the sexes remains very much part of the European racing scene, and contributes to its interest. Across the Atlantic, however, a dedicated programme of graded events has long been in place which means that the best fillies and mares rarely need to, or are asked to, compete in open company. But when they do, and they come out on top, the novelty value of such successes means that they capture the American racing public's imagination to a far greater extent than they would in Europe. It was remarkable, therefore, that in the same season, the three-year-old filly **Rachel Alexandra** and the five-year-old mare **Zenyatta**, should each prove themselves the best of their respective generations by being campaigned against, and beating, male rivals. In any other year, the achievements of either of them, neither of whom were beaten all year, would have won her Horse of the Year honours hands down, but the fact they both presented similar claims gave the Eclipse award voters a headache. As well being the most anticipated clash of the year, a meeting between the two would have gone a long way to resolving the issue. It was never likely to come off, though. Zenyatta did all her racing in 2009 in California, and therefore on synthetic tracks, while Rachel Alexandra was kept to the traditional dirt surfaces. The Breeders' Cup ought to have been the culmination of the campaigns of both horses, though Rachel Alexandra's owner, Jess Jackson, made it clear as early as the summer that she wouldn't be racing on what he termed the 'plastic' surface at Santa Anita, his position no doubt influenced by the defeat of his champion colt Curlin in the Breeders' Cup Classic at the same track in 2008. Rachel Alexandra's connections could hardly be accused of ducking challenges, though, with three Grade 1 victories over male rivals, including older horses, to her name by the end of her campaign, making her a deserved winner of the Horse of the Year title—even if Zenyatta was more widely expected to take the honour.

Breeders' Cup Classic, Santa Anita—Zenyatta (noseband) extends her unbeaten run to fourteen, quickening to catch Gio Ponti inside the final furlong with British challenger Twice Over in third and the blinkered Summer Bird fourth

Zenyatta's connections had shown more reluctance to race her in open company—'the boys play a lot rougher' in the words of her trainer John Shirreffs before the 2008 Breeders' Cup. Zenyatta had ended her four-year-old season with an impressive win in the Ladies' Classic at the Breeders' Cup, which sealed her the Eclipse award as best older filly, and was kept to races (each of which she had won in 2008 as well) for her own sex in the latest season until the Breeders' Cup came round again, although an earlier run against males in the Pacific Classic had been under consideration. After an easy reappearance success in a Grade 2 at Hollywood, Zenyatta reeled off three more Grade 1 wins before the Breeders' Cup, giving around a stone all round in the Vanity Handicap at the same track, getting up in the last stride under an extremely confident ride in the upgraded Clement L. Hirsch Stakes at Del Mar, and then coasting home with more to spare again in the Lady's Secret Stakes at Santa Anita. Starting favourite, Zenyatta rounded off her season in the Breeders' Cup Classic with a memorable display, still with only one behind her as she turned in on the rail before easing out to make her usual wide late run in the straight and quickening to lead in the last fifty yards. Zenyatta became the first of her sex to win North America's richest race but was only the fourth to have tried after the French-trained pair Triptych and Jolypha (sixth in 1986 and third in 1992 respectively), and Azeri, who was fifth in 2004, two years after becoming the last female to win the Horse of the Year title. Zenyatta's unbeaten record of fourteen wins (eight at Grade 1 level and four at Grade 2) took her past the previous best by a female Grade 1 winner, Personal Ensign, who also won eight times at the top level, notably the 1988 Breeders' Cup Distaff and a defeat of male opponents in the Whitney Handicap. Like Personal Ensign, Zenyatta's achievements will also be commemorated by having a Grade 1 race, the Lady's Secret, renamed in her honour. For the record, Lady's Secret in 1986 was herself the last female Horse of the Year before Azeri, and as well as that year's Breeders' Cup Distaff, her record eight Grade 1 wins that season (from a career total of eleven) also included the Whitney Handicap, one of four wins she gained that year against male rivals. Although 'retired' after the Breeders' Cup, Zenyatta returned to track work late in the year, prompting rumours that she would stay in training in 2010, something which was confirmed in January.

Rachel Alexandra had no unbeaten record to protect but after ending her two-year-old season with a Grade 2 success in the Golden Rod Stakes at Churchill Downs, she developed into a high-class filly at three with eight wins from as many starts which made her the best of her generation, male or female. Beginning the year with a non-graded win and two successes in Grade 2 company, Rachel Alexandra made a spectacular debut at Grade 1 level with a twenty-length drubbing of an admittedly substandard field in the Kentucky Oaks. Bought privately by Jess Jackson afterwards and transferred from Hal Wiggins to Steve Asmussen, Rachel Alexandra was promptly supplemented for the Preakness Stakes a fortnight later when she became the first filly to win the second leg of the Triple Crown since Nellie Morse in 1924. Her length win came at the chief expense of Kentucky Derby winner **Mine That Bird**, justifying jockey Calvin Borel's decision, as the regular rider of both horses, to stick with the filly. Rachel Alexandra maintained her overwhelming dominance over her fellow three-year-old fillies when almost matching her Kentucky Oaks-winning margin against just two rivals in the Mother Goose Stakes at Belmont on her next start, doing so in stakes-record time. Another good performance on the clock followed in the Haskell Invitational at Monmouth back against top male company where she went clear in a matter of strides from the home turn to give a six-length beating (in receipt of 5 lb) to the Belmont winner **Summer Bird**. She faced a tougher battle on her final outing of the year when taking on older male rivals for the first time but rounded off a sensational campaign by gamely holding on for a head win over Macho Uno, becoming the first filly ever (and the first three-year-old since Holy Bull in 1994) to win the Woodward Stakes at Saratoga. Rachel Alexandra stays in training in 2010 when the Breeders' Cup, to be held at Churchill Downs where she was so impressive in the Kentucky Oaks, ought to be very much on her schedule this time—and hopefully at least one clash with Zenyatta. For the second year running, and the third time in all, Steve Asmussen set a new trainers' record for number of wins (650) during a season.

While neither Summer Bird nor Mine That Bird were any match for Rachel Alexandra, the two sons of the 2004 Belmont winner Birdstone proved the best male representatives

Kentucky Derby (presented by Yum! Brands), Churchill Downs—the withdrawal of so many fancied runners in the weeks before the race makes for an unsatisfactory renewal, but the race produces a remarkable winner in rail-hugging 50/1-shot Mine That Bird, the only gelding in the field

of the three-year-old generation. The gelded Mine That Bird had been voted Canada's top two-year-old male, though had finished last at the Breeders' Cup that year and was given a Kentucky Derby preparation well off the beaten track of usual Triple Crown contenders, beaten in a couple of non-graded stakes at Sunland Park in New Mexico. Even in a field missing a number of leading fancies from earlier in the spring, Mine That Bird was sent off at more than 50/1 at Churchill Downs, but became the second longest-priced winner in the history of the race, trailing the field early on but coming right away in the straight in the sloppy conditions to beat the Santa Anita Derby winner **Pioneerof The Nile** by nearly seven lengths, a margin that hadn't been exceeded since 1946. Although placed in the two other legs of the Triple Crown, Mine That Bird never quite repeated his Kentucky Derby form and was below his best in three subsequent starts, finishing only ninth in the Breeders' Cup Classic.

Unraced at two, Summer Bird was another long-shot in the Kentucky Derby, finishing sixth on what was his Grade 1 debut, but went on to prove himself a high-class colt when blinkered for his remaining starts. Having skipped the Preakness and beaten Mine That Bird into third in the Belmont, his only defeat from then on prior to the Breeders' Cup came against Rachel Alexandra in the Haskell. Summer Bird ran out a decisive winner of the Travers Stakes (another race won by his sire) at Saratoga from **Hold Me Back** and **Quality Road** and had the latter colt placed behind him again when following up, again in sloppy conditions, in the Jockey Club Gold Cup at Belmont. Summer Bird fared much the best of the three-year-olds in the line-up when fourth to Zenyatta on his synthetic track debut in the Breeders' Cup Classic. Summer Bird is expected to return in 2010 despite fracturing a leg in Japan when preparing for an intended run in the Japan Cup Dirt. Quality Road should have been in the field at Santa Anita as well but delayed the start by causing a deal of trouble both behind the stalls and once eventually loaded, lashing out wildly and ultimately having to be withdrawn. Although he began the year well, beating the subsequent Belmont runner-up **Dunkirk** into second in the Florida Derby in March, little went right for Quality Road afterwards. He was one of the notable Kentucky Derby absentees when ruled out with a quarter crack, and also required surgery for a leg fracture before a Grade 2 win at Saratoga and those placed efforts behind Summer Bird.

Notable absentees from the Kentucky Derby included the Wood Memorial winner **I Want Revenge** (taken out with an ankle problem on the morning of the race) and **The Pamplemousse** who had won a couple of Grade 3 events at Santa Anita early in the year. **Friesan Fire** started favourite for the Kentucky Derby after completing a hat-trick in graded stakes at the Fair Grounds but was well beaten at both Churchill Downs (where he suffered a hoof injury) and in the Preakness and was well below his best again on his return in allowance company late in the year. Others failed to make it past the Triple Crown races; Pioneerof The Nile was retired to stud after finishing well beaten in the Preakness, **Musket Man** missed the rest of the year after finishing third in the Kentucky

Derby and the Preakness, while the Preakness was also the last race of the season for **General Quarters**, who had finished in mid-field in the Kentucky Derby for his one-horse stable after beating Hold Me Back in the Blue Grass Stakes. Godolphin was doubly represented by three-year-olds in the Breeders' Cup Classic, and though neither **Regal Ransom** nor **Girolamo** managed to figure there, each had put up good performances at Grade 2 level. Regal Ransom added to his UAE Derby success with an easy win in the Super Derby at Louisiana Downs, while Girolamo won all three of his starts beforehand, notably the Jerome Handicap at Belmont. The Super Derby was the only defeat for runner-up **Blame** in his last five starts, and he looks the sort to make an impact at Grade 1 level in 2010 after accounting for a smart field in the Grade 2 Clark Handicap at Churchill Downs on his final outing. A couple of notable successes for European-trained three-year-olds on the pro-ride at Santa Anita came from **Gitano Hernando** (Marco Botti) who upset some good older horses as well as Mine That Bird in the Goodwood Stakes, while **Man of Iron** (Aidan O'Brien) was another to leave his home form behind when narrowly winning the Breeders' Cup Marathon which was run over a mile and three quarters for the first time.

Over shorter trips, the three-year-old colts were headed by exuberant front runner **Zensational**. A Grade 1 hat-trick on synthetic surfaces in the Triple Bend Handicap, Bing Crosby Handicap and Pat O'Brien Stakes made him a short-priced favourite for the Breeders' Cup Sprint but he was unable to get his own way in front at Santa Anita and finished only fifth in what proved his final start before retiring to stud. **Midshipman** and **Vineyard Haven**, who had both been leading two-year-olds, maintained a similar level of form in the latest season for Godolphin. 2008 Breeders' Cup Juvenile winner Midshipman managed only two runs but came back from a lengthy absence to win in allowance company before finishing a good third in the Breeders' Cup Dirt Mile. Vineyard Haven, on the other hand, missed the Breeders' Cup for the second year running in favour of a dirt-track campaign and passed the post first in the King's Bishop Stakes at Saratoga (demoted to second behind **Capt Candyman Can**) and the Frank J. de Francis Memorial Dash over a barely adequate six furlongs before finishing third in the Cigar Mile. **M One Rifle** made into a very smart performer by the end of the year, making all in the Malibu Stakes on his graded stakes debut.

Blackberry Preakness Stakes, Pimlico—the fifth of eight wins in an unbeaten campaign for the supplemented Rachel Alexandra, the first filly to win the Preakness since 1924; Mine That Bird is about to pass Kentucky Derby third Musket Man for second

Rachel Alexandra apart, the latest generation of three-year-old fillies was a weak one. **Stardom Bound**, the 2008 Breeders' Cup Juvenile Fillies winner, began the year well enough with two more Grade 1 wins at Santa Anita in the Las Virgenes Stakes and Santa Anita Oaks but an odds-on reverse in the Ashland Stakes in April (behind **Hooh Why**, whom she'd beaten the time before) proved to be her final outing for nearly eight months before just a fair return when fifth in the Gazelle Stakes late in the year. Canadian-trained **Careless Jewel** compiled a good record prior to the Breeders' Cup, her most notable win coming at Saratoga with an eleven-length win in the Alabama Stakes, but she went off far too fast before finishing last when sent off favourite for the Breeders' Cup Ladies' Classic. The only other three-year-old filly of note on dirt was **Flashing** (a remote last of three to Rachel Alexandra in the Mother Goose), whose wins in the Test Stakes at Saratoga and Gazelle Stakes at Aqueduct were among nine Grade 1 wins for the Godolphin operation in the USA, all of them gained from August onwards.

On turf, **Courageous Cat** disappointed at odds on for his first try at Grade 1 level when third to the Secretariat Stakes winner **Take The Points** in the Jamaica Handicap at Belmont but went on to put up just about the best effort by a three-year-old on that surface in North America all year when chasing home Goldikova in the Breeders' Cup Mile. The Breeders' Cup undercard saw a win for gelding **The Usual Q T** in the Grade 2 Oak Tree Derby before he beat the ex-British colt **Battle of Hastings** into second again, but with more to spare, to complete a five-timer in the Hollywood Derby, in which Take The Points was below form. Some of the most noteworthy performances from three-year-old fillies on turf came from British-trained visitors, with **Midday** taking the Breeders' Cup Filly & Mare Turf against mainly older rivals and **Lahaleeb** and **Rainbow View** finishing first and second in the E. P. Taylor Stakes at Woodbine. On the same day as the E. P. Taylor, **Hot Cha Cha** put up the best effort by a US-trained three-year-old filly on turf when a clear-cut winner of the Queen Elizabeth II Challenge Cup on soft ground at Keeneland from a field that included Grade 1 winners **Gozzip Girl** (American Oaks) and **Miss World** (Garden City Handicap).

There was no dominant older male horse in the nine/ten-furlong division on dirt and synthetic tracks to the extent that none was able to win more than one Grade 1 contest on those surfaces. Arguably the best performance in the division came outside North America when **Well Armed**, third to Curlin the year before, put up an apparently stunning effort to win the Dubai World Cup by fourteen lengths, making all. Donn Handicap winner **Albertus Maximus**, the shortest-priced American contender, was a below-form sixth in a substandard renewal, and Well Armed finished last in a Grade 2 at Del Mar on his subsequent outing four months later. Perhaps the strongest race outside the Breeders' Cup in this division was the Pacific Classic at Del Mar in September which went to one of the outsiders, **Richard's Kid**. He showed improved form once joining Bob Baffert and ran respectably at Santa Anita later in the autumn, finishing third to Gitano Hernando in the Goodwood Stakes and sixth in the Breeders' Cup Classic. Well Armed's stable-companion **Colonel John** contested the same three races in a light campaign, running fifth to Richard's Kid in the Pacific Classic but finishing one place ahead of him in both races at Santa Anita, going one better than the year before to finish fifth in the Breeders' Cup Classic on his final outing before retiring to stud. Hollywood Gold Cup winner **Rail Trip** was third in the Pacific Classic, for which he started favourite, but had to miss the Breeders' Cup with a foot problem. Seven-year-old **Einstein** did most of his racing on turf in his early days and won the Woodford Reserve Turf Classic at Churchill Downs in May for the second year running, but he was campaigned largely on dirt and synthetic tracks in the latest season, proving his versatility with a win in the Santa Anita Handicap. Einstein was well beaten there in the Breeders' Cup Classic but otherwise held his form really well all year and, as well as finishing second in the Pacific Classic, he was also third in the Donn Handicap, the Stephen Foster Handicap (behind **Macho Again** and **Asiatic Boy**) and the Grade 2 Clark Handicap at Churchill Downs. The Stephen Foster winner Macho Again was missing from the Breeders' Cup (below form both starts on synthetic tracks) but put up a couple of good efforts on the dirt at Saratoga, going down to **Bullsbay** in the Whitney Handicap and coming closest to spoiling Rachel Alexandra's unbeaten record for the year when beaten a head in the Woodward Stakes, with Bullsbay third.

A muddling renewal of the Breeders' Cup Dirt Mile went to **Furthest Land**, making a winning debut at Grade 1 level, from another outsider **Ready's Echo**. **Kodiak Kowboy** put up at least as good a performance to win the Cigar Mile Handicap at Aqueduct from the Metropolitan Handicap winner **Bribon** and retired to stud with Grade 1 wins to his name over three different trips after earlier successes in the Carter Handicap over seven furlongs (by a head, in receipt of 5 lb from runner-up **Fabulous Strike**) and the Vosburgh Stakes over six on level terms against the same rival. A dual Grade 2 winner (including a defeat of the previous year's winner **Benny The Bull** in the True North Stakes at Belmont) in between those defeats, Fabulous Strike, like Kodiak Kowboy, was absent from the Breeders' Cup Sprint which saw the tighest finish of the meeting, with a nose, head and nose splitting **Dancing In Silks**, **Crown of Thorns**, **Cost of Freedom** and **Gayego**. The long-priced winner showed improved form on his first outing in a graded stakes, whereas the three others had all met over course and distance the previous month in the Ancient Title Stakes when Godolphin's Gayego had come out on top ahead of Crown of Thorns. The previous year's Ancient Title winner (fourth this time) Cost of Freedom only just failed to make all in the Breeders' Cup Sprint, having been ruled out by the track vet the year before. As well as Gayego, Godolphin was represented over shorter trips by **Pyro**, who had beaten Kodiak Kowboy and Ready's Echo in the seven-furlong Forego Stakes at Saratoga, but failed to give his running in the Breeders' Cup Dirt Mile for the second year running.

With the previous year's winner Zenyatta going for the Classic instead, no Rachel Alexandra, and a poor run from the three-year-old favourite Careless Jewel, the latest Breeders' Cup Ladies' Classic lacked strength, while there was also a suspicion the first two were flattered in coming from well off a strong pace. Winner **Life Is Sweet** had been beaten on three occasions by her stable-companion Zenyatta during the season (she'd also finished third against males in the Hollywood Gold Cup despite being below her best) but returned to top form at the Breeders' Cup after completing a hat-trick in graded stakes at Santa Anita early in the year in the Santa Margarita Invitational Handicap. Ladies' Classic runner-up **Mushka** had previously been awarded the Spinster Stakes on the demotion of French import **Proviso**, fourth behind her at Santa Anita. Godolphin's **Music Note** was third in the Ladies' Classic for the second year but wasn't at her best this time, though wins earlier in the season, routing her field in the seven-furlong Ballerina Stakes at Saratoga and following up with a minimum of fuss from **Unbridled Belle** in the Beldame Stakes at Belmont over nine, were as good as any by an older filly all year on dirt. The ex-British filly **Icon Project** showed plenty of improvement switched to dirt, with both her graded wins gained by margins of around thirteen lengths, including a defeat of the subsequent Ruffian Handicap winner **Swift Temper** in the Personal Ensign Stakes at Saratoga. The Ruffian runner-up **Seventh Street** disappointed in the Filly & Mare Sprint at the Breeders' Cup but was hard to fault otherwise, winning the Apple Blossom and Go For Wand Handicaps and finishing a good second to **Seattle Smooth** in the Ogden Phipps Handicap in between.

Breeders' Cup Dirt Mile, Santa Anita—run on pro-ride, not dirt, on this occasion; a third win at the meeting for jockey Julien Leparoux on Furthest Land ('R' on cap and blinkers), while the favourite Mastercraftsman (right) stumbles and collides with the rail, eventually dropping back to fourth, and the leader Midshipman (noseband) finishes third

Ventura started odds on to claim a second consecutive success in the Breeders' Cup Filly & Mare Sprint and was unlucky not do so, left with considerably more to do than the winner **Informed Decision** from the home turn, though Informed Decision had also had the better of the argument (narrowly, in receipt of weight) when the pair first met in the upgraded Madison Stakes at Keeneland in April. Both compiled excellent records during the year. Informed Decision won six graded races in all, her other Grade 1 success coming in the Humana Distaff Stakes at Churchill Downs and her only defeat when third to Music Note in the Ballerina. Ventura proved equally adept at seven furlongs on synthetic tracks and at a mile on turf. She too won three times at Grade 1 level, the Santa Monica Handicap at Santa Anita early in the year and the Woodbine Mile (against males) and Matriarch Stakes either side of her Breeders' Cup defeat. Retired to stud after the Matriarch, Ventura's success was a fitting one for her trainer Humberto Ascanio who had been assistant to Robert Frankel until his death just weeks earlier. The Matriarch figured eight times among numerous Grade 1 successes during Frankel's training career which earned him a record five Eclipse Awards. The 2008 Filly & Mare Sprint runner-up **Indian Blessing**, another with a win and place record that was hard to fault, was retired before the latest Breeders' Cup but had proved herself as good as ever when second in the Dubai Golden Shaheen and when bowing out with a Grade 2 win at Belmont in September. In between, she had been another notable scalp for Music Note when second in the Ballerina Stakes at Saratoga.

Behind Zenyatta, the result of the Breeders' Cup Classic was notable for the performances of 'turf horses' **Gio Ponti** and **Twice Over** in second and third, lending support to the view that synthetic surfaces bear more similarity to turf than traditional dirt. The Henry Cecil-trained Champion Stakes winner Twice Over was having his first start off the turf, while Gio Ponti, although a minor stakes winner on the Santa Anita pro-ride late in 2008, had established himself as America's top grass performer prior to the Breeders' Cup. However, a defeat to shock winner **Interpatation** over a mile and a half (on soft ground) at Belmont in the Joe Hirsch Turf Classic steered connections towards the Classic instead of the Turf at the Breeders' Cup. Prior to that, Gio Ponti had completed a four-timer in Grade 1 company at distances from a mile to eleven furlongs, beginning with a narrow defeat of an unlucky Ventura in the Frank E. Kilroe Mile Handicap at Santa Anita. Better efforts followed over longer trips at Belmont in the Manhattan Handicap (from **Marsh Side**) and Man o'War Stakes before a decisive success over Rainbow View's half-brother **Just As Well** in the Arlington Million. It was left instead to the six-year-old gelding **Presious Passion** to provide the stiffest home defence in a field of just seven for the Breeders' Cup Turf, though a career-best effort at Santa Anita was only good enough to see him into second place behind the 2008 winner **Conduit**. Otherwise, Presious Passion's usual trail-blazing tactics had carried him to a second successive win in the United Nations Stakes (breaking the Monmouth track record) and another Grade 1 success in the Clement L. Hirsch Memorial Turf Championship at Santa Anita. **Champs Elysees** would have been worth his place in the Breeders' Cup Turf but had been retired to stud by then following a career-best effort to win the Canadian International in October. In so doing he turned the tables on Marsh Side (demoted to fourth), Just As Well, and the German-trained **Quijano** who all finished in front of him in the Northern Dancer Turf Stakes over the same course and distance at Woodbine the previous month. **Grand Couturier** was below his best in Grade 1 company in 2009, including when going for repeat wins in both the Sword Dancer Invitational (won by rank outsider **Telling**) and Joe Hirsch Turf Classic, but showed something closer to his best when winning the Grade 2 Bowling Green Handicap at Belmont in September.

For the second year running America's best milers on turf proved no match for **Goldikova** who stays in training in a bid to become the first triple Breeders' Cup winner in 2010. **Justenuffhumour** won his first six starts, including a couple of Grade 2 events at Saratoga, before disappointing on soft ground behind **Court Vision** in the Shadwell Turf Mile, but proved his Keeneland running all wrong when finishing a good third in the Breeders' Cup Mile, having to weave through from last place. Court Vision was only a head behind Justenffhumour at Santa Anita and proved at least as well suited dropped to a mile as he had been over nine and ten furlongs earlier in the year. His earlier runs included a third place to 2008 Breeders' Cup Mile runner-up **Kip Deville** (who was below

Man o' War Stakes, Belmont Park—North America's top turf performer Gio Ponti (far left) is on his way to the third of four Grade 1s in a row

form afterwards) in the Gulfstream Park Turf Handicap and other good efforts to reach the frame in the Woodford Reserve Turf Classic and the Manhattan Handicap. **Cowboy Cal** disappointed in the Breeders' Cup Mile but he had a good record at Santa Anita, winning two Grade 2 events on pro-ride there early in the year and another on turf when beating the Eddie Read Handicap winner **Global Hunter** in the Oak Tree Handicap prior to the Breeders' Cup. Cowboy Cal also went down by a head to Einstein in the Woodford Reserve Turf Classic and ran Justenuffhumour to half a length in another Grade 2 event at Saratoga, winding up his campaign with a creditable third to **Fluke** and **Ever A Friend** in the Citation Handicap at Hollywood.

Things went more the local horses' way in the Breeders' Cup Turf Sprint, and it was probably no coincidence on the idiosyncratic downhill turf track at Santa Anita that the first two, **California Flag** and the mare **Gotta Have Her**, were course and distance winners on their most recent starts, the winner having things his own way in front. California Flag had been well beaten in the race the year before behind **Desert Code**, who himself was behind in the latest renewal after losing his form since a Grade 3 win over the same course and distance in February. **Cannonball** took third in the Turf Sprint, though ran his best race all year when beaten a neck in the Golden Jubilee Stakes at Royal Ascot.

The mare **Diamondrella** found the Turf Sprint a bit too much of a test of speed, but had a good record on turf otherwise, with Grade 1 wins at a mile on softer ground in the Just A Game Stakes at Belmont and the First Lady Stakes. **Forever Together** was placed in both those contests and, while successful in the Diana Stakes at Saratoga for the second year running, she had to settle for third when attempting a repeat win as favourite for the Breeders' Cup Filly & Mare Turf. **Pure Clan** had run the only poor race of her career behind Forever Together at the Breeders' Cup in 2008, but made amends with a much better performance to finish second to Midday in the Filly & Mare Turf this time, though like Forever Together she was at a disadvantage in being held up compared with the winner. Pure Clan had earlier finished third to **Dynaforce** (last at Santa Anita) in the Beverly D Stakes before winning the Flower Bowl Invitational at Belmont. Ex-British filly **Magical Fantasy** finished fifth in the Filly & Mare Turf after a hat-trick of Grade 1 wins, beating Gotta Have Her in the John C. Mabee Handicap at Del Mar in between defeats of another ex-British filly, Visit (rated 115), in the Gamely Stakes at Hollywood and the Yellow Ribbon Stakes at Santa Anita. Visit, incidentally, finished fourth in the Filly & Mare Turf, reaching the frame for the second year running, this time effectively acting as pacemaker for her same owner's Midday.

Less than a length covered the first four home in the Breeders' Cup Juvenile, with Godolphin's **Vale of York** another example of a horse making a successful switch from turf to the pro-ride surface. He did well to overcome some brief trouble in the straight but more credit should go to the runner-up and favourite **Lookin At Lucky** who was unfortunate to lose his unbeaten record in coming from further back off the ordinary pace than the other principals. He had already won twice in Grade 1 company, the Del Mar Futurity and the Norfolk Stakes, before the Breeders' Cup and confirmed his superiority over Juvenile third **Noble's Promise** when beating that rival into second, with a bit in hand, in the Cashcall Futurity at Hollywood in December. Lookin At Lucky has plenty going for him at three, though has done all his racing so far on synthetic surfaces. Noble's Promise and **Piscitelli**, first and fifth in the Breeders' Futurity on Keeneland's polytrack, completed the frame in the Breeders' Cup Juvenile ahead of the Breeders' Futurity runner-up **Aikenite** in fifth. **Dublin** (Hopeful Stakes, in which Aikenite was third) and **Homeboykris** (Champagne Stakes) gained their Grade 1 wins on dirt, and while their best form was on a par with the Santa Anita principals, subsequent defeats for both of them in lesser graded stakes suggests they weren't missed at the Breeders' Cup. **D'Funnybone** did take his chance at Santa Anita after impressing with Grade 2 wins on dirt in the Saratoga Special Stakes and Futurity Stakes at Belmont (from subsequent Champagne runner-up **Discreetly Mine**) but finished last in the Breeders' Cup Juvenile, lack of stamina possibly as much an issue as the different surface. **Aspire**, placed in the Hopeful and the Champagne, was another to come unstuck on his synthetic track debut in the Breeders' Cup Juvenile in which he had only D'Funnybone behind him. **Make Music For Me** was absent from the Breeders' Cup but was placed three times behind Lookin At Lucky in graded company, his best run when a close third in the Cashcall Futurity. Among colts with more progressive profiles later in the year, Champagne Stakes fourth **Super Saver** made all for a five-length win in the Grade 2 Kentucky Jockey Club Stakes at Churchill Downs, while **Buddy's Saint** was successful in a couple of Grade 2 contests at Aqueduct, beating Homeboykris into fifth in the Remsen Stakes. British-trained youngsters took three of the first five places in the Breeders' Cup Juvenile Turf won by the John Gosden-trained **Pounced**. **Interactif**, who was third, looked to have the strongest claims of the American colts beforehand, and the form took a knock when runner-up **Bridgetown**, who dictated a steady pace, was beaten at odds on into fourth in the Grade 3 Generous Stakes at Hollywood next time.

Long before the Breeders' Cup, one of the best performances by a US-trained two-year-old filly had come at Royal Ascot. Queen Mary Stakes winner **Jealous Again** was part of a five-strong raiding party of juveniles (plus older sprinter Cannonball) at the Royal meeting launched by trainer Wesley Ward, who also struck with the gelding Strike The Tiger (rated 98), 33/1 winner of the Windsor Castle Stakes twenty-four hours earlier—the first American-trained horses to win on the Flat in Britain. The trainer rated Aegean (102), who'd beaten Jealous Again in a Grade 3 at Churchill Downs, as his best hope at Ascot, though she proved disappointing in the Albany Stakes. Jealous Again joined Godolphin afterwards but was not seen out again.

The Breeders' Cup Juvenile Fillies was another closely-fought affair (three lengths covered the first seven), with trouble in running behind the first three also playing its part. The Alcibiades Stakes at Keeneland proved the key trial to the Juvenile Fillies in which the Alcibiades runner-up **She Be Wild** squeezed through on the rail to beat **Beautician**, fifth behind her at Keeneland. Things were less straightforward for the Alcibiades winner **Negligee**, who veered badly right in the straight before finishing sixth, just in front of **Zilva** (fourth at Keeneland) who was persistently denied a clear run on the rail. Canadian filly **Biofuel**, fourth past the post, did well despite being another to suffer interference, being badly hampered by Negligee. Of the other principals, **Blind Luck** failed to make it eight winning favourites in a row in the race but ran up to her previous best in third, two places in front of **Always A Princess** whom she'd beaten into second in the Oak Leaf Stakes over course and distance the time before. However, Frizette Stakes winner **Devil**

May Care, a half-sister to Regal Ransom, was another dirt winner to fail to cut any ice. There was a much more clear-cut result when the placed horses from the Juvenile Fillies, Beautician and Blind Luck, met again in the Hollywood Starlet Stakes in December. While Beautician ran too poorly to be true, Blind Luck routed her field by upwards of seven lengths, improving on previous efforts to top the two-year-old filly division. Of the fillies missing from the Breeders' Cup, **Mi Sueno** was retired after fracturing a leg in training following her beating of Blind Luck in the Debutante Stakes at Del Mar, while **Hot Dixie Chick** boasted two defeats of Beautician at Saratoga, including in the Spinaway Stakes. **Awesome Maria** had impressed in winning the Grade 2 Matron Stakes at Belmont and remains one to do better having suffered a troubled run when narrowly beaten by Devil May Care in the Frizette. It will be a surprise if the latest Golden Rod winner fares anything like so well as Rachel Alexandra, but **Sassy Image** left earlier efforts in the Spinaway and Alcibiades well behind when stringing out her rivals at Churchill Downs, while **Quiet Temper** lost her maiden tag with a near eight-length win on a wet track in the Grade 3 Delta Princess Stakes. In the Breeders' Cup Juvenile Fillies' Turf, **Tapitsfly** and **Rose Catherine** dominated throughout before finishing clear, the latter subsequently finishing well held on her synthetic track debut in the Hollywood Starlet.

European-trained horses who showed or reproduced their best form in North America are included in this list

Two-Year-Olds

120 Blind Luck (f)
119 Jealous Again (f)
117p Lookin At Lucky
117 †Vale of York
116 D'Funnybone
116 Dublin
116 Mi Sueno (f)
116 She Be Wild (f)
115 Hot Dixie Chick (f)
115 Negligee (f)
115 Noble's Promise
115 Piscitelli
114p Awesome Maria (f)
114p Buddy's Saint
114 Aikenite
114 Beautician (f)
114 Homeboykris
114 Zilva (f)
113+ Biofuel (f)
113 Devil May Care (f)
113 Make Music For Me
113 Quiet Temper (f)
113 Super Saver
113 Tapitsfly (f)
113 Worstcasescenario (f)
112 Always A Princess (f)
112 †Pounced
112 Rose Catherine (f)
112 Sassy Image (f)
112 The Program
111 Aspire
111 Discreetly Mine
110 Ailalea (f)
110 Bridgetown
110 Interactif
109 Dixie Band
109 Hidden Expression (f)
109 Pulsion
109 Rule
108 Amen Hallelujah (f)
108 †Awesome Act
108 Smiling Tiger
108 Uh Oh Bango
108 Western Smoke

DIRT/SYNTHETIC SURFACES

Three-Year-Olds

130 †Rachel Alexandra (f)
126 Summer Bird
125 Mine That Bird
124 †Gitano Hernando
124 Quality Road
124 Zensational
123 †Man of Iron
122 Careless Jewel (f)
122 Friesan Fire
122 *Regal Ransom
121 Blame
121 Dunkirk
121 The Pamplemousse
120 Hold Me Back
120 M One Rifle
119 Capt Candyman Can
119 Flashing (f)
119 General Quarters
119 *Vineyard Haven
118 Evita Argentina (f)
118 Girolamo
118 Midshipman
118 Misremembered
118 Munnings
118 Musket Man
118 Old Fashioned
117 Gabby's Golden Gal (f)
117 Gone Astray
117 I Want Revenge
117 Kensei
117 Pioneerof The Nile
117 Sara Louise (f)
117 Stardom Bound (f)
117 Win Willy

---

115 Funny Moon (f)
114 Hooh Why (f)
111 Cat Moves (f)

Older Horses

131 †Zenyatta (f)
130 †Gio Ponti
129 †Well Armed
127 †Twice Over
123 Fabulous Strike
123 Gayego
123 Music Note (f)
123 Richard's Kid
122 Albertus Maximus
122 *Asiatic Boy
122 Georgie Boy
122 Life Is Sweet (f)
122 Macho Again
122 Rail Trip
121 Benny The Bull
121 Colonel John
121 Cost of Freedom
121 Crown of Thorns
121 Dancing In Silks
121 Icon Project (f)
121 Informed Decision (f)
121 In Summation
121 Kodiak Kowboy
121 Pyro
120 Fatal Bullet
120 Furthest Land
120 Indian Blessing (f)
120 Informed
120 Magnum
120 Smooth Air
119 Bullsbay
119 Mast Track
119 Parading
119 Seattle Smooth (f)
118 Bribon
118 Coal Play
118 Commentator
118 Finallymadeit
118 It's A Bird
118 Kinsale King
118 Nownownow

118 †Proviso (f)
118 Ready's Echo
118 Secret Getaway
118 Unbridled Belle (f)
117 Awesome Gem
117 Bribon
117 Delta Storm
117 Dry Martini
117 My Pal Charlie
117 Tiago
117 Tizway

---

116 Santa Teresita (f)
115 Game Face (f)
115 Seventh Street (f)
115 Swift Temper (f)

TURF

Three-Year-Olds

124 Courageous Cat
122 †Midday (f)
121 †Lahaleeb (f)
120 Hot Cha Cha (f)
120 †Rainbow View (f)
119 The Usual Q T
117 Take The Points

---

116 Gozzip Girl (f)
116 Miss World (f)
112 Internallyflawless (f)

Older Horses

132 †Goldikova (f)
130 †Conduit
130 †Gio Ponti
124 California Flag
124 Champs Elysees
124 Presious Passion
123 Cloudy's Knight
123 †Jukebox Jury
122 Cannonball
122 Einstein
122 Ventura (f)
121 Cowboy Cal
121 Grand Couturier
121 Interpatation
121 Justenuffhumor
121 Kip Deville
120 Cosmonaut
120 Court Vision
120 Diamondrella (f)
120 Forever Together (f)
120 Marsh Side
120 Midships
120 Monterey Jazz
120 Pure Clan (f)
120 †Quijano
120 Rahy's Attorney
120 Thorn Song
119 †Buccellati
119 Ever A Friend
119 Ferneley
119 Global Hunter
119 Karelian
119 Proudinsky
119 Storm Military
118 Dynaforce (f)
118 Fluke
118 Hyperbaric
118 Just As Well
118 †Loup Breton
118 Marchfield
118 †Stotsfold
118 Telling
118 Whatsthescript
117 Better Talk Now
117 Gotta Have Her (f)
117 Magical Fantasy (f)
117 Sailor's Cap
117 Soldier's Dancer
117 Spice Route
117 Tizaqueena (f)

---

116 Mr Sidney

JAPAN The last few seasons have been remarkable for the emergence of some top racemares in various parts of the world. In Japan, **Vodka** has made a similar mark to the exploits of her female contemporaries Zenyatta and Rachel Alexandra in America and Zarkava and Goldikova in France. Already the champion two-year-old filly, Vodka first made a name for herself more widely the following year when becoming only the third filly to win the Tokyo Yushun (Japanese Derby), while in both subsequent seasons she has earned Horse of the Year honours, becoming the first of her sex to gain that award twice. She was arguably a more deserving winner of that title in 2009 than she had been the year before, capping her season by becoming the first Japanese-trained filly or mare to win the Japan Cup after finishing fourth and then third in the two previous editions. Vodka held on by only a matter of inches from the previous year's Kikuka Sho (St Leger) winner **Oken Bruce Lee**, and while a mile and a half is an absolute maximum for her, she is at least as effective at a mile or ten furlongs. Earlier in the season she gained a seven-length victory against her own sex in the Victoria Mile and followed up with a second successive win over the same trip in the Yasuda Kinen against males with an easy defeat of the previous season's Derby winner and Japan Cup runner-up **Deep Sky**. With record earnings and number of Group 1 wins (seven) for a Japanese mare, Vodka is due to have a final run in Dubai in 2010 before retiring to stud; she was below form in two runs there in the latest season after finishing fourth in the 2008 Dubai Duty Free on her only other start outside Japan.

Despite her excellent record, strictly on form Vodka was not Japan's best horse; taking her sex allowance into account, she was not even the best horse in the Japan Cup. Runner-up Oken Bruce Lee, the winner of a Group 2 contest at Kyoto earlier in the autumn, was arguably an unlucky loser in the Japan Cup, finishing strongly from last place to lose out by a nose. Five-year-old **Dream Journey** had strong claims to being the top performer, with Group 1 successes in the Takarazuka Kinen in June (from **Sakura Mega Wonder** and Deep Sky) and the Arima Kinen in December in which Japan Cup fifth **Air Shady** took third for the second year running. Another leading performer was **Company** who proved better than ever at the age of eight, becoming the first horse of his age to win at Group 1 level in Japan, doing so twice. Contesting the Tenno Sho (Autumn) for the fourth time (he was a close fourth to Vodka in 2008), he came out on top in the latest renewal in what was the best-contested race in Japan all year, with the previous year's Japan Cup winner **Screen Hero**, Vodka and Oken Bruce Lee completing the frame

Japan Cup, Tokyo—a very popular victory for the five-year-old mare Vodka, winning her seventh Group 1 (equalling the record for a Japanese-trained horse), though, in the end, she has only a nose to spare over the strong-finishing Oken Bruce Lee (white face); British-trained Conduit (light colours) keeps on for fourth

and Dream Journey sixth. That was Company's second defeat of Vodka on the bounce after a Group 2 win over nine furlongs at Tokyo, and he retired to stud after gaining his other Group 1 win in the Mile Championship from **Meiner Falke** and the French-trained Sun Chariot Stakes winner Sahpresa.

Meiner Kitz staked his claim to being the best stayer with a win in the two-mile Tenno Sho (Spring) and wasn't discredited when eighth in the Japan Cup later in the year. Chief among his rivals in the Tenno Sho were Dream Journey (third) and **Jaguar Mail** (fifth), the latter going on to finish in the frame in the Hong Kong Vase for the second year running, not beaten far in fourth. The shock 2007 Arima Kinen winner **Matsurida Gogh** has been below form in both subsequent renewals of that race but improved his record at Nakayama still further when winning a Group 2 event, the eleven-furlong Sankei Sho All Comers, for the third year running, beating Dream Journey and subsequent Tenno Sho (Autumn) fifth **Shingen**. Among the sprinters, **Laurel Guerreiro** completed the double in Japan's two Group 1 six-furlong contests, the Takamatsunomiya Kinen in March and the Sprinters Stakes in October (by just a nose from **B B Guldan**), but for the second year running finished down the field in the Hong Kong Sprint.

A new name emerged at the top of the dirt division in **Espoir City**, winner of the Japan Cup Dirt. As well as having former winner **Vermilion** down the field in that race, he also managed to turn the tables on fourth-placed **Success Brocken** who had had Espoir City back in fourth in the February Stakes, where **Casino Drive** and **Kane Hekili** had filled the places. Casino Drive, incidentally, became Japan's latest challenger to disappoint in the Dubai World Cup despite starting third favourite.

Three-year-old colts **Silk Mobius** and **Golden Ticket** were placed in the Japan Cup Dirt but some of their leading turf counterparts met with injury. **Logi Universe** won a soft-ground Tokyo Yushun (Derby) on what proved his final start of the year but is expected to return in 2010; his only defeat so far in six starts came in the Satsuki Sho (2000 Guineas) won by **Unrivaled**. A more serious injury was suffered by the Kikuka Sho (St Leger) winner **Three Rolls** who broke down in the Arima Kinen. Other prominent three-year-olds included **Forgettable**, beaten a nose in the Kikuka Sho and fourth in the Arima Kinen, **Seiun Wonder**, third in both the Guineas and St Leger, and Derby runner-up **Reach The Crown** whose ninth place in the Japan Cup wasn't a bad effort.

On the whole though, it was the fillies who made more of an impact in the big all-aged events later in the year. There was little between the top two in the classics, with **Buena Vista** getting the better of **Red Desire** in their first two encounters, winning the Oka Sho

(1000 Guineas) by half a length and the Yushun Himba (Oaks) by a nose. However, in the third leg of the fillies' triple crown in the autumn, the Shuka Sho, it was Red Desire who was a nose in front of Buena Vista who was subsequently demoted to third. Buena Vista went on to be a fast-finishing third to older mare **Queen Spumante** in the Queen Elizabeth II Commemorative Cup before an excellent second in the Arima Kinen, while Red Desire also excelled herself with third place in the Japan Cup.

While recent seasons have seen less success for Japanese horses on the international front, there were a couple of important developments domestically which virtually complete the process of opening up racing in Japan to foreign interests. For the first time in 2010, all JRA pattern races, the classics included, will be open to foreign-trained horses. That development comes nearly thirty years after the Japan Cup was instituted in 1981 as a means of testing Japanese bloodstock against foreign opposition. The other step forward came in November when Sheikh Mohammed became the first non-Japanese resident to be accepted as an owner with the JRA—his wife Princess Haya and son Sheikh Hamdan were also among the first foreign owners to be registered following a relaxing of the rules governing ownership.

Three-Year-Olds
122 Buena Vista (f)
122 Logi Universe
121 Red Desire (f)
119 Forgettable
119 Three Rolls
118 Jo Cappuccino
118 Silk Mobius
118 Unrivaled
117 Seiun Wonder
117 Testa Matta
116 Golden Ticket
116 I Ko Piko
116 Transcend
116 Wonder Acute
115 Antonio Barows
115 Reach The Crown
115 Suni

Older Horses
128 Company
127 Oken Bruce Lee
126 Dream Journey
125 Deep Sky
125 †Vodka (f)
124 Espoir City
124 Screen Hero
123 Success Brocken
122 Casino Drive
122 Matsurida Gogh
122 Vermilion
121 Kane Hekili
120 Jaguar Mail
120 Sakura Mega Wonder
119 Furioso
119 Super Hornet
118 Air Shady
118 Axion
118 B B Guldan
118 Faridat
118 Laurel Guerreiro
118 Meiner Falke
118 Meiner Kitz
118 Miyabi Ranveli
118 Tascata Sorte
117 Al Nasrain
117 Asakusa Kings
117 Bamboo Ere
117 Captain Thule
117 Eishin Deputy
117 Kinshasa No Kiseki
117 Never Bouchon
117 Suzuka Causeway
116 Ferrari Pisa
116 Higher Game
116 Hikaru Kazabue
116 Makoto Sparviero
116 Shadow Gate
116 Smart Falcon
116 Smile Jack
116 Tamamo Support
116 Tosho Courage
115 Absolute
115 Namura Crescent
115 Osumi Grass One
115 Queen Spumante (f)
115 Shingen
115 Smart Gear
115 Sunrise Max
115 Wonder Speed

HONG KONG The vast majority of Hong Kong's racehorses are geldings which means that, with no stud career awaiting them, the best performers are able to stay around to compete for several seasons and can establish a popular, and in some cases, fanatical following, provided, of course, that they stay sound. It was therefore for the third year running that sprinter Sacred Kingdom, miler Good Ba Ba and middle-distance performer Viva Pataca each figured as leading performers in their respective categories.

After sustaining a hairline fracture to a leg in 2008 (causing him to miss the International meeting that December), **Sacred Kingdom** re-established himself as not just Hong Kong's, but the world's, best sprinter in 2009. He took a while to return to his best but followed up a defeat of **Regency Dragon** and **One World** in the Group 2 Sprint Cup in May with a top-class effort to defeat Singapore's hitherto unbeaten sprinter Rocket Man (rated 125) in the Krisflyer International Sprint at Kranji later that month. Moving on to Royal Ascot where he was supplemented for the Golden Jubilee Stakes, Sacred Kingdom got worked up in the preliminaries and failed to give his running in fifth behind Art Connoisseur but it was a different story back home against another international line-up at Sha Tin in December. There, he regained his Hong Kong Sprint title, not having to show the same form as when successful in 2007, but still winning with plenty of authority in a race dominated by the locally trained sprinters. Coming off a strong pace, One World, **Joy And Fun** (a dual Group 3 handicap winner over seven furlongs earlier in 2009) and the previous year's runner-up **Green Birdie** completed the frame. **Inspiration**, who had caused an upset in the Hong Kong Sprint in Sacred Kingdom's absence in 2008 was down the field this time, though he'd had Sacred Kingdom back in fourth in the Centenary Sprint Cup earlier in the year and had carried joint top weight to victory ahead of One World in the Group 3 Premier Bowl Handicap in October. One of Hong Kong's most progressive horses, and a potential successor to Sacred Kingdom's sprint title, was **Happy Zero**, though whether he continues to be campaigned as a sprinter remains to be seen. Happy Zero won seven of his first eight starts in Hong Kong from five to seven furlongs, including a defeat of One World in the Group 3 Sha Tin Sprint Trophy Handicap in October before accounting for Sacred Kingdom and several other leading sprinters in the Group 2 International Sprint Trial. However, instead of the Sprint at the International meeting in December, Happy Zero was stepped up in trip to contest the Hong Kong Mile, for which he started odds on. The move all but paid off as he was collared only close home to be beaten half a length by **Good Ba Ba**.

Good Ba Ba thus completed an historic hat-trick of wins in the Hong Kong Mile, becoming the first horse to win three races at the International meeting. While he has avoided the injury which has prevented Sacred Kingdom completing a similar treble in the Sprint, it has not all been plain sailing for Good Ba Ba. He did win a second successive Stewards' Cup in January, from **Fellowship**, but wasn't in peak form for much of the year during which he changed stables from Andreas Schutz to Derek Cruz. Fellowship again finished behind Good Ba Ba when third in the Hong Kong Mile, though beforehand, in receipt of weight, he came out on top in the International Mile Trial in which Good Ba Ba was only third. Hong Kong's other international Group 1 mile event, the Champion's Mile in April, saw a close finish between **Sight Winner** and front-running **Egyptian Ra**, the pair dominating throughout and having Good Ba Ba back in fourth. Sight Winner's only similar form came when runner-up in the International Mile Trial but Egyptian Ra enjoyed a couple of group-race wins over seven furlongs, notably a defeat of Good Ba Ba and Fellowship in the Queen's Silver Jubilee Cup in March, while he also made the frame in the Hong Kong Mile for the second year running, finishing fourth.

If Hong Kong's Horse of the Year title were decided at the end of the calendar year, the 2009 winner would surely have been either Good Ba Ba (the 2007/8 winner) or Sacred

Cathay Pacific Hong Kong Sprint, Sha Tin—another win for a great local favourite as Sacred Kingdom adds to his win in the same race in 2007 (denied a run in 2008 by a leg injury)

Cathay Pacific Hong Kong Mile, Sha Tin—Good Ba Ba wins this race for the third year in a row, challenging on the outside to lead in the last strides; odds-on Happy Zero (striped cap), Fellowship (spots) and Egyptian Ra are also in the photo

Kingdom (voted the Most Popular Horse), but with the voting taking place at the end of the 2008/9 season in June, the honour went to **Viva Pataca** who enjoyed a good first half of the year, winning two more Group 1 events. He gained a second successive victory in the Hong Kong Gold Cup in February with a defeat of **Packing Winner**, while his win in the Champions & Chater Cup, over a mile and a half in May, was his third in the race in four seasons (Packing Winner had denied him in 2008). Viva Pataca also fared best of the local horses when runner-up to Presvis in the Queen Elizabeth II Cup in April (**Thumbs Up** a close third and Packing Winner fifth), placed for the second time since his win in 2007. One of Viva Pataca's best efforts all year came in defeat when fourth to Packing Winner in the Group 3 Sha Tin Trophy Handicap in October, conceding 8 lb to the winner over a barely adequate mile. Having made the frame in three consecutive Hong Kong Cups, Viva Pataca contested the Vase at the International meeting for the first time, and though finishing only sixth behind the French-trained winner Daryakana, was the first home among the locally-trained horses.

Viva Pataca's future dominance of the middle-distance scene in Hong Kong looks likely to be threatened most by his own stable-companion **Collection**. A former winner of the Hampton Court Stakes at Royal Ascot for William Haggas, Collection won the Hong Kong Derby in March and finished third behind Viva Pataca in the Champions & Chater Cup. However, his two best performances came at the end of the year, a win in the International Cup Trial (on a day which celebrated the 125th anniversary of the Hong Kong Jockey Club) coming ahead of another high-class effort to split European visitors Vision d'Etat and Presvis in the Hong Kong Cup itself.

130	†Sacred Kingdom	120	Joy And Fun	117	Jackpot Delight
126	†Good Ba Ba	120	Sight Winner	117	More Bountiful
125	Collection	120?	Yellow Diamond	116	Sunny Power
125	Happy Zero	119	Enthused	115	Able One
123	Egyptian Ra	119	Packing Winner	115	Medic Power
122	Fellowship	118	Dim Sum	115	Regency Dragon
122	Inspiration	118	Green Birdie	115	Special Days
122	Viva Pataca	118	Thumbs Up		
121	One World	117	*Eagle Mountain		

AUSTRALIA AND NEW ZEALAND Australia's highest-rated horse of 2008 **Weekend Hussler** (then rated 130) was forced out of action after only one race in 2009, when dead-heating for fourth in the first Group 1 of the year, the Lightning Stakes at Flemington in January. In his absence, the Timeform ratings at the end of 2009 were headed by the veteran globe-trotting sprinter **Takeover Target** and the five-year-old **Scenic Blast**, who won the Lightning and the Newmarket Handicap before emulating Takeover Target and going on to success in the King's Stand Stakes at Royal Ascot. Takeover Target actually recorded the highest-rated performance in Australia in 2009 (equalled by Scenic Blast's at Royal Ascot) when demolishing a top field in the T. J. Smith Stakes at Randwick in April. He followed up in the Goodwood Handicap at Morphettville on his only other start at home, conceding weight all round, before running well below his best in the Krisflyer International Sprint in Singapore on the way to making a fourth visit to Britain. After missing Royal Ascot—for the first time in four years—with a high temperature, worse followed when Takeover Target cracked his near-hind cannon bone in the July Cup, an injury that required the insertion of five screws and forced his retirement. Takeover Target won twenty-one races in four countries—he also won in Singapore and Japan—from forty-one starts after his owner/trainer Joe Janiak bought him as an unraced four-year-old for the equivalent of £500 at a disposal sale. He won eight times at Group 1 level and was only the second horse in history to win in every major racing state in Australia. Jay Ford rode Takeover Target in all but two of his races, Nash Rawiller riding him for the only time when he won the T. J. Smith in the latest season. Scenic Blast finished tenth (three places behind Takeover Target) when a short-priced favourite for the July Cup. He wasn't the same horse as he had been when winning the King's Stand in breathtaking fashion, putting up a performance that day at least on a par with those of previous Australian winners of the King's Stand (Takeover Target's win was sandwiched between those of Choisir and Miss Andretti). Scenic Blast failed to produce anything like his best in the Sprinters Stakes in Japan (where he suffered interference in running) or in the Hong Kong Sprint. He bled at Sha Tin and has been sent to continue his career in California. **Apache Cat**, another who ranks among the best Australian sprinters of the last decade, broke down in the Hong Kong Sprint (a race in which he had come third in 2008) and was retired. He won twice at Group 1 level in his final season, taking the Australia Stakes and the Doomben 10,000 (for a second time), bringing his career total of Group 1 wins to eight. **All Silent**, who started second favourite but managed only eighth to local hero Sacred Kingdom in a strongly-contested Hong Kong Sprint, looks set to assume the mantle

BMW Caulfield Cup (Handicap), Caulfield—
Viewed defies top weight to win his first race since the previous year's Melbourne Cup

Emirates Melbourne Cup, Flemington—
Shocking gets on top in the closing stages to edge out the Godolphin runner Crime Scene (blinkers, mostly obscured by winner), with the staying-on Mourilyan in third

of Australia's top international sprinter. He won three times from eight runs in 2009, putting up his best performance when slamming his field in the Victoria Racing Club Stakes at the Melbourne Cup Carnival. Another up-and-coming sprinter **Nicconi**, who scored his first Group 1 victory with an impressive display in The Galaxy at Randwick in April, has been pencilled in for a Royal Ascot challenge in 2010.

Moving towards the other end of the distance spectrum, the highest-rated stayers of the year were **Viewed**, the previous year's Melbourne Cup winner, and **Scenic Shot** (trained like Scenic Blast by Dan Morton). Scenic Shot had an excellent year, winning three Group 2s in Queensland, the Doomben Cup (ten furlongs), the P. J. O'Shea Stakes (eleven furlongs) and the Brisbane Cup (mile and a half), before landing the Group 1 Mackinnon Stakes (ten furlongs) at Flemington on Victoria Derby day. Viewed recorded a career-best effort to win the Caulfield Cup (mile and a half) under top weight, becoming only the third to win the Caulfield after a Melbourne Cup win the previous year. He ran another fine race in the two-mile Melbourne Cup, carrying top weight into a very creditable seventh after suffering plenty of interference behind **Shocking**. Shocking was trained by Mark Kavanagh who had to retire his stable star, the C. F. Orr Stakes winner **Maldivian** (winner of the Cox Plate in 2008), after he was injured in the Turnbull Stakes at Flemington in October. Shocking won the Hotham Handicap at Flemington on Derby day three days before the Cup in which he put up a smart performance to win from Crime Scene who gave Godolphin its third second place in Australia's most famous race, following Central Park and Give The Slip (Beekeeper finished third in the royal blue colours). The Melbourne Cup third Mourilyan was saddled by South African Herman Brown but he had finished second in the Goodwood Cup on his fourth start in 2009 when trained in Britain. Viewed's Caulfield Cup victory was one of six Group 1s during the year for eighty-two-year-old

Hall of Fame trainer Bart Cummings. The other successes came from **Roman Emperor** (AJC Derby), **Russeting** (Winter Stakes), **Allez Wonder** (Toorak Handicap), **So You Think** (Cox Plate) and **Faint Perfume** (VRC Oaks). Roman Emperor, who finished second to Viewed in the Caulfield Cup, gave Cummings his fifth AJC Derby winner (still four behind the late Tommy Smith's record of nine). So You Think caused an upset in Australia's premier weight-for age classic the Cox Plate, having only his fifth run and his first against older rivals at Moonee Valley. He was only the seventh three-year-old (**Manhattan Rain** made it a one, two for the youngsters) to win the Cox Plate since 1970 (his trainer has now won the race on four occasions) and his winning time of 2m 3.98sec was the second fastest in the history of the race. Among the other three-year-olds, **Wanted** was the top-rated sprinter in the age group (he also ran a fine race against All Silent in the Victoria Racing Club Stakes), **Phelan Ready** joined Dance Hero (in 2004) as one of only two horses to complete the Magic Millions/Golden Slipper double, **Starspangled-banner**, who is set to join the Coolmore/Ballydoyle team in Ireland, won the Caulfield Guineas (defeating So You Think, among others) and **More Joyous** was the highest-rated filly, one of her four victories coming in effortless style in the Group 1 Flight Stakes over a mile at Randwick. Another exciting three-year-old filly, the unbeaten **Black Caviar**, beat Wanted in a tight finish in the Group 2 Danehill Stakes at Flemington, despite suffering an injury to her chest when almost coming down at the start (she was off the course afterwards). The New Zealand-trained three-year-old **Monaco Consul** caused an upset in the Spring Champion Stakes at Randwick on heavy going but proved that win was no fluke when winning the Victoria Derby. The Blue Diamond winner **Reward For Effort** was off with injury after the Golden Slipper Stakes.

The 2008 Caulfield Guineas winner **Whobegotyou** shared top spot among the four-year-olds in 2009 with **Heart of Dreams**. The pair met five times during the year with Whobegotyou holding a three-two advantage at the end. Whobegotyou won the Yalumba Stakes (ten furlongs) at Caulfield (defeating Heart of Dreams) while Heart of Dreams, who also won the Australian Guineas at Flemington in March, beat Whobegotyou in the Underwood Stakes (nine furlongs) at Caulfield. **Predatory Pricer**, a half-brother to Takeover Target, is making his mark as more of a stayer. He went down narrowly to the 2007 Melbourne Cup winner **Efficient** in the Turnbull Stakes (ten furlongs) at Flemington after coming a close third to Heart of Dreams and Whobegotyou in the Underwood Stakes and an unlucky third to Roman Emperor in the AJC Derby. **Metal Bender** failed to stay in the AJC Derby but won the first two legs of the triple crown, the Randwick Guineas (mile) and the Rosehill Guineas (mile and a quarter). Metal Bender was trained by Jack Denham who died in December at the age of eighty-five. He trained the winners of forty-nine Group 1 races, his best-known champion being Might And Power, winner of the Caulfield and Melbourne Cups in 1997 and the Cox Plate in 1998. The leading four-year-old filly **Typhoon Tracy** was the highest-rated filly or mare in training. She won six of her nine starts in 2009 including two Group 1s at around a mile, the Coolmore Classic at Rosehill and the Myer Classic at Flemington, recording the biggest winning margin (four and three quarter lengths) in the history of the last-named. The highest-rated older females were **Hot Danish**, who didn't win a Group 1 but was mostly consistent, and **Tuesday Joy**, who won the Group 2 Apollo Stakes over seven furlongs and the Group 1 Chipping Norton Stakes over a mile. The two-year-old ratings are, as usual, based on a limited number of races but **Run For Wilson** topped the list at the end of the year after making an impressive debut in the Breeders' Plate at Randwick. **Secession**, who made a winning debut at Sandown Park, was another to make an early impression. Secession is owned by Darley which, in a new move, sent a number of its best horses, headed by Spring Champion Stakes winner **Sousa**, to join the Godolphin stable for the 2010 Dubai Carnival.

Ratings and text for Australia and New Zealand are supplied courtesy of Gary Crispe (www.racingandsports.com.au) The ages listed below are as at 31st December 2009

Two-Year-Olds

116	Run For Wilson
114	General Truce
114	Intertidal
114+	Secession
113p	Gybe (f)
113+	Solar Charged (f)
113	Military Rose (f)
113	Sweet Cheeks (f)
112	Mafia Miss (f)
112	Marking Time
111	Jantzen
111	Stirling Grove
110p	Brightexpectations
110	Jigsaws
110	Spirit of Boom

110 Startsmcup

Three-Year-Olds
125p So You Think
124 Wanted
123p Denman
123p Starspangledbanner
123 Phelan Ready
123 Real Saga
122p More Joyous (f)
122 Manhattan Rain
122? Onemorenomore
121p Reward For Effort
120+ Black Caviar (f)
119p Monaco Consul
119p Trusting
119 Shellscrape
118p More Than Great
118 Delago Bolt
118 Rostova (f)
118 Tickets
117+ King Pulse
117 Definitely Ready
117 Melito (f)
116 Stryker
115+ Shamoline Warrior
115 Avenue (f)
115 Extra Zero
115 Faint Perfume (f)
115 Headway (f)
115 Irish Lights (f)
115 Rarefied
114 Carrara
114 Demerit
114 Indian Ocean (f)
114? God Has Spoken
113 Funtantes (f)
113 Horizons (f)
113 Hus der Lieften
113 Kidnapped
113 Lovemelikearock (f)
113 Paprika (f)
113 Purdey
113? Tollesprit

Four-Year-Olds
127 Heart of Dreams
127 Whobegotyou
126 Mic Mac
126 Predatory Pricer
124 Nicconi
124 Typhoon Tracy (f)
123 Metal Bender
123 Sousa
122 Duporth
122 Ortensia (f)
122 Rock Kingdom
122 Roman Emperor
122 Wilander
122 Youthful Jack
121 Caymans
121 Harris Tweed
121 Northern Meteor
120p First Command
120 Aichi
120 All American
120 Cats Whisker (f)
120 Fully Fledged
119 Desuetude
119 Fravashi
119 Pre Eminence
119 Shocking
119? Von Costa de Hero
118p O'Lonhro
118 Eagle Falls
118 Tavistock (f)
118 Time Thief
117+ Tobique
117? Naval Escort
116 Gold Water (f)
116 *Marchinski
(renamed Vital Flyer)
116 Old Jock
116 Portillo (f)
116 Purple (f)
116 Rock Me Baby (f)
116 Samantha Miss (f)
116 Swift Alliance
116? Glowlamp (f)
115p Battlefield
115 Allez Wonder (f)
115 Back Off
115 Bhutane Dane
115 Coniston Bluebird
115 Geeza
115 Grand Nirvana
115 Romneya (f)
115? Leapfrog
115? Lucky Thunder

Older Horses
128 †Scenic Blast
128 †Takeover Target
127 All Silent
126 Apache Cat
126 Racing To Win
126 Scenic Shot
126 Viewed
125 Danleigh
125 Efficient
125 Maldivian
124 Lucky Secret
124 Niconero
124 Pompeii Ruler
124 Theseo
124? Fiumicino
123 Alamosa
123 Bank Robber
123 Black Piranha
123 El Segundo
123 Light Fantastic
123 Royal Discretion
123 Sarrera
123 Swiss Ace
123? Zagreb
122 Road To Rock
122 Vision And Power
121p Rangirangdoo
121 Sniper's Bullet
122? Triple Honour
122? Typhoon Zed
121 Baughurst
121 Danny Beau
121 Dao Dao
121 Master O'Reilly
121 (Mr) Baritone
121 Red Ruler
121 Zipping
121? Moatize
120 Vigor
119 Grand Duels
119 Hot Danish (f)
119 Vosne Romanee
118+ Alcopop
118+ Weekend Hussler
118 Megatic
118 Burdekin Blues
118 C'Est La Guerre
118 El Cambio
118 Falaise
118 (King) Mufhasa
118 Raheeb
118 Swick
118 Turffontein
118 The Jackal
118 Tuesday Joy (f)
118? Sir Slick
117 Forensics (f)
117 Here de Angels
117 Kroner
117 Mentality
117 Secret Flyer
117 Solo Flyer
117 Valedictum
117 Zarita (f)
116 Court Command
116 Dante's Volonte
116 Diplomatic Force
116 Ginga Dude
116 Ice Chariot
116 Illuminates (f)
116 Keen Commander
116 Largo Lad
116 Light Vision
116 Maco'Reilly
116 Marasco
116 Musket
116 Neroli (f)
116 Nom du Jeu
116 Serious Speed (f)
116 Speed Gifted
116 Tarzi
116 The Fuzz
116 Zavite
116? Culminate (f)
116? Pinnacles
115 Chasm
115 Ista Kareem
115 Maxisun
115 Miss Maren (f)
115 Newport
115 Orange County
115 Posadas
115 Sea Battle
115 Spin Around
115? Magical Pearl

*(f) fillies and mares; *horse trained in the country for only part of the season; † (sections outside Europe and UAE) horse has a commentary in main section.*

INDEX TO PHOTOGRAPHS

PORTRAITS & SNAPSHOTS

Siyouni	2 b.c Pivotal – Sichilla	*Bertrand*	1000
Spanish Moon	5 b.h El Prado – Shining Bright	*Ed Byrne*	1019
Special Duty	2 ch.f Hennessy – Quest To Peak	*Bertrand*	1024
Sri Putra	3 b.c Oasis Dream – Wendylina	*Clare Williams*	1032
Stacelita	3 b.f Monsun – Soignee	*Ed Byrne*	1036
St Nicholas Abbey ...	2 b.c Montjeu – Leaping Water	*Peter Mooney*	1050
Tanoura	3 b.f Dalakhani – Takarouna	*Peter Mooney*	1082
Termagant	2 b.f Powerscourt – Rock Salt	*Peter Mooney*	1092
The Miniver Rose	3 b.f High Chaparral – Bloemfontain	*Clare Williams*	1101
Twice Over	4 b.c Observatory – Double Crossed	*Ed Byrne*	1136
Varenar	3 ch.c Rock of Gibraltar – Visor	*Bertrand*	1153
Virtual	4 b.c Pivotal – Virtuous	*Clare Williams*	1160
Xtension	2 br.c Xaar – Great Joy	*Alec Russell*	1201
Zacinto	3 b.c Dansili – Ithaca	*Ed Byrne*	1216

RACE PHOTOGRAPHS

Race and Meeting	*Copyright*	Page
Abu Dhabi International Stakes (Heritage Handicap) (Ascot)	*John Crofts*	55
Addleshaw Goddard Dee Stakes (Chester)	*Alec Russell*	1014
Addleshaw Goddard Stakes (Heritage Handicap) (York)	*John Crofts*	891
Amethyst Stakes (Leopardstown)	*Caroline Norris*	1063
Ascot Stakes (Handicap) (Royal Ascot)	*Ed Byrne*	553
At The Races Curragh Cup (the Curragh)	*George Selwyn*	842
Audemars Piguet Queen Elizabeth II Cup (Sha Tin)	*George Selwyn*	832
Audi Pretty Polly Stakes (the Curragh)	*Peter Mooney*	289
betchronicle.com Ormonde Stakes (Chester)	*Alec Russell*	176
Betfair Cup (Lennox) (Goodwood)	*George Selwyn*	390
Betfair Gordon Stakes (Goodwood)	*George Selwyn*	474
betfred.com Old Borough Cup (Heritage Handicap) (Haydock)	*Alec Russell*	1207
betfred.com Temple Stakes (Haydock)	*Alec Russell*	631
Betfred Silver Bowl (Heritage Handicap) (Haydock)	*Alec Russell*	304
Betfred Sprint Cup (Haydock)	*Alec Russell*	874
bet365 Lancashire Oaks (Haydock)	*Alec Russell*	120
BGC Sussex Stakes (Goodwood)	*John Crofts*	885
bluesquare.com Stewards' Cup (Heritage Handicap) (Goodwood)	*Ed Byrne*	425
Blue Square Brigadier Gerard Stakes (Sandown)	*George Selwyn*	236
Blue Square Henry II Stakes (Sandown)	*Ed Byrne*	426
Blue Square Heritage Handicap (Newmarket)	*John Crofts*	392
Blue Square Nassau Stakes (Goodwood)	*Ed Byrne*	691
Blue Square Premier Stakes (Thoroughbred) (Goodwood)	*John Crofts*	1214
boylesports.com Irish 1000 Guineas (the Curragh)	*Caroline Norris*	35
boylesports.com Irish 2000 Guineas (the Curragh)	*Peter Mooney*	669
Breeders' Cup Juvenile Turf (Santa Anita)	*George Selwyn*	826
Breeders' Cup Marathon Stakes (Santa Anita)	*Bill Selwyn*	660
Britannia Stakes (Heritage Handicap) (Royal Ascot)	*George Selwyn*	378
Call Stan James 08000 351135 Stakes (Handicap) (Newmarket)	*John Crofts*	478
Camas Park & Ashton House Studs Phoenix Stakes (the Curragh)	*Caroline Norris*	49
Cathay Pacific Hong Kong Cup (Sha Tin)	*Frank Sorge*	1163
Cathay Pacific Hong Kong Vase (Sha Tin)	*George Selwyn*	294
CGA Geoffrey Freer Stakes (Newbury)	*Ed Byrne*	589
CGA Hungerford Stakes (Newbury)	*Ed Byrne*	114
Connaught Access Flooring Abernant Stakes (Newmarket)	*George Selwyn*	1087
Coolmore Fusaichi Pegasus Matron Stakes (Leopardstown)	*Ed Byrne*	856
Coolmore Nunthorpe Stakes (York)	*Ed Byrne*	161
Coral Challenge (Heritage Handicap) (Sandown)	*John Crofts*	28
Coral Distaff (Sandown)	*John Crofts*	1054
Coral-Eclipse (Sandown)	*John Crofts*	950
Coral Rockingham Stakes (York)	*Alec Russell*	611
Coral Sprint Trophy (Heritage Handicap) (York)	*Alec Russell*	560
Coronation Stakes (Royal Ascot)	*Frank Sorge*	431
Criterium de Saint-Cloud (Saint-Cloud)	*Bertrand*	795
Criterium International (Saint-Cloud)	*Bertrand*	535
Coutts Glorious Stakes (Goodwood)	*Bill Selwyn*	513
Coutts Goodwood Cup (Goodwood)	*George Selwyn*	939
Coventry Stakes (Royal Ascot)	*Frank Sorge*	189
Cuisine de France Summer Stakes (York)	*Alec Russell*	966

totesport Victoria Cup (Heritage Handicap) (Ascot)	*Bill Selwyn*	1071
totesuper7 Zetland Gold Cup (Heritage Handicap) (Redcar)	*Alec Russell*	573
TVG Breeders' Cup Mile (Santa Anita)	*Bill Selwyn*	452
Veuve Clicquot Vintage Stakes (Goodwood)	*John Crofts*	1200
Victor Chandler Challenge Stakes (Newmarket)	*Bill Selwyn*	75
Virgin Money Chester Vase (Chester)	*Alec Russell*	448
Watch The Last 2 Races On Racing UK Acomb Stakes (York)	*John Crofts*	350
Weatherbys Insurance £300,000 2-Y-O Stakes (Doncaster)	*George Selwyn*	1072
Weatherbys Ireland Greenlands Stakes (the Curragh)	*Bill Selwyn*	1144
Weatherbys Super Sprint (Newbury)	*Bill Selwyn*	716
William Hill (Ayr) Bronze Cup Handicap (Ayr)	*Alec Russell*	113
William Hill (Ayr) Gold Cup (Heritage Handicap) (Ayr)	*Alec Russell*	546
williamhill.com Doonside Cup Stakes (Ayr)	*Alec Russell*	838
williamhill.com - Play Poker Brocklesby Stakes (Doncaster)	*Alec Russell*	481
William Hill Great St Wilfrid Stakes (Heritage Handicap) (Ripon)	*Alec Russell*	664
William Hill Lincoln (Heritage Handicap) (Doncaster)	*Alec Russell*	366
Willmott Dixon Bengough Memorial Stakes (Ascot)	*John Crofts*	908
Willmott Dixon Cornwallis Stakes (Ascot)	*George Selwyn*	783
Windflower March Stakes (Goodwood)	*John Crofts*	726
Windsor Castle Stakes (Royal Ascot)	*Frank Sorge*	1058
Windsor Forest Stakes (Royal Ascot)	*Ed Byrne*	1016
Wokingham Stakes (Heritage Handicap) (Royal Ascot)	*John Crofts*	495
Wolferton Handicap (Royal Ascot)	*Alec Russell*	806
Woodlands Stakes (Naas)	*Caroline Norris*	525

ADDITIONAL PHOTOGRAPHS

The following photographs appear in the Introduction:– montage page 5 (photos taken by George Selwyn), Yeats after the Gold Cup (John Crofts), Queen Elizabeth II Stakes and Champion Stakes (Bill Selwyn), the Godolphin team (Bill Selwyn), Mark Johnston and Michael Kinane (George Selwyn)

Credits for the photographs in 'Top Horses Abroad' are as follows:– Preis der Diana (Frank Sorge), Premio Presidente della Republicca (Stefano Grasso), UAE Derby (Frank Sorge), Breeders' Cup Classic (George Selwyn), Kentucky Derby (Bill Selwyn), Preakness Stakes (International Racing Photos), Breeders' Cup Dirt Mile (Frank Sorge), Man o'War Stakes (Adam Coglianese), Japan Cup (Frank Sorge), Hong Kong Sprint (George Selwyn), Hong Kong Mile (Frank Sorge), Caulfield Cup and Melbourne Cup (both Bronwen Healy).

ERRATA & ADDENDA

Extended Pedigrees	The dam of grandsire Green Desert is Foreign **Courier** — p753 Racehorses of 2004; p751 Racehorses of 2005; p892 Racehorses of 2006; p972 Racehorses of 2008

'Racehorses of 2008'

Introduction	p10, 23 lines down, **one hundred and eighty-nine wins**
2008 Statistics	p15/16 Trainers' tables, R. Hannon, races won **189**
	p16 Jockeys' tables, Richard Hughes, races won **127**
Elnawin	p340, 16 lines down, Hannon stable which won a **hundred and eighty-nine races** in Britain (Rebecca de Winter was disqualified from a claimer at Lingfield following a disciplinary panel inquiry held on Feb 26th 2009 after *Racehorses* had gone to press)
Indian Lady	was not a maiden
Readily	awarded claimer at Lingfield on disqualification of Rebecca de Winter (seventh start)
Visit	promoted to third in Breeders' Cup Filly & Mare Turf

'Racehorses of 2009'

Fajita	disqualified (failed dope test) at an inquiry in February 2010 from win at Newmarket in August, race awarded to Dove Mews

NOTNOWCATO
By INCHINOR -
RAMBLING ROSE
by Cadeaux Genereux